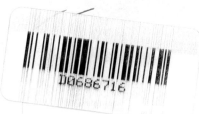

For Reference

Not to be taken from this room

THE OXFORD-HARRAP
STANDARD
GERMAN-ENGLISH
DICTIONARY

THE OXFORD-HARRAP
STANDARD
GERMAN-ENGLISH
DICTIONARY

Edited by
TREVOR JONES

VOLUME I
A-E

CLARENDON PRESS · OXFORD

Oxford University Press, Walton Street, Oxford OX2 6DP

OXFORD   LONDON   GLASGOW
NEW YORK   TORONTO   MELBOURNE   WELLINGTON
IBADAN   NAIROBI   DAR ES SALAAM   LUSAKA   CAPE TOWN
KUALA LUMPUR   SINGAPORE   JAKARTA   HONG KONG   TOKYO
DELHI   BOMBAY   CALCUTTA   MADRAS   KARACHI

First published in Great Britain in 1963 by
George G. Harrap and Co. Ltd., 182 High Holborn, London WC1V 4AX
Published by Oxford University Press 1977

Reprinted with corrections 1978

British Library Cataloguing in Publication Data
The Oxford-Harrap Standard German-English Dictionary
  Vol. 1: A-E
  1. German Language – Dictionaries – English
  I. Jones, Trevor, b. 1908
  433′.2′1   PF3640   77–30137
  ISBN 0–19–864129–X
  (formerly 0–245–57662–2)

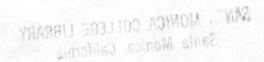

Printed in Great Britain by
William Clowes & Sons, Limited, London, Beccles and Colchester

Preface

IN the years following the last war there was an ever-increasing need for precise and adequate translations from German into English and *vice versa*. Those who had to make such translations found little help from the bilingual dictionaries then available. It was inevitable that many new words and phrases did not appear in them; but it was disquieting to discover their inadequacy within their own limits. They clung to confused and confusing methods of presentation inherited from the nineteenth century; they often offered translations which made no sense when used in a continuous context, or windy explanatory phrases which a translator could not use at all, or else they offered a variety of translations without any adequate indication of differences in nuance and stylistic level, with the result that an utterance conscientiously translated with the aid of a dictionary emerged as a grotesque patchwork of incompatible elements. Furthermore, any translator with expert knowledge in a particular field inevitably hit upon entirely false translations that had been repeated from dictionary to dictionary and thus acquired a spurious air of authority. Such experiences made it clear that a large, reliable German-English and English-German dictionary was urgently needed; it was also evident that such a dictionary would have to start again from first principles, accept no traditional shibboleths, and aim above all at offering the translator really workable equivalents, together with an indication of the kind of context in which they could safely be used and any grammatical information required for their correct employment.

A similar situation had already existed with regard to the French language after the first World War. This had been recognized by J. E. Mansion.[1] His profound knowledge of the language and matchlessly fine sense of linguistic values made it possible for him to create a model of what a bilingual dictionary ought to be. Long experimenting with a mass of German material showed that the principles of Mansion's lucid and practical methodology could also be applied to a German dictionary, if certain modifications were made to conform with the differing pattern of the German language. After initial discussions, Messrs George G. Harrap and Company Ltd agreed to the plan for producing a German counterpart to their *Standard French and English Dictionary*; staff were assembled, and work began in 1950.

---

[1] *Harrap's Standard French and English Dictionary*, London 1934, Preface, pp. v–vii.

Since that date, a lexicographical team has been working continuously on the compilation of the Dictionary. The personal composition of the team has, inevitably, fluctuated from time to time. It has, however, been the rule that it should comprise British as well as German nationals (the latter drawn from a variety of German speech-areas), together with at least one Austrian. It is thus possible thoroughly to discuss and test proposed translations on the spot, and especially to guard against any misunderstandings of words and phrases with a regional colouring. The material of the present volume has also been checked in the United States for the purpose of verifying all examples of North-American usage and adding any further renderings desirable for the American or Canadian user. In view of the marked fluidity of contemporary English usage, both at home and on the North-American continent, it is manifestly not feasible for a bilingual dictionary to indicate *all* the current variations in usage between the two main areas of the English-speaking world. For this reason, American terms are listed only where the native English locution would be incomprehensible, or else would convey a false nuance, in an American or Canadian context. In order to avoid undue expenditure of space, American translations are usually given only under the entries for the simplex (*e.g.* **Ähre, Benzin**); it is assumed that American users will check with the simplex entries when they find only English translations given for a German compound.

In selecting the material it was necessary to consider the needs of very diverse types of reader, such as the academic student of German language and literature, the translator of present-day German literary works and newspaper articles, the historian concerned with German sources, and the scientist reading German scientific articles. If the Dictionary were to be of the greatest benefit to the greatest number of readers, then it was clear that the seventeenth century and much of the eighteenth must be neglected, in order to make room for indispensable modern matter. It was therefore decided to exclude words and phrases that had lost currency by about 1800, unless they were of especial importance as concepts in the development of German civilization, literature, art, music, law, etc.; an exception was also made for certain words and phrases in major authors writing before 1800—*e.g.* Kant, Lessing, Wieland, Goethe and Schiller—the sense of which would not be apparent to a modern reader. Regional variations in modern German usage have been noted throughout. The selection of dialect words and expressions has been restricted to those which appear in literary works of some importance and those which the visitor is likely to encounter in local speech.

The material of the Dictionary has been collected primarily from purely German sources, such as *Grimm's Deutsches Wörterbuch*, the various Duden publications, *Meyer's Konversationslexikon* and *Der Große Brockhaus*, from specialized textbooks, from periodicals and newspapers, and also from trade catalogues and lists supplied by experts in various fields. The English translations are checked against the *Oxford English Dictionary*, *Webster's Third New International Dictionary*, the *Encyclopaedia Britannica*, *Chambers's Encyclopaedia*, and also appropriate English textbooks, catalogues, brochures, etc.; if any doubt remains, the opinion of an expert or practical worker in the relevant field is sought. Recent bilingual dictionaries have been carefully examined; but no entry in a bilingual dictionary has been accepted as

evidence in itself without confirmation from actual contexts. It may be useful to the reader to note that there have appeared in recent years some good specialized bilingual glossaries (the best among them being Leo Herland's *Dictionary of Mathematical Sciences*, New York 1951, which is a model of precise definition, compression and effective lexical arrangement), but that many of the smaller 'technical' dictionaries published since 1945 are of little practical use; they are often loaded with non-technical entries that have no place in a specialized dictionary, and often their terminology is exact in the one language but dubious in the other.

The German language has almost limitless possibilities of forming simple nominal compounds, and also analogy-compounds of both nouns and verbs. The inclusion of all possible compounds would make a word-list far beyond the scope of a manageable dictionary. For this reason, self-evident compounds (*i.e.* those whose total sense is merely the sum of the senses of their elements) have been omitted, except where the compound is very widely used, or represents an important technical concept, or else where the appropriate sense of any one component might be difficult to discover in a complicated article (*e.g.* **Abflugleistung**). Special articles on combining forms are provided to indicate the possible uses of certain words in combinations. Prefixes and suffixes are also treated in such a way as to show their possible implications in an unlisted word, and the possible uses of the various verbal prefixes (**ab-, ent-, ge-, ver-,** etc.) are illustrated in considerable detail in the relevant articles. Words ending in **-keit** or **-heit** have been listed only when the word concerned is stylistically useful, or when it offers a variety of possibilities in English translation.

Many German dictionaries deliberately (and exasperatingly) evade any treatment of the 'Fremdwort' (*i.e.* word borrowed from another language). In this Dictionary, those 'Fremdwörter' have been included which have general currency and have acquired a special flavour in German usage. Such Latin, French and Italian phrases as are common coin among all the European nations have been omitted. The Italian musical terminology has also been omitted, except where there is some peculiarity in its use in Germany, or where the reader might wish to know the German gender and plural forms (*e.g.* of **Adagio** and **Andante** used as nouns). With regard to Latin words and phrases, the English reader should be forewarned that the educated German's stock of Latin tags differs considerably from his own, that a familiar Latin tag may be used by a German with a flavour strange to us, and further that words of Latin origin may acquire a totally unexpected significance in Austrian usage. The German reader might also be reminded that the English have little acquaintance with Italian, and that Italian phrases forming part of the German commercial and financial terminology are not used in England. Any such words or phrases are listed in their alphabetical order.

Names of towns, districts, rivers, etc. have been omitted unless they have important literary, historical or political associations, or have some difference of spelling in the two languages. Designations of less important minerals, formed from a proper name by adding the suffix -ite in English and the masculine suffix **-it** in German, have usually been listed only when there are variant designations in either language.

The following explanations should be found helpful in using the Dictionary:

ORDER OF ENTRIES: Unlike many large bilingual dictionaries, this work maintains a strictly alphabetical order throughout, with the one exception of the arrangement of the parts of the verb in the verb-articles.

NOMINAL COMPOUNDS: The genitive and plural forms of nominal compounds are not given; these forms are identical with those for the final element of the compound and will be found by looking up this element in its alphabetical order in the Dictionary.

ORTHOGRAPHY AND PUNCTUATION: The Duden *Rechtschreibung* and the *Oxford English Dictionary* have been used as guides for German and English orthography.

The genitive forms of proper names are indicated as follows:

(i) **-s** indicates that the genitive takes **s** when the name is used without an article, but remains uninflected after the article (*e.g.* **Adam**; **Adams Fall**, but **der Fall des Adam**).

(ii) **[']** with names ending in **s, ß, z, tz** or **x** indicates that the genitive is written with an apostrophe when the name is used without an article, but remains uninflected after the article (*e.g.* **Achilles**; **Achilles' Schild**, but **der Schild des Achilles**).

Certain German adjectives with either a capital letter or a small letter according to the context (*e.g.* **deutsch, englisch, achäisch, dorisch**) have for convenience been printed with a small letter in the head-word; illustrations are given in the articles of contexts in which a capital letter is required.

Spellings with **ph** have been preferred to those with **f** in accordance with Duden principles. German spelling usage with **C, K** and **Z** fluctuates; words not found under **C** should be sought under **K** or **Z** and *vice versa*.

The English style of quotation-marks has been used throughout the work.

The use of the hyphen in contemporary English raises insoluble problems for the lexicographer. North-American English seems in great measure to have rejected the hyphen. Many hyphenated words listed in the *Oxford English Dictionary* now seem unnatural in present-day English, which clearly prefers two separate words (e.g. *love affair, dog racing*) or else a closed compound written as one word (e.g. *bathtub, horserace, textbook*). There is, however, one pattern in which there is still general agreement about the use of the hyphen, namely the three-word nominal compound in which the hyphen serves to clarify the relation of the second element (e.g. *return-flue boiler*). Apart from this, there are no definable rules for the use of the hyphen in present-day English; it can only be noted that there is a marked avoidance of it in administrative, industrial and scientific contexts. In the present work, hyphenated forms have been used only when they seemed natural to a present-day English reader.

A note on the use of punctuation in individual articles will be found in the section *Conventions employed in the Dictionary* (item 6).

GERMAN PRONUNCIATION: Native German words normally have the stress on the first syllable; none the less, nouns ending in **-ei** have the stress on the final syllable (see the article on **-ei**), and the prefixes **be-, ent-, ge-, ver-,** etc., are unstressed (see the individual articles for the various prefixes). For further information on pronunciation, the reader is referred to the note attached to the *Table of Phonetic Symbols*.

CONVENTIONS EMPLOYED IN THE DICTIONARY

1. Verbs having the strong conjugation are indicated as such; if there is no indication of conjugation, it is to be assumed that the verb has the weak conjugation. Compound verbs are conjugated in the same manner as the simplex, unless there is an explicit statement to the contrary.

2. In the *vbl s.* (verbal substantive) section of a verb-article, the convention *in vbl senses* has been used to indicate that English verbs given as translations in the earlier part of the article have parallel substantive forms ending in *-ing* (e.g. *age, ageing; burn, burning*).

3. At the end of a *vbl s.* entry there will sometimes be found a reference to a masculine or feminine noun derived from the verb (*e.g.* III. *vbl s.* **1. Ablassen,** *n.* . . . . /**2. Ablassung,** *f.* . . . . *Cp.* **Ablaß**; III. *vbl s.* **Angeben,** *n.* . . . *Cp.* **Angabe**). Such references should be taken as indicating that there is a certain overlapping between the usages of **Ablassen** and **Ablaß, Angeben** and **Angabe,** etc., and that other useful translations may be found by consulting the article to which the reader is referred.

4. The convention **etwas** *gen.* has been used to avoid any possible misunderstandings which might arise from the conventional **einer Sache** which has been used in other dictionaries. Here **etwas** stands in lieu of possible nouns; these may frequently be verbal nouns, for which **Sache** cannot be a proper substitute—for example, in the phrase **etwas** *gen.* **kundig sein,** the **etwas** may stand for **des Lesens, des Schreibens,** etc., which are not **Sachen.**

5. In verb-articles, *esp.* should be taken to mean 'in a special sense'. In other articles, *esp.* signifies 'in particular'; *e.g.* **Dreesch,** *m.* **-es/-e, Dreeschbrache,** *f. Agr:* green fallow, *esp.* used for pasture, **Eisenhut,** *m.* **2.** *Bot:* aconite, *esp.* monk's-hood, mean respectively 'green fallow, and in particular a green fallow used for pasture', 'aconite, and in particular the variety of aconite known as monk's-hood'.

6. It will be noticed that in the sub-sections of the articles in this Dictionary the various translations are separated sometimes by commas, sometimes by semicolons. A group of translations separated from one another by commas may be regarded as virtually interchangeable in the same English context; but the semicolon normally indicates that there is a significant shift of nuance or usage away from that of the preceding word or phrase. This arrangement precludes the showing of the initial capital letter in such locutions as *Dear Sir, Oh dear!* (which have to appear as *dear Sir, oh dear!*), but this should not be taken as a deviation from the rule that demands a capital letter at the start of any isolated locution. A semicolon is also

occasionally used to break up a complicated entry which might otherwise be confusing to the reader.

7. Some of the classification-labels used in the body of the Dictionary are printed with a single stop instead of a colon. This has been done with double classifications, e.g. *Hist. & F:* or *Hist. of Med:* The single stop has also been used in a label such as *A.Hist:* which stands for Ancient History, whereas *Hist: A:* implies not only that the German word represents an historical concept, but also that the word itself is now antiquated.

8. Matter printed in italics and enclosed in brackets (usually preceding the translation) is intended only as an explanation and not as part of the suggested translation: *e.g.* '**bedeuten.** I. *v.tr.* **1.** (*a*) (*of word, phrase, etc.*) to mean, signify', which conveys the information that when the subject of the verb **bedeuten** is a word, a phrase, etc., then the appropriate translation is 'to mean' or 'to signify'; '**bäh,** *int.* (i) (*bleat of sheep*) baa; (ii) (*mocking*) yah! boo to you!' where the italicized explanation defines the specific sense of the word in each of its applications.

Matter printed in roman type and enclosed in brackets is used as follows:

(i) to indicate an optional element in the translation—*e.g.* '**Barsoi,** *m.* -s/-s, borzoi (hound)', where either 'borzoi' or 'borzoi hound' is equally correct in English;

(ii) to indicate an element of definition which may be desirable for unequivocal translation but can be omitted in contexts where the nature of the concept is already evident—*e.g.* '**Bauscht,** *m.* -(e)s/-e. *Paper m:* post (of 180 sheets)'; '**Auerhahn,** *m. Orn:* (cock) capercaillie'; '**Auerhenne,** *f. Orn:* (hen) capercaillie';

(iii) to indicate the kind of noun to which an adjective normally applies, or the kind of noun which can be the object of a verb used in a specific sense—*e.g.* '**deutschsprachig,** *a.* German-speaking (population, etc.)'; '**anfechten.** I. *v.tr. sep.* (*strong*) to contest, dispute (opinion, statement, s.o.'s right, etc.)'. In verb-entries of this type, it should be noted that the sample object-nouns are usually given without the article, as the translator's context may demand 'a', 'the', 'his', 'any', etc.

9. Where there are possible variants of a combining form, *e.g.* **Buch-** and **Bücher-,** the compounds have generally been listed only in the form most frequently encountered—*e.g.* **Buchladen, Bücherwissen.** In order to save the space that would be wasted by repetitive entries for **Bücherladen, Buchwissen,** etc., cross-references have been given (*e.g.* **Buch-,** *comb.fm. cp.* **Bücher-,...**; and **Bücher-,** *comb.fm. cp.* **Buch-**), to inform the reader that the compound listed in one form will be identical in meaning with its unlisted counterpart.

10. The symbol = is used not only to refer the reader to a synonym listed elsewhere, but also occasionally to indicate a correspondence between German and English institutions, where the terms thus brought together cannot strictly be regarded as translations one of the other.

Thus: **Amtsrichter,** *m. Jur:* district court judge (= English county court judge); **Arnim-Paragraph, der.** *Jur:* = the Official Secrets Act. In practice, German terms of this kind may conveniently be left untranslated, and the indicated correspondence used as an explanatory footnote.

11. In case of doubt about the use of the classification-labels *F: P:* etc., the reader should be informed that they apply primarily to the German head-word when they appear immediately after it, but that a subsequent *F:* or *P:* refers only to the following English translation—*e.g.* in the article '**anranzen,** *v.tr. sep. F:* to give (s.o.) a dressing-down, *F:* to blow (s.o.) up, tell (s.o.) off', it is to be understood that the word **anranzen** is in itself a familiar usage in German, 'to give someone a dressing-down' is standard English, 'to blow someone up', 'to tell someone off' are familiar usage in English.

12. Proverbs, common sayings, etc., are generally entered either under the first important word or under the word that forms the point of interest.

13. As the Dictionary is to appear in several parts, it is impossible to complete all the cross-reference entries until the work of compilation is finished. For this reason, in a few places blanks have been left in this volume where cross-references will be given in the completed work. The *List of Abbreviations* will appear at the end of the final German-English volume of the Dictionary.

We are greatly indebted to Dr E. Rosenbaum for her invaluable contribution in arranging and editing the material; to Miss E. L. R. Goodwin for her tireless organization of our team-work, and to our past and present staff of assistant lexicographers. For valuable assistance in providing a comprehensive list of European and other bird-names for inclusion in the Dictionary, we extend our thanks to three eminent experts, Dr W. Przygodda, Dr H. Frieling and Mr H. T. Porter. We also wish to record our gratitude to Mr J. L. M. Trim for establishing our procedure with phonetic transcriptions; to Dr E. Myers (Cultural Attaché, United States Embassy, London) and Professor B. Q. Morgan for their help with American terms; to Professor G. Bing and Mr J. C. T. Oates for their astringent reading of galley proofs and their valuable suggestions for improvements; to Mr W. Schapiro for his help with reading the proofs, and to Messrs William Clowes & Sons Ltd for their admirable handling of our intricate printing problems.

We owe thanks to Messrs D. C. Heath of Boston, U.S.A., for providing us with an American reader, and to the London Library for allowing us to use Van Wijk's monumental *Dictionary of Plant Names.* We gratefully acknowledge the constant co-operation we have received from the Duden Verlag des Bibliographischen Instituts, Mannheim, and the help that has been given us in recruiting staff members by the German and Austrian Universities, by the English University Appointments Boards, and especially by Professor Dr P. L. Jaeger, Leiter der Englisch-Amerikanischen Abteilung, Auslands- und Dolmetscherinstitut der Universität Mainz in Germersheim.

We are particularly indebted to Professor L. W. Forster and Mr C. H. Barker, who have for many years submitted patiently to the exploiting of their own learning by the Editor and also led him to the solution of many lexical problems.

Mr R. P. L. Ledésert has given most generous guidance in the organization of the work from its inception, and we count ourselves fortunate to have been able to draw upon his lexicographical experience and wisdom.

Lastly, we offer our thanks to the host of other experts, craftsmen, and friendly citizens at home and abroad who have, wittingly or unwittingly, yielded up their special knowledge to the benefit of this Dictionary.

1963   TREVOR JONES

Vorwort

In den Jahren nach dem letzten Kriege wurden genaue und verläßliche Übersetzungen aus dem Deutschen ins Englische und umgekehrt in immer stärkerem Maße erforderlich. Demjenigen, der solche Übersetzungen anzufertigen hatte, boten die damals vorhandenen zweisprachigen Wörterbücher wenig Hilfe. Daß viele neue Wörter und Ausdrücke in ihnen nicht vorkamen, schien unvermeidlich, doch wiesen sie selbst in ihrem eigenen Rahmen erschreckende Mängel auf. Sie klebten an unklaren, verwirrenden Darstellungsmethoden, die sie aus dem 19. Jahrhundert übernommen hatten. Häufig brachten sie Übersetzungen, die keinerlei Sinn ergaben, wenn man sie im Textzusammenhang verwenden wollte, oder langatmige Erklärungen, die für den Übersetzer vollkommen nutzlos waren, oder aber sie boten eine Vielzahl von Übersetzungen ohne ausreichende Angabe der Bedeutungsnuancierungen und Stilunterschiede, mit dem Ergebnis, daß eine an Hand eines Wörterbuches gewissenhaft übersetzte Aussage als groteskes Flickwerk nicht zusammen passender Teile erschien. Weiterhin mußte jeder Fachübersetzer ständig auf ganz und gar falsche Übersetzungen stoßen, die von einem Wörterbuch ins andere mitgeschleppt worden waren und so einen zweifelhaften Anspruch auf Gültigkeit erworben hatten. Solche Erfahrungen ließen ein großes, zuverlässiges deutsch-englisches und englisch-deutsches Wörterbuch dringend notwendig erscheinen. Dabei war es klar, daß ein Wörterbuch dieser Art von Grund auf neu gestaltet werden mußte, keine veralteten Vorstellungen anerkennen durfte und vor allem darauf auszugehen hatte, dem Übersetzer praktisch verwendbare Entsprechungen anzubieten, zusammen mit Angaben über den Zusammenhang, in dem sie ohne Bedenken benutzt werden können, und Hinweisen über die richtige grammatische Behandlung.

J. E. Mansion[1] hatte eine ähnliche Situation im Bereich der französischen Sprache bereits nach dem ersten Weltkrieg erkannt. Dank seiner profunden Sprachkenntnis und seinem außergewöhnlich feinen Gefühl für die Erfassung linguistischer Werte war er in der Lage, das Vorbild eines zweisprachigen Wörterbuches zu schaffen. Langjährige Versuche mit einer Fülle deutschen Materials hatten erwiesen, daß Mansions klare und praktische Methodik sich grundsätzlich auch auf ein deutsches Wörterbuch anwenden ließe, wenn dem abweichenden Aufbau der

---

[1] *Harrap's Standard French and English Dictionary*, London 1934, Vorwort, S. v–vii.

deutschen Sprache durch gewisse Änderungen Rechnung getragen würde. Nach einleitenden Verhandlungen stimmte der Verlag Harrap schließlich dem Plane zu, ein deutsches Gegenstück zu seinem französisch-englischen Standardwörterbuch herzustellen. Eine Redaktionsabteilung wurde eingerichtet, in der im Jahre 1950 die planmäßige Arbeit begann.

Seither ist eine Gruppe lexikographischer Mitarbeiter ständig mit der Zusammenstellung des Wörterbuches beschäftigt. Die personelle Zusammensetzung dieser Gruppe muß sich natürlich von Zeit zu Zeit verschieben. Grundsätzlich gehören ihr jedoch immer sowohl englische als auch deutsche Mitarbeiter an. Die letzteren stammen aus den verschiedensten deutschen Sprachgebieten und werden jeweils durch mindestens einen österreichischen Kollegen ergänzt. Auf diese Weise ist es möglich, Übersetzungsvorschläge an Ort und Stelle zu besprechen bzw. zu erproben und insbesondere zu vermeiden, daß Wörter oder Ausdrücke regionalen Charakters mißverstanden werden.   Unter demselben Gesichtspunkt wurde das Wortmaterial des vorliegenden Bandes auch in den Vereinigten Staaten durchgesehen. Alle für den nordamerikanischen Sprachgebrauch angegebenen Beispiele wurden überprüft und weitere Übersetzungen, die vom Standpunkt des amerikanischen oder kanadischen Benutzers aus wünschenswert erschienen, hinzugefügt. Angesichts der ausgeprägten Veränderlichkeit des heutigen englischen Sprachgebrauchs in Großbritannien und auf dem nordamerikanischen Kontinent liegt es auf der Hand, daß ein zweisprachiges Wörterbuch unmöglich alle heutigen Gebrauchsunterschiede zwischen den beiden Hauptgebieten der englischsprechenden Welt angeben kann. Aus diesem Grunde werden amerikanische Ausdrücke nur da aufgeführt, wo die britische Entsprechung im amerikanischen oder kanadischen Bereich unverständlich oder irreführend wäre. Ebenso geben wir aus Gründen der Raumersparnis amerikanische Übersetzungen gewöhnlich nur unter dem Simplex (z.B. **Ähre, Benzin**). Es wird erwartet, daß der amerikanische Benutzer den jeweiligen Simplex-Artikel zu Hilfe zieht, wenn er unter einem deutschen Kompositum nur britische Übersetzungen vorfindet.

Bei der Auswahl des aufzunehmenden Materials mußten die Anforderungen eines sehr unterschiedlichen Benutzerkreises berücksichtigt werden: des wissenschaftlichen Erforschers deutscher Sprache und Literatur, des Übersetzers zeitgenössischer deutscher Literatur und journalistischer Arbeiten, des mit deutschem Quellenmaterial beschäftigten Historikers, des Naturwissenschaftlers, der das deutschsprachige wissenschaftliche Schrifttum studiert, usw. Sollte das Wörterbuch der größtmöglichen Leserzahl den größtmöglichen Nutzen bringen, dann war klar, daß das siebzehnte Jahrhundert und der größte Teil des achtzehnten Jahrhunderts unberücksichtigt bleiben mußte, damit unerläßliches neueres Material nicht aus Platznot verlorenging. Wir entschlossen uns daher, Wörter und Redewendungen nicht aufzunehmen, wenn sie um etwa 1800 nicht mehr gebräuchlich waren, es sei denn, es handele sich um besonders wichtige Begriffe in der Entwicklung deutscher Kultur, Literatur, Kunst, Musik, des deutschen Rechtswesens usw. Eine weitere Ausnahme bilden Wörter und Redewendungen aus den Werken bedeutender Schriftsteller vor 1800 (wie Kant, Lessing, Wieland, Goethe und Schiller), die dem **heutigen** Leser nicht ohne weiteres verständlich wären. Regionale Unterschiede im deutschen

Sprachgebrauch sind überall berücksichtigt. Die Auswahl mundartlicher Wörter und Ausdrücke ist jedoch auf solche beschränkt, die in einigermaßen bedeutenden literarischen Werken vorkommen oder aber dem ausländischen Besucher in der mundartlich gefärbten Unterhaltung begegnen könnten.

Das aufgenommene Material stammt in erster Linie aus rein deutschen Quellen wie Grimms Deutschem Wörterbuch, den verschiedenen Veröffentlichungen des Dudenverlages, aus Meyers Konversationslexikon und dem Großen Brockhaus, aus Fachbüchern, Zeitungen und Zeitschriften sowie aus Firmenkatalogen und Aufstellungen, die uns Fachleute auf den verschiedensten Gebieten zur Verfügung stellten. Die englischen Übersetzungen werden nachgeprüft an Hand des Oxford English Dictionary, von Webster's Third New International Dictionary, der Encyclopaedia Britannica und Chambers's Encyclopaedia sowie einschlägigen englischen Fachbüchern, Katalogen, Broschüren usw. Wenn dann noch Zweifel bestehen, werden sie Sachverständigen bzw. auf dem jeweiligen Gebiet praktisch tätigen Fachleuten zur Begutachtung vorgelegt. Neuere zweisprachige Wörterbücher werden sorgfältig durchgesehen, doch wird kein Eintrag in einem zweisprachigen Wörterbuch für richtig erachtet, der sich nicht außerdem durch Textbelege nachweisen läßt. Es ist vielleicht angebracht, den Leser an dieser Stelle darauf hinzuweisen, daß in den letzten Jahren einige gute zweisprachige Fachglossarien erschienen sind (das beste davon Leo Herlands Wörterbuch der Mathematischen Wissenschaften, New York 1951, ein Musterbeispiel klarer Definition, straffer Gliederung und wirkungsvoller lexikalischerAnlage), daß jedoch viele der seit 1945 erschienenen kleineren Spezialwörterbücher kaum von praktischem Nutzen sind. Häufig sind sie mit nichttechnischen Einträgen überladen, für die ein Fachwörterbuch nicht der richtige Ort ist, und oft trifft die Terminologie zwar in einer Sprache zu, ist aber in der anderen nicht verläßlich.

In der deutschen Sprache gibt es nahezu unbegrenzte Möglichkeiten für die Bildung einfacher substantivischer Zusammensetzungen wie auch für Analogiebildungen aus Substantiven und Verben. Alle möglichen Komposita aufzunehmen ginge weit über den Rahmen eines einigermaßen handlichen Wörterbuches hinaus. Aus diesem Grunde werden selbstverständliche Komposita nicht aufgenommen (d.h. solche, deren Gesamtbedeutung sich aus der Summe der Bedeutungen der Einzelelemente ergibt), außer wo das Kompositum als solches sehr gebräuchlich ist oder einen wichtigen technischen Begriff darstellt bzw. wo der zutreffende Sinn eines Bestandteils in einer komplizierten Zusammensetzung schwer erkennbar sein könnte (z.B. **Abflugleistung**). Zahlreiche Zusammensetzungselemente erscheinen in Form von selbständigen Stichwortartikeln, in denen der Benutzer Auskunft über die Gebrauchsmöglichkeiten bestimmter Wörter in Zusammensetzungen erhält. Präfixe und Suffixe werden ebenfalls derart behandelt, daß ihre möglichen Bedeutungen als Teil eines nicht aufgeführten Wortes ohne weiteres erkennbar sind. Sehr gründlich werden die Anwendungsformen der verschiedenen Verbalpräfixe (**ab-, ent-, ge-, zer-** usw.) in den entsprechenden Artikeln dargestellt. Auf **-keit** oder **-heit** endende Wörter werden nur dann gesondert aufgeführt, wenn sie stilistischen Wert haben oder wenn sie im Englischen auf verschiedene Weise wiedergegeben werden können.

Es ist für den Benutzer oft ärgerlich festzustellen, wie in vielen deutschen Wörterbüchern

die Behandlung des Fremdwortes mit Absicht vermieden wird. In diesem Wörterbuch werden solche Fremdwörter berücksichtigt, die allgemein geläufig sind und im deutschen Sprachgebrauch eine eigene Färbung angenommen haben. Ausgelassen sind lateinische, französische und italienische Redewendungen, die zum Gemeingut aller europäischen Völker gehören. Auch auf die italienische Musikterminologie wird verzichtet, außer in Fällen, wo deutsche Gebrauchseigentümlichkeiten vorliegen bzw. wo im Deutschen eine Angabe des Genus und der Pluralformen im Interesse des Benutzers wünschenswert ist (z.B. für die substantivische Verwendung von **Adagio** und **Andante**). Was lateinische Wörter und Redewendungen betrifft, so sei der englische Leser warnend darauf hingewiesen, daß darin der sprachliche Vorrat des gebildeten Deutschen beträchtlich von seinem eigenen abweicht, daß eine bekannte lateinische Redensart in der deutschen Verwendung bisweilen einen ihm fremden Klang besitzt, und ferner, daß Wörter lateinischen Ursprungs im österreichischen Sprachgebrauch sogar eine vollkommen unerwartete Bedeutung annehmen können. Der deutsche Leser sollte seinerseits daran denken, daß der Engländer allgemein mit dem Italienischen wenig vertraut ist und daß die in der deutschen Wirtschaftsterminologie üblichen italienischen Ausdrücke in England ungebräuchlich sind. Wörter oder Ausdrücke dieser Art erscheinen an alphabetischer Stelle.

Namen von Städten, Gebieten, Flüssen usw. werden nicht angegeben, außer wenn sie in literarischem, historischem oder politischem Zusammenhang von Bedeutung sind bzw. wenn sie in den beiden Sprachen orthographische Unterschiede aufweisen. Bezeichnungen von weniger wichtigen Mineralien, gebildet aus einem Eigennamen unter Anfügung des Suffixes *-ite* im Englischen und dem maskulinen Suffix **-it** im Deutschen, werden gewöhnlich nur dann aufgeführt, wenn in einer der beiden Sprachen abweichende Bezeichnungen auftreten.

Die folgenden Erläuterungen sind als Hilfe für die Benutzung des Wörterbuches gedacht:

REIHENFOLGE DER STICHWÖRTER: Im Unterschied zu vielen großen zweisprachigen Wörterbüchern hält *Harrap's Standard German and English Dictionary* überall eine streng alphabetische Reihenfolge ein. Die einzige Ausnahme bilden abgewandelte Verbformen, die jeweils unter dem Infinitiv des Verbs erscheinen.

ZUSAMMENGESETZTE SUBSTANTIVE: Genitiv- und Pluralendungen werden bei zusammengesetzten Substantiven nicht angegeben. Sie stimmen mit den entsprechenden Formen des letzten Zusammensetzungsgliedes überein und können unter dem jeweiligen Simplex an alphabetischer Stelle nachgeschlagen werden.

ORTHOGRAPHIE UND INTERPUNKTION: Als Richtlinien für die deutsche und englische Orthographie liegen die Duden-Rechtschreibung und das Oxford English Dictionary zugrunde.

Die Genitive von Eigennamen werden folgendermaßen angegeben:

a) **-s** bedeutet, daß der Name im Genitiv ein angehängtes **s** hat, wenn er ohne Artikel gebraucht wird, daß er jedoch in Verbindung mit einem Artikel unverändert bleibt (z.B. **Adam; Adams Fall,** aber **der Fall des Adam**).

b) **[']** bei auf **s, ß, z, tz** oder **x** endenden Namen bedeutet, daß der Genitiv beim Gebrauch

ohne Artikel durch einen Apostroph bezeichnet wird, nach einem Artikel jedoch mit dem Nominativ übereinstimmt (z.B. **Achilles; Achilles' Schild**, aber **der Schild des Achilles**).

Deutsche Adjektive, die je nach Zusammenhang groß oder klein geschrieben werden (z.B. **deutsch, englisch, achäisch, dorisch**) erscheinen der Einfachheit halber im Stichworteintrag mit kleinem Anfangsbuchstaben. Anwendungsbeispiele für die Großschreibung werden innerhalb des Artikels gegeben.

Den geltenden Grundsätzen des Dudens entsprechend wird die **ph**-Schreibweise der **f**-Schreibweise vorgezogen. Zwischen **C, K** und **Z** schwankt die deutsche Rechtschreibung. Wörter, die unter dem Buchstaben **C** nicht erscheinen, sind unter **K** oder **Z** nachzuschlagen und umgekehrt.

Anführungszeichen werden durchgehend nach englischer Art (oben) gesetzt.

Der Gebrauch des Bindestrichs (*hyphen*) im heutigen Englisch wirft für den Lexikographen unlösbare Probleme auf. Das nordamerikanische Englisch scheint den Bindestrich großenteils schon verworfen zu haben, und viele im Oxford English Dictionary aufgeführte Bindestrichformen können im modernen Gebrauch nicht mehr als natürliche Schreibweise angesprochen werden. Man gibt den Vorzug jetzt eindeutig der getrennten Schreibung (z.B. *love affair*, *dog racing*) bzw. der Zusammenschreibung (z.B. *bathtub*, *horserace*, *textbook*). Eine übereinstimmende Handhabung des Bindestrichs besteht allerdings immer noch bei den aus drei Wörtern gebildeten substantivischen Zusammensetzungen, wo der Bindestrich das Verhältnis zwischen Grund- und Bestimmungselement klärt (z.B. *return-flue boiler*). Abgesehen davon gibt es keine festliegenden Regeln für den Gebrauch des Bindestrichs im heutigen Englisch. Es kann nur darauf hingewiesen werden, daß er in der Sprache der Verwaltung, Wirtschaft und Naturwissenschaft auffallend häufig vermieden wird. In diesem Wörterbuch werden Bindestrichformen nur da verwandt, wo sie der heutige englische Leser als natürlich empfindet.

Zur Interpunktion innerhalb der einzelnen Artikel vergleiche man den Abschnitt *Zur Einrichtung des Wörterbuches* (Punkt 6).

DEUTSCHE AUSSPRACHE: Rein deutsche Wörter werden gewöhnlich auf der ersten Silbe betont. Auf **-ei** endende Substantive tragen den Ton jedoch auf der letzten Silbe (siehe den Artikel **-ei**). Die Präfixe **be-, ent-, ge-, ver-** usw. bleiben unbetont (siehe die jeweiligen Präfix-Artikel). Im übrigen sei der Leser auf die Bemerkungen zur Liste der phonetischen Umschrift (*Table of Phonetic Symbols*) verwiesen.

ZUR EINRICHTUNG DES WÖRTERBUCHES

1. Stark konjugierte Verben sind als solche bezeichnet. Das Fehlen einer Konjugationsangabe bedeutet, daß das betreffende Verb schwach konjugiert wird. Zusammengesetzte Verben werden wie das Simplex konjugiert, wenn nicht ein ausdrücklicher Hinweis auf abweichende Behandlung vorliegt.

2. In den Abschnitten über die Verbalsubstantive (*vbl s.*) innerhalb der Verbartikel wird die Angabe *in vbl senses* benutzt, um darauf hinzuweisen, daß englische Verben, die vorher in

demselben Artikel als Übersetzungen erscheinen, parallele Substantivformen auf *-ing* besitzen (z.B. *age, ageing; burn, burning*).

3. Am Ende eines Verbalsubstantiv-Eintrages erscheint bisweilen ein Hinweis auf ein maskulines oder feminines Substantiv, das von demselben Verb abgeleitet ist (z.B. III. *vbl s.* **1. Ablassen,** *n.* . . . /**2. Ablassung,** *f.* . . . *Cp.* **Ablaß;** III. *vbl s.* **Angeben,** *n.* . . . *Cp.* **Angabe**). Solche Verweise bedeuten, daß sich der Gebrauch von **Ablassen** und **Ablaß,** von **Angeben** und **Angabe** usw. hier und da überschneidet und der Benutzer unter dem Artikel, auf den er verwiesen wird, u.U. weitere Übersetzungsmöglichkeiten nachschlagen kann.

4. Die Formel **etwas** *gen.* wird verwandt, um Mißverständnissen vorzubeugen, die bei dem in anderen Wörterbüchern üblichen **einer Sache** leicht möglich sind. **etwas** vertritt hier Substantive, die häufig in Form von Verbalsubstantiven auftreten, für die **Sache** kaum die gegebene Abkürzung wäre. So kann in der Wendung **etwas** *gen.* **kundig sein** das **etwas** anstelle von **des Lesens, des Schreibens** usw. stehen, was also keineswegs Sachen sind.

5. *esp.* lese man in Verbartikeln als ‚in speziellem Sinne‘. In anderen Artikeln bedeutet *esp.* ‚insbesondere‘. Z.B. **Dreesch,** *m.* **-es/-e, Dreeschbrache,** *f. Agr:* green fallow, *esp.* used for pasture (hier wird darauf hingewiesen, daß der mit ‚green fallow‘ wiedergegebene deutsche Terminus sich insbesondere auf Weideland bezieht) oder **Eisenhut,** *m.* . . . **2.** *Bot:* aconite, *esp.* monk's-hood (d.h. die englische Entsprechung des deutschen Pflanzennamens ist ‚aconite‘ und insbesondere die als ‚monk's-hood‘ bekannte Abart davon).

6. Sobald innerhalb eines Artikels bzw. seiner Unterabteilungen mehrere Übersetzungen angegeben sind, werden sie entweder durch Komma oder Semikolon voneinander getrennt. Durch Komma voneinander getrennte Übersetzungen dürfen im gleichen englischen Kontext als austauschbar angesehen werden. Ein Semikolon zeigt jedoch gewöhnlich an, daß in bezug auf den vorhergehenden Ausdruck eine bedeutende Nuancen- oder Gebrauchsverschiebung vorliegt. Eine solche Anordnung verhindert leider die exakte Verwendung des großen Anfangsbuchstabens in Wendungen wie *Dear Sir, Oh dear!* (die als *dear Sir, oh dear!* verzeichnet werden müssen), was nicht als Abweichung von der Regel zu werten ist, die am Anfang jeder selbständigen Aussage Großschreibung verlangt. Gelegentlich dient ein Semikolon auch einfach dazu, eine komplizierte Aufzählung für den Leser übersichtlicher zu machen.

7. Einige der in diesem Wörterbuch zur Klassifizierung der Stichwörter benutzten Abkürzungen sind anstelle eines Doppelpunktes mit einem Punkt versehen. Dies ist der Fall bei doppelten Klassifizierungen, z.B. *Hist. & F:* oder *Hist. of Med:* Der Punkt wird auch in Klassifizierungen wie *A.Hist:* verwandt, was als ‚Ancient History‘ (Alte Geschichte) zu lesen ist, während *Hist: A:* bedeutet, daß das bezeichnete deutsche Wort einen historischen Begriff darstellt und darüberhinaus als Wort selbst heute veraltet ist.

8. Kursiver Text in Klammern (gewöhnlich der Übersetzung vorangestellt) ist lediglich als Erklärung gedacht, nicht aber als Teil der vorgeschlagenen Übersetzung. In dem Beispiel ‚**bedeuten.** I. *v.tr.* **1.** (*a*) (*of word, phrase, etc.*) to mean, signify‘ soll dem Benutzer mitgeteilt werden, daß wenn ein Wort, eine stehende Wendung usw. als Subjekt zu dem Verb **bedeuten** tritt, die zutreffende Übersetzung ‚to mean‘ oder ‚to signify‘ ist. In dem Beispiel ‚**bäh,** *int.*

(i) (*bleat of sheep*) baa; (ii) (*mocking*) yah! boo to you!' definiert die kursiv gedruckte Erklärung den spezifischen Sinn des Wortes in jeder seiner Anwendungen.

Eingeklammerter Text in Antiqua wird folgendermaßen verwandt:

a) zur Bezeichnung eines dem Benutzer freigestellten Übersetzungszusatzes, z.B. ,**Barsoi, *m.* -s/-s,** borzoi (hound)' (wo ,borzoi' oder ,borzoi hound' gleich richtige englische Entsprechungen sind);

b) zur Bezeichnung eines definierenden Zusatzes, der u.U. für die eindeutige Übersetzung wünschenswert ist, aber dort weggelassen werden kann, wo der Begriff vom Zusammenhang her bereits unmißverständlich festliegt, z.B. ,**Bauscht,** *m.* -(e)s/-e. *Paperm:* post (of 180 sheets)'; ,**Auerhahn,** *m. Orn:* (cock) capercaillie'; ,**Auerhenne,** *f. Orn:* (hen) capercaillie';

c) zur Bezeichnung der Kategorie von Substantiven, auf die sich ein Adjektiv gewöhnlich bezieht, oder von Substantiven, die zu einem in bestimmtem Sinne gebrauchten Verb als Objekt treten können—z.B. ,**deutschsprachig,** *a.* German-speaking (population, etc.)'; ,**anfechten.** I. *v.tr. sep.* (*strong*) to contest, dispute (opinion, statement, s.o.'s right, etc.)'. In Verbeinträgen dieser Art werden die Beispielobjekte meist ohne Artikel angegeben, da die Übersetzung je nach Zusammenhang ,a', ,the', ,his', ,any' usw. verlangt.

9. Wenn ein Zusammensetzungselement verschiedene Formen annehmen kann, z.B. **Buch-** und **Bücher-,** dann werden die Komposita im allgemeinen nur in der häufiger auftretenden Form angegeben: z.B. **Buchladen, Bücherwissen.** Um nicht durch unnötige Wiederholungen (**Bücherladen, Buchwissen** usw.) Platz zu verschwenden, werden Querverweise gegeben (z.B. **Buch-,** *comb.fm. cp.* **Bücher-,** ...; und **Bücher-,** *comb.fm. cp.* **Buch-**), die dem Benutzer sagen sollen, daß das in der einen Form aufgeführte Kompositum mit der nicht angegebenen Variante bedeutungsgleich ist.

10. Das Symbol = wird nicht nur verwandt, um den Benutzer auf ein an anderer Stelle aufgeführtes Synonym zu verweisen, sondern gelegentlich auch, um eine gewisse Übereinstimmung zwischen deutschen und englischen Institutionen da anzudeuten, wo die auf solche Weise nebeneinandergestellten Termini genau genommen nicht als gegenseitige Übersetzungen anzusprechen sind. So etwa: **Amtsrichter,** *m. Jur:* district court judge (=English county court judge); **Arnim-Paragraph, der.** *Jur:*=the Official Secrets Act. In der Praxis wird der Übersetzer eine deutsche Bezeichnung dieser Art meist unübersetzt lassen und die angegebene Entsprechung in einer erklärenden Fußnote verwenden.

11. Um keine Zweifel über die Verwendung der Abkürzungen *F:*, *P:* usw. aufkommen zu lassen, sei dem Leser mitgeteilt, daß sie sich in erster Linie auf das deutsche Stichwort beziehen, wenn sie unmittelbar danach erscheinen, daß aber ein innerhalb des Artikels folgendes *F:* oder *P:* nur für die nachstehende englische Übersetzung gilt. Der Artikel ,**anranzen,** *v.tr. sep. F:* to give (s.o.) a dressing-down, *F:* to blow (s.o.) up, tell (s.o.) off' ist zum Beispiel so zu verstehen, daß das Wort **anranzen** selber der deutschen Umgangssprache angehört, daß ,to give someone a dressing-down' ein durchaus normaler englischer Ausdruck ist, während ,to blow someone up' und ,to tell someone off' als umgangssprachlich anzusehen sind.

12. Sprichwörter, sprichwörtliche Redensarten usw. werden unter dem ersten wichtigen oder unter dem hauptsächlich interessierenden Wort angegeben.

13. Da das Wörterbuch in mehreren Teilbänden erscheinen soll, ist es nicht möglich, vor Fertigstellung der Arbeit sämtliche Querverweise einzutragen. In diesem Bande sind deshalb hier und da Lücken gelassen, an deren Stelle im vollständigen Werk die entsprechenden Verweise stehen werden. Eine Liste deutscher Abkürzungen folgt am Ende des letzten deutsch-englischen Teilbandes.

Unser besonderer Dank gilt Frau Dr. E. Rosenbaum, die mit ihrer Bemühung um die Einrichtung und redaktionelle Bearbeitung des Materials entscheidenden Anteil am Erfolg der Arbeit hat. Gleicher Dank gebührt Miß E. L. R. Goodwin für ihre organisatorische Leistung bei der Koordinierung der Redaktionsaufgaben und mit ihr allen früheren and jetzigen lexikographischen Mitarbeitern. Wertvolle Hilfe bei der Herstellung einer umfassenden Liste europäischer und anderer Vogelnamen für die Verarbeitung in diesem Wörterbuch erfuhren wir von drei hervorragenden Fachleuten, Dr. W. Przygodda, Dr. H. Frieling und Mr. H. T. Porter, denen wir hiermit unseren Dank aussprechen. Ebenso verpflichtet sind wir Mr. J. L. M. Trim für die Erstellung unseres phonetischen Umschriftsystems, den Herren Dr. E. Meyers (Kulturattaché an der Botschaft der Vereinigten Staaten in London) und Professor B. Q. Morgan für ihre beratende Unterstützung bei der Aufnahme amerikanischer Ausdrücke, Frau Professor Dr. G. Bing und Mr. J. C. T. Oates für die kritische Durchsicht der Korrekturfahnen und ihre wertvollen Verbesserungsvorschläge, Mr. W. Schapiro für seine Hilfe beim Lesen der Korrekturen und der Firma William Clowes & Sons Ltd für die hervorragende Bewältigung unserer komplizierten setz- und drucktechnischen Probleme.

Wir danken der Firma D. C. Heath in Boston, U.S.A., für ihre vermittelnde Hilfe im Zusammenhang mit der Überprüfung des Manuskriptes in den Vereinigten Staaten und der London Library für die Überlassung von Van Wijks umfangreichem Dictionary of Plant Names. Dankbar erwähnen müssen wir ferner die ständige Unterstützung durch den Dudenverlag des Bibliographischen Instituts, Mannheim, und die Hilfe bei der Einstellung sprachlicher Fachkräfte, die uns von deutschen, österreichischen und englischen Universitäten zuteil wurde, insbesondere von Herrn Professor Dr. P. L. Jaeger, Leiter der Englisch-Amerikanischen Abteilung am Auslands- und Dolmetscherinstitut der Universität Mainz in Germersheim.

Viel zu verdanken haben wir Herrn Professor Dr. L. W. Forster und Mr. C. H. Barker, auf deren reiches Wissen der Herausgeber seit vielen Jahren immer wieder zurückgreifen darf und die ihm bei der Lösung mancher lexikalischer Probleme entscheidende Hilfe gewährten.

Mr. R. P. L. Ledésert hat das Werk von Anfang an großzügig gefördert. Wir schätzen uns glücklich, seine Erfahrung und sein Können auf dem Gebiete der Lexikographie zu unserer ständigen Verfügung zu haben.

Zum Schluß danken wir der großen Zahl von Fachleuten aus allen Berufen und vielen anderen freundlichen Helfern im In- und Ausland, die auf unsere Bitte oder auch rein zufällig ihre besonderen Kenntnisse in den Dienst dieses Wörterbuches gestellt haben.

1963   TREVOR JONES

Representation of the Pronunciation

T H E pronunciation recorded in this Dictionary follows closely the 'Bühnenaussprache' as defined in Th. Siebs, *Deutsche Hochsprache*, 18th revised edition, Berlin 1961, to which the reader is referred for a more exhaustive treatment of the subject of German pronunciation.

The notation adopted in the Dictionary is constructed according to the principles of the International Phonetic Association. It is a 'word' notation, using the smallest number of symbols required to represent the pronunciation of words unambiguously. An exception is made, however, in the case of 'half-long' vowels. The German long vowels iː, oː, uː, yː and øː have a different quality from their short counterparts, the tongue being higher and more tense. In certain environments, particularly in unstressed syllables, long vowels are considerably shortened without any change in their quality; in these cases the reduction in length is indicated by the use of a single raised sign (ˑ), e.g. iˑ, øˑ. The stress is indicated by strong and secondary accents (ˈ) (ˌ) which precede the stressed syllables: **Ablativ** [ˈaplaˑtiːf]; **Analysis** [aˈnaːlyˑzis]; **Analyse** [anaˑˈlyːzə]; **antediluvianisch** [ˌanteˑdiˑluˑvĭˈaːniʃ].

Phonetic transcriptions are given for foreign words and German words with peculiarities of pronunciation, but not for compounds of these forms. No phonetic transcription is given for the plural or genitive forms, unless there is a shift of stress or a change in pronunciation caused by the addition of a final vowel, consonant or syllable.

TABLE OF PHONETIC SYMBOLS

VOWELS

a	hat	hat		u	rund	runt
aˑ	deklamieren	deˑklaˑˈmiːrən		uˑ	kulinarisch	kuˑliˑˈnaːriʃ
aː	Wagen	ˈvaːgən		uː	Kugel	ˈkuːgəl
eˑ	deklamieren	deˑklaˑˈmiːrən		ŭ	Betschuane	bɛtʃŭˈaːnə
eː	Ehre	ˈeːrə		ɛ	Feld	fɛlt
ə	fehlen	ˈfeːlən		ɛˑ	Mätresse	mɛˑˈtrɛsə
ĭ	ist	ist		ɛː	Ähre	ˈɛːrə
iˑ	bipolar	biˑpoˑˈlaːr		ø	völlig	ˈføliç
iː	wieder	ˈviːdər		øˑ	Ökonom	øˑkoˑˈnoːm
i	Adoption	aˑdoptsĭˈoːn		øː	böse	ˈbøːzə
o	Holz	holts		y	Fülle	ˈfylə
oˑ	Oboe	oˑˈboːə		yˑ	Dynamit	dyˑnaˑˈmiːt
oː	ohne	ˈoːnə		yː	lügen	ˈlyːgən

DIPHTHONGS

ai	frei	frai		oy	treu	troy
au	Haus	haus				

VOWEL SYMBOLS IN FOREIGN PRONUNCIATIONS

æ	Jamboree	dʒæmboˈriː		ɛ̃ː	Azilien	aˈziˑlĭˈɛ̃ː
ã˙	} Arrangement	arã˙ʒəˈmãː		õː	Affront	aˈfrõː
ãː				œ̃ː	Parfum	parˈfœ̃ː
əː	Merchandising	ˈməːtʃəndaiziŋ		ɔː	Crawl	krɔːl

CONSONANTS

b	Benzin	bɛnˈtsiːn		ŋk	Dank	daŋk
ç	ich	iç		p	Person	pɛrˈzoːn
d	Doktor	ˈdoktor			abnehmen	ˈapneːmən
f	für	fyːr		r	Rede	ˈreːdə
	von	fon			aber	ˈaːbər
g	ganz	gants		r	Homeruler	ˈhoumruːlər
h	Hase	ˈhaːzə		s	Maus	maus
j	Jot	jot		ʃ	Tisch	tiʃ
k	Kahn	kaːn		t	trinken	ˈtriŋkən
	Tag	taːk			rund	runt
ks	boxen	ˈboksən		v	was	vas
kv	Qual	kvaːl			Villa	ˈvila
	Akquisition	akviˑziˑtsĭˈoːn		w	Gangway	ˈgæŋweː
l	lachen	ˈlaxən		x	lachen	ˈlaxən
m	Mann	man		z	Hase	ˈhaːzə
n	naß	nas		ʒ	Blamage	blaˈmaːʒə
ŋ	lang	laŋ		θ	Bathoolit	baːθˑoˑrˈliːt
	singen	ˈziŋən		ð	Rutherford	ˈraðərfəd
ŋg	fingiert	fiŋˈgiːrt				

OTHER SYMBOLS

ˈ	Wagen	ˈvaːgən		ʔ	Alleinheit	alʔˈlainhait
(stress mark)	archimedisch	ˌarçiˑˈmeːdiʃ		(glottal stop)		

NOTE: the stress mark (ˈ) has also been used to indicate significant stress in English utterances, *e.g.* it ˈdoes matter.

Strong Verbs and Verbs with Anomalous Conjugation Forms

ONLY the strong and anomalous conjugation forms are included in the following list. In modern educated usage a considerable number of German verbs have both strong and weak conjugation or mixed weak and strong forms or alternative forms of limited use. In some instances these verbs are without distinction in meaning; sometimes they have minor distinctions in meaning or usage, and sometimes there is an essential distinction in meaning between the forms. Such verbs are indicated by an asterisk in the following list (*e.g.* *** backen**) and information on usage will be found in the relevant articles in the main body of the Dictionary. Where, however, verbs of different etymology or meaning have identical spellings and the strong conjugation or the variation in conjugation occurs only in one form of the verb, the entry in the verb table is marked with the superior number of the corresponding article in the dictionary (*e.g.* **bewegen**[2]).

At the colloquial speech-level, usage may be found to fluctuate between strong and weak forms. The town-dweller may avoid the strong form of the imperfect (*e.g.* **buk, molk**) because he feels it to have an archaic or pedantic flavour; he may nevertheless maintain it in a Biblical or pseudo-Biblical utterance. Regional or country speech, even at a highly-educated level, may consistently prefer strong forms that would seem incorrect to speakers of academic standard German.

There is, however, general agreement at all levels that the imperfect subjunctive of the strong verb (apart from everyday forms such as **ginge, käme**) has a markedly pedantic or rhetorical flavour and should be avoided in unpretentious utterances.

The following notes may be found helpful in using the list:

1. When a prefix (**be-, ent-, ver-, zusammen-,** etc.) is added to the simple strong verb, the conjugation forms are unaltered.

   The English reader should, however, be mindful of the existence of certain verbs constructed on the pattern *prefix+noun+*(e)n, *e.g.* **beinhalten** (=**be-Inhalt-en**), **veranlassen** (=**ver-Anlaß-en**). Such verbs have the weak conjugation, even though their last element appears to be identical with a strong verb.

2. The past participle normally has the augment **ge-**; for exceptions to this rule see the article **ge-** in the main body of the Dictionary.

3. The so-called 'modal auxiliaries' or 'auxiliaries of mood' (**dürfen, können, mögen, müssen, sollen, wollen**) have two forms of the past participle, one of them being identical with the infinitive; the choice of form depends on the construction. In modern colloquial German there is a growing tendency to use certain other verbs (*e.g.* **lernen, sehen**) with a similar second past participle form, identical with the infinitive. On this question the reader is advised to consult a good Grammar, *e.g. Der Große Duden: Die Grammatik der deutschen Gegenwartssprache;* G. O. Curme, *A Grammar of the German Language* (Frederick Ungar Publishing Company); F. J. Stopp, *Manual of Modern German* (University Tutorial Press Ltd).

4. In modern usage, the singular form of the imperative in speech or reported speech is normally without a final **e** (*e.g.* **spring!** is preferred, rather than **springe!**); the spelling with an apostrophe (*e.g.* **spring'!**) is to be avoided.

   The second person plural of the imperative and of the present tense are formed by adding **t** to the verb stem. They are accordingly identical in spelling with the third person singular of the present tense, except where the third person singular present undergoes a vowel change.

Verb Table

STRONG AND ANOMALOUS CONJUGATION FORMS

Infinitive	Present Tense 2nd pers. sg.	Present Tense 3rd pers. sg.	Imperative 2nd pers. sg.	Imperfect Indicative 3rd pers. sg.	Imperfect Subjunctive 3rd pers. sg.	Past Participle (see Notes 2, 3)
*backen	bäckst	bäckt	back(e)!	buk	büke	gebacken
befehlen	befiehlst	befiehlt	befiehl!	befahl	befähle, beföhle	befohlen
befleißen (sich)	befleiß(es)t	befleißt	befleiß(e)!	befliß	beflisse	beflissen
beginnen	beginnst	beginnt	beginn(e)!	begann	begänne begönne	begonnen
beißen	beiß(es)t	beißt	beiß(e)!	biß	bisse	gebissen
*beklemmen	—	—	—	—	—	beklommen
bergen	birgst	birgt	birg!	barg	bärge, bürge	geborgen
*bersten	birst	birst	birst!	barst occ. borst	bärste occ. börste	geborsten
betrügen	betrügst	betrügt	betrüg(e)!	betrog	betröge	betrogen
bewegen[2]	bewegst	bewegt	beweg(e)!	bewog	bewöge	bewogen
biegen	biegst	biegt	bieg(e)!	bog	böge	gebogen
bieten	bietest A: beutst	bietet A: beut	biet(e)! A: beut!	bot	böte	geboten
binden	bindest	bindet	bind(e)!	band	bände	gebunden
bitten	bittest	bittet	bitte! bitt!	bat	bäte	gebeten
blasen	bläs(es)t	bläst	blas(e)!	blies	bliese	geblasen
bleiben	bleibst	bleibt	bleib(e)!	blieb	bliebe	geblieben
*bleichen	bleichst	bleicht	—	blich	bliche	geblichen
*braten	brätst	brät	brat(e)!	briet	briete	gebraten
*brechen	brichst	bricht	brich!	brach	bräche	gebrochen
brennen	brennst	brennt	brenn(e)!	brannte	brennte	gebrannt
bringen	bringst	bringt	bring(e)!	brachte	brächte	gebracht
denken	denkst	denkt	denk(e)!	dachte	dächte	gedacht
*dingen	dingst	dingt	ding(e)!	occ. dang A: dung	occ. dänge A: dünge	gedungen
dreschen	drischst	drischt	drisch!	drosch A: drasch	drösche A: dräsche	gedroschen
dringen	dringst	dringt	dring(e)!	drang	dränge	gedrungen
*dünken	—	es deucht mich, mir, usw.	—	deuchte	deuchte	gedeucht
dürfen	darfst	darf	—	durfte	dürfte	gedurft; dürfen
empfangen	empfängst	empfängt	empfang(e)!	empfing	empfinge	empfangen
empfehlen	empfiehlst	empfiehlt	empfiehl!	empfahl	empfähle empföhle	empfohlen
empfinden	empfindest	empfindet	empfind(e)!	empfand	empfände	empfunden
*erbleichen	erbleichst	erbleicht	erbleich(e)!	erblich	erbliche	erblichen
*erkiesen	erkies(es)t	erkiest	erkies(e)!	erkor	erköre	erkoren
erlöschen	erlisch(e)st	erlischt	erlisch!	erlosch	erlösche	erloschen
*erschallen	erschallst	erschallt	erschall(e)!	erscholl	erschölle	erschollen
*erschrecken	erschrickst	erschrickt	erschrick!	erschrak	erschräke	erschrocken
*erwägen	erwägst	erwägt	erwäg(e)!	erwog	erwöge	erwogen
essen	ißt, issest	ißt	iß!	aß	äße	gegessen
fahren	fährst	fährt	fahr(e)!	fuhr	führe	gefahren
fallen	fällst	fällt	fall(e)!	fiel	fiele	gefallen
fangen	fängst	fängt	fang(e)!	fing	finge	gefangen
fechten	fichtst, fichst	ficht	ficht!	focht	föchte	gefochten
finden	findest	findet	find(e)!	fand	fände	gefunden
flechten	flichtst, flichst	flicht	flicht!	flocht	flöchte	geflochten
fliegen	fliegst A: fleugst	fliegt A: fleugt	flieg(e)! A: fleug!	flog	flöge	geflogen
fliehen	flieh(e)st A: fleuch(e)st	flieht A: fleucht	flieh(e)! A: fleuch!	floh	flöhe	geflohen
fließen	fließ(es)t A: fleußt	fließt A: fleußt	fließ(e)! A: fleuß!	floß	flösse	geflossen
*fragen	Dial: frägst	Dial: frägt	—	Dial: frug	Dial: früge	—
fressen	frißt, frissest	frißt	friß!	fraß	fräße	gefressen
frieren	frierst	friert	frier(e)!	fror	fröre	gefroren
*gären	gärst	gärt	gär(e)!	gor	göre	gegoren
*gebären	gebierst	gebiert	gebier!	gebar	gebäre	geboren
geben	gibst	gibt	gib!	gab	gäbe	gegeben
gedeihen	gedeihst	gedeiht	gedeih(e)!	gedieh	gediehe	gediehen
gehen	gehst	geht	geh(e)!	ging	ginge	gegangen
gelingen	—	gelingt	geling(e)!	gelang	gelänge	gelungen
gelten[1]	giltst	gilt	gilt!	galt	gälte, gölte	gegolten
genesen	genes(es)t	genest	genes(e)!	genas	genäse	genesen
genießen	genieß(es)t	genießt	genieß(e)!	genoß	genösse	genossen
geraten	gerätst	gerät	gerat(e)!	geriet	geriete	geraten
geschehen	—	geschieht Dial: geschicht	—	geschah	geschähe	geschehen

Infinitive	Present Tense		Imperative	Imperfect		Past Participle (see Notes 2, 3)
	2nd pers. sg.	3rd pers. sg.	2nd pers. sg.	Indicative	Subjunctive	
				3rd pers. sg.		
gewinnen	gewinnst	gewinnt	gewinn(e)!	gewann	gewänne gewönne	gewonnen
gießen	gieß(es)t *A:* geuß(es)t	gießt *A:* geußt	gieß(e)! *A:* geuß!	goß	gösse	gegossen
gleichen	gleichst	gleicht	gleich(e)!	glich	gliche	geglichen
gleißen	gleiß(es)t	gleißt	gleiß(e)!	*A:* gliß	*A:* glisse	*A:* geglissen
*gleiten	gleitest	gleitet	gleit(e)!	glitt	glitte	geglitten
*glimmen	glimmst	glimmt	glimm(e)!	glomm	glömme	geglommen
graben	gräbst	gräbt	grab(e)!	grub	grübe	gegraben
greifen	greifst	greift	greif(e)!	griff	griffe	gegriffen
haben	hast	hat	hab(e)!	hatte	hätte	gehabt
halten	hältst	hält	halt(e)!	hielt *A:* hätte	hielte	gehalten
A: hangen	hangst, hängst	hangt, hängt	hang(e)! häng(e)!	hing	hinge	gehangen
*hängen	hängst	hängt	häng(e)!	hing	hinge	gehangen
*hauen	haust	haut	hau(e)!	hieb	hiebe	gehauen
heben	hebst	hebt	heb(e)!	hob, *A:* hub	höbe, *A:* hübe	gehoben
*heißen[1]	heiß(es)t	heißt	heiß(e)!	hieß	hieße	geheißen *occ.* gehießen; heißen
helfen	hilfst	hilft	hilf!	half	hülfe, *occ.* hälfe	geholfen; helfen
kennen	kennst	kennt	kenn(e)!	kannte	kennte	gekannt
*kiesen	kies(es)t	kiest	kies(e)!	kor	köre	gekoren
*kleiben	kleibst	kleibt	kleib(e)!	*A:* klieb	*A:* kliebe	*A:* gekloben
*klieben	kliebst	kliebt	klieb(e)	klob	klöbe	gekloben
*klimmen	klimmst	klimmt	klimm(e)!	klomm	klömme	geklommen
klingen	klingst	klingt	kling(e)!	klang	klänge	geklungen
kneifen	kneifst	kneift	kneif(e)!	kniff	kniffe	gekniffen
*kneipen	kneipst	kneipt	kneip(e)!	knipp	knippe	geknippen
kommen	kommst, *A. &* *Dial:* kömmst	kommt, *A. &* *Dial:* kömmt	komm(e)!	kam	käme	gekommen, *A. &* *Dial:* kommen
können	kannst	kann	—	konnte	könnte	gekonnt; können
*kreischen	kreisch(e)st	kreischt	kreisch(e)!	*Dial:* krisch	*Dial:* krische	*Dial:* gekrischen
kriechen	kriechst *A:* kreuchst	kriecht *A:* kreucht	kriech(e)! *A:* kreuch!	kroch	kröche	gekrochen
*küren	kürst	kürt	kür(e)!	kor	köre	gekoren
laden[2]	lädst	lädt	lad(e)!	lud	lüde	geladen
laden[3]	lädst	lädt	lad(e)!	lud	lüde	geladen
lassen	läßt, lässest	läßt	laß! lasse!	ließ	ließe	gelassen; lassen
laufen	läufst	läuft	lauf(e)!	lief	liefe	gelaufen
leiden	leidest	leidet	leid(e)!	litt	litte	gelitten
leihen	leihst	leiht	leih(e)!	lieh	liehe	geliehen
lesen	lies(es)t	liest	lies!	las	läse	gelesen
liegen	liegst	liegt	lieg(e)!	lag	läge	gelegen
*löschen[1]	lisch(e)st	lischt	lisch!	losch	lösche	geloschen
lügen	lügst	lügt	lüg(e)!	log	löge	gelogen
*mahlen						gemahlen
meiden	meidest	meidet	meid(e)!	mied	miede	gemieden
*melken	milkst	milkt	milk!	molk	mölke	gemolken
messen	mißt, missest	mißt	miß!	maß	mäße	gemessen
mißlingen		mißlingt	—	mißlang	mißlänge	mißlungen
mögen	magst	mag	—	mochte	möchte	gemocht; mögen
müssen	mußt	muß	—	mußte	müßte	gemußt; müssen
nehmen	nimmst	nimmt	nimm!	nahm	nähme	genommen
nennen	nennst	nennt	nenn(e)	nannte	nennte	genannt
pfeifen	pfeifst	pfeift	pfeif(e)!	pfiff	pfiffe	gepfiffen
*pflegen	pflegst	pflegt	pfleg(e)!	pflog *A:* pflag	pflöge *A:* pfläge	gepflogen
preisen	preis(es)t	preist	preis(e)!	pries	priese	gepriesen
*quellen	quillst	quillt	quill!	quoll	quölle	gequollen
Dial: quillen						
*rächen	—	—	—	—	—	*A.&Hum:* gerochen
raten	rätst	rät	rat(e)!	riet	riete	geraten
reiben	reibst	reibt	reib(e)!	rieb	riebe	gerieben
*reihen[1]	reih(e)st	reiht	reih(e)!	rieh	riehe	geriehen
reißen	reiß(es)t	reißt	reiß(e)!	riß	risse	gerissen
reiten	reitest	reitet	reit(e)!	ritt	ritte	geritten
rennen	rennst	rennt	renn(e)!	rannte	rennte	gerannt
riechen	riechst	riecht	riech(e)!	roch	röche	gerochen
ringen	ringst	ringt	ring(e)	rang	ränge	gerungen
rinnen	rinnst	rinnt	rinn(e)!	rann	ränne, *occ.* rönne	geronnen
rufen	rufst	ruft	ruf(e)!	rief	riefe	gerufen
*salzen						gesalzen
saufen	säufst	säuft	sauf(e)!	soff	söffe	gesoffen
*saugen	saugst	saugt	saug(e)!	sog	söge	gesogen
schaffen[1]	schaffst	schafft	schaff(e)!	schuf	schüfe	geschaffen
*schallen	schallst	schallt	schall(e)!	scholl	schölle	geschallt
scheiden	scheidest	scheidet	scheid(e)!	schied	schiede	geschieden
scheinen	scheinst	scheint	schein(e)!	schien	schiene	geschienen
scheißen	scheiß(es)t	scheißt	scheiß(e)!	schiß	schisse	geschissen
*schelten	schiltst	schilt	schilt!	schalt	schölte	gescholten
*scheren[1]	*A:* schierst	*A:* schiert	*A:* schier!	schor	schöre	geschoren
schieben	schiebst	schiebt	schieb(e)!	schob	schöbe	geschoben
schießen	schieß(es)t	schießt	schieß(e)!	schoß	schösse	geschossen
*schinden	schindest	schindet	schind(e)!	schund	schünde	geschunden
schlafen	schläfst	schläft	schlaf(e)!	schlief	schliefe	geschlafen
schlagen	schlägst	schlägt	schlag(e)!	schlug	schlüge	geschlagen
schleichen	schleichst	schleicht	schleich(e)!	schlich	schliche	geschlichen
schleifen[2]	schleifst	schleift	schleif(e)!	schliff	schliffe	geschliffen
*schleißen	schleiß(es)t	schleißt	schleiß(e)!	schliß	schlisse	geschlissen

| Infinitive | Present Tense | | Imperative | Imperfect | | Past Participle (see Notes 2, 3) |
| | 2nd pers. sg. | 3rd pers. sg. | 2nd pers. sg. | Indicative | Subjunctive | |
				3rd pers. sg.		
schliefen	schliefst	schlieft	schlief(e)!	schloff	schlöffe	geschloffen
schließen	schließ(es)t	schließt	schließ(e)!	schloß	schlösse	geschlossen
	A. & Poet: schleuß(es)t	*A. & Poet:* schleußt	*A. & Poet:* schleuß(e)!			
schlingen	schlingst	schlingt	schling(e)!	schlang	schlänge	geschlungen
*schmalzen	—					geschmalzen
*schmeißen	schmeiß(es)t	schmeißt	schmeiß(e)!	schmiß	schmisse	geschmissen
*schmelzen	schmilz(es)t	schmilzt	schmilz!	schmolz	schmölze	geschmolzen
*schnauben	schnaubst	schnaubt	schnaub(e)!	schnob	schnöbe	geschnoben
schneiden	schneid(e)st	schneidet	schneid(e)!	schnitt	schnitte	geschnitten
*schrecken	schrickst	schrickt	schrick!	schrak	schräke	geschrocken
schreiben	schreibst	schreibt	schreib(e)!	schrieb	schriebe	geschrieben
schreien	schreist	schreit	schrei(e)!	schrie	schriee	geschrie(e)n
schreiten	schreitest	schreitet	schreit(e)!	schritt	schritte	geschritten
A: schrinden	schrind(e)st	schrindet	—	schrund	schründe	geschrunden
*schroten						*A:* geschroten
*schwären	—	*A:* es schwiert	*A:* schwier!	*A:* schwor	*A:* schwöre	*A:* geschworen
schweigen	schweigst	schweigt	schweig(e)!	schwieg	schwiege	geschwiegen
*schwellen	schwillst	schwillt	schwill!	schwoll	schwölle	geschwollen
schwimmen	schwimmst	schwimmt	schwimm(e)!	schwamm	schwämme schwömme	geschwommen
schwinden	schwindest	schwindet	schwind(e)!	schwand	schwände	geschwunden
schwingen	schwingst	schwingt	schwing(e)!	schwang	schwänge	geschwungen
*schwören	schwörst *occ.* schwurst	schwört *occ.* schwurt	schwör(e)!	schwor, schwur	schwüre	geschworen
sehen	siehst	sieht	sieh(e)!	sah	sähe	gesehen; sehen
sein	bist	ist	sei!	war	wäre	gewesen
*senden	sendest	sendet	send(e)!	sandte	sendete	gesandt
*sieden	siedest	siedet	sied(e)!	sott	sötte	gesotten
singen	singst	singt	sing(e)!	sang	sänge	gesungen
sinken	sinkst	sinkt	sink(e)!	sank	sänke	gesunken
sinnen	sinnst	sinnt	sinn(e)!	sann	sänne, sönne	gesonnen
sitzen	sitz(es)t	sitzt	sitz(e)!	saß	säße	gesessen
sollen	sollst	soll	—	sollte	sollte	gesollt; sollen
*spalten	spaltest	spaltet	spalt(e)!	spaltete	spaltete	gespalten
*speien	speist	speit	spei(e)!	spie	spie	gespie(e)n
spinnen	spinnst	spinnt	spinn(e)!	spann	spänne, spönne	gesponnen
*spleißen	spleiß(es)t	spleißt	spleiß(e)!	spliß	splisse	gesplissen
sprechen	sprichst	spricht	sprich!	sprach	spräche	gesprochen
sprießen	sprieß(es)t	sprießt	sprieß(e)!	sproß	sprösse	gesprossen
springen	springst	springt	spring(e)!	sprang	spränge	gesprungen
stechen	stichst	sticht	stich!	stach	stäche	gestochen
*stecken	steckst	steckt	steck(e)!	stak	stäke	gesteckt
stehen	stehst	steht	steh(e)!	stand *A:* stund	stände, stünde	gestanden
stehlen	stiehlst	stiehlt	stiehl!	stahl	stähle, stöhle	gestohlen
steigen	steigst	steigt	steig(e)!	stieg	stiege	gestiegen
sterben	stirbst	stirbt	stirb!	starb	stürbe	gestorben
*stieben	stiebst	stiebt	stieb(e)!	stob	stöbe	gestoben
stinken	stinkst	stinkt	stink(e)!	stank	stänke	gestunken
stoßen	stöß(es)t	stößt	stoß(e)!	stieß	stieße	gestoßen
streichen	streichst	streicht	streich(e)!	strich	striche	gestrichen
streiten	streitest	streitet	streit(e)!	stritt	stritte	gestritten
tragen	trägst	trägt	trag(e)!	trug	trüge	getragen
treffen	triffst	trifft	triff!	traf	träfe	getroffen
treiben	treibst	treibt	treib(e)!	trieb	triebe	getrieben
treten	trittst	tritt	tritt!	trat	träte	getreten
*triefen	triefst	trieft	trief(e)!	troff	tröffe	getroffen
trinken	trinkst	trinkt	trink(e)!	trank	tränke	getrunken
trügen	trügst	trügt	trüg(e)!	trog	tröge	getrogen
tun	tust	tut	tu(e)!	tat *A:* tät	täte	getan
verbleichen	verbleichst	verbleicht	verbleich(e)!	verblich	verbliche	verblichen
verderben	verdirbst	verdirbt	verdirb!	verdarb	verdürbe	verdorben
verdrießen	verdrieß(es)t	verdrießt	verdrieß(e)!	verdroß	verdrösse	verdrossen
vergessen	vergißt vergissest	vergißt	vergiß!	vergaß	vergäße	vergessen
verlieren	*Poet:* verlierst	verliert	verlier(e)!	verlor	verlöre	verloren
*verlöschen	verlischst	verlischt	verlisch!	verlosch	verlösche	verloschen
*verschallen	verschallst	verschallt	verschall(e)!	verscholl	verschölle	verschollen
*wachsen[1]	wächs(es)t	wächst	wachs(e)!	wuchs	wüchse	gewachsen
*wägen	wägst	wägt	wäg(e)!	wog	wöge	gewogen
waschen	wäsch(e)st	wäscht	wasch(e)!	wusch	wüsche	gewaschen
*weben	webst	webt	web(e)!	wob	wöbe	gewoben
weichen[1]	weichst	weicht	weich(e)!	wich	wiche	gewichen
weisen	weis(es)t	weist	weis(e)!	wies	wiese	gewiesen
*wenden	wendest	wendet	wend(e)!	wandte	wendete	gewandt
werben	wirbst	wirbt	wirb!	warb	würbe	geworben
werden	wirst	wird	werd(e)!	wurde *Poet:* ward	würde	geworden; worden
werfen	wirfst	wirft	wirf!	warf	würfe	geworfen
wiegen[2]	wiegst	wiegt	wieg(e)!	wog	wöge	gewogen
winden[1]	windest	windet	wind(e)!	wand	wände	gewunden
*winken						*occ.* gewunken
wissen	weißt	weiß	wisse!	wußte	wüßte	gewußt
wollen	willst	will	wolle!	wollte	wollte	gewollt; wollen
wringen	wringst	wringt	wring(e)!	wrang	wränge	gewrungen
*zeihen	zeihst	zeiht	zeih(e)!	zieh	ziehe	geziehen
ziehen	ziehst	zieht	zieh(e)!	zog	zöge	gezogen
	A: zeuchst	*A:* zeucht	*A:* zeuch!			
zwingen	zwingst	zwingt	zwing(e)!	zwang	zwänge	gezwungen

Labels and Abbreviations used in the Dictionary

a.	adjective	Adjektiv
A.	ancient	alt
A:	Archaism; in former use	Archaismus, veraltet
abbr.	abbreviation	Abkürzung
abs.	absolutely, absolute use	absolut, absolut gebraucht
Ac:	Acoustics	Akustik
acc.	accusative	Akkusativ
adj. adjs	adjective; adjectival; adjectives	Adjektiv; adjektivisch; Adjektive
Adm:	Administration	Verwaltung
adv. advbs	adverb; adverbial; adverbs	Adverb; adverbial; Adverbien
adv.acc.	adverbial accusative	adverbialer Akkusativ
Advertising:	Advertising	Werbung
adv.phr.	adverbial phrase	adverbiale Wendung
Aer:	Aerodynamics; Aeronautics	Aerodynamik; Aeronautik
Agr:	Agriculture	Landwirtschaft
A.Hist:	Ancient History	alte Geschichte
Air-conditioning	Air-conditioning	Klimatechnik
Alch:	Alchemy	Alchemie
Alg:	Algebra	Algebra
Algae:	Algae	Algen
Amph:	Amphibia	Amphibien
Anat:	Anatomy	Anatomie
Ann:	Annelida, etc.	Ringelwürmer, usw.
Ant:	Antiquity; Antiquities	Altertum; Altertümer
Anthr:	Anthropology	Anthropologie
Ap:	Apiculture	Bienenzucht
approx.	approximately	ungefähr
Ar:	Arithmetic	Arithmetik
Arach:	Arachnida	Spinnentiere
Arb:	Arboriculture	Baumzucht
Arch:	Architecture	Architektur
Archeol:	Arch(a)eology	Archäologie
Archery:	Archery	Bogenschießen
Arm:	Armour	Rüstung
art.	article	Artikel
Art:	Art	Kunst
Artil:	Artillery	Artillerie
Astr:	Astronomy	Astronomie
Astrol:	Astrology	Astrologie
Astro-Ph:	Astrophysics	Astrophysik
Atom.Ph:	Atomic Physics	Atomphysik
attrib.	attributive	attributiv
Austr:	Australian	australisch
Austrian:	Austrian	österreichisch
Austrian Dial:	Austrian Dialect	österreichischer Dialekt
Aut:	Automobilism	Kraftfahrwesen
aux.	auxiliary	Hilfs-; Hilfsverb
Av:	Aviation	Flugwesen
B:	Biblical, Bible	biblisch, Bibel
Bac:	Bacteriology	Bakteriologie
Bak:	Baking	Bäckerei
Ball:	Ballistics	Ballistik
Bank:	Banking	Bankwesen
Basketm:	Basket-making	Korbmacherei
B.Hist:	Bible History	biblische Geschichte
Bib:	Bibliography	Bibliographie
Bill:	Billiards	Billard
Bio-Ch:	Bio-Chemistry	Biochemie
Biol:	Biology	Biologie
Bleach:	Bleaching	Bleicherei
Bookb:	Bookbinding	Buchbinderei
Book-k:	Book-keeping	Buchführung
Bootm:	Bootmaking	Schuhmacherei
Bot:	Botany	Botanik
Box:	Boxing	Boxen
Breed:	Breeding	Tierzucht
Brew:	Brewing	Brauerei
Brickm:	Brickmaking	Ziegelherstellung
Cards:	Cards	Kartenspiel

Carp:	Carpentry	Zimmerhandwerk
Cav:	Cavalry	Kavallerie
Cer:	Ceramics	Keramik
Ch:	Chemistry	Chemie
Ch. of Eng:	Church of England	Anglikanische Kirche
Chr:	Chronology	Chronologie
Cin:	Cinematography	Kinowesen
Civ.D:	Civil Defence	zivile Verteidigung
Civ.E:	Civil Engineering	Bauwesen; Tiefbau
Civil:	Civilization	Kultur
Cl:	Classical	klassisch
Cl.Lit:	Classical Literature	klassische Literatur
Clockm:	Clockmaking	Uhrmacherei
Coel:	Coelenterata	Hohltiere
cogn.acc.	cognate accusative	Akkusativ des Inhalts
Cokem:	Cokemaking	Koksherstellung
coll. Coll.	collective	kollektiv, Kollektivum
Com: Com.	Commerce; commercial	Handel; Handels-
comb.fm.	combining form	Zusammensetzungselement
Comest:	Comestibles	Lebensmittel
comp.	comparative	Komparativ
Computing:	Computing	Computertechnik
Conch:	Conchology	Konchyliologie
condit.	conditional	konditional; Konditional
conj. conjs	conjunction; conjunctive; conjunctions	Konjunktion; konjunktional; Konjunktionen
conj. like	conjugated like	konjugiert wie
Constr:	Construction	Hochbau
Coop:	Cooperage	Böttcherei
Corr:	Correspondence	Korrespondenz
Cost:	Costume	Tracht
Cp. cp.	compare	vergleiche
Cr:	Cricket	Kricket
Crust:	Crustacea	Krustentiere
Cryst:	Crystallography	Kristallographie
Cu:	Culinary; cuisine	kulinarisch; Kochkunst
Cust:	Customs (i.e. C. & Excise)	Zoll
Cy:	Cycles; cycling	Fahrräder; Radfahren
Cy.-Rac:	Cycle-racing	Radrennsport
Danc:	Dancing	Tanz
dat.	dative	Dativ
decl.	declined; declension	dekliniert; Deklination
def.	definite	bestimmt
def.	defective	unvollständig
dem.	demonstrative	hinweisend
Dent:	Dentistry	Zahnheilkunde
Dial:	Dialect	Dialekt
dim.	diminutive	verkleinernd; Diminutiv
Dipl:	Diplomacy	Diplomatie
Dist:	Distilling	Destillation
Dom.Ec:	Domestic Economy	Hauswirtschaft
Draw:	Drawing	Zeichnen
Dressm:	Dressmaking	Damenschneiderei
Dy:	Dyeing	Färberei
Dyn:	Dynamics	Dynamik
E.	East	ost-; Osten
E:	Engineering	Technik
Ecc:	Ecclesiastical	kirchlich, Kirchen-; geistlich
Echin:	Echinodermata	Stachelhäuter
e.g.	exempli gratia, for example	zum Beispiel
Egypt.	Egyptian	ägyptisch
El:	Electricity; electrical	Elektrizität; Elektro-
El.Ch:	Electro-Chemistry	Elektrochemie
Electronics:	Electronics	Elektronik
ellipt.	elliptical(ly)	elliptisch
Eng.	English; England	englisch; England
Engr:	Engraving	Gravierkunst
Ent:	Entomology	Insektenkunde
epith.	epithet (adjective)	Beiname
Equit:	Equitation	Reitkunst
esp.	especially	besonders
etc.	et cetera	und so weiter
Eth:	Ethics	Ethik

Ethn:	*Ethnology*	Völkerkunde
excl.	*exclamation; exclamatory*	Ausruf; Ausrufe-
Exp:	*Explosives*	Sprengstoffe
f.	*feminine*	weiblich; Femininum
F:	*Familiar*	umgangssprachlich
Farr:	*Farriery*	Hufschmiedehandwerk
Fb:	*Football*	Fußball
Fenc:	*Fencing*	Fechtkunst
Ferns:	*Ferns*	Farne
Fin:	*Finance*	Finanz
Fish:	*Fishing*	Fischerei; Angeln
Folkl:	*Folklore*	Volkskunde
For:	*Forestry*	Forstwesen
Fort:	*Fortification*	Festungsbau
Fr.	*French; France*	französisch; Frankreich
Free-masonry:	*Freemasonry*	Freimaurerei
Fuel:	*Fuel*	Brennstoff
Fung:	*Fungi*	Pilze
Furn:	*Furniture*	Möbel
fut.	*future*	Zukunft; Zukunfts-
G.	*German*	deutsch
Gaming:	*Gaming*	Glücksspiel
Gasm:	*Gasmaking*	Gasherstellung
gen.	*genitive*	Genitiv
Genetics:	*Genetics*	Genetik
Geog:	*Geography*	Geographie
Geol:	*Geology*	Geologie
Geom:	*Geometry*	Geometrie
ger.	*gerund*	Gerundium
G.Hist:	*German History*	deutsche Geschichte
Glassm:	*Glassmaking*	Glasherstellung
Goldmin:	*Gold-mining*	Goldbergbau
Gr.	*Greek*	griechisch
Gr.Alph:	*Greek Alphabet*	griechisches Alphabet
Gram:	*Grammar*	Grammatik
Gr.Ant:	*Greek Antiquity*	griechisches Altertum
Gr.Civ:	*Greek Civilization*	griechische Kultur
Gr.Hist:	*Greek History*	griechische Geschichte
Gr.Myth:	*Greek Mythology*	griechische Mythologie
Gym:	*Gymnastics*	Gymnastik; Turnen
Haird:	*Hairdressing*	Friseurhandwerk
Harn:	*Harness*	(Zugtier-)Geschirr
Hatm:	*Hatmaking*	Hutmacherei
Hep:	*Hepaticae*	Lebermoose
Her:	*Heraldry*	Heraldik
Hist:	*History; historica*	Geschichte; geschichtlich
Hor:	*Horology*	Zeitmessung
Hort:	*Horticulture*	Gartenbau
Hum:	*Humorous*	scherzhaft
Husb:	*Husbandry*	Acker- und Viehwirtschaft
Hyd:	*Hydraulics; Hydrostatics*	Hydraulik; Hydrostatik
Hyd.E:	*Hydraulic Engineering*	Wasserbau
Hyg:	*Hygiene*	Hygiene
i.	*intransitive*	intransitiv
I.C.E:	*Internal Combustion Engines*	Verbrennungsmotoren
Ich:	*Ichthyology*	Fischkunde
i.e.	*id est, that is*	das heißt
Ill.E:	*Illuminating Engineering*	Beleuchtungstechnik
imp.	*imperative*	Imperativ
impers.	*impersonal*	unpersönlich
ind.	*indicative*	Indikativ; Indikativ-
Ind:	*Industry*	Industrie
indef.	*indefinite*	unbestimmt
inf.	*infinitive*	infinitiv; Infinitiv-
in infl. style	*in inflated style*	in schwülstigem Stil
Ins:	*Insurance*	Versicherungswesen
insep.	*inseparable*	fest zusammengesetzt
int.	*interjection*	Interjektion
Internat.Jur:	*International Law*	Völkerrecht
interr.	*interrogative*	Fragewort; Frage-
intr.	*intransitive*	intransitiv
inv.	*invariable*	unveränderlich
Iron:	*ironical(ly)*	ironisch
Ital.	*Italian*	italienisch
j-d		jemand
Jew:	*Jewish*	jüdisch
Jewel:	*Jewellery*	Schmuck
j-m	—	jemandem
j-n	—	jemanden
Join:	*Joinery*	Tischlerei
Journ:	*Journalism*	Zeitungswesen
j-s		jemand(e)s
Jur:	*Jurisprudence; Law*	Rechtswissenschaft; **Recht**
Lap:	*Lapidary Arts*	Edelsteinbearbeitung
Laund:	*Laundering*	Wäscherei
Leath:	*Leatherwork*	Lederarbeit
Leg:	*Legislation*	Gesetzgebung
Library:	*Library*	Bibliothek
Ling:	*Linguistics*	Linguistik
Lit:	*Literary use; Literature; literary*	gewählte Ausdrucksweise; Literatur; literarisch
Lith:	*Lithography*	Lithographie
Locksm:	*Locksmithery*	Schlosserei
Log:	*Logic*	Logik
Lt.	*Latin*	Latein; lateinisch
m.	*masculine*	männlich; Maskulinum
Machine-Tls:	*Machine Tools*	Werkzeugmaschinen
Magn:	*Magnetism*	Magnetismus
Mapm:	*Map-making*	Kartographie
masc.	*masculine*	männlich; Maskulinum
Matchm:	*Match-making*	Streichholzfabrikation
Mch:	*Machines (steam-engines, boilers, etc.)*	Dampfkraftmaschinen, Dampfkessel usw.
Meas:	*Weights & Measures*	Maße und Gewichte
Mec:	*Mechanics*	Mechanik
Mec.E:	*Mechanical Engineering*	Maschinenbau
Med:	*Medicine*	Medizin
Mediev:	*Medieval*	mittelalterlich
Metall:	*Metallurgy*	Metallurgie
Metalw:	*Metalworking*	Metallbearbeitung
Metaph:	*Metaphysics*	Metaphysik
Meteor:	*Meteorology; meteorological*	Meteorologie; meteorologisch
Microscopy:	*Microscopy*	Mikroskopie
Mil:	*military*	militärisch; Militär-
Mill:	*Milling*	Müllerei
Min:	*Mining & Quarrying*	Bergwerks- und Steinbruchwesen
Miner:	*Mineralogy*	Mineralogie
M.Ins:	*Marine Insurance*	Seeversicherung
Mint:	*Minting*	Münzwesen
Moham.Rel:	*Mohammedan Religion*	mohammedanische Religion
Moll:	*Molluscs*	Weichtiere
Moss:	*Mosses & Lichens*	Moose und Flechten
Mount:	*Mountaineering*	Bergsteigen
Mth:	*Mathematics*	Mathematik
Mus:	*Music*	Musik
Myr:	*Myriapoda*	Tausendfüßler
Myth:	*Myth & legend; Mythology*	Sage und Legende; Mythologie
n.	*neuter*	sächlich; Neutrum
N.	*North*	nord-; Norden
N.Arch:	*Naval Architecture*	Schiffbau
Nat.Hist:	*Natural History*	Naturgeschichte
Nau:	*Nautical*	nautisch; Marine-, See-, Schiffs-
Nav:	*Navigation*	Navigation
Navy:	*Navy*	Kriegsmarine
Needlew:	*Needlework*	Näh-, Handarbeit
neg.	*negative*	negativ
neut.	*neuter*	sächlich; Neutrum
nom.	*nominative*	Nominativ
North G.Dial:	*North German Dialect*	norddeutscher Dialekt
Num:	*Numismatics*	Münzkunde
num.a.	*numeral adjective*	Zahladjektiv
obj.	*object*	Objekt
Obst:	*Obstetrics*	Geburtshilfe

Oc:	Oceanography	Meereskunde
occ. Occ.	used occasionally	gelegentlich gebraucht
Oil Technology:	Oil Technology	Erdölgewinnung und -verarbeitung
Onomat:	Onomatopoeia	Lautmalerei
Opt:	Optics	Optik
Orn:	Ornithology	Ornithologie
Ost:	Ostreiculture	Austernzucht
p.	(i) Participle; (ii) past	(i) Partizip; (ii) Vergangenheits-
P:	Popular; slang	derbe Umgangssprache; Slang
Paint:	Painting trade	Maler- und Anstreicher-gewerbe
Pal:	Pal(a)eography	Handschriftenkunde
Paleont:	Pal(a)eontology	Paläontologie
Paperm:	Papermaking	Papierherstellung
Parl:	Parliament	Parlament
Path:	Pathology	Pathologie
Pej: pej.	Pejorative	pejorativ, abfällig
perf.	perfect	Perfekt; perfektivisch
pers.	person; personal	Person; persönlich
Ph.	Physical	physikalisch
Ph:	Physics	Physik
Pharm:	Pharmacy	Pharmazie
Ph.Geog:	Physical Geography	physikalische Geographie
Phil:	Philosophy	Philosophie
Phonetics:	Phonetics	Phonetik
Phot:	Photography	Photographie
Phot.Engr:	Photo-Engraving	photomechanische Repro-duktion
phr.	phrase	Redewendung
Phren:	Phrenology	Phrenologie
Physiol:	Physiology	Physiologie
Pisc:	Pisciculture	Fischzucht
pl.	plural	Mehrzahl
Plastics:	Plastics	Kunststoffe
Plumb:	Plumbing	Klempnerarbeit
P.N:	Public Notices	Öffentliche Bekannt-machungen und Hinweise
Poet:	Poetical	dichterisch
Pol:	Politics	Politik
Pol.Ec:	Political Economy	Volkswirtschaft
poss.	possessive	besitzanzeigend
Post:	Postal Service	Postwesen
p.p.	past participle	Partizip Perfekt
pr.	present	Präsens; Gegenwarts-
pred.	predicate; predicative; predicatively	Prädikat; prädikativ
pref.	prefix	Präfix
Prehist:	Prehistory	Vorgeschichte (Prähistorie)
prep. preps	preposition, prepositions	Präposition, Präpositionen
prep.phr.	prepositional phrase	präpositionale Wendung
Print:	Printing	Druckerei
Pr.n.	Proper name	Eigenname
Prof:	Profession	(gelehrter, freier) Beruf; Stand
pron.	pronoun; pronominal	Pronomen; pronominal
Pros:	Prosody	Prosodie
Prot:	Protozoa	Urtiere
Prov:	Proverb	Sprichwort
pr.p.	present participle	Partizip Präsens
Psy:	Psychology	Psychologie
Psychics:	Psychics	Psychik
p.t.	past tense	Vergangenheit(sform)
Publ:	Publishing	Verlagswesen
Pyr:	Pyrotechnics	Pyrotechnik
q.v.	quod vide, which see	siehe dieses
Rac:	Racing	Rennsport
Rad.-A:	Radio-activity	Radioaktivität
Radar:	Radar	Radar
Radio-therapy:	Radiotherapy	Radiotherapie
Rail:	Railways	Eisenbahn
R.C.Ch:	Roman Catholic Church	Römisch-Katholische Kirche
refl.	reflexive	reflexiv
rel.	relative	relativ; Relativ
Rel:	Religion(s)	Religion(en)
Rel.Hist:	Religious History	Religionsgeschichte
Rept:	Reptilia	Reptilien
Rh:	Rhetoric	Rhetorik
Rocketry:	Rocketry	Raketen
Rom.	Roman	römisch
Ropem:	Ropemaking	Seilerei
Row:	Rowing	Rudersport
(R.t.m.)	Registered trade mark	eingetragene Schutzmarke
Rubberm:	Rubber manufacture	Gummiherstellung
Russ.	Russian	russisch
S.	South	süd-; Süden
s. sb.	substantive; substantival	Substantiv; substantivisch
Sch:	Schools and Universities	Schulen und Universitäten
Scot:	Scottish	schottisch
Sculp:	Sculpture	Bildhauerkunst
sep.	separable	unfest zusammengesetzt
Ser:	Sericulture	Seidenzucht
sg.	singular	Einzahl
Skating:	Skating	Eislauf
Ski:	Ski-ing	Skisport
Sm.a:	Small arms	Handwaffen
s.o.	someone	jemand
Soapm:	Soapmaking	Seifenfabrikation
Soc.Hist:	Social History	Sozialgeschichte
South G.Dial:	South German Dialect	süddeutscher Dialekt
Sp:	Sport	Sport
Space:	Space research	Raumforschung
Spong:	Sponges	Schwämme
St.Exch:	Stock Exchange	Börse
sth.	something	etwas
Stonew:	Stoneworking	Steinbearbeitung
sub.	subjunctive	Konjunktiv
subst.	substantival	substantivisch; Substantiv-
suff.	suffix	Suffix
Sug-R:	Sugar-refining	Zuckerraffinerie
sup.	superlative	Superlativ
Surg:	Surgery	Chirurgie
Surv:	Surveying	Vermessungswesen
Swim:	Swimming	Schwimmsport
Swiss:	Swiss	schweizerisch
Swiss Dial:	Swiss Dialect	schweizerischer Dialekt
syll.	syllable	Silbe
Tail:	Tailoring	Schneiderei
Tan:	Tanning	Gerberei
Tape-recording:	Tape-recording	Tonbandtechnik
Tchn:	technical	Technik
Telecom:	Telecommunications	Fernmeldewesen
Ten:	(i) Tennis; (ii) Lawn Tennis	(i) Tennis; (ii) Lawn-Tennis
Ter:	Teratology	Teratologie
Tex:	Textiles	Textilien; Textil-
Tg:	Telegraphy	Telegraphie
Th:	Theatre	Theaterwesen
Theol:	Theology	Theologie
thg	thing	Ding, Sache
Tinplating:	Tinplating	Verzinnung
Tls:	Tools	Werkzeuge
Toil:	Toilet	Toilettenartikel; Körperpflege
Torp:	Torpedoes	Torpedos
Tp:	Telephony	Fernsprechwesen
tr.	transitive	transitiv
Tram:	Tramways	Straßenbahn
Trans:	Transport	Transport
Trig:	Trigonometry	Trigonometrie
Turb:	Turbines	Turbinen
Turf:	Turf, Horse-racing	Pferderennsport
Turk:	Turkish; Turkey	türkisch; Türkei
TV:	Television	Fernsehen
Typewr:	Typewriting	Maschinenschreiben
U.S:	United States; American	Vereinigte Staaten; US-amerikanisch
usu.	usually	gewöhnlich
usw.	—	und so weiter

v.	*verb*	Verb
V:	*Vulgarism*	ungebildete, unfeine, geschmacklose, Ausdrucksweise
vb vbs	*verb, verbs*	Verb, Verben
vbl	*verbal*	verbal
vbl pref.	*verbal prefix*	Verbalpräfix
vbl s.	*verbal substantive*	Verbalsubstantiv
Veh:	*Vehicles*	Fahrzeuge
Ven:	*Venery*	Jagd
Vet:	*Veterinary science*	Tierheilkunde
v.i.	*verb intransitive*	intransitives Verb
Vit:	*Viticulture*	Weinbau
voc.	*Vocative*	Vokativ
v.tr.	*verb transitive*	transitives Verb
W.	*West*	west-; Westen
W:	*Wireless, Radio*	Radio

Wine-m:	*Wine-making*	Weinherstellung
Woodw:	*Woodworking*	Holzbearbeitung
Wr:	*Wrestling*	Ringen
W.Tel:	*Wireless Telephony & Telegraphy, U.S: Radio & Telegraphy*	drahtlose Telephonie und Telegraphie
W.Tg:	*Wireless Telegraphy*	drahtlose Telegraphie
W.Tp:	*Wireless Telephony*	drahtlose Telephonie
X-Rays:	*X-rays*	Röntgenologie
Y:	*Yachting*	Segelsport
Yiddish:	*Yiddish*	Jiddisch
Z	*Zoology*	Zoologie

A

A, a [a:], n. -/- (*in speech only* -s/-s [a:s]). **1.** (the letter) A, a; **großes A**, capital A; **kleines a**, small a; **es wird mit zwei a geschrieben**, it is spelt with two a's; *Tp:* **A wie Anton**, A for Andrew; **etwas von A bis Z kennen**, to know something from A to Z, thoroughly, inside out; **noch im großen A sein**, to be a mere beginner, a tyro (in business, a science, etc.); *Prov:* **wer A sagt, muß auch B sagen**, in for a penny in for a pound; *B:* **ich bin das A und das O, der Anfang und das Ende**, I am Alpha and Omega, the beginning and the end; **das A und O** (einer Wissenschaft, usw.), the essence (of a science, etc.). **2.** *Mus:* (the note) A; **A-dur, A-Dur, a-moll, a-Moll, (-Tonart)**, (key of) A major, A minor; **die A-Saite**, the A string (of violin, etc.). **3.** Ia=A1; (i) *Com:* (*read as:* 'eins a' [ainsᵓ¹a:], *or:* 'prima' ['pri:ma]), 'first quality', 'top grade'; (ii) *Sch:* Ia [ains¹a:] (*as mark on exercise*) 'alpha', 'excellent'; (iii) *Mil:* Ia [ainsᵓ¹a:] (**beim Stabe**), General Staff Officer (Intelligence). *See also List of Abbreviations.*

Ä, ä (*occ.* Ae-, ae) [ɛ:], n. -/- & -s/-s, (the letter) Ä, ä; A, a, modified; *F:* Ä, a, umlaut; *Tp:* **Ä wie Ärger**, A for Andrew, E for Edward.

à, *prep.* (Fr.) (*occ. wrongly without accent*) *Com:* =@, at (the price of)..., at...a piece; **fünf Schachteln Zigaretten à 2 Mark**, five boxes of cigarettes at 2 marks (each). *Note:* à condition, on condition, *and other set expressions are listed in alphabetical order.*

a, *prep.* (Lt. & Ital.) *used in various set phrases, e.g.* **a conto**, on account. (*Listed in alphabetical order.*)

a, *num. a. & indef. art.* South G. *Dial:*=ein¹ I, II.

A- (*abbr. of* Atom), atom..., atomic...; **die A-Bombe**, the atom bomb, *F:* the A-bomb.

Aachen. *Pr.n.n.* -s. *Geog:* Aix-la-Chapelle, Aachen.

Aachener. 1. *m.* -s/-. *Geog:* inhabitant, native, of Aix-la-Chapelle, of Aachen. **2.** *inv.a.* of Aix-la-Chapelle, of Aachen; *Hist:* **der A. Friede**, the Peace of Aix-la-Chapelle.

Aal, *m.* -(e)s/-e. (*a*) *Ich:* eel; *Cu:* **Aal gekocht**, stewed eels; **Aal blau**, boiled eels; **Aal in Sülze, in Gelee**, jellied eels; *F:* **er ist glatt, schlüpfrig, wie ein Aal**, he is as slippery as an eel; (*b*) *Navy: F:* torpedo.

Aalbank, *f. Navy: F:* torpedo depot.

Aalbeere, *f. Hort:* black currant.

Aalbricke, *f. Cu:* small pickled eel.

Aalbrut, *f. Pisc:* eel-fry; elvers, young eels.

Aalbutt, *m. Ich:* pleuronectes cynoglossus, *F:* witch.

aalen, *v.* **1.** *v.i.* (haben) to fish for eels. **2. sich aalen,** (*a*) to stretch oneself, one's limbs; (*b*) to idle (away one's time), to slack, to loaf; to laze in bed, in the sun; to laze about.

Aalfang, *m.* **1.** eel-catching. **2.** eel-trap, -pot.

aalförmig, *a.* anguilliform, eel-like.

Aalgabel, *f.* eel-prong.

aalglatt, *a. F:* **er ist a.**, he is as slippery as an eel; he is a slippery customer.

Aalhamen, *m.* eel-trap.

Aalharke, Aalharpune, *f.* eel-spear, -prong.

Aalhaut, *f.* eel-skin.

aalig, *a.*=aalglatt.

Aalkiste, *f.* eel-trap.

Aalkorb, *m.* eel-basket, -pot.

Aalmolch, *m. Amph:* Congo snake.

Aalmutter, *f. Ich:* viviparous blenny.

Aalpastete, *f. Cu:* eel-pie.

Aalpuppe, *f. Fish:* bob (of worms for eel-fishing).

Aalquappe, *f. Ich:* **1.**=Aalmutter. **2.**=Aalraupe.

Aalquaste, *f.*=Aalpuppe.

Aalraupe, *f. Ich:* eel-pout, burbot.

Aalreuse, *f. Fish:* eel-trap.

Aalrutte, *f.*=Aalraupe.

Aalschlange, *f. Ich:* conger(-eel).

Aalspeer, Aalstecher, *m.* eel-spear, -prong.

Aalstreifen, Aalstrich, *m.* dark stripe (along back of horse, cow, deer, etc.).

Aalteich, *m.* eel-bed, -pond, -preserve.

Aaltierchen, *n.* **1.** *Ann:* nematode, eel-worm, anguillule. **2.** *Prot:* infusorian; *pl.* infusoria.

Aar, *m.* -(e)s/-e. *Poet:* eagle.

Aarbeere, *f. Bot:* sorb-apple.

Aarkirsche, *f. Bot: F:* (*a*) sorb(-apple); (*b*) service-tree, sorb-apple tree.

Aaron ['a:rɔn]. *Pr.n.m.* -s. *B.Hist:* Aaron; *B:* **der Stab Aarons**, Aaron's rod.

Aaronitisch [a:ro¹ni:tiʃ], *a.* **der Aaronitische Segen**, Aaron's blessing.

Aaron(s)stab, *m.*, **Aaron(s)wurz,** *f. Bot:*=Aron(s)stab, Aron(s)wurzel.

Aarweih, *m.*, **Aarweihe,** *f. Orn:* kite.

Aas, *n.* -es/-e & Äser. **1.** (*a*) carrion, decaying carcass; (*b*) meat unfit to eat; (*c*) *Leath:* fleshings, scrapings (from hides). **2.** *Ven:* bait. **3.** *P:* scoundrel; dirty swine. **4.** (*occ. used as term of endearment*) **du kleines Aas**, you little rogue.

Aasanger, *m.* garbage-heap (of slaughter-house, etc.).

Aasblume, *f. Bot:* stapelia, *esp.* stapelia asterias, *F:* carrion-flower.

aasen, *v.i.* (haben) **1.** to scavenge. **2.** *Ven:*=äsen. **3.** *F:* (*a*) **mit dem Zucker a.**, to waste the sugar; to be heavy on the sugar; (*b*) *F:* **mit einer Arbeit a.**, to bungle, to botch, a piece of work. **4.** *Fish: Ven:* to lay bait. **5.** *v.tr. Leath:* to flesh (hides).

Aaser, *m.* -s/-. *Swiss Dial:* knapsack.

Aasfliege, *f. Ent:* carrion fly.

aasfressend, *a. Z:* necrophagous.

Aasgeier, *m.* **1.** *Orn:* vulture, *esp.* griffon-vulture. **2.** *F:* exploiter; *F:* shark.

Aasgeruch, Aasgestank, *m.* (*a*) smell, odour, of putrefaction; (*b*) *F:* filthy smell.

Aasgrube, *f.* garbage-pit (of slaughter-house, etc.).

aashaft, aasig, *a.* (*a*) carrion-like; (*b*) (smell) of carrion; *F:* offensive; (*c*) *P:* **er war aasig zu ihr**, he treated her abominably, he was a swine to her.

Aasjäger, *m. Pej:* pot-hunter, tuft-hunter.

Aaskäfer, *m. Ent:* carrion-beetle, silpha.

Aaskrähe, *f. Orn:* carrion crow.

Aaspflanze, *f.*=Aasblume.

Aasrabe, *m. Orn: F:* raven.

Aasseite, *f. Leath:* flesh side (of hide).

aaßen, *v.i.* (haben) *Ven:* (of deer) to graze.

Aastier, *n.* carrion-devouring animal *or* bird.

Aasvogel, *m. Orn:* vulture.

ab. I. (*abs. use*) (*a*) **ab!** off! off with you! off you go! go! go away! *F:* **ab nach Kassel! ab mit Schaden!** off with you! *F:* buzz off! scram! **Hut ab!** hat(s) off! off with your hat(s)! *Mil.Av:* (*order to jump from aircraft*) **ab!** jump! *Mil:* **Gewehr ab!** order arms! (*b*) **wir waren nur etwa hundert Meter ab** (vom Ziel), we had only about a hundred yards to go, we were within a hundred yards of our goal.

II. ab, *prep.* **1.** (+*dat.*) from; from...on, onwards; (*a*) (*indicating starting point in space*) (i) **ab Wien, von Wien ab**, from Vienna onwards; **ab hier**, from here (on); (ii) *Com:* ex; **ab Bahnhof**, ex rail; **ab Stuttgart**, ex Stuttgart; (*b*) (*indicating starting point in time*) (i) **ab drei Uhr**, from three o'clock on, onwards; **ab Ostern, von Ostern ab**, from Easter onwards; (ii) as from, with effect from; **der Vertrag gilt ab 1. Januar**, the agreement takes effect, runs, from January 1st; **die Lieferungen beginnen ab 1. März**, deliveries will take place on and after March 1st. **2.** (+*gen.*) (=abzüglich) *Com:* less...;

ab Diskonto, less discount. **3.** (*a*) *A. & Lit:* (+*dat.*) from, by; **das Vieh ab der Weide holen**, to drive in the cattle from the pasture; (etwas) **ab der Post erhalten**, to receive (sth.) by post; (*b*) (*combined with* von) (*separation*) **wir sind ab von ihm**, we have dropped him, we have become estranged (from him).

III. ab, *adv.* (*a*) (*time and space*) **von da ab**, (i) from that time forward, from then on, thenceforward, thenceforth; (ii) from there on, *Lit:* from thence, thence; **ab und zu**, (i) from time to time, now and then; occasionally; (ii) to and fro; (*b*) (*time*) **ab und an**, off and on, now and then, from time to time, at odd times, on occasion, occasionally, *Lit:* ever and anon; **von jetzt ab, von nun ab**, from now on, henceforth; (*c*) (*space*) **auf und ab**, up and down, backwards and forwards, to and fro; **im Zimmer auf und ab gehen**, to walk up and down the room; (*of ship*) **ab und an kreuzen**, to stand off and on; **wir sind vom Wege ab**, we are off the track, we have lost our way; (*d*) *subst.phr.*, **das Auf und Ab des Lebens**, the ups and downs of life; **das Auf und Ab der Wege**, the ups and downs of the roads (in the hills); **das Ab und Zu von Reisenden, Gästen, usw.**, the coming and going of travellers, guests, etc.

IV. ab. (*ellipt. use, verbal or nominal element understood*) **1.** (*in timetables*) **Ab — An** (= Abfahrt — Ankunft), departure—arrival; **Hamburg ab..., Hannover an...**, train departs from Hamburg at..., arrives at Hanover at.... **2.** off; **ein Knopf, ein Rad, ein Fleck, die Farbe, der Schmutz, ist ab** (=abgegangen), a button, a wheel, one spot, the paint, the dirt, is off, has come off; **ich habe den Flecken, den Schmutz, den Staub, usw., ab** (= abgebürstet, abgerieben, abgewaschen), I have got the stain, dirt, dust, etc., off, out; I have brushed, rubbed, washed, off the stain, dirt, dust, etc.; **die Spitze ist ab** (=abgebrochen), the point (of pencil, needle, etc.) is off, broken (off); **das Nähgarn ist ab** (=abgerissen), the cotton has broken (off), the thread has snapped. **3. ab sein**, (*of pers.*) to be exhausted, worn out, played out, finished, *F:* all in, whacked; **er ist völlig, ganz und gar, ab**, he is completely exhausted, played out, he is dead-beat; **er ist ab als** (ein) **Bergmann, Politiker, usw.**, he is finished as a miner, he is finished (in his profession) as a politician, etc.; *see also* **absein, abhaben**.

ab-, *vbl pref. Note: Separable in all purely German verbs where it occurs as the first element without other prefix; such verbs have the augment* -ge- *in the p.p.* (*e.g.* absetzen, *p.t.* setzte ab, *p.p.* abgesetzt). *May be combined with inseparable prefixes; when* ab- *is the first element, the verb is separable but has p.p. without the augment* -ge- (*e.g.* abvermieten, *p.t.* vermietete ab, *p.p.* abvermietet); *when* ab- *is the second element, the verb is inseparable* (*e.g.* beabsichtigen, *p.t.* beabsichtigte, *p.p.* beabsichtigt).

Hybrid verbs with ab+Lt. *or* Fr. *verbal element are separable; when they end in* -ieren *they have p.p. without the augment* -ge- (*e.g.* abmontieren, *p.t.* montierte ab, *p.p.* abmontiert); *the augment* -ge- *is also dropped when it would be cacophonous* (*e.g.* abkonterfeien, *p.t.* konterfeite ab, *p.p.* abkonterfeit). *In some verbs of Latin origin the distinction between the Latin and the German* ab- *has become blurred, e.g.* abnegieren *may have p.t.* negierte ab.

Denotes in verbs: **1.** (*downward motion*) **abgleiten**, to slip down; **abstürzen**, to crash (down). **2.** (*departure, removal, separation*) **abfahren**, to depart; **abbrechen**, to break off (branch from tree, etc.); **abtrennen**, to separate. **3.** (*deviation from a norm*) **abweichen**, to deviate; **abarten**, to

deviate from type. 4. (*wearing away*) **abtragen,** to wear out (clothes); **abreiben,** to wear (sth.) away (by rubbing). 5. (*reversal of the sense expressed in the verb*) **abbauen,** to dismantle, demolish; **abbestellen,** to countermand (an order). 6. (*copying, reproduction*) **abbilden,** to take a likeness of (s.o., sth.); **abdrücken,** to take an impression, make a mould, of (sth.). 7. (*causing s.o. to part with sth.*) **j-m etwas abringen,** to wrest sth. from s.o. 8. (*completion of the action expressed in the verb*) **abschließen,** to conclude; **abregnen,** to stop raining. 9. (*excessive action*) **sich (mit Arbeit) abrackern,** to work oneself to death. 10. (*denoting negation in subst. & adj.*) **Abgott** *m*, idol; **Abgrund** *m*, abyss; **abgründig,** abysmal.

-ab, *suff. denoting* (*a*) (*space*) **fernab,** far away; **linksab,** (away) to the left; (*b*) (*time*) **fortab,** from now on; (*c*) (*manner*) **kurzab,** abruptly; **schnellab,** rashly.

abaasen, *v.tr. sep. Leath:* to flesh (hides).

Abaddon [a·ba'do:n]. *Pr.n.m.* **-s.** *B:* Abaddon; (*a*) the angel of the bottomless pit; (*b*) the bottomless pit; Hell.

Abaisseur [a·bɛ·'sø:r], *m.* **-s/-s.** *Anat:* depressor (muscle).

abaissieren [a·bɛ·'si:rən], *v.tr. insep.* 1. to lower (arm, etc., by muscular action). 2. to abase (s.o.). 3. *Her:* **abaissiert,** abased.

Abaka [a'ba:ka:], *m.* **-/-.** *Bot:* abaca; Manilla hemp plant.

Abakus ['a:ba·kus], *m.* **-/-.** 1. *Mth:* abacus, counting-frame. 2. *Arch:* abacus.

abänderbar, abänderlich, *a.* (*a*) modifiable, alterable; (*b*) *Jur:* commutable (sentence); (*c*) *Gram:* declinable; variable.

abändern. I. *v.tr. sep.* (*a*) to alter, change, modify (**etwas in etwas anderes,** sth. into sth. else); (*b*) *Pol:* to amend (law, draft bill).

II. *vbl s.* **Abänderung,** *f.* (*a*) alteration, modification; (*b*) *Pol: etc:* amendment (to bill, etc.); **eine A. beantragen,** to move an amendment.

Abänderungsantrag, *m.* (proposed) amendment; **einen A. stellen,** to move an amendment; **Zusatz zu einem A.,** amendment to an amendment.

abänderungsfähig, *a.* alterable; modifiable.

Abänderungsplan, *m.* plan for alterations (to building, etc.); *Pol:* proposal for amendment (to bill, etc.).

Abandon [abã·'dõ:], *m.* **-s/-s.** *Ins: Nau:* abandonment (of insured goods, ship, etc.).

abandonnieren [abã·do'ni:rən], *v.tr. Ins: Nau:* to abandon (ship, cargo, etc.) to an insurer.

abängstigen, *v.tr. sep.* 1. to harass, torment, worry; to bother. 2. **sich abängstigen,** to be uneasy; to fret, worry; to bother.

abarbeiten. I. *v.tr. sep.* 1. (*a*) to rough out (design, plan); (*b*) to work off (relief, etc.) (*for re-carving*); (*c*) to trim, to rough down (timber); to rough-plane (timber); (*d*) to rough-dress, to scabble (stone). 2. to complete (task). 3. **eine Schuld a.,** to work off a debt; to work out a debt; **seine Überfahrt a.,** to work one's passage. 4. (*a*) to wear, tire, (s.o.) out; to exhaust (s.o.); **sich a.,** to wear, tire, oneself out, to exhaust oneself; **abgearbeitet sein,** (*of pers.*) to be tired out, to be spent (with fatigue), *F:* to be fagged, dead-beat, done up; (*of horse*) to be knocked up; (*b*) **sich** *dat.* **die Finger a.,** to work one's fingers to the bone. 5. *Nau:* to refloat, to set afloat, to float off (ship); to claw off (ship). 6. *v.i.* (*haben*) (*of wine*) to cease fermenting.

II. *vbl s.* 1. **Abarbeiten,** *n. in vbl senses.* 2. **Abarbeitung,** *f.* (*a*)=II. 1; *also:* completion (of task); (*b*) *Art:* **das Relief hat mehrere Abarbeitungen,** the relief shows several worked-off places.

abärgern, *v.tr. sep.* 1. to annoy, provoke, vex, aggravate (s.o.). 2. **sich abärgern,** to be consumed with vexation; to fret oneself.

Abart, *f.* (*a*) variety (of flower, etc.); (*b*) degenerate species, type.

abarten. I. *v.i. sep.* (*sein*) (*a*) to deviate from type; (*b*) to degenerate.

II. *vbl s.* **Abartung,** *f.* (*a*) deviation from type; (*b*) degeneration, degeneracy.

abartig, *a.* abnormal; freakish; (*of bees, etc.*) degenerate.

Abartling, *m.* **-s/-e.** *Biol:* (*a*) freak, sport; (*b*) degenerate type.

abäsen, *v.tr. sep.* (*of deer, etc.*) to feed upon (leaves, etc.); to crop (grass).

abästen, *v.tr. sep.* to cut away, lop off, break off, the branches from (tree); to prune, trim; to strip; to poll (tree).

abätmen. I. *v.tr. sep. Metall:* to anneal; to cupel.

II. *vbl s.* **Abätmen** *n.*, **Abätmung** *f. in vbl senses; also:* cupellation.

abätzen, *v.tr. sep.* 1. to corrode, eat away. 2. to burn off (with caustic); *Med:* to cauterize. 3. *A:*=**abäsen.**

abbacken, *v.tr. sep.* (*conj. like* **backen**) (*a*) to bake (a loaf, etc.) dry; to over-bake; **abgebackenes Brot,** loaf in which the crust has parted from the crumb; (*b*)=**backen** 1 (*a*).

abbaden, *v.tr. sep.* to wash off (dirt, etc.) (from sth.); *A:* **die Kinder a.,** to give the children their baths.

abbaken, *v.tr. sep. Nau:* to beacon, mark out (channel).

abbalgen, abbälgen, *v.tr. sep.* 1. (*a*) to flay, skin (animal); (*b*) *Dial:* to shell (peas). 2. **sich abbalgen,** to tire oneself out (with struggling, wrestling, etc.).

abbangen (sich), *v.refl. sep.*=**abängstigen** 2.

abbasten, *v.tr. sep.* (*a*) to strip the bast, the (inner) bark, off (tree); (*b*) to strip, scutch, swingle (flax, hemp, etc.).

Abbau, *m.* **-(e)s/.** 1. demolition; pulling down (of structure); dismantling, dismantlement (of machine, factory, etc.). 2. *Adm: Ind:* (*a*) retrenchment; (*b*) dismissal (of personnel); reduction (of staff); laying off (of hands); (*c*) reduction (of prices, etc.). 3. *Min:* (*a*) exploitation, exploiting, working (of minerals); (*b*) (*place*) working. 4. (*pl.* **Abbauten**) outbuilding. 5. *Agr:* **den Boden in A. bringen,** to lay land fallow. 6. *Biol: Physiol:* catabolism. 7. (*a*) *Ch:* decomposition; (molecular) disintegration; (*b*) *Ch: etc:* analysis (of organic compound, etc.).

Abbaubetrieb, *m. Min:* workings.

abbauen. I. *v.tr. sep.* 1. to demolish, pull down (structure); to dismantle (machine, factory, fortifications, etc.); *Mil: A:* to withdraw (troops). 2. *Adm: Ind:* to dismiss (personnel); to reduce (staff); to lay off (hands); *F:* to axe (officials, officers); *F:* to give (s.o.) the sack, to sack (s.o.); to reduce (taxes, prices, etc.); *abs.* **a.,** to reduce one's staff; (*of pers.*) **abgebaut werden,** to get the sack; to lose one's job; *Com:* **einen Geschäftszweig a.,** to drop a line of business. 3. *Min:* (*a*) to exploit, work (minerals); (*b*) to abandon (mine); (*c*) to drain off (water). 4. *Ch:* (*a*) to decompose, disintegrate (compound); (*b*) to analyse (organic compound, etc.). 5. to divide (estate) up into smallholdings. 6. *abs. F:* (*a*) to clear out; to pack up; (*b*) to faint, pass out.

II. *vbl s.* **Abbauen** *n.*, *occ.* **Abbauung** *f. in vbl senses; cp.* **Abbau** 1, 2, 3 (*a*), 7.

Abbaufeld, *n. Agr:* fallow field.

Abbauförderstrecke, *f. Min:* hauling gallery.

Abbaugerechtigkeit, *f. Min:* mining right; right of exploitation.

Abbauhammer, *m. Min:* pick-hammer.

Abbauort, *n. Min:* working.

Abbauprodukt, *n. Biol:* catabolic product.

Abbaupunkt, *m. Min:* working face.

Abbauschacht, *m.* (mine-)working; working pit.

Abbausohle, *f. Min:* level.

Abbaustelle, *f. Min:* working face.

Abbaustoß, *m. Min:* working face; coal-face.

Abbaustrecke, *f. Min:* panel entry, *U.S:* gangway; (*in bord and pillar system*) bord(way); headway, wall; (*in British longwall system*) heading, stall; gate.

Abbaustufe, *f. Ch:* stage in decomposition.

abbauwürdig, *a. Min:* workable (seam).

abbeeren, *v.tr. sep.* (i) to strip (bush, etc.) of berries; (ii) **eine Traube a.,** to pick off grapes from a bunch.

abbefehlen, *v.tr. sep.* (*strong*) 1. to countermand the order for (sth.). 2. to recall (s.o.) (from his post).

abbefördern. I. *v.tr. sep.* to transport away; *Mil:* to evacuate (wounded, etc.).

II. *vbl s.* **Abbefördern** *n.*, **Abbeförderung** *f. in vbl senses; also: Mil:* evacuation.

abbeißen, *v.tr. sep.* (*strong*) to bite (sth.) off; to nip (sth.) off; to snap (sth.) off; *F:* **da(von) beißt die Maus keinen Faden ab, da(von) beißt keine Maus einen Faden ab,** it can't be altered; there's nothing to be done about it.

Abbeizdruck, *m. Tex:* discharge printing (of calico).

abbeizen. I. *v.tr. sep.* 1. (i) to remove stain from (surface); (ii) to stain (wood, etc.). 2. *Tan:* to dress (skins). 3. *Metalw:* to pickle, dip. 4. *Med: A:* to cauterize (with caustic).

II. *vbl s.* **Abbeizen** *n.*, **Abbeizung** *f. in vbl senses; also:* removal (of paint, etc.); *Med: A:* cauterization (with caustic).

Abbeizmittel, *n.* (*a*) paint-stripper; varnish-remover; (*b*) corrosive; (*c*) *Metalw:* pickle.

abbekommen, *v.tr. sep.* (*strong*) 1. to get; **sein Teil a.,** to get, come in for, one's share; **einen Schlag a.,** to get a blow; *F:* **er hat eins abbekommen,** (i) something, someone, has hit him; (ii) he is wounded, *F:* he has stopped a bullet; **eine Rüge a.,** to get a reprimand. 2. to get (sth.) off; **eine Schraubenmutter a.,** to get a nut off.

abberufen. I. *v.sep.* (*strong*) 1. *v.tr.* (*a*) to recall (s.o.); to call, summon, (s.o.) back; **einen Gesandten a.,** to recall an ambassador, an envoy; (*b*) **Gott hat ihn abberufen,** God has called him home. 2. *v.i.* (*haben*) *Jur: A:* to appeal to a higher court.

II. *vbl s.* 1. **Abberufen,** *n. in vbl senses.* 2. **Abberufung,** *f.*=II. 1; *also:* recall; *Mil:* recall to the colours (of reservists); *Jur: A:* appeal (to a higher court).

Abberufungsschreiben, n. *Dipl:* letters of recall.

abbestellen, *v.tr. sep.* (*a*) to countermand an order for (sth.); **eine Zeitung a.,** to cancel one's subscription to a paper, *F:* to stop a paper; (*b*) to cancel; to put off (party, dance, etc.).

abbeten, *v.tr. sep.* 1. (*a*) to recite (prayer); **den Rosenkranz a.,** to tell one's beads; (*b*) *F:* to gabble through (a lesson, etc.); *F:* to reel off (verses, a list, etc.). 2. to expiate (a sin) by prayer. 3. to avert (sth.) by prayer. 4. **dem Teufel eine Seele a.,** to wrest a soul from the devil by prayer.

abbetteln, *v.tr. sep.* **j-m etwas a.,** to get sth. out of s.o. by begging, to wheedle sth. out of s.o.

abbetten, *v.tr.* to divert (watercourse, etc.).

abbezahlen, *v.tr. sep.* to pay off (debt) by instalments.

abbiegen. I. *v.sep.* (*strong*) 1. *v.tr.* (*a*) to bend (sth.) aside; to deflect (sth.); (*b*) *Hort:* to layer; (*c*) *F:* to avert, ward off (danger); to parry (awkward question). 2. *v.tr.* to break (sth.) off (by bending it). 3. *v.i.* (*sein*) **von einer Straße a.,** to turn off a road; **er bog in eine Seitenstraße ab,** he turned down a side street; **wo die Straße abbiegt,** (i) where the road branches off; (ii) where the road bends.

II. *vbl s.* 1. **Abbiegen,** *n. in vbl senses.* 2. **Abbiegung,** *f.*=II. 1; *also: Geol:* anticlinal flexure.

Abbild, *n.* 1. image; likeness; portrait; representation. 2. reflection.

abbilden. I. *v.tr. sep.* 1. (*a*) to copy, reproduce; to represent, figure; to make a cast, model, mould, of (statue, etc.); to take a likeness of (s.o., sth.); (*b*) to portray, depict; to paint. 2. **sich abbilden,** to be reflected (in sth.).

II. *vbl s.* 1. **Abbilden,** *n. in vbl senses.* 2. **Abbildung,** *f.* (*a*)=II. 1; (*b*) picture; figure, illustration; cut; image; reproduction (of work of art); (*c*) *Geom: etc:* representation; diagram.

Abbildungsfehler, *m. Opt:* defect (of image).

Abbildungsgüte, *f. Opt: etc:* definition.

Abbildungsvermögen, *n. Opt:* resolving power (of lens).

abbimsen, *v.tr.* 1. to pumice; to polish, clean, (metal, etc.) with pumice-stone. 2. *Leath:* (i) to stone, (ii) to fluff, frizz (skin).

abbinden, *v.sep.* (*strong*) I. *v.tr.* 1. (*a*) to untie, undo, unbind; **seinen Schlips a.,** to undo, take off, one's tie; (*b*) *Surg:* to ligature, tie; to remove (wart, etc.) by ligature; (*c*) *Husb:* to wean (calf); (*d*) *Ch:* to remove (element) by causing a chemical combination. 2. (*a*) *Carp:* to assemble, to join (up); *Coop:* to hoop (cask); (*b*) *Av: El.E:* to bond (screening to earth-system of aircraft).

II. **abbinden,** *v.i.* (*haben*) (*of cement*) to set; **langsam, schnell, abbindender Zement,** slow-, quick-setting cement.

Abbindewärme, *f.* heat of setting (of cement); **Zement mit geringer A.,** low-heat cement.

Abbindezeit, *f.* setting time (of cement).

Abbiß, *m.* 1. (*a*) bite; (*b*) *Ven:* bough(s) nibbled by deer. 2. *Bot:*=**Abbißkraut.**

Abbißkraut, *n. Bot:* blue scabious, devil's-bit scabious.

Abbitte, *f.* **j-m, bei j-m, A. tun,** to make due apology, to make a full apology, to s.o.; **öffentliche A. tun,** to make a public apology.

abbitten. I. *v.tr. sep.* (*strong*) 1. **j-m etwas a.,** (*a*) to make due apology, to make a full apology, to s.o.; **ich glaube, ich habe ihm etwas abzubitten,** I think I have done him an injustice; (*b*) to beg sth. of s.o. 2. *A:* to seek to avert (divine wrath, etc.) by prayer; *A:* to deprecate.

II. *pr.p. & a.* **abbittend,** (*a*) apologetic; *adv.* apologetically; (*b*) deprecatory.

Abblasehahn, *m. Mch:* blow-off gear; pet-cock.

abblasen, *v.tr. sep. (strong)* **1.** (*a*) to blow off, away; **den Staub a.,** to blow off, away, the dust; (*b*) *Mch:* **Dampf a.,** to blow off steam; *Mil:* **Gas a.,** to release gas. **2.** (*a*) *Ven:* **(die Jagd) a.,** to call off the hounds; (*b*) *F:* to call off (strike, meeting, etc.); to cancel (meeting, dance, etc.); **die ganze Sache ist abgeblasen,** *F:* the whole thing is off. **3.** *abs. Mil: A:* to sound the retreat.

Abblaserohr, *n. Mch:* blow-off pipe.

Abblaseventil, *n. Mch:* blow-off valve, pet-cock; blow-down valve.

abblassen, *v.i. sep. (sein)* to fade, pale; (*of colours*) to fade, go off.

abblatten, *v.tr. sep.* **1.** to thin out the leaves of (vine, etc.). **2.** (*of deer*) to browse on the foliage of (tree, etc.). **3.** *Carp:* to bevel (panel, etc.).

abblättern. I. *v.sep.* **1.** *v.tr. Bot: Med:* to exfoliate; *Med:* to desquamate; *Bot:* to defoliate. **2.** *v.i. (sein)* (*of paint, skin, etc.*) to scale, shell off, flake (off), peel (off); *Bot:* to defoliate, exfoliate; *Med:* to desquamate. **3. sich abblättern = sich entblättern,** *q.v. under* **entblättern.**

II. *vbl s.* **1. Abblättern,** *n. in vbl senses; also: Bot: Med:* exfoliation; *Med:* desquamation; *Bot:* defoliation. **2. Abblätterung,** *f.* (*a*) = II. 1; (*b*) scales, flakes (of paint, skin, etc.).

abbläuen, *v.tr. sep.* (*a*) to blue (linen, etc.); to tint (sth.) blue; (*b*) = **abbleuen.**

abbleiben, *v.i. sep. (strong) (sein)* (*a*) to fall behind; to fall away; **wo ist er abgeblieben?** what has become of him? (*b*) **vom Wege a.,** to stray (away) from the path, road, etc.

abbleichen, *v.sep.* **1.** *v.i. (strong) (sein)* = **abblassen. 2.** *v.tr. (weak)* to bleach; *Bot:* to etiolate.

abblenden. I. *v.tr. sep.* **1.** (*a*) to screen (light); to black out (room, etc.); *abs.* **a.,** *Navy:* to darken ship; (*b*) *Aut:* **die Scheinwerfer a.,** *abs.* **a.,** (i) to dip, (ii) dim, the headlights; **abgeblendet fahren,** *Aut:* to drive with, on, (i) dipped, (ii) dimmed, (head)lights; *Nau:* to sail, steam, without lights. **2.** *Cin:* to black out; *Cin: W.Tel:* to fade out. **3.** *Phot:* to stop down (lens).

II. *vbl s.* **Abblenden** *n.,* **Abblendung** *f. in vbl senses; also: Cin:* fade-out, black-out, dissolve out, wipe; *see also* **spiralförmig.**

Abblendfaden, *m. Aut:* dip filament.

Abblendhaube, *f. Aut:* anti-dazzle cap.

Abblendlicht, *n. Aut:* (*a*) dipped beam, low beam; (*b*) anti-dazzle headlight.

Abblendscha ltr, *m. Aut:* dip switch.

Abblendvorrichtung, *f. Aut:* dipping *or* dimming device (for headlights).

Abblendwiderstand, *m. El.E:* dimmer.

abbleuen, *v.tr. sep.* to beat (s.o.) black and blue, to give (s.o.) a drubbing.

abblitzen, *v.i. sep. (sein)* **1.** (*a*) *A:* (*of gun*) to misfire; to flash in the pan; (*of powder, etc.*) to go off with a flash. **2. (bei j-m) a.,** to be unsuccessful; to be snubbed; to meet (with) a rebuff; **einen Freier a. lassen,** to turn a suitor down (flat); **j-n a. lassen,** to send s.o. packing; to send s.o. away with a flea in his ear. **3.** *v. impers.* **es hat (sich) abgeblitzt,** the lightning has stopped, is over, it has stopped lightning.

abblühen. I. *v.i.* (*a*) *(haben)* (*of tree, etc.*) to finish, cease, flowering; to lose, shed, its blossom; (*b*) *(sein)* to wither, fade.

II. *vbl s.* **Abblühen,** *n. in vbl senses; also:* fall of the blossom.

abbohren, *v.tr. sep.* (*a*) to finish (i) drilling, (ii) boring; (*b*) to drill through (sth.); (*c*) *Min:* **ein Gelände a.,** to make borings (for minerals).

Abbohrer, *m. Min: Tls:* long borer.

abborgen, *v.tr. sep.* **j-m etwas a.,** to borrow sth. from s.o.

abborken, *v.tr. sep.* to bark (tree).

abböschen. I. *v.tr. sep. Civ.E: etc:* to slope (ditch, etc.); to embank (track); to batter (wall).

II. *vbl s.* **1. Abböschen,** *n. in vbl senses.* **2. Abböschung,** *f.* (*a*) = II. 1; (*b*) = **Böschung,** *q.v. under* **böschen** II.

abbossieren, *v.tr. sep.* (*p.p.* **abbossiert**) = **bossieren.**

Abbrand, *m. Metalw:* **1.** loss of weight (in working); melting loss. **2.** slag. **3.** *El:* fusing (of wires, etc.).

abbrassen, *v.tr. sep. Nau:* to brace back.

abbraten, *v.tr. sep. (strong)* (*a*) to roast (joint, etc.) thoroughly; **gut abgebraten,** well done; (*b*) = **braten** 1.

abbrauchen, *v.tr. sep.* **1.** (*a*) to use up, consume (sth.); (*b*) to wear (sth.) out, down, away. **2. sich abbrauchen,** to wear (out). **3.** *p.p. & a.* **abgebraucht,** shabby, threadbare, worn-out (garment); trite, stale (joke, etc.).

abbraunen, abbräunen, *v.tr. sep.* = **bräunen** 1.

abbrausen. I. *v.sep.* **1.** *v.i. (haben)* (*of liquid*) to cease fermenting. **2.** *v.i. (sein) F:* (*of pers.*) to rush off; (*of vehicle, etc.*) to roar off, to go off with a roar. **3.** *v.tr.* (*a*) to give (s.o.) a shower-bath, *F:* a shower; **sich a.,** to take a shower-bath, *F:* to have a shower; (*b*) *Cokem:* to quench, spray (coke).

II. *vbl s.* **Abbrausen,** *n. in vbl senses; also:* (*a*) (*of liquids*) cessation of fermenting; (*b*) **das A. ist immer erfrischend,** it's always refreshing to have a shower(-bath).

abbrechen. I. *v.tr. sep. (strong)* **1.** (*a*) to break (sth.) off; **die Spitze a.,** to break the point off (a pencil, etc.); *F:* **brich dir ja keine Verzierungen ab!** keep your shirt on! **einem Argument die Spitze a.,** to take the point out of s.o.'s argument; (*b*) to pick, pluck (flowers, fruit, etc.); (*c*) **etwas kurz a.,** to break, snap, sth. off short; (*d*) **die Hufeisen a.,** to unshoe a horse; (*e*) **sich** *dat.* **etwas vom Munde a.,** to stint oneself of sth. **2.** (*a*) (*discontinue; terminate*) **Beziehungen, Unterhandlungen, a.,** to break off relations, negotiations; **seine Rede kurz a.,** to break off, end, one's speech abruptly; **das Gefecht a.,** to stop, cease, fighting; to break off the engagement; **eine Belagerung a.,** to raise a siege; **die Arbeit a.,** to break off (work), *F:* to knock off; (*b*) to demolish, pull down (house, bridge, etc.); to break up (ship); **alle, die, Brücken hinter sich a.,** to burn one's boats; (*c*) *Mil: etc:* **die Zelte a.,** to strike tents; **das Lager a.,** to strike camp, break camp; *F:* to fold one's tent. **3.** *Print:* to divide (word at end of line); **nicht a.,** to run on (the matter).

II. **abbrechen,** *v.i. sep. (strong)* **1.** (*a*) *(sein)* to break off, snap off; **mein Messer brach kurz ab,** my knife snapped off short; (*b*) *(haben)* **mit j-m a.,** to break (off) with s.o.; (*c*) *(haben)* **(mitten) in einer Rede a.,** to break off in (the middle of) a speech; **kurz a.,** to stop short (in speech, etc.). **2.** *(sein) Mil:* **zu zweien a.,** to fall in two deep; **zu zweien brecht ab!** form up two deep! **zur Kolonne a.,** to reform column. **3.** *(haben) A. & Lit:* (*with dative object*) = **Abbruch tun,** *q.v. under* **Abbruch** 4.

III. *vbl s.* **Abbrechen** *n.,* **Abbrechung** *f. in vbl senses; also:* (*a*) cessation, discontinuance; (*b*) demolition (of house, etc.); (*c*) *Mil:* **Abbrechen des Lagers,** striking, breaking, camp; (*d*) *Print:* division (of word at end of line). *Cp.* **Abbruch.**

IV. *p.p. & a.* **abgebrochen,** *in vbl senses; esp.* (*of speech, style, etc.*) abrupt; jerky; disconnected; **abgebrochene Sätze,** disjointed sentences; incoherent phrases; *adv.* disconnectedly, disjointedly, incoherently; (ending) abruptly.

abbreiten, *v.tr.* to stretch out, spread out; *Metalw:* to beat out (copper, etc.).

abbremsen. I. *v.sep.* **1.** *v.i. (haben) Aut: etc:* to brake, to put on the brakes; to slow down. **2.** *v.tr.* (*a*) *Aut: etc:* to halt, stop (vehicle); to slow down (vehicle); (*b*) *Atom.Ph:* to slow down, moderate (particles); (*c*) *Ind:* **einen Motor a.,** to brake-test a motor; (*d*) *Av:* **den Motor a.,** to run the engine on the chocks, on the ground; to rev up the engine; (*e*) **einen Streik a.,** to prevent an impending strike.

II. *vbl s.* **1. Abbremsen,** *n. in vbl senses.* **2. Abbremsung,** *f.* = II. 1; *also:* brake-test (of motor); running-up test, ground-test (of aircraft); *Atom.Ph:* moderation (of particles).

abbrennbar, *a.* combustible.

abbrennen. I. *v.sep. (conj. like* **brennen**) **1.** *v.tr.* (*a*) to burn away, off (metal, rust, weeds, etc.); **Farbe a.,** to burn off paint (with blow-torch); (*b*) to sear; to singe; to corrode; to calcine (gypsum, etc.); (*c*) *Nau:* to bream (ship); (*d*) *Metall:* to refine (in the furnace); *Metalw:* to scour, pickle, dip; to harden, temper (steel); (*e*) *Cer:* to give the final firing (to the ware); (*f*) to burn down (house, etc.); (*g*) *Ch:* (i) to deflagrate, (ii) to distil (sth.) off, out; (*h*) **ein Feuerwerk a.,** to let off, set off, fireworks; *A:* **eine Flinte a.,** to fire (off) a gun. **2.** *v.i. (sein)* (*a*) (*of candle, fire, etc.*) to burn down, away; (*of paint, etc.*) to burn off; **ein Streichholz a. lassen,** to let a match burn down; **abgebranntes Streichholz,** spent, used, match; (*b*) (*of house, etc.*) to burn down, to be burnt down, consumed by fire; *F:* (*of pers.*) **abgebrannt sein,** to be hard up (for money), *F:* to be cleaned out, stony-broke, on the rocks, on one's beam ends; (*c*) *A:* (*of powder*) to flash in the pan; (*of gun*) to hang fire, to misfire; (*d*) *Ch:* to deflagrate; (*e*) to cease, finish, burning. **3. sich (von, in, der Sonne) abbrennen lassen,** to get brown (in the sun).

II. *vbl s.* **Abbrennen** *n.,* **Abbrennung** *f. in vbl senses; also:* conflagration; *Ch:* (i) deflagration, (ii) distillation; *Ind:* calcination (of gypsum, etc.); *A:* **Abbrennen (des Pulvers),** flash in the pan, misfire.

Abbrenner, *m. Ch:* deflagrator.

Abbrennglocke, *f. Ch:* deflagrating jar.

Abbrennlampe, *f.* (painter's) blow-lamp.

Abbrennlöffel, *m. Ch:* deflagration spoon.

Abbrennschweißung, *f. Metalw:* flash welding.

Abbreviation [abreˑviaˑtsĭˈoːn], *f.* **-/-en,** abbreviation; abridg(e)ment; abridging.

Abbreviator [abreˑvĭˈaːtor], *m.* **-s/-en** [-vĭaˑˈtoːrən]. **1.** abridger (of texts, etc.). **2.** *Ecc:* drafter of Papal briefs; abbreviator.

Abbreviatur [abreˑvĭaˑˈtuːr], *f.* **-/-en,** abbreviation; abridg(e)ment.

abbreviieren [abreˑviˑˈiːrən], *v.tr.* to abbreviate; to abridge.

abbringen. I. *v.tr. sep. (conj. like* **bringen**) **1.** (*a*) to remove (sth.); to take (sth.) away; to remove, get (dirt, stains, etc.) out, off; to get (stiff nut, tight lid, etc.) off; (*b*) *Nau:* to heave off, refloat, set afloat (stranded ship); (*c*) *Com:* **Waren a.,** to find a customer for goods. **2.** to divert, turn aside; **j-n von etwas a.,** to dissuade s.o. from doing sth.; to argue s.o. out of doing sth.; to put s.o. off doing sth.; **j-n vom rechten, richtigen, Wege a.,** to lead s.o. astray; to put s.o. on the wrong track; **die Hunde von der Fährte, Spur, a.,** to throw the hounds off the scent, put the hounds on the wrong scent; **davon läßt er sich nicht a.,** he cannot be dissuaded from it, *F:* he won't budge.

II. *vbl s.* **Abbringen,** *n. in vbl senses; also:* removal (of nut, lid, stain, etc.).

abbröckeln, *v.sep.* **1.** *v.tr.* to crumble. **2.** *v.i.* *(sein, haben), occ. v.refl.* to crumble (away); (*of paint, plaster, etc.*) to peel (off); (*of wall, ceiling*) to scale (off); *Com:* (*of prices*) to drop (away); *St. Exch:* (*of rates*) to ease off; *F:* (*of customers, members, etc.*) to drop away, off.

Abbruch, *m.* **1.** (*a*) demolition; pulling down (of house, etc.); **auf A. verkaufen,** to sell (building, etc.) at demolition value; to sell (machinery, etc.) as junk; (*b*) breaking away, crumbling (of earth, etc.). **2.** (*a*) remains, wreckage, debris, fragments; (metal) scrap; (*b*) *Geol:* river deposits; ice-fall. **3.** breaking off, discontinuance; **A. der Verhandlungen,** breaking off, rupture, of negotiations. **4.** detriment, injury, damage, prejudice; **A. erleiden,** to suffer damage, injury; to be damaged, injured; **j-m A. tun,** to wrong, damage, s.o.; to inflict an injury, a loss, on s.o.; (*of action*) to be prejudicial to s.o.'s interests; **das würde unseren Interessen A. tun,** that would be detrimental, prejudicial, to our interests; *F:* **das tut der Liebe keinen A.,** that needn't stand between us. **5.** *Ven:* **A. tun,** to thin out (game).

abbrüchig, *a.* **1.** (*of brick, etc.*) friable, crumbly, brittle. **2.** *occ:* prejudicial, injurious, detrimental (**für,** to); *Jur:* derogatory (clause).

Abbruchlinie, *f. Geol: etc:* line of cleavage.

abbruchreif, *a.* (*of building*) due for demolition; (*of machinery, etc.*) due to be scrapped.

Abbruch(s)arbeit, *f.* demolition (work).

abbruchtuend, *a.* derogatory (statement, etc.); harmful, injurious (act, etc.).

abbrühen, *v.tr. sep. Cu:* (*a*) to boil (vegetables, etc.); (*b*) to scald (poultry, etc.), to blanch (vegetables, etc.). *See also* **abgebrüht.**

abbrüllen, *v.tr. sep.* **1.** to bawl, bellow out (a song). **2. sich abbrüllen,** to bawl, shout, oneself hoarse.

abbrummen, *v.tr. sep. F:* **seine Strafe a.,** to serve one's sentence, *F:* to do a stretch, to do one's time; **sechs Monate a.,** to serve a sentence of six months, *F:* to do six months.

abbuchen. I. *v.tr. sep.* **1.** *Book-k:* to debit (an amount). **2.** (*a*) *Fin:* to write down (capital); to write off (capital); (*b*) *Com:* **eine zweifelhafte,** *F:* **faule, Schuld a.,** to write off a bad debt; (*c*) *Mil.Av: F:* **ein Flugzeug, eine Besatzung, a.,** to write off an aircraft, aircrew (*after crash*).

II. *vbl s.* **1. Abbuchen,** *n. in vbl senses.* **2. Abbuchung,** *f.* (*a*) = II. 1; (*b*) *Book-k:* debit-entry.

abbügeln, *v.tr. sep.* to iron (out) (clothes, etc.); **eine Naht a.,** to press a seam.

abbürsten, *v.tr. sep.* (*a*) to brush off (dirt, etc.); (*b*) to brush; to clean (sth.) with a brush; *F:* **j-n a.,** to give s.o. a good talking-to, a (good) dressing-down; to haul s.o. over the coals.

abbüßen. I. *v.tr. sep.* to expiate, atone for, pay the penalty of (sin, etc.); **ein Vergehen mit Geld a.,** to pay a fine for an offence; **er hat es schwer a. müssen,** *F:* he paid for it up to the

hilt; **eine Strafe a.,** to serve a sentence, *F:* to do time, to do a stretch.

II. *vbl s.* **Abbüßen** *n.*, **Abbüßung** *f. in vbl senses; also:* expiation; *Theol:* atonement.

ABC, Abc [aːbeːˈtseː], *n.* **-/- & -s/-s.** **1.** alphabet, ABC. **2.** rudiments, elements (of a science).

Abc-Bank, *f. Sch:* **auf der A.,** in the infants' class.

Abc-Code, *m. Tg: etc:* telegraphic code; ABC code.

Abc-Schütz(e), *m.* **-(e)n/-(e)n,** child learning to read.

ABC-Staaten, *pl. only*=Argentine, Brazil, Chile.

ABC-Waffen, *f.pl. Mil:* ABC weapons.

Abdach, *n. Constr:* (*a*) penthouse; lean-to roof; (*b*) coping (of wall).

abdachen. I. *v.tr. sep.* **1.** (*a*) to roof (house, etc.); (*b*) *occ:* to unroof (house, etc.); *cp.* **abdecken. 2.** (*a*) *Civ.E: etc:* to slope (ditch, etc.); to batter (wall); *Fort:* to (e)scarp; *Arch:* **einen (gotischen) Strebepfeiler a.,** to finish a (Gothic) buttress with a coping; (*b*) **sich a.,** to slope down, shelve; *Civ.E:* to batter.

II. *vbl s.* **1. Abdachen,** *n. in vbl senses.* **2. Abdachung,** *f.* (*a*)=II. 1; (*b*) declivity, slope, incline, gradient; *Civ.E: etc:* bank, embankment, slope, ramp; *Fort:* escarpment; (*c*) *Constr:* coping.

abdachig, *a.* sloping, shelving (ground, etc.).

Abdachungswinkel, *m.* angle of slope.

abdämmen. I. *v.tr. sep.* **1.** to dam up (river, etc.); to dam (stream); *Mil:* to block (up), close (road); **den Lauf der Ereignisse a.,** to stay, stem, the course of events. **2.** to impound (water). **3.** to dike, dyke (land); to (em)bank (river, etc.).

II. *vbl s.* **1. Abdämmen,** *n. in vbl senses.* **2. Abdämmung,** *f.* (*a*)=II. 1; (*b*) bank; embankment; dike; *Hyd.E:* (coffer-)dam, caisson.

Abdampf, *m. Mch:* exhaust steam, waste steam, dead steam.

Abdampf-, *comb. fm. Mch:* waste-steam . . . ; exhaust-; *Ch:* evaporating . . . ; **Abdampfgefäß** *n*, evaporating vessel, dish, basin, pan.

Abdampfapparat, *m. Ind: etc:* evaporator.

abdampfen. I. *v.sep.* **1.** *v.i.* (*sein*) (*of train, ship*) to steam away, off; *F:* (*of pers.*) to take oneself off, *F:* to clear off, sling one's hook, make oneself scarce. **2.** *v.i.* (*haben, sein*) (*of liquids*) to evaporate; (*of solids*) to volatilize. **3.** *v.tr.* to evaporate, boil down (liquid); to volatilize (solid).

II. *vbl s.* **1. Abdampfen,** *n.* (*a*) evaporation, vaporization; (*b*) departure (of train, ship); steaming off, out, away (of ship). **2. Abdampfung,** *f.*=II. 1 (*a*).

abdämpfen. I. *v.tr. sep.* **1.** to evaporate, boil down (liquid). **2.** *Cu:* to stew (meat, etc.); to steam (fish, potatoes, etc.). **3.** to deaden, muffle, *Cin:* to damp (sound).

II. *vbl s.* **Abdämpfen** *n.*, **Abdämpfung** *f. in vbl senses; also:* (*a*) *Cin: etc:* (sound-)damping; (*b*) evaporation (of liquid).

Abdampfflansch, *f. Mch:* steam outlet.

Abdampfleitung, *f. Mch:* waste-steam pipe; exhaust-pipe.

Abdampfmaschine, *f.* **1.** *Ind:* evaporator. **2.** *Cer:*=**Abdampfofen.**

Abdampfofen, *m. Cer:* slip-kiln.

Abdampfrohr, *n.*=**Abdampfleitung.**

Abdampfrückstand, *m.* solid residue from evaporation.

Abdampfturbine, *f.* waste-steam turbine.

Abdampfverwertung, *f.* utilization of waste steam.

Abdampfvorrichtung, *f.*=**Abdampfapparat.**

abdanken. I. *v.sep.* **1.** *v.tr.* (*a*) *A:* to discharge, dismiss, *F:* sack, turn off (servant, employee); *Mil: A:* to dismiss (officer) from the service, to cashier (officer); **er ist abgedankt,** he is out of employment; (*b*) to retire (s.o.), pension (s.o.) off, superannuate (s.o.); *Mil: Navy: A:* to retire (officer); **abgedankter Major,** retired major; **abgedankter Feldwebel,** pensioned-off sergeant-major; (*c*) *A:* to disband (troops, workmen); *Navy: A:* pay off (ship's crew); to put (ship) out of commission. **2.** *v.i.* (*haben*) (*a*) to resign office; to resign one's post, *F:* to throw up one's appointment; *Mil: Navy: A:* to take one's discharge, to leave the service; (*b*) (*of monarch*) to abdicate.

II. *vbl s.* **Abdanken** *n.*, **Abdankung** *f. in vbl senses; also:* **1.** (*a*) discharge, dismissal (of employee); (*b*) superannuation (of official, officer); **um seine Abdankung bitten,** to ask to be relieved of one's duties. **2.** resignation, retirement (of official); abdication (of monarch). **3. Abdankung,** *Swiss:* funeral (ceremony).

Abdankungsdekret, *n.*, **Abdankungsurkunde,** *f.*, instrument of abdication.

abdarben, *v.tr. sep.*=**absparen.**

abdarren, *v.tr. sep.* (*a*) to (kiln-)dry, to kiln (hops, etc.); to cure (flax, etc.) (by drying); to desiccate (fruit, etc.); (*b*) *Ch: Metall:* to liquate (copper, lead, etc.).

Abdarrtemperatur, *f. Brew:* finishing temperature (of malt).

abdasseln, *v.tr. sep. Vet:* to dewarble, remove warble(-fly) from (cattle).

abdechseln, *v.tr. sep. Nau:* to dub (deck-planking).

abdecken. I. *v.tr. sep.* **1.** to uncover, take the covering off (sth.); to unroof, untile (house); to untile, strip (roof); **(den Tisch) a.,** to clear the table, to clear away; to remove the (table-)cloth; **das Bett a.,** (i) to take off the bed cover; (ii) *occ.* to strip the bed. **2.** to flay (ox, horse, etc.). **3.** (*a*) to cover (sth.) (up, over); *Phot:* to mask (negative, transparency); *Phot: Engr:* to stop out (parts of negative, plate); (*b*) to put a protective covering on (sth.); *Phot:* to cap (lens); *Constr:* (i) to cope (wall); (ii) to cover (up) (wall, etc.) (with protective material, etc.); to face, plate (surface) (with sheet-iron, etc.); (iii) to tile *or* slate *or* thatch (wall, roof, house) ; *Tchn:* to cover, conceal, case in (pipes, etc.); to protect, board over (machinery, etc.); to enclose (electrical apparatus, etc.); *Mil:* to camouflage (guns, vehicles, etc.). **4.** *Com: Fin:* to cover (overdraft, etc.); to meet, settle (debt); to repay (credit); to make up, make good (deficit).

II. *vbl s.* **1. Abdecken,** *n. in vbl senses.* **2. Abdeckung,** *f.* (*a*)=II. 1; *also: Com: Fin:* settlement (of debt); repayment (of credit); (*b*) (protective) cover(ing); *Constr: etc:* (i) coping (of wall); (ii) (straw, bitumen, etc.) covering; (metal) plating.

Abdecker, *m.* (*a*) knacker; (*b*) flayer.

Abdeckerei, *f.* **-/-en,** knacker's yard; *Leath:* rendering establishment.

Abdeckerhäute, *f.pl. Leath:* hides from rendering establishments; *F:* renderers.

Abdeckflügel, *m. Cin:* obscuring blade, masking blade (of shutter).

Abdeckplatte, *f. Constr: etc:* cover-plate, covering plate.

Abdeckscheibe, *f.* cover-plate (of accumulator, etc.).

Abdeckstein, *m.* coping-stone (of wall).

Abdeckung, *f. see* **abdecken** II. 2.

abdeichen, *v.tr. sep.* **1.** to dam up (river, etc.); to dam (stream). **2.** to impound (water). **3.** to dike, dyke (land).

Abderit [apdeˑˈriːt], *m.* **-en/-en.** **1.** *A.Hist:* Abderite. **2.** *Lit: F:* Abderite; Gothamite; simpleton.

abderitisch [apdeˑˈriːtiʃ], *a.* **1.** *A.Geog:* Abderitan. **2.** *Lit: F:* simple, foolish, Abderite.

abdestillieren, *v.tr. sep.* (*a*) to distil; (*b*) to distil (sth.) off, out.

abdichten. I. *v.tr. sep.* (*a*) to make (sth.) (water-, air-, steam-, gas-)tight; to caulk, hammer (boiler seams, etc.); *Nau:* to caulk (ship, seams); *Mec.E: Mch:* to pack (gland, etc.); *Ind: etc:* to lute (retort, crucible, etc.); (*b*) to block up, stop (up) (chinks); to seal (up) (window); **ein Zimmer a.,** to make a room draught-proof.

II. *vbl s.* **1. Abdichten,** *n. in vbl senses.* **2. Abdichtung,** *f.* (*a*)=II. 1; *also:* **metallische A.,** metal-to-metal joint; (*b*)=**dichten**[1] II. 2 (*b*), (*d*).

III. *p.p. & a.* **abgedichtet,** *in vbl senses; esp.* (*of joint, etc.*) (made) tight; (*of container*) watertight; air-tight; (*of boat, etc.*) watertight.

Abdichtungsmaterial, *n.* caulking; packing; sealing (material).

Abdichtungsring, *m.*, **Abdichtungsscheibe,** *f.* packing washer; expanding washer.

abdicken, *v.tr. sep.* to reduce, boil down (solution); to concentrate (syrup); inspissate (liquid); *Cu:* to thicken by boiling; to reduce (fruit-juice) to a syrup.

abdielen, *v.tr. sep.* **1.** (*a*) to plank (floor, etc.); (*b*) to floor (room, etc.). **2.** to board off, partition (off) (room, etc.).

abdienen, *v.tr. Mil: etc:* **seine Zeit a.,** to do one's (military) service; to serve one's time (in the Forces).

Abdikation [apdiˑkaˑtsĭˈoːn], *f.* **-/-en,** abdication (of throne); renunciation, surrender (of authority, rights, etc.).

abdingen, *v.tr. sep.* (*conj. like* **dingen**) **j-m etwas a.,** to purchase *or* hire sth. from s.o.; to do a deal with s.o. for sth.

abdizieren [apdiˑˈtsiːrən], *v.insep.* (*a*) *v.tr.* to abdicate (throne); to renounce, surrender (rights, etc.); (*b*) *v.i.* (*haben*) to abdicate; to renounce, surrender, one's rights, etc.

abdocken, *v.tr. sep.* to unwind (wool, etc.) (from the skein).

Abdomen [apˈdoːmɛn], *n.* **-s/- & -mina** [-minaː]. *Anat: etc:* abdomen.

abdominal [apdoˑmiˑˈnaːl], *a. & comb.fm. Anat: etc:* abdominal.

Abdominaltyphus, *m. Med:* typhoid (fever), enteric fever.

abdonnern, *v.sep.* (*a*) *v.i.* (*sein*) (*of racing car, aeroplane, etc.*) to roar off; (*b*) *v.impers.* (*only in the phrase*) **es hat (sich) abgedonnert,** the thunder has stopped, is over, it has stopped thundering.

abdorren, *v.i. sep.* (*sein*) (*of fruit, etc.*) to wither up; to wither and fall.

abdörren, *v.tr. sep.* **1.** to desiccate (fruit, vegetables, etc.). **2.** *Metall:* to sweat, roast (lead and silver ore).

Abdörrofen, *m. Metall:* refining furnace.

Abdraht, *m. Metalw:* turnings (from a lathe).

abdrängen. I. *v.tr. sep.* **1.** (*a*) to push, thrust, shove, (s.o.) aside; (*b*) to supplant (s.o.); (*c*) (*of wind*) to deflect (ship, aircraft) from its course. **2. j-m etwas a.,** to worry, badger, sth. out of s.o.

II. *vbl s.* **1. Abdrängen,** *n., in vbl senses.* **2. Abdrängung,** *f.* (*a*)=II. 1; (*b*) *Av:Nau:* drift; deflection from course.

Abdrängungsmesser, *m. Av: A:*=**Abtriftmesser.**

abdrechseln, *v.tr. sep.* (*a*) to turn off (irregularities, etc.) (with the lathe); (*b*) to turn (sth.); to round (sth.) off (with the lathe); to copy (sth.) on the lathe; (*c*) *p.p. & a.* **abgedrechselt,** *F:* (*of courtesies, etc.*) stiff; over-formal; affected; *see also* **Redensart.**

abdrehen, *v.sep.* **1.** *v.tr.* (*a*) to turn off, twist off; **eine Schraubenmutter a.,** to unscrew, twist off, a nut; **das Gewinde von einer Mutter a.,** to strip (the thread from) a nut; **einem Huhn den Hals a.,** to wring a fowl's neck; *F:* **j-m den Hals a.,** to wring s.o.'s neck; *F:* **j-m etwas a.,** to trick, *F:* do, diddle, twist, s.o. out of sth.; (*b*) to turn off (tap, water, gas); to turn out (light); to switch off (electric light); (*c*) to turn, fashion, shape, (sth.) on the lathe; to turn off (irregularities, etc.) (with the lathe); (*d*) **sein Gesicht a.,** to turn away one's face (from sth.). **2.** *v.i.* (*haben*) (*of aircraft, ship*) to turn away (from the target, from enemy aircraft, ship); to sheer off; *F:* (*of pers.*) to sheer off, clear off.

abdreschen, *v.tr. sep.* (*strong*) *Husb:* to thresh (corn). *See also* **abgedroschen.**

Abdrift, *f. Nau:*=**Abtrift.**

abdringen, *v.tr. sep.* (*strong*) to extort (money); to exact (promise). *Cp.* **abnötigen.**

abdrohen, *v.tr. sep.* **j-m etwas a.,** to bully sth. out of s.o.; to get sth. out of s.o. by threats.

abdrosseln, *v.tr. sep.* (*a*) *Mch: I.C.E:* to throttle (steam, engine); *abs.* **a.,** to throttle down; *Ind:* **Produktion a.,** to cut back, *F:* to taper off, production; (*b*) *El:* to choke (out).

Abdruck[1], *m.* **-(e)s/-e.** **1.** *Print:* (*a*) printing (off), striking off; **A. von tausend Stück,** run, printing, of a thousand (copies); (*b*) proof; **erster A.,** first proof; (*c*) text (of passage, letter, article, etc.) printed as part of the material of a book; **ein A. des Gedichtes in der Urfassung befindet sich im Anhang,** the original text of the poem will be found in the appendix; (*d*) reprint, re-impression (of book); (*e*) separate reprint (of magazine article, etc.); offprint (of learned article, etc.); (*f*) *A:* copy (of book). **2.** (*a*) *Engr:* proof; **erster A.,** first state; **A. vor der Schrift,** proof before the letter, before letters; **A. nach der Schrift,** proof after letters, letter proof; (*b*) *Phot:* proof (of photograph); (*c*) *Phot.Engr:* phototype.

Abdruck[2], *m.* **-(e)s/⸗e.** **1.** (*a*) impress(ion), (im)print, mark, stamp; **A. eines Siegels,** impression of a seal; **A. in Gips,** plaster cast; **A. in Wachs,** wax impression; *Archeol:* squeeze (of seal, coin, inscription); *Paleont:* mould (of fossil); (*b*) *A:* image, counterpart; **die Natur ist der A. der Gottheit,** Nature is the image of the deity. **2.** *Sm.a:* (*a*) trigger; (*b*) pressing, pulling, of the trigger.

Abdruckbild, *n. F:* transfer(-picture).

abdrucken, *A. & South G.Dial:* **abdrücken**[1]. I. *v.tr. sep.* **1.** (*a*) *Print:* to print (off), to strike off; **tausend Stück a.,** to strike off a thousand copies; **ein Buch (wieder) a.,** to reprint a book; (*b*) to reproduce (document, etc.) (*by manifolding, etc.*); (*c*) to transfer (design, coloured picture, etc.); (*d*) to print (passage, letter, article, etc.) (*as part of the material of a book*); **dieser Brief isthier zum**

ersten Mal vollständig abgedruckt, this letter is printed here in its entirety for the first time. **2.** *Print:* **sich abdrucken,** to mackle, macle.

II. *vbl s.* **Abdrucken,** *n. in vbl senses; cp.* **Abdruck**[1] 1 (*a*).

abdrücken[2]. **I.** *v.tr. sep.* **1.** (*a*) to take an impression, make a mould of (sth.); to make, take a (plaster-)cast of (statue, etc.); *Archeol:* to squeeze, to take a squeeze of (coin, seal, inscription); (*b*) *Adm:* **einen Stempel auf etwas** *acc.* **a.,** to impress a stamp on, to stamp, sth. **2. eine Feder a.,** to release, snap, a spring; **ein Schloß a.,** to snap a (spring-)lock; *Sm.a:* **(ein Gewehr) a.,** to fire a gun, a rifle; **(den Hahn) a.,** to pull, press, the trigger; **einen Pfeil a.,** to let fly, let off, loose, an arrow; to speed an arrow (from a bow). **3.** (*a*) to crush (crystals, etc.); to squeeze (rubber sac, etc.); (*b*) to force out, drive out (nail, pin, etc.); to squeeze off, force off (collar from rod, etc.); (*c*) **es drückt mir das Herz ab,** it wrings my heart; it grieves me to the heart; (*d*) **j-n herzlich a.,** to give s.o. an affectionate hug, squeeze. **4. sich abdrücken,** to leave an impression, a print, an imprint, a mark; **auf seinem Gesicht drückte sich die Freude, der Schmerz, ab,** his face showed joy, grief; joy, grief, was plain, imprinted, on his face.

II. *vbl s.* **Abdrücken,** *n. in vbl senses; cp.* **Abdruck**[2] 2 (*b*).

Abdruckmasse, *f. Ind: etc:* (*a*) moulding substance; (*b*) substance to be moulded.

Abdruckrecht, *n. Publ:* right of reproduction.

Abdruckschraube, *f. Mec.E:* set screw.

Abdruckstempel, *m. Phot.Engr:* block.

abdudeln, *v.tr. sep. F:* to drool out (a song); to play (a piece) monotonously; *F:* to churn out (a piece).

Abduktion [apduktsɪˈoːn], *f.* **-/-en. 1.** *Physiol: Surg:* abduction. **2.** *Log:* transition (from one proposition to another).

Abduktor [apˈduktor], *m.* **-s/-en** [-ˈtoːrən]. *Anat:* abductor (muscle); abducent muscle.

abdunkeln, *v.sep.* **1.** *v.tr.* (*a*) to darken, deaden, deepen, dull, dim; *Dy: Paperm:* to sadden (colour); (*b*) to black out (room). **2.** *v.i.* (*haben*) (*of colour, substance*) to grow darker, deeper; to darken, deepen.

abdunsten. I. *v.i. sep.* (*sein*) to evaporate.

II. *vbl s.* **Abdunsten** *n.,* **Abdunstung** *f.,* evaporation.

abdünsten. I. *v.tr. sep.* **1.** to evaporate, dry off (liquid); to graduate (brine). **2.** *Cu:* to steam (vegetable, fish, etc.); to stew (fruit, meat, fish).

II. *vbl s.* **Abdünsten** *n.,* **Abdünstung** *f. in vbl senses; also:* evaporation (of liquids); graduation (of brine).

abduzieren [apduˈtsiːrən], *v.tr. insep. Physiol: Surg:* to abduct.

Abe [a·ˈbeː, ˈa·beː], *m. & n.* **-s/-.** *South G.Dial:* (= **Abort**) lavatory.

abebben, *v.i. sep.* (*sein*) to ebb away; (*of tide*) to ebb; (*of flood, passions, etc.*) to abate; (*of passion, etc.*) to die down, die away.

abeb(e)nen, *v.tr. sep.* = **ebnen.**

Abece [aːbeːˈtseː], *n.* **-s/-s,** alphabet, ABC.

Abecedarier [aːbeːtseːˈdaːriər], *m.* **-s/-. 1.** child learning to read. **2.** *Hist: F:* anabaptist.

abecelich, *a.* = **alphabetisch.**

abecken, *v.tr. sep. Tchn: Carp:* **etwas a.,** to take off the edges, the corners, of sth.; **etwas nach dem rechten Winkel a.,** to square sth.

abeggen, *v.tr. sep. Agr:* to harrow, drag (field).

abeichen, *v.tr. sep.* = **eichen**[3].

abeifern (sich), *v.refl. sep.* = **ereifern (sich).**

abeilen, *v.sep.* **1.** *v.i.* (*sein*) to hurry off, away. **2. sich abeilen,** to be in a hurry, in a rush.

abeisen, *v.tr. sep.* = **enteisen.**

-abel [ˈaːbəl], *a.suff.* (*in words taken from French*) -able; **adorabel,** adorable; **diskutabel,** debatable; **miserabel,** miserable; **respektabel,** respectable.

Abelbaum [a·bˈeːl-], *m.,* **Abele** [a·ˈbeːlə], *f.* **-/-n.** *Bot:* white poplar, abele.

Abelmosch, *m.* **-es/,** **Abelmoschus,** *m. Bot:* abel-musk, musk-mallow (of India).

Abelmoschuskörner, *n.pl. Toil:* musk-seed, ambrette.

abelsch, *a. North G.Dial:* silly, stupid.

Abend, *m.* **-s/-e** (*in certain contexts spelt with a small a*). **1.** (*a*) evening; **guten A.!** good evening! good night! *F:* **'n A., Willi!** *F:* evening, Willie! *see also* **gut**[1]; **heute a., diesen A.,** this evening, tonight; **bis heute a.!** I shall be seeing you again this evening, *F:* see you tonight! **morgen a.,** tomorrow night; **gestern a.,** yesterday evening, last night; **Montag a.,** Monday evening; **am A.,** in the evening; **am vorigen A., am A. vorher,** on the evening before, on the previous evening; **an jenem A., jenen A.,** on that evening; **am folgenden, nächsten, A.,** on the next evening, on the evening of the next day; **des Abends,** in the evening(s); **er macht des Abends einen Spaziergang,** he takes a walk in the evening(s), of an evening; **eines schönen Abends im Sommer,** one, on a, fine summer evening; **es geht auf, gegen, den A. zu, es wird A., es will A. werden,** evening is drawing on; day is drawing to a close; *Poet:* night is drawing nigh; **zu A. essen, speisen,** to have supper; to dine; **nicht zu A. essen,** to go without supper, dinner; to go supperless; **es ist noch nicht aller Tage A.,** (i) we must abide the end; (ii) we are not yet out of the wood; (iii) don't count your chickens before they are hatched; *see also* **Tag;** (*b*) *Dial:* afternoon; (*c*) *Lit:* **der A. des Lebens,** the evening of life; **am A. seines Lebens,** in his declining years; in the evening of his life; (*d*) **freier A.,** free evening; evening off; **ich habe für Wochen keinen freien A.,** I shan't have an evening to myself for weeks to come; I shall have no free evening for some time to come. **2.** (evening) party; at-home; social evening; **bunter A.,** social (evening with varied entertainments); **Bach-A.,** musical evening, evening concert, with works by Bach; Bach concert. **3.** eve, preceding day; **der A. vor Weihnachten, der Heilige A.,** Christmas Eve. **4.** the west; **gegen,** *Poet:* **gen, A.,** westwards, to the west; **gegen A. gelegen,** lying to the west, in the west; westward.

Abend-, *comb.fm.* **1.** evening . . . . **2.** west . . . ; westerly . . . ; occidental . . . .

Abendandacht, *f. Ecc:* evening prayer; evening service; evensong.

Abendanzug, *m.* (man's) evening dress(-suit).

Abendbeleuchtung, *f.* evening light(ing); *Art:* evening effect.

Abendbesuch, *m.* (*a*) evening visit; (*b*) evening visitor(s); **wir haben heute A.,** we have visitors, a visitor, this evening.

Abendbrot, *n.* supper.

Abenddämmerung, *f.* (evening) twilight, dusk, nightfall; **in der A.,** at dusk, in the dusk of evening, in the gloaming.

Abenddunkel, *m.* gloom of the evening; dusk.

abenden, *v.impers.* (*occurs only in the phr.*) **es abendet,** evening is drawing on, day is drawing to a close; *Poet:* night is drawing nigh.

Abendessen, *n.* dinner; supper; evening meal; **j-m zum A. einladen,** to ask, invite, s.o. to dinner *or* supper; to ask s.o. to dine (with one).

Abendfalter, *m. Ent:* = **Nachtfalter.**

Abendfrische, *f.* cool of the evening.

abendfüllend, *a.* full-length (film, etc.); **abendfüllendes Programm,** full-length programme, programme that fills a whole evening.

Abendgebet, *n.* (*a*) evening prayer(s), evening devotion; bedtime prayer(s); (*b*) = **Abendandacht.**

Abendgeläut(e), *n.* (pealing of) evening bells; *A:* curfew.

Abendgesellschaft, *f.* (evening) party.

Abendglanz, *m.* sunset glow, glow of the setting sun.

Abendglocke, *f.* evening bell; angelus(-bell); *A:* curfew.

Abendglut, *f.* = **Abendglanz.**

Abendgottesdienst, *m. Ecc:* evening service; evensong; *R.C.Ch:* vespers.

Abendgrauen, *n.* dusk; (the) shadows of evening, (the) shades of night.

Abendkasse, *f. Th:* box office (for the current evening performance).

Abendkleid, *n.* (lady's) evening dress, *U.S:* evening gown, formal gown.

Abendkurs(us), *m.* evening classes.

Abendland, das, the West, the Occident.

Abendländer, *m.* **-s/-.** Westerner, Occidental.

abendländisch, *a.* Western (country, civilization, etc.); Occidental; **die abendländische Kirche,** the Western church; the Roman Catholic church.

abendlich. 1. (*a*) *a.* of the evening; in the evening; evening . . . ; **ein abendlicher Besuch,** an evening visit; **in abendlicher Ruhe,** in the peace of evening; (*b*) *adv.* at evening; in the evening(s). **2.** *a.* western; westerly; occidental.

Abendlichtnelke, *f. Bot:* white campion.

Abendluft, *f.* evening air; **die (frische) A.,** (i) the cool of evening; (ii) the evening breeze.

Abendmahl, *n.* **1.** *A:* supper. **2.** (*a*) **das A.,** the Last Supper; (*b*) *Ecc:* **das (heilige) A.,** (Holy) Communion, the Sacrament, the Lord's Supper; **j-m das A. reichen,** to administer Holy Communion to s.o., to communicate s.o.; **ich will das A. darauf nehmen,** I swear to God that it is true.

Abendmahlsbrot, *n. Ecc:* (eucharistic) host.

Abendmahlsbulle, die. *Ecc.Hist:* the papal bull 'In coena Domini'.

Abendmahlsfeier, *f.* communion service.

Abendmahlsgänger, Abendmahlsgast, *m.* communicant.

Abendmahlsgemeinschaft, *f.* intercommunion.

Abendmahlskelch, *m.* communion cup; chalice.

Abendmahlsstreit, *m. Ecc.Hist:* controversy about the dogma of transubstantiation.

Abendmahlstisch, *m.* communion table; the Lord's Table.

Abendmahlswein, *m.* communion wine, sacramental wine.

Abendmahlzeit, *f.* evening meal; supper; dinner.

Abendmusik, *f.* serenade.

Abendnachrichten, *f.pl. W.Tel:* evening news (bulletin).

Abendpfauenauge, *n. Ent:* eyed hawk-moth.

Abendpunkt, *m. Astr: A:* true west.

abendrot[1], *a.* **abendroter Himmel,** sunset glow; afterglow; red evening sky.

Abendrot[2], *n.,* **Abendröte,** *f.* sunset glow; red evening sky; *Prov:* **Abendrot Gutwetterbot',** red sky at night, shepherd's delight.

abends, *adv.* (*a*) in the evening; *esp. U.S:* evenings; of an evening; **um neun Uhr a.,** at nine o'clock in the evening; **a. spät, spät a.,** late in the evening, in the late evening; **neulich a.,** the other evening; a few evenings ago; **a. am ersten Mai,** on the evening of the first of May; (*b*) (regularly) in the evenings; **er geht a. spazieren,** he takes a walk in the evening(s), of an evening; **montags a.,** Monday evenings, nights; **von früh bis a. arbeiten,** to work from morning to night; to work morning, noon and night.

Abendschein, Abendschimmer, *m.* (*a*) gleam of the evening sky; (*b*) = **Abendrot**[2].

Abendschule, *f.* evening school; evening classes; night school.

Abendseite, *f.* west(ern) side.

Abendsonne, *f.* (*a*) setting, *Lit:* westering, sun; (*b*) evening sun; evening sunshine.

Abendstern, der. *Astr:* the evening star; Hesper; Hesperus; Venus; *Dial:* the shepherd's lamp.

abendstill, *a. Poet:* **die abendstillen Felder,** the fields (i) in the still of the evening, (ii) quiet as though evening had fallen.

Abendstille, *f.* peace, quiet, stillness, of the evening.

Abendstimmung, *f.* **1.** evening mood. **2.** *Art:* evening effect.

Abendtau, *m.* evening dew; (*in tropical countries*) serein.

Abendtisch, *m.* (*a*) supper; evening meal; (*b*) supper-table; **guter Mittags- und A.,** good board.

Abenduhr, *f.* sundial (with its surface turned to the west).

Abendvogel, *m. Dial: Ent:* = **Nachtfalter.**

Abendwache, *f. Nau:* dog-watch.

abendwärts, *adv. A. & Poet:* westwards.

Abendweite, *f. Astr:* western amplitude (of a star).

Abendwind, *m.* **1.** (*a*) evening breeze; (*b*) *Meteor:* (*in mountain areas*) katabatic valley-wind. **2.** *A. & Poet:* west(erly) wind.

Abendzeit, *f.* evening; the evening hours; **zur A.,** at evening; *Poet:* at eve, at eventide.

abenken, *v.tr. sep. Hort:* to layer.

Abenteuer, *n.* **-s/-. 1.** (*a*) adventure; exploit; **A. suchen, auf A. ausgehen, ausziehen,** to go in quest, search, of adventure; **ein A. bestehen, erleben,** to meet with, have, an adventure; **das große A.,** the great adventure, *esp.* the one memorable happening in an otherwise uneventful life; (*b*) **(galantes, kleines) A.,** intrigue, (love) affair, (amorous) adventure. **2.** venture. **3.** *A:* marvel; **wilde Tiere und sonstige A. für Geld sehen lassen,** to put on show wild animals and other marvels.

abenteuerhaft, *a.* adventurous (experience, etc.).

Abenteuerin, *f.* **-/-innen.** *Pej:* adventuress.

Abenteuerleben, *n.* life of adventure; adventurous life.

abenteuerlich, *a.* **1.** adventurous (act, life, person); venturesome (person, act); **abenteuerliches Unternehmen,** hazardous, risky, undertaking; *adv.* adventurously, venturesomely. **2.** strange, curious, odd; **eine abenteuerliche Geschichte,** a curious business; a most remarkable affair.

Abenteuerlichkeit, *f.* **1.** (*a*) adventurousness, venturesomeness; (*b*) quixotry; knight-errantry. **2.** (*a*) oddity; strangeness (of an event, affair); (*b*) odd happening; curious adventure.

Abenteuerlust, *f.* spirit of adventure; delight in adventure(s); venturesomeness.
abenteuerlustig, *a.* adventurous, venturesome.
abenteuern, *v.i.* (*haben*) to go adventuring; to lead an adventurous life; *A:* (*of knight*) to quest for adventures; **abenteuernder Ritter,** knight-errant.
Abenteuerroman, *m.* novel of adventure; adventure story; romance of chivalry.
Abenteuertum, *n.* **-s/.** (*a*) adventuring; adventure; adventurous existence *or* way of life; (*b*) quixotry; knight-errantry.
Abenteurer, *m.* **1.** adventurer; adventurous man. **2.** man who lives by his wits; adventurer; soldier of fortune; sharper.
Abenteurergeist, *m.* spirit of adventure; adventurous spirit; venturesomeness.
Abenteurerin, *f.* **-/-innen=Abenteuerin.**
aber. 1. *conj.* (*coordinating and adversative*) (*a*) but; **ärmlich, aber anständig gekleidet,** poorly but respectably dressed; (*b*) but; however; yet; (*after a negative,* **aber** *is used when the two halves of the statement are not mutually exclusive; cp.* **sondern***; exceptional use,* **nicht er, aber ich,** not he, but I); **ich mißtraue ihm, aber mehr noch seinem Bruder,** I distrust him, but I distrust his brother even more; **er ist nicht hier, aber er wird, (er) wird aber, bald zurückkommen,** he is not here, but, however, he will be back soon; **er ist ein intelligenter Mann, seine Frau aber ist ungewöhnlich dumm,** he is an intelligent man; his wife, however, is extraordinarily stupid; **ich fühle mich nicht wohl, krank aber bin ich auch nicht,** I am not well, but, yet, I am not ill; *see also* **zwar;** (*c*) (i) **nun aber,** now; *Lit:* **nun aber er gekommen ist, . . . ,** now that he has come . . . ; (ii) **oder aber,** or else, otherwise; **er muß die Miete bezahlen oder aber das Zimmer räumen,** he must pay the rent or else give up the room; he must pay the rent, otherwise he will have to give up the room. **2.** *conj.* (*coordinating*) and, but; *B:* **Jesus aber sprach zu ihm,** (and) Jesus said unto him; **da es aber Herodes hörte,** but when Herod heard thereof; *Lit:* **Isegrim aber der Wolf begann die Klage . . . ,** and Isegrim the wolf began his complaint. . . . **3.** *emotive particle* (*a*) (*with nuance of emphasis*) **es ist aber wahr,** but it is true; it is true indeed; **ich hab's aber mit eigenen Augen gesehen!** but I tell you I saw it (with my own eyes)! **aber ˈja!** why, certainly! but yes! **aber ˈnein!** (i) not at all! by no means! (ii) I can't believe it; **das ist aber herrlich,** but that's wonderful; that's just splendid; *F:* **ich hab's ihm aber gegeben,** I gave him what for; **nun ist's aber genug!** that's quite enough of it, *F:* stow it! *see also* **doch** III. 2 (*b*), **schon** , **wohl** ; (*b*) (*nuance of warning*) **tu's aber (ja) nicht!** don't do it! (—you'll regret it); don't risk it; **daß du mir aber (ja) nicht wieder zu spät kommst,** but mind you don't come late again; **du kriegst aber Haue!** look out, you'll get a beating! (*c*) (i) **aber doch,** (*with nuance of reassurance or desire for certainty*) **er wird dir aber doch ˈschreiben, nicht wahr?** but he will write to you, won't he? (ii) **doch aber,** (*more tinged with anxiety than* **aber doch**) **er wird doch aber schreiben?** he will write, I hope? (*d*) **aber, aber!** (i) (*soothing*) there, there; (ii) (*warning*) now, now! now then! come, come! (*humorous disgust*) tut, tut! **aber Kinder!** (*with nuance of impatience*) for heaven's sake! (*with nuance of indignation*) really, children! **4.** *adv.* again; **aber und abermals,** over and over again; **Tausende und aber Tausende,** thousands upon thousands; **hundert und aber hundert . . . ,** hundreds upon hundreds of . . . , hundreds and hundreds of (times); *A:* **selig und aber selig,** blessed and once more blessed. **5. Aber,** *n.* **-s/-(s), es ist ein Aber dabei,** there is one objection, criticism, to be made; there is a but (about it); **dein(e) Wenn(s) und Aber(s),** your ifs and buts; **hier gibt es kein Aber,** don't start arguing; and that's flat! *A. & Hum:* but me no buts. *See also* **wenn.**
Aber-, aber-, *pref. denotes:* **1.** *repetition;* **Aberahn** *m,* great-great-grandfather; **abermalig,** repeated; **Abername** *m,* nickname (*i.e. additional name*); **Tausende und Abertausende,** thousands upon thousands; **Abersaat** *f,* aftercrop. **2.** *distortion or falsification of the sense expressed in the noun or adj.* (*cp.* **After-** 4); **Aberglaube** *m,* superstition; **Aberkönig** *m,* spurious king; pretender; **Aberwitz** *m,* frenzy.
Aberacht, *f. G.Mediev.Hist:* double ban (imposed one year after original ban).
Aberahn, *m.* great-great-grandfather.
Aberbann, *m.*=**Aberacht.**
aberben, *v.tr. sep.* to inherit the estate of (s.o.) to inherit from (s.o.).
Aberglaube, *m.* superstition.
abergläubig, *a.*=**abergläubisch.**
abergläubisch, *a.* superstitious; *adv.* -ly.
Abergunst, *f. A:* false, treacherous, favour.
aberkennen. I. *v.tr. sep.* (*conj. like* **kennen**) **j-m etwas a.,** to deny, disallow, s.o.'s right to sth.; to declare s.o. to have forfeited his right to sth.; to deprive, dispossess, s.o. of sth. (by decree); *Jur:* **j-m die bürgerlichen Ehrenrechte a.,** to deprive s.o. of civil rights; **j-m die (deutsche) Staatsangehörigkeit a.,** to deprive s.o. of (German) citizenship.
II. *vbl s.* **Aberkennen** *n.,* **Aberkennung** *f.,* dispossession, deprivation (by decree); disallowing (of s.o.'s right to sth.); *Jur:* loss (of a right); disallowance (of costs, etc.); **Aberkennung der bürgerlichen Ehrenrechte, der Staatsangehörigkeit,** deprivation of civil rights, of citizenship.
aberklug, *a.* conceited; priggish; too clever by half.
abermal, *adv.*=**abermals.**
abermalig, *a.* repeated (attempts, etc.); second (revision, etc.); renewed (request).
abermals, *adv.* (once) again, once more; *see also* **aber** 4.
Abername, *m.* nickname.
abernten, *v.sep.* **1.** *v.tr.* to reap (corn, field, etc.); to harvest, gather (crops); to crop (land, fields). **2.** *v.i.* (*haben*) to complete the harvest, to finish harvesting.
Aberration [abɛraˈtsĭˈoːn], *f.* **-/-en.** *Astr: Opt:* aberration; *see also* **chromatisch, sphärisch.**
Aberraute, *f. Bot:*=**Eberraute.**
aberregen. I. *v.tr. sep. El:* to de-energize.
II. *vbl s.* **Aberregen** *n.,* **Aberregung** *f. El:* de-energization.
aberrieren [abɛˈriːrən], *v.i.* (*sein*) *Astr: Opt:* to produce aberration; to aberrate.
abertausend. 1. *inv.a.* thousands and thousands of . . . . **2.** *n.pl.* **Tausende und Abertausende von . . . ,** thousands upon thousands of . . .
Aberwille, *m.*=**Widerwille.**
Aberwitz, *m.* **-es/.** *A:* frenzy, madness, raving; foolishness, craziness, senselessness, silliness.
aberwitzig, *a. A:* frenzied, crazed, lunatic, mad, out of one's wits, raving; foolish, senseless, silly.
Aberzahn, *m. Vit:* axillary, lateral, shoot.
abessen, *v.sep.* (*strong*) **1.** *v.tr.* to eat (sth.) up entirely; to eat one's way through (a large meal); to eat (a dish) clean; to pick (a bone). **2.** *v.i.* (*haben*) to finish eating; **als sie abgegessen hatten,** when they had finished their meal; *F:* **er hat bei uns abgegessen,** we have finished with him; he will get nothing further from us. **3.** *occ.* **sich an einer Speise a.**=**überessen.**
Abessinien [aˑbɛˈsiːnĭən]. *Pr.n.n.* **-s.** *Geog:* Abyssinia.
Abessinier [aˑbɛˈsiːnĭər], *m.* **-s/-. 1.** *Geog:* Abyssinian. **2.** *F:*=**Abessinierbrunnen.**
Abessinierbrunnen, *m. Hyd.E:* driven well, drive-well; tube-well.
abessinisch [aˑbɛˈsiːniʃ], *a. Geog:* Abyssinian.
abfachen, *v.tr. sep.* to divide (sth.) into compartments; *Constr:* to frame; to half-timber (wall).
abfädeln, *v.tr. sep.* **1.** to unstring, unthread (beads, pearls, etc.). **2.** *Cu:* to string (beans).
abfaden, *v.tr. sep. Nau:* to sound, fathom.
abfadmen, abfadnen, *v.tr. sep.* **1.** *Dial:*=**abfädeln. 2.** *Nau:*=**abfaden.**
abfahrbar, *a.* removable, transportable (machine, etc.).
abfahren, *v.sep.* (*strong*) **I.** *v.i.* (*sein*) **1.** (*a*) (*of vehicle, of pers. in vehicle*) to depart, leave, start; to go off; (*of carriage, motor-car, etc., or pers. in it*) to drive off, away; (*of cyclist, motor-cyclist*) to ride off, away; (*of cyclist*) to cycle off, to pedal off, away; (*of ship*) to sail (away), to move off; (*of ship, train*) to steam off, out; (*of train*) to pull out; (*of motor transport column*) to move off; **wir fahren morgen nach München ab,** we leave, start, for Munich to-morrow; **der Zug, das Schiff, fährt um zehn Uhr ab,** the train leaves, starts, goes, the ship leaves, starts, goes, sails, at ten; **abfahren!** (i) off you go! (ii) *Rail: etc:* right away! (*b*) *F:* to make off, decamp, make oneself scarce; to clear out, *U.S:* beat it; **fahr ab!** hop it! *U.S:* beat it! **j-n a. lassen,** to send s.o. about his business, send s.o. packing; to snub s.o.; *F:* to send s.o. to the right-about, give s.o. his marching orders, send s.o. away with a flea in his ear; **einen Freier a. lassen,** to turn a suitor down (flat), *F:* to show a suitor the door; **er fuhr übel ab mit seiner Werbung,** his was a luckless wooing; (*c*) *F:* to die; *A. & Lit:* **aus, von, diesem elenden Leben a.,** to depart (from) this miserable life. **2.** to slip; **der Meißel fuhr ihm ab,** the chisel slipped out of his hands. **3.** to descend; *Ski:* to run downhill; *see also* **Hocke**[1], **Schuß.**
II. **abfahren,** *v.tr.* **1.** to cart away, off; to carry away; to transport (away). **2. sich abfahren,** (*of tyres*), to wear (out); **die Hinterreifen fahren sich schon ab,** the back tyres are wearing (out), are wearing smooth, *F:* are going; **stark, arg, abgefahrene Reifen,** badly worn tyres; **abgefahrener Wagen,** worn-out car. **3.** (*a*) to tear (sth.) off, to knock (sth.) down (*by driving vehicle against it*); (*b*) **bei einem Autounfall wurde ihm ein Bein abgefahren,** he was run over by a car and lost a leg. **4.** (*a*) to travel over, to traverse; **er hat die ganze Schweiz abgefahren,** he has travelled all over Switzerland, *F:* he has covered the length and breadth of Switzerland; (*b*) to drive, travel, the whole length of (road, etc.); (*of police car, etc.*) to patrol (road, etc.); (*c*) *Rail: abs.* to work a train.
III. *vbl s.* **Abfahren,** *n. in vbl senses; cp.* **Abfahrt, Abfuhr.**
Abfahrt, *f.* **1.** (*a*) start; departure (of person, vehicle, train, etc.); sailing (of ship); **schon bei der A. war er sehr müde,** he was very tired even at the start of the journey; (*b*) way out, exit (for vehicles); (*c*) *F:* death, decease, *F:* demise (of s.o.). **2.** descent; going down, downward journey (of lift, mountain railway, etc.); *Ski:* (i) slope; (ii) run; (iii) downhill running.
abfahrtbereit, *a.* ready to depart; (*of ship*) ready to sail, with steam up; (*of pers.*) *F:* all set to go.
abfährten, *v.i. sep.* (*haben*) *Ven:* to follow the trail, traces, track (of animal); to follow the slot (of deer); **rein a.,** to follow a clearly distinguishable trail.
Abfahrt(s)flagge, *f.* **1.** *Nau:*=**Abfahrt(s)signal** 1. **2.** *Sp:* starting-flag.
Abfahrt(s)hafen, *m. Nau:* port of sailing, of departure.
Abfahrtshaltung, *f. Ski:* running position.
Abfahrtslauf, *m. Ski:* downhill race.
Abfahrt(s)schuß, *m.* starting-gun, -shot, -signal.
Abfahrt(s)signal, *n.* **1.** *Nau:* the Blue Peter. **2.** starting-signal; *Rail:*=guard's green flag *or* whistle.
Abfahrt(s)zeichen, *n.* starting-signal.
Abfahrt(s)zeit, *f.* time of departure, departure time; *Nau:* time of sailing.
Abfall, *m.* **1.** (*a*) falling (off), dropping (off) (of leaves, etc.); falling, dropping (of water from fountain, etc.); (*b*) *Clockm:* drop; **den A. einstellen,** to put in beat. **2.** slope, incline, declivity, gradient; **steiler A.,** sudden dip (in ground, sea-bed); *Arch:* pitch, slope (of roof). **3.** wastage; decrease, diminution; drop, dropping (away); *El.E:* drop, decrease (in current, potential, voltage); (*of trade, etc.*) **in A. kommen, geraten,** to decline, drop away, decay. **4.** (*a*) defection, desertion, falling away; **A. von einer Partei, von einer Sache,** defection from, desertion of, falling away from, a party, a cause; **A. von einem Glauben, von einer Religion,** apostasy; falling away from a faith, a religion; backsliding; *A:* **A. zum Feinde,** desertion (to the enemy); (*b*) revolt, rebellion; *Hist:* **der A. der Niederlande,** the revolt of the Netherlands. **5.** contrast (**gegen,** to, with); **welcher A. gegen früher!** what a contrast with previous conditions! *F:* what a come-down! **6.** (*a*) deficiency, shortage (in weight, measure, etc.) (**an**+*dat.,* in); **A. an Gewicht,** underweight, short weight; (*b*) *Agr:* failure (of crops). **7.** *Nau:* drift (of ship). **8. Abfall,** *pl.* **Abfälle,** waste, refuse, rubbish; litter; (household, town) refuse; chips (of stone, wood, diamonds); chippings (of stone, marble, metal); cuttings (of wood, metal, etc.); garbage; (butcher's, leather) offal; parings (of vegetables, leather); scraps; shavings (of wood, metal); trimmings (of wood, iron, paper, etc.; *Cu:* of meat); *Cin:* film waste; *Ind:* waste products, by-products; *Ind: F:* junk; *Metalw:* (i) waste metal, scrap (metal); (ii) turnings; (iii) filings; *Mill: Husb:* refuse grain, tail-corn, tailings; *Min:* tailings; *Nau:* shakings (of rope, sailcloth); *Tex:* **A. vom Kämmen,** combing waste.
Abfallasche, *f.* riddlings.
Abfallauge [ˈapfalˀlaugə], *f. Paperm: etc:* spent lye, waste lye.
Abfallbrennstoff, *m.* refuse fuel.
Abfallbunker, *m. Cokem:* breeze bunker.
Abfalldünger, *m. Agr:* offal (used as) manure.

Abfallecke, *f. Clockm:* delivery edge.

Abfalleimer, *m.* refuse-bin, dustbin, *U.S:* ashcan.

Abfalleisen, *n.* scrap-iron, iron scrap.

abfallen. I. *v.i. sep.* (*strong*) (*sein*) **1.** (*a*) (*of leaves, etc.*) to fall (off), drop (off); (*of water from fountain, shavings from wood, etc.*) to fall, drop; (*b*) (*of pers.*) to fall off; (*c*) **j-n a. lassen,** to drop s.o.'s acquaintance, *F:* to drop s.o.; **bei j-m a.,** to be rebuffed, snubbed, *F:* sent to the right-about, by s.o.; (*d*) *Clockm:* **die Uhr fällt ungleich ab,** the clock is off the beat, out of beat; (*e*) *Print:* (*of letters*) to fall, drop, out of place; (*f*) *Sp:* (*running, motor-racing, etc.*) to fall behind, back; (*g*) (*of profits*) **bei einem solchen Geschäft fällt nicht viel (Gewinn) ab,** that sort of business does not yield much profit; **nur keine Angst, es fällt etwas für dich ab,** don't worry, you'll get your share, *F:* your whack; *F:* there'll be something in it for you; *U.S. & F:* you'll get your cut. **2.** (*of ground, road*) to slope (down); to dip (away); (*of ground*) to shelve; **steil a.,** to drop (away), fall away; **schroff a.,** to drop, fall, precipitously; **das Ufer fällt gegen das Meer ab,** the shore shelves down to the sea. **3.** to break away; (*a*) **vom Glauben, von seiner Religion a.,** to apostatize, become an apostate; to renounce one's faith; **von einer Partei, einer Sache a.,** to fall away from, desert (from), a party, a cause; **von j-m a.,** to forsake, desert s.o., to throw s.o. over; (*b*) to rebel, revolt (**von,** against); **von Gott a.,** to rebel against God; (*c*) *Mil: A:* **zu zweien a.,** to form up two deep. **4.** *Nau:* (*of ship*) (i) to fall off; to fall (off) to leeward; (ii) **nach Backbord a.,** to cast to port. **5.** (*a*) to fall away, off; to decrease, diminish; to drop away, off; to decline; to wane; to decay; to deteriorate; *El.E:* (*of voltage, potential*) to drop, fall; (*b*) (*of living being*) to lose weight, flesh; to become emaciated, to waste away; **(stark) abgefallen,** emaciated, wasted (figure, face, etc.). **6. gegen j-n, etwas, a.,** to come off badly by comparison with s.o., sth.; to compare badly with s.o., sth. **7.** to be wasted; to be waste; *Ind:* to come off as waste, as a waste product, as a by-product; **bei einem Verfahren abfallende Säure,** waste acid resulting from a process. **8.** *Ven:* (*of birds*) to fly off (from tree); (*of hound*) to lose the scent; (*of stag*) to descend from the hind. **9.** *v.tr.* **sich** *dat.* **ein Bein a.,** to lose a leg by a fall.

II. *vbl s.* **Abfallen,** *n. in vbl senses; also: Bot:* deciduousness; *Nat.Hist:* caducity; *Nau:* lee lurch, drift (of ship); *cp.* **Abfall** 1 (*a*), 2, 3, 4.

III. *pr.p. & a.* **abfallend,** *in vbl senses; esp.* **1.** sloping, shelving (ground, etc.); **steil a.,** steeply inclined, sloping; **schroff a.,** precipitous. **2.** *Nat.Hist:* caducous (membrane, etc.); deciduous (leaf).

IV. *p.p. & a.* **abgefallen,** *in vbl senses; esp.* **Abgefallene** *m, f,* deserter, renegade, turncoat; apostate (from a religion).

abfällen, *v.tr. sep. Ch:* to precipitate (out) (a solid).

Abfallenergie, *f.* waste energy.

Abfaller, *m.* -s/-. *Swim:* dead man's drop.

Abfallerzeugnis, *n.* = **Abfallprodukt.**

Abfallfaß, *n.* refuse-bin, dustbin, *U.S:* ashcan.

Abfallgrenze, *f.* lower limit (of drop); *El.E: etc:* critical limit.

Abfallgut, *n. Ind:* material recovered from waste; *Coal-Min:* waste washings.

Abfallholz, *n.* waste wood; *For:* refuse wood.

abfällig, *a.* **1.** ready, likely, to fall; apt to fall off, drop off; *Nat.Hist:* caducous (membrane, etc.); *Bot:* deciduous (leaf); **abfälliges Obst,** (i) fruit ready to drop; (ii) *occ.* windfalls. **2.** inclined, sloping (ground, etc.); shelving (ground, coast). **3.** *A:* = **abtrünnig. 4.** unfavourable (opinion, answer); adverse (criticism, judgment, opinion); disparaging, depreciatory (remarks). **5.** *A:* = **fällig. 6.** *Com:* (*of goods, etc.*) rubbishy, trashy; of inferior quality. **7.** *adv.* **sich über j-n, etwas, a. äußern,** to speak disparagingly of s.o., sth.; **etwas a. beurteilen,** to pass an adverse, unfavourable, judgment on sth.; **j-n a. bescheiden,** to give s.o. an unfavourable answer; to rebuff s.o.

Abfälligkeit, *f.* -/-en. **1.** declivity, slope (of ground, etc.). **2.** *A:* desertion; *Rel:* apostasy. **3.** derogatory, depreciatory, nature (of remarks, judgment).

Abfallkalk, *m. Ind:* by-product lime.

Abfallkohle, *f.* **1.** waste coal, refuse coal. **2.** waste charcoal.

Abfallkoks, *m.* coke breeze, waste coke.

Abfallkübel, *m.* refuse-bin, dustbin, *U.S:* ashcan.

Abfallmarke, *f. Dy:* off-shade.

Abfallmoment, *n. Mec:* breaking-down moment.

Abfallpapier, *n.* waste paper.

Abfallprahm, *m. Nau: etc:* refuse disposal lighter.

Abfallprodukt, *n. Ind:* waste product; by-product.

Abfallrinne, *f.* drainage channel *or* outlet.

Abfallrohr, *n.,* **Abfallröhre,** *f.* **1.** drain-pipe, waste-pipe, discharge pipe, outlet pipe. **2.** *Constr:* downpipe, rain(-water) pipe, fall-pipe. **3.** *Tchn:* suction-pipe.

Abfallrücken, *m. Hyd.E:* ogee curve.

Abfallsäure, *f. Ch: etc:* residuary acid; waste acid; spent acid; *esp. Ind:* spent sulphuric acid.

Abfallschneider, *m. Metalw:* waste-cutter.

Abfallschraube, *f. Clockm:* beat screw (of crutch-fork).

Abfallstoff, *m.* (*a*) waste material; (*b*) *pl.* **Abfallstoffe,** sewage.

Abfallstoffaufbereitung, *f. Paperm:* preparation of waste for pulping.

Abfallstoffverwertung, *f.* = **Abfallverwertung.**

Abfallstrom, *m. El.E:* releasing current; waste current.

Abfallstück, *n. Ind: etc:* reject, *F:* throw-out, waster; piece of waste material; scrap (of cloth, leather, etc.).

Abfallvernichter, *m.* refuse destructor; incinerator; *Dom.Ec:* waste disposal unit.

Abfallvernichtungsanlage, *f.* refuse destruction plant; refuse destructor; incinerator (plant).

Abfallverwertung, *f.* utilization of waste.

Abfallverwertungsanlage, *f.* waste utilization plant.

Abfallware, *f. Ind:* reject(s), *F:* throw-out(s), waster(s).

Abfallwasser, *n.* **1.** waste water. **2.** sewage.

Abfallwirtel, *m. Ropem:* tapered whirl.

Abfallzeit, *f. El.E:* (pulse) decay time.

abfälschen, *v.tr. sep. Sp:* to put spin on (ball); to slice (ball).

abfalzen, *v.tr. sep. Leath:* to scrape, skive (skin).

Abfangautomatik, *f.* = **Abfang(s)vorrichtung.**

abfangen. I. *v.tr. sep.* (*strong*) **1.** (*a*) to catch (s.o., sth.); to seize (s.o., sth.); to trap, snare (animal); *Mil:* to capture (enemy patrol); (*b*) to collect (water); to catch, impound, pipe (water); to divert (watercourse); (*c*) *Metall:* to tap (molten metal from furnace); (*d*) to intercept (s.o., letter, etc.; *Navy: Mil.Av:* ship, aircraft); to head off (fugitives, etc.); (*e*) **einen Angriff, usw., a.,** to foil, thwart, frustrate, an attack, etc.; *Sp:* **einen Gegner a.,** to thwart an opponent (runner) (by putting on a spurt); *Fenc:* **einen Stoß a.,** to parry a thrust; (*f*) *Sp: etc:* to catch up (with) (another runner, etc.); to catch (s.o.) up; **wenn du läufst, wirst du ihn vielleicht a.,** you may catch him if you run. **2.** *Ven:* to dispatch (wounded animal); to give (stag, boar, etc.) the coup de grâce. **3.** *Constr: etc:* to stay; to prop (up), shore (up) (wall, etc.); to underpin (wall, etc.); *Min:* to timber (gallery, etc.). **4.** to bring (vehicle, etc.) back to normal course; to right (vehicle); (*a*) *Aut:* **einen schleudernden Wagen a.,** to get a skidding car under control, to pull a car out of a skid, side-slip; (*b*) *v.tr. & i.* (*haben*) *Av:* to pull (an aircraft) out of a dive, to flatten out; to right (an aircraft); *Navy:* to trim (submarine). **5. j-m etwas a.,** to deprive s.o. of sth. by catching it; **j-m die Kaninchen a.,** to poach s.o.'s rabbits; **j-m die Kunden a.,** to steal s.o.'s customers; **j-m das Wasser a.,** to divert s.o.'s water supply (to one's own use); *Nau:* **einem Schiff den Wind a.,** to get the weather gauge of a ship, to luff a ship.

II. *vbl s.* **Abfangen,** *n. in vbl senses; also:* capture (of s.o.); interception (of letter, aircraft, etc.); diversion (of s.o.'s water supply).

Abfangjäger, *m. Mil.Av:* interceptor-fighter, interceptor.

Abfangkanal, *m. Civ.E:* branch sewer, interception sewer.

Abfangkeile, *m.pl. Tls:* slips (for handling tubes).

Abfangrinne, *f. Hyd.E:* catch-drain.

Abfangseil, *n. Av:* check cable.

Abfang(s)vorrichtung, *f. Av:* pull-out device (of dive-bomber).

Abfang(ungs)taktik, *f. Mil: etc:* interception tactics.

Abfangverfahren, *n. Ch:* interception process.

Abfangwalze, *f. Mil:* climbing roller (of tank).

Abfarad, *n. El.Meas:* abfarad.

abfärben, *v.sep.* **1.** *v.tr.* to finish the dyeing of (sth.). **2.** *v.i.* (*a*) (*sein*) to fade, to lose colour; to grow dull, dim; *Dy:* (*of dyes, dyed materials*) to bleed; **diese Stoffe färben bald ab,** the colour soon comes out of these materials; (*b*) (*haben*) to impart colour (**auf** + *acc.,* to); **der Schlips hat auf das Hemd abgefärbt,** the colour of the tie has run on to the shirt; **sein Stil färbt schon auf mich ab,** my style is beginning to be coloured by his, *F:* I am catching his tricks of style.

abfasen. I. *v.tr. sep. Carp: Stonew: etc:* to chamfer, bevel; *Farr:* to shape (horseshoes).

II. *vbl s.* **1. Abfasen,** *n. in vbl senses.* **2. Abfasung,** *f.* (*a*) = II. 1; (*b*) chamfer, chamfered edge, bevel, bevel-edge.

abfasern, *v.sep.* **1.** *v.tr.* (*a*) to ravel out, unravel, tease out; (*b*) to fray (material); (*c*) *Cu:* to string (beans). **2.** *v.i.* (*haben*) & **sich abfasern,** (*of material*) to fray (out), to unravel.

abfassen, *v.tr. sep.* **1.** to draw up, draft, word, write (out) (agreement, report, letter, etc.); to write (article, essay); to compose, pen (sermon, etc.); *A:* to indite (letter); **dieser Artikel ist gemeinverständlich abgefaßt,** this article is written, couched, in a popular style. **2.** to catch (thief, etc.); **j-n dabei, bei einer Tat, a.,** to catch s.o. in the act, red-handed. **3.** *A:* to weigh out, measure out (corn, etc.).

abfaulen, *v.i. sep.* (*sein*) to rot off, away.

abfedern. I. *v.sep.* **1.** *v.tr.* (*a*) to pluck (poultry); (*b*) to fit (sth.) with springs; to spring (carriage, car, undercarriage of aircraft, etc.); **abgefederter Wagen,** sprung carriage; (*c*) to absorb (shock); to take up (bumps, jolts); *Aut: Av:* (*of wheel, tail-skid, etc.*) **abgefedert,** fitted with shock-absorbers; (*d*) *Ven:* to dispatch, kill, (wounded bird) (by piercing brain). **2.** *v.i.* (*haben*) to lose, shed, feathers; (*of bird*) to moult.

II. *vbl s.* **1. Abfedern,** *n. in vbl senses; also:* absorption (of shock). **2. Abfederung,** *f.* (*a*) = II. 1; (*b*) *Veh:* suspension, springing, springs (of car, etc.).

abfegen, *v.tr. sep.* **1.** to sweep, wipe, off (sth.); to clean; **den Staub von einem Tisch a.,** to wipe the dust off a table. **2.** *Ven:* (*of deer*) to fray (its head).

abfeilen, *v.tr. sep.* (*a*) to file (sth.) off, away; (*b*) to file (sth.) down; to clip (coin); to rough (sth.) out with a file; to file up (surface to be soldered).

abfeilschen, *v.tr. sep.* **1. j-m etwas a.,** to bargain, haggle, chaffer, with s.o. for sth. **2. j-m zwanzig Mark a., vom Preise zwanzig Mark a.,** to get s.o. to reduce his price by twenty marks, knock twenty marks off his price; to beat the price down by twenty marks; **er läßt sich keinen Heller a.,** he won't take a halfpenny less than his price.

abfeimen, *v.tr. sep.* to scum, skim (soup, molten glass, molten metal, etc.); *see also* **abgefeimt.**

abfertigen. I. *v.tr. sep.* **1.** (*a*) (*of post-office official, warehouse official, etc.*) to get (sth.) ready for sending off, for dispatch; to dispatch (goods, etc.); to attend to (letter, parcel, goods, etc.); *Rail:* **einen Zug a.,** to start a train; *Nau:* **ein Schiff a.,** to dispatch, clear, a ship; *Cust:* **Güter (zollamtlich) a., Zollgüter a.,** to clear goods; (*b*) to carry out, deal with, attend to (business, etc.); to deal with, attend to (application, order, complaint, etc.); *Com:* **einen Auftrag a.,** to deal with, attend to, an order, to carry out an order; **Anträge von Mitgliedern werden bevorzugt abgefertigt,** applications from members are dealt with first, are given priority, preference; **seine Beschwerde wurde als bloße Schikane abgefertigt,** his complaint was dismissed as mere malice; **etwas eilig a.,** to deal with sth. quickly; to expedite sth.; (*c*) *A:* to let (s.o.) go; to set (s.o.) on his way, *A:* to bring (s.o.) on his journey. **2.** (*a*) to serve, attend to (customer, etc.); **einen Boten a.,** to attend to, deal with, a messenger; **er fertigte die letzten Kunden ab, dann schloß er das Geschäft,** he served the last customers, then he closed the shop; (*b*) to deal with, get rid of (s.o.); to get (s.o.) out of the way; **j-n derb, grob, schroff, a.,** to deal roughly with s.o.; to send s.o. packing; to snub s.o.; *F:* to send s.o. away with a flea in his ear; **j-n kurz a.,** to be brusque, short, off-hand, with s.o.; to treat s.o. in an off-hand(ed) manner; **ich lasse mich nicht so a.,** I won't be dealt with like that, I won't be snubbed like that; I'm not going to let myself be put off like that; (*c*) to pay (s.o.) off (on dismissal).

II. *vbl s.* **1. Abfertigen,** *n. in vbl senses.* **2. Abfertigung,** *f.* (*a*) = II. 1; *also:* dispatch (of goods, etc.); *Cust:* clearance; (*at post-office counter, etc.*) **'hier keine A.',** 'position closed', *U.S:* 'closed'; (*b*) rebuff; **j-m eine A. erteilen,** to

rebuff s.o., to send s.o. packing; **j-m eine kurze, schroffe, A. erteilen,** to be brusque, short, with s.o.; **von j-m eine A. erhalten,** to be rebuffed, sent packing, by s.o.; (*c*) **seine A. erhalten,** to get one's documents, papers (after dismissal); (*d*) *Post: Rail: Com:* dispatching office *or* counter; forwarding office.

Abfertigungsbeamte, *m.* (*decl. as adj.*) *Rail:* luggage-office clerk, *U.S:* baggage clerk.

Abfertigungsdienst, *m. Com:* dispatch service.

Abfertigungsschein, *m.* **1.** *Com:* dispatch note; way-bill. **2.** *Cust:* customs declaration (form).

Abfertigungsstelle, *f. Rail: Post: Com:* dispatching office *or* counter; forwarding office.

Abfett, *n.* waste fat; waste grease; *Ind:* skimmings.

abfetten, *v.sep.* **1.** *v.tr.* (*a*) *Ind: etc:* to skim; *Cu:* **die Suppe a.,** to skim the fat off the soup; (*b*) *F:* to grease (machine, etc.). **2.** *v.i.* (*haben*) (*of greasy matter*) (**auf etwas** *acc.*) **a.,** to leave, make, grease-marks (on sth.); to go through (paper, etc.).

Abfeuergriff, *m. Artil:* firing handle.

abfeuern. I. *v.sep.* **1.** *v.tr.* to discharge, fire (off), let off, shoot (firearm, etc.); to fire (rocket); **Geschütze wurden abgefeuert,** guns were being fired, were going off; **einen Revolverschuß auf j-n a.,** to fire, shoot, at s.o. with a revolver; **sein Gewehr auf j-n a.,** to discharge, let off, fire (off), one's gun at s.o., *F:* to let fly at s.o. **2.** *v.i.* (*haben*) (*a*) *Artil: etc:* to fire; *Ind: etc:* to cease firing, heating; to let the fire(s) down, drop.

II. *vbl s.* **1. Abfeuern,** *n. in vbl senses; also:* discharge (of firearm, shot). **2. Abfeuerung,** *f.* (*a*)=II. 1; (*b*) *Artil:* firing mechanism; trigger.

Abfeuerungshebel, *m. Artil:* firing lever.

abfiedeln, *v.tr. sep.* **1. eine Melodie a.,** to scrape out a tune (on the fiddle). **2.** *Metall:* to skim off (dross from molten metal).

abfiedern, *v.sep.* **1.** *v.tr.* to trim off the edges of (glass). **2.** *v.i.* (*haben*)=**abfedern** I. 2.

abfieren, *v.tr. sep. Nau:* (*a*) to slack, slacken, ease, pay out (rope); **a. und holen,** to veer and haul; (*b*) to lower (away) boat; to lower (yard, cargo into hold).

abfiltern, *v.tr. sep.*=**abfiltrieren.**

abfiltrieren. I. *v.tr. sep.* to filter off, out.

II. *vbl s.* **Abfiltrieren** *n.*, **Abfiltrierung** *f.* filtering off, out; filtration.

abfinden. I. *v.sep.* (*strong*) **1.** *v.tr.* (*a*) to satisfy, pay off (creditor); to buy out (partner); (*b*) **sich a. lassen,** to compound, compromise; to accept proffered terms; **er läßt sich leicht a.,** he is easy, not difficult, to satisfy; he is easily satisfied; (*c*) to indemnify, compensate; **j-n für einen Verlust a.,** to compensate, recoup, s.o. for a loss, to make good a loss to s.o.; (*d*) *Com:* **seine Gläubiger (durch Vergleich) a.**= **sich mit seinen Gläubigern a.,** *q.v. under* 2; (*e*) *Jur:* (i) to pay (s.o.) compensation (for relinquished share of inheritance); (ii) to settle a separate portion on (son, daughter); (*f*) *Hist:* **einen Prinzen, Fürsten, a.,** (i) to compensate a prince (for relinquished rights); (ii) to endow a prince with an ap(p)anage; **abgefundener Prinz, Fürst,** ap(p)anagist. **2. sich abfinden,** (*a*) **sich mit etwas a.,** to accommodate oneself to sth.; to make the best of sth.; to make shift, put up, with sth.; to compound, compromise, with sth.; to reconcile oneself to sth.; to acquiesce in (a doctrine, etc.); **ich kann mich nicht damit a.,** I can't put up with that; I can't reconcile myself to that; (*b*) **sich mit j-m a.,** (i) to compound, compromise, effect a compromise, with s.o.; (ii) to come to an agreement, to an arrangement, to terms, with s.o.; *F:* to fix things up with s.o.; *Com:* **sich mit seinen Gläubigern a.,** to compound, make a composition, come to terms, make an arrangement, with one's creditors; (*c*) to return the compliment; to reciprocate; to do s.o. a favour, send s.o. a present, in one's turn.

II. *vbl s.* **1. Abfinden,** *n. in vbl senses; also:* satisfaction (of creditor); compensation, indemnification (of s.o. for loss, etc.); (*action of*) compromise, agreement, settlement. **2. Abfindung,** *f.* (*a*)=II. 1; (*b*) (*accomplished fact*) (i) agreement, settlement, compromise, arrangement; (ii) composition, arrangement (with creditors); (iii) compensation, indemnity, indemnification; (iv); *Jur:*=**Abfindungsvertrag;** (*c*) (*sum, etc.*) (i) compensation, indemnity; (ii) *Com:* payment to creditor(s) under a scheme of composition; (iii) *Jur:* separate portion settled on son, daughter; (iv) *Hist:* ap(p)anage (of a prince)

Abfindungsgeld, *n.*=**Abfindungssumme.**

Abfindungsquantum, *n.* (sum paid as the) share of compensation *or* indemnity; dividend paid to each creditor (of bankrupt estate, etc.).

Abfindungssumme, *f.* pecuniary compensation; (*a*) (*for loss sustained*) indemnity, indemnification, compensation; (*b*) money paid to s.o. in consideration of relinquishing a claim.

Abfindungsvertrag, *m. Jur:* settlement arrived at by parties *inter se*; settlement out of court compromise.

abfingern, *v.tr. sep.* **1.** to count (things, days, etc.) on one's fingers; *F:* **das läßt sich leicht a., das kann ich mir bald a.,** that's not hard to guess. **2.** to finger (guitar, etc.).

abfinnen, *v.tr. sep. Metalw:* to beat out (metal) with a peen-hammer, to peen metal.

abfischen, *v.tr. sep.* (*a*) to clear (river, etc.) of fish; to unstock, draw (pond); (*b*) **das Beste von etwas a.,** to take the cream of sth., to skim the cream off sth.

abfitzen, *v.tr. sep.* **1.** *Tex:* to bundle (yarn) into hanks. **2.** *Constr:* to smooth (plaster, etc.) with a sprinkling-brush. **3.** *Cu: Dial:* (i) to string (beans); (ii) to slice (beans).

abflachen. I. *v.sep.* **1.** *v.tr.* to make (sth.) flat, to flatten (sth.) out; to flatten, smooth (surface, etc.); to level, even up (surface, road, etc.); to bevel (edge); to blunt (angle). **2. sich abflachen,** (*a*) to become flat, to flatten out; to become level, to level out; to become smooth; (*of road*) to grow smoother, easier; (*of hills, undulations*) to subside; (*b*) *Nau:* (*of coast, sea-bed*) to shoal. **3.** *v.i.* (*sein*) *Nau:* (*of water, coast*) to shoal. **4.** *p.p. & a.* **abgeflacht,** (*a*) flattened, flat; level(led); smooth(ed); (*b*) *Nau:* shoaling (coast, sea-bed); (*c*) bevel(led) (edge); blunt (angle); flattened (curve); *Geom:* **(an den Polen) abgeflachtes Ellipsoid, usw.,** oblate (ellipsoid, etc.); *see also* **Kugel.**

II. *vbl s.* **1. Abflachen,** *n. in vbl senses.* **2. Abflachung,** *f.* (*a*)=II. 1; (*b*) (i) flat; flat part (of sth.); level ground; (ii) bevel (of crystal, etc.); (iii) *Nau:* shoal.

abflattern, *v.i. sep.* (*sein*) to flutter off, away; to take wing; (*of bird, F: of pers.*) to fly off.

abflauen. I. *v.sep.* **1.** *v.tr.* to wash, rinse (cloth, etc.); *Min:* to wash, buddle (ore). **2.** *v.i.* (*sein, haben*) (*a*) (*of wind*) to slacken, slack off; to drop, die down, subside; *Mil:* (*of artillery fire*) to ease off; (*of interest, zeal, etc.*) to diminish, fail, flag; **sein Interesse flaut ab,** his interest is flagging, is failing; **sein Talent flaut ab,** his talent is falling off; (*b*) *Com: Fin:* (*of prices, etc.*) to drop, weaken; **die Preise, Kurse, flauen ab,** prices are sagging, going down, becoming easier; **die Geschäfte flauen ab,** business is slackening, falling off.

II. *vbl s.* **Abflauen,** *n. in vbl senses; also: St.Exch:* reaction.

Abflaufaß, *n.* washing-, rinsing-tub; *Min:* buddle, sluice-box.

Abflauherd, *m. Min:* buddle-head.

Abfleischeisen, *n. Leath:* fleshing-iron, -knife.

abfleischen, *v.tr. sep. Leath:* to flesh, scrape (hides).

Abfleischmesser, *n. Leath:* fleshing-iron, -knife.

abflensen, *v.tr. sep.* to remove the blubber from (carcass of whale); to flench, flense (whale).

abfliegen. I. *v.sep.* (*strong*) **1.** *v.i.* (*sein*) (*a*) (*of bird*) to fly away, fly off; to take flight; to take wing; *Ven:* to flush; *Bot:* (*of winged seed*) to fly away; **Tauben a. lassen,** to release pigeons; (*b*) (*of aircraft*) to take off, fly off; (*c*) (*of hat, etc.*) to blow off; (*d*) *For:* (*of wood*) to grow dry and drop; (*e*) *F:* to meet with a rebuff; to be sent packing. **2.** *v.tr. Av:* to patrol (an area, etc.).

II. *vbl s.* **Abfliegen,** *n. in vbl senses; cp.* **Abflug** 1, 2 (*a*).

abfließen. I. *v.i. sep.* (*strong*) (*sein*) (*a*) (*of water, etc.*) to flow away, off, out; to run away, off, out; to drain away, off; **das Wasser a. lassen,** to run off, drain off, the water; *Ind:* **abfließendes Wasser,** waste water; (*b*) (*of river, etc.*) to empty, flow, pour, discharge (**in** + *acc.*, into); (*c*) (*of tide*) to ebb, go out; (*of sea*) to recede; (*d*) *El:* (*of current*) to flow off, leak off; to discharge.

II. *vbl s.* **Abfließen,** *n. in vbl senses; cp.* **Abfluß** 1.

abflitzen, *v.i. sep.* (*sein*) *F:* to make off, dash off, shoot off.

abflößen, *v.tr. sep.* **1.** to raft, float, (timber) downstream. **2.** *Dial:* to skim, take the cream off (milk).

abfluchten, *v.tr. sep.* to align, line up (objects); to lay out, set, (objects) in a line.

Abflug, *m.* **1.** (*a*) (i) flight; taking flight, taking wing (of birds); (ii) *Av:* take-off, start; **A. mit Starthilfe,** assisted take-off; (*b*) release (of pigeons, etc.); (*c*) departure, migration (of swallows, etc.); (*d*) downward flight; descent; *Av:* **A. aufs Wasser,** descent, alighting, on water. **2.** *Bot:* (*a*) flying off (of winged seeds); (*b*) **A. der Bäume,** winged seeds (borne by the wind); *cp.* **abfliegen.**

Abflugbahn, *f. Av:* runway; the tarmac.

Abflugdeck, *n. Navy:* flight deck (of aircraft carrier).

Abfluggeschwindigkeit, *f. Av:* take-off speed.

Abflugleistung, *f. Av:* take-off power.

Abflugplatz, *m. Av:* (*a*) take-off area; (*b*) airfield of departure, airfield from which an aircraft takes off.

Abfluß, *m.* **1.** (*a*) outflow, flow, flowing, discharge (of liquid, gas, etc.); draining off (of water); efflux (of liquid); *Med:* drainage (of lymph, etc.); (*b*) *Hyd.E: etc:* flow, run-off; discharge (of weir, etc.); outfall, outflow, discharging (of sewer); effluent (of sewer, etc.); *Ind:* waste water; (*c*) *Ph.Geog:* drainage; **Gebiet ohne A.,** inland drainage area; (*d*) *Aer:* airflow; **glatter A.,** laminar flow, smooth airflow; (*e*) *Fin:* **A. des Kapitals,** outflow of capital; **A. von Gold ins Ausland,** efflux, draining off, of gold from the country; **der A. unserer Goldreserven,** the drain on our gold reserves. **2.** (*a*) waste-pipe; overflow-pipe; escape-pipe; (*b*) outlet, outflow (of pond, etc.); *Ph.Geog:* **See ohne A.,** lake with no outlet; (*c*) *Constr: etc:* drain; drain-pipe; gutter; sink; gully; *Agr:* drain; *Civ.E:* channel (draining water into a roadside ditch); (*d*) **der Stallboden hat nicht genügend A.,** the floor of the stable has not sufficient slope for the water to drain away.

Abflußdeckel, *m. Nau: Mch:* outlet door (of filter-box).

Abflußdruck, *m.* flow-pressure; flowing pressure (of oil-well, etc.).

Abflußgebiet, *n. Ph.Geog:* drainage area (of sea *or* ocean); catchment area, basin (of river).

Abflußgraben, *m.* drain, (drainage) ditch, trench, gutter, channel; *Dial:* rill.

Abflußgrube, *f. Metall:* (*a*) crucible (of furnace); (*b*)=**Abflußrinne** 2.

Abflußhahn, *m.* drain-cock; discharge cock; delivery cock.

Abflußkanal, *m.* (*a*) *Hyd.E:* waste channel; tail-race; (*b*) *Civ.E:* effluent drain.

Abflußkasten, *m.* drain-tank; draining-trap.

Abflußkühler, *m. Ind:* efflux condenser.

Abflußleitung, *f.* (*a*) waste-pipe, drain-pipe, outlet pipe, discharge pipe, escape-pipe; (*b*) *Ind:* flow-line (from oil-well, etc.).

Abflußloch, *n. Constr:* drain-hole; weep-hole (in wall), *F:* weeper.

abflußlos, *a. Ph.Geog:* **abflußloser See,** lake with no outlet; **abflußloses Gebiet,** inland drainage area.

Abflußmenge, *f.* amount of discharge; *Hyd.E:* delivery (of stream, weir, etc.); discharge, flow (of stream, lake); run-off (of weir, etc.).

Abflußmengenkurve, *f. Hyd.E:* hydrogram.

Abflußmesser, *m. Hyd.E: etc:* flow-meter.

Abflußrinne, *f.* **1.** (*a*) *Hyd.E: etc:* overflow, overflow channel; waste-channel; (drainage) trench; outfall, outlet (of culvert, etc.); (*b*) *Civ.E:* gutter, gully; runnel, kennel. **2.** *Metall:* runner (of a casting).

Abflußrohr, *n.*, **Abflußröhre,** *f.* waste-pipe, drain-pipe, outlet pipe, discharge pipe, escape-pipe; downpipe (from roof); soil-pipe (of W.C.).

Abflußschacht, *m. Civ.E: etc:* gully.

Abflußschleuse, *f. Hyd.E:* outlet sluice; waste-gate.

Abflußventil, *n.* escape valve, outlet valve, discharge valve; draining valve; exhaust valve.

Abflußwasser, *n.* (*a*) waste water; (*b*) *Hyg:* sewage; cess-water.

abfluten, *v.i. sep.* (*sein*) to flow off, away; (*of waters*) to fall, subside.

Abfolge, *f.* series, sequence; order; succession; **in rascher A.,** in quick, rapid, succession.

abfolgen, *v.tr. sep.* **1.**=**verabfolgen. 2.** *Com: A:* **j-m etwas a. lassen,** to let s.o. have sth. on credit, on trust; **Sie dürfen ihm alles, was er fordert, a. lassen,** you may deliver to him whatever he requires; **Sie sollen ihm bis 500 Mark auf mein Konto a. lassen,** you are to pay him up to 500 marks and charge it to my account.

abfordern. I. *v.tr. sep.* **1. j-m etwas a.,** to demand, require, sth. of, from, s.o.; **j-m Rechnung a.,** to call s.o. to account; *see also* **Rechnung; j-m die Parole a.,** to demand the pass-

word of s.o.; *A:* **j-m den Degen a.,** to demand s.o.'s sword; to make s.o. one's prisoner. **2.** *(a)* to recall (s.o.); to call, summon, (s.o.) back; **einen Botschafter a.,** to recall an ambassador; *(b)* **von der Welt abgefordert werden,** to die, to be called home; **Gott hat ihn abgefordert,** God has called him home.

II. *vbl s.* **Abfordern** *n.*, **Abforderung** *f. in vbl senses; also:* demand, requirement; recall (of general, ambassador, etc.); summoning away.

Abforderungsbrief, *m.*, **Abforderungsschreiben,** *n.* summons to return; *Dipl:* letters of recall.

abformen. I. *v.tr. sep.* to mould; to model, form, fashion, shape; to cast (statue, etc.).

II. *vbl s.* **1. Abformen,** *n. in vbl senses.* **2. Abformung,** *f.* *(a)*=II. 1; *(b)* cast (of statue, etc.); shape; duplicate.

Abformer, *m. Cer: Metall: etc:* moulder.

Abformmasse, *f.* moulding material, modelling material.

abforschen, *v.tr. sep.* **j-m etwas a.,** to elicit sth. from s.o.; **j-m die Wahrheit a.,** *F:* to screw the truth out of s.o.

abforsten. I. *v.tr. sep.* to deforest, untimber (land); to clear (country) of trees.

II. *vbl s.* **Abforsten** *n.*, **Abforstung** *f.* deforestation.

Abfrageapparat, *m. Tp:* operator's head-set.

Abfragebetrieb, *m. Tp:* direct trunking.

Abfrageklinke, *f. Tp:* answering jack, home jack, calling jack.

abfragen, *v.sep.* **1.** *v.tr.* *(a)* **j-m, j-n, etwas a.,** to question, examine, s.o. about sth.; **einen, einem, Schüler die Grammatik a.,** to question a pupil on grammar, to examine a boy in grammar; **die Kinder, den Kindern, die Aufgaben a.,** to hear the children repeat their lessons; *(b)* **j-m seine Geheimnisse a.,** to pump s.o., to worm secrets out of s.o. **2.** *v.tr.* **eine Klasse a.,** to question a class, to examine a class (orally), to ask questions round a class, *U.S:* to quiz a class. **3.** *v.i.* *(haben)* *Tp:* to accept the call; to inquire; to answer.

Abfrageplatz, *m. Tp:* outgoing position.

Abfrageschalter, *m. Tp:* listening key; speaking key.

Abfragestöpsel, *m. Tp:* answering plug.

Abfragetaste, *f.*=**Abfrageschalter.**

abfräsen, *v.tr. sep. Mec.E:* to cut away (edges, etc.) (with a milling-machine, etc.); *Metalw: Stonew:* to mill away (edges, etc.); *Bootm:* to trim away (edges, etc.).

abfressen, *v.tr. sep.* *(strong)* **1.** *(a)* *(of animals)* to browse on (grass, foliage); to crop (grass); *(of cattle)* to graze down (grass); *(b)* to eat (sth.) bare; **einen Knochen a.,** to gnaw a bone; **die Heuschrecken haben die Bäume abgefressen,** the locusts have stripped the trees, eaten the trees bare; *(c)* to eat (sth.) up; to consume (sth.). **2.** *(a)* *(of acid, rust, etc.)* to corrode; to pit; to eat away (metal); **der Rost frißt Eisen ab,** rust eats away, attacks, iron; *(b)* **vom Meer abgefressene Küste,** coast eaten away, eroded, by the sea; **vom Krebs abgefressene Nase,** nose eaten away by cancer; *(c)* **Sorge, die einem das Herz abfrißt,** consuming, tormenting, grief; *Lit:* carking care; **das wird ihm das Herz a.,** that will break his heart. **3.** to remove (surface of metal, etc.) by applying caustics.

abfrieren, *v.i. sep.* *(strong)* *(sein)* *(a)* *(of plants, etc.)* to be nipped, killed, by the frost; to be frost-bitten; **abgefrorene Knospen,** frost-nipped buds; *(b)* *(of limb, etc.)* to become frost-bitten; to be lost through frost-bite; **ihm ist ein Finger abgefroren,** he lost a finger through frost-bite.

abfrischen, *v.tr. sep. Brew: etc:* **das Wasser a.,** to change the water.

abfügen, *v.tr. sep.* *A:* *(a)* to trim off the edges of (glass, etc.); *(b)* to plane (wood) smooth.

abfühlen, *v.tr. sep.* **1.** *(a)*=**abtasten** I. 1; *(b)* to search, *U.S:* to frisk (s.o.). **2.** *A:* **j-m die Gedanken a.,** to read s.o.'s thoughts; **j-m den Wunsch a., etwas zu tun,** to sense s.o.'s desire to do sth.

Abfühlnadel, *f. Tg:* pecker (of tape transmitter).

Abfuhr, *f.* -/-en. **1.** *(a)* cartage, carriage; removal, transport, by waggon; carting away (of felled timber, etc.); *(b)* (i) **A. der Abfälle,** removal of refuse, of rubbish; scavenging; (ii) **A. (der Fäkalien),** voidance, draining, emptying, of cesspools, etc. **2.** *(a)* *Fenc:* disablement; putting (of one's opponent) hors de combat, out of action; **bis zur A. fechten,** to fight until disabled, until hors de combat; **den Gegner zur A. bringen, dem Gegner eine A. erteilen,** to disable one's opponent, to put one's opponent hors de combat, out of action; *(b)* *(no pl.)* **j-m eine A. erteilen,** (i) to send s.o. packing, to send s.o. to the right-about; *F:* to send s.o. away with a flea in his ear, to put s.o. in his place; (ii) to give s.o. a trouncing (in a contest, etc.); **eine (schwere) A. erleiden,** (i) *(in contest, etc.)* to be badly beaten, to get a trouncing; (ii) to be sent packing; **sich eine A. holen,** (i) to meet with a rebuff; *F:* to be turned down flat; (ii) to meet with defeat, to get a trouncing (in a contest, etc.).

Abführ-, *comb.fm., cp.* **Abführungs-.**

Abfuhranstalt, *f.*=**Abfuhrgesellschaft.**

Abführarbeit, *f. Metalw:* wire-drawing.

Abfuhrdünger, *m. Hyg:* night-soil.

Abführeisen, *n. Metalw:* draw-plate.

abführen, *v.sep.* I. *v.tr.* **1.** *(a)* to lead, take, (s.o.) away; **er wurde abgeführt,** he was arrested, taken away in custody; **j-n in die Knechtschaft a.,** to carry s.o. off into slavery; *(b)* *Mil:* to evacuate (wounded, prisoners of war); to relieve (guard). **2.** *(a)* to convey (goods); to lead, take, carry, away (s.o., sth.); *(b)* **j-n vom Wege a.,** to lead, take, s.o. out of his way; **j-n vom rechten Wege a.,** to lead s.o. astray; *(c)* **j-n vom Thema a.,** to lead, get, s.o. away from the subject; *(d)* (i) to divert (watercourse); (ii) **das Wasser aus einem Teich a.,** to drain a pond; **abführender Graben,** draining-ditch, -channel; **abführender Kanal,** drain-canal; *(e)* to exhaust (waste steam, etc.); to lead off (noxious gases, etc.); *Ph:* to dissipate (heat). **3.** *(a)* *Med:* to purge, evacuate (impurities) (from the system); *A.Med:* **die Feuchtigkeiten a.,** to expel the humours; *(b)* *Physiol:* **abführender Gang, Kanal,** efferent duct, excretory duct. **4. eine Schuld a.,** to discharge, pay off, a debt; **eine Summe (Geld) a.,** to pay out a sum (of money); **Zinsen, Steuern, a.,** to pay (off) taxes. **5.** *(a)* *Fenc:* to disable (one's opponent), to put (one's opponent) hors de combat, out of action; *(b)* *F:* **j-n a.=j-m eine Abfuhr erteilen,** *q.v. under* **Abfuhr** 2 *(b)*. **6.** *Metalw:* **Draht a.,** to draw wire. **7.** *Min:* **Gezähe a.,** to blunt, wear down, tools. **8.** *Nau:* **ein Tau a.,** to slip a cable, a rope. **9.** *Ven:* to train (retriever, etc.). **10. sich abführen,** *(a)* *A:* to take oneself off, to depart without ceremony; *(b)* *A. & F:* to die.

II. **abführen,** *v.i.* *(haben)* *Med:* *(of medicine, etc.)* to have a purgative *or* laxative effect; to clear the bowels; **Rhabarber führt ab,** rhubarb acts as an opening medicine, loosens the bowels; **abführendes Mittel=Abführmittel.**

III. *vbl s.* **1. Abführen,** *n. in vbl senses; also:* *Med:* evacuation; *F:* **A. haben,** to have diarrhoea. **2. Abführung,** *f.* *(a)*=III. 1; *also:* arrest; diversion (of watercourse); *Mch:* exhaust; *Ph:* dissipation (of heat); discharge (of debt); *Fenc:* disablement (of one's opponent); *cp.* **Abfuhr** 2; *Min:* **A. des Gezähes,** blunting, wearing down, of tools; *(b)* outlet pipe; *El.E:* *(in electric motor)* outlet (for cooling air).

Abführer, *m. Metalw:* *(pers.)* wire-drawer.

Abfuhrgesellschaft, *f.* scavenging company, cesspool clearing company.

Abfuhrkarren, *m.* *(a)* night-cart; *(b)* dust-cart.

Abfuhrkosten, *f.pl.* transport charges; charges for carting, conveying, (sth.) away.

Abführlatwerge, *f.*, **Abführmus,** *n.* *Pharm:* laxative electuary.

Abführmittel, *n. Med:* purgative, purge; opening medicine, aperient; cathartic; **mildes A.,** laxative; **drastisches, starkes, A.,** (drastic) purgative, purge; **ein A. einnehmen,** to take a purgative, *F:* to take medicine, a pill.

Abführpille, *f. Pharm:* laxative pill, cathartic pill; purgative pill.

Abfuhrrollgang, *m. Metalw:* delivery roller conveyor.

Abführsalz, *n. Pharm:* aperient salt.

Abfuhrsystem, *n. Hyg:* scavenging system; cesspool clearing system.

Abführtisch, *m. Metalw:* wire-drawing bench.

Abführungs-, *comb. fm., cp.* **Abführ-.**

Abführungsgang, Abführungskanal, *m. Physiol:* efferent duct; excretory duct.

Abführungsrohr, *n.* discharge pipe, outlet pipe.

Abführungsschlauch, *m.* exhaling tube (of breathing apparatus).

Abfüllanlage, *f. Brew: etc:* racking plant; filling plant.

Abfüllapparat, *m.* emptying *or* drawing-off apparatus; *Brew: Wine-m:* racking, filling, apparatus; racker.

abfüllen. I. *v.tr. sep.* **1.** to decant (liquid); to draw off, rack (beer, wine, etc.); to fill up (container, etc.); to empty (barrel, etc.); **Wein auf Fässer a.,** to draw wine off into casks; **Bier, Wein, usw., in, auf, Flaschen a.,** to bottle beer, wine, etc. **2.** *Ind:* to fill (container, etc.).

II. *vbl s.* **1. Abfüllen,** *n. in vbl senses.* **2. Abfüllung,** *f.* *(a)*=II. 1; *(b)* *Wine-m:* bottled wine; **'eigene A.,'** 'bottled by the grower'.

Abfüllflasche, *f.* receiving bottle, receiver.

Abfüllgefäß, *n.* receiving vessel, receiver.

Abfüllhahn, *m. Brew: Wine-m:* filling tap.

Abfüllkeller, *m. Brew:* filling, cleansing, cellar.

Abfüllmaschine, *f.* *(a)* *Brew: etc:* bottling, drawing-off, racking, machine; *(b)* *Ind:* filling machine (for filling containers).

Abfüllpipette, *f. Ch: etc:* delivery pipette.

Abfüllpumpe, *f.* pump for drawing liquid from barrels; *Brew:* racking-pump.

Abfüllraum, *m. Brew:* racking room; bottling room.

Abfüllschlauch, *m. Brew: etc:* racking hose, racking pipe; filling-up pipe; **A. aus Darm,** racking gut.

Abfüllspund, *m. Brew:* drawing-off bung.

Abfülltrichter, *m.* (filling) funnel.

Abfüllung, *f. see under* **abfüllen** II.2.

Abfüllvorrichtung, *f. Brew: etc:* racking apparatus.

abfurchen, *v.sep.* I. *v.tr.* to divide up (field, etc.) by furrows; **sich a.,** *Biol:* to segment; to undergo segmentation *or* cleavage.

II. *vbl s.* **Abfurchen** *n.*, **Abfurchung** *f.* division by furrows; *Biol:* segmentation.

abfüttern. I. *v.tr. sep.* **1.** *(a)* *Husb:* to feed (cattle, etc.); *(b)* to give (cattle, etc.) the last feed of the day; *(c)* *F:* **die Gäste a.,** to give the guests a feed, a spread, a blow-out. **2.** to line (garment, container, etc.).

II. *vbl s.* **Abfüttern** *n.*, **Abfütterung** *f. in vbl senses; also:* *F:* feed, spread, blow-out, bean-feast.

Abgabe, *f.* **1.** *(a)* delivery (of letter, parcel, goods, shares, etc.); handing over (of sth.) **(an j-n,** to s.o.); *(b)* *Post:* posting, *U.S:* mailing (of letter, parcel); handing in (of telegram); *(c)* leaving (of visiting card, message, etc.); *(d)* *Rail: etc:* **A. des Gepäcks,** depositing, leaving, of luggage at the left-luggage office, etc., *U.S:* checking of baggage in the baggage room, etc.; registering of luggage, *U.S:* checking of baggage (to be forwarded); *(e)* *Adm:* **A. von Schriftstücken an eine andere Behörde oder Abteilung,** passing of documents to another authority or department; *Fb: etc:* pass; passing (of the ball); *Nau:* sending, transmitting (of signal); *(f)* **A. der Stimme (bei einer Wahl),** casting of one's vote (at an election); voting, polling; **A. einer Meinung, eines Urteils,** delivering of an opinion, pronouncing of judgment; *Jur:* **A. einer Offerte,** making of an offer; **A. eines Schusses,** firing of a shot; *(g)* paying, payment (of taxes, etc.); *cp.* 2; *(h)* *Ch:* giving off, emission, liberation, escape (of gases); *Mch: etc:* generation (of steam); *El.E:* power output (of motor, generator, etc.); *Med: Physiol:* discharging (of corpuscles, etc.); passing (of water); disposing (of impurities, etc.); **unter A. von . . . ,** by loss of . . . ; (i) *Com:* drawing (of bill of exchange); buying (of bill of exchange); *(j)* sale (of shares, etc.); *St.Exch:* **größere Abgaben,** heavy sales, heavy selling; *Com:* disposal (of goods); selling; *(k)* giving up, parting with, conceding, concession (of sth.) (to s.o.); relinquishing, laying down (of functions, office, etc.); getting rid (of sth.); *(l)* sharing (in sth.). **2.** *(a)* *Adm:* (direct *or* indirect) tax; duty, due; toll; excise tax (on consumer goods); *Hist:* impost; **hohe Abgaben (be)zahlen,** to pay heavy taxes, to be heavily taxed; **A. vom, auf das, Grundvermögen,** levy on real estate; **A. für einen wohltätigen Zweck,** contribution to charity; *see also* **drücken** V. 1; *(b)* *Min:* **Abgaben (an den Staat),** royalties; *(c)* *Jur:* **Abgaben,** fees (to be deducted); *(d)* *Nau:* **(Hafen-)Abgaben,** (port) dues; *(e)* *Com:* bill of exchange; draft; negotiable instrument; *F:* bill **3.** counter (for depositing clothes, etc.); **(Garderoben-)A.,** cloak-room. *Cp.* **abgeben.**

Abgabekurs, *m. Fin:* issue price.

Abgabemeßvorrichtung, *f. Ind: etc:* delivery gauge (on storage tank, etc.).

abgabenfrei, *a.* *(of goods, etc.)* free of tax, tax-free, exempt from tax; free from duty, duty-free, exempt from duty.

Abgabenpächter, *m. Hist:* farmer of revenue, of taxes, tax-farmer.

abgabenpflichtig, *a.* taxable, assessable; rateable; dutiable; liable to tax, duty, toll.

Abgabenverteilung, *f. Pol: Adm:* (*a*) allocation of revenue; (*b*) classification of duties; (*c*) graduation of tax(ation).

Abgabenwesen, *n.* (system of) taxation.

Abgabepreis, *m.* selling price; (gas-, electricity-, water-)rate; *Fin:* issue price.

Abgabespannung, *f. El.E:* discharge voltage (of battery).

Abgang, *m.* **1.** (*a*) departure; start (of vehicle); sailing (of ship); dispatch (of mail, messenger); (*b*) *A. & Lit:* **sein A. aus diesem Leben,** his departure from this life; his demise; (*c*) *Th:* (i) **A. (eines Schauspielers) von der Bühne,** exit (of an actor); (ii) actor's final words before his exit, *F:* exit line; (*d*) *Gym:* finish, completion (of exercise). **2.** leaving (for good); retirement, retiral (of official); **nach dem A. von der Schule ging er in ein Büro,** on leaving school he went into an office; **beim A. des Ministers,** on the retirement of the minister; *Th: occ.* **A. (eines Schauspielers) von der Bühne,** retirement (for good) (of an actor) from the stage; (*cp.* 1 (*c*)); **sich einen guten A. verschaffen,** to retire gracefully. **3.** *Com:* sale (of goods); **diese Ware hat guten A., findet raschen A.,** this article sells well, quickly; **diese Ware hat keinen A.,** this article does not sell at all; there is no sale, demand, for this article. **4.** *Anat:* offset (of branch); *Tp: Tg:* junction. **5.** (*a*) waste, wastage, loss; leakage (of liquid, gas), escape (of gas); *Mil:* decrease in strength (of unit); wastage (of men); (*b*) *Com:* depreciation, loss in value (owing to damage or waste); **im Sommer ist beim Fischhandel viel A.,** the fish trade loses considerably during the summer through fish going bad; (*c*) **A. am Gewicht,** shortage, deficiency, in weight, *U.S:* wantage; (*d*) *A:* **A. an Kräften,** diminishing of strength; (*e*) *A:* **in A. der Nahrung kommen,** to be in a poor way of business; (*f*) *A:* **in A. kommen, geraten,** to fall, pass, into disuse; to fall into desuetude; to become a dead letter; (*of custom*) to go out of fashion; (*of law*) to be no longer enforced, to fall into abeyance. **6.** *Med:* flux (of blood, etc.); disgorging (of bile, etc.); passing (of stools); discharge (of urine); **unfreiwilliger A. von Urin,** incontinence of urine; **A. der (Leibes-)Frucht,** miscarriage; abortion. **7.** *usu.pl.* **Abgänge,** (*a*) waste, refuse; (kitchen) scraps; slops; (butcher's) offal; *Ind: etc:* chips, shavings (of wood); chips, chippings (of stone); clippings, trimmings (of cloth, leather, etc.); (metal) filings; scrap (metal); (gold) parings; tailings (of grain, ore, etc.); *Print:* waste (paper), spoilage; (*b*) *Mil:* losses, casualties. *Cp.* **abgehen.**

abgängig, *a.* **1.** (*of object*) lost, missing; mislaid; untraceable; *Post:* (*of letter, parcel*) lost; gone astray (*through loss or misdirection*); *Mil:* (*of soldier*) missing. **2.** *Com:* **abgängige Waren,** saleable, marketable, vendible, goods; goods that sell well, easily. **3.** deteriorating; decaying; (*of meat*) going bad, going off; (*of garment*) wearing out, worn out; (*of horse*) worn out, knocked up; *Vit:* **abgängiger Weinberg,** exhausted vineyard; **a. werden,** (*of custom, etc.*) to disappear, fall into disuse, go out of fashion; *A:* (*of business*) to decline, decay.

Abgangsamt, *n. Post:* (postal) office of dispatch; *Tg:* office of origin; *Rail: etc:* forwarding office; dispatch office.

Abgangsbahnhof, *m. Rail:* (*a*) station of dispatch (of goods); (*b*) departure station.

Abgangsbesteck, *n. Nau:* departure; **das A. nehmen,** to take (a bearing of) the departure.

Abgangsdampf, *m. Mch:* dead steam; exhaust steam.

Abgangsfehler, Abgangsfehlerwinkel, *m. Ball:* (angle of) jump.

Abgangshafen, *m. Nau:* port of sailing.

Abgangskurs, *m. Artil:* line of departure.

Abgangsprüfung, *f. Sch:* leaving examination; *U.S:* final examination, *F:* finals.

Abgangswinkel, *m. Ball:* angle of departure (of projectile); *Ph: W.Tel:* **A. einer Welle,** angle of departure of a wave, wave angle.

Abgangszeit, *f.* time of departure (of train, vehicle); time of sailing (of ship); *Telecom:* time of dispatch (of telegram, signal).

Abgangszeugnis, *n. Sch:* leaving certificate; *U.S:* diploma.

Abgas, *n. Mch: I.C.E:* exhaust gas; *Ind:* waste gas; flue gas.

Abgasaustritt, *m. I.C.E: etc:* exhaust outlet.

Abgasbrodem, Abgasbrüden, *m. I.C.E: Mch: etc:* exhaust vapour; exhaust fumes.

Abgasheizung, *f.* waste-gas heating.

Abgaskanal, *m.* (*a*) *Metall:* waste-gas main; (*b*) exhaust passage (of diesel engine).

Abgaskessel, *m. Mch:* exhaust-heat boiler.

Abgaslader, *m. Av:* exhaust-driven supercharger, turbo-supercharger.

Abgasleitung, *f. I.C.E:* exhaust-pipe; exhaust manifold.

Abgasluftverdichter, *m. Av: I.C.E:* exhaust-driven (air-)compressor.

Abgasreinigungsanlage, *f.* waste-gas purifying plant.

Abgasring, *m.* = **Abgassammelring.**

Abgasrohr, *n. I.C.E: etc:* exhaust-pipe; *Av:* exhaust branch-pipe.

Abgassammelleitung, *f. I.C.E:* exhaust manifold.

Abgassammelring, *m. Av: I.C.E:* exhaust ring; circular exhaust manifold.

Abgassammler, *m. I.C.E:* exhaust manifold.

Abgasschalldämpfer, *m. Aut:* silencer.

Abgasspeicherofen, *m. Ind: Mch:* regenerator, recuperator; hot-blast stove.

Abgasstutzen, *m. Av: I.C.E:* exhaust stub-pipe.

Abgasturbine, *f. Av:* exhaust-driven turbine.

Abgasturbolader, *m. Av:* exhaust-driven turbo-supercharger.

Abgasventil, *n. I.C.E: Mch:* exhaust valve; blow-through valve.

Abgasverwertung, *f. Ind: etc:* utilization of waste gases.

Abgasverwertungsanlage, *f. Ind: etc:* waste-gas utilizing plant.

Abgasvorwärmer, *m. Mch:* (fuel) economizer; **Dampfmaschine mit A.,** exhaust-gas engine.

Abgaswärme, *f.* heat of *or* from exhaust gases.

Abgaswärmeverwertung, *f.* utilization of heat from exhaust gases.

abgattern, *v.tr. sep.* **1.** *A:* = **abgittern.** **2.** *Dial:* **j-m etwas a.,** to wheedle sth. out of s.o.

abgaunern, *v.tr. sep.* **j-m etwas a.,** to swindle, *F:* diddle, do, s.o. out of sth.

abgautschen, *v.tr. sep. Paperm:* to couch (paper).

abgeben, *v.sep.* (*strong*) I. *v.tr.* **1.** (*a*) to deliver, hand over (letter, parcel, etc.); to hand in (parcel, etc.) (at private house, office); **j-m ein Telegramm a.,** to hand a telegram to s.o.; **würden Sie bitte dieses Paket bei Mrs Smith a.?** would you please leave, drop, this parcel at Mrs Smith's? **ist etwas für mich abgegeben worden?** has anything been left for me? (*b*) *occ.* to post, *U.S:* mail (letter, etc.); to hand in (telegram); (*c*) **bei j-m seine Karte a.,** to leave a card on s.o.; (*d*) to deposit (article) (for safe keeping); *Rail:* **sein Gepäck a.,** to leave one's luggage at the left luggage office, *U.S:* to check one's baggage in the baggage-room. **2.** to pass, to transmit; (*a*) *Adm:* **Schriftstücke an eine andere Behörde oder Abteilung a.,** to pass documents to another authority *or* department; (*b*) *Fb: etc:* **(den Ball) a.,** to pass (the ball); (*c*) *Nau:* to send, transmit (signal). **3.** (*a*) to give, deliver (opinion, etc.); **ein Gutachten a.,** to give an expert opinion; **ein Urteil über etwas** *acc.* **a.,** to pass judgment, give one's judgment, on sth.; **eine Erklärung a.,** to make a declaration; (*b*) to cast (vote); **die Zahl der abgegebenen Stimmen,** the number of votes cast; (*c*) *Com: Jur:* **eine Offerte a.,** to make an offer; (*d*) **einen Schuß a.,** to fire a shot. **4.** to pay (an amount) as tax; **die Engländer geben viel an Steuern ab,** the English pay heavy taxes; **große Summen für Wohltätigkeitszwecke a.,** to give, contribute, large sums to charity. **5.** (*a*) *Ph: Ch: etc:* **Wärme a.,** to give off, give out, emit, radiate, heat; **. . . Kalorien werden abgegeben, . . .** calories are given off; **Gas a.,** to give off gas, **Sauerstoff a.,** to yield up oxygen; *Mch: etc:* **Dampf a.,** to generate steam; (*b*) *El:* to deliver (current); **abgegebene Leistung,** output; (*c*) *Med: Physiol:* to discharge (corpuscles, etc.); to pass (water); to dispose of (impurities, etc.); (*d*) (*of soil*) **eine gute Ernte a.,** to yield a good crop. **6.** *Com:* **(einen Wechsel) über 500 Mark auf j-n a.,** to draw a bill, *abs.* to draw, (up)on s.o. for 500 marks; **Geld auf Wechsel a.,** to buy bills of exchange; *see also* **Sicht**. **7.** (*a*) *Com:* to sell, supply, furnish (goods); to dispose of (stock, etc.); **er gibt seine Waren billig ab,** he sells his goods cheap, lets his goods go cheaply; **Sie dürfen diese Partie zu verminderten Preisen a.,** you may dispose of this lot at reduced prices; **ich habe nur einen kleinen Vorrat und kann Ihnen nichts davon a.,** I have only a small stock and cannot let you have any of it; (*b*) *Fin:* to sell (shares); *see also* **blanko.** **8.** (*a*) to give up, part with, concede, cede (**j-m,** to s.o.); **er hat seinem Sohn den Laden abgegeben,** he has given up the shop to his son; (*b*) to give up, relinquish (functions, office, command, etc.), to lay down (office); (*c*) to get rid of (sth.). **9.** (*a*) **a. von etwas,** to give away part of sth.; **gib mir etwas von deiner Schokolade ab,** give me a piece of your chocolate; (*b*) *F:* **j-m eins a.,** *F:* to let s.o. have it, to give it to s.o., to give s.o. a rap on the knuckles; **einem Hund, einem Kind, eins a.,** to give a dog, a child, a whack, to give a child a smack, a slap. **10.** to serve as (sth.); to play the part of (sth.); **er würde einen guten Soldaten, Offizier, Schauspieler, a.,** he would make a good soldier, officer, actor; he is cut out for a soldier, an officer, an actor; **einen Narren a.,** to play the fool; **das Gelände würde einen guten Spielplatz a.,** this site would be very suitable for a playground, would make a good playground; *A:* **er gab einen Professor zu Leipzig ab,** he was a professor at Leipzig.

II. **abgeben,** *v.impers.* to happen, come about, ensue; **es wird heute (noch) Schnee a.,** we shall have snow (before the day is out); **es wird (unter ihnen) Streit a.,** it will come to a quarrel (between them); **benimm dich, sonst gibt's was ab!** behave yourself, or there'll be trouble!

III. **sich abgeben,** (*a*) **sich mit etwas a.,** to engage in sth.; to occupy, busy, oneself with sth.; to concern oneself with, about, in, sth.; (*of book, author*) to deal with (a subject); **er gibt sich viel mit Astrologie ab,** he interests himself, dabbles, in astrology; **geben Sie sich mit solchen Dingen nicht ab!** don't meddle with such things! **ich habe mich nie mit Politik abgegeben,** I've never bothered about politics; (*b*) **sich mit j-m a.,** to have dealings, relations, with s.o.; **sie gibt sich gern mit Kindern ab,** she loves to be among, to look after, children; **ich will mich nicht mit ihm a.,** I don't want to have anything to do with him; **er gibt sich zu viel mit Tänzerinnen ab,** he spends too much of his time with chorus-girls.

IV. **abgeben,** *v.i.* (*haben*) **1.** *Cards:* to deal last. **2.** to retire (from business, etc.); **der alte Bauer hat voriges Jahr abgegeben,** the old farmer retired last year.

V. *vbl s.* **Abgeben,** *n. in vbl senses; cp.* **Abgabe 1.**

Abgeber, *m. Com:* seller, drawer (of bill).

abgebrannt, *p.p. & a. see* **abbrennen.**

abgebrochen, *p.p. & a. see* **abbrechen IV.**

abgebrochenblätt(e)rig, *a. Bot:* abruptifolious, (plant) with truncated, abruptly terminating, leaves.

Abgebrochenheit, *f.* abruptness (of speech, style); disconnectedness (of conversation, etc.); disjointedness (of speech); jerkiness (of style, etc.).

abgebrüht, *p.p. & a.* (*of pers.*) callous; past shame, lost to all (sense of) shame, *F:* case-hardened. *See also* **abbrühen.**

abgedroschen, *p.p. & a.* hackneyed, trite (subject, story, joke); stale (joke). *See also* **abdreschen.**

Abgedroschenheit, *f.* banality, triteness.

Abgefallene, *m., f.* (*decl. as adj.*) *see* **abfallen IV.**

abgefäumt, *p.p. & a.* = **abgefeimt.**

abgefeimt, *p.p. & a.* artful, wily, guileful, crafty, sly, sharp, *F:* foxy; **abgefeimter Schurke, Spitzbube,** unmitigated scoundrel; villain of the deepest dye; out-and-out, utter, rogue; arch-rogue. *See also* **abfeimen.**

Abgefeimtheit, *f.* artfulness, wiliness, craftiness, knavery, *F:* foxiness.

abgegriffen, *p.p. & a. see* **abgreifen.**

abgehaart, *p.p. & a.* hairless; *Nat.Hist:* glabrous. *See also* **abhaaren.**

abgehackt, *p.p. & a.* jerky (speech, gait); *F:* staccato (speech). *See also* **abhacken.**

abgehen, *v.sep.* (*strong*) I. *v.i.* (*sein*) **1.** (*a*) to depart, leave, start; to set out, off; to go off; to go away; (*of ship*) to sail (away), to leave port; (*of train, ship*) to steam off, away; (*of motor vehicle*) to move off; (*of pers.*) to take one's departure; (*b*) (*of letter, telegram, messenger, ship, etc.*) to be dispatched, to go off; **die Post geht um fünf Uhr ab,** the post, *U.S:* mail, goes at five o'clock; **jede Woche geht ein Schiff nach Rio ab,** there is a ship to Rio, a ship leaves for Rio, every week; **einen Boten, einen Brief, a. lassen,** to dispatch, send off, a messenger, a letter; *Nau:* **ein Schiff a. lassen,** to dispatch a ship; *W.Tel:* **der Spruch ist schon abgegangen,** the message has gone off, has already been dispatched; **'17.25 abgegangen',** 'time of dispatch 17.25'; (*c*) **mit (dem) Tode a.,** to die, to depart this life; *see also* **Armee;** (*d*) *Th:* to make one's exit, *F:* to exit; to go off; **Macbeth geht ab,** exit Macbeth; **alle gehen ab,**

exeunt omnes; (*e*) **von der Schule a.**, to leave school; (*f*) **(von einem Amt) a.**, to give up a post; (*of official*) to retire; to resign; (*of minister*) to go out (of office); (*of employee*) to leave one's employment; to be dismissed; **ein abgegangener Beamter**, a retired, former, official, an ex-official; *occ.* (*of actor*) **von der Bühne a.**, to retire from the stage, to leave the stage (for good). **2.** to end, finish; to go off, pass off; **es ist alles (noch) gut, glatt, abgegangen**, everything went off well, passed off smoothly; things have turned out well; **es wird übel a.**, it will end in trouble; **es geht doch nicht ohne Schläge ab**, they will come to blows before they have finished; it will end in a fight. **3.** (*a*) (*of button, wheel, paint, fabric, stain, dirt, etc.*) to come off; (*of stain, spot*) to come out; **der Fleck ist abgegangen**, the spot has come out, is out, has disappeared; (*b*) (*of colour*) (i) to fade; (ii) to come out; (iii) to wear off. **4.** *Com:* (*of article*) to sell, to go; **gut, rasch, reißend, a.**, to sell readily, to go well, to find a ready sale; to be in great demand; *see also* **Semmel**. **5.** (*a*) to deviate; to diverge; to depart; to stray (**von**, from); **von einer Regel a.**, to deviate from a rule; **von seiner Meinung a.**, to alter, change, one's opinion; **er geht von seinem Vorhaben nicht ab**, he persists in, sticks to, his plan; **davon kann ich nicht a.**, I must insist upon that; **geh nicht von der Sache ab!** keep to the point! (*b*) (*of path, road*) to branch off, turn off, fork off, go off; to diverge. **6.** (*a*) **diese Eigenschaft geht ihm ab**, he lacks this quality; **was ihm an Intelligenz abgeht, ersetzt er durch Fleiß**, what he lacks in intelligence he makes up for by hard work; **er läßt sich** *dat.* **nichts a.**, he does himself well, *F:* he does himself proud; he denies himself nothing, he does not stint himself of anything; **es gehen mir fünf Mark ab**, I am five marks short (of the amount); **dir soll nichts a.**, you shan't go short; *F:* you'll be looked after; (*b*) **die Kinder sind im Internat gut aufgehoben, aber das Familienleben geht ihnen sehr ab**, the children are well looked after at boarding-school, but they miss family life very much. **7.** *Com: etc:* to be deducted, taken off; **Summe, die vom Rechnungsbetrag abgeht**, sum to be deducted from the total; **bei Barzahlung gehen 5 v.H., 5 Prozent, ab**, there is a reduction, discount, rebate, of 5 per cent for cash; **etwas vom Preise a. lassen**, to abate sth. of the price. **8.** *A:* (*of buildings, etc.*) to decay, depreciate; (*of customs, etc.*) to decay, drop away, fall into disuse; **abgegangener Ort**, deserted settlement. **9.** *Com:* to be lost by waste *or* damage; *Ind:* to be lost in processing; **vom Obst geht beim Transport viel ab**, fruit suffers heavy wastage in transit; **bei diesem Verfahren geht viel vom Metall ab**, much of the metal is lost in this process. **10.** *Med:* to be evacuated, discharged, voided (from the body); (*of stools, worms*) to pass; **es ging ihm viel Blut ab**, he lost a lot of blood. **11.** (*of path*) to go down; (*of river-bank, etc.*) to slope (away). **12. ab- und zugehen**, to come and go, to go to and fro; *see also* **auf III. 2.**

II. **abgehen**, *v.tr.* (*sein, haben*) **1. eine Entfernung a.**, to pace (out, off) a distance, to step (out, off) a distance; to measure (out, off) a distance by pacing. **2.** to go, walk, over, round; to inspect (tracks, fields, etc.); *Rail:* **der Streckenwärter geht die Gleise ab**, the trackman inspects the tracks; **der Bauer geht seine Felder ab**, the farmer takes a look round his fields; *Mil:* **das Gelände a.**, to patrol the terrain. **3.** *F:* **sich** *dat.* **die Beine (nach etwas) a.**, *F:* to walk one's legs off (looking for, trying to get, sth.).

III. *vbl s.* **Abgehen**, *n. in vbl senses; also:* deviation (from a rule); departure (from a custom, principle); inspection (of fields, etc.); *Mil:* patrolling (of terrain); **ihr Ab- und Zugehen**, their comings and goings; **es war ein ständiges Ab- und Zugehen**, there was continual coming and going, *F:* to-ing and fro-ing. *Cp.* **Abgang** 1, 2, 5 (*a*), 6.

IV. *pr.p. & a.* **abgehend**, *in vbl senses; esp.* **1.** (*a*) outgoing (mail, post, telephone call, wireless message, etc.); departing (train); *Nau:* **abgehende Ladung**, outward cargo; (*b*) *El.E:* outgoing (cable, telephone line); (*c*) **abgehender Minister**, outgoing, retiring, minister. **2.** descending; **steil abgehendes Ufer, usw.**, steeply-sloping bank, etc.

abgeizen, *v.sep.* **1.** *v.tr.* **dem Boden, Feld, eine (doppelte) Ernte a.**, to wrest a (double) crop from the soil, field. **2. sich** *dat.* **etwas für seine Kinder a.**, to pinch and scrape for one's children.

abgeklappert, *p.p. & a. F:* (*of pers.*) doddery; (*of thg*) ramshackle; (*of joke, etc.*) trite, stale. *See also* **abklappern**.

abgeklärt, *p.p. & a. see* **abklären**.

Abgeklärtheit, *f.* serenity, tranquillity (of mind, character, etc.); limpidity, limpidness, pellucidity, pellucidness, clarity (of style, etc.); clearness (of liquid, etc.).

Abgeld, *n. Fin:* discount.

abgelegen, *p.p. & a. see* **abliegen**.

Abgelegenheit, *f.*, **Abgelegensein**, *n.*, remoteness, isolation, seclusion, solitariness, loneliness (of a place).

abgeloben, *v.tr. sep.* to abjure, forswear (sth.).

abgelten. I. *v.tr. sep.* (*strong*) (*a*) to settle (obligations) in full; to make full payment for (sth.); to make compensation for (sth.); to requite (sth.); to settle, satisfy (claim); (*b*) *Ind:* **Überstunden a.**, to take time off in order to compensate for previous overtime.

II. *vbl s.* **1. Abgelten**, *n. in vbl senses.* **2. Abgeltung**, *f.*=II. 1; *also:* compensation, settlement.

abgemessen, *p.p. & a. see* **abmessen**.

Abgemessenheit, *f.* precision; ceremoniousness; stiffness, starchiness (of manner); reserve (in one's bearing).

abgeneigt, *p.p. & pred.a.* **etwas** *dat.*, **gegen etwas, a. sein**, to be averse to, from, sth.; to be disinclined to sth., for sth.; **j-m a. sein**, to be ill-disposed toward s.o.; to have an aversion to, for, s.o.; **a. sein, etwas zu tun**, to be disinclined to do sth.; to be reluctant, loath, to do sth.; to be averse to doing sth.; to feel an aversion to doing sth.; **sich** *dat.* **j-n a. machen**, to alienate s.o.'s sympathies; to estrange s.o. (from oneself); **das hat ihn mir sofort a. gemacht**, that turned him against me at once; **wie sehr er auch gegen das Schreiben a. war**, however reluctant, loath, he was to write; however averse he was to writing, however great was his aversion to writing; **er war dem Plan nicht a.**, his attitude to the plan was not unfavourable; he was not unfavourably disposed towards the plan; **ich bin gar nicht a., dem Verein beizutreten**, I am not at all averse to joining the society; I feel quite inclined to join the society. *See also* **abneigen**.

Abgeneigtheit, *f.* **A. gegen etwas, vor etwas** *dat.*, disinclination to sth., for sth.; aversion to, from, sth.; dislike of, for, sth.; distaste for sth.; repugnance to, against, sth.; **A. gegen j-n**, dislike for s.o.; aversion for s.o.; **seine A. gegen das Schreiben**, his reluctance to write; his aversion to writing.

abgenicken, *v.tr. sep. Ven: occ.* to dispatch (wounded animal).

abgenutzt, *p.p. & a. see* **abnutzen**.

Abgenutztheit, *f.* shabbiness (of garment); bluntness (of tool, pencil, etc.).

Abgeordnete, *m., f.* (*decl. as adj.*) **1.** deputy, delegate. **2.** *Pol:*=representative; (*in Germany*) member of the Bundestag, Landtag, *Hist:* Reichstag, etc.; (*in England*) Member of Parliament, M.P; parliamentary representative; (*in France*) deputy; (*in U.S.*) representative, Member of the House of Representatives; congressman; congresswoman.

Abgeordnetenhaus, *n.*, **Abgeordnetenkammer**, *f.* house of deputies; parliament; *G.Hist:* (*in Prussia*) Chamber of Deputies; (*in England*) House of Commons; (*in France*) Chamber of Deputies; (*in U.S.*) House of Representatives.

Abgeordnetenwahl, *f.* parliamentary election.

abgerben, *v.tr. sep.* **1.** (*a*) *Leath:* to tan (hide) (thoroughly); (*b*) *F:* **j-n a.**, to give s.o. a thrashing, a tanning, a leathering, a hiding, *F:* to tan s.o.'s hide. **2.** *South G.Dial:* to press (corn) out of the husk; to husk (corn).

abgerissen, *p.p. & a. see* **abreißen**.

Abgerissenheit, *f.* (*a*) jerkiness, abruptness (of speech, style, etc.); disjointedness (of speech); disconnectedness (of conversation); (*b*) irregularity (of breathing).

abgerundet, *p.p. & a. see* **abrunden**.

Abgerundetheit, *f.* roundness; perfection; finish.

Abgesandte, *m., f.* (*decl. as adj.*) (*a*) delegate; envoy; emissary; plenipotentiary; (*b*) *A:*=**Gesandte**.

Abgesandtin, *f.* -/-innen. *A:* ambassador's wife.

Abgesang, *m. Pros:* **1.** (*a*) third and last section of the strophe in the Middle High German lyric; (*b*) third and last section of the strophe in the 'Meistergesang' following the two 'Stollen'; *cp.* **Aufgesang**. **2.** burden (of hymn).

abgeschieden, *p.p. & a.* **1.** *Ch: etc:* isolated; separated; disengaged; (*of metals*) refined; **abgeschiedener Stoff**, precipitate. **2.** remote, retired, secluded, sequestered (spot); *Lit:* **in eines Gartens abgeschiedener Stille**, in the quiet seclusion of a garden; *adv.* **ganz a. leben**, to live retired, in (complete) retirement; to lead a sequestered life; to live in seclusion. **3.** (*of pers.*) deceased, defunct, departed; **die Abgeschiedenen**, the departed; **abgeschiedene Seelen, Geister**, departed spirits. **4.** *B:* divorced (woman); **wer eine Abgeschiedene freiet**, whosoever shall marry her that is divorced, that is put away. *See also* **abscheiden**.

Abgeschiedenheit, *f.* (*a*) remoteness, isolation, seclusion, loneliness (of a place); (*b*) retirement, seclusion; secluded, retired, sequestered, life.

abgeschliffen, *p.p. & a. see* **abschleifen**.

Abgeschliffenheit, *f.* polish, refinement; (good) breeding; urbanity; polished manners.

abgeschlossen, *p.p. & a. see* **abschließen**.

Abgeschlossenheit, *f.*, **Abgeschlossensein**, *n.* **1.** isolation; seclusion. **2.** completeness; **Abgeschlossensein in sich (selbst)**, completeness within itself; compactness. **3.** *Mth:* closure.

abgeschmackt, *a.* in bad taste; tasteless; tactless; inappropriate; **ein abgeschmackter Witz**, a joke in bad taste, a tasteless joke; a tactless joke; **abgeschmackte Äußerungen machen**, to make inept remarks.

Abgeschmacktheit, *f.* bad taste; tastelessness; tactlessness; inappropriateness, ineptitude.

abgesondert, *p.p. & a. see* **absondern**.

Abgesondertheit, *f.* (*a*) separateness; detachedness (**von**, from); (*b*) isolation; seclusion; loneliness.

abgespannt, *p.p. & a.* (*of pers.*) fatigued, weary, exhausted, tired (out), *F:* dead-beat, done up; whacked, fagged out; **ich bin (ganz) a.**, *F:* I'm (absolutely) all in. *See also* **abspannen**.

Abgespanntheit, *f.* enervation, exhaustion, languor; *Med:* atony, want of tone, low physical condition.

abgestanden, *p.p. & a.* (*a*) stale (bread, fish, beer, milk, etc.); musty (food, etc.); flat (beer, wine); dead (wine); spoilt (fruit); (flowers, etc.) that are not fresh, that have lost their freshness; stagnant (water in pond, etc.); perished (rubber, steel, metal plate); (*b*) outworn, stale, *F:* musty (ideas, etc.); *Husb:* **abgestandene Kuh**, worn-out, useless, cow. *See also* **abstehen**.

Abgestemme, *n.* -s/. *Min:* stepped working; offset.

abgestorben, *p.p. & a. see* **absterben**.

Abgestorbenheit, *f.* (*a*) deadness, numbness (of limb, etc.); (*b*) torpor; apathy, listlessness; insensitiveness (**für**, to).

abgestumpft, *p.p. & a. see* **abstumpfen**.

Abgestumpftheit, *f.*, **Abgestumpftsein**, *n.* **1.** (*a*) bluntness (of pointed instrument, edged tool); dullness (of edge, edged tool); (*b*) dullness, deadness (of senses, etc.). **2.** (*a*) apathy; listlessness; dullness, obtuseness; (*b*) indifference, insensitivity, callousness (**gegen**, to).

abgetakelt, *p.p. & a. F:* **abgetakelte Person**, seedy, shabby, down-at-heel, individual; wreck. *See also* **abtakeln**.

abgetan, *p.p. & a. see* **abtun**.

abgetrennt, *p.p. & a. see* **abtrennen**.

Abgetrenntheit, *f.*, **Abgetrenntsein**, *n.* separateness, detachedness.

abgewettert, *p.p. & a.* weather-beaten (person, countenance); *see also* **abwettern**.

abgewinnen. I. *v.tr. sep.* (*strong*) (*a*) **j-m etwas a.**, to win, gain, sth. from s.o.; **j-m im Spiel Geld a.**, to win money from s.o. at cards, etc.; **j-m Liebe, Achtung, a.**, to win, gain, s.o.'s affection, esteem; **einer Dame ein Lächeln a.**, to win a smile from a lady; (*b*) **j-m einen Vorsprung a.**, to get the start of s.o.; to forestall s.o.; to **steal a** march on s.o.; *Nau:* **einem Schiff**, *F:* **j-m, den Wind a.**, to get the weather gauge of a ship, *F:* of s.o.; to get to windward of a ship, *F:* of s.o.; (*c*) **der Wüste Ernten a.**, to win, wrest, crops from the desert; *Min: etc:* to win, extract (metal from ore, etc.); **das dem Erz abgewonnene Metall**, the metal won, extracted, from the ore; (*d*) **etwas** *dat.* **Geschmack a.**, to take, find, pleasure in sth.; to have a taste for sth.

II. *vbl s.* **Abgewinnen** *n.*, **Abgewinnung** *f. in vbl senses; also: Min:* extraction.

abgewogen, *p.p. & a. Aer:* (*of airship*) buoyant; *see also* **abwägen, abwiegen**.

Abgewogenheit, *f.* balance; equilibrium; symmetry.

abgewöhnbar, *a.* curable (habit).

abgewöhnen. I. *v.tr. sep.* **1. j-m etwas a.**, to disaccustom s.o. to sth.; **j-m das Rauchen, usw., a.**, to break s.o. of, get s.o. out of the habit of, smoking, etc.; to make s.o. leave off, to cure

s.o. of, smoking, etc.; **sich** *dat.* **das Rauchen, usw., a.,** to break oneself of the habit of smoking, etc.; to give up, leave off, cure oneself of, smoking, etc. **2.** *occ.* **j-n von j-m a.,** to estrange s.o. from s.o.; to wean s.o. from the company of s.o.

II. *vbl s.* **Abgewöhnen** *n.*, **Abgewöhnung** *f. in vbl senses; also: Hum:* **'noch ein Glas—zum Abgewöhnen!'** approx.='just one for the road!'

abgezehrt, *p.p. & a. see* **abzehren** IV.

Abgezehrtheit, *f.* emaciated, wasted, state; painful thinness (of face, figure); gauntness, haggardness (of face).

abgezogen, *p.p. & a. see* **abziehen.**

Abgezogenheit, *f.* **1.** *Phil:* abstraction. **2.** *A:* seclusion; retirement; isolation.

abgieksen, *v.tr. sep. Dial:* to slaughter, cut the throat of (pig, etc.).

abgieren, *v.i. sep.* (*haben*) (*of ship*) to sheer off, to sheer off course.

abgießen. I. *v.tr. sep.* (*strong*) **1.** (*a*) to pour off (liquid, etc.); (*b*) *Ch: etc:* to decant (liquid); (*c*) *Metall:* **das Metall a.,** to pour the metal; **geschmolzenes Metall in eine Form a.,** to pour, run, molten metal into a mould; **das Metall stehend, waagerecht, a.,** to pour the metal on end, horizontally; **das Metall fallend, steigend, a.,** to top-pour, to bottom-pour, the metal; (*d*) *Mil:* **Kampfstoffe aus Flugzeugen a.,** to spray chemical warfare agents, gas, from aircraft. **2.** to cast, found (iron, etc.); **eine Statue in Bronze, in Gips, a.,** to cast a statue in bronze, to make a plaster cast of a statue. **3.** *Cu:* to strain (off), to drain (vegetables). **4.** *occ.* **sich abgießen,** to take a shower-bath, *F:* to have a shower.

II. *vbl s.* **Abgießen** *n., occ.* **Abgießung** *f. in vbl senses; cp.* **Abguß** 1.

Abgießer, *m. Metall: etc:* caster, pourer, founder, foundry hand.

Abgift, *f. A:*=**Abgabe** 2 (*a*).

abgipfeln, *v.tr. sep. For:* to top, pollard (tree).

abgisch(t)en, *v.i. sep.* (*haben*) (*of liquids*) to cease foaming, fermenting.

abgittern, *v.tr. sep.* to rail (sth.) off; to fence (sth.) off; **abgegitterter Raum,** railed-in, -off, space.

Abglanz, *m.* **1.** reflection; (*a*) reflected light; **der A. der Abendsonne,** the reflection, reflected light, of the setting sun; **der A. der Sonne im Wasser,** the gleam, reflection, shimmer, of the sun on the water(s); **farbiger A.,** play of (iridescent) colours; (*b*) reflected glory, splendour; **die Poesie ist der verklärte A. des Lebens,** poetry is the exalted reflection of life; (*c*) **das Bild ist nur ein schwacher A. des Originals,** the picture is but a pale reflection, a pale reflex, of the original; the picture is only a feeble copy; **sein Ruhm ist nur ein schwacher A. von dem seines Vaters,** his fame is but a pale reflection, a pale reflex, of his father's. **2.** *Ch: Ind:* **A. eines Öls,** cast, bloom, of an oil.

abglänzen, *v.tr. sep. Metalw:* to polish, finish.

abglasen, *v.tr. sep. Leath:* to glass, glaze (leather).

abglätten, *v.tr. sep.* **1.** to smooth, gloss, polish (stone, etc.); to glaze (paper, etc.); to surface (board, paper, etc.); to sleek, slick (leather); to burnish (metals). **2.** *F:* (*a*) **j-n a.,** to polish up s.o.'s manners; (*b*) **sich a.,** (*of pers.*) to lose one's uncouth ways, to acquire polish.

Abglätter, *m.* (*pers.*) polisher (of stone, marble, etc.).

Abgleich, *m.* **-s/-e. 1.** balance; equilibrium; counterpoise (of forces, weights, etc.); alignment (of spindles, etc.). **2.**=**abgleichen** II. 1.

Abgleich-, *comb.fm. Tchn:* balancing . . . ; equalizing . . . ; adjusting . . . ; balance . . . .

abgleichen. I. *v.tr. sep.* (*strong*) **1.** (*a*) to level, smooth, even up (surface, piece of ground, etc.); to make (surface, ground, etc.) even; to level down (wall, etc.); to make (wall) level, even; to planish (metal); (*b*) to bring (timbers, etc.) to the same level; to level up (two walls, etc.); to make flush; to align; **abgeglichene Oberfläche,** flush surface. **2.** to equalize, adjust, balance, equilibrate (forces, weights, values, etc.); **die Rechnung a., Schulden und Forderungen a.,** to balance, square, accounts; *Clockm:* to equalize (wheel, fusee); to equipoise (balance-wheel); *El.E: W.Tel:* to balance (circuits, etc.); *Print:* to justify, adjust (type, line, length of column).

II. *vbl s.* **1. Abgleichen,** *n. in vbl senses; also:* (*a*) alignment (of walls, spindles, etc.); (*b*) equalization, equilibration, adjustment (of forces, etc.); *Clockm:* equalization; *Print:* justification (of type, line). **2. Abgleichung,** *f.* (*a*)=II. 1; (*b*)=**Abgleich** 1.

Abgleichfehler, *m. El.E: Tg:* unbalance; balance error.

Abgleichfeile, *f. Tls:* smoothing-file.

Abgleichfrequenz, *f. W.Tel:* balancing frequency.

Abgleichkondensator, *m. W.Tel:* trimming condenser.

Abgleichprüfer, *m. Tp: Tg:* balance tester.

Abgleichpunkt, *m. Tchn:* balance-point.

Abgleichschaltung, *f. Tp: Tg:* balancing two-way repeaters.

Abgleichstange, *f. Clockm:* adjusting rod.

Abgleichverfahren, *n. El.E:* method of, procedure for, balancing (of circuits).

Abgleichwa(a)ge, *f.* proving-scale, testing-scale (for coins, etc.).

Abgleichzirkel, *m.* (pair of) dividers.

abgleiten. I. *v.i. sep.* (*strong*) (*sein*) **1.** (*a*) to slip off, down; to slide off, down; to glide off, down; *Med:* (*of epiphysis, etc.*), *Surg:* (*of bandage, etc.*) to slip; (*b*) **vom Pfad der Tugend a.,** to stray from the path of virtue, *F:* to go astray; (*c*) (*of knife, sword, etc.*) to glance aside, off; **das Schwert glitt an seinen Rippen ab,** the sword glanced off his ribs; (*d*) (*of water*) to run off (an oilskin, a duck's back); **alle seine Verführungskünste glitten an ihr ab,** she was proof against all his blandishments; **alle Ermahnungen gleiten an ihm ab,** he is deaf, irresponsive, to all exhortations. **2.** *Aut: etc:* to skid, to side-slip. **3.** *St.Exch:* (*of prices*) to fall away (gradually), to decline; to slump; *Fin:* **die Mark ist abgeglitten,** the mark has slumped, has gone down.

II. *vbl s.* **Abgleiten** *n.*, **Abgleitung** *f. in vbl senses; also:* slip; (moral) slip; *Aut: etc:* skid(ding), side-slip; *St.Exch: etc:* decline (in prices).

Abgleitschiene, *f.* (*a*) *Aut:* splash-protector; (*b*) *Mil:* (*on armoured car, etc.*) (bullet) deflector strip.

abgliedern. I. *v.sep.* **1.** *v.tr.* (*a*) to dismember (sth.); (*b*) *Av:* **einen Fesselballon a.,** to cast off a captive balloon (from winch). **2.** *v.i.* (*haben*) to form shoots, suckers; to joint off; *Biol:* to segment off.

II. *vbl s.* **1. Abgliedern,** *n. in vbl senses; also:* dismemberment; *Biol:* adjunction. **2. Abgliederung,** *f.* (*a*)=II. 1; (*b*) offshoot; outgrowth.

abglimmen, *v.i. sep.* (*strong & weak*) (*sein*) (*of fire, candle*) to die (out); to burn itself out.

abglitschen, *v.i. sep.* (*sein*) *A. & F:*=**abgleiten** I. 2.

Abglitt, *m.* **-(e)s/e.** *Ling:* off-glide.

abglühen, *v.sep.* **1.** *v.i.* (*sein*) to cease glowing; to cool down (*esp. from a red heat*). **2.** *v.tr.* (*a*) to bring (metal) to a red heat; **abgeglühtes Eisen,** red-hot iron; (*b*) to anneal (steel, glass); to temper (steel).

Abgott, *m.* idol; (*a*) **Abgöttern dienen,** to worship false gods; (*b*) **der A. der Familie,** the idol of the family; **das Geld zu seinem A. machen,** to worship money, to make a god of money; **sein eigener A. sein,** (i) to worship oneself; to idolize oneself; (ii) to be full of, eaten up with, self-conceit.

Abgottanbeter, *m.*=**Götzendiener.**

Abgottdienst, *m.*, **Abgötterei,** *f.* **-/-en**=**Götzendienst.**

abgöttisch, *a.* (*a*) idolatrous (cult, etc.); (*b*) **zu j-m eine abgöttische Liebe hegen,** *adv.* **j-n a. lieben,** to idolize, worship, s.o.; to be passionately fond of s.o.

Abgottschlange, *f. Rept:* boa-constrictor.

Abgrabearbeiten, *f.pl. Civ.E: etc:* levelling (works).

abgraben, *v.tr. sep.* (*strong*) **1.** to dig (sth.) away; to level (mound, etc.). **2.** to mark off, surround, line, with ditches; **ein Feld a.,** to surround a field with ditches, to ditch (in) a field; **einen Weg a.,** to dig a ditch along a road. **3. einen Teich, einen Sumpf, a.,** to drain a pond, a marsh. **4.** *A:* **einer Stadt das Wasser a.,** to cut off, to divert, the water supply of a town; *F:* **j-m das Wasser a.,** to cut the ground from under s.o.'s feet; to work the ruin of s.o., s.o.'s ruin.

abgrämen (sich), *v.refl. sep.* to be taken up with worry; to be anxious; to become careworn; to pine away, to waste away; **sie sah abgegrämt aus,** she had a careworn expression.

abgrasen, *v.tr. sep.* **1.** (*of cattle, etc.*) to graze on (field, etc.); **eine Weide a.,** to browse in a meadow. **2.** *F:* (*a*) **die ganze Stadt, das ganze Gebiet, nach etwas a.,** to scour the town, the district, for sth.; (*b*) *Com:* **einen Markt, ein Gebiet, a.,** to exhaust a market, a selling area; (*c*) to exhaust the possibilities of (field of research, etc.); **dieses Gebiet ist schon gehörig abgegrast (worden),** this field has already been thoroughly worked over; there isn't much left to do in this field; this field is about worked out.

abgraten. I. *v.tr. sep. Metalw:* to remove the burr from (metal), to take the burrs off (metal); to trim (forgings, etc.).

II. *vbl s.* **Abgraten** *n.*, **Abgratung** *f.*, edge-finishing; removal of the burr; trimming (of forgings, etc.).

Abgratmaschine, *f. Metalw:* burr-removing machine, edge-finishing machine; trimming machine.

Abgratmatrize, *f. Metalw:* trimming die.

Abgratpresse, *f. Metalw:* burr-removing press, edge-finishing press; trimming press.

abgrätschen, *v.i. sep.* (*haben*) *Gym:* to scissor-jump off (apparatus).

abgreifen, *v.tr. sep.* (*strong*) **1.** (*a*) to wear out (book, hat, etc.) with handling; **abgegriffene Münzen,** worn coins; **ein abgegriffener Hut,** a worn, shabby, hat; **ein abgegriffenes Buch,** a well-worn, well-thumbed, book; **abgegriffene Seiten,** dog-eared pages; **abgegriffene Redensarten,** well-worn, trite, hackneyed, phrases; (*b*) to feel (sth.) all over. **2.** to span (distance, etc.); (*a*) *Mus:* **eine Oktave a.,** to span, stretch, an octave; (*b*) **eine Entfernung auf einer Karte (mit dem Zirkel) a.,** to measure (off) a distance on a map (with compasses). **3.** *El.E:* to tap (circuit, etc.).

Abgreifklemme, *f.* clip (for radio wiring, rubber tubing, etc.).

abgrenzbar, *a.* capable of delimitation; delimitable; definable; distinguishable.

abgrenzen. I. *v.tr. sep.* (*a*) to delimit, demarcate; to mark the boundaries of (territory, etc.); to mark out (field, vineyard, etc.); to peg out, stake (claim); (*b*) to define (powers, rights, duties, etc.); to circumscribe (powers, field of action); (*c*) to divide, keep apart, keep distinct, distinguish, demarcate (**gegen, von,** from); **einen Gegenstand gegen einen anderen a.,** to distinguish, demarcate, one subject from another; to keep one subject distinct from another; **klar abgegrenzte Begriffe,** clearly defined, clearly distinguished, clear-cut, notions.

II. *vbl s.* **Abgrenzen** *n.*, **Abgrenzung** *f. in vbl senses; also:* (*a*) delimitation, demarcation (of field, etc.); (*b*) definition (of powers, notions, etc.).

abgrenzungsfähig, *a.* capable of delimitation; delimitable.

Abgrenzungslinie, *f.* dividing line, line of demarcation; boundary line.

Abgriff, *m. El.E:* tap, branch (from circuit).

Abgrund, *m.* (*a*) gulf, pit, chasm, abyss, unfathomable depth(s); *occ.* whirlpool; **gähnender A.,** yawning chasm; *B:* **. . . und warf ihn in den A.,** . . . and cast him into the bottomless pit; (*b*) precipice; **am Rande eines jähen, steilen, Abgrundes,** on the edge, brink, of a plunging precipice; (*c*) **er war am Rande des Abgrundes,** he was on the verge, the brink, the edge, of ruin, of destruction, of disaster; **in einem A. der Verzweiflung, des Elends,** in the depths of despair, of affliction; engulfed in despair, in misery; (*d*) *Geol:* swallow(-hole); (*e*) *Oc:* cauldron.

abgründig, *a.* abysmal; unfathomable (depth); deep (bitterness, etc.); **ein abgründiger Charakter,** an unfathomable character; **er ist ein abgründiger Charakter,** he's a deep one, *F:* a dark horse.

abgrundtief, *a.* abysmal; infinitely deep; unfathomable (depth).

abgrundwärts, *adv.* toward the abyss; down (the side of) a precipice; over (the edge of) a precipice.

abgucken, *v.tr. sep.* (*a*) **j-m etwas a.,** to learn sth. by watching, observing, s.o.; to copy (habit, behaviour) from s.o.; to pick up (a habit) from s.o.; **wenn ich ihm doch das Kunststück a. könnte!** if I could only spot how he does it! (*b*) *Sch:* **von einem anderen Schüler die Antwort a.,** to copy, crib, the answer from another boy; *abs.* **a.,** to copy, crib.

abgünstig, *a. A:*=**mißgünstig.**

abgurgeln, *v.tr. sep.* **j-n a.,** (i) to cut, slit, s.o.'s throat; (ii) to throttle s.o.

abgurten, *v.tr. sep.* to ungirth, take the girths off (horse).

abgürten, *v.tr. sep.* **1.** *Lit:* to ungird (s.o.); **sich a.,** *Lit:* to ungird oneself. **2.**=**abgurten.**

Abguß, *m.* **1.**=*vbl s. in vbl senses of* **abgießen** I. 1–3. **2.** (*a*) cast *or* mould(ing); casting; **einen A. von etwas machen,** to take, make, a cast of sth.; **A. in Gips, Bronze, Wachs,** plaster cast, cast in bronze, wax; (*b*) *Print:* (stereotyped) plate, stereotype, *F:* stereo. **3.** decanted liquid;

Cu: vegetable, etc., water. **4.** gutter; drain; sink.

abgußfertig, *a.* ready for casting *or* moulding.

Abgußgerät, *n.* casting *or* moulding equipment.

Abgußkasten, *m. Tchn:* trap, drain.

abhaaren, *v.sep.* **1.** *v.tr.* to depilate, to remove the hair from (sth.); *Tan:* to unhair, scrape, grain (skins). **2.** *v.i.* (*haben*) (*a*) (*of animal*) to lose its hair, its fur; to shed, cast, its coat; (*b*) **dieser Pelzmantel haart ab,** this fur coat is wearing thin; the hair is coming off this fur coat. *See also* **abgehaart.**

abhaben, *v.tr. sep.* (*conj. like* **haben**) **1.** to have (garment, shoes, hat) off; **er hatte den Hut schon ab,** he already had his hat off. **2. etwas von etwas a.,** to have sth. of sth.; to get one's share, one's due, of sth.; *F:* **ich möchte, will, auch etwas von dem Kuchen a.,** I want a bit of the cake, too; **er will auch etwas a.,** he wants his share, *F:* his cut, whack. *See also* **ab** IV. 2.

abhacken, *v.tr. sep.* (*a*) to hack off, strike off, cut off, chop off; (*b*) to cut down, hew down, chop down, cut away, clear (trees). *See also* **abgehackt.**

abhageln, *v.sep.* **1.** *v.tr.* (*usu. only in p.p.*) **die Blüten sind abgehagelt,** the hail has damaged, stripped off, the blossom, the blossom has been damaged by, with, the hail. **2.** *v.impers.* **es hat (sich) abgehagelt,** the hail has stopped, is over, it has stopped hailing.

abhagern, *v.i. sep.* (*sein*) (*of pers.*) to grow thin; to lose flesh; to become emaciated, to waste away.

abhaken, *v.tr. sep.* **1.** to unhook; to unfasten, undo (dress, etc.); to take down (coat, etc.) (from a hook); to take off, lift (telephone receiver); to uncouple, disconnect (railway carriages, etc.); **eine Spange a.,** to undo a clasp. **2.** *Hort:* **eine Pflanze a.,** to fasten down layers from a plant; to layer a plant. **3.** to tick off, *U.S:* check (off) (list, items in list, etc.); to tick (name, etc.), to put a tick, *U.S:* check (mark), against (name, etc.).

abhaldig, *a. A:* rifted (ground, etc.).

abhalftern, *v.tr. sep.* **1. ein Pferd a.,** to take the halter off a horse. **2.** *F:* **einen Beamten a.,** *F:* to sack an official; **abgehalftert,** dismissed, sacked, *U.S:* fired.

abhalsen, *v.tr. sep.* **1.** *Ven:* to slip, unleash, uncouple (hounds). **2.** to hug (s.o.). **3.** *F:* **sich** *dat.* **etwas, j-n, a.,** to get rid of, to rid oneself of, sth., s.o.; *F:* to get shot of sth.

abhalten, *v. sep.* (*strong*) I. *v.tr.* **1.** (*a*) **j-n von etwas a.,** to keep s.o. away from sth., off sth.; **Landstreicher von seinem Gut a.,** to keep tramps off one's estate; **den Feind (vom eigenen Gebiet) a.,** to hold off the enemy (from one's territory); (*b*) **j-n von einem dummen Streich a.,** to restrain s.o. from a stupid action; to stop, keep, s.o. from doing something silly; **ich will Sie nicht von der Arbeit a.,** I don't want to keep you from your work; **lassen Sie sich nicht a.!** please don't disturb yourself; **der Schnee wird mich nicht a.,** the snow won't stop me, deter me; the snow won't keep me away. **2.** (*a*) **etwas (von) j-m a.,** to keep sth. (away) from s.o.; **er hielt alle Unannehmlichkeiten von seiner Frau ab,** he kept all unpleasantness away from his wife; (*b*) **etwas von sich a.,** to hold (sth.) away from oneself. **3. ein Kind a.,** to put a child on, hold a child over, its pot; to hold out a child. **4.** to keep out; to hold back (water, etc.); **das Dach hält den Regen ab,** the roof keeps out the rain. **5.** *occ.* to withstand, resist (wear, fatigue, sickness, etc.); **das Kind hält wenig, nicht viel, ab,** the child has little resistance; the child is delicate. **6. eine Versammlung, Sitzung, Prüfung, Auktion, Parade, usw., a.,** to hold a meeting, an examination, an auction, a parade, etc.; (*of Parliament, law court, etc.*) **eine Sitzung a.,** to sit; *Ecc:* **den Gottesdienst a.,** to celebrate, conduct, perform, take, Divine Service; to hold a service; *see also* **Gerichtstag, Truppenschau.**

II. **abhalten,** *v.i.* (*haben*) *Nau:* to bear away, to fall off; (*a*) **vom Lande a.,** to bear off from the land; (*b*) **auf ein Schiff a.,** to bear down upon a ship; to run down a ship; **auf ein Vorgebirge a.,** to bear away for a point.

III. *vbl s.* **1. Abhalten,** *n. in vbl senses; also:* celebration (of service). **2. Abhaltung,** *f.* (*a*)= III. 1; (*b*) *usu. pl.* **Abhaltungen,** engagements (elsewhere); **er konnte nicht kommen, er hatte anderweitige Abhaltungen,** he could not come, he had other business to attend to, he was otherwise engaged.

Abhaltepunkt, *m. Surv:* fixed point.

Abhalter, *m. Nau: etc:* guy(-rope).

Abhaltungsmittel, *n.* means of prevention; deterrent.

abhämmern, *v.tr. sep.* to hammer (sth.) off, to knock (sth.) off with a hammer.

abhandeln. I. *v.tr. sep.* **1.** to negotiate; **das ist zwischen ihnen abgehandelt worden,** they have settled it between them. **2.** (*a*) to handle (business); **das Übrige wird morgen abgehandelt werden,** the remaining business will be handled, dealt with, tomorrow; (*b*) to discuss, handle, deal with (subject); to treat (of) (subject); to discourse upon, *Lit:* to dissertate on (subject). **3.** (*a*) **j-m etwas a.,** to purchase sth. from, of, s.o.; to do a deal with s.o. for sth.; (*b*) **j-m zwanzig Mark a.,** to get s.o. to reduce his price by twenty marks, to knock twenty marks off s.o.'s price; to beat s.o. down by twenty marks; **er läßt sich keinen Heller a.,** he won't take a halfpenny less than his price; **er fordert zehn Pfund und er läßt sich nichts a.,** *F:* his price is ten pounds and he won't come down; **er läßt sich von seinen Bedingungen nichts a.,** he cannot be persuaded to modify his conditions.

II. *vbl s.* **Abhandeln,** *n. in vbl senses; cp.* **Abhandlung.**

abhanden, *adv.* (*a*) **a. kommen,** to be, get, lost; to go astray; to be mislaid; **Ihr Scheck ist a. gekommen,** your cheque has been mislaid, has gone astray; *Fin:* **a. gekommene Wertpapiere, Effekten,** lost, missing, securities; (*b*) **a. sein,** to be lost, to be missing; **einer meiner Kragen ist a.,** one of my collars is missing, *F:* I'm a collar short.

Abhandenkommen, *n.* loss (of document, umbrella, etc.).

Abhandlung, *f.* **1.** treatise, dissertation; paper; (written) discourse (**über** *acc.*, *A:* **von,** on, upon); **kleine Abhandlungen,** short essays; (short) tracts; articles; **gelehrte A.,** learned treatise, learned essay; **(gesammelte) Abhandlungen einer gelehrten Gesellschaft, einer Forschungsgesellschaft,** transactions, proceedings, memoirs, of a learned society, of a research organization; (*Note: in academic contexts, booksellers' catalogues, etc.,* **Abhandlung** *is usu. employed to describe treatises other than doctoral dissertations*). **2.** (oral) discourse, discussion (**über** *acc.*, about, on, upon).

Abhang, *m.* (*a*) slope, incline; declivity; *Civ.E: Rail: etc:* gradient; **jäher, steiler, A.,** steep descent; steep incline, slope; declivity; (*b*) **A. eines Hügels,** side, slope, of a hill; hillside; **A. eines Gebirges,** slope, slide, versant, of a mountain-range; (*c*) *Fort:* glacis.

abhängen, *occ.* **abhangen,** *v.sep.* (*conj. like* **hängen**) I. *v.i.* (*haben*) **1.** (*of ground*) to slope, fall away; (*of surface*) to shelve; **die Straße hängt gegen Süden ab,** the road falls away to the south. **2. von etwas a.,** to hang down, be suspended, from sth.; *A. & Poet:* to depend from sth. **3. von etwas a.,** to hang away, out, from sth.; **es hängt nicht weit genug vom Feuer ab,** it isn't hanging far enough away from the fire, it hangs too near (to) the fire; **die Birnen hingen von der Mauer ab,** the pears hung out from the wall. **4. von etwas, j-m, a.,** to depend on, upon, sth., s.o.; to be dependent on sth., s.o.; **die Ernte hängt vom Wetter ab,** crops depend upon, are dependent on, the weather; **das hängt von seiner Genehmigung ab,** that depends upon, is subject to, his approval; it depends whether he approves; **ich hänge geldlich von meinem Onkel ab,** I am financially dependent on my uncle; **alles hängt von den Umständen ab,** it all depends on circumstances; **alles hängt von seiner Antwort ab,** everything depends, hangs, hinges, turns, on his answer; **das hängt ganz von Ihnen ab,** that depends entirely on you; that is entirely for you to decide; **sein Schicksal hängt von Ihnen ab,** his fate lies in your hands, rests with you; **wir hängen alle vom Schicksal ab,** we are all at the mercy of fortune. **5.** *Cu:* (*of meat, game, etc.*) to hang (until tender).

II. **abhängen,** *v.tr.* **1.** (*a*) to unhook, take down (coat) (from peg, etc.); to detach (sth.) (from hook, etc.); (*b*) *Mil: etc:* **den Tornister a.,** to unsling, take off, one's pack; (*c*) to disconnect; to uncouple (railway carriages, etc.); *Rail:* **der Speisewagen wird in München abgehängt,** the dining-car is taken off at Munich; (*d*) *Tp:* **(den Hörer) a.,** (i) to take off, lift, the receiver; (ii) to ring off; *F:* **er wurde frech, ich habe also einfach abgehängt,** he got cheeky, so I just hung up on him. **2. etwas von etwas a.,** to hang sth. at a distance from, well away from, sth. **3.** *Cu:* to hang (meat, game, etc.). **4.** *F:* to get rid of (companion, collaborator, etc.); to shake off (unwanted companion, pursuer, *Sp:* competitor, *Mil.Av:* enemy aircraft); to leave (competitor) behind; to outdistance, outstrip, outrun, outpace (s.o.); to outsail (s.o., ship).

III. *vbl s.* **Abhängen,** *n. in vbl senses; also:* disconnection; *cp.* **Abhang.**

IV. *pr.p. & a.* **abhängend,** *occ.* **abhangend,** *in vbl senses; esp.* (*a*) hanging, suspended, pendent; (*b*) sloping (road, etc.); shelving (surface); (*c*) dependent.

V. *p.p. & a.* **abgehangen,** *in vbl senses; esp. Cu:* hung (meat, game).

abhängig, *a.* **1.** inclined, sloping (road, ground, etc.); shelving (surface); **abhängige Straße,** street, road, on the slope; **ein Blumenbeet a. machen,** to slope a flower-bed. **2.** dependent; **voneinander abhängige Funktionen,** functions dependent on each other, interdependent functions. **3.** dependent; subordinate; (*a*) (*of pers.*) **in abhängiger Stellung sein,** to be in a subordinate, dependent, position; **abhängiges Gebiet,** dependency (of a State); (*b*) *Mth:* **abhängige Veränderliche, abhängige Variable,** dependent variable; *Gram:* **abhängiger Satz,** subordinate, dependent, clause; **abhängiger Kasus,** oblique case; **abhängige Rede,** indirect speech, reported speech, oblique oration. **4.** (*a*) **von etwas a. sein,** to be dependent on sth., to depend (up)on sth.; **die Ernten sind vom Wetter a.,** crops depend upon, are dependent on, the weather; **ich bin von seiner Gnade a.,** I am dependent on his favour; **er ist vom Geschäft a.,** he is dependent on his business; he has no other source of income beside his business; (*b*) **von j-m a. sein,** to be dependent on s.o., *esp.* to be financially dependent on s.o. **5.** (*of event, etc.*) **von etwas a. sein,** to be conditional on sth., contingent on sth., subject to sth.; **die Versteigerung ist von seiner Genehmigung a.,** the auction is subject to his consent. **6. etwas von etwas a. machen,** to make sth. dependent on, subordinate to, conditional on, subject to, sth.

Abhängigkeit, *f.* **1.** declivity, slope; sloping nature (of ground, etc.). **2.** (*a*) dependence, dependency (**von,** on, upon); subordination, subjection (**von,** to); **A. der Kinder von ihren Eltern,** dependence of children on their parents; **in A. geraten,** to lose one's independence; **A. einer Wirkung von einer Ursache,** dependence of an effect upon a cause; **A. des Einzelnen vom Staat,** dependence of the individual (up)on the State; subordination, subjection, of the individual to the State; *Tchn:* **in unmittelbarer A. von . . . funktionieren,** to operate in direct relation(ship) to . . . ; (*b*) *Gram:* subordination.

Abhängigkeitsgefühl, *n.* feeling of dependence, of dependency; feeling that one is not one's own master.

Abhängigkeitsverhältnis, *n.* (*a*) condition of dependence (**zu,** upon); condition of subjection (**zu,** to); (*b*) dependent relation(ship) (**zu, to**).

Abhängling, *m.* -s/-e. *Arch:* pendant.

Abhangsfortsatz, *m. Anat:* clinoid process.

abhären, *v.tr. sep.*=**abhaaren** 1.

abharken, *v.tr. sep.* **1.** to rake (sth.) off, away; to clear (sth.) away with a rake. **2.** (*a*) to rake (ground, etc.); (*b*) to hoe; to scuffle (path, etc.).

abhärmen (sich), *v.refl. sep.* (*a*) to pine away, waste away, with grief; to become careworn; (*b*) **sich wegen etwas, über etwas** *acc.*, **a.,** to grieve, fret, over sth.; (*c*) *p.p. & a.* **abgehärmt,** (*of pers.*) consumed with grief; careworn, haggard (face, appearance); **sie sah abgehärmt aus,** she had a careworn look.

abhärten. I. *v.sep.* **1.** *v.tr.* (*a*) to harden, toughen, indurate; *Metall:* to temper (steel); (*b*) to harden, inure (s.o.); to toughen (s.o.) (up); **j-n gegen Strapazen a.,** to inure s.o. to hardships, fatigue; (*c*) *Hort:* **Sämlinge a.,** to harden (off) seedlings. **2. sich abhärten,** (*a*) to harden, become hard, to indurate, toughen; (*b*) (*of pers.*) to become hardened, callous; (*c*) (*of pers.*) to become hardened, fit, tough; to toughen (up); **sich gegen etwas a.,** to inure, harden, oneself to sth.; **sich durch kalte Bäder a.,** to toughen oneself, keep oneself fit, by cold baths; **ein abgehärteter Mensch,** a hardy person; **gegen Strapazen abgehärtet,** inured, hardened, to fatigue.

II. *vbl s.* **Abhärten** *n.*, **Abhärtung** *f. in vbl senses; also:* induration; inurement (**gegen,** to).

abharzen, *v.tr. sep.* to tap (fir-trees, etc.) for resin.

abhaschen, *v.tr. sep.* **j-m etwas a.,** to snatch, get, sth. away from s.o.

Abhaspelmaschine, *f.* reeling-machine, winder.

abhaspeln, *v.sep.* **1.** *v.tr.* (*a*) *Tex: etc:* (i) to unwind; (ii) to reel, wind off, spool (thread, etc.); (*b*) *F:* to reel off, rattle off, gabble out (poetry, a list, etc.). **2. sich abhaspeln,** to wear oneself out (with hard work), to work oneself to a standstill.

Abhaspelungsmaschine, *f.*=**Abhaspelmaschine.**

abhasten, *v.tr. sep.* **1.** to do (sth.) hastily; to scamp (piece of work); to gallop through, rattle off (prayers, piece of work, etc.). **2. sich abhasten,** to hustle; to bustle along.

Abhau, *m. Min:* downward working.

abhauben, abhäuben, *v.tr. sep. Ven:* to unhood (falcon, hawk).

abhauchen, *v.tr. sep.* **1.** to blow the dust off (sth.). **2.** to breathe (words) softly.

abhauen, *v. sep.* (*conj. like* **hauen**) **I.** *v.tr.* (*a*) to fell, cut down, hew down, cut away, clear (trees); to cut (corn); to lop off, cut off, chop off (branch, etc.); (*b*) to strike off, lop off, cut off, *F:* chop off (head, limb); **j-m den Kopf a.,** to behead, decapitate, s.o., to cut off, *F:* chop off, s.o.'s head.

II. **abhauen,** *v.i.* (*sein*) *F:* to make off; to push off; to hop it, sling one's hook, *U.S:* beat it; **hau ab!** be off! clear off! take yourself off! hop it! *U.S:* beat it! scram!

III. *vbl s.* **Abhauen,** *n. in vbl senses; also: F:* hasty departure.

abhäufeln, *v.tr. sep.*=**häufeln.**

abhausen, *v.tr. sep.*=**verwohnen.**

abhäuten, *v.tr. sep.* **1.** (*a*) to skin (eel, rabbit, etc.); to flay (large animal); (*b*) to excoriate; to peel off the skin from (finger, etc.); (*c*) *Metall:* to scum, skim (molten metal). **2. sich abhäuten,** (*a*) (*of pers., nose, animal*) to peel; (*b*) (*of snake*) to cast its slough, its skin; (*of reptile, insect*) to slough its skin.

Abhebegabel, *f. Tp:* receiver-hook, cradle (of desk telephone).

Abhebemaschine, *f. Ind:* lifting-machine; *esp. Metall:* drawing-machine (to remove patterns, moulding boxes).

abheben. I. *v.tr. sep.* (*strong*) **1.** (*a*) to lift off, take off, take away, remove; **den Deckel von einem Kasten a.,** to lift, take, the lid off a box, to remove the lid from a box; *Tp:* **den Hörer a.,** to lift, take off, the receiver; *Knitting:* **eine Masche a.,** to slip a stitch; *Metall:* **ein Modell, einen Formkasten, a.,** to draw, withdraw, a pattern, a moulding box; *Metalw:* **Späne a.,** to remove chips; **ein Werkzeug vom Werkstück a.,** to clear a tool from the work; (*b*) **den Rahm von der Milch a.,** to skim the cream off the milk, to skim the milk; (*c*) *Civ.E: etc:* **die Bodenoberschicht a.,** to strip off the top-soil; *Surg:* **die Haut vom Gewebe a.,** to lift off, strip off, the skin from the tissues. **2.** *Av:* **das Flugzeug a.,** to get the aircraft away, pull the aircraft up, *F:* to hoick the aircraft off. **3.** *v.i.* (*haben*) (*a*) *Cards:* to cut (the cards); **wer hebt ab?** whose turn is it to cut? **zum Geben a.,** to cut for deal; **um Plätze, zum Bestimmen der Plätze, a.,** to cut for partners; (*b*) (*with string, etc.*) to play cat's cradle. **4. Geld a.,** to withdraw, draw, money (from the bank, etc.); *Fin:* **Dividenden a.,** to collect dividends; **abgehobene Dividenden,** dividends collected. **5.** *Ch: etc:* **zwei Flüssigkeiten (von einander) a.,** to separate two liquids. **6.** *Hyd.E:* **den Fundationsgrund a.,** to bare the foundations. **7. sich abheben,** to stand out (in relief); **sich von einem Hintergrund, vom Himmel, a.,** to stand out against a background, against the sky; (*of pers., thg*) **sich von den anderen (stark) a.,** to stand out from the others; to stand out in sharp contrast to the others.

II. *vbl s.* **Abheben** *n., occ.* **Abhebung** *f. in vbl senses; also:* removal; cut (of cards); withdrawal (of money from bank, etc.); collection (of dividends); separation (of two liquids); **Abheben spielen,** to play cat's cradle.

abhebern, *v.tr. sep.* (*a*) to siphon off (liquid, *F:* excessive profits); (*b*) **Wein a.,** to take a sample of wine (with sampling tube).

abhecheln, *v.tr. sep. Tex:* to hackle (flax, hemp).

abheften, *v.tr. sep.* **1.** to file (letters, etc.). **2.** *Needlew:* to tack; to pin.

abheilen, *v.i. sep.* (*sein, haben*) (*of wound*) to heal (up); to skin over, scar (over).

abheischen, *v.tr. sep.* **j-m etwas a.,** to demand sth. of, from, s.o.

abhelfen. I. *v.i. sep.* (*strong*) (*haben*) **1. j-m (vom Pferde, Fahrrad, usw.) a.,** to help a person down (from a horse, bicycle, etc.). **2. etwas** *dat.* **a.,** to remedy sth.; **einem Fehler a.,** to rectify, correct, an error; **einem Unrecht a.,** to redress a wrong; **einem Übel, einem Übelstand, a.,** to cure, redress, an evil; to put a trouble right; to redress a grievance; to put, set, a bad state of things right; **dem ist nicht mehr abzuhelfen,** it is past, beyond, remedy; it is past mending; there's nothing (more) to be done about it; **ein Unrecht, dem nicht mehr abgeholfen werden kann,** a wrong that cannot be righted; an injury beyond, past, redress; **dem kann leicht abgeholfen werden, dem ist leicht abgeholfen, abzuhelfen,** that can easily be remedied, cured; we can easily do something about that; **abhelfende Maßnahmen,** remedial measures.

II. *vbl s.* **Abhelfen,** *n. in vbl senses; also:* rectification (of error); *cp.* **Abhilfe.**

abhellen, *v.tr. sep.* (*a*)=**abklären** I. 1 (*a*); (*b*)=**aufhellen** I. 1.

abherzen, *v.tr. sep.* to hug (and kiss) (s.o.); to load, smother, (s.o.) with caresses.

abhetzen, *v.tr. sep.* **1.** (*a*) *Ven:* to hunt down, run down (stag, boar, etc.); to bring (stag, boar) to bay; (*b*) **j-n a.,** to harass s.o.; to drive s.o. hard; to exhaust s.o.; to tire s.o. out; to work s.o. to death; *F:* to make s.o. work like a slave, like a nigger; to keep s.o. on the run; (*c*) *Ven:* to exhaust, over-hunt, jade (hounds); **die Hunde sind abgehetzt,** the hounds are jaded. **2. sich abhetzen,** to rush, hurry (*to get somewhere, to do sth.*); to tire oneself out (with scurrying around); to exhaust oneself, to wear oneself out. **3. abgehetzt sein,** to be tired out, worn out, dog-tired, dead-tired, *F:* fagged out, done up, dead-beat; (*of runner*) to be winded.

Abhetzerei, *f.* (*a*) (continual) harassing (of s.o.); harassment; (*b*) *F:* harassing, nerve-racking, business; **mein Vormittag war eine einzige A.,** my morning was just one big rush.

abheuern, *v.tr. sep.* **j-m etwas a.,** to hire sth. from s.o.

abheulen, *v.tr. sep.* **1.** to howl out, roar out, bawl out (song). **2. sich abheulen,** to cry one's eyes out, *F:* to howl, bawl, one's head off.

Abhieb, *m.* **1.** *For:* felling, cutting (down), chopping down (of trees in a wood). **2.** *Min:* (*a*) cut, undercut; (*b*) cutting, undercutting.

Abhieb(s)fläche, *f. For:* cutting area, felling area.

abhier, *adv.* from here (on), from this place; *Com:* (communication, delivery) from our end; (delivery) ex works, ex store; **frei abhier,** no delivery charge; free on rail; **Preise abhier,** prices free of delivery charges; prices free on rail, *abbr.* f.o.r.; *U.S:* free on board, f.o.b.

Abhilfe, *f.* remedy (**für,** for); **A. für ein Unrecht, einen Übelstand,** redress for a wrong, remedy for an evil; **A. für einen Fehler,** rectification, correction, of an error; **für etwas A. schaffen, leisten, bringen,** to remedy sth.; to cure (an evil); to redress (a wrong, a grievance); **dem kann man leicht A. schaffen,** that can easily be remedied, cured; **wir müssen sofort A. schaffen,** we must take remedial measures at once; **er sinnt auf A.,** he is seeing what can be done about it, what can be done to help; **diese Situation verlangt sofortige A.,** this state of affairs demands immediate action, will have to be remedied at once; **ein Unrecht ohne A.,** an injury beyond, past, redress; **Mittel** *n pl* **zur A.,** remedial measures. *Cp.* **abhelfen** II.

abhinken, *v.i. sep.* (*sein*) to limp away, off; to hobble away, off.

Abhitze, *f.* (*also comb. fm.*)=**Abwärme.**

abhobeln, *v.tr. sep.* **1.** (*a*) to plane off (edges, irregularities, etc.); to shave off (edges); (*b*) **ein Brett (rauh) a.,** to rough-plane a plank; **eine Fläche fein a.,** to smooth a surface, plane a surface smooth. **2.** *F:* **j-n a.,** to polish s.o. up, to civilize s.o., *F:* to knock the corners off s.o., to lick s.o. into shape. **3.** *F:* **sich abhobeln,** to acquire polish, to become civilized, to lose one's uncouth ways.

abhocken, *v.sep.* **1.** *occ. v.tr.* to take (burden, child) off one's back. **2.** *v.i.* (*sein*) *Gym:* to squat-jump off (apparatus); *Ski:* to crouch (low); to run in a (low) crouch.

abhold, *a.* (*a*) **j-m a. sein,** to be ill-disposed towards s.o.; to feel an aversion to, for, s.o.; **die Dame ist mir a.,** the lady does not care for me; **er ist den Frauen nicht a.,** he is not averse to women; (*b*) **etwas** *dat.* **a. sein,** to be averse to sth., to have no liking for sth.; **er ist dem Biertrinken nicht a.,** he is not averse to, *F:* he doesn't mind, a glass of beer.

abholen. I. *v.tr. sep.* **1.** to (go and *or* come and) fetch, to get (sth., s.o.); (*a*) **ich werde Ihr Gepäck vom Hotel a.,** I'll (go and) fetch, get, your luggage from the hotel; I'll call at, go to, the hotel for your luggage; **Gepäck wird vom Bahnhof abgeholt,** luggage is collected, fetched, from the station; **Gepäck wird vom Hause abgeholt,** luggage is called for, collected; **sein Gepäck von der Gepäckaufbewahrung a.,** to claim one's luggage from the left-luggage office, *U.S:* one's baggage from the baggage room; *Th: etc:* **vorbestellte Karten müssen 5 Minuten vor Beginn der Vorstellung abgeholt werden,** tickets booked, *U.S:* reserved, in advance must be claimed 5 minutes before the start of the performance; **etwas a. lassen,** to send for sth.; **bitte a. lassen,** kindly call, send, for it; **'wird abgeholt',** 'to be (left until) called for'; *Post:* **seine Briefe (von der Post) a.,** to fetch, collect, one's letters from the post office, from one's post-office box; **wann wird abgeholt?** what time is the collection? when is the box, are the letters, cleared? (*b*) **ich werde Sie vom Hotel a.,** I'll call for you at the hotel, I'll come to the hotel to meet you; **ich werde abgeholt,** someone is calling, coming, for me; I am being called for; **j-n am Bahnhof a.,** to go to meet s.o. at the station; *F:* to meet s.o. off the train; **j-n am Bahnhof a. lassen,** to arrange for s.o. to be met at the station; *Nau:* **die Mannschaft von einem Schiff a.,** to take off the crew from a ship; (*of police*) **j-n a.,** to arrest s.o. at his home, *F:* to (come and) take s.o. away. **2.** *Nau:* **ein Schiff (vom Strand) a.,** to refloat, set afloat, a stranded ship; to heave, get, a stranded ship off the shore.

II. *vbl s.* **Abholen** *n.,* **Abholung** *f. in vbl senses; also: Post:* collection, clearance.

Abholer, *m.* **-s/-.** *Post:* caller (*esp.* for mail from private box).

Abholkommando, *n.* **1.** *Mil:* fetching party; party detailed to fetch equipment, etc. **2.** *Mil.Av:* aircraft ferrying detachment.

Abholungsfach, *n.* post-office box, P.O. box (for letters to be called for).

Abhol(ungs)zeit, *f. Post:* time of collection, of clearance.

Abholz, *n. For:* waste wood, refuse (wood); loppings.

abholzen. I. *v.tr. sep.* to deforest, untimber (land); to clear (hillside, etc.) of trees; to fell, cut down, clear (trees).

II. *vbl s.* **Abholzen** *n.,* **Abholzung** *f. in vbl senses; also:* deforestation.

abholzig, *a.* (*of trees*) (*a*) *Bot:* tapering; (*b*) *For:* yielding little timber.

Abhörapparat, *m.* **1.** *Mil: Navy:* listening device; sound-detection device. **2.** *Cin: W.Tel: Tp:* monitoring device, apparatus.

Abhörbox, *f. Cin.*=**Abhörraum** 2.

abhorchen. I. *v.tr. sep.* **1. j-m ein Geheimnis a.,** to learn a secret from s.o. by eavesdropping, to overhear sth. said secretly by s.o. **2.** (*a*) *Med:* to sound, auscultate (patient, the chest); to examine (s.o.) by auscultation; (*b*) *Navy: etc:* to follow the movements of (submarine, etc.) by means of a sound-detection device.

II. *vbl s.* **Abhorchen,** *n. in vbl senses; also: Med:* auscultation; *Mil: Navy:* listening.

Abhorchgerät, *n. W.Tel: etc:* listening apparatus, *esp. Navy:* anti-submarine listening device; Asdic.

Abhorchstelle, *f. Mil: Navy:* listening-post, -station.

Abhördienst, *m.* (*a*) *Tp: W.Tel:* monitoring service; (*b*) *Mil:* (telephone) interception service.

abhören. I. *v.tr. sep.* **1.** (*a*) **j-m etwas a.,** to learn sth., to pick up a piece of information, by listening to s.o.; (*b*) *Sch:* **einem Kind seine Aufgabe a., ein Kind a.,** to hear a child's lesson. **2.** *Jur:* **die Zeugen a.,** to hear the witnesses. **3.** (*a*) to overhear, eavesdrop on (conversation); (*b*) *Cin: Tp: W.Tel:* to monitor; (*c*) *Mil:* to intercept, listen in to (message, telephone conversation); to tap, *F:* milk (land-line); *abs.* to listen in.

II. *vbl s.* **Abhören** *n.,* **Abhörung** *f. in vbl senses; also: Mil:* interception.

Abhörer, *m.* **1.** *Cin:* monitor man; sound engineer. **2.** (*a*) *Tg: Tp:* wire-tapper; (*b*) *W.Tel:* monitor (of foreign broadcasts, etc.).

Abhörlautsprecher, *m.* control loud-speaker; *Cin:* projection-room monitor.

Abhörraum, *m.* **1.** *W.Tel:* control-room. **2.** *Cin:* monitor room; **fahrbarer A.,** transportable monitor room.

abhorrent [aphoˈrɛnt], *a.* abhorrent, disgusting, loathsome, repugnant, *F:* horrid.

Abhorreszenz [aphorɛsˈtsɛnts], *f.* **-/-en,** abhorrence, disgust, loathing, horror, repugnance.

abhorreszieren [aphorɛsˈtsiːrən], **abhorrieren** [aphoˈriːrən], *v.tr. insep.* to abhor, loathe, abominate (sth.); to hold (sth.) in abhorrence.

Abhörstelle, *f. Mil: etc:* listening-post, -station; *W.Tel:* monitoring station.

Abhortation [aphorta·tsi'oːn], *f.* **-/-en,** solemn warning; dissuasion.

abhortieren [aphor'tiːrən], *v.tr. insep.* to give (s.o.) a solemn warning; to dissuade (s.o.).

Abhörung, *f. see* **abhören** II.

Abhörvorrichtung, *f.* (secret) listening device; **es sind Abhörvorrichtungen in diesem Zimmer,** *F:* this room is wired, *U.S:* bugged.

Abhörzelle, *f. W.Tel:* control-room.

Abhub, *m.* **1.** *Metalw:* clearing (of tool) from the work. **2.** waste; *Soapm: etc:* scum, skimmings; *Metall:* dross, scoria; *Min:* waste; *Gold-Min:* spent dirt. *Cp.* **abheben** II.

Abhubkiste, *f. Min: A:* rake.

abhucken, *v.tr. sep.*=**abhocken** 1.

abhülsen, *v.tr. sep.*=**enthülsen.**

abhumpeln, *v.i. sep. (sein)* to hobble away, off; to limp away, off.

abhungern (sich), *v.refl. sep.* (*a*) to starve oneself; (*b*) to starve; **abgehungert sein, aussehen,** to be, look, famished, (half-)starved.

abhupen, *v.i. sep. (haben)* to hoot, sound, a horn as a starting-signal.

abhüpfen, *v.i. sep. (sein) (of child)* to skip, hop, away; *(of bird, etc.)* to hop away; *F: (of pers.)* to hop off.

abhuschen, *v.i. sep. (sein)* to whisk away; to slip away.

abhusten (sich), *v. refl. sep.* to exhaust oneself with coughing.

abhüten, *v.tr. sep. Husb:* **eine Wiese a.,** to graze, pasture (a meadow).

abhütten, *v.tr. sep. Min: A:* **1.** to abandon (mine). **2.** to spoil (mine) by bad working.

abi, *adv. South G.Dial:*=**ab, herab.**

Abichit [abi·'çiːt], *m.* **-(e)s/.** *Miner:* clinoclasite, clinoclase.

äbich(t), *a. A. & Dial:* **1. die äbichte Seite eines Tuchs,** the wrong side, reverse, back, of a material. **2.** (lying) on the northern side, slope; away from the sun. **3.** unpleasant; awkward; cross-grained (character).

Abietin [a·bi·e·'tiːn], *n.* **-s/.** *Ch:* abietin(e).

Abietinsäure, *f. Ch:* abietic acid.

Abigail [a·bi·'gaːil]. *Pr.n.f.* **-s.** *B.Hist:* Abigail.

Abigeat [abi·ge·'aːt], *m.* **-(e)s/-e.** *Jur:* theft of cattle; cattle-stealing, -lifting.

Abig(e)ator [abi·g(e·)aː'tor], *m.* **-s/-en** [-a·'toːrən]. *Jur:* cattle-thief, -lifter.

abigieren [abi·'giːrən], *v.tr. insep. Jur:* to drive away; to steal, lift (cattle).

Abiogenesis [a·bi·o·'geːne·zis], *f.* **-/.** *Biol:* abiogenesis, spontaneous generation.

Abiologie [a·bi·o·lo·'giː], *f.* **-/.** study of inanimate things.

Abiose [a·bi·'oːzə], *f.* **-/.** *Biol:* abiosis.

Abiostatik [a·bi·o·'staːtik], *f.* **-/.** study of the properties of inanimate things.

abiotisch [a·bi·'oːtiʃ], *a. Biol:* abiotic.

abirren. I. *v.i. sep. (sein)* (*a*) to deviate, stray, wander, err (**von,** from); to lose one's way, to go astray; to go off the track; to go adrift; **vom rechten Weg a.,** to wander, err, from the straight path, the right way; **vom Pfad der Tugend a.,** to stray, wander, from the path of virtue; **vom Thema a.,** to stray, wander, from the subject; to digress; to wander (away) from the point; (*b*) *Astr: Opt: (of ray, etc.)* to deviate.

II. *vbl s.* **Abirren** *n.,* **Abirrung** *f. in vbl senses; also:* deviation; **Abirrung des Verstandes,** aberration of the mind, mental aberration; *Astr: Opt:* aberration. *Cp.* **Aberration.**

äbisch, *a.*=äbich(t).

Abitur [a·bi·'tuːr], *n.* **-s/-e.** *Sch:* school-leaving examination (qualifying for university entrance); *(in England)* examination for the General Certificate of Education; *U.S:* final examination; **das, sein, A. ablegen, machen,** to take one's school-leaving certificate; to pass one's school-leaving examination; **das A. bestehen,** to get one's school-leaving certificate, to pass one's school-leaving examination; *U.S:* to graduate; **er hat kein A. (gemacht),** he has not taken his (school-) leaving certificate; he has not had a secondary education; *U.S:* he has not graduated.

Abiturient [a·bi·tu·ri'ɛnt], *m.* **-en/-en,** (*a*) candidate for the school-leaving examination; *(in England)* candidate for the General Certificate of Education; (*b*) person who has passed the school-leaving examination; *(in England)* person who has (got) the General Certificate of Education; *U.S:* graduate (of senior high school).

Abiturientenexamen, *n.,* **Abiturientenprüfung,** *f.*=**Abitur.**

Abiturium [a·bi·'tuːrium], *n.* **-s/-ria** *&* **-rien**=**Abitur.**

abjagen, *v.sep.* I. *v.tr.* **1.** *Ven:* **ein Revier a.,** (i) to shoot over an area, a preserve; to hunt over a district; (ii) to kill all the game in an area, in a preserve. **2.** (*a*) to override, overstrain, overwork, founder, knock up, exhaust, jade (horse, hounds); (*b*)=**abhetzen** 1 (*b*). **3. j-m etwas a.,** to retrieve sth. from s.o.; **seinem Feind die Beute (wieder) a.,** to retrieve, recover, snatch back, the booty from one's enemy. **4. sich abjagen**=**abhetzen** 2.

II. **abjagen,** *v.i. (haben) Ven:* to leave off, cease, hunting.

abjäten, *v.tr. sep.* to weed (field, garden, etc.) (thoroughly).

abjochen, *v.tr. sep.* to unyoke (oxen).

Abjudikation [apju·di·ka·tsi'oːn], *f.* **-/-en.** *Jur:* abjudication; deprival by judicial sentence.

abjudizieren [apju·di·'tsiːrən], *v.tr. insep. Jur:* **j-m etwas a.,** to deprive s.o. of sth. by judicial sentence.

Abjuration [apju·ra·tsi'oːn], *f.* **-/-en,** abjuration; renunciation (on oath); recantation.

abjurieren [apju·'riːrən], *v.tr. insep.* to abjure, forswear; to renounce (on oath); to recant, retract.

abkaffen, *v.tr. sep. Constr: etc:* to slant, slope, (sth.) off at the apex.

abkalben, *v.i. sep. (haben) (of cow)* to cease calving.

abkalken. I. *v.tr. sep. Ind: etc:* to delime (substance), to free (substance) from lime.

II. *vbl s.* **Abkalken** *n.,* **Abkalkung** *f. in vbl senses; also:* removal of lime.

abkälten, *v.tr. sep.* to cool (down), refrigerate; to chill (liquids, etc.).

abkämmen, *v.tr. sep.* **1.** to comb (sth.) off. **2.** *Tex:* to card, comb (wool, etc.). **3.** (*a*) **einen Wald nach vermißten Kindern a.,** to comb a wood for missing children; *Mil:* **ein Gelände mit Maschinengewehren a.,** to rake an area with machine-gun fire; (*b*) *Mil: A:* to cut down (parapet, etc.) (by gun-fire).

abkämpfen[1], *v.tr. sep.* **1. j-m etwas a.,** to wrest sth. from s.o. (in battle, struggle); *Nau:* **einem Schiff den Wind a.,** to get the weather-gauge of a ship. **2.** *Ven: (of stag in rutting season)* to drive away, fight off (rivals). **3.** *Ven: (of stag)* **ein Ende a.,** to lose a branch of its antlers (by fighting). **4. sich abkämpfen,** to exhaust oneself (with) fighting; *(of troops)* **abgekämpft,** exhausted, worn out, with fighting; battle-weary.

abkämpfen[2], *v.tr. sep. Constr:* to furnish (arch, abutment) with an impost moulding.

abkandeln, *v.tr. sep. Carp: etc:* to flute, channel; **Stuhl mit abgekandelten Beinen,** chair with fluted legs.

abkanteln, *v.tr. & i. (haben) sep.*=**abkanten** I. 1 (*a*), 3.

abkanten. I. *v.tr. sep.* **1.** (*a*) *Carp: etc:* to chamfer, bevel; (*b*) *Metalw:* to bend, fold (sheet-metal). **2.** *Tex: etc:* **Tuch, Tapetenpapier, a.,** to cut off the selvedge of cloth, of wallpaper. **3.** *v.i. (haben) Knitting:* to cast off.

II. *vbl s.* **1. Abkanten,** *n. in vbl senses.* **2. Abkantung,** *f.* (*a*)=II. 1; (*b*) chamfer, chamfered edge, bevel-edge; bend, fold (of metal sheet).

Abkantmaschine, *f. Metalw:* (*a*) (sheet-metal) bending machine; edging machine; **Abkant- und Falzmaschine,** bending and folding machine; (*b*) nut-bevelling machine; (*c*) *Carp:* (i) squaring machine; (ii) bevelling machine.

Abkantpresse, *f. Metalw:* bending press, *esp. U.S:* press brake.

abkanzeln, *v.tr. sep.* **1.** *A:* (*a*) to deliver (warning, etc.) from the pulpit; (*b*) to reprimand (s.o.) from the pulpit. **2.** *F:* to lecture (s.o.), read (s.o.) a lecture; to give (s.o.) a rating, a (good) talking-to; *F:* to tell, tick, (s.o.) off; to haul s.o. over the coals; to blow (s.o.) up; *U.S:* to call (s.o.) down, *F:* to bawl (s.o.) out.

abkapiteln, *v.tr. sep.*=**abkanzeln** 2.

abkappen, *v.tr. sep.* **1.** to chop off, cut off; *Nau:* to cut (cable); to cut away (mast, cordage). **2.** *F:* to snub (s.o.); to send (s.o.) packing. **3.** *For:* to top, pollard (tree). **4.** *Ven:* to unhood (hawk).

abkapseln. I. *v.tr. sep.* to enclose (sth.) in a capsule; *Biol:* to encapsulate (organism); *Ling:* to incapsulate (element); **sich a.,** *Biol: Med: (of parasite, tumour, etc.)* to encyst itself, to become encysted; *(of pers.)* to retire into one's shell.

II. *vbl s.* **1. Abkapseln,** *n. in vbl senses.* **2. Abkapselung,** *f.* (*a*)=II. 1; *also: (process of)* incapsulation, *Biol: Med:* encystation, encystment; (*b*) *(condition)* encystment.

abkarren, *v.tr. sep.* to cart (sth.) away, off.

abkarteln, *v.tr. sep. South G.Dial:*=**abkarten.**

abkarten, *v.tr. sep.* to prearrange (statements, etc.); to concert, arrange, plan (sth.) in collusion; **sie haben es miteinander, unter sich, abgekartet,** they are acting in collusion; **ein abgekartetes Spiel,** a prearranged affair, *F:* a put-up job; a plant, a rig; *Jur:* **die Zeugenaussagen sind abgekartet,** the evidence is collusive.

abkasteien (sich), *v.refl. sep.* to mortify the body, the flesh; to deny oneself.

abkauen, *v.tr. sep.* **1.** to chew (sth.) away, off; to gnaw (sth.) away, off. **2. (sich** *dat.***) die Nägel a.,** to bite one's nails (to the quick).

Abkauf, *m.* purchase (=act of purchasing); *cp.* **abkaufen** II.

abkaufen. I. *v.tr. sep.* **1. j-m etwas a.,** to buy, purchase, sth. from s.o.; *F:* **man muß ihm jedes Wort a.,** you have to drag every word out of him. **2. eine Strafe a.,** to pay a fine for an offence.

II. *vbl s.* **Abkaufen,** *n. in vbl senses; cp.* **Abkauf.**

Abkäufer, *m.* purchaser, buyer; *Jur:* vendee.

abkäuflich, *a. A:* **1.** purchasable. **2.** (punishment) that can be avoided by payment of a fine.

abkehlen. I. *v.tr. sep.* **1. ein Tier a.,** to cut the throat of an animal; to stick, bleed (pig, sheep, etc.). **2.** to groove, channel (wood, cornice, etc.).

II. *vbl s.* **1. Abkehlen,** *n. in vbl senses.* **2. Abkehlung,** *f.* (*a*)=II. 1; (*b*)=**Kehle** 2 (*b*).

Abkehr, *f.* **-/.** estrangement (from God, from friends, from a cause); *A:* aversion; withdrawal (from the world, from society); *see also* **abkehren**[1] II.

abkehren[1]. I. *v.sep.* **1.** *v.tr.* to turn away, avert (one's face, eyes). **2. sich von etwas, j-m, abkehren,** to turn away, aside, from sth.; to withdraw from, dissociate oneself from, a cause, etc.; to become estranged from (s.o., sth.); to take no further interest in (s.o., sth.); **sich vom Irdischen a.,** to turn away from earthly things; **sich von der Welt a.,** to turn one's back on the world; to stand aloof from the world; to withdraw from society; **er hat sich von seinen Kindern abgekehrt,** he has lost interest in, no longer has any interest in, his children; he has become estranged from his children. **3.** *v.i. (sein) Min:* to leave the pit (for good), to give up one's employment.

II. *vbl s.* **Abkehren,** *n. in vbl senses; see also:* **Abkehr.**

abkehren[2], *v.tr. sep.* **1.** (*a*) to sweep out (room, etc.); to sweep (floor, carpet); to clean out (furnace, etc.); (*b*) to sweep up (dirt, etc.); *Metall:* **die Schlacken a.,** to skim off the slag (from molten metal); (*c*) *A:* to brush (hat, clothes, etc.). **2.** to wear out (broom); **der Besen ist abgekehrt,** the broom is worn out.

Abkehrschein, *m. Min:* licence for a miner to leave a pit.

abkeilen, *v.tr. sep.* **1.** to split (sth.) with a wedge. **2.** *F:* to give (s.o.) a beating, a thrashing.

abkeltern, *v.sep.* **1.** *v.tr.* **Trauben, Äpfel, a.,** to press grapes (for wine), apples (for cider). **2.** *v.i. (haben)* to finish pressing.

abketteln, *v.tr. sep. Tex:* to fasten the stitches of (knitted material); *Knitting:* to cast off.

abketten, *v.tr. sep.* (*a*) to unchain, to let loose (dog, etc.); (*b*) **die Tür a.,** to put the chain on the door; (*c*)=**abketteln.**

abkimmen, *v.tr. sep. Coop:* to cut off the chime (of a barrel).

abkippen, *v.sep.* **1.** *v.tr.* (*a*) to nip off (point, nail, wire, etc.); (*b*) **eine Münze a.,** to clip a coin. **2.** *v.tr.* to tip, dump (contents from truck, etc.). **3.** *v.i. (sein)* (*a*) to tilt (over), cant (over); to tip over; to topple over; (*b*) *F: (of aircraft, submarine)* to dive; (*c*) *Av:* **wegen Kopflastigkeit a.,** to pitch down by the nose.

abkitzeln, *v.tr. sep.* to tickle (s.o.) thoroughly, give (s.o.) a good tickling.

abklammern, *v.tr. sep.* **1.** to unpeg, to take down (washing from line). **2.** to fasten (sth.) with a clip; *Surg:* to clamp, tie (an artery).

Abklang, *m.* fading sound; faint echo (of happier times, etc.); closing stages (of a development, etc.).

abklappen, *v.sep.* **1.** *v.tr.* to swing (the flaps of sth.) down; to let down (tip-up seat, leaf of table, etc.). **2.** *v.i. (sein) F:* (*a*) *(of pers.)* to flop; **abgeklappt sein,** to feel flat; (*b*) *(of performance, etc.)* to deteriorate, to tail off.

abklappern, *v.tr. sep. F:* to walk over (fields, etc.); to walk through (streets, shops, etc.); **die ganze Gegend (nach etwas) a.,** to scour the

district (for sth.); **die Läden nach etwas a.,** to chase round the shops looking for sth.; **die Straßen a.,** *F:* to traipse, trapes, round the streets; **ich habe alles abgeklappert,** I've searched everywhere. *See also* **abgeklappert.**

abklären. I. *v.tr. sep.* **1.** (*a*) to clarify, clear (liquid); to fine (wine, beer); *Ch: etc:* to decant (liquid); *Sug-R: Pharm:* to defecate, clarify, purify; (*b*) to clarify (ideas, etc.); (*c*) to bring serenity to (s.o.'s mind); (*d*) *Swiss:* =**aufklären** I. 1 (*b*). **2. sich abklären,** (*a*) (*of liquid*) to become clear, to clear, to clarify; to settle; (*b*) (*of ideas, etc.*) to clarify (themselves), to become clarified; (*c*) (*of mind*) to gain, attain, serenity.

II. *vbl s.* **Abklären** *n.*, **Abklärung** *f. in vbl senses; also:* clarification (of liquid, of ideas, etc.); *Ch: etc:* decantation; *Pharm: Sug-R:* defecation, clarification; **Abklärung des Geistes,** attainment, attaining, of serenity of mind.

III. *p.p. & a.* **abgeklärt,** *in vbl senses; esp.* (*of pers., character*) serene; tranquil; (*of style*) limpid, pellucid; (*of liquid, wine*) clarified, cleared; (*of wine*) fined.

Abklärflasche, *f.*, **Abklärgefäß,** *n. Ch: etc:* decanting bottle, vessel, jar.

Abklärmittel, *n.*=**Abklärungsmittel.**

Abklärtopf, *m.*=**Abklärflasche.**

Abklärungsflasche, *f.*, **Abklärungsgefäß,** *n. Ch: etc:* =**Abklärflasche.**

Abklärungsmethode, *f.* method of clarification; *Wine-m: Brew:* method of fining.

Abklärungsmittel, *n.* clarifier, clarifying agent; *Wine-m: Brew:* fining agent.

Abklärungstopf, *m.*=**Abklärflasche.**

Abklatsch, *m.* **-es/-e. 1.** *A:* casting (of a pattern, letters, etc.) (in liquid metal). **2.** *Print:* (*a*) (brush-)proof; (*b*) (stereotyped) plate, stereotype, *F:* stereo. **3.** *Archeol:* squeeze (of coin, inscription, etc.). **4.** servile imitation; **seine Verse sind ein bloßer A. Georges,** in his verses he merely apes George. **5.** *Th: A:* understudy.

abklatschen, *v.tr. sep.* **1.** *A:* to cast (letters, pattern, etc.) (in liquid metal). **2.** *Print:* (*a*) to stereotype; (*b*) to dab; (*c*) **einen Korrekturbogen a.,** to take off, pull off, strike off, a (brush-) proof. **3.** *Archeol:* to squeeze, take a squeeze of (coin, inscription, etc.). **4.** *Cer:* to imprint (coloured picture) (on the ware). **5.** to make an exact copy of (sth.); to produce a servile imitation of (sth.). *See also* **dritte(r)** 1.

Abklatscher, *m.* **-s/-. 1.** *Print:* proof-puller. **2.** *Engr: Print:* dabber. **3.** *Art: Lit: F:* slavish imitator.

abklauben, *v.tr. sep.* **1.** to pick (sth.) off. **2.** *A:* **j-m etwas a.,** to filch sth. from s.o.

abkleckern, *v.i. sep.* (*sein*) (*of paint, etc.*) to drip.

abklecksen, *v.sep.* **1.** *v.tr.* to daub (picture). **2.** *v.i.* (*haben*) (*of ink, etc.*) to smudge.

abkleiden, *v.tr. sep.* **1.** *Constr:*=**verkleiden. 2.** *Nau:* to unserve, remove the serving from (a rope).

abklemmen, *v.tr. sep.* **1.** to pinch (sth.) off. **2.** to clip, clamp (tube, etc.).

abklimpern, *v.tr. sep.* to strum (a tune) (on piano, guitar).

abklingeln, *v.i. sep.* (*haben*) *Tp:* to ring off.

abklingen, *v.i. sep.* (*strong*) (*sein*) **1.** (*of sounds*) (*a*) to die away, to fade (away); (*b*) *W.Tel:* to fade out. **2.** (*of colours, emotions*) to fade (away); (*of pain, excitement*) to die down; (*of pain, illness*) to ease off; *Med:* (*of anaesthesia*) to wear off; *Poet:* **abgeklungene Liebe,** love long since faded, love long grown cold.

Abklopfbürste, *f. Print:* letter-brush.

abklopfen, *v.tr. sep.* **1.** to knock, beat, hammer (sth.) off; to chip off (rust, scale, etc.); *Mch: etc:* **den Kesselstein a.,** to chip, knock, off the boiler scale, to scale off the boiler, the pan. **2.** (*a*) to beat (the dust from) (carpet, clothes, etc.); (*b*) *F:* **j-n a.,** to give s.o. a beating, a drubbing, *F:* to dust s.o.'s jacket (for him), to give s.o. a dusting. **3.** to beat (sth.) thoroughly; *Cu:* **Fleisch a.,** to beat, *U.S:* pound, meat (to make it tender). **4.** (*a*) *Med:* to sound, tap (chest, etc.); to percuss; (*b*) *Mec.E: Rail:* to sound, tap (wheel, etc.) (for defects); (*c*) **eine Wand nach Hohlräumen a.,** to sound a wall for cavities. **5.** *Print:* (*a*) **einen Korrekturbogen a.,** to strike off a (brush-)proof; (*b*) **eine Form a.,** to plane (down) a forme. **6.** *F:* (*of beggar, etc.*) **eine Gegend a.,** to work a district; (*of shopper*) **alle Läden nach etwas a.,** to scour all the shops for sth. **7.** *abs. Mus:* (*of conductor*) to rap with the baton (*as signal to orchestra to stop*); **der Kapellmeister klopfte ab,** the conductor stopped the orchestra.

abklöppeln, *v.tr. sep.* **1.** *Tex:* **ein Muster a.,** to copy a pattern on the bobbins. **2.** *El.E:* to unbraid (cable).

abklören, *v.tr. sep. Ind:* to decolo(u)rize, bleach; *Dy:* to boil out (material).

abknabbern, *v.tr. sep.* (*a*) (*of rabbits, etc.*) to nibble, gnaw (sth.) (bare); (*b*) (*of pers.*) to nibble (sth.) away; to nibble off (corner of slice of bread, etc.).

abknallen. I. *v.sep.* **1.** *v.tr.* (*a*) to detonate, explode (charge); to discharge, let off, fire (off) (gun); *Ch:* to detonate; to fulminate; (*b*) *F:* to shoot down, bring down, pick off (man, bird, etc.). **2.** *v.i.* (*sein*) (*of charge*) to explode, go off, burst; (*of gun*) to go off; *Ch:* to detonate; to fulminate.

II. *vbl s.* **Abknallen,** *n. in vbl senses; also:* detonation (of explosive charge); discharge (of fire-arm); *Ch:* detonation; fulmination.

abknappen, *v.tr. sep.* **1.** *A:* to break (sth.) off in small pieces. **2. j-m, sich** *dat.*, **etwas a.,** to stint s.o., oneself, of sth.; to keep s.o., oneself, short of (food, money, etc.).

abknappern, *v.tr. sep. Dial:*=**abknabbern.**

abknapsen, *v.tr. sep.* **1.** to break (sth.) off (short); to break off, nip off, the end *or* top of (sth.). **2.** to deduct, take off, dock (sth.) (from wages, etc.); **man hat mir ein Pfund vom Lohn abgeknapst,** my wages have been cut (down) by a pound; they have docked, *F:* knocked, a pound off my wages; **sich** *dat.*, **j-m, etwas a.,** to stint oneself, s.o., of sth.

abkneifen, *v.tr. sep.* (*strong*) **1.** to nip (sth.) off, to pinch (sth.) off; *Hort:* **ein Auge, eine Knospe, a.,** to nip off, pinch off, a bud. **2.** *Nau:* **(den Wind) a.,** to work, ply, to windward; to haul the wind; **einem Schiff den Wind a.,** to get to windward of a ship, to luff a ship.

Abkneifer, *m.* nipping device; *Metalw:* cut-off.

abkneipen, *v.tr. sep.* (*weak; occ. strong*) *A. & Dial:* =**abkneifen.**

abknicken, *v.sep.* **1.** *v.tr.* (*a*) to snap off, break off (end of matchstick, etc.); (*of wind, etc.*) to break down (plants), to break (flower-stem); (*b*) *Ven:* to break *or* wring the neck of (hare, etc.); (*c*) *Surg:* to kink (intestine); to produce a greenstick fracture of (bone). **2.** *v.i.* (*sein*) (*a*) to snap off, break off (sharply, but with only a slight sound); (*of flower stem*) to break; (*of plants*) to be broken down (by wind, etc.); (*b*) *Gym: etc:* **in der Hüfte a.,** to bend from the hips.

abknippen, *v.tr. sep.*=**abknipsen** 1.

abknipsen, *v.tr. sep.* **1.** to snip off (the corner, end, of sth.), to cut off (the end of a cigar). **2.** to flick, flip, fillip (sth.) (with the finger). **3.** *F:* (*a*) **einen Film a.,** to finish off, use up, a film; (*b*) **meine Wochenkarte ist abgeknipst,** my weekly season ticket has expired (=*all the sections have been clipped*).

abknistern. I. *v.sep. Ch:* **1.** *v.tr.* to decrepitate (a salt). **2.** *v.i.* (*haben*) (*of salt*) to decrepitate.

II. *vbl s.* **Abknistern** *n.*, **Abknisterung** *f. Ch:* decrepitation.

abknöpfen, *v.tr. sep.* **1.** to unbutton (skirt, etc.) (from bodice, etc.). **2.** *F:* **j-m Geld a.,** to get money out of s.o., *F:* to sting s.o. for money.

abknüpfen, *v.tr. sep.* to unknot, unbind; to undo (knot); to untie, undo, loose (bootlace, scarf, etc.); to undo, take off (bonds, string, etc.).

abknuppern, *v.tr. sep.*=**abknabbern.**

abknutschen, *v.tr. sep.* to hug, cuddle (s.o.); *P:* to paw (a woman); to maul (a woman) about.

abkochecht, *a.*=**kochecht** (*a*).

abkochen. I. *v.tr. sep.* **1.** to boil (drinking water, vegetables, etc.); to scald (milk). **2.** *Pharm: etc:* to make a decoction of (herbs, etc.). **3.** *abs.* (*of soldiers, boy scouts, etc.*) to cook in the open air; to cook over the camp-fire.

II. *vbl s.* **1. Abkochen,** *n.* (*a*) *in vbl senses; also: Pharm:* (*process*) decoction; (*b*) camp(-fire) cookery. **2. Abkochung,** *f.* (*a*) *occ.*=II. 1 (*a*); (*b*) *Pharm: etc:* decoction.

Abkochmittel, *n. Pharm: etc:* liquid used for a decoction; decoction medium.

abkohlen, *v.tr. sep. Min:* to brush, break, get, the coal from (section).

abkommandieren. I. *v.tr. sep.* (*p.p.* **abkommandiert**) *Mil: etc:* **1.** *A:* to countermand the order for (sth.). **2.** to detail (s.o., personnel); to detach, second (officer); **einen Offizier an eine Einheit a.,** to second an officer to a unit; **einen Offizier zum Dienst bei j-m a.,** to detach an officer to serve with s.o., to lend an officer to s.o.; **zu einem Lehrgang abkommandiert sein,** to be detached for a course of instruction, *F:* to be on a course; *Adm:* **Beamter, der an eine andere Abteilung abkommandiert ist,** official seconded to, temporarily attached to, on loan to, another department.

II. *vbl s.* **Abkommandieren** *n.*, **Abkommandierung** *f. in vbl senses; also:* detachment; secondment (of officer, personnel).

Abkommdreieck, *n. Artil:* triangular aiming point.

Abkomme, *m.* **-n/-n,** descendant; scion, offspring (of a family).

abkommen. I. *v.i. sep.* (*strong*) (*sein*) **1. von etwas a.,** to get away from, get off (one's route, one's subject); **vom Wege a.,** to lose one's way; to lose oneself; to go astray; **von der Fährte, von der Spur, a.,** to lose the trail, to be thrown off the trail; **vom rechten Pfad a.,** to stray from the right path; *Nau: Av:* **vom Kurs, von der Fahrt, a.,** *abs.* **a.,** to deviate from, get off, one's course; *Nau:* **vom Wind a.,** to drop, fall, to leeward. **2. von einer Idee, usw., a.,** to get away from, forsake, an idea, etc.; **ich bin von solchen Ideen längst abgekommen,** I have long since got away from, abandoned, dropped, such ideas; **von dieser Vorstellung ist man längst abgekommen,** this idea was dropped long ago; this idea became obsolete, went out, long ago; **er ist von seinem Vorhaben abgekommen,** he has given up his intention; he has changed his mind. **3.** (*a*) **von einer Gewohnheit, Vorstellung, usw., a.,** to get rid of a habit, an idea, etc.; to get away from an idea; **er kann nicht von diesen Gewohnheiten a.,** he cannot break himself of these habits; (*b*) **(vom Geschäft, usw.) a. können,** to be able to get away (from business, etc.); **ich könnte auf zwei Tage a.,** I could get away for two days; I could manage to get two days off; **er kann (heute) nicht a.,** he cannot (manage to) get away (today); (*c*) *Sp:* **gut a.,** to make a good start; (*of horse, runner*) to get away well; (*of runner*) to get off the mark well; (*d*) *Artil:* (i) to lay the gun; (ii) to be on the mark; (*e*) *Mil: Sm.a:* (*of marksman, gun-aimer*) to be on the mark; **gut, schlecht, a.,** to aim well, badly; **hoch, tief, rechts, links, a.,** to aim high, low, to the right, to the left; (*f*) *Nau:* (*of ship, boat*) to get afloat, to get off (*after running aground*); (*g*) *A:* **gut, billig, davon a.,** to come off, get off, cheaply; to get well out of it. **4.** (*of clothes, customs, etc.*) to go out of fashion; (*of fashion*) to go out, die out; (*of customs, etc.*) to fall into disuse, to become obsolete, to die out; (*of law*) to fall into abeyance, into desuetude; to become a dead letter. **5.** *A:*=**abstammen.**

II. *vbl s.* **Abkommen,** *n.* **1.** (*a*) *in vbl senses; also: Sp:* start; *cp.* **Abkunft;** (*b*) *Mil: etc:*= **Abkommpunkt. 2.** (*a*) *Com: etc:* agreement; **mit j-m ein A. treffen,** (i) to enter into, conclude, an agreement with s.o.; (ii) *Jur:* to come to a settlement with s.o.; **mit seinen Gläubigern ein A. treffen,** to make a composition, an arrangement, with one's creditors; **ein gütliches A.,** an amicable settlement; (*b*) *Pol:* (international) agreement; convention; **das A. über die Sicherheit des menschlichen Lebens auf See,** the Convention for Safety of Life at Sea; *see also* **Genfer, Haager.**

Abkommenschaft, *f.* **-/.** offspring, issue, progeny, posterity, descendants.

Abkommkanone, *f. Artil:* sub-calibre gun (*for practice*).

Abkommlauf, *m. Sm.a:* (*a*) Morris tube; (*b*) aiming rifle.

abkömmlich, *a.* dispensable; **er ist heute gut a.,** we can easily do without him, dispense with him, spare him, today; we don't need him today; he can manage to get away for the day.

Abkömmling, *m.* **-s/-e. 1.** descendant; scion, offspring (of a family); **er ist ohne (männliche) Abkömmlinge gestorben,** he died without (male) issue; **A. eines edlen Geschlechts,** scion of a noble house; **seine unzähligen Abkömmlinge,** his innumerable progeny. **2.** *Ch: Ind:* derivative; **Abkömmlinge des Kohlenteers,** coal-tar derivatives.

Abkommpunkt, *m. Artil: Sm.a:* point at which the muzzle of the weapon is actually directed when firing; point of aim.

Abkommrohr, *n. Artil:* sub-calibre barrel.

Abkommschießen, *n. Artil: Sm.a:* sub-calibre practice.

abkonterfeien, *v.tr. sep.* (*p.p.* **abkonterfeit**) to make, paint, a portrait of (s.o.); to portray, *A:* to limn (s.o.); to draw a likeness of (s.o.).

abköpfen, *v.tr. sep.*=**köpfen** I. 1.

abkopieren, *v.tr. sep.* (*p.p.* **abkopiert**)=**kopieren** I. 1.

abkoppeln, *v.tr. sep.* **1.** to uncouple (horses); *Ven:* to slip, unleash, uncouple (hounds). **2.** to unbuckle, unbelt (one's sword).

abkragen, *v.tr. sep. Arch:* to bevel off (top of wall, etc.).
abkramen, *v.tr. sep. A:* to clear away (things from table, etc.); to clear (table, etc.).
abkrämpeln, *v.tr. sep. A:*=**abkrempeln.**
abkrämpen, *v.tr. sep. A:*=**abkrempen.**
Abkratzbürste, *f.* stiff brush, *esp.* wire brush (for removing mud, etc.).
Abkratzeisen, *n.* **1.** *Tls:* scraper. **2.** shoe-scraper, boot-scraper, door-scraper.
abkratzen, *v.sep.* I. *v.tr.* **1.** to scrape off (mud, paint, etc.). **2.** (*a*) to scrape down (a wall, etc.). (*b*) *Leath: etc:* to scrape, flesh (hide, skin, of animal).
II. **abkratzen,** *v.i.* (*sein*) *F:* **1.** to make off, to clear off, to make oneself scarce, to hop it, *U.S:* to beat it. **2.** to die, *F:* to peg out.
abkrauten, *v.tr. sep.* to weed (garden, etc.); to clean (a field, etc.).
abkreisen, *v.tr. sep.* to mark (sth.) off with a circle; to surround (sth.) with a circle.
abkrempeln, *v.tr. sep. Tex:* to card (wool, etc.) (thoroughly).
abkrempen, *v.tr. sep.* to turn down the brim of (hat).
abkreuzen, *v.sep. Nau:* **1.** *v.i.* (*haben*) **(vom Legerwall) a.,** to beat off (the lee-shore), to claw off. **2.** *v.tr.* to cruise over, across (a sea, etc.).
Abkreuzung, *f. Constr:* cross-beams (of wall, etc.).
abkriechen, *v.i. sep.* (*strong*) (*sein*) to creep away; to crawl away.
abkriegen, *v.tr. sep.* **1.** *A:* **j-m etwas a.,** to conquer sth. from s.o.; to gain sth. from s.o. by force of arms. **2.** *F:*=**abbringen I.** 1 (*a*), (*b*). **3.** *F:*=**abbekommen.**
abkröpfen, *v.tr. sep. Mec.E:* to crank (shaft).
abkrücken, *v.tr. sep. Metall:* to rabble (molten iron).
abkrümeln, *v.sep.* **1.** *v.tr.* to crumble (sth.) off. **2.** *v.i.* (*sein*) **& sich abkrümeln,** to crumble (away); (*of mortar, etc.*) to crumble off; (*of wall*) to scale.
abkrümmen, *v.sep.* **1.** *v.tr.* to bend (sth.) down; to bend (sth.) away, off; to curve (a pipe, etc.); *abs. Sm.a:* to press, pull, squeeze, the trigger; to fire. **2. sich abkrümmen,** to bend down; to bend away; to curve off; to curl.
abkrusten, *v.tr. sep.* (*a*) to cut the crust off (bread); (*b*) to remove the incrustation from (sth.); to scale (boiler, tube, etc.).
abkugeln, *v.i. sep. A:* (*haben*) to vote (by white or black balls); to ballot.
Abkühlapparat, *m. Ind: etc:* cooler; cooling device; refrigerator; refrigerating machine.
abkühlen. I. *v.sep.* **1.** *v.tr.* (*a*) to cool (air etc.); (*b*) to cool (liquid, etc.) (towards freezing-point); *Ind: etc:* to chill, to refrigerate (foodstuffs, etc.); *Cu:* **Wasser mit Eis a., Getränke, eine Melone, in Eis a.,** to ice water, drinks, a melon; (*c*) *Ind:* to cool (sth.) down, to cool (sth.) off (*from high temperature*); *Metalw:* to cool (steel); *Glassm:* to anneal (glass); *Oil Technology:* to quench (heavy oil) (in cracking process); (*d*) to cool, chill (s.o.'s love, friendship, zeal); to cool, damp, dash (s.o.'s enthusiasm); to calm, quiet, moderate (s.o.'s anger). **2.** *v.i.* (*sein*) **& sich abkühlen,** (*a*) (*of liquid, air, etc.*) to cool, to grow cold; (*of pers.*) to cool down, off (*under a shower, after exertion, etc.*); **es, die Luft, hat sich abgekühlt, ist abgekühlt,** it, the weather, has turned cooler; (*b*) *Ind: etc:* (*of foodstuffs, etc.*) to chill, to refrigerate; (*c*) *Ind:* (*of heated metal, glass, etc.*) to cool (down), to cool off; (*d*) (*of passion, friendship, zeal*) to cool; **seine Zuneigung ist, hat sich, stark abgekühlt,** his affection has cooled considerably.
II. *vbls s.* **Abkühlen** *n.*, **Abkühlung** *f. in vbl senses; also:* refrigeration.
III. *pr.p. & a.* **abkühlend,** *in vbl senses; esp.* **1.** (*a*) cooling (effect, etc.); (*b*) *Ind: Med:* refrigerant. **2.** calming, moderating (effect). **3.** *adv.* **a. wirken,** (*a*) to have a cooling effect; (*b*) to have a calming, moderating, effect.
Abkühler, *m.*=**Abkühlapparat.**
Abkühlfaß, *n.* **1.** *Ind:* cooling-vat. **2.** *Glassm:* annealing-oven.
Abkühlgeschwindigkeit, *f. Metalw: etc:* cooling speed.
Abkühlofen, *m. Glassm:* annealing-oven.
Abkühlpumpe, *f. Oil Technology:* quench-pump (of cracking plant).
Abkühlung, *f. see* **abkühlen II.**
Abkühlungsfläche, *f.* cooling surface; radiating surface (of cooler).
Abkühlungsmittel, *n.* **1.** *Med:* (*a*) cooling medicine; (*b*) refrigerant. **2.** cooling medium; cooling fluid; *I.C.E: etc:* coolant. **3.** *Ind:* refrigerant.
Abkühlungsraum, *m.* **1.** *Ind:*=**Kühlraum. 2.** *Glassm:* annealing-oven.
Abkühlverlust, *m. Ch: Ind:* cooling loss, loss by cooling.
abkummern, *v.tr. sep. Min:* **ein Flöz a.,** to remove the overburden.
abkündigen, *v.tr. sep.* **1.** (*a*) to proclaim, publish, announce (sth.) (publicly); *esp.* to announce (birth, death, etc.) from the pulpit; (*b*) **ein Brautpaar a.,** to publish, put up, the banns (of a couple to be married). **2.**=**absagen** I.
Abkunft, *f.* -/. **1.** descent, lineage, extraction; ancestry; race; birth (of person, family, nation); origin (of person, family); **Leute (von) hoher A.,** people of high birth; **(von) hoher A. sein,** to be high-born; **(von) adeliger A.,** of noble descent, lineage; **(von) fürstlicher A.,** of princely blood, lineage; (born) of a princely line; **(von) bürgerlicher A. sein,** to be a commoner; **(von) niedriger A.,** of humble birth, parentage; **(von) gemeiner A.,** of low birth, of low extraction; base-born; **Einwanderer slawischer A.,** immigrants of Slav, *U.S:* Slavic, blood. **2.** (*pl.* **Abkünfte**) *A:*=**abkommen II.** 2.
abkuppelbar, *a. Mec.E:* detachable (part, etc.); free (drum of crane, etc.).
abkuppeln, *v.tr. sep.* to uncouple (trucks, a machine, etc.); to disengage (parts of machine).
abkürzen. I. *v.tr. sep.* (*a*) to shorten; to make shorter; to reduce the length of (sth.); to abridge, curtail; to cut down; to cut (speech, visit, etc.) short; **den Weg a.,** to take a short cut; **ein Verfahren a.,** to shorten a procedure, process; *Ling:* **eine Silbe a.,** to shorten a syllable; (*b*) **j-m etwas am Lohn a.,** to deduct sth. from s.o.'s wages; (*c*) to abridge, epitomize, cut down, condense (book, etc.); to shorten (text); **abgekürzte Ausgabe eines Werkes,** abridged, concise, edition of a work; (*d*) **ein Wort a.,** to abbreviate *or* contract a word.
II. *vbl s.* **1. Abkürzen,** *n. in vbl senses.* **2. Abkürzung,** *f.* (*a*)=II. 1; (*b*) abbreviation *or* contraction (of word); abridgment (of work); (*c*) short cut.
III. *pr.p. & a.* **abkürzend,** *in vbl senses; esp.* abbreviatory.
Abkürzer, *m.* -s/-, abridger (of texts, etc.).
Abkürzsäge, *f. Tls:* cross-cut saw.
Abkürzungsbuchstabe, *m.* (initial) letter used as abbreviation; *Pal:* sigla.
Abkürzungssprache, *f.* abbreviated language, language of abbreviation.
Abkürzungsweg, *m.* short cut.
Abkürzungszeichen, *n.* mark of abbreviation; mark of suspension; *Pal:* sigla.
abküssen, *v.tr. sep.* (*a*) to kiss (s.o.) over and over again, to keep on kissing (s.o.); **sie küßten sich ab,** they kept on kissing; *F:* they were kissing away; they were billing and cooing; (*b*) **j-m die Tränen a.,** to kiss s.o.'s tears away.
abkutschen, abkutschieren, *v.i. sep.* (*sein*) *A:* to drive away, off (*usu. in a coach*).
Ablade-, *comb.fm., cp.* **Abladungs-.**
Abladefrist, *f. Com:* time allowed for unloading, for discharging (goods).
Abladegebühr, *f. Com:* unloading charges; discharging fees.
Abladegewicht, *n. Com:* shipping weight (of hides, etc.).
Abladekommando, *n. Mil:* unloading party *or* detachment.
Abladelohn, *m. Com:* unloading charges; discharging fees.
abladen, *v.tr. sep.* (*strong*) **1.** (*a*) to unload (cart, etc.); to unlade, discharge (ship); to unship, discharge (cargo); to off-load (material, passengers) (from bus, etc.); *Mil:* to debus *or* detrain (troops); **eine Fuhre Kies a.,** to tip, to dump down, to shoot, a cartload of gravel; **Schutt a.,** to tip, shoot, dump, rubbish; (*b*) **die Verantwortung für etwas auf j-n a.,** to shift the responsibility for sth. to s.o. else; **seine Sorgen bei j-m a.,** to unburden, unbosom, one's sorrows to s.o; (*c*) *abs. P:* to pay up, *F:* to fork out, stump up, cough up; **jetzt lad ab!** come on, cough up! (*d*) *P:* **ein Kind a.,** to give birth to a child, *esp.* an illegitimate child. **2.** *Com:* **Güter an j-n a.,** to ship goods to s.o.
Abladeort, Abladeplatz, *m.* (*a*) unloading place; *Mil:* unloading point; *Nau:* wharf; unlading place; (*b*) *Nau:* unlading port; port of discharge; (*c*) dump, dumping-ground, tip (for refuse).
Ablader, Abläder, *m.* -s/-. **1.** unloader; (*a*) market porter; heaver (of coal, etc.); (*b*) *Nau:* (i) dock-labourer, docker, lumper, stevedore, *U.S:* longshoreman; (ii) lighterman. **2.** *Com:* shipper (of goods). **3.** unloading machine.
Abladerlohn, *m.*=**Abladelohn.**
Abladestelle, *f.*=**Abladeort.**
Abladungs-, *comb. fm., cp.* **Ablade-.**
Abladungsboot, *n. Nau:* lighter.
Abladungshafen, *m. Nau:* unlading port; port of discharge.
Abladungskosten, *pl.* unloading charges; discharging fees.
Abladungsschein, *m. Nau: etc:* certificate of discharge.
Ablage, *f.* (*a*) depot, store, depository, repository; warehouse; yard, *esp.* timber yard; *Mil: etc:* dump; (*b*) (=**Kleiderablage**) cloakroom (of theatre, etc.); (*c*) *Rail:*=**Gepäckablage**; (*d*) (letter-, newspaper-)rack (*in hotel, etc.*); (*e*) filing tray. *Cp.* **ablegen III.**
ablagern, *v. sep.* I. *v.tr.* **1.** to mature (sth.) (by keeping); to mature, age, mellow (wine); to mature (cigars); to season (wood, cigars, etc.); to hang (meat). **2.** (*a*) (*of liquid*) to deposit (sediment); (*of wine, etc.*) to throw (down), deposit, cast (sediment); (*b*) *Geol:* to deposit (mud, etc.); to lay down (deposit). **3.** *Hyd.E:* to decant, draw off. **4. sich ablagern,** (*of matter*) to settle; to be deposited; to form a deposit; **der Bodensatz lagert sich ab,** the sediment is deposited; *Physiol:* **Kalk lagert sich in den Arterienwänden ab,** calcareous deposits are formed in the walls of the arteries.
II. **ablagern,** *v.i.* (*sein*) to mature; (*of wine*) to mature, age, grow mellow; (*of cigars*) to mature; (*of wood, cigars*) to season; **etwas a. lassen,** to mature sth.; to age (wine); to season (wood, cigars); *Leath:* **Häute a. lassen,** to age hides; **geschmiertes Leder a. lassen,** to lay leather away in grease.
III. *vbl s.* **1. Ablagern,** *n. in vbl senses; also:* deposition (of sediment); *Geol: Hyd.E:* sedimentation; *Hyd.E:* decantation. **2. Ablagerung,** *f.* (*a*)=III. 1; (*b*) sediment; *Geol:* deposit; bed, layer, stratum; *Physiol:* deposit.
IV. *p.p. & a.* **abgelagert,** (*a*) (*of wood, wine, cigars*) seasoned; (*of wine, cigars*) matured; (*b*) *Geol: etc:* deposited (matter); **abgelagertes Material,** sediment; (*c*) *Hyd.E:* decanted, drawn off.
Ablagerungsbassin, *n. Hyd.E:* settling tank *or* reservoir.
ablaken, *v.tr. sep. Dial:* to put (meat) in brine, in pickle.
Ablaktation [aplaktatsĭ'oːn], *f.* -/-en, weaning; *Hort:* inarching; grafting by approach.
ablaktieren [aplak'tiːrən], *v.tr. insep.* to wean; *Hort:* to inarch; **Ablaktieren** *n*, grafting by approach; inarching.
ablammen, *v.i. sep.* (*haben*) *Husb:* (*of ewe*) to cease lambing, yeaning.
ablandig, *a. Nau:* off-shore; **ablandiger Wind,** off-shore wind, land-wind, land-breeze; *adv.* **der Wind steht a.,** the wind is off-shore.
ablangen, *v.tr. sep.* (*a*) to fetch, reach, get, (sth.) down (from shelf, hook, etc.); (*b*) *F: A:* to arrest, *F:* to nab (s.o.).
ablängen, *v.tr. sep.* (*a*) to cut (plank, etc.) into lengths; (*b*) to cut (beam, joist, rails, etc.) to length; (*c*) *Min:* **einen Stollen a.,** to dig lengthwise.
Ablängsäge, *f. Tls: Carp:* cross-cut saw; chain-saw (*for cutting joists, etc., to length*).
ablappen, *v.tr. sep. Ven:* **ein Revier a.,** to hang a covert with rags (*to frighten back deer, etc.*).
ablaschen, *v.tr. sep. For:* to mark, blaze (trees).
Ablaß, *m.* -lasses/-lässe. **1.** (*a*) outlet; drain(-hole, -pipe) (of sink, boiler, etc.); vent (of barrel, etc.); *Hyd.E:* sluice-gate; drainage-hole, shut-off (of pond, etc.); side-sluice (of water-mill); *Mch: etc:*=**Ablaßhahn, -leitung, -ventil, -vorrichtung;** (*b*) discharged water, steam, etc.; water, steam, etc., let off. **2.** *Com:* **A. vom Preise,** deduction from, abatement of, allowance off, the price; rebate. **3.** *R.C.Ch:* indulgence; **vollkommener, unvollkommener, A.,** plenary, partial, indulgence. *Cp.* **ablassen III.**
Ablaßbrief, *m. R.C.Ch:* bull *or* letter of indulgence.
ablassen, *v. sep.* (*strong*) I. *v.tr.* **1.** (*a*) to leave (hat, lid, nut, etc.) off; (*b*) **die Hand von etwas a.,** to keep one's hands off sth.; to leave sth. alone. **2.** (*a*) to drain off (liquid); to draw off, run off (liquid), to let (liquid) run off, drain off; to let off (liquid, steam, etc.); **Wein (vom Faß) a.,** to draw off, rack, wine; **eine Tonne, ein Faß, a.,** to draw off the contents of a barrel, a cask; to empty a barrel, a cask; *Hyd.E:* **das Wasser aus einem Teich a., einen Teich a.,** to drain (the

water from) a pond; **das Wasser von, aus, einer Schleuse a.,** to let the water out of a lock; *Mch:* **Dampf a.,** to let off, blow off, steam; **Schlamm a.,** to blow off, blow out, drain, sludge (from boiler); **den Kessel a.,** to empty, blow down, blow off, the boiler; *Metall:* **den Ofen a.,** to tap the furnace; **Schlacken a.,** to tap off slag; (*b*) *Med:* **j-m Blut a.,** to draw, let, blood from s.o.; to bleed s.o. **3.** to start (sth., s.o.) (off); to set (sth., s.o.) going; to release (sth.); to dispatch (s.o., sth.); **einen Brief, ein Telegramm, einen Boten, a.,** to dispatch, send off, a letter, a telegram, a messenger; **Tauben a.,** to release pigeons; *Rail:* **einen Zug a.,** to start a train; *N.Arch:* **ein Schiff vom Stapel a.,** to launch a ship. **4.** *Com:* **j-m Waren a.,** to let s.o. have goods; **j-m etwas billig a.,** to let s.o. have sth. cheap, at a cheap rate; **Waren billig a.,** to let goods go cheaply. **5.** *Com:* **etwas (vom Preise) a.,** to give a discount, to deduct sth. from the price; to take, knock, sth. off the price; to allow sth. off the price, to make an allowance; to give a rebate; to abate sth. of the price; **ich kann keinen Heller a.,** I can't take a penny off. **6.** *Tchn:* (*a*) to let (sth.) cool; *Metalw: Glassm:* to anneal (steel, glass); *Glassm:* **den Ofen a.,** to let the oven cool, let the oven down; (*b*) to cut (leather, etc.) to a thin edge; *Bootm:* to feather (sole, welt).

II. **ablassen,** *v.i.* (*haben*) (*a*) to stop, cease; **a., etwas zu tun,** to stop doing sth.; **laß ab, mich zu plagen!** stop bothering me! **laß ab!** stop it! (*b*) **von etwas a.,** to desist from sth.; to give sth. up; to stop doing sth.; **von einer Gewohnheit a.,** to get out of, leave off, give up, a habit; **er will nicht von seinem Vorsatz a.,** he will not desist from, budge from, give up, his intention; **von j-m a.,** to give s.o. up; to break with s.o.; to turn away from s.o.; **sie läßt nicht von ihm ab,** she won't give him up; she remains faithful to him; she sticks by him.

III. *vbl s.* **1. Ablassen,** *n. in vbl senses; also:* discharge (of liquid); dispatch(ing) (of letter, telegram, messenger). **2. Ablassung,** *f. in vbl senses of* I. *Cp.* **Ablaß.**

Ablasser, *m.* **-s/-. 1.** *Rac:* starter. **2.** *Bootm:* feathering knife *or* device.

Ablaßgeld, *n. Hist:* money paid for an indulgence.

Ablaßgraben, *m. Agr: Hort:* (drainage) trench, ditch, drain.

Ablaßgrube, *f. Ind:* sump; blow-down pit.

Ablaßhahn, *m. Mch:* (*a*) blow-down cock, blow-off gear, pet-cock; (*b*) mud-cock, sludge-cock; (*c*) draw-off cock, drain-cock, drip-cock; (oil, petrol, etc.) waste tap.

Ablaßhandel, *m. Hist:* sale of indulgences.

Ablaßhändler, *m. Hist:* seller of indulgences; pardoner.

Ablaßjahr, *n. R.C.Ch:* jubilee (year).

Ablaßkante, *f. Bootm:* feather (of sole).

Ablaßkram, *m.*=**Ablaßhandel.**

Ablaßkrämer, *m.*=**Ablaßhändler.**

Ablaßleitung, *f.* (*a*) drain-pipe; (*b*) *Ind:* bleeder (of boiler, etc.).

Ablaßpfennig, *m. Hist:* **1.**=**Ablaßgeld. 2.** medal (with an effigy of a saint) blessed by the Pope.

Ablaßpfropfen, *m.* drain-plug, draw-off plug.

Ablaßpunkt, *m. Rac:* starting-point; (*in pigeon-racing*) release point.

Ablaßrohr, *n.,* **Ablaßröhre,** *f.* outlet pipe; escape-pipe; drain-pipe; *Hyd.E: etc:* waste-pipe.

Ablaßschlauch, *m.* (flexible) escape-pipe, escape-tube (for steam, etc.).

Ablaßschraube, *f. I.C.E: Mch: etc:* drain-plug, draw-off plug.

Ablaßschütz, *n.,* **Ablaßschütze,** *f. Hyd.E:* sluice-gate, water-gate.

Ablaßstopfen, *m.* drain-plug, draw-off plug.

Ablaßtag, *m. R.C.Ch:* day on which indulgences are granted.

Ablaßtrichter, *m.* discharging funnel (of spraying device, etc.).

Ablaßventil, *n.* (*a*) escape-valve (for steam, etc.); *Mch:* blow-off (gear, cock); (*b*) *Ind:* drain-valve, bleeder; (*c*) *Mch:*=**Ablaßhahn.**

Ablaßvorrichtung, *f. Ind:* draining device; bleeder.

Ablaßwoche, *f. R.C.Ch:* Corpus Christi week.

Ablaßzettel, *m. R.C.Ch:* letter of indulgence.

Ablast [a·ˈblast], *m.* **-s/.** *Biol:* suppression, non-development (of an organ).

Ablastebogen, *m. Arch: Civ.E:* relieving arch.

ablasten, *v.tr. sep.* (*a*)=**abladen** 1 (*a*); (*b*) to relieve the strain on (sth.), to take the strain off (sth.).

Ablation [apla·tsĭˈoːn], *f.* **-/-en. 1.** *Surg:* ablation. removal, excision (of part, tumour, etc.). **2.** *Geol:* (*a*) ablation (of glacier); (*b*) erosion (of land surface).

Ablativ [ˈapla·tiːf, abla·ˈtiːf], *m.* **-s/-e** [-tiːvə]. *Gram:* ablative (case).

Ablativsatz, *m. Gram:* ablative absolute.

Ablativus [apla·ˈtiːvus], *m.* **-/-ve.** *Gram:* ablative (case).

ablatschen, *v.tr. sep. Dial:* to wear out (shoe); **abgelatschter Schuh,** worn-out, down-at-heel, shoe.

ablatten, *v.tr. sep.* to remove the laths from (wall, ceiling, etc.).

ablauben, *v.tr. sep.* to remove the leaves, the foliage, from (bush, tree); to thin out the leaves of (fruit-tree, vine).

Ablauf, *m.* **1.** (*a*) running off, run-off, outflow, draining (away, off) (of water, etc.); (*b*) *Hyd.E: etc:*=**Abfluß** 1 (*b*); (*c*) liquid discharged *or* drained off; jet (from pump, etc.); *Ch: Ind:* filtrate; *Ind:* effluent; *Dist:* run; (*d*) *Lit:* ebb (-tide); ebbing, reflux (of the sea). **2.** (*a*) outlet; *Hyd.E: etc:* drain(-pipe); drainage channel; (*b*) *Constr:*=**Ablaufrohr;** (*c*) *Arch: etc:* drain-hole. **3.** (*a*) *Rac: Equit: etc:* start; (*b*) *Ski:* (i) run, running down; (ii) (*slope*) run. **4.** *N.Arch:* launch, launching (of ship). **5.** (*a*) expiration, expiry, lapse (of a period of time); **vor A. des Jahres,** before the end, the close, of the year; before the year is out; **nach (dem) A. von drei Monaten,** after three months had passed, elapsed; after a lapse of three months; **nach A. der Frist von zehn Jahren,** at the end of the (agreed, appointed) period of ten years; on the expiration of the term of ten years; *Jur:* **A. der Frist, des Termins,** effluxion of time; (*b*) expiry, expiration, termination, end (of lease, insurance policy, term of office, etc.); **bei A.,** on, upon, expiry; **bei, nach, A. des Mietvertrags, des Pachtvertrags,** on expiry of the lease; when the lease expires, expired, runs out, ran out; *Jur:* **A. eines Vertrags,** determination of a contract; *St.Exch:* **A. der Bezugsrechte,** expiration of subscription rights; (*c*) *Com:* maturing, falling due (of bill of exchange); **bei A. des Wechsels,** when the bill matures, falls due; at maturity of the bill. **6.** running down (of clockwork mechanism). **7.** course (of a process, a procedure, an illness, events, etc.); **der gewöhnliche A. der Ereignisse,** the usual course, sequence, of events; **der A. der Verhandlungen war sehr befriedigend,** the negotiations went off, passed off, very satisfactorily. **8.** (*a*) taper; *Mec.E:* run-off (of cutting tool); back taper (of screw-tap); (*b*) tapered part *or* end; *Arch:* (e)scape, spring; congé; apophyge (of column); (*c*) *Arch:* grooved moulding (at top of wall, etc.); (*d*) *Civ.E:* batter (of buttress, etc.).

Ablaufbacken, *m.* trailing shoe (of brake).

Ablaufbahn, *f.* **1.** *N.Arch:* slip-way. **2.** *Av: A:* (=**Rollbahn**) runway.

Ablaufbalken, *m. N.Arch:* (launching) cradle.

Ablaufberg, *m. Rail:* hump (in marshalling yard).

Ablaufbetrieb, *m. Rail:* hump shunting.

ablaufen, *v. sep.* (*strong*) I. *v.i.* (*sein*) **1.** (*a*) (*of water, etc.*) to run off; to flow out; to flow off; to drain off, away; **das Wasser läuft aus dem Teich ab,** the water flows out of, drains from, the pond; **der Teich ist abgelaufen,** the pond has drained away; **das Wasser aus dem Waschbecken a. lassen,** to let the water out of the wash-basin; to drain the water off from the wash-basin; (*b*) (*of water on oilskin, on a duck's back*) to run off; *F:* **ihre Worte liefen an ihm ab wie Wasser von einer Ente,** her words ran off him like water off a duck's back; **Wasser lief von der Wand ab,** the wall was running, dripping, with water; (*c*) (*of sea*) to flow back, recede; to ebb. **2.** *Rac: Equit: etc:* to start. **3.** *Nau:* (*of ship*) (*a*) (=**auslaufen**) to (set) sail, to leave port; (*b*) **(vor dem Winde) a.,** to fetch to windward. **4.** *N.Arch:* (*of ship*) to be launched, to come off the stocks; **ein Schiff a. lassen,** to launch a ship. **5.** (*a*) *Fenc:* **den Gegner a. lassen,** to parry, ward off, a thrust from one's opponent; (*b*) *A:* **j-n a. lassen,** to snub s.o.; to rebuff s.o.; to send s.o. packing, send s.o. about his business; **(gut) abgelaufen sein,** *F:* to be sent off with a flea in one's ear. **6.** (*a*) (*of thread, film, from spool; of rope from drum, etc.*) to unwind; to be paid out; to run off (the spool, the drum, etc.); to run out; **den Faden a. lassen,** to pay out, run out, run off, the thread; (*b*) **die Spule ist abgelaufen,** the spool is used up, finished; the spool has run out. **7.** (*a*) (*of period of time*) to expire, come to an end, elapse; **die Frist, der Termin, ist abgelaufen,** the (agreed, appointed) period has expired; the time is up; **seine Zeit ist abgelaufen,** his (last) hour has come, has struck; (*b*) (*of lease, insurance policy, term of office, etc.*) to expire, terminate, run out; (*of insurance policy*) to lapse; *Jur:* (*of contract*) to determine; (*c*) *Com:* (*of bill of exchange*) to mature, fall due, become due. **8.** (*of clock, watch, clockwork mechanism*) to run down; **abgelaufene Uhr,** (i) run-down clock; (ii) *A:* (*of hour-glass*) hourglass from which the sands have run out. **9.** *Tp:* (*of telephone dial*) to return to the normal position. **10.** (*of process, procedure, illness, etc.*) to take its course; (*of business, etc.*) to go off (well, badly, etc.); **die Sache ist gut, übel, abgelaufen,** the affair went off well, badly; **die ganze Sache ist schief abgelaufen,** the whole affair went wrong; **die Sache wird übel, nicht gut, a.,** the affair will end badly; there will be trouble before the business is over; **die Verhandlungen liefen reibungslos ab,** the negotiations went off, passed off, smoothly; **die Versteigerung ist gut abgelaufen,** the auction went well, showed good results. **11.** (*a*) to go off at an angle; (*of side-road, ramification, etc.*) to branch off; (*b*) (*of ground, etc.*) to incline, slope; (*of column, of edge of tool, etc.*) to taper.

II. **ablaufen,** *v.tr.* **1.** (*a*) *Sp:* **eine Strecke a.,** to run over (the whole length of) a course; (*b*) **die Läden, die ganze Stadt, nach etwas a.,** to scour the shops, the whole town, for sth. **2.** (*a*) **sich** *dat.* **die Schuhe, die Schuhsohlen, a.,** to wear out the soles of one's shoes; (*b*) **sich** *dat.* **die Beine nach etwas a.,** to wear oneself out chasing after sth., to do one's utmost to get sth., *F:* to run one's legs off trying to get sth.; (*c*) *F:* **das hab' ich mir längst an den Schuhen, an den Schuhsohlen, abgelaufen,** I know all about that, *F:* I know that inside out. *See also* **Horn** 1 (*a*). **3. j-m den Rang a.,** to prevail over, get the better of, s.o.; to best s.o.; to leave s.o. behind; to outrun, outdistance, outrival, outstrip, s.o.; to get the start of s.o., to forestall s.o. **4.** *A:* (*of knight, in tourney, etc.*) **den Gegner a.,** to unseat, unhorse, dismount, one's opponent. **5. sich ablaufen,** to wear oneself out with running *or* walking; to run *or* walk oneself to a standstill; to get winded, blown, *F:* puffed.

III. *vbl s.* **Ablaufen,** *n. in vbl senses; cp.* **Ablauf** 1 (*a*), (*b*).

IV. *pr.p. & a.* **ablaufend,** *in vbl senses; esp.* **1.** *Nau:* **das ablaufende Meer, Wasser,** the outgoing tide, the ebb(-tide). **2.** *Bot:* decurrent (leaves, etc.).

Ablaufenlassen, *n. N.Arch:* launching (of ship).

Abläufer, *m.* **1.** *Tex: etc:*=**Ablaufspule. 2.** *Civ.E: etc:* (*a*) guard-stone, fender (at edge of road, etc.); (*b*) (ice-)fender, starling (of bridge pier). **3.** *Tex:* thread run out of place. **4.** *Nau: pl.* **Abläufer,** scuppers.

Ablauffrist, *f. Fin: Com:* (date of) maturity, due date, date of falling due (of a bill); date of expiration (of agreement, etc.).

Ablaufgerüst, *n. N.Arch:* (launching) cradle.

Ablaufgleis, *n. Rail:* running-down track.

Ablaufkammer, *f. Ind: El.E:* outlet chamber (o sulphuric acid plant, etc.; of generator).

Ablaufkanal, *m. Hyd.E: etc:* drainage channel; drain; gutter; gully.

Ablaufknagge, *f. Mec.E:* slip-catch, slip-dog (of winch-shaft, etc.).

Ablaufkrone, *f. Civ.E: etc:* swift (of cable-drum).

Ablaufkurs, *m. Nau: Av:* **auf A. gehen,** to sheer off.

Ablauflinie, *f.* starting-line (for runners, cars, armoured fighting vehicles, etc.).

Ablauföl, *n.* (*a*) *Ind:* run oil; used oil; waste oil; (*b*) *Com: Ind:* expressed oil (from nuts, etc.).

Ablaufrinne, *f.* (*a*) *Hyd.E: etc:* drainage channel; gutter; gully; (*b*) *Nau:* scupper.

Ablaufrohr, *n.,* **Ablaufröhre,** *f. Hyd.E: etc:* outlet pipe; drain-pipe; escape-pipe; waste-pipe (of bath, etc.); soil-pipe, cesspipe (of W.C.).

Ablaufrollgang, *m. Metalw:* delivery roller train; delivery roller conveyor.

Ablaufs-, *comb. fm., cp.* **Ablauf-.**

Ablaufschleuse, *f. Hyd.E:* way-gate, tail-race.

Ablaufschlitten, *m. N.Arch:* (launching) cradle.

Ablaufseite, *f. Mec.E:* **A. eines Nockens,** trailing edge of a cam.

Ablaufspule, *f. Tex: etc:* winding-off spool.

Ablauf(s)tag, *m.* day, date, of expiration (of agreement, etc.).

Ablauftermin, *m.*=**Ablauffrist.**

Ablauftrichter, *m.* discharging funnel (of spraying device, etc.).

Ablaufwinkel, *m. Biol: Bot: etc:* angle of departure; angle between a branch and the plane *or* axis from which it departs.

Ablaufzeit, *f.* **1.**=**Ablauffrist. 2.** *Tchn:* running-down time (of clockwork device).

Ablauge, *f. Ch: Paperm: etc:* spent lye, waste lye; *Dy:* waste liquor.

ablaugen. I. *v.tr. sep.* **1.** (*a*) to wash, steep (linen, yarn, etc.) in lye; to buck, boil (linen); (*b*) *Ch: etc:* to lixiviate (wood-ashes, etc.). **2.** *Tex: etc:* to rinse off, wash out, the lye from (yarn, etc.).

II. *vbl s.* **Ablaugen,** *n. in vbl senses; also: Ch: etc:* lixiviation (of wood-ashes, etc.).

ablauschen, *v.tr. sep.* **1. j-m etwas a.,** to learn sth. from s.o. by listening *or* watching intently; **der Natur ihre Geheimnisse a.,** to watch Nature patiently until one learns her secrets. **2.** *Mil: W.Tel:* to pick up (an enemy signal).

ablausen, *v.tr. sep.*=**entlausen.**

Ablaut, *m. Ling:* vowel gradation, ablaut, apophony.

Ablautbasis, *f. Ling:* gradation basis.

ablauten, *v.i. sep.* (*sein*) *Ling:* (*of word*) to undergo ablaut, to change its vowel by ablaut.

abläuten, *v.sep.* **1.** *v.tr.* **einen Zug, ein Schiff, usw., a.,** to ring a bell to announce that a train, a ship, etc., is about to start; to ring the bell for departure; *abs.* **es wird abgeläutet,** the departure bell is ringing. **2.** *v.tr. Rac:* **ein Rennen a.,** to stop a race because of a false start. **3.** *v.i.* (*haben*) *Tp:* to ring off.

Abläuterfaß, *n.,* **Abläuterkiste,** *f. Min:* buddle, sluice-box.

abläutern. I. *v.tr. sep.* (*a*) to clarify, clear (liquid); to fine (down) (beer, wine); to strain, filter (liquid); (*b*) to purify (wax, etc.); to refine (sugar); (*c*) *Min:* to buddle, sluice, wash (ore).

II. *vbl s.* **Abläutern** *n.,* **Abläuterung** *f. in vbl senses; also:* clarification, filtration (of liquid); purification (of wax).

Abläutezeichen, *n. Tp:* ring-off signal.

Ablautverb, *n. Ling:* verb that undergoes ablaut in its conjugation, *F:* ablaut verb.

ableben. I. *v. sep.* **1.** *v.tr. A:* to live through (the years, etc.); to live out (the winter, etc.); *Poet:* **in abgelebten Zeiten,** in (the) days of yore. **2. sich ableben,** (*a*) to cease to have real existence; **diese Anschauungen haben sich abgelebt,** these views are obsolete, have had their day; (*b*) (*of pers.*) to wear oneself out (*esp.* with fast living); *F:* to burn the candle at both ends; **ein abgelebter Greis,** a decrepit old man. **3.** *v.i.* (*sein*) (*used only in p.p.*) **er ist abgelebt,** he has died; he has departed (from this life); he has passed away; (*in official language*) he is deceased.

II. *vbl s.* **Ableben,** *n.* death, decease, *Jur:* demise; **ich muß ihn vom A. des Herrn X in Kenntnis setzen,** I must inform, notify, him of the death, decease, of Mr. X; **nach dem A. seines Vaters übersiedelte er nach Schottland,** on his father's death, when his father died, he went to live in Scotland.

ablecken, *v.tr. sep.* (*a*) to lick (sth.) off; **die Marmelade vom Löffel a.,** to lick the jam off the spoon; (*b*) to lick (sth.) (thoroughly, all over); **den Teller a.,** to lick the plate clean; *F:* **sich** *dat.* **die Lippen a.,** to lick one's lips, *F:* one's chops; *see also* **Finger.**

abledern, *v.tr. sep.* **1.** to flay (large animal); to skin (small animal). **2.** to strip the leather from, off (chair-seat, etc.). **3.** to polish (sth.) with a leather. **4. j-n a.,** (*a*) to give s.o. a beating, a drubbing, *F:* to give s.o. a hiding, a leathering, a tanning, a good belting; to leather s.o., belt s.o., to tan s.o.'s hide (for him); (*b*) to give s.o. a (good) dressing-down, *F:* to tell, tick, s.o. off.

ableeren, *v.tr. sep.* to empty (dish, etc.); to clear (plate, table, etc.); **die Felder a.,** to clear the fields of crops; **abgeleerte Felder,** fields empty after harvest.

ablegbar, *a.* discardable.

Ablegeapparat, *m. Print:* (type-)distributor.

Ablegefehler, *m. Print:* printer's error, misprint, literal (error).

Ablegekasten, *m.* (*on desk*) letter-tray.

Ablegekorb, *m.* (*on desk*) letter-basket; letter-tray.

Ablegemappe, *f.* (letter-)file; filing jacket.

Ablegemaschine, *f. Print:* automatic (type-)distributor.

ablegen, *v.sep.* I. *v.tr.* **1.** (*a*) to take off (garments, accoutrements); to lay aside (garments); **den Mantel, die Handschuhe, a.,** to take off, pull off, one's overcoat, one's gloves; *abs.* **a.,** to take off one's (hat and) coat; **bitte, legen Sie ab!** (do) please take your coat off! *F:* (do) please take your things off! **den Tornister a.,** to take off one's haversack, *Mil:* one's pack; (*b*) to leave off, cast off, discard (garments, etc.) (for good); **abgelegte Kleider,** left-off, cast off, discarded, clothing, *F:* cast-offs; **die Kinderschuhe a.,** to emerge from childhood; **er hat die Kinderschuhe abgelegt,** he is no longer a child, he is grown up now; **die Trauer a.,** to come out of mourning; **die Maske a.,** to throw off the mask, to throw off all disguise; (*c*) **die Waffen, die Rüstung, a.,** to lay down one's arms; **sein Schwert a.,** to lay one's sword aside; (*d*) *Surg:* to discard (truss, etc.); (*e*) (*of reptile*) **die alte Haut a.,** to slough, to cast its skin. **2.** to get rid of (sth.); to cast (sth.) off; to drop (sth.); to discard (sth.); (*a*) **einen Namen a.,** to drop, give up using, a name; **veraltete Fachausdrücke a.,** to discard obsolete terminology; **Sorge, Kummer, a.,** to put away care; **die Sünde a.,** to cease from sinning; **einen Fehler a.,** to cure oneself, rid oneself, of a failing; **seine Fehler a.,** to mend one's ways; **eine Gewohnheit a.,** to give up, discontinue, a habit, to break oneself of a habit; **er hat seine barsche Art abgelegt,** he has overcome his brusqueness, his brusqueness has left him; **er legte den Schulmeister so weit als möglich ab,** he did his best to get rid of his schoolmasterish ways; *B:* **lasset uns a. die Werke der Finsternis,** let us cast off the works of darkness; *B. & F:* **den alten Menschen a.,** to put off the old man, *F:* to cast off the old Adam; *see also* **Hülle** 1 (*b*); (*b*) *Cards:* to discard, throw away (card); *abs.* **a.,** to discard. **3.** to do (sth.) in due form; to perform; to execute; to deliver; (*a*) *A:* **bei j-m einen Besuch a.,** to pay a visit to s.o., to call on s.o.; **eine Predigt a.,** to deliver a sermon; **eine Schuld a.,** to pay a debt; (*b*) **einen Eid a.,** to take an oath; to be sworn (before s.o.); *see also* **Eid; ein Gelübde a.,** to make, take, a vow; (*of monk*) **seine Gelübde a.,** to take the vows; **eine Prüfung a.,** to take an examination; **ein Bekenntnis a.,** to make a confession, to confess; **Zeugnis a.,** to testify, bear witness, give evidence, *Jur:* to depose; **Zeugnis über etwas** *acc.* **a.,** to give evidence about sth.; **Zeugnis für etwas a.,** to bear testimony to sth., to bear witness to, of, sth.; to testify to sth.; **Zeugnis für j-n a.,** to give evidence in s.o.'s favour; **Zeugnis gegen, wider, j-n a.,** to give evidence against s.o.; **eine Probe von etwas a.,** to give, furnish, proof of sth.; **Proben von seiner Freundschaft a.,** to give proofs, signs, tokens, of one's friendship; **über etwas** *acc.* **Rechenschaft, Rechnung, a.,** to give, render, account of sth., to account for sth. **4.** (*a*) to lay down (burden, etc.); (*b*) *Biol: Geol: etc:* to deposit (coating, layer, etc.). **5.** to lay (sth. coiled, twisted *or* folded) out flat. **6.** *Dial: P:* **ein Kind a.,** to bear a child, *esp.* an illegitimate child; (*cp.* II. 1). **7.** *Hort: Vit:* to layer (carnations, a vine, etc.). **8.** *Print:* **den Satz a.,** to distribute, *F:* to dis, the (composed) type. **9.** *Adm: Com:* **Akten a.,** to file *or* pigeon-hole documents; **die (einkommende) Post a.,** to file the (incoming) correspondence. **10.** *Ap:* **einen Bienenstock a.,** to divide a hive (so as to produce a second swarm). **11.** *Nau:* to bring (ship) into the roads. **12.** *Min:* **Arbeiter a.,** to pay off, lay off, discharge, workmen; **eine Grube a.,** to shut down, close down, a mine. **13.** *Dial:* **j-n a.,** to let s.o. down; to leave s.o. in the lurch, *F:* to ditch s.o.

II. **ablegen,** *v.i.* (*haben*) **1.** (*a*) (*of animal*) to bring forth, drop, throw (young); (*b*) *Dial: P:* (*of woman*) to bear a child, *esp.* an illegitimate child; (*cp.* I. 6). **2.** (*of dog*) to sit; to lie down; **leg ab!** sit! **3.** *Nau:* to put out to sea; to get under way. **4.** *A:* (*of eyes, memory, etc.*) to grow weak, grow feeble; to fail; **seine Augen legen (ihm) ab,** his sight is failing.

III. *vbl s.* **Ablegen** *n., occ.* **Ablegung** *f. in vbl senses; also: Print:* distribution (of type). *Cp.* **Ablage.**

Ableger, *m.* **-s/-. 1.** (*a*) *Hort:* runner, sucker; (*b*) *Hort: Vit:* layer; **Nelken durch Ableger vermehren,** to propagate carnations by layering; (*c*) plant produced by layering *or* grafting; plant not raised from seed; *Vit: etc:* layered branch *or* stock; (*d*) *Hort:* slip, cutting; scion (for grafting); (*e*) *Bot:* shoot; offshoot (of a plant); *F:* offshoot (of an organization, an activity, etc.); *Com:* **dieses Geschäft ist ein A. unserer Firma,** this business is an offshoot, a subsidiary, a satellite, of our firm; (*f*) *Ap:* second swarm (produced by dividing a hive). **2.** *Print:* (*a*) (*pers.*) distributor (of type); (*b*)=**Ablegeapparat.**

Ablegesatz, *m. Print:* dead matter; type to be distributed.

Ablegespan, *m. Print:* distributing stick.

Ablegetisch, *m.* (work-)rest (on sewing-machine, etc.).

ablehnbar, *a.* refusable.

ablehnen. I. *v.tr. sep.* (*a*) to refuse, decline, reject (sth.); to decline, refuse (invitation); to decline (responsibility, liability, obligation, commission); to set aside, throw out, rule out, dismiss, reject (proposal); to turn down (offer, proposal); to reject, refuse to accept (theory, thinker, writer); **er lehnte (es) ab, zu unterschreiben,** he refused, declined, to sign; **er lehnte höflich ab,** he refused, declined, courteously; he gave a courteous, civil, refusal; **einen Antrag durch Abstimmung a.,** to vote down a motion; **der Antrag wurde abgelehnt,** the motion was lost; the noes had it; *Parl:* **einen Gesetzentwurf a.,** to reject, throw out, a bill; **wir lehnen Nietzsche als Philosophen ab,** (i) we do not agree with Nietzsche's philosophy, (ii) we cannot accept Nietzsche as a philosopher; (*b*) *Jur:* to challenge, take exception to, take objection to, object to (a witness, a juror, an arbitrator); to impugn (evidence); **eine Gerichtsbarkeit a.,** to refuse to acknowledge a jurisdiction; (*c*) *Jur:* **eine Erbschaft a.,** to renounce, relinquish, a succession *or* an inheritance.

II. *vbl s.* **Ablehnen** *n.,* **Ablehnung** *f. in vbl senses; also:* (*a*) refusal, rejection (of sth.); rejection (of proposal, of motion, of a theory, philosophy); refusal to accept (poet, philosopher, etc.); (*b*) *Jur:* **Ablehnung eines Zeugen, eines Geschworenen, eines Schiedsrichters,** challenge of, exception to, objection to, a witness, a juror, an arbitrator; **Ablehnung des Zeugnisses,** impugnment of evidence; **Ablehnung einer Gerichtsbarkeit,** refusal to acknowledge a jurisdiction; **Ablehnung einer Erbschaft,** renunciation, relinquishing, relinquishment, of a succession *or* an inheritance.

III. *pr.p. & a.* **ablehnend,** *in vbl senses; esp.* (*a*) containing *or* implying a refusal; **ablehnende Antwort,** negative answer; refusal; **eine ablehnende Haltung einnehmen,** *adv.* **sich a. verhalten,** to take up a negative attitude (**zu,** to); to refuse to be a party (to sth.); (*b*) *Jur:* declinatory (plea, etc.).

Ablehnungserklärung, *f. Jur:* declinatory plea.

Ablehnungsfall, *m.* **im A.,** in case of refusal; if the invitation, etc., is declined; if the proposal, etc., is rejected.

ablehren, *v.tr. sep.* (*a*) *Metalw:* to gauge, *U.S:* gage (dimensions of a casting, etc.); (*b*) *Mec.E:* to true (up) (machine parts).

ableiern, *v.tr. sep.* **1.** to play (tune) in a mechanical manner; to recite (sth.) in a sing-song manner; *Th:* **seine Rolle, a.,** to recite one's part mechanically. **2.** to unscrew, twist off (nut, etc.).

ableinen, *v.tr. sep.* to take the lead off, to unleash (dog).

ableisten[1]. I. *v.tr. sep.* **1.** *Jur:* **einen Eid a.,** to take an oath; to be sworn (before s.o.). **2. den Militärdienst, die Wehrpflicht, a.,** to do one's military service; **die Wehrpflicht abgeleistet haben,** to have done one's military service, to have served one's time (as a conscript).

II. *vbl s.* **Ableisten** *n.,* **Ableistung** *f.* **1.** *Jur:* taking (of an oath). **2. A. des Militärdienstes, der Wehrpflicht,** completion of one's military service, serving of one's time (as a conscript).

ableisten[2], *v.tr. sep. Bootm:* to take (boot, shoe) off the last.

ableitbar, *a.* **1.** (word, etc.) that can be derived (from a source); derivable (word, etc.). **2.** (river, etc.) that can be diverted; (liquid, etc.) that can be carried off.

ableiten. I. *v.tr. sep.* **1.** (*a*) to turn (s.o., sth.) away, aside; **j-n vom richtigen Weg, von der rechten Bahn, a.; j-n vom Guten a.,** to lead s.o. astray; (b) to divert (watercourse, etc.); to divert, tap, the course of (running water, etc.); to deflect (lightning); *Hyd.E:* **Hochwasser a.,** to discharge floods; *Med:* **Blut a.,** to draw away blood (from diseased part); *A.Med:* **die Feuchtigkeiten a.,** to draw off the humours from one part of the body to another; *El.E:* **den Strom a.,** to shunt, branch (current); (*c*) to drain off (liquid); to carry off, lead off (liquid, gases, etc.); *Ph:* **Wärme a.,** to conduct heat; to carry off heat by conduction *or* convection; *El:* **Elektrizität a.,** to conduct electricity; **den Strom in die Erde a.,** to carry off the current to earth. **2.** *Ling: Mth:* to derive (**aus, von,** from); **abgeleitet werden,** to derive, to be derived; **abgeleitetes Wort,** derivative; **aus dem, vom, Lateinischen abgeleitetes Wort,** word derived

from Latin; *Mth:* **abgeleitete Funktion, Kurve,** derived function, curve; **eine Gleichung a.,** to obtain the differential (coefficient) of an equation; *Chem:* **abgeleiteter Körper,** derivate. **3.** to deduce (information, formula, etc.); to infer (answer, conclusion, etc.); to educe (information, etc.) (aus, von, from). **4.** to trace (sth.) back (von, to a source); **er leitet seine Herkunft von den Normannen ab,** he traces his descent, his family, back to the Normans; he claims to be of Norman descent, to be descended from the Normans. **5. sich ableiten,** (a) to issue, spring, be derived, proceed (aus, von, from); *Ling:* **das Wort leitet sich aus dem, vom, Lateinischen ab,** the word is derived, derives, from Latin; (b) (of pers., family)=**seine Herkunft a.,** q.v. under **4.** See also **Bastard 2.**
    II. *vbl s.* **1. Ableiten,** n. in vbl. senses. **2. Ableitung,** f. (a)=II. 1; also: diversion (of watercourse); *Hyd.E:* discharge (of floods); *Mch:* eduction (of steam); *El.E:* leakage (of current); *Ph:* **A. der Wärme,** (i) conduction, (ii) convection, of heat; **A. der Elektrizität,** conduction of electricity; *Ling:* derivation, etymology (of word); *Mth:* derivation (of function, curve); deduction (of information, formula, etc.); eduction (of information from data); *Agr: Hyd.E:* **A. des Wassers,** drainage; (b) derivation (aus, von, from); (c) (i) diversion (in watercourse, etc.); branch (of pipe, etc.); (ii) *El.E:* branch circuit; *W.Tel:* by-pass; (iii) *El.E:* (=**Erdleitung**) earth-lead; (iv) *Hyd.E: etc:* drainage channel; drain; (v) *Mth:* derivative, esp. differential coefficient; (vi) deduction; educt, eduction.
    III. *pr.p. & a.* **ableitend,** in vbl senses; esp. *Med:* revulsive; counter-irritant; **ableitendes Mittel,** counter-irritant (agent).
Ableiter, m. **1.** (a) *El:* conductor; (b) *El.E:* (i) lightning-arrester, lightning-protector (for electrical apparatus); (ii) lightning-conductor. **2.** *I.C.E:* compression tap. **3.** *Ling:*=**Ableitungssilbe. 4.** *Vit:* layer (from vine).
Ableiterohr, n.=**Ableitungsrohr.**
Ableitung, f. see **ableiten** II. 2.
Ableitungsangriff, m. *Mil:* diversion; feint (attack).
Ableitungsdraht, m. *El.E:* (a) branch wire; (b) earth(-wire).
Ableitungsgewebe, n. *Bot:* conducting tissue.
Ableitungsgraben, m. **1.** *Agr: Hyd.E:* drainage ditch; drain; drainage channel. **2.** *Mil:* evacuation trench.
Ableitungskanal, m. *Hyd.E:* drainage channel; drain; outlet (of reservoir, lake, etc.); outfall (of sewer).
Ableitungsmittel, n. *Med:* counter-irritant (agent); revulsive.
Ableitungsrechnung, f. *Mth: A:* differential calculus.
Ableitungsrinne, f. drain-pipe; *Constr:* gutter.
Ableitungsrohr, n., **Ableitungsröhre,** f., (a) waste-pipe; by-pass (of valve, etc.); (b) delivery pipe or tube.
Ableitungssilbe, f. *Ling:* derivative syllable; formative syllable ; affix.
Ableitungsstange, f. lightning-rod.
Ableitungstabelle, f. *Ling:* table of derivations; etymological table.
Ableit(ungs)widerstand, m. *El.E:* leakage resistance.
Ableitungswort, n. -(e)s/-wörter. *Ling:* derivative.
Ablenk-, comb. fm. *Tchn:* deflection . . . , deflecting . . . , deflector . . . ; esp. *El.E:* **Ablenkelektrode** f, deflecting electrode; **Ablenkspule** f, deflecting, deflection, deflector, coil. Cp. **Ablenkungs-.**
ablenkbar, a. (a) that can be diverted, turned aside; that can be deflected; *Opt:* that can be diffracted; (b) (of pers.) leicht a., easily distracted.
ablenken, I. *v.sep.* **1.** *v.tr.* (a) to turn (sth., s.o.) aside; to divert (watercourse, etc.); to avert, ward off (danger, suspicion); to avert, divert (suspicion); to turn (activity, conversation, thoughts) into a different channel; to turn (s.o.'s thoughts) in another direction; to distract, divert (s.o.'s thoughts) (from sth.); (cp. 2 (a)); to provide (s.o.) with distraction, diversion, amusement; **den Verdacht von sich a.,** to divert suspicion from oneself; **j-s Aufmerksamkeit (von etwas) a.,** to divert, distract, s.o.'s attention (from sth.); to take s.o.'s attention, mind, off sth.; **j-n von seiner Arbeit a.,** to distract s.o. from his work; **j-n von seinem Vorhaben a.,** to divert, dissuade, s.o. from his intention; **j-n von seinen Sorgen a.,** to take s.o.'s mind off his worries; **die Kinder langweilen sich; wir müssen**

sie a., the children are getting bored; we must find something to amuse them; (b) *Fenc:* to parry, ward off (thrust); (c) *Magn:* to cause a deviation of (magnetic needle); *El:* to deflect (coil, etc.); (d) *Opt:* to deflect (rays); to diffract (beam). **2.** *v.i.* (haben) (a) to turn aside, turn away; to deviate (von, from); **vom Thema, von der Sache, a.,** to digress, wander, from the subject; **er lenkte rasch (vom Thema) ab,** he hastily changed the subject; (b) abs. to create a diversion; (c) *Aut: Veh:* to turn (into a side-road, etc.); to turn off (the main road); (d) (of rays) to deviate; to diverge.
    II. *vbl s.* **1. Ablenken,** n. in vbl senses. **2. Ablenkung,** f. (a) in vbl senses of I. 1; also: diversion (of watercourse, of s.o.'s thoughts, attention, of suspicion); distraction (of s.o.'s attention); dissuasion (of s.o. from his design); *El:* deflection (of coil, etc.); *Opt:* deflection (of rays); diffraction (of beam); (b) in vbl senses of I. 2; also: digression (from the subject); *Opt: etc:* deviation, divergence (of rays, etc.); (c) *Fenc:* parry; (d) *Magn:* deviation (of magnetic needle); (e) *Mil: etc:* diversion; (f) distraction, diversion; change; amusement; **für Kranke ist irgendeine Form der A. unbedingt notwendig,** it is absolutely necessary for invalids to have some form of distraction; **er arbeitet immer; er braucht A.,** he is always working; he needs a change; **die Kinder brauchen A.,** the children need something to amuse them.
    III. *pr.p. & a.* **ablenkend,** in vbl senses; esp. diverting (action); distracting (activity); deflecting (force, action); *Opt:* diffracting, diffractive (effect, etc.); *El:* **ablenkende Wirkung eines Stroms,** deflecting action of a current.
Ablenker, m. *El.E: etc:* deflector; *Mec.E:* baffle, baffle-plate.
Ablenkfeld, n. *El:* deflecting field.
Ablenkfrequenz, f. *TV:* sweep frequency.
Ablenkplatte, f. **1.** *El.E:* deflector plate, deflecting plate. **2.** *Mec.E:* baffle, baffle-plate, deflector.
Ablenkspannung, f. *El:* deflecting voltage.
Ablenkstrom, m. *El:* deflection current.
Ablenkung, f. see **ablenken** II. 2.
Ablenkungs-, comb. fm. *Tchn:* deflecting . . . , deflection . . . ; esp. *El.E:* **Ablenkungsmagnet** m, deflection magnet; *El: Ph: etc:* **Ablenkungskraft** f, deflecting force; deflecting power. Cp. **Ablenk-.**
Ablenkungsangriff, m. *Mil:* diversion; feint (attack).
Ablenkungsmanöver, n. *Mil: etc:* diversion; feint; *F:* **ein A. machen,** to draw a red herring across the path.
Ablenkungsmesser, m. *Magn:* deflectometer, declinometer; declination compass.
Ablenkungsrolle, f. *Mec.E:* deviation pulley, deviation roller.
Ablenkungswiderstand, m. *Av:* resistance (of aircraft) to turning.
Ablenkungswinkel, m. *Ph: etc:* angle of deflection (of rays, etc.).
Ablepsie [a'blɛp'siː], f. -/-n [-'siːən], (physical or mental) blindness.
ablernen, v.tr. sep. **j-m etwas a.,** to learn sth. from s.o.; to learn from s.o. how to do sth., to pick up the knack of sth. from s.o.
ablesbar, a. *Tchn:* readable (value) (as registered by instrument).
Ablesefehler, m. *Tchn:* reading error, error in reading (precision instrument, etc.).
Ablesefernrohr, n. *Ind: etc:* reading telescope (for precision observations); cathetometer.
Ablesegerät, n. *Tchn:* (direct-)reading instrument.
ablesen. I. *v.tr. sep.* (strong) **1.** to pick (sth.) off; to gather, pick (fruit, etc.); **die Raupen von den Obstbäumen a.,** to pick the caterpillars off the fruit-trees, to clear the fruit-trees of caterpillars. **2.** (a) to read off, read out (announcement, poem, list, etc.); to read (a speech); to call over (list of names); to read (off) (values, from precision instrument); (b) to read (barometer, gas-meter, precision instrument); to take readings from (precision instrument); (c) **j-m etwas am Gesicht, an den Augen, a.,** to read sth. in s.o.'s face; **ich kann es dir an den Augen a., daß . . . ,** I can tell from your face that . . . ; **das liest man dir am Gesicht ab,** it shows in your face; **er las ihr jeden Wunsch an den Augen ab,** he anticipated her every wish; (d) **von den Lippen, vom Munde, a.,** to lip-read; **er las ihr die Worte von den Lippen ab,** (i) he made out the words by the movement of her lips; (ii) he hung on her words, on her lips.

    II. *vbl s.* **1. Ablesen,** n. in vbl senses. **2. Ablesung,** f. reading (taken from precision instrument, gas-meter, etc.).
Ablesestrich, m. graduation mark (on scale, instrument dial).
Ablesevorrichtung, f. *Tchn:* reading device.
Ablesungsfehler, m.=**Ablesefehler.**
ableuchten, v.tr. sep. to shine a light along (wall, etc.); to inspect (machinery, cellar, etc.) with a lamp.
Ableuchtlampe, Ableuchtlaterne, f, inspection lamp.
ableugnen. I. *v.tr. sep.* (a) **eine Tatsache a.,** to deny, *Jur:* to traverse, a fact; **der Angeklagte leugnet die Tat, seine Schuld, ab,** the accused denies the charge, pleads not guilty; (b) to deny (paternity, responsibility, etc.); to disclaim (authorship, etc.); to disown (offspring); **seine Unterschrift a.,** to deny, disown, one's signature; **a., etwas gesagt zu haben,** to deny having said sth.; (c) **etwas eidlich a.,** to deny sth. on oath; to abjure, forswear, sth.; to renounce sth. on oath; **seinen Glauben a.,** to abjure, renounce, one's religion.
    II. *vbl s.* **Ableugnen** n., **Ableugnung** f. (a) denial, *Jur:* traverse (of a fact); (b) disavowal (of action); denial (of paternity, responsibility, one's signature, etc.); disclaimer (of authorship, etc.); disowning (of offspring, one's signature); (c) eidliche **Ableugnung von etwas,** abjuration, forswearing, of sth.; renunciation of sth. on oath; **A. seines Glaubens,** abjuration, renouncing, of one's religion.
Ableugnungseid, m. (a) denial on oath; (b) renunciation on oath.
ablichten, v.tr. sep. **1.** *Dy:* to lighten, clear, reduce (colour); to strip (dyed material). **2.** to make a photostat of (document, etc.), to photostat (document, etc.); **Ablichtung** f, photostatic copy, photostat.
Abliefer-, comb. fm., cp. **Ablieferungs-.**
Ablieferer, m. (a) deliverer (of goods); delivery-man; (b) bearer (of a letter); (c) supplier, furnisher, purveyor; contractor; (d) *Com: Fin:* deliverer (of documents, stocks, etc.).
abliefern. I. *v.tr. sep.* (a) to deliver (goods, letter, etc.); **die Waren sind sofort abzuliefern,** the goods are to be delivered forthwith; (b) to supply, furnish (goods); (c) to hand over, deliver up; to surrender (sth.) (dat., an+acc., to); *Com: Fin:* to deliver (documents, shares); *Fin:* **Kupons a.,** to surrender coupons; **Getreide, ausländische Währungen, usw., den Staatsbehörden a.,** to surrender, hand over, grain, foreign currency, etc., to the government authorities; **Waffen a.,** to surrender weapons.
    II. *vbl s.* **Abliefern** n., **Ablieferung** f. in vbl senses; also: (a) delivery (of goods, letter, shares, etc.); **bei Ablieferung, nach (erfolgter) Ablieferung,** on delivery; (b) surrender(ing) (of produce, foreign currency, weapons, etc.; *Fin:* of coupons).
Ablieferungsbuch, n. *Com:* delivery book (of shop, etc.).
Ablieferungsfrist, f. *Com: etc:* (a) delivery date; (b) period allowed for delivery.
Ablieferungsgewicht, n. *Com:* delivery weight.
Ablieferungskontingent, n. *Adm: Ind: etc:* delivery quota.
Ablieferungspflicht, f. *Adm:* obligation to surrender (certain) produce, etc., to the authorities.
Ablieferungsprämie, f. *Adm: Ind: etc:* (delivery) bonus; bounty; subsidy.
Ablieferungsschein, m. *Com:* (a) delivery note; (b) certificate of delivery.
Ablieferungstermin, m. **1.** *Com: Fin:*=**Ablieferungsfrist. 2.** *St.Exch:* settling day.
Ablieferungszeit, f.=**Ablieferungstermin.**
abliegen. I. *v.i.sep.* (strong) (haben) **1.** to lie at a distance, to be distant; to be well away (von, from); **weit, fern, a.,** to be remote (from town, etc.); **das Haus liegt weit von der Straße ab,** the house is a long way from, well off, the road; **das Dorf liegt weit ab, ist sehr abgelegen,** the village is very remote, very out-of-the-way, very isolated; **eine abgelegene Stelle,** a remote, lonely, secluded, sequestered, an unfrequented, spot; **diese Erwägungen liegen ganz, sehr, ab,** these considerations are wide of the mark, are irrelevant. **2.** (of wine, etc.) to mature; to improve with keeping; (of fruit) to ripen with keeping; to ripen in store, in the storeroom; **abgelegener Wein,** wine old in bottle or in cask.
    II. *pr.p & a.* **abliegend,** in vbl senses; esp. *N.Arch:* **abliegende Platte,** outer strake.
ablisten, v.tr. sep. **j-m etwas a.,** to trick, *F:* do,

s.o. out of sth.; **j-m sein Geld a.,** *F:* to do, diddle, twist, s.o. out of his money.

ablocken, *sep. v.tr.* **1. j-n von etwas a.,** to entice, lure, coax, s.o. away from sth. **2.** (*a*) **j-m etwas a.,** to wheedle, coax, sth. out of s.o.; **j-m ein Geständnis a.,** to draw a confession from s.o.; to wheedle a confession out of s.o.; **j-m Tränen a.,** to bring tears to s.o.'s eyes; **mir kannst du mit dieser Geschichte keine Träne a.,** you can't move me, you won't get any sympathy from me, with a story like that; (*b*) **einem Musikinstrument Töne a.,** to draw, extract, sounds from a musical instrument.

ablohnen, ablöhnen. I. *v.tr sep.* (*a*) to pay (workman, servant, etc.), to pay (his *or* her) wages to (s.o.); (*b*) to pay off, discharge (workmen, troops); to dismiss (workman, servant, etc.).

II. *vbl s.* **1. Ablohnen, Ablöhnen,** *n. in vbl senses; also:* payment (of workman, etc.); dismissal, discharge (of workman, servant, etc.). 2. **Ablohnung, Ablöhnung,** *f.* (*a*)=II. 1; (*b*) (i) payment; (ii) dismissal, discharge.

Ablokation [aplo·ka·tsiˈoːn], *f.* **-/-en.** *Jur: A:* location, (i) letting (of house, etc.), (ii) leasing (of land, farm).

ablösbar, *a.* **1.** detachable; removable; separable. **2.** *Fin:* redeemable (stock, annuity, etc.).

Ablösbarkeit, *f.* **1.** separability; detachability; removability. **2.** *Fin:* redeemability (of stock, annuity, etc.).

ablöschen, *v.tr. sep.* **1.** (*a*) to slake, slack, kill (lime); (*b*) *Metall:* to quench (red-hot iron, etc.); to temper (steel); (*c*) *Cokem:* to quench (coke). **2.** (*a*) to blot (page written in ink); to blot (up) (ink); (*b*) **etwas a.,** to rub sth. out; to wipe sth. off (the slate, the blackboard, etc.); **eine Rechnung, eine Schuld, a.,** to wipe out a bill, a debt; (*c*) to wipe (slate, blackboard, etc.) clean.

Ablöschflüssigkeit, *f.,* **Ablöschwasser,** *n.* *Metall:* quenching liquid; quenching water.

Ablöse, *f.* **-/-n.** **1.** *Austrian:*=**Abstandsgeld** 4. **2.**=**Ablösegeld.**

Ablösegeld, *n. Sp:* transfer fee (for player).

ablösen. I. *v.tr. sep.* **1.** (*a*) to detach, separate, remove, disjoin (**von,** from); **einen Teil von etwas a.,** to split off, strip off, a part of sth.; **die Rinde von einem Baum, die Haut von einer Frucht, die Tapete von einer Wand, a.,** to strip off, peel off, the bark from a tree, the skin from a fruit, the paper from a wall; **die Sohle von einem Schuh a.,** to take the sole off a shoe, to strip the sole from a shoe; **die Briefmarke von einem Umschlag, das Etikett von einer Flasche, usw., a.,** to remove, unstick, the stamp from an envelope, the label from a bottle, etc.; **einen Backstein von der Mauer a.,** to remove, loosen, prise out, prize out, a brick from the wall; *Fin:* **Kupons a.,** to detach coupons; *Dent:* **das Zahnfleisch a.,** to bare, expose, a tooth *or* teeth; (*b*) *Ch:* *etc:* to dissolve (sth.) (out); to eliminate (sth); (*c*) *A:* **ein Boot vom Ufer a.,** to cast off from the shore. **2.** (*a*) to relieve (troops, a sentry); **die Wache a.,** (i) *Mil:* to relieve the guard, (ii) *Nau:* to relieve the watch; *Nau:* **den Mann am Ruder, am Steuer, a.,** to relieve the man at the wheel; (*b*) **j-n a.,** to take s.o.'s place (at a duty); to take over (from s.o.); (*c*) **j-n von seinem Dienst a.,** to relieve s.o. of his duties, of his office; (*d*) **sich, einander, a.,** (*of pers.*) to take (it in) turns; to relieve one another (at a duty); to work in relays; *Ind: etc:* to work in shifts; (*of phenomena, ideas, etc.*) to alternate (with one another); to come by turns; **Glück und Unglück lösten sich bei ihm ab,** he was happy and unhappy by turns; he alternated between happiness and unhappiness. **3.** *Fin: Com: etc:* (*a*) to withdraw (capital) (**von,** from); (*b*) to redeem (annuity, etc.); (*c*) to discharge (obligation, debt); to redeem, pay off, extinguish, amortize (debt); (*d*) to settle (running accounts, postal charges, freight charges, etc.) by block payments. **4. sich ablösen,** (*a*) to break off, come off, break loose, come loose; to become detached; to disengage itself; to separate; (*of skin, paint, wallpaper, etc.*) to peel off; (*of scab, sore*) to slough; (*of incrustation, etc.*) to scale off; (*of catch, fastening, link, etc.*) to slip off, come undone; (*of label, stamp, etc.*) to come off, come unstuck; *Phot:* (*of gelatine coating*) to frill; **die Rinde löst sich (vom Baum) ab,** the bark is stripping (from the tree); **ein Backstein hat sich von der Mauer abgelöst,** a brick has come out of the wall; **ein mächtiger Stein löste sich von der Felswand ab,** a great stone broke away from the cliff-face; (*b*) *Ch: etc:* (*of gas, vapour*) to come off, be released; (*of solid, etc.*) to dissolve (out); to be eliminated.

II. *vbl s.* **1. Ablösen,** *n. in vbl senses.* **2. Ablösung,** *f.* (*a*)=II. 1; *also:* separation, detachment; *Ch: etc:* elimination; release (of gas, vapour); relief (of troops, sentry, *Nau:* of watch, man at wheel, *Ind:* of outgoing shift); *Ind: etc:* **mit A. arbeiten,** to work in shifts; *Fin: Com: etc:* (i) withdrawal (of capital); (ii) redemption (of annuity, etc.); (iii) redemption, extinguishment, extinction, amortization (of debt); (*b*) settling (of running accounts, postal *or* freight charges, etc.) by block payments; *Post:* **'frei durch A.',** 'official paid'; *A:* **'frei durch A. Reich'**='On His, Her, Majesty's Service', *abbr.* O.H.M.S.; (*c*) *Jur:* commutation (of a punishment); (*d*) relief (for worker *or* shift); relieving party; *Ind:* oncoming shift; **ich warte auf meine A.,** I am waiting for my relief, for the man who relieves me.

III. *pr.p. & a.* **ablösend,** *in vbl senses; esp.* **1.** relieving (troops, sentry, etc.); *Ind:* oncoming (shift, personnel); **die Ablösenden,** the oncoming shift. **2.** *Ch:* resolvent (agent).

ablöslich, *a.*=**ablösbar.**

Ablöslichkeit, *f.*=**Ablösbarkeit.**

Ablösungsanleihe, *f. Fin:* redemption loan.

Ablösungsfläche, *f.* (*a*) *Geol: Miner: Cryst:* cleavage surface; cleavage-plane; (*b*) *Geol:* joint(ing)-plane.

Ablösungsfonds, *m. Fin:* sinking fund; redemption fund.

Ablösungsmannschaft, *f. Mil: Nau:* relief; *Mil:* relieving party; new guard, relieving guard; *Nau:* relieving watch; *Ind:* oncoming shift.

Ablösungsrichtung, *f. Cryst:* cleavage-plane.

Ablösungsschicht, *f. Ind:* oncoming shift.

Ablösungssumme, *f. Fin:*=**Ablösungsfonds.**

Ablösungswert, *m. Ins:* surrender value (of policy).

Abloteinstrument, *n. Surv: etc:* (any) instrument for measuring vertical distances; *Nau:* sounder, sounding apparatus *or* machine; depth-finder.

abloten, *v.tr. sep.* **1.** *Constr:* **eine Mauer a.,** to plumb a wall; to take the plumb of a wall. **2.** *Nau:* to sound; **die Küste a.,** to take soundings along the coast; **abgeloteter Grund,** sounded bottom. **3.** *Surv:* to locate points in the same vertical plane; to measure vertical distances.

ablöten, *v.tr. sep. Metalw:* to unsolder.

Abloter, *m.* **-s/-**=**Abloteinstrument.**

ablotsen, *v.tr. sep. F:* **j-m etwas a.,** to manœuvre s.o. out of sth.

ablozieren [aplo·ˈtsiːrən], *v.tr. insep. Jur: A:* to let (sth.) for hire; to let (house, etc.); to lease (land, farm, etc.).

abluchsen, *v.tr. sep.* **1. j-m etwas a.,** to cheat, swindle, trick, *F:* to do, bamboozle, s.o. out of sth.; **j-m sein Geld a.,** *F:* to do, diddle, twist, s.o. out of his money. **2. j-m ein Geheimnis, usw., a.,** to worm a secret, etc., out of s.o.

Abluentia [aplu·ˈɛntsĭa], *pl. Med: Pharm:* abstergents.

Abluft, *f.* **-/.** bad, foul, air; vitiated air; *Ind: etc:* waste air, outgoing air; *I.C.E: etc:* exhaust air.

Abluftgitter, *n.* air exhaust louvre (of armoured vehicle, etc.).

Abluftkanal, *m.* air exhaust duct.

Abluftlutte, *f. Min:* foul air duct.

Abluftrohr, *n.* air exhaust pipe; air outlet tube.

Abluftschlot, *m. Ind:* air exhaust chimney.

Abluftstutzen, *m.* (exhaust) air outlet (of electric motor, etc.).

abluieren [aplu·ˈiːrən], *v.tr. insep.* to wash, cleanse.

ablutieren [aplu·ˈtiːrən], *v.tr. sep.* (*p.p.* **ablutiert**) *Ch: Cer:* to unlute.

Ablution [aplu·tsiˈoːn], *f.* **-/-en,** washing, cleansing; *Ecc:* ablution.

abmachen. I. *v.tr. sep.* **1.** to detach, remove (sth.) (from sth.); to take (sth.) off, down; to pull (sth.) off; to strip (sth.) off. **2.** (*a*) to arrange, settle (business, an affair); to agree on (price, course of action, etc.); to conclude (bargain, etc.); **mit j-m etwas a.,** to arrange sth. with s.o.; to come to an agreement, arrive at an understanding, with s.o. about sth.; *F:* to fix things up with s.o.; **es ist so gut wie abgemacht,** it's as good as settled; **eine Sache gütlich, im Guten, in Güte, mit j-m a.,** to arrange a matter amicably with s.o.; to come to an amicable arrangement, agreement, with s.o. about a matter; **das müssen Sie miteinander a.,** you will have to arrange, settle, that between yourselves; **das muß er mit sich selbst a.,** he will have to settle that on his own, make his own decisions about that; **er hatte es bei sich abgemacht, daß er . . . würde,** he had made up his own mind that he would . . . ; **das ist also abgemacht,** well, that's settled, arranged; **abgemacht!** agreed, *F:* it's a bargain, *F:* done! **abgemachter Preis,** agreed, stipulated, price; *see also:* **vertragsmäßig;** (*b*) to complete (work, piece of business, etc.); **die Sache war schnell abgemacht,** it was done quickly; it was a quick business; it was quickly over; **verschiedene Erledigungen auf einmal a.,** to do various errands, jobs, at one go; to get various errands, jobs, done at the same time; (*c*) **eine Schuld a.,** to discharge, settle, a debt; **eine Rechnung a.,** (i) to settle an account, (ii) to close, wind up, an account; (*d*) **einen Streit a.,** to settle a quarrel; to compose, settle, adjust, a dispute; (*e*) *A:* **der Lehrling hatte seine Zeit abgemacht,** the apprentice had served his time.

II. *vbl s.* **1. Abmachen,** *n. in vbl senses; also:* completion (of work, piece of business, etc.); *F:* **das ist ein A.,** that can be done at the same time. **2. Abmachung,** *f.* (*a*) *in vbl senses;* (*b*) agreement; arrangement; settlement; compact; **Abmachungen über etwas** *acc.* **treffen,** to make arrangements about, for, sth.; *Jur:* **vertragliche, vertragsmäßige, A.,** stipulation; *Pol:* **internationale, zwischenstaatliche, Abmachungen,** international conventions; international agreements; *see also* **binden** I. 5 (*a*).

abmagern. I. *v.i. sep.* (*sein*) to grow thin; to lose flesh, to fall away in flesh; to waste away; to become emaciated.

II. *vbl s.* **Abmagern** *n.,* **Abmagerung** *f. in vbl senses; also:* loss of flesh; emaciation.

Abmagerungskur, *f. Med:* reducing diet *or* treatment; slimming diet *or* treatment; slimming course.

abmähen, *v.tr. sep.* to mow, cut, reap (field, hay, corn, etc.); to mow off (grass, etc.)

abmahnen, *v.tr. sep. A:* **j-n von etwas a., j-n davon a., etwas zu tun,** to dissuade s.o. from sth., from doing sth.; to warn s.o. against doing sth.

abmaischen, *v.tr. sep. Brew:* to mash off (malt).

abmalen, *v.tr. sep.* **1.** (*a*) to make, paint, a portrait of (s.o.), to portray (s.o.); to draw a likeness of (s.o.); *F:* **da möcht' ich nicht abgemalt sein,** I should hate to be there; (*b*) to depict, picture, describe (s.o., sth.). **2.** to copy, reproduce (painting, etc.).

abmallen, *v.tr. sep. N.Arch:* to shape, mould (keel, etc.).

abmarken. I. *v.tr. sep.* to delimit, demarcate; to mark the boundaries of (territory, etc.); to mark out (field, vineyard, etc.).

II. *vbl s.* **Abmarken** *n.,* **Abmarkung** *f. in vbl senses; also:* delimitation, demarcation (of territory).

Abmarkungslinie, *f.* dividing line, line of demarcation; boundary line.

Abmarsch, *m. Mil:* **1.** marching off (of troops); moving off, start (of column, vehicles); **den A. antreten,** to march off; **Befehl zum A.,** marching orders, order to march; **zum A. blasen,** to sound the bugle for departure. **2.** *A:* cavalry section (of four troopers).

abmarschbereit, *a.* ready to march, to move off, to start.

abmarschieren, *v.i. sep.* (*sein*) (*p.p.* **abmarschiert**) (*of troops*) to march off; (*of column, vehicles*) to move off, to start; **einzeln a.,** to file off.

Abmarschzeit, *f. Mil:* departure time, starting time.

abmartern, *v.tr. sep.* **1.** (*a*)=**martern;** (*b*) **sein Gehirn a.,** to rack, cudgel, one's brains. **2. sich abmartern,** to torture, torment, oneself; to fret, worry.

Abmaß, *n. Mec.E:* deviation (from prescribed dimensions); tolerance, allowance, margin, limit.

Abmaßtabelle, Abmaßtafel, *f. Mec.E:* (limit) gauge table.

abmatten, *v.sep.* **1.** *v.tr.* (*a*) to weary (s.o., s.o.'s limbs); (*b*) to mat, dull (metals, etc.). **2.** *v.i.* (*sein*) (*a*) (*of pers., limbs*)=**ermatten** I. (*a*); (*b*) (*of metals, etc.*) to grow dull.

abmeiern. I. *v.tr.sep.* (*a*) **einen Pächter a.,** to turn out, *Jur:* evict, dispossess, a tenant farmer; (*b*) *F: A:* **j-n a.,** to send s.o. about his business, to send s.o. packing; to give s.o. a dressing-down.

II. *vbl s.* **Abmeiern** *n.,* **Abmeierung** *f. in vbl senses; also: Jur:* eviction, dispossession (of a tenant farmer).

abmeißeln, *v.tr. sep.* **1.** to chisel (sth.) off; to chip (sth.) off. **2.** to chisel (sth.); to shape, fashion, (sth.) with a chisel.

Abmeldeformular, *n. Adm:* official form for giving notice of one's departure from a town *or* district; form for notification of removal.

abmelden. I. *v.tr. sep.* **1.** to cancel, *F:* call off (visit, engagement, etc.). **2. j-n, sich, a.,** (*a*) to notify s.o. that s.o., one, cannot attend (function, meeting, class, etc.); to have s.o.'s, one's, name removed, taken off (from list of participants, candidates, etc.); **einen Schüler a.,** to give notice of the withdrawal, removal, of a pupil (from school); *F:* **er ist bei mir abgemeldet,** I don't want to have any more to do with him; I have finished with him; (*b*) to notify s.o. of s.o.'s, one's, departure; to sign off, *U.S:* to check out; *Adm:* **j-n, sich, polizeilich a.,** to give notice to the police of s.o.'s, one's, departure (from town *or* district); to report change of address to the police. **3.** *Rail:* **einen Zug a.,** to signal the departure of a train (by telegraph *or* acoustically).

II. *vbl s.* **Abmelden** *n.*, **Abmeldung** *f. in vbl senses; also:* cancellation (of visit, engagement, etc.); withdrawal (of pers. from engagement, from list of participants, candidates, etc.); notice of non-attendance (at function, meeting, class, etc.); notice of withdrawal, of removal (of pupil); notification of departure; *Adm:* **polizeiliche Abmeldung,** report of change of address (to police).

Abmeldeschein, *m.* = **Abmeldeformular.**

Abmeldesignal, *n. Rail:* (acoustic *or* telegraphic) starting-signal.

Abmelkwirtschaft, *f.* system of dairying restricted to keeping cows that are in milk.

abmergeln, *v.tr. sep.* = **ausmergeln.**

abmeßbar, *a.* (*a*) measurable, mensurable; **in abmeßbarer Zeit,** within measurable time; (*b*) commensurable (**an** + *dat.*, with, to).

Abmeßbarkeit, *f.* (*a*) measurability, mensurability; (*b*) commensurability (**an** + *dat.*, with, to).

abmessen. I. *v.tr. sep.* (*strong*) **1.** (*a*) to measure (dimensions, quantity); to measure out (corn, liquid, etc.); to survey (land); to measure up (wood, land); to measure off (cloth, etc.); to measure out (tennis-court, etc.); *Constr:* to level (wall); *Civ.E: Constr:* to survey (for quantities, for amount of work done); *Mec.E: etc:* to gauge; *Surv:* to lay out, stake out, mark out (line, piece of ground, etc.); *Cust:* **den Inhalt einer Teekiste a.,** to bulk a chest of tea; (*b*) **seine Schritte a.,** to measure one's steps; to walk with measured tread; **seine Worte a.,** to weigh one's words; **abgemessen,** precise, ceremonious, formal, stiff (manner, etc.); reserved (manner); **(streng) abgemessene Bewegungen,** precise movements. **2. etwas nach etwas a.,** (*a*) to measure sth. by sth.; (*b*) to proportion, adjust, adapt, sth. to sth.; to conform sth. to sth.; (*c*) to estimate, judge, sth. by sth. **3. (zwei) Dinge gegeneinander a.,** (i) to compare (two) things (for height, size, etc.); (ii) to balance (the height, size, of) (two) things; **verschiedene Möglichkeiten gegeneinander a.,** to assess various possibilities.

II. *vbl s.* **1. Abmessen,** *n. in vbl senses; also:* (*a*) mensuration; (*b*) **A. von etwas nach etwas,** (i) adjustment of sth. to sth.; (ii) estimation, judgment, of sth. by sth. **2. Abmessung,** *f.* (*a*) = **II. 1**; (*b*) (proper) balance (of parts); (*c*) dimension, size; **die Abmessungen einer Kiste,** the dimensions, size, of a box.

Abmesser, *m.* (*a*) (land-)surveyor; (*b*) quantity-surveyor.

abmieten, *v.tr. sep.* to rent (house, etc.); to hire (car, etc.); **(j-m, von j-m,** from s.o.).

abmildern, *v.tr. sep.* to moderate (heat, etc.); to temper (heat, conditions, etc.); to tone down (contrast, colour, effect, etc.); to subdue (light, etc.).

abmontieren, *v.sep.* (*p.p.* **abmontiert**) **1.** *v.tr.* to take down, take to pieces, dismantle; to disassemble (machine, etc.); to strip (gun, etc.). **2.** *v.i.* (*sein*) *Av: F:* (*of aircraft*) to break up in the air.

abmühen (sich), *v.refl. sep.* (*a*) to wear oneself out; to drudge, to toil, *F:* to toil and moil; (*b*) **sich a., (etwas zu tun),** to take trouble, take pains, be at great pains (to do sth.).

abmurksen, *v.tr. sep. F:* to kill, murder, (s.o.) in a barbarous manner, *F:* to do away with (s.o.), to knock (s.o.) off; to butcher (animal).

abmüßigen, *v.tr. sep. A:* **1. j-m etwas a.,** (*a*) to extort, force, sth. from s.o.; (*b*) to steal sth., take sth. away, from s.o. **2. sich abmüßigen (von einer Beschäftigung),** to take time off (from work), to stop (work) for a moment.

abmustern, *v.sep.* **1.** *v.tr. Tex:* to pattern (material). **2.** *Nau:* (*a*) *v.tr.* to pay off, discharge (crew); (*b*) *v.i.* (*haben*) (*of member of crew*) to sign off.

abnabeln, *v.tr. sep. Obst:* **ein Kind a.,** to cut a child's umbilical cord.

abnageln, *v.tr. sep.* to stud (sth.) with nails.

abnagen, *v.tr. sep.* (*a*) to gnaw (sth.) away, off; **einen Knochen a., das Fleisch von einem Knochen a.,** (*of pers.*) to pick a bone, (*of dog*) to gnaw a bone; (*b*) **der Gram nagte ihr das Herz ab,** she was tormented, consumed, with grief; she was eating her heart out; sorrow gnawed at her heart.

abnähen, *v.tr. sep.* (*a*) to quilt (petticoat, counterpane, etc.); (*b*) **einen weißen Kragen, usw., rot a.,** to stitch a white collar, etc., with red; (*c*) **Biesen a.,** to take (in), make, tucks; to tuck; (*d*) **einen Rock, usw., a.,** to make darts in a skirt, etc.; to dart a skirt, etc.

Abnäher, *m.* **-s/-.** *Dressm:* (*a*) tuck; (*b*) dart.

Abnahme, *f.* **-/-n.** **1.** removal, removing; taking off; taking away; breaking (of seal); *Surg:* removal (of dressing, etc.); amputation, cutting off (of limb, etc.); *Art:* **die A. (Christi) vom Kreuz,** the Descent from the Cross. **2.** *El.E:* (= **Stromabnahme**) collecting, intake (of current). **3.** (*a*) *Com:* acceptance, taking delivery (of goods); purchase (of goods); *Fin:* delivery (of shares, etc.); **vor A.,** before taking delivery; **die Restzahlung erfolgt bei A. der Maschine,** the balance will be paid on taking delivery of the machine; **bei A. größerer Mengen wird ein Abschlag von 10 Prozent gewährt,** ten per cent discount is allowed if larger quantities are taken; **sich zur A. der ganzen Reihe verpflichten,** to agree to take, undertake to purchase, the whole series (of books, etc.); **diese Ware findet keine A.,** this article does not sell, there is no demand for this article; (*b*) *Ind:* acceptance (of machine, casting, gun, etc.) (*by inspector*); taking over (of machine, bridge, railway-line, etc.); (*c*) *Jur:* **A. eines Eides,** administering of an oath; (*d*) *Com:* **A. einer Rechnung,** auditing of an account; (*e*) *Mil:* **A. einer Parade,** (holding of a) review; reviewing of the troops. **4.** diminution, decrease (*gen.*, of; **an** + *dat.*, in); lessening; reduction; lowering (of strength, etc.); depreciation (in value); abatement (of flood, fever, etc.); fall, falling, subsidence, going down, ebb(ing), retirement (of the waters); retreat (of the waters, of glacier); decline (of strength, of empire, etc.); weakening (of strength, power, etc.); wane (of the moon); waning (of the moon, of powers, empire, etc.); slackening, decrease (of speed, etc.); falling off (of speed, talents, etc.); slowing down, slowing up (of a movement, etc.); fall, drop (in temperature, *El:* in voltage); diminution (of pressure); shrinkage (of requirements, resources, etc.); drawing in, shortening (of the days); **A. der Dicke (einer Säule, usw.),** tapering (of column, etc.); **A. der Breite,** narrowing; **A. des Gewichts,** loss of weight, decrease in weight; **A. der Kräfte,** falling off of strength; decline of (s.o.'s) powers; enfeeblement; *Med:* debility; **A. der Gesundheit,** failure, failing, of (s.o.'s) health; **wegen der A. seiner Gesundheit,** on account of his failing health; **A. des Eifers,** abatement, cooling, flagging, of zeal; **A. der Geschäfte,** falling off of, decline in, business; **allgemeine A. des Reichtums,** general falling off in wealth; **in A. kommen, geraten,** (i) to fall off, to decline; (*of powers, empire, etc.*) to wane; (ii) (*of custom, etc.*) to fall, pass, into disuse; to fall into desuetude; **in A. (begriffen) sein,** to be declining, to be on the decline; (*of moon, of empire, etc.*) to be on the wane. **5.** *Metalw:* reduction, draughting (of metal, in rolling). *Cp.* **abnehmen III.**

Abnahmebeamte, *m.* (*decl. as adj.*) *Ind:* (quality) inspector; *Mil:* acceptance inspector; acceptance official.

Abnahmebeschuß, *m. Artil:* (gun) trials; proof firing.

Abnahmedienststelle, *f. Mil:* acceptance depot.

Abnahmekontrolle, *f. Ind:* quality control; quality inspection.

Abnahmelehre, *f. Ind:* inspection gauge; acceptance gauge.

Abnahmepflicht, *f. Jur:* obligation of the purchaser to accept delivery of goods.

Abnahmeprobe, Abnahmeprüfung, *f. Ind:* inspection test; acceptance test *or* trial; taking-over test.

Abnahmeraum, *m. Ind:* inspection department.

Abnahmeschein, *m.* **1.** *Fin:* receipt (for shares, etc.). **2.** *Ind:* acceptance certificate.

Abnahmetoleranz, *f. Ind:* acceptance tolerance.

Abnahmeversuch, *m.* = **Abnahmeprobe.**

Abnahmeverweigerung, *f. Ind:* rejection (of articles not up to specification).

Abnahmevorschrift, *f. Ind:* specification(s) for acceptance; quality specification(s).

Abnarbeisen, *n. Tls: Leath:* (buffing) slicker.

abnarben, *v.tr. sep. Leath:* to shave, buff (hides).

Abnegation [apne·ga·tsĭ'oːn], *f.* **-/-en,** abnegation, denial; rejection (of claims, etc.).

abnegieren [apne·'giːrən], *v.tr. insep.* (*p.t. occ. & incorrectly* **negierte ab**) to abnegate, deny; to reject (claims, etc.).

abnehmbar, *a.* removable, detachable.

abnehmen, *v. sep.* (*strong*) I. *v.tr.* **1.** to remove, take away, take off; (*a*) **den Deckel a.,** to remove, take off, the lid; **den Mantel a.,** to take off, pull off, to doff, one's overcoat; **den Hut a.,** to remove, take off, pull off, one's hat; **vor j-m den Hut a.,** to take off, to raise, lift, *Lit:* to doff, one's hat to s.o.; **den Schnurrbart a.,** to shave off, take off, one's moustache; **sich** *dat.* **den Bart a. lassen,** to have, get, one's beard shaved off, taken off; **die Larve, die Maske, a.,** to throw off, drop, the mask; to unmask; **die Siegel a.,** to break the seals; **die Speisen a.,** to clear (the table); **das Tischtuch a.,** to remove the cloth; **das Obst a.,** to pick, gather, the fruit; *Cards:* **die Karten a.,** *abs.* **a.,** to cut (the cards); *Knitting:* **Maschen a.,** *abs.* **a.,** *abs.* to decrease; **eine Masche a.,** to decrease one stitch; *Surg:* **Verbände, usw., a.,** to remove, take off, dressings, etc.; **ein Glied, usw., a.,** to amputate, cut off, take off, a limb, etc.; *Tp:* **den Hörer a.,** to take off, lift, the receiver; (*b*) **etwas von etwas a.,** to take sth. away from sth., off sth.; to remove sth. from sth.; **ein Bild von der Wand a., die Steppdecke vom Bett a., die Wäsche von der Leine a.,** to take a picture off the wall, the quilt off the bed, the washing off the line; **den Deckel von etwas a.,** to take the lid off sth., remove the lid from sth.; **die Speisen vom Tisch a.,** to clear the table, *abs.* to clear (away); **das Obst vom Baum a.,** to pick, gather, the fruit from the tree; **den Rahm von der Milch a.,** to take the cream off the milk; to cream, skim, the milk; **einem Pferd den Sattel a.,** to take the saddle off a horse, to unsaddle a horse; **einem Pferd die Hufeisen a.,** to unshoe a horse; **Stieren das Joch a.,** to unyoke oxen; **von etwas eine Kleinigkeit a.,** to take a little off sth.; to reduce sth. by a trifle; (*c*) **j-m etwas a.,** to take sth. (away) from s.o.; to take sth. off s.o.; **j-m den Hut a.,** to take s.o.'s hat from him; **das Hausmädchen hat mir den Brief (an der Tür) abgenommen,** the maid took the letter from me (at the door), the maid took the letter in; **j-m Geld a.,** to take money from, of, off, s.o.; **j-m sein Geld a.,** to take s.o.'s money off him; to rob s.o. of his money; to swindle s.o. out of his money; to fleece s.o.; **er hat mir zuviel abgenommen,** he charged me too much, overcharged me; **dem Feind eine Stellung wieder abnehmen,** to retake, recapture, a position from the enemy; **j-m die Larve, die Maske, a.,** to unmask s.o.; **einem Betrüger die Larve a.,** to expose, show up, an impostor; **j-m die Waffen a.,** to take s.o.'s arms, weapons, from him; to disarm s.o.; *Surg:* **j-m die Verbände, usw., a.,** to take the dressings, etc., off s.o.; **j-m ein Bein a.,** to amputate, cut off, take off, s.o.'s leg; **einer Frau die linke Brust a.,** to remove a woman's left breast; (*d*) **j-m eine Last, eine Mühe, eine Verantwortung, a.,** to relieve s.o. of a burden, a trouble, a responsibility; to take a burden, a responsibility, off s.o.'s shoulders; **er hat mir den Gang in die Stadt abgenommen,** he relieved me of the necessity of going into town, *F:* he saved me the trip to town. **2. Strom a.,** (*a*) to use electricity; (*b*) *El.E:* to collect current. **3.** (*a*) *A:* to depict (s.o., a landscape); **von j-m ein Bild a.,** to take a likeness of (s.o.); *Phot: A:* to photograph, take a photograph of (s.o.); (*b*) **eine Totenmaske a.,** to make a death-mask (of s.o.). **4.** (*a*) to infer, conclude, deduce (sth.) **(aus,** from); **aus den Berichten konnte man a., was wirklich geschehen war,** one could infer, deduce, gather, from the reports what had really happened; (*b*) **das kann ich dir nicht a.,** I cannot accept what you say. **5.** (*a*) *Com:* to purchase, buy, take (goods); to take delivery of (goods); **er nimmt mir viel ab,** he buys a good deal from me, he is a good customer of mine; **es gibt eine Preisermäßigung, wenn Sie den ganzen Posten a.,** there is a reduction if you take the whole lot; **der Käufer muß sich verpflichten, die ganze Reihe abzunehmen,** the buyer must undertake to purchase the whole series; **wir werden die**

Waren hier a., we will take delivery of the goods here; (*b*) *Ind:* to accept (machine, casting, gun, etc.) (*after inspection*); to take over (machine, bridge, railway-line, etc.). **6.** (*a*) **j-m ein Versprechen a.**, to make s.o. promise sth.; to obtain a promise from s.o.; (*b*) *Jur:* **j-m einen Eid a.**, to swear s.o.; to administer an oath to s.o.; (*c*) *Com:* **eine Rechnung a.**, to audit an account; (*d*) *Mil:* **die Parade a.**, to inspect the troops.

II. **abnehmen,** *v.i.* (*haben*) to diminish, decrease (**an**+*dat.*, in); to lessen, grow less; to depreciate (in value); (*of flood, storm, fever, zeal, etc.*) to abate; (*of waters*) to fall, subside, go down, abate, retire; (*of waters, glacier*) to retreat; (*of strength, empire, etc.*) to decline; (*of strength, power, etc.*) to weaken; (*of health, memory, sight, hearing*) to fail, to grow weak, grow feeble; (*of strength, courage, resolution*) to fail, flag; (*of body, pers.*) to grow thin(ner); (*of pers.*) to lose weight, to lose flesh; (*of swelling*) to go down; (*of the moon*) to wane; (*of light*) to fail, wane, dwindle; (*of speed, etc.*) to slacken, decrease; (*of speed, talents, etc.*) to fall off; (*of a movement, etc.*) to slow down, slow up; (*of temperature, pressure, El.E: of voltage*) to drop; (*of pressure*) to diminish; (*of resources, etc.*) to shrink, dwindle; (*of members, receipts*) to drop off, fall off, fall away; (*of prices*) to drop, fall away; (*of demand*) to fall off; (*of winter days*) to draw in, shorten, grow shorter; (*of column, etc.*) **an Dicke a.**, to taper; (*of groove, etc.*) **an Breite a.**, to narrow; **an Gewicht a.**, to lose weight; **am, an, Wert a.**, to depreciate (in value); **der Wind nimmt ab**, the wind is abating, is dropping, is going down; **seine Gesundheit, sein Gesicht, sein Gehör, nimmt ab**, his health, his sight, his hearing, is failing, *F:* is going; **sein Mut, sein Eifer, nimmt ab**, his courage, his zeal, is failing, is flagging; **der Mond nimmt ab, wir haben abnehmenden Mond**, the moon is waning, is on the wane; **sein Ruhm, seine Beliebtheit, nimmt ab**, his fame, his popularity, is waning, dwindling, declining, is on the decline: **die Aufwärtsbewegung, die Abwärtsbewegung, (der Preise) nimmt ab**, the upward movement, downward movement, (of prices) is slowing down, *F:* is tapering off; *Mth:* **abnehmende Reihe,** descending, decreasing, series. *See also* **zusehends.**

III. *vbl s.* **Abnehmen,** *n. in vbl senses; also:* **im A. (begriffen) sein,** to be declining, on the decline; to be decreasing, on the decrease; to be waning, on the wane; to be on the down-grade; **der Mond ist im A.**, the moon is waning, on the wane. *Cp.* **Abnahme.**

Abnehmer, *m.* **1.** (*a*) *Com: etc:* buyer, purchaser, taker (of goods, etc.); customer; consumer; **diese Ware findet, für diese Ware findet man, keine Abnehmer,** there are no customers for this article; this article does not sell, is unsaleable, finds no sale; **Lohnsteigerungen werden letzten Endes durch den A. bestritten,** wage-increases are ultimately paid by the consumer; **A. einer Zeitung,** subscriber to anewspaper; (*b*) **A. (von Gestohlenem),** receiver (of stolen goods), *F:* fence. **2.** picker, gatherer (of fruit).

Abnehmerland, *n.* customer (country).

Abnehmerstange, *f. El.E:* contact-rod.

abneigen, *v.tr. sep.* **1.** *A:* (*a*)=**abgeneigt machen,** *q.v. under* **abgeneigt;** (*b*)=**abwenden** I. 1. **2. sich von etwas abneigen,** *Lit:*=**abwenden** I. 2.

Abneigung, *f.* **1.** *A:* turning away, deviation (**von,** from); declination (of needle, etc.). **2.** aversion (**gegen, vor,** to, for); dislike (**gegen, vor,** of, for); distaste (**gegen, vor,** for); repugnance (**gegen, vor,** towards, for); disinclination (**gegen, vor,** for); reluctance (**gegen**+*vbl noun,* to do sth.); **eine A. gegen j-n, vor j-m, haben,** to feel an aversion to, for, s.o.; **eine A. gegen etwas bekommen, fassen,** to conceive a distaste for sth.; to take a dislike to, conceive a dislike for, sth.; **das, er, flößt mir A. ein,** it, he, is distasteful to me; I find it, him, distasteful; it, he, fills me with distaste.

abnieten, *v.tr. sep.* **1.** to unrivet. **2.** to unclinch (nail).

abnorm [ap'nɔrm], *a.* abnormal, irregular; anomalous (type, case, etc.); *adv.* abnormally.

abnormal [ˌapnɔr'maːl], *a. Occ. & Swiss:*=**abnorm.**

Abnormalität [apnɔrmaˑliˑ'tɛːt], *f. Occ. & Swiss:* =**Abnormität.**

Abnormität [apnɔrmiˑ'tɛːt], *f.* **-/-en. 1.** abnormality, irregularity; anomaly. **2.** freak (of nature); *Biol:* sport.

abnötigen. I. *v.tr. sep.* to extort; **j-m Geld a.**, to extort money from s.o., *F:* to screw money out of s.o.; **j-m ein Versprechen, ein Geständnis, eine Entschuldigung, a.**, to wring a promise, a confession, an apology, from s.o.; to force s.o. to make a promise, a confession, an apology.

II. *vbl s.* **Abnötigen** *n.*, **Abnötigung** *f. in vbl senses; also:* extortion (of money, a promise, a confession, etc.).

abnutschen, *v.tr. sep.* (*a*) *Ind: etc:* to suck (sth.) off; to draw off (moisture from crystals, etc.) by suction; to extract (moisture, etc.) with a hydro-extractor; (*b*) *Ch: etc:* to filter (liquid) by suction.

Abnutzbarkeit, *f. Ind: etc:* liability, proneness, (of materials) to wear; **hohe A., geringe A.**, poor, good, wearing qualities.

abnutzen, abnützen. I. *v.tr. sep.* **1.** (*a*) to use up, consume (sth., one's strength); (*b*) *Jur: A:* to have the use, the usufruct, of sth.; (*c*) to wear (sth.) out, down, away; to wear out (coins, clothes); to abrade (bearings, coins, etc.); **abgenutzte Kleider,** shabby, threadbare, worn-out, clothes; **abgenutzter Bleistift, Bohrer, usw.**, blunt pencil, drill, etc. **2. sich abnutzen,** *occ.* **a.**, *v.i.* (*sein*) to wear (out); (*of bearings, coins, etc.*) to abrade; *Artil:* (*of gun*) to wear; *A. Artil:* (*of bronze gun*) **sich (an der Mündung) a.**, to wear, run, spew, at the muzzle.

II. *vbl s.* **1. Abnutzen, Abnützen,** *n. in vbl senses.* **2. Abnutzung, Abnützung,** *f.* (*a*) wear (and tear) (of furniture, machinery, etc.); depreciation (of equipment, furniture, etc.); wear (of coin); *Geol:* erosion, detrition; *Mch:* erosion (of boiler); *Mec.E: etc:* **A. eines Lagers,** abrasion of a bearing; *Mec.E: etc:* **einseitige A.**, one-sided wear(ing); *Artil:* **A. eines Geschützrohres,** wear(ing), erosion, of a gun-barrel; *Jur:* **gewöhnliche, normale, A.**, fair wear and tear; (*b*) *Jur: A:* usufruct; life interest.

Abnutzer, *m.* **-s/-.** *Jur: A:*=**Nutznießer.**

Abnutzungserscheinung, *f.* sign of wear; sign, symptom, of attrition.

Abnutzungsgröße, *f. Mec.E: etc:* degree of wear.

Abnutzungskampf, *m. Mil:* battle of attrition; wearing-down engagement.

Abnutzungssatz, *m.* **1.** rate of depreciation (of machinery, furniture, etc.). **2.** *For:* annual yield (of a forest).

aböden, *v.tr. sep.* to lay waste, devastate (a region, etc.).

Abohm, *n.* **-s/-.** *El.Meas:* abohm.

abohrfeigen, *v.tr. sep.* **j-n a.**, to box s.o.'s ears soundly.

Aböl, *n.* waste oil; *Mch: etc:* used oil.

abölen, *v.tr. sep.* **1.** to remove the oil from (sth.). **2.** to oil (sth.) thoroughly.

abolieren [aboˑ'liːrən], *v.tr.* to abolish, suppress; **die Klassenunterschiede a.**, to make an end of, do away with, class-distinctions.

Abolition [aboˑliˑtsi'oːn], *f.* **-/-en. 1.** abolition, abolishment; suppression. **2.** *Jur: A:* amnesty; annulment (of verdict, etc.).

Abolitionismus [aboˑliˑtsĭoˑ'nismus], *m.* **-/.** *Hist:* abolitionism.

Abolitionist [aboˑliˑtsĭoˑ'nist], *m.* **-en/-en.** *Hist:* abolitionist.

Abolitionsbrief, *m. Jur: A:* (declaration of) amnesty.

A-Bombe, *f.* A-bomb.

abominabel [aboˑmiˑ'naːbəl], *a.* abominable, loathsome; heinous (crime); *F:* wretched, beastly (weather, etc.).

abondieren [abɔn'diːrən], *v.i. insep.* (*haben*) to abound (**an**+*dat.*, in); to be plentiful.

Abonnement [abɔnə'mɑ̃ː], *n.* **-s/-s,** (*a*) subscription (**auf**+*acc.*, to a newspaper, etc., for a series of performances, etc.); **im A.**, by subscription; **Konzerte im A.**, subscription concerts; **'Tannhäuser' wird heute Abend bei, mit, aufgehobenem A. gegeben,** season tickets are not valid for this evening's performance of Tannhäuser; **im A. essen,** to take one's meals regularly (at restaurant) at reduced prices; *see also* **erneuern** I. 1 (*b*), II. 2 (*a*); (*b*)=**Abonnementskarte;** (*c*) *Tp:* (*in Switzerland*) (telephone) subscriber's contract.

Abonnementsbillett, *n. A:*=**Abonnementskarte** (*a*).

Abonnementskarte, *f.* (*a*)=**Dauerkarte, Zeitkarte;** (*b*) luncheon voucher; book of luncheon vouchers; *U.S:* (reduced-price) meal ticket.

Abonnementsliste, *f.* list of subscribers (to periodical, etc.).

Abonnementspreis, *m.* subscription price; subscription rate (for periodicals, etc.); (*at restaurant*) reduced price for regular customers.

Abonnent [abo'nɛnt], *m.* **-en/-en. 1.** subscriber (to newspaper, etc.). **2.** *Th: etc:* season-ticket holder. **3.** regular customer (of restaurant) taking meals at reduced prices. **4.** *Tp:* (*in Switzerland*) (telephone-)subscriber.

Abonnentenversicherung, *f. Journ:* free insurance scheme for newspaper readers.

abonnieren [abɔ'niːrən]. **1.** *v.tr.* to enrol (s.o.) on a list of subscribers; **j-n auf eine Zeitung a.**, to take out a subscription to a paper in favour of s.o.; **auf eine Zeitung abonniert sein,** to subscribe to, take, a paper; **im Theater, in der Oper, abonniert sein,** to have a season-ticket for the theatre, for the opera; *F. & Dial:* (*esp. Swiss*): **auf der Eisenbahn, auf der Straßenbahn, abonniert sein,** to have a season-ticket on the railway, on the trams, *U.S:* to have a commutation ticket. **2.** *v.i.* (*haben*) **& sich abonnieren,** (*a*) **(sich) auf eine Zeitung a.**, to subscribe, become a subscriber, to a paper; (*b*) *Th: etc:* to buy a season-ticket, a subscriber's ticket; (*c*) (*at restaurant*) to buy (a book of) luncheon vouchers, *U.S:* meal tickets; to take one's meals regularly (at restaurant) at reduced prices; (*d*) *Tp:* (*in Switzerland*) to become a (telephone) subscriber.

aboral [apoˑ'raːl], *a. Z:* aboral; at the opposite extremity from the mouth.

abordern, *v.tr. sep. Mil: etc:*=**abkommandieren.**

abordnen. I. *v.tr. sep.* **1.** to delegate (s.o.); to depute (s.o.), to appoint (s.o.) as deputy, as delegate (**zu,** to); to detail, detach (s.o.) (for duty). **2.** *A:* to countermand.

II. *vbl s.* **1. Abordnen,** *n. in vbl senses.* **2. Abordnung,** *f.* (*a*)=II. 1; (*b*) delegation, deputation; body of representatives, of delegates.

Abort[1] [a'bɔrt, 'abɔrt], *m.* **-(e)s/-e. 1.** *A. & occ. Dial:* retired, out-of-the-way, spot; remote place. **2.** lavatory, toilet, (water-)closet, privy; *Mil: etc:* latrine; *Mil: Sch: F:* the lats, the rear(s); *Nau: F:* the heads; **auf den A. gehen,** to go to the lavatory.

Abort[2] [a'bɔrt], *m.* **-(e)s/-e.** *Biol:*=**Abortus.**

Abortanlagen, *pl. Hyg:* lavatory installations; lavatories; *Mil: etc:* latrines.

Abortgrube, *f.* (*a*) *Hyg:* cesspool, soil-tank; (*b*) *Mil:* latrine (pit).

abortieren [abɔr'tiːrən], *v.i.* (*haben*) **1.** *Biol:* to abort; *Med:* to miscarry. **2.** (*of animals*) to slip, slink, cast (young). **3.** *Bot:* to develop imperfectly; to fail to ripen; to abort.

abortiv [abɔr'tiːf], *a.* **1.** *Biol: etc:* abortive. **2.** *Bot:* abortive (fruit); (fruit) that has developed imperfectly. **3.** *adv. Med:* **eine Krankheit a. abwehren,** to apply abortive treatment to a disease, to abort a disease.

Abortivei, *n.* (*a*) *Biol:* abortive ovum; (*b*) *Obst:* false conception.

Abortivfrucht, *f.* **1.** *Bot:* abortive fruit. **2.** *Obst:* mola, mole; false conception.

Abortivkur, *f. Med:* abortive treatment (of disease).

Abortivum [abɔr'tiːvum], *n.* **-s/-va.** *Obst:* abortifacient (drug).

Abortus [a'bɔrtus], *m.* **-/-,** (*a*) *Biol:* abortion; (*b*) *Obst:* miscarriage; **einen (künstlichen) A. einleiten,** to procure an abortion; to bring on a miscarriage; **krimineller A.**, (procured) abortion, 'illegal operation'.

aboxydieren, *v.tr. sep.* (*p.p.* **aboxydiert**) *Ch: etc:* to oxidize (sth.) off, to remove (sth.) by oxidation.

abpaaren, *v.sep.* **1.** *v.tr.* to arrange (dancers, etc.) in pairs, in couples; to sort (gloves, etc.) into pairs. **2. sich abpaaren,** to pair off; to separate into pairs, into couples. **3.** *v.i.* (*haben*) *Parl:* (*of political opponents*) to pair; **sich a. lassen,** to apply for a pair; to arrange for a pair.

abpachten. I. *v.tr. sep.* **(von) j-m einen Bauernhof a.**, to rent, lease, a farm from s.o.; **(von) j-m ein Geschäft, usw., a.**, to take a business, etc., from s.o. on contract.

II. *vbl s.* **1. Abpachten,** *n. in vbl senses.* **2. Abpachtung,** *f.* (*a*)=II. 1; (*b*) lease.

Abpackanlage, *f. Ind:* packing plant.

abpacken, *v.tr. sep.* **1.** to unload (cart, etc.). **2.** *Com:* to pack (up) (groceries, etc.); *Ind:* to pack (goods).

Abpacker, *m.* **1.** unpacker. **2.** *Com: Ind:* packer.

abpälen, *v.tr. sep. Leath:* to unhair, depilate (hide); to scrape off the hair from (hide).

abparieren, *v.tr. sep.* (*p.p.* **abpariert**)=**parieren.**

abpassen, *v.tr. sep.* **1.** to adjust, fit; to trim (panel, piece of material, etc.) to the required size; *Dressm:* to adjust the length of (dress,

material). **2. j-n a.**, to lie in wait for, to be on the look-out for, to watch for, s.o.; **die Gelegenheit a.**, to watch one's opportunity; **die Zeit a.**, to bide one's time; **das war gut abgepaßt**, that was neatly timed.

abpatrouillieren, *v.tr. sep.* (*p.p.* **abpatrouilliert**) *Mil: Navy: etc:* to patrol (area, streets, sea area, etc.).

abpellen, *v.tr. sep.* to remove (skin *or* peel); to peel (potatoes, etc.); to skin (vegetables, fruit); (*of skin*) **sich a.**, to peel; to come off.

abpelzen, *v.tr. sep.* **1.** to skin (animal). **2.** *F:* to thrash (s.o.) severely, *F:* to take the hide off (s.o.).

abpfählen, *v.tr. sep.* **1.** to stake out, mark out, lay out (line, piece of ground, etc.); to peg (out) (claim). **2.** to palisade; to fence in, rail in; to enclose (ground).

abpfänden, *v.tr. sep.*=**pfänden.**

abpfeifen, *v.tr. sep.* (*strong*) **1.** to whistle (tune). **2.** (*a*) *Navy:* **die Mannschaft a.**, to pipe the hands away, down; (*b*) *Ind:* **die Arbeit a.**, *abs.* **a.**, to blow the whistle to stop work; (*c*) *Fb: etc:* (*of referee*) **das Spiel a.**, *abs.* **a.**, (i) to blow the final whistle; (ii) to blow his whistle, to stop play.

abpferchen, *v.tr. sep.* to pen (cattle); to fold (sheep).

Abpfiff, *m. Fb: etc:* final whistle.

abpflöcken, *v.tr. sep.* **1.** to peg out, mark out, stake out, lay out (line, piece of ground, etc.); to peg (out) (claim). **2.** to unpeg; *Carp:* to remove the pegs, the dowels, from (framework, etc.).

abpflücken, *v.tr. sep.* (*a*) to gather, pick, pluck, *Lit:* to cull (flowers, fruit); (*b*) to strip (tree) (of fruit).

abpflügen. **1.** *v.tr.* (*a*) to plough off (tree-roots, strip from field, etc.); (*b*) *abs. F:* **dem Nachbar a.**, to plough off a piece of one's neighbour's land. **2.** *v.i.* (*haben*) *Dial:* to finish ploughing.

abpicken, *v.tr. sep.* (*a*) (*of bird*) to peck (sth.) off; (*b*) (*of pers.*) to pick (sth.) off; *Mch:* to chip off (scale from boiler); to scale (boiler).

abpipettieren, *v.tr. sep.* (*p.p.* **abpipettiert**) *Ch:* to draw off (liquid) with a pipette, to pipette off (liquid).

abplacken (sich), *v.refl. sep.* to wear oneself out (with work).

abplagen, *v.tr. sep.* **1.** to torment, harass, worry, *F:* plague, bother (s.o.). **2. sich abplagen**, (*a*) to exhaust oneself; to tire oneself out; to toil (and moil) **(mit, an**+*dat.*, at); (*b*) **sich a., (um) etwas zu tun**, to be at great pains to do sth.

abplaggen, *v.tr. sep.* **Rasen a.**, to cut turf; to cut sods.

abplanken, *v.tr.* to board up, board over (hole, etc.).

abplärren, *v.tr. sep.* **1.** to bawl (out) (song); to drone out (prayer, etc.) (in a high voice). **2. sich abplärren**, (*of child*) to bawl till it is blue in the face, to bawl itself blue in the face.

abplatten. I. *v.tr. sep.* (*a*) to make (sth.) flat, to flatten (sth.) (out); *Geom:* **(an den Polen) abgeplattetes Ellipsoid, usw.**, oblate ellipsoid, etc.; (*b*) *Woodw:* to bevel (edges).

II. *vbl s.* **1. Abplatten,** *n. in vbl senses.* **2. Abplattung,** *f.* (*a*)=II. 1; (*b*) *Geom:* oblateness (of an ellipsoid, etc.).

abplätten, *v.tr. sep. Metalw:* to laminate, flat(ten), roll (metal).

Abplattmaschine, *f. Tls: Woodw:* bevelling machine.

abplatzen, *v.i. sep.* (*sein*) (*of part of boiler, etc.*) to burst off; (*of button, rivet-head, etc.*) to fly off, come off.

abplätzen, *v.tr. sep. For:* to mark, blaze (trees).

abplündern, *v.tr. sep.* **1. j-m etwas a.**, to plunder, rob, s.o. of sth. **2. einen Obstbaum, einen Weihnachtsbaum, a.**, to strip a tree (of fruit), a Christmas tree (of edible decorations).

abpochen, *v.tr. sep.* (*a*) *Min:* to stamp, pound, crush (ore); (*b*) *Metalw:* to hammer (copper plates, etc.).

abpolieren, *v.tr. sep.* (*p.p.* **abpoliert**) **1.** to polish off (stain, etc.), to remove (stain, etc.) by polishing. **2.**=**polieren.**

abprägen, *v.tr. sep.* (*a*)=**prägen**; (*b*) (*of thg*) **sich auf etwas** *acc.* **a.**, to make an impress(ion), imprint, on sth., to imprint, impress, stamp, itself on sth.

Abprall, *m.* **-s/-e**, (*a*) rebound(ing) (of a solid body); bounce (of ball, etc.); reverberation (of sound); reflection, reverberation (of light); (*b*) ricochetting; ricochet (of bullet, shell, etc.).

abprallen. I. *v.i. sep.* (*sein*) (*a*) (*of solid body*) to rebound; (*of ball, etc.*) to bounce (off); (*of missiles, hailstones, etc.*) to glance off; (*of sound, light*) to be reverberated; to reverberate **(von**, from); (*b*) (*of ideas, etc.*) **an j-m a.**, to make no impression on s.o.; **alle Vorwürfe prallen (wirkungslos) an ihr ab**, she is impervious to reproaches; (*c*) (*of bullet, shell, etc.*) to ricochet.

II. *vbl s.* **Abprallen** *n.*, *occ.* **Abprallung** *f.*= **Abprall.**

Abpraller, *m.* **-s/-**, (*a*) *Artil: Sm.a:* ricochet; **das Ziel mit einem A. treffen**, to make an indirect hit; (*b*) *Artil:* ricochet air-burst.

Abprallwinkel, *m.* angle of rebound; angle of bounce (of ball); angle of reflection (of light, heat); *Artil: Sm.a:* angle of ricochet.

abprellen, *v.sep.* **1.** *v.tr.* to make (sth.) rebound; to make (ball, etc.) bounce back; to repel (sth., s.o.) (violently); to send (sth.) flying, hurtling, back. **2.** *v.i.* (*sein*)=**abprallen** I. (*a*).

abpreschen, *v.sep.* **1.** *v.tr.* to overstrain, overwork, override, founder (horse). **2.** *v.i.* (*sein*) *F:* (*of pers.*) to hurry off, scurry off, rush off.

abpressen. I. *v.tr. sep.* **1.** (*a*) **j-m Geld, ein Geständnis, usw., a.**, to extort money, etc., from s.o., to wring, force, a confession, etc., from s.o.; (*b*) to squeeze (sth.) off; *Mec.E:* to unwedge, unkey. **2.** to squeeze (sth.) in a press; *Bookb:* **den Falz a.**, to shape the shoulder of a book.

II. *vbl s.* **Abpressen** *n.*, **Abpressung** *f. in vbl senses; also:* extortion (of money, a confession, etc.).

Abpreßmaschine, *f. Bookb:* nipping-press.

Abpreßwalze, *f. Bookb: etc:* pressing roller.

abpricken, *v.tr. sep.* to prick off, mark off (points on map, chart, etc.).

Abprodukt, *n. Ind:* (*a*) by-product; (*b*) waste product.

abprotzen, *v.tr. sep.* **1.** (*a*) *Artil:* to unlimber (gun); (*b*) *Fire-fighting:* **die Spritze a.**, to take the (manual) fire-engine off its cart. **2.** *abs. Mil: P:* to relieve oneself.

Abprotzspritze, *f.* dismountable manual fire-engine.

abprügeln, *v.tr. sep.*=**verprügeln.**

abpuffen, *v.sep. A:*=**abdecken** I. 2.

Abpuffer, *m.* **-s/-**. *A:*=**Abdecker.**

abpumpen, *v.tr. sep.* **1.** to pump off (liquid, gas). **2.** *F:* **j-m Geld a.**, to borrow money from s.o., *F:* to touch s.o.; **er hat mir zehn Schilling abgepumpt**, he touched, tapped, me for ten bob.

abpusten, *v.tr. sep.*=**abblasen** 1 (*a*).

Abputz, *m.*=**Verputz.**

abputzen, *v.tr. sep.* **1.** (*a*)=**putzen**; (*b*) to clean (sth.) (off); to wipe (off) (dust, etc.); to brush (off), to scrub (off), to swab (off) (dirt); to scrape (off) (mud, dirt); **die Stiefel a.**, to scrape one's boots; **den Schmutz von den Stiefeln a.**, to scrape the mud off one's boots; **putz erst den Schmutz ab!** first scrape off the mud! **ein Kind, sich, a.**, to wipe a child, oneself; to wipe a child's, one's, behind. **2.** *Carp:* **einen Balken a.**, to trim up a (roughly dressed) beam. **3.** *Constr:* to rough-cast (wall); to plaster (wall). **4.** *F:* **j-n a.**, to tell s.o. off, to tick s.o. off; to snub s.o.; to put s.o. in his place; to sit on s.o.

Abputzer, *m.* **1.** (*pers.*) plasterer. **2.** *F:* snub; telling-off; ticking-off; **einen A. bekommen**, to get snubbed; to get told off, ticked off; **j-m einen A. erteilen**=**j-n abputzen**, *q.v. under* **abputzen** 4.

abquälen, *v.tr. sep.* **1. j-m etwas a.**, to pester, torment, s.o. for sth., s.o. into giving one sth. **2. sich abquälen**, (*a*) to torment oneself; to fret, worry; *F:* to bother; (*b*) **sich (mit etwas) a.**, to take great pains (with sth.); to labour (at, over, sth.).

abquellen, *v.tr. sep. Dial:* to boil (potatoes) in their jackets.

abquetschen, *v.tr. sep.* (*a*) to squeeze (sth.) off; to pinch (sth.) off; (*b*) **es wurde ihm bei einem Unfall ein Finger, eine Zehe, abgequetscht**, he got a finger, a toe, crushed in an accident.

abquicken, *v.tr. sep. Metall:* **1.** to extract (gold) from an amalgam. **2.** to cool down (cupelled silver) with water.

abquirlen, *v.tr. sep.*=**quirlen.**

abrackern (sich), *v.refl. sep.* to drudge; to toil (and moil); to slave **(mit**+*dat.*, **über**+*acc.*, at); to work oneself to death.

abradeln, *v.i. sep.* (*sein*) to cycle off, away; to pedal off, away.

abradieren [ˈapraˌdiːrən], *v.tr. sep.* (*p.p.* **abradiert**), to scrape (sth.) off; to scratch (sth.) off; to scratch out (words, figures); to erase (writing, etc.); *esp.* to rub out (writing, etc.) (with rubber eraser).

abraffen, *v.tr. sep.* to snatch up, sweep up (coins from table, etc.).

Abraham [ˈaːbraˑham]. *Pr.n. m.* **-s.** Abraham.

Abrahamit [aˑbraˑhaˑˈmiːt], *m.* **-en/-en.** *Rel.Hist:* Abrahamite (*member of a Bohemian sect in the 18th century*).

Abrahamsbaum, Abrahamsstrauch, *m. Bot:* agnus-castus, chaste-tree, Abraham's balm.

Abrahamskuh, *f. South G.Dial: F:* nanny-goat.

abrahmen, *v.tr. sep.* (*a*) to skim, cream (milk); **abgerahmte Milch**, skim-milk; (*b*) *F:* **die Milch a.**, to take the best part, the cream, of sth.

abrainen, *v.tr. sep. Agr:* to separate (one field from another) by a ridge.

Abrakadabra [aˑbraˑkaˑˈdaːbraː], *n.* **-s/.** (*a*) abracadabra; magic keyword; (*b*) twaddle; meaningless talk.

abraken, *v.tr. sep. Nau:* to heave off, float off, get off, refloat, set afloat (stranded ship).

abrändeln, abranden, abrändern, *v.tr. sep.* **1.** to trim, clip, pare, cut, cut down, the edges of (sth.); **eine Münze a.**, to clip a coin. **2.** *Num:* to mill (coin).

Abrandkraut, *n. Bot:* southernwood, *F:* boy's-love, lad's-love.

abranken, *v.tr. sep. Hort:* to thin out (a creeper); *Vit:* to thin out the shoots of (vine).

abrasen[1], *v.tr. sep.* to remove, dig away, the turf from (patch of ground); to strip (lawn).

abrasen[2] **(sich)**, *v.refl. sep.* **1.** to wear oneself out with rushing around. **2.** to exhaust one's rage; to rave oneself out; (*of storm*) to rage itself out, to spend its rage.

abrasieren, *v.tr. sep.* (*p.p.* **abrasiert**) (*a*) to shave off (beard, etc.); (*b*) to raze (building, etc.) to the ground.

Abrasion [abraˑziˈoːn], *f.* **-/-en.** **1.** abrasion, attrition. **2.** *Geol:* coastal erosion.

abraspeln, *v.tr. sep.* to rasp (off) (wood, etc.); to grate off (crust from bread, cheese from lump, etc.).

abraten, *v.sep.* (*strong*) **1.** *v.tr. & i.* (*haben*) **j-m etwas a., j-m von etwas a.**, to advise s.o. against sth.; to dissuade s.o. from sth.; **j-m a., etwas zu tun**, to advise s.o. against doing sth.; to dissuade s.o. from doing sth.; **man riet ihm von der Reise ab**, he was advised not to make the journey; **er rät entschieden ab**, he advises strongly against it; **ich werde versuchen, ihm von diesem Vorhaben abzuraten**, I shall try to put him off this plan. **2.** *v.tr. A:* **j-m sein Geheimnis, seine Gedanken, a.**, to guess s.o.'s secret, s.o.'s thoughts.

abrauchen, *v.i. sep.* (*sein*) to go off in smoke, in vapour, in fumes; (*of liquid*) to (fume and) evaporate; to evaporate completely; **Abrauchen** *n, Ch:* evaporation (accompanied by fuming).

Abrauchraum, *m. Ch:* evaporating chamber.

Abrauchschale, *f. Ch:* evaporating dish.

abrauhen, *v.tr. sep.* to trim; to remove the roughnesses from (sth.); *Metall:* to dress (casting, etc.); to fettle (casting).

Abraum, *m.* **-s/.** **1.** refuse, rubbish, waste matter; remnants, remains; chips, chippings (of wood, stone); rubble (from demolished building, etc.); *For:* waste wood, refuse wood; slashings, loppings; *Min:* rubbish. **2.** (*at colliery, etc.*) dump(-heap), (rubbish-)tip. **3.** *Min:* overburden (of a seam). **4.** *Occ:*=**Abräumung** *q.v. under* **abräumen** II.

Abraumarbeiter, *m. Min:* clearing pitman.

Abraumdecke, *f. Min:* overburden (of a seam).

abraumen, *v.tr. sep. For: Min:*=**abräumen.**

abräumen. I. *v.tr. sep.* (*a*) to clear away, to remove; **(die Speisen, das Geschirr, den Tisch) a.**, to clear the table, to clear away (the things); **Schutt a.**, to clear away, to shift, rubble; *For:* **Abholz a.**, *abs.* **a.**, to clear away loppings, waste wood; (*b*) *Min:* **ein Flöz a.**, to remove the overburden (from a seam); **einen Gang a.**, to clear a gallery.

II. *vbl s.* **Abräumen** *n.*, **Abräumung** *f. in vbl senses; also:* removal.

Abräumer, *m.* **1.** (*pers.*) remover, clearer (of snow, rubbish, etc.); person who clears away (dirty dishes, etc.); cleaner; sweeper. **2.** *Rail:* guard-iron, life-, rail-guard, *U.S:* cowcatcher, pilot.

Abraumgebirge, *n. Min:*=**Abraumdecke.**

Abraumsalze, *n.pl. Geol: Ind:* (salts contained in the) saline deposits above the rock-salt at Staßfurt and elsewhere, *F:* abraum salts.

Abraumstoff, *m.* waste substance, waste material; waste; *pl.* **Abraumstoffe**, waste, refuse; trash.

abraupen, *v.tr. sep.* to clear (fruit-trees, etc.) of caterpillars.

abrauschen, *v.i. sep.* (*sein*) to roar off, away; to

rush away; (*of bird among trees, woman in taffeta dress, etc.*) to rustle away.

abreagieren. I. *v.tr. sep.* (*p.p.* **abreagiert**) *Psy:* to abreact, *F:* to work off (complexes, etc.).

II. *vbl s.* **Abreagieren,** *n. in vbl senses; also:* abreaction.

abrechen, *v.tr. sep.* **1.** to rake (sth.) off, away; to clear (sth.) away with a rake; *Husb:* to rake up (hay, etc.). **2.**=**abharken** 2.

abrechnen. I. *v.sep.* **1.** *v.tr.* (*a*) *Com: etc:* to deduct; **5 Prozent a.,** to take off, allow, deduct, 5%; **seine Unkosten a.,** to deduct one's expenses; **Verluste abgerechnet,** making allowance for losses; **die Tara a.,** to make allowance for the tare; (*b*) *abs. Artil:* to shorten the range; (*c*) to leave (sth.) out of account, out of consideration; **die Lage abgerechnet, ist das Haus ganz gut,** it is quite a good house apart from, except for, its position; **das abgerechnet, könnte ich . . . ,** apart from that, were it not for that, I could . . . . **2.** *v.tr. Com: Fin:* (*a*) **ein Konto a.,** to settle, balance, clear, an account; **Konten a.,** to calculate, reckon (up); (*b*) **j-m einen Betrag a.,** to debit *or* credit a sum to s.o.'s account. **3.** *v.i.* (*haben*) to balance, square, clear, accounts; **wir müssen a.,** we must square accounts, we must square up (with one another); **mit j-m a.,** (i) to settle (accounts) with s.o., to square up with s.o.; (ii) *F:* to pay s.o. out; to get even with s.o.; **ich habe mit ihm abgerechnet,** (i) I've settled, squared up, with him; (ii) *F:* I'm even, quits, with him; we're quits; I've had my own back.

II. *vbl s.* **1. Abrechnen,** *n. in vbl senses.* **2. Abrechnung,** *f.* (*a*)=II. 1; *also: Com: Fin:* (i) deduction (of expenses, losses, etc.); **nach A. der Spesen,** after deduction of charges; when charges have been deducted; (ii) **wöchentliche A.,** weekly settlement (of accounts); **jährliche A.,** annual balance (of business, bank, etc.); **mit j-m A. halten**=**mit j-m abrechnen,** *q.v. under* I. 3; (iii) clearing; *Fin:* **A. der Provinzbanken,** country clearing; (iv) final settlement; liquidation (of account); (v) **einen Betrag in A. bringen,** to debit *or* credit a sum; **im voraus bezahlte Beträge in A. bringen,** to allow for sums paid in advance; **auf A. bezahlter Betrag,** sum paid on account; (*b*) (statement of) account; bill; **j-m eine A. über ein Geschäft erteilen,** to render s.o., present s.o. with, an account in respect of a piece of business; (*c*) *St.Exch:* contract note.

Abrechner, *m. Jur: A:* liquidator.

Abrechnungsblatt, *n.*, **Abrechnungsbogen,** *m. Book-k:* summary sheet.

Abrechnungsbörse, *f. Fin: Com:* clearing-house.

Abrechnungsbüro, *n. Com: Fin:* clearing office; clearing-house.

Abrechnungsgenossenschaft, *f. Com:* clearing-house (*esp.* of the German Booksellers' Association).

Abrechnungshaus, *n. A:* clearing-house, *esp.* railway clearing-house.

Abrechnungsintendantur, *f. Mil:* headquarters accounts office.

Abrechnungskontor, *n. Fin:* clearing-house.

Abrechnungsstelle, *f. Fin:* clearing-house; *Mil: etc:* accounts office.

Abrechnungstag, *m. St.Exch:* settling day, account day.

Abrechnungsverfahren, *n. Fin:* clearing (procedure).

Abrechnungsverkehr, *m. Fin:* clearing (business).

Abrechte, *f. Tex:* wrong side, reverse, back (of a material).

Abrede, *f.* **1.** denial; **etwas in A. stellen,** to contest, dispute, question (point, right, etc.). **2.** agreement, understanding, pact, contract; **mit j-m eine A. treffen,** to come to an agreement, an understanding, with s.o.; **der A. gemäß handeln,** to keep to the terms of the agreement; **das ist wider, gegen, die A.,** that contravenes, is contrary to, breaks, infringes, our agreement; *A:* **einmütig A. nehmen,** to agree unanimously, to be of one accord.

abreden, *v.sep.* **1.** *v.tr. & i.* (*haben*) **mit j-m a.,** to come to an agreement, an understanding, with s.o.; to make a pact, a covenant, with s.o.; **mit j-m etwas a.,** to arrange sth. with s.o.; to come to an agreement, an understanding, with s.o. about sth.; *A:* **einen Kauf a.,** to make, strike, a bargain; *A:* **Tag und Stunde a.,** to appoint, fix, the day and hour (for meeting, etc.); *A:* **die abgeredeten Punkte,** the articles (of an agreement); *A:* **ein abgeredetes Spiel,** a preconcerted, clandestinely arranged, business; *F:* a put-up job. **2.** *v.tr.* **j-n von etwas a.,** to dissuade s.o. from sth.; to talk s.o. out of sth.

Abredung, *f. occ.*=**Abrede** 2, **Verabredung.**

Abrégé [abre·ˈzeː], *n.* **-s/-s. 1.** abridgment, précis, summary, epitome, abstract. **2.** *Mus:* tracker (of organ).

abregen, *v.tr. sep. F:* **sich a.,** to calm down; **reg dich ab!** calm down!

abregieren [abre·ˈziːrən], *v.tr. insep.* to abridge, epitomize, cut down (book, etc.); to summarize (speech, etc.).

abregnen, *v.sep.* **1.** *v.tr.* (*usu. only in p.p.*) **die Blüten sind abgeregnet (worden),** the rain has stripped off the blossom. **2.** *v.tr. Mil. Av:* **Kampfstoffe a.,** to spray gas from aircraft. **3.** *v.impers.* **es hat (sich) abgeregnet,** the rain has stopped, is over, it has stopped raining; it has rained itself out.

abreiben. I. *v.tr. sep.* (*strong*) **1.** to rub (sth.) off; to scrape (sth.) off; to scour off (rust, etc.); *Cu:* to grate off (crust from bread, etc.). **2.** (*a*) to scrape (sth.); to scour (sth.); to rub (sth.) smooth; **Holz mit Sandpapier a.,** to smooth wood with sandpaper, to sandpaper wood; *see also* **Bimsstein;** *Paint:* **die Farbe, eine Wand, a.,** to rub down the paint, a wall; *Constr:* **den Verputz a.,** to float the plaster; (*b*) to rub (s.o.) down; to rub down (horse); to give (s.o., horse) a rub-down; **j-n, sich, kalt a.,** to give s.o., oneself, a cold rub-down; **j-n, sich, naß a.,** to sponge s.o., oneself, down, to give s.o., oneself, a sponge-down; **ein Pferd mit einem Strohwisch a.,** to wisp down a horse; (*c*) *F:* **j-n a.**=**j-m eine Abreibung geben,** *q.v. under* II. 2 (*b*); (*d*) *Nau:* **ein Schiff a.,** to clean a ship's bottom, to hog a ship. **3.** (*a*) to wear (sth.) away, down (by rubbing); to rub (cloth); to abrade (metal, etc.); to chafe, rub (a rope); to chafe (the skin); to gall, graze, rub off (the skin); (*b*) to grind (sth.) (to powder); to triturate (sth.). **4. sich abreiben,** to be worn away by friction; to wear down, away; (*of cloth*) to rub; (*of metal, etc.*) to abrade, become abraded; (*of rope*) to chafe, rub; (*of skin*) to get chafed; to get rubbed off.

II. *vbl s.* **1. Abreiben,** *n. in vbl senses; also:* abrasion, attrition. **2. Abreibung,** *f.* (*a*)=II. 1; (*b*) rub-down; **kalte A.,** cold rub-down; *F:* **die Nachricht wirkte auf ihn wie eine kalte A.,** the news came to him like a cold douche; **nasse A.,** sponge-down; *F:* **j-m eine A. geben,** (i) to give s.o. a dressing-down; (ii) to give s.o. a beating, a thrashing, *F:* a licking, a drubbing.

abreifen[1], *v.tr. sep.* to unhoop (cask, etc.).

abreifen[2], *v.tr. sep. Metalw:* to file, file off, take off.

Abreise, *f.* departure, setting out, starting (**nach,** for); going away (on a journey); **seine A. von Rom,** his departure from Rome; **vor der A.,** before leaving, departing, going away; before one's departure; **er stand gerade vor der A. nach Berlin,** he was on the point of starting, leaving, for Berlin; **nach meiner A.,** after I have gone; after I had gone; after my departure.

abreisen, *v.i. sep.* (*sein*) to depart, leave, start; to take one's departure; to set out (on a journey); to go off; to go away; **von Rom a.,** to leave, go away from, Rome; **nach Köln a.,** to leave, set out, for Cologne; **wir reisen morgen ab,** we leave, start, tomorrow; **wir reisen mit dem nächsten Schiff ab,** we are sailing, leaving, by the next boat.

Abreißblock, *m.* tear-off pad (of paper).

Abreißbremse, *f. Veh:* automatic braking device (for trailer that has broken away from towing vehicle).

abreißen, *v. sep.* (*strong*) I. *v.tr.* **1.** to tear (sth.) off; to pull (sth.) off; to rip off (bandage, paper, label, etc.); to wrench off (handle, lock, etc.); **ein Blatt vom Block a.,** to tear a sheet off the pad; **den Kalender a.,** to tear the (out-of-date) page off the calendar; **die Tapete von einer Wand a.,** to strip a wall. **2.** (*a*) to pull down (house, etc.); to demolish (house, bridge, fortifications, etc.); to dismantle (fortifications); (*b*) *Hyd.E:* to unprime (siphon). **3.** (*a*) to break (off), snap (thread, string, shoelace, etc.); (*b*) *South G.Dial:*=**zerreißen. 4.** *occ:* to trace, sketch, outline (plan, pattern, etc.).

II. **abreißen,** *v.i.* (*sein*) **1.** (*occ.* **sich abreißen**) (*of thg*) to break off, away; to break loose; to snap off; to become detached; (*of parts*) to come apart, asunder, *F:* adrift. **2.** (*a*) (*of activity, etc.*) to cease (suddenly); to come to an end; to be cut short; to be interrupted; (*of patience, etc.*) to give out; **die Geduld riß ihm ab,** his patience was exhausted, gave out, was at an end; he was at the end of his patience; **das Gespräch riß (plötzlich) ab,** the conversation stopped (abruptly), broke off (suddenly); *F:* **es reißt nicht ab,** it goes on interminably, for ever; there's no end to it; **das Briefschreiben reißt bei ihr nicht ab,** she is eternally, for ever, writing letters; there's no end to her letter-writing; (*b*) *Av:* **Geschwindigkeit, bei der die Strömung abreißt,** speed at which stalling occurs, stalling speed. **3.** *Veh:* (*of trailer*) to break away from the towing vehicle.

III. *vbl s.* **Abreißen** *n.*, *occ.* **Abreißung** *f. in vbl senses; also:* demolition (of house, bridge, fortifications, etc.); dismantlement (of fortifications); cessation; interruption (of an activity); *Rad.-A:* quenching (of discharge in Geiger counter); *Av:* **Abreißen der Strömung,** stalling; **Geschwindigkeit, bei der das Abreißen der Strömung eintritt,** stalling speed.

IV. *p.p. & a.* **abgerissen,** *in vbl senses; esp.* **1.** shabby, worn-out (clothes); *F:* **ich bin völlig a.,** I am (very) badly off for clothes; I look shabby; I haven't a thing fit to wear. **2.** (*a*) abrupt, disconnected, jerky (style, speech); incoherent (conversation); **abgerissene Sätze,** disjointed sentences; incoherent phrases; (*b*) **abgerissener Atem,** irregular breathing; gasping breath **3.** *Her:* erased. **4.** *adv.* disconnectedly, disjointedly, incoherently; (to speak) brokenly.

Abreißer, *m. Tls:* scriber, scribing-awl, -tool.

Abreißfeder, *f.* **1.** *Mch:Mec.E:* return-spring, drawback-spring; antagonistic spring; retractile spring. **2.** *Av:* rip-cord spring (of parachute).

Abreißfunken, *m. El.E:* break-spark.

Abreißhebel, *m. I.C.E:* interrupter.

Abreißkalender, *m.* block-calendar, tear-off calendar.

Abreißklinke, *f. El.E:* contact-breaking catch.

Abreißknopf, *m.* **1.** *Av:* rip-cord button (of parachute). **2.** *Exp:* button of the igniter cord (of grenade).

Abreißrolle, *f.* tear-off roll (of paper).

Abreißschnur, *f.* **1.** *Av:* breaking-cord; rip-cord (of parachute). **2.** *Exp:* igniter cord, pull-out cord (of grenade).

Abreißspannung, *f. Mec:* tearing stress.

Abreißvorrichtung, *f.* **1.** *Av:* breaking device, rip device (of parachute). **2.** *I.C.E:* make-and-break. **3.** *Exp:* firing device (of grenade).

Abreißzettel, *m. & pl.*=**Abreißblock.**

Abreißzünder, *m.* **1.** *I.C.E:* make-and-break igniter, electric igniter. **2.** *Exp:* friction igniter.

Abreißzündung, *f. I.C.E:* coil ignition, make-and-break ignition.

abreiten, *v.sep.* (*strong*). **1.** *v.tr.* (*a*) **ein Landgut, usw., a.,** to ride over an estate, etc.; (*b*) *Mil:* (*of general, etc.*) **die Front a.,** to ride past the troops; (*c*) *Nau:* **einen Sturm, das Wetter, a.,** to ride out a storm, a gale. **2.** to override (horse). **3.** *v.i.* (*sein*) (*a*) to ride away, off; **vom Wege a.,** to ride off the road; (*b*) *Ven:* (*of large birds*) to fly off; to rise.

Abreiter, *m.*=**Rüttelsieb.**

abrennen. I. *v.sep.* (*conj. like* **rennen**) **1.** *v.tr.* (*a*) **die ganze Stadt (nach etwas) a.,** to scour the whole town (for sth.); (*b*) **die ganze Strecke a.,** to cover the whole distance, the whole course. **2. sich** *dat.* **die Schuhsohlen a., sich** *dat.* **(fast) die Beine a.,** to scurry, rush, around; *F:* to run oneself off one's legs; to wear one's legs to stumps. **3. sich abrennen,** (*a*) to wear oneself out with running *or* racing; (*b*) *F:* to scurry, rush, around. **4.** *v.i.* (*sein*) (*a*) to run off, away; to race off, away; (*b*) *Rac:* to start.

II. *vbl s.* **Abrennen,** *n. in vbl senses; also: Rac:* start.

abresten, *v.tr. sep. Brew:* to decant; to clear (liquid) of dregs.

Abrichte- *see* **Abricht-.**

abrichten. I. *v.tr. sep.* **1.** (*a*) to train (animal); to break (in) (horse, foal); **ein Pferd zum Ziehen a.,** to break a horse to harness; **einen Hund auf Hühner, auf die Hühnerjagd, a.,** to train a dog to retrieve game birds; *Ven:* **einen Jagdhund a.,** (i) to break in, train, a retriever, hound, etc.; (ii) to enter a (fox-)hound; **einen Falken a.,** to train, man, a hawk; (*b*) **j-n a.,** to drill, coach, s.o.; *Mil. & F:* to teach s.o. the drill; *Adm. & F:* to indoctrinate s.o.; **j-n auf etwas, zu etwas, a.,** to drill s.o. in sth.; to teach s.o. how to do sth.; **er ist gut (darauf) abgerichtet,** he has learned the knack of it; he knows his cue; *Mil. & F:* he knows the drill. **2.** *Tchn:* to smooth (surface); to dress (surface); to plane (wood); to planish (metal); to face (metal, etc.); *Constr:* to level (wall). **3.** *Mec.E: etc:* (*a*) to adjust to fit (parts); to set (apparatus, tool, etc.); (*b*) to true (sth.) up; to true, dress (grindstone).

II. *vbl s.* **Abrichten** *n.*, **Abrichtung** *f. in vbl senses; also: Mec.E: etc:* adjustment.

Abrichter, *m.* **1.** (*a*) trainer (of animals); (*b*) horse-breaker, rough-rider. **2.** *Tchn:* (*a*) (*pers.*) adjuster; truer(-up) (of grindstones, etc.); dresser (of grindstones); (*b*) adjusting tool *or* device; truing-tool; truing device; dressing tool (for grindstones); (*c*)=**Abricht(hobel)maschine.**

Abrichthammer, *m. Tls:* planishing hammer; (large) dressing hammer.

Abrichthobel, *m. Tls: Carp:* smoothing-plane.

Abricht(hobel)maschine, *f. Carp: Metalw:* (smooth-)planing machine.

Abrichtkunst, *f.* (*a*) (art of) training animals; (*b*) art of the horse-breaker.

Abrichtlauge, *f. Soapm:* second liquor; weak caustic liquor.

Abrichtschleifmaschine, *f. Mec.E:* disc grinder.

Abrichtstock, *m. Metalw:* planishing anvil.

Abrichtvorrichtung, *f. Mec.E:* truing device.

Abrieb, *m.* **-s/. 1.** abrasion, attrition; *Mec.E:* (**mechanischer**) **A.,** abrasion, wear. **2.** rubbings; (*from grinding*) grit, dust, grindings; *Coal-Min: Cokem:* breeze, fines.

abriegeln. I. *v.tr. sep.* **1.** to bolt (door, window); to bar (door); to bolt, bar, the door of (room). **2.** (*a*) to barricade, *Mil:* to block (road); (*b*) to cut off, isolate (area, etc.); (*c*) *Mil:* to seal off (sector); *Artil:* to box-barrage (sector, etc.); (*d*) *Mil:* **einen Angriff a.,** to contain an attack. **3.** *Constr:* to fit (sth.) with cross-bars *or* rails.

II. *vbl s.* **Abriegeln** *n.*, **Abriegelung** *f. in vbl senses; also:* isolation (of an area, etc.).

Abriegelungsfeuer, *n. Artil:* box-barrage; defensive barrage.

abrieseln, *v.i. sep.* (*sein*) **1.** (*of liquid*) to trickle down; (*of rain*) to drizzle down. **2.** (*of crumbling mortar, etc.*) to powder off.

abriffeln, *v.tr. sep.* (*a*) to remove (seeds from flax, etc.) with a ripple; (*b*) to pill, ripple (flax).

abrinden, *v.tr. sep.*=**entrinden.**

abrindern, *v.i. sep.* (*haben*) (*of cow*) to go off heat.

abringen[1], *v.tr. sep.* to remove, detach, the ring(s) from (sth.).

abringen[2], *v.tr. sep.* (*strong*) **j-m, etwas** *dat.*, **etwas a.,** to wrest sth. from s.o., from sth.; to wrench sth. from s.o.; to wring sth. from, out of, s.o.; to gain sth. from s.o. after a (bitter) struggle; **dem Meer abgerungenes Land,** land wrested, won back, from the sea; **j-m ein Geständnis a.,** to wring, extort, a confession from s.o., *F:* to screw a confession out of s.o.; **sich ein Geständnis a.,** to force oneself into a confession.

abrinnen, *v.i. sep.* (*strong*) (*sein*) (*of liquid*) (*a*) to run off; (*b*) to flow off; (*b*) to run down; to flow down; (*c*) to trickle away.

abrispen, *v.sep. Husb:* **1.** *v.tr.* to remove the panicles from (oats, etc.). **2.** *v.i.* (*sein*) (*of oats*) to drop out of the panicles.

Abriß, *m.* **1.** (*a*) draft, design, sketch; skeleton, outline; (*b*) *Surv:* lay-out. **2.** summary; abstract; epitome; précis (of document, etc.); compendium (of a science); digest (of legal problems, etc.); **A. der organischen Chemie,** a concise organic chemistry; **A. der deutschen Literaturgeschichte,** a short history of German literature; outline(s) of German literature.

Abrißpunkt, *m. Surv:* bench-mark.

Abrißzone, *f. Bot:* zone of abscission.

Abritt, *m.* riding away, off; departure (on horseback).

Abrivent [abri·ˈvɛnt], *m. & n.* **-s/-s. 1.** (wind-)screen; wind-break. **2.** *Mil:* sentry-box; (look-out man's) shelter.

Abrogation [apro·ga·tsĭˈoːn], *f.* **-/-en,** (*a*) abrogation, rescission, repeal (of law, etc.); (*b*) *Com:* cancellation (of order).

abrogieren [ap-, abro·ˈgiːrən], *v.tr. insep. a*) to abrogate, annul, repeal, rescind (law, decree); (*b*) *Com:* to cancel (order).

abrohren, *v.tr. sep. Constr:* to line (wall, ceiling) with reeds.

Abrollapparat, *m.* reeling machine; *Nau: etc:* paying-out device (for cable, etc.); reel.

Abrollbock, *m. Rail:* tipping bracket.

Abrollebene, *f. Mec:* rolling plane.

abrollen, *v. sep.* I. *v.tr.* **1.** (*a*) to roll (sth.) off, away; (*b*) to cart away (goods); to convey (goods) away; (*c*) to roll down (stone, etc.); (*d*) to unroll (blind, map, etc.); to unwind, unreel, wind off (cable, thread, etc.); to reel off (thread); to uncoil (wire, etc.); **ein Kabel, ein Tau, a. lassen,** to pay out a cable, a rope; **einen Film a. lassen,** to run off a film. **2. sich abrollen,** (*a*) (*of map, etc.*) to come unrolled, to unroll; (*of cable, thread, etc.*) to come unwound, to unwind; (*b*) to unfold, to develop; **das Drama rollt sich vor unseren Augen ab,** the drama unfolds before our eyes.

II. **abrollen,** *v.i.* (*sein*) **1.** (*of stone, etc.*) to roll down, off; to roll away. **2.** (*a*) (*of wheeled vehicle*) to move off, start; (*of train*) to move off; to steam away, off; *F:* to pull out (of the station); (*b*) *Av:* (*of aircraft*) to taxi off. **3.** (*a*) (*of time*) to pass, elapse; **die Jahre rollten ab,** the years rolled by, rolled on; (*b*) **die Ereignisse rollten in rascher Folge ab,** the events followed quickly upon each other. **4.**=**sich abrollen** *q.v.* I. 2 (*b*). **5.** *Ind:* (*of manufactured goods, etc.*) to come off, roll off, the conveyor-belt, the assembly-line.

III. *vbl s.* **1. Abrollen,** *n. in vbl senses; also:* development (of drama, etc.); departure (of wheeled vehicle); sequence (of events). **2. Abrollung,** *f.* (*a*) *occ.*=III. 1; (*b*) *Mec.E:* rolling movement *or* action.

Abrollspule, *f. Tex:* revolving *or* rolling bobbin.

Abrollvorrichtung, *f.*=**Abrollapparat.**

Abrollwalze, *f. Metalw:* (*in rolling-mill*) pull-off roll.

Abrome, *f.* **-/-n.** *Bot:* abroma.

Abromfaser, *f. Com:* Indian hemp.

Abrotanum, Abrotonum [aˈbrota·num, aˈbro-to·num], *n.* **-s/.** *Bot:* abrotanum, southernwood, boy's-love, lad's-love, old man.

abrotzen, *v.i. sep.* (*sein*) *Nau: P:* (*of ship*) to sink, to go down; to founder (*in bad weather*).

abrubbeln, *v.tr. sep. F:*=**abreiben** I. 2.

abrücken. I. *v.sep.* **1.** *v.tr.* (*a*) to move, push, (sth.) away; **die Stühle vom Tisch a.,** to draw back, pull back, push back, set back, the chairs from the table; **den Schrank von der Wand a.,** to move, pull, push, the cupboard away from the wall; (*b*) *Print:* **die Zeilen (voneinander) a.,** to lead the lines. **2.** *v.i.* (*sein*) (*a*) *Mil:* (*of troops*) to depart, move off; to march away; to retire; (*b*) *F:* (*of pers.*) to clear out; to push off; to sheer off; (*c*) **von j-m, etwas, a.,** to draw away, draw back, from s.o., sth., (i) (*of seated pers.*) to move, push, one's chair further away from s.o., sth.; (ii) to dissociate oneself from s.o., sth.

II. *vbl s.* **Abrücken,** *n. in vbl senses; also: Mil:* departure; retirement.

abrudern, *v.sep.* **1.** *v.i.* (*sein*) to row off, away. **2.** *v.tr.* to row (boat) away; to push (boat) out (from the shore).

Abruf, *m.* **1.** recall (of general, ambassador, etc.); calling away (of s.o., from post, etc.); *Adm:* **Beamte auf A.,** official subject to recall; official whose appointment can be terminated without notice. **2.** (*a*) *Com: Fin:* calling in (of sum advanced, etc.); call (for funds); **Gelder auf A.,** money on, at, call; (*b*) *Com:* request for delivery (of goods); **Lieferung erfolgt auf A., Waren sind lieferbar auf A.,** goods are deliverable on call.

Abrufauftrag, *m. Com:* order for goods to be delivered on demand; order with provision for staggered deliveries; *U.S:* make-and-take order.

abrufen. I. *v.tr. sep.* (*strong*) **1.** (*a*) to recall (s.o.); to call, summon (s.o.) back; to call (s.o.) away; **einen General, einen Gesandten, a.,** to recall a general, an ambassador; **j-n von der Arbeit, von seinem Posten, a.,** to call s.o. away from his work, from his post; **der Tod, Gott, hat ihn abgerufen,** death has called him away, has taken him (from us); God has called, summoned, him home; (**vom Tode**) **abgerufen werden,** to die; to depart this life; *A:* **j-n a. lassen,** to send for s.o.; (*b*) *Ven:* to call off (hounds). **2.** (*a*) *Fin:* to call up (capital); to call in (sum advanced, etc.); (*b*) *Com:* to request delivery of (previously ordered goods). **3.** (*a*) to announce (sth.); to proclaim (sth.); *Rail:* **einen Zug a.,** to announce a train; *A:* (*of watchman*) **die Stunden a.,** to cry, call, the hours; (*b*) *v.i.* (*haben*) to give the last call. **4.** *A:* **das Schiff läßt sich a.,** the ship is within hailing distance, within hail. **5.** *v.i.* (*haben*) *Tp:* (*esp. Mil:*) to ring off.

II. *vbl s.* **Abrufen** *n.*, **Abrufung** *f. in vbl senses; also:* recall; summons to return; *Com:* request for delivery (of goods); announcement (of trains, etc.). *Cp.* **Abruf.**

Abrufungsbrief, *m.*, **Abrufungsschreiben,** *n.*, *Dipl:* letters of recall.

Abrufungsschuß, *m. Nau: A:* (gun fired as) recall signal.

abrühren, *v.tr. sep. Cu:* **die Milch mit einem Ei a.** to beat an egg into the milk.

abrunden. I. *v.tr. sep.* **1.** (*a*) to round (sth.) (off); to make (sth.) round; **einen Winkel, eine Ecke, sein Vermögen, sein Gut, a.,** to round off an angle, a corner, one's fortune, one's estate; (*b*) **einen Betrag nach oben, nach unten, a.,** to bring an amount up to, down to, round figures; **einen Betrag auf Zehner a.,** to round off an amount to the nearest ten. **2.** *Tchn:* **einen Schleifstein a.,** to true (up), dress, a grindstone; **eine Linse a.,** to nibble a lens; **einen Getriebezahn a.,** to chamfer a gear-tooth.

II. *vbl s.* **1. Abrunden,** *n. in vbl senses; also: Tchn:* chamfer(ing) (of gear-tooth). **2. Abrundung,** *f.* (*a*)=II. 1; (*b*) roundness; sphericity (of globe, etc.); careful finish (of style).

III. *p.p. & a.* **abgerundet,** *in vbl senses; esp.* **abgerundete Leistung,** *Mus:* **abgerundetes Spiel,** finished performance. *See also* **Knierohr.**

abrupfen, *v.tr. sep.* **1.** to pluck (hairs, feathers, etc.); to pluck out (hair); to pluck off (leaf from plant). **2.** to pluck (poultry); *F:* to fleece (s.o.).

abrupt [ap-, abˈrupt], *a.* abrupt (style, speech, etc.); short, blunt, brusque (answer); *adv.* abruptly.

Abruption [abruptsĭˈoːn], *f.* **-/-en. 1.** breaking away, off (of part). **2.** breaking off, abrupt ending (of speech).

Abrusbohnen, *f.pl. Bot:* jequirity beans, rosary-peas, crab's-eyes.

abrußecht, *a. Leath: etc:* (article) from which the colour does not rub off; (article, colour) fast to rubbing; non-crocking (article, colour).

abrußen, *v.i. sep.* (*haben*) *Leath: etc:* (*of colour*) to rub off, to crock; (*of article*) to lose its colour through rubbing, to crock; **diese Handschuhe rußen ab,** the colour rubs off, comes off, these gloves.

abrüsten. I. *v.sep.* **1.** *v.tr.* (*a*) *Constr: Civ.E:* to remove the scaffolding from (house, etc.); **einen Bogen a.,** to strike, remove, the centring of, to discentre, an arch; (*b*) to take down, dismantle, disassemble (machine); to unrig, strike (shears); (*c*) to take the equipment off (sth., troops); to lay up, pay off, de-store, de-ammunition (ship); to put (ship) out of commission; to unrig (sailing-ship); to dismantle (aircraft); to disarm (military *or* naval forces). **2.** *v.i.* (*haben*) to disarm; to disband one's naval *or* military forces.

II. *vbl s.* **Abrüsten** *n.*, **Abrüstung** *f. in vbl senses; also:* (*a*) *Constr: Civ.E:* removal of the scaffolding, of the centring of an arch; dismantlement (of machine); (*b*) disarmament.

Abrüstungskonferenz, *f.* disarmament conference.

Abrüstwagen, *m. Mil:* break-down lorry, *U.S:* wrecker.

abrutschen. I. *v.i. sep.* (*sein*) **1.** to slip off, down; to slide off, down; to slither off, down. **2.** *Av:* (*of aircraft*) **seitlich a.,** to side-slip, to skid; to stall; **nach hinten a.,** to tail-slide. **3.** *Geol: etc:* (*of earth, ground*) to slip. **4.** *F:* to come down in the world.

II. *vbl s.* **Abrutschen,** *n. in vbl senses; also: Av:* **seitliches A.,** side-slip, skid; stall, stalling; **A. nach hinten,** tail-slide; *Geol: etc:* (land)slip.

abrütteln, *v.tr. sep.* to shake (sth.) off.

Abruzzen, die. *Pr.n.pl. Geog:* the Abruzzi.

absäbeln, *v.tr. sep.* **1.** to cut (sth.) off with a sabre. **2.** *F:* to hack off, slash off (piece of bread, meat, etc.).

absacken[1]. I. *v.tr. sep.* **1.** *A:* to unload (beast of burden). **2.** (*a*) to put (corn, etc.) into sacks; to sack (corn, etc.); to bag (coal, ore, etc.); to pack (goods) in bags; (*b*) to enclose (sth.) in a bag *or* capsule. **3. sich absacken,** *Biol:* to encyst itself, to become encysted.

II. *vbl s.* **Absacken** *n.*, *occ.* **Absackung** *f. in vbl senses; also: Biol:* encystation, encystment.

absacken[2]. I. *v.i. sep.* (*sein*) **1.** to sink down; (*a*) (*of ground*) to subside, sink; (*of loose mass*) to settle (down); to sink down; to shrink (in volume); *Nau:* **das Wasser sackt ab,** the tide is falling; (*b*) (*of ship, aircraft in sea*) to sink, to go down; (*c*) *Av:* (*of aircraft*) to pancake; to stall; **wegen Schwanzlastigkeit a.,** to pitch down by the tail. **2.** (*of boat*) to drift with the stream, with the current. **3.** *F:* (*of pers.*) to succumb; to go under.

II. *vbl s.* **Absacken** *n.*, *occ.* **Absackung** *f. in vbl senses; also:* subsidence (of ground).

Absackmaschine, *f. Ind:* sacking machine; bagging machine.

Absackwaage, *f. Ind:* bagging and weighing machine.

Absage, *f.* **1.** announcement that meeting, etc., will not take place; cancellation, calling off (of meeting, etc.). **2.** refusal, declining (of an invitation); **er hat eine A. geschickt,** he has written to say that he cannot come, he has sent an apology (for not accepting the invitation).

3. *A:* **A. an j-n,** renunciation, repudiation, of s.o.; **eine A. an die Frauen,** a declaration of enmity against women. 4. *W.Tel:* lead-out, *F:* sign-off (by announcer).

Absagebrief, *m.* 1. letter cancelling an engagement; letter refusing, declining, an invitation; letter of apology (for not accepting an invitation). 2. *A:* letter breaking off friendly relations; letter of defiance.

absagen, *v.sep.* 1. *v.tr.* (*a*) to cancel, call off (visit, engagement, meeting, etc.); **das Konzert ist abgesagt,** the concert is cancelled, is off; **eine Einladung a.,** to cancel an invitation; (*b*) **j-m die Freundschaft a.,** to break with s.o. 2. *v.i.* (*haben*) (*a*) to announce that one cannot come, cannot keep an engagement; **ich habe (bei) dem Zahnarzt abgesagt,** I have cancelled my appointment with the dentist; **(auf eine Einladung) a.,** to decline, refuse, an invitation; to say that one is unable to attend; (*b*) **seinen Gästen a. (lassen),** to put off one's guests. 3. *v.i.* (*haben*) (*a*) **j-m, etwas** *dat.*, **a.,** to renounce, repudiate, s.o., sth.; **dem Vergnügen, der Welt, dem Teufel, a.,** to renounce pleasure, the world, the devil; **einer Lehre** (*occ.* **eine Lehre**) **a.,** to repudiate, renounce, a doctrine; **seinem Glauben a.,** to abjure, renounce, one's faith; (*b*) *A:* **j-m a.,** to declare oneself at enmity with s.o.; to defy s.o.; to set s.o. at defiance; **abgesagter Feind,** declared, avowed, sworn, enemy; **abgesagter Feind der Kirche,** open, professed, enemy of the Church.

absägen, *v.tr. sep.* 1. to saw off (branch, piece of wood, etc.); *F:* **den Ast a., auf dem man sitzt,** to bring about one's own downfall, *F:* to saw off the branch one is sitting on. 2. *F:* to dismiss (s.o.); to give (s.o.) the sack, *U.S. & F.:* to axe (s.o.); to get rid of (s.o.); **einen Beamten a.,** to discharge, *F:* to sack, an official.

Absageschein, *m. Com: South G.Dial:* protest (of a bill of exchange).

Absageschreiben, *n.*=**Absagebrief.**

Absagesignal, *n. Rail:* 'train cancelled' signal.

absahnen, *v.tr. sep.* to cream, skim (milk).

absaigern, *v.tr. sep. Surv:*=**abloten.**

absatteln, *v.tr. sep.* 1. (*a*) to unsaddle (horse); *abs.* to off-saddle; (*b*) to take the pack-saddle off, to unsaddle (pack-horse, mule). 2. *Civ.E:* to support (girder, etc.) (temporarily) with a saddle.

Absatteltrupp, *m. Mil:* unsaddling party (at horse-ferry, etc.).

absättigen. I. *v.tr. sep. Ch:* to saturate (solution, acid); to neutralize (acid).

II. *vbl s.* **Absättigen** *n.*, **Absättigung** *f. Ch:* saturation (of solution, acid); neutralization (of acid).

Absatz, *m.* 1. interruption; intermission; pause; break; breaking off; **ohne A.,** without interruption, uninterruptedly. 2. *Print: etc:* (*a*) paragraph, *F:* para; **in diesem A. behauptet der Verfasser, daß . . .,** in this paragraph the author maintains that . . . ; (*b*) break (between paragraphs); new paragraph; **mit A.,** starting a new paragraph, a new line; **einen A. machen,** to start a new line; **'ohne A.',** 'run on'; (*in dictating*) **'A.',** 'new paragraph'; 'new line', 'next line'; (*c*) sub-paragraph (of statutory order, etc.); (*d*) *A:* **A. (in einem Lied),** stanza, stave. 3. **A. (an einem Berge),** shelf (in a mountain); **A. im Gelände,** (natural) terrace. 4. *Tchn:* (*a*) *Arch: Mec.E: Physiol:* offset; *Arch:* set-off (of wall, etc.); (*b*) *Arch:* landing (of stairs), stair-head, *F:* floor; (*c*) *Civ.E: Constr:* step (of embankment, of foot of wall); (*d*) *Civ.E:* berm; set-off; bench (with footpath); *Fort:* berm, foreland; (*e*) *Min:* niche, landing-place; *A:* shamble (in adit). 5. heel (of boot, shoe); **Schuhe mit hohen, mit niedrigen, Absätzen,** high-heeled, low-heeled, shoes; **einen A. aufnageln,** to heel (a shoe); **sich auf dem A. herumdrehen,** to turn on one's heel; *Geog: F:* **der A. (am Stiefel Italien),** the heel of Italy. 6. *Com:* sale, disposal (of goods); **Ware mit sicherem A.,** goods certain to sell, with a ready sale, with a ready market; **dieser Artikel hat, findet, reißenden A.,** this article is in great demand, sells very rapidly, *F:* sells like hot cakes; **für einen Artikel schnellen A. finden,** to find a quick sale for an article; **diese Ware hat nur kleinen A., findet schlechten A., findet schwer A.,** there is little demand, little sale, for these goods; **das findet gar keinen A.,** that does not sell at all; there is no demand at all for that; **großer A., kleiner Nutzen,** small profits, quick returns. 7. deposit, sediment (from liquid); *Geol:* **mechanische Absätze,** mechanical deposits.

Absatzahle, *f. Bootm:* pegging-awl.

Absatzaufnagelmaschine, *f. Bootm:* heeling machine.

Absatzausglasmaschine, *f. Bootm:* heel-scouring machine.

Absatzbar, *f.* heel bar (in large store, etc.).

Absatzbassin, *n. Ind:* settling tank.

Absatzbereich, *m.*=**Absatzgebiet.**

Absatzeisen, *n. Bootm:* heel-tip.

absatzfähig, *a.* saleable, marketable (goods).

Absatzfeld, *n.*=**Absatzgebiet.**

Absatzferkel, *n.* weaner, weanling (pig).

Absatzfleck, *m. Bootm:* lift (of heel); heel-tap.

Absatzfräser, *m. Bootm:* 1. *Machine-Tls:* (*a*) heel-trimmer; (*b*) heel-trimming machine. 2. (*pers.*) heel-trimmer.

Absatzfront, *f. Bootm:* heel breast.

Absatzgebiet, *n. Com:* marketing area, selling area, sales area, trading area, *U.S:* territory; **neue Absatzgebiete eröffnen, erschließen,** to open up new marketing areas, new markets; to find new export markets, new outlets for exports.

Absatzgefäß, *n. Ind:* settling tank.

Absatzgenossenschaft, *f.* co-operative marketing society.

Absatzgestein, *n. Geol:* aqueous rock, sedimentary rock; stratified rock.

Absatzglasmaschine, *f. Bootm:* heel-scouring machine.

Absatzhonorar, *n. Publ:* royalty.

absätzig, *a. Min:* **die Erzführung ist a.,** the lode is broken, gives out, peters out, goes dead.

Absatzkanal, *m. Com:* channel for trade; marketing channel; channel of distribution; opportunity for sales; outlet (for export goods).

Absatzkosten, *pl. Com:* distribution costs.

Absatzkreis, *m.*=**Absatzgebiet.**

Absatzlenkung, *f. Com:* control(ling) of the market.

Absatzmarkt, *m.*=**Absatzgebiet.**

Absatzmöglichkeit, *f. Com:* opening (for sales, for trade).

Absatzmuffe, *f. Mec.E: etc:* reducing coupling, reducer (for pipes).

Absatzort, *m. Bootm:*=**Absatzahle.**

Absatzpflock, *m. Bootm:* (wooden) heel-peg.

Absatzplatte, *f. Bootm:* heel-tap.

Absatzquelle, *f.*=**Absatzkanal.**

Absatzreparatur, *f. Bootm:* heel repair, heeling.

Absatzsäge, *f. Tls:* =**Absetzsäge 1.**

Absatzsporn, *m. Ski:* heel-plate (on ski-boot).

Absatzstatistik, *f. Com:* marketing statistics, statistics of sales; sales-chart(s).

Absatzstockung, *f. Com:* stagnation of the market; flagging, slowing down, of sales.

Absatzstück, *n. Mec.E: etc:*=**Absatzmuffe.**

Absatztank, *m. Ind:* settling tank.

Absatzvorbaumaschine, *f. Bootm:* heel-building machine.

Absatzweg, *m.*=**Absatzkanal.**

absatzweise, *adv.* (*a*) at intervals; step by step; (*b*) *Print: etc:* paragraph by paragraph; one paragraph at a time.

Absatzzeichen, *n. Print:* paragraph mark.

Absauberer, *m. Min: Civ.E: etc:* screen jigger.

absäubern, *v.tr. sep.*=**säubern.**

absäuern, *v.tr. sep.* to acidify; to acidulate; to sour.

absaufen, *v.sep.* (*strong*) 1. *v.tr.* (*of pers., animal*) to drink off (part of liquid); to drink off, drain (whole of liquid). 2. *v.i.* (*sein*) (*a*) *F: Nau:* (*of ship*) to sink, go down, go to the bottom; to founder (in bad weather); *Av:* (*of aircraft*) to sink (in the sea); (*b*) *F:* (*of pers.*) to drown, be drowned; (*c*) *Av:* (*of aircraft in flight*) to lose height.

Absauganlage, *f.* (*a*) *Ch: Ind:* suction apparatus; (*b*) *Ind:* induced draught plant.

Absaug(e)flasche, *f.*, **Absaug(e)kolben,** *m. Ch:* filtering-flask.

Absaug(e)leitung, *f. Ch: Ind:* suction-pipe, -piping; suction-line.

absäugeln, *v.tr. sep. Hort:* to inarch.

absaugen. I. *v.tr. sep.* (*weak & strong*) (*a*) to suck (sth.) off; to exhaust, suck up, draw off (water, etc.); to aspirate (a gas, a liquid); *Ch: Ind:* to extract (moisture) with a hydro-extractor, *F:* to hydro-extract (moisture); (*b*) *Ch: etc:* to filter (liquid) by suction; (*c*) *Ind:* to dry (textiles, etc.) with a hydro-extractor.

II. *vbl s.* **Absaugen** *n.*, **Absaugung** *f. in vbl senses; also:* (*a*) aspiration (of a gas, a liquid); *Ch: Ind:* extraction (of moisture) with a hydro-extractor, *F:* hydro-extraction; (*b*) *Ch: etc:* filtration by suction.

Absaugentfeuchter, *m.* centrifugal dryer.

Absaug(e)pumpe, *f.* vacuum-pump.

Absauger, *m. Ind:* (*a*) centrifugal extractor; hydro-extractor; (*b*) suction-fan; (*c*) (dust-) exhauster; (*d*) *Paperm:* suction-box (under the machine-wire).

absäumen, *v.tr. sep. For:* to clear a strip between (sections) of forest allocated for use at different dates.

abscedieren, Absceß=**abszedieren, Abszeß.**

Abschab(e)eisen, *n. Tls:* scraper, scraping-iron, -tool; *Paperm: Print: etc:* doctor.

abschaben, *v.tr. sep.* 1. (*a*) to scrape (sth.) off; to grate (sth.) off; (*b*) to scrape (skin, horn, carrot, etc.); to abrade (skin, etc.); to rasp the crust off (bread); to clean off the soft surface of (quarry stone); *Dent:* to scale (teeth); *Leath:* to scrape, flesh (hides). 2. **sich abschaben,** (*of garments, etc.*) to wear out; to become threadbare, shabby, *F:* shiny.

Abschabsel, *n.* -s/-, scrapings (of wood, horn, leather, brick, etc.); *Leath:* fleshings.

Abschach, *n. Chess:* double check.

abschachern, *v.tr. sep.* **j-m etwas a.,** to buy sth. from s.o. at a trifling price, for a (mere) song.

abschachteln, *v.tr. sep.* to rub, polish, (woodwork, etc.) with a scouring-rush.

abschachten, *v.tr. sep. Min:* to line, timber, tub (bore-hole, etc.).

abschaffen. I. *v.tr. sep.* (*weak*) 1. (*a*) to abolish, do away with (law, tax, office, institution, etc.); to abrogate, annul, repeal, rescind (law, decree); to put down, put an end to, *Jur:* to abate (an abuse); (*b*) *South G.Dial:* to stop, put a stop to (sth.). 2. (*a*) **j-n, etwas, a.,** to get rid of s.o., sth.; **wir haben unser Hausmädchen abgeschafft,** we no longer keep a maid, we are doing without a maid now; **wir haben unser Auto abgeschafft,** we have given up our car, we are no longer running a car; *A:* **Soldaten, Truppen, a.,** to disband troops; (*b*) *Austrian:*=**abschieben** I. 3. 3. **sich abschaffen,** *Dial. & F:*=**abarbeiten** I. 4 (*a*), **abmühen** (*b*).

II. *vbl s.* **Abschaffen** *n.*, **Abschaffung** *f. in vbl senses; also:* abolition, abolishment (of law, tax, office, institution, etc.); abrogation, annulment, repeal, rescission (of law, decree); suppression, *Jur:* abatement, abating (of an abuse).

abschäkeln, *v.tr. sep. Nau:* to unbend (cable); to unshackle (anchor, etc.).

abschälen. I. *v.tr. sep.* 1. to decorticate; to peel (fruit, vegetables); to pare (apple, etc.); to shell (nuts); to blanch (almonds); to debark, disbark (timber); to bark (tree); to peel (twig); to exfoliate (bark, cuticle, etc.); to excoriate (skin, etc.). 2. **sich abschälen,** (*of skin, bark, etc.*) to peel off, to come off; (*of bark, skin, bone, rock, etc.*) to scale off; *Bot: Med: Miner:* to exfoliate; *Med:* (*of cuticle, etc.*) to desquamate.

II. *vbl s.* **Abschälen** *n.*, **Abschälung** *f. in vbl senses; also:* decortication; exfoliation (of bark, cuticle, etc.); excoriation (of skin, etc.); *Bot: Med: Miner:* exfoliation; *Med:* desquamation (of cuticle, etc.).

Abschallklappe, *f. I.C.E:* exhaust-valve.

abschaltbar, *a. El.E:* that can be disconnected; disconnectible.

abschalten. I. *v.tr. sep.* (*a*) *El.E:* to disconnect; to switch (a lamp, etc.) off; to cut off (current); to cut out (battery, etc.); (*b*) *W.Tel:* to cut out (part of radio programme).

II. *vbl s.* **Abschalten** *n.*, **Abschaltung** *f. in vbl senses; also: El.E:* disconnection, disconnexion.

Abschaltmagnet, *m. El.E:* disconnecting magnet.

Abschaltstellung, *f. El.E:* 'off' position.

Abschaltstromstärke, *f. El.E:* current on breaking.

Abschaltzelle, *f. El.E:* spare cell.

abschärfen, *v.tr. sep.* 1.=**schärfen.** 2. (*a*) *Carp: Constr: etc:* to bevel, chamfer (edge, cornice, etc.); to round off (corner); *Bookb:* to pare (binding, corner); (*b*) to thin down, pare (wood); (*c*) *Leath:* to pare (skin); (*d*) to taper; to cut, make, (sth.) into a point; *N.Arch:* to fair (hull) 3. to mark, nick, fake (playing cards.)

Abschärfmesser, *n. Bootm: etc:* paring-knife.

Abschärfstein, *m.* whetstone; hone; grindstone.

abscharren, *v.tr. sep.* to scrape (sth.) off; to scrape away (earth, etc.).

abschatten. I. *v.tr. sep.* 1. to shade (drawing). 2. *Lit:*=**abschattieren** I. 3. *Lit:* to silhouette, outline (figure, etc.). 4. *Lit:* **sich abschatten,** to cast a shadow; **die Blätter der Reben schatteten sich ab auf seinem Antlitz,** the foliage of the vines cast its shadow on his face.

II. *vbl s.* 1. **Abschatten,** *n. in vbl senses.* 2. **Abschattung,** *f.* (*a*)=II. 1; (*b*) *Lit:* (i) silhouette,

outlines; (ii)=**Abschattierung,** *q.v. under* **abschattieren** II. 2 (*b*).

abschattieren. I. *v.tr. sep.* to shade (off) (colours); to graduate (colours), to express faint differences, nuances, in (characters in a novel, etc.).

II. *vbl s.* **1. Abschattieren,** *n. in vbl senses.* **2. Abschattierung,** *f.* (*a*)=II. 1; (*b*) shading; shade; nuance; degree.

abschätzbar, *a.* appreciable; rateable; appraisable, assessable (goods, property); foreseeable, calculable (consequences, development, etc.); *adv.* appreciably.

Abschätzbarkeit, *f.* rateability; calculability.

abschätzen. I. *v.tr. sep.* **1.** to value (**auf**+*acc.,* at); to appraise (goods, property, etc.); to estimate, form an estimate of, the value of (sth.); to assess (damages, capabilities, etc.); to estimate, reckon, calculate (value, weight, number, etc.); *Adm:* to assess (property) (*for purposes of taxation*); *Adm:* to classify, grade (agricultural land); *Jur:* to tax (costs, bill of costs); **etwas unter dem Wert a.,** to under-value, underrate, sth.; **j-s Vermögen a.,** *A:* **j-n nach seinem Vermögen a.,** to estimate s.o.'s fortune; **sein Vermögen wird auf £100 000 abgeschätzt,** his fortune is estimated at, assessed at, £100,000; **j-s Fähigkeiten a.,** to assess s.o.'s capabilities, *F:* to take s.o.'s measure; to size s.o. up; **die Wirkung einer Rede a.,** to gauge, calculate, estimate, the effect of a speech. **2.** *A:* to depreciate, disparage, belittle; to pass an adverse judgment on (s.o., sth.).

II. *vbl s.* **1. Abschätzen,** *n. in vbl senses.* **2. Abschätzung,** *f.* (*a*)=II. 1; (*b*) valuation, appraisement, appraisal (of property, etc.); assessment (of damage, capabilities, etc.); estimate (of value, weight, number, etc.); *Adm:* assessment (of property) (*for taxation*); *Adm:* classification, grading (of agricultural land); **nach ungefährer, oberflächlicher, A.,** at, on, a rough estimate.

abschätzend, *a. & adv. A:*=**abschätzig.**

Abschätzer, *m.* valuer, appraiser; *Adm:* assessor (of land-values, etc.); *M.Ins:* **A. für Havarien,** average adjuster.

abschätzig. **1.** *a.* unfavourable (opinion); adverse (judgment); disparaging (criticism, remarks); depreciatory (remarks). **2.** *adv.* **etwas a. beurteilen,** to pass an adverse, derogatory, judgment on sth.; to dismiss sth. contemptuously; **sich über j-n, etwas, a. aussprechen,** to speak disparagingly, depreciatingly, of s.o., sth.; **j-n a. behandeln,** to treat s.o. in a contemptuous, derogatory, manner.

Abschätzungsbeamte, *m* (*a*) valuation officer; official valuer; official appraiser; (*b*) official charged with the classifying of agricultural land.

Abschätzungskommission, *f.* (*a*) assessment committee; (*b*) committee for the classification of agricultural land.

abschauen, *v.tr. & i. sep.* (*haben*)=**absehen.**

abschaufeln, *v.tr. sep.* to shovel (sth.) away, off.

Abschaum, *m.* (*a*) scum (on soup, etc.); **der A. der Menschheit,** the off-scourings, the (very) dregs, of humanity; the scum of the earth; (*b*) *Metall:* dross, scum; (*c*) skimmings.

abschäumen, *v.tr. sep.* **1.** to skim off (impurities, grease from soup, etc.). **2.** to scum, skim (soup, molten metal, etc.).

Abschäumer, *m.* **-s/-.** **1.** (*pers.*) skimmer; one who scums (soup, molten metal, etc.). **2.** skimming device; skimmer.

Abschaumhahn, *m. Mch:* blow-off (gear, cock), scum-cock; *Nau:* brine-cock.

Abschaumventil, *n. Mch:* blow-off valve, scum-valve; *Nau:* brine-valve.

abscheidbar, *a.* separable; isolable; that can be isolated, segregated; precipitable (substance), (substance) that can be precipitated; (gas) that can be disengaged, liberated; *Physiol:* eliminable (matter).

Abscheidegefäß, *n. Ch:* separating vessel.

Abscheidekammer, *f. Ch:* separating chamber.

abscheiden, *v. sep.* (*strong*) I. *v.tr.* **1.** (*a*) to separate, part, disjoin, sever, sunder (one thing from another); (*b*) to isolate (element, species, etc.); to segregate. **2.** *Ch:* (*a*) to precipitate (substance); (*b*) to disengage, liberate (oxygen, hydrogen, etc.). **3.** *Metalw:* to deposit (metal, by galvanic process). **4.** *Metall:* (*a*) to separate, part (silver from lead, etc.); (*b*) to refine (gold, silver). **5.** *Physiol:* (*a*) to excrete (waste matter); to eliminate (toxic matter); (*b*) (*of gland*) to secrete (bile, etc.); (*c*) *Med:* to discharge (pus, etc.).

II. **sich abscheiden.** **1.** (*a*) to separate, to be separated; to divide, to be divided; to part, to be parted; (*b*) to be isolated; to be segregated. **2.** *Ch:* (*a*) (*of substance*) to precipitate, to be precipitated; to form a precipitate; (*b*) (*of gas*) to disengage, be disengaged; to be liberated, given off; **Sauerstoff scheidet sich ab,** oxygen is given off. **3.** *Metalw:* (*of metal, in galvanic process*) to be deposited. **4.** *Metall:* (*of metals*) to separate, part. **5.** *Physiol:* (*of waste matter*) to be excreted; (*of toxic matter*) to be eliminated; (*of bile, etc.*) to be secreted.

III. **abscheiden,** *v.i.* (*sein*) (*of pers.*) **1.** to depart, take one's departure; **von j-m, einem Ort, a.,** to take one's leave of s.o., of a place. **2.** **(von dieser Welt, diesem Leben) a.,** to die; to depart this life. *See also* **abgeschieden.**

IV. *vbl s.* **1. Abscheiden,** *n.* (*a*) *in vbl senses; also:* severance; isolation; segregation; *Ch:* precipitation, deposition (of substance); liberation (of gas); *Metall: etc:* separation; *Metalw:* deposition (of metal) (*in galvanic process*); *Physiol:* excretion (of waste matter); elimination (of toxic matter); secretion (of bile, etc.); *Med:* discharge (of pus); (*b*) death, demise, decease. **2. Abscheidung,** *f.* (*a*)=IV. 1 (*a*); (*b*) *Ch: etc:* deposit; *Metalw:* (galvanic) deposit; *Physiol:* excreted, eliminated, matter; secretion (from gland); *Med:* discharge; discharged pus.

Abscheider, *m.* **1.** *Tchn:* (*a*) separator; (*b*) *Mch: etc:* steam separator. **2.** *Metall:* (*pers.*) refiner.

Abscheidungsmittel, *n. Ch: etc:* separating agent; means by which separation is effected; precipitant.

Abscheidungsprodukt, *n. Physiol:* secretory product; secretion; excretory product.

Abscheidungsverfahren, *n. Ch: Metall:* separation process, separating process.

Abscheidungsvorrichtung, *f. Tchn:* separating device, separator.

Abschein, *m. A:*=**Abglanz** I.

abschelfern, *v. sep.*=**abschilfern.**

Abscherblock, *m. Mec.E: etc:* shearing block.

Abscherbolzen, *m. Mec.E: etc:* shearing bolt.

abscheren[1], *v.sep.* I. *v.tr.* (*strong*) **1.** to shear (sth.) off; to cut (sth.) off (*with shears, scissors, clippers*); to cut off, clip off (hair); to cut off, shave off (beard); to clip (wool); **abgeschorene Wolle,** shearings, clip. **2.** to shear (sheep).

II. **abscheren,** *v.* (*weak*) *Mec:* (*a*) *v.tr.* (*of stress*) to shear (bolt, plate, etc.); (*b*) *v.i.* (*sein*) (*of bolt, plate, etc.*) to shear.

III. *vbl s.* **1. Abscheren,** *n. in vbl senses.* **2. Abscherung,** *f.* (*a*)=II. 1; (*b*)=**Abscherkraft.**

abscheren[2], *v.i. sep.* (*weak*) (*sein*) *Nau:* to sheer off; to slacken moorings; **abscheren!** fend off!

Abscherfestigkeit, *f. Mec:* shearing strength.

Abscherkraft, *f. Mec:* shearing (stress), shear.

Abscherkupplung, *f. Mec.E:* pin coupling, safety coupling.

Abscherquerschnitt, *m. Mec:* shearing section.

Abscherstift, *m. Mec.E:* shear pin.

Abscherung, *f. see under* **abscheren**[1] III.

Abscherungs- *see* **Abscher-.**

Abscheu, *m.* **-s/.** **A. vor j-m, etwas** *dat.,* repugnance (to s.o., sth.), disgust (for s.o., sth.), abhorrence (of, for, s.o., sth.), horror (of s.o., sth.); distaste, loathing (for s.o., sth.); **sich mit A. wegwenden,** to turn away in disgust; **A. vor j-m, etwas, haben,** to have a horror of s.o., sth.; to hate, detest, abhor, abominate, s.o., sth.; to loathe, have a loathing for, sth.; to find s.o., sth., repugnant; to be repelled by s.o., sth.; **j-m A. einflößen,** to disgust, horrify, s.o.; to fill s.o. with disgust, with horror; **j-m ein A. sein,** to be held in abhorrence by s.o.; **Knoblauch ist mir ein A.,** I detest, loathe, garlic; **sie ist mir ein A.,** I cannot bear her, *F:* I can't stand her, I hate the sight of her; *A.Ph:* **die Natur hat A. vor dem Leeren,** Nature abhors a vacuum.

abscheuern. I. *v.tr. sep.* **1.** to scour off (dirt, etc.). **2.** (*a*) to scour, clean, cleanse (pots and pans, etc.); (*b*) to wear (sth.) away with scouring *or* rubbing; to rub (sth.) away; *Nau:* to chafe, fret (rope, etc.). **3. sich abscheuern,** to wear away; *Nau:* (*of rope etc.*) to chafe, fret; *F:* (*of pers.*) to lose one's uncouth ways.

II. *vbl s.* **Abscheuern** *n.,* **Abscheuerung** *f. in vbl senses; also:* attrition.

abscheuerregend, *a.*=**ekelerregend.**

abscheulich, *a.* disgusting, revolting, repulsive; loathsome, detestable, abominable, execrable, hateful; odious (action, behaviour); heinous (crime, action); **das war a. von dir,** that was a nasty thing to do, to say; *F:* that was horrid, beastly, of you; that was a nasty, filthy, trick; **du Abscheulicher!** you horror! *adv.* **das hat a. weh getan,** it hurt abominably, dreadfully; **sich a. benehmen,** to behave abominably, outrageously.

Abscheulichkeit, *f.* **1.** disgusting, execrable, revolting, character, quality (of sth.); repulsiveness, loathsomeness, detestableness, hatefulness. **2.** abominable deed, act; disgusting, revolting, thing *or* incident; **das Buch ist voller Abscheulichkeiten,** the book is full (i) of horrors, (ii) of disgusting incidents.

abschichten. I. *v.tr. sep.* **1.** to arrange, dispose, (sth.) in layers; to layer; *Geol: etc:* to stratify. **2. sich abschichten,** to separate into, settle in, layers; *Geol: etc:* to stratify. **3.** *Jur:* **einen Erben a.,** to make an immediate payment to an heir on condition that he relinquishes the right of inheritance; to buy off the claims of an heir.

II. **Abschichten** *n.,* **Abschichtung** *f. in vbl senses; also: Geol: etc:* stratification.

abschicken. I. *v.tr. sep.* (*a*) to send (off), despatch, dispatch (letter, telegram, parcel, goods); to post, mail (letter, parcel), to forward (letter, parcel, goods); to consign, *U.S:* ship (goods); to remit (money); (*b*) to send, despatch, dispatch (messenger); *A:* **einen Gesandten a.,** to send, despatch, an envoy.

II. *vbl s.* **Abschicken** *n.,* **Abschickung** *f. in vbl senses; also:* despatch, dispatch.

abschieben, *v.sep.* (*strong*) I. *v.tr.* **1.** to push (sth.) off, away. **2.** *Husb:* (*of foal, heifer, lamb, etc.*) **(die ersten Zähne) a.,** to shed its milk-teeth. **3.** *Adm:* to expel (vagrant, etc.); to deport (alien). **4. eine Schuld von sich a.,** to exculpate oneself; to exonerate oneself, clear oneself (from blame); to deny a charge; **eine Verantwortung von sich a.,** to refuse a responsibility; to get rid, *F:* get shot, of a responsibility.

II. **abschieben,** *v.i.* (*sein*) *F:* to push off, shove off, to slope off; to clear off; to clear out; **schieb ab!** (i) off with you! get going! *U.S:* on your way! (ii) clear off! buzz off! get lost!

III. *vbl s.* **1. Abschieben,** *n. in vbl senses; also: Adm:* expulsion (of vagrant, etc.); deportation (of alien); **A. einer Schuld,** exculpation (of oneself); exoneration (of oneself) (*from blame*); denial of a charge; **A. einer Verantwortung,** refusal of a responsibility. **2. Abschiebung,** *f.* (*a*)=III. 1; (*b*) *Geol: Min:* (normal) fault.

Abschied, *m.* **-(e)s/-e.** **1.** (*a*) departure, farewell, parting, leave-taking; **A. nehmen,** to take one's leave, departure; to depart, leave, go away; **von j-m A. nehmen,** to take leave of s.o.; to bid farewell to s.o.; to say good-bye to s.o.; **sie nahmen liebevoll A. voneinander,** they bade each other a fond farewell; **beim A.,** at, on, parting; when saying good-bye, farewell; on taking (one's) leave; **der A. von seinen Freunden fiel ihm schwer,** the parting from his friends saddened him; he parted from his friends with a heavy heart; **ohne A. weggehen,** (i) to go, slip away, without saying good-bye; (ii) to take French leave; (*b*) **vom Leben A. nehmen,** to depart (from) this life; to die; **A. vom Leben,** decease, demise, death. **2.** (*a*) retirement; **seinen A. nehmen,** to resign (one's appointment); to retire; to quit office; *Mil: Navy:* to resign one's commission; to be placed on the retired list; to take one's discharge; to quit the service; **einen ehrenvollen A. erhalten,** to be honourably retired; **j-m den A. erteilen, bewilligen,** to retire s.o., pension s.o. off, superannuate s.o.; *see also* **einkommen**[1] 2, **einreichen;** (*b*) discharge, dismissal; **j-m den A. geben,** to discharge, dismiss, s.o.; **seinen A. erhalten,** to be discharged, dismissed; *Mil: Navy:* **schlichter A.,** cashiering, dismissal from the service; **mit schlichtem A. entlassen werden,** to be cashiered, to be dismissed the service; *Mil: A:* **einem Regiment den A. geben,** to disband a regiment. **3.** *A:* (*a*) **(gerichtlicher) A.,** decree; statute; ordinance; (*b*) *Hist:* recess, ordinance (of the Imperial Diet, of the Diet of the Hanseatic League).

Abschiednehmen, *n.* leave-taking; **beim A.,** when saying good-bye, farewell; on taking one's leave.

Abschiedsaudienz, *f.* farewell audience (of retiring minister, etc.); parting visit (of ambassador).

Abschiedsbesuch, *m.* farewell call, parting visit.

Abschiedsbrief, *m.* **1.** farewell letter. **2.** *A:* letter of discharge, of dismissal. **3.** *A:* testimonial; certificate of (an employee's) conduct.

Abschiedsessen, *n.* farewell dinner, valedictory dinner.

Abschiedsfeier, *f.* farewell celebration, *F:* send-off.

Abschiedsgeleit, *n.* **j-m das A. geben,** to see s.o. on his way; *F:* to give s.o. a (friendly) send-off.

Abschiedsgesuch, *n.* request to be retired, to be placed on the retired list, to be relieved of one's duties, to be allowed to resign, to be superannuated; *see also* **einreichen.**

Abschiedsgruß, *m.* (words, gesture, of) farewell.

Abschiedskuß, *m.* parting kiss, farewell kiss.

Abschiedsrede, *f.* farewell speech; valedictory address, *U.S:* valedictory.

Abschiedsschmaus, *m.* = **Abschiedsessen.**

Abschiedsstunde, *f.* the hour of parting.

Abschiedstrunk, *m.* stirrup-cup; farewell glass.

Abschiedswort, *n.* -(e)s/-e, parting word(s); word(s) of farewell; farewell speech.

abschiefern. I. *v.sep.* **1.** *v.tr.* to peel off; to flake off, scale-off; *Geol: etc:* to exfoliate; to laminate. **2.** *v.i.* (*haben*) & **sich abschiefern,** to peel (off); to flake off, scale (off); (*of rock, etc.*) to exfoliate; to laminate.

II. *vbl s.* **Abschiefern** *n.*, **Abschieferung** *f. in vbl senses; also: Geol:* exfoliation, lamination.

abschienen, *v.tr. sep.* **1.** *Surg:* (i) to splint, (ii) to remove the splint from (fractured leg, etc.). **2.** *Min: A:* to survey (mine).

Abschiener, *m.* -s/-. *Min: A:* mine surveyor.

abschießen, *v. sep.* (*strong*) I. *v.tr.* **1.** to shoot (sth.) off, away; **es wurde ihm ein Fuß abgeschossen,** he had a foot shot off, shot away; a shot took off his foot. **2.** to discharge, fire (off), let off, shoot (firearm, projectile, etc.); to launch, fire (rocket); **einen Pfeil, den Bogen, a.,** to launch, loose, speed, let fly, an arrow; **seine ganze Munition a.,** to exhaust, shoot away, one's ammunition. **3.** (*a*) to shoot down, bring down, pick off, kill (man, bird, etc.); **den Vogel a.,** to win the prize (*originally by hitting the clay bird at a shooting-match*); to bear away the bell; *F:* to ring the bell; to be far and away the best, the most successful; *U.S: F:* to take the rag off the bush; **mit dieser Bemerkung hat er den Vogel abgeschossen,** his remark hit the nail on the head; (*b*) *Mil: Av:* to shoot down, bring down (aircraft); *Mil:* **einen Feindpanzer a.,** to knock out an enemy tank; *F:* **j-n a.,** to kick s.o. out (of his job). **4.** *Ven:* **ein Revier a.,** to shoot over an area, a preserve.

II. **abschießen,** *v.i.* (*sein*) **1.** (*of waterfall, etc.*) to shoot down, rush down; (*of rock, etc.*) to descend perpendicularly, sheer; to sheer; **Kliff, das in die See abschießt,** cliff that falls, drops, sheer into the sea. **2.** to shoot off; to dart away. **3.** *A:* (*of colour, stuff*) to fade.

abschiffen, *v.sep.* **1.** *v.tr.* to ship (goods). **2.** *v.i.* (*sein*) to set sail; to sail.

abschilfern. I. *v. sep.* **1.** *v.tr.* to peel off, scale off, flake off; to excoriate (skin, etc.); *Bot: Med: etc:* to exfoliate. **2.** *v.i.* (*haben*) & **sich abschilfern,** to peel (off), scale (off), flake off; to desquamate; *Bot: Med: etc:* to exfoliate.

II. *vbl s.* **Abschilfern** *n.*, **Abschilferung** *f. in vbl senses; also:* desquamation; excoriation (of skin, etc.); *Bot: Med: etc:* exfoliation.

abschinden, *v.tr. sep.* (*strong*) **1.** (*a*) to strip off (skin) (from animal); to flay (large animal); to skin (rabbit, etc.); **einem Ochsen die Haut a.,** to flay an ox; (*b*) to abrade, gall, graze, chafe, rub off (the skin); **sich** *dat.* **den Ellbogen, das Schienbein, a.,** to graze, bark, one's elbow, one's shin; *Med:* **abgeschundene Stelle,** abrasion, excoriation (of the skin); gall; *Vet:* **abgeschundene Stelle unter dem Sattel,** saddle-gall. **2.** (*a*) = **schinden;** (*b*) **sich a.,** to slave, drudge, toil and moil; to work one's fingers to the bone.

Abschirmbecher, *m. W.Tel:* screen.

Abschirmblech, *n. Mil.Veh:* metal shield (of armoured vehicle, etc.).

abschirmen. I. *v.tr. sep.* (*a*) to screen (sth.) off; to screen, protect, shield (s.o., sth.) (**gegen,** against, from); *W.Tel: Atom.Ph:* to screen; (*b*) *Mil:* to cover (battery, unit, etc.).

II. *vbl s.* **1. Abschirmen,** *n. in vbl senses; also:* protection; *W.Tel:* **A. von Störungen,** suppression of interference. **2. Abschirmung,** *f.* (*a*) = II. 1; (*b*) screen, screening substance *or* device; protection; shield.

Abschirmhaube, *f. W.Tel:* screen.

Abschirmungszahl, *f. Atom.Ph:* screening number.

Abschirmvorrichtung, *f.* (*a*) *W.Tel: Atom.Ph:* screening device; (*b*) *W.Tel:* (*in motor-car, etc.*) (interference) suppressor.

abschirren, *v.tr. sep.* to unharness (horse, etc.).

abschlachten. I. *v.tr. sep.* **1.** (*a*) to slaughter (cattle); (*b*) to butcher, massacre, slaughter (persons). **2.** *Nau:* to break up (ship).

II. *vbl s.* **Abschlachten** *n.*, **Abschlachtung** *f. in vbl senses; also:* slaughter (of cattle, etc.).

abschlacken, *v.tr. sep. Metall:* to skim off the slag from (molten metal).

Abschlag, *m.* -s/⸗e. **1.** (*a*) *For:* felling, cutting down, clearing (of forest, trees); (*b*) cuttings, chips, chippings (of wood, etc.); *For:* loppings, *U.S:* slash. **2.** *Sp:* (*a*) opening stroke *or* hit; *Golf:* drive; *Hockey:* bully; *Fb:* **A. vom Tor,** goal kick; (*b*) *Golf:* tee. **3.** rebound(ing), bounce (of a ball); **der Tennisplatz,** *Bill:* **die Bande, hat einen guten A.,** the court, *Bill:* the cushion, is lively. **4.** (*a*) *Com:* reduction (in price); allowance, rebate, discount, abatement; **einen A. gewähren,** to make an allowance, allow a rebate, allow a discount; **mit 10% A.,** less 10%; **ohne A.,** without reduction, discount; net(t); (*b*) *Fin:* discount (*esp.* difference between actual and nominal value of shares); (*c*) *Com:* first instalment, part(ial) payment, payment on account, down payment; **auf A.,** on account, in part payment (of a sum); **100 Mark auf A. bezahlen,** to pay 100 marks on account; **eine Rechnung auf A. bezahlen,** to pay an account by instalments. **5. A. der Kälte, der Hitze,** abating of the cold, of the heat. **6.** *Com: Fin:* **A. der Preise, in den Preisen, im Kurs,** drop, fall, decline, in prices; sinking, lowering, of prices; **die Preise sind in A. geraten,** prices have dropped, fallen, declined, sunk; **das Korn ist wieder in A. geraten,** (the price of) wheat has fallen again. **7. A. einer Bitte,** refusal of a request. **8.** (*a*) striking (of coin, medal); stamping, impressing (of pattern, letters, etc.); (*b*) impress(ion), (im)print, stamp; *Metall: Print: etc:* matrix. **9.** *Hyd.E:* (*a*) outlet, discharge pipe, waste-pipe, drain(-pipe); (*b*) discharged water, waste water; overflow; outflow. **10.** *Constr:* partitioned-off space; compartment; closet (in room, etc.).

Abschlagblech, *n. Paperm:* beater plate.

Abschlageisen, *n. A:* wrought iron.

abschlagen, *v. sep.* (*strong*) I. *v.tr.* **1.** to knock (sth.) off; to beat out (dust, etc.); to hammer (sth.) off; to cut, chop, strike, hew, (sth.) off; **die Nüsse a.,** to knock down the nuts, knock the nuts off a tree; **den Henkel von einem Krug a.,** to knock, break, the handle off a jug; **j-m den Kopf a.,** to decapitate, behead, s.o.; to cut off, strike off, *F:* chop off, s.o.'s head; **j-m den Arm, die Hand, a.,** to cut off, *A:* strike off, s.o.'s arm, hand. **2.** (*a*) to knock, beat, (sth.) down; (*b*) *For:* to fell, cut down (tree, etc.); to clear (a forest). **3.** (*a*) *Com:* to lower, bring down (price); to bring down the price, lower the value, of (goods, etc.); **das Korn a.,** to cheapen wheat, to bring down the price of wheat; (*b*) **eine Münze a.,** to depreciate a coinage. **4.** to beat back (s.o., sth.); to repulse, repel, beat off (the enemy, an attack); to ward off, parry (blow, thrust); (*in race*) **abgeschlagen sein,** to be left behind. **5. eine Bitte, ein Anerbieten, a.,** to refuse a request, an offer; **er hat es mir glatt, rund(weg), abgeschlagen,** he flatly refused it me, refused it me outright; **mir hat niemals jemand etwas abgeschlagen,** I have never been refused (anything); **ich lasse es mir nicht a.,** I will not be denied, I will take no refusal; I won't take no for an answer. **6.** (*a*) *Hyd.E:* to drain off, let off (water); to divert, tap, the course of (running water); (*b*) (*of pers.*) **sein Wasser a.,** to make water, to urinate. **7.** *Constr:* to partition off (space, compartment). **8.** to undo; to take to pieces, to dismantle (bed, etc.); to take down, pull down (scaffolding, etc.); *Mil: etc:* **ein Zelt a.,** to strike a tent; **das Lager a.,** to strike camp; *Nau:* **ein Segel a.,** to unbend a sail; *Print:* **das Format a.,** to unlock the form(e). **9. einen Meiler a.,** to cover a charcoal-clamp with turf. **10.** (*a*) *Metalw:* to beat out (iron, gold, etc.); (*b*) *Ind:* to beat (pulp, etc.). **11.** (*a*) to impress, imprint, stamp (pattern, letters, etc.); (*b*) *Num:* to strike off (coin, medal); (*c*) *Print:* **einen Bürstenabzug a.,** to take off a (brush-)proof; (*d*) *N.Arch:* **ein Schiff auf dem Schnürboden a.,** to lay off a ship on the mould-loft. **12.** *Games:* to have, tag, tig (s.o.); **Dritten a.,** to play twos-and-threes; **Abgeschlagene,** *m, f,* tagged player.

II. **abschlagen,** *v.i.* **1.** (*haben*) *Sp:* to make the opening stroke *or* hit; *Golf:* to drive (off); *Hockey:* to bully (off). **2.** (*sein*) (*of ball, esp. billiard-ball*) to rebound; to bounce. **3.** (*sein, haben*) *A:* (*of plan, etc.*) to fail; to go wrong; *Cards:* **diese Karte ist, hat, abgeschlagen,** that was a losing card. **4.** (*sein, haben*) (*a*) *Com:* (*of prices*) to fall; to come down, go down; to decline, to sink; (*of goods*) to go down (in price), to become cheaper; **das Korn schlägt (im Preise) ab,** (the price of) wheat is going down; (*b*) (*haben*) *Husb:* (*of cow*) to give less milk.

III. *vbl s.* **1. Abschlagen,** *n. in vbl senses; also:* (*a*) *Com:* drop, fall, decline (in price); (*b*) depreciation (of a currency); (*c*) refusal (of request, offer); (*d*) repulse (of the enemy); (*e*) *Sp:* = **Abschlag** 2 (*a*). **2. Abschlagung,** *f. in vbl senses of* I. 4, 5; *also:* refusal (of request, offer); repulse (of the enemy).

Abschläger, *m. Paperm:* (converting) cutter.

abschlägig, *a.* unfavourable (answer); **abschlägige Antwort, abschlägiger Bescheid,** refusal; rebuff; *adv.* **j-n a. bescheiden,** to give s.o. an unfavourable answer; to rebuff s.o.; **j-m ein Gesuch a. bescheiden,** to refuse, turn down, s.o.'s request; **a. beschieden werden,** to get an unfavourable answer, to be refused, to meet with a refusal; to meet with, suffer, a rebuff.

abschläglich, *a.* **1.** (sum, payment) as an instalment, on account; **abschlägliche Zahlung,** instalment, part(ial) payment, payment on account; *adv.* on account, in part payment, as an instalment; by instalments. **2.** *A:* = **abschlägig.**

Abschlagmaschine, *f. Ind:* splint-cutting machine (for manufacture of match-sticks, etc.).

Abschlag(s)dividende, *f. Fin:* interim dividend.

Abschlag(s)verteilung, *f.* distribution of dividend (to creditors of bankrupt estate).

Abschlag(s)zahlung, *f.* (*a*) instalment, part(ial) payment, payment on account; **etwas auf A. kaufen,** to buy sth. on hire-purchase; (*b*) payment by instalments; (*c*) advance payment.

Abschlämmaschine, *f.* road-sweeping, road-scraping, machine.

abschlämmen. I. *v.tr. sep.* (*a*) to cleanse, to clear, (streets, etc.) of mud *or* slime; to wash out (container); **einen Abzugskanal a.,** to sluice a sewer; **einen Wasserbehälter a.,** to clean out a cistern; (*b*) *Min:* to wash (coal, ore); to trunk, clean, sluice, buddle (ore); (*c*) *Mch:* **einen Kessel a.,** to blow down, blow off, a boiler; (*d*) *Ch: etc:* to decant (liquid); to elutriate (solid).

II. *vbl s.* **Abschlämmen** *n.*, **Abschlämmung** *f. in vbl senses; also: Ch: etc:* decantation (of liquid); elutriation (of solid).

Abschlämmventil, *n. Mch:* blow-down cock; blow-off (gear, cock).

abschleifen. I. *v.tr. sep.* (*strong*) **1.** to grind (sth.) off; to smooth off, rub off (irregularities, etc.). **2.** (*a*) to grind (marble, glass, diamonds, etc.); to polish (metal, etc.) (with pumice-stone, etc.); to rough-polish (gems, marble, etc.); to rub down (paint); to sandpaper (walls, wood, etc.); (*b*) to abrade; to wear (sth.) away (by friction); (*c*) *F:* to polish, refine (s.o.'s style, manners, etc.); **j-n a.,** to polish s.o. up, to knock the corners off s.o., to lick s.o. into shape; (*d*) **sich a.,** (i) (*of idea, metaphor, etc.*) to lose its freshness, its individuality; (ii) *F:* (*of pers.*) to lose one's uncouth ways, to acquire polish. **3.** to grind (knife, axe, etc.); to sharpen, set, whet, give an edge to, put an edge to, put an edge on (knife, tool); to regrind (tool).

II. *vbl s.* **Abschleifen** *n.*, **Abschleifung** *f. in vbl senses; also:* abrasion; attrition; refinement (of style, manners, of pers.).

III. *p.p. & a.* **abgeschliffen,** *in vbl senses; esp.* **1.** smooth; ground (smooth); polished (marble, etc.); burnished, bright (steel, etc.). **2.** polished (style); polite, civil, urbane (manners).

Abschleifer, *m.* (*pers.*) grinder; polisher; rubber-down (of paint).

abschleimen, *v.tr. sep.* to rid, clear, (sth.) of slime, *Bot: Med:* of mucus; *Sug-R:* to clarify, defecate.

abschleißen, *v.tr. sep.* (*strong*) to wear (sth.) away; to abrade (sth.).

abschlemmen, *v.tr. sep.* **1.** = **abschlämmen. 2.** (*of river, etc.*) to wash away (sand, etc.).

abschlendern, *v.i. sep.* (*sein*) to saunter off.

Abschleppdienst, *m. Aut:* breakdown service, towing service, *U.S:* wrecking service (for disabled vehicles); *Mil:* recovery service.

abschleppen, *v.tr. sep.* **1.** (*a*) to drag (sth., s.o.) away, off; to carry, lug, (sth.) away; (*b*) to tow off (ship); to tow off, tow away (damaged vehicle). **2.** *F:* to take (sth.) away furtively, by stealth. **3. sich mit einer Last abschleppen,** to trail, toil, along with a heavy burden.

Abschleppkommando, *n. Mil:* (vehicle) recovery section.

Abschleppkran, *m. Aut:* breakdown crane salvage crane, *U.S:* wrecking crane.

Abschleppmannschaft, *f. Aut:* breakdown gang, *U.S:* wrecking crew.

Abschleppwagen, *m. Aut:* breakdown lorry, *U.S:* wrecking car, wrecker; tow car, towing truck.

Abschleudermaschine, *f. Ind:* centrifugal (machine), centrifuge; hydro-extractor.

abschleudern, *v.tr. sep.* **1.** to fling (off), hurl (off), throw (off); (*of horse*) to throw (rider). **2.** to centrifugalize, centrifuge (a liquid); to hydro-extract (textiles, etc.). **3.** *Av:* to catapult (aircraft) (from carrier, etc.).

abschlichten, *v.tr. sep.* to smooth (surface); to plane (wood); to planish (metal).

Abschlichthammer, *m. Tls: Metalw:* planishing hammer.

abschlicken, *v.tr. sep.* to dredge, unsilt; to clear (harbour).

abschließbar, *a.* **1.** that can be locked; that can be closed (off), sealed (off). **2.** that can be concluded.

abschließen, *v. sep.* (*strong*) I. *v.tr.* **1.** to lock (door, cupboard, etc.); to lock up (house, room, etc.). **2.** to shut (sth.) up; to seal (up) (mouth of tube, etc.); **hermetisch abgeschlossen,** hermetically sealed. **3.** (*a*) to shut (sth.) off; to cut (sth.) off; to separate (sth.) off; to isolate (s.o., sth.); to seal (sth.) off; to seclude (s.o., sth.) **(von,** from); **von der Außenwelt abgeschlossen,** cut off, shut off, secluded, from the outside world; **sie lebt abgeschlossen,** she lives in seclusion, lives a secluded life; (*b*) to shut off, cut off, interrupt, stop; *Mch:* **den Dampf a.,** to shut off, cut off, the steam, to shut down steam. **4.** (*a*) to end, conclude, finish (off), complete (work, book, investigation, etc.); to bring (speech, etc.) to an end, to a close, to a conclusion; to end, finish (speech, etc.); to close (debate); to wind up (affair, debate); to settle (quarrel); to adjust, compose, end (dispute); (*b*) to conclude, effect, finalize (an agreement, etc.); to come to terms, come to an agreement, about (bargain, contract, etc.); **einen Frieden, einen Waffenstillstand, a.,** to conclude peace, an armistice; to arrange a peace, an armistice; **einen Vertrag a.,** to effect, come to, an agreement; to enter into an agreement, a contract; to sign an agreement, a contract; to finalize an agreement; to conclude a treaty, enter into a treaty (with s.o.); **ich habe mit ihm noch nichts abgeschlossen,** I have as yet made no definite agreement with him; **einen Handel, ein Geschäft, a.,** to drive, strike, clinch, a bargain; **abgeschlossene Händel gelten,** a bargain's a bargain; *Com: Fin:* **abgeschlossene Geschäfte,** business done, (already) transacted; **einen Kauf, einen Verkauf, eine Versicherung, a.,** to effect a purchase, a sale, an insurance; **eine Anleihe a.,** to contract a loan; **mit seinen Gläubigern einen Vergleich a.,** to compound, come to terms, with one's creditors; (*c*) *Com:* **eine Rechnung a.,** to adjust, settle, an account; **nicht abgeschlossene Rechnungen,** unsettled accounts; *Book-k:* **die Bücher a.,** to close, make-up, balance, the books. **5. sich abschließen,** to seclude oneself; **sich (von der Außenwelt) a.,** to cut oneself off from the (outer) world, to retire within oneself; to keep oneself to oneself; **sich von der Gesellschaft a.,** to cut oneself off, seclude oneself, hold oneself aloof, from society; to avoid all company; **sich gegen alle Einflüsse von außen a.,** to screen oneself from, guard oneself against, all external influences.

II. **abschließen,** *v.i.* (*haben*) **1.** to end, come to an end; **der Abend schloß mit patriotischen Liedern ab,** the evening concluded with patriotic songs; **das Finanzjahr schließt mit dem 5. April ab,** the financial year ends, closes, on the 5th of April; **der Bericht schließt mit der Revolution ab,** the account ends with, breaks off at, the revolution. **2.** (*a*) **mit j-m a.,** to come to an agreement, to terms, with s.o.; **ich habe mit ihm für 1000 Mark abgeschlossen,** I closed with him for 1000 marks; **für diesen Preis kann ich nicht mit ihm a.,** I cannot do business with him at that price; (*b*) **mit j-m, mit etwas, a.,** to be, have, done with sth., s.o.; **mit einer Sache a.,** to bring a matter to an issue, to settle a matter once and for all, to set a matter at rest; **ich habe mit ihm abgeschlossen,** I've done, finished, with him; **er hat mit dem Leben, mit der Welt, abgeschlossen,** he has done, finished, with life.

III. *vbl s.* **Abschließen** *n.*, **Abschließung** *f.* *in vbl senses; also:* closure (of debate); conclusion (of peace, armistice, agreement); completion (of preparations, etc.); *Com:* adjustment, settlement (of account); *cp.* **Abschluß.**

IV. *pr.p & a.* **abschließend,** *in vbl senses; esp.* (*a*) conclusive, final, definite, definitive, positive (judgment, answer); (*b*) *adv.* in conclusion, in concluding, in closing; **a. bemerkte er, daß . . .,** in conclusion he remarked that . . . .

V. *p.p. & a.* **abgeschlossen,** *in vbl senses; esp.* (*a*) complete, completed; (*b*) **abgeschlossene Wohnung,** self-contained flat; **in sich selbst a.,** (i) self-contained; (ii) complete within itself; perfect; (*c*) *Mth:* closed.

abschlingern, *v.tr. sep. Nau:* **das Schiff hatte die Masten abgeschlingert,** the ship had rolled away her masts.

Abschluß, *m.* **1.** = **Verschluß** . **2. oberer A.,** top (part); upper termination; **rückwärtiger, hinterer, A.,** rear (end), back (end); **seitlicher A.,** side (part); **unterer A.,** bottom (part). **3.** (*a*) conclusion, termination; close, end (of speech, meeting, examination, etc.); winding up (of affair, debate); closure (of debate); settling (of quarrel); composing, adjusting, ending (of dispute); **zum A. kommen,** to terminate, conclude, close; to draw to a close, an end; **mit j-m zum A. kommen** = **mit j-m abschließen,** *q.v. under* **abschließen** II. 2 (*a*); **etwas zum A. bringen,** to end, finish, terminate, sth.; to bring (speech, etc.) to an end, to a close, to a conclusion; to complete (piece of work, book, etc.); **eine Sache zu einem befriedigenden A. bringen,** to bring a matter to a satisfactory conclusion; **mit einer Sache zum A., zu einem endgültigen A., kommen** = **mit einer Sache abschließen,** *q.v. under* **abschließen** II. 2 (*b*); (*b*) concluding, conclusion (of treaty, armistice, agreement); effecting (of agreement, insurance, etc.); finalizing (of agreement); *Com: Fin:* **A. (eines Geschäfts),** transaction, deal, bargain; sale; contract; commitment; **mit j-m einen A. machen,** to do a deal with s.o.; to drive, strike, clinch, a bargain with s.o.; **den A. eines Kaufs tätigen,** to conclude, effect, a purchase; **Abschlüsse machen, tätigen,** to enter into commitments; to do business; **einen A. über 5000 Meter Stoff machen,** to make a contract for 5,000 metres of material; **es fanden nur wenige Abschlüsse statt, es waren nur wenige Abschlüsse zu verzeichnen, zu berichten,** very few sales took place, were effected; little business was done, there was little business to report. **4.** (*a*) *Com:* adjusting, adjustment, settling, settlement (of account); *Book-k:* closing, making up (of account, of books); balancing (of books); **beim A. der Bücher,** on, when, balancing, closing, making up, the books; (*b*) *Book-k:* balance; **jährlicher A.,** annual balance; **den A. machen,** to balance the books, to strike a balance; **den A. vorlegen,** to disclose one's balance-sheet; *Jur:* to file one's petition (in bankruptcy). *Cp.* **abschließen III.**

Abschlußbilanz, *f. Com:* (annual) balance-sheet.

Abschlußblech, *n.* (metal) cap (of bearing, etc.).

Abschlußblende, *f. Phot:* front diaphragm.

Abschlußborte, *f.* border; frieze (of wallpaper).

Abschlußdeckel, *m.* sealing cover; cover plate.

Abschlußdichtung, *f.* seal(ing) (of joint, seam, etc.).

Abschlußhahn, *m.* stopcock.

Abschlußimpedanz, *f. El.E:* terminal impedance.

Abschlußkabel, *n. El.E:* **1.** terminal cable. **2.** waterproof cable.

Abschlußkante, *f.* = **Abschlußborte.**

Abschlußkappe, *f. El.E:* cap (end) (of cable).

Abschlußklasse, *f.* final-year class (at school).

Abschlußkondensator, *m. W.Tel:* block condenser.

Abschlußkurs, *m. Fin:* agreed price.

Abschlußleiste, *f. Av:* **hintere A.,** trailing edge (of wing, etc.).

Abschlußmeldung, *f.* final report.

Abschlußmuffe, *f. El.E:* terminal box (of cable).

Abschlußnadel, *f. Hyd.E:* needle-plunger (of needle-valve).

Abschlußnota, *f. Com: Fin:* contract note.

Abschlußplatte, *f. Mec.E: etc:* closing plate; protecting plate; cover-plate; *Arch:* top (part, band, etc.) (of entablature, etc.).

Abschlußprovision, *f. Com: Fin:* final commission (paid to agent).

Abschlußprüfer, *m. Com: Fin:* auditor.

Abschlußprüfung, *f.* **1.** *Sch:* leaving examination; *U.S:* final examination, *F:* finals. **2.** *Com: Fin:* audit.

Abschlußrahmen, *m. Mec.E: etc:* end-frame.

Abschlußrechnung, *f. Com: Fin:* final account.

Abschlußscheibe, *f. Mec.E: etc:* cover-plate.

Abschlußscheinwiderstand, *m.* = **Abschlußimpedanz.**

Abschlußschieber, *m. Mch:* slide-valve.

Abschlußsignal, *n. Rail:* home signal.

Abschlußstichtag, *m. Com:* delivery date.

Abschlußtag, *m. St.Exch:* settling day, account-day.

Abschlußventil, *n.* stop-valve.

Abschlußwechsel, *m. Com: Fin:* remittance to balance account, in settlement of account.

Abschlußwiderstand, *m. El:* terminal resistance.

Abschlußzahlung, *f.* final payment; final instalment.

Abschlußzettel, *m.* = **Abschlußnota.**

Abschlußzeugnis, *n. Sch:* leaving certificate; *U.S:* diploma.

abschmecken, *v.tr. sep. Cu:* to season (with salt, pepper, etc.); *abs.* to season to taste.

abschmeicheln, *v.tr. sep.* **j-m etwas a.,** to get sth. from s.o. by flattery; to coax, cajole, sth. out of s.o.; to blandish s.o. into giving one sth.

Abschmeißer, *m.* **-s/-,** buck-jumper, bucker; vicious horse.

Abschmelzdraht, *m. El.E:* fuse-wire.

abschmelzen. I. *v.sep.* **1.** *v.tr.* (*strong, occ. weak*) (*a*) to melt (sth.) off; (*b*) *Metall:* to separate (metals) by fusion; to liquate (metals); to liquate out (lead, etc.); (*c*) to melt (snow, wax, metal, etc.); to melt down (metal, etc.); to fuse (metal, glass, etc.); *El:* **eine Sicherung a.,** to blow a fuse; (*d*) to seal (off) (glass tube, etc.). **2.** *v.i.* (*strong*) (*sein*) (*a*) to melt off; (*b*) to melt; (*of snow, glacier, etc.*) to melt away; (*of metal, glass*) to fuse; *El:* **die Sicherung schmilzt ab,** the fuse blows (out).

II. *vbl s.* **1. Abschmelzen,** *n. in vbl senses; also: Ch: Metall:* liquation; fusion (of metal, glass); *Geol:* ablation (of glacier). **2. Abschmelzung,** *f. in vbl senses of* I. 1.

Abschmelzschweißung, *f.* flash-welding; fusion welding.

Abschmelzsicherung, *f. El.E:* safety-fuse, cut-out.

Abschmelzstreifen, *m. El.E:* safety strip, fuse strip; cartridge fuse.

Abschmelzstrom, *m. El.E:* fusing current, *F:* blowing current.

abschmiegen, *v.tr. sep. Carp: etc:* to bevel, chamfer (edges).

abschmieren, *v.sep.* I. *v.tr.* **1.** (*a*) to copy (sth.) hurriedly, carelessly; to scrawl, scribble off (copy, letter, etc.); to scamp (exercise, etc.); (*b*) *F: Lit:* to plagiarize (work); *Sch:* to copy, crib (exercise, etc.). **2.** *Com: P:* to wipe out (item, etc.); to write off (bad debt, etc.); *Mil. Av: F:* **ein Flugzeug a.,** to write off an aircraft (after crash *or* after being shot down); **eine Besatzung a.,** to write off an aircrew. **3.** (*a*) to lubricate, (oil and) grease (axle, car, etc.) (thoroughly); (*b*) *F:* **j-n a.,** to give s.o. a thrashing, a drubbing, a hiding. **4.** to remove the grease from (sth.); to remove stains, smears, from (sth.). **5.** *Mil: F:* **den Feind a.,** to beat off, repel, the enemy.

II. **abschmieren,** *v.i.* **1.** (*haben*) to make (grease-)stains *or* smears; to stain, maculate, spot. **2.** (*sein*) (*a*) *Av: F:* (*of aircraft*) to crash; *Mil.Av:* to be shot down; (*b*) *Av:* to skid, to side-slip.

Abschmierer, *m.* (*a*) slovenly transcriber, copyist (of document, etc.); (*b*) *F: Lit:* plagiarist; *Sch:* boy who copies, cribs.

abschminken, *v.tr. sep. Th: etc:* to take the paint off (s.o.'s) face; to remove (actor's, woman's) make-up; **sich a.,** (*of actor, woman*) to take off, remove, one's make-up.

abschmirgeln, *v.tr. sep.* to rub, grind, polish, (sth.) with emery.

Abschmutzbogen, *m. Print:* offset blanket; set-off sheet.

abschmutzen. I. *v.i. sep.* (*haben*) to soil; to maculate; to blot; to stain, spot; *Print:* (*of wet ink*) to set off; **auf etwas** *acc.* **a.,** to soil, stain, blot, sth.

II. *vbl s.* **Abschmutzen,** *n. in vbl senses; also:* maculation.

Abschmutzmakulatur, *f.*, **Abschmutzpapier,** *n. Print:* set-off paper, *U.S:* offset paper.

abschnäbeln (sich), *v.refl. sep.* to bill and coo.

abschnallen, *v.tr. sep.* **1.** (*a*) to unbuckle (belt, etc.); (*b*) to take off (rucksack, pack, etc.); *abs.* **a.,** to unload; *F:* to dump one's gear; (*c*) to unstrap (roll of bedding from rucksack, parcel from bicycle carrier, etc.). **2.** *A:* (*students' slang*) **j-m etwas a.,** to beg sth. from s.o.; to pester s.o. into giving one sth.

abschnappen, *v. sep.* **1.** *v.tr.* (*a*) to release (spring, catch); **ein Schloß a.,** to release the spring of a

lock; (*b*) *Dial:* **einen Karren a.,** to tip the load from a cart. **2.** *v.i.* (*sein*) (*a*) (*of spring*) to become slack, to slacken, relax; (*of catch, lock*) to slip; (*b*) to stop short, stop dead; (*c*) *F:* (*of pers.*) to die, *F:* to peg out.

Abschneideapparat, *m.* cutting machine *or* device; cutter.

Abschneidegesenk, *n. Metalw:* cutting die, trimming die; cut-off.

Abschneidemaschine, *f.* cutting machine, cutter.

Abschneidemesser, *n.* cutter (of cutting machine, etc.).

abschneiden, *v. sep.* (*strong*) I. *v.tr.* **1.** (*a*) to cut off; to carve off; to slice off; to lop off, lop away, shear off (branch, limb, etc.); **sich** *dat.* **ein Stück Kuchen a.,** to cut oneself a piece of cake; (*b*) to truncate (tree, *Geom:* cone, etc.); (*c*) to sever; **j-m den Hals, die Kehle, a.,** to cut s.o.'s throat; *see also:* **Hals** 1 (*a*); **j-m den Kopf a.,** to cut off s.o.'s head, to decapitate, behead, s.o.; **einem Huhn den Hals a.,** to cut a fowl's throat, to kill a fowl; **j-m ein Bein a.,** to cut off, take off, s.o.'s leg; *Surg:* **einen Knochen a.,** to resect a bone; (*d*) **einen Gehenkten (vom Strick) a.,** to cut down a man who has been hanged; *P:* **er sah aus wie vom Strick abgeschnitten,** he looked like death warmed up. **2.** (*a*) to cut off, snip off, detach; **j-m das Haar a.,** to cut off s.o.'s hair; *Fin: etc:* **Kupons a.,** to detach coupons; (*b*) to clip, trim, pare, cut down; **sich** *dat.* **die Nägel a.,** to cut, pare, one's nails; **einem Vogel die Flügel a.,** to clip a bird's wings; **einem Tier,** *F:* **j-m, die Krallen a.,** to pare, clip, an animal's, *F:* s.o.'s, claws; **den Docht a.,** to trim the wick (of lamp, etc.); *Carp: etc:* **Kanten, usw., schräg a.,** to bevel, chamfer, edges, etc. **3.** to cut off, interrupt, stop; (*a*) **dieser Pfad schneidet (ein Stück Weges) ab,** this path provides, is, a short cut; (*of pers.*) **den Weg a.,** to take a short cut; (*b*) **j-m den Weg a.,** to cut off, bar, s.o.'s way; to head s.o. off; **j-m den Rückzug, die Flucht, a.,** to cut off, intercept, s.o.'s retreat; **einer Stadt die Zufuhr, dem Feind den Nachschub, a.,** to cut off a town's, the enemy's, supplies; *Mch:* **den Dampf a.,** to shut down steam, to shut off, cut off, the steam; *Aut:* **das Benzin a.,** to cut off the petrol supply, *U.S:* gas; **j-m das Wort, die Rede, a.,** to interrupt s.o., to cut s.o. short; (*c*) **diese Büsche schneiden unseren Garten von dem nächsten ab,** these bushes divide, mark off, our garden from the next one; **ein vom Meer abgeschnittenes Volk,** a people cut off from, with no outlet to, the sea; **sie waren von aller Verbindung abgeschnitten,** all their communications were cut off; **sie lebt hier von allem Verkehr abgeschnitten,** she lives here in complete isolation; (*d*) **die Bäume schneiden den Wind ab,** the trees break the wind. **4. j-m etwas a.,** to deprive s.o. (decisively) of sth.; **j-m alle Möglichkeiten des Handelns a.,** to deprive s.o. of all opportunity for action; **j-m die Ehre a.,** to speak ill of s.o.; to slander, libel, vilify, backbite, s.o.; to ruin s.o.'s good name; to blacken, destroy, s.o.'s reputation; *Lit:* to denigrate s.o.; *Lit:* **das Schicksal schnitt ihm den Lebensfaden ab,** Fate cut, severed, the thread of his life. **5.** *A:* **sich abschneiden,** to stand out, show up, project (**gegen,** against).

II. **abschneiden,** *v.i.* (*haben*) **1.** = I. 5. **2.** *Min:* **der Erzgang schneidet ab,** the lode gives out (suddenly). **3. gut, schlecht, a.,** to do well, badly (in an examination, a contest, etc.); **in einem Examen am besten a.,** to come out best, to come out top, in an examination; **im Spiel am besten a.,** to have, get, the best of the game; **er hat in dieser Auseinandersetzung besser abgeschnitten als sein Gegner,** in this argument he came out, showed up, acquitted himself, better than his opponent.

III. *vbl s.* **Abschneiden,** *n. in vbl senses; also: Surg:* resection (of bone); abscission (of soft part); truncation (of tree, cone, etc.); interception (of s.o.'s retreat); **gutes, schlechtes, A.,** good, bad, performance (in an examination, a contest, etc.).

IV. *pr.p & a.* **abschneidend,** *in vbl senses; esp. Constr: Metalw:* **abschneidende Fläche, Fuge,** flush surface, joint.

V. *p.p. & a.* **abgeschnitten,** *in vbl senses; esp.* **1.** *Her:* **gerade a.,** couped. **2.** *Geom:* **abgeschnittener Kegel, abgeschnittene Pyramide,** truncated cone, pyramid; **schief abgeschnittener Zylinder(stutz), Kegel(stutz),** ungula of a cylinder, cone.

Abschneider, *m.* **1.** (*pers.*) cutter. **2.** (*a*) *Tls:* cutter; cutting device; (*b*) = **Zigarrenabschneider;** (*c*) *Metalw:* anvil chisel; set.

Abschneideschere, *f. Tls:* shears; *Metalw:* cutter, shears.

Abschneideweg, *m.* short cut.

abschneien, *v.sep. impers.* to cease snowing; **es hat (sich) abgeschneit,** the snow has stopped, is over, it has stopped snowing.

abschnellen, *v.sep.* **1.** *v.tr.* (*a*) to shoot, let fly, loose (an arrow); to speed (an arrow) (from the bow); to launch, hurl (javelin, etc.); (*b*) to flip (sth.) away; to fillip (sth.); (*c*) to snap (spring). **2.** *v.i.* (*sein*) (*a*) (*of arrow*) to speed (from the bow); to be launched, loosed; (*of javelin, etc.*) to dart, speed, away; (*b*) (*of spring*) to snap back, fly back, flip back.

abschneuzen, *v.tr. sep.* to snuff (candle).

abschnippe(l)n, *v.tr. sep.* to chip at (sth.); to clip, trim, pare; to snip off pieces from (sth.).

Abschnitt, *m.* **1.** (*a*) portion cut off; cutting; chip (of wood, etc.); shred (of cloth, leather, etc.); **Abschnitte** *pl*, scraps, trimmings, cuttings (of cloth, leather, etc.); (*b*) = **Stoffmuster;** (*c*) coupon (of ration-book, etc.); counterfoil, stub (of cheque, receipt, ticket, etc.); (*d*) *Metalw:* slug (of metal). **2.** *Com: Fin:* (*a*) bill (of exchange); (*b*) item; **£10 000 (Wechsel) in zehn Abschnitten,** ten bills totalling £10,000. **3.** part, portion, section (of whole); (*a*) *Geom: etc:* segment (of circle, sphere, of a set of integers, etc.); intercept (of axis); **A. auf der x-Achse,** x-intercept; *Num:* exergue; (*b*) paragraph; section (of page, column, chapter, etc.); part, section (of regulations, etc.); division (of book); *Print:* new paragraph; 'break'; (*c*) phase, stage (*in a development*); **mit seiner Ankunft in Weimar begann ein neuer A. in seinem Leben,** his arrival in Weimar opened a new chapter in his life; *Geol: Hist:* period; epoch; (*d*) *Mil:* (i) sector; (ii) frontage. **4.** *Fort: A:* entrenchment; trench.

Abschnittgestänge, *n. Tp: Tg:* transposition pole.

Abschnittlinie, *f. Print: etc:* cutting line; 'cut here' line.

Abschnittpunkt, *m. Tp: Tg:* transposition point.

Abschnittschein, *m.* coupon.

Abschnittsgrenze, *f. Mil:* sector boundary.

Abschnittsleitung, *f. Mil:* sector control.

Abschnittsreserve, *f. Mil:* local reserve (of troops).

abschnittsweise, *adv. & a.* **1.** *Print: etc:* (arranged, arrangement, etc.) by sections; by paragraphs. **2.** (to occur, etc.) in phases. **3.** *Mil:* by, in, sectors; **a. gegliedert,** organized in sectors; *a.* **abschnittsweise Gliederung,** organization in sectors.

Abschnittszeichen, *n. Print:* section mark (§).

Abschnitzel, *n., occ. m.* = **Schnitzel** l.

abschnitze(l)n, *v.tr. sep.* **1.** to pare off, trim off; to chip off; to whittle off. **2.** to whittle away (stick, etc.).

abschnorren, *v.tr. sep. F:* **j-m etwas a.,** to cadge, scrounge, sth. from s.o.

abschnüren. I. *v.tr. sep.* **1.** to unlace; to loosen (corset). **2.** (*a*) *Surg:* to ligature, tie (artery, etc.); to apply a tourniquet to (arm, leg); to string (a wart); (*b*) to cut off (area, etc.); *Ph.Geog:* **abgeschnürtes Meeresbecken,** enclosed sea-basin; (*c*) to constrict, strangle; *Mil:* **den Feindhandel a.,** to strangle, throttle, the enemy's commerce; (*d*) **sich a.,** *Biol:* to segment. **3.** (*a*) to mark (sth.) out, measure (sth.) off, with a string; **ein Grundstück a.,** to line out, mark out, a piece of ground; *N.Arch:* **die Schiffslinien a.,** to mark out the lines of a ship (in shipyard); (*b*) to rope off (an area, etc.).

II. *vbl s.* **Abschnüren** *n.*, **Abschnürung** *f. in vbl senses; also: Surg:* ligation (of artery, etc.); constriction (of the breathing, etc.); *Biol:* segmentation.

abschnurren, *v.sep.* **1.** *v.tr.* to rattle off (prayer, etc.); to reel off (story, verses, etc.). **2.** *v.i.* (*sein*) (*of wheel, spool*) to whirr off, rattle off; (*of arrow*) to whirr away (from the bow). **3.** *v.tr.* = **abschnorren.**

abschöpfen. I. *v.tr. sep.* to skim off (fat from soup, etc.); to ladle out (superfluous liquid); **den Rahm, die Milch, a.,** to skim the cream off the milk, to cream, skim, the milk; *F:* **den Rahm (von etwas) a.,** to take the best part of (sth.), *F:* to skim the cream off (sth.); *Com: Adm:* **Gewinn a.,** to siphon off profits.

II. *vbl s.* **1. Abschöpfen,** *n. in vbl senses.* **2. Abschöpfung,** *f. in vbl senses; also:* price-adjustment levy; (*in E.E.C.*) (import) levy (on a product of a third country), 'skimming' levy.

Abschoß, *m.* **-sses/⸗sse.** *Hist:* **1.** removal tax, emigration tax. **2.** tax on an inheritance; legacy duty.

abschotten, *v.tr. sep.* to partition off; to divide up, subdivide (ship's hold, etc.) (by bulkheads).

abschrägen. I. *v.tr. sep.* **1.** to slant; to bevel, chamfer (edge); to taper (end, edges); *Lap:* to bezel; *Metalw:* to scarf (edges to be welded). **2.** to slope (ground, etc.); *Civ.E:* to batter (embankment, etc.). **3. sich abschrägen,** (*of ground, roof, etc.*) to slope (away).

II. *vbl s.* **1. Abschrägen,** *n. in vbl senses.* **2. Abschrägung,** *f.* (*a*) = II. 1; (*b*) bevelled edge, bevel-edge, bevel, chamfered edge, chamfer, feather-edge; *Lap:* bezel; *Metalw:* scarf (for welding); (*c*) slope (of ground, roof, etc.); *Civ.E:* batter (of embankment, etc.).

abschrämen, *v.tr. sep. Min:* to hew, cut (coal).

abschrammen, *v.sep.* **1.** *v.tr.* to scratch off (sth.). **2.** *v.i.* (*sein*) *F:* (*a*) to clear off, hop it, *U.S:* to beat it, scram; (*b*) *P:* = **abkratzen** 2.

abschränken, *v.tr. sep.* **1.** *A:* to enclose, fence in (pasture, etc.). **2.** *Glassm:* to run (molten glass) into cold water.

abschrappen, *v.tr. sep.* to scrape off, scratch off (sth.).

abschrauben, *v.tr. sep.* **1.** (*a*) to unscrew (bolt, machine, etc.); to screw out (tap, etc.); (*b*) to take the screws out of, to unscrew (lock, etc.). **2. sich abschrauben,** to come unscrewed.

Abschreckalterung, *f. Metall:* quench ageing.

Abschreckbad, *n. Metall:* quenching bath.

abschrecken. I. *v.tr. sep.* **1.** to intimidate, frighten (s.o.); to discourage, dishearten (s.o.); to startle, scare away, frighten away (animal); **j-n von etwas a.,** to deter s.o. from sth.; **j-n davon a., etwas zu tun,** to deter s.o. from, put s.o. off, doing sth.; **er läßt sich durch nichts a.,** nothing will deter him; **er läßt sich leicht a.,** he is easily discouraged, put off; **er wurde vom Versuch abgeschreckt,** he was scared out of the attempt; **er schreckt jedermann ab mit seinem herrischen Auftreten,** he puts everybody off by his lordly airs. **2.** (*a*) to make (liquid) lukewarm, (i) to cool down (hot liquid, by adding cold water); (ii) to take the chill off (liquid, by adding warm water); **abgeschrecktes Wasser,** lukewarm water; (*b*) to cool, chill, (sth. hot) by means of cold water; *Metall:* to quench (metal); (*c*) *Cu:* (i) to rinse (spaghetti, etc.); (ii) **ein Ei a.,** to dip an egg in cold water (*to loosen the shell*). **3.** *Cu:* **den Kaffee a.,** to clear the coffee with a dash of cold water; **die Suppe a.,** to bring the fat to the surface by adding a dash of cold water.

II. *vbl s.* **Abschrecken** *n.*, **Abschreckung** *f. in vbl senses; also:* intimidation; **zur Abschreckung dienende Strafe,** exemplary punishment.

III. *pr.p & a.* **abschreckend,** *in vbl senses; esp.* (*a*) repulsive, repellent, loathsome, dreadful; intimidating; **eine Frau von abschreckendem Aussehen, Äußeren,** a woman of forbidding, repulsive, appearance; **es ist nichts Abschreckendes an ihm,** (i) there is nothing repulsive about him, (ii) he is not in any way intimidating; *adv.* **a. häßlich,** repulsively, *F:* dreadfully, frightfully, ugly; (*b*) deterrent; **ein abschreckendes Beispiel,** a deterrent example, a warning, *F:* a horrid warning; **Strafe, die als abschreckendes Beispiel dienen soll,** exemplary punishment; punishment intended to serve as a deterrent.

Abschreckhärtung, *f. Metall:* quench hardening.

Abschreckungsmittel, *n.* **1.** deterrent; **als A. gegen Verbrechen dienen,** to serve as a deterrent to crime. **2.** chilling, cooling, agent; *Metall:* quenching agent.

Abschreckungssystem, *n. Jur:* system of intimidation.

Abschreckungstheorie, *f. Jur:* theory of the deterrent value of punishment.

Abschreckwirkung, *f.* **1.** deterrent effect (of punishment, etc.). **2.** *Tchn:* chilling, cooling, effect (of liquid).

Abschreibegebühr, *f.*, **Abschreibegeld,** *n. Jur: etc:* copying fee(s).

Abschreibemaschine, *f.* copying machine, copying-press.

abschreiben. I. *v.tr. sep.* (*strong*) **1.** (*a*) to copy, transcribe, to make, write, a copy of (manuscript, document, etc.); to write out (poem, passage from book, etc.); (*b*) (i) = **plagiieren;** (ii) *Sch:* to copy, crib (answer, exercise, etc.). **2.** (*a*) to wipe out, off, to cancel (debt, etc.); *Com: Fin:* to write off (capital, bad debt); **Kapital teilweise a.,** to write down capital; (*b*) to delete (s.o.'s) name from the records; to cross (s.o.) off the books; *F:* to write off (friend, member, etc.) as a dead loss; **dieses Mitglied, diesen Kunden, können wir a.,** we can regard this member, this customer, as lost; (*c*) *Mil: Av: etc:* to write off (a unit, etc., **as lost;** an aircraft, an aircrew, after crash *or* after being

shot down); (*d*) *Com: Ind:* to depreciate, allow for depreciation of, write off (plant, machinery, etc.), (*cp.* 3). **3.** *Com: Fin:* to deduct (sum from account); **die 500 Mark werden wir Ihnen a.,** we will credit you with the 500 marks; **Verluste a.,** to deduct, charge off, losses; *Com: Ind:* **für Büroeinrichtungen, für Maschinen, 10 000 Mark a.,** to allow 10,000 marks for depreciation of office equipment, of machines. **4.** (*a*) to countermand, revoke (order, etc.); to cancel (invitation) (in writing); *Com:* **einen Auftrag a.,** to write cancelling an order; (*b*) *v.i.* (*haben*) **j-m a.,** to write to s.o. cancelling an engagement, (i) to write to s.o. saying that one cannot come, (ii) to write asking s.o. not to come; **ich habe ihm a.,** (i) I have written to tell him that I cannot come; I have sent him an apology (for not coming); (ii) I have written asking him not to come; I have put him off; I have written to tell him that the meeting, the dinner, etc., is off. **5. einen Bleistift a.,** to wear down a pencil; **die Mine a.,** to use up the lead; **eine Feder(spitze) a.,** to wear out a nib; *F:* **sich** *dat.* **(fast) die Finger a.,** to write until one's fingers are sore, numb. **6. sich abschreiben,** (*of pencil*) to wear down; (*of lead in a propelling pencil*) to be used up; (*of nib*) to wear out.

II. *vbl s.* **1. Abschreiben,** *n. in vbl senses; also: Com: Fin:* deduction (of sum from account). **2. Abschreibung,** *f.* (*a*)=II. 1; (*b*) *Com: Fin:* deduction, sum deducted (for losses, etc.); write-off, sum written off (for bad debts); *Com: Ind:* (sum allowed for) depreciation; **jährliche A. an Maschinen,** annual depreciation of machinery; **Rückstellung für Abschreibungen,** allowance (in balance-sheet) for depreciation. *Cp.* **Abschrift.**

Abschreiber, *m.* (*a*) copyist, transcriber; (*b*) *Sch:* pupil who copies, cribs.

Abschreiberei, *f.* -/-en. *Sch: etc:* copying, cribbing.

abschreien, *v.tr. sep.* (*strong*) (*a*) **sich** *dat.* **die Kehle a.,** to shout, bawl, oneself hoarse; (*b*) **sich a.,** (i)=(*a*); (ii) *F:* (*of child*) to tire itself out with crying, howling, squalling.

abschreiten, *v.sep.* (*strong*) **1.** *v.tr.* **eine Entfernung a.,** to pace (off) a distance, to step off, out, a distance; *Mil:* **die Front a.,** to pass down the ranks (at a parade); **eine Ehrenwache a.,** to inspect a guard of honour. **2.** *v.i.* (*sein*) to stride off; to stalk away.

abschricken, *v.tr. sep. Nau:* to ease off and belay (rope); **die Schoten a.,** to check the sheets; **ein um das Gangspill laufendes Tau a.,** to surge a rope round the capstan.

Abschrift, *f.* (*a*) copy (of letter, text, exercise, etc.); *Typewr:* carbon (copy); typewritten copy; transcript, transcription (of speech, notes, etc.); **eine A. von einem Brief nehmen, machen,** to take a copy of a letter; **den Brief füge ich in A. bei,** I attach a copy of the letter; (*b*) *Jur:* copy; **A. einer Akte,** duplicate (copy) of a deed; **gleichlautende A.,** true copy, copy corresponding to the original; **'für gleichlautende A.', 'A. beglaubigt,'** 'certified true copy'; **(gerichtlich) beglaubigte A.,** certified copy, exemplified copy, exemplification.

abschriftlich. 1. *a.* copied; in duplicate. **2.** *adv.* (*a*) in duplicate; as a copy; (*b*) by (means of, sending, etc.) a copy.

abschröpfen, *v.tr. sep.* **1.** *Med:* **j-m Blut a.,** to cup s.o. **2.**=**schröpfen**

Abschrot, *m.* **1.**=**Abschröter. 2.** *occ.*=**Schrot.**

abschroten, *v.tr. sep.* **1.** to chop off (metal, etc.); to chisel off (metal, stone, etc.); to saw off (wood, with cross-cut saw). **2.** to trim (metal, stone). **3.**=**schroten. 4.** *occ.* **Fässer a.,** to roll down barrels (*esp.* into cellar).

Abschröter, *m. Tls: Metalw:* anvil chisel, blacksmith's hardy.

Abschrotmeißel, *m.*=**Schrotmeißel.**

abschrubbe(r)n, *v.tr. sep.* **1.** (*a*) to scrub (sth.) (down); to scour (pots, pans, etc.); (*b*) *Nau:* to hog, scrub (ship's bottom). **2.**=**abschruppen** 2 (*a*).

abschruppen, *v.tr. sep.* **1.**=**abschrubbe(r)n 1. 2.** *Carp:* (*a*) to rough-plane; to trim (wood) with a jack-plane; (*b*) to rough-turn (on the lathe).

Abschub, *m.* **1.** pushing away, off (of sth.). **2.** trace, mark, track; scratch (left by sth. pushed away). **3.** (*a*) *Adm:* deportation, expulsion (of undesirables); (*b*) *Mil:* transporting away (of material, from battle area).

Abschubstelle, *f. Mil:* evacuation station.

abschuften (sich), *v.refl. sep.* to wear oneself out; to work oneself to death; to work like a nigger, like a navvy, like a horse; to slave.

abschultern, *v.tr. sep.* to unshoulder (rifle, etc.).

abschuppen. I. *v.sep.* **1.** *v.tr.* to scale (fish). **2.** *v.i.* (*haben*) & **sich abschuppen,** to scale off, peel off, flake off; *Med:* to desquamate, *F:* to scale, peel; *Geol: etc:* to laminate.

II. *vbl s.* **Abschuppen** *n.*, **Abschuppung** *f. in vbl senses; also: Med:* desquamation; *Geol: etc:* lamination.

Abschur, *f.* (*a*) shearing (of sheep); (*b*) clipping (of animals).

abschürfen, *v.tr. sep.* **I. 1.** to scrape, graze (skin, finger, etc.); to abrade (skin); to excoriate (skin, hands, etc.); **sich die Schienbeine a.,** to bark one's shins. **2.** *Min:* to dig out (ore, coal).

II. *vbl s.* **1. Abschürfen,** *n. in vbl senses; also:* excoriation (of skin, hands). **2. Abschürfung,** *f.* (*a*)=II. 1; (*b*) scrape, graze (on hand, etc.); abrasion (on skin).

Abschuß, *m.* **1.** discharge, firing (of firearm); launching, firing (of rocket). **2.** shooting down, bringing down (of bird, aircraft, etc.); *Mil:* knocking out (of tank); *Mil. Av:* **die Gruppe hat schon 50 Abschüsse verzeichnet,** the squadron already has 50 victories to its credit, has already shot down 50 enemy aircraft. **3.** *Ven:* total bag (for the season). **4.** *Ven:* shooting off (of superfluous game). *Cp.* **abschießen.**

Abschußentfernung, *f. Anti-aircraft Artil:* range of the aircraft at the moment of firing, 'present slant range'.

Abschußgerät, *n. Mil:* firing apparatus; launching apparatus, launcher (for grenades, rockets, etc.).

Abschußgerüst, *n.* launching gantry (for rocket).

Abschußhirsch, *m. Ven:* stag with deformed antlers.

abschüssig, *a.* (*a*) sloping, shelving (ground); steep (slope, etc.); precipitous (descent, etc.); **das Gelände ist a.,** the ground shelves, falls away (rapidly); **abschüssige Felswand,** precipice; *F:* (*of pers.*) **auf die abschüssige Bahn kommen, geraten,** to go downhill; *adv.* in a slope, slopingly; steeply; precipitously; (*b*) **Pferd mit abschüssiger Kruppe,** goose-rumped horse.

Abschüssigkeit, *f.* sloping, shelving, nature (of ground); steepness (of slope); precipitousness (of slope, cliff).

Abschußkandidat, *m.* (*pers.*) possible failure (*in examination*).

Abschußpunkt, *m. Anti-aircraft Artil:* position of the aircraft at the moment of firing, 'present position'.

Abschußrampe, *f.* launching platform (for rockets, etc.).

Abschußvorrichtung, *f. Mil:* launching device (for rockets, etc.).

abschütteln, *v.tr. sep.* (*a*) to shake off; **den Staub von etwas a.,** to shake the dust off sth.; *F:* **den Staub von den Füßen a.,** to shake off the dust from one's feet; to depart indignantly; **j-n a.,** to shake s.o. off; to get rid of s.o.; **er schüttelte den Angreifer (von sich) ab,** he shook off his assailant, flung his assailant from him; **das Joch a.,** to shake off, fling off, cast off, the yoke; **die Ketten a.,** to throw off one's chains; **die Sorgen a.,** to cast away care; **Furcht, Zweifel, a.,** to put aside one's fears, doubts; (*b*) to shake down (fruit, etc.).

abschütten, *v.tr. sep.* to pour out, tip out (grain from sack, etc.); to pour out (liquid); to pour off (liquid).

abschützen, *v.tr. sep.* **1.** (*a*) *Hyd.E:* **das Wasser a.,** *abs.* **a.,** to close the flood-gate(s); (*b*) *abs. Metall:* to cut off the blast. **2.** *A:* **einen Teich a.,** to drain a pond.

Abschützer, *m. Tchn:* cut-off (esp. for air-blast).

abschwächen. I. *v.sep.* **1.** *v.tr.* (*a*) to weaken, lessen, diminish, reduce, attenuate; to tone down (expression, colour, contrast, sound); to dilute (acid, etc.); to soften (expression, impression, contrast); to reduce (contrast); to break (fall); to break the force of, soften (blow, impact); to deaden (shock); to qualify (statement, etc.); **eine abschwächende Erklärung geben,** to give a palliative explanation; *Med:* **ein Virus a.,** to attenuate a virus; *Ph:* **Schwingungen a.,** to damp down, damp out, oscillations; *Com: St.Exch:* **das wird die Preise bedeutend a.,** that will weaken prices considerably; (*b*) *Phot:* **ein Negativ a.,** to reduce (the density of) a negative; (*c*) *Leath:* to mellow (leather). **2.** (*a*) *v.i.* (*sein*) & **sich abschwächen,** *Com: St.Exch:* (*of prices*) to ease off, weaken, sag; **die Preise schwächen (sich) ab,** prices are sagging, going down, becoming easier; **die Preise sind etwas abgeschwächt,** prices have eased off a little, *F:* a fraction; **die Börse ist abgeschwächt,** the market is weaker; (*b*) **sich a.**=**schwach werden,** *q.v. under* **schwach**

II *vbl s.* **Abschwächen** *n.*, **Abschwächung** *f. in vbl senses; also:* diminution, attenuation.

Abschwächer, *m.* -s/-. *Phot:* reducer, reducing agent.

abschwären, *v.i. sep.* (*sein*) *Med:* to fester away.

abschwarten, *v.tr. sep.* **1.** (*a*) *Cu:* to skin (ham, bacon); (*b*) *Ven:* to skin (boar, badger). **2.** to slab (timber). **3.** *F:* **j-n a.,** to give s.o. a hiding, a leathering.

abschwatzen, abschwätzen, *v.tr. sep.* **j-m etwas a.,** to cajole sth. out of s.o.; to wheedle (money, promise) out of, from, s.o.; **j-m sein Geld a.,** to talk s.o. out of his money.

abschweben, *v.i. sep.* (*sein*) to float off, away; to float down.

abschwefeln. I. *v.tr. sep. Ch: Ind:* **1.** to desulphurize. **2.** *occ.* to impregnate (sth.) with sulphur. **3.** *A:* to coke (coal).

II. *vbl s.* **Abschwefeln** *n.*, **Abschwefelung** *f. in vbl senses; also:* desulphurization.

Abschweif, *m. A. & Dial:* digression.

abschweifen. I. *v.sep.* **1.** *v.i.* (*sein*) to deviate, stray; (*a*) **vom Weg a.,** to stray off the road; **vom Ziel a.,** to wander away from one's objective; (*b*) to digress, wander (*from the subject*); **vom Thema, vom Gegenstand, a.,** to wander away, stray, from the point, from the subject; **seine Gedanken schweiften ab,** his thoughts strayed; **bitte schweifen Sie nicht ab!** please keep to the point, to the subject! **abschweifende Bemerkungen,** digressive remarks. **2.** *v.tr. Carp:* to cut (sth.) into a curve.

II. *vbl s.* **1. Abschweifen,** *n. in vbl senses.* **2. Abschweifung,** *f.* (*a*)=II. 1; (*b*) deviation; digression.

abschweißen, *v.tr. sep. Metalw:* **1.** to weld. **2.** to reopen (a welded seam).

Abschweißwärme, *f. Metall:* sweating heat.

abschwelen, *v.tr. sep. Ch: Ind:* to calcine; to roast (ore).

abschwellen, *v.i. sep.* (*strong*) (*sein*) (*a*) (*of swelling*) to go down, to subside; **meine Wange schwillt ab,** the swelling in my cheek is going down; (*b*) (*of sound*) to die down; to die away; to diminish; (*of noise*) to subside; *Ling:* **abschwellende Betonung,** falling stress.

abschwemmen, *v.tr. sep.* **1.** (*of river, etc.*) to float, carry (wood) (downstream); to sweep away, carry off, to wash away *or* down (gravel, earth, etc.); *see also* **anlanden** II. 2 (*b*). **2.** to wash (ore, etc.); to purify, scour, cleanse (wool, leather, etc.); to rinse (yarn, etc.). **3. die Pferde a.,** to water the horses, to take the horses to water.

abschwenden, *v.tr. sep. Agr:* **1.**=**schwenden. 2.** to burn off (grass, etc.).

abschwenken. I. *v.sep.* **1.** *v.tr.* to rinse off, wash off, away (dirt, etc.); to rinse (washing, etc.). **2.** *v.i.* (*sein*) to change direction; *Mil:* to wheel; **rechts a.,** to wheel to the right; **rechts abgeschwenkt!** right wheel! **halbrechts a.,** to incline to the right; **halbrechts abgeschwenkt!** right incline! **von der Straße a.,** to wheel off the road.

II. *vbl s.* **Abschwenken** *n.*, **Abschwenkung** *f. in vbl senses; also: Mil:* wheel.

abschwimmen, *v.i. sep.* (*strong*) **1.** (*sein*) (*a*) (*of pers.*) to swim away, off; (*of thg*) to float away, off; (*b*) *F:* to clear out, hop it, hook it, *U.S:* beat it; **schwimm ab!** hop it! *U.S:* beat it! **2.** (*sein, haben*) **eine Strecke a.,** to swim a distance; **eine Stunde a.,** to swim for an hour.

abschwindeln, *v.tr. sep.* **j-m etwas a.,** to swindle, do, *F:* diddle, twist, s.o. out of sth.; to humbug s.o. out of sth.

abschwingen, *v.sep.* (*strong*) **I.** *v.tr.* **1.** to shake (sth.) off. **2.** (*a*) *Husb:* to fan, winnow, sift (grain); (*b*) *Ind:* to centrifuge; to hydro-extract. **3. sich von etwas abschwingen,** to swing oneself off sth., to leap off sth.; **sich vom Pferd a.,** to swing oneself off one's horse; to vault from one's horse, from the saddle; (*of acrobat*) **er schwang sich vom Trapez ab,** he swung off the trapeze.

II. abschwingen, *v.i.* (*haben*) **1.** (*of note, sound*) to grow fainter. **2.** *Golf:* to finish the shot; to follow through.

abschwirren, *v.sep.* **1.** *v.i.* (*sein*) (*a*) (*of bird, insect, arrow, etc.*) to whirr away, off; to whizz away, off; (*of bee, etc.*) to buzz away, fly off with a buzz; (*b*) *F:* (*of pers.*) to buzz off, hop it. **2.** *v.tr. Ind:* to centrifuge.

abschwitzen, *v.tr. sep.* **1.** to sweat off (fat, etc.). **2.** *Tan:* to sweat (leather); to depilate (hides) (by heating). **3. sich abschwitzen,** (*a*) to

sweat off one's fat; (*b*) *F:*=**abschuften (sich).**

abschwören. I. *v.tr. sep.* (*conj. like* **schwören**) **1.** (*a*) *A:* to take (oath); (*b*) *F:* **er würde dem Teufel, des Teufels Großmutter, ein Bein a.,** he would cheerfully swear to anything. **2.** (*a*) to deny (sth.) (on oath); **ein Verbrechen, seine Schuld, a.,** to deny one's guilt, to declare oneself innocent; *Jur:* to plead not guilty; **seine Unterschrift a.,** to deny one's signature; (*b*) to abjure, forswear; to renounce (on oath); **seinen Glauben a.,** to abjure, renounce, one's faith; **einen Irrtum a.,** to renounce an error; to recant an error (of doctrine); (*c*) *v.i.* (*haben*) **j-m, einer Partei, a.,** to cast off one's allegiance to s.o., to a party; to break irrevocably with s.o., with a party; **einem Laster a.,** to renounce a vice.

II. *vbl s.* **Abschwören** *n.*, **Abschwörung** *f. in vbl senses; also:* denial (of guilt, of one's signature); abjuration, renunciation (of one's faith, of an error, etc.); recantation (of an error of doctrine).

Abschwung, *m.* **1.** swinging off; swinging down; downward swing; vault (from saddle, etc.); *Gym:* swing, leap (from trapeze, etc.). **2.** *Golf:* follow-through.

abscindieren, Absciß, Abscisse=**abszindieren, Absziß, Abszisse.**

absegeln. I. *v.sep.* **1.** *v.i.* (*sein*) (*a*) to sail out, away, off; to set sail, depart; to put (out) to sea; to get under way; (*b*) *F:* to get on one's way. **2.** *v.tr.* to sail along (coast, etc.); to sail over (sea, etc.); **eine gegebene Strecke a.,** to sail a given distance.

II. *vbl s.* **Absegeln,** *n. in vbl senses; also:* departure (of ship).

absehbar, *a.* (*a*) within the range of vision; within sight; (*b*) foreseeable; **in absehbarer Zeit,** in the not-too-distant, foreseeable, *F:* visible, future; within measurable time; **die Folgen sind nicht absehbar,** one cannot foresee the consequences, cannot tell what the consequences will be.

Absehebene, *f.*=**Absehlinie.**

absehen. I. *v.tr. sep.* (*strong*) **1.** to see the whole extent of (sth.); to regard (sth.) in its entirety; **eine Entfernung, die das Auge nicht a. kann,** a distance that the eye cannot compass, that is beyond the range of vision. **2.** to perceive the (possible) extent of (sth.); to foresee; **den Verlauf einer Entwicklung a.,** to foresee the course of a development; **das Ende, der Ausgang, der Sache läßt sich nicht a.,** the outcome of the affair is unpredictable; one cannot say how the affair will end; **es ist gar nicht abzusehen, was geschehen wird,** there is no saying, telling, what will happen. **3. etwas auf j-n, auf etwas, a.,** to aim sth. at s.o., sth.; (*a*) **die Bemerkung war auf dich abgesehen,** the remark was aimed at, intended for, meant for, you; **das ist auf dich abgesehen,** *F:* that's a hit at you; **auf wen hast du es abgesehen?** *F:* who are you getting at? (*b*) **es auf j-n, auf etwas, abgesehen haben,** to have one's eye on s.o., sth.; to have designs on s.o., sth.; to have sth. in view; **sie haben's auf dich abgesehen,** they are after you, *F:* they are after, out for, your blood; **er hat es auf eine Professur abgesehen,** he is aiming at, has his eye on, a professorship; **er hat es auf ihr Geld abgesehen,** he has designs on, is after, her money; **es darauf abgesehen haben, etwas zu tun,** to be intent, bent, on doing sth.; to have made up one's mind to do sth. **4.** (*a*) **j-m etwas a.,** to learn sth. by watching, observing, s.o.; **ich habe ihm das Kunststück abgesehen,** I learned the trick by watching him; I've spotted how he does the trick; (*b*) **j-m etwas an den Augen a.,** to read sth. in s.o.'s eyes; **sie sieht mir jeden Wunsch an den Augen ab,** she knows what I want even before I speak; she anticipates my every wish; (*c*) *Sch:* **etwas von j-m, von etwas, a.,** *abs.* **a.,** to copy, crib (sth. from s.o., from sth.).

II. **absehen,** *v.i.* (*haben*) **1.**=**wegsehen**

2. (*a*) **von etwas, von j-m, a.,** to leave sth., s.o., out of account, of consideration; to disregard sth., s.o.; **wenn wir von ihm absehen,** leaving him out (of consideration, of account, *F:* of it); **wenn man von den Unkosten absieht,** if one disregards, takes no account of, the expenses; **abgesehen davon, davon abgesehen,** apart from, not to mention, without regard to, not counting, *U.S:* aside from, the fact; these considerations aside; **es ist nicht nötig, daß man das Grundstück kauft, (ganz) abgesehen davon, daß ich das Bargeld nicht habe,** there is no need to buy the ground, quite apart from the fact that I haven't got the ready money; (*b*) **von etwas a.,** to refrain from (a course of action, etc.); **diesmal werden wir von einer Bestrafung a.,** we will refrain from punishment, impose no punishment, this time.

III. *vbl s.* **Absehen,** *n. in vbl senses; also:* (*a*) complete perception (of sth.); **da ist kein A.,** it's endless, there's no end to it; (*b*) *A:*=**Absicht** 1; (*c*) *A:*=**Absehlinie.**

Absehlinie, *f.* (*a*) *Opt: Surv:* line of collimation, line of sight; (*b*) *A. & Dial: Sm.a:* line of sight.

Abseide, *f. Tex:* floss(-silk).

abseifen, *v.tr. sep.* **1.** to wash (sth.) with soap; to soap (the washing, etc.). **2.** *Ind: etc:* **eine luftdichte Naht a.,** to test an airtight joint with soapy water.

abseigern. I. *v.tr. sep.* **1.**=**abloten** 3. **2.** *Metall:* to liquate (copper, lead, etc.).

II. *vbl s.* **Abseigern** *n.*, **Abseigerung** *f. in vbl senses; also: Metall:* liquation.

Abseihbier, *n.* residue (of beer in cask).

Abseihebeutel, *m.* filter-bag; straining-bag.

abseihen. I. *v.tr. sep.* to filter, strain (liquid); to percolate (liquid); to decant (wine, etc.).

II. *vbl s.* **Abseihen** *n.*, **Abseihung** *f. in vbl senses; also:* filtration.

abseilen, *v.tr. sep.* **1.** (*a*) to lower (s.o., oneself) on a rope; to let (s.o., oneself) down with a rope; (*b*) *Mount:* **sich a.,** to come down on a doubled rope, to rope down; **Abseilen** *n*, roping-down. **2.** to unrope (s.o., sth.); to cast loose (buoy, balloon, etc.).

absein, *v.i. sep.* (*sein*) (*conj. like* **sein**) *F:* (*of pers.*) to be exhausted, worn out, played out. *See also* **ab** III (*c*); IV. 2, 3.

abseit[1], *adv. & prep.*=**abseits.**

Abseit[2], *n.* **-s/-.** *Fb: Hockey:* off-side.

Abseite, *f.* **1.** (*a*) back, rear (of building, etc.); (*b*) northern side (of hill, etc.). **2.** *Num:* (*a*) reverse (of coin); (*b*) exergue. **3.** *Ecc.Arch:* (side-)aisle. **4.** sloping side (of road, roof, etc.); *Constr:* side, panel (of roof); sloping wall (of garret); *Dial:* attic, garret.

Abseiter, *m.* **-s/-,** outsider.

abseitig, *a.* **1.** standing aside, on one side, apart; aloof; solitary, secluded (existence, etc.). **2.** (remark, etc.) off the point.

Abseitigkeit, *f.* solitariness; secludedness, seclusion; solitary, secluded, existence.

Abseitregel, *f. Fb: Hockey:* off-side rule.

abseits. **1.** *adv.* (*a*) aside, on one side, apart; **a. vom Wege,** off the road; **a. gehen,** to step aside; **sich a. halten,** to keep out of the way, in the background; to hold, stand, aloof; **bei einem Streit a. bleiben, stehen,** to keep out of, hold aloof from, a dispute; (*b*) *Fb: Hockey:* off-side. **2.** *prep.* (+*gen.*) aside from, on one side of, apart from (sth.); **a. des Weges,** off the road.

Absence [ap'sã:s(ə)], *f.* **-/-n.** *Med:* (*a*) (fit of) absent-mindedness; (fit of) abstraction; (*b*) epileptic vertigo.

absenden. I. *v.tr. sep.* (*conj. like* **senden**) (*a*) to send (off), despatch, dispatch (letter, telegram, parcel, goods), to post, mail (letter, parcel), forward (letter, parcel, goods); to consign, *U.S:* ship (goods); to remit (money); *W.Tel:* to send (message); (*b*) to send, despatch, dispatch (messenger, ambassador, etc.); *see also* **Abgesandte.**

II. *vbl s.* **Absenden** *n.*, **Absendung** *f. in vbl senses; also:* despatch, dispatch (of letter, parcel, goods, messenger, ambassador, etc.); consignment, *U.S:* shipment (of goods).

Absender, *m.* (*a*) sender (of letter, telegram, goods, etc.); forwarder (of goods, letter, etc.); addresser (of letter); *W.Tel:* sender, originator (of message); (*on envelope, parcel, etc.*) **'A. J. Schmidt',** 'from J. Schmidt'; (*b*) *Com:* consigner, consignor, *U.S:* shipper (of goods).

Absendestelle, *f.* (*a*) *Com: etc:* forwarding point *or* station; *Post:* office of despatch; *Tg:* office of origin; *W.Tel:* station of origin; (*b*) *Mil.A:* release point (for messenger pigeons).

absengen, *v.tr. sep.* **1.** to singe off (hair, down, from fowl, etc.). **2.** to singe (hair, fowl, cloth, etc.); to scorch (linen, etc.); (*of heat, frost*) to sear (leaves, grain, etc.).

absenkbar, *a.* that can be lowered; *Hyd.E:* **absenkbare Klappe,** folding gate.

absenkeln, *v.tr. sep.*=**abloten** 1.

absenken, *v.tr. sep.* **1.** (*a*) to lower (a flap, etc.); (*b*) **sich a.,** (*of ground*) to slope (down); to shelve. **2.** *Min: etc:* to sink (shaft, well); to bore (well). **3.** *Hort: Vit:* to layer; **Erdbeerableger in Töpfe a.,** to set strawberry runners in pots. **4.** *Constr:* to discentre (arch, etc.).

Absenker, *m.* **1.** *Hort:* (*a*) runner, sucker; (*b*) layer; plant produced by layering; *Vit:* layered branch *or* stock; (*c*) slip, cutting. **2.** *F:* offshoot (of a society, etc.); scion (of a family).

absensen, *v.tr. sep.* to scythe, mow (grass, corn, etc.).

absent[1] [ap'zɛnt], *a.* absent; not present.

Absent[2], *m.* **-en/-en,** absentee.

Absentation [apzɛnta·tsi'o:n], *f.* **-/-en,** absenting of oneself; absence.

Absentenliste, *f.* list of absentees, absentee list.

Absenter [ap'zɛntər], *m.* **-s/-s.** *Hist:* absentee (landlord).

absentieren (sich) [apzɛn'ti:rən], *v.refl. insep.* to absent oneself; **sich von der Schule a.,** to stay, stop, away from school.

Absentismus [apzɛn'tismus], *m.* **-/.** *Hist:* absenteeism.

Absenz [ap'zɛnts], *f.* **-/-en,** absence; **A. von der Schule,** absence from, non-attendance at, school; *Jur:* **in A. verhandeln,** to hear the case in the absence of the defendant; **in A. verurteilt,** sentenced in his, her, absence.

Absenzgelder, *n.pl. Ecc.Hist:* fees paid to a bishop for dispensing an ecclesiastic from residence in his benefice.

Absenzliste, *f.*=**Absentenliste.**

absetzbar, *a.* **1.** removable (official); subject to dismissal. **2.** saleable, marketable, vendible (article, etc.); *Fin:* **absetzbare Wertpapiere,** marketable securities.

Absetzbarkeit, *f.* **1.** removability (of an official). **2.** marketability, marketableness (of an article, *Fin:* of securities); saleability, saleableness, vendibility (of an article, etc.).

Absetzbassin, *n.*, **Absetzbehälter,** *m. Ind:* settling tank.

Absetzbewegung, *f. Mil:* disengaging movement.

Absetzbottich, *m. Dy: etc:* settling vat, settling tub.

Absetzdock, *n. Nau:* depositing dock.

absetzen, *v. sep.* I. *v.tr.* **1.** (*a*) to lay, put, set, (sth.) down; (*b*) to set down, put down, drop (s.o.) (from a vehicle); **der Autobus wird Sie am Bahnhof a.,** the bus will put you down at the station; **ich werde Sie vor Ihrer Tür a.,** I will drop you at your door; (*c*) *Mil.Av:* **Luftlandetruppen, Fallschirmspringer, a.,** to land airborne troops, to drop parachutists (from aircraft); (*d*) *Nau:* **den Lotsen a.,** to drop the pilot. **2. j-n (von seinem Amt) a.,** to dismiss, discharge, s.o.; to dethrone (monarch); to depose (monarch, president, etc.); **einen Beamten a.,** to remove an official (from office); *Mil:* **einen Offizier a.,** to cashier, break, an officer. **3.** (*a*) (*of liquid*) to deposit (sediment); **Wein setzt Hefe ab,** wine throws (down), deposits, a sediment, a crust; (*b*) (*of roasting meat*) **Fett a.,** to yield dripping. **4.** to remove (sth.) from its normal position of activity; (*a*) **den Kessel vom Gasherd a.,** to take the kettle off the gas-stove; **den Geigenbogen a.,** to lift the bow from the (violin-)strings; **das Glas, die Flöte, a.,** to take the glass, the flute, from one's lips; **die Feder a.,** to lift one's pen from the paper; (*cp.* IV. 1 (*a*)); (*b*) *Mil:* **das Gewehr a.,** to bring the rifle down to the ready (after aiming *or* firing); **Seitengewehre a.,** to unfix bayonets; **die Gasmaske a.,** to take off one's gas mask; *abs.* **setzt ab!** ground arms! **5.** to wean (animal, *A. & occ.* child). **6.** to push (sth.) off, away; *Nau:* **ein Boot vom Kai a.,** *abs.* **a.,** to push off from the quay; **ein Boot vom Schiff a.,** *abs.* **a.,** to shove off, bear off, sheer off. **7.** (*a*) to break, cut, (sth.) apart; to disarticulate; to cut off, amputate (limb, etc.); (*b*) **die Zeile a.,** to begin a new paragraph, a new line. **8.** to bring out, set off (colours, etc.); *Paint:* to set off (one colour with another); to line in (a contour); *Dressm:* **ein rotes Kleid mit Weiß a.,** to set off a red dress with white; to trim a red dress with white; **einen grünen Fensterrahmen weiß a.,** to pick out a green window-frame with white; *Bookb:* **mit Fileten a.,** to fillet; to ornament (binding) with a fillet. **9.** *Mus:* **die Töne (voneinander) a.,** to detach the notes; **'abgesetzt',** '*staccato*'. **10.** (*a*) to strike out, remove (item from list, etc.); to deduct (sum); **eine Summe vom Haushalt a.,** to strike a sum off, from, the budget; *Th:* **ein Stück (vom Spielplan) a.,** to take off, withdraw, a play; **einen Punkt von der Tagesordnung a.,** to remove, cut out, an item from the agenda; *Book-k:* **einen Posten a.,** to cancel an entry; **Spesen a.,** to deduct expenses; *St.Exch:* **Aktien von der Notierung a.,** to remove shares from the official price-list; (*b*) to cancel (previously arranged date, intended proceedings, etc.). **11.** *Com:* to sell, dispose of, get rid of (goods); **Waren, die leicht abzusetzen sind, die sich leicht a. lassen, leicht abzusetzende Waren,** goods that sell well, readily; goods with a ready sale; **diese Ware läßt sich überhaupt**

nicht a., there is no sale at all for these goods. **12.** *Print:* **ein Manuskript a.,** to compose a manuscript, to set up a manuscript (in type). **13.** *Constr: Mec.E: etc:* to offset. **14.** (*a*) to transfer (pattern on to paper, measurement from one plane to another, etc.); (*b*) *Nau:* **den Schiffsort auf der Karte a.,** to prick off the ship's position on the chart; *abs.* **a.,** to prick the chart; *Nau:* **einen Kurs a.,** to shape a course.

II. **sich absetzen. 1.** (*a*) (*of solid matter*) to settle, to form a deposit; (*b*) (*of liquid*) to set. **2.** to stand out in relief (**von, gegen,** against); to contrast (strongly) (**von, gegen,** with); **sich gegen den Himmel a.,** to stand out against the sky. **3.** *Mil:* to break away (from the enemy); to disengage. **4.** *Min:*=IV. 1 (*c*).

III. **absetzen,** *v. impers.* **es wird Hiebe a.,** (i) there will be trouble; (ii) this will end in a fight, *F:* in a scrap; *F:* **es wird was a.,** there's trouble brewing, *F:* there'll be ructions.

IV. **absetzen,** *v.i.* (*haben*) **1.** (*a*) to pause, break, stop (short); **mitten in seiner Ansprache setzte er ab,** he broke off in the middle of his address; **ohne abzusetzen,** without pausing, straight off, at one go; at one stretch; **er trank das Glas aus ohne abzusetzen,** he emptied the glass at a draught, at one gulp, at one go; **er schrieb zwei Kapitel ohne abzusetzen,** he wrote two chapters straight off, without a break, at a stretch; (*b*) to come to an end; **das Gebirge setzt hier ab,** the mountain-range ends, finishes, here; (*c*) *Min:* **der Erzgang, das Erz, setzt ab,** the lode is broken, gives out, peters out, goes dead. **2.** *Mil:*=II. 3. **3.** *Av:* to increase the distance between the aircraft (in a flying formation). **4.** *Min:* (*of rock*) to crumble.

V. *vbl s.* **1. Absetzen,** *n. in vbl senses; also:* removal (of sum from budget, item from list, etc.); pause, break (in speech); *Mil:* disengagement. **2. Absetzung,** *f.* dismissal (of official, etc.); removal (of official) from office; dethronement (of monarch); deposing, deposition (of monarch, president, etc.); amputation (of limb, etc.); *Mil:* cashiering, breaking (of officer); *Th:* withdrawal (of play); **einstweilige A.,** suspension (of official). *Cp.* **Absatz.**

Absetzer, *m.* **1.** *Mil.Av:* despatcher, jump-master. **2.** *Civ.E: etc:* dumper; dumping device.

Absetzferkel, *n.*=**Absatzferkel.**

Absetzgebiet, Absetzgelände, *n. Mil.Av:* landing area (for airborne troops, parachutists).

Absetzlinie, *f.* **1.** *Paint:* colour stripe. **2.** *Bookb:* fillet.

Absetzkasten, *m. Paperm: etc:* draining-tank.

Absetzplatz. *m. Mil.Av:*=**Absetzgebiet.**

Absetzsäge, *f. Tls: Carp:* **1.** medium-size framed saw with fine teeth. **2.** grooving saw with a fixed fence, *U.S:* rabbet saw.

Absetzteich, *m. Ind:* settling trough.

Absetztubbe, *f. Dy: etc:* settling tub.

Absetzzeit, *f. Ch: Ind:* settling time; time required for a deposit to settle.

Absetzzisterne, *f.* settling cistern (for rain-water, etc.).

absicheln, *v.tr. sep.* to cut, reap, (corn, etc.) with a sickle.

Absicht, *f.* -/-en. **1.** (*a*) intention, purpose, motive, design; *Jur:* intent; **die A. haben, etwas zu tun,** to intend to do sth., to mean to do sth.; **ich habe nicht die geringste, leiseste, A., dabei zu sein,** I have not the slightest intention of, I wouldn't dream of, being present; **er tat es ohne besondere A.,** he did it without any particular motive; **ich habe nicht die A., zu kommen,** I don't intend, mean, to come; **das war nicht meine A., das lag nicht in meiner A.,** I didn't mean (to do) it, I didn't do it on purpose; **in, mit, der A.,** with the object of, with the intention of, with a view to; with, for, the purpose of; **in welcher A. tun Sie das?** to what end are you doing this? what is your objective? what have you in mind? **etwas mit (voller) A. tun,** to do sth. deliberately, designedly, on purpose; to do sth. with intent; **seine A. erreichen,** to attain, achieve, one's end; **mit redlicher A.,** with honesty of purpose, with honourable intentions; **etwas in bester A. tun,** to do sth. with the best (of) intentions; **er hat die besten Absichten,** he means well; **man läßt die A. für die Tat gelten,** it is the intention that counts; **man merkt die A., und man wird verstimmt,** the intention is all too obvious; **ohne A.,** without intention, unintentionally, undesignedly; **die Bemerkung hat er nicht ohne A. gemacht,** there was a purpose behind this remark, his remark was not made at random; **in, mit, böswilliger A.,** with malicious intent, *Jur:* with malice aforethought, with, of, through, malice prepense; **in, mit, betrügerischer A.,** with intent to defraud; **böse Absichten,** evil intentions; **seine Absichten wurden vereitelt,** his plans were frustrated; his schemes, his designs, failed; (*b*) **auf j-n, etwas** *acc.*, **Absichten haben,** to have designs on s.o., sth.; **er hat Absichten auf ihre Tochter,** he has an eye on her daughter; he is interested in marrying her daughter; *F:* **er hat Absichten,** (i) he has his eye on something; (ii) he is up to something. **2.** *A: prep. phr.* **in A. auf j-n, etwas, in A.**+*gen.*, (i) as regards, with respect to, with regard to, s.o., sth., (ii) with a view to sth.

absichtlich, *a.* intentional; deliberate (action, omission, etc.); wilful (action); **absichtliche Beleidigung,** deliberate insult, studied insult; *Jur:* **absichtlicher Mord,** wilful murder; *adv.* **ich bin a. gekommen, um ihn zu sehen,** I came on purpose, purposely, to see him; **er hat es nicht a. getan,** he didn't mean (to do) it, he didn't do it on purpose.

Absichtlichkeit, *f.* deliberateness (of an insult, etc.); wilfulness (of an action); deliberate intention; *Jur:* premeditation.

absichtslos, *a.* unintentional; undesigned (action, etc.); *adv.* unintentionally, undesignedly.

Absichtslosigkeit, *f.* unintentional, undesigned, character (of an action, etc.).

Absichtssatz, *m. Gram:* final clause, *U.S:* clause of purpose.

absichtsvoll, *a.* deliberate, designed, (fully) intentional; *adv.* deliberately, designedly, intentionally.

absickern, *v.i. sep.* (*sein*) to ooze, seep, drip (down); to trickle (down).

absieben, *v.tr. sep.* to separate (sth.) by sifting; **Kiesel von Sand a.,** to sift out pebbles from sand.

absieden, *v.tr. sep.* (*conj. like* **sieden**) **1.** To boil (sth.) (thoroughly). **2.** *Pharm: etc:* to make a decoction of (herbs, etc.). **3.** To extract (sth.) by boiling; to boil out (solid) (from a liquid). **4.** *Tex:* to boil off (raw silk).

absingen, *v.tr. sep.* (*strong*) **1. ein Lied (vom Notenblatt) a.,** to sing a song at sight, to sight-read a song. **2.** (*a*) to sing (patriotic song); (*b*) *Ecc:* to chant (litany, etc.). **3.** to wear out (voice) with singing; **eine abgesungene Stimme,** a worn-out voice.

absinken. I. *v.sep.* (*strong*) **1.** *v.i.* (*sein*) to sink down, sink away; (*of speed*) to drop. **2.** *v.tr. Min:*=**abteufen.**

II. *vbl s.* **Absinken,** *n. in vbl senses;* **A. der Geschwindigkeit,** drop in speed.

absintern, *v.i. sep.* (*sein*)=**absickern.**

Absinth [ap'zint], *m.* -(e)s/-e. **1.** *Bot:* wormwood. **2.** absinth(e).

absinthartig, *a. Ch: etc:* absinthine.

Absinthismus [apzin'tismus], *m.* -/. *Med:* absinthism.

Absitzbecken, *n. Ind:* settling tank; *Hyd.E:* settling reservoir.

Absitzbütte, *f. Brew:* settling tub.

absitzen, *v. sep.* (*strong*) I. *v.i.* **1.** (*haben*) **von j-m, etwas, a.,** to sit away from s.o., sth.; **weit vom Fenster a.,** to sit well away from the window. **2.** (*sein*) (*a*) to dismount (from horse, motorcycle, etc.); to get down from one's horse, to alight from horseback; *Mil:* (*order to cavalry, motor-cyclists, men in lorries, etc.*) **'absitzen!' 'abgesessen!'** 'dismount!'; (*b*) *A:* **bei j-m a.,** to visit s.o.; to stop, stay, with s.o.; to rest at s.o.'s house (when on a journey). **3.** (*sein*) *Min:* (*of earth*) to slip.

II. **absitzen,** *v.tr.* **1.** to wear out (trousers, etc.) by sitting. **2.** to sit out (a set period of time); (*a*) **die drei Stunden der Vorstellung a.,** to sit out the three hours of the performance; *Hum:* **ich werde mein Eintrittsgeld a.,** I've paid my money and I'm going to stick it out; (*b*) **die Schulzeit a.,** to get through one's schooling; to pass through school; (*c*) **eine Strafe a.,** to serve a sentence of imprisonment; to do time; **seine Strafe a.,** to serve one's sentence, *F:* one's time, *F:* to do a stretch, to do one's time; *A:* **eine Schuld a.,** to be imprisoned for debt.

absolut [apzo·'lu:t], *a.* absolute; (*a*) **absolute Höhe,** altitude, vertical elevation, height above sea-level; **absolute Mehrheit,** absolute, clear, majority; **absolute Malerei,** abstract painting; **absolute Musik,** absolute, abstract, music; *Mus:* **absolutes Gehör,** absolute pitch, perfect pitch; **absolute Geschwindigkeit.** (i) *Mec:* absolute velocity, (ii) *Av:* air-speed; *Ph:* **absoluter Nullpunkt,** absolute zero; **absolute Leere,** perfect vacuum; *Ph.Meas:* **absolutes Maß(system),** absolute system of units; C.G.S. (centimetre-gramme-second) system; *Mth:* **absoluter Betrag, Wert,** absolute value; modulus (of a complex quantity); **absolute Monarchie,** absolute monarchy; *adv.* **a. herrschen,** to rule absolutely; *s.n. Phil:* **das Absolute,** the Absolute; (*b*) **absolute Verneinung, Weigerung,** absolute, flat, denial, refusal; *adv.* **etwas a. verneinen,** to deny sth. absolutely, flatly; **a. trocken,** bone-dry; **a. unbrauchbar,** completely, utterly, useless; **sie will a. nicht wiederkommen,** she simply won't return; **das verstehe ich a. nicht,** I just don't understand it at all.

Absoluteffekt, *m. Mec:* amount of energy taken up (by a machine).

Absolutglied, *n. Mth:* absolute term (in an equation).

Absolution [apzo·lu·tsi'o:n], *f.* -/-en. **1.** *Ecc:* absolution; **j-m A. erteilen,** to grant s.o. absolution. **2.** *Jur: A:* acquittal, discharge.

Absolutismus [apzo·lu·'tismus], *m.* -/. *Pol:* absolutism.

Absolutist [apzo·lu·'tist], *m.* -en/-en, absolutist.

absolutistisch [apzo·lu·'tistiʃ], *a.* absolutist.

Absolutorialprüfung [apzo·lu·to·ri'a:l-], *f. Sch: A:* leaving examination.

absolutorisch [apzo·lu·'to:riʃ], *a.* absolutory.

Absolutorium [apzo·lu·'to:rium], *n.* -s/-rien. **1.** *Jur:* acquittal, discharge. **2.** *Sch: A. & Austrian:*=**Absolutorialprüfung.**

Absoluttrocken-, *comb. fm. Ch: etc:* bone-dry (state, weight).

Absolutwert, *m. Mth:* absolute value; modulus (of a complex quantity).

Absolvent [apzol'vɛnt], *m.* -en/-en, **A. eines Lehrgangs, einer Ausbildung,** person who has completed a course of study, a period of training; **A. einer Prüfung,** candidate who has passed an examination; **A. einer Schule,** pupil *or* student who has completed his studies at school, *U.S:* graduate (from a school).

absolvieren [apzol'vi:rən]. I. *v.tr. insep.* **1.** to absolve (s.o.) (from blame); to acquit, exonerate (s.o.). **2.** to complete (task, course of study, training, etc.); to do (exercise, training, etc.); to fulfil (duty, etc.); to pass (examination, etc.); to complete one's studies at, to finish, *U.S:* to graduate from (school, etc.).

II. *vbl s.* **Absolvieren** *n.*, **Absolvierung** *f. in vbl senses; also:* (*a*) absolution (of s.o.); acquittal, exoneration (of s.o.); (*b*) completion (of task, course of study, training, etc.); *U.S:* graduation (from school, etc.).

absonderbar, *a.* **1.** separable; detachable. **2.** that can be isolated; *Ch:* isolable. **3.** *Physiol:* that can be secreted.

Absonderheit [ap'zondərhait], *f.*=**Absonderlichkeit.**

absonderlich [ap'zondərliç], *a.* (*a*) exceptional, unusual, uncommon, remarkable (merit, virtue, etc.); **ein Käfer von absonderlicher Größe,** a beetle of uncommon, extraordinary, exceptional, size; (*b*) odd, curious, strange, queer, singular (person, behaviour, custom, fact, etc.); out-of-the-way (idea, etc.); **absonderlicher Brauch,** quaint, odd, custom; **absonderliche Gebärden,** peculiar, odd, gestures; **die Situation ist etwas a.,** the situation is somewhat out of the common, is rather odd; **das Absonderliche an der Sache ist, daß . . . ,** the strange part of, the queer thing about, the affair is that . . . ; *adv.* **sich a. betragen,** to behave strangely, oddly, queerly; (*c*) *A:* particular, special; *adv.* (e)specially, (more) particularly, in particular.

Absonderlichkeit, *f.* **1.** particularity; particular, special, nature (of sth.). **2.** (*a*) peculiarity, unusualness, uncommonness, remarkableness; (*b*) oddness, oddity, curiousness, strangeness, queerness, singularity (of person, behaviour, custom, fact, etc.); quaintness (of custom, etc.).

absondern. I. *v.tr. sep.* **1.** to separate, detach, divide; to disjoin; to isolate (**von,** from); to put (sth.) apart; to segregate (species, etc.); *Ch:* to isolate (element, etc.). **2.** (*a*) *Physiol:* to secrete (bile, etc.); to excrete (waste matter); to discharge (pus, hormones, etc.); (*b*) (*of plant*) to excrete (juice). **3.** *Phil: A:* to abstract (concepts). **4.** *Jur:* (*a*) **die Forderung eines Gläubigers a.,** to treat a creditor's claim as preferential; **abgesonderte Befriedigung,** settlement of preferential claims; satisfaction of preferential creditors; **Recht auf abgesonderte Befriedigung,** preferential rights; (*b*) *A:* **einen Erben a.,** to pay off, buy off, an expectant heir. **5. sich absondern,** (*a*) to separate, part (**von,** from); to withdraw (from sth.); to dissociate oneself (from s.o., sth.); **sich von der Welt a.,** to detach oneself, retire, from the world; to withdraw into solitude; to seclude oneself, hold

aloof, from society; *Com:* **sich von einem Teilhaber a.,** to dissolve a partnership (with s.o.); (*b*) to be, become, isolated; (*of a species, etc.*) to segregate; (*c*) *Physiol:* to be secreted; to be excreted; to be discharged.

II. *vbl s.* **1. Absondern,** *n. in vbl senses; also:* separation; division; isolation (**von,** from); segregation (of species); *Physiol:* secretion (of bile, etc.); excretion (of waste matter); discharge (of pus, hormones, etc.); *Phil: A:* abstraction (of concepts); *Jur:* preferential treatment (of a creditor's claim). **2. Absonderung,** *f.* (*a*)=II. 1; (*b*) (*state*) separation; division; isolation; segregation; (*c*) *Physiol:* (*resulting matter*) secretion; excretion; discharge; *Phil: A:* abstract concept, abstraction.

III. *pr.p. & a.* **absondernd,** *in vbl senses; esp. Physiol:* secreting, secretive, secretory; excreting, excretive, excretory.

Absonderungsanspruch, *m. Jur:* creditor's preferential claim; claim made by a secured creditor.

absonderungsberechtigt, *a. Jur:* preferential or secured (creditor); **ein Absonderungsberechtigter,** a preferential creditor; a secured creditor.

Absonderungsbläschen, *n. Biol:* vacuole.

Absonderungsdrüse, *f. Anat:* secretory gland.

Absonderungsfläche, *f. Geol:* joint(ing)-plane.

Absonderungsflüssigkeit, *f. Physiol:* secretory fluid; excretory fluid.

Absonderungsgraben, *m.* boundary ditch.

Absonderungsgefäß, *n.*=**Absonderungsorgan** (*b*).

Absonderungsorgan, *n. Anat:* (*a*) secretory organ; (*b*) excretory organ.

Absonderungsrecht, *n. Jur:* preferential right (of a creditor).

Absonderungsstoff, *m. Physiol:* secreted matter, product of secretion; *pl.* secreta.

Absorber [apˈzorbər], *m.* **-s/-.** *Ch: Ph:* absorber.

absorbierbar [apzorˈbiːrbaːr], *a.* absorbable.

Absorbierbarkeit, *f.* absorbability.

absorbieren [apzorˈbiːrən]. I. *v.tr. insep.* **1.** *Ch: Ph: etc:* to absorb; **das Gas wird von der Flüssigkeit absorbiert,** the gas is absorbed by the liquid; **absorbierendes Mittel,** absorbent; **absorbierende Fähigkeit,** absorptive power. **2.** to absorb, engross; **seine Arbeit absorbiert ihn ganz, er wird, ist, ganz von seiner Arbeit absorbiert,** he is engrossed, entirely absorbed, in his work; his work engrosses him completely, takes up all his time; he is entirely taken up by his work.

II. *vbl s.* **Absorbieren** *n.,* **Absorbierung** *f. in vbl senses; also:* absorption.

Absorptiometer [apzorptsioˈmeːtor], *n.* **-s/-.** *Ch:* absorptiometer.

Absorption [apzorptsiˈoːn], *f.* **-/-en,** absorption; (*a*) absorbing; (*b*) absorbed state of mind.

Absorptions-, *comb.fm.* (*a*) absorption . . . ; . . . of absorption; **Absorptionsrohr** *n,* absorption tube; **Absorptionswärme** *f,* heat of absorption; (*b*) absorbent . . . ; absorptive . . . ; **Absorptionsmittel** *n,* absorbent (substance); **Absorptionskraft** *f,* absorptive power.

absorptionsfähig, *a.* absorbent (substance); absorptive (gland, etc.).

Absorptionsfähigkeit, *f.* absorptive power.

Absorptionsgas, *n. Ch:* absorbed, occluded, gas.

Absorptionsgewebe, *n. Biol:* absorbing, absorptive, tissue.

Absorptionsindex, Absorptionskoeffizient, *m. Ch: Ph:* coefficient of absorption.

Absorptionskraft, *f.* absorptive power.

Absorptionslinie, *f. Opt:* absorption line.

Absorptionsmittel, *n.* absorbent.

Absorptionsspektrum, *n. Ph:* absorption spectrum.

Absorptionsstreifen, *m. Ph:* absorption band.

Absorptionsvermögen, *n.* absorptive power.

absorptiv [apzorpˈtiːf], a. absorptive.

abspalten. I. *v.tr. sep.* (*conj. like* **spalten**) **1.** to split off, cleave off; to separate; *Biol: etc:* to segregate; *Ch:* to eliminate. **2.** to cleave, split; to fissure (rock, etc.); *Ch:* to break down (compound); to decompose (double salts, etc.); *Ind:* to crack (heavy oil, etc.). **3. sich abspalten,** (*a*) to split off, to separate; to segregate (**von,** from); (*b*) to cleave (asunder); to split; (*of rock, etc.*) to fissure; *Ch:* (*of compound*) to break down.

II. *vbl. s.* **1. Abspalten,** *n. in vbl senses.* **2. Abspaltung,** *f.,* (*a*)=II. 1; *also:* separation; *Biol: etc:* segregation; *Ch:* elimination; *Ch:* decomposition (of double salts, etc.); (*b*) piece split off; *Pol:* splinter group.

abspänen, *v.tr. sep.* **1.** *Metalw:* to clear (work, etc.) of shavings, of turnings. **2.** to clean (sth.) by rubbing it with metal shavings, with steel wool.

Abspanndraht, *m.* stay-wire, bracing wire; span-wire; stretching wire, stretcher; anchoring wire.

abspannen. I. *v.tr. sep.* **1.** (*a*) to relax, slacken, loosen (sth. that is taut); to unstring (bow); to unbrace (drum); to uncock (firearm); **eine Feder a.,** (i) to let down, slacken, (ii) to release, a spring; **ein Seil a.,** to slacken a rope; (*b*) to unclamp; to release (sth.) from a clamp *or* vice; (*c*) *Mch:* **den Dampf a.,** to cut off, shut off, the steam; (*d*) *abs. El.E:* to step down the voltage. **2.** to unhitch, take out (horse(s)); to unhook (team); to unyoke (oxen); **die Pferde, den Wagen, a.,** *abs.* **a.,** to take the horses out (of the shafts). **3.** (*a*) to guy, stay, brace; *Tg: etc:* to rig (pole, mast); (*b*) *Tg:* **die Leitungen a.,** to strain back the wires. *See also* **abgespannt.**

II. *vbl s.* **1. Abspannen,** *n. in vbl senses.* **2. Abspannung,** *f.* (*a*)=II. 1; (*b*) guys, stay-wires, span-ropes, bracing (wires *or* ropes); (*c*)=**Abgespanntheit.**

Abspanner, *m. El.E:* step-down transformer.

Abspanngestänge, *n. Tg: etc:* guyed *or* strutted pole.

Abspannisolator, *m. El.E:* strain insulator.

Abspannklemme, *f. El.E:* anchoring clamp.

Abspannmast, *m.* **1.** *Tg:* terminal mast. **2.** *Civ.E: etc:* pylon.

Abspannseil, *n.* guy(-rope); span-rope.

Abspannstange, *f. Tg:* terminal pole.

Abspannstütze, *f. Tg:* terminal spindle.

Abspannung, *f. see* **abspannen** II.

Abspannwerk, *n. El.E:* (step-down) transformer station.

absparen, *v.tr. sep.* **sich** *dat.* **etwas a.,** to deny oneself sth.; to go short of sth. (*in order to save for a special purpose*); **sich das Studium am, vom, Munde a.,** to pinch and scrape in order to study.

abspateln, *v.tr. sep.* to remove (sth.) with a spatula.

abspeisen, *v.sep.* **1.** *v.tr.* (*a*) *A:* to feed (s.o.), to give (s.o.) a meal; **die Diener a.,** to give the servants their dinner; (*b*) **j-n mit schönen Worten, mit Ausreden, a.,** to put s.o. off with fine words, with excuses; **ich lasse mich nicht so a.,** I won't be put off, fobbed off, like that; *see also* **Bauch** 2. **2.** *v.i.* (*haben*) *A. & Dial:* to finish one's meal; **die Herren hatten abgespeist,** the gentlemen had finished dining, had had their dinner.

abspenstig, *a.* **j-m j-n a. machen,** to entice, lure, seduce, s.o. away from s.o.; **j-m seine Kunden a. machen,** to entice away, steal, s.o.'s customers; **er hat mir mein Mädchen a. gemacht,** he has stolen, *F:* pinched, my girl; **j-m, von j-m, a. werden,** to desert s.o.; *Pol:* **seiner Partei a. werden,** to desert one's party, *F:* to rat.

absperren. I. *v.tr. sep.* **1.** to bar, obstruct (the way); to close, block (up), barricade (road); to obstruct, stop (up), block (pipe, etc.); to stop, block (traffic, trade, progress). **2.** to isolate, shut off, cut off (area, etc.); to cordon off (area, etc.); to wall off (room, etc.); *Ch: Ind:* to confine, seal off (gas, etc.). **3. das Wasser a.,** to turn off, shut off, the water; *Hyd.E:* (i) to shut off, (ii) to dam up, the water; *Mch:* **den Dampf a.,** to shut down steam, to shut off, cut off, the steam; *Aut: Av:* **das Benzin, die Benzinzufuhr, a.,** to cut off the petrol supply, *U.S:* gas. **4.** *Ind:* **Holz a.,** to laminate wood, to make plywood. **5. sich absperren,** to shut oneself up, away, off; to seclude oneself; **dieses Land hat sich gegen alle westlichen Einflüsse abgesperrt,** this country has shut, sealed, itself off from all western influences; **sich von der Außenwelt a.,** to cut oneself off from the outer world; to retire within oneself; to keep oneself to oneself.

II. *vbl s.* **1. Absperren,** *n. in vbl senses; also:* obstruction (of way, pipe, etc.); isolation (of an area, etc.); *Ind:* lamination (of plywood). **2. Absperrung,** *f.* (*a*)=II. 1; (*b*) barrier; barricade; (road-)block; obstruction; stoppage; cordon.

Absperrflüssigkeit, *f.* sealing fluid (of gas-holder, etc.).

Absperrglied, *n. Tchn:* shut-off; cut-off.

Absperrhahn, *m.* stopcock.

Absperrklappe, *f. Tchn:* clack(-valve); stop-valve, check-valve.

Absperrklinke, *f. Mec.E:* pawl.

Absperrorgan, *n. Tchn: esp. Hyd.E:* shut-off.

Absperrposten, *m.pl. Mil:* cordon of sentries.

Absperrschieber, *m.* gate-valve, slide-valve; *Hyd.E:* sluice-valve; check-valve; *Mch:* stop-valve; cut-off valve.

Absperrsicherung, *f. El.E:* safety-fuse, cut-out.

Absperrsystem, *n. Rail:*=**Blocksystem.**

Absperrungssystem, *n. Pol.Ec:* system of prohibition of imports.

Absperrventil, *n.* stop-valve; shut-off valve; *Mch:* cut-off valve; *Mch: Hyd.E:* check-valve.

Absperrvorrichtung, *f.* (*a*) *Hyd.E: etc:* shut-off; *Mch: etc:* cut-off (device); (*b*) sealing device (of gas-holder, etc.).

abspiegeln, *v.tr. sep.* to reflect, mirror.

abspielen, *v.tr. sep.* **1.** *Mus:* **(ein Stück) vom Blatt a.,** to sight-read (a piece). **2.** (*a*) *Mus:* to play (piece) (right through, to the end); (*b*) **eine Schallplatte a.,** to play (over) a gramophone record; **eine Tonbandaufnahme a.,** to play back a tape-recording. **3.** (*a*) *Games:* **den Ball a.,** to put the ball into play; (*b*) *Bill:* **den Ball von der Bande a.,** to play off the cushion. **4.** (*a*) to wear out (sth.) with playing; *Cin:* to wear out (film) with repeated showing; **abgespielte Schallplatte, abgespielte Karten,** worn-out record, worn-out cards; (*b*) **eine Melodie a.,** to repeat a tune until it becomes wearisome; *F:* to play a tune to death; **abgespielte Melodie,** hackneyed, *F:* threadbare, tune. **5. sich abspielen,** to take place, to happen; to be enacted; to pass off, go off; **die Geschichte spielt sich in Deutschland ab,** the scene of the story is laid in Germany; *Th:* **der zweite Akt spielt sich auf der Straße ab,** the second act is set in the street; **die Ereignisse, die sich in Rußland abspielen,** the events that are being enacted, that are taking place, in Russia; **die Zeremonie hat sich gut abgespielt,** the ceremony went off, passed off, well.

abspinnen, *v.tr. sep.* (*strong*) (*a*) to spin (off) (thread, wool); **den Rocken, die Wolle vom Rocken, a.,** to empty the distaff; (*b*) *F:* **ein Garn a.,** to spin a yarn, tell a tale.

abspitzen, *v.tr. sep.* **1.** (*a*) to sharpen (sth.), to put a point on (sth.); **einen Bleistift a.,** to point, sharpen, a pencil; *A:* **eine Schreibfeder a.,** to nib a (quill-)pen; (*b*) **ein Epigramm a.,** to point an epigram. **2.** to blunt (sth. sharp); to break the point off (sth.); **Steine a.,** to smooth the surface of stones. **3.** (*a*) **eine Bemerkung, usw., auf j-n a.,** to aim a remark, etc., at s.o.; (*b*) *F:* **es auf j-n, auf etwas, a.,** to have one's eye on s.o., sth.; to have sth. in view.

abspleißen, *v.tr. sep.* (*strong*) *Nau:* to unlay (rope).

Abspliß, *m.* **-splisses/.** *Nau:* unlaying (of rope).

absplittern, *v.sep.* **1.** *v.tr.* to split (sth.) off; to splinter (sth.) off. **2.** *v.i.* (*sein*) to split off; to come off, fly off, in splinters.

Absprache, *f.* (*a*) **(mündliche) A.,** verbal arrangement, agreement; (*b*) arrangement, agreement (by correspondence, etc.); *Com:* **laut (unserer) A.,** in accordance with our agreement; as per arrangement, agreement.

absprachegemäß, *adv. Com:* in accordance with the, our, agreement; as per arrangement, agreement.

absprechen. I. *v.sep.* (*strong*) **1.** *v.tr. Jur:* **j-m etwas a.,** to deprive s.o. of sth. (by judicial sentence); **j-m ein Gut a.,** (i) to dispossess s.o. of an estate, (ii) to adjudicate against a claimant to an estate; *Lit:* **j-m das Leben, den Kopf, das Haupt, a.,** to condemn, sentence, s.o. to death, to pass sentence of death on s.o. **2.** *v.tr.* **j-m etwas a.,** to deny s.o. the possession of sth.; **j-m ein Recht a.,** to deny s.o. a right; **ich spreche ihm das Recht auf Berufung nicht ab,** I do not deny, question, his right of appeal; **j-m alles Talent a.,** to deny, refuse to admit, that s.o. has any talent; **seine Fähigkeiten lassen sich nicht a.,** one cannot deny, dispute, question, his capabilities; **das Bild ist Vermeer abgesprochen worden,** it has been decided that the picture is not by, can no longer be ascribed to, Vermeer. **3.** *v.tr.* **etwas mit j-m a.,** to discuss (matter of business, etc.) with s.o.; **das ist schon abgesprochen,** that is already arranged, settled, agreed. **4. sich mit j-m absprechen,** to come to an agreement, an arrangement, with s.o. **5.** *v.i.* (*haben*) **über j-n, etwas, a.,** to speak of, to judge, s.o., sth., unfavourably.

II. *vbl s.* **Absprechen,** *n., in vbl senses; also: Jur:* sentence of deprival, of dispossession; denial (of a right, etc.). *Cp.* **Absprache.**

III. *pr.p. & a.* **absprechend,** *in vbl senses; esp.* (*a*) unfavourable, adverse (judgment, criticism); (*b*) derogatory (judgment); disparaging (criticism, tone, manner); censorious (tone, manner); **in absprechendem Ton über j-n, etwas, reden,** to speak disparagingly of s.o., sth.; (*c*) peremptory (judgment); dogmatic (judgment, *F:* tone, manner).

Absprecherei, *f.* **-/-en,** (*a*) censorious, disparaging,

criticism; (*b*) peremptory *or* dogmatic judgment(s).

absprecherisch, *a.*=**absprechend,** *q.v. under* **absprechen** III. (*b*).

abspreizen. I. *v.tr. sep. Constr: etc:* (*a*) to brace, stay, strut; (*b*) to shore up, prop (excavation).

II. *vbl s.* **1. Abspreizen,** *n. in vbl senses.* **2. Abspreizung,** *f.* (*a*)=II. 1; (*b*) brace(s), stay(s), strut(s); shoring, props (of excavation).

absprengen, *v.sep.* I. *v.tr.* **1.** to blow (sth.) off (with explosives); to blast away (rock, etc.). **2.** to split off (rock, etc.) (with wedge, crowbar, etc.); to break off, cut off (piece of glass). **3.** *Mil:* **Truppen (vom Gros) a.,** to cut off troops from the main body; **Abgesprengte** *pl*, troops cut off from the main body; stragglers. **4.** *Constr:* to erect (arch, etc.) on the cantilever principle. **5.** to water (flowers, plants, dusty road).

II. **absprengen,** *v.i.* (*sein*) (*of horseman*) to gallop off, away.

Absprenger, *m. Tls:* glass-cutter.

absprenkeln, *v.tr. sep.* to spray (sth.) down; to spray (insecticides, etc.) from aircraft.

abspringen. I. *v.i. sep.* (*strong*) (*sein*) **1.** (*a*) to jump down, off; to leap down, off; **vom Pferd a.,** to jump off, leap off, leap from, one's horse; **von einem Felsen a.,** to jump, leap, from a rock; **von einem fahrenden Zug a.,** to jump out of a moving train; (*b*) *Av:* (*of parachutist*) to jump, make a jump; (*of pilot, etc.*) to bale, *U.S:* bail, out. **2.** (*of deer, etc.*) to bound away; to gallop off. **3.** (*a*) **vom Thema a.,** to break away suddenly from the subject; to make a sudden digression; to change the subject abruptly; (*b*) **(von einem Vorhaben) a.,** to abandon, to withdraw from, one's intention (suddenly); *F:* **von j-m a.,** to desert s.o., leave s.o. in the lurch; *Pol:* **von einer Partei a.,** to desert a party; *F:* to rat. **4.** (*a*) (*of button, rivet-head, etc.*) to come off, fly off; (*of jug-handle, etc.*) to come off, break off, snap off; (*of window-pane, watch-glass, etc.*) to shatter; (*b*) (*of paint, lacquer, etc.*) to come off, crack off, flake off. **5.** to rebound; (*of ball, etc.*) to bounce (off). **6.** (*of compass-needle*) to spin. **7.** (*of timber*) to warp; to start. **8.** *Metall:* (*of iron*) to be red-short, hot-short, brittle.

II. *vbl s.* **Abspringen,** *n. in vbl senses; also:* (sudden) digression; sudden change of subject, of plan; desertion (of s.o.), from a party. *Cp.* **Absprung.**

abspritzen, *v.tr. sep.* (*a*)=**spritzen** ; (*b*) to spray (plants, etc.) (with insecticide, etc.); to wash down (car, yard, street, etc.); to wash (sth.) off, away (with hose *or* jet); (*c*) *Constr:* to roughcast, parget (wall); (*d*) *Paint:* to spray (wall, etc.) with a paint-gun.

Absprung, *m.* **1.** (*a*) jump, leap (from horse, rock, etc.); *Av:* parachute descent, jump, (live) drop; baling, *U.S:* bailing, out (by pilot, etc.); (*b*) spring, bound; (*c*) *Sp:* take-off (for jump, etc.). **2.** bound (of escaping deer, etc.); **Absprünge machen,** (*of hunted animal*) to double; to dodge. **3.** (*a*) rebound; bounce (of ball); (*b*) *Ph:* reflection (of rays). **4.** offshoot; **Absprünge** *pl*, *For:* (i) lateral shoots; (ii) fallen shoots (of conifers). *Cp.* **abspringen.**

Absprungbalken, *m. Sp:* take-off (strip) (for long jump).

Absprunghafen, *m. Mil.Av: Navy:* operational base (for launching a special operation).

Absprunghöhe, *f. Av:* jumping height; height from which a parachute jump is made.

Absprungtisch, *m. Ski:* platform, take-off.

abspulen, *v.tr. sep.* to unwind; to reel off, wind off, spool off (thread, etc.).

abspülen. I. *v.tr. sep.* (*a*) to rinse (sth.); to swill (the floor, etc.); to flush (lavatory, drain); to wash up (dishes); (*b*) to rinse, wash, away (impurities); (*of stream, rain*) to wash away, erode (soil).

II. *vbl s.* **Abspülen** *n.*, **Abspülung** *f. in vbl senses; also:* erosion (of soil, by stream or rain).

Abspuler, *m. Tex:* reeler, wind(st)er.

Abspülwasser, *n.* dirty water (from washing); dish-water.

abspüren, *v.tr. sep. Ven:* **die Fährten a.,** to track game.

abstammen, *v.i. sep.* (*sein*) **1.** to be descended **(von,** from); **er stammt von einem Bauerngeschlecht ab,** he comes of peasant stock. **2.** *Ling: Ch:* to derive, to be derived **(von,** from).

Abstammung, *f.* **1.** descent, lineage, ancestry, origin, parentage, extraction; **von hoher A.,** of noble descent, of noble birth; high-born; **von königlicher A.,** of royal descent, sprung of a royal line; **er ist (von) deutscher A.,** he is of German extraction, origin; *Biol:* **die A. des Menschen,** the descent of man. **2.** (*a*) *Ling:* (i) derivation, (ii) etymology; (*b*) *Ch:* derivation.

Abstammungsachse, *f. Bot:* central axis (of plant).

Abstammungsgemeinschaft, *f.* ethnically homogeneous community.

Abstammungsklage, *f. Jur:* (action for) affiliation.

Abstammungslehre, *f. Biol:* doctrine, theory, of evolution, of the origin of species; theory of descent.

Abstammungstafel, *f.* family-tree; genealogical table, tree; pedigree.

Abstand, *m.* **1.** (*a*) distance away (from a given point, etc.); **in einem A. von drei Fuß von . . . ,** three feet away, back, from . . . ; **der zweite Wagen folgte in einem A. von hundert Metern, in hundert Meter A.,** the second car followed a hundred metres behind, at a distance of a hundred metres; **(seinen) A. halten, wahren,** to keep one's distance; **von etwas A. nehmen, halten,** to stand away, back, from sth.; to place oneself at a distance from sth.; **A. nehmen!** stand back! stand clear! keep back! *Sp:* take your distance! *Mil: Sp:* **nach rechts A. nehmen!** extend to the right! *Astr:* (angular) distance; **A. von der Sonne,** elongation; *Mth:* **von gleichem A.,** equidistant; (*b*) distance apart (of two points, etc.); gap, clearance, interval (between bars, etc.); space, distance (between two trees, etc.); **A. der Bäume, der Säulen, usw.,** spacing of trees, columns, etc.; **A. zwischen den Zeilen,** space between the lines; spacing of the lines; **A. der Radzähne, der Schraubengänge,** pitch of the cogs, of the screw-threads; **in gleichmäßigen Abständen,** at regular intervals; **in Abständen von hundert Metern,** at intervals of a hundred metres; **in Abständen von zehn Minuten,** at ten-minute intervals; **er ist mit (weitem) A. der beste von ihnen,** he is far and away the best of them; (*c*) disparity; (marked) difference; **trotz des (gesellschaftlichen) Abstandes zwischen ihnen,** in spite of the disparity of their circumstances. **2. von etwas A. nehmen,** to refrain from sth.; to desist from sth.; **von einer Forderung A. nehmen,** to relinquish, forego, abandon, waive, a claim; *Jur:* **A. (von einer Forderung),** waiving, abandonment, renunciation, of a claim. **3.**=**Abstandsgeld.**

Abständer, *m.* **1.** *For:* decayed tree. **2.** *Husb:* weakly *or* diseased animal; runt.

abständig, *a.* **1.** *For:* decayed (tree, wood). **2.** (*of goods*) **a. werden,** to deteriorate, spoil (with keeping). **3.**=**abgestanden.**

Abstandsflansch, *m. Mch: etc:* thimble (joining two tubes).

Abstandsgeld, *n.* **1.** compensation, indemnification. **2.** forfeit, penalty (for not fulfilling contract, etc.). **3.** *St.Exch:* option money. **4.** key-money (paid by a person taking a flat *or* house).

abstandsgleich, *a.* equidistant.

Abstand(s)halter, *m. Constr: Mec.E:* distance piece.

Abstand(s)hülse, *f. Mec.E:* spacer; distance piece.

Abstandslinie, *f. Astr:* line of apsides.

Abstand(s)messer, *m. Artil:* position-finder.

Abstandspunkt, *m. Astr:* apsis.

Abstandsrücklicht, *n. Mil:* rear light (of vehicle travelling in convoy).

Abstand(s)stück, *n. Constr: Mec.E:* distance piece.

Abstand(s)summe, *f.*=**Abstandsgeld.**

Abstandstrebe, *f. Av:* drag-strut.

Abstandswinkel, *m. Astr:* angle of elongation.

Abstandwerfen, *n. Mil.Av:* pattern-bombing.

abstapeln, *v.tr. sep.* to unstack (timber, etc.).

abstatten. I. *v.tr. sep.* to render, give, make, pay; (*a*) **j-m einen Besuch a.,** to pay, make, a call on s.o., to pay s.o. a visit; to call on s.o.; **j-m seinen Dank (für etwas) a.,** to thank s.o. (for sth.); to give, render, thanks, to extend, offer, express, one's thanks, to s.o. (for sth.); (*b*) **einen Bericht über etwas** *acc.* **a.,** to make, render, present, deliver, send in, a report on sth.; (*c*) *A:* **eine Schuld a.,** to pay, discharge, a debt; **j-m seine Schuldigkeit a.,** to discharge one's obligation to s.o.

II. *vbl s.* **Abstatten** *n.*, **Abstattung** *f.*, *in vbl senses; also:* expression (of thanks); delivery (of a report).

Abstaub, *m.* flying dust (from machine, etc.).

abstäubecht, *a. Leath: etc:* non-crocking (colour); (colour) that does not come off.

abstauben, abstäuben, *v.sep.* **1.** *v.tr.* to brush, wipe, the dust off (sth.); to beat the dust from (clothes, carpet, etc.); to dust (furniture, etc.). **2.** *v.tr. F:* to steal, *F:* to pinch, lift, snaffle, sneak (sth.). **3.** *v.i.* (*sein*) (*a*) to come off, fly off, as, in, dust; (*b*) *Leath: etc:* (*of colour*) to come off, crock.

Abstauber, Abstäuber, *m.* **-s/-.** **1.** person who dusts, duster. **2.** (*thg*) duster.

abstauen, *v.tr. sep. Hyd.E:* to dam up (water, watercourse).

Abstech(dreh)bank, *f. Tls:* slicing lathe, cutting-off lathe.

Abstecheisen, *n.* **1.** *Hort:* edging-iron, -tool. **2.** *Mec.E:*=**Abstechstahl.**

abstechen, *v. sep.* (*strong*) I. *v.tr.* **1.** to cut off (part of sth., with chisel, spade, etc.); *Metalw:* **eine Eisenstange a.,** to cut the end off, to crop, an iron bar; **Rost a.,** to chip off rust; **Soden, Torf, a.,** to cut sods, peat; *Hort:* **den Rasen a.,** to trim the edges of the lawn. **2.** to mark (sth.) out by cutting lines *or* making holes; (*a*) to cut (design, etc.); to engrave (drawing, etc.); to copy (engraving); (*b*) **ein Muster auf Papier a.,** to prick out a pattern on paper; (*c*) **einen Bauplatz a.,** to mark out a building site (with a trench). **3.** to tap; to drain liquid from (sth.); (*a*) **einen Teich a.,** to drain a pond; (*b*) **ein Faß a.,** to broach, tap, a cask; **den Wein a.,** (i) to rack, to draw off, the wine from the lees; (ii) to broach the wine; (iii) to sample the wine; (*c*) *Metall:* **den Hochofen a., das flüssige Metall a.,** to tap the furnace, to tap off the molten metal. **4.** to remove (sth.) with a pointed instrument; (*a*) *A:* (*at tilting-match*) **den Ring a.,** to get the lance into the ring; (*b*) *Husb:* **Heu a.,** to unload hay with a pitchfork. **5.** to cut the throat of (animal); to stick, bleed (pig, sheep, etc.); *Ven:* to stab (animal); to give (stag, boar, etc.) the coup de grâce; *see also* **Kalb** 1. **6. j-n a.,** (*a*) *Cards:* to beat, take, trump *or* overtrump, s.o.'s card; (*b*) (*at games, shooting*) to outpoint s.o., to beat s.o.'s score; *A:*=**ausstechen** 3. **7.** (*a*) *A:* (*in tourney*) to unhorse, unseat (rider); (*b*) *A:* (*in student duel*) to disable (opponent). **8.** *Nau:* **einem Schiff den Wind a.,** to get the weather-gauge of a ship. **9.** *Ven:* **die Büchse a.,** to put on the safety-catch of one's gun.

II. **abstechen,** *v.i.* (*haben*) **1.** (*of colours, characteristics, etc.*) **gegen, von, etwas a.,** to contrast (strongly) with sth.; to stand out clearly against sth.; **dieses Rot sticht zu sehr ab,** this red stands out too much, is too great a contrast; **Grün sticht gegen Rot ab,** green contrasts with red; **Charaktere, die scharf gegeneinander abstechen,** strongly contrasted characters; **ihre Güte sticht sehr von der unfreundlichen Natur ihres Mannes ab,** her kindliness is in marked contrast with, to, the unfriendly nature of her husband; **grell gegen etwas a.,** to clash, jar, with sth. **2.** *Nau:* to shove off, bear off, sheer off. **3.** *occ.*=**einen Abstecher machen,** *q.v. under* **Abstecher** 2.

III. *vbl s.* **Abstechen,** *n. in vbl senses; also:* contrast (of colours, characteristics, etc.); **grelles A.,** clash. *Cp.* **Abstich** 2.

Abstecher, *m.* **1.** (*a*) (*pers.*) cutter; (*b*) *Ind:* (i)=**Abstechmaschine;** (ii)=**Abstechstahl;** (*c*) (*pers.*) *Metall:* tapper. **2.** (*a*) detour; **einen A. nach einem Ort machen,** to make a detour, leave one's route, go a roundabout way, in order to visit a place; **da wir etwas Zeit übrig hatten, machten wir einen A. nach Venedig,** having some time to spare we made a detour to Venice; (*b*) excursion, outing, trip; (short) boat-trip; **einen A. nach London machen,** to take a trip to London; (*c*) digression, *F:* excursion (in a speech, etc.); (*of scholar*) **einen A. in ein anderes Fach machen,** to make a brief excursion into another subject.

Abstechgrube, *f. Metall:* casting-pit.

Abstechmaschine, *f. Ind:* cutting-off machine.

Abstechmeißel, *m. Tls:* (*a*) chipping chisel; cutting chisel; (*b*) *Mec.E:*=**Abstechstahl.**

Abstechmesser, *n.* slaughterman's knife, slaughtering-knife.

Abstechpflug, *m. Agr:* paring-plough; breast-plough.

Abstechstahl, *m. Tls: Mec.E:* cutting-off tool, parting-tool.

Abstechsupport, *m. Mec.E:* cut-off rest (of lathe).

Absteckeisen, *n.* (iron) stake; surveyor's (levelling-)rod.

abstecken, *v.tr. sep.* **1.** to unpin; to undo; to untie; **sich** *dat.* **das Haar a.,** to let one's hair down, to undo one's hair; *Nau: etc:* **ein Tau a.,**

to untie, unbend, a rope. **2.** *Husb:* to wean (animal). **3.** (*a*) *Surv:* to lay out, stake out, mark out (line, piece of ground, etc.); to trace out (building site, etc.); to tape off (line, etc.); to mark (out) (boundaries); (*b*) *Av:* **den Kurs a.,** to plot the course; (*c*) *Artil: etc:* **das Ziel a.,** to pinpoint the target. **4.** *Dressm:* (*at a fitting*) **ein Kleid a.,** to fit a dress (*with the aid of pins*); **den Saum, die Weite, a.,** to pin up the hem; to adjust the width (*by pinning*).

Absteckfähnchen, *n.* marker flag; surveyor's flag.

Absteckkette, *f.* surveying-, measuring-chain; land-chain.

Absteckleine, *f. Surv: etc:* tracing-line.

Absteckinie, *f. Surv:* trace; lay-out (of building, etc.); lie (of a road).

Absteckpfahl, Absteckpflock, *m.* (*a*) (surveyor's) staff, pole, stake, rod; (*b*) *Mil:* tracing picket, alignment picket.

Absteckschnur, *f.* = **Absteckleine.**

Absteckstab, *m.,* **Absteckstange,** *f.* = **Absteckpfahl** (*a*).

Absteckrupp, *m. Mil:* marking-out party.

abstehen, *v. sep.* (*strong*) I. *v.i.* **1.** (*sein*) *Ven:* (*of large birds*) to come down, fly away, from the trees. **2.** (*haben*) (*a*) to stand away, apart, aside; to be at a distance (**von,** from); **das Pfarrhaus steht hundert Meter von der Kirche ab,** the parsonage stands a hundred metres (away) from, at a distance of a hundred metres from, the church; **die Häuser stehen weit voneinander ab,** the houses are far apart; **der Schreibtisch steht zu weit vom Fenster ab,** the desk is too far away, too far back, from the window; (*b*) to stand out; to protrude; **die Ohren stehen ihm vom Kopf ab, er hat abstehende Ohren,** his ears stick out; **abstehend,** *Bot:* spreading; patulous (boughs, flowers); *Nat.Hist:* squarrose (scales, etc.). **3.** (*sein, haben*) **von etwas a.,** to desist from sth.; to refrain from sth.; to hold aloof from (a plan, etc.); **von einer Forderung a.,** to relinquish, forego, abandon, waive, a claim; **ich stehe davon ab, eine persönliche Meinung auszudrücken,** I refrain from expressing a personal opinion. **4.** (*a*) (*sein*) (*of fish, plants, flowers*) to die (off); (*b*) (*of foodstuffs*) to spoil with keeping; to become stale; to go bad; (*of milk*) to turn sour; (*of beer*) to go flat; (*of water*) to become stagnant; *usu. only in p.p. & a.* **abgestanden,** *q.v.*

II. **abstehen,** *v.tr.* **1.** *A:* **j-m etwas a.,** to surrender, yield up, give up, sth. to s.o. **2. eine Stunde a.,** to stand for an hour (on end); *Mil:* **seine zwei Stunden Wache a.,** to stand guard for two hours, to do one's two hours on guard. **3. sich** *dat.* **die Beine, die Füße, a.,** to stand until one's legs are weary; to grow weary with waiting.

III. *vbl s.* **Abstehen,** *n. in vbl senses; also:* abandonment, renunciation (of a claim). *Cp.* **Abstand.**

Absteher, *m. Jur: A:* = **Abtreter.**

abstehlen, *v.tr. sep.* = **stehlen;** *see also* **Herrgott.**

Absteifbalken, *m. Constr:* truss (of girder, etc.).

absteifen. I. *v.tr. sep. Constr: etc:* to stay, brace, strut; to stiffen; to prop (up), shore (up) (wall, etc.); *Min:* to timber (gallery, etc.).

II. *vbl s.* **1. Absteifen,** *n. in vbl senses.* **2. Absteifung,** *f.* (*a*) = II. 1; (*b*) stays, braces, struts; props, shores; *Min:* timbers.

Absteige, *f.* (*a*) chance accommodation; (*b*) = **Absteigequartier** 1.

absteigen. I. *v.i. sep.* (*strong*) (*sein*) **1.** to descend; to come down, go down; *Fb:* (*of team*) to go, move, down, to drop (to next division); **von einem Berg, einem Baum, a.,** to come down from a mountain, from a tree; **von einer Leiter a.,** to get off, get down from, a ladder. **2.** (*a*) **von einem Wagen a.,** to alight from a carriage; **vom Pferd, Fahrrad, usw., a.,** to get off one's horse, bicycle, etc., to dismount; (*b*) **in einem Gasthof a.,** to put up at a hotel; **bei Verwandten a.,** to stop, stay, with relations.

II. *vbl s.* **Absteigen** *n., occ.* **Absteigung** *f. in vbl senses; also:* descent. *Cp.* **Abstieg.**

III. *pr.p. & a.* **absteigend,** *in vbl senses; esp.* (*a*) descending (curve, branch, etc.); *Mus:* **absteigende Tonleiter,** descending scale; *Astr:* **absteigende Zeichen,** descendent signs (of the zodiac); **absteigender Knoten,** descending node (of the orbit of a planet, etc.); *Bot:* **absteigende Achse,** descending axis; *Ball:* **absteigender Ast der Geschoßbahn,** descending branch of the trajectory; (*b*) (*of person, family, nation, etc.*) **auf dem absteigenden Ast sein,** to be on the down-grade, to be going downhill. *See also* **Linie.**

Absteigequartier, *n.* **1.** (*a*) (overnight) accommodation; (*b*) *A:* **bei j-m sein A. nehmen,** to stop, stay, with s.o. **2.** shady hotel; lodgings used for immoral purposes; house of call.

Abstellbahn, *f. Av: Nau:* parking bay (for shipborne aircraft).

Abstellbahnhof, *m. Rail:* sidings; stabling station.

abstellbar, *a.* **1.** that can be removed. **2.** (machine, etc.) that can be stopped, put out of action; (electric device) that can be switched off. **3.** (law) that can be repealed, abrogated; remediable, reformable (abuse, etc.); redressable (grievance).

Abstellbrett, *n.* shelf (for storage).

abstellen. I. *v.tr. sep.* **1. etwas von etwas a.,** to place sth. at a distance from sth.; **einen Stuhl von der Wand a.,** to place a chair away from the wall. **2.** (*a*) to put down, set down (a burden); (*b*) to put (sth.) away; to park (car, bicycle); to put (bicycle) in the rack; *Av:* to park (aircraft); **Flugzeuge luftangriffsicher a.,** to disperse aircraft (for protection against air attack); (*c*) *Rail:* to shunt (carriage, wagon, train) on to a siding; to sidetrack (train), to stable (wagons); (*d*) *Mil:* to detail off (men, vehicles). **3.** to stop (clock, machine, gramophone, etc.); to shut down (machine); to put (machine, pump) out of action; to draw off the water of (a pump); to turn off (tap, the gas, the water, the heating, the electricity); to disconnect (electric device); *Tp:* to disconnect (line, telephone); to cut off (telephone); **das Radio a.,** to switch off, turn off, the wireless; **stell ab!** switch off! *Mch:* **den Dampf a.,** to shut down steam, to shut off, cut off, the steam; *I.C.E:* **die Zündung, die Gaszufuhr, a.,** to cut off, switch off, the ignition; **den Motor a.,** to switch off the engine. **4.** to put an end to (sth.); **einen Mißbrauch a.,** to remedy, reform, amend, put an end to, stop, put down, an abuse. **5. es auf etwas** *acc.* **a.,** to intend (to do) sth.; to aim at sth.; **die Gesellschaft ist ausschließlich auf die Förderung der Wissenschaft abgestellt,** the sole aim of the society is the advancement of scholarship.

II. *vbl s.* **Abstellen** *n.,* **Abstellung** *f. in vbl senses; also:* disconnection (of electric device, telephone, line).

Abstellgeleise, Abstellgleis, *n. Rail:* siding, side-track.

Abstellhahn, *m.* stopcock.

Abstellhebel, *m.* **1.** *Mec.E:* stopping lever; locking-lever. **2.** *Typewr:* line-space lever.

Abstellhof, *m. Rail:* = **Abstellbahnhof.**

Abstellkammer, *f.* store-room.

Abstelloch, *n. Constr: etc:* socket (to receive end of beam, etc.).

Abstellplatz, *m.* **1.** parking place (for cars, bicycles, aircraft). **2.** *Mil.Av:* (small) dispersal airfield; (*on airfield*) dispersal bay.

Abstellraum, *m.* store-room.

Abstelltisch, *m.* (*a*) stand (on which to lay down work, etc.); (*b*) dumb-waiter.

Abstellvorrichtung, *f.* stopping device; cut-off (device); stop-gear, stop-motion; (*in pipe-line, etc.*) shut-off (device); *Typewr:* releasing device.

abstemmen, *v.tr. sep.* to chisel (sth.) off.

abstempeln. I. *v.tr. sep.* (*a*) to stamp (weights, etc.); to hall-mark (metal objects); (*b*) to stamp (document, passport, etc.); to stamp the postmark on (letter); (*c*) to cancel, deface (stamp).

II. *vbl s.* **Abstempeln** *n.,* **Abstempelung** *f. in vbl senses; also:* cancellation, defacement (of a stamp).

Abstention [apstɛntsĭˈoːn], *f.* **-/-en. 1.** abstention, abstaining (**von,** from). **2.** *Jur:* renunciation of an inheritance. **3.** *Jur:* removal (of criminal) from the scene of the crime.

absteppen, *v.tr. sep.* to stitch; to quilt (petticoat, counterpane, etc.).

absterben. I. *v.i. sep.* (*strong*) (*sein*) **1.** (*a*) (*of pers.*) to expire; to be (gradually) dying; (*of trees, plants, flowers*) to die off; to wither away, decay; (*of friendship*) to fade; **abgestorben,** dead; (*b*) (*of limb*) to mortify; (*c*) (*of limb, etc.*) to become insensible, insensitive; to lose all feeling; to go numb; **meine Finger sind abgestorben,** my fingers have gone dead, gone numb; (*d*) (*of pers.*) **j-m, etwas** *dat.,* **a.,** to become indifferent to s.o., sth., insensible to sth.; to lose all feeling for, all interest in, s.o., sth.; **der Welt a.,** to withdraw from, *Theol:* to die to, the world; *Theol:* **der Sünde a.,** to die to sin. **2.** (*of lime*) to slack by exposure to air, to air-slack. **3.** *Sug-R:* to turn into opaque crystals.

II. *vbl s.* **Absterben,** *n. in vbl senses; also:* death, decease (of s.o.); mortification (of a limb).

Abstergens [apˈstɛrgɛns], *n.* **-/-gentia** [-ˈgɛntsĭaː], **-gentien** & **-genzien** [-ˈgɛntsĭən]. *Med: Pharm:* abstergent; purge.

abstergieren [apstɛrˈgiːrən], *v.tr. insep. Med:* to cleanse; to purge.

Abstersion [apstɛrzĭˈoːn], *f.* **-/-en,** abstersion.

abstersiv [apstɛrˈsiːf], *a.* abstersive.

Absteuer, *f. Hist:* = **Abzugssteuer.**

absteuern, *v.sep.* **1.** *v.tr.* to steer (ship, boat) away, off (from the shore, etc.); *F:* to divert (s.o.) from, steer (s.o.) off (an intention). **2.** *v.i.* (*haben*) to steer off, away (**von,** from); *Nau:* to bear off from the land.

Abstich, *m.* **1.** = **abstechen** III. **2.** (*a*) drawing off (of liquid); *Winem:* **erster, zweiter, A.,** first, second, racking; (*b*) running off (of molten metal); *Metall:* tap, run-off. **3.** (*a*) pattern pricked out on paper; (*b*) *A:* engraved copy (of drawing, etc.).

Abstichloch, *n. Metall:* tap-hole, tapping hole.

Abstichöffnung, *f.* = **Abstichloch.**

Abstichrinne, *f. Metall:* runner.

Abstichseite, *f.* **1.** *Metall:* tapping side (of furnace). **2.** *Metalw:* cropped end (of bar, etc.), crop-end.

absticken, *v.tr. sep.* to copy (design, etc.) in embroidery.

abstieben, *v.i. sep.* (*strong*) (*sein*) **1.** (*of dust, sparks, etc.*) to fly off. **2.** *Ven:* (*of birds*) to fly off; to scatter.

abstiefeln, *v.i. sep.* (*sein*) *F:* to go away; to make off; to march off.

Abstieg, *m.* **-s/-e,** descent; coming down, going down (from a height); decline (of family, nation); *Fb:* (*of team*) relegation, drop (to the next division); **Auf- und Abstieg,** ascent and descent; going up and coming down; rise and decline (of family, nation).

Abstiegstollen, *m. Min:* entry; adit.

abstillen, *v.tr. sep.* to wean (child).

Abstimm-, *comb.fm. W.Tel:* tuning . . .

abstimmen. I. *v.sep.* **1.** *v.tr.* (*a*) **etwas auf etwas anderes a.,** to harmonize sth. with sth. else; *Lit:* to attune sth. to sth.; **ein fein abgestimmtes Urteil,** a nicely balanced judgment; **Berichte, usw., aufeinander a.,** to collate reports, etc., to check reports, etc., against one another; (*b*) *W.Tel:* to syntonize; to tune in (set) (**auf,** to); **abgestimmter Empfänger,** syntonic, tuned, receiver; *El.E: W.Tel:* **einen Kreis auf einen anderen a.,** to tune one circuit to another; **abgestimmte Kreise,** tuned circuits; (*c*) *I.C.E:* to tune up (engine). **2.** *v.i.* (*haben*) to vote, *esp. U.S:* ballot; (*in Parliament*) to come to a division; to divide; **über etwas** *acc.* **a.,** to vote on sth.; **über etwas** *acc.* **a. lassen,** to put a question to the vote, to the meeting; to take a vote on a question; **durch Handzeichen a.,** to vote by (a) show of hands.

II. *vbl s.* **1. Abstimmen,** *n. in vbl senses; also: W.Tel:* syntonization. **2. Abstimmung,** *f.* (*a*) = II. 1; (*b*) *W.Tel:* syntony, syntonism; (*c*) vote; voting, ballot(ing), poll; (*in Parliament*) division; **geheime A.,** secret ballot; **A. durch Handzeichen,** show of hands; **eine A. vornehmen,** to take a vote; **zur A.!** take a vote! (*in Parliament*) divide! **bei der A.,** during the voting; at the poll; on a vote being taken; (*in Parliament*) on division; **eine Maßnahme durch A. beschließen,** to vote a measure; (*d*) plebiscite.

Abstimmfähigkeit, *f. W.Tel:* selectivity.

Abstimmknopf, *m. W.Tel:* tuning knob *or* control.

Abstimmschärfe, *f. W.Tel:* selectivity; sharpness of tuning.

Abstimmung, *f. see* **abstimmen II.**

Abstimmungs-, *comb.fm.* **1.** *W.Tel:* tuning . . . ; *cp.* **Abstimm-. 2.** *Adm:* voting . . . .

Abstimmungsergebnis, *n. Adm:* result of a, the, poll.

Abstimmungsleiter, *m.* polling-clerk.

Abstimmungsrecht, *n.* right to vote; *Adm:* franchise; **das A. haben,** to have a vote.

Abstimmungsumschlag, *m.* envelope enclosing the voting paper.

Abstimmungszettel, *m.* voting paper, *U.S:* ballot (papcr).

Abstimmvorrichtung, *f. W.Tel:* tuning device, tuner.

abstinent [apstiˑˈnɛnt], *a.* abstemious; abstinent.

Abstinenz [apstiˑˈnɛnts], *f.* **-/.** abstinence; (*a*) *Ecc:* abstınence from meat; (*b*) abstemiousness; (*c*) (total) abstinence (from alcohol); temperance; teetotalism.

Abstinenzbewegung, *f.* temperance movement.

Abstinenzler [apstiˑˈnɛntslər], *m.* **-s/-**, (total) abstainer (from alcohol); teetotal(l)er.

Abstinenztag, *m. Ecc:* day of abstinence.

abstolzieren, *v.i. sep.* (*sein*) (*p.p.* **abstolziert**), to strut away, off; to stalk off; *F:* to sail off.

abstoppeln, *v.tr. sep. Agr:* **einen Acker a.,** to clear a field of stubble, to stubble a field.

abstoppen, *v.sep.* **1.** (*a*) *v.tr.* to stop (car, mechanism, etc.); **ein Schutzmann stoppte den Wagen ab,** a policeman stopped, halted, the car; **die Produktion a.,** to put the brake on production; (*b*) *v.i.* (*haben*) to stop; to come to a stop; to halt; to pull up; *Aut:* to put on the brake. **2.** *v.tr. Sp: etc:* to time (race, runner, etc.) (with a stop-watch).

abstöpseln, *v.tr. sep.* to uncork, open (bottle); to unstopper (scent-bottle, jar, etc.).

Abstoß, *m.* **1.** repulsion; rebound. **2.** *Sp:* throw (of skittle, etc.); put (of the weight). **3.** *Fb:* goal kick. **4.** *Sp:* push-off; **zum A. fertig,** ready to push off.

Abstoßbetrieb, *m. Rail:* fly shunting.

Abstoßeisen, *n. Tls:* scraper; chipping-chisel; burr(-cutter).

abstoßen. I. *v.tr. sep.* (*strong*) **1.** (*a*) to knock (sth.) off; to break (sth.) off; to chip, scrape, shave, plane, (sth.) (off); to dress, hew (stone); *Leath:* to degrain, shave, buff (skins); **den Kalk von der Wand a.,** to chip, scrape, the plaster off the wall; **die Ecke(n) von etwas a.,** to break, chip, *Carp:* to plane, the corner(s) off sth.; *Carp:* **die Kanten von einem Brett a.,** to plane the edges off a board; to chamfer a board; (*b*) **sich** *dat.* **die Hörner a.,** to sow one's wild oats; (*c*) **j-m das Herz a.,** to break s.o.'s heart; to rend s.o.'s heart; to cut s.o. to the heart; to grieve s.o. most deeply; (*d*) *A:* **j-m den Kopf, den Arm, a.,** to cut off s.o.'s head, arm; **einem Hirsch das Genick a.,** to give a stag the coup de grâce; (*e*) to chafe, graze, scrape; **sich** *dat.* **die Haut a.,** to graze, chafe, one's skin; **sich** *dat.* **den Ärmel a.,** to chafe, fray, one's sleeve. **2.** to push (sth.) away, off; *Nau:* **ein Boot a.,** to push off (from the land); to shove off (from ship); *Bill:* **den Ball a.,** to bring the ball off the cushion. **3.** *Sp:* to throw (skittle, etc.); **den Stein a.,** to put the weight. **4.** (*a*) to repel; *El:* **gleichnamige Pole stoßen einander ab,** like poles repel one another; (*b*) to be repellent to (s.o.); to repel (s.o.); *abs.* **das Werk stößt ab,** the work is repulsive, repels one. **5.** *Rail:* to bump (wagon); **'nicht a.',** 'shunt with care'. **6.** (*a*) to get rid of (sth.); to discard (sth.); **die Milchzähne a.,** to shed, lose, one's milk-teeth; (*b*) **eine Schuld a.,** to discharge, pay off, a debt. **7.** *Com: Fin:* to dispose of, sell (goods, shares, etc.); *esp. Com:* **Waren (unter Preis) a.,** to sell off, clear, goods (at a reduced price); *St.Exch:* **Aktien in größeren Posten a.,** to unload stock on the market. **8.** *Mus:* **die Töne a.,** to detach the notes, to play the notes *staccato*; **die Töne mit der Zunge a.,** to tongue a passage (on the flute, etc.); **(kurz) abgestoßen,** *staccato,* detached. **9.** *Husb:* to wean (animal). **10. sich abstoßen,** to get battered; (*of garment*) to fray. **11.** (*a*) *v.i.* (*haben, sein*) *Nau:* to push off (from the land); to shove off (from ship); (*b*) **sich a.,** to push off.

II. *vbl s.* **1. Abstoßen,** *n. in vbl senses; also:* repulsion; *Com: Fin:* disposal (of goods, shares, etc.). **2. Abstoßung,** *f.* (*a*)=II. 1; (*b*) *El:* repulsion (of poles).

III. *pr.p. & a.* **abstoßend,** *in vbl senses; esp.* repulsive, repellent (character, manner, appearance); unprepossessing (manner); uninviting (appearance); disgusting (ways).

Abstoßfett, *n. Leath:* grease scraped from hides.

Abstoßlinie, *f. Sp:* the mark (for putting the weight).

Abstoßmesser, *n. Leath:* shaving-knife; fleshing-knife.

Abstoßstange, *f.* raftsman's pole.

Abstoßzange, *f. Tls:* burr-cutter, -nipper.

abstottern, *v.tr. sep. Hum:* to pay for (sth.) by instalments, to buy (sth.) on the 'never-never'.

abstract [apˈstrakt], *a. A:*=**abstrakt;** *Lt.phr:* **in abstracto,** in the abstract.

abstrafen, *v.tr. sep.* to punish, chastise, castigate; to correct, administer correction to (child, etc.).

abstrahieren [apstraˑˈhiːrən], *v.tr. insep.* **1.** to abstract; to separate; to consider (sth.) apart (from sth.); **abstrahierend,** *Phil:* abstractive. **2.** *A:* to give (sth.) up.

Abstrahl, *m.* reflected ray; reflected beam.

abstrahlen. I. *v.sep.* **1.** *v.tr.* (*a*) to reflect (light); (*b*) *Ph:* to radiate. **2.** *v.i.* (*sein*) (*a*) to be reflected; (*b*) *Ph:* to radiate.

II. *vbl s.* **Abstrahlen** *n.,* **Abstrahlung** *f.* (*a*) reflection; (*b*) *Ph:* radiation.

Abstrahlungswinkel, *m. Ph:* angle of reflection; radiation angle.

abstrakt [apˈstrakt]. **1.** *a.* (*a*) *Phil:* abstract (idea, etc.); **das Abstrakte,** the abstract; (*b*) **abstrakte Zahl,** abstract number; **abstrakte Kunst, Musik,** abstract art, music; **abstrakte Wissenschaften,** abstract sciences; **in abstrakte Theorien versunken,** lost in abstract speculations; **er ist ein abstrakter Kopf,** he is of an abstract, academic, turn of mind. **2.** *adv.* abstractly; in the abstract; **etwas a. betrachten,** to consider sth. in the abstract.

Abstrakte [apˈstraktə], *f.* **-/-n.** *Mus:* tracker (of organ).

Abstraktion [apstraktsiˈoːn], *f.* **-/-en.** *Phil:* abstraction.

Abstraktionsvermögen, *n. Phil:* faculty of abstraction, abstractive faculty.

Abstraktum [apˈstraktum], *n.* **-s/-ta,** (*a*) *Phil:* abstract idea; abstraction; (*b*) *Gram:* abstract noun.

abstrampeln, *v.tr.* **1.** (*of baby*) **die Decke a., sich a.,** to kick off the coverings, bedclothes. **2.** *F:* **sich abstrampeln,** to pedal, cycle, furiously; to exhaust oneself cycling.

abstrapazieren, *v.tr. sep.* (*p.p.* **abstrapaziert**) **1.** to wear (sth.) out (with hard usage). **2. sich abstrapazieren,** to exhaust oneself; to drudge (and slave).

Abstränze, *f.* **-/-n.** *Bot:* black masterwort.

Abstrebekraft, *f. Ph:* centrifugal force.

abstreben[1], *v.i. sep.* (*haben*) **von etwas a.,** to tend away from sth.; to tend to diverge from sth.

abstreben[2]. I. *v.tr. sep. Constr: etc:* to brace (platform, etc.) with struts; *Av:* to strut, brace (wing); **abgestrebter Flügel, abgestrebte Tragfläche,** strutted, semi-cantilever, wing.

II. *vbl s.* **1. Abstreben,** *n. in vbl senses.* **2. Abstrebung,** *f.* (*a*)=II. 1; (*b*) *Constr:* struts, braces; *Av:* (wing-)bracing.

abstrecken, *v.tr. sep. Metalw:* to reduce (metal) (by rolling).

Abstreich, *m.* **1. (Zuschlag im) A.,** awarding, knocking down, (of sth.) to the lowest bidder; **(Verkauf im) A.,** Dutch auction. **2.**=**Abstreicher.**

Abstreichblei, *n.*=**Abstrichblei.**

Abstreicheisen, *n. Tls:* scraping iron; scraper.

abstreichen, *v. sep.* (*strong*) I. *v.tr.* **1.** to wipe (sth.) off; to take off, wipe off, the top layer *or* excess of (sth.); (*a*) **die Asche von der Zigarre a.,** to knock the ash off one's cigar; **den Schaum vom Bier a., ein Glas Bier a.,** to take the froth, the head, off a glass of beer; **eine Eistüte a.,** to trim off the top of an ice-cream cone; (*b*) **das Korn, das Maß, a.,** to strike the corn, the measure; to make the corn level with a strickle; (*c*) *Glassm:* to skim, scum (molten glass); *Metall:* to dross. **2.** to scrape; **die Schuhe, die Füße, a.,** to scrape (the mud off) one's boots; *Leath:* **ein Fell a.,** to scrape, flesh, a skin; *Print:* **die Walze a.,** to scrape down the roller. **3.** to strop, set (razor). **4.** (*a*) to cancel; to strike off, deduct (item from account); **etwas von der Rechnung a.,** to knock sth. off the bill; (*b*) **das hat er gesagt, aber davon mußt du viel a.,** that's what he said, but you must take it with a grain of salt. **5.** (*a*) to tick off, *U.S:* check (off) (items in list); (*b*) *Ar:* to point off (decimals). **6.** (*a*) *Ven:* **das Feld a.,** to beat for game; (*of bird of prey*) **die Flur a.,** to scour the plain (for prey); (*b*) **das Gelände mit einem Scheinwerfer a.,** to sweep the ground with a searchlight. **7.** *A:* to beat (s.o.) with rods.

II. **abstreichen,** *v.i.* **1.** (*sein*) (*a*) (*of bird*) to fly away, to fly off; to take flight; to take wing; *Ven:* to flush; (*of young birds*) to leave the nest; (*b*) *F:* (*of pers.*) to slip away; to steal off; to make oneself scarce. **2.** (*haben*) (*of fish*) to finish spawning. **3.** (*haben*) **an etwas** *dat.* **auf- und abstreichen,** to pass one's hand up and down sth.

III. *vbl s.* **Abstreichen** *n., occ.* **Abstreichung** *f. in vbl senses; also:* cancellation; deduction (of item from account).

Abstreicher, *m.* (*a*) scraper, scraping-tool; (*b*) shoe-scraper, boot-scraper, door-scraper; scraper-mat; (*c*) *Pharm: Surg: etc:* spatula; (*d*)=**Abstreichmesser.**

Abstreichgitter, *n.* scraper-mat (at door, entrance).

Abstreichholz, *n. Meas:* strickle, strike; straight-edge.

Abstreichlatte, *f.* strickle.

Abstreichlöffel, *n.* skimming ladle, skimmer.

Abstreichmaß, *n.* corn-measure.

Abstreichmesser, *n.* (*a*) scraping-knife; (*b*) *Paperm: Print: Tex:* doctor.

Abstreichriemen, *m. Tls:* (razor-)strop.

abstreifbar, *a.* that can be stripped off; (habit) that can be thrown off.

abstreifen, *v.sep.* I. *v.tr.* **1.** (*a*) to strip off; to take off, pull off; **einen Handschuh, einen Strumpf, a.,** to take off, pull off, a glove, a stocking; **sie streifte ihr Kleid ab,** she slipped off her dress; **einen Ring vom Finger a.,** to take a ring off one's finger; **das Laub von einem Baum a., die Beeren von einem Zweig a.,** to strip a tree of its leaves, a branch of its berries; **die Asche von der Zigarre a.,** to knock the ash off one's cigar; (*b*) **einem Fuchs den Balg a.,** to skin, flay, a fox; (*c*) (*of reptile, etc.*) **die Haut a.,** to cast its skin, its slough; to slough; (*d*) *I.C.E:* **das Öl a.,** to scrape off the oil; (*e*) *Metall:* **ein Gußstück a.,** to strip a casting. **2. etwas (von sich) a.,** to divest, rid, oneself of (characteristic, etc.); to rid oneself of (habit); to throw off (bad habit); **er streifte seine Vergangenheit von sich ab,** he cast off his past. **3.** *Mil: etc:* to patrol (area, road, etc.).

II. **abstreifen,** *v.i.* (*sein*) **1.** to deviate; **vom Weg a.,** to stray from, wander off, the road. **2.** (*of projectile*) to glance off.

Abstreifer, *m.* **1.** *Metall:* stripper. **2.** *I.C.E:*=**Abstreifring. 3.**=**Abstreicher. 4.**=**Abstecher 1.**

Abstreifkran, *m. Metall:* stripping crane, stripper crane.

Abstreifmesser, *n.*=**Abstreichmesser.**

Abstreifölung, *f. I.C.E:* friction lubrication.

Abstreifring, *m. I.C.E:* scraper-ring.

Abstreifschmierung, *f.*=**Abstreifölung.**

abstreiten, *v.tr. sep.* (*strong*) **1. j-m etwas a.,** to wrest sth. from s.o.; *esp.* to gain sth. from s.o. by a lawsuit. **2. j-m etwas a.,** to dispute, contest, s.o.'s right to sth.; **j-m das Recht a., etwas zu tun,** to contest s.o.'s right to do sth.; **er läßt es sich nicht a.,** he won't give up his point; he sticks to it; he stands by it; **das lasse ich mir nicht a.,** I won't be argued out of it; I am quite positive on that point. **3.** to deny (facts, guilt, etc.); **eine Schuld a.,** to refuse to acknowledge a debt.

abstreuen, *v.tr. sep. Mil:* **das Gelände a.,** to sweep, spray, the ground with fire, *esp.* with machine-gun fire.

Abstrich, *m.* **1.** (*a*) (*in writing*) down-stroke; (*b*) *Mus:* (*violin-playing, etc.*) down-bow. **2.** deduction; amount struck off; (*a*) *Com:* reduction (in price); allowance, rebate, abatement, discount; **einen A. (vom Preis) machen,** to make a reduction; to knock something off the price; (*b*) **A. von den Unkosten,** curtailing, curtailment, cutting down, of expenses. **3.** (*a*) scraping off; scumming, skimming; (*b*) scum, scummings, skimmings; *Metall:* slag, cinders, scoria; dross. **4.** *Med:* (*a*) swab (from throat, etc.); (*b*) smear (of blood, etc.) (for microscopic slide).

Abstrichblei, *n. Metall:* lead recovered from dross.

abstricken, *v.tr. sep. Knitting:* to work (stitch); **eine Nadel a.,** to finish a row, needle (of knitting).

abstriegeln, *v.tr. sep.* **1.** to curry(comb), rub down, groom (horse). **2.** *F: A:* to give (s.o.) a thrashing, a drubbing, a licking.

Abstrom, *m.* outflow, flow, flowing (off, out, away), discharge (of liquid, gas, etc.); *Hyd.E:* flow, run-off; *Av:* downwash.

abströmen, *v.sep.* **1.** *v.i.* (*sein*) (*a*) (*of liquid, etc.*) to stream (forth, out); to flow away, out; to pour out; **die Menge strömte schnell ab,** the crowd (i) flowed out, streamed out, poured out, (ii) dispersed rapidly; (*b*) *Nau: etc:* to be carried away, to be borne away, along, to be swept away, along, by the current; to drift (away). **2.** *v.tr.* (*of river*) to wash away, sweep away, carry away (bank, etc.).

abstrus [apˈstruːs], *a.* abstruse, recondite (reasoning, knowledge, etc.).

abstufen. I. *v.tr. sep.* **1.** (*a*) to arrange (sth.) in steps; to arrange, lay out, (garden, etc.) in terraces; to terrace (garden, etc.); to range (seats, etc.) in tiers; (*b*) *Min:* **Erz a.,** to work ore in steps. **2.** (*a*) to graduate (exercises, taxes, etc.); to grade (staff, etc.); (*b*) to shade off (colours); to graduate (colours, light); to gradate (colours); to distinguish (characters in novel, etc.) by delicate nuances. **3. sich abstufen,** (*a*) to be arranged in steps; (*of garden, etc.*) to descend *or* rise in terraces; (*of seats, etc.*) to rise in tiers; (*b*) (*of exercises, taxes, etc.*) to be

graduated; (*of staff, etc.*) to be graded; (*c*) (*of colours*) to shade off; to be graduated, to gradate; (*of characters*) to be (subtly) differentiated.

II. *vbl s.* **1. Abstufen,** *n. in vbl senses; also:* graduation (of colours, light, etc.); gradation (of colours); (subtle) differentiation (of characters in novel, etc.). **2. Abstufung,** *f.* (*a*)=II. 1; (*b*) terrace; tier; (*c*) *Mth:* **geometrische A.,** geometrical progression; (*d*) *Ling:* vowel gradation, ablaut, apophony; (*e*) shade (of colour).

abstumpfen. I. *v.tr. sep.* **1.** (*a*) to blunt (edge, point, tool, pencil, angle); to dull (edge, tool); to take the edge off (knife, tool); to break the point off (pencil, etc.); to round, smooth off (angle); (*b*) *Geom:* to truncate (cone, prism); **abgestumpfter Kegel, abgestumpfte Pyramide,** truncated cone, pyramid; frustum of a cone, pyramid. **2.** (*a*) to dull, deaden (the mind, the senses); to blunt (the senses); **den Geschmacksinn a.,** to blunt one's sense of taste; to cloy the palate; (*b*) to make (s.o.) indifferent (**gegen,** to). **3.** *Ch:* to neutralize, saturate (acid). **4. sich abstumpfen,** (*of tool, etc.*) to lose its edge *or* point, its keenness; (*of razor*) to get dull; (*of senses*) to become blunted, dull, less keen; (*of pers.*) to become, grow, indifferent (**gegen,** to); to become blasé.

II. *vbl s.* **1. Abstumpfen,** *n. in vbl senses.* **2. Abstumpfung,** *f.* (*a*)=II. 1; *also: Cryst: etc:* truncation; *Ch:* neutralization, saturation (of acid); (*b*) dullness, deadness (of mind, the senses); apathy; indifference (of s.o.) (**gegen,** to); lack of sensitivity.

abstürmen, *v.i. sep.* (*sein*) to rush away, off.

Absturz, *m.* **1.** (heavy, headlong) fall; crash; plunge; downrush (of water, avalanche); *Av:* crash; **ein Flugzeug zum A. bringen,** to bring down, shoot down, an aircraft. **2.** abrupt descent; steep slope; precipice; cliff, bluff, steep.

abstürzen[1], *v.sep.* **1.** *v.i.* (*sein*) to fall (heavily); to plunge (down); to crash (down); (*of water, avalanche*) to rush down; *Av:* (*of aircraft, pilot, crew*) to crash; (*of aircraft*) **in Flammen a.,** to come down in flames. **2.** *v.i.* (*sein*) (*of ground*) to fall away abruptly, steeply, precipitously; to sheer. **3.** *v.tr.* (*a*) *A:* to hurl (s.o., sth.) down; (*b*) *Ind:* to dump (coal, slag, etc.).

abstürzen[2], *v.tr. sep. A:* to take the lid off (crucible, etc.).

Abstürzrinne, *f.,* **Absturzschacht,** *m. Hyd.E: Ind: etc:* chute, shoot.

Abstützbock, *m.* trestle, support.

abstutzen. I. *v.tr. sep.* **1.**=**stutzen**[1]. **2.** *Geom: Cryst: Arch: etc:* to truncate (cone, prism, column, etc.). **3.** (*a*) to pollard, top (tree); to head down (tree); (*b*) to prune (tree).

II. *vbl s.* **Abstutzen** *n.,* **Abstutzung** *f. in vbl senses; also: Geom: Cryst: Arch: etc:* truncation.

abstützen. I. *v.tr. sep.* **1.** *Constr: etc:* to support; to stay, brace, strut; to prop (up), to shore (up) (wall, deck, etc.); to underpin (building); *N.Arch:* to undershore (the deck, booms, etc.). **2.** to push (sth.) away; **sich von der Felswand a.,** to push oneself away from the rock-face (when descending by a rope).

II. *vbl s.* **1. Abstützen,** *n. in vbl senses.* **2. Abstützung,** *f.* (*a*)=II. 1; (*b*) support(s); stay(s), brace(s), strut(s); shore(s), shoring; underpinning (of building); *N.Arch:* shores (of deck, booms, etc.).

Abstützvorrichtung, *f. Mec.E: etc:* supporting *or* bracing device; support.

absuchen, *v.tr. sep.* **1.** to find and pick (off); **Raupen von einem Obstbaum, Flöhe von einem Hund, a.,** to pick caterpillars off a fruit-tree, fleas off a dog. **2.** to search; **die Brombeersträucher a.,** to pick over the blackberry-bushes; **eine Schublade a.,** to ransack a drawer; **einen Schrank a.,** to search, rummage, (in) a cupboard; **j-s Gepäck a.,** to go through s.o.'s luggage; **einen Wald a.,** to search, scour, a wood; *Ven:* to beat a wood (for game); **das Gelände a.,** to search the ground; *Ven:* to beat for game; **das Gelände, den Himmel, (mit einem Scheinwerfer) a.,** to sweep the ground, the sky, with a searchlight; **den Horizont mit einem Fernrohr a.,** to sweep, scan, the horizon with a telescope; **die ganze Gegend nach j-m a.,** to scour, *F:* comb, the whole district for s.o. **3. sich absuchen,** (*a*) to search oneself (for sth.); (*b*) **sich halbtot nach j-m, etwas, a.,** to wear oneself out searching for s.o., sth.

Absud, *m.* **1.** *Pharm: etc:* (*a*) (*process*) decoction; (*b*) (*resulting liquid*) decoction; extract. **2.** *Dy:* mordant. **3.** *Num:* brightening (of coins, by boiling with dilute acid).

absurd [ap'zurt]. **1.** *a.* absurd, preposterous, nonsensical, irrational; **das Absurde an einer solchen Situation,** the absurdity of such a situation. **2.** *adv.* absurdly, preposterously, nonsensically, irrationally.

Absurdität [apzurdi·'tɛːt], *f.* **-/-en,** absurdity, preposterousness, unreasonableness; **lauter Absurditäten reden,** to talk utter nonsense.

absurren, *v.i. sep.* (*sein*) *F:* to clear off, buzz off.

absüßen, *v.tr. sep.* **1.** (*a*) to sweeten (liquid, etc.); to edulcorate (powdered substance, etc.); (*b*) to purify (liquid); to remove acid *or* salt from (liquid). **2.** *Ch:* to wash out (precipitate).

Absüßkessel, *m. Ind:* edulcorating vessel.

Absüßwasser, *n. Sug-R:* sweet water.

Absynt(h) [ap'zint], *m.* **-(e)s/-e**=**Absinth** 1.

abszedieren [apstse·'diːrən], *v.i. insep.* (*sein*) **1.** to move away; to lose contact. **2.** *Med:* to form an abscess.

Abszeß [aps'tsɛs], *m. & Austrian: n.* **-zesses/-zesse.** *Med:* abscess; gathering; **einen A. aufstechen,** to lance, drain, an abscess.

abszindieren [apstsin'diːrən], *v.tr. insep.* to cut off.

Absziß [aps'tsis], *m.* **-zisses/-zisse.** *Geom:* segment (*esp.* of a circle).

Abszisse [aps'tsisə], *f.* **-/-n.** *Mth:* abscissa.

Abszissenachse, *f. Mth:* x-axis.

Abt, *m.* **-(e)s/Äbte,** abbot; *F:* **den Abt reiten lassen,** to throw off all restraint, *F:* to let oneself go.

abtafeln, *v.i. sep.* (*haben*) *A:* to finish one's meal; to finish dining; to rise from table.

abtäfeln, *v.tr. sep.*=**täfeln.**

abtakeln, *v.tr. sep.* **1.** *Nau:* to dismantle, unrig, strip (ship, mast, etc.); to lay up (ship). **2.** (*a*) *F:* to discharge, dismiss, *F:* sack (employee, official); (*b*) *F. & North G.Dial:* to blow (s.o.) up, dress (s.o.) down, tick (s.o.) off. *See also* **abgetakelt.**

abtanzen, *v.sep.* **1.** *v.tr.* (*a*) to dance (a dance, a figure); (*b*) **sich** *dat.* **die Schuhe, die Sohlen, a.,** to wear out one's shoes with dancing; (*c*) **sich a.,** to exhaust oneself, wear oneself out, with dancing; to dance oneself to a standstill. **2.** *v.i.* (*sein*) to dance off, away; **die Girls tanzten von der Bühne ab,** the chorus-girls danced off the stage.

Abtastdose, *f. Gramophones:* pick-up; *Cin:* pick-up, sound-unit.

abtasten. I. *v.tr. sep.* **1.** to feel (sth.) (all over); to explore, try, test (sth.) (with fingers *or* instrument); to probe; to prod; *Med:* to explore (organ, wound); to probe (wound). **2.** *Cin: TV:* to scan, hunt (sound-track, image).

II. *vbl s.* **Abtasten** *n.,* **Abtastung** *f. in vbl senses; also:* exploration (of sth., *Med:* of organ, wound) (with instrument *or* fingers).

Abtaster, *m. TV:* scanner.

Abtastperiode, *f. TV: Radar:* time-base.

Abtaststrahl, *m. TV:* scanning beam.

Abtastvorrichtung, *f. Cin: TV:* scanning device, scanner, hunting device.

abtauen, *v.sep.* **1.** *v.i.* (*sein*) (*of snow, ice, etc.*) to thaw; to thaw off. **2.** *v.tr.* to thaw, melt (snow, ice, etc.).

Abtausch, *m. Com: etc:* exchange, barter, *F:* swap, truck (**von etwas gegen etwas,** of sth. for sth.).

abtauschen. I. *v.tr. sep.* (*a*) *Com: etc:* to exchange, barter, *F:* swap, truck (**etwas gegen etwas,** sth. for sth.); (*b*) *Chess:* **Läufer, Bauern, a.,** to exchange bishops, pawns; *abs.* **a.,** to exchange pieces.

Abtei [ap'tai], *f.* **-/-en. 1.** abbey. **2.** benefice of an abbey; abbacy.

Abteikirche, *f.* abbey church, abbey.

Abteil [ap'tail], *n. Rail:* compartment.

abteilbar, *a.* **1.** (*a*) divisible; (room, ship's hold, etc.) that can be partitioned, divided into compartments; (*b*) classifiable. **2.** that can be divided off, partitioned off.

abteilen. I. *v.tr. sep.* **1.** to divide, separate (**in**+*acc.,* into); (*a*) to divide, split up (word into syllables, garden into plots, goods into lots, etc.); *Com:* to parcel out (goods); *Constr: N.Arch:* to partition (room, hold, etc.); to divide (hold, etc.) into compartments; **ein Meßgerät in Grade a.,** to graduate, calibrate, a measuring instrument; (*b*) to classify (species, museum exhibits, etc.); (*c*) **das Haar (in der Mitte) a.,** to part one's hair (in the middle). **2.** to divide off; to partition off (space, compartment).

II. *vbl s.* **1. Abteilen,** *n. in vbl senses.* **2. Abteilung** ['aptailuŋ], *f.*=II. 1; *also:* division, separation (**in**+*acc.,* into); **A. in Grade,** graduation, calibration (of measuring-instrument); classification. **3. Abteilung** [ap'tailuŋ], *f.* part, portion, section (of whole); (*a*) compartment (of cupboard, shop-window, ship's hold, etc.); division (of drawer, etc.); *Nau:* **wasserdichte A.,** watertight compartment; (*b*) (administrative) department, branch; section (of administrative department); department (in shop); ward (of hospital); *Sch:* (*at university*) department (of a faculty); (*at school*) division, section (of school, form); **die germanistische A.,** the Department of German, the German Department; *see also* **Leiter**[1]; **die höhere A. der Schule,** the upper school; (*c*) *Mil:* (i) detachment; (ii) (signals, armoured, etc.) battalion; (artillery) battery; (iii) (specialist) unit; (*d*) category; class, classification; rubric; head; **in derselben A.,** under the same head; (*e*) column (of newspaper, etc.); (*f*) *Mth:* **A. von drei Stellen,** group, period, of three figures (in the decimal notation); (*g*) *Ven:* hunting district.

Abteilungschef, *m.*=**Abteilungsleiter.**

Abteilungsfeuer, *n. Mil: A:* rifle fire concentrated on one target.

Abteilungskommandeur, *m. Mil:* (*a*) commander of a detachment; (*b*) unit commander; *Artil:* battery commander.

Abteilungsleiter, *m.* **1.** *Adm:* head of a department, departmental head; head of a section. **2.** *Com:* head of a department.

Abteilungsrennen, *n.* (horse-)race run in heats.

Abteilungsschott, *n. N.Arch:* athwartship bulkhead.

Abteilungsschreiber, *m. Mil:* orderly room clerk.

Abteilungsunterricht, *m. Sch:* teaching of ungraded classes (containing pupils of widely differing levels of attainment).

Abteilungsvorrichtung, *f. Mec.E:* separating device; *Rail:* uncoupling device, slipping device.

Abteilungsvorstand, *m.*=**Abteilungsleiter** 1.

Abteilungsvorsteher, *m.*=**Abteilungsleiter.**

Abteilungswand, *f.* partition.

Abteilungszeichen, *n.* **1.** *Print:* hyphen. **2.** (*on road*) milestone.

Abteilventil, *n.* block-valve (in pipe-line, etc.).

abtelegraphieren ['apte·le·gra·,fiːrən], *v.i. sep.* (*haben*) (*p.p.* **abtelegraphiert**) **j-m a.,** to telegraph, wire, to s.o. to cancel an engagement; to cancel an engagement by telegram.

abtelephonieren ['apte·le·fo·,niːrən], *v.i. sep.* (*haben*) (*p.p.* **abtelephoniert**) **j-m a.,** to ring s.o. up in order to cancel an engagement; to cancel an engagement by telephone.

Abtestat ['aptesta·t], *n. Sch:* professor's *or* lecturer's signature (in student's record-book to prove attendance at the end of a course of lectures).

abtestieren ['aptestiːrən], *v.i. sep.* (*haben*) (*p.p.* **abtestiert**) *Sch:* (*of professor, lecturer*) to sign student's record-book (as proof of attendance at the end of a course of lectures).

abteufen, *v.tr. sep. Min: etc:* to sink, bore (mine-shaft, well); to deepen (mine-shaft).

Abteufkübel, *m. Min:* skip (for removing soil from sinking of shaft, etc.).

Abteufpumpe, *f. Min:* drainage pump (used when sinking shaft).

Abtgraf, *m. Ecc.Hist:* secular abbot.

abtiefen, *v.tr. sep.* (*a*) to deepen (hole, etc.); to excavate (canal, etc.); (*b*)=**abteufen.**

abtilgen, *v.tr. sep.* **1.**=**tilgen**[1]. **2. eine Schuld a.,** to discharge, settle, pay (off), clear (off), a debt.

Abtin, *f.* **-/-innen.** *A. & Poet:*=**Äbtissin.**

abtippen, *v.tr. sep. F:* to type out (letter, etc.).

Äbtissin [ɛp'tisin], *f.* **-/-innen,** abbess.

äbtlich, *a.* abbatial.

Abton[1], *m.* **-(e)s/.** *Ling:* falling tone.

Abton[2], *n.* **-(e)s/.** *Bot: A:*=**Widerton.**

abtönen. I. *v.tr. sep.* to tone down (colours); to shade off, graduate, gradate (colours); to blend, shade (colours) (**mit,** with); *Paint:* to tint (colour); *Phot:* to vignette; *Lit:* to distinguish (characters in a novel, etc.) by delicate nuances.

II. *vbl s.* **1. Abtönen,** *n. in vbl senses; also:* graduation, gradation (of colours). **2. Abtönung,** *f.* (*a*)=II. 1; (*b*) shade (of colour, character); tint; nuance (of colour, character); (*c*) *Ling:* qualitative gradation (of vowels).

Abtönfarbe, *f. Paint:* tint; *Art:* **Abtönfarben,** shading-off tints.

Abtönvignette, *f. Phot:* vignetter.

abtöten. I. *v.tr. sep.* **1.** (*a*) to destroy, kill (off) (bacteria, etc.); (*b*) **den Zahnnerv a.,** to kill the nerve of a tooth; (*c*) **die Gefühle a.,** to deaden, subdue, the emotions; **seine Leidenschaften a.,** to deaden, mortify, extinguish, one's passions;

den Ehrgeiz a., to kill ambition; **das Fleisch a.**, to mortify the flesh. **2. sich abtöten**, to deny oneself.

II. *vbl s.* **Abtöten** *n.*, **Abtötung** *f. in vbl senses; also:* destruction (of bacteria, etc.); mortification (of passions, of the flesh).

Abtpräses, *m. R.C.Ch:* president of a monastic congregation.

Abtprimas, *m. R.C.Ch:* president of the Benedictine congregation.

Abtrab, *m.* **-(e)s/-e.** *Mil: A:* cavalry detachment.

abtraben, *v.i. sep.* (*sein*) to trot off, away; to go off at a trot.

Abtrag, *m.* **-(e)s/⸗e. 1.**=**abtragen II. 1. 2.** (*a*) spoil earth, dug earth; excavated material; (*b*) *A:* scraps, leavings (from the table); (*c*) instalment; payment on account. **3.** compensation; indemnification (for loss sustained); **j-m A. leisten,** *A:* **tun,** to compensate, indemnify, s.o. **4. j-m A. tun,** to do s.o. harm, to hurt s.o., to do s.o. an injury, to injure s.o.; to damage s.o.'s cause, business, reputation. **5.** *Mth:* difference (between two quantities). **6.** *Dial: esp. Swiss:* (=**Ertrag**) yield (from investment, etc.); profits (from business, etc.).

abtragen. I. *v.tr. sep.* (*strong*) **1.** to carry (sth.) off, away; to take, bear, (sth.) away; to remove (sth.); (*a*) *Civ.E: Rail: etc:* to excavate, cut (earth); to clear away, dig away (earth, etc.); to level (hill, ground); to demolish, pull down (structure, bridge); *Mil:* to raze (fortifications); *Constr:* **eine Mauer um zwei Schichten a.**, to lower a wall, reduce the height of a wall, by two courses; (*b*) **die Speisen, die Schüsseln, a.; den Tisch, die Tafel a.**, to remove, clear away, the dishes from the table; to clear the table; *abs.* to clear away, to take away; (*c*) *Surg:* to excise, remove, ablate (part, tumour, etc.); (*d*) *Geol:* to erode; to denude; (*e*) *Ven:* to take (hound) off a false scent. **2.** (*a*) to transfer (design on to paper, etc.); (*b*) *Geom:* to mark off, lay off (distance, etc.). **3.** (*a*) **eine Schuld, eine Hypothek, a.**, to discharge, settle, wipe off, pay, a debt; to redeem a mortgage; to pay off, clear off, a debt, a mortgage; *Fin:* to redeem, extinguish, amortize, a debt; **Steuern, Zinsen, a.**, to pay taxes, interest; (*b*) **j-m seinen Dank a.**, to render, give, (due) thanks to s.o. **4.** to wear out (clothes, shoes). **5.** *Dial: esp. Swiss:* (=**eintragen**) to bring in, yield, produce; **das Geschäft trägt viel ab**, the business yields a good profit; **das trägt nicht (viel) ab**, it doesn't pay. **6.** *Ven: A:* to train (hawk, etc.). **7. sich abtragen,** (*a*) (*of tree*) to become exhausted; **die Birnbäume haben sich abgetragen,** the pear-trees are past bearing; (*b*) (*of clothes*) to wear out; (*of clothes, F: ideas*) to grow threadbare.

II. *vbl s.* **1. Abtragen,** *n. in vbl senses; also:* removal (of sth.); excavation (of earth); demolition (of structure, etc.); *Surg:* excision, removal, ablation (of part, tumour, etc.); discharge, settlement (of debt); redemption (of mortgage); payment (of taxes, interest); *Fin:* redemption, extinction, amortization (of debts). **2. Abtragung,** *f.* (*a*)=II. 1; (*b*) *Geol:* erosion, detrition, denudation.

III. *pr.p. & a.* **abtragend,** *in vbl senses; esp. Agr:* **abtragende Frucht,** final crop in the rotation.

IV. *p.p. & a.* **abgetragen,** *in vbl senses; esp.* **abgetragene Kleider,** threadbare, worn-out, shabby, clothes; *Lit:* **ein alter, abgetragener Mann,** a worn-out old man; **alte, abgetragene Witze,** hackneyed, threadbare, well-worn, jokes; stale jokes.

abträglich, *a.* **1.** unfavourable, adverse (remark, consequence, etc.); **etwas** *dat.* **a. sein,** to be detrimental, injurious, to (health, friendship, etc.); to be prejudicial, harmful, to (s.o.'s interests, etc.); to detract from (s.o.'s looks, etc.); *adv.* **a. von j-m sprechen,** to speak unfavourably of s.o. **2.** *Dial: esp. Swiss:* profitable (business, etc.).

Abtragsböschung, *f. Rail:* bank, slope, of a cutting.

Abtragungsgebiet, *n. Geol:* erosion zone.

abtrampeln, *v.tr. sep.* **1.** to trample (sth.) down. **2.** to wear (sth.) away *or* off by continual trampling.

abtränken, *v.tr. sep. Leath:* **die Grube a.**, to fill the tan-pit with liquor.

Abtransport, *m.* transport(ing) away; carting off, away; carrying away (of goods); *Mil:* evacuation (of wounded, prisoners).

abtransportieren, *v.tr. sep.* (*p.p.* **abtransportiert**) to transport (away); to cart away, off; to carry away (goods); *Mil:* to evacuate (wounded, prisoners).

abträufe(l)n, *v.i. sep.* (*haben*) to drip, trickle; to fall drop by drop.

Abtreibanker, *m. Av:* drag, drogue.

Abtreibeherd, *m. Metall:* refining hearth.

Abtreibehütte, *f. Metall:* (re)finery, (re)fining works.

Abtreibemeister, *m. Metall:* master refiner.

Abtreibemittel, *n.* (*a*) *Ch: Pharm:* expulsive agent; *esp. Pharm:* purge; (*b*) *Obst:*=**Abtreibungsmittel.**

abtreiben, *v. sep.* (*strong*) I. *v.tr.* **1.** (*a*) to drive away, drive off (cattle, etc.); to drive out (swarm of bees, etc.); **die Tiere aus einem Wald a.**, to drive the animals out of a wood; **das Vieh von der Alm a.**, to drive, bring, down the cattle from the mountain pasture; (*b*) to repulse, repel (enemy); to avert (an evil); (*c*) (*of current, wind*) to drive (ship, aircraft) out of its course; to carry (swimmer) out of his direction; to force (ship, swimmer) away from the shore. **2.** to drive out, expel (s.o.); to eject (s.o.); to turn (s.o.) out; to oust (s.o.) (**von,** from); **j-n von einem Gut a.**, to evict, eject, s.o. from an estate; to dispossess, *Jur:* disseize, s.o. of an estate. **3.** *Med:* (*a*) **ein Gift (aus dem Körper) a.**, to expel a poison from the body; (*b*) **Würmer, einen Bandwurm, a.**, to purge off worms, a tapeworm; *F:* **j-m ein Würmchen a.**, to take it out of s.o.; (*c*) **die Milch (von den Brüsten) a.**, to express the milk (from the breasts); (*d*) **ein Kind, die Leibesfrucht, a.**, to procure abortion; to bring on a miscarriage. **4.** *Ch:* (*a*) to expel (gas); (*b*) to separate (substance) by distillation. **5.** *Metall:* to (re)fine (gold, silver) (by cupellation); to cupel (gold, silver). **6.** *Min:* to quarry, split off (stone). **7.** *Min: Civ.E:* to drive (gallery, tunnel). **8.** *For:* (*a*) to clear (a wood); to deforest, untimber (land); (*b*) to fell (trees). **9.** *Husb:* **eine Weide (mit der Herde) a.**, to graze a pasture. **10.** *Ven:* **einen Wald a.**, to beat a wood (for game). **11.** to overwork; to exhaust; to override, overdrive, jade (horse); **seine Arbeiter a.**, to work one's men too hard; to overwork, (over)drive, exploit, sweat, one's men.

II. **abtreiben,** *v.i.* (*sein*) *Nau: Av:* (*of ship, airship*) to drift; to be driven out of its course; *Nau:* **leewärts a.**, to fall off (the wind), to fall to leeward.

III. *vbl s.* **1. Abtreiben,** *n. in vbl senses.* **2. Abtreibung,** *f.*=II. 1; *also:* (*a*) expulsion, eviction, ejection (of s.o.); (*b*) *Med:* expulsion (of poison from the body); **Abtreibung (der Leibesfrucht),** (procured) abortion, 'illegal operation', foeticide; (*c*) *Ch:* (i) expulsion (of gas); (ii) separation (of substance) by distillation; (*d*) *Metall:* cupellation (of gold, silver).

IV. *pr.p. & a.* **abtreibend,** *in vbl senses; esp. Obst:* abortive; abortifacient (drug).

Abtreibeofen, *m. Metall:* refining furnace, fining-furnace; cupel furnace.

Abtreibgas, *n. Ch:* expelled gas.

Abtreibkupelle, *f. Ch: Metall:* cupel, test.

Abtreibung, *f. see* **abtreiben III.**

Abtreibungsmittel, *n. Obst:* abortifacient (drug).

abtrennbar, *a.* separable, detachable, severable; *Fin:* detachable (coupon); **nicht a.**, non-detachable.

Abtrennbarkeit, *f.* separability, detachability

abtrennen. I. *v.tr. sep.* **1.** (*a*) to detach; to separate, disjoin (**von,** from); **ein Stück von etwas a.**, to detach, cut off, break off, a piece from sth.; **den Kopf vom Rumpf a.**, to sever the head from the body; **einen Scheck vom Scheckbuch a.**, to tear a cheque out of the book; *Pol:* **abgetrennte Gebiete,** detached territories; *Fin:* **einen Kupon von einem Bond a.**, to detach a coupon from a bond; (*b*) *El.E:* to disconnect (a lead, etc.); (*c*) **den Besatz von einem Kleid a.**, to take the trimmings off a dress; (*d*) to separate, divide off; fence off (garden, etc.); to partition off, wall off (part of room, etc.). **2. sich abtrennen,** (*of things*) to separate (**von,** from); to be, become, separated; to become detached; to become isolated.

II. *vbl s.* **Abtrennen** *n.*, **Abtrennung** *f. in vbl senses; also:* separation, disjunction (**von,** from); severance (from sth.); *El.E:* disconnection.

abtrennlich, *a.*=**abtrennbar.**

abtreppen. I. *v.tr. sep.* to terrace (hillside, garden, etc.); *Constr: Hyd.E:* to step, bench (foundation, spillway, etc.); **abgetreppt,** terraced (garden, hillside, etc.); stepped, benched (spillway, foundation, etc.).

II. *vbl s.* **1. Abtreppen,** *n. in vbl senses.* **2. Abtreppung,** *f.* (*a*)=II. 1; (*b*) terrace; *Constr: Hyd.E:* step (in foundation, spillway, etc.).

abtretbar, *a. Jur:* (territory, etc.) that can be ceded; transferable, assignable (estate, etc.); (*of pension, etc.*) negotiable.

Abtretbarkeit, *f. Jur:* transferability, assignability (of estate, etc.); negotiability (of pension, etc.).

abtreten, *v.sep.* (*strong*) I. *v.tr.* **1.** (*a*) to wear out (step, mat, etc.) (by walking over it); **seine Schuhe, sich** *dat.* **die Schuhe, a.**, to wear out one's shoes; **seine Absätze, sich** *dat.* **die Absätze, a.**, to wear one's heels down, to wear one's shoes down at the heels; (*b*) **sich a.**, (*of carpet, etc.*) to wear; **sich nicht leicht a.**, to stand hard wear; (*c*) to damage (sth.) by treading on it; **einer Dame die Schleppe a.**, to tread on and tear off a lady's train; **j-m die Zehe a.**, to tread on and sever s.o.'s toe; (*d*) to trample (sth.); to make (earth) firm by treading it down; **Beete a.**, to divide up a (flower-)bed by treading paths across it. **2. den Schmutz, den Schnee, von den Schuhen a., (sich** *dat.***) die Schuhe, die Füße, a.**, to wipe the mud, the snow, off one's shoes; to wipe one's shoes, one's feet. **3.** to resign (a possession, etc.); to give (sth.) up; to yield (a right) (*dat.*, to); to transfer, make over, assign; to surrender (right, goods); to convey (an estate, etc.); to cede (a territory, a province) (**an**+*acc.*, to); **ein verpfändetes Gut a.**, to abandon a mortgaged estate; **einen Besitz durch Unterschrift a.**, to sign away a possession; **abgetretene Gebiete,** ceded territories.

II. **abtreten,** *v.i.* (*sein*) **1.** (*a*) to step aside, draw aside, move aside; to retire, withdraw; (*b*) (*as euphemism*) to retire (in order to relieve oneself); (*c*) *Mil:* to fall out; **die Mannschaften a. lassen,** to dismiss the men, the parade; **abtreten!** dismiss! fall out! (*d*) *Th:* **(von der Bühne) a.**, to make one's exit, *F:* to exit; to go off; **Macbeth tritt ab,** exit Macbeth; **alle treten ab,** exeunt omnes; (*e*) **vom Schauplatz a.**, (i) to retire from the scene, (ii) *F:* to die, *F:* to quit the scene. **2.** *A:* **bei j-m a.**, to stop, stay, with s.o.; **ie einem Wirtshaus a.**, (i) to alight at, (ii) to put up at, an inn. **3. von etwas a.**, to renounce, give up, relinquish, sth.; **vom Amt a.**, to resign, quit, lay down, office; to give up one's post; to demit office; to retire from office; *abs.* to resign, retire; **von einer Partei, von einem Glauben, a.**, to renounce a party, a faith; *A:* **vom Thron a.**, to renounce the throne; to abdicate.

III. *vbl s.* **1. Abtreten,** *n. in vbl senses; also:* (*a*) retirement; withdrawal; *Th:* **A. (von der Bühne),** exit; (*b*) renunciation (of sth.); **A. vom Amt,** resignation from, laying down of, office; *A:* **A. vom Throne,** renunciation of the throne; abdication. **2. Abtretung,** *f. in vbl senses of* I. 1, 3; *also:* resignation, resigning (of a possession); *Jur:* transfer, assignation, assignment (of property, etc.); surrender (of right, goods); conveyance, conveying (of an estate, etc.); cession (of a right, etc.); abandonment, abandoning (of mortgaged estate); **A. eines Besitzes durch Unterschrift,** signing away of a possession.

Abtreter, *m.* **1.** door-mat; scraper-mat. **2.** *Jur:* assignor, transferor transfer(r)er (of property, shares, etc.); grantor (of an annuity, etc.).

Abtretungsurkunde, *f. Jur:* (*a*) (deed of) conveyance; (deed of) transfer, assignation, assignment; (*b*) deed of assignation, of assignment (in favour of creditors).

Abtrieb, *m.* **1.** *For:* (*a*) (clear-)felling; (*b*) (yield of) felled timber; (*c*) clearing (in forest). **2.** *Husb:* **A. (des Viehs von der Alm),** bringing down, driving down, of the cattle from the mountain pasture. **3.** (*a*) *Mec:* downward force; (*b*) *Aer:* negative buoyancy, negative lift. **4.** *Nau:*=**Abtrift 1. 5.** *Jur:* (*a*) eviction, ejection (of s.o., from a property); (*b*)=**Abtriebsrecht.**

Abtriebanker, *m. Av:* drag, drogue.

Abtriebsalter, *n. For:* felling age (of trees).

Abtriebsrecht, *n. Jur:* prior claim (to a property, etc.).

Abtriebswert, *m. For:* potential value (of forest, etc.) as timber.

abtriefen, *v.i. sep.* (*strong & weak*) (*sein*) to drip, trickle; to fall drop by drop.

Abtrift, *f.* **1.** *Nau:* leeway, drift; *Av:* drift. **2.** *Jur:* (*a*) grazing rights, common of pasture, of pasturage; *Scot:* pasturage. **3.** *Jur: A:*=**Abtriebsrecht.**

Abtriftmesser, *m. Av:* drift indicator.

abtrinken, *v.tr. sep.* (*strong*) to drink, sip, the top off liquid); **die Sahne vom Kaffee, die Blume**

vom Bier, a., to sip the cream off the top of one's coffee, the head off one's beer.

abtrippeln, *v.i. sep.* (*sein*) to trip away.

Abtritt, *m.* **1.**=**abtreten** III. 1; *A:* **seinen A. nehmen**, to withdraw, retire, depart; **A. vom Leben**, departure from this life; demise, death. **2.** lavatory; *Mil: etc:* latrine; **auf den A. gehen**, to go to the lavatory. **3.** *Ven:* traces left by a stag in underwood, etc.; *A:* abature.

Abtritt(s)dünger, *m. Agr:* night-soil used as manure; (*in powder form*) poudrette.

Abtritt(s)grube, *f. Hyg:* cesspool, soil-tank.

Abtritt(s)rohr, *n. Constr:* soil-pipe, cesspipe (of water-closet).

Abtrittstoffe, *m.pl. Hyg: etc:* faecal matter; night-soil.

abtrocknen, *v.sep.* **1.** *v.tr.* to dry (sth.) (off, out); to dry (dishes, etc.); to wipe, rub, (sth.) dry; **das Geschirr a.**, *abs.* **a.**, to dry up, to do the drying up; **sich** *dat.* **die Hände a.**, to wipe, dry, one's hands; **sich** *dat.* **die Tränen a.**, to dry (away), wipe away, one's tears; **sich** *dat.* **den Schweiß von der Stirn a.**, to wipe, mop, the sweat from one's brow. **2. sich abtrocknen**, (*a*)=3; (*b*) to dry oneself, rub oneself down, (after bath, etc.). **3.** *v.i.* (*a*) (*sein*) to dry (off, out, up); to become dry; (*of plant*) to wilt; (*of plant, leaves*) to wither away, to shrivel; (*of leaves*) to wither and drop off; (*b*) *v. impers.* (*haben*) to dry up; **es wird schnell wieder a.**, it will soon dry up again (after the rain).

abtrollen, *v.i. sep.* (*sein*) **1.** *Ven:* (*of stag, etc.*) to trot off, away; to canter away. **2.** *F:* (*of pers.*) to go away, take oneself off, *F:* to clear off, push off.

abtrommeln, *v.sep.* **1.** *v.tr.* **einen Marsch a.**, to play, beat out, a march on the drum; **eine Tatsache a.**, to announce a fact by beat of drum, *A:* by tuck of drum. **2.** *v.i.* (*haben*) (*a*) *A:* to cease drumming; (*b*) *Mil:* to beat the retreat.

Abtropf, *m.*=**Abtropfbank, Abtropfbrett.**

Abtropfbank, *f.* drainer; draining-rack (for bottles, etc.).

Abtropfblech, *n. Mec.E: etc:* drip-pan.

Abtropfbrett, *n.* draining-board, drainer; *Dom. Ec:* plate-rack.

abtröpfeln, *v.i. sep.* (*sein*) **1.**=**abtropfen** 1. **2.** (*a*) (*of moisture, blood, etc.*) to ooze, seep; (*of moisture*) to sweat, distil; (*of sweat, moisture*) to exude (**von**, from); (*b*) **die Bäume tröpfeln ab**, the rain is dripping from the trees.

abtropfen, *v.i. sep.* (*sein*) **1.** (*of liquid*) to drip, trickle; to fall drop by drop. **2.** (*of dishes, vegetables, etc.*) to drain.

Abtropfer, *m.* drainer.

Abtropfgefäß, *n.* **1.** drainer. **2.** *Tin-plating:* list-pot.

Abtropfgestell, *n.* draining-rack, drainer; *Dom. Ec:* plate-rack.

Abtropfkasten, *m. Paperm: etc:* draining-tank.

Abtropfpfanne, *f.*=**Abtropfgefäß, Abtropfschale.**

Abtropfschale, *f.* **1.** drainer. **2.** *Mec.E: etc:* drip-pan; *Mch:* save-all (to collect dripping oil).

Abtropfstein, *m.* draining slab (of kitchen sink).

abtrotzen, *v.tr. sep.* **j-m etwas a.**, to bully, hector, sth. out of s.o.; to get sth. out of s.o. by sheer persistence; to extort, wring, (money, a promise, etc.) out of, from, s.o.

abtrudeln, *v.i. sep.* (*sein*) **1.** *Av:* to go into, come down in, a spin; **über den Schwanz a.**, to go into a tail-spin. **2.** *North G.Dial:* to take oneself off, *F:* to push off, clear off.

abtrumpfen, *v.tr. sep.* **1.** *Cards:* to overtrump. **2.**=**abblitzen lassen** *q.v. under* **abblitzen** 2.

abtrünnig, *a.* unfaithful, faithless, false (**von**, to); (*a*) **von seinem Herrscher a.**, unfaithful, disloyal, to one's ruler; **von einer Partei, von einer Sache, a. werden**, to desert from a party, a cause; *F:* to turn one's coat, to rat; (*b*) *Rel:* apostate; renegade (monk, Christian); **von seinem Glauben a. werden**, to apostatize, to renounce, one's faith; (*c*) *B:* rebellious; **weh den abtrünnigen Kindern**, woe to the rebellious children; **die abtrünnige Israel**, (the) backsliding Israel; **a. werden von . . .**, to rebel against . . . ; **jene sind a. worden vom Licht**, they are those that rebel against the Lord.

Abtrünnige, *m., f.* (*decl. as adj.*) (*a*) deserter, renegade (from a party, a cause), *F:* turncoat; *Mil: A:* deserter to the other side; (*b*) *Rel:* (i) apostate, renegade, *F:* turncoat; (ii) back-slider.

Abtrünnigkeit, *f.* defection, falling away (from allegiance *or* cause), desertion (of allegiance *or* cause); disloyalty (to one's ruler, etc.); desertion, *F:* ratting (from a party); *Rel:* apostasy.

Abt(s)stab, *m.* abbot's crook; crosier, crozier, pastoral staff.

Abtswürde, *f.* abbacy, office of abbot.

abtummeln, *v.tr. sep.* **1.** to override, knock up (horse). **2. sich abtummeln**, to tire oneself with romping.

abtun, *v.tr. sep.* (*strong*) **1.** (*a*) *F:* to take off, pull off, remove (garment, ring, etc.); (*b*) *A:* **die Hand von j-m a.**, to withdraw one's aid from s.o.; to cast s.o. off. **2.** *A:* (*a*) to kill (s.o., animal, fowl); to slaughter (cattle); to cut the throat of, *F:* stick (pig, sheep); to execute (s.o.); to put (criminal, etc.) to death; to make away, do away, with (s.o.); to dispose of (s.o.); to despatch, dispatch, (criminal, animal, fowl); (*b*) to vanquish, dispose of (opponent); (*c*) to demolish (sth.). **3.** *A. & Lit:* (*a*) to abolish, do away with (law, tax, custom, abuse, etc.); to suppress (custom, abuse, etc.); to abrogate, annul, repeal, rescind (law, decree); **den Haß a.**, to make an end of, do away with, hatred; (*b*) to throw off, get rid of (habit, characteristic); **eine üble Gewohnheit a.**, to throw off, get rid of, break off, a bad habit; **alle Eitelkeit a.**, to throw aside, cast aside, all vanity; *B:* **da ich aber ein Mann ward, tat ich ab, was kindisch war**, but when I became a man, I put away childish things. **4.** (*a*) to finish, complete (task, piece of work); **das Tagwerk ist abgetan**, the day's work is done, is over; (*b*) to settle (question, matter, quarrel, etc.; *A:* debt, account); to dispose of (question, matter); to adjust, settle (dispute, difference); to close (investigation, etc.); to dismiss (excuses, etc.); **einen Streit gütlich a.**, to settle a dispute amicably; **sie wollte meine Erklärung als bloße Ausrede a.**, she tried to dismiss my explanation as mere evasion; **die Sache ist abgetan**, the matter is settled, closed; the whole thing is over and done with; **das ist mit zwei Worten abgetan**, that's soon, easily, settled; **mit einer bloßen Geldentschädigung ist das noch nicht abgetan**, the matter cannot be settled, disposed of, by mere pecuniary compensation; **damit ist's noch nicht abgetan**, we haven't heard the last of it; the matter will not rest there. **5.** *A:* **sich etwas** *gen.*, **von etwas, a.**, to get rid of sth., to rid oneself of sth.; **sich seiner Schulden a.**, to get clear of one's debts. **6. sich abtun**, *Ven: A:* (*of sick or wounded animal*) to withdraw from the herd; to seek solitude.

abtünchen, *v.tr. sep.*=**tünchen.**

abtupfen, *v.tr. sep.* **1.** to mop up, sponge up (liquid); to remove liquid by dabbing (*esp. Med:* with lint); **den Schweiß (mit dem Taschentuch) von der Stirn a.**, to mop one's brow (with one's handkerchief). **2.** to dab (surface) (with pad); to sponge (surface); *Med:* to dab (wound, etc.) with lint; (**sich** *dat.*) **die Stirn a.**, to mop one's brow.

abtürmen, *v.i. sep.* (*haben*)=**türmen.**

abtuschen, *v.tr. sep.* (*a*) to draw (sth.) with Indian ink; (*b*) to shade in (drawing) with Indian ink.

Abtwahl, *f. Ecc:* election of an abbot.

Abukir [a·bu·ˈkiːr], *Pr.n.n.* -s. *Geog:* Abukir; *Hist:* **die Seeschlacht bei A.**, the Battle of the Nile.

Abulie [a·bu·ˈliː], *f.* -/-n [-ˈliːən]. *Med:* abulia, aboulia.

abulienhaft, *a. Med:* abulic, aboulic.

abundant [abunˈdant], *a.* abundant, copious, plentiful.

Abundanz [abunˈdants], *f.* -/-en, abundance, plenty.

abundieren [abunˈdiːrən], *v.i. insep.* (*haben*) to abound (**an**+*dat.*, in); to be plentiful.

aburteilbar, *a. A:* subject to a legal decision.

aburteilen. I. *v.sep.* **1.** *v.tr.* **j-m etwas a.**, to deprive s.o. of sth. by judicial sentence. **2.** *v.tr.* **j-n, etwas, a.**, to pass a final, definitive, judgment on s.o., sth.; *Jur: A:* to decide (case); to condemn (criminal). **3.** *v.i.* (*haben*) (*a*) *A:* (*of court, judge*) to pass a final judgment; **das Gericht urteilte zugunsten des Angeklagten ab**, the court decided in favour of, found for, the defendant; (*b*) **über j-n, etwas, a.** (i) to pass summary judgment on s.o., sth.; to condemn s.o., sth., out of hand; to reject sth. summarily, (ii) to pass a hasty, peremptory, ill-considered, harsh, judgment on s.o., sth.; **ich will ihn nicht a.**, I do not want to judge him too hastily, too harshly.

II. *vbl s.* **1. Aburteilen**, *n. in vbl senses.* **2. Aburteilung**, *f.* (*a*)=II. 1; *also:* (i) deprivation by judicial sentence; (ii) *Jur: A:* deciding (of case); condemnation (of criminal); (*b*) final, definitive, judgment (*gen.*, on); (*c*) **A. über j-n, etwas, A. in einer Sache**, hasty, peremptory, ill-considered, harsh, judgment on s.o., sth., in a matter.

abusiv [abu·ˈziːf]. **1.** *a.* improper, contrary to usage. **2.** *adv.* improperly, wrongly.

Abusus [abˈuːzus], *m.* -/-, abuse; corrupt practice; evil custom *or* usage.

abverdienen, *v.tr. sep.* **1. j-m Geld a.**, to earn money from s.o.; **Gott seine Gnade a.**, to earn God's grace. **2. eine Schuld a.**, to work out, work off, a debt.

abverlangen, *v.tr. sep.* **j-m etwas a.**, to demand sth. of, from, s.o.; to require sth. of s.o.

abvermieten, *v.tr. sep.* to let off, sublet (room).

abvieren, *v.tr. sep.* **1.** (*a*) to square (timber, stone, etc.); (*b*) *A:* to rub the corners off (boor, etc.). **2.** *Nau: A:*=**abfieren.**

abvisieren [ˈapvi·ziːrən], *v.tr. sep.* (*p.p.* **abvisiert**) **1.** *Surv:* to survey (ground); to line out, mark out (plot of ground); to measure the height of (tree, hill, etc.) by optical methods. **2.** to gauge (cask).

Abvolt [ˈapvolt], *n. El.Meas:* abvolt.

abvotieren [ˈapvo·tiːrən], *v.tr. sep.* (*p.p.* **abvotiert**) **1.** to vote down (a motion). **2.** to outvote (s.o.).

abwackeln, *v.sep.* **1.** *v.tr. A:* to give (s.o.) a beating, a thrashing, a drubbing. **2.** *v.i.* (*sein*) *F:* to totter off, away.

Abwage, *f. Surv:* relative altitude; difference in level between two points.

Abwägeinstrument, *n.*=**Abwägungsinstrument.**

Abwägekunst, *f.*=**Abwägungskunst.**

abwägen. I. *v.tr. sep.* (*strong, occ. weak*) **1.** (*a*) to weigh (sth.) (with balance, scales); to weigh out (goods); **etwas nach Pfund und Lot a.**, to weigh sth. in pounds and ounces; **alles nach Gewinn und Verlust a.**, to estimate everything as a matter of profit and loss; (*b*)=**abwiegen** 1 (*b*). **2.** (*a*) **etwas gegen etwas anderes a., zwei Dinge gegeneinander a.**, to weigh one thing against another, to balance two things against one another; **das Für und Wider a.**, to weigh the pros and cons; (*b*) to balance, counterpoise (forces, powers); to proportion, balance, adjust (parts of a whole, *esp.* the parts of a work of art); *see also* **abgewogen. 3.** to ponder, weigh (matter, arguments, consequences); to weigh (sth.) (up) in one's mind; to consider (matter) well, carefully; **seine Worte a.**, to weigh one's words. **4.** *Surv:* to take the level of, to level, survey, contour (ground); to bone.

II. *vbl s.* **Abwägen** *n.*, **Abwägung** *f. in vbl senses; also:* adjustment (of parts of a whole); consideration (of a matter).

Abwäger, *m.* -s/-. *Surv:* (*pers.*) leveller.

abwägsam, *a.* circumspect, prudent, careful, serious-minded (person); (person) who weighs his words.

Abwägungsinstrument, *n. Surv:* level, *esp.* water-level.

Abwägungskunst, *f.* (art of) levelling; (art of) surveying, contouring (land).

Abwahl, *f.* removal (of s.o.) (from office) by a majority vote.

abwählen, *v.tr. sep.* to vote (s.o.) out (of office).

abwalken, *v.tr. sep.* **1.** *Tex:* to full (cloth). **2.** *F:* to give (s.o.) a thrashing, a beating, a drubbing, a hammering.

abwallen, *v.i. sep.* (*sein*)=**herabwallen.**

abwällen, *v.tr. sep. Cu:* to bring (water, vegetables) to the boil; to blanch (vegetables, etc.).

abwalzen, *v.sep.* **1.** *v.tr.* to roll (road, lawn, metal, etc.); to roll down (surfacing of road, etc.). **2.** *v.i.* (*sein*) to waltz off, away.

abwälzen. I. *v.tr. sep.* **1.** to roll away (stone, barrel, etc.); *F:* **das hat mir einen Stein vom Herzen abgewälzt**, that has taken a load off my mind, off my heart. **2.** to shift (blame, responsibility, work, etc.) (from oneself); **eine Steuer von sich a.**, to get out of paying a tax; **eine Anklage, eine Schuld, von sich a.**, to exculpate, exonerate, oneself (from blame); to clear oneself from blame, of an accusation; **die Schuld auf andere a.**, to shift the blame on to others; to cast, lay, the blame on others; **ein Verbrechen auf einen anderen a.**, to lay a crime at s.o. else's door, to s.o. else's charge; **eine Verantwortung auf j-n a.**, to throw, shift, a responsibility on to s.o.; **eine Arbeit auf einen anderen a.**, *F:* to push a job off on to s.o. else. **3.**=**abwalzen** 1. **4.** *Mec.E:* to hob (gear-wheel, etc.).

II. *vbl s.* **Abwälzen** *n.*, **Abwälzung** *f. in vbl senses; also:* **A. der Schuld, der Anklage**, exculpation, exoneration, clearing, of s.o.

Abwälzer, *m.*, **Abwälzfräser,** *m.*, **Abwälzfräsmaschine,** *f. Mec.E:* hobber, hobbing machine.

abwamsen, *v.tr. sep.* *A:* to give (s.o.) a beating, a thrashing, a drubbing, *A:* to drub, cudgel (s.o.).

abwandelbar, *a. Gram:* declinable (noun, etc.); (word) that can be inflected; (verb) that can be conjugated.

abwandeln, *v. sep.* I. *v.tr.* **1.** to modify, vary (theme, etc.); to change (sth.); **in leicht abgewandelter Form,** in a slightly different form; in a slightly modified form. **2.** *Gram:* to decline (noun, etc.); to inflect (word); to conjugate (verb); **sich a.,** to be declined, to decline; to be inflected, to inflect; to be conjugated, to conjugate. **3.** *Jur:* *A:* (*a*) to punish (crime); (*b*) to atone for (a fault).

II. **abwandeln,** *v.i.* (*sein*) **1.** to walk off, away. **2. auf- und abwandeln,** to pace, walk, up and down.

III. *vbl s.* **1. Abwandeln,** *n. in vbl senses.* **2. Abwand(e)lung,** *f.* (*a*)=III. 1. *also: Gram:* declension (of noun, etc.); inflexion (of word); conjugation (of verb); (*b*) modification, variation; **Abwandlungen des gleichen Themas,** modifications of, variations on, the same theme.

abwand(e)lungsfähig, *a.* **1.** modifiable, variable. **2.** *Gram:*=**abwandelbar.**

abwandern. I. *v.i.* (*sein*) **1.** to move away; **vom Land a.,** (*of pers.*) to migrate from the country (into a town); (*of population*) to migrate, drift away, from the country. **2.** to wander away; to deviate; (*of projectile, etc.*) to drift.

II. *vbl s.* **1. Abwandern,** *n. in vbl senses; also:* deviation; drift (of projectile, etc.). **2. Abwanderung,** *f.* (*a*)=II. 1; (*b*) **A. vom Land,** migration (of pers.) from the country (into the town); migration, drift, flight, (of population) from the country (into the town).

Abwärme, *f. Ph:* lost heat; *Ind:* waste heat; *cp.* **Abhitze.**

Abwärmeanlage, *f. Ind:*=**Abwärmeverwertungsanlage.**

Abwärmekanal, *m. Ind:* waste-heat flue.

Abwärmekessel, *m. Ind:* waste-heat boiler.

abwärmen, *v.tr. sep.* **1.** to heat (furnace, etc.) (gradually). **2.** *Glassm:* to let (oven) cool down gradually.

Abwärmerückgewinnung, *f.* recovery of waste heat.

Abwärmeverwerter, *m. Ind:* (*a*)=**Abwärmeverwertungsanlage;** (*b*) waste-heat recuperator.

Abwärmeverwertung, *f. Ind:* utilization of waste heat.

Abwärmeverwertungsanlage, *f. Ind:* waste-heat (utilization) plant.

abwarnen, *v.tr. sep.* **j-n von etwas a.,** to caution, warn, s.o. against sth.

Abwart, *m. Swiss:* attendant; caretaker (of flats, school, etc.).

abwarten. I. *v.sep.* **1.** *v.tr. & i.* (*haben*) to wait for, await (sth.); **das Ende von etwas a.,** (i) to await the end, the outcome, the upshot, of sth., (ii) to stay to the end, the conclusion, of a play, a meeting, etc.; **die Gelegenheit, den (günstigen) Augenblick, a.,** to bide one's time; to watch one's opportunity, one's time; **die Zeit a.,** to temporize; to put off action deliberately; to wait for the right moment; **geduldig, ruhig, a., in Geduld a.,** to exercise patience, to possess one's soul in patience; **ich werde es ruhig a.,** I shall wait and see (what happens); **das bleibt abzuwarten,** that remains to be seen; **es muß abgewartet werden, ob . . . ,** it remains to be seen, we must wait and see, whether . . . ; only time will tell whether . . . ; *F:* **a. und Tee trinken!** don't be impatient! don't be in too much of a hurry! *F:* don't rush things! easy does it! **2.** *A:*=**warten** . **3. sich abwarten,** *A:*=**sich pflegen,** *q.v. under* **pflegen**

II. *pr.p. & a.* **abwartend,** *in vbl senses; esp.* (*a*) expectant (attitude, etc.); (*b*) temporizing; cautious; **abwartende Haltung,** waiting, *F:* wait-and-see, attitude; **eine abwartende Haltung einnehmen, bewahren,** to temporize; to hold back; *F:* to sit on the fence, to wait and see.

abwärts, *adv.* **1.** downward(s), down; downhill; (*in relation to river*) downstream; **der Weg führt a.,** the road runs downwards, downhill, slopes down, away; **a. steigen,** to descend; **sich a. bewegen,** to move down(wards); (*of prices*) to come down, to fall; **es geht a. mit ihm,** (i) his fortunes are on the decline, *F:* he is coming down in the world; he is on the downward path; he is in a bad way; things have taken a bad turn with him; (ii) (*of ageing man*) he is on the decline (of life), his sands are running out; (iii) he, his health, is failing; (*of invalid*) he is sinking; **es geht a. mit seiner Gesundheit,** his health is failing; **mit seinem Geschäft geht's a.,** his business is going down, *F:* is in a bad way, is going to the bad; *Her:* **a. gebogen,** arched and reversed. **2.** *A. & Dial:* away, aside, off. **3.** *prep.* (+*gen.*) *Dial:* under, below.

Abwärtsbewegung, *f.* downward movement (*esp. Com: Fin:* of prices).

abwärtsgerichtet, *a.* directed, pointing, *or* slanted, downwards; inverted (arrow, etc.).

abwärtsschalten, *v.i. sep.* (*haben*) *Aut:* to change down, *U.S:* to shift down.

Abwärtstransformator, *m. El.E:* step-down transformer.

Abwärtstransformierung, *f. El.E:* stepping down.

Abwasch, *m.* **-es/.** **1.** washing up, dish-washing. **2.** dirty dishes.

abwaschen. I. *v.tr. sep.* (*strong*) (*a*) to wash (sth.) (away); to wash off (dirt, etc.); to wash out (dirt, stain, colour, etc.); to cleanse; to rinse (glasses, etc.); to bathe (wound, eyes); (*of river*) to wash away (earth, etc.); **den Schmutz mit einem Schwamm a.,** to sponge off the dirt; **wasch dir den Schmutz vom Gesicht ab!** wash the dirt off your face! **das Geschirr a.,** *abs.* **a.,** to wash, *U.S:* do, the dishes, *abs.* to wash up; (*b*) *B:* **laß a. deine Sünden,** wash away thy sins; *Lit:* **eine Beleidigung mit Blut a.,** to wipe out an insult in blood.

II. *vbl s.* **1. Abwaschen,** *n. in vbl. senses; also: Dom.Ec:* washing-up, *U.S:* dish washing; *F:* **das ist ein A.,** we can make a single job of that; we can do it all at one go. **2. Abwaschung,** *f.* (*a*)=II. 1; (*b*) ablution; **kalte Abwaschung(en),** cold rub-down, sponge-down; (*c*) *Ecc:* ablution, purification.

Abwaschlappen, *m.* dish-cloth, *F:* dish-clout.

Abwaschmagd, *f.* scullery maid, *F:* washer-up.

Abwaschseife, *f.* kitchen soap.

Abwaschtisch, *m.* washing-up table.

Abwaschtuch, *n.*=**Abwaschlappen.**

Abwaschwasser, *n.* **1.** (dirty) dish-water, (dirty) washing-up water. **2.** *F:* thin, watery, washy, beer, soup, etc.; *F:* dish-water, slops, *P:* hogwash, wish-wash.

Abwasser, *n.* **-s/¨.** **1.** *Ind:* waste water; effluent. **2.** *Hyg:* sewage; cess-water; effluent.

Abwasseranlage, *f.* **1.** *Ind:* waste-water disposal plant. **2.** *Hyg:* sewage disposal plant.

Abwasserklärung, *f.* **1.** *Ind:* purification of waste water. **2.** *Hyg:* purification of sewage.

Abwasserleitung, *f. Ind:* drain(-pipe), waste-pipe.

abwassern. I. *v.i. sep.* (*sein*) *Av:* (*of seaplane, flying-boat*) to take off (from water).

II. *vbl s.* **Abwassern** *n.*, **Abwasserung** *f.* *Av:* take-off, taking-off (of seaplane, flying-boat, from water).

abwässern. I. *v.tr. sep.* **1.** to drain (ground, marsh, etc.); *Ch: etc:* to free (substance) from water. **2.** *Constr:* to slope (window-sill, buttress, etc.) to allow the rain-water to run off. **3.**=**wässern** .

II. *vbl s.* **Abwässern** *n.*, **Abwässerung** *f. in vbl senses; also:* drainage (of land, marsh, etc.).

Abwasserrohr, *n.*=**Abwasserleitung.**

Abwässerungsgebiet, *n. Ph.Geog:* drainage-area, -basin.

Abwechsel, *m. A:*=**Abwechs(e)lung,** *q.v. under* **abwechseln** II.

abwechseln. I. *v.sep.* **1.** *v.i.* (*haben*) (*a*) *A:*= **wechseln** ; (*b*) to alternate; to come alternately, by turns; **Sturm und Stille wechseln (miteinander) ab,** storm and calm succeed one another, come by turns; (*c*) to take turns (**mit, in**+*noun of action,* in+*ger.*); to take turn and turn about (**mit, in**+*noun of action,* to+*inf.,* in+*ger.*); to take it in turns (**mit, in**+*noun of action,* to+*inf.*); **sie wechseln im Dienst ab,** they take it in turns to go on duty, they go on duty alternately; they relieve one another; **er wechselt mit den anderen im Wachen ab,** he takes turns with the others in sitting up; *Mil: A:* **die Wache, das Regiment, wechselte ab,** the guard, the regiment, was relieved; (*d*) *occ.* **in etwas** *dat.* **a.,** to vary (sth.); to make variations in (sth); to give variety to (sth.). **2.** *v.tr.* (*a*) *A:* to change, exchange (sth.); *Mil: A:* **die Wachen a.,** to change, relieve, the guard; (*b*) to alternate (sth.) (**mit,** with); to vary (sth.); to make variations in (sth.); to give variety to (menu, etc.).

II. *vbl s.* **1. Abwechseln,** *n. in vbl senses; also:* alternation; succession (of the seasons, etc.). **2. Abwechs(e)lung,** *f.* (*a*)=II. 1; (*b*) variety ,diversity; change; **A. in eine Tätigkeit, ein Gespräch, usw., (hinein)bringen,** to diversify, vary, an occupation, a conversation, etc.; **zur A.,** for a change; **etwas zur A., der A. wegen, halber, tun,** to do sth. for a change, by way of a change, for the sake of variety; **diese Tätigkeit bietet keinerlei A.,** this is a monotonous, humdrum, occupation; **Sie haben A. nötig,** you need a change; **A. ist die Seele des Lebens,** variety is the spice of life.

III. *pr.p. & a.* **abwechselnd,** *in vbl senses; esp.* (*a*) alternate, alternating; *Med:* intermittent (symptoms, etc.); *Pros:* **abwechselnde Reime,** alternate rhymes; *adv.* alternately; by turns, in turn, turn and turn about, one after another; **etwas a. tun,** to do sth. turn (and turn) about; (*b*) *Mec.E:* reciprocating (motion); (*c*) *occ.* changeable, variable; (*d*) *occ.*=**abwechs(e)lungsreich.**

abwechs(e)lungsreich, *a.* diversified, varied; lively, animated (scene, etc.); (scene, conversation, etc.) full of, with plenty of, variety.

abwechs(e)lungsweise, *adv.* alternately; by turns.

abwedeln, *v.tr. sep.* **von etwas den Staub, die Fliegen, a.,** to fan away the dust on sth., the flies from sth.

Abweg, *m.* (*a*) side-road, by-path, by-way; (*b*) detour; circuitous, roundabout, devious, way; (*c*) wrong way, road, track; **auf Abwege geraten,** (i) to take the wrong road, to mistake the way, to lose oneself, lose one's way, (ii) to be on the wrong track, on the wrong tack; to go right off the track; to be entirely mistaken; to go the wrong way (about sth.), (iii) to go astray (morally); to stray from the right path, from the path of virtue *or* duty; to go to the bad; **j-n auf Abwege führen,** (i) to mislead s.o.; to lead s.o. astray; to put s.o. on the wrong track; (ii) to seduce s.o. from virtue *or* from his duty; to lead s.o. astray (morally).

abwegig, *a.* erroneous, wrong, mistaken (view, conclusion, etc.); false (idea, belief, etc.); irrelevant (consideration, idea, etc.); (*of remark, etc.*) off the point.

Abwegigkeit, *f.* erroneousness, wrongness, mistakenness; falsity (of idea, belief, view, etc.); irrelevance (of remark, etc.).

abwegs, *adv. A:* off the road; off the path; off the track.

abwehen, *v.sep.* (*of wind*) **1.** *v.tr.* to blow away, blow off (leaves, hat, etc.); to blow away, dissipate (fog). **2.** *v.i.* (*haben*) (*a*) to drop, die down, subside; to slacken, slack off; (*b*) **der Wind wehte vom Land ab,** the wind was blowing from the shore; there was an off-shore wind, a land-breeze.

Abwehr, *f.* **-/.** **1.** warding off (of blows, thrust, danger, illness); averting (of danger, accident, misfortune); fending off (of blows, etc.); staving off (of danger, disease); parrying (of blow, thrust); repelling (of attack, enemy); keeping off (of flies, etc.); **zur A. eines Angriffs,** in order to ward off an attack; **bei der A.,** when on the defensive. **2.** (*a*) **A. (gegen),** defence (against); resistance (to); safeguarding (against); (*b*) *Box: Fenc:* defence; *Mil:* resistance; **die A. des Gegners, die gegnerische A., war schwach,** *Box: Fenc:* the opponent's defence was weak; *Mil:* the enemy offered only weak resistance; (*c*) *Mil:* (i) security; (ii) **die A.,** military intelligence; the counter-espionage service; (*d*) *Sp:* **die A.,** the defence. **3.** (*a*)=**Abwehrmaßnahme;** (*b*)=**Abwehrmittel.**

Abwehrangelegenheiten, *f.pl. Mil:* matters of security.

Abwehrbereitschaft, *f. Mil:* stand-by; readiness to take defensive measures.

Abwehrdienst, *m. Mil:* counter-espionage service.

abwehren. I. *v.tr. sep.* (*a*) to ward off (danger, illness); to avert (danger, accident, misfortune); to fend off (blow, etc.); to stave off (danger, disease); to turn (weapon) aside; *Box: Fenc: etc:* to parry, ward off (blow, thrust); *Mil:* to repulse, repel, ward off (attack, enemy); *see also* **abortiv** 3; (*b*) **j-m etwas a., etwas von j-m a.,** to keep sth. off s.o.; to protect s.o. against sth.; **eine Gefahr von j-m a.,** to keep s.o. safe from a danger; **einem Verwundeten die Fliegen a.,** to keep the flies off a wounded man; **Unannehmlichkeiten, usw., von sich a.,** to push away, aside, unpleasant things, etc.

II. *vbl s.* **Abwehren** *n.*, *occ.* **Abwehrung** *f. in vbl senses; cp.* **Abwehr** 1.

Abwehrferment, *n. Physiol:* defensive enzyme.

Abwehrfeuer, *n. Mil:* defensive fire.

Abwehrflugzeug, *n.*=**Abwehrjäger.**

Abwehrgeschütz, *n.*=**Abwehrkanone.**

Abwehrgraben, *m. Mil:* support trench.

Abwehrgranate, *f. Artil:* armour-piercing shell, *esp.* anti-tank shell.

Abwehrgriff, *m. Life-saving:* (rescuer's) release method (*when clutched by drowning person*).

Abwehrjäger, *m. Mil.Av:* interceptor (fighter).

Abwehrkampf, *m. Mil:* defensive battle; defensive fighting.

Abwehrkanone, *f. Artil:* anti-aircraft gun.

Abwehrkörper, *m. Physiol:* antibody.

Abwehrmanöver, *n. Mil.Av:* **ein A. ausführen,** to take avoiding action.

Abwehrmaßnahme, *f.* defensive measure; protective, preventive, measure; measure of protection.

Abwehrmechanismus, *m. Psy:* defence mechanism.

Abwehrmittel, *n.* means of defence; preventive, preventative; preservative (against a danger, etc.); *Med:* prophylactic.

Abwehrneurose, *f. Psy:* defensive neurosis.

Abwehroffizier, *m. Mil:* security officer.

Abwehrschlacht, *f. Mil:* defensive battle.

Abwehrspieler, *m. Sp:* defending player, defender.

Abwehrstelle, *f. Mil:* **1.** *A:* anti-aircraft post. **2.** (*a*) office of the security control; (*b*) office of the counter-espionage service.

Abwehrstoff, *m. Physiol:* = **Abwehrkörper.**

Abwehrvorrichtung, *f.* protective device; safety device.

Abwehrwaffen, *f.pl. Mil:* defensive weapons; defensive armament (of aircraft, etc.).

Abwehrzauber, *m.* protective magic; apotropaic, protective, charm *or* amulet.

Abwehrzoll, *m. Pol.Ec:* protective tariff; safeguarding duty.

Abwehrzone, *f. Mil:* defence area.

abweichen[1]. I. *v.i. sep.* (*strong*) (*sein*) **1.** to deviate, diverge, swerve, depart (**von,** from); to differ, vary (**von,** from); **er weicht nie von seinen Grundsätzen ab,** he never deviates, never departs, never swerves, from his principles; **ich weiche keinen Finger breit ab,** I won't budge an inch; **vom rechten Weg a.,** to swerve, stray, from the straight path, from the path of duty; **von einer Regel a.,** (i) to depart from a rule, (ii) to be an exception to a rule; **von der Wahrheit a.,** to deviate, stray, from the truth; **vom Typus a.,** to deviate from the norm; **von j-s Ansicht a.,** to differ from s.o.; to dissent from s.o.'s opinion; **voneinander a.,** to diverge (from one another); to vary; **diese beiden Resultate weichen stark voneinander ab,** there is a marked difference, discrepancy, variation, between these two results. **2.** to deviate (from the true line); to deflect; (*a*) *Ball:* (*of projectile*) to deviate, to be deflected, to drift; (*b*) *Magn:* to deviate; (*of compass-needle*) **senkrecht a.,** to dip; **Kompaß, der um 3° abweicht,** compass that has a deviation, a variation, of 3°; (*c*) *Ph:* (*of beam, ray*) to deviate; (*d*) *Nau: Av:* (*of ship, aircraft*) **vom Kurs a.,** to go off course. **3.** *A:* (*of time*) to elapse, to go by; **das abgewichene Jahr,** the past year; the year that has (just) ended, (just) drawn to a close.

II. *vbl s.* **1. Abweichen,** *n. in vbl senses; also:* deviation; divergence; swerving (from principles, duty); departure (from principles, rules, one's duty, etc.); digression (in an argument, etc.). **2. Abweichung,** *f.* (*a*) = II. 1; (*b*) deviation (from the true line); deflection; *Ball:* deflection, deviation, *Artil:* drift (of projectile); **unerlaubte A.,** error; **erlaubte, gestattete, A.,** allowance (for deviation); *Mec.E:* **erlaubte A.,** tolerance; (*c*) *Magn:* declination; **senkrechte A.,** dip (of magnetic needle); **A. eines Kompasses,** variation, deviation, of a compass; (*d*) *Ph:* deflection (of beam, ray); *Astr: Opt:* aberration; *see also* **chromatisch, sphärisch;** (*e*) *Astr:* declination (of star); (*f*) *Nau:* departure (eastwards *or* westwards); *Nau: Av:* **A. (vom Kurs),** deviation from normal course; *Civ.E: Min: etc:* **(seitliche) A. einer Bohrung,** (lateral) drift of a boring; (*g*) variation; difference; discrepancy (in results, etc.); *Gram:* **A. von einer Regel,** exception to a rule.

III. *pr.p. & a.* **abweichend,** *in vbl senses; also:* (*a*) deviating; divergent, diverging; different, differing; varying, variant; dissenting, dissentient (opinion); discrepant (results, etc.); (*b*) exceptional; abnormal; aberrant; anomalous (case, etc.); *Gram:* irregular, anomalous (declension, etc.); (*c*) *adv.* divergently, differently (**von,** from); exceptionally; abnormally; irregularly; anomalously.

abweichen[2]. I. *v.sep.* (*weak*) **1.** *v.tr.* (*a*) to soften (sth.) (*esp.* by soaking); to soak, steep; to macerate (herbs, etc.); (*b*) to soak off (mud, *Surg:* dressing, etc.); (*c*) *South G.Dial:* (*of medicine, food, etc.*) to have a laxative effect; to loosen the bowels. **2.** *v.i.* (*sein*) (*a*) to soften, to become soft; to soak, steep; (*of herbs, etc.*) to macerate; (*b*) (*of mud, Surg: of dressing, etc.*) to soften and come off; to come off with soaking.

II. *vbl s.* **Abweichen** *n.,* **Abweichung** *f. in vbl senses; also:* (*a*) maceration (of herbs, etc.); (*b*) *South G.Dial:* diarrhoea; looseness of the bowels.

III. *pr.p. & a.* **abweichend,** *in vbl senses; esp.* softening; *adv.* with softening effect; *South G.Dial:* laxative (medicine, effect); *adv.* with laxative effect; as a laxative.

Abweichungsinstrument, *n. Surv:* trough-compass.

Abweichungskompaß, *m.* declination compass, declinometer; azimuth compass.

Abweichungskreis, *m. Astr:* declination circle.

Abweichungsmesser, *m. Civ.E: Min: etc:* driftmeter.

Abweichungswinkel, *m.* **1.** angle of deviation; angle of divergence; angle of deflection. **2.** *Astr:* anomaly (of a star).

abweiden, *v.tr. sep.* **1.** (*of cattle, etc.*) to graze (on) (meadow). **2.** (*of pers.*) to take, drive, (cattle) to pasture; to feed, graze (cattle).

abweifen, *v.tr. sep.* to reel off, wind off, spool off (yarn, etc.).

abweinen (sich), *v.refl. sep.* (*a*) to wear oneself out with crying; (*b*) to cry one's eyes out.

Abweiseblech, *n. Constr:* (rain-water) shoot (on chimney, etc.).

abweisen. I. *v.tr. sep.* (*strong*) **1.** to send, turn, (s.o.) away; to refuse, reject, (s.o.'s) request *or* application; to refuse to see (s.o.); to decline to receive (s.o.); *Sch:* **einen Prüfling, einen Kandidaten, a.,** to reject, refuse, a candidate (at an examination); **sie läßt sich nicht a.,** she won't take no for an answer; she will take no refusal; she won't be put off; **j-n schroff, kurz, a.,** to send s.o. packing, send s.o. to the right-about, send s.o. about his business; to rebuff, snub, s.o.; to be very short with s.o.; **schroff, kurz, abgewiesen werden,** to meet with, suffer, a rebuff; to get snubbed, suffer a snub; **abgewiesen werden,** to be turned away; to meet with a refusal; to be refused, turned down; *Jur:* **er ist mit seiner Forderung abgewiesen worden,** his claim has been rejected, dismissed, set aside. **2.** (*a*) to turn (sth.) away, aside; to keep (sth.) off; to deflect (bullets, etc.); **einen Angriff a.,** to repulse, repel, beat off, an attack; **Buhne, die die Wellen abweist,** groyne that keeps off the waves; (*b*) to reject (sth.); to refuse to acknowledge (sth.); **eine Bitte a.,** to refuse a request; **ein Gesuch a.,** to reject, turn down, an application; **ein Anerbieten a.,** to reject, decline, an offer; to dismiss an offer; **einen Vorschlag von sich a.,** to reject a proposal (decisively); to refuse to entertain a proposal; **j-s Ansprüche a.,** to reject, turn down, dismiss, s.o.'s claims; **seine Ansprüche wurden glatt abgewiesen,** his claims were rejected out of hand, *F:* were turned down flat; **eine Beschuldigung a.,** to deny an accusation; *Com:* **einen Wechsel a.,** to dishonour a bill; to protest a bill; *Jur:* **eine Klage a.,** to dismiss, reject, a suit; **j-s Klage a.,** to dismiss s.o.'s claim, to nonsuit s.o.; **eine Berufung a.,** to dismiss an appeal; **eine Forderung a.,** to set a claim aside.

II. *vbl s.* **1. Abweisen,** *n. in vbl senses.* **2. Abweisung,** *f.* = II. 1; *also:* (*a*) **schroffe, kurze, A.,** rebuff; snub; (*b*) rejection (of offer, application, claim, etc.); refusal (of request, application, etc.); dismissal (of offer); **A. einer Beschuldigung,** denial of an accusation; *Com:* **A. eines Wechsels,** dishonouring, protesting, non-acceptance, of a bill; *Jur:* **A. einer Klage,** dismissal, rejection, of a suit; nonsuiting of a plaintiff; **A. einer Berufung,** dismissal of an appeal; **A. einer Forderung,** setting aside of a claim.

III. *pr.p. & a.* **abweisend,** *in vbl senses; esp.* adverse, unfavourable (judgment, etc.); unfriendly (manner); **abweisende Geste, Worte, usw.,** gesture, words, etc., of refusal; brusque gesture, words, etc.

Abweiser, *m.* **1.** (*pers.*) rejecter (of claim, offer, etc.); refuser (of offer, etc.). **2.** (*a*) *Tchn:* deflector, deflecting device, *esp. Mil:* bullet-deflector; (*b*) *Artil:* recoil guard (on gun); (*c*) *Civ.E:* = **Abweisstein;** *Constr:* corner-, angle-post; (*d*) *Hyd.E:* groyne; breakwater; (*e*) *N.Arch:* rubbing-strake.

Abweisstein, *m.* guard-stone, fender (at edge of road, etc.); kerb-stone, *U.S:* curb(stone).

Abweisungsbescheid, *m. Jur:* (judgment of) nonsuit; **den A. geben,** to direct a nonsuit.

Abweisungsschreiben, *n.* letter of refusal; letter rejecting an application, etc.

Abweisungsurteil, *n. Jur:* dismissal (of an appeal).

Abweitung, *f. Nau:* departure (eastwards *or* westwards).

abwelken, *v.sep.* **1.** *v.i.* (*sein*) (*of flowers, etc.*) to wither, wilt, fade; (*of beauty, youth*) to fade; (*of flowers, leaves*) to wither and drop off. **2.** *v.tr. Leath:* to sam, sammy (leather); to dry (leather) partially.

Abwelkmaschine, *f. Leath:* samm(y)ing machine.

Abwelkpresse, *f. Leath:* samm(y)ing press, drying press.

abwellen, *v.tr. sep. Cu:* to boil (meat, vegetables) briskly.

abwendbar, *a.* avertable, avertible; preventable, preventible; (blow) that can be parried.

Abwendbarkeit, *f.* avertability, preventability.

abwenden. I. *v.tr. sep.* (*conj. like* **wenden**) **1.** (*a*) to turn (sth.) aside, away; **das Gesicht, die Augen, den Blick, a.,** to turn away, avert, one's face, one's eyes, one's gaze, (**von,** from); **seine Aufmerksamkeit von etwas a.,** to divert one's attention from sth.; *B:* **warum wendest du deine Hand ab?** why withdrawest thou thy hand? **sein, das, Herz von j-m, von einer Sache, a.,** to become estranged from s.o., a cause; to lose interest in s.o., a cause; (*b*) **j-n (von) j-m, von einer Sache, a.,** to alienate, estrange, s.o. from s.o., from a cause; to draw s.o. away from a cause. **2. sich abwenden** (*usu.* **wandte ab; abgewandt**) to turn away, turn aside; **sich von j-m a.,** to turn away from s.o.; to break away, become alienated, from s.o.; to withdraw one's friendship from s.o.; **sie wandte sich mit Ekel von ihm ab,** she turned (away) from him in disgust; **sich von der Welt a.,** to turn one's back on the world; **sich von der Wahrheit a.,** to turn one's back on the truth, *B:* to turn from the truth. **3.** to avert, prevent (danger, accident, war, etc.); to ward off, stave off (danger); **einen Hieb, einen Stoß, (von sich) a.,** to parry, ward off, avert, a blow, a thrust; **j-s Zorn a.,** to turn away s.o.'s wrath.

II. *vbl s.* **Abwenden** *n.,* **Abwendung** *f. in vbl senses; also:* prevention (of danger, etc.).

abwendig, *pred. a.* **1. j-n (von) j-m a. machen,** to alienate, estrange, s.o. from s.o.; **j-m seine Kunden a. machen,** to entice away s.o.'s customers. **2.** *A:* (*a*) **j-m etwas a. machen,** to take sth. from s.o., to deprive s.o. of sth.; (*b*) **j-n von seinem Vorhaben a. machen,** to dissuade, turn, s.o. from his intention.

abwerben, *v.tr. sep.* (*strong*) to seduce (s.o.) to leave service; to entice (s.o.) away from his job (*esp. from the German Democratic Republic*); **Abwerbung** *f,* enticing, enticement, (of employee, etc.) to leave his job.

abwerfbar, *a.* **1.** that can be thrown off, cast off. **2.** *Av:* jettisonable (fuel tank, etc.).

abwerfen. I. *v.tr. sep.* (*strong*) **1.** (*a*) to throw (sth.) off; to fling (sth.) off; to cast (sth.) off; to cast, shed (clothes); **den Überzieher a.,** to throw off one's overcoat; **die Maske a.,** to throw off, drop, the mask; to throw off all disguise; **das Joch, die Fesseln, a.,** to shake off, cast off, throw off, fling off, the yoke, one's fetters; (*of horse*) **den Reiter a.,** to throw, unseat, its rider; **sein Pferd warf ihn ab,** his horse threw him, bucked him off; (*b*) (*of animal*) to shed, cast (skin, horns); (*of tree*) to shed its leaves; (*of snake, etc.*) **die Haut a.,** to cast, throw, its skin; to cast its slough, to slough; **der Hirsch wirft sein Geweih, sein Gehörn, ab,** *abs.* **wirft ab,** the stag sheds, casts, its antlers, its horns; *B:* **gleichwie ein Feigenbaum seine Feigen abwirft,** even as a fig tree casteth her untimely figs; (*c*) *Lit:* **die Materie a.,** to put off material things; to throw off the fetters of the material world; *see also* **Hülle** 1 (*b*). **2.** (*of animals*) **Junge a.,** *abs.* **a.,** to bring forth, drop, throw, young. **3.** to throw (sth.) down; to throw (sth.) out; *Av:* to drop (bombs, mail-bags, pamphlets, etc.) (from aircraft); to jettison, drop (fuel tank, etc.); to jettison, get rid of (bombs); *see also* **blind** 2 (*b*). **4.** to knock (sth.) down; *Sp:* **die Latte a.,** to knock down the bar (in high jump); *A:* **eine Brücke a.,** to break down, demolish, a bridge. **5.** *Sp:* **einen Spieler a.,** (*in ball-games*) to get a man out (by a throw of the ball). **6.** *Cards:* **die Fehlblätter a.,** to throw away, discard, one's useless cards; **Herz a.,** to get rid of one's hearts; to clear one's hand of hearts. **7.** *Ling:* to elide (vowels).

8. (*a*) *Metall:* **Schlacken a.,** to run off slag; (*b*) *Tinplating:* **das überflüssige Zinn a.,** to melt off the list. 9. *Dicing: A:* (*a*) **j-n a.,** to throw higher than s.o.; (*b*) *abs.* to throw last, take the last throw. 10. (*a*) *A:* (*of tree*) **Früchte a.,** to drop its fruit; to yield fruit; (*b*) (*of investment, business, etc.*) to bring in, bear, yield, produce (profit); **Kapitalanlage, die fünf Prozent abwirft,** investment that brings in, bears, returns, five per cent; **das Geschäft wirft einen schönen Gewinn ab,** the business yields a handsome profit; **ein Geschäft, das viel abwirft,** a lucrative, paying, business; **Boden, der viel abwirft,** land that pays well; **das wirft nicht viel ab,** there's not much profit in it; **das wirft nichts ab,** it doesn't pay. **11. sich abwerfen,** (*a*) *Cards:* = **die Fehlblätter a.,** *q.v. under* 6; (*b*) *A:* **sich mit j-m, mit etwas, a.,** to come into conflict with s.o., sth.; to fall out with s.o.; to be at odds, at variance, with s.o.

II. *vbl s.* **Abwerfen,** *n. in vbl senses; also: Ling:* elision (of vowel).

Abwerfofen, *m. Metall:* refining furnace.

Abwerfpfanne, *f. Tinplating:* list-pot.

Abwerg, *m. & n., Dial:* **Abwerk,** *n.* (waste) tow.

abwerten. I. *v.tr. sep.* 1. to estimate; to value, appraise (goods, etc.). 2. (*a*) *Pol.Ec:* to devaluate, devalue, devalorize (currency); (*b*) to depreciate, *F:* devalue (ideals, etc.).

II. *vbl s.* **Abwerten** *n.*, **Abwertung** *f. in vbl senses; also:* 1. estimation (of the value of sth.); valuation (of goods, etc.). 2. (*a*) *Pol.Ec:* devaluation, devalorization (of currency); (*b*) depreciation, *F:* devaluation (of ideals, etc.).

Abwesen, *n. A:* = **Abwesenheit** 1, *esp.* (*c*).

abwesend, *a.* 1. (*a*) absent, away (**von,** from); **von der Arbeit, von der Schule, a.,** absent from work, from school; **er ist (vom Hause, vom Büro) a.,** he is away (from home, from the office); *Hist:* **abwesender Gutsherr,** absentee (landlord); (*b*) *Jur:* defaulting (defendant, etc.); **vorsätzlich a.,** contumacious (person). 2. (*of pers.*) absent-minded; (*of thoughts*) far away; **er ist (wie) a.,** his mind is, his thoughts are, far away, elsewhere; he is wool-gathering; **seine Gedanken sind manchmal a.,** he is liable to be absent-minded; his mind wanders at times; he has fits of abstraction. **3. Abwesende,** *m., f.* (*decl. as adj.*) (*a*) absent person; (the) absent one; absentee (from work, school, etc.); **die Abwesenden,** the absent; the absentees; **Liste der Abwesenden,** absentee list, list of absentees; *Prov:* **die Abwesenden haben immer unrecht, der Abwesende muß immer herhalten, muß Haare lassen,** the absent are always in the wrong; (*b*) *Jur:* defaulter; person who has failed to appear (in court); **vorsätzlich Abwesender, Abwesende,** contumacious person.

Abwesenheit, *f.* 1. (*a*) absence (**von,** from); **in, während, meiner A.,** in, during, my absence; **in A. seines Vaters, in seines Vaters A.,** in his father's absence; **A. von der Schule,** absence from non-attendance at, school; **A. von der Arbeitsstelle,** absenteeism (from work); **ihre A. wird niemandem auffallen,** no one will miss them; *F:* **durch A. glänzen,** to be conspicuous by one's absence; *Prov:* **A. tötet die Liebe,** out of sight, out of mind; long absent, soon forgotten; *Hist:* **A. der Gutsherren,** absenteeism (of landlords); (*b*) *Jur:* **seine A. (vom Tatort) nachweisen,** to establish an alibi; (*c*) *Jur:* non-appearance (in court); default; **vorsätzliche A.,** contumacy; **in A. verurteilt,** sentenced in his, her, absence. 2. (*pl.* **Abwesenheiten**) absence of mind, abstraction.

Abwesenheitspfleger, *m. Jur:* curatorship for an absent person.

Abwesenheitspflegschaft, *f. Jur:* trusteeship in the absence of parents *or* guardians.

Abwesenheitsprotest, *m. Com:* protesting of a bill when the drawee is inaccessible *or* untraceable.

abwettern, *v.sep.* 1. *v. impers.* **es wettert (sich) ab,** the storm is abating, dying down. 2. *v.tr. Nau:* **einen Sturm a.,** to weather (out), ride out, a storm, a gale. 3. *v.tr. A:* to beat off, repel, repulse (the enemy, an attack). 4. *v.tr. Constr:* = **abwässern** 2. *See also* **abgewettert.**

abwetzen, *v.tr. sep.* 1. to whet, sharpen, grind (tool, knife); (*of bird*) **den Schnabel a.,** to whet its beak. 2. (*a*) to wear out (tool) by constant sharpening; (*b*) to blunt (point of knife, etc.); (*c*) **den Rost von einer Klinge a.,** to rub off, grind off, the rust from a blade. 3. *F:* to wear out the seat of (trousers); **abgewetzte Hosen,** worn-out trousers; trousers badly worn at the seat.

abwichsen, *v.tr. sep.* 1. to polish (shoes, etc.) thoroughly, to give (shoes, etc.) a good polishing. 2. *F:* to give (s.o.) a thrashing, a drubbing, a hiding.

abwickelbar, *a.* 1. that can be unrolled, unwound; that unrolls. 2. *Geom:* developable (surface); *Mth:* rectifiable (curve).

Abwickelkassette, *f. Cin:* feed magazine; cassette.

Abwickelmaschine, *f. Tex: etc:* reeling machine; winding *or* unwinding machine.

abwickeln. I. *v.tr. sep.* 1. (*a*) to unwind, unreel (thread, cable, etc.); to reel off, wind off, spool off (thread, etc.); *Cin:* **den Film a.,** to pay out, deliver, feed, the film; (*b*) to unravel, disentangle (thread, etc.). 2. (*a*) to settle (matter, transaction, etc.); **Schulden a.,** to clear, settle, liquidate, debts; **eine Aktiengesellschaft, ein Unternehmen, a.,** to wind up, liquidate, a company, a business; (*b*) *Mil:* to disperse (unit); to wind up (unit); *A:* to demobilize (unit). 3. *Geom:* to develop (surface); to rectify (curve). **4. sich abwickeln,** to develop; (*of affair*) to run its course; **die Sache hat sich glatt abgewickelt,** the affair has gone off smoothly.

II. *vbl s.* **1. Abwickeln,** *n. in vbl senses.* **2. Abwick(e)lung,** *f.* = II. 1; *also: Com:* settling, settlement, liquidation (of debts); liquidation, winding up, *U.S:* wind-up (of company, business); *Mil:* winding up, dispersal (of a unit); *A:* demobilization; *Geom:* development (of surface); rectification (of curve).

Abwickelspule, *f. Ind: etc:* feed reel, feed spool; *Cin:* upper spool, delivery spool, pay-out spool, feed spool.

Abwickler, *m. Com: Jur:* liquidator.

Abwicklungskurve, *f. Geom: A:* evolvent.

Abwicklungsmaschine, *f.* = **Abwickelmaschine.**

Abwicklungsstelle, *f. Mil: A:* dispersal station; demobilization station.

Abwieg(e)ler, *m.* **-s/-,** *occ:* appeaser, pacifier.

abwiegeln, *v.tr. sep. occ:* to appease, pacify, calm down (mob, angry creditors, etc.).

abwiegen, *v.tr. sep.* (*strong*) 1. (*a*) to weigh (sth.) (in the balance); to weigh out (sugar, etc.); (*b*) **etwas mit der Hand a.,** to feel, try, the weight of sth.; to weigh sth. in one's hand; *Dial. & U.S:* to heft (packet, etc.). 2. = **abwägen** 2(*b*), 3; *see also* **abgewogen.**

abwimmeln, *v.tr. sep.* 1. *Dial:* to gather, pick (grapes). 2. *F:* (*a*) **j-n a.,** to get rid of s.o.; to shake s.o. off; *F:* to choke s.o. off, *U.S:* to brush s.o. off; **j-n mit einer Ausrede a.,** to put s.o. off, fob s.o. off, with an excuse; (*b*) *Sch: A:* **einen Studenten, einen Schüler, a.,** to send a student down; to expel a pupil; (*c*) *Mil: A:* **einen Unteroffizier a.,** to reduce an N.C.O. (to the ranks); (*d*) *Cards:* = **abwerfen** 6.

Abwind, *m.* 1. *Meteor:* katabatic wind; down wind, down-current. 2. *Av:* downwash.

Abwinde, *f. Tex: etc:* reel, winder, spool.

abwinden, *v.tr. sep.* (*strong*) 1. (*a*) to unwind, wind off, unreel, reel off, spool off (thread, yarn, etc.); to uncoil (cable); *Nau:* to pay out (cable); **sich a.,** (*of thread, etc.*) to unwind, to come unwound; to wind off; (*of cable*) to uncoil; (*b*) to disentangle, unravel (thread, etc.). 2. *Nau:* **das Spill a.,** to walk back, heave back, the capstan. 3. to lower (sth.), let (sth.) down (with windlass, block and tackle, etc.).

Abwinder, *m.* 1. *Tex:* (*pers.*) reeler, wind(st)er. 2. *Tex: etc:* winder; reeling-machine; reel, spool.

Abwindwinkel, *m. Av:* downwash angle.

abwinken, *v.i. sep.* (*haben*) 1. to make a gesture, a sign, of refusal; **j-m a.,** to gesture, make a sign, to s.o. to go away *or* to refrain from doing sth.; **er winkte dem Kellner ab,** he motioned, made motions, signed, to the waiter to go away; **ich wollte ihm einen Kognak anbieten, aber er winkte (mir) ab,** I was going to offer him a brandy, but he made a gesture of refusal, but he refused; **er wollte eintreten, aber der Schupo winkte ihm ab,** he was about to walk in, but the policeman motioned him away, signed to him not to enter. 2. to give a hint of discouragement; **j-m a.,** to give s.o. a hint not to do sth.; to let s.o. see that his presence *or* intentions will not be welcomed; to put s.o. off doing sth.; **er wollte dich besuchen, aber ich habe ihm abgewinkt** (*Hum:* **abgewunken**), he wanted to call on you, but I put him off.

abwipfeln, *v.tr. sep. Arb:* to pollard, top (tree); to head down (tree).

abwirbeln, *v.tr. sep.* 1. (*of wind, etc.*) to whirl (sth.) away. 2. *occ.* **einen Rhythmus (auf der Trommel) a.,** to beat out, play, a (fast) rhythm on the drum. 3. *occ.* **die Saiten a.,** to slacken, loosen, the strings (of violin, etc.).

abwirtschaften, *v.sep.* 1. *v.tr. Agr:* to exhaust (soil); **der Boden ist abgewirtschaftet,** the soil is exhausted, worked out. 2. *v.tr. & i.* (*haben*) to ruin (one's business, domestic life, etc.) by bad management; *F:* **er hat abgewirtschaftet,** (i) he's done for, down and out, *F:* he's finished, (ii) he's at the end of his tether, at his wits' end. **3. sich abwirtschaften,** to ruin one's business; to make a mess of one's affairs; to be unable to keep one's household together.

abwischen, *v.tr. sep.* (i) to wipe off (dust, etc.), (ii) to wipe (sth.) clean (with rag, etc.); **den Staub von einem Stuhl a., einen Stuhl a.,** to wipe off the dust from a chair; to wipe a chair; **das Geschriebene von der Tafel a., die Tafel a.,** to clean the blackboard; **den Schmutz mit einem Schwamm a.,** to take off the dirt with a sponge, to sponge off the dirt; **sich die Tränen a.,** to wipe away one's tears; to wipe, dry, one's eyes; **sich den Schweiß von der Stirn a., sich die Stirn a.,** to mop one's brow; **sich den Mund a.,** to wipe one's mouth.

Abwischer, *m.*, **Abwischlappen,** *m.*, **Abwischtuch,** *n.* duster; cleaning-rag; (kitchen) rubber; floor-cloth.

Abwitterung, *f.* weathering (of rocks).

Abwitterungshalde, *f. Geol:* weathered, disintegrated, slope.

abwohnen, *v.tr. sep.* 1. to depreciate the condition of (house, etc.) (by living in it); **dieses Haus ist sehr abgewohnt,** this house badly needs redecoration, *F:* badly needs doing up, *U.S:* over; **ich habe mein Zimmer ziemlich abgewohnt,** I have let my room get rather shabby; my room looks rather the worse for wear. 2. to get the value (of money paid) by living in house, etc.; **einen Baukostenzuschuß a.,** to work off the cost of a contribution to the building (of rented house, etc.) by living rent free for a determined period; **ich habe zwanzig Pfund für den Monat bezahlt, und ich werde die Miete a.,** I've paid twenty pounds for the month and I'm going to stay out my time.

Abwolle, *f. Tex:* 1. wool from dead sheep. 2. waste wool.

abwracken, *v.tr. sep. Nau:* to break up (ship).

abwuchern, *v.tr. sep.* **j-m Geld a.,** to get money from s.o. by usury; to wring, extort, money from s.o.

abwürdigen, *v.tr. sep.* = **herabwürdigen.**

Abwurf, *m.* 1. = **abwerfen** II. 2. *Sp:* (*a*) throwing out (of ball); (*b*) finish of a throw. 3. *Civ.E:* dumping (of sand, gravel, etc.). 4. object (*esp.* mail-bag, container) dropped from an aircraft. 5. (*a*) rubbish; refuse; thing thrown away *or* cast aside; (*b*) *Ven:* cast, shed, antlers (of stag). 6. *Constr:* rough-cast. 7. return, profit (of transaction); yield (of investment, etc.).

Abwurfautomat, *m. Av:* automatic bomb-release.

Abwurfbehälter, *m. Av:* (*a*) drop-tank, jettisonable fuel-tank; (*b*) container (for dropping supplies, etc., from aircraft).

Abwurfgerät, *n. Av:* bomb-release mechanism.

Abwurfgeschoß, *n. Av:* projectile dropped from an aircraft, *esp.* bomb.

Abwurfmeldung, *f. Mil: etc:* message dropped from an aircraft.

Abwurfmunition, *f. Av:* projectiles for dropping from an aircraft, *esp.* bombs.

Abwurfsendung, *f. Post:* mail dropped from an aircraft.

Abwurfstelle, *f. Av: Mil: Post:* point where messages, mail, supplies, etc., are dropped from an aircraft; dropping point.

Abwurftasche, *f. Mil.Av:* message-bag; *Post:* mailbag dropped from an aircraft.

Abwurfvorrichtung, *f.* 1. *Av:* (*a*) bomb-release mechanism; (*b*) dropping device (for mailbag, etc.); jettisoning device (for fuel-tank, etc.). 2. *Civ.E: etc:* dumping device (for sand, gravel, etc.).

Abwurfwagen, *m. Ind:* throw-off carriage (of conveyor-belt).

abwürgen. I. *v.tr. sep.* 1. (*a*) to strangle, throttle, choke (s.o.); (*b*) *Pol:* **die Opposition a.,** to stifle the opposition; (*c*) *Aut:* **den Motor a.,** to stall the engine. **2. sich abwürgen,** (*of pers.*) to choke. 3. (*a*) to slaughter, butcher (s.o.); (*b*) **ein Huhn a.,** to wring a fowl's neck.

II. *vbl s.* **Abwürgen** *n.*, **Abwürgung** *f. in vbl senses; also:* strangulation; slaughter, *F:* butchery (of human beings).

abyssisch [a'ˈbysiʃ], *a.* **1.** abysmal. **2.** *Oc:* abyssal; **abyssische Region,** abyssal zone; *Geol:* **abyssische Gesteine,** plutonic rocks.

Abyssus [a'ˈbysus], *m.* -/. abyss.

abzahlen. I. *v.tr. sep.* to pay off; (*a*) **eine Schuld a.,** to pay a debt by instalments; **eine Schuld monatlich, in monatlichen Raten, a.,** to pay a debt by monthly instalments; **eine Schuld nach und nach, in kleinen Raten, a.,** to pay a debt little by little, in small instalments; **soundsoviel auf eine Schuld a.,** to pay so much on account; (*b*) **eine Schuld ganz a., das Ganze a.,** to settle, discharge, clear off, a debt; to pay (off) the whole amount, to pay in full.

II. *vbl s.* **1. Abzahlen,** *n.* paying off; (*a*) payment (of debt) by instalments; (*b*) settlement, clearing off (of debt), payment (of debt) in full. **2. Abzahlung,** *f.* (*a*)=II. 1; (*b*) instalment, part(ial) payment, payment on account; **Verkauf auf A.,** hire-purchase, sale on the instalment, deferred payment, system; **Möbel auf A. kaufen,** to buy furniture on the instalment system, by instalments.

abzählen. I. *v.sep.* **1.** (*a*) *v.tr.* to count (up), enumerate, number, *A:* tell (persons, thgs); to count (over) (one's money, etc.); to count out (money); *abs.* **a.,** (i) (*in children's games*) to count out; (ii) *Rocketry: etc:* to count down; **die Stimmen a.,** to count, tell, the votes; **Tage, usw., an den Fingern a.,** to count days, etc., on one's fingers; *F:* **das kann ich mir an den Fingern a.,** that's not hard to guess; **er hatte das Geld abgezählt in der Hand,** he had the exact amount of money in his hand; **'das Fahrgeld ist abgezählt bereitzuhalten',** 'please have the exact fare ready'; (*b*) *v.i.* (*haben*) *Mil: etc:* to number (off); **abzählen!** number! **zu vieren a.,** to form fours; **zu vieren a.!** form fours! **2.** *v.tr.* to subtract.

II. *vbl s.* **Abzählen,** *n. in vbl senses; also:* subtraction; *Rocketry: etc:* count-down.

Abzählreim, *m.* counting-out rhyme.

Abzahlungsgeschäft, *n.* **1.** hire-purchase; sale on the instalment system, plan, on the deferred payment system. **2.** hire-purchase firm.

Abzahlungskauf, *m.* hire-purchase; purchase by instalments, on the instalment system, plan, on the deferred payment system.

Abzahlungssystem, *n.* hire-purchase (system); instalment system, plan; deferred payment system.

abzahnen, *v.sep.* **1.** *v.tr.* to indent; to tool, tooth (stone); to tooth, cog, ratch (wheel, etc.). **2.** *v.i.* (*haben*) (*of child*) to finish teething.

abzanken, *v.tr. sep.* **1.** to give (s.o.) a scolding, a rating; *A. & U.S:* to berate (s.o.). **2. sich (gegenseitig) abzanken,** to scold one another; **als die beiden Weiber sich abgezankt hatten,** when the two women had finished scolding each other.

abzapfen, *v.tr. sep.* **1. ein Faß a.,** to broach, tap, a cask, to set a cask abroach; **einen Teich a.,** to let the water out of a pond; *Tchn:* **eine Gasleitung, einen Stromkreis, usw., a.,** to tap a gas main, a circuit, etc.; *Surg:* **eine Lunge, einen Wassersüchtigen, a.,** to tap a lung, a dropsical patient. **2.** (*a*) to tap, draw off (liquid); **den Wein a.,** to broach, tap, draw, the wine; (*b*) *Med:* **j-m Blut a.,** to bleed s.o.; to draw, let, blood from s.o.; *F:* **j-m Geld a.,** to extort, squeeze, *F:* extract, money from s.o.; *F:* to bleed, fleece, s.o.; (*c*) *A:* **seine Kräfte a.,** to drain one's strength; to exhaust one's powers.

Abzapfer, *m.* **1.** (wine-, beer-)drawer, tapster. **2.** *Surg: A:* catheter.

abzappeln (sich), *v.refl. sep.* (*of small child*) to tire itself by wriggling about; (*of fish, puppy, etc.*) to exhaust itself by struggling *or* floundering about; *F:* (*of pers.*) to exhaust one's nervous energy.

abzäumen, *v.tr. sep.* to unbridle (horse, etc.).

abzäunen. I. *v.tr. sep.* to fence (sth.) off, in; to rail in (garden, etc.); to enclose, to hedge in, off (piece of ground, etc.); **von der Straße abgezäunt,** hedged, fenced, railed, off from the road; **abgezäunte Ecke eines Feldes,** railed-off corner of a field.

II. *vbl s.* **1. Abzäunen,** *n. in vbl senses.* **2. Abzäunung,** *f.* (*a*)= II. 1; (*b*) fence, fencing; enclosure, enclosing fence *or* hedge; railing(s); barrier; *Jur:* close. **3.** enclosure, close, enclosed piece of ground.

abzausen, *v.tr. sep.* **1.** to pull, tear, (sth.) off roughly; to snatch (sth.) off. **2.** to dishevel, rumple, tousle (s.o.'s hair); to disorder, tumble, crumple (s.o.'s dress). **3.** *F:* to knock, bash, (s.o.) about; to handle (s.o.) roughly, *F:* to rough-house (s.o.).

abzehren. I. *v.sep.* **1.** *v.tr.* (*a*) to consume; to make thin; to emaciate, waste (s.o., the body); **das Fieber hat ihn abgezehrt,** the fever has wasted him; the fever has sapped his strength, undermined his health; **der Kummer zehrt ihn ab,** he is pining away with grief; (*b*) to corrode, erode, eat away (metal, stone, etc.). **2. sich abzehren** & *v.i.* (*sein*) to grow, become, thin(ner); to lose flesh, fall away in flesh; to become emaciated; to waste (away), pine away; to go into a decline, *esp.* to go into consumption; **sich vor Kummer a.,** to pine away with grief.

II. *vbl s.* **1. Abzehren,** *n. in vbl senses of* I. 1. **2. Abzehrung,** *f.* (*a*)=II. 1; (*b*) wasting (away), growing thin, loss of flesh, emaciation; pining away; (*c*)=**Auszehrung,** *q.v. under* **auszehren** 2; (*d*) corrosion, erosion, eating away (of metal, stone, etc.).

III. *pr.p. & a.* **abzehrend,** *in vbl senses; esp.* **abzehrende Krankheit,** wasting disease, *esp. F:* consumption.

IV. *p.p. & a.* **abgezehrt,** *in vbl senses; esp.* emaciated, wasted (body, face, pers.); attenuated (frame); haggard, gaunt, worn, drawn (face, features).

Abzeichen, *n.* **1.** (*a*) distinguishing mark, mark of distinction; badge (on arm, uniform, blazer, etc.); *Pol:* party badge; (*at election, etc.*) favour; *Av:* (aircraft) marking, *esp.* nationality marking; *Mil:* badge, *esp.* badge, insignia, of rank, *U.S:* stripe; marking(s) (on tank, etc.); **die Offiziere trugen keine Abzeichen,** the officers wore no badges (of rank), no markings; (*b*) *Com:* (firm's) distinctive mark *or* label; *Adm: etc:* ear-mark. **2.** *Z:* mark *or* spot of different colour (on animal's body).

abzeichnen. I. *v.tr. sep.* **1.** (*a*) to draw, sketch (sth.); to copy, reproduce (picture, etc.); to draw a plan (of sth.); to plot, set out (curve, graph); (*b*) to mark off (line, area, etc.). **2. sich gegen etwas, von etwas, abzeichnen,** to contrast, stand in contrast, with sth.; to form a contrast to sth.; to stand out (sharply) against sth.; **der Baum zeichnet sich gegen den, von dem, Himmel ab,** the tree stands out against the sky; **das Standbild zeichnet sich gegen einen, von einem, dunklen Hintergrund ab,** the statue stands out (in relief) against a dark background; **die Berge zeichnen sich scharf gegen den, von dem, Himmel ab,** the mountains are sharply, boldly, outlined against the sky, stand out in bold relief against the sky; **ihre Hüften zeichneten sich durch das, unter dem, Kleid ab,** her dress revealed the line of her hips. **3.** *Adm: etc:* **ein Schriftstück a.,** to initial a document.

II. *vbl s.* **1. Abzeichnen,** *n. in vbl senses.* **2. Abzeichnung,** *f.* (*a*)=II. 1; (*b*) copy, reproduction (of picture, etc.); (*c*) **(scharfe) A. der Umrisse,** sharpness, boldness, of outline.

abzerren, *v.tr. sep.* to pull, wrench, tear, (sth.) off; to tug (sth.) away.

abzetteln, *v.tr. sep. Tex:* to unweave, undo the warp of (cloth).

abzeugen, *v.tr. sep. Nau:*=**abtakeln** 1.

Abziehapparat, *m.* **1.** *Print:* proof-press. **2.** *Ch: etc:* distilling apparatus. **3.** sharpener (for knives, etc.).

abziehbar, *a.* (number, sum, etc.) that can be subtracted.

Abziehbild, *n.* transfer(-picture); *Cer: etc:* decalcomania.

Abziehbilderdruck, *m.* transfer printing, process; *Cer: etc:* decalcomania.

Abziehblase, *f. Ch:* retort, still, *A:* alembic.

Abziehbogen, *m. Print:* tympan-sheet.

Abziehbürste, *f. Print:* letter-brush.

Abziehdraht, *m. Artil:*=**Abzugsleine.**

abziehen, *v.sep.* (*strong*) I. *v.tr.* **1.** (*a*) to remove, take off (garment, etc.); **den Hut, die Schuhe, die Handschuhe, a.,** to remove, take off, pull off, one's hat, shoes, gloves; to draw off one's gloves; **einen Ring (vom Finger) a.,** to take off, pull off, draw off, a ring (from one's finger); **die Kleider a.,** to take off one's clothes, to undress; **j-m die Kleider a.,** to undress s.o.; **j-m die Maske a.,** to unmask s.o.; **einem Betrüger die Maske a.,** to expose, show up, an impostor; (*b*) to remove, strip off (skin); **die tote Haut von einer Blase a.,** to pull off the dead skin from a blister; **einem Tier die Haut, das Fell, a., ein Tier a.,** to skin an animal; to flay a horse, an ox, etc.; *Leath:* **schlecht abgezogene Haut,** badly flayed hide; (*c*) **den Kopfkissenbezug, das Kopfkissen, a.,** to take off, to remove, the pillow-case; **das Bett a.,** to strip the bed; (*d*) **eine Saite von einem Musikinstrument a.,** to remove a string from an instrument; **die Saiten a.,** to unstring the instrument; *Aut:* **ein Rad a.,** to remove, take off, a wheel; *Av:* **die Luftschraube a.,** to dismount, remove, take off, the airscrew; (*e*) *Carp:* **eine Kante, usw., a.,** to plane off an edge, etc.; (*f*) *Cu:* **die Fäden von Bohnen a., Bohnen a.,** to string beans; (*g*) **den Schaum von einer Flüssigkeit a., eine Flüssigkeit a.,** to skim (the froth off) a liquid. **2.** (*a*) to pull, draw, take, (sth.) out; to withdraw (sth.); **den Schlüssel vom Schloß a.,** to withdraw the key from, take the key out of, the lock; (*b*) **Kapital a.,** to withdraw capital; **Geld von der Bank a.,** to withdraw money, make a withdrawal, from the bank; (*c*) **die Hand a.,** to draw back one's hand, draw one's hand away; **die, seine, Hand von j-m a.,** to withdraw one's support, one's aid, one's favour, from s.o.; to leave s.o. to his own devices; *B:* **Gott der Herr wird mit dir sein, und wird die Hand nicht a., noch dich verlassen,** the Lord God will be with thee, He will not fail thee nor forsake thee. **3.** to turn (s.o., sth.) away; to draw (s.o.) away; to lead (s.o.) away; to divert (s.o., attention, etc.) (von, from); **seinen Blick von etwas a.,** to avert one's eyes, one's gaze, from sth.; **seine Gedanken von etwas a.,** to turn one's thoughts away from sth.; **j-s Blick, j-s Gedanken, j-s Aufmerksamkeit, von etwas a.,** to divert, distract, draw off, s.o.'s attention from sth.; to abstract s.o.'s attention; **ich werde versuchen, ihn von diesem Vorhaben abzuziehen,** I shall try to put him off this plan. **4.** (*a*) *Ar:* to subtract, deduct, take away (sum); **eine Zahl von der anderen a.,** to take one number from another; **zieh(e) drei von sieben ab,** deduct, take away, three from seven; **drei abgezogen von sieben gibt vier,** three from seven leaves four; **abzuziehend,** (sum) to be deducted; *Mth:* subtractive (number, etc.); **die abzuziehende Zahl,** the number to be subtracted, the subtrahend; (*b*) *Com: etc:* **etwas vom Preise a.,** to deduct sth. from the price; to take, knock, sth. off the price; to allow sth. off the price; to make an allowance; to give a rebate; **soundsoviel für den Transport a.,** to allow so much for carriage, *U.S:* shipping; **eine Summe zuvor a.,** to deduct a sum in advance; **10% von einer Summe zuvor a.,** to make a previous deduction of 10% from a sum of money; *Ind: etc:* **(für Versicherung, usw.) fünf Prozent vom Lohn a.,** to deduct five per cent from wages (for insurance, etc.); **fünfzehn Mark von j-s Lohn a.,** to keep back, withhold, fifteen marks from s.o.'s wages; to dock fifteen marks off s.o.'s wages; to stop fifteen marks out of s.o.'s wages. **5.** to shoot, fire, let off (firearm, etc.); *abs.* **a.,** to press, squeeze, the trigger; to fire. **6.** *Physiol: Surg:* to abduct (organ, etc.). **7.** (*a*) to sharpen whet, put an edge on (knife, tool, etc.); to grind (knife, tool, etc.); to hone (tool, razor); to stone (down) (tool); to strop, set (razor); to true (up), dress (grindstone); (*b*) to polish, glaze (knife, tool). **8.** (*a*) *Print:* to pull, print, strike off (proof, engraving); to take off (proof); to work off (sheets); **den Satz in Fahnen a.,** to take proofs in galley; (*b*) *Cin: Phot:* to print (film); (*c*) to transfer (design, coloured picture). **9.** (*a*) to draw off, drain off, tap off (liquid); to draw off, lead off (smoke, gas, etc.); **das Wasser von einem Teich a., einen Teich a.,** to draw off the water from a pond, to drain a pond; (*b*) to draw off, rack (wine, beer, etc.); **Wein, Bier, auf Flaschen a.,** to bottle wine, beer; (*c*) to decant, pour off (liquid, from sediment). **10.** *Ch: Ind:* to abstract; to extract (sth.) by distillation; to distil (spirits, etc.); **Weingeist stark a.,** to rectify, re-distil, spirits. **11.** *Phil: etc:* to abstract (a quality, a conception, a rule); to formulate (rule). **12.** (*a*) to lighten, freshen (colour); (*b*) *Dy:* **die Farbe a.,** to boil out, strip (off), the colour. **13.** *Tex:* **Rohseide a.,** to boil off, degum, raw silk. **14.** *Clockm:* **eine neue Uhr a.,** to check the working of, to test, a new clock. **15.** *Cu:* **die Suppe (mit einem Ei) a.,** to blend, stir, an egg into the soup.

II. **abziehen,** *v.i.* (*sein*) **1.** (*a*) to depart, leave; to go away; to go off; *F:* to clear off; *F:* **aus der Wohnung, usw., a.,** to clear out (of the flat, etc.); **heimlich a.,** to sneak off; to slink away; (*of servant*) **aus dem Dienst a.,** to leave his, her, place, situation; to leave service; (*b*) *Mil:* (*of troops*) to withdraw, retire; to march off; **von der Wache a.,** to come off guard,

off duty; **die Wache zog ab,** the guard was relieved; **die abziehende Wache,** the old guard (about to be relieved); **der Feind zog von der belagerten Stadt ab,** the enemy raised the siege; (*c*) **leer a.,** to return empty-handed, *F:* to draw a blank; **unverrichteter Sache a.,** to fail to achieve one's purpose, to be disappointed (in one's design); *F:* **mit langem Gesicht, langer Nase, a.,** to go away disappointed, with a long face; **mit Schimpf und Schande a.,** to go away in disgrace; to leave under a cloud. **2.** (*a*) (*of steam, smoke, etc.*) to go off; to clear; to find an outlet; to escape (from vent, etc.); (*b*) (*of thunderstorm, cloud*) to move on.

III. *vbl s.* **Abziehen** *n., occ.* **Abziehung** *f. in vbl senses; also:* (*a*) removal (of garment, etc.); *Aut:* **Abziehen eines Rades,** removal, taking off, of a wheel; *Av:* **Abziehen der Luftschraube,** removal, dismounting, taking off, of the air-screw; (*b*) withdrawal (of key from lock, money from bank); (*c*) *Ar:* subtraction, deduction; (*d*) *Com: etc:* deduction (of sth. from the price); allowance (of so much for carriage, etc.); *Ind: etc:* deduction (of insurance payment, etc.); (*e*) *Physiol: Surg:* abduction (of organ, etc.); (*f*) transfer (of design, coloured picture); (*g*) *Ch: Ind:* distillation (of spirits, etc.); rectification (of spirits); (*h*) *Phil: etc:* abstraction (of a quality, a conception, a rule); formulation (of a rule); (*i*) escape (of steam, smoke, etc.). *Cp.* **Abzug I.** 2 (*a*).

Abzieher, *m.* **1.** (*a*) *Print:* proof-puller; (*b*) *Cin: Phot:* printer. **2.** *Anat.*=**Abziehmuskel.**

Abziehfeile, *f. Tls:* smooth file.

Abziehflasche, *f. A.Ch:* cucurbit (of an alembic).

Abziehhalle, *f. Brew: Wine-m:* racking-room; bottling-room.

Abziehklinge, *f.* (sharpening) steel; knife-sharpener.

Abziehkolben, *m. Ch: Ind:* retort; still, *A:* alembic.

Abziehlatte, *f. Constr:* (plasterer's) long float.

Abziehleder, *n.*=**Abziehriemen.**

Abziehmaschine, *f.* **1.** *Brew:* bottling, racking, machine. **2.** road-sweeping machine.

Abziehmesser, *n.* **1.** scraper. **2.** flaying knife.

Abziehmittel, *n. Dy:* agent used for lightening a colour; stripping agent.

Abziehmuskel, *m. Anat:* abductor (muscle), abducent muscle.

Abziehpapier, *n.* **1.** transfer-paper. **2.** *Print:* proof-paper.

Abziehpflug, *m. Agr:* draining plough.

Abziehpresse, *f. Print:* proof-press; galley-press.

Abziehriemen, *m. Tls:* (razor-)strop.

Abziehstahl, *m. Tls:* (sharpening) steel.

Abziehstein, *m.* **1.** whetstone; oilstone; hone. **2.** *Mec.E:*=**Abziehwerkzeug 1.**

Abziehvorrichtung, *f. Aut:* wheel-brace.

Abziehwerkzeug, *n.* **1.** *Mec.E:* (wheel-)dresser, dressing tool. **2.** tool for removing wheels, etc.; *Aut:* wheel-brace.

Abziehzahl, *f. Mth:* subtrahend.

Abziehzünder, *m. Exp: etc:* friction igniter.

abzielen, *v.tr. & i. sep.* (*haben*) **auf j-n, etwas, a.,** to aim at s.o., sth.; to have sth. in view; **seine Bemerkung zielte auf dich ab, er hat seine Bemerkung auf dich abgezielt,** his remark was aimed at you, was intended, meant, for you; **die neuen Maßnahmen zielen auf eine Verminderung der Unkosten ab,** the new measures are designed, intended, to cut, reduce, expenses.

abzirkeln. I. *v.tr. sep.* **1.** to measure off (distance) with compasses *or* dividers. **2.** to be precise in (one's speech, behaviour, etc.); **er zirkelt seine Worte ab,** he chooses his words with great care; he is finical, very precise, very particular, in his speech; **er zirkelt alles genau ab,** he is a very punctilious, precise, gentleman; he is finicky, *F:* he likes everything just so, he is very 'just so'.

II. *vbl s.* **Abzirkeln,** *n.,* **Abzirkelung,** *f.* **1.** measuring (with compasses *or* dividers). **2.** preciseness (of speech); formality, setness, stiffness (of manner, etc.).

III. *p.p. & a.* **abgezirkelt,** *in vbl senses; esp.* (*a*) carefully 'measured; precise (judgment, utterance); well-considered (words); (*b*) over-precise, over-exact (manner, expression); stiff, formal (manner).

Abzucht, *f.* -/⸗e, (*a*) *Swiss Dial:* outlet pipe; discharge pipe; drainage ditch; drain; *Hyg:* sewer; (*b*) *Min: etc:* air-shaft, ventilating shaft, ventilation shaft.

Abzug, *m.* I. **1.** *occ.*=**abziehen III. 2.** (*a*) deduction, abstraction (of one quantity *or* sum from another); **nach A. von . . . ,** after deducting . . . , after deduction of . . . ; **nach A. der Unkosten,** after deducting charges, *Com:* 'charges deducted'; **unter A. von . . . ,** deducting . . . ; subject to the deduction of . . . ; *Com:* **eine Summe, einen Diskont, in A. bringen,** to deduct a sum, a discount; **Summe, die von . . . in A. kommt,** sum that falls to be deducted from . . . ; (*b*) *Com: etc:* deduction (from price); allowance, abatement, rebate; discount; **einen A. gewähren,** to make a reduction, allow a rebate; to allow a discount; **5% A. bei Barzahlung,** 5% discount for cash, 5% cash discount, *F:* 5% off for cash; **'Preise verstehen sich ohne A.',** 'terms (strictly) net(t) cash', 'prices net(t)'; *Fin:* **A. von Zinsen,** discount on interest (for prompt payment); (*c*) *Com:* **A. vom Gewicht,** tare; (*d*) sum kept back, stoppage, deduction (from payment, wages); **A. für Versicherung, für Steuer,** deduction for insurance, for tax; **einen A. von 5% am, vom, Lohn machen,** to stop, deduct, 5% from the wages; *Com: Fin:* **die Zahlung beträgt 1000 Mark ohne A., ohne Abzüge, frei von Abzügen,** the payment amounts to 1,000 marks net(t), clear, free from deductions; *Hum:* **sie haben mir lauter Abzüge ausgezahlt,** when they had made all their deductions there was nothing left (of my wages, etc.). **3.** *Fin:* withdrawal (of capital, of money from bank). **4.** (*a*) *Print:* proof, pull; **erster A., A. in Fahnen,** slip-proof, galley-proof; **unkorrigierter A., verschmutzter A.,** foul proof; **reiner A.,** clean proof; (*b*) *Print:* offset, set-off; (*c*) *Engr:* impression, proof; **A. vor der Schrift,** proof before the letter, before letters; **A. nach, mit, der Schrift,** letter proof; proof after letters; (*d*) *Phot:* positive; print; copy; (*e*) *Cer: etc:* transfer (picture *or* design). **5.** (*a*) *Sm.a: Artil:* trigger; (*b*) *Mec.E:* pawl, catch.

II. **Abzug,** *m.* **1.** departure; (*a*) *occ. in vbl senses of* **abziehen** II. 1 (*a*); (*b*) *Mil:* (i) marching off; striking of camp, (ii) withdrawal, retirement; retreat; **der Besatzung freien, ehrenvollen, A. gewähren,** to allow the garrison (of a fortress) to leave with all the honours of war; **zum A. blasen, trommeln,** to sound, beat, the retreat. **2.** (*a*) outflow, flow, flowing, discharge (of liquid, steam, etc.); going off, escape, escaping (of steam, smoke); (*b*) outlet (for water, gases, steam, etc.); vent (for air, steam, smoke); *Agr:* drain, furrow-drain, (drainage) ditch; (drainage) trench; gutter; channel; rill; culvert; *Hyg:* sewer; *Mec.E:* cut, groove (for oil, etc.); *Min: etc:* air-shaft, ventilating shaft, ventilation shaft; **das Wasser, der Rauch, findet keinen A.,** the water, the smoke, finds no outlet.

Abzughechel, *f. Tex:* coarse flax-comb; coarse heckle, hackle, hatchel; coarse rougher, ruffer.

abzüglich, *prep.* (+*gen. & acc.*) deducting, less; *Com:* **a. 5%,** less 5%; **a. aller, alle, Unkosten,** all charges deducted, deducting all charges.

Abzugpapier, *n.* (*a*) duplicating paper, duplicator paper; manifold paper; mimeograph paper; (*b*) *Print:* proof-paper.

Abzugsblei, *n. Metall:* lead recovered from dross.

Abzugsbogen, *m. Print:* proof-sheet; proof, pull.

Abzugsbügel, *m. Sm.a:* trigger-guard.

Abzugsdampf, *m.* vapour carried off; escaping vapour; *Mch:* exhaust (steam), dead steam; waste steam.

Abzugseinrichtung, *f. Sm.a: Artil:*=**Abzugsvorrichtung 1.**

abzugsfähig, *a.* deductible (expenses, etc.).

Abzugsfeder, *f. Sm.a: Artil:* sear-spring.

Abzugsflagge, *f. Nau: A:* (the) Blue Peter.

Abzugsfreiheit, *f. Hist:* freedom to emigrate, right of emigration (without paying emigration tax).

Abzugsfurche, *f. Agr:* gutter; (drainage) rill; furrow-drain.

Abzugsgas, *n.* exhaust gas; *Ind:* waste gas; escape-gas; flue-gas.

Abzugsgeld, *n. Hist:* emigration tax.

Abzugsgerinne, *n. Hyd.E:* outlet sluice; tail-race (of mill).

Abzugsgraben, *m.* **1.** drain, (drainage) ditch, (drainage) trench, gutter, channel; (open) culvert; *Hyd.E:* conduit; *Civ.E:* (open) sewer. **2.** *Mil:* evacuation trench.

Abzugsgrube, *f. Hyg:* cesspool, cesspit; sink-hole.

Abzugshebel, *m.* (*a*) *Sm.a: Artil:* trigger-arm, -lever; sear; (*b*) *Artil:* firing-lever.

Abzugskamin, *m. Constr:* flue.

Abzugskanal, *m.* **1.** (*a*)=**Abzugsgraben 1;** (*b*) *Civ.E:* **überwölbter, überdeckter, A.,** closed-in culvert; barrel-drain. **2.** outlet (channel), discharge channel (for steam, gas, etc.); *Ind: etc:* flue (of furnace, etc.); *Mch:* exhaust-pipe, eduction-pipe; *I.C.E: etc:* exhaust-port, eduction-port.

Abzugskupfer, *n. Metall:* copper recovered from dross.

Abzugsleine, *f. Artil:* (firing) lanyard.

Abzugsloch, *n. Constr:* **1.** drain-hole; weep-hole (in wall), *F:* weeper; draining-channel (of bridge). **2.** ventilation-hole (in roof, etc.).

Abzugspapier, *n.*=**Abzugpapier.**

Abzugsraum, *m.* **1.** hood (of forge, laboratory, over fireplace). **2.** *Ch: Ind:* room *or* laboratory with hoods.

Abzugsrecht, *n. Hist:* right of a government to levy a tax on emigrants *or* on property sent abroad.

Abzugsrinne, *f.* gutter, gully; channel (conducting water into roadside ditch, etc.).

Abzugsrohr, *n.,* **Abzugsröhre,** *f.* (*a*) waste-pipe, drain-pipe, outlet-pipe, discharge pipe, escape-pipe; soil-pipe, cesspipe (of W.C.); (*b*) *Mch: etc:* exhaust-pipe, eduction-pipe; (*c*) *Ind: Cin:* vent-stack.

Abzugsschach, *n. Chess:* discovered check.

Abzugsschacht, *m.* ventilation-shaft, ventilating-shaft (of mine, laboratory hood, etc.); flue (of furnace, etc.).

Abzugsschalter, *m. Exp:* firing-switch (for blasting-charge, etc.).

Abzugsschleuse, *f.* (*a*) *Hyd.E:* waste-gate; way-gate; outlet sluice; tail-lock; tail-race; (*b*) *Constr:* sewer.

Abzugsschnalle, *f. Mec.E: Clockm:* detent, stop.

Abzugsschnur, *f.*=**Abzugsleine.**

Abzugsschrank, *m. Ch:* fume-cupboard, -chamber.

Abzugssicherung, *f. Sm.a:* safety-catch.

Abzugssteuer, *f. Hist:*=**Abzugsgeld.**

Abzugsstollen, *m. Sm.a:* sear.

Abzugsventil, *n. Mch: etc:* exhaust-valve, eduction-valve; outlet-valve; escape-valve.

Abzugsvorrichtung, *f.* **1.** *Sm.a: Artil:* trigger mechanism. **2.** *Hyd.E:* (*a*) draining apparatus; escape (apparatus); overflow-shoot (of tank, etc.); (*b*) constant-level apparatus (of reservoir, etc.).

Abzugswärme, *f. Ph: etc:* lost heat; waste heat.

Abzugswasser, *n. Hyd.E:* down-stream water; tail-water (below water-wheel).

Abzugszahl, *f. Mth:* subtrahend.

Abzugszoll, *m. Hist:*=**Abzugsgeld.**

abzupfen, *v.tr. sep.* **1.** to pluck off, pull off (leaf, petal, etc.); to pluck out (hair). **2.** to unravel, ravel out, tease out (silk, etc.).

abzurren, *v.tr. sep. Nau: etc:* (*a*) to unlash (piece of equipment, hammock, etc.); (*b*) to unclamp (instrument, etc.).

abzwacken, *v. tr. sep.* (*a*) to nip (sth.) off; to pinch (sth.) off; (*b*) *A:* to excise, cut out (items from list, etc.); (*c*)=**abknapsen** 2.

abzwecken, *v.i. sep.* (*haben*) **auf etwas a.,** to aim at sth., to have sth. in view; *cp.* **abzielen.**

Abzweig, *m. Tchn:* **1.**=**Abzweigrohr. 2.** *El.E:* (*a*)=**Abzweigleitung;** (*b*)=**Abzweigklemme.**

Abzweigdose, *f. El.E:* junction-box; distributing box; connecting box (for cables).

abzweigen. I. *v.tr. sep.* **1.** to cut away, lop off, break off, the branches from (tree); to lop, prune, trim (tree). **2.** (*a*) to fork, bifurcate; to branch; to tap (gas-main, etc.); *El.E:* to branch, tap (circuit); to shunt, branch (current); **einen Strom von einer Leitung a.,** to take off a current from a circuit; (*b*) *Com: etc:* to divert (capital); to turn (money) to other uses; (*c*) *Mil:* to detach (unit); **eine Einheit an die Westfront a.,** to transfer, switch, a unit to the Western front. **3.** *v.i.* (*haben*) & **sich abzweigen,** to fork, bifurcate; to branch off.

II. *vbl s.* **1. Abzweigen,** *n. in vbl senses; also:* bifurcation; *Com:* diversion (of capital); *Mil:* diversion (of unit) (to a different front). **2. Abzweigung,** *f.* (*a*)=II. 1; (*b*) branch; (i) ramification; bifurcation; offshoot; (ii) road-junction, fork (of road); (iii) branch-road; *Rail:* branch-line; (iv) diffluent, divarication (of watercourse); (*c*) *El.E:* branch circuit; branch.

III. *pr.p & a.* **abzweigend,** *in vbl senses; esp.* branching; *Anat:* **abzweigende Ader,** emissary vein.

Abzweigklemme, *f. El.E:* branch terminal.

Abzweigleitung, *f. El.E:* branch circuit; *Tg: Tp:* branch line.

Abzweigmuffe, *f. El.E:* connecting box (for cables).

Abzweigrohr, *n.,* **Abzweigröhre,** *f.* branch-pipe.

Abzweigschraube, *f. El.E:*=**Abzweigklemme.**

Abzweigstecker, *m. El.E:* connection plug.

Abzweigstelle, *f. Rail:* branching-off point.

Abzweigstrom, *m. El.E:* derived, shunted, current.

Abzweigstromkreis, *m. El.E:* derived, shunted, circuit; branch circuit.

abzwicken, *v.tr. sep.*=**abzwacken** (*a*).

abzwingen, *v.tr. sep.* (*strong*) **j-m etwas a.,** to wrest, wring, sth. from s.o.; to extort sth. from s.o.; to force sth. out of s.o.; **j-m Geld a.,** to extort money from s.o.; **j-m ein Geständnis a.,** to wring, wrest, extort, draw, a confession from s.o.; **j-m ein Lächeln a.,** to force a smile out of s.o.

abzwirnen, *v.tr. sep.* to unwind, wind off (thread).

Aca-, aca- *see* **Aka-, aka-.**

Acaj(o)u [akaˈʒuː], *m.* -s/-s. *Bot:*=**Acaj(o)ubaum.**

Acaj(o)uapfel, *m. Bot:* cashew nut.

Acaj(o)ubaum, *m. Bot:* anacardium, cashew (-tree).

Acaj(o)uholz, *n.* mahogany.

Acaj(o)unuß, *f. Bot:* cashew nut.

Acca [ˈakaː]. *Pr.n.n.* -s. *Geog:* Acre.

Acca-, acca- *see* **Akka-, akka-.**

Acce-, acce-, Acci-, acci- *see* **Akze-, akze-, Akzi-, akzi-.**

Accl-, accl- *see* **Akkl-, akkl-.**

Acco-, acco- *see* **Akko-, akko-.**

Accon [ˈakɔn]. *Pr.n.n.* -s. *Geog:* Acre.

Accr-, accr-, Accu, accu- *see* **Akkr-, akkr-, Akku-, akku-.**

Ace-, ace- *see* **Aze-, aze-.**

Ach[1], *f.* -/-en. *South G.Dial:* brook, burn, (small) stream.

-ach[2], *s.suff.* (*in place-names*) (*indicating proximity to running water*)=-brook, -burn, -beck.

ach[3]. **1.** *int.* (*a*) oh! ah! **ach, wie nett!** oh, how nice! **ach, das ist aber anders,** oh, ah, but that's different; **ach, daß, wenn, sie kommen würde!** (oh,) if only she would come! (*indicating annoyance*) **ach, gehen Sie weg!** oh, go away! (*indicating surprise and dismay*) **ach, ich habe es fallen lassen!** oh, I've dropped it! **ach je!** oh dear! **ach Gott!** oh Lord! good Lord! oh dear! **ach ja!** (i) (*on being reminded of sth.*) yes, of course! (yes) naturally! (ii) (*on recollecting sth.*) ah, oh, yes (I remember)! oh yes, of course! **er ist ja vor fünf Jahren gestorben!—ach ja, ich habe einen Kranz geschickt,** but he died five years ago!—ah yes, (of course,) I sent a wreath; **ach nein!** oh no! (*expressing disbelief, astonishment*) no! you don't say so! well, I never! not really! **ach, was Sie nicht sagen!** well, just fancy that! well, you do surprise me! (*indicating sudden enlightenment*) **ach so!** oh, I see! so that's it! (*expostulation*) **ach geh!** come, come! (*indignant repudiation*) **ach was!** (i) nonsense! rubbish! (ii) (*expressing extreme impatience*) oh for heaven's sake! **ach wo!** what nonsense! of course not! (*b*) alas! ah! **das war das Ende meines ach so kurzen Glückes,** that was the end of my happiness, which was, alas, so brief! **2.** *s.* **Ach,** *n.* -/-, lament, (cry of) lamentation; **sein ewiges Weh und Ach,** his continual lamentations; *B:* **Klage, Ach und Wehe,** lamentations, and mourning, and woe; **ach und weh schreien** (*in this phr. usu. with small letter*), to make a shrill protest, to give vent to one's indignation, to make a hullabaloo, *F:* to shout, cry, blue murder; *F:* **er hat das Examen mit Ach and Krach bestanden,** he passed the exam, but it was a narrow squeak; **wir kamen mit Ach und Krach den Berg 'rauf,** we got up to the top of the hill by the skin of our teeth.

Achäer [aˈxɛːər], *m.* -s/-. *A.Hist:* Achaean, Achaian; *Gr. Lit:* (*in Homer*) Greek.

achäisch [aˈxɛːiʃ], *a.* Achaean, Achaian; *A.Hist:* **der Achäische Bund,** the Achaean League.

Achaia, Achaja [aˈxaːjaː]. *Pr.n.n.* -s. *A.Geog:* Achaea, Achaia.

Achäne [aˈxɛːnə], *f.* -/-n. *Bot:* achene, achenium.

acharnieren [aʃarˈniːrən], *v.tr.* **1.** *A:* **einen Hund a.,** to flesh, blood, a dog. **2. j-n a.,** to make s.o. keen in pursuit; to infuriate s.o.

Achat [aˈxaːt], *m.* -(e)s/-e. **1.** *Miner:* agate. **2.** *Print: A:*=**Achatschrift.**

achaten [aˈxaːtən], *a.* composed, made, of agate; **achatene Schale,** agate cup.

achathaltig, *a. Miner:* agatiferous, agate-bearing.

achatisieren [axaˑtiˑˈziːrən], *v.tr.* to agatize, (i) *Geol:* to transform (rock) into agate, (ii) *Ind:* to give an agate-like appearance to (flints, etc.).

Achatkiesel, *m. Lap:* Egyptian pebble.

Achatmandel, *f. Miner:* agate found in the cavity of an amygdaloid.

Achatschnecke, *f. Moll:* achatina, *F:* agate-shell.

Achatschrift, *f. Print: A:* ruby (type); *U.S:* agate.

Ache, *f.* -/-n=**Ach**[1].

Achel, *f.* -/-n. **1.** *Bot:* beard, awn, arista (of ear of wheat, barley, etc.). **2.** *Tex:* shreds detached from the flax-stalk.

Achelfahrt, *f.* (*in beggars' language*) expedition to beg a meal.

acheln, *v.i.* (*haben*) *Yiddish:* to eat; *esp.* to eat heartily, *F:* to guzzle.

Achene [aˈxeːnə], *f.* -/-n. *Bot:*=**Achäne.**

Acheron [ˈaxərɔn]. *Pr.n.m.* -s, (*a*) *A.Geog: Myth:* Acheron; (*b*) *Lit:* the underworld; Acheron.

acherontisch [axəˈrɔntiʃ], *a.* (*a*) *A.Geog: Myth:* of Acheron; (*b*) *Lit:* of the underworld; of Acheron.

Acheuléen, das [aʃøˑleˑˈɛ̃ː], -s. *Paleont:* (the) Acheulean culture.

acheuleisch [aʃøˑˈleːiʃ], *a.* Acheulean.

Achill [aˈxil]. *Pr.n.m.* -s. Achilles.

Achillea, Achillee [axiˈleːaː, axiˈleːə], *f.* -/-leen [-leːən]. *Bot:* achillea, milfoil, yarrow.

Achilleis [axiˈleːis], *f.* -/. *Lit:* song, epic, about Achilles.

achilleisch [axiˈleːiʃ], *a.* **1.** *Myth:* of Achilles. **2.** Achillean; invulnerable, invincible.

Achillenkraut, *n. Bot:*=**Achillea.**

Achilles [aˈxilɛs]. *Pr.n.m.* -'. Achilles.

Achillesferse, *f. Myth:* heel of Achilles; *F:* **Algebra ist seine A.,** algebra is his heel of Achilles, is his weak spot.

Achillessehne, *f. Anat:* Achilles tendon, tendon of Achilles.

Achilleus [aˈxiloys]. *Pr.n.m.* -'. Achilles.

Achim. *Pr.n.m.* -s. (*abbr. of* **Joachim**) Joachim.

Achiver [aˈxiːvər], *m.* -s/-. *A.Hist:*=**Achäer.**

Ach-Laut, Achlaut, *m. Ling:* (the) sound of **ch** following **a, o, u;** voiceless [x].

Achromasie [aˑkroˑmaˑˈziː], *f.* -/. *Opt:* achromatism.

Achromat [aˑkroˑˈmaːt], *m.* -(e)s/-. *Opt: Phot:* achromatic lens.

Achromatin [aˑkroˑmaˑˈtiːn], *n.* -s/. *Biol:* achromatin.

achromatisch [aˑkroˑˈmaːtiʃ], *a. Opt:* achromatic.

achromatisieren [aˑkroˑmaˑtiˑˈziːrən], *v.tr. Opt:* to achromatize (lens, etc.).

Achromatismus [aˑkroˑmaˑˈtismus], *m.* -/. *Opt:* achromatism.

Achromatopsie [aˑkroˑmaˑtɔpˈsiː], *f.* -/. colour-blindness, achromatopsy.

achronistisch [aˑkroˑˈnistiʃ], *a. Ling:* timeless (verb-form).

Achs-, *comb.fm. Veh:* axle-; *cp.* **Achsen-.**

Achsabstand, *m. Veh: Aut: Rail:* wheel-base; distance between the axles.

Achsantrieb, *m. Aut:* axle drive.

Achsband, *n. Veh:* axle-clip; guard-plate (of axle).

Achsblech, *n. Veh:* clout (of axle).

Achsbruch, *m.*=**Achsenbruch.**

Achsbüchse, *f.* axle box, grease-box.

Achsdruck, *m. Veh: Rail:* load on the axle, axle pressure.

Achse, *f.* -/-n. **1.** *Veh: Aut: Rail:* axle(-tree); **drehbare A.,** live axle; **feste A.,** dead, fixed, axle; **gekröpfte A.,** cranked axle, bent axle; **fliegende A.,** floating axle; *Av:* **Fahrgestell mit durchgehender A.,** cross-axle undercarriage; **Fahrgestell mit geteilter A.,** split undercarriage. *Com:* **Güter per A., auf A., mit A., schicken,** to send goods by road *or* rail, *A:* to send goods by wagon; **die Waren sind auf der A.,** the goods are on their way; *F:* **er ist immer auf der A.,** he is always travelling; he spends his time travelling. **2.** *Mec.E:* shaft, spindle, axle; *Clockm: etc:* arbor. **3.** (*a*) axis (of sphere, crystal, plant, lens, etc.); *Mec.E: Civ.E:* centre-line (of wheel, bridge, etc.); **die Erde dreht sich um ihre eigene A.,** the earth revolves about its own axis; *Opt:* **optische A.,** axis of vision, optical axis; *Geom:* **große A. einer Ellipse,** major axis of an ellipse; **kleine A.,** minor axis; (*b*) *Hist:* **die A. (Rom-Berlin),** the (Rome–Berlin) Axis.

Achseisen, *n. Veh:* axle-bar.

Achsel, *f.* -/-n. **1.** shoulder; **die Achseln, mit den Achseln, zucken,** to shrug (one's shoulders); **j-n über die A. ansehen,** to look over one's shoulder at s.o.; *F:* to look down on s.o.; **ein Kind auf den Achseln reiten lassen,** to give a child a flying-angel, a ride on one's shoulders; **eine Entscheidung auf seine A., auf seine Achseln, nehmen,** to take the responsibility for a decision; *F:* **etwas auf die leichte A. nehmen,** to make light of sth.; to do sth. without care *or* exertion, to make easy work of sth.; **er nimmt alles auf die leichte A.,** he takes things very easily; *F:* **auf beiden Achseln tragen,** to sit on the fence; to run with the hare and hunt with the hounds; to blow hot and cold; **er trägt auf beiden Achseln,** he is a double-dealer, he is given to double-dealing. **2.** *Bot:* axil(la); *Nat.Hist:* axilla; **Achsel-,** *comb.fm.* axillary . . . **3.** *Tchn:* shoulder (of tenon, etc.).

Achselader, *f. Anat:* axillary vein.

Achselband, *n.* **1.** *Mil: etc:* aiguillette; shoulder-knot. **2.** *Cost:* (*a*) shoulder-strap; (*b*) shoulder-piece. **3.** *Constr:* brace, strut, angle-brace.

Achselbein, *n. Anat:* shoulder-blade.

Achselblick, *m.* contemptuous look; **j-m einen A. geben,** to look down on s.o.

Achselfeder, *f. Nat.Hist:* axillary feather.

Achselgriff, *m.* hold under the armpits; **beim Retten eines Ertrinkenden ist der A. ratsam,** when rescuing a drowning man it is advisable to hold him under the armpits.

Achselgrube, *f.* armpit.

Achselhaar, *n. coll.* armpit hair, *F:* hair under the arms.

Achselhemd, *n. Cost:* (man's) sleeveless shirt; (woman's) sleeveless chemise.

Achselhöhle, *f.* armpit; *Anat: Nat.Hist:* axilla.

Achselklappe, *f. Mil: etc:* shoulder-strap.

Achselkleid, *n. Ecc:* amice.

Achselknochen, *m.*=**Achselbein.**

achseln, *v.tr.* **1.** to shoulder (burden, etc.). **2.** *abs. A:*=**auf beiden Achseln tragen,** *q.v. under* **Achsel 1.**

ächseln, *v.tr. Carp:* to shoulder (tenon, beam).

Achselschnur, *f. Mil:* **1.**=**Achselband 1. 2.**=**Achseltroddel.**

Achselschutz, *m.* (protective) shoulder-pad (*esp. of student duellist*).

Achselsproß, *m. Bot:* axillary shoot.

achselständig, *a. Bot:* axillary (leaf, etc.).

Achselstreifen, *m.*, **Achselstück,** *n. Cost:* shoulder-piece (of garment).

Achseltroddel, *f. Mil:* lanyard (worn by certain units round the left shoulder).

Achseltuch, *n. Ecc:*=**Achselkleid.**

Achselzucken, *n.* shrug (of the shoulders).

Achsen-, *comb.fm.* **1.** *Veh:* axle-; *cp.* **Achs-. 2.** . . . of the axis; axial . . .; **Achsenebene** *f,* axial plane; **Achsenverhältnis** *n,* axial ratio; **Achsenwinkel** *m,* axial angle.

achsen, *v.tr.* **1.** to fit (vehicle, etc.) with an axle *or* axles. **2.** to provide (sth.) with an axis.

Achsenabschnitt, *m. Mth:* axial intercept; intercept on an axis of co-ordinates.

Achsenarm, *m.*=**Achsschenkel.**

Achsenbecher, *m. Bot:* hypanthium.

achsenbildend, *m. Bot:* axile.

Achsenbruch, *m. Veh: Rail:* breaking of an axle; **bei A.,** if an axle breaks; **der Wagen hat einen A.,** the car, *Rail:* the carriage *or* wagon, has a broken axle.

Achsendrehung, *f.* rotation; revolution about an axis.

Achsenfaden, *m. Anat:*=**Achsenzylinder.**

Achsengeld, *n.* **1.** money paid for carriage (of goods). **2.** toll (levied on vehicle, for use of road, bridge, etc.); *A:* wheelage.

Achsenhals, *m.* axle-neck.

Achsenkreuz, *n. Mth:* system of co-ordinates.

Achsenmessung, *f.* axonometry.

Achsenneigung, *f. Astr:* axial inclination (of the planets); obliquity of the ecliptic.

Achsenregler, *m. Mec.E:* shaft governor.

Achsenschere, *f. Veh:* futchel.

Achsenschmiere, *f.* axle-grease; cart-grease.

Achsenschnitt, *m.* **1.** axial section. **2.**=**Achsenabschnitt.**

Achsenstrang, *m. Biol:* notochord.

Achsensymmetrie, *f. Geom:* axial symmetry.

Achsenzylinder, *m. Anat:* axon cylinder, axis cylinder.

Achsfederung, *f. Veh:* axle suspension.

achsfliehend, *a. Ph:* centrifugal.

Achsfutter, *n. Veh:* axle-bed.

Achsgehäuse, *n. Veh: Rail:* axle-box; axle casing, housing.

achsial [aksiˈaːl], *a.* (*incorrect*)=**axial.**

-achsig, *comb.fm. a.* **1.** -axial; **zweiachsig,** biaxial; **dreiachsig,** triaxial. **2.** *Veh:* -axled; **einachsig,** single-axled; **zweiachsig,** two-axled.

Achskappe, *f. Veh:* axle-cap; linchcap.

Achskilometer, *n.pl. Rail:* actual distance covered by carriage *or* wagon in a given time; =mileage covered.

Achskopf, *m. Veh:*=**Achssitz.**

Achslager, *n.* **1.** *Veh:* axle-bearing. **2.** *Mec.E:* journal-bearing.

Achslagerkasten, *m. Rail:*=**Achsbüchse.**

Achsmotor, *m. El.E:* direct-drive motor.

Achsnagel, *m. Veh:* axle-pin, linchpin.

Achsprobe, *f. Veh:* axle test.

achsrecht, *a.* axial.

Achsriegel, *m. Veh:* transom.

Achsring, *m. Veh:* washer (on axle).

Achsschenkel, *m.* axle-rod, spindle (of axle); axle-arm, -neck, axle-journal; *Aut:* stub-axle; steering-knuckle.

Achsschenkelbolzen, *m. Aut:* king-pin, -bolt, (steering) swivel pin.

Achsschenkelträger, *m. Aut:* steering-head.

Achsschnitt, *m.*=Achsenschnitt 1.

Achsschwenkung, *f. Mil: A:* pivoting movement; change of front.

Achssitz, *m. Veh:* wheel-seat.

Achsstand, *m.*=Achsabstand.

Achssturz, *m. Aut: Veh:* canting, inward slant, of the wheels.

Achsstütze, *f. Veh:* axle-stay; axle bracket.

Achstrichter, *m. Aut:* banjo.

Achswelle, *f. Aut: etc:* axle-shaft.

Achszapfen, *m. Mec.E:* pivot; *Aut:* king-pin, -bolt.

acht[1], *F:* **achte. 1.** *cardinal num.a.* eight; (*a*) **a. Mark fünfzig,** eight marks and fifty pfennigs; **wir frühstücken um a. (Uhr),** we breakfast at eight (o'clock); **der Zug, der um a. Uhr dreißig fährt,** the train that goes at eight-thirty, the eight-thirty train; **a. Jahre alt sein,** to be eight years old; **ein Junge von a. Jahren,** a boy of eight, an eight-year-old boy; **eine Familie von achten,** a family of eight; **eine Mutter von a. Kindern, von achten,** a mother of eight; **a. von meinen Schülern,** eight of my pupils; **a. kleine Jungen,** eight little boys; **wir waren unser acht(e),** **wir waren zu achten,** there were eight of us; **es sind a. Mann, es sind ihrer acht(e),** there are eight of them; **Seite a., Kapitel a.,** page eight, chapter eight; **mit achten fahren,** to drive with eight horses; **Größe a. in Handschuhen haben,** to take eights in gloves; *Num: Hist:* **ein Stück von achten,** a piece of eight (reals); peso; (*b*) **a. Tage,** eight days; a week; **a. Tage Urlaub,** a week's holiday, *Mil: etc:* a week's leave; **etwa a. Tage fort sein,** to be away about a week; **er ist auf a. Tage verreist,** he has gone away for a week; **(heute) vor a. Tagen,** a week ago (today); **gestern vor a. Tagen,** yesterday week; **Samstag vor a. Tagen,** last Saturday week; **(heute) über a. Tage, in acht Tagen,** a week from now, today week, this day week; **morgen, Dienstag, über a. Tage,** tomorrow week, Tuesday week; **alle a. Tage,** every week; **once a week; binnen a. Tagen,** within the, a, week; in the course of the week; *Adm: Com:*=within seven days; *Jur:* **einen Fall auf a. Tage zurückstellen,** to adjourn a case for a week; **auf a. Tage in die Untersuchungshaft zurückgeschickt,** remanded for eight days, for a week. **2.** *s.f.* **Acht, -/-en,** *F:* **Achte, -/-n,** (figure) eight; **eine A., zwei Achten** (*occ.* **zwei Acht**), **schreiben,** to write an eight, two eights; *F:* **eine lange A.,** a tall, lanky, individual; *Skating:* **Achten fahren, laufen,** to cut eights, figures of eight; *F:* **eine A. bauen,** to fall, to have a spill, to come a cropper, a purler; *Ent:* **gelbe, goldene, A.,** sulphur (butterfly); pale clouded yellow. **3. acht-, Acht-,** *comb.fm.* (*a*) (*in numerals*) **achtundzwanzig,** twenty-eight; **achthundert,** eight hundred; (*b*) eight-, oct(a)-, oct(o)-; **Achtflächner** *m,* octahedron; **achtkantig,** eight-sided, octagonal; **achtklauig,** eight-clawed, octodactylous. *See also* **achte(r)**[1].

Acht[2], *f. -/-.* (*when used in phrases without definite article usu.* **acht,** *with small letter*) heed, attention; **etwas in a. nehmen,** to take care of, look after, sth.; **seine Gesundheit in a. nehmen,** to take (good) care of one's health; **seine Gesundheit nicht in a. nehmen,** to take no heed of, to neglect, one's health; **etwas aus der A., außer a., lassen,** to leave sth. out of account, of consideration; to disregard sth.; **etwas außer aller A. lassen,** to disregard sth. entirely; **alle Vorsicht außer a. lassen,** to throw all discretion to the winds; **sich in a. nehmen,** to be careful, cautious; to beware, to be wary, to be on one's guard, *F:* to mind one's P's and Q's; **nimm dich in a.!** look out! mind yourself! *F:* mind your eye! watch your step! **du mußt dich höllisch in a. nehmen,** you'll have to walk very warily, *P:* to be damned careful; **sich vor j-m, etwas** *dat.,* **in a. nehmen,** to beware of, be on one's guard against, s.o., sth.; to be wary of s.o., sth.; to look out for, watch out for (swindlers, etc.); **nimm dich in a. vor blonden Frauen!** beware of blondes! **nimm dich in a. vor den Nesseln!** look out for the nettles! mind the nettles! **sich in a. nehmen, daß man etwas nicht tut,** to take care, to be careful, not to do sth.; **nimm dich in a., daß du nicht fällst!** mind you don't fall! **sich in a. nehmen, daß ... nicht ...,** to be careful lest (sth. should happen); *see also* **achtgeben, achthaben, achtpassen.**

Acht[3], *f. -/-.* *Hist:* outlawry; banishment; ban; proscription; *Hist. & F:* ostracism; *F:* boycott; **j-n in die A. erklären, tun; j-n in A. und Bann tun,** (i) *Hist:* to outlaw, banish, proscribe, s.o.; to ostracize s.o.; (ii) *F:* to boycott s.o.; to ostracize s.o., to send s.o. to Coventry; **er ist in A. und Bann,** he is ostracized; he has been sent to Coventry.

achtbar, *a.* respectable; worthy of respect; estimable (person); reputable (family, profession, etc.); **achtbare Firma,** firm of high standing.

Achtbarkeit, *f.* (*a*) respectability; good repute; (*b*) standing (of a firm).

achtblumig, *a. Bot:* octopetalous.

Achtbreiter, *m. -s/-.* *Husb:* five-year-old sheep.

Achtbrief, *m. Hist:* writ of outlawry, of banishment, of proscription.

achte, *num.a. see* (i) *pred.* **acht**[1]; (ii) **achte(r)**[1].

Achteck, *n. Geom:* octagon.

achteckig, *a.* octagonal, eight-angled.

acht(e)halb, *inv.a.* seven and a half.

achteinhalb, *cardinal num. a.inv.* eight and a half.

Achtel. I. *n. -s/-.* **1.** (*a*) eighth (part); **drei A.,** three eighths; **ein A. vom Kilo,** an eighth of a kilogramme; *see also* **-tel;** (*b*) *Mus:*=Achtelnote. **2. Achtel-,** *comb.fm. Ch: A:* (*in names of compounds*) octo-; **Achtelschwefeleisen** *n,* octoferric sulphide.

  II. achtel, *inv.a.* **Achtel-,** *comb.fm.* eighth (part) of ...; **ein a. Kilo, ein Achtelkilo,** an eighth part of a kilogramme.

Achtelband, *m. Print:* octavo; in eights.

Achtelcicero, *f. Print:* eight to pica (spacing).

Achtelektrodenröhre, *f. W.Tel:* =Achtpolröhre.

Achtelformat, *n.,* **Achtelgröße,** *f. Print:*=Achtelband.

Achtelkilo, *n. Meas:* eighth of a kilogramme,= 4·41 ounces.

Achtelkreis, *m. Geom: Astr:* octant.

Achtelkugel, *f. Geom:* octant of a sphere.

Achtelliter, *n. Meas:* eighth of a litre,=a little less than a quarter of a pint.

Achtelmeter, *n. Meas:* eighth of a metre.

achteln, *v.tr.* to divide (sth.) into eighths, into eight (equal) parts.

Achtelnote, *f. Mus:* quaver, *U.S:* eighth note.

Achtelpause, *f. Mus:* quaver rest, *U.S:* eighth rest.

Achtelpetit, *f. Print:* twelve to pica (spacing); hair-lead.

Achtelschlag, *m. Arch: Constr:* angle of forty-five degrees.

Achteltakt, *m. Mus:* time of a quaver, *U.S:* an eighth note; length of a quaver, *U.S:* an eighth note.

Achtelton, *m. Mus:*=Achtelnote.

Achtelzentner, *m. Meas:* eighth of a (German) hundredweight,=*approx.* 13·78 lbs.

achten, *v.* **1.** *v.tr.* (*a*) to deem, consider, regard; **j-n, etwas, für etwas a.,** to hold, deem, consider, s.o., sth., to be sth.; to regard s.o., sth., as sth.; (*cp.* **erachten, halten I. 1** 1(*b*)); (*b*) to esteem (s.o.); to value (s.o., sth.); to have a high opinion of (s.o., sth.); to respect, have regard for (s.o., sth.); **ich achte ihn, aber ich könnte ihn nie lieben,** I respect him, think highly of him, but I could never be fond of him; **ich achte sein Urteil,** I value, respect, his judgment; **ich muß seine Beweggründe a.,** I cannot but respect his motives; **etwas, j-n, nicht a., etwas, j-n, für nichts a.,** to despise sth., s.o.; to hold sth., s.o., in contempt; to set little value on, little store by, sth.; to make light of sth.; **kein Ansehen der Person a.,** to be no respecter of persons; **er achtet das Geld nicht,** he sets little store by money; he does not value money; **er achtet das Geld für nichts,** he despises money; money means nothing to him; **die Gefahr nicht a.,** to despise danger; to take no heed of danger; **sein Leben nicht a.,** to hold one's life of little account, to hold life cheap; *F:* **einer acht's, der andre verlacht's,** tastes differ, and you can't tell how people will react; *Prov:* **wer's nicht achtet, dem tut's nicht weh,** it's easy to do without things you set no great store by. **2.** *A:* **sich nach etwas a.,** to act in accordance with sth.; to accommodate oneself to sth.; to allow oneself to be guided by sth. **3.** *v.i.* (*haben*) **auf etwas** *acc.* **a., einer Sache** *gen.* **a.,** to pay attention to, pay heed to, pay regard to, take notice of, sth.; to mind sth.; **achte auf meine Worte!** mark me! mark you! mark my words! **auf j-s Befehle nicht a.,** to take no notice of, no heed of, to disregard, s.o.'s orders; **man achtete nicht auf seinen Rat,** his advice was disregarded, was not heeded; **ertat es, ohne auf meine Einwände zu a.,** he did it regardless of, in spite of, my objections; **auf alles a.,** (i) to attend to everything, (ii) to keep a sharp look-out; **auf nichts a.,** to pay no attention to anything; **achte auf das Baby!** watch the baby! look after, mind, the baby! **darauf a., daß ...,** to take care, to be careful, that ...; **achte darauf, daß die Tür geschlossen ist,** take care (that), make sure (that), the door is shut; **achte darauf, daß sie ruhig bleibt,** mind (that) she keeps quiet.

ächten. I. *v.tr.* to outlaw, proscribe, banish (s.o.); *Gr.Ant. & F:* to ostracize (s.o.); *F:* to boycott (s.o., an organization, etc.); to send (s.o.) to Coventry; **einen Gebrauch ä.,** to do away with, *F:* to taboo, a practice; **ein Wort ä.,** to forbid the use of a word; **den Alkohol ä.,** to ban, forbid, the use of alcohol.

  II. *vbl s.* **1. Ächten,** *n.* in vbl senses. **2. Ächtung,** *f.* (*a*)=II. 1; (*b*) *Hist:* outlawry, proscription, banishment.

Achtender, *m. Ven:* four-pointer, stag with eight tines (*cp.* **Achter**[2] 5 (*b*)).

achtens, *adv.* eighthly, in the eighth place.

achtenswert, *a.* (*a*) estimable, respectable, worthy of respect; (*b*) considerable (achievement, etc.).

achte(r)[1], **achte, achte(s),** *ordinal num.a.* eighth; **achte Seite, achtes Kapitel,** eighth page, eighth chapter; page eight, chapter eight; **zum achten,** eighthly, in the eighth place; **Sie sind der siebente oder achte, der mir diese Frage gestellt hat,** you are the seventh or eighth who has asked me that question; **es ist heute der achte April,** today is the eighth of April; **am achten April,** on the eighth of April; **der Achte (des Monats),** the eighth of the month; (*date at head of letter*) **den 8. Juni 1953,** 8th June 1953; **Heinrich der Achte,** Henry the Eighth; **die Regierung Heinrichs des Achten,** the reign of Henry the Eighth. *See also* **Stufe.**

Achter[2], *m. -s/-.* **1.** (*a*) (figure) eight; **einen A. schreiben,** to write an eight, a figure eight; (*b*) figure of eight; *Skating:* **Achter fahren, laufen, zeichnen,** to cut figures of eight. **2.** *Mil:* soldier of the 8th Regiment. **3.** wine of the '08 vintage. **4.** *Num:* eight-pfennig piece; eight-kreuzer piece; eight-groschen piece. **5.** (*a*) eight-oared boat; *Row: F:* eight; (*b*) *Ven:*= **Achtender; ewiger A.,** stag that never grows more than eight tines; (*c*) anything with eight parts, etc., *e.g.* eight-wheeled vehicle, eight-cylinder car; *Pros:* octave, eight-line stanza. **6. Achter-,** *comb.fm.* ... of eight; **Achterperiode** *f,* period of eight (elements).

achter[3]. *North G.Dial.* **1.** (*a*) *a.* rear, hinder; *Nau:* after(-hold, etc.); (*b*) *adv.* behind; at the rear; *Nau:* aft. **2.** *prep.* (+*dat.*) behind; *Nau:* aft of, abaft; **a. dem Mast,** aft of the mast, abaft the mast.

Achter-, *comb.fm. Nau:* (*a*) (*in names of parts of ship, ship's equipment*) after-; **Achterbrassen** *fpl,* after-braces; **Achterdeck** *n,* after-deck; (*b*) (*in names of sails*) miz(z)en-; **Achterbramstagsegel** *n,* miz(z)en-topgallant staysail; **Achtermittelstagsegel** *n,* miz(z)en-middle staysail.

Ächter, *m. -s/-.* **1.** proscriber, banisher. **2.** *A:* (=Geächteter) outlaw.

achteraus, *adv. Nau:* astern; **Schiff gerade a.,** ship right astern; **Schiff etwas a.,** ship slightly astern; **a. gehen,** to go, come, astern; **einem Schiff a. folgen,** to follow astern of a ship; **Fahrt a.,** stern-way; astern motion, motion astern; **volle Kraft a.! Volldampf a.!** full speed astern!

Achterbahn, *f.* figure-eight railway; switchback, scenic railway; *F:* big dipper.

Achterbramrah(e), *f. Nau:* miz(z)en-topgallant yard.

Achterbramsegel, *n. Nau:* miz(z)en-topgallant sail.

Achterdeck, *n. Nau:* after-deck; quarter-deck; *Dial: F:* **j-m das A. kalfatern,** to tan s.o.'s backside.

Achtereinmaleins, das. *Mth:* the eight times table.

Achterende, *n. Nau:* aft end, rear end.

Achterflicken, *m. North G.Dial:* heel(-piece) (of shoe, boot).

Achtergruppe, *f.* group of eight.

Achterkastell, *n. N.Arch: A:* sterncastle.

Achterklaue, *f. Constr:* =Afterklaue 2.

Achterkreis, *m. Tg: Tp:* double phantom circuit.

Achterladeraum, *m. Nau:* after-hold.

Achterlast, *f. Nau:* (*a*) (excessive) load at the stern; (*b*)=Achterlastigkeit.

achterlastig, *a. Nau:* (ship) heavy by the stern,

by the tail, (ship) down by the stern, tail-heavy (ship).
Achterlastigkeit, *f. Nau:* tail-heaviness; heaviness by the stern.
Achterlaterne, *f. Nau:* stern-light.
achterlei, *inv.a.* of eight kinds, sorts, varieties; **a. Kuchen,** eight kinds of cake.
Achterleine, *f. Nau:* stern-rope, stern-fast.
achterlich, *a. & adv. Nau:* aft; (coming from) astern; **einen achterlichen Wind, eine achterliche Brise, haben,** to have the wind astern, dead aft; to have the wind behind one; **(drei Strich) achterlicher als dwars,** (three points) abaft the beam.
Achterliek, *n. Nau:* after-leech (of sail).
Achterluke, *f. Nau:* after-hatch(way).
Achtermann, *m.* **-(e)s/-männer. 1.=Hintermann** 1 (*a*), (*b*). **2.** *Pr.n. Geog:* **der A.,** the Achtermann mountain (in the Harz).
Achtermannschaft, *f. Row:* eight; crew of an eight.
Achtermast, *m. Nau:* after-mast.
achtern, *adv. Nau:* (*a*) aft, abaft; **der Kapitän ist a.,** the captain is aft; **a. schlafen,** to berth aft; **ganz a.,** right aft, right abaft; **a. vom Mast,** aft of the mast, abaft the mast; **a. (im Boot),** in the sternsheets (of a small boat); (*b*) astern; **von a.,** from astern; **a. von einem Schiff passieren,** to pass astern of a ship.
Achterraum, *m. Nau:* after-hold.
Achterrennen, *n. Row:* eights (race).
Achterschale, *f. Atom.Ph:* eight-electron shell.
Achterschiff, *n. Nau:* after-body; stern.
Achtersegel, *n.pl. Nau:* after-sails.
Achterstek, *m.***=Achterstich.**
Achtersteven, *m. Nau:* stern-post.
Achterstich, *m. Nau:* figure-of-eight knot.
Achterzelt, *n. Mil: etc:* eight-man tent.
achtfach, *a.* (*a*) eightfold, octuple; eight times; (*b*) **sechzehn ist das Achtfache von zwei,** sixteen is eight times two; **sich um das Achtfache vermehren,** to increase eightfold.
achtfällig, *a.* subject to, condemned to, outlawry, proscription; outlawed, proscribed.
achtfältig, *a.* eightfold, octuple.
Achtflach, *n.* **=Achtflächner.**
achtflächig, *a.* octahedral.
Achtflächner, *m. Geom:* octahedron.
Achtfußkraken, *m. Moll:* octopod; octopus.
Achtfüß(l)er, *m.* **-s/-.** *Moll:* octopod.
achtgeben, *v.i. sep.* (*strong*) (*haben*) to pay attention, give heed, take care; **gib acht! achtgeben!** take care! have a care! be careful! look out! watch out! mind yourself! **a., daß man etwas nicht tut,** to take care, to be careful, not to do sth.; **gib acht, daß du es nicht verlierst!** mind you don't lose it! be sure not to lose it! **auf j-n, etwas, a.,** to take care of s.o., sth., (i) to look after s.o., sth.; (ii) to beware of s.o., sth.; **auf seine Gesundheit a.,** to take (good) care of, to watch, one's health; **gib auf das Baby acht!** keep an eye on, look after, the baby! **gib acht auf das Baby!** mind the baby! **gib acht auf die Stufe!** mind the step!
achtgliedrig, *a.* eight-membered, with eight members.
Achtgroschenjunge, *m. F:* informer, (police) spy, *F:* (copper's) nark.
achthaben, *v.i. sep.* (*strong*) (*haben*) (*a*)**=achtgeben;** (*b*) *Austrian: Mil:* **'habt acht!'** 'attention!' ''shun!'; (*c*) *Lit:* to pay attention, give heed (*gen.*, to s.o.); **niemand hat seiner acht,** no one heeds, nobody takes any notice of, him.
achthundert, *num.a.inv.* eight hundred.
achtjährig, *a.* **1.** eight-year-old (child, animal, etc.); **ein achtjähriger Junge, ein Achtjähriger,** a boy of eight, an eight-year-old boy, *F:* an eight-year-old. **2.** lasting (for) eight years; octennial.
achtjährlich. 1. *a.* eight-yearly, octennial (event, etc.). **2.** *adv.* every eight years.
Achtkant, *m.* **-s/-e.** *Geom:* octahedron.
Achtkanteisen, *n. Mec.E:* octagon iron bar.
achtkantig, *a.* eight-sided; octagonal (nut, etc.); *F:* **j-n a. herauswerfen,** to throw s.o. out for good and all.
Achtkantmaterial, *n. Mec.E:* octagon bars, *F:* octagons.
Achtkantmutter, *f. Mec.E:* octagonal nut, octagon nut.
Achtknoten, *m.***=Achterstich.**
achtlos, *a.* (*a*) inattentive (**auf**+*acc.*, to); unobservant, careless, heedless (**gegen, auf**+*acc.*, of); indifferent (**gegen, auf**+*acc.*, to); **a. auf die Leiden anderer Menschen, den Leiden anderer Menschen gegenüber,** heedless of, indifferent to, the sufferings of others; (*b*) negligent, careless; (*c*) casual, nonchalant; **a. an etwas** *dat.*, **j-m, vorübergehen,** to pass sth., s.o., without paying any attention to it, him.
Achtlosigkeit, *f.* (*a*) inattention (**gegen, auf**+*acc.*, to); carelessness, heedlessness, negligence, unobservance (**gegen, auf**+*acc.*, of); disregard (**gegen, auf**+*acc.*, of, for); indifference (**gegen, auf**+*acc.*, to); (*b*) inattentiveness, carelessness, negligence; (*c*) casualness, nonchalance.
achtmal, *adv.* eight times.
achtmalig, *a.* (announcement, etc.) made eight times; eight (attempts, etc.).
achtmännig, *a. Bot:* octandrous (plant).
achtmonatig, *a.* **1.** lasting (for) eight months; (stay, etc.) of eight months. **2.** (child) of eight months, eight-month(s)-old (child).
Achtmonatskind, *n. Obst:* eight-month baby.
achtpassen, *v.i. sep.* (*haben*)**=achtgeben, aufpassen.**
Achtpfünder, *m. A.Artil:* eight-pounder.
achtpolig, *a. El.E:* eight-pole, octopolar (stator, etc.).
Achtpolröhre, *f. W.Tel:* octode; eight-electrode valve, *U.S:* tube.
Achtpunktschrift, *f. Print:* eight-point type; brevier.
Achtrad, *n.* (*a*) eight-wheeled car, vehicle; (*b*) *Mil:***=Achtradpanzer.**
Achtradpanzer, *m. Mil:* eight-wheeled armoured car.
Achtruderer, *m.* eight-oared boat; *Row: F:* eight.
achtruderig, *a. Row:* eight-oared (boat).
achtsam, *a.* attentive (**auf**+*acc.*, to); heedful, mindful (**auf**+*acc.*, of); careful (**auf**+*acc.*, of); circumspect, prudent, cautious, wary, guarded.
Achtsamkeit, *f.* attention (**auf**+*acc.*, to); carefulness, care, heedfulness, mindfulness (**auf**+*acc.*, of); circumspection, circumspectness, caution, wariness.
achtsäulig, *a. Arch:* having eight columns.
Achtschaufler, *m. Husb:* five-year-old sheep.
achtseitig, *a.* **1.** eight-sided. **2.** (pamphlet, etc.) of eight pages.
Achtserklärung, *f.* sentence of outlawry, of banishment, of proscription.
achtsilbig, *a.* octosyllabic (word, verse).
Achtstein, *m.* amber.
Achtstek, Achtstich, *m.***=Achterstich.**
achtstellig, *a. Mth:* eight-figure (number); eight-place (decimal).
achtstemp(e)lig, *a. Bot:* octogynous.
Achtstundentag, *m. Ind:* (the) eight-hour day.
achtstündig, *a.* lasting (for) eight hours; eight-hour (rest, working day, etc.).
achtstündlich. 1. *a.* eight-hourly (intervals, bulletins, etc.). **2.** *adv.* every eight hours.
Achttageuhr, *f.* eight-day clock.
achttägig, *a.* (event, etc.) lasting (for) (i) eight days, (ii) a week; **ein achttägiger Urlaub,** a week's holiday, *Mil: etc:* a week's leave.
achttäglich. 1. *a.* (i) (visits, etc.) at eight day intervals; (ii) weekly (visits, etc.). **2.** *adv.* (i) every eight days; (ii) weekly.
achttausend, *cardinal num.a.inv.* eight thousand.
achtteilig, *a.* having eight parts.
Achtuhr-, *comb.fm.* eight o'clock . . .; **Achtuhrvorstellung** *f*, eight o'clock performance; **Achtuhrzug** *m*, eight o'clock train.
achtund-, *comb.fm. num.a.inv.* -eight; **achtundzwanzig,** twenty-eight; **achtundneunzig,** ninety-eight; **achtundvierzig Stunden,** forty-eight hours; two days.
Achtundneunziger, *m. Ent: F:* red admiral (butterfly).
Achtundvierziger, *m.* **1.** *G. & Fr. Hist: F:* revolutionary of 1848. **2.** wine of the '48 vintage.
Achtundvierzigstelformat, *n. Print:* forty-eightmo, forty-eights.
Achtung, *f.* **1.** attention, heed; **auf j-n, etwas, A. geben, haben,** to pay attention to, pay heed to, take notice of, s.o., sth.; to mind s.o., sth.; to look after, see to, s.o., sth.; **Achtung!** *Dial. & F:* **paß(t) A.!** look out! take care! have a care! beware! mind yourself! *F:* mind out! **Achtung!** *Mil:* attention! *F:* 'shun! *Nau:* stand by! *Nau:* **A. beim Steuer!** mind the helm! **A., Stufe!** mind the step! *P.N:* **'A. Steinschlag!'** 'beware of, caution, falling rock!' **2.** esteem, regard, respect; **j-m (große, viel) A. erweisen, entgegenbringen,** to show (high) regard for s.o., to show s.o. (great) respect; **A. vor j-m haben,** to have respect for s.o., to hold s.o. in respect; **große, viel, A. vor j-m, für j-n, vor etwas** *dat.*, **haben,** to have a great regard for, to think highly of, s.o., sth.; **in j-s A. steigen, sinken,** to go up, to rise, to go down, to fall, in s.o.'s esteem; **A. vor dem Gesetz haben,** to respect the law; **große A. genießen,** to be held in high respect, esteem, to be greatly respected, highly esteemed; **sich** *dat.* **A. erwerben, gewinnen,** to earn, win, respect, to gain esteem; **A. gebieten,** to command respect; **sich** *dat.* **A. verschaffen,** to make oneself respected; **er wußte sich A. zu verchaffen,** he was able to make himself, his authority, respected; **sich bei j-m in A. setzen,** to gain s.o.'s respect, s.o.'s esteem; **bei j-m in A. stehen,** to stand well with s.o., to stand high in the opinion, the estimation, of s.o.; **etwas aus A. für j-n, gegen j-n, vor j-m, tun,** to do sth. out of respect for s.o., out of regard for s.o.; **ich sage es mit aller (schuldigen) A. vor Ihnen,** I say it with all (due) respect to you; **alle A. vor seiner Wahl!** I admire his choice; **alle, allerhand, A.!** that's admirable! *F:* I take off my hat to that, to you! *see also* **abgewinnen, einflößen.**
Achtung, *f. see* **ächten** II. 2.
achtunggebietend, *a.* imposing (personality, figure, etc.); commanding (personality, air, etc.).
Achtungsbeweis, *m.***=Achtungsbezeugung.**
Achtungsbezeigung, *f.***=Achtungsbezeugung.**
Achtungsbezeugung, *f.* mark, token, of respect; mark, proof, of one's esteem.
Achtungserfolg, *m.* **1.** success based on respect for s.o.'s performance *or* technique; *succès d'estime.* **2.** *Sp: etc:* victory worthy of respect.
Achtungsgesetze, *n.pl.* proscriptive laws.
achtungslos, *a.* disrespectful.
Achtungsverletzung, *f.* disrespect, irreverence; *Mil: etc:* wilful defiance (of authority); insubordination.
achtungsvoll, *a.* respectful (**gegen,** to); *Corr:* **a. J. Schmidt,** (I am, Sir,) yours (very) truly J. Schmidt; (I remain) yours respectfully J. Schmidt.
achtungswert, *a.***=achtenswert** (*a*).
achtungswidrig, *a.* disrespectful, irreverent (behaviour, etc.); *Mil: etc:* insubordinate (act, etc.).
Achtungswidrigkeit, *f.* disrespect(fulness), irreverence; *Mil: etc:* insubordination.
achtungswürdig, *a.***=achtungswert.**
achtweibig, *a. Bot:* octogynous.
achtwertig, *a. Ch:* octovalent, octavalent.
achtwink(e)lig, *a.* octagonal.
achtzählig, *a.* having *or* consisting of eight parts *or* members; *Nat. Hist:* octamerous (flower, etc.).
achtzehn. 1. *cardinal num.a.* eighteen; **sie ist a. (Jahre alt),** she is eighteen (years old). (*For other phrases cp.* **acht**[1]) **2.** *s.f.* **Achtzehn, -/-en,** (number) eighteen.
Achtzehnender, *m. Ven:* (*stag*) eighteen-pointer.
Achtzehner, *m.* **-s/-. 1.** *Mil:* soldier of the 18th Regiment. **2.** wine of the '18 vintage. **3.** *Ven:* **=Achtzehnender. 4. Achtzehner-,** *comb.fm.* . . . of eighteen; **Achtzehnergruppe** *f*, group of eighteen.
achtzehnjährig, *a.* **1.** eighteen-year-old (pers., etc.); **ein achtzehnjähriger Junge, ein Achtzehnjähriger,** a boy of eighteen, an eighteen-year-old boy, *F:* an eighteen-year-old. **2.** lasting (for) eighteen years; eighteen-year (period, etc.).
Achtzehntel, *n.* eighteenth (part); *see also* **-tel.**
Achtzehntelformat, *n.*, **Achtzehntelgröße,** *f. Print:* decimo-octavo, eighteenmo.
achtzehnte(r), achtzehnte, achtzehnte(s), *ordinal num.a.* eighteenth; **das achtzehnte Haus,** the eighteenth house; **am achtzehnten Mai,** on the eighteenth of May; **Ludwig der Achtzehnte,** Louis the Eighteenth. (*For other phrases cp.* **achte(r)**[1]).
achtzeilig, *a.* (stanza, paragraph, etc.) of eight lines; *Pros:* **achtzeilige Strophe,** eight-line stanza, octave, *esp.* ottava rima.
achtziff(e)rig, *a. Mth:* eight-figure (number).
achtzig. 1. *cardinal num.a.* eighty, *A. & Lit:* fourscore; **Seite a.,** page eighty; **a. Jahre alt,** eighty years old; *Dial: esp. Austrian:* **in den a. sein,** to be in one's, the, eighties. **2.** *s.f.* **Achtzig, -/- & -en,** (number) eighty; **er ist in die A. gekommen, gegangen,** he is, has, turned eighty; **er ist in den Achtzigen,** *occ.* **in den achtzigen,** he is in his, the eighties; **sie ist Mitte A.,** she is in the, mid, middle, eighties; **an die A. sein,** to be getting on for, *U.S:* going on, eighty. *Cp.* **achtzigste(r).**
achtziger. 1. *inv.a.* (*a*) of *or* relating to the group, series, etc., characterized by the number 80; (*b*) (*of pers.*) octogenarian; (*c*) **die a. Jahre,** (i) the eighties (of s.o.'s age); **er war in den a. Jahren,** he was in his, the, eighties; **er war hoch in den a. Jahren=er war in den hohen Achtzigern,** *q.v. under* 2 (*b*); (ii) the eighties (of a century); **die a. Jahre,** *occ.* **die Achtzigerjahre, des vergangenen Jahrhunderts,** the eighties of the last century; **der Gesellschaftsroman der a. Jahre,** the social novel of the eighties. **2.** *s.m.* **Achtziger,**

-s/-, (*a*) octogenarian, *A. & Lit:* man of fourscore (years); **er war ein hoher A., sie war eine hohe Achtzigerin**=**er, sie, war in den hohen Achtzigern,** *q.v. under* (*b*); (*b*) *pl*, **die Achtziger,** the eighties (of s.o.'s age); in **den Achtzigern sein,** to be in one's, the, eighties; **er ist (in der) Mitte der Achtziger,** he is in the, mid, middle, eighties; **er, sie, war in den hohen Achtzigern,** he, she, was well on in the eighties, was in his, her, the, late eighties; he, she, was getting on for ninety; (*c*) wine of the '80 vintage; (*d*) man born in the year '80; (*e*) *Mil:* soldier of the 80th Regiment.

Achtzigerjahre, die, the eighties (of s.o.'s age).

achtzigjährig, *a.* eighty-year-old (pers., etc.); octogenarian; **ein Achtzigjähriger, eine Achtzigjährige,** an eighty-year-old man, woman; an octogenarian; *A. & Lit:* a man, woman, of fourscore (years).

Achtzigstel. I. *n.* -s/-, eightieth (part); **ein A., zwei Achtzigstel, des Wertes verlieren,** to lose one eightieth, two eightieths, of the value.

II. **achtzigstel,** *inv.a.* eightieth (part) of. . . .

achtzigste(r), achtzigste, achtzigste(s), *ordinal num.a.* eightieth; **das achtzigste Haus,** the eightieth house; **der achtzigste Teil (von etwas),** the eightieth (part) (of sth.); **der Achtzigste in der Liste,** the eightieth on the list.

Achtzylinder, *m. Aut: F:* eight-cylinder car, *F:* eight.

Achtzylindermotor, *m. I.C.E:* eight-cylinder engine.

ächzen. I. *v.i.* (*haben*) to groan, moan, wail; to whimper, whine; (*of hinge, door, floor-boards, etc.*) to creak; **vor Schmerzen ä.,** to groan, moan, with, in, pain; **vor Müdigkeit ä.,** to groan with fatigue; **der Wind ächzte im Walde,** the wind was moaning through the forest; **der Karren ächzte unter der Last,** the cart groaned under the load; **das alte Auto ächzte den Hügel hinauf,** the old car went creaking up the hill.

II. *vbl s.* **Ächzen,** *n.* groan(ing), moan(ing), wail(ing); whimper(ing), whining, whine; creaking (of door, floor-boards, etc.).

Ächzer, *m.* -s/-, (*a*) groan, moan, wail; whimper; (*b*) creak (of door, floor-board, etc.).

Aci-, aci-. 1. *see* **Azi-, azi-.** 2. (*words of Greek derivation*) *see* **Aki-, aki-;** *e.g.* **Acinesie**=**Akinesie.**

acinös [a·tsi·ˈnøːs], *a. Anat: Bot:* acinose, acinous; aciniform; *Anat:* **acinöse Drüsen,** acinous glands.

Acker, *m.* -s/=. 1. (*a*) field, *esp.* ploughed, cultivated, field; **den A. bauen, bestellen,** to plough, till, cultivate, the ground; *Prov:* **kein A. ohne Disteln,** no rose without a thorn; every rose has its thorn; (*b*) *Agr:*=**Ackerbeet;** (*c*)=**Ackerfläche.** 2. *A.Meas:* (German) acre (*varying between 2,200 and 6,500 square metres*); **ein A. Landes,** an acre of land. 3. **Acker-,** *comb.fm. in botanical names, often equates with the Latin . . . arvensis, e.g.* **Ackerdistel** *f, carduus arvensis,* corn thistle; **Ackergauchheil** *n, anagallis arvensis,* scarlet pimpernel.

Ackerarbeit, *f.* agricultural work; work in the fields; farm-work.

Ackerbaldrian, *m.*=**Ackersalat.**

ackerbar, *a.* arable, tillable, cultivable (land); plough(-land).

Ackerbau, *m.* agriculture; husbandry; farming; cultivation, tillage, tilling (of the soil); **A. treiben,** to cultivate, till, the soil; to practise agriculture; to farm the soil, *abs.* to farm; **A. und Viehzucht,** farming and stockbreeding.

Ackerbauchemie, *f.* agricultural chemistry.

ackerbauend, *a.*=**ackerbautreibend.**

Ackerbauer, *m.* farmer; agriculturist; husbandman; tiller of the soil.

Ackerbaugerät, *n.*=**Ackergerät.**

Ackerbaugesellschaft, *f.* agricultural society, association.

Ackerbaukunde, *f.*=**Ackerbauwissenschaft.**

Ackerbauschule, *f.* agricultural college.

Ackerbautechnik, *f.* agricultural technology; (the) science of agriculture.

ackerbautreibend, *a.* agricultural, farming (people, community); (nation) of farmers.

Ackerbauwissenschaft, *f.* (the) science of agriculture.

Ackerbeere, *f. Bot:* dewberry.

Ackerbeet, *n. Agr:* land (*i.e.* space between water-furrows).

Ackerbestellung, *f.* cultivation, tillage, tilling (of the soil).

ackerbewohnend, *a.* 1. rustic (people); agricultural (population). 2. *Bot: Ent: etc:* agrest(i)al.

Kckerboden, *m.* arable, tillable, land; plough-land, (land in) tillage; **fruchtbarer A.,** fertile soil.

Ackerbohne, *f. Bot: Agr:* field bean, horse-bean.

Ackerbrachweide, *f.* fallow pasture.

Ackerbrombeere, *f.*=**Ackerbeere.**

Ackerbürger, *m.* townsman owning a farm in the country; *F:* city farmer.

Äckerchen, *n.* -s/-, little, tiny, field; scrap, patch, (small) plot (of land).

Ackerdistel, *f. Bot:* corn thistle, creeping thistle, cursed thistle, *U.S:* Canada thistle.

Ackerdoppe, *f.*=**Eckerdoppe.**

Ackerehrenpreis, *m. Bot:* field speedwell.

Ackerer, *m.* -s/-. 1. tillage farmer. 2.=**Ackermann.**

Ackererbse, *f.*=**Felderbse.**

Ackererde, *f.* 1.=**Ackerboden.** 2.=**Ackerkrume.**

Ackereule, *f. Ent:* turnip-moth, common dart-moth.

Ackerfeld, *n.* tilled field, *esp.* ploughed field; field in, under, cultivation; plough-land, ploughed land.

Ackerfläche, *f.* land, fields, under cultivation; plough-land.

Ackerfuchsschwanz, *m. Bot:* slender foxtail (grass).

Ackerfurche, *f.* (open) furrow.

Ackerfutterpflanze, *f.* (cultivated) fodder plant.

Ackergänsedistel, *f.*=**Ackersaudistel.**

Ackergare, *f.*=**Bodengare.**

Ackergauchheil, *n. Bot:* scarlet pimpernel, *F:* poor man's, shepherd's, weather-glass.

Ackergaul, *m.* farm horse, plough-horse, *F:* dobbin.

Ackergerät, *n.* (*a*) agricultural, farming, implement; (*b*) *coll.* agricultural, farming, implements; tillage implements.

Ackergerätschaft, *f.* = **Ackergerät.**

Ackergesetz, *n. Jur:* agrarian law, land-act, land-law.

Ackergrenze, *f. Agr:* field boundary.

Ackergünsel, *m. Bot:* ground-pine, yellow bugle.

Ackerhahnenfuß, *m. Bot:* corn crowfoot, hunger-weed, *F:* buttercup.

Ackerholler, *m. Bot: F:* aegopodium, bishop's weed, gout-weed.

Ackerholunder, *m. Bot:* bloodwort, danewort, dwarf-elder.

Ackerholz, *n. Agr:* wood from land cleared for cultivation.

Ackerhornkraut, *n. Bot:* field, meadow, chick-weed.

Ackerhuhn, *n. Orn:* partridge.

Ackerkamille, *f. Bot:* corn camomile.

Ackerklee, *m. Bot:* hare's foot trefoil.

Ackerklette, *f. Bot:* bastard parsley, hedge-parsley.

Ackerknecht, *m.* ploughman, plough-boy; farm-hand, farm-labourer, hind.

Ackerkohl, *m.* 1. field cabbage. 2. =**Ackersenf.**

Ackerkrähe, *f. Orn:* rook.

Ackerkratzdistel, *f. Bot:*=**Ackerdistel.**

Ackerkrume, *f. Agr:* surface-soil, topsoil, tilth.

Ackerkrummhals, *m. Bot:* (corn, field) bugloss.

Ackerkult, *m.* cult of the fields; religious practices intended to protect crops.

Ackerland, *n.* arable land; ploughland.

Ackerlattich, *m. Bot:* coltsfoot.

Ackerlaus, *f. Bot: Austrian Dial:*=**Ackerwinde.**

Äckerlein, *n.* -s/-=**Äckerchen.**

Ackerlerche, *f. Orn:* skylark.

Ackerleute, *pl. see* **Ackermann.**

Ackerlohn, *m.* ploughman's wages; farm-labourer's wages.

Ackerlöwenmaul, *n. Bot:* corn snapdragon.

Ackermähre, *f.* (*a*) plough-mare; (*b*) *F:* old mare, jade; screw, crock.

Ackermann, *m.* -(e)s/-leute, (*a*) farmer; cultivator, agriculturist, husbandman; (*b*) farmhand; farm-labourer, *esp.* ploughman; *Lit:* **der A. aus Böhmen,** *F:* **der A.,** Death and the Ploughman.

Ackermännchen, *n. Orn:* white wagtail.

Ackermaß, *n. Meas:* land-measure.

Ackermaus, *f. Z:*=**Erdmaus.**

Ackermennig, *m.* -(e)s/-e. *Bot:* (common) agrimony.

Ackerminze, *f. Bot:* corn-mint.

Ackermohn, *m. Bot:* rough-headed poppy.

ackern. I. *v.* 1. *v.tr.* to cultivate, till, *esp.* to plough (land). 2. *v.i.* (*haben*) *F:* to labour, toil, drudge, *F:* to grind (away) (*esp.* at writing). 3. *v.i.* (*haben*) *Fb: F:* to dribble.

II. *vbl s.* **Ackern** *n.*, **Ackerung** *f. in vbl senses; also:* (*a*) cultivation, tillage; (*b*) *F:* labour, toil, drudgery, *F:* grind.

Ackernahrung, *f. Agr:* land sufficient to support a family.

Ackernuß, *f. Bot:* tuberous pea, earth-nut pea.

Ackernüßchen, *n. Bot:* neslia, neslea.

Ackerparzelle, *f.* plot, patch, parcel, of (arable) land.

Ackerpferd, *n.*=**Ackergaul.**

Ackerpflug, *m. Agr:* plough.

Ackerrade, *f. Bot:* agrostemma (githago), corn-cockle.

Ackerrain, *m. Agr:* balk, baulk; strip of un-ploughed ground between two fields.

Ackerraute, *f. Bot:* fumitory, fumaria.

Ackerrettich, *m. Bot:* wild radish, jointed, joint-podded, charlock.

Ackerrittersporn, *m. Bot:* wild larkspur.

Ackerrixe, *f.* -/-n. *Orn:* landrail, corncrake.

Ackerröte, *f. Bot:* sherardia, field-madder.

Ackersalat, *m. Bot:* lamb's lettuce, corn-salad.

Ackersaudistel, *f. Bot:* corn sow-thistle.

Ackerschachtelhalm, *m. Bot:* field horsetail.

Ackerschädling, *m.* agricultural pest.

Ackerschirmling, *m. Fung:* flayed parasol.

Ackerschleife, Ackerschleppe, *f. Agr:* drag; clod-breaker, -crusher.

Ackerschlepper, *m. Husb:* (agricultural) tractor.

Ackerschmiele, *f. Bot: F:* agrostis, bent(-grass).

Ackerschnabelkraut, *n. Bot:* erodium (cicutarium), stork's bill.

Ackerschnecke, *f. Moll:* (small) slug, *esp.* field slug.

Ackerscholle, *f.* clod, lump of earth.

Ackerschöterich, *m. Bot:* treacle-mustard.

Ackerschwertel, *m. Bot:* corn-flag, (common) gladiolus.

Ackersenf, *m. Bot:* (*a*) charlock, wild mustard; (*b*) wild radish, jointed, joint-podded, charlock.

Ackerskabiose, *f. Bot:* field scabious, meadow scabious.

Ackersleute, Ackersmann=**Ackerleute, Ackermann.**

Ackerspark, Ackerspörgel, *m. Bot:* corn spurrey.

Ackersteinsame(n), *m. Bot:* corn gromwell, bastard alkanet.

Ackerstiefmütterchen, *n. Bot:* heart's-ease, wild pansy.

Ackerstrehl, *m. Bot:* scandix, shepherd's needle.

Ackertäschelkraut, *n.*, **Ackertaschenkresse,** *f. Bot:* penny-cress.

Ackertrespe, *f. Bot:* field brome-grass.

Ackertrolle, *m.* -n/-n. *F:* (country) bumpkin, yokel, clodhopper, *U.S:* hick, hayseed.

Ackerveilchen, *n.*=**Ackerstiefmütterchen.**

Ackervieh, *n.* farm animals, farm cattle.

Ackervorbau, *m. Agr:* catch-crop, snatch-crop.

Ackerwachtelweizen, *m. Bot:* field cow-wheat.

Ackerwagen, *m.* farm-cart.

Ackerwalze, *f. Agr:* roller.

Ackerweide, *f. Agr:* green fallow used for pasture.

ackerweise, *adv.* 1. *A. & Dial:* acre by acre. 2. in plots, in parcels; field by field; **Land a. verkaufen,** to sell land in plots, in parcels.

Ackerweizen, *m. Bot:* 1. (common) couch-grass, creeping wheat-grass, twitch, *U.S:* quack grass. 2.=**Ackerwachtelweizen.**

Ackerwerbel, *m.* -s/-. *Ent: F:* mole-cricket.

Ackerwerk, *n.*=**Ackerbau, Ackerwirtschaft.**

Ackerwerkzeug, *n.*=**Ackergerät.**

Ackerwiese, *f. Agr:* meadow surrounded by plough-land.

Ackerwinde, *f. Bot:* field bindweed, corn-bind, convolvulus.

Ackerwirtschaft, *f.* agriculture; farming; husbandry.

Ackerwurm, *m. Ent: F:* cockchafer-grub.

Ackerwurz, *f. Bot:* sweet calamus, sweet flag, sweet rush.

Ackerzeit, *f. Agr:* ploughing-time; (the) ploughing season.

Ackerzins, *m.* rent (of farm *or* land).

Ackerzweizahn, *m. Bot:* bidens tripartita, water hemp.

Ackerzwiebel, *f. Bot:* star of Bethlehem.

Ackt, *f.* -/-en. *Swiss Dial:*=**Abzucht.**

Acme, Acne, *f.* -/.=**Akme, Akne.**

Aco- *see* **Ako-.**

à condition [a kõ·di·sĭˈõː]. *Fr.phr.* (*abbr.* **à cond.** *Com:* on sale or return; *Publ: abbr:* O/S.

a conto [a· ˈkontoː]. *Ital.phr. Com:* on account *see also* **Akontozahlung, Konto.**

acquirieren, Acquis, Acquisition, *etc. see* **akquirieren, Akquis, Akquisition,** *etc.*

Acr-, acr-, Act-, act-, Acu, acu- *see* **Akr-, akr-, Akt-, akt-, Aku-, aku-**

acyclisch, acyklisch, *a.* = azyklisch.

ada-ada-gehen, *v.i.* (*sein*) (*nursery language*) to go ta-tas, go for a ta-ta

ad acta [at ˈaktaː]. *Lt.phr.* **(einen Bericht, eine Bitte, usw.) ad acta legen = zu den Akten legen,** *q.v. under* **Akte.**

adagio [a·ˈdaːdʒoː]. *Mus:* **1.** *adv.* adagio, slow. **2.** *s.* **Adagio,** *n.* -s/-s, adagio (movement).

Adam. *Pr.n.m.* -s. **1.** Adam; **der alte A.,** the old Adam, the old man; original sin; **den alten A. ausziehen, ablegen,** to cast off the old Adam, to put off the old man; to mend one's ways; *F:* **A. und Eva spielen,** to undress completely, to strip to the buff. **2.** *F:* **der A.,** (*a*) (*barber's name for*) the razor-strop; (*b*) *Mil: F:* the relief (man).

Adamit [a·da·ˈmiːt], *m.* -en/-en. **1.** *Rel.Hist:* Adamite. **2.** *pl.* **Adamiten** human, beings, *Lit:* sons of men.

adamitisch [a·da·ˈmiːtiʃ], *a.* **1.** Adamic (race, etc.). **2.** *Rel.Hist:* Adamitic.

Adamsapfel, *m.* **1.** *Anat:* Adam's apple. **2.** *Bot: F:* (*a*) banana; (*b*) pompelmoose, shaddock; grapefruit.

Adamsbiß, *m.* = **Adamsapfel** 1.

Adamsbrücke, die. *Geog:* Adam's Bridge (*submerged ridge between Ceylon and India*).

Adamsbutzen, *m.* = **Adamsapfel** 1.

Adamsfeige, *f. Bot:* Egyptian sycamore, oriental sycamore, sycamore-fig.

Adamsholz, *n.* ice-age wood washed up by the sea.

Adamsit [a·damˈziːt], *n.* -(e)s/. *Exp:* adamsite.

Adamskind, *n.* descendant of Adam; human being; **wir sind alle Adamskinder,** we are all descended from Adam.

Adamskostüm, *n.* (*of man*) **im A.,** stark naked, mother naked, in nature's garb, *F:* in his birthday suit.

Adamsnadel, *f. Bot: F:* yucca, *F:* Adam's needle.

adaptabel [a·dapˈtaːbəl], *a.* adaptable.

Adaptation [a·dapta·tsiˈoːn], *f.* -/-en, adaptation, adjustment, accommodation; *esp. Physiol:* adaptation (of the eye).

Adapter [a·ˈdaptər], *m.* -s/-. *El.E: Phot:* adaptor, adapter.

Adaptibilität [a·dapti·bi·li·ˈtɛːt], *f.* -/-en = **Adaptionsfähigkeit.**

adaptieren [a·dapˈtiːrən]. **1.** *v.tr.* to adapt (sth.). **2.** *vbl s.* **Adaptierung,** *f.* (*a*) adapting; (*b*) = **Adaptation.**

Adaption [a·daptsiˈoːn], *f.* -/-en = **Adaptation.**

Adaptionsfähigkeit, *f.* adaptability (*esp. Physiol:* of the eye).

adaptiv [a·dapˈtiːf], *a.* adaptive.

adäquat [adɛ·ˈkvaːt], *a.* adequate, sufficient.

adäquieren [adɛ·ˈkviːrən], *v.tr.* to make (sth.) adequate, sufficient; to equalize.

a dato [a· ˈdaːtoː]. *Lt.prep.phr.* (*abbr.* **a d.**) *Com:* from date.

Addel, *m.* -s/. *Dial: Husb:* liquid manure.

addeln. *Dial:* **1.** *v.i.* (*haben*) (*of cattle*) to stale, urinate. **2.** *v.tr. Husb:* to manure (field) with liquid manure.

Addelpfuhl, *m. Dial: Husb:* urinarium, urinary, liquid-manure pit *or* sump.

Addend [aˈdɛnt], *m.* -en/-en [-ˈdɛndən/-ˈdɛndən]. *Mth:* addend, summand.

Addenda [aˈdɛndaː], *n.pl.* addenda.

Adder, *f.* -/-n. *North G.Dial:* viper, adder.

addierbar [aˈdiːrbaːr], *a.* addible; (sum, etc.) that can be added.

addieren [aˈdiːrən], *v.tr.* to add (a figure, etc.); to add up, cast up, total up, *F:* tot up (figures, expenses, etc.); **falsch a.,** to make a mistake in adding, in addition; **Addierung** *f.* adding, addition.

Addiermaschine, *f.* adding-machine.

Addierwerk, *n.* adding device (in taximeter, etc.).

Addis Abeba [adis ˈaːbe·baː]. *Pr.n.n.* -s. *Geog:* Addis Ababa.

Addition [adi·tsiˈoːn], *f.* -/-en, addition, adding up, totting up; **eine A. ausführen,** to perform an addition.

additional, additionell [adi·tsio·ˈnaːl, -ˈnɛl], *a.*, **Additional-,** *comb.fm.* additional.

additionsfähig, *a.* **1.** = **addierbar. 2.** *Ch:* additive; (compound) capable of addition.

Additionsfehler, *m.* error in addition, mistake in adding.

Additionsmaschine, *f.* adding-machine.

Additionsreaktion, *f. Ch:* additive reaction.

Additionsverbindung, *f. Ch:* addition compound.

Additionszeichen, *n. Mth:* plus (sign).

additiv[1] [adi·ˈtiːf], *a.* additive.

Additiv[2], *n.* -s/-e [-ˈtiːvə]. *Ch: etc:* additive.

Additivität [adi·ti·vi·ˈtɛːt], *f.* -/. *Ch:* additivity.

addizieren [adi·ˈtsiːrən], *v.tr.* **j-m etwas a.,** to adjudge award, allocate, sth. to s.o.

Adduktion [aduktsiˈoːn], *f.* -/-en. *Physiol:* adduction.

Adduktor [aˈduktor], *m.* -s/-en [-ˈtoːrən]. *Anat:* adductor, adducent muscle.

adduzieren [adu·ˈtsiːrən], *v.tr.* **1.** to adduce. **2.** *Physiol:* to adduct (muscle, etc.).

ade [a·ˈdeː]. **1.** *int.* adieu, good-bye, farewell; **j-m ade sagen,** to bid s.o. farewell, adieu; to say good-bye to s.o.; *F:* **das Glück hat mir ade gesagt,** fortune has forsaken me; *A:* **der Welt ade sagen,** (i) to retire from the world, (ii) to depart this life; to die. **2.** *s.* **Ade,** *n.* -s/-s, farewell, good-bye; parting, leave-taking; **als alle Ades gesagt waren,** when all the good-byes had been said.

Adebar, *m.* -s/-e. *Dial: esp. North G:* stork.

Adebarsschnabel, *m. Bot: Dial:* geranium, crane's-bill.

Adel, *m.* -s/-. **1.** nobility (and gentry); aristocracy; **der hohe A.,** (i) the higher nobility, (ii) (*in England*) the nobility, *F:* the peerage; **der niedere A.,** (i) the lesser nobility, (ii) (*in England*) the gentry. **2.** (*a*) noble birth, nobility; **von A. sein,** *A:* **von gutem A. sein, gut von A. sein,** to be of noble descent, of noble birth; **ein Venezianer von A.,** a noble Venetian, a Venetian nobleman; **eine Engländerin von A.,** a titled English lady; **er ist von altem A.,** he belongs to the old nobility; **er ist von hohem A.,** he comes of a titled family; **Familie von altem A.,** gentilitial family; *Prov:* **A. verpflichtet,** the nobly born must nobly do; *noblesse oblige*; (*b*) noble rank, nobility; **j-m den A. verleihen,** to ennoble s.o., raise s.o to noble rank; to confer a title on s.o.; (*in England*) to raise s.o. to the peerage. **3.** nobility, nobleness (of heart, behaviour, style, etc.); **innerer A., A. des Geistes, A. der Gesinnung,** nobility, nobleness, of mind; high-mindedness, noble-mindedness; loftiness of mind; **der A. der Arbeit,** the dignity of labour; *Prov:* **A. sitzt im Gemüt, nicht im Geblüt,** handsome is that, as, handsome does. **4.** *Min:* metallic content (of ore).

Adelaide. *Pr.n.* **1.** [aːdəla·ˈiːdə] *f.* -s. Adelaide. **2.** [ˈædəleːid] *n.* -s. *Geog:* Adelaide.

Adelbeere, *f. Bot: F:* sorb, service-apple.

Adelbonde, *m. Dial:* (*in Schleswig-Holstein*) landed proprietor, landowner.

Adele [a·ˈdeːlə]. *Pr.n.f.* -s. Adela.

Adelesche, *f. Bot: F:* sorb, service-tree.

Adelgras, *n. Bot:* **1.** meadow-grass, *U.S:* spear-grass. **2.** alpine plantain.

Adelheid. *Pr.n.f.* -s. Adelaide.

Adelherr, *m. A:* aristocrat.

adelherrisch, *a. A:* aristocratic, lordly.

Adelhof, *m. Hist:* domain; manor.

Adeliepinguin [a·ˈdeːliə-], *m. Orn:* Adélie penguin.

ad(e)lig, *A:* **ad(e)lich. 1.** *a.* (*a*) noble (pers., family, descent); aristocratic (family); (pers.) of noble birth *or* rank; **er ist a.,** he has a title, he is a noble(man); **sie ist a.,** she is a lady of title, a noblewoman; **er ist nicht a.,** he is a commoner; **von ad(e)liger Geburt,** of noble birth, nobly born, of noble descent; **seine ad(e)lige Geburt mütterlicherseits,** his noble birth on his mother's side; (*b*) of *or* belonging to a noble; **ein ad(e)liges Wappen,** a nobleman's coat of arms; **ein ad(e)liges Gut,** (i) a nobleman's estate, (ii) *Hist:* a domain; a manor; (*c*) noble (heart, sentiments, deeds, figure, etc.); lofty (soul, demeanour, sentiments); high-minded (action, nature). **2.** *s.* **Ad(e)lige,** *m., f.* (*decl. as adj.*) (i) person of noble birth *or* rank; member of the nobility; aristocrat, member of the aristocracy; noble(man), *f.* noblewoman, lady of title; (ii) (*in England*) peer, *f.* peeress; **die Ad(e)ligen,** the nobles; the nobility, the aristocracy; persons of title.

adeln[1]. I. *v.tr.* **1.** to ennoble (s.o.), to raise (s.o.) to noble rank; (*in England*) to raise (s.o.) to the peerage; **kürzlich geadelte Familie,** family recently ennobled. **2.** to ennoble (action, character, etc.); to elevate, uplift (the mind, etc.); *abs.* **(die) Arbeit adelt,** work is ennobling; **die adelnde Gewalt der Poesie,** the ennobling power of poetry; *Prov:* **Tugend adelt,** virtue is the only true nobility; handsome is that, as, handsome does.

II. *vbl s.* **1. Adeln,** *n. in vbl senses.* **2. Adelung,** *f. in vbl senses; also:* ennoblement (*gen.*, of); conferring of a title (*gen.*, on); (*in England*) raising to the peerage.

adeln[2], *v.i.* (*haben*) & *tr. South G.Dial:* = **addeln.**

Adelsanmaßung, *f. Jur:* assumption of a spurious title (of nobility).

Adelsbrief, *m.* patent of nobility.

Adelsbuch, *n.* peerage(-book, -list).

Adelschaft, *f.* -/. (the) nobility; aristocracy; (*in England*) the peerage.

Adelsdiplom, *n.* = **Adelsbrief.**

Adelserhebung, *f.* = **Adelung,** *q.v. under* **adeln**[1] **II.**

Adelsgenossenschaft, *f.* **die Deutsche A.,** the Association of the German Nobility.

Adelsherrschaft, *f.* (government by the) aristocracy.

Adelshof, *m. Hist:* domain; manor.

Adelskammer, . *Hist:* upper chamber, upper house (of legislative assembly); (*in England*) House of Lords, *F:* the Lords.

Adelskrone, *f.* coronet.

Adelslexikon, *n.* = **Adelsbuch.**

Adelsmarschall, *m. Hist:* Earl Marshal.

Adelspartikel, *f.* nobiliary particle (*e.g. the German* **von,** *the French* **de**).

Adelsprobe, *f.* proof(s) of nobility.

Adelsrang, *m.* noble rank.

Adelsregister, *n.* = **Adelsbuch.**

Adelsstand, *m.* nobility; aristocracy; **j-n in den A. erheben,** to ennoble s.o.; to confer a title on s.o.; (*in England*) to raise s.o. to the peerage; **Erhebung einer Person in den A.,** ennoblement of s.o.; conferring of a title on s.o.; (*in England*) raising of s.o. to the peerage.

adelsstolz[1], *a.* proud of one's noble birth *or* rank.

Adelsstolz[2], *m.* pride of birth; aristocratic pride.

Adelstitel, *m.* title (of nobility).

Adelsurkunde, *f.* **1.** = **Adelsbrief. 2.** *pl.* **Adelsurkunden,** titles of nobility.

Adelsverleihung, *f.* ennoblement; conferring of a title.

Adelsverschub, *m. Min:* metallic content (of a lode); grade, content (of ore).

Adeltum, *n.* -s/. aristocracy, nobility; (the) aristocratic world, (the) world of the nobility.

Adelwild, *n. Ven: A:* deer.

Adenitis [a·de·ˈniːtis], *f.* -/. *Med:* adenitis, inflammation of a gland.

adenoid [a·de·no·ˈiːt], *a. Anat:* adenoid; *Med:* **adenoide** [a·de·no·ˈiːdə] **Wucherungen,** adenoid growths, *F:* adenoids.

Adenom [a·de·ˈnoːm], *n.* -s/-e. *Med:* adenoma, glandular tumour.

adenomatös [a·de·no·ma·ˈtøːs], *a. Biol: Med:* adenomatous; glandular.

Adept [aˈdɛpt], *m.* -en/-en, adept.

Ader, *f.* -/-n. **1.** (*a*) *Anat:* vein; artery; blood-vessel; **j-n zur A. lassen, j-m eine, die, A. schlagen, j-m eine A. öffnen,** to bleed s.o., (i) *Med:* to draw, let, blood from s.o.; to phlebotomize s.o.; (ii) *F:* to extort money from s.o.; (*b*) *Med: A: F:* **goldene, güldene, A.,** haemorrhoids, piles. **2.** (*a*) (traffic) artery; (*b*) *El.E:* core, conductor (of a cable). **3.** (*a*) *Bot: Ent:* vein, rib, nerve, nervure (of leaf, insect-wing); (*b*) vein (in wood, marble, etc.); (*c*) *Min:* vein, seam, lode, lead (of metal, etc.); reef (of gold); streak of ore; (*d*) flaw (in glass, gem); cloud (in precious stones). **4.** strand (of rope). **5.** (*a*) trait (of character); streak (in s.o.'s character); **er hat eine falsche A.,** there is a treacherous streak in him; he has a treacherous nature; **es ist keine falsche A. an ihm,** he's a thoroughly honest man, he's as honest as the day; there is not a grain of deceit in him; he's as straight as a die; **sie hat eine leichte A.,** there is a frivolous streak in her; she is inclined to be frivolous; **er hat eine komische A.,** he's a humorous fellow; (*b*) vein, inspiration; talent, gift; **die dichterische, poetische, A.,** the poetic vein, poetic inspiration; **er hat eine musikalische A.,** he has a talent, a gift, a natural bent, for music.

aderblättrig, *a. Bot:* inophyllous.

Aderbruch, *m. Med:* rupture, bursting, of a blood-vessel; **einen A. bekommen,** to burst, rupture, a blood-vessel.

Äderchen, *n.* -/-. (*dim. of* **Ader**) **1.** (*a*) *Anat:* veinlet, venule; arteriole; small vein *or* artery; (*b*) *Ent:* venule (of wing). **2.** *Min:* stringer, thread (of ore).

Aderentzündung, *f. Med:* phlebitis.

aderflügelig, *a. Ent:* hymenopterous.

Aderflügler, *m.pl. Ent:* hymenoptera.

aderförmig, *a.* vein-like; in the form of veins.

Adergeflecht, *n. Anat: Physiol:* vascular plexus, *esp.* choroid plexus.

Adergeschwulst, *f. Med:* angioma.

Aderhaut, *f. Anat:* choroid coat, choroid (of the eye).

Aderhäutchen, *n. Biol: Obst:* chorion.

Aderhautspanner, *m. Anat:* ciliary muscle, choroid muscle.

Aderholz, *n.* wood cut with, along, the grain.

ad(e)rig, äd(e)rig, *a.* (*a*) full of veins; veiny (wood, etc.); veined (marble, etc.); (*b*) *Bot: Ent:* venose (leaf, insect-wing); *Physiol:* vascular (tissue, etc.); (*c*) (*of gem*) flawed; clouded, cloudy.

Aderknoten, Aderkropf, *m. Med:* varix, varicosity; varicose vein.

Aderlaß, *m.* **-lasses/-lässe.** *Med:* bleeding, phlebotomy, venesection, *A:* blood-letting; *Vet:* bleeding.

Aderlaßeisen, *n.* **1.** *Med: A:* lancet. **2.** *Vet:* fleam.

Aderlassen, *n.* **-s/.=Aderlaß.**

Aderlasser, *m.* **-s/-. 1.** *Med:* phlebotomist, *A:* blood-letter. **2.** *Med: Vet:* **=Aderlaßeisen.**

Aderlaßkunst, *f.* (art, technique, of) phlebotomy, venesection.

Aderlaßmann, *m.* **-(e)s/-männer, Aderlaßmännchen,** *n. A.Med:* depiction of the male body showing where blood may be let; blood-letting diagram, blood-letting man.

Aderlaßtechnik, *f.* **=Aderlaßkunst.**

adern, ädern. I. *v.tr.* to make veins on, in (sth.); to vein, grain (door, etc.).

II. *vbl s.* **1. Ädern,** *n. in vbl senses.* **2. Äderung,** *f.* (*a*)=II. 1; (*b*) veining, veins (of wood, marble, etc.); *Bot: Ent:* venation, veining.

Adernetz, *n.* network of veins; *Anat: Physiol:* venous network.

Adernetzschlagader, *m. Anat:* choroid artery.

Aderpresse, *f. Surg:* tourniquet.

aderreich, *a.* full of veins; (richly) veined.

Aderriß, *m. Med:* rupture of an artery, *esp.* through aneurism.

Aderschlag, *m.* **1.** *Physiol:* pulsation, pulse (-beat). **2.** *Med:* **=Aderlaß.**

Äderung, *f. see* **adern, ädern II.**

Aderverkalkung, *f. Med:* arteriosclerosis.

Aderwasser, *n. Physiol:* lymph; blood serum.

Adessiv [adɛˈsiːf], *m.* **-s/-e** [-s/-ˈsiːvə]. *Gram:* adessive (case).

adhärent [athɛˈrɛnt]. **1.** *a.* adherent (**an**+*dat.*, to). **2.** *s.* **Adhärent,** *m.* **-en/-en,** adherent, supporter (of a cause, party, etc.), partisan.

Adhärenz [athɛˈrɛnts], *f.* **-/-en,** (*a*) adherence, adhesion; (*b*) adhering substance; adhesion; appendage.

adhärieren [athɛˈriːrən], *v.i.* (*haben*) to adhere, stick, cling (**an**+*dat.*, to); (*of wheels*) to grip the rails *or* the road, *abs.* to grip.

Adhäsion [athɛziˈoːn], *f.* **-/-en,** adhesion, sticking; *Mec: Med: Surg:* adhesion.

Adhäsionsbahn, *f.* adhesion railway, friction railway.

Adhäsionsfähigkeit, *f.* adhesive capacity, adhesiveness.

Adhäsionskraft, *f.* **1.** force of adhesion. **2.=Adhäsionsfähigkeit.**

Adhäsionsvermögen, *n.***=Adhäsionsfähigkeit.**

adhäsiv [athɛˈziːf], *a.* adhesive.

Adheritanz [atheriˈtants], *f.* **-/.** *Jur:* appointment of an heir.

adheritieren [atheriˈtiːrən], *v.tr. Jur:* to appoint (s.o.) as an heir.

adhibieren [athiˈbiːrən], *v.tr.* to adhibit; to apply, employ (remedies, etc.).

adhortativ [athortaˈtiːf], *a.* hortative, hortatory.

adhortieren [athorˈtiːrən], *v.tr.* to exhort, urge.

Adiabate [adiaˈbaːtə], *f.* **-/-n.** *Ph:* adiabatic curve.

adiabatisch [adiaˈbaːtiʃ], *a. Ph:* adiabatic.

Adiaphora [adiˈaforaː], *n.pl. Phil: Theol:* things indifferent, non-essential things.

adieu [aˈdiøː]. **1.** *int.* good-bye, farewell; **j-m a. sagen,** to say good-bye to s.o., to bid s.o. farewell. **2.** *s.* **Adieu,** *n.* **-s/-s,** farewell, good-bye; parting, leave-taking.

Ädikula [ɛˈdiːkulaː], *f.* **-/-lä.** *Arch:* niche, aedicule.

Ädil [ɛˈdiːl], *m.* **-s & -en/-en.** *Rom.Ant:* aedile.

Ädil(en)amt, *n.* aedileship.

ädilisch [ɛˈdiːliʃ], *a.* aedilitian.

Ädilität [ɛdiliˈtɛːt], *f.* **-/.** aedileship.

adip(id)ieren [adiˈpiːrən, adipiˈdiːrən], *v.tr.* to grease; to render (sth.) greasy.

Adipinsäure [adiˈpiːn-], *f. Ch:* adipic acid.

adipös [adiˈpøːs], *a.* *Physiol:* adipose, fatty (tissue, etc.).

Adipsie [adiˈpsiː], *f.* **-/.** *Med:* adipsy, absence of thirst.

Aditiv [adiˈtiːf], *m.* **-s/-e** [-ˈtiːvə]. *Gram:* aditive (case).

adjazent[1] [atjaˈtsɛnt], *a.* adjacent, contiguous; neighbouring (property, etc.).

Adjazent[2], *m.* **-en/-en. 1.** neighbour. **2.** riverside dweller, riparian, riverain; *Jur:* adjacent owner, riparian owner.

adjazieren [atjaˈtsiːrən], *v.i.* (*haben*) to be adjacent, contiguous.

Adjektion [atjɛktsiˈoːn], *f.* **-/-en.** *Jur:* additional sum (offered).

adjektiv[1] [atjɛkˈtiːf], *a. Tex: etc:* **adjektive Farben, Farbstoffe,** adjective colours, dyes, indirect dyestuffs, acid dyestuffs.

Adjektiv[2] [ˈatjɛktiːf], *n.* **-s/-e** [-tiːvə]. *Gram:* adjective; **als A. gebraucht,** used as an adjective, used adjectivally.

adjektivisch [ˈatjɛktiːviʃ, atjɛkˈtiːviʃ], *a.* adjectival; *adv.* adjectivally; *see also* **Partizip.**

Adjektivsatz, *m. Gram:* adjectival clause.

Adjektivum [atjɛkˈtiːvum], *n.* **-s/-va=Adjektiv**[2].

adjes [adˈjɛs], *int. Dial:*=**adieu 1.**

Adjudikation [atjudikatsiˈoːn], *f.* **-/-en.** *Adm: Com: Jur:* adjudication, allocation, award.

adjudizieren [atjudiˈtsiːrən], *v.tr.* **j-m etwas a.,** to adjudge, award, allocate, sth. to s.o.

Adjunkt [atˈjuŋkt], *m.* **-en/-en,** (*a*) *Adm: Sch: A:* assistant; (*b*) *Austrian:* junior civil servant.

Adjunkte [atˈjuŋktə], *f.* **-/-n.** *Mth:* co-factor.

Adjunktion [atjuŋktsiˈoːn], *f.* **-/-en,** adjunction; adjoining, adding.

adjüs [atˈjys, atˈʃys], *int. Dial:*=**adieu 1.**

Adjustage [atjusˈtaːʒə], *f.* **-/-n.** *Ind:* **1.** finishing; adjusting. **2.** finishing-shop; adjusting shop.

Adjustieramt [atjusˈtiːr-], *n.***=Eichamt.**

adjustieren [atjusˈtiːrən]. **I.** *v.tr.* **1.** (*a*) to adjust, set (apparatus, mechanism, tool, etc.); to regulate (mechanism); **Gewichte a.,** to adjust, to try, weights; (*b*) *Ind:* to true (sth.) up; to finish (piece); to size (piece, coin); to gauge (metal plate, etc.); (*c*) *Artil: etc:* to correct (scale reading). **2.** *Austrian:* to equip (soldier) with uniform and accoutrements.

II. *vbl s.* **1. Adjustieren,** *n. in vbl senses.* **2. Adjustierung,** *f.*=II. 1; *also:* adjustment (of apparatus, etc.); regulation (of a mechanism); *Artil: etc:* **A. (der Skalenablesungen),** scale correction.

Adjustierschraube, *f.* adjusting screw, set screw; regulating screw, regulation screw.

Adjutant [atjuˈtant], *m.* **-en/-en. 1.** *Mil:* (*a*) adjutant; (*b*) (*in Swiss army*) sergeant-major. **2. (persönlicher) A.,** (i) *Mil:* aide-de-camp, *U.S:* aide, (ii) *Navy:* flag-lieutenant.

Adjutantenstelle, *f.* adjutancy; place as adjutant.

Adjutantur [atjutanˈtuːr], *f.* **-/-en.** *Mil:* **1.** adjutancy. **2.** adjutant's office. **3.** *A:* military household (of a sovereign). **4.** branch of the General Staff dealing with administrative routine.

Adlatus [atˈlaːtus], *m.* **-/-ti & -ten,** assistant.

Adler, *m.* **-s/-. 1.** (*a*) *Orn:* eagle; **junger A.,** eaglet; **kühn wie ein A.,** as bold as a lion; *Prov:* **Adler fangen keine Fliegen,** eagles catch no flies; the great do not seek after trifles; (*b*) *Astr:* **der A.,** (the constellation) Aquila. **2.** (*a*) *Her:* eagle; **kleiner A.,** eaglet; **A. mit ausgebreiteten Flügeln,** eagle displayed, spread-eagle; **gestümmelter A.,** alerion, eagle without beak or legs; **A. mit Krallen,** eagle armed; **A. mit Beinen,** eagle membered; (*b*) **der Gasthof zum A.,** *F:* **der A.,** the Eagle hotel, *F:* the Eagle. **3.** *Hist:* eagle, standard; **die römischen Adler,** the Roman eagles; **der schwarze A. Preußens,** the Black Eagle of Prussia. **4.** *Hist:***=Adlerorden.**

Adlerauge, *n.* keen eye, keen sight, *F:* eagle eye; **Adleraugen haben,** to have eyes like a hawk, to be hawk-eyed.

adleräugig, *a.* eagle-eyed; hawk-eyed; keen-eyed.

Adlerbaum, *m. Bot:* aquilaria, eagle-wood tree, aloe.

Adlerbein, *n. Her:* eagle's claw.

Adlerblick, *m.* keen, penetrating, glance; **mit seinem A.,** with his eagle eye.

Adlerbussard, *m. Orn:* long-legged buzzard.

Adlereule, *f. Orn:* eagle-owl.

Adlerfarn, *m. Bot:* bracken, brake, eagle-fern.

Adlerfibel, *f. Prehist: Art:* eagle-brooch.

Adlerfisch, *m. Ich:* meagre, bar.

Adlerflügel, *m.* eagle's wing, *Lit:* eagle's pinion; **mit Adlerflügeln,** eagle-winged.

Adler-Fregattvogel, *m. Orn:* Ascension frigate bird.

Adlerfuß, *m. Her:* eagle's claw winged.

Adlergedanken, *m.pl.* soaring ideas; inspired thoughts.

Adlerholz, *n.* eagle-wood, aloes-wood.

Adlerhorst, *m.* eyrie (of eagle).

Adlerkopf, *m.* eagle's head; *Her:* **gekrönter A.,** eagle crowned.

Adlermöwe, *f. Orn:* black-headed great gull.

Adlernase, *f.* aquiline nose, Roman nose, *F:* eagle's beak.

Adlerorden, *m. Hist:* (*in Prussia, until 1919*) **der Schwarze, der Rote, A.,** the Order of the Black, the Red, Eagle.

Adlerplakette, *f.* plaquette with an eagle design (*esp. as trophy for sport, etc.*).

Adlerpult, *n. Ecc. Art:* lectern with an eagle-shaped rest; eagle.

Adlerrochen, *m. Ich:* eagle-ray, *F:* sea-eagle.

Adlerschild, *m.* shield with an eagle design (*esp. as prize or distinction*).

Adlerstein, *m. Geol:* aetites, eagle-stone.

Adlervitriol, *n.***=Doppelvitriol.**

Adlerzange, *f. Tls: Civ.E: etc:* stone tongs.

ad libitum [at ˈliːbitum]. *Lt.adv.phr. Mus:* ad libitum.

adlig, *a. see* **ad(e)lig.**

Admet [atˈmeːt]. *Pr.n.m.* **-s.** *Gr.Lit:* Admetus.

Administration [atministratsiˈoːn], *f.* **-/-en. 1.** (*a*) administration, direction, management (of business, of public affairs, etc.); (*b*) administration (of town, etc.); (*c*) *Jur:* trusteeship. **2.** (*a*) governing board, board of directors, management; (*b*) government service. **3.** administering, dispensing (of justice, of the sacrament).

Administrations-, *comb.fm.***=Verwaltungs-.**

administrativ [atministraˈtiːf], *a.* administrative; **die administrative** [atministraˈtiːvə] **Staatsgewalt, die Administrative,** the administrative power.

Administrator [atminisˈtraːtor], *m.* **-s/-en** [-straˈtoːrən]. **1.** administrator (of business, parish, etc.). **2.** *Jur:* trustee (of estate, etc.); receiver (in bankruptcy).

administrieren [atminisˈtriːrən], *v.tr.* **1.** to administer, direct, manage, conduct (business, undertaking, estate); to govern (country). **2.** to administer, dispense (justice, the sacrament).

admirabel [atmiˈraːbəl], *a.* admirable, wonderful.

Admiral [atmiˈraːl], *m.* **-s/-e & -räle. 1.** *Navy:* admiral, flag-officer. **2.** *Ent:* red admiral (butterfly). **3.** *Conch:* admiral-shell. **4.** (*drink*) egg-flip, egg-nog (*made with red wine and cloves*).

Admiralität [atmiraliˈtɛːt], *f.* **-/-en.** (*office*) Admiralty, *esp.* the British Admiralty, *U.S:*= the Navy Department.

Admiralitätsanker, *m. Nau:* anchor with a stock.

Admiralitätsgericht, *n.* Court of Admiralty.

Admiralitätsinseln, die. *Pr.n. Geog:* the Admiralty Islands.

Admiralitätskarte, *f. Nau:* admiralty chart.

Admiralitätskollegium, *n.* Board of Admiralty.

Admiralsbarkasse, *f. Navy:* admiral's barge.

Admiralschaft, *f.* **-/-en.** *A:* admiralship; *esp. Hist:* leadership of a body of unprotected merchant vessels.

Admiralschnecke, *f.***=Admiral 3.**

Admiralsschiff, *n. Navy:* flagship.

Admiralstab, *m.* naval staff.

Admiralstabschef, *m.* Chief of the Naval Staff.

Admiration [atmiratsiˈoːn], *f.* **-/.** admiration.

Admission [atmisiˈoːn], *f.* **-/-en. 1.** admission. **2.** *Mch: I.C.E:* admission; intake; inlet; induction.

Admissionsdampf, *m. Mch:* live steam.

admiszieren [atmisˈtsiːrən], *v.tr.* to admix.

admittieren [atmiˈtiːrən], *v.tr.* **1.** to admit; to let (s.o.) in, let (s.o.) enter. **2.** to admit, admit of, permit, allow (sth.).

admonieren [atmoˈniːrən], *v.tr.* to admonish.

Admonition [atmonitsiˈoːn], *f.* **-/-en,** admonition, admonishment.

Adnex [atˈnɛks], *m.* **-es/-e,** (*a*)**=Annex;** (*b*) *Anat:* appendant, appendage, accessory part (of an organ).

Adnexorgane, *n.pl. Anat:* accessory organs, *esp.* the ovary and Fallopian tube.

adnominal [atnomiˈnaːl], *a. Ling:* adnominal.

Adnomination [atnominatsiˈoːn], *f.* **-/-en.** *Rh: Ling:* paronomasia.

ad notam [at ˈnoːtam]. *Lt.adv.phr.* **etwas ad n. nehmen,** to take due note of sth.

ad oculos [at ˈoːkuloːs]. *Lt.adv.phr.* **etwas ad o. demonstrieren,** to give a visible demonstration of sth.; **Demonstration ad o.,** visible demonstration.

Adoleszenz [adolɛsˈtsɛnts], *f.* **-/.** adolescence, youth.

Adolf. *Pr.n.m.* **-s.** Adolphus.

Adonis [aˈdoːnis]. **1.** *Pr.n.m.* **-'.** *Myth:* Adonis. **2.** *m.* **-/-se.** *F:* handsome, good-looking, man, *F:* Adonis; **er ist ein richtiger A.,** he is a regular Adonis; **er ist kein A.,** he is no beauty, *F:* he's no oil-painting. **3.** (*a*) *m.* **-/-.** *Ent:***=Adonisfalter;** (*b*) *f.* **-/-.** *Bot:***=Adonisröschen.**

Adonisblume, *f.***=Adonisröschen.**

adonisch [aˈdoːniʃ], *a.* (*a*) of Adonis; Adonis-like; (*b*) *Pros:* **adonischer Vers,** Adonic verse, Adonic.

Adonisfalter, *m. Ent:* adonis (butterfly); Clifton blue, Clifden blue; mazarine (blue).

Adonisgarten, *m.* (*a*) *Gr.Ant:* garden of Adonis; (*b*) (*set before altar, etc., in Italian church*) miniature flower garden.

Adoniskraut, *n. Bot:* adonis vernalis, spring pheasant's-eye.

Adonisröschen, *n. Bot:* adonis, pheasant's-eye.

Adoptator [adop'taːtor], *m.* **-s/-en** [-ta·'toːrən]. *Jur:* adopter; adoptive parent.

adoptierbar [adop'tiːrbaːr], *a.* adoptable.

adoptieren [adop'tiːrən], *v.tr.* **1.** to adopt (child). **2.** to adopt, take up, embrace (a cause); to adopt, take over (an organisation, s.o.'s ideas, etc.).

Adoptierte [adop'tiːrtə], *m., f.* (*decl. as adj.*) adopted child, adoptive child; *Jur:* adoptee.

Adoption [adoptsi'oːn], *f.* **-/-en,** adoption.

adoptiv [adop'tiːf], *a.,* **Adoptiv-,** *comb.fm.* adoptive . . . , adopted . . . ; **Adoptivkind** *n,* **Adoptivsohn** *m,* **Adoptivtochter** *f,* adopted, adoptive, child, son, daughter; **Adoptiveltern** *pl,* adoptive parents, *Jur:* adopters; **Adoptivvater** *m,* **Adoptivmutter** *f,* adoptive father, mother; *Jur:* adopter; **Adoptivbruder** *m,* **Adoptivschwester** *f,* adoptive brother, sister; brother, sister, by adoption.

adoral [ado·'raːl], *a. Nat.Hist:* adoral; situated near the mouth.

Adorant [ado·'rant], *m.* **-en/-en,** (*a*) adorer, worshipper, votary (of a god); (*b*) *Art:* praying figure.

Adoration [ado·ra·tsi'oːn], *f.* **-/-en. 1.** adoration, worship (of a god). **2.** *R.C.Ch:* adoration (of the Cross, of the Pope).

adorieren [ado·'riːrən], *v.tr.* to adore, worship (a god).

adossieren [ado'siːrən], *v.tr.* to slope, bank up (earth, etc.).

adoucieren [adu·'siːrən]. I. *v.tr.* **1.** to sweeten (medicine, etc.); to edulcorate (powdered substance, etc.). **2.** to soften, tone down (colour). **3.** *Metall:* (*a*) to anneal, temper; (*b*) to soften (iron, steel); (*c*) to decarbonize, decarburize (cast iron).

II. *vbl s.* **Adoucieren,** *n. in vbl senses; also:* decarbonization, decarburization (of cast iron).

Adoucierofen [adu·'siːr-], *m. Metall:* annealing furnace, tempering-furnace.

ad referendum [at re·fe·'rɛndum]. *Lt.adv.phr.* (*abbr.* **ad. ref.**) *Adm:* 'for information.'

Adrenalin [adre·na·'liːn], *n.* **-s/.** *Med:* adrenalin.

adrenocorticotrop [a·ˌdreːno·korti·ko·'troːp], *a. Physiol:* **adrenocorticotropes Hormon,** adrenocorticotropic hormone (ACTH).

Adressant [adrɛ'sant], *m.* **-en/-en,** sender, addresser, originator (of letter); forwarder (of parcel, goods); consignor (of goods).

Adressat [adrɛ'saːt], *m.* **-en/-en,** addressee, recipient (of letter, etc.); consignee (of goods).

Adreßbuch [a'drɛs-], *n.* (*a*) (postal) directory; (*b*)=**Adressenbuch.**

Adreßbüro, *n.*=**Adressenbüro.**

Adreßdebatte, *f.* (*in British Parliament*) debate on the Address.

Adresse [a'drɛsə], *f.* **-/-n. 1.** (*a*) address (of pers., letter); direction, destination (of letter); **wie lautet Ihre A.?** what is your address? **dieser Brief ist an Ihre A. (gerichtet),** this letter is directed, addressed, to you; **schreibe mir per A.** (*occ.* **unter A.**) **Frau X, p.A. Frau X,** write to me care of Mrs X, c/o Mrs X, *U.S:* in care of Mrs X; **einen Brief an die betreffende A. befördern,** to forward a letter to its destination; **der Brief ist endlich an die richtige A. gelangt,** the letter reached its destination at last; *F:* **diese Bemerkung war an Ihre A. gerichtet,** that remark was directed at you; **Sie sind an die falsche A. gekommen,** you have mistaken your man; you have come to the wrong person, *F:* to the wrong shop; (*b*) *Computing:* address. **2.** (formal) address (to assembly *or* personage); address of congratulation, condolence, etc.; **j-m eine A. überreichen,** to present an address to s.o. **3.** *A:* skill, dexterity, adroitness, *A:* address.

Adressenbuch, *n.* address-book.

Adressenbüro, *n.* **1.** address bureau, information bureau. **2.** registry office.

Adressenheft, *n.* address-book.

adressieren [adrɛ'siːrən], *v.tr.* **1.** (*a*) to address, direct (letter, parcel, etc.); to label (parcel); to consign (goods) (**an**+*acc.,* to); **falsch adressierter Brief,** misdirected letter; (*b*) *Nau:* **ein Schiff an j-n a.,** to address a ship to s.o. **2. sich an j-n adressieren,** to address oneself, to apply, to s.o.

Adressiermaschine, *f.* addressing-machine; addressograph.

Adreßkarte, *f.* business card.

Adreßrecht, *n. Pol: A:* right of address (to the monarch).

Adreßzettel, *m.* label; docket.

adrett [a'drɛt], *a.* **1.** dext(e)rous, deft, skilful, handy; smart, sharp, wide-awake. **2.** *F:* (*of pers., dress*) neat, smart, *F:* natty; (*of pers.*) dapper, spruce, trim, well turned out, spick and span; **sie war a. wie ein Püppchen,** she was as neat as a new pin, she looked as if she had just stepped out of a bandbox.

Adria, die ['aːdri·aː]. *Pr.n.* **-.** *Geog:* the Adriatic.

Adrianopel [a·dri·a·'noːpəl]. *Pr.n.n.* **-s.** *Geog:* Adrianople.

Adrianopelrot, *n. Dy:* Turkey red, Adrianople red.

adriatisch [a·dri·'aːtiʃ], *a. Geog:* Adriatic; **das Adriatische Meer,** the Adriatic.

adrig, ädrig, *a. see* **ad(e)rig, äd(e)rig.**

Adrittura [adri'tuːraː], *n.* **-/.** *Com:* direct drawing of a bill.

Adscharien [at'ʃaːrĭən], **Adscharistan** [at'ʃaːrista·n]. *Pr.n.n.* **-s.** *Geog:* Adzharia.

adskribieren [atskri·'biːrən], *v.tr.* to ascribe; to append, add (sth.) (to document, etc.).

Adskription [atskriptsi'oːn], *f.* **-/-en,** ascription; addition (to document, etc.).

adskriptiv [atskrip'tiːf], *a.* ascriptitious; appended, added (to document, etc.).

Adsorbat [atzor'baːt], *n.* **-(e)s/-e.** *Ph:* adsorbate.

adsorbieren [atzor'biːrən], *v.tr. Ph:* to adsorb.

Adsorption [atzorptsi'oːn], *f.* **-/-en.** *Ph:* adsorption.

Adstringens [at'striŋgɛns], *n.* **-/-genzien** & **-gentien** [-'gɛntsĭən] & **-gentia** [-'gɛntsĭa]. *Med:* astringent.

adstringieren [atstriŋ'giːrən], *v.tr.* to astringe; *abs.* **a.,** to act as an astringent, to have an astringent effect; *Med:* **adstringierendes Mittel,** astringent.

Äduer ['ɛːdŭər], *m.* **-s/-.** *Hist:* Aeduan; **die Äduer,** the Aedui.

Adular [a·du·'laːr], *m.* **-s/-e.** *Miner: Lap:* adularia, moonstone.

Adultera [a'dultəraː], *f.* **-/-rä.** *A:* adulteress.

adumbrieren [adum'briːrən], *v.tr.* **1.** to adumbrate; to sketch out, outline (plan, etc.). **2.** *Lit:* to palliate, gloss over (faults).

A-dur, A-Dur, *n. Mus:* (key of) A major.

Advaloremzoll [atva·'loːrɛm-], *m. Cust:* ad valorem duty.

Advent [at'vɛnt], *m.* **-(e)s/-e. 1.** *Ecc:* Advent. **2.** *Theol: A:* advent (of Christ); coming (of the Messiah).

Adventist [atvɛn'tist], *m.* **-en/-en.** *Rel.Hist:* Adventist; **A. des siebenten Tags,** Seventh-day Adventist.

adventiv [atvɛn'tiːf], *a.,* **Adventiv-,** *comb.fm.* adventitious, (*a*) casual, accidental; (*b*) accessory.

Adventivauge, *n. Bot:*=**Adventivknospe.**

Adventivfieder, *f. Bot:* accessory pinna.

Adventivknospe, *f. Bot:* adventitious bud.

Adventivpflanze, *f. Bot:* adventitious weed, casual weed.

Adventivwurzel, *f. Bot:* adventitious root.

Adventskranz, *m. Folkl:* Advent garland (*usu. made of fir-twigs*).

Advent(s)sonntag, *m.* Advent Sunday.

Adventszeit, *f.* Advent (season); **in der A.,** during Advent.

Adverb [at'vɛrp], *n.* **-s/-ien** [-'vɛrbĭən]. *Gram:* adverb; **als A. gebraucht,** used adverbially.

adverbial [atvɛrbi'aːl], *a. Gram:* adverbial; **adverbiale Bestimmung,** adverbial element; adverbial phrase; *adv.* adverbially.

Adverbialsatz, *m. Gram:* adverbial clause.

Adverbium [at'vɛrbĭum], *n.* **-s/-bia** & **-bien**=**Adverb.**

Adversarien [atvɛr'zaːrĭən], *n.pl.* (*a*) jottings; rough notes; (*b*) *Com:* day-book; *A:* waste-book.

adversativ [atvɛrza·'tiːf], *a. Gram:* adversative (conjunction, etc.).

Advokat [atvo·'kaːt], *m.* **1. -en/-en,** (*a*) lawyer; *Prov:* **gute Advokaten, schlechte Nachbarn,** a good lawyer makes a bad neighbour; (*b*) *Jur:* (*now generally superseded by the appellation* **Anwalt,** *q.v.*) barrister(-at-law), counsel, *Scot:* advocate; **beratender A.,** counsel in chambers, chamber-counsel, consulting barrister; (*c*) pleader, advocate, intercessor. **2. -s/-,** advokaat (liqueur); brandy with egg-yolks.

Advokatenbirne, *f. Bot:* avocado pear, alligator pear.

Advokatengebühr, *f.* lawyer's fee.

Advokatengriff, *m. A:*=**Advokatenkniff.**

Advokatenhonorar, *n.* lawyer's fee; retainer.

Advokatenkniff, *m. F:* lawyer's trick, legal trick; piece of sharp practice.

Advokatenkunststück, *n. F:* (*a*)=**Advokatenkniff;** (*b*) piece of special pleading.

Advokatenstand, der, the bar; *F:* the legal profession.

Advokatenzunft, die, (*a*) *A:*=**Advokatenstand;** (*b*) *Pej:* the legal fraternity; attorneydom.

advokatorisch [atvo·ka·'toːriʃ], *a.* advocatory; (activity, etc.) of, as, a barrister.

Advokatur [atvo·ka·'tuːr], *f.* **-/-en. 1.** advocacy. **2.**=**Advokatenstand. 3.** *occ.* (barrister's) practice.

Adynamie [a·dy·na·'miː], *f.* **-/.** *Med:* adynamia; prostration.

adynamisch [a·dy·'naːmiʃ], *a. Med: Ph:* adynamic.

Adyton ['aːdy·ton], *n.* **-s/-ta,** (*a*) *Gr.Ant:* adytum; (*b*) *Ecc:* holy of holies.

Ae-, ae- [ɛ·-]. *Tg: occ. Print:*=**Ä-, ä-.**

aeriform [a·e·ri·'form], *a.* aeriform; gaseous.

aerob [a·e·'roːp], *a. Biol:* aerobic, aerobian (organism).

Aerobat [a·e·ro·'baːt], *m.* **-en/-en,** tight-rope walker; acrobat.

Aerobion [a·e·'roːbion], *n.* **-s/-bien, Aerobiont** [a·e·ro·bi'ont], *m.* **-en/-en.** *Biol:* aerobe.

aerobiontisch [a·e·ro·bi'ontiʃ], **aerobisch** [a·e·'roːbiʃ], *a.*=**aerob.**

Aerobium [a·e·'roːbĭum], *n.* **-s/-bien**=**Aerobion.**

Aerodynamik [a·e·ro·dy·'naːmik], *f.* **-/.** aerodynamics.

aerodynamisch [a·e·ro·dy·'naːmiʃ], *a.* aerodynamic.

Aerogengas [a·e·ro·'geːn-], *n. Ch:* aerogene gas.

Aerogramm [a·e·ro·'gram], *n.* **-(e)s/-e.** *Post: Austrian:* air letter, aerogramme.

Aerograph [a·e·ro·'graːf], *m.* **-en/-en,** aerographer.

Aerographie [a·e·ro·gra·'fiː], *f.* **-/.** aerography.

Aeroklinoskop [a·e·ro·kli·no·'skoːp], *n.* **-(e)s/-e.** *Meteor:* aerograph; storm-warning device.

Aeroklub [a·'eːro·-], *m.* Aero (Sports) Club, Flying Club.

Aerolith [a·e·ro·'liːt], *m.* **-(e)s/-e.** *Meteor:* aerolite, aerolith, meteorite.

Aerologie [a·e·ro·lo·'giː], *f.* **-/.** aerology; meteorology.

Aeromechanik [a·e·ro·me·'çaːnik], *f.* **-/.** aerodynamics and aerostatics.

Aerometer [a·e·ro·'meːtər], *n.* **-s/-.** *Ph:* aerometer, air-poise.

Aeronaut [a·e·ro·'naut], *m.* **-en/-en. 1.** *A:* aeronaut. **2.** aeronautics expert.

Aeronautik [a·e·ro·'nautik], *f.* **-/.** aeronautics.

aeronautisch [a·e·ro·'nautiʃ], *a.* aeronautical.

Aerophagie [a·e·ro·fa·'giː], *f.* **-/.** *Med:* aerophagia.

Aerophobie [a·e·ro·fo·'biː], *f.* **-/.** aerophobia; dislike of fresh air.

Aerophor [a·e·ro·'foːr], *m.* **-s/-e,** breathing apparatus, *esp.* underwater breathing apparatus.

Aerophyt [a·e·ro·'fyːt], *m.* **-en/-en.** *Bot:* epiphyte.

Aeroplan [a·e·ro·'plaːn], *m.* **-(e)s/-e.** *A:* aeroplane, aircraft.

Aeroskop [a·e·ro·'skoːp], *n.* **-(e)s/-e.** *Bac: Meteor:* aeroscope.

Aeroskopie [a·e·ro·sko·'piː], *f.* **-/-n** [-'piːən], aeroscopy.

Aerostat [a·e·ro·'staːt], *m.* **-(e)s/-e,** aerostat; lighter-than-air craft.

Aerostatik [a·e·ro·'staːtik], *f.* **-/.** aerostatics.

Aerotherapie [a·e·ro·te·ra·'piː], *f.* **-/.** aerotherapeutics.

Aetit [a·e·'tiːt], *m.* **-(e)s/-e.** *Geol:* aetites, eaglestone.

affabel [a'faːbəl], *a.* affable, kindly, gracious.

Affabilität [afa·bi·li·'tɛːt], *f.* **-/.** affability, graciousness.

Affäre [a'fɛːrə], *f.* **-/-n. 1.** (*a*) (serious, difficult) affair, business; **sich aus der A. ziehen,** to get out of one's difficulties, *F:* to save one's bacon; to get out from under; (*b*) (love) affair. **2.** *A:* (*a*) duel; affair (of honour); (*b*) *Mil:* engagement, encounter.

Äffchen, *n.* **-s/-,** (*dim. of* **Affe**) (*a*) young, small, monkey; young ape; (*b*) (*little girl*) vain little monkey; pert little creature.

Affe, *m.* **-n/-n. 1.** (*a*) *Z:* (**großer, schwanzloser**) **A.,** ape; (**langschwänziger**) **A.,** monkey; (*b*) *F:* **frieren wie ein A.,** to be frozen stiff, to be frozen to the marrow; **er saß da wie der A. auf dem Stangenbohrer, auf dem Schleifstein,** he sat there like a monkey on a stick; **er sah aus wie der A. im Frack,** he was ridiculously overdressed; **eitel wie ein A.,** as vain as a peacock; **er rannte wie ein vergifteter, wildgewordener, A.,** he ran off like a scalded cat; **ich dachte, mich laust der A.,** I was completely flabbergasted; you could have knocked me down with a feather. **2.** *F:* (*a*) ape, imitator; (*b*) fool, clown, simpleton; conceited ass; jackanapes; fop; **ein alter A.,** a silly old fool; **kommt dieser A. auch?** is that idiot coming too? **du A.!** you clown! you

big ape! *Prov:* **jeder A. liebt seine Jungen,** all parents are fools about their children. **3.** *F:* (*a*) **seinen Affen füttern, seinem Affen Zucker geben,** to be in a carefree, sprightly, exuberant, irresponsible, mood; to let oneself go; *Pej:* to have a fit of silliness; (*b*) **einen Affen an j-m gefressen haben,** to be infatuated with, to dote upon, s.o.; *F:* to be keen on, gone on, s.o., to have a crush on s.o.; (*c*) **einen Affen haben,** to be drunk, tipsy, *F:* tight; **einen kleinen Affen haben,** to be half-seas-over; **sich einen Affen kaufen,** to get drunk, *F:* to (go and) get tight. **4.** *Mil: F:* knapsack; (soldier's) pack. **5.** *Draw: F:* pantograph, pantagraph.

Affekt [a'fɛkt], *m.* **-(e)s/-e. 1.** emotion; passion; **im A. gesprochene Worte, im A. gefaßtes Urteil,** words spoken in anger; judgment formed in the heat of the moment; impulsive words, judgment; **im A. begangene Tat,** deed committed under the impulse of, in the heat of, the moment; *esp.* crime due to jealousy; *crime passionel*; **mit A. gesprochene Worte,** words spoken with emotion, with warmth (of feeling); *A:* **die Affekte,** the emotions. **2.** *Ling:* emotive charge, emotive associations (of word).

Affektation [afɛkta·tsĭ'o:n], *f.* **-/-en,** (*a*) affectation, pretence; (*b*) affectedness.

affektbeladen, *a. Ling:* (word) charged with emotive associations.

Affektbetonung, *f. Ling:* emphatic stress.

Affekthandlung, *f.* act motivated by anger, fear, despair.

affektieren [afɛk'ti:rən], *v.tr.* to affect, pretend, feign, simulate.

affektiert [afɛk'ti:rt], *a.* (*a*) affected; **das Affektierte an seinem Stil,** the affectedness of his style; the affectations of his style; (*b*) affected, pretended, feigned, simulated (indifference, interest, etc.).

Affektiertheit, *f.* affectedness, affectation.

Affektion [afɛktsĭ'o:n], *f.* **-/-en. 1.** affection, fondness, liking, attachment (**für,** for); *A:* **j-n, etwas, in A. nehmen,** to become attached, to take a fancy, to s.o., sth. **2.** *Med:* affection, disease, complaint.

affektioniert [afɛktsĭo·'ni:rt], *a.* affectionate, loving; *A:* (*at end of letter*) **Ihr wohl affektionierter . . . ,** your affectionate . . . , affectionately yours . . .

Affektionswert, *m.* sentimental value.

affektiv [afɛk'ti:f], *a.* affective; emotional, emotive.

Affektivität [afɛkti·vi·'tɛ:t], *f.* **-/.** susceptibility; emotional sensitivity.

affektlos, *a.* **1.** dispassionate, unimpassioned. **2.** *Ling:* (word) without emotive associations.

Affektlosigkeit, *f.* **1.** dispassionateness. **2.** *Ling:* absence of emotive associations.

äffen, *v.tr.* **1.** to ape, mimic (s.o.); to take (s.o.) off. **2.** (*a*) to mock, make fun of, make game of, make sport of (s.o.); to poke fun at (s.o.); to chaff, banter (s.o.); (*b*) to fool, gull, dupe (s.o.); to hoax (s.o.); to take (s.o.) in.

Affenadler, *m. Orn:* monkey-eating eagle.

Affenart, *f.* **1.** variety, species, of monkey *or* ape. **2.** *adv.phr.* **nach A.,** like a monkey, like monkeys; like an ape, like apes; monkey-fashion; ape-fashion.

affenartig, *a.* **1.** *Z:* simian (type, etc.). **2.** monkey-like, ape-like; apish (face, grimace, etc.); *F:* **mit affenartiger Geschwindigkeit,** with lightning speed, like lightning, *F:* like greased lightning. **3.** *adv.* like an ape; apishly; like a monkey; monkey-fashion.

Affenbeere, *f. Bot: F:* (*a*) crowberry, heath-berry; (*b*) whortleberry, bilberry.

Affenblume, *f. Bot:* mimulus, monkey-flower.

Affenbrotbaum, *m. Bot:* baobab(-tree), monkey-bread.

Affenfratze, *f.* (*a*) monkey-like, ape-like, apish, grimace; (*b*)=**Affengesicht.**

Affengang, *m. Gym:* (the) elephant-walk.

Affengeschlecht, *n.* tribe, family, of monkeys *or* apes; **das A.,** the simian race.

Affengesicht, *n.* monkey-like, ape-like, apish, face, *F:* monkey-face.

affenhaft, *a.*=**affenartig.**

Affenhaus, *n.* monkey-house; apery.

Affenhaut, *f. Tex:* frieze.

Affenhitze, *f. F:* insufferable, scorching, heat; **es war eine A. an dem Tag,** it was a scorching hot day, the day was baking-hot.

Affenhocke, *f. Gym:* monkey-crouch.

Affenjäckchen, *n.* (*a*) (circus monkey's) short jacket; (*b*) *F:* short jacket, *F:* monkey-jacket (*worn by hussar, waiter, etc.*); (schoolboy's) Eton jacket.

affenjung, *a. A:* very young (and inexperienced); of tender years.

Affenkäfig, *m.*=**Affenhaus.**

Affenkasten, *m.* (*a*)=**Affenhaus;** (*b*) *F:* **dieses Büro ist der reinste A.,** this office is like the monkey-house at the zoo.

Affenklettern, *n. Gym:* climbing monkey-fashion (using the soles of the feet).

Affenkomödie, *f.* **1.**=**Affenpossen. 2.** *F:*= **Affentanz.**

Affenkönig, *m. Z:* coaita, red-faced spider-monkey.

Affenliebe, *f. F:* ridiculously exaggerated affection; **sie hat eine A. zu ihren Kindern,** she dotes upon her children.

affenmäßig, *a.*=**affenartig.**

Affenmensch, *m.* **1.** *Paleont:* pithecanthrope; (Java) ape-man; *F:* the 'missing link'. **2.** *Ter:* microcephalus, microcephalic.

Affennase, *f.* pug-nose.

affennasig, *a.* pug-nosed.

Affenparadies, *n.* (*at zoo*) walled-in *or* ditched-in enclosure for monkeys; monkey-run.

Affenpinscher, *m.* **1.** *Breed:* griffon (terrier). **2.** *F:* silly fool.

Affenpossen, *f.pl.* (apish) antics; monkey-tricks, *U.S:* monkey-shines; buffoonery, tomfoolery, clownery.

Affenschande, *f. F:* **es ist eine A.!** it's a (proper) scandal! it's a sin and a shame! **es ist eine A., daß . . . ,** it's a crying shame that . . .

Affenschaukeln, *f.pl. F:* (*young girl's hair-style*) looped plaits.

Affenschwanz, *m.* **1.** monkey's tail. **2.** *F:* endless string (of words, excuses, etc.); rigmarole (of words). **3.** *F:* (silly) idiot.

Affenspektakel, *m.* hullabaloo, uproar.

Affenspiel, *n.*=**Affenpossen.**

Affenstreich, *m.* apish trick; silly, stupid, clownish, trick; piece of buffoonery, of tomfoolery, of clownery; *pl.* monkey-tricks.

Affentanz, *m.*, **Affentheater,** *n. F:* ludicrous, farcical, performance; **die Sitzung war ein richtiges Affentheater,** the meeting was an utter farce, was sheer foolery.

Affentopf, *m. Bot:* (*a*) monkey-pot; (*b*) monkey-pot (tree), sapucaia(-tree).

Affenvolk, *n.* (*a*) (crowd of) monkeys *or* apes; (*b*) simian race.

Affenweibchen, *n. Z:*=**Äffin.**

Affenzahn [ˌafən'tsa:n], *m.* (*usu. only in phr.*) *F:* **mit einem A.,** at a breakneck speed; **einen A. draufhaben,** to go at a breakneck speed.

Äfferei, *f.* **-/-en,** (*a*) (monkey-like, grotesque) imitation; (*b*) apishness; (*c*) mockery, banter.

Affiche [a'fi:ʃə], *f.* **-/-n,** placard; poster, bill.

Afficheur [afi·'ʃø:r], *m.* **-s/-e,** bill-sticker, bill-poster.

affichieren [afi·'ʃi:rən], *v.tr.* to post (up), stick (up), placard (notice); *abs.* **a.,** to post (up) bills; to stick bills.

Affidat [afi·'da:t], *m.* **-en/-en.** *Hist:* liegeman, vassal.

Affidavit [afi·'da:vit], *n.* **-s/-s.** *Jur:* affidavit.

affig, *a.* (*a*)=**äffisch;** (*b*) affected; mincing; (*of man*) foppish; **affiges Wesen,** affected, *F:* la-di-da, manner.

affigieren [afi·'gi:rən], *v.tr.* (*a*) to affix; (*b*)= **affichieren.**

Affigkeit, *f.* affectedness, affectation; foppishness, foppery.

Affiliation [afi·lĭa·tsĭ'o:n], *f.* **-/-en. 1.** affiliation (**an**+*acc.*, to, with). **2.** *Jur:* adoption (of child).

affiliieren [afi·li·'i:rən], *v.tr.* **1.** to affiliate (*dat.*, to, with). **2.** *Jur:* to adopt (child). **3. ein Ehrenzeichen einem Orden a.,** to attach a decoration to an order.

affin [a'fi:n], *a. Mth: Geom:* affine (transformation); *adv.* **a. ähnlich,** in a corresponding ratio.

Äffin, *f.* **-/-innen.** *Z:* she-monkey, female monkey; she-ape, female ape; *F:* **eine alte Ä.,** a silly old fool.

Affinade [afi·'na:də], *f.* **-/-n.** *Sug-R:* washed sugar.

Affinage [afi·'na:ʒə], *f.* **-/-n, Affination** [afi·na·tsĭ'o:n], *f.* **-/-en,** (re)fining (of precious metals); refining (of sugar, etc.).

Affinerie [afi·nə'ri:], *f.* **-/-n** [-'ri:ən]. **1.**= **Affinage. 2.** refinery, *esp.* metal (re)finery.

Affinieranstalt [afi·'ni:r-], *f.*=**Affinerie 2.**

affinieren [afi·'ni:rən]. **I.** *v.tr. Ind:* to refine; *esp.* to (re)fine (gold) with sulphuric acid; to refine (raw sugar) by washing.

II. *vbl s.* **Affinieren** *n.*, **Affinierung** *f.*= **Affinage.**

affiniert [afi·'ni:rt], *a. Metall: etc:* refined (gold, etc.).

Affinierwasser, *n. Ind:* caustic water; washing fluid; solvent.

Affinität [afi·ni·'tɛ:t], *f.* **-/-en,** affinity (**mit, zu,** with, to); (*a*) relationship by marriage; (*b*) resemblance, similarity of character; **A. zweier Dinge miteinander,** affinity between two things; (*c*) *Ch:* **A. für einen Körper,** affinity for a body.

Affirmation [afirma·tsĭ'o:n], *f.* **-/-en,** affirmation; assurance.

affirmativ [afirma·'ti:f], *a.* affirmative; *adv.* affirmatively, in the affirmative.

Affirmativa [afirma·'ti:va:], *n.pl. Gram:* affirmative forms.

Affirmative [afirma·'ti:və], *f.* **-/-n,** (*a*) *Gram: etc:* affirmative; (*b*) affirmative opinion; assent, acquiescence.

affirmieren [afir'mi:rən], *v.tr.* to affirm; to state (sth.) positively.

äffisch, *a.* apish; ape-like; monkey-like; **äffisches Wesen,** apishness.

Affix [a'fiks], *n.* **-es/-e.** *Ling:* affix.

Affixion [afiksĭ'o:n], *f.* **-/-en.** *Ling: etc:* affixion, affixture.

Affixum [a'fiksum], *n.* **-s/-xa**=**Affix.**

affizierbar [afi·'tsi:rba:r], *a.* susceptible, impressionable; sensitive; easily moved, easily affected.

Affizierbarkeit, *f.* susceptibility, impressionability, impressibility; sensitivity.

affizieren [afi·'tsi:rən], *v.tr.* (*a*) to affect, move, touch (s.o.); **er ist leicht affiziert,** he is easily moved, easily affected; he is emotional; (*b*) *Med:* to affect (an organ, etc.); **die Lunge ist leicht affiziert,** the lung is slightly affected; **Affizierung** *f*, affection.

Affluenz [aflu·'ɛnts], *f.* **-/-en. 1.** flowing, flood (of water, etc.). **2.** affluence, abundance, plenty.

affluieren [aflu·'i:rən], *v.i.* (*sein*) to flow in.

Affner, *m.* **-s/-.** *Tex: F:* reed, slay.

Affodill [afo·'dil], *m.* **-s/-e.** *Bot:* asphodel; **weißer A.,** king's spear, silver rod; **zweigblütentragender A.,** branched lily, king's rod.

Affodill-Lilie, *f. Bot:* hemerocallis, day-lily.

Affrikata, Affrikate [afri·'ka:ta:, -tə], *f.* **-/-ten & -tä.** *Ling:* affricate, affricative.

Affront [a'frõ:, a'front], *m.* **-s/-s** [a'frõ:s] **& -e** [a'frontə], affront, indignity, insult, snub, slight, *F:* slap in the face; **das ist ein A.!** it's an insult! **j-m einen A. antun,** to insult s.o.; to slight s.o.; to snub s.o.; to put an affront upon s.o., to offer an affront to s.o.

affrontieren [afron'ti:rən] *v.tr.* to insult (s.o.) openly, to affront (s.o.).

affrös [a'frø:s], *a.* frightful, hideous, atrocious, ghastly (appearance, dress, etc.).

Afghane [af'ga:nə], *m.* **-n/-n, Afghanin,** *f.* **-/-innen.** *Ethn:* Afghan.

afghanisch [af'ga:niʃ], *a.* Afghan.

Afghanistan [af'ga:nistan]. *Pr.n.n.* **-s.** *Geog:* Afghanistan.

à fonds perdu [a 'fõ: pɛr'dy:]. *Fr.adv.phr. Fin:* without right to repayment of the capital; outright (payment, subsidy, etc.) (*with no expectation of repayment or compensation*); **Leibrente à fonds perdu,** life annuity without repayment of capital.

Afrika ['afri·ka:]. *Pr.n.n.* **-s.** *Geog:* Africa.

Afrika(a)nder [a·fri·'ka:ndər], *m.* **-s/-** *Geog:* Afrikander, Afrikaner, *esp.* Boer.

Afrikaans [afri·'ka:ns], *n.* **-/.** *Ling:* Afrikaans, Cape Dutch, 'the taal'.

afrikaansch [afri·'ka:nʃ]. **1.** *a.* Afrikaans, Afrikander. **2.** *s.* **Afrikaansch,** *n. Ling:* Afrikaans, Cape Dutch, 'the taal'.

Afrikafeldzug, der. *Mil.Hist:* the African campaign.

Afrikaforscher, *m.* (*a*) African explorer, explorer of Africa; (*b*) research worker in the field of African ethnology, etc.

Afrikane [afri·'ka:nə], *f.* **-/-n.** *Bot:* African marigold.

Afrikaner [afri·'ka:nər], *m.* **-s/-.** *Ethn: Geog:* African.

afrikanisch [afri·'ka:niʃ], *a.* African.

Afrikareisende, *m.* African explorer, traveller; traveller in Africa.

afro-asiatisch [afro·ˀa·zĭ'a:tiʃ], *a.* Afro-Asian.

aft, *adv. Nau:*=**achter(n).**

After[1], *m.* **-s/-. 1.** (*a*) *Anat:* anus; (*b*) *F:* bottom. **2.** back (of saddle).

After[2], *n.* **-s/-.** *A:* (*a*) waste matter; residue; *Butchery: Mill:* offal; *Mill: Min:* tailings; (*b*) excrement, ordure, dung.

After-, *comb.fm.* **1.** *Anat: Nat.Hist:* anal . . . ; **Afterborste** *f,* anal bristle. **2.** (*a*) rear(ward) . . . , back . . . ; **Aftertür** *f,* back door, rear door;

(b) subsequent...; after-; **Afterzeit** f, after-time; (c) secondary...; **Afterbildung** f, secondary growth. 3. residual..., waste...; **Afterholz** n, waste wood. 4. false..., spurious..., pseudo-; **Afterberedsamkeit** f, spurious eloquence; **Afteraufklärung** f, pseudo-enlightenment.

Afterahorn, m. Bot: sycamore (maple), great maple.

Afteranhang, m. Ent: anal appendage; cercus.

Afteranwalt, m. unqualified lawyer, hedge lawyer.

Afterarzt, m. quack (doctor).

Afterassel, f. Crust: anisopod.

Afterbein, n. Nat.Hist: spurious leg.

afterbelehnen, v.tr. insep. Hist: to enfeoff (s.o.) as an under-vassal.

Afterbelehnte, m. (decl. as adj.) Hist:=Afterlehnsmann.

Afterbiene, f. Ent: andraena, solitary bee.

Afterbildung, f. 1. Med: etc: malformation. 2. Biol: etc: secondary formation, secondary growth. 3. pseudo-culture, pseudo-education.

Afterblatt, n. Bot: stipule.

Afterblattlaus, f. Ent: phylloxera.

Afterblech, n. back-plate (of saddle).

Afterbruch, m. Med: proctocele.

Afterchrist, m. pseudo-Christian.

Afterdarm, m. Anat: rectum.

Afterdecke, f. Ent: Crust: pygidium.

Afterdeich, m. Hyd.E: rearward, secondary, dike.

Afterdichter, m. poetaster, rhymester.

Afterdolde, f. Bot: cyme.

Afterdrüse, f. Z: anal gland (of skunk, etc.).

Afterentzündung, f. Med: proctitis.

Afterfeld, n. Echin: periproct.

Afterflosse, f. Ich: anal fin.

Afterflügel, m. Orn: alula, bastard wing.

Afterfüße, m.pl.=Bauchfüße.

Aftergebilde, n. Biol:=Aftergewebe.

Aftergeburt, f. Obst: afterbirth, secundines.

Aftergefälle, n. Min: sump.

Aftergelehrsamkeit, f. pseudo-scholarship; sciolism.

Aftergelehrte, m. (decl. as adj.) pseudo-scholar; sciolist.

Aftergewebe, n. Biol: heteroplasm, heteroplastic tissue.

Aftergröße, f. A: pretended greatness; false grandeur.

Afterhaut, f. Nat.Hist: 1. anal membrane. 2. false membrane.

Afterhuf, m. Z:=Afterklaue 1.

Afterjucken, n. Med: pruritus ani, itching.

Afterkamel, n. Z: llama.

Afterkegel, m. Geom: A: conoid.

Afterkind, n. A: 1. posthumous child. 2. illegitimate, natural, child. 3. occ: last child, F: baby, Benjamin (of large family).

Afterklappe, f. Ent: cercus.

Afterklaue, f. 1. Z: dew-claw (of certain mammals). 2. Constr: rear lap (of rafter, etc.).

Afterkohle, f. 1. small (coal), smalls; slack. 2. A: lignite, brown coal.

Afterkristall, m. Miner: pseudomorph.

Afterkritik, f. pseudo-criticism.

Afterkugel, f. A: spheroid, esp. oblate spheroid.

Afterkünstler, m. would-be artist, pseudo-artist.

Afterleder, n. 1. Bootm: heel-piece (inside boot or shoe). 2. leather seat (of breeches). 3. A: waste leather.

Afterleh(e)n, n. Hist: arriere-fee, arriere-fief.

Afterlehnsherr, m. Hist: mesne lord.

Afterlehnsmann, m. -(e)s/-leute. Hist: under-vassal, rear vassal.

Afterlücke, f. Echin:=Afterfeld.

Aftermehl, n. Mill: coarse flour; second flour; pollard; middlings.

Aftermiete, f.=Untermiete.

Aftermieter, m.=Untermieter.

Aftermoos, n. Bot: alga.

Aftermuse, f. Lit: false Muse; false, spurious, art.

Aftermutter, f. A: (a) stepmother; (b) bad, unnatural, mother.

Aftern, f.pl. Ven: (=Afterklauen) dew-claws (of deer).

äftern, v.i. (haben) Ven: (of deer) to leave traces of dew-claws.

Afterpacht, f. sub-lease, sub-let; underlease (of land).

Afterpächter, m. underlessee, sub-lessee; under-lessee (of land).

Afterphilosophie, f. pseudo-philosophy.

Afterquendel, m. Bot: peplis, water-purslane.

Afterraupe, f. Ent: pseudo-caterpillar, esp. larva of the saw-fly.

Afterrede, f. backbiting, calumny.

afterreden, v.i. insep. (haben) von j-m a., to backbite, calumniate (s.o.).

Afterreif, m. Harn: tail-case.

Afterriemen, m. Harn: tail-leather.

Afterrüßler, m. -s/-. Ent: rhynchites.

Afterschirm, m. Bot: cyme.

Afterschlag, m. 1. after-effects (of illness, etc.). 2. For: loppings (from felled trees).

Afterschließer, m. Anat: anal sphincter.

Afterschörl, m. Miner: axinite.

Aftersilber, n. impure silver; mixture of silver and dross.

Afterskorpion, m. Arach: false scorpion, chelifer.

Afterspinne, f. Arach: harvester, harvest-spider, U.S: daddy-long-legs.

aftervermieten, v.tr. insep.=untervermieten.

Aftervermieter, m.=Untervermieter.

afterverpachten, v.tr. insep. (a)=untervermieten; (b) to underlease (land).

Aftervorfall, m. Med: proctocele.

Afterweisheit, f. spurious wisdom; affectation of wisdom; philosophism.

Afterwelt, f. 1. A: (the) after-world; posterity. 2. occ. A: demi-monde.

Afterwesen, n. inferior creature; sub-normal being; F: abortion.

Afterwind, m. Nau: A: wind from astern.

Afterwissenschaft, f. (a) pseudo-scholarship; (b) pseudo-science.

Afterwitz, m.=Aberwitz.

afterwitzig, a.=aberwitzig.

Afterwurm, m. Med: A: ascaris, F: thread-worm.

Afterzehe, f. Z:=Afterklaue.

Afterzeit, f. A: after-time; time to come; (the) future.

Afterzwang, m. Med: tenesmus.

Aga ['a:ga:], m. -s/-s. Turk.Civil: ag(h)a.

Ägadisch [ɛ'ga:diʃ], a. Geog:=Ägatisch.

Ägäis, die [ɛ'gɛ:is]. Pr.n. -. Geog: the Aegean (Sea).

Ägäisch [ɛ'gɛ:iʃ], a. Geog: das Ägäische Meer, the Aegean (sea).

Agallocheholz [a'ga·loʃ-], n. Com: eaglewood, aloes-wood.

agam [a'ga:m], a.=agamisch.

Agame [a'ga:mə], f. -/-n. Rept: agama; agamoid.

Agami [a'ga:mi:], m. -s/-s. Orn: agami, trumpeter.

Agamie [aga·'mi:], f. -/. (a) A: celibacy; (b) Bot: cryptogamy.

agamisch [a'ga:miʃ], a. (a) A: celibate; (b) Biol: Bot: agamic, agamous; Bot: cryptogamic, cryptogamous.

Agamist [aga·'mist], m. -en/-en. A. & Lit: celibate; bachelor.

Agape [a'ga:pə], f. -/-n. 1. Rel.Hist: agape, love-feast. 2. occ. brotherly love.

Agapeten [aga·'pe:tən]. Rel.Hist: (i) m.pl. agapeti; (ii) f.pl. agapetae.

Agar-Agar ['a:gar·'a:ga:r], m. -s/. agar-agar, Bengal isinglass, Ceylon moss.

Agaricin [a'ga·ri:tsi:n], n. -s/. Ch: agaricine.

Agarizinsäure, f. Ch: agar(ic)ic acid.

Agatha [a'ga:ta:, 'aga:ta:], **Agathe** [a'ga:tə]. Pr.n.f. -s & Lit: -thens. Agatha.

Agathabrot, n. R.C.Ch: 'Saint Agatha's bread'; bread blessed on Saint Agatha's day.

Agathodämon [a'ga·to:'dɛ:mon], m. agathodemon; good divinity; good genius.

Ägatisch [ɛ'ga:tiʃ], a. Geog: die Ägatischen Inseln, the Aegades.

Agave [a'ga:və], f. -/-n. Bot: agave; American aloe, sisal plant, pita, F: century plant.

Agavefaser, f. Com: aloe-fibre, Tampico fibre, sisal-grass, sisal-hemp, pita fibre, pita hemp.

-age [-'a:ʒə], s.suff. f. -/n, (a) (in nouns borrowed from French=Fr. -age) Courage, courage; Dressage, training (of horse, etc.); Adjustage, finishing; adjusting; (b) (added to German roots, and occ. to French roots where it does not appear in French) Takelage, cordage, rigging; Stellage, fitment; fitting; rack; Blamage, fiasco; disgrace.

Agenda [a'gɛnda:], f. -/-den. 1. agenda (of meeting, etc.). 2. Com: etc: agenda-, note-, memorandum-book; Com: price-list.

Agende [a'gɛndə], f. -/-n. 1. Ecc: agenda, ritual(-book). 2.=Agenda 2.

Agenesie [a'gene·'zi:], f. -/-n [-'zi:ən]. Biol: 1. agenesis (of organ). 2. sterility (of female).

Agens ['a:gens], n. -/-genzien [a'gentsiən]. 1. active force; agency; active cause; motive force. 2. Ch: agent.

Agent [a'gɛnt], m. -en/-en, (a) Com: etc: agent; representative; (b) geheimer A., geheime Agentin, secret (service) agent.

Agentengebühr, f. Com: (agent's) commission.

Agentie [a'gɛntsi:], f. -/-n [-'tsi:ən], office of the Danube Steamship Company.

Agentschaft, f. -/-en=Agentur (b).

Agentur [a'gɛn'tu:r], f. -/-en, (a) agency (office);

bureau; (b) agency (für eine Firma, for a firm).

Agenzien, n.pl. see Agens.

Agglomerat [aglo·me·'ra:t], n. -s/-e. Geol: etc: agglomerate.

Agglomeration [aglo·me·ra·tsi'o:n], f.-/-en, agglomeration. 1. massing together; packing (of snow, etc.). 2. (a) mass, cluster; (b) centre of population; built-up area.

agglomerieren [aglo·me·'ri:rən]. 1. v.tr. to agglomerate; to mass (people, etc.) together. 2. v.i. (haben) to agglomerate; to cohere, to bind; to cake; (of particles, etc.) to cluster (together).

agglutinieren [aglu·ti·'ni:rən], v.tr. to agglutinate; to bind; **agglutinierend**, agglutinant; Ling: agglutinating, agglutinative (language); **agglutiniert**, agglutinated; agglutinate.

Agglutiniermittel, n. agglutinant.

Agglutinin [aglu·ti·'ni:n], n. -s/-e, agglutinin, agglutinant.

Aggravation [agra·va·tsi'o:n], f. -/-en. 1. aggravation (of crime, disease, etc.). 2. augmentation (of penalty).

aggravieren [agra·'vi:rən], v.tr. 1. to aggravate (crime, disease); to render (offence) more heinous. 2. to increase, augment (penalty); to increase, aggravate (difficulties).

Aggregat [agre·'ga:t], n. -(e)s/-e. 1. Mth: Ch: Geol: etc: aggregate. 2. Ind: etc: (a) set, unit (of machinery, electrical equipment); power unit; (b) El.E: (=Ladeaggregat) charging set, charging unit.

Aggregatform, f. physical form, state (of a substance).

Aggregation [agre·ga·tsi'o:n], f. -/-en. Ph: etc: aggregation.

Aggregatsveränderung, f. Ph: change of state.

Aggregatzustand, m. Ph: state; fester, gasförmiger, A. eines Körpers, solid, gaseous, state of a substance.

aggregieren [agre·'gi:rən], v.tr. 1. to mass together; to assemble; Ph: to aggregate. 2. A: to admit, incorporate (s.o.); Mil. A: aggregierte Offiziere, officers attached to a unit.

Aggression [agrɛsi'o:n], f. -/-en, aggression; unprovoked assault (gegen, upon).

aggressiv [agrɛ'si:f], a. aggressive, provocative (policy, manner, act, etc.); adv. aggressively.

Aggressor [a'grɛsor], m. -s/-en [-'so:rən], aggressor; assailant.

Agha ['a:ga:], m. -s/-s=Aga.

Agid [a'gi:t]. Pr.n.m. -s=Ägidius.

Ägide [ɛ'gi:də], f. -/. (a) Gr.Myth: aegis; (b) protection; unter der Ä. von..., under the auspices of..., Lit: under the aegis of...

Ägidius [ɛ'gi:di̯us]. Pr.n.m. -'. Giles.

agieren [a'gi:rən]. 1. v.i. (haben) (a) to act; to be active; (b) Th: to act; F: to play one's part; mit den Händen a., to gesticulate; er hat in dieser Angelegenheit gut agiert, he played his part well in this matter. 2. v.tr. eine Rolle a., to act, play, a part.

agil [a'gi:l], a. agile, nimble.

Agilität [a'gi·li·'tɛ:t], f. -/. agility, nimbleness.

Ägina ['ɛ:gi·na:, ɛ'gi:na:]. Pr.n. A.Geog: (i) f. -s. (the island of) Aegina; (ii) n. -s. (the town of) Aegina.

Äginete [ɛ·gi·'ne:tə], m. -n/-n. 1. Geog: Aeginetan. 2. Archeol: die Ägineten, the Aeginetan Marbles.

äginetisch [ɛ·gi·'ne:tiʃ], a. Aeginetan.

Agio ['a:ʒi̯o:], n. -s/. Fin: (a) agio, (exchange) premium; A. auf Gold, premium on gold; (b) (percentage) difference between actual and face value of a security; diese Papiere genießen A., these securities are at a premium.

Agiogewinn, m. Fin: speculative profit.

Agiojäger, m. St.Exch: F: premium-hunter, stag.

Agiokonto, n. Fin: agio account.

Agiopapiere, n.pl. Fin: premium bonds.

Agiotage [a·ʒi̯o·'ta:ʒə], f. -/-n. Fin: agiotage, stock-jobbing; gambling (on the Stock Exchange).

Agioteur [a·ʒi̯o·'tø:r], m. -s/-e. Fin: speculator, gambler (on the Stock Exchange); premium-hunter; stock-jobber.

agiotieren [a·ʒi̯o·'ti:rən], v.i. (haben) to speculate, gamble (on the Stock Exchange); U.S: to play the market.

Ägis ['ɛ:gis], f. -/. Gr.Myth: aegis.

Agitakel [a·gi·'ta:kəl], n. -s/-. Ch: stirrer, stirring-rod, glass rod.

Agitation [a·gi·ta·tsi'o:n], f. -/-en, agitation. 1. (a) shaking, stirring (of sth.); Pol: agitating; F: rabble-rousing. 2. (state of) perturbation, excitement.

Agitator [a·gi·'ta:tor], m. -s/-en [-ta·'to:rən].

1. (political) agitator, *F:* rabble-rouser. 2. *Ch: Ind:* stirring-machine, agitator, mixer.

agitatorisch [a·gi·ta·ˈto:riʃ], *a.* 1. agitating. 2. *Pol:* intended, tending, to produce agitation; *F:* rabble-rousing (speech, etc.); **agitatorische Tätigkeit,** stirring up of the masses, *F:* rabble-rousing.

agitieren [a·gi·ˈti:rən], *v.* 1. *v.tr.* (*a*) to agitate, shake (sth.); (*b*) to stir (mixture); (*c*) to agitate, excite, disturb (s.o.); to perturb (s.o.); (*d*) **die Volksmenge a.,** to stir up the masses. 2. *v.i.* (*haben*) **für etwas a.,** to agitate for sth.; **gegen j-n, gegen etwas a.,** to agitate against s.o., sth.

Aglaia, Aglaja [a·ˈgla:ja:]. *Pr.n.f.* **-s.** *Gr.Myth:* Aglaia.

Aglei, *f.* **-/-en.** *Bot:* aquilegia, *F:* columbine.

Aglobulie [a·glo·bu·ˈli:], *f.* **-/.** *Physiol:* diminished proportion of red corpuscles in the blood.

Aglobulose [a·glo·bu·ˈlo:zə], *f.* **-/.** *Med:* pernicious anaemia.

Agnat [aˈgna:t], *m.* **-en/-en.** *Rom.Jur:* agnate.

Agnation [agna·tsĭˈo:n], *f.* **-/-en,** agnation.

agnatisch [aˈgna:tiʃ], *a.* agnatic; agnate.

Agnes [ˈaŋnɛs, ˈagnɛs]. *Pr.n.f.* **-'.** Agnes.

Agnition [agni·tsĭˈo:n], *f.* **-/-en,** acknowledgement, recognition.

Agnomen [aˈgno:mɛn], *n.* **-s/- & -mina** [aˈgno:mi·na:]. *Rom.Ant:* agnomen.

Agnostiker [a·ˈgnostikər], *m.* **-s/-.** *Phil:* agnostic.

agnostisch [a·ˈgnostiʃ], *a.* *Phil:* agnostic.

Agnostizismus [a·gnosti·ˈtsismus], *m.* **-/.** *Phil:* agnosticism.

agnoszieren [agnosˈtsi:rən], *v.tr.* to acknowledge, recognize.

Ago, *n.* **-s/.** *Bootm:* ago cement (*solution of celluloid in acetone*).

Agogik [aˈgo:gik], *f.* **-/.** *Mus:* agogics.

agogisch [aˈgo:giʃ], *a.* *Mus:* agogic(al).

Agon [a·ˈgo:n], *m.* **-s/-e,** struggle, contest, *esp. Gr.Ant:* athletic contest.

agonal [a·go·ˈna:l], *a.* 1. *Med:* dying (person), (person) in the death-agony. 2. agonistic, athletic (ideal, upbringing, etc.).

Agone [a·ˈgo:nə], *f.* **-/-n.** *Magn:* agonic line.

Agonie [a·go·ˈni:], *f.* **-/-n** [-ˈni:ən], agony, *esp.* death-agony, death-struggle, pangs of death.

agonisieren [a·go·ni·ˈzi:rən], *v.i.* (*haben*) to be dying, to be at the point of death.

Agonistik [a·go·ˈnistik], *f.* **-/.** competitive athletics.

agonistisch [a·go·ˈnistiʃ], *a.* agonistic(al).

Agora [a·go·ˈra:], *f.* **-/.** *Gr.Ant:* agora.

Agoraphobie [a·go·ra·fo·ˈbi:], *f.* **-/.** *Med:* agoraphobia.

Ägospotamoi [ɛ·gosˈpota·moy]. *Pr.n.m.* **-.** *A.Geog: Hist:* Aegospotami.

Agoverfahren, *n.* *Bootm:* 'stuck-on' method of manufacture (*without nails or stitching*).

Agraffe [aˈgrafə], *f.* **-/-n.** 1. agraffe, clasp. 2. (*a*) *Constr:* clamp, cleat; cramp, cramp-iron; (*b*) casement fastener, hasp *or* catch (of window, etc.); (*c*) *Bootm:* lacing hook (of boot). 3. *Mec.E:* belt-fastener. 4. *Arch:* (ornamental) keystone (of arch).

Agram [ˈa:gram]. *Pr.n.n.* **-s.** *Geog:* Agram, Zagreb.

Agrar- [a·ˈgra:r-], *comb.fm.* agrarian (law, society, etc.); agricultural (bank, country, crisis, etc.).

Agrarbank, *f.* *Fin:* agricultural bank; land-bank.

Agrargemeinschaft, *f.* (*in Austria*) common land.

Agrargesetz, *n.* *Jur:* agrarian law, land-act, land-law.

Agrarier [a·ˈgra:rĭər], *m.* **-s/-.** 1. agriculturist; farmer. 2. *Pol:* agrarian.

agrarisch [a·ˈgra:riʃ], *a.* agrarian.

Agrarkommunismus, *m.* *Pol.Ec:* collective farming.

Agrarkrise, *f.* agricultural crisis.

Agrarland, *n.* agricultural country.

Agrarreform, *f.* *Pol.Ec:* agrarian reform.

Agrarstaat, *m.* *Pol.Ec:* agrarian state, agricultural state.

agreabel [agre·ˈa:bəl], *a.* agreeable, pleasant, pleasing, nice; prepossessing, winsome (manner, countenance).

Agrément, Agrement [agre·ˈmã:], *n.* **-s/-s.** 1. (*a*) assent; approval, approbation; (*b*) *Dipl:* intimation that an ambassador, etc., is acceptable. 2. (*a*) ornament(ation), embellishment; (*b*) *pl.* **Agréments,** *Mus:* grace-notes, ornaments, *A:* graces.

Agrest[1] [aˈgrɛst], *m.* **-(e)s/-en.** *Cu: A:* verjuice.

Agrest[2] [ˈagrɛst], *f.* **-/-en.** *Swiss Dial:* magpie.

Agrigent [a·gri·ˈgɛnt]. *Pr.n.n.* **-s.** *Geog:* Agrigento, Girgenti, *A:* Agrigentum.

Agrikultur [a·gri·kulˈtu:r], *f.* **-/.** agriculture; husbandry; farming; *cp.* **Ackerbau, Landwirtschaft** 1.

Agrikulturstaat, *m.* = **Agrarstaat.**

Agronom [a·gro·ˈno:m], *m.* **-en/-en,** agronomist, scientific agriculturalist, rural economist.

Agronomie [a·gro·no·ˈmi:], *f.* **-/.** agronomy, husbandry.

agronomisch [a·gro·ˈno:miʃ], *a.* agronomic(al).

Agrume [aˈgru:mə], *f.* **-/-n.** *Bot:* 1. citrus. 2. *pl.* **Agrumen, Agrumi,** citrus fruits.

Agstein, *m.* = **Agtstein.**

Agtstein, *m.* *South G.Dial:* amber.

Aguti [aˈgu:ti:], *m.* & *n.* **-s/-s.** *Z:* agouti, agouty.

Ägypten [ɛ·ˈgyptən]. *Pr.n.n.* **-s.** *Geog:* Egypt; *see also* **Fleischtopf.**

Ägyptenland. *Pr.n.n. B:* the land of Egypt.

Ägypter [ɛ·ˈgyptər], *m.* **-s/-.** Egyptian.

Ägypterblau, *n.* *Dy:* Egyptian blue.

ägyptisch [ɛ·ˈgyptiʃ], *a.* Egyptian; *B.Lit. & F:* **ägyptische Finsternis,** intense darkness, Egyptian darkness; *Med:* **ägyptische Augenentzündung,** trachoma, granular conjunctivitis; *see also* **Bleichsucht, Plage.**

Ägyptologe [ɛ·gypto·ˈlo:gə], *m.* **-n/-n.** Egyptologist.

Ägyptologie [ɛ·gypto·lo·ˈgi:], *f.* **-/.** Egyptology.

ah, (*a*) *int.* ah! oh! **ah so!** (i) (oh,) I see; I understand; all right; (ii) (*said reflectively*) oh, I (begin to) understand; oh, so that's the answer; (oh,) that's what it is; **seine Frau hat ihn verlassen; —ah so!** his wife has left him;—oh, that's what it is! so that's what's up! that explains a lot! *cp.* **Ach** 1 (*a*); (*b*) *s.* **Ah,** *n.* **-s/-s,** ah, oh; **laute Ahs ausstoßen,** to exclaim with admiration.

äh, *int.* (*a*) (*expressing disgust*) ugh! (*expressing annoyance*) (oh) bother! (*b*) (*expressing doubt*) h'm; (*c*) *A:* (*in the Wilhelmine age*) *the* '**eh**' *sound uttered at the beginning of a sentence as an affectation of military incisiveness.*

aha [a·ˈha:], *int.* (*a*) aha! oho! (*b*) there you are! I told you so! (*c*) (oh), I see.

Ahab [ˈa:hap]. *Pr.n.m.* **-s.** *B.Hist:* Ahab.

Ahas [ˈa:has]. *Pr.n.m.* **-'.** *B.Hist:* Ahaz.

Ahasja [a·ˈha:sja:]. *Pr.n.m.* **-s.** *B.Hist:* Ahaziah.

Ahasver [a·ˈhasve·r], **-s, Ahasverus** [a·hasˈve:rus], **-'.** *Pr.n.m.* 1. *B.Hist:* (King) Ahasuerus. 2. Ahasuerus (the Wandering Jew).

Ahlbaum, *m.* *Bot:* bird-cherry tree, hagberry.

Ahlbeere, *f.* *Hort:* black currant.

Ahle, *f.* **-/-n.** *Tls:* 1. (*a*) awl; **flache A.,** bradawl; (*b*) punch; *Coop: etc:* broach; (*c*) *Print:* bodkin, point. 2. whetstone, hone; oilstone.

Ahleisen, *n.* point of an awl.

ahlförmig, *a.* awl-shaped, pointed; *Nat.Hist:* acuminate, subulate.

Ahlkirsche, *f.* = **Ahlbaum.**

Ahm, *n.* **-(e)s/-e.** *Dial:* 1. *Meas: West German:* = **Ohm**[2]. 2. *North German:* = **Ahming.**

ahmen, *v.tr.* *Dial:* to gauge (cask).

Ahming, Ahmung, *f.* **-/-e.** 1. *Nau:* draught-marks. 2. *North G.Dial:* turning-place (for the plough), headland; turn (of the plough).

Ahn, *m.* **-(e)s & -en/-en,** (*a*) ancestor, forefather, forbear; **seine Ahnen,** his ancestors, *coll.* his ancestry; *Lit:* **ich rechne ihre Tugend für Ahnen,** in my eyes her virtue makes her noble, even without noble birth; *Her:* (*of pers.*) **acht Ahnen nachweisen,** to have eight quarterings; (*b*) *A. & South G.Dial:* grandfather; *pl.* **Ahnen,** grandparents.

ahnbar, *a.* (danger, development, etc.) of which one can have a presentiment, a foreboding.

ahnden. I. *v.tr.* 1. to punish (offence, etc.); to avenge (offence, crime, insult, etc.); *A. & Lit:* **ein Verbrechen an j-m a.,** to punish s.o. for a crime; **seine Verbrechen werden an ihm geahndet werden,** he will pay the penalty of his crimes, be brought to book (for his crimes). 2. *A:* = **ahnen.**

II. *vbl s.* 1. **Ahnden,** *n. in vbl senses.* 2. **Ahndung,** *f.* (*a*) *in vbl senses; also:* punishment (of offence); (*b*) *A:* = **Ahnung** 1.

ahndevoll, *a.* *A:* = **ahnungsvoll.**

Ahndl, *m.* **-s/Ähndel.** *South G.Dial:* grandfather.

Ahne[1], *m.* **-n/-n** = **Ahn.**

Ahne[2], *f.* **-/-n.** 1. ancestress. 2. *A. & South G.Dial:* grandmother.

Ahne[3], *f.* **-/-n.** *Dial:* chaff (from corn); waste, refuse (from flax, hemp).

ähneln, *v.i.* (*haben*) **j-m, etwas** *dat.*, **ä.,** to show, bear, a (certain) resemblance to s.o., sth., to resemble s.o., sth. (in some degree); to be (somewhat) like s.o., sth.; **wem ähnelt er?** whom is he like? **die beiden Fälle ähneln sich,** the two cases bear a certain resemblance, are somewhat alike.

ahnen, I. *v.* 1. *v.tr.* (*a*) to have a presentiment, a foreboding, of (sth.); **Gefahr a.,** to have a presentiment, a premonition, of danger; **höhere Wesen, die wir ahnen,** higher beings whom we instinctively feel to exist; **etwas a. lassen,** to forebode, foreshadow, portend, foretoken, sth.; **das Kommende läßt sich a.,** one can guess what is coming (next); (*b*) to suspect, surmise, guess (sth); **er ahnt etwas,** he suspects something, *F:* he smells a rat; **er ahnt nichts,** he has no suspicions; he has no inkling of the matter; **ich habe deine Antwort schon geahnt,** I guessed what your answer would be; **nichts ahnend, ohne etwas zu a., hatte er sein Geheimnis verraten,** without suspecting it, all unawares, he had betrayed his secret; **ich habe es geahnt!** I knew it was going to happen! I knew it! (*c*) **etwas von einem Gegenstand a.,** to have some idea, an inkling, of a subject; **jetzt ahnt er schon etwas von unseren Methoden,** he has now got some idea of our methods; **von etwas nichts a.,** to have no idea of sth., to be completely in the dark about sth.; **du ahnst nicht, wie glücklich sie ist,** you have no idea how happy she is; *F:* **(ach,) du ahnst es nicht!** (i) (*expressing astonishment*) who would believe it! (ii) (*surprise and dismay*) oh Lord! *F:* **that's** torn it! (*d*) to sense (the nearness of s.o., sth.); **im Nebel konnten sie doch schon die Küste a.,** despite the fog they sensed that they were nearing land. 2. *v.i.* (*haben*) & *impers.* (*with dat. of pers.*) (*a*) **mir ahnt, es ahnt mir, nichts Gutes;** *A. & Lit:* **meinem Herzen ahnt ein Unglück,** I have forebodings, misgivings; I fear the worst; **es ahnte ihm, ihm ahnte, daß . . .,** he had a presentiment that . . . ; **das ahnte mir,** I had a presentiment, a feeling, that it would happen; (*b*) **mir ahnte so etwas,** I guessed, thought, as much.

II. *vbl s.* **Ahnen,** *n. in vbl senses; cp.* **Ahnung** 1.

Ahnenbild, *n.* picture, figure, of an ancestor *or* of ancestors; **Ahnenbilder** *pl*, ancestral, family, portraits, figures.

Ahnendünkel, *m.* (overweening) pride in one's ancestry.

Ahnengalerie, *f.* gallery of ancestral, family, portraits.

Ahnengut, *n.* *Jur: A:* entailed property.

Ahnenkeimplasma, *n.* *Biol:* germ-plasm.

Ahnenkult, *m.* ancestor-worship.

Ahnenpaß, *m.* (*in Nazi period*) certified family tree (*proving Aryan descent*).

Ahnenplasma, *n.* = **Ahnenkeimplasma.**

Ahnenprobe, *f.* proof(s) of one's ancestry; proofs of nobility.

Ahnenreihe, *f.* **eine lange A.,** a long line of ancestors.

Ahnensaal, *m.* (*a*) ancestral hall; (*b*) = **Ahnengalerie.**

ahnenstolz[1], *a.* proud of one's ancestry.

Ahnenstolz[2], *m.* pride in one's ancestry; pride of birth.

Ahnentafel, *f.* family tree, genealogical table, genealogical tree; pedigree.

Ahnenträger, *m.* latest descendant (of a family).

Ahnfrau, *f.* (first) ancestress.

Ahnherr, *m.* (first) ancestor.

Ahnin, *f.* **-/-innen** = **Ahne**[2].

ähnlich. 1. *a.* (*a*) (i) more or less alike, bearing some resemblance, having a certain similarity (*dat.*, to); quite like, more or less like, (ii) alike; similar (*dat.*, to); like; **ähnliche Fälle, Begriffe,** analogous, similar, cases, concepts; **ähnliche Gedanken, Ideen,** similar thoughts, ideas; **Ihr Fall ist dem meinen ä.,** your case resembles mine; **Ihr Fall ist dem meinen sehr ä.,** your case is very like, is very similar to, closely resembles, mine; **etwas ganz Ähnliches,** something very similar, something very much like it; **ich habe nie etwas Ähnliches gesehen,** I have never seen the like (of it), anything like it; **sie trug ein ähnliches Kleid wie dieses,** she wore a dress rather like this one; **. . . und ähnliches,** . . . and similar matter, articles, cases, etc.; . . . *et hoc genus omne*; . . . *etcetera*; **etwas ä. machen,** to make sth. similar; to assimilate sth. (*dat.*, to); *Geom:* **ähnliche Dreiecke,** similar triangles; *Alg:* **ähnliche Glieder,** similar terms; (*b*) **j-m ä. sein, sehen,** to resemble, look like, be like, s.o.; **er ist, sieht, seinem Vater ä.,** he resembles, is like, his father; **wem ist, sieht, er ä.?** whom does he resemble? whom is he like? **das Bild ist sprechend, zum Sprechen, ä.,** the portrait is a speaking likeness; **er sieht seinem Vater sprechend, täuschend, zum Verwechseln, ä.,** he is the very image, the living image, *F:* the very spit, the dead spit, of his father; **sie sehen sich sprechend, täuschend, zum Verwechseln, ä.,** they are as like as two peas; *see also* **Ei**[2] 1 (*a*);

er sieht sich gar nicht mehr ä., he has altered past recognition; *F:* **das sieht ihm, dir, ä.!** that's just like him, you! that's him, you, all over! that's just what one would expect from him, you; **ich hatte es ganz vergessen!—das sieht dir ä.!** I quite forgot—(naturally,) you would (forget)! **das sieht ihm gar nicht ä.,** it isn't like him at all. **2.** *adv.* similarly, likewise; in (a) like manner; **ich dachte ä. wie Sie,** I thought like you, (much) the same as you; **ich hätte ä. gehandelt,** I should have done much the same; *Geom:* **ä. gelegene, ä. liegende, Figuren,** homothetic figures; *see also* **perspektivisch.**

-ähnlich, *comb.fm. a.* (*combined with nouns*) -like, like . . .; resembling . . .; **holzähnlich,** wood-like, like wood, resembling wood; **beinähnlich,** bone-like; bony; shaped like a leg; leg-like; **faserähnlich,** fibre-like; fibriform; fibrous; **katzenähnlich,** catlike.

ähnlichen. 1. *v.i.* (*haben*)=**ähneln. 2.** *v.tr.*=**anähneln.**

Ähnlichkeit, *f.* (*a*) resemblance, likeness; **eine Ä. mit j-m, mit etwas, haben, aufweisen,** to bear, show, a resemblance to s.o., sth.; **große, viel, Ä., eine starke Ä., mit j-m, mit etwas, haben,** to bear a strong resemblance to s.o., sth.; **eine sprechende Ä.,** a speaking likeness; **sie haben eine entfernte Ä. miteinander,** there is a distant, a faint, resemblance between them; (*b*) similarity, similitude, likeness (**mit,** to); affinity (**mit,** with, to); *Geom:* similarity (of triangles, etc.); (*c*) *Log:* analogy.

Ähnlichkeitsbeweis, *m. Log:* proof, argument, by analogy.

Ähnlichkeitspunkt, *m.* **1.** point of resemblance. **2.** *Geom:*=**Ähnlichkeitszentrum.**

Ähnlichkeitsschluß, *m. Log:* argument by analogy.

Ähnlichkeitstransformation, *f. Geom:* **1.** similarity transformation. **2.** homothetic transformation.

Ähnlichkeitsverhältnis, *n.* **1.** *Log: etc:* analogy. **2.** *Geom: etc:* ratio of similarity.

Ähnlichkeitszeichen, *n.* (*a*) mark, sign, of similarity; (*b*) *Mth:* 'is similar to' sign; ~.

Ähnlichkeitszentrum, *n. Geom:* centre of similarity.

Ahnung, *f.* **1.** presentiment, forewarning; presage; foreboding; misgiving; premonition (of danger); **ich habe so eine A., als ob . . .,** I have a feeling that . . ., *U.S:* I've got a hunch that . . .; **eine A. von etwas haben,** to have an intuition, a presentiment, of sth.; **eine bange A.,** a premonition of danger; dire forebodings. **2.** (*a*) idea, conception, notion; inkling; suspicion; **ich habe nicht die geringste A. (davon),** *F:* **ich habe keine blasse A. (davon),** I haven't the least idea, *F:* the remotest conception, the ghost of a notion; **ich habe keine A.,** *F:* **keine blasse A., von Algebra,** I don't know a thing, the first thing, about algebra; **ohne die leiseste A. von etwas zu haben,** without having the least inkling of sth.; **ich hatte keine A., daß er da war,** I had no suspicion, no thought, no idea, that he was there; **keine A. haben, wer jemand ist,** not to know s.o. from Adam; **hast du eine A., wo er wohnt?** have you any idea where he lives? do you know where he lives? *F:* **hast du eine A.!** that's what you think! **weißt du, wie das heißt?—keine A.!** *F:* **keine blasse A.!** do you know what that is called?—I haven't the faintest idea, *F:* I haven't the foggiest (idea)! *F:* **er hat von Tuten und Blasen keine A.,** he doesn't know the first thing about it; he's an ignoramus; (*b*) *F:* **gehst du in den Vortrag?—keine A.!** are you going to the lecture?—no fear! not likely!

ahnungsbang, *a.* =**ahnungsvoll 1** (*b*).

ahnungslos, *a.* **1.** unsuspecting, unsuspicious; unconscious of danger; *adv.* unsuspectingly; (all) unawares. **2.** (*a*) innocent; (*b*) ignorant.

Ahnungsvermögen, *n.* (premonitory) instinct; *Psy:* second sight.

ahnungsvoll, *a.* **1.** (*a*) *A:* (*of pers.*) gifted with foreknowledge, with second sight; (*b*) (*of pers., feelings*) apprehensive, fearful, anxious; *adv.* apprehensively. **2.** *Lit:* (*of event, etc.*) mysterious, uncanny; full of presage; ominous (signs, silence, etc.).

ahoi [aˑˈhoy], *int. Nau:* **Boot, Schiff, a.!** boat, ship, ahoy!

Ahorn, *m.* -(e)s/-e. *Bot:* (*a*) maple(-tree); (*b*) **eschenblättriger A.,** box-elder.

ahornen, *a.* made of maple(-wood); **ein ahornener Tisch,** a maple-wood table.

Ahorngewächse, *n.pl. Bot:* aceraceae.

Ahornholz, *n.* maple(-wood).

Ahornmaser, *f.* (*wood*) bird's-eye maple.

Ahornmelasse, *f.* maple syrup.

Ahornsäure, *f. Ch:* aceric acid.

Ahornzucker, *m.* maple sugar.

Ährchen, *n.* -s/-. *Bot:* spikelet, spicula, spicule.

Ährchenachse, *f. Bot:* pedicel, pedicle.

ährchenblumig, *a. Bot:* (plant) bearing spikelets, spicules.

Ährchenspindel, *f. Bot:* rachilla.

Ähre, *f.* -/-n, ear, head (of grain); spike (of flower, grass); (*of grain*) **in Ähren schießen,** to ear, to head; **Korn in Ähren,** corn, *U.S:* wheat, in the ear; **Ähren lesen,** to glean.

Ähren-, *comb.fm. Bot:* **1.** spiked (plant, etc.); **Ährenaloe** *f,* spiked aloe. **2.** spike-like . . .; **Ährentraube** *f,* spike-like cluster.

ähren[1], *v.* **1.** *v.tr.* to glean (corn, field); *abs.* to glean. **2. sich ähren,** (*of grain*) to ear, to head; *see also* **geährt.**

ähren[2], *v.tr. Dial:* to plough (land).

Ährenblüte, *f. Bot:* spike-flower; floret.

Ährenbund, *n. Agr:* sheaf (of corn).

Ährenbüschel, *n.* bunch of corn-ears; bunch of gleanings.

Ährenfeld, *n.* (*a*) *Agr:* field of corn in the ear; (*b*) *Lit:* field of (ripening, ripe) corn.

Ährenfisch, *m. Ich:* atherine.

ährenförmig, *a. Bot:* spiciform; spicate, spicated (flower, etc.).

Ährenfrucht, *f.* grain, cereal; **Ährenfrüchte** *pl,* cereals, bread-stuffs, grain.

Ährengräser, *n.pl.* cereal plants, cereals.

Ährenkranz, *m.* crown, garland, of corn-ears.

Ährenkurve, *f. Geom:* épi.

Ährenlese, *f.* **1.** *Agr:* gleaning. **2.** *Lit:* anthology.

Ährenlesen, *n.*=**Ährenlese 1.**

Ährenleser, *m.* gleaner.

Ährenlilie, *f. Bot:* bog asphodel, Lancashire asphodel.

Ährenmeer, *n. Lit:* sea of corn.

Ährenmonat, *m.* (month of) August.

Ährenrapunzel, *f. Bot:* spiked rampion.

ährenreich, *a. Lit:* (land) rich in corn.

Ährensammler, *m.*=**Ährenleser.**

Ährensieb, *n.* (grain-)sieve; winnowing-basket.

Ährenspitze, *f. Bot:* glume; beard, awn, arista (of ear of wheat, barley, etc.).

ährenständig, *a. Bot:* spicate, spicated (flower).

Ährenstein, *m. Miner:* asbestos with chaff-like fibres.

Ährenstoppler, *m.*=**Ährenleser.**

ährentragend, *a.* spicate, spicated (flower, etc.); spiked (plant); eared (corn).

Ährenverband, *m. Surg:* spica (bandage).

Ährenweiderich, *m. Bot:* willow-herb.

ährig, *a.* **1.** *occ.*=**geährt. 2. -ährig,** *comb.fm.* -eared; **langährig,** long-eared (corn); (**grass**) with long spikes; **vollährig,** full-eared.

ahumanistisch [aˑhuˑmaˑˈnistiʃ], *a.* ahumanist, non-humanist (art, etc.).

Ai [ˈaːiː], *n.* -s/-s. *Z:* ai, three-toed sloth.

Aich-, *comb.fm.,* **aichen,** *v.tr. A:*=**Eich-, eichen**[3].

Aide [ˈɛːdə], *m.* -/-s & -n/-n, (*a*) assistant, helper; *Games:* partner; (*b*) **A. de camp** [ˈɛːdə də ˈkãː] (*pl.* **Aides de camp),** *Mil:* aide-de-camp, *U.S:* aide.

Aide-Memoire [ɛːdmeˑmoˑˈaːr], *n.* -/-. **1.** *A:* memorandum-book, pocket-book (of formulae, etc.). **2.** *Dipl.:* aide-mémoire.

Aigrette [ɛˑˈgrɛtə], *f.* -/-n. **1.** (*a*) aigrette (of heron, egret); (*b*) *Cost:* aigrette, plume; tuft (of feathers); osprey (as head ornament); *Mil:* shaving-brush plume; (*c*) spray of diamonds. **2.** *Orn:* egret; tufted heron.

Ailant(h)us [aiˈlantus], *m.* -/-. *Bot:* ailantus, *esp.* tree of heaven, varnish-tree, lacquer-tree.

Air [ɛːr], *n.* -s/-s. **1.** appearance, look, air; **er hat ein Air,** he has an air about him; **sich** *dat.* **ein Air geben,** to give oneself airs, to put on airs. **2.** *Mus:* tune, air, melody.

Airedale [ˈɛːrdeːl], *m.* -s/-s, **Airedaler** [ˈɛːrdeːlər], *m.* -s/-=**Airedaleterrier.**

Airedaleterrier, *m.* Airedale (terrier).

ais, Ais [ˈaːis], *n.* -/-. *Mus:* (the note) A sharp, A♯; **Ais-dur, Ais-Dur, ais-moll, ais-Moll,** (**-Tonart**), (key of) A sharp major, A sharp minor.

aisis, Aisis [ˈaːizis], *n.* -/-. *Mus:* (the note) A double sharp.

Aitel, *m.* -s/-. *Ich: F:* chub.

Aixeröl [ˈɛːksər-], *n. Com:* olive oil (from Aix-en-Provence).

Aja [ˈaːjaː]. **1.** *Pr.n.f.* -s. Aja; *Lit:* **Frau Aja,** (*Goethe's mother*) Frau Aja. **2.** *f.* -s/-s. *A:* (children's) nurse, governess.

Ajas, Ajax [ˈaːjas, ˈaːjaks]. *Pr.n.m.* -'. *Gr.Lit:* (*a*) **A. (der Große),** Ajax, son of Telamon; (*b*) **A. der Kleine,** Ajax the Less.

à jour [aˑ ˈʒuːr]. *Fr.adv.phr.* **1.** *Com: etc:* up to date; *Book-k:* **meine Bücher sind à j.,** my books are up to date, are posted up. **2.** *Tex: Constr: etc:* (done) in open-work; **à j. gefaßte Edelsteine,** jewels in an open-work setting.

Ajour- [aˑˈʒuːr-], *comb.fm.* open-work (balustrade, stockings, etc.).

Ajourarbeit, *f.* open-work.

ajouriert [aˑʒuˑˈriːrt], *a.* (done in) open-work.

ajustieren [aˑjusˈtiːrən], *v.tr.*=**adjustieren.**

Akademie [aˑkaˑdeˑˈmiː], *f.* -/-n [-ˈmiːən]. **1.** *Gr.Phil:* **die A. (Platos),** the Academy (of Plato). **2.** (*a*) academy, society (of letters, science, art, etc.); **A. der Wissenschaften, der Künste,** Academy of Sciences, of Arts; **A. für deutsches Recht,** Academy of German Law; (*b*) college, institute (of university standing, providing for specialized studies *or* research), *e.g.* **Bergakademie,** college of mining; (*c*) school, academy (of riding, dancing, fencing, etc.), *e.g.* **Reitakademie,** riding-school, riding-academy.

Akademiestück, *n. Art:* study from the nude; academy-figure.

Akademiker [aˑkaˑˈdeːmikər], *m.* -s/-. **1.** academician, member of an academy. **2.** (*a*) academically trained person; man who has had a university education, university man; (*b*) university teacher *or* (senior) research worker; *F:* (*at Oxford and Cambridge*) don; (*c*) (professional) scholar. **3.** *Art:* painter of the old school; traditionalist; conventionalist.

Akademikerin, *f.* -/-innen, woman who has had a university education, university woman.

akademisch [aˑkaˑˈdeːmiʃ], *a.* **1.** academical; academic; **akademische Bildung,** academic(al) training; university, higher, education; **akademischer Unterricht,** university teaching; higher education; **akademische Laufbahn,** academic career; **akademischer Grad,** university degree; **akademische Würde,** (i) dignity of an academic person, of a university man; (ii) university degree; **die akademische Jugend,** the student generation, the young students; **akademischer Bürger,** (student) member of a university; **akademische Tracht,** academic(al) dress, academicals; (*in England*) cap and gown; **akademische Freiheit,** academic freedom, *esp.* student's right to choose his own course of study; academic privilege (of university); **das akademische Viertel,** the quarter of an hour's grace allowed for late starting of a lecture; **akademische Abhandlung,** academical dissertation; *see also* **Austauschdienst;** *adv.* academically; **er war a. gebildet,** he had received an academic(al) training, he had had a university education; **er spricht sehr a.,** he talks very learnedly, *F:* he talks like a professor. **2.** (*a*) academic, theoretical (discussion, methods, etc.); (theories, etc.) without practical application; (*b*) *Art:* conventional (artist, piece of work); traditional (technique).

Akadien [aˑˈkaːdiən]. *Pr.n.n.* -s. *Geog: A:* Nova Scotia, *A:* Acadia.

Akadier [aˑˈkaːdiər], *m.* -s/-. *Geog: A:* Nova-Scotian, *A:* Acadian.

akadisch [aˑˈkaːdiʃ], *a. Geog: A:* Nova-Scotian, *A:* Acadian.

Akajou [akaˈʒuː], *m.* -s/-s=**Acaj(o)u.**

Akalephe [aˑkaˑˈleːfə], *f.* -/-n. *Coel:* acaleph, acalepha, jelly-fish.

Akanthit [aˑkanˈtiːt], *m.* -(e)s/-e. *Miner:* acanthite.

Akanthus [aˑˈkantus], *m.* -/-. **1.** *Bot:* acanthus, brank-ursine, *F:* bear's-breech. **2.** *Art:* acanthus.

Akanthusblatt, *n. Art:* acanthus leaf.

Akariden [aˑkaˑˈriːdən], **Akarinen** [aˑkaˑˈriːnən], *f.pl. Arach:* acaridae, acarina, arachnids, mites.

Akarinose [aˑkaˑriˑˈnoːzə], *f.* -/. *Agr: Vit:* curl, rust (caused by acaridae).

Akaroidharz [aˑkaˑroˑˈiːt-], *n.* acaroid resin; *Com:* yellow-gum.

Akarpie [aˑkarˈpiː], *f.* -/. *Bot:* sterility.

akatalektisch [aˑkataˑˈlɛktiʃ], *a. Pros:* acatalectic; complete in its syllables.

Akatalepsie [aˑkataˑlɛpˈsiː], *f.* -/. **1.** *Phil:* acatalepsy, incomprehensibility. **2.** *Med:* inability to comprehend.

Akatholik [aˑkaˑtoˑˈliːk], *m.* -en/-en. *Ecc:* non-Catholic.

akatholisch [aˑkaˈtoːliʃ], *a.* non-Catholic.

akaustisch [aˑˈkaustiʃ], *a.* incombustible; fire-proof.

Akazie [aˈkaːtsĭə], f. -/-n. Bot: (a) acacia; (b) (falsche, unechte, weiße) A., robinia, false acacia, common locust-tree; rote A., rose acacia; (c) F: es ist, um auf die Akazien zu klettern, it's enough to drive one crazy, F: to send one up the wall.

Akaziengummi, n. gum acacia, gum-arabic.

Akazienholz, n. Com: acacia.

Akelei [aˈkəˈlai], f. -/-en. 1. Bot: aquilegia, F: columbine. 2. Med: whitlow.

Akephale [aˈkeˈfaːlə], m. -n/-n. 1. Moll: acephalan. 2. Ter: acephalous foetus, foetus without a head.

akephalisch [aˈkeˈfaːliʃ], a. Nat.Hist: acephalous; headless.

Akinesie [aˈkiˈneˈziː], f. -/. Med: akinesia.

Akineten [aˈkiˈneːtən], pl. Prot: acinetae.

akinetisch [aˈkiˈneːtiʃ], a. akinetic.

Akka [ˈakaː]. Pr.n.n. -s. Geog: Acre.

akkablieren [akaˈbliːrən], v.tr. to overpower, overwhelm, crush; F: to floor (opponent).

Akkader [aˈkaːdər], m. -s/-. A. Civil: Accadian.

akkadisch [aˈkaːdiʃ]. 1. a. A. Civil: Accadian. 2. s. Akkadisch, n. Ling: Accadian.

Akklamation [aklamaˈtsĭoːn], f. -/-en, acclamation; cheering; durch A. angenommen, gewählt, carried, elected, by acclamation.

akklamieren [aklaˈmiːrən], v.tr. to acclaim; to applaud, cheer; to greet (s.o.) with cheers; abs. a., to applaud, cheer; to shout approval.

Akklimatisation [aklimatiˈzaˈtsĭoːn], f. -/-en, acclimatization (in einem Land, to life in a country).

akklimatisieren [aklimatiˈziːrən], v.tr. to acclimatize; sich a., to get, become, acclimatized (in einem Land, to life in a country); Akklimatisierung f, acclimatization.

Akkolade [akoˈlaːdə], f. -/-n. 1. accolade; j-m die A. erteilen, to confer the accolade, a knighthood, on s.o., to dub s.o. a knight. 2. Mus: Print: brace, bracket, accolade.

akkolieren [akoˈliːrən], v.tr. to join side by side, to couple; Mus: Print: to brace, bracket.

Akkommodation [akomoˈdaˈtsĭoːn], f. -/-en. 1. (a) adapting, accommodation; (b) Physiol: accommodation (of the eye). 2. Com: accommodation, loan.

Akkommodationslähmung, f. Med: paralysis of accommodation (of the eye).

akkommodieren [akomoˈdiːrən], v.tr. 1. (a) to adapt, accommodate (an+acc., to); Physiol: to accommodate (eye); (b) to arrange, dispose (furniture, etc.); (c) A: to dress, cook (food); (d) A: to dress (hair). 2. sich akkomodieren, to adapt, accommodate, oneself (an etwas acc., to sth.); Physiol: (of eye) to accommodate itself.

Akkompagnement [akompanjəˈmãː], n. -s/-s. Mus: accompaniment.

akkompagnieren [akompanˈjiːrən], v.tr. to accompany; (a) A: to go, come, with (s.o.); (b) Mus: to accompany (s.o., solo, etc.).

Akkon [ˈakon]. Pr.n.n. -s. Geog: Acre.

Akkord [aˈkort], m. -(e)s/-e [-s, aˈkordəs/ aˈkordə]. 1. (a) Mus: chord; einen A. anschlagen, to strike a chord (on the piano); einen A. auflösen, to break, spread, a chord; (b) harmony, accord, concord, agreement; in schönem A. leben, to dwell in perfect harmony, to live in concord. 2. (a) agreement, bargain, compact, settlement; (mit j-m) einen A. schließen, to make a compact, come to an agreement (with s.o.); (b) Com: composition, settlement, agreement (with creditors); mit seinen Gläubigern einen A. schließen, to compound with, come to terms with, one's creditors; gerichtlicher A., legal settlement; (bankrupt's) certificate; A. von 50 Prozent, composition of ten shillings in the pound. (c) Ind: contract; Arbeit in A., auf A., übernehmen, to contract for work; auf A. arbeiten, to work by contract, by agreement; (of workman) in A., im A. arbeiten, to be on piece-work, to do job-work; F: er ißt wie im A., he eats like a good one, he is a good trencherman.

Akkordarbeit, f. Ind: 1. piece-work; job-work. 2. contract work, work on contract.

Akkordarbeiter, m. Ind: piece-worker; job-worker, jobber.

Akkordbedingungen, f.pl. Ind: terms of the contract, of the agreement.

Akkordeon [aˈkordeon], n. -s/-s. Mus: accordion.

akkordieren [akorˈdiːrən], v.i. (haben) mit j-m über etwas acc. a., to agree, come to an agreement, come to terms, with s.o. concerning sth.; Com: mit seinen Gläubigern a., to compound with, come to terms with, one's creditors.

Akkordion [aˈkordĭon], n. -s/-s = Akkordeon.

Akkordlohn, m. Ind: piece-wage, wage for piece-work.

Akkordoir [akordoˈaːr], m. -s/-s. Mus: 1. (piano) tuning-key, -hammer. 2. tuning-cone (for organ). 3. tuning-fork.

Akkordsatz, m. Ind: rate for piece-work; rate for the job.

Akkouchement [akuˈʃəˈmãː], n. -s/-s. 1. bringing forth (of child); delivery; confinement, lying-in; labour; accouchement. 2. Surg: A. der Linse, removal of a cataract (from the eye).

akkreditieren [akreˈdiˈtiːrən], v.tr. 1. einen Gesandten bei einer Regierung a., to accredit an ambassador to a government. 2. Com: Fin: to open a credit for s.o., a credit account in s.o.'s favour; to provide s.o. with a letter of credit; to accredit s.o.; Herrn X bei der Firma Schmidt mit, für, 5000 M a., to provide Mr X with a letter of credit for 5,000 marks on the firm of Schmidt; j-n bei einer Bank a., to give s.o. a bank credit.

Akkreditiv [akreˈdiˈtiːf], n. -(e)s/-e [-s, -ˈtiːvəs/ -ˈtiːvə]. 1. credentials (of ambassador, Com: of representative). 2. Com: Fin: (a) letter of credit; see also revolvierend; (b) credit; j-m ein A. eröffnen = j-n akkreditieren, q.v. under akkreditieren 2.

Akkreszenz [akrɛsˈtsɛnts], f. -/-en, continuous growth; accretion.

Akkretionskatalog [akreˈtsĭˈoːns-], m. = Akquisitionskatalog.

Akku [ˈakuː], m. -s/-s. El.E: = Akkumulator (a).

Akkumobil [akuˈmoˈbiːl], n. -s/-e. El.E: battery-driven machine or vehicle.

Akkumulat [akuˈmuˈlaːt], n. -(e)s/-e. Geol: agglomerate.

Akkumulation [akuˈmuˈlaˈtsĭoːn], f. -/-en, accumulation; collection; pile.

Akkumulator [akuˈmuˈlaːtor], m. -s/-en [-laˈtoːrən], (a) El: accumulator, (storage-) battery; A. mit gepasteten Platten, mit Masseplatten, pasted-plate accumulator; see also gelatinieren; (b) Hyd.E: Mch: etc: accumulator; hydraulischer A., hydraulic accumulator.

Akkumulatorenbatterie, f. El: storage battery; battery of accumulators.

Akkumulatorenprüfer, m. El: acid-tester (for accumulators); accumulator capacity indicator.

Akkumulatorenraum, m. Ind: Navy: etc: accumulator room, battery room.

Akkumulatorensäure, f. El: accumulator acid; electrolyte.

Akkumulatorenwagen, m. El.E: battery-driven vehicle.

Akkumulatorplatte, f. El: accumulator plate.

akkumulieren [akuˈmuˈliːrən]. 1. v.tr. to accumulate, amass; to heap (up), pile up. 2. v.i. (sein) & sich akkumulieren, to accumulate; to pile up.

akkurat [akuˈraːt]. 1. a. meticulous, punctilious (person); careful, painstaking, exact (workman etc.); precise, neat (work, handwriting, etc.). 2. adv. (a) carefully, with care; a. arbeiten, to work carefully, with exactitude; (b) exactly, precisely; es ist a. so, wie er sagt, it is precisely as he says.

Akkuratesse [akuˈraˈtɛsə], f. -/. (a) exactness, exactitude; carefulness; precision; (b) punctiliousness, meticulosity, meticulousness.

Akkusativ [ˈakuːzaˈtiːf, ˈakuˈzaˈtiːf, akuˈzaˈtiːf], m. -s/-e [-tiːvə]. Gram: accusative (case).

Akkusativobjekt, n. Gram: direct object.

Akkusativus [akuˈzaˈtiːvus], m. -/-vc. Gram: accusative (case).

Akkusator [akuˈzaːtor], m. -s/-en [-zaˈtoːrən], accuser, indicter, impeacher, arraigner.

akkusatorisch [akuzaˈtoːriʃ], a. accusatory, accusing.

Akline [aˈkliːnə], f. -/. Magn: aclinic line, magnetic equator.

aklinisch [aˈkliːniʃ], a. Magn: aclinic; aklinische Linie = Akline.

Akme [ˈakmeː, akˈmeː], f. -/. 1. acme, summit (of fame, etc.); esp. prime of life; height of career. 2. Med: crisis (of a disease).

Akmit [akˈmiːt], m. -(e)s/-e. Miner: acmite, akmite.

Akne [ˈakneː], f. -/. Med: acne.

Akoluth [aˈkoˈluːt], m. -en & -s/-en. Ecc: acolyte.

Akon [ˈakoːn], n. -s/. Com: silk-cotton (from the asclepias, etc.).

Akonit [aˈkoˈniːt], n. -(e)s/-e. Bot: Pharm: aconite.

Akonitin [aˈkoˈniˈtiːn], n. -s/. Ch: aconitine.

Akonitsäure, f. Ch: aconitic acid.

Akkordion [aˈkordĭon], n. -s/-s = Akkordeon.

Akontozahlung [aˈkonto-], f. Com: Fin: payment on account, part payment.

Akosmismus [aˈkosˈmismus], m. -/. Phil: acosmism.

akquirieren [akviˈriːrən], v.tr. to acquire, obtain, secure.

Akquis [aˈkiː], m. & n. -/. acquired knowledge, attainments, experience; (acquired) skill, deftness.

Akquisiteur [akviˈziˈtœrr], m. -s/-e, (a) A: commercial traveller, representative (of a firm), U.S: drummer; advertisement agent.

Akquisition [akviˈziˈtsĭˈoːn], f. -/-en, acquisition; (a) acquiring; (b) thing bought or obtained; purchase.

Akquisitionskatalog, m. catalogue of recent acquisitions (by museum, library, etc.).

Akquisitionsnummer, f. = Akzessionsnummer.

Akquisitor [akviˈziˈtor], m. -s/-en [-ziˈtoːrən], acquirer, purchaser, buyer.

Akquisitum [akviˈziˈtum], -s/-ta & -ten, acquisition; purchase.

Akra [ˈakraː]. Pr.n.n. -s. Geog: Acre.

akral [aˈkraːl], a. situated at the point or summit.

Akranier [aˈkraːnĭər], m. -s/-. Nat. Hist: acranial vertebrate.

Akribie [aˈkriˈbiː], f. -/. (extreme) precision (of measurements, methods of work, handwriting, etc.).

Akridier [aˈkriːdĭər], m. -s/-. Ent: locust.

Akridin [akriˈdiːn], n. -s/. Ch: Dy: acridine.

akritisch [aˈkriːtiʃ], a. Phil: uncritical.

akroamatisch [aˈkroaˈmaːtiʃ], a. (a) Phil: acroamatic; (b) Sch: oral (method of teaching).

Akrobat [aˈkroˈbaːt], m. -en/-en, acrobat, A: tumbler.

Akrobatik [aˈkroˈbaːtik], f. -/. acrobatics.

akrobatisch [aˈkroˈbaːtiʃ], a. acrobatic.

Akrodynie [aˈkroˈdyˈniː], f. -/. Med: pink disease.

akrokarp [aˈkroˈkarp], a. Bot: acrocarpous.

Akrokephale [aˈkroˈkeˈfaːlə], m. -n/-n. Anthr: acrocephalous person, person with a lofty skull.

Akromion [aˈkroːmĭon], n. -s/-mien & -mia. Anat: acromion (process).

akronitisch [aˈkroˈniːtiʃ], akronychisch [aˈkroˈnyːçiʃ], akronyktisch [aˈkroˈnyktiʃ], a. Astr: acronychal.

Akronym [aˈkroˈnyːm], n. -s/-e, acronym.

akropetal [aˈkroˈpeˈtaːl], a. Bot: acropetal.

Akrophonie [aˈkroˈfoˈniː], f. -/. Ling: acrophony.

Akropolis [aˈkroˈpoˈlis], f. -/-len [aˈkroˈpoːlən], acropolis.

Akrostichon [aˈkrostiçon], n. -s/-chen & -cha, acrostic.

akrostisch [aˈkrostiʃ], a. acrostic.

Akroter [aˈkroˈteːr], m. -s/-e, Akroterion [aˈkroˈteːrĭon], Akroterium [aˈkroˈteːrĭum], n. -s/-rien. Arch: acroterium.

Akrozephale [aˈkroˈtseˈfaːlə], m. -n/-n = Akrokephale.

Akrylsäure [aˈkryːl-], f. Ch: acrylic acid.

äks, int. ugh!

Akt[1], m. -(e)s/-e. 1. (a) act, action, deed; ein Akt der Gerechtigkeit, der Menschenliebe, der Verzweiflung, an act of justice, of charity, of despair; (b) ceremonial act; ceremonial meeting (of a body). 2. Th: act (of a play). 3. sexual act. 4. Art: nude, (i) nude figure, posed nude, (ii) study from the nude; academy (figure); einen Akt zeichnen, malen, to draw, paint, from the nude. 5. (a) esp. Austrian: (Austrian pl. -en) = Akte 1; (b) von etwas Akt nehmen, to take (legal) cognizance of sth.; to note sth.

Akt[2], m. -(e)s/-e. Swiss Dial: = Abzucht.

Aktäon [akˈtɛːon]. 1. Pr.n.m. -s. Myth: Actaeon. 2. m. -s/-. Moll: actaeon.

Aktbild, n. Art: (picture from the) nude; drawing or painting from the nude; nude photograph.

Akte, f. -/-n. 1. Adm: etc: (a) document; Jur: instrument, deed; proof in writing; notarielle A., deed or document executed and authenticated by a notary; notarial deed; (b) coll. A., pl. Akten, documents, papers (relating to the matter); file, dossier; record(s); etwas in die Akten eintragen, to put sth. on the record; diese Forderung ist nicht in den Akten, this claim is not on the record; ein Schriftstück zu den Akten legen, to file a document; 'zu den Akten', 'z.d.A', 'to be filed', 'files'; F: einen Bericht, ein Gesuch, usw., zu den Akten legen, to shelve, pigeon-hole, a report, a request, etc.; mein Gesuch ist zu den Akten gelegt worden, my request has been shelved; F: das legen wir zu den Akten, let us drop the subject, let us say no more about it. 2. Adm: act, decree; esp. (British) Act of Parliament.

Aktei [akˈtai], f. -/-en = Aktenzimmer.

Aktenbock, *m. Adm: Com:* stand (for documents *or* correspondence).
Aktendeckel, *m.* jacket (for document(s)); folder, cover.
Aktenheft, *n.* file, dossier.
Aktenhefter, *m. Com:* (index-)file, jacket-file. filing jacket.
Aktenkammer, *f.* **1.** *A:* (public) record office; (*in England*) the Rolls. **2.** = **Aktenzimmer.**
Aktenmappe, *f.* **1.** portfolio (for documents); folder; binder. **2.** (*a*) (lawyer's) portfolio (carried under the arm); (*b*) = **Aktentasche.**
aktenmäßig, *a. Jur:* authentic (document, etc.); documentary (proof, etc.).
Aktenmensch, *m. F:* bureaucrat.
Aktenreiter, *m. F:* (pettifogging) bureaucrat.
Aktenschrank, *m.* filing-cabinet.
Aktenschreiber, *m.* copying clerk, *esp.* lawyer's clerk.
Aktenschwanz, *m.* tab (in document-file).
Aktenständer, *m.* set of pigeon-holes; shelf *or* shelves for documents.
Aktenstaub, *m.* dust from (old) documents; **im A. des Advokatenzimmers**, in the musty atmosphere of a lawyer's office.
Aktenstoß, *m.* pile of documents; file (of documents), dossier.
Aktenstück, *n.* (*a*) document; (*b*) *Jur:* instrument, deed; (*c*) file (of documents); *Jur:* **das A. des Prozesses**, the documents pertaining to the case before the court; (*d*) *Adm: Jur:* copy for filing, file copy (of document).
Aktentasche, *f.* briefcase, satchel, dispatch-case.
Aktenumschlag, *m.* = **Aktendeckel.**
Aktenvernichter, *m.* = **Aktenwolf.**
Aktenwesen, *n.* procedure with regard to documents; *Adm:* filing procedure.
aktenwidrig, *a. Jur:* not authentic; not in accordance with the documents *or* records.
Aktenwolf, *m.* shredding machine (for destroying confidential documents).
Aktenzeichen, *n. Adm: Com:* file number, reference number, reference.
Aktenzimmer, *n. Adm: etc:* filing room; (*in lawyer's office*) storage room for deeds.
-akter, *comb.fm. m.* **-s/-.** (*with num. prefixed*) *Th:* . . . -act play; **Zweiakter**, two-act play; **Vierakter**, four-act play.
Akteur [ak'tøːr], *m.* **-s/-e.** *Th:* actor; player.
Aktgemälde, *n. Art:* painting from the nude.
Aktie ['aktsĭə], *f.* **-/-n.** *Fin:* share; **Aktien** *pl*, shares, *F:* scrip, *U.S:* stock; **gewöhnliche A.**, ordinary share; **voll eingezahlte, vollbezahlte, A.**, fully paid-up share; **teilweise eingezahlte, teilweise bezahlte, A.**, partly-paid-up share; *F:* **seine Aktien steigen, fallen**, his stock is going up, going down.
Aktienabschnitt, *m. Fin:* dividend-warrant.
Aktienausgabe, *f.* issue (of shares).
Aktienbank, *f.* joint-stock bank.
Aktienbesitz, *m.* shareholdings, *U.S:* stock-holdings.
Aktienbesitzer, *m.* = **Aktieninhaber.**
Aktienbier, *n.* beer from a joint-stock brewery.
Aktienbörse, *f.* stock exchange.
Aktienbräu, *m.* **1.** = **Aktienbrauerei. 2.** = **Aktienbier.**
Aktienbrauerei, *f.* joint-stock brewery.
Aktienbuch, *n.* stock-register, register of shareholders.
Aktiengesellschaft, *f.* (*abbr.* AG, A.G., A.-G.) *Com: Ind:* joint-stock company, *U.S:* corporation.
Aktiengesetz, *n. Jur:* law governing the operation of joint-stock companies.
Aktienhandel, *m.* dealing in stocks and shares.
Aktienhändler, *m. St.Exch:* dealer in stocks and shares.
Aktieninhaber, *m. Fin:* shareholder, *U.S:* stock-holder.
Aktienkapital, *n. Com:* share-capital.
Aktienkupon, *m.* = **Aktienabschnitt.**
Aktienkurs, *m. St.Exch:* market price; quotation.
Aktienkurszettel, *m. St.Exch:* share-list.
Aktienmakler, *m.* stockbroker.
Aktienmarkt, *m.* stock-market.
Aktiennotierung, *f. St.Exch:* quotation.
Aktienpaket, *n. St.Exch: etc:* block, parcel, of shares.
Aktienpromesse, *f. Fin:* share-certificate, (provisional) scrip.
Aktienprospekt, *m. Com: Fin:* prospectus.
Aktienrecht, *n. Jur:* laws governing the operation of joint-stock companies.
Aktienschien, *m. Fin:* share-certificate, *F:* scrip, *U.S:* stock certificate.
Aktienschwindel, *m. Fin: St.Exch:* (*a*) market-rigging; (*b*) share-pushing.
Aktienschwindler, *m. Fin: St.Exch:* (*a*) market-rigger; (*b*) share-pusher.
Aktiensparen, *n.* saving by investment through a savings-bank.
Aktienspekulant, *m. St.Exch:* speculator.
Aktienspekulation, *f.*, **Aktienspiel**, *n. St.Exch:* speculation, *Pej:* stock-jobbing, playing the (stock-)market.
Aktienspieler, *m.* = **Aktienspekulant.**
Aktienurkunde, *f.* = **Aktienschein.**
Aktienzeichnung, *f. Fin:* subscription (for shares).
Aktienzertifikat, *n.* = **Aktienschein.**
Aktinie [ak'tiːnĭə], *f.* **-/-n.** *Coel:* actinia, sea-anemone.
aktinisch [ak'tiːniʃ], *a. Ph:* actinic.
Aktinismus [akti'nismus], *m.* **-/.**, **Aktinität** [aktiniˈtɛːt], *f.* **-/.** *Ph:* actinism.
Aktinium [ak'tiːnĭum], *n.* **-s/.** *Ch:* actinium.
Aktinochemie [aktiˑnoˑçeˑ'miː], *f.* actino-chemistry, actinology.
Aktinograph [aktiˑnoˑ'graːf], *m.* **-en/-en.** *Phot:* actinograph, recording actinometer.
Aktinolith [aktiˑnoˑ'liːt], *m.* **-(e)s/-e & -en/-en.** *Miner:* actinolite.
Aktinometer [aktiˑnoˑ'meːtər], *n.* **-s/-.** *Ph: Phot:* actinometer.
aktinomorph [aktiˑnoˑ'morf], *a. Nat.Hist:* actinomorphous; radiate.
Aktinomykose [aktiˑnoˑmyˑ'koːzə], *f.* **-/.** **1.** *Vet: Med:* actinomycosis; *Vet: F:* big-jaw. **2.** *Hort:* potato-scab.
Aktinotherapie [aktiˑnoˑteˑraˑ'piː], *f.* **-/.** *Med:* sunlight treatment.
Aktion [aktsĭ'oːn], *f.* **-/-en.** **1.** (*a*) action, act; activity; **in A. treten**, to come into action; (*b*) action, motion, working, functioning (of machine, etc.). **2.** *A:* action (of horse); action, gesture(s) (of orator, etc.). **3.** (important) occurrence, event; **das ist eine A.!** it's quite an event. **4.** *Jur:* (civil) action, lawsuit, civil trial. **5.** (*a*) *Mil:* action, fight, engagement; operation; (*b*) **-aktion**, *comb.fm.* (i) . . . operation(s); **Rettungsaktion**, rescue operation(s); **Säuberungsaktion**, *Mil:* mopping-up operation(s); *Pol:* purge; (ii) *Adm:* scheme, plan; campaign, drive; **Sparaktion**, savings campaign; economy drive. **6.** *Ling: Gram:* = **Aktionsart.**
Aktionär [aktsĭoˑ'nɛːr], *m.* **-s/-e.** *Fin:* shareholder, *U.S:* stockholder.
Aktionärin [aktsĭoˑ'nɛːrin], *f.* **-/-innen.** *Fin:* shareholder; **die Firma X ist die alleinige A.**, the firm X is the sole shareholder.
Aktionärversammlung, *f. Fin:* shareholders' meeting.
Aktionsart, *f. Ling: Gram:* aspect (of verb).
Aktionsbereich, *m.* sphere of action; range of action.
Aktionsmalerei, *f. Art:* action painting.
Aktionsradius, *m.* radius of action; range of action; range (of aircraft, submarine, etc.).
Aktionsschaufel, *f.* impulse blade (of turbine).
Aktionsstrom, *m. Physiol:* action current.
Aktionsturbine, *f.* impulse turbine.
aktiv[1] [ak'tiːf], *a.* (*a*) active (supporter, drug, disease, etc., *Ch:* carbon, acid, etc., *Gram:* verb, voice, etc.); *Com:* **aktiver** [ak'tiːvər] **Teilhaber**, active, working, partner; *Pol: etc:* **bei einem Verein, bei einer Partei, a. sein**, to be an active member of, to be actively associated with, a club, a party; *Sch:* **a. sein, werden**, to be an active member of, to join, a students' association; *Mil:* **aktives Heer**, regular, standing, army; **aktive Dienstzeit**, (period of) service with the colours; **aktiver Soldat**, regular (soldier); **aktiver Offizier**, regular officer; *Pol.Ec:* **aktive (Handels-)Bilanz** = **Aktivbilanz**; *see also* **Wahlrecht**; (*b*) active, brisk, sprightly, agile (person); (*c*) *adv.* actively; *Mil:* **er hat a. gedient**, he has served with the colours.
Aktiv[2] ['aktiːf, ak'tiːf], *n.* **-s/-e** [-tiːvə]. *Gram:* active voice; active form.
Aktiva [ak'tiːvaː], *n.pl.* (*a*) *Com: Fin:* assets; **A. und Passiva**, assets and liabilities; (*b*) *Jur:* (bankrupt's) estate.
Aktivbestand, *m.* = **Aktivstand.**
Aktivbilanz, *f. Pol.Ec:* favourable balance of trade.
Aktiven, *n.pl. Com:* = **Aktiva.**
Aktivforderung, *f.* outstanding claim.
Aktivgeschäft, *n. Com: Fin:* financing of business (by bank, etc.) to create assets.
Aktivhandel, *m. Pol.Ec:* export trade (based on country's own resources).
aktivieren [akti'viːrən], *v.tr.* **1.** to put (sth.) into action; to get (business, etc.) going; to activate (digestion, etc.); to hasten, expedite, accelerate (piece of work, etc.). **2.** *Ph:* to activate (substance); **Aktivierung** *f*, activation.
Aktivismus [akti'vismus], *m.* **-/.** *Pol:* activism; militancy.
Aktivist [akti'vist], *m.* **-en/-en.** *Pol:* activist; militant.
aktivistisch [akti'vistiʃ], *a. Pol:* activist(ic); militant.
Aktivität [aktiˑviˑ'tɛːt], *f.* **-/.** activity.
Aktivkapital, *n.* (*a*) *Fin:* assets; capital; (*b*) = **Aktivmasse.**
Aktivkohle, *f. Ch:* active carbon.
Aktivmasse, *f. Jur:* (bankrupt's) total estate; assets.
Aktivposten, *m. Fin: Book-k:* item among the assets.
Aktivsaldo, *n. Com: Fin:* credit balance.
Aktivschulden, *f.pl. Com:* outstanding debts; debts due to the firm; *Jur:* book-debts ranking as assets.
Aktivstand, *m.* **1.** (*a*) *Com: Fin:* assets; (*b*) *Jur:* = **Aktivmasse. 2.** *Mil:* effective strength (of army).
Aktivtruppen, *f.pl. Mil:* regular troops, regulars.
Aktivum [ak'tiːvum], *n.* **-s/-va. 1.** *Gram:* = **Aktiv**[2]. **2.** *Com: Fin:* asset.
Aktivvermögen, *n. Com: Fin:* assets.
Aktivzinsen, *m.pl. Fin:* interest to be received from debtors.
Aktklasse, *f. Art: Sch:* life class.
Aktmodell, *n. Art:* nude model.
Aktrice [ak'triːsə], *f.* **-/-n.** *Th:* actress.
Aktsaal, *m. Art: Sch:* room where the life class is held.
Aktstudie, *f. Art:* study from the nude.
aktualisieren [aktuˑaˑliˑ'ziːrən], *v.tr.* to make (subject, etc.) topical.
Aktualität [aktuˑaˑliˑ'tɛːt], *f.* **-/-en. 1.** actuality, reality; contemporary significance; *F:* up-to-dateness (of book, film, etc.). **2.** (*a*) question, event, of the (present) day, of the moment; **Aktualitäten** *pl*, current events, passing events; (*b*) *Cin: W.Tel: etc:* topical item.
Aktualitätenkino, *n. Cin:* news theatre.
Aktualitätsfilm, *m. Cin:* news film, topical film.
Aktuar [aktu'aːr], *m.* **-s/-e.** *Jur:* **1.** clerk (of the court); registrar. **2.** *A:* = **Referendar.**
Aktuariat [aktuˑaˑrĭ'aːt], *n.* **-s/-e.** *Jur:* office of the clerk of the court; record-office (of court), registry(-office).
Aktuarius [aktu'aːrĭus], *m.* **-/-rien** = **Aktuar.**
aktuell [aktu'ɛl], *a.* **1.** actual, real (value, etc.); *Mec:* **aktuelle Energie**, kinetic energy, active energy, actual energy. **2.** (*a*) (now) existing; actual; present-day, of the (present) day, of the moment; **die aktuelle Sachlage**, the present, actual, state of affairs; **die aktuellen Zustände**, present-day conditions, conditions now prevailing, current conditions; **aktuelle Frage**, present-day question; question of present, current, interest; topic of the day; **diese Frage ist immer a.**, this question is always with us; (*b*) topical (book, film, etc.); *F:* up-to-date (book, film, report, etc.); **seine Artikel sind immer sehr a.**, his articles are always right up to the minute.
Aktus ['aktus], *m.* **-/.** (*a*) ceremonial, formal, meeting (of a body); (*b*) *Sch:* speech-day.
Aktzeichnen, *n. Art:* (art of) drawing from the nude.
Aktzeichnung, *f. Art:* drawing, sketch, from the nude.
akuieren [aˑku'iːrən], *v.tr.* to sharpen; to stress (syllable) sharply; *Pros:* **akuierte Silbe**, acute syllable.
Akuität [aˑkuˑi'tɛːt], *f.* **-/.** sharpness; acuteness, high pitch (of a sound).
Akuleat [aˑkuˑleˑ'aːt], *n.* **-(e)s/-en.** *Ent:* aculeate hymenopter; **Akuleaten** *pl*, aculeata.
akuminiert [aˑkuˑmiˑ'niːrt], *a. Nat.Hist:* acuminate.
Aku(o)meter [aˑkuˑ(oˑ)'meːtər], *n.* **-s/-.** *Med: etc:* acoumeter, acousimeter.
Akupressur [aˑkuˑprɛ'suːr], *f.* **-/-en.** *Med:* styptic.
akupunktieren [aˑkuˑpuŋk'tiːrən], *v.tr. Surg:* to acupuncture.
Akupunktur [aˑkuˑpuŋk'tuːr], *f.* **-/-en.** *Surg:* acupuncture.
Akusimeter [aˑkuˑziˑ'meːtər], *n.* **-s/-** = **Aku(o)meter.**
Aküsprache, *f. F:* = **Abkürzungssprache.**
Akustik [a'kustik], *f.* **-/.** acoustics; (*a*) **die A. ist die Wissenschaft vom Schall**, acoustics is the science of sound; (*b*) **dieser Saal hat eine ausgezeichnete A.**, the acoustics of this hall are excellent.
Akustiker [a'kustikər], *m.* **-s/-**, acoustician.

Akustikon [aˈkustiˑkon], n. -s/-ka, ear-trumpet.
Akustikus [aˈkustiˑkus], m. -/. Anat: auditory nerve.
akustisch [aˈkustiʃ], a. acoustic (studies, properties, effect, etc.); **akustisches Signal**, sound signal; Med: **akustisches Mittel**, hearing aid; Hvd.E: **akustische Aufnahme**, auscultation.
akut[1] [aˈkuːt], a. (a) acute (problem, danger, shortage, etc.); (b) Med: acute (attack, illness, inflammation, case, etc.); **akutes Stadium einer Krankheit**, acute stage of a disease; **akutes Abdomen**, acute abdomen.
Akut[2], m. -(e)s/-e. Gram: acute accent.
Akyanoblepsie [aˑkyˑaˑnoˑblɛpˈsiː], f. -/. Med: blue-blindness.
akzedieren [aktseˈdiːrən], v.i. (haben) (+dat.) to accede to, join (a party, etc.); to accede, assent, agree, to (a request, etc.).
Akzeleration [aktseˑleˑraˈtsiˑoːn], f. -/-en. 1. (a) Astr: Aut: acceleration; (b) gradual gaining (of clock). 2. hastening, speeding up, pushing on (of work, etc.).
Akzelerator [aktseˑleˈraːtor], m. -s/-en [-raˈtoːrən]. Aut: accelerator.
akzelerieren [aktseˑleˈriːrən], v.tr. 1. to accelerate; to hasten, speed up, expedite (work, etc.). 2. v.i. (haben) Aut: to accelerate.
Akzent [akˈtsɛnt], m. -(e)s/-e. 1. Ling: (a) accent, stress; **starkgeschnittener A.**, close stress; **schwachgeschnittener A.**, open stress; (b) (grammatical) accent, diacritic; accent sign. 2. accent, pronunciation; **Deutsch mit englischem A. sprechen**, to speak German with an English accent; **irischer A.**, Irish brogue; **er spricht (ganz) ohne A.**, he speaks without (any) accent. 3. **auf eine Tatsache den A. legen**, to lay stress, particular stress, on a fact. 4. tone of voice; **er sagte es mit einem solchen A., daß nichts mehr zu antworten war**, he said it in a tone of voice that admitted of no reply. 5. Mus: (melodic. etc.) accent.
akzentfrei, a. (pronunciation, etc.) free from foreign accent; **er spricht akzentfreies Deutsch**, adv. **er spricht a. Deutsch**, he speaks German without (any foreign) accent.
akzentlos, a. 1. Ling: unstressed, unaccented (syllable, etc.). 2. adv. **er spricht a.**, he speaks without (any) accent.
Akzenttaste, f. Typewr: accent key.
Akzentträger, m. Ling: accented syllable or vowel; stressed syllable.
Akzentuation [aktsɛntuˑaˈtsiˑoːn], f. -/-en= akzentuieren II.
akzentuieren [aktsɛntuˈiːrən]. I. v.tr. 1. (a) to stress (word, syllable, note, etc.); to accent (syllable, vowel, etc.); **akzentuierte Silbe**, accented, stressed, syllable; (b) to accentuate; to mark (vowel, etc.) with a grammatical accent. 2. to emphasize, lay stress on (fact, etc.). II. vbl s. **Akzentuieren** n., **Akzentuierung** f. in vbl senses; also: accentuation.
Akzentwechsel, m. Ling: accentual gradation.
Akzentzeichen, n. (a) Ling: accent sign, grammatical accent, diacritic(al sign); stress-mark; (b) Mus: accent mark, e.g. <.
Akzepisse [aktseˈpisə], n. -/- & -s/-n. Com: (acknowledgement of) receipt.
Akzept [akˈtsɛpt], n. -(e)s/-e. Com: (a) acceptance (of a bill); **einen Wechsel zum A. vorlegen**, to present a bill for acceptance; **das A. verweigern**, to refuse acceptance; **mangels A. zurückgegangener Wechsel**, draft returned (under protest) for non-acceptance; **A. ehrenhalber**, acceptance for honour, acceptance supra protest; see also **einlösen**; (b) accepted bill, honoured bill.
akzeptabel [aktsɛpˈtaːbəl], a. acceptable.
Akzeptabilität [aktsɛptaˑbiˑliˈtɛːt], f. -/. acceptability, acceptableness.
Akzeptant [aktsɛpˈtant], m. -en/-en. Com: acceptor, drawee (of a bill); **A. eines Ehrenakzeptes**, acceptor for honour, acceptor supra protest.
Akzeptation [aktsɛptaˈtsiˑoːn], f. -/-en. Com:= Akzept (a).
Akzeptbank, f. Fin: acceptance house.
Akzeptbuch, n. Com:= Akzeptobligobuch.
akzeptfähig, a. Fin: bankable, negotiable (draft).
Akzeptgeschäfte, n.pl. Fin: acceptance business; (bill-)broking, brokerage.
Akzepthaus, n.=Akzeptbank.
akzeptieren [aktsɛpˈtiːrən]. I. v.tr. (a) to accept, acknowledge; to agree to, acquiesce in (claims, proposals, etc.); (b) Com: **einen Wechsel a.**, (i) to accept, sign, a bill, (ii) to honour a bill; **einen Wechsel nicht a.**, to dishonour a bill. II. vbl s. 1. **Akzeptieren**, n. in vbl senses;

also: acceptance; acknowledgement. 2. **Akzeptierung**, f. (a)=II. 1; (b)=**Akzept** (a). III. p.p. & a. **akzeptiert**, Com: accepted, honoured (bill); **nicht akzeptierter Wechsel**, unaccepted, dishonoured, bill.
Akzeptkredit, m. Com: acceptance credit; blank credit.
Akzeptobligobuch [ak,tsɛptʔobliˑgoˑ-], n. Com: bills-payable book, bill-book.
Akzeptprovision, f. Fin: acceptance commission.
Akzeptvermerk, m. Com: acceptance, endorsement (on a bill).
Akzeptverweigerung, f. Com: non-acceptance (of a bill).
Akzeß [akˈtsɛs], m. -zesses/-zesse. 1. access, approach. 2. Adm: Jur: A. & Austrian: admission as an unpaid assistant.
akzessibel [aktsɛˈsiːbəl], a. accessible.
Akzession [aktsɛsiˈoːn], f. -/-en. 1. (a) accession (to power, to the throne, etc.); (b) Dipl: A. **zu einem Vertrag**, accession to a treaty. 2. new acquisition (in collection, museum); accession (to library).
Akzessionskatalog, m. (in museum, etc.) catalogue of new acquisitions; (in library) catalogue of accessions; accession(s) book.
Akzessionsnummer, f. (in library, museum, etc.) accession number.
Akzessionsvertrag, m. Dipl: treaty of accession.
Akzessist [aktseˈsist], m. -en/-en. Adm: Jur: A. & Austrian: unpaid assistant.
Akzessit [akˈtsɛsit], n. -/- & -s/-s. Sch: etc: 'proxime accessit'; honourable mention; certificate of merit.
Akzessorietät [aktsɛsoˑrieˈtɛːt], f. -/-en. 1. accessibility. 2. admissibility (of candidate, etc.).
akzessorisch [aktsɛˈsoːriʃ], a. accessory.
Akzessorium [aktsɛˈsoːriʊm], n. -s/-rien, accessory; appurtenance; adjunct; appendage; concomitant.
Akzidens [ˈaktsiˑdɛns], n. -/-dentien & -denzien [-ˈdɛntsiən]. 1. accident; Phil: accidental property, accident; attribute. 2. Mus: accidental. 3. pl. Akzidenzen, casual earnings; fees (in addition to fixed salary); perquisites, F: perks; F: pickings.
Akzident [ˈaktsiˑdɛnt], m. -s/-s. Swiss Dial: accident, mishap.
Akzidentalia, Akzidentalien [aktsiˑdɛnˈtaːliaˑ, -liən], n.pl. accidental, fortuitous, circumstances; Jur: non-essential clauses (of agreement, etc.).
Akzidentalpunkt, m. Art: accidental point (in perspective).
akzidentell, akzidentiell [aktsiˑdɛnˈtɛl, -tsiˈɛl], a. accidental, casual, fortuitous; adventitious; Med: etc: concomitant (symptoms, etc.).
Akzidentien, n.pl. see Akzidens.
Akzidenz [aktsiˈdɛnts], f. -/-en. Print: (a) job; (b) pl. Akzidenzen=Akzidenzarbeit.
Akzidenzarbeit, f. Print: job-work, jobbing work.
Akzidenzdruck, m. Print: job-printing.
Akzidenzdrucker, m. Print: job-printer, jobbing printer.
Akzidenzdruckerei, f. Print: jobbing-firm, -house; job-office.
Akzidenzhaus, n. F: A: pawnshop.
Akzidenzien, n.pl. see Akzidens.
Akzidenzschrift, f. Print: display type.
Akzidenzsetzer, m. Print: job-compositor.
akzisbar [akˈtsiːsbaːr], a. (a) Adm: excisable (goods); (b) Hist: (goods) subject to town dues.
Akzise [akˈtsiːzə], f. -/-n. 1. (a) Adm: excise; (b) Hist: town dues, city toll (on goods to be consumed); octroi. 2.=Akzisenamt.
Akzisenamt, n. Adm: Excise Office.
akzisfrei, a. (a) Adm: free of excise duty; (b) Hist: free of town dues.
akzisieren [aktsiˈziːrən], v.tr. (a) Adm: to excise, to levy excise duty on (goods); (b) Hist: to collect town dues on (goods).
Akzisor [akˈtsiːzor], m. -s/-en [-tsiˈzoːrən]. Excise officer; exciseman.
akzispflichtig, a. (goods) subject to excise duty, excisable (goods).
à la [a la]. Fr.phr. after the manner of ... ; **à la ...** ; **er schreibt à la George**, he imitates George's style, writes à la George.
alaaf [aˈlaːf], int. Dial: (in Cologne area) hurrah! hurray! bravo!
Alabaster [aˑlaˈbastər], m. -s/. alabaster.
alabasterartig, a. alabastrine, resembling alabaster.
Alabastergips, m. Com: best quality plaster of Paris.
Alabasterglas, n. Glassm: milk-glass, opal glass, opaline.

Alabasterhand, f. Poet: hand as white as alabaster; lily-white hand.
alabastern, a. 1. (made) of alabaster; **eine alabasterne Vase**, an alabaster vase. 2.= alabasterweiß.
Alabasterpapier, n. Paperm: frosted paper.
alabasterweiß, a. as white as alabaster; Lit: alabastrine.
Alad(d)in [ˈaˑlaˑdiˑn]. Pr.n.m. -s. Aladdin; **Aladdins Wunderlampe**, Aladdin's lamp.
Alaktaga [aˈlaktaˑgaː], m. -s/-s. Z: Siberian five-toed jerboa, jumping mouse (of the steppes).
Alamannen [aˑlaˈmanən], m. pl. Hist:=**Alemannen**, q.v. under Alemanne.
Alamodewesen [alaˈmoːdə-], n. Hist: imitation of French manners and costume.
Alamodezeit, f. Hist: period of imitation of the French (esp. in the seventeenth century).
Aland, m. -(e)s/-e. 1. Ich: ide, orfe. 2. Bot:= Alant 1.
Alander, m. -s/-. Ich: smelt, sparling.
Alang-Alang [ˈaˑlaŋʔˈaˑlaŋ], n. -s/. Bot: steppe grass.
Alant, m. -(e)s/-e. 1. Bot: inula; **echter A.**, elecampane, horse-heal, scab-wort. 2. Ich:= Aland 1.
Alantbeere, f. Hort: Dial: black currant.
Alantkampfer, m. Ch: helenin.
Alantöl, n. Pharm: elecampane oil.
Alantwein, m. elecampane wine (made from the root).
Alapurin [aˑlaˑpuˈriːn], n. -s/. Ch: Pharm: lanoline.
Alarich [ˈaːlaˑriç]. Pr.n.m. -s. Hist: Alaric.
Alarm [aˈlarm], m. -(e)s/-e. 1. (a) alarm; **A. geben, blasen, schlagen**, to give, sound, the alarm; **blinder A.**, false alarm; (b) Mil: Civ.D: alert, warning; Mil: **stiller A.**, silent alert; **(den) A. geben**, to give the alert; **Alarm!** (i) Mil: fall in at the double! A: up! to arms! (ii) Civ.D: alert! A. aus! all clear! **den A. aufheben**, to give the 'all clear'. 2. alarm (bell or device); warning device.
Alarmanlage, f. alarm system; Civ.D: warning system.
Alarmapparat, m. alarm; warning apparatus or device.
alarmbereit, a. Mil: etc: in constant readiness; on the alert; standing by.
Alarmbereitschaft, f. Mil: etc: (state of) constant readiness; stand-by; **die Truppen sind in A.**, the troops are in constant readiness, are standing by.
Alarmeinrichtung, f. alarm; alarm system; warning device.
Alarmgebiet, n. Mil: danger area.
Alarmgerät, n. alarm; warning apparatus or device; Civ.D: etc: warning equipment.
Alarmgeschütz, n. alarm-gun.
Alarmglocke, f. alarm-bell, (i) warning bell (of safety device, etc.), (ii) tocsin.
Alarmhupe, f. (a) alarm siren; (b) alarm-hooter; alarm-whistle.
alarmieren [alarˈmiːrən], v.tr. 1. to give the alarm to (s.o.); to put (troops, police) on the alert, to alert (troops, police); to turn out (troops); **die Feuerwehr a.**, to call out the fire brigade. 2. to alarm, frighten, startle (s.o.); **alarmierende Nachrichten**, alarming, startling, news.
Alarmkanone, f.=Alarmgeschütz.
Alarmpfeife, f. alarm-whistle.
Alarmplatz, m. Mil: alarm station, alarm-post.
Alarmposten, m. Mil: alarm sentry.
Alarmquartier, n.=Alarmunterkunft.
Alarmsammelplatz, m. Mil: alarm (assembly) post.
Alarmschuß, m. shot fired as an alarm-signal.
Alarmsirene, f. alarm siren, warning siren; Civ.D: **bei der A.**, at the alert.
Alarmstart, m. Mil.Av: scramble.
Alarmtauchen, n. Navy: crash-dive (of submarine).
Alarmthermometer, n. Ind: alarm thermometer; thermic alarm-device.
Alarmunterkunft, f. Mil: quarters occupied by men in constant readiness.
Alarmventil, n. Mch: sentinel-valve.
Alarmvorrichtung, f. alarm device, alarm.
Alarmwort, n. Mil: password.
Alarmzeichen, n. alarm-signal.
Alarmzustand, m. Mil: stand-to.
Alaun [aˈlaun], m. -s/-e, alum; **eigentlicher A.**, potash alum; Miner: **römischer A.**, Roman alum.
alaunartig, a. aluminous.
Alaunbad, n. Phot: alum bath.
Alaunbeize, f. (a) Tan: (i) alum steep, (ii) steeping

(of skins) in alum solution; (*b*) *Dy:* alum mordant.
Alaunbergwerk, *n.* alum mine.
Alaunbruch, *m.* alum quarry, alum mine.
Alaunbrühe, *f.* alum solution; *Tan:* alum steep.
alaunen [a·ˈlaunən], *v.tr. Dy: etc:* to alum.
Alaunerde, *f. Miner:* alumina.
alaunerdehaltig, *a.* aluminiferous.
Alaunerdemetall, *n. A:* = **Aluminium.**
Alaunerz, *n.,* **Alaunfels,** *m. Miner:* alunite, alum-stone.
alaungar, *a. Tan:* tawed (leather).
Alaungerber, *m. Tan:* tawer.
Alaungerberei, *f. Tan:* **1.** tawing, dressing (of skins) with alum. **2.** tawery.
Alaungerbung, *f.* = **Alaungerberei 1.**
alaunhaltig, *a.* aluminous; *Miner:* alumniferous.
Alaunhütte, *f.* alum works.
alaunieren [a·lauˈniːrən], *v.tr.* = **alaunen.**
alaunig [a·ˈlauniç], *a.* aluminous.
Alaunkies, *m. Miner:* aluminous pyrites.
alaunsauer, *a. Ch:* aluminate of . . . ; **alaunsaures Magnesium,** magnesium aluminate; **alaunsaures Salz,** aluminate.
Alaunschiefer, *m. Miner:* alum shale.
Alaunsieden, *n.* alum-making, manufacture of alum.
Alaunsieder, *m.* alum manufacturer.
Alaunsiederei, *f.* alum works.
Alaunspat, *m.* = **Alaunstein 1.**
Alaunstein, *m.* **1.** *Miner:* alunite, alum-stone. **2.** *Toil:* shaving-block.
Alaunwerk, *n.* alum works.
Alaunwurzel, *f. Bot: Pharm:* alum-root.
Alb[1], *m.* **-(e)s/-en.** **1.** (mischievous) sprite, imp, elf, (hob)goblin; brownie. **2.** nightmare, incubus; **vom Alb gedrückt sein,** to have a nightmare, to be troubled with nightmares; **der Gedanke an die Prüfung liegt mir wie ein Alb auf der Brust,** the thought of the examination haunts me, is a nightmare to me. **3.** *F:* simpleton, booby, noodle, *F:* fathead, halfwit.
Alb[2], *f.* **-/-en.** *Dial:* = **Alp**[2]; *Geog:* **die Schwäbische Alb,** the Swabian Alps.
Alba[1]. *Pr.n.f.* **-s.** *A.Geog:* Alba (Longa).
Alba[2]. *Pr.n.n. Hist:* **der Herzog von A.,** the Duke of Alva.
Alba[3], *f.* **-/-ben.** *Ecc: Cost:* alb.
Alba[4], *f.* **-/-ben.** *Mediev.Lit:* dawn-song.
Albane [alˈbaːnə], *m.* **-n/-n.** *Geog:* Albanian.
Albaner [alˈbaːnər], *m.* **-s/-.** *Geog:* **1.** inhabitant, native, of Albano. **2.** Albanian.
Albanerberge, die, Albanergebirge, das. *Geog:* the Alban Hills.
Albanerhemd, *n. Cost:* fustanelle, fustanella, (Greek) kilt.
Albanese [alba·ˈneːzə], *m.* **-n/-n, Albanesin,** *f.* **-/-innen.** *Geog:* Albanian.
albanesisch [alba·ˈneːziʃ], *a.* Albanian.
Albanien [alˈbaːniən]. *Pr.n.n.* **-s.** *Geog:* Albania.
Albanier [alˈbaːniər], *m.* **-s/-.** *Geog:* Albanian.
albanisch [alˈbaːniʃ], *a.* Albanian.
Albatros [ˈalba·tros], *m.* **-/-se.** **1.** *Orn:* albatross; **schwarzbrauner A.,** black-browed albatross; **buntschnäbliger A.,** grey-headed albatross; **gemeiner A.,** wandering albatross, great albatross; **gewellter A.,** waved albatross; **rußbrauner, dunkelmanteliger, A.,** sooty albatross; **scheuer A.,** shy albatross. **2.** *Hist. of Av:* Albatross (aircraft).
Albdruck, *m.,* **Albdrücken,** *n.* nightmare.
Albe[1], *f.* **-/-n.** *Ecc.Cost:* alb.
Albe[2], *f.* **-/-n.** *Ich:* bleak; ablet.
Albe[3], *f.* **-/-n.** *Bot:* = **Alber**[1].
Albedo [alˈbeːdoː], *f.* **-/.** *Opt: Astr:* albedo; whiteness (of planet).
Albeere [ˈaːlbeːrə], *f. Hort: Dial:* black currant.
alben, *v.i.* (*haben*) *Dial:* (*of ghost*) to walk; (*of pers.*) to wander about at night; to prowl.
Alber[1], *f.* **-/-n** *&* *m.* **-s/-n.** *Bot:* white poplar, silver poplar.
alber[2], *a. occ.* = **albern**[1].
Alberei, *f.* **-/-en,** foolery; foolish, stupid, act.
Albergine [alberˈgiːnə], *f.* **-/-n.** *Bot:* aubergine, egg-plant, brinjal; *Cu:* aubergine.
albern[2], *a.* silly, stupid (person, etc.); mawkish (person, behaviour, conversation, etc.); silly, childish (behaviour, remark); puerile (answer, remark, etc.); insipid, vapid, silly (conversation, etc.); pointless (joke); absurd, ridiculous (question, answer, idea); vacuous (remark, laugh); vacant (expression); **sie ist ein albernes Ding,** she's a silly creature, a little ninny, a little goose, *F:* she's a dumb one; **albernes Wesen,** silliness, foolishness; **albernes Zeug reden,** to talk nonsense; to twaddle; to make silly, vacuous, remarks; *Scot:* to blether; **albernes Geschwätz, Gerede,** twaddle, *Scot:* blether.
albern[2], *v.i.* (*haben*) (*a*) to play the fool, the ass, *F:* to ass about; (*b*) to talk nonsense; to twaddle; to make silly, vacuous, remarks; *Scot:* to blether.
Albernheit, *f.* stupidity (of pers., etc.); insipidity, insipidness, vapidness, vapidity (of conversation, etc.); silliness, foolishness (of remark, etc.); childishness (of remark, behaviour); absurdity, puerility (of question, answer, idea, etc.); mawkishness (of compliments, etc.); pointlessness (of remark, joke).
Albert. *Pr.n.m.* **-s.** Albert; *Mediev.Hist:* **A. der Große,** Albertus Magnus.
Albertina, die [alberˈtiːnaː]. *Pr.n.f.* **-.** **1.** the University of Königsberg. **2.** the Albertina (*in Vienna*).
Albertiner [alberˈtiːnər], *pl. G.Hist:* (members of) the Albertine line, the royal house of Saxony.
albeszieren [albɛsˈtsiːrən], *v.i.* (*haben*) to turn, grow, white.
Albigenser [albi·ˈgɛnzər], *m.* **-s/-.** *Geog:* inhabitant, native, of Albi; *Hist:* **die Albigenser,** the Albigenses.
Albigenserkriege, die, *m.pl. Hist:* the Albigensian Crusade.
albigensisch [albi·ˈgɛnziʃ], *a. Geog:* of Albi; *Hist:* Albigensian.
Albinismus [albi·ˈnismus], *m.* **-/.** albinism.
Albino [alˈbiːnoː], *m.* **-s/-s,** albino.
albinotisch [albi·ˈnoːtiʃ], *a. Med:* albino (eye, etc.).
Albion [ˈalbiɔn]. *Pr.n.n.* **-s.** *A.Geog:* Albion, Britain.
Albit [alˈbiːt], *m.* **-(e)s/-e.** *Miner:* albite, white feldspar.
Albrecht. *Pr.n.m.* **-s.** Albert.
Albugo [alˈbuːgoː], *n.* **-s/.** *Med: Fung:* albugo.
Album, *n.* **-s/Alben,** album.
Albumblatt, *n.* **1.** page of an album. **2.** poem, etc., written in *or* for an album; 'album piece'.
Albumen [ˈalbuˑmən], *n.* **-s/.** *Biol: Bot:* albumen.
Albumin [albu·ˈmiːn], *n.* **-s/-e.** *Biol: Ch:* albumin; **technisches A.,** albumin for industrial purposes (*as adhesive, clearing agent, etc.*).
albuminartig, *a.* albuminoid.
Albuminat [albu·mi·ˈnaːt], *n.* **-s/-e.** *Ch:* albuminate.
albuminisiert [albu·mi·ni·ˈziːrt], *a.* albumenized (paper, etc.).
Albuminoid [albu·mi·no·ˈiːt], *n.* **-s/-e** [-ˈiːdə], albuminoid.
albuminös [albu·mi·ˈnøːs], *a.* albuminose, albuminous.
Albuminpapier, *n. Phot:* albumenized paper.
Albuminstoff, *m. Ch:* albuminous substance; *Ch: Physiol:* protein.
Albuminurie [albu·mi·nu·ˈriː], *f.* **-/.** *Med:* albuminuria.
Albumose [albu·ˈmoːzə], *f.* **-/-n.** *Ch: Physiol:* albumose.
Albumvers, *m.* poem written in *or* for an album.
alcäisch [alˈkɛːiʃ], *a.* = **alkäisch.**
Alchemie [alçe·ˈmiː], *f.* **-/.** alchemy.
Alchemille [alçe·ˈmilə], *f.* **-/-n.** *Bot:* alchemilla, lady's mantle.
Alchemist [alçe·ˈmist], *m.* **-en/-en,** alchemist.
alchemistisch [alçe·ˈmistiʃ], *a.* alchemic(al), alchemistic(al).
Älchen, *n.* **-s/-.** **1.** *Ich:* elver; young eel; grig. **2.** *Ann:* anguillule.
Alchimie [alçi·ˈmiː], *f.* **-/.** alchemy.
Alchimist [alçi·ˈmist], *m.* **-en/-en,** alchemist.
alchimistisch [alçi·ˈmistiʃ], *a.* alchemic(al), alchemistic(al).
Alcyone [alˈtsyːo·neː]. *Pr.n.f.* **-s** = **Alkyone.**
alcyonisch [altsy·ˈoːniʃ], *a.* = **alkyonisch.**
Aldehyd [alde·ˈhyːt], *m. & n.* **-(e)s/-e** [-s, -ˈhyːdəs/-ˈhyːdə]. *Ch:* aldehyde.
Aldermann, *m.* **-(e)s/-männer,** alderman; councillor.
Aldina [alˈdiːnaː], *f.* **-/-nen.** *Print.Hist:* Aldine edition.
Aldine [alˈdiːnə], *f.* **-/-n.** *Print.Hist:* **1.** Aldine (italic). **2.** = **Aldina.**
Ale [ˈeːl], *n.* **- & -s/.** ale.
aleatorisch [a·le·a·ˈtoːriʃ], *a.* aleatory (contract, etc.); depending on contingencies; hazardous.
Alemanne [a·ləˈmanə], *m.* **-n/-n,** (*a*) *Hist:* native, inhabitant, of Alemannia; **die Alemannen,** the Alemanni; (*b*) *Ling:* native of the Alemannic speech-area.
Alemannien [a·ləmˈaniən]. *Pr.n.n.* **-s.** *A.Geog:* Alemannia.
alemannisch [a·ləˈmaniʃ], *a.* (*a*) *Hist:* Alemannic, Alemannian; (*b*) *Ling:* Alemannic; **das Alemannische,** the Alemannic dialect.
Alençonspitzen [alɑ̃ˈsɔ̃ː-], *f.pl.* Alençon point, lace.
Alepine [a·le·ˈpiːnə], *f.* **-/-n.** *Tex: A:* alepine, alapeen, bombasine.
Aleppobeule [a·ˈlɛpoː-], *f. Med:* endemic ulcer, *F:* Aleppo ulcer, boil *or* gall; Biskra button; Dehli sore.
Aleppokiefer, *f. Bot:* Aleppo pine.
Aleppонuß, *f. Bot: Com:* pistachio (nut).
alert [aˈlɛrt], *a.* alert, brisk, quick, agile.
Aleuron [a·ˈloyron], *n.* **-s/.** *Bot: Ch:* aleuron(e); protein grains.
Aleuten, die [a·le·ˈuːtən]. *Pr.n.pl. Geog:* the Aleutian Islands, *F:* the Aleutians; **Bewohner(in) der A.,** Aleutian.
Aleutenseeschwalbe, *f. Orn:* Aleutian tern.
Alex [ˈa·lɛks]. **1.** *Pr.n.m.* **-ens & -'.** (*abbr. of* **Alexander**) Alex, Alec. **2.** *F:* **der A.,** the Alexanderplatz (*in Berlin*).
Alexander [a·lɛˈksandər]. *Pr.n.m.* **-s.** Alexander.
Alexanderroman, *m. Lit:* Alexander romance.
Alexandersittich, *m. Orn:* **kleiner A.,** green parakeet (*psittacula krameri*).
Alexandria [a·lɛˈksandri·aː], **Alexandrien** [a·lɛˈksandriən]. *Pr.n.n.* **-s.** *Geog:* Alexandria.
Alexandriner [a·lɛksanˈdriːnər], *m.* **-s/-.** **1.** *A.Hist: Geog:* Alexandrian. **2.** *Pros:* alexandrine (line).
Alexandrinertum, *n.* **-s/.** *F:* (*a*) merely derivative scholarship; (*b*) remoteness from reality.
alexandrinisch [a·lɛksanˈdriːniʃ], *a. A.Hist: Geog:* Alexandrian; *A.Hist:* **die Alexandrinische Bibliothek,** the Alexandrian Library; *Phil:* **die Alexandrinische Schule,** the Alexandrian School; *see also* **Kodex.**
Alexios [a·ˈlɛksios], **Alexis** [a·ˈlɛksis], **Alexius** [a·ˈlɛksius]. *Pr.n.m.* **-'.** Alexis.
Alfa, *f.* **-/., Alfagras,** *n. Bot: Paperm:* alfa(-grass).
Alfanz [ˈalfants], *m.* **-en/-en.** *A:* **1.** buffoon, clown, fool, jester. **2.** = **Alfanzerei.**
Alfanzerei [alfantsəˈrai], *f.* **-/-en,** (*a*) *A:* buffoonery; clownery; (*b*) *occ. & A:* humbug.
alfanzig [alˈfantsiç], *a.* (*a*) *A:* farcical, nonsensical; clownish (trick, etc.); (*b*) *South G.Dial:* self-willed, stubborn.
Alfenid [alfe·ˈniːt], *n.* **-(e)s/.** [-s, -ˈniːdəs]. *Metall:* nickel silver coated with silver.
Alfons. *Pr.n.m.* **-'.** Alfonso, Alphonso.
alfonsinisch [alfonˈziːniʃ], *a. Astr:* **die alfonsinischen Tafeln,** the Alphonsine tables.
Alfred. *Pr.n.m.* **-s.** Alfred.
Algaroba [alga·ˈroːbaː], *f.* **-/-ben.** *Bot:* algarroba (tree).
Alge, *f.* **-/-n.** *Bot:* alga; seaweed.
Algebra [ˈalge·braː], *f.* **-/.** algebra.
algebraisch [alge·ˈbraːiʃ], *a.* algebraic; **algebraisches Symbol, Vorzeichen,** algebraic symbol, sign; *adv.* algebraically.
Algebraist [alge·bra·ˈist], *m.* **-en/-en,** algebrist, algebraist.
algenähnlich, algenartig, *a. Bot:* algoid.
Algenkunde, *f.* algology.
Algenpilze, *m.pl. Fung:* phycomycetes, phycomycetea.
Algenschleim, *m. Ind:* mucilage obtained from algae.
Algerien [alˈgeːriən]. *Pr.n.n.* **-s.** *Geog:* Algeria.
Algerier [alˈgeːriər], *m.* **-s/-.** Algerian.
algerisch [alˈgeːriʃ], *a.* Algerian.
-algie [-alˈgiː], *comb.fm. f.* **-/-n** [-ˈgiːən]. *Med:* -algia, -algy; **Koxalgie,** coxalgia, coxalgy; **Neuralgie,** neuralgia; **Odontalgie,** odontalgia, odontalgy.
Algier [ˈalʒiːr]. *Pr.n.n.* **-s.** *Geog:* Algiers.
Algierer [alˈʒiːrər], *m.* **-s/-.** Algerian, Algerine; native, inhabitant, of Algiers.
Algin [alˈgiːn], *n.* **-s/., Alginsäure,** *f. Ch: Phot:* algin(e).
-algisch, *a.suff. Med:* -algic; **neuralgisch,** neuralgic; **odontalgisch,** odontalgic.
Algol [alˈgol]. *Pr.n.m.* **-s.** *Astr:* Algol; the Demon star.
Algolfarbe, *f. Dy:* algol dye.
Algologe [algo·ˈloːgə], *m.* **-n/-n,** algologist.
Algologie [algo·lo·ˈgiː], *f.* **-/.** algology.
Algonkium, das [alˈgoŋkium], **-s.** *Geol:* the Algonkian age.
Algorithmus [algo·ˈritmus], *m.* **-/.** algorism, algorithm.
Algraphie [algra·ˈfiː], *f.* **-/.** *Print:* algraphy, printing from aluminium plates.
Alhidade [alhi·ˈdaːdə], *f.* **-/-n.** *Surv: etc:* alidad(e).
alias [ˈaːlias], *adv.* (*usu. used of criminal*) alias; otherwise (known as . . .); **Herr Meyer, a. Schmidt,** Mr Meyer, alias Schmidt.
Alibi [ˈaːli·biː], *n.* **-s/-s.** *Jur:* alibi; **ein A. bei-**

bringen, erbringen, to produce an alibi; **ein A. beweisen, nachweisen,** to establish an alibi.

Alibibeweis, *m. Jur:* (evidence, proof of an) alibi; **Alibibeweise vorbringen,** to fall back on, set up, plead, an alibi.

Alicante [a·li·ˈkantə]. **1.** *Pr.n.n.* **-s.** *Geog:* Alicante. **2.** *m.* **A., -/., Alicant(e)wein,** *m.* Alicante wine.

Alice [ˈali·s, aˈliːsə]. *Pr.n.f.* **-s.** Alice.

alienabel [a·lĭe·ˈnaːbəl], *a. Jur:* alienable, transferable.

Alienation [a·lĭe·na·tsĭˈoːn], *f.* **-/-en. 1.** *Jur:* alienation, transfer (of property, rights, etc.). **2.** alienation, derangement, of mind; insanity.

alienieren [a·lĭe·ˈniːrən], *v.tr. Jur:* to alienate, part with, transfer (property, rights, etc.).

Alignement [alinjəˈmãː], *n.* **-s/-s,** alignment, alinement; line (of wall, etc.); building line (of street).

alignieren [alinˈjiːrən], *v.tr.* to align, aline, line up; to lay out (houses, etc.) in a line; to line out, mark out (plot of ground).

Aliment [a·li·ˈmɛnt], *n.* **-(e)s/-e.** *Jur: usu. pl.* **Alimente,** alimony, allowances for necessaries; allowance for maintenance (of wife, child).

alimentär [a·li·mɛn·ˈtɛːr], *a. Physiol:* alimentary.

Alimentation [a·li·mɛnta·tsĭˈoːn], *f.* **-/-en. 1.** alimentation, feeding, nourishing. **2.** *Jur:* (*a*) maintenance (of wife, child); (*b*) = **Alimente,** *q.v. under* **Aliment.**

alimentationsberechtigt, *a. Jur:* entitled to maintenance; (wife) entitled to alimony.

Alimentationsgelder, *n.pl. Jur:* = **Alimente,** *q.v. under* **Aliment.**

Alimentationskosten, *pl. Jur:* maintenance expenses.

Alimentationspflicht, *f. Jur:* obligation to pay alimony *or* maintenance.

alimentationspflichtig, *a. Jur:* obliged to pay alimony *or* maintenance.

Alimentenklage, *f. Jur:* claim for alimony; claim for maintenance (of child).

alimentieren [a·li·mɛn·ˈtiːrən], *v.tr.* **1.** to feed, nourish (s.o.). **2.** *Jur:* **seine Frau a.,** to provide (i) maintenance, (ii) alimony, for one's wife; **ein Kind a.,** to maintain a child.

a limine [a· ˈliːmi·neː]. *Lt.phr.* **eine Bitte a l. abweisen, einen Vorschlag a l. ablehnen,** to refuse a request, reject a proposal, out of hand.

Alinea [a·ˈliːne·aː], *n.* **-s/-s.** *Print:* **1.** first line of paragraph, indented line. **2.** (new) paragraph, *F:* para.

Alineazeichen, *n. Print:* paragraph (mark).

alineieren [a·li·ne·ˈiːrən], *v.i.* (*haben*) *Print:* to begin a new paragraph.

aliphatisch [a·li·ˈfaːtiʃ], *a. Ch:* aliphatic (compound, series); fatty (series).

aliquant [a·li·ˈkvant], *a. Mth:* aliquant (part).

Aliquante [a·li·ˈkvantə], *f.* **-/-n.** *Mth:* aliquant part.

aliquot [a·li·ˈkvoːt], *a. Mth:* aliquot (part).

Aliquote [a·li·ˈkvoːtə], *f.* **-/-n.** *Mth:* aliquot (part).

Alisma [a·ˈlismaː], *n.* **-s/-men.** *Bot:* alisma, water-plantain.

Alit [aːˈliːt], *n.* **-(e)s/-e.** *Metall:* alite (cement).

alitieren [a·li·ˈtiːrən], *v.tr. Metalw:* to alitize, calorize.

Alizarin [a·li·tsa·ˈriːn], *n.* **-s/.** *Ind: Ch:* alizarin, madder dye.

alizyklisch [a·li·ˈtsyːkliʃ], *a. Ch:* alicyclic (compound, etc.).

Alk, *m.* **-en/-en** & **-(e)s/-e.** *Orn:* auk.

alkäisch [alˈkɛːiʃ], *a. Pros:* alcaic (strophe, etc.); **alkäische Verse,** alcaics.

Alkalde [alˈkaldə], *m.* **-n/-n.** *Spanish Adm:* alcalde, justice, sheriff.

Alkaleszenz [alka·lɛsˈtsɛnts], *f.* **-/.** *Ch:* alkalescence.

alkaleszierend [alka·lɛsˈtsiːrənt], *a.* alkalescent.

Alkali [alˈkaːliː], *n.* **-s/-en** [-ˈkaːlĭən]. *Ch:* alkali.

alkaliartig, *a.* alkaloid.

alkalibeständig, *a.* alkali-resisting.

Alkalibeständigkeit, *f.* alkali-resistance.

alkaliecht, *a. Dy:* fast to alkali.

Alkalimesser, *m. Ch:* alkalimeter.

Alkalimessung, *f. Ch:* alkalimetry.

Alkalimetall, *n. Ch:* alkaline metal.

alkalinisch [alka·ˈliːniʃ], *a.* = **alkalisch.**

Alkalinität [alka·li·ni·ˈtɛːt], *f.* **-/.** *Ch:* alkalinity.

Alkalinitätsgrad, *m.* alkali strength (of solution, etc.).

alkalisch [alˈkaːliʃ], *a. Ch:* alkaline; **a. werdend,** alkalescent; **alkalische Metalle, Erden,** alkaline metals, earths; *adv.* **a. reagieren,** to give an alkaline reaction.

alkalisieren [alka·li·ˈziːrən], *v.tr. Ch:* to alkalize, to alkalify, to make (solution, etc.) alkaline; **sich a.,** to become alkalized; **Alkalisierung** *f,* alkalization.

Alkalität [alka·li·ˈtɛːt], *f. Ch:* (degree of) alkalinity.

Alkaloid [alka·lo·ˈiːt], *n.* **-(e)s/-e** [-s, -ˈiːdəs/-ˈiːdə], alkaloid.

alkaloidisch [alka·lo·ˈiːdiʃ], *a.* alkaloid.

Alkanna [alˈkanaː], *f.* **-/.** *Bot:* **1.** alkanet, dyer's bugloss. **2.** *A:* henna.

Alkannarot, *n.* = **Alkannin.**

Alkannawurzel, *f. Dy:* alkanet (root).

Alkannin [alkaˈniːn], *n.* **-s/.** *Ch: Dy:* anchusin.

Alkäos, Alkäus [alˈkɛːos, -us]. *Pr.n.m.* **-'.** *Gr.Lit:* Alcaeus.

Alkestis [alˈke·stis]. *Pr.n.f.* **-'.** *Gr.Lit:* Alcestis.

Alkibiades [alki·ˈbiːa·dɛs]. *Pr.n.m* **-'.** *Gr.Hist:* Alcibiades.

Alkohol [ˈalko·hol, alko·ˈhoːl], *m.* **-s/-e** [-ˈhoːlə], alcohol; **absoluter A.,** absolute, pure, alcohol; **denaturierter A.,** denatured alcohol, methylated spirit; *F:* **j-n unter A. setzen,** to make s.o. drunk; **sich unter A. setzen,** to get drunk.

alkoholarm, *a.* with a low alcoholic content.

Alkoholat [alko·ho·ˈlaːt], *n.* **-s/-e.** *Ch:* alcoholate.

Alkoholdruck, *m. F:* (*of pers.*) **unter A.,** in liquor, under the influence of drink, *F:* under the influence.

alkoholfrei, *a.* (*a*) free from alcohol; non-alcoholic (beverage); (*b*) **alkoholfreies Restaurant,** temperance restaurant.

Alkoholgehalt, *m.* alcohol content; alcoholic content (of beverage).

alkoholhaltig, *a.* containing alcohol; alcoholic (beverage, etc.).

Alkoholiker [alko·ˈhoːlikər], *m.* **-s/-,** (*a*) alcoholic, habitual drinker; (*b*) *Med:* alcoholic patient.

Alkoholisation [alko·ho·li·za·tsĭˈoːn], *f.* **-/-en,** alcoholization.

alkoholisch [alko·ˈhoːliʃ], *a.* alcoholic (content, etc.); **alkoholische Getränke,** alcoholic liquors, *esp.* spirits.

alkoholisieren [alko·ho·li·ˈziːrən], *v.tr.* to alcoholize; **Alkoholisierung** *f,* alcoholization.

Alkoholismus [alko·ho·ˈlismus], *m.* **-/.** *Med:* alcoholism.

alkohollöslich, *a.* soluble in alcohol.

Alkoholmesser, *m.* = **Alkoholometer.**

Alkoholmessung, *f.* alcoholometry.

Alkoholnachweis, *m. Med:* blood-test for alcohol.

Alkoholometer [alko·ho·lo·ˈmeːtər], *n.* **-s/-,** alcoholometer.

Alkoholometrie [alko·ho·lo·me·ˈtriː], *f.* **-/.** alcoholometry.

Alkoholthermometer, *n.* alcohol thermometer.

Alkoholverbot, *n.* prohibition of sale and consumption of alcoholic liquors, *F:* prohibition.

Alkoholvergiftung, *f. Med:* alcoholic poisoning; alcoholism.

Alkoven [alˈkoːvən, ˈalko·vən], *m.* **-s/-,** alcove, (bed-)recess; bed-closet.

Alkosol [alko·ˈzoːl], *n.* **-s/-e.** *Ch:* alcosol.

Alkuin [ˈalku·iːn]. *Pr.n.m.* **-s.** *Hist:* Alcuin.

Alkyl [alˈkyːl], *n.* **-s/-e.** *Ch:* alkyl.

alkylieren [alky·ˈliːrən], *v.tr. Ch:* to alkylate.

Alkyone [alˈkyːo·neː]. *Pr.n.f.* **-s.** *Myth: Astr:* Alcyone.

alkyonisch [alky·ˈoːniʃ], *a. Lit:* **alkyonische Tage,** halcyon days.

all, aller, alle, alles. I. *a.* **1.** (*a*) (*noun particularized in sg.*) all; **alle Ruhe war hin,** all peace was gone; **alle Welt,** everybody, everyone; **für alle Zeit,** for all time; (*usu. inv. when followed by poss. or dem. adj. with strong decl.*) **all sein Stolz,** all his pride; **all dies(es) Lachen,** all this laughter; **all Ihr Schmerz,** all your pain; **all(e) meine Habe,** all my possessions; **all mein Geld,** all my money; **bei all(er) meiner Mühe,** with, in spite of, all my trouble; **trotz all(er) seiner Liebe,** in spite of all his love; **all sein Leben,** all his life; (*emphatic form* **alle,** *inv.,*+*dat. pron.*) **mit, bei, alle diesem,** with all this; **alle dem,** *see* **alledem**; (*b*) (*noun particularized in pl*) all; all the; **alle Menschen,** all men; all mankind; **auf, für, alle Fälle,** in any case, at all events; at all hazards; **vor allen Dingen,** first of all; especially; in the first place; **alle Passagiere waren an Bord,** all the passengers were aboard; **alle Verwandten waren da,** all the relatives were there; **alle Leute,** *Lit:* **all(e) die Leute,** all the people; everybody, everyone; **alle Freunde, all die Freunde, die . . . ,** all the friends who . . . ; (*emphatic, following the noun*) **die anderen alle,** all (of) the others; **von des Lebens Gütern allen . . . ,** of all the things that life can offer . . . ; (*followed by adj. with weak decl.; the strong decl. is also used, but is less favoured*) **alle guten Christen,** *occ.* **alle gute Christen,** all good Christians; **alle anderen, alle übrigen,** (*less frequently*) **alle andere, alle übrige,** all the others, all the rest; **alle, all** (*inv., followed by poss. adj. with strong decl.*), **alle, all, meine Freunde,** all my friends; **alle, all, seine Felder,** all his fields. **2.** (*a*) every; (*after* **ohne**) any; **aller Anfang ist schwer,** all beginnings are difficult; everything is difficult at first; **Bücher aller Art,** every kind of book, all sorts of books; **bei aller und jeder Gelegenheit,** at every possible opportunity; *A:* **allen Augenblick,** (at) every moment; *A:* (*in nom. only*) **alles Ding,** everything; **alles Ding hat seine Zeit,** there is a time for everything; **ohne allen Zweifel,** without any doubt; **ohne allen Grund,** without any reason, quite without reason; **ohne alle Mühe,** without any trouble; effortlessly; (*with pl noun*) **alle Tage,** every day, daily; **alle Jahre,** every year; **alle Augenblicke,** (at) every moment; **aus aller Herren Länder,** from all over the world; from far and wide; (*b*) **alles and(e)re, alles übrige,** everything else; all the rest (of it); **er ist alles andere, nur kein Lehrer,** he is anything but a teacher; whatever he is, he is not a teacher; **vor allem andern,** above all, above all things, first and foremost; most of all; **alles Gute,** everything good, all good things; **j-m alles Gute wünschen,** to wish s.o. all the best; **alles Gute!** all the best! **die Wurzel alles Übels, allen Übels,** the root of all evil. **3.** (*with numerals*) (*a*) **alle beide,** both; the pair of them; **alle drei, alle fünf,** all three, all five; (*b*) **alle zwei Tage,** *Dial:* **aller zwei Tage,** every other day; **alle,** *Dial:* **aller, zwei oder drei Tage,** every second or third day; **alle acht Tage,** once a week; **alle vierzehn Tage,** once a fortnight; **alle fünfzehn Minuten,** every fifteen minutes, every quarter of an hour; **alle fünf Schritt(e),** every five paces, at every fifth pace; **alle zehn Meilen,** every ten miles; *see also* **neun, vier. 4.** (*intensive*) **in aller Eile,** with all (possible) speed, at speed; post-haste, in hot haste, in a great hurry; **in aller Frühe,** early in the morning, in the early morning; **in aller Stille,** very quietly, without any fuss, unobtrusively; *F:* on the quiet; **die Beerdigung fand in aller Stille statt,** he, she, was buried very quietly; **zu allem Unglück . . . ,** as a crowning misfortune . . . , to crown all . . . ; **mit aller Kraft, Gewalt,** with all one's might and main; **mit aller Macht,** with all one's might; **allen Ernstes,** *A:* **alles Ernstes,** in all seriousness; *F:* **was in aller Welt wird er tun?** what on earth, what in the world, will he do? **wer in aller Welt kommt noch zu dieser Stunde?** who on earth can be coming at this hour?

II. *indef. pron.* **1.** *sg.* (*a*) **aller, all** (*inv.*), each, every one, each one; **aller, all, und jeder,** each and every person, one and all, all and sundry; **allem, all, und jedem,** to one and all, to all comers, to all and sundry; (*b*) *coll.* **alles,** everybody, everyone, all; **alles einsteigen!** take your seats! all aboard! **alles aussteigen!** all change! **alles aufpassen!** (pay) attention, everybody! **alles herhören!** listen, all of you! **alles war geflohen,** everyone had fled. **2.** *sg.* (*neuter*) (*a*) **alles,** everything, all; all things; **das ist alles,** that is all; **wenn das alles ist,** if that is, be, all; if it is no more than that; **Geld ist nicht alles,** money is not everything; **alles hat seine Zeit,** there is a time for everything; all in good time; **alles und jedes,** anything and everything; **er ist alles, nur kein Lehrer,** he is anything but a teacher; **es geht um alles oder nichts,** it is neck or nothing; **da hört,** *F:* **hört sich, doch alles auf!** that's the limit! *F:* that puts the lid on it! **damit ist alles gesagt,** I need say no more; **das geht ihm über alles,** he values that more than anything, above all (things), above all else; **sie gilt mir alles,** she is everything , all in all, to me; **alles zusammen,** all together; **alles auf einmal,** all at once; **alles in allem (zusammengenommen), alles eingerechnet,** (taking it) all in all, (taking it) by and large, all told, on the whole, altogether; everything, all things, considered; taking all things into consideration; when all is said and done; **das tu' ich um alles (in der Welt) nicht,** I wouldn't do it on any account; I wouldn't do it for (all) the world, for worlds, *F:* for anything; *F:* **Mädchen für alles,** maid of all work; *Hum:* general factotum; (*b*) (*with prepositions*) **in allem,** (i) in everything, (ii) in all, all told; **dreißig Mann in allem,** thirty men in all, all told; **(alles) in allem habe ich hundert Mark ausgegeben,** I spent a hundred marks in all; all told, I spent a hundred marks; **vor allem,** above all, first and foremost; most of all; **bei allem, trotz allem,** in spite of everything, of all;

with all that; **zu allem fähig,** capable of anything; (*c*) **das alles, das . . . alles, alles das,** all that; all this; **ich kenne das alles,** I know all that, I know it all; **das alles ist Unsinn, das ist alles Unsinn,** all that is nonsense, that is all nonsense; **was soll das alles?** what does it all mean? what's it all about? what's all this about? **alles das, das alles, gehört mir,** all that, that all, belongs to me; (*d*) (*intensive*) **und was alles (noch),** and all the rest of it; and so on; and so forth; **Kaviar, Sekt und wer weiß, Gott weiß, was alles,** caviare, champagne and goodness, heaven, Lord, knows what else, *F:* and what have you, and I don't know what all; **was sind das alles für Menschen?** whatever sort of people are they? whoever are these people? **wer war denn alles da?** who was there altogether? **ich weiß nicht, was er alles getan hat,** I don't know everything he's done; *F:* **da ist, war, (aber) alles dran,** (i) it's, it was, just perfect, *F:* the last word; (ii) *Pej:* it's, it was, the limit; it couldn't be, couldn't have been, worse; **ich habe gestern ein Auto gesehen, da war alles dran,** I saw a car yesterday that had just everything, that was just perfect; (*e*) **alles, was . . . ,** all that . . . , everything that . . . ; **alles, was ich tat,** all, everything, (that) I did; **alles, was ich besitze,** all, everything, (that) I possess; **es ist nicht alles Gold, was glänzt,** all that glitters is not gold; **ist das alles, was Sie mir zeigen können?** is that all you can show me? **ist das alles, was Sie an Gepäck mitnehmen?** is that all the luggage you are taking? (*f*) **mein alles,** my all; **ich habe dir mein alles gegeben,** I have given you my all; **ich war sein alles,** I was everything to him; **mein ein und (mein) alles,** my all in all; my little all; **ihre Tochter war ihr ein und (ihr) alles,** her daughter was all in all to her. **3.** *pl.* (*a*) **alle,** all, everybody, everyone; **wir alle,** all of us; **Sie müssen alle Ihre Pflicht tun,** you must all do your duty; **wir lieben ihn alle,** we all love him; **alle für einen und einer für alle,** all for each and each for all; **alle, die ich sah,** all whom I saw, everyone I saw; **die kenne ich alle,** I know them all; **ich kenne sie alle nicht,** I don't know any of them; **ich kenne sie nicht alle,** I don't know them all; **so sind sie alle!** they're all like that! **so machen's alle,** everybody does it; **alle und jeder,** one and all, all and sundry; **allen und jedem,** to one and all, to all and sundry; to all comers; **alle ohne Ausnahme,** all without exception, every single one of them; **alle, nur er nicht,** all but he; **alle zusammen,** all together; **alle auf einmal,** all at once; **'an alle',** (i) (*heading of circular, etc.*) 'general notice', 'to all concerned', (ii) *Mil: Navy:* (*signal*) 'to all units'; **vor aller Augen,** before everyone's eyes, in sight of everybody; *B:* **aller Augen warten auf dich,** the eyes of all wait upon thee; *Com:* **'das Kaufhaus für alle',** 'the popular store'; *Th:* **alle ab,** exeunt omnes; (*b*) **all,** *inv. Poet:* (*following the noun, in nom. and acc. only*) **die Rosen welken all,** the roses are all fading, *Poet:* the roses all are fading; **die Schönheit lockt uns all,** beauty lures us all.

III. all, alle, *adv. or pred. a. F:* (*a*) **alle,** *A. & Dial:* **all, werden,** to come to an end; (*of money, stock, supplies, etc.*) (i) to run out, give out, (ii) to run low; **der Zucker wird alle,** the sugar is coming to an end, is running low; **die Dummen werden nicht alle,** fools are always with us; (*b*) **alle sein,** to be finished, exhausted, at an end; **ich bin ganz alle,** I'm exhausted, *F:* done up, dead-beat, all in; **unser Geld ist alle,** our money has run out, we have no money left, *F:* we're broke; **der Zucker ist alle,** the sugar is finished, there is no sugar left, *F:* we are out of sugar; (*in restaurant*) **Huhn ist alle,** chicken is off, *U.S:* no more chicken; (*c*) **etwas alle machen,** to make an end of sth.; to finish off (piece of work, etc.); to finish up, polish off (dish, meal); to exhaust (money, resources); to get rid of (one's money); **j-n alle machen,** to eliminate s.o.; to put s.o. out of action; to put (competitor) out of the running.

IV. all, alle, *adv. A. & Dial:* altogether; entirely; very; **das ist all gut,** that is very good.

V. All, das, -s, the universe; *Lit:* the sum of things.

all-, *comb.fm.* **1.** (*a*) all-; omni-; **allmächtig,** all-powerful, omnipotent; **Allmacht** *f*, omnipotence; **allwissend,** all-knowing, omniscient; **Allwissenheit** *f*, omniscience; **allumfassend,** all-embracing; (*b*) pan-; **alldeutsch,** *Hist:* pan-German; *see also* **alldeutsch**; (*c*) every; **alltäglich,** *a.* daily, *adv.* every day, daily; *see compounds listed below.* **2.** (*intensifying*) (*a*) supremely . . . ; **allwichtig,** supremely important; (*b*) universally . . . ; **allverhaßt,** universally hated; (*c*) (*lending a slight emphasis, but otherwise almost meaningless*) **allda,** there; **allhier,** here; **allüberall,** everywhere.

allabendlich [alˀ'aːbəntliç]. **1.** *a.* occurring every evening; **sein allabendlicher Besuch,** his regular evening visit. **2.** *adv.* every evening.

allabends [alˀ'aːbənts], *adv.* every evening.

Allah ['alaː]. *Pr.n.m.* **-s.** Allah.

allargieren [allar'giːrən], *v.tr.* to broaden, enlarge.

Allasch ['alaʃ], *m.* **-(e)s/-e.** *Dist:* allasch; kümmel.

Allativ ['alatiːf, ala'tiːf], *m.* **-s/-e** [-tiːvə]. *Gram:* (*in Turkish, etc.*) allative (case).

allbarmherzig, *a.* all-merciful.

allbekannt, *a.* universally known; notorious (fact); **es ist a., daß . . . ,** it is a matter of common, public, knowledge that . . . ; it is notorious that . . .

allbeliebt, *a.* universally popular; generally liked, liked by everybody.

Allbesamung, *f. Biol:* pansperm(at)ism, panspermy.

allda [al'daː], *adv.* there; at that (very) spot.

alldeutsch, *a.* **1.** *Hist:* pan-German; **der Alldeutsche Verband,** the Pan-German League. **2.** all-German; (policy, etc.) for the whole of Germany. **3.** *s.* **Alldeutsche,** *m., f.* (*decl. as adj.*) *Hist:* pan-Germanist, pan-German.

Alldeutschland, *n. Hist:* pan-Germany.

Alldeutschtum, *n. Hist:* pan-Germanism.

alldieweil [aldiˑ'vail], *conj. A. & Hum:* because, *Lit:* forasmuch as.

alldort [al'dɔrt], *adv.*=**allda.**

alle *see* **all.**

allebendig, *a.* instinct with life; full of life, lively.

alledem [alə'deːm], *indef.pron.* **trotz a.,** in spite of all (that); nevertheless; **bei, mit, a.,** for, with, all that; nevertheless.

Allee [a'leː], *f.* **-/-n** [a'leːən]. **1.** avenue (lined with trees); (tree-lined) walk. **2.** *A:* lane, double line (of soldiers, drawn swords, etc.).

Allegat [aleˑ'gaːt], *n.* **-(e)s/-e,** quotation, citation.

Allegation [aleˑgaˑtsi'oːn], *f.* **-/-en. 1.** citing, quoting (of passage, etc.). **2.**=**Allegat.**

Allegatstrich, *m. A:*=**Anlagestrich.**

allegieren [aleˑ'giːrən], *v.tr. esp. Jur:* to cite, quote (passage, law, etc.); to adduce (written proof).

Allegorie [aleˑgoˑ'riː], *f.* **-/-n** [-'riːən], allegory.

allegorisch [aleˑ'goːriʃ], *a.* allegorical; *adv.* allegorically.

allegorisieren [aleˑgoˑriˑ'ziːrən], *v.tr. & i.* (*haben*) to allegorize; **Allegorisierung** *f*, allegorizing; allegorization.

Allegorist [aleˑgoˑ'rist], *m.* **-en/-en,** allegorist.

Allegretto [aleˑ'grɛtoː]. *Mus:* **1.** *adv.* allegretto. **2.** *s.* **Allegretto,** *n.* **-s/-s,** allegretto (movement).

allegro [a'leːgroː]. *Mus:* **1.** *adv.* allegro. **2.** *s.* **Allegro,** *n.* **-s/-s,** allegro (movement).

allein [a'lain]. **1.** (*occ. emphatic* **alleine**) *inv.pred. a. & adv.* (*a*) alone; **er war a. im Zimmer,** he was alone, the only person, in the room; **ich bin heute ganz a.,** I am all alone, *F:* all on my own, today; **er lebt (ganz) a.,** he lives (all) alone, by himself; *B. & F:* **es ist nicht gut, daß der Mensch a. sei,** it is not good, *B:* that the man, *F:* that man, should be alone; **a. stehen,** (*of farm, house, etc.*) to stand alone; to stand on its own; to be isolated; to stand apart; (*of house*) to be detached; (*of pers.*) to live alone; to be alone in the world; (*of man, woman*) to be without dependants, without family ties, family encumbrances; to be single, unmarried; **a. stehend,** (*of farm, house, etc.*) standing alone; standing on its own; isolated; standing apart; (*of house*) detached; *cp.* **alleinstehend**; **sie steht a. (da), sie ist a. auf der Welt,** she is alone in the world, is entirely on her own; *Lit: Hum:* **a. auf weiter Flur,** all alone; *Lit:* alone in the wide landscape; *Hum:* in splendid isolation; in solitary state; left to one's own devices; **für sich a.,** apart, separately; **für sich a. leben,** to live solitarily, alone; **er möchte Sie a. sprechen,** he would like to talk to you alone, privately; **ich habe das (ganz) allein(e) getan,** I did it (by) myself, alone, single-handed; *Hum:* alone I did it; **ich kann nicht a. damit fertigwerden,** I cannot cope with it alone, single-handed, singly, on my own; *Lit:* **der Starke ist am mächtigsten a.,** the strong man is strongest when he is alone; **das Kind kann jetzt allein(e),** *F:* **von alleine, gehen,** the child can now walk by itself; **du brauchst mich nicht anzutreiben, ich gehe schon von allein(e),** you don't have to push me, I'll go myself; **das brauchst du mir nicht zu sagen, das weiß ich (schon) (von) allein(e),** you don't have to tell me that, I know it myself; *F:* **diese Angelegenheit läuft von alleine,** that matter will take care of itself; *Th:* **Posa a.,** Posa alone, Posa solus; *Prov:* **ein Unglück kommt selten a.,** misfortunes never come singly; it never rains but it pours; (*b*) (*following the noun or pron.*) alone; mere; only; **Gott a. kann uns helfen,** God alone, only God, can help us; **er a. ermutigte uns,** he was the only one who encouraged us, he alone encouraged us; **er a. hat mehr als alle anderen getan,** he alone did more, he did more by himself, than all the others put together; **einem a. alles anvertrauen,** to entrust everything to one person alone, to one and the same person; **Mut a. genügt nicht,** courage alone, mere courage, is not enough; **an seinem Gesichtsausdruck a. wußte ich schon alles,** the mere look on his face told me all; *B:* **der Mensch lebet nicht vom Brot a.,** man shall not live by bread alone; (*c*) mere; **a. der Gedanke, der Gedanke a., macht mich schon wütend,** the bare, mere, very, thought of it makes me furious. **2.** *adv.* (*a*) merely, only; solely; **sie lebt a. für ihre Kinder,** she lives solely, only, for her children; (*b*) **nicht a. . . . , sondern auch . . . ,** not only, not merely . . . , but also . . . ; (*c*) **einzig und a.,** solely, entirely, uniquely; **es ist einzig und a. seinen Bestrebungen zu verdanken, daß . . . ,** it is due entirely, solely, to his efforts that . . . **3.** *conj.* but, yet, however, nevertheless; **ich war oft in ihrem Hause, a. ich sah sie nie,** I was often in her house, but, yet, however, nevertheless, I never (actually) saw her; **ich hatte völliges Vertrauen in ihn, a. ich wurde von ihm betrogen,** I had full confidence in him, but, nevertheless, (and) yet, I was deceived by him.

Alleinberechtigung, *f.* exclusive, sole, right.

Alleinbesitz, *m.* **1.** exclusive possession. **2.** sole property.

alleine [a'lainə], *see* **allein 1.**

Alleinflug, *m. Av:* solo flight.

Alleingang, *m.* single-handed effort; solo attempt; lone attempt; **einen A. machen,** to make a solo attempt, an individual effort; **etwas im A. unternehmen,** to do sth. on one's own; to play a lone hand; **einen Berg im A. bezwingen,** to conquer a mountain alone; *Fb: etc:* **ein Tor im A. erzielen,** to score a goal on one's own.

Alleinhaft, *f. occ.*=**Einzelhaft.**

Alleinhandel, *m.*, **Alleinhandelsrecht,** *n.* monopoly.

Alleinhändler, *m.* monopolist.

alleinheilig, *a.* **der alleinheilige Gott,** the one holy God, the alone holy God.

Alleinheit[1] [a'lainhait], *f.* **1.**=**Alleinsein. 2.** detached state *or* existence; isolation.

Alleinheit[2] [alˀ'ainhait], *f. Phil:* unity (of God, the universe).

Alleinheitslehre [alˀ'ainhaits-], *f. Phil:* monism; monistic doctrine.

Alleinherr, *m.*=**Alleinherrscher.**

Alleinherrschaft, *f.* (*a*) sole reign; (*b*) autocracy; absolute monarchy; dictatorship.

Alleinherrscher, *m.* (*a*) sole ruler; (*b*) autocrat, absolute monarch; dictator.

alleinig [a'lainiç], *a.* **1.** sole, exclusive (use, etc.); sole, only, single (reservation, exception, etc.); **alleinige Rechte,** sole rights; **alleiniger Vertreter,** sole agent. **2.** *South G.Dial: pred.a.* alone.

Alleinigkeitslehre [alˀ'ainiçkaits-], *f. Theol: A:* monotheism.

Alleinmädchen, *n.* general maid.

Alleinsein, *n.* solitariness, solitude, loneliness.

alleinseligmachend, *a.* **der alleinseligmachende Glaube, die alleinseligmachende Kirche,** the true faith, the true church, in which alone salvation is to be found.

Alleinspiel, *n.* (*a*) *Mus:* solo; (*b*) (*in variety performance, etc.*) solo act, monologue; one-man act; single act.

alleinstehend, *a.* (person) living alone; (person) alone in the world; (man, woman) without dependants, without family ties, family encumbrances; **alleinstehende Witwe,** widow without (family) encumbrances. *Cp.* **allein 1** (*a*).

Alleinverkauf, *m.* exclusive sale (of goods); monopoly.

Alleinvertreter, *m. Com:* sole representative; sole agent.

Alleinvertrieb, *m.* monopoly; exclusive sale (of goods); **wir sind zum A. dieser Ware berechtigt,** we are the sole agents for, the sole distributors of, this article.

Allel [a'leːl], *n.* **-s/-e, Allelomorph** [aleˑloˑ'mɔrf], *n.* **-es/-e.** *Biol:* allelomorph.

Alleluja(h) [ale·ˈluːjaː]. *Ecc:* **1.** *int.* hallelujah, alleluia(h); *F:* thank heavens! **2.** *s.* **Alleluia(h),** *n.* -s/-s & -/-, (cry of) hallelujah, alleluia(h); *F:* shout of joy.

allemal, *adv.* **1.** every time, always; **a. wenn . . . ,** as often as, every time that . . . ; **ein für a.,** once (and) for all; **eine Sache ein für a. erledigen,** to settle a question once and for all. **2.** in any case; however; certainly; **es ist a. wahr!** indeed, it's true!

allemalig, *a.* (occurring, arising, etc.) on all occasions.

Allemande [aləˈmã·də], *f.* **-/-n.** *A.Danc: Mus:* allemande.

Allemannen [aləˈmanən], *m. pl.*=**Alemannen,** *q.v. under* **Alemanne.**

allenfalls, *adv.* **1.** (*a*) if need be, if really necessary, if the worst comes to the worst, *F:* at a pinch, *U.S:* in a pinch; **wir könnten a. das Haus verkaufen,** if the worst came to the worst, we could (always) sell the house; (*b*) possibly; **ich könnte seine Antwort a. in acht Tagen haben,** I might possibly have his answer in a week. **2.** by chance; **wenn er a. sterben sollte;** *conj. A:* **a. er sterben sollte,** if he should chance to die, *A:* if perchance, if peradventure, he should die.

allenthalben, *adv.* (*a*) everywhere, on all sides, in every direction; (*b*) in all respects, in every respect, in every way, on every account.

aller *see* **all.**

aller-, *comb.fm.* (+*superlative*) most (+*adj.*) of all; (*superlative*+) of all; -most; **am allerärgsten,** worst of all; **das Allerschwierigste,** the most difficult thing of all; **der, die, das, allerhöchste . . . ,** the highest . . . of all; the topmost (peak, etc.); **die allerweitesten Berge,** the furthest mountains of all, the furthermost mountains.

allerart, *inv.a.*=**allerlei** 1 (*a*).

alleräußerstens, *adv.* at the most.

alleräußerste(r), -äußerste, -äußerste(s), *a.* utmost, uttermost, extreme (importance, necessity, etc.); most extreme (case, measures, etc.); very last (extremity); **das Alleräußerste,** the extreme limit; the utmost.

Allerbarmer, der [alˀɛrˈbarmər], **-s,** the All-Merciful; the God of Mercy.

allerbeste(r), -beste, -beste(s), *a.* best . . . of all; very best; **die allerbesten Stellen,** the (very) best positions, the best jobs (of all); **das allerbeste wäre, zu . . . ,** (the) best of all would be to . . . ; **das ist das Allerbeste,** that's the best of all, *F:* that's the pick of the bunch, of the basket; **und das allerbeste (daran) ist (noch), daß . . . ,** and the best of it all is that . . . ; **der Arzt hat sie aufs allerbeste behandelt,** the doctor could not have treated her better; *F:* (*to pers.*) **mein Allerbester,** my dear fellow, chap; old chap.

allerchristlichst, *a. Hist:* **Seine Allerchristlichste Majestät,** his Most Christian Majesty (of France).

allerdinge [alərˈdiŋə], *adv. A. & B:* (*a*) by all means; altogether; (*b*) **a. nicht,** not at all.

allerdings [alərˈdiŋs], *adv. & emotive particle* (*a*) certainly; **es ist a. so,** it is certainly so; (*strong affirmative*) **glaubst du, ich sollte hingehen? — a. glaube ich das!** do you think I should go there?—certainly I think you should! **hast du ihn entlassen?—a.!** did you sack him?—I certainly did! *U.S:* I sure did! **hat er dich denn betrogen? — a.!** did he really cheat you?—he certainly did! I'll say he did! **kennst du diesen Menschen?—a. kenne ich ihn!** do you know this man?—I certainly do! indeed I do! *F:* rather! you bet I do! (*b*) (*with concessive nuance*) (=**zwar**) **das ist a. wahr, aber . . . ,** that is indeed, of course, admittedly, true, but . . .; I grant you that that is true, but . . . ; **ich habe das a. gesagt, aber . . . ,** I did indeed, certainly, say that, but . . . ; (*c*) (*restrictive nuance*) **er kann nach Deutschland zurückkehren, a. darf er nicht öffentlich auftreten,** he can return to Germany, but he is not allowed to appear in public.

allerdurchlauchtigst, *a.* (Most) Serene (Highness).

allerenden [alərˀˈɛndən], *adv. A:*=**allerorten.**

allererste(r), -erste, -erste(s), (*a*) *a.* first . . . of all, very first; foremost; **der allererste Flieger,** the first aviator of all, the very first aviator; **er war als allererster da,** he was the very first to arrive; (*b*) *adv.* **zu allererst**=**zuallererst.**

Allergie [alɛrˈgiː], *f.* **-/-n** [-ˈgiːən]. *Med:* allergy.

Allergiker [aˈlɛrgikər], *m.* **-s/-.** *Med:* allergic subject; patient suffering from an allergy.

allergisch [aˈlɛrgiʃ], *a. Med:* allergic.

allergnädigst, *a.* most gracious; *adv.* most graciously.

Allerhalter, der [alˀɛrˈhaltər], the Preserver (of All).

allerhand, *inv.a.* (*a*) of all sorts, of all kinds; **a. Fragen,** all sorts, all kinds, all manner, of questions; *F:* **das ist a. Geld,** that's a lot of money, *F:* a packet, a deal, *U.S:* a pile, a heap, of money; *see also* **Achtung** 2; (*b*) *F:* (*elliptic use*) **tausend Mark sind a.,** a thousand marks is a lot of money; **das ist a. für einen Schilling,** that's good value, a lot, for a shilling; that's a good shillingsworth; **das ist ja a.!** that's the limit! **allerhand!** that's really good, *F:* that's something like; **das ist schon a.,** that's quite an achievement; *F:* that's quite something; **er kann a.,** he can do all sorts of, lots of, no end of, things; **er hat a. los,** there's something, there's good stuff, in him; **es gehört a. dazu,** it takes, wants, some doing; **es gehörte a. dazu, es zu finden,** it took some finding; **es gehört schon a. dazu, seinen besten Freund zu betrügen,** it takes a lot of nerve to deceive one's best friend; **es gehört a. dazu, seinem Vorgesetzten die Meinung zu sagen,** it takes a lot of courage, nerve, to speak one's mind to one's superior.

Allerheiligen [alərˈhailiˑgən], *n.inv.* All Saints' Day, All Hallows' Day, All-Hallows; Hallowmas.

Allerheiligenaster, *f.* (garden) chrysanthemum.

Allerheiligenbild, *n. Ecc.Art:* (picture of) (the) Adoration of the Trinity, of the Lamb *or* of Christ, by all the saints (and the faithful).

Allerheiligenfest, *n.*=**Allerheiligen.**

Allerheiligenkraut, *n. Bot:* hedge hyssop.

Allerheiligentag, *m.*=**Allerheiligen.**

allerheiligste(r), -heiligste, -heiligste(s), *a.* most holy (of all); **die allerheiligste Jungfrau, die Allerheiligste,** the Blessed Virgin (Mary); **der allerheiligste Vater,** the Holy Father; the Pope; **das Allerheiligste,** (i) the Holy of Holies; the sanctuary, (ii) the (Most) Blessed Sacrament; the host.

allerhöchst, *a.* (*a*) highest . . . of all; **die allerhöchste Spitze,** the highest peak of all, the topmost peak; **die allerhöchste Autorität,** the supreme authority; **die allerhöchsten Eide,** the most sacred oaths; **der Allerhöchste,** the Most High; Almighty God; **im allerhöchsten Grade, aufs allerhöchste,** in the highest degree; (*b*) **an Allerhöchster Stelle ist man der Meinung, daß . . . ,** His, Her, Majesty is of the opinion that . . . ; **auf Allerhöchsten Befehl,** by royal command, by command of His, Her, Majesty; by command of the Head of the State; *adv.* **Ihre Majestät hat,** *A:* **haben, a. verfügt, daß . . . ,** Her Majesty is graciously pleased to command that . . .

Allerhöchstderselbe, *m.,* **Allerhöchstdieselbe,** *f. Hist:* His Majesty, Her Majesty.

allerkatholischst, *a. Hist:* **Seine Allerkatholischste Majestät,** his Catholic Majesty (of Spain).

allerlei. 1. *inv.a.* (*a*) of all sorts, of all kinds; **a. Gutes,** all sorts, all manner, of good things; **a. Leute,** all sorts, all manner, of people; people of all kinds; all sorts, all manner, of men; **er weiß a.,** he knows all sorts of things; *B:* **a. Tier, a. Gewürm, a. Vögel,** every beast; every creeping thing, and every fowl; (*b*) *B:* **ich bin jedermann a. worden,** I am become all things to all men; (*c*) *F:* (*elliptic use*)=**allerhand** (*b*); **das ist a.!** (i) that's really good! *F:* that's something like! (ii) *F:* it's a bit thick! **2.** *s.* **Allerlei,** *n.* **-s/-s,** (*a*) *Cu:* hotchpotch; salmagundi; **(Leipziger) A.,** mixed vegetables, macédoine of vegetables (*esp.* peas, carrots, and asparagus); (*b*) *Mus:* pot-pourri, medley; selections; *Lit:* medley, miscellany (of extracts, etc.); (*c*) *Pej:* farrago, hotchpotch, olio, medley, *A. & F:* gallimaufry.

allerletzte(r), -letzte, -letzte(s), (*a*) *a.* last of all, very last; final (page, effort, etc.); latest (news, novelties); **im allerletzten Augenblick,** at the very last moment; **er ist der allerletzte in der Klasse,** he is (the very) bottom, *U.S:* at the bottom, of the class; **er war der allerletzte,** he was the last of all; (*b*) *adv.* **zu allerletzt**=**zuallerletzt.**

allerliebst, *a.* (*a*) dearest of all; **du bist mir der allerliebste,** you are dearest of all to me, I like you best of all; (*b*) charming, delightful; **es ist ein allerliebstes Kind,** he, she, is a little darling; **was für ein allerliebstes Kind!** what a love of a child! (*c*) *F:* (*said sardonically*) **das ist ja a.!** that's a nice state of affairs! that's a pretty kettle of fish! (*d*) *adv.* **am allerliebsten,** for preference; as one's first choice; **j-n, etwas, am a. haben,** to like s.o., sth., best of all; **am a. aber besuchte er die Großmutter,** but best of all he liked to go and see his grandmother; **am allerliebsten trinke ich deutsche Weine,** I like German wines best of all, my first preference is for German wines.

Allermannsfreund, *m.* friend of any and everybody.

Allermannsharnisch, *m. Bot:* **1.** allium victoriale, *F:* long-rooted garlic. **2.** Solomon's seal.

allermeist, *a.* (*a*) most; very most; **das allermeiste, was ich tun kann,** the very most, the utmost, I can do; **das hat mir die allermeiste Freude gemacht,** that gave me (the) most pleasure (of all); (*b*) **die allermeisten . . . ,** most . . . ; the greater part (of . . .); the greatest number (of . . .); **die allermeisten (von ihnen),** most of them; **die allermeisten Menschen glauben . . . ,** the generality, the great majority, of men believe . . . ; **das allermeiste hat er abgeschrieben,** most of it he has copied; (*c*) *adv.* **am allermeisten,** *A. & Lit:* **a.,** most of all; chiefly, principally.

allermeistens, *adv.* most often; more often than not.

allermindestens, *adv.* at the very least; at the lowest estimate, at the lowest figure.

allernächst, *a.* very next; (very) nearest (neighbour, town, etc.); *adv.* in close proximity; close at hand, close by, hard by.

allernächstens, *adv.* very shortly; very soon; in the immediate future.

allerneu(e)stens, *adv.* very recently; only a very short time ago; **a. tragen die Frauen wieder kurze Kleider,** it is the latest thing for women to wear short dresses again.

allerneu(e)ste(r), -neu(e)ste, -neu(e)ste(s), *a.* very newest; most recent; very latest (fashion, news).

allernötigst, *a.* indispensable (articles, etc.); **ich habe mich auf das Allernötigste beschränkt,** I confined myself to bare necessaries, to the bare necessities.

allerorten [alərˀˈortən], **allerorts** [alərˀˈorts], *adv.* everywhere.

Allerschaffer, der [ˈalˀɛrʃafər], the Creator (of all things), the Maker of all.

Allerseelen [alərˈzeːlən], *n.,* **Allerseelenfest,** *n.,* **Allerseelentag,** *m.* All Souls' Day.

allerseits, *adv.* (*a*) on all sides; far and wide; (*b*) **guten Morgen a.!** good morning everyone! **ich empfehle mich a.,** good-bye everyone, I wish you all good-bye.

alleruntertänigst, *a.* most obedient, most humble (servant); *adv.* most obediently, most humbly.

allerwärts, *adv.* everywhere.

allerwege(n) [alərˈveːgə(n)], *adv.* **1.** (*a*) everywhere; (*b*) *A:* always; for ever. **2.** *Dial:* in any case, at all events.

Allerweltheil, *n. Bot: popular name for various plants, esp.* (*a*) centaury; (*b*) meadowsweet; (*c*) crosswort gentian; (*d*) herb bennet; helianthemum.

Allerweltsfreund [alərvɛltsˈfroynt], *m.* friend of everyone; person who is *or* tries to be everybody's friend.

Allerweltskerl [alərˈvɛltskɛrl], *m. F:* (*a*) person who can do anything, person (i) who can turn his hand to anything, (ii) who is at home in many fields; (*b*) fantastic chap, *U.S:* hell of a guy; (*c*) clever, smart, chap, *U.S:* smart guy.

Allerweltswort [alərˈvɛltsvort], *n.* word that is in everybody's mouth; household word.

allerwenigstens, *adv.* at the very least.

allerwenigste(r), -wenigste, -wenigste(s), (*a*) *a.* very few; (the) smallest part (of . . .); **die allerwenigsten Menschen,** only very few people; only the smallest part of mankind; **das allerwenigste, was er tun konnte,** the very least he could do; (*b*) *adv.* **am allerwenigsten,** least of all.

allerwerteste(r), -werteste, -werteste(s), (*a*) *a.* most precious; dearest; (*b*) *Hum:* **der Allerwerteste,** the backside, behind, bottom, posterior.

alles *see* **all.**

allesamt, *adv.* all together; one and all.

Allesfresser, *m.* (*a*) pantophagist, omnivorous animal; (*b*) *Hum:* guzzler, *F:* greedy-guts.

Alleskleber, *m.* general-purpose adhesive.

Alles-oder-Nichts-Sicherung, *f. Clockm:* repeating spring; all-or-nothing piece.

Alleswisser, *m.* **-s/-,** know-all; *U.S:* know-it-all, wise guy.

allewege [aləˈveːgə], *adv.*=**allerwege(n).**

alleweil(e), *adv.* **1.** *A:* (*a*) just now, only a few minutes ago; (*b*) now, at present, at the moment. **2.** always. **3.** *F:* **gib's a. her!** come on, give it to me!

allezeit, *adv.* always; for ever; for ever and ever, for evermore.

allfällig, (*a*) *a.* possible, contingent, liable to happen; **allfällige Verluste,** any losses which

may occur; (*last item on agenda*) **'Allfälliges'**, 'any other business'; (*b*) *adv.* possibly, contingently; should the occasion arise.
allfarb, allfarbig, *a.* iridescent.
Allgegenwart, *f.* omnipresence, ubiquity.
allgegenwärtig, *a.* omnipresent, ubiquitous.
Allgeist, *m. Phil:* universal spirit.
allgemach, *adv.* gradually, by degrees, little by little; gently, cautiously, without haste; *Prov:* **a. kommt nach,** (i) little and often fills the purse; little strokes fell great oaks, (ii) gently does it!
allgemein [ˈalgəˈmain, algəˈmain]. **1.** *a.* (*a*) general (rule, ideas, etc.); common (belief, etc.); public (welfare, etc.); universal (application, character, etc.); **die allgemeine Meinung,** the prevailing, general, opinion; **etwas zur allgemeinen Kenntnis bringen,** to bring sth. to the notice of the public, to make sth. public; to bring sth. to everyone's notice; **das allgemeine Beste,** the general weal, the public weal; **zum allgemeinen Besten arbeiten,** to labour for the common good; **etwas a. machen,** to make sth. general, common; to spread (habit, etc.); to generalize (custom, etc.); **allgemeine Anwendung eines Prinzips,** universal application of a principle; **allgemeines Wahlrecht,** universal suffrage; **allgemeine Wehrpflicht,** universal military service; conscription; **im allgemeinen nimmt man heute an, daß . . .,** it is generally assumed today that . . . ; *Ecc:* **allgemeine Kirchenversammlung,** general council; oecumenical council; (*in creed*) **allgemeine christliche Kirche,** catholic church; (*b*) general (statement, state, etc.); **(viel) zu allgemeine Behauptung,** sweeping statement, sweeping generalization; **aus etwas allgemeine Schlüsse ziehen,** to draw general conclusions, to generalize, from sth.; **das Allgemeine im Auge haben,** to take a general view of things, to look at things all round; **sich im Allgemeinen bewegen,** to confine oneself to generalities, to speak in general terms; **im allgemeinen,** in general, generally, taken all round; **im allgemeinen und im besonderen,** in general and in particular; **im allgemeinen gesagt, genommen,** generally speaking, broadly speaking, as a general thing, by and large, in the main, for the most part; **allgemeine Bildung**=**Allgemeinbildung. 2.** *adv.* generally; universally; commonly; **ein a. hochgeschätzter Mann,** a man generally esteemed; **er ist a. beliebt,** he is a general, universal, favourite; **es ist a. bekannt, daß . . .,** it is widely, generally, known, it is common knowledge, that . . . ; **a. gültig,** universally valid; **der Beschluß wurde a. angenommen,** the decision was generally, universally, accepted; **a. gebrauchtes Wort,** (i) word in general use; (ii) word used in a general sense; **a. verbreitete Meinung,** widespread opinion; **es wird a. geglaubt, angenommen, man glaubt a., daß . . .,** it is commonly, generally, believed, that . . . ; **a. gesprochen**=**im allgemeinen gesagt,** *q.v. under* 1 (*b*); *see also* **anerkannt.**
Allgemeinbefinden [algəˈmain-], *n.* general state (of health), general health.
Allgemeinbegriff, *m.* general idea, general notion; *Phil:* concept; universal.
allgemeinbildend, *a.* (book, work) of general cultural value.
Allgemeinbildung, *f.* general, all-round, education; general knowledge; general culture.
allgemeingültig, *a.* universally valid.
Allgemeingültigkeit, *f.* universal validity.
Allgemeingut, *n.* **1.** communal property; public property. **2. das ist A.,** (i) that is a matter of common knowledge, (ii) that is an open secret, that is common property.
Allgemeinheit, *f.* **1.** (*a*) generality; (*b*) universality, universalness. **2. die A.,** (i) the general public, the public at large; people at large; (ii) the community.
allgemeinverbindlich, *a.* (*of contract, etc.*) generally binding.
allgemeinverständlich, *a.* popular (work, treatise); (work) intelligible to the layman, to the ordinary man.
Allgemeinwohl, *n.* public welfare, public well-being; (the) general weal, (the) public weal, (the) common good.
Allgewalt, *f.* omnipotence (*esp.* of God); (God's) almighty power; universally constraining power (of love).
allgewaltig, *a.* almighty, omnipotent, all-powerful.
Allgewürz, *n.* **1.** *Bot:* pimento, Jamaica pepper, allspice, bayberry. **2.** *Cu:* pimento, red pepper.
allgütig [alˈgyːtiç], *a.* (*of God*) infinitely kind, infinitely good.
allhaft, *a.* universal.
Allheilmittel [alˈhailmitəl], *n.* panacea; *F:* heal-all; cure-all.
Allheit, *f. Phil: etc:* totality.
allhier [alˈhiːr], *adv.* here; in this place; locally; *A:* (*on addresses*) **'a.',** 'local'.
Allianz [aliˈants], *f.* **-/-en,** (*a*) alliance; *Hist:* **die Heilige A.,** the Holy Alliance; (*b*) alliance, union (*by marriage*).
Allianzwappen, *n. Her:* united arms of husband and wife.
Alliebe [alˈliːbə], *f.* (God's) infinite love.
alliebend, *a.* (*of God*) infinitely loving.
Alligation [aliˑgaˑtsiˈoːn], *f.* **-/-en.** *Ar: Metall:* alligation; *Metall:* alloy; alloying.
Alligationsrechnung, *f. Ar:* alligation.
Alligationsregel, *f. Ar:* alligation; the rule of mixtures.
Alligator [aliˈgaːtor], *m.* **-s/-en** [-gaˑˈtoːrən]. *Rept:* alligator.
Alligatorbirne, *f. Bot:* alligator pear, avocado pear.
alligieren [aliˑˈgiːrən], *v.tr.* to alligate; *Metall:* to alloy.
alliieren (sich) [aliˑˈiːrən], *v.refl.* to ally oneself (**mit,** with, to).
alliiert, *a.* allied; *Hist:* **die alliierten Streitkräfte,** the Allied Forces; **der Alliierte,** the ally; **die Alliierten,** the Allies.
Alliteration [aliteˑraˑtsiˈoːn], *f.* **-/-en,** alliteration.
alliterieren [aliteˑˈriːrən], *v.i.* (*haben*) to alliterate; to use alliteration; **alliterierend,** alliterative.
alljährig [alˈjɛːriç], *a.*=**alljährlich.**
alljährlich [alˈjɛːrliç]. **1.** *a.* annual, yearly. **2.** *adv.* annually, yearly, every year, year by year.
Allmacht, *f.* omnipotence; (God's) almighty power.
allmächtig [alˈmɛçtiç], *a.* almighty, omnipotent, all-powerful; **der allmächtige Gott, der Allmächtige,** Almighty God, God Almighty; **Allmächtiger, wir bitten dich . . .,** Almighty God, we pray thee . . . ; *int. F:* **Allmächtiger!** God almighty! good Lord!
allmählich [alˈmɛːliç]. **1.** *a.* gradual. **2.** *adv.* gradually, by degrees, little by little; bit by bit; **ganz a.,** very gradually, by slow degrees; inch by inch; *F:* **die Polizisten sahen a. besorgt aus,** the policemen were beginning to look anxious; **ich denke, wir gehen a. nach Hause,** it's about time we were going home, *F:* it's time we were moving, time to make a move.
Allmende [alˈmɛndə], **Allmeinde** [alˈmaində], *f.* **-/-n. 1.** common land, common; communal pasture; communal forest. **2.** *Swiss Dial:* ground between two houses.
allmonatlich [alˈmoːnaˑtliç]. **1.** *a.* monthly. **2.** *adv.* monthly, each month, every month.
allmorgendlich, allmorgens [alˈmorgəntliç, -ˈmorgəns], *adv.* (regularly) every morning.
Allmutter, die, (Nature, Night,) the mother of all things.
allnächtlich [alˈnɛçtliç], *a. & adv.* nightly.
Allod [aˈloːt], *n.* **-(e)s/-e** [-s,- ˈloːdəs/-ˈloːdə]. *Hist:* allodium; freehold (estate).
allodial [aloˑdiˈaːl], *a.*, **Allodial-,** *comb.fm. Hist:* allodial, freehold (estate, etc.).
Allodialbesitz, *m.*, **Allodialgut,** *n. Hist:* freehold estate, allodium, freehold.
Allodium [aˈloːdium], *n.* **-s/-dien**=**Allod.**
Allogamie [aloˑgaˑˈmiː], *f.* **-/.** *Bot:* allogamy, cross-fertilization.
allogamisch [aloˑˈgaːmiʃ], *a.* allogamous.
allogen [aloˑˈgeːn], *a.* allogeneous.
Allokution [aloˑkuˑtsiˈoːn], *f.* **-/-en,** allocution; ceremonial address.
Allomorphie [aloˑmorˈfiː], *f.* **-/.** *Cryst: etc:* allomorphism.
Allonge [aˈlõːʒə], *f.* **-/-n,** (*a*) lengthening-piece; extension; (*b*) *Com: Fin:* allonge (to a bill of exchange, etc.); (*c*) *Equit:* lunging rein, longe, lunge.
Allongeperücke, *f.* full-bottomed wig.
Allopath [aloˑˈpaːt], *m.* **-en/-en.** *Med:* allopathist.
Allopathie [aloˑpaˑˈtiː], *f.* **-/.** *Med:* allopathy.
allopathisch [aloˑˈpaːtiʃ], *a. Med:* allopathic.
allothigen [aloˑtiˑˈgeːn], *a. Geol:* allothogenic, allothogenous.
Allotria [aˈloːtriˑaː], *n.pl.* trivialities; unimportant matters, matters of no significance; **A. treiben,** to fool around; to trifle, waste time on trifles; to fiddle-faddle; to frivol.
allotrop [aloˑˈtroːp], *a. Ch:* allotropic.
Allotropie [aloˑtroˑˈpiː], *f.* **-/-n** [-ˈpiːən]. *Ch:* allotropy.
Allotropismus [aloˑtroˑˈpismus], *m.* **-/.** *Ch:* allotropism.
Allradantrieb, *m. Aut:* all-wheel drive.
Allradlenkung, *f. Aut:* all-wheel steering.
allrussisch, *a.* pan-Russian.
allseitig, (*a*) *a.* all-round (knowledge, mind, improvement); comprehensive (knowledge); (*b*) *adv.* all round; from every angle; **eine Angelegenheit a. betrachten,** to look at a matter all round, in all its bearings, from all points of view, from every angle.
Allseitigkeit, *f.* all-round character (of s.o.'s knowledge, etc.); all-round ability.
allseits, *adv.* **1.**=**allerseits. 2.** from every angle; from all points of view; in all respects.
allsogleich, *adv. A:*=**sogleich.**
Allstrom-, *comb.fm. El.E:* for alternating or direct current; A.C./D.C. (wireless receiver, etc.); all-mains (receiver).
allstündlich [alˈʃtyntliç], (*a*) *a.* hourly; (*b*) *adv.* hourly, every hour, hour by hour.
Alltag, *m.* **1.** work-day, working day; ordinary day; weekday; *adv.phr.* **des Alltags**=**alltags. 2.** (*a*) monotonous, uneventful, unexciting, period; (*b*) monotony; **der graue A.,** colourless, unrelieved, monotony, *esp.* the dull monotony of daily life; the daily grind, 'the daily round, the common task'. **3.**=**Alltagsleben.**
alltäglich. 1. [alˈtɛːkliç] (*a*) *a.* daily (task, wants, etc.); everyday (occurrence, etc.); (event, etc.) of daily occurrence; **sein alltäglicher Gang durch die Stadt,** his daily walk through the town; (*b*) *a.* usual, ordinary; customary, accustomed; common (happening, experience, etc.); banal, trite, trivial (remark, etc.); **das ist (bei ihm) etwas Alltägliches,** it happens (to him) every day; it's nothing out of the ordinary, out of the way (for him), it's a normal thing (to him); it's a commonplace (to him); **das ist nichts Alltägliches,** it's something out of the ordinary; it's something out of the usual (run of things); (*c*) *adv.* daily, every day. **2.** *a.* [ˈalteˑkliç] dull (existence, etc.); humdrum (existence); workaday (existence, clothes, etc.); matter-of-fact (manner, etc.); **ein alltäglicher Mensch,** an ordinary, average, undistinguished, person; a very ordinary person.
Alltäglichkeit, *f.* **1.** dullness (of existence, etc.); banality, triteness, triviality (of remark, etc.); ordinariness (of character, display, etc.). **2.** (i) everyday happening, everyday occurrence; normal thing; (ii) commonplace; platitude; banal remark, banality; trivial remark, triviality; **das sind für ihn Alltäglichkeiten,** it's nothing out of the ordinary, out of the way, for him; these are everyday happenings to him; **seine Rede enthielt nichts als Alltäglichkeiten,** his speech consisted of nothing but commonplaces, platitudes.
alltags, *adv.* **1.** *occ.* daily, every day. **2.** on working days; on weekdays; on ordinary days.
Alltagsbeschäftigung, *f.* daily task; everyday occupation; routine occupation; the daily routine.
Alltagsgeschwätz, Alltagsgewäsch, *n.* (mere) commonplaces; empty chatter.
Alltagskleid, *n.* everyday dress, ordinary dress; **Alltagskleider** *pl*, ordinary clothes, everyday clothes; (man's) workaday clothes.
Alltagskost, *f.* ordinary fare, everyday fare; ordinary meal(s).
Alltagsleben, *n.* everyday life; ordinary, workaday life; humdrum daily life; the daily round, the daily routine.
Alltagsmensch, *m.* ordinary, average, undistinguished, person; **der A.,** the ordinary man, the common man.
Alltagssorgen, *f.pl.* everyday cares; worries of daily life.
Alltagswelt, *f.* everyday world, workaday world.
Alltagswort, *n.* household word; word that is in everybody's mouth.
allüberall, *adv.* (just) everywhere; here, there, and everywhere.
alludieren [aluˑˈdiːrən], *v.i.* (*haben*) to allude (**an**+*acc.*, to).
allum, all um [alˈˀum], *adv.* all round, round about.
allumfassend, *a.* all-embracing; universal (mind, intellect); comprehensive, encyclopaedic (knowledge); all-round (knowledge, education); wide (knowledge, culture).
Allüre [aˈlyːrə], *f.* **-/-n. 1.** gait, paces, action (of horse). **2.** *pl.* **Allüren,** manners; behaviour; mannerisms; **sie hat seltsame Allüren,** she behaves in a strange way; **die Allüren eines Filmstars,** the ways and manners of a film star; the grand airs of a film star.

Allusion [aluˑzĭ'oːn], *f.* -/-en, allusion (**an**+*acc.*, to).

allusiv [aluˑ'ziːf], **allusorisch** [aluˑ'zoːriʃ], *a.* allusive.

alluvial [aluˑvĭ'aːl], *a.*, **Alluvial-**, *comb.fm. Geol:* alluvial.

Alluvialboden, *m.* alluvial soil; alluvium.

Alluvialland, *n.* alluvial (tract of) land; alluvium.

Alluvion [aluˑvĭ'oːn], *f.* -/-en. **1.** *Geol:* alluvion; (*a*) river deposits; (*b*) accretion through, by, alluvion. **2.** *esp. Jur:* alluvion.

Alluvionsrecht, *n. Jur:* right to (land made by) alluvion.

Alluvium [a'luːvĭum], *n.* -s/-vien. *Geol:* **1.** alluvium; alluvial deposit(s); alluvial land *or* soil. **2. das A.**, the Holocene (series, epoch), the Recent (series, epoch).

Allvater, der, (God, *G.Myth:* Wotan) the Father of All.

allverehrt [ˌalvɛr'eːrt], *a.* revered by all; universally venerated.

allweg, *adv.*=**allewege.**

allweil, *adv.*=**alleweile.**

allweise [al'vaizə], *a.* all-wise; supremely wise.

Allwellenempfänger, *m. W.Tel:* all-wave receiver.

allwissend [al'visənt], *a.* omniscient; (*of God*) all-knowing.

Allwissenheit, *f.* omniscience.

allwo [al'voː], *rel.adv. A:* where.

allwöchentlich [al'vœçəntliç], *a.* weekly; hebdomadal (meeting, etc.).

Allyl [a'lyːl], *n.* -s/. *Ch:* allyl.

allzeit, *adv.*=**allezeit.**

allzu, *adv.*, **allzu-**, *comb.fm.* (+*adj. or adv.; usu. separately as adv. when heavily stressed*) all too; only too; much too; altogether too, far too, too ... by far; excessively; over-; **ich kenne ihn a. gut, allzugut,** I know him all, only, too well; **ist es wahr?—ja, a. wahr,** is it true?—yes, only too true; **allzubald,** all, only, too soon; **das tue ich allzugern(e),** I am only too willing to do it; **er hat a. lange, allzulange, gezögert,** he hesitated far too long; **er kam allzufrüh,** he came much, far, too early; **er war allzugut zu mir,** he was excessively, much too, far too, kind to me; **a. vorsichtig,** excessively cautious; over-cautious, *adv.* over-cautiously.

allzuhauf, *adv.* all in a heap.

allzumal, *adv.* all together; one and all; *B:* **ihr seid a. Kinder des Höchsten,** all of you are children of the Most High.

allzusammen, *adv.* all together.

allzusehr, *adv.* excessively, overmuch; inordinately; **dieser Schriftsteller ist a. gelobt worden,** this author has been excessively praised, praised overmuch; **sich a. anstrengen,** to exert oneself overmuch, to over-exert oneself; **j-n a. lieben,** to be inordinately fond, over-fond, of s.o.; to idolize s.o.

allzuviel, *adv.* & *quasi-sb.* (far) too much; overmuch; **a. ist ungesund,** all excess does one harm; *Prov:* enough is as good as a feast.

Allzweck-, *comb.fm.* all-purpose ... ; general-purpose ... ; universal (tool, appliance, etc.); **Allzweckfahrzeug** *n*, all-purpose, general-purpose, vehicle; utility vehicle; **Allzweckflugzeug** *n*, all-purpose, general-purpose, aircraft; **Allzweckmotor** *m*, all-purpose engine *or* motor; **Allzwecktisch** *m*, all-purpose table; *Mec.E:* **Allzweckhebezeug** *n*, all-purpose, universal, hoisting gear; *Tls:* **Allzweckbohrgerät** *n*, all-purpose, universal, boring *or* drilling tool; **Allzweckzange** *f*, all purpose, universal, pliers.

Alm[1], *m.* -(e)s/. *Agr:* marl (from lakes).

Alm[2], *f.* -/-en, alpine pasture, alpine meadow, alp.

Almabfahrt, *f.* driving down of the cattle from the alpine pastures.

Almagest [alma'gɛst], *m.* -/. *A.Astr:* almagest.

Alma mater ['almaː 'maːtər], *f.* -/. university; Alma Mater.

Almanach ['almaˑnax], *m.* -(e)s/-e. **1.** almanac; calendar; *Astr:* ephemeris. **2.** year-book, annual; directory, guide.

Almandin [alman'diːn], *m.* -s/-e. *Miner:* almandine, almandite.

Almanger, *m. Swiss Dial:* alpine meadow (by cowherd's hut).

Almauftrieb, *m.*=**Almfahrt.**

Almdudler, *m. Dial: & F:* wine and soda-water, wine shandy.

Alme[1], *f.* -/-n. *Ind:* drying-kiln (esp. *for cardboard*).

Alme[2], **Almeh** [al'meː], *f.pl.* alma(h)s, almehs; (Egyptian) dancing-girls.

Almei [al'mai], *n.* -s/. *Metall: etc:* tutty; crude zinc oxide.

Almende [al'mɛndə], *f.* -/-n=**Allmende.**

Almenrausch, *m.*=**Almrausch.**

Almer[1], *m.* -s/-. *Swiss Dial:*=**Älmler.**

Almer[2], *f.* -/-n, **Almerei**, *f.* -/-en. *South G.Dial:* **1.** cupboard. **2.** *Ecc:* muniment chest; muniment room.

Almfahrt, *f.* driving up of the cattle to the alpine pastures.

Almge, *f.* -/-n. *Swiss Dial:*=**Allmende.**

Almhütte, *f.* alpine (cowherd's) hut.

Almiranten, die [almiˑ'rantən]. *Pr.n.f.pl.*= **Amiranten.**

Älmler, *m.* -s/-. dweller in the alpine pastures; alpine cowherd.

Almosen ['almoːzən], *n.* -s/-, (*a*) alms, dole; **j-m ein A. geben,** to give alms to s.o.; **j-n um ein A. bitten,** to ask an alms of s.o.; to beg from s.o.; (*b*) *pl.* **Almosen,** alms, charity; **von A. leben,** to live on charity, on doles; **auf A. angewiesen sein,** to be reduced to beggary; to have to live on charity; *B:* **wenn du A. gibst,** when thou doest alms.

Almosenamt, *n.* almonry; alms-house.

Almosenanstalt, *f.* charitable institution.

Almosenbeutel, *m.* alms-bag.

Almosenbüchse, *f.* alms-box; poor-box.

Almosenempfänger, *m.* (*a*) receiver of alms, of charity; almsman; (*b*) *F:* pauper.

Almosengeben, *n.* alms-giving.

Almosengeber, *m.* alms-giver.

Almosengeld, *n.* alms(-money).

Almosenhaus, *n.* alms-house.

Almosenier [almoˑzeˑ'niːr], *m.* -s/-e, almoner.

Almosenkasse, *f.*, **Almosenkasten**, *m.*=**Almosenbüchse.**

Almosenpflege, *f.* (*a*) alms-giving; (*b*) *Adm:* poor-relief.

Almosenpfleger, *m.* (*a*) almoner; *cp.* **Großalmosenpfleger**; (*b*) *Adm: A:* guardian, overseer, of the poor.

Almosensammler, *m.* alms-collector; collector of contributions for the poor.

Almosensammlung, *f. Ecc: etc:* collection (for the poor).

Almosenstock, *m.*=**Almosenbüchse.**

Almosentasche, *f. A:* (*a*) alms-purse; (*b*) *F:* (lady's) purse; mesh-bag.

Almosenverteilung, *f.* distribution of alms; alms-giving.

Almrausch, *m.*, **Almrose**, *f. Bot:* rhododendron; alpine rose.

Almwiese, *f.* alpine meadow.

Almwirtschaft, *f.* **1.** alpine dairy-farming. **2.** alpine inn.

Almzeit, *f.* period during which the cattle can be left on the alpine pastures.

Aloe ['aːloˑeː], *f.* -/-n [-ən]. **1.** *Bot:* (*a*) aloe; (*b*) **hundertjährige A.,** American aloe, century plant. **2.** *Pharm:* aloes.

Aloebitter, *n. Pharm:* bitter aloes.

Aloeextrakt, *m. Pharm:* aloes.

Aloefaser, *f. Com:* aloe-fibre, sisal-grass, -hemp.

aloehaltig, *a. Pharm:* aloetic.

Aloehanf, *m.*=**Aloefaser.**

Aloeholz, *n. Com:* aloes-wood, eagle-wood.

Aloemittel, *n. Pharm:* aloetic.

Aloesaft, *m. Pharm:* aloes.

Aloesäure, *f. Ch:* aloetic acid.

Aloetinktur, *f. Pharm:* (tincture of) aloes.

Aloetinsäure [aˑloˑeˑ'tiːn-], *f.*=**Aloesäure.**

aloetisch [aˑloˑ'eːtiʃ], *a. Pharm:* aloetic.

Alogie [aˑloˑ'giː], *f.* -/. illogicality, irrationality.

alogisch [aˑ'loːgiʃ], *a.* illogical, irrational.

Alois ['aːloˑiːs], **Aloisius** [aˑloˑ'iːzĭus]. *Pr.n.m.* -'. Aloysius.

aloof [ə'luːf], *adv. Nau:* to windward.

Alopekie [aˑloˑpeˑ'kiː], **Alopezie** [aˑloˑpeˑ'tsiː], *f.* -/. *Med:* alopecia, baldness.

Alose [aˑ'loːzə], *f.* -/-n. *Ich:* alosa; *esp.* alose, shad, allice-shad.

Alp[1], *m.* -(e)s/-e=**Alb**[1].

Alp[2], *f.* -/-en, (*a*) alpine meadow, alpine pasture; (*b*) *Dial:* alps, mountains, highlands; *see also* **Alpen.**

Alpaka [al'paˑkaː], *n.* -s/-s. *Z: Tex:* alpaca.

Alpakawolle, *f. Tex:* alpaca wool.

Alpak(k)a [al'pakaː], *n.* -s/. *Metall:* German silver, nickel silver.

al pari [al 'paːriː]. *Ital. phr. Fin:* at par.

Alpbalsam, *m. Bot:*=**Alpenrose.**

Alpdruck, *m.*, **Alpdrücken**, *n.* nightmare.

Alpe, *f.* -/-n. *Dial: esp. Austrian:*=**Alp**[2].

älpeln, *v.i.* (*haben*) to work a small alpine dairy-farm.

Alpen[1], *pl. Geog:* alps; **die A.,** the Alps; **die Schweizer A.,** the Swiss Alps; *see also* **diesseits, jenseits.**

Alpen-, *comb.fm.* alpine ... ; **Alpenbärlapp** *m*, alpine club-moss; **Alpenfauna** *f*, alpine fauna.

alpen[2], *v.i.* (*haben*) to live on the alpine pastures; to work on an alpine dairy-farm.

alpen[3], *v.i.* (*haben*)=**alben.**

alpenartig, *a.* alpine (scenery, etc.).

Alpenbahn, *f.* alpine railway, mountain railway.

Alpenbewohner, *m.* inhabitant of, dweller in, the Alps.

Alpenbirke, *f. Bot:* dwarf birch.

Alpenbirkenzeisig, *m. Orn:* lesser redpoll.

Alpenbraunelle, *f. Orn:* alpine accentor.

Alpencharakter, *m. Geol: etc:* alpine characteristics.

Alpendistel, *f. Bot:* **1.** carduus defloratus, long-stalked (alpine) thistle. **2.**=**Alpenmannstreu.**

Alpendohle, *f. Orn:* alpine chough.

Alpenflora, *f. Bot:* alpine flora.

Alpenflühvogel, *m. Orn:* alpine accentor.

Alpenführer, *m.* **1.** (*pers.*) alpine guide. **2.** (*book*) guide to the Alps.

Alpengarten, *m. Hort:* garden of alpine plants; rock-garden.

Alpenglöckchen, *n. Bot:* soldanella.

Alpenglühen, *n.* alpenglow.

Alpengras, *n. Bot:* alpine carex.

Alpenheide, *f. Bot:* alpine azalea.

Alpenhelm, *m. Bot:* alpine bartsia.

Alpenhirt, *m.* alpine cowherd.

Alpenhorn, *n.* **1.**=**Alphorn. 2.** *occ.* peak (of mountain).

Alpenhütte, *f.* alpine hut; chalet.

Alpenjäger, *m.* **1.** hunter in the Alps. **2.** *Mil:* (*a*) mountain rifleman; (*b*) *pl.* **Alpenjäger,** (i) (French) Chasseurs Alpins, (ii) (Italian) Alpini.

Alpenkette, *f.* alpine chain, chain of alps.

Alpenkrähe, *f. Orn:* chough.

Alpenkresse, *f. Bot:* hutchinsia.

Alpenland, *n.* alpine region(s).

Alpenlattich, *m. Bot:* purple-flowered wild lettuce.

Alpenlerche, *f. Orn:* shore lark.

Alpenliebstöckel, *n. Bot:* lovage.

Alpenlinse, *f. Bot:* alpine milk-vetch.

Alpenmannstreu, *f. Bot:* alpine sea-holly, alpine eringo.

Alpenmauerläufer, *m. Orn:* wall-creeper.

Alpenmolch, *m. Amph:* alpine newt.

Alpennelke, *f. Bot:* alpine pink.

Alpenpaß, *m.* alpine pass, pass in the alps.

Alpenpflanze, *f. Bot:* alpine plant, alpestrine plant.

Alpenrausch, *m. Bot:*=**Alpenrose.**

Alpenrebe, *f. Bot:* alpine clematis.

Alpenringamsel, **Alpenringdrossel**, *f. Orn:* alpine ring-ouzel.

Alpenrose, *f. Bot:* rhododendron; alpine rose; **(behaarte, bewimperte) A.,** (hairy) alpine rose; **rostrote A.,** rusty-leaved alpine rose.

Alpenrot, *n.* red snow.

Alpensalamander, *m. Amph:* (black) alpine salamander.

Alpenscharte, *f. Bot:* **1.** saussurea, alpine saw-wort. **2.** alpine knapweed.

Alpenschneehuhn, *n. Orn:* ptarmigan; *U.S:* rock-ptarmigan.

Alpensegler, *m. Orn:* alpine swift.

Alpenskabiose, *f. Bot:* small scabious.

Alpensteiger, *m.* alpine climber, alpinist.

Alpensteinbock, *m. Z:* ibex, steinbock (of the Alps).

Alpenstock, *m.* alpenstock.

Alpenstrandläufer, *m. Orn:* dunlin.

Alpenstraße, *f.* alpine road, road over the alps.

Alpenveilchen, *n. Bot:* cyclamen, sowbread.

Alpenverein, *m.* Alpine Club.

Alpenvorland, das. *Geog:* the Alpenvorland; the South German plateau; the foot-hills of the Alps.

Alpenwirtschaft, *f.* **1.** (*a*) alpine (dairy-)farming; (*b*) alpine (dairy-)farm. **2.** alpine inn.

Alpfahrt, *f.*=**Almfahrt.**

Alpfuß, *m.* pentagram, pentacle.

Alpgeld, *n.*=**Alpzins.**

Alpha ['alfaː], *n.* -s/-s. *Gr.Alph:* alpha.

Alphabet [alfa'beːt], *n.* -(e)s/-e. **1.** alphabet. **2.** *Bookb: Print: A:* twenty-three consecutive quires.

alphabetisch [alfa'beːtiʃ], (*a*) *a.* alphabetical; (*b*) *adv.* alphabetically; **a. geordnet,** arranged in alphabetical order.

alphabetisieren [alfaˑbeˑtiˑ'ziːrən], *v.tr.* to arrange (a list, etc.) alphabetically, in alphabetical order, to alphabetize.

Alphabetist [alfaˑbeˑ'tist], *m.* -en/-en, abecedarian; child learning the rudiments.

Alphabetschloß, *n.* combination-lock, letter-lock, puzzle-lock.

alphaft, *a.* alpine (scenery, etc.).

Alphard [ˈalfaˑrt], *m.* -/. *Astr:* Alphard; Cor Hydrae.

Alphastrahlen, *m.pl. Ph:* alpha rays.

Alphirt, *m.* alpine cowherd.

Alphof, *m.* alpine (dairy-)farm.

Alphorn, *n. Mus:* alpine horn, alp-horn, alpenhorn.

Alphütte, *f.* alpine hut; chalet.

alpin [alˈpiːn], **alpinisch** [alˈpiːniʃ], *a.* alpine; **alpiner Verein**, Alpine club; *Ethn:* **alpine Rasse**, alpine race.

Alpinismus [alpiˑˈnismus], *m.* -/. alpinism, alpine climbing.

Alpinist [alpiˑˈnist], *m.* **-en/-en**, alpinist, alpine climber.

Alpinistik [alpiˈnistik], *f.* **-/.=Alpinismus.**

Alpinum [alˈpiːnum], *n.* **-s/-na=Alpengarten.**

alpisch, *a. occ.*=**alpin.**

Alpkraut, *n. Bot:* **(purpurblütiges) A.**, trumpet-weed, *U.S:* kidney-root.

Alpkreuz, *n.*=**Alpfuß.**

Älpler, *m.* **-s/-**, (*a*) dweller in the alpine pastures; (*b*) alpine (dairy-)farmer; alpine cowherd.

Älpner, *m.* **-s/-=Älpler.**

Alpranke, *f. Bot: F:* **1.** woody nightshade, bittersweet. **2.** mistletoe.

Alprauch, *m. Bot:* fumitory.

Alprute, *f. Bot:* club-moss.

Alptraum, *m.* nightmare.

Alpwirtschaft, *f.*=**Alpenwirtschaft.**

Alpzins, *m.* (*in Switzerland*) rent paid for grazing rights on alpine pastures.

Alpzopf, *m.* elf-lock.

Alraun [alˈraun], *m.* **-(e)s/-e, Alräunchen** [alˈrɔynçən], *n.* **-s/-, Alraune** [alˈraunə], *f.* **-/-n.** *Bot:* **1.** mandragora, *F:* mandrake. **2.** *F:* **wilder Alraun,** allium victoriale, *F:* long-rooted garlic.

alraunenhaft, *a.* resembling a mandrake; (*a*) (object) endowed with magic powers; (*b*) shrivelled, shrunken; wizened (little man, woman).

Alraunwurzel, *f. Bot:* mandrake(-root).

als. I. *adv.* **1.** (*relative, introducing a predicative complement*) (*a*) as; for; by way of; **der Wert des Romans als Literatur,** the value of the novel as literature; **j-n als Lehrer haben,** to have s.o. as, for, a teacher; **j-n als seinen Sohn anerkennen,** to recognize s.o. as one's son; **j-n als einen Freund betrachten,** to consider, regard, s.o. as a friend; **sein Taschentuch als Flagge benutzen,** to use one's handkerchief as a flag; **etwas als Geschenk schicken,** to send sth. as a present; **als Einleitung, Warnung, Belohnung,** as, by way of, introduction, warning, reward; *see also* **dienen** 5 (*b*), **gelten[1], zulassen;** (*b*) (*with temporal nuance*) **als Kind war er häufig krank,** he was often ill as a child, in his childhood; **schon als Knabe hatte er zeichnerisches Talent,** even as a boy, in his boyhood, he had a talent for sketching; **noch als alter Mann,** even as an old man; (*c*) as, considered as, regarded as; *qua;* **der Mensch als Säugetier (betrachtet),** man as a mammal; **der Mensch als Mensch,** man *qua* man; **die Franzosen als Volk,** the French as a nation; *see also* **solch;** (*d*) as, in the guise of; *Th:* in the rôle of; **als Page gekleidet sein,** to be dressed as a page; (*e*) as; being; in the capacity of, in one's capacity as; **das sage ich Ihnen als Freund,** I tell you this as a friend; **als alter Freund Ihres Vaters . . . ,** as, being, an old friend of your father's . . . ; **meine Rechte als Vater,** my rights as a father; **als guter Christ,** as a good Christian; **als Engländer trank er ausschließlich Bier,** being an Englishman he drank nothing but, *F:* stuck to, beer; **als Athlet taugt er nicht viel,** he is not much good as an athlete, not much of an athlete; **als Freiwilliger dienen,** to serve as a volunteer; **eine Stellung als Sekretär,** a post as secretary; **als Dolmetscher fungieren,** to act as interpreter; **ich handelte in meiner Eigenschaft als Friedensrichter,** I acted in my capacity as a Justice of the Peace; *see also* **Eigenschaft** 2; (*f*) (*often not translated*) **er starb als Katholik,** he died a Catholic; **er kehrte aus Afrika als Kranker zurück,** he returned from Africa an invalid; **er zeigte sich als guter Freund,** he showed himself a good friend; **sie begannen als Freunde und endeten als Feinde,** they started (as) friends and ended (as) enemies; **er wurde als Vorsitzender gewählt,** he was elected chairman; **er war als Erster da,** he was there first, was the first to arrive; **es hat sich als wahr, als unmöglich, erwiesen,** it has proved true, impossible; *for further examples, see under the verbs* **ausrufen** I. 1 (*b*), **bekennen** I. 2 (*b*), **betrachten** I. 1 (*d*), **erweisen** I. 1 (*a*), *etc.* **2.** *A:* (=**also**) thus, so; **als hatte der König befohlen,** the king had commanded thus. **3.** *West G.Dial:* (=**immer**) **als weiter gehen,** to go on and on.

II. **als,** *conj.* **1.** (*a*) (*in comparison of inequality*) than; **ich habe mehr, weniger, als Sie,** I have more, less, than you; **er ist mehr als zwanzig Jahre alt,** he is more than, over, twenty; **er ist größer als ich,** he is taller than I; **er ist älter als Sie denken,** he is older than you think; **ich kenne Sie besser als ihn,** I know you better than (I know) him; **ich wollte lieber sterben als ihn um Geld bitten,** I would rather die than ask him for money; **lieber tot als Sklave!** better death than slavery! (*b*) **zu . . . , als daß . . . ,** too . . . +*inf.*; **sie ist zu dumm, als daß sie es verstehen könnte,** she is too stupid to understand it; **ich bin viel zu alt, als daß ich noch heiraten könnte,** I am much too old to marry now; **das Loch war zu eng, als daß eine Ratte hätte durchkommen können,** the hole was too narrow for a rat to get through; (*c*) but, except; **nichts als die Wahrheit,** nothing but the truth; **niemand, kein anderer, als er,** none but he, nobody else but he; **wer anders als er?** who else but he? **was hätte ich ander(e)s tun können, als lachen?** how could I do anything else but laugh? *see also* **anders** 2; **es bleibt (mir, uns) nichts anderes übrig, als Ihnen zu danken,** there remains nothing more but to thank you; **es bleibt mir nichts anderes übrig, als sie zu heiraten,** I have no choice but to marry her; (*d*) *A. & occ.* (*in comparison of equality*) (=**wie**); **genau so gut als er,** just as good as he; **so viel als,** as much as; **so viele als,** as many as; *B:* **seine Kleider wurden weiß als ein Licht,** his raiment was white as the light; (*pleonastic use*) **als wie der Donner,** just like thunder; **so klug als wie zuvor,** no wiser than before; (*e*) **sowohl . . . als (auch);** *see* **sowohl;** (*f*) (*relative use*) **als (da sind) . . . ,** such as . . . ; **die üblichen Schulfächer, als (da sind) Latein, Mathematik, Geographie,** the usual school subjects, such as, like, (as) for example, Latin, mathematics, geography. **2. als** (+*past subj. with inverted order*), **als ob, als wenn** (+*past subj. with dependent order*), as if, as though; **er redet, als wäre er betrunken, als ob, als wenn, er betrunken wäre,** he talks as if he were drunk; **es sieht so aus, als wenn, als ob, er fort wäre,** it looks as though he has gone; **es sieht aus, als wollte es regnen, als ob es regnen wollte,** it looks like rain; **es ist nicht, als ob sie es übelnehmen würden,** it is not as if they would mind; **als wäre es alles wahr,** as though it were all true; **als wäre nichts geschehen,** as though nothing had happened; *F:* **(so) tun als ob,** to pretend; to be pretending; to feign, simulate, interest, enthusiasm, etc.; to pretend to agree; *F:* to put on an act, *U.S:* to play along; *see also* **Als Ob. 3.** (*temporal use, with past tenses only*) (*a*) (*with pluperfect*) after, when; **ich kam, als er gegangen war,** I came after he had gone, after he went, when he had gone; **er sprach, als ich geendet hatte,** he spoke when, after, I had finished; **als sie ihre Mahlzeit beendet hatten, gingen sie in den Garten,** after, when, they had finished their meal they went into the garden; (*b*) (*with imperfect*) when; as; **als der Krieg vorbei war,** when the war was over; **als es Frühling wurde,** when spring came; **als er heiratete,** when he married, got married; **als ich jung war,** when I was young, in my young days; **zu der Zeit, als . . . ,** at the time when . . . ; **als er noch auf der Schule war,** when (he was) still at school; **seine Gedanken wanderten zu der Zeit zurück, als er noch studierte,** his mind went back to (the time) when he was still a student; **kaum hatte ich die Tür geöffnet, als . . . ,** I had hardly opened the door when . . . ; **als er noch arbeitete,** when, while, he was still working; **eines Tages, als ich im Garten saß, . . . ,** one day when, as, I was sitting in the garden . . . ; **gerade als ich das Zimmer betrat, ging er hinaus,** he went out just as I came, was coming, into the room; **es waren noch keine zwei Sekunden vergangen, als ich einen Schuß hörte,** barely two seconds had elapsed when I heard a shot; **er wich zurück, als ich näher kam,** he drew back as I advanced; **er wurde nachsichtiger, als er älter wurde,** he grew more charitable as he grew older.

alsbald, *adv.* immediately, directly, at once, forthwith, without delay, without loss of time.

alsbaldig, *a.* immediate (answer, etc.).

alsdann. 1. *adv.* afterwards, after that, then, thereupon; **(und) a. sagte er mir . . . ,** and then, afterwards, he said to me . . . ; **und a. verließ er uns,** thereupon, whereupon, he left us. **2.** *int.* well then!

Alse, *f.* **-/-n.** *Ich:* alosa, shad, allice-shad.

Alsem, *m.* **-s/.** *Dial: Bot:* wormwood.

alsgemach, *a. & adv. Dial:*=**allmählich.**

also. 1. *adv. A. & Lit:* thus, so; in, after, this manner; **es sei also!** so be it! **es ist nicht also,** it is not so; **also steht geschrieben,** thus, so, it is written; **also sprach Zarathustra,** thus spoke Zoroaster; *B:* **also ward vollendet Himmel und Erde,** thus the heavens and the earth were finished. **2.** (*a*) *conj.* therefore, accordingly, so, consequently, then; **ich denke, also bin ich,** I think, therefore I am; **er war nicht da, also bin ich zurückgekommen,** he wasn't there, so I came back again; **das Leben ist teuer, wir müssen also sparen,** living is dear, therefore, so, we must economize; **ich wäre also dankbar, wenn Sie . . . würden,** I should therefore be glad if you would . . . ; (*verging on 'emotive particle' nuance; cp.* 2 (*b*)) **die ganze Welt wartete also auf den Messias,** the whole world, then, was awaiting the Messiah; (*b*) (*emotive particle*) so, then, well; **da bist du also!** so there you are! **wir wollen also versuchen . . . ,** let us then, therefore, try . . . ; well, let us try . . . ; **du kommst also nicht?** so you aren't coming? you aren't coming then? **Sie sind (denn) also aus Berlin hergekommen?** so you've come from Berlin. (have you)? **es ist also wahr?** it's true then? then it's true? **also gehen Sie schon (in Gottes Namen), wenn Sie unbedingt wollen!** if you are so anxious to go, well then for Heaven's sake go! **also, gehen Sie!** go then! **also los!** (i) fire away! get on with it! *F:* get cracking! (ii) come on! let's go! (iii) off with you! **also gut!** all right (then)! *U.S. & F:* O.K.! **also, es bleibt dabei,** well, all right, that's settled, that's fixed, (then); **nun also!** now then! well then! **na also,** there you are! I told you so! what did I tell you? **schließe die Augen!—(na) also?** shut your eyes!—well, (what now)? (*c*) (*meaningless, used to attract attention*) **also, meine Herren . . . ,** well, gentlemen . . . ; **also, heute werden wir . . . ,** now, well, today we will . . . ; **bist du bereit? also!** are you ready? well, here goes!

Als Ob, Als-ob, *n.* **-/.** *Phil:* fiction; **die Philosophie des Als Ob,** the philosophy of fictions.

alsobald, alsofort, alsogleich [alzoˑˈbalt, -ˈfort, -ˈglaiç], *adv. A:*=**alsbald, sofort, sogleich.**

Alster[1], *f.* **-/-n.** *Dial:*=**Elster.**

Alster[2], **die.** *Pr.n.* **-.** *Geog:* the (river) Alster (running through Hamburg).

Alsterauge, *n. Dial:*=**Elster(n)auge.**

alt[1], *a.* (*see also* **älter, älteste(r)**) **1.** (*a*) old, aged; **mein alter Vater,** my old father; **alt an Körper, jung an Geist,** old in body, young in mind; **ziemlich alt,** getting on; oldish; rather old; quite old; **alt werden,** to grow old; to be growing, getting, old; to age; **er wird nicht alt werden,** he won't live long; he's not long for this world; he won't make old bones; **seine Krankheit hat ihn alt gemacht,** his illness has aged him; *F:* **er ist alt wie Methusalem,** he is as old as Methuselah, as Adam, as the hills; **man ist so alt, wie man sich fühlt,** one is as old as one feels; **zu alt für, zu, etwas sein, zu alt sein, etwas zu tun,** to be too old for sth., to do sth.; to be past doing sth.; **ich bin zu alt zum Tanzen,** I'm past dancing; **zu alt sein, Kinder zu haben,** to be too old to have children, to be past child-bearing; **ein alter Mann, ein Alter,** an old man; **eine alte Frau, eine Alte,** an old woman; **der alte Johann,** old John; **die alte Frau Schmidt,** old Mrs Schmidt; **der alte Goethe,** the aged Goethe, Goethe in his old age; **der Alte vom Berge,** the Old Man of the Mountains; **der Alte der Tage,** the Ancient of Days; *Hist:* **der Alte vom Sachsenwald,** Bismarck; **alte Leute, die Alten,** old people, old folk(s); the aged; *pl. inv.* **alt und jung,** old and young; **in seinen alten Tagen,** in his old age; in his older days; **auf meine alten Tage muß ich das erleben!** and this has to happen to me in my old age, at my time of life! (*b*) *Turf:* **altes Pferd,** horse above six years old; (*c*) *Min:* **alter Mann,** (i) attle, deads, gang(ue), leavings, (ii) old working. **2.** (*of thgs*) (*a*) old (house, tree, picture, etc.); ancient (monument); (*b*) matured; **alter Wein, Kognak,** old wine, brandy; **alter Käse,** hard ripened cheese; (*c*) stale; **altes Brot,** stale, old, bread; **altes Bier,** stale, flat, beer; (*d*) worn-out; useless, unserviceable; cast-off (clothes); second-hand (books, clothes, furniture, etc.); **altes Eisen,** old iron, scrap-iron; **altes Zeug,** old stuff; rubbish, lumber, junk, *U.S:* trash; **ich habe die Kamera alt gekauft,** I bought the camera second-hand; (*e*) **das alte Jahr,** the old year. **3. wie alt sind Sie?** how old are you? **für wie alt halten,**

schätzen, Sie ihn? how old would you take him to be? **er sieht nicht so alt aus, wie er ist,** he does not look his age; **er ist genau so alt wie ich,** he is just my age, just the same age as myself; **fünf Jahre alt sein,** to be five years old; **alt genug sein, um etwas zu tun,** to be old enough to do sth.; **Nachrichten, die schon eine Woche alt sind,** news a week old. **4.** (*a*) old, long-established, long-standing; **eine alte Familie,** an old family; **eine Familie von altem Adel,** a noble old family; **ein alter Bekannter,** an old acquaintance; **alte Liebe rostet nicht,** old love endures; love never grows old; **ein alter Wunsch,** a long-cherished wish; **alte Schuld,** old debt; **eine alte Geschichte,** an old story; (*b*) old, experienced; **alter Krieger,** old soldier, old campaigner; (*c*) inveterate, persistent; **ein altes Übel,** an inveterate evil; **alter Sünder,** hardened sinner; **alter Verbrecher,** old, persistent, offender; **alter Säufer,** confirmed drunkard. **5.** (*a*) former, late, old, ex- (teacher, pupil, etc.); **alter Schüler,** former pupil, old boy (of school), *U.S:* alumnus, (old) graduate; **alter Staatsbeamter,** former civil servant; **der alte Bürgermeister,** the former mayor, the ex-mayor (*cp.* 7); *Sch:* **alter Herr,** former member (of students' association); (*b*) ancient, old, olden, early, bygone, past, of yore; **in alten Zeiten,** in times past, *Lit:* in olden days, in days of yore; **in alten Tagen,** in the old days, in former times; **die Alte Welt,** (i) the Old World, (ii) *occ.* the ancient world; **das Alte Testament,** the Old Testament (*see also* **Bund** 1); *B. & F:* **den alten Menschen ablegen, ausziehen,** to put off the old man; **(die) Alte Geschichte,** ancient history; **die Alten,** (i) the ancients, (ii) *occ.* our forefathers, our forbears, our ancestors; **die alten Germanen,** the ancient Germans, the old Teutons; **das alte Rom,** ancient Rome; **das alte London,** old, historic, London; (*c*) previous; former; **das Alte,** (i) the old things, (ii) the former, old, state of affairs; **das Alte und das Neue,** the old and the new; **es bleibt beim alten,** everything is just the same, remains as it was (before); 'no change'; **wir lassen alles beim alten,** we are leaving things just as they are; **wir bleiben die alten,** we are just the same; **er ist nicht mehr der alte,** he has changed completely; he is no longer the same person; he's not the man he was; **er ist immer (noch) der alte,** he hasn't changed at all, he is the same as ever; **er ist wieder ganz der alte,** he is, looks, quite himself again; **der alte Lauf des Flusses,** the old, former, course of the river; *see also* **Gang**[1] 2. **6.** *F:* (*a*) **der alte, mein alter, Herr,** my father; **die, meine, alte Dame,** my mother; **der Alte,** the old man, (i) the old 'un, the old chap, (ii) (the, my) father, (iii) the master; the proprietor; *F:* the boss, the governor, *P:* the guv'nor, (iv) *Nau:* the captain, (v) *Mil:* the commanding officer, (vi) *Sch:* the headmaster; the form-master; **die Alte,** (i) (the, my) mother, (ii) the mistress (of the house); the proprietress, (iii) = **meine Alte,** (iv) (*of animal*) the mother; the old sow, bitch, vixen, etc.; **mein Alter,** (i) my father, *F:* my old man, my, the, governor, *P:* the guv'nor, (ii) my husband, *F:* my old man; **meine Alte,** my wife, *F:* my old woman, my better half, *P:* my old girl, my old dutch; **meine Alten,** my parents; (*b*) (*affectionate*) **alter Junge, alter Knabe, alter Schwede,** (*students' language*) **altes Haus,** old man, old boy, old fellow, old chap, old pal, *P:* old cock; **na, meine Alte!** well, old dear, *P:* old girl! **der gute, liebe, alte Schmidt!** good, dear, old Schmidt! (*c*) *Pej:* (*of pers.; cp.* 4 (*c*)) **ein alter Fuchs,** a sly old fox; **ein alter Ochse, ein alter Tropf,** a stupid old fool; **ein alter Schwätzer,** a garrulous old fool, *F:* a proper old windbag; **alter Esel!** silly ass! **er ist ein altes Weib, Waschweib,** he is nothing but an old woman, *P:* he's a proper old washerwoman. **7. Alt-,** *comb.fm.* (*with adjectival force; cp.* 1, 2, 4, 5) (*a*) old; **Altengland** *n,* Old England; *Hist:* **Altbayern** *n,* the original Bavaria (*but cp.* **Alt-Bayern,** historic Bavaria); *Ling:* **Altfranzösisch** *n,* **Altirisch** *n,* **Altspanisch** *n,* etc., Old French, Old Irish, Old Spanish, etc.; (*b*) former, ex-; **der Altbürgermeister,** the former mayor, the ex-mayor; *esp. Swiss:* **Altprofessor** *m,* emeritus, retired, professor; **Dr. Gremli, Altbundesrat,** Dr Gremli, formerly Federal Councillor; (*c*) *Ind: etc:* waste; scrap; **Altmetall** *n,* scrap-metal; **Altpapier** *n,* waste-paper; (*d*) (trade, tradesmen) concerned with second-hand articles; *see* **Altbinder, Altflicker, Althändler,** e c.

Alt[2], *m.* -(e)s/-e. *Mus:* alto, counter-tenor (voice); (*female voice*) contralto.

altad(e)lig, *a.* of (the) old nobility; noble old (family, name); gentilitial (family).

Altai, der [al'tai]. *Pr.n.* -s. *Geog:* the Altai.

altaisch [al'taːiʃ], *a. Ethn: Ling:* Altaic.

Altait [alta'iːt], *m.* (e)s/. *Miner:* altaite.

Altammann, *m.* former mayor, ex-mayor.

Altan [al'taːn], *m.* -(e)s/-e, **Altane** [al'taːnə], *f.* -/-n. *Arch:* (*a*) balcony, gallery; (*b*) flat roof (of house).

Altar [al'taːr], *m.* -s/-̈e. **1.** altar; **dem A. dienen,** to be a priest; **eine Braut zum A. führen,** to lead a bride to the altar; **alles auf dem A. des Vaterlandes opfern,** to sacrifice everything for the sake of one's country; *R.C.Ch:* **das Sakrament des Altares** = **das Altarsakrament,** *q.v.* **2.** *Astr:* **der A.,** Ara; the Altar.

Altaraufsatz, *m.* retable, altar-piece, superaltar.

Altarbehang, *m.* altar frontal; antependium.

Altarbekleidung, *f.* (*a*) altar-cloth; altar-linen; (*b*) altar-facing, altar frontal, antependium.

Altarbild, *n. Ecc: Art:* altar-piece; altar-panel.

Altarbildschirm, *m.* altar-screen, reredos.

Altarblatt, *n.* (painted) altar-piece, altar-panel.

Altarbuße, *f. A:* penance of kneeling at the altar.

Altardecke, *f.* altar-cloth.

Altargemälde, *n. Ecc: Art:* altar-piece.

Altargerät, *n.* altar-furniture.

Altargitter, *n.* altar-rail.

Altarhimmel, *m.* canopy (of an altar)

Altarplatte, *f.* = **Altartisch.**

Altarplatz, Altarraum, *m.* sanctuary.

Altarsakrament, *n.* Holy Communion, the Sacrament, the Lord's Supper; *R.C.Ch:* **das (heilige) A.,** the Blessed Sacrament, the eucharist.

Altarschranke, *f.* altar-rail.

Altarschrein, *m.* central shrine of a winged altar.

Altarssakrament, *n.* = **Altarsakrament.**

Altartisch, *m.* altar-table; altar-slab, -stone.

Altartuch, *n.* altar-cloth.

Altarvorderteil, *m.* altar-facing, altar frontal.

Altazimut [alt$^{\circ}$a'tsi'muːt], *m.* -(e)s/-e. *Astr:* altazimuth.

altbacken, *a.* stale (bread, *F:* joke, etc.); *F:* out-of-date (ideas, etc.).

Altbau, *m.* -(e)s/-ten, old building.

Altbauer, *m.* **1.** old farmer (*cp.* **Jungbauer**). **2.** farmer on traditional peasant land (*cp.* **Neubauer**).

Altbäuerin, *f.* wife of an 'Altbauer' (*q.v.*).

Altbauwohnung, *f.* flat, *U.S:* apartment, in an old building.

altbegründet, *a.* long-, old-established.

altbekannt, *a.* long-known, well-known, familiar.

altberühmt, *a.* of ancient fame; of old renown; famous old (town, etc.).

Altbesitz, *m. Jur:* property acquired before 1st July, 1920.

altbewährt, *a.* long-standing; (friendship, etc.) of long standing; well-tried (remedy); **die altbewährten Methoden,** the old approved methods, the methods that have stood the test of time.

Altbinder, *m.* barrel-mender, -repairer.

Altbundesrat, *m.* (*in Switzerland*) former Federal Councillor.

Altbürgermeister, *m.* ex-mayor, former mayor.

Altchen, *n.* -s/-. *F:* (*as form of address*) old dear.

altchristlich, *a.* early Christian (art, etc.).

altdeutsch, *a.* old, ancient, German; *esp.* medieval German.

Altdeutschland, *n.* old, ancient, Germany.

Altdünung, *f. Nau:* diminishing swell (after storm).

Alte, *m., f. see* **alt**[1], 1, 5, 6.

altehrwürdig, *a.* venerable, time-honoured (custom, etc.).

alteingesessen, *a.* old-, long-established (family, farmers, etc.) (*in a particular place*); **die Alteingesessenen,** the old-established inhabitants.

Alteisen, *n.* old iron, scrap-iron.

Alteltern, *pl.* grandparents.

alten, *v.i.* (*sein, haben*) *Lit:* = **altern** 1 (*a*).

altenglisch. 1. *a.* old English; Old English, Anglo-Saxon (language). **2.** *s.* **Altenglisch,** *n. Ling:* Old English, Anglo-Saxon. **3.** *Print:* **altenglische Schrift, Altenglisch,** *f.* -/. Gothic type, Old English, black letter, German text.

Altenheim, *n.* = **Altersheim.**

Altenteil, *m.* **1.** *Jur:* provision made for a retiring farmer on handing over the farm to his heir *or* successor. **2.** house *or* part of the house in which the retired farmer lives.

Altenteiler, *m.* retired farmer who receives the 'Altenteil'.

Alter[1], *m. see* **alt**[1], 1, 5, 6.

Alter[2], *n.* -s/-. **1.** (*a*) age; **im A. von zwanzig Jahren,** at the age of twenty, at twenty years of age; (person) aged twenty; **er ist genau in meinem A.,** he is just my age, just the same age as myself; **sie sind im selben A.,** they are the same age, are of an age; **das erforderliche, gesetzliche, A., noch nicht erreicht haben,** to be under (the required, legal) age; **über das vorgeschriebene A. hinaus sein,** to be over (the required) age; *F:* **über das A. hinaus sein,** to be too old; to be past (doing sth.); (*in amorous pursuits*) (*of man*) to be past it, (*of woman*) to be too old; **über das A. hinaus sein, Kinder zu bekommen,** to be too old to have children, to be past child-bearing; **über das arbeitsfähige A. hinaus sein,** to be too old to work, to be past work; **im frühen A.,** at an early age, in early youth; **Mann mittleren Alters,** man of middle age, middle-aged man; **das reife A.,** the years of maturity; **im besten, blühendsten, A.,** in the prime, heyday, of life; **das gefährliche A.,** the dangerous age; **in meinem (jetzigen) Alter,** at my time of life, *F:* of day; **in Ihrem A. hatte ich . . . ,** at your age, when I was your age, I had . . . ; **man sieht ihm sein A. nicht an,** he does not look his age; (*b*) seniority, (i) in years, (ii) (= **Dienstalter**) by length of service; priority (of claim); **dem A. nach befördert werden,** to be promoted (i) in order of age, (ii) by seniority; (*c*) **(hohes) A.,** (old) age; **sechzig — das ist (gar) kein A.!** sixty —that's not old! *F:* that's no age at all! **er spart für sein A.,** he is saving for his old age; **im hohen A. stehen,** to be well on in years; to be at an advanced age, advanced season of life; **in hohem A. sterben,** to die at a good old age; **ein hohes A. erreichen, bis ins hohe A. leben,** to live to an old age, to live to be old; **ein sehr hohes A., ein biblisches A., erreichen,** to live to a great age, a ripe old age; *Prov:* **A. schützt vor Torheit nicht,** even old men make fools of themselves; *Prov:* there's no fool like an old fool; (*d*) old people; **das A. soll man ehren,** age should be held in honour; old people are entitled to respect; (*e*) age, decrepitude (of thgs); **das Haus zerfällt vor A.,** the house is falling to pieces with age; (*f*) **hohes A.,** antiquity; **Inschriften von sehr hohem A.,** inscriptions of great antiquity, of very ancient date; **ich schätze das A. dieser Skulptur auf etwa fünfhundert Jahre,** I estimate that this sculpture is about five hundred years old. **2.** (= **Zeitalter,** *q.v.*) age, period, epoch.

älter, *a.* (*comp. of* **alt**[1]) **1.** (*a*) (*of pers.*) older; senior; more advanced in years; (*of thg*) older; **er, der Baum, das Bild, ist ä., als du denkst,** he, the tree, the picture, is older than you think; **ä. werden,** to grow older; to age; **er sieht aus, als wäre er fünf Jahre ä. geworden, er sieht fünf Jahre ä. aus,** he looks five years older; **ich bin ä. als er,** I am older than he; **er ist zehn Jahre ä. als ich,** he is ten years older than I, he is my senior by ten years, ten years my senior, ten years senior to me; (*b*) (*of work of art, etc.*) older, earlier; **ältere Fassung,** earlier, older, version; (*c*) older; elder; senior; **mein älterer Bruder,** my elder brother; **welcher ist der ältere?** which is the elder? **Plinius der Ältere,** Pliny the Elder; **Herr Müller der Ältere,** Mr Müller senior, the elder Mr Müller; **die älteren Schüler, Schülerinnen, die Älteren,** the elder, older, senior, boys, girls; the bigger boys, girls; the seniors; **du sollst denen gehorchen, die älter sind als du!** obey your elders! **2.** (*a*) elderly; oldish; **ein älterer Herr, eine ältere Dame,** an elderly, oldish, gentleman, lady; **ältere Leute,** elderly people; people getting on in years; **eine ältere Verkäuferin,** (i) an elderly saleswoman; (ii) a saleswoman with considerable experience; (*b*) earlier; early; older; **die ältere deutsche Dichtung,** early German literature.

Alterantia [alte'rantsiaː], *n.pl. Med:* alteratives.

Alteration [alte'ratsi'oːn], *f.* -/-en. **1.** alteration, change; variation. **2.** excitement; emotion, *esp.* consternation *or* chagrin. **3.** *Mus:* inflection, inflecting (of note).

Alterativa [altera'tiːvaː], *n.pl. Med:* = **Alterantia.**

Alterchen, *n.* -s/-, little old man.

alter ego ['alter 'eːgoː], *n.inv.* (*Lt.phr. used as s.*) alter ego; **er ist mein alter ego,** he is my second self.

alterieren [alte'riːrən], *v.tr.* **1.** (*a*) to alter, change; to vary; *Med:* **alterierendes Mittel,** alterative; (*b*) *Mus:* to inflect (note); **alterierter Akkordton,** inflected note. **2.** to excite (s.o.); to put (s.o.) into a state of violent emotion; **sich (über etwas** *acc.***) a.,** to get worked up, *F:* het up (over sth.); to make a fuss (about sth.).

-alterig *see* **-altrig.**

Ältermann, *m.* -(e)s/-männer. *A:* elder; officer (of guild).

Ältermutter, *f. A. & Dial:* ancestress; great-grandmother.

altern. I. *v.i.* (*haben, sein*) (*a*) to age, to grow old; to be growing, getting, older; **ich fand ihn sehr gealtert,** I found him greatly aged; **alternd,** ageing; (*b*) *Metall: Magn:* to age.
II. *vbl s.* **Altern** *n.*, **Alterung** *f.* ageing, growing old; *Metall: Magn:* ageing.

Alternanz [altɛrˈnants], *f.* -/-en, alternation; *esp. Bot:* alternation of leaves.

Alternat [altɛrˈnaːt], *n.* -(e)s/-e, (*a*) alternation; (*b*) *Dipl:* rotation in precedence (in signing treaties, etc.).

Alternation [altɛrnaˑtsĭˈoːn], *f.* -/-en, (*a*)= **Alternanz**; (*b*)=**Alternat** (*b*).

alternativ [altɛrnaˑˈtiːf], *a.* **1.** alternative. **2.** alternate; *adv. Bot:* **a. stehende Blätter,** alternate leaves.

Alternative [altɛrnaˑˈtiːvə], *f.* -/-n, alternative; option; choice; **vor die A. gestellt werden, vor der A. stehen,** to be faced with the alternative; to be forced to make a choice; **j-m die A. überlassen,** to leave s.o. to make his own choice; **keine A. haben,** to have no alternative, no option, no choice; **keine andere A. haben,** to have no other alternative.

Alternator [altɛrˈnaːtor], *m.* -s/-en [-naˑˈtoːrən]. *El.E:* alternating-current generator; alternator.

alternieren [altɛrˈniːrən], *v.i.* (*haben*) to alternate (**mit,** with).

alternierend, *a.* **1.** alternate (colours, layers, etc.; *Bot:* leaves). **2.** alternating; *El.E:* **alternierender Strom,** alternating current; *Med:* **alternierendes Fieber,** intermittent fever; *Mth:* **alternierende Reihe,** alternating series; *Pros:* **alternierender Vers,** accentual verse.

alters, *adv.* **vor a.,** in the olden time, in olden times, in the days of old, in the days of yore; long, long ago; **von a. her, seit a.,** from time immemorial; time out of mind; **von a. her ist es so gewesen,** it was ever thus.

Altersaufbau, *m.* age-group structure (of population).

Altersbestimmung, *f. Biol: etc:* determination of age.

Altersblödsinn, *m. Med:* senile dementia.

Altersbrand, *m. Med:* senile gangrene.

Altersdialekt, *m. Ling:* characteristic speech of a particular age-group.

Altersentartung, *f.* senile decay.

Alterserscheinung, *f.* symptom of old age, manifestation of senility.

Altersfolge, *f.* order of seniority.

Altersfürsorge, *f.* care of the aged.

Altersgenoß, Altersgenosse, *m.*, **Altersgenossin,** *f.* man, woman, of the same age as oneself; contemporary; **meine Altersgenossen,** my contemporaries; **er ist mein Altersgenosse, wir sind Altersgenossen,** we are of an age, we are contemporaries, we are of the same generation; we are of the same age.

Altersgewicht, *n. Turf:* weight to be carried by a horse of specified age.

Altersgliederung, *f.*=**Altersaufbau.**

altersgrau, *a.* grey with age; hoary; (*of buildings, etc.*) of hoary antiquity, age-old.

Altersgrenze, *f.* age-limit; **die A. erreichen,** to reach, attain, the age-limit.

Altersgruppe, *f.* age-group.

Altersheim, *n.* old people's home, home for the aged.

Altersjahr, *n. Swiss:*=**Lebensjahr.**

Altersklasse, *f.* age-class; age-group.

Altersmarasmus, *m. Med:* senile marasmus, senile decay.

Alterspension, *f.* old age pension.

Alterspräsident, *m.* chairman by seniority; oldest member (of a learned society, etc.).

Altersrente, *f.* **1.** annuity (paid in old age). **2.** old age pension.

Altersring, *m.* **1.** *Bot:* age-ring, annual ring (of tree). **2.** white ring in the eye (of aged person *or* animal).

Altersschicht, *f.* age-group.

altersschwach, *a.* decrepit; broken down, worn out, with age; old and infirm; senile; *F:* decrepit old (car); rickety old (furniture); crumbling old (house).

Altersschwäche, *f.* decrepitude; feebleness of age; infirmity through age; senility; senile decay; **an A. sterben,** to die of old age; *F:* **das Auto kann vor A. nicht mehr weiter,** the car is too decrepit to go any further; **das Haus bricht vor A. fast zusammen,** the house is so old it's almost falling to pieces.

Alterssichtigkeit, *f. Med:* long-sightedness, far-sightedness, (caused by age).

Altersstil, *m.* style of the ageing artist; style of (an artist's) last years, old age.

Altersstufe, *f.* place on the age-scale; age; age-class; stage of life; **in verschiedenen Altersstufen wird das Kind . . . ,** at different ages the child will . . .

Alterstod, *m.* death from old age; **den A. sterben,** to die of old age.

Altersunterschied, *m.* difference in age.

Altersveränderung, *f. Biol:* senile change.

Altersversicherung, *f.* old age insurance.

Altersversorgung, *f.* **1.** *Adm:* provision for the aged. **2.**=**Alterspension.**

Altersversorgungsanstalt, *f.*=**Altersheim.**

Altersversorgungskasse, *f.* old-age pension fund.

Alterswerk, *n.* (artist's) late work, work produced towards the end of (artist's) life, in (artist's) late period; **Rembrandts Alterswerke,** Rembrandt's last works, works from Rembrandt's later years, late period.

Alterszulage, *f.* (*addition to pay*) (*a*) age bonus; (*b*) seniority bonus; seniority increment.

Altertum, *n.* **1.** -(e)s/. (*a*) antiquity, ancient times; **das graue A.,** the remote past, the earliest times, distant ages; (*b*) **das klassische A.,** classical antiquity; **die Kunst des Altertums,** the art of antiquity, ancient art, classical art; (*c*) **das germanische A.,** early Germanic civilization; the early history of the Germanic peoples. **2.** -(e)s/⸗er, ancient relic; *usu. pl.* **Altertümer,** antiquities.

Altertümelei, *f.* -/-en. **1.** archaizing. **2.** archaism.

altertümeln, *v.i.* (*haben*) to archaize; **altertümelnder Stil,** archaizing style.

Altertümerpflege, *f.* conservation of antiquities.

altertümlich, *a.* (*a*) ancient, pertaining to the ancients, of the ancient world; (*b*) of olden times; old-time, old-world (ceremonial, etc.); (*c*) old-fashioned, antiquated; archaic (style, etc.); antique (furniture, etc.).

Altertümlichkeit, *f.* (*a*) antiquity, antiqueness, ancientness; (*b*) old-fashionedness; archaism; archaic character (of style, etc.).

Altertumsforscher, *m.* (*a*) student of antiquity, *esp.* Graeco-Roman antiquity; (*b*) archeologist; (*c*) antiquary, antiquarian.

Altertumsforschung, *f.* (*a*) study of, research into, antiquity, *esp.* Graeco-Roman antiquity; (*b*) archeology; (*c*) antiquarian researches.

Altertumshändler, *m. Com:* dealer in antiquities; antique-dealer.

Altertumskenner, *m.* (*a*) person with a scholarly knowledge of antiquity, of ancient civilizations; classical scholar; (*b*) antiquary, antiquarian.

Altertumskunde, *f.* (*a*) the study of antiquity; *esp.* **klassische A.,** the study of classical, Graeco-Roman, history and civilization; classical studies; (*b*) archeology.

Altertumskundler, *m.* (*a*) student of antiquity, *esp.* classical antiquity; classical scholar; (*b*) archeologist.

Altertumsstück, *n.* antique; relic of the past.

Altertumswissenschaft, *f.*=**Altertumskunde.**

Alterung, *f. see* **altern** II.

Ältervater, *m.* ancestor, forefather, forbear.

Altesse [alˈtɛsə], *f.* -/-n, (*title*) Highness.

Ältestenkollegium, *n. A:* (board of) syndics (of a corporation); governing body.

Ältestenrat, *m.* **1.** *Hist: Ecc:* council of elders. **2.** *Parl:* standing (advisory) committee.

Ältestenrecht, *n. Jur:* right of primogeniture.

Ältestenwürde, *f.* eldership.

älteste(r), älteste, älteste(s), *a.* (*sup. of* **alt**[1]) **1.** (*a*) oldest; eldest (son, daughter, brother); **der älteste Freund, den ich habe,** the oldest friend I have; **mein ältester Sohn, mein Ältester, meine älteste Tochter, meine Älteste,** my eldest son, daughter; my eldest; **das älteste Mitglied des Vereins,** the oldest, the senior, member of the society; (*b*) earliest (times, poets, literature, etc.); **die ältesten Urkunden,** the earliest, oldest, records; **meine ältesten Erinnerungen,** my earliest recollections. **2.** *s.* **Älteste,** *m. Hist: Jew. Rel:* elder.

Altflicker, *m.* mender, repairer, *esp.* cobbler.

Altflöte, *f. Mus:* bass flute.

altfränkisch, *a. F:* old-fashioned; quaint (style, etc.); antiquated (clothes, language, etc.); old-world (village, etc.); *F:* frumpish (pers., clothes).

altfranzösisch. 1. *a.* old French, Old French (language). **2.** *s.* **Altfranzösisch,** *n. Ling:* Old French.

altgedient, *a.* veteran; grown old in service.

Altgedinge, *n.*=**Altenteil.**

Altgeige, *f. Mus:* viola, tenor violin.

Altgesell(e), *m. Ind:* foreman; charge-hand; *Civ.E:* ganger.

altgewohnt, *a.* (long-)accustomed (procedure, journey, etc.).

altgläubig, *a. Rel:* orthodox.

Altgläubigkeit, *f. Rel:* orthodoxy.

Altgold, *n.* **1.** *Com:* old gold (*from discarded jewellery, etc.*). **2.** (*colour*) old gold.

Altgriechenland. *Pr.n.n. A.Geog:* ancient Greece.

altgriechisch. 1. *a.* ancient Greek. **2.** *s.* **Altgriechisch,** *n. Ling:* ancient, classical, Greek.

Altgummi, *n.* scrap rubber.

Altgut, *n.* second-hand goods; old goods *or* material; *F:* junk.

Althäa [alˈtɛːaː]. *Pr.n.f.* -s. *Gr.Myth:* Althaea.

Althäe, Althee [alˈtɛːə, alˈteːə, alˈteː], *f.* -/-n. *Bot:* althaea, marsh-mallow; **gemeine A.,** hollyhock, rose mallow.

Althandel, *m.* second-hand trade, business.

Althändler, *m.* second-hand dealer (*esp. in old clothes and furniture*); **etwas beim A. kaufen,** to buy sth. in a junk shop.

Alt-Hellas. *Pr.n.n. A.Geog:* ancient Greece, Old Hellas.

althergebracht, altherkömmlich, *a.* traditional; customary (ceremonies, etc.); long-standing (custom).

althiebig, *a. For:* mature (timber).

althochdeutsch. 1. *a.* Old High German (period, literature, etc.). **2.** *s.* **Althochdeutsch,** *n. Ling:* Old High German.

Altholz, *n. For:* (*a*) old growth; (*b*) mature timber.

Altholzbestand, *m. For:* mature stand (of timber-trees).

Altholzstamm, *m. For:* veteran (tree).

Altist [alˈtist], *m.* -en/-en. *Mus:* alto (singer).

Altistin [alˈtistin], *f.* -/-innen. *Mus:* contralto (singer); alto (singer).

Altjahrsabend, Altjahrstag, *m.* New-Year's Eve.

altjüngferlich, *a.* old-maidish, spinsterish.

Altjungfernstand, *m.* spinsterhood, old-maid(en)-hood.

Altkanzler, *m.* ex-, former, Chancellor; *esp. Hist:* **der A.,** Bismarck (*after his retirement from office*).

Altkastilien. *Pr.n.n. Geog:* Old Castile.

Altkatholik, *m. Ecc:* Old Catholic.

altkatholisch, *a. Ecc:* Old Catholic.

Altkleiderhändler, *m.* old-clothes-man; wardrobe dealer.

altklug, *a.* precocious.

Altklugheit, *f.* precociousness, precocity.

Altknecht, *m.* foreman, head man (on a farm).

Altkultur, *f. Biol:* ageing culture.

Altkunst, *f.* old (objects of) art.

Altlander, *m.* -s/-, native, inhabitant, of the Altes Land (*district on the Lower Elbe*).

Altlatein, *n. Ling:* early Latin.

altlateinisch. *Ling:* **1.** *a.* early, archaic, old, Latin. **2.** *s.* **Altlateinisch,** *n.* early Latin.

Altliberalen, die. *Prussian Hist:* the Moderate Liberals of 1848.

ältlich, *a.* elderly, oldish; **ein etwas ältliches Fräulein,** a dried-up, middle-aged, spinster.

Altmaterial, *n. Ind:* scrap.

Altmeister, *m.* **1.** (*a*) *A:* master, president (of guild, corporation); (*b*) past-master (in an art, etc.); doyen (of artists, scientists); *F:* Grand Old Man (of an art, science, sport); **Goethe, der A. der deutschen Dichtung,** Goethe, the patriarch, *F:* the Grand Old Man, of German letters; **der A. der Biologie,** the doyen of the biologists, *F:* the Grand Old Man of biology; **ein A. des Rudersports,** a famous old rowing man; *F:* one of the grand old men of rowing; (*c*) *Sp:* (*f.* **Altmeisterin**) ex-, former, champion. **2.** past-master (of masonic lodge).

altmelk, *a. Husb:* (cow) that has long been in milk.

Altmensch, *m. Anthr:* primitive man.

Altmetall, *n.* scrap(-metal).

altmodisch, *a.* old-fashioned, out of fashion; obsolete, antiquated, out-of-date (clothes, ideas, theories, etc.); outmoded (ideas, etc.).

Altmutter, *f. A. & Dial:* great-grandmother; ancestress.

Altniederdeutsch, *n. Ling:* Old Low German.

altnordisch. 1. *a.* old Norse (literature, civilization, etc.); Old Norse (language). **2.** *s.* **Altnordisch,** *n. Ling:* Old Norse.

Alto [ˈaltoː], *m.* -/Alti. *Mus:*=**Alt**[2].

Altoboe, *f. Mus:* cor anglais, English horn, tenor oboe.

Altostratus [altoˑˈstraːtus], *m.* -/-ti. *Meteor:* altostratus.

Altpapier, *n.* waste paper.
Altphilologe, *m.* (*a*) classical philologist; classical scholar; (*b*) (university) student reading Classics.
Altphilologie, *f.* classical philology; classical studies, Classics.
Altposaune, *f. Mus:* alto trombone.
Altpreußen. *Pr.n.n. Hist:* the old Prussia (before 1815).
altpreußisch. **1.** *a.* old Prussian. **2.** *s.* **Altpreußisch,** *n. Ling:* Old Prussian (*extinct Baltic language*).
Altreich, das. *Hist:* Germany before 1938.
Altreichskanzler, *m. Hist:*=**Altkanzler.**
-altrig, *comb.fm.* of . . . age(s); **gleichaltrig,** of the same age; **verschiedenaltrig,** of different ages.
Alt-Rom. *Pr.n.n.* (*a*) *Hist:* ancient Rome; (*b*) historic Rome; the old parts of Rome.
altrömisch, *a.* ancient Roman; of ancient Rome.
Altrot, *n. Dy:* Turkey red, Adrianople red.
Altruismus [altru·ˈismus], *m.* -/. altruism; unselfishness.
Altruist [altru·ˈist], *m.* **-en/-en,** altruist.
altruistisch [altru·ˈistiʃ], *a.* altruistic; selfless, unselfish; *adv.* altruistically.
altsächsisch. **1.** *a.* old Saxon; Old Saxon (language). **2.** *s.* **Altsächsisch,** *n. Ling:* Old Saxon.
Altsänger, *m.*, **Altsängerin,** *f.*=**Altist, Altistin.**
Altsaxophon, *n. Mus:* alto saxophone; **A. in Es,** tenor saxophone in E flat.
Altsche, *f.* -n/-n. *F:* old woman; *Pej:* old hag.
Altschlüssel, *m. Mus:* alto clef.
Altschneider, *m.* **1.** clothes-repairer; tailor who does repairs. **2.** *Husb:* old gelded animal.
Altschrift, *f. Print:* roman type.
Altsilber, *n. Com:* oxidized silver.
Altsitz, *m.* dwelling *or* property of a retired farmer; *cp.* **Altenteil** 2.
Altsitzer, *m.*=**Altenteiler.**
Altsolo, *n. Mus:* (*male voice*) alto solo; (*female voice*) contralto solo.
altsprachlich, *a.* (study, etc.) of dead languages, *esp.* Greek and Latin; classical (studies).
Altstadt, *f.* original town, old part(s) of a town; **die Nürnberger A.,** the old town of Nuremberg; **die Londoner A.,** the City (of London).
Altstahl, *m.* steel scrap, scrap-steel.
Altsteinzeit, die. *Prehist:* the Palaeolithic Age.
Altstimme, *f. Mus:* (*male*) alto voice; (*female*) contralto voice.
Altstoff, *m.* waste material, waste, *F:* junk.
altsyrisch. *Ling:* **1.** *a.* Syriac. **2.** *s.* **Altsyrisch,** *n. Ling:* Syriac.
Alttestamentler, *m.* -s/-. Old Testament scholar; Professor of Old Testament Studies.
alttestamentlich, *a.* of the Old Testament; Old Testament (characters, studies, etc.).
Alttier, *n. Ven:* mother animal, *esp.* hind, doe.
Alttum, *n.* -s/⸚er, *occ.* obsolete, outmoded, institution, etc.; 'a thing of the past'.
altüberliefert, *a.*=**althergebracht.**
Altung, *m.* -s/-e & *f.* -/-en. *Min:* old working.
Altvater, *m.* **1.** patriarch (*esp.* of the Old Testament, of the Church); **die Altväter der (ersten) Kirche,** the Fathers of the Church. **2.** progenitor, ancestor, forefather, forbear.
altväterisch. **1.** old-fashioned, antiquated, out-of-date. **2.** old-time (comfort, etc.); old-world (appearance, etc.); (house, room) of old-world character.
altväterlich, *a.* (*a*) patriarchal (appearance, etc.); (*b*) ancestral (hall, etc.).
Altvaterrecht, *n.*=**Altenteil** 1.
altvettelisch, *a. A:* old-womanish; *B:* **altvettelische Fabeln,** old wives' fables.
Altvordern, *pl.* ancestors, forefathers, forbears, progenitors, predecessors.
Altwaren, *f.pl.* second-hand goods, articles.
Altwarenhändler, *m.* second-hand dealer.
Altwasser, *n. Ph.Geog:* dead arm (of river); ox-bow (lake).
Altweiberfabel, Altweibergeschichte [altˈvaibər-], *f.*=**Altweibermärchen.**
Altweibergeschwätz, Altweibergewäsch, *n.* gossip, tittle-tattle, silly chatter.
altweiberhaft, *a.* old-womanish, *Lit:* anile.
Altweiberknoten, *m. Nau: etc:* granny knot.
Altweibermärchen, *n.* old wives' tale.
Altweibersommer, *m.* **1.** Indian summer, St Martin's summer, St Luke's summer. **2.** gossamer.
Altweltaffen, *m.pl. Z:* catarrhine monkeys.
altweltlich, *a.* old-world (*as distinct from* (i) *the modern world,* (ii) *America*).
Altwerden, *n.* ageing, growing old.
Altzeit, *f.* primeval times.
Alumen [a·ˈluːmɛn], *n.* -s/. alum.
alumetieren [a·lu·me·ˈtiːrən], *v.tr. Metalw:* to alumetize, to spray (metal) with an aluminium coating.
Alumia [a·ˈluːmĭaː], *f.* -/. *Miner:* alumina.
Aluminat [a·lu·mi·ˈnaːt], *n.* -(e)s/-e. *Ch:* aluminate.
Aluminit [a·lu·mi·ˈniːt], *m.* -(e)s/-e. *Miner:* aluminite, websterite.
Aluminium [a·lu·ˈmiːnĭum], *n.* -s/. aluminium, *U.S:* aluminum.
Aluminiumblech, *n.* aluminium sheet, sheet aluminium.
Aluminiumbronze, *f.* aluminium bronze.
Aluminiumdruck, *m. Print:* aluminography, algraphy.
Aluminiumfarbe, *f. Paint:*=**Aluminiumlackfarbe.**
Aluminiumfolie, *f.* aluminium foil; *F:* silver paper.
aluminiumhaltig, *a.* aluminous; containing aluminium.
Aluminiumlackfarbe, *f.* aluminium enamel, aluminium paint.
Aluminiummessing, *n.* aluminium brass.
Aluminiumpulver, *n.* aluminium powder.
Aluminiumzelle, *f. El.E:* aluminium cell (of rectifier, etc.).
Aluminodruck [a·lu·ˈmiːno·-], *m.* =**Aluminiumdruck.**
aluminös [a·lu·mi·ˈnøːs], *a.* aluminous.
Aluminothermie [a·lu·mi·no·tɛrˈmiː], *f.* -/. *Metall: Ind:* aluminothermy.
Alumnat [a·lumˈnaːt], *n.* -(e)s/-e. **1.** (endowed free) boarding school. **2.** *esp. Austrian:* (theological) seminary.
Alumne [a·ˈlumnə], *m.* -n/-n, **Alumnus** [a·ˈlumnus], *m.* -/-nen. *Sch:* **1.** boarder. **2.** *esp. Austrian:* pupil of a (theological) seminary.
Alundum [a·ˈlundum], *n.* -s/. *Ind:* alundum.
Alunit [a·lu·ˈni·t], *m.*- (e)s/-e. *Miner:* alunite, alumstone.
Alunogen [a·lu·no·ˈgeːn] *m.* -s/. *Miner:* alunogen, feather alum, hair salt; halotrichite.
alveolar [alve·o·ˈlaːr], *a.* **1.** alveolate; cellular; honeycombed. **2.** *Anat:* (*usu. comb.fm.* **Alveolar-**) alveolar (nerve, etc.). **3.** *Ling:* alveolar gingival (sound). **4.**=**alveolär.**
alveolär [alve·o·ˈlɛːr], *a. Anat:* alveolar, vesicular (gland).
Alveolarabszeß, *m. Med:* abscess at the root of a tooth.
Alveolarfortsatz, *m. Anat:* alveolar process *or* ridge.
Alveolarpyorrhöe, *f. Med:* pyorrhea alveolaris.
Alveole [alve·ˈoːlə], *f.* -/-n. **1.** (*a*) alveole, alveolus; cell (of honeycomb, etc.); (*b*) *Anat:* alveolus, air-cell (of the lung); (*c*) *Anat:* alveolus (of gland). **2.** *Anat:* alveolus, socket (of tooth).
Alyssum [a·ˈlysum], *n.* -/. *Bot:* alyssum, madwort.
Alzbeere, *f.* -/n. *Dial:*=**Elsbeere** 2 (*a*).
am, *prep.* (*contraction of* **an dem**; *cp.* **an I**) (*Notes:* (i) **an dem** *introducing a relative clause can never be contracted to* **am**; (ii) *in constructions where the article has a demonstrative nuance, both* **am** *and* **an dem** *can be used in writing, but* **am** *is preferred in speech;* **er ist am Fieber gestorben,** he died of (the) fever; **er ist an dem Fieber, am Fieber, gestorben,** it was the fever that killed him (not anything else); **Flecken am Kleid sind ein Zeichen von Liederlichkeit,** spots on one's dress are signs of slovenliness; **die Flecken an dem Kleid werden nie mehr abgehen,** the marks will never come off that dress; **am Tage, wo . . . ,** on the day when . . . ; **an dem Tage, wo . . . , an dem Tage, an dem . . . ,** on that day, the day, when, on which, . . . ; (iii) **an dem** *is sometimes substituted for* **am** *when the noun is more closely qualified;* **er hatte etwas am Auge,** he had something on his eye; **an dem, am, linken Auge hatte er den Star,** he had a cataract in his left eye (not his right); **am Ende des Seiles,** at the end of the rope; **an dem einen, am einen, Ende des Seiles,** at one end of the rope; (iv) *the choice between* **am** *and* **an dem** *is often decided by purely rhythmic considerations; in a simple statement the monosyllable is preferred, e.g.* **das Haus liegt am Fluß,** *but in a more complex rhythm-pattern the disyllable is felt to be more effective, e.g.* **das Haus liegt an dem Ufer eines reißenden Stroms.**) **1.** (*in adv. phrases*) (*resolution into* **an dem** *is possible in some cases, see Notes above*) (*a*) (*time*) **am Morgen, am Nachmittag, am Abend,** in the morning, afternoon, evening; **am Mittwoch,** on Wednesday; **am Tage,** (i) by day, in the daytime, (ii) on the day (of . . . , when . . .); **am fünften April, am 5. April,** on the fifth of April, on April 5th; **am Schluß,** at the close, at the finish; (*b*) (*space*) (i) on the, at the, by the; **am Wege,** by the road(side); on the road; **am Scheidewege,** at the crossroads; **am Boden,** on the floor, ground; **ein Haus am See,** a house by, on, the lake; **das Schloß am Meer,** the castle by the sea; **der Garten am Berge,** the garden on the mountainside, the mountain garden; **am Fluß,** by, on, the river; **Reben wachsen am Rhein,** vines grow by, along, the Rhine; (*in place-names*) **Bonn am Rhein,** Bonn on the Rhine; **Frankfurt am Main,** Frankfurt-on-Main; (ii) **am Arm, am Finger, am Bein, am Kopf, usw.,** on one's arm, finger, leg, head, etc.; (iii) **am Hofe,** at (the royal) court; **er ist am Gericht(shof) angestellt,** he is employed at the law-courts; (*c*) (*with verbs and verbal phrases*) (*resolution into* **an dem** *would sound stilted*) **am Scharlach erkranken,** to fall ill with scarlet fever; **am Schlagfluß sterben,** to die of apoplexy; **sie taten sich am Wein gütlich,** they drank their fill of the wine; **j-m am Rockschoß hängen,** to cling to s.o.'s coat-tails; **j-n am Bändel haben,** *F:* to have s.o. on a string; *see also* **Bändel. 2.** (*with vbl s.; can never be resolved into* **an dem**) in the act of, engaged in (doing sth.); **er war (gerade) am Unterschreiben,** he was in the act of signing, was just signing; **er war am Sterben,** he was dying, on the point of death, at death's door; **er war am Verhungern,** he was dying of starvation; **ist er noch am Leben?** is he still alive, still living? *see also individual verbs.* **3.** (*used to form superlative adv. phrase; can never be resolved into* **an dem**) **am meisten,** (the) most; **am deutlichsten, am klarsten,** (the) most clearly; **er schreibt am besten, am schnellsten,** he writes (the) best, (the) fastest; **sie ist mir am teuersten,** she is (the) dearest (of all) to me; **er wohnt am weitesten von uns weg,** he lives furthest (away) from us; **wir täten am besten hier zu bleiben,** it would be best for us to stay here; **die Rosen sind am besten im Juni,** the roses are at their best, look their best, in June.
Amadine [a·ma·ˈdiːnə], *f.* -/-n. *Orn:* thick-billed weaver(-bird).
Amadis [ˈa·ma·dis]. *Pr.n.m.* -'. *Lit:* **A. von Gaula,** Amadis of Gaul.
Amalek [ˈa·ma·lɛk]. *Pr.n.m.* -s. *B.Hist:* Amalek.
Amalekiter [a·ma·le·ˈkiːtər], *m.* -s/-. *B.Hist:* Amalekite.
amalfitanisch [a·malfi·ˈtaːniʃ], *a. Geog:* Amalfitan, Amalphitan.
Amalgam [a·malˈgaːm], *n.* -s/-e, amalgam.
Amalgamation [a·malga·ma·tsĭˈoːn], *f.* -/-en. **1.** amalgamation (of mercury with metal); *Goldmin:* amalgamation process. **2.** amalgamation, blending (of two races, etc.).
Amalgambad, *n. Ind:* amalgam solution.
Amalgamier- [a·malga·ˈmiːr-], *comb.fm. Metall:* amalgamating (apparatus, pan, etc.).
amalgamieren [a·malga·ˈmiːrən], *v.tr.* **1.** *Metall:* to amalgamate (gold, silver). **2.** to amalgamate, blend (races, parties, etc.). **3. sich amalgamieren,** to amalgamate. **4. amalgamierend,** *Metall:* amalgamating; *Ling:* amalgamating, amalgamate (language).
Amalgamierer [a·malga·ˈmiːrər], *m.* -s/-. *Metall:* amalgamator.
Amalgamierung, *f.*=**Amalgamation.**
Amalgamierwerk, *n.* amalgamating mill.
Amalia, Amalie [a·ˈmaːliaː, -liə]. *Pr.n.f.* -s & *Lit:* **-liens.** Amelia.
Amalinsäure [a·ma·ˈliːn-], *f. Ch:* amalic acid.
Amandine [a·manˈdiːnə], *f.* -/-n. *Orn:*=**Amadine.**
Amant [a·ˈmɑ̃ː], *m.* -s/-s, lover.
Amanuensis [a·ma·nu·ˈɛnzis], *m.* -/-sen & **-ses,** amanuensis; secretary.
Amarant[1] [a·ma·ˈrant], *m.* -(e)s/-e. **1.** *Bot:* amarant(h); love-lies-bleeding; **(Garten-)A.,** cockscomb. **2.** *Orn:* **(kleiner) A., (roter) A.,** Senegal fire finch, red-billed fire finch.
amarant[2]. (*colour*) **1.** *a.* amarant(h); (amaranth-) purple; purplish; *Lit:* amarant(h)ine. **2.** *s.* **Amarant,** *n.* -(s)/. amarant(h); (amaranth-) purple.
amaranten [a·ma·ˈrantən], *a.*=**amarant**[2] 2.
Amarantfarbe, *f.*=**amarant**[2] 2.
amarantfarben, *a.*=amarant[2] 1.
Amarantholz, *n. Com:* king-wood, violet-wood, purple-wood.
Amarelle [a·ma·ˈrɛlə], *f.* -/-n. *Hort:* morello (cherry).
Amarellkraut, *n. Bot:* yellow gentian, bitterwort.
Amaryl [a·ma·ˈryl], *m.* -s/-e. *Lap:* synthetic light green sapphire.
Amaryllis [a·ma·ˈrylis]. **1.** *Pr.n.f.* -'. Amaryllis. **2.** *f.* -/-en. *Bot:* amaryllis (belladonna), belladonna lily.
amassieren [a·maˈsiːrən], *v.tr.* to amass; to heap up, pile up.

A-Mast, m. Tg: A-pole.
Amata [aˈmaːta:]. Pr.n.f. -s & Lit: -tens. Amy.
Amateur [amaˈtøːr], m. -s/-e, amateur; comb.fm. Amateur-, amateur (boxer, boxing, photographer, etc.).
Amateurbaukasten, m. Com: home construction kit.
Amateurfunker, m. W.Tel: radio amateur, F: (radio) ham.
Amaul [aˈmaul], n. -(e)s/꞊er. South G.Dial: Ich: pike-perch.
Amaurose [amauˈroːzə], f. -/. Med: amaurosis.
amaurotisch [amauˈroːtiʃ], a. Med: amaurotic.
Amause [aˈmauzə], f. -/-n. Lap: imitation gem; paste.
Amazonas, der [amaˈtsoːnaˑs]. Pr.n. -. Geog: the (river) Amazon.
Amazonasmandel, f. Brazil-nut, Para-nut.
Amazone [amaˈtsoːnə], f. -/-n. 1. (a) Myth. & F: Amazon; (b) Equit: woman show-jumper. 2. Orn: green parrot.
Amazonenfluß, der = Amazonas, der.
amazonenhaft, a. Amazon-like, Amazonian.
Amazonenkleid, n. A: (lady's) riding-habit.
Amazonenstein, m. Miner: Amazon-stone, amazonite.
Amazonenstrom, der = Amazonas, der.
Amazonien [amaˈtsoːniən]. Pr.n.n. -s. Geog: the Amazon country.
amazonisch [amaˈtsoːniʃ], a. 1. = amazonenhaft. 2. Geog: Amazonian; of the Amazon country.
Amazonseeschwalbe [amaˈtsoːn-], f. Orn: Amazon tern.
Ambacht, f. -/-en. 1. A: = Amt. 2. Swiss Dial: guild; corporation.
Ambachtslehen, n. Mediev.Hist: fief granted to a court official.
Ambak [ˈambak], m. -s/. = Ambatsch.
Ambassadeur [ambasaˈdøːr], m. -s/-e. A: ambassador.
Ambatsch [ˈambatʃ], m. -es/. Bot: sola.
Ambe [ˈambə], f. -/-n, combination of two elements; (in gambling) combination of two numbers.
Amber, m. -s/-(n). 1. = Ambra. 2. A: (gelber) A., yellow amber.
Amberbaum, m. Bot: sweet gum, liquidambar.
Amberfett, Amberharz, n. Ch: ambreine.
Amberkörbchen, n. Bot: (yellow) sweet sultan.
Amberkraut, n. Bot: cat-thyme.
Amberstoff, m. = Amberfett.
ambidexter [ambiˈdɛkstər]. 1. a. ambidextrous. 2. s. Ambidexter, m. -s/-, ambidexter.
Ambidextrie [ambidɛksˈtriː], f. -/. ambidexterity, ambidextrousness.
Ambient [ambiˈɛnt], m. -en/-en. A: candidate for, seeker after, an office.
ambieren [amˈbiːrən], v.tr. A: to desire, seek after (an office, etc.)
Ambiguität [ambiguiˈtɛːt], f. -/-en, ambiguity.
Ambition [ambiˈtsioːn] f. -/-en, ambition; (große) Ambitionen haben, to have (great) ambitions.
ambition(n)ieren [ambiˈtsioˈniːrən], v.tr. to be ambitious of, eager for (sth.); to covet (sth.).
ambitiös [ambiˈtsiøːs], a. ambitious.
ambivalent [ambivaˈlɛnt], a. Psy: etc: ambivalent.
Ambivalenz [ambivaˈlɛnts], f. -/-en. Psy: etc: ambivalency.
Amblyopie [amblyoˈpiː], f. -/. Med: amblyopia.
Ambo [ˈamboː], m. -s/-nen [-ˈboːnən]. Ecc.Arch: ambo.
Amboina [amboˈiːna]. Pr.n.n. -s. Geog: (die Insel) A., Amboyna.
Amboinabeule, f. Med: = Aleppobeule.
Amboinaholz, n. Com: Amboyna wood.
Ambon[1] [ˈamboːn], m. -s/-en [-ˈboːnən] = Ambo.
Ambon[2] [amˈboːn]. Pr.n.n. -s. Geog: = Amboina.
Ambonoklast [amboˈnoˈklast], m. -en/-en. Ecc. Hist: opponent of church music.
Amboß, m. -bosses/-bosse. 1. (a) Metalw: etc: anvil; zweihörniger A., two-beaked anvil, two-horned anvil; beak-iron, stake; F: zwischen Hammer und A. sein, to be between the devil and the deep sea; to be in a dilemma, to be between the upper and the nether millstone; Lit: du mußt A. oder Hammer sein, you must either strike the blow or take it; Prov: when you are an anvil, hold you still; when you are a hammer, strike your fill; (b) Clockm: etc: stake; (c) Exp: anvil (of cartridge, primer). 2. Anat: incus, anvil (of inner ear).
Amboßbahn, f. anvil face.
Amboßbucht, f. Anat: incudal fossa.
Amboßelnsatz, m. anvil-tool.
Amboßfalte, f. Anat: incudal fold.
Amboßfutter, n. anvil-bed, -block, -stand, -stock.

Amboßhorn, n. anvil-beak, beak-iron.
Amboßklotz, m. = Amboßfutter.
Amboßkontakt, m. El.E: Aut: anvil contact.
Amboßstock, Amboßuntersatz, m. = Amboßfutter.
Ambozeptor [amboˈtsɛptor], m. -s/-en [-ˈtoːrən]. Biol: amboceptor.
Ambra, f. -/-s, occ. m. -s/-s. 1. ambergris. 2. A: (gelber) A., yellow amber.
Ambraholz, n. Com: yellow sandalwood.
Ambrakraut, n. = Amberkraut.
Ambrettekörner [amˈbrɛtə-], n.pl. Toil: ambrette; musk-seed.
ambrieren [amˈbriːrən], v.tr. to amber; to scent (sth.) with amber(gris).
Ambroid [ambroˈiːt], n. -(e)s/. [-s, -ˈiːdəs] Ind: ambroid.
Ambrosia [amˈbroːzia:], f. -/. Myth: Bot: ambrosia.
Ambrosiana, die [ambroˈziˈaːna:], -, the Ambrosian Library (at Milan).
ambrosianisch [ambroˈziˈaːniʃ], a. Ambrosian, esp. Ecc.Mus: Ambrosianische Liturgie, Ambrosian rite; Ambrosianischer Gesang, Ambrosian chant; der Ambrosianische Lobgesang, the Te Deum.
ambrosisch [amˈbroːziʃ], a. ambrosial.
Ambrosius [amˈbroːzius]. Pr.n.m. -'. Ambrose; der heilige A., Saint Ambrose.
Ambrotypie [ambroˈtyˈpiː], f. -/-n [-ˈpiːən]. Phot: ambrotype; photograph on glass.
Ambulakralfeld [ambuˈlaˈkraːl-], n. Echin: ambulacrum.
Ambulakralfüßchen, n.pl. Echin: ambulacral feet, tube-feet.
Ambulakralsystem, n. Echin: ambulacral system, water-vascular system.
Ambulakrum [ambuˈlaːkrum], n. -s/-kra & -kren. 1. Echin: ambulacrum. 2. Ecc.Arch: ambulatory.
ambulant [ambuˈlant], a. 1. itinerant, peripatetic; ambulatory; perambulating, strolling; ambulanter Gewerbebetrieb, street trading; door-to-door trading. 2. Med: ambulante Behandlung, out-patient treatment; ambulanter Typhus, ambulant typhoid fever; adv. j-n a. behandeln, to treat s.o. as an out-patient; a. behandelter Patient, out-patient.
Ambulanz [ambuˈlants], f. -/-en. 1. Mil: A: ambulance. 2. out-patients' department (of hospital). 3. Veh: ambulance.
ambulatorisch [ambulaˈtoːriʃ], a. 1. occ. = ambulant 1. 2. Med: = ambulant 2.
Ambulatorium [ambulaˈtoːrium], n. -s/-rien. Med: = Ambulanz 2.
ambulieren [ambuˈliːrən], v.i. (sein) to (per)-ambulate; to move around.
Ameise, f. -/-n. Ent: (a) ant; geflügelte A., winged ant, ant-fly; B: geh hin zur A., du Fauler, go to the ant, thou sluggard; see also fleißig; (b) weiße A., termite, white ant.
ameiseln, v.i. (haben) F: 1. to swarm like ants. 2. to itch; to feel as though ants were crawling on one.
Ameisenaldehyd, m. & n. Ch: A: formaldehyde.
Ameisenäther, m. Ch: ethyl formate, formic ether.
Ameisenbär, m. Z: ant-eater.
Ameiseneier, n.pl. F: ant-eggs, ants' eggs.
Ameisenfluß, m. F: = Ameisenkriechen.
ameisenfressend, a. Z: ant-eating, myrmecophagous.
Ameisenfresser, m. Z: ant-eater; großer A., great ant-eater, ant-bear.
Ameisenfreund, Ameisengast, m. Ent: myrmecophile.
Ameisengeist, m. Pharm: spirit of ants.
Ameisenhaufen, m. ant-hill, -heap.
Ameisenigel, m. Z: porcupine ant-eater.
Ameisenjungfer, f. Ent: myrmeleon, (full-grown) ant-lion.
Ameisenkriechen, Ameisenlaufen, n. Med: formication; paraesthesia, paraesthesis; F: pins and needles.
Ameisenlöwe, m. Ent: ant-lion.
Ameisennest, n. ants' nest.
Ameisenpflanze, f. Bot: myrmecophyte, myrmecophilous plant.
ameisensauer, a. Ch: formate of . . . ; ameisen-saures Salz, formate.
Ameisensäure, f. Ch: formic acid.
Ameisenscharrer, m., **Ameisenschwein**, n. Z: Cape aardvark, Cape ant-eater.
Ameisenspiritus, m. = Ameisengeist.
Ameisenvogel, m. Orn: (South American) ant-bird.
Amelioration [ameˈlioˈraˈtsioːn], f. -/-en, amelioration, improvement, betterment; esp. Agr: soil improvement.

ameliorieren [ameˈlioˈriːrən], v.tr. to ameliorate, to better, to improve; Agr: to improve (the soil).
Amelkorn, n. Agr: amelcorn, emmer.
Amelmehl, n. Dial: starch.
amen [ˈaːmɛn], int. & s. Amen, n. -s/-, amen; so be it; sein A. zu etwas geben, ja und a. zu etwas sagen, to assent, consent, to sth.; dazu sagen wir alle ja und a., F: and we all say amen to that; F: so sicher wie ein A., das A., in der Kirche, as sure as fate, as death, F: as sure as eggs is eggs; ein A. lang, for one brief moment.
Amendement [amãˈdəˈmãː], n. -s/-s. Pol: etc: A: amendment (to a bill, etc.); ein A. stellen, to move an amendment.
Amenie [ameˈniː], f.-/., **Amenorrhöe** [ameˈnoˈrøː], f. -/. Med: amenorrhoea.
Amentum [aˈmentum], n. -s/-ten. Bot: amentum, ament, catkin.
Americ(i)um [aˈmeːriˈkum, aˈmeːriˈtsium], n. -s/. Ch: americium.
Amerika [aˈmeːriˈkaˑ]. Pr.n.n. -s. Geog: America; die Vereinigten Staaten von A., the United States of America, the U.S.(A.); see also Mittelamerika, Nordamerika, Südamerika.
Amerikadeutsche, m., f. (decl. as adj.) German-American; German living in America.
amerikafeindlich, a. anti-American.
amerikafreundlich, a. pro-American.
Amerikakabel, n. El.E: transatlantic cable.
Amerikakunde, f. Sch: American studies.
Amerikaner [ameˈriˈkaɪnər], m. -s/-. 1. American. 2. Veh: American phaeton. 3. Cu: small iced cake. 4. Cy: (non-competing) pace-maker.
amerikanern [ameˈriˈkaɪnərn], v.i. (haben) (p.p. amerikanert) to adopt American habits; to behave like an American.
Amerikanerzange, f. Clockm: split chuck.
amerikanisch [ameˈriˈkaɪniʃ]. 1. a. American; die amerikanische Sprache, the American language, American English; see also Duell, Nuß, Orgel. 2. s. Amerikanisch, n. Ling: American English.
amerikanisieren [ameˈriˈkaniˈziːrən], v.tr. to Americanize; Amerikanisierung f, Americanization.
Amerikanismus [ameˈriˈkaˈnismus], m. -/-men. 1. Ling: Americanism, (i) (modern) American usage imported into English, (ii) American Indian word taken over into English. 2. der A., Americanism; American style or influence; the American way of life.
Amerikanist [ameˈriˈkaˈnist], m. -en/-en. 1. Americanist. 2. specialist in United States language and literature.
Amerikanistik [ameˈriˈkaˈnistik], f. -/. 1. Americanistics; the study of American archaeology and early history. 2. (modern) American studies, esp. (study of) United States language and literature.
Amerikareise, f. American journey, transatlantic journey; journey to or through America.
a metà [a meˈta]. Italian phr. Com: Fin: sharing profit and loss equally; (deal) on joint account.
Ametabole [ameˈtaˈboːlə], n. -/-n. Ent: ametabolian; die Ametabolen, the ametabola.
Ametall [ˈaˈmeˈtal], n. -s/-e. Ch: non-metal.
amethodisch [ˈaˈmeˈtoːdiʃ], a. unmethodical; adv. unmethodically, without method.
Amethyst [ameˈtyst], m. -(e)s/-e, amethyst.
amethystartig, a. amethystine, amethyst-like.
amethystfarben, amethystfarbig, a. amethystine, amethyst-coloured, violet-purple.
Ametrie [ameˈtriː], f. -/-n [-ˈtriːən], disproportion(ateness).
ametrisch [aˈmeːtriʃ], a. disproportionate, out of proportion.
Ametropie [ameˈtroˈpiː], f. -/. Med: ametropia.
Ameublement [aˈmøˈbləˈmãː], n. -s/-s. 1. furnishing (of house, office, etc.). 2. (set or suite of) furniture.
amharisch [aˈmaːriʃ]. 1. a. Amharic (language, etc.). 2. s. Amharisch, n. Ling: Amharic.
Amherstfasan [ˈɛm(h)ørst-], m. Orn: Lady Amherst's pheasant.
Ami[1] [aˈmiː], m. -s/-s, man- or boy-friend; lover, sweetheart.
Ami[2] [ˈamiː]. F: 1. m. -s/-s, American, F: Yankee, P: Yank. 2. f. -s/-s, American cigarette.
Amiant [aˈmiˈant], m. -s/-e. Miner: amiant(h)us; asbestos.
Amid [aˈmiːt], n. -(e)s/-e [-s,-ˈmiːdəs/-ˈmiːdə]. Ch: 1. amide. 2. -amid, comb. fm. -amide; Azetamid, acetamide; Oxamid, oxamide; Zyanamid, cyanamide.

Amidgruppe, f. *Ch:* amido, amino, group; amidogen.
amidieren [a·mi·'diːrən], v.tr. *Ch:* to amidate; Amidierung f, *Ch:* amidation.
Amidin [a·mi·'diːn], n. -s/-e. *Ch:* amidin.
Amido- [a·'miːdo·-], comb.fm. *Ch:* amido-; amino-; **Amidoschwefelsäure** f, amidosulphuric acid; **Amidobenzol** n, aminobenzene; **Amido-essigsäure** f, aminoacetic acid.
Amidoazo- [a·mi·do·a·'tso:-], comb.fm. *Ch: Dy:* aminoazo (dye, etc.).
Amidol [a·mi·'doːl], n. -s/. *Phot:* amidol.
Amid(o)säure, f. *Ch:* amidic acid, amic acid, amide acid.
amikroskopisch [ˌa·mi·kro·'sko:piʃ], a. ultra-microscopic.
Amikt [a·'mikt], m. -(e)s/-e. *Ecc.Cost:* amice.
Amin [a·'miːn], n. -s/-e. *Ch:* amine; -amin, comb.fm. -amine; **Äthylamin,** ethylamine; **Methylamin,** methylamine; **Phenylamin,** phenylamine.
aminieren [a·mi·'niːrən], v.tr. *Ch:* to aminate.
Amino- [a·'miːno·-], comb.fm. *Ch:* amino(-); **Aminosäure** f, amino acid; **Aminoverbindung** f, amino compound.
Aminoplast, n. -(e)s/e, amino-plastics.
Aminsäure, f. *Ch:* amino acid; amidic, amic, acid.
Amiranten, die [a·mi·'rantən]. *Pr.n.f.pl. Geog:* the Amirante Islands, the Amirantes.
Amitose [a·mi·'toːzə], f. -/-n. *Biol:* amitosis.
Ammann, m. -s/-männer. *North G. Dial: & Swiss:* district magistrate; mayor; *A:* bailiff.
Ammarelle [ama·'rɛlə], f. -/-n. *South G.Dial:* apricot.
Amme, f. -/-n. 1. (a) (wet-)nurse; **die Universität, die A. aller Wissenschaft,** the university, the nurse of all scholarship; (b) (children's) nurse, *F:* nanny. 2. foster-mother. 3. *Dial:* mother. 4. occ. midwife. 5. *Biol:* asexual organism.
Ammei, f. -/. *Bot:* ammi, bishop('s)-weed.
Ammeli, n. -/-. *Swiss Dial:* (infant's) feeding-bottle.
Ammelkorn, Ammelmehl, n.=**Amelkorn, Amelmehl.**
ämmeln, v.i. (haben) 1. to act as a wet-nurse. 2. *Dial:* to curve.
ammenhaft, a. (a) like a (wet-)nurse; (b) big-, broad-bosomed (woman).
Ammenlied, n. nursery rhyme.
Ammenmärchen, n. 1. nursery tale; fairy-story, -tale. 2.=**Altweibermärchen.**
Ammenzeugung, f. *Biol:* asexual reproduction.
Ammer[1], m. -s/. *Agr:*=**Emmer**[2].
Ammer[2], f. -/-n, occ. m. -s/-. *Orn:* bunting; **kleinasiatische A.,** cinereous bunting, grey-headed bunting.
Ammer[3], f. -/-n. *Hort:* morello (cherry).
Ämmerling, m. -s/-e. *Orn:*=**Ammer**[2].
Ammon[1] ['amo·n]. *Pr.n.m. -s. Myth:* Ammon.
Ammon[2] [a'mo·n], m. -s/. *Ch:* ammonium; **Ammon-,** comb.fm.=**Ammonium-.**
Ammonal [amo·'naːl], n. -s/. *Exp:* ammonal.
Ammonalaun, m. ammonia alum.
Amoniak [amo·ni'ak], n. -s/-e. *Ch:* 1. (a) ammonia (gas); (b) flüssiges, wässeriges, A., ammonia hydrate, ammonia solution, *F:* ammonia. 2. **Ammoniak-,** comb.fm. (in older nomenclature)=**Ammon(ium)-.**
Ammoniakalaun, m. *Ch:* ammonia alum.
ammoniakalisch [amo·ni·a·'ka:liʃ], a. ammoniacal.
Ammoniakbase, f. *Ch:* amine.
Ammoniakflüssigkeit, f. *Ch: Ind:* ammonia liquor, ammonia water.
Ammoniakgummi, m. *Pharm: etc:* (gum) ammoniac.
ammoniakhaltig, a. *Ch:* ammoniacal.
Ammoniakharz, n.=**Ammoniakgummi.**
Ammoniaklösung, f. *Ch: etc:* ammonia solution; wässerige A., ammonia hydrate, *F:* ammonia.
Ammoniakpflanze, f. *Bot:* ammoniac fennel, ammoniac plant.
Ammoniaksalpeter, m.=**Ammonsalpeter.**
Ammoniakwasser, n. *Ch:* ammonia water; *Ind:* ammonia liquor.
Ammonit[1] [amo·'niːt], m. -en/-en. *Paleont:* ammonite.
Ammonit[2], m. -(e)s/-e. *Exp:* (any) ammonium nitrate explosive.
Ammoniter [amo·'niːtər], m. -s/-. *B.Hist:* Ammonite.
Ammonium [a'mo·niʊm], n. -s/. *Ch:* ammonium.
Ammoniumchlorid, n. *Ch:* ammonium chloride, sal ammoniac.
Ammoniumkarbonat, n. *Ch:* ammonium carbonate.
Ammoniumnitrat, n. *Ch:* ammonium nitrate.
Ammoniumrest, m. *Ch:* ammonium radical.

Ammoniumzinnchlorid, n. *Ch:* ammonium chlorostannate, *Tex:* pink salt.
Ammonpulver, n. *Exp:* ammonal.
Ammonsalpeter, m. *Ch: Exp:* ammonium nitrate.
Ammonshorn ['amons-], n. *Paleont:* ammonite.
Ammonzinnchlorid, n.=**Ammoniumzinnchlorid.**
Amnesie [amne·'ziː], f. -/-n [-'ziːən]. *Med:* amnesia.
amnesisch [am'neːziʃ], a. *Med:* amnesic.
Amnestie [amnɛs'tiː], f. -/-n [-'tiːən], (a) amnesty, general pardon, act of oblivion; (b) amnesty ordinance.
amnestieren [amnɛs'tiːrən], v.tr. to amnesty, pardon.
Amnion ['amni̯on], n. -s/-nien. *Obst:* amnion, *F:* water-bag.
Amnionwasser, n. *Obst:* amniotic fluid.
Amöbe [a·'møːbə], f. -/-n. *Prot:* amoeba.
amöbenförmig, a. amoebiform.
Amöbenruhr, f. *Med:* amoebic dysentery.
amöboid [a·mø·bo·'iːt], a. amoeboid.
Amok ['a:mok, a·'mok], m. -s/-, amok, amuck; **A. laufen,** to run amok, to run amuck.
Amoklaufen, n. running amok, running amuck.
Amokläufer, m. person who runs amok, amuck.
a-moll, a-Moll, n. *Mus:* (key of) A minor.
amollieren [a·mo·'liːrən], v.tr. to soften; to weaken, enervate (mind, courage, etc.).
Amom [a·'mo:m], n. -s/-e, **Amome** [a·'mo:mə], f. -/-n. *Bot:* amomum.
amön [a·'møːn], a. agreeable; charming; graceful.
Amor ['a:mo·r]. 1. *Pr.n.m. -s.* Cupid, Eros, the God of Love. 2. occ. pl. **Amoren,** Cupids.
amoralisch ['a·mo·ra:liʃ], a. amoral, non-moral, unmoral.
Amoralismus [a·mo·ra·'lismus], m. -/. amoralism; abstention from moral judgments.
Amoralität [a·mo·ra·li·'tɛːt], f. -/-en, amoral character (of sth.); amoral action.
Amorce [a'morsə], f. -/-n & -s. 1. (a) *Exp: A:* fuse; primer, detonator; (b) *Sm.a: A:* percussion cap, cartridge cap; (c) *Toys:* (snap) cap (for toy pistol). 2. *Constr:* toothing (of wall). 3. *Fish: Ven: etc:* bait.
Amorette [a·mo·'rɛtə], f. -/-n. *Art:* amoretto, (little) Cupid.
Amoriter [a·mo·'riːtər], m.pl. *B.Hist:* Amorites.
amorph [a·'morf], a. *Biol: Ch: etc:* amorphous (form, state, substance, etc.).
Amorphie [a·mor'fiː], f. -/. amorphism.
amorphisch [a·'morfiʃ], a.=**amorph.**
Amorphismus [a·mor'fismus], m. -/.=**Amorphie.**
amortisabel [a·morti·'za:bəl], a.=**amortisierbar.**
Amortisation [a·morti·za·tsi'o:n], f. -/-en, (a) *Fin:* amortization, redemption (of stocks, obligation); paying off, liquidation (of debt, etc.); (b) *Ind:* (amount written off for) depreciation.
Amortisationsfonds, m., **Amortisationskasse,** f. sinking-fund; redemption fund.
Amortisationsplan, m. redemption table; terms for redemption, for amortization.
Amortisationsrate, f. amortization quota; amortization instalment.
amortisierbar [a·morti·'ziːrba·r], a. *Fin:* redeemable (stock, etc.).
amortisieren [a·morti·'ziːrən], v.tr. (a) *Fin:* to amortize, redeem (stocks, obligation); to pay off, extinguish (debt, etc.); (b) *Ind:* to allow for depreciation of, to write off (plant).
Amortisierung, f.=**Amortisation.**
Amour [a·'muːr], f. -/-s & -en, amour; (love-)affair; intrigue.
Amourettengras [a·mu·'rɛtəngra:s], n. *Bot:* (common) quaking-grass, lady's hair.
Amp, n. -s/-. *F:*=**Ampere.**
Ampel, f. -/-n. 1. hanging lamp. 2. hanging flower-pot. 3.=**Ampulle.** 4.=**Verkehrsampel.**
ampeln, v.i. (haben) nach etwas a., to struggle hard for sth.
Ampelographie [ampe·lo·gra·'fiː], f. -/. ampelography; description of (the varieties of) the vine.
Ampelopsis [ampe·'lopsis], f. -/. *Bot:* ampelopsis, Virginia creeper.
Ampelpflanze, Ampelranke, f. *Hort:* plant suitable for a hanging pot; hanging plant.
Ampere [ã·'pɛːr], n. -(s)/-. *El.Meas:* ampere, *F:* amp.
Amperemeter [ã·pɛ·r'meːtər], n. -s/-. *El:* ammeter, amperemeter; aperiodisches A., dead-beat ammeter.
Amperesekunde, f. *El.Meas:* ampere-second.
Amperestunde, f. *El.Meas:* ampere-hour.
Amperewindung, f. *El:* ampere-turn.
Amperezahl, f. *El:* amperage.
Ampfer, m. -s/-. *Bot:* sorrel; dock; **krausblättriger A.,** krauser A., yellow dock, curled dock.
ampferig, a. *Dial:* sour, tart.

Ampferklee, m. *Bot:* oxalis, wood-sorrel.
Amphi-, amphi- [amfi·-], pref. amphi-; **Amphiarthrosis** f, amphiarthrosis; **Amphibrach** m, amphibrach; **amphikarpisch,** amphicarpous; **Amphitheater** n, amphitheatre.
Amphibie [am'fiːbi̯ə], f. -/-n, (a) *Nat.Hist:* amphibian; **die Amphibien,** the amphibians, the amphibia; (b) *Bot:* amphibious plant.
Amphibienfahrzeug, n. amphibious vehicle.
Amphibienpanzerwagen, m. *Mil:* amphibious tank, amphibian tank.
amphibisch [am'fiːbiʃ], a. amphibious (animal, plant, vehicle, aircraft, etc.); *Mil:* **amphibische Operationen,** amphibian operations; combined operations.
Amphibium [am'fiːbi̯um], n. -s/-bien. 1. = **Amphibie** (a). 2. *Av: Veh:* amphibian.
Amphibol [amfi·'bo:l], m. -s/-e, **Amphibolfels,** m. *Miner:* amphibolite, hornblende rock.
Amphibolie [amfi·bo·'liː], f. -/-n [-'liːən], amphibology, ambiguity.
amphibolisch [amfi·'bo:liʃ], a. amphibological, ambiguous.
Amphibolit [amfi·bo·'liːt], m. -(e)s/-e=**Amphibol.**
Amphibrach [amfi·'brax], m. -s/-en. *Pros:* amphibrach.
Amphigonie [amfi·go·'niː], f. -/. amphigony, sexual reproduction.
Amphigurie [amfi·gu·'riː], f. -/-n [-'riːən]. *Lit:* amphigouri, amphigory; (piece) of nonsense-verse.
amphigurisch [amfi·'guːriʃ], a. *Lit:* amphigoric; rambling (discourse).
Amphiktyone [amfikty·'o:nə], m. -n/-n. *Gr.Hist:* Amphictyon.
Amphiktyonie [amfikty·o·'niː], f. -/-n [-'niːən]. *Gr.Hist:* amphictyony, amphictyonic council.
Amphioxus [amfi·'oksus], m. -/. *Ich:* amphioxus, lancelet.
Amphipode [amfi·'po:də], m. -n/-n. *Crust:* amphipod, sand-flea.
Amphitheater [am'fiːte·a·tər], n. *Arch: Th: etc:* amphitheatre.
amphitheatralisch [amfi·te·a·'tra:liʃ], a. rising all round; amphitheatr(ic)al (valley, etc.).
Amphitrite [amfi·'triːte:]. *Pr.n.f. -s. Gr.Myth:* Amphitrite.
amphitropisch [amfi·'tro:piʃ], a. *Biol: Bot:* amphitropal, amphitropous.
Amphitryon [am'fiːtry·on]. 1. *Pr.n.m. -s. Myth:* Amphitryon. 2. m. -s/-en, Amphitryon, (a) cuckold; (b) (from Molière's play) host, entertainer.
Amphora ['amfo·ra:], f. -/-ren ['amfo·rən, am'fo·rən]. *Archeol: etc:* amphora.
amphorisch [am'fo·riʃ], a. *Med:* amphoric (sound, cough, etc.).
amphoter [amfo·'teːr], a. *Ch:* amphoteric.
Amplifikation [amplifi·ka·tsi'o:n], f. -/-en, amplification, development, expansion (of idea, etc.).
amplifizieren [amplifi·'tsiːrən], v.tr. to amplify, develop, expand, enlarge (idea, etc.).
Amplitude [ampli·'tuːdə], f. -/-n. *Astr: Ph:* amplitude.
Amplitudenmodulation, f. *W.Tel:* amplitude modulation, frequency modulation.
Amplitudenverfahren, n. *Cin:* variable width recording.
Ampulle [am'pulə], f. -/-n. 1. (a) *Rom.Ant: Ecc:* ampulla; (b) phial; (c) *Pharm:* ampoule. 2. *Anat:* ampulla (of duct, canal, etc.).
ampullenförmig, a. *Bot: etc:* ampullaceous.
ampullös [ampu·'løːs], a. 1.=**ampullenförmig.** 2. *A:* pompous, pretentious (words, etc.).
Amputation [ampu·ta·tsi'o:n], f. -/-en. *Surg:* amputation.
Amputationsbesteck, n. set of amputation instruments.
amputieren [ampu·'tiːrən]. I. v.tr. *Surg:* to amputate (leg, etc.).
II. vbl s. **Amputieren** n., **Amputierung** f. amputation.
Amputierte, m. (decl. as adj.) person who has had one or more limbs amputated, amputee.
Ämse, f. -/-n. *Dial:*=**Ameise.**
Amsel, f. -/-n. 1. *Orn:* blackbird. 2. *Her:* (gestümmelte) A., martlet.
Amselbeere, f. *Bot:* buckthorn berry.
Amselfeld, das. *Geog:* Kossovo Kolje, the field of Kossovo; *Hist:* **die Schlacht auf dem A.,** the battle of Kossovo.
Amselmöwe, f. *Orn:* black tern.
Amstelkraut, n. *Bot:* meadow-rue, meadow-rhubarb.
Amsterdam [amstər'dam]. *Pr.n.n. -s. Geog:* Amsterdam; see also **Neu-Amsterdam.**
Amsterdamer [amstər'damər, 'amster-]. 1. m.

-s/-. *Geog:* inhabitant, native, of Amsterdam. **2.** *inv.a.* of Amsterdam, Amsterdam . . .; **eine A. Zeitung,** an Amsterdam newspaper.

Amt, *n.* -(e)s/⸗er. **1.** (*a*) office, function; employment, post, place, appointment, situation; **hohes Amt,** high, important, office; **öffentliches Amt,** public office; **geistliches Amt,** ecclesiastical office, ecclesiastical function; **das Amt eines Bischofs, eines Sekretärs,** the office of bishop, of secretary; *Pol:* **das Amt eines Finanzministers,** the office of Minister of Finance; **im Amte sein,** to be in office, to hold office; **ein Amt bekleiden,** to hold office; to hold an appointment, a position; **in Amt und Würden sein,** to be in an established position, to be a man of position and authority; **von Amts wegen handeln,** to act in virtue of one's office, ex officio; **sich um ein Amt bewerben,** to be a candidate for office, to seek office; **j-n in ein Amt einsetzen,** to put s.o. into office; to admit (s.o.) to (an) office, install s.o. (in an office); **das Amt antreten,** to take office, to come into office; **sein Amt niederlegen, vom Amt zurücktreten, aus dem Amte scheiden,** to leave, resign, office; to resign one's post; *Prov:* **wem der Herr ein Amt gibt, dem gibt er auch Verstand,** heaven suits the back to the burden; (*b*) functions; duty, duties; province; **seines Amtes walten; tun, was seines Amtes ist,** to perform one's functions, the duties of one's office; **tu, was deines Amtes ist!** do your duty! **das ist nicht seines Amtes,** that is not (within) his province, that is beyond (the scope of) his authority; **es ist nicht meines Amtes, das zu tun,** it is not my business, my place, to do it; **was deines Amtes nicht ist, da lasse deinen Vorwitz!** mind your own business! **2.** *Ecc:* (*a*) (*Protestant*) Divine Service; **das Amt halten,** to take, conduct, the service; (*b*) *R.C.Ch:* sung mass. **3.** *Adm:* (*a*) government office; government department; section (of a ministry); *U.S:* bureau; **Amt für Wetterdienst,** Meteorological Office, *U.S:* Weather Bureau; **Amt für Statistik,** Office, *U.S:* Bureau, of Statistics; *see also* **auswärtig;** (*b*) **das Amt,** the administrative authorities, the administration. **4.** (*a*) *Adm:* office; post-office, telegraph-office, tax-office, etc.; *Tp:* (telephone) exchange, *U.S:* central; **das Amt anrufen,** to call the exchange; **'das Amt, bitte',** 'exchange, please'; (*b*) *Jur:* (magistrate's) court; official residence of a magistrate. **5.** (*a*)= **Amtsbezirk;** (*b*)=**Amtmannschaft** 2. **6.** *A:* (*a*) board of management; (*b*) corporation; (craftsmen's) company.

Ämtchen, *n.* -s/-, (*dim. of* **Amt**) minor, unimportant, office; *Prov:* **Ä. bringt Käppchen,** all officials have their pickings.

Amtei, *f.* -/-en. **1.**=**Amtslokal. 2.**=**Amtsbezirk.**

amten, *v.i.* (*haben*)=**amtieren.**

Ämterhandel, *m.* (*a*) *Pol:* office-jobbing; (*b*) *Ecc:* simony.

Ämterjagd, *f.* place-hunting; seeking after office.

Ämterjäger, *m.* office-seeking politician, office-seeker; place-hunter.

Ämterkauf, *m.* purchasing of offices; *Ecc:* simony.

ämtersüchtig, *a.* office-seeking, place-hunting (politician).

Ämtertausch, *m. Adm:* exchange of posts (between two officials).

amtfrei, *a.*=**amtsfrei.**

Amthaus, *n.* (*a*) office (of local administration); court-house; official residence of the 'Amtmann', *q.v.*; (*b*) *Hist:* bailiff's house.

amtieren [am'tiːrən]. I. *v.i.* (*haben*) **1.** to hold office, to be in office; to exercise one's functions; **als Sekretär a.,** to act as secretary, to perform the office of secretary; **amtierender Präsident,** acting president. **2.** *Ecc:* to officiate (at a service); to celebrate a religious ceremony, *abs.* to celebrate; **amtierender Geistlicher,** officiating minister, officiant; celebrant.

II. *vbl s.* **Amtieren** *n.*, **Amtierung** *f.*, exercise of one's (official) functions; *Ecc:* officiation; celebration (of religious ceremony).

amtlich, *a.* (*a*) official; **amtliches Schreiben,** official letter; **amtliche Kreise,** official circles; **von amtlichen Stellen,** from official quarters; by the authorities; (*b*) official, authentic; **amtliche Nachrichten,** official news; **das ist a.!** it's official! *Fin:* **amtliche Notierung,** official quotation; *adv.* officially; **a. bestätigt,** officially confirmed; **a. handeln,** to act officially, in one's official capacity, ex officio.

amtlos, *a.* without office; (*of politician*) out of office, out of place.

Amtmann, *m.* -(e)s/-männer & -leute. **1.** district administrator; district magistrate; *Hist:* bailiff. **2.** agent, steward, bailiff, *Scot:* factor (of estate). **3.** senior clerk (in middle grade of German civil service).

Amtmannschaft, *f.* **1.** rank, office, of a district administrator; magistrateship; *Hist:* rank, office, of a bailiff. **2.** area under the jurisdiction of an administrator; *Hist:* bailiwick.

Amtmeister, *m.* master, president (of guild, craftsmen's company, etc.).

Amtsadel, *m.* nobility whose titles derive from the holding of public offices.

Amtsalter, *n.* seniority (in office).

Amtsanmaßung, *f. Jur:* unauthorized assumption of authority; fraudulent exercise of a public office.

Amtsanruf, *m. Tp:* call to *or* from the exchange.

Amtsantritt, *m.* accession to office, assumption of office.

Amtsanwalt, *m. Jur:* Public Prosecutor (in lower courts).

Amtsarzt, *m. Adm:* medical officer of health.

Amtsbefugnis, *f. Jur:* competence, competency, authority (of official).

Amtsbeleidigung, *f. Jur:* (*a*) insult to, insulting of, an official while on duty; (*b*) attack on s.o.'s professional integrity.

Amtsbericht, *m.* official report; return.

Amtsbewerber, *m.* candidate for (an) office.

Amtsbezeichnung, *f. Adm:* (authorized) designation, description, title, style (of official).

Amtsbezirk, *m.* (*a*) administrative district; (*b*) *Jur:* jurisdiction; **A. eines Richters, eines Beamten,** area within, under, the jurisdiction of a judge, an official.

Amtsblatt, *n.* gazette.

Amtsbote, *m. Jur:* **1.** messenger. **2.** *occ.*= **Amtsdiener** (*a*).

Amtsbruder, *m.* colleague, *esp. Ecc:* brother-minister, fellow-clergyman.

Amtsbürgermeister, *m.* district administrator (exercising mayoral functions for several villages).

Amtscharakter, *m.* **1.** official character, official nature (of visit, procedure, etc.). **2.**=**Amtsbezeichnung.**

Amtsdauer, *f.* duration of office; period, term, of office, *U.S:* term.

Amtsdelikt, *n.*=**Amtsverbrechen.**

Amtsdiener, *m. Jur:* (*a*) process-server; bailiff; (*b*) court usher; (*c*) *A:* beadle.

Amtsehrenbeleidigung, *f.*=**Amtsbeleidigung.**

Amtseid, *m.* oath of office; **j-m den A. abnehmen,** to swear s.o. in, to administer the oath (of office) to s.o.; **den A. ablegen,** to be sworn in.

Amtseinkünfte, *f.pl.* emoluments, salary.

Amtsenthebung, *f.* (*a*)=**Amtsentsetzung;** (*b*) **zeitweilige A.,** suspension (of official).

Amtsentsetzung, *f.* dismissal, removal (of official).

Amtsfolge, *f.* **1.** *Adm:* rotation (in office). **2.** *Jur:* **A. leisten,** to comply with the order of a court, of a magistrate.

amtsfrei, *a.* **1.** *A:* not holding any (public) office; **amtsfreie Person,** private person. **2.** (pers., hours, etc.) off duty; off-duty (hours, etc.).

Amtsfreizeichen, *n. Tp:* dialling tone, *U.S:* dial tone.

Amtsführung, *f.* administration.

Amtsgebühr, *f. Adm:* charge, fee.

Amtsgeheimnis, *n.* **1.** official secret. **2.** official secrecy.

Amtsgehilfe, *m. Adm:* assistant.

amtsgemäß, *a.* official; *adv.* officially.

Amtsgenosse, *m.* colleague, fellow-official.

Amtsgericht, *n. Jur:* local court; *approx.*=(i) county court; (ii) magistrates' court.

amtsgerichtlich, *a. Jur:* (decision, etc.) of, by, a local court; **amtsgerichtliches Verfahren,** local court procedure.

Amtsgerichtsrat, *m.* official rank of 'Amtsrichter' (*q.v.*).

Amtsgeschäfte, *n.pl.* official business; official duties.

Amtsgewalt, *f.* (official) authority.

Amtsgewand, *n.* robe of office; (judge's, lawyer's) gown.

Amtsgruppe, *f. Mil.Adm:* branch (of department in war ministry).

Amtshaftung, *f. Jur:* responsibility of an official for the legality of his actions.

amtshalber, *adv.* officially.

Amtshandlung, *f.* (*a*) official act; (*b*) *Ecc:* ministration; religious ceremony.

Amtshauptmann, *m. A:* district administrator.

Amtshauptmannschaft, *f. A:* administrative district.

Amtshaus, *n.*=**Amthaus.**

Amtsherr, *m.* **1.**=**Amtmann** 1. **2.** *Hist:* feudal lord.

Amtshoheit, *f.* official dignity; dignity of office.

Amtsinhaber, *m.* holder of an office; *Ecc:* incumbent.

Amtsjäger, *m.* =**Ämterjäger.**

Amtsjahr, *n.* year of office (of mayor, etc.).

Amtskette, *f.* chain of office.

Amtskleid, *n.*, **Amtskleidung,** *f.*=**Amtstracht.**

Amtskörperschaft, *f.* official body.

Amtskosten, *pl. Adm:* charges, fees.

Amtsleiter, *m. Adm:* head of a section.

Amtslokal, *n.* office, *esp.* magistrate's office; administrative office.

amtsmäßig, *a.* official; *adv.* officially.

Amtsmeister, *m.*=**Amtmeister.**

Amtsmiene, *f.* official air; solemn, severe, look; **eine A. aufstecken, aufsetzen,** to put on a solemn look, to look as solemn as a judge.

Amtsmißbrauch, *m. Jur:* (*a*) undue use of (administrative) authority; misuse, abuse, of authority; (*b*)=**Amtsverbrechen.**

amtsmüde, *a.* weary of the cares of office.

Amtsperson, *f.* official; official personage; *Lit:* functionary.

Amtspflicht, *f.* official duty; obligations of an office.

Amtsrat, *m.* (*civil service grade*) *approx.*=chief executive officer.

Amtsreise, *f.* tour (of official); circuit (of judge).

Amtsrichter, *m. Jur:* local court judge; *approx.* =(i) county court judge; (ii) magistrate.

Amtssache, *f.* official matter, official business.

Amtssasse, *m. Hist:* person under the jurisdiction of a bailiff.

amtssässig, *a. Hist:* living within the jurisdiction (of a bailiff).

Amtsschimmel, *m.* bureaucracy, officialism, *F:* red tape; *F:* **den A. reiten,** to be fond of red tape.

Amtsschreiber, *m.* **1.** *Jur:* clerk (of the court). **2.** clerk to the agent, to the steward (of estate).

Amtssiegel, *n.* official seal; official stamp.

Amtssitz, *m.* official residence.

Amtssprache, *f.* official language, *F:* officialese.

Amtsstelle, *f.* official position; public office.

Amtsstube, *f.*=**Amtslokal.**

Amtsstunden, *f.pl.* office hours.

Amtstag, *m. Jur:* court-day; *A:* (magistrate's) audience day.

Amtstätigkeit, *f.* exercise of an office, of official functions; (*of official*) **in A. sein,** to be in active employment; **j-n außer A. setzen,** to relieve s.o. of his office, of his duties.

Amtstitel, *m.*=**Amtsbezeichnung.**

Amtstracht, *f.* official dress; robe(s) of office; (judge's, lawyer's, etc.) gown; **geistliche A.,** canonical dress, canonicals.

Amtsträger, *m.* office-bearer, *U.S:* office-holder.

Amtsüberschreitung, *f.*=**Amtsmißbrauch.**

Amtsübung, *f. Ecc:* **A., Amtsübungen,** ministrations.

Amtsuntersagung, *f. Adm:* suspension from duty.

Amtsunterschlagung, *f. Jur:* embezzlement, malversation.

Amtsverbrechen, Amtsvergehen, *n. Jur:* dereliction of duty; misuse, abuse, of authority; maladministration; malversation, malpractice; malfeasance.

Amtsverlust, *m.* loss of office; degradation.

Amtsvermittlung, *f. Tp:* (telephone) exchange.

Amtsverrichtung, *f.* exercise of one's (official) functions.

Amtsverschwiegenheit, *f.* official secrecy.

Amtsvertreter, *m.* deputy, substitute (of official); locum-tenens (for clergyman).

Amtsverwalter, *m.* **1.** administrator; *Hist:* bailiff. **2.**=**Amtsvertreter.**

Amtsverwaltung, *f.* administration.

Amtsverweser, *m.* deputy, substitute (of official); *Hist:* deputy bailiff.

Amtsvogt, *m. Hist:* bailiff.

Amtsvogtei, *f. Hist:* **1.** bailiwick. **2.** office of bailiff.

Amtsvorgänger, *m.* predecessor, precursor (in office).

Amtsvormund, *m. Jur:* officially appointed guardian (of orphan, etc.).

Amtsvormundschaft, *f. Jur:* official guardianship.

Amtsvorstand, *m. Adm:* head of a section.

Amtsvorsteher, *m. Adm:* **1.** overseer of the local constabulary. **2.** manager (of a local government office, etc.).

Amtswechsel, *m.* **1.** change of office. **2.** *Adm:* rotation (in office).

Amtsweg, *m. Adm:* **auf dem Amtswege,** officially,

through official channels; conforming to official regulations; **den A. einhalten,** to act through the proper, the usual, channels.

amtswegen, von amtswegen=**von Amts wegen,** *q.v. under* **Amt** 1.

amtswidrig, *a.* (action) constituting a breach, dereliction, of duty.

Amtswidrigkeit, *f.* breach, dereliction, of duty.

Amtswohnung, *f.* official residence.

Amtszeichen, *n.* **1.** *Adm:* official stamp. **2.** *Tp:* dialling tone, *U.S:* dial tone.

Amtszeit, *f.* **1.** period, term, of office. **2.** office hours.

Amtszimmer, *n.*=**Amtslokal.**

Ämulation [ɛ·mu·la·tsĭ'oːn], *f.* **-/-en,** emulation, rivalry, competition.

Amulett [a·mu·'lɛt], *n.* **-s/-e,** amulet, (lucky) charm; talisman.

ämulieren [ɛ·mu·'liːrən], *v.tr.* to emulate.

amüsant [amy·'zant], *a.* amusing, entertaining, diverting, funny; **er ist sehr a.,** he is very amusing, he is great fun.

Amüsement [amy·zə'mãː], *n.* **-s/-s,** amusement; recreation, pastime; diversion.

Amusie [a·mu·'ziː], *f.* **-/.** lack of aesthetic sensibility.

amüsieren [amy·'ziːrən], *v.tr.* to amuse, entertain, divert; **sich a.,** (*a*) to amuse, enjoy, oneself; to have a good time; **wir werden uns a.,** we are going to enjoy ourselves, we shall have fun; **ich habe mich amüsiert wie noch nie,** I had the time of my life; **wir haben uns herrlich, köstlich, amüsiert,** we had a grand time, a (perfectly) lovely time; we enjoyed ourselves immensely, enormously; we had lots of fun; **sich über etwas** *acc.* **a.,** to be amused at, by, entertained by, sth.; to laugh at, over, sth.; **sich über j-n a.,** to laugh at s.o.; to make fun, make game, of s.o.; (*b*) to see life, to have a good time; *F:* to step out, to go places; to go on the spree; to be on the spree, on the binge.

amusisch [a·'muːziʃ], *a.* without aesthetic sensibilities.

Amygdalin [a·mykda·'liːn], *n.* **-s/.** *Ch:* amygdalin.

Amygdalinsäure, *f. Ch.* amygdalic acid.

Amyl [a·'myːl], *n.* **-s/.** *Ch:* amyl.

Amylalkohol, *m. Ch:* amyl alcohol.

Amylazetat, *n. Ch:* amyl acetate.

Amylen [a·my·'leːn], *n.* **-s/-e.** *Ch:* amylene.

Amyloid [a·my·lo·'iːt], *n.* **-(e)s/-e** [-s, -'iːdəs/-'iːdə]. *Bio-Ch:* amyloid.

Amyloidentartung, *f. Med:* amyloidosis; amyloid, waxy, degeneration (of the liver, of the spleen).

Amylolyse [a·my·lo·'lyːzə], *f.* **-/.** *Ch:* amylolysis; saccharization of starch.

Amylon ['aːmy·lon], *n.* **-s/.** *Ch: etc:* starch.

Amylose [a·my·'loːzə], *f.* **-/.** *Ch:* amylose.

Amyloxyhydrat [a·ˌmy·loksy·hy·'draːt], *n. Ch:*= **Amylalkohol.**

an. I. *prep.* **1.** (+*dat.*) (*cp.* **am**) (*a*) in (lateral) contact with; (leaning, lying) against; attached to; on; **die Leiter steht an der Mauer,** the ladder is standing against the wall; **die Tapete an der Wand,** the paper on the wall; **die Blätter an den Bäumen,** the leaves on the trees; **die Scheinwerfer an einem Wagen,** the headlights on a car; **die Entenmuscheln an einem Schiffsrumpf,** the barnacles on the hull of a ship; **Seite an Seite,** side by side; **Kante an Kante,** edge to edge; **Rücken an Rücken,** backed against one another, back to back; (*of ships*) **Bord an Bord,** alongside (one another); (*b*) at; on; in; by, near, close to, adjacent to; **an der Tür,** at the door; **an der Grenze,** (i) at, on, the frontier, (ii) near the frontier; **an seiner rechten Seite,** at his right hand, on his right; **an dem Ufer,** on the bank, on the shore; **an dem Rand des Sees,** at, on, the edge of the lake; **an jenem Ort,** at, in, that place; **an seiner Stelle,** in his place; **an erster Stelle,** in the first place; **an der Wand sitzen,** to sit by the wall; **ein Platz an der Sonne,** a place in the sun; **an . . . entlang,** *see* **entlang; an . . . vorbei,** *see* **vorbei;** (*of pers.*) **schmal an den Hüften,** narrow at the hips; *Geog:* **an der Nordsee,** by the North Sea; on (the coast, the shores, of) the North Sea; **an der Donau, an der Weichsel,** on the Danube, on the Vistula; *Nau: Av:* **an Bord,** aboard; on the ship; in the aircraft; (*c*) (*with parts of the body*) (i) on; **an dem Finger, an der Zehe,** on one's finger, toe; **Muttermal an der Wange,** mole on the cheek; (ii) (*injury*) **Wunde an der Brust,** wound on the breast; **Verletzung an den Rippen,** injury to the ribs; (iii) **an allen Gliedern zittern, wund sein,** to tremble, to be sore, in every limb; (*d*) on the (permanent) staff of (an institution); **Professor, Dozent, an der Universität München,** professor, lecturer, at the University of Munich; **Lehrer, Lehrerin, an einer Schule,** master, mistress, at a school; (*e*) on; **an Krücken gehen,** to walk on crutches; **einen Hund an der Leine führen,** to keep a dog on the lead; (*f*) by; **j-n an der Kehle packen,** to seize s.o. by the throat; **j-n an der Hand führen,** to lead s.o. by the hand; **einen Hut an der Krempe anfassen,** to catch hold of a hat by the brim; (*g*) (*suspension*) **an einem Seile hängen,** to hang on, by, from, a rope; to be suspended by a rope; **an einem Faden hängen,** to hang by a thread; **an dem Galgen,** on the gallows; (*h*) **Arbeit an einem Neubau, an einem Jahresbericht, usw.,** work on a new building, on an annual report, etc.; **Reparaturen an einem Dach,** repairs to a roof; *Surg:* **Operation an der Leber,** operation on the liver; (*i*) in the (very) act of; engaged in; **an der Arbeit,** at work; (*j*) **an einem Ort ankommen,** to arrive at, in, a place; **an seinem Ziel angelangt sein,** to have reached one's goal; **an der letzten Seite eines Buches sein,** to be on, to have reached, to have got to, the last page of a book; (*k*) falling to the responsibility of (s.o.); **die Schuld ist an ihm,** the fault lies, is, with him; it is his fault; **es liegt an mir,** it is up to me (to do it); **es ist an dir, die Sache besser zu machen,** it is up to you to do better; **es ist nicht an mir,** it is not my responsibility, not my place (to do it); **es ist nicht an mir zu entscheiden,** it is not for me to decide; **soviel an mir liegt, ist,** for my part; as far as lies in my power; (*l*) about; in; **was ich an ihm bewundere, ist . . .,** what I admire about him is . . . ; **das Merkwürdige an der Sache ist, daß . . .,** the remarkable thing about the affair is that . . . ; **es ist gar nichts Gemeines an ihm,** there is nothing common about him; **er hat nichts vom Schulmeister an sich,** there is nothing schoolmasterish about him; **es ist nichts Wahres an der Nachricht,** there is no truth in the report; **es ist nichts an der Sache,** there is nothing in it; **es ist nicht an dem,** that is not so; **weißt du, was an dem ist?** do you know the facts about it? do you know if there is any truth in it? (*m*) **an sich,** in itself; in themselves; as such; **Fleiß an sich genügt nicht,** diligence by itself, as such, is not enough; **ein an sich lobenswerter Versuch,** an attempt praiseworthy in itself; **an und für sich,** by itself alone; without extraneous considerations; basically; actually; **der Staat an und für sich betrachtet,** the State regarded purely as such, viewed in the abstract, regarded as an abstraction; *Phil:* **das Ding an sich,** the noumenon; **das Schöne an sich,** absolute beauty; (*n*) **du hast einen treuen Freund an ihm gefunden,** you have found a faithful friend in him; **an etwas, an j-m, ein Geschäft machen,** to make a profit out of sth., s.o.; to turn sth. to one's profit; to make a good thing out of sth., s.o.; (*o*) with respect to; with regard to; in the way of; in; **an Gewicht zunehmen, abnehmen,** to increase, decrease, in weight; **j-m an Begabung gleich sein,** to be s.o.'s equal in talent, to be just as gifted as s.o.; **an Größe gleich,** of equal size *or* greatness; **ist das alles, was Sie an Gepäck haben?** is that all you have in the way of luggage? **drei, acht, an der Zahl,** three, eight, in number; *Com:* (*on bill*) **'an Waren 500 Mark',** 'to goods (supplied) 500 marks'; (*p*) **krank an der Leber,** suffering from a disease of the liver; **krank an Leib und Seele,** sick in soul and body; **müde an Körper und Geist,** weary in body and spirit; (*q*) **an (der) Grippe erkrankt,** ill with influenza; **an einer Krankheit, an Kopfweh, leiden,** to suffer from an illness, from headaches; (*r*) (*temporal use*) **an jenem Tage, Morgen, Nachmittag, Abend,** (on) that day, morning, afternoon, evening; **an einem schönen Frühlingstage,** on a fine spring day; **am Tage, an dem . . .,** on the day when, on which, . . . ; **an Sonn- und Feiertagen,** on Sundays and public holidays; **es ist an der Zeit, (daß . . .),** it is (high) time (that . . .); (*s*) **Turm an Turm ragte empor,** tower rose by tower; tower after tower arose; **Haus an Haus stürzte ein,** the houses collapsed one after another, one by one. *For other uses in verbal constructions see under the verbs* **arbeiten, befestigen, begehen, erkennen, festhalten, freuen, handeln, hindern, kennen, leiden**[1]**, messen, nagen, rächen, sterben, teilnehmen, vergreifen, verzweifeln, zweifeln,** *etc.* **2.** *with acc.* (*Note: in colloquial usage* **an das** *is frequently contracted to* **ans.**) (*a*) (*of letter, remark, etc.*) (directed) to (s.o.); intended for (s.o.); **ein Brief an einen gewissen Herrn,** a letter to a certain gentleman; **eine Mahnung an alle,** an admonition, a warning, to all; **des Königs Aufruf an sein Volk,** the king's appeal to his people; (*b*) (*in various verbal constructions, with underlying sense of motion towards sth.*) (i) to; **an die Arbeit gehen,** to go to work, to set to work; **an das Fenster treten,** to step over to the window; **an den Galgen kommen,** to come to the gallows; **an die richtige Adresse gelangen,** to reach, get to, the right address; **wir gehen nächsten Monat an die See,** we're going to the seaside next month; **einen Brief an j-n richten,** to direct, address, a letter to s.o.; **an j-n schreiben,** to write to s.o.; **j-m einen Ring an den Finger stecken,** to put a ring on s.o.'s finger; **etwas an j-n verkaufen,** to sell sth. to s.o., sell s.o. sth.; **Geld an j-n verlieren,** to lose money to s.o. (*at cards, etc.*); **an . . . heran,** *see* **heran; bis an,** *see* **bis**[1] 1; *Mil:* **an die Front gehen,** to go to the front; (ii) *Nau:* **an Bord gehen,** to go aboard, on board; **an Land gehen,** to go ashore; to leave the ship; (iii) on; on to; **etwas an etwas binden, heften, nageln,** *etc.*, to tie sth. on to sth.; to stick *or* pin sth. on to sth.; to nail sth on to sth., *etc.*; **etwas an einen Haken, an die Wand, hängen,** to hang sth. on a hook, on the wall; **an eine Tür klopfen, schlagen,** to knock, to beat, on a door; **an etwas (fest)frieren,** to freeze on to sth.; (iv) at; **j-m etwas an den Kopf werfen,** to throw sth. at s.o.'s head; **der Regen peitschte an die Fenster,** the rain was lashing at the windows; (v) (up) against (wall, etc.); **einen Stuhl, einen Jungen, usw., an die Wand stellen,** to put, stand, a chair, a boy, etc., (up) against the wall; **ein Brett an ein anderes lehnen,** to lean one board (up) against another; **der Wagen fuhr rückwärts an die Mauer (an),** the car ran back against, ran back(wards) into, the wall. *For other uses in verbal constructions see under the verbs* **bringen, denken, erinnern, glauben,** *etc.* (*Note: in some verbal constructions there may occur a fluctuation between* **an**+*acc. and* **an**+*dat.; the choice is usually conditioned by the general association of the dative with a state of repose and of the accusative with motion towards sth.*); (*c*) (*approximation*) **an (die) hundert Mann,** about, approximately, a hundred men; **das wird dich an (die) tausend Mark kosten,** it will cost you somewhere about, somewhere round, something like, round about, up to, a thousand marks; **das wird an die zehn Tage dauern,** it will take something like ten days, some ten days; **sie ist an die sechzig,** she is (round) about sixty.

II. **an,** *adv.* **1.** on; (*a*) **er stand da mit dem Mantel an,** he stood there with his coat on; **sie hatte fast nichts an,** she had hardly anything on; (*b*) **das Gas, das Licht, usw., ist an,** the gas, the light, etc., is (turned) on; **der Ofen ist an,** the fire is alight, in, *U.S:* on; the (electric) fire is on. **2.** (*place*) **von Köln an,** from Cologne on(wards); **von da an führt der Weg durch einen Wald,** from there on the path leads through a wood. **3.** (*temporal use*) on(wards), forth; **von jetzt an,** from now on(wards), henceforward, henceforth, from this time forth; hereafter; **von heute an,** (as) from today, from today onwards, from this day forth; **von jenem Tage an, von der Zeit an, von da an,** from that day on(wards), from that day forth, from then on(wards), thenceforward; **ab und an,** *see* **ab III.**

an-[1], *verbal pref.; usu. sep., but with a few verbs, e.g.* **anberaumen, anempfehlen, anerbieten, anerkennen,** *usage varies between sep. and insep. Denotes in verbs:* **1.** (*forward motion or approach*) (*Note: in older German the prefix* **an-** *is frequently used where* **heran-** *is now more usual; verbs of this type are now generally used as p.p. with* **kommen.**) **anbringen,** to fetch, bring; **sich annähern,** to approach, draw near; **angeflattert kommen,** to come fluttering along; **angeflogen kommen,** to come flying along, to fly up; **angelaufen kommen,** *A:* **anlaufen,** to come running along, up; to come up at a run; **angefahren kommen,** *A:* **anfahren,** to come driving along, up; to drive up; **angerast kommen,** to come tearing along, up; **angerasselt kommen,** to come rattling along; **angeschritten kommen,** to come striding along. **2.** (*addressing activity to s.o.; directing activity towards s.o., sth.*) **anbellen,** to bark at (s.o., sth.); **anbeten,** to adore, worship; **anbieten,** to offer; **anblicken,** to look at (s.o., sth.); **andonnern,** to thunder, roar, at (s.o.); **angreifen,** to attack; **anmelden,** to announce; *Nau: etc:* **anpeilen,** to take a bearing on (sth.); *W.Tel:* **ansagen,** to announce. **3.** (*fastening, fixing, attaching*) **anbinden,** to tie (sth.) up; **anbolzen,** to bolt (sth.) on; **anbringen,** to attach, affix (sth.); **anhaken,** to hook (sth.) on; **anhämmern,** to hammer (sth.) on; **anringen,** to fasten (sth.) with a ring *or* to a ring; **anschweißen,** to weld (sth.) on. **4.** (*applying of*

oil, paint, etc.; coating of sth.) **anfeuchten,** to moisten, damp; **anölen,** to oil, lubricate; **anschmieren,** to smear, daub; **anschwärzen,** to blacken; **anstreichen,** to coat (sth. with sth.); to paint; **anteeren,** to coat with tar, to tar. **5.** (*acquiring, assimilation, attraction*); **annehmen,** to receive; **anähneln, anarten,** to assimilate; **sich** *dat.* **etwas aneignen,** to acquire sth.; to adopt sth.; **sich** *dat.* **etwas anmaßen,** to arrogate sth, to oneself; **sich** *dat.* **etwas anschaffen,** to procure sth.; to provide oneself with sth; **sich** *dat.* **Mut antrinken,** to drink to give oneself courage; **anlocken,** to entice; **anziehen,** to attract. **6.** (*beginning of an activity; partial application of a process, with slight effect*) **anfangen,** to begin, start; **anbacken,** to bake lightly, partly; **anbläuen,** to tinge with blue; **anbraten,** to roast lightly; to seal (steak, etc.); **anbrennen,** (*of thg*) to catch fire; **anfahren,** (*of vehicle*) to start; **anfaulen,** to begin to rot; **anfressen,** to corrode, eat away (metal, etc.); **anfühlen,** to touch, finger; **anraspeln,** to give (sth.) a touch of the rasp; **ansengen,** to singe slightly; **anzünden,** to set fire to (sth.), to ignite. **7.** (*activity restricted to a spot or an area*) **anschwellen,** to swell; **anhäufen,** to heap up, pile up; **ansammeln, to accumulate. 8.** (*continuous activity*) **andauern, anhalten,** to last, endure, continue, persist. **9.** (*adverbial use*) **den Mantel, die Bluse, den Hut, usw., anhaben, anbehalten,** to have, keep, one's coat, one's blouse, one's hat, etc., on.

an-[2], An-, *pref.* (*a*) an-; **anhydrisch,** anhydrous; **Anazidität** *f*, anacidity; (*b*) in-; **anorganisch,** inorganic.

-an, *adv.suff.* **1.** (*a*) up; **bergan,** uphill; up the mountainside; (*b*) up towards; **himmelan,** towards the sky, skywards; towards heaven, heavenwards. **2.** (*proximity*) **nebenan,** at the side; close by; next door. **3.** (*temporal use*) **fortan,** henceforth, henceforward.

Ana [ˈaːnaː], *f.* -/-s. *Lit.Hist:* ana; **Anas sammeln,** to collect anas.

Ana-, ana- [anaˑ-], *pref.* ana-; *Rh:* **Anadiplosis** *f*, anadiplosis; *Opt:* **anakamptisch,** anacamptic; *Pharm:* **anakathartisch,** anacathartic.

-ana [-ˈaːnaː], *s.suff.n.pl. Lit.Hist:* -ana; **Goetheana,** Goetheana.

Anabaptismus [anaˑbapˈtismus], *m. Rel.Hist:* anabaptism.

Anabaptist [anaˑbapˈtist], *m. Rel.Hist:* anabaptist.

anabaptistisch [anaˑbapˈtistiʃ], *a.* anabaptistical.

Anabasis [aˈnaˑbaˑzis], *f.* -/. *Gr.Hist:* anabasis.

anabatisch [anaˑˈbaːtiʃ], *a. Med: A:* anabatic (fever).

Anabiose [anaˑbiˈoːzə], *f.* -/. *Biol:* anabiosis, reanimation.

anabiotisch [anaˑbiˈoːtiʃ], *a. Biol:* anabiotic.

Anachoret [anaxoˑˈreːt, -çoˑˈreːt], *m.* **-en/-en,** anchorite, recluse.

anachoretisch [anaxoˑˈreːtiʃ, -çoˑˈreːtiʃ], *a.* anchoretic (life, etc.); (life, etc.) of a recluse.

anachromatisch [anaˑkroˑˈmaːtiʃ], *a. Phot:* anachromatic, soft-focus (lens).

Anachronismus [anaˑkroˑˈnismus], *m.* **-/-men,** anachronism.

anachronistisch [anaˑkroˑˈnistiʃ], *a.* anachronistic.

anaerob [anaˑeˑˈroːp], *a. Bac:* anaerobic.

Anaerobe [anaˑeˑˈroːbə], *f.* **-/-n, Anaerobiont** [anaˑeˑroˑbiˈont], *m.* **-en/-en, Anaerobium** [anaˑeˑˈroːbium], *n.* **-s/-bien.** *Bac:* anaerobe.

Anagallis [anaˑˈgalis], *f.* -/-. *Bot:* anagallis, pimpernel.

Anaglyphe [anaˑˈglyːfə], *f.* **-/-n.** *Art: Opt: Phot:* anaglyph.

Anaglyptik [anaˑˈglyptik], *f.* -/. *Art:* anaglyptics; carving in low relief.

Anagoge [anaˑˈgoːgə], *f.* **-/-n.** *Theol:* anagoge, anagogy; mystical interpretation.

Anagogie [anaˑgoˑˈgiː], *f.* -/. *Theol:* anagogy; spiritual evaluation.

anagogisch [anaˑˈgoːgiʃ], *a. Theol:* anagogic(al).

Anagramm [anaˑˈgram], *n.* -(e)s/-e, anagram.

anagrammatisch [anaˑgraˑˈmaːtiʃ], *a.* anagrammatic(al); *adv.* anagrammatically.

Anagrammatist [anaˑgramaˑˈtist], *m.* **-en/-en,** anagrammatist.

anähneln, anähnlichen, *v.tr. sep.* (*a*) **etwas etwas anderem a.,** to make sth. similar to, like, sth. else; to assimilate sth. to sth. else; (*b*) *Ling:* **einen Konsonanten einem anderen a.,** to accommodate, partially assimilate, one consonant to another.

Anähnlichung, *f.* assimilation; *Ling:* accommodation, partial assimilation (of consonants).

Anakarde [anaˑˈkardə], **Anakardie** [anaˑˈkardiə], *f.* **-/-n.** *Bot:* anacardium, cashew(-tree).

anaklastisch [anaˑˈklastiʃ], *a. Opt:* anaclastic (curve, etc.).

Anakoluth [anaˑkoˑˈluːt], *m.* **-(e)s/-e.** *Gram:* anacoluthon.

Anakonda [anaˑˈkondaː], *f.* **-/-s.** *Rept:* anaconda.

Anakreon [aˈnaˑkreˑon]. *Pr.n.m.* **-s.** Anacreon.

Anakreontiker [anaˑkreˑˈontikər], *m.* **-s/-.** *Lit.Hist:* anacreontic poet, Anacreontic.

anakreontisch [anaˑkreˑˈontiʃ], *a.* anacreontic.

Anakrusis [anaˑˈkruːzis], *f.* **-/-sen.** *Pros: Mus:* anacrusis.

anal [aˑˈnaːl], *a.* **Anal-,** *comb.fm. Anat:* anal.

Analanhang, *m. Ent:* anal appendage.

Analdrüse, *f. Ent:* anal gland.

Analekten [anaˑˈlɛktən], *pl. Lit:* analecta, analects; gleanings.

Analemma [anaˑˈlɛmaː], *n.* **-s/-s.** *Geom: Astr:* analemma; planisphere.

Analeptikum [anaˑˈlɛptiˑkum], *n.* **-s/-ka.** *Med:* analeptic; building-up food.

analeptisch [anaˑˈlɛptiʃ], *a. Med:* analeptic, building-up (diet, etc.); **analeptisches Mittel**= **Analeptikon.**

Analgegend, *f. Anat:* anal region.

Analgesie [anʔalgeˑˈziː], *f.* -/. *Med:* analgesia.

Analgetikum [anʔalˈgeːtiˑkum], *n.* **-s/-ka.** *Med:* analgesic, analgetic.

analgetisch [anʔalˈgeːtiʃ], *a.* analgesic, analgetic.

Analgie [anʔalˈgiː], *f.* -/. *Med:*=**Analgesie.**

anallagmatisch [anʔalakˈmaːtiʃ], *a. Mth:* anallagmatic (curve, etc.).

anallaktisch [anʔaˈlaktiʃ], *a.* invariable.

analog [anaˑˈloːk], *a.* **1.** analogous (*dat.*, to, with); similar (*dat.*, to); **zeigen, daß zwei Fälle a. sind,** to show that two cases are analogous, are on all fours. **2.**=**analogisch.**

Analogie [anaˑloˑˈgiː], *f.* **-/-n** [-ˈgiːən], analogy (**zu,** to, with; **zweier Dinge zueinander,** between two thgs); counterpart (**zu,** of); **nach A. schließen,** to argue from analogy; **Entscheidung nach A. eines anderen Falles,** decision analogous to, on all fours with, that of another case; **etwas in A. zu . . . behandeln,** to treat sth. analogously to . . . ; **nach A. von . . . , als A. nach . . . ,** on the analogy of . . . , by analogy with . . . ; **das findet seine A. in . . . ,** that has its counterpart in . . .

Analogiebildung, *f.* (*a*) analogy-formation; (*b*) analogical form, analogy-form.

Analogieform, *f. Ling:*=**Analogiebildung** (*b*).

Analogiegerät, *n. Electronics:* analogue, *U.S:* analog, computer.

Analogieschluß, *m.* argument by, from, analogy.

Analogiezauber, *m.* homoeopathic magic, imitative magic.

analogisch [anaˑˈloːgiʃ], (*a*) *a.* analogical; (*b*) *adv.* analogically; **etwas a. darstellen, erklären,** to analogize sth.; **a. nach . . . ,** on the analogy of . . . , by analogy with . . .

analogisieren [anaˑloˑgiˑˈziːrən], *v.tr.* to analogize.

Analogismus [anaˑloˑˈgismus], *m.* **-/-men**= **Analogieschluß.**

Analogon [aˈnaːloˑgon], *n.* **-s/-ga,** analogue, parallel, counterpart.

Analphabet [ˈanʔalfaˑˌbeːt], *m.* **-en/-en,** illiterate person, illiterate.

analphabetisch [ˈanʔalfaˑˌbeːtiʃ], *a.* illiterate, analphabetic.

Analphabetismus [anʔalfaˑbeˑˈtismus], *m.* -/. illiteracy.

Analysator [anaˑlyˑˈzaːtor], *m.* **-s/-oren** [-zaˑˈtoːrən]. *Ph:* analyser (of polariscope).

Analyse [anaˑˈlyːzə], *f.* **-/-n,** analysis; (*a*) *Ch: Ph: etc:* **eine A. vornehmen,** to make an analysis; *Ch:* **quantitative A.,** quantitative analysis; *see also* **qualitativ; A. auf feuchtem Wege,** wet analysis; **A. auf trockenem Wege,** dry analysis; (*b*) *Log: Gram:* **A. eines Satzes,** (i) parsing, (ii) analysis, of a sentence.

Analysen-, *comb.fm. Ch:* analytical (apparatus, report, weight, etc.).

analysenfertig, *a. Ch:* ready for analysis.

analysenrein, *a. Ch:* analytically pure.

Analysenwaage, *f.* chemical, analytical, balance.

analysierbar [anaˑlyˑˈziːrbaˑr], *a.* analysable.

analysieren [anaˑlyˑˈziːrən], *v.tr.* to analyse (facts, substance, etc.); **einen Satz a.,** (i) to parse, (ii) to analyse, a sentence.

Analysierende, *m., f.* (*decl. as adj.*) analyser.

Analysis [aˈnaːlyˑzis], *f.* -/. *Mth:* analysis; **höhere A.,** infinitesimal calculus; **A. situs** [ˈsiːtus], analysis situs; topology.

Analytik [anaˑˈlyːtik], *f.* -/. analytics; *Phil:* **die Aristotelische, die Kantische, A.,** Aristotle's, Kant's, Analytics.

Analytiker [anaˑˈlyːtikər], *m.* **-s/-.** *Ch: etc:* analyst.

analytisch [anaˑˈlyːtiʃ], *a.* analytic(al); **analytische Chemie,** analytical chemistry; **analytische Geometrie,** analytical geometry; **analytische Sprachen,** analytic languages; *adv.* analytically.

Anämie [anɛˑˈmiː], *f.* -/. anaemia; **perniziöse A.,** pernicious anaemia.

anämisch [aˈnɛːmiʃ], *a.* anaemic.

Anamnese [anamˈneːzə], *f.* **-/-n.** *Med: Ecc:* anamnesis.

Anamorphose [anaˑmorˈfoːzə], *f.* **-/-n.** *Bot: Opt:* anamorphosis.

Anamorphot [anaˑmorˈfoːt], *m.* **-(e)s/-e.** *Cin: Phot:* anamorphic lens, anamorphic.

anamorphotisch [anaˑmorˈfoːtiʃ], *a. Cin: Phot:* anamorphic (lens).

Ananas [ˈaˑnaˑnas], *f.* **-/-.** *Bot:* pineapple, ananas (*plant or fruit*).

Ananasbatist, *m. Com:* pineapple cloth.

Ananasbeet, *n.* pinery.

Ananaserdbeere, *f. Bot: Hort:* pine-strawberry.

Ananasfaser, *m. Bot: Com:* pineapple fibre.

Ananasfeld, *n.* pinery.

Ananasgewächs, *n. Bot:* bromeliad.

Ananaskirsche, *f. Bot:* Cape gooseberry.

Ananastreibhaus, *n.* pinery.

Ananasvogel, *m. Orn: F:* colibri; humming-bird.

anandrisch [anʔˈandriʃ], *a. Bot:* anandrous.

Ananias [aˑnaˑˈniːas]. *Pr.n.m.* **-'.** *B.Hist:* Ananias.

Ananke [aˈnaŋkeː]. *Pr.n.f.* **-s.** *Gr.Myth:* Ananke; (blind) Fate.

anankern, *v.sep.* **1.** *v.i.* (*haben*) *Nau:* to anchor; to moor. **2.** *v.tr. Constr: etc:*=**ankern I. 1** (*b*).

Anapäst [anaˑˈpɛːst], *m.* **-(e)s/-e.** *Pros:* anapaest.

anapästisch [anaˑˈpɛːstiʃ], *a. Pros:* anapaestic.

Anaphase [anaˑˈfaːzə], *f. Biol:* anaphase, diaster stage.

Anapher [aˈnaˑfɛr], *f.* **-/-n. 1.** *Rh:* anaphora. **2.** *Astr:* rising of the celestial bodies.

Anaphora [aˈnaˑfoˑraː], *f.* **-/-rä**=**Anapher.**

anaphorisch [anaˑˈfoːriʃ], *a. Gram:* anaphoric (pronoun, etc.).

Anaphrodisiakum [anʔafroˑdiˑˈziːaˑkum], *n. Pharm:* anaphrodisiac.

Anaphrodisie [anʔafroˑdiˑˈziː], *f.* -/. *Med:* anaphrodisia.

anaphrodisisch [an'afroˑˈdiːziʃ], *a.* anaphrodisiac.

Anaphylaxie [anaˑfyˑlakˈsiː], *f.* -/. *Med:* anaphylaxis.

anarbeiten, *v.sep.* **1.** *v.i.* (*haben*) **gegen etwas a.,** to bear against, bear on, sth. **2.** *v.tr.* **etwas an etwas** *acc.* **a.,** to work sth. on to sth.

Anarchie [anarˈçiː], *f.* **-/-n** [-ˈçiːən], anarchy; lawless condition.

anarchisch [aˈnarçiʃ], *a.* anarchic(al); *adv.* anarchically.

Anarchismus [anarˈçismus], *m.* -/. anarchism.

Anarchist [anarˈçist], *m.* **-en/-en,** anarchist.

anarchistisch [anarˈçistiʃ], *a.* anarchistic; anarchist (writer, etc.).

anärgern, *v.tr. sep.* **sich** *dat.* **einen Nervenanfall, usw., a.,** to fret oneself into a fit of nerves, etc.

anarten, *v.sep.* **1.** *v.tr.* to assimilate. **2.** *v.i.* (*sein*) & **sich anarten,** to assimilate, be assimilated (*dat.*, to). **3. angeartet,** (*of quality, etc.*) innate, inborn.

Anasarka [anaˑˈzarkaː], *f.* -/. *Med: Vet:* anasarca.

Anastaltikon [anaˑˈstaltiˑkon], *n.* **-s/-ka.** *Med:* styptic, astringent.

anastaltisch [anaˑˈstaltiʃ], *a. Med:* styptic, astringent.

anastatisch [anaˑˈstaːtiʃ], *a. Engr: Print:* anastatic (printing, etc.).

Anästhesie [anɛs-, anʔɛsteˑˈziː], *f.* -/. anaesthesia; *Surg:* **allgemeine, lokale, A.,** general, local, anaesthesia.

anästhesieren [anɛs-, anʔɛsteˑˈziːrən], *v.tr. Med:* to anaesthetize; **Anästhesierung** *f*, anaesthetization.

Anästhesist [anɛs-, anʔɛsteˑˈzist], *m.* **-en/-en,** anaesthetist.

Anästhetikum [anɛs-, anʔɛsˈteːtiˑkum], *n.* **-s/-ka,** anaesthetic.

anästhetisch [anɛs-, anʔɛsˈteːtiʃ], *a.* anaesthetic; **anästhetisches Mittel,** anaesthetic.

Anastigmat [anʔaˑ-, anaˑstigˈmaːt], *n.* **-s/-e.** *Opt: Phot:* anastigmat.

anastigmatisch [anʔaˑstigˈmaːtiʃ], *a. Opt: Phot:* anastigmatic.

anastomisieren [anastoˑmiˑˈziːrən], *v.i.* (*sein*) *Anat:* to anastomose, inosculate.

Anastomose [anaˑstoˑˈmoːzə], *f.* -/. *Anat:* anastomosis, inosculosis, inosculation.

Anastrophe [aˈnastroˑfeː], *f.* **-/-n** [-ˈstroːfən]. *Rh:* anastrophe.

Anateden [anaˑˈteːdən], *pl. Orn:* anatidae.

Anathem [anaˑˈteːm], *n.* **-s/-e,** anathema, ban,

curse; **das A. über j-n aussprechen,** to pronounce an anathema against s.o., to anathematize s.o.

Anathema [a'na·te·maː], *n.* -s/-ta [ana·'teːma·taː] & /-s. **1.** anathema; person *or* thing accursed. **2.** = **Anathem.**

anathematisieren [ana·te·ma·ti·'ziːrən], *v.tr.* to anathematize, curse; **Anathematisierung** *f,* anathematization.

anational ['a·natsio·naːl], *a.* non-nationalistic.

anatmen, *v.tr. sep.* to breathe (up)on (sth., s.o.).

Anatolien [ana·'toːliən]. *Pr.n.n.* **-s.** *Geog:* Anatolia.

anatolisch [ana·'toːliʃ], *a. Geog:* Anatolian.

Anatom [ana·'toːm], *m.* **-en/-en,** anatomist.

Anatomie [ana·to·'miː], *f.* -/-n [-'miːən]. **1.** (science of) anatomy; **vergleichende A.,** comparative anatomy. **2.** dissecting-room; anatomical theatre, anatomy theatre.

anatomieren [ana·to·'miːrən], *v.tr.* to anatomize, dissect.

Anatomiker [ana·'toːmikər], *m.* **-s/-,** anatomist, *esp.* university teacher *or* student of anatomy.

anatomisch [ana·'toːmiʃ], *a.* anatomical; **anatomisches Theater,** anatomical theatre, anatomy theatre; **in anatomischer Hinsicht,** anatomically; **vom anatomischen Standpunkte aus gesprochen . . .,** from the anatomist's point of view . . .

Anatomist [ana·to·'mist], *m.* **-en/-en = Anatom.**

Anatozismus [anato·'tsismus], *m.* -/. *Fin:* anatocism; (taking of) compound interest.

anatrop [ana'troːp], *a. Bot:* anatropous (ovule).

Anatto [a'natoː], *m.* **-s/.** **1.** *Dy:* anatto, roucou. **2.** *Bot:* anatto(-tree), roucou(-tree).

Anattostrauch, *m. Bot:* = **Annato** 2.

anätzen, *v.tr. sep.* **1.** (*a*) to (begin to) etch (copper plate, etc.); (*b*) (*of acid, etc.*) to bite into (metal, etc.); (*c*) *Med:* to cauterize (wound, etc.). **2.** to etch on (design, calibration, etc.).

anäugeln, *v.tr. sep.* **1.** to ogle (s.o.); to make (sheep's) eyes at (s.o.). **2.** *Hort:* to bud, graft a bud on to (tree).

anbacken[1], *v.sep.* (*conj. like* **backen**) **1.** *v.tr.* (*strong*) to bake (sth.) lightly, partly. **2.** (*a*) *v.tr.* (*strong*) **etwas an etwas** *acc.* **a.,** to bake sth. on to sth.; (*b*) *v.i.* (*sein, haben*) **an etwas** *acc.* **a.,** to bake on to sth.; (*of earth, etc.*) to stick (on) to sth.; to cake on sth.

anbacken[2], *v.tr. sep.* (*weak*) **das Gewehr a.,** to level one's rifle, one's gun; to take aim.

anbahnen. I. *v.tr. sep.* to pave, smooth, the way for (relations, undertaking, etc.); to prepare, clear, the ground for (negotiations, undertaking, etc.); **ein Gespräch a.,** to make an opening for a conversation; **neue Handelsbeziehungen a.,** to open up new trade channels, new markets; **eine Ehe a.,** to facilitate the arranging of a marriage; **Beziehungen bahnen sich an,** relations are already being established; relations are opening up.

II. *vbl s.* **Anbahnen** *n.,* **Anbahnung** *f. in vbl senses; also:* **Anbahnung einer Ehe,** facilitation of, smoothing the way to, a marriage; introducing of prospective marriage partners to one another (by a marriage bureau).

anballen (sich), *v.refl. sep.* to conglobate, conglobe; to form into a ball *or* mass.

Anbändelei, *f.* **-/-en,** attempt to strike up an acquaintance.

anbändeln, *Dial:* **anbandeln,** *v.i. sep.* (*haben*) **1. mit j-m a.,** to make advances to s.o., to make up to s.o.; to scrape acquaintance with s.o.; to pick up with s.o., to pick s.o. up (as a casual acquaintance); *F:* to get off with s.o. **2. mit j-m a.,** *A: v.tr.* **mit j-m einen Streit a.,** to pick a quarrel with s.o.

anbanden, *v.tr. sep. Bill:* to cushion (ball).

Anbau, *m.* **-(e)s/.** **1.** (*a*) cultivation, tillage, tilling (of the soil); (*b*) cultivation, cultivating, culture, growing (of plants); (*c*) *A:* cultivation (of an art, a literary genre, etc.). **2.** (*a*) enlarging, enlargement, extending, extension (of building); (*b*) (*pl.* **Anbauten**) (i) addition (to building); annex(e), outbuilding, outlying building; new wing (of building); extension (of factory, library, etc.), (ii) lean-to (building); penthouse; (iii) new area (of town). **3.** *A:* (*a*) colonization, settling; (*b*) (*pl.* **Anbauten**) colony, settlement.

anbauen. I. *v.tr. sep.* **1.** (*a*) to bring (land) into cultivation; to cultivate, farm, till (the soil, etc.); (*b*) to cultivate, grow (plants); **Getreide a.,** to cultivate, raise, grow, rear, cereals; (*c*) *A:* to cultivate (an art, a literary genre, etc.); **bei den Deutschen ist diese Dichtungsart nur selten angebaut worden,** this genre has been little cultivated in Germany. **2.** to build on (**an** + *acc.,* to); to add (to existing building); **einen neuen Flügel an ein Hotel a.,** to build a new wing on to a hotel; **drei neue Zimmer an sein Haus a.,** to add three new rooms to one's house; **angebaut,** built-on (room, etc.); **angebauter Schuppen,** lean-to shed. **3.** *A:* **eine Gegend a.,** to colonize, settle, a region. **4. sich in einem Ort anbauen,** to settle (down) in a locality.

II. *vbl s.* **Anbauen** *n.* = **Anbau** 1, 2 (*a*), 3 (*a*).

Anbauer, *m.* **-s/-.** **1.** cultivator, grower; farmer. **2.** colonist, settler; pioneer; planter; (*in U.S. and Australia*) squatter.

Anbaufläche, *f. Agr:* area under cultivation; arable land.

Anbaugebiet, *n.* (*a*) = **Anbaufläche;** (*b*) area intended for cultivation.

Anbaumöbel, *n. pl.* unit furniture.

Anbauschrank, *m.* cupboard unit.

Anbaustoffwechsel, *m. Biol:* anabolism.

anbefehlen, *v.tr. sep.* (*strong*) (*a*) **j-m etwas a.,** to recommend sth. to s.o.; to enjoin (prudence, secrecy, etc.) on s.o.; **seine Seele Gott, einem Heiligen, a.,** to commend one's soul to God, to a saint; (*b*) **j-m a., etwas zu tun,** to charge, instruct, enjoin, order, command, s.o. to do sth.; to bid s.o. do sth.

Anbeginn, *m.* beginning, first beginnings, commencement; **von A.,** from the very beginning, from the outset.

anbeginnen, *v.tr. sep.* (*strong*) *occ.* = **anfangen** 1.

anbehalten, *v.tr. sep.* (*strong*) to keep (garment) on.

anbei [an'bai], *adv. Com:* herewith, enclosed; (*of memorandum, etc.*) (hereto) annexed; **a. (sende ich den) Scheck über 50 Mark,** herewith cheque, enclosed please find cheque, for 50 marks.

Anbeiß, *m.* **-es/-e.** *Ich:* perch.

anbeißen. I. *v.sep.* (*strong*) **1.** *v.tr.* (*a*) to bite into (sth.); to take the first bite of (cake, etc.); (*b*) **vom Frost angebissen,** frost-bitten. **2.** *v.i.* (*haben*) (*a*) (*of fish, animal*) to take the bait; (*of fish*) to nibble at, rise to, swallow, the bait; **die Fische bissen gerne an,** the fish were biting, rising, well; (*b*) (*of pers.*) to respond to s.o.'s advances; to be caught, to take the bait; *F:* to bite; to swallow the bait; to rise to the fly; **er, sie, will nicht a.,** *F:* he, she, won't bite, won't play, isn't having any.

II. *vbl s.* **Anbeißen** *n.* (*a*) *in vbl senses, esp. F:* **sie ist zum A. schön,** she is most appetizing to look at, *F:* she looks nice enough to eat; (*b*) *Jew:* first meal after the fast.

anbelangen, *v.impers. sep.* to concern, affect; (*usu. only in the phr.*) **was ihn, Sie, mich, anbelangt . . .,** as far as he is, you are, I am, concerned; as for him, you, me . . .; **was mich anbelangt, so werde ich nichts dergleichen tun,** as far as I am concerned, for my part, as for me, (speaking) for myself, I shall do nothing of the sort.

anbelfern, *v.tr. sep.* (*of pers.*) to snarl, *F:* bark, at (s.o.).

anbellen, *v.sep.* **1.** *v.tr.* (*a*) (*of dog*) to bark at (s.o., sth.); **den Mond a.,** to bark at, bay (at), the moon; (*b*) (*of pers.*) = **anbelfern.** **2.** *v.i.* (*in p.p. only*) **der Hund kam angebellt,** the dog came up barking.

anbequemen, *v.tr. sep.* to accommodate, adapt (+*dat.,* to); **sich den Verhältnissen a.,** to accommodate, adapt, oneself to circumstances; to make the best of the circumstances.

anberaumen, *v.tr. sep., occ. insep.* **einen Termin a.,** to appoint, fix, settle, a date; **eine Sitzung a.,** to call, fix, a meeting (**auf einen gewissen Tag,** for a certain day).

anberegt, *a. A:* aforementioned, aforenamed, aforesaid.

anbeten. I. *v.tr. sep.* (*a*) to worship (idol, a god, etc.); **Gott a.,** to worship, adore, God; *A. & Lit: abs.* **a.,** to worship; (*b*) *F:* to worship (s.o., money, etc.); to adore, idolize (s.o.).

II. *vbl s.* **1. Anbeten,** *n. in vbl senses.* **2. Anbetung,** *f.* = II. 1; (*a*) *also:* adoration, worship (of a god); (*b*) adoration, profound admiration (of s.o.).

anbetenswert, *a.* adorable.

Anbeter, *m.* **1.** adorer, worshipper, votary (of a god). **2.** adorer, ardent admirer (of s.o.).

Anbetracht, *m.* (*only in prep. phr.*) **in Anbetracht** + *gen.,* in consideration of, on account of, in view of; **in Anbetracht der Umstände,** considering, in view of, the circumstances; **in Anbetracht (dessen), daß . . .,** in view of, in consideration of, the fact that . . .

Anbetreff, *m.* (*only in prep. phr.*) **in Anbetreff** (+ *gen.*), with regard to, regarding; with respect to, respecting.

anbetreffen, *v.impers. sep.* (*strong*) (*a*) = **anbelangen;** (*b*) to concern, affect (sth.); to relate to (sth.).

anbetreffs, *prep.* (*with gen.*) = **in Anbetreff.**

Anbettelei, *f.* soliciting (of alms); begging.

anbetteln, *v.tr. sep.* to beg from (s.o.), to solicit alms of (s.o.); to importune (s.o.).

anbetungswert, anbetungswürdig, *a.* adorable; *Rel:* worthy of adoration.

anbiedern. I. *v. sep.* **1.** *occ. v.tr.* to address, approach, (s.o.) in a free and easy, familiar, manner. **2. sich anbiedern,** to behave in a free and easy manner; **er biedert sich überall an,** he is at his ease, makes himself at home, everywhere; **sich bei, mit, j-m a.,** (i) to become familiar, get on good terms, with s.o.; *F:* to chum up, pal up, with s.o., (ii) to hobnob with s.o., (iii) to ingratiate oneself with s.o.; to insinuate oneself into s.o.'s favour; to curry favour with s.o., *P:* to suck up to s.o.

II. *vbl s.* **Anbiedern** *n.,* **Anbiederung** *f.* (*a*) *in vbl senses;* (*b*) = **Anbiederungsversuch.**

Anbiederungsversuch, *m.* attempt at familiarity; attempt to ingratiate oneself.

anbiegen, *v.tr. sep.* (*strong*) **1. etwas an etwas** *acc.* **a.,** to bend, fold, sth. on to, towards, sth. **2.** *Adm: Com: A:* to enclose, annex, attach (document, etc.); **angebogen,** enclosed, annexed, attached.

anbieten. I. *v. sep.* (*strong*) **1.** *v.tr.* (*a*) to offer, to proffer; to tender (one's services, sum of money, etc.); **j-m etwas a.,** to offer s.o. sth., offer sth. to s.o., to make an offer of sth. to s.o.; **es wurde ihm eine Stelle angeboten,** he was offered a post; **sie bot mir eine Ohrfeige an,** she threatened to box my ears; **einer Dame die Hand a.,** to propose (marriage), make an offer (of marriage), to a lady; **Waren (zum Verkauf) a.,** to offer goods (for sale), **angebotene Waren,** goods offered (for sale), goods on offer; (*b*) **sich a.,** to offer oneself (**als,** as); **sich zum Dienste a.,** to offer one's services; **sich a., etwas zu tun,** to offer to do sth. **2.** *v.i.* (*haben*) (*a*) (*at auction-sale*) to open, start, the bidding, to make the first bid; (*b*) *Fb: etc:* to open up (for the attack); (*c*) *F:* to seek a quarrel; to act provocatively.

II. *vbl s.* **Anbieten** *n.,* **Anbietung** *f. in vbl senses; also:* offer; tender (of services, sum of money, etc.); proposal.

Anbieter, *m.* person making an offer; (*at sale*) first bidder.

Anbild, *n. A:* (*a*) = **Abbild;** (*b*) = **Vorbild.**

anbilden, *v.tr. sep.* **1.** to adapt (+*dat.,* to); to mould (+*dat.,* on to). **2. j-m etwas a.,** to instil sth. into s.o.

Anbindekalb, *n. Husb:* weanling calf.

anbinden, *v.sep.* (*strong*) I. *v.tr.* **1.** (*a*) to bind, fasten, tie (up) (**an** + *acc. or dat.,* to); to tie up (horse, dog, etc.); to tether (horse, sheep, etc.); to chain up (dog); *Hort:* to tie up, fasten up (trailing plants, wall-trees, etc.); *Nau:* (i) to bend (sail), (ii) to make fast, tie up, moor (boat, ship); **die Grammatik ist von jeher allzusehr an die Logik angebunden,** grammar has always been too much tied up with, too closely linked with, logic; *F:* **ich bin heute sehr angebunden,** my time is fully taken up, *F:* I am completely tied up, today; *F:* **j-n kurz a.,** to take care not to allow s.o. too much rope; to keep a tight hold on s.o.; (*b*) **gegen j-n kurz angebunden sein,** to be abrupt, brusque, curt, short, sharp, with s.o.; to be off-hand(ed) with s.o.; **er ist immer sehr kurz angebunden,** he is always very abrupt, brusque, snappish, snappy; **j-m kurz angebunden antworten,** to answer s.o. abruptly, brusquely, curtly, shortly, sharply; (*c*) *Carp:* to join, frame (up) (parts of a structure, etc.); (*d*) **der zweite Band ist angebunden,** the second volume is bound up (together) with the first. **2.** *Husb:* (*a*) to rear, *U.S:* raise (animal); (*b*) to wean (calf, etc.). **3.** *A:* (*a*) to make a present to (s.o.); (*b*) to make (s.o.) give presents (*esp. on a ceremonial occasion*); **ein Angebundener,** someone who has received a present, *esp.* a birthday present. **4.** *F:* = **aufbinden.**

II. **anbinden,** *v.i.* (*haben*) *F:* **mit j-m a.,** (i) to pick a quarrel with s.o., (ii) to make advances, approaches, to s.o.; to make up to s.o.

Anbindezeit, *f.* setting time (of cement).

Anbindezettel, *m.* tie-on label.

Anbindling, *m.* **-s/-e.** *Husb:* weanling.

Anbiß, *m.* **1.** first bite; place where a bite has been taken (out of sth.). **2.** bait.

anblaffen, *v.tr. sep.* **1.** (*of dog*) to bark at (s.o.). **2.** *F:* (*of pers.*) to snap at (s.o.); to go for (s.o.).

anblaken, *v.tr. sep.* to blacken (sth.) (with smoke, soot).

anblasen, *v.tr. sep.* (*strong*) **1.** (*a*) (*of wind*) to blow (up)on (s.o., sth.); (*of pers.*) to blow on (surface, mirror, etc.); (*b*) *F:* (*of pers.*) to storm at (s.o.); *F:* to blow (s.o.) up, to go for (s.o.);

to tell, tick (s.o.) off (properly). **2.** (*a*) to blow (up) (the fire); to fan (fire, passion, discontent, etc.); to stir up (hatred, discord, etc.); (*b*) *Metall:* to blow in (blast-furnace); (*c*) *v.i.* (*haben*) *Navy:* to blow the tanks (of a submarine). **3.** *Mus:* to intone (wind instrument, note). **4.** (*a*) **die Jagd a.,** to blow the horn for the hunt to begin; (*b*) *A:* **j-n a.,** to greet s.o. with a flourish of trumpets. **5.** (*a*) *A:* **j-m eine Krankheit a.,** to pass an infection on to s.o. unconsciously; (*b*) (*of sickness, pain, etc.*) **wie angeblasen kommen,** to happen, come on, suddenly (and unaccountably). **6.** *Ind: etc:* to seal on, fix on, by blast.

Anblaseventil, *n. Navy:* blow-valve (of submarine).

anblatten. I. *v.tr. sep. Carp: etc:* to scarf, to halve and lap.

II. *vbl s.* **1. Anblatten,** *n.* scarfing, halving (and lapping). **2. Anblattung,** *f.* (*a*)=II, 1; (*b*) scarf-joint, halved joint, half-lap.

anbläuen, *v.tr. sep.* **1.** to tinge (sth.) with blue. **2.** *Laund: Ind:* to blue.

anblecken, *v.tr. sep.* (*of animal, pers.*) to show its, one's, teeth to (s.o.), to bare its, one's, teeth at (s.o.).

anbleiben, *v.i. sep.* (*strong*) (*haben*) to stay on, remain on.

Anblick, *m.* **1.** (*a*) *A. & occ.* look, glance, gaze; **ein freundlicher A. erfreut das Herz,** a kindly look gladdens the heart; (*b*) sight, view (of s.o., sth.); **beim ersten A.,** at first sight, at first view, off-hand, *F:* at the first blush; **sein bloßer A. macht mich zittern,** the very sight of him makes me tremble; **beim A.**+*gen.*, at the sight of . . . ; **beim A. dieses Bildes blieb er stehen,** he stopped at the sight of this picture; **bei seinem, ihrem, A.,** at the sight of him, her; **er war in den A. der Statue versunken,** he was lost, absorbed, in contemplation of the statue. **2.** sight; spectacle; appearance; aspect; **trauriger A.,** sad sight; sorry spectacle; **freudiger A.,** joyful, *Lit:* joyous, sight, spectacle; **es war ein herrlicher A.,** it was a noble sight, a magnificent spectacle; **einen kläglichen A. darbieten,** to present a lamentable appearance.

anblicken, *v.tr. sep.* to look at (s.o., sth.); to gaze at (s.o., sth.), to gaze on, upon (sth.); to contemplate (s.o., sth.); **j-n, etwas, flüchtig a.,** to glance at s.o., sth.; **j-n starr a.,** to stare at s.o.; **j-n prüfend a.,** to give s.o. a questioning look; to look inquiringly at s.o.; **j-n schief, von der Seite, a.,** to look askance at s.o.; **j-n zornig a.,** to glare at s.o.; **j-n finster a.,** to frown at s.o.; to give s.o. a threatening look, *F:* a dirty look; **j-n mißtrauisch a.,** to eye s.o. suspiciously; *Poet:* **von tausend Blumen angeblickt,** gazed upon by a thousand flowers.

anblinken, *v.tr. sep.* (*of light, star, etc.*) to wink, twinkle, at (s.o., sth.); **das Leuchtfeuer blinkte ihn an,** the beacon was winking at him.

anblinze(l)n, *v.tr. sep.* to wink at (s.o.), give (s.o.) a wink; (*of eyes*) to twinkle at (s.o.).

anblitzen, *v.tr. sep.* (*a*) to give (s.o.) a furious look; to cast a withering glance at (s.o.); (*b*) to attack (s.o.) furiously, *F:* to go for (s.o.) bald-headed.

anblöken, *v.tr. sep.* **1.** (*of sheep*) to bleat at (s.o.); (*of cattle*) to low at (s.o.); *F:* (*of cow*) to moo at s.o. **2.** *F:* (*of pers.*) to blow (s.o.) up; to go for (s.o.).

anbluten, *v.i. sep.* (*haben*) (*of dye*) to bleed, run.

anbohren. I. *v.tr. sep.* **1.** (*a*) to pierce; to bore, make, a hole in (sth.); to bore into (sth.); **ein Faß a.,** to broach, tap, a cask; to set a cask abroach; (*b*) *Metalw:* to drill, bore; (*c*) **einen Baum a.,** to tap a tree (for resin); (*d*) *F:* **j-n a.,** (*also v.i.* **bei j-m a.**) (i) to borrow (money) from s.o., *F:* to tap, touch, s.o.; (ii) to sound s.o. (about sth.); to pump s.o. (for information). **2.** *Nau:* to scuttle (ship).

II. *vbl s.* **Anbohren** *n.*, **Anbohrung** *f. in vbl senses.*

anbolzen, *v.tr. sep. Mec.E:* to bolt (sth.) on (**an**+*acc.*, to).

anborden, *v.tr. sep. Nau:* to board (ship); *A:* to grapple with (ship in a fight).

anborgen, *v.tr. sep.* to borrow money from (s.o.).

Anbot, *n.* **-(e)s/-e. 1.**=**Angebot** (*a*). **2.** *South G.Dial:* share in a mine.

anbrachen, *v.tr. sep. Leath:* to repair (damaged furs, etc.).

anbrassen, *v.tr. sep. Nau:* to brace (up) (the yards).

anbraten, *v. sep.* (*strong*) *Cu:* **1.** *v.tr.* to roast (meat, etc.) lightly; to start (meat, etc.) roasting; to seal (steak, etc.) (by exposure to a fierce fire). **2.** *v.i.* (*sein*) to stick to the pan.

anbräunen, *v.tr. sep.* (*a*) *Cu: etc:* to brown; (*b*) to brown, *F:* bronze (skin) (in the sun); **angebräunt werden,** to get browned, *F:* bronzed.

anbrausen, *v.i. sep.* (*sein*) to dash up, roar up; **angebraust kommen,** (*of vehicle*) to dash up; (*of train, etc.*) to come roaring along.

Anbrechbohrer, *m. Min:* borer, drill, chisel.

anbrechen, *v. sep.* (*strong*) I. *v.tr.* **1.** (*a*) to break into (provisions, stocks, etc.); to cut into, make the first cut in (loaf, etc.); to start (loaf, bottle, pot of jam, box of cigars, packet of notepaper, etc.); to open (bottle, box of cigars, etc.); **noch nicht angebrochen,** uncut (loaf, etc.); unopened, untouched (bottle of wine, box of cigars, etc.); (*b*) *Civ.E: etc:* **den Boden a.,** to break ground; *Min:* **ein Erzlager a.,** to open up a lode; (*c*) to break a piece off the edge of (sth.); to notch (sth.), make a notch in (sth.); to gap (metal plate, etc.); to chip (cup, plate, etc.); **angebrochene Mauer,** tumble-down wall; (*d*) to crack (cup, plate, stick, bone, etc.). **2.** to break into (one's day, evening); **angebrochener Abend,** evening already broken into, already partially taken up (with engagements, commitments).

II. **anbrechen,** *v.i.* (*sein*) **1.** (*a*) (*of day*) to dawn, break; **der Tag bricht an,** day is dawning, breaking; dawn is breaking; **der Tag wollte gerade a.,** day was about to break, was just breaking; **bei, mit, anbrechendem Tage,** at break of day, at daybreak, at dawn; *Lit:* **der Frühling bricht an,** spring is coming in; **eine neue Zeit bricht an,** a new era is dawning; (*b*) (*of night*) to fall, close in; to come on; **die Nacht bricht an,** night is falling, closing in; **bei, mit, anbrechender Nacht,** at nightfall, when night closes in. **2.** *Dial:* (*of wine, fish, meat, etc.*) to go bad, to go off; (*of fruit, fish, etc.*) to spoil.

III. *vbl s.* **Anbrechen,** *n. in vbl senses; also:* **bei A. des Tages,** at break of day, at daybreak, at dawn.

anbrennen, *v.sep.* (*conj. like* **brennen**). **1.** *v.tr.* (*a*) to set fire to (sth.), to set (sth.) on fire, afire; to set (sth.) alight; to ignite (sth.); to light (fire, candle, cigar, etc.); to kindle (fire, wood, etc.); (*b*) to scorch; (*c*) *Ch: Ind:* to calcine; (*d*) **einen Pfahl a.,** to harden a stake in the fire. **2.** *v.i.* (*sein*) (*a*) to catch, take, fire; to catch alight; to ignite; to (begin to) burn; **die Kohlen wollen nicht a.,** the coal will not burn, catch; *F:* **nichts a. lassen,** to be on the alert, on the look-out, on the qui-vive; (*b*) *A:* (*of pers.*) **angebrannt sein,** to be inflamed with passion; (*c*) (*of fabric, etc.*) to scorch; (*d*) *Ch: Ind:* to calcine; (*e*) *Cu:* to stick to the pan; to burn; **leicht a.,** to catch; **die Milch ist angebrannt,** the milk has caught, has burnt; **das Gemüse ist angebrannt,** the vegetables have stuck to the pan; **das Fleisch ist angebrannt,** the meat is burnt.

Anbrennholz, *n.* firewood, kindling.

anbringen. I. *v.tr. sep.* (*conj. like* **bringen**) **1.** to bring, fetch; *Ven:* (*of dog*) to retrieve (game). **2.** (*a*) to install; to place (sth.) in position, get (sth.) into position; to fix (sth.) (in position); to mount (apparatus, machine, etc.); to put in, to place (nails, rivets, etc.); to lay (carpet, rails, pipes, etc.); to rig (sth.) up; **etwas (an etwas** *dat.*, **auf etwas** *dat.*) **a.,** to affix sth. (to sth.); to apply sth. (to sth.); to attach (label, fitment, etc.) (to sth.); to put up (sign, name-plate, notice, etc.); to post (up) (notice, bill); **einen Haken an der Wand a.,** to fix a hook on the wall; **einen Stiel an einem Besen a.,** to fit, fix, a handle to a broom; (*b*) **ich kann den Schuh, den Handschuh, nicht a.** I cannot get the shoe, the glove, on. **3.** (*a*) **eine Bitte, ein Gesuch, a.,** to make, prefer, put forward, a request; **eine Bemerkung a.,** to put in one's word; to put a word in; to have one's say; **ein Wort für j-n a .,** to put in a word for s.o.; **eine Beschwerde a.,** to lodge, make, a complaint; *Jur:* **eine Klage gegen j-n a.,** to lodge a complaint against s.o.; to lay an information against s.o.; *F: A:* **j-n a.,** to denounce, expose, s.o.; to inform against s.o.; *F:* to give s.o. away; *Sch: F:* to sneak on s.o.; (*b*) *Fenc. & F:* **einen Stoß a.,** to make, score, *F:* register, a hit; (*c*) *F:* to display (one's knowledge, etc.); to get in (joke, bon mot, etc.) (aptly, neatly); **das kannst du bei mir nicht a.,** you can't put that across me, put that over on me; it's no use your trying that on with me. **4.** (*a*) *Com:* **Waren a.,** to sell, dispose of, get rid of, goods; **leicht anzubringende Waren,** goods easily disposed of, that have a ready sale; saleable goods; **schwer anzubringender Artikel,** article difficult to get rid of; slow-moving article; (*b*) **Geld a.,** (i) to place, invest, money; (ii) *F:* to spend, get rid of, money. **5.** (*a*) **j-n a.,** to find a place, employment, a berth, for s.o.; *F:* to get s.o. into a job; (*b*) **seine Tochter a.,** to marry off, settle, one's daughter; to find a husband for one's daughter; to get one's daughter off (one's hands); **sie hat ihre Tochter noch nicht angebracht,** she has not got her daughter married off yet.

II. *vbl s.* **1. Anbringen,** *n. in vbl senses; esp.* (*a*) installation, erection; (*b*) *Com:* disposal (of goods). **2. Anbringung,** *f.* (*a*)=II. 1; (*b*) *F: A:* denunciation (of s.o.); informing (against s.o.).

III. *p.p. & pred.a* **angebracht. 1.** *in vbl senses.* **2.** appropriate, proper, suitable, fitting, befitting; well-timed, seasonable, timely; (*of remark, expression*) apt; (*of action, remark, etc.*) opportune; **die Maßnahmen, die bei dieser Lage a. sind,** the measures appropriate to, called for by, the situation; **seine Bemerkung war gut, wohl, sehr, a.,** his remark was very apt, was very opportune, was well-timed; **der Rat war wohl a.,** the advice was timely; **seine Vorschläge waren sehr a.,** his suggestions were very much to the purpose; **wäre hier ein Trinkgeld a.?** would it be proper, fitting, desirable, in order, to offer a tip? is a tip called for, do you think? **es würde a. sein, zu . . . ,** it would be appropriate, fitting, proper, desirable, to . . . ; it would be advisable, be well, to . . . ; **seine Bemerkung war falsch, schlecht, a.,** his remark was ill-timed, misplaced, out of place, uncalled for; **der Verweis war übel a.,** the rebuke was uncalled for, undeserved; **ihr Vertrauen war falsch, übel, a.,** her confidence was misplaced; **der Rat war bei ihm nicht a.,** the advice was lost on him; **solche Empfehlungen sind bei ihm schlecht a., nicht a.,** such recommendations are out of place, won't do, won't work, with him.

Anbringer, *m. A:*=**Angeber** 2.

Anbringerei, *f.* **-/-en.** *A:*=**Angeberei 2.**

Anbruch, *m.* **1.** (*a*) starting (of sth.); breaking into (sth.); *Min:* opening up (of mine lode); (*b*) commodity, batch, that has been started *or* broken into; *Min:* lode just opened up; first ore (from new lode); *Com:* job lot, *U.S:* broken lot; **das Faß liegt im A.,** the cask has already been broached. **2.** crack (in stick, bone, plate, cup, etc.); chip (in plate, cup, etc.). **3.** break (of day); dawn(ing) (of day, of a new era); closing in (of night); **bei, mit, A. des Tages,** at dawn, break of day, daybreak; **bei, mit, A. der Nacht,** at nightfall; when night (i) closes in, (ii) closed in. **4.** decay; putrescence; *For:* (i) decayed, rotten, wood, (ii) decayed spot (in tree). **5.** *Vet:* anaemia (in sheep).

anbrüchig, *a.* decaying; putrescent; rotting, rotten (wood, fruit, etc.); carious (tooth, bone); unsound (wood, fruit, etc.).

anbrühen, *v.tr. sep.* (*a*)=**abbrühen** (*b*); (*b*)= **aufbrühen.**

anbrüllen, *v.tr. sep.* to bellow, roar, bawl, at (s.o.).

anbrummen, *v.tr. sep.* to growl, grumble, *F:* grouse, at (s.o.); to speak gruffly, surlily, to (s.o.).

anbrüten, *v.tr. sep.* (*of hen*) to begin to hatch (egg); **angebrütetes Ei,** egg that has been sat on; addle(d) egg.

Anchovibirne [an'ʃoːviˑbirnə], *f. Bot:* anchovy-pear.

Anchovis [an'ʃoːvis], *f.* **-/-.** *Ich: Cu:* anchovy.

Anciennität [ãˑsieniˑ'tɛːt], *f.* **-/-en.** (*a*) *Sch:* seniority; (*b*) *Adm: Mil: A:* seniority (in rank, office); *cp.* **Dienstalter.**

Andacht, *f.* **-/-en. 1.** devotion; devout meditation; **mit A. beten,** to pray devoutly, with devotion; **in A. versunken,** wrapped in devout meditation. **2.** devotions, prayers; (short) religious service; **seine A. halten, verrichten,** to be at one's devotions; to say one's prayers; **es wird jeden Morgen eine A. gehalten,** a short service is held every morning.

Andächtelei, *f.* **-/-n,** pretended devotion, pretence of devotion; sanctimoniousness.

andächteln, *v.i. insep.* (*haben*) to make a pretence of devotion.

andächtig, *a.* devout, pious; reverent (person, state of mind); meditative; profoundly attentive; rapt (person, state of mind); *Ecc:* (*address to congregation*) **meine andächtigen Zuhörer!**= dear(ly beloved) brethren; *adv.* **a. beten,** to pray devoutly, with devotion; **j-m a. zuhören,** to listen to s.o. reverently, with rapt attention.

Andächtler, *m.* **-s/-,** hypocrite; sanctimonious person.

Andachtsbild, *n.* devotional picture; (*in Eastern countries*) icon.

Andachtsbuch, *n.* devotional book.

andacht(s)los, *a.* undevout, indevout; irreverent; *adv.* -ly.

Andacht(s)losigkeit, *f.* indevotion; irreverence.

Andachtsübung, *f.* devotional, religious, exercise; **Andachtsübungen** *pl*, devotions.

andacht(s)voll, *a.* devout, pious; reverent (person, state of mind).

Andalusien [anda·ˈluːzɪən]. *Pr.n.n.* **-s.** *Geog:* Andalusia.

Andalusier, *m.* **-s/-.** *Geog:* Andalusian.

andalusisch [anda·ˈluːziʃ], *a.* Andalusian.

Andamanen, die [andaˈmaːnən]. *Pr.n.pl. Geog:* the Andaman Islands.

Andamaner, *pl. Ethn:* Andamanese.

andämmen, *v.tr. sep. Hyd.E: etc:* to dam up.

andampfen, *v.sep.* **1.** *v.tr.* (*a*) to send vapours toward (s.o., sth.); to steam on (s.o., sth.); to blow vapour, smoke, at (s.o., sth.); (*b*) *Ch: etc:* to deposit (substance) by evaporation. **2.** *v.i.* (*sein*) (*a*) to steam up; **angedampft kommen,** (*of train, ship*) to come steaming along; *F:* (*of pers.*) to come rushing along; to rush up; (*b*) *Ch: etc:* (*of substance*) to be deposited by evaporation.

andante [anˈdanteː]. *Mus:* **1.** *adv.* andante. **2.** *s.* **Andante,** *n.* **-s/-s,** andante (movement).

Andantesatz, *m. Mus:* andante (movement).

andantino [andanˈtiːnoː]. *Mus:* **1.** *adv.* andantino. **2.** *s.* **Andantino,** *n.* **-s/-s,** andantino (movement).

Andauche, *f.* **-/-n.** *Swiss Dial:* = **Abzucht.**

Andauer, *f.* = **andauern II.**

andauern. I. *v.i. sep.* (*haben*) to last, endure, continue, go on; (*of fever, effect, etc.*) to persist; **das hat jahrelang angedauert,** this has gone on for years; **der Regen hat drei Tage angedauert,** the rain did not stop, it kept on raining, for three days; **wenn die Kälte andauert,** if it stays cold.

II. *vbl s.* **Andauern,** *n. in vbl senses; also:* endurance; continuance; persistence (of fever, effect, etc.).

III. *pr.p. & a.* **andauernd,** *in vbl senses; esp.* continuous; uninterrupted, unintermitting; constant, continual; sustained, steady; persistent; **andauernder Regen,** constant, continual, rain; steady downpour; *Com:* **andauernde Nachfrage nach . . . ,** steady, persistent, demand for . . . ; *adv.* constantly, continually; uninterruptedly, without interruption, without intermission.

Andel, *f.* **-/-n, Andelgras,** *n. Bot:* **1.** sea-plantain. **2.** (*on North Sea and Baltic coast*) atropis thalassica.

Anden, die. *Pr.n.pl. Geog:* the Andes; **Anden-,** *comb.fm.* Andean (region, flora, etc.).

Andenbär, *m.* = **Brillenbär.**

andenken. I. *v.i. sep.* (*usu. only in the phr.*) **denk (mal) an!** just think! just fancy!

II. *vbl s.* **Andenken,** *n.* **1.** **-s/.** remembrance, memory (**an**+*acc.*, of); **zum A. an . . . ,** in memory, remembrance, of . . . ; as a souvenir of (visit, etc.); **der König seligen Andenkens,** the late king, of blessed memory; **sein A. ist uns teuer,** his memory is dear to us; **j-m ein liebendes A. bewahren,** to cherish s.o.'s memory, keep s.o.'s memory green; **er behält Sie in freundlichem A.,** he has a very pleasant memory of you; **bei j-m in gutem A. stehen,** to be remembered kindly by s.o. **2.** **-s/-,** (*a*) token of remembrance; keepsake; souvenir (of visit, journey, etc.); (*b*) memento, memorial; **das wird ein A. an Sie sein,** that will be something to remember you by.

Andenmöwe, *f. Orn:* Andean gull.

Andentanne, *f. Bot:* araucaria, Chile pine, *F:* monkey-puzzle.

Andenwellenläufer, *m. Orn:* Hornby's storm-petrel.

änderbar, *a.* changeable, variable; alterable.

anderenfalls, *adv.* = **andernfalls.**

anderenteils, *adv.* = **andrerseits.**

andere(r), andere, andere(s), *a. & pron.* (*colloquially* **andre(r), andre, andre(s); andern, anderm.**) **1.** (*a*) other (of two); **der andere,** the other (one); **die andere Hälfte,** the other half; **das andere Ufer,** the other bank; the farther shore; **am anderen Ende,** at the other end; **die andere Seite,** the other side (of road, etc.); the wrong side, the reverse (of cloth); **die andere Welt,** the other world; the beyond; (*b*) (immediately) following; next; second; **am anderen Tag, Morgen,** (on) the next, the following day, morning; on the day, morning, after; **zum anderen,** secondly, in the second place; **ein Jahr über, um, das andere; einen Tag über, um, den anderen, einen über, um, den anderen Tag,** every second, every other, year, day; in alternate years; on alternate days; *Lit:* **ein Jahr geht um das andere hin, ein Tag geht um den anderen hin,** year after year, day after day, goes by; *B:* **da ward aus Abend und Morgen der andere Tag,** and the evening and the morning were the second day; (*c*) other, further (persons, items, etc., not already specified); **andere gute Leute,** other good people; **unter anderen,** among(st) others; **unter anderem,** among other things; **und anderes mehr,** and so on, and so forth; **die anderen Bilder,** the other pictures; the rest of the pictures; **die anderen Anwesenden,** the other persons present; **ich und ein anderer,** myself and another (person), and one other; **irgendeine andere Frau,** some other woman; **die beiden anderen, die anderen beiden,** the two others, the other two; **die vier anderen,** the other four; **andere haben es gesehen,** other people have seen it; **noch viele andere,** many more besides; **die Fehler anderer Leute, anderer Leute Fehler,** the failings of others; **Kohl und anderes Gemüse,** cabbage and other vegetables; **er war ein Tourist wie jeder andere,** he was just an ordinary tourist; **es gibt noch andere wie er,** there are others like him; (*d*) **der eine . . . , der andere,** one . . . , the other; **der eine sagt dies, der andere sagt das,** one says this and the other says that; **ich kenne weder den einen noch den anderen,** I don't know either of them; **ist sie glücklich oder unglücklich?—weder das eine noch das andere,** is she happy or unhappy?—neither (the one nor the other); (*e*) **ich habe es im Verlauf der Woche von dem einen und (dem) anderen gehört,** I have heard it from one and another during the week; **der eine oder andere von uns wird es besorgen,** one or other of us will see to it; (*f*) **ihr seid einer wie der andere,** you are all alike; (*g*) **sie kamen einer nach dem anderen herein,** they came in one after another, one by one; **einer um den anderen,** alternately, in turn, by turns; **er las eine Seite nach der anderen,** he read page after page; **eine Dummheit nach der anderen, über, um, die andere, begehen,** to commit blunder after blunder, one blunder after, upon, another; **eins kommt zum anderen,** one thing comes on top of another; **ein Wort gab das andere,** one word led to another; (*h*) **eins in das andere, zum anderen, gerechnet kommen wir knapp aus,** taking one thing with another, we just manage. **2.** (*a*) other, different; **nehmen Sie diese Tasse weg und bringen Sie mir eine andere,** take this cup away and bring me another (one); **ein anderes Kleid anziehen,** to put on another, a different, dress; to change one's dress; **sie ist jetzt eine ganz andere Frau,** she is now quite a different, new, woman; she has changed completely; **das ist eine ganz andere Sache, das ist ganz etwas anderes,** that is quite another matter, quite a different matter; **das ist etwas anderes,** that's different; **ich bin ganz anderer Meinung, Ansicht, als Sie,** I am of an altogether different opinion from you; **ich wurde bald anderer Ansicht,** I soon changed my opinion; **ich hatte ganz andere Gründe, zu glauben, daß . . . ,** I had quite other reasons for believing that . . . ; *see also* **belehren I, besinnen I.** 1; *Prov:* **andere Zeiten, andere Sitten,** other days other ways; manners change with the times; **andere Länder, andere Sitten,** other people have other ways of doing things; when in Rome do as Rome does, as the Romans do; (*b*) (*of woman*) **in anderen Umständen sein,** to be pregnant, *F:* to be in the family way, to be expecting; (*c*) (someone, something) else; **irgendein anderer,** anyone else; **ein anderer,** someone else; **fragen Sie einen anderen!** ask someone else, somebody else; **das glaube ein anderer!** *F:* tell that to the marines! *see also* **weismachen; kein anderer wußte davon als er,** no one else but he, none but he, knew of it; **anderes, etwas anderes,** something else; anything else; **Fisch mag ich nicht, kann ich etwas anderes bekommen?—wir haben leider nichts anderes, anderes haben wir leider nicht,** I don't like fish, can I have anything else, something else?—sorry, we have nothing else, we haven't anything else; **nichts anderes als . . . ,** nothing else but . . . ; **er konnte nichts anderes tun als gehorchen,** he could not but obey, could not do otherwise than obey; **alles andere,** everything else; **Bemerkungen, die alles andere als schmeichelhaft sind,** remarks that are anything but complimentary, that are the reverse of complimentary; *cp.* **jemand 1.**

andererseits, *adv.* = **andrerseits.**

Andergeschwisterkind, *n. A:* second cousin.

Anderheit, *f.* difference; different nature (of sth.).

Anderkonto, *n. Fin:* bank account in the name of a trustee, trustee account.

anderlei, *inv.a.* of another, a different, kind.

andermal, *adv.* **ein a.,** another time; (at) some other time.

andermalig, *a.* **1.** (interview, opportunity, etc.) at some other time. **2.** *A:* second (attempt, etc.).

ändern. I. *v.* **1.** *v.tr.* (*a*) to alter (sth.) (**zu,** into); **er änderte die 6 zu einer 8,** he altered the 6 into an 8; **das ändert den Sinn,** that alters the sense; *Dressm:* **ein Kleid ä.,** to alter a dress; **etwas an einem Kleid ä.,** to make an alteration to a dress; (*b*) to change, alter, modify; **seine Meinung ä.,** to change one's mind, alter one's opinion; **seine Pläne ä.,** to alter, change, modify, one's plans; **seinen Standpunkt ä.,** to change, shift, one's ground; **seinen Ton ä.,** to change, alter, one's tone, *F:* to change one's tune; *Nau: Av:* **den Kurs ä.,** to alter course; (*c*) to alter (circumstances, etc.); **die Lage ä.,** to alter the situation; **das wird nichts an der Lage ä.,** it won't alter matters in any way; **das ändert die Sache,** that alters matters, alters the case; **das ist nicht zu ä., das läßt sich nicht ä., daran läßt sich nichts ä.,** it cannot be altered (now); it can't be helped, there is no help for it; there's nothing to be done (about it); **ich kann es nicht ä.,** I can't help it, can't do anything about it; **etwas zum Vorteil, zum Nachteil, ä.,** to change, alter, sth. for the better, for the worse; *Prov:* **geschehene Dinge sind nicht (mehr) zu ä.; was man nicht kann ä. muß man lassen schlendern,** what is done cannot be undone; what can't be cured must be endured; it's no use crying over spilt milk. **2.** *v.i.* (*haben*) **& sich ändern,** to change, alter; (*of wind, opinions, prices, etc.*) to vary; (*of wind*) to shift; (*of weather*) to change; (*of prices, markets*) to fluctuate; (*of pers.*) **sich zu seinem Vorteil ä.,** to change for the better; **er hat sich sehr geändert,** he has greatly altered, he is greatly changed; **die Zeiten haben sich geändert,** times have changed; **die Sache kann sich ä.,** things may change, alter; **das Wetter wird sich ä.,** there is going to be a change in the weather.

II. *vbl s.* **1.** **Ändern,** *n. in vbl senses.* **2.** **Änderung,** *f.* (*a*) = II. 1; *also:* alteration (of dress, text, plans, etc.); modification (of plans, etc.); variation (of prices, etc.); (*b*) change (of plan, circumstances, in prices, in the weather, etc.); alteration (in plans, to dress, etc.); modification (to plan, etc.); variation (in wind, prices, etc.); fluctuation (in prices, markets, etc.); shift (of the wind); **eine Ä. machen, vornehmen,** to make, effect, a change; (*on price list, timetable, etc.*) **'Änderungen vorbehalten',** '(all prices, times, etc., are) subject to alteration'.

andernfalls, *adv.* otherwise, (or) else.

ander(n)orts, *adv.* elsewhere, somewhere else.

anderntags, *adv.* (on) the next, the following, day; (on) the day after.

andernteils, *adv.* = **andrerseits.**

anders, *adv.* **1.** (*a*) (*used as adj.*) different (**als,** from; to); **das ist a.,** that's different; **das ist ganz a.,** that's quite different, quite a different matter; **in dem Kleid siehst du ganz a. aus,** that dress makes you look quite different; (*of pers., situation, weather, etc.*) **a. werden,** to change; **sie ist ganz a. geworden,** she has changed completely; (*b*) *F:* **mir wird a.,** I feel ill, unwell; **mir wird ganz a., wenn ich daran denke,** I feel quite ill when I think of it, it makes me feel quite ill to think of it. **2.** (*a*) differently, in a different way (**als,** from); otherwise (**als,** than); **er spricht a. als Sie,** he speaks differently from you; **ich denke a.,** I think otherwise; **ich denke a. als Sie,** I think differently from you; I am of a different opinion from you, from yours; **ich habe es ganz a. begonnen,** I set about it in quite a different way; **können wir das nicht a. machen?** can't we do it some other way? **ich sah es ganz a. als vorher,** I saw it quite differently from before; **wenn die Dinge a. liegen sollten,** should it be otherwise, should things turn out otherwise; **es ist ganz a. gekommen, als ich erwartet hatte,** it turned out quite different(ly) from what I expected; **das ist nun (ein)mal nicht a.,** well, that's how matters stand; that's how, that's the way, things are; well, there it is (and nothing can be done about it); *F:* **es ist gerade a. herum, rum,** it's just the other way about, the other way round; **ich kann nicht a.,** I cannot do otherwise; I have no choice; **ich kann nicht a., ich muß lachen,** I can't help laughing; **er kann nicht a., er muß gehen,** he can't avoid going; **er konnte nicht a., er mußte gehorchen,** he could not but obey, could not do otherwise than obey;

ich konnte nicht a. als+*inf.*, I could not do otherwise than, I could not do other than, I could do no other than ...; **ich habe es mir a. überlegt,** I changed my mind; *see alo* **besinnen** I. 1; (*b*) *Lit:* **wenn a. ...,** if indeed, if however ...; provided that ...; insofar as ... **3.** else; **jemand a.,** someone else, somebody else; **fragen Sie jemand a.!** ask someone else, somebody else; **niemand a.,** no one else, nobody else; **niemand a. wußte davon als er,** no one else but he, none but he, knew of it; **wer a.?** who else? **wo anders?** where else? **irgendwo a.,** somewhere else; **nirgendwo a.,** nowhere else; **es war kaum a. zu erwarten,** one would hardly have expected anything else.

andersartig, *a.* of another kind; different, of a different kind (**als,** from).

andersbürtig, *a.* born elsewhere, of alien birth, not a native.

andersdenkend, *a.* (person) of a different opinion; dissenting, dissident, dissentient (sect, party, etc.); **Andersdenkende** *m, f,* person of a different opinion; dissenter, nonconformist.

anderseitig, *a.* different; divergent; contrary (opinion, etc.).

anderseits, *adv.*=**andrerseits.**

andersfarbig, *a.* of another, a different, colour.

andersgeartet, *a.* of a different character.

andersgerichtet, *a.* differently orientated.

andersgesinnt, *a.* of a different opinion; **Andersgesinnte** *pl,* persons who think otherwise, who hold other opinions.

andersgestaltet, *a.* differently formed; *Bot: Ent: Ch:* heteromorphous, heteromorphic.

andersgläubig, *a.* of a different faith; heterodox, unorthodox; heretical; dissenting; **Andersgläubige** *m, f,* person of a different faith; dissenter, nonconformist; *R.C. Ch:* non-Catholic.

Andersgläubigkeit, *f.* heterodoxy.

andersmeinend, *a.*=**andersdenkend.**

Anderssein, *n.* state of being different; difference (in nature).

anderssprachig, *a.* speaking a different language.

anderswertig, *a. Ch:* (element) of another valency.

anderswie, *adv.* in some other way.

anderswo, *adv.* elsewhere, somewhere else.

anderswoher, *adv.* from elsewhere, from somewhere else.

anderswohin, *adv.* to some other, another, place; **a. gehen,** to go elsewhere, somewhere else.

anderthalb, *inv.a.* (*a*) one and a half; **a. Jahre, a. Stunden,** a year, an hour, and a half; **a. Kilo,** a kilogramme and a half, one and a half kilogrammes; (*b*) **anderthalb-,** *comb.fm. Ch: etc:* sesqui-; *Ch:* **anderthalbkohlensaures Ammonium,** sesquicarbonate of ammonia.

anderthalbbasisch, *a. Ch:* sesquibasic.

Anderthalbdecker, *m. Av:* sesquiplane.

anderthalbfach, *a. & adv.* one and a half times; *Ch:* sesqui-; **anderthalbfaches Salz,** sesquisalt; **anderthalbfaches Fluorür,** sesquifluoride; **anderthalbfaches Oxyd,** sesquioxide.

anderthalbig, *a. Mth:* sesquialter.

anderthalbmal, *adv.* **a. soviel,** one and a half times as much; *Mth:* sesquialter.

Anderthalbmaster, *m. Nau:* (sailing-)ship with normal foremast and one short mast aft.

anderthalbschläfrig, *a.* **anderthalbschläfriges Bett,** three foot six bed.

Änderung, *f. see* **ändern** II.

Änderungsantrag, *m. Pol: etc:* amendment.

änderungsfähig, *a.* changeable, alterable, modifiable.

Änderungsgeschwindigkeit, *f.* rate of change.

Änderungssucht, *f.* mania for changing things about.

Änderungsvorschlag, *m.*=**Änderungsantrag.**

anderwärtig, *a.* in, from, another place; further (information, instructions, etc.).

anderwärts, *adv.* elsewhere; in another, some other, place.

anderweit, *adv.* **1.**=**anderwärts. 2.** otherwise.

anderweitig. 1. *a.* further; other (dispositions, measures, etc.); (help, etc.) from another quarter. **2.** *adv.* elsewhere; otherwise; **man hat a. darüber verfügt,** it has been otherwise disposed of.

andeuten. I. *v.tr. sep.* (*a*) to indicate; to suggest; to allude to (sth.); **nur die Hauptpunkte a.,** to indicate only the main points; **die vergilbenden Blätter deuten den Herbst an,** the yellowing leaves show that autumn is on the way; **etwas flüchtig a., etwas andeutend erwähnen,** to make a passing allusion to sth., to allude to sth. in passing; (*b*) to imply; to hint at (sth.); to insinuate; **a., daß ...,** to imply that ...; to throw out, drop, let fall, a hint that ...; **wollen Sie etwa a., daß ...?** do you mean to insinuate that ...? are you trying to suggest that ...? **j-m etwas a.,** to intimate sth. to s.o.; **j-m a., daß ...,** to intimate, suggest, hint, to s.o. that ...; to give s.o. to understand that ...; (*c*) to give a (mere) hint of (sth.); *Lit:* **eine protestierende Gebärde a.,** to make a vague gesture of protest; **indem er es sagte, deutete er ein Lächeln an,** he said it with a hint, *F:* a ghost, of a smile; (*d*) *Art: Lit:* to outline, sketch (features, plot, etc.).

II. *vbl s.* **1. Andeuten,** *n. in vbl senses.* **2. Andeutung,** *f.* (*a*) indication, suggestion, hint (**von,** of); **ohne jede A. von Stolz,** without any suggestion, hint, trace, of pride; **A. eines Lächelns,** hint, *F:* ghost, of a smile; (*b*) allusion (**an, auf**+*acc.*, to); (*c*) intimation, suggestion (**daß ...,** that ...); hint (**über**+*acc.*, about; **daß ...,** that ...); **j-m eine A. machen,** to give, drop, s.o. a hint; **eine A. machen, daß ...,** to throw out, drop, let fall, a hint that ...; (*d*) implication; innuendo; **(beleidigende, geheimnisvolle) Andeutungen machen,** to throw out innuendos.

andeutungsweise, *adv.* (*a*) allusively; (*b*) by way of a suggestion; (*c*) by way of innuendo.

andichten, *v.tr. sep.* **1. j-m etwas a.,** to attribute sth. (falsely) to s.o.; to impute (fault, action, etc.) to s.o.; **man dichtet mir Meinungen an, die ich nie gehabt habe,** I am credited with opinions (that) I have never held. **2.** *Lit:* to address verses to (one's beloved, etc.).

andienen. I. *v.tr. sep.* **1.** *Nau: A:* **das Land, einen Hafen, a.,** to make land, a port, to put into a port. **2.** *Com:* **j-m etwas a.,** to offer s.o. sth.; to tender (payment, documents, goods *or* services in fulfilment of contract) to s.o.; to offer s.o. (immediate) delivery of (goods); to deliver up, hand over, (foreign exchange, government-controlled produce, etc.) (to the authorities, the official buyers, etc.); to notify s.o. of (intended shipment, means of shipment, etc.); **die Reederei kann uns ein anderes Schiff a.,** the owners can offer, tender, us shipment by another vessel.

II. *vbl s.* **Andienung** *f, in vbl senses; also:* offer; tender; delivery; notification.

andonnern, *v.tr. sep.* **1.** (*of pers.*) to thunder at (s.o.); to roar at (s.o.); to fulminate against (s.o.). **2. wie angedonnert dastehen,** to be thunderstruck.

Andorn, *m.* -(e)s/-e & -̈er. *Bot:* marrubium; (*a*) **(weißer) A.,** hoarhound, horehound; (*b*) **schwarzer A.,** ballota, black horehound.

Andrang, *m.* -(e)s/. **1.** (*a*) press, crowd, throng, multitude, concourse, mob (of people); dense mass (of traffic); (*b*) rush (**zu,** to a place, performance; **nach,** for sth.); run (**zu, nach,** on); **der A. zu der Abendvorstellung ist immer groß,** there is always a rush for the evening performance, people always crowd to the evening performance; *Fin:* **A. zu einer Bank,** run on a bank; *Com:* **A. nach den Frühlingsmoden,** rush for, run on, the spring fashions. **2.** *Med:* **A. des Blutes,** afflux, rush, of blood; congestion.

andrängen, *v.tr. sep.* **1. j-n an etwas** *acc.* **a.,** to push, thrust, s.o. against sth. **2. sich an j-n andrängen,** (*a*) to push up against s.o.; (*b*) to obtrude oneself on s.o.; to thrust, force, foist, oneself upon s.o.

andre *see* **andere(r).**

Andreas [an'dre:as]. *Pr.n.m.* -'. Andrew.

Andreaskraut, *n. Bot: F:* (Scotch) thistle.

Andreaskreuz, *n.* (i) St Andrew's cross; (ii) *Her:* saltire.

Andreasorden, *m. Hist:* Order of St Andrew; (*in Scotland*) Order of the Thistle.

andrehen, *v.tr. sep.* **1.** (*a*) to turn (crank); to turn on (a tap, gas, water, radio, electric light); to switch on (light, radio); *abs.* **a.,** *El:* to switch on (the current); *Aut: etc:* **den Motor a.,** to start (up) the engine; **einen Wagen mit der Kurbel a.,** to crank up a car; *Av:* **die Luftschraube a.,** to swing the propeller; *Tp:* **(die Wählscheibe) a.,** to dial; (*b*) *F:* **etwas a.,** to contrive to do sth.; **ich weiß gar nicht, wie ich es a. soll,** I just don't know how to set about it. **2.** *F:* **j-m etwas a.,** to fob off, palm off, sth. (up)on s.o.; to foist, *F:* unload, sth. on s.o.; to work sth. off on s.o.; to land s.o. with sth.

Andrehkurbel, *f. Aut: etc:* starting-handle, starting crank.

Andrehvorrichtung, *f. Aut: etc:* starting device; starting-gear.

andrer *see* **andere(r).**

andrerseits, *adv.* on the other hand; *cp.* **einerseits.**

andres *see* **andere(r).**

andringen, *v.i. sep.* (*strong*) (*sein*) to thrust forward; to rush forward; **auf, gegen, j-n a.,** to rush at, on, s.o., to make a rush at s.o.; **auf den Feind a.,** to rush at the enemy; *Med:* (*of blood*) to rush, flow (**gegen,** to).

Androgyn [andro·'gy:n], *m.* -s/-e. *Bot: Z:* androgyne, hermaphrodite.

Androgynie [andro·gy·'ni:], *f.* -/. *Bot: Z:* androgyny, hermaphroditism.

androgynisch [andro·'gy:niʃ], *a. Bot: Z:* androgynous, hermaphrodite.

androhen. I. *v.tr. sep.* **j-m etwas a.,** to threaten, *Lit:* to menace, s.o. with sth.

II. *vbl s.* **Androhen** *n.*, **Androhung** *f.* threat, *Lit:* menace; **bei, unter, Androhung einer Strafe, des Todes,** on pain, under penalty, of a punishment, of death.

Andromanie [andro·ma·'ni:], *f.* -/. *Med:* nymphomania.

Andromeda [an'dro:me·da:]. **1.** *Pr.n.f.* -s. *Myth: Astr:* Andromeda. **2.** *f.* -/. *Bot:* andromeda, (lesser) wild rosemary.

Andrözeum [andrø·'tse:um], *n.* -s/-zeen. *Bot:* androecium.

Andruck, *m.* -(e)s/-e. **1.** *Print:* pull, proof (*esp.* of picture, engraving). **2.** *Print:* beginning of the printing; going to press.

andrücken, *v.sep.* **1.** *v.tr.* (*a*) **etwas an etwas** *acc.* **a.,** to press, squeeze, sth. against sth.; (*b*) to press, squeeze (two things) together; (*c*) to apply pressure to (sth.); to damage (sth.) by pressure. **2.** *v.i.* (*haben*) *Av:* to put on speed.

Andrückfenster, *n. Cin:* pressure gate.

Andruckmaschine, Andruckpresse, *f. Print:* proof-press.

Andrückrolle, *f.* (*a*) *Typewr: Tg: etc:* feed-roll (of typewriter, recording instrument, etc.); (*b*) *Cin:* pressure roller; idler.

Andrückwalze, *f.*=**Andrückrolle** (*a*).

andudeln (sich), *v.refl. sep. F:* to get drunk, *F:* merry, tight, plastered.

anduften, *v.tr. sep.* (*of flower*) to spread its fragrance, waft its scent, towards s.o.

andunkeln, *v.i. sep.* (*haben*) to grow darker, deeper (in colour); to darken; (*of colour*) to deepen.

Äneas [ɛ·'ne:as]. *Pr.n.m.* -'. *Lt.Lit:* Aeneas.

Äneasratte, *f. Z:* mouse-opossum, murine opossum, marmose.

anecken, *v.sep. F:* **1.** *v.tr.* **j-n a.,** to push, *F:* shove, up against s.o.; to knock against s.o. **2.** *v.i.* (*sein*) (*a*) **irgendwo a.,** to knock up against something; (*b*) *F:* **bei j-m, überall, a.,** to rub s.o., everyone, up the wrong way.

Äneide, die [ɛ·ne·'i:də], -. *Lt.Lit:* the Aeneid.

aneifern. I. *v.tr. sep.* to stimulate (s.o.); to incite (s.o.); to spur (s.o.) on.

II. *vbl s.* **Aneifern** *n.*, **Aneiferung** *f. in vbl senses; also:* incitement, incitation.

aneignen. I. *v.tr. sep.* **sich** *dat.* **etwas a. 1.** (*a*) to acquire sth.; **sich eine Sprache, eine Kunst, a.,** to acquire, learn, a language, an art; **sich eine Gewohnheit a.,** to acquire, contract, a habit; (*b*) to adopt sth.; **sich einen Namen, j-s Meinung, a.,** to adopt a name, s.o.'s opinion; (*c*) to appropriate sth. (to oneself); to seize sth.; to lay hands on sth.; (*improperly, illegally*) to misappropriate sth.; to usurp sth.; **sich die Macht, einen Titel, den Thron, (widerrechtlich) a.,** to usurp power, a title, the throne; to seize power, the throne; **sich Geldsummen (widerrechtlich) a.,** to misappropriate money, *Jur:* to convert funds to one's own use; (*d*) *F:* to pinch, bag, lift, swipe, sth.; **irgend jemand hat sich meinen Tabak angeeignet,** someone's bagged, swiped, my tobacco. **2.** *Physiol: etc:* to assimilate (sth.).

II. *vbl s.* **Aneignen** *n.*, **Aneignung** *f. in vbl senses; also:* **1.** adoption (of opinion, name); appropriation; usurpation (of power, title, throne, etc.); seizure (of property, power, throne, etc.); **(widerrechtliche) Aneignung von Geldsummen,** misappropriation of money, *Jur:* conversion of funds to one's own use; improper conversion of funds. **2.** *Physiol: etc:* assimilation.

aneinander [an^ai'nandər], *pron. adv.* (*a*) by one another; to one another; adjacent to one another; (*esp. with verbs*) together; (*b*) **a. vorbei,** past one another; **a. vorbeigeben,** to pass one another; **a. vorbeireden,** (i) to talk at cross-purposes; (ii) to talk to each other without really communicating; to talk past one another.

aneinanderbinden, *v.tr. sep.* (*strong*) to tie, bind, fasten, (thgs) together.

aneinanderflechten, *v.tr. sep.* (*strong*) to twist, plait, (threads, etc.) together; to splice (cordage).

aneinanderfügen. I. *v.tr. sep.* to fit (thgs) together; to join (two words, etc.); to join up (parts, two thgs); to join (timbers, etc.) end to end; *Carp: etc:* to assemble (parts).

II. *vbl s.* **Aneinanderfügen** *n.*, **Aneinanderfügung** *f. in vbl senses; also: Carp: etc:* assembly.

aneinandergeraten, *v.i. sep. (strong) (sein)* (*a*) (*of thgs*) to meet; to touch; (*b*) (*of opposing forces*) to come to grips with one another; (*c*) to have a confrontation, to clash, with one another.

aneinandergrenzen. I. *v.i. sep.*(*sein*) (*of gardens, etc.*) to adjoin, touch; to be contiguous; to be adjacent (to one another); **die beiden Länder grenzen aneinander,** the two countries border on one another; **aneinandergrenzend,** adjoining, adjacent; contiguous.

II. *vbl s.* **Aneinandergrenzen,** *n.* contiguity; adjacency.

aneinanderhängen, *v.sep.* (*conj. like* **hängen**) **1.** *v.tr.* to string (objects, sentences, etc.) together; to connect up (parts, coaches, etc.). **2.** *v.i.* (*haben*) (*of objects, sentences, etc.*) to be strung together; (*of parts, etc.*) to be connected together.

aneinanderkleben. I. *v.sep.* **1.** *v.tr.* to stick (thgs) together; to agglutinate; to conglutinate. **2.** *v.i.* (*haben*) to stick together; to bind; to agglutinate; to conglutinate.

II. *vbl s.* **Aneinanderkleben,** *n. in vbl senses; also:* agglutination; conglutination.

aneinanderkommen, *v.i. sep. (strong) (sein)* (*of thgs*) to touch; to meet.

Aneinanderlagerung, *f.* juxtaposition; *Anat: Surg:* apposition.

aneinanderlegen, *v.tr. sep.* to place (thgs) in juxtaposition; to range (thgs) side by side; *Surg:* to bring (ends of broken bone, etc.) into apposition.

aneinanderliegen, *v.i. sep. (strong) (haben)* to lie together, contiguous with one another; to lie side by side; to be in juxtaposition; **aneinanderliegend,** juxtaposed.

aneinanderprallen. I. *v.i. sep. (sein)* to collide; to clash; to cannon against one another.

II. *vbl s.* **Aneinanderprallen,** *n. in vbl senses; also:* collision; shock; impact, clash (of two thgs, etc.).

aneinanderreiben. I. *v.sep. (strong)* **1.** *v.tr.* to rub (two thgs) together. **2.** *v.i.* (*haben*) to rub, chafe (against one another).

II. *vbl s.* **Aneinanderreiben,** *n. in vbl senses; also: Mec.E: etc:* friction.

aneinanderreihen, *v.tr. sep.* to line (thgs) up; to set (thgs) in a row; to range (thgs) side by side; to string (beads, pearls); to string (sentences, etc.) together; to connect up (parts, etc.).

aneinanderrücken, *v.sep.* **1.** *v.tr.* to move (chairs, etc.) closer together. **2.** *v.i.* (*sein*) to move (closer) together.

aneinanderschlagen. I. *v.sep. (strong)* **1.** *v.tr.* to strike, knock, (two thgs) together. **2.** *v.i.* (*sein*) to strike, knock, against one another; to collide.

II. *vbl s.* **Aneinanderschlagen,** *n. in vbl senses; also:* (*a*) concussion; (*b*) impact, collision.

aneinanderschließen, *v.tr. sep. (strong)* to connect, join.

aneinanderstoßen, *v.sep. (strong)* **1.** *v.tr.* to push, knock, (two thgs) together. **2.** *v.i.* (*sein*) (*a*) = **aneinanderprallen;** (*b*) = **aneinandergrenzen;** *Her:* **aneinanderstoßend,** conjoined.

aneinanderwachsen, *v.i. sep. (strong)* to grow together; (*of edges of wound*) to coalesce; (*of bones*) (i) to knit; (ii) to become anchylosed.

Äneis[1], **die** [ɛ·ˈneːis], **-.** *Lt.Lit:* the Aeneid.

Äneis[2] [ɛˈnais, ˈɛːnais], *m.* **-es/-e.** *Dial:* = **Anis.**

Anekdote [anɛkˈdoːtə], *f.* **-/-n,** anecdote.

anekdotenartig, *a.* anecdotal, anecdotic(al).

Anekdotenerzähler, *m.* anecdotist, teller of anecdotes.

anekdotenhaft, anekdotisch, *a.* = **anekdotenartig.**

anekeln, *v.tr. sep.* **1.** (*a*) to be repugnant, distasteful, to (s.o.); to disgust, sicken, nauseate (s.o.); **Ohrwürmer ekeln mich an,** I loathe, detest, earwigs; earwigs revolt me, turn my stomach; I find earwigs disgusting, revolting; **sie fühlte sich durch seine Schmeicheleien angeekelt,** she felt disgusted by his flattery, his flattery disgusted her, *F:* made her (feel) sick; (*b*) *impers.* **es ekelt mich an, das zu tun,** it is repugnant to me, it goes against me, I am reluctant, to do it; I shrink from doing it; I am lo(a)th to do it; I loathe doing it. **2.** *F:* to make oneself offensive to (s.o.); to pester (s.o.).

Anemie [aneˑˈmiː], *f.* **-/.** = **Anämie.**

Anemograph [aneˑmoˑˈgraːf], *m.* **-en/-en.** *Meteor:* anemograph.

anemographisch [aneˑmoˑˈgraːfiʃ], *a.* anemographic.

Anemometer [aneˑmoˑˈmeːtər], *n.* **-s/-.** *Meteor:* anemometer, windgauge.

Anemometrie [aneˑmoˑmeˑˈtriː], *f.* **-/.** *Meteor:* anemometry.

anemometrisch [aneˑmoˑˈmeːtriʃ], *a.* anemometric.

Anemone [aneˈmoːnə], *f.* **-/-n.** *Bot:* anemone, wind-flower.

Anemonin [aneˑmoˑˈniːn], *n.* **-s/., Anemonkampfer** [aneˑˈmoːn-], *m. Ch:* anemonin.

Anemonsäure, *f. Ch:* anemonic acid.

anemophil [aneˑmoˑˈfiːl], *a. Bot:* anemophilous.

anempfehlen. I. *v.tr. sep. & insep. (strong)* (*a*) **j-m etwas a.,** to recommend sth. to s.o.; (i) to commend sth. to s.o., to s.o.'s care; to recommend sth. to the care of s.o.; (ii) to recommend (goods, a remedy, etc.) to s.o. (iii) **j-m (die) Vorsicht a.,** to recommend prudence to, to enjoin prudence on, s.o.; (*b*) **j-m a., etwas zu tun,** to recommend, advise, charge, instruct, enjoin, s.o. to do sth.; **mir ist anempfohlen worden, zu Ihnen zu kommen,** I have been recommended (to come) to you; **meiner Mutter wurde anempfohlen, diese Pillen zu versuchen,** my mother was recommended to try these pills; **j-m dringend a., etwas zu tun,** to urge s.o. to do sth.; **ich empfehle Ihnen dringend an, ich anempfehle Ihnen dringend, zu . . . ,** I strongly advise you to . . . .

II. *vbl s.* **Anempfehlen** *n.*, **Anempfehlung** *f. in vbl senses; also:* recommendation; advice; injunction.

anempfinden (sich), *v.refl. sep. (strong) A:* **sich j-m a.,** to assimilate one's emotions, opinions, to s.o. else's; **anempfindende Persönlichkeit,** personality easily swayed by the emotions, opinions, of others; **anempfunden,** (*of emotions, opinions*) spurious, not genuine; **anempfundene Begeisterung,** factitious, simulated, enthusiasm.

-aner, *m.* **-s/-, -anerin,** *f.* **-/-anerinnen,** *s.suff.* **1.** -an; **Franziskaner,** Franciscan; **Puritaner,** Puritan. **2.** -an, -ian; native, inhabitant, of . . . ; **Amerikaner,** American; **Neapolitaner,** Neapolitan; **Hannoveraner,** Hanoverian; **Liliputaner,** Lilliputian; **Münsteraner,** native, inhabitant, of Munster. *See also* **Primaner, Sextaner.**

Anerbe, *m. Jur:* principal heir; heir to entailed property.

anerben, *v.tr. sep.* **j-m etwas a.,** to transmit sth. to s.o. by inheritance, as a heritage; **es ist ihm angeerbt,** it is his inheritance, his heritage; it is his by right of birth.

Anerbengericht, *n. Jur:* court for settlement of questions involving entailed property.

Anerbenrecht, *n. Jur:* law of entail.

anerbieten. I. *v.tr. sep., occ. insep. (strong)* = **anbieten;** *esp. Com: Jur:* to offer; to tender.

II. *vbl s.* **Anerbieten** *n.*, **Anerbietung** *f. in vbl senses; also:* offer; proposal, proposition; *Com: Jur:* tender.

anerkannt, *a. & adv. see* **anerkennen** I. 3.

anerkanntermaßen, *adv.* admittedly; confessedly; by common consent; **a. unrichtig,** admittedly incorrect; **a. schwierig,** confessedly difficult; **sie ist a. begabt,** everyone admits, agrees, that she has talent.

Anerkanntheit, *f.* recognized (high) quality; high repute; established reputation (of sth.).

anerkennbar, *a.* acknowledgeable; recognizable; admissible (proof, etc.).

anerkennen. I. *v.tr. sep. & insep.* (*conj. like* **kennen**) **1.** (*a*) to acknowledge, recognize (s.o., truth, right, claim, authority, etc.); to allow (claim); to own (s.o., s.o.'s authority); **ein Kind, einen armen Verwandten, a.,** to acknowledge, own, a child, a poor relation; **ein Kind nicht a.,** to disown, disavow, a child; **j-n als seinen Bruder a.,** to acknowledge, own, s.o. as one's brother; **j-n als König a.,** to recognize, acknowledge, own, s.o. as king; to acknowledge s.o. to be king; **sie wollten den König nicht a.,** they refused to own the king; **ein Werk als vortrefflich a.,** to recognize, acknowledge, a work to be excellent; **eine Lehre nicht a.** (**wollen**), to refuse to recognize a doctrine; to disavow a doctrine; **einen Anspruch nicht a.,** to disallow, refuse to admit, a claim; **einen Vertrag, eine Schuld, nicht a.,** to repudiate an agreement, a debt; **seine Unterschrift nicht a.,** to deny, disown, one's signature; **die Verantwortung (durchaus) nicht a.,** to deny, disclaim, (all) responsibility; *Com:* **einen Wechsel a., nicht a.,** to accept, honour, a bill; to refuse, dishonour, a bill; *Sp:* **ein Meeting a.,** to recognize a meeting; **einen Rekord a.,** to recognize, confirm, a record; (*b*) to appreciate (merit, virtue, good thing); to recognize (merit, etc.); to approve (of), give one's approval to (sth.); **man erkennt schon seine Verdienste an,** his merits are indeed recognized, appreciated. **2.** *pr.p. & a.* **anerkennend,** (*a*) (letter, etc.) of acknowledgement; (act, gesture, etc.) of recognition; (*b*) appreciative; approving; *adv.* appreciatively; approvingly. **3.** *p.p. & a.* **anerkannt,** (*a*) acknowledged, recognized; accepted (usage, custom, doctrine, authority, etc.); admitted (truth, etc.); received (doctrine, pronunciation, etc.); **allgemein anerkannte Tatsache,** accepted, established, fact; fact universally admitted; *Ling:* **allgemein anerkannte Hochsprache,** received standard (language); *Jur:* **gerichtlich anerkannte Schuld,** judgment debt; **gerichtlich anerkannter Gläubiger,** judgment creditor; *Sp:* **anerkanntes Meeting,** recognized meeting; **anerkannter Rekord,** recognized, official, record; (*b*) *adv.* (i) = **anerkanntermaßen;** (ii) **anerkannt guter Gasthof,** hotel of established reputation.

II. *vbl s.* **1. Anerkennen,** *n. in vbl senses.* **2. Anerkennung,** *f. in vbl senses; also:* (*a*) acknowledgement (of sth.); recognition (of s.o., sth.) (**als,** as); **A. des Königs durch das ganze Volk,** recognition of the king by all the people; *Com:* **A. eines Wechsels,** acceptance of a bill; *Jur:* **gesetzliche A. (eines Kindes),** legitimation (of a child); **gerichtliche A.,** legalization; authentication, certification (of document, signature); **A. einer Klage,** cognovit; **auf A. eines Testaments klagen,** to propound a will; *Jur: Hist:* **A. eines Konsuls,** consul's exequatur; (*b*) approbation, approval; appreciation; recognition, acknowledgement; **bei j-m A. finden,** to meet with s.o.'s approval; **beim Publikum A., A. seitens des Publikums, gewinnen,** to earn the approbation of the public; **seine Bestrebungen fanden keine A.,** his efforts were not appreciated; **als A. für . . . ,** in recognition of . . . , in acknowledgement of (a service, etc.).

anerkennenswert, *a.* that merits recognition; laudable, praiseworthy; commendable (**wegen,** for).

Anerkenntnis, *n.* **-nisses/-nisse** & *f.* **-/-nisse,** (*a*) *Fin: Jur:* (= **Anerkennung**) acknowledgement; (*b*) *Jur:* (= **Schulderkenntnis**) recognizance.

Anerkennung, *f. see* **anerkennen** II. 2.

Anerkennungsschreiben, *n.* letter of acknowledgement.

Anerkennungsurkunde, *f. Jur:* act of ratification and acknowledgement.

anerkennungswert, anerkennungswürdig, *a.* = **anerkennenswert.**

Aneroid [aneˑroˑˈiːt], *n.* **-(e)s/-e** [-s, -ˈiːdəs/-ˈiːdə], **Aneroidbarometer,** *n.* aneroid barometer, *F:* aneroid.

anerschaffen. I. *v.tr. sep. (strong)* **etwas, j-m, eine Eigenschaft a.,** to endow sth. with a quality at its creation; to implant a quality in s.o. at birth.

II. **anerschaffen,** *a.* innate, inborn (quality, etc.).

anerziehen, *v.tr. sep. (strong)* **j-m etwas a.,** to inculcate sth. upon s.o.; to instil sth. into s.o.; **die Höflichkeit war ihm anerzogen,** he had been brought up to be courteous; **ein anerzogener Geschmack,** an acquired taste.

Aneth [aˑˈneːt], *n.* **-s/.** *Bot: Pharm:* dill.

Anetikon [aˈneːtiˑkon], *n.* **-s/-ka.** *Med:* palliative; soothing medicament.

anetisch [aˈneːtiʃ], *a.* palliative; soothing.

Aneurie [anoyˈriː], *f.* **-/.** *Med:* nervous debility.

Aneurisma, Aneurysma [anoyˈrismaː, anoyˈrysmaː], *n.* **-s/-men.** *Med:* aneurism, aneurysm.

aneurismatisch [anoyrisˈmaːtiʃ], **aneurysmatisch** [anoyrysˈmaːtiʃ], *a.* aneurismal, aneurysmal.

Anewand, *f.* **-/⸗e, Anewende,** *f.* **-/-n,** ridge, balk (between two fields).

anfächeln, *v.tr. sep.* to fan.

anfachen, *v.tr. sep.* to blow (up) (the fire); to fan (fire, discontent, hatred, etc.); to inflame, excite, kindle, rouse (passions); to stir up, foment (hatred, discord, etc.); **eine Leidenschaft zu heller Glut a.,** to fan a passion into flame.

anfädeln, *v.tr. sep.* **1.** to thread, string (beads, etc.). **2.** to begin, start; to open (a conversation); **mit j-m ein Gespräch a.,** to strike up a conversation with s.o.

anfahrbar, *a.* passable, negotiable (road, etc.); *Nau:* navigable (channel, etc.).

anfahren, *v.sep. (strong)* I. *v.tr.* **1.** (*a*) to cart (up), carry (up); to bring up (coal, building materials, etc.) (in vehicle, barge, etc.); (*b*) *F:* to bring (on) (drinks, cigars, etc.). **2.** (*a*) (*of vehicle*) to approach (building, etc.); (*b*) *Nau:* **einen Hafen a.,** to put in, touch, call, at a port. **3.** *Aut: Rail: etc:* (**j-n, etwas**) **a.,** to run into (s.o.,

sth.); to collide with (sth.); to run foul of, to foul (carriage, car, *Nau:* another ship). **4.** (*a*) (*of dog*) to make a rush at (s.o.), to go for (s.o.); (*b*) (*of pers.*) j-n (**hart, grob**) **a.,** to go for s.o.; to snap at s.o.; '**wo warst du gestern abend?**' **fuhr sie ihn an,** 'where were you last night?' she snapped at him. **5.** *Hort:* **Kartoffeln a.,** to hoe (between the rows of) potatoes.
　　II. **anfahren,** *v.i.* (*sein*) **1.** (*of vehicle, pers. in vehicle*) to drive up; (*of cyclist*) to ride up; (*of ship*) to sail up; to steam up; **ein Wagen kam angefahren,** a car, a carriage, drove up. **2.** (*of car, train*) to start (off); **der Wagen fuhr weich an,** the car started smoothly; **der Zug fuhr sachte an,** the train gently gathered speed. **3.** (*of vehicle*) **an, auf, etwas** *acc.* **a.=etwas a.,** *q.v.* under I. 3. **4.** *Min:* to descend the (mine-) shaft, to go down the mine(-shaft).
　　III. *vbl s.* **Anfahren,** *n. in vbl senses; also:* (*a*) cartage; carriage, conveyance, transport (of coal, building materials, etc.); *cp.* **Anfahrt, Anfuhr;** (*b*) *Aut:* start; **A. am Berg,** hill-start.
Anfahrschacht, *m. Min:* descending shaft; winze.
Anfahrt, *f.* **1.** arrival (of vehicle, train, ship). **2.** *Min:* descent into the mine; going down the mine(-shaft). **3.=Anfuhr. 4.** (*a*) approach (to house, station, harbour, etc.); (carriage-) drive; avenue; (*traffic sign*) 'way in', 'entrance'; (*b*) *Nau:* landing-place, -stage; landing jetty; quay.
Anfahrweg, *m.=***Anfahrt 4** (*a*).
Anfall, *m.* **1.** assault, attack, onslaught; *Mil:* rush attack, surprise attack; raid. **2.** fit, attack, bout (of malady); (apoplectic) seizure; outburst (of temper); fit (of laughter, merriment); *F:* paroxysm (of rage, laughter); **der erste A. einer Krankheit,** the first onset of a disease; **A. von Fieber,** attack, bout, of fever; **A. von Gicht, von Schwindel,** attack of gout, of dizziness; **A. von Wahnsinn, von Schwermut,** fit of madness, of melancholy; **leichter A. von Fieber, von Gicht,** touch of fever, of gout; *see also* **epileptisch, hysterisch. 3.** *Jur:* **A.** (**einer Erbschaft**), inheritance; succession, reversion (of an estate); **durch den A. einer Erbschaft,** by accession to an inheritance, an estate. **4.** *Fin: Ind: etc:* amount (of money) accruing; amount (of money, material, etc.) coming in; incomings; yield (of interest, products, etc.); *Ch:* amount (of substance) formed *or* collected; *pl.* **Anfälle,** *Adm: etc:* revenue. **5.** *Min:* prop, stay, shore. **6.** *Arch:* impost, springer (of arch).
anfallen, *v.sep.* (*strong*) I. *v.tr.* to assail, assault, attack, beset; **den Feind a.,** to fall (up)on the enemy; **von einer Krankheit angefallen werden,** to be attacked by a disease, to catch a disease; **anfallende Art,** aggressive manner.
　　II. **anfallen,** *v.i.* (*sein*) **1.** j-m **a.,** to fall to s.o.'s share, to s.o.'s lot; *Jur:* (*of property*) to devolve upon, to, s.o. **2.** to accumulate; (*of moneys, etc.*) to accrue; (*of material, etc.*) to come in; to come to hand; to become available; *Ch:* (*of substance*) to be obtained; to be yielded; to be given off; **anfallendes Material,** material becoming available, as it becomes available; **Material, wie es anfällt,** unselected material, *F:* material just as it comes; *Ind:* **anfallende Nebenprodukte,** resulting by-products.
anfällig, *a.* prone to disease; *F:* shaky (in health); **a. gegen, für, eine Krankheit,** susceptible to a disease.
Anfälligkeit, *f.* proneness to disease; *F:* shakiness (in, of, health); **A. gegen, für, eine Krankheit,** susceptibility to a disease.
Anfallrecht, *n. Jur:* **1.** remainder; reversionary interest (in an estate). **2.** right of escheat.
Anfallssteuer, *f. Adm:* probate duty; estate duty; *F:* death duty.
anfallsweise, *adv.* fitfully.
Anfang, *m.* (*a*) beginning, start, commencement, outset; **am, im, zu, A.,** at the start; at the outset; at first; *Lit:* in the beginning; *B:* **im A. war das Wort,** in the beginning was the Word; **am A. ist diese Arbeit schwer,** this work is difficult at the start; **gleich am A.,** at the very start, beginning; right at the start; **am, im, zu, A.+** *gen.,* at the beginning of . . . ; **am A. des neunzehnten Jahrhunderts,** at the beginning of the, in the early, nineteenth century; **am A. seiner Laufbahn,** at the outset of, early in, his career; **zu A. des Winters,** at the beginning of winter; early in the winter; **vor A. des Winters,** before winter begins; **A. Juni,** at the beginning of June; in the early part of, early in, June; **A. dieser, nächster, Woche,** at the beginning of this week, next week; early this week, next week; **sie ist**

A. vierzig, A. der Vierziger, she is in the, her, early forties; she is not much more than forty; (**gleich**) **von A. an,** from the (very) beginning, from the (very) start, from the outset; *F:* all along; **von A. bis zu Ende,** from beginning to end, from start to finish, from first to last; *F:* **das ist der A. vom Ende,** it is the beginning of the end; **den A. machen,** to make a beginning, a start; to begin, start (off) (**mit,** with); **wer macht den A.?** who's going to start (off)? who's going first? **zu A. muß ich Ihnen sagen . . . ,** to begin with, first of all, I must tell you . . . ; **für den A. werden Sie hier arbeiten,** you will work here for a start; **einen neuen A. machen,** to make a fresh start; to start again, start afresh; **noch im A. sein,** to be a mere beginner, a tyro (*in a science, business, etc.*); (*of development, game, disease, etc.*) **seinen A. nehmen,** to begin, start; **der A., die Anfänge, des Lebens,** the beginnings, the origin, of life; **die ersten Anfänge der Kultur,** the first beginnings, the rudiments, the dawn, of civilization; *Th:* '**A. der Vorstellung 7 Uhr',** 'performance begins, commences, at 7 o'clock'; *Prov:* **aller A. ist schwer,** all beginnings are difficult; everything is difficult at the start; (*b*) inception, initiation, opening; outbreak, commencement (of hostilities); **A. der Verhandlungen,** opening of negotiations; (*c*) exordium; introduction, beginning (of discourse); opening (of poem, letter, play, conversation, etc.); (*d*) front (place), head (of vanguard, column, etc.); (*e*) *Arch:* spring (of pillar, arch); (*f*) **die Anfänge einer Wissenschaft,** the rudiments, elements, first principles, of a science.
anfangen, *v.sep.* (*strong*) **1.** *v.tr.* (*a*) to begin, start, commence; to undertake; to set (sth.) going; to set (sth.) in train; to open (conversation, debate, etc.); to set (enquiries, etc.) on foot; **seine Arbeit a.,** to begin, start, one's work; **eine Aufgabe a.,** to begin, start (up)on, a task; **ein Geschäft a.,** to start a business; to start, set up, in business; to set up shop; **ein Hauswesen a.,** to set up house, *esp. U.S:* to set up housekeeping; **Verhandlungen a.,** to open, start, negotiations; **ein neues Leben a.,** to start afresh, to turn over a new leaf; **die Feindseligkeiten a.,** to begin, open, hostilities; **einen Krieg a.,** to start a war; **einen Briefwechsel mit j-m a.,** to begin, open, a correspondence with s.o., to enter into correspondence with s.o.; **einen Streit mit j-m a.,** to pick, start, a quarrel with s.o.; **einen Prozeß mit j-m a.,** to bring, commence, an action against s.o.; **er fängt zuviel(erlei) an,** he tries to do too many things at once; *F:* he has too many irons in the fire; (*b*) to take (sth.) in hand; to set one's hand to, address oneself to (task); to set about (task); **wie man es a. muß, soll,** how to go about it, set about it; **ich weiß nicht, wie ich es a. soll,** I don't know how to set about it, how to do it; **du fängst es falsch, verkehrt, an,** you are setting, going, about it the wrong way; you are going the wrong way to work; you are doing it wrong; **du mußt es anders a.,** you must set about it differently; you must find another way of doing it; (*c*) to manage, contrive, to do (sth.); to do (sth.); **was soll ich damit a.?** what am I to do with it? **mit ihm ist nichts anzufangen,** it is impossible to deal with him; there is nothing to be done with him; *F:* he's useless, hopeless; **mit ihm kann ich gar nichts a.,** I can't do anything with him at all; *F:* I can't get anywhere with him; **ich weiß nicht, was ich a. soll,** I don't know what to do; I don't know which way, where, to turn; **sie wußte nicht, was sie (vor Freude, vor Verlegenheit) anfangen sollte,** she didn't know what to do with herself (for joy, for embarrassment). **2.** *v.i.* (*haben*) (*a*) to begin, start, commence; **die Vorstellung fängt um 7 Uhr an,** the performance starts, begins, commences, at 7 o'clock; **das Stück fängt mit einem Prolog an,** the play begins, starts, commences, opens, with a prologue; **mit Suppe a.,** to start with soup; **die Heide fängt am Ende dieser Straße an,** the heath starts, begins, at the end of this road; **der Regen hat gerade angefangen,** it has just started raining, started to rain; it has just come on to rain; **die Schule fängt morgen (wieder) an,** school, term, starts tomorrow; **er hatte als Arzt angefangen,** he had started as a doctor; **früh a.,** to make an early start; **mit nichts a.,** to start from nothing; to rise from nothing; *F:* to start from scratch; **von vorn a.,** (i) to begin at the beginning; (ii)=**wieder von vorn a.; wieder von vorn a., von neuem a.,** to start again, start afresh, make a fresh start; **für sich a.,** to set up for oneself; **da fängt sie (schon) wieder an!** there she goes

again! she's at it again! (*i.e. crying, etc.*); **sie fängt immer wieder davon an,** she keeps on talking about it; she's always harping on it, *F:* she's always on about it; (*to quarrelling children, etc.*) **wer hat angefangen?** who started it? *see also* **klein;** (*b*) **a., etwas zu tun,** to begin, start, to do sth.; to begin, start, doing sth.; **er fing zu schreiben an,** he began, started, to write; he began, started, writing; **es fängt an zu regnen,** it is beginning, starting, to rain; it is coming on to rain; **damit a., etwas zu tun,** to begin, start, by doing sth. **3.** *occ. & Dial:* **sich anfangen,** to begin; **mit vierzig fängt sich das Leben an,** life begins at forty.
Anfänger, *m.* **1.** beginner, tyro; novice, learner; **ein A. in etwas** *dat.* **sein,** to be a beginner at sth., a novice at, in, sth.; *see also* **blutig 2, Lesebuch. 2.** *Arch:* springer (of arch).
Anfängerkurs, *m. Sch:* elementary course; course for beginners; introductory course.
Anfängerübung, *f. Sch:* elementary class; (practical) class for beginners; *Mus:* elementary exercise.
anfänglich, (*a*) *a.* initial; incipient (state, etc.); original, first; early (attempts, symptoms, etc.); (*b*) *adv.=***anfangs.**
anfangs. 1. *adv.* at the start; at, *Lit:* in, the beginning; at the outset; at first; initially; originally; to begin with; to start with; **a. war er sehr schüchtern,** he was very shy at first, at the start, to begin with; **gleich a.,** at the very start, beginning; right at the start, beginning, outset. **2.** *prep.* (+*gen*) *A. & occ.* **a. Juni,** at the beginning of June.
Anfangs-, *comb.fm.* (*a*) initial state, position, voltage, velocity, value, etc.); first (position, equation, symptoms, etc.); early (growth, stage, etc.); opening (stages, etc.); (*b*) elementary, rudimentary (instruction, etc.).
Anfangsbuchstabe, *m.* (*a*) initial (letter); **kleiner A.,** small initial letter, *Print:* lower case initial letter; **großer A.,** capital (letter), *Print: F:* cap; (*b*) *pl.* **Anfangsbuchstaben,** initials (of name, etc.).
Anfangsbully, *m. Hockey:* bully-off.
Anfangsfeld, *n. Rail:* starting point of a block section.
Anfangsfestigkeit, *f. Mec: Constr: etc:* initial strength (of materials, etc.).
Anfangsgehalt, *n.* starting, initial, salary.
Anfangsgeschwindigkeit, *f.* initial velocity; *Ball:* muzzle velocity.
Anfangsgründe, *m.pl.* rudiments, elements, first principles (of a science, etc.); **in den Anfangsgründen einer Sache stecken,** to be only at the ABC of a subject; *Sch:* **A. der Algebra,** elementary algebra.
Anfangskurs, *m. St.Exch:* opening price.
Anfangspunkt, *m.* starting-point; origin; *Arch: Mth: etc:* point of origin (of curve, etc.).
Anfangsstadium, *n.* early stage; initial stage.
Anfangstermin, *m.* commencing date; date on which a legal ruling, etc., comes into force.
Anfangsunterricht, *m.* elementary instruction; introductory teaching; **einen guten A. in Latein gehabt haben,** to have (had) a good grounding, *U.S:* to have a good foundation, in Latin.
Anfangszeile, *f.* first line.
anfärben, *v.tr. sep.* to tinge; to colour; *Dy:* to dye.
anfassen, *v. sep.* I. *v.tr.* **1.** to touch (s.o., sth.); to handle (s.o., sth.); to grasp; to seize; to grab; to lay hold, take hold, catch hold, of (s.o., sth.); to set about (task); **nicht anfassen!** don't touch! **sie faßte ihn am Arm an,** she seized him by the arm; she caught hold of, grabbed, his arm; (*reciprocal use*) **sie faßten einander sich, an, um den Fluß zu durchwaten,** they joined hands to ford the stream; **etwas fest a.,** to take a firm hold of, on, sth.; to grip sth.; **etwas richtig a.,** to set about, tackle, sth. the right way; **etwas verkehrt a.,** to go about sth. the wrong way, *F:* to put the cart before the horse; *see also* **Ende 1** (*a*), **falsch**[1]: **1, 5; ich weiß nie, wie ich sie a. soll,** I never know how to manage, handle, her; **j-n grob, sanft, a.,** to handle, treat, s.o. roughly, gently; *F:* **j-n mit (Glacé-)Handschuhen a.,** to handle s.o. with great tact, *F:* with kid gloves; to treat s.o. with the utmost consideration. **2.** *Turf: etc:* (*of rider*) **sein Pferd a.,** to press one's horse hard. **3.** **sich anfassen,** to feel; **es faßt sich hart, weich, kalt, an,** it feels hard, soft, cold; **Tuch, das sich rauh anfaßt,** cloth that is rough to the touch.
　　II. **anfassen,** *v.i.* (*haben*) **1.** to take hold; to grip. **2.** (*of plant, tree*) to take root, strike root. **3.** **mit a.,** to lend a hand, bear a hand (**bei,** with, in); **bei der Arbeit mit a.,** to take a hand in the work oneself.

III. *vbl s.* **Anfassen,** *n. in vbl senses; also:* treatment.

Anfasser, *m. Dom.Ec:* kettle-holder; cloth, pad, *U.S:* pot holder, used for handling hot pans, etc.; oven-cloth; holder (for flat-iron, etc.).

anfauchen, *v.tr. sep.* (*a*) (*of cat*) to spit at (s.o., another animal); (*b*) (*of pers.*)=**anfahren** I. 4 (*b*).

anfaulen, *v.i. sep.* (*sein*) to (begin to) decay, rot; (*of fruit, fish, etc.*) to spoil, go bad; (*of fish, meat*) to go off; **anfaulend,** putrescent; **angefaultes Fleisch,** tainted, bad, meat; **angefaultes Obst,** spoilt, damaged, fruit; (*of pers.*) **(moralisch) angefault,** (morally) vitiated.

anfechtbar, *a.* contestable; questionable; disputable; controversial (statement, opinion); (idea, procedure, etc.) that is open to objections, to criticism; impeachable (motive, conduct, witness, evidence, etc.); impugnable (declaration, evidence, etc.); *Jur:* voidable, defeasible (contract, etc.); contestable (decision, will, etc.).

Anfechtbarkeit, *f.* contestableness; questionableness; *Jur:* defeasibility.

anfechten. I. *v.tr. sep.* (*strong*) **1.** to contest, dispute (opinion, statement, s.o.'s right, etc.); to call, bring, (sth.) in question; to attack, impugn (s.o.'s opinion, course of action, etc.); to impugn (s.o.'s veracity); to impeach (s.o.'s honour, s.o.'s veracity; *Jur:* witness, evidence); to challenge (statement, right, s.o.'s honour, etc.); *Jur:* to contest (decision, etc.); (to try, to take measures) to avoid (contract); to oppose (patent); to challenge, object to (witness, etc.); to take exception to (witness, evidence); to impugn (evidence); **einen Geschworenen a.,** to challenge a juror; **ein Testament a.,** to contest a will, to dispute the validity of a will; **eine Ehe a.,** to contest the validity of a marriage; to petition for nullity of marriage. **2.** (*a*) to disquiet, trouble, disturb, bother, worry (s.o.); **er ließ sich's nicht a.,** he didn't let it worry him; he didn't bother himself about it; **laß dich das nicht a.!** never mind that! don't bother, worry, about that! **was ficht dich an?** what's the matter with you? what's wrong with you? what's up with you? *F:* what's biting you? **was ficht mich das an?** what does it matter to me? why should I mind? (*b*) (*of Satan*) to tempt (s.o.).

II. *vbl s.* **1. Anfechten,** *n. in vbl senses.* **2. Anfechtung,** *f.* (*a*) *in vbl senses; also:* contestation (of right, etc.); taking of measures to avoid, avoidance of (contract); **A. eines Patents,** opposing of, opposition to, a patent; impeachment (ot s.o.'s honour, veracity, *Jur:* of witness, evidence); *Jur:* challenge (of juror, witness); objection (to witness); impugnment (of statement; *Jur:* of witness, evidence); (*b*) temptation; **gegen alle Anfechtungen gefeit,** proof against all temptations.

Anfechtungsklage, *f. Jur:* action to invalidate a contract; opposition proceedings *or* interference proceedings (against a patent); action to set aside a will, etc.; petition for nullity (of marriage), nullity suit; bastardy case.

anfeilen, *v.tr. sep.* to give (sth.) a touch of the file.

anfeinden. I. *v.tr. sep.* to show hostility, enmity, ill-will, towards (s.o.); to be hostile to, at enmity with (s.o.); to bear malice towards (s.o.), bear (s.o.) malice; to persecute (s.o.).

II. *vbl s.* **Anfeindung,** *f.* hostility; ill-will; persecution.

anfertigen. I. *v.tr. sep.* to manufacture, make (goods, clothing, etc.); to produce (goods); to make (up) (suit, dress, etc.); *see also* **Maß**[1] 3 (*b*); to prepare, draw up (document, list, etc.); to draft (agreement, deed, etc.); to write (article, fair copy, etc.); to make (copy, draft, list, etc.); **einen Anzug, ein Ersatzteil, eine Liste, eine Übersetzung, usw., a. lassen,** to have a suit, a spare part, a list, a translation, etc., made.

II. *vbl s.* **Anfertigen** *n.,* **Anfertigung** *f. in vbl senses; also:* manufacture; production; preparation.

Anfertiger, *m.* manufacturer; producer; maker.

Anfertigungskosten, *pl.* cost of production; manufacturing costs.

anfesseln, *v.tr. sep.* to chain up, tie up (s.o.); **j-n an etwas** *acc.* **a.,** to chain, tie, s.o. to sth.; *F:* **an seinen Schreibtisch angefesselt,** chained to one's desk, tied to one's work.

anfetten, *v.tr. sep.* to grease; to oil; to lubricate.

anfeuchten, *v.tr. sep.* to damp, moisten, wet; to spray, sprinkle (seedlings, etc.); *Ind:* to spray (pulp, etc.); **Wäsche a.,** to damp, sprinkle, linen (*for ironing*); *F:* **(sich** *dat.***) die Kehle a.,** to wet one's whistle.

Anfeuchter, *m.* **-s/-,** moistening *or* wetting appliance, brush *or* machine; moistener; damper (*for stamps, labels, etc.*); sprinkler (*for plants, etc.*).

Anfeuchtgrube, *f. Paperm:* sizing-vat.

Anfeuchtmaschine, *f.* moistening machine; wetting machine; *Paperm:* spray-damper.

Anfeuchtpinsel, *m.* damping brush; moistening brush.

anfeuern. I. *v.tr. sep.* **1.** to heat (oven, etc.); to stoke, fire (up) (furnace, boiler). **2.** *Pyr:* to prime (rocket). **3.** to animate, excite (s.o.); to fire (s.o.); to fire (s.o.) with, rouse (s.o.) to, enthusiasm; to fire, kindle, (s.o.'s) enthusiasm; to encourage (s.o.); to inflame (s.o.'s) courage; **j-n zu etwas a.,** to incite s.o. to sth.

II. *vbl s.* **1. Anfeuern,** *n. in vbl senses.* **2. Anfeuerung,** *f.* (*a*) *in vbl senses; also:* animation; excitement; encouragement; incitement **(zu,** to); (*b*) *Tchn:* fire-lighting material; *Pyr:* priming (of rocket).

anfinden (sich), *v.refl. sep.* (*strong*) to be found (again); **dein Schirm ist dir abhanden gekommen? reg dich nicht auf, er wird sich schon wieder a.,** you've lost your umbrella? don't get excited, it will turn up.

anfirnissen, *v.tr. sep.* to varnish, to give (sth.) a coat of varnish.

anflammen, *v.tr. sep. A:*=**entflammen** 1.

anflehen. I. *v.tr. sep.* to supplicate, implore (s.o.); to beseech, entreat (s.o.); **j-n um etwas a.,** to supplicate s.o. for sth., to implore sth. of s.o.; **j-n um Schutz a.,** to implore, beg for, crave, s.o.'s protection; **j-n um Gnade a.,** to beg s.o. for mercy; to cry to s.o. for mercy; **j-n a., etwas zu tun,** to implore, entreat, beg, beseech, s.o. to do sth.

II. *vbl s.* **Anflehen** *n.,* **Anflehung** *f. in vbl senses; also:* supplication, imploration; entreaty.

anfletschen, *v.tr. sep.*=**anblecken.**

anflicken, *v.tr. sep.* (*a*) to patch, put a patch on, to piece (garment, etc.); (*b*) **etwas an etwas** *acc.* **a.,** (i) to patch sth. on to sth.; to put, sew, stick, (piece of material) on to sth.; (ii) *F:* to tack, tag, sth. on to sth.; (*c*) *F:* **j-m etwas a.,** to pin (theft, etc.) on s.o.

anfliegen, *v. sep.* (*strong*) I. *v.tr.* **1.** (*of aircraft*) (*a*) to approach, make for, head for (airport, town, etc.); (*b*) to call at, land at (airport). **2.** (*a*) *Lit:* **eine Röte flog ihre Wangen an,** a blush suffused, mounted to, her cheeks; she coloured up; (*b*) (*of weakness, etc.*) to come over (s.o.) suddenly, momentarily; **eine Schwäche flog ihn an,** he had a sudden feeling of weakness; **was fliegt ihn an?** what has come over him? what is wrong with him?

II. **anfliegen,** *v.i.* (*sein*) **1.** (*a*) (*of bird, insect*) **angeflogen kommen,** to come flying along; to fly up; (*b*) (*of seeds, esp. winged seeds*) **a., angeflogen kommen,** to be disseminated by the wind, to be wind-borne; **angeflogene Pflanzen, angeflogenes Holz,** plants, trees, from wind-borne seeds. **2.** *Ch: Min:* to effloresce; (*of surface, etc.*) **angeflogen,** encrusted, incrusted. **3.** (*a*) (*of illness*) **wie angeflogen kommen,** to come on without apparent cause, unexpectedly, without warning; **die Krankheit kam (über ihn) wie angeflogen,** a sudden illness overtook him, he suddenly fell ill; (*b*) (*of knowledge, success, etc.*) **j-m a., j-m angeflogen kommen,** to come to s.o. easily, without effort; **Griechisch fliegt ihm nur so an,** Greek comes easily to him; Greek is mere child's-play to him.

III. *vbl s.* **Anfliegen,** *n. vbl senses; also: Av:* approach (to airport, etc.). *Cp.* **Anflug.**

anflößen. I. *v.tr. sep.* **1.** to bring (timber) in rafts; to bring (goods, etc.) on rafts. **2.** (*of sea*) to wash up (wreckage, etc.); (*of river*) to deposit (sand, soil).

II. *vbl s.* **1. Anflößen,** *n. in vbl senses.* **2. Anflößung,** *f.* (*a*) *in vbl senses;* (*b*) alluvium, alluvial deposit; alluvion.

Anflug, *m.* **1.** (*a*) approach (of bird, aircraft); *Av:* run-up; (*b*) arrival (of aircraft at airport). **2.** rising flight, soaring (of bird); *Av: A:* start of the flight; take-off. **3.** *Bot:* plants, trees, from wind-borne seeds, *esp.* trees from winged seeds. **4.** *For:* young wood, small wood; copse, coppice. **5.** thin coating, thin surface layer; incrustation; film (of verdigris, etc.); bloom (on fruit); down (on peach, etc.; on s.o.'s chin, etc.); *Ch: Min:* efflorescence; bloom (of sulphur on rubber). **6. ein A. von etwas,** just a little of sth.; a (mere) suggestion of sth.; a slight indication of sth.; shade, touch, tinge (of malice, of jealousy); fit (of jealousy, generosity, etc.); spasm (of jealousy); **es war ein A. von Röte auf ihren Wangen,** there was a slight flush on her cheeks, a touch of colour in her cheeks; **A. von Bart, von Schnurrbart,** downy beard, moustache; incipient beard, moustache; smudge of moustache; **A. von Lächeln,** hint, trace, suspicion, ghost, of a smile; **A. von Ironie,** hint, touch, tinge, suspicion, of irony; **A. von Furcht,** momentary feeling of fear; **in einem A. von Mitleid sagte er ihr . . . ,** suddenly moved to pity, in a sudden access of pity, he told her. . . .

Anflugweg, *m. Av:* approach path; approach lane.

anflunkern, *v.tr. sep. F:*=**anlügen.**

Anfluß, *m.* **1.** afflux; **A. des Wassers,** influx, inflow(ing), of the water; rising of the tide. **2.** *Geol:* alluvium, alluvial deposit.

anfluten, *v.i. sep.* (*of water, waves, etc.*) **1.** to come flooding in; to flow in. **2.** to swell (to a flood).

anfordern. I. *v.tr. sep.* **1.** (*a*) to demand, require (**von j-m,** from s.o.); *Mil:* to claim the services of (personnel); to requisition (foodstuffs, etc.); (*b*) to request, ask for, call for (funds, etc.); **weitere Vorschüsse wurden angefordert,** a request was made for further advances. **2.** (*a*) *Com: Ind:* to order (article); to request delivery of (article); (*b*) *Mil: Adm:* **etwas bei j-m a.,** to indent on s.o. for sth.

II. *vbl s.* **1. Anfordern,** *n. in vbl senses.* **2. Anforderung,** *f.* (*a*) *in vbl senses;* (*b*) demand, requirement; claim; request; *Mil: etc:* requisition; **große, übermäßige, Anforderungen an j-n, an etwas, stellen,** to make great, excessive, demands upon s.o., sth.; **alle Anforderungen erfüllen, allen Anforderungen genügen,** to meet, fulfil, all requirements; to satisfy all the conditions; (*c*) *Com: Ind:* order **(von etwas,** for sth.); request for delivery; (*d*) *Mil: Adm:* indent.

Anforderungsbeamte, *m. Adm:* official responsible for supply, *U.S:* procurement officer.

Anfrage, *f.* **1.** enquiry; **eine A. an j-n richten,** to address an enquiry to s.o., to make enquiries of s.o. **(über etwas** *acc.***, wegen etwas,** about sth.); **auf A. erfuhren wir, daß . . . ,** on enquiry we learned that . . . **2.** *Parl:* **(kleine) A.,** question; interpellation; **eine A. an j-n richten,** to put a question to s.o.

anfragen, *v.i. sep.* (*haben*) **bei j-m a.,** to enquire of s.o., make enquiries of s.o., ask s.o. **(über etwas** *acc.***, wegen etwas, nach etwas,** about sth.); to apply to s.o. (for information); **a., ob . . . , wie . . . ,** to enquire whether . . . , if . . . , how . . . .

anfressen, *v.sep.* (*strong*) I. *v.tr.* **1.** to gnaw; to nibble, nibble at (sth.); **von Ratten angefressen,** attacked by rats; rat-eaten, rat-gnawed (fruit, etc.); **von Motten angefressen,** moth-eaten; **von Würmern angefressen,** worm-eaten (book, wood, etc.); **angefressenes Obst,** worm-eaten, *Lit:* cankered, fruit; *F:* **vom Laster angefressen,** (person) tainted with vice. **2.** (*of acid, rust, etc.*) to corrode; to erode, attack, pit, eat away (metal, etc.); (*of decay*) to attack (bone, tooth, etc.); (*of cancer*) to eat away (flesh, etc.); **anfressende Wirkung,** corrosive action; **angefressenes Metall,** corroded, pitted, metal; **vom Meer angefressene Kliffe,** cliffs eaten away, eroded, by the sea; **angefressener Zahn,** decayed, carious, tooth; **angefressene Nase,** nose partially eaten away. **3.** *P:* (*a*) **sich a.,** to fill one's belly, to stuff oneself; (*b*) **sich** *dat.* **einen Bauch a.,** to grow stout, *F:* to develop a corporation.

II. **anfressen,** *v.i.* (*haben*) *Mec.E: etc:* (*of part*) to seize; to bind, jam.

III. *vbl s.* **1. Anfressen,** *n. in vbl senses.* **2. Anfressung,** *f.* (*a*) *in vbl senses; also:* corrosion; erosion; (*b*) *Med:* decay, caries (of bone, tooth).

anfreunden (sich), *v.refl. sep.* **sich mit j-m a.,** to form, strike up, a friendship with s.o.; to make friends with s.o.; to become intimate with s.o.; **sich (miteinander) a.,** to become friends, to make friends.

anfrieren, *v.i. sep.* (*strong*) (*sein*) **1. an etwas** *acc. or dat.* **a.,** to freeze on to sth. **2.** to begin to freeze; to freeze partially; *Cu:* **Angefrorenes** *n,* soft, partially frozen, ice-cream.

anfrischen. I. *v.tr. sep.* **1.**=**auffrischen** I. 1. **2.** *Metall:* to reduce (metallic oxide); to refine (metal).

II. *vbl s.* **Anfrischen** *n.,* **Anfrischung** *f. in vbl senses; also: Metall:* reduction; refinement.

Anfrischherd, Anfrischofen, *m. Metall:* refining furnace.

Anfuge, *f. A:* enclosure (*with a letter*); **in der A.,** enclosed, subjoined.

anfugen, *v.tr. sep. Carp: etc:* to join on, joint on (a piece, etc.).

anfügen. I. *v.tr. sep.* **1.** to join, attach (sth.) (**an**+*acc.*, to); to annex, join, append, attach (document, etc.) (**einem Brief, an einen Brief,** to a letter); to subjoin (list, etc.); to affix, append (signature, seal); **das Ihrem Brief angefügte Muster,** the sample attached to, enclosed with, your letter; **das Angefügte,** the enclosure; **seine Unterschrift, sein Siegel, an ein Dokument a.,** to set one's hand, one's seal, to a document, to append, affix, one's signature, one's seal, to a document. **2. sich j-m, etwas, anfügen=sich j-m, etwas anpassen,** *q.v. under* **anpassen** I. 1 (*a*). **3.** *Ling:* **anfügende Sprache,** agglutinating, agglutinative, language.

II. *vbl s.* **1. Anfügen,** *n. in vbl senses.* **2. Anfügung,** *f. in vbl senses; also:* (*a*) addition; (*b*) **wir bitten um Rückantwort unter A. der Verzeichnisse,** we request a reply enclosing the lists.

anfühlen, *v.tr. sep.* (*a*) to feel, touch, finger, handle (sth.); **mein Gesicht ist so heiß — fühl's mal an!** my face is so hot—just feel (it)! (*b*) to sense (sth.); **man fühlt es ihm an, daß er . . . ,** one senses, feels, has a feeling, that he . . . ; (*c*) (*of thg*) **sich hart, weich, a.,** to feel hard, soft, to be hard, soft, to the touch; **die Mauer fühlte sich heiß an,** the wall felt hot.

Anfuhr, *f.* **-/-en,** cartage, carting, haulage, carriage; delivery (of coal, potatoes).

anführbar, *a.* quotable, citable (passage, etc.); adducible (example, etc.); (passage, etc.) that can be quoted, cited.

anführen. I. *v.tr. sep.* **1.** (*a*) to be at the head of, to head (party, column, etc.); to lead (party, movement, troops, etc.); to command, be in command of (army, fleet, etc.); **den Tanz a.,** to lead the dance; **von zwei Herolden angeführt,** preceded by two heralds; **Truppen zum Kampf a.,** to lead troops into battle; **einen Aufstand, eine Meuterei, a.,** to lead a revolt, a mutiny; (*b*) *occ:*=**anleiten** I. 1. **2.** to quote (author, passage, authority, proof, etc.); to cite (passage, author, authority); to adduce, bring forward (reasons, argument, proof); to allege (reasons); to advance (pretext, reasons); **oben angeführter Schriftsteller,** author quoted above; **am angeführten Orte,** *abbr.* **a.a.O.,** loco citato, loc. cit.; **einen Schriftsteller, eine Stelle, falsch a.,** to misquote an author, a passage, **ein Beispiel für etwas a.,** to give an example of sth.; to quote an instance of sth.; **j-n, etwas, als Beispiel a.,** to quote s.o., sth., as an example; **vieles läßt sich zugunsten dieser Erfindung a.,** there is much to be said for, in favour of, this invention; **etwas als, zum, Beweis a.,** to adduce sth. as proof; to bring sth. forward as evidence; *Jur:* **zum Beweis a., daß . . . ,** to put in evidence that . . . ; **eine Entschuldigung a.,** to offer an excuse; **etwas als, zur Entschuldigung a.,** to make sth. one's excuse; *Jur:* to plead sth. (in one's defence); **seine Unwissenheit als Entschuldigung a.,** to plead ignorance; **was kannst du zu deiner Entschuldigung a.?** what have you to say for yourself? **3.** to trick, dupe, deceive, fool, gull (s.o.); to take (s.o.) in; **er wurde schön von ihr angeführt,** he was properly taken in by her; **sich a. lassen,** to (let oneself) be imposed upon; to be taken in; **er läßt sich leicht a.,** he is gullible, easily taken in. **4.** *South G.Dial:*=**anfahren** I. 1.

II. *vbl s.* **1. Anführen,** *n. in vbl senses.* **2. Anführung,** *f. in vbl senses; also:* (*a*) guidance, direction; leadership; lead; command (of army, etc.); conduct (of campaign); (*b*) quotation, citation (of author, passage, authority); adduction (of facts, reason, authority).

Anführer, *m.* leader; chief, chieftain (of tribe, clan, etc.); leader, *U.S:* boss (of political party); ringleader (of plot, revolt, mutiny); *Mil:* commander; *Sp:* leader, captain (of team).

Anführerschaft, *f.*=**Führerschaft.**

Anführungsstriche, *m.pl.,* **Anführungszeichen,** *n.pl. Print: etc:* quotation-marks, inverted commas, quotes; **halbe Anführungszeichen,** single quotation-marks, single quotes; **ein Wort, eine Stelle, in A. setzen,** to put a word, a passage, in inverted commas, in quotation-marks; to quote a word, a passage; (*in dictating*) **'A. unten',** 'begin inverted commas', 'quote'; **'A. oben',** 'close inverted commas', 'unquote'.

anfüllen, *v.tr. sep.* to fill (up) (**mit,** with); **der Saal war mit Leuten angefüllt,** the hall was full of, crowded with, people; **etwas wieder a.,** to refill sth.; to replenish (container, lamp, etc.); **sich a.,** (i) (*of tank, reservoir, etc.*) to fill (up); (ii) *F:* (*of pers.*) **sich (mit Essen) a.,** to fill oneself up, cram oneself, with food; to stuff (oneself), to gorge; **sich mit Kenntnissen a.,** to cram, stuff, one's head with knowledge.

anfunken, *v.tr. sep.* to send a wireless, radio, message to (s.o.), to wireless to, radio to (s.o.).

Anfurt, *f. Nau:* landing-place; wharf.

Angabe, *f.* **1.** (*a*) indication (*gen. or* **von,** of); (piece of) information (**über**+*acc.*, about); **unter A. des genauen Tages,** indicating, quoting, giving, the exact date; **ohne A. von Gründen,** without giving (any) reasons; (*of book*) **ohne A. der Jahreszahl,** with no indication of date, 'no date'; *Com:* **um A. der Preise wird gebeten,** please quote prices; **nähere Angaben,** particulars, details; **nähere Angaben über etwas erbitten,** to ask for fuller particulars about, of, sth.; (*b*) *pl.* **Angaben,** *Mth: etc:* data; given information (of problem, etc.); (*c*) *pl.* **Angaben,** instructions, directions, specifications; **nach unseren Angaben angefertigt,** made in accordance with our instructions, directions; made to our specifications. **2.** (*a*) declaration, statement, assertion; *Jur:* testimony, evidence, deposition; **nach seiner A., seiner A. nach, gemäß,** according to his statement; by, according to, what he said; according to him; *Jur:* **nach A. des Zeugen,** according to the witness's statement, testimony; **falsche, betrügerische, A.,** false, fraudulent, statement; misrepresentation; (*b*) *Adm:* return; (*c*) *Cust:* **A. (beim Zollamt),** (customs) declaration, (bill of) entry. **3.** *Jur:* **A. eines Verbrechens (bei Gericht),** laying of an information. **4.** *F:* boasting, bragging; showing off. **5.** *Com:* (*a*) part payment in advance; down payment; earnest money; (*b*) article given in part exchange. **6.** *Sp:* putting of the ball into play; *Ten:* service.

angaffen, *v.tr. sep.* to gape, *F:* gawk, at (s.o., sth.); to stare open-mouthed at (s.o., sth.).

angähnen, *v.tr. sep.* to yawn at (s.o.); (*of gulf, etc.*) to yawn before (s.o.), at (s.o.'s) feet.

Angang, *m.* **1.** first encounter with another person (in the morning, new year, etc.); *Ven:* first animal sighted. **2.** *occ.* beginning, commencement.

angängig, *occ.* **angänglich,** *pred. a.* (*a*) feasible, practicable, possible; **wenn irgend a.,** if it is at all possible; (*b*) permissible.

Angarienrecht [aŋˈgaːriən-], *n. Internat. Jur:* (right of) angary.

Angebäude, *n.*=**Anbau** 2 (*b*).

angebbar, *a.* that can be indicated; assignable (cause, reason, etc.).

angeben, *v.sep.* (*strong*) I. *v.tr.* **1.** (*a*) to indicate; to appoint, name, state (a day, etc.); to set (a date, a day); to give, state (name, reasons, etc.); to assign (reason, cause); *Com:* to quote (prices); **auf die angegebene Weise,** in the manner indicated; **seinen Namen a.,** to give, state, one's name; **das Datum a.,** to give, *Adm: Com:* to quote, the date; **eine Stunde für eine Sitzung a.,** to fix the time of, appoint a time for, a meeting; **Gründe für etwas a.,** to give, state, assign, reasons for sth.; to account for sth.; **etwas als Grund a.,** to give sth. as a reason; to give sth. as a pretext; to make sth. one's excuse; **welche Gründe können Sie für eine solche Handlung a.?** what cause can you show, what reasons can you give, for such an action? **etwas genau a.,** to state sth. precisely; to specify sth.; **näher a.,** to give details of, to specify (conditions, etc.); to particularize (causes, etc.); **der Wert des Hauses wird mit 20 000 M. angegeben,** the value of the house is given as, put at, 20,000 marks; **seine Einkünfte, usw., zu hoch, zu niedrig, a.,** to overstate, to understate, one's income, etc.; *Com:* **zu den angegebenen Preisen,** at the prices quoted; *Nau: Av:* **angegebener Kurs,** indicated course; (*b*) *Adm:* to return (sth.), make a return of (sth.); (*c*) *Cust:* to declare, enter (goods); *Cust: Post:* **den Wert eines Pakets a.,** to declare the value of a parcel; (*d*) *Mus:* **einen Ton a.,** to sound a note; **den Ton a.,** (i) to sound the key-note, strike the note, give the lead (to singers, etc.); (ii) *F:* to give the lead, set the fashion; to set the tone (*of a society, etc.*). **2.** *A:* **sich als, für, etwas a.,** to represent oneself as sth. **3.** (*a*) **a., daß . . . ,** to declare, state, assert, that . . . ; to allege, claim, that . . . ; **der Zeuge gab an, daß er den Angeklagten gesehen habe,** the witness declared, stated, alleged, that he had seen the accused; the witness claimed to have seen the accused; **a., ob . . . ,** to state whether . . . ; (*b*) **a., wie etwas gemacht werden soll,** to indicate, to give directions, instructions, how sth. is to be done. **4.** (*a*) *Jur:* to denounce (s.o.); to inform against (s.o.), *F:* to give (s.o.) away, to split on (s.o.); **sich selbst a.,** to give oneself up; (*b*) *Sch: F:* to tell on, sneak on, snitch on, *U.S:* tattle on (s.o.). **5.** *Com:* (*a*) to give (sum) as part payment in advance, as a deposit, as earnest money; (*b*) to give (article) in part exchange. **6.** *A:* to do; **was gebt ihr heute an?** what are you doing today? **Dummheiten, Späße, a.,** to do silly, funny, things; to play silly, funny, tricks. **7.** *South G.Dial:* **j-m etwas a.,** to delude s.o. into believing sth.

II. **angeben,** *v.i.* (*haben*) **1.** (*a*) *Cards:* to deal first; (*b*) *Sp:* to put the ball into play; *Ten:* to serve. **2.** (*a*) **diese Feder will nicht a.,** this pen won't write; (*b*) **die Flöte will nicht a.,** the flute won't play; **Hammer (im Klavier), der nicht a. will,** piano-note that does not sound; dead key. **3.** *F:* (*of pers.*) to boast, brag; to draw the long bow; to fuss, make a fuss; to show off; to give oneself airs, put on airs; to be bumptious; *F:* to swank; to put it on; to shoot a line; **einer, der gern angibt,** a man who likes to show off, *F:* a line-shooter.

III. *vbl s.* **Angeben,** *n. in vbl senses; also:* **1.** indication; specification (of details, etc.). **2.** (*a*) *Jur:* denunciation, delation; (*b*) talebearing. **3.** *Cards:* first deal. **4.** *F:* **das wäre etwas zum A.,** that would be something to boast about, brag about. *Cp.* **Angabe.**

Angeber, *m.* **1.** *occ.* author (of project, proposal, etc.). **2.** (*a*) *Jur:* informer, denouncer; *P:* nark; (*b*) *Sch: etc: F:* sneak, talebearer, tell-tale. **3.** *F:* boaster; swaggerer; braggart; person who likes to show off; person who puts on side; pretender; poseur; *F:* swank; line-shooter, show-off, *U.S: F:* blowhard.

Angeberei, *f.* **-/-en.** **1.** (*a*) informing, (persistent) denunciation; (*b*) (*in school, etc.*) sneaking, talebearing. **2.** *F:* boasting, bragging; showing off.

angeberisch, *a.* **1.** denunciatory, denunciative; *F:* talebearing; **auf angeberische Art,** like, in the manner of, an informer. **2.** *F:* (*of pers.*) given to showing off; (*of pers., manner*) pretentious; *F:* swanky; uppish; **er ist a.,** he likes to show off; he puts on side.

Angebinde, *n.* **-s/-,** present, gift, *esp.* birthday *or* anniversary present.

angeblich. **1.** *a.* (*a*) supposed; reputed; alleged (reason, claim, culprit, thief, etc.); ostensible (purpose, etc.); pretended (claim, claimant, etc.); so-called (improvements, etc.); would-be (connoisseur, etc.); *Jur:* reputed (father); putative (father, marriage); **angeblicher Wert,** nominal value; *Fin:* face-value (of a bill, etc.); **dieser angebliche Dichter,** *F:* this alleged poet; (*b*) *A:*=**angebbar.** **2.** *adv.* supposedly; ostensibly; *Jur: etc:* reputedly; **er ist a. reich,** he is supposed, reputed, to be wealthy; **er ist a. gestorben,** he is reported to be dead; **er ist a. der Schuldige,** he is said to be the culprit; **a. hat er gesagt, daß . . . ,** he is reported as saying that . . . ; **er ging hinaus, a. um Tabak zu kaufen,** he went out, ostensibly to buy tobacco.

angeboren, *a.* (*a*) (*of quality, etc.*) innate, inborn (*dat.*, in); inherent (*dat.*, in); natural (*dat.*, to), **angeborene Gabe, Güte,** innate, natural, gift, goodness; inherent goodness; **dem Menschen angeborene Tugenden,** virtues innate, inherent, in man; **unsere angeborenen Rechte,** our natural rights, *F:* the rights we are born with; **die Fröhlichkeit ist ihm a.,** he is naturally cheerful, cheerful by nature; *Phil:* **angeborene Begriffe,** innate, connate, ideas; (*b*) congenital (weakness, idiocy, etc.).

Angebot, *n.* (*a*) (*at auction sale*) bid, *esp.* first bid, opening bid, starting bid; *cp.* **Gebot**[1] 2; (*b*) *Com: Fin:* offer ((i) to buy, (ii) to sell); tender; **ein A. für etwas machen,** to make s.o. an offer for sth.; to make, put in, send in, a tender for sth.; **das ist mein äußerstes A.,** that is the best offer I can make; **ein A. auf etwas** *acc.* **machen,** to make an offer for sth.; (*c*) *Com: Fin:* (amount of) goods, shares, etc., on offer; supply; **das laufende A. an Zucker,** the current supply of sugar, supplies of sugar currently available; *Pol.Ec:* **A. und Nachfrage,** supply and demand.

angebracht, *p.p. & pred.a. see* **anbringen** III.

angebunden, *p.p. & a. see* **anbinden.**

angedeihen, *v.i. sep.* (*strong*) (*usu. only in the phr.*) **j-m etwas a. lassen,** to grant sth. to s.o., to grant s.o. sth.; to bestow sth. on s.o.; **j-m Schutz a. lassen,** to grant s.o. protection; **seinen Kindern eine gute Erziehung a. lassen,** to give one's children a good education.

Angedenken, *n.* **-s/.** *A. & Poet:*=**andenken** II; **der König seligen Angedenkens,** the late king, of blessed memory.

angedudelt, *a.*=**angeduselt.**

angeduhnt, *a. North G.Dial:* = **angeduselt.**

angeduselt, *a. F:* slightly the worse for drink, slightly tipsy; *F:* half-tight.

Angefälle, *n.* **1.** inheritance. **2.** *Arch:* abutment (of wall, arch); buttress.

angeführt, *p.p. & a. see* **anführen**

angegeben, *p.p. & a. see* **angeben.**

angegriffen, *p.p. & a. see* **angreifen.**

Angegriffenheit, *f.* weariness, exhaustion; low physical condition.

Angehänge, *n.* pendant (worn round the neck); hanging ornament (on chandelier, etc.); appendage.

Angehäufe, *n.* **-s/-,** agglomeration; conglomeration; *Ch: Miner:* aggregate.

angeheiratet, *a.* **angeheirateter Onkel, Vetter,** uncle, cousin, by marriage.

angeheitert, *a. F:* enlivened by drink; slightly tipsy, *F:* (slightly) elevated, happy, merry, lit up.

angehen, *v.sep.* (*strong*) I. *v.i.* (*sein*) **1. angegangen kommen,** to come walking along. **2. gegen j-n, etwas, a.,** to attack, make an attack on, s.o., sth.; to fight against sth.; **Sie müssen dagegen a.,** you must fight against it; you must resist it. **3.** (*of garment, shoe, lid, etc.*) to go on; **leicht a.,** to go on easily; **schwer a.,** to be difficult to get on, put on; **die Schuhe gehen schwer an,** these shoes are hard to get on. **4.** (*of road, path, etc.*) to slope up; to ascend, rise; **steil angehende Straße,** steeply inclined road, road with a sharp slope. **5.** (*a*) *F:* to begin, start, commence; (*of night*) to come on; (*of dawn*) to appear; (*of winter, etc.*) to set in; **wann geht das Semester an?** when does term, *U.S:* semester, school, begin? **die Unruhen gingen bald wieder an,** the troubles soon started, broke out, again; *Fin:* **die Zinsen gehen vom 1. Juni an,** interest accrues from June 1st; (*b*) **angehend,** incipient; (that is) in the early, initial, stages; on-coming (night, winter, etc.); (winter, etc.) that is setting in; (intending doctor, lawyer, etc.) just beginning his training; (poet, barrister, etc.) in embryo; *F:* budding (poet, lawyer, etc.); **angehender Bart, Schnurrbart,** incipient beard, moustache; **bei angehender Nacht,** at nightfall; in the gathering darkness; **das angehende neunzehnte Jahrhundert,** the early (years of the) nineteenth century; the dawning nineteenth century; **ein angehender Sechziger,** (i) a man just turned, just over, sixty, (ii) a man verging on sixty; a man entering upon his sixtieth year; **eine angehende Neigung zu j-m,** a dawning affection for s.o. **6.** (*a*) (*of fire*) to catch; (*of wood, coal, etc.*) to catch fire, take fire; **das Feuer will nicht a.,** the fire won't burn, won't light; **die Kohlen wollen nicht a.,** the coal won't catch, won't burn; (*b*) (*of machine, engine, motor*) to start (up); **der Motor will nicht a.,** the engine, the motor, won't start; (*c*) (*of plant*) to take root, strike root; (*d*) *Med:* (*of vaccination*) to take. **7.** (*of meat*) to go bad, go off; *Cu:* (*of game*) to get high; **schon angegangenes Fleisch,** tainted meat; meat that is slightly off; *Cu:* **stark angegangenes Wildbret,** high game. **8. es geht an,** it will do; it is tolerable, passable; it is not too bad; **das geht nicht an,** that won't do; that won't pass; **es geht nicht an, es geht kaum an, daß ich wegbleibe,** it won't do, it would hardly do, for me to stay away; I can't very well stay away; **wie ist's mit Ihrem Rheuma? — es geht an,** how is your rheumatism?—not too bad; it might be worse.

II. **angehen,** *v.tr.* **1.** (*a*) (*of animal*) to rush at, make a rush at (s.o.), *F:* to go for (s.o.); (*b*) (*of horse, rider, etc.*) **ein Hindernis a.,** to go at an obstacle; **eine Frage, ein Problem, a.,** to approach, tackle, a question, a problem. **2.** (*of pers.*) to approach (s.o.); **j-n um Geld, Hilfe, usw., a.,** to apply to s.o. for money, help, etc. **3.** to concern, affect (s.o.); to regard (s.o.); **das geht mich kaum an,** that hardly affects, concerns, me; **das geht dich gar nichts an,** that is none of your business, that is no business, no concern, of yours; it's nothing to do with you; **sie geht mich gar nichts an,** she is no concern of mine; she is nothing to do with me; **was mich angeht . . . ,** as far as I am concerned . . . , (speaking) for myself . . . ; **was dich angeht . . . ,** as far as you are concerned . . . ; as for you, as to you . . . ; regarding you . . . , as far as regards you . . . ; **was geht mich das an?** what business, what concern, is it of mine? what has it to do with me? what do I care? **eine Frage, die die Wohlfahrt des Landes angeht,** a question which bears upon, affects, the welfare of the country.

angehören, *v.i. sep.* (*haben*) to belong (*dat.*, to); **einer Familie, einer Gesellschaft, a.,** to belong to, to be a member of, a family, a society; (*of pers.*) **dem deutschen Staat a.,** to be a member of the German State, a German national, a German citizen.

angehörig. 1. *a.* belonging (*dat.*, to); **einer Familie a.,** belonging to a family; (*of pers.*) related to a family. **2.** *s.* **Angehörige,** *m., f.*(*decl. as adj.*) (*a*) member (of family, society, etc.); **die Angehörigen eines Staates,** the nationals of a country; (*b*) relative, relation; **meine Angehörigen,** my relatives; my kin; my family.

Angehörigkeit, *f.* **1.** membership (**zu,** of). **2.** relationship, kinship.

angeifern, *v.tr. sep.* **1.** to slaver over, to slobber over, on (s.o.). **2.** *F:* to vent one's spite on (s.o.).

Angeklagte, *m., f.* (*decl. as adj.*) *Jur:* (*a*) person accused of a crime; (the) accused; (*in court*) defendant; prisoner at the bar; (*b*) (*in civil case*) defendant; (*esp. in divorce case*) respondent.

Angel, *f.* **-/-n. 1.** *Fish:* (i) (fish-)hook, (ii) fishing-tackle; fishing-rod; **die A. auswerfen,** to cast, throw, the line; to make a cast (**nach,** for). **2.** (*a*) hinge (of door); **eine Tür aus den Angeln heben,** to unhinge, unhang, a door; *see also* **Tür;** (*b*) pivot, pin, axis, spindle, pintle; axis (of the earth); *Lit:* **die Welt ist aus den Angeln,** the times are out of joint; (*c*) *Tchn:* tang, tongue, fang (of tool, blade, etc.); (*d*) (= **Fußangel**) mantrap. **3.** *Dial:* sting (of bee, wasp, etc.).

angelangen, *v.i. sep.* (*sein*) to arrive.

Angelausrüstung, *f.* = **Angelgerät.**

Angelband, *n.* (butt-)hinge.

Angelbissen, *m. Fish:* bait.

Angelblei, *n. Fish:* sinker.

angelborstig, *a. Bot:* glochidiate.

Angeld, *n.* part payment in advance; first instalment; down payment; earnest money.

Angeldraht, *m. Mil:* trip-wire.

angelegen, *p.p. & a. see* **anliegen** III.

Angelegenheit, *f.* (*a*) affair, concern, matter; business; **das ist meine A.,** that is my affair, my business; **das ist nicht meine A.,** that is not my business, not my concern; **geschäftliche Angelegenheiten,** business matters; **in welcher A. wollen Sie ihn sprechen?** in what connection do you want to speak to him? **ich komme in einer privaten A., in einer geschäftlichen A.,** I have come on a private matter, on a matter of business; (*b*) *Jur:* cause, case, suit, action.

angelegentlich, (*a*) *a.* pressing, urgent (request); earnest, fervent (desire); cordial (recommendation, greetings); (*b*) *adv.* **angelegentlich(st),** *adv. phr.* **aufs angelegentlichste,** pressingly, urgently; earnestly, fervently; cordially; **sich a. bemühen, etwas zu tun,** to strive hard, do one's utmost, spare no pains, to do sth.; **etwas aufs angelegentlichste empfehlen,** to recommend sth. heartily, cordially; **sich j-m a., aufs angelegentlichste, empfehlen,** to send s.o. (very) cordial greetings; **empfehlen Sie mich ihnen a.,** remember me kindly to them, give them my kind remembrances.

angelfest, *a.* firmly pinned; securely fixed (in).

Angelfischer, *m.* angler, line-fisherman.

Angelfischerei, *f.* angling, line-fishing; rod-fishing.

Angelfliege, *f. Fish:* fly.

angelförmig, *a. Nat.Hist:* unciform, uncinate, hook-like.

Angelgerät, *n.* fishing tackle, apparatus, outfit.

Angelglied, *n. Ent:* cardo, hinge (of maxilla).

Angelhaken, *m.* fish-hook.

Angelika [aŋ'geːli·kaː]. **1.** *Pr.n.f.* **-s.** Angelica. **2.** *f.* **-/.** *Bot: Cu:* angelica; *Bot:* **wilde A.,** aegopodium, gout-weed, bishop's weed.

Angelikaöl, *n. Ch:* angelica oil.

Angelikasäure, *f. Ch:* angelic acid.

Angeliter [aŋə'liːtər], *m.* **-s/-,** native, inhabitant, of Angel.

Angelleine, *f.* fishing-line.

Angelmächte, *f.pl.* **die A.,** the decisive powers; the pivotal forces; the powers on which everything depends, turns.

Angeln[1], *m.pl. Ethn: Hist:* Angles.

Angeln[2]. *Pr.n.n.* **-s.** *Geog:* Angel.

angeln[3]. I. (*a*) *v.i.* (*haben*) to angle; to fish (with rod and line) (**nach,** for); **nach Forellen a.,** to fish for trout; **in der Elbe angelt es sich gut,** there is good fishing in the Elbe; *F:* **nach Komplimenten a.,** to fish, angle, for compliments; (*of woman*) **nach einem Mann a.,** to angle for a husband; to set one's cap at a man, to try to hook a man; (*b*) *v.tr.* to hook, catch (fish, *F:* a husband); *F:* **sie hat ihn geangelt,** she has hooked him, got her hooks into him.

II. *vbl s.* **Angeln,** *n.* (*a*) angling, line-fishing; rod-fishing; **A. mit künstlichen Fliegen,** fly-fishing; (*b*) *F:* angling (for a husband, etc.).

angeloben, *v.tr. sep. A. & Lit:* = **geloben.**

Angelolatrie [aŋgəlo·la·'triː], *f.* **-/.** angelolatry, angel-worship.

Angelpunkt, *m.* (*a*) pivot; central point; the point on which everything turns; **die Angelpunkte,** the cardinal points; **London ist der A. der Finanzwelt,** London is the hub of the financial world; **dieses Bündnis ist der A. unserer Politik,** our whole policy turns, hinges, upon this alliance; (*b*) *Astr:* pole.

Angelring, *m.* (bearing-)ring (of rudder, door, etc.); crapaudine.

Angelrute, *f.* fishing-rod.

Angelsachse, *m.*, **Angelsächsin,** *f.* Anglo-Saxon.

angelsächsisch. 1. *a.* Anglo-Saxon. **2.** *s.* **Angelsächsisch,** *n. Ling:* Anglo-Saxon, Old English.

Angelschein, *m.* fishing licence, permit.

Angelschnur, *f.* fishing-line.

Angelstange, *f.* fishing-pole, (one-piece) fishing-rod.

Angelstern, *m. Lit:* pole-star, lodestar.

Angeltugend, *f.* cardinal virtue.

Angelus ['aŋgəlus], *m., occ. n.* **-/.** *Ecc:* (*a*) angelus-bell, ave-bell; (*b*) the Ave Maria, the Hail Mary.

Angelusläuten, *n.* angelus-bell, ave-bell.

angelweit, *adv.* (*of door, etc.*) **a. offen,** wide open; **die Tore a. aufreißen,** to fling the gates wide open.

Angelwind, *m.* cardinal wind, wind blowing from one of the four cardinal points.

Angelzapfen, *m.* hinge-pin.

Angelzeug, *n.* = **Angelgerät.**

angemessen. 1. *a.* appropriate, adapted (*dat.*, to); suitable (*dat.*, for, to), suited (*dat.*, to); conformable (*dat.*, to); consistent, consonant (*dat.*, with); proper, fit, fitting, befitting, becoming (behaviour, etc.); apt (word, expression, etc.); compatible (*dat.*, with); adequate (*dat.*, to); proportionate (*dat.*, to); **es für a. halten, zu . . . ,** to judge proper to . . . , to think, deem, it fitting, proper, suitable, advisable, to . . . ; **das angemessene Wort,** the appropriate, proper, fitting, word; **angemessenes Verhalten,** proper, (be)fitting, conduct; **angemessenes Verfahren,** suitable, fit, proper, procedure; **einen angemessenen Preis verlangen,** to ask a fair, reasonable, price; **seine Handlungen sind seinen Grundsätzen a.,** his actions conform with, are consistent with, in conformity with, his principles. **2.** *adv.* appropriately; suitably, properly, fittingly, fitly; compatibly (*dat.*, with); conformably (*dat.*, to); in conformity (*dat.*, with); adequately; proportionately, proportionally. *See also* **anmessen.**

Angemessenheit, *f.* appropriateness, suitability, suitableness; conformity; consonance; propriety (of an expression, etc.); fitness, aptness (of remark, etc.); compatibility; adequacy, adequateness (of measures, etc.); proportionateness.

angenehm, *a.* (*a*) pleasant, pleasing, agreeable, nice; prepossessing, winsome, engaging (manner, countenance); gratifying (memory, etc.); comfortable (warmth, sensation, situation, etc.); **sich bei j-m a. machen,** to make oneself pleasant, agreeable, to s.o., to ingratiate oneself with s.o.; **a. im Geschmack,** pleasant-tasting, pleasant to the taste; **es ist a., (etwas zu tun),** it is pleasant, good, nice (to do sth.); **es ist mir sehr a., das zu hören,** I am very pleased, gratified, to hear it; **es wäre uns sehr a., zu . . . ,** we should be very pleased, it would afford us great pleasure, to . . . ; **es ist ihm sehr a., gelobt zu werden,** he very much likes to be praised; **wenn es Ihnen a. ist,** if you care to; if you like; **das Angenehme mit dem Nützlichen verbinden,** to combine the pleasant with the useful; **angenehme Reise!** pleasant journey! *bon voyage!* **gute Nacht, angenehme Ruhe!** good night, sleep well! pleasant dreams! (*on being introduced to s.o.*) **(sehr) a.!** pleased to meet you; *adv.* **a. überrascht,** pleasantly, agreeably, surprised; **a. aussehend,** of pleasant appearance, pleasant-looking; **a. riechend,** pleasant-smelling, pleasantly scented; (*b*) welcome (guest, etc.); acceptable (offer, gift, etc.); **er ist mir stets a.,** I am always glad to see him; **Opfer, das Gott a. ist,** sacrifice acceptable to God; *Com:* **ein angenehmer Artikel,** a popular article.

angenommen, *p.p. & a. see* **annehmen.**

Anger, *m.* **-s/-. 1.** (*a*) pasture, grazing-ground; meadow; (*b*) green, sward, greensward; strip of grass (between ploughed fields); (*c*) common (meadow); village green. **2.** (*a*) = **Schindanger;** (*b*) *A:* execution-ground.

Angerblümchen, *n. Bot:* (common) daisy.

angeregt, *a.* animated, spirited, lively (discussion, mood, etc.); *see also* **anregen.**
Angeregtheit, *f.* animation, liveliness, briskness.
Angergras, *n. Bot:* (annual) meadow-grass.
Angerkraut, *n. Bot: F:* plantain.
Angerling, *m.* **-s/-e.** *Fung:* meadow mushroom, field mushroom.
angeschrieben, *p.p. & a. see* **anschreiben.**
Angeschuldigte, *m., f. (decl. as adj.)* (*a*) accused (before appearance in court); (*b*) suspect.
angesehen, *a.* esteemed, respected (person); (person) of influence, of standing; notable, distinguished (personality); reputable, respectable (firm); (firm) of good standing; **bei j-m a. sein,** to be (highly) esteemed by s.o.; to be in good repute with s.o.; **bei j-m schlecht a. sein,** to be in bad repute with s.o. *See also* **ansehen.**
Angesehenheit, *f.* high reputation, repute; good standing (of firm).
angesessen, *a.* (*of pers., family*) settled; **in einem Ort a.,** resident in, domiciled at, a place.
Angesicht, *n.* **1.** *Lit:* (=**Gesicht**) face, countenance, visage; **j-n von A. zu A. sehen,** to see, meet, s.o. face to face; to come face to face with s.o.; **er hat dem Tod ins A. geschaut,** he has looked death in the face; *B:* **im Schweiß deines Angesichts sollst du dein Brot essen,** in the sweat of thy face shalt thou eat bread; *F:* **im Schweiße seines Angesichts,** by the sweat of one's brow. **2.** sight; view; **im A.** (+*gen.*)=**angesichts.**
angesichts, *prep.* (+*gen.*) in (full) sight of, in (full) view of; in face of; **a. der Altäre,** in full view of the altars; **a. des Todes,** in face of death, faced with death; in the presence of death; **a. dieser Tatsachen,** in view of these facts, faced with these facts, with these facts before one; **a. der Tatsache, daß . . . ,** in view of, in consideration of, considering, the fact that . . . .
angestammt, *a.* hereditary (property); ancestral (castle, etc.); inherited (property, character, instinct, etc.); traditional (beliefs, etc.); *F:* **mit deinem angestammten Leichtsinn,** with your habitual light-heartedness.
Angestellte, *m., f. (decl. as adj.)* employee (*receiving salary or fixed wage*); (*in office, bank, etc.*) clerk; (*in shop*) assistant; (=**Hausangestellte**) domestic (servant); (*female*) maid; **die Angestellten dieser Firma,** the employees, staff, of this firm.
Angestelltenverband, *m. Adm:* Union of (German) Salaried Employees.
Angestelltenversicherung, *f. Adm:* insurance scheme for salaried employees.
angestiefelt, *p.p. F:* (*only in the phr.*) **a. kommen,** to come (striding) along; to come (walking) up.
angestochen, *p.p. & a. see* **anstechen.**
angetan, *p.p. & a. see* **antun.**
angetrunken, *p.p. & a. see* **antrinken.**
angewandt, *p.p. & a. see* **anwenden.**
Angewende, *n.*=**Anewand.**
angewiesen, *p.p. & a. see* **anweisen.**
angewinnen, *v.tr. sep. (strong) A. & Dial:* **j-m etwas a.,** to wrest sth. from s.o.
angewöhnen. I. *v.tr. sep.* **j-m etwas a.,** to accustom, habituate, s.o. to sth.; to train s.o. in (good manners, etc.); **sich** *dat.* **etwas a.,** to become habituated to sth.; to inure oneself to (opium, etc.); to train oneself in (good manners, etc.); (*with verbal noun*) to get into the habit of doing sth.; **j-m, sich, a., etwas zu tun,** to accustom s.o., oneself, to doing sth.; to get s.o., oneself, into the habit of doing sth.; **sich eine schöne Schrift a.,** to cultivate a good hand; **sich das Trinken a.,** to get into the habit of drinking; to take to drink, to drinking.
II. *vbl s.* **Angewöhnen** *n.,* **Angewöhnung** *f. in vbl senses; also:* habituation (*gen.,* to); inurement (to opium, etc.).
Angewohnheit, *f.* habit; **Schnupfen ist eine üble A.,** snuff-taking is a nasty habit; **er hat die A., sich die Nase zu kratzen,** he has a habit of scratching his nose; **etwas aus (purer) A. tun,** to do sth. from mere habit, by sheer force of habit.
angießen, *v.tr. sep. (strong)* **1.** to damp, moisten; to water (plants, etc.); to infuse (tea, herbs). **2.** to start (liquid) running; *Metall:* to pour, run (the metal). **3.** (*a*) to mould (sth.) on; *Metall:* to cast (flange, etc.) integrally with the piece; **angegossene Flanschen,** integrally cast flanges; (*b*) (*of garment*) **es sitzt, paßt, dir wie angegossen,** it fits you like a glove, to a nicety, to a T.
Angina [aŋˈgiːnaː], *f.* **-/-nen.** *Med:* **1.** (i) pharyngitis; (ii) tonsillitis; *A. & U.S:* angina. **2. A. pectoris** [ˈpɛktoˑris], angina pectoris, *F:* angina.
anginös [aŋgiˈnøːs], *a. Med:* anginose, anginous.
angiokarp [aŋgioˑˈkarp], *a. Bot:* angiocarpous.
Angiom [aŋgiˈoːm], *n.* **-s/-e, Angioma** [aŋgiˈoːmaː], *n.* **-s/-ta** [-maˑtaː]. *Med:* angioma.
Angiosperme [aŋgioˑˈspɛrmə], *f.* **-/-n.** *Bot:* angiosperm.
angirren, *v.tr. sep.* (*of dove, F: of pers.*) to coo at (s.o.).
Anglaise [ãˑˈglɛːzə], *f.* **-/-n.** *Danc:* anglaise.
angleichen. I. *v.tr. sep. (strong)* (*a*) to assimilate (*dat.,* **an**+*acc.,* to, with); (*b*) **(aneinander) a.,** to match (up) (parts, etc.); (*c*) **sich etwas** *dat.* **a.,** to become assimilated to sth.; to adapt oneself, itself, to sth.
II. *vbl s.* **Angleichen** *n.,* **Angleichung** *f.* (*a*) assimilation (**an**+*acc.,* to, with); (*b*) matching (up).
Angler[1], *m.* **-s/-**=**Angeliter.**
Angler[2], *m.* **-s/-.** **1.** angler, line-fisherman. **2.** *Ich:*=**Anglerfisch.**
Anglerfisch, *m. Ich:* angler-fish, *F:* sea-devil.
angliedern. I. *v.tr. sep.* to link (on), join (on), attach; to annex, append (*dat.,* **an**+*acc.,* to); **eine Gesellschaft an eine andere a.,** to affiliate one society to, with, another; **sich a.,** (*of thg*) to attach itself, become attached (*dat.,* **an,** to); to link up (*dat.,* **an,** with); (*of pers., society, etc.*) **sich einer Organisation a.,** to affiliate (oneself, itself) to an organization; *Mil:* **Truppen einem Verband a.,** to attach troops to a formation.
II. *vbl s.* **1. Angliedern,** *n. in vbl senses.* **2. Angliederung,** *f.* (*a*) *in vbl senses; also:* affiliation; (*b*) affiliated organisation.
Anglikaner [aŋ(g)liˑˈkaːnər], *m.* **-s/-.** *Ecc:* Anglican.
anglikanisch [aŋ(g)liˑˈkaːniʃ], *a. Ecc:* Anglican; **die Anglikanische Kirche,** the Church of England, the Anglican Church.
Anglikanismus [aŋ(g)liˑkaˑˈnismus], *m.* **-/.** *Rel. Hist:* Anglicanism.
anglimmen, *v.i. sep. (weak & strong) (haben, sein)* to begin to glow; to (begin to) smoulder; to take fire slowly.
anglisieren [aŋ(g)liˑˈziːrən], *v.tr.* **1.** to anglicize; **sich a.,** to adopt English manners, to become anglicized. **2. ein Pferd a.,** to nick a horse's tail; **anglisiertes Pferd,** horse with a nicked tail.
Anglist [aŋˈglist], *m.* **-en/-en,** student *or* teacher of English; English scholar, Anglicist.
Anglistik [aŋˈglistik], *f.* **-/.** *Sch:* (study of) English language and literature, English studies.
Anglizismus [aŋ(g)liˑˈtsismus], *m.* **-/-men.** *Ling:* Anglicism.
Angloamerikaner [ˈaŋ(g)loˑaˑmeˑriˑˈkaːnər], *m.* Anglo-American.
angloamerikanisch [ˈaŋ(g)loˑaˑmeˑriˑˈkaːniʃ], *a.* Anglo-American (parentage, etc.).
Anglofranzösisch [ˈaŋ(g)loˑfranˈtsøːziʃ], *n.*—**Anglonormannisch** 2.
Angloinder [ˈaŋ(g)loˑˀˈindər], *m.* Anglo-Indian, (i) Eurasian; (ii) Englishman born in India.
Anglokatholik [ˈaŋ(g)loˑkatoˑˈliːk], *m. Rel.Hist:* Anglo-Catholic.
anglokatholisch [ˈaŋ(g)loˑkaˈtoːliʃ], *a.* Anglo-Catholic.
Anglomane [aŋ(g)loˑˈmaːnə], *m., f.* **-n/-n** *& decl. as adj.* Anglomaniac.
Anglomanie [aŋ(g)loˑmaˑˈniː], *f.* **-/.** Anglomania.
Anglonormanne [ˈaŋ(g)loˑnorˈmanə], *m.* Anglo-Norman.
anglonormannisch [ˈaŋ(g)loˑnorˈmaniʃ]. **1.** *a.* Anglo-Norman. **2.** *s.* **Anglonormannisch,** *n. Ling:* Anglo-Norman, Norman French.
anglophil [aŋ(g)loˑˈfiːl], *a.* Anglophile.
Anglophile [aŋ(g)loˑˈfiːlə], *m., f.* **-n/-n** *& decl. as adj.* Anglophile.
anglophob [aŋ(g)loˑˈfoːp], *a.* Anglophobe.
Anglophobe [aŋ(g)loˑˈfoːbə], *m., f.* **-n/n** *& decl. as adj.* Anglophobe.
Anglophobie [aŋ(g)loˑfoˑˈbiː], *f.* **-/.** Anglophobia.
anglotzen, *v.tr. sep.* to gaze open-eyed at (s.o.); to stare round-eyed at (s.o.); to goggle at (s.o.).
anglühen, *v.sep.* **1** *v.tr.* to make (sth.) glow; to heat (metal) red-hot, bring (metal) to red-heat; **angeglühtes Eisen,** red-hot iron, iron brought to red-heat. **2.** *v.i.* (*sein*) (*of metal*) to (begin to) glow, to become red-hot. **3.** *v.tr. F:* to gaze at (s.o.) with glowing eyes.
Angolaerbse [aŋˈgoːlaː-], *f. Bot:* **1.** Angola-pea, pigeon-pea. **2.** Bambar(r)a ground-nut.
Angolaner [aŋgoˑˈlaːnər], *m.* **-s/-.** Angolan.
angolisch [aŋˈgoːliʃ], *a.* Angolan.
Angora [aŋˈgoːraː]. *Pr.n.n.* **-s.** *Geog: A:* Ankara, *A:* Angora.
Angorahaar, *n. Tex:* angora wool.
Angorakaninchen, *n. Z:* angora rabbit.
Angorakatze, *f. Z:* (i) Persian cat; (ii) angora cat.
Angorawolle, *f. Tex:* (*a*) angora wool; (*b*) angora (cloth), mohair.
Angoraziege, *f. Z:* angora goat.
Angostura [aŋgoˈstuːraː], *m.* **-s/-s.** *Pharm: etc:* angostura.
Angosturabitter, *m.* angostura bitters.
angreifbar, *a.* **1.** assailable (town, fortress, etc.). **2.** contestable, assailable (opinion, etc.). **3.** attackable (metal, etc.).
angreifen. I. *v.tr. sep. (strong)* **1.** (*a*) to touch (sth.); to grasp; to seize; to lay hold, take hold, catch hold, get hold, of (s.o., sth.); *Fb:* **einen Gegner a.,** to tackle an opponent; *Prov:* **wer Pech angreift, besudelt sich,** you can't touch pitch without being defiled; (*b*) (*of cloth, etc.*) **sich rauh, weich, a.,** to feel rough, soft; to be rough, soft, to the touch; (*c*) *v.i.* (*haben*) (*of force*) to act, to come into play. **2.** to set one's hand to, address oneself to, set about (task); to begin, to tackle, *F:* to wire into (subject, piece of work); to grapple with, tackle (problem, etc.); *v.i.* (*haben*) **selbst mit a.,** to lend a hand; to take a hand in the work oneself. **3.** to break into (reserves, etc.); **sein Kapital a.,** to break into, dip into, one's capital; **die Kasse a.,** to break into the till. **4.** (*a*) *Mil: etc:* to attack, assail (enemy, fort, etc.); to set upon (s.o., enemy); to assault (s.o.); to commit an act of aggression against (country); *v.i.* (*haben*) to attack; to take the offensive; (*b*) **j-n in einer Zeitung a.,** to attack s.o. in a newspaper; **j-n bei, an, der Ehre a.,** to impeach s.o.'s honour; (*c*) (*of disease, illness*) to attack (organ, tissue, etc.); to affect (s.o., organ, etc.); (*of exertion, etc.*) to strain (s.o., nerves, etc.); to fatigue, exhaust (s.o.); to sap (s.o.'s) vitality; **die Lunge ist schon angegriffen,** the lung is already affected; **angegriffener Körperteil,** affected part (of the body); **angegriffene Gesundheit,** poor, weak, health; **die Krankheit hat sie sehr angegriffen,** her illness has left her very low, *F:* has taken it out of her; **diese Beleuchtung, der kleine Druck, greift die Augen an,** this light, the small print, tries, is trying to, one's eyes; **diese Arbeit greift einen an,** *abs.* **greift an,** this is exhausting, trying, work; **ich fühle mich sehr angegriffen,** I feel thoroughly exhausted, thoroughly worn out; **sie sieht angegriffen aus,** she looks worn out, very tired; she looks ill; **sich a.,** to exert oneself (to the utmost); to strain oneself (to the limit); (*d*) (*of acid, etc.*) to attack, corrode, eat into, bite into (metal, etc.); **Rost greift Eisen an,** rust attacks iron.
II. *vbl s.* **Angreifen,** *n. in vbl senses; also:* **1.** *Fb:* tackle. **2.** (*a*) *Mil: etc:* attack; (*b*) corrosion (of metal). *Cp.* **Angriff.**
III. *pr.p. & a.* **angreifend. 1.** (*a*) *Mil: etc:* attacking (troops); aggressive, offensive (measures, etc.); **der angreifende Teil, der Angreifende,** the aggressor; **angreifender Staat,** aggressor nation; (*b*) *Hyd.E:* **angreifendes Wasser,** aggressive water. **2.** fatiguing, exhausting, tiring, *F:* back-breaking, killing (work, journey, etc.); trying (work, light, etc.).
Angreifer, *m.* **1.** aggressor; assailant, attacker. **2.** (*device, rag, etc.*) holder.
angreiferisch, *a.* aggressive (manner, etc.).
angrenzen. I. *v.i. sep.* (*haben*) **an etwas** *acc.* be to be in touch, in contact, with sth.; to **a.,** contiguous to sth.; to border on sth.; to adjoin sth.; to be adjacent to sth.; to abut on sth.; **Haus, das an meines angrenzt,** house adjoining mine; **an ein Land a.,** to border upon, be contiguous to, a country; **angrenzend,** contiguous, adjacent; adjoining, neighbouring (house, room, etc.); conterminous (areas, etc.); **an etwas** *acc.* **angrenzend,** contiguous to sth.; bordering on sth.; abutting on sth.
II. *vbl s.* **Angrenzen** *n.,* **Angrenzung** *f.* contiguity, adjacency, neighbouring position; juxtaposition (of two surfaces, etc.).
Angrenzer, *m.* immediate neighbour, next-door neighbour; *Jur:* abutting owner, abutter.
Angriff, *m.* **1.** (*a*) laying hold (of sth.); beginning, taking in hand (of task); **eine Arbeit, einen Plan, in A. nehmen,** to set one's hand to, address oneself to, set about, a task; to take, put, a piece of work in hand; to put a plan into action; (*b*) **A. einer Kraft,** action, coming into play, of a force; (*c*) *Tchn:* notch (in lock-bolt). **2.** (*a*) attack, onslaught, assault, onset, onrush; *Mil: Sp:* attack; **einen A. auf j-n, etwas** *acc.,* **machen,** to make an attack upon s.o., sth.; **zum A. übergehen,** to take, go over to, assume, the offensive; **zum A. vorgehen,** to push forward to the attack; **einen A. abbrechen,** to break off an attack; **erneuerter A.,** renewed attack; **einen erneuerten A. machen, den A. erneuern,** to return to the attack, *F:* to the charge; *Prov:* **A. ist die**

beste Verteidigung, attack is the best defence; (*b*) aggression (**auf**+*acc.*, against, upon); (*c*) **A. auf, gegen, j-n in der Presse,** attack upon s.o. in the newspapers; **A. auf j-s Ehre,** attack upon, impeachment of, s.o.'s honour.

angriffig, *a. Swiss Dial:* enterprising; skilful, deft.

Angriffsaufstellung, *f. Mil:* attack formation; **in A.,** in battle array.

Angriffsbewegung, *f. Mil:* offensive movement; offensive.

Angriffsboxer, *m. Box:* aggressive fighter, *esp.* boxer who prefers infighting.

Angriffsbündnis, *n.* offensive alliance.

Angriffsfläche, *f.* (*a*) place where one can get a hold, a grip, a purchase; **er bot mir keine A.,** I could find no chink in his armour; I couldn't get at him at all; (*b*) *Mec.E:* working surface.

Angriffsfront, *f. Mil:* battle front.

Angriffsgeist, *m.* aggressive spirit; aggressiveness; *Mil:* offensive spirit.

Angriffshandlung, *f. Mil:* offensive.

Angriffskrieg, *m.* offensive war; war of aggression.

Angriffslust, *f.* aggressiveness.

angriffslustig, *a.* aggressive.

Angriffspunkt, *m.* **1.** *Mil: etc:* point of attack; point attacked *or* to be attacked. **2.** point of application (of a force); point where a force acts; *Mec.E:* working point. **3.** point at which one can get a hold, a grip, on sth.

Angriffsreihe, *f. Fb: etc:* forward-line, forwards.

Angriffsspieler, *m. Fb: etc:* forward.

Angriffsstelle, *f.* (*a*)=**Angriffspunkt;** (*b*) *Min:* working face.

Angriffstag, *m. Mil:* day set for the attack; zero day.

Angriffswaffe, *f. Mil:* **1.** offensive weapon. **2.** offensive, assaulting, arm.

angriffsweise, *adv.* aggressively; offensively.

Angriffswelle, *f. Mil:* assault wave.

Angriffszeit, *f. Mil:* zero hour.

Angriffsziel, *n. Mil:* objective.

Angriffszwischenziel, *n. Mil:* intermediate objective.

angrinsen, *v.tr. sep.* to grin at (s.o.); to smirk at (s.o.).

angrob(s)en, *v.tr. sep. F:* to be rude to (s.o.); to say rude things to (s.o.).

angrunzen, *v.tr. sep.* (*of pig*) to grunt at (s.o.); *F:* (*of pers.*) to grunt, growl, at (s.o.).

Angst. I. *f.* -/⸚e, fear, fright, dread; (mental) anguish; anxiety; *Psy:* angst; **die A. vor dem Tode,** the fear of death; **A. haben, in A. sein,** to be, feel, afraid, frightened; to be apprehensive; to be alarmed; to be anxious, in a state of anxiety; **in großer A. sein,** to be very much afraid; to be badly frightened, scared; to be full of apprehension; **in tödlicher A.,** in an agony of fear; in mortal fear; **aus A. vor . . . ,** for fear of . . . ; **aus A., daß . . . ,** for fear that . . . ; **A. bekommen, in A. geraten,** to get frightened, alarmed, scared, to take fright, alarm, *F:* to get the wind up; **A. vor j-m, etwas, haben,** to be afraid, frightened, of s.o., sth.; to be, stand, in fear of s.o., sth.; **große A. vor j-m, etwas, haben,** to dread s.o., sth., to be, stand, in dread of s.o., sth.; to be terrified of s.o., sth.; **A. um j-n, etwas, haben,** to be anxious, worried, concerned, about s.o., sth.; to be nervous on s.o.'s account; to fear for s.o., sth.; **in tausend Ängsten sein, schweben,** to be very, terribly, worried; **j-n in A. versetzen,** to alarm, scare, s.o.; to give s.o. a fright, a scare; **A. (davor) haben, etwas zu tun,** (i) to be afraid, frightened, scared, to do sth.; (ii) to be afraid of doing sth.; **es mit der A. zu tun bekommen,** *F:* **kriegen,** to become, get, scared, *F:* to get the wind up; **ich habe keine A. vor dir, vor ihm,** I'm not afraid, scared, of you, of him; **(nur) keine A.,** (i) don't be afraid; don't be alarmed, scared; don't worry; (ii) *Iron:* no fear; don't (you) worry.

II. **angst,** *inv. a.* **j-m a. machen,** to frighten s.o.; to alarm, scare, s.o.; *F:* to put the wind up s.o.; **mir ist a.,** I am frightened, scared, afraid (**vor**+*dat.*, of); I am anxious, worried, concerned (**um,** about); **ihm war, wurde, a. und bange,** he was, he got, really alarmed, scared; *F:* he really got, he really had got, the wind up; **der Gedanke an die Operation macht mir a.,** the thought of the operation frightens, scares, me, I'm frightened, scared, at the thought of the operation.

angstbeklommen, *a.* weighed down by anxiety; oppressed by fears; fearful.

ängsten, *v.tr.*=**ängstigen.**

Angster[1], *m.* -s/-, glass drinking-vessel with a narrow twisted neck.

Angster[2], *m.* -s/-. *Num: A:* (*Swiss copper coin*) angster.

angsterfüllt, *a.* full of anxiety; full of fear(s); fearful.

Ängsterling, *m.* -s/-e =**Angsthase.**

Angstgefühl, *n.* (feeling of) anxiety, distress; *Med:* sense of oppression.

Angstgeschrei, *n.* cry, cries, of alarm, of terror.

Angsthase, *m. F:* funk, coward.

ängstig, *a. A:*=**ängstlich.**

ängstigen, *v.tr.* (i) to frighten (s.o.); to alarm, scare (s.o.); (ii) to worry (s.o.); to cause (s.o.) worry; **sich ä.,** (i) to be frightened, afraid, scared (**vor j-m, etwas** *dat.*, of s.o., sth.); (ii) to worry, to be worried (**um j-n, etwas,** about s.o., sth.); **sich zu Tode ä.,** (i) to be frightened, scared, to death; (ii) to worry oneself, to be worried, to death.

Angstklausel, *f. Fin: Jur:* 'without recourse' clause (on bill of exchange).

ängstlich, *a.* (*a*) easily frightened (pers., etc.); (pers., etc.) of a nervous disposition; timid (child, etc.); anxious (mother, look, etc.); frightened, scared (look, etc.); **ä. sein,** (i) to be easily frightened; to be nervous; to be timid; (ii) to be afraid, frightened, scared; (iii) to be worried, to worry (**um j-n, etwas,** about s.o., sth.); **ihm wurde ä. zumute,** he grew frightened, scared; he began to feel uneasy; **wenn die Kinder allein zu Hause sind, bin ich ä.,** I worry, I get worried, when the children are alone in the house; **nur nicht so ä.!** don't be afraid, frightened, scared! **seine Eltern wachten über ihn mit ängstlicher Sorge,** his parents watched over him with anxious care; *adv.* **er war ä. besorgt um die Gesundheit seiner Frau,** he was most solicitous for his wife's health; (*b*) worrying (situation, etc.); (*c*) scrupulous, meticulous (care, accuracy, etc.); **mit etwas ä. sein,** to be scrupulous about (paying one's bills, etc.); to be fussy about (one's car, camera, etc.); **er borgt gern, aber mit dem Zurückzahlen ist er nicht so ä.,** he's quick enough to borrow but he's not so anxious to repay; **mit dem Bezahlen ist es nicht so ä,** there's no great hurry about paying; *adv.* **ein ä. gehütetes Geheimnis,** an anxiously guarded secret; **ä. bemüht sein, etwas zu tun,** to be anxious to do sth.; to be at great pains to do sth.

Ängstlichkeit, *f.* (*a*) (i) nervous disposition; timidity; (ii) anxiety; (iii) uneasiness; (*b*) scrupulousness, meticulousness.

Ängstling, *m.* -s/-e =**Angsthase.**

Angstmann, *m.* -(e)s/-männer. *F:* hangman, executioner.

Angstmeier, *m. F:*=**Angsthase.**

Angstneurose, *f. Psy:* anxiety neurosis.

Angströhre, *f. F:* top hat, silk hat, *F:* topper, high hat, chimney-pot hat, stove-pipe hat.

Ångströmeinheit [ˈɔŋstrøːm-], *f. Ph:* Angström unit.

Angstruf, Angstschrei, *m.* cry of alarm, of terror.

Angstschweiß, *m.* cold sweat.

Angsttraum, *m.* bad dream, nightmare.

angstvoll, *a.* anxious, fearful; (voice, etc.) full of anxiety; *adv.* anxiously, fearfully; with anxiety; with trepidation.

angstzitternd, *a.* shaking, quaking, with fear, *F:* shaking in one's shoes.

Angstzustand, *m. Psy:* anxiety state.

angucken, *v.tr. sep.* (*a*) to look at (s.o., sth.); (*b*) to peep at (s.o., sth.); to cast a (sidelong) glance at (s.o., sth.); to eye (s.o.).

Anguillulide [aŋgviluˈliːdə], *f.* -/-n. *Ann:* anguillule.

angular [aŋguˈlaːr], *a.* angular.

angurten, *v.tr. sep.* **1.** *Harn:* to girth (on) (saddle, etc.). **2.**=**angürten.**

angürten, *v.tr. sep.* to gird on, buckle on (sword, etc.).

Anguß, *m.* **1.** (*a*) pouring on (of liquid); watering, moistening; (*b*) *Metall:* pouring, running (of metal); *cp.* **angießen. 2.** *Metall:* deadhead (of casting); sullage piece, (feed-)head, sprue, runner; *Print:* jet, sprue (of cast type). **3.** *Cer:* (*a*) coating with slip; (*b*) slip.

Angußfarbe, *f. Cer:* coloured slip.

anhaben, *v.tr. sep.* (*conj. like* **haben**) **1.** (*a*) to have on, to be wearing (garment, shoes, hat, etc.); **sie hatte ein neues Kleid an,** she had on, was wearing, a new dress; **er hatte die Schuhe schon an,** he already had his shoes on; (*b*) **sie hatten die Heizung, alle Lichter, an,** they had the heating, all the lights, on. **2. j-m etwas a. können,** to be able to affect, damage, harm, s.o.; **das kann mir nichts a.,** that can't affect, hurt, me; **er kann mir nichts a.,** he can't harm me, can't do anything to me; *U.S. & F:* he's got nothing on me; **man kann ihm nichts a.,** there's no (way of) getting at him.

anhacken, *v.sep.* **1.** *v.tr.* to hack at (sth.); (*of bird*) to peck at (sth.). **2.** *v.i.* (*haben*) *Dial:*=**anhaften 1.**

anhaften. I. *v.i. sep.* (*haben*) **1.** to adhere, stick, cling (*dat.*, to); **anhaftender Schmutz,** adhering, clinging, dirt. **2.** (*a*) to attach (*dat.*, to); **ihm haftet keine Schuld an,** no blame attaches to him; (*b*) to be inherent (*dat.*, in); **die Mängel, die unserem Erziehungssystem anhaften,** the inherent shortcomings of our educational system; **anhaftende Schwäche,** inherent weakness.

II. *vbl s.* **Anhaften,** *n. in vbl senses; also:* adhesion.

anhägern (sich), *v.refl. sep. North G.Dial:* (*of sand in estuary, etc.*) to bank up, form banks; **Anhägerung** *f,* sandbank.

anhäkeln, *v.tr. sep.* **1.** to crochet (sth.) on. **2.** to hook, hitch, (sth.) on.

anhaken, *v.tr. sep.* **1.** (*a*) to hook, hitch, (sth.) on (**an**+*acc.*, to); to fasten sth. by means of a hook; *Tp:* **den Hörer a.,** to replace, hang up, the receiver; (*b*) to hook (floating object, etc.); *Nau: A:* **ein Schiff a.,** to grapple with a ship; (*c*) *v.i.* (*haben*) *F:* to get off (with a girl). **2.** to tick (off), *U.S:* check (off), to mark with a tick, *U.S:* check; to put a tick, *U.S:* check (mark), against (name, etc.).

anhalftern, *v.tr. sep.* to halter (up) (a horse).

Anhall, *m. Ac:* build-up of sound.

Anhalldauer, *f. Ac:* duration of the build-up of sound.

Anhalt[1], *m.* **1.** (*a*) support, prop, stay; (*b*) hold (for hand *or* foot); **einen A. finden, gewinnen,** to get a foothold, to gain a footing. **2.** datum-point; guiding point, guide (**für,** for); support (for a line of thought, etc.); **er hat keinen A. für diese Behauptung,** he has no supporting evidence for this assertion; **einen A. für eine Erklärung gewähren,** to offer a clue to an explanation. **3.** *Rail: etc:* (*a*) stop; (*b*) stopping-place, stop, halt; *Nau:* place of call.

Anhalt[2]. *Pr.n.n.* -s. *Geog:* Anhalt; *Hum:* **er ist aus A.,** he is close-fisted.

Anhaltelager, *n. Austrian:* detention camp; concentration camp.

anhalten, *v.sep.* (*strong*) I. *v.tr.* **1. etwas an etwas** *acc.* **a.,** to hold sth. up against sth.; **sich an etwas** *acc. or dat.*, **an j-n, a.,** to hold fast to sth.; to hold on to s.o., sth. **2. j-n zu etwas a.,** to get s.o. into the way of doing sth.; to oblige, constrain, s.o. to be, to do, sth.; **j-n zur Arbeit a.,** to urge s.o. (on) to work; **j-n zum, zu, Gehorsam, zur Pflicht, a.,** to urge s.o. to be obedient, dutiful; to keep s.o. to his duty. **3.** *Mus:* **einen Ton a.,** to hold, sustain, dwell on, a note; *adv.* **anhaltend,** *sostenuto.* **4.** to stop (s.o., sth.); to bring (train, etc.) to a standstill; to halt (train, etc.); to hinder, impede; to detain; to delay; to hold (s.o.) up; to arrest (criminal); **ein Pferd a.,** to stop, pull up, hold in, a horse; **den Verkehr a.,** to stop, hold up, block, the traffic; **eine Maschine a.,** to stop a machine; to put a machine out of action; **eine Uhr a.,** to stop a clock, a watch; **die Arbeit a.,** to stop, interrupt, work; **den Atem a.,** to hold one's breath; **mit angehaltenem Atem,** with bated breath, hardly daring to breathe; *Adm:* **Waren a.,** to hold up goods; to seize goods; *Med:* (*of food, medicine*) **(den Stuhlgang) anhaltend,** binding. **5. j-n um etwas a.,** (i)=**bei j-m um etwas a.,** *q.v. under* II. 3; (ii) to ask s.o. (repeatedly, insistently) for sth.

II. **anhalten,** *v.i.* (*haben*) **1.** to stop, to come to a stop, to a standstill; (*of vehicle, horseman, cyclist*) to pull up; **der Wagen hielt vor meiner Tür an,** the car stopped, pulled up, drew up, at my door; (*of driver*) **mit dem Wagen a.,** to pull up; *Nau:* **an einem Hafen a.,** to call at a port. **2.** to last, endure, continue, persist; (*of weather*) to hold; **wenn der Regen anhält,** if it keeps on raining, if the rain continues; **das Fieber hält an,** the fever continues, pursues its course. **3. bei j-m um etwas a.,** to apply to s.o. for sth.; to solicit s.o. for sth., sth. from s.o.; **um eine Stelle a.,** to apply for a post; **um ein Mädchen, um die Hand eines Mädchens, a.,** to ask for a girl's hand in marriage, to sue for a girl's hand.

III. *vbl s.* **Anhalten,** *n. in vbl senses; also:* **1.** stop; stoppage. **2.** continuance; persistence, persistency. **3. A. um eine Stelle,** application, candidature, for a post; **A. um ein Mädchen,** request for a girl's hand in marriage.

IV. *pr.p. & a.* **anhaltend,** *in vbl senses; esp.* (*a*) continuous, unbroken, uninterrupted, un-

ceasing, ceaseless, unintermitting, constant; continual; persistent; sustained, continued (interest, attack, etc.); unremitting (attention, efforts, rain, etc.); **anhaltender Beifall,** prolonged, sustained, applause; *adv.* continuously, continually, uninterruptedly, without interruption, ceaselessly, constantly; persistently; unintermittingly; (*b*) persevering; dogged (effort, etc.); *adv.* perseveringly; doggedly.

Anhalteort, *m.*=**Anhaltepunkt** 1.

Anhaltepunkt, *m.* **1.** *Rail: etc:* stopping-place, stop, halt; *Nau:* place of call. **2.** point of support. **3.** *Surv: etc:* datum-point, reference point. **4.** *Mus:* fermata.

Anhalter[1], *m. Tchn:* arresting device, stopping device, stop, *Mec.E:* detent.

Anhalter[2], *m. F:* **1.** hitch-hiker. **2.** (*usu. in the phr.*) **per A. fahren,** to hitch-hike.

Anhalter[3]. **1.** *m.* **-s/-.** *Geog: Hist:* native, inhabitant, of Anhalt. **2.** *inv.a.* (*a*) of Anhalt, Anhalt . . . ; (*b*) **der A. Bahnhof,** the Anhalter (railway-)station (in Berlin).

Anhalterzeichen, *n. Aut: F:* sign indicating that one wants a lift; **das A. geben,** to signal for a lift; to (try to) thumb a lift, *U.S:* a ride.

Anhaltestelle, *f.*=**Anhaltepunkt** 1.

Anhaltestift, *m. Mec.E:* stop-pin; stop-bolt; detent-pin.

Anhaltevorrichtung, *f.*=**Anhalter**[1].

Anhalteweg, *m. Aut: etc:* overall stopping distance.

Anhaltiner [anhal'tiːnər], *m.* **-s/-**=**Anhalter**[3] 1.

anhaltinisch [anhal'tiːniʃ], **anhaltisch** ['anhaltiʃ], *a. Geog: Hist:* of Anhalt.

Anhaltspunkt, *m.* **1.** guiding point, guide; guiding principle (for comprehension, action); clue (**für,** to); **einen A. für eine Erklärung gewähren,** to offer a clue to an explanation; **j-m einen A. geben,** to give s.o. a clue, a lead, to give s.o. something to go on; **der einzige A.,** the only thing to go by, (up)on; **ich habe keinerlei Anhaltspunkte,** I have nothing to go by. **2.**=**Anhaltepunkt** 3.

Anhaltswert, *m.* value, figure, used as a rough basis for calculation; approximate value, figure.

anhand [an'hant], *prep.*=**an Hand,** *q.v. under* **Hand** 3 (*a*).

Anhang, *m.* **1.** (*a*) appendage; *Anat:* apophysis; appendix; appendant, appendage, accessory part (of an organ); (*b*) supplement, appendix (to book, report, etc.); addition, addendum (to book, document); *Jur:* rider (to document, bill, etc.); schedule (to act); codicil (to will); *Com: Fin:* allonge, rider (to a bill of exchange); slip. **2.** (*a*) following; followers, adherents, supporters; **Idee, die A. gewinnt,** idea that is gaining adherents; (*b*) near relatives, *esp.* children; **Witwe ohne A.,** widow without (family) encumbrances.

Anhängeadresse, *f.* tie-on label, address-tag.

Anhängeetikett, *n.*=**Anhängezettel.**

anhangen, *v.i. sep.* (*strong*) *occ.*=**anhängen III.**

anhängen, *v.sep.* (*conj. like* **hängen**) **I.** *v.tr.* **1.** to hang (sth.) up; **den Hut, den Mantel, (am Haken) a.,** to hang up one's hat, one's coat; *Tp:* **(den Hörer) a.,** to replace, hang up, the receiver, *U.S: & F:* to hang up; to ring off. **2. j-m, sich** *dat.*, **eine Medaille a.,** to put, hang, a medal on s.o.'s, one's chest. **3.** *F:* **j-m etwas a.,** (*a*) to burden, saddle, s.o. with sth.; to inflict sth. on s.o.; *F:* to land s.o. with sth.; **einem Kunden alte Ladenhüter a.,** to fob off, palm off, unload, old stock on a client; **j-m eins a.,** to impose on s.o.; to play a trick on s.o.; *F:* to pull a fast one on s.o.; (*b*) to cast aspersions on s.o.; **er hat mir allerhand angehängt,** he has brought all sorts of accusations against me; **er hat mir immer etwas anzuhängen,** he is always finding fault with me; (*c*) *F:* **angehängt sein,** to be tied up (with work, domestic responsibilities, etc.). **4.** (*a*) to affix, attach, join (on), fasten; to annex, join, append, attach (document, etc.); to subjoin (list, etc.); to add (clause, etc.) (*dat.*, **an**+*acc.*, to); **ein Siegel an ein Dokument a.,** to affix, append, a seal to a document; **einen Zettel an ein Paket a.,** to tie a label on a parcel; **Nullen an eine Zahl a.,** to add (on) noughts, *U.S:* zeros, to a figure; (*b*) *Rail: Aut:* to couple (on) (coach, *U.S:* car, vehicle as trailer); *Rail:* **einen Wagen an den Zug a.,** to couple, hitch, a coach on to the train; **der Speisewagen wird in Köln angehängt,** the dining car comes on at Cologne; (*c*) *Mec.E:* **einen Maschinenteil an einen anderen a.,** to connect (up) two parts of a machine.

II. sich anhängen, (*a*) **sich an etwas** *acc.* **a.,** to fasten on to, cling to, sth.; to hang on to sth.; to adhere to sth.; (*b*) **sich an j-n a.,** (i) to attach oneself to s.o.; (ii) to foist, thrust, force, oneself upon s.o., *F:* to inflict oneself, one's company, on s.o.; to tack, tag, on to s.o.; (*c*) *Nau:* **sich an ein Schiff a.,** to hang on to a ship, to follow a ship closely.

III. anhängen, *occ.* **anhangen,** *v.i.* (*haben*) **1. (an) etwas** *dat.* **a.,** (*a*) to hang on (to) sth.; to be suspended from sth.; *Anat:* **anhängende Teile eines Organs,** appendages of an organ; *Com:* **das anhängende Muster,** the attached sample; (*b*) to be attached to sth.; to adhere, stick, cling, to sth.; **anhängend,** adherent, adhesive; (*c*) (*of pers.*) to adhere, cleave, hold (to opinion, etc.). **2. j-m, einer Partei, einer Philosophie, a.,** to be an adherent of s.o., a party, a philosophy; **einer Überzeugung a.,** to adhere to a conviction. **3.** *Nau:* (*of ship*) (i) to follow (another ship) closely; (ii) to be in tow.

IV. *vbl s.* **Anhängen,** *n. in vbl senses; also:* **1.** adherence, adhesion (**an etwas** *acc.*, to sth.). **2.** adherence, attachment (**an eine Partei, usw.,** to a party, etc.).

Anhänger, *m.* **1.** adherent, supporter, partisan (of a party, etc.); disciple (of s.o., of a sect); follower (of s.o., of a custom, etc.); advocate, upholder (of a custom, etc.); *Pol:* backer, henchman; **zahlreiche Anhänger haben,** to have a numerous following. **2.** *Veh:* trailer (*behind car, tram-car, etc.*). **3.** pendant (of necklace, etc.); trinket, *esp.* watch-trinket. **4.**=**Anhängeschildchen, Anhängezettel.** **5.** *Hort:* graft, scion, slip. **6.** (*a*) hanger; hook; (*b*) loop, hanger (on coat, etc.).

Anhängerschaft, *f.* following; followers, adherents, disciples.

Anhängeschildchen, *n.* tag.

Anhängeschloß, *n.* padlock.

Anhängesilbe, *f. Ling:* suffix.

Anhängewagen, *m.*=**Anhänger** 2.

Anhängewort, *n. Gram:* enclitic.

Anhängezettel, *m.* tie-on label; tag.

anhängig, *a.* **1.** *A:* (*a*) attached, annexed; adherent; (*b*) dependent (**an**+*dat.*, on). **2.** *Jur:* (*of lawsuit*) pending, pendent; undecided; **einen Fall (vor Gericht) a. machen,** to begin legal proceedings; **eine Klage gegen j-n a. machen,** to take, institute, initiate, proceedings against s.o.; **der Fall wird bald a.,** proceedings will soon begin, be initiated.

anhänglich, *a.* devoted (friend, husband, etc.); staunch, loyal (friend, etc.); affectionate (pet); **an j-n a. sein,** to be attached, devoted, to s.o.

Anhänglichkeit, *f.* devotion, attachment; loyalty (**an j-n,** to s.o.).

Anhangsdrüse, *f. Anat:* appendicular gland.

Anhängsel, *n.* **1.** (*a*) appendage (*gen.*, to); accessory; adjunct; *Anat: Nat.Hist:* appendage; *Bot:* **kleines A.,** appendicle; (*b*) unimportant addition; passage, clause, tacked on (to document, etc.). **2.** *Jewel:*=**Anhänger** 3. **3.** *F:* **er ist ein bloßes A.,** he is a mere hanger-on (*of a party, etc.*); *F:* he doesn't really belong; **ein lästiges A.,** a tiresome encumbrance.

Anhangsgebilde, *n. Anat: Nat.Hist:* appendage.

Anhangskraft, *f.* adhesive force; power of adhesion.

Anhangsmuskel, *m. Anat:* suspensor(y) muscle.

anhangsweise, *adv.* as a supplement, by way of supplement; in an appendix *or* excursus.

Anhau, *m. For:* first cutting, first felling (of timber).

Anhauch, *m.* **1.** (light) breath. **2.** *Lit:* afflatus; inspiration. **3.** blur (of breath on mirror, etc.); thin film (of vapour, moisture); trace, tinge, (mere) suggestion (of colour, melancholy, etc.); delicate touch (of colour); **ein A. von Vanille,** just a suspicion of vanilla.

anhauchen, *v.tr. sep.* **1.** to breathe (up)on (s.o., sth.); **einen Spiegel a.,** to breathe upon a mirror; **die Finger a.,** to breathe, blow, on one's fingers. **2.** *Lit:* **von den Göttern angehaucht,** under the divine afflatus; inspired by the Gods. **3. angehauchte Farben,** extremely delicate colours; **rosig angehaucht,** of a delicate pink, delicately tinged with pink; **bläulich angehaucht,** with a slight tinge, a faint touch, a (mere) suggestion, of blue. **4.** *F:* **j-n a.,** to tell, tick, s.o. off; to blow s.o. up.

anhauen, *v.tr. sep.* (*conj. like* **hauen**) **1.** to start cutting, chopping (sth.); to start hewing (stone); *For:* **einen Forst a.,** to start cutting, felling, (timber in) a forest. **2.** *F:* **j-n a.,** to approach, make approaches, to s.o.; to accost s.o.; **j-n um zehn Mark a.,** to tap, touch, s.o. for ten marks.

anhäufeln, *v.tr. sep. Hort: Agr:* to earth up, ridge, hill (plants, *esp.* potatoes).

anhäufen. **I.** *v.tr. sep.* to accumulate, pile up, heap up; to bank (up) (stones, etc.); to stack (packing-cases, etc.); to increase (stocks, etc.); to amass (money); to hoard (money, etc.); to stockpile (supplies); to mass (troops, etc.); to agglomerate (particles, etc., *Ling:* words); to cluster (particles, etc., *Mth:* points); *Ph:* to aggregate; **sich a.,** to accumulate; to pile up; to gather (together, in masses); (*of crowds, etc.*) to collect; (*of troops, crowds, etc.*) to mass; (*of particles, etc., Ling: of words*) to agglomerate; (*of particles, Mth: of points*) to cluster; *Ph:* to aggregate; **anhäufend,** *Ling: etc:* agglomerative; **angehäuft,** accumulated; *Ling: etc:* agglomerated, agglomerate.

II. *vbl s.* **1. Anhäufen,** *n. in vbl senses; also:* accumulation; agglomeration; aggregation. **2. Anhäufung,** *f.* (*a*)=II. 1; (*b*) accumulation; collection, heap, pile; hoard (of money, etc.); clutter (of furniture, etc.); agglomeration (of particles, words, etc.); cluster (of particles, *Mth:* of points); *Ph:* aggregation.

anheben, *v.sep.* (*strong*) **1.** *v.tr.* (*a*) to lift (sth.) (**an etwas** *acc.*, up to sth.); *Tchn:* to jack up (vehicle, etc.); (*b*) to raise (prices); (*c*) **eine Pumpe a.,** to start a pump going; to prime, fetch, a pump. **2.** *Lit:* to begin; (*a*) *v.tr.* **ein Lied a.,** to strike up a song; (*b*) *v.i.* (*haben*) to begin to speak; **der Redner hob an,** *A. & Lit:* **hub an, 'meine Freunde . . . ',** the speaker began, 'my friends . . . '; **zu singen a.,** to begin to sing; to strike up; to break into song.

Anhebevorrichtung, *f. Tchn:* lifting device; jack.

anhefteln, *v.tr. sep.* to pin (sth.) on.

anheften. **I.** *v.tr. sep.* **1.** to attach, affix, fix on, fasten; (i) to stick (sth.) on; (ii) to stitch, sew, (sth.) on; to tack on (piece of material, etc.); (iii) to pin (sth.) on; (iv) to clip (sth.) on (*dat. or* **an**+*acc.*, to); **eine Bekanntmachung a.,** to put up a notice; **angeheftet,** (*of coupons, etc.*) attached; *F:* **j-m etwas a.**=**j-m etwas anhängen,** *q.v. under* **anhängen** I. 3. **2.** (*a*) **sich etwas** *dat.*, **an etwas** *acc.*, **a.,** to stick, cling, adhere, to sth.; (*b*) *F:* **sich j-m, an j-n, a.,** to stick closely to s.o.; to cling to s.o.; to dog s.o.'s footsteps.

II. *vbl s.* **Anheften** *n.*, **Anheftung** *f. in vbl senses; also:* **1.** attachment (*esp. Nat.Hist:* of part, member). **2.** adherence.

anheilen, *v.sep.* **1.** *v.tr.* to heal (up) (wound); to knit (bones). **2.** *v.i.* (*sein*) (*of wound*) to heal up; (*of lips of wound*) to join, unite; (*of bones*) to knit.

anheim [an'haim], *adv. A:*=**heim**[2].

anheimeln, *v.tr. sep.* (*of atmosphere, house, etc.*) to make (s.o.) feel (as though he, she, were) at home; to give (s.o.) a sense of ease, of friendliness; **er fühlte sich dort angeheimelt,** he felt at home there; **anheimelnd,** homelike; friendly (town, room, atmosphere, etc.).

anheimfallen, *v.i. sep.* (*strong*) (*sein*) (*a*) **j-m a.,** (*of inheritance, etc.*) to devolve to, upon, s.o.; to fall to s.o.; (*b*) **etwas** *dat.* **a.,** to fall a prey to sth.; to be delivered over to sth.; **der Vergessenheit, der Vergangenheit, a.,** to fall into oblivion; **der Fürsorge a.,** to be reduced to (living on) charity.

anheimgeben, *v.tr. sep.* (*strong*)=**anheimstellen;** **das geben wir dem Schicksal anheim,** we'll leave that to Fate (to decide).

anheimstellen, *v.tr. sep.* **j-m die Sache a.,** to leave it to s.o.; **es j-m a., etwas zu tun,** to leave it to s.o., leave s.o., to do sth.; to rely on s.o. to do sth.; **ich stelle es Ihnen anheim, das Geld zu verteilen,** I leave it to you, leave you, to distribute the money; I put the distribution of the money entirely in your hands; **es ist Ihnen anheimgestellt, zu entscheiden,** the decision rests (entirely) with you; it is for you, up to you, to decide.

Anheirat, *f.* **(Verwandtschaft durch) A.,** relationship by marriage; affinity.

anheiraten, *v.tr. sep.* to acquire (relations, fortune, etc.) by marriage; *see also* **angeheiratet.**

anheischig, *pred. a.* (*only in the phr.*) **sich a. machen, etwas zu tun,** to engage, undertake, pledge one's word, bind oneself, to do sth.

anheizen, *v. sep.* **1.** *v.tr.* **einen Kessel, eine Lokomotive, a.,** to stoke up, fire up, a boiler, an engine; to raise steam; **den Ofen a.,** to set the stove going; to stoke up the furnace. **2.** *v.i.* (*haben*) (*in building*) to start up the heating.

anher [an'heːr], *adv. A:*=**her; bis a.**=**bisher.**

anhero [an'heːroː], *adv. A:*=**bisher.**

anherrschen, *v.tr. sep.* to shout at (s.o.) imperiously.

anhetzen, *v.tr. sep.* = **aufhetzen.**

anheuern, *v. sep. Nau:* **1.** *v.tr.* to sign on (seaman). **2.** *v.i.* (*haben*) (*of seaman*) to sign on.

anhexen, *v.tr. sep.* **j-m etwas a.,** to bring (illness, etc.) upon s.o. by witchcraft, by a spell; **wie angehext,** (i) as if by witchcraft; (ii) spellbound.

Anhidrose [anhiˑˈdroːzə], *f.* -/. *Med:* inadequate perspiration.

Anhieb, *m.* -(e)s/. (*a*) first blow, first stroke, first cut; **etwas auf (den ersten) A. tun,** to do sth. at the first attempt, first go (off), at the first go, at the first shot; (*b*) *For:* = **Anhau.**

anhimmeln, *v.tr. sep. F:* to gaze adoringly at (s.o.); to go into raptures over (s.o.); to gush over (s.o.).

Anhinga [anˈhiŋgaː], *f.* -/-s & -gen. *Orn:* darter.

Anhöhe, *f.* high ground, rise (of the ground), rising ground; elevation, eminence, height; hill; knoll, hillock, mound.

anholen, *v.tr. sep.* **1.** = **heranholen, herbeiholen.** **2.** to draw (cord) tight; *Nau:* to haul (rope, sail) taut, to tauten (rope, sail).

anhören. I. *v.tr. sep.* **1.** (*a*) to listen (patiently) to (s.o., sth.); to hear (witnesses, a sermon, etc.); (*b*) to listen, h(e)arken, to (s.o.); to attend to (s.o.); **hören Sie mich an!** listen to me! give me a hearing! attend to me! **j-n nicht a. wollen,** to refuse to listen to s.o., to turn a deaf ear to s.o.; **man wollte ihn nicht a.,** he was refused a hearing, they refused to hear him; (*c*) **sich** *dat.* **etwas a.,** to listen to sth.; **was hast du gestern getan? — ich habe mir ein Konzert angehört,** what did you do yesterday?—I listened to a concert; **hör dir bloß das Geschrei an!** just listen to the shouting! **es ist nicht anzuhören,** one can't bear to listen to it; it's intolerable. **2. seine Reden lassen sich a., hören sich gut an,** his speeches are (well) worth listening to; **das hört sich gut an in einer Rede,** that sounds well in a speech; **seine Worte hörten sich wie ein Versprechen an,** his words sounded like a promise. **3. man hört (es) ihm (an der Stimme) an, daß . . . ,** one can tell from his voice, from the way he speaks, that . . . ; **man hört ihm den Iren sofort an,** he's an Irishman—you can tell at once from his accent; **man hörte ihm die Erkältung an,** you could hear that he had a cold; **man hörte ihm die Enttäuschung gar nicht an,** his tone gave no hint of his disappointment.

II. *vbl s.* **Anhören** *n.*, **Anhörung** *f. in vbl senses; esp:* **1.** *Jur:* hearing (of witnesses); **nach A. der Zeugen,** after hearing the witnesses. **2. es ist nicht zum Anhören = es ist nicht anzuhören,** *q.v. under* I. 1.

Anhub, *m. Mec.E:* lift (of clack-valve, etc.).

Anhydrid [anhyˑˈdriːt], *n.* -(e)s/-e [-s, -ˈdriːdəs/-ˈdriːdə]. *Ch:* anhydride.

Anhydrie [anhyˑˈdriː], *f.* -/. *Ch:* anhydrous state.

anhydrisch [anˈhyːdriʃ], *a. Ch:* anhydrous.

anhydrisieren [anhyˑdriˑˈziːrən]. I. *v.tr. Ch: Ind:* to render (substance) anhydrous; to dehydrate.

II. *vbl s.* **Anhydrisieren** *n.*, **Anhydrisierung** *f.* anhydration, dehydration.

Anhydrisierungsmittel, *n. Ch: Ind:* dehydrating agent.

Anhydrit [anhyˑˈdriːt], *m.* -(e)s/. *Miner:* anhydrite.

Änigma [ɛˑˈnigmaː], *n.* -/-men & -mata [-maˑtaː], enigma, riddle.

änigmatisch [ɛnigˑˈmaːtiʃ], *a.* enigmatic(al).

anil[1] [aˈniːl], *a.* anile; imbecile.

Anil[2], *m.* -/. *Bot:* anil, indigo-plant.

Anilid [aˑniˑˈliːt], *n.* -(e)s/-e [-s, -ˈliːdəs/-ˈliːdə]. *Ch:* anilide, phenylamide.

Anilin [aˑniˑˈliːn], *n.* -s/. *Ch:* aniline, phenylamine.

Anilinfarben, *f.pl.* aniline dyes.

Anilinrot, *n.* aniline red; magenta.

Anilismus [aˑniˑˈlismus], *m.* -/. *Med:* anil(in)ism, aniline poisoning.

animalisch [aˑniˑˈmaːliʃ], *a.* **1.** animal (matter, etc.). **2.** animal, sensual, brutal (instinct, etc.).

animalisieren [aˑniˑmaˑliˑˈziːrən], *v.tr.* to animalize. **1.** *Physiol:* to convert (food) into animal matter. **2.** to sensualize, brutalize (passion, etc.).

Animalismus [aˑniˑmaˑˈlismus], *m.* -/. **1.** *Biol:* animalism. **2.** *Anthr:* zoolatry. **3.** sensualism.

Animalität [aˑniˑmaˑliˑˈtɛːt], *f.* -/. animality, animal nature.

Animierbankier [aˑniˑˈmiːrbaŋkĭˌeː], *m. F:* shady banker, shady financier.

Animierdame [aˑniˑˈmiːrˌdaːmə], *f. F:* partner, hostess (in dubious bar, night-club, etc.).

animieren [aˑniˑˈmiːrən], *v.tr.* (*a*) to animate, quicken; to endow with life; to give life to (s.o., sth.); (*b*) to liven (s.o.) up, brisk (s.o.) up; to excite (s.o.); to animate, quicken, enliven, liven up (conversation, etc.); to stir up (feelings); **animiert,** (i) (*of discussion*) animated, lively; (*of pers.*) in high spirits; (ii) *F:* (*of pers.*) slightly tipsy, *F:* slightly elevated.

Animierkneipe, *f.*, **Animierlokal,** *n. F:* bar, café, with hostesses; (dubious) night-club; *U.S. & F:* honky-tonk.

Animiermädchen, *n.* = **Animierdame.**

Animismus [aˑniˑˈmismus], *m.* -/. *Phil:* animism.

Animist [aˑniˑˈmist], *m.* -en/-en. *Phil:* animist.

animistisch [aˑniˑˈmistiʃ], *a. Phil:* animistic.

animos [aˑniˑˈmoːs], *a.* hostile; spiteful.

Animosität [aˑniˑmoˑziˑˈtɛːt], *f.* -/-en, animosity, animus, spite (**gegen,** against).

Animus [ˈaːniˑmus], *m.* -/. **1.** (*a*) mind; (*b*) intention. **2.** *F:* **einen A. (von etwas) haben,** to have an inkling, a (vague) suspicion (of sth.).

Anion [ˈanˀion], *n.* -s/-en [-iˀoːnən]. *El:* anion.

Anis [aˈniːs, ˈaːnis], *m.* -es/-e [-ˈniːzəs/-ˈniːzə]. **1.** *Bot:* anise. **2.** aniseed.

Anisaldehyd, *m. & n. Ch:* anisaldehyde.

Anisbaum, *m. Bot:* anise-tree.

Anischampignon, *m. Fung:* horse mushroom.

Anisett [aniˑˈzɛt], *m.* -s/-e, **Anisette** [aniˑˈzɛtə], *f.* -/-n, anisette (cordial).

Anisgeist, *m.* = **Anisette(e).**

Aniskuchen, *m. Cu:* aniseed cake.

Anislikör, *m.* = **Anisett(e).**

Anisöl, *n.* oil of anise, aniseed oil.

anisomer [anˀiˑzoˑˈmeːr], *a. Ch:* anisomeric.

anisometrisch [anˀiˑzoˑˈmeːtriʃ], *a. Geom: etc:* anisometric.

anisophyllisch [anˀiˑzoˑˈfyliʃ], *a. Bot:* anisophyllous.

anisosthen [anˀiˑzoˑˈsteːn], *a. Med:* anisosthenic.

anisotrop [anˀiˑzoˑˈtroːp], *a. Ph:* anisotropic.

Anisotropie [anˀiˑzoˑtroˑˈpiː], *f.* -/. *Ph:* anisotropy.

Anissamen, *m.* aniseed.

Anissäure, *f. Ch:* anisic acid.

Anisschnaps, *m.*, **Aniswasser,** *n.* = **Anisett(e).**

Anjagd, *f. Ven:* start of the hunt; (*with hounds*) throw-off.

anjagen, *v.sep.* **1.** *v.tr. Ven:* to start (stag, etc.). **2.** *v.i.* (*sein*) to rush up; **angejagt kommen,** to come rushing up; to come up (at) full tilt, (at) full pelt.

anjammern, *v.tr. sep.* to moan at (s.o.); to whine at (s.o.); *F:* to weep on (s.o.'s) shoulder.

anjetzt, anjetzo, *adv. A:* = **jetzt.**

anjochen, *v.tr. sep.* to yoke (oxen).

ankämpfen, *v.i. sep.* (*haben*) to struggle, contend, fight (**gegen j-n, etwas,** against, with, s.o., sth.); **gegen den Wind, den Brand, a.,** to battle with the wind, the fire; **gegen den Strom a.,** to battle with the current; to stem the tide; **gegen die Wellen a.,** to wrestle with the waves, to buffet (with) the waves; **gegen Schwierigkeiten a.,** to contend, wrestle, with difficulties; **gegen Müdigkeit a.,** to fight against weariness; **gegen einen Mißbrauch a.,** to make a stand against an abuse.

Ankauf, *m.* purchase. **1.** purchasing, buying; acquiring; acquisition (by purchase). **2.** thing bought; acquisition.

ankaufen. I. *v.tr. sep.* **1.** to purchase, buy, acquire (goods, house, plot of land, etc.). **2. er hat sich in Holstein angekauft,** he has bought himself a property, a house, in Holstein.

II. *vbl s.* **Ankaufen,** *n.* = **Ankauf** 1.

Ankäufer, *m.* purchaser, buyer, acquirer; *Jur:* vendee.

Ankaufspreis, *m.* purchase price.

Ankaufssumme, *f.* purchase-money.

Ankaufszettel, *m. Com:* purchase-note.

Anke[1], *m.* -n/. *Swiss Dial:* butter.

Anke[2], *m.* -n/-n. *Dial: Ich:* salmon-trout.

Anke[3], *f.* -/-n. *South G.Dial:* **1.** rowing-boat, skiff. **2.** *Metalw:* (*in swaging*) sheet of metal with round depressions; swage-block. **3.** = **Ankel.**

ankehren, *v.sep. Swiss Dial:* **1.** *v.tr.* = **anwenden** I. (*b*). **2.** *v.i.* (*sein*) = **einkehren** (*a*).

ankehrig, *a. Swiss Dial:* clever, deft, skilful.

ankeifen, *v.tr. sep.* to nag, rail, at (s.o.); to scold, chide (s.o.).

ankeilen, *v.tr. sep.* **1.** *Mec.E:* to wedge, key, cotter (crank to shaft, etc.). **2.** *F:* **j-n a.,** to approach, make approaches to, s.o.

Ankel, *m.* -s/-n. *Dial:* ankle(-bone); knuckle.

Anken[1], *m.* -/. *Swiss Dial:* = **Anke**[1].

anken[2], *v.tr. Swiss Dial:* to butter.

anken[3], *v.i.* (*haben*) *Dial:* to complain; to moan, groan.

Ankenblume, *f. Swiss Dial:* marsh-marigold.

ankennen, *v.tr. sep.* (*conj. like* **kennen**) *Dial:* **j-m das schlechte Gewissen, usw., a.,** to see from s.o.'s appearance that he has a bad conscience, etc.

Anker, *m.* -s/-. **1.** *Nau:* anchor; **erster A., zweiter A.,** best bower, second bower; **den A. (aus)werfen, den A. fallen lassen,** to let go, drop, the anchor; **vor A. gehen, zu A. gehen, das Schiff vor A. legen,** to cast, drop, anchor; to anchor; to moor; **ein Schiff vor A. legen,** to anchor, moor, a ship; **vor A. liegen,** to lie, ride, at anchor; **bequem vor A. liegen,** to ride easy; **der A. ist auf und nieder,** the anchor is apeak, is up and down; *Nau: Her:* **unklarer A.,** foul anchor. **2.** *Constr: etc:* anchor-tie, anchor-iron, anchor; cramp-iron, tie, tie-plate (of wall, furnace, etc.); brace, stay (of pole, boiler, etc.); *Mec.E: etc:* tie-bolt; tie-rod. **3.** *Clockm:* pallet. **4.** *El:* keeper (of horseshoe magnet); armature (of magneto, dynamo); rotor (of dynamo); *see also* **Stabwicklung, Trommelwicklung.** **5.** *Meas: A:* anker (*approx. 8 gallons*).

Ankerbalken, *m. Nau:* cathead.

Ankerbandage, *f. El.E:* armature binding.

ankerben, *v.tr. sep.* **1.** to notch, nick (stick, etc.). **2.** to notch (sth.) up (on a tally); *F:* **das werde ich dir a.!** I'll remember that! I'll chalk that up against you!

Ankerblech, *n. El.E:* armature stamping.

Ankerbohrung, *f. El.E:* armature gap.

Ankerboje, *f. Nau:* anchor-buoy.

Ankerbolzen, *m. Constr: etc:* tie-bolt, tie-rod, truss-rod; *Mec.E:* stay, brace, stay-rod.

Ankerbüchse, *f. El.E:* armature spider.

Ankerdeck, *n. Nau:* anchor-deck.

Ankerdraht, *m.* stay-wire.

Ankeregge, *f. Nau:* grapnel, hook, grappling-anchor.

Ankereisen, *n.* **1.** *Nau:* grappling-iron, grapnel. **2.** *El:* = **Ankerkern.**

Ankerfeld, *n. El:* armature field.

ankerfest, *a. Nau:* (*of ship*) (safely) anchored, at anchor.

Ankerfliege, *f.* = **Ankerflügel.**

Ankerflott, *n. Nau:* = **Ankerboje.**

Ankerflügel, *m. Nau:* fluke, palm, of an anchor.

Ankergang, *m. Clockm:* = **Ankerhemmung.**

Ankergebühren, *f.pl.*, **Ankergeld,** *n. Nau:* anchorage dues.

Ankergeschirr, *n. Nau:* ground-tackle.

Ankergrund, *m. Nau:* anchorage, anchoring-ground.

Ankerhaken, *m.* **1.** *Civ.E: etc:* holdfast; guy-hook. **2.** *Nau:* (= **Katthaken**) cat-hook.

Ankerhals, *m. Nau:* throat *or* trend of an anchor.

Ankerhand, *f.* = **Ankerflügel.**

Ankerhelm, *m.* = **Ankerrute.**

Ankerhemmung, *f. Clockm:* lever escapement; **A. in gerader Linie,** straight-line lever escapement; **A. mit Rechen und Trieb,** rack lever escapement.

Ankerit [aŋkəˈriːt], *m.* -(e)s/. *Miner:* ankerite.

Ankerkatt, *f. Nau:* cat(-tackle, -purchase).

Ankerkern, *m. El:* armature core.

Ankerkette, *f. Nau:* cable; *see also* **schlippen.**

Ankerklaue, *f. Clockm:* pad; pallet.

Ankerkloben, *m. Clockm:* pallet cock.

Ankerklotz, *m. Civ.E: etc:* stay-block.

Ankerklüse, *f. Nau:* hawse-hole, -pipe.

Ankerkörper, *m. El.E:* rotor (body); armature spider.

Ankerkreuz, *n.* **1.** *Nau:* crown of an anchor. **2.** *Her:* cross moline; cross sarcelly; **eingerolltes A.,** cross resarcelée, resarcelled.

Ankerlicht, *n. Nau:* anchor-light, riding-light.

ankerlos, *a. Nau:* (*of ship*) adrift.

Ankermast, *m. Aer:* mooring mast.

Ankermine, *f. Navy:* moored mine.

Ankermöglichkeit, *f. Nau:* possible, available, anchorage.

Ankermutter, *f. Mec.E:* stay-nut; stay-bolt nut (of boiler, etc.).

ankern. I. *v.* **1.** *v.tr.* (*a*) *Nau: etc:* to anchor (ship, mine); to moor (ship, buoy, mine, airship); (*b*) *Constr: etc:* to brace, stay, tie, anchor (chimney, engine, boiler, etc.). **2.** *v.i.* (*haben*) to anchor, cast anchor; to moor; **auf der Höhe von Cuxhaven, vor Cuxhaven, a.,** to anchor off Cuxhaven. **3.** *v.i.* (*haben*) *Dial:* **nach etwas a.,** to strive for sth.; to struggle for sth.

II. *vbl s.* **Ankern,** *n. in vbl senses; also: Nau:* **Achtung! klar zum A.!** stand by the anchor!

Ankernut, *f. El.E:* armature slot.

Ankerpalette, *f. Clockm:* pallet; pad.

Ankerpfahl, *m.* **1.** *Nau:* anchor-stake. **2.** *Civ.E. etc:* anchor-stake; anchor-pile; stay-block.

Ankerpflug, *m.* = **Ankerflügel.**

Ankerplatte, *f. Constr: Civ.E:* anchor-plate; tie-plate.

Ankerplatz, *m. Nau:* (anchoring) berth, anchorage; **es gibt einen sicheren A. in, zu . . . ,** there is a safe anchorage at . . . ; **den A. wechseln, verlegen,** to change anchorage; to shift berth; **den A. verfehlen,** to miss the anchorage.

Ankerring, *m. Nau:* anchor-ring.

Ankerrödel, *m. Mil: Civ.E:* anchoring lines (of temporary bridge).

Ankerrohr, *n.* stay-tube (of boiler).

Ankerröhrung, *f. Nau:* pudd(en)ing (of anchor-ring).

Ankerrute, *f.,* **Ankerschaft,** *m. Nau:* shank, shaft, of an anchor.

Ankerschäkel, *m. Nau:* anchor-shackle, Jew's-harp.

Ankerschaufel, *f. Nau:*=**Ankerflügel.**

Ankerscheibe, *f. Constr: Civ.E:* anchor-plate, -ring; tie-plate.

Ankerscheuer, *f. Nau:* bill-board.

Ankerschraube, *f.* (*a*) *Carp: etc:* coach-screw, lag-screw; (*b*) *Mec.E: etc:* foundation-bolt.

Ankerseil, *n.* **1.** anchor-rope (of small anchor). **2.** *Civ.E: etc:* stay-rope; stay-wire; anchor-stay (of mast, etc.).

Ankerspaten, *m. Nau:*=**Ankerflügel.**

Ankerspill, *n. Nau:* capstan, windlass, winch.

Ankerspitze, *f. Nau:* (anchor-)bill.

Ankerspule, *f. El.E:* armature coil.

Ankerstab, *m. El.E:* armature bar.

Ankerstange, *f. Her:* anchor shank.

Ankerstelle, *f.*=**Ankerplatz.**

Ankerstern, *m. El.E:* armature spider.

Ankerstock, *m. Nau: Her:* anchor-stock.

Ankerstocknuß, *f. Nau:* nut of an anchor-stock.

Ankerstocksplint, *m. Nau:* forelock of an anchor-stock.

Ankerstrom, *m. El:* armature current.

Ankertakel, *n. Nau:* fish-tackle.

Ankertau, *n. Nau:* **1.** *A:* (anchor) cable. **2.** (*a*) mooring-rope; (*b*) (=**Stromankertau**) warp.

Ankertonne, *f. Nau:* anchor-buoy.

Ankertrosse, *f.*=**Ankertau.**

Ankeruhr, *f. Clockm:* lever watch, watch with lever escapement.

Ankerwache, *f. Nau:* anchor-watch.

Ankerwelle, *f.* **1.** *El.E:* armature shaft. **2.** *Clockm:* pallet staff.

Ankerwicklung, *f. El.E:* armature winding.

Ankerwinde, *f.,* **Ankerwinsch,** *m.*=**Ankerspill.**

Ankerzahn, *m. El.E:* armature tooth.

Ankerzeichen, *n. Nau:* mooring buoy.

anketteln, *v.tr. sep.* **1.** to attach (sth.) by a small chain (**an**+*acc.*, to); to moor (boat) by a chain. **2.** *Needlew: etc:* to stitch (sth.) on (**an**+*acc.*, to).

anketten, *v.tr. sep.* to chain (**an etwas** *acc.*, to sth.); to chain up (dog).

ankeuchen, *v.i. sep.* (*usu. only in*) **angekeucht kommen,** to come panting along.

ankirren, *v.tr. sep.* to allure, entice, decoy, inveigle (animal, person).

ankitschen, *v.tr. F:* to chip (cup, plate, etc.).

ankitten, *v.tr. sep.* to cement (sth.) on; to fix (sth.) on with putty (**an**+*acc.*, to).

ankläffen, *v.tr. sep.* (*of dog, F: of pers.*) to yap at s.o.

anklagbar, *a.* (*of pers.*) accusable; chargeable; impeachable; *Jur:* prosecutable; (*of pers., act*) indictable; (*of act, remark, etc.*) actionable.

Anklage, *f.* **1.** accusation, charge; inculpation; *Parl:* arraignment; impeachment; **A. gegen j-n erheben,** to raise, bring, an accusation against s.o.; **A. gegen j-n wegen etwas erheben,** to charge, tax, s.o. with sth.; **A. gegen j-n erheben, etwas getan zu haben,** to charge, tax, s.o. with doing sth. **2.** *Jur:* accusation, charge, indictment; **A. wegen Diebstahls,** indictment for theft, on a charge of theft; prosecution for theft; **j-n unter A. wegen Mordes stellen,** to charge s.o. with murder; to arraign, indict, s.o. for murder; to bring s.o. to trial for murder; **unter A. wegen Mordes stehen,** to stand accused of murder, to be charged with murder, to be on trial for murder; (*of barrister*) **die A. vertreten,** to prosecute; **Vertreter der A.,** counsel for the prosecution, prosecuting counsel; **als Vertreter der A. sagte Dr. X . . . ,** for the prosecution Dr X said . . . ; *see also* **vorbringen.**

Anklageakte, *f.*=**Anklageschrift.**

Anklagebank, *f. Jur:* dock; **auf der A. sitzen,** to be in the dock.

Anklageerhebung, *f. Jur:* indictment, action of indicting (s.o.).

Anklagejury, *f. Jur:* (*English*) Grand Jury.

Anklagemonopol, *n. Jur:* sole right of the State to institute criminal proceedings.

anklagen, *v.tr. sep.* **1.** to accuse, inculpate (s.o.); **j-n wegen etwas a., j-n etwas** *gen.* **a.,** to accuse s.o. of sth.; to indict s.o. for sth.; to charge, tax, s.o. with sth.; **j-n des, wegen, Hochverrats a.,** to accuse s.o. of, *Parl:* to arraign, impeach, s.o. for, high treason; **j-n a., etwas getan zu haben,** to charge, tax, s.o. with doing sth.; **anklagend,** accusing, accusatory; *adv.* accusingly. **2.** *Jur:* (*a*) to indict (s.o.) (**wegen** *or gen.,* for); to charge (s.o.) (**wegen** *or gen.,* with); to arraign (s.o.) (**wegen** *or gen.,* for); to prosecute (s.o.) (**wegen** *or gen.,* for); **j-n wegen schwerer tätlicher Beleidigung a., j-n a., einen Diebstahl begangen zu haben,** to charge s.o. with assault and battery, with committing a theft; **j-n des Mordes an seiner Frau a.,** to charge s.o. with, indict s.o. for, the murder of his wife; *see also* **Angeklagte;** (*b*) **j-n bei der Polizei a.,** to report, denounce, s.o. to the police.

Anklagepunkte, *m.pl. Jur:* counts of an indictment; heads of a charge.

Ankläger, *m.* **1.** (*a*) accuser, *Parl:* impeacher, arraigner; (*b*) *Jur:* prosecutor, indicter; **der öffentliche A.,** the Public Prosecutor; (*c*) *Jur:* plaintiff, complainant. **2.** informer, denouncer.

Anklagerede, *f.* accusatory oration; *Jur:* speech for the prosecution, prosecuting counsel's speech.

anklägerisch, *a.* accusatory, accusing.

Anklageschrift, *f. Jur:* indictment; bill of indictment; *Mil:* charge-sheet.

Anklagestück, *n. Th:* accusatory drama; drama directed against an abuse.

Anklagevertreter, *m. Jur:* counsel for the prosecution, prosecuting counsel.

Anklagezustand, *m. Jur:* **j-n in A. versetzen,** to arraign s.o., to commit s.o. for trial.

anklammern, *v.tr. sep.* **1.** to clip (sth.) on (**an**+*acc.*, to). **2.** **sich an etwas** *acc.*, **an j-n, a.,** to fasten on to, clutch, sth., s.o.; to cling (on) to, hold on to, hang on to, keep tight hold of, sth., s.o.; *F:* to latch on to sth., s.o.; **sich an eine Hoffnung a.,** to cling to a hope.

Anklammerungspunkt, *m.* **1.** point where sth. is clipped on. **2.** point to which one clings; *Mil:* strong point.

Anklang, *m.* **1.** *Mus:* accord. **2.** echo, reminiscence (**an**+*acc.*, of); **in diesem Werk findet man viele Anklänge an Goethe,** in this work one notices many echoes of Goethe. **3.** *Pros:* (*a*) alliteration; (*b*) assonance. **4.** (**bei j-m**) **A. finden,** (*of ideas, work, etc.*) to be sympathetically received (by s.o.); to find favour (with s.o.); **dieser Roman findet bei den Engländern keinen A.,** this novel has no appeal for the English, does not appeal to the English imagination, stirs no chord in the English mind; *Com:* **Artikel, die bei den Damen A. finden,** articles that appeal to, find favour with, the ladies.

anklatschen, *v.sep.* **1.** *v.tr.* to slap on (paint, grease, etc.). **2.** *v.i.* (*a*) (*haben*) (*of waves*) **am, ans, Ufer a.,** to lap against the shore; (*b*) (*sein*) (*of garment, etc.*) to cling (damply) (**an**+*dat.*, to); **angeklatschte Haare,** sleek hair; **angeklatschtes Badekostüm,** bathing-costume that clings to the figure. **3.** *v.tr. Sch: F:* **j-n a.,** to sneak, *F:* snitch, *U.S:* tattle, on s.o.

ankleben, **I.** *v.sep.* **1.** *v.tr.* to stick (sth.) on; to paste, glue, gum (sth.) on (**an**+*acc.*, to); *Ch: etc:* to agglutinate; **ein Plakat an eine Wand a.,** to stick a bill on a wall; to paste up, post up, a bill; *F:* **sich an j-n a.,** to cling to s.o.; to hang around s.o. (continually); to stick to s.o. (like a limpet, like a leech). **2.** *v.i.* (*haben, sein*) to stick, adhere, cling (**an**+*acc.*, to); *Ch: etc:* to agglutinate; **anklebend,** adhesive; agglutinant, agglutinative. **II.** *vbl s.* **Ankleben,** *n. in vbl senses; also:* bill-posting, -sticking; **A. verboten!** stick, *U.S:* post, no bills!

Ankleber, *m.* (*pers.*) gluer; paster, *esp.* bill-sticker, billposter.

anklecksen, *v.tr. sep.* to daub, smear (surface, page, etc.); to splash, (be)spatter (s.o. with mud, page with ink, etc.).

Ankleidekabine, *f.* (*at baths*) cubicle; (*in shop*) fitting-room; trying-on room *or* cubicle.

Ankleidekabinett, *n. A:* dressing-room.

ankleiden, **I.** *v.tr. sep.* to dress, *Lit:* attire (s.o.); to clothe (s.o.); to robe (priest, etc.); **sich a.,** to dress (oneself), to put one's things on; to clothe oneself; *Lit:* to make one's toilet; (*of priest, judge, etc.*) to robe; **sie kleidet sich an,** she is dressing; **sie ist noch nicht angekleidet,** she is, has, not yet dressed; **sich zum Abendessen a.,** to dress for dinner; **sich anders a.,** to dress differently; to put on different, other, clothes.

II. *vbl s.* **1. Ankleiden,** *n. in vbl senses; also:* **j-m beim A. helfen,** to help s.o. to dress. **2. Ankleidung,** *f.* (*a*) *in vbl senses;* (*b*) *A:* dress, attire, apparel, *Lit:* toilet.

Ankleidepuppe, *f.* (*a*) cut-out paper doll; (*b*) doll that can be dressed.

Ankleider, *m.,* **-s/-,** **Ankleiderin** *f.* **-/-innen.** *Th:* dresser.

Ankleideraum, *m.* dressing-room; changing-room (of sports pavilion, etc.); robing-room (of judges, etc.); *Th:* (artist's) dressing-room.

Ankleidespiegel, *m.* dressing mirror, full-length mirror; full-length dressing-table mirror; cheval-glass.

Ankleidezimmer, *n.*=**Ankleideraum.**

ankleistern, *v.tr. sep.* to paste, stick, (sth.) on (**an**+*acc.*, to).

anklemmen, *v.tr. sep.* **1. etwas an etwas** *acc.* **a.,** to jam, squeeze, sth. up against sth. **2. ein Stück, ein Rohr, an etwas** *acc.* **a.,** to clamp a piece, a pipe, on to sth.; to clip a tube on to sth.

anklingeln, *v.tr. sep.* **1.** *v.i.* (*haben*) (*a*) **bei j-m a.,** to ring at s.o.'s door, to ring s.o.'s door-bell; (*b*) *Tp:* to ring up. **2.** *v.tr. Tp:* to ring, *U.S:* call, (s.o.) up.

anklingen, *v.i. sep.* (*strong*) (*haben*) **1.** (*of sound*) to become audible. **2. mit den Gläsern a.,** *occ. v.tr.* **die Gläser a.,** to clink glasses. **3. an etwas** *acc.* **a.,** to sound like an echo of sth.; to remind one of sth.; to awaken, stir up, memories of sth.; **in diesem Gedicht klingt vieles an Schiller an,** there are many echoes of Schiller in this poem; much of this poem reminds one of Schiller; **dieses Lied läßt Erinnerungen aus alter Zeit a.,** this song calls up, awakens, memories of other days.

Anklingzeit, *f. Tp: Tg:* onset time (of audible signal).

anklopfen, *v.sep.* **1.** *v.tr.* to hammer (sth.) on. **2.** *v.tr. Med:* to sound (chest, etc.) by percussion; to percuss. **3.** *v.i.* (*haben*) (*a*) **an die Tür a.,** to knock, rap, at the door; **bei j-m a.,** to knock at s.o.'s door; *B:* **klopfet an, so wird euch aufgetan,** knock, and it shall be opened unto you; (*b*) *F:* (**wegen etwas**) **bei j-m a.,** to sound s.o. (about sth.); **wegen einer Anleihe bei j-m a.,** *F:* to try to tap, touch, s.o. (for a loan).

Anklopfer, *m.* door-knocker.

Anklopfmaschine, *f. Bootm:* pounder, knocker-up.

Anklopfring, *m.* ring door-knocker.

ankneifen, *v.tr. sep.* (*strong*) to squeeze (sth.) on (**an**+*acc.*, to).

ankneipen, *v.tr. sep.* **1.** *occ.*=**ankneifen.** **2.** (*only in p.p.*) **angekneipt,** slightly drunk, tipsy; (somewhat) fuddled, *F:* tiddly.

anknipsen, *v.tr. sep. El:* to switch on, turn on, put on (light, radio, etc.); to snap on (a switch, the light, etc.).

anknöpfbar, *a.* button-on (hood, etc.).

anknöpfen, *v.tr. sep.* to button (sth.) on (*dat.*, **an**+*acc.*, to); **die Kapuze wird an den Mantel angeknöpft, knöpft sich an den Mantel an,** the hood buttons on to the coat.

anknüpfen, **I.** *v.sep.* **1.** *v.tr.* (*a*) **etwas an etwas** *acc.*, **etwas etwas** *dat.*, **a.,** to fasten, tie, attach, sth. to sth.; to knot sth. to sth.; (*b*) **einen Satz an einen anderen, eine Frage an eine andere, a.,** to link up, connect, one clause, one question, with another; **anknüpfend,** connecting; *Gram:* conjunctional; (*c*) to begin, commence, start (conversation, relations, etc.); to initiate (relations, etc.); **ein Gespräch mit j-m a.,** to start, open, a conversation, to enter into conversation, with s.o.; to engage s.o. in conversation; **ein Gespräch wieder a.,** to resume, restart, a conversation, to carry on a conversation (where it was broken off); **eine Bekanntschaft mit j-m a.,** to strike up, form, an acquaintance with s.o.; **einen Briefwechsel mit j-m a.,** to open a correspondence, enter into correspondence, with s.o.; **den Briefwechsel mit j-m wieder a.,** to resume correspondence with s.o.; **Beziehungen zu j-m a.,** to enter into, establish, relations with s.o.; **die engen Beziehungen (zueinander), die wir angeknüpft haben,** the close relations that we have established (between us); **geschäftliche Verbindungen, Geschäfte, mit j-m a.,** to enter into business relations with s.o. **2.** *v.i.* (*haben*) (*a*) (*of pers.*) **mit j-m a.,** to enter into, establish, relations with s.o.; (*b*) (*of thg*) **an etwas** *acc.* **a.,** to be connected with sth.; to link on to, link up with, sth.; **diese Frage knüpft an eine andere an,** this question links up, is linked up, with another, depends on another; (*c*) (*of pers.*) to refer to sth.; **anknüpfend an die Worte des Redners sagte er . . . ,** taking up the remarks, the words,

of the speaker he said . . . ; **anknüpfend an unser Gespräch . . .**, referring to, with reference to, *Adm: Com:* further to, our conversation . . . ; (*d*) **an den Faden seiner Rede wieder a.**, to resume the thread of one's discourse.

II. *vbl s.* I. **Anknüpfen,** *n. in vbl senses; also:* connection. 2. **Anknüpfung,** *f.* (*a*)=II. 1; (*b*) connection, link; **in A. an . . .**, (i) referring to . . . , with reference to . . . ; (ii) following . . . ; *Gram:* **relative, relativische, A.**, relative connection.

Anknüpfungspunkt, *m.* **1.** point of contact; point of linkage; link; **es bestehen keine Anknüpfungspunkte zwischen ihnen,** they have no points of contact; they have no common interests. **2.** starting-point (of discourse, etc.).

anknurren, *v.tr. sep.* (*of dog, F: of pers.*) to growl, snarl, at (s.o.).

ankobern (sich), *v.refl. sep. Yiddish:* **sich mit j-m a.**=**sich mit j-m anbiedern,** *q.v. under* **anbiedern** I. 2.

ankochen, *v.tr. sep. Cu: etc:* to partly boil, parboil (meat, vegetables, etc.).

anködern, *v.tr. sep.* to decoy (fish, animal); to decoy (s.o.) (with promises, etc.); to lure (s.o.) on.

ankohlen, *v.tr. sep.* to char (sth.) partially, slightly; *F:* **j-n a.**, to tell s.o. a pack of lies.

ankommen. I. *v.i. sep.* (*strong*) (*sein*) **1.** (*of pers., vehicle, ship, letter, etc.*) to arrive (**in einem Ort,** at, in, a place); **zu Hause a.**, to arrive home, get (back) home; **er ist eben aus Paris angekommen,** he has just arrived, got here, from Paris; **ich erwarte, daß er morgen (hier, dort) a. wird,** I expect he'll arrive (here, there) tomorrow; **er wird voraussichtlich nächste Woche a.**, he is expected to arrive next week; **sobald er in Köln angekommen war,** as soon as he arrived at, in, reached, Cologne; **der Zug kommt um 7.30 in Zürich an,** the train arrives, is due, at Zürich at 7.30; **in London ankommende Züge, Fahrgäste,** trains, travellers, arriving in London; **ankommende Briefe,** incoming letters; *El.E:* **ankommende Leitungen,** incoming cables, *Tp:* incoming lines; *F:* **bei ihnen ist ein kleines Mädchen angekommen,** they've just had a baby girl. **2.**=**herankommen. 3.** (*a*) *F:* **man kann ihm gar nicht a.**, it's impossible to get at him; **damit kannst du mir nicht a.**, it's no use trying that on with me, that won't go down with me, that won't get you anywhere with me; (*b*) **(bei j-m) gut a.**, to be well received (by s.o.); to be successful (with s.o.); **übel a.**, to be ill received; **er kam übel an mit seiner Bitte,** his request was ill, not well, received; *Iron:* **da kam er (aber) schön an!** he got more than he bargained for; he met with a warm reception, found he had caught a Tartar; (*c*) **gegen j-n, etwas, nicht a. (können),** to be powerless against s.o., sth.; (*d*) **(bei einer Firma) a.**, to find employment; to be taken on, to get a job; **sie ist bei Kunz als Verkäuferin angekommen,** Kunz's have taken her on as a salesgirl; (*e*) *Com:* **(bei einem Geschäft) gut, schlecht, a.**, to make a profitable, unprofitable, deal. **4.** (*of play, piece of stage business, exhortation, etc.*) to have the desired effect on the audience, *F:* to get across, get over; to register; **diese Erklärung wird bei den Schülern nicht a.**, this explanation won't get home to, get across to, the pupils, won't register with the pupils; *Th:* **das Stück ist unten nicht angekommen,** the play failed to get across (the footlights); *Cin: Th:* **wird das auch unten a.?** will that get across (with the audience)? **5.** (*a*) **auf j-n, auf etwas** *acc.*, **a.**, to depend on s.o., sth; **es, das, kommt (ganz) auf Sie an,** that depends entirely on you; **es kommt nur auf die Zeit an,** it is merely a question of time, simply a matter of time; **es kommt darauf an, ob Sie es eilig haben oder nicht,** it depends on whether you are in a hurry or not; **es kommt (ganz) d(a)rauf an,** that depends, it all depends; (*b*) **es kommt darauf an zu . . .**, what matters is to . . . **es kommt darauf an, zu wissen, ob . . .**, the question is whether . . . ; **es kommt mir darauf an, zu . . .**, it is (a matter) of importance to me to . . . ; **darauf kommt es (nicht) an,** that's (not) the point; **als es darauf ankam,** when it came to the point; **es kommt auf die Minute an,** every minute counts; **ihm kommt es nur auf das Geld an,** money counts with him more than anything; **es kommt ihm nicht auf die Ausgaben an,** he doesn't mind the expense; **es kommt ihm mehr auf lange Ferien als auf hohes Gehalt an,** long holidays matter more to him than a high salary; **auf zwanzig Mark, auf ein paar Tage, soll es mir nicht a.**, twenty marks or so, a few days, will make no difference to me; **es kommt mir nicht so sehr darauf an,** I am not very particular, not over-particular, about it; **darauf soll es nicht a.**, never mind about that, that need be no obstacle; **er ist einer, dem es nicht darauf ankommt,** he is a happy-go-lucky fellow; (*c*) **es auf j-n, auf j-s Entscheidung, a. lassen,** to leave it to s.o. (to decide), to rely on s.o.; **es darauf, auf gut Glück, a. lassen,** to trust to luck, to chance; **ich lasse es darauf a.**, I'll chance it, risk it. **6.** *v.tr. & i.* (*sein*) (*of desire, emotion, etc.*) **j-n, j-m, a.**, to come to s.o.; to come over s.o., come upon s.o.; **was kommt dich, dir, an?** what's the matter with you? **was kommt ihn, ihm, an?** what has come over him? what's up with him now? **der Schlaf kam ihn, ihm, an,** sleep came upon him, sleepiness overcame him; **es kommt mich, mir, hart, schwer, sauer, an, zu . . .**, it comes hard on me to . . . , I find it a hard matter to . . . .

II. *vbl s.* **Ankommen,** *n. in vbl senses; also:* arrival. *Cp.* **Ankunft.**

Ankömmling, *m.* **-s/-e. 1.** (*a*) new-comer; new, recent, arrival; (*b*) *F:* new-born child; **der A.**, *F:* the new arrival, the little stranger. **2.** *Bot:* adventitious weed, casual weed. **3.** *Ch: Ind:* new product; novel product.

anköpfen, *v.tr. sep.* to put a head on (sth.); to head (pin, nail, etc.).

ankoppeln, *v.tr. sep.* **1.** *Ven:* to couple (hounds); *Husb:* to yoke (oxen). **2.** to couple (railway wagons, trailers, *El:* batteries, circuits, etc.); **Ankopplung** *f*, coupling.

ankören, *v.tr. sep.* to test *or* attest (cattle) (intended for breeding).

ankörnen, *v.tr. sep.* **1.** to decoy, lure, (birds) with seeds, with grain. **2.** *Metalw:* to mark (surface) with a centre-punch.

Ankörner, *m. Tls:* centre-punch.

ankrallen, *v.tr. sep.* **1.** (*of bird of prey, etc.*) to claw at (sth.); to seize (sth.) in its claws, *F:* to claw on to (sth.). **2.** *F:* (*of pers.*) **j-n a.**, to buttonhole s.o.; to accost s.o. **3. sich (verzweifelt) ankrallen,** to hang on, hold on (like grim death) (**an**+*acc.*, to).

ankränkeln, *v.tr. sep.* to enervate, weaken (person, character, etc.); **angekränkelt,** sickly, weakly; (*of style, etc.*) emasculated; *Lit:* **von des Gedankens Blässe angekränkelt,** sicklied o'er with the pale cast of thought.

ankratzen, *v.tr. sep. F:* **1. j-n a.**, to strike up an acquaintance with s.o. **2.** (*of woman*) **sich** *dat.* **einen Mann a.**, to catch a husband.

ankreiden, *v.tr. sep.* **1.** to chalk (sth.); to mark (line, etc.) with chalk; to write (sth.) up with chalk, to chalk (sth.) up. **2.** *F:* (*a*) **die Zeche a.**, to chalk up, score up, the drinks, to put the drinks on the slate; **seine Getränke, sein Essen, a. lassen,** to have one's drinks, one's meal, chalked up to one, put on the slate; to get one's drinks, one's meal, on tick; (*notice in bar*) **'hier wird nichts angekreidet'**, 'no credit given here', 'no tick'; (*b*) **diese Bemerkung wird er dir ankreiden,** he will score up that remark against you; **das werde ich ihm schon a.!** I won't forgive him that in a hurry!

Ankreis, *m. Mth:* escribed circle, excircle.

ankreischen, *v.tr. sep.* to screech at (s.o.).

Ankreismittelpunkt, *m. Mth:* centre of an escribed circle, excentre.

ankreuzen, *v.tr. sep.* to mark (items in a list, etc.) with a cross.

ankriechen, *v.sep.* (*strong*) **1.** *v.tr.* to creep, crawl, on to (sth.). **2.** *v.i.* (*only in p.p.*) **angekrochen kommen,** to creep up, crawl up; to come creeping, crawling, along.

ankriegen, *v.tr. sep. F:* to get on (one's shoes, etc.); **ich kann diese Schuhe nicht a.**, I can't get these shoes on.

ankündigen, *occ.* **ankünden.** I. *v.tr. sep.* **1.** (*a*) to announce (sth.), give notice of (sth.), to give (sth.) out; to make (sth.) known; to proclaim, declare, publish (sth.); *A:* to declare (war); (*b*) to advertise (sale, etc.); (*c*) **j-m etwas a.**, to notify s.o. of sth., to give s.o. notice of sth.; to inform, apprise, advise, s.o. of sth.; to make sth. known to s.o., to bring sth. to s.o.'s knowledge; to warn s.o. of sth.; to intimate sth. to s.o. **2.** to promise, foretell, forebode, portend, augur, herald; **alles kündigt Erfolg an,** everything points to, seems to promise, success; **Ereignis, das eine neue Epoche ankündigt,** event that heralds, ushers in, a new era; **ein Gewitter kündigte sich an,** a storm announced itself; **eine neue Epoche kündigt sich an,** a new epoch is heralded.

II. *vbl s.* **1. Ankündigen,** *n. in vbl senses.* **2. Ankündigung,** *f.* (*a*) *in vbl senses;* (*b*) announcement; proclamation; notification, notice; warning; intimation; *A:* **A. des Krieges,** declaration of war; (*c*) advertisement.

Ankündiger, *m.* **-s/-. 1.** announcer; *Lit:* harbinger. **2.** advertiser (of sale, etc.).

Ankündigungskommando, *n. Mil:* warning order; warning part of a word of command.

Ankündigungsschreiben, *n. Com: A:* letter of advice, advice-note.

Ankündigungssignal, *n. Tp: Tg:* warning signal.

Ankunft, *f.* **-/. 1.** (*a*) arrival, coming; advent (of s.o., of spring, etc.); *Rail: Nau: Av:* arrival; *Rail:* **A. und Abfahrt der Züge,** arrivals and departures; **bei (der) A. (einer Person, eines Zuges, usw.)** on arrival (of s.o., of a train, etc.); **glückliche, gute, A.**, safe arrival; **'A. voraussichtlich 7 Uhr'**, 'probable time of arrival 7 o'clock'; (*b*) *F:* **die A. eines Jungen, eines Mädchens, anzeigen,** to announce the birth, *F:* the arrival, of a son, a daughter. **2.** *Theol:* advent (of Christ); coming (of the Messiah); **die zweite A.**, the second Advent, the Second Coming.

Ankunftsbahnsteig, *m. Rail:* arrival platform.

Ankunftshafen, *m. Nau:* port of arrival.

Ankunftshalle, *f. Rail:* arrival side (of station).

Ankunftsort, *m.*, **Ankunftsstelle,** *f.* place of arrival; *Nau:* port of arrival.

Ankunftszeit, *f.* time of arrival, arrival time.

ankuppeln, *v.tr. sep.* to couple up, on (**an**+*acc.*, to); *esp. Rail:* **einen Wagen an den Zug a.**, to couple, hitch, a coach, a wagon, *U.S:* car, freight car, on to the train.

ankurbeln, *v.tr. sep.* **1.** to crank up (machine, engine); to wind up (gramophone); to start (up) (engine, car, etc.). **2.** (*a*) to liven up, *F:* to boost (industry, the economy); *U.S. & F:* to give (the economy) a shot in the arm; (*b*) *abs. F:* to get a move on, to get moving, *F:* to get cracking.

Ankurbelungskredit, *m. Fin: Pol.Ec:* loan to establish an industry *or* a business.

Ankylose [aŋky·ˈlo:zə], *f.* **-/-n.** *Med:* anchylosis.

Ankylostomiasis [aŋky·losto·ˈmi:a·zis], *f.* **-/.** *Med:* ankylostomiasis, hookworm disease, miner's anaemia, tunnel disease.

Ankyra [ˈaŋky·ra:]. *Pr.n.n* **-s.** *A.Geog:* Ancyra.

anlächeln, *v.tr. sep.* to smile at, (up)on (s.o.); to give (s.o.) a smile.

anlachen, *v.tr. sep.* **1.** to smile at (s.o.); to beam at, on (s.o.). **2.** *F:* **sich** *dat.* **ein Mädchen, einen Mann, a.**, to get off with, pick up, a girl, a man.

Anlage, *f.* **1.** construction (of factory, mine-shaft, etc.); building (of factory, etc.); erection (of building, plant, etc.); installing, installation (of plant, apparatus, etc.); establishing, establishment (of factory, etc.); laying out (of construction, network, etc.); *cp.* **anlegen** III. **2.** *Fin:* investment, (i) investing (of capital), (ii) invested capital, money invested; **vorteilhafte A.**, good investment; **das wäre eine vorteilhafte A. Ihres Geldes,** that would be a good way of investing your money. **3.** (*a*) design, plan, outline; (rough) sketch (of picture); draft, draught, drawing (of construction); skeleton, outline, design, rough draft (of novel, etc.); (*b*) arrangement, order(ing), disposition (of house, garden, etc.); lay-out (of house, garden, gear-box, etc.); construction, structure (of play, novel); composition (of play, novel, picture). **4.** *Constr: Ch: Civ.E: El.E: etc:* installation; equipment; *Ch: etc:* (large) apparatus; *Ind:* (i) plant; (ii) factory; *W.Tel:* station; *Ind:* **A. zur Herstellung von Salpetersäure,** nitric acid (production) plant; **schwere Anlagen,** heavy installations, heavy plant. **5.** (public) garden (laid out with walks); ornamental strip with flower-beds, trees, etc. (*before public building, at bus-stop, along sides or middle of traffic-road, etc.*); *esp.* (public) park, (public) pleasure-ground; promenade, (public) walk; **in diesen Anlagen,** in these grounds; in this park; **städtische Anlagen,** municipal parks. **6.** (*a*) *Com:* enclosure (**zu einem Schreiben,** to, with, a letter); **in der A.**, herewith, hereto (annexed), subjoined; enclosed; **in der A. senden wir Ihnen die Quittung,** please find receipt attached; enclosed please find receipt; **A. beachten!** see enclosure, see attached; (*at end of letter*) **A.**, enclosure, *abbr.* encl.; (*b*) appendix (to report, etc.); annex, annexure (to document); rider (to document). **7.** *Biol:* germ (of an organism); rudiment; *Bot:* meristem. **8.** (*a*) predisposition (**zu,** to); natural inclination, tendency (**zu,** to); *Med:* diathesis; **A. zur Arthritis,** predisposition to arthritis, arthritic diathesis; **A. zu, zur, Schwindsucht, zur Tuber-**

kulose, haben, to have a tendency to consumption, to be a consumptive subject; **A. zur Korpulenz,** inclination, tendency, to stoutness; **verbrecherische Anlagen,** criminal tendencies; (*b*) (natural) disposition, (natural) aptitude, aptness (**zu,** for); **A. zum Malen haben,** to have an aptitude, a natural gift, a turn, a bent, for painting; **A. zur Musik,** natural bent for music; **dichterische A.,** poetic gift, poetic talent; **er hat A. zum Geschäftsmann,** he has a natural aptitude, a turn, for business; **Junge, der gute Anlagen hat,** naturally gifted youth; **er hat, besitzt, keine A. zu . . . ,** he has no (real) aptitude, no (great) turn, for . . . **9.** *Adm:* (tax) assessment. **10.** *Sm.a:* butt(-end) (of gun). **11.** *Fort:* **A. einer Böschung,** (angle of) slope of an escarpment.

Anlageblatt, *n.*=**Anlage** 6 (*b*).

Anlagegüter, *n.pl. Com: Fin:* capital goods; capital equipment.

Anlagekapital, *n.* **1.** (*a*) *Fin:* invested capital, capital invested; (*b*) *Com: Fin:* fixed capital; permanent assets. **2.** capital to be invested, available for investment.

Anlagekonto, *n. Fin:* investment ledger.

Anlagekosten, *pl. Ind: etc:* **1.** cost of construction (of factory, etc.); cost of installation (of plant, etc.). **2.** promotion costs (of enterprise), promotion money; initial outlay.

Anlagekredit, *m. Fin:* investment credit; (long-term) credit for the establishing of an enterprise.

Anlagepapier, *n.*=**Anlagewert.**

Anlageplan, *m.* lay-out (diagram).

anlagern. I. *v.tr. sep.* **1.** (*a*) to accumulate; (*b*) *Ch:* (*of compound*) to add on, take up (element, another compound). **2. sich anlagern,** (*a*) (*of matter*) to accumulate; to settle, to form a deposit; (*b*) *Ch:* (*of element, compound*) to be added, taken up.

II. *vbl s.* **1. Anlagern,** *n. in vbl senses.* **2. Anlagerung,** *f. in vbl senses; also:* (*a*) accumulation; (*b*) deposit; (*c*) *Ch:* addition (of element *or* compound); (*d*) *Geol:* juxtaposition (of deposits, strata).

Anlagerungsverbindung, *f. Ch:* addition compound.

Anlagestrich, *m.* horizontal line (in margin of letter) drawing attention to an encloures.

Anlagetypus, *m. Biol:* genotype.

Anlagevermögen, *n. Com: Fin:* fixed capital, fixed assets; permanent assets.

Anlagewert, *m. Fin:* (investment) security, *U.S:* bond; **Anlagewerte** *pl,* securities, investments, *U.S:* bonds.

anlallen, *v.tr. sep.* to babble at (s.o.); (*of baby*) to lisp at (s.o.).

Anlände, *f.* **-/-n,** (*a*) landing-place; (*b*) landing-stage; jetty, pier, quay, wharf.

anlanden. I. *v.i. sep.* (*sein*) **1.** *Nau:* (*a*) to land (**in**+*dat.,* at); to arrive (by water); to touch, make, land; to go ashore, to disembark; (*b*) *v.tr.* to bring (boat) to land, to ground (boat), to run (boat) ashore. **2.** (*of river-bank*) to increase through alluvion.

II. *vbl s.* **1. Anlanden,** *n. in vbl senses; also:* disembarkation. **2. Anlandung,** *f.* (*a*)=II. 1; (*b*) (i) alluvium, alluvial deposit(s); river deposits; (ii) accretion through alluvion; *Geol:* aggradation; *Jur:* **A. eines Ufergrundstücks,** gaining of land through (i) alluvion, (ii) avulsion; **A. eines abgeschwemmten Ufergrundstücks,** (gaining of land through) avulsion.

Anlandeplatz, *m.,* **Anlandestelle,** *f.* landing-place.

Anländung, *f.*=**Anlandung,** *q.v. under* **anlanden** II. 2 (*b*).

anlangen, *v.sep.* **1.** *v.i.* (*sein*) **in einem Ort a.,** to arrive at, to reach, a place; **kaum war er dort angelangt, als . . . ,** hardly had he arrived there, got there, when . . . ; **wir sind schon beim achten Buch des Euklid angelangt,** we have already got to the eighth book of Euclid. **2.** *v.impers.*=**anbelangen; was mich anlangt,** as far as I am concerned; (speaking) for myself; *acc.*+**anlangend,** concerning . . . ; with respect to, with regard to . . . ; in regard to . . . , as far as . . . is concerned.

anlaschen, *v.tr. sep.* **1.** *Civ.E: Rail: etc:* to fasten (sth.) on with a fish-plate *or* butt-strap. **2.** *For:* to mark, blaze (tree).

Anlaß, *m.* **-lasses/-lässe,** (*a*) occasion (**zu,** for, to; **etwas zu tun,** to do sth.); motive, ground(s) (**zu,** for; **etwas zu tun,** for doing sth.); reason, cause (**zu,** for; **etwas zu tun,** to do sth., for doing sth.); incentive (**zu,** to; **etwas zu tun,** to do sth.); **A. zu einem Streit,** motive, cause, of a dispute; **A. zu Mißvergnügen,** cause, grounds, for discontent; **ich habe keinen A. zur Klage, zu klagen,** I have no cause, no grounds, for complaint, I have no cause, no reason, to complain; **sie hat mir nie den geringsten A. zur Klage gegeben,** she has never given me the slightest grounds, cause, for complaint; **ich habe allen A. zu glauben, daß . . . ,** I have every reason to suppose that . . . ; **aus diesem A.,** on these grounds, for this reason; **aus A. der Jahrhundertfeier,** on the occasion of the centenary; **ohne allen, jeden, A.,** without any reason, for no reason at all, without any cause (whatsoever); **Beleidigung ohne jeden A.,** gratuitous insult; **j-n ohne jeden A. beleidigen,** to insult s.o. gratuitously; **den A. zu etwas bilden,** to be the cause of sth., to give rise to sth.; **A. zu etwas geben,** to give occasion for, to, sth.; to give cause for sth.; to be the cause of sth.; to give rise to sth.; to be the motive for, the incentive to, sth.; **die Lage gibt A. zu Befürchtungen,** the situation gives cause for apprehension; **zu einem Ausbruch öffentlicher Entrüstung A. geben,** to give occasion to, give rise to, an outburst of popular indignation; **zu Gerede A. geben,** to give occasion for, give rise to, scandal; **Vorrecht, das zu Mißbräuchen A. gibt,** privilege that gives rise to, lends itself to, abuses, that opens the door to abuses, that creates a dangerous precedent; **j-m A. geben, etwas zu tun,** to give s.o. occasion to do sth.; **A. nehmen, etwas zu tun,** to avail oneself of, to take, to seize, the opportunity to do sth.; to take (the) occasion to do sth.; (*b*) **auf A.**+*gen.,* (acting) on instructions from . . . ; at, by, the instigation of . . . ; prompted by . . . ; on orders from, by order of (the town council, etc.).

Anlaßblech, *n. Clockm:* blueing pan.

Anlaßdruckknopf, *m. Aut: etc:* starter-button.

Anlaßdüse, *f. Aut:* pilot-jet, slow-running jet.

Anlaßeinspritzung, *f. I.C.E:* priming.

anlassen. I. *v.tr. sep.* (*strong*) **1.** to leave, keep (garment, etc.) on; **du hast das Licht, den Hahn, angelassen,** you've left the light, the tap, on. **2.** *Metall:* to anneal, temper (steel); to anneal (glass); to draw (steel) to the temper; to let down (steel) to quenching temperature; **Stahl blau a.,** to blue steel. **3. j-n barsch, hart, rauh, übel, a.,** to be sharp, rude, uncivil, with s.o.; to speak harshly to s.o.; to treat s.o. snappishly, with scant courtesy; to snub s.o.; to rate, scold, s.o.; to browbeat s.o.; to give s.o. a dressing-down; *F:* to jump down s.o.'s throat; to sit (up)on s.o. **4.** (*a*) **das Wasser a.,** to turn on the water; *Mch:* **den Dampf a.,** to turn on the steam, to put steam on; (*b*) **einen Teich a.,** to let the water into a pond, to fill a pond. **5.** (*a*) **eine Maschine a.,** to start (up) a machine, to set a machine going; *Aut: Av: etc:* **den Motor a.,** to start (up) the engine; (*b*) **einen Hochofen a.,** to blow in a blast-furnace. **6.** *Ven:* **die Hunde a.,** to slip the hounds; **die Hunde auf ein Tier, auf j-n, a.,** to set the hounds at an animal, at s.o. **7. sich gut, schlecht, anlassen,** to make a good, bad, start; to promise well, ill, to give promise, no great promise; **das Wetter läßt sich gut an,** the weather is hopeful, it looks like being fine; **die Ernte läßt sich gut an,** the harvest looks promising, is coming on; the crops are shaping well, look well, *F:* are coming along nicely; **das Geschäft läßt sich gut an,** the business looks promising, promises well, bids fair to succeed; **es läßt sich an, als würde es . . . ,** there is (a) promise that it will . . . , it bids fair to . . . ; **Sache, die sich sehr gut anläßt,** affair of great promise; **junger Mann, der sich gut anläßt,** promising, likely, young man; **der neue Mann läßt sich ganz gut an,** the new man is quite promising, *F:* the new man is getting along nicely, is doing quite nicely, is not doing at all badly.

II. *vbl s.* **Anlassen,** *n. in vbl senses; esp. Aut: etc:* **leichtes A.,** easy, smooth, starting.

Anlasser, *m.* **-s/-.** *Aut: Av: El.E: etc:* starter.

Anlasserfußschalter, *m.* foot-starter, kick-starter (of motor-cycle, etc.).

Anlasserknopf, *m. Aut: etc:* starter-button.

Anlaßfarbe, *f. Metall:* tempering colour.

Anlaßhahn, *m. Mch:* starting-cock.

Anlaßhebel, *m. Aut: etc:* starting-lever; starting-handle.

Anlaßkontakt, *m. Aut: etc:* starter-button.

Anlaßkraftstoff, *m. I.C.E:* priming fuel, primer fuel.

Anlaßkurbel, *f. Aut: etc:* starting-handle.

anläßlich, *prep.* (+*gen.*) (*a*) on the occasion of; **a. seines Geburtstags, der Jahrhundertfeier,** on the occasion of his birthday, of the centenary; (*b*) *occ.* (*as pseudo-adverb*) on occasion occasionally.

Anlaßmagnet, *m. I.C.E:* starting magneto.

Anlaßmoment, *n. Mec:* starting torque.

Anlaßmotor, *m. Av: etc:* starting-motor.

Anlaßofen, *m.* annealing furnace, tempering furnace.

Anlaßschalter, *m. Aut: El.E: etc:* starting switch, starter-switch; *Aut:* starter-button.

Anlaßschieber, *m. Mch:* starting-valve.

Anlaßspule, *f. Av:* booster coil (of ignition system).

Anlaßventil, *n. Mch:* starting-valve.

Anlaßvorrichtung, *f. I.C.E: etc:* starting device *or* system; starting-gear; **selbsttätige A.,** self-starter, automatic starter.

Anlaßwiderstand, *m. El.E:* starting resistance.

anlasten, *v.tr. sep. Com: Fin:* **j-m die Spesen, die Postgebühren, usw., a.,** to charge (up) the expenses, the postage, etc., to s.o.

anlatschen, *v.i. sep.* (*sein*) to shuffle, slouch, up; **er kam angelatscht,** he came shuffling, slouching, along.

Anlauf, *m.* **1.** (*a*) dash, start; *Sp:* run-up, run, take-off (**zu einem Sprung,** for a jump); *Ski:* approach run; **einen A. zu einem Sprung nehmen,** to run up, to take off, for a jump; *F:* **einen guten A. nehmen,** to make a good start; *F:* **er nahm einen A. zu einer Rede,** he prepared to deliver himself of a speech; **im ersten A.,** directly, at the very first, right away, straight off, *F:* first go (off); (*b*) *Av:* take-off run; (*c*) *Mil:* rush, charge; onset; **die Stellung wurde im ersten A. genommen,** the position was taken at the first onset, in the first rush. **2.** starting (up) (of machine). **3.** rising, swelling (of waters, etc.). **4.** slope, *Civ.E:* batter (of embankment, etc.). **5.** (*a*) *Arch:* congé, apophyge, escape (of column); (*b*) *N.Arch:* fore-foot, gripe (of ship's stem). **6.** tarnish (on metal, mirror); mist, cloud (on glass); film (on metal, glass). **7.** *Metall:* tempering colour.

Anlaufbahn, *f.* **1.** *Sp:* run-up track; *Ski:* approach. **2.** *Av:* runway.

Anlauf(dreh)moment, *n. Mec:* starting torque.

anlaufen, *v.sep.* (*strong*) I. *v.i.* (*sein*) **1.** (*a*) to run up; **angelaufen kommen,** to come running up; to rush up; *Sp:* **zum Sprung a.,** to run up, take off, for the jump; (*b*) *Av:* (*of aircraft*) to make its take-off run, to run up for the take-off; (*c*) *Ven:* (*of animal*) (i) to come within (easy) range; (ii) to make a rush; **einen Eber a. lassen,** to let a boar run on to the spear; (*d*) **gegen etwas a.,** (i) to rush at sth.; to run (slap) into sth.; to collide with sth.; (ii) to run counter to sth.; **mit dem Kopf gegen etwas a.,** to knock, strike, bump, run, one's head against sth.; **das läuft gegen die Vorschriften an,** that is contrary to, goes against the regulations; (*e*) **übel bei j-m a.,** to be ill received by s.o.; to be rebuffed by s.o.; **er war mit seiner Bitte übel angelaufen,** his request was ill, not well, received; *Iron:* **da sind wir schön angelaufen!** we're in a nice mess! here's a pretty go! (*f*) *F:* **j-n a. lassen,** (*deliberately*) to let s.o. get into trouble, *F:* to let s.o. put his foot in it. **2.** (*a*) (*of machine*) to start (up); **eine Maschine a. lassen,** to start (up) a machine, to set a machine going; (*b*) *Cin:* (*of film*) to start, to come on. **3.** (*of embankment, mine-gallery, etc.*) to slope upwards, to rise. **4.** (*a*) (*of waters, etc.*) to rise, swell; (*of puddles, etc.*) to collect; (*of interest, debts, etc.*) to mount up; **seine Schulden sind auf 10 000 Mark angelaufen,** his debts amount to, add up to, 10,000 marks; **Rechnungen a. lassen,** to run up bills; (*b*) (*of limb, etc.*) to swell (up); **angelaufen,** swollen. **5.** (*a*) to take on a coating, a film (of moisture, deposit, etc.); (*of metal, mirror*) to tarnish, to grow dull, dim; (*of coin, etc.*) to become discoloured; (*of glass, mirror, spectacles*) to cloud over, mist over, film over; (*of bread, etc.*) to mildew, turn mouldy; **angelaufenes Metall,** tarnished, discoloured, metal; **Brillengläser schwarz a. lassen,** to darken, smoke, spectacle-lenses; (*b*) *Metall:* (*of steel*) to become, turn, blue; **Stahl (blau) a. lassen,** to blue steel; to temper steel; (*c*) (*of limb, swelling, etc.*) **blau, rot, grün, usw., a.,** to turn blue, purple, green, etc.; (*of pers.*) **er war vor Kälte, vor Wut, ganz blau angelaufen,** he was blue with cold, purple with rage; **sie lief vor Scham rot an,** she blushed with, for, shame.

II. **anlaufen,** *v.tr.* **1.** to make a run, a rush, at (s.o.), to rush at (s.o.). **2.** *F:* **j-n (beständig) a.,** to importune, bother, pester, *F:* badger, s.o. **3.** *Nau:* **eine Küste a.,** to make for, run for,

a coast; **einen Hafen a.,** to call at, put into, a port; to touch at a port.
III. *vbl s.* **Anlaufen,** *n. in vbl senses; also:* discolo(u)ration; *cp.* **Anlauf.**
Anlauffarbe, *f. Metall:* tempering colour.
Anlaufgestell, *n. Navy:Av:* launching cradle (for shipborne aircraft).
Anlaufhafen, *m. Nau:* port of call.
Anlaufmoment, *n. Mec:* starting torque.
Anlaufpalette, *f. Clockm:* warning-piece.
Anlaufrad, *n.* 1. *Mec.E:* starting-wheel. 2. *Clockm:* warning-wheel.
Anlaufstreifen, *m. Cin:* leader.
Anlauftemperatur, *f. Metalw:* tempering temperature.
Anlaufwippe, *f. Clockm:* flirt.
Anlaufzeit, *f.* 1. *Mec:* starting time (of machine). 2. *Hyd.E: etc:* time required to fill a tank, pipe, etc.
Anlaut, *m. Ling:* first phoneme, initial sound (of word, syllable); **a, r, usw., im A.,** a, r, etc., in the first position, initial a, r, etc.
anlauten, *v.i. sep.* (*haben*) (*a*) (*of vowel, consonant*) to be in the initial position; **anlautendes r,** initial r; (*b*) (*of word, syllable*) **mit a, r, usw., a,** to begin with a, r, etc.
anläuten, *v.tr. sep.* 1. to ring the bell(s) for the beginning of (church service, etc.). 2. *Tp:* **j-n a.,** *v.i.* (*haben*) **bei j-m a.,** to ring, *U.S:* call, s.o. up.
anlecken, *v.tr. sep.* to lick (stamp, label, etc.).
Anlegeapparat, *m. Print:* feeding apparatus, feeder.
Anlegebrett, *n. Print:* = **Anlegetisch.**
Anlegebrücke, *f. Nau:* landing-stage, jetty.
Anlegegebühren, *f.pl. Nau:* mooring dues, moorage.
Anlegegoniometer, *n. Cryst:* contact goniometer.
Anlegehafen, *m. Nau:* port of call.
Anlegemarke, *f. Print:* lay-mark.
Anlegemaschine *f. Tex:* spreading-machine, spreader.
anlegen, *v.sep.* I. *v.tr.* 1. (*a*) to put on, lay on; to apply; **etwas an etwas** *acc.* **a.,** to put, lay, sth. on sth.; to apply sth. to sth.; **eine Leiter (an die Wand) a.,** to set a ladder against the wall, to put up, set up, a ladder; **einen Hund (an die Kette) a.,** to put a dog on the chain, to chain up a dog; **einen Säugling (an die Brust) a.,** to give a child the breast, to suckle a child; **Feuer an etwas a.,** to set fire to sth., to set sth. on fire; **Kohlen, usw., (ans Feuer) a.,** to put coal, etc., on the fire; **das Feuer a.,** to lay the fire; *Carp:* **den Winkel an eine Kante a.,** to put the square to, lay the square against, an edge; *Med:* **einen Breiumschlag, einen Verband, a.,** to apply a poultice, a dressing; *Print:* **den Bogen a.,** to lay on, feed, stroke in, the paper; *Min:* **Arbeiter a.,** to take on hands; *Ven:* **die Hunde a.,** to put the hounds on the scent; *Dominoes:* **einen Stein a.,** to pose, play (a piece); (*b*) **sich an etwas a.,** (i) (*of pers.*) to lie close to sth.; to flatten oneself against sth.; (ii) (*of thg*) to attach itself to sth., to fix on to sth.; *Ch:* (*of matter*) **sich (an etwas) a.,** to settle, to form a deposit (on sth.); (*c*) **j-m, etwas** *dat.,* **etwas a.,** to put sth. on s.o., sth.; **j-m ein Kleid, ein Gewand, a.,** to put a garment on s.o., *Lit:* to clothe s.o. in a garment; **j-m die Kleider a.,** to dress s.o.; **j-m Fesseln, Ketten, a.,** to put s.o. in fetters, in irons, in chains, to fetter s.o.; *Coop:* **einem Faß die Reifen a.,** to put the hoops on, to hoop, a barrel; (*d*) to put on (clothes), to put (clothes) on, (*in slightly mannered style*) to don (coat, uniform, etc.); **alle seine Orden a.,** to put on all one's decorations; **Trauer a.,** to go into mourning; *Dial:* **sich a.,** to put on one's clothes, to dress (oneself); (*e*) *Nau:* **ein Schiff an den Kai, an ein anderes Schiff, a.,** to lay, berth, moor, a ship alongside the quay; to lay a ship alongside another ship; (*f*) *Sm.a:* **das Gewehr a.,** to bring the gun to the shoulder, to the firing position; *abs.* **a.,** to level one's gun, to take aim; **auf j-n a.,** to level one's gun at, against, s.o., to point a gun at s.o., to aim at s.o.; *F:* (*of remark, etc.*) **das war auf dich angelegt,** that was aimed at you, that was meant, intended, for you; (*g*) **es darauf a., etwas zu tun,** to aim at doing sth.; to make it one's aim, one's object, to do sth.; to make a point of doing sth.; *F:* to be (dead) set on doing sth.; **er legt es darauf an, dich zu ruinieren,** he is bent on, intent upon, ruining you; **er legt es geradezu darauf an, den Leuten grob zu begegnen,** he will go out of his way to be rude to people; **er scheint es darauf anzulegen, sich zu verletzen,** he seems to go out of his way to get hurt; *F:* **er legt's drauf an!** he's asking for

it! (*h*) **sich mit j-m a.,** to get into trouble with s.o.; *F:* to get in wrong with s.o. 2. (*a*) *Fin:* **Geld, Kapital, a.,** to invest money, capital; **Geld auf Zinsen a.,** to put money out to, *U.S:* at, interest; **Geld zu 5 Prozent a.,** to invest money at 5%; **sein Geld in Wertpapieren, in Grundbesitz, a.,** to invest one's money in stock, in real estate; **Kapital fest a.,** to lock up, tie up, capital; **sein Geld vorteilhaft, gewinnbringend, nutzbringend, a.,** to invest one's money profitably, to lay out one's money to advantage; **mein Privatvermögen ist im Geschäft angelegt,** my private means are invested in the business; (*b*) **Geld für etwas a.,** to spend, lay out, money on sth.; **wieviel, was, wollen Sie a.?** how much, what, do you want to pay, to give (for it)? **soviel können wir nicht a.,** we cannot afford to pay such prices; (*c*) **seine Zeit gut, vorteilhaft, a.,** to employ, use, one's time to advantage, to make good use of one's time. 3. (*a*) to dispose, set out, arrange; to establish (factory, wireless station, new town, enterprise, etc.); to found (new town, enterprise); to build, construct (dam, railway, etc.); to lay down (railway); to set up (factory, etc.); to put up (building); to set up, put up (scaffolding, etc.); to install, fix up, put in (machinery, etc.); to install, lay on, put in (electricity, gas, the telephone); to fit up, equip (factory, etc.); to design, plan (out) (garden, house, etc.); to plan (new town, suburb, etc.); to lay out (garden, road, avenue, new town, etc.); *Hist:* **eine Kolonie a.,** to establish, found, a colony; *Constr:* **eine Bauarbeit a.,** to lay out a piece of (building) work; *N.Arch:* **ein Schiff (zum Bau) a.,** to lay a ship on the stocks, to lay down a ship; (*b*) to sketch out (plan, picture, etc.); to draw up, work out (plan, project); to hatch (plot); to weave (intrigue); **groß angelegt,** on a grand scale; **groß angelegter Plan,** ambitious plan; grandiose plan; **der Plan ist darauf angelegt, zu . . . ,** the plan is designed to . . . , the purpose of the plan is to . . . .
II. **anlegen,** *v.i.* (*haben*) 1. *Nau:* (*a*) to make fast, to moor; (*b*) to put ashore, to land; (*c*) **an den Kai, an ein Schiff, a.,** to come, draw, alongside the quay, a ship. 2. *Mil:* **A: anlegen!** present (arms)! *cp.* I. 1 (*f*).
III. *vbl s.* **Anlegen** *n.,* **Anlegung** *f. in vbl senses; also:* (*a*) application (**an etwas** *acc.,* to sth.); (*b*) investment (of money, capital); (*c*) disposition; construction (of dam, railway, factory, etc.); installation (of machinery, electricity, gas, the telephone, etc.). *Cp.* **Anlage** 1.
Anlegeplatz, *m.* = **Anlegestelle.**
Anleger, *m.* -s/-. *Print:* 1. (*pers.*) layer-on, feeder, stroker-in. 2. = **Anlegeapparat.**
Anlegeschloß, *n.* padlock.
Anlegespan, *m. Print:* (*a*) reglet; (*b*) side-stick.
Anlegesteg, *m.* 1. *Nau:* = **Anlegebrücke.** 2. *Print:* side-stick *or* head-stick; *pl.* **Anlegestege,** furniture.
Anlegestelle, *f. Nau:* landing-place; landing-stage, jetty; wharf; quay.
Anlegetisch, *m. Print:* laying-on table, feeding bench, horse.
Anlehen, *n.* -s/-, (*a*) = **Anleihe;** (*b*) = **Darleh(e)n.**
anlehnen. I. *v.tr. sep.* 1. (*a*) to lean, rest, support; **etwas an etwas** *acc.* **a.,** to lean, rest, support, sth. against, on, sth.; **eine Leiter an die Wand a.,** to lean a ladder, prop a ladder (up), against the wall; (*of pers.*) **sich an j-n, etwas** *acc.,* **a.,** (i) to lean, rest, against, on, s.o., sth.; (ii) to rely on s.o., sth.; to base oneself on s.o., sth.; to look to s.o., sth., for support; to be dependent on s.o., sth.; to use s.o., sth., as authority; to lean on s.o. (for aid); to follow s.o.; to imitate (author, artist, artist's style, etc.); **sich mit dem Rücken an die Wand a.,** to lean back against the wall; (*of thg*) **sich an etwas** *acc.* **a.,** to lean, rest, against, on, sth.; (*of document, work of art, opinion, etc.*) to be based on sth.; (*b*) *Mil:* (*of unit, body of troops*) **sich an eine Einheit a., an eine Einheit angelehnt sein,** to be supported, covered, by a unit; **beiderseits angelehnt, supported on both flanks, with both flanks covered.** 2. **die Tür, das Fenster, a., angelehnt lassen,** (i) to set the door ajar; to leave the door, window, open just a crack; (ii) to leave the door, the window, on the latch; **die Tür war angelehnt,** the door was (i) ajar, open just a crack, pushed to, (ii) on the latch.
II. *vbl s.* 1. **Anlehnen,** *n. in vbl senses.* 2. **Anlehnung,** *f.* (*a*) = II. 1; (*b*) dependence (**an** + *acc.,* on); **enge A.,** close dependence; (close) imitation; **wörtliche A. an einen Autor,**

literal borrowing from, literal following of, an author; **in A. an . . . ,** (i) referring back to . . . ; (ii) following (author, etc.); in imitation of (author, etc.); under the influence of (author, etc.); (*c*) *Mil:* support.
Anlehnungsbedürfnis, *n.* need to lean on someone; **ein starkes A. haben,** to be badly in need of someone to lean on.
anlehnungsbedürftig, *a.* in need of support, *esp.* of moral support; needing to lean on someone.
Anleihe, *f.* (*a*) loan (of money); **bei j-m eine A. machen,** to borrow money of, from, s.o.; *Fin:* **kurzfristige, langfristige, A.,** short (-term), long-term, loan; **gesicherte A.,** secured loan; **ungesicherte, nicht gesicherte, A.,** unsecured loan; **hypothekarische A.,** mortgage loan; **öffentliche A.,** government *or* municipal loan; **konsolidierte A.,** consolidated funds, *F:* consols; (*of the State, a municipality*) **eine A. aufnehmen, auflegen, aufgeben,** to raise a loan; **eine A. vermitteln,** to negotiate a loan; (*b*) *pl.* **Anleihen,** *Fin:* government *or* municipal stock, bonds; *U.S:* government *or* municipal bonds; (*c*) (literary, artistic) borrowing; **er hat oft bei Goethe eine A. gemacht,** he has often borrowed (an idea, a phrase) from Goethe.
Anleiheablösung, *f. Fin:* redemption of a loan, of loans.
Anleihekapital, *n. Fin:* capital raised by way of loan(s); bonded debt.
Anleihelos, *n. Fin:* lottery bond, premium bond.
Anleihemarkt, *m. Fin:* market in government *or* municipal bonds, securities.
Anleihepapiere, *n.pl. Fin:* government *or* municipal securities; stock *or* bonds, *U.S:* government *or* municipal bonds.
Anleiheschuld, *f. Fin:* bonded debt; funded debt.
Anleihevertrag, *m. Nau:* respondentia.
anleimen, *v.tr. sep.* to glue (sth.) on; to stick (sth.) on (**an** + *acc.,* to); *F:* **er saß da wie angeleimt,** he sat tight; he refused to budge; he showed not the slightest sign of moving, of going away; *Ling:* **anleimende Sprachen,** agglutinating, agglutinative, languages.
anleinen, *v.tr. sep.* to put (dog) on the lead, on the leash; to leash (dog).
anleiten. I. *v.tr. sep.* 1. (*a*) *A:* **j-n zu etwas a.,** to guide, lead, s.o. to sth.; (*b*) **j-n zu etwas a., j-n (dazu) a., etwas zu tun,** to give s.o. a lead to sth., to give s.o. a lead, give s.o. hints, about the way sth. should be done; **man sollte die Kinder zur Höflichkeit a., man sollte die Kinder (dazu) a., höflich zu sein,** children should be given a lead about polite behaviour; children should be given (helpful) hints on politeness, on how to be polite; **j-n in einem Fach a.,** to introduce s.o. to, to give s.o. an introduction to, initial guidance in, a subject; **unsere Studenten sind oft nicht fähig, selbständig an die Quellen heranzugehen, man muß sie ein wenig a.,** our students are often not capable of an independent approach to the sources; one has to give them (something of) a lead, some initial guidance, some hints how to go about it. 2. *Hort:* to train (plant, tree).
II. *vbl s.* 1. **Anleiten,** *n. in vbl senses.* 2. **Anleitung,** *f.* (*a*) = II. 1; (*b*) direction; guidance; (*c*) (preliminary) instruction; introduction; **j-m Anleitungen geben, wie man etwas macht, wie etwas gemacht werden soll,** to give s.o. a lead, to give s.o. hints, about the way sth. should be done; **j-s, den, Anleitungen folgen,** to follow s.o.'s, the, instructions; (*d*) (*book*) introduction; **eine A. zur Photographie,** an introduction, a guide, to photography; **eine A. zur Physik,** an introduction to physics, a first course in physics.
Anleiter, *m.* instructor, teacher; guide.
Anlernberuf, *m.* occupation involving a period of training (but no formal apprenticeship); skilled occupation.
anlernen, *v.tr. sep.* 1. **sich** *dat.* **etwas a.,** to learn sth.; to pick sth. up; **bloß angelernter Trick, bloß angelernte Fertigkeit,** mechanical trick, mechanical dexterity. 2. *Ind:* to train (apprentice, new hand); **angelernter Arbeiter,** semi-skilled worker.
Anlernling, *m.* -s/-e. *Ind:* trainee.
Anlernwerkstätte, *f. Ind:* training shop, training establishment.
Anlernzeit, *f. Ind:* training period, period of training.
anlesen, *v.tr. sep.* (*strong*) 1. **ein Buch a.,** to begin (reading) a book (and not finish it); to read only the opening pages, chapters, of a book. 2. **sich** *dat.* **Kenntnisse a.,** to acquire, pick up, knowledge from books, by reading;

angelesenes Wissen, knowledge culled, picked up, from books.

anleuchten, *v.tr. sep.* to direct a beam of light on to (sth.); to spotlight (sth., s.o.); *Mil: Av:* to turn a searchlight on (sth.); (*of searchlight*) to pick up (aircraft, etc.).

anliefern. I. *v.tr. sep. Com: Ind:* **1.** (*a*) to deliver (goods); (*b*) to supply (goods). **2.** *occ.* **j-n mit etwas a.,** to supply s.o. with sth.
II. *vbl s.* **Anliefern** *n.,* **Anlieferung** *f.* (*a*) delivery (of goods); (*b*) supply(ing) (of goods).

Anlieferungsschein, *m. Com: Nau:* shipping-note.

anliegen. I. *v.i. sep.* (*strong*) (*haben*) **1.** (*a*) to be adjacent, contiguous; **an etwas** *dat.* **a.,** to be next to, close to, adjacent to, contiguous to, sth.; to abut on sth.; to adjoin sth.; to border on sth.; **zwei Häuser, die aneinander a.,** two houses next (door) to one another, abutting on one another; two adjoining houses; **Haus, das an der Straße anliegt,** house abutting on the street; house fronting on the street; **Gebäude, das an zwei Straßen anliegt,** building with frontages on two streets; **anliegend,** adjacent, adjoining, contiguous; abutting; neighbouring; bordering; **anliegende Felder,** neighbouring, abutting, fields; **am Fluß anliegende Wiese,** meadow adjoining the river; *Geom:* **anliegender Winkel,** adjacent, adjoining, angle; **anliegende Seite,** adjacent side; (*b*) *Com:* **anliegend,** (*of letter, document, etc.*) attached, annexed, enclosed; **anliegend schicken wir Ihnen . . . ,** we send you herewith . . . , enclosed please find . . . **2. es liegt mir, ihm, an,** it is a matter of consequence, of concern, to me, to him. **3.** (*of pers.*) (*a*) **j-m a.,** *occ. v.tr.* **j-n a.,** to importune, pester, *F:* bother, s.o. (with requests); to urge s.o. (to do sth.); (*b*) *Ven:* **einem Tier a.,** to lie in wait for an animal. **4.** (*a*) (*of garment*) to fit, sit; **gut, glatt, schlecht, a.,** to fit well, sit well; to fit smoothly; to fit, sit, badly; to be a good, smooth, bad, fit; **eng a.,** to fit close, tight(ly), snugly; to be a close, tight, snug, fit; to fit to the figure; to fit like a glove; **eng anliegendes Kleid,** close-fitting, tight-fitting, form-fitting, dress; **eng, knapp, anliegende Hosen,** tight(-fitting) trousers; (*b*) *Bot:* **anliegende Keimblätter,** accumbent cotyledons. *See also* **Platte** . **5.** *Nau:* (*of gear, article of cargo, etc.*) to be in its proper place; to be properly stowed; to be 'home'. **6.** *v.tr. & i. Nau:* (*of ship*) **seinen Kurs a.,** to lie her course; **einen Punkt a.,** to head for, bear away for, a point; **Ost, ostwärts, a.,** to head (to the) east, to stand to the east, to steer a course to the east; **seewärts a.,** to stand out to sea; to stand off; **landwärts a.,** to stand in to land, stand in for (the) land.
II. *vbl s.* **Anliegen,** *n.* **1.** *in vbl senses; also:* (*a*) contiguity (**an**+*dat.,* with), adjacency (**an**+*dat.,* to); proximity (**an**+*dat.,* to), vicinity (**an**+*dat.,* to, with); (*b*) fit, sit (of garment). **2.** (*a*) concern; **mein, sein, A.,** the matter, the affair, about which I am, he is, concerned; my, his concern; what I have on my mind, what he has on his mind; **mein A. heute abend ist, zu besprechen . . . ,** what I should like to discuss this evening is . . . ; *B:* **wirf dein A. auf den Herrn,** cast thy burden upon the Lord; (*b*) petition, request, suit, entreaty; desire, wish; **ein A. vorbringen,** to make, prefer, put forward, a request; to express a wish, a desire; **ich habe ein dringendes A. an Sie,** I have an urgent request to make of you.
III. *p.p. &* a. **angelegen,** important, of importance, of consequence; **sich etwas a. sein lassen,** to make sth. one's concern; to put (all) one's heart into sth.; **es sich a. sein lassen, etwas zu tun,** to make it one's duty, one's business, one's concern, to do sth.; to make every endeavour to do sth.; to make a point of doing sth.; **er hatte nichts Angelegeneres zu tun, als . . . ,** his only concern was to . . . , he was above all concerned to . . .

Anliegenheit, *f.*=**anliegen** III. 2.

Anlieger, *m.* **1.** *Jur:* abutter, abutting owner; **die Anlieger an dieser Straße,** the residents of this road. **2.** (next-door) neighbour.

Anliegersiedlung, *f. Agr:* group of small holdings forming an agricultural entity.

Anliegerstaaten, *m.pl.* neighbouring states, *esp.* states lying along the same river, mountain-range, etc.

Anliegerverkehr, *m. P.N:* **keine Einfahrt, ausgenommen A.,** no entry, residents only.

anlieken, *v.tr. sep. Nau:* to rope (sail).

anloben, *v.tr. sep.*=**geloben.**

anlocken. I. *v.tr. sep.* (*a*) to decoy (bird, animal); to lure (bird, animal, fish); to allure (bird, animal); (*b*) to attract, allure (s.o.) (with promises, etc.); to lure, lead, entice, (s.o.) on (with promises, etc.); **Kunden a.,** to attract, allure, draw, entice customers.
II. *vbl s.* **1. Anlocken,** *n. in vbl senses.* **2. Anlockung,** *f.* (*a*)=II. 1; *also:* attraction, allurement; (*b*)=**Anlockungsmittel.**

Anlockungsmittel, *n.* (*a*) decoy (for birds); (*b*) bait; lure, allurement.

anlöten, *v.tr. sep. Metalw:* to solder (sth.) on (**an**+*acc.,* to).

anludern, *v.tr. sep. Ven:* to lure (animal) with a bait.

anlüften, *v.tr. sep.* (*a*) to lift; (*b*) *Aer:* to lift (balloon); to let (balloon) rise from the ground.

anlügen, *v.tr. sep.* (*strong*) to lie to (s.o.).

anlupfen, *v.tr. sep. South G.Dial:* to lift.

anlustern, *v.tr. sep.* to gaze at (s.o.) with desire; to look lustfully at (s.o.).

anluven, *v.i. sep.* (*haben*) *Nau:* to luff; to round to.

anmachen. I. *v.tr. sep.* **1.** (*a*) to attach; to fasten, fix, (sth.) on (**an**+*acc.,* to); to put up, fix (up) (curtain, etc.); to hang (bell); **einen Hund an die Kette a.,** to put a dog on the chain, to chain up a dog; (*b*) *occ.* **sich an j-n a.,** to make up to s.o. **2.** to prepare, mix (*esp. with addition of liquid*); *Cu:* **den Teig a.,** to mix the dough; to knead, work, the dough; **den Salat a.,** to dress the salad; **Salat mit Essig, Öl und Zwiebeln a.,** to make a salad dressing or vinegar, oil and onions, to dress salad with vinegar and oil flavoured with onions; **Gemüse mit Sahne, usw., a.,** to prepare vegetables with cream, etc.; *Civ.E: etc:* **Beton, Mörtel, a.,** to mix concrete, mortar; **Kalk a.,** to slake, slack, lime; *Art: etc:* **Farben (mit Öl, usw.) a.,** to temper colours (with oil, etc.). **3.** to adulterate, *F:* fake, doctor (wine, a product, etc.); **angemachter Wein,** doctored wine. **4. Feuer a.,** to light, kindle, a fire; **das Feuer a.,** to light the fire; **(das) Licht a.,** to light the lamp(s); to switch on, put on, the light; to light up.
II. *vbl s.* **Anmachen,** *n. in vbl senses; also:* adulteration (of wine, product).

Anmachholz, *n.* firewood, kindling.

Anmachwasser, *n. Civ.E: etc:* water for mixing (concrete, mortar, etc.).

anmähen, *v.i. sep.* (*haben*) to begin reaping *or* mowing, to begin cutting the corn, the hay.

anmahnen, *v.tr. sep.* (*a*) to exhort, admonish; **j-n zu etwas a.,** to urge sth. upon s.o.; to exhort, urge, s.o. to do sth.; (*b*) *Com: Fin:* to warn, notify (s.o.) (that payment is due); **Steuern, rückständige Beträge, usw., a.,** to issue a warning to pay taxes, outstanding accounts, etc.

Anmal, *n. Swiss Dial:* birthmark.

anmalen, *v.tr. sep.* **1.** (*a*) to cover (wall, etc.) with a coat of paint; to paint (wall, etc.); to colour (in) (drawing, etc.); **eine Wand grün a.,** to paint a wall green; (*b*) to bedaub; (*c*) *F:* to paint (one's face, fingernails, etc.); **sich a.,** to paint one's face. **2.** to paint on (name, etc.); to paint up (name); **etwas an die Wand a.,** to paint sth. on the wall.

Anmarsch, *m. Mil:* approach (march); advance; *Navy: Mil.Av:* approach (of ships, aircraft); **im A. sein,** (*of troops*) to be advancing; to be on the march; (*of ships, aircraft*) to be approaching.

anmarschieren, *v.i. sep.* (*sein*) (*p.p.* **anmarschiert**) *Mil:* (*of troops*) to advance; *Navy: Mil.Av:* (*of ships, aircraft*) to approach; (*of troops, pers.*) **anmarschiert kommen,** to come marching along, up.

Anmarschweg, *m.* (*a*) *Mil:* route of advance; *Navy: Mil.Av:* approach route; (*b*) **einen weiten A. haben,** to have a long journey, a long way to go (to work, school, etc.).

anmaßen. I. *v.tr. sep.* **1. sich** *dat.* **etwas a.** (*also A:* **sich** *acc.* **etwas** *gen.* **a.**), to arrogate sth. to oneself; **sich ein Recht, ein Vorrecht, a.,** to arrogate a right, a privilege, to oneself; to assume a right; **sich die Gewalt a.,** to assume power; **sich den Thron, einen Titel, a.,** to usurp the throne; to usurp, assume, a title; **angemaßter Titel,** usurped, assumed, title. **2. sich** *dat.* **etwas a.; sich** *dat.* **a., etwas zu sein, etwas zu tun,** to pretend to sth.; to assume, claim, lay claim to, sth.; to pretend, claim, to be sth.; to presume to do sth.; to take it upon oneself to do sth.; **ich maße mir kein Urteil an,** I will not presume to give an opinion; I do not feel entitled to an opinion, qualified to give an opinion; **sich a., etwas zu wissen,** to claim to know sth., to lay claim to knowledge; **sich a., ein Philosoph zu sein,** to claim, to pretend, to be a philosopher; to set up for a philosopher; **angemaßter Philosoph,** pretended, would-be, self-styled, philosopher; **sich das Recht a., etwas zu tun,** to take upon oneself the right to do sth.; **er maßt sich vieles an,** he takes a good deal upon himself.
II. *vbl s.* **Anmaßung,** *f.* **1.** arrogation (of sth.); usurpation (of throne, title, etc.); assumption (of power, title); **A. der Autorität,** unwarranted assumption of authority. **2.** arrogance; overbearing manner; presumption, presumptuousness; overweening confidence; pretentiousness, pretension; insolence, effrontery, *F:* cheek; **das war eine A.,** that was a piece of effrontery, *F:* of cheek.
III. *pr.p. & a.* **anmaßend,** arrogant; overbearing; presumptuous, overweening; pretentious; insolent; **anmaßendes Wesen,** arrogance; overbearing manner; presumption; overweening confidence; **es wäre a., wenn ich sagen würde . . . ,** it would be presumptuous of me, it would be presumption on my part, to say . . . ; *adv.* arrogantly, presumptuously; pretentiously; insolently.

anmaßlich, *a.*=**anmaßend,** *q.v. under* **anmaßen** III.

anmästen, *v.tr. sep.* **1.** to fatten (animals); to cram (fowls). **2.** *F:* **sich** *dat.* **ein Bäuchlein a.,** to grow stout, *F:* to develop a corporation, *P:* to put on a pot.

Anmeldeamt, *n.* **1.**=**Meldeamt 1. 2.** *Tp:* originating exchange.

Anmeldeformular, *n.*=**Anmeldungsformular.**

Anmeldefrist, *f.* time allowed for application(s) *or* entries; **A. bis zum 1. Mai,** closing date for applications *or* entries May 1.

Anmeldegebühr, *f.* registration fee; entrance fee (for competition, etc.).

anmelden. I. *v.tr. sep.* **1.** to announce (s.o., sth.); (*a*) **sich (bei j-m) a. lassen,** to send in one's name (to s.o.); **wen soll ich a.?** what name, who, shall I say? **sind Sie bei Dr. X angemeldet?** have you an appointment with Dr X? is Dr X expecting you? **ich bin angemeldet,** I am here by appointment, I have an appointment, I am expected; **sich a.,** (i) to announce oneself; to give in, send in, one's name; (ii) to make an appointment; (*b*) **einen Besuch a.,** to announce, give notice of, a visit; **eine Grippe meldete sich (bei ihm) an,** he showed the first signs of influenza. **2.** (*a*) *Adm:* **etwas bei einer Behörde a.,** to notify an authority of sth.; to give notice of sth. to an authority; **ein Kind beim Standesamt a.,** to register a (new-born) child (at the registrar's office), *U.S:* to register the birth of a child; **einen Todesfall beim Standesamt a.,** to report a death (to, at, the registrar's office, *U.S:* to the authorities); **j-n, j-s Ankunft, bei der Polizei a.,** to notify the police of s.o.'s arrival (at hotel, boarding house, etc.); **sich a.,** (i) **sich bei der Polizei, sich polizeilich, a.,** to register (oneself) with the police; to notify the police of one's arrival, of one's (new) address; to report to the police; (ii) (*in hotel, etc.*) to register; to fill up a registration form; *Tp:* **ein Ferngespräch a.,** to book, place, a trunk call, a long-distance call; (*b*) **einen Anspruch a.,** to make, put forward, a claim; *Jur:* **eine Forderung a.,** to lodge a claim; (*c*) *Cust:* to declare (goods); **eine Ladung a.,** to manifest a cargo; **ein Schiff (zum Zoll) a.,** to report a vessel; (*d*) *Mil:* **sich a.,** to report to one's unit, to headquarters. **3.** to enrol(l) (s.o.); to enter (s.o.'s) name; **ein Kind zur, bei der, in der, Schule, a., einen Schüler a.,** to enter a pupil at school, to enter a child as a pupil; **sich bei einem Verein a.,** to apply for membership of a society; **sich zu einem Kursus a.,** to enter, to put down one's name, to enrol(l), for a course; **sich persönlich zu einem Seminar a.,** to present oneself for interview (with professor, etc.) before joining a seminar; **sich zu einem Wettbewerb a.,** to enter for, go in for, a competition; **ich bin zum Hochsprung angemeldet,** I am down for the high jump.
II. *vbl s.* **1. Anmelden,** *n. in vbl: senses.* **2. Anmeldung,** *f. in vbl senses; also* (*a*) announcement; notice (of visit, etc.); (making of an) appointment; **j-n ohne (vorherige) A. besuchen,** to visit s.o. without (previous) notice, without an appointment; (*b*) notification (of arrival, new address, etc.); notice (of arrival, etc.); *Adm:* registration (of new-born child, hotel guest, etc.); **A. zum Patent,** application for a patent; **polizeiliche A.,** registration with the police; *Cust:* **A. (zum Zoll),** (customs) declaration; *Jur:* **A. des Konkurses,** filing of a petition in bankruptcy; (*c*) registration office; (*in hotel, etc.*) **'Anmeldung', 'Reception'.**

Anmeldepflicht, *f. Adm:* obligation to register with the police, to notify the police of one's address; obligation (on hotel-keeper, etc.) to report new arrivals; compulsory registration.

Anmeldeschein, *m.* = **Anmeldungsformular.**

Anmeldestelle, *f. Adm:* registration office; registry (office); register office; registrar's office.

Anmeldungsformular, *n.* (*a*) *Adm:* registration form; (*b*) application form; entry-form (for competition, etc.).

anmengen, *v.tr. sep.* to mix (dough, mortar, etc.); to dress (salad).

anmerken. I. *v.tr. sep.* **1.** (*a*) to take, make, a note of (sth.); to make a memorandum of (sth.), to note (sth.) down, jot (sth.) down; (*b*) to mark (sth.); **einen Passus rot a.,** to mark a passage in red, with a red line; **Bäume zum Fällen a.,** to mark trees for felling; (*c*) **j-m das schlechte Gewissen, usw., a.,** to see from s.o.'s appearance that he has a bad conscience, etc.; **man merkt ihm die Geistesabwesenheit an,** one can see, cannot fail to notice, how absent-minded he is; **man merkt seiner Arbeit die Nachlässigkeit an,** his work is evidently careless; **man merkt ihm die Anstrengung nicht an,** he shows no outward signs of strain; **sie läßt sich nichts a.,** she does not show anything; she conceals her (deeper) feelings; she does not give herself away; **laß dir nichts a.!** don't give yourself away, *F:* don't give the game, the show, away; don't let the cat out of the bag. **2. a., daß . . . ,** to remark, observe (*orally*), that . . .

II. *vbl s.* **Anmerkung,** *f.* **1.** note; foot-note; annotation; **Anmerkungen zu einem Text machen, einen Text mit Anmerkungen versehen,** to write notes to a text; to annotate a text; **Text mit Anmerkungen,** text with notes; annotated text; text with commentary. **2.** (*spoken*) remark, observation.

anmessen, *v.tr. sep.* (*strong*) **1. j-m einen Anzug, usw., a.,** to take s.o.'s measurements, measure s.o., for a suit, etc.; **ich werde mir einen Überzieher a. lassen,** I am going to be measured for an overcoat. **2.** *occ.* to adjust (*dat.*, to). *See also* **angemessen.**

anmustern, *v.sep. Nau:* **1.** *v.tr.* to sign on (seaman). **2.** *v.i.* (*haben*) (*of seaman*) to sign on.

Anmut, *f.* grace, gracefulness; charm; attractiveness; sweetness of manner; pleasantness (of person, manner, place, etc.); elegance, grace, graciousness (of style, etc.); amenity (of place); **das verleiht der Landschaft A.,** it adds charm, lends (a) charm, to the landscape; **etwas mit A. tun,** to do sth. gracefully, with grace; **etwas ohne A. tun,** to do sth. ungracefully, without grace, awkwardly.

anmuten. I. *v.tr. sep.* **1.** (*a*) *A:* to please (s.o.), to be pleasing to (s.o.); (*b*) to give (s.o.) a feeling, a sense (of strangeness, familiarity, etc.); **es mutet mich seltsam an,** it seems odd to me; **es mutete ihn heimatlich an,** he felt (as though he were) at home; it seemed just like home to him; **holländisch anmutende Szenen,** scenes that make one think, put one in mind, of Holland; scenes that have something Dutch about them. **2.** *A:* = **zumuten.**

II. *vbl s.* **Anmutung,** *f. A. & Dial:* **1.** (*a*) attractiveness, attraction; charm; (*b*) **A. für etwas,** liking for sth. **2.** = **Zumutung,** *q.v. under* **zumuten** II.

anmutig, *a.* graceful (pers., gesture, etc.); charming (pers., manner, smile, etc.); attractive (pers., etc.); agreeable, pleasant (manner, place, etc.); **eine anmutige Gegend,** a delightful, smiling, countryside; *adv.* gracefully; **etwas a. tun,** to do sth. gracefully, with grace.

Anmutigkeit, *f.* = **Anmut.**

anmutlos, *a.* (*of pers.*) ungraceful; graceless; unlovely, charmless, devoid of charm; (*of pers., style, etc.*) uncouth, awkward; *adv.* ungracefully, awkwardly.

anmutsvoll, *a.* = **anmutig.**

Anna[1]. *Pr.n.f.* **-s** *& Lit:* **Annens.** Anna, Ann(e).

Anna[2], *s.m.* **-(s)/-(s).** *Num:* ($\frac{1}{16}$ *rupee*) anna.

annageln, *v.tr. sep.* (*a*) to nail (sth.) on, to fasten (sth.) with nails (**an**+*acc.*, to); to nail up (notice, picture, etc.); (*b*) *F:* (*of pers.*) **wie angenagelt stehen,** to stand stock still, remain rooted to the spot.

annagen, *v.tr. sep.* to gnaw, gnaw at (sth.); to nibble, nibble at (sth.).

annahen, *v.i. sep.* (*sein*) *occ.* = **herannahen.**

annähen, *v.tr. sep.* to sew on (button, fastener, etc.) (**an**+*acc.*, to); to put on (button).

annähern. I. *v.tr. sep.* **etwas etwas** *dat.*, **an etwas** *acc.*, **a.,** to bring sth. nearer, closer, to sth.; *Mth: etc:* **einen Fall, einen Wert, dem anderen a.,** to approximate a case, a value, to another; **sich a.,** (i) to draw near, come near (**j-m, etwas** *dat.*, to s.o., sth.); to approach (**j-m, etwas** *dat.*, s.o., sth.); (ii) *Mth:* (*of lines*) to converge; to approach one another; (iii) *Mth: etc:* (*of values, etc.*) **sich etwas** *dat.* **a.,** to approximate sth., to approach sth.; (*of values*) **sich einem Grenzwert a.,** to converge towards a limit.

II. *vbl s.* **1. Annähern,** *n.* (*a*) *in vbl senses; also: Hort:* **(Veredelung durch) A.,** grafting by approach; inarching; (*b*) = II. 2 (*a*), (*b*), (*c*). **2. Annäherung,** *f. in vbl senses; also:* (*a*) approach; *esp. Mil:* approach (of troops, to the front); (*b*) convergence (of lines, values) (**an**+*acc.*, **gegen,** towards); (*c*) approximation (**an**+*acc.*, to); **genaue, rohe, A.,** close, rough, approximation; (*d*) rapprochement; understanding; reconciliation; **zwischen zwei Gegnern, zwei Staaten, eine A. herbeiführen, zustande bringen,** to bring about a rapprochement, an understanding, between two opponents, two states; to bring two opponents, two states, together.

III. *pr.p. & a.* **annähernd,** *in vbl senses; esp. Mth: etc:* (*a*) **(sich) annähernde Linien,** converging lines; (*b*) approximate (value); rough (estimate, calculation); **annähernde Berechnung,** approximation; *adv.* approximately, roughly; **a. gleich,** approximately, roughly, equal, *F:* pretty nearly equal (*dat.*, to); **nicht a. . . . ,** nowhere near . . . , nothing like . . . ; **sie ist nicht a. so hübsch wie du,** she is nowhere near, nothing like, as pretty as you; **das ist nicht a. genug,** it's nothing like, nowhere near, enough, it isn't anything like enough.

IV. *p.p. & a.* **angenähert,** *in vbl senses; esp. Mth:* approximate (value).

Annäherungsgraben, *m. Mil:* approach trench.

Annäherungsmaßstab, *m. Surv: etc:* approximate scale.

Annäherungsschlag, *m. Golf:* approach shot.

Annäherungsschläger, *m. Golf:* (mid-)iron.

Annäherungsverfahren, *n. Mth:* method of approximation, approximation method.

Annäherungsversuch, *m.* attempt at a rapprochement; **bei j-m Annäherungsversuche machen,** to make approaches, advances, overtures, to s.o., *Pol: etc:* to seek a rapprochement with s.o.

Annäherungsweg, *m. Mil:* line, route, of approach.

annäherungsweise, *adv.* approximately, approximatively; *occ. a.* approximate, approximative.

Annäherungswert, *m. Mth: etc:* approximate value; approximate figure; approximation.

Annahme, *f.* **-/-n. 1.** (*a*) acceptance, accepting (of gift, proposal, play for presentation, etc.); receipt, receiving (of letters, luggage to be deposited, etc.; *Fin:* of deposits); acceptance, appointment (of applicant); adoption (of opinion, theory, doctrine, etc.); (*of theory, doctrine, etc.*) **bei j-m A. finden,** to find acceptance with s.o., to be accepted, believed, by s.o.; (*b*) *Com:* (i) acceptance, taking delivery (of goods); (ii) acceptance (of bill of exchange); **die A. der Waren verweigern,** to refuse to accept (delivery of) the goods; **einen Wechsel zur A. vorlegen,** to present a bill for acceptance; **die A. eines Wechsels verweigern,** to refuse acceptance of a bill; **mangels A. zurückgegangener Wechsel,** bill returned (under protest) for non-acceptance; **A. ehrenhalber,** acceptance for honour, acceptance supra protest; *Post:* **(die) A. verweigern,** to refuse to accept (delivery of) letter, etc.; *see also* **bedingen** III; (*c*) *Jur:* **A. (eines Jungen, eines Mädchens) an Kindes Statt,** adoption (of a boy, a girl); (*d*) *Pol:* **A. einer Gesetzesvorlage,** passage, passing, carrying, adoption, of a bill. **2.** (*a*) = **Annahmestelle;** (*b*) *Rail:* 'deposits' section *or* counter (of luggage-office). **3.** supposition, assumption; hypothesis; theory; **unbegründete A.,** gratuitous assumption, unfounded supposition; **wir haben Grund zur A., daß . . . ,** we have (good) reason to assume, suppose, that . . . ; **in, unter, der A., daß . . . ,** on the assumption, supposition, that . . .

Annahmepflicht, *f. Jur:* obligation to accept legal tender.

Annahmestelle, *f. Post: Rail: etc:* receiving-office (for letters, parcels, etc.).

Annahmevermerk, *m. Com:* acceptance, endorsement (on a bill).

Annahmeverweigerung, *f. Com:* non-acceptance (of goods, bill); *Post:* refusal to accept (delivery of) letter, etc.

Annalen [aˈnaːlən], *pl.* annals; (historical) records.

Annalin [anaˑˈliːn], *n.* **-s/.** *Ch: Paperm:* annaline (gypsum).

Annalist [anaˑˈlist], *m.* **-en/-en,** annalist.

annalistisch [anaˑˈlistiʃ], *a.* annalistic.

Annam [ˈanam]. *Pr.n.n.* **-s.** *Geog:* Annam.

Annamit [anaˑˈmiːt], *m.* **-en/-en.** Annamese, Annamite.

annamitisch [anaˑˈmiːtiʃ], (*a*) *a.* Annamese, Annamite; (*b*) *s.* **Annamitisch,** *n. Ling:* Annamese.

annässen, *v.tr. sep.* = **annetzen.**

Annaten [aˈnaːtən], *pl.* **1.** *Ecc:* annates, first-fruits. **2.** *R.C.Ch:* (*masses*) annals.

Annatto [aˈnatoː], *m.* **-s/.** = **Anatto.**

Ännchen. *Pr.n.n. & f.* **-s.** (*dim. of* **Anna**) Annie.

Anne[1]. *Pr.n.f.* **-s.** Anna, Ann(e).

Anne[2], *f.* **-/-n.** *Husb:* woody stalk (of flax).

annehmbar, *a.* **1.** acceptable, receivable; reasonable, acceptable (offer, price, etc.); allowable, admissible (opinion, doctrine, etc.); plausible (statement, opinion, etc.); passable, respectable (article, etc.); (article) of acceptable, tolerable, quality; *adv.* acceptably; **sie spielt ganz a.,** she plays quite acceptably, quite respectably, quite tolerably. **2.** assumable, supposable.

Annehmbarkeit, *f.* acceptability, acceptableness; admissibility (of opinion, doctrine, etc.).

annehmen. I. *v.tr. sep.* (*strong*) **1.** (*a*) to accept (gift, title, proposal, offer, bet, invitation, office, etc.); to take (employment, offer, bet, etc.); to take on (responsibility, piece of work, bet, etc.); to undertake (commission, work, etc.); to receive (visit); to accept, take on (applicant); to agree to (proposal); **ein Geschenk gnädig a.,** to be graciously pleased to accept a present; (*of deity*) **eine Gabe, ein Opfer, gnädig a.,** graciously to accept an offering; **er hat den Brief nicht angenommen,** he refused to accept the letter; **eine Einladung zum Abendessen a.,** to accept an invitation to dinner; *abs.* **er nahm dankend an,** he accepted with thanks; **ich werde nicht a.,** I shall not accept; I shall decline (the invitation); **sie nimmt heute keinen Besuch an,** she is not receiving (visitors) today; **Schüler a.,** to take pupils; **Sommergäste a.,** to take (in) summer visitors; **einen Namen a.,** to adopt, take, assume, a name; **eine Herausforderung a.,** to take up, accept, a challenge; **Rat von j-m a.,** to take s.o.'s advice; **er will keinen Rat a.,** he won't take any advice; **ein Kind a.,** to adopt a child; *Jur:* **j-n an Kindes Statt a.,** to adopt s.o.; *Pol: etc:* **eine Gesetzesvorlage, eine Resolution, a.,** to pass, carry, adopt, a bill, a resolution; **einstimmig angenommen,** carried, agreed, unanimously; **die Gesetzesvorlage wurde nicht angenommen,** the bill was rejected, thrown out; **der Antrag wurde nicht angenommen,** the motion was lost; *Ven:* (*of hound*) **die Fährte a.,** to pick up the scent, to get on the scent; (*of large animal*) **den Jäger a.,** to make a rush at the hunter; (*b*) *Com:* **Waren a.,** to accept (delivery of) goods, take delivery of goods; **einen Wechsel a.,** (i) to accept, sign, a bill; (ii) to honour a bill; **einen Wechsel nicht a.,** to dishonour a bill; (*c*) to adopt (view, religion, etc.); to embrace (cause, doctrine, faith); **die christliche Religion a.,** to embrace Christianity; **Vernunft, Verstand, a.,** to listen to reason; **wenn er keine Vernunft a. will,** if he won't listen to reason, if he doesn't see reason; (*d*) to take on, assume (appearance, attitude, tone, etc.); to acquire, develop, contract (habit); to take on, acquire (patina); (*of town, etc.*) **ein festliches Aussehen a.,** to take on a holiday appearance, to put on, assume, a festive look; **die Bäume nehmen herbstliche Farben an,** the trees take on autumn tints; (*of pers.*) **eine drohende Haltung a.,** to assume, take up, a threatening attitude; **einen strengen Ton a.,** to assume, put on, a tone of severity; **eine feierliche Miene a.,** to assume, put on, a solemn expression; **einen südlichen Akzent a.,** to acquire a southern accent; **einen Geschmack für etwas a.,** to acquire, develop, a taste for sth.; **die Maske der Tugend a.,** to put on a semblance of virtue. **2. sich j-s, etwas** *gen.*, **a.,** to take care of s.o., sth.; to take s.o., sth., under one's care; to take s.o. under one's protection, to extend one's protection to s.o.; to take s.o. up; to look after s.o., sth.; to accept responsibility for s.o., sth.; **sich der Sache der Heimatlosen a.,** to take up, espouse, adopt, the cause of the homeless; **ich werde mich der Sache a.,** I will look after, attend to, the matter, I will see to it. **3.** (*of substance*) to take (dye, etc.); **Pergament, das die Tinte nicht annimmt,** parchment that

will not take the ink; **Baumwolle nimmt Farben nicht gut an,** cotton does not take dyes well, kindly, cotton does not dye well. **4.** to assume, suppose, presume; **eine Behauptung, usw., als wahr a.,** to assume, presume, a statement, etc., to be true; to accept a statement, etc. as true; **ich nehme an, daß . . . ,** I suppose that . . . , I assume, presume, that . . . , I take it that . . . ; **ich nahm an, er wollte sagen . . . ,** I understood him to mean . . . , I took it that he meant . . . ; **man nimmt an, daß er in Paris ist,** he is supposed to be in Paris; **man nimmt an, er kommt nicht wieder,** it is assumed that he won't come back; **man nimmt allgemein an, daß . . . ,** it is generally assumed, believed, that . . . ; it is a common assumption that . . . ; **wird das Buch bald erscheinen? — ich nehme an,** will the book appear soon?—I suppose so, think so, I presume it will; **wir nehmen es als selbstverständlich, als ausgemacht, an, daß . . . ,** we take it for granted, as settled, that . . . ; **nehmen wir an, wir wollen a., daß . . . ,** let us take it that . . . , let us assume, presume, that . . . ; **angenommen, daß . . . ,** suppose that . . . , supposing that . . . ; **angenommen, daß es sich so verhält, . . . ,** supposing that is the case . . . , if we take that to be the case . . . ; granting that it is so . . . ; **das einmal angenommen, . . . ,** granting this, this being granted . . . ; **angenommen, er ist schuldig, . . . ,** assuming he is, assuming him to be, guilty; **angenommen, die Geschichte wäre wahr, . . . ,** supposing the story were true . . . , assuming the truth of the story . . . ; **gut, angenommen, es wäre wahr, was dann?** well, say, supposing, it were true, what then? **II.** *vbl s.* **Annehmen,** *n.* (a) *in vbl senses;* (b)=**Annahme.** **III.** *p.p. & a.* **angenommen,** *in vbl senses; esp.* **angenommenes Kind,** adopted, adoptive, child, *Jur:* adoptee; **angenommener Name,** assumed name; pseudonym; (author's) nom de plume, pen-name; **angenommene Lehre,** accepted, received, recognized, doctrine.
annehmenswert, *a.*=**annehmbar** 1.
Annehmer, *m.* **1.** accepter, receiver (of a present, etc.). **2.** *Com:* acceptor, drawee (of bill); transferee, assignee.
annehmlich, *a.*=**annehmbar** 1.
Annehmlichkeit, *f.* **1.** acceptability, acceptableness. **2.** (a) agreeableness, attractiveness, pleasantness, charm; (b) *pl.* **Annehmlichkeiten,** amenities (of place, home life, etc.); charms, delights (of home life, etc.); **die Annehmlichkeiten des Lebens,** the amenities, conveniences, comforts, sweets, sweet things, of life.
annektieren [anɛk'ti:rən]. **I.** *v.tr.* **1.** to annex (territory). **2.** *F:* to commandeer, bag, snaffle (chairs, places, etc.). **II.** *vbl s.* **Annektieren** *n.,* **Annektierung** *f.* annexation.
Annelide [ane'li:də], *f.* -/-n. *Nat. Hist:* annelid.
annetzen, *v.tr. sep. Constr: etc:* to moisten, damp, wet (plaster, etc.).
Annetzer, *m. Constr: etc:* sprinkling-brush, sprinkler.
Annex [a'nɛks], *m.* -es/-e. **1.** annexed document, annex; annexure (to report, letter, etc.); appendix (to report, etc.); rider (to document, etc.); enclosure (with letter). **2.** annex(e), outbuilding, outlying building, outlier.
Annexbau, *m.*=**Annex** 2.
Annexion [anɛksi'o:n], *f.* -/-en, annexation.
Annexionist [anɛksio'nist], *m.* -en/-en. *Pol:* annexationist.
anniesen, *v.tr. sep.* **1.** to sneeze at (s.o.); to sneeze all over (s.o.). **2.** *F:* to tell (s.o.) off, tick (s.o.) off.
annieten, *v.tr. sep.* to rivet (sth.) on.
Annihilation [anihila'tsi'o:n], *f.* -/-en. **1.** annihilation. **2.** *Jur:* annulment.
Annihilator [anihi'la:tor], *m.* -s/-en [-la'to:rən], hand fire-extinguisher.
annihilieren [anihi'li:rən], *v.tr.* **1.** to annihilate, destroy (army, will-power, etc.). **2.** *Jur:* to annul, cancel (decision, will, etc.). **3.** *vbl s.* **Annihilierung,** *f.*=**Annihilation.**
Anniversarium [ani'vɛr'za:rĭum], *n.* -s/-rien. **1.** anniversary. **2.** *Ecc:* anniversary service; *R.C.Ch:* anniversary (mass).
Anno[1]**, anno** ['ano:]. *Lt.s. A.* **1740,** in the year 1740; **A. Domini** ['do:mi'ni:] **1660,** in the year of Our Lord 1660, in the year of grace 1660, in A.D. 1660; *F:* **a. dazumal,** in olden times, in the days of yore, in the dim and distant past; **von a. dazumal (her), von a. Tobak (her),** time out of mind, *F:* since the year dot.
Anno[2]**. Pr.n.m.** -s. *Hist:* Anno.

annoch [a'nox], *adv. A:* still; as yet; up to now.
Annonce [a'nõ:sə], *f.* -/-n, advertisement, *esp.* small advertisement, *F:* small ad.
Annoncenblatt [a'nõ:sən-], *n.*=**Anzeigenblatt.**
Annoncenbüro [-by'ˌro:], *n.,* **Annoncenexpedition** [-ɛkspe'di'tsio:n], *f.* advertising agency.
Annoncenmann, *m.* -(e)s/-männer. *F:* sandwich-man.
Annoncenwesen, *n.* advertising; publicity.
Annonceuse [anõ'sø:zə], *f.* -/-n. *Th:* (female) announcer (in a revue), *F:* commère.
annoncieren [anõ'si:rən]. **I.** *v.tr.* to announce (sth.). **2.** (a) *v.tr.* to advertise (sth.); (b) *v.i.* (haben) to advertise, to put in an advertisement (für etwas, for sth.).
Annotation [anota'tsi'o:n], *f.* -/-en, annotation, note.
Annuale [anu'a:lə], *f.* -/-n. *R.C.Ch:* annual.
Annuarium [anu'a:rĭum], *n.* -s/-rien, annual, year-book.
annuell [anu'ɛl], *a.* annual, yearly; *Bot:* **annuelle Pflanze,** annual.
Annuität [anui'tɛ:t], *f.* -/-en, annuity; **lebenslängliche A.,** life annuity; **ewige, unendliche, A.,** perpetual annuity; **A. mit begrenzter Laufzeit, A. auf bestimmte Zeit,** terminable annuity; **aufgeschobene A.,** deferred annuity.
Annullation [anula'tsi'o:n], *f.* -/-en. *Jur:*=**Annullierung,** *q.v. under* **annullieren** II.
annullierbar [anu'li:rba:r], *a. Jur:* voidable, defeasible (contract, etc.); that can be annulled, cancelled, quashed.
annullieren [anu'li:rən]. **I.** *v.tr.* to annul, to nullify; (a) *Jur:* to render void, repeal, quash, set aside, rescind (law, will, judgment, etc.); to abate (writ, etc.); to revoke (order, decree); (b) *Com:* to cancel (contract, order, etc.); to revoke, countermand, withdraw (order). **II.** *vbl s.* **Annullierung,** *f. in vbl senses; also:* annulment, nullification; (a) *Jur:* repeal, rescission (of judgment, etc.); abatement (of writ, etc.); revocation (of order, decree); (b) *Com:* cancellation (of contract, order, etc.); revocation, withdrawal (of order).
Anode [a'no:də], *f.* -/-n. *El:* anode, positive pole; plate (of battery, valve).
anöden, *v.tr. sep.* (a) to bore, weary (s.o.); **sie ödet mich an,** I get dreadfully tired of her, *F:* she bores me stiff; (b) to pull s.o.'s leg; to take a rise out of s.o.
Anodenbatterie [a'no:dənbatə,ri:], *f. El:* high-tension battery, *U.S:* B-battery.
Anodenbelastung, *f.*=**Anodenverlustleistung.**
Anodenentladung, *f. El:* discharge at the anode.
Anodenfall, *m. El:* anode fall, drop.
Anodengleichrichter, *m. W.Tel:* anode bend detector.
Anodengleichrichtung, *f. W.Tel:* anode (bend) rectification.
Anodenkreis, *m. El: W.Tel:* anode circuit.
Anodenschlamm, *m. El.-Ch:* anode mud, slime.
Anodenschutznetz, *n. W.Tel:* anode screen.
Anodenspannung, *f. El: W.Tel:* anode voltage; plate voltage.
Anodenstrahlen, *m.pl. El:* anode rays.
Anodenstrom, *m. El:* anode current; plate current.
Anodenverlustleistung, *f. El: W.Tel:* anode dissipation.
Anodenwiderstand, *m. El: W.Tel:* anode resistor, anode load.
Anodenzerstäubung, *f. El:* anode sputtering.
anodisch [a'no:diʃ], *a. El:* anodic, anodal; *El.-Ch:* **anodische Oxydation,** anodic oxidation, anodizing; **a. behandeln,** to anodize (aluminium, etc.).
Anodynie [ano'dy'ni:], *f.* -/. painless state; freedom from pain.
Anökumene, die [an'ø'ku'me:nə], *f.* -. *Geog:* the uninhabited portions of the earth.
anölen, *v.tr. sep.* to oil, lubricate.
Anolis [a'no:lis], *m.* -/-. *Rept:* anolis; anole.
anomal [ano'ma:l], *a.* **1.** anomalous (case *Gram:* verb, etc.). **2.** (often incorrectly)= **anormal.**
Anomalie [ano'ma'li:], *f.* -/-n [-'li:ən]. *Biol: Astr: etc:* anomaly.
anomalisch [ano'ma:liʃ], *a.*=**anomal.**
anomalistisch [a·no·ma·'listiʃ], *a. Astr:* anomalistic (year, month).
Anomie [ano'mi:], *f.* -/. lawlessness, disregard of law.
anomisch [a'no:miʃ], *a.* lawless.
Anonazeen [a·no·na·'tse:ən], *f.pl. Bot:* anonaceae.

Anone [a·'no:nə], *f.* -/-n, (a) *Bot:* anona; (b) *Com:* (fruit) custard-apple.
anonenartig [a·'no:nən-], *a. Bot:* anonaceous.
Anonengewächse, *n.pl. Bot:* anonaceae.
anonym [ano'ny:m], *a.* anonymous (writer, letter, etc.); unnamed (benefactor, etc.); *adv.* anonymously.
Anonymität [ano·ny·mi·'tɛt], *f.* -/. anonymity.
Anonymus [a'no:ny·mus], *m.* -/-mi [a'no:ny·mi:] & -men [ano·'ny:mən], anonymous person, *esp.* anonymous writer.
Anopheles [a·'no:fe·les], *f.* -/-. *Ent:* anopheles.
Anorak ['ano·rak], *m.* -s/-s. *Cost:* anorak, ski jacket.
anordnen. I. *v.tr. sep.* **1.** to arrange (sth.); to dispose, set out (objects in order, position); to set (books, etc.) in rows; to dispose, draw up, array, marshal (troops, etc.); to order (troops, furniture, words in sentence, etc.); to put, set, (thgs, sth.) in order; to regulate, direct (procedure, etc.); to dispose, arrange (rooms in house, furniture in room, etc.); to arrange, group, place (figures in picture, etc.); to lay out (rooms, gear-box, etc.); **Truppen zur Schlacht a.,** to draw up troops in battle array; **die Gestalten im Bilde sind vortrefflich angeordnet,** the arrangement, grouping, placing, of the figures in the picture is excellent; **schlecht angeordnete Sätze,** ill-arranged, ill-balanced, sentences; **alles vorausschauend a.,** to plan everything ahead, to arrange everything in advance. **2.** (a) to order (sth.); to command (sth.); to decree (sth.); **der Arzt hat Luftveränderung angeordnet,** the doctor has ordered him, her, a change of air; **der General ordnete den Rückzug an,** the general ordered the retreat; (b) **a., daß etwas getan wird,** to order sth. to be done; to give orders for sth. to be done, that sth. should be done; to arrange, make arrangements, for sth. to be done; **ich werde a., daß die Sitzung rechtzeitig eröffnet wird,** I will arrange for the meeting to start, I will see (to it) that the meeting starts, promptly. **II.** *vbl s.* **1.** **Anordnen,** *n. in vbl senses.* **2.** **Anordnung,** *f.* (a) *in vbl senses; also:* arrangement; disposition (of troops, objects, furniture, words in sentence, etc.); disposal (of troops, objects); order (of rooms in house, etc.); regulation, direction (of procedure, etc.); adjustment (of parts of machine, etc.); (b) layout (of room, gearbox, etc.); **A. des Ganzen,** (general) structure, (general) lay-out; composition (of picture); **räumliche A.,** configuration, spatial relationships (of parts of building); (c) *usu.pl.* **Anordnungen,** arrangements, dispositions; **Anordnungen treffen,** to make arrangements, to take (one's) dispositions; **wir haben in diesem Sinne Anordnungen getroffen,** we have made provisions to this effect; (d) order, command; instruction, direction; **auf A.+gen.,** on instructions from . . . , by direction of . . . , by order of . . . ; **auf A. des Arztes,** on doctor's orders; **Anordnungen geben, treffen,** to give orders, instructions, directions (wegen etwas, about sth.; **daß etwas getan wird,** for sth. to be done, that sth. should be done).
Anordner, *m.* director, arranger; person in charge of the arrangements (for festival, etc.).
Anordnungsplan, *m.* lay-out (plan, diagram).
Anordnungsrecht, *n. Adm:* right to issue instructions.
Anorexie [ano·rɛ'ksi:], *f.* -/. *Med:* anorexia; loss of appetite.
Anorganiker ['an·or,ga:nikər], *m.* inorganic chemist.
anorganisch ['an·or,ga:niʃ], *a.* inorganic (body, chemistry, etc.).
anormal ['a·norma:l], *a.* abnormal; irregular, anomalous (type, case, etc.); *cp.* **abnormal.**
Anorthit [anor'ti:t], *m.* -(e)s/-e. *Geol:* anorthite, lime-feldspar.
Anosmie [an·os'mi:], *f.* -/. *Med:* anosmia; loss of the sense of smell.
anoxydieren ['an·oksy·di:rən], *v.tr. sep.* (p.p. **anoxydiert**) *Ch: etc:* to oxidize.
anpaaren, *v.tr. sep. Breed:* to pair (a male and a female animal).
anpacken, *v.tr. sep.* to seize; to grasp, grip; to lay hold, take hold, catch hold, grasp hold, grab hold, of (s.o., sth.); to tackle (s.o., sth.); to grab (s.o., sth.); **j-n am Arm a.,** to seize, catch, grab, clutch, s.o. by the arm; to grasp, grab, clutch, (at) s.o.'s arm; **j-n beim Kragen a.,** to seize s.o. by the collar, to collar s.o.; **j-n an der Gurgel a.,** to seize, catch, grip, pin, s.o. by the throat; **j-n, ein Tier, am Genick a.,** to catch, seize, s.o., an animal, by the scruff of the neck; **ein Problem a.,** to tackle, attack, a problem;

eine Frage, eine Schwierigkeit, a., to tackle a question, a difficulty.

anpappen, *v.tr. sep.* to paste, stick, (sth.) on.

Anpaß, *m.* **-passes/.** *Mec.E:* shoulder (of axle).

anpassen. I. *v.tr. sep.* **1.** (*a*) **etwas etwas** *dat.* **a.,** (i) to fit, adjust, conform, sth. to sth.; (ii) to adapt, accommodate, suit, sth. to sth.; to make sth. suitable for sth.; **seinen Stil den Zuhörern a.,** to suit one's style to one's audience; **seine Rede war der Gelegenheit gut angepaßt,** his speech was well suited to the occasion, was very fitting (for the occasion); **sich j-m, etwas** *dat.*, **an j-n, an etwas** *acc.*, **a.,** to adapt, adjust, oneself to s.o., sth.; to accommodate oneself to sth.; to conform to sth.; **sich den Verhältnissen a.,** to adapt, accommodate, oneself to circumstances; to make the best of circumstances; **sich seiner, an seine, Umgebung a.,** to adapt oneself to one's environment, to fit oneself (in)to one's surroundings; **sich j-s Meinung a.,** to fall in with s.o.'s opinion; (*b*) *El.E:* to accommodate, to match (circuits, etc.). **2.** to try on, fit on (garment); **j-m ein Kleid a.,** to fit, try, a dress on s.o.; *abs.* **der Schneider kann nächste Woche a.,** the tailor can manage a fitting next week; (*of optician*) **eine Brille a.,** to fit a pair of spectacles.

II. *vbl. s.* **1. Anpassen,** *n. in vbl senses.* **2. Anpassung,** *f. in vbl senses; also:* (*a*) adaptation (**an**+*acc.*, to); adjustment (**an**+*acc.*, to); conformation (**an**+*acc.*, to); conformity (**an**+*acc.*, to, with); accommodation (**an**+*acc.*, to); *Biol:* adaptation; *El.E:* accommodation (of circuits, etc.); *Ling:* accommodation, partial assimilation (of consonants); (*b*) *Tail: etc:* fitting (on), fitting on, try-on (of garment).

Anpaßraum, *m. Tail: etc:* fitting-room; trying-on room *or* cubicle.

Anpassungsbuchse, Anpassungsbüchse, *f. W.Tel:* (plug-)socket.

anpassungsfähig, *a.* adaptable (**an**+*acc.*, to); adaptive; (*of pers.*) accommodating; conformable; (*of character, pers.*) supple; (*of character, language, etc.*) flexible; *Biol:* adaptable; **geistig a.,** versatile.

Anpassungsfähigkeit, *f.* adaptability (**an**+*acc.*, to); adaptiveness; suppleness (of character, pers.); flexibility (of character, language, etc.); *Biol:* adaptability; **geistige A.,** versatility; **wirtschaftliche A.,** economic adaptiveness.

Anpassungsmerkmal, *n. Biol:* adaptive characteristic.

Anpassungspolitik, *f.* policy adapted to circumstances; opportunist, *Pej:* time-serving, policy.

Anpassungsschaltung, *f. El.E: Tp:* accommodating connection.

Anpassungstransformator, *m. El.E:* matching transformer.

Anpassungsvermögen, *n.* adaptability; adaptiveness.

anpasten, *v.tr. sep. Pharm:* to work up (ointment, salve).

anpatschen, *v.sep.* **1.** *v.tr.* (*of pers.*) to dab at (sth.) (with one's hand). **2.** *v.i.* (*usu. only in*) **angepatscht kommen,** to come splashing, floundering, along.

anpeilen, *v.tr. sep. Nau: W.Tel:* to take a bearing on (sth.).

anpetzen, *v.tr. sep. F:* to sneak, tell, *F:* split, snitch, *U.S:* tattle, on s.o.

Anpfahl, *m. Min:* (pit-)prop; shore.

anpfählen, *v.tr. sep.* to fasten (sth.) to a stake *or* stakes; to prop, stake (vine, etc.).

anpfeffern, *v.tr. sep. F:* to hot up, pep up (song, revue, etc.).

anpfeifen, *v.sep.* (*strong*) **1.** *v.tr. Fb: etc:* (*of referee*) **das Spiel a.,** *abs.* **a.,** to blow the whistle for the start of play. **2.** *v.tr. F:* **j-n a.,** to tick, tell, s.o. off; to let fly at s.o. **3.** *v.i.* (*of engine, etc.*) **angepfiffen kommen,** to come whistling along.

Anpfiff, *m.* **1.** *Fb: etc:* whistle (*from referee*) for the start of play. **2.** *F:* ticking-off, telling-off; **einen A. kriegen,** to get ticked off, to get a wigging.

anpflanzen. I. *v.tr. sep.* **1.** to plant, grow (trees, etc.); to cultivate (land, garden); **eine Baumallee a.,** to lay out an avenue of trees. **2. sich anpflanzen,** to settle (*esp. Hist:* in new colony).

II. *vbl s.* **1. Anpflanzen,** *n. in vbl senses.* **2. Anpflanzung,** *f.* (*a*) *in vbl senses; also:* cultivation; (*b*) *Hist:* plantation, settlement (in new colony); (new) colony.

Anpflanzer, *m.* (*a*) planter, grower (of trees, etc.); (*b*) cultivator; (*c*) planter, settler (in new colony).

anpflaumen, *v.tr. sep. F:* to take a rise out of (s.o.); to pull (s.o.'s) leg; to chip (at) (s.o.); to kid (s.o.).

anpflöcken, *v.tr. sep.* to peg (sth.) on (**an**+*acc.*, to); to tether (goat) to a post.

anpflügen, *v.i. sep.* (*haben*) *Dial:* to begin ploughing.

anpfropfen, *v.tr. sep.* **1.** *Arb:* to graft on; **eine Art an eine andere a.,** to graft one variety on, upon, another. **2.** *Carp:* to lengthen, join a lengthening-piece to (beam, etc.).

anpichen, *v.tr. sep.* to coat (sth.) with pitch; to pitch (planks, etc.).

anpicken, *v.tr. sep.* to peck at (sth.); **angepicktes Obst,** fruit that has been pecked (by birds).

anpinseln, *v.tr. sep. F:* to brush (sth.) over (with varnish, etc.); to paint (sth.); to varnish (one's fingernails).

anpirschen (sich), *v.refl.sep.*=**heranpirschen (sich).**

anplacken, *v.tr. sep.* (*a*) to stick, paste, (sth.) on; (*b*) to put up (notice).

anplärren. *v.tr. sep.* (*esp. of child*) to bawl, *F:* squawk, at (s.o.).

anplätzen, *v.tr. sep. For:* to blaze, mark (tree).

anpöbeln, *v.tr. sep.* to behave rudely towards (s.o.); to use abusive language to (s.o.); (*of angry crowd*) to mob (s.o.).

anpochen, *v.i. sep.* (*haben*) **an etwas** *acc.* **a.,** to knock on, at, sth.; **an die Tür a.,** to knock at the door; **bei j-m a.,** to knock at s.o.'s door.

anpolieren, *v.tr. sep.* (*p.p.* **anpoliert**) *Ind:* to give a rough polishing to (furniture, etc.); **anpolierte Stühle,** rough-polished chairs.

anpoltern, *v.i. sep.* (*haben*) **1. an die Tür a.,** to hammer at, on, the door. **2. sie kamen angepoltert,** they came up making a great commotion, a great racket, an awful row.

Anprall, *m.* impact (**gegen, auf**+*acc.*, on, upon); impingement (of body); collision (**gegen, auf**+*acc.*, with); shock; brunt (of attack); **A. eines Körpers gegen, auf, einen anderen,** impact of one body on, against, another; collision of one body with another; **den A. des feindlichen Angriffs aushalten,** to withstand the onslaught, onset, of the enemy; to bear the brunt of the enemy's attack.

anprallen, *v.i. sep.* (*sein*) **an, gegen, etwas** *acc.* **a.,** to strike (forcibly) against sth.; to impact with, against, sth., to impinge on, upon, sth.; to collide with sth.; to knock against sth., to run against, into, sth.; *F:* to cannon into, against sth.

Anprallpunkt, *m.* point of impact.

anprangern, *v.tr. sep.* to pillory (s.o., an abuse, etc.); to denounce (malpractice, etc.).

anpreien, *v.tr. sep. Nau:* to hail (ship).

anpreisen. I. *v.tr. sep.* (*strong*) to commend (s.o., sth.); to extol, praise, laud (s.o., sth.); to cry up, *F:* crack up (s.o., sth.); to puff, boost (sth.).

II. *vbl s.* **1. Anpreisen,** *n. in vbl senses.* **2. Anpreisung,** *f.* (*a*) *in vbl senses;* (*b*) commendation; (high) praise; puff, boost.

Anpreiser, *m.* praiser; extoller (of a political system, etc.); puffer, crier up, booster (of merchandise, etc.).

anprellen, *v.i. sep.* (*sein*)=**anprallen.**

anpressen, *v.tr. sep.* **etwas an etwas** *acc.* **a.,** to press, squeeze, sth. against sth.

Anpreßteller, *m. Mec.E:* pressure-plate (of coupling).

Anprobe, *f. Tail: etc:* fitting (on), trying on, try-on (of clothes); **ich kann nächste Woche zur A. kommen,** I can come for a fitting next week.

anprobieren, *v.tr. sep.* (*p.p.* **anprobiert**) to try on (garment, clothes); **wann kann ich a.?** when can I come for a fitting?

anpudern, *v.tr. sep.* to powder (sth.); to dust (sth.) (with powder).

anpumpen, *v.tr. sep. F:* to borrow money from (s.o.), *F:* to touch (s.o.); **j-n um zehn Mark a.,** to touch, tap, s.o. for ten marks.

Anpumper, *m. F:* (constant) borrower.

anpusten, *v.tr. sep.* to puff, blow, at (sth.); to breathe on (mirror, etc.).

Anputz, *m.* **1.** *A:* finery; fine clothes; *F:* pretties, 'buttons and bows'. **2.** *Constr:* plastering, plaster.

anputzen, *v.tr. sep.* **1.** (*a*) to adorn (s.o.); to dress, get, (s.o.) up; **sich a.,** to adorn oneself, bedeck oneself, deck oneself out; to dress, get, oneself up; to titivate, *F:* to tog oneself up; (*b*) to adorn, decorate (sth.). **2.** *Constr:* to plaster (wall). **3.** *F:* to tell, tick, (s.o.) off.

anqualmen, *v.tr. sep.* (*of smoker*) to blow, puff, clouds of smoke at (s.o.).

anquatschen, *v.tr. sep. F:* (*a*) to accost (s.o.) (in street, train, etc.); to talk to (stranger); (*b*) to jaw away at (s.o.); to blether at (s.o.).

anquellen, *v.sep.* **1.** *v.i.* (*strong*) (*sein*) (*of seeds*) to sprout. **2.** *v.tr.* (*weak*) to make (seeds) sprout.

anquicken, *v.tr. sep.* to amalgamate (gold, silver).

Anquickfaß, *n. Metall:* amalgamating tub.

anradeln, *v.i. sep.* (*sein*) to cycle up, pedal up; to ride up (on bicycle); **er kam angeradelt,** he came pedalling along; he pedalled up.

anrainen, *v.tr. & i. sep.* (*haben*) **(an) j-n, j-s Grundstück, a.,** to be s.o.'s neighbour; **mein Feld, Grundstück, raint an seines an, ich raine an ihn an,** I am his neighbour, he is my neighbour; his land abuts on mine; **anrainende Grundstücke,** abutting, adjoining, plots of land.

Anrainer, *m.* **-s/-,** *esp. Agr:* neighbour; owner *or* tenant of adjacent land; *pl.* **Anrainer,** abutting owners *or* tenants of property adjoining a road.

Anrainerstaaten, *m.pl.*=**Anliegerstaaten.**

Anrand, Anrang, *m.* **-(e)s/.** *South G.Dial:*= **Anlauf 1** (*a*).

anranken (sich), *v.refl. sep.* (*of climbing or creeping plant*) **sich an etwas** *acc.* **a.,** to fasten its tendrils to sth., to cling to sth.; to creep over (wall, etc.).

anranzen, *v.tr. sep. F:* to give (s.o.) a dressing-down, *F:* to blow (s.o.) up, tell (s.o.) off, tick (s.o.) off; to bite (s.o.'s) head off; to go for (s.o.).

anraspeln, *v.tr. sep.* to rasp (sth.) slightly; to give (sth.) a touch of the rasp.

anrasseln, *v.i. sep.* (*sein*) (*usu. only in p.p.*) **angerasselt kommen,** to come rattling, clattering, along; **der alte Wagen kam angerasselt,** the old car rattled up, clattered up.

Anrat, *m.* counsel, (piece of) advice.

anraten. I. *v.tr. sep.* (*strong*) **j-m etwas a.,** to recommend (course of action, etc.) to s.o.; **j-m Geduld, Vorsicht, a., j-m a., geduldig, vorsichtig, zu sein,** to advise, recommend, *Lit:* counsel, s.o. to be patient, cautious.

II. *vbl s.* **Anraten,** *n., A:* **Anratung,** *f.* advice, recommendation, *Lit:* counsel; **auf j-s A.** *acc.*, at, by, on, s.o.'s advice; **auf A. des Arztes,** on the advice of, on advice from, the doctor; on medical advice.

anrauchen, *v.tr. sep.* **1.** to smoke (sth.); to blacken (wall, paper, glass, etc.) with smoke; **angeraucht,** (*of wall, window, etc.*) smoke-blackened. **2.** (*of pers.*) **j-n a.,** to blow, puff, smoke into s.o.'s face. **3.** (*a*) **eine Zigarre a.,** to light (up), start, a cigar, to get a cigar going; (*b*) **eine Pfeife a.,** (i) to break a pipe in, smoke a pipe in, (ii) to season, colour, a pipe. **4.** *F:* **angeraucht,** half-drunk, fuddled, tipsy.

anräuchern, *v.tr. sep.* **1.** (*a*) to smoke (ham, etc.) (lightly); (*b*) to fumigate, smoke (plants, etc.). **2.** to perfume (sth.) with incense. **3.** *vbl s.* **Anräucherung,** *f. in vbl senses; also:* fumigation.

Anraum, *m.* **-(e)s/.** *Dial:* white frost.

anrauschen, *v.i. sep.* (*sein*) (*usu. only in p.p.*) **angerauscht kommen,** (*of wind*) (i) to come roaring, rushing, blustering, (ii) to blow, to come rustling (through the trees, etc.); (iii) (*of woman*) to come rustling up.

anrechnen. I. *v.tr. sep.* **1.** (*a*) *Com: Fin:* **j-m einen Betrag a.,** (i) to credit a sum to s.o., to credit s.o. with a sum; to enter, put a sum to s.o.'s credit; to allow s.o. a sum, to make s.o. an allowance (of so much); (ii) to charge s.o. a sum; to charge a sum (up) to s.o., to debit s.o. with a sum, to enter, put, a sum down to s.o.'s account; **j-m 20 M für einen Artikel a.,** to charge s.o. 20 marks for an article; **j-m zuviel a.,** to overcharge s.o.; **er hat es mir billig angerechnet,** he let me have it cheap; **eine Zahlung auf eine gewisse Schuld a.,** to apply a payment to a particular debt; **wir können für Ihren alten Kühlschrank 200 M a.,** we can allow you, make you an allowance of, 200 marks on your old refrigerator; *Jur:* **etwas aufs Erbteil a.,** to add sth. to the estate; to bring sth. into hotchpot; (*b*) *Adm: etc:* **j-m fünf Jahre Dienstzeit a.,** to allow, grant, give, s.o. five years' seniority; *Jur:* **die Untersuchungshaft a.,** to take into account the time already spent in custody. **2. j-m etwas als Verdienst a.,** to count sth. to s.o.'s credit, to give s.o. credit for sth.; **wir rechnen ihm seine Hilfe hoch an,** we greatly appreciate his help; **ich rechne es mir zur Ehre an, Ihnen zu dienen,** I count, consider, *Lit:* deem, it an honour to serve you; **j-m etwas als Sünde a.,** to count sth. to s.o. for a sin.

II. *vbl s.* **1. Anrechnen,** *n. in vbl senses.* **2. Anrechnung,** *f.* (*a*) *in vbl senses; also:* **in A. bringen,** (i) to take (sum, etc.) into account; (ii) to take sth. into consideration; to allow for, make allowance(s) for (circumstances, etc.);

das alte Radio in A. bringen, (*of dealer*) to take the old radio in part exchange; to make an allowance, allow something, on, for, the old set; (*b*) deduction (**auf**+*acc.*, from); allowance (**auf einen Artikel,** on, for, in respect of, an article).

Anrecht, *n.* title, claim, right (**auf**+*acc.*, to); **ein A. auf etwas haben,** to have a right to sth., to be entitled to sth.; **auf sein A. auf etwas verzichten,** to renounce one's claim to sth., one's interest in sth.; **ich habe kein A. auf Ihre Hilfe,** I have no right to claim your help, I have no claim on you.

Anrede, *f.* **1.** (*a*) address; harangue (to crowd); allocution (by general to army; by Pope to the Church, etc.); charge (by bishop to clergy; by judge to jury); (*b*) approach (to s.o.), addressing (of s.o.); **bei dieser A. blieb er stehen,** hearing himself thus addressed, he stopped; (*c*) *Gram:* apostrophe. **2.** form of address (*gen.*, **an**+*acc.*, to); (*in a letter*) salutation; **die richtige A. für den Rektor, des Rektors, einer deutschen Universität ist 'Magnifizenz',** the proper form o address to the Rector of a German university is, the Rector of a German university should be addressed as, 'Magnifizenz'; **die A. 'Sie',** the polite, conventional, form of address; **die A. 'Du',** the familiar form of address; **die A. in einem Brief an einen Unbekannten ist 'sehr geehrter Herr',** the salutation in a letter, *F:* the way to start a letter, to a stranger is 'Dear Sir'.

Anredefall, *m. Gram:* vocative (case); nominative of address.

Anredeform, *f.* (*a*)=**Anrede** 2; (*b*) *Gram:* vocative (case).

anreden, *v.tr. sep.* **1.** (*a*) to address (s.o.), to speak to (s.o.); **j-n freundlich, grob, a.,** to speak amiably, rudely, to s.o.; **j-n feierlich a.,** to address s.o. ceremoniously; to apostrophize s.o.; **sie redete mich englisch an,** she spoke to me, addressed me, in English; **j-n mit 'Sie' a.,** to address s.o. as, to call s.o., 'Sie'; to use the polite, conventional form of address to s.o.; **j-n mit 'Du' a.,** to address s.o. as, to call s.o., 'du'; to use the familiar form of address to s.o.; **er redete mich (mit) 'Herr Oberst' an,** he addressed me as 'Colonel'; (*b*) to deliver, give, an address to (company, etc.); to address, harangue (crowd). **2. j-n um etwas a.,** to approach s.o. with a request for sth.; to ask a favour of s.o.; **j-n auf etwas hin a.,** to (go and) ask s.o. about sth.; to tackle s.o. about (the truth of rumour, etc.).

Anredeweise, *f.* (*a*) manner, way, of addressing someone; (*b*)=**Anrede** 2.

anregbar, *a.* that can be stimulated, excited; *El: Physiol:* excitable.

anregen. I. *v.tr. sep.* **1.** (*a*) to actuate; to get (s.o., sth.) going; to incite, instigate (s.o.); **j-n zu etwas a., j-n a., etwas zu tun,** to stimulate, incite, encourage, prompt, s.o. to sth., to do sth.; to bring s.o. to do sth.; **durch ein Gefühl des Mitleids, des Interesses, angeregt,** prompted by a feeling of pity, of interest; **j-n zu neuen Ideen a.,** to give s.o. a fresh impetus to thought; *abs.* **das wird zu neuen Bestrebungen a.,** that will give rise to, give occasion for, fresh efforts; (*b*) to suggest (sth.); to give an impetus to, to start (discussion, etc.); to give the initial idea(s) for (essay, article, etc.); to initiate (negotiations, scheme, etc.); to originate (scheme, etc.); **ein Thema a.,** to bring a subject up (for consideration, for discussion); to raise a subject, a question; **ich werde das a.,** I'll bring it up; I'll suggest it, make a suggestion about it; **a., daß etwas getan wird, daß etwas geschieht,** to make suggestions that sth. be done, that sth. should happen; to make the first move to get sth. done; *Sch:* **Herr Professor X regte das Dissertationsthema an,** the subject of the dissertation was suggested by Professor X; the dissertation was inspired by a suggestion from Professor X. **2.** (*a*) to stimulate (digestion, thirst, desire, etc.); to activate (digestion, etc.); to excite (thirst, desire, etc.); to stir up (desire); to animate, quicken, enliven, stimulate (conversation, etc.); to animate, stimulate (s.o.); *Ch:* to activate; *Physiol:* to stimulate (organ, nerve, etc.); to excite (nerve); *El:* to excite (substance, etc.); *Radiotherapy:* to stimulate; **den Appetit a.,** to stimulate, excite, whet, *F:* put an edge on, the appetite; **j-s Ideen a.,** to stimulate s.o.'s ideas; to make s.o. think; *abs.* **starker Tee regt an,** strong tea stimulates, acts as a stimulant; **das Buch regt an, ist anregend,** the book is stimulating, makes one think, gives one food for thought; **anregend,** stimulating, stimulative; stirring (speech, book, melody, etc.); **seine Reden wirken anregend,** his speeches are stimulating; **er weiß, anregend zu reden,** he knows how to arouse interest in an audience, how to get his listeners interested; *Med:* **anregendes Mittel,** stimulant; excitant; (*b*) *Ven:* to start, flush, rouse (game).

II. *vbl s.* **1. Anregen,** *n. in vbl senses.* **2. Anregung,** *f.* (*a*) *in vbl senses; also:* (i) actuation; stimulation (**zu**, to); encouragement, incitement, incitation (**zu**, to); instigation (**zu**, to); (ii) initiation (of negotiations, scheme, etc.); (iii) animation; *Ch: etc:* activation; *Physiol:* stimulation; excitement; *Ph: Physiol:* excitation; (*b*) suggestion; **j-m eine A., Anregungen, geben,** to give s.o. a suggestion, suggestions; to give s.o. the initial idea(s) (for dissertation, article, etc.); to prompt s.o.; **auf j-s A. (hin),** at, on, the suggestion of s.o.; by, at, the instigation of s.o.; *occ.* **ein Thema in A. bringen**=**ein Thema anregen,** *q.v. under* I. 1; (*c*) stimulant, stimulus (**zu**, to).

III. *p.p. & a.* **angeregt,** *in vbl senses; esp.* animated, spirited, lively (discussion, etc.); brisk (discussion); (*of pers.*) lively.

Anreger, *m.* **-s/-,** instigator (of deed, etc.); initiator, originator (of proposal, scheme, etc.); promoter (of scheme, etc.).

Anregungsmittel, *n. Med:* stimulant; excitant.

Anregungsspannung, *f. El:* excitation potential.

anreiben, *v.tr. sep.* (*strong*) **1.** to grind (colours); **Farben mit Wasser a.,** to dilute, moisten, colours. **2.** to rub (sth.) on; *Metalw:* to apply (silvering, gilding, etc.) with a rag; *Bookb:* to paste on (the covering). **3. ein Streichholz a.,** to strike a match.

anreichern. I. *v.tr. sep.* to enrich; *Ch: Min:* to concentrate (solution, ore); to strengthen (solution).

II. *vbl s.* **Anreichern** *n.*, **Anreicherung** *f. in vbl senses; also:* enrichment; concentration.

anreihen. I. *v.tr. sep.* **1.** to add (objects, figures, etc.) to a series; **etwas etwas** *dat.*, **an etwas** *acc.*, **a.,** to attach, add, sth. to sth.; to join sth. to sth.; *Gram:* **Sätze aneinander a.,** to co-ordinate clauses; **anreihende Verbindung,** copulative conjunction; **anreihende Satzverbindung,** copulative construction; **sich a.,** to follow on; to line up; (*of persons, cars, etc.*) to join a queue, *U.S:* a line; (*of figures, etc.*) to continue a series; **diese Stiftung reiht sich würdig denen der Vergangenheit an,** this foundation takes a worthy place beside those of the past, ranks worthily with those of the past. **2.** *Dressm: etc:* to tack on, baste on (braid, lining, etc.).

II. *vbl s.* **1. Anreihen,** *n. in vbl senses.* **2. Anreihung,** *f.* (*a*) *in vbl senses; also: Gram:* co-ordination; (*b*) series; sequence; chain (of events, etc.).

Anreim[1], *m.* alliteration.

Anreim[2], *m.* **-(e)s/.**=**Anraum.**

anreimen, *v.i. sep.* (*haben*) to alliterate.

Anreise, *f.* journey (to a conference, etc.); **es ist eine lange A.,** it takes a long time to get there.

anreisen, *v.i. sep.* (*sein*) to make the journey (to place of conference, etc.); to arrive (at a place); *F:* **angereist kommen,** to arrive; **da kommt sie schon angereist,** there she comes; **Angereiste** *m, f,* person arriving; arrival; **die Angereisten,** the new arrivals, the new-comers.

anreißen, *v.tr. sep.* (*strong*) **1.** (*a*) to tear (paper, etc.) slightly; to make a (small) tear in (paper, etc.); to tear the edge of (page, etc.); (*b*) to cut into (sth.); to notch (tree, etc.); (*c*) to break into (stocks, one's capital, savings, etc.); to start (box of cigars, etc.); (*c*) *P:* **j-n a.,** to borrow money from s.o., *F:* to tap, touch, s.o.; (*d*) *F:* **angerissen,** half-drunk, tipsy. **2.** *Com: F:* to press (s.o.) to buy; to tout (s.o.) for his custom. **3.** to scratch (a mark on) (sth.); *Carp: Metalw:* to mark (wood, metal); to trace, mark (out), scribe, a line on (wood, metal). **4. ein Zündholz a.,** to strike a match.

Anreißer, *m.* **1.** *Com: etc: F:* (*a*) tout; *U.S. & F:* barker (in front of booth, etc.); (*b*) (street-) hawker; cheap-jack. **2.** *Ind: etc:* (*a*) (*pers.*) tracer; (*b*) *Tls:* (i) scraping-tool, scraper; (ii) marking-tool.

Anreißerei, *f.* **-/-en.** *Com: F:* touting, *U.S. & F:* drumming (for custom); 'high-pressure salesmanship'.

Anreißnadel, *f. Tls:* scriber, scribe(-awl); marking-tool.

Anreißteilmaschine, *f. Mec.E:* graduating machine, graduator.

Anreißwerkzeug, *n.* marking-tool.

anreiten, *v.sep.* (*strong*) **1.** *v.i.* (*sein*) (*a*) to ride up (on horse, camel, etc.); **angeritten kommen,** to come riding up, along; (*b*) *Mil: A:* (*of cavalry*) to charge; (*c*) **an etwas** *acc.* **a.,** to ride against, into, sth. **2.** *v.tr.* (*a*) to ride up to (s.o.); to ride at (s.o., fence, etc.); to ride into (s.o., sth.); *Mil: A:* (*of cavalry*) to charge (the enemy). **3.** *v.tr.* to break in (horse); **angerittenes Pferd,** horse that has been broken in.

Anreiz, *m.* **1.** incentive, incitement, stimulus (**zu**, to); inducement (**zu**, to); **der wahre A. zur wissenschaftlichen Forschung,** the true incentive to scientific research; **die Arbeitslosigkeit ist ein A. zum Verbrechen,** unemployment is an incentive to crime. **2.** attraction; **sexueller A.,** sexual attraction, *F:* sex-appeal.

anreizen. I. *v.tr. sep.* to stimulate (s.o., desires, the senses, etc.); **j-n zu etwas a., j-n a., etwas zu tun,** to stimulate s.o. to sth., to do sth.; to incite, prompt, s.o. to sth., to do sth.; to instigate s.o. to do sth.; to tempt s.o. to sth., to do sth.; **j-n zum Diebstahl a.,** to instigate, incite, s.o. to steal; **j-n zum Trinken a.,** to egg s.o. on to drink; to tempt, entice, s.o. to drink; **sie wollte ihn zur Liebe a.,** she tried to inflame his passions; *abs.* **die Aussicht reizt an,** the prospect is tempting, alluring, enticing; **anreizend,** (i) stimulating, (ii) enticing, tempting, alluring; provocative (ways, gestures, etc.).

II. *vbl s.* **1. Anreizen,** *n. in vbl senses.* **2. Anreizung,** *f.* (*a*)=II. 1; (*b*)=**Anreiz.**

anrempeln, *v.tr. sep.* **1.** *F:* to jostle, hustle (s.o.); to barge into (s.o.); to shoulder (s.o.); *Fb:* **den Gegner a.,** to barge one's opponent. **2.** *F:* to molest (s.o.); to accost (s.o.).

anrennen, *v.sep.* (*conj. like* **rennen**) **1.** *v.i.* (*sein*) (*a*) **angerannt kommen,** to come running up, along; (*b*) **gegen j-n, gegen, an, etwas, a.,** to rush, charge, at s.o., sth.; (*unintentionally*) to run into s.o., sth.; (*c*) *F:* **übel angerannt sein,** to come off badly; to get more than one bargained for; to find that one has caught a Tartar; (*d*) *F:* **gegen etwas a.,** to fight tooth and nail against sth. **2.** *v.tr.* (*a*) to run into (s.o., sth.); to collide with (s.o., sth.); (*b*) to rush at (s.o., sth.); **j-n mit dem Arm, mit der Schulter, a.,** to elbow s.o.; to shoulder s.o.; to jostle s.o.

Anrichte, *f.* **-/-n.** **1.** (*in dining-room*) sideboard, buffet; (*in kitchen*) cabinet; (*in refectory, etc.*) serving table. **2.** (butler's) pantry; *Nau:* pantry.

anrichten, *v.tr. sep.* **1.** to prepare (sth.); (*a*) to get (sth.) ready for use; *Ind:* to dress (timber, ore, etc.); (*b*) *Cu:* to arrange (food) (on serving dish); to dress, *F:* do up (food); to dress (a salad); to garnish (dish, salad); to get (dinner, etc.) ready for serving; **Kalbfleisch mit weißer Sauce angerichtet,** veal served in a white sauce; **es ist angerichtet,** dinner is served. **2.** to cause, give rise to (confusion, disaster, discord, etc.); to sow (discord); **großen Schaden a.,** to do great damage, much harm; **viel Unheil a.,** to do much mischief; **der Frost hat in den Weinbergen Verwüstung angerichtet,** the frost has wrought havoc in, made havoc of, played havoc among, the vineyards; *Iron:* **da hast du was Nettes, was Schönes, angerichtet,** you've made a nice mess of it! now you've put your foot in it! now you've gone and done it! you're in a pretty pickle!

Anrichter, *m.* **1.** *Ind:* preparer; dresser (of timber, ore, etc.). **2.** *Cu:* preparer, dresser (of food); server.

Anrichtetisch, *m.*=**Anrichte** 1.

Anrichtezimmer, *n.* (butler's) pantry.

Anrichtstift, *m. Mec.E:* steady-pin.

anriechen, *v.tr. sep.* (*strong*) **1.** to smell (at) (sth.); **eine Rose a.,** to smell, sniff (at), a rose. **2. j-m etwas a.,** to smell sth. on s.o., s.o.'s breath, s.o.'s clothes, etc.; **man riecht es ihm an, daß er Whisky getrunken hat, man riecht ihm den Whisky an,** you can smell the whisky on his breath; he smells of whisky.

Anriß, *m.* **1.** small tear (in paper, etc.); notch (in wood); (small) crack (in surface of material); (superficial) scratch (on metal, etc.). **2.** *Row:* start of the stroke.

Anritt, *m. A:* **1.** approach (of rider); *Mil:* charge (of cavalry). **2.** first exercises in equitation.

anritzen, *v.tr. sep.* to scratch, make a scratch on (sth.).

anroden, *v.tr. sep. Agr:* to clear, grub (land for cultivation); to bring (land) into cultivation.

anrollen, *v.sep.* **1.** *v.i.* (*sein*) (*a*) (*of ball, barrel, etc.*) to roll up; (*b*) (*of pers.*) **a., angerollt kommen,** to arrive (in carriage); to drive up; (*c*) *Av:* (*of aircraft*) to taxi up; (*d*) *Mil: etc:* (*of supplies*) to be brought up (by road *or* rail);

die Güter sind im Anrollen, the goods are on their way. **2.** *v.tr.* (*a*) to roll up (ball, barrel, etc.); (*b*) to convey (goods) (by road *or* rail).

anrosten, *v.i. sep.* (*sein*) **1.** to rust, get rusty. **2. an etwas** *acc.* **a.,** to rust on to sth.; **die Mutter ist an die Schraube angerostet,** the nut has rusted on to the screw.

anrüchig, *a.* disreputable (pers., place, etc.); (pers., place, etc.) of bad reputation, of, in, bad, ill, repute; **ein anrüchiger Mensch,** a person of bad reputation; a disreputable, shady, character; **anrüchiges Benehmen,** disreputable, questionable, shady, conduct; **eine anrüchige Angelegenheit,** an unsavoury, *F:* a fishy, business; **anrüchiger Gasthof,** disreputable, dubious, hotel; hotel with a bad reputation, of bad repute; **anrüchiges Wort,** word with a bad meaning, with unpleasant associations; *F:* dirty word; **'Arbeit' ist für ihn ein anrüchiges Wort,** to him 'work' is a dirty word.

Anrüchigkeit, *f.* disreputableness, disrepute; ill-repute, bad reputation; shadiness (of pers., conduct, etc.); questionableness (of conduct, etc.); dubious character (of hotel, etc.); *F:* fishiness (of affair, etc.).

anrücken. I. *v.sep.* **1.** *v.tr.* **etwas an etwas** *acc.* **a.,** to bring, draw, move, sth. nearer to sth.; **einen Stuhl an den Tisch a.,** to draw up a chair (to the table); **einen Schrank an die Wand a.,** to push a cupboard against the wall. **2.** *v.i.* (*sein*) to approach, draw near; (*of troops, etc.*) to move forward, to advance; to move up; **gegen den Feind a.,** to advance on the enemy; **angerückt kommen,** to come moving up. **3.** *v.i.* (*haben*) (*of clock*) to be about to strike.

II. *vbl s.* **Anrücken,** *n. in vbl senses; also:* approach; advance.

anrucks, *adv. Swiss Dial:* immediately, straight away, forthwith.

anrudern, *v.sep.* **1.** *v.i.* (*sein*) & *tr.* to row along, up; to row towards (sth.); **angerudert kommen,** to row up, to come rowing up, along; **ans Ufer a., das Ufer a.,** to row, pull, for the shore. **2.** *v.i.* (*haben*) *Row:* to go on the first outing (of the season); to go on the river for the first time; **Anrudern** *n,* first outing (of the season); first time on the river.

Anruf, *m.* **1.** (*a*) call; *Nau: etc:* hail; *Mil:* (sentry's) challenge; **A. um Hilfe,** call for help; appeal for help; (*b*) *Lit:* invocation. **2.** (*a*) *Tp:* (telephone) call; ring (on the telephone); **danke für den A.,** thanks for ringing, *U.S:* calling (me); (*b*) *W.Tel: A:* call-sign.

Anrufbetrieb, *m. Tp:* direct trunking.

anrufen. I. *v.tr. sep.* (*strong*) **1.** to call, call to (s.o.); to call, hail (taxi); *Nau:* to hail (ship); *Mil:* (*of sentry*) to challenge (s.o.). **2.** (*a*) **j-n um Hilfe a.,** to appeal to s.o. for help, to call upon s.o.'s help; **die höheren Mächte a.,** to call upon, invoke, (the aid of) the higher powers; **den Herrn a.,** to call upon the Lord; **Gott um Gnade a.,** to implore God's mercy; (*b*) *Jur:* **j-n zum Zeugen a.,** to call s.o. to witness; **den Beistand der Gesetze a., das Gericht a.,** to appeal to the law; to seek legal redress; **eine höhere Instanz a.,** to appeal to a higher court. **3.** *Tp:* to telephone (to) (s.o.), *F:* to 'phone (to) (s.o.), to 'phone (s.o.) up; to ring, *U.S:* call, (s.o.) (up); **ich werde dich a.,** I'll give you a ring, a call; I'll ring you (up), 'phone you; **bitte, können Sie diese Nummer für mich a.?** can you ring, get, *U.S:* call, this number for me, please?

II. *vbl s.* **1. Anrufen,** *n. in vbl senses.* **2. Anrufung,** *f. in vbl senses; also:* (*a*) appeal (*gen.*, to s.o.); invocation (*gen.*, of a deity, etc.); (*b*) *Jur:* **A. einer höheren Instanz,** appeal to a higher court; **A. eines Schiedsgerichts,** reference, referring, of a question to arbitration; submission of an affair to arbitration.

Anrufer, *m.* **1.** (*a*) caller; person who calls; (*b*) invoker (of higher powers, etc.). **2.** *Jur: A:* appellant.

Anrufglocke, *f. Tp: etc:* call-bell.

Anrufklappe, *f. Tp:* call-indicator, call-disc (of annunciator-board).

Anruflampe, *f. Tp: etc:* call-lamp.

Anrufsucher, *m. Tp:* (*device*) call-finder.

Anrufwecker, *m. Tp:* call-bell.

Anrufzeichen, *n. Tp:* calling signal.

anrühmen, *v.tr. sep.*=**anpreisen.**

anrühren. I. *v.tr. sep.* **1.** (*a*) to touch (s.o., sth.); **rühre mich nicht an!** don't touch me! keep your hands off me! **etwas nicht a.,** not to touch sth.; to let, leave, sth. alone; **rühre meine Werkzeuge nicht an!** leave my tools alone! don't meddle with my tools! **nicht a.!** don't touch! (keep your) hands off! **ich rühre keinen Wein an,** I never touch wine; **sie kann heute keinen Bissen a.,** she can't eat at all today, *F:* she can't touch a thing, can't look at food, today; (*b*) **ein Thema a.,** to touch on a subject. **2.** to stir; to mix, temper (mortar, cement, colours, etc.); *Cu:* to mix (flour, etc.) (with liquid); **Mehl mit Wasser a.,** to mix a thin paste of flour and water.

II. *vbl s.* **Anrühren,** *n. in vbl senses; also:* **A. verboten!** do not touch! hands off!

anrußen, *v.tr. sep.* to coat (sth.) with soot, to soot.

ans, *prep.* (*contraction of* **an das**; *cp.* **an** I. 2) to the; **ans Fenster treten,** to step over to the window; **ans Ufer kommen,** to come to (the) shore.

ansäen, *v.tr. sep. Agr:* to sow (seeds, a field); **Felder mit Weizen a.,** to sow fields with wheat, to put fields under wheat.

Ansage, *f.* **1.** announcement; notification, notice (of meeting, etc.); *Rail: Sp: Th: etc:* announcement (of trains, results, variety turns, etc.); *W.Tel:* announcement; lead-in (of broadcast). **2.** *Cards:* declaration; (first) call; **Sie haben die A.,** it's your call.

Ansagemikrophon, *n.* announcing, announcer's, microphone.

ansagen, *v.tr. sep.* **1.** (*a*) to announce (**j-m etwas,** sth. to s.o.); **eine Sitzung ist für, auf, Mittwoch angesagt,** a meeting has been announced for Wednesday; **j-n, sich, (zu einem, zum, zu, Besuch) bei j-m a.,** to tell s.o., to let s.o. know, that s.o., one, is going to visit him; **er hat sich bei uns zum Mittagessen angesagt,** he has told us he is coming to lunch; (*b*) *W.Tel: etc:* to announce; *Rail:* **die Züge a.,** to announce the trains; *Sp:* **die Resultate a.,** to announce the results; *Th:* **die Spielfolge a.,** to announce the items, the turns (in revue, etc.). **2.** *Cards:* (*in Skat*) to announce; **die Trumpffarbe, eine Farbe, a.,** to declare trumps, a suit; **Sie sagen an,** it's your call; **kein Spiel a.,** to pass; to leave the call to one's partner. **3.** *v.i. Lit:* & *Poet:* **sag an, . . . , sagt an, . . . ,** say, . . . , speak, . . . , tell us, (pray), . . .

ansägen, *v.tr. sep.* to make a saw-cut in (sth.), to cut into (sth.), to nick (sth.) (with a saw).

Ansager, *m.* **-s/-.** *Rail: Sp: W.Tel: TV: etc:* announcer; *Th:* announcer, compère (in a revue).

Ansagerin, *f.* **-/-innen,** (woman) announcer; *Th:* announcer, *F:* commère.

ansammeln. I. *v.tr. sep.* (*a*) to collect, gather (together); to accumulate, amass; to hoard up, store up; to heap (up), to pile up; *Mil:* to concentrate (troops); *Ph:* to concentrate, focus (rays); (*b*) **sich a.,** to accumulate, to pile up; (*of dust, water*) to collect, accumulate; (*of deposit, crowds, etc.*) to collect, gather; (*of troops*) to concentrate; (*of troops, crowds*) to mass.

II. *vbl s.* **1. Ansammeln,** *n. in vbl senses.* **2. Ansammlung,** *f.* (*a*) *in vbl senses; also:* collection, accumulation; concentration (of troops, *Ph:* of rays); (*b*) collection; accumulation; hoard, store; heap, pile; (*c*) concourse, assemblage, gathering, mass, throng (of people); concentration (of troops, *Ph:* of rays).

ansässig, *a.* resident, domiciled (**in**+*dat.*, in); **a. werden, sich a. machen,** to take up one's residence, one's abode, to establish oneself, to settle (**in einem Ort,** in a place); **ein Ansässiger, eine Ansässige,** a resident; **die Ansässigen,** the residents; the local inhabitants.

Ansässigkeit, *f.* domiciliation; (permanent) residence (in a place); **wegen seiner A. in London,** by reason of his being resident, domiciled, in London.

Ansatz, *m.* **1.** (*a*) immediate preparations for an action; initial stages of an action; *Sp:* (i) stance; initial position (of arms, legs, body); (ii) take-off (**zu einem Sprung,** for a jump); **einen A. zum Sprung machen,** to get into position for a jump; to be on the point of jumping; *F:* **er machte einen A. zum Reden,** he made an attempt to speak; he prepared to deliver himself of a speech; **einen A. zu einer Versöhnung machen,** to make the first attempt, to start an attempt, at reconciliation; **auf den ersten A.,** right away, straight off, *F:* first go (off); (*b*) *usu. pl.* **Ansätze,** initial, rudimentary, stages (of a development); **Ansätze zur Kultur,** rudiments, first beginnings, of civilization; *F:* **in den Ansätzen steckenbleiben,** to get stuck, bogged down, at the very outset. **2.** *Mus:* attack; embouchure, lipping (*i.e.* lip position, attack of the note, etc., on wind instrument). **3.** (*a*) *Bot:* germ; spore (of plant); meristem; (*b*) *Biol:* rudiment; **Ansatz zu einem Daumen, zu einem Schwanz,** rudiment of a thumb, of a tail; (*c*) *Bot:* young shoot, sprout; (*d*) **A. von Bauch,** beginnings of a corporation. **4.** (*a*) evaluation; *Com: etc:* estimate (of value, charges, etc.); (*b*) *Com: Fin:* account; item (of account); charge, amount charged; **j-m einen Betrag in A. bringen,** to charge a sum to s.o., to debit s.o. with a sum, to enter a sum to s.o.'s account; **die Ansätze des Bücherrevisors,** the accountant's charges; **die Ansätze des Tarifs,** the tariff rates; (*c*) *Mth:* statement (of problem); **A. einer Gleichung,** arrangement, set-up, setting up (of an equation). **5.** deposit, sediment; crust, incrustation; coating (of dirt, etc.); crust (in wine-bottle); fur (in boiler, radiator, etc.); *Mch:* (boiler) scale; *Geol:* **A. von Land,** alluvial deposit(s), alluvium, alluvion. **6.** (i) added piece, extension; component extending from main structure; (ii) part of component that emerges from *or* joins on to main structure; (*a*) lengthening-piece, eking-piece; extension(-piece); *Dressm: etc:* strip of material (used to lengthen dress, etc.); *Furn:* (extra) leaf, extension leaf (of table); (*b*) *Mus:* mouthpiece (of wind instrument); (*c*) *Av:* root (of wing); (*d*) *Av:*=**Ansatzfläche**; (*e*) shoulder (of knife, sword-blade, pulley-block, etc.); beading, bead (of pneumatic tyre); *Mec.E: etc:* lug, flange; stop, stopper; tappet. **7.** (*place where something begins*) (*a*) **Narbe gerade am A. des Haars,** scar just where the hair begins, just on the hair-line; (*b*) *Tail: Dressm:* point of attachment (of sleeve, etc.); line (of collar, sleeve, etc.); **der A. des Kragens ist nicht richtig,** the line of the collar is wrong. **8.** *Anat:* (*a*) apophysis *or* epiphysis (of bone); (*b*) attachment, insertion (of muscle). **9.** (*a*) setting (of seeds); (*b*) striking, taking root. *Cp.* **ansetzen III.**

Ansatzbad, *n. Dy:* first bath.

Ansatzfeile, *f. Tls:* flat file.

Ansatzfläche, *f. Av:* extension (of control surface).

Ansatzpunkt, *m.* **1.** (*a*) starting-point; (*b*) boring site (for oil-well). **2.** point of attachment.

Ansatzrohr, *n.* **1.** extension pipe, tube; attached pipe, tube; nozzle. **2.** *Anat: Phonetics:* **das A.,** the supraglottic passages.

Ansatzschraube, *f.* set screw.

Ansatzstelle, *f.* point of attachment; joint; *Anat:* attachment, insertion (of muscle).

Ansatzstück, *n.* (*a*) extension(-piece); lengthening-piece, eking-piece; *Dressm: etc:* strip of material (used to lengthen dress, etc.); *Furn:* (extra) leaf, extension leaf (of table); *Min:* lengthening-rod (of borer); (*b*) connecting piece; (*c*) attachment.

Ansatzteil, *m.* (*a*) attachment; nozzle (of spraying device); rose (of watering-can); (*b*)=**Ansatzstück.**

ansäuern, *v.tr. sep.* **1.** to acidify, sour; to acidulate (drink, etc.); **Ansäuerung** *f,* acidification. **2.** *Bak:* to put yeast in (dough), to leaven (dough).

ansaufen, *v.tr. sep.* (*strong*) *P:* **sich** *dat.* **einen a.,** to get very drunk; **er hatte sich einen angesoffen,** he had had a skinful.

Ansaugegerät, *n.* suction apparatus; *Ind: etc:* aspirator.

Ansaugehub, *m. I.C.E:* suction stroke, induction stroke.

ansaugen. I. *v.sep.* (*weak & strong*) **1.** *v.tr.* (*a*) to suck in, suck up (liquid, air, gas); to draw (up) (water, etc.); *Ph:* to adsorb; (*b*) **einen Schlauch a.,** to suck a tube full of liquid (*for transference to another container, etc.*). **2. sich (an etwas** *acc.*) **ansaugen,** to fasten on, to adhere, (to sth.) (by suction). **3.** *v.i.* (*haben*) to start sucking; (*a*) **das Kind will nicht a.,** the child won't suck, won't take the breast; (*b*) **eine Pumpe a. lassen,** to prime, fetch, a pump.

II. *vbl s.* **Ansaugen** *n.*, **Ansaugung** *f. in vbl senses; also:* suction; *I.C.E:* induction (of gases); *Med:* aspiration (of gas, liquid); *Ph:* adsorption.

Ansäugen, *n. Hort:* grafting by approach; inarching.

Ansaug(e)periode, *f. I.C.E:*=**Ansaugehub.**

Ansaug(e)rohr, *n.* suction pipe, tube; *I.C.E:* induction pipe.

Ansaug(e)stutzen, *m. I.C.E:* branch suction pipe.

Ansaugheber, *m.* siphon.

Ansaugleitung, *f.* suction pipe(s); *I.C.E:* induction manifold.

Ansaugpumpe, *f.* suction pump.

Ansaugraum, *m.* receiver (of suction apparatus); *Mch:* steam cone.

Ansaugschlot, *m. Ind:* air intake shaft.

Ansaugvorrichtung, *f.* suction apparatus *or* device; *Ind: etc:* aspirator.

ansäuseln, *v.tr. sep.* **1.** (*of breeze, etc.*) to fan (s.o.). **2.** *F:* **sich** *dat.* **einen a.,** to get slightly tipsy; (*of pers.*) **angesäuselt,** half-drunk, tipsy, *F:* tiddly.

ansausen, *v.i. sep.* (*sein*) to rush, roar, along; to come rushing, roaring, along; **angesaust kommen,** to come rushing up, along; (*of train, car, etc.*) to come roaring up, along.

anschaffen. I. *v.tr. sep.* (*weak*) **1.** (*a*) **j-m etwas a.,** to procure, obtain, get, sth. for s.o.; to provide, furnish, supply, s.o. with sth.; **sich** *dat.* **etwas a.,** to provide, furnish, equip, oneself with sth.; to acquire, purchase, sth.; to procure sth.; **sich einen Vorrat Wäsche a.,** to lay in a stock of linen; to buy linen; **sich Kleider a.,** to provide oneself with clothes, to fit oneself out (with clothing); **wir wollen uns einen Hund a.,** we're going to get a dog; *F:* **sich eine Krankheit a.,** to get, catch, a disease; *Com:* **Waren a.,** to procure, buy, goods; to lay in (a stock of) goods; (*b*) **sie muß das Geld irgendwie a.,** she will have to procure, get, the money somehow. **2.** *Com: Fin:* (*a*) **Geld für etwas a.,** to provide funds for sth., to make provision for sth.; *see also* **decken** III. 2 (*f*); (*b*) to remit; **einen Betrag bei einer Bank a.,** to remit a sum to a bank. **3.** *Austrian:* **j-m etwas a.,** to make s.o. do sth.; to land s.o. with (unwanted task); **wer hat dir das angeschafft?** who (on earth) landed you with that job?

II. *vbl s.* **1. Anschaffen,** *n. in vbl senses.* **2. Anschaffung,** *f.* (*a*) *in vbl senses; also:* procurement, procuration; provision; acquirement, purchase; (*b*) *Com: Fin:* provision (of funds, of cover); (*c*) *Com: Fin:* remittance (**bei einer Bank,** to a bank); (*d*) thing acquired, acquisition, purchase; **wir haben letztes Jahr so viele Anschaffungen gemacht, daß wir jetzt sparen müssen,** we bought so much last year that we shall have to save from now on.

Anschaffungskosten, *pl. Com:* price delivered.

Anschaffungspreis, *m. Com:* full price, list price.

anschäften, *v.tr. sep.* (*a*) to fix a handle to, to haft, to helve (axe, etc.); (*b*) to stock (rifle); (*c*) *Bootm:* to put the top on (boot).

anschalmen, *v.tr. sep. For:* to mark, blaze (trees).

anschalten, *v.tr. sep. El:* to switch on (lamp, circuit); *Tp: Tg:* to connect (circuit, line).

Anschaltklinke, *f. Tp: Tg:* jack.

anschärfen, *v.tr. sep.* **1.** to sharpen. **2.** *Metalw:* to scarf (weld).

anschauen. I. *v.tr. sep.* **1.** to look at, *Lit:* upon (s.o., sth.); to view (s.o., sth.); *Lit:* to gaze at, upon (s.o., sth.); to contemplate (s.o., sth.); **wie man die Sache auch anschaut,** whichever way, however, one looks at, regards, views, the matter. **2.** *Phil:* (*a*) to have an intuition, an intuitive conception, of (sth.); (*b*) to have a visual image of (sth.).

II. *vbl s.* **1. Anschauen,** *n. in vbl senses; also:* (*a*) contemplation; *Lit:* **in, im, A. versunken,** lost in contemplation; (*b*) *Phil:* intuition. **2. Anschauung,** *f.* (*a*) *in vbl senses; also:* contemplation; *Theol:* **A. Gottes,** seeing God face to face; (*b*) *Art: Lit:* **das ist eine ganz andere Art der A.,** that is an entirely different kind of vision; (*c*) visual perception; **auf A. gerichtete Lehrmethoden,** visual methods of teaching; teaching by demonstration with visual aids; **ein Phänomen zur A. bringen,** to make a phenomenon understandable by means of a concrete illustration; (*d*) *Phil:* (i) perception; (ii) **(intuitive) A.,** intuition; (*e*) **A. von etwas,** idea, notion, conception, of sth.; **er hat eine merkwürdige A. von (der) Pflicht,** he has a curious idea, notion, of duty; (*f*) opinion; view; point of view; **A. über etwas** *acc.*, idea(s), notion(s), about sth.; idea, notion, of sth.; opinion about, of, sth.; view of sth.; way of seeing sth., of looking at sth.; outlook upon (life, politics, etc.); **sie haben verschiedene Anschauungen,** their views differ, they have different ideas; **nach meiner A.,** in my view, from my point of view; as I see it; in my opinion; **ich kann Ihre A. nicht teilen,** I do not share your opinion; I cannot agree with your view; I see the matter differently from you.

III. *pr.p. & a.* **anschauend.** **1.** *in vbl senses; esp.* (*a*) contemplative; (*b*) *Phil:* intuitive. **2.** *A:* = **anschaulich.**

anschaulich, *a.* **1.** (*a*) forming a clear visual image; **anschauliches Bild,** (clear) visual image; visual picture; visual illustration (of phenomenon, etc.); **j-m etwas a. machen,** to give s.o. a clear (mental) picture of sth.; to make sth. clear to s.o. by a visual, concrete, illustration; **durch diese Beispiele wird das Ganze a. gemacht,** these examples make the whole thing vivid, bring the whole thing to life; with the help of these examples one can see the whole thing clearly, vividly; **etwas a. erklären,** to explain sth. in visual terms; to explain sth. vividly; (*b*) vivid (style, narrative, etc.); graphic (description, style, etc.); plastic (style); **er schreibt sehr a.,** he has a very vivid style; he writes vividly; his style has marked visual, plastic, qualities. **2.** *Phil:* intuitive (thinking, etc.).

Anschaulichkeit, *f.* visual quality; plastic quality, plasticity (of style, of s.o.'s prose, etc.); graphic quality (of description, etc.); vividness (of description, exposition, style, etc.).

Anschauungsbegriff, *m. Phil:* notion of intuition.

Anschauungsbild, *n. Psy:* mental image; **eidetische Anschauungsbilder,** eidetic images.

Anschauungskraft, *f. Phil:* (power of) intuition.

Anschauungskreis, *m.* **1.** *Phil:* sphere of intuition. **2.** mental horizon.

Anschauungsmaterial, *n.* illustrative material; *esp. Sch:* demonstration material; visual aids.

Anschauungsunterricht, *m.* (*a*) *Sch:* visual instruction, instruction with visual aids; object-teaching, -system; (*b*) *F:* object-lesson.

Anschauungsurteil, *n.* intuitive judgment.

Anschauungsvermögen, *n. Phil:* (faculty of) intuition, intuitive faculty.

Anschauungsweise, *f.* kind of vision; mental outlook; attitude of mind; point of view; *F:* way of looking at things.

Anschein, *m.* appearance, semblance, look; (outward) show; **das Haus hat, erweckt, den A., als sei es behaglich,** the house looks as though it would be comfortable; the house has an air, a look, of comfort about it; **es hat den A., als wollte es regnen,** it looks like rain; **es hat ganz den A., als würde es morgen schön,** it has every appearance of being fine, there is every likelihood of its being fine, tomorrow; **dem A. nach, allem A. nach,** apparently, seemingly; **nach dem äußeren A. zu urteilen, dem äußeren A. nach, ist das eine wohlhabende Familie,** judging by outward appearances, it is a rich family; **sich** *dat.* **den A. geben, etwas zu sein,** to feign, pretend, make believe, to be sth.; **sie gibt sich den A., fromm zu sein,** she puts on a pretence of piety, she pretends, makes believe, to be pious.

anscheinen, *v.tr. sep.* (*strong*) (*of sun, etc.*) to shine (up)on (s.o., sth.).

anscheinend, (*a*) *a.* apparent, seeming; **anscheinende Besserung,** apparent, seeming, improvement; **anscheinende Frömmigkeit,** apparent, ostensible, piety; (*b*) *adv.* apparently, seemingly.

anscheinlich, *adv.* = **anscheinend** (*b*).

anscheißen, *v.tr. sep.* (*strong*) *P:* **1.** to excrete on, to befoul (sth.). **2.** to swindle, *F:* do, diddle (s.o.). **3.** to tell, tick, (s.o.) off.

Anschere, *f. Tex:* warp(ing)-frame.

anscheren, *v.tr. sep.* (*strong*) **1.** to start shearing (sth.); to shear, cut, into (sth.). **2.** *Tex:* to warp (linen, cloth). **3.** *F:* to make fun of (s.o.); to chip (s.o.).

anschichten, *v.tr. sep.* to pile (sth.) up in layers; to layer; to stack (wood, coal, cases, etc.); *Geol: etc:* to stratify.

anschicken (sich), *v.refl. sep.* **sich zu etwas a., sich a., etwas zu tun,** to get ready, make ready, for sth., to do sth.; to prepare for sth., to do sth.; to set about doing sth.; **sich zu einer Reise a.,** to get, make, ready for a journey, to make preparations for a journey; **er schickte sich an, weiterzugehen, er schickte sich zum Weitergehen an,** he prepared, was preparing, to move on; **sich zu einer Arbeit a.,** to set about a piece of work; **er schickt sich gut dazu an,** he goes about it the right way, he goes the right way to work; **sich zum Kampf a.,** to prepare for the struggle, *Lit. & F:* to gird oneself for the fray.

anschieben, *v.sep* (*strong*) **1.** *v.tr.* **etwas an etwas** *acc.* **a.,** to push sth. up against sth. **2.** *v.tr.* to start (car, etc.) moving; to give (car, etc.) a shove off. **3.** *v.i.* (*haben*) (*at skittles*) to throw off, bowl off; to throw, bowl, first. **4.** *Bak:* **angeschobenes Brot,** batch-bread; batch-loaf.

Anschieber, *m.* **1.** *Furn:* (extra) leaf, extension leaf (of table). **2.** *Bak:* kissing-crust (of loaf).

Anschiebestück, *n.* = **Anschieber** 1.

Anschiebetisch, *m. Furn:* extending table, table with an extra leaf.

Anschiebsel, *n.* -s/-, added piece, piece added on; addition; extension.

anschielen, *v.tr. sep.* **1.** to squint at (s.o., sth.). **2.** (*a*) to cast a sidelong glance at (s.o.); (*b*) to ogle, make eyes at (s.o.); (*c*) to look askance at (s.o., sth.).

anschienen, *v.tr. sep.* **1.** *Surg:* to put (limb) in splints, to splint (limb). **2.** *Constr: etc:* to fasten (sth.) with metal bands.

anschießen, *v.sep.* (*strong*) I. *v.tr.* **1.** to shoot at and wound (s.o., sth.); *Ven:* to wound (game); to wing (bird); **angeschossen,** (*of game*) wounded; (*of bird*) winged; *F:* (*of pers.*) (i) in love, *F:* smitten; (ii) crazy, cracked. **2.** *A:* to fire a salute for (guest); to fire off guns to celebrate (the new year); to fire off guns to mark the opening of (festival). **3.** to test, try (out) (firearm); *Tchn:* to prove (firearm, cannon). **4.** *Bak:* to push (loaves) close together (in the oven). **5.** *Print:* to add (pages) (to book). **6.** *Tail:* to tack in (sleeve).

II. **anschießen,** *v.i.* **1.** (*sein*) to shoot, dart, along; **angeschossen kommen,** to come shooting, darting, along; to dart up; (*of wild beast, etc.*) **auf j-n a.,** to dart at, upon, s.o. **2.** (*haben*) (*at shooting match, etc.*) to fire first, to fire the first shot. **3.** (*sein*) (*of substance*) to crystallize; (*of crystals*) to form.

III. *vbl s.* **Anschießen,** *n. in vbl senses; also:* **1.** trial, (firing) test (of firearms, cannon). **2.** crystallization.

Anschießfaß, Anschießgefäß, *n. Ch: Ind:* crystallizing vessel.

anschiffen, *v.sep.* **1.** *v.i.* (*sein*) *Nau: A:* to land; to touch land, to make land; **an eine Sandbank a.,** to ground on a sand-bank. **2.** *v.tr.* to bring (goods, etc.) by water, by ship; to land (goods). **3.** *v.tr. F:* to urinate, *F:* to piddle, pee, on (sth.).

anschiften, *v.tr. sep. Carp: etc:* to join up; to nail (rafters, etc.) together; to glue (pieces of wood) together; to mend (broken wooden article).

anschimmeln, *v.i. sep.* (*sein*) to go mouldy; to mildew.

anschirren, *v.tr. sep.* to harness (horse); to hook in (horse); to put (horses) to.

Anschiß, *m. P:* **1.** swindle; swindling. **2.** ticking off, telling off.

Anschlag, *m.* **1.** (*a*) striking, impact (**an etwas** *acc.*, **gegen etwas,** on, against, sth.); **A. der Wellen gegen die Mole,** beating, breaking, of the waves against the mole; (*b*) stroke, striking (of bell, clock); (*c*) *Ten: A:* (= **Aufschlag**) service; (*d*) *Knitting:* casting on; (*e*) *esp. Ven:* bark, barking, baying (of dogs, hounds); *cp.* **anschlagen** III. **2.** touch; touching; (*a*) *Mus:* touch (of pianist, of piano); (pianist's) attack; **dieses Klavier hat einen schweren A.,** this piano has not got a good touch; (*of pers.*) **einen leichten A. haben,** to have a light touch (on the piano); **sie hat einen wunderbaren A.,** she has a lovely touch; she has a magnificent attack; (*b*) *Typewr:* touch; tension (of key); **240 Anschläge in der Minute schreiben,** to type at (approx.) 50 words per minute; (*c*) *Swim:* touching of the side, the end, of the bath (when turning *or* at finish of race); (*d*) *Games:* **A. spielen,** to play tig, to play tag, to play touch. **3.** notice; placard, poster, bill; **einen A. an einer Mauer machen,** to post (up), stick (up), a bill, a notice, on a wall; **einen A. am schwarzen Brett machen,** to put up, post (up), a notice on the (notice-)board; **eine Versteigerung durch A. bekanntmachen,** to advertise, bill, post up, a sale. **4.** *Sm.a:* aiming position (with rifle, etc.); **das Gewehr im A. haben, halten; im, in, A. sein,** to hold the rifle in the aiming position; **im A. auf j-n, auf etwas** *acc.*, **sein,** to be aiming at s.o., sth.; **in A. gehen,** to level the rifle; to take aim (**auf j-n, etwas,** at s.o., sth.). **5.** (*a*) design, plan, scheme, project; (*b*) plot, machination, intrigue (**gegen j-n,** against s.o.); **Anschläge gegen j-n machen,** to plot, scheme, conspire, against s.o.; to have designs against s.o.; (*c*) (criminal) attempt; attack (upon s.o., public institution); (organized) attempt (on s.o.'s life); plot, conspiracy (to assassinate s.o.); outrage; **einen A. auf j-n machen,** to make an attempt on s.o.'s life. **6.** evaluation; valuation; estimate (of value, cost, etc.); assessment (of value, charges, damages, etc.); **einen A. der Kosten machen,** to make an estimate of, to estimate, the costs; *Pol: etc:* **A. der Einnahmen und Ausgaben,** estimates; **nach ungefährem A.,** at a rough estimate; roughly calculated; **etwas in A. bringen,** to take sth. into account, into consideration; to make allowance(s) for sth., to allow for sth.; **wir müssen seine Jugend in A. bringen,** we must make allowances for, must consider, his youth; **in A. kommen,** to be taken into account, into consideration. **7.** *Tchn:*

(*a*) butt (of rifle); stock (of carpenter's square, T-square, etc.); (*b*) stop (of door, machine, microscope, telephone dial, etc.); check; buffer; wall rebate (for window-frame); rebate (at the junction of windows); lug; stop-pin; (*c*) *Nau:* tabling, edging (of sail).

Anschlagarten, *f.pl. Mil:* aiming positions (with rifle).

Anschlagbändsel, Anschlagbindsel, *n.pl. Nau:* rope-bands, robands.

Anschlagbrett, *n.* notice-board, *U.S:* bulletin board.

Anschlagdraht, *m. Mec.E:* stop-wire.

anschlagen, *v.sep.* (*strong*) I. *v.tr.* **1.** (*a*) to strike, hit, knock (sth.); to tap (sth.); to strike, sound (bell); **seinen Kopf, sich** *dat.* **den Kopf, (an etwas** *dat.* & *acc.*) **a.,** to bump one's head (against sth.); (*of clock*) **die Stunden a.,** to strike the hours; *Mus:* **einen Ton a.,** to strike, hit, a note (on piano); **eine Saite a.,** to touch, strike, a string (on guitar, etc.); **den richtigen Ton a.,** to strike, hit, the right note; *F:* **einen anderen Ton a.,** to change one's tune; *see also* **Lache**[1]; *Typewr:* **eine Taste a.,** to strike, hit, a key; (*b*) *Games:* (*in game of tig, of touch*) to touch (s.o.); (*c*) *Swim:* (**die Beckenwand**) **a.,** to touch the edge of the bath (when turning *or* at finish of race). **2. Feuer a.,** to strike a light. **3. eine Pumpe a.,** to prime, fetch, a pump. **4.** (*a*) to break into (stock, block of sth., etc.); **ein Faß a.,** to broach, tap, a cask, to set a cask abroach (*cp.* 5 (*b*)); **ein Thema a.,** to broach a subject; **ein Thema wieder a.,** to return, revert, recur, to a subject; (*b*) to make a break, a breach, in (sth.); to chip (cup, plate, etc.); **angeschlagene Tassen,** chipped cups; (*c*) to damage (s.o., sth.); **schwer angeschlagen,** (*of house, etc.*) badly damaged; (*of pers.*) badly knocked about, *F:* groggy; *Box:* **den Gegner a.,** to get one's opponent groggy. **5.** (*a*) to attach, fix, fasten (**etwas an etwas** *acc.*, sth. to sth.); *Carp:* to nail on (board, etc.); *Tail: Dressm:* **einen Ärmel a.,** to tack on, baste on, a sleeve; (*b*) to secure (sth.) with cords; *Constr: Nau: etc:* to sling (burden for hoisting); **ein Faß a.,** to sling, rope, a cask (*cp.* 4 (*a*)); *Nau:* **ein Segel a.,** to bend a sail; (*c*) *Knitting:* **eine Masche a.,** to cast on a stitch; to make one; **zwei Maschen a.,** to make two; (*d*) **Feuchtigkeit hat sich angeschlagen,** a film of moisture has formed. **6.** to post (up), stick (up), placard, display (bill, notice, etc.); **ein Plakat an eine Mauer a.,** to stick, post (up), a bill on a wall; **eine Versteigerung a.,** to advertise, bill, post up, a sale. **7.** *Sm.a:* to bring (rifle, etc.) to the aiming position; **das Gewehr auf j-n, auf etwas** *acc.*, **a.,** to level one's rifle, one's gun, at s.o., sth.; to take aim at s.o., sth.; *Mil: A:* **schlagt an!** present! **8.** to value; to estimate (value, costs, etc.); to assess (value, charges, damages, etc.); **sein Vermögen wird auf £10 000 angeschlagen,** his fortune is estimated at £10,000; **etwas hoch a.,** to set a high value, a high price, upon sth.; to rate sth. high; to set great store by sth.; **wie hoch schlagen Sie es an?** what value, what price, do you set on it? what would you put it at, assess it at? how high do you rate it? **die Kosten zu hoch a.,** to overestimate the costs, to put the costs too high; **seine Kräfte zu hoch a.,** to overestimate, overrate, one's powers, one's strength; **man darf seine Fähigkeiten nicht zu gering a.,** one must not underestimate, underrate, his capabilities.

II. **anschlagen,** *v.i.* (*haben*) **1.** to strike, knock, bump (**an etwas** *acc.*, against sth.); **mit dem Kopf an etwas a.,** to knock, bump, one's head against sth.; to run one's head into, against, sth.; **die Wellen schlagen an das Ufer an,** the waves are (i) beating, breaking, (ii) lapping, on the shore. **2.** (*a*) to strike first, to strike the first blow; (*b*) *Sp:* to take the first stroke; *Ten: A:* (= **aufschlagen**) to serve. **3.** (*of bell, clock*) to strike. **4.** (*a*) *esp. Ven:* (*of dogs, hounds*) to bark; to give tongue, to bay; (*b*) (*of nightingale, etc.*) to start singing, to burst into song; (*c*) (*of drummer*) to start drumming; to strike up. **5.** (*a*) (*of plant*) to take root, to strike (root); (*of graft*) to take; (*b*) *Med:* (*of remedy*) to take effect, to work, to operate; (*of physic, inoculation*) to take; (*of food*) to do one good; to make flesh; **der Impfstoff hat nicht angeschlagen,** the vaccine has not taken; **bei ihm schlägt nichts an,** his food does him no good; he stays thin however much he eats; **bei ihm schlägt nichts mehr an,** nothing works with him any more; he is past curing, past all help; (*c*) *F:* (*of joke, etc.*) **nicht a.,** to misfire.

III. *vbl s.* **Anschlagen,** *n. in vbl senses; cp.* **Anschlag.**

Anschläger, *m.* **1.** (*pers.*) *Ind: Min:* hooker, hitcher; *Min:* putter, trammer. **2.** *Tchn:* striking device; *Mus: A:* jack (of harpsichord).

Anschlagerad, *n. Clockm:* striking wheel.

Anschlagfaden, *m.* tacking thread, basting thread.

Anschlagholz, *n. Mill:* clapper (of mill-hopper).

anschlägig, *a.* **1.** (*of pers.*) skilful; deft, dext(e)rous, handy; resourceful; **ein anschlägiger Kopf,** a resourceful, inventive, mind. **2.** (*of food*) beneficial, body-building.

Anschlagklotz, *m. Mec.E:* stop-piece; *Clockm:* banking-piece.

Anschlagleine, *f. Nau:* (furling) gasket.

Anschlagplatte, *f. Mec.E:* impact plate; stop-plate.

Anschlagrandsteller, *m. Typewr:* margin stop.

Anschlagregler, *m. Typewr:* touch (control) regulator.

Anschlagsäule, *f.* advertising pillar.

Anschlagschiene, *f.* **1.** *Rail:* stock-rail. **2.** *Draw:* T-square, tee-square.

Anschlagschraube, *f.* stop-screw; locking screw, clamp(ing) screw; set screw; *Clockm:* banking screw.

Anschlag(s)höhe, *f. Mil: etc:* breast-height.

Anschlagstift, *m. Mec.E:* stop-pin; *Clockm:* banking-pin.

Anschlagstück, *n. Mec.E:* stop-piece.

Anschlagtafel, *f.* notice-board.

Anschlagvorrichtung, *f. Mec.E:* stop (device).

Anschlagwert, *m.* **1.** estimated value. **2.** body-building value (of food).

Anschlagwinkel, *m. Tls:* try-square.

Anschlagzettel, *m.* notice; poster, bill, placard.

Anschlagzünder, *m. Artil: etc:* percussion-fuse.

anschlämmen, *v.tr.* **1.** (*a*) to cover (sth.) with slime, with mud; *Geol:* to deposit mud on (land); (*b*) to silt; to choke up (canal, etc.) with mud; **sich a.,** (*of harbour, etc.*) to silt up. **2.** *Ch:* to elutriate (chalk, etc.).

anschleichen, *v.i. sep.* (*strong*) (*sein*) & **sich anschleichen,** to steal up, slink up, sneak up; **angeschlichen kommen,** to come stealing, slinking, sneaking, along, up; *Ven:* **(sich) an das Wild,** *Mil:* **an den Feind, a.,** to stalk the game, the enemy; to creep up on the game, the enemy.

anschleifen, *v.sep.* I. *v.tr.* (*strong*) **1.** (*a*) to grind, set an edge on (knife, etc.); (*b*) *Lap:* to start cutting (precious stone); (*c*) **eine Spitze an ein Werkzeug a.,** to point a tool; to sharpen a tool to a point. **2.** to polish (surface).

II. **anschleifen,** *v.tr.* (*weak*) **1.** to drag, trail, (sth., s.o.) along, up; **(j-m) etwas, j-n, a., angeschleift bringen,** (i) to drag sth., s.o., along, up (to s.o.); (ii) *F:* to lug, trail, sth., s.o., (along) (to s.o.). **2.** to tie (sth.) on with a slip-knot (**an** + *acc.*, to).

anschlendern, *v.i. sep.* (*sein*) (*usu. only in*) **angeschlendert kommen,** to come dawdling, lounging, sauntering, along.

anschleppen, *v.tr. sep.* to drag, haul, (s.o., sth.) along, up.

anschlicken, *v.i. sep.* (*sein*) (*of harbour, etc.*) to silt up.

anschließen, *v.sep.* (*strong*) I. *v.tr.* **1.** to padlock (bicycle, etc.); to chain (up) (s.o., dog, bicycle, etc.) (**an** + *acc.*, to). **2.** (*a*) to connect, join (up); *El:* to connect (up); **etwas etwas** *dat.*, **an etwas** *acc.*, **a.,** to join (up), attach, sth. to sth.; to annex sth. to sth.; to add sth. (on) to sth.; to link sth. up with sth.; **ein Dokument einem Brief a.,** to attach a document to, enclose a document with, a letter; **hier angeschlossen,** enclosed herewith, attached herewith; **zwei Maschinenteile aneinander a.,** to connect up, join up, two parts of a machine; **einen Verein an eine Organisation a.,** to affiliate a society to an organization; *El.E:* **eine Lampe an eine Batterie a.,** to connect a lamp to a battery; **eine Klingel an den Beleuchtungsstromkreis a.,** to run a bell off the light circuit; **an das Stadtnetz a.,** to connect up with the town supply; *W.Tel:* **Sender a.,** to link (up) transmitters, (transmitting) stations; **angeschlossen,** *El.E:* (*of power stations*) connected up; *W.Tel:* (*of transmitters*) linked (up); **München und die angeschlossenen Sender,** Munich and other stations relaying the (same) programme; **angeschlossen alle deutschen Sender,** (programme) relayed by all German stations; (*b*) *Tchn:* to tap (gas-main, electric circuit, etc.). **3. sich anschließen,** (*a*) (i) *Mil:* to close the ranks; to close up; *abs.* **anschließen! angeschlossen!** close up! **rechts, links, a.!** on the right, left, close! (ii) (*in queue, etc.*) to close up; to get closer together; (*in tram, U.S: streetcar, etc.*) **bitte nach vorne a.!** pass along the car, please! *U.S:* step forward, please! (*b*) **sich j-m, an j-n, a.,** to attach oneself to s.o., (i) to join company with s.o., to join s.o.; (ii) to form, strike up, a friendship with s.o., to make friends with s.o.; to take up with s.o.; (iii) to side, take sides, with s.o.; to throw in one's lot with s.o.; **wollen Sie sich uns, unserer Gesellschaft, a.?** will you join us, join our party? **sich j-m auf dem Weg a.,** to join s.o. on his way; to accompany s.o. (on his way), to go along with s.o.; **sich dem Zuge a.,** to join the procession; **er schließt sich leicht, schwer, an,** he makes, does not make, contacts easily; he is, is not, a sociable person; **sich einem Verein a.,** to join a society; **sich einer Partei a.,** to accede to, attach oneself to, rally to, join, a party; to throw in one's lot with a party; **sich der Mehrheit a.,** to come into line with the majority; **sich einer Ansicht a.,** to concur in, subscribe to, an opinion; to come round to an opinion; to adopt a view; **sich j-s Meinung a.,** to fall in with, come over to, s.o.'s opinion; to concur, acquiesce, in the opinion of s.o.; to agree with s.o.'s opinion; **ich schließe mich Ihrer Meinung an,** I concur in your opinion, I concur with you; **sich einem Vorschlag, j-s Wünschen, a.,** to accede to, fall in with, comply with, a proposal, s.o.'s wishes; **sich einem Antrag, einem Unternehmen, a.,** to associate oneself with a proposal, with an undertaking; (*c*) (*of thg*) **sich an etwas** *acc.* **a.** (*also occ. v.i.*) (i) to join (up) with sth.; to connect with sth.; to link on to sth., to link up, in, with sth.; (ii) to follow sth. (immediately); (iii) to adjoin sth.; to be adjacent to sth.; **an die Versammlung schloß sich ein Konzert an,** the meeting was followed by a concert, (immediately) after the meeting there was a concert (*cp.* IV); **an den Schulhof schließt sich ein Sportfeld an,** a playing-field adjoins the school yard; (*d*) (*of text, work of art, etc.; of author*) **sich an ein Vorbild a.,** to follow a model closely.

II. **anschließen,** *v.i.* (*haben*) **1.** (*of garment*) (**gut**) **a.,** to fit (well); **eng a.,** to fit tightly, closely, to be a tight, close, fit; to cling to the figure; to fit like a glove; **eng anschließendes Kleid,** tight-fitting, close-fitting, clinging, dress. **2.** *occ.* (*of trains*) **an** (+*acc.*) **. . . a.,** to connect with . . . ; **die Züge schließen nicht gut an,** there is not a good connection, *F:* the trains don't fit.

III. *vbl s.* **Anschließen** *n.*, **Anschließung** *f. in vbl senses; cp.* **Anschluß** 1.

IV. **anschließend. 1.** *pr.p.* & *a. in vbl senses.* **2.** *adv.* subsequently; (immediately) afterwards; **a. an die Versammlung fand ein Konzert statt,** the meeting was followed by a concert, (immediately) after the meeting there was a concert; *F:* (*said by waiter, waitress*) **a. Käse?** and cheese to follow?

Anschließer, *m. Anat:* adductor, adducent muscle.

Anschliff, *m.* polish; polished surface (of marble, metal, etc.).

anschlingen, *v.tr. sep.* (*strong*) **etwas an etwas** *acc.* **a.,** to fasten sth. to sth. with a noose, with a loop; to loop sth. on to sth.

anschlitzen, *v.tr. sep.* to make a slit in (sth.), to slit (sth.).

Anschlitzung, *f. Carp:* groove-and-tongue joint; *Carp: Mec.E: etc:* slit-and-tongue junction.

Anschluß, *m.* **1.** (*a*) connecting (up), connection (**an** + *acc.*, to, with); attaching, attachment (**an** + *acc.*, to); annexing (**an** + *acc.*, to); adding, addition (**an** + *acc.*, to); linking (up) (**an** + *acc.*, with); *El.E: Mec.E: etc* connecting up (of cables, pipes, etc.); **A. eines Vereins an eine Organisation,** affiliation of a society to an organization; **A. eines Staates an eine Union,** joining of a union by a state, accession of a state to a union; **A. eines Staates an einen anderen,** (political) union of one state with another; *esp. Hist:* **der A.** (**Österreichs an das Deutsche Reich**), the Union of Austria with Germany (*1938*), the *Anschluss*; *Gram:* **relativer, relativischer, A.,** relative connection; (*b*) **im A. an die Versammlung fand ein Konzert statt,** the meeting was followed by a concert, after the meeting there was a concert; *Com:* **im A. an unser Schreiben vom 20. . . . ,** with further reference to, further to, referring to, our communication of the 20th . . . ; (*c*) *Art: Lit: etc:* **im A. an ein Vorbild,** following a model closely; **im A. an die Bibel schreibt hier Goethe . . . ,** here, closely following the (text of the) Bible, Goethe writes . . . **2.** (*a*) connection, contact (with persons); **er findet leicht, schwer, A.,** he makes,

does not make, contacts easily; he is, is not, a sociable person, *F:* a good mixer; **sie sucht A.**, (i) she is trying, wants, to get to know (some) people, to make (some) friends; (ii) *F:* she is trying to find herself a man; **'gebildete Dame sucht A.'**, 'cultured lady wishes to meet gentleman (with a view to matrimony)'; *Com:* **wir haben in London, an Londoner Firmen, keinen A. gefunden,** we have not established any connections in London, with London firms; (*b*) *Mil:* contact, touch; **Einheit X hat A. an Einheit Y,** unit X is in contact, in touch, with unit Y. **3.** *Rail:* connection (between trains, between train and boat); **A. an** (+*acc.*) ... **haben,** (*of train or boat*) to connect with ...; (*of train*) to run in connection with ...; **dieser Zug hat A. nach X,** this train has a connection with, to, X; **ich habe den A. in Köln versäumt, verpaßt, verfehlt, gerade noch erreicht,** I missed, only just got, my connection at Cologne; *F:* **sie hat den A. verpaßt, versäumt,** she has missed her chance (of marriage); *F:* she has missed the boat. **4.** (*a*) *Tp:* connection, communication (with subscriber); connection (with telephone system); **A. (an j-n) bekommen,** to get one's connection (with s.o.), to get through, to be put through (to s.o.); **haben Sie A.?** (i) have you been connected, put through? (ii) **haben Sie (Telephon-)A.?** have you a telephone? are you on the telephone? **das Büro hat sieben Anschlüsse,** the office has seven (telephone) lines; (*b*) *El.E: etc:* connection with a mains supply; **die Wohnung hat keinen elektrischen A., hat keinen A. an die Wasser-, Gasleitung,** the flat is not connected to the electricity supply, to the water mains, to the gas mains; the flat has no electricity, water, gas, laid on; (*c*) *W.Tel:* **A. eines Senders an einen anderen,** linking (up), link-up, of one transmitter with another; relaying by one station of the programme broadcast by another. **5.** *Ling:* **fester A.,** close stress; **loser A.,** open stress. **6.** *Constr: Mec.E: etc:* joint; connection, junction (of pipes, cables, etc.); union (of pipes, wires, etc.); coupling (of pipes); (water, gas) connection; plug (of fire hydrant, etc.); *El.E: W.Tel:* connection; terminal; plug; socket; *Rail:* (i) junction; (ii) = **Anschlußbahn, -gleis, -linie, -schiene.** **7.** *occ.* enclosure (with letter); annexed, attached, document. **8. Anschluß-,** *comb.fm. Tchn:* connecting ..., connection ...; joining ..., joint ...; **Anschlußblech** *n*, **Anschlußplatte** *f*, connecting plate, connection plate; joining plate, joint plate; **Anschlußdraht** *m*, connecting wire.

Anschlußbahn, *f. Rail:* branch-line; junction line, loop-line.

Anschlußbahnhof, *m. Rail:* connecting station.

Anschlußbereich, *m. Tp:* telephone area.

Anschlußbüchse, *f. El.E:* socket.

Anschlußbuchstaben, *m.pl. Print:* abutting letters, ablated sorts.

Anschlußdose, *f. El.E:* (*a*) junction-box; connecting box; (*b*) (wall) socket, wall plug, point.

Anschlußgeleise, *n.*, **Anschlußgleis,** *n. Rail:* (*a*) siding; side-line (leading to factory, etc.); (*b*) junction line, loop-line.

Anschlußkabel, *n. El.E:* connecting cable; lead; *Tp:* subscriber's cable.

Anschlußkasten, *m. El.E:* junction-box; connecting box.

Anschlußklemme, *f. El.E:* (*a*) terminal clamp, terminal; (*b*) (cable-)connecter.

Anschlußklinke, *f. El.E:* jack; *esp. Tp:* operator's jack.

Anschlußleitung, *f.* **1.** *Tp:* subscriber's line. **2.** *Mec.E: etc:* connecting pipe, joint-pipe.

Anschlußlinie, *f. Rail:* = **Anschlußbahn.**

Anschlußmann, *m.* **-(e)s/-männer.** *Mil:* connecting file.

Anschlußpunkt, *m.* **1.** junction-point; *Rail:* junction. **2.** *Surv: Artil:* reference point; *Artil:* reference object.

Anschlußrohr, *n.* connecting pipe; joint-pipe; coupling pipe.

Anschlußschema, *n. El.E:* wiring diagram; lay-out (of wireless set, etc.).

Anschlußschiene, *f. Rail:* junction-rail.

Anschlußschnur, *f. El.E:* flexible lead, *F:* flex, *U.S:* connecting cord.

Anschlußstation, *f. Rail:* junction (station).

Anschlußstecker, *m. El.E:* (connecting-up) plug.

Anschlußstelle, *f.* **1.** junction-point. **2.** *El.E:* (point of) connection; terminal.

Anschlußstöpsel, *m. Tp:* (operator's) plug.

Anschlußstück, *n. Mec.E: etc:* joining piece, joint; coupling (piece); connecting piece, connection.

Anschlußteil, *m. Mec.E: etc:* (*a*) = **Anschlußstück;** (*b*) fitting.

Anschlußtor, *n.* **das A. erzielen,** to score the goal that leaves the side only one down.

Anschlußtreffer, *m.* = **Anschlußtor.**

Anschlußzug, *m. Rail:* connecting train; **ich habe den A. verpaßt, der A. war schon weg,** I missed my connection.

Anschlußzwang, *m. Adm:* compulsory participation in public service schemes.

anschmachten, *v.tr. sep.* to look at (s.o.) languishingly, with languishing eyes; *F:* to make sheep's eyes at (s.o.).

Anschmack, *m.* **-(e)s/.** *Dial:* **ein A. von etwas,** a sample of sth. (to taste), a taste of sth.

anschmeicheln, *v.tr. sep.* **1. j-m etwas a.,** to force sth. upon s.o. by flattery. **2. sich bei j-m a.,** to ingratiate oneself with s.o.; to insinuate oneself into s.o.'s good graces; to curry favour with s.o.; *F:* to blarney s.o.

anschmelzen, *v.sep.* **1.** *v.tr.* (*strong, occ. weak*) to solder (sth.) on; to weld, braze, (sth.) on (**an**+*acc.*, to). **2.** *v.i.* (*strong*) (*sein*) to melt on (**an etwas** *acc.*, to sth.).

Anschmelzherd, *m. Metall:* melting-furnace; (*for ore*) smelt(ing)-furnace.

anschmieden, *v.tr. sep.* **1.** *Metall:* to forge (sth.) on (**an**+*acc.*, to). **2.** to rivet fetters on (s.o.); to fetter, shackle (s.o.).

anschmiegen. I. *v.tr. sep.* **1. etwas etwas** *dat.*, **etwas an etwas** *acc.*, **a.,** to press sth. close against sth.; to adapt, fit, sth. to the shape, to the contours, of sth.; to fit sth. closely, smoothly, snugly, to sth.; **die Katze schmiegte ihren Kopf an mein Knie an,** the cat snuggled its head against my knee. **2. sich anschmiegen,** (*a*) (i) (*of pers., animal*) **sich an j-n, an etwas** *acc.*, **a.,** to snuggle up to s.o., sth.; to nestle close (up) to s.o., sth.; (ii) *A:* (*of pers.*) **sich j-m, an j-n, a.,** to be complaisant with s.o.; **sich etwas** *dat.* **a.,** to conform to, with, sth.; to conform, accommodate, oneself to a custom, etc.; (*b*) (*of thg*) **sich an etwas** *acc.* **a.,** to fit exactly to sth.; to take on the exact shape of sth.; **der Weg schmiegt sich an die Küstenlinie an,** the road hugs the coastline; **das Kleid schmiegt sich an den Körper an,** the dress clings to the figure, fits snugly, fits like a glove; *Geom:* (*of curve*) **sich an eine Linie a.,** to osculate with a line.

II. *vbl. s.* **Anschmiegen** *n.*, **Anschmiegung** *f. in vbl senses; also:* (*a*) adaptation (**an**+*acc.*, to); (*b*) *Geom:* osculation (**an**+*acc.*, with).

anschmiegsam, *a.* (*a*) cuddlesome (pers., animal); (*b*) *A:* pliant, pliable; supple; (*of pers., character, etc.*) docile, tractable, accommodating; complaisant.

anschmieren, *v.tr. sep.* **1.** (*a*) to smear; to daub; to dirty (one's face, etc.); (*b*) **etwas an etwas** *acc.* **a.,** to smear, daub, sth. on(to) sth. **2.** *F:* (*a*) **j-n a.,** to cheat, diddle, bamboozle, s.o.; to take s.o. in, to do s.o.; **da bist du schön angeschmiert worden!** you've been properly had! you've been done brown, been sold a pup! **j-n mit etwas a., j-m etwas a.,** to fob off, palm off, sth. (up)on s.o., to foist sth. on s.o.; to work sth. off on s.o.; *F:* to land, *U.S:* to stick, s.o. with sth.; (*b*) **sich bei j-m a.** = **sich bei j-m anschmeicheln,** *q.v. under* **anschmeicheln.**

anschmitzen, *v.tr. sep.* **1.** to strike (s.o., sth.) sharply; to give (horse) a cut (with the whip). **2.** to soil, dirty (sth.).

anschmucken (sich), *v.refl. sep. South G.Dial:* = **sich anschmiegen,** *q.v. under* **anschmiegen I. 2.**

anschmunzeln, *v.tr. sep.* to smirk at (s.o.); to smile at (s.o.) (i) in a self-satisfied manner, (ii) roguishly.

anschmutzen, *v.tr. sep.* to soil, dirty (sth.) (slightly); *Com:* (*of goods*) **leicht angeschmutzt,** slightly soiled, shop-soiled, *U.S:* shopworn.

anschnallen, *v.tr. sep.* to buckle on (belt, spurs, sword, etc.); to gird on (sword); to fasten (ski); to do up (skating-boot); to strap (s.o., sth.) in, down; **sich a.,** to fasten one's seat-belt; to buckle, strap, oneself in.

Anschnallgurt, *m.* (waist-)belt (with buckle); *Aut: etc:* safetybelt.

Anschnallsporen, *m.pl. Equit:* buckled spurs.

anschnarchen, *v.tr. sep.* **1.** to snore at (s.o.). **2.** *F:* = **anschnauzen.**

anschnauben, *v.sep.* (*conj. like* **schnauben**) **1.** (*a*) *v.tr.* (*of horse*) to snort at (s.o., sth.); (*b*) *v.i.* (*sein*) **angeschnaubt kommen,** (i) (*of horse*) to come snorting up; (ii) *F:* (*of pers.*) to come snorting up; to come up puffing and blowing; (*of locomotive*) to come puffing along. **2.** *v.tr. F:* = **anschnauzen.**

anschnauzen, *v.tr. sep. F:* to tell (s.o.) off, tick (s.o.) off; to blow (s.o.) up; to jump down (s.o.'s) throat; to bite, snap, (s.o.'s) head off; to go for (s.o.); to brow-beat (s.o.); *U.S. & F:* to bawl (s.o.) out.

Anschnauzer, *m. F:* reprimand, wigging, scolding; jawing, slanging, blowing up; telling-off, ticking-off; **einen A. bekommen,** to get a good dressing-down; to get hauled over the coals; to get told off, ticked off.

Anschneideergebnisse, *f.pl. Surv: Artil:* cross-bearings.

Anschneidemesser, *n. Dom.Ec:* carving-knife, carver.

anschneiden, *v.tr. sep.* (*strong*) **1.** (*a*) to cut into, make the first cut in (loaf, cheese, joint, etc.); to cut the first piece from, to start (roll of cloth, etc.); **angeschnittenes Brot,** loaf which has been already started, cut; (*b*) **ein Thema a.,** to broach, start, a subject. **2.** *A:* **etwas (auf dem Kerbholz) a.,** to notch sth. up (on the tally-stick); to score sth. up. **3.** (*a*) *Surv: etc:* to get (object) in the cross-wires of the telescope; to train the instrument on (object); (*b*) *Surv: Artil:* to get cross-bearings on (sth.). **4.** *Games: Ten: etc:* **den Ball a.,** to put spin on the ball; to put side on the ball. **5.** (*of yacht, etc.*) to cut close to (point, buoy, etc.). **6.** *Ven:* (*of hounds*) **das Wild a.,** to begin to eat the game. **7.** *Dressm: Tail:* to cut (collar, sleeve, etc.) in one piece with the garment, etc.; **angeschnittener Ärmel,** sleeve cut in one piece with the garment; dolman sleeve.

Anschneidetrupp, *m. Artil:* flash-spotting troop.

anschniegeln (sich), *v.refl. sep.* to make oneself smart; to dress, get, oneself up; to titivate (oneself).

Anschnitt, *m.* **1.** (*a*) (action of) cutting (into sth.); **Tuch, das hart im A. ist,** cloth that is hard to cut, that cuts hard; (*b*) **etwas im A. verkaufen,** to sell sth. by the piece; to sell sth. (by) retail; **'Wildbret heute im A.'**, 'cuts of venison today'. **2.** first cut, outside slice (of loaf, joint, etc.). **3.** cut, nick (in piece of wood, etc.); *A:* notch, nick, score (on tally-stick). **4.** *pl.* **Anschnitte,** *Surv: Artil:* cross-bearings.

anschnüffeln, *v.tr. sep.* (*of dog, etc.*) to sniff at (s.o., sth.); *F:* (*of candidate for an appointment*) **er kommt morgen, um angeschnüffelt zu werden,** he's coming tomorrow to be interviewed, *F:* to be looked over.

anschnüren, *v.tr. sep.* to tie (sth.) on (**an**+*acc.*, to).

anschoppen. I. *v.tr. sep. Med:* to congest; to engorge (blood vessels, etc.); **sich a.,** to become congested, to congest; (*of blood vessels, etc.*) to become engorged.

II. *vbl s.* **Anschoppung,** *f. in vbl senses; also:* congestion; engorgement.

Anschove [an'ʃo:və], *f.* **-/-n, Anschovis** [an'ʃo:vis], *f.* **-/-.** *Ich: Cu:* anchovy.

Anschovisbirne, *f. Bot:* anchovy-pear.

anschrauben, *v.tr. sep.* to screw (sth.) on (**an**+*acc.*, to).

Anschraubgewinde, *n. Mec.E:* screw thread.

Anschreibeblatt, *n. Games: Sp:* score-card, *U.S:* tally (sheet).

Anschreibebuch, *n.* (*a*) note-book; memorandum-book; (*b*) *Com:* credit sales book; (bakery, dairy, etc.) roundsman's book; (*c*) *Games: Sp:* score-book.

anschreiben. I. *v.tr. sep.* (*strong*) **1.** (*a*) to write (sth.) down, to put (sth.) down, set (sth.) down (in writing); **eine Formel an, auf, die Tafel a.,** to write (up) a formula on the blackboard; **etwas an etwas** *acc.* **mit Kreide a.,** to chalk (up) sth. on sth.; *Games: Sp:* **die Punkte a.,** to keep the score, to score; (*b*) **er ist gut, schlecht, angeschrieben,** he is well, badly, reported on; he is, is not, thought well of; **bei j-m gut angeschrieben sein,** to be in s.o.'s good books, good graces; to stand well with s.o.; **bei j-m schlecht, übel, nicht gut, angeschrieben sein,** to be in s.o.'s bad books, black books; to be out of favour with s.o.; (*c*) *Com:* **j-m etwas a.,** to put sth. on s.o.'s account; to debit sth. to s.o.; to charge sth. up to s.o.; **etwas a. lassen,** to have sth. charged to one's account; to buy sth. on credit, on trust, *F:* on tick; **bitte schreiben Sie es an! bitte a.!** please charge it up to my account, to me; please put it down to me; please enter it; **die Getränke a. lassen,** *F:* to have the drinks chalked up, put on the slate. **2. einen neuen Füller a.,** to break in a new fountain-pen. **3.** *Mth:* **angeschriebener Kreis,** escribed circle, excircle; **Mittelpunkt des angeschriebenen Kreises,** excentre.

II. *vbl s.* **Anschreiben,** *n.* **1.** *in vbl senses*

2. *A:* communication, *esp.* official communication; circular (letter).
Anschreiber, *m. Games: Sp:* scorer; marker.
Anschreibetafel, *f. Games: Sp:* score-board.
anschreien, *v.tr. sep. (strong)* to shout at (s.o.); to bawl, roar, at (s.o.); to scream at (s.o.); *Nau:* to hail (ship).
anschreiten, *v.i. sep. (strong) (usu. only in)* **angeschritten kommen,** to come striding along.
Anschrift, *f.* address (of letter, pers.); direction (of letter); **falsche A.,** wrong address, misdirection (on letter); **genaue A. angeben!** give exact postal address.
Anschriftenbuch, *n.* address-book; directory.
Anschriftenbüro, *n.* address bureau, information bureau.
Anschriftenmaschine, *f.* addressing-machine, addressograph.
Anschriftenplatte, *f.* address-plate.
Anschrot, *n.* **-(e)s/.,** **Anschrote,** *f.* **-/.** *Tex:* selvedge, list (of cloth).
anschroten, *v.tr. sep.* **1.** *Tex:* to put a selvedge, a list, on (cloth). **2.** to roll up, trundle up (barrel).
Anschub, *m. Skittles:* first bowl, first throw; **wer hat den A.?** who bowls first?
anschuhen, *v.tr. sep. Tchn:* to tip (sth.) (with metal); to shoe (a pile, etc.).
anschuldigen. I. *v.tr. sep.* **j-n eines Verbrechens, eines Vergehens, a.,** to accuse s.o. of a crime, of an offence; to indict s.o. for a crime; to charge s.o. with a crime, with an offence; to (in)criminate, inculpate, s.o.; to tax s.o. with an offence; **der, die, Angeschuldigte,** the accused; *(in court)* the defendant; prisoner at the bar.
II. *vbl s.* **1. Anschuldigen,** *n. in vbl senses; also:* accusation; (in)crimination; inculpation. **2. Anschuldigung,** *f. (a)*=II. 1; *(b)* accusation; indictment; charge; imputation; **Anschuldigungen gegen j-n schleudern,** to hurl accusations at s.o.; **falsche A.,** false accusation; *Jur:* malicious prosecution.
anschüren, *v.tr. sep.* **1.** to stir (up), poke (up), *Mch: etc:* to stoke (fire); to fan (flame). **2.** to stir up (passions, discontent, etc.); to fan (passions) (to a flame); to foment (feelings, discord).
Anschürer, *m.* agitator, trouble-maker; fomenter of discord, *Lit:* fire-brand.
Anschuß, *m.* **1.** first shot; **den A. haben,** to have the first shot; to shoot, fire, first. **2.** *Ven: (a)* shot-wound; position of the shot-wound on the game; *(b)* place where the game stood when shot. **3.** shooting, rushing (in) (of flood-water, cataract, etc.). **4.** *Cryst: (a)* crystalization, forming of crystals; *(b)* crop of crystals.
Anschußgefäß, *n. Ch: Ind:* crystallizing vessel.
anschütten, *v.tr. sep.* **1.** *(a)* **Wasser, Sand, usw., an etwas** *acc.* **a.,** to pour water, sand, etc., on to sth.; *(b)* **Getreide an die Wand a.,** to heap up grain against the wall. **2.** *Civ.E: etc: (a)* to fill up, pack (sunk part of ground, etc.); *(b)* to embank, to bank (up) (road, etc.).
anschützen, *v.tr. sep. Hyd.E:* **1. das Staumauer a.,** to open the flood-gate(s). **2. eine Staumauer a.,** to provide a dam with sluices.
anschwängern, *v.tr. sep. Ch: etc:* to impregnate, saturate (substance) **(mit,** with); **Anschwängerung** *f,* impregnation, saturation.
anschwanken, *v.i. sep. (sein) (usu. only in)* **angeschwankt kommen,** to come tottering along, up.
anschwänzeln, *v.i. sep. (sein) (usu. only in)* **angeschwänzelt kommen,** (i) *(of dog)* to come up wagging its tail; (ii) *F: (of pers.)* to approach in an ingratiating *or* affected manner.
anschwänzen, *v.tr. sep. Brew: Dist:* to sprinkle, sparge (draff).
anschwärmen, *v.sep.* **1.** *v.i. (haben) (a) (of bees)* to start swarming; *(b) (of bees, etc.; F: of visitors, etc.)* **angeschwärmt kommen,** to arrive in swarms; to come swarming in. **2.** *v.tr.* to adulate; to fawn on (s.o.); *F:* to gush at, *U.S:* over, (s.o.); *F:* to have a crush on (s.o.).
anschwärzen. I. *v.tr. sep.* **1.** to blacken; to make (sth.) black; to black (leather, etc.). **2. j-n bei j-m a.,** to blacken s.o.'s character to s.o.; to talk scandal to s.o. about s.o.; to disparage s.o., to speak disparagingly of s.o., to s.o.; **er hat mich überall, bei allen Leuten, angeschwärzt,** he's been running me down, *F:* crabbing me, all over the place.
II. *vbl s.* **1. Anschwärzen,** *n. in vbl senses.* **2. Anschwärzung,** *f. (a) in vbl senses; also:* disparagement (of s.o.); *(b)* backbiting.
Anschwärzerei, *f.* **-/-en,** *(a)* (continual) disparagement, *F:* crabbing; *(b)* backbiting.
anschwatzen, *v.tr. sep.* **j-m etwas a.,** to talk s.o. into (i) accepting, (ii) buying, sth.
anschweben, *v.i. sep. (sein) (a)* to come gliding along, in; to come floating along, in; *(b) Av: (of aircraft)* to glide in.
anschwefeln, *v.tr. sep.* to treat (sth.) with sulphur; to sulphurize; *esp.* to fumigate (sth.) with sulphur.
Anschweif, *m. Tex:* **1.** warp. **2.** end-list, end-selvedge (of piece of cloth).
anschweifen, *v.tr. sep. Tex:* to warp (cloth).
Anschweifrahmen, *m. Tex:* warp(ing)-frame.
anschweißen, *v.tr. sep.* **1.** *Metalw:* to weld; **etwas an etwas** *acc.* **a.,** to weld sth. (on) to sth.; **zwei Metallstücke a.,** to weld two pieces of metal (together). **2.** *Ven:* to wound (game).
Anschweißstelle, *f.* welding point.
anschwellen, *v.sep.* I. *v.i. (strong) (sein)* to swell (up); to become distended; to become inflated; to swell out; *(of face)* to grow puffy; *(of difficulties, expenses, etc.)* to swell, to increase; *Med:* to swell, to tumefy; *Mus: (of note, voice)* to swell; to rise in a crescendo; *Nau: (of sail)* to fill, to swell out; to bag, belly, bunt; **der Fluß schwillt an,** the river is rising; **der Fluß ist angeschwollen,** the river is swollen, is in spate; **sein Arm schwillt an,** his arm is swelling (up); **seine Backe ist angeschwollen,** his cheek is swollen, he has a swollen cheek; *Mus:* **einen Ton a. lassen,** to swell a note; **anschwellend,** swelling; *Med:* intumescent; *Ling:* **anschwellende Betonung,** rising stress; **angeschwollen,** swollen (river, limb, cheek, etc.); puffy (face); *Med:* tumid, intumescent.
II. **anschwellen,** *v.tr. (weak) (a)* to swell; to cause (sth.) to swell; to inflate (sth.); to distend (sth.); to puff (sth.) up; to make (face) puffy; *Med:* to swell, to tumefy; **der Regen hat den Fluß angeschwellt,** the rain has swollen the river; **die Schwierigkeiten, die Unkosten, a.,** to swell, increase, the difficulties, the expenses; *Nau: (of wind)* **die Segel a.,** to fill, swell (out), belly (out), the sails; *(b) Dial:* to boil (meat, etc.).
III. *vbl s.* **1. Anschwellen,** *n. in vbl senses; also:* increase; *Mus:* swell: crescendo; *Med:* intumescence. **2. Anschwellung,** *f. (a)*=III. 1; *(b)* swelling; protuberance; *Med:* swelling, intumescence.
anschwemmen. I. *v.sep.* **1.** *v.tr. (of river, sea)* to wash (sth.) up, ashore; to float (sth.) ashore; *Geol:* to deposit (alluvium); *Geol:* **angeschwemmtes Land,** alluvion; *Nau:* **angeschwemmtes Wrackgut,** wreckage washed up by the sea; **angeschwemmte Leiche,** (i) corpse washed ashore; (ii) *Mil: P:* elderly (re-employed) officer, *F:* dug-out, blimp. **2.** *v.i. (sein) Dial: (of alluvium)* to be deposited. **3.** *v.i. (sein) Dial:* =**anschwimmen.**
II. *vbl s.* **1. Anschwemmen,** *n.*=II. 2 *(a).* **2. Anschwemmung,** *f. (a) in vbl senses; also: Geol:* (accretion through) alluvion; aggradation; silting; *(b) Geol:* alluvial deposit(s), alluvium; sediment.
anschwimmen, *v.sep. (strong)* **1.** *v.tr.* to swim towards (sth.); **das Ufer a.,** to swim towards, for, the shore. **2.** *v.i. (sein) (a)* **ans Ufer a.,** to swim ashore; **angeschwommen kommen,** *(of pers.)* to come swimming along; to swim up; *(of thg)* to come floating along, up; *(b)* **gegen den Strom a.,** (i) to swim against the current, against the tide, against the stream; (ii) *F:* to struggle against the trend; to go against the majority. **3.** *v.i. (haben)* to open the swimming season; **Anschwimmen** *n,* first event of the swimming season.
anschwindeln, *v.tr. sep.* to lie (to s.o.); to tell (s.o.) a fib *or* fibs.
anschwingen, *v.i. sep. (strong) (haben)* to start swinging; to start oscillating; to start rocking.
anschwöden, *v.tr. sep. Tan:* to paint (hide) with lime.
Anschwung, *m.* start of the swinging, of the oscillation, of the rocking; initial impetus (causing sth. to oscillate); push-off.
Anse, *f.* **-/-n. 1.** *Veh:* (pair of) shafts, thills. **2.** *Art: etc:* ansa. **3.** *Astr:* ansa (of Saturn's ring).
ansegeln. *v.sep.* **1.** *v.i. (sein)* **a., angesegelt kommen,** *(of ship, F: of pers.)* to come sailing along, up. **2.** *v.tr. (a)* to sail towards, make for (a point); **einen Hafen a.,** (i) to make for a port, (ii) to put into a port; **das Land a.,** (i) to make for land, (ii) to touch land, to land; *(b)* to run foul of (another craft); to run on to (reef). **3.** *v.i. (haben)* to open the sailing season; **Ansegeln** *n,* first event of the sailing season.
Ansegelungsboje, Ansegelungstonne, *f. Nau:* entrance buoy.
ansehen. I. *v.tr. sep. (strong)* **1.** *(a)* to look at (s.o., sth.); to inspect (sth.); **sich** *dat.* **etwas a.,** to have, take, a look at sth.; **darf ich es (mir mal) a.?** may I look (at it)? may I have a look (at it)? **sich ein Theaterstück a.,** to see a play; **sieh nur das Pärchen an!** just look at that couple! **sieh, seht, das nur an!** *abs.* **sieh, seht, mal an! sieh mal einer an!** (i) just look at this! (ii) well, well! well, to be sure! well I never! you don't say so! who'd have thought it! fancy that! bless my soul! **schön anzusehen,** fair to look upon, good to look at; **j-n, etwas, gerade a.,** to look straight at s.o., sth.; to look s.o. in the face, in the eye; **j-n, etwas, starr, mit unverwandten Augen, a.,** to stare at s.o., sth.; to gaze (fixedly) at s.o., sth.; **j-n, etwas, scharf a.,** to look hard at s.o., sth.; to give s.o. a sharp look; **etwas näher a.,** to look closely at sth.; to inspect sth.; to consider sth. carefully; **j-n von der Seite a.,** to cast a sidelong glance at s.o.; **j-n scheel, schief, a.,** to look askance at s.o.; **j-n bös, finster, sauer, a.,** to give s.o. a nasty look, a black look, a sour look, *F:* a dirty look; **j-n argwöhnisch a.,** to eye s.o. suspiciously; **j-n prüfend a.,** to look searchingly at s.o., to give s.o. a searching look; **j-n erstaunt, verwundert, a.,** to look, gaze, at s.o. in astonishment; **j-n von oben bis unten a.,** to look s.o. up and down, to eye s.o. from head to foot; **j-n verliebt a.,** to make sheep's eyes at s.o.; **etwas auf seine Brauchbarkeit hin a.,** to look at sth. with an eye to its usefulness, to see whether it can be used; *(b)* **das sieht sich gut an,** it looks well; it has style about it; **das sieht sich schön an,** it's a handsome, pretty, sight; it's a pleasure to the eye, *F:* it's easy on the eye; *(c)* **etwas mit a.,** to be a spectator, a witness, an eye-witness, of sth.; to look on at sth.; **etwas stillschweigend mit a.,** to look on passively at sth.; to look on without participating *or* without intervening; **ich kann es nicht länger mit a.,** I can't bear to watch this any longer; I can't endure, stand, put up with, watching this any longer; **ich verstehe nicht, wie er das ruhig, stillschweigend, mit ansehen konnte,** I just don't understand how he could see that going on without doing something about it; *(d)* **j-m das schlechte Gewissen, usw., a.,** to see from s.o.'s appearance that he has a bad conscience, etc.; **man sieht ihm seine Schwäche nicht an,** you cannot detect his weakness by looking at him; one does not notice, he does not show, his weakness; his weakness is not noticeable; **man sieht ihm sein Alter, seine Jahre, nicht an,** he does not look his age, his years; **man sieht ihm an, daß er ein Deutscher ist, man sieht ihm den Deutschen an,** you can see (at once) that he's a German; **man sieht's ihr an den Augen an, daß sie verliebt ist,** the very look in her eyes tells you that she's in love; *F:* **man sieht dir an der Nasenspitze an, daß du lügst,** it's written in your face that you're lying; *cp.* **anmerken** I. 1; *(e)* to see (sth.) (mentally); to look at, consider, contemplate (a matter, etc.); **die Geschehnisse anders a.,** to take a different view of events; **so sehe ich die Sache nicht an,** I see, view, the matter differently; I do not look on, do not view, the matter in that light; **ich sehe das Problem mit anderen Augen an,** I look upon the problem with a different eye, I see the problem in quite another light; **wie man es auch a. mag,** however, whichever way, one looks at it; in whatever light one regards it; whichever way you take it; **wie ich die Sache ansehe . . . ,** in my view . . . ; to my mind . . . ; as it strikes me . . . ; to my way of thinking . . . , as I see the matter . . . ; **wir sehen es ernst an,** we take a grave view of it, we regard it seriously; **etwas von der falschen Seite a.,** to see sth. in a false light; to take a wrong view of sth.; **etwas von der schlimmsten Seite a.,** to look on the dark side of sth.; to see sth. in the worst, the most unfavourable, light. **2. j-n, etwas, als,** *occ.* **für, etwas a.,** to regard, consider, s.o., sth., as sth.; to look upon s.o., sth., as sth.; to deem s.o., sth., to be sth.; to take s.o., sth., for sth., to be sth.; **ich sehe es als eine Ehre an, Ihnen dienen zu dürfen,** I (ac)count it, deem it, an honour to serve you; **etwas als ein Verbrechen, als gesetzwidrig, a.,** to regard, look (up)on, sth. as a crime, as illegal; **ich sehe es als meine Pflicht an, zu . . . ,** I regard it, look upon it, as my duty to . . . ; I deem it (to be) my duty to . . . ; **ich sehe das als etwas ganz Belangloses an,** I regard that as, hold that to be, something quite unimportant; **er sah das**

Haus als sein eigenes an, he regarded, looked upon, the house as his own; **früher sah ich ihn als meinen treusten Freund an,** I used to consider him, look upon him as, my most faithful friend; **ich sah sie als seine Schwester an,** I took her to be his sister; I (mis)took her for his sister; **wofür siehst du mich eigentlich an?** what do you take me for? what do you think I am? **3.** (*a*) to regard, respect (persons); **die Person nicht a.,** to be no respecter of persons; *B:* **meinet ihr, er werde eure Person a.?** will he regard your persons? *B:* **die Person a. im Gericht ist nicht gut,** it is not good to have respect of persons in judgment; (*b*) **etwas nicht a.,** to attach no importance to sth.; **sie sehen keine Kosten an,** they take no heed of expense; **sie sieht das Geld nicht an,** she does not bother about money, money is no object to her.

II. *vbl s.* **1. Ansehen,** *n.* (*a*) *in vbl senses; also:* sight, look; **j-n von A. kennen,** to know s.o. by sight; **das Bild ist nicht des Ansehens wert,** the picture is not worth looking at; **(das) A. kostet nichts,** looking costs nothing; *Com:* 'inspection invited—no obligation to purchase'; **vom bloßen A. wird man nicht satt,** a feast for the eye is no comfort to the stomach; (*b*) (outward) appearance, look, semblance; mien; complexion (of affairs); **dem A. nach,** to all appearances; **sich ein (vornehmes, großes) A. geben,** to give oneself airs, to put on a high-and-mighty manner, *F:* to put on side, to put it on; **die Sache hat jetzt ein ganz anderes A. gewonnen,** the affair has now assumed quite a different complexion; **die Sache hat ein übles A. (bekommen),** things are shaping badly, are looking black, are looking ugly; **die Sache hat jetzt ein besseres A.,** things are looking up; (*c*) **ohne A. der Person,** without respect of persons; **bei, vor, Gott ist kein A. der Person,** God is no respecter of persons; (*d*) (high) reputation, (high) standing, repute, credit; distinction; prestige (of country, etc.); **Leute von A.,** persons of distinction, of note, of standing, of repute; reputable persons; eminent persons; notabilities; **hohes A. genießen, in hohem A. stehen,** to enjoy a high reputation; to be highly respected, highly esteemed; to be held in high repute; to be thought much of; **wenig A. genießen,** to be little esteemed, held in no esteem; to be of little account; to be thought little of; **sich** *dat.* **A. verschaffen,** to get, make, oneself respected; to acquire, make, gain, a reputation (for oneself); **seine Tätigkeit als Schiedsrichter hat ihm großes A. verschafft,** he has made, gained, a great reputation as an arbitrator; **sein A. (bei j-m) verlieren,** to fall into discredit (with s.o.); **sein A. einbüßen,** to lose (people's) esteem, to lose face. **2. Ansehung,** *f.* (*a*) **in A.+** *gen.*, in consideration of . . . , considering . . . , having regard to . . . , in view of . . . , with respect to . . . ; **in A. der hohen Studentenzahl . . . ,** considering, taking into consideration, bearing in mind, the large number of students . . . ; (*b*) *occ.* **ohne A. der Person,** without respect of persons.

III. *p.p. & a.* **angesehen,** (*of pers., etc.*) **(bei j-m) a. sein,** to be highly respected, to be held in high esteem (by s.o.); **die angesehensten Bürger der Stadt,** the most respected, esteemed, citizens of the town; the most eminent, distinguished, notable, noted, citizens of the town; the notabilities of the town; **eine sehr angesehene Firma,** a very reputable, respectable, firm; a noted firm; a firm of high standing, of excellent reputation; **ein angesehener Gelehrter,** a scholar of high, established, reputation; an eminent scholar; a distinguished scholar; **er ist bei seinen Mitbürgern schlecht angesehen,** his fellow-citizens have a poor opinion of him, do not think much of him.

ansehnlich, *a.* **1.** good-looking; good to look at, fair to look upon, handsome, sightly; **ein ansehnlicher Mann, eine ansehnliche Frau,** a handsome man, woman; a fine figure of a man, of a woman. **2.** considerable, important, large (sum, etc.); handsome (sum, fortune, salary, dowry, etc.); (very) respectable (sum, fortune, etc.); *Lit:* goodly (fortune, heritage, etc.); *F:* sizeable (sum, fortune, etc.); **ein ansehnliches Besitztum,** a handsome property; **eine ansehnliche Leistung,** a very respectable achievement. **3.** notable (pers., etc.); (pers.) of reputation, of importance; respected (pers.); (scholar, etc.) of standing; (*opening of address*) **'ansehnliche Versammlung!'** = 'ladies and gentlemen of this distinguished assembly . . . '.

Ansehnlichkeit, *f.* **1.** handsomeness, sightliness. **2.** importance, considerable size (of sum, etc.); respectable quality (of achievement, etc.). **3.** importance; reputation, repute; eminence (of pers.).

anseilen, *v.tr. sep.* to attach (sth.) by a rope; to rope (boat, etc.); *Mount:* to rope (climbers) (together); **sich a.,** to rope, to put on the rope; **sich mit j-m a.,** to rope oneself to s.o.

Anseite, *f.* adjacent side; near side.

ansengen, *v.tr. sep.* **1.** to singe (sth.) (slightly). **2. der Reif hat die Knospen angesengt,** the frost has nipped the buds.

Ansetzblatt, *n.* **1.** *Bot:* newly sprouted leaf. **2.** *Bookb:* end-paper.

Ansetzblech, *n. Metall:* shutter (of furnace).

ansetzen, *v. sep.* I. *v.tr.* **1.** (*a*) **etwas an etwas** *acc.* **a.,** to apply sth. to sth.; to put sth. on sth., to sth.; **ein Stück an etwas a.,** to add, join, fix, put, a piece on to sth.; **ein Stück an einen Rock a.,** to put a piece on a skirt; *Dominoes:* **einen Stein a.,** to pose, play, a piece; (*b*) to put (sth.) into position (for action); **er setzte das Glas an,** *abs.* **er setzte an,** he lifted, raised, put, set, the glass to his lips; **die Feder a.,** to put one's pen to paper, to set pen to paper; to start writing; **das Messer, den Pinsel, a.,** to apply the knife, the brush; to start cutting, painting; **bevor man das Messer, den Pinsel, ansetzt . . . ,** before applying the knife, the brush . . . ; **den Spaten a.,** to insert the spade; to start digging; *Mil:* **das Gewehr a.,** to bring the rifle to the shoulder; *Mus:* **ein Blasinstrument a.,** to set a wind instrument to one's lips, to put a wind instrument to one's mouth; (*violin-playing*) **den Bogen a.,** to put, place, hold, the bow in (the bowing) position. **2.** (*a*) to put (sth.) into position; to set (sth.); **eine Leiter a.,** to put up, set up, a ladder; *Civ.E:* **Pflaster a.,** to set paving-stones, to lay set(t)s; (*b*) *Nau:* **eine Wante a.,** to fleet a shroud; *see also* **Blutegel. 3.** to start (sth.); to set (sth.) going; (*a*) **einen Spürhund a.,** to lay on a bloodhound; to put, set, a bloodhound on the trail; (*b*) **einen Hochofen a.,** to charge a furnace; (*c*) *Mil:* **einen Angriff a.,** to launch an attack; (*d*) *Min:* **ein Bohrloch a.,** to start a boring. **4.** *Cu:* **die Suppe, das Gemüse, usw., a.,** to put the soup, the vegetables, etc., on (to boil). **5.** *Cu: Dist: etc:* to make, prepare (vinegar, spirits, etc.); to mix the ingredients of (a composition, etc.); to put the ingredients of (drink, etc.) to work; **eine Bowle a.,** to start a *Bowle* (*q.v.*); **Branntwein mit Fruchtsaft a.,** to blend, mingle, flavour, spirits with fruit-juice. **6.** *Mth:* **eine Gleichung a.,** to set up, arrange, an equation; **ein Problem a.,** to state a problem. **7.** to fix, determine; to set (time); (*a*) **eine Sitzung auf,** *occ.* **für, drei Uhr a.,** to fix a meeting for three o'clock; **einen Termin a.,** to fix, appoint, a date; **einen Tag a.,** to fix, appoint, name, a day; **der Tag ist noch anzusetzen,** the day remains to be settled, fixed, decided upon; **seine Abfahrt war auf Montag angesetzt,** his departure was fixed for Monday; **die Ankunft des Bürgermeisters war auf drei Uhr angesetzt,** the arrival of the Mayor was timed for three o'clock; **die Abfahrt des Zuges war auf Mittag angesetzt,** the train was timed, *U.S:* scheduled, to leave at midday; (*b*) *Com: etc:* **einen Preis a.,** to fix, settle, a price; to quote, name, a price; **den Preis zu hoch a.,** to put the price too high, to ask too high a price; (*c*) to fix a rate for (sth.); **die Einkommensteuer auf (+***acc.***) . . . a.,** to fix the (rate of) income-tax at . . . ; *Com:* **das zweite Hundert wird Ihnen mit 20 M pro Stück angesetzt,** you will be charged 20 marks apiece for the second hundred; (*d*) to estimate, assess (**auf+***acc.*, at); to date, assign a date to (manuscript, work of art, etc.); **den Gewinn zu hoch a.,** to make too high an estimate of the profits. **8.** (*a*) (*of trees, etc.*) **Blätter a.,** to put forth leaves, to come into leaf, to leaf; **Knospen a.,** to put forth buds, to bud; to be in bud; *Lit:* to burgeon; **Blüten a.,** to put forth blossoms, to blossom; **Wurzeln a.,** to put forth, shoot forth, shoot out, roots; to strike, take, root, to root; **Früchte a.,** (*of tree*) to put forth fruit; to bear fruit; (*of blossom*) to set; (*of tree*) **Ringe a.,** to put on (annual) rings; (*b*) **Fleisch a.,** (*of pers., animal*) to put on flesh; (*of pers.*) to grow stout; **Fett a.,** (*of body, pers.*) to become adipose; (*of pers.*) to put on fat; (*c*) (*of liquid*) to deposit (matter); (*of river*) **Schwemmerde a.,** to deposit alluvium; (*of wine*) **eine Kruste a.,** to form, throw, a crust; (*of iron*) **Rost a.,** to get rusty, to rust; (*of paper, leather, etc.*) **Schimmel a.,** to become mildewed, to mildew; (*of milk*) **Rahm a.,** to cream; *see also* **Kesselstein; sich a.,** (*of substance*) to accumulate; to form a deposit; to form a crust (**an etwas** *acc.*, on sth.); (*of rust, mildew, etc.*) to form; (*of dust*) to settle; (*of sugar, etc.*) to granulate; *Ch:* (*of a salt*) to effloresce; to crystallize. **9.** (*of pers.*) **sich in einem Ort a.,** to settle (down) in a locality.

II. **ansetzen,** *v.i.* (*haben*) **1.** to raise one's glass to one's lips; *Mus:* to set the (wind) instrument to one's lips; *cp.* I. 1. **2.** (*of fruit*) to set, knit; **die Birnen, die Tomaten, haben gut angesetzt,** the pears, the tomatoes, have set well, promise well. **3.** (*of pers.*) = **Fleisch a.,** *q.v. under* I. 8 (*b*). **4.** *Cu:* to catch (in the pan). **5.** (*a*) to begin, start; to make a start; *Chess: etc:* to make the first move; **mit einer Arbeit a.,** to start (on, upon) a task; **noch einmal a.,** to start afresh, to make a fresh start, to start all over again; to have another go (**mit etwas,** at sth.); **beim Empirestil setzt die Taille unmittelbar unter dem Busen an,** in the Empire style the waist starts immediately below the bust; (*b*) **zum Sprung a.,** to get ready to jump; **er setzte zum Sprechen an,** he got ready to speak. **6.** *Min:* (*of ore*) to appear in increasing quantities.

III. *vbl s.* **Ansetzen** *n.*, **Ansetzung** *f. in vbl senses; also:* **1.** (*a*) application (**einer Sache an etwas** *acc.*, of sth. to sth.); insertion (of spade); (*b*) *Mus:* = **Ansatz** 2. **2.** assessment, estimation (**auf+***acc.*, at); dating; assigning of a date (to manuscript, work of art, etc.); **bei einer so frühen Ansetzung . . . ,** if we assign so early a date . . . , if we date the work so early . . . ; **eine so frühe Ansetzung ist unmöglich,** so early a date would be impossible. **3.** accumulation (of dust, etc.); granulation (of sugar, etc.); *Ch:* efflorescence; crystallization (of a salt). *Cp.* **Ansatz.**

Ansetzer, *m. Artil:* rammer.

Ansetzkolben, *m. Sm.a:* ramrod.

Ansetzpunkt, *m.* = **Ansatzpunkt.**

Ansetzstück, *n.* = **Ansatzstück.**

Ansetzungsstelle, *f.* = **Ansatzstelle.**

Ansicht, *f.* -/-en. **1.** *Com:* **zur A.,** for inspection; **Waren zur A. (schicken),** (to send) goods on approval, on approbation, *F:* on appro. **2.** (*a*) view, prospect, outlook; **die A. der Stadt,** the prospect of the town, the outlook on the town; (*b*) *Art: etc:* view; **Ansichten von Köln,** views of Cologne. **3.** point of view; view (**über eine Sache,** of a matter); views (**über+***acc.*, on); opinion (**über+***acc.*, of, on, about); **Goethes Ansichten über die Kunst,** Goethe's view of, views on, ideas about, opinions about, art; **eine A. über etwas haben,** to have an opinion, to hold views, about sth.; **(sich** *dat.***) eine A. über etwas bilden,** to form an opinion on sth.; **eine A. äußern,** to give, advance, express, put forward, an opinion; **meiner A. nach . . . ,** in my opinion . . . , in my view . . . ; to my mind . . . ; as it strikes me . . . ; to my way of thinking . . . , as I see the matter . . . ; **was ist Ihre A. darüber?** what are your views on the matter? **ich bin der A., daß . . . ,** I am of (the) opinion that . . . ; **ich vertrete die A., daß . . . ,** I take the standpoint that . . . ; **ich bin ganz Ihrer A., ich teile Ihre A., ich bin derselben A. wie Sie,** I am entirely of your opinion, I agree with you, I concur with you (in your view); I share your views; **ich bin anderer A. als Sie,** I differ, am of a different opinion, from you; I take a different view from yours; I see, view, the matter differently; **mit seiner A. zurückhalten,** to refrain from expressing an opinion; **darüber sind die Ansichten verschieden, geteilt,** views, opinions, differ about that; there is more than one opinion about that.

ansichtig. 1. *pred. a.* **j-s, einer Sache, a. werden,** to catch sight, get a sight, of s.o., sth., *F:* to clap eyes on s.o., sth. **2. -ansichtig,** *comb.fm.* (*with numeral prefixed*), **einansichtig, zweiansichtig,** (*of sculptured group, etc.*) intended to be seen from one side, from the front, only; intended to be seen from two angles.

Ansichts(post)karte, *f.* picture postcard, view-card.

Ansichtssache, *f.* matter of opinion.

Ansichtsseite, *f.* **1.** façade, front(age) (of building); front (of sculpture). **2.** (*in book*) plate with a view of a town, etc.

Ansichtssendung, *f. Com:* article(s) sent on approval, *F:* on appro.

Ansichtsskizze, *f. Art:* (perspective) sketch, view, *A:* prospect (of town, etc.).

ansiedeln, *v.sep.* I. *v.tr.* (*a*) to settle (population, colonists, etc.); (*b*) **sich in einem Ort a.,**

to settle (down) in a locality; to establish oneself, take up one's abode, in a place; (*of colonists*) **sich in einem Gebiet a.**, to colonize, settle, a region.

II. *vbl s.* **1. Ansiedeln,** *n.*=II. 2 (*a*). **2. Ansiedlung,** *f.* (*a*) *in vbl senses; also:* settlement; colonization; (*b*) settlement, colony.

ansieden, *v.tr. sep.* (*conj. like* **sieden**) (*a*) to boil; (*b*) *Metall:* to scorify, slag.

Ansiedler, *m.* settler; colonist; **unbefugter A., A. ohne Rechtstitel,** squatter.

ansiegeln, *v.tr. sep.* **1.** *A:* to seal (document, etc.). **2.** to attach, affix (sth.) with a seal, to seal (sth.) on.

ansingen, *v.tr. sep.* (*strong*) *Lit:* to sing to (s.o.); to address a, one's, song to (s.o.).

ansinnen. 1. *v.tr. sep.* (*strong*) **j-m etwas a., es j-m a., etwas zu tun,** to expect sth. of s.o.; to expect s.o. to do sth. **2.** *vbl s.* **Ansinnen,** *n.* (unreasonable) request, (unexpected, surprising, unjustified) demand; **du willst, daß ich schon um fünf Uhr aufstehen soll? — was für ein merkwürdiges Ansinnen!** you want me to be up at five?—fancy asking that of me! **ein Ansinnen an j-n stellen,** to request sth. unexpected, unreasonable, of s.o.; to ask s.o. to do sth. unreasonable.

ansintern, *v.i. sep.* (*sein*) to sinter; to form concretions; *Geol:* to form stalactites *or* stalagmites.

Ansitz, *m. Ven:* (hunter's) hiding-, lurking-place; hide; post for lying in wait.

ansitzen, *v.i. sep.* (*strong*) (*haben*) **1.** *Ven:* to lie in wait, in ambush. **2.** *see* **angesessen. 3.** (*a*) to adhere; to cling (**an**+*dat.*, to); (*of garment*) to fit closely; **eng ansitzende Jacke,** tight-fitting jacket; (*b*) (*of persons*) to sit close (together).

ansohlen, *v.tr. sep. F:* **j-n a.,** to hoax s.o., have s.o. on, pull s.o.'s leg.

ansonst(en) [an'zɔnst(ən)], *adv.*=**sonst.**

Anspann, *m. A:* team (of horses, oxen, etc.); pair (of horses, of oxen); yoke (of oxen).

Anspanndraht, *m.* span-wire, bracing-wire, stay-wire.

anspannen. I. *v.tr. sep.* **1.** to stretch, tighten (spring, rope, etc.); to draw (rope, etc.) tight, to tauten (rope, etc.); to tense (muscle, etc.); **den Bogen, die Sehne, a.,** to bend the bow; *cp.* **spannen. 2.** to brace, strain (nerves, etc.); to apply, exert (powers, faculties); **alle (seine) Kräfte a.,** to apply all one's energies; *F:* to go at it hammer and tongs, with might and main; to go hard at it, to buckle to, to put one's back into it; **sich a.,** to stiffen one's will, to brace oneself; **sich aufs äußerste, aufs höchste, a.,** to exert oneself to the utmost, to make the utmost effort, to strain every nerve; *Fin:* **seinen Kredit, den Geldmarkt, a.,** to strain one's credit, the money market. **3.** (*a*) to put, harness, (horses, etc.) to the carriage, etc.; to yoke (oxen) (to the plough, etc.); *abs.* **a.,** to put the horses to; **ein Pferd an den Wagen a.,** to put, harness, a horse to the carriage, cart; **einen Wagen a.,** to put, harness, a horse *or* horses to a carriage, a cart; **dem Kutscher sagen, er soll a.,** to tell the coachman to put to; (*b*) *F:* **j-n zu einer Aufgabe a.,** *F:* to put s.o. to a task; **j-n a., etwas zu tun,** to put s.o. (on) to do sth., to rope s.o. in to do sth.

II. *vbl s.* **1. Anspannen,** *n. in vbl senses; esp.* putting to (of horses); hooking on (of additional horse); **das A. befehlen,** to order the horses to be put to. **2. Anspannung,** *f. in vbl senses; also:* **etwas mit A. aller Kräfte tun,** to throw all one's energies into doing sth.; *Fin:* **A. seines Kredits,** strain on one's credit; **A. des Geldmarktes,** strain on the money market; tightening of money conditions.

III. *p.p. & a.* **angespannt,** *in vbl senses; also:* tense, taut, tight; **aufs äußerste a.,** stretched, strained, to the utmost; at full stretch; **mit angespannten Sehnen zog er . . . ,** with his sinews taut, tense(d), he was pulling . . . ; **mit angespannter Aufmerksamkeit,** with the utmost, with rapt, attention; **mit angespannten Sinnen,** with all senses alert; with every nerve taut, tensed; *adv.* **a. arbeiten,** to work intensively.

Anspänner, *m.* **-s/-,** small farmer, small-holder.

anspazieren, *v.i. sep.* (*sein*) (*usu. only in the phr.*) **anspaziert kommen,** to come walking along, up.

anspeichern, *v.tr. sep.*=**aufspeichern.**

anspeien, *v.tr. sep.* (*strong*) to spit upon (s.o.); to spit at (s.o.); to spit in (s.o.'s) face.

anspeile(r)n, *v.tr. sep. Cu:* to skewer (fowl, etc.).

Anspiel, *n.* (*a*) *Games:* start of play; first turn; *Fb:* kick-off; *Golf:* first drive, drive-off; *Ten:* (first) service; *Basketball: etc:* first throw; (*b*) *Cards:* lead; **das A. haben,** to have the lead.

anspielen. I. *v.sep.* **1.** (*a*) *v.i.* (*haben*) *Games:* to start playing; to play first; to have the first stroke, shot, throw, etc.; *Fb:* to kick off; *Golf:* to drive off; *Ten:* to serve (first); *Basketball: etc:* to throw off; *Bill:* to lead off, to break; (*b*) *v.tr. & i.* (*haben*) *Cards:* to lead; to have the lead; **eine Karte a.,** to lead a card; **Treff a.,** to lead clubs; **wer spielt an?** whose lead is it? **Sie spielen an,** your lead! **2.** *v.tr. Mus:* to play (instrument) for the first time; to try (out) (instrument); to begin to play (piece of music); to run over the first few bars of (piece). **3.** *v.i.* (*haben*) **auf etwas** *acc.*, **auf j-n, a.,** to allude, make an allusion, to sth., to s.o.; to refer, make a reference, to sth., to s.o.; to advert to sth.; to hint at sth.; to insinuate sth.; **anspielend,** (*of remark, style, etc.*) allusive.

II. *vbl s.* **1. Anspielen,** *n. in vbl senses; also: Cards:* lead. **2. Anspielung,** *f.* allusion, reference (**auf**+*acc.*, to); hint (**auf**+*acc.*, at); innuendo; insinuation; **Stil voller Anspielungen,** allusive style; **mit A. auf etwas** *acc.*, in allusion to sth.; alluding, referring, to sth.; **das war eine A. auf dich,** *F:* that was a hit, a dig, at you.

anspießen, *v.tr. sep.* (*a*) *Cu:* to spit, to put (meat, fowl, etc.) on the spit; (*b*) to run (s.o., animal) through with a spear, lance, sword, etc.; *F:* to spit, impale (s.o., animal).

anspinnen, *v.tr. sep.* (*strong*) **1.** *Tex:* **einen Faden a.,** to join a thread (on) (**an einen anderen,** to another). **2. sich anspinnen,** (*of spider*) to spin its web; (*of caterpillar*) to spin its cocoon. **3.** (*a*) **mit j-m eine Unterhaltung a.,** to enter into, engage in, conversation with s.o.; **mit j-m Verbindungen a.,** to establish relations with s.o.; **ein Liebesverhältnis a.,** to engage in a love-affair; **Ränke a.,** to weave intrigues; to hatch plots; **sich a.,** (*of relations, etc.*) to develop, to come into being; (*of friendship, etc.*) to spring up; **es spinnen sich Ränke an,** there are intrigues going on; there is treachery afoot; (*b*) **den Faden seiner Rede wieder a.,** to resume the thread of one's discourse; **die Fäden einer Geschichte wieder a.,** to gather up the threads of a story.

Anspinner, *m. Tex:* piecer, piecener.

anspitzen, *v.tr. sep.* to point, to give a point to, to put a point on (tool, pencil, etc.); to sharpen (tool) to a point; to sharpen (pencil).

Anspitzer, *m.* sharpener (for pointed tools, etc.); *esp.* pencil-sharpener.

anspleißen, *v.tr. sep.* (*strong*), **ansplissen,** *v.tr. sep. Nau: etc:* to splice (rope, etc.) (on) (**an**+*acc.*, to).

Ansporn, *m.* spur, incentive, stimulus (**zu etwas, etwas zu tun,** to sth., to do sth.); whet (to appetite, etc.); **A. zum Handeln,** incentive, encouragement, to action, to act.

anspornen, *v.tr. sep.* **1. sein Pferd a.,** to spur, set spurs to, one's horse. **2. j-n a.,** to spur s.o. on, urge s.o. on (**zu etwas, etwas zu tun,** to sth., to do sth.); to incite, encourage, s.o. (**zum Handeln, zu handeln, usw.,** to action, to act, etc.); to rouse s.o.; to stir s.o. up; **j-s Eifer a.,** to spur on s.o.'s zeal; **vom Ehrgeiz angespornt,** spurred on by ambition.

Ansprache, *f.* **1.** speech, address; allocution; **eine A. halten,** to deliver, give, an address (**an**+*acc.*, to). **2.** response (of musical instrument, of aircraft to controls, etc.); **Klavier mit leichter A.,** piano with a light touch; (*of pers.*) **keine A. finden,** (i) to meet with no response, to be disregarded; (ii) *F:* to have nobody to talk to.

ansprechen, *v.sep.* (*strong*) I. *v.tr.* **1.** (*a*) to speak to (s.o.), to address (s.o.); to approach (s.o.); to accost (s.o.); *Nau:* to hail, speak (a ship); **j-n um etwas a.,** to approach s.o., apply to s.o., for sth.; to ask s.o. for sth.; *abs.* **ich werde bei ihm a.,** I will approach him (on the matter); I will ask him about it; (*b*) **j-n als Herrn X a.,** (i) to address s.o. (erroneously) as, (ii) to (mis)take s.o. for, Mr X. **2.** *Golf: etc:* to address (the ball, the target). **3.** (*a*) **etwas als etwas a.,** to regard sth. as sth.; **die Forderung muß als fingiert angesprochen werden,** the claim must be regarded as fictitious; (*b*) *Jur: A:* **etwas (als sein Eigentum) a.,** to lay claim to, to claim, sth. **4.** (*of thg*) **j-n a.,** to appeal to s.o., to please s.o.; *cp.* II. 2.

II. **ansprechen,** *v.i.* (*haben*) **1.** to respond, answer (**auf**+*acc.*, to); (*a*) *Mus:* **Ton (auf dem Klavier, usw.), der nicht anspricht,** (i) note that does not respond, answer, sound, *F:* dead note, (ii) note that sounds badly; **das Klavier, die Flöte, spricht leicht, schwer, an,** the piano has a light, a heavy, touch; the flute speaks, does not speak, easily; (*b*) *Av:* **das Flugzeug spricht auf die Steuerung an,** the aircraft answers, responds, to the controls; (*c*) (*of pers.*) **auf einen Anreiz, die Behandlung, usw., a.,** to respond, react, to a stimulus, to treatment, etc. **2.** (*of play, book, scenery, character, etc.*) to appeal, to make, have, an appeal; to please, to be pleasing; (*of play, theory, etc.*) to meet with a good response, *F:* to catch on, take on.

III. *vbl s.* **Ansprechen,** *n. in vbl senses; also:* response; reaction (**auf**+*acc.*, to).

IV. *pr.p. & a.* **ansprechend,** *in vbl senses; esp.* appealing, pleasing, pleasant, attractive; engaging, prepossessing, winning (manners, etc.); **ein ansprechendes Äußeres,** a pleasing, engaging, appearance.

Ansprechzeit, *f.* operating time (of brakes, etc.).

ansprengen, *v.sep.* **1.** *v.tr. & i.* (*sein*) (*of horseman*) **j-n a., auf j-n a.,** to gallop up to s.o.; (*of cavalry*) **den Feind a.,** to charge the enemy; **angesprengt kommen,** to come galloping along, up; to come charging along, up. **2.** *v.tr.* to sprinkle (lawn, linen, etc.) (with water); to water (plants); to spray (seedlings, lawn, etc.). **3.** *v.tr.* to blast (rock, etc.).

anspringen, *v.sep.* (*strong*) I. *v.i.* **1.** (*sein*) to bound along, up; (*usu. only in the phr.*) **angesprungen kommen,** (*of pers., animal*) to come bounding along, up; to come skipping along. **2.** (*haben*) *Sp: etc:* to jump first, to take the first jump. **3.** (*sein*) (*of trotting horse*) to break into a gallop. **4.** (*sein*) *Aut: Av: etc:* (*of engine, motor, Hyd.E: of siphon*) to start (up); **endlich sprang der Motor an,** at last the engine started, *F:* came to life; **der Motor sprang nicht an,** the engine wouldn't start, refused to start, failed to start; *Hyd.E:* **einen Siphon a. lassen,** to prime a siphon. **5.** (*sein*) (*of glass, china, etc.*) to crack; **die Vase ist angesprungen,** the vase is cracked, has a crack in it; **ein angesprungener Teller,** a cracked plate.

II. **anspringen,** *v.tr.* (*of pers.*) to jump, leap, at (sth., s.o.); to spring at (s.o.); to pounce on (s.o.); (*of dog, etc.*) to jump up, leap up, at (s.o.).

Anspringnase, *f. Hyd.E:* priming nose (of siphon).

anspritzen, *v.sep.* **1.** *v.tr.* (*a*) to spray, sprinkle (seedlings, lawn, etc.); to syringe (flowers, etc.); (*b*) **einen Whisky a.,** to dilute a whisky with soda water, to mix a whisky and soda. **2.** *v.tr. & i.* (*sein*) **j-n, etwas, a.; an j-n, an etwas** *acc.* **a.,** (*of liquid*) to splash, squirt, spurt, on to s.o., sth.; (*of mud, etc.*) to (be)spatter s.o., sth.; (*of pers., etc.*) **j-n mit Wasser a.,** to splash water on, over, s.o.

Anspruch, *m.* **1.** *Jur:* **A. auf etwas** *acc.*, right, title, fair claim, to sth.; **rechtmäßiger A. auf etwas,** legal claim to sth.; **älterer A.,** prior claim; **A. auf etwas haben,** to have a claim, a right, a title, to sth., to be entitled to sth.; **A. darauf haben, etwas zu tun,** to be entitled, have a right, to do sth.; **seine Ansprüche auf etwas geltend machen,** to assert one's claims to sth.; to establish one's rights to sth.; **seine Ansprüche aufgeben,** to waive, renounce, one's claims, one's rights. **2.** (*a*) *Jur: etc:* claim, demand (**an j-n,** upon s.o.; **auf etwas** *acc.*, for sth.); **etwas (als sein Eigentum) in A. nehmen; A. auf etwas** *acc.* **erheben, machen,** to lay claim to sth., to claim sth.; to set up a claim for sth.; **seine Rechte in A. nehmen,** to vindicate one's rights; **A. auf Schadenersatz erheben,** to make, put in, a claim for damages; (*b*) pretension, claim (**auf etwas** *acc.*, to sth.); **ich mache keinen A. auf Gelehrsamkeit,** I have no pretensions, I do not lay claim, to learning; I do not pretend to be learned; **das Werk macht keinen A. auf wissenschaftliche Genauigkeit,** the work does not claim to be scientifically accurate; (*c*) **auf j-n A. haben,** to have a claim on s.o.; **ich habe gewisse Ansprüche auf seine Freundschaft,** I have some claims on his friendship. **3. Ansprüche machen,** to make demands; **er macht große Ansprüche,** he is demanding, exacting, hard to please; **er machte keine großen Ansprüche,** he is not at all demanding, exacting, he is easy to please; **nur bescheidene Ansprüche an j-n stellen,** to be moderate in one's demands upon s.o.; **Hotel, das allen Ansprüchen genügt,** hotel that satisfies all possible requirements. **4. j-n, etwas, in A. nehmen,** to make claims on, demands upon, s.o., sth.; **j-s Dienste, j-s Hilfe, in A. nehmen,** to call upon *or* avail oneself of s.o.'s services; to enlist the services of s.o.; to call upon s.o. for aid; **j-s Tatkraft, j-s Güte, sehr in A. nehmen,** to make great demands upon s.o.'s energy, upon s.o.'s good nature; **j-s Aufmerksamkeit in A. nehmen,** to engage, claim, s.o.'s attention; **j-s Geduld allzusehr in A. nehmen,** to

make excessive demands upon s.o.'s patience; to try, tax, s.o.'s patience; **j-s Mittel, j-s Kräfte, sehr in A. nehmen,** to be a strain on s.o.'s resources, on s.o.'s powers; **die Unterhaltung zweier Häuser hat meinen Geldbeutel zu sehr in A. genommen,** the upkeep of two houses was too great a drain upon my purse; **er nimmt seine Angestellten stark in A.,** he makes considerable demands upon, expects a good deal from, his employees; **meine Zeit ist sehr in A. genommen,** I have many demands upon, claims on, my time; **ich bin heute morgen sehr in A. genommen,** I am very busy, very much taken up, this morning; **er ist von seiner Arbeit völlig in A. genommen,** his work takes up all his attention, occupies all his time; he is entirely absorbed in his work; **die Arbeit nahm viel Zeit in A.,** the work took (up) a lot of time; **die Bauarbeiten werden mindestens drei Jahre in A. nehmen,** the construction work will occupy, require, take, at least three years.

anspruchsfrei, *a.*=**anspruchslos.**

anspruchslos, *a.* (*a*) modest; simple; (*of pers., manner*) unassuming, unpresuming, unpresumptuous; (*of pers., manner, thg*) unpretentious, unostentatious; (*of style, narrative, etc.*) straightforward; (*b*) (*of pers.*) modest in one's requirements; not difficult to please; (*of way of life*) frugal.

Anspruchslosigkeit, *f.* modesty, simplicity; unpretentiousness; unostentatiousness; frugality.

anspruchsvoll, *a.* (*a*) (*of pers., style, manner, etc.*) pretentious; presumptuous; (*of pers., manner*) assuming; **anspruchsvolles Wesen,** pretentious manner, ways; pretentiousness; (*b*) (*of pers.*) exacting, exigent, demanding; (*of pers., taste*) fastidious; difficult to please; exacting; *Com:* **'für den anspruchsvollen Kunden',** 'for the exacting customer'.

Anspruchswappen, *n. Her:* escutcheon of pretence.

Ansprung, *m.* **1.** spring, bound, leap; *Gym:* leap on to the apparatus. **2.** *Med: F:* impetigo, *F:* milk-blotch, -crust, -scab.

anspucken, *v.tr. sep.* to spit at (s.o.); to spit upon (s.o.).

anspulen, *v.tr. sep. Tex:* to wind, spool (thread).

anspülen, *v.sep.* **1.** *v.i.* (*haben*) (*of waves, ripples*) **an das Ufer a.,** to wash against the shore. **2.** *v.tr.* (*of river, etc.*) to wash (sth.) ashore; to wash up (driftwood, etc.); to deposit (sand, etc.); **angespültes Land,** alluvial soil, alluvium. **3.** *vbl s.* **Anspülung,** *f.* (*a*) *in vbl senses; also:* (accretion by) alluvion; (*b*) alluvial deposit.

anspüren, *v.tr. sep.* **j-m etwas a.,** to notice, sense, sth. about s.o.; **man spürt es ihr an, daß sie müde ist,** you can tell that she is tired.

anstacheln, *v.tr. sep.* **1.** to goad, prod (oxen). **2.** to goad (s.o.) on; to incite (s.o.); to stimulate (s.o.); **j-n zur Wut a.,** to goad s.o. into a fury; **j-n zur Rache a.,** to incite s.o. to revenge; **j-n a., etwas zu tun,** to goad s.o. on to do sth.; **er wurde durch Ehrgeiz zum Handeln angestachelt,** he was goaded into, driven to, action, by ambition.

anstählen, *v.tr. sep. Metalw:* to steel (tool, etc.); to coat *or* edge (tool, etc.) with steel.

Anstalt, *f.* -/-en. **1.** (*a*) *Hist: etc:* (public) institution; *Lit:* **die Schaubühne als moralische A.,** the theatre as a moral institution; (*b*) institution; institute; (educational, etc.) establishment; hospital; home; (=**Irrenanstalt**) mental hospital; (=**Besserungsanstalt**) reform school, reformatory; (=**Strafanstalt**) prison; **typographische A.,** printing establishment, printing office, press; **das Mädchen ist in einer A. untergebracht worden,** the girl has been taken to an institution, to a home; **j-n in, auf, die A. bringen,** to put s.o. in a mental hospital, *F:* to have s.o. put away. **2.** *pl.* **Anstalten,** arrangements, dispositions; **Anstalten zu etwas machen, für etwas treffen,** to make preparations, arrangements, for sth.; **Anstalten machen, etwas zu tun,** to prepare to do sth.; to get ready to do sth.; to be about to do sth.; **er machte Anstalten zu gehen,** he prepared to leave; he was about to leave; he made as if to go; **nach drei Stunden machten sie immer noch keine Anstalten zu gehen,** after three hours they still showed no sign of going; **die nötigen Anstalten treffen,** to make all necessary arrangements; to take the necessary steps.

Anstaltsbehandlung, *f. Med:* institutional treatment.

anstammen *see* **angestammt.**

Anstand, *m.* **1.** *Ven:*=**Ansitz; auf den A. gehen,** (i) to take up one's position; to go to one's hide; (ii) to go to watch the game; **auf dem A. stehen, sein,** to lie in wait; to be in one's hide. **2.** (*no pl.*) (*a*) bearing, behaviour, carriage, deportment; good manners, good breeding; dignity; tact; civility, politeness, courtesy; etiquette; **er hat keinen A.,** he lacks breeding, he has no manners, he is ill-mannered; he does not know how to behave; he is awkward, loutish; **ich werde ihm A. beibringen!** I'll teach him how to behave! I'll teach him manners! **der bloße A. hätte es erfordert, daß . . . ,** mere good manners demanded that . . . ; **aus lauter A. habe ich noch ein Glas getrunken,** I took another glass (merely) out of politeness; **etwas mit A. tun,** to do sth. decently, with decency, with decorum; to do sth. becomingly, in a becoming manner, with a good grace; **der A. fordert, daß . . . ,** etiquette demands that . . . , it is etiquette to . . . ; (*b*) propriety, decency, decorum, seemliness; respectability; **ein Gefühl, Sinn, für A.**=**Anstandsgefühl; bürgerlicher A.,** middle-class propriety; middle-class respectability; **den A. wahren,** to observe the proprieties, the decencies; **den A. verletzen, gegen den A. verstoßen,** (i) (*of pers.*) to forget one's manners, to fail in good breeding, to commit a breach of decorum, to behave indecorously; (ii) (*of action, thg*) to offend against decorum, against common decency; **Verstoß gegen den A.,** breach of decorum; offence against common decency; **den A. beiseitesetzen,** to defy convention; **etwas aus A. unterlassen,** to refrain from (doing) sth. for decency's sake. **3.** (*a*) delay; demur, hesitation, reluctance; **ohne A.,** without delay; without hesitation, without demur(ring); **er zahlte ohne A.,** he paid up readily, without demur(ring), without (any) more ado, without further ado; **A. nehmen, etwas zu tun,** to hesitate, be reluctant, to do sth.; to be shy of doing sth.; to be backward in doing sth.; to hold back (from doing sth.); to shilly-shally; **er willigte ein, ohne A. zu nehmen,** he did not hesitate to accept; he accepted without further ado, without any fuss; he made no demur, made no bones, about accepting; (*b*) *pl.* **Anstände,** difficulties; **ich will keine Anstände beim Steueramt haben,** I don't want any difficulties, any trouble, with the tax-office; **es wurden keine Anstände gemacht,** no objections were raised.

anständig, *a.* **1.** befitting, becoming, appropriate, proper; **das ist für ein Schulmädchen nicht a.,** that's not becoming, not the proper thing, for a schoolgirl; **es ist nicht a. von ihr, so etwas zu tun,** it's not becoming, not proper, not (be)fitting, for her to do such a thing. **2.** (*a*) decent, well-behaved (person); respectable (person, society, behaviour, etc.); seemly, decorous (conduct, costume, etc.); gentlemanly (conduct, etc.); ladylike (conduct, etc.); modest (behaviour, dress, etc.); reputable (person, firm, etc.); **er sah sehr a. aus,** he looked very respectable; **anständige Leute,** respectable, decent, people; **das ist nicht a.,** that's not respectable, not proper, not correct; it (just) isn't done; **sei a.!** behave yourself! *adv.* decently, with decency; respectably; decorously, with propriety; **sich a. benehmen,** to behave decently, with propriety; (*b*) (*of word, joke, etc.*) decent, proper, not improper; **ein anständiger Witz,** *F:* a clean joke; **nicht a.,** indecent, improper. **3.** *F:* (*a*) (*indicating approval*) decent; respectable; **ein (sehr) anständiger Kerl,** a good, decent, chap, a (very) decent (sort of) fellow; **das war sehr a. von ihm,** that was very decent of him; **anständiges Gehalt, Vermögen,** decent, respectable, tidy, salary, fortune; sizeable fortune; **eine anständige Leistung,** a respectable performance, achievement; **eine anständige Mahlzeit,** a decent meal; **der Wein ist ganz a.,** the wine is quite decent, is not at all bad, is pretty good; *adv.* **er behandelt seine Angestellten sehr a.,** he treats his employees very decently; (*b*) (*intensive*) considerable; proper; **das ist eine anständige Entfernung,** that's quite a distance, a tidy distance, quite a long way; **eine anständige Tracht Prügel bekommen,** to get a proper hiding; *adv.* **es regnet ganz a.,** it's raining pretty heavily; it's raining now and no mistake.

Anständigkeit, *f.* propriety, decency, decorum; seemliness; respectability.

Anstandsbesuch, *m.* formal call; duty call.

Anstandsbissen, *m.* piece left (on one's plate or on the dish) for manners.

Anstandsdame, *f.* chaperon; **die A. spielen,** to play (the) chaperon, *A:* to play propriety; *F:* to play gooseberry.

Anstandsgefühl, *n.* sense of decency; sense of propriety, of decorum; sense of delicacy; tact.

anstandshalber, *adv.* for decency's sake; for the sake of appearances; out of politeness, for politeness' sake.

Anstandslehre, *f. A:* deportment; manners.

Anstandslehrer, *m. A:* teacher of deportment.

anstandslos, *a.* unhesitating (acceptance, etc.); *adv.* readily, without hesitation; **er zahlte a.,** he paid up readily, without demur(ring), without (any) more ado, without further ado; **er hat es a. getan,** he did it without the slightest hesitation, without the slightest objection.

Anstandsperson, *f.*=**Anstandsdame.**

Anstandsregeln, *f.pl.* rules of good form, of decorum; etiquette; social conventions; usages of polite society.

Anstandsrock, *m. A:* petticoat.

Anstandsrolle, *f. Th:* aristocratic rôle.

Anstandsübungen, *f.pl. A:* lessons in deportment, in manners.

anstandsvoll, *a. A:* graceful (manners, walk, etc.).

Anstandswauwau, *m. F:* third person present for the sake of respectability; chaperon, *F:* gooseberry.

anstandswidrig, *a.* (*a*) unseemly, indecorous; impolite; unbecoming; (*b*) improper; indecent.

anstapeln, *v.tr. sep.*=**aufstapeln.**

anstarren, *v.tr. sep.* to stare at (s.o., sth.); to look, gaze, fixedly at (s.o., sth.).

anstatt [anˈʃtat]. **1.** *prep.* (+*gen.*) instead of, in place of (s.o., sth.); in (s.o.'s) place, stead; in lieu of (sth.). **2.** *conj.* instead of (doing sth.); **a. uns zu besuchen, a., daß er uns besuchte, schrieb er . . . ,** instead of visiting us he wrote . . . .

anstäuben, *v.tr. sep.* to powder, dust.

anstauchen, *v.tr. sep. Metalw:* to upset (bolt-head, etc.).

anstauen, *v.tr. sep.* to dam (up), to stem (water, watercourse); to impound (water); **sich a.,** (*of water*) to collect; (*of water, traffic*) to pile up; (*of feelings*) to be, get, bottled up; **Anstauung** *f,* (i) *in vbl senses;* (ii) artificial lake; reservoir.

anstaunen, *v.tr. sep.* to gaze, look, at (s.o., sth.) in astonishment, in wonder, in surprise, in amazement; to stare open-mouthed at (s.o., sth.).

anstechen, *v.tr. sep.* (*strong*) **1.** (*a*) to puncture (sth.); to stab (sth., animal); to prick (sth.); **etwas mit etwas a.,** to stick sth. into sth.; **das Obst ist von den Wespen angestochen,** the fruit has been eaten into, pitted, by the wasps, *F:* the wasps have been at the fruit; *F:* **rennen wie ein angestochenes Kalb,** to run like a scalded cat; (*b*) *A:* to spur on (horse); *v.i. F:* (*of pers.*) **angestochen kommen,** to arrive, appear; to turn up; (*c*) **ein Faß a.,** to broach, tap, a barrel; to set a barrel abroach; **'heute frisch angestochen',** 'new barrel started, tapped, today'. **2.** *F:* **angestochen,** (*of pers.*) (i) tipsy, slightly drunk; (ii) (slightly) crazy, *F:* (slightly) cracked, dotty, barmy; (iii) disreputable, *F:* shady. **3.** *Dial:*=**anstecken** I. 2.

Ansteckärmel, *m. Dressm: Tail:* tacked-on sleeve.

Ansteckartikel, *m.pl. Com:* button-hole favours, button-holes; rosettes; fancy lapel-pins, badges, etc.

anstecken. I. *v.tr. sep.* **1.** (*a*) to pin (sth.) on; to fasten (sth.) on (with a pin, a prong, etc.) (**an**+*acc.*, to); **sich** *dat.* **eine Blume a.,** (*of man*) to put a flower in one's button-hole; (*of woman*) to pin a flower on (one's dress); (*b*) **einen Ring a.,** to put a ring on one's finger, to put on a ring. **2.** to light (lamp, fire, pipe, cigar, cigarette, etc.); to kindle, ignite, set fire to (sth.); **ein Haus a.,** to set fire to a house, to set a house on fire, afire, ablaze. **3. ein Faß a.**=**ein Faß anstechen,** *q.v. under* **anstechen** 1. **4.** (*a*) *Med:* to infect; **j-n mit einer Krankheit a.,** to infect s.o. with a disease, to give s.o. a disease; to communicate a (contagious) disease to s.o.; *abs.* **a.,** (*of disease*) to be infectious, contagious, *F:* catching; **er hat mich mit seiner Erkältung angesteckt,** he gave me his cold; (*of pers.*) **angesteckt werden, sich a.,** to become infected; to catch, get, take, the infection; *F:* **j-n mit einer Meinung, mit einem Glauben, a.,** to infect s.o. with an opinion, with a belief; **von der allgemeinen Begeisterung für etwas angesteckt werden,** to be infected, *F:* bitten, with the general enthusiasm for sth.; **die Meuterei steckte die anderen Regimenter an,** the mutiny spread to the other regiments; **das Gelächter steckte die ganze Versammlung an,** the laughter infected, spread over, the whole meeting; *abs.* **Gähnen steckt an,** yawning is infectious, catching; **ansteckend,** (*of disease, laughter, good humour*) contagious; infectious; *F:* catching; (*of disease*) communicable; (*of pers.*) infectious; **hochgradig ansteckende Krankheit,** virulent disease; (*b*) to contaminate to pollute (s.o.,

s.o.'s mind, morals, etc.); to taint (s.o.'s mind, morals, etc.).

II. *vbl s.* **1. Anstecken,** *n. in vbl senses.* **2. Ansteckung,** *f. in vbl senses; also:* (*a*) *Med:* infection; contagion; communication of (contagious) disease; *F:* infection, contagion (of enthusiasm, laughter, etc.); *Med:* **durch A. verbreitete Krankheit,** disease spread by contagion; (*b*) *Ling:* contagion.

Anstecker, *m.* **1.** *Carp: etc:* lengthening-piece, eking-piece; extension(-piece). **2.** (*pers.*) lamp-lighter.

Ansteckhahn, *m.* tap, spigot (on beer-barrel, etc.).

Ansteckiampe, *f. El:* plug-in lamp.

Ansteckmagazin, *n. Sm.a:* detachable magazine.

Anstecknadel, *f.* (*a*) decorative pin; fancy lapel-pin; rosette; (*b*) badge; flag (*sold on flag-day*).

ansteckungsfähig, *a. Med:* (*of pers.*) liable (i) to spread infection, (ii) to catch the infection.

Ansteckungsfähigkeit, *f. Med:* (i) liability to spread infection; contagiousness; (ii) liability to infection.

Ansteckungsgefahr, *f.* danger of infection; **bei A.,** when there is danger of infection.

Ansteckungsgrad, *m. Med:* degree of infectiousness, of virulence; **hoher A. einer Krankheit,** virulence of disease.

Ansteckungsherd, *m. Med:* centre, focus, source, of infection.

Ansteckungskraft, *f. Med:* virulence (of disease).

Ansteckungskrankheit, *f. Med:* contagious, infectious, communicable, *F:* catching, disease.

Ansteckungsquelle, *f. Med:* source of infection.

Ansteckungsstoff, *m. Med:* infectious matter; virus; contagium, contagion.

Ansteckungsvermögen, *n. Med:* infectiousness.

anstehen, *v.i. sep.* (*strong*) (*haben*) **1. an etwas** *dat.* **a.,** to stand, be, close to sth.; to be contiguous to sth.; to be next to sth.; **die Kommode steht zu nahe an der Wand an,** the chest of drawers is too close to the wall. **2.** *Geol: Min:* (*of stratum, seam*) to crop out, to outcrop, to basset; **anstehender Gang,** outcropping seam; **anstehendes Gestein,** (i) outcropping rock; (ii) live, living, rock; solid rock. **3.** *Ven:* (**auf Wild** *acc.*) **a.,** to lie in wait (for game); to be in one's hide. **4.** to stand in a line, in a queue; to queue (up), line up, form up; **nach Eintrittskarten a.,** to queue (up) for tickets; **diese Probleme stehen zur Debatte an,** these problems are down for, awaiting, debate. **5.** (*of engagement, date, etc.*) to be fixed, settled. **6.** (*of matter*) to be delayed, put off, held over; to stand over; **das kann vorläufig noch a.,** that can stand over, can wait, for the time being; **etwas a. lassen,** to postpone sth., put sth. off, hold sth. over; to let sth. stand over; to defer, hold over, payment of (debt). **7. a., etwas zu tun,** to delay in doing sth.; to hesitate, waver, about doing sth.; **ich stehe nicht an zu sagen, daß . . . ,** I have no hesitation in saying that . . . ; I am quite prepared to say that . . . . **8. j-m a.** (*a*) (*of garment*) to look well on s.o.; (*b*) (*of manner, behaviour, etc.*) to become, befit, s.o.; to be fitting, proper, seemly, for s.o.; **etwas mehr Höflichkeit würde ihm wohl a.,** it wouldn't be amiss for him, *F:* it wouldn't do him any harm, to show rather more politeness; **es steht Ihnen schlecht, übel, an, zu . . . ,** it does not become you, it is not becoming for you, to . . . ; it is unbecoming of you, it ill becomes you, to . . . ; it is not proper, fitting, seemly, for you to . . . ; **es steht mir nicht an, mich in die Sache einzumischen,** it would not be proper for me, it is not my place, to interfere; (*c*) (*of employment, house, etc.*) to suit s.o.'s requirements, wishes; to suit s.o.; **eine solche Stelle würde ihm wohl a.,** a post like that would suit him well, would be just what he wants, would be just right for him.

ansteifen, *v.tr. sep.* **1.** to starch, stiffen (linen, etc.). **2.** *Constr:* to stiffen, prop (up), stay (wall, etc.).

ansteigen. I. *v.i. sep.* (*strong*) (*sein*) **1.** (*of pers.*) (*a*) to ascend, mount, climb (up); (*b*) *F:* **angestiegen kommen,** to come stalking along. **2.** (*of ground, road, etc.*) to rise, to slope up; (*of road, path*) to ascend, to climb; (*of water*) to rise; (*of number, debt, etc.*) to increase, swell, mount up; (*of prices*) to increase, rise; **sanft ansteigendes Gelände,** gently rising ground; **steil, schroff, ansteigender Hang,** steep, precipitous, abrupt, slope.

II. *vbl s.* **Ansteigen,** *n. in vbl senses; also:* **A. der Preise,** increase, rise, in prices. *cp.* **Anstieg.**

Anstellbottich, *m. Brew:* pitching tub

anstellen. I. *v.tr. sep.* **1.** (*a*) to stand, place (sth.) (**an etwas** *acc.*, against sth.); **die Leiter a.,** to put the ladder in position, to put up the ladder; **einen Schrank näher an die Wand a.,** to put, set, a cupboard closer to the wall; (*b*) (*of pers.*) **sich a.,** to take up one's position, to take one's place; **sich (in einer Reihe) a.,** to stand in a line, in a queue; to queue (up), line up, form up; **sich nach Eintrittskarten a.,** to queue (up) for tickets. **2.** *Com:* **Waren a.,** to offer goods (for sale). **3.** to give (s.o.) (regular) employment, to take (s.o.) into one's employ, to employ (s.o.); to engage, take on, sign on, *U.S:* to hire (workman, etc.); to appoint (s.o.) (to an office, a post); **j-n (zu einer Arbeit) a.,** to set s.o. to work (doing sth., at sth.); **angestellt werden,** to be engaged, taken on; to be appointed (to an office, a post); to find employment, a situation, a post; to get a job; **angestellt sein,** to be in (regular) employment; to be in a situation, a post, a job; **er ist bei unserer Firma angestellt,** he is employed by, in the employ of, our firm; he is one of our firm's employees; he is with our firm; **j-n fest a.,** to make s.o. a permanent member of the staff, to put s.o. on the establishment, to establish s.o.; to confirm s.o. in his post, his appointment; **fest angestellt,** on the regular staff; employed under contract; permanently appointed; established; *see also* **Angestellte. 4.** to start (up) (machinery); to switch on (electric current, light, wireless, vacuum cleaner, etc.); to turn on (water, gas, heating, wireless, etc.); to put on (gramophone, heating, etc.). **5.** *Brew:* **die Würze a.,** to pitch the wort. **6.** (*a*) to make, carry out (experiments, etc.); **Versuche über etwas** *acc.* **a.,** to carry out experiments on sth.; **Betrachtungen über etwas** *acc.* **a.,** to reflect, meditate, on sth.; to make observations (up)on sth.; **tiefsinnige Betrachtungen über die Nichtigkeit alles Irdischen a.,** to meditate profoundly on the vanity of all earthly things; **einen Vergleich zwischen . . . und . . . a.,** to make, draw, a comparison, to draw a parallel, between . . . and . . . ; *Jur:* **einen Prozeß gegen j-n a.,** to initiate, institute, proceedings against s.o.; (*b*) to contrive (to do) (sth.); to manage (to do) (sth.); **ich weiß gar nicht, wie ich es a. soll,** I've no idea how to set, go, about it, how to manage it; **er hat es so schlau angestellt, daß . . . ,** he has managed matters so cunningly that . . . ; **was sie auch a. mag, sie wird nicht . . . können,** no matter what she does she won't be able to . . . ; *F:* **etwas a.,** (i) to do something silly; (ii) to do something troublesome; to make trouble; **da hast du ja was Schönes angestellt!** (i) now you've (been and) gone and done it! (ii) now you've put your foot in it! (iii) you've made a pretty mess, haven't you! **wenn er mit dir etwas anstellt . . . ,** if he tries anything on with you, starts anything, any of his tricks, with you . . . ; **was hat er (bloß) angestellt?** (just) what has he been up to? **7. sich anstellen,** to behave; to act; (*a*) **sich klug, geschickt, ungeschickt, dumm, bei, zu, etwas a.,** to set about, go about, get about, sth. cleverly, skilfully, clumsily, stupidly; (*b*) **sie ist nicht krank, sie stellt sich nur an,** she isn't ill, she's only putting it on, putting on an act; **er stellt sich an, als ob er nichts wüßte,** he acts, behaves, as though he did not know anything; **stell dich nicht an, als ob du nichts verstündest!** don't act as if you didn't understand! **sie konnte sich a., wie sie wollte . . . ,** however she behaved . . . ; **stell dich nicht so an!** don't make so much fuss! *A:* **sich krank, fromm, a.,** to pretend to be ill, pious; to feign illness, piety; to put on an air of piety.

II. *vbl s.* **1. Anstellen,** *n. in vbl senses.* **2. Anstellung,** *f.* (*a*) *in vbl senses of* I. 3, 4, 5; *also:* engagement, appointment, employment (of personnel); (*b*) situation, post, place, appointment; office; *F:* job; **feste A.,** permanent appointment, established post, post on the establishment, on the regular staff.

Ansteller, *m.* employer (of labour).

Anstellerei, *f.* **-/-en,** (*a*) pretence (*of illness, piety, etc.*); (*b*) fussing, making of a good deal of fuss; putting on of a woebegone, long-suffering, air; **es ist pure A. bei ihr,** she's just shamming, *F:* she's just putting on an act; (*c*) queueing (up).

Anstellhefe, *f. Brew:* pitching yeast.

anstellig, *a.* dext(e)rous, deft, skilful, handy, clever; adroit.

Anstelligkeit, *f.* dexterity, deftness, skilfulness, skill; cleverness; adroitness.

Anstelltemperatur, *f. Brew:* pitching temperature.

Anstellungsbüro, *n.* employment agency, bureau, office; (servants') registry office.

Anstellwinkel, *m. Aer:* angle of incidence (of wing, airscrew blade, etc.).

anstemmen, *v.tr. sep.* **den Rücken, den Fuß, den Arm, usw., gegen etwas a.,** to brace one's back, one's foot, one's arm, etc., against sth.; **sich (gegen etwas) a.,** (i) to brace oneself (against sth.); to shove hard (against sth.); (ii) to offer stubborn resistance (to sth.); *F:* to dig one's toes, one's heels, in.

ansterben, *v.i. sep.* (*strong*) (*sein*) *Jur: A:* **j-m a.,** to devolve upon s.o. by death; **sein Gut ist seinem Vetter angestorben,** on his death his estate passed to his cousin.

ansteuern. 1. *v.tr. sep. Nau: Av:* to steer, head, make, for (sth.); to shape a course, set (the) course, for (sth.); *Nau:* to close (a ship, etc.); *Av:* to approach (airfield). **2.** *vbl s.* **Ansteuern** *n.*, **Ansteuerung** *f. in vbl senses; also: Av:* approach (*gen.*, to).

Ansteuerungsboje, *f. Nau:* entrance buoy.

Ansteuerungsfeuer, *n. Av:* location beacon; landing beacon.

Ansteuerungstonne, *f. Nau:* entrance buoy.

Anstich, *m.* **1.** (*a*) broaching, tapping (of cask, barrel); starting (of cask, barrel, block of butter, etc.); (*b*) **frischer A.,** newly tapped beer, wine, etc.; beer, wine, etc., from a fresh barrel. **2.** puncture; pit (*in fruit, caused by wasp, etc.*); pitting (of fruit). **3.** (*a*) first insertion of the spade; digging of the first spit, *U.S:* spadeful; (*b*) *Fenc:* first thrust.

Anstichhahn, *m.* tap, spigot (for beer-barrel, etc.).

anstiefeln, *v.i. used only in p.p.* **angestiefelt,** (*q.v.*).

Anstieg, *m.* **-(e)s/-e. 1.** (*a*) ascent; rise; climb; **sein A. zum Erfolg,** his rise, climb, to success; (*b*) **A. der Preise,** rise, increase, in prices; **die Preise sind im A.,** prices are rising, are on the rise, are going up. **2.** *Mount:* ascent (route); way up.

Anstiegsskizze, *f. Mount:* sketch showing an ascent route.

anstieren, *v.tr. sep.* to stare fixedly at (s.o., sth.); to glare, glower, at (s.o., sth.).

anstiften. I. *v.tr. sep.* **1.** (*a*) to cause, bring about (confusion, a quarrel, etc.); to occasion (confusion, mischief, a rising, etc.); to instigate (crime, revolt, etc.); to foment (sedition, discord, a quarrel, etc.); to promote (disorder); to foster (discord, sedition, etc.); to abet (crime); *F:* **da hast du was Schönes angestiftet!** (i) a nice mess you've made of it! (ii) now you've started something! (*b*) **j-n zu etwas a.; j-n a., etwas zu tun,** to incite s.o. to sth.; to induce, instigate, incite, s.o. to do sth.; to egg s.o. on to do sth.; **j-n zum Verbrechen a.; j-n a., ein Verbrechen zu begehen,** to instigate s.o. to crime; to incite s.o. to (a) crime, to commit a crime; to abet s.o. in a crime; **j-n zum Diebstahl a.,** to incite s.o. to steal, to (a) theft; to abet s.o. in a theft; **ein Kind zu einem Streich a.,** to egg a child on to do mischief. **2.** *Tchn:* to pin, peg, bolt, (sth.) on (**an**+*acc.*, to).

II. *vbl s.* **Anstiften** *n.*, **Anstiftung** *f. in vbl senses; also:* instigation; incitement; fomentation (of discord, etc.); **Anstiftung eines Verbrechens, Anstiftung zu einem Verbrechen,** instigation of a crime, incitement to a crime; **auf Anstiftung j-s,** at, by, the instigation of s.o.

Anstifter, *m.* instigator (*gen.*, of); inciter (*gen.*, to); abettor (of a crime, of disorders); ringleader (in mischief, etc.); *Jur:* accessory before the fact.

anstimmen, *v.tr. sep. Mus:* **1.** (*a*) *abs.* to give the lead (to singers, etc.); **sie stimmten an und sangen,** they began to sing; **ein Lied a.,** to begin to sing (a song); to break into (a) song; to strike up a song; *F:* **einen anderen Ton a.,** to change one's tune, to begin to sing another tune; *F:* **er stimmt immer wieder das alte Lied an,** he is always harping on the same string, on the same note; he is always singing the same song; *see also* **Klagelied;** (*b*) *Ecc.Mus:* to intone (opening phrases of chant, etc.). **2.** *vbl s.* **Anstimmen** *n.*, **Anstimmung** *f. in vbl senses; also: Ecc.Mus:* intonation.

anstolpern, *v.i. sep.* (*sein*) **1. an etwas** *acc.* **a.,** to stumble against sth. **2. angestolpert kommen,** to come stumbling along, up.

anstolzieren, *v.i. sep.* (*usu. only in the phr.*) **anstolziert kommen,** to come strutting along, up.

Anstoß, *m.* **1.** (*a*) impact; shock; knock, blow, bump; **A. eines Körpers gegen einen anderen,** impact of one body on, against, another; collision of one body with another; **A. mit dem Ellenbogen,** push with one's elbow; nudge; (*b*) hesitation; difficulty; check; hitch; **ohne A.,** without hesitating: without a hitch. without

upset; **ohne A. sprechen, lesen,** to speak, read, fluently, without hesitancy, without faltering, without stumbling. **2.** (*a*) *Mec:* impulse; **einem Pendel einen A. geben,** to set a pendulum swinging; (*b*) impulse, impulsion, impetus; **den A. zu etwas geben,** to give an impetus to sth.; to start sth. off; to set sth. going; **Herr X hat den ersten A. zu diesem Unternehmen gegeben,** this undertaking was initiated, originated, by Mr X; Mr X gave the first impetus to this undertaking, took the initiative in this undertaking. **3.** *Fb:* kick-off; **wer hat den A.?** whose kick-off is it? **4.** offence; **(bei j-m) A. erregen, geben,** to cause, give, offence (to s.o.); **wenn ich das sagen darf, ohne A. zu erregen,** if I may say so without (giving) offence; **ich wollte keinen A. erregen,** I meant no offence; I did not mean to hurt anyone's feelings; **an etwas** *dat.* **A. nehmen,** to take offence at sth., be offended by sth.; to be shocked, scandalized, at, by, sth.; to take umbrage at sth.; **Stein des Anstoßes,** source of offence. **5.** (*a*) joint; *Carp: etc:* butt-joint; (*b*) *Needlew:* = **Anstoßnaht**; (*c*) *Bak:* = **Anstoßkruste**; (*d*) *Dial:* boundary (between two properties, etc.); (*e*) piece joined on.

anstoßen, *v.sep.* (*strong*) I. *v.tr.* **1.** (*a*) to strike, knock, bump (**etwas an etwas** *acc.*, sth. against sth.); **j-n a.,** to give s.o. a push; **j-n mit dem Ellenbogen a.,** to nudge s.o.; **angestoßen,** (*of fruit*) bruised; (*of glass, china*) damaged, chipped; (*b*) *v.tr. & i.* (*haben*) **die Gläser a., (mit den Gläsern) a.,** to clink glasses (before drinking); to touch glasses; **auf j-s Wohl a.,** to touch, clink, glasses and drink to s.o., s.o.'s health. **2.** *abs. Fb:* to kick off. **3.** (*a*) to join (timbers, pipes, etc.) end to end; to butt(-joint); (*b*) *Needlew:* to fine-draw (seam, etc.); **ein Stück Tuch an ein anderes a.,** to fine-draw two pieces of cloth. **4.** *Ind: etc:* to crush (material). **5.** *A:* (*of illness, fever, dizziness, etc.*) to attack (s.o.). **6.** *A:* to set fire to (timber, etc.); to kindle (fire).

II. **anstoßen,** *v.i.* (*sein, haben*) **1.** (*sein*) (*a*) **an etwas** *acc.* **a.,** to strike, knock, bump, against sth.; to collide with sth.; **mit dem Kopf an die Wand a.,** to run one's head against the wall; **mit dem Fuß an einen Stein a.,** to stub one's foot, to stumble, against a stone; (*b*) (*of horse*) to stumble, to flounder. **2.** (*haben*) to falter, stumble (in speaking, reading, etc.); **mit der Zunge a.,** to lisp; **er stößt im Reden sehr an,** he is very hesitant in his speech; his speech is very faltering; **er redete diesmal ganz ohne anzustoßen,** this time he spoke fluently, without faltering at all, without the slightest hesitancy. **3.** (*sein, haben*) (*a*) to cause, give, offence; (*b*) (*of pers.*) to be awkward (in society, etc.); **mit seinem etwas bäurischen Benehmen stößt er überall an,** his somewhat countrified behaviour doesn't go down well (with people). **4.** (*haben*) **an etwas** *acc.* **a.,** to be contiguous, adjacent, to sth.; to adjoin sth.; to abut on sth.; to border on sth.; **Haus, das an das meine anstößt,** house adjoining mine; **die Länder, die an Deutschland a.,** the countries bordering on Germany; (*of house, piece of timber, piece of cloth, etc.*) **das stößt nicht ganz an,** it doesn't quite join (up), it doesn't quite meet (*with the next house, piece of timber, with the edge of another piece of cloth, etc.*); **anstoßend,** adjoining, adjacent (room, house, etc.); contiguous (area, etc.); abutting (houses, fields, etc.); conterminous (areas, etc.).

III. *vbl s.* **Anstoßen,** *n. in vbl. senses; also:* **1.** collision (of one body with another). **2.** hesitancy (in speaking, etc.); lisp.

Anstößer, *m.* (next-door) neighbour.

anstößig, *a.* offensive; objectionable; obnoxious (behaviour, remarks, etc.); shocking, scandalous (behaviour, etc.); improper, unseemly, unbecoming, indecorous (behaviour, remarks, etc.); scabrous (topic, tale, etc.); *adv.* **sich a. benehmen,** to behave offensively, objectionably, obnoxiously.

Anstößigkeit, *f.* **1.** offensiveness; objectionableness; obnoxiousness; scandalousness, scandalous nature (of behaviour, remarks, etc.); impropriety, unseemliness, (indecorousness of behaviour, remarks, etc.); scabrousness (of topic, tale, etc.). **2.** *pl.* **Anstößigkeiten,** improprieties; offensive, objectionable, words *or* actions.

Anstoßkruste, *f. Bak:* kissing-crust (of loaf).

Anstoßnaht, *f. Needlew:* fine-drawn seam.

anstrahlen. I. *v.tr. sep.* **1.** (*of sun*) to shed its rays, its radiance, on (sth.); (*of sun, lamp, etc.*) to shine (up)on (sth.); (*of searchlight, projector, etc.*) to cast its beam on (sth); to illuminate (sth.); (*of pers.*) **etwas mit einer Taschenlampe, usw., a.,** to shine a torch, *U.S:* flashlight, etc., on sth.; to fix sth. in the beam of a torch, etc.; **ein Gebäude, usw., (mit Scheinwerfern) a.,** to floodlight a building, etc. **2.** *F:* (*of pers.*) to beam at (s.o.).

II. *vbl s.* **Anstrahlen** *n.*, **Anstrahlung** *f. in vbl senses; also:* illumination (of sth.); flood-lighting (of building, etc.).

ansträngen, *v.tr. sep.* to put, harness, (horse) to a carriage.

Anstrebekraft, *f. Ph:* centripetal force.

anstreben, *v.sep.* **1.** *v.tr.* to aspire to, after (sth.); to be hoping to get (sth.); *F:* to be after (sth.); **es wird angestrebt, daß . . . ,** it is hoped to . . . , our aim is to . . . ; **ein Ziel a.,** to strive for, after, an end; to strive to attain an end; **Einfluß a.,** to be eager to gain influence. **2.** *v.i.* (*haben*) **gegen etwas a.,** to strive against, with, sth.; to struggle against, with, sth.; to wrestle with sth.; to resist sth.

anstrebenswert, *a.* (end, position, etc.) worth striving for.

anstreichen. I. *v.tr. sep.* (*strong*) **1.** to coat (sth.) (**mit,** with); *esp.* to cover (wall, etc.) with a coat of paint; to paint (wall, house, etc.); to dope (aircraft wings); **eine Tür grün a.,** to paint a door green; **eine Tür zweimal a.,** to give a door two coats of paint; **'(Achtung!) frisch angestrichen!'** 'wet paint', 'mind the paint!' **eine Wand mit Tünche a.,** to whitewash a wall; to colour-wash, distemper, a wall; **etwas mit Firnis a.,** to put a coat of varnish on sth., to apply a coat of varnish to sth., to varnish sth.; **einen Zaun mit Teer a.,** to coat a fence with tar, to tar a fence; **etwas mit Farbe grob a.,** to (be)daub, smear, sth. with paint, with colour; *F:* **sich a., sein Gesicht a.,** to paint one's face. **2.** (*a*) to make a (pencil) mark against (name, passage in book, etc.); to mark (name, date, passage, etc.); to side-line (passage); to underline, underscore (word, passage); **etwas rot a.,** to mark sth. in red, with a red pencil; *F:* **den Tag werde ich rot a.,** I'll make that a red-letter day; (*b*) *F:* **das werde ich dir a.!** I'll pay you out, serve you out, for that! I'll get my own back on you! I'll be even with you yet! **3. ein Zündholz a.,** to strike a match.

II. *vbl s.* **Anstreichen,** *n. in vbl senses; cp.* **Anstrich** 1.

Anstreicher, *m.* (*a*) house-painter; (house) decorator; (*b*) whitewasher; (*c*) *Art: F:* dauber, daubster; inferior artist.

Anstreichgerät, *n.* (*a*) painting equipment; whitewashing *or* distempering equipment; (*b*) = **Anstreichpistole.**

Anstreichpistole, *f.* spray-gun; paint-gun, -sprayer; air-brush.

anstreifen, *v.tr. sep.* to touch (sth.) lightly; to graze, brush (sth.); to skim (the surface of the water).

anstrengen. I. *v.tr. sep.* **1.** (*a*) to exert; to strain; **seinen Geist a.,** to exert one's mind, one's mental powers; to set one's mind to work; **alle seine Kräfte a. (etwas zu tun),** to do all one can, to do one's utmost, to use, make, every effort, to make every endeavour, to strain every nerve, to try one's hardest (to do sth.); **dieser Druck strengt die Augen sehr an, ist sehr anstrengend für die Augen,** this print strains, tries, one's eyes, is (very) trying to the eyes; **anstrengend,** (*of work, activity, etc.*) arduous, laborious, exacting, requiring all one's energies; trying; **die Sitzung war sehr anstrengend für mich,** the meeting was a severe strain on me; I found the meeting very fatiguing, very trying; *abs.* **Korrekturlesen strengt an,** proof-reading is trying work; (*b*) **sich a.,** to make an effort, to exert oneself; **sich a., etwas zu tun,** to make an effort, to endeavour, strive, to do sth.; **du mußt dich mehr a.,** you must make greater efforts, try harder, work harder, put more energy into it; **sich über seine Kräfte a.,** to over-exert oneself; to overtax one's strength; to overstrain oneself; to overdo it; to work too hard; *F:* **der Klub ist in Geldschwierigkeiten — die Mitglieder werden sich a. müssen,** the club is in financial difficulties —the members will have to make a special effort. **2.** *Jur:* **einen Prozeß gegen j-n a.,** to initiate, institute, proceedings against s.o.; to bring an action against s.o.

II. *vbl s.* **1. Anstrengen,** *n. in vbl senses.* **2. Anstrengung,** *f.* (*a*) = II. 1; *also:* exertion, application (of one's powers, faculties); (*b*) effort; exertion; strain; **es ist für mich eine große A., zu . . . ,** it is a great effort, exertion, for me, a severe strain on me, to . . . ; **die Sitzung war eine große A. für mich,** the meeting was a severe strain on me, meant a considerable effort for me; I found the meeting very trying; **die größten, alle möglichen, Anstrengungen machen, etwas zu tun,** to use, make, every effort, to strain every nerve, to do one's utmost, to do sth.; **größere Anstrengungen machen,** to increase one's efforts, make greater efforts, try harder, work harder; **trotz aller Anstrengungen,** in spite of every effort, despite all his, her, their, exertions; whatever pains they took; **ohne A.,** easily, without effort, effortlessly; without exertion; without (any) strain.

III. **angestrengt,** *p.p. & a. in vbl senses; esp.* assiduous, strenuous (work, efforts); sedulous (efforts, attention); intense (labour); intensive (work); persistent, unremitting (labour, toil); close, concentrated (attention); *adv.* **a. arbeiten,** to work strenuously, assiduously, sedulously, unremittingly; to work hard.

Anstrich, *m.* **1.** coating (with paint, varnish, etc.); painting; varnishing; doping (of aircraft wings); whitewashing; limewashing; colour-washing, distempering; *cp.* **anstreichen** II. **2.** (coat of) paint, colour; (coat of) varnish; dope (on aircraft wings); (coat of) limewash; (coat of) whitewash; (coat of) colour-wash, distemper; wash (of distemper, etc.); *Paint:* **erster A.,** first coat, ground coat, undercoat, priming, grounding; **letzter A.,** final coat; **einer Tür einen neuen A. geben,** to give a door a fresh coat of paint, to repaint a door. **3.** colour, hue, tinge, tincture; semblance, appearance, (outward) show; **seinen Handlungen einen gesetzmäßigen A. geben,** to put a varnish of legality upon one's actions, to cover one's actions with a gloss of legality, to give one's actions a semblance of legality; **einen A. von etwas haben,** to have a tinge, a tincture, of sth.; to be tinged with sth.; **die Sache hat einen geheimnisvollen A.,** the affair has a tinge of mystery about it; there is an air of mystery about the business; (*of pers.*) **einen A. von Bildung haben,** to have a veneer, a semblance, of culture; (*of pers., speech, etc.*) **einen ironischen, usw., A. haben,** to have a tinge, a streak, of irony, etc.; **Rede ohne jeden A. von Pedanterie,** speech untinged with, without any flavour of, pedantry; **ein gelehrter A., ein A. von Gelehrsamkeit,** a veneer, a smattering, of scholarship; (*of thg*) **einen vornehmen A. haben,** to look elegant *or* genteel; (*of pers.*) **sich** *dat.* **einen vornehmen A. geben,** to put on (genteel) airs; to put on a semblance of gentility. **4.** *Mus:* (*violin-playing*) first touch (of the bow).

Anstrichfarbe, *f. Paint:* painting colour; colour of the paint; colour in which sth. is, is to be, painted.

Anstrichstoff, *m.* (special) paint *or* varnish *or* wash; composition to be applied; *Av: etc:* dope.

anstricken, *v.tr. sep.* to knit (sth.) on (**an** + *acc.*, to); to lengthen (knitted sleeve, etc.); **einen Strumpf a.,** (i) to foot, (ii) to re-foot, new-foot, a stocking.

anströmen, *v.sep.* **1.** *v.tr.* to stream, flow, towards (sth.); to wash against (sth.); (*of river*) to wash (bank, etc.). **2.** *v.tr.* (*of river*) to carry, bring down, bear down (sand, driftwood, etc.). **3.** *v.i.* (*sein*) (*usu. in the phr.*) **angeströmt kommen,** (*of water, etc.*) to come streaming, rushing, along, in; to come pouring in; (*of people*) to come streaming along, in; to stream in; to come crowding, flocking, thronging, up, in; (*of people, letters, etc.*) to pour in, to come pouring in.

anstücke(l)n, *v.tr. sep.* to add a piece to (sth.); to lengthen (garment, etc.); **etwas an etwas** *acc.* **a.,** to piece sth. on to sth.

Ansturm, *m.* (*a*) *Mil: etc:* assault; onset; onslaught (**auf** + *acc.*, on); charge, rush (**auf** + *acc.*, against, upon); onrush (of the enemy, of the waters); **etwas in einem A. tun,** to do sth. in one rush, *F:* at one go; (*b*) **sobald die Leute vom Ausverkauf hörten, gab es einen richtigen A. auf den Laden,** as soon as people heard about the sale they made a wild rush, there was a wild rush, for the shop; *Fin:* **A. auf eine Bank,** run on a bank.

anstürmen, *v.sep.* **1.** *v.i.* (*sein*) (*a*) *Mil:* to charge; to attack; to make a rush; **auf, gegen, den Feind, eine Stellung, a.,** to charge, attack, the enemy; to storm, attack, a position; (*b*) **auf, gegen, j-n, einen Laden, usw., a.,** to rush at s.o.; to make a rush at, to rush, s.o., a shop, etc.; to make a dash at s.o.; (*c*) **das Meer stürmte gegen das Ufer an,** the sea was raging against the shore; (*d*) (*of pers.*) to come charging, rushing, dashing, pelting, along, up; to come up at full pelt. **2.** *occ. v.tr.* to attack (the enemy); to make a rush, a dash, at (s.o., sth.).

Ansturz, *m.* onrush, rush.

anstürzen, *v.i. sep.* (*sein*) (*usu. only in the phr.*) **angestürzt kommen,** to come dashing, pelting, along, up; to come up at full pelt; to rush up, dash up.

ansuchen. I. *v.i. sep.* (*haben*) **bei j-m um etwas a.,** to solicit s.o. for sth., sth. from s.o.; to apply, make application, to s.o. for sth.; to ask s.o. for sth.; to request sth. of s.o.; *Lit:* to crave sth. from, of, s.o.; to sue to s.o. for sth.; **bei j-m um Erlaubnis a., etwas zu tun,** to ask, beg, s.o.'s permission, s.o.'s leave, to do sth.; **beim Gericht um etwas a.,** to petition the court for sth.

II. *vbl s.* **Ansuchen,** *n.* request, application, solicitation; suit; entreaty; petition; **auf j-s A.** *acc.*, **auf A. von j-m,** at s.o.'s request, at the request of s.o.; on s.o.'s application; **auf mein dringendes A.,** at my earnest entreaty, at my urgent request; **auf A. von zehn Mitgliedern,** on application from, upon a requisition by, ten members; **ein A. an das Gericht stellen,** to petition the court, to make application to the court.

Ansucher, *m.* petitioner; solicitant; applicant (**um,** for).

Ansuch(ungs)schreiben, *n.* (written) petition.

Ansud, *m.* **1.** boiling (up); partial boiling. **2.** boiled-up liquid.

ansummen[1], *v.sep.* **1.** *v.tr.* (*of insect, etc.*) to hum, buzz, at (s.o.). **2.** *v.i.* (*sein*) (*usu. only in the phr.*) **angesummt kommen,** to come humming, buzzing, along.

ansummen[2], *v.tr. sep.* to sum up, total up, tot up (numbers, etc.); **sich a.,** (*of expenses, etc.*) to mount up, to run up, tot up.

ansumpfen, *v.tr. sep.* to swamp (field, etc.); to make (land, etc.) marshy, boggy, swampy.

ansüßen, *v.tr. sep.* to sweeten; to edulcorate (powdered substance, etc.).

Ant, *f.* **-/-en.** *North G.Dial:* duck.

Ant-, ant- [ant-]. *Gr.pref.* (*used before a vowel*) = **Anti-, anti-.**

antagonisieren [ant(ʔ)a·go·niˈziːrən], *v.tr.* to antagonize.

Antagonismus [ant(ʔ)a·go·ˈnismus], *m.* **-/-men,** antagonism.

Antagonist [ant(ʔ)a·go·ˈnist], *m.* **-en/-en,** antagonist, opponent.

antagonistisch [ant(ʔ)a·go·ˈnistiʃ], *a.* antagonistic, opposed; *Physiol:* **antagonistische Muskeln,** antagonistic muscles.

antakeln, *v.tr. sep. Nau:* to rig (vessel, mast).

Antakije [anˈtaːkijə]. *Pr.n.n.* **-s.** *Geog:* Antioch.

Antalgikum [antʔˈalgi·kum], *n.* **-s/-ka.** *Med:* antalgic, analgesic.

antalgisch [antʔˈalgiʃ], *a. Med:* antalgic, analgesic.

Antananarivo [anta·na·naˈriːvoː]. *Pr.n.n.* **-s.** *Geog:* Antananarivo, Tananarivo.

antanzen, *v.i. sep.* (*sein*) to dance up; **angetanzt kommen,** (i) to come dancing along, up; (ii) *F:* to come along, to turn up; **da kommt sie endlich angetanzt!** here she is at last! *F:* **j-n a. lassen,** to send for s.o. (*to warn him, reprimand him, etc.*).

Antaphrodisiakum [antʔafro·di·ˈziːa·kum], **Antaphroditikum** [antʔafro·ˈdiːti·kum], *n.* **-s/-ka.** *Pharm:* antaphrodisiac.

antaphroditisch [antʔafro·ˈdiːtiʃ], *a. Pharm:* antaphrodisiac.

Antapoplektikum [antʔapo·ˈplɛkti·kum], *n.* **-s/-ka.** *Med:* antapoplectic.

antapoplektisch [antʔapo·ˈplɛktiʃ], *a. Med:* antapoplectic.

antappen, *v.i. sep.* (*sein*) (*usu. only in the phr.*) **angetappt kommen,** to come groping along.

Antares [anˈtaːrɛs]. *Pr.n.m.* **-'.** *Astr:* Antares; the Scorpion's Heart.

Antarktik, die [antʔˈarktik]. *Pr.n.f.* **-.** *Geog:* the Antarctic Ocean.

Antarktika [antʔˈarkti·kaː]. *Pr.n.f.* **-s.** *Geog:* Antarctica, the Antarctic Continent.

Antarktis, die [antʔˈarktis]. *Pr.n.f.* **-.** *Geog:* the Antarctic.

antarktisch [antʔˈarktiʃ], *a.* Antarctic.

Antarthritikum [antʔarˈtriːti·kum], *n.* **-s/-ka.** *Med:* antarthritic.

antarthritisch [antʔarˈtriːtiʃ], *a. Med:* antarthritic.

antasten. I. *v.tr. sep.* **1.** to feel, touch; to finger, handle (material, etc.); **nicht a.!** don't touch! hands off! **2.** (*a*) to encroach upon, break into, touch (money, funds); **wir dürfen das Kapital nicht a.,** we are not allowed to touch the capital; (*b*) **j-s Rechte, j-n, a.,** (i) to cast doubt upon, to impugn, s.o.'s rights; (ii) to encroach upon s.o.'s rights; **j-s Ehre, j-s guten Namen, j-n, a.,** to cast aspersions, a slur, on s.o.'s honour; to detract from s.o.'s reputation; to reflect on, impugn, s.o.'s honour; **er kann dich nicht a.,** he can't do you any damage, hurt you, *F:* touch you.

II. *vbl s.* **1. Antasten,** *n. in vbl senses.* **2. Antastung,** *f.* (*a*) = II. 1; *also:* **A. meiner Ehre,** impugnment of my honour; **A. meiner Rechte,** (i) impugnment of my rights; (ii) encroachment upon my rights; (*b*) damage (to reputation, etc.).

antasthmatisch [antʔastˈmaːtiʃ], *a. Med:* antasthmatic.

antatschen, *v.tr. sep.* to finger, feel (sth.).

antaumeln, *v.i. sep.* (*sein*) (*usu. only in the phr.*) **angetaumelt kommen,** to come reeling, staggering, along.

Antäus [anˈtɛːus]. *Pr.n.m.* **-'.** *Myth:* Antaeus.

Ante-, ante- [ˌante·-], *pref.* ante-.

Ante [ˈantə], *f.* **-/-n.** *Arch:* anta.

antedatieren [ˌante·da·ˈtiːrən], *v.tr.* (*a*) to postdate (document, etc.); (*b*) to antedate, foredate (document, etc.).

Antediluvianer [ˌante·di·lu·viˈaːnər], *m.* **-s/-,** antediluvian.

antediluvianisch [ˌante·di·lu·viˈaːniʃ], *a.* antediluvian.

anteeren, *v.tr. sep.* to coat (sth.) with tar, to tar.

Antefixum [antəˈfiksum], *n. Arch:* antefix.

Anteflexion [antəflɛksiˈoːn], *f. Med:* anteflexion (of the uterus).

anteigen, *v.tr. sep.* to make a paste of (sth.); to work (sth.) up into a paste.

Anteil, *m.* **1.** (*a*) share, part, portion; quota; contingent (of troops, etc.); **ihr A. der Erbschaft,** her share of the inheritance, *Jur:* her portion; **A. am Gewinn,** share, percentage, of the profits; **A. am Gewinn haben,** to have a share, an interest, in the profits; to share, participate, in the profits; **A. an einem Geschäft haben,** to have an interest, a share, in a business; **seinen A. an der Rechnung bezahlen,** to pay one's share of the bill; *F:* to pay one's scot, one's shot; **seinen verhältnismäßigen A. beitragen,** to contribute one's appropriate share, one's quota; to contribute *pro rata;* **A. an einer Tätigkeit haben,** to participate, share, take (a) part, in an activity; **großen, tätigen, A. an einem Unternehmen haben,** to play a large part, an active part, in an undertaking; (*b*) *Fin:* share (in a company, etc.); **A. am Konsortium,** underwriting share. **2.** interest (**an** + *dat.*, in); sympathy (**an** + *dat.*, with, for); **A. nehmen an etwas** *dat.*, to take an interest in sth.; to be concerned about sth.; to sympathize with sth.; **ich nehme innigen A. an ihrem Wohlergehen,** I take a deep interest in, am deeply concerned for, her welfare; **ich nehme aufrichtigen A. an seinem Unglück,** I sympathize sincerely with him in his misfortune.

Anteilgebühr, *f.* proportionate charge; percentage (of takings, etc.).

Anteilhaber, *m.* = **Teilhaber.**

anteilig, *a.* & *adv.* = **anteilmäßig.**

anteillos, *a.* unsympathetic, unconcerned; indifferent.

Anteillosigkeit, *f.* lack of sympathy, of concern; indifference.

anteilmäßig, *a.* proportionate, proportional; (contribution, distribution, etc.) *pro rata; adv.* proportionately, proportionally; *pro rata.*

Anteilnahme, *f.* **-/.** sympathy (**für j-n,** for s.o.; **an j-s Unglück, usw.** *dat.*, with s.o.'s misfortune, etc.); concern (**an etwas** *dat.*, about sth.; **für j-n,** for s.o.); **ich möchte meine aufrichtige A. ausdrücken,** I should like to express my sincere sympathy; **er hat keine A. für sie,** he feels no concern for her.

Anteilschein, *m. Fin:* share-certificate, *F:* scrip, *U.S:* stock certificate.

Anteilscheinbesitzer, Anteilseigner, *m. Fin:* shareholder, stockholder.

Anteilshypothek, *f. Fin:* share in a mortgage.

Anteil(s)verschreibung, *f.* = **Anteilschein.**

Anteilwirtschaft, *f. Agr:* half-share farming; 'métayage' system (by which farmer pays half the yield as rent); *U.S:* share-crop system.

Anteilzahl, *f.* contingent; (numerical) quota.

antelephonieren [ˈante·le·fo·ˌniːrən], *v.tr. sep.* (*p.p.* **antelephoniert**) to telephone (to) (s.o.), to phone (s.o.), to ring, *U.S:* call (s.o.) (up); **ich werde dich a.,** *abs.* **ich werde a.,** I'll give you a ring, I'll ring you (up).

Antenne [anˈtɛnə], *f.* **-/-n.** **1.** *Nat. Hist:* antenna, *F:* feeler, horn (of insect, etc.). **2.** *W.Tel:* aerial, antenna. **3.** *Nau: A:* lateen yard.

Antennen-, *comb.fm.* **1.** *Nat. Hist:* antennal . . . , . . . of the antenna. **2.** *W.Tel:* aerial . . . , antenna . . . ; . . . of the aerial; **Antennendraht** *m*, aerial wire, antenna wire; **Antennenkreis** *m*, aerial circuit, antenna circuit; **Antennenanordnung** *f*, arrangement, set-up, of the aerial.

Antennenableitung, *f. W.Tel:* down lead, (aerial) lead-in.

Antennenabstimmspule, *f. W.Tel:* (aerial) tuning inductance, tuning-coil.

Antennendrüse, *f. Nat.Hist:* antennal gland.

Antennendurchführung, *f. W.Tel:* aerial fair-lead.

Antenneneinführung, *f. W.Tel:* (aerial) lead-in.

Antennenmast, *m. W.Tel:* aerial mast, wireless mast, radio mast.

Antennenspule, *f. W.Tel:* antenna coil.

Antennenturm, *m. W.Tel:* aerial tower; pylon.

Antennenzuführung, Antennenzuleitung, *f.* = **Antennenableitung.**

Antentempel [ˈantən-], *m. Arch:* temple with antae.

Antepänultima [ˌante·pɛ·nˈulti·maː], *f.* **-/-men & -mä.** *Pros:* antepenultimate, antepenult.

Antependium [ante·ˈpɛndium], *n.* **-s/-dien.** *Ecc:* antependium, altar frontal.

anteponieren [antəpo·ˈniːrən], *v.tr.* (*a*) *Gram:* to put (word, etc.) before, in front; (*b*) to prefer.

Antestat [ˈantɛstaːt], *n. Sch:* professor's *or* lecturer's signature (in student's record-book) to prove attendance at the beginning of a course of lectures.

antestieren [ˈantɛstiːrən], *v.i. sep.* (*haben*) (*p.p.* **antestiert**) *Sch:* (*of professor, lecturer*) to sign student's record-book (as proof of attendance at the beginning of a course of lectures).

Antezedens [ˌante·ˈtseːdɛns], *n.* **-/-denzien** [-tse·ˈdɛntsiən]. **1.** *Gram:* antecedent. **2.** *pl.* **Antezedenzien,** antecedents; previous history; past record.

Anthelium [anˈteːlium], *n.* **-s/-lien.** *Meteor:* anthelion, glory; circle of Ulloa.

Anthelminthikum [antelˈminti·kum], *n.* **-s/-ka.** *Pharm:* anthelmint(h)ic, vermifuge.

Anthemion [anˈteːmion], *n.* **-s/-mien.** *Art:* anthemion.

Anthemis [ˈante·mis], *f.* **-/.** *Bot:* anthemis, Paris daisy, marguerite.

Anthere [anˈteːrə], *f.* **-/-n.** *Bot:* anther.

Antherenbrand [anˈteːrən-], *m. Bot:* anther smut.

antherentragend, *a. Bot:* antheriferous.

Antheridium [ante·ˈriːdium], *n.* **-s/-dien.** *Bot:* antheridium.

Antholith [anto·ˈliːt], *m.* **-en/-en.** *Geol:* antholite.

Anthologie [anto·lo·ˈgiː], *f.* **-/-n** [-ˈgiːən], anthology; **A. auf das Jahr 1782,** anthology for the year 1782.

anthologisch [anto·ˈloːgiʃ], *a.* anthological.

Anthologist [anto·lo·ˈgist], *m.* **-en/-en,** anthologist.

Anthoskraut [ˈantos-], *n. Bot:* rosemary.

Anthozoen [anto·ˈtsoːən], *n.pl. Geol:* anthozoa.

Anthozyan [anto·tsy·ˈaːn], *n.* **-s/.** *Ch:* anthocyan(in).

Anthrachinon [antra·çi·ˈnoːn], *n.* **-s/.** *Ch:* anthraquinone.

Anthraknose [antra·ˈknoːzə], *f.* **-/.** *Agr:* anthracnose.

Anthrakonit [antra·ko·ˈniːt], *m.* **-(e)s/-e.** *Miner:* anthraconite.

Anthrakose [antra·ˈkoːzə], *f.* **-/.** *Med:* anthracosis, *F:* miner's phthisis, collier's lung.

Anthrax [ˈantraks], *m.* **-/.** **1.** *Med: A:* anthrax; malignant carbuncle. **2.** *Med: Vet:* anthrax. **3.** *Ent:* anthrax.

Anthrazen [antra·ˈtseːn], *n.* **-s/-e.** *Ch:* anthracene.

Anthrazenfarbstoffe, *m.pl.* anthracene dyes.

Anthrazit [antra·ˈtsiːt], *m.* **-(e)s/-e.** *Min:* anthracite, stone coal, glance coal, blind coal.

anthrazitartig, *a. Geol:* anthracitous, anthracitic.

anthrazithaltig, *a. Geol:* anthraciferous, anthracitic.

Anthropo-, anthropo- [antro·po·-], *comb.fm.* anthropo-.

anthropogen [antro·po·ˈgeːn], *a.* of human origin; made, caused, by human agency.

Anthropogenie [antro·po·ge·ˈniː], *f.* **-/.** anthropogeny.

Anthropogeographie [antro·po·ge·o·gra·ˈfiː], *f.* anthropogeography, human geography.

Anthropographie [antro·po·gra·ˈfiː], *f.* **-/.** anthropography.

anthropoid [antro·po·ˈiːt], *a.* anthropoid.

Anthropoide [antro·po·ˈiːdə], *m.* **-n/-n.** *Z:* anthropoid (ape).

Anthropologe [antro·po·ˈloːgə], *m.* **-n/-n,** anthropologist.

Anthropologie [antro·po·lo·ˈgiː], *f.* **-/.** anthropology.

anthropologisch [antro·po·ˈloːgiʃ], *a.* anthropological.

Anthropometer [antro·po·ˈmeːtər], *n.* **-s/-,** anthropometer.

Anthropometrie [antro·po·me·'triː], f. -/. anthropometry.

anthropometrisch [antro·po·'meːtriʃ], a. anthropometric(al).

anthropomorph [antro·po·'morf], a. anthropomorphic; anthropomorphous.

Anthropomorphe [antro·po·'morfə], m. -n/-n. Z: anthropoid (ape).

anthropomorphisch [antro·po·'morfiʃ], a. anthropomorphic; anthropomorphous.

anthropomorphisieren [antro·po·morfi·'ziːrən], v.tr. to anthropomorphize.

Anthropomorphismus [antro·po·'mor'fismus], m. -/. Rel.Hist: anthropomorphism.

Anthropomorphist [antro·po·mor'fist], m. -en/-en, anthropomorphist.

anthropomorphistisch [antro·po·mor'fistiʃ], a. anthropomorphic.

Anthropomorphit [antro·po·mor'fiːt], m. -en/-en. Rel.Hist: anthropomorphite.

Anthroponymie [antro·po·ny·'miː], f. -/. study of family names.

Anthropophage [antro·po·'faːgə], m. -n/-n, cannibal, man-eater; pl. anthropophagi.

Anthropophagie [antro·po·fa·'giː], f. -/. anthropophagy, cannibalism.

Anthropophobie [antro·po·fo·'biː], f. -/. anthropophobia.

Anthroposoph [antro·po·'zoːf], m. -en/-en, anthroposophist.

Anthroposophie [antro·po·zo·'fiː], f. -/. anthroposophy.

anthroposophisch [antro·po·'zoːfiʃ], a. anthroposophical.

anthropozentrisch [antro·po·'tsɛntriʃ], a. Phil: anthropocentric.

anthropozoisch [antro·po·'tsoːiʃ], a. Geol: anthropozoic.

Anthypnotikum [anthyp·'noːti·kum], n. -s/-ka. Pharm: antihypnotic; drug to prevent sleep.

Anti-, anti- [anti·-], pref. (i) anti-; (ii) F: (used as prep.) anti, against; **anti alles**, anti everything; **ich war immer anti**, I was always against (it).

Antialkoholbewegung [anti·alko·'hoːl-], f. temperance movement, abstinence movement.

Antialkoholiker [anti·alko·'hoːlikər], m. (a) advocate of temperance, of abstinence (from alcohol); (b) teetotaller, (total) abstainer.

Antiar [anti·'aːr], m. -s/-e. Bot: antiar, upas-tree.

Antibarbarus [anti·'barba·rus], m. -/-ri. Lit: opponent of barbarism.

Antibiotikum [anti·bi·'oːti·kum], n. -s/-ka. Med: Pharm: antibiotic.

antibiotisch [anti·bi·'oːtiʃ], a. Med: Pharm: antibiotic.

antichambrieren [anti·ʃam·'briːrən], v.i. (haben) to haunt the ante-chambers (of influential people); to dance attendance (on great folk); to lobby (members of parliament, etc.).

Antichlor [anti·'kloːr], n. Tex: etc: antichlor.

Anticholerikum [anti·ko·'leːri·kum], n. -s/-ka. Pharm: anticholeraic.

anticholerisch [anti·ko·'leːriʃ], a. Pharm: anticholeraic.

Antichrese [anti·'kreːzə], f. -/-n, antichresis.

antichretisch [anti·'kreːtiʃ], a. antichretic.

Antichrist ['anti·krist], m. 1. B: etc: Antichrist. 2. antichristian.

antichristlich [anti·'kristliç], a. antichristian.

anticken, v.tr. sep. to set (clock, pendulum, metronome) going; to give (pendulum, etc.) a flick.

antideutsch [anti·'doytʃ], a. anti-German.

Antidot [anti·'doːt], n. -(e)s/-e, **Antidoton** [an'tiː·do·ton], n. -s/-ta, antidote (**gegen**, for, to, against).

Antidumping [anti·'dampiŋ, anti·'dɔmpiŋ], n. -s/. Pol.Ec: measure(s) to prevent dumping (of manufactured goods).

Antidumpinggesetz, n. Pol.Ec: law to prevent dumping.

Antiemetikum [anti·e·'meːti·kum], n. Pharm: drug to counteract vomiting.

Antiepileptikum [anti·e·pi·'lɛpti·kum], n. -s/-ka. Pharm: drug to alleviate epilepsy.

Antifaschismus [anti·fa·'ʃismus], m. anti-Fascism.

Antifaschist [anti·fa·'ʃist], m. anti-Fascist.

Antifäulnisfarbe, f. Nau: anti-fouling composition.

Antifebrilium [anti·fe·'briːlium], n. -s/-lia. Pharm: antefebrile (drug), drug to reduce fever.

Antifebrin [anti·fe·'briːn], n. -s/. Pharm: antifebrin.

Antifeminismus [anti·fe·mi·'nismus], m. anti-feminism.

Antifeminist [anti·fe·mi·'nist], m. antifeminist.

Antiferment [anti·fɛr·'mɛnt], n. Ch: antiferment.

Antifoulingfarbe [anti·'fauliŋ-], f. Nau: = Antifäulnisfarbe.

Antifreudianer [anti·froydi·'aːnər], m. anti-Freudian.

Antifreudianismus [anti·froydia·'nismus], m. -/. Psy: anti-Freudism, anti-Freudianism.

Antifriktions- [anti·friktsiˈoːns-], comb.fm. Mec.E: anti-friction (device, curve, etc.).

Antifriktionsmetall, n. Mec.E: antifriction metal; Babbit metal, babbit, white metal.

Antifritter [anti·'fritər], m. -s/-. W.Tel: anticoherer.

antigallisch [anti·'galiʃ], a. A: anti-French.

Antigefrierfett [anti·gə·'friːr-], n. Mec.E: antifreeze, non-freezing, lubricant.

Antigen [anti·'geːn], n. -s/-e. Med: antigen.

Antigoa [an'tiː·goa:]. Pr.n. n. -s. Geog: = Antigua.

Antigone [an'tiː·go·neː]. Pr.n.f. -s. Antigone.

Antigua [an'tiː·gua:]. Pr.n. n. -s. Geog: (die Insel) A., Antigua.

Antihektika [anti·'hɛkti·ka:], n.pl. Med: medicines against consumption.

antik [an'tiːk], a. (a) classical (art, literature, etc.); Graeco-Roman; ancient; of the ancient world; pertaining to the ancients; **die antike Gesellschaftsordnung**, ancient society; (b) antique (furniture, etc.); (c) old-fashioned, antiquated; F: **eine antike Schönheit**, an aged beauty.

Antikaglien [anti·'kaljən], n.pl. (small) antiquities.

Antikardion [anti·'kardion], n. -s/. Anat: epigastrium, pit of the stomach.

Antikatalysator [anti·kata·ly·'zaːtor], m. Ch: anticatalyst.

antikatalytisch [anti·kata·'lyːtiʃ], a. Ch: anti-catalytic.

antikatarrhalisch [anti·kata·ra·liʃ], a. Med: Pharm: anticatarrhal.

Antikatarrhalium [anti·kata·'raːlium], n. -s/-lia. Pharm: anticatarrhal.

Antikathode [anti·ka·'toːdə], f. El: anticathode.

antikatholisch [anti·ka·'toːliʃ], a. anticatholic.

Antikbronze, f. Com: 'antique' bronze; bronze with (artificial) patina.

Antikdruckpapier, n. Paperm: antique laid paper.

Antike[1], die [an'tiː·kə], -. antiquity; the ancient world; esp. classical antiquity; the Graeco-Roman world; **die Kunst der A.**, classical art, ancient art, esp. Greek and Roman art; **griechische, römische, klassische, A.**, Greek, Roman, classical, antiquity; **in der A.**, in antiquity; **das Rom der A.**, ancient Rome; **berühmte Städte der A.**, famous cities of antiquity, of the ancient world; **die A. nachahmen**, to imitate the style of classical art; **das Nachleben der A.**, the survival of antiquity.

Antike[2], f. -/-n, (a) classical work of art; esp. classical sculpture; (b) antique; antique work of art; **Antiken** pl, antiques, antiquities.

Antikengrün [an'tiː·kən-], n. Miner: verd-antique.

Antikenhändler, m. antique dealer.

Antikenhandlung, f., **Antikenladen,** m. antique shop.

antikisch [an'tiː·kiʃ], a. in the manner of classical antiquity, of the ancients.

antikisieren [anti·ki·'ziːrən], v.i. (haben) to imitate classical antiquity, classical art; to copy the style of the ancients; **antikisierender Stil**, style modelled on the ancients.

Antikleder, n. Com: 'antique' leather; embossed leather.

antiklerikal [anti·kle·ri·'kaːl], a. anticlerical.

Antiklerikale [anti·kle·ri·'kaːlə], m., f. (decl. as adj.) anticlerical.

Antiklerikalismus [anti·kle·ri·ka·'lismus], m. -/. anticlericalism.

Antiklimax [anti·'kliːmaks], f. Rh: anticlimax.

antiklinal [anti·kli·'naːl], a. Geol: anticlinal.

Antiklinalachse, f. Geol: anticlinal line, axis; saddleback.

Antiklinale [anti·kli·'naːlə], f. -/-n. Geol: anticline, saddle.

Antiklinallinie, f. Geol: anticlinal line; saddleback.

Antiklopfmittel [anti·'klopf-], n. I.C.E: anti-knock agent.

Antikohärer [anti·ko·'hɛːrər], m. -s/-. W.Tel: anticoherer.

Antikommunist [anti·komu·'nist], m. anti-communist.

antikommunistisch [anti·komu·'nistiʃ], a. anti-communist.

Antikompounddynamo [anti·'kompaund,dyna·moː], f. El.E: differential compound-wound dynamo.

antikonstitutionell [anti·konsti·tu·tsio·'nɛl], a. anti-constitutional.

antikonzeptionell [anti·kontsɛptsio·'nɛl], a. contraceptive.

Antikörper ['anti·kørpər], m. Physiol: antibody.

Antikritik [anti·kri·'tiːk], f. counter-criticism.

antiliberal [anti·li·be·'raːl], a. Pol: antiliberal.

Antillen, die [an'tilən]. Pr.n.f.pl. Geog: the Antilles, the West Indies; **die Großen, Kleinen, A.**, the Greater, Lesser, Antilles.

Antilogarithmus [anti·lo·ga·'ritmus], m. Mth: antilogarithm.

Antilogie [anti·lo·'giː], f. -/-n [-'giːən]. Log: antilogy.

antilogisch [anti·'loːgiʃ], a. antilogous.

Antilope [anti·'loːpə], f. -/-n. Z: antelope.

Antimachiavell [anti·makia·'vɛl], m. -s/. Lit: Anti-Machiavelli.

antimagnetisch [anti·ma·'gneːtiʃ], a. antimagnetic; non-magnetizable (watch, etc.).

Antimakassar [anti·ma·'kasa·r], m. -s/-s. A: antimacassar.

Antimaterie [anti·ma·'teːriə], f. -/. Atom.Ph: antimatter.

antimephitisch [anti·me·'fiːtiʃ], a. Med: anti-mephitic.

Antimilitarismus [anti·mi·li·ta·'rismus], m. anti-militarism.

Antimilitarist [anti·mi·li·ta·'rist], m. antimilitarist.

Antimon [anti·'moːn], n. -s/. Ch: antimony.

antimonarchisch [anti·mo·'narçiʃ], a. anti-monarchical.

Antimonarchismus [anti·mo·nar'çismus], m. anti-monarchism.

Antimonarchist [anti·mo·nar'çist], m. anti-monarchist.

Antimonat [anti·mo·'naːt], n. -(e)s/-e. Ch: antimoniate.

Antimonblei, n. Ch: Ind: antimonial lead, hard lead.

Antimonblende, f. Miner: antimony blende, kermesite.

Antimonblüte, f. Miner: antimony bloom, white antimony, valentinite.

Antimonbutter, f. Ch: anhydrous antimony chloride, A: butter of antimony.

Antimonglanz, m. Miner: antimony-glance, grey antimony; stibnite.

Antimonglas, n. Ch: glass of antimony.

antimonhaltig, a. Ch: Pharm: antimonial; containing antimony.

Antimonhütte, f. antimony works.

Antimoniakum [anti·mo·ni·'aːkum], n. -s/-ka. Pharm: antimonial medicine, antimonial.

antimonig [anti·'moːniç], a. Ch: antimonious.

Antimonigsäure, f. Ch: antimonious acid.

antimonisch [anti·'moːniʃ], a. Ch: etc: antimonial; antimonic.

Antimonium [anti·'moːnium], n. -s/. = Antimon.

Antimonkermes, m. Miner: Pharm: kermes mineral.

Antimonpentoxyd, n. Ch: antimony pentoxide.

antimonsauer, a. Ch: antimoniate of ....

Antimonsäure, f. Ch: antimonic acid.

Antimonsulfid, n. Ch: antimony sulfide, black antimony.

Antimonwasserstoff, m. Ch: antimoniuretted hydrogen; stibine.

Antimonzinnober, m. Miner: Pharm: kermes mineral.

antimoralisch [anti·mo·'raːliʃ], a. antimoral.

antinational [anti·na·tsio·'naːl], a. antinational.

Antinaturalismus [anti·na·tu·ra·'lismus], m. anti-naturalism.

antinephritisch [anti·ne·'friːtiʃ], a. Pharm: anti-nephritic.

Antineutron [anti·'noytron], n. -s/-en [-'troːnən]. Atom.Ph: antineutron.

Antinomianer [anti·no·mi·'aːnər], m. -s/-. Rel.Hist: antinomian.

Antinomie [anti·no·'miː], f. -/-n [-'miːən], anti-nomy.

antinomisch [anti·'noːmiʃ], a. antinomic.

Antinomismus [anti·no·'mismus], m. Rel.Hist: antinomianism.

Antinomist [anti·no·'mist], m. -en/-en. Rel.Hist: antinomian.

antiochenisch [anti·o·'xeːniʃ], a. A.Geog: Antiochian; Theol: Antiochene (liturgy); **die Antiochenische Schule**, the Antiochian School.

Antiochia [anti·o·'xiːa:, anti·'oxia:], **Antiochien** [anti·'oxiən]. Pr.n.n. -s. A.Geog: Antioch.

Antipapismus [anti·pa·'pismus], m. antipopery.

Antipapist [anti·pa·'pist], m. antipapist.

antipapistisch [anti·pa·'pistiʃ], a. antipapal; antipapist; Hist: **antipapistische Aufruhre**, no-popery riots.

antiparallel [anti·paraˈleːl], *a. Geom:* antiparallel.

Antiparallele [anti·paraˈleːlə], *f. Geom:* antiparallel.

Antiparallelogramm [anti·parale·lo·ˈgram], *n. Geom:* antiparallelogram, isosceles trapezoid.

Antipassat [anti·paˈsaːt], *m. Nau:* anti-trade (wind).

Antipathie [anti·pa·ˈtiː], *f.* -/-n [-ˈtiːən], antipathy (**gegen**, to, against, for).

antipathisch [anti·ˈpaːtiʃ], *a.* antipathetic (**gegen**, to).

Antipatriot [anti·pa·tri·ˈoːt], *m.* antipatriot.

antipatriotisch [anti·pa·tri·ˈoːtiʃ], *a.* antipatriotic.

Antipatriotismus [anti·patri·o·ˈtismus], *m.* antipatriotism.

Antiperistaltik [anti·pe·ri·ˈstaltik], *f.* -/. *Physiol:* antiperistalsis, antivermicular motion.

antiperistaltisch [anti·pe·ri·ˈstaltiʃ], *a. Physiol:* antiperistaltic, antivermicular.

Antiphon[1] [anti·ˈfoːn], *n.* **-s/-e**, ear-plug.

Antiphon[2], *f.* **-/-en.** *Ecc.Mus:* antiphon.

Antiphonale [anti·fo·ˈnaːlə], *n.* **-/-n, Antiphonar** [anti·fo·ˈnaːr], *n.* **-s/-e.** *Ecc:* antiphonary.

Antiphone [anti·ˈfoːnə], *f.* **-/-n, Antiphonie** [anti·fo·ˈniː], *f.* **-/-n** [-ˈniːən]. *Ecc:* antiphon.

antiphonisch [anti·ˈfoːniʃ], *a. Ecc:* antiphonal.

Antiphrase [anti·ˈfraːzə], *f. Rh:* antiphrasis.

Antiphthisikum [anti·ˈftiːzi·kum], *n.* **-s/-ka.** *Med:* antitubercular medicine.

antiphthisisch [anti·ˈftiːziʃ], *a. Med:* antitubercular.

Antiplanet [anti·pla·ˈneːt], *m. Phot:* antiplanat; antiplanatic lens.

Antipode [anti·ˈpoːdə], *m.* **-/-n.** 1. person diametrically opposite to another person on the earth's surface; dweller in the antipodes; *Geog:* **die Antipoden,** the antipodes. 2. *F:* person of diametrically opposed views.

antipodisch [anti·ˈpoːdiʃ], *a.* 1. *Geog:* antipodal; antipodean. 2. diametrically opposed.

Antipol [ˈanti·poːl], *m. Mth:* antipole.

antippen, *v.tr. & i. sep.* (*haben*) **j-n, etwas, a., an etwas** *acc.* **a.,** to tap, touch, s.o., sth. (lightly); to give s.o., sth., a (light) tap; *F:* **ein Thema a.,** to touch (lightly) on a subject; **bei j-m a.,** to sound s.o.

Antiprohibitionist [anti·pro·hi·bi·tsi̯o·ˈnist], *m. Pol:* antiprohibitionist.

Antiprotektionist [anti·pro·tɛktsi̯o·ˈnist], *m. Pol:* antiprotectionist.

Antiproton [anti·ˈproːton], *n.* **-s/-en** [-pro·ˈtoːnən]. *Atom.Ph:* antiproton.

Antipyretikum [anti·py·ˈreːti·kum], *n.* **-s/-ka.** *Med:* antipyretic.

antipyretisch [anti·py·ˈreːtiʃ], *a. Med:* antipyretic.

Antipyrin [anti·py·ˈriːn], *n.* **-s/.** *Pharm:* antipyrin(e).

Antiqua [anˈtiːkvaː], *f.* **-/.** *Print:* roman type; **Umdruck in A.,** romanization.

Antiquabuchstaben, *m.pl. Print:* roman characters, roman letters; roman type.

Antiquar [anti·ˈkvaːr], *m.* **-s/-e,** (*a*) second-hand bookseller; antiquarian bookseller; (*b*) antiquarian; curio-dealer.

Antiquariat [anti·kva·riˈaːt], *n.* **-(e)s/-e,** second-hand bookshop; antiquarian bookshop.

Antiquariatsbuchhändler, *m.*=**Antiquar** (*a*).

Antiquariatsbuchhandlung, *f.*=**Antiquariat.**

antiquarisch [anti·ˈkvaːriʃ], *a.* 1. historical (method, characteristics, etc.); antiquarian. 2. second-hand (book, bookshop); antiquarian (bookshop); *adv.* **ein Buch a. kaufen,** to buy a book second-hand, to buy a second-hand copy of a book.

Antiquarium [anti·ˈkvaːri̯um], *n.* **-s/-rien,** antiquarium; collection of antiquities.

Antiquaschrift [anˈtiːkvaː-], *f.* 1. (*written or incised*) Trajan lettering. 2. *Print:* roman type; roman letters, roman characters.

antiquieren [anti·ˈkviːrən]. 1. *v.i.* (*sein*) to become antiquated, obsolete; to go out of use, out of fashion; to become out-of-date; **antiquiert,** antiquated, obsolete, out-of-date. 2. *occ. v.tr.* to render (sth.) obsolete.

Antiquität [anti·kvi·ˈtɛːt], *f.* **-/-en,** antique; **Antiquitäten** *pl*, antiques, (i) old curiosities, (ii) antiquities.

Antiquitätenhandel [anti·kvi·ˈtɛːtən-], *m.* trade in antiques, antique trade.

Antiquitätenhändler, *m.* antique dealer; curio-dealer.

Antiquitätenhandlung, *f.*, **Antiquitätenladen,** *m.* antique shop; curio-shop.

Antiquitätensammler, *m.* antiquarian; collector of antiques; curio-collector, curio-hunter.

antirachitisch [anti·raˈxiːtiʃ], *a. Med:* antirachitic (vitamin, etc.).

Antirepublikaner [anti·re·pu·bli·ˈkaːnər], *m.* antirepublican.

antirepublikanisch [anti·re·pu·bli·ˈkaːniʃ], *a.* antirepublican.

antirevolutionär[1] [anti·re·vo·lu·tsi̯o·ˈnɛːr], *a.* antirevolutionary.

Antirevolutionär[2], *m.* antirevolutionary.

Antirrhinum [anti·ˈriːnum], *n.* **-s/.** *Bot:* antirrhinum, snapdragon.

Antisemit [anti·ze·ˈmiːt], *m.* anti-Semite.

antisemitisch [anti·ze·ˈmiːtiʃ], *a.* anti-Semitic.

Antisemitismus [anti·ze·mi·ˈtismus], *m.* anti-Semitism.

Antisepsis [anti·ˈzɛpsis], *f. Med:* antisepsis.

Antiseptikum [anti·ˈzɛpti·kum], *n.* **-s/-ka.** *Med:* antiseptic.

antiseptisch [anti·ˈzɛptiʃ], *a. Med:* antiseptic.

Antiserum [anti·ˈzeːrum], *n. Med:* antiserum.

Antisklavereibewegung, *f. Hist:* antislavery movement, *U.S:* abolitionist movement.

Antiskorbutikum [anti·skorˈbuːti·kum], *n.* **-s/-ka.** *Pharm:* antiscorbutic.

antiskorbutisch [anti·skorˈbuːtiʃ], *a. Pharm:* antiscorbutic.

antisozial [anti·zo·tsi̯ˈaːl], *a.* antisocial.

Antistrophe [anti·ˈstroːfə], *f.* antistrophe.

Antiteilchen [ˈanti·tailçən], *n. Atom.Ph:* antiparticle.

Antitetanikum [anti·te·ˈtaːni·kum], *n.* **-s/-ka.** *Med:* antitetanic.

antitetanisch [anti·te·ˈtaːniʃ], *a. Med:* antitetanic.

Antithese [anti·ˈteːzə], *f.* 1. antithesis; counterthesis; *esp. Phil:* antithesis (in the Hegelian triad). 2. antithesis, direct contrast (**zu, von,** to, of).

Antithetik [anti·ˈteːtik], *f.* **-/.** 1. *Phil:* antithetics. 2. use, arrangement, of contrasting ideas.

antithetisch [anti·ˈteːtiʃ], *a.* antithetic(al); in strong contrast.

Antitoxin [anti·toˈksiːn], *n. Med:* antitoxin.

Antitoxineinheit, *f. Med:*=**Immunitätseinheit.**

Antitrinitarier [anti·tri·ni·ˈtaːriər], *m. Rel:* Antitrinitarian.

antitrinitarisch [anti·tri·ni·ˈtaːriʃ], *a. Rel:* antitrinitarian.

Antitrustgesetz [anti·ˈtrast-], *n.* anti-trust law.

Antitypus [ˈanti·ˌty·pus], *m.* antitype.

Antiwagnerianer [anti·vaːgne·riˈaːnər], *m.* anti-Wagnerite.

antizipando [anti·tsi·ˈpandoː], *adv. Com: Fin:* in anticipation; (to pay) in advance; **Zahlung a.,** advance payment, prepayment.

Antizipandozinsen, *m.pl. Fin:* anticipated interest; interest paid before it is due.

Antizipation [anti·tsi·pa·tsi̯ˈoːn], *f.* **-/-en,** (*a*) anticipation; (*b*) *Mus:* anticipation (of harmony); (*c*) *Rh: Gram:* prolepsis.

antizipativ [anti·tsi·pa·ˈtiːf], *a.* anticipatory, anticipative; **antizipative** [anti·tsi·pa·ˈtiːvə] **Zahlung,** advance payment, prepayment.

antizipieren [anti·tsi·ˈpiːrən], *v.tr.* to anticipate; **antizipierende, antizipierte, Zahlung,** advance payment, prepayment.

Antizyklone [anti·tsy·ˈkloːnə], *f. Meteor:* anticyclone.

antizyklonisch [anti·tsy·ˈkloːniʃ], *a.* anticyclonic.

Antizymotikum [anti·tsy·ˈmoːti·kum], *n.* **-s/-ka,** anti-fermentation agent.

Antlaßtag, *m. South G.Dial:* Maundy Thursday.

Antlitz, *n.* **-es/-e.** *B. & Lit:* face, *Lit:* countenance, visage; *B:* **das Licht seines Antlitzes,** the light of his countenance; **Gott lasse uns sein A. leuchten,** God cause his face to shine upon us.

antoben, *v. sep.* 1. *v.i.* (*haben*) **gegen etwas a.,** to rage at, against, sth. 2. *v.i.* (*sein*) (*usu. only in the phr.*) **angetobt kommen,** (i) to come raging along, up; (ii) to come along making a great commotion, an awful row.

Antöken [anˈtøːkən], *m.pl. Geog:* antoeci, antoecians.

Anton [ˈantoːn]. *Pr.n.m.* **-s.** Ant(h)ony; **Mark A.,** Marcus Antonius, Mark Antony.

antönen, *v.i. sep.* (*haben*) to sound; (*of trumpet, etc.*) to resound, *Lit:* to sound forth.

Antonia, Antonie [anˈtoːniaː, -ni̯ə]. *Pr.n.f.* **-s** & *Lit:* **-niens.** Antonia, Antoinette.

Antoninen, die [anto·ˈniːnən]. *Pr.n.m.pl. Rom. Hist:* the Antonines.

Antoninus [anto·ˈniːnus]. *Pr.n.m.* **-'.** Antoninus; *Rom.Hist:* **A. Pius,** Antoninus Pius.

Antonius [anˈtoːni̯us]. *Pr.n.m.* **-'.** Antonius, Ant(h)ony; **Marcus A.,** Marcus Antonius, Mark Antony; *Rel.Hist:* **der heilige A. (von Padua),** St Anthony (of Padua); **der heilige A. der Große,** *F:* **mit der Sau,** St Anthony the Great.

Antoniusfeuer, *n. Med: A:* erysipelas, *F:* the rose; St Anthony's fire.

Antoniuskraut, *n. Bot: F:* willow-herb, rose bay, French willow.

Antoniuskreuz, *n. Her:* St Anthony's cross, tau-cross.

Antonomasie [anto·no·ma·ˈziː], *f.* **-/-n** [-ˈziːən]. *Rh:* antonomasia.

Antonskraut, *n.*=**Antoniuskraut.**

Antonym [anto·ˈnyːm], *n.* **-s/-e,** antonym.

antraben, *v.i. sep.* (*sein*) 1. (*usu. in the phr.*) **angetrabt kommen,** to come trotting along, up. 2. to start trotting; to break into a trot.

Antrag, *m.* **-(e)s/⸗e.** 1. (*a*) proposal, proposition; (*in assembly*) motion; **einen A. stellen, einbringen,** to propose, bring forward, a motion; to make a proposal; to move a resolution; **einen A. unterstützen,** to second a motion; **einen A. annehmen,** to carry a motion; to adopt a resolution; **einen A. durchbringen,** to get a resolution adopted; **der A. wurde angenommen, ging durch,** the motion was carried; **der A. wurde abgelehnt, fiel durch,** the motion was rejected, was lost; **auf A.** *acc.* **des Herrn X (hin),** on the motion, on the proposal, of Mr X; **A. auf etwas** *acc.*, motion for sth., to do sth.; **A. auf Abstimmung,** motion, proposal, to put the matter to the vote; **den A. auf Vertagung stellen,** to put the motion for adjournment, to adjourn; (*b*) *Parl:*= **Gesetzesantrag;** (*c*) application, *Jur:* petition, request, (**auf**+*acc.*, for); **einen A. stellen,** to make an application, to apply; *Jur:* to enter a petition; **auf j-s A.** *acc.* **(hin),** on application by, from, s.o.; at the request of s.o.; *Jur:* at the suit of s.o.; *Jur:* **A. auf Konkurs,** petition in bankruptcy. 2. offer, overture; *esp.* offer, proposal, of marriage; **einem Mädchen einen A. machen,** to propose to a girl.

antragen, *v.sep.* (*strong*) 1. *v.tr.* (*a*) to bring (sth.) along; to bring, carry up (earth, timber, etc.); *Ven:* (*of dog*) to retrieve (game); (*b*) to apply (coating, veneer, etc.); (*c*) to offer; **j-m ein Amt a.,** to offer s.o. an official post; **einem Mädchen seine Hand a.,** to propose to a girl. 2. *v.i.* (*haben*) **auf etwas** *acc.* **a.,** (i) to propose sth.; (ii) *Dial:* to strive after sth.

Antragsdelikt, *n. Jur:* offence punishable only on the petition of the injured party.

Antragsformular, *n.* application form, *U.S:* application blank.

Antragsteller, *m.* (*a*) mover of a proposal; proposer of a motion; (*b*) applicant; *Jur:* petitioner.

antrauen, *v.tr. sep.* **j-n j-m a.,** to marry s.o. to s.o.; **mein angetrautes Weib, das mir angetraute Weib,** my wedded wife.

antreffen, *v.tr. sep.* (*strong*) 1. (*a*) to meet, fall in with (s.o.); to find (s.o.); *esp.* to find (s.o.) at home; **j-n bei etwas** *dat.* **a.,** to catch, find, s.o. doing sth.; **ich ging zu seiner Wohnung und traf ihn glücklicherweise an,** I went to his flat and was fortunate enough to find, catch, him in; **wir hoffen, diese Zeilen treffen Euch bei guter Gesundheit an,** we hope this finds you in good health; (*b*) to encounter, find, meet with, come across (s.o., sth.); **solche Männer trifft man selten an,** such men are seldom found, seldom met with; one rarely encounters such men. 2. *A:* to affect (s.o.); **das trifft mich nicht an,** that does not affect me.

antreiben, *v.sep.* (*strong*) I. *v.tr.* 1. to drive (sth.) along; to goad on (cattle); to urge (horse, cattle) along; (*of waters, sea*) to carry (sth.) along; to float, wash, (sth.) ashore. 2. (*a*) to impel, propel (ship, etc.); to actuate (machine); to drive (machine, vehicle); **die Maschine wird durch Dampfkraft angetrieben,** the machine is driven, worked, by steam; **antreibende Kraft,** impulsive force, impelling force; (*b*) to drive, impel, urge, actuate (s.o.); **j-n zu etwas a.; j-n a., etwas zu tun,** to urge s.o. (on) to sth., to do sth.; to egg s.o. on to sth., to do sth.; to goad s.o. into doing sth.; to prompt s.o. to sth., to do sth.; to induce, instigate, s.o. to do sth.; to stimulate s.o. to sth., to do sth.; **j-n zum Fleiß a.,** to urge s.o. to be diligent; **durch geheime Beweggründe angetrieben,** impelled, actuated, by secret motives; (*c*) *Hort:* to force (plants). 3. to drive (sth.) on; to drive (sth.) in; **einen Keil a.,** to drive (in) a wedge; *Coop:* **einen Faßreifen a.,** to drive on a barrel hoop; **ein Faß a.,** to drive on the hoops of a barrel, to hoop, truss, a barrel.

II. **antreiben,** *v.i.* 1. (*sein*) (*of ice-floes, driftwood, etc.*) to drift up; to be washed up; to be washed ashore. 2. (*haben*) (*of plants*) to put forth shoots.

III. *vbl s.* **Antreiben** *n.*, **Antreibung** *f. in vbl senses; also:* impulsion; stimulation; incitement, incitation (**zu** to). *Cp.* **Antrieb.**

Antreiber, *m.* **1.** prompter; impeller; urger (on); inciter, instigator (**zu,** to). **2.** *Coop:* hooper.

Antreibesystem, *n. Hist: Ind:* system of exploiting the workers; sweating system.

Antreibmaschine, *f. Coop:* hooping machine.

antreten, *v.sep.* (*strong*) I. *v.i.* (*sein*) **1.** (*a*) *A:* **zu j-m a.,** to walk up to s.o.; (*b*) **bei j-m a.,** to wait upon, call upon, s.o., to report to s.o. **2.** to take one's place (in a rank, for a dance, at work, etc.); *Mil: etc:* to fall in, to form up, to line up; *F:* to toe the line, the mark; **zum Tanz a.,** to take one's place in the dance, to join the dancers; **er muß Punkt fünf Uhr in der Fabrik a.,** he has to be in his place at the factory, *F:* he has to clock in, *U.S:* he has to punch the clock, at five o'clock sharp; *Mil: etc:* **antreten! angetreten!** fall in! form up! **ich muß in zehn Minuten a.,** I'm on parade in ten minutes' time; **zum Dienst a.,** to assume one's duties; to report for duty; *Sp:* **zum Hundertmeterlauf a.,** to line up, get on the mark, for the hundred metres; *F:* **mit a.,** to do one's share (of the work). **3.** to step off; **mit dem linken Fuß a.,** to step off with the left foot. **4.** *Cy:* to tread (hard) on the pedals; to put on speed, *F:* to step on it. **5.** *Sp:* to limber up (before a race, etc.).

II. **antreten,** *v.tr.* **1.** (**sich** *dat.*) **Erde an den Schuh a.,** to get earth on one's shoe; **Erde a.,** to tread down earth. **2. ein Motorrad a.,** to start a motor-cycle (with kick-starter). **3.** *A:* to step up to (s.o.); to approach (s.o.); to accost (s.o.); *Lit:* **rasch tritt der Tod den Menschen an,** death swiftly steals upon us. **4.** (*a*) to enter upon (sth.); to begin (sth.); **ein Amt a.,** to enter upon, accede to, an office; **sein Amt a.,** to take, assume, office; to enter upon, take up, one's duties; **Bismarck hat 1871 das Reichskanzleramt angetreten,** Bismarck assumed office as Imperial Chancellor in 1871; **die Macht a.,** to assume power; to come into power, into office; **die Regierung a.,** (i) (*of monarch*) to begin his reign, to come to the throne; (ii) (*of party*) to come into power, into office; **einen Beruf a.,** to enter (upon) a profession; **ein Geschäft a.,** to embark on a business; **eine Stelle a.,** to take up a position, to start an employment, to start in a (new) job; **eine Reise a.,** to start on, set out on, set off on, a journey; **das neue Jahr a.,** to begin the New Year; **er hat sein sechzigstes Jahr angetreten,** he has entered upon, is already in, his sixtieth year; **ein Erbe, eine Erbschaft, den Besitz eines Gutes, a.,** to enter upon an inheritance; to come into, take possession of, an inheritance, an estate; *Jur:* **seine Strafe, die Haft, a.,** to begin (serving) one's sentence; (*b*) *Jur:* **den Beweis a.,** to offer proof (**für,** of).

III. *vbl s.* **Antreten,** *n. in vbl senses; cp.* **Antritt.**

Antreteplatz, *m.* parade area (for troops, etc.).

Antrieb, *m.* **1.** *Mec:* impulse; impulsion; impulsive, impelling, force; propulsion; propulsive, propelling, force. **2.** *Mec.E:* drive; driving-gear; **Maschine, Wagen, mit elektrischem A.,** electrically driven machine; electrically driven, propelled, car; **seitlicher, rückwärtiger, A.,** lateral, rear, drive; **Rakete mit neuartigem A.,** rocket with a new method of propulsion, with a new type of drive. **3.** impulse, impulsion, impetus, urge; stimulus, incentive, inducement; **etwas aus eigenem A., aus freiem A., tun,** to do sth. of one's own accord, spontaneously, of one's own free will, of one's own volition; **aus natürlichem A.,** instinctively, by, from, instinct; **aus innerem A.,** from an inner, inward, urge; from inner compulsion; **sie fühlte nicht den geringsten A., sich mit ihm zu versöhnen,** she felt not the slightest impulse, inclination, she did not feel at all impelled, to make it up with him; **dem Handel einen neuen A. geben,** to give a stimulus, an impulse, a fillip, to trade; **die Geschäfte haben einen neuen A. bekommen,** business has received fresh impetus, shows renewed activity; **es fehlt heute jeder A. zum Sparen,** today there is no incentive, inducement, at all to save.

Antriebs-, *comb.fm. Mec.E: Mch: El.E:* driving . . . ; **Antriebsmagnet** *m,* driving magnet; **Antriebsmotor** *m,* driving motor; **Antriebsspindel** *f,* driving spindle; **Antriebsstange** *f,* driving rod.

Antriebsabteil, *n. Veh:* gear-box compartment.

Antriebsachse, *f. Mec.E:* live axle; *Aut: Rail:* driving axle.

Antriebsbahn, *f. Rocketry:* powered trajectory.

Antriebsdeckenvorgelege, *n. Mec.E:* overhead driving gear.

Antriebskasten, *m. Aut:* gear-box.

Antriebskegelrad, *n. Aut:* bevel pinion.

Antriebskette, *f. Mec.E:* driving chain.

Antriebsmaschine, *f.* driving engine; **die Antriebsmaschinen,** (i) *Mec.E:* the driving machinery; (ii) *Nau:* the propelling machinery, the engines.

Antriebsmittel, *n.* **1.** means of propulsion; propelling agent. **2.** incentive.

Antriebsrad, *n. Mec.E:* driving wheel, driver.

Antriebsriemen, *m. Mec.E:* driving belt.

Antriebsriemenscheibe, *f. Mec.E:* driving pulley.

Antriebsritzel, *n. Mec.E:* driving pinion.

Antriebsscheibe, *f. Mec.E:* driving pulley.

Antriebsstrang, *m. Ind:* driving line.

Antriebsvorrichtung, *f. Mec.E:* driving gear.

Antriebswelle, *f. Mec.E:* driving shaft, power shaft, engine shaft, main shaft; *Aut:* clutch shaft; *I.C.E:* feed shaft.

Antriebszahnrad, *n. Mec.E:* driving pinion.

antrinken, *v.sep.* (*strong*) **1.** *v.tr.* (*a*) to start drinking (glass of wine, etc.); **angetrunkenes Glas,** glass that has (already) been drunk from; (*b*) **sich** *dat.* **einen (Rausch, Spitz) a.,** to get tipsy, fuddled, *F:* tight; **sich** *dat.* **Mut a.,** to drink to give oneself courage; to stiffen one's courage with drink, *F:* to take a drop of Dutch courage; (*c*) **angetrunken sein,** to be partially intoxicated; **in angetrunkenem Zustand,** in a state of partial intoxication; **stark angetrunken sein,** to be much the worse for drink. **2.** *v.i.* (*haben*) to drink first, take the first drink.

Antritt, *m.* **1.** (*a*)=**antreten** III; (*b*) *Cy:* burst (of speed); spurt (*cp.* **antreten** I. 4). **2.** beginning, starting; entering (upon sth.); entrance (into sth.); **A. eines Amtes,** accession to, assumption of, entrance into, an office; entrance upon one's duties; **A. der Macht,** assumption of power, accession to power; **A. der Regierung,** (i) (*monarch's*) accession to the throne, beginning of his *or* her reign; (ii) (*party's*) accession to power; **A. einer Stelle,** taking up of a post, a position; **A. einer Reise,** setting off, out, starting, on a journey; departure; **A. eines Erbes, einer Erbschaft,** entering into possession, taking possession, of an inheritance; accession to an estate. **3.** (*a*) first step, bottom step (of staircase, flight of steps); (*b*) short ladder.

Antrittsaudienz, *f.* first audience (of minister, etc.).

Antrittsbesuch, *m.* first visit, formal call.

Antrittsgeld, *n.* **sein A. bezahlen,** (i) to pay one's admission fee, one's entrance fee; (ii) to pay one's footing.

Antrittspredigt, *f.* (newly-appointed clergyman's) first sermon.

Antrittsrede, *f.* inaugural address.

Antrittsrolle, *f. Th:* (*a*) part played by an actor at his first appearance; first part; (*b*) inaugural part; part played at the opening of a theatre, beginning of a season, etc.

Antrittsschmaus, *m.* dinner to celebrate (s.o.'s) appointment to an office.

Antrittsvorlesung, *f. Sch:* inaugural lecture, *F:* inaugural.

antrocknen, *v.i. sep.* (*sein*) to begin to dry; **die Wäsche a. lassen,** to let the washing part-dry; **an etwas** *acc.* **a.,** to dry on to sth.

Antrunk, *m.* first drink; **den A. haben,** to take the first drink, to drink first.

antun. I. *v.tr. sep.* (*strong*) **1.** to put on, *A:* to don (garment). **2.** (*a*) **j-m etwas a.,** to do sth. to s.o.; **j-m Ehre a.,** to do honour to, to honour, s.o.; **j-m Gutes, Liebes, a.,** to do s.o. a kindness, to act kindly towards s.o.; **j-m Böses a.,** to do s.o. harm, to harm, hurt, s.o.; **j-m Schimpf a.,** to put an affront upon s.o., to offer an affront to s.o.; **j-m Schande a.,** to disgrace s.o., bring disgrace upon s.o.; **du würdest kaum wagen, mir das anzutun!** you would hardly dare to do such a thing to me! **j-m, etwas** *dat.,* **Gewalt a.,** to do violence to s.o., sth.; **einem Mädchen, einer Frau, Gewalt a.,** to ravish, violate, outrage, force, rape, a girl, a woman; **dem Sinne eines Wortes, einer Stelle, Gewalt a.,** to force, strain, twist, wrench, wrest, the sense of a word, the meaning of a passage; **sich** *dat.* **Zwang a.,** (i) to restrain oneself; to keep one's feelings in check; to hold back; (ii) to compel oneself (to do sth.); to overcome one's reluctance; **sich** *dat.* **keinen Zwang a.,** to put no restraint on oneself; to let oneself go; to be free and easy; **sich** *dat.* **ein Leid(s),** *F:* **etwas, a.,** to lay violent hands on oneself, to commit suicide; (*b*) **es j-m a.,** to fascinate, captivate, charm, s.o.; to take, please, s.o.'s fancy; **er hat es ihr sofort angetan,** *F:* she fell for him at once.

II. *p.p. & pred.a.* **angetan,** *in vbl senses; esp.* **1.** dressed, apparelled; **a. mit ihrem ganzen Staat,** dressed out, *F:* tricked out, got up, in all her finery; **lächerlich a.,** ridiculously dressed, *F:* in a ridiculous get-up. **2.** (*of facts, situation, etc.*) **danach, dazu, a., zu . . . ,** of a nature, of a kind, calculated, to . . . ; **die Verhältnisse sind (ganz) danach a., uns die Ferien zu verleiden,** conditions are such that they are (very) likely to, will (very) probably, spoil our holiday for us; **die Situation ist nicht danach a., die Aktionäre zu erfreuen,** the situation shows little likelihood, little promise, of pleasing the shareholders. **3. von j-m, etwas, a. sein,** to have a liking, a fancy, a fondness, for s.o., sth.; to be taken with s.o., sth.; **er ist sehr von sich angetan,** he has a very high opinion of himself, *F:* he fancies himself.

antupfen, *v.tr. sep.* to dab, pat (sth.) (with finger, cloth, sponge, etc.).

antuschen, *v.tr. sep. Art:* to tint (a drawing) with a wash, to wash (a drawing).

Antvogel, *m. North G.Dial:* duck.

Antwerpen [ˈantvɛrpən, antˈvɛrpən]. *Pr.n.n.* **-s.** *Geog:* Antwerp.

Antwerpener, Antwerper. 1. *m.* **-s/-,** inhabitant, native, of Antwerp. **2.** *inv.a.* of Antwerp, Antwerp . . .

Antwort, *f.* **-/-en,** (*a*) answer, reply; response (**auf**+*acc.,* to); **schlagfertige A.,** retort; pat answer, *U.S. & F:* snappy answer, quick comeback; **eine A. geben,** to give an answer, to make a reply; **j-m eine A. geben,** *A. & Poet:* **j-m A. sagen,** to return s.o. an answer, to answer s.o., to make a reply, to reply, to s.o.; **eine freche A. geben,** to give an impudent, *F:* a cheeky, answer; to answer back; **sie gab keine A.,** she gave no answer, made no reply, no response; **als A. auf diese Bemerkung . . . ,** in answer, in reply, to this remark . . . ; **als A. zeigte er auf die Tür,** for answer he pointed to the door; **als einzige A. brach sie in Schluchzen aus,** her only answer was to break into sobs; **keine A. schuldig bleiben, um keine A. verlegen sein,** to have, find, an answer for everything; never to be at a loss for an answer; **er ist immer gleich mit einer A. bei der Hand,** he is always ready with an answer; he always answers pat, has an answer pat; **j-m (über etwas** *acc.***) Rede und A. stehen,** to give s.o. a full account (of sth.); to answer to s.o. (for sth.); **A. auf einen Brief, auf eine Einladung,** answer, reply, to a letter, to an invitation; acknowledgement of a letter; **umgehende A.,** answer by return (of post); **der Brief bedarf keiner A.,** the letter needs no answer, there is no need to answer the letter; **um A. wird gebeten, (u.A.w.g.),** an answer is requested, (R.S.V.P.); *Com:* **in A. auf Ihr geehrtes Schreiben vom 20. d.M. . . . ,** in answer to your letter of the 20th inst. . . . ; *Tg:* **A. bezahlt,** reply paid, *U.S:* answer prepaid; *Tp:* **Ich bekam keine A.,** I got no reply, no one answered (the telephone); **'keine A.',** 'no reply'; *Prov:* **keine A. ist auch eine A.,** (i) silence gives consent; (ii) silence means 'no'; (*b*) response (**auf einen Anreiz, usw.,** to a stimulus, etc.); (*c*) *Ecc:* response; (*d*) *Mus:* real answer (*in fugue*).

antworten. 1. *v.i.* (*haben*) (*a*) to answer, reply; to respond (**auf**+*acc.,* to); **auf eine Frage a.,** to answer, reply to, a question; **j-m a.; auf j-s Frage a., j-m auf seine Frage a.,** to answer s.o.; to reply to s.o.'s question, to a question from s.o.; **mit ja, mit nein, a.,** to answer yes, no; **er antwortete mit einem Nicken,** he nodded in answer; he gave an answering nod; **sie antwortete nicht,** she did not answer; she gave no answer, made no reply, no response; **der Junge antwortete frech,** the boy gave an impudent, *F:* a cheeky, answer; the boy answered back; **auf meine Frage antwortete sie, daß . . . ,** in reply to my question she said that . . . ; her answer to my question was that . . . ; **er antwortete, daß ich unrecht habe,** he answered, replied, that I was wrong; **auf einen Brief, auf eine Einladung, a.,** to answer, reply to, a letter, an invitation; to acknowledge a letter; **umgehend auf einen Brief a.,** to answer a letter by return (of post); *Ecc:* **dem (Messe lesenden) Priester a.,** to make the responses (at Mass); *Mil:* **auf das Feindfeuer a.,** to answer the enemy's fire; *abs.* **a.,** *Tp:* to answer (the telephone); **man antwortet nicht,** they do not answer, there is no reply; (*b*) to respond (**auf einen Anreiz, usw.,** to a stimulus, etc.). **2.** *v.tr.* **etwas a.,** to make some reply; **ich habe nichts geantwortet,** I made no reply, no answer; **kein einziges Wort a.,** to answer not a (single) word; **was haben Sie darauf zu antworten?** what have you to say in reply?

Antwortgesang, *m. Ecc:* (sung) response.

Antwortkarte, *f. Post:* reply card.

antwortlich, *prep.* (+ *gen.*) in answer, in reply (to a communication).
Antwortpostkarte, *f. Post:* reply postcard.
Antwortschein, *m. Post:* **internationaler A.,** international reply coupon.
Antwortsignal, *n. Nau: Tp: etc:* answering signal.
Antwort(s)schreiben, *n.* (written) answer, reply; answering letter.
Antwort(s)schrift, *f.* (*a*) = **Antwort(s)schreiben;** (*b*) (*in controversy*) rejoinder, reply.
Antwortzeichen, *n. Tp: etc:* answering signal.
anüben, *v.tr. sep.* **sich** *dat.* **eine Fertigkeit a.,** to acquire a skill (by practice); **angeübte Fertigkeit,** acquired skill.
anulken, *v.tr. sep. F:* to make fun of (s.o.); to hoax (s.o.); to pull (s.o.'s) leg; to take a rise out of (s.o.); to rag (s.o.).
-anum, *s.suff.n.* (*suffixed to proper name*) . . . Institute; **Goetheanum,** Goethe Institute.
An- und Abfuhr, *f.* -/-en, cartage, carting, haulage, carriage.
Anundfürsichsein, *n. Phil:* noumenal existence.
Anuren [aˈnuːrən], *n.pl. Amph:* an(o)ura.
Anurie [anˀuˑˈriː], *f.* -/. *Med:* anuresis, anuria.
Anus [ˈaːnus], *m.* -/-. *Anat:* anus.
anvertrauen. I. *v.tr. sep.* **1. j-m etwas a.,** to (en)trust s.o. with sth., to entrust sth. to s.o., to entrust, commit, consign, sth. to s.o.'s care, to entrust s.o. with the care of sth., to place sth. in s.o.'s charge; *Jur:* to deliver sth. to s.o. in trust; **die ihm anvertraute Stelle,** the position entrusted to him; **wagst du, ihm soviel Geld anzuvertrauen?** do you dare to trust him with that much money? **j-n j-m a., j-n der Obhut j-s a.,** to entrust s.o. to s.o.'s care, to commit, consign, s.o. to s.o.'s care, to the charge of s.o.; **j-m eine Aufgabe, eine Angelegenheit, a.,** to (en)trust, charge, s.o. with a task, to entrust a task to s.o.; to put a matter in the hands of s.o.; **sich etwas** *dat.* **a.,** to trust in sth., to put one's trust in sth.; **sich der Vorsehung a.,** to trust to Providence; **sich, seine Seele, Gott a.,** to commit one's soul to God; *Jur: etc:* **anvertrautes Gut,** (property held in) trust. **2. j-m etwas a.,** to confide sth. to s.o.; to tell s.o. sth. in confidence, to disclose, impart, sth. to s.o. in confidence; **j-m ein Geheimnis a.,** to entrust s.o. with a secret, to tell s.o. a secret; **sich j-m a.,** to confide in s.o.; to unbosom oneself, open one's heart, to s.o.
II. *vbl s.* **Anvertrauen** *n.*, **Anvertrauung** *f. in vbl senses; also:* consignment, commitment (to s.o.'s care).
anverwandeln, *v.tr. sep.* **sich** *dat.* **etwas a.,** to assimilate sth.; **Anverwandlung** *f,* assimilation.
anverwandt, *a.* related (*esp.* by marriage) (*dat.,* to); **sie ist mir a.,** she is a relative, a relation, of mine; **einer Familie a. sein,** to be related to a family; to be connected with a family (by marriage).
Anverwandte, *m.,f.* (*decl. as adj.*) relative, relation (*esp. by marriage*); connection; kinsman, kinswoman.
Anverwandtschaft, *f.* kinship, relationship; connection (by marriage).
anvettern (sich), *v.refl. sep.* **sich bei j-m a.,** to try to become intimate with s.o., to make up to s.o., to curry favour with s.o., *F:* to try to get in with s.o.
anvisieren, *v.tr. sep.* to aim, take aim, at (s.o., sth.); *Surv:* to sight; to take a sight on (sth.).
Anwachs, *m.* **-es/. 1.** (*a*) growth, growing (of plant, etc.); (*b*) increase, increasing; rising, swelling (of waters, river, etc.); *Fin:* accumulation, accruing (of interest); *Geol: Jur:* accretion (of land by alluvion); *Jur:* accretion (of legacy). **2.** (*a*) (amount of) increase, growth; (*b*) *Fin:* accumulated interest, accrued interest; *Geol: Jur:* accreted land; alluvion; *Jur:* (amount of) increase in a legacy through accretion; accession to a legacy.
anwachsen. I. *v.i. sep.* (*strong*) (*sein*) **1.** to begin to grow; (*of plant*) to take (root), strike (root). **2. (an etwas** *acc.*) **a.,** to grow on (to sth.); to adhere (to sth.); **die Haut ist an den Knochen angewachsen,** the skin has adhered to the bone; *F:* **ihm war die Zunge wie angewachsen,** he was tongue-tied, speechless, (as though) struck dumb; **ihm ist die Zunge nicht angewachsen,** he has a glib, ready, tongue; he is never at a loss for words; **er saß da wie angewachsen,** he sat there stock still; he sat tight; he wouldn't budge; **er stand da wie angewachsen,** he stood there as if rooted to the spot; **steh nicht da wie angewachsen!** come on, don't stand there like a wooden image! *Bot:* **angewachsener Staubbeutel,** adnate anther. **3.** to grow, increase, augment; to increase in volume; (*of waters, river, etc.*) to rise, swell; (*of snow*) to thicken, get thicker; (*of sound*) to swell; *Fin:* (*of interest*) to accumulate, accrue; **die Bevölkerung ist rasch angewachsen,** the population has increased, grown, gone up, rapidly; **das Geräusch war zu einem Dröhnen angewachsen,** the noise had swollen to a rumble, into a rumbling; *Mus:* **einen Ton a. lassen,** to swell a note.
II. *vbl s.* **1. Anwachsen,** *n. in vbl senses; also:* (*a*) growth, increase; accumulation (of interest); accretion (of a legacy); **im A. sein,** to be on the rise, on the increase; (*b*) adhesion (**an**+*acc.*, to). **2. Anwachsung,** *f.* (*a*) = II. 1; (*b*) = **Anwachs** 2. *Cp.* **Anwachs, Anwuchs.**
Anwachsstreifen, *m.pl. Z:* lines of growth (on snail-shell, etc.).
anwackeln, *v.i. sep.* (*sein*) (*usu. only in the phr.*) **angewackelt kommen,** to come waddling along, up; (*of an old car, etc.*) to come wobbling along.
Anwalt, *m.* -(e)s/=e. **1.** *Jur:* lawyer; (i) (**plädierender**) **A.,** barrister(-at-law), counsel, *Scot:* advocate, *U.S:* counselor; (ii) solicitor, *Scot:* law-agent, *A. & U.S:* attorney(-at-law); **durch einen A. vertreten sein,** to be represented by counsel; **einen A. befragen,** to take counsel's opinion; **eine Angelegenheit einem A. übergeben,** to put a matter in the hands of a lawyer; **sich** *dat.* **einen A. nehmen,** to retain a barrister, a counsel. **2.** authorized representative *or* agent; attorney. **3.** pleader, intercessor, advocate; **zum A. einer Sache werden,** to become the advocate of a cause; **ein begeisterter A. der Verstaatlichung,** an enthusiastic advocate of nationalization.
Anwaltsassessor, *m.* **1.** intending lawyer undergoing three years' training in lawyer's office; = articled clerk. **2.** *Adm:* (clerk in the) initial grade of the State Legal Service.
Anwaltsbüro, *n.* **1.** lawyer's office. **2.** firm of solicitors, of lawyers.
Anwaltschaft, *f.* -/. **1. die A.,** (*a*) the legal profession, the bar; (*b*) the barristers entitled to plead at a particular court. **2.** activity as an agent *or* representative; attorneyship.
Anwaltsfirma, *f.* firm of solicitors, of lawyers.
Anwaltsgebühr, *f.* lawyer's fee; solicitor's *or* barrister's fee.
Anwaltshonorar, *n.* lawyer's fee; solicitor's fee; barrister's honorarium.
Anwaltskammer, *f.* (German) Bar Association.
Anwaltsprozeß, *m. Jur:* case in which the parties are obliged to be legally represented.
Anwaltsstand, *m.* **der A.,** the legal profession.
Anwaltstätigkeit, *f.* activity as a lawyer, as a solicitor *or* barrister; advocacy.
Anwaltsvorschuß, *m.* retaining fee, retainer (paid to lawyer).
Anwaltszwang, *m. Jur:* obligation to be legally represented in the courts.
anwalzen, *v.i. sep.* (*sein*) (*usu. only in the phr.*) **angewalzt kommen,** (i) to come rolling along; (ii) (*of pers.*) to come waltzing along, up.
anwälzen, *v.tr. sep.* to roll up (stone, etc.); **etwas an etwas** *acc.* **a.,** to roll sth. up against sth.
Anwand, *f.* = **Anewand.**
anwandeln. I. *v.sep.* **1.** *v.i.* (*sein*) (*usu. only in the phr.*) **angewandelt kommen,** to come up at a leisurely pace; to approach in a dignified manner. **2.** *v.tr.* (*of emotion*) to come over (s.o.); (*of emotion, illness*) to seize (s.o.); **ein plötzliches Schwindelgefühl wandelte sie an,** (a fit of) dizziness came over her, she was seized with dizziness; **ein Gefühl der Ohnmacht wandelte sie an,** a feeling of faintness came over her, she felt faint; **eine plötzliche Furcht wandelte ihn an,** fear suddenly came upon him; **was wandelt dich an?** what has come over you? what is the matter, *F:* what's up, with you?
II. *vbl s.* **Anwandlung,** *f.* fit; touch, (slight) attack (of illness); **sie hatte eine A. von Schwindel,** (a fit of) dizziness came over her, she was seized with dizziness; **in einer A. von Zorn,** in a fit of anger, of temper, *Lit:* in an access of rage; **in einer A. von Furcht . . . ,** seized with fear . . . ; **in einer (plötzlichen) A. von Großmut,** moved by a generous, magnanimous, impulse; in a sudden fit of generosity, of magnanimity; **er hat manchmal sonderbare Anwandlungen,** he sometimes has strange impulses, strange desires.
Anwänder, *m.* -s/-. *Dial:* neighbouring farmer; neighbour.
anwandern, *v.i. sep.* (*sein*) (*usu. only in the phr.*) **angewandert kommen,** to come walking along; to arrive on foot.
anwanken, *v.i. sep.* (*sein*) (*usu. only in the phr.* **angewankt kommen,** to come tottering along, up; to come up unsteadily.
Anwärmeapparat, *m.* (*a*) warming device, (*b*) *Mch:* = **Vorwärmer.**
Anwärmeherd, *m. Metall: etc:* warming furnace.
anwärmen, *v.sep.* **1.** *v.tr.* to warm (sth.) slightly; to take the chill off (wine, etc.); to warm up (liquid, engine, etc.); to heat up (metal, engine, etc.); *Mch:* to preheat (feed-water). **2.** *occ. v.i.* (*sein*) to warm up.
Anwärmeschuß, *m. Artil:* **einen A. abgeben,** to fire a warming shot.
Anwärter, *m.* **1.** aspirant (**auf eine Stelle, usw.,** to, after, a post, etc.); candidate (**auf eine Stelle,** for a post); *Adm: etc:* employee, official, not yet established; probationer; *Mil:* cadet, officer candidate. **2.** *Jur:* **A. (auf eine Erbschaft),** reversioner, expectant (of an inheritance); expectant heir, heir in expectancy.
Anwartschaft, *f.* -/-en. **1. A. auf eine Stelle,** expectation of a post; **die A. auf eine Stelle erwerben,** to qualify as a probationer for a post. **2.** *Jur:* (right of) reversion; remainder; **A. auf ein Erbe,** expectation, expectancy, of an inheritance; reversion of an inheritance; **bedingte A.,** contingent remainder. **3.** *Ins:* qualifying period (between payment of premiums and receipt of benefit).
anwartschaftlich, *a. Jur:* reversionary (interest, etc.).
Anwartschaftsrecht, *n. Jur:* **ein A. auf ein Gut haben,** to have a reversionary interest in an estate.
Anwartschaftsrente, *f.* deferred, reversionary, annuity.
anwassern, *v.i. sep.* (*sein*) *Av:* to alight, land (on water, on the sea).
anwässern, *v.tr. sep.* to moisten (sth.) (with water).
anwatscheln, *v.i. sep.* (*sein*) (*usu. only in the phr.*) **angewatschelt kommen,** (*of duck, F: of pers.*) to come waddling along, up.
anwecken, *v.tr. sep. Tp:* to ring, *U.S:* call, (s.o.) up.
anwedeln, *v.tr. sep.* **1.** to fan (s.o.). **2.** (*a*) (*of dog*) to wag its tail at (s.o.); (*b*) *F:* (*of pers.*) to fawn upon (s.o.); to toady to (s.o.).
anwehen, *v.sep.* **1.** *v.tr.* (*of wind, etc.*) (*a*) to blow (up)on (s.o., sth.); to breathe (up)on (s.o., sth.); **hier fühlen wir uns von dem Hauch der Vergangenheit angeweht,** here we feel the breath of the past upon us, feel the past still living and breathing; **hier weht es mich heimatlich an,** the atmosphere here reminds me of home; **j-n mit dem Hauch der Begeisterung a.,** to inspire, infuse, s.o. with enthusiasm; **vom Hauch der Götter angeweht,** under the divine afflatus; (*b*) **Schneemassen, Sandmassen, a.,** to drift snow, sand. **2.** *v.i.* (*sein*) (*a*) (*of snow, sand*) to drift; (*b*) (*of leaf, etc.*) **angeweht kommen,** to come drifting along; to be wafted along.
anweichen, *v.tr. sep.* to soften (sth.); to soak (sth.) slightly.
anweisbar, *a.* assignable, transferable; (sum) that can be remitted.
anweisen. I. *v.tr. sep.* (*strong*) **1** to give directions, instructions, to (s.o.); **j-n a., etwas zu tun,** to direct, instruct, order, s.o. to do sth., to give s.o. instructions, orders, to do sth.; **seine Bank a., einen Betrag gutzuschreiben,** to instruct one's bank to credit a sum. **2. j-m etwas a.,** to assign sth. to s.o.; to allocate, allot, sth. to s.o.; **j-m einen Platz a.,** to assign a place, a position, to s.o.; (*in cinema, theatre, at festival, sports meeting, etc.*) to show s.o. to a seat; **j-m ein Zimmer a.,** to assign a room to s.o., assign s.o. a room; to give s.o. a room (in hotel, hostel, etc.). **3. j-m einen Betrag a.,** to remit a sum of money to s.o.; **Geld auf j-n, auf eine Bank, a.,** to remit money to s.o., to a bank; **wir haben den Betrag auf Ihr Konto a. lassen,** we have had the sum credited to your account.
II. *vbl s.* **Anweisung,** *f.* **1.** *in vbl senses; also:* instruction, direction (of s.o.); guidance (of s.o.); assignation, assignment (of sth.) (**an j-n,** to s.o.); allocation, allotment (of money, supplies, etc.) (**an j-n,** to s.o.). **2.** (*a*) direction, instruction, order; *Adm: etc:* directive; **j-m Anweisungen zum Gebrauch einer Sache geben,** to give s.o. instructions how to use sth.; **j-m Anweisungen, eine A., geben, erteilen, daß . . . ,** to give s.o. directions, instructions, orders, that . . . ; *Adm:* to issue a directive to s.o. that . . . ; **wir haben Anweisungen erhalten, zu . . . ,** we have received directions, instructions, orders, to . . . , we have been directed, instructed, ordered, to . . . ; **auf A. des Stadtrats,** by order of, on, under, instructions from, the Town Council; (*b*) allocation, allotment (of supplies,

etc.); (*c*)=**Anweiseschein**; (*d*) remittance; draft; (money) order; **A. auf 50 M,** draft, order, for 50 marks.

III. *p.p. & a.* **angewiesen. 1.** *in vbl senses; esp.* **a. sein, etwas zu tun,** to have instructions, orders, to do sth. **2. auf j-n, auf etwas** *acc.*, **a. sein,** to have to rely on s.o., sth.; to have no other resource but s.o., sth.; to be entirely dependent on s.o., sth.; to be thrown back upon s.o., sth.; **Gott sei Dank bin ich nicht auf dich angewiesen!** thank Heaven I haven't got to rely entirely, I'm not entirely reliant, on you! **auf Almosen a. sein,** to be dependent on alms; to be reduced to charity; **auf sich selbst a. sein,** to be entirely dependent on oneself; to be thrown upon one's own resources.

Anweiser, *m.* **1.** instructor. **2.**=**Platzanweiser. 3.** assigner; remitter (of money).

Anweiseschein, *m. Adm:* assignment note, allocation note.

anweißen, *v.tr. sep.* to whiten; to whitewash (wall, etc.).

Anweisung, *f. see* **anweisen II.**

Anweisungsschein, *m.*=**Anweiseschein.**

anwendbar, *a.* (*a*) applicable (**auf**+*acc.*, to); (rule, etc.) that can be applied, that applies; **diese Regel ist a. auf alle Fälle, ist allgemein a.,** this rule applies to all cases, is of general, universal, application; (*b*) that can be used, employed (**für, zu,** for); (*of means, remedy, expedient, etc.*) usable, employable; applicable; practicable; (*of word, description, etc.*) applicable.

Anwendbarkeit, *f.* (*a*) applicability (**auf**+*acc.*, to); (*b*) usability, usableness; possibility of use; practical usefulness (**für, zu,** for); practicability (of means, procedure, etc.); **dieses Heilmittel hat nur bedingte A.,** the possible uses of this medicament are limited.

anwenden. I. *v.tr. sep.* (*conj. like* **wenden**) (*a*) to apply (rule, law, etc.) (**auf**+*acc.*, to); **Regel, die man a. kann, die sich a. läßt,** rule that can be applied, that is applicable; **diese Regel läßt sich auf alle Fälle a.,** this rule applies, is applicable, to all cases, is of general, universal, application; **ein Gesetz auf einen besonderen Fall a.,** to apply a law to, bring a law to bear upon, a particular case; **ein Prinzip, ein System, praktisch a.,** to apply a principle, a system, to put, carry, a principle, a system, into practice; **die Algebra auf die Geometrie a.,** to apply algebra to geometry; **die angewandten Wissenschaften,** the applied sciences; **angewandte Mathematik,** applied mathematics; **angewandte Chemie,** applied, experimental, chemistry; **angewandte Künste,** applied, decorative, arts; (*b*) to employ, use (sth.) (**für, zu,** for); to apply (pressure, remedy, etc.) (**auf**+*acc.*, to); **etwas gut, nützlich, a.,** to make good use of sth., put sth. to good use; to turn, put, sth. to account; **etwas schlecht a.,** to use sth. badly, make bad use of sth.; to put sth. to (a) bad use; **etwas falsch, verkehrt, a.,** to use sth. wrongly, incorrectly; to misapply sth.; **alle möglichen Mittel a.,** to use all possible means; **ein Verfahren a.,** to use, make use of, a procedure; **Wort, das man a. kann, das sich a. läßt,** word that can be used; applicable word; **ein Wort falsch a.,** to use a word wrongly, incorrectly, improperly, in a wrong sense; **falsch angewandtes Wort,** word improperly used, word that is out of place (in the context); **sein Geld zum Kauf von Büchern a.,** to use one's money to buy books, to lay out, spend, one's money on books; **mehr kann ich leider nicht a.,** unfortunately I can't (afford to) spend more than that; **sein Geld gut a.,** to spend one's money wisely; **seine Zeit gut a.,** to make good use of, the most of, one's time; **sein Geld, seine Zeit, schlecht a.,** to mis-spend one's money, one's time; to misapply one's time; **alle (seine) Kräfte a., um zu . . .,** to use every effort, strain every nerve, do one's utmost, to . . . ; **Gewalt a.,** to use, employ, force; to resort to force; **bei einer Handlung Vorsicht a.,** to use caution in doing sth.; **bei einer Aufgabe Fleiß a.,** to take pains over a task; **das ist bei ihm schlecht angewandt,** it's no use trying that with him; *Pharm:* **'äußerlich anzuwenden',** 'for external, outward, application', 'not to be taken'.

II. *vbl s.* **Anwendung,** *f. in vbl senses; also:* (*a*) application (of rule, law, system, etc.) (**auf**+*acc.*, to); **eine Regel, ein System, in A. bringen,** to apply a rule, a system (**auf**+*acc.*, to); to put a rule, a system, into practice; **diese Regel findet keine A. auf solche Fälle,** this rule does not apply, is not applicable, has no application, to such cases; **entsprechende A. finden,** (*of principle, law, etc.*) to apply mutatis mutandis; (*b*) employment, use (**für, zu,** for); utilization; application (of pressure, remedy, etc.) (**auf**+*acc.*, to); **etwas (für, zu, etwas) in A. bringen,** to employ, use, sth. (for sth.); **falsche, verkehrte, A.,** misuse, misapplication (of word, remedy, etc.); **Rohstoffe, die keine A. finden,** raw materials that have, for which there is, no use; *Pharm:* **äußerliche A. eines Heilmittels,** external, outward, application of a remedy.

Anwendungsbereich, *m.* field of application; scope (of law, rule).

Anwendungsweise, *f.* manner of using (sth.); method of application (of medicament, etc.).

anwerben, *v.tr. sep.* (*strong*) *Mil:* to enlist (men, recruits); to recruit (men); **sich a. lassen,** to enlist; *Ind:* **Arbeitskräfte a.,** to recruit labour; **Anwerbung** *f, in vbl senses; also:* enlistment, recruitment.

anwerfen, *v.sep.* (*strong*) **1.** *v.i.* (*haben*) (*at dice, skittles, etc.*) to throw first, have the first throw. **2.** *v.tr.* **etwas an etwas** *acc.* **a.,** to throw, fling, sth. on to, against, sth.; **Putz an eine Wand a.,** to fling plaster on a wall; to rough-cast a wall; *F:* **j-m etwas a.,** to throw, fling, sth. at s.o.; **sie hat es mir angeworfen,** (i) she flung it at me; (ii) she made offensive remarks about me, *F:* she threw dirt at me. **3.** *v.tr. Aut: Av: etc:* **den Motor a.,** to start (up) the engine; *Av:* to rotate, turn, the engine; **den Motor mit der Hand, von Hand, a.,** to start the engine by hand; to crank (up) the engine, swing the engine over; *Av:* **die Luftschraube a.,** to swing the airscrew. **4.** *v.tr. Tail:* to tack in (sleeves); to put in (sleeves).

Anwerfer, *m. Aut: etc:* (*device*) starter.

Anwerfkurbel, *f. Aut: etc:* starting-handle.

Anwerfvorrichtung, *f. Aut: etc:* starting device, starter.

Anwesen, *n.* property; estate; premises; *Jur:* messuage (*e.g.* farm together with farm-house).

anwesend, *a.* present; **bei einer Feier, bei einer Sitzung, usw., a. sein,** to be present at a ceremony, at a meeting, etc.; to attend a meeting; **die anwesenden Herren,** the gentlemen present.

Anwesende, *m., f.* (*decl. as adj.*) person present; man, woman, present; **die Anwesenden,** those present; (i) the audience, the company, (ii) the spectators, the onlookers; **alle Anwesenden,** everyone present, all (those) present; **jeder A. hat es gehört,** all present heard it; **Anwesende, die Anwesenden, (stets, immer) ausgenommen,** present company excepted; (*in address*) **'verehrte Anwesende!'**='ladies and gentlemen . . .'.

Anwesenheit, *f.* presence; attendance (**bei einer Sitzung, usw.,** at a meeting, etc.); **in j-s A.,** in the presence of s.o.; **sage nichts darüber in seiner A.!** say nothing about it in his presence; **bei A. aller Aktionäre,** in the presence of all the shareholders, all the shareholders being present; **bei seiner A. in London,** during his presence, while he is, was, in London; **die A. von Metallteilchen, usw., feststellen,** to establish the presence of metallic particles, etc.

Anwesenheitsliste, *f.* attendance sheet.

Anwesenheitsverzeichnis, *n.* attendance register.

anwettern, *v.tr. sep.* to storm at (s.o.); *F:* to go for (s.o.) bald-headed; **angewettert werden,** *F:* to get a thorough ticking-off, telling-off.

anwetzen, *v.i. sep.* (*sein*) *F:* (*usu. only in the phr.*) **angewetzt kommen,** (*of pers.*) to come tearing along, dashing along; (*of aircraft*) to swoop down, come swooping down; *F:* to come tearing in.

anwidern, *v.tr. sep.*=**anekeln 1; anwidernd,** (*of behaviour, etc.*) offensive, disgusting; (*of appearance, etc.*) repulsive, repellent, loathsome.

anwiehern, *v.tr. sep.* (*of horse*) to whinny at (s.o., sth.); to neigh at (s.o., sth.).

anwimmern, *v.tr. sep.* (*of pers., child*) to whimper at (s.o.); to snivel, whine, at (s.o.).

anwinseln, *v.tr. sep.* (*of dog, F: pers., child*) to whimper at (s.o., sth.); to whine at (s.o., sth.); (*of pers.*) to snivel at (s.o.).

anwirken, *v.tr. sep. Tex:* (*a*) to weave (piece, etc.) on (**an**+*acc.*, to); (*b*) **Strümpfe a.,** to foot stockings.

anwohnen, *v.i. sep.* (*haben*) **einem Fluß a.,** to live on the banks of a river; **einem Fluß anwohnend,** riparian, riverain.

Anwohner, *m.* **-s/-,** person living nearby; person living near to (airport, etc.); *Jur:* adjacent owner; **die Anwohner dieser Straße,** the residents of this road. **A. eines Flusses,** river-side resident; riparian owner; riverian; **die Anwohner der Donau,** the borderers on, the countries bordering on, the Danube.

Anwohnerschaft, *f.* **-/. die A.,** the neighbouring inhabitants; the neighbours; the residents (of a road); (*by a river*) the riparian proprietors; *Jur:* the adjacent owners; **meine, seine, A.,** my, his neighbours.

Anwuchs, *m.* **1.** (*a*) growth, growing (of a plant, etc.); (*b*) increase, increasing; growth (of population, etc.). **2.** *For:* stand of young trees; coppice, copse. **3.** *Nau:* fouling (of ship's hull by marine growths); **ein Mittel gegen A.,** an antifouling composition. *Cp.* **Anwachs.**

Anwunsch, *m. A:* good wish(es).

anwünschen, *v.tr. sep.* (*a*) **j-m Böses, eine Plage, ein Unglück, usw., a.,** to wish something evil, a plague, a disaster, etc., upon s.o.; (*b*) *A:* **j-m alles Gute a.,** to wish s.o. well.

Anwurf, *m.* **1.** *Games: Sp:* first throw; throw-off; (*at dice*) first cast; **den A. haben,** to throw first, have the first throw; to throw off. **2.** *Aut: etc:* starting (up) (of engine). **3.** *Constr:* plaster, *esp.* rough coat of plaster; rough-cast. **4.** offensive remark; slanderous remark. **5.** *A:* (*a*) proposal, proposition; (*b*) payment on account; deposit(-money); earnest money.

anwürfeln, *v.i. sep.* (*haben*) (*at dice*) to throw first, to have the first throw, the first cast.

Anwurfmotor, *m. I.C.E:* starting-motor, -engine.

anwurzeln, *v.i. sep.* (*sein*) & **sich anwurzeln,** (*of plant*) to take root, strike root; **er stand wie angewurzelt da,** he stood stock still, remained rooted to the spot, stood nailed to the spot.

Anzahl, *f.* **-/.** number, quantity; **eine A. Leute, von Leuten,** a number of people; **eine A. von Bildern,** a number, a quantity, of pictures; **eine große A. (Leute) war, waren, bei der Sitzung anwesend,** there were a large number of, a lot of, a good many, people at the meeting, there was a good attendance at the meeting; **eine große A. der Bevölkerung,** a large part, a large proportion, of the population; **eine kleine A. der Studenten ist, sind, noch hier,** a small number, a small proportion of the students are still here.

Anzahlbegriff, *m. Mth: Phil:* concept of number.

anzahlen. I. *v.tr. sep.* to pay (a sum) on account; to pay (a sum as) a deposit, a first instalment, to make a down payment (of so much) (**auf einen Artikel,** on an article).

II. *vbl s.* **1. Anzahlen,** *n. in vbl senses.* **2. Anzahlung,** *f.* (*a*)=II. 1; (*b*) sum paid on account, part payment; earnest money; deposit, first instalment, down payment (**auf einen Artikel,** on an article); **j-m eine A. leisten, machen,** to pay s.o. a sum on account; to pay s.o. a deposit, a first instalment; to pay s.o. so much down.

Anzapfdampfmaschine, *f. Mch:* extraction steam-engine.

anzapfen. I. *v.tr. sep.* **1.** (*a*) **ein Faß a.,** to broach, tap, a barrel, a cask; (*b*) **einen Baum a.,** to tap a tree (for resin, etc.); (*c*) *Tchn:* to tap (gas-main, water-main, *El.E:* a circuit, etc.); *Mch:* to extract, *F:* to bleed (steam). **2.** *F:* **j-n a.,** (*a*) to get money out of (s.o.); **j-n um zwanzig Mark a.,** to tap, touch, s.o. for twenty marks; (*b*) **j-n über eine Angelegenheit a.,** to make s.o. talk, *F:* to pump s.o., about a matter; (*c*) to pull (s.o.'s) leg; to take a rise out of (s.o.); to chaff (s.o.); to chip (s.o.); to rag (s.o.), *U.S:* to razz (s.o.).

II. *vbl s.* **1. Anzapfen,** *n. in vbl senses; also: Mch:* extraction (of steam). **2. Anzapfung,** *f.* (*a*)= II. 1; tap (on extraction turbine).

Anzapfhahn, *m.* (barrel) tap, spigot.

Anzapfturbine, *f.* extraction turbine, bleeder turbine.

Anzapfventil, *n. Mch:* extraction valve, *F:* bleeder valve.

anzaubern, *v.tr. sep.* **1.** (*a*) *A:* to bewitch (s.o.); to cast a spell on (s.o.); (*b*) **er stand da wie angezaubert,** he stood there as though bewitched, spellbound. **2.** (*a*) **j-m eine Krankheit, einen Schönheitsfehler, usw., a.,** to bring a disease, a blemish, upon s.o. by witchcraft, by a spell; (*b*) **j-m etwas a.,** to procure sth. for s.o. by magic; *F:* **das kann ich dir nicht a.,** (you'll just have to do without,) I can't get it for you by magic.

anzäumen *v.tr. sep.*=**aufzäumen.**

anzechen (sich), *v.refl. sep.* to get drunk.

Anzeichen, *n.* indication, sign; mark, token; augury, omen, presage, foreboding; *Med: etc:* symptom (of an illness, etc.); prognostic; **ein plötzliches Sinken des Barometers ist ein A. für Sturm,** a sudden fall in the barometer is a sign, an indication, of a storm; **A., daß es regnen wird,** sign that it will rain, sign of rain; **Anzeichen eines schlechten Charakters, für einen schlechten Charakter,** signs, indications, marks, of a bad

character; **die A. eines nahenden Krieges,** the signs, omens, symptoms, of an approaching war; **alle A. deuten darauf hin, daß . . . ,** there is every indication that . . . ; **es liegen keine A. für ein Verbrechen vor,** there are no indications that a crime has been committed; **es liegen alle A. für eine baldige Besserung vor,** there is every indication, every sign, of a speedy recovery; **wenn nicht alle A. trügen . . . ,** if we read the signs correctly . . . ; if appearances do not deceive us, are not deceptive . . . ; **die ersten A. einer Krankheit,** the first signs of a disease; **die A. dieser Krankheit, für diese Krankheit, sind . . . ,** the symptoms of this disease are . . . ; **er hat, trägt, alle A. dieser Krankheit an sich,** he shows all the symptoms, has all the marks, of this disease.

anzeichnen, *v.tr. sep.* to mark (sth.), to make, put, a mark against (sth.).

Anzeige, *f.* **-/-n.** **1.** (*a*) indication (*gen.*, of); *Min:* **A. auf Erz** *acc.*, indication of the presence of ore; (*b*) *Tchn:* reading (on measuring instrument). **2.** (*a*) announcement, notice, notification, intimation; letter *or* card announcing a death, marriage, etc.; *Com:* (i) (letter of) advice, advice-note; (ii) acknowledgement (of receipt); **schriftliche A.,** written notice, notice in writing; **A. bei einer Behörde,** declaration to an authority; notification (of fact, case of infectious disease, etc.) to an authority; **A. von einer Tatsache bei der Behörde machen,** to notify the authorities of a fact, to report a fact to the authorities; (*b*) *Jur:* information; denunciation; **A. gegen j-n erstatten,** to lay an information against s.o. (with the police), to inform against s.o.; to report s.o. to the police; to denounce s.o. to the authorities. **3.** (*in newspaper, etc.*) (*a*) advertisement, *F:* advert; announcement, notice (of death, marriage, etc.); **kleine Anzeigen,** small advertisements, *F:* small ads; **eine A. in einer Zeitung aufgeben,** to insert, put, an advertisement in a paper; to put a notice in a paper; (*b*) notice *or* short review (of a book); **kurze A.,** short notice; (*c*) (*in learned periodical*) note; (short) notice.

Anzeigeamt, *n. A:* registry office.

Anzeigebereich, *m.* indicating range, range of indication (of a measuring instrument).

Anzeigeblatt, *n.*=**Anzeigenblatt.**

Anzeigebrett, *n. El.E: etc:* indicator (board).

Anzeigebrief, *m.* notice (announcing a wedding, death, etc.); intimation (of wedding, etc.).

Anzeigefehler, *m.* error (of a measuring instrument).

Anzeigegerät, Anzeigeinstrument, *n.* indicating instrument, indicator.

Anzeigelampe, *f. El.E: Ind: etc:* tell-tale lamp, signal lamp, pilot lamp.

Anzeigematerial, *n. Jur:* information provided by an informer; relation.

Anzeigemittel, *n. Ch:* indicator.

anzeigen, *v.tr. sep.* **1.** (*a*) (*of recording instrument*) to indicate, show (sth.), to give a reading of (so many degrees, volts, etc.); **das Thermometer zeigt dreißig Grad an,** the thermometer registers, records, reads, thirty degrees; the thermometer stands at 30°; **das Barometer zeigt Regen, schönes Wetter, an,** the barometer points to rain, to set fair; *Tchn:* **anzeigendes Gerät,** indicating instrument; (*b*) *abs. Mil: etc:* to mark (*at butts, at shooting competition*); (*c*) to indicate, show, the presence of (sth.); to indicate, show, denote, mark; to signify; to betoken, give token of (sth.); **Symptome, die eine Krankheit a.,** symptoms that indicate, denote, a disease; *Gram:* **anzeigendes Fürwort,** demonstrative pronoun; (*d*) to indicate, presage, (fore)bode, portend, augur, betoken; **Gefahr a.,** to indicate danger; **das zeigt nichts Gutes an,** it bodes, augurs, no good; **das zeigt schönes Wetter an,** that is a sign, an indication, of good weather, that shows that good weather is on the way; (*e*) **etwas für angezeigt halten,** to regard (procedure, etc.; *Med:* treatment) as advisable, as desirable, as expedient; **es für angezeigt halten, zu . . . ,** to deem it expedient to . . . ; to judge, deem, it proper, to think proper, to . . . ; to think fit, see fit, to . . . ; **strenge Maßnahmen schienen angezeigt,** strong measures were clearly indicated; **es scheint angezeigt, zu schreiben,** it seems desirable to write, *F:* a letter seems indicated; **Fall, bei dem eine gewisse Behandlung angezeigt ist,** case in which a certain treatment is indicated; (*f*) **sich a.,** (*of phenomenon, etc.*) to show (itself); to manifest itself; *A:* (*of dead person*) **sich j-m a.,** to appear to s.o. (as a ghost). **2.** (*a*) to announce (sth.); to give notice of (sth.); **j-m etwas a.,** to announce sth. to s.o.; to inform, *Lit:* apprise, s.o. of sth.; to intimate sth. to s.o.; to advise s.o. of sth.; to acquaint s.o. with (a fact); **eine Tatsache bei der Behörde a.,** to notify the authorities of a fact, to report a fact to the authorities; **einen Einbruch bei der Polizei a.,** to report a burglary to the police; *Com:* **Preise a.,** to quote prices; **den Empfang a.,** to acknowledge receipt; **eine Tratte a.,** to advise a draft; (*b*) *Jur:* **j-n (bei der Polizei, bei Gericht, bei der Behörde) a.,** to lay an information against s.o. (with the police), to inform against s.o.; to report s.o. to the police, to the authorities; to denounce s.o. to the authorities; *F:* to give s.o. away; *Sch:* **j-n (beim Lehrer) a.,** to tell, *F:* sneak, on s.o.; **sich selbst a.,** (i) (*of criminal*) to give oneself up; (ii) to provoke an indictment in order to clear one's own name; (iii) (*of tax offender*) to make a voluntary admission of tax evasion; **Anzeigung** *f. in vbl senses; also:* denunciation. **3.** (*a*) to advertise (sth.) (in newspaper, etc.); to publish a notice of (sth.); to announce (death, wedding, engagement, etc.) (by cards *or* in newspaper); (*b*) **ein Buch a.,** to publish a notice of a book; to notice a book; (*c*) *Com:* **als insolvent angezeigt werden,** to be gazetted bankrupt, *U.S:* to be publicly named as bankrupt.

Anzeigenblatt, *n.* **1.** advertiser, advertising sheet. **2.** advertisement page (in newspaper).

Anzeigenfachmann, *m.* advertising expert.

Anzeigengebühren, *f.pl.* advertising charges; advertisement rates.

Anzeigenmittler, *m.*=**Anzeigenvermittler.**

Anzeigensteuer, *f.* advertisement tax.

Anzeigenteil, *m.* advertisement pages, advertisement section (in newspaper).

Anzeigenvermittler, *m.* advertising agent.

Anzeigenvermittlung, *f.* advertising agency.

Anzeigenwesen, *n.* advertising, publicity.

Anzeigepflicht, *f. Jur:* obligation to report a crime *or* intended crime to the police; *Adm:* obligation to notify the authorities (of facts, case of infectious disease, etc.).

anzeigepflichtig, *a. Jur:* (crime) that must be reported to the police; *Adm:* (fact, etc.) of which the authorities must be notified; notifiable (disease).

Anzeiger, *m.* **1.** (*pers.*) (*a*) indicator (*gen.*, of); (*b*) *Mil:* marker (at the butts); (*c*) *Jur:* informer; (*d*) advertiser (in newspaper, etc.). **2.** (*newspaper*) gazette, advertiser. **3.** (*device*) indicator; pointer; *Tp:* annunciator.

Anzeigesystem, *n. El.E: Ind: etc:* indicating system.

Anzeigetafel, *f.* **1.** advertisement board. **2.** *El.E: etc:* indicator-board, tell-tale board; *Tp:* annunciator-board.

Anzeigevorrichtung, *f.* indicating device, indicator.

anzementieren, *v.tr. sep.* to cement (sth.) on.

anzeps [ˈantsɛps], *a. Pros:* (syllable) that can be either short or long.

Anzettel, *m. Tex: A:* warp.

anzetteln, *v.tr. sep.* **1.** *Tex: A:* to warp (cloth). **2.** to hatch, weave (plot, intrigue); to concoct (plot); to scheme, plot, machinate, contrive (piece of knavery, etc.); **eine Verschwörung a.,** to hatch a conspiracy; **seine Frau hat das Ganze angezettelt,** it is all his wife's doing; his wife is responsible for the whole business.

Anzettler, *m.* **-s/-,** machinator, hatcher, author (of plot, etc.); schemer, intriguer.

anziehbar, *a.* **1.** attractable. **2.** (*of dress, etc.*) wearable.

anziehen, *v.sep.* (*strong*) I. *v.tr.* **1.** *A:*=**heranziehen 1** (*b*). **2.** (*a*) to pull (at) (sth.); **eine Türglocke a.,** to pull a door-bell; (*of horse*) **einen Wagen a.,** to pull a cart; (*b*) **die Tür a.,** to pull the door to, to close the door; **die Vorhänge a.,** to draw the curtains (to); (*c*) **die Knie, die Beine, a.,** to draw up one's knees, one's legs; (*d*) *Physiol:* (*of muscle*) to adduct (thumb, thigh, etc.). **3.** (*a*) to quote, cite (passage, example, etc.); to adduce (example, instance); to mention, use, (sth.) as an example; (*b*) *Dial:* **sich** *dat.* **etwas a.,** to take sth. to heart. **4.** to stretch, strain (sth.); to pull (sth.) tight; to tighten (rope, screw, etc.); to tauten (rope), to haul (rope) taut; **einen Bogen a.,** to bend, draw, a bow; **einen Riemen a.,** to tighten a strap; *Mec.E:* to stretch, tighten, a belt; **eine Geigensaite a.,** to tighten a violin-string; **eine Feder a.,** to tighten a spring; to set a spring; **die Bremse a.,** to set, put on, the (hand-)brake; **eine Schraube (gut, fest) a.,** to tighten a screw right up; **eine Schraubenmutter gut a.,** to tighten a nut up, down, hard; *F:* **die Schrauben a.,** to apply pressure, to put on the screw; *Equit:* **die Zügel a.,** to draw rein; *F:* **bei j-m die Zügel straff a.,** to keep a tight rein on s.o. a tight hand on, over, s.o. **5.** (*a*) (*of magnet, body, etc.*) to attract, draw; (*of pers., etc.*) to attract, have an attraction for (s.o.); **ein Magnet zieht Eisen an,** a magnet attracts iron; **die Himmelskörper ziehen einander an, ziehen sich gegenseitig an,** the heavenly bodies attract one another; **durch eine Kraft angezogener Körper,** body attracted by a force; **Wasser zieht Mücken an,** water attracts midges; **Schauspieler, der ganz London anzieht,** actor who draws the whole of London; **Kunden a.,** to attract, draw, customers; **der Plan zieht ihn gar nicht an,** the plan does not attract him, has no attractions for him; **sie zieht ihn nicht an,** she does not attract him, he is not attracted to her; **sich von j-m angezogen fühlen,** to feel attracted to s.o., drawn toward s.o.; to feel a liking, a sympathy, for s.o.; *Prov:* **Gegensätze ziehen sich an,** there is a mutual attraction between opposites, opposites appeal to one another; *cp.* IV. 1; (*b*) (*of pump, etc.*) to suck up, suck in, draw (up) (water, etc.); (*of salt, etc.*) **Feuchtigkeit a.,** to take up moisture; **die Butter hat den Zwiebelgeruch angezogen,** the smell of onions has got into the butter, the onions have tainted the butter. **6.** (*a*) to put on, *Lit:* to don (garment, uniform, gloves, shoes, stockings, etc.); to draw on (gloves, garment); to pull on (gloves, stockings, boots, garment); **j-m helfen, den Mantel anzuziehen,** to help s.o. on with, help s.o. (to get) into, his overcoat; *B:* **denn dies Verwesliche muß a. die Unverweslichkeit,** for this corruptible must put on incorruption; *B:* **den neuen Menschen a.,** to put on the new man; *F:* **einen neuen Menschen a.,** to start afresh, to start a new life; to become a new man; to turn over a new leaf; to mend one's ways; (*b*) to dress (s.o.); to clothe, *Lit:* attire (s.o.); **halb angezogen,** half-dressed; **schwarz angezogen,** dressed, clad, in black; **gut, einfach, sauber, angezogen sein,** to be well, plainly, neatly, dressed; **dürftig angezogen,** poorly dressed; thinly clad; **warm angezogen sein,** (i) to be warmly dressed, clad; to be well wrapped up; (ii) *F:* to be in easy circumstances, to be comfortably off, *U.S:* to be well fixed; **sie war bei aller Einfachheit tadellos angezogen,** she was simply but faultlessly dressed; **sich a.,** (i) to dress (oneself); to put on one's clothes, put one's things on, (ii) to dress (for dinner, for the evening); **sich schwarz a.,** to dress in black, to put on black (clothes); **sich geschmackvoll, sorgfältig, a.,** to dress with taste, with care; **sie weiß sich anzuziehen,** she knows how to dress.

II. **anziehen,** *v.i.* **1.** (*haben*) (*of cart-horse*) to start pulling, to pull; **das Pferd wollte nicht a.,** the horse refused to pull, the horse jibbed. **2.** (*haben*) *Chess: etc:* to move first, have the first move. **3.** (*sein*) (*a*) *A:* (*of army, troops*) to march up; to move in; **gegen den Feind a.,** to march against the enemy; (*b*) *A:* (*of servant*) to start (in a situation); (*c*) (*of pers.*) **angezogen kommen,** to arrive; to approach; to come along, up; to come marching along, up; **mit etwas angezogen kommen,** to come along with sth. **4.** (*haben*) (*of weather*) to get, grow, colder; **es zieht an,** it is getting cold, it is turning cold. **5.** (*haben*) (*of screw, cog-wheel, etc.*) to grip; (*of screw*) to bite; (*of cement*) to bind, set; to take; (*of glue*) to stick, grip; **Schraube, die nicht a. will,** screw that won't bite, that doesn't grip; **Schraube, die gut anzieht,** screw with a good bite. **6.** (*haben*) *Com: Fin:* (*of prices, rates*) to go up, move up, rise, advance; (*of prices, market*) to improve, harden; (*of rates*) to stiffen; **die Preise ziehen an,** prices are hardening, advancing, on the advance, on the rise; **die Preise ziehen scharf, stark, an,** prices are going up sharply, there is a sharp advance in prices; **Weizen zieht an,** the price of wheat is hardening, there is an advance on wheat; *cp.* IV. 2.

III. *vbl s.* **1. Anziehen,** *n. in vbl senses; also:* (*a*) **sie ist (gerade) beim A.,** she is (just) dressing; **sie war bald fertig mit dem A.,** she had soon finished dressing, she was soon dressed; (*b*) *Com: Fin:* **A. der Preise, des Marktes,** rise, improvement, in prices; improvement of the market. **2. Anziehung,** *f.* (*a*) *A: in vbl senses as in* I. 3 (*a*); *also:* citation (of authority, etc.); (*b*) attraction (of magnet, body, etc.; of pers.); pull (of magnet, heavenly body, etc.); **magnetische, molekulare, A.,** magnetic, molecular, attraction; **A. des Eisens durch einen Magneten,** attraction of iron by a magnet; **A. der Schwere,** attraction, force, of gravity; gravitational pull; (*c*) *Physiol:* adduction.

IV. *pr.p. & a.* **anziehend,** *in vbl senses; esp.*

1. attractive; (*of personality, manner, etc.*) engaging, winning, prepossessing; (*of plan, offer, prospects, etc.*) inviting, alluring, tempting; **sie hat ein anziehendes Wesen,** she has an attractive nature, personality; she has engaging ways; she is a likeable person; **sein Aussehen war gar nicht a.,** his appearance was uninviting, unprepossessing, not at all prepossessing; **das Anziehende an ihr ist ihre Freundlichkeit,** the attractive thing about her is her friendliness; her charm lies in her friendliness; *adv.* **etwas a. darstellen,** to present sth. attractively, in an attractive manner. 2. *Com: Fin:* **anziehender Markt,** rising market, seller's market; **bei anziehenden Preisen, Kursen, verkaufen,** to sell on, in a rising market.

Anzieher, *m.* 1. (*a*) shoe-horn, -lift; boot-hook; (*b*) button-hook. 2. *Anat:* = **Anziehmuskel.** 3. *Mec.E: etc:* tightener.

Anziehmaschine, *f. Coop:* trussing-machine.

Anziehmuskel, *m. Anat:* adductor, adducent muscle.

Anziehung, *f. see* **anziehen** III.

Anziehungsbereich, *m. Magn:* field of attraction.

Anziehungskraft, *f.* attractive force, attraction, drawing power (of magnet, etc.); pull (of magnet, heavenly body, etc.); attraction, attractiveness (of pers., etc.); appeal (of play, actor, etc.); **eine starke A. auf j-n, auf etwas** *acc.*, **ausüben,** to exert a strong attraction on, have a strong attraction for, s.o., sth., to attract s.o., sth., strongly.

Anziehungspunkt, *m.* centre of attraction; **der A. der Ausstellung,** the chief attraction, *F:* the real draw, of the exhibition.

Anziehungsvermögen, *n.* attractive power, (power of) attraction.

anzielen, *v.tr. sep.* to aim at (sth.); *Surv: etc:* to take a sight on (sth.).

anzinnen, *v.tr. sep. Metalw:* to tin (copper, etc.).

anzischen, *v.tr. sep.* to hiss at (s.o.).

anzotteln, *v.i. sep.* (*sein*) *F:* (*usu. only in the phr.*) **angezottelt kommen,** to come jogging along.

Anzucht, *f.* 1. -/⸚e. *Dial:* (*a*) drainage ditch; drain; (*b*) sewer. 2. (*a*) cultivation, rearing (of plants); breeding, rearing (of animals); *A:* bringing up (of children); (*b*) *coll.* **die A.,** the young from a deliberate breeding (of animals, birds).

anzuckern, *v.tr. sep.* to sugar (mixture, etc.) slightly; to sprinkle (cake, etc.) with sugar.

Anzug, *m.* 1. approach, drawing near; advance; **im A. sein,** (i) (*of army*) to be approaching; (ii) (*of storm*) to be gathering; (*of trouble, danger*) to be impending, imminent; **der Feind ist im A.,** the enemy is approaching, is advancing, is on the march; **ein Gewitter ist im A.,** a storm is gathering, threatening, brewing, is coming up, is on the way; *F:* **es ist etwas im A.,** there's something up, something in the wind, something brewing, something afoot. 2. *A:* settling; coming into residence (in a place); (*of servant*) starting in a situation. 3. *Chess: etc:* first move, opening move; **den A. haben,** to have the first move, to move first. 4. starting (of machine, etc.). 5. (*a*) *Civ.E:* batter (of a wall, etc.); (*b*) *Clockm:* draw (of lever escapement). 6. (*a*) dress; costume; **in vollem A.,** in full dress, *F:* in full rig, fig; (*b*) suit (of clothes); *Mil:* uniform; **dreiteiliger A.,** three-piece suit; **fertiger A.,** ready-made, *F:* off-the-peg, suit; **sich** *dat.* **einen A. machen lassen,** to have a suit made (for one).

Anzugbolzen, *m. Mec.E: etc:* draw-in bolt.

anzüglich, *a.* (*a*) pointed (remark, question, etc.); **a. werden,** to make pointed remarks; *adv.* **sich a. räuspern,** to clear one's throat pointedly; **a. husten,** to cough pointedly; (*b*) suggestive (joke, etc.).

Anzüglichkeit, *f.* 1. (*a*) pointedness (of remark, question, etc.); (*b*) suggestiveness (of joke, etc.). 2. pointed remark; **sich** *dat.* **Anzüglichkeiten erlauben,** to make pointed remarks.

Anzugmutter, *f. Mec.E: etc:* tightening nut.

Anzugordnung, *f. Mil:* dress regulations.

Anzugsdrehmoment, *n. Mec:* starting torque.

Anzugsgeld, *n. A:* tax on new settlers; tax on persons coming into residence.

Anzugskraft, *f. Mec:* starting power.

Anzugsstoff, *m. Com:* (gentleman's) suiting.

Anzugsvermögen, *n.* (*a*) *Mec:* starting power; (*b*) *Aut:* acceleration; **ein Motorrad hat mehr A. als ein Wagen,** a motor-cycle has better acceleration than a car.

Anzugszeit, *f. El.E:* starting time (of relay).

anzünden, *v.tr. sep.* (*a*) to light (lamp, fire, gas, pipe, etc.); to kindle, ignite, set fire to (sth.); to set (house, forest, etc.) on fire; to fire (sth.); **das Licht a.,** to put on the light; **ein Streichholz a.,** to strike a match, *F:* a light; to light a match; **sich** *dat.* **eine Zigarette, eine Pfeife, a.,** to light a cigarette, a pipe; *F:* to light up; (*b*) to inflame, kindle, fire, excite (passions, etc.).

Anzünder, *m.* 1. (*pers.*) lighter, *esp.* lamplighter. 2. (*a*) lighting device; lighter (for gas, cigarettes, etc.); igniter; (*b*) *Dom.Ec:* firelighter.

anzwängen, *v.tr. sep.* to force on (tight shoe, garment, etc.).

anzwecken, *v.tr. sep.* to fasten (sth.) on with sprigs *or* tacks; to sprig, tack, (sth.) on; *Bootm:* to peg (sole, heel).

anzweifeln, *v.tr. sep.* to call (sth.) in question; to question (sth.); to cast doubts upon (sth.); to have (one's) doubts about (sth.).

anzwinkern, *v.tr. sep.* to blink at (s.o., sth.); to wink at (s.o.); to flutter one's eyelids at (s.o.).

Äol [ˈɛːol]. *Pr.n.m.* -s. *Gr.Myth:* Aeolus.

Äoler [ɛˑˈoːlər], *m.* -s/-. *A.Geog:* Aeolian.

Äolien [ɛˑˈoːlĭən]. *Pr.n.n.* -s. *A.Geog:* Aeolis, Aeolia.

Äolier [ɛˑˈoːlĭər], *m.* -s/-. *A.Geog:* Aeolian.

Äolipile [ɛˑoˑliˑˈpiːlə], *f.* -/-n. 1. *Ph:* aeolipile, -pyle. 2. soldering lamp, blow-lamp.

Äolis [ˈɛːoˑlis]. *Pr.n.n.* -'. *A.Geog:* Aeolis, Aeolia.

äolisch [ɛˑˈoːliʃ], *a. A.Geog:* Aeolian; *Mus:* **äolische Tonart,** Aeolian mode.

Äolsharfe [ˈɛːols-], *f. Mus:* Aeolian harp.

Äolus [ˈɛːoˑlus]. *Pr.n.m.* -'. *Gr.Myth:* Aeolus.

Äon [ɛːˈoːn], *m.* -s/-en, aeon.

äonenlang [ɛˑˈoːnən-], *a.* lasting for aeons; eternal; *adv.* during aeons upon aeons; eternally.

Aorist [aˑoˑˈrist], *m.* -(e)s/-e. *Gram:* aorist.

aoristisch [aˑoˑˈristiʃ], *a. Gram:* aorist.

Aorta [aˑˈortaː], *f.* -/-ten. *Anat:* aorta.

Aorten- [aˑˈortən-], *comb.fm. Anat:* aortic . . . ; . . . of the aorta; **Aortenbogen** *m*, arch of the aorta; **Aortenstamm** *m*, aortic trunk; **Aortenwand** *f*, wall of the aorta.

Aorteninsuffizienz, *f. Med:* aortic insufficiency, aortic incompetence.

Aortenkammer, *f. Anat:* left ventricle (of the heart).

Apache [aˑˈpaxə], *m.* -n/-n. 1. *Ethn:* Apache. 2. *F:* apache, ruffian (*esp.* of Paris).

Apagoge [apᵓaˑˈgoːgə, apᵓagoˑˈgɛː], *f.* -/-n. *Log:* apagoge; abduction.

apagogisch [apᵓaˑˈgoːgiʃ], *a. Log:* apagogic(al); **apagogischer Beweis,** reductio ad absurdum.

Apalachicolabai, die [apalatʃiˈkolaˑˌbai]. *Pr.n.f. Geog:* Apalachee Bay.

Apanage [apaˑˈnaːʒə], *f.* -/-n. *Hist:* ap(p)anage (of a prince).

apanagieren [apaˑnaˑˈʒiːrən], *v.tr. Hist:* to endow (a prince) with an ap(p)anage.

apart [aˈpart]. 1. *adv.* apart; **Spaß a.,** joking apart; **etwas a. legen,** to put sth. aside. 2. *a.* distinctive (clothes, pers., face, etc.); smart, stylish (hat, dress, etc.); striking, unusual (face, pers., etc.); original (personality, etc.); **aparte Abendkleidung,** distinctive evening clothes, evening clothes of distinction; **a. aussehen,** to have a distinctive appearance.

Aparte [aˈpartə], *n.* -/-s. *Th:* aside, stage-whisper.

Apartheid [aˑˈparthait], *f.* -/. apartheid.

Apathie [aˑpaˑˈtiː], *f.* -/. apathy, listlessness.

apathisch [aˑˈpaːtiʃ], *a.* apathetic, listless.

Apatit [apaˈtiːt], *m.* -s/-e. *Miner:* apatite.

Apennin, der [apɛˈniːn] -s, **Apenninen, die** [apɛˈniːnən] *m.pl. Pr.n.Geog:* the Apennines.

Apenninenhalbinsel, die. *Geog:* The Italian peninsula.

apenninisch [apɛˈniːniʃ], *a. Geog:* Apennine.

Apenrade [apənˈraːdə]. *Pr.n.n.* -s. *Geog:* Aabenraa.

Apepsie [aˑpɛpˈsiː], *f.* -/. *Med:* apepsy, indigestion, dyspepsia.

aper [ˈapər], *a. South G.Dial:* clear of snow.

Aperçu [apɛrˈsyː], *n.* -s/-s. 1. aperçu, summary; conspectus. 2. flash of insight. 3. witty saying; *jeu d'esprit.*

Aperiens [aˑˈpeːrĭɛns], *n.* -/-entia [aˑpeˑrĭˈɛntsĭa]. *Pharm:* aperient.

aperiodisch [aˑpeˑrĭˈoːdiʃ], *a. Mec: El:* aperiodic; dead-beat (galvanometer, voltmeter, etc.).

Aperitif [apeˑriˑˈtiːf], *m.* -s/-s, aperitif, appetizer.

apern [ˈapərn], *v.i.* (*haben*) *South G.Dial:* to become clear of snow.

Apertur [aˑpɛrˈtuːr], *f.* -/-en. 1. (*a*) *esp. Anat:* aperture, opening; (*b*) *Opt: Phot:* aperture; **numerische A.,** numerical aperture. 2. *A.Jur:* reversion (of lands).

Aperwind [ˈapər-], *m. South G.Dial:* westerly wind (causing thaw).

Apetale [aˑpeˈtaːlə], *f.* -/-n. *Bot:* plant with apetalous flowers.

apetal(isch) [aˑpeˈtaːl(iʃ)], *a. Bot:* apetalous.

Apex [ˈaːpɛks], *m.* -/**Apizes** [ˈaːpiˑtseːs]. 1. apex (of cone, tower, curve, etc.); tip (of cone, spire, etc.); *Astr:* **A. der Sonnenbewegung,** apex of the sun's motion. 2. (priest's) conical hat. 3. (*a*) *Mus:* (stress) accent; (*b*) *Gram: Pros:* length mark (over vowel).

Apfel, *m.* -s/⸚. 1. apple; **wilder A.,** crab-apple; **fauler A.,** rotten apple; **j-n mit faulen Äpfeln bewerfen** = to pelt s.o. with rotten tomatoes; **der A. der Zwietracht,** the apple of discord; *F:* **etwas für einen Apfel und ein Ei kaufen, verkaufen,** to buy, sell, sth. for a mere trifle, for a (mere) song; **in den sauren A. beißen (müssen),** to (have to) swallow the (bitter) pill, to (have to) take one's medicine; **es konnte kein A. zur Erde (fallen),** (it was so crowded that) there wasn't room to move an elbow, to breathe; **der A. fällt nicht weit vom Stamm,** (i) *Prov:* like father like son; what's bred in the bone will come out in the flesh; (ii) he's a chip of, off, the old block. 2. orb (of regalia). 3. (horse-) dropping, *P:* turd. 4. dapple (on horse's hide).

apfelartig, *a.* like, resembling, an apple; *Bot:* pomaceous, malaceous.

Apfeläther, *m. Ch:* synthetic apple oil.

Apfelausstecher, *m. Dom.Ec:* apple-corer.

Apfelbäckchen, *n.pl.* (*of pers.*) **mit A.,** apple-cheeked.

Apfelbaum, *m.* apple-tree; **wilder A.,** crab(-apple) tree, wild apple-tree.

Apfelbeere, *f. Bot:* choke-berry.

Apfelblattsauger, *m. Ent:* psylla mali, apple psylla.

Apfelblüte, *f.* apple-blossom.

Apfelbohrer, *m. Ent:* apple weevil.

Apfelbranntwein, *m.* apple-brandy; (*French*) calvados; *U.S:* apple-jack.

Äpfelbrater, *m.* -s/-. *A:* (*pers.*) molly-coddle.

apfelbraun, *a.* dappled bay (horse).

Apfelbrecher, *m. Tls:* apple-picker.

Apfelbrei, *m.* (*a*) *Cu:* apple sauce; (*b*) *Cu:* apple purée; (*c*) *Com:* apple pulp.

Apfelcharlotte, *f. Cu:* apple charlotte.

Apfeldorn, *m. Bot:* crab-tree, wild apple-tree.

Apfelfalbe, *m.* (*decl. as adj.*) dappled light-bay horse.

Apfelfrau, *f.* apple-woman.

Apfelfrucht, *f. Bot:* pome.

Apfelfuchs, *m.* dappled chestnut horse.

Apfelgarten, *m.* apple-orchard.

Apfelgebackenes, *n. Cu:* apple turnover.

Apfelgehäuse, *n.* apple-core.

Apfelgelee, *n.* apple jelly.

apfelgrau, *a.* dapple-grey (horse).

Apfelgriebs, *m.* apple-core.

apfelgrün. 1. *a.* apple-green. 2. *s.* **Apfelgrün,** *n.* apple-green (colour).

apfelig, *a.* dappled (horse, sky, etc.).

Apfelkammer, *f.* store-room for apples; apple-loft.

Apfelkelter, *m.* cider-press.

Apfelkern, *m.* apple-pip.

Apfelkloß, *m. Cu:* (steamed) apple pudding; apple dumpling.

Apfelkompott, *n. Cu:* (*a*) stewed apples; (*b*) apple sauce; (*c*) apple purée.

Apfelkrapfen, *m. Cu:* apple-fritter.

Apfelkraut, *n. Cu:* thickened apple syrup.

Apfelkreuz, *n. Her:* cross pommetty, pommelly.

Apfelkuchen, *m. Cu:* apple flan, *U.S:* apple cake.

Apfelmade, *f. Ent:* **große A.,** caterpillar of the codling-moth.

Apfelmost, *m.* 1. (unfermented) apple-juice. 2. new cider.

Apfelmotte, *f. Ent:* codling-moth.

Apfelmus, *n. Cu:* (*a*) apple purée; (*b*) apple sauce.

äpfeln, *v.i.* (*haben*) (*of horse*) to drop dung, to dung.

Apfelpfannkuchen, *m. Cu:* pancake made with sliced apples; apple-fritters.

Apfelpresse, *f.* cider-press.

Apfelquitte, *f. Hort:* apple-quince, round quince.

Apfelringe, *m.pl.* (*a*) *Com:* dried apple rings; (*b*) *Cu:* apple-fritters.

Apfelsaft, *m.* apple-juice.

Apfelsalbe, *f. A:* pomade, pomatum.

apfelsauer, *a. Ch:* malate of . . . ; **apfelsaures Salz,** malate.

Apfelsauger, *m.* = **Apfelblattsauger.**

Apfelsäure, *f. Ch:* malic acid.

Apfelschale, *f.* apple-peel.

Apfelschimmel, *m.* dapple-grey horse.

Apfelschnecke, *f. Conch:* apple-shell.

Apfelschnittchen, *n.pl.* 1. slices of apple. 2. *Com:* = **Apfelschnitzel.** 3. *Cu:* apple-slices.

Apfelschnitzel, *n.pl. Com:* dried apple sections.

Apfelschorf, *m. Hort:* apple scab.

Apfelschuß, *m.* (William Tell's) shooting at the apple (on his son's head).

Apfelsine [apfəl'ziːnə], *f.* -/-**n,** (sweet) orange; *A:* China orange.

Apfelsinenbaum, *m.* orange-tree.

Apfelsinensaft, *m.* orange-juice.

Apfelsinenschale, *f.* orange-peel.

Apfelspinner, *m. Ent:* apple-tree bombyx.

Apfelstecher, *m.* **1.** *Dom.Ec:* apple-corer. **2.** *Ent:* apple weevil.

Apfelstrudel, *m. Cu:* apple strudel.

Apfeltasche, *f. Cu:* (*a*) apple turnover; (*b*) apple puff.

Apfeltorte, *f.* apple tart; apple flan; **gedeckte A.,** apple pie.

äpfeltragend, *a. Bot:* pomiferous.

Apfelwein, *m.* cider.

Apfelwickler, *m. Ent:* codling-moth.

Aphärese [afɛ·'reːzə], *f.* -/-**n.** *Ling:* aphaeresis, aphesis.

Aphasie [a·fa·'ziː], *f.* -/-**n** [-'ziːən]. *Med:* aphasia.

Aphasiker [a·'faːzikər], *m.* -**s**/-. *Med:* aphasiac.

aphasisch [a·'faːziʃ], *a. Med:* aphasiac, aphasic.

Aphel [a·'feːl], *n.* -**s**/-**e, Aphelium** [a·'feːlium], *n.* -**s**/-**lien.** *Astr:* aphelion.

Aphidide [a·fi·'diːdə], *f.* -/-**n.** *Ent:* aphid.

Aphis ['aːfis], *f.* -/. *Ent:* aphis.

Aphongetriebe [a·'foːn-], *n. Aut:* synchromesh (gearing).

Aphonie [a·fo·'niː], *f.* -/-**n** [-'niːən]. *Med:* loss of voice; aphonia, aphony.

aphonisch [a·'foːniʃ], *a. Med: etc:* aphonic, aphonous; *Ling:* voiceless.

Aphorismus [afo·'rismus], *m.* -/-**men,** aphorism.

aphoristisch [afo·'ristiʃ], *a.* aphoristic; *adv.* aphoristically.

Aphrodisiakum [afro·di·'ziːa·kum], *n.* -**s**/-**ka,** aphrodisiac.

aphrodisisch [afro·'diːziʃ], *a.* (*a*) concerning love; concerning Aphrodite; like Aphrodite; (*b*) aphrodisiac.

Aphrodite [afro·'diːtə]. *Pr.n.f.* -**s.** *Gr.Myth:* Aphrodite.

aphroditisch [afro·'diːtiʃ], *a. occ.* = **aphrodisisch.**

Aphthe ['aftə], *f.* -/-**n,** (*a*) *Med: Vet:* aphtha; aphthous pustule; (*b*) *pl.* **Aphthen,** *Med:* aphthous stomatitis; (*in infants*) thrush.

Aphthenseuche ['aftən-], *f. Vet:* aphthous fever, *F:* foot-and-mouth disease.

aphthös [af'tøːs], *a. Med: Vet:* aphthous.

Aphylle [a·'fylə], *f.* -/-**n.** *Bot:* aphyllous plant.

aphyllisch [a·'fyliʃ], *a. Bot:* aphyllous, leafless.

apikal [a·pi·'kaːl], *a. & comb.fm.* **Apikal-,** *Geom: Bot: etc:* apical.

Apikultur [ˌaːpi·kul'tuːr], *f.* apiculture, bee-keeping, bee-rearing.

Apiol [a·pi'oːl], *n.* -**s**/. *Pharm:* apiol, parsley-camphor.

Apirie [a·pi·'riː], *f.* -/. inexperience.

Apis ['aːpis], *m.* -/. *Egypt. Ant:* apis, sacred bull.

Aplanat [a·pla·'naːt], *m.* -**s**/-**e.** *Phot:* aplanat; aplanatic lens.

aplanatisch [a·pla·'naːtiʃ], *a. Phot:* aplanatic.

Aplanatismus [a·pla·na·'tismus], *m.* -/. *Opt:* aplanatism.

aplastisch [a·'plastiʃ], *a. Biol:* (*of blood, deposits, etc.*) aplastic.

Aplit [a·'pliːt], *m.* -**s**/. *Miner:* aplite.

Aplomb [a'plõː], *m.* -**s**/. aplomb; self-confidence, self-assurance.

Apnoe [a'pnoːeː], *f.* -/. *Med:* apnoea.

Apochromat [apo·kro·'maːt], *m. Phot:* apochromat.

apochromatisch [apo·kro·'maːtiʃ], *a. Phot:* apochromatic (lens).

apodeiktisch [apo·'daiktiʃ]. *Log: Phil:* apod(e)ictic, clearly demonstrable, indisputable; *adv.* apod(e)ictically.

Apodeixis [apo·'daiksis], *f.* -/. *Log: Phil:* apod(e)ixis, clear demonstration, absolute proof.

apodiktisch [apo·'diktiʃ], *a.* (*a*) = **apodeiktisch;** (*b*) (*of pers., statement*) dogmatic.

apodisch [a·'poːdiʃ], *a. Z:* apodal; (*a*) apodous, footless; **apodisches Tier,** apod; (*b*) *Ich:* without ventral fins; **apodischer Fisch,** apodan.

Apodosis [a'podo·zis], *f.* -/-**dosen** [apo'doːzən]. *Gram:* apodosis, 'then'-clause.

Apogamie [apo·ga·'miː], *f.* -/. *Bot:* apogamy.

Apogäum [apo·'gɛːum], *n.* -**s**/-**äen.** *Astr:* apogee.

Apokalypse [apo·ka·'lypsəl, *f.* -/-**n,** apocalypse; *B.Lit:* **die A.,** the Book of Revelation, the Apocalypse (of St John).

Apokalyptik [apo·ka·'lyptik], *f.* -/. **1.** apocalyptic ideas; apocalyptic studies. **2.** leaning towards apocalyptic ideas.

Apokalyptiker [apo·ka·'lyptikər], *m.* -**s**/-, (*a*) believer in the Apocalypse; (*b*) expert on, scholar with special knowledge of, the Apocalypse; (*c*) *occ.* (any) one of the Four Horsemen of the Apocalypse.

apokalyptisch [apo·ka·'lyptiʃ], *a.* **1.** apocalyptic; **die Apokalyptischen Reiter,** the Four Horsemen of the Apocalypse; **die apokalyptische Zahl,** the apocalyptic number, 666; *B.Lit:* the number of the beast. **2.** (outlook, etc.) coloured by apprehensions of impending disaster; gloomy (view of life); **apokalyptische Stimmung,** atmosphere of impending disaster.

apokarp(isch) [apo·'karp(iʃ)], *a. Bot:* apocarpous.

Apokatastase [apo·kata·'staːzə], *f.* -/. apocatastasis; return to a previous condition *or* position.

Apokope [apo·'koːpə], *f.* -/-**n.** *Ling:* apocope.

apokopieren [apo·ko·'piːrən], *v.tr. Ling:* to apocopate, cut off; **apokopiert,** apocopated.

Apokryph [apo·'kryːf], *n.* -**s**/-**en,** apocryphal book; *B.Lit:* **die Apokryphen,** the Apocrypha; **die neutestamentlichen Apokryphen,** the New Testament Apocrypha.

apokryph(isch) [apo·'kryːf(iʃ)], *a.* apocryphal.

apolar [a·po·'laːr], *a. Biol: Anat:* apolar (cell).

apolitisch [a·po·'liːtiʃ], *a.* non-political.

Apoll [a'pol]. *Pr.n.m.* -**s.** *Myth:* Apollo; *Art:* **der A. vom Belvedere,** the Apollo (of the) Belvedere; *F:* **Bruder in A.,** brother-artist, brother-poet; **er ist schön wie A., er ist der reinste A.,** he is as handsome as a Greek god.

apollinisch [apo'liːniʃ], *a.* Apolline, Apollinic.

Apollo [a'poloː]. **1.** *Pr.n.m.* -**s.** *Myth:* Apollo. **2.** *m.* -**s**/-**s** = **Apollofalter.**

Apollofalter, *m. Ent:* Apollo butterfly.

Apollon [a'poloːn]. *Pr.n.m.* -**s.** *Myth:* Apollo.

Apolog [apo·'loːk], *m.* -**s**/-**e** [-'loːgə]. *Lit:* apologue, fable.

Apologet [apo·lo·'geːt], *m.* -**en**/-**en,** apologist.

Apologetik [apo·lo·'geːtik], *f.* -/. *Theol:* apologetics.

apologetisch [apo·lo·'geːtiʃ], *a.* (*of book, etc.*) apologetic(al); *adv.* apologetically.

Apologie [apo·lo·'giː], *f.* -/-**n** [-'giːən], apology, apologia (*gen.,* for); defence, vindication, (written) justification (*gen.,* of).

Aponeurose [apo·noy'roːzə], *f. Anat:* aponeurosis, fascia.

aponeurotisch [apo·noy'roːtiʃ], *a. Anat:* aponeurotic, fascial.

Apophthegma [apo·'ftɛgmaː], *n.* -**s**/-**men** [-mən] *&* -**mata** [-ma·taː], apophthegm.

Apophyge [apo·'fyːgə], *f.* -/-**n.** *Arch:* scape, spring, apophyge (of column).

Apophyse [apo·'fyːzə], *f.* -/-**n,** apophysis; **1.** *Anat:* process; **2.** *Bot:* offshoot; **3.** *Geol:* outgrowth.

Apoplektiker [apo·'plɛktikər], *m.* -**s**/-. *Med:* apoplectic.

apoplektisch [apo·'plɛktiʃ], *a. Med:* apoplectic.

Apoplexie [apo·plɛ'ksiː], *f.* -/-**n** [-'ksiːən]. *Med:* apoplexy, cerebral haemorrhage.

Aporie [apo·'riː], *f.* -/-**n** [-'riːən]. *Rh:* aporia.

Aposiopese [apo·zi·o·'peːzə], *f.* -/-**n.** *Rh:* aposiopesis.

Apostasie [apo·sta·'ziː], *f.* -/-**n** [-'ziːən], apostasy.

apostasieren [apo·sta·'ziːrən], *v.i.* (*haben*) to apostatize, to become an apostate; to renounce one's party, one's principles.

Apostat [apo·'staːt], *m.* -**en**/-**en,** apostate.

apostatisch [apo·'staːtiʃ], *a.* apostate.

Apostel [a'postəl], *m.* -**s**/-, apostle.

Apostelakten, *n.pl. B.Lit:* **die apokryphen A.,** the apocryphal acts of (certain of) the apostles.

Apostelamt [a'postəl-], *n.* apostolate, apostleship.

Apostelbrief, *m. B.Lit:* epistle.

Apostelgeschichte, *f. B:* **die A.,** the Acts of the Apostles.

Apostelkollegium, *n.* the Twelve Apostles.

Apostelkonzil, das, *B.Hist:* the gathering of the Apostles (at Jerusalem).

Apostelkrug, *m.* jug decorated with figures of the Apostles, apostle jug.

Apostellöffel, *m.* apostle spoon.

Aposteltum, *n.* -**s**/. = **Apostelamt.**

Apostelwürde, *f.* = **Apostelamt.**

Apostem [apo'steːm], *n.* -**s**/-**e.** *Med:* apostem(e), abscess.

a posteriori [a· poste·ri·'oːriː]. *Lt.adv.phr. Log:* a posteriori.

Aposteriori, *n.* -**s**/-. *Log:* principle established a posteriori, empirical principle.

aposteriorisch [a·poste·ri·'oːriʃ], *a.* empirical (knowledge, etc.), (knowledge, etc.) a posteriori.

Apostolat [aposto·'laːt], *n.* -(**e**)**s**/-**e,** apostolate, apostleship.

Apostoliker [apos'toːlikər], *m.pl. Rel.Hist:* Apostolics.

Apostolikum [apos'toːli·kum], *n.* -**s**/. *Ecc:* **das A.,** the Apostles' Creed.

apostolisch [apos'toːliʃ], *a.* **1.** apostolic (church, doctrine, etc.); **das Apostolische Glaubensbekenntnis,** the Apostles' Creed; **der Apostolische Segen,** the apostolic benediction; *Rel.Hist:* **die Apostolischen Väter,** the Apostolic Fathers; **apostolische Nachfolge, Sukzession,** apostolic succession. **2.** apostolic, papal; **apostolischer Legat,** papal legate; *Hist:* **seine Apostolische Majestät,** (i) the King of Hungary, (ii) the Emperor of Austria; *see also* **Stuhl, Vikar.**

Apostolizität [aposto·li·tsi·'tɛːt], *f.* -/. apostolicity; apostolic character *or* origin.

Apostroph [apos'troːf, apo·'stroːf], *m.* -**s**/-**e.** *Gram:* apostrophe.

Apostrophe [a'postro·feː, apo·'stroːfə], *f.* -/-**n** [-'stroːfən]. *Rh:* apostrophe.

apostrophieren [apostro·'fiːrən], *v.tr.* **1.** to apostrophize (s.o.). **2.** to apostrophize, put an apostrophe after (a word).

apothekarisch [apo·te·'kaːriʃ], *a.* pharmaceutical.

Apotheke [apo·'teːkə], *f.* -/-**n,** (*a*) (dispensing) chemist's shop, *U.S:* drugstore; pharmacy; *A:* apothecary's shop; (*b*) (*in hospital, etc.*) dispensary.

Apotheker [apo·'teːkər], *m.* -**s**/-, pharmacist, pharmaceutist; dispensing chemist, dispenser, *U.S: & Scot:* druggist; (pharmaceutical) chemist; apothecary.

Apothekerbuch [apo·'teːkər-], *n.* pharmacopoeia; dispensatory.

Apothekergewicht, *n.* apothecaries' weight.

Apothekerkunst, *f.* = **Apothekerwissenschaft.**

Apothekerladen, *m.* = **Apotheke** (*a*).

Apothekerlatein, *n. F:* dog-Latin; vile Latin.

apothekern [apo·'teːkərn], *v.i.* (*haben*) **1.** to dispense medicines. **2.** *F: A:* to dose oneself.

Apothekerordnung, *f.* dispensatory; instructions for dispensing.

Apothekerpräparate, *n.pl. Com:* pharmaceutical preparations; drugs.

Apothekerpreis, *m. F:* exorbitant price, *F:* stiff, steep, price.

Apothekerrechnung, *f.* (*a*) chemist's bill; (*b*) *F:* exorbitant bill, *F:* stiff, swingeing, bill.

Apothekerrose, *f. Bot:* Provence rose.

Apothekerschaft, *f.* -/. **die deutsche A.,** the German Pharmaceutical Society.

Apothekerschwamm, *m.* bath-sponge.

Apothekerskink, *m. Rept:* adda, medicinal skink.

Apothekerwaren, *f.pl. Com:* pharmaceutical goods, drugs.

Apothekerwarenhändler, *m.* wholesale druggist.

Apothekerwissenschaft, *f.* pharmacy, pharmaceutics.

Apothem [apo·'teːm], *n.* -**s**/-**e.** *Geom:* apothem.

Apotheose [apo·te·'oːzə], *f.* -/-**n,** apotheosis; deification.

apotheosieren [apo·te·o·'ziːrən], *v.tr.* to apotheosize; to deify; **Apotheosierung** *f,* apotheosis; deification.

Apotropaion [a·po·tro·'paion], *n.* -**s**/-**paia** = **Apotropäum.**

apotropäisch [a·po·tro·'pɛːiʃ], *a.* apotropaic, protective (effect, etc.); protective (charm, amulet, etc.).

Apotropäum [a·po·tro·'pɛːum], *n.* -**s**/-**päen,** apotropaion; protective amulet *or* charm.

Appalachen, die [apa·'laxən]. *Pr.n.pl. Geog:* the Appalachian Mountains.

Appalachentee, *m. Bot:* yaupon; (*beverage*) black drink.

appalachisch [apa·'laxiʃ], *a.* Appalachian; **das Appalachische Gebirge,** the Appalachian Mountains.

Apparat [apa·'raːt], *m.* -(**e**)**s**/-**e.** **1.** (*a*) apparatus, outfit; equipment; *Ind:* plant; **chirurgischer A.,** surgical apparatus; **der A. des primitiven Menschen,** the equipment of primitive man; (*b*) (*in library*) research material(s); books in use for a particular piece of research, etc.; **den A. zusammenstellen,** to get one's books together; **'A. — bitte nicht entfernen!'** 'books in constant use—please do not remove'. **2.** *Lit:* **kritischer A. (zu einem Text),** critical apparatus, apparatus criticus (of a text). 3. device, appliance, (piece of) apparatus; instrument; contrivance; gadget; *esp.* (*a*) *Tp:* (telephone) instrument; **j-n an den A. rufen,** to call s.o. to the telephone; **'ist Herr X da?' — 'am A.',** 'is Mr X there?'—'speaking'; **bleiben Sie bitte am A.!** hold the line, hold on, please; **A. (Nummer) 3,** extension 3; (*b*) (radio, television) set; (*c*) (**photographischer**) **A.,** camera; (*d*) (= **Lichtbildapparat**) lantern; projector; (*e*) (= **Rasierapparat**) safety-razor *or*

electric razor, shaver. **4.** (*a*) *F:* array, pomp, show; trappings; **etwas mit großem A. tun,** to do sth. in style, with all possible display, *F:* with all the trimmings; (*b*) machinery (of government, administration, etc.); paraphernalia.

Apparatebau, *m. Ind:* light engineering, *esp.* apparatus construction.

Apparatebrett, *n. Ind: etc:* apparatus board; instrument board; instrument panel.

Apparatetisch, *m. Ind: etc:* instrument table.

apparativ [apa·ra·ˈtiːf], *a.* (*a*) forming part of the apparatus; (*b*) (matters, etc.) relating to the apparatus.

Apparatur [apa·ra·ˈtuːr], *f.* -/-en, apparatus; equipment; outfit.

apparent [apa·ˈrɛnt], *a.* **1.** obvious, evident, apparent. **2.** (*of movement, size, etc.*) apparent, not real.

Apparenz [apa·ˈrɛnts], *f.* -/. (*a*) appearance, look; semblance (of truth, etc.); (*b*) *Com:* look, appearance, *F:* eye appeal (of an article).

Apparition [apa·ri·tsĭˈoːn], *f.* **-/-en. 1.** *Astr:* appearance, appearing (of star). **2.** apparition, ghost, spectre.

Appartement [apartəˈmãː], *n.* **-s/-s** *& Swiss:* **-e,** apartment; suite *or* set of rooms.

Appassionata, die [apasĭo·ˈnaːtaː], **-.** *Mus:* the Appassionata.

Appel, *m.* **-s/⁼.** *F. & Dial:* apple.

Äppelkahn, *m. Dial: Hum:* (*a*) (*boat*) old tub; (*b*) bed; (*c*) *pl.* **Äppelkähne,** big boots, *F:* beetle-crushers.

Appell [aˈpɛl], *m.* **-s/-e. 1. A. an j-n, an etwas** *acc.*, appeal to s.o., to sth.; **einen A. an j-n richten,** to make an appeal to s.o.; **A. an die Vernunft,** appeal to reason; **A. an die Waffen,** appeal to arms; recourse to arms. **2.** *Mil:* roll-call, call over; parade; inspection (of equipment, etc.); **A. abhalten,** to call (over) the roll, to take the call-over; to hold an inspection; **zum A. blasen,** to sound the (call for) fall-in; **zum A. antreten,** to fall in for roll-call, for inspection; to answer the roll-call; **beim A. fehlen,** to be absent from roll-call. **3.** *Fenc:* appel, alarm. **4.** *Ven:* **Hund, der A., keinen A., hat,** dog that obeys, does not obey, orders; well-trained, badly trained, dog.

appellabel [apɛˈlaːbəl], *a. Jur:* appealable (action).

Appellant [apɛˈlant], *m.* **-en/-en.** *Jur:* appellant.

Appellat [apɛˈlaːt], *m.* **-en/-en.** *Jur:* defendant, respondent (before court of appeal).

Appellation [apɛla·tsĭˈoːn], *f.* **-/-en.** *Jur:* appeal.

Appellationsgericht, *n. Jur:* court of appeal.

Appellativ [apɛla·ˈtiːf], *n.* **-s/-e** [-ˈtiːvə]. *Gram:* appellative; common noun.

appellativisch [apɛla·ˈtiːviʃ], *a, Gram:* appellative.

Appellativum [apɛla·ˈtiːvum], *n.* **-s/-va = Appellativ.**

appellfähig [aˈpɛl-], *a. Mil:* fit to appear on parade.

appellierbar [apɛˈliːrbaːr], *a. Jur:* appealable (action).

appellieren [apɛˈliːrən], *v.i.* (*haben*) **1. an j-n, an etwas** *acc.*, **a.,** to appeal, make an appeal, to s.o., sth.; to call on, invoke, s.o., sth. **2.** *Jur:* to appeal; **die appellierende Partei,** the party appealing, the appellant.

Appellstärke, *f. Mil:* parade state (of unit).

Appendektomie [apɛndɛkto·ˈmiː], *f.* **-/-n** [-ˈmiːən]. *Surg:* appendicectomy, removal of the appendix, *U.S:* appendectomy.

appendikular [apɛndi·ku·ˈlaːr], *a. Nat.Hist:* appendicular.

Appendikularien [apɛndi·ku·ˈlaːrĭən], *f.pl. Moll:* appendicularia.

Appendix [aˈpɛndiks], *m.* **-/-dizes** [-di·ˌtseːs] & **-es/-e. 1.** appendix, supplement (to book, etc.). **2.** annex(e), appendage (to building). **3.** *also f.* **-/-dizes** & **-dices.** *Anat:* (vermiform) appendix.

appendizieren [apɛndi·ˈtsiːrən], *v.tr.* to append (document, note, etc.).

Appendizitis [apɛndi·ˈtsiːtis], *f.* -/. *Med:* appendicitis.

Appertinens [apɛrti·ˈnɛns], *n.* **-/-nenzien** [-ˈnɛntsĭən], appurtenance.

Apperzeption [apɛrtsɛptsĭˈoːn], *f.* **-/-en. 1.** *Psy:* apperception. **2.** perception.

apperzeptiv [apɛrtsɛpˈtiːf], *a.* **1.** *Psy:* apperceptive. **2.** perceptive.

apperzipieren [apɛrtsi·ˈpiːrən], *v.tr. Psy:* to apperceive.

Appetanz [ape·ˈtants], *f.* -/. *Orn:* appetitive behaviour.

Appetit [ape·-, apa·ˈtiːt], *m.* **-(e)s/-e,** appetite; **(einen) guten A. haben,** to have a good, a hearty, appetite; **mit (gutem) A. essen,** to eat heartily, with relish, with zest; **guten A.!** I hope you enjoy it; **einen Spaziergang machen, um A. zu bekommen,** to go for a walk to get up an appetite; **A. auf etwas** *acc.*, **nach etwas, haben,** to have an appetite for sth.; **hättest du A. auf ein Schweinskotelett?** would you fancy, could you manage, a pork chop? **ich habe keinen rechten A.,** I'm off my food; **j-m den A. anregen,** to give s.o. an appetite; **j-m den A. verderben, nehmen,** to spoil, take away, s.o.'s appetite; *Prov:* **der A. kommt beim, mit dem, Essen,** (i) once you start eating you soon get hungry, (ii) the more a man gets the more he wants; the appetite grows with what it feeds on.

appetitanregend, *a.* appetizing (food, etc.); (medicine, etc.) that stimulates the appetite, that gives one an appetite.

Appetitbissen, *m.* = **Appetithappen.**

Appetitbrötchen, *n. Cu:* canapé; (savoury) snack; cocktail savoury.

appetiterregend, *a.* appetizing.

Appetiterreger, *m.* appetizer.

Appetithappen, *m.* (*a*) tasty morsel, savoury morsel; titbit; (*b*) = **Appetitbrötchen.**

appetitiv [ape·ti·ˈtiːf], *a.* appetitive.

appetitlich [ape·ˈtiːtliç], *a.* (*of food*) appetizing, tempting, dainty, savoury, tasty; (*of girl*) attractive-looking; dainty; wholesome-looking; (*of room, etc.*) attractive, inviting, pleasing; **ein appetitlicher Bissen,** a savoury, tasty, toothsome, morsel; **ein Gericht a. machen,** to make a dish appetizing, attractive; *adv.* appetizingly; daintily; attractively.

Appetitlosigkeit, *f.* lack of appetite; loss of appetite; *Med:* inappetence, anorexia.

Appisch [ˈapiʃ], *a. Rom.Ant:* **die Appische Straße,** the Appian Way.

applanieren [apla·ˈniːrən], *v.tr.* (*a*) to flatten, level, smooth (surface, etc.); (*b*) to settle (dispute).

applaudieren [aplauˈdiːrən], *v.tr. & i.* (*haben*) to applaud, clap (s.o., sth.); to greet (s.o., sth.) with applause.

Applaus [aˈplaus], *m.* **-es/-e** [-ˈplauzə], applause, clapping; **donnernder A.,** thunderous applause, loud applause; **A. spenden,** to applaud; **A. bekommen, erhalten,** to meet with, be greeted with, applause.

applikabel [apli·ˈkaːbəl], *a.* applicable; employable; serviceable.

Applikant [apli·ˈkant], *m.* **-en/-en,** applicant; candidate (for a job).

Applikation [apli·ka·tsĭˈoːn], *f.* **-/-en. 1.** application (**einer Sache an etwas** *acc.*, of sth. to sth.). **2.** request, application (for a job, etc.). **3.** assiduity, diligence, application. **4.** *Needlew:* appliqué (trimmings).

Applikationsarbeit [apli·ka·tsĭˈoːns-], *f. Needlew:* appliqué work; appliquéd ornament.

Applikationsstickerei, *f. Needlew:* appliqué work.

Applikatur [apli·ka·ˈtuːr], *f.* **-/-en. 1.** *Mus:* fingering (of piece of music). **2.** *occ.* = **Applikationsstickerei.**

Appliqué [apli·ˈkeː], *n.* **-s/-s.** *Metall:* (kind of) German silver.

applizieren [apli·ˈtsiːrən], *v.tr.* to apply (medicament, paint, etc.); to administer (remedy, etc.); *F:* **j-m eine Ohrfeige a.,** to give s.o. a box on the ear.

Appoggiatura [apodʒa·ˈtuːraː], *f.* **-/-ren.** *Mus:* appoggiatura.

Appoint [apo·ˈɛ̃ː], *m.* **-s/-s.** *Com:* small note; draft for the balance due; **per A. trassieren,** to draw for the exact amount.

Appoloniakraut [apo·ˈloːnĭaː-], *n. Bot:* monk's-hood, wolf's-bane, blue rocket.

apponieren [apo·ˈniːrən], *v.tr.* to appose; to affix; to attach, annex (document, etc.).

apport[1] [aˈport], *int.* (*order to dog*) fetch!

Apport[2], *m.* **-s/-e. 1.** *Com: Ind:* contribution (of equipment, etc.). **2.** *Psychics:* apport.

apportieren [aporˈtiːrən], *v.tr. & i.* (*haben*) to fetch (sth.); (*of dog*) (i) *Ven:* to retrieve (game); (ii) to fetch (stick, etc.); *v.i.* to fetch and carry (for s.o.).

Apportierhund [aporˈtiːr-], *m. Ven:* retriever.

Apposition [apo·zi·tsĭˈoːn], *f.* **-/-en.** *Gram: etc:* apposition; **als A. stehendes Wort,** word in apposition.

appositionell [apo·zi·tsĭo·ˈnɛl], *a. Gram:* appositional.

Appositionsauge, *n. Ent:* apposition eye.

appositiv [apo·zi·ˈtiːf], *a. Gram:* appositive (word, complement); (word) in apposition.

Apprehension [apre·hɛnzĭˈoːn], *f.* **-/-en,** (*in all senses*) apprehension.

apprehensiv [apre·hɛnˈziːf], *a.* apprehensive.

Appret [aˈpreː], *m. & n.* **-s/-s.** *Tex:* dressing; stiffening (agent).

Appreteur [apre·ˈtøːr], *m.* **-s/-e.** *Ind:* finisher, dresser (of fabrics, etc.).

appretieren [apre·ˈtiːrən], *v.tr.* (*a*) *Tex:* to dress, finish, stiffen (fabrics); (*b*) *Bootm:* to put the finish on (boots, shoes).

Appretierer [apre·ˈtiːrər], *m.* **-s/- = Appreteur.**

Appretur [apre·ˈtuːr], *f.* **-/-en. 1.** (*process*) (*a*) *Tex:* dressing, finishing, stiffening (of fabrics); (*b*) *Bootm:* finishing (of boots, shoes). **2.** (*a*) *Tex:* dressing, stiffening (agent); (*b*) *Bootm:* finishing liquid, finish.

Appreturmaschine, *f. Tex:* finishing-machine.

Approbation [apro·ba·tsĭˈoːn], *f.* **-/-en.** *Adm:* (formal) State approval (of newly qualified doctor, chemist, etc.); certificate of State approval.

approbieren [apro·ˈbiːrən], *v.tr. Adm:* to give (formal) State approval to (newly qualified doctor, chemist, etc.); **approbierter Apotheker,** State-registered chemist.

Approche [aˈprɔʃə], *f.* **-/-n.** *Mil: A:* communication trench, approach trench.

approchieren [aproˈʃiːrən], *v.i.* (*sein*) **1.** to approach. **2.** *Mil: A:* to dig approach trenches.

approfondieren [apro·fonˈdiːrən], *v.tr.* to go deeply, thoroughly, into (sth.); to study (sth.) thoroughly.

Appropriation [apro·pri·a·tsĭˈoːn], *f.* **-/-en,** appropriation (of property, etc.).

appropriieren [apro·pri·ˈiːrən], *v.tr.* to appropriate.

approvisionieren [apro·vi·zĭo·ˈniːrən], *v.tr.* to provide with stores; to provision; to victual; to cater for (s.o.).

Approximation [aproksi·ma·tsĭˈoːn], *f.* **-/-en.** *Mth: etc:* approximation; *Mth:* **geometrische A.,** geometric exhaustion.

Approximationsmethode, *f. Mth:* method of approximation; **geometrische A.,** method of geometric exhaustion.

approximativ [aproksi·ma·ˈtiːf], *a.* approximate; approximative; *adv.* approximately; approximatively.

Approximative [aproksi·ma·ˈtiːvə], *f.* **-/-n.** *Mth:* approximation.

approximieren [aproksi·ˈmiːrən], *v.tr. & i.* (*haben*) to approximate.

Appunto [aˈpuntoː], *m.* **-s/-ti.** *Com:* = **Appoint.**

Apraxie [a·pra·ˈksiː], *f.* -/. *Med:* apraxia.

Aprikose [a·pri·ˈkoːzə], *f.* **-/-n. 1.** apricot. **2.** (*a*) *Hort:* apricot-tree; (*b*) *Bot: F:* **wilde A.,** cannon-ball tree.

Aprikosenbaum, *m.* apricot-tree.

Aprikosenfarbe, *f.* apricot (colour).

Aprikosenpflaume, *f.* apricot-plum.

Aprikosenschnaps, *m. Dist:* apricot-brandy; (*Hungarian*) barack.

April [a·ˈpril], *m.* **-s** & **-/-e.** April; **im A.,** in April; **im Monat A.,** in the month of April; **am siebenten A.,** on the seventh of April, on April (the) seventh; **der erste A.,** (i) the first of April, (ii) April Fool(s') Day, All Fools' day; **j-n in den A. schicken,** to make an April-fool of s.o.; **A.! A.!** April-fool! (*of pers.*) **launisch wie der A.,** capricious, fitful, as April weather; *Prov:* **April tut was er will,** April weather is fickle.

Aprilblume, *f. Bot: F:* wood-anemone.

Aprilfliege, *f. Ent: F:* sand-fly.

Aprilgeschenk, *n.* dummy present (intended to make an April-fool of s.o.); First of April hoax.

Aprilglück, *n.* precarious happiness; short-lived happiness; brief (spell of) good fortune.

Aprilregen, *m.* April showers; *Prov:* **A., Maisegen,** April showers bring forth May flowers.

Aprilschein, *m.* April moon.

Aprilscherz, *m.* April-fool joke, First of April hoax.

April(s)geck, *m.* April-fool.

April(s)narr, *m.* April-fool.

Aprilwetter, *n.* April weather; April showers; changeable, fitful, weather.

a priori [a· pri·ˈoːriː]. *Lt.adv.phr.* a priori.

Apriori, *n.* **-/-,** a priori concept.

apriorisch [a(·)pri·ˈoːriʃ], *a.* a priori (concept, etc.).

Apriorismus [a(·)pri·o·ˈrismus], *m.* **-/-men,** apriorism, (i) a priori reasoning, (ii) a priori idea *or* doctrine.

Apriorist [a(·)pri·o·ˈrist], *m.* **-en/-en,** a priori reasoner, apriorist.

aprioristisch [a(·)pri·o·ˈristiʃ], *a.* a priori (reasoning, reasoner).

apropos, à propos [apro·ˈpoː]. **1.** *adv.* (*a*) **a., haben Sie dieses Buch schon gelesen?** by the way, that reminds me, have you read this book?

a. Bücher, . . . , talking of books . . . ; (*b*) opportunely, seasonably; at the right moment; **die Bemerkung kam sehr a.,** the remark was very apt, very much to the point; the remark came just at the right moment. **2.** *pred.a.* (*of remark, etc.*) opportune, seasonable; apposite; apt.

Apside [ap'si:də], *f.* -/-n. **1.** *Ecc.Arch:* apse. **2.** *Astr:* apsis.

Apsidenlinie, *f. Astr:* line of apsides.

Apsidiole [apsi·di·'o:lə], *f.* -/-n. *Ecc.Arch:* apsidiole, apsidal chapel.

Apsis ['apsis], *f.* -/**Apsiden** [ap'si:dən]. *Ecc.Arch:* apse.

Aptere [ap'te:rə], *f.* -/-n. *Nat.Hist:* apteran; **die Apteren,** the aptera.

aptieren [ap'ti:rən], *v.tr.* to adapt; to adjust; **Aptierung** *f,* adaptation; adjustment.

Aptyalismus [apty·a·'lismus], *m.* -/. *Physiol: Med:* aptyalism.

Apulien [a·'pu:liən]. *Pr.n.n.* -s. *Geog:* Apulia.

Apulier [a·'pu:liər], *m.* -s/-. *Geog:* Apulian.

apulisch [a·'pu:liʃ], *a.* Apulian.

apyretisch [a·py·'re:tiʃ], *a. Med:* apyre(c)tic; free from fever.

Apyrexie [a·py·rɛ·'ksi:], *f.* -/. *Med:* apyrexia; abatement of fever.

apyrisch [a·'py:riʃ], *a.* apyrous; *Cer: etc:* fireproof; *Ch: Min:* refractory.

aqua destillata ['a·kva· desti·'la:ta:], *f.* -/. *Pharm: etc:* distilled water.

Aquädukt [a·kve·'dukt], *m.* -(e)s/-e. *Civ.E:* aqueduct.

Aquafortist [a·kva·for'tist], *m.* -en/-en. *Engr:* etcher, aquafortist.

äqual [ɛ·'kva:l], *a.* equal (*esp.* in age *or* seniority).

Äqualität [ɛ·kva·li·'tɛ:t], *f.* -/. equality (*esp.* in age *or* seniority).

Aquamanile [a·kva·ma·'ni:lə], *n.* -(s)/-. *Ecc:* ewer.

Aquamarin [a·kva·ma·'ri:n]. **1.** *m.* -s/-e. *Miner:* aquamarine. **2.** *n.* -s/. (*colour*) aquamarine, sea-green.

aquamarin², *a.* aquamarine, sea-green.

Äquanimität [ɛ·kva·ni·mi·'tɛ:t], *f.* -/. equanimity.

Aquaplan [a·kva·'pla:n], *m.* -(e)s/-e. *Sp:* surfboard.

Aquarell [a·kva·'rɛl], *n.* -(e)s/-e. *Art:* water-colour (painting); aquarelle.

Aquarelldruck, *m. Print:* reproduction of water-colour (by lithographic *or* offset process).

Aquarellfarbe, *f. Art:* water colour.

Aquarellgemälde, *n.* water-colour painting.

aquarellieren [a·kva·rɛ·'li:rən], *v.tr. & i.* (*haben*) to paint in water-colours.

Aquarellist [a·kva·rɛ·'list], *m.* -en/-en, **Aquarellmaler,** *m.* painter in water-colours, water-colourist; aquarellist.

Aquarellmalerei, *f.* painting in water-colours, water-colour painting.

Aquarianer [a·kva·ri·'a:nər], *m.* -s/-, keeper of an aquarium; fish-breeder, pisciculturist.

Aquarienfische [a·'kva:riən-], *m.pl.* aquarium fish.

Aquarium [a·'kva:riʊm], *n.* -s/-rien, aquarium.

Aquatinta [a·kva·'tinta:], *f.* -/-ten. *Engr:* aquatint.

Äquation [ɛ·kva·tsi·'o:n], *f.* -/-en, equation.

Äquationstafel, *f. Astr:* table showing the transits of the sun (across the meridian).

Äquationsuhr, *f.* clock showing both mean time and true solar time.

aquatisch [a·'kva:tiʃ], *a.* **1.** aquatic. **2.** marshy, watery (land).

Äquator [ɛ·'kva:tor], *m.* -s/. **1.** *Astr:* equator; equinoctial (line). **2.** *Geog:* equator; **unter dem Ä.,** at the equator; **den Ä. überqueren,** to cross the line; **der magnetische Ä.,** the magnetic eqnator; *Meteor:* **thermischer Ä.,** thermal equator.

Äquatoreal [ɛ·kva·to·re·'a:l], *n.* -(e)s/-e, equatorial telescope.

Äquatorhöhe [ɛ·'kva:tor-], *f. Astr:* angle between the equator and the horizon.

äquatorial [ɛ·kva·to·ri·'a:l], *a. & comb.fm.* **Äquatorial-,** equatorial.

Äquatorialkalmen, *f.pl. Nau:* equatorial doldrums.

Äquatorialuhr, *f. Astr:* equatorial clock.

Äquatorkalmen [ɛ·'kva:tor-], *f.pl.*=**Äquatorial- kalmen.**

Äquatorprojektion, *f. Mapm:* equatorial projection.

Äquatortaufe, *f. Nau:* ducking on 'crossing the line'.

Aquavit [a·kva·'vi:t], *m.* -(es)/. *Dist:* (*a*) aqua vitae, eau-de-vie; (*b*) kümmel.

äqui-, Äqui- [ɛ·kvi·-], *comb.fm.* equi-; **äquipollent,**

equipollent; **äquivok,** equivocal; **Äquilibrium** *n,* equilibrium; **Äquivalenz** *f,* equivalence.

äquidistant [ɛ·kvi·dis'tant], *a.* equidistant.

Äquidistanz [ɛ·kvi·dis'tants], *f.* -/-en. *Geom:* equidistance.

Aquilarie [a·kvi·'la:riə], *f.* -/-n. *Bot:* aquilaria, aloe, eagle-wood tree

äquilateral [ɛ·kvi·la·tə·'ra:l], *a. Geom:* equilateral.

Äquilaterum [ɛ·kvi·'la:tərum], *n.* -s/-ra. *Geom:* equilateral figure.

äquilibrieren [ɛ·kvi·li·'bri:rən], *v.tr.* to equilibrate.

Äquilibrismus [ɛ·kvi·li·'brismus], *m.* -/. **1.** theory of equilibrium. **2.** *Phil:* doctrine of mental equilibrium.

Äquilibrist [ɛ·kvi·li·'brist], *m.* -en/-en, equilibrist; rope-walker; acrobat.

äquilibristisch [ɛ·kvi·li·'bristiʃ], *a.* equilibristic.

Äquilibrium [ɛ·kvi·'li:briʊm], *n.* -s/-rien, equilibrium, balance.

äquimolekular [ɛ·kvi·mo·le·ku·'la:r], *a. Ch:* equimolecular.

Aquin [a·'kvi:n]. *Pr.n.n.* -s. **Thomas von A.,** Saint Thomas Aquinas.

Aquinas [a·'kvi:na:s], *a.* **Thomas A.,** Saint Thomas Aquinas.

Aquinate, der [a·kvi·'na:tə], -n. Saint Thomas Aquinas.

Aquino [a·'kvi:no:]. *Pr.n.n.* -s. *Geog:* Aquino; **Thomas von A.,** Saint Thomas Aquinas.

äquinoktial [ɛ·kvi·noktsi·'a:l], *a. & comb.fm.* **Äquinoktial-,** equinoctial.

Äquinoktialgegenden, die, *f.pl. Geog:* the tropics.

Äquinoktialgezeiten, *f.pl.* equinoctial tides.

Äquinoktialkreis, *m.,* **Äquinoktiallinie,** *f. Astr:* equinoctial line; equator.

Äquinoktialsturm, *m.* equinoctial gale.

Äquinoktium [ɛ·kvi·'noktsiʊm], *n.* -s/-tien, equinox.

äquipollent [ɛ·kvi·po'lɛnt], *a.* equipollent.

Äquipollenz [ɛ·kvi·po'lɛnts], *f.* -/-en, equipollence, equipollency.

äquipotential [ɛ·kvi·po·tɛntsi·'a:l], *a. El:* equipotential.

Äquipotentialfläche, *f. El:* equipotential surface.

äquipotentiell [ɛ·kvi·po·tɛntsi·'ɛl], *a.* of equal power.

Aquitanien [a·kvi·'ta:niən]. *Pr.n.n.* -s. *A.Geog:* Aquitaine.

aquitanisch [a·kvi·'ta:niʃ], *a. A.Geog:* Aquitanian.

Äquität [ɛ·kvi·'tɛ:t], *f.* -/-en, equity.

äquivalent¹ [ɛ·kvi·va·'lɛnt], *a.* equivalent.

Äquivalent², *n.* -(e)s/-e, equivalent (**für,** of).

Äquivalentgewicht, *n. Ch:* equivalent weight; combining weight.

Äquivalenz [ɛ·kvi·va·'lɛnts], *f.* -/-en, equivalence.

Äquivalenzparität, *f. Pol.Ec:* parity of exchange.

äquivok [ɛ·kvi·'vo:k], *a.* equivocal.

Äquivokation [ɛ·kvi·vo·ka·tsi·'o:n], *f.* -/-en, equivocation.

Ar [a:r], *n. & m.* -s/- & -e. *Meas:* are (*land-measurement unit of* 100 *square metres,* 119.6 *square yards*).

Ara¹ ['a:ra:], *m.* -s/-s. *Orn:* ara, macaw.

Ara², *f.* -/. *Astr:* Ara, the Altar.

Ära ['ɛ:ra:], *f.* -/**Ären** ['ɛ:rən], era.

Araber ['a·ra·bər, a·'ra:bər], *m.* -s/-. **1.** *Ethn:* Arab. **2.** Arab (horse).

arabesk [a·ra·'bɛsk], *a.* arabesque.

Arabeske [a·ra·'bɛskə], *f.* -/-n. *Arch: Mus: etc:* arabesque.

Arabien [a·'ra:biən]. *Pr.n.n.* -s. Arabia; **das Glückliche A.,** Arabia Felix; **das peträische A.,** Arabia Petraea.

Arabin [a·ra·'bi:n], *n.* -s/. *Ch:* arabin.

Arabinsäure, *f. Ch:* arabic acid.

arabisch [a·'ra:biʃ]. **1.** *a.* Arabic (language, numerals, etc.); Arabian, Arab (customs, etc.); *Geog:* **der Arabische Meerbusen,** the Arabian Gulf; **die Arabische Wüste,** the Arabian Desert. **2.** *s.* **Arabisch,** *n. Ling:* Arabic.

arabisieren [a·ra·bi·'zi:rən], *v.tr.* (*a*) *Ling:* to Arabianize (word, etc.); (*b*) to Arabize (institutions, etc.).

Arabist [a·ra·'bist], *m.* -en/-en. Arabist, Arabic scholar.

Arabistik [a·ra·'bistik], *f.* -/. Arabic studies; Arabic scholarship.

Arachinsäure [a·ra·'xi:n-], *f. Ch:* arachic acid, butic acid.

Arachis [a·'raxis], *f.* -/-. *Bot:* peanut, earth-nut, ground-nut.

Arachisöl, *n. Com:* peanut oil, earth-nut oil.

Arachnide [a·rax·'ni:də], *f.* -/-n. *Nat. Hist:* arachnid.

Arachnoide [a·raxno·'i:də], *f.* -/-n. **1.** *Anat:* arachnoid (membrane). **2.** =**Arachnide.**

Arachnologie [a·raxno·lo·'gi:], *f.* -/. arachnology, araneology.

Aragonese [a·ra·go·'ne:zə], *m.* -n/-n. *Geog:* Aragonese.

Aragonien [a·ra·'go:niən]. *Pr.n.n.* -s. *Geog:* Aragon.

Aragonier [a·ra·'go:niər], *m.* -s/-. *Geog:* Aragonese.

aragonisch [a·ra·'go:niʃ], *a.* Aragonese.

Aragonit [a·ra·go·'ni:t], *m.* -(e)s/-e. *Miner:* aragonite.

Arak ['arak], *m.* -s/-s & -e. *Dist:* arrack.

Aralie [a·'ra:liə], *f.* -/-n. *Bot:* aralia.

Aramäa [a·ra·'mɛa:]. *Pr.n.n.* -s. *A.Geog:* Aramaea.

Aramäer [a·ra·'mɛɪər], *m.* -s/-. *Ethn:* Aramaean.

aramäisch [a·ra·'mɛ:iʃ]. **1.** *a. Ethn:* Aramaean. **2.** *s.* **Aramäisch,** *n. Ling:* Aramaic.

Arancini [a·ran'tsi:ni:], *pl. Austrian:* (sugar-coated *or* chocolate and sugar-coated) crystallized orange peel.

Araneologie [a·ra·ne·o·lo·'gi:], *f.* -/.=**Arachnologie.**

Aräometer [a·rɛo·'me:tər], *n.* -s/-. *Ph: etc:* areometer, hydrometer.

Ärar [ɛ·'ra:r], *n.* -s/-e & (*in Austria*) -ien [-iən], (*a*) *Rom.Ant:* imperial treasury; (*b*) (*esp. in Austria*) Treasury, Exchequer; (*c*) (church, parish, etc.) treasury.

Arara [a·'ra:ra:], *m.* -s/-s & *f.* -/-s. *Orn:* ara, macaw.

ärarial [ɛ·ra·ri·'a:l], *a. & Ärarial-,* comb.fm. fiscal; of *or* connected with the Treasury, the Exchequer; **ärariale Ausgaben,** public expenditure.

Ärarialschatz, *m.*=**Ärarialvermögen.**

Ärarialschuld, *f.* public debt.

Ärarialvermögen, *n.* public funds, State funds, Exchequer (funds).

ärarisch [ɛ·'ra:riʃ], *a.* fiscal; connected with the Treasury.

Ärarium [ɛ·'ra:riʊm], *n.* -s/-rien=**Ärar.**

Araukaner [a·rau·'ka:nər], *m.* -s/-. Araucanian.

Araukanien [a·rau·'ka:niən]. *Pr.n.n.* -s. *Geog:* Araucania.

araukanisch [a·rau·'ka:niʃ], *a.* Araucanian.

Araukarie [a·rau·'ka:riə], *f.* -/-n. *Bot:* araucaria, Chile pine, *F:* monkey-puzzle.

Arbe, *f.* -/-n. *Bot: Swiss:* Swiss stone-pine.

Arbeit, *f.* -/-en. **1.** (*a*) work; labour; toil; exertion; effort; trouble; **an selbständige A. gewöhnt sein,** to be accustomed to working on one's own, to working independently; **A. an etwas** *dat.,* work on sth.; **körperliche A.,** physical work, bodily labour; **von seiner Hände A. leben,** to earn one's living with one's hands; to live by the sweat of one's brow; **geistige A.,** intellectual work, brain-work, head-work; **A. auf dem Gebiet der Archäologie,** work in the archaeological field; **schwere, harte, saure, A.,** hard work, uphill work; **gute A. machen, leisten,** to do good work; **ganze A. machen,** to make a good job of it; **nützliche A. leisten,** to perform useful work; **die A. gehen, sich an die A. machen,** to set to work; **eifrig an die A. gehen,** to set to, to buckle to, *F:* to get down to it, *U.S:* to get down to it; **an, bei, der A.,** at work; **er war tüchtig bei der A.,** he was hard at work, *F:* hard at it; **die A. geht ihm leicht von der Hand, von den Händen,** he's a quick worker, a hustler; he makes the work fly; **die A., sich vor der A., scheuen,** to dislike work, to be work-shy; *F:* **er hat die A. nicht erfunden,** he's a lazy beggar; **die A. einstellen,** (i) to stop work, (ii) to down tools, *U.S:* to quit working; **j-m A. machen, verursachen,** to make work for s.o.; **ich habe damit viel A. gehabt,** I had a good deal of trouble with it; it was heavy going, uphill work; **das ist verlorene A.,** it's wasted effort, a waste of time; *Min:* **A. unter Tage,** work underground; *Prov:* **A. macht das Leben süß,** work is the real recipe for happiness; work (is what) makes life enjoyable; **erst die A., dann das Spiel, dann's Vergnügen,** work first and play afterwards; business before pleasure; (*b*) *Pol: Pol.Ec:* labour; **Kapital und A.,** capital and labour; **der Tag der A.,** Labour Day, the First of May; (*c*) *Mec: Ph:* work; **Wärme in A. umsetzen,** to convert heat into work; **Einheit der A.,** unit of work; (*d*) working, functioning (of machine, pump, the digestion, etc.); operation (of machine, etc.); fermentation, fermenting, working (of wine); (*of wine*) **in A. sein,** to be fermenting, working; (*e*) occupation, employment, work; **j-m A. geben, j-n in A. nehmen,** to give s.o. employment, to give s.o. a job; to take s.o. on; **A. nehmen,** to take, accept, employment; **A. haben,** to be employed, in employment, in work, in a job; to have a job; **keine A. haben, ohne A. sein,** to be unemployed, out of employment, out of a job, jobless; **A. suchen,** to look for work, to try to find work, a job; **auf die, zur,**

A. gehen, to go to (one's) work; **auf A. gehen,** to go out to work; (*f*) piece of work (*to be done*); task, job; **j-m eine A. aufgeben,** to set, assign, s.o. a task; to give s.o. a job to do; **seine A. tun,** to perform one's task, to do one's job; **eine saure A.,** a stiff piece of work; a stiff, gruelling, task; a tough job; **eine langweilige A.,** a boring, dreary, job, *U.S. & F:* a chore; **die zwölf Arbeiten des Herkules, Herakles,** the twelve labours of Hercules; (*g*) **in A. sein,** (*of article*) to be in hand, in the making, in process of manufacture; **ein Möbelstück, ein Paar Schuhe, usw., in A. haben,** to have a piece of furniture, a pair of shoes, etc., in hand; **wir haben die Stühle schon in A.,** we have the chairs in hand, have already started (work) on the chairs; *F:* (*of author*) **ein neues Buch in A. haben,** to have a new book in preparation, in hand, on the stocks; **etwas in A. nehmen,** to take sth. in hand, to start work on sth., *F:* to put sth. on the stocks; **wir werden die Vorhänge sofort in A. geben,** we will put the curtains in hand, have work started on the curtains, at once. **2.** (*a*) (*finished*) piece of work; handiwork; achievement; **das ist seine A.,** that is his handiwork, (all) his own work; (*b*) needlework; embroidery; crochet-work; (*c*) (craftsman's) work; (piece of) workmanship; **getriebene A.,** hammer-wrought work; **zisilierte, gestochene, A.,** chased work; **die Schüssel ist wohl italienische A.,** the dish is probably Italian work, of Italian workmanship; **es ist zwar Gold, aber die A. ist nichts Besonderes,** it is certainly gold, but the workmanship isn't up to much. **3.** *Sch:* exercise; essay; *U.S:* theme, composition; (*at University*) (i) paper, *U.S:* article, written for a seminar, etc., (ii) dissertation, thesis (for a degree); **schriftliche Arbeiten,** written work; **sie schreibt an einer A. über Hebbel,** she is writing, working on, (i) a paper, (ii) a dissertation, on Hebbel. **4.** *pl.* **Arbeiten,** (constructional, etc.) works; *Adm:* **öffentliche Arbeiten,** public works.

arbeiten. I. *v.i.* (*haben*) **1.** (*a*) to work; to labour; to toil; **für seine Familie a.,** to work for, to work to maintain, one's family; **auf dem Land a.,** to work on the land, on the soil; **mit den Händen a.,** to work with one's hands, to do manual work; **mit dem Kopf a.,** to work with one's brain; to be a brain-worker; **mit der Nadel a.,** to do needlework; **a. gehen,** to go out to work; **selbständig a.,** to work independently, on one's own; **die arbeitenden Klassen,** the working classes; **wir a. samstags nicht,** we do not work on Saturday(s); **schwer a.,** to work hard; **tüchtig a.,** to work hard, conscientiously; to do good work; **wie ein Pferd a.,** to work like a horse, like a nigger; **für zwei a.,** to do two men's work, the work of two men; **mit Händen und Füßen a.,** to exert oneself; **er arbeitete mit Händen und Füßen, um aus der Grube zu kommen,** he tried to clamber out, struggled to get out, of the pit; **an etwas** *dat.* **a.,** to work at, on, sth.; **er arbeitet an einem Roman,** he is working, at work, on a novel; **ich habe bis Mittag daran gearbeitet,** I was at it till noon; **umsonst a.,** to work for nothing, (i) to work without payment, (ii) to get nothing out of it, to have all one's trouble for nothing; **in Leder, in Messing, a.,** to work in leather, in brass; **j-n a. lassen,** (i) to allow, permit, s.o. to work, (ii) to let s.o. do the work, (iii) to set s.o. to work; **ein Pferd a. lassen,** to work a horse, put a horse to work; **bei welchem Schneider lassen Sie a.?** who is your tailor? where do you get your clothes made? **für sich a.,** to work for oneself, on one's own account; **j-m in die Hände a.,** to play into the hands of s.o.; **bei, in, einer Firma a.,** to work for, with, a firm; to be employed by a firm; **er arbeitet nicht,** (i) he does not work, (ii) he is unemployed, out of work; **er arbeitet nicht mehr,** he has given up work; he has retired; (*b*) (*of performing animals, etc.*) to go through their performance, to perform. **2.** (*a*) (*of ship*) to labour, to strain; (*of wood*) to warp, to shrink; (*of wine, beer*) to ferment, to work; (*of dough*) to rise; (*of volcano*) to be active; (*of money*) to earn interest; **sein Geld a. lassen,** to put one's money out at interest, to employ one's capital to advantage; (*b*) **sein ganzes Gesicht arbeitete,** his whole face was working; **man sah an seinem Gesicht, wie es in ihm arbeitete,** one could see from his face that his mind was in a ferment. **3.** (*of machine, pump, organ, the digestion, etc.*) to work, to function; (*of machine, business firm, etc.*) to operate; (*of firm*) to do business (**mit j-m,** with s.o.); **eine Maschine a. lassen,** to work, operate, a machine; **arbeitende Teile,** working parts (of a machine); *Med:* **die Nieren a. normal,** the kidneys are functioning, working, normally.

II. **arbeiten,** *v.tr.* **1.** to work, fashion, shape (wood, iron, etc.); to make (suit, piece of furniture, carpet, etc.); *A:* to till (the soil); *Needlew:* to work (a cushion, a cloth, etc.); to make (handkerchief, etc.); *Tail:* **j-m einen Anzug a.,** to make s.o. a suit; *Carp: Metalw: etc:* **gearbeitet,** worked, wrought; **in Messing, in Stein, gearbeitet,** worked, wrought, fashioned, in brass, in stone; made of brass, of stone; (*of piece of furniture, suit, carpet, etc.*) **gut gearbeitet,** well made. **2.** (*a*) **j-n, ein Tier, zu Tode a.,** to work s.o., an animal, to death; **sich zu Tode a.,** to kill oneself with work, to work oneself to death; **sich krank a.,** to work oneself ill; (*b*) **sich durch den Schlamm a.,** to work one's way, to labour, through the mud; **sich von seinen Fesseln frei a.,** to work oneself free from one's fetters; (*c*) **hier läßt es sich gut a.,** this is a good place to work in; **es arbeitet sich schlecht, es läßt sich schlecht a., bei solchen Zuständen,** one can't work properly in such conditions.

III. *vbl s.* **Arbeiten,** *n. in vbl senses; also:* **1.** work; labour; toil; **an selbständiges A. gewöhnt sein,** to be used, accustomed, to working independently, on one's own. **2.** fermentation.

Arbeiter, *m.* **-s/-,** (*a*) worker; **flinker, langsamer, A.,** deft, slow, worker; **geistiger A.,** brain-worker; (*b*) *Ind: etc:* worker; workman; working man; artisan, craftsman, tradesman; mechanic; hand, operative; **gelernter A.,** skilled workman, skilled tradesman; **ungelernter A.,** unskilled worker; **die A.,** the workers; the toilers; the working class(es); (*c*) *Ent:* = **Arbeiterameise, Arbeiterbiene.** *Cp.* **Arbeiterin.**

Arbeiterameise, *f. Ent:* worker ant.

Arbeiterausschließung, *f. Ind:* lock-out.

Arbeiterausschuß, *m.* workers' committee.

Arbeiterausstand, *m. Ind:* strike, *U.S:* walk-out.

Arbeiterbevölkerung, *f.* working population.

Arbeiterbewegung, *f. Hist: Pol:* Labour movement.

Arbeiterbiene, *f. Ent:* worker bee.

Arbeiterbildung, *f.* workers' education.

Arbeiterbund, *m.* workers' association; trade union.

Arbeiterfahrkarte, *f. Rail:* workman's ticket.

Arbeiterfamilie, *f.* working-class family.

Arbeiterfrage, *f.* labour question

Arbeiterführer, *m. Pol:* workers' leader; labour leader.

Arbeiterin, *f.* **-/-innen,** (*a*) worker; **unser Mädchen ist eine gute A.,** our maid is a good worker; (*b*) *Ind: etc:* (female, woman) worker; work-woman; working woman *or* girl; (female) hand, operative; **wir Arbeiterinnen,** we working women; (*c*) *Ent:* worker bee; worker ant. *Cp.* **Arbeiter.**

Arbeiterklasse, *f.* working class.

Arbeiterkolonie, *f.* **1.** workers' settlement. **2.** labour colony (for unemployed, etc.).

Arbeiterpartei, *f. Pol:* workers' party; (*in England*) **die A.,** the Labour party.

Arbeiterrat, *m.* (*esp. communist*) workers' council.

Arbeiterrückfahrkarte, *f. Rail:* cheap return ticket (issued for travel between place of work and official residence).

Arbeiterschaft, *f.* **-/.** *Coll.* workers; the working class(ses).

Arbeiterschutz, *m.* protection of the workers, of labour; *Hist:* **der internationale A.,** the International Association for the Protection of Labour.

Arbeitersiedlung, *f.* workers' settlement; housing estate.

Arbeitersperre, *f. Ind:* lock-out.

Arbeiterstand, *m.* working class(es); the workers.

Arbeitertum, *n.* **-s/.** = **Arbeiterschaft.**

Arbeiterverband, Arbeiterverein, *m.* workers' association; trade union.

Arbeiterversicherung, *f.* industrial insurance.

Arbeitervertretung, *f. Pol:* (parliamentary) representation of Labour; *Ind:* representation of the workers.

Arbeiterviertel, *n.* working-class quarter (of town).

Arbeiterwohnungen, *f.pl.* workers' flats; *A:* workmen's dwellings, tenements.

Arbeitgeber, *m.* employer (of labour); **A. und Arbeitnehmer,** employers and employed; the masters, *F:* the bosses, and the men.

Arbeitgeberhut, *m. F:* homburg (hat).

Arbeitgeberverband, *m.* employers' association, organization of employers.

Arbeitnehmer, *m.* employee; *cp.* **Arbeitgeber.**

Arbeits-, *comb.fm.* (*a*) working (man, group, party, etc.); *Mil:* fatigue (duty, party, etc.); (*b*) working . . . ; . . . of work; **Arbeitsbedingungen** *f pl,* working conditions, conditions of work; **Arbeitsmethode** *f,* working method, method of work; **Arbeitsprozeß** *m,* working process, process of work; **Arbeitsverfahren** *n,* working procedure; (*c*) *Mec.E: El: etc:* working . . . ; operating . . . ; **Arbeitsdruck** *m,* working pressure; operating pressure; **Arbeitsmoment** *n,* working moment; **Arbeitsstrom** *m,* working current; (*d*) . . . for use at work; working . . . ; work-; **Arbeitskleid** *n,* working clothes; **Arbeitsgerät** *n,* working equipment; **Arbeitskorb** *m,* work-basket; (*e*) *Ind:* . . . to be worked; **Arbeitsstück** *n,* piece to be worked, piece of work; (*f*) . . . of the work; **Arbeitsmuster** *n,* sample of the work; (*g*) (payment, etc.) for work (done); **Arbeitsentgelt** *n,* remuneration for work; (*h*) *Pol.Ec: Ind:* labour . . . ; . . . of labour; industrial . . . ; **der Arbeitsmarkt,** the labour market; **Arbeitslenkung** *f,* direction of labour; **Arbeitsprobleme** *n pl,* labour problems; industrial problems; (i) *Adm: etc:* employment . . . ; **Arbeitsbeschaffung** *f,* creation of employment; **Arbeitsmöglichkeiten** *f pl,* opportunities for employment; **Arbeitsplatzwechsel** *m,* change of employment.

arbeitsam, *a.* (*of pers.*) industrious, diligent, hard-working; painstaking, assiduous, sedulous; laborious; (*of workman, pupil, etc.*) persevering, steady; (*of pupil, etc.*) studious.

Arbeitsameise, *f. Ent:* worker ant.

Arbeitsamkeit, *f.* industry, industriousness, diligence, application, assiduousness, assiduity, sedulousness, sedulity; perseverance, steadiness (in work, study); studiousness (of pupil, etc.).

Arbeitsamt, *n. Adm:* (*a*) employment exchange, labour exchange; (*b*) **das Internationale A.,** the International Labour Office.

Arbeitsanzug, *m.* (*a*) suit, clothes, one wears to work; working clothes; workaday clothes; (*b*) *Ind:* overalls; dungarees, boiler-suit; (*c*) *Mil:* fatigue dress, denims.

Arbeitsäquivalent, *n. Ph:* **A. der Wärme,** mechanical equivalent of heat.

Arbeitsaufnahme, *f. Mec:* absorption of energy.

Arbeitsaufwand, *m.* (*a*) expenditure of work, of labour; (*b*) work (involved); effort (involved).

Arbeitsausschuß, *m. Adm: etc:* (*a*) working committee; (*b*) study group.

Arbeitsbank, *f.* (work-)bench.

Arbeitsbasis, *f.* working basis; **ein Unternehmen auf eine A. stellen,** to put an undertaking on a working basis.

Arbeitsbeginn, *m.* beginning, starting, of work; *Ind:* **den A. registrieren,** to clock in, on; to sign on, *U.S:* to punch the clock.

Arbeitsbereich, *m.* **1.** scope (of administrative department, etc.); field of action; sphere of action, of activity. **2.** *Mec.E:* **A. eines Krans,** radius of a crane-jib.

Arbeitsbeschaffung, *f.* creation of employment; providing, provision, of employment.

Arbeitsbeschaffungsmaßnahme, *f. Adm:* measure to create employment.

Arbeitsbeschaffungsprogramm, *n. Adm:* employment programme; employment scheme.

Arbeitsbeutel, *m.* (*a*) tool-bag; wallet of tools; (*b*) (lady's) work-bag.

Arbeitsbiene, *f. Ent:* worker bee, working bee; *F:* (*of pers.*) **sie ist eine richtige A.,** she's a real busy bee.

Arbeitsbörse, *f.* employment exchange, labour exchange.

Arbeitsbreite, *f. Tex:* working width.

Arbeitsbuch, *n. Adm:* worker's *or* employee's record book (showing details of training and previous employment).

Arbeitsbühne, *f. Ind:* working platform; *Glassm:* siege (of melting-furnace).

Arbeitsdienst, *m.* **1.** (*a*) labour service; (*b*) *Mil:* fatigue (duty). **2.** *Hist:* **der A.,** the Labour Service.

Arbeitsdienstpflicht, *f.* liability for labour service.

Arbeitseffekt, *m. Mec:* power (of an engine, a motor).

Arbeitseinheit, *f. Mec:* unit of work.

Arbeitseinkommen, *n.* earned income.

Arbeitseinsatz, *m. Adm: Pol.Ec:* **1.** planned utilization, deployment, of labour. **2.** (total) labour force; labour pool. **3. zum A. nach X befohlen werden,** to be sent to X for labour duties.

Arbeitseinstellung, *f. Ind:* cessation of work; stoppage, *U.S:* tie-up; (*in factory*) shut-down.

Arbeitserlaubnis, *f.* permission to work; *Adm:* labour permit, work permit.
arbeitsersparend, *a.* labour-saving.
Arbeitsersparnis, *f.* saving of labour, labour-saving.
Arbeitsexemplar, *n.* working copy (of book); copy on which notes *or* corrections are made.
arbeitsfähig, *a.* (*of pers.*) able-bodied; able to work, capable of work(ing); (*of horse*) fit for work; (*of pers.*) fit for work, for duty, for service; *Parl: etc:* **arbeitsfähige Mehrheit**, working majority.
Arbeitsfähigkeit, *f.* ability to work; fitness for work, for duty, for service; capacity for work.
Arbeitsfeld, *n.* field of action; sphere of action, of activity; scope (of administrative department, etc.); (scholar's, etc.) (special) subject, field.
Arbeitsfläche, *f.* working area; *Mec.E:* bearing surface, working surface.
Arbeitsflugzeug, *n. Mil.Av:* army co-operation aircraft.
Arbeitsfrau, *f.* workwoman.
Arbeitsfreude, *f.* pleasure in, enjoyment of, one's work; enthusiasm for one's work.
arbeitsfreudig, *a.* taking pleasure, finding enjoyment, in one's work; happy in one's work; **er ist wirklich a.**, he is a keen worker, his heart is really in his work.
Arbeitsfront, *f. Hist:* **die Deutsche A.**, the German Labour Front.
Arbeitsfuge, *f. Civ.E: Hyd.E:* construction joint (in timber-work).
Arbeitsgang, *m. Ind:* (individual) process; series of operations; stage (of manufacture); **in einem A. ausgeführt**, done in one continuous process.
Arbeitsgebiet, *n.*=**Arbeitsfeld.**
Arbeitsgemeinschaft, *f.* **1.** (*a*) syndicate, combine; *Adm:* joint association (**für**, for); (*b*) (working) team (of students, scholars, investigators, etc.); *Adm: Sch:* study group; *Sch:* seminar group. **2.** *Com: Ind:* (co)partnership (of employers and employees).
Arbeitsgenehmigung, *f. Adm:* labour permit, work permit.
Arbeitsgerät, *n.* (working) equipment; tools.
Arbeitsgericht, *n.Jur:* industrial (relations) court, labour court.
Arbeitsgerichtsbarkeit, *f. Jur:* jurisdiction in industrial matters.
Arbeitsgeschütz, *n. Artil:* roving gun.
Arbeitsgleis, *n. Rail:* (temporary) line serving construction works.
Arbeitsgrad, *m.* efficiency (of work).
Arbeitsgruppe, *f.* working group; working party.
Arbeitshaus, *n. Adm:* house of correction; penitentiary; *U.S:* workhouse.
Arbeitsholz, *n.* timber.
Arbeitshose, *f. Cost:* working trousers; workman's trousers; *U.S: F:* jeans.
Arbeitshub, *m. Mch: I.C.E:* power stroke.
Arbeitshypothese, *f.* working hypothesis.
Arbeitskammer, *f.* **1.** work-room; *Ch:* laboratory. **2.** working chamber (of compressed air apparatus).
Arbeitskarte, *f.* **1.** *Ind:* instruction card (issued to workman). **2.** *Adm:* juvenile's employment permit.
Arbeitskästchen, *n.*, **Arbeitskasten**, *m.* (*a*) toolbox; (*b*) (*lady's*) work-box.
Arbeitskittel, *m. Cost:* (*a*) overall; (*b*) working clothes.
Arbeitskleid, *n.*, **Arbeitskleidung**, *f.* working clothes; overall; overalls; dungarees, boiler-suit.
Arbeitsklima, *n.*=**Betriebsklima.**
Arbeitskommando, *n. Mil:* working party; fatigue party, *U.S:* work detail.
Arbeitskontakt, *m. El.E:* make contact, front contact.
Arbeitskorb, *m.* (*a*) tool-basket; (*b*) (lady's) work-basket.
Arbeitskraft, *f.* **1.** working power; capacity (for work). **2.** worker; **Arbeitskräfte** *pl*, personnel, workers; *Ind:* hands; operatives; manpower; **gelernte Arbeitskräfte**, skilled hands, skilled labour; **Mangel an Arbeitskräften**, shortage of labour.
Arbeitskreis, *m.* working party; study group.
Arbeitslager, *n.* labour camp; work camp.
Arbeitsleistung, *f.* **1.** amount of work done; quota (of work); output (of machine, factory, etc.). **2.** efficiency (of machine, factory, personnel); power (of engine, motor).
Arbeitsleute *see* **Arbeitsmann.**
Arbeitslohn, *m.* **1.** wage(s), pay. **2.** (*item in account, etc.*) labour charges; charge for work done.
arbeitslos, *a.* unemployed, out of work, out of a job, idle; **a. werden**, to lose one's employment, one's job, to be thrown out of work; **j-n a. machen**, to throw s.o. out of work; **Arbeitslose** *m, f*, unemployed person; man, woman, without a job; **die Arbeitslosen**, the unemployed, the workless, the jobless.
Arbeitslosenhilfe, *f. Adm:* unemployment relief.
Arbeitslosenunterstützung, *f. Adm:* unemployment benefit, unemployment pay; **A. beziehen**, to draw unemployment benefit, *F:* to be on the dole.
Arbeitslosenversicherung, *f. Adm:* unemployment insurance.
Arbeitslosigkeit, *f.* unemployment; idleness.
Arbeitslust, *f.* (*a*) eagerness to work; (*b*)=**Arbeitsfreude.**
Arbeitsmaid, *f. Hist:* (*Nazi*) Labour Service girl.
Arbeitsmangel, *m.* lack of work; shortage of work.
Arbeitsmann, *m.* **1.** (*pl.* **-leute**) workman, working man; artisan; labourer; **Arbeitsleute**, workpeople. **2.** (*pl.* **-männer**) *Hist:* private in the (Nazi) Labour Service.
Arbeitsmarkt, *m. Pol.Ec:* labour-market.
Arbeitsmaterial, *n.* working material; materials.
Arbeitsminister, *m.* Minister of Labour, *U.S:* Secretary of Labour.
Arbeitsministerium, *n.* Ministry of Labour, *U.S:* Department of Labour.
Arbeitsmoral, *f.* (*of workers in factory, etc.*) morale.
Arbeitsnachweis, *m.* **1.** (bulletin of) information about available employment. **2.** employment bureau, employment agency.
Arbeitsnot, *f.* lack of employment, shortage of work.
Arbeitsordnung, *f.* **1.** (*a*) *Adm:* organization of labour; (*b*) *Ind:* (*in factory, etc.*) organization, regulation, of work. **2.** *Ind:* (factory, etc.) regulations.
arbeitsparend, *a.* labour-saving.
Arbeitspause, *f. Ind: etc:* break (from work), *U.S:* recess, intermission.
Arbeitspferd, *n.* **1.** draught-horse; cart-horse. **2.** *F:* tireless worker, *F:* slogger; **er ist ein richtiges A.**, he works like a cart-horse.
Arbeitspflicht, *f.* obligation (*esp.* on the citizen) to work; **die A. anerkennen**, to recognize that it is one's duty to work.
Arbeitsphysiologie, *f.* physiology of effort.
Arbeitsplatz, *m.* **1.** (*a*) desk, place, bench, etc., at which one works; (*in library, laboratory, etc.*) place for a worker; *Ind:* bay (in workshop); *Tp:* operating position; (*b*) place of employment, place of work. **2.** job; **Arbeitsplätze schaffen**, to make, create, new jobs; **Wechsel des Arbeitsplatzes**, change of employment.
Arbeitspsychologie, *f.* industrial psychology.
Arbeitsraum, *m.* (*a*) workroom; *Ch: etc:* laboratory; (*b*) office.
Arbeitsrecht, *n. Jur:* labour legislation.
arbeitsreich, *a.* busy, active (existence, etc.).
Arbeitsrichter, *m. Jur:* judge in an industrial court, in a labour court.
Arbeitssaal, *m.* workroom.
arbeitsscheu[1], *a*, work-shy, reluctant to work; lazy, idle; **Arbeitsscheue** *m, f*, idler, slacker, shirker, lazybones, *F:* (artful) dodger.
Arbeitsscheu[2], *f.* dislike of work, reluctance to work; laziness, idleness, *F:* dodging (of work).
Arbeitsschiene, *f. El.Rail:* conductor rail, live rail, third rail.
Arbeitsschluß, *m.* end, close, of work; *Ind:* **den A. registrieren**, to clock off, out; to sign off.
Arbeitsschule, *f. Sch:* Froebel-type school.
Arbeitsschutz, *m. Adm:* protection of labour.
Arbeitssitzung, *f.* work(ing) session (of conference).
Arbeitssperre, *f. Ind:* lock-out.
Arbeitsspiel, *n. I.C.E:* cycle.
Arbeitsstab, *m. Mil:* planning staff.
Arbeitsstätte, *f.* (*a*) place of work; place of employment; (*b*) workshop; *Constr: etc:* yard.
Arbeitsstelle, *f.*=**Arbeitsplatz 1** (*b*), 2.
Arbeitsstreckung, *f. Ind:* short-time working to maintain the number of workers employed.
Arbeitsstrom, *m. El.E:* working current, operating current; open-circuit current.
Arbeitsstrombetrieb, *m.Tg:* open-circuit working.
Arbeitsstube, *f.* (*a*) (small) work-room; (*b*) study.
Arbeitsstufe, *f. Ind:* stage, phase (of manufacture, of a process); (individual) process.
Arbeitsstunden, *f.pl.* (*a*) hours of work; **die Herstellungskosten in A. berechnen**, to calculate the cost of production in man-hours; (*b*) working hours.
Arbeitstag, *m.* working day, work-day.
Arbeitstakt, *m.* (*a*) working tempo; rate of work; (*b*) *I.C.E:* stroke power.
Arbeitstarifvertrag, *m. Ind:* wage agreement.
Arbeitsteilung, *f.* division of labour.
Arbeitstherapie, *f.* = **Beschäftigungsbehandlung.**
Arbeitstisch, *m.* (*a*) desk; *Ind: etc:* bench; (*b*) (lady's) work-table.
Arbeitsuchende, *m., f.* (*decl. as adj.*) person seeking work, seeking employment.
arbeitsunfähig, *a.* unable to work; unfit, not fit, for work; **vorübergehend a.**, temporarily incapacitated; **dauernd a.**, permanently disabled.
Arbeitsunfähigkeit, *f.* inability to work; unfitness for work; incapacitation for, from, work; **vorübergehende A.**, temporary incapacitation; **dauernde A.**, permanent disablement.
Arbeitsunterricht, *m. Sch:* teaching (of children) by the Froebel method.
Arbeitsurlaub, *m. Mil:* leave from the armed forces to carry on one's own employment.
Arbeitsvereinigung, *f.* co-ordination of labour, of effort.
Arbeitsverhältnis, *n.* contractual relation between employer and employee.
Arbeitsvermittlung, *f.* **1.** negotiation of employment; advising workers of possible employment. **2.** (i) employment bureau, office, agency; (ii) *Adm:* employment exchange, labour exchange.
Arbeitsvermögen, *n.* capacity for work; *Ph:* kinetic energy.
Arbeitsvertrag, *m. Jur:* contract of employment.
arbeitsverwendungsfähig, *a. Mil:* (*of man*) fit for labour duties only.
Arbeitsweise, *f.* (*a*) manner of working; method (of working); mode of operation, *modus operandi;* (*b*) functioning, working (of a machine).
Arbeitswert, *m.* value in terms of work; *Ph:* mechanical equivalent (of heat).
Arbeitswille, *m.* willingness to work.
arbeitswillig, *a.* willing to work; *Ind:* **die Streikenden und die Arbeitswilligen**, the strikers and those willing, prepared, to work.
Arbeitswissenschaft, *f.* scientific study of labour methods and problems.
Arbeitszeit, *f.* working time; time spent on a piece of work; hours of work; working hours; **die A. ist von 9 bis 5**, the hours of work are, the working day is, from 9 to 5; **während der A.**, during, in, working hours; during, in, business hours.
Arbeitszettel, *m. Ind:* (workman's) time-sheet.
Arbeitszeug, *n.* (kit of) tools; (working) gear.
Arbeitszimmer, *n.* (*a*) study; (*b*) workroom.
Arbeitszoll, *m. Constr:* (*in measuring stone*) allowance for working; 'the extra inch'.
Arbeitszug, *m. Rail:* train carrying track-laying materials.
Arbeitszylinder, *m.* (*a*) working cylinder (of machine); (*b*) *Av:* jack (of undercarriage).
Arbiter ['arbiˑtər], *m.* **-s/-**, arbiter; *Jur:* arbitrator, referee, adjudicator; **a. elegantiarum**, arbiter of taste.
Arbitrage [arbiˑ'traːʒə], *f.* **-/-n.** **1.** *Fin:* arbitrage; arbitration of exchange. **2.** *Com: Jur:* arbitration.
Arbitragerechnung, *f. Fin:* (*in foreign exchange transactions*) arbitration of exchange.
Arbitrageur [arbiˑtraˑ'ʒøːr], *m.* **-s/-e.** *Fin:* arbitragist.
arbiträr [arbiˑ'trɛːr], *a.* arbitrary; *Mth:* **arbiträre Größen**, arbitrary constants, arbitraries (of an equation).
Arbitrator [arbiˑ'traːtor], *m.* **-s/-en** [-traˑ'toːrən]. *Jur:* arbitrator, referee, adjudicator.
arbitrieren [arbiˑ'triːrən], *v.tr.* & *i.* (*haben*) **1.** to arbitrate. **2.** *Fin:* (*a*) *v.tr.* to assess (sum) by arbitrage; (*b*) *v.i.* to do arbitrage business.
Arbitrium [ar'biːtrĭum], *n.* **-s/-ria**, judgment, decision; power to choose; *Phil:* **a. liberum**, free will.
arboreszent [arboˑrɛs'tsɛnt], *a. Bot:* arborescent.
Arboretum, [arboˑ'reːtum], *n.* **-s/-ta** & **-ten**, arboretum.
Arborikultur [arboˑriˑkul'tuːr], *f.* **-/.** arboriculture.
Arbuse [ar'buːzə], *f.* **-/-n.** **1.** *Hort:* water-melon. **2.** *Bot:* arbutus, cane-apple, strawberry-tree.
Archaikum, das [ar'çaˑiˑkum], **-s.** *Geol:* the archaean (system, period).
archaisch [ar'çaːiʃ], *a.* archaic.
archäisch [ar'çɛːiʃ], *a. Geol:* archaean.
archaisieren [arçaˑiˑ'ziːrən], *v.tr.* & *i.* (*haben*) to archaize; **archaisierend**, archaizing; archaistic.
Archaismus [arçaˑ'ismus], *m.* **-/-men**, archaism.
archaistisch [arçaˑ'istiʃ], *a.* archaistic.

Archangel(sk) [arˈçaŋəl(sk)]. *Pr.n.n.* **-s.** *Geog:* Archangel.
Archäologe [arçɛ·o·ˈloːgə], *m.* **-n/-n,** archaeologist, *esp.* classical archaeologist.
Archäologie [arçɛ·o·lo·ˈgiː], *f.* **-/.** archaeology, *esp.* classical archaeology.
Archäologin [arçɛ·o·ˈloːgin], *f.* **-/-innen,** (woman) archaeologist, *esp.* classical archaeologist.
archäologisch [arçɛ·o·ˈloːgiʃ], *a.* archaeological.
Archäozoikum, das [arçɛ·o·ˈtsoːi·kum], **-s.** *Geol:* the archaeozoic age.
Arche, *f.* **-/-n. 1.** ark; *(a)* **die A. Noah(s), die A. Noä,** Noah's ark; *(b)* **die A.,** the Ark of the Covenant. **2.** chest, coffer; trunk; casket. **3.** *Fish:* eel-trap. **4.** *Hyd.E:* strengthening of river-bank; coffer-dam; dike; breakwater; groyne. **5.** *Moll:* = **Archenmuschel. 6.** *Mus:* wind-chest (of organ). **7.** *Mus:* string-plate, wrest-plank (of piano).
Archenmuschel, *f. Moll:* arca Noae, Noah's ark.
Archetyp [arçe·ˈtyːp], *m.* **-s/-en, Archetypus** [arçe·ˈtyːpus], *m.* **-/-typen** & **-typi,** archetype, prototype.
archetypisch [arçe·ˈtyːpiʃ], *a.* archetypal, prototypal.
Archi-, archi- [ˌarçi·-], *pref.* arch- archi-; **Archidiakon** *m,* archdeacon; **archiepiskopal,** archiepiscopal.
Archidiakon [ˈarçi·di·a·ˈkoːn], *m. Ecc:* archdeacon; **der Sprengel eines Archidiakons,** an archdeaconry.
Archidiakonat [ˌarçi·di·a·ko·ˈnaːt], *n. Ecc:* **1.** archdeaconship, archdeaconate, archdeaconry. **2.** *(residence)* archdeaconry.
archidiakonisch [ˌarçi·di·a·ˈkoːniʃ] *a.* archidiaconal.
Archidiakonus [ˌarçi·di·ˈaːko·nus], *m.* **-/-nen** & **-ne** = **Archidiakon.**
-archie [-arˈçiː], *s.suff. f.* **-/-n** [-arˈçiːən], -archy; **Hierarchie,** hierarchy; **Oligarchie,** oligarchy; **Tetrarchie,** tetrarchy.
archiepiskopal [ˌarçi·e·pisko·ˈpaːl], *a. Ecc:* archiepiscopal.
Archiepiskopus [ˌarçi·e·ˈpisko·pus], *m.* **-/-pi,** archbishop.
Archigonie [arçi·go·ˈniː], *f.* **-/.** *Biol:* abiogenesis, spontaneous generation.
Archihierarch [ˌarçi·hi·eˈrarç], *m.* **-en/-en,** archpriest.
Archimandrit [ˌarçi·manˈdriːt], *m.* **-en/-en.** *Ecc:* archimandrite.
archimedisch [ˌarçi·ˈmeːdiʃ], *a.* Archimedean; **das Archimedische Prinzip,** the Archimedean principle; *Mec:* **archimedische Schraube,** Archimedean screw; *Tls:* **archimedischer Bohrer,** spiral drill.
Archipel [arçi·ˈpeːl], *m.* **-s/-e. 1.** *Geog:* archipelago. **2.** *A.Geog:* **der A.** = **der Archipelagus.**
Archipelagus, der [arçi·ˈpɛ·la·gus]. *Pr.n.* **-.** *A.Geog:* the Archipelago; the Aegean sea.
Archipresbyter [ˌarçi·ˈprɛsby·tər], *m. R.C.Ch:* archpriest.
Architekt [arçi·ˈtɛkt], *m.* **-en/-en,** architect.
Architektin [arçi·ˈtɛktin], *f.* **-/-innen,** (woman) architect.
Architektonik [arçi·tɛkˈtoːnik], *f.* **-/.** architectonics, tectonics.
architektonisch [arçi·tɛkˈtoːniʃ], *a.* architectonic; architectural.
Architektur [arçi·tɛkˈtuːr], *f.* **-/-en. 1.** architecture. **2.** structure, building.
Architrav [arçi·ˈtraːf], *m.* **-(e)s/-e** & **-en/-en** [-ˈtraːvə(n)]. *Arch:* architrave.
Archiv [arˈçiːf], *n.* **-(e)s/-e** [-s, -ˈçiːvəs/ -ˈçiːvə]. **1.** *(documents, etc.)* archives; records; library (of films, gramophone records); *Com: etc:* files. **2.** *(building or room)* archives; *Adm:* record office; *Com: etc: (in office)* filing room.
Archivalien [arçi·ˈvaːliən], *n.pl.* documents in the archives; archives; records.
archivalisch [arçi·ˈvaːliʃ], *a.* documentary (proof, etc.); **archivalische Urkunde,** original document *or* deed (lodged in the archives); *adv.* **etwas a. beweisen,** to prove sth. by reference to the archives, to the official records
Archivar [arçi·ˈvaːr], *m.* **-s/-e,** *(a)* archivist; keeper of public records; keeper of the records (of a society, etc.); *(b) Com: etc: F:* clerk in charge of records; filing clerk.
Archivbeamte [arˈçiːf-], *m.* archivist.
Archivexemplar, *n. Publ:* file-copy.
Archivolte [arçi·ˈvoltə], *f.* **-/-n.** *Arch:* archivolt.
Archon [arˈçoːn], *m.* **-s/-e, Archont** [arˈçont], *m.* **-en/-en.** *Gr.Hist:* archon.
Archontat [arçonˈtaːt], *n.* **-(e)s/-e.** *Gr.Hist:* archonship; archontate.
Arcus [ˈarkus], *m.* **-usses/-usse** = **Arkus.**
Ardennen, die [arˈdɛnən]. *Pr.n.pl. Geog:* the Ardennes.
Ardenner [arˈdɛnər], *inv.a.* **der A. Wald,** the Ardennes.
Area [ˈaːre·aː], *f.* **-/-s** & **Areen** [ˈaːre·ən], area; open space; courtyard (of house); (threshing-, etc.) floor.
Areal [a·re·ˈaːl], *n.* **-s/-e. 1.** area (of field, triangle, building, etc.). **2. Areale von schäumendem Wasser,** stretches, patches, of foaming water.
Arekanuß [a·ˈreːka·-], *f. Bot:* areca-nut, betel-nut.
Arekapalme, *f. Bot:* areca palm(-tree).
Aremorika [a·re·ˈmoːri·kaː]. *Pr.n.f.* **-s.** = **Armorika.**
Arena [a·ˈreːnaː], *f.* **-/-nen,** arena; (circus, bull-) ring; *F:* **die A. der Politik,** the political arena; **in die A. hinabsteigen,** to enter the arena, the lists, the fray.
Areometer [a·re·o·ˈmeːtər], *n.* **-s/-** = **Aräometer.**
Areopag [a·re·o·ˈpaːk]. *Pr.n.m.* **-s** & *s.m.* **-s/-e.** *Gr.Hist:* Areopagus.
Areopagit [a·re·o·pa·ˈgiːt], *m.* **-en/-en.** *Gr.Hist:* Areopagite.
Ares [ˈaːreːs]. *Pr.n.m.* **-'.** *Gr.Myth:* Ares; *(Roman)* Mars.
Arethusa [a·re·ˈtuːzaː]. *Pr.n.f.* **-s.** *Gr.Myth:* Arethusa.
aretinisch [a·re·ˈtiːniʃ], *a.* Aretine; *Hist. of Mus:* **die aretinischen Silben,** Guido's hexachords.
arg. I. **1.** *a.* **(ärger; ärgst)** *(a) (in biblical and quasi-biblical uses)* evil, wicked; **ein arges Geschlecht,** a wicked, an evil, generation; **diese arge Welt,** this wicked, evil, world; **arge Gedanken,** wicked, evil, thoughts; **der Arge,** (i) the wicked man, (ii) the Evil One, the Devil; **das Arge,** evil, wickedness; *B:* **hasset das Arge,** hate that which is evil; **die ganze Welt liegt im Argen,** the whole world lieth in wickedness; *(b)* evil, ill (thought, etc.); wicked (person); harmful, hurtful, malicious (intentions, etc.); **arge Gedanken,** evil thoughts, thoughts of evil; **mein ärgster Feind,** my worst, bitterest, enemy; **ein arger Geselle,** a bad character, *F:* a bad lot, a bad egg; **er hatte nichts Arges im Sinne, er dachte sich** *dat.* **nichts Arges dabei,** he meant no harm (by it); he had no evil intentions; **an nichts Arges denken,** (i) to mean no harm; (ii) to suspect nothing, to be unsuspecting, to have no suspicions; **ich sehe nichts Arges darin, dabei,** I see no harm in it; **es ist nichts Arges an ihm** = **er ist ohne Arg,** *q.v. under* II; *(c)* bad; damaging; distressing; painful; troublesome; severe (punishment, illness, etc.); *F:* awful, dreadful, terrible (cold, confusion, etc.); **arger Winter,** hard winter; bad, trying, winter; **arges Versehen,** bad, grave, grievous, mistake; *F:* bad slip, nasty slip; **arger Verdruß,** great, serious, annoyance; great, serious, worry; **in arge Verlegenheit kommen,** to get into serious, grave, difficulties; to run into serious trouble; **arges Mißverständnis,** serious, bad, *F:* nasty, misunderstanding; *(of affairs, etc.)* **(sehr) im argen liegen,** to be badly neglected; to be in a bad way; **es ist ziemlich arg,** it's pretty bad; **das ist (denn doch) zu arg!** that's too bad! that's altogether too much! that's the limit! **so arg ist es doch nicht,** it's not as bad as all that, not as bad as you think; **es ist ärger als je,** it's worse than ever; **ärger werden,** to grow, get, worse; to worsen; **es wird immer ärger,** it's getting worse and worse; things are going from bad to worse; **ein Übel (noch) ärger machen,** to make an evil (even, still,) worse, to aggravate, worsen, an evil; **das Ärgste dabei ist, daß . . . ,** the worst of it is that . . . ; **das Ärgste befürchten,** to fear the worst; **das Ärgste kommt noch,** the worst is still to come; **im ärgsten Falle, wenn es zum Ärgsten kommt,** at (the) worst; if it comes to the worst; if the worst comes to the worst; **sein Husten ist morgens am ärgsten,** his cough is worst in the mornings; *see also* **Hand** 4 *(b)*; *(d) (of pers.)* **arger Raucher,** inveterate, heavy, smoker; **arger Säufer,** heavy drinker; inveterate, confirmed, drunkard; **arger Schwätzer,** inveterate, constant, chatterer; **arger Spieler,** inveterate, confirmed, gambler; **arger Narr,** utter fool; **arger Sünder,** hardened, persistent, sinner; *(e) Dial:* **mir, ihr, ist arg danach,** I am, she is, keen on it. **2.** *adv. (a)* badly; ill; severely; *(of thg)* **arg abgenutzt,** badly worn; *(of pers.)* **j-m arg mitspielen,** to treat s.o. badly, to use s.o. ill; *F:* to give s.o. a rough time; **es zu arg machen, treiben,** to go too far, carry things too far; **j-n arg strafen,** to punish s.o. severely; **sie wurden arg geschlagen,** they were badly beaten; **er wurde ärger behandelt als je,** he was treated worse than ever; **der Mann, der sie am ärgsten beschwindelte,** the man who duped her worst of all; *(b) F. & Dial:* very, *F:* awfully, dreadfully, terribly; **der Zug war arg besetzt,** the train was very crowded, *F:* was packed; **sie ist arg jung,** she is very, *F:* awfully, young; **arg dumm,** deplorably stupid; **arg schön,** really, *F:* absolutely, just too, lovely.
II. *s.* **Arg,** *n.* **-s/.** malice, spitefulness; guile; **er ist ohne Arg, es ist kein Arg an, in, ihm,** there is no harm in him; he is without malice; he is without, free from, guile.
Argala [ˈarga·laː], *m.* **-s/-s.** *Orn:* adjutant, adjutant-bird.
Argali [ˈarga·liː], *m.* **-s/-.** *Z:* argali, wild sheep (of Asia).
Arganbaum [arˈgaːn-], *m. Bot:* argan(-tree).
Argandbrenner [arˈgãː-], *m.* argand lamp.
argdenkend, *a.* evil-, ill-intentioned, ill-meaning.
Argental [argɛnˈtaːl], *n.* **-s/.** *Metall:* argental (aluminium-silver alloy).
Argentan [argɛnˈtaːn], *n.* **-s/.** German silver, nickel silver.
argentieren [argɛnˈtiːrən], *v.tr.* to silver (sth.); to coat (sth.) with silver.
Argentinien [argɛnˈtiːniən]. *Pr.n.n.* **-s.** *Geog:* the Argentine (Republic), Argentina.
Argentinier [argɛnˈtiːniər], *m.* **-s/-.** Argentine.
argentinisch [argɛnˈtiːniʃ], *a. Geog:* Argentine, of Argentina; **die Argentinische Republik** = **Argentinien.**
Argentit [argɛnˈtiːt], *m.* **-(e)s/.** *Miner:* argentite, silver-glance.
ärger [1], *a. & adv. see* **arg I.**
Ärger [2], *m.* **-s/.** *(a)* annoyance; irritation; vexation; *F:* aggravation; **seinem Ä. Luft machen,** to give vent to one's irritation; **seinen Ä. an j-m auslassen,** to vent one's irritation on s.o., *F:* to take it out on s.o.; **seinen Ä. verbeißen,** to swallow one's annoyance; **zu meinem großen Ä. kam er nicht,** to my great annoyance he did not come; *(b)* trouble; **der tägliche Ä.,** (i) the daily irritations; (ii) the irritations, vexations, of daily life; **j-m Ä. machen,** (i) to annoy s.o.; (ii) to make trouble for s.o.; to get s.o. into trouble (with the police, etc.); **mit j-m, etwas, Ä. haben,** to have trouble with s.o.; **mit der Polizei, den Behörden, Ä. bekommen,** *F:* **kriegen,** to get into trouble with the police, the authorities; **sie hat viel Ä. mit ihren Untermietern gehabt,** she has had a lot of trouble with her tenants; **ich habe mit dem Auto nichts als Ä. gehabt,** I have had nothing but trouble with that car; **Geld bringt oft nichts als Ä. und Sorge,** money often brings nothing but trouble and worry; *F:* **mach keinen Ä.,** (i) don't make trouble; (ii) don't be silly.
ärgerlich, *a. (a) (of pers.)* annoyed, cross (expression, remark, etc.); **ein ärgerliches Gesicht machen,** to look annoyed, cross; **ä. werden,** to get annoyed, cross; **auf j-n ä. sein,** to be annoyed, cross, with s.o.; **über etwas** *acc.* **ä. sein,** to be annoyed, cross, about sth.; *(of action, remark, etc.)* **j-n ä. machen,** to annoy s.o., to make s.o. cross; *adv.* **ä. antworten,** to answer crossly, with annoyance; *(b)* irritating (incident, matter, etc.); tiresome, troublesome (matter, delay, etc.); vexing (matter, incident, etc.); **die Verzögerung war höchst ä.,** the delay was extremely annoying; **die Sache ist doch zu ä.! es ist doch eine zu ärgerliche Sache!** the whole thing is just too annoying! **es ist sehr ä., daß der Scheck noch nicht gekommen ist,** it's very annoying that the cheque hasn't arrived yet; **wie ä.!** how annoying, *F:* aggravating! what a nuisance!
Ärgerlichkeit, *f.* **1.** *(a)* annoyance, crossness; *(b)* annoying, irritating, nature (of matter, incident, etc.). **2.** *pl.* **Ärgerlichkeiten,** annoyances; irritations; vexations; troubles, worries.
ärgern, *v.tr.* **1.** *(a) (of action, remark, etc.)* to annoy, irritate, vex, *F:* aggravate (s.o.); to make (s.o.) cross; **sich ä.,** to be *or* get annoyed, cross **(über j-n,** with s.o., **über etwas** *acc.,* about sth.); **es ärgert mich, ich ärgere mich darüber, daß er immer zu spät kommt,** it annoys me, it makes me cross, that he is always late; **ich könnte mich krank, schwarz, ä., daß ich es vergessen habe,** I am really annoyed, cross, furious, with myself, *F:* I could kick myself, for forgetting it; **über den Jungen kannst du dich manchmal krank, schwarz, ä.,** at times that boy can drive you to despair, *F:* round the bend, up the wall; **ärgere dich doch nicht darüber,** don't let it annoy you, don't let it make you cross; don't get annoyed, cross, about it; *F:* **ihn ärgert die Fliege an der Wand,** everything, every little thing, annoys him; *(b)* **sich mit etwas ä.,** to struggle with (difficult text, sewing machine, etc.); **ich ärgere mich schon zwei Stunden lang mit dieser Übersetzung,** I've been struggling with this translation for two hours; **ich möchte kein Lehrer**

sein und mich dauernd mit anderer Leute Kinder ä., I wouldn't want to be a teacher and let other people's children make my life a misery; (*c*) to tease (s.o., animal, etc.); to annoy (s.o.); **den Lehrer ä.,** to annoy the teacher, to play the teacher up; **ich sagte es bloß, um sie zu ä.,** I only said it to annoy her; **hört auf, den Hund zu ä.,** stop teasing the dog. **2.** *Lit:* to cause offence to (s.o.); to scandalize (s.o.); *B:* **ärgert dich deine rechte Hand, so hau sie ab,** if thy right hand offend thee, cut it off; **und wer der Kleinen einen ärgert,** but whosoever shall offend one of these little ones.

Ärgernis, *n.* **-nisses/-nisse,** *A:f.* **-/. 1.** annoyance; offence; **Ä. an etwas** *dat.* **nehmen,** to take offence at sth.; **Ä. erregen, geben,** to cause annoyance; to give offence; *Jur:* **öffentliches Ä. erregen,** to create a public nuisance; *B:* **weh dem Menschen, durch welchen Ä. kommt,** woe to that man by whom the offence cometh. **2.** (cause of) offence; source of annoyance; nuisance; scandal; *Jur:* **öffentliches Ä.,** public nuisance.

arggesinnt, *a.* evil-, ill-intentioned; ill-meaning.

argherzig, *a.* evil-hearted; wicked.

Argiver [arˈgiːvər], *m.* **-s/-.** *A.Geog:* Argive.

argivisch [arˈgiːviʃ], *a. A.Geog:* Argive.

Arglist, *f.* malice; craft, cunning, guile; wiles; *Jur:* malice; malicious intent.

arglistig, *a.* malicious (pers., act); crafty, cunning, guileful, wily, *F:* foxy (pers.); *Jur:* malicious (act, intent); **arglistige Täuschung,** wilful deceit.

Arglistigkeit, *f.* maliciousness, malice; craftiness, cunning(ness), guile(fulness), wiliness, *F:* foxiness.

arglos, *a.* (*a*) without malice; ingenuous; guileless, without guile; simple, artless, naïve, innocent; (*b*) unsuspecting; *adv.* **etwas a. tun,** to do sth. unsuspectingly, all unsuspecting, innocently, in all innocence.

Arglosigkeit, *f.* (*a*) ingenuousness; guilelessness; simplicity, artlessness, naïveté, innocence; (*b*) unsuspecting nature *or* state of mind; innocence.

Argo [ˈargoː]. *Pr.n.f.* **-s. 1.** *Gr.Myth:* Argo. **2.** *Astr:* Argo, the Ship.

Argofahrer [ˈargo·-], *m. Myth:* Argonaut.

Argolis [ˈargo·lis]. *Pr.n.n.* **-'.** *A.Geog:* Argolis.

Argon [arˈgoːn, ˈargo·n], *n.* **-s/.** *Ch:* argon.

Argonaut [argo·ˈnaut], *m.* **-en/-en. 1.** *Myth:* Argonaut. **2.** *Moll:* argonaut, paper nautilus.

Argonautenzug, der. *Myth:* the voyage of the Argonauts; the quest of the Golden Fleece.

Argonnen, die [arˈgonən]. *Pr.n.pl. Geog:* the Argonne.

Argonner [arˈgonər], *inv.a.* **der A. Wald,** the Argonne.

Argos [ˈargos]. *Pr.n.n.* **-'. 1.** *A.Geog:* Argos. **2.** *Gr.Myth:* Argus.

Argot [arˈgoː], *n.* **-s/.** argot, slang.

ärgste(r), ärgste, ärgste(s) *see* **arg I.**

arguieren [argu·ˈiːrən]. **1.** *v.i.* (*haben*) to argue (**mit j-m,** with s.o.). **2.** *v.tr.* to argue (case, etc.).

Argument [argu·ˈmɛnt], *n.* **-(e)s/-e. 1.** argument (**für, gegen,** for, in favour of, against). **2.** summary, argument, plot (of Greek *or* Latin play). **3.** *Mth:* *Astr:* *etc:* argument; independent variable.

Argumentation [argu·mɛnta·tsĭˈoːn], *f.* **-/-en,** argumentation.

argumentieren [argu·mɛnˈtiːrən], *v.i.* (*haben*) to argue.

Argus [ˈargus]. **1.** *Pr.n.m.* **-'.** *Gr.Myth:* Argus. **2.** *s.m.* **-/.** *F:* watchful guardian, Argus. **3.** *s.m.* **-/.** (*a*) = **Argusfalter;** (*b*) = **Argusfasan.**

Argusaugen, *n.pl.* (*of pers.*) **mit A.,** Argus-eyed; **j-n mit A. bewachen,** to keep a watchful eye on, over, s.o.

argusäugig, *a.* Argus-eyed.

Argusfalter, *m. Ent:* argus (butterfly); **blauer A.,** mazarine blue; holly-blue.

Argusfasan, Arguspfau, *m. Orn:* argus (pheasant).

Argwille, *m.* malevolence, ill-will; spite.

Argwohn, *m.* **-s/.** suspicion; mistrust, distrust (**gegen j-n, etwas,** of s.o., sth.); **A. erregen,** to arouse suspicion; **j-s A. erregen, wecken,** to arouse, awaken, s.o.'s suspicions; **A. gegen j-n, etwas, hegen, haben,** to have, entertain, suspicions about s.o., sth.; to suspect s.o., sth.; to be mistrustful of s.o., sth.; **A. fassen, schöpfen,** to become, grow, suspicious.

argwöhnen, *occ.* **argwohnen,** *v.tr.* to be suspicious of (sth.), to suspect (sth.); to mistrust, be mistrustful of (sth.); **a., daß . . . ,** to suspect, have a suspicion, that . . . .

argwöhnisch, *a.* suspicious; mistrustful, distrustful; *adv.* suspiciously.

Argyrie [argy·ˈriː], *f.* **-/.** *Med:* argyria, silver poisoning.

Argyrol [argy·ˈroːl], *n.* **-s/.** *Pharm:* argyrol.

Ariadne [a·ri·ˈadnə]. *Pr.n.f.* **-s.** *Gr.Myth:* Ariadne.

Ariadnefaden, der. *Gr.Myth:* Ariadne's clew.

Arianer [a·ri·ˈaːnər], *m.* **-s/-.** *Rel.Hist:* Arian.

arianisch [a·ri·ˈaːniʃ], *a. Rel.Hist:* Arian.

Arianismus [a·ri·a·ˈnismus], *m.* **-/.** *Rel.Hist:* Arianism.

arid [a·ˈriːt], **aride** [a·ˈriːdə], *a.* arid, dry, barren (country, discourse, subject, etc.).

Aridität [a·ri·di·ˈtɛːt], *f.* **-/.** aridity, aridness, dryness, barrenness (of country, discourse, etc.).

Arie [ˈaːrĭə], *f.* **-/-n.** *Mus:* aria.

Arier [ˈaːrĭər], *m.* **-s/-. 1.** *Ethn:* Aryan; **die A.,** the Aryas, the Aryans. **2.** *F:* non-Semitic, 'Aryan'.

Arierparagraph, der. *Hist:* the (Nazi) anti-Jewish legislation.

Aries [ˈaːri·ɛs]. *Pr.n.m.* **-'.** *Astr:* Aries, the Ram.

Ariette [a·ri·ˈɛtə], *f.* **-/-n.** *Mus:* arietta.

Arimathäa [a·ri·ma·ˈtɛːaː], **Arimathia** [a·ri·ma·ˈtiːaː]. *Pr.n.n.* **-s.** *A.Geog:* Arimathaea.

arioso [a·ri·ˈoːzoː]. *Mus:* **1.** *adv.* arioso. **2.** *s.* **Arioso,** *n,* **-s/-s** *&* **-si,** arioso.

Ariost [a·ri·ˈost]. *Pr.n.m.* **-s.** *Lit.Hist:* Ariosto.

Ariovist [a·rĭo·ˈvist]. *Pr.n.m.* **-s.** *Hist:* Ariovistus.

arisch [ˈaːriʃ], *a.* **1.** *Ethn:* Aryan. **2.** *F:* non-Semitic, 'Aryan'.

arisieren [a·ri·ˈziːrən], *v.tr. F:* to 'Aryanize'; to remove Jewish elements from (State, business, etc.); **Arisierung** *f,* Aryanization.

Aristarch [a·riˈstarç]. *Pr.n.m.* **-s.** *Gr.Ant:* Aristarchus.

Aristides [a·riˈstiːde·s]. *Pr.n.m.* **-'.** *Gr.Hist:* Aristides.

Aristipp [a·riˈstip]. *Pr.n.m.* **-s.** *Gr.Ant:* Aristippus.

Aristippos, Aristippus [a·riˈstipos, -us]. *Pr.n.m.* **-'.** *Gr.Ant:* Aristippus.

Aristokrat [a·risto·ˈkraːt], *m.* **-en/-en,** aristocrat.

Aristokratie [a·risto·kra·ˈtiː], *f.* **-/-n** [-ˈtiːən], aristocracy.

aristokratisch [a·risto·ˈkraːtiʃ], *a.* aristocratic (air, person, etc.); aristocratical (government).

Aristolochie [a·risto·loˈxiː], *f.* **-/-n** [-ˈloxĭən]. *Bot:* aristolochia, birthwort.

Aristophanes [a·riˈstoːfa·ne·s]. *Pr.n.m.* **-'.** *Gr.Lit:* Aristophanes.

aristophanisch [a·risto·ˈfaːniʃ], *a.* (*a*) by, of, Aristophanes; (*b*) Aristophanic.

Aristoteles [a·riˈstoːtele·s]. *Pr.n.m.* **-'.** *Gr.Phil:* Aristotle.

Aristoteleshirsch, *m. Z:* sambur, sambar.

Aristoteliker [a·risto·ˈteːlikər], *m.* **-s/-.** Aristotelian.

aristotelisch [a·risto·ˈteːliʃ], *a.* Aristotelian.

Arithmetik [a·ritˈmeːtik, a·ritme·ˈtiːk], *f.* **-/.** arithmetic.

Arithmetiker [a·ritˈmeːtikər], *m.* **-s/-,** arithmetician.

arithmetisch [a·ritˈmeːtiʃ], *a.* arithmetical.

Arithmogriph [a·ritmo·ˈgriːf], *m.* **-en/-en,** arithmetical puzzle; number-puzzle.

Arithmometer [a·ritmo·ˈmeːtər], *n.* **-s/-,** arithmometer; calculating machine.

Arkade [arˈkaːdə], *f.* **-/-n. 1.** *Arch:* arcade; arcading. **2.** arched (style of) handwriting.

Arkadien [arˈkaːdĭən]. *Pr.n.n.* **-s.** *A.Geog: Lit. & F:* Arcadia.

Arkadier [arˈkaːdĭər], *m.* **-s/-.** *A.Geog: Lit. & F:* Arcadian.

arkadisch [arˈkaːdiʃ], *a. A.Geog: Lit. & F:* Arcadian; **arkadische Dichtung,** (i) Arcadian poetry; pastoral poetry, (ii) pastoral (poem).

Arkandisziplin, die [arˈkaːn-]. *Rel.Hist:* the Discipline of the Secret.

Arkanum [arˈkaːnum], *n.* **-s/-na,** arcanum; secret; mystery.

Arkatur [arka·ˈtuːr], *f.* **-/-en.** *Arch:* arcading.

Arkebusade [arke·bu·ˈzaːdə], *f.* **-/-n.** *Mil.Hist:* (h)arquebusade.

Arkebuse [arke·ˈbuːzə], *f.* **-/-n.** *Mil.Hist:* (h)arquebus.

Arkebusier [arke·bu·ˈziːr], *m.* **-s/-e.** *Mil.Hist:* (h)arquebusier.

Arkesilaos [arke·ˈziːla·os, -ˈlaːos]. *Pr.n.m.* **-'.** *Gr.Phil:* Arcesilaus.

Arko [ˈarkoː], *n.* **-s/.** *Metall:* crude brass.

Arkograph [arko·ˈgraːf], *m.* **-en/-en.** *Draw:* arcograph, cyclograph.

Arkose [arˈkoːzə], *f.* **-/.** *Miner:* arkose, fel(d)-spathic sandstone.

Arkosol [arko·ˈzoːl], *n.* **-s/-ien** [-ˈzoːlĭən], **Arkosolium** [-ˈzoːlĭum], *n.* **-s/-lien.** *Art:* (*in catacomb*) wall-tomb, arcosolium.

Arktiker [ˈarktikər], *m.* **-s/-. 1.** *Geog:* inhabitant of the Arctic. **2.** Arctic explorer *or* specialist in Arctic matters.

Arktis, die [ˈarktis]. *Pr.n.f.* **-.** *Geog:* the arctic circle, the Arctic.

arktisch [ˈarktiʃ], *a. Geog: etc:* arctic; **das Arktische Meer,** the Arctic Ocean.

Arktogäa, die [arkto·ˈgɛːaː], **-.** *Geog:* Arctogaea.

Arktur [arkˈtuːr], **-s, Arkturus** [arkˈtuːrus], **-'.** *Pr.n.m. Astr:* Arcturus.

Arkuballiste [arku·baˈlistə], *f.* **-/-n.** *Mil.Hist:* arbalest.

Arkus [ˈarkus], *m.* **-/-,** *occ.* **-kusses/-kusse.** *Mth:* arc (of an angle); *comb.fm.* arc . . . ; **Arkuskosinus** *m,* arc cosine; **Arkustangens** *m,* arc tangent.

Arm[1], *m.* **-(e)s/-e. 1.** (*a*) arm (of pers., ape, cuttlefish, etc., *Farr:* of horse); **einen Korb am Arm haben,** to have a basket on one's arm; **ein Kind auf dem Arm tragen,** to carry a child on one's arm; **ein Kind, ein Mädchen, im Arm haben,** to have a child, a girl, in one's arms; **ein Kind auf den Arm nehmen,** to pick a child up on one's arm; **etwas unter dem Arm tragen,** to carry sth. under one's arm; **etwas mit ausgestreckten Armen von sich halten,** to hold sth. at arm's length; **j-n am Arm haben,** to have s.o. on one's arm; **j-n am Arm führen,** to lead s.o. by the arm; to have s.o. on one's arm; **j-m den Arm bieten, reichen,** to give, offer, one's arm to s.o.; **j-s Arm nehmen,** to take s.o.'s arm; **Arm in Arm gehen,** to walk arm in arm; **den Arm um j-n legen,** to put one's arm round s.o.; **j-n in die Arme schließen, nehmen,** to fold, take, clasp, s.o. in one's arms; **sie schlossen sich in die Arme,** they clasped, embraced, each other; **sie lief mir in die Arme,** she ran into, to, my arms; **j-n mit offenen Armen, j-n offenen Armes, empfangen,** to receive, greet, s.o. with open arms, to receive s.o. open-armed; **sich j-m in die Arme werfen,** to throw oneself into s.o.'s arms; **sich dem Laster in die Arme werfen,** to abandon oneself to vice; **j-m in den Arm fallen,** (i) to seize s.o. by the arm; (ii) to stay s.o.'s hand; to prevent, stop, s.o. (from doing sth.); **mit verschränkten Armen zusehen,** to look on with folded arms; to make no attempt to interfere; **einen langen Arm haben,** (i) to have a long arm; (ii) to have far-reaching influence; **j-m unter die Arme greifen,** (i) to lift s.o. up; to give s.o. a hoist (up), (ii) *F:* to give s.o. support; to give s.o. a lift; to give s.o. a leg up; **j-m mit zwanzig Mark unter die Arme greifen,** to help s.o. out with twenty marks; *F:* **die Beine unter die Arme nehmen,** to pick up one's heels; to put on a spurt; to put one's best foot forward; *F:* **j-n auf den Arm nehmen,** to pull s.o.'s leg, to have s.o. on; *U.S:* to take s.o. for a ride; (*b*) (*of pers.*) **der beste, stärkste, Arm,** (i) the best worker, (ii) the strongest man; (*c*) **der Arm des Gesetzes,** (i) the arm of the law, (ii) the secular arm. **2.** arm (of chair, anchor, balance, lever, crank, signal, etc.); beam (of balance); jib (of crane); limb (of cross); branch (of candelabra); web (of crank, crankshaft); (gas, electric light) bracket; *Constr: etc:* cross-piece, arm; bracket; *Veh:* shaft; shaft-bar; futchel; **Arm des Meeres,** arm of the sea, sound; **Arm eines Flusses,** arm, branch, of a river.

arm[2], *a.* (**ärmer; ärmst**) **1.** (*a*) poor; needy, in want, penurious; **ein armer Mann,** a poor man; an indigent man; **ein Armer, eine Arme,** a poor man, woman, *Adm:* a pauper; **die Armen,** the poor, the indigent; **für die Armen sorgen,** to help the poor; **die ärmeren Klassen,** the poorer classes; **arm wie eine Kirchenmaus,** as poor as a church mouse, as Job; **ich bin um hundert Mark ärmer,** I am a hundred marks worse off, I am the poorer by a hundred marks, I am a hundred marks down; **geistig arm,** wanting, lacking, in intellect; of inferior intellect; simple, slow-witted; **die Armen im Geiste,** (i) the poor in spirit; (ii) *F:* those, people, of limited intelligence; those who are slow in, on, the uptake; the dunces, *F:* the duffers; *B:* **selig sind, die da geistlich arm sind,** blessed are the poor in spirit; (*b*) poor, wretched, mean, sorry, miserable; **ein armer Tropf,** a poor, wretched, miserable, creature; **ein armer Teufel,** a poor devil, a poor wretch; **ein armer Sünder,** (i) a miserable sinner; a miserable wretch; (ii) a condemned criminal; *see also* **Ritter** ; (*c*) poor, unfortunate, to be pitied; **der Arme!** poor fellow! poor chap! **ich Armer!** poor me! *Lit:* woe is me! **wir Armen!** poor us! how unfortunate we are! **die Arme! die Ärmste!** poor woman! poor girl! poor dear! **du Armer! du Ärmster!** poor you! **das arme Ding!** poor thing! **die**

armen Kleinen! poor little things! (*d*) (*deceased*) **meine arme Frau,** my late wife; my poor dear wife. **2.** (*a*) of poor quality; deficient; **armer Boden,** poor, infertile, unproductive, soil; **armes Erz,** poor, low-grade, ore; **armes Gas,** weak, lean, gas; **arme Kohle,** lean coal; *Aut:* **armes Gemisch,** poor, weak, mixture; (*b*) **arm an**+*dat.*, poor in . . . , deficient in . . . , lacking in . . . ; with a low content of . . . ; **arm an Geist,** lacking in wit; of inferior intellect; **arm an Geld,** poor in money; **arm an Kohle, an Bäumen,** poor in coal, in trees; **-arm,** *comb.fm.* poor in . . . ; with a low content of . . . ; **ammoniakarm,** poor in ammonia; **metallarmes Erz,** ore poor in metal, low-grade ore; **alkoholarmes Getränk,** beverage with a low alcoholic content, containing little alcohol; **nikotinarmer Tabak,** tobacco with a low nicotine content, with little nicotine; **stärkearme Brötchen,** starch-reduced rolls; (*of pers.*) **ideenärmer werden,** to become poorer in ideas.

Armada [arˈmaːdaː], *f.* **-/-den & -s,** armada; *Hist:* **die spanische A.,** the Spanish Armada.

Armadill [armaˑˈdil], *n.* **-s/-e. 1.** *Z:* armadillo, tatu. **2.** *Crust:* armadillo (wood-louse).

Armagnac, Armagnak [armanˈjak], *m.* **-s/-.** *Dist:* armagnac (brandy).

Armarbeit, *f. Sp:* arm-action (of swimmer, runner, rower, etc.).

Armarium [arˈmaːrĭum], *n.* **-s/-rien.** *Furn:* cupboard; bookcase; *esp. Ecc:* ambry.

Armatur [armaˑˈtuːr], *f.* **-/-en. 1.** *Mil: A:* (soldier's) accoutrements. **2.** (*a*) *usu. pl.* **Armaturen,** valves and fittings (of boiler, etc.); fittings (of tap, gauge, etc.); mountings (of apparatus); (*b*) armouring (of electric cable); (*c*) *occ.* armature (of magnet). **3.** *Her:* arms shown beneath the shield.

Armaturenbrett, *n. Aut: Av:* instrument-board, -panel, dash-board, fascia-board.

Armauflage, *f.* elbow-rest, arm-rest (*for marksman, etc.*).

Armband, *n.* (*a*) bracelet; bangle; wristlet; (*worn above elbow*) armlet; watch-strap; (*b*) brassard; arm-band, (cloth) armlet.

Armbanduhr, *f.* wrist-watch; wristlet-watch.

Armbein, *n.* arm-bone; *Anat:* humerus.

Armbeuge, *f.* **1.** bend, crook, of the arm. **2.** *Gym:* 'arms bend'.

Armbeugen, *n. Gym:* 'arms bend' exercises.

Armbewegung, *f.* movement of the arm; *Sp:* arm-movement (of runner, rower, etc.); *Swim:* (arm-)stroke.

Armbiege, *f.* bend, crook, of the arm.

Armbinde, *f.* (*a*) arm-band, armlet; brassard; (*b*) *Med:* sling.

Armblatt, *n. Cost:* dress-shield, -preserver.

Armblei, *n. Metall:* desilverized lead.

Armbruch, *m. Surg:* fracture of the arm; **einen A. haben,** to have a fractured, broken, arm.

Armbrust, *f.* cross-bow, *A:* arbalest.

Ärmchen, *n.* **-s/-,** (*dim. of* **Arm**) little, small, arm.

armdick, *a.* as thick as one's arm.

Armee [arˈmeː], *f.* **-/-n** [arˈmeːən]. *Mil:* army (*in modern military terminology usu. component army within the total* **Heer,** *q.v.*); *Hist:* **die Große A.,** the Grand Army; *F: A:* **zur großen A. abgehen, abgerufen werden,** to die, *F:* to join the (great) majority.

Armeeabteilung, *f. Mil: A:* army group.

Armeegruppe, *f. Mil:* army group.

Armeekorps, *n. Mil:* army corps.

Armeeoberkommando, *n. Mil:* army headquarters staff.

Ärmel, *m.* **-s/-,** sleeve (of coat, dress, etc.); **Kleid mit Ärmeln,** dress with sleeves, sleeved dress; **Kleid mit langen, kurzen, Ärmeln,** long-sleeved, short-sleeved, dress; **Kleid ohne Ä.,** sleeveless dress; **j-n am Ä. zupfen,** to pluck s.o.'s sleeve; **sich** *dat.* **etwas in den Ä. stecken,** to put sth. up one's sleeve; *F:* **etwas aus dem Ä. schütteln,** to do sth. off-hand, *F:* straight off the bat, *U.S:* off the cuff; **ich kann diesen Aufsatz nicht aus dem Ä. schütteln,** I can't write that essay off-hand, *F:* I can't produce that essay out of a hat; **das kann man nicht so aus dem Ä. schütteln,** that takes, requires, some doing; that can't be done off-hand, *F:* straight off the bat; one can't do it just like that.

Ärmelabzeichen, *n. Mil: etc:* sleeve-badge.

Ärmelaufschlag, *m.* cuff (of coat sleeve); *Mil:* cuff facing.

Ärmelausschnitt, *m.* arm-hole, sleeve-hole (of dress, etc.).

Ärmelbrett, *n. Dom.Ec:* sleeve-board.

Ärmeleinsatz, *m. Dressm:* **1.** setting in of a sleeve. **2.** arm-hole, sleeve-hole (of coat, dress, etc.).

Armeleute-, *comb.fm.* poor people's . . . ; poor man's . . . ; **Armeleuteessen** *n,* poor man's meal.

Armeleuteviertel, *n.* slum quarter, poor quarter (of town).

Ärmelhalter, *m.pl.* sleeve-bands.

-ärmelig, *a. comb.fm.* -sleeved; **langärmelig,** long-sleeved; **kurzärmelig,** short-sleeved.

Ärmelkanal, der. *Geog:* the (English) Channel.

Ärmelloch, *n.* arm-hole, sleeve-hole (of coat, dress, etc.).

ärmellos, *a.* sleeveless (dress, etc.).

Ärmelmeer, das=**Ärmelkanal, der.**

Ärmelpatte, *f. Mil:* cuff-patch.

Ärmelschoner, *m.* oversleeve, cuff-protector, sleeve-protector.

Ärmelstreifen, *m. pl. Navy:* **goldene Ä.,** (officer's) gold rings (on sleeve).

Ärmelweste, *f. Cost:* sleeve-waistcoat, sleeved vest; *U.S. & F:* lumberjack.

Armenanstalt, *f. A:* poor-law institution; public assistance institution; *A. & F:* workhouse, poorhouse.

Armenanwalt, *m. Jur:* barrister, counsel (representing a person who has been granted legal aid).

Armenapotheke, *f. A:* (charitable, public) dispensary.

Armenarzt, *m. A:* doctor giving free treatment to the poor; *Adm:* public assistance doctor.

Armenasyl, *n. A:* pauper asylum; *A. & F:* workhouse, poorhouse.

Armenaufseher, *m. A:*=**Armenpfleger.**

Armenbehörde, *f. Adm: A:* Public Assistance Authority; Relieving Authority; Poor-Law Authority; *A:* Board of Guardians.

Armenbibel, *f. Mediev.Lit:* biblia pauperum.

Armenbüchse, *f. A:* poor-box, *A:* alms-box.

Armenfürsorge, *f.*=**Armenpflege.**

Armengebühr, *f. A:* contribution to charity (included in price of admission-ticket, etc.).

Armengeld, *n. A:* (*a*) contribution(s) to charity; *A:* alms; (*b*) *F:*=**Armensteuer.**

Armengesetzgebung, *f. Jur:* legislation for the relief of the poor; *A:* poor-law.

Armenhaus, *n. A. & F:* workhouse, poorhouse.

Armenien [arˈmeːnĭən]. *Pr.n.n.* **-s.** *Geog:* Armenia.

Armenier [arˈmeːnĭər], *m.* **-s/-.** *Ethn: Geog:* Armenian.

armenisch [arˈmeːniʃ]. **1.** *a.* Armenian; *A.Pharm:* **armenischer Bol(us),** Armenian bole, bole armeniac. **2.** *s.* **Armenisch,** *n. Ling:* Armenian (language).

Armenkasse, *f. A:* (poor-)relief fund.

Armenpflege, *f.* assistance of the poor; *Adm:* poor relief, public assistance.

Armenpflegeausschuß, *m. Adm: A:* Relief Committee; *A:* Board of Guardians.

Armenpfleger, *m. Adm: A:* relieving officer; welfare officer; *A:* guardian, overseer, of the poor.

Armenrat, *m. A:* Board of Guardians.

Armenrecht, *n. Jur:* right to sue *in forma pauperis;* right (of a poor person) to legal aid; **unter A. klagen,** to sue *in forma pauperis;* **unter A. Klagende(r),** litigant appearing as a poor person; pauper; **das A. erlangen,** to obtain legal aid; **einen Antrag auf Erteilung des Armenrechts stellen,** to apply for legal aid; to petition for leave to sue *in forma pauperis.*

Armenschule, *f. A:* charity-school.

Armensteuer, *f. Adm: A:* poor-rate.

Armenstock, *m. A:* poor-box, *A:* alms-box.

Armenunterstützung, *f. Adm: A:* poor-relief; **A. empfangen,** to be in receipt of relief, to receive public assistance.

Armenverwaltung, *f. Adm: A:* poor-law administration; public assistance.

Armenviertel, *n.* slum; poor quarter (of a town); **im A. wohnen,** to live in the slums; **die Pariser Armenviertel,** the slums of Paris.

Armenvogt, Armenvorsteher, *m. A:*=**Armenpfleger.**

Armenwesen, *n. Adm: A:* poor-law administration.

ärmer *see* **arm**².

Armeria [armeˑˈriːaː], *f.* **-/-rien,** armoury; arsenal.

Armerie [arˈmeːrĭə], *f.* **-/.** *Bot:* armeria, thrift.

Armesin [armeˑˈziːn], *n.* **-s/-e.** *Tex: A:* armozeen, sarsenet, sarcenet.

Armesünder-, *comb.fm.* . . . of a condemned criminal; **Armesünderhemd** *n,* shirt, garment, worn by a condemned criminal; execution shirt.

Armesünderblume, *f. Bot. F:* wild chicory.

Armesündergesicht, *n.*=**Armesündermiene.**

Armesünderglocke, *f.,* **Armesünderglöcklein,** *n. A:* death knell (rung at an execution); execution bell.

Armesündermiene, *f. F:* **eine A. haben,** to wear a hang-dog look, a look of abject misery; to have the look of a gallows-bird.

Armesünderstuhl, *m. A:* stool of repentance; *F:* **auf dem A. sitzen,** to be under cross-examination; *F:* to be on the carpet.

Armesünderzelle, *f. A:* condemned cell.

Armfeile, *f. Tls:* rubber (file).

Armflor, *m.* mourning-band, (mourning) arm-band.

Armflosser, *m.* **-s/-.** *Ich:* pediculate (fish); **die Armflosser,** pediculates, pediculati.

armförmig, *a.* arm-shaped; *Anat:* brachial; *Bot:* brachiate.

Armfüß(l)er, *m.* **-s/-.** *Moll:* brachiopod.

Armgeflecht, *n. Anat:* brachial plexus.

Armgeige, *f. Mus:* viola, tenor violin.

Armgelenk, *n. Anat:* elbow-joint.

Armgrube, *f.* **1.** armpit. **2.** *Bot:* axil(la).

Armgurt, *m. Veh:* arm-loop, -sling, -strap.

armhaarig, *a. Nat.Hist:* with scanty hair.

Armheber, *m. Anat:* deltoid (muscle).

Armhöcker, *m. Anat:* olecranon.

Armhöhle, *f.* **1.** armpit. **2.** *Bot:* axil(la).

armieren [arˈmiːrən]. **I.** *v.tr.* **1.** (*a*) to arm; to provide (s.o., sth.) with arms; (*b*) to equip, fit out (ship, etc.). **2.** to reinforce, fortify, strengthen; **armierter Balken, Träger,** trussed, reinforced, beam *or* girder; **ein Kabel a.,** to sheathe, armour, a cable; **einen Magneten a.,** to arm, cap, a magnet.

II. *vbl s.* **1. Armieren,** *n. in vbl senses.* **2. Armierung,** *f.* (*a*)=II. 1; (*b*) armament; equipment; reinforcement (for beam, for girder, in concrete); sheathing, armouring (of cable).

Armierungsbataillon, *n. Mil: A:* labour battalion.

Armierungssoldat, *m. Mil: A:* soldier in a labour unit.

-armig, *comb.fm. a.* -armed; **kurzarmig,** short-armed; **langarmig,** long-armed; **dreiarmig,** three-armed.

Armilla [arˈmilaː], *f.* **-/-lä. 1.**=**Armille. 2.** *A.Astr:* armilla.

Armillarsphäre [armiˈlaːr-], *f. A.Astr:* armillary sphere.

Armille [arˈmilə], *f.* **-/-n.** *Prehist:* armilla, bracelet.

Arminianer [armiˑnĭˈaːnər], *m.* **-s/-.** *Rel.Hist:* Arminian.

arminianisch [armiˑnĭˈaːniʃ], *a.* Arminian.

Arminianismus [armiˑnĭaˑˈnismus], *m.* **-/.** *Rel.Hist:* Arminianism.

Armkachel, *f. Mediev. Arm:* elbow cop.

Armkiemer, *m.* **-s/-.** *Moll:* brachiopod.

Armknochen, *m.* arm-bone; *Anat:* humerus.

Armkorb, *m.* handbasket.

Armkraft, *f.* strength of arm; *Mec.E:* man-power, hand-power; **etwas mit (bloßer) A. tun,** to do sth. by strength of arm, by sheer strength, by brute force.

Armkreuz, *n. Mec.E: etc:* spider (of wheel).

Armlampe, *f.* bracket-lamp.

armlang, *a.* as long as one's arm.

Armlänge, *f.* length of arm, arm-length; **auf A.,** at arm's length; **j-n auf A. herankommen lassen,** to let s.o. approach to within arm's length.

Armlehne, *f.* arm (of a chair); elbow-rest, arm-rest.

Armleuchter, *m.* **1.** candelabrum; branched candlestick, cluster-candlestick. **2.** *Bot:* stone-wort, chara. **3.** *P:* objectionable *or* contemptible person; swine, skunk, louse; nit, twerp.

Armleuchteralgen, *f.pl.,* **Armleuchtergewächse,** *n.pl. Bot:* stoneworts.

ärmlich, *a.* poor; miserable (dwelling, clothing, circumstances, etc.); humble (dwelling, gift, contribution, etc.); poor (furniture); sparse (furnishings); poorly-furnished (room); meagre, *F:* skimpy (gift, contribution, furnishings, etc.); **ärmliches Kleid,** (i) poor dress; (ii) *F:* dress that isn't much to look at; (*of pers.*) **(von) ärmlicher Herkunft sein,** to come from a poor family; **in ärmlichen Verhältnissen leben,** to live in poor, *F:* narrow, circumstances; **ärmliche Kost,** poor, frugal, fare; **ein ärmliches Aussehen haben,** (*of pers., house, etc.*) to look poor; *Agr:* **ärmlicher Boden,** poor, penurious, soil; *adv.* poorly; miserably; **ä. gekleidet,** poorly dressed, poorly clad; **ä. leben,** to live humbly, very simply; **ä. essen,** to eat frugally, to eat frugal meals; **ä. aussehendes Kind,** poor-looking child; puny-, weakly-looking child.

Ärmlichkeit, *f.* poorness; miserableness, misery; poor appearance (of room, furniture, etc.); humbleness (of room, gift, etc.); *F:* skimpiness (of gift, etc.); **Ä. des Bodens,** poorness of the soil.

Ärmling¹, *m.* **-s/-e.** *Cost:* oversleeve; cuff-, sleeve-protector.

Ärmling², *m.* **-s/-e,** poor person, *F:* pauper.

Armloch, *n.* arm-hole, sleeve-hole (of dress, etc.).

Armmolch, *m. Rept:* siren; mud-iguana.

Armmuskel, *m.* arm muscle.

Armnervengeflecht, *n. Anat:* brachial plexus.

Armorial [armoˑriˈaːl], *n.* **-s/-e,** armorial, book of heraldry.

Armorika [arˈmoːriˑkaː]. *Pr.n.f.* **-s.** *A.Geog:* Armorica.

Armorikaner [armoˑriˑˈkaːnər], *m.* **-s/-.** *Ethn: Geog:* Armorican.

armorikanisch [armoˑriˑˈkaːniʃ], *a.* Armorican; *Ling:* **die armorikanische Sprache,** Breton; *Geog:* **das Armorikanische Gebirge,** the Armorican chain.

Armpolster, *n.* upholstery of a chair-arm; (upholstered) arm-rest, elbow-rest.

Armprothese, *f. Surg:* artificial arm.

Armrand, *m. Orn:* bend of the wing.

Armreichschalter, *m. I.C.E:* (*device*) mixture control.

Armreif(en), Armring, *m.* bangle.

Armröhre, *f. Anat:* humerus.

Armsäule, *f.* sign-post, finger-post.

Armschiene, *f.* **1.** *Mediev:* arm-guard (*of armour*); (*for upper arm*) brassard; rerebrace; (*for forearm*) vambrace. **2.** *Surg:* arm-splint.

Armschild, *m.* **1.** *Hist:* small shield worn on the arm; buckler. **2.** = **Armspiegel.**

Armschlag, *m. Swim:* (arm-)stroke.

Armschlagader, *f. Anat:* brachial artery.

Armschützer, *m.* **1.** *Archery: etc:* arm-guard. **2.** *Cost:* oversleeve.

Armschwinge, *f. Orn:* secondary (feather).

armsdick, *a.* as thick as one's, as an, arm.

armselig, *a.* miserable; wretched (person); pitiful, piteous, lamentable (figure, state, etc.); wretched, mean, sorry (appearance, dwelling, etc.); paltry, despicable, beggarly (gift, sum, wage, etc.); **ein armseliges Städtchen,** a mean, miserable, *F:* beggarly, wretched, little town; **ein armseliger Versuch,** a pitiable effort; a miserable, wretched, attempt; *occ.* **Armseligkeiten,** trifles, bagatelles.

Armsessel, *m.* armchair, easy-chair.

Armsignal, *n.* arm-, hand-signal; *Mil: Nau: Rail:* semaphore signal.

Armspange, *f.* bangle; bracelet.

Armspeiche, *f. Anat:* radius.

Armspiegel, *m.* arm-badge, sleeve-badge.

Armspindel, *f. Anat:* radius.

ärmste(r), ärmste, ärmste(s) *see* **arm**[2].

Armstern, *m. Mec.E: etc:* spider (of wheel).

Armstuhl, *m.* armchair, easy-chair.

Armstulp, *m.*, **Armstulpe,** *f.*, gauntlet (of fencing glove, etc.); (large) cuff (on sleeve).

Armstumpf, *m.* stump (of an amputated arm); arm-stump (of statue, etc.).

Armstütze, *f.* arm-rest, elbow-rest.

Armsünder-, *comb.fm. cp.* **Armesünder-.**

armunklar, *a. Nau:* (anchor) fouled by the flukes.

Armut, *f.* **-/.** (*a*) poverty, indigence, want; penury; **äußerste A.,** extreme, abject, poverty; destitution; pauperism; **drückende A.,** dire, wretched, poverty; **in A. geraten,** to be reduced to poverty, to penury; to come to want; **in A. leben,** to live in poverty; to be living in want; *Prov:* **A. tut weh, A. ist ein schlimmer Gast,** poverty hurts, is hard to bear; **A. schändet nicht, A. ist keine Schande,** poverty is no disgrace, no crime, no sin, no vice; (*b*) **geistige A.,** poverty of intellect; (*c*) poverty, poorness, barrenness (of language, etc.); baldness (of style, etc.); **A. des Bodens,** poorness, poverty, of the soil; **A. an+** *dat.*, poverty in . . . ; lack, want, of . . . ; **A. des Bodens an Phosphaten,** poverty of the soil in phosphates; lack, want, of phosphates in the soil; **A. an Ideen,** poorness, poverty, penury, of ideas.

Armutszeugnis, *n.* **1.** *Adm:* certificate of poverty; *Jur:* certificate of entitlement to legal aid. **2.** *F:* **sich** *dat.* **ein A. ausstellen,** to betray one's ignorance *or* incompetence; to give oneself away (badly, completely).

Armvoll, *m.* **-s/-,** armful.

armvollweise, *adv.* in armfuls, by the armful.

Armzeichen, *n. Mil: Nau: etc:* arm signal, semaphore signal; **eine Mitteilung durch A. übermitteln,** to transmit a message by arm signals, to semaphore a message.

Armzeichengebung, *f.* arm signalling, semaphoring.

Armzeug, *n. Mediev:* arm-guard, brassard (of armour).

Arnaut(e) [arˈnaut(ə)], *m.* **-(e)n/-(e)n.** *Ethn:* Arna(o)ut, Albanian.

Arnheim. *Pr.n.n.* **-s.** *Geog:* Arnhem.

Arnheimer. 1. *m.* **-s/-,** (*a*) *Geog:* inhabitant, native, of Arnhem; (*b*) *A:* (steel) safe. **2.** *inv.a.* of Arnhem, Arnhem . . .

Arnika [ˈarniˑkaː], *f.* **-/.** *Bot: Pharm:* arnica.

Arnim-Paragraph, der. *Jur:* = the Official Secrets Act.

Arnulfinger, die [arnulˈfiŋgər], *m.pl. Hist:* the descendants of Arnulf; the Carolingians, the Carlovingians.

Arom [aˑˈroːm], *n.* **-(e)s/-e, Aroma** [aˑˈroːmaː], *n.* **-s/-men** & **-mata,** *occ.* **-maten** [aˑroˑˈmaːtən], aroma; fragrance; bouquet (of wine); *Cu:* (aromatic) essence.

Aromalith [aˑroˑmaˑˈliːt], *m.* **-s/-e.** *Miner:* (any) aromatic stone.

Aromaten [aˑroˑˈmaːtən]. **1.** *m.pl.* aromatic substances, aromatics. **2.** *occ. n.pl. see* **Aroma.**

aromatisieren [aˑroˑmaˑtiˑˈziːrən], *v.tr.* to give aroma to (sth.); to aromatize (soap, drug, etc.).

aromatisch [aˑroˑˈmaːtiʃ], *a.* aromatic; *Ch:* **aromatische Reihe,** aromatic series; **aromatische Verbindungen,** aromatic compounds, aromatics.

Aron [ˈaːron]. **1.** *Pr.n.m.* **-s.** *B.Hist:* Aaron. **2.** *m.* **-s/.** *Bot:* arum.

Aron(s)stab, *m. Bot:* arum; **gefleckter A.,** wake-robin, cuckoo-pint, lords-and-ladies.

Aron(s)wurz, *f. Bot:* wake-robin, cuckoo-pint, lords-and-ladies.

Arpeggiatur [arpɛdʒaˑˈtuːr], *f.* **-/-en.** *Mus:* series of arpeggios, of arpeggiated, broken, chords.

arpeggieren [arpɛˈdʒiːrən], *v.tr. Mus:* to arpeggio (passage, accompaniment); **arpeggierter Akkord,** arpeggiated chord.

Arpeggio [arˈpɛdʒoː], *n.* **-s/-s.** *Mus:* arpeggio; spread, broken, *or* arpeggiated chord.

Arrak [ˈarak], *m.* **-s/-e** & **-s.** *Dist:* arrack.

Arrangement [arãˑʒəˈmãː], *n.* **-s/-s,** (*a*) arrangement; ordering; order; (*b*) arrangement, agreement; **Arrangements treffen,** to make arrangements; **mit j-m ein A. treffen,** to make an arrangement, come to an arrangement, to terms, with s.o.; **ein A. mit seinen Gläubigern treffen,** to come to an arrangement, to compound, make a composition, with one's creditors; (*c*) (*in Switzerland*) 'en pension' terms (at hotel); (*d*) *Mus:* **A. für Klavier, für Geige,** arrangement, setting, for piano, for violin; (*e*) basket *or* (large) bouquet of flowers.

Arrangeur [arãˑˈʒøːr], *m.* **-s/-e,** (*a*) arranger, contriver (of an entertainment, etc.); director (of a festival); (*b*) *Mus:* arranger (of score, etc.).

arrangieren [arãˑˈʒiːrən]. **I.** *v.tr.* **1.** (*a*) to arrange, set in order; (*b*) *Mus:* to arrange, set (song for violin, etc.). **2.** to arrange, contrive; to fix (sth.) up; to arrange for, organize, get up (entertainment, festival, etc.); **wenn du ein Zimmer brauchst, so kann ich das a.,** if you need a room I can make the necessary arrangements, I can fix it up for you. **3. (sich) mit seinen Gläubigern a.,** to come to an arrangement, to compound, make a composition, with one's creditors.

II. *vbl s.* **Arrangieren,** *n. in vbl senses; also:* arrangement.

Arras [ˈaras]. **1.** *Pr.n.n.* **-'.** *Geog:* Arras. **2.** *m.* **-/.** *Tex: A:* (cloth of) arras.

Arre, *f.* **-/-n.** *North G.Dial:* slow-worm, blind-worm.

Arrendator [arɛnˈdaːtor], *m.* **-s/-en** [-daˑˈtoːrən] = **Pächter.**

Arrende [aˈrɛndə], *f.* **-/-n** = **Pacht.**

arrendieren [arɛnˈdiːrən], *v.tr.* **1.** = **pachten. 2.** = **verpachten.**

Arrest [aˈrɛst], *m.* **-(e)s/-e. 1.** *Jur:* seizure, impounding, attachment (of goods); distraint (of property of debtor); arrest, detention (of ship); embargo (on ship); **dinglicher A.,** attachment; **etwas mit A. belegen, A. auf etwas** *acc.* **legen,** to attach, seize, sth.; **ein Schiff unter A. stellen,** to arrest a ship; to order the detention of a ship; to lay an embargo on a ship; (*in bankruptcy proceedings*) **offener A.,** stopping of all payments, deliveries, etc., to a debtor. **2.** (*a*) arrest; confinement; detention (of pers.); **j-n in A. schicken,** to have s.o. detained; to put s.o., have s.o. put, under arrest; **A. haben, im A. sein,** to be under arrest; **j-n mit A. bestrafen,** to punish s.o. by detention; to put s.o. under arrest; *Mil: Navy:* **leichter A.,** open arrest; **strenger A.,** (i) close arrest, (ii) solitary confinement; **verschärfter A.,** detention on bread-and-water diet; (*b*) (*in Austria*) imprisonment; **einfacher A.,** ordinary imprisonment (*with certain privileges*); **strenger A.,** imprisonment with hard labour; (*c*) *Sch: A:* detention, keeping in; **einen Schüler mit A. bestrafen,** to keep a pupil in, to detain a pupil, to give a pupil detention, put a pupil in detention.

Arrestanstalt, *f. Mil:* military prison; *Navy:* detention barracks.

Arrestant [arɛsˈtant], *m.* **-en/-en. 1.** prisoner; *Mil: Navy:* man under arrest; man in detention. **2.** *Jur:* seizing party; distrainer, *Scot:* arrester.

Arrestat [arɛsˈtaːt], *m.* **-en/-en. 1.** *Jur:* distrainee, person distrained. **2.** *occ.* = **Arrestant 1.**

Arrestation [arɛstaˑtsĭˈoːn], *f.* **-/-en,** arrest; arresting.

Arrestbruch, *m. Jur:* illegal interference with attached property.

arrestieren [arɛsˈtiːrən], *v.tr.* = **arretieren.**

Arrestlokal, *n. Mil:* guard-room.

Arrestvollziehung, *f. Jur:* seizure (of goods); (levying of) distraint.

Arrestzelle, *f. Mil:* detention cell.

arretieren [areˑˈtiːrən]. **I.** *v.tr.* **1.** to arrest, apprehend, seize (malefactor); to detain (s.o.). **2.** *Jur:* to seize, impound, attach (s.o.'s goods); to arrest (ship), to place (ship) under arrest. **3.** to arrest, stop (sth.); *Mec.E:* to lock, clamp (piece of machinery).

II. *vbl s.* **1. Arretieren,** *n. in vbl senses.* **2. Arretierung,** *f.* (*a*) = II. 1; *also:* arrest (of pers., ship); apprehension (of pers.); detention (of pers.); seizure, attachment (of s.o.'s goods); (*b*) *Mec.E:* (*device*) stop, catch, check; detent.

Arretierfalle [areˑˈtiːr-], *f. Mec.E:* catch, check; stop-piece; stop-bolt, -pin; detent(-pin).

Arretierhebel, *m. Mec.E:* locking-lever; catch.

Arretierscheibe, *f. Mec.E:* locking-disc.

Arretierstange, *f. Mec.E:* locking-bar; stop-bar.

arretinisch [arɛˈtiːniʃ], *a.* Arretine; **Arretinische Keramik, Arretinische Gefäße,** Arretine ware.

Arrêtstoß [aˈrɛː-], *m. Fenc:* stop-thrust.

Arrhythmie [arytˈmiː], *f.* **-/-n** [-ˈmiːən]. *Med:* arrhythmia, arrhythmy.

arrhythmisch [aˈrytmiʃ], *a.* arrhythmic (pulse).

Arrieregarde [ariˈɛːrˌgardə], *f.* **-/-n.** *Mil: A:* rear-guard.

Arrierepensee [ariɛːrpãˑˈseː], *f.* **-/-s,** arrière-pensée; (*a*) mental reservation; (*b*) dissembled thought; ulterior motive.

arrivieren [ariˑˈviːrən], *v.i.* (*sein*) to get on; to succeed; **der wird a.,** he is a man who will get on, *F:* will arrive.

Arrivierte [ariˑˈviːrtə], *m., f.* (*decl. as adj.*) man, woman, who has achieved success, who has got on (in the world); **er ist ein Arrivierter,** *F:* he is a made man, he has arrived.

Arröder, *m.* **-s/-.** *Dial:* farm-labourer, -hand.

arrodieren [aroˑˈdiːrən], *v.tr.* to erode; *Med:* (*of diseased part*) to destroy (neighbouring bone *or* tissue).

arrogant [aroˑˈgant], *a.* arrogant; overbearing (person, manner, etc.).

Arroganz [aroˑˈgants], *f.* **-/-en. 1.** arrogance; overbearing manner; overbearingness. **2.** arrogant remarks, etc.

arrondieren [arõˑˈdiːrən], *v.tr.* to round off (territory, property, etc.).

Arrosement [aroˑzəˈmãː], *n.* **-s/-s, Arrosierung** [aroˑˈziːruŋ], *f.* **-/-en.** *Fin:* additional payment (on shares, etc.).

Arrosion [aroˑziˈoːn], *f.* **-/-en,** erosion; *Med:* destruction of neighbouring bone *or* tissue.

Arrowroot [ˈɛroruːt, ˈærouruːt], *n.* **-s/.** *Com: Cu:* arrowroot.

Arsakiden [arzaˑˈkiːdən], **Arsaziden** [arzaˑˈtsiːdən], *pl. Hist:* Arsacids.

Arsch, *m.* **-es/⸗e,** (*a*) (*not in polite use*) arse, bum, backside, fanny, *U.S:* ass; **sich auf den A. setzen,** *F:* to take the weight off one's feet, *P:* to park one's arse; **den ganzen Tag auf dem A. sitzen,** to spend the whole day sitting down, *P:* to sit on one's arse, one's bum, one's fanny, all day long; **man kann nicht mit einem A. auf zwei Hochzeiten sitzen,** you can't eat your cake and have it; you can't have it both ways; **über A. gehen,** to go head over heels, *F:* base over apex, *P:* arse over tip; **einem Jungen den A. vollhauen,** to give a boy a good hiding, to tan a boy's backside, *P:* a boy's arse; **j-m einen Tritt in den A. geben, versetzen, j-n in den A. treten,** to give s.o. a kick on the backside, *P:* on the bum, up the arse; to kick s.o.'s backside, *P:* to kick s.o. up the arse, *U.S:* ass; **mit dem Scheck kannst du dir den A. wischen; den Scheck kannst du dir in den A. stecken,** *P:* you can put the cheque where the monkey puts its nuts; **j-m in den A. kriechen,** to curry favour with s.o., *F:* to lick s.o.'s boots, to suck up to s.o.; **du kannst mich am A. lecken!** (*usu. elliptically* **du kannst mich (mal)!**), nothing doing! what a hope! go and take a running jump at yourself! to hell with you! *P:* balls to you! **er soll mich mal (am A. lecken)!** to hell with him! (*of thg, money, etc.*) **im A. sein,** to be a dead loss, *F:* to be down the drain, up the spout; (*of thg*) **in den A. gehen,** to get smashed up; to go to pot;

see also **Grundeis**; (*b*) *Arch:* foundation (of column).
Arschbacke, *f. P:* buttock; *P:* cheek of the arse; *P:* **die Arschbacken zusammenklemmen,** to brace oneself; to force oneself to stick it out; to grit one's teeth.
Arschfell, *n.*=**Arschleder.**
Arschfinger, *m. A:* middle finger.
Arschgesicht, *n. P:* fat, puffy face; **jener Junge mit dem A.,** *P:* that bum-faced youth.
-ärschig, *comb.fm. a.* (*of pers.*) -arsed; **dick-ärschig,** squat, *P:* short-arsed.
Arschitze, *f.* **-/-n.** *Bot:* (*in Austria*) sorb, service-tree.
Arschkriechen, *n.*, **Arschkriecher,** *m.*, **Arsch-kriecherei,** *f.*=**Arschlecken, Arschlecker, Arsch-leckerei.**
Arschlecken, *n. P:* sycophancy, *F:* boot-licking, *P:* arse-licking, bum-sucking.
Arschlecker, *m. P:* sycophant, *F:* boot-licker, *P:* arse-licker, bum-sucker.
Arschleckerei, *f.*=**Arschlecken.**
Arschleder, *n.* **1.** leather seat (of miner's apron); (miner's) apron with a leather seat. **2.**=**Arsch** (*a*).
ärschlings, *adv. P:* (to fall, slide, etc.) on one's backside, *P:* on one's arse; **ä. den Berg hinunter-rutschen,** to slither down the hill on one's backside, *F:* on one's hunkers.
Arschloch, *n.* **1.** *P:* anal orifice, *P:* arse-hole. **2.** (*a*) *P:* (*pers.*) swine, skunk, louse; nit, twit, twerp; *P:* shit; (*b*) (*in South G., as a term of rude affection*) **du altes A.!** you old scoundrel!
Arschpauker, *m. P:* schoolmaster.
Arschwisch, *m. P:* lavatory-paper, toilet-paper; (*lavatory-paper or writing-paper*) *P:* bumfodder, bumf.
Arsen[1] [arˈzeːn], *n.* **-s/.** *Ch:* arsenic; **Arsen-,** *comb.fm.* (*in names of certain compounds*) arsenide of ...; **Arseneisen** *n*, iron arsenide; **Arsenkupfer** *n.* copper arsenide; **Arsenzink** *n*, zinc arsenide.
Arsen[2] [ˈarzən], *f.pl. see* **Arsis.**
Arsen[3] [arˈzeːn]. *Pr.n.m.* **-s.** Arsenius.
Arsenal [arzəˈnaːl], *n.* **-s/-e. 1.** *Hist:* arsenal; military storehouse; naval dockyard. **2.** *Lit:* arsenal, storehouse (of arguments, ideas, etc.).
Arsenblende [arˈzeːn-], *f. Miner:* arsenic blende; **gelbe A.,** orpiment; **rote A.,** realgar.
Arsenblüte, *f. Miner:* arsenic bloom; arsenolite.
Arsenchlorid, *n. Ch:* arsenic chloride.
Arseneisensinter, *m. Miner:* pitticite, pittizite.
Arsenfahlerz, *n. Miner:* tennantite.
arsenführend, *a. Miner:* arseniferous.
Arsenglas, *n.*=**Arsenikglas.**
arsenhaltig, *a.* containing arsenic; *Ch: etc:* arsenical.
Arseniat [arzeˑniˈaːt], *n.* **-s/-e.** *Ch:* arsen(i)ate.
Arsenid [arzeˑˈniːt], *n.* **-(e)s/-e** [-s, -ˈniːdəs/-ˈniːdə]. *Ch:* arsenide.
arsenig [arˈzeːniç], *a. Ch:* arsenious (acid, etc.).
arsenigsauer, *a. Ch:* combined with arsenious acid; **arsenigsaures Salz,** arsenite.
Arsenigsäure, *f. Ch:* arsenious acid.
Arsenik [arˈzeːnik], *n.* **-s/.** *Ch:* arsenious oxide, arsenic trioxide, *Com: etc:* (white) arsenic.
Arsenikalien [arzeˑniˑˈkaːliən], *n.pl. Com: Pharm:* arsenical preparations, preparations of arsenic.
arsenikalisch [arzeˑniˑˈkaːliʃ], *a. Ch: etc:* arsenical.
Arsenikbleispat, *m. Miner:* mimetite.
Arsenikblüte, *f.*=**Arsenblüte.**
Arsenikesser, *m. Med:* arsenic-eater.
Arsenikglas, *n. Ch:* arsenic glass, vitreous arsenic trioxide.
arsenikhaltig, *a.* containing arsenic; *Ch: etc:* arsenical.
Arsenikhütte, *f. Ind:* arsenic works.
Arsenikkalk, *m. Miner:* arsenolite.
Arsenikkies, *m.*=**Arsenkies.**
Arsenikmehl, *n. Com:* (**weißes**) **A.,** white arsenic, flaky arsenic, flowers of arsenic.
Arsenit [arzeˑˈniːt], *n.* **-(e)s/-e.** *Ch:* arsenite.
Arsenkies, *m. Miner:* arsenopyrite; mispickel, arsenical pyrites.
Arsennickel, *n. Ch:* nickel arsenide; *Miner:* niccolite, kupfernickel.
Arsenolith [arzeˑnoˑˈliːt], *m.* **-es/-e** & **-en/-en.** *Miner:* arsenolite.
Arsenopyrit [arzeˑnoˑpyˑˈriːt], *m.* **-(e)s/.** *Miner:* arsenopyrite; mispickel, arsenical pyrites.
Arsenpräparat, *n. Com: Pharm:* arsenical preparation, preparation of arsenic.
Arsenrubin, *m. Miner:* realgar, ruby arsenic.
arsensauer, *a. Ch:* combined with arsenic acid; arsen(i)ate of ...; **arsensaures Kalium,** potassium arsen(i)ate.
Arsensäure, *f. Ch:* arsenic acid.
Arsensilberblende, *f. Miner:* proustite, light-red silver ore, ruby silver.
Arsentrioxyd, *n. Ch:* arsenic trioxide, arsenious oxide, white arsenic.
Arsentrisulphid, *n. Ch:* arsenious trisulphide, *Miner:* orpiment, yellow arsenic.
Arsenvergiftung, *f.* arsenic poisoning; *Med:* arsenical intoxication, arseniasis.
Arsenwasserstoff, *m. Ch:* arseniuretted hydrogen, arsine.
Arsin [arˈziːn], *n.* **-s/-e.** *Ch:* arsine.
Arsis [ˈarzis], *f.* **-/Arsen** [ˈarzən]. *Mus: Pros:* arsis.
Arsonvalisation [arzoˑnvaˑliˑzaˑtsiˈoːn], *f.* **-/.** *Med:* treatment by diathermy.
Art[1], *f.* **-/-en. 1.** (*a*) *Nat.Hist:* species (of plants, animals); **die Entstehung der Arten,** the origin of species; (*b*) type (of pers., animal); breed, race (of dogs, horses, etc.); variety (of flower, etc.); **Waldtiere aller Arten,** forest animals of all types, of all kinds; **das letzte seiner Art,** the last of its type, of its kind; **das einzige seiner Art,** the only one of its kind; **ein Hund, ein Pferd, von guter Art,** a dog, a horse, of a good breed; (*of pers.*) **er ist von guter Art,** he is a man of (real) breeding; he is a (true) gentleman; **aus der Art schlagen,** (i) to degenerate; not to remain true to type; to be a freak, a sport; (ii) (*of pers.*) to develop unexpected tendencies *or* abilities; **er ist aus der Art geschlagen,** he has not run true to type; he is different from all the rest of his family; *Prov:* **Art läßt nicht von Art,** (i) what's bred in the bone will come out in the flesh; (ii) like will to like; birds of a feather flock together; (*c*) *A. & B:* generation (of people); *B:* **das ist eine arge Art,** this is an evil generation; **o du ungläubige und verkehrte Art,** O faithless and perverse generation; (*d*) *A:* origin; descent; ancestry; **von göttlicher Art,** of divine origin. **2.** (*a*) kind, sort; nature; class (of people, etc.); type (of wine, etc.); **welcher Art, von welcher Art, ist es?** of what kind is it? **ein Buch (von) der besten Art,** a book of the best kind; **welche Art (von) Baum ist das?** what kind, sort, of tree is this? **er ist die Art (von) Mensch, er ist ein Mensch (von) der Art, die sich wehrt,** he is the kind, the sort, of man who will hit back; **ein Schuft (von) der schlimmsten Art,** a scoundrel of the worst type, of the worst description; **Leute (von) Ihrer Art,** people of your sort, of your kind, *F:* of your kidney; **diese Art Männer ist ..., Männer dieser Art sind ...,** men of this kind, this sort, are ...; **aller Art,** of all kinds, of all sorts; **Menschen aller Art,** people of all kinds, of all types; all kinds, all sorts, all manner, of people; **das war eine ganz andere Art Empfang, als ich erwartet hatte,** it was quite a different kind of reception from what I had expected; **er ist so eine Art Finanzmann,** he is a financier of some kind (or other), he is some sort of financier; *Pej:* he is a financier of sorts; **eine primitive Art (von) Pflug,** a primitive kind, type, of plough; **eine verbesserte Art (von) Feuerzeug,** an improved type of cigarette-lighter; **die Bäume bildeten eine Art Bogen,** the trees formed a sort of arch; **für gewisse Leute ist der Besuch des Kinos eine Art Andacht,** for some people, going to the cinema is a kind of religious exercise; *Com:* **ungarischer Wein — gute Art,** Hungarian wine—superior character; **Wein nach Art des Sauternes,** wine of the Sauternes type; (*b*) nature, disposition, character (of pers.); **es lag nicht in seiner Art (zu ...),** it was not his way (to ...), it was not in his nature (to ...); **sie handeln ihrer Art gemäß,** they act in accordance with their nature, *A. & Lit:* they act after their kind. **3.** (i) (*often pleonastically* **Art und Weise**) manner, mode, way (of acting, speaking, etc.); (ii) (artistic, literary, etc.) style, manner; **seine Art zu handeln, zu denken, zu sprechen; die Art, in der er handelt, denkt, spricht,** his manner, his way, of acting, thinking, speaking; the way he acts, thinks, speaks; **er hat eine angenehme Art sich auszudrücken,** he expresses himself in an agreeable manner; **diese Art zu denken,** this way of thinking; this manner, mode, of thought; **die Art (und Weise), in der er schreibt, wie er schreibt, seine Art (und Weise) zu schreiben,** his manner, style, of writing; the way he writes; **die billigste Art zu leben,** the cheapest way of living; **auf irgendeine, irgendwelche, Art,** in some way; **auf die eine oder die andere Art,** in one way or another; **auf jede (mögliche) Art (und Weise),** in every possible way; **auf ähnliche Art, in ähnlicher Art,** in a similar way, manner, fashion; in like manner; **in einer (gewissen) Art,** in a (certain) way; **das Buch ist gut in seiner Art,** the book is good in its way; (*of thg*) **vollkommen in seiner Art,** perfect of its kind; (*of pers., thg*) **einzig in seiner Art,** unique (of his, its, kind); **er ist in seiner Art freundlich, er ist freundlich nach seiner Art,** he is amiable in his (own) way, after his (own) fashion; **das ist so seine Art,** it is his way, that's his way, *F:* that's the way he is, he's like that; **das ist nicht meine Art,** that's not my way (of doing things); **nun, das ist eben die englische Art,** well, that's the English way (i) of thinking, of looking at things, (ii) of behaving; that's the way the English mind works; **nach Art der Behandlung wird man entweder ... oder ...,** according to, in accordance with, the type of treatment one will either ... or ...; **nach französischer Art,** in the French manner; in the French style; *à la française;* **nach der Art Goethes, in der Art Goethes, nach goethescher Art,** in the manner, in the style, of Goethe; **in der Art Watteaus gemalt,** painted in the manner of Watteau; *Lit:* **'von deutscher Art und Kunst',** 'on the German way of life and German art'; *Cu:* **Lendenbraten nach englischer Art,** roast sirloin (à l'anglaise); **Kartoffeln nach Lyoner Art,** lyonnaise potatoes, sauté potatoes with onions; (*also comb.fm.*) **Seezunge nach Müllerinart,** sole meunière; **Hammelkeule nach Hausfrauenart,** leg of mutton bonne femme; **Tournedos nach Jägerart,** tournedos chasseur; *Gram:* **adverbiale Bestimmung der Art und Weise,** adverbial element of manner. **4.** (*a*) (good) behaviour, (good) manners; **er hat keine Art,** he has no manners; **das ist doch keine Art!** that's no way to behave! that's no way to talk! **was ist das für eine Art!** what a way to behave! where are your manners? (*b*) *F:* **es regnet, daß es nur so eine Art hat,** it's raining with a vengeance, *F:* like billy-o(h), like old boots; **er arbeitete, daß es (nur so) eine Art hatte,** he worked with a will, *F:* he put plenty of vim into it.
Art[2], *f.* **-/-en.** *Agr: A:* **1.** ploughing. **2.** ploughed field; ploughed land, plough-land.
Artacker, *m. Agr: A:* ploughed field.
Artanfang, *m. Biol:* (*a*) emergence of a species; (*b*) species just coming into being.
artbar, *a. A:* arable (land).
Artbastard, *m. Biol:* species hybrid.
Artbegriff, *m.* **1.** *Nat.Hist:* concept of a, the, species. **2.**=**Artcharakter.**
Artcharakter, *m.* typical character; common characteristics (of things, etc., belonging to a group).
Artefakt [arteˑˈfakt], *n.* **-(e)s/-e.** *Prehist: etc:* artifact.
arteigen, *a.* characteristic of the species *or* race; native (culture, etc.).
Artemisia [arteˑˈmiːziaː]. **1.** *Pr.n.f.* **-s.** *A.Hist:* Artemisia. **2.** *f.*=**Artemisie.**
Artemisie [arteˑˈmiːziə], *f.* **-/-n.** *Bot:* artemisia; *U.S. & F:* sage-brush, -bush.
Artemisiengewächse, *n.pl. Bot:* artemisias.
arten[1], *v.i.* (*sein*) **nach j-m, nach etwas, a.,** to take after s.o.; to partake of the nature of sth.; **die Menschen sind so geartet, daß sie ...,** human nature is such that people ...; it is only human nature for people to ...; **er ist ganz anders geartet als sein Bruder,** he is of quite a different disposition from his brother; his nature is altogether different from his brother's; **seine Tochter ist gar nicht nach ihm geartet,** his daughter does not take after him at all; **das Kind ist gut geartet,** the child has a nice disposition, nature, is good-natured; *cp.* **gutgeartet**; *A. & Lit:* **diese Pflanze artet hier nicht gut,** this plant won't thrive, prosper, flourish, here.
arten[2], *v.tr. A:* to plough (land), to put (land) under the plough.
Arterialisation [arteˑriaˑliˑzaˑtsiˈoːn], *f.* **-/.** *Physiol:* arterialization (of venous blood).
arterialisieren [arteˑriaˑliˑˈziːrən], *v.tr. Physiol:* to arterialize (venous blood).
Arterie [arˈteːriə], *f.* **-/-n.** *Anat:* artery.
arteriell [arteˑriˈɛl], *a. Physiol:* arterial.
Arteriendruck, *m. Physiol:* arterial pressure, blood-pressure.
Arterienentzündung, *f. Med:* arteritis.
Arterienerweiterung, *f. Med:* aneurism, aneurysm.
Arterienkammer, *f. Anat:* left ventricle (of the heart).
Arterienöffnung, *f. Surg:* arteriotomy.
Arterienstiel, *m. Anat:* arterial trunk.
Arterienverkalkung, *f. Med:* arteriosclerosis, *F:* hardening of the arteries.
Arteriitis [arteˑriˈiːtis], *f.* **-/.** *Med:* arteritis.

Arteriole [arte·ri'o:lə], *f.* **-/-n.** *Anat:* arteriole, small artery.
Arteriorhexis [arte·rio·'rεksis], **-/.** *Med:* arterial haemorrhage.
arteriös [arte·ri'ø:s], *a. Physiol:* arterial.
Arteriosklerose [arte·rio·skle·'ro:zə], *f. Med:*= **Arterienverkalkung.**
arteriosklerotisch, *a.* [arte·rio·skle·'ro:tiʃ], *a.* arteriosclerotic.
Arteriotomie [arte·rio·to·'mi:], *f.* **-/-n** [-'mi:ən]. *Surg:* arteriotomy.
Arteritis [arte·'ri:tis], *f.* **-/.**=**Arteriitis.**
artesisch [ar'te:ziʃ], *a.* **1.** *Geog:* Artesian; of Artois. **2.** *Hyd.E:* **artesischer Brunnen,** artesian well; *Geol:* **artesischer Strom,** artesian layer.
Artfeld, *n. Agr: A:* ploughed field.
artfremd, *a.* alien (characteristics, culture, etc.); foreign (culture).
artgleich, *a.* of identical type(s); of identical character; of the same species.
arthaft, *a.* **1.** *occ.* characteristic; peculiar; individual. **2.** *A:* productive (soil, etc.); arable (land).
Arthralgie [artral'gi:], *f.* **-/.** *Med:* arthralgia; pain in the joints.
arthralgisch [ar'tralgiʃ], *a. Med:* arthralgic.
Arthritiker [ar'tri:tikər], *m.* **-s/-,** person suffering from arthritis; *Med:* arthritic patient.
Arthritis [ar'tri:tis], *f.* **-/.** *Med:* arthritis.
arthritisch [ar'tri:tiʃ], *a. Med:* arthritic.
Arthro-, arthro- [artro·'-], *comb.fm.* arthro-; **Arthroplastik** [artro·'plastik] *f,* arthroplasty; **arthrozoisch** [artro·'tso:iʃ], arthrozoic.
Arthropode [artro·'po:də], *m.* **-n/-n.** *Nat. Hist:* arthropod; **die Arthropoden,** the arthropoda, the arthropods.
Arthrose [ar'tro:zə], *f.* **-/-n.** *Med:* arthrosis.
Arthrospore [artro·'spo:rə], *f.* **-/-n.** *Bot:* arthrospore.
Arthrotomie [artro·to·'mi:], *f.* **-/.** *Surg:* arthrotomy.
artifiziell [arti·fi·tsi'εl], *a.* artificial.
artig, *a.* (*a*) (*of child*) well-behaved, nicely-behaved, good; **sei a.!** behave yourself! be a good child, a good boy, a good girl! **die Kinder waren heute abend sehr a.,** the children behaved beautifully, were as good as gold, this evening; *adv.* **sich a. benehmen, betragen,** to behave well, to behave nicely, to be good; (*b*) *Lit:* (*of pers.*) polite, courteous, civil; amiable, agreeable, kind, nice; (*of pers., manner*) well-bred; (*of manner*) pleasant, pleasing, agreeable; (*of address*) kind(ly), friendly; **das war a. von dir, daß du . . . ,** it was very nice of you to . . . ; **er hat mir viel Artiges über meine Skizzen gesagt,** he said a lot of kind, nice, things to me, he was very complimentary, about my sketches; *adv.* **sie haben uns sehr a. behandelt,** they treated us very kindly; they were very kind, very nice, to us; **a. sprechen,** to speak nicely.
-artig, *comb.fm. a.* (*a*) (*combined with noun*) -like; resembling . . . ; **apfelartig,** apple-like; like, resembling, an apple; *Bot:* pomaceous; **krebsartig,** (i) crab-like; crustaceous (animal); (ii) cancerous (tumour, etc.); **steinartig,** stone-like, stony (substance, etc.); **traubenartig,** like a bunch, a cluster, of grapes; clustering, clustered; *Bot:* racemose; **wollartig,** wool-like, woolly (substance, etc.); *adv.* like (a) . . . ; **tigerartig gestreift,** striped like a tiger; **marmorartig geädert,** veined like marble; (*b*) (*combined with adj.*) -natured; of a(n) . . . kind; **bösartig,** (*of pers.*) ill-natured; (*of tumour*) malignant; **gutartig,** (*of pers.*) good-natured, kindly; (*of tumour*) non-malignant; **verschiedenartig,** of a different kind; of different, various, kinds; heterogeneous; *adv.* in different, various, ways.
Artigkeit, *f.* **1.** (*a*) good behaviour; (*b*) politeness, courtesy, courteousness, civility; niceness (of pers., manner); daintiness (of girl, behaviour); kindliness, friendliness (of address). **2.** *pl.* **Artigkeiten,** civilities; polite attentions; gracious words; kind words; **j-m Artigkeiten sagen,** to say nice things to s.o.; to pay s.o. compliments.
Artikel [ar'ti·kəl], *m.* **-s/-.** **1.** (*a*) article, clause (of contract, constitution, etc.); *Theol:* article (of faith, religion); (*b*) article (in newspaper, etc.). **2.** *Com:* article, commodity, *pl* goods, wares; **diesen A. führen wir nicht,** we don't keep that article, we don't deal in that line. **3.** *Gram:* **bestimmter, unbestimmter, A.,** definite, indefinite, article.
artikular [arti·ku·'la:r], *a. Nat.Hist: Med:* articular.
Artikulat [arti·ku·'la:t], *n.* **-en/-en.** *Nat. Hist:* articulate (animal); *pl.* articulata, articulates.
Artikulation [arti·ku·la·tsi'o:n], *f.* **-/-en. 1.** *Anat: etc:* articulation; joint. **2.** *Dent:* articulation (of upper and lower teeth). **3.** *Ling:* articulation; utterance; (manner of) speech.
Artikulationsbasis [arti·ku·la·tsi'o:ns-], *f. Ling:* basis of articulation.
Artikulationsfläche, *f. Nat.Hist:* articular surface.
artikulieren [arti·ku·'li:rən]. **1.** *v.tr.* (*a*) *Anat: etc:* to articulate; to hinge, joint, to connect by joints; **artikuliert,** articulated; *Z:* articulate (body, animal, etc.); (*b*) *Ling:* to articulate; to utter, pronounce, distinctly; **artikuliert,** (*of sounds*) articulated; articulate; **artikulierte Sprache,** articulate language; *adv.* **artikuliert sprechen,** to speak articulately. **2.** *v.i.* (*haben*) *Dent:* (*of upper and lower teeth*) to articulate.
Artillerie [artilə'ri:], *f.* **-/-n** [-'ri:ən], (*a*) (*guns, gunnery, or one of the arms of the service*) artillery; **leichte A.,** light artillery; field artillery; **schwere A.,** medium artillery; **überschwere A.,** heavy artillery; *see also* **Kraftzug, Pferdebespannung;** (*b*) (*guns; usu. only in administrative contexts*) ordnance; *esp. in comb.fm., e.g.* **Artilleriewerkstatt** *f,* ordnance factory.
Artillerieabteilung [artilə'ri:-], *f. Mil:* artillery battery.
Artillerieaufklärer, *m.,* **Artillerieaufklärungsflugzeug,** *n. Mil.Av:* artillery spotting aircraft, artillery spotter.
Artilleriebatterie, *f. Mil:* artillery troop.
Artilleriebekämpfung, *f. Artil:* firing against enemy artillery; counter-battery firing.
Artilleriefeuer, *n.* artillery fire.
Artillerieflieger, *m.,* **Artillerieflugzeug,** *n.*= **Artillerieaufklärer.**
Artillerieführer, *m. Mil:* divisional artillery commander.
Artilleriekampf, *m.* artillery battle, artillery duel.
Artilleriekolonne, *f. Mil:* artillery supply column.
Artillerieleitstand, *m. Mil:* artillery command post; *Navy:* fire control tower.
Artilleriemechaniker, *m. Navy:* gunnery artificer.
Artillerieoffizier, *m. Mil:* artillery officer; *Navy:* gunnery officer.
Artilleriepark, *m. Mil:* artillery park.
Artillerieprüfungsausschuß, *m. Mil:* ordnance proving committee.
Artillerieschnellboot, *n. Navy:* motor gunboat.
Artillerieschulschiff, *n. Navy:* gunnery (training) ship.
Artillerieverbindungsflugzeug, *n.*=**Artillerieaufklärer.**
Artilleriewerkstatt, *f.* ordnance factory.
Artilleriezielschiff, *n. Navy:* (gunnery) target-ship, -vessel.
Artilleriezug, *m. Mil:* artillery section.
Artillerist [artilə'rist], *m.* **-en/-en,** artilleryman; gunner.
artilleristisch [artilə'ristiʃ], *a.* (questions, etc.) relating to artillery; *Artil.Surv:* **artilleristischer Punkt,** trigonometrical point; bearing picket; *adv.* **a. betrachtet,** seen from the artillery point of view.
Artiodaktyl [arti·o·dak'ty:l], *n.* **-s/-e.** *Z:* artiodactyl.
Artischocke [arti·'ʃokə], *f.* **-/-n.** *Bot: Hort:* globe artichoke, leaf artichoke.
Artischockenboden, Artischockenkäse, *m. Cu:* artichoke-bottom.
Artist [ar'tist], *m.* **-en/-en, Artistin** [-'tistin], *f.* **-/-innen. 1.** *Sch: A:* student in the Faculty of Arts, arts student. **2.** (circus, variety) artiste, *U.S:* performer.
Artistenfakultät [ar'tistən-], *f. Sch: A:* Faculty of Arts.
Artistik [ar'tistik], *f.* **-/.** (circus *or* variety stage) artistry.
artistisch [ar'tistiʃ], *a.* artistic (performance, etc.); *adv.* artistically; with artistry.
Artkennzeichen, *n.pl.* typical characteristics.
Artkreuzung, *f. Biol: Breed:* crossing of two species.
Artland, *n. Agr: A:* ploughed land, plough-land.
Artmann, *m.* **-(e)s/-männer.** *A:* ploughman.
Artnummer, *f. Mil:* (soldier's) number on the war establishment of the unit.
Artokarp [arto·'karp], *m.* **-(e)s/-en.** *Bot:* artocarpad; tree of the bread-fruit group.
artrein, *a.* pure-bred.
Artur. *Pr.n.m.* **-s.** Arthur.
Artus. *Pr.n.m.* **-'.** *Hist:* (King) Arthur.
Artushof, *m. Hist:* **der A.,** the court of King Arthur; **ein A.,** a court pursuing Arthurian ideals.
Artusroman, *m. Lit.Hist:* Arthurian romance.
Artusrunde, die, -. *Hist:* the Round Table.
Artverband, *m. Nat.Hist:* group(ing) of species.
artverwandt, *a.* of the same nature and origins; kindred; akin (**mit,** to).
Arvalen, die [ar'va:lən], *m.pl. Rom.Ant:* the Arval Brethren.
Arve, *f.* **-/-n.** *Bot:* Swiss stone-pine.
arytänoideisch [a·ry·tε·no·i·'de:iʃ], *a. Anat:* arytenoid (cartilage, muscle).
Arz(e)nei, *f.* **-/-en,** medicine, physic; medicament; drug; **A. (ein)nehmen,** to take medicine; **die himmlische A.,** the holy sacrament; *F:* **eine gute A. gegen Langeweile,** a good antidote to boredom; **die bittere A. schlucken,** to take, swallow, one's medicine; to swallow the bitter pill.
Arzneibuch, *n.* pharmacopoeia.
Arzneifläschchen, *n.,* **Arzneiflasche,** *f.* medicine-bottle; phial.
Arzneigemisch, *n. Pharm:* mixture.
Arzneiglas, *n.* (*a*) medicine-bottle; phial; (*b*) medicine-glass.
Arzneikraut, *n.* (*a*) medicinal plant; officinal plant; (*b*) *pl.* **Arzneikräuter,** medicinal herbs, simples.
Arzneikunde, *f.* (*a*) pharmacology; (*b*) pharmaceutics.
Arzneimischung, *f. Pharm:* mixture.
Arzneimittel, *n.* medicine; medicament; drug; pharmaceutical preparation.
Arzneimittellehre, *f.* pharmacology.
Arzneipflanze, *f.* medicinal plant; officinal plant.
Arzneischrank, *m.* medicine-cabinet, -chest.
Arzneistoff, *m.* pharmaceutical preparation; medicament; ingredient.
Arzneitaxe, *f. Adm:* list of controlled prices for medicines and drugs.
Arzneitrunk, *m. Med:* draught, potion.
Arzneiverordnung, Arzneivorschrift, *f. Med:* medical prescription.
Arzneiware, *f.* pharmaceutical preparation; (proprietary) medicine *or* drug.
Arzneiwarenkunde, *f.* pharmaceutics.
Arzneiwasser, *n. Pharm:* lotion.
Arzneiwissenschaft, *f.* pharmaceutics.
Arzt, *m.* **-es/⸚e,** doctor, medical man, medical practitioner; physician *or* surgeon; *Mil:* medical officer, M.O.; **praktischer A.,** general practitioner, G.P.; **zum A. gehen,** to go to the doctor; **einen A. konsultieren, befragen,** to consult a doctor; **sich an den A. wenden,** to take medical advice; **der himmlische A.,** the Divine Healer; Christ; *B:* **A., hilf dir selber!** physician, heal thyself! **die Gesunden bedürfen des Arztes nicht,** they that are whole need not a physician; *Prov:* **ein guter A. bedarf keiner Posaune,** competence is the best advertisement; *Prov:* good wine needs no bush.
Ärztekammer, die, *approx.*=the General Medical Council.
Ärzteschaft, *f.* **-/. die Ä.,** (*a*) the medical profession, the (medical) Faculty; (*b*) the body of medical practitioners (in a country, district, etc.).
Ärztezeitung, *f.* Medical Journal.
Arzthilfe, *f.* doctor's nurse-secretary.
Ärztin, *f.* **-/-innen,** (woman, lady) doctor.
ärztlich, *a.* medical; **ärztliche Behandlung,** medical treatment; **ärztliche Bemühungen,** medical attention; **ärztliche Hilfe in Anspruch nehmen,** to have medical attention; to call in medical aid; *see also* **Gutachten, Zeugnis;** *adv.* medically; by a doctor, by the doctors; **j-n ä. behandeln,** to give s.o. medical treatment; **ä. verordnet,** prescribed by a doctor; **ä. empfohlen,** recommended by doctors, by the medical profession.
Arztrechnung, *f.* doctor's bill.
As[1] [as], *n.* **Asses/Asse. 1.** *Cards: Dice:* ace. **2.** *Av: etc:* (*of pers.*) ace.
As[2], *n.* **-/-.** *Rom.Ant:* (*coin*) as.
as[3], **As,** *n.* **-/-.** *Mus:* (the note) A flat, A♭; **As-dur, As-Dur, as-moll, as-Moll, (-Tonart),** (key of) A flat major, A flat minor.
Asa foetida [ˌa:za· 'føːtida·], *f.* **-/.** *Pharm:* asafoetida.
Asant ['a:zant], *m.* **-(e)s/.** *Bot: Pharm:* **(stinkender) A.,** asafoetida.
asas, Asas ['asas], *n.* **-/-.** *Mus:* (the note) A double flat.
Asbest [as'bεst], *m.* **-(e)s/-e.** *Miner:* asbestos.
Asbestdichtung [as'bεst-], *f. Mec.E: etc:* asbestos packing; asbestos joint.
Asbestpappe, *f.* asbestos-board, -sheet.
Asbestzement, *m. Constr:* asbestos cement.
Asbolan [asbo·'la:n], *m.* **-s/.** *Miner:* asbolite, asbolan; earthy cobalt; wad; bog manganese.
Asch, *m.* **-es/⸚e.** *Dial:* **1.** *Cu: etc:* bowl; basin; dish; tin. **2.** *Ich:*=**Äsche. 3.** *Dial:*=**Asche.**

Asch-, *comb.fm. cp.* **Aschen-.**
Aschanti [aˈʃanti·]. **1.** *Pr.n.n.* **-s.** *Geog:* Ashanti, Ashantee. **2.** *m., f.* **-/-.** *Ethn:* Ashanti, Ashantee. **3.** *n.* **-/.** *Ling:* Ashanti.
Aschantinuß, *f. Bot:* peanut, ground-nut, *F:* monkey-nut.
Aschbecher, *m.* ashtray.
Aschbehälter, *m.* (*a*)=**Ascheimer**; (*b*) ash-pan (in stove, etc.).
Aschblei, *n. Miner: A:* bismuth.
aschbleich, *a.*=**aschfahl.**
aschblond, *a.* ash-blond.
Asche, *f.* **-/-n.** **1.** (*a*) ash (of coal, cigarette, etc.); ashes (of coal, wood, etc.); cinders (of coal, wood, etc.; for racing-track, etc.); **vulkanische A.,** volcanic ash; **etwas zu A. (ver)brennen, in A. verwandeln,** to reduce, burn, sth. to ashes; to incinerate sth.; **eine Stadt in (Schutt und) A. legen,** to reduce a town to ashes; **die Stadt ist aus der A. erstanden,** the town has risen again from its ashes; **sich** *dat.* **A. aufs Haupt streuen,** to strew one's head with ashes; to do penance; to mourn; *see also* **glimmen, Sack, Staub;** (*b*) *F:* **ungebrannte A.,** a beating, a thrashing; (*c*) *F:* money, *F:* dust. **2.** (*of the dead*) ashes, dust, mortal remains; **bis ich A. werde,** till my body turns to dust; **Friede seiner A.!** peace (be) to his ashes!
Äsche, *f.* **-/-n.** *Ich:* grayling, umber.
Ascheimer, *m.* ash-bucket; ash-bin, ash-can; dust-bin.
Aschejektor, *m. Nau: etc:* ash-ejector, -hoist.
Aschejektorhahn, *m. Nau:* ash-cock.
Aschel, Äschel, *m.* **-s/-.** *Metall:* **1.** sullage; slag, cinders, scoria. **2.** ash-spot (in iron, steel).
aschen, *v.tr. Metall:* to ash (a mould).
Aschen-, *comb.fm. cp.* **Asch-.**
Aschenaufzug, *m.* ash-hoist.
Aschenausbläser, *m. Nau: etc:* ash-ejector.
Aschenauswurf, *m.* **1.** (*from volcano*) volcanic ash. **2.** *Nau:* ash-shoot.
Aschenbahn, *f. Sp:* dirt-track; cinder-path, -track; **Motorradrennen auf der A.,** (i) dirt-track racing; (ii) dirt-track race.
Aschenbahnrennen, *n.* (*a*) dirt-track racing; (*b*) dirt-track race.
Aschenbecher, *m.* ashtray.
Aschenbestandteile, *m.pl.* ash constituents (of a plant, etc.).
Aschenbestimmung, *f. Ch:* determination of ash content, ash determination (of a fuel, etc.).
Aschenbrödel. **1.** *Pr.n.n.* **-s.** Cinderella. **2.** *n.* **-s/.** (household) drudge, *F:* slavey, skivvy.
Aschenbrot, *n. Cu:* bread baked under the ashes; (*in Australia*) damper.
Aschendünger, *m. Agr:* ash manure, cinereal manure.
Ascheneimer, *m.*=**Ascheimer.**
Aschenermittlung, *f.*=**Aschenbestimmung.**
Aschenfall, *m.*=**Aschfall.**
Aschenfleck, *m. Metall:* ash-spot (in iron, steel).
Aschengehalt, *m.* ash content (of a fuel, etc.).
Aschengrittel, *n.* **-s/.**=**Aschenbrödel.**
Aschengrube, *f.* ash-pit, ash-hole.
Aschenhaufen, *m.* ash-heap; dust-heap.
Aschenkegel, *m. Geol:* cinder cone (of volcano).
Aschenkraut, *n.*=**Aschkraut.**
Aschenkrug, *m. Ant:* cinerary urn, cinerary vase.
Aschenkuchen, *m. Cu:* cake baked under the ashes, *U.S:* ash-cake; (*in Australia*) damper.
Aschenkugel, *f. Furn:* spherical ash-tray (*usu.* on stand).
Aschenlauge, *f.* lye (from ashes).
Aschenloch, *n. Metall:*=**Aschenfleck.**
Aschenpflanze, *f. Bot:* cineraria.
Aschenprahm, *m. Nau:* ash-lighter, ash-boat.
Aschenputtel, *n.* **-s/.**=**Aschenbrödel.**
Aschenregen, *m.* rain of ashes, *esp.* rain of volcanic ash.
Aschensalz, *n. Ch: A:* potash.
Aschentrecker, *m. Miner: A:* tourmalin(e).
Aschenurne, *f. Ant: etc:* cinerary urn, cinerary vase.
Aschenwolke, *f.* ash-cloud (over volcano).
Aschenzacken, *m. Metall:* back-plate (of fining-furnace).
Aschenzieher, *m. Miner: A:* tourmalin(e).
Ascher, *m.* **-s/-.** **1.** ash-tray. **2.**=**Äscher** 1, 2.
Äscher, *m.* **-s/-.** **1.** *Agr: Glassm: etc:* buck-ashes, lye-ashes. **2.** (*a*) *Tan:* milk of lime; (*b*) *Tan:* lime-pit; lime-tub. **3.** *Vit:* mildew (on vines).
Äscherfaß, *n. Tan:* lime-tub.
Äschergrube, *f. Tan:* lime-pit.
Äscherich, *m.* **-s/.** *Vit:* mildew (on vines).
Äscherkalk, *m. Tan:* milk of lime.
Aschermittwoch, *m. Ecc:* Ash Wednesday.
äschern, *v.tr.* **1.** to strew (sth.) with ashes *or* cinders; to cinder (path, track); *Ind:* to treat (sth.) with ashes; *Metall:* to ash (a mould). **2.** (*a*) *Dom.Ec:* to wash (linen, etc.) in lye; to buck (linen); (*b*) *Ind:* to treat (sth.) with lye; (*c*) *Tan:* to lime (skins).
Äschertuch, *n. Dom.Ec:* bucking-cloth.
aschfahl, *a.* ashen (grey); ashy (pale).
Aschfall, *m. Mch: etc:* ash-pit, ash-hole (of furnace).
Aschfalldämpfer, *m.* damper, register (of furnace).
aschfarben, *a.* ash-coloured, ash-grey, ashy; cinereous (plumage, etc.).
aschgrau, *a.* (*a*) ash-grey, ashy; ashen (complexion); cinereous (plumage, etc.); (*b*) *F:* **das geht ins Aschgraue,** there's no end to it; that's too much of a good thing; **das ist schon a.!** that's a bit thick!
Aschheißvorrichtung, *f. Nau: etc:* ash-hoist.
Aschhuhn, *n. Orn:* water-rail.
aschig, *a.* ashy; full of ashes; cindery; gritty; dusty; soiled with ashes.
Äschines [ˈɛːsçi·ne·s]. *Pr.n.m.* **-'.** *Gr.Hist:* Aeschines.
Aschitze, *f.* **-/-n.** *Bot:* sorb, service-tree.
Aschkasten, *m.* **1.** ash-pan (of stove); ash-box (of locomotive). **2.** ash-bin, dust-bin.
Aschkastenklappe, *f.* damper, register (of stove).
Aschkraut, *n. Bot:* cineraria.
Aschkuchen, *m. Cu:* **1.** cake baked in a dish *or* tin. **2.**=**Aschenkuchen.**
Aschkühlhahn, *m. Nau:* ash-cock.
Aschlauch, *m.*=**Eschlauch.**
Aschmeise, *f. Orn:* marsh tit(mouse).
Aschraum, *m.* ash-pit, ash-hole.
Äschrig, *m.* **-s/-e.** **1.**=**Äscher** 1. **2.** *Dom.Ec:* washing-bag.
Aschschütte, *f. Nau:* ash-shoot.
Aschur [ˈaʃu·r], *m.* **-s/-.** *Bot:* yercum (bush), mudar.
Aschwinde, *f. Nau: etc:* ash-hoist.
Aschwurz, *f. Bot:* **1.** (white) dittany. **2.** carline thistle.
äschyleisch [ɛ·ʃy·ˈleːiʃ], *a.* Aeschylean; of Aeschylus.
Äschylus [ˈɛ·ʃylus]. *Pr.n.m.* **-'.** *Gr.Lit:* Aeschylus.
Ascites [asˈtsiːtes], *f.* **-/.** *Med: Vet:* ascites, abdominal dropsy.
Äsculin [ɛsku·ˈliːn], *n.* **-s/.** *Ch:* esculin.
Ase, *m.* **-n/-n.** *Norse Myth:* As; divinity of the race of Odin; **die Asen,** the Aesir.
Asebie [a·ze·ˈbiː], *f.* **-/.** impiety.
äsen. **I.** *v.i.* (*haben*) *Ven:* (*of deer*) to graze; to browse.
II. *vbl s.* **1. Äsen,** *n. in vbl senses; also:* **zum Ä. kommen,** to come to graze, feed, browse. **2. Äsung,** *f.* (*a*)=II. 1; (*b*) feed, fodder.
Asepsis [a·ˈzɛpsis], *f.* **-/.** *Med:* asepsis; asepticism, aseptic treatment.
Aseptik [a·ˈzɛptik], *f.* **-/.** *Med:* asepticism.
aseptisch [a·ˈzɛptiʃ], *a. Med:* aseptic.
Äser[1], *pl. see* **Aas.**
Äser[2], *m.* **-s/-,** knapsack.
Aserbeidschan [a·zɛrˈbaidʃa·n]. *Pr.n.n.* **-s.** *Geog:* Azerbaijan.
asexual(isch) [a·zɛksu·ˈaːl(iʃ)], *a. Biol:* asexual.
Asexualität [a·zɛksu·a·li·ˈtɛːt], *f.* **-/.** asexuality.
Asgard. *Pr.n.n.* **-s.** *Norse Myth:* Asgard.
Asiat [a·ziˈaːt], *m.* **-en/-en.** Asiatic, Asian.
asiatisch [a·ziˈaːtiʃ], *a.* Asiatic, Asian.
Asien [ˈaːziən]. *Pr.n.n.* **-s.** *Geog:* Asia.
Askanien [asˈkaːniən]. *Pr.n.n.* **-s.** *A.Geog:* Ascania.
Askanier [asˈkaːniər], *m.* **-s/-.** **1.** *A.Hist:* Ascanian. **2.** *Hist:* member of the Ascanian line of princes (of Anhalt).
Askanius [asˈkaːnius]. *Pr.n.m.* **-'.** *Lt.Lit:* Ascanius.
Askari [asˈkaːriː], *m.* **-s/-s.** *Hist:* Askari; native soldier serving in the forces of a European power in East Africa.
Askaris [asˈkaːris], *f.* **-/-riden** [-ka·ˈriːdən]. *Med:* ascaris, roundworm; **die Askariden,** the ascaridae.
Askese [asˈkeːzə], *f.* **-/.** asceticism.
Asket [asˈkeːt], *m.* **-en/-en,** ascetic.
Asketik [asˈkeːtik], *f.* **-/.** asceticism, ascetical theology.
Asketiker [asˈkeːtikər], *m.* **-s/-,** author of ascetical treatises; preacher of asceticism.
asketisch [asˈkeːtiʃ], *a.* ascetic; ascetical (theology, etc.); **asketische Schriften,** ascetic books; **ein asketisches Leben führen,** *adv.* **a. leben,** to lead an ascetic, austere, life; to live ascetically.
Askii [a·ˈskiːiː], *m.pl. Geog:* ascians.
Asklepiadazee [asklе·pia·da·ˈtseːə], *f.* **-/-n** [-ˈtseːən]. *Bot:* asclepiad.
Asklepiades [askle·ˈpiːa·de·s]. *Pr.n.m.* **-'.** *Gr.Ant:* Asclepiades.
Asklepiadeus [askle·pia·ˈdeːus], *m.* **-/-deen** [-ˈdeːən]. *Pros:* asclepiad.
asklepiadisch [askle·piˈaːdiʃ], *a.* of, concerning, Asclepiades; *Pros:* **asklepiadischer Vers,** asclepiad.
Asklepie [asˈkleːpiə], *f.* **-/-n.** *Bot:* asclepias, milk-weed.
Asklepios [asˈkleːpios]. *Pr.n.m.* **-'.** *Myth:* Aesculapius.
Askomyzeten [asko·my·ˈtseːtən], *m.pl. Fung:* ascomycetes.
Askorbinsäure [askorˈbiːn-], *f. Bio-Ch:* ascorbic acid, vitamin C.
Askospore [askoˈspoːrə], *f.* **-/-n.** *Fung:* ascospore.
Äskulap [ˈɛ·sku·la·p]. *Pr.n.m.* **-s.** *Myth:* Aesculapius.
äskulapisch [ɛ·sku·ˈlaːpiʃ], *a.* Aesculapian; medical.
Äskulapnatter, *f. Rept:* Aesculapius snake.
Äskulapschlange, *f.* **1.**=**Äskulapnatter.** **2.**=**Äskulapstab.**
Äskulapstab, *m.* Aesculapius's staff (*esp.* as a badge).
Äskulin [ɛsku·ˈliːn], *n.* **-s/.** *Ch:* esculin.
Askus [ˈaskus], *m.* **-/Asken.** *Fung:* ascus.
Asmodäus [asmoˈdeːus]. *Pr.n.m.* **-'.** *Lit:*=**Asmodi.**
Asmodi [asˈmoːdiː]. *Pr.n.m.* **-s.** *B:* Asmodeus.
asomatisch [a·zo·ˈmaːtiʃ], *a.* asomatous, incorporeal.
Äsop [ɛ·ˈzoːp]. *Pr.n.m.* **-s.** *Gr.Lit:* Aesop.
äsopisch [ɛ·ˈzoːpiʃ], *a.* Aesopic; **die Äsopischen Fabeln,** Aesop's Fables.
Asow [ˈaːzof]. *Pr.n.n.* **-s.** *Geog:* Azov.
Asowsche Meer, das [ˈaːzofʃə]. *Pr.n. Geog:* the Sea of Azov.
asozial [ˈa·zo·tsi̯aːl], *a.* asocial (attitude, etc.).
Asozialität [a·zo·tsia·li·ˈtɛːt], *f.* **-/.** asocial character *or* attitude.
Aspalatholz [aspa·ˈlaːt-], *n. Bot: Com:* aspalathus (wood).
Asparagin [aspa·ra·ˈgiːn], *n.* **-s/-e.** *Ch:* asparagine.
Asparaginsäure, *f. Ch:* aspartic acid.
Asparagus [aˈspa·ra·gus], *m.* **-/.** *Bot: Hort:* asparagus-fern.
Aspe, *f.* **-/-n.** *Bot:* aspen, trembling poplar.
Aspekt [aˈspɛkt], *m.* **-(e)s/-e.** **1.** aspect; **die verschiedenen Aspekte einer Sache berücksichtigen,** to consider the various aspects of a matter; **von diesem A. her,** from this aspect, from this point of view. **2.** (*pl. usu.* **-en**) *Astrol:* aspect, relative position (of stars). **3.** *Ling:* aspect (of verb).
Asperges [aˈspɛrgɛs], *n.* **-/.** *R.C.Ch:* asperges.
aspergieren [aspɛrˈgiːrən], *v.tr.* to sprinkle, *esp.* with holy water; *A:* to asperse.
Aspergill [aspɛrˈgil], *n.* **-s/-e.** *Ecc:* aspergillum, holy-water sprinkler.
Aspergillus [aspɛrˈgilus], *m.* **-/.** *Fung:* aspergillus.
Aspermatismus [a·spɛrma·ˈtismus], *m.* **-/., Aspermie** [a·spɛrˈmiː], *f.* **-/.** *Bot: Physiol:* aspermatism.
aspermisch [a·ˈspɛrmiʃ], *a. Bot:* aspermous.
Aspersion [aspɛrziˈoːn], *f.* **-/-en.** *Ecc:* sprinkling (of holy water).
Aspersorium [aspɛrˈzoːrium], *n.* **-s/-rien.** *Ecc:* aspersorium.
Asphalt [asˈfalt, ˈasfalt], *m.* **-(e)s/-e.** *Miner; Civ.E:* asphalt; **eine Straße mit A. bestreichen,** to asphalt a road, to cover a road with asphalt.
Asphaltbeton, *m.* asphalt(ic) concrete.
asphalthaltig, *a.* asphaltic, containing asphalt.
asphaltieren [asfalˈtiːrən], *v.tr.* to asphalt (road, etc.); to cover (road, etc.) with asphalt.
asphaltisch [asˈfaltiʃ], *a.* asphaltic.
Asphaltkitt, *m.* asphalt cement; asphalt mastic.
Asphaltlack, *m.* asphalt lacquer *or* varnish; black japan.
Asphaltmastix, *m.* asphalt mastic.
Asphaltpappe, *f. Constr:* asphalt board, tar-board.
Asphaltpech, *n.* bituminous mineral pitch.
Asphaltpresse, *f. F:* metropolitan newspapers that aim at large street sales, *F:* the yellow press.
Asphaltstein, *m. Miner:* native asphalt.
Asphaltverputz, *m.* asphalt coating.
asphärisch [a·ˈsfɛːriʃ], *a. Opt:* non-spherical (lens).
Asphodelos [asˈfoːde·los], *m.* **-/.** *Bot:* asphodel.
Asphodeloswiesen, *f.pl. Poet:* meads of asphodel; Elysian fields.
Asphodelus [asˈfoːde·lus], *m.* **-/.** *Bot:* asphodel.
Asphodill [asfo·ˈdil], *m.* **-s/-e.** *Bot:* asphodel.
asphyktisch [a·ˈsfyktiʃ], *a. Med:* **asphyktischer Zustand,** (state of) asphyxia.
Asphyxie [a·sfy·ˈksiː], *f.* **-/-n** [-ˈksiːən], asphyxia.
Aspidistra [aspi·ˈdistraː], *f.* **-/-tren.** *Bot:* aspidistra.
Aspik [aˈspi·k], *m.* (*in Austria also n.*) **-s/-e.** *Cu:* aspic (jelly).

Aspirant [aspi'rant], *m.* -en/-en. **1.** candidate (for a post, etc.); *Mil: A:* officer candidate. **2.** *Ecc:* aspirant (to noviciate).

Aspirantin [aspi'rantin], *f.* -/-innen. *Ecc:* aspirant (to noviciate).

Aspirata [aspi'ra:ta:], *f.* -/-ten & -tä. *Ling:* aspirate.

Aspirateur [aspira'tø:r], *m.* -s/-e. *Ind:* suction-fan; dust-exhauster.

Aspiration [aspira'tsi'o:n], *f.* -/-en. **1.** aspiration, yearning. **2.** *Ling:* aspiration, rough breathing. **3.** suction; exhaustion.

Aspirationsinstrument, *n. Meteor:* aspirated instrument.

Aspirationsvorrichtung, *f. Ch: Ind:* suction device; aspirator.

Aspirationswind, *m. Meteor:* wind blowing towards an area of low pressure.

Aspirator [aspi'ra:tor], *m.* -s/-en [-ra·'to:rən]. **1.** *Ph:* aspirator. **2.** *Ind:*=**Aspirateur.**

aspiratorisch [aspira·'to:riʃ], *a.* aspiratory.

aspirieren [aspi·'ri:rən], *v.tr.* **1.** to aspire to, after (sth.). **2.** to suck up, suck in, draw (up) (water, dust, etc.); to exhaust (dust, etc.). **3.** *Ling:* to aspirate, breathe (a sound); **aspirierter Laut,** aspirate.

Aspirin [aspi·'ri:n], *n.* -s/. (*R.t.m.*) *Pharm:* aspirin.

Aspirintablette, *f.* aspirin tablet; **nehmen Sie zwei Aspirintabletten,** *F:* take two aspirins.

Aspis ['aspis], *f.* -/**Aspiden** [-'pi:dən]. *Rept:* (Egyptian) asp, hooded serpent.

Aspisviper, *f. Rept:* asp.

aß *see* **essen.**

Assagai [asa·'gai], *m.* -s/-e, assegai.

Assaipalme ['asai-], *f. Bot:* (assai-palm).

assaisonnieren [asɛzo·'ni:rən], *v.tr. Cu:* to season.

Assala ['asa·la·], *f.* -/-s. *Rept:* African rock python.

Assam ['asam]. *Pr.n.n.* -s. *Geog:* Assam.

assamisch [a'sa:miʃ], *a. Geog:* Assamese.

Assamit [asa·'mi·t], *m.* -en/-en. *Geog:* Assamese.

assanieren [asa·'ni:rən], *v.tr.* to make (sth.) healthier; to cleanse, purify (atmosphere, etc.).

Assassinat [asasi·'na:t], *n.* -s/-e, assassination.

Assassinator [asasi·'na:tor], *m.* -s/-en [-na·'to:rən], assassin.

Assassinen [asa·'si:nən], *m.pl. Hist:* Assassins.

assassinieren [asasi·'ni:rən], *v.tr.* to assassinate.

Assaut [a'so:], *m.* -s/-s. **1.** assault, attack, onslaught. **2.** *Fenc:* assault at arms.

äße *see* **essen.**

Assekuradeur [asɛku·ra·'dø:r], *m.* -s/-e, **Assekurador** [asɛku·ra·'do:r], *m.* -s/-e. *Com: Ins:* (*a*) insurer; (*b*) underwriter.

Assekurant [asɛku·'rant], *m.* -en/-en, insurer.

Assekuranz [asɛku·'rants], *f.* -/-en. **1.** insurance, assurance. **2.** insurance company.

Assekuranzbrief, *m.,* **Assekuranzpolice,** *f.* insurance policy.

Assekurat [asɛku·'ra:t], *m.* -en/-en. *Ins:* (*a*) policy-holder; insuree; insured; (*b*) *Adm:* insured person.

Assekurator [asɛku·'ra:tor], *m.* -s/-en [-ra·'to:rən], (*a*) *Com:* insurer; (*b*) *M.Ins:* underwriter.

assekurieren [asɛku·'ri:rən], *v.tr.* to insure.

Assel, *f.* -/-n. **1.** *Crust:* (*a*) isopod; **die Asseln,** the isopods, the isopoda; (*b*) woodlouse, slater, *U.S:* sow-bug. **2.** *Myr:* (=**Bandassel**) scolopendra.

Asselspinne, *f. Nat. Hist:* pycnogonid.

Assemblee [asã·'ble:], *f.* -/-n [-'ble:ən], assembly.

Assembleur [asã·'blø:r], *m.* -s/-e. *Bookb:* gatherer; collator (of sheets).

aßen *see* **essen.**

Assensus [asɛn'sus], *m.* -/-, assent; approval.

assentieren [asɛn'ti:rən]. **1.** *v.i.* (*haben*) to assent, give one's assent. **2.** *v.tr.* (*in Austria*) to declare (man) fit for military service.

asserieren [asɛ·'ri:rən], *v.tr.* to assert.

Assertion [asɛrtsi'o:n], *f.* -/-en, assertion.

assertorisch [asɛr'to:riʃ], *a.* assertory, assertive.

Asservat [asɛr'va:t], *n.* -(e)s/-e, article *or* property confided to s.o.'s keeping; charge.

Asservation [asɛrva·tsi'o:n], *f.* -/-en, preservation, (safe-)keeping.

asservieren [asɛr'vi:rən], *v.tr.* to preserve, keep, safeguard (sth.); to have charge of (sth.).

Assessor [a'sɛsor], *m.* -s/-en [-'so:rən], **Assessorin** [-'so:rin], *f.* -/-innen. **1.** *Jur:* assessor (to magistrate, etc.). **2.** *Adm:* 'assessor' (title of Higher Civil Service probationer (*e.g.* secondary school teacher) and of member of the legal profession having passed the second State Examination).

assessoral [asɛso·'ra:l], **assessorisch** [asɛ'so:riʃ], *a. Adm: Jur:* assessorial (functions, etc.).

Assessorstelle, *f.* assessorship.

Asseveration [asɛve·ra·tsi'o:n], *f.* -/-en, asseveration.

Assibilation [asi·bi·la·tsi'o:n], *f.* -/-en. *Ling:* (as)sibilation.

assibilieren [asi·bi·'li:rən], *v.tr. Ling:* to (as)sibilate (a sound).

Assiduität [asi·du·i·'tɛːt], *f.,* -/. assiduousness, assiduity.

Assiette [asi'ɛtə], *f.* -/-n. **1.** (*a*) position; established position; **er sitzt in einer guten A.,** he is in a good position; he is well off; *Equit:* **eine gute, schlechte, A. haben,** to have a good, bad, seat (on horseback); (*b*) frame of mind; humour. **2.** (*a*) dinner-plate; (*b*) *Cu:* (*in Austria*) hors-d'œuvre.

Assignant [asig'nant], *m.* -en/-en. *Com: Fin:* drawer (of bill).

Assignat [asig'na:t], *m.* -en/-en. *Com: Fin:* drawee (of bill).

Assignatar [asigna·'ta:r], *m.* -s/-e. *Fin:* payee (of draft, etc.); assignee (of shares, funds, etc.).

Assignate [asig'na:tə, asin'ja:tə], *f.* -/-n. *Fr.Hist:* assignat.

Assignation [asigna·tsi'o:n], *f.* -/-en. *Fin:* assignment, transfer (of shares, funds, etc.) (an+*acc.,* to).

assignieren [asig'ni:rən], *v.tr. Fin:* to assign, transfer (shares, funds, etc.) (*dat.,* an+*acc.,* to).

Assimilant [asi·mi·'lant], *m.* -en/-en, conformist, *esp.* Jew who conforms to Gentile customs.

Assimilat [asi·mi·'la:t], *n.* -(e)s/-e. *Bio-Ch:* assimilation product.

Assimilation [asi·mi·la·tsi'o:n], *f.* -/-en. **1.** (*making or becoming alike*) assimilation (an+*acc.,* to, with). **2.** *Physiol: etc:* assimilation (of food, etc.).

assimilatorisch [asi·mi·la·'to:riʃ] *a.* assimilatory, assimilative.

assimilierbar [asi·mi·'li:rba:r], *a.* assimilable.

assimilieren [asi·mi·'li:rən], *v.tr.* to assimilate (*dat.,* to, with); *Physiol:* to assimilate (food, etc.); *Ling:* to assimilate (sound); **sich a.,** to assimilate (*dat.,* to, with); **assimilierend,** assimilative, assimilatory; **Assimilieren** *n,* **Assimilierung** *f,* assimilation.

Assimilierungsprozeß, *m.* process of assimilation, assimilative process.

Assise [a'si:zə], *f.* -/-n, session, sitting (of official body); **Assisen** *pl, Jur:* assizes; (*of judge*) **Assisen abhalten,** to go on circuit; *Hist:* **die Assisen von Jerusalem,** the Assizes of Jerusalem.

Assisenhof, *m. Jur:* assize-court, court of assizes.

Assistent [asis'tɛnt], *m.* -en/-en, **Assistentin,** *f.* -/-innen. *Adm: etc:* (*a*) assistant; *Sch:* assistant (in university department); assistant director (of university institute); **medizinisch-technische Assistentin,** laboratory assistant; (*b*) *comb. fm.* **-assistent, -assistentin,** assistant . . . ; **Bibliotheksassistent,** assistant librarian; *Sch:* **Direktorialassistent, Oberassistent,** assistant director (of university institute).

Assistenz [asis'tɛnts], *f.* -/-en. **1.** assistance; **unter A. von . . . ,** with the assistance of . . . . **2.** presence, attendance (*esp.* of official personage). **3.** (*pers.*) assistant; *coll.* **A.,** assistants.

Assistenzarzt, *m.* assistant-surgeon; medical assistant; doctor's assistant; *Mil:* assistant medical officer (=Lieutenant, R.A.M.C.).

Assistenzfigur, *f. Art:* attendant figure.

Assistenzprediger, *m. Ecc:* assistant minister; curate.

assistieren [asis'ti:rən], *v.i.* (*haben*) **1.** j-m a., (i) to assist, help, s.o. (**bei etwas,** with sth.); (ii) to be s.o.'s assistant. **2. bei etwas a.,** to attend sth., to be present at sth.

Associé [aso·si'e:], *m.* -s/-s. *Com:* partner.

Assonanz [aso·'nants], *f.* -/-en. *Pros:* assonance.

assonieren [aso·ro·'ni:rən], *v.i.* (*haben*) *Pros:* to assonate; **assonierend,** assonant.

assortieren [asor'ti:rən], *v.tr. Com:* to assort (goods); **sein Lager a., sich a.,** to lay in stock; **assortiert,** assorted (goods); (goods) of various kinds; **Laden mit wohl assortiertem Lager,** well-stocked shop.

Assortiment [asorti·'mɛnt], *n.* -(e)s/-e. *Com:* assortment (of goods); selection of goods of various kinds.

assouplieren [asu·'pli:rən], *v.tr.* to make (sth.) supple; to supple, soften (leather).

Assoziation [aso·tsia·tsi'o:n], *f.* -/-en. **1.** (*a*) association (of ideas, words, etc.); (*b*) *Ch:* association, coupling (of molecules). **2.** (*a*) association; society, company; (*b*) *Com:* partnership.

Assoziationspsychologie, *f.* association psychology.

Assoziationsrecht, *n. Jur:* right of association.

Assoziationszentren, *n.pl. Physiol:* association centres (of the brain).

assoziativ [aso·tsia·'ti:f], *a.* associative.

assoziieren [aso·tsi·'i:rən], *v.tr.* to associate; **Ideen a.,** to associate, connect, ideas; *Com:* **sich mit j-m a.,** to become associated with s.o.; to enter into partnership with s.o.

assumieren [asu·'mi:rən], *v.tr.* to assume.

Assumption [asum(p)tsi'o:n], *f.* -/-en. **1.** *Log:* assumption. **2.**=**Assumtion.**

Assumptionist [asum(p)tsio·'nist], *m.* -en/-en. *R.C.Ch:* Assumptionist.

assumptiv [asum(p)'ti:f], *a. Log:* assumptive.

Assumtion [asumtsi'o:n], *f.* -/-en. **1.** Assumption (of the Virgin Mary). **2.** *Art:* picture of the (Virgin's) Assumption.

Assunta [a'sunta:], *f.* -/-ten=**Assumtion**[2].

Assyrien [a'sy:riən]. *Pr.n.n.* -s. *A.Geog:* Assyria.

Assyrier [a'sy:riər], *m.* -s/-. *A.Hist:* Assyrian.

Assyriologe [asy·rio·'lo:gə], *m.* -n/-n, Assyriologist.

Assyriologie [asy·rio·lo·'gi:], *f.* -/. Assyriology.

assyrisch [a'sy:riʃ], *a.* Assyrian.

Ast, *m.* -(e)s/ẜe. **1.** (*a*) branch, bough, limb (of a tree); **einen Ast durchsägen,** (i) to saw through a branch, (ii) *F:* to snore; *F:* **den Ast absägen, auf dem man sitzt,** to saw off the branch one is sitting on; to bring about one's own downfall; (*b*) branch, ramification (of river, nerve, etc.); branch (of stag's antlers); **sich in Äste teilen,** to ramify, branch out; (*c*) branch, leg (of tube); (*d*) branch of (curve); *Ball:* **aufsteigender, absteigender, Ast der Flugbahn,** ascending, descending, branch of the trajectory; *F:* (*of pers., business, etc.*) **auf dem absteigenden Ast sein,** to be going downhill, to be on the down-grade, to be in a bad way; (*of pers.*) to be past one's prime. **2.** knot, knur(l), knag (in timber). **3.** *F:* hump (of hunchback); knob (on surface, forehead, etc.); *see also* **lachen**[1] 2. **4.** *F:* task; piece of drudgery, *F:* chore.

Astarte [a'startɛ]. *Pr.n.f.* -s. *Myth:* Astarte.

Astasie [asta·'zi:], *f.* -/-n [-'zi:ən]. *Med:* astasia.

astasieren [asta·'zi:rən], *v.tr. Magn:* to astatize, make astatic.

astatisch [a·'sta:tiʃ], *a. El:* astatic; **astatisches Nadelpaar,** astatic needles.

Ästchen, *n.* -s/-, small branch; twig, sprig.

Asteismus [aste·'ismus], *m.* -/-men, (*a*) urbanity; (*b*) asteism; polished wit.

asten, *v.i.* (*haben*) **1.**=**ästen** I. **2.** *F:* (*of pers.*) to work hard, to toil.

ästen. I. *v.* **1.** *v.i.* (*haben*) (*of tree*) to put forth branches. **2.** *v.tr.* (*of pers.*) to lop the branches of (tree). **3. sich ästen,** to ramify, branch out. II. *p.p.* & *a.* **geästet,** (*a*) in *vbl senses;* (*b*) branchy, branching, ramifying; *Nat.Hist:* ramose.

Aster [‚'astər], *f.* -/-n. *Bot:* aster.

-aster [-'astər], *s.suff. m.* -s/-, *usu. Pej:* -aster; **Kritikaster,** criticaster; **Medikaster,** medicaster; **Poetaster,** poetaster.

Asterias [a'ste:rias], *m.* -/-. *Echin:* asterias, star-fish.

Asterie [a'ste:riə], *f.* -/-n. *Geol:* fossil star-fish.

asterisch [a'ste:riʃ], *a.* **1.** *A:* (influence, etc.) of the stars; astral (influence, etc.). **2.** star-like; *Miner:* asteriated.

Asteriskus [aste·'riskus], *m.* -/-ken. *Print:* asterisk (*esp. Ling: to mark a conjectural form*).

Asterismus [aste·'rismus], *m.* -/. *Astr: Cryst:* asterism.

asteroid[1] [aste·ro·'i:t], *a.* asteroid; star-like.

Asteroid[2] [aste·ro·'i:t], *m.* -(e)s & -en/-en [-s, -'i:dəs & -'i:dən/-'i:dən]. *Astr:* **1.** asteroid. **2.** planetoid, minor planet.

Asteroide [aste·ro·'i:də], *f.* -/-n. *Geom:* astroid.

Asteroidee [aste·ro·i·'de:ə], *f.* -/-n [-'de:ən]. *Echin:* asteroid.

Asterstadium, *n. Bot:* aster stage.

Astfänger, *m. Paperm:* knotter.

Astfäule, *f. Arb:* branch-rot.

Astflechte, *f. Moss:* reindeer-moss.

astfrei, *a.* (*of timber*) free from knots.

Asthenie [aste·'ni:], *f.* -/-n [-'ni:ən]. *Med:* asthenia; debility.

Astheniker [as'te:nikər], *m.* -s/-. *Med:* person suffering from asthenia.

asthenisch [as'te:niʃ], *a. Med:* asthenic.

Asthenopie [aste·no·'pi:], *f.* -/. *Med:* asthenopia, weakness of sight.

Ästhesie [ɛste·'zi:], *f.* -/. (capacity of) feeling.

Ästhesiometer [ɛste·zio·'me:tər], *n.* -s/-. *Physiol:* aesthesiometer.

Ästhesis [ɛ·ˈsteːzis], *f.* -/. aesthezis, perception through the senses.
Ästhet [ɛ·ˈsteːt], *m.* **-en/-en,** aesthete.
Ästhetentum, *n.* **-s/.** aestheticism.
Ästhetik [ɛ·ˈsteːtik], *f.* -/. aesthetics.
Ästhetiker [ɛ·ˈsteːtikər], *m.* **-s/-,** aesthetician, aestheticist; aesthete.
ästhetisch [ɛ·ˈsteːtiʃ], *a.* aesthetic.
ästhetisieren [ɛ·ste·ti·ˈziːrən]. **1.** *v.tr.* to aestheticize. **2.** *v.i.* (*haben*) to talk about aesthetics; to talk like an aesthete.
Ästhetizismus [ɛ·ste·ti·ˈtsismus], *m.* -/. aestheticism.
Asthma [ˈastmaː], *n.* **-s/.** asthma.
Asthmatiker [astˈmaːtikər], *m.* **-s/-,** asthmatic (subject).
asthmatisch [astˈmaːtiʃ], *a.* asthmatic(al).
Astholz, *n.* (*a*) branches, boughs (of trees); (*b*) *For:* small wood; loppings.
Asti [ˈastiː], *m.* **-s** *&* **-/-.** Asti (white wine).
astig, ästig, *a.* **1.** branchy, branching, ramifying; *Nat.Hist:* ramose. **2.** (*of wood*) knotty; (*of stem*) gnarled.
astigmatisch [a·stig·ˈmaːtiʃ], *a.* *Opt:* *Med:* astigmatic.
Astigmatismus [astigma·ˈtismus], *m.* -/. *Opt: Med:* astigmatism.
Astik [ˈastik], *m.* **-s/-e.** *Bootm: Mil: etc:* polishing stick.
ästimabel [ɛ·sti·ˈmaːbəl], *a.* estimable; worthy of esteem.
Ästimation [ɛ·sti·ma·tsĭˈoːn], *f.* **-/-en. 1.** estimation (of the value, price, of sth.); valuing, appraising (of goods, etc.). **2.** esteem, regard.
ästimatorisch [ɛ·sti·ma·ˈtoːriʃ], *a.* estimatory; *Jur:* **ästimatorischer Eid,** sworn statement of the value (of sth.).
ästimieren [ɛ·sti·ˈmiːrən], *v.tr.* **1.** to estimate; to value, appraise (goods, etc.). **2.** to esteem (s.o.).
Ästivoautumnalfieber [ɛ·ˌstiːvo·autum·ˈnaːl-], *n.* *Med:* tropical fever.
Astknorren, Astknorz, *m.*=**Ast** 2.
Astkreuz, *n.* *Her:* cross of untrimmed branches (*frequently fork-shaped*).
Ästlein, *n.* **-s/-**=**Ästchen.**
Ästling, *m.* **-s/-e. 1.**=**Ästchen. 2.** young bird able to hop from branch to branch, *A:* brancher.
Astloch, *n.* knot-hole (in timber).
astlochfrei, *a.* (timber) free from knot-holes.
astlos, *a.* **1.** branchless, without branches. **2.** (timber) free from knots *or* knot-holes.
Astmoos, *n.* *Moss:* hypnum; feather-moss.
astomisch [a·ˈstoːmiʃ], *a.* *Bot:* astomous (moss).
Astpalme, *f.* *Bot:* doum, doom(-palm).
Astputzer, *m.* *Tls: Hort:* pruning-scissors; secateurs.
Asträa [asˈtrɛːaː]. *Pr.n.f.* **-s.** *Myth:* Astraea.
Astrachan [astraˈxaːn]. **1.** *Pr.n.n.* **-s.** *Geog:* Astrak(h)an. **2.** *m.* **-s/-s,** (*a*) *Com:* astrak(h)an (fur); (*b*) *Tex:* (imitation) astrak(h)an.
Astragal [astra·ˈgaːl], *m.* **-s/-e. 1.** *Anat:* astragalus, ankle-bone, talus. **2.** *Arch: etc:* astragal, bead(-moulding); bead and reel moulding.
Astragalus [astra·ˈgaːlus], *m.* -/. *Bot:* astragalus, milk-vetch.
astral [asˈtraːl], *a.*, **Astral-,** *comb.fm.* astral.
Astrallampe, *f.* astral lamp.
Astralleib, *m.* astral body.
Astrallicht, *n.*, **Astralschein,** *m.* *Astr:* interstellar light (of the Milky Way).
astrein, *a.* **1.** (*of timber*) free from knots. **2.** *F:* **etwas ist nicht ganz a.,** there's something fishy about it, it's not on the level.
Astrild [asˈtrilt], *m.* **-(e)s/-e.** *Orn:* thin-billed weaver(-bird).
Astrograph [astro·ˈgraːf], *m.* **-en/-en.** *Astr:* camera telescope.
Astrographie [astro·gra·ˈfiː], *f.* **-/-n** [-ˈfiːən], astrography.
Astroide [astro·ˈiːdə], **Astrois** [aˈstro·is], *f.* **-/-iden** [astro·ˈiːdən]. *Geom:*=**Asteroide.**
Astrolab [astro·ˈlaːp], *n.* **-s/-ien** [-s/-ˈlaːbĭən], **Astrolabium** [astro·ˈlaːbĭum], *n.* **-s/-bien.** *Astr:* astrolabe.
Astrologe [astro·ˈloːgə], *m.* **-n/-n,** astrologer.
Astrologie [astro·lo·ˈgiː], *f.* **-/-n** [-ˈgiːən], astrology.
astrologisch [astro·ˈloːgiʃ], *a.* astrological.
Astronaut [astro·ˈnaut], *m.* **-en/-en,** astronaut.
Astronautik [astro·ˈnautik], *f.* -/. astronautics.
astronautisch [astro·ˈnautiʃ], *a.* astronautical.
Astronavigation [ˌastro·na·vi·ga·tsĭˈoːn], *f.* -/. *Av:* astronavigation.
Astronom [astro·ˈnoːm], *m.* **-en/-en,** astronomer.
Astronomie [astro·no·ˈmiː], *f.* **-/-n** [-ˈmiːən], astronomy.
astronomisch [astro·ˈnoːmiʃ], *a.* astronomic(al); **astronomischer Ort,** astronomical position; **astronomisches Jahr,** astronomical, sidereal, year; **astronomische Uhr,** astronomical clock; *Av:* **astronomische Ortung,** astronavigation; *F:* **astronomische Zahlen,** astronomical figures.
astrophisch [a·ˈstroːfiʃ], *a.* *Pros:* (poem) not divided into strophes.
Astrophotographie [ˌastro·fo·to·gra·ˈfiː], *f.* -/. astrophotography.
Astrophysik [astro·fy·ˈzi·k], *f.* -/. astrophysics.
astrophysikalisch [ˌastro·fy·zi·ˈkaːliʃ], *a.* astrophysical.
Astsäge, *f.* *Tls: Hort:* pruning-saw.
Astschere, *f.* *Tls: Hort:* **1.** tree-pruner, averruncator. **2.** pruning-scissors, -shears; secateurs; lopping-shears.
astständig, *a.* *Bot:* ramose.
Ästuar [ɛ·stu·ˈaːr], *n.* **-s/-ien** [-rĭən], **Ästuarium** [ɛ·stu·ˈaːrĭum], *n.* **-s/-rien,** estuary.
Asturien [asˈtuːrĭən]. *Pr.n.n.* **-s.** *Geog:* Asturias.
Asturier [asˈtuːrĭər], *m.* **-s/-.** *Geog:* Asturian.
asturisch [asˈtuːriʃ], *a.* Asturian.
Astwerk, *n.* **1.** branches, boughs, foliage. **2.** *Art:* Gothic ornament in the form of branches.
Astwurzel, *f.*=**Ast** 2.
Äsung, *f.* *see* **äsen** II.
Aswan [asŭˈaːn]. *Pr.n.* **-s.** *Geog:* Assouan, Aswan.
Asyl [a·ˈzyːl], *n.* **-s/-e. 1.** asylum, sanctuary; **politisches A.,** political asylum. **2.** shelter, home, (place of) refuge; **ohne A.,** homeless; **A. für Obdachlose,** night-shelter, *F:* doss-house, *U.S:* flophouse; *Adm:* casual ward (of public assistance institution).
Asylrecht, *n.* right of asylum; *Ecc.Jur:* right of sanctuary; **politisches A.,** right of political asylum.
Asymmetrie [a·zyme·ˈtriː], *f.* **-/-n** [-ˈtriːən], asymmetry.
asymmetrisch [a·zy·ˈmeːtriʃ], *a.* asymmetrical, unsymmetrical.
Asymptote [a·zym·ˈptoːtə], *f.* **-/-n.** *Mth:* asymptote.
asymptotisch [a·zym·ˈptoːtiʃ], *a.* *Mth:* asymptotic; *adv.* **sich a. nähern,** to approach asymptotically.
asynchron [a·zyn·ˈkroːn], *a.* *Mec:* asynchronous.
Asynchronismus [a·zynkro·ˈnismus], *m.* -/. *Mec:* asynchronism.
Asynchronmotor, *m.* *El.E:* asynchronous motor.
Asyndese [a·zyn·ˈdeːzə], *f.* **-/-n.** *Rh:* asyndeton.
asyndetisch [a·zyn·ˈdeːtiʃ], *a.* *Rh:* asyndetic.
Asyndeton [a·ˈzynde·ton], *n.* **-s/-ta.** *Rh:* asyndeton.
Asynergie [a·zynˀɛr·ˈgiː], *f.* **-/-n** [-ˈgiːən]. *Med:* asynergy.
Aszendent [astsɛnˈdɛnt], *m.* **-en/-en. 1.** *Astrol:* ascendant. **2.** *Genealogy:* ascendant, ancestor.
Aszendenz [astsɛnˈdɛnts], *f.* **-/-en. 1.** ascent, ascension; *Astrol:* **Stern in der A.,** star in the ascendant. **2.** *Genealogy:* ascending line, ancestry.
Aszendenztafel, *f.* genealogical table, family-tree.
Aszendenztheorie, *f.* *A.Miner:* ascension theory.
aszendieren [astsɛnˈdiːrən], *v.i.* (*sein*) (*a*) *esp. Astr: Astrol:* to ascend; **aszendierender Stern,** star in the ascendant; (*b*) (*of pers.*) to ascend in rank; to be promoted.
Aszension [astsɛnzĭˈoːn], *f.* **-/-en.** *Astr: Astrol: Ecc:* ascension.
Aszensionaldifferenz [astsɛnzĭo·ˈnaːl-], *f.* *Astr:* ascensional difference.
Aszese [asˈtseːzə], **Aszet** [asˈtseːt], **Aszetik** [asˈtseːtik], **Aszetiker** [asˈtseːtikər], **aszetisch** [asˈtseːtiʃ]=**Askese, Asket, Asketik, Asketiker, asketisch.**
Aszidie [asˈtsiːdĭə], *f.* **-/-n. 1.** *Bot:* ascidium, vasculum, *F:* pitcher. **2.** *Moll:* ascidian; sea-squirt.
Aszites [asˈtsiːte·s], *f.* -/.=**Ascites.**
-at [-ˈaːt]. **1.** *s.suff.* -ate; (*a*) *n.* **-(e)s/-e** (*denoting function*) **Kaliphat,** caliphate; **Mandat,** mandate; **Syndikat,** syndicate; (*b*) *m.* **-en/-en** (*denoting pers.*) **Advokat,** advocate; **Delegat,** delegate; (*c*) *n.* **-(e)s/-e.** *Ch:* **Azetat,** acetate; **Sulfat,** sulphate. **2.** *a.suff.* -ate; **disparat,** disparate; **separat,** separate.
Atakamit [a·ta·ka·ˈmiːt], *m.* **-(e)s/-e.** *Miner:* atacamite.
ataktisch [a·ˈtaktiʃ], *a.* *Med:* ataxic.
Atalante [a·ta·ˈlantə]. *Pr.n.f.* **-s.** *Gr.Myth:* Atalanta.
Ataman [a·ta·ˈmaːn], *m.* **-en/-en,** (Cossack) ataman, hetman.
Ataraxie [a·ta·ra·ˈksiː], *f.* -/. *Phil: Med:* ataraxy.
Atavismus [a·ta·ˈvismus], *m.* **-/-men,** atavism.
atavistisch [a·ta·ˈvistiʃ], *a.* atavistic, atavic.
Ataxie [a·ta·ˈksiː], *f.* **-/-n** [-ˈksiːən]. *Med:* ataxy, ataxia; tabes.
Ate [ˈaːteː]. *Pr.n.f.* **-s.** *Gr.Myth:* Ate.
Ateknie [a·tɛkˈniː], *f.* -/. childlessness, barrenness.
atektonisch [a·tɛkˈtoːniʃ], *a.* (*of work of art, etc.*) loosely constructed.
Atelier [atəlˈjeː], *n.* **-s/-s.** *Art: Cin: Phot:* studio.
Atelieraufnahme, *f.* *Cin:* studio shot; *Phot:* studio photograph.
Atellanen [atɛˈlaːnən], *f.pl.* *Rom.Ant:* Atellanae, Atellans.
Atem, *m.* **-s/.** (*a*) breath; respiration, breathing; **geruchlosen, reinen, A. haben,** to have an odourless, a sweet, breath; **übelriechenden A. haben,** to have (a) bad breath; **er leidet an übelriechendem A.,** he suffers from halitosis; **der A. des Frühlings, der Götter,** the breath of spring, of the gods; **den A. anhalten,** to hold one's breath; **mit verhaltenem A. lauschen,** to listen with bated breath; **in einem A.,** (i) all in the same breath, in one and the same breath, at a breath; (ii) at one go; **man darf sie nicht in einem A. nennen,** they are not to be mentioned in the same breath; **bis zum letzten A.,** to the last breath; **seinen letzten A. aushauchen,** to breathe one's last; (*b*) breath, wind; **langen, guten, A. haben,** to have plenty of wind, *F:* to have a good pair of lungs; *F:* **wir haben einen längeren A.,** we can hold out longer (than they can), we have more staying-power; **kurzen A. haben,** to be short-winded; (*of horse*) to be broken-winded; **A. holen, schöpfen,** to draw breath, take breath; *F:* to take a breather; **laß mich A. holen,** give me time to breathe, to take breath; **tief A. holen,** to breathe deeply, take a deep breath; **j-n, ein Pferd, A. schöpfen lassen,** to give s.o. time to breathe, *F:* to give s.o. a breather; to let a horse get its wind, to breathe a horse; **kaum A. holen können,** to breathe with difficulty, to have difficulty in breathing; **ich kann kaum A. holen,** I find it very hard to get my breath; **der A. ging uns aus,** our breath was beginning to fail; **der A. geht ihm schnell aus,** he soon gets out of breath; (*of orator, etc.*) he is soon at the end of his tether, he soon runs dry, *F:* he can't stay the course, he is soon pumped out; **dem wird der A. bald ausgehen,** he won't last out; **den A. verlieren, außer A. kommen, geraten,** to get out of breath, to lose one's breath; **außer A. sein,** to be short of breath, out of breath; to be winded, blown, *F:* puffed; **j-n, ein Pferd, außer A. bringen,** to blow, wind, s.o., a horse; **sich außer A. laufen,** to run till one is out of breath, to run oneself out of breath, to run till one is winded, blown, *F:* puffed; **j-m den A. nehmen, rauben,** to take s.o.'s breath away; to make s.o. gasp, *F:* to flabbergast s.o.; **zu A. kommen,** to get one's breath; **ich bin heute gar nicht zu A. gekommen,** I've hardly had time to breathe today, I've been on the run, *F:* on the hop, all day; **laß mich zu A. kommen,** give me time to breathe, to take breath; **wieder zu A. kommen,** to recover one's breath, to get one's second wind; **j-n in A. halten,** (i) to hold s.o. breathless, to hold s.o.'s attention, to keep s.o. on the alert, in suspense; (ii) to keep s.o. busy; *F:* to keep s.o. at it, on the go.
atembar, *a.* breathable, respirable.
Atembeklemmung, *f.* shortness of breath, breathlessness, difficulty in breathing.
atemberaubend, *a.* breath-taking (beauty, etc.); breathless (suspense, speed, etc.).
Atemeinsatz, *m.* *Mil:* drum, filter-canister (of gas-mask).
Atemgerät, *n.* *Min: etc:* breathing apparatus, *esp.* oxygen breathing apparatus; respirator.
Atemgeräusch, *n.* sound of breathing; breath-sound; *Med:* **abgeschwächtes A.,** diminished vesicular murmur; *see also* **vesikulär.**
Atemgymnastik, *f.* (deep-)breathing exercises.
Atemhöhle, *f.* *Bot:* *Z:* respiratory cavity, air-chamber.
Atemholen, *n.* respiration; breathing; **nach mehrmaligem A.,** after taking several breaths.
Atemkanal, *m.* *Anat:* respiratory duct; *Anat: Bot:* stoma.
Atemloch, *n.* *Anat: Bot:* stoma; *Ent:* spiracle, stigma.
atemlos, *a.* breathless; **atemlose Spannung,** breathless excitement *or* suspense; **atemlose Stille,** dead silence; breathless hush; **ganz a.,** quite out of breath.
Atemmesser, *m.* spirometer, pulmometer.
Atemnot, *f.* difficulty in breathing; dyspnoea; **einen Anfall von schwerer A. haben,** to have a severe spasm of breathlessness.
Atemöffnung, *f.* breathing aperture; *Anat: Bot:* stoma.
Atemorgan, *n.* respiratory organ.
Atempause, *f.* (*a*) breathing-space, -spell, -time, *F:* breather; **j-m eine kleine A. gewähren,** to give s.o. a moment's respite, *F:* to give s.o. a breather;

(*b*) *Mus:* (*for phrasing*) breathing-time, breathing point.

a tempo [a· ˈtɛmpoː]. *Ital.adv.phr.* (*a*) in good time; at the proper time; in the nick of time; (*b*) simultaneously; (*c*) *Mus:* a tempo.

atemraubend, *a.*=**atemberaubend.**

Atemrohr, *n.*, **Atemröhre,** *f.* breathing-tube; respiratory tube; *Nat. Hist:* siphon.

Atemschlauch, *m.* breathing-tube; connecting-tube (of respirator).

Atemschutzgerät, *n.* breathing apparatus, respirator; *esp.* (fireman's, etc.) smoke-helmet.

Atemübung, *f.* breathing exercise.

Atemwurzel, *f. Bot:* pneumatophore.

Atemzentrum, *n. Anat:* respiratory centre.

Atemzug, *m.* breath; respiration; **einen tiefen A. tun,** to draw a deep, long, breath; **in einem A.,** all in the same breath, in one and the same breath, at a breath; **ich werde bis zum letzten A. Widerstand leisten,** I will resist to my last breath, to the last gasp; **seinen, den, letzten A. tun,** to draw one's last breath, to breathe one's last; **in den letzten Atemzügen liegen,** to breathe one's last, to be at one's last gasp; to be *in extremis;* **mit seinem letzten A. ließ er mich schwören . . . ,** with his dying breath he made me swear . . . .

Atemzunge, *f.*, **Atemzünglein,** *n. Anat:* uvula.

Äternat [ɛtɛrˈnaːt], *n.* -(e)s/. **1.** state of affairs fixed for all time. **2.** *Rom.Ant: etc:* irreducible minimum establishment (of army).

äternieren [ɛtɛrˈniːrən], *v.tr.* to eternize, perpetuate.

Äthal [ɛ·ˈtaːl], *n.* **-s/.** *Ch:* cetyl, ethal.

Athalja [a·ˈtaljaː]. *Pr.n.f.* **-s.** *B.Hist:* Athalia.

Äthan [ɛ·ˈtaːn], *n.* **-s/-e.** *Ch:* ethane, dimethyl; **Äthane** *pl,* paraffin hydrocarbons of the ethane series.

Athanasianisch [a·ta·na·ziˈaːniʃ], *a.* Athanasian; **das Athanasianische Glaubensbekenntnis,** the Athanasian Creed.

Athanasie [a·ta·na·ˈziː], *f.* **-/.** athanasy, immortality.

Athanasius [a·ta·ˈnaːzius]. *Pr.n.m.* **-'.** *Rel.Hist:* Athanasius.

Atheismus [a·te·ˈismus], *m.* **-/.** atheism.

Atheist [a·te·ˈist], *m.* **-en/-en,** atheist.

atheistisch [a·te·ˈistiʃ], *a.* atheistic(al).

athematisch [a·te·ˈmaːtiʃ], *a. Gram:* athematic (verb).

Athen [a·ˈteːn]. *Pr.n.n.* **-s.** *Geog:* Athens; *see also* **Eule** 1.

Äthen [ɛ·ˈteːn], *n.* **-s/.** *Ch:* ethene, ethylene.

Athenäum [a·te·ˈnɛːum], *n.* **-s/-näen. 1.** *Gr.Ant:* athenaeum. **2.** (*academy*) athenaeum. **3.** *Lit. Hist:* **das A.,** the Athenaeum (*periodical edited by the brothers Schlegel, 1798–1800*).

Athene [a·ˈteːnə]. *Pr.n.f.* **-s.** *Gr.Myth:* Athene.

Athener [a·ˈteːnər]. **1.** *m.* **-s/-.** *Geog: etc:* Athenian. **2.** *inv.a. Geog: etc:* Athenian, of Athens.

Athenienser [a·te·niˈɛnzər], *m.* **-s/-.** *Geog: etc:* Athenian.

atheniensisch [a·te·niˈɛnziʃ], *a. Geog: etc:* Athenian.

athenisch [a·ˈteːniʃ], *a. Geog: etc:* Athenian.

Äther [ˈɛːtər], *m.* **-s/. 1.** *Ph: Ch: Med:* ether; *Ch: Com:* **gewöhnlicher Ä.,** sulphuric ether, ethyl oxide. **2.** *A. & Poet:* **der Ä.,** the ether; the upper air.

ätherähnlich, *a.* ether-like; *Ch:* (*of liquid*) ethereal.

Ätherarten, *f.pl. Ch:* ethers.

ätherartig, *a. Ch:* (*of liquid*) ethereal.

Äthergruppe, *f. Ch:* ether group, ether grouping.

ätherifizieren [ɛ·te·ri·fi·ˈtsiːrən], *v.tr. Ch:* to etherify; **Ätherifizierung** *f,* etherification.

ätherisch [ɛ·ˈteːriʃ], *a.* **1.** ethereal (body, regions, etc.); airy (regions, etc.). **2.** *Ph: Ch:* ethereal; *Ch:* **ätherisches Öl,** essential oil; volatile oil.

ätherisieren [ɛ·te·ri·ˈziːrən]. **1.** *v.i.* (*haben*) to use ether. **2.** *v.tr.* (*a*) *Med:* to etherize (patient); (*b*) *Hort:* to force (plant) with ether; (*c*) *Pharm:* to etherize, mix with ether; **Ätherisierung** *f,* etherization.

Ätherleib, *m. Anthroposophy:* ethereal body.

atherman [a·tɛrˈmaːn], *a. Ph:* athermanous; impervious to radiant heat.

äthern, *v.tr. Pharm:* to etherize, mix with ether.

Atherom [a·təˈroːm], *n.* **-s/-e.** *Med:* atheroma, sebaceous cyst, wen.

Ätherschwingungen, *f.pl. Ph:* vibrations in the ether.

Ätherweingeist, *m. Pharm:* spirit of ether.

Ätherwellen, *f.pl. Ph:* waves in the ether.

Athethese [a·te·ˈteːzə], *f.* **-/-n,** athethesis; rejection (*esp. Lit:* of a passage as spurious).

athethieren [a·te·ˈtiːrən], *v.tr.* to reject, throw out (passage, etc.) (as spurious).

Äthin [ɛ·ˈtiːn], *n.* **-s/.** *Ch:* acetylene, ethine.

Äthionsäure [ɛ·tiˈoːn-], *f. Ch:* ethionic acid.

Äthiopien [ɛ·tiˈoːpiən]. *Pr.n.n.* **-s.** *Geog:* Ethiopia; Abyssinia.

Äthiopier [ɛ·tiˈoːpiər], *m.* **-s/-.** Ethiopian; Abyssinian.

äthiopisch [ɛ·tiˈoːpiʃ], *a.* (*a*) Ethiopian; Abyssinian; (*b*) Ethiopic (language, church, etc.).

Athlet [atˈleːt], *m.* **-en/-en,** athlete.

Athletik [atˈleːtik], *f.* **-/.** athletics.

Athletiker [atˈleːtikər], *m.* athlete; *Anthr:* athletic type.

athletisch [atˈleːtiʃ], *a.* athletic.

Athor [ˈaːto·r]. *Pr.n.f.* **-s.** *Egypt.Myth:* Hathor.

Athos [ˈaːtos]. *Pr.n.m.* **-'.** *Geog:* **der (Berg) A.,** Mount Athos.

Athoskloster, *n.* monastery on Mount Athos.

Äthyl [ɛ·ˈtyːl], *n.* **-s/.** *Ch:* ethyl.

Äthylalkohol, *m. Ch:* ethyl alcohol.

Äthylamin [ɛ·ty·la·ˈmiːn], *n.* **-s/.** *Ch:* ethylamine.

Äthyläther, *m. Ch:* ethyl ether, ethyl oxide; *Com:* sulphuric ether, *F:* ether.

Äthylen [ɛ·ty·ˈleːn], *n.* **-s/.** *Ch:* ethylene.

Äthylenreihe, *f. Ch:* ethylene series.

Ätiologie [ɛ·tio·lo·ˈgiː], *f.* **-/.** aetiology.

ätiologisch [ɛ·tio·ˈloːgiʃ], *a.* aetiological.

Atlant [atˈlant], *m.* **-en/-en. 1.** *Arch:* atlas, telamon; **Atlanten** *pl,* atlantes, telamones (supporting entablature). **2.** atlas, book of maps.

Atlantenformat, *n.*=**Atlasformat.**

Atlantiden [atlanˈtiːdən], *f.pl. Myth:* Atlantides, daughters of Atlas.

Atlantik, der [atˈlantik]. *Pr.n.* **-(s).** *Geog:* the Atlantic (Ocean).

Atlantikcharta, die. *Hist:* the Atlantic Charter.

Atlantikdampfer, *m. Nau:* Atlantic liner.

Atlantikpakt, der. *Hist:* the Atlantic Pact.

Atlantis [atˈlantis]. *Pr.n.f.* **-'.** *Myth:* Atlantis.

atlantisch [atˈlantiʃ], *a.* Atlantic; *Geog:* **der Atlantische Ozean,** the Atlantic (Ocean); *El.E:* **atlantisches Kabel,** Atlantic cable.

Atlas[1] [ˈatlas]. **1.** *Pr.n.m.* **-'.** *Gr.Myth:* Atlas. **2.** *m.* **-& -lasses/Atlanten** [atˈlantən] **& Atlasse,** (*a*) *Anat:* atlas, the first cervical vertebra; (*b*) (*book of maps, charts, etc.*) atlas; (*c*)=**Atlasformat. 3.** *Pr.n.m.* **-.** *Geog:* **der A.,** the Atlas mountains.

Atlas[2], *m.* **- & -lasses/-lasse.** *Tex:* satin; *see also* **Florentiner** 1.

atlasartig, *a. Tex:* satin-like; satiny.

Atlasband[1], *m.* atlas; atlas volume (of encyclopaedia, scientific work, etc.); *Bookb:* atlas folio.

Atlasband[2], *n.* satin ribbon.

Atlasbeere, *f. Bot:*=**Elsbeere** 2 (*a*).

Atlasbindung, *f. Tex:* satin-weave.

Atlasbirne, *f. Bot:* wild service-tree.

Atlasblume, *f. Bot:* lunaria, *F:* satin-flower.

Atlaserz, *n. Miner:* malachite.

Atlasfink, *m. Orn:* combassou.

Atlasformat, *n. Paperm: Bookb:* atlas size; large folio size; **ein Foliant in A.,** an atlas folio.

Atlasgebirge, das. *Pr.n. Geog:* the Atlas mountains.

Atlasgips, *m. Miner:* satin gypsum, satin spar.

Atlasholz, *n. Com:* satin-wood.

Atlaspapier, *n. Paperm:* glazed paper, satin paper.

Atlasseide, *f. Tex:* satin.

atlassen [ˈatlasən], *a.* satin; made of satin.

Atlasspat, *m. Miner:* satin spar, satin gypsum.

Atlasspinner, *m. Ent:* atlas-moth.

Atlasstein, *m. Miner:*=**Atlasspat.**

Atlaszeder, *f. Bot:* Atlas cedar, silver cedar.

atmen. I. **1.** *v.i.* (*haben*) to breathe; *Physiol: Bot:* to respire; **tief a.,** to breathe deeply; to draw a deep breath, a long breath; **frei a.,** to breathe freely; **jetzt kann ich wieder frei a.,** now I can breathe again; **leise a.,** to breathe gently, softly; **schwer a.,** to breathe heavily; to breathe hard; to breathe with difficulty; to gasp for breath; **mühsam a.,** to breathe with difficulty; **alles, was atmet,** all that breathes; all living creatures; **solange ich atme,** as long as I live; while I still have breath (in my body); *v.impers.* **es atmet sich leichter hier oben als in der Stadt,** one can breathe more easily up here than in the city. **2.** *v.tr.* (*a*) to breathe; to inhale (air, etc.); *Physiol: Bot:* to respire; **die Luft der Heimat a.,** to breathe one's native air; **eine reinere Luft a.,** to breathe purer air; (*b*) **hier atmet alles Frieden,** here everything breathes peace; **die Häuser atmen den Geist der alten Zeit,** the houses breathe with the spirit of former days; the houses are redolent of the past; **die Blumen atmeten süßen Duft,** the flowers exhaled their fragrance, perfume, were perfuming the air.

II. *vbl s.* **1. Atmen,** *n.* breathing. **2. Atmung,** *f.* breathing; *Physiol: Bot:* respiration.

ätmen, *v.tr. Metall:*=**abätmen.**

-atmig, *comb.fm.* -winded; **kurzatmig,** short-winded; **langatmig,** long-winded.

Atmolyse [atmo·ˈlyːzə], *f.* **-/-n.** *Ph:* atmolysis.

Atmometer [atmo·ˈmeːtər], *n.* **-s/-.** *Ph:* atmidometer, evaporimeter.

Atmosphäre [atmoˈsfɛːrə], *f.* **-/-n. 1.** (*a*) atmosphere; (*b*) *F:* air; atmosphere; ambience, ambiency; environment; **gespannte A.,** tense atmosphere; **die A. war mit Elektrizität geladen,** the air was electric; sparks were about to fly; **die A. reinigen,** to clean the air; **mit Streit geladene A.,** quarrelsome atmosphere, *Lit:* ambience, ambiency, of strife; **lasterhafte A.,** vicious atmosphere; vicious environment; *Lit:* ambience, ambiency, of vice. **2.** (i) *Ph:* **(physikalische, alte) A.,** *abbr.* **atm,** *A:* **Atm,** atmosphere (*pressure of 760 mm. of mercury or 1.033 kg. per sq. cm.*); (ii) *Tchn:* **(technische, neue, metrische) A.,** *abbr.* **at,** metric atmosphere (*pressure of 735.5 mm. of mercury or 1 kg. per sq. cm.*).

Atmosphärendruck, *m.* atmospheric pressure.

Atmosphärilien [atmosfɛ·ˈriːliən], *n.pl. Ph: Ch:* atmospheric influences.

atmosphärisch [atmoˈsfɛːriʃ], *a.* atmospheric; **atmosphärischer Druck,** atmospheric pressure; **atmosphärische Elektrizität,** atmospheric electricity; *Bot:* **atmosphärische Pflanze,** epiphyte; *Mch: A:* **atmosphärische (Dampf-)Maschine,** atmospheric engine; *Mch:* **atmosphärische Linie,** atmospheric line (of indicator-card); *Ph:* **atmosphärische Linien,** atmospheric lines (*seen in spectroscope*); *Rail: A:* **atmosphärische Bahn,** atmospheric railway; *W.Tel:* **atmosphärische Störungen,** atmospherics.

Atmungs-, *comb.fm.* respiratory . . . breathing . . . ; **Atmungsorgan** *n,* respiratory organ; **Atmungsrohr** *n,* breathing tube, respiratory tube; *cp.* **Atem-.**

Atmungsapparat, *m.* breathing apparatus; respirator.

Atmungsbeschwerden, *f. pl.* difficulty in breathing; **A. haben,** to have difficulty in breathing.

Atmungsgerät, *n.*=**Atemgerät.**

Atmungsgeräusch, *n.*=**Atemgeräusch.**

Atmungsgröße, *f. Bot:* respiratory quotient.

Atmungsorgan, *n. Anat:* respiratory organ.

Atmungsstoffwechsel, *m. Biol:* respiratory exchange.

Atmungsweg, *m. Anat:* respiratory duct.

Atmungswerkzeug, *n. Anat:* respiratory organ; respiratory apparatus.

Atmungszentrum, *n. Anat:* respiratory centre.

Ätna, der [ˈɛtnaː]. *Pr.n.* **-(s).** *Geog:* (Mount) Etna.

Ätolien [ɛ·ˈtoːliən]. *Pr.n.n.* **-s.** *A.Geog:* Aetolia.

Ätolier [ɛ·ˈtoːliər], *m.* **-s/-.** *A.Geog:* Aetolian.

ätolisch [ɛ·ˈtoːliʃ], *a. A.Geog:* Aetolian.

Atoll [a·ˈtol], *n.* **-s/-e.** *Geog:* atoll, lagoon-reef; coral-island.

Atom [a·ˈtoːm], *n.* **-s/-e,** (*a*) *Ch: Ph:* atom; *Atom. Ph:* **leichtes, schweres, A.,** light, heavy, atom; **das A. zertrümmern,** to split, *F:* smash, the atom; (*b*) **etwas in Atome auflösen, zerspalten,** to reduce sth. to atoms; *F:* **nicht ein A. Wahrheit,** not an atom, not a jot, grain, particle, scrap, of truth; **es ist nicht ein A. Stolz in ihm,** there's not an atom, not a grain, morsel, scrap, of pride in him; **ein A. Salz in eine Speise tun,** to put (just) a trace of salt in a dish.

Atom-, *comb.fm. Ch: Ph:* atom . . . ; atomic . . . ; nuclear . . . ; **Atombewegung** *f,* atomic motion; **Atomgeschütz** *n* atom gun, atomic gun; **Atomspaltung** *f,* atomic, nuclear, fission; **Atomspektrum** *n,* atom, atomic, spectrum; **Atomwaffe** *f,* atomic, nuclear, weapon; **Atomzeichen** *n,* atomic symbol.

Atomabfall, *m. Atom.Ph:* atomic waste; by-products of atomic disintegration.

Atomangriff, *m. Mil:* attack with atomic weapons, atomic attack.

Atomanlage, *f.*=**Atomkraftanlage.**

Atomantrieb, *m.* atomic propulsion (of rocket, submarine, etc.); atomic drive.

atomar [a·to·ˈmaːr], *a.* atomic (energy, etc.).

Atomaufbau, *m. Atom.Ph:* **(künstlicher) A.,** artificial building up of atoms.

Atombatterie, *f. Atom.Ph:* atomic pile.

Atombau, *m. Ch: Atom.Ph:* atomic structure.

Atombeschießung, *f. Mil:* atomic bombardment.

atombetrieben, *a.* nuclear-, atom(ic)-powered.

Atombindungsvermögen, *n. Ch:* atomic combining power, valency.

Atombombe, *f. Mil:* atomic bomb, atom bomb, A-bomb.
Atombomber, *m. Mil.Av:* atom bomber, A-bomber.
Atombrenner, *m. Atom.Ph:* atomic pile.
Atomenergie, *f.* atomic, nuclear, energy.
Atom-Epoche, die, the atomic age.
Atomforschung, *f.* atomic research.
Atomforschungsanstalt, *f.* atomic research station.
Atomgewicht, *n. Ch:* atomic weight.
Atomgramm, *n. Ch:* gramme-atom.
Atomhülle, *f. Atom.Ph:* electron cloud.
Atomigkeit, *f. Ch:* atomicity; valency.
Atomingenieur, *m.* atomic engineer.
atomisch [aˑˈtoːmiʃ], *a.* indivisible.
atomisieren [aˑtoˑmiˑˈziːrən], *v.tr.* to atomize; to reduce (sth.) to atoms.
Atomismus [aˑtoˑˈmismus], *m.* -/. *A.Phil:* atomism.
Atomist [aˑtoˑˈmist], *m.* -en/-en. *A.Phil:* atomist.
Atomistik [aˑtoˑˈmistik], *f.* -/. *A.Phil:* atomism.
atomistisch [aˑtoˑˈmistiʃ], *a. A.Phil:* atomistic.
Atomizität [aˑtoˑmiˑtsiˑˈtɛːt], *f.* -/-en. *Ch:* atomicity; valency.
Atomkern, *m. Atom.Ph:* atomic nucleus.
Atomkernforschung, *f. Atom.Ph:* nuclear research.
Atomkraft, *f.* atomic, nuclear, power; atomic energy.
Atomkraftanlage, *f.* (*a*) atomic energy plant; atomic pile; (*b*) nuclear power station.
Atomkraftwerk, *n.* nuclear power station.
Atomkrieg, *m.* (*a*) atomic war, nuclear war; (*b*) atomic warfare, nuclear warfare.
atomlich, *a.* atomic.
Atommacht, *f. Pol:* power in possession of atomic weapons, *F:* atomic power.
Atommaschine, *f.* **1.** atomic machine *or* device; vehicle, etc., driven by atomic power. **2.** *Atom. Ph:* atom-disintegrating device; particle-accelerating device.
Atommeiler, *m. Atom.Ph:* atomic pile; nuclear reactor.
Atommodell, *n. Atom.Ph:* atom model.
Atommüll, *m. Atom.Ph:* atomic waste.
Atomnummer, *f. Ch:* atomic number (of element).
Atomphysik, *f.* atomic physics.
atomphysikalisch, *a.* . . . of, in relation to, in connection with, atomic physics; atomic physics . . . ; **atomphysikalische Forschung,** research in atomic physics; **atomphysikalische Masseneinheit,** atomic mass unit (*abbr.* amu).
Atomphysiker, *m.* atomic physicist.
Atomreaktor, *m. Atom.Ph:* nuclear reactor, atomic reactor.
Atomrumpf, *m. Atom.Ph:* (atomic) core, atomic kernel, *U.S:* rumpf.
Atomsäule, *f. Atom.Ph:* atomic pile.
Atomschutt, *m.* fallout (from atomic explosion).
Atomspaltung, *f. Atom.Ph:* atomic fission, nuclear fission.
Atomsprengkopf, *m. Mil:* atomic, nuclear, warhead (on rocket).
Atomstrahlen, *m.pl. Atom.Ph:* atomic rays.
Atomstrahlung, *f. Atom.Ph:* atomic radiation.
Atomtheorie, *f.* atomic theory.
Atom-U-Boot, *n. Navy:* nuclear(-powered), atomic(-powered), submarine.
Atomuhr, *f.* atomic clock.
Atomumwandlung, *f. Atom.Ph:* nuclear disintegration.
Atomumwandlungsmaschine, *f. Atom.Ph:* atom-disintegrating machine *or* device; transmutation plant.
Atomverkettung, *f. Ch:* atomic linkage; bond.
Atomvolumen, *n. Ch:* atomic volume.
Atomwaffe, *f. Mil:* atomic, nuclear, weapon.
Atomwärme, *f. Ch:* atomic heat.
Atomwertigkeit, *f. Ch:* (atomic) valency.
Atomzahl, *f.* **1.** number of atoms. **2.** *Ch:* atomic number (of element).
Atomzeitalter, das, the atomic age.
Atomzerfall, *m. Atom.Ph:* atomic decay, atomic disintegration, (natural) disintegration of the atom.
Atomzertrümmerung, *f. Atom.Ph:* (artificial) disintegration, splitting, of the atom, *F:* atom-smashing.
atonal [aˑtoˑˈnaːl], *a. Mus:* atonal.
Atonalität [aˑtoˑnaˑliˑˈtɛːt], *f.* -/. *Mus:* atonality.
Atonie [aˑtoˑˈniː], *f.* -/. *Med:* atony, want of tone, low physical condition.
atonisch [aˑˈtoːniʃ], *a.* **1.** *Ling:* atonic, unstressed. **2.** *Med:* atonic, lacking tone.
Atonon [ˈaːtoˑnon], *n.* -s/**Atona.** *Ling:* atonic (word).
Atout [aˈtuː], *n.* (*in Austria also m.*) -s/-s. *Cards:* trump.
atoxisch [aˑˈtoksiʃ], *a.* non-toxic, non-poisonous.
atramentieren [aˑtraˑmɛnˈtiːrən], *v.tr. Metall:* to treat (steel) by the atrament process.
Atramentstein [aˑtraˑˈmɛnt-], *m. Miner:* ink-stone, native copperas.
Atramentverfahren, *n. Metall:* atrament process.
Atresie [aˑtreˑˈziː], *f.* -/-n [-ˈziːən]. *Med:* atresia; stoppage (of a passage).
Atreus [ˈaːtroys]. *Pr.n.m.* -ʼ. *Gr.Lit:* Atreus.
Atrichie [aˑtriˑˈçiː], *f.* -/. *Med:* hairlessness, absence of hair, *Med:* atrichia.
Atriden, die [aˑˈtriːdən]. *Pr.n.m.pl. Gr.Lit:* the Atridae.
Atrium [ˈaːtrium], *n.* -s/-rien. *Arch: Anat:* atrium.
Atropa [ˈaːtroˑpaː], *f.* -/. *Bot:* atropa, *esp.* belladonna, deadly nightshade.
Atropasäure, *f. Ch:* atropic acid.
Atrophie [aˑtroˑˈfiː], *f.* -/. atrophy.
atrophisch [aˑˈtroːfiʃ], *a.* atrophic, atrophous.
Atropin [aˑtroˑˈpiːn], *n.* -s/. *Ch: Pharm:* atropine.
Atropinvergiftung, *f. Med:* atropine poisoning, atrop(in)ism.
Atropos [ˈaːtroˑpos]. **1.** *Pr.n.f.* -ʼ. *Gr.Myth:* Atropos. **2.** *m.* -/-. *Ent:* acherontia atropos, death's-head moth.
Atrozität [aˑtroˑtsiˑˈtɛːt], *f.* -/-en, atrocity.
ätsch, *int.* (*a*) (*derision*) yah, boo! **ä., ich habe aber ein neues Kleid!** but I've got a new dress, see! (*b*) (*mild disgust*) bah!
Atschin [ˈatʃin]. *Pr.n.n.* -s. *Geog:* Achin.
Atschinese [atʃiˑˈneːzə], *m.* -n/-n. *Geog:* inhabitant, native, of Achin, of North-West Sumatra.
Attaché [ataˑˈʃeː], *m.* -s/-s. *Dipl: etc:* attaché.
Attachement [ataʃəˈmãː], *n.* -s/-s, attachment (**an j-n,** to s.o.), affection (**an j-n,** for s.o.).
attachieren [ataˈʃiːrən], *v.tr.* to attach; **einen Beamten einer Behörde a.,** to attach an official to an authority; **sich j-m, einer Partei, a.,** to attach oneself to s.o., to a party.
Attacke [aˈtakə], *f.* -/-n, (*a*) *Mil:* cavalry charge; **eine A. (auf den Feind) reiten,** to charge (the enemy); (*b*) *F:* attack; **eine A. gegen j-n reiten,** to make an attack upon s.o.; (*c*) *Med: F:* attack, bout (of illness); (*d*) *Mus:* attack.
attackieren [ataˈkiːrən], *v.tr.* **1.** to attack; *Mil:* (*of cavalry*) to charge (the enemy). **2.** *Equit:* to spur, put spurs to (horse).
attalisch [aˈtaːliʃ], *a. Hist:* of Attalus; **die attalischen Schätze,** the treasures of Attalus.
Attentat [atɛnˈtaːt, ˈatəntaˑt], *n.* -(e)s/-e, (politically motivated) attack, attempt, on s.o.'s life; outrage; **ein A. auf j-n begehen, verüben,** (i) to make an attempt on s.o.'s life, to try to assassinate s.o.; (ii) to assassinate s.o.; **A. auf die Freiheit,** attempt upon, against, liberty; *F:* **ich habe ein A. auf dich vor,** I'm going to put a strain on your good nature.
Attentäter [atɛnˈtɛːtər, ˈatəntɛˑtər], *m.* -s/-, perpetrator of an outrage; author of a murderous attack; (would-be *or* successful) assassin.
Attention [atɛntsiˈoːn], *f.* -/-en, attention; **Attention!** (pay) attention! look out!
Attentismus [atɛnˈtismus] *m.* -/. wait-and-see attitude.
Attenuation [ateˑnuˑaˑtsiˈoːn], *f.* -/. attenuation.
attenuieren [ateˑnuˑˈiːrən], *v.tr.* to attenuate; **sich a.,** to become attenuated.
Atter, *f.* -/-n. *Dial:* snake.
Attest [aˈtɛst], *n.* -(e)s/-e, attestation, certificate; **ärztliches A.,** doctor's, medical, certificate; **j-m ein A. ausstellen,** to write s.o. a certificate.
Attestat [atɛsˈtaːt], *n.* -(e)s/-e, *occ.*=**Attest.**
attestieren [atɛsˈtiːrən], *v.tr.* to attest; to certify.
Ätti, *m.* -s/-. *Swiss:* father.
Attich, *m.* -s/-e, **Attichholunder,** *m. Bot:* dwarf-elder, bloodwort, danewort.
Attika [ˈatiˑkaː]. **1.** *Pr.n.n.* -s. *A.Geog:* Attica. **2.** *f.* -/-ken. *Arch:* attic.
Attikageschoß, *n. Arch:* attic (storey).
Attila [ˈatiˑlaː]. **1.** *Pr.n.m.* -s. *Hist:* Attila. **2.** *m.* -s/-s & *f.* -/-s. *Mil.Cost: A:* hussar's (frogged) tunic.
attisch [ˈatiʃ], *a.* Attic, Athenian; **attisches Salz,** Attic salt, wit; *Arch:* **attische Basis,** Attic base.
attisieren [atiˑˈziːrən], *v.i.* (*haben*) & *v.tr.* to atticize.
Attitüde [atiˑˈtyːdə], *f.* -/-n, attitude; posture; **A. gegen j-n,** attitude towards s.o.
Attizismus [atiˑˈtsismus], *m.* -/-men. *Ling: Lit:* atticism.
Attizist [atiˑˈtsist], *m.* -en/-en, atticist.
attizistisch [atiˑˈtsistiʃ], *a.* atticizing (style, etc.).
Attraktion [atraktsiˈoːn], *f.* -/-en. **1.** attraction; pull; *Ling:* attraction. **2.** *Th: etc:* attraction; **die große A.,** the great attraction, *F:* the big draw.
attraktiv [atrakˈtiːf], *a.* attractive.
attraktorisch [atrakˈtoːriʃ], *a.* attractile (force).
Attrappe [aˈtrapə], *f.* -/-n. **1.** dummy; sham; *Com:* article made for display purposes only; dummy (article, box, etc.); *Mil:* dummy (vehicle, tank, etc.); *Av:* dummy bomb; *Ind:* mock-up (of aircraft, etc,); *F:* **das ist alles bloß A.,** that's all window-dressing, all sham, all eyewash. **2.** trap; catch, *F:* do.
attrappieren [atraˈpiːrən], *v.tr.* to catch (s.o.); to take (s.o.) in, *F:* to do (s.o.).
attribuieren [atriˑbuˑˈiːrən], *v.tr.* to attribute, to ascribe (*dat.*, **an**+*acc.*, to).
Attribut [atriˑˈbuːt], *n.* -(e)s/-e. **1.** (*a*) attribute, essential characteristic, inherent property; *Phil:* attribute; (*b*) attribute (of gods, saints, etc.). **2.** *Gram:* attributive adjunct, attributive modifier, attribute.
Attribution [atriˑbuˑtsiˈoːn], *f.* -/-en, attribution, attributing, assigning, ascription (**an**+*acc.*, to).
attributiv [atriˑbuˑˈtiːf], *a. Gram:* attributive (adjective, clause); *adv.* **a. gebraucht, verwendet,** used attributively.
Attributivsatz, *m. Gram:* attributive clause.
Attrition [atritsiˈoːn], *f.* -/-en. **1.** *Theol:* attrition. **2.** *occ.* attrition; abrasion; wear caused by friction.
atypisch [aˑˈtyːpiʃ], *a. Med: etc:* atypic(al).
Ätz, *m.* -es/.=**Atzung,** *q.v. under* **atzen** II. 2.
Ätz-, *comb.fm.* (*a*) corrosive . . . ; **Ätzgas** *n,* corrosive gas; **Ätzwirkung** *f,* corrosive action; (*b*) *Ch:* caustic . . . ; **Ätzalkalien** *npl,* caustic alkalis; **Ätzkalk** *m,* caustic lime; (*c*) *Engr:* etching . . . ; **Ätzgrund** *m,* etching-ground; **Ätznadel** *f,* etching-needle; (*d*) *Tex: Calico-printing:* discharge . . . ; **Ätzartikel** *mpl,* discharge (-printed) goods; **Ätzverfahren** *n,* discharge process.
Ätzammoniak, *n. Ch:* caustic ammonia; ammonia water, ammonia liquor.
Ätzbad, *n. Engr:* etching-bath.
ätzbar, *a.* (*a*) (metal, etc.) that can be corroded; (*b*) *Engr:* (surface) that can be etched; (*c*) *Dy:* dischargeable (fabric), (fabric) from which the colour can be bleached out.
Ätzbeizdruck, *m.*=**Ätzdruck** 2.
Ätzbeize, *f. Dy: etc:* mordant; *Calico-printing:* discharge.
Ätzbild, *n. Engr:* etching.
Ätzdruck, *m.* **1.** *Engr:* (proof of an) etching. **2.** *Tex:* discharge printing (of calico).
Ätze, *f.* -/-n. **1.**=**Ätzung,** *q.v. under* **ätzen**[1] II. 2. **2.** *Engr:* etching fluid; *Tex:* (chemical used as) discharge.
Atzel, *f.* -/-n. **1.** *Orn:* magpie. **2.** *A.Cost: F:* pied wig, piebald wig.
atzen. I. *v.* **1.** *v.i.* (*haben*) (*of animal*) to feed; (*of cattle, deer*) to graze. **2.** *v.tr.* (*a*) to feed (child, animal); to cram (goose); **sich a.**=I. 1; (*b*) *Ven:* to lure (animal) with a bait.
II. *vbl s.* **1. Atzen,** *n. in vbl senses.* **2. Atzung,** *f.* (*a*)=II. 1; (*b*) food; (*for animals*) fodder, feed; *Ven:* bait.
ätzen[1]. I. *v.tr.* (*a*) (*of acid, etc.*) to corrode, attack, eat into, eat away, bite into (metal, etc.); to etch (glass, metal); (*b*) *Engr:* to etch; **eine Platte ä.,** to etch a plate; (*c*) *Med:* to cauterize, sear (wound, etc.); (*d*) *Tex:* to discharge, bleach the colour out of (a fabric).
II. *vbl s.* **1. Ätzen,** *n.*=II. 2. **2. Ätzung,** *f.* (*a*) *in vbl senses; also:* corrosion; *Med:* cauterization, cautery; *Tex:* discharge; (*b*) *Engr: Print:* (i) etched plate; (ii) etching; *Print:* line-block.
III. *pr.p. & a.* **ätzend,** *in vbl senses; esp.* corrosive (liquid, poison, etc.); caustic (liquid, etc.); mordant, biting, caustic, pungent (wit, remark, etc.).
ätzen[2] *v.*=**atzen.**
Ätzer, *m.* -s/-. *Art:* etcher, aquafortist.
Ätzfigur, *f.* (*a*) *Engr:* etched figure; (*b*) *Cryst:* etching-figure.
Ätzgas, *n.* corrosive gas.
Ätzgift, *n.* corrosive poison; caustic poison.
Ätzgrund, *m. Engr:* etching-ground.
atzi, *int. Hum:* (*sneeze*) atishoo!
Ätzkali, *n. Ch:* caustic potash.
Ätzkalilauge, *f.* caustic potash lye, *Ind:* potassium lye.
Ätzkalk, *m. Ch: Ind:* caustic lime, *esp.* (**gebrannter**) **Ä.,** quicklime; **gelöschter Ä.,** slaked, slack(ed), lime.
Ätzkalklösung, *f. Pharm: etc:* lime-water.
Ätzkasten, *m. Engr:* etching-bath, -trough.
Ätzkraft, *f.* (*a*) corrosive power; corrosiveness; (*b*) *Ch:* causticity.
Ätzkunst, *f.* (art of) etching.
Ätzlack, *m. Engr: etc:* etching-varnish; resist.
Ätzlauge, *f. Ind:* caustic (potash *or* soda) lye.

Ätzmanier, *f.* (technique of) etching.
Ätzmittel, *n.* (*a*) corrosive; (*b*) *Ch: Med:* caustic; (*c*) *Tex: Calico-printing:* (chemical used as) discharge.
Ätznadel, *f. Engr:* etching-needle.
Ätznatron, *n. Ch:* caustic soda.
Ätznatronlauge, *f.* caustic soda lye.
Ätzpapp, *m. Tex: Calico-printing:* resist.
Ätzprobe, *f. Ind:* (*a*) etching test; (*b*) sample for an etching test.
Ätzschicht, *f. Engr: Phot.Engr:* resist.
Ätzsilber, *n. Ch: Med:* lunar caustic, (fused) silver nitrate.
Ätzspitze, *f. Tex:* burnt-out lace (*with holes made by chemical processes*).
Ätzstein, *m.* **1.**=**Ätzkali. 2.**=**Ätzsilber.**
Ätzstift, *m. Med: etc:* stick of caustic.
Ätzstoff, *m.* (*a*) corrosive; (*b*) *Ch:* caustic.
Ätzsublimat, *n. Ch:* corrosive sublimate, mercuric chloride.
Ätztinte, *f. Engr:* etching ink.
Atzung, *f. see* **Atzen II.**
Ätzung, *f. see* **Ätzen II.**
Ätzverfahren, *n.* (*a*) *Ch: Ind:* corrosive process; caustic process; (*b*) *Engr:* etching process; (*c*) *Tex: Calico-printing:* discharge process.
Ätzwasser, *n.* (*a*) *Engr:* etching fluid, *esp.* aqua fortis, nitric acid; (*b*) *Dy: etc:* mordant.
Ätzwirkung, *f.* corrosive action.
Ätzzeichnung, *f. Engr:* etching, etched engraving.
Au[1], *f.* **-/-en**=**Aue.**
au[2], *int.* (*a*) (*expressing pain or annoyance*) ouch! ow! oh! (*b*) (*pained astonishment*) **au (weh)!** oh! oh dear! (*c*) **au Backe!** you don't say! did you ever! *P:* blimey! crikey! (*d*) (*enthusiastic approval*) **au fein!** oh, lovely!
Aubade [o·ˈbaːdə], *f.* **-/-n.** *Mus:* (*a*) aubade; (*b*) dawn-song.
Aubergine [o·bɛrˈʒiːnə], *f.* **-/-n.** *Bot:* aubergine, egg-plant, brinjal; *Cu:* aubergine.
Auboden, *m. Agr:* river-meadow; well-watered meadow (soil).
auch. 1. *adv.* (*a*) (*in addition*) also; too; as well; **du kommst a.,** you are coming too, as well, you are also coming; **wir sind a. eingeladen,** we have been invited also, too; we have also been asked; **er ist Dichter und a. Maler,** he is a poet and also a painter; **diese darfst du a. behalten,** you may keep these as well, too, you may also keep these; **es ist schwierig und manchmal a. gefährlich,** it is difficult and sometimes (also) dangerous; **ich kann nicht, ich will (aber) a. nicht,** I can't, and what's more I won't, I don't want to; **nicht nur . . . sondern a. . . . ,** not only . . . but also; (*b*) (*equality*) also; too; as well; *Lit:* likewise; **er hat es a. gesehen,** he also, too, saw it, he saw it too, as well, *Lit:* he likewise saw it; **a. ich war in Arkadien geboren,** I too was born in Arcadia; **ich will a. etwas davon haben,** I want some too, as well; **soviel Verstand habe ich a.!** I've got enough sense to know that too! **wenn er es darf, dann darf ich's a.,** if he may do it, then I may too, (then) so may I; if he is allowed to do it, (then) so am I; **wenn du nicht kommst, so komme ich a. nicht,** if you don't come I won't (come) either; I won't come if you don't; **wie bei uns, so a. bei ihnen,** as with us, so it is with them, *Lit:* so also, so likewise, with them; **sein Bruder war bankrott, und a. er war in bedrängter Lage,** his brother was bankrupt and he too was in sore straits; **a. so einer,** another of the same kind, such another; **er ist a. so einer,** *F:* he's just (such) another; **sowohl . . . als a. . . . , . . .** as well as . . . ; **sowohl Männer als a. Frauen sind . . . ,** men as well as women, men and women alike, are . . . ; **sowohl er als a. seine Eltern waren . . . ,** he, as well as his parents, was . . . , he, like his parents, was . . . ; (*c*) (*as response to a statement*) **ich a.,** so am I, so can I, so do I, so shall I, so did I, so was I, *etc.*; **ich bin müde — ich a.,** I'm tired—so am I; **mich friert — mich a.,** I'm cold—so am I. **ich werde zurückkommen — ich a.,** I shall come back—so shall I; **ich habe es satt — ich a.,** I'm fed up with it—so am I, *F:* same here, me too! **er hat abgelehnt — und sein Partner a.,** he refused—and so did his partner; **er darf nicht gehen — du a. nicht,** he is not to go—nor are you, nor you either; **sie kann nicht singen — ihre Schwester a. nicht,** she can't sing—nor, neither, can her sister, (and) her sister can't (sing) either; **du warst nicht dabei? — wir a. nicht,** you weren't there?—neither, nor, were we, we weren't there either; **du bist unverschämt! — du a.!** you're impudent!—so are you! **du bist ein Schwein! — du a.!** you're a pig!—so are you! you're another! *F:* (the) same to you! (*d*) too; even; **a. Heiden glauben an eine Gottheit,** heathens too believe in a divinity; **a. du wirst mich einmal betrügen,** you too will one day betray me; **a. du, mein Sohn Brutus!** *et tu Brute!* **a. seine Feinde lieben,** to love even one's enemies; **a. in Kriegszeiten,** even in time of war; **a. die flüchtigste Reue,** even the most transitory remorse; **a. nicht ein Zeichen, das geringste Zeichen, der Liebe,** not even, never, a sign, the faintest sign, of love; **a. nicht das Beste ist vollkommen,** even the best is not perfect, not even the best is perfect; **a. nicht einer,** not a single one, never a one; **er ging fort, ohne a. nur auf Wiedersehen zu sagen,** he went away without even, without so much as, saying goodbye. **2.** *adv. & conj.* (*concessive*) **wäre es a. wahr . . . ,** even if it were true . . . ; **wie dem a. sei . . . ,** however that may be . . . , be that as it may . . . , at all events . . . ; **a. wenn . . . , wenn . . . a. . . . ,** even if . . . , even though . . . ; **a. wenn es ihm mißlänge,** even if, even though, he failed; **wenn er a. nicht durchkommt,** even if he does not get through; *Lit:* **ob er a. gleich ein König ist . . . ,** even though he be a king . . . ; **wäre es a. verfehlt zu glauben, daß . . . ,** even if, even though, it were a mistake to believe that . . . ; **wenn er a. noch so mutig ist, sei er a. noch so mutig, so mutig er a. ist,** however brave he is, *Lit:* be he never so brave; **mag sie a. noch so fähig sein, ich habe sie doch nicht gern,** however capable she is, I still don't care for her, *F:* she can be as capable as she likes, but I still don't care for her; **soviel sie a. lachten, er gab es nicht auf,** however much they laughed, he still went on trying; **so lang es a. dauern mag,** however long it lasts, may last; **so reizvoll London a. ist . . . ,** delightful as London is . . . ; **was . . . a. (immer), whatever . . . ; was er a. immer sagen mag, was er a. sagt,** whatever he says, may say; for all he may say; **was a. immer geschehen mag, was a. geschieht, bleibe ruhig,** whatever happens, keep calm; **was du a. hören magst, sage nichts,** whatever you hear, say nothing; **was es a. immer kosten mag,** whatever, however much, it costs; **was immer du a. wählen magst, du hast ein gutes Geschäft gemacht,** whichever you choose, you have a good bargain; **wer . . . a. immer,** whoever; **wer er a. immer sein mag,** whoever he may be; **wo es a. immer sein mag,** wherever it is, may be; **wann immer er a. kommen mag, er ist stets willkommen,** whenever he chooses to come, he is always welcome. **3.** *conj.* also, in addition; **a. möchte ich darauf hinweisen, daß . . . ,** I should also like, in addition I should like, to draw attention to the fact that. . . . **4.** *emotive particle* (*a*) (*often not translated*) **a. gut! a. recht!** oh, all right! just as you like! **man kann es (aber) a. anders machen,** yes, but it can (also) be done differently; **oder könnte man es a. anders machen?** or could it be done some other way? (*b*) (*unstressed; inviting a reassuring answer*) really; **hörst du a. zu?** are you really listening **bist du a. bereit, das zu tun?** are you really prepared, are you sure you're prepared, to do it? **ist es (aber) a. bewiesen?** is it really proved? **kann ich mich (aber) a. auf ihn verlassen?** can I really rely on him? (*c*) really; **er hat es vorausgesagt, und es ist a. geschehen,** he predicted it and it really happened; **er versprach, uns zu besuchen, und er ist a. gekommen,** he promised to visit us and he really came; **ich habe es versprochen, und ich will a. Wort halten,** I've promised and I'm going to keep my word, and I'm really going to do it; (*d*) (*nuance of exasperation*) **den Teufel a.!** damn it all, no! **er hätte (doch) a. antworten können,** he could have answered, couldn't he? surely he could have answered? **warum hast du dich a. so schlecht benommen?** why did you behave so badly? **man hat doch a. seine Rechte,** after all, one has one's rights; one has one's rights, hasn't one? (*nuance of remonstrance*) **so krank bist du a. (wieder) nicht,** you're not as ill as all that; (*e*) (*not translated*) **wozu (denn) a.? weshalb a.?** why (on earth) should you? what (earthly) use would it be? **was hätte es a. für einen Sinn gehabt?** what would have been the point of it? (*f*) **danke a.!** (oh) thank you! much obliged (I'm sure)!
Auchbuchhändler, *m. Com:* shopkeeper (*chemist, U.S: druggist, draper, etc.*) selling books as a sideline.
Auchchrist, *m.* nominal Christian.
Audh [aud]. *Pr.n.n.* **-s.** *Geog:* Oudh.
Audienz [audiˈɛnts], *f.* **-/-en,** audience, hearing; (*a*) (*of king, etc.*) **j-m eine A. gewähren, erteilen, j-n in A. empfangen,** to grant s.o. an audience; **eine A. beim König erhalten, beim König zur A. vorgelassen werden,** to have an audience of the King; (*b*) *Jur: A:* hearing (by the court); sitting, session.
Audienzsaal, *m.,* **Audienzzimmer,** *n.* audience chamber, presence-chamber.
Audiometer [audio·ˈmeːtər], *n.* **-s/-,** audiometer.
Audion [ˈaudiɔn], *n.* **-s/-s & -en** [audiˈoːnen]. *W.Tel:* audion, vacuum tube.
Audionempfänger, *m. W.Tel:* audion receiver.
Audionröhre, *f. W.Tel:* audion, vacuum, valve.
audio-visuell [ˌaudio·vi·zu·ˈɛl], *a. Sch:* audio-visual.
Audiphon [audi·ˈfoːn], *n.* **-s/-e,** audiphone.
Auditeur [audi·ˈtøːr], *m.* **-s/-e.** *Mil.Jur: A:* judge advocate (at court martial).
auditiv [audi·ˈtiːf], *a.* (*of pers.*) especially sensitive to sound-impressions; given to auditory images.
Auditor [auˈdiːtor], *m.* **-s/-en** [-di·ˈtoːrən]. **1.** hearer, listener, auditor. **2.** (*a*) *Ecc.Jur:* auditor; (*b*)=**Auditeur;** (*c*) *Jur: A:* assessor.
Auditorium [audi·ˈtoːrium], *n.* **-s/-rien. 1.** *Sch: etc:* lecture-room, -hall, -theatre; **das A. maximum der Hochschule,** the great (lecture-) hall of the university. **2.** (*assembly*) audience.
Aue[1], *f.* **-/-n. 1.** *A:* (*surviving only in place-names*) river; watercourse. **2.** (river-)island. **3.** well-watered meadow(s) *or* meadowland; river-meadow(s); *Poet:* **grünende Auen,** verdant meadows, meads.
Aue[2], *m.* **-/-n.** *Dial:* ewe.
Aueboden, *m.*=**Auboden.**
Auengrün, *n.* (*colour*) grass-green.
Auenhederich, *m. Bot:* treacle-mustard.
Auenwald, *m.* wood in a river-valley.
Auer, *m.* **-s/-**=**Auerochs.**
Auerbrenner, *m.* Auer burner; Welsbach type burner; mantle gas-burner.
Auerhahn, *m. Orn:* (cock) capercaillie, wood grouse, great grouse.
Auerhenne, *f. Orn:* (hen) capercaillie, (hen of the) wood grouse, great grouse.
Auerhuhn, *n. Orn:* (*generic*) capercaillie, wood grouse, great grouse.
Auerkalb, *n. Z:* young aurochs, young urus.
Auerlicht, *n.*=**Auerbrenner.**
Auermetall, *n.* Auer metal (*cerium-iron alloy used in gas-lighters, etc.*).
Auerochs, *m. Z:* aurochs, urus, wild ox.
Auerwild, *n. Ven:* (*sg. or coll.*) capercaillie, wood grouse, great grouse.
auf[1]. I. *abs. use.* **auf!** up! get up! come on! **frisch auf!** come along! come on! let's be off! **Glück auf!** (*esp. as traditional miners' greeting*) good luck! **'Auf!'** (*sign on lift*) 'Up'.

II. **auf,** *prep.* (*see also* **aufs**). **1.** (+*dat., answering question* '*where?*') (*a*) (up)on, on top of (sth.); **sie saß auf dem Stuhl,** she was sitting on the chair; **das Päckchen liegt auf dem Tisch,** the parcel is lying on the table; **du wirst die Vase auf dem Schrank finden,** you'll find the vase on top of the cupboard; **auf der Bühne,** on the stage; **auf dem Fahrrad,** on one's bicycle; **auf dem Pferde,** on horseback; *Aut: Rac:* **auf (einem) Mercedes,** in a Mercedes; **er stand auf dem Berg,** he was standing on the (top of the) mountain; **seine Felder sind auf dem Berg,** his fields are on the mountain-side; (*b*) **auf einer Insel,** on an island; **auf Capri,** on Capri; **auf den Britischen Inseln,** in the British Isles; **auf der Straße,** in, *U.S:* on, the street; **auf dem Hof,** in the courtyard; **auf dem Wege, auf dem Felde, auf der Wiese,** on the path, in the field, meadow; **auf der Welt,** in the world; **auf dem Flur,** in the hall; **auf dem Kirchhof,** in the churchyard; **auf dem Markt,** at, in, the market; (*esp. in hotel*) **auf seinem Zimmer sein,** to be in one's room; **auf dem Lande,** in the country; **auf dem Bild,** in the picture; **auf dem Relief,** in the relief; (*c*) at (an institution, etc.); **auf der Post,** at the post-office; **auf der Schule,** at school; **auf der Universität,** (studying) at the University; **auf dem Feste,** at the party; (*d*) **auf der Lauer sein,** to lie in wait; **sei auf der Hut!** be on your guard! **auf der Wache,** on guard, on the look-out; **auf der Reise,** on the journey; while travelling; **ich habe es auf der Reise gelesen,** I read it during the journey; **auf der Reise sein,** to be on a journey; to be travelling; **auf (der) Wanderschaft,** on one's travels; **auf Urlaub,** on leave, holiday, *U.S:* vacation; **auf der Jagd sein,** to be hunting; (*e*) in; on; **blind auf einem Auge,** blind in one eye; **taub auf einem Ohr,** deaf in one ear; **lahm auf einer Seite,** paralysed on one side; (*f*) **es hat nichts auf sich,** it doesn't mean anything, there's nothing in it; it's nothing; **hat es etwas auf sich?** does it mean anything? is there anything in it? **2.** (+*acc., answering question*

'*where to?*') (*a*) on (to); on top of; up; **sie setzte sich auf den Stuhl,** she sat down on the chair; **ich legte das Buch auf den Tisch,** I put the book (down) on the table; **das Kind kletterte auf das Fensterbrett,** the child climbed (up) on to the window-sill; **er stellte die Vase auf den Schrank,** he put the vase on top of the cupboard; **auf ein Pferd steigen,** to get on (to), to mount, a horse; **auf den Berg gehen,** to go up the mountain; **auf das Schloß, auf die Burg, gehen,** to go (up) to the castle; **auf die Bühne gehen,** to appear on the stage, to come, go, on to the stage (*cp.* (*d*)); (*b*) (in)to; **sie ging auf die Straße, auf den Hof, auf das Feld, auf die Wiese, auf den Kirchhof,** she went into the street, the yard, the field, the meadow, the churchyard; **auf die Insel Wight fahren,** to go to the Isle of Wight; **auf den Markt gehen,** to go to (the) market; **auf sein Zimmer gehen,** to go to one's room; **sich auf den Weg machen,** to set out, to start on one's way; **ein Kind auf die Welt bringen,** to bring a child into the world; **auf die Welt kommen,** to come into the world; (*c*) **auf j-n, etwas, zugehen, losgehen,** to go towards, up to, s.o., sth.; **als er mich sah, kam er gleich auf mich zu,** when he saw me he came straight towards, up to, me; **er lief auf das Ziel los,** he ran towards the goal; **es geht auf Mitternacht zu,** it's getting on for, *U.S:* going on, midnight; **es geht auf den Winter (zu),** it will soon be winter, winter will soon be here; (*d*) to (an institution, etc.); **auf die Post gehen,** to go to the post-office; **auf die Schule, auf die Universität, gehen,** to go to school, to the University; **auf das Gemeindeamt gehen,** to go to the council offices; **auf die Bühne gehen,** to go on the stage, to become an actor, an actress (*cp.* (*a*)); (*e*) **auf Reisen gehen,** to go on a journey; **auf die Wanderschaft gehen,** to set off on one's travels; **auf die Jagd gehen,** to go hunting; **sich auf die Lauer legen,** to lie in wait (for s.o.); (*f*) (*in grammatical terminology*) **Feminina enden auf -a,** feminines end in -a; **Wörter, die auf -us enden,** words ending in -us. **3.** (*+acc.; the uses of* '*auf*' *as a link between verb or adj. and its complement are shown under the respective words that take this construction, e.g. for* **stolz auf etwas sein** *see* **stolz**) (*a*) **auf j-n herabsehen,** to look down on s.o.; **er blickte mit Wohlgefallen auf das Werk seiner Hände,** he looked complacently at his handiwork; **auf die Uhr sehen,** to look at the clock; **auf j-n, etwas, hören,** to listen to s.o., sth.; **du solltest auf seinen Rat hören,** you ought to listen to his advice; **auf etwas lauschen,** to listen to, for, sth.; **j-s Blick, j-s Aufmerksamkeit, auf etwas lenken,** to direct, call, s.o.'s attention to sth.; **seinen Blick, seine Aufmerksamkeit, auf etwas richten, wenden,** to direct, to turn, one's attention to sth.; **auf etwas achten,** to take notice of sth., to pay attention to sth.; **auf etwas hinweisen, zeigen,** to point to sth., to point sth. out; (*b*) to; down to; **sie haben den Preis auf drei Mark herabgesetzt,** they have reduced the price to three marks; **die Truppe wurde auf die Hälfte reduziert,** the troop was reduced to half its number; **eine Schuld auf Heller und Pfennig bezahlen,** to pay a debt to the last penny; *Mth:* **Brüche auf einen gemeinsamen Nenner bringen,** to reduce fractions to a common denominator; *see also* **bis**[1] I. 4 (*b*); (*c*) **auf Abenteuer ausgehen,** to go out in search of adventure, *A:* to quest for adventure; **etwas auf Druckfehler hin durchlesen,** to read sth. through for, in search of, misprints; **auf Geld aus sein,** to be out for, to be after, money; *F:* **sich auf etwas spitzen,** to be keen on (getting) sth.; **die Bemerkung war auf dich abgesehen,** the remark was intended for, aimed at, you; **sich auf den Krieg rüsten,** to prepare for war; *see also* **aus** II. 3, **herauskommen** 6; (*d*) **etwas auf etwas ausdehnen,** to extend sth. to sth., to extend sth. to include sth.; **seinen Handel auf Asien ausdehnen,** to extend one's trade to Asia; **sich auf etwas erstrecken,** to extend to sth.; (*e*) **sich auf Gnade und Ungnade ergeben,** to surrender unconditionally; **j-m auf Gnade und Ungnade ausgeliefert sein,** to be at s.o.'s mercy; **auf Tod und Leben kämpfen,** to fight to the death; **es geht auf Tod und Leben,** it's a matter of life and death; *F:* **es geht auf Biegen oder Brechen,** it's neck or nothing; (*f*) **auf ihre Anfrage antwortete ich, daß . . . ,** in reply to her inquiry I said that . . . ; **sich auf etwas freuen,** to look forward to sth.; **auf etwas hoffen,** to hope for sth.; **auf eine Frage antworten,** to answer, to give an answer to, a question; **auf etwas zielen,** to aim at sth.; **sich auf etwas einlassen,** to agree to do sth.; **sich auf etwas, j-n, verlassen,** to depend, rely, on sth., s.o.; **auf etwas sinnen,** to be thinking about, of, sth.; **er sann auf Rache,** he was meditating revenge, he was thinking how to get his revenge; **sich auf etwas besinnen,** to remember sth.; **wie kam er auf den Gedanken?** how did he come to think of that? what gave him that idea? (*g*) **das tat er auf Befehl seines Vaters,** he did that at his father's command; **auf seine Bitte ging ich mit,** at his request I went with him; **auf ihr Versprechen hin,** on the strength of her promise; **auf ein bloßes Gerücht (hin),** on the strength of a mere rumour. **4.** (*time*) (*+acc.*) (*a*) for; **auf ewig,** for ever; **ich muß auf einige Wochen nach Frankreich fahren,** I have to go to France for a few weeks; **entschuldigen Sie mich bitte auf einen Augenblick,** excuse me (for) a moment, please; **er ist auf vierzehn Tage hier,** he is here for a fortnight; he intends to stay here for a fortnight; *see also* **Dauer**; (*b*) until, till; **wir werden es auf Montag verschieben,** we'll postpone it till Monday; **sie mußten die Diskussion auf eine bessere Gelegenheit verschieben,** they had to postpone the discussion till a more convenient time; **auf Wiedersehen,** goodbye; **auf Morgen,** till tomorrow; **auf später,** till later; *see also* **bis**[1] I. 2 (*b*); (*c*) **die Nacht von Montag auf Dienstag,** the night from Monday to Tuesday; **von heute auf morgen,** from one day to the next; at very short notice; (*d*) after, upon; **auf Regen folgt Sonne,** sun comes after rain; **er trank Glas auf Glas des feurigen Weines,** he drank glass after glass, glass upon glass, of the fiery wine; **es folgte Katastrophe auf Katastrophe,** one disaster followed the other, disaster followed disaster. **5.** (*mode*) (*+acc.*) (*a*) **auf diese Weise,** in this way; **ich tue es auf meine Weise,** I do it my own way, *U.S:* I do it in my own way, I do it my way; **auf den ersten Blick,** at first sight, at first glance; **auf Sicht,** at sight; **auf einen Schlag,** at a blow; **sieben auf einen Streich,** seven at one blow, at a blow; **etwas auf Anhieb tun,** to do sth. first go; **das Glas auf einen Zug leeren,** to empty the glass at a draught; **etwas auf gut Glück tun,** to do sth. at a venture; **ich bin auf gut Glück hingegangen,** I took a chance and went; **auf eigene Gefahr,** at one's own risk; **auf eigene Kosten,** at one's own expense; **auf Kredit,** on credit; *F:* **auf Borg, auf Pump,** on loan, *F:* on tick; (*b*) **auf Deutsch, auf Englisch,** in German, in English; **auf gut Deutsch,** (i) in good German; (ii) *F:* plainly, forthrightly, in plain language; (*c*) (*with superlative*) (*usually* **aufs,** *q.v.*) **auf das beste,** as well as possible; **wir werden sie auf das schönste bewirten,** we shall entertain them as nicely as possible; (*d*) **auf jeden Fall, auf alle Fälle,** in any case; **das sollst du auf keinen Fall machen,** you mustn't do that on any account. **6.** (*a*) **auf Ehre, auf sein Wort, schwören,** to swear on one's honour; **auf die Bibel schwören,** to swear on the Bible, on the Book; **sie schwört auf diese Medizin,** she swears by this medicine; (*b*) **auf j-s Gesundheit trinken,** to drink to s.o., to drink s.o.'s health; **auf bessere Tage!** to better days! **auf Ihr Wohl! auf Ihre Gesundheit!** your health! **auf j-n ein Gedicht machen,** to write a poem to s.o.; **ein Gedicht auf die Freundschaft,** a poem to friendship.

III. **auf,** *adv.* **1.** on(wards); **von Kindheit, von klein, auf,** from one's childhood (on, onwards); **von Jugend auf,** from one's youth. **2.** up(wards); **auf und nieder,** up and down; **die Äste schwangen im Winde auf und nieder,** the branches swung up and down in the wind; **auf und ab,** up and down; backwards and forwards, to and fro; **auf und ab rennen,** to run up and down, to and fro; **im Zimmer auf und ab gehen,** to walk up and down the room; **es geht sehr auf und ab mit ihm,** (i) his affairs are very unsettled; (ii) his health is very uncertain, *F:* he's very up and down; **auf und davon gehen,** to go away; **sich auf und davon machen,** to make off. **3.** (*elliptical use with vbl element understood*) **die Tür ist auf** (=**aufgegangen**), the door is open; **endlich hatte ich die Kiste auf** (=**aufbekommen**), at last I had the box open; *see also* **aufhaben, aufsein. 4.** *subst. phr.* **das Auf und Ab des Lebens,** the ups and downs of life; **das Auf und Ab der Wege,** (*in hilly country*) the ups and downs of the roads; **das Buch hat ein Auf und Ab erlebt,** the book has had (its) ups and downs.

IV. *conj.* **auf daß,** so that; *B:* **du sollst deinen Vater und deine Mutter ehren, auf daß du lange lebest . . . ,** honour thy father and thy mother: that thy days may be long . . .; *see also* **daß** 5 (*c*).

auf- I. *vbl pref. sep.* (*cp. Note to* **ab-**) *denoting:* **1.** (*a*) (*position on top*) **einen Hut aufhaben,** to have a hat on; (*b*) (*placing on top*) **einen Hut aufsetzen,** to put a hat on; **j-m etwas aufbürden,** to burden s.o. with sth., to impose sth. on s.o.; **Bücher, usw., aufhäufen,** to pile up books, etc. **2.** (*a*) (*upward motion*) **aufstehen,** to get up; **etwas aufhängen,** to hang sth. up; **etwas aufheben,** to pick sth. up; **auftauchen,** to appear; **aufspringen,** to jump up; (*b*) (*upright position*) **aufsein,** to be up; **aufbleiben,** to stay up; **aufragen,** to tower. **3.** (*distension*) **etwas aufblähen, aufblasen,** to blow sth. up, inflate sth., distend sth.; **einen Reifen aufpumpen,** to blow up, inflate, a tyre; **aufgehen,** to swell, to expand. **4.** (*separation*) **einen Stoff auflösen,** to dissolve a substance; **eine Naht auftrennen,** to undo, *U.S:* rip, a seam. **5.** (*a*) (*starting of an action*) **aufhorchen,** to prick up one's ears; **aufbrüllen,** to give a (loud) roar *or* bellow; **aufleuchten,** to flash; to shine out; (*b*) (*awakening or startling of s.o., animal, etc.*) **aufscheuchen,** to disturb (wild animal, bird); to start (hare, etc.); **aufregen,** to excite (s.o.); **aufwecken,** to awaken (s.o.); to rouse (s.o.); **aufwachen,** to awake(n), to wake (up); **aufschrecken,** to startle (s.o., game, etc.); to start, to jump, to be startled. **6.** (*completion of action expressed in the verb*) **etwas aufbrauchen,** to use sth. up; **etwas aufessen,** to eat sth. up; **Geld aufwenden,** to use, spend, money; **das Geschirr aufwaschen,** to wash up the dishes. **7.** (*a*) (*opening, state of being open*) **aufsein, aufbleiben,** to be open, to stay open; **die Tür aufmachen, aufschließen,** to open, to unlock, the door; **die Tür ist auf,** the door is open; **etwas aufbrechen, aufstechen,** to break, prick, sth. open; (*b*) (*in connexion with* **zu-**) **die Tür, usw., auf- und zumachen, auf- und zuschließen,** to open and close the door, to unlock and lock the door; **das Kind macht die Tür ständig auf und zu,** the child keeps opening and closing the door.

II. **Auf-, auf-.** (*prefixed to nouns, adjs, advbs.*) **1. aufeinander,** on (top of) one another. **2. Auffahrt,** *f.* ascension; **aufwärts,** upwards; **auf- und abwärts,** up(wards) and down(wards); **aufrecht,** upright; **aufrichtig,** upright, upstanding, honest.

-auf, *suff.* **1. wohlauf!** come on! **2.** (*upward motion*) **herauf, hinauf,** up here, up there; **bergauf,** uphill; up the mountain; **stromauf,** upstream; **treppauf,** up the stairs.

Auf[2], *m.* -(e)s/-e. *Dial: Orn:*=**Uhu.**

aufächzen, *v.i. sep.* (*haben*) (laut) **a.,** to give, utter, a (loud) groan, moan, wail.

aufackern, *v.tr. sep.* (*a*) to plough up (field, etc.); to plough (land); to break (ground); **den Boden leicht a.,** to scratch, rake over, the soil; (*b*) to turn up (bones, coins, etc.) (with the plough).

aufarbeiten. I. *v.tr. sep.* **1.** (*a*) to get through, finish off, *F:* polish off (accumulated work, etc.); **Rückstände a.,** to clear off arrears of work; to get up to date with one's work; (*b*) to use up, finish up, get through (provisions, etc.). **2.** (*a*) to get (sth.) open; **einen Deckel a.,** to prize, prise, up a lid, to prize, prise, a lid open; (*b*) **ich habe mir die Hände aufgearbeitet,** my hands are sore from working. **3. sich aufarbeiten,** to work oneself up; to work one's way up. **4.** (*a*) to work up (raw material) (**zu,** into); to process (material); (*b*) to recondition, renovate (sth.); to do (sth.) up; to refurbish (furniture, etc.).

II. *vbl s.* **Aufarbeiten** *n.*, **Aufarbeitung** *f. in vbl senses; also:* renovation.

aufästen, *v.tr. sep. Arb:* to head (down) (tree).

aufatmen, *v.i. sep.* (*haben*) (*a*) to draw breath; to fetch one's breath; (*b*) to breathe again; to heave, fetch, draw, a sigh; to sigh (with relief, etc.); **ich atmete wieder auf,** I breathed again; I sighed with relief; **jetzt kann ich wieder a.,** now I can breathe (freely) again, now I am free to breathe; **er atmete erleichtert auf,** he breathed, heaved, a sigh of relief.

aufätzen[1], *v.tr. sep.* to open (sth.) with caustic *or* corrosive; to take the skin off (arm, face, etc.) with a caustic *or* corrosive.

aufätzen[2], *v.tr. sep. Husb:* to feed up (animal); to cram (geese).

aufbacken, *v.* (*conj. like* **backen**) I. *v.tr.* **1.** to bake (sth.) on (**auf**+*acc.*, to). **2.** to re-bake; to warm up (bread, vegetables, etc.); to crisp (rolls, etc.) in the oven. **3. sämtliche Mehlvorräte a.,** to use up all one's stocks of flour for baking.

II. **aufbacken,** *v.i.* (*sein*) **auf etwas** *acc.* **a.,** to bake on to sth.; (*of earth, mud, etc.*) to cake on(to) sth.

aufbahren. *v.tr. sep.* to put (body, coffin) on the bier; to lay out (corpse); to put (body) to lie in

state; **aufgebahrt sein,** to lie (in mortuary, chapel, before the altar, etc.); (*of body of notable personage*) to lie in state; **Aufbahrung** *f* **eines Königs,** lying in state of a king.

Aufbahrungshalle, *f.* mortuary (at cemetery).

aufbänken, *v.tr.sep. Mch: Nau:* to bank (up) (fires).

Aufbau, *m.* -(e)s/. **1.** (*a*) constructing, construction; erecting, erection; organizing, organization (of a society, etc.); setting up (of organization, etc.); building up (of structure, organization, new social order, etc.); *Sch:* **Schule, Abteilung einer Schule, die im A. (begriffen) ist,** school, school stream, in which further classes are being progressively introduced; (*b*) **sozialer A.,** social improvement; (*c*) *Ch:* synthesis (of compound); (*d*) *Atom.Ph:* artificial building up (of atoms); (*e*) = **Wiederaufbau. 2.** (*pl.* **Aufbauten**) structure, construction (of edifice, machine, organization, literary work, sonata, etc.); composition (of society, age-group, etc.); organization (of the State, etc.); build-up (of organization, etc.); *Pol.Ec: etc:* **horizontaler, vertikaler, A.,** horizontal, vertical, structure. **3.** (*pl.* **Aufbauten**) *Arch: Civ.E: Constr: etc:* superstructure; *Furn:* top (part) (of piece of furniture); *Veh:* body (of car, railway coach, etc.); *Av:* framework (of aircraft); **Aufbauten** *pl*, *N.Arch:* superstructures, upper works (of ship); *Th: Cin: etc:* sets.

Aufbauarbeit, *f.* construction work; constructive work; **(soziale) A.,** (work of) social improvement.

Aufbaueinheit, *f.* standardized unit *or* attachment (for machine-tool, etc.).

aufbauen. I. *v.tr. sep.* **1.** to build up; to erect; to construct; to put up (tent, booth, etc.); to set up (tent, booth, organization, etc.); to assemble, rig (machine, aircraft, etc.); to pile up, stack up (boxes, etc.) (in a heap); to build up (organization, new social order, etc.); to organize (society, etc.); *Ch:* to synthesize (compound); *Atom.Ph:* to build up (atoms) artificially; **ein (neues) Stockwerk (auf ein Haus) a., ein Haus a.,** to add a storey to a house; **ein Gebäude schnell a.,** to run up a building; **andere Gesellschaften bauen sich anders auf,** other societies are differently organized, have a different structure; **die Symphonie ist nach dem Prinzip der Sonate aufgebaut,** the symphony is constructed on the principle of the sonata; **der Roman ist geschickt aufgebaut,** the novel is cleverly constructed; **wieder a., neu a.,** to rebuild; to reconstruct; to refashion, reorganize (society, etc.); **aufbauend,** (i) constructive (methods, policy, criticism, etc.); (ii) *Ch:* synthetic (method, process, etc.); *F:* (*of pers.*) **sich a.,** to draw oneself up to one's full height; to stand, stiffly to attention. **2.** to base, found (a theory, etc.) (**auf** + *acc.*, on); **sich auf etwas** *dat. or acc.* **a., auf etwas** *dat. or acc.* **aufgebaut sein,** to be based, founded, on sth.; **er baut seine Theorie auf gewisse Beobachtungen auf,** he bases his theory on certain observations.

II. *vbl s.* **Aufbauen,** *n. in vbl senses; also:* construction; erection; *Ch:* synthesis. *Cp.* **Aufbau** 1.

Aufbauform, *f. Sch:* **höhere Schule in A.** = **Aufbauschule.**

Aufbauklassen, *f.pl. Sch:* continuation classes (in an elementary school).

aufbaumen, *v.i. sep.* (*sein*) *Ven:* (*of beast*) to climb a tree, to tree; (*of bird*) to perch on a tree.

aufbäumen, *v.tr. sep.* **1.** *Tex:* to beam (warp, yarn); to take up (the cloth) (in weaving). **2. sich aufbäumen,** (*of horse, etc.*) to rear; (*of pers., conscience, etc.*) **sich gegen etwas a.,** to jib at sth., to rise in protest against sth., to rebel against sth.; **sein Stolz bäumte sich dagegen auf,** his pride rebelled at it.

Aufbauprinzip, *n.* structural principle; principle governing the construction (of sth.).

Aufbauprozeß, *m.* constructive process; process of construction; *Ch:* synthetic process; *Biol:* anabolic process.

Aufbausalze, *n.pl. Physiol:* nutrient salts.

aufbauschen, *v.sep.* **1.** *v.tr.* (*a*) (*of wind, etc.*) to puff (sth.) out, swell (sth.) out; to cause (sth.) to bulge out; (*of wind*) to balloon (out) (dress, sail, etc.); to belly (out) (sail); (*b*) (*of pers.*) to exaggerate (a matter, piece of news, etc.); to inflate the importance of, to magnify (incident, etc.). **2.** *v.i.* (*sein*) & **sich aufbauschen,** to bulge (out); (*of dress, etc.*) to puff (out), swell out; (*with puff of wind*) to balloon out; (*of sail*) to balloon, belly.

Aufbauschule, *f. Sch:* secondary school based on six *or* seven years of elementary school preparation.

Aufbauten *see* **Aufbau** 2, 3.

Aufbauzug, *m. Sch:* continuation-class stream, *U.S:* continuation course group (in elementary school).

aufbegehren, *v.i. sep.* (*haben*) to protest; to bristle up, bridle up (in protest); *F:* to get one's back up, to kick (at sth.); **gegen j-n a.,** to rebel against s.o.; **gegen etwas a.,** to revolt at, against, sth.; to kick at, against, sth.; to be up in arms against sth.

aufbehalten, *v.tr. sep.* (*strong*) **1.** to keep (sth.) on; **den Hut a.,** to keep one's hat on, not to remove one's hat. **2.** to keep (sth.) open; **sie konnte die Augen kaum a.,** she could hardly keep her eyes open, keep her eyes from closing.

aufbeißen, *v.tr. sep.* (*strong*) to bite (sth.) open; to open (sth.) with one's teeth; to crack (nut) with one's teeth.

aufbeizen, *v.tr. sep.* **1.** = **aufätzen**[1]. **2.** to freshen (sth.) up with a mordant; to improve the appearance of (wood, etc.) by staining; to re-stain (wood, etc.).

aufbekommen, *v.tr. sep.* (*strong*) **1.** to get (door, flap, etc.) open. **2.** *Sch:* **wir haben heute zwanzig Seiten Geschichte aufbekommen,** today we were set, given, *U.S:* assigned, twenty-pages of history (to do). **3.** to eat up, finish (food); **ich kann die Suppe nicht a.,** I can't finish the soup.

aufbereiten. I. *v.tr. sep. Ind:* to prepare, process (raw material); *Min:* to dress, prepare (ore); **Erz naß a.,** to dress ore by the wet method; to wash ore; **Erz magnetisch a.,** to separate ore magnetically; *Economics: etc:* **Tabellen, usw., a.,** to prepare tables, etc.; **Zahlen a.,** to tabulate figures; **statistisches Material a.,** to process statistical material.

II. *vbl s.* **Aufbereiten** *n.*, **Aufbereitung** *f. in vbl senses; also:* preparation; separation (of ore); tabulation (of figures).

Aufbereitungsanlage, *f. Ind: Min:* preparing plant; *Min:* dressing plant.

Aufbereitungsmaschine, *f. Ind: Min:* preparing machine; *Min:* dressing machine.

aufbersten, *v.i. sep.* (*strong*) (*sein*) to burst open; (*of bark, skin, etc.*) to split (open); to crack; (*of lips*) to chap; (*of flower*) to burst into bloom.

aufbessern. I. *v.tr. sep.* (*a*) to ameliorate; to better; to improve; to raise, increase (salary, wages); *Fin:* to improve (prices, rates); (*b*) to recondition, renovate (sth.); to do (sth.) up; to refurbish (furniture, etc.).

II. *vbl s.* **Aufbesserung,** *f.* (*a*) *in vbl senses; also:* amelioration; betterment; improvement; (*b*) **A. des Gehalts,** increase of, in, salary; rise, *U.S:* raise, (in salary); *Fin:* **A. der Kurse,** improvement of, in, prices, rates; (*c*) renovation.

aufbewahren. I. *v.tr. sep.* to keep (sth.); to store (provisions, luggage, furniture, etc.); to lay (sth.) by; to preserve (documents, records, etc.), *Com:* to keep (records) on file; to have (documents, etc.) in one's keeping; to have custody of (documents, etc.); to hold (securities, etc.) on trust; **das wollen wir für die Zukunft, für später, a.,** we'll keep that, save that (up), for the future, for later on; **diese Äpfel lassen sich gut a.,** these apples keep well; **Dokumente bei einer Bank a. lassen,** to place documents on deposit, in safe custody, to deposit documents, with a bank; **das Elfenbeinkreuz wird in der Sakristei der Pfarrkirche zu X aufbewahrt,** the ivory cross is preserved in the sacristry of the parish church at X; **gut aufbewahrt,** (*of provisions, furniture, etc.*) safely stored; (*of document, etc.*) in safe-keeping, in safe custody; **sein Gepäck a. lassen,** to have one's luggage stored; *Rail:* to leave one's luggage at the cloak-room, *U.S:* to check one's baggage.

II. *vbl s.* **1. Aufbewahren,** *n.* = II. 2 (*a*). **2. Aufbewahrung,** *f.* (*a*) *in vbl senses; also:* storage (of provisions, luggage, furniture, etc.); preservation (of documents, records, etc.); custody (of documents, etc.); safe custody, safe-keeping; **j-m etwas zur A. geben,** to entrust s.o. with the care of sth.; to get s.o. to keep, mind, sth. for one; to leave sth. in s.o.'s custody; to deposit a document with a solicitor, etc.; (*b*) *Rail:* left luggage office, cloak-room, *U.S:* baggage room.

Aufbewahrer, *m.* custodian (of documents, etc.); depositary; trustee; holder (of securities) on trust; *Jur:* bailee.

Aufbewahrungsgebühr, *f.* charge(s) for storage; charge(s) for safe custody *or* safe-deposit services; *Rail:* cloak-room fee, *U.S:* checkroom fee.

Aufbewahrungsort, *m.* (*a*) depository, repository; store; depot; (*b*) **A. von Kunstgegenständen,** place where art treasures are housed, preserved; (*in catalogue, etc.*) **'(derzeitiger) A.',** 'present location'; **'A. unbekannt',** 'whereabouts unknown'.

Aufbewahrungspflicht, *f. Com: Jur:* obligation (on merchant, etc.) to preserve business records for a period of ten years.

Aufbewahrungsraum, *m.* storage room, store (-room); depository, repository; *Rail:* luggage-room, cloak-room, *U.S:* baggage room.

Aufbewahrungsschein, *m.* safe-custody receipt; *Rail: etc:* receipt for left luggage, *U.S:* (baggage) check.

Aufbewahrungszimmer, *n.* = **Aufbewahrungsraum.**

aufbiegen, *v.tr. sep.* (*strong*) **1.** to bend (sth.) up, upwards. **2.** to bend (sth.) open.

aufbieten. I. *v.tr. sep.* (*strong*) **1. ein Brautpaar a.,** to call the banns (of an engaged couple); (*of couple to be married*) **aufgeboten werden,** to have their banns published, called, *F:* to be asked in church. **2.** (*a*) to summon, call together; *Mil: A:* to call up (troops); to levy (troops); to raise (an army); **das (gesamte) Volk a.,** to call the nation to arms; (*b*) to summon up (one's courage, strength, etc.); to call forth (one's courage, etc.); to bring (one's influence, etc.) to bear; **seinen ganzen Mut a.,** to summon up, muster up, call on, call forth, all one's courage; **alle Kräfte a.,** to summon up all one's strength; to put forth all one's strength; to bring, call, all one's forces into play; **seine (ganze) Beredsamkeit zugunsten** + *gen.* **a.,** to summon up, exert, all one's eloquence in favour of . . . ; **sie mußte ihren ganzen Scharm a., um zu . . . ,** she had to exert, put forth, all her charm, she had to avail herself of all her charm, bring all her charm into play, in order to . . . ; **alle Mittel, alles (Mögliche), a., um etwas zu tun,** to use every possible means, to put, set, everything in motion, to bring every influence to bear, to leave no stone unturned, in order to do sth.

II. *vbl s.* **Aufbietung,** *f. in vbl senses; esp.* (*a*) **A. (eines Brautpaars),** publication of the banns; (*b*) summons; *Mil: A:* call to arms; levy (of troops); **A. des gesamten Volkes, A. in Masse,** levy in mass, *levée en masse;* (*c*) **unter, mit, A. aller Kräfte vermochte er, zu . . . ,** with the utmost effort, by exerting himself to the utmost, he was able to . . . . *Cp.* **Aufgebot.**

aufbinden, *v.tr. sep.* (*strong*) **1.** to tie (sth.) up; to tuck up (one's skirt, apron, etc.); to bind up (sheaf); to bind (corn) (into sheaves); **(sich** *dat.***) das Haar a.,** to tie up, fasten up, do up, bind (up), one's hair (*cp.* 3). **2.** (*a*) **j-m etwas a.,** to burden s.o. with sth. (as a duty, responsibility, etc.); *see also* **Rute;** (*b*) *F:* **j-m etwas, eins, a.,** to impose (up)on s.o.; to take a rise out of s.o.; to have s.o. on; to pull s.o.'s leg; to take s.o. in; *F:* to put one over on s.o., to pull a fast one on s.o., to make a sucker out of s.o., *U.S. & F:* to take s.o. for a ride; **j-m ein Märchen a.,** to tell s.o. a tall story, a thumping lie, a whopper; *see also* **Bär** 1; **sich** *dat.* **etwas a. lassen,** to allow oneself to be taken in, to swallow the bait; **er läßt sich alles a.,** he is easily taken in; he'll swallow anything; *F:* he's a (proper) sucker. **3.** to unknot; to untie, undo, loose (knot, scarf, bootlace, bonds, etc.); **sich** *dat.* **das Haar a.,** to undo, let down, unbind, one's hair (*cp.* 1).

Aufbiß, *m.* snack (taken with spirits).

aufblähen. I. *v.sep.* **1.** *v.tr.* (*a*) to inflate, distend; to puff out, blow out, bulge (one's cheeks); to blow up (bladder, etc.); (*of wind*) **die Segel a.,** to fill, belly (out), the sails; **sich a.,** (i) to become inflated, distended; to distend; (*of sail, etc.*) to balloon out; (*of sail*) to fill, to belly; (ii) (*of pers.*) to puff oneself up, to give oneself airs; (*b*) *Med:* to distend (stomach); to make (abdomen) flatulent; *Vet:* to distend (abdomen of cattle, sheep); to blow, hove (cattle, sheep); (*of stomach*) **sich a.,** to become distended; (*b*) *Pol.Ec:* to inflate (currency) **2.** *v.i.* (*sein*) *Vet:* (*of cattle, sheep*) to become hoven, blown, blasted; **häufig aufblähende Tiere,** animals frequently suffering from bloat, blast.

II. *vbl s.* **1. Aufblähen,** *n.* (*a*) = II. 2 (*a*); (*b*) *Vet:* bloat, hoove, blast. **2. Aufblähung,** *f.* (*a*) *in vbl senses; also:* inflation, distension; (*b*) *Med:* distension (of stomach); flatulence; (*c*) *Pol.Ec:* inflation (of currency).

III. *p.p. & a.* **aufgebläht,** *in vbl senses; esp.*

(*a*) (*of cheeks. etc.*) bulging, bulgy; (*of sail*) full; (*b*) (*of pers.*) puffed up (with pride); (*c*) *Vet:* (*of cattle, sheep*) hoven, blown, blasted.

aufblasen. I. *v.tr. sep.* (*strong*) **1.** (*a*) to inflate, blow up (balloon, tyre, etc.); to pump up (tyre); to distend (balloon, one's cheeks, etc.); to puff out, bulge (one's cheeks); **sich a.**, (*of pers.*) to puff oneself up, give oneself airs; (*b*) to magnify, inflate (the importance of) (incident, rumour, etc.). **2.** to blow (up) (fire).

II. *p.p. & a.* **aufgeblasen,** *in vbl senses; esp.* **aufgeblasener Stil,** inflated, turgid, flatulent, style; (*of pers.*) **a. sein,** to be puffed up (with pride), *F:* blown up with pride; *F:* to suffer from a swollen head, *U.S:* to get the swelled head; **ein aufgeblasener Kerl,** a puffed-up, *F:* swollen-headed, individual; a chap with a great idea, no small idea, of himself, a chap who thinks no small beer of himself.

aufblatten, *v.tr. sep. Carp:* = **anblatten.**

aufbleiben, *v.i. sep.* (*strong*) (*sein*) **1.** (*of pers.*) to stay up, stop up; to stay out of bed; to sit up. **2.** (*of door, shop, etc.*) to remain, stay, open.

aufblenden, *v.tr. sep.* **1.** *Cin:* to dissolve in, fade in (a scene); **Aufblendung** *f*, dissolve; dissolve-in, fade-in; *see also* **spiralförmig. 2.** *Arch:* to face (wall) (with blind arcades, etc.). **3.** *Aut:* **die Scheinwerfer a.,** *abs.* **a.,** to switch (the head-lights) to main beam.

Aufblick, *m.* **1.** upward look, upward glance (**zu,** at); lifting up, raising, of the eyes (**zu,** to). **2.** *Metall:* gleam, shine (of silver, gold) (at end of cupelling process), *A:* fulguration.

aufblicken, *v.i. sep.* (*haben*) **1.** (*a*) to look up, glance up (**zu,** at); to lift (up), raise, one's eyes (**zu,** to); **sie blickte von ihrer Stickerei auf,** she looked up, lifted her eyes, from her needlework; **zum Himmel a.,** (i) to look up at the sky, (ii) to lift up, cast up, one's eyes to heaven; (*b*) **zu j-m a.,** to look up to s.o.; to respect s.o.; to revere s.o. **2.** *Metall:* (*of silver, gold*) to gleam, shine (at end of cupelling process), *A:* to fulgurate.

aufblitzen, *v.i. sep.* (*sein, haben*) (*of light, diamond, etc.*) to flash; (*of diamond, etc.*) to sparkle (suddenly); (*of light*) to gleam out; (*of star, light*) to appear (suddenly); (*of searchlight, beacon, etc.*) to flare up, flash up; **der Gedanke blitzte in mir auf, daß . . . ,** it flashed upon me, across my mind, that . . . .

aufblocken, *v.i. sep.* (*haben*) *Ven:* (*of bird of prey*) to perch, settle, on a rock *or* crag.

aufblühen. I. *v.i. sep.* (*sein*) (*a*) (*of flower*) to open, blossom (out); (*of plant, flower*) to bloom, blossom, blow; to come, burst, into bloom, into flower, *Lit:* to effloresce; **aufblühende Pflanze,** plant just coming into bloom, *Bot:* efflorescent plant; **voll aufgeblühte Blume,** flower in full bloom, full-blown flower; **eine aufblühende Schönheit,** a budding beauty; (*b*) (*of country, town, industry, etc.*) to be on the rise; to be thriving; to show increasing prosperity; **eine aufblühende Stadt, Industrie,** a rising, thriving, town, industry; *F:* **der Handel blüht wieder auf,** trade is looking up.

II. *vbl s.* **Aufblühen,** *n. in vbl senses; also:* (*a*) *Bot:* efflorescence; (*b*) rise (to prosperity); **im A. sein,** to be on the rise; *F:* to be up and coming.

Aufblühzeit, *f. Bot:* flowering period, (period of) efflorescence.

aufbocken, *v.tr. sep.* (*a*) to mount (sth.) on a trestle; (*b*) to jack up (car, aircraft); to lay up (car); **wenn wir kein Benzin bekommen, müssen wir den Wagen a. lassen,** if we can't get any petrol we shall have to have the car laid up.

aufbohren, *v.tr. sep.* **1.** to bore (sth.) open. **2.** to bore (hole); to bore out (aperture).

aufbojen, *v.tr. sep. Nau:* to buoy up, float (an object).

aufborgen, *v.tr. sep.* to borrow (money); to raise (funds) by borrowing.

aufbrassen, *v.tr. & i. sep.* (*haben*) *Nau:* (**ein Schiff**) **a.,** to bring a vessel by the lee.

aufbraten, *v.tr. sep.* (*strong*) *Cu:* to roast (meat) up again; to fry up (left-overs); to fry up (fish, potatoes, etc.) again.

aufbrauchen, *v.tr. sep.* to use up, exhaust, consume (provisions, ammunition, one's strength, etc.); **aufgebraucht,** (*of provisions, etc.*) used up, exhausted, consumed; (*of strength, ammunition*) spent, exhausted.

aufbrausen. I. *v.i. sep.* **1.** (*sein, haben*) (*a*) (*of liquid*) to effervesce; to bubble (up), boil up, seethe, froth up; (*of sea*) to surge; (*b*) (*of wind, sea*) to rise to a roar. **2.** (*sein*) (*of pers.*) to flare up; to fire up, blaze up, in a moment; **er braust leicht, schnell, auf,** he is easily enraged; he flares up at the least thing; it doesn't take much to make him flare up.

II. *vbl s.* **Aufbrausen,** *n. in vbl senses; also:* effervescence; seethe.

III. *pr.p. & a.* **aufbrausend,** *in vbl senses; esp.* (*a*) (*of liquid*) effervescent; (*b*) (*of pers., nature*) **leicht a.,** easily enraged; easily put into a passion.

aufbrechen, *v.sep.* (*strong*) I. *v.tr.* **1.** to lever up, prise up, prize up (stone, etc.). **2.** (*a*) *Agr:* to break up, plough (ground); (*b*) *Civ.E: etc:* to break up (road); to take up (paving, road surface); to strip (road). **3.** *Nau:* to break up (ship). **4.** to break open (door, safe, case, lid, etc.); to unseal, open, break open (letter); to force (door, lock, safe, etc.); to force open (door, etc.); to pick, break open (lock). **5.** *Ven:* to slit up the belly of (stag, etc.); to eviscerate, disembowel (stag, etc.).

II. **aufbrechen,** *v.i.* (*sein*) **1.** to break open; (*of door, lid, etc.*) to burst open; (*of bud*) to burst; (*of flower*) to open, to blossom (out); (*of abscess*) to burst; (*of wound*) to open (again); (*of skin*) to crack, chap; (*of road surface*) to burst, crack (through frost); (*of ice*) to break (up). **2.** *Nau:* (*of stranded ship*) to break up. **3.** to start on one's way, to set out, to make a start; to be off; *Mil:* to break (up), strike, camp; **zu einer Reise a.,** to start off, set out, on a journey; **nach Frankreich a.,** to set out for France; **es ist Zeit aufzubrechen; es wird Zeit, nun ist es (aber) Zeit, daß wir a.,** it's time we were going, were moving, were on our way, were off; it's time we left, time for us to leave, time we got going.

III. *vbl s.* **Aufbrechen,** *n. in vbl senses; also: Ven:* evisceration (of stag, etc.). *Cp.* **Aufbruch.**

aufbreiten, *v.tr. sep.* to spread out, lay out (linen to dry, articles for inspection, etc.); **das Tischtuch a.,** to spread the cloth over the table, to lay the cloth.

aufbrennen, *v.sep.* (*conj. like* **brennen**) I. *v.tr.* **1.** to burn up, consume (fuel, etc.). **2.** to open (wound, etc.) with caustic; to take the skin off (arm, etc.) with caustic. **3.** (*a*) **j-m, einem Tier, ein Zeichen, ein Mal, a.,** to brand s.o., an animal; (*b*) **j-m eine Kugel,** *F:* **j-m eins, a.,** to fire a shot at s.o.; *F:* **j-m eins a.,** to inflict a punishment on s.o. **4.** (*a*) to freshen up (silver, etc.) by burning; *Metall:* to refine (metal); (*b*) *Winem:* to sulphur (wine).

II. **aufbrennen,** *v.i.* (*sein*) (*a*) to burn up; to burst into flame; to go up in flames; to flare up; (*b*) (*of pers.*) to fly into a passion, a temper; to flare up; (*of passion, etc.*) to be aroused, excited; to kindle.

Aufbrief, *m. Nau:* certificate of tonnage (of ship) (with details of dimensions and carrying capacity).

aufbringen. I. *v.tr. sep.* (*conj. like* **bringen**) **1.** to get (sth.) up; to raise (sth.) (with an effort); to lift up, hoist (weight); to set (sth.) upright; to set up (structure). **2. ein Kind a.,** to bring up, rear, a child. **3.** *Ven:* to put up, flush, start (game). **4.** *Nau:* **ein feindliches Schiff a.,** to capture, seize, take, an enemy ship. **5.** to bring up (subject, question, etc.); to bring (sth.) into fashion, into favour, into vogue; to bring (word, etc.) into currency, into circulation; to introduce, bring in (custom, fashion, new word, idea, etc.); to start (fashion, custom, etc.); **ein Gerücht a.,** to start a rumour, to set a rumour about. **6.** (*a*) to collect, gather (resources, persons, for a purpose, etc.); to raise, procure, find (money, capital); to get (money) together; (*of ruler, etc.*) to raise, levy (troops); (*of government, etc.*) to levy (taxes); to find, procure (adherents, witnesses); **die Kosten a.,** to (find the money to) meet the expenses; **das Geschäft ist so schlecht, daß wir kaum die Steuern a. können,** business is so bad that we can hardly meet the taxes, raise the money to pay our taxes; (*b*) to summon up (courage, strength, determination); to muster up (courage, etc.); **er konnte den Mut nicht a., zu . . . ,** he could not summon up, muster up, (the) courage, he could not pluck up, screw up, (his) courage, to . . . ; **mit aller Geschicklichkeit, die er a. konnte,** with all the skill he could command, call up, summon up. **7.** to anger (s.o.), to make (s.o.) angry; to infuriate, incense (s.o.); to exasperate, irritate, exacerbate (s.o.); to make (s.o.) indignant, to rouse (s.o.) to indignation; to get (s.o.'s) temper up; **j-n gegen sich a.,** to get s.o.'s back up; **er hat jedermann gegen sich aufgebracht,** he has set everyone against him; (**über etwas** *acc.*, **j-n**) **aufgebracht sein,** to be angry (at, about, sth., with s.o.); to be infuriated (by, at, sth., by, with, s.o.); to be incensed, *Lit:* wroth (at sth.); to be exasperated, irritated (by, at, sth.); to be, feel, indignant (about, at, sth., with s.o.); to be in a temper (about sth.); **aufgebracht werden,** to get angry, incensed, *Lit:* to wax wroth; to lose one's temper; to get, fly, into a temper, a passion, a rage; **er war ganz aufgebracht,** he was all worked up; his blood was up; he was in a rage, a fury. **8.** to get (sth.) open; **ich kann die Schublade, die Tür, nicht a.,** I can't get the drawer, the door, (to) open.

II. *vbl s.* **Aufbringen** *n.*, **Aufbringung** *f. in vbl senses; also:* **1.** capture (of enemy ship). **2.** introduction (of custom, fashion, etc.).

Aufbringer, *m. Nau:* captor, capturer (of enemy ship).

aufbrodeln, *v.i. sep.* (*sein*) (*of liquid*) to bubble up, boil up; to seethe.

Aufbruch, *m.* **1.** *Agr:* (*a*) ploughing up, breaking (of ground); (*b*) newly-ploughed land. **2.** *Civ.E: etc:* (*a*) breaking up (of road); stripping (of road); taking up (of road surface); (*b*) stretch of road taken up; portion of road damaged by frost. **3.** (*a*) opening, breaking open (of abscess, etc.); (*b*) breaking up, break-up (of ice); (*c*) breaking up (of dinner-party, etc.). **4.** (*a*) starting (out), start, setting off, departure; **kurz vor ihrem A. nach Paris,** shortly before their departure, before they set out, for Paris; **beim A. zur Jagd, zur Reise, hörten sie . . . ,** as they were starting off, setting out, for the hunt, just as they were setting out, setting forth, on their journey, they heard . . . ; **zum A. rüsten,** to prepare for (one's) departure, to get ready to leave; (*b*) complete re-orientation (of national policy, habits of thought, etc.); spiritual uprising (of a nation). **5.** *Ven:* entrails, *F:* guts (of stag, etc.); *A:* numbles (of stag).

aufbrühen, *v.tr. sep. Cu:* to boil (sth.) up; to brew (tea, coffee).

aufbrüllen, *v.i. sep.* (*haben*) to give a (loud) roar *or* bellow.

aufbrummen, *v.sep.* **1.** *v.i.* (*haben*) to give a growl. **2.** *v.tr. F:* **j-m eine Strafe a.,** to inflict a punishment on s.o.; **sie haben mir sieben Tage aufgebrummt,** they gave me seven days (imprisonment), *F:* they sent me up for seven days; **sie haben mir die Kosten aufgebrummt,** they let me in for, landed me with, the expenses; *Sch:* **der Lehrer hat mir drei Seiten aufgebrummt,** the master gave me a three-page imposition, *U.S:* the teacher penalized me with a three-page assignment; *A:* (*students' slang*) **j-m einen dummen Jungen a.,** to pick a quarrel with s.o., force a quarrel on s.o.

aufbuckeln, *v.tr. sep.* (*a*) to take (burden) on one's back; to shoulder (burden); (*b*) **j-m eine Last a.,** to lay a burden on s.o., put a burden on s.o.'s back.

aufbügeln, *v.tr. sep.* to press (jacket, trousers, etc.); to iron (up) (hat, clothes); **Aufbügeln** *n*, pressing; ironing; **seine Hosen zum Aufbügeln geben,** to take *or* send one's trousers to be pressed.

aufbumsen, *v.i. sep.* (*sein*) (*of heavy object, head, etc.*) **auf etwas** *acc.* **a.,** to bump, thud, on, against, sth.; **er bumste mit dem Kopf auf den Tisch auf,** he bumped his head on the table.

aufbürden, *v.tr. sep.* **j-m etwas a.,** to saddle s.o. with sth., saddle sth. on s.o.; to burden s.o. with sth., to impose sth. on s.o.; to impute (fault, action, guilt, etc.) to s.o.; to lay, put, cast, the blame for sth. upon s.o.; **j-m eine Last a.,** to saddle s.o. with a burden, to lay a burden upon s.o.; **sich** *dat.* **eine Verantwortung a.,** to burden oneself, saddle oneself, with a responsibility; to let oneself in for a responsibility; **j-m die Schuld a.,** to lay the blame on s.o., at s.o.'s door.

aufbürsten, *v.tr. sep.* (*a*) to brush (sth.) up; to give (hat, etc.) a brush-up; to freshen up (hat, etc.) (by brushing); (*b*) **sich** *dat.* **das Haar a.,** to brush one's hair up.

aufdämen, *v.tr. sep. Draughts:* to crown (a piece).

aufdämmern, *v.i. sep.* (*sein*) (*a*) (*of daylight*) to dawn, break; **der Morgen dämmert auf,** day(break) is at hand; (*b*) **die Ahnung, der Gedanke, dämmerte (in) ihm auf, daß . . . ,** it began to dawn on him that . . . ; **endlich dämmerte es (in) mir auf, daß . . . ,** at length it dawned on me that . . . ; **die Hoffnung dämmerte wieder in ihr auf,** she felt hope reviving within her; hope rose again in her breast; **aufdämmernde Hoffnung,** reviving hope.

aufdarren, *v.tr. sep. Ind:* to kiln(-dry) (grain, etc.); to desiccate (fruit, etc.).

aufdecken, I. *v.tr. sep.* **1. das Tischtuch a.,** to

spread the cloth (over the table); to lay the cloth, the table. **2.** to uncover; (*a*) to remove the cover, the covering, from (sth.); **die Betten a.,** to turn down the beds; (*of pers. in bed*) **sich a.,** to throw off the bedclothes, to uncover oneself; (*b*) to reveal, lay bare (abuse, crime, plot, etc.); to oxpose (plot, abuse, etc.); to disclose (secret, etc.); *Cards:* **die Karten a.,** to show one's cards, one's hand; *F:* **seine Karten a.,** to show one's hand; *Chess:* **aufgedecktes Schach,** discovered check.

II. *vbl s.* **Aufdecken** *n.*, **Aufdeckung** *f. in vbl senses; also:* revelation (of abuse, crime, plot, etc.); exposure (of plot, abuse, etc.); disclosure (of secret, etc.).

aufdingen, *v.tr. sep.* (*conj. like* **dingen**) *A:* **j-n j-m als Lehrling a.,** to bind s.o. apprentice to s.o.

aufdocken, *v.tr. sep.* **1.** to bundle up (thread, etc.); to bundle (yarn, etc.) into hanks. **2.** *Agr:* to shock (up) (corn).

aufdonnern (sich), *v.refl. sep. F:* to dress oneself up; to get oneself up (to the nines, to kill); to doll oneself up; to tog oneself up; **aufgedonnert,** (all) dressed up, dolled up, togged up, got up to the nines; got up, done up, to kill.

aufdornen, *v.tr. sep. Mec.E:* to enlarge (hole); to drift (rivet-hole).

aufdörren, *v.tr. sep.*=**aufdarren.**

aufdrängeln, *v.tr. sep.*=**aufdrängen** 2.

aufdrängen, *v.tr. sep.* **1.** to thrust open, force open, burst open (door, etc.). **2. j-m etwas a.,** to force, thrust, sth. (up)on s.o.; **j-m ein Geschenk a.,** to force, thrust, a present on s.o.; to force, compel, s.o. to accept a present; **j-m seine Ansicht a.,** to force, thrust, foist, one's opinion on s.o.; **sich j-m a.,** to force, thrust, foist, oneself upon s.o.; to obtrude (oneself) upon s.o.; (*of question, etc.*) to force itself, obtrude itself, upon s.o.'s attention; (*of thought, conviction, suspicion, etc.*) to force its way into s.o.'s mind; **der Gedanke, der sich mir aufdrängte,** the thought that forced itself upon me, that intruded into my mind, that was borne in upon me; **es, der Gedanke, drängte sich ihm immer stärker auf, daß . . . ,** it was more and more borne in upon him that . . . ; **der Verdacht drängte sich ihm auf, daß . . . ,** the suspicion was borne in upon him that . . . .

aufdrehen, *v.sep.* I. *v.tr.* **1.** (*a*) to turn (sth.) up(wards); *Row:* **ein Ruder a.,** to feather an oar; (*b*) **j-m, sich** *dat.*, **die Haare a.,** to put s.o.'s, one's, hair in curlers. **2.** to screw (sth.) on (*dat.*, **auf etwas** *acc.*, (to) sth.); to screw on (screw-cap, etc.); *F:* **j-m etwas a.,** to hoax s.o., *F:* to have s.o. on (with an invented story, etc.). **3.** (*a*) to wind (up) (clock, watch); to wind up (gramophone, musical box, etc.); (*b*) *F:* (*of pers.*) **aufgedreht sein,** (i) to be full of verve, *F:* of go; to be in capital form; (ii) to be worked up (*after a gay party, etc.*); **die Kinder waren so aufgedreht, daß wir sie kaum zu Bett bringen konnten,** the children were so wound up, worked up, that we could scarcely get them to bed. **4.** (*a*) to unscrew (bolt, nut, screw-cap, etc.); to loosen (screw); to screw out (bolt, etc.); (*b*) to turn on (tap, gas, etc.); (*c*) to untwist, untwine, unravel (cord, etc.); to unlay (rope); (*of cord, rope*) **sich a.,** to unravel, untwist; to become frayed, fagged; to fray; **aufgedrehtes Tauende,** fag-end (of rope).

II. **aufdrehen,** *v.i.* (*haben*) **1.** *Nau:* (*of ship*) to haul, hug, the wind. **2.** *Aut: Sp:* to increase speed; to put on a burst (of speed), to put on a spurt; *Aut. & F:* to step on the gas, on it; *F:* to get a move on; *F:* **dreh mal auf!** (come on,) get a move on! step on it! put some pep into it! get cracking!

aufdrieseln, *v.tr. sep.*=**aufdrehen** I. 4 (*c*).

aufdringen, *v.sep.* **1.** *v.i.* (*sein*) to rise up, **(zu,** to). **2.** *v.tr.*=**aufdrängen.**

aufdringlich, *a.* (*of pers., manner*) importunate; obtrusive; pushful, pushing; officious; insistent; **ein aufdringlicher Kerl,** a pestering fellow: a pushful person; *F:* a nuisance of a man; **aufdringliche Reklame,** insistent advertisement; **aufdringliche Farben,** loud, flashy, gaudy, flaring, insistent, colours; **aufdringliche Musik,** insistent music; music that forces itself upon the ear.

Aufdringlichkeit, *f.* importunity; obtrusiveness; pushfulness; officiousness; insistence; flashiness, gaudiness (of colours).

aufdröseln, *v.tr. sep.* to untwist, untwine, unravel (cord, etc.); *F:* to unravel (story).

Aufdruck, *m.* **1.** *Print: Tex:* printing (of sth. on sth.). **2.** impress(ion), imprint; stamp; printed words, printing; legend (on map, coin, etc.); *Post:* (i) print, legend (on postage stamp); (ii) surcharge, over-print; **Marke mit A.,** surcharged, over-printed, stamp.

aufdrucken, *v.tr. sep.* **etwas auf etwas** *acc.* **a.,** to (im)print sth. on sth.; to print *or* stamp (initials, address, etc.) on sth.

aufdrücken, *v.tr. sep.* **1.** to impress, imprint, stamp (**auf**+*acc.*, on); **ein Pflaster auf eine Wunde a.,** to stick a plaster on a wound; **ein Siegel auf Wachs a.,** to impress a seal upon wax; **sein Siegel auf eine Akte a.,** to impress one's seal upon, set one's seal to, a deed; **j-m einen Kuß auf die Lippen, auf die Stirn, a.,** to impress a kiss on s.o.'s lips, on s.o.'s forehead; *F:* **etwas** *dat.* **sein Siegel, seinen Stempel, a.,** to leave one's mark upon sth.; to set one's seal, one's stamp, upon sth. **2.** to press (sth.) open; to squeeze (sth.) open; to push open (door); *F:* to open (lid, etc.) by pressing the catch *or* spring; to open (door) by pressing the button. **3. die Feder, den Bleistift, (aufs Papier) a.,** *v.i.* **mit der Feder, mit dem Bleistift, (aufs Papier) a.,** *abs.* **a.,** to press one's pen, one's pencil, on the paper, *abs.* to press on one's pen, one's pencil (*while writing*); **drück nicht so sehr auf!** don't press so hard!

aufducken, *v.i. sep.* (*sein*) (*of pers.*) to bob up; to pop up.

aufduften, *v.i. sep.* (*haben*) to give off (a) scent, (a) fragrance; to give off an odour, to become odorous.

aufdunsen, *v.i. sep.* (*sein*) *A:* (*usu. only in present tense & p.p.* **aufgedunsen**) to swell up; to become puffed up; (*of face*) to grow puffy; (*of pers., face*) to become bloated; *see also* **aufgedunsen.**

aufdunsten, *v.sep.* **1.** *v.i.* (*sein*) (*of liquid, perfume, etc.*) to evaporate; **Aufdunstung** *f*, evaporation. **2.** *v.tr.* to reheat, warm up (food).

aufdünsten, *v.tr. sep.*=**aufdunsten** 2.

aufeinander [aufʔai'nandər], *pron. adv.* **1.** one upon *or* above another, the other; one on top of another, the other; on top, atop, of one another; **a. gehäufte Säcke,** piled-up, stacked(-up), sacks. **2.** one after another, the other. **3.** (*action, influence, etc.*) upon, on, one another; **Einfluß zweier Bewegungen a.,** influence of two movements on each other; interaction of two movements.

Aufeinanderfolge, *f.* succession; sequence, series (of ideas, sounds, days, etc.).

aufeinanderfolgen, *v.i. sep.* (*sein*) to follow one another; to succeed one another; **die Tage folgen aufeinander,** the days follow one another; day follows, succeeds, day; **aufeinanderfolgend,** successive; consecutive; **an drei aufeinanderfolgenden Tagen,** on three consecutive days; three days running.

aufeinanderlegen, *v.tr. sep.* to lay (things) one on top of the other; to superimpose (boards, etc.); to superpose (things) (upon, on, one another); *Geom:* **zwei Dreiecke a.,** to superpose two triangles; **Aufeinanderlegen** *n*, **Aufeinanderlegung** *f, in vbl senses; also:* superimposition; *Geom: etc:* superposition.

aufeinanderliegen, *v.i. sep.* (*strong*) (*haben*) to lie on top, atop, of one another; to be superimposed; to be superposed (on, upon, one another); **aufeinanderliegend,** lying on top, atop, of one another; superimposed; superposed (on, upon, one another).

aufeinanderplatzen, *v.i. sep.* (*sein*) (*of opinions, etc.*) to clash (with one another); **Aufeinanderplatzen** *n* **der Meinungen,** clash of opinions.

Aufeinanderprall, *m.*=**Aufeinanderstoß.**

aufeinanderprallen, *v.i. sep.* (*sein*)=**aufeinanderstoßen.**

Aufeinanderstoß, *m.* collision; impact (of two bodies); clash, clashing (of opinions, wills, etc.).

aufeinanderstoßen, *v.i. sep.* (*strong*) (*sein*) (*of bodies, vehicles, ships, etc.*) to collide; (*of two bodies*) to impact with, against, one another; (*of ships*) to run foul of one another; (*of opinions, wills, etc.*) to clash.

aufeinandertreffen, *v.i. sep.* (*strong*) (*sein*) **1.** to encounter, meet, one another. **2.**=**aufeinanderstoßen.**

aufeinandertreiben, *v.i. sep.* (*strong*) (*sein*) *Nau:* (*of ships*) to run foul of one another.

aufeinandertürmen, *v.tr. sep.* to pile up, stack up (objects); to rear a pile of (stones, etc.); **Berge, die sich a.,** mountains towering upon mountains.

aufeinanderwirken, *v.i. sep.* (*haben*) to act upon one another; to interact.

aufeisen, *v.tr. sep.* to break the ice on (pond, etc.); to free (harbour, road, etc.) from ice; to open up (ice-bound harbour, etc.).

Aufelektron, *n. Atom.Ph:* outer electron.

aufentern, *v.i. sep.* (*sein*) *Nau:* (*of sailor*) to go aloft.

Aufenthalt, *m.* -(e)s/-e. **1.** (*a*) stop; halt; *Nau:* stay (of ship in port); (*unforeseen*) wait, delay; **Reise ohne A.,** non-stop journey; **ohne A. reisen,** to make a journey non-stop, without a break; *Rail: etc:* **zehn Minuten A.,** ten minutes' stop, halt; **der Zug hat in X keinen A.,** the train (stops but) does not wait at X; **wieviel A. hat der Zug, der Bus? wie lange hat der Zug, hat der Bus, haben wir, hier A.?** how long does the train, the bus, stop, wait, here? **der Verkehr war so stark, daß es an allen Stationen längere Aufenthalte gab,** the traffic was so heavy that there were long delays, waits, at every station; **wir hatten zwei Stunden A. in Köln,** we stopped for two hours in Cologne; we had a two-hour wait at Cologne; we were delayed for two hours at Cologne; (*b*) stay, sojourn; **bei seinem A. in Berlin, während seines Berliner Aufenthalts,** during his stay in Berlin; while he is, was, (staying) in Berlin; **A. von vierzehn Tagen, vierzehntägiger A.,** fortnight's stay; **A. in einem Ort nehmen,** to stay, stop, reside, *Lit:* sojourn, in, at, a place; **nur einen kurzen A. in einem Ort nehmen,** to make only a short stay in a place. **2.** (place of) abode; residence; domicile; **er hat jetzt festen A. in X,** he is now settled, domiciled, at X; **ohne festen A.,** with no fixed abode; *Adm:* **j-m den A. verweigern,** to refuse s.o. permission to reside.

Aufenthaltsbeschränkung, *f. Adm:* limitation of (period of) residence.

Aufenthaltsdauer, *f.* (*a*) period, length, of (s.o.'s) stay (in a place); (*b*) length of stop (of train, bus, etc.).

Aufenthaltserlaubnis, Aufenthaltsgenehmigung, *f. Adm:* (*a*) permission to reside; **Verlängerung der A.,** extension of stay; (*b*) residence permit.

Aufenthaltskarte, *f. Adm:* residence permit.

Aufenthaltsort, *m.* (place of) abode; residence; domicile; **sein jetziger A. ist unbekannt,** his present location is unknown; nobody knows his whereabouts; **j-s A. ermitteln,** to discover s.o.'s whereabouts; to find out where s.o. is (at the moment); **ohne festen A.,** with no fixed abode.

Aufenthaltsraum, *m.* (*in hostel*) day-room; (*in hotel*) lounge.

aufer-, *compound vbl pref. Note: although* **auf-** *in this combination is theoretically separable, German usage avoids any form demanding separation; e.g.* **als er Lazarus auferweckte** *is felt to be acceptable, but not* **er erweckte Lazarus auf.**

auferbauen, *v.tr. sep. Lit:* to erect, set up (temple, etc.).

auferlegen. I. *v.tr. sep.* **j-m etwas a.,** to impose sth. on, upon, s.o.; to lay (an obligation, a penalty, a fine, etc.) upon s.o.; to enjoin (silence, etc.) on s.o.; **j-m Bedingungen a.,** to impose conditions (up)on s.o.; to lay down conditions to s.o.; to dictate conditions to s.o.; **j-m einen Eid a.,** to put s.o. on his, her, oath; to make s.o. take an oath; **j-m Schweigen, Gehorsam, a.,** to enjoin, impose, silence, obedience, on s.o.; to enforce silence, obedience, on s.o.; **j-m eine Steuer a.,** to impose, lay, a tax on s.o.; **j-m eine Geldstrafe a.,** to impose, inflict, a fine on s.o.; to lay a fine upon s.o.; **j-m eine Buße a.,** to impose (a) penance on s.o.; to enjoin penance (up)on s.o.; **j-m die Pflicht a., etwas zu tun,** to impose (up)on s.o., lay on s.o., the duty of doing sth.; **sich** *dat.* **die Pflicht a., zu . . . ,** to make it a duty, one's duty, to . . . ; **die Verpflichtung, die ihm auferlegt wurde,** the obligation laid upon him; **j-m, sich** *dat.*, **Beschränkungen a.,** to impose restrictions upon s.o., upon oneself; **sich** *dat.* **Zwang a.,** to restrain oneself, put a restraint on oneself; to control oneself; to keep oneself, one's feelings, in check; to do violence to one's feelings.

II. *vbl s.* **Auferlegung,** *f. in vbl senses; also:* imposition (of a duty, penalty, etc.); infliction (of penalty, fine, etc.).

auferstehen. I. *v.i. sep.* (*strong*) (*sein*) to rise again; **(von den Toten, aus dem Grabe) a.,** to rise (again) from the dead; **Christus ist auferstanden,** Christ is risen; **der auferstandene Christus,** the risen Christ; *B:* **so die Toten nicht a., so ist Christus auch nicht auferstanden,** if the dead rise not, then is not Christ raised; **daß die Toten a., hat auch Mose gedeutet,** that the dead are raised, even Moses shewed.

II. *vbl s.* **Auferstehung,** *f.* resurrection; rising again, rising from the dead; **die A. Christi,** the resurrection of Christ; *Theol:* **die A. des Fleisches, des Leibes,** the resurrection of the body;

B: **ich bin die A. und das Leben,** I am the resurrection and the life; *Ecc:* **(das Fest der) A., Chrsti A.,** the Feast of the Resurrection; Easter.

Auferstehungsfest, das. *Ecc:* the Feast of the Resurrection; Easter.

Auferstehungspflanze, *f. Bot:* selaginella lepidophylla, resurrection plant.

auferwachen, *v.i. sep. (sein) Lit:* to rise from the dead; to awake(n) (from the sleep of death).

auferwecken. I. *v.tr. sep.* **1.** *B: (in Old Testament)* to raise up (judges, prophets, etc.). **2.** *(a) B:* to raise (s.o.) from the dead; **in dem Namen Jesu, den Gott von den Toten auferwecket hat,** in the name of Jesus, whom God raised from the dead; **Gott, der die Toten auferwecket,** God which raiseth the dead; *(b) Lit:* to bring (a nation, etc.) to life again; to bring about the resurgence of (a nation, etc.).

II. *vbl s.* **Auferweckung,** *f. (a)* raising (of s.o.) from the dead; **die A. des Lazarus, der Tochter des Jairus,** the raising of Lazarus, of Jairus's daughter; **die A. der Totengebeine,** the resurrection of the dry bones; *(b) Lit:* spiritual rebirth; resurgence (of a nation, etc.).

auferziehen, *v.tr. sep. (strong)* to bring up, rear (child); to educate (child); to breed (animals); to raise (animals, plants, *U.S:* children); **Auferziehung** *f, in vbl senses; also:* upbringing, education.

aufessen, *v.tr. sep. (strong)* to eat up (sth.); to finish (food); *abs.* **a.,** to finish one's food; to finish; **iß deine Suppe auf, sonst bekommst du kein Fleisch,** finish up your soup or you won't get any meat; *F:* **iß deinen Teller auf,** clear your plate.

auffädeln, *Dial:* **auffädmen,** *v.tr. sep.* to string, thread (beads, etc.); **Isolatoren, usw., auf einen Draht a.,** to string insulators, etc., on a wire.

auffahren, *v.sep. (strong)* I. *v.i. (sein)* **1.** to rise (up); to ascend; to mount; *(of dust, flames, etc.)* to rise up; *(of eagle, etc.)* to mount (into the sky); **Jesus fuhr auf gen Himmel,** Jesus ascended to Heaven; *B:* **er schied von ihnen und fuhr auf gen Himmel,** he was parted from them and carried up into heaven; *Min: (of miner)* **(aus dem Schacht) a.,** to come up out of the mine, to come to the surface. **2.** to start (involuntarily); to give a jump, a (sudden) start; **vom Stuhl a.,** to start up, jump up, from one's chair; **aus dem Schlaf a.,** to wake up with a start, to start out of one's sleep. **3.** to flare up; to snap; **'nein!' fuhr er auf,** 'no!' he snapped; **du brauchst nicht gleich aufzufahren,** you needn't snap at me like that. **4.** to drive up; to arrive *(in a vehicle)*; *(of vehicle)* to draw up (before a house, etc.); *(of vehicles)* to take up their stations; to draw up, range themselves, in order; **der Wagen fuhr vor der Stadthalle auf,** the car drew up before, drove up to, the town hall. **5.** *(a) (of vehicle)* **auf ein anderes Fahrzeug a.,** to run into another vehicle; *(b) Nau: (of ship)* to run aground; to ground; **das Schiff fuhr auf die Felsen auf,** the ship ran on (to), struck, the rocks. **6.** *(of door, etc.)* to fly open, spring open, burst open.

II. **auffahren,** *v.tr.* **1.** *(a)* to bring up (earth, timber, etc.) *(in vehicles)*; *(b)* **Erde auf einen Damm, usw., a.,** to deposit (truck-)loads of soil on an embankment, etc. **2.** *(a)* **Fahrzeuge, Flugzeuge, a., a. lassen,** to bring vehicles, aircraft, into position; to park vehicles, aircraft (in line, in formation); *Mil:* **Geschütze a.,** to bring guns into action; **die Batterie a.,** to form the battery; *F:* **schwerstes Geschütz, seine schwersten Geschütze, a. (lassen),** to bring weighty arguments to bear, *F:* to bring up one's heavy artillery; *(b) F:* **er ließ Sekt a.,** he had champagne brought on; **ein ganzes Schwein wurde aufgefahren,** a whole pig was brought on, served up; **sie haben alles aufgefahren, was sie im Hause hatten,** they brought out everything they had in the house (in the way of food and drink). **3.** *Min:* **einen Stollen a.,** to drive a gallery. **4.** *(of vehicles)* to cut up, churn up, *F:* plough up (road, ground, grass, etc.); **arg aufgefahrene Straße,** badly cut-up road; **durch Panzer aufgefahrene Straße,** road ploughed up by tanks.

Auffahrt, *f.* **1.** ascent; ascension; rising; ascent, upward journey (of lift, mountain railway, etc.); **Christi A.,** the Ascension (of Christ). **2.** *(a) Civ.E: Fort:* ramp; *Nau:* slope, slip (of quay); *(b)* (carriage-)drive; approach (to a house, etc.).

Auffahrtstag, *m. Swiss:* Ascension Day.

auffallen, *v.sep. (strong)* I. *v.i. (sein)* **1.** *(a)* **auf den Boden, auf eine Fläche, usw., a.,** to fall upon, hit, strike ,the floor, a surface, etc.; to impinge on a surface; **er war mit dem Kopf aufgefallen,** he had fallen on his head; **er fiel mit dem Kopf auf einen Stein auf,** he fell and hit his head on a stone; *Opt:* **auffallender Lichtstrahl, auffallendes Licht,** incident ray, light; *(b) Ven: (of large bird)* to swoop (down); *(c) Ven: (of hound)* **auf die Fährte a.,** to hit off the scent. **2.** to be conspicuous; to attract attention; to attract notice; to be (very) noticeable; *(of fact, etc.)* to be evident; *(of likeness, etc.)* to be striking; **Fehler, der sofort auffällt,** mistake that is noticed at once; **es fiel allgemein auf,** it attracted general notice, was noticed by everyone; **fällt es sehr auf?** is it very noticeable? is it conspicuous? does it notice (much)? does it show (much)? **der Unbekannte fiel in der Menge gar nicht auf,** the stranger was not at all conspicuous, attracted no attention, was not noticed, in the crowd; **angenehm a.,** to be noticed with approval; to make a good impression; **unangenehm a.,** to attract unfavourable notice; to make a bad impression; **er fällt durch seine vorlauten Bemerkungen überall unangenehm auf,** he makes a bad impression everywhere with his forward remarks; *F:* **er fällt immer auf,** he always steps off on the wrong foot; **j-m a.,** to strike s.o.; to draw, catch, s.o.'s attention; to be noticed by s.o.; **es fiel ihm auf, daß . . . ,** it struck him, he noticed, that . . . ; **was mir am meisten auffiel, war . . . ,** what struck, impressed, me most was . . . ; **es ist mir nie aufgefallen,** it has never struck me; I have never noticed it; **es scheint niemandem aufzufallen,** it does not seem to strike anyone; nobody seems to notice it; **dem Auge a.,** to strike, catch, draw, the eye; **den Augen eines Künstlers fällt das sofort auf,** an artist will notice, *F:* spot, that at once; **auffallend,** (i) striking, remarkable; conspicuous; (ii) gaudy, loud, garish (colour, dress, etc.); showy (dress, etc.); **auffallende Schönheit,** striking, remarkable, beauty; **auffallende Ähnlichkeit,** striking likeness; **auffallendes Abweichen von der Regel,** remarkable departure from the rule; **auffallende Kleidung,** (i) striking dress, (ii) showy, garish, dress; *adv.* **auffallend schön,** strikingly beautiful; **auffallend gekleidet,** (i) strikingly dressed, (ii) showily, garishly, dressed.

II. **auffallen,** *v.tr.* **sich** *dat.* **den Kopf a.,** to cut, *F:* crack, one's head in a fall.

auffällig, *a.* (i) conspicuous; striking; gaudy, loud, garish (colour, dress, etc.); showy (dress, etc.); ostentatious (behaviour, dress, etc.); blatant (behaviour, manners); (ii) peculiar; remarkable; odd; **auffälliges Benehmen,** (i) ostentatious behaviour; conduct that attracts unfavourable notice; (ii) peculiar, remarkable, odd, behaviour; **das Auffällige daran ist . . . ,** (i) the striking thing, (ii) the peculiar thing, the odd thing, about it is . . . ; **du hättest es nicht so a. machen sollen, daß du dich gelangweilt hast,** you shouldn't have made it so obvious that you were bored; *adv.* **sich a. kleiden,** to dress showily; to be ostentatious in one's dress; **sich a. benehmen,** (i) to make oneself conspicuous; to (try to) get oneself noticed; to (try to) show off; (ii) to behave oddly, strangely, peculiarly; **wenn du es so a. machst, merkt er es gleich,** if you are so obvious about it he will notice straight away.

Auffälligkeit, *f.* conspicuousness (of uniform, etc.); gaudiness, loudness, garishness (of colour, dress, etc.); ostentatiousness, ostentation (of behaviour, dress, etc.); blatancy (of behaviour, manners); strangeness, oddness (of behaviour).

auffalten, *v.tr. sep.* **1.** to unfold; **sich a.,** *(of flower)* to unfold, open out. **2.** to fold (sth.) up; to fold (sth.) together. **3.** *Geol: (of strata)* **sich auffalten,** to fold upward.

Auffangbehälter, *m. Ch: Ind:* collecting vessel, collector; receiver.

Auffange-, *comb.fm.* = **Auffang-.**

auffangen, *v.tr. sep. (strong) (a)* to catch (sth.) up; to catch (flying ball, falling object, person about to fall, etc.); *(of birds)* to snap up, seize, snatch, catch (insects, etc.); *(of dog)* to catch (morsel, etc.) in mid-air; *Mil: etc:* to head off (fugitives); to round up (fugitives, deserters); *(b)* to collect (rainwater, liquid, gas, etc.); to catch (dripping water, blood, etc.); *(c) Box: Fenc:* **einen Schlag, einen Hieb, a.,** to parry, ward off, a blow, a thrust; *(d)* to pick up (expression, news, information); *(e)* to catch (words, sounds); **ich habe nur ein paar Worte des Gesprächs a. können,** I could only catch a few words of the conversation; *(f)* **j-s Blick a.,** to catch s.o.'s eye; **ihr Blick fing den meinen auf,** her eyes, her glance, caught mine; *(g)* to intercept (letters, etc.); *Tg: Tp:* **ein Gespräch, ein Telegramm, a.,** to intercept a telephone conversation, a telegram; to tap a telegraph wire; *F* to milk a message, milk the wire.

Auffänger, *m. Ch: Ind:* collector (for liquid); receiver (for gas, liquid).

Auffanggebiet, *n. Rocketry:* recovery area.

Auffanggefäß, *n. Ch: Ind:* collecting vessel, collector; receiver.

Auffangglas, *n. Opt:* object-glass, objective (of microscope, etc.).

Auffangkommando, *n. Mil:* rounding-up party.

Auffanglager, *n.* reception camp (for refugees).

Auffangröhr, *n.*, **Auffangröhre,** *f. Ch: Mec.E: etc:* collecting tube *or* pipe.

Auffangschale, *f. Ch: etc:* collecting dish; *Mec.E:* drip-pan; *Mch: etc:* drip-cup.

Auffangstange, *f.* lightning-rod (of lightning-conductor).

Auffangtrichter, *m.* collecting funnel; *Ind:* receiving hopper.

Auffangvorrichtung, *f.* **1.** *Ch: Mec.E: etc:* collecting device. **2.** lightning-rod (of lightning-conductor).

auffärben, *v.tr. sep.* to freshen up, touch up, the colour(s) of (sth.); to touch up (painting, etc.); to re-dye (material).

auffasern, *v.tr. sep.* to fray, unravel, ravel out.

auffassen. I. *v.tr. sep.* **1.** to pick up, take up (sth.). **2.** *(a)* to comprehend, understand (sth.); to grasp (idea, meaning, etc.); to take in (s.o.'s words, etc.); **das ist leicht aufzufassen,** that is easy to understand, comprehend; that is easily grasped; **schnell, rasch, a.,** to understand quickly; to be quick of apprehension, of understanding; to be nimble-minded, quick in, on, the uptake; **schwer a.,** to be slow of apprehension, of understanding; to be slow-witted, slow in, on, the uptake; *(b)* **etwas als etwas a.,** to understand sth. as sth.; to interpret sth. as sth.; to view, see, sth. as sth.; **wenn wir die Natur als göttlich a. . . . ,** if we regard, consider, conceive of, Nature as divine . . . ; **etwas richtig a.,** to understand sth. correctly, properly, aright; to put the right construction on (a passage, s.o.'s words, etc.); to interpret (a passage, a part, etc.) correctly; **etwas falsch a.,** to misunderstand sth.; to misinterpret, misconstrue (a passage, s.o.'s words, etc.); to put a wrong construction on (a passage, etc.); to put a false construction on (s.o.'s actions, etc.); to misconceive (word, passage, etc.); **etwas anders a.,** to see, take, view, sth. differently; to see sth. in another, a different, light; to put a different construction on (a passage, etc.); to interpret (a passage, a part, etc.) differently; **j-n falsch a.,** to misconstrue s.o.'s words *or* actions; to misunderstand s.o., *F:* to get s.o. wrong; **j-n richtig a.,** to understand s.o. correctly; **wie fassen Sie die Lage auf?** how do you understand, view, the situation? what is your view of, what are your views on, the situation? **wie ich die Sache auffasse . . . ,** in my view . . . ; to my mind, to my way of thinking . . . ; as it strikes me . . . ; as I take it, see it . . . ; **die Dinge richtig a.,** to take a right view of things; **er faßt immer alles falsch auf,** he always takes a wrong view of things; he always misunderstands; he always takes things the wrong way.

II. *vbl s.* **Auffassung,** *f.* **1.** *(a)* comprehension, understanding; interpretation, reading (of a passage, a part, etc.); view (of affairs, situation, etc.); **um zu einer richtigen A. dieser Stelle zu gelangen . . . ,** to arrive at a right understanding of this passage . . . ; **falsche A.,** misconception; misconstruction (of words, etc.); misinterpretation (of a passage, a part, etc.); **ich habe eine ganz andere A. von der Sache,** I take an entirely different view of the matter; I see the matter quite differently, in quite a different light; **nach meiner A.,** in my view, to my mind, to my way of thinking, as it strikes me, as I take it, as I see it; *(b)* conception; *Phil:* concept; **eine hohe A. von seiner Pflicht haben,** to have a high conception, idea, of one's duty. **2.** = **Auffassungsgabe.**

Auffassungsart, *f.* way of looking at things; point of view; *Psy:* type of apprehension.

Auffassungsgabe, *f.*, **Auffassungskraft,** *f.*, **Auffassungsvermögen,** *n.* faculty of perception; perceptive faculty, faculties; perceptiveness, perceptivity; (faculty of) apprehension; understanding; **rasche Auffassungsgabe,** swiftness of perception; quickness of mind; **gute Auffassungsgabe, gutes Auffassungsvermögen, haben,** to be quick to grasp things, to be quick in, on, the uptake; to be perceptive.

Auffavorit [ˈaufˀfaˈvoˑˌriːt], *m. Turf:* odds-on favourite; **als A. starten,** to start odds-on.

auffegen, *v.tr. sep.* to sweep up (dirt, etc.).

auffeilen, *v.tr. sep.* **1.** to file up (surface); to touch (piece) up with a file; to file (sth.) again. **2.** to file (sth.) open.

auffeuern, *v.i. sep. (haben) Mch:* to fire up.

auffieren, *v.tr. sep. Nau:* to slack, slacken, ease (rope).

auffindbar, *a.* findable, discoverable; traceable; detectable; **nirgends a.,** not to be found, discovered, anywhere.

auffinden, *v.tr. sep. (strong)* **1.** to find, discover (s.o., sth.); to discover the whereabouts of (sth.); to trace, ferret out (lost object); to unearth (old manuscript, etc.); to detect (weak spot, leakage of gas, etc.); *Ven: (of dog)* to find (game). **2.** *vbl s.* **Auffinden** *n.*, **Auffindung** *f. in vbl senses; also:* discovery; detection; *Ecc:* **die Auffindung des Kreuzes,** the Invention of the Cross.

auffischen, *v.tr. sep.* to fish up; to take (sth.) out of the water; **eine Leiche a.,** to fish up, out, a dead body; **eine Mine a.,** to fish up a mine; *F:* **wo hast du das aufgefischt?** where did you pick that up? where did you get hold of that?

aufflackern, *v.i. sep. (sein) (of candle, flame, etc.)* to flicker up; *(of candle, flame, passion, revolt, etc.)* to flare up; *Ch: (of substance)* to deflagrate; **Aufflackern** *n*, flickering (up); flicker (of light, flame, *Lit:* of life); flaring up; flare-up; *Ch:* deflagration.

aufflammen, *v.i. sep. (sein)* **1.** to flame up; to burst, break, into flame(s); to go up in flames; to blaze up; to flare up; *(of fire)* to blaze out; *(of passions, etc.)* to flame out; *Ch: (of substance)* to deflagrate; **der Aufruhr war wieder aufgeflammt,** the revolt had flared up, blazed up, broken out, again. **2.** *vbl s.* **Aufflammen,** *n. in vbl senses; also:* flare-up; *Ch:* deflagration.

aufflattern, *v.i. sep. (sein)* to flutter up.

aufflechten, *v.tr. sep. (strong)* **1.** to untwist, untwine, unravel (yarn, etc.); to undo (hair, wickerwork, rush matting, etc.); to unplait (hair); to unbraid (hair); to unlay (rope). **2.** to plait (hair, etc.) up(wards); **sie trägt ihr Haar aufgeflochten,** she wears her hair plaited up (on her head).

auffliegen, *v.i. sep. (strong) (sein)* **1.** *(of dust, etc.)* to fly up; *(of bird)* to fly up (through the air); to take wing, to soar; *(of bird, aircraft, balloon)* to ascend; to mount; *(of aircraft)* to be in upward flight; *Ven: (of birds)* to rise; **auffliegender Adler,** soaring eagle, *Her:* eagle soarant. **2.** *(of mine, etc.)* to explode; *(of powder-magazine, mine, ship, etc.)* to blow up; *(of boiler)* to burst; *(of firm, etc.)* to go smash; *(of project, etc.)* to fail; to collapse; *F:* to go up in smoke. **3.** *(of door, etc.)* to fly open. **4.** *vbl s.* **Auffliegen,** *n. in vbl senses; also:* explosion (of mine, etc.); **ein Pulvermagazin zum Auffliegen bringen,** to blow up a powder-magazine; **ein Unternehmen zum Auffliegen bringen,** to cause the failure, bring about the collapse, of an undertaking.

aufflimmern, *v.i. sep. (haben) (of light)* to (begin to) glimmer; *(of object)* to (begin to) glitter; *(of star)* to (begin to) twinkle.

Aufflug, *m.* **1.** *(a) (of birds)* taking flight, taking wing; flying up; *(b)* flight, soaring (of bird); ascent (of balloon, aircraft); upward flight (of aircraft). **2.** *Ven:* covey of young birds.

auffordern. I. *v.tr. sep.* **j-n a., etwas zu tun; j-n zu etwas a.,** to invite s.o. to do sth.; to ask, request, s.o. to do sth.; to summon s.o. to do sth.; to bid s.o. to do sth.; to call upon, on, s.o. (to speak, etc.); **ich forderte ihn auf zu kommen,** I asked him to come; **j-n a., ein paar Worte über etwas** *acc.* **zu sagen,** to ask, request, invite, s.o. to say a few words about sth.; to call upon s.o. to say a few words about sth.; **j-n zum Trinken a.,** to encourage s.o. to have a drink; **er forderte seine Gäste auf zuzugreifen,** he urged his guests to help themselves; **eine Dame zum Tanz a.,** to ask a lady to dance; **darf ich Sie zum nächsten Tanz a.?** may I have the pleasure of the next dance? *F:* **hat er dich eingeladen oder aufgefordert?** is it on him, or do you have to pay for yourself? **j-n zur Mitarbeit a.,** to ask s.o. to co-operate; to call upon s.o. to give assistance; **j-n a., den Hörsaal zu verlassen,** to call upon s.o., to ask s.o., to leave the lecture-room; **die Glocke, die sie zum Gebet aufforderte,** the bell that called, summoned, bade, them to prayers; **j-n zur Zahlung a.,** to call upon s.o. to pay; to apply to s.o. for payment; **j-n dringend zur Zahlung a.,** to press s.o. for payment; to dun s.o.; **j-n zur Erfüllung eines Vertrags a.,** to summon s.o. to perform a contract; to call upon s.o. to fulfil a contract; **j-n zum Duell a.,** to challenge s.o. to a duel; to call s.o. out; *Mil:* **eine Stadt zur Übergabe a.,** to summon a town to surrender; *Cards:* **Trumpf a.,** to call for trumps; *Jur:* **j-n gerichtlich a.,** to summon s.o.

II. *vbl s.* **1. Auffordern,** *n. in vbl senses.* **2. Aufforderung,** *f.* *(a)* invitation, request; summons; demand; **die A. an j-n richten, etwas zu tun,** to ask, request, call upon, s.o. to do sth.; **A. an j-n, etwas zu tun,** request to s.o. to do sth.; summons to, call upon, s.o. to do sth.; **A. zum Tanz,** invitation to the dance; **A. zur Zahlung,** application, demand, for payment; **A. zum Duell,** challenge to a duel; *Fin:* **A. zur Einzahlung (auf Aktien),** calling up of capital; call; *Jur:* **gerichtliche A.,** summons; *Mil:* **A. zur Übergabe,** summons to surrender; *(b)*=**Aufforderungsschreiben.**

auffördern, *v.tr. sep. Min:* to bring (ore, etc.) to the surface.

Aufforderungsbefehl, *m. Jur:* writ of summons.

Aufforderungssatz, *m. Gram:* clause of command, entreaty *or* exhortation.

Aufforderungsschreiben, *n.* *(a)* (formal) summons; letter requesting (s.o.'s) attendance; *(b)* (letter of) invitation; letter (inviting the recipient to do sth.).

aufforsten, *v.tr. sep. For:* to (re)afforest; to retimber, restock (land); **Aufforstung** *f*, (re)afforestation; retimbering, restocking.

auffressen, *v.tr. sep. (strong)* *(a) (of animal)* to eat up (food); to devour (prey); *P: (of pers.)* to devour, eat greedily, gobble up, wolf (food); **die Katze fraß die Maus mit Haut und Haaren auf,** the cat gobbled up the mouse bones and all; *F:* **nur keine Angst, sie wird dich nicht a.,** don't be afraid, she won't eat you; *(b) (of acid, etc.)* to corrode (metal, etc.).

auffrieren, *v.i. sep. (strong) (sein) (of plant)* to be forced up by frost.

auffrischen. I. *v.sep.* **1.** *v.tr.* to freshen (sth.) up; to refresh (sth.); to revive (colour, painting, etc.); to retouch, touch up (painting, paintwork); to brighten up (colour); to do up, renovate (clothes, furniture, etc.); to refurbish (clothes, furniture, etc.); **j-s Gedächtnis a.,** to refresh, jog, s.o.'s memory; **seine Erinnerung an etwas** *acc.* **a.,** to refresh one's memory of, about, sth.; **sein Englisch, seine englischen Kenntnisse, a.,** to brush up, rub up, one's English; *Surg:* **eine Wunde a.,** to refresh a wound. **2.** *v.i. (sein) (of wind)* to freshen.

II. *vbl s.* **1. Auffrischen,** *n. in vbl senses.* **2. Auffrischung,** *f.*=II. 1; *also:* **zur A. Ihres Gedächtnisses,** (in order) to refresh your memory.

Auffrischungskursus, *m. Sch:* refresher course.

auffugen, auffügen, *v.tr. sep. Carp: etc:* to joint, fit, (sth.) on (**auf**+*acc.*, to).

aufführbar, *a. Th:* performable, playable, stageable; **schwer, leicht, a.,** difficult, easy, to produce, to stage.

aufführen. I. *v.tr. sep.* **1.** to erect, set up (wall, building, etc.); to raise (mound, rampart, etc.); to throw up (mound, etc.); **ein Gerüst a.,** to put up a scaffolding. **2.** *Mil: A:* to post (sentry, guns); **die Wache a.,** to bring up the (relieving) guard. **3.** *(a) A:* **einen Zeugen a.,** to produce, bring forward, a witness; **j-n als Autorität, als Zeugen, a.,** to quote, cite, s.o. as an authority, as a witness; **eine Stelle a.,** to quote, cite, a passage; *(b)* to list (names, sums, etc.); to enter (names, sums, etc.) (in a list); **Posten in einer Rechnung a.,** to list, enter, items in an account; **bitte die verschiedenen Sendungen in der Rechnung einzeln a.,** please list the various deliveries separately, please itemize the various deliveries, in the account. **4.** *(a) Th: etc: (of management, company)* to put on, to give (play, opera, ballet); to put (play) on the stage, to stage (play); to present (play, opera, ballet, film); *(of company)* to play (drama); to perform (play, opera, ballet); *(of concert-hall management, musical society, conductor, etc.)* to put on, give (concert, oratorio, etc.); **in diesem Konzert wurden Werke junger Komponisten aufgeführt,** works by young composers were performed, played, at this concert; *(b) F:* **was er heute aufgeführt hat, war unglaublich,** it was incredible the way he carried on today. **5.** *A:* **j-n bei j-m a.,** to present s.o. to s.o.; to introduce s.o. to s.o. **6. sich aufführen,** to behave, act; to conduct oneself; **sich gut, anständig, a.,** to behave well, with decency; **sich schlecht a.,** to behave (oneself) badly, to misbehave; to misconduct oneself; **sich wie ein Feigling a.,** to behave, act, like a coward.

II. *vbl s.* **1. Aufführen,** *n. in vbl senses.* **2. Aufführung,** *f.* *(a)*=II. 1; *also:* erection (of wall, building, etc.); *Com:* **A. der einzelnen Posten in einer Rechnung,** itemination of an account; *Th:* **bei der A. des Stückes . . .,** when the play was performed, presented . . .; **ein Schauspiel zur A. bringen,** to put a play on the stage; **ein Oratorium zur A. bringen,** to get an oratorio performed; **er hat sich besondere Verdienste erworben, indem er Werke zeitgenössischer Komponisten zur A. brachte,** he has acquired special merit by getting the works of contemporary composers performed; *(b) Th: etc:* performance (of play, opera, ballet, etc.); presentation (of play, film, etc.); **von allen Aufführungen des 'Tell', die ich gesehen habe . . .,** of all the performances I have seen of 'Tell' . . .; **eine hervorragende, miserable, A.,** an outstanding, a wretched, performance; *(c)* behaviour, conduct; way of acting.

Aufführungsrecht, *n. Th: etc:* right of performance; performing rights.

Aufführungsserie, *f. Th: etc:* run (of performances); series of performances of plays by one author.

auffüllen, *v.tr. sep.* *(a)* to fill up, top up (container, etc.); to fill (up) (gap); to fill (up) the gaps in (sth.); to replenish (container, stocks, etc.); *Civ.E:* to fill (up), pack (sunk part of ground, etc.); *(b)* **Wein a.,** (i) to bottle wine, (ii) to put wine in casks.

auffüttern, *v.tr. sep. Husb:* to rear, *U.S:* raise (animals); to feed up (animals, *F:* children, etc.).

Aufgabe, *f.* **1.** *(a) Post:* posting, *U.S:* mailing (of letter, parcel); handing in (of telegram); *Rail:* registering, registration, booking (of luggage), *U.S:* checking (of baggage); sending (of luggage, *U.S:* baggage) in advance; *(b)* **A. einer Anzeige (in der Zeitung),** insertion, inserting, of an advertisement in the paper; *(c) Com:* **A. einer Bestellung,** giving, placing, sending, of an order. **2.** *(a) Ind: Metall:* charging, feeding (of furnace, conveyor, etc.); *(b) Metall:* throat (of blast-furnace). **3.** *Com: Fin:* *(a)* advice; instructions; **laut A., Ihrer A. gemäß,** as per advice, in accordance with your instructions; *(b)* indication (of costs, price, etc.); quotation (of price). **4.** propounding, posing, setting (of problem, riddle, etc.). **5.** *(a)* task; duty; job; function, mission; *U.S. & Mil:* assignment; **seine A. erfüllen,** to perform, carry out, one's task; to fulfil one's task, one's duty; **es sich** *dat.* **zur A. machen, etwas zu tun,** to make it one's duty, to make every endeavour, to do sth.; to undertake to do sth.; to make a point of doing sth.; to make it one's business to do sth.; **es ist meine A., zu . . .,** it is my duty to . . .; it is my business to . . .; I have to . . .; it is up to me to . . .; **es ist die A. der Eltern, zu . . .,** it is the task, the duty, the part, of parents to . . .; **es ist nicht deine A., sie zu trösten,** it is not your business, your duty, your responsibility, it is not up to you, *F:* it is not your job, to console her; **ich habe die A., zu . . .,** it is my task, my duty, to . . .; **sie hält es für die A. ihres Lebens, zu . . .,** she thinks her mission in life is to . . .; **die soziale A. der Kirchen,** the social mission, task, of the Churches; **j-m eine A. stellen,** to set s.o. a task; **seiner A. gewachsen sein,** to be equal to, to be able to cope with, one's task, *F:* to be up to one's job; **dieses Gesetz hat eine doppelte A.,** this law has a double function, a double purpose, (to fulfil); *(b) Mth:* problem; **j-m eine A. stellen,** to set s.o. a problem; **eine A. lösen,** to solve a problem; *(c) Sch: usu. pl.* **Aufgaben,** homework; *F:* prep; *U.S:* assignment(s); **seine Aufgaben machen,** to do one's homework, *F:* one's prep; **schriftliche Aufgaben,** written homework; **mündliche Aufgaben,** reading *or* learning homework. **6.** giving up (of sth.); abandoning, abandonment (of sth.); leaving off (of a habit); relinquishing, relinquishment (of rights, a claim, an office, etc.); resigning, resignation, renouncing, renunciation, surrendering, surrender, waiving, *Jur:* waiver (of a right); *Sp:* giving up; retirement, retiral (from race, etc.); **A. des Amtes,** giving up of office, retirement, retiral (from office), resignation from office; **A. des Geschäfts,** giving up of, retirement from, business; **'wegen A. des Geschäfts geschlossen',** 'closed—proprietor given up, gone out of, retired from, business'; *Jur:* **A. einer Klage,** discontinuance of an action; abandoning of a prosecution; *Mil:* **A. einer Stellung,** abandoning, abandonment, of a position.

Aufgabeamt, *n. Post:* office of dispatch; *Tg:* office of origin.

aufgabeln, *v.tr. sep.* **1.** to lift (sth.) with a fork. **2.** *F:* to pick (s.o., sth.) up; **wo hast du das**

aufgegabelt? where did you pick that up? where did you get hold of that?
Aufgabenbereich, *m.* field of duties; (extent of the) functions (of an organization, etc.); scope (of a science, etc.); terms of reference (of committee of enquiry).
Aufgabenbuch, *n.*, **Aufgabenheft,** *n. Sch:* book for homework notes, prep book.
Aufgabengebiet, *n.* = **Aufgabenbereich.**
Aufgabensammlung, *f. Sch:* set of exercises; *Mth:* collection, set, of problems.
Aufgabenverteilung, *f.* allocation of tasks; *Mil:* distribution of assignments.
Aufgabeort, *m.* place where a letter was posted, *U.S:* mailed; place where a telegram was handed in; place where luggage was registered, *U.S:* checked.
Aufgaberutsche, *f. Ind:* charging chute (of furnace, etc.).
Aufgabeschein, *m.* receipt (for registered luggage, etc.), *U.S:* (claim) check.
Aufgabestation, *f. Rail:* station where registered luggage was accepted, *U.S:* where baggage was checked.
Aufgabestempel, *m. Post:* stamp of office of dispatch; *Tg:* stamp of office of origin; *Rail:* stamp of accepting office.
Aufgabetrichter, *m. Metall:* blast-furnace cone.
Aufgabeventil, *n. Mec.E:* delivery valve; charging valve.
Aufgabevorrichtung, *f. Ind: Metall:* charging device, charger, feeder (of blast-furnace, etc.).
Aufgabezeit, *f.* time of posting, *U.S:* mailing (of letter, etc.); time of handing in, of acceptance (of telegram).
Aufgalopp ['aufga·lɔp], *m. Turf:* trial gallop.
Aufgang, *m.* **1.** going up; rising; ascent; **A. der Sonne,** rising of the sun, sunrise; **A. eines Gestirns,** rising, ascension, of a star; *Mch: I.C.E:* **A. des Kolbens,** up-stroke of the piston. **2.** *A. & Poet:* **der A.,** the Orient, the East (of the earth). **3.** (*a*) way up; (flight of) steps; staircase; stairs; (*b*) slope up; ascent; gradient; acclivity. **4.** breaking up, break-up, of the ice; thaw. **5.** *Ven:* beginning of the open season.
aufgären, *v.i. sep.* (*conj. like* **gären**) (*sein*) to ferment (and rise); to seethe up, froth up.
aufgattern, *v.i. sep.* (*haben*) *Dial:* **j-m a.,** to lie in wait for s.o.; to waylay s.o.
aufgeben. I. *v.tr. sep.* (*strong*) **1.** (*a*) *Post:* to post, *U.S:* mail (letter, packet, parcel); to hand in (telegram); *Rail:* to register, book (luggage), *U.S:* to check (baggage); to send (luggage, *U.S:* baggage) in advance; **aufgegebenes Gepäck,** registered luggage, *U.S:* checked baggage; (*b*) **eine Anzeige (in der Zeitung) a.,** to insert, put, an advertisement in the paper; to put a notice in the paper; (*c*) *Com:* **eine Bestellung a.,** to give, place, send, an order. **2.** to serve (food); **darf ich Ihnen noch etwas Suppe a.?** may I give you a little more soup? **3.** *Ind: Metall:* to put (fuel, ore, etc.) on (furnace, conveyor, etc.); **Brennstoff (am Ofen) a.,** *abs.* **a.,** to charge, feed, the furnace. **4.** *Com: Fin:* **j-m etwas a.,** to give s.o. notice of sth.; to advise s.o. of sth.; to inform s.o. of sth.; **j-m eine Auskunft über etwas** *acc.* **a.,** to inform s.o., furnish s.o. with information, about, sth.; **einen Preis a.,** to quote a price. **5. j-m eine Arbeit a.,** to set s.o. a task, to assign s.o. a task, to assign a task to s.o.; **j-m a., etwas zu tun,** to set, assign, give, s.o. the task of doing sth.; to commission, order, set, s.o. to do sth.; **j-m ein Problem a.,** to set s.o. a problem; **j-m ein Rätsel a.,** (i) to ask s.o. a riddle; (ii) *F:* to perplex, puzzle, s.o. (*by one's actions, etc.*); *Sch:* **Hausarbeiten a.,** to set, give, *U.S:* assign, homework; **einen Hausaufsatz a.,** to set an essay as homework; **der Lehrer hat uns heute viel aufgegeben,** the teacher has set, given, *U.S:* assigned, us a lot of homework today. **6.** to give up (sth.); to abandon (sth.); to leave off (habit); to relinquish (rights, a claim, an office, etc.); to resign, renounce, surrender, *Jur:* to waive (a right); *abs. Sp. & F:* to give up (the race, the contest); to retire; (*of runner*) to drop out; (*of boxer, etc.*) to throw up, throw in, *F:* chuck up, the sponge; *F:* to pack up; **den Geist a.,** to give up the ghost, to render up one's spirit; **das Rauchen] a.,** to give up, leave off, *F:* cut out, smoking; **allen Luxus a.,** to give up luxuries; **seine Stelle a.,** to give up, throw up, leave, one's job; **sein Amt a.,** to give up, resign from, one's office; **den Dienst a.,** to give up, leave, quit, the service; **das Geschäft a.,** to give up, retire from, go out of, business; **(das) Latein a.,** to give up, drop, Latin; **den Kampf a.,** to give up the struggle; to cease fighting; **den Versuch als hoffnungslos a.,** to abandon the attempt (in despair), to give it up as a bad job; **jede Hoffnung a.,** to abandon all hope; **den Verkehr mit j-m a., j-n a.,** to drop s.o.'s acquaintance, to drop s.o.; **der Arzt hat ihn aufgegeben,** the doctor has given him up, has given up hope for him; **das Rennen a.,** (i) *Sp:* to give up the race, to drop out of the race; (ii) *F:* to throw up, to throw in, the sponge; *Cards & F:* **das Spiel a.,** to throw in one's cards, one's hand; *F:* to give it up (as hopeless, as a bad job), to pack up, to pack (it) in; **ich gebe es auf!** I give up! *Jur:* **eine Klage a.,** to discontinue an action; to abandon a prosecution; *Mil:* **eine Stellung a.,** to abandon a position.
II. *vbl s.* **Aufgeben,** *n. in vbl senses; cp.* **Aufgabe** 1, 2, 4, 6.
Aufgeber, *m.* **1.** sender (of letter, telegram, etc.). **2.** *Ind:* furnace-feeder.
Aufgebetrichter, *m.* = **Aufgabetrichter.**
aufgeblasen, *p.p. & a. see* **aufblasen.**
Aufgeblasenheit, *f.* **1.** swollen condition, state; puffiness (of the face, etc.). **2.** vanity, self-importance, (self-)conceit, bumptiousness. **3.** inflation, turgidity, flatulence, flatulency (of style).
Aufgebot, *n.* **1.** (*a*) *Jur:* public notice to persons having claims against an estate, a bankrupt, etc.; **A. der Gläubiger,** calling of a meeting of creditors; (*b*) *Ecc:* banns (of marriage); *Adm:* notice of an intended marriage; **das A. bestellen,** to put up the banns (*for marriage in church*); to give notice of an intended marriage (*at registry office*); **das A. verlesen,** to call the banns; **das A. aushängen,** to display the announcement of an intended marriage; **'erstes A.',** 'this is the first time of asking'. **2.** (*a*) *Mil:* levy(ing) (of troops); calling up (of recruits, reservists); call to arms; call-up; **allgemeines A.,** levy in mass, *levée en masse*; (*b*) body (of troops, personnel, etc.); contingent (of troops, competitors, etc.); mass (of cars, etc.); **ein starkes A. von Polizisten,** a strong body, a strong force, a large posse, of police; **ein starkes A. von Tänzerinnen,** a whole host of dancers; (*c*) **das erste und das zweite A.,** (i) *G.Hist:* the first and second age-groups of the *Landwehr*; (ii) *Fr.Hist:* the ban and the arrière-ban. **3. unter, mit, A. aller Kräfte konnte er . . . ,** summoning up all his strength, (by) exerting himself to the utmost, with the utmost exertion, by straining every nerve, he was able to . . . .
aufgebracht, *p.p. & a. see* **aufbringen.**
aufgedunsen, *p.p. & a.* puffed (up), swollen; puffy (face, features); bloated (face, corpse of drowned person, etc.); inflated, turgid, flatulent (style).
Aufgedunsenheit, *f.* puffiness (of face, etc.); bloated state (of face, corpse of drowned person, etc.); inflation, turgidity, flatulence (of style).
aufgehen, *v.sep.* (*strong*) I. *v.i.* (*sein*) **1.** (*of sun, moon, star, etc.*) to rise; **die Sonne, der Mond, Mars, ist aufgegangen,** the sun, the moon, Mars, has risen, is up; *Nau:* **eine steife Brise ging auf,** a stiff breeze was rising, springing up, getting up. **2. j-m a.,** (*of idea, meaning, etc.*) to become apparent to s.o.; to become clear to s.o.; **mir ging ein Licht,** *Hum:* **eine Stallaterne, auf,** I realized; I saw through it; I saw light, daylight; it (suddenly) dawned on me; *F:* the penny dropped; **endlich ging mir auf, daß . . . ,** at length I realized, understood, became aware, that . . . ; **die Wahrheit ging ihm auf,** he realized the truth; **die Bedeutung seiner Worte ging mir plötzlich auf,** I suddenly saw, realized, became aware of, the meaning of his words. **3.** (*of seed*) to come up; to spring up; to shoot; to sprout. **4.** (*a*) (*of cake, etc.*) to rise; (*of noodles, etc.*) to swell (up); (*of lime*) to swell, expand; *F:* **sie ist aufgegangen wie eine Dampfnudel,** she has got as fat as a pig; (*b*) **ihm ging das Herz auf,** his heart swelled, warmed (with joy); **ein Anblick, der einem das Herz a. läßt,** a sight that gladdens one's heart. **5.** (*a*) (*of door, lid, eyes, etc.*) to open; *Th:* (*of curtain*) to rise, to go up; **das Fenster ging plötzlich auf,** the window opened suddenly, flew open; **ihm ging eine neue Welt auf,** a new world opened before his eyes; **die Schublade, die Flasche, will nicht a.,** the drawer, the bottle, won't open; **ihm gingen die Augen auf,** his eyes were opened; he perceived the true state of affairs, *Lit:* the scales fell from his eyes; **mir sind die Augen aufgegangen,** I have had my eyes opened; *Th:* **ehe der Vorhang aufgeht,** before the curtain rises, goes up, before the rise, the rising, of the curtain; (*b*) *Ven:* **die Jagd geht nächsten Monat auf,** the open season starts next month; (*c*) (*of flower, bud*) to open; (*of bud*) to burst; (*d*) (*o ice*) to break (up); to thaw. **6.** (*of clothes, packet, knot, string, sewing, etc.*) to come undone; (*of garment, envelope, etc.*) to come open; (*of sewing, etc.*) to come apart; (*of flap of envelope, etc.*) to come unstuck; (*of wound*) to open; (*of abscess, boil*) to burst, break. **7.** (*a*) **in etwas** *dat.* **a.,** to merge, become merged, in, into, sth.; **mehrere kleine Länder gingen im Reich auf,** several small states were, became, merged in the Empire; **etwas in etwas** *dat.* **a. lassen,** to merge sth. in, into, sth.; (*b*) (*of pers.*) **in etwas** *dat.*, **in j-m, (ganz, völlig) a.,** to live entirely for sth., s.o., to live for nothing else but sth., s.o.; to be entirely devoted, wholly given up, to sth., s.o.; to be permanently taken up with sth., s.o.; to be (utterly) absorbed, engrossed, in sth., s.o.; **er geht ganz, völlig, in seiner Arbeit auf,** he is utterly devoted to his work; he is engrossed, wrapped up, in his work; **völlig in seiner Familie a.,** to devote one's whole existence to one's family; to have no life apart from one's family; (*c*) **in Flammen a.,** to go up in flames; **in Rauch a.,** to go up in smoke; to end in smoke; **in Dampf a.,** (*of liquid*) to pass into, turn to, vapour. **8.** *Mth:* (*of number*) **in einer anderen Zahl (restlos, ohne Rest) a.,** to divide another number exactly, with no remainder; **drei geht in zwölf auf,** three goes into twelve, divides twelve, twelve is divisible by three, divides by three; **zwei geht in allen geraden Zahlen auf,** two divides all even numbers, all even numbers divide, are divisible, by two; **die Rechenaufgabe geht genau auf,** the calculation comes out, works out, exactly; **die Gleichung geht auf,** the equation comes out; **die Aufgabe ging nicht auf,** the problem did not resolve itself, did not work out; **es geht gerade, genau, auf,** it works out exactly, just right; *F:* **seine Rechnung ging nicht auf,** he had miscalculated.
II. **aufgehen,** *v.tr.* **sich** *dat.* **die Füße a.,** to make one's feet sore with walking, to walk one's feet sore.
III. *vbl s.* **Aufgehen,** *n. in vbl senses; also:* (*a*) *Th:* **vor dem A. des Vorhangs,** before the rise, the rising, of the curtain; before the curtain rises, rose, goes up, went up; (*b*) **völliges A. in seiner Arbeit,** complete devotion to, absorption in, one's work; (*c*) *Jur:* **A. eines Besitzes in einem anderen,** merger. *Cp.* **Aufgang** 1.
aufgeien, *v.tr. sep. Nau:* to take in, clew (up), brail (up) (sail).
aufgeklärt, *p.p. & a. see* **aufklären.**
Aufgeklärtheit, *f.* (*a*) enlightened state of mind; enlightenment; broad-mindedness; (*b*) enlightenment about sexual matters, acquaintance with the facts of life.
Aufgeld, *n.* **1.** advance; earnest money. **2.** (*a*) additional charge; premium; (*b*) *Fin:* agio. **3.** *London St.Exch:* contango.
aufgelegt, *p.p. & a. see* **auflegen.**
aufgeräumt, *p.p. & a.* good-humoured; merry, cheerful, gay; in good spirits, in a good humour. *See also* **aufräumen.**
Aufgeräumtheit, *f.* good humour; cheerfulness; good spirits; gaiety.
aufgeregt, *p.p. & a. see* **aufregen.**
Aufgeregtheit, *f.* nervousness; nervous state; (state of) excitement; anxiety; *F:* edginess.
Aufgesang, *m. Pros:* (*a*) the first two sections of the strophe in the Middle High German lyric; (*b*) the two 'Stollen' comprising the first section of the strophe in the 'Meistergesang'.
aufgeschlagen, *p.p. & a. Her:* turned up.
aufgeschlossen, *p.p. & a.* open-minded; receptive (**für,** to). *See also* **aufschließen.**
Aufgeschlossenheit, *f.* open-mindedness; receptivity, receptiveness (**für,** to).
aufgeschmissen. **1.** *p.p. see* **aufschmeißen.** **2.** *a. F:* (*of pers.*) **(schön) a. sein,** to be in a proper, an awful, fix; to be in a proper, an awful, mess; to be in a quandary; to be up a gum-tree; **wenn er nicht bald kommt, sind wir a.,** if he doesn't turn up soon we've had it; **vier Gäste kamen, und wir hatten gar nichts im Hause — da waren wir schön a.,** four guests turned up and we had nothing at all in the house—we were in an awful fix, in an awful hole.
aufgetrieben, *p.p. & a. see* **auftreiben.**
Aufgetriebenheit, *f.* distension (of stomach, etc.); *Med:* intumescence (of spleen, etc.).
aufgeweckt, *p.p. & a.* bright, sharp, smart (child, etc.). *See also* **aufwecken.**
Aufgewecktheit, *f.* brightness, sharpness (of child, etc.).
aufgichten, *v.tr. sep. Metall:* to charge, feed (blast-furnace).
aufgießen, *v.tr. sep.* (*strong*) **1. eine Flüssigkeit auf etwas** *acc.* **a.,** to pour a liquid on sth. **2.** to

infuse (tea, herbs); to brew (tea); to make (tea, coffee); **Aufgießen** *n, in vbl senses; also;* infusion; *cp.* **Aufguß.**

aufgleisen, *v.tr. sep. Rail:* to rerail (locomotive); **Aufgleisen** *n,* **Aufgleisung** *f,* rerailing, rerailment.

Aufgleisungskran, *m. Rail:* rerailing crane, break-down crane.

Aufgleisungsschuh, *m. Rail:* rerailing ramp.

Aufgleisungsvorrichtung, *f. Rail:* rerailing device, rerailer.

aufgliedern, *v.tr. sep.* **1.** to arrange (material) in groups, under headings; to arrange (text, literary work) (in chapters, paragraphs, etc.); to classify (information, material, etc.); to process (figures, statistical material); **Aufgliederung** *f, in vbl senses; also:* arrangement; classification. **2.** to break (sth.) up into its component parts; to dismember (sth.).

aufglimmen, *v.i. sep.* (*weak & strong*) (*sein*) (*of fire, light*) to (begin to) glimmer; (*of light, dying fire, hope*) to flicker up; **wieder a.,** (*of fire, hope*) to (begin to) revive.

aufglühen, *v.i. sep.* (*sein*) to begin to glow.

aufgraben, *v.tr. sep.* (*strong*) **1.** to dig up (the earth, flower-bed, etc.); to break up (road). **2.** to dig up, unearth (buried object, etc.).

aufgreifen, *v.tr. sep.* (*strong*) (*a*) to pick (sth.) up; to take (sth.) up; to snatch (sth.) up; (*b*) to catch, seize (fugitive, criminal); to take up, adopt (idea, suggestion, proposal, etc.); **den Faden seiner Rede wieder a.,** to pick up the thread of one's discourse again; *Ven:* (*of hound*) **die Fährte a.,** *abs.* **a.,** to hit off the scent.

aufgrund, *prep.* (+*gen.*) on the basis of; on account of; *cp.* **Grund.**

aufgucken, *v.i. sep.* (*haben*) to look up; to glance up.

aufgürten, *v.tr. sep.* **1. einem Pferd den Sattel a.,** to girth the saddle on a horse. **2.** *A:* **sein Kleid a., sich a.,** to tuck up one's dress. **3.** *abs.* to slacken (horse's) girths.

Aufguß, *m.* **1.** pouring on (of liquid); sprinkling (with liquid); infusing, infusion (of tea, herbs); brewing (of tea). **2. zweiter A.,** second brew (of same tea); second boiling (of same coffee).

Aufgußapparat, *m. Ind:* sprinkler; *Brew:* sparger.

Aufgußtierchen, *n. Prot:* infusorian; *pl.* infusoria.

Aufgußverfahren, *n. Ch: Ind:* infusion process.

aufhaben, *v.tr. sep.* (*conj. like* **haben**) **1. einen Hut, eine Mütze, usw., a.,** to have a hat, a cap, etc., on; to wear, to be wearing, a hat, cap, etc. **2.** *Nau: etc:* **Dampf a.,** to have steam up. **3.** *Sch:* to have homework to do; **wir haben am Montag immer viel auf,** we always have a lot of homework on Mondays. **4.** (*a*) **den Mund, die Bluse, usw., a.,** to have one's mouth, one's blouse, etc., open; (*b*) **den Laden a.,** to have one's shop open; *abs.* (*of shop, etc.*) to be open; **wir haben heute bis sieben Uhr auf,** we are open till seven today.

aufhacken, *v.tr. sep.* (*a*) to dig up (ground, etc.) with a pick; to pick (ground); to break up (road, pavement); to hoe up (ground); (*b*) to chop (sth.) open; (*of bird*) to peck (sth.) open; **das Eis a.,** to chop a hole in the ice.

aufhaken, *v.tr. sep.* **1.** to unhook, unfasten, undo (garment, etc.); to unclasp (bracelet, buckle, etc.); to unbuckle (belt, etc.); **sich a.,** (*of garment, etc.*) to come unhooked, unfastened, undone; (*of bracelet, buckle, etc.*) to come unclasped, undone. **2.** to hook up (curtain, etc.); to put (sth.) on a, the, hook; to hang (sth.) up.

aufhalsen, *v.tr. sep. F:* **j-m etwas a.,** to saddle s.o. with sth., to saddle sth. on s.o., to land s.o. with (a responsibility, a task, an office, etc.); **sich** *dat.* **anderer Leute Sorgen a.,** to saddle oneself, burden oneself, with other people's troubles; **er hat eine Witwe geheiratet und sich** *dat.* **dabei fünf Stiefkinder aufgehalst,** he married a widow and landed himself with five stepchildren.

Aufhalt, *m.* stop; check; pulling up, pull-up (of horse, bicycle, etc.).

Aufhaltekraft, *f. Ball:* stopping power (of projectile).

Aufhaltelinie, *f. Mil:* stop-line.

aufhalten. I. *v.tr. sep.* (*strong*) **1.** to stop (s.o., sth.); to halt (s.o., vehicle, etc.); to arrest (motion, etc.); to check (motion, the enemy, etc.); to hold up (s.o., car, the enemy, etc.); to hinder, impede (s.o., sth.); to retard (progress, motion, etc.); to detain, delay (s.o., ship, etc.); to stay (procedure, process, etc.); to stay the progress of (s.o., sth.); **ein Pferd a.,** to stop, pull up, a horse; **einen Wagen a.,** to stop, hold up, halt, a car; to make a car pull up; **den Verkehr a.,** to hold up, block, obstruct, the traffic; (*of policeman*) to hold up, stop, the traffic; **j-s Fall a.,** to break s.o.'s fall; **einen Schlag a.,** to stop a blow; to break the force of a blow; **den Feind a.,** to stop, hold up, the enemy; to check the enemy; to hold the enemy in check; **das Wasser a.,** to stem the waters; **den Lauf der Ereignisse a.,** to stay, stem, the course of events; **ein Schüler, der die ganze Klasse aufhält,** a boy who holds up the whole class, who is a drag on the class; **den Fortschritt a.,** to arrest, block, progress; to retard progress; **ich brauche Sie nicht länger aufzuhalten,** I don't need to detain you, keep you, any longer; **ich will, ich möchte, Sie nicht a.,** (i) I don't want to hold you up, to take up your time; (ii) I don't want to detain you; don't let me keep you; *Mus:* **aufgehaltener Ton,** suspended note; *Navy:* **ein Schiff a.,** to intercept a ship. **2. sich aufhalten,** (*a*) **sich in, an, einem Ort a.,** to stay, stop, *Lit:* to sojourn, tarry, in a place; **sich bei j-m a.,** to stay, stop, with s.o.; **sie hielten sich tagsüber, eine Stunde, im Garten auf,** they stayed in the garden all day, for an hour; they spent the whole day, an hour, in the garden; (*b*) **sich bei, mit, einem Gegenstand a.,** to dwell on a subject; to linger over, upon, a subject; to enlarge upon a subject; **wir brauchen uns nicht länger bei dieser Stelle aufzuhalten,** we need not dwell on this passage any longer, we need not spend any further time on this passage; **ich habe keine Zeit, mich bei, mit, solchen Dummheiten aufzuhalten,** I have no time to waste on such fooleries; (*c*) **sich über j-n, über etwas** *acc.*, **a.,** to get worked up about s.o., sth., s.o.'s behaviour, views, etc. **3.** to hold (sth.) open; to keep (sth.) open; **j-m die Tür a.,** to hold the door open for s.o.; **den Laden, das Büro, a.,** to keep the shop, the office, open; **ich kann die Augen kaum a.,** I can hardly keep my eyes open; **die Hand a.,** to hold out one's hand (*to receive sth.*); **der Staat hält immer die Hand auf,** the State is forever wanting money.

II. *vbl s.* **1. Aufhalten,** *n. in vbl senses; also:* (*a*) stoppage; check; obstruction (of traffic); retardation (of progress, etc.); detention (of s.o.); *Mus:* suspension (of note); *Navy:* interception (of ship). **2. Aufhaltung,** *f.* (*a*)= II. 1; (*b*) delay; **ich habe allerlei Aufhaltungen gehabt,** all sorts of things have delayed me, held me up.

Aufhalter, *m.* **1.** *Mec.E:* stopping device; stop; check; brake. **2.** *Harn:* =**Aufhalteriemen.**

Aufhalteriemen, *m. Harn:* breeching, breech-band.

Aufhaltewucht, *f.*=**Aufhaltekraft.**

aufhämmern, *v.tr. sep.* **1.** to hammer (sth.) on (auf+*acc.*, to). **2.** to hammer (sth.) open.

Aufhänge-, *comb.fm.* **1.** *Mec.E:* suspension . . . ; **Aufhängedraht** *m,* suspension wire; **Aufhängeeisen** *n,* suspension iron. **2.** *Laund: Paperm: etc:* drying . . . ; **Aufhängegelände** *n,* drying ground; **Aufhängeleine** *f,* drying line. **3.** *Anat: Surg:* suspensory (ligament, bandage, etc.).

Aufhängeachse, *f. Mec.E:* suspension shaft.

Aufhängeband, *n.* **1.** *Anat:* suspensory ligament. **2.** *Surg:* suspensory bandage, *A:* suspensor.

Aufhängeboden, *m. Laund: etc:* drying-room, -loft.

Aufhängebügel, *m. Mec.E: etc:* suspension loop.

Aufhängegestänge, *n. Mec.E:* suspension rods.

Aufhängehaken, *m.* (*a*) *Mec.E: etc:* suspension hook; lifting-hook; (*b*) hanger.

Aufhängekreuz, *n. Paperm: Print: etc:* peel.

Aufhängeleine, *f. Dom.Ec:* clothes-line; *Tchn: Laund:* drying line.

Aufhängemuskel, *m. Anat:* levator (muscle).

aufhängen. I. *v.tr. sep.* (*conj. like* **hängen**[2]) **1.** (*a*) to hang (sth.) up; to hang (picture, meat, etc.); *Tchn:* to suspend (sth.) (an+*dat.*, on, from); **den Hut, den Mantel, a.,** to hang up one's hat, one's coat; **die Wäsche (zum Trocknen) a.,** to hang out the washing (to dry); **ein Bild an der Wand a.,** to hang a picture on the wall; **eine Lampe an der Decke a.,** to hang, suspend, a lamp from the ceiling; *Mec.E:* **frei beweglich aufgehängt,** freely suspended; *see also* **kardanisch;** *Aut:* **einen Wagen a.,** to spring a car, to fit the springing, the springs, the suspension, of a car; (*b*) **j-n a.,** to hang s.o. (**am Galgen,** on the gallows); **sich a.,** to hang oneself. **2.** *F:* **j-m etwas a.,** to saddle s.o. with sth., to saddle sth. on s.o.; to fob off, palm off, sth. (up)on s.o.; to foist, *F:* unload, sth. on s.o.; to work sth. off on s.o.; to land s.o. with (a responsibility, an unwanted article, etc.); **j-m einen Prozeß a.,** to involve s.o. in, let s.o. in for, a lawsuit; **j-m eine Lüge a.,** to tell s.o. a (thumping) lie; **da hast du dir was Schönes a. lassen,** you've been had; *P:* **einem Mädchen ein Kind a.,** to put a girl in the family way.

II. *vbl s.* **1. Aufhängen,** *n. in vbl senses; also:* suspension. **2. Aufhängung,** *f.* (*a*)=II. 1; (*b*) *Mec.E: etc:* suspension (device, arrangement); **federnde A.,** elastic suspension; *see also* **kardanisch;** *Aut:* **A. eines Wagens,** suspension, springing, springs, of a car; *Aut: etc:* mounting (of engine, etc.).

Aufhängenase, *f. Mec.E:* suspension lug.

Aufhängepunkt, *m. Mec.E: etc:* point of suspension.

Aufhänger, *m.* **1.** (*pers.*) hanger. **2.** (*device*) (*a*) hanger; (*b*) (*inside collar, for hanging up coat, etc.*) loop, hanger. **3.** (*a*) hook, (clothes) peg; (*b*) *F:* peg (on which to hang ideas).

Aufhängeseil, *n.* (*a*) *Mec.E:* suspension cable; (*b*)=**Aufhängeleine.**

Aufhängestange, *f. Mec.E:* suspension rod.

Aufhängevorrichtung, *f. Mec.E:* suspension device *or* arrangement.

Aufhängsel, *n.*=**Aufhänger** 2 (*b*).

Aufhängungs-, *comb.fm.*=**Aufhänge-.**

Aufhängungsfeder, *f. Mec.E: Aut:* suspension spring.

aufharken, *v.tr. sep.* to rake (sth.) up; to scuffle (path, etc.).

aufhaschen, *v.tr. sep.* to snatch (sth.) up; to grab (sth.).

aufhaspeln, *v.tr. sep.* to hoist, raise (with a windlass); to windlass.

Aufhau, *m. Min:* upward working.

aufhauen, *v.sep.* (*conj. like* **hauen**) **1.** *v.tr.* (*a*) to chop, hew, (sth.) open; to cut (sth.) open; *Min:* to open (up) (a coal-face, etc.); (*b*) to chop up, cut up (side of meat, etc.); (*c*) **eine Feile a.,** to recut a file; (*d*) *abs. F:* to spend money lavishly (*on an entertainment, etc.*), *F:* to do the grand. **2.** *v.i.* (*haben*) *Min:* to work upwards.

Aufhauer, *m. Tls:* cold chisel.

aufhäufeln, *v.tr. sep.* (*a*) to pile (sth.) up in (small) heaps; *Hort:* to hill (earth); (*b*) *Hort:* to earth up, ridge up, hill (plants).

aufhäufen. I. *v.tr. sep.* to heap (up), pile (up), bank (up) (earth, stones, etc.); to gather (thgs) (in a heap); to accumulate (goods capital, etc.); to amass (money, etc.); to hoard, pile up (goods, money, etc.); **ein Vermögen a.,** to amass a fortune; **ein Maß a.,** to fill a measure to overflowing; **aufgehäuftes Maß,** heaped measure; **sich a.,** to pile up; to collect; to gather (in a heap); to accumulate; (*of snow*) to drift.

II. *vbl s.* **1. Aufhäufen,** *n. in vbl senses; also:* accumulation. **2. Aufhäufung,** *f.* (*a*)=II. 1; (*b*) heap, pile; accumulation; drift (of snow); hoard (of goods, money, etc.).

aufheben. I. *v.tr. sep.* (*strong*) **1.** (*a*) to lift (sth., s.o.) up; to raise (weight, arm, skirt, etc.); to pick (sth., s.o.) up; to take (sth.) up; **die Augen a.,** to lift, raise, one's eyes; to look up; **die Hand a.,** to lift, raise, one's hand (i) to take an oath, to vote, etc., (ii) to deliver a blow; **die Hand gegen j-n a.,** to lift one's hand against s.o.; **etwas, j-n, (vom Boden) a.,** to lift sth., s.o., up (from the ground); to pick sth., s.o., up; to help s.o. up, help s.o. to his feet; **sich a.,** to pick oneself up, to get up; *see also* **Handschuh;** (*b*) **die Tafel a.,** (*of host*) to rise from table, to leave the table. **2.** (*a*) to keep (sth.); **etwas für j-n a., j-m etwas a.,** to keep sth. for s.o.; to save sth. (up) for s.o.; **sie hebt alle Briefe auf,** she keeps all her letters; **die Papiere sind sicher, gut, aufgehoben,** the papers are in a safe place, are safely put away; the papers are in good hands, are in safe keeping; **dein Geheimnis ist bei mir gut aufgehoben,** your secret is safe with me; **das werde ich für magere, schlechte, Zeiten a.,** I'll keep it, save it up, for a rainy day; (*b*) (*of pers.*) **gut aufgehoben sein,** to be in good hands; to be well looked after; to be kept safe from harm; **der Alte ist bei seinem Enkel gut aufgehoben,** the old man is well looked after in his grandson's home; **Kinder sind am besten bei der Mutter aufgehoben,** the best place for a child is with its mother; **die Kinder wären besser in einem Heim aufgehoben,** the children would be better off in a home; (*of invalid*) **im Himmel wäre sie am besten aufgehoben,** death would be a merciful release for her. **3.** *A:* to take (criminals, conspirators, etc.) by surprise; to capture, seize (criminals, insurgents, etc.); to raid (gambling-den, nest of conspirators, etc.). **4.** to raise (siege, interdict); to dissolve (assembly, meeting, etc.); to break up (meeting); to suppress (institution, etc.); to dissolve, break (partnership); to annul (law, agreement, contract, marriage, etc.); to rescind (law, judgment,

contract, etc.); to revoke (decree, edict, etc.); to abrogate, repeal (law, decree); to nullify, invalidate (contract, etc.); to abolish, do away with (law, tax, etc.); to cancel, terminate, *Jur:* avoid (agreement, contract); *Jur:* to render void, to quash, to set aside (judgment); to disaffirm (judgment, agreement, contract); **ein Lager a.,** to abandon a camp; **ein Kloster a.,** to dissolve a monastery *or* nunnery; **eine Verlobung a.,** to break off an engagement; **eine Ehe a.,** to annul a marriage; to dissolve a marriage; **ein Verbot a.,** to cancel, lift, a prohibition; to lift, take off, an embargo; **eine Beschränkung a.,** to remove, lift, a restriction; **die Beschränkungen des Handels a.,** to lift the restrictions on trade; **aufgeschoben ist nicht aufgehoben,** there is always another time; it is only a pleasure deferred; *Jur:* **eine Klage a.,** to withdraw an action; **eine Beschlagnahme a.,** to restore goods (taken in distraint); to grant replevin; **aufhebende Entscheidung,** annulment of a court decision (by a higher court); *Nau:* **das Embargo auf ein Schiff a.,** to take off the embargo on a ship; *Pol:* **einen Vertrag, einen Waffenstillstand, a.,** to denounce a treaty, an armistice. **5.** to neutralize (effect, advantage, etc.); to balance out (loss, gain, etc.); to counter-balance (force, etc.); to offset (fault, advantage, etc.); to compensate for (fault etc.); *Mth:* to cancel (term, etc.); **sich (gegenseitig) a., einander a.,** to neutralize one another; (*of loss and gain*) to balance out; (*of forces*) to counterbalance one another; *Mth: etc:* (*of terms, etc.*) to cancel out, to cancel one another; *Opt:* **Farben, die sich a.,** complementary colours.

II. *vbl s.* **1. Aufheben,** *n.* (*a*)=II. 2; (*b*) **über etwas** *acc.,* **von etwas, viel Aufhebens, großes A., ein großes Aufhebens, machen,** to make a great fuss, a great to-do, a great pother, much ado, about sth.; to pay too much attention to sth.; to attach too much importance to sth.; **von diesem Erfolg wurde zu viel Aufhebens gemacht,** this success was too much noised abroad; too much was made of, too much fuss was made about, this success; too much importance was attached to this success; **kein großes A. von etwas, um etwas, machen,** to make very little fuss about sth.; not to make too much of sth.; **viel Aufhebens um nichts machen,** to make much ado about nothing. **2. Aufhebung,** *f.* *in vbl senses; also:* (*a*) dissolution (of assembly, meeting, partnership, institution, marriage, etc.); suppression (of institution); annulment (of agreement, contract, partnership, marriage, etc.); rescission (of law, judgment, contract, etc.); reversal (of judgment); disaffirmation (of judgment, agreement, contract); revocation (of decree, edict); abrogation, repeal (of law, decree, etc.); removal (of restriction); nullification, invalidation (of contract, etc.); abolition, abolishment (of law, tax, etc.); **A. eines Klosters,** dissolution of a monastery *or* nunnery; *Jur:* **A. einer Klage,** withdrawal of an action; **A. der ehelichen Gemeinschaft,** judicial separation; *Pol:* **A. eines Vertrags, eines Waffenstillstands,** denunciation, denouncing, of a treaty, of an armistice; (*b*) *A:* seizure (of conspirators, etc.); (*c*) neutralization (of effect, advantage, etc.).

Aufhebungsgericht, *n. Jur:* court of cassation; court of appeal.

Aufhebungsgründe, *m.pl. Jur:* grounds for annulment (of judgment, marriage, contract, etc.).

Aufhebungsklage, *f. Jur:* petition for annulment (of marriage, contract, etc.).

Aufhebungszeichen, *n. Mus:* (*sign*) natural, ♮.

aufhefteln, *v.tr. sep.* **1.** to pin (sth.) on. **2.** to un-hook, unfasten, undo (dress, etc.).

aufheften, *v.tr. sep.* **1.** to fasten (sth.) on (**auf**+*acc.,* to); *Needlew:* to tack on, baste on (lining, etc.). **2.** to pin up, tuck up (one's skirt, etc.). **3.** *Needlew:* to undo (tacked-on lining, etc.); to take apart (tacked-together garment, etc.).

aufheißen, *v.tr. sep. Nau: etc:* to hoist (up) (sail, flag, heavy object, etc.); to trice (up) (sail); to run up (flag); to sway up (yard); **heiß auf!** up with it! hoist away! *Nau:* sway away!

aufheitern. I. *v.tr. sep.* to cheer (s.o.) up; to brighten up, liven up, enliven (s.o., a conversation, situation, etc.); **er war ganz aufgeheitert,** he had become quite cheerful, quite gay; **sich a.,** (*of pers.*) to cheer up; (*of sky, weather*) to clear (up); to become bright(er); (*of pers., face, sky, weather*) to brighten up; **sein Gesicht heiterte sich auf,** his face brightened (up), lit up; his brow cleared; **der Himmel, das Wetter, heitert sich auf,** the sky, the weather, is

clearing (up), is becoming bright(er), is brightening.

II. *vbl s.* **Aufheiterung,** *f.* (*a*) *in vbl senses; also:* **etwas zu j-s A. tun,** to do sth. to cheer s.o. up; **sie las den Kindern zur A. eine lustige Geschichte vor,** she read the children a funny story to cheer them up; (*b*) **A. suchen,** to try to find something to cheer one up; to seek diversion, amusement, distraction.

aufhelfen, *v.i. sep.* (*strong*) (*haben*) **1. j-m a.,** to help s.o. up; to help s.o. to get up; *F:* to give s.o. a lift; to give s.o. a leg up; *F:* **dem ist nicht mehr aufzuhelfen,** there's nothing more to be done for him. **2. j-m eine Last a.,** to help s.o. to shoulder a burden.

aufhellen. I. *v.tr. sep.* **1.** to lighten (colour); to brighten (up) (colour, etc.); to lighten the colour of (substance, hair, etc.); to clarify (liquid, wine, beer); to fine (wine, beer); **sich a.,** (*of colour, substance*) to lighten; to grow, get, lighter; (*of sky, weather*) to clear (up), brighten (up); **sein Gesicht hellte sich auf,** his face brightened (up), lit up; his brow cleared. **2.** to elucidate, clear up (question, mystery, etc.); to throw, shed, light on (subject, mystery, crime, situation, etc.); to clarify (question, etc.); to illuminate (subject, question).

II. *vbl s.* **Aufhellen** *n.,* **Aufhellung** *f. in vbl senses; also:* clarification (of liquid, wine, beer, question, etc.); elucidation (of question, mystery, etc.); illumination (of subject, question).

Aufhellungsmittel, *n.* **1.** *Ch: Brew: etc:* clearing agent. **2.** brightener (for colours).

aufhenken, *v.tr. sep.* to hang (s.o.) (on the gallows).

aufhetzen. I. *v.tr. sep.* **1.** *Ven:* to start (stag, etc.). **2. j-n a.,** to goad s.o. into a rage; to rouse s.o. to fury; to incite s.o.; **den Pöbel a.,** to stir up the mob; to rouse the rabble; **j-n zur Revolte a.,** to incite s.o., egg s.o. on, to revolt; *abs. zur Revolte a.,** to instigate revolt; **j-n gegen j-n a.,** to set s.o. against s.o.; **Arbeiter gegen die Arbeitgeber a.,** to incite workmen against their employers; **Leute gegeneinander a.,** to set people at loggerheads, set people by the ears, get people at daggers drawn (with one another); to stir up mutual hatred among people; **auf-hetzende Reden halten,** to make provocative, inflammatory, *F:* rabble-rousing, speeches.

II. *vbl s.* **Aufhetzen** *n.,* **Aufhetzung** *f. in vbl senses; also:* incitement; (political) agitation; *F:* rabble-rousing; **A. zur Revolte,** instigation to revolt.

Aufhetzer, *m.* inciter; instigator; agitator; firebrand; (political) trouble-maker; *F:* rabble-rouser.

Aufhetzerei, *f.* agitation; stirring up of (political) trouble; rousing of (popular) fury; *F:* rabble-rousing.

aufhetzerisch, *a.* provocative (actions, speech, etc.); inflammatory, *F:* rabble-rousing (speech, etc.).

aufhissen, *v.tr. sep.*=**aufheißen.**

aufhocken. I. *v.sep.* **1.** *v.tr.* to take (burden, child, etc.) on one's back; to give (s.o.) a pick-a-back; *F:* **er muß alles a.,** he has to carry all the burdens. **2.** *v.i.* (*sein*) (*a*) *Gym:* to squat on (to horizontal bar, etc.); (*b*) to climb on s.o.'s back. **II.** *vbl s.* **Aufhocken,** *n.* **1.** *in vbl senses.* **2.**=**Aufhockspiel.**

Aufhocker, der. *Myth:* the Old Man of the Sea.

Aufhockspiel, *n. Games:* high-, hey-cockalorum.

aufhöhen, *v.tr. sep.* **1.** to raise, to increase the height of (wall, house, mound, etc.); *Arch:* to stilt (arch). **2.** to enhance, heighten, set off (colour).

aufholen, *v.tr. sep.* **1.** to pull (sth.) up; to haul (sth.) up; to hoist (sth.) up; to run up (flag); *Nau:* **ein Segel, einen Baum, a.,** to trice (up) a sail, a boom. **2. die Verspätung a.,** to make up for lost time; **das Versäumte a.,** to make up for what one has missed; to catch up again; *abs.* **a.,** to make up for lost time; to catch up; to make up leeway; *Rac:* to catch up on the man ahead; to close the gap; *Rail:* (*of train*) to make up time; **er muß tüchtig a.,** he will have to work hard to catch up; he has considerable leeway to make up; **wenn Sie ihm Zeit gäben, würde er aufholen,** if you gave him time he would catch up; *Rac:* **er holte in der Kurve schnell auf,** he caught up fast, came up well, at the bend.

Aufholer, *m.* -s/-. *Nau:* tricing-line, -rope; tripping-line.

aufhorchen, *v.i. sep.* (*haben*) to prick up one's ears; to cock one's ears; to listen attentively; to be all ears, all attention; to keep one's ears open.

aufhören. I. *v.i. sep.* (*haben*) **1.** *A:* to listen (attentively). **2.** to cease; to leave off; to stop, come to a stop; to end, come to an end; to finish; (*of speaker, singer, incomplete text, etc.*) to break off; **er hörte mitten in einem Satz auf,** he stopped, broke off, in the middle of a sentence; **wenn der Regen nicht aufhört,** if the rain does not stop, leave off; **er hörte nicht auf, bis sie errötete,** he did not stop, he kept on, until she was blushing; **wo haben wir aufgehört?** where did we leave off? **gestern hörten wir bei Seite 30 auf,** we stopped, left off, yesterday at page 30; **das hört nicht auf,** there's no end to it; **die Hügel hören bei X auf,** the hills fall away at X; **plötzlich a.,** to stop short, dead; **mitten in einer Rede plötzlich a.,** to stop short in the middle of a speech; **der Pfad hörte plötzlich auf,** the path came to a dead end; **der Pfad hörte allmählich auf,** the path petered out; **hör auf!** (i) stop! (ii) **hör (doch) auf!** (do) be quiet! (do) leave off! have done with it! give over! *F:* stop it! drop it! lay off! *F:* **da hört (sich) doch alles auf!** that beats everything! that's the limit! that's a bit stiff! that's a bit thick! that's a bit off! **a., etwas zu tun,** **mit etwas a.,** to cease (from) doing sth.; to stop, leave off, doing sth.; to discontinue sth., doing sth.; **a. zu arbeiten, mit der Arbeit a.,** to cease, leave off, stop, work; to stop, cease, finish, working; to knock off (work); **er hört nie auf, dumme Fragen zu stellen,** he keeps on asking, never stops asking, silly questions; **er hört nie auf mit seinen Klagen,** he keeps on, never stops, is constantly, complaining; **hör mit dem Weinen auf!** stop crying! have done (with) crying!; **a. zu zahlen, mit der Zahlung a.,** to stop paying, to stop, suspend, cease, payment; to discontinue the payments; **mit seinen Besuchen a.,** to discontinue, stop, one's visits.

II. *vbl s.* **Aufhören,** *n. in vbl senses; also:* cessation; discontinuation; stoppage (of work, etc.); **Zeichen zum A.,** signal to stop, to finish; **ohne A.,** without cease, unceasingly, ceaselessly; constantly; (to work, etc.) without intermission.

aufhucken, *v.tr. sep.* to take (s.o.) on one's back; to give (s.o.) a pick-a-back.

aufhüpfen, *v.i. sep.* (*sein*) to jump (up); to skip; (*of bird, insect, etc.*) to hop (up); (*of ball, etc.*) to bounce.

aufhusten. 1. *v.tr.* to cough up (blood, phlegm, etc.). **2.** *v.i.* (*haben*) to give a (short) cough.

Aufhütte, *f. Ven:* crow-shooting hut.

aufjagen, *v.tr. sep.* to rout out (*Ven:* animal, *F:* s.o.); to rouse (*Ven:* game, *F:* s.o.); *Ven:* to start (stag, hare, bird, etc.); to put up (partridge, etc.); to flush (birds); to draw (fox); to unearth (fox); *F:* **sie haben mich heute morgen schon um sechs Uhr aufgejagt,** they routed me out of bed at six this morning.

aufjammern, *v.i. sep.* (*haben*) to break out into lamentations; to set up a wail.

aufjauchzen, *v.i. sep.* (*haben*) to burst out into cries of joy; to shout for joy; to jubilate.

aufjubeln, *v.i. sep.* (*haben*) to burst out into jubilation; to jubilate, exult; *F:* to raise a cheer.

aufkaden, *v.i. sep.* (*haben*) *Dial:* to heighten the dike(s) (with sandbags, etc.); **Aufkadung** *f,* (i) heightening of the dike(s); (ii) line of sand-bags, etc., laid along the top of the dike(s).

aufkämmen, *v.tr. sep.* **1.** to comb up (hair, etc.); to comb (hair) upwards; to comb out ((tangled) hair); to freshen up (fur, etc.) by combing; **aufgekämmtes Haar,** hair combed upwards. **2.** *Carp:* to fit together (structure) with cog-joints, notch-joints.

aufkanten, *v.tr. sep.* to set (sth.) on edge; to set, lay, (sth.) edgeways, edgewise.

aufkappen, *v.tr. sep. Ven:* to hood (hawk).

aufkatten, *v.tr. sep. Nau:* to cat (anchor).

Aufkauf, *m.* buying up (of commodity, lands, etc.); *Hist:* forestalling (of a commodity); *Com:* **A. des gesamten Angebotes (an einer Ware),** cornering of a commodity.

aufkaufen, *v.tr. sep.* to buy up (commodity, lands, etc.); *Hist:* to forestall (a commodity); *abs.* to forestall; *Com:* **im voraus a.,** to buy in anticipation, to buy ahead; **den Markt a.,** to corner the market; **das gesamte Angebot an Weizen a.,** to corner, make a corner in, wheat.

Aufkäufer, *m.* buyer-up (of commodities, food, etc.); *Hist:* forestaller.

aufkehren, *v.tr. sep.* to sweep up (dust, etc.).

aufkeilen, *v.tr. sep. Mec.E:* to key on (wheel, pulley, etc.); **eine Rolle auf eine Spindel a.,** to key a pulley on, to, a spindle.

aufkeimen, *v.i. sep.* (*sein*) to germinate; (*of plant, etc.*) to shoot, spring up, sprout; (*of hope, love,*

etc.) to spring up, to dawn; **aufkeimende Knospe,** newly-formed bud; **aufkeimende Liebe, Leidenschaft,** budding love, passion; **aufkeimende Hoffnung,** dawning hope; **Aufkeimen** *n*, **Aufkeimung** *f, in vbl senses; also:* germination.

Aufkimmung, *f. N.Arch:* rise, upsweep (of floor-timbers, etc.).

aufkitten, *v.tr. sep.* to cement (sth.) on; to putty (sth.) on; to stick (sth.) on with mastic *or* lute (**auf**+*acc.*, to).

aufklaffen, *v.i. sep.* (*a*) (*haben*) (*of hole, seam, etc.*) to gape (open); (*of chasm*) to yawn; (*b*) (*sein*) (*of earth, rock*) to open.

aufklaftern, *v.tr. sep.* to stack (up), cord (firewood).

Aufklang, *m.* (*a*) opening bars (of piece of music); (*b*) opening words *or* initial proceedings (of ceremony, etc.); beginning (of ceremony, friendship, etc.); **das gab der Feier einen festlichen A.,** that started the celebration on a joyful note.

aufklappbar, *a.* (lid, flap, hood of car, etc.) that can be raised; (lid) that can be opened; (hinged structure) that can be opened out; hinged (flap, lid); (chair, etc.) that can be unfolded.

aufklappen, *v.sep.* **1.** *v.tr.* (*a*) to raise (hinged object); to put up (hood of car, flap of table, etc.); to turn up (brim of hat); (*b*) to open (book, piano, folding chair, clasp-knife, etc.); to unfold (folding chair, etc.). **2.** *v.i.* (*sein*) (*of lid, etc.*) to open with a click, a snap; to snap open; to jerk open.

aufklaren, *v.sep.* **1.** *v.tr. Nau:* to clear (up) (deck, etc.); to clear away, tidy up (ropes, etc.); **alles ist aufgeklart,** everything is ship-shape. **2.** *v.i.* (*haben*) **das Wetter, es, klart auf,** the weather, it, is clearing (up); (*in weather-forecast*) **bewölkt, später aufklarend,** overcast, clearing later.

aufklären. I. *v.tr. sep.* **1.** (*a*) (*of wind, etc.*) to clear up (sky, weather); **sich a.,** (*of sky, weather*) to clear (up), to become bright(er); **sein Gesicht klärte sich auf,** his face brightened (up), lit up; his brow cleared; (*b*) to clear up, elucidate (question, mystery, etc.); to throw, shed, light on (situation, mystery, crime, etc.); to clarify (question, etc.); to illuminate (subject, question); **die Lage hat sich aufgeklärt,** the situation has clarified, cleared (up). **2.** (*a*) to enlighten (s.o.) (**über einen Gegenstand, über etwas** *acc.*, on a subject, as to sth.); to instruct, inform (s.o.) (**über etwas** *acc.*, about sth.); *Lit: Rel:* to illuminate, illumine (s.o.'s mind); **ich habe ihn über die Sachlage aufgeklärt,** I have enlightened him as to the situation; I have explained the situation, made the situation clear, to him; I have informed him of, about, the situation; (*b*) to enlighten (s.o.) about sexual matters, to tell (s.o.) the facts of life. **3.** *Mil: Navy: Av:* to reconnoitre, *F:* recce (ground, sea area, etc.); (*of aircraft*) to spot (enemy guns, movements, etc.); *abs.* to reconnoitre, *F:* recce; to scout.

II. *vbl s.* **1. Aufklären,** *n.*=II. 2 (*a*). **2. Aufklärung,** *f.* (*a*) *in vbl senses; also:* elucidation (of question, mystery, etc.); clarification (of question, etc.); illumination (of subject, question, *Lit: Rel:* of s.o.'s mind); imparting of information about sexual matters; education in sexual matters; (*b*) *Mil: Navy: Av:* reconnaissance, *F:* recce; (*c*) *Hist. of G.Lit. & Phil:* **die (deutsche) A.,** the (German) Enlightenment, the 'Aufklärung'; **das Zeitalter der A.,** the Age of Enlightenment; (*d*)=**Aufgeklärtheit.**

III. *p.p. & a.* **aufgeklärt,** *in vbl senses; esp.* enlightened; broad-minded; liberal-minded; free from prejudices; free from superstitions; **a. werden,** to become enlightened, to find enlightenment, *F:* to see the light.

Aufklärer, *m.* **-s/-. 1.** enlightener (of s.o.; of question, subject). **2.** (*a*) *Hist. of G.Lit. & Phil:* spreader of enlightenment; representative of the Age of Enlightenment; (*b*) rationalist. **3.** *Mil: Navy: Av:* scout; *Navy:* reconnoitring vessel; scouting vessel; look-out ship; *Av:* reconnaissance, *F:* recce, aircraft.

Aufklärerei, *f.* **-/-en.** *Hist. of G.Lit. & Phil: Pej:* pseudo-enlightenment; shallow rationalism.

aufklärerisch, *a.* striving towards enlightenment; **aufklärerische Bestrebungen,** tendencies towards enlightenment; attempts to combat ignorance *or* superstition.

Aufklaricht, *n.* **-s/-e**=**Aufklärerei.**

Aufklärungs-, *comb.fm.* **1.** *Lit: Phil: etc:* . . . of enlightenment; **die Aufklärungszeit, das Aufklärungszeitalter,** the Age of Enlightenment. **2.** *Mil: Navy: Av:* reconnaissance, *F:* recce . . . ; reconnoitring . . . ; scouting . . . ; **Aufklärungskräfte** *pl*, reconnaissance forces; *Mil:* **Aufklärungsabteilung** *f*, reconnaissance, *F:* recce, unit; **Aufklärungstruppe** *f*, reconnaissance, *F:* recce, troops; *Navy:* **Aufklärungsfahrzeuge** *n pl*, reconnoitring craft, scout craft, scouts; *Av:* **Aufklärungsbomber** *m*, reconnaissance, *F:* recce, bomber.

Aufklärungsbuch, *n.* sex education book.

Aufklärungsfahrt, *f. Navy: Av.* reconnaissance (patrol); *Navy:* reconnaissance cruise.

Aufklärungsflieger, *m. Mil.Av:* **1.**=**Aufklärungsflugzeug. 2.** pilot *or* member of the crew of a reconnaissance aircraft.

Aufklärungsflugzeug, *n. Mil.Av:* reconnaissance, *F:* recce, aircraft; observer aircraft.

Aufklärungspflicht, *f. Jur:* duty (of the presiding judge) to ensure that the facts of the case are fully and clearly presented to the court.

Aufklärungsraum, *m. Mil: Navy: Av:* reconnaissance, *F:* recce, sector.

Aufklärungsspähtrupp, *m. Mil:* reconnaissance, *F:* recce, patrol; reconnoitring party.

Aufklärungsstreife, *f. Mil:* reconnaissance, *F:* recce, patrol.

Aufklärungsstreifen, *m. Mil: Mil.Av:* reconnaissance, *F:* recce, sector.

Aufklärungstätigkeit, *f. Mil: Navy: Av:* reconnaissance, *F:* recce, activity.

aufklatschen, *v.sep.* **1.** *v.tr.* **etwas auf etwas** *acc.* **a.,** to slap sth. on sth.; **Tünche auf die Wand a.,** to slap distemper on the wall. **2.** *v.i.* (*sein*) (*of heavy object*) **aufs Wasser, auf den Boden, a.,** to hit the water with a splash; to fall on the ground *or* floor with a smack, *F:* to fall smack on the ground *or* floor; (*of rain*) **aufs Pflaster a.,** to splash on the pavement; *Swim:* (**mit dem Bauch aufs Wasser) a.,** to do a belly-flop.

aufklauben, *v.tr. sep.* to pick (sth.) up; **seine Ideen da und dort a.,** to pick up, glean, garner, an idea here and there.

aufklebbar, *a.* that can be stuck on; stick-on (label); adhesive (stamp, label, etc.).

aufkleben, *v.tr. sep.* to stick (sth.) on; to paste *or* glue (sth.) on; **eine Briefmarke auf einen Brief a.,** to stick, put, a stamp on a letter.

Aufkleber, *m.* **1.** (*pers.*) paster. **2.**=**Aufklebezettel.**

Aufklebezettel, *m.* stick-on label, *U.S:* sticker.

aufkleistern, *v.tr. sep.* to paste (sth.) on (**auf**+*acc.*, to).

aufklinken, *v.tr. sep.* to unlatch (door); to turn the handle of (door).

aufklotzen. I. *v.tr. sep.* **1.** to mount (sth.) on a block *or* blocks. **2.** (*a*) *N.Arch: etc:* to support (sth.) by a chock *or* chocks; (*b*) *N.Arch:* to bolt dead-wood on to (keel, etc.).

II. *vbl s.* **1. Aufklotzen,** *n.*=II. 2 (*a*). **2. Aufklotzung,** *f.* (*a*) *in vbl senses;* (*b*) mounting; *N.Arch: etc:* chock; (*c*) *N.Arch:* dead-wood.

aufknacken, *v.tr. sep.* to crack (sth.) open; to crack (nut, etc.).

aufknöpfbar, *a. Cost:* that can be buttoned on; button-on (collar, etc.).

aufknöpfen, *v.tr. sep.* **1.** to unbutton (garment); to undo (the buttons of) (dress, etc.); **sich a.,** (*of garment*) to come unbuttoned; *F:* (*of pers.*) **aufgeknöpft sein,** to be in an expansive mood; to be free and easy; *Hum:* **die Ohren, die Augen, a.,** to keep one's ears, one's eyes, open; *Hum:* to keep one's eyes peeled. **2.** to button (sth.) on; **einen Kragen, eine Manschette, auf ein Kleid a.,** to button a collar, a cuff, on to a dress.

aufknospen, *v.i. sep.* (*sein*) to bud, shoot; to come out (in bud); *Lit:* to burgeon.

aufknoten, *v.tr. sep.* **1.** to unknot (string, etc.); to untie, undo (parcel, etc.); *occ.* **sein Haar a.,** to undo, let down, untie, one's hair. **2. aufgeknotetes Haar,** hair done up in a knot *or* bun.

aufknüpfen, *v.tr. sep.* **1.** to tie (sth.) up; *F:* **j-n a.,** to string s.o. up; to hang s.o. (on the gallows). **2.** to untie, undo (knot, parcel, string, etc.); to unknot (string, etc.).

aufkochen, *v.sep.* **1.** *v.tr.* to boil (sth.) up; to bring (sth.) to the boil; to boil (milk); **wieder a.,** to reboil (jam, syrup, etc.). **2.** *v.i.* (*haben, sein*) to come to the boil; **etwas a. lassen,** to bring sth. to the boil; **etwas kurz a. lassen,** to bring sth. quickly to the boil.

Aufkochgefäß, *n. Ch: Ind:* boiler.

aufkohlen, *v.tr. sep. Metall:* to carburize, cement (wrought iron); **Aufkohlung** *f*, carburization, cementation.

aufkommen. I. *v.i. sep.* (*strong*) (*sein*). **1.** (*of pers.*) (*a*) to get up (from the ground); to get on one's feet, rise to one's feet; (*b*) (**wieder**) **a.,** to get up (from sick-bed); to recover (from an illness), to get well again; to pull round. **2.** (*a*) (*of plant*) to come up, grow, grow up, spring up; (*of new generation, etc.*) to arise, to spring up; (*b*) (*of wind*) to rise, get up, spring up; (*of squall*) to spring up; **schlechtes Wetter kam auf,** bad weather was setting in; (*c*) (*of custom, idea, doubts, rumours, etc.*) to arise, to spring up; (*of new invention, etc.*) to come into being, into existence; (*of custom, style*) to come into fashion, into vogue; to become fashionable; to become established; (*of custom, fashion, rumour, etc.*) to start; (*of fashion, style, etc.*) to come in; to appear; (*of ideas, desires, doubts*) **in j-m a.,** to arise, rise, in s.o.'s mind; **diese Mode ist im fünfzehnten Jahrhundert aufgekommen,** this fashion came in, was introduced, in the fifteenth century; **der Gedanke, der gerade in ihm aufkam,** the idea that was just forming, rising, in his mind; **Zweifel kamen in ihm auf, ihm kamen Zweifel auf,** he began to have (his) doubts; **Zweifel, Verdacht, a. lassen,** to give rise to doubts, to suspicion; **um keinen Zweifel a. zu lassen . . . ,** in order that no doubts shall arise . . . ; to forestall any doubts about the matter . . . ; **das läßt keinen Zweifel a.,** that admits of no doubt; **eine aufkommende Mode,** a rising fashion. **3. gegen j-n, etwas, a.,** to make headway against s.o., sth.; to stand up against s.o., sth.; **gegen j-n, etwas, nicht a. können,** to be unable to prevail against s.o., sth.; to be unable to stand (up) against s.o., sth.; **gegen eine solche Konkurrenz können wir gar nicht a.,** we cannot stand against, cope with, such competition; we can do nothing against, in the face of, such competition; **er läßt niemanden neben sich a.,** he allows, brooks, no competition. **4. für etwas a.,** to accept responsibility for sth.; to make oneself responsible, answerable, for sth.; **j-m für etwas a.,** to be responsible to s.o. for sth.; to answer, be answerable, to s.o. for sth.; **für den Schaden a.,** to be responsible for (making good) the damage; **die Direktion kann für etwa entstehende Schäden nicht a.,** the management cannot be held responsible for any damage that may occur; **wir mußten für den Verlust a.,** we had to make good the loss; we had to stand the loss; **ihr Vater wird für die (Ausgaben der) Hochzeitsreise a.,** her father will pay for the honeymoon; **für j-s Unkosten a.,** to pay, defray, s.o.'s expenses; **er wird für meine Ausgaben a. müssen,** he will have to settle my expenses for me. **5.** (*of money*) to come in (*as yield of taxes, collection, etc.*); **aus den freiwilligen Beiträgen ist sehr wenig aufgekommen,** the voluntary subscriptions have produced, yielded, very little. **6.** (*a*) *Nau:* (*of ship*) to approach; to gain (on another ship); to come up (with another ship); **der Schlepper kam schnell auf,** the tug was coming up fast; (*b*) *Sp:* (*of runner, etc.*) to make headway; to gain (on competitors); to come up (with competitors).

II. *vbl s.* **Aufkommen,** *n. in vbl senses; also:* **1.** recovery (from illness); **man zweifelt an seinem A.,** his recovery is (very) doubtful. **2.** rise (of custom, fashion, etc.); emergence (of custom, etc.). **3.** yield (of tax, etc.).

Aufkömmling, *m.* **-s/-e,** parvenu, upstart; self-made person.

aufkorken, *v.tr. sep.* to uncork, open (bottle).

aufkratzen, *v.tr. sep.* **1.** (*of birds, etc.*) to scratch up (seeds, etc.). **2.** (*a*) to open (sth.) by scratching; to scratch; **die Haut a.,** to scratch, abrade, the skin; **den Boden a.,** to scratch, rake over, the soil; **ein Feuer a.,** to stir up, rake up, a fire; (*b*) *Tex:* to card (wool, etc.); to teasel, to raise (the nap of), to nap (cloth). **3.** *F:* **j-n a.,** to cheer s.o. up; to buck s.o. up; **er war sehr aufgekratzt,** he was very cheery; he was in high spirits, in high feather, in fine fettle, in fine form. **4.** *A:* **eine Melodie a.,** to scrape out a tune (on the fiddle).

aufkräusen, *v.i. sep.* (*haben*) (*of beer*) to form a head.

aufkreischen, *v.i. sep.* (*haben*) to give a scream, a shriek, a screech; to scream, shriek, screech; **vor Schmerz a.,** to scream (out), shriek (out), screech, with pain.

aufkrempeln, *v.tr. sep.* **1.** to turn up, roll up (sleeve, trousers, etc.); to tuck up (shirt-sleeve, etc.). **2.**=**aufkrempen.**

aufkrempen, *v.tr. sep.* **den Hutrand, den Hut, a.,** to turn up the brim of one's hat; to cock one's hat.

aufkreuzen, *v.sep.* **1.** *v.tr. Breed:* to improve (breed) by cross-breeding; to grade (up) (breed). **2.** *v.i. Nau:* (*haben*) to work, ply, to windward; to beat up; *F:* (*of pers.*) to heave in sight; to show up.

Aufkreuzer, *m. Nau:* ship that sails well to windward.

aufkriegen, *v.tr. sep.* = **aufbekommen.**

aufkrimpen, *v.i. sep.* (*haben*) *Nau:* (*of wind*) to back.

aufkühlen, *v.tr. sep. Ind: etc:* to cool; to aerate.

aufkündigen, *v.tr. sep.* to give notice to terminate (sth.); to cancel (sth.); **einen Vertrag a.,** to annul, rescind, cancel, terminate, a contract; to withdraw from a contract; **j-m die Freundschaft a.,** to withdraw one's friendship from s.o.; **j-m den Gehorsam a.,** to refuse further obedience to s.o.; to disown one's allegiance to s.o.

Aufkunft, *f.* **-/⸗e.** *A:* = **Aufkommen,** *q.v. under* **aufkommen** II. 1, 3.

auflachen, *v.i. sep.* (*haben*) to give a laugh; **laut a.,** to burst into a loud laugh.

Aufladegebläse, *n. I.C.E:* supercharger.

Aufladegebühr(en), *f.(pl.) Nau: Rail: etc:* loading charges.

Aufladekommando, *n. Mil:* loading detachment; entraining detachment; embussing detachment.

aufladen, *v.tr. sep.* (*strong*) **1.** (*a*) to load (goods, etc.); *Mil:* to entrain *or* embus (personnel); **Güter (auf einen Wagen, Zug, usw.) a.,** to put goods aboard (a vehicle, train, etc.); *Mil.Av:* **die Bomben a.,** to stow the bombs; to bomb up; **Aufladung** *f* **der Bomben,** bombing-up; (*b*) to load (up) (vehicle); (*c*) **j-m etwas a.,** to burden s.o. with sth.; to saddle s.o. with sth., to saddle sth. on s.o.; **sich** *dat.* **eine Verantwortung a.,** to saddle oneself with a responsibility; to take a responsibility upon oneself, to shoulder a responsibility. **2.** *El:* to charge (battery, accumulator). **3.** *I.C.E:* to boost (engine); **Aufladung** *f,* boosting, supercharging.

Auflader, *m.* loader; porter; (*at docks*) lumper, stevedore.

Auflage, *f.* **1.** (*a*) condition (attached to gift, permission to do sth., etc.); *Jur:* obligation (*esp.* attached to a gift *or* bequest); (*b*) *A:* tax, impost; (*c*) *Jur: A:* accusation. **2.** *Print: Publ:* (*a*) edition; issue; impression; **dritte A.,** third edition; third impression; third printing; **neue unveränderte A.,** reprint, new impression; **verbesserte und vermehrte A.,** revised and enlarged edition; **das Werk hat schon zehn Auflagen erlebt,** the work has already gone through ten editions; *F:* **er ist eine zweite A. seines Vaters,** he is a second edition of his father; (*b*) edition (of so many copies); number of copies printed; *Journ:* circulation; **das Buch hatte nur eine kleine A., eine A. von nur 500 (Stück),** only a small number of copies, only 500 copies, of the book were printed; **wie hoch, groß, war die zweite A.?** how many copies of the second edition were printed? **Zeitung mit einer ungeheuren A.,** newspaper with an enormous circulation. **3.** *Cu:* garnishing. **4.** *For:* annual growth. **5.** (*a*) upper layer (in mattress); (*b*) overlay (mattress). **6.** rest (for arm, tools, etc.); hand-rail; *Tchn:* support, rest (of lathe, etc.). **7.** *A. & Dial:* meeting, assembly (of craftsmen, etc.). **8.** *A:* collection (of money).

Auflagefläche, *f. Mec.E: etc:* bearing surface; working surface.

Auflagegestell, *n. Mil:* aiming-rest.

Auflagepunkt, *m. Constr: etc:* point of support; point on which beam, etc., rests; *Veh:* point of contact between wheel and ground.

Auflager, *n.* (*a*) *Constr: etc:* support; bearer; bearing (of steel bridge); *Arch:* springer (of arch); impost (of bearing arch); (*b*) *Mec.E:* bearing.

Auflagerdruck, *m. Constr:* bearing pressure.

auflagern, *v. sep.* **1.** *v.tr.* (*a*) to store up (goods); (*b*) *Geol: etc:* to aggregate (matter). **2.** *v.tr. Geol:* to superpose; **aufgelagerte Schichten,** superposed strata; **Auflagerung** *f,* superposition. **3.** *v.i.* (*sein*) (*of matter*) to aggregate, form an aggregate.

Auflagerplatte, *f. Mec.E:* bed-plate; *Civ.E: etc:* bearing-plate.

Auflagerschuh, *m. Arch: Civ.E:* coussinet, cushion (of arch-pier, etc.).

Auflageschiene, *f.* hand-rail (of gangway, etc.).

Auflagetisch, *m. Mec.E:* table, bed (of machine-tool).

auflanden, *v.i. sep.* (*haben*) *Geol:* (*of river-bank, etc.*) to increase through alluvial deposits; to be increased by silting; **Auflandung** *f,* accretion through alluvion; aggradation; silting.

auflandig, *a.* **auflandiger Wind,** wind coming off the sea; sea-breeze.

Auflanger, *m.* **-s/-.** *N.Arch:* timber, futtock; timber-head.

auflassen. I. *v.tr. sep.* (*strong*) **1.** (*a*) **einen Kranken nicht a.,** not to let an invalid get up; to keep an invalid in bed; (*b*) to release (carrier *or* racing pigeons, balloon, etc.). **2. den Hut a.,** to keep one's hat on. **3.** to leave (door, one's coat, blouse, etc.) open. **4.** to abandon, shut down (mine, factory, etc.); *Hist:* to abandon (camp, fortress, etc.); *Min:* **aufgelassene Grube,** abandoned, disused, shut-down, mine. **5.** *Jur:* to transfer, make over, cede, assign, convey (a property, etc.) (**an j-n,** to s.o.).

II. *vbl s.* **Auflassen** *n.,* **Auflassung** *f. in vbl senses; also:* **1.** abandonment (of mine, factory, camp, fortress, etc.). **2.** *Jur:* transfer, assignation, assignment, conveyance (of a property, etc.).

auflässig, *a. Min:* abandoned, disused, shut-down (mine).

Auflau(e)rer, *m.* waylayer; spy, watcher; lurker.

auflauern, *v.i. sep.* (*haben*) **j-m a.,** to lie in wait, to be on the look-out, on the watch, for s.o.; to waylay s.o.; to spy (up)on s.o.

Auflauf, *m.* **1.** *Mec.E: etc:* running up, run-up (of conveyor belt, etc.). **2.** *Constr: etc:* bridge; gang-plank (*leading up to scaffolding, etc.*). **3.** concourse, crowd, gathering, assemblage (of persons in street, etc.); *Jur:* (i) unlawful assembly; (ii) riot; **einen A. verursachen,** (i) to cause a crowd to gather, (ii) *Jur:* to cause a riot. **4.** *Fin:* accumulation (of charges, debts, interest); accruing (of interest). **5.** *Cu:* savoury dish (consisting of pre-cooked ingredients) *or* sweet baked in a mould; baked pudding; (*with eggs*) soufflé.

Auflaufbacken, *m.* leading shoe (of brake).

Auflaufbremse, *f. Veh:* overrun brake.

auflaufen, *v.sep.* (*strong*) I. *v.i.* (*sein*) **1.** (*a*) (*of conveyor belt, etc.*) to run up; (*b*) *Ven:* (*of boar*) to charge. **2.** (*a*) *Nau:* to run aground, ashore; to ground; to get stranded; **auf eine Sandbank aufgelaufenes Schiff,** ship aground on a sandbank; **ein Schiff a. lassen,** to run a ship aground; to strand a ship; to beach a ship; (*b*) *Aut: F:* (*of car*) to get stuck (so that the wheels do not grip); *Mil:* (*of tank*) to get stuck (so that the tracks do not grip); to be bellied; **einen Panzer a. lassen,** to belly a tank. **3.** (*a*) to become distended; (*of dough, veins, etc.*) to swell (up); (*of waters, tide, dough, pastry*) to rise; (*b*) *Fin:* (*of charges, credits, interest, etc.*) to accumulate; to mount up, run up (**auf** + *acc.,* to); (*of interest*) to accrue; (*of debts*) to run on; **aufgelaufene Zinsen,** accumulated, accrued, interest; **Auflaufen der Zinsen,** accumulation, accruing, of interest.

II. **auflaufen,** *v.tr.* **sich** *dat.* **die Füße a.,** to make one's feet sore with running *or* walking; to walk one's feet sore; **sich** *acc.* **a.,** to make one's legs sore with walking.

Aufläufer, *m.* **1.** *Ind:* blast-furnace stoker. **2.** *Nau:* ordinary seaman; apprentice.

Auflaufform, *f. Cu:* baking-mould; soufflé dish.

auflavieren, *v.i. sep.* (*haben*) (*p.p.* **auflaviert**) *Nau:* to work, ply, to windward.

aufleben, *v.i. sep.* (*sein*) (**wieder**) **a.,** to revive; to come to life again; (*of ideas, etc.*) to be revived; to gain fresh force; *Mil:* (*of fighting, fire, etc.*) to become more active; **das Geschäft lebt wieder auf,** business is looking up; **einen alten Brauch wieder a. lassen,** to revive an old custom; *vbl s.* **Aufleben** *n, in vbl senses; also:* revival; renascence (of ideas, etc.).

auflecken, *v.tr. sep.* to lick up (spilt milk, etc.); (*of cat, dog, etc.*) to lap (up) (water, milk, etc.).

Auflegegestell, *n.* support; rest; *esp. Mil:* aiming-rest.

Auflegematratze, *f.* overlay (mattress).

auflegen. I. *v.tr. sep.* (*a*) to lay (sth.) on; to put on (coating, paint, rouge, table-cloth, gramophone record, etc.); to apply (coating, paint, poultice, etc.); **etwas auf etwas** *acc.* **a.,** to lay sth. on sth.; to put sth. on sth.; to apply (paint to surface, plaster to wound, etc.); **Kohlen, Holz (aufs Feuer) a.,** to put coal, wood, on the fire; **das Tischtuch a.,** to put the cloth on (the table), to put on, lay, the cloth; **ein Gedeck a.,** to lay a place (at table); **leg noch ein Gedeck auf!** lay another place, lay for one more; **drei Gedecke a.,** to lay for three, to set (the table) for three; **einem Pferd den Sattel a.,** to put the saddle on a horse, to saddle a horse; **Stieren das Joch a.,** to yoke oxen; **den, die, Ellbogen, die Arme, (auf den Tisch) a.,** to put one's elbows on the table, to lean on one's elbow, elbows; **die Ellbogen, sich mit den Ellbogen, auf etwas** *acc.* **a.,** to rest one's elbows on sth.; *Ecc:* **j-m die Hand a.,** to lay, impose, hands on s.o.; *Tp:* **den Hörer a.,** to replace, hang up, the receiver; to ring off; *abs.* **a.,** to hang up; to ring off; (*b*) *Mil:* **das Gewehr a.,** to lay the rifle on an aiming-rest; to support the rifle; **ein Schiff a.,** (i) *Nau:* to lay up a ship; to put a ship out of commission; (ii) *N.Arch:* **ein Schiff (zum Bau) a.,** to lay a ship on the stocks, to lay down a ship; *Aut:* **einen Wagen a.,** to lay up a car; (*c*) **j-m eine Last a.,** to lay a burden upon s.o.; **j-m eine Steuer a.,** to impose a tax on s.o.; **j-m eine Strafe a.,** to impose a penalty on s.o.; to inflict a penalty, a punishment, on s.o.; *Prov:* **Gott legt uns nicht mehr auf, als wir tragen können,** Heaven suits the back to the burden; God tempers the wind to the shorn lamb; (*d*) (*of animals*) **Fett a.,** to grow fat; to thrive; (*e*) **ein Faß Bier a.,** to set up a cask of beer (for drinking); (*f*) to lay out, display (articles for inspection, etc.); to lay out, put out, set out (books, periodicals) for perusal; **eine Liste a.,** to make a list available for inspection; to put out a list (for signatures *or* inspection); **eine Subskriptionsliste a.,** to open a subscription-list; *Cards:* **seine Karten a.,** to lay down one's cards, put one's cards on the table; to show one's hand; *Fin:* **eine Anleihe (zur Zeichnung) a.,** to invite subscriptions to a loan; to float a loan; (*g*) *Publ:* to publish, print (an edition of) (a work); **ein Werk wieder, neu, a.,** to republish a work; to issue a new edition of a work.

II. *vbl s.* **Auflegen** *n.,* **Auflegung** *f. in vbl senses; also:* **1.** application (of coating, paint, poultice, etc.); *Ecc:* imposition (of hands). **2.** imposition (of tax, penalty); infliction (of penalty, punishment).

III. *p.p. & a.* **aufgelegt.** **1.** *in vbl senses; esp.* (*a*) *Nau: Aut:* laid-up (ship, car); (*b*) *Mil:* **aufgelegtes Gewehr,** rifle laid on an aiming-rest; rifle with support; *adv.* **liegend a. schießen,** to fire from the lying position with support; (*c*) *F:* **ein aufgelegter Schwindel,** an obvious, unmistakable, *F:* barefaced, swindle. **2.** (*of pers.*) **gut a. sein,** to be in a good humour, a good mood; to be in a happy frame of mind; to be in good trim; **schlecht a. sein,** to be in a bad humour, a bad mood; to be out of humour; to be out of sorts, out of trim; **heute ist sie aber schlecht a.!** how bad-tempered she is today! **wie bist du heute a.?** what sort of mood are you in today? **zu etwas a. sein; a. sein, etwas zu tun,** to be in the mood, the vein, for sth., to do sth.; to feel like sth., like doing sth.; **zum Lesen a. sein,** to be in the mood for reading, in a reading mood; **ich bin nicht zum Lachen a.,** I am in no humour for laughing, in no laughing humour; I am in no mood to laugh; I don't feel like laughing.

Aufleger, *m.* **-s/-.** (*pers.*) **1.** layer-on; *Metall: etc:* (furnace-)stoker, feeder; *Print:* layer-on, feeder. **2.** imposer (of penalty); inflictor (of penalty, punishment).

auflehnen. I. *v.sep.* **1.** *v.tr.* & **sich auflehnen, die Ellbogen, sich mit den Ellbogen, auf den Tisch a.,** to put, lean, rest, one's elbows on the table; **sich auf etwas** *acc.* **a.,** to lean on sth. **2. sich auflehnen,** (*a*) (*of horse*) to rear; (*b*) (*of pers.*) **sich gegen etwas a.,** to rise in protest against sth.; to offer resistance to sth.; to jib at sth.; to rebel, to rise (in rebellion), to revolt, against sth.; to kick at (fate, etc.); **sich gegen j-n a.,** to rebel, revolt, against s.o.; **sich gegen die Staatsgewalt a.,** to rebel against the authority of the state.

II. *vbl s.* **Auflehnung,** *f.* rebellion, revolt, insurrection (**gegen,** against).

aufleimen, *v.tr. sep.* to glue, stick, (sth.) on (**auf** + *acc.,* to); to glue (painted picture, etc.) on to a canvas backing; to line (painted picture).

auflesen, *v.tr. sep.* (*strong*) to pick (sth.) up; to collect, gather (up) (thgs); **Ähren a.,** to glean ears of corn; **Holz a.,** to gather, pick up, sticks (for firewood); *F:* **Ideen a.,** to pick up ideas; **eine Krankheit a.,** to catch, take, *F:* pick up, an illness; **Flöhe a.,** to pick up, get, fleas; **wo hast du denn diesen Kerl aufgelesen?** where on earth did you pick up this fellow?

aufleuchten, *v.i. sep.* (*haben*) (*of light*) to flash; to shine out; (*of face, eyes*) to light up; (*of face*) to brighten (up); (*of beacon, searchlight, etc.*) to flash up, flare up, blaze up; *Artil:* (*of gun*) to flash; **Aufleuchten** *n, in vbl senses; also;* flash (of light, gun).

auflichten, *v.tr. sep.* to brighten (up) (colours, picture, room, etc.); **der Himmel, die Zukunft, lichtet sich auf,** the sky, the future, is looking a little brighter.

Auflieferer, *m. Com: Rail:* consignor, sender (of goods).

aufliefern, *v.tr. sep. Com: Rail:* to consign, send, dispatch, *U.S:* ship (goods); **Auflieferung** *f,*

consigning, consignment, sending, dispatch, *U.S:* shipping.

aufliegen, *v.sep.* (*strong*) I. *v.i.* (*haben*) (*a*) to lie; to rest; to be supported (**auf etwas** *dat.*, on sth.); (*b*) *Nau:* (*of ship*) to be laid up; to be out of commission; (*c*) (*of responsibility, etc.*) **j-m a.,** to be incumbent on s.o.; to be part of s.o.'s duty; **der Gedanke daran, daß . . . , liegt mir schwer auf,** the thought that . . . weighs upon my mind; **die Verantwortung lag ihm schwer auf,** the responsibility weighed heavily on him; *F:* **das Essen liegt mir schwer auf,** my dinner lies heavy on my stomach; (*d*) (*of articles*) to be put out, laid out, set out, for inspection; (*of books, periodicals*) to be laid out for perusal; (*of list*) to be available for signatures *or* inspection; **alle größeren Tageszeitungen liegen im Vorsaal auf,** all the more important newspapers are available for reading in the anteroom; **eine Subskriptionsliste liegt auf,** a subscription-list has been opened; *Com:* (*of goods*) **zum Verkauf a.,** to be exposed for sale; *Fin:* **die Anleihe liegt (zur Zeichnung) auf,** subscriptions are invited to the loan.
II. **sich aufliegen,** to get sore with lying; (*of invalid*) to get bed-sores.
III. *vbl s.* **Aufliegen,** *n.* (*a*) *in vbl senses;* (*b*) *Med:* decubitus, bed-sores.

auflockern. I. *v.tr. sep.* (*a*) to loosen (sth.); to slacken, ease (knot, etc.); to relax (restrictions, controls, etc.); to loosen up (muscles); to ease (tightly packed articles, etc.); to break the monotony of (an arrangement, etc.); to open out (ranks); to break up, to (begin to) disintegrate (rock, tissue, etc.); *Agr:* to loosen, break up, mellow (the soil); *Tex: Paperm:* to break, willow (rags, etc.); (*b*) (*of pers.*) **aufgelockert, relaxed; sie ist etwas aufgelockerter als bisher,** she is rather more relaxed than she was; (*c*) **sich a.,** (*of knot, etc.*) to loosen; to come undone; (*of muscles*) to loosen up; (*of crowd*) to begin to break up; (*of ranks*) to open out; (*of rock, tissue, etc.*) to (begin to) break up, to (begin to) disintegrate; (*of morals*) to grow lax, loose.
II. *vbl s.* **1. Auflockern,** *n. in vbl senses; also:* relaxation (of restrictions, controls, etc.). **2. Auflockerung,** *f.* (*a*)=II. 1; (*b*) (incipient) disintegration; **A. der Sitten,** laxity of morals.
Auflockerungsübungen, *f.pl.* limbering-up exercises; (*for muscles, etc.*) loosening-up exercises.

auflodern. I. *v.i. sep.* (*sein*) (*of fire, quarrel, rage, etc.*) to blaze up, to flare up; (*of embers, etc.*) to burst into flame.
II. *vbl s.* **Auflodern,** *n. in vbl senses; also:* flare-up.

auflösbar, *a.* **1.** (*a*) *Ph: Ch: etc:* (*of substance*) soluble, dissoluble (**in**+*dat.*, in); **nicht auflösbarer Körper,** insoluble body; (*b*) *Mth:* solvable (group); *Astr:* **auflösbarer Nebelfleck,** resolvable nebula. **2.** dissolvable (assembly, association, contract, etc.); dissoluble (contract, marriage, etc.); annullable, cancellable, terminable (contract). **3.** solvable, soluble (problem); resolvable, resoluble (problem); **nicht auflösbares Problem,** unsolvable, insoluble, problem.
Auflösbarkeit, *f.* **1.** (*a*) solubility, dissolubility (of substance); (*b*) *Mth:* solvability (of group). **2.** dissolubility (of contract, marriage, etc.). **3.** solvability (of problem).
Auflöse-, *comb.fm.*=**Auflösungs-.**
Auflöseapparat, *m. Ch: Ind:* dissolving apparatus, dissolver.

auflösen. I. *v.tr. sep.* **1.** to loosen (knot); to disentangle (cord, etc.); to untie, undo, loose (knot, etc.); **sein Haar a.,** to let down, untie, unbind, one's hair; **aufgelöstes Haar,** hair falling loose; dishevelled hair; **sich a.,** (*of knot, etc.*) to come undone. **2.** (*a*) to break (sth.) up; to split (sth.) up; to disintegrate, decompose (body, etc.); **etwas in etwas** *acc.* **a.,** to resolve, dissolve, break up, sth. into sth.; **etwas in seine Bestandteile a.,** to resolve sth. into its component parts, its elements; *Ch:* to analyse (substance); **Körper, der sich in seine Bestandteile a. läßt,** body resoluble into its elements; *Mth:* **eine Gruppe a.,** to solve a group; **die Klammern a.,** to get rid of the brackets; *Rail:* **einen Zug a.,** to split up a train; **sich a.,** to break up; to split up; (*of body, etc.*) to disintegrate, to decompose; (*of human frame*) to break up; (*of crowd*) to break up; to disperse; (*of formation of aircraft, etc.*) to split up, to separate; *Mil:* (*of formation*) to go into open order; **aufgelöst,** in open order; *adv.* **aufgelöst vorgehen,** to advance in open order; (*b*) *Mus:* **einen Akkord a.,** to spread, break, a chord; **eine Dissonanz a.,**

to resolve a discord; **ein Versetzungszeichen a.,** to cancel an accidental; **ein Kreuzchen a.,** to cancel a sharp; to restore a note; (*c*) to solve, resolve (problem, equation); to clear up (difficulty, mystery). **3.** (*a*) **einen Stoff in einer Flüssigkeit a.,** to dissolve, melt, a substance in a liquid; (*of sugar, etc.*) **sich in Wasser** *dat.* **a.,** to dissolve, melt, in water; **die Seife hatte sich im Wasser aufgelöst,** the soap had dissolved in the water; **die Seele löst sich im All auf,** the soul merges into the universe; **auflösend,** (dis)solvent; **auflösendes Mittel,** solvent, dissolvent; **aufgelöste Salze,** salts in solution; (*b*) (*of cloud, fog, snow*) **sich in Regen** *acc.* **a.,** to dissolve into rain; **ihr Schmerz löste sich in Tränen** *acc.* **auf,** her pain found an outlet in tears; (*of hopes, ambitions, etc.*) **sich in blauen Dunst a.,** to melt, vanish, into thin air; **sich in nichts a.,** to dissolve into nothingness; to come to nothing; **alles hat sich in Wohlgefallen aufgelöst,** it all passed off happily; the whole business straightened, sorted, itself out; (*of pers.*) **sich in Tränen** *acc.* **a.,** to melt, dissolve, in(to) tears; **in Tränen aufgelöst,** in a flood of tears; *Lit:* **er war in Wehmut aufgelöst,** he was suffused with tender melancholy; (*c*) *F:* (*of pers.*) **aufgelöst sein,** (i) to be worked up, upset; (ii) to be dishevelled; **aufgelöst aussehen,** (i) to look upset; (ii) to look dishevelled. **4.** (*a*) to dissolve (society, assembly, parliament, marriage, etc.); to dissolve, break up (firm, partnership); to wind up (company); to annul, cancel, terminate (contract); **eine Verlobung a.,** to break off an engagement; *Mil:* **ein Heer, eine Einheit, a.,** to disband an army, a unit; to demobilize an army, a unit; *Jur:* **auflösende Bedingung,** condition subsequent; (*b*) *Bank: etc:* to close (account). **5. sich auflösen,** (*of society, assembly, parliament, etc.*) to dissolve; (*of firm, partnership*) to dissolve, to break up; (*of company*) to wind up; (*of formation of aircraft, etc.*) to split up, to separate, to break formation.
II. *vbl s.* **1. Auflösen,** *n.*=II. 2. **2. Auflösung,** *f. in vbl senses; also:* (*a*) disentanglement; *Th:* **A. des Knotens,** dénouement; (*b*) disintegration, decomposition (of a body); dissolution (of the human frame); resolution (of sth. into its component parts); *Ch:* analysis; (*c*) *Mus:* **A. einer Dissonanz,** resolution of a discord; **A. eines Versetzungszeichens,** cancellation of an accidental; **A. eines Kreuzchens,** cancellation of a sharp; restoration of a note; (*d*) *Mth: etc:* solution (of problem, equation); resolution (of problem, equation); (*e*) *Ph: Ch: etc:* solution; (*f*) dissolution (of society, assembly, parliament, marriage, etc.); cancellation, termination (of contract); winding up, *U.S:* wind-up (of a business); *Com:* closing, *U.S:* elimination (of an account); *Mil:* disbandment (of army, unit); demobilization (of army, unit).
Auflöser, *m.* -s/-. *Ch: Ind:* dissolving apparatus, dissolver.
auflöslich, *a.*=**auflösbar** 1, 2.
auflösungsfähig, *a.*=**auflösbar** 1, 3.
Auflösungsfähigkeit, *f.*=**Auflösbarkeit** 1, 3.
Auflösungsgefäß, *n. Ch: Ind:* dissolving vessel, dissolver.
Auflösungsgrenze, *f. Opt:* limit of resolution (of lens, microscope).
Auflösungskoeffizient, *m. Ph: Ch:* coefficient of dissociation.
Auflösungskraft, *f.*=**Auflösungsvermögen.**
Auflösungsmittel, *n.* solvent, dissolvent.
Auflösungsprodukte, *n.pl. Ch: Geol: etc:* disintegration products; *Mill:* reduction products.
Auflösungsstab, *m. Mil:* demobilization staff.
Auflösungsvermögen, *n.* **1.** *Ph: Ch: etc:* dissolving power. **2.** *Opt:* (**optisches**) **A.,** resolving power (of lens, microscope).
Auflösungswärme, *f. Ph: Ch:* heat of solution.
Auflösungszeichen, *n.* **1.** *Mil: Av:* signal to break formation. **2.** *Mus:* (*sign*) natural, ♮.
auflöten, *v.tr. sep. Metalw:* to solder (sth.) on (*dat.*, **auf**+*acc.*, to); **einen Flansch (hart) a.,** to braze on a flange.
aufluven, *v.i. sep.* (*haben*) *Nau:* to luff.
aufmachen, *v.sep.* I. *v.tr.* **1.** *Mch:* **Dampf a.,** to raise steam, to get up steam. **2.** (*a*) *Com:* to make up (account, etc.); to make out (invoice, etc.); **eine Rechnung a.,** to make up, make out, draw up, an account; to state, make a statement of, an account; **die Bücher a.,** to make up the books; *M.Ins:* **eine Havarie a.,** to adjust an average; (*b*) *Tex:* to make up (material); (*c*) to arrange (sth.) for effect; to get (sth.) up (to impress, to appeal to the eye); to dress (s.o.)

up, to get (s.o.) up; *Publ:* to get up (book); **einen Bericht tendenziös a.,** to give a report a tendentious flavour; to work up a report for tendentious effect; **sie war als Kleopatra aufgemacht,** she was got up, done up, as Cleopatra; *Com:* **einen Artikel zum Verkauf a.,** to get up an article for sale; **hübsch aufgemachte Geschenkartikel,** articles in attractive gift packings. **3.** to open (door, box, parcel, book, bottle, etc.); to undo (knot, parcel, one's dress, etc.); to untie (knot, parcel, etc.); to open, unseal (letter); to undo *or* unlace (corset); to unfasten (door, one's dress, etc.); to unbutton (coat, etc.); to unpick, unstitch, *U.S:* rip (seam); to uncork (bottle); to crack (nut); to open, put up (umbrella); to turn on (tap); **die Tür halb a.,** to half open the door; **j-m die Tür a.,** *abs.* **j-m a.,** to open the door to s.o.; to let s.o. in; *abs.* **a.,** to open the door; to answer the door, *U.S:* the (door)bell; **aufmachen!** open the door! *U.S: & F:* open up! **den Mund a.,** (i) to open one's mouth; (ii) *F:* to speak (up); **die Augen a.,** to open one's eyes; **mach die Augen, die Ohren, auf!** keep your eyes, ears, open! use your eyes! **den Laden a.,** to open the shop; *abs.* **wir machen um neun (Uhr) auf,** we open at nine; **die Läden, die Banken, machen heute um zehn auf,** the shops, the banks, open at ten today; **ein Geschäft a.,** to open a shop, a business; to set up shop; *Com: F:* **ein Konto a.,** to open an account.
II. **sich aufmachen. 1.** (*a*) *A. & B:* to get up, to rise up, to arise; (*b*) to start on one's way; to go off, *F:* to be off; to set out; **sich nach Frankreich a.,** to set out for France. **2.** (*of wind*) to rise, get up, spring up. **3.** to dress oneself up, get oneself up; (*of woman*) to make (oneself) up, to put on one's make-up; **er hatte sich als Matrose aufgemacht,** he had got himself up as a sailor; **eine elegant aufgemachte Empfangsdame,** an elegantly got-up, turned-out, receptionist; **schwer aufgemacht,** heavily made up.
III. *vbl s.* **1. Aufmachen,** *n. in vbl senses.* **2. Aufmachung,** *f.* (*a*)=III. 1; *also: Com:* **A. einer Rechnung,** statement of an account; *M.Ins:* **A. der Havarie,** average adjustment; (*b*) get-up (of pers., book, goods, newspaper article, etc.); presentation (of book); lay-out (of book, page, etc.); (woman's) make-up; *Com:* packaging; **Artikel in hübscher A.,** nicely got-up article, attractively packaged article; **Damen in eleganter A.,** elegantly dressed, elegantly turned-out, ladies; *Journ:* **eine Nachricht in großer A. bringen,** to splash, play up, a piece of news; *F:* **das ist alles bloß A.,** that's all mere window-dressing, all eyewash.
aufmalen, *v.tr. sep.* **1.** to paint (sth.) on (**auf**+*acc.*, to). **2.** *Art:* to touch up, retouch (picture).
Aufmarsch, *m. Mil:* **1.** parade; (ceremonial) march. **2.** assembly (in battle array); (strategic) concentration; forming up for deployment.
Aufmarschgebiet, *n. Mil:* assembly area; concentration area; deployment area.
aufmarschieren, *v.i. sep.* (*p.p.* **aufmarschiert**) (*sein*) **1.** *Mil:* to parade; to form up in line; **die Truppen a. lassen,** to parade the troops. **2.** (*a*) *Mil:* to assemble in battle array; to form up for deployment; **Truppen a. lassen,** to assemble troops (for deployment); to array troops; (*b*) *Lit:* **seine Argumente, Gründe, a. lassen,** to deploy one's arguments.
Aufmarschlinie, *f. Mil:* line of march (toward assembly area).
Aufmarschplan, *m. Mil:* assembly plan.
aufmaschen, *v.tr. sep.* to re-mesh (net); to mend a ladder, *U.S:* run, in (stocking).
Aufmaß, *n.* heaped measure.
aufmeißeln, *v.tr. sep.* to chisel (sth.) open; to pierce (sth.) with a chisel; *Surg:* to chisel open (jawbone, frontal bone, etc.).
aufmerken, *v.sep.* **1.** *v.tr.* to note (sth.) (down); to take, make, a note of sth.; to jot (sth.) down. **2.** *v.i.* (*haben*) to listen attentively; to prick up one's ears; *F:* to be all attention; **aufgemerkt!** attention! **auf j-n a.,** to pay attention to s.o., to give, pay, heed to s.o., to take careful notice of s.o., to mind s.o.; **j-m a.,** to keep a watchful, sharp, eye on s.o.
aufmerksam, *a.* (*a*) attentive; **ein aufmerksamer Hörer,** an attentive listener; **bei diesen Worten wurde er a.,** at these words he pricked up his ears; **auf etwas** *acc.* **a. werden,** to notice sth.; to become conscious of sth; **j-n auf etwas** *acc.* **a. machen,** to call, attract, draw, s.o.'s attention to sth.; to point out sth. to s.o.; to bring sth. to s.o.'s notice; **j-n auf eine Gefahr a. machen,** to draw s.o.'s attention to a danger; to make s.o. conscious, warn s.o., of a danger; **auf einen**

Fehler a. machen, to call attention to a fault; *adv.* a. zuhören, to listen attentively, intently, *F:* to be all attention; a. zuschauen, to watch closely, intently, carefully; einer Beweisführung a. folgen, to follow an argument closely, carefully; (*b*) gegen j-n a. sein, to be attentive to s.o.; to be full of attentions for s.o.; ein aufmerksamer junger Mann, an attentive young man.

Aufmerksamkeit, *f.* **1.** attention; attentiveness; mit großer, gespannter, A. zuhören, to listen attentively, intently; etwas *dat.*, j-m, seine A. schenken, to pay attention, give one's attention to sth., s.o.; etwas *dat.*, j-m, seine ganze A. schenken, to give one's whole attention to sth., s.o.; seine A. auf etwas *acc.* richten, to direct, turn, one's attention to sth.; j-s A. auf etwas *acc.* lenken, to call, attract, draw, s.o.'s attention to sth.; to point out sth. to s.o.; to bring sth. to s.o.'s notice; A. auf sich *acc.* ziehen, to attract attention; to draw attention to oneself (durch, by); j-s A. fesseln, to engage, arrest, catch, hold, s.o.'s attention; to win s.o.'s attention; j-s A. ablenken, to divert, distract, draw away, s.o.'s attention (von, from); beständige A., constant attention. **2.** (*a*) attentiveness (gegen j-n, to s.o.); (*b*) (kind) attention; Aufmerksamkeiten, attentions; j-n mit Aufmerksamkeiten überhäufen, to shower attention(s) on s.o.; to be all attention(s) to s.o.; to wait on s.o. hand and foot; (*c*) mark, token, of one's regard; gift; wir erlauben uns, Ihnen als kleine A. eine Flasche Champagner zu überreichen, as a mark of our regard we are making you a small gift of a bottle of champagne.

aufmessen, *v.tr. sep.* (*strong*) **1.** to measure, survey (land); *Husb:* to measure and store (grain). **2.** j-m einen Mantel, usw., a., to take s.o.'s measurements, to measure s.o., for a coat, etc.; *F:* j-m eins a., to strike s.o. a blow, to hit s.o.

aufmöbeln, *v.tr. sep. F:* **1.** to cheer (s.o.) up, brighten (s.o.) up, buck (s.o.) up; eine Tasse Tee wird dich a., a cup of tea will buck you up. **2.** sich aufmöbeln, to dress oneself up, *F:* doll oneself up.

aufmontieren, *v.tr. sep.* (*p.p.* aufmontiert) to set up, fit up, erect (machine, apparatus, etc.); to assemble, put together (apparatus, etc.); etwas auf etwas *acc.* a., to mount sth. on sth.

aufmucken, *v.i. sep.* (*haben*) to bristle up, bridle up (in protest); to get one's back up, *F:* to kick, jib; gegen etwas a., to kick against sth.; to jib at sth.; to be up in arms against sth.

aufmuntern. I. *v.tr. sep.* to cheer, *F:* buck, (s.o.) up; to brighten (s.o.) up; to put new heart, new life, into (s.o.); to rouse (s.o.) (from lethargy); to animate, liven up, enliven (guests, etc.); j-n zur Arbeit a., to encourage, incite, s.o. to work; ein aufmunternder Brief, a cheering letter. **II.** *vbl s.* **1.** Aufmuntern, *n. in vbl senses.* **2.** Aufmunterung, *f.* (*a*)=II. 1; (*b*) eine kleine A. nötig haben, to need something to cheer one up.

aufmutzen, *v.tr. sep.* **1.** *Dial:* to arrange (articles); to hang up, fix up (articles). **2.** *F:* j-m etwas a., to put, lay, the blame for sth. on s.o.; to tax s.o. with sth.; to rebuke s.o. for sth.; to reproach s.o. with sth.

aufnageln, *v.tr. sep.* to nail (sth.) on; etwas auf etwas *acc.* a., to nail sth. on to sth.; den Deckel auf eine Kiste a., to nail down the lid on a box.

aufnagen, *v.tr. sep.* to gnaw (sth.) open.

Aufnäharbeit, *f. Needlew:* appliqué work.

aufnähen, *v.tr. sep.* **1.** to sew (sth.) on; etwas auf etwas *acc.* a., to sew sth. on to sth. **2.** sich *dat.* die Finger a., to make one's fingers sore by sewing.

Aufnäher, *m.* -s/-. *Dressm:* tuck; einen A. in einen Rock machen, to put, make, take up, a tuck in a skirt.

Aufnahme, *f.* -/-n. **1.** taking up (of discussion, work, etc.); adoption (of plan); A. der diplomatischen Beziehungen, establishing of diplomatic relations; A. der Verbindung mit j-m, establishing of contact with s.o.; A. der Verhandlungen mit j-m, entering into, upon, negotiations with s.o. **2.** raising (of money, loan). **3.** (*a*) taking in, intake (of food, etc.); accepting, acceptance (of sth.); absorbing, absorption (of sth.); inclusion (of sth.); A. von Nahrung in den Darm, intake of food into the bowel; Maßnahmen zur A. des Getreideüberschusses, measures to absorb the surplus wheat; A. eines Fremdworts in die Sprache, absorption of a foreign word into the language; A. eines Tanzes in das Programm, eines Wortes ins Lexikon, inclusion

of a dance in the programme, of a word in the dictionary; (*b*) *El:* input. **4.** assimilation (of knowledge); taking in, absorbing, absorption (of details, impressions, etc.). **5.** (*a*) reception (into heaven); (*b*) taking in (of s.o.) (into one's house, etc.); reception (of s.o., sth.); admission (of s.o.) (into a society, hospital, etc.); affiliation (of s.o.) (to, with, a society); seine A. in den Verein, his admission to the club; (*c*) (*department in hospital, etc.*) reception (office); (*d*) reception; eine warme, kühle, A. finden, to meet with a warm, a cool, reception; die günstige A. eines Theaterstücks, the favourable reception of a play; (*e*) in A. kommen, to (begin to) come into fashion, to become popular. **6.** (*a*) recording, writing down (of speech, etc.); recording (of voice, etc.); photographing (of object, etc.); taking of a photograph; shooting (of a film); A. des Protokolls, recording of evidence, of proceedings; keeping of the minutes (at a meeting); A. der Bestände, taking of an inventory of the stocks; *Cin:* Achtung, A.! action! (*b*) *Civ.E:* survey, surveying (of land, building, etc.); *Adm:* A. der Bevölkerung, taking of a census of the population; *see also* akustisch. **7.** (*a*) photograph; exposure (on roll of film); *Cin: TV:* shot, take; eine A. machen, to take a photograph; (*b*) (sound) recording.

Aufnahmeapparat, *m. Cin:* cine-camera, film camera, *U.S:* motion-picture camera, movie camera; *Gramophones:* recorder, recording machine.

Aufnahmeatelier, *n.* **1.** photographer's studio. **2.** recording studio.

aufnahmebereit, *a.* **1.** (*a*) (*of pers., mind*) receptive; für neue Ideen a. sein, to be receptive to, of, new ideas; (*b*) ready to receive, take in (guests, visitors, etc.). **2.** *Cin:* ready to shoot, for shooting.

aufnahmefähig, *a.* **1.** capable of absorbing, of absorption; der Markt ist nicht mehr a., the market is saturated. **2.** (*of pers.*) receptive (für, to); ich bin abends nicht mehr a., I can't take in anything more in the evening; ich bin heute nicht sehr a. für Musik, I don't feel very receptive to music today; nachdem er den ganzen Tag im Museum gewesen war, war er nicht mehr a., after spending the whole day in the museum he was incapable of taking in any more.

Aufnahmefähigkeit, *f.* **1.** capacity for absorption. **2.** receptiveness, receptivity (of mind); abends ist meine A. beschränkt, in the evening my capacity for taking things in is limited; die A. der Kinder nimmt nachmittags ab, children's minds are less receptive by the afternoon.

Aufnahmegebühr, *f.* admission fee, fee for admission, entry fee (to society, school, etc.), (society, school, etc.) registration fee.

Aufnahmegelände, *n. Cin:* lot.

Aufnahmegerät, *n.* (*a*) camera; photographic outfit; (*b*) recorder, recording machine.

Aufnahmeleiter, *m. Cin:* **1.** director of photography. **2.** recording manager.

Aufnahmeprüfung, *f.* entrance examination.

Aufnahmeraum, *m. W.Tel: etc:* recording-room, studio.

Aufnahmeröhre, *f. TV:* camera tube, pick-up tube.

Aufnahmesilo, *m. Ind:* receiving silo, (receiving) hopper.

Aufnahmestellung, *f. Mil:* delaying position; rallying position.

Aufnahmevermögen, *n.*=Aufnahmefähigkeit.

Aufnahmewagen, *m. W.Tel: etc:* recording van, *U.S:* car.

Aufnahms-, *comb.fm. cp.* Aufnahme-.

Aufnähnadel, *f. Bootm: etc:* sewing awl.

aufnehmen, *v.sep.* (*strong*) **I.** *v.tr.* **1.** (*a*) to pick up (stone, etc.); ein Buch (vom Tisch) a., to take up, pick up, a book (from the table); ein Kind a., to take a child from its bed; to pick up a child; to pick, take, a child up in one's arms; (*b*) to take up (carpet, floorboards, etc.); (*c*) to mop up (water, etc.); to wash (floor), to wash the floor of (room); (*d*) *Ven. & F:* die Spur, die Fährte, a., to get on the scent, to pick up the scent. **2.** (*a*) to take up (work, discussion, etc.); einen Plan a., to adopt a plan; Beziehungen mit j-m a., to enter into relations with s.o.; Verbindung mit j-m a., to establish contact with s.o.; Verhandlungen (mit j-m) a., to enter into, upon, negotiations (with s.o.); den Betrieb a., to start operating; to begin work(ing); (*of business, etc.*) to open; (*b*) den Fehdehandschuh a., to take up the gauntlet, the challenge, to accept the challenge; die Fehde a., to start a feud; den Kampf a., to give battle, to take up the

cudgels; den Kampf gegen etwas, j-n, a., to go into battle against sth., s.o.; den Kampf mit j-m a., to give battle to s.o.; den Kampf für j-n a., to take up the cudgels on s.o.'s behalf; einen Streit a., to take up a quarrel; Feindseligkeiten wieder a., to reopen hostilities; es mit j-m a. (können), to be a match for s.o., to be as good as s.o., to be s.o.'s equal; im Schwimmen kann ich es mit ihm jederzeit a., I can take him on any time at swimming; mit ihm kann ich es nicht a., I'm no match for him; die Arbeit wieder a., to resume, restart, work, to start work again; eine Arbeit wieder a., to take up a piece of work again, to return to a piece of work; eine Frage wieder a., to reopen a question; den Faden einer Diskussion wieder a., to pick up the thread of a discussion again; sein Studium wieder a., to resume one's studies; das Schiff nahm seine Fahrt wieder auf, the ship resumed its voyage; einen Plan wieder a., to return to a plan; *see also* Betrieb 1 (*a*); (*c*) to raise (money, loan); Geld auf ein Haus, usw., a., to raise money on a house, etc. **3.** *Lit:* to take up, to receive up (s.o., s.o.'s soul) (into heaven); möge ihre Seele in den Himmel aufgenommen werden, may her soul be received into heaven; *B:* bis an den Tag, da er aufgenommen ward, until the day in which he was taken up. **4.** (*a*) to receive, accept (sth.); to take in (food, etc.); to include (sth.) (in a list, etc.); etwas (in sich *acc.*) a., to absorb sth.; das Meer nahm die Ertrunkenen in seine Tiefe auf, the sea received the drowned into its bosom; die Dunkelheit nahm ihn auf, he was swallowed up by the darkness; wir haben viele französische Wörter in unsere Sprache aufgenommen, we have absorbed many French words into our language; ein Wort ins Lexikon a., to put, include, a word in the dictionary; einen Tanz in ein Programm a., to include a dance in a programme; (*b*) *Breed:* (*of mare, etc.*) to take (stallion, etc.); *abs.* to conceive; (*c*) (*of pers., mind*) to take (sth.) in; sein Gedächtnis konnte so viele Einzelheiten nicht a., his mind could not take in, absorb, so many details; Wissen in sich *acc.* a., to assimilate knowledge; Eindrücke (in sich) a., to absorb impressions; (*d*) etwas gut, übel, a., to take sth. well, badly; (*e*) to take (s.o.) in; to receive (s.o.); to accept (sth.); j-n in sein Haus a., to take s.o. in; to put s.o. up, to accommodate s.o., to have s.o. to stay; einen Flüchtling, eine Waise, in sein Haus a., to take in a refugee, an orphan; j-n (als Mitglied) in eine Gesellschaft, einen Verein, a., to admit s.o. to, to receive s.o. into, a society, an association; to affiliate s.o. to, with, a society; sich in eine Gesellschaft, usw., a. lassen, to join a society, etc.; to affiliate (oneself) to, with, a society, etc.; einen Artikel in eine Zeitschrift a., to accept an article for publication in a periodical; (*f*) j-n freundlich a., to receive s.o. kindly; to give s.o. a kind, friendly, warm, reception; to make s.o. welcome; freundlich, kühl, aufgenommen werden, to be kindly, coolly received, to meet with a friendly, a cool, reception, to meet with a warm, a cold, welcome; das Buch ist günstig aufgenommen worden, the book had a favourable reception; das Publikum hat seine Rede sehr ungünstig aufgenommen, the audience gave his speech a very hostile reception; die Kritiker haben das Stück beifällig aufgenommen, the critics applauded the play, received the play favourably, gave the play a favourable reception; (*g*) *W.Tel:* to pick up, receive (signal). **5.** (*a*) to record (sth.); to take, write, (sth.) down; to commit (sth.) to writing; ein Diktat a., to take (sth.) down from dictation; ein Stenogramm a., to take (sth.) down in shorthand; die Bestände a., to take an inventory of the stocks; (*b*) ein Gebiet a., to survey a district (*as a preliminary to making a map*); ein Gebäude a., to make the survey of a building; die Bevölkerung a., to take a census of the population; (*c*) wir haben seine Stimme (auf Tonband) aufgenommen, we have recorded his voice (on tape), made a (tape-)recording of his voice; seine Stimme läßt sich nicht gut a., his voice does not record well; (*d*) to photograph, take a photograph of (s.o., sth.); to shoot (film). **II.** aufnehmen, *v.i.* (*haben*) *Av:* to gain speed. **III.** *vbl s.* Aufnehmen, *n. in vbl senses; also:* acceptance (of sth.); absorption (of sth.); inclusion (of sth.); reception (of s.o.); admission (of s.o.) (into a society, etc.); affiliation (of s.o.) (to, with, a society, etc.).

Aufnehmer, *m.* **1.** receiver (of steam-engine). **2.** floor-cloth.

äufnen, *v.tr. Swiss:* to increase (sth.); to pile (sth.) up.

aufnieten, *v.tr. sep.* to rivet (sth.) on; **etwas auf etwas** *acc.* **a.,** to rivet sth. on to sth.

aufnorden, *v.* **1.** *v.tr. sep.* to restore *or* impart Nordic characteristics to (people, etc.); *F:* to Nordicize. **2. sich aufnorden,** *(a)* to acquire *or* reacquire Nordic characteristics; *(b) F:* (*in Nazi period*) to make oneself look Nordic; (*esp. of women*) to peroxide one's hair.

aufnotieren, *v.tr. sep.* to note (sth.) down, to make a note of (sth.).

aufnötigen, *v.tr. sep.* **j-m etwas a.,** to force sth. (up)on s.o.; to insist that s.o. shall take, shall accept, sth.; to force s.o. to take, accept, sth.; **einem Kranken Nahrung a.,** to force a patient to eat.

aufoktroyieren ['aufoktroa,ji:rən], *v.tr. sep.* **j-m seine Ideen, usw., a.,** to force, thrust, one's ideas, etc., (up)on s.o., to force s.o. to accept one's ideas, etc.; **einem Volk eine Verfassung a.,** to force a constitution on a people.

aufopfern. I. *v.tr. sep.* *(a)* to offer (sth.) as a sacrifice (to God); to sacrifice (sth.) (to God); **gute Werke a.,** to offer up good works; **seine Schmerzen Gott a.,** to bring one's sufferings as a sacrifice to God; *(b)* **sich (für j-n, etwas) a.,** to sacrifice oneself (for s.o., sth.); **seine Zeit für j-n, etwas, a.,** to give up, devote, one's time to s.o., sth.; **sich, alles, für seine Kinder a.,** to give up everything for one's children; **sein Leben für sein Vaterland a.,** to lay down one's life for one's country.

II. *vbl s.* **1. Aufopfern,** *n. in vbl senses.* **2. Aufopferung,** *f. (a) in vbl senses; also:* sacrifice (of sth., oneself); *(b)* self-sacrifice.

III. *pr.p. & a.* **aufopfernd,** *in vbl senses; esp.* devoted (affection, loyalty, etc.); unselfish (love, devotion, etc.).

aufopferungsfähig, *a.* capable of self-sacrifice; capable of devotion.

Aufopferungsgeist, *m.* spirit of self-sacrifice.

aufpacken, *v.tr. sep.* to load (sth.) **(auf etwas** *acc.*, on to sth.); **einem Tragtier eine Last a.,** to put a load on a pack-animal's back, to load a pack-animal; *F:* **j-m etwas a.,** to saddle s.o. with sth.; **da habe ich mir was Schönes aufgepackt!** now I've landed myself with something!

aufpäppeln, *v.tr. sep.* to feed (s.o., animal) up (*after illness, etc.*).

aufpassen, *v.sep.* **1.** *v.i.* (*haben*) to attend, to pay attention; to be on the alert; to take care; **in der Schule a.,** to be attentive, alert, in school; **a. wie ein Schießhund,** to watch like a hawk; to keep one's eyes (and ears) open (all the time); **paß auf! aufgepaßt!** (i) look (here)! listen! pay attention! (ii) be careful! look out! take care! mind (out)! **paß auf, was du (da) machst!** mind what you're doing! **paß auf, daß er dich nicht sieht,** take care that, mind, he doesn't see you; **auf etwas** *acc.* **a.,** to keep an eye on sth., to give an eye to sth.; **auf j-n a.,** to take care of, look after, s.o.; to keep an eye on s.o. **2.** *v.tr.* to fit (sth.) on; **etwas auf etwas** *acc.* **a.,** to fit sth. on sth.; **j-m einen Hut a.,** to fit a hat on s.o.'s head.

Aufpasser, *m.* **-s/-.** *(a)* one who watches, spies; watcher; spy; look-out (man); *F:* watch-dog; *(b)* busybody.

aufpeitschen, *v.tr. sep.* to whip (s.o.) up, stir (s.o.) up, to excite (s.o., s.o.'s passions, etc.); **aufpeitschende Musik,** music which whips up, excites, the passions; **sich durch Rauschgift a.,** to excite oneself by means of drugs.

aufpfählen, *v.tr. sep.* to impale (sth., s.o.).

aufpflanzen, *v.tr. sep.* *(a) Mil:* to fix (bayonet); **mit aufgepflanzten Seitengewehren,** with fixed bayonets; *(b) F:* to set (sth.) up; to plant (sth.); to plant, stick, set (stake, etc.) in the ground; **sich (vor j-m) a.,** to plant oneself (in front of s.o.).

aufpflastern, *v.tr.sep.* **1.** to pave (road). **2. etwas (auf etwas** *acc.***) a.,** to stick sth. on (sth.); to plaster sth. on (to sth.).

aufpflöcken, *v.tr. sep.* **etwas (auf etwas** *acc.***) a.,** to peg sth. on (to sth.), to fasten sth. on (to sth.) with pegs.

aufpflügen, *v.tr. sep.* to plough up (land, weeds, etc.).

aufpfropfen, *v.tr. sep.* to graft (sth.) on; *Carp:* to graft, scarf (timbers); *Arb:* **eine Art auf eine andere a.,** to graft one variety on, upon, another.

aufpicken, *v.tr. sep.* (*of bird*) *(a)* to peck up (crumbs, etc.); *(b)* to peck (sth.) open.

aufpinseln, *v.tr. sep.* to brush (sth.) on, to put (sth.) on with a brush.

aufplätten, *v.tr. sep.*=**aufbügeln.**

aufplatzen, *v.i. sep.* (*sein*) to burst (open); to crack, split.

aufplumpsen, *v.tr. sep.* **(auf etwas** *acc.*, **j-n) a.,** to plump (on to sth., s.o.), to fall plump (on to sth., s.o.).

aufplustern, *v.tr. sep.* (*of bird*) **sein Gefieder a., sich a.,** to ruffle (up) its feathers; *F:* (*of pers.*) **sich a.,** to puff oneself up.

aufpolieren, *v.tr. sep.* to polish (sth.) up; to rub up (table, etc.).

aufpolstern, *v.tr. sep.* to upholster (chair, etc.).

aufprägen, *v.tr. sep.* **etwas auf etwas** *acc.* **a.,** *(a)* to impress, imprint, stamp, sth. on sth.; to put the impress of sth. on sth.; **eine Figur auf eine Medaille a.,** to impress a figure on a medal; **eine Münze mit aufgeprägtem Adler,** a coin with the picture of an eagle stamped on it; **Grausamkeit ist seinem Gesichte aufgeprägt,** his face bears the impress of cruelty, cruelty is stamped on his face; **seiner Umgebung seinen Charakter, den Stempel seines Charakters, a.,** to impress one's character on one's surroundings; *(b)* to superimpose (design) (on coin, etc.).

Aufprall, *m.* impact (of missile, etc.) **(auf etwas** *acc.*, on sth.); **beim A.,** at the moment of impact, of striking.

aufprallen, *v.i. sep.* (*haben*) (*of missile, etc.*) **(auf etwas** *acc.***) a.,** to strike (sth.).

Aufpreis, *m.* additional price, cost.

aufpressen, *v.tr. sep.* **1.** to impress (pattern, etc. **(auf etwas** *acc.*, on sth.). **2.** to press (sth.) open.

aufprobieren, *v.tr. sep.* to try on (hat, etc.); **sich** *dat.*, **j-m, einen Hut a.,** to try on a hat; to try a hat on s.o.

aufprotzen, *v.tr. sep. Artil:* to limber (gun).

aufpullen, *v.tr. sep.* to pull up (horse).

aufpulvern, *v.tr. sep. F:* to buck (s.o.) up, ginger (s.o.) up; to pull (s.o.) together; **eine Tasse Tee wird dich a.,** a cup of tea will buck you up, pull you together, pick you up.

aufpumpen, *v.tr. sep.* **1.** to pump up (water, etc.). **2.** to pump up, inflate, blow up (tyre, etc.); **das Fahrrad a.,** to pump up one's bicycle tyres.

aufputschen, *v.tr. sep.* **1.** to rouse (s.o.), to incite (s.o.), to stir (s.o.) up; **j-n a., etwas zu tun,** to incite s.o. to sth., to do sth.; **das Volk (mit Reden) a.,** to rouse the (mob by making speeches). **2.** *F:* to stimulate (s.o.), *F:* to buck (s.o.) up, to pep (s.o.) up; **sich mit Kaffee a.,** to take coffee as a stimulant, *F:* to buck oneself up by drinking coffee.

Aufputz, *m.* dress, costume, attire, get-up; finery; **sie ging in ihrem schönsten A. zum Ball,** she went to the ball in all her finery.

aufputzen, *v.tr. sep.* **1.** to dress (s.o., oneself) up, to deck (s.o., oneself) out, to adorn (s.o., oneself), to attire (s.o., oneself), to get (s.o., oneself) up; **sich mit allerhand Flitter a.,** to deck oneself out in all kinds of frippery. **2.** to polish, rub, (sth.) up; to brush (sth.) up; to clean (sth.) up; to brighten (sth.) up. **3.** to mop up (dirt, water, etc.).

Aufputzverlegung, *f. El.E: Constr:* surface wiring system.

aufquellen, *v.i. sep.* (*strong*) (*sein*) **1.** (*of water*) to well up; to spring. **2.** (*of grain, etc.*) to swell (up); (*of earth, lime, wood, etc.*) to swell (up), to expand (*when moistened*); (*of part of body*) to swell; to become puffy; **Erbsen a. lassen,** to soak (dried) peas.

aufquirlen, *v.tr. sep. Cu:* to whisk (batter, etc.); **Eier und Milch zusammen a.,** to whisk, beat, eggs and milk together.

aufraffen, *v.tr. sep.* **1.** to gather (thgs) up; to pick (thgs) up. **2.** to pick up (one's skirts). **3. sich aufraffen,** *(a)* to get on to one's feet, to pull oneself up (on to one's feet); to struggle to one's feet; (*after fall*) to get on to one's feet again, *F:* to pick oneself up; *(b)* to pull oneself together, to collect oneself; to summon (up), muster (up), one's energy; **sich a., etwas zu tun,** to find the energy to do sth.; to bring oneself to do sth.; **ich konnte mich nicht dazu a.,** I couldn't find, summon up, muster, the energy, I couldn't be bothered, to do it; **er konnte sich nicht einmal dazu a., sich auszuziehen,** he even lacked the energy to get undressed; **du mußt dich zu einem Entschluß a.,** you must pull yourself together and make a decision, you must bring yourself to make a decision.

aufragen, *v.i. sep.* (*haben*) to tower (up); to stand high; to jut up; **das Gebirge ragte vor uns auf,** the mountains rose before us; *see also* **Himmel** 1 *(a)*.

Aufrahmung, *f.* natural separation of cream and milk.

aufranken, *v.i. sep.* (*sein*) & **sich aufranken,** (*of plant*) to creep, to climb; **der Efeu rankte sich am Hause auf,** the ivy was climbing, creeping, up the walls of the house.

aufrappeln (sich), *v.refl. sep. F:* *(a)* to pull oneself together, to collect oneself; to summon (up), muster (up), one's energy; **sich a., etwas zu tun,** to find the energy to do sth.; **ich kann mich nicht dazu a.,** I can't be bothered to do it; *(b)* to pull round; to get oneself on one's feet again, to pick up again (*after illness, etc.*).

aufraspe(l)n, *v.tr. sep.* to open (sth.) with a rasp, to rasp (sth.) open.

aufrauchen, *v.tr. sep.* to finish (cigarette, etc.); to finish, use up (tobacco); **hast du deine Zigarette schon aufgeraucht?** have you smoked, finished, your cigarette already? **ich habe meinen ganzen Tabak aufgeraucht,** I have finished, smoked, used up, all my tobacco.

aufräufeln, *v.tr. sep.* to undo, unravel (knitting, etc.).

aufrauhen, *v.tr. sep.* to roughen (surface); *Tex:* to nap, raise, dress (cloth).

aufräumen, *v.tr. sep.* **1.** *(a)* to clear (up), tidy (up), straighten (up) (room, desk, papers, etc.); to tidy away, put away, clear away (objects); *abs.* **a.,** to clear up, to tidy up; to make a clearance; **ein Zimmer, in einem Zimmer, a.,** to tidy (up), clear (up), straighten (up), a room, to put a room straight; **du mußt deine Sachen a.,** you must put, tidy, clear, away your things; you must tidy, clear, up your things; **räum auf, damit wir essen können,** clear the table so that we can have our meal; **wir müssen hier ein wenig a.,** we must do some tidying up here, we must tidy this place up a bit, we must make a bit of a clearance here; *Com:* **sein Lager a.,** to clear, sell off, one's stock; *(b) abs.* **die Seuche hat in der Stadt, unter der Bevölkerung, furchtbar aufgeräumt,** the epidemic has greatly thinned out the population of the town, has taken terrible toll of the population; *(c) abs.* **mit einem Mißbrauch a.,** to do away with, get rid of, abolish, an abuse; **mit diesen veralteten Ideen muß bald aufgeräumt werden,** we shall have to get rid of, do away with, these obsolete ideas soon. **2.** to ream (out), enlarge, open out, broach (a hole). *See also* **aufgeräumt.**

Aufräumer, *m.* **1.** person who tidies up. **2.** *Tls:* broach, reamer(-bit).

Aufräumerin, *f.* **-/-innen,** charwoman, *F:* char, *U.S:* cleaning woman.

Aufräumungsarbeiten, *f.pl.* clearance work.

aufrechnen. I. *v.tr. sep.* **1.** to add (thgs) up. **2. etwas gegen etwas a.,** to balance, set off, reckon, one thing against another; to compensate sth. by sth.; *Jur:* to balance, set off (one claim against another); **einen Posten gegen einen anderen a.,** to set off one item against another; **das Gute gegen das Böse a.,** to balance, set off, the good against the bad, to reckon up the good against the bad. **3. j-m etwas a.,** *(a)* to charge, reckon, sth. to s.o.'s account; to charge sth. to s.o.; *(b)* to lay, put, the blame on s.o. for sth., to blame s.o. for sth.

II. *vbl s.* **Aufrechnung,** *f. in vbl senses; esp. Jur:* balancing off, setting off, set-off (of claims).

aufrecht, *a.* **1.** upright; erect; on end; **etwas a. stellen,** to put, set, stand, sth. upright, on end; **eine Kiste a. stellen,** to set a box on (its) end; **a. stehen,** to stand upright, erect, straight; (*of thg*) to stand on end; **a. stehend,** (standing) upright, erect, straight; (*of thg*) (standing) on end; **etwas a. halten,** (i) to hold sth. upright, on end; (ii) to maintain (argument, etc.); **den Kopf a. halten,** to hold up one's head, to hold one's head erect; **j-n a. halten,** to hold s.o. up, to support s.o.; **sich a. halten,** to stay, keep, upright; to keep oneself from falling; **a. sitzen,** to sit up(right); **a. im Bett sitzen,** to sit up in bed; **a. auf seinem Stuhl sitzen,** to sit upright on one's chair; **a. auf seinem Stuhl,** sitting upright on one's chair. **2.** (*of character, mind, etc.*) upright, honourable, honest, straight; **ein aufrechter Mensch,** an upright man, a man of upright character, of integrity.

aufrechterhalten. I. *v.tr. sep.* to maintain (sth.). to keep (sth.) up, to uphold (sth.); **die öffentliche Ordnung a.,** to maintain, uphold, law and order; **den Frieden a.,** to keep the peace; **eine Freundschaft a.,** to maintain, keep up, a friendship; **die Beziehung mit j-m a.,** to maintain, keep up, one's relationship with s.o., to keep up with s.o.; **einen Brauch a.,** to stick to, abide by, a custom; **seine Ansicht, seinen Standpunkt, eine Behauptung, a.,** to maintain, uphold, stick to, adhere to, one's opinion, one's view, an assertion; **eine Entscheidung a.,** to abide by, uphold, a decision; **ein Angebot a.,** to abide by an offer,

II. *vbl s.* **1. Aufrechterhalten,** *n. in vbl senses.* **2. Aufrechterhaltung,** *f.*=II. 1; *also:* maintenance (of law and order); adherence (to an opinion, etc.).

aufrecken, *v.tr. sep.* to stretch (neck, etc.); to stretch (sth.) up(wards); **die Hände zum Himmel a.,** to stretch out, up, one's hands towards Heaven; **sich a.,** to stretch up(wards); to straighten up.

aufreden, *v.tr. sep.*=**aufschwatzen.**

aufregen. I. *v.tr. sep.* to excite (s.o.); to upset (s.o.); to agitate (s.o.); **diese Nachricht hat uns alle sehr aufgeregt,** (i) this piece of news excited us all very much, made us all very excited; (ii) this piece of news upset, worried, us all very much, made us all very upset, worried; **sich (über etwas** *acc.*) **a.,** to get excited, worked-up (about sth.); to become, get, upset (about sth.), to upset oneself (about sth.); **regen Sie sich bitte nicht auf!** please don't upset yourself, don't get upset! please don't worry! please don't get excited! **wir wollen uns nicht weiter darüber a.,** we mustn't worry about it any more; **reg dich nicht darüber auf!** don't get worried, don't fret (yourself), don't fuss, don't get fussed, *F:* don't take on, don't get into a stew, about it! **die kleinste Sache regt ihn auf,** the least thing upsets him, he gets upset, worried, flustered, flurried, fussed, at the least thing; **sie wird sich sehr a., wenn sie hört, daß du kommst,** she will get very (i) excited, (ii) upset, agitated, if she hears you are coming; **Sie dürfen den Kranken nicht a.,** you mustn't excite the patient; **er war sehr aufgeregt,** he was very excited; he was very upset, agitated, flurried, flustered, he was in a great flurry, fluster, *F:* he was in a great state, stew, taking; **eine aufregende Nachricht,** (i) an exciting piece of news; (ii) an upsetting piece of news.

II. *vbl s.* **Aufregung,** *f.* **1.** excitement; agitation; flurry, fluster; **sie geriet in heftige A.,** she became very excited, upset, agitated; **in heftiger A. sein,** to be in a state of great excitement, to be very excited; to be in a state of great agitation, to be in a great flurry, fluster; to be very upset; **vor lauter A. ließ sie das Tablett fallen,** she was so (i) excited, (ii) upset, that she dropped the tray; **in der allgemeinen A. hat man es nicht gemerkt,** in the general excitement it passed unnoticed; **wir kommen aus der A. gar nicht mehr heraus,** we have one excitement after the other. **2.** excitement; exciting event, etc; **sie hat in letzter Zeit so viele Aufregungen gehabt,** she has had so many excitements, so much excitement, recently; **die geringste A. würde dem Kranken schaden,** the smallest excitement would harm the patient.

aufreiben, *v.tr. sep.* (*strong*) **1.** to abrade, gall, graze, chafe, rub off, excoriate (skin, etc.); **ein Kragen, der die Haut aufreibt,** a collar that chafes the skin; **bei dieser Arbeit reibt man sich** *dat.* **die Hände auf,** this work makes one's hands sore, takes the skin off one's hands. **2.** to ream (out), open out, enlarge, widen, broach (hole). **3.** to grate (whole of cheese, etc.). **4.** to cut up (enemy troops, etc.); to cut, hew (army) to pieces. **5.** to wear (s.o.) out; to exhaust (s.o.); to fret (s.o.); to irritate (s.o.); *F:* to get (s.o.) down; **j-s Kräfte a.,** to wear down, sap, s.o.'s strength; **diese Sorgen reiben seine Gesundheit auf,** these worries are making him ill, are undermining his health; **der unaufhörliche Lärm reibt meine Nerven auf,** the constant noise frays my nerves; **er reibt sich in dieser Stellung auf,** this job is getting him down, fraying his nerves; **aufreibende Arbeit,** wearing, tiring, exhausting, work; **einen aufreibenden Tag hinter sich haben,** to have had a tiring, trying, gruelling, day.

Aufreiber, *m. Tls:* reamer(-bit); broach.

aufreihen, *v.tr. sep.* (*a*) to string, thread (beads, etc.); **Perlen auf einen Faden a.,** to thread beads, to put beads on a thread; (*b*) to put (people, thgs) in a row, to line up (people, thgs).

aufreißen, *v. sep.* (*strong*) **1.** *v.tr.* (*a*) to tear open, rip open (envelope, etc.); to cut (sth.) open, to split (sth.); **sich** *dat.* **den Finger a.,** to tear, rip, one's finger open; **aufgerissene Schuhe,** cracked shoes; **die Kälte hat mir die Haut an den Händen aufgerissen,** the cold has cracked the skin on my hands; (*b*) to tear open (door, etc.), to open (door, etc.) suddenly; **die Tür war weit aufgerissen,** the door was wide open, was flung wide; (*c*) **die Augen a.,** to open one's eyes wide; **den Mund a.,** (i) to open one's mouth wide; (ii) *F:* to talk big; to be a great talker. **2.** *v.tr.* to tear up, take up (floor-boards, etc.); **die Straße a.,** (*of workmen*) to tear up the road-surface; (*of tank, etc.*) to rip up the road. **3.** *v.i.* (*sein*) to crack; to split (open); to burst (open); (*of stone, wood, etc.*) to split, to crack; (*of wound*) to reopen; **die Naht ist aufgerissen,** the seam has split.

aufreiten, *v. sep.* (*strong*) **1.** *v.i.* (*sein*) to ride up; to come riding up; to ride up in line. **2.** *v.tr.* **sich a.,** to become chafed by riding.

aufreizen. I. *v.tr. sep.* **1.** to incite, instigate, urge on (s.o.); to rouse (s.o.), to stir (s.o.) up; to fire (s.o., s.o.'s passions); **die Masse zur Empörung, Seeleute zur Meuterei, a.,** to incite the masses to revolt, sailors to mutiny; **er hat mich dazu aufgereizt,** he urged me on, prompted me, *F:* egged me on, to do it; **die Leidenschaften der Masse a.,** to rouse, stir up, fire, the passions of the crowd. **2.** (*a*) to excite (s.o., the senses); **aufreizende Kleidung,** provocative, *F:* sexy, clothes; **sich aufreizend anziehen,** to wear provocative, *F:* sexy, clothes; **aufreizende Musik,** music which excites the senses; (*b*) to madden, infuriate (s.o., animal); **sie hat ein aufreizendes Benehmen, Lächeln,** her behaviour is maddening, infuriating, she has a maddening, an infuriating, smile; **ihre Faulheit ist aufreizend,** her indolence drives one mad.

II. *vbl s.* **Aufreizen** *n.*, **Aufreizung** *f. in vbl senses; also:* incitement, instigation (of s.o.).

aufrennen, *v.i. sep.* (*conj. like* **rennen**) (*sein*) *Nau:* (*of ship*) to run aground.

aufribbeln, *v.tr. sep. F:* to unravel (knitting, etc.).

aufrichten. I. *v.sep.* **1.** *v.tr.* (*a*) to put, set, stand (sth.) upright, on end; to erect (sth.); *Nau:* to right (boat, ship); **sich a.,** to straighten; to become erect; **einen Mast a.,** to erect, to step, a mast; **Säulen wieder a.,** to set up, re-erect, columns; (*b*) to help (s.o.) to his feet, to pick (s.o.) up (*after a fall*); to raise (s.o.) (*from a kneeling, sitting, lying, position*); **sich a.,** (*of pers.*) to straighten (up), (*of animal*) to stand on its hind legs; **sich wieder a.,** (*of pers.*) to get to one's feet, to pick oneself up (*after a fall*); **sich hoch a.,** to draw oneself up (to one's full height); **sich (stolz) a.,** to draw oneself up (proudly); **sich im Bett a.,** to sit up in bed; **den Kopf a.,** to raise, lift up, one's head; **die Schlange richtete sich auf,** the snake reared its head; *Her:* **aufgerichteter Löwe,** lion rampant; (*c*) **j-n a.,** to put fresh heart into s.o.; to hearten s.o.; to raise s.o.'s morale; **er hat mich durch seine Worte wieder aufgerichtet,** his words gave me fresh heart; **nach solchem Kummer kann man sich nicht so schnell wieder a.,** it takes time to pull up again after troubles like these. **2.** *v.i.* (*haben*) (*of ship*) to right (itself); *Av:* to straighten up, out, to flatten out.

II. *vbl s.* **Aufrichten** *n.*, **Aufrichtung** *f. in vbl senses; also:* erection (of sth.).

aufrichtig, *a.* sincere, straightforward; upright, honest; frank, candid; sincere (admiration, regret, etc.); frank, candid, honest (opinion); **ein aufrichtiger Mensch,** a sincere, straightforward, honest, person; *adv.* **a. gesagt,** frankly, to be frank, candid; **sag mir a., was du davon denkst,** tell me frankly, honestly, what you think about it; **sich a. bemühen, etwas zu tun,** to make honest, sincere, efforts to do sth.

Aufrichtigkeit, *f.* sincerity, straightforwardness; honesty; frankness, candour.

aufriegeln, *v.tr. sep.* to unbolt (door).

aufriffeln, *v.tr. sep.*=**aufribbeln.**

aufriggen, *v.tr. sep. Nau:* to rig (mast, etc.).

aufringeln, *v.tr. sep.* (*a*) to curl up (hair, etc.); to coil up (hair, etc.); (*b*) **sich a.,** (i) (*of snake*) to coil (itself) up; (ii) (*of smoke*) to curl upwards.

Aufriß, *m.* (*a*) *Arch: Geom:* vertical projection, elevation (of building, etc.); **ein Gebäude im A. darstellen,** to draw the elevation of a building; (*b*) outlines (of literary history, etc.).

Aufritt, *m.* **1.** ride up. **2.** chafing from riding.

aufritzen, *v.tr. sep.* to slit (sth.) open; to scratch (skin, etc.); **sich** *dat.* **die Haut a.,** to get scratched.

aufrollen, *v.tr. sep.* **1.** (*a*) to roll up (map, sleeves, etc.); to furl (flag, scroll, etc.); *Mil:* **die feindliche Front a.,** to roll up the enemy front; (*b*) **sich a.,** to roll up; (*of paper, etc.*) to roll up; to curl up; (*of kitten, etc.*) to roll up into a ball; to curl up. **2.** (*a*) to unroll (sth.); to unfurl (flag, scroll, etc.); (*b*) **sich a.,** to unroll; to come unrolled; to unfurl, to come unfurled. **3.** to bring up (subject, question) (for discussion); to go into (subject, question); **eine Geschichte a.,** to unfold a tale.

aufrücken, *v.sep.* **1.** *v.tr. A:* **j-m etwas a.,** to reproach, tax, s.o. with sth. **2.** *v.i.* (*sein*) (*a*) to move up; to close up; *Mil: etc:* to close the ranks, to close up; **eins a.,** to move up one; (*b*) to move up ; to be promoted; **in eine höhere Stelle a.,** to be promoted (to a better position), to rise to a better position; **zum Hauptmann a.,** to be promoted (to be) captain, to a captaincy, to rise to be a captain; *Sch:* **in eine höhere Klasse a.,** to be moved up (in)to a higher form, *U.S:* class, to move into a higher form, to move up.

Aufruf, *m.* **1.** calling, call, exhortation, appeal; *Mil: etc:* calling-up (of certain age-group); *Fin:* calling-in (of bank-notes, etc.); **A. zu den Waffen,** call to arms; *Jur:* **A. der Sache, der Zeugen,** calling of the case, of witnesses. **2. A. an das Volk,** appeal to the nation; proclamation; **öffentlicher A.,** proclamation.

aufrufen. I. *v.tr. sep.* (*a*) *Sch:* to call upon (s.o.) (to translate, etc.); **j-n (in der Schule, usw.) a.,** to call (out) s.o.'s name (in school, etc.); **die Schüler a.,** to call over the pupil's names, to call the roll; *Mil:* **einen Jahrgang a.,** to call up an age-group; *Jur:* **die Sache, die Zeugen, a.,** to call the case, the witnesses; **j-n zum Zeugen a.,** to call s.o. as witness; *Fin:* to call in (bank-notes, etc.); (*b*) **j-n a., etwas zu tun,** to call on s.o., to exhort s.o., to appeal to s.o., to do sth.; **die Bevölkerung a., an ihre Arbeitsplätze zurückzukehren,** to call upon, appeal to, the public to return to work.

II. *vbl s.* **Aufrufen** *n.*, **Aufrufung** *f.*= **Aufruf** 1.

Aufruhr, *m.* (*a*) commotion, disorder; uproar, turmoil, tumult; **A. der Elemente, der Leidenschaften, usw.,** turmoil, tumult, of the elements, of the passions, etc.; **sein Blut war in A.,** his pulse was racing; he was in a turmoil, in a fever (of excitement); **die ganze Stadt ist in A.,** the whole town is in a (state of) turmoil, in (a state of) commotion; **eine Stadt, ein Land, in A. bringen, versetzen,** to throw a town, a country, into disorder, commotion, turmoil, uproar (*cp.* (*b*)); **in A. geraten,** to be thrown into a (state of) turmoil, into commotion; (*b*) revolt, rebellion, riot, (up)rising, insurrection; *Mil: etc:* mutiny; **ein Land in A. bringen, versetzen,** to stir up, excite, rouse, a country to rebellion, to revolt; **das Land, das Volk, gegen j-n, etwas, in A. bringen, versetzen,** to raise the country, the people, against s.o.; **den A. unterdrücken,** to suppress, put down, the revolt, riot, rebellion, rising; *F:* **in hellem A. gegen j-n, etwas, sein,** to be up in arms against s.o., sth.

aufrühren, *v.tr. sep.* to stir up (dregs, mud, etc.); to rouse, stir up (passions); **eine alte Geschichte wieder a.,** to stir up, revive, rake up, old troubles, old scandal, etc.; *F:* to rip up old grievances, sores, etc.; **das Land, das Volk, a.,** to stir up, rouse, the country, the people (to rebellion).

Aufrührer, *m.* **-s/-.** **1.** agitator, incendiary; revolutionary. **2.** rebel, rioter, insurgent, insurrectionist; *Mil: etc:* mutineer.

aufrührerisch, *a.* **1.** seditious, incendiary (speech, activities, etc.). **2.** rebellious, rioting, insurgent (populace, etc.); *Mil: etc:* mutinous (elements, etc.).

Aufruhrstifter, *m.* (political) agitator.

Aufruhrversicherung, *f.* riot and civil commotion insurance.

aufrunden, *v.tr. sep.* **eine Summe, einen Betrag, (nach oben) a.,** to bring an amount up to a round figure.

aufrüsten. I. *v.tr. sep.* to arm (country, etc.); to rearm (country, etc.); *abs.* (*of country*) to arm; to rearm.

II. *vbl s.* **1. Aufrüsten,** *n. in vbl senses.* **2. Aufrüstung,** *f.* (*a*)=II. 1; (*b*) armament; rearmament; **moralische A.,** moral rearmament.

aufrütteln, *v.tr. sep.* to shake (s.o.) up, to rouse (s.o., country, etc.); **j-n aus dem Schlaf a.,** to shake s.o. out of his sleep, to rouse s.o. from his sleep; **j-n aus seiner Gleichgültigkeit a.,** to shake s.o. out of his apathy, to rouse s.o. from his apathy, to rouse, shake, s.o. up.

aufs, *prep.* (*contraction of* **auf das,** *cp.* **auf** II.) (*for usage of* **aufs** *and* **auf das** *cp. notes to* **am**) **1.** (*a*) **das Kind kletterte aufs Fensterbrett,** the child climbed on to the window-sill; (*b*) **aufs Gemeindeamt gehen,** to go to the council offices; **aufs Büro gehen,** (i) to go to the office; (ii) to work in an office. **2.** (*a*) **aufs Geratewohl,** at random, hit or miss; (*b*) (*with superlative*) **wir müssen ihn aufs schnellste, aufs eiligste, einholen,** we must catch up with him as quickly as possible; *see also* **beste(r)** 3 (*b*).

Aufsage, *f.* withdrawal (of friendship, etc.); cancellation (of contract, etc.).

aufsagen. I. *v.tr. sep.* **1.** to recite, repeat (poem, etc.). **2.** to withdraw, cancel (sth.); **einen Vertrag a.,** to annul, rescind, cancel, terminate, a contract, to withdraw from a contract; **j-m den Dienst a.,** to give s.o. one's notice; **(j-m) die**

Freundschaft a., to withdraw one's friendship (from s.o.); *abs.* **j-m a.**, to break off relations with s.o.; to give s.o. notice.

II. *vbl s.* **1. Aufsagen,** *n. in vbl senses; also:* (*a*) recitation, repetition (of poem, etc.); (*b*) annulment, rescission, cancellation, termination (of contract), withdrawal (from contract); withdrawal (of friendship). **2. Aufsagung,** *f.*= II. 1 (*b*).

aufsägen, *v.tr. sep.* **1.** to saw (sth.) open. **2.** to saw up (wood, all available wood).

aufsammeln, *v.tr. sep.* to gather (thgs) up, to collect (thgs) up.

aufsässig, *a.* (*a*) rebellious; **a. werden,** to rebel, become rebellious; **gegen etwas, j-n, a. werden, sein,** to rebel against sth., s.o., to be in revolt against sth., s.o.; (*b*) *A:* **etwas** *dat.*, **j-m, a. sein,** to be hostile to sth., s.o., to be against sth., s.o.; to bear s.o. ill-will; to have a grudge against s.o.

Aufsässigkeit, *f.* rebelliousness.

aufsatteln, *v.tr. sep.* **1.** *abs.* to saddle. **2.** *Aut:* to couple (on) (trailer). **3.** *Min:* to raise (mouth of shaft).

Aufsatz, *m.* **1.** (i) top piece of a structure; superstructure; (ii) piece of machinery, etc., made to be attached *or* placed on top of main structure; (*a*) (ornamental) structure (above door, on chair, cupboard, sofa, etc.); (*b*)=**Altaraufsatz;** (*c*) centre-piece (on dinner table), epergne; (*d*) (*in organ*) resonator (on reed pipe); (*e*) *Artil:* sight; (*f*) *A:* head-dress. **2.** *A:* piece of material, etc., sewn, appliquéd, on (to garment, etc.). **3.** (*a*) *Golf:* tee; (*b*) *Mec.E:* chuck (on lathe). **4.** essay; (learned) article, paper; *Sch:* composition, essay, *U.S:* theme.

Aufsatzbacke, *f. Tls:* face jaw (of anvil).

Aufsatzband, *n. Carp: Constr: etc:* (surface type) counter-flap hinge.

Aufsatzbohle, *f. Skittles:* starting board.

Aufsatzfehler, *m. Artil:* error in range.

Aufsatzhammer, *m.* set-hammer.

Aufsatzhöhe, *f. Artil:* elevation.

Aufsatzkränze, *m.pl. Min:* tubbing rings.

Aufsatzplatte, *f.* added plate, plinth, etc.

Aufsatzringe, *m.pl. Min:* tubbing rings.

Aufsatzschrank, *m.* court cupboard.

Aufsatzstange, *f.* **1.** *Min:* lengthening-rod. **2.** *Artil:* sight-bar.

Aufsatzthema, *n.* essay-subject.

Aufsatzwinkel, *m. Ball:* tangent elevation; angle of sight.

aufsaufen, *v.tr. sep.* (*strong*) (*of animal*) to drink up (water, etc.); *F:* (*of pers.*) to swig, toss off, gulp down (drink).

aufsaugen. I. *v.tr. sep.* (*strong & weak*) to suck up (liquid, etc.); (*of plant*) to absorb, imbibe (moisture); (*of sponge, cotton wool, etc.*) to absorb, imbibe, soak up (moisture); **aufsaugendes Mittel,** absorbent; **aufsaugende Wirkung,** absorbent effect.

II. *vbl s.* **Aufsaugen** *n.*, **Aufsaugung** *f. in vbl senses; also:* absorption (of moisture, etc.).

Aufsauger, *m. Ch: Ph:* absorber.

aufschärfen, *v.tr. sep. Ven:* to cut open (skin of game).

aufscharren, *v.tr. sep.* (*of hen, etc.*) to scratch up (earth, flower-bed, etc.); (*of dog, etc.*) to dig up (earth, buried object, etc.).

aufschauen, *v.i. sep.* (*haben*) to look up; **zum Himmel a.,** to look up at the sky; **von seiner Arbeit a.,** to look up from one's work; **zu j-m a.,** (i) to look up at s.o.; (ii) to look up to s.o.

aufschaufeln, *v.tr. sep.* to shovel up (earth, etc.).

aufschäumen, *v.i. sep.* (*sein*) to froth up; to bubble up, to effervesce.

aufscheinen, *v.i. sep.* (*strong*) (*sein*) *Austrian:*= **erscheinen I.** 1(b).

aufscheuchen, *v.tr. sep.* to disturb (wild animal, bird); to start (hare, etc.); *F:* to rout (s.o.) out (of bed, etc.), to make (s.o.) get up (from chair, etc.); **j-n aus seiner Ruhe a.,** to rouse, wake, s.o. from his tranquillity.

aufscheuern, *v.tr. sep.* **1.** to clean, scour (sth.). **2.** to abrade, graze, chafe, excoriate (skin); **er hat sich** *dat.* **die Haut an den Händen aufgescheuert,** he has grazed the skin on his hands, taken the skin off his hands.

aufschichten, *v.tr. sep.* to pile (thgs.) up in layers *or* tiers; to stack up (timber, crates, etc.); *Geol:* (*of natural forces*) to stratify (rock, etc.); **sich a.,** to pile up (in layers); *Geol:* (*of rock, etc.*) to stratify; **aufgeschichtete Erde,** earth in layers; layers of earth; *Geol:* **aufgeschichtetes Gestein,** stratified rock; **Aufschichtung** *f, in vbl senses; also: Geol:* stratification.

aufschiebbar, *a.* **1.** (*a*) (bolt, etc.) which can be pushed up; (*b*) sliding (door, etc.). **2.** postponable; (decision, business, payment, etc.) which can be postponed, delayed, deferred, put off.

aufschieben. I. *v.tr. sep.* (*strong*) **1.** to push (sth.) up; to push up, back (bolt, etc.); to slide open (door, window, etc.). **2.** to postpone, defer, delay, adjourn, put off (sth.); to hold over (decision, etc.); **eine Reise, einen Besuch, a.,** to postpone a journey, visit, etc.; **etwas auf, für, später a.,** to postpone sth. till later, to defer sth. to a later date, to put sth. off till another time; **wir schieben diese Frage für später auf,** we'll leave that question till later; **sie haben die Entscheidung bis, auf, Montag aufgeschoben,** they have postponed, put off, making a decision till Monday; **eine Sache (für) eine Woche a.,** to postpone sth. for a week; **Geschäfte, die man nicht a. kann,** business which cannot be deferred; **die Zahlung a.,** to defer, delay, postpone, put off, payment; **die Sache läßt sich nicht (länger) a.,** the matter cannot be deferred, delayed, any longer, the matter brooks no delay; **das Schreiben a.,** to put off writing; **er schiebt immer alles auf,** he always puts everything off, he always procrastinates; **aufgeschoben ist nicht aufgehoben,** there is always another time; it is only a pleasure deferred; **einen Termin a.,** to extend a time-limit; to fix a later date; *Jur:* **aufschiebende Bedingung,** condition precedent. *See also* **Annuität.**

II. *vbl s.* **Aufschieben** *n.*, **Aufschiebung** *f. in vbl senses; also:* postponement, deferment, adjournment (of sth.); extension (of time-limit).

Aufschiebling, *m.* **-s/-e.** *Constr:* sprocket (piece).

aufschiefern (sich), *v.refl. sep.* (*of wood, etc.*) to split.

aufschießen, *v.sep.* (*strong*) **1.** *v.tr. Nau:* **ein Tau a.,** to coil (down) a rope. **2.** *v.i.* (*sein*) (*a*) (*of flame, water, etc.*) to shoot up(wards); (*of water*) to gush, spout, forth; (*of flame*) to leap (up); (*of pers.*) to leap up, jump up; (*b*) (*of plant, child*) to shoot up; **lang, hoch, aufgeschossen sein,** (*of child*) to have grown (suddenly) lanky; (*of plant*) to have shot up (high).

aufschimmern, *v.i. sep.* (*sein, haben*) to (begin to) shimmer, glimmer.

aufschirren, *v.tr. sep.* to harness (horse).

Aufschlag, *m.* **1.** striking (of missile, etc.); impact (of missile, aircraft in crash-landing, etc.); thud (of falling object, bouncing ball, etc.). **2.** turn-up (on trousers, etc.); (upturned) cuff (on sleeve); facing (on coat, etc.); lapel (of coat, etc.); **Aufschläge an einem Rock, Mantel,** facing, revers, lapels, of a jacket, coat; **Aufschläge auf einen Rock setzen,** to face a jacket. **3.** (*a*) *Mus:* (*in conducting*) arsis; (*b*) *Ten:* service, serve; **amerikanischer A.,** American service; **A. von oben,** overarm service; **wer hat A.?** whose service is it? **4.** *Com:* additional, extra, charge; surcharge; supplementary charge; supplement; *Adm:* additional tax *or* duty. **5.** *For:* plants growing from hard fruit.

Aufschlagball, *m. Ten:* (i) ball which has been served; (ii) ball to be served; **das Recht auf einen zweiten A. haben,** to have the right to serve a second ball.

Aufschlagbrand, *m. Av:* fire caused by a crash (-landing).

aufschlagen, *v.sep.* (*strong*) I. *v.tr.* **1.** (*a*) to cast up (one's eyes); **die Augen zum,** *Lit:* **gen, Himmel a.,** to cast up one's eyes to Heaven; **die Augen (fragend, usw.,) zu j-m a.,** to look up at s.o. (questioningly, etc.); (*b*) to turn up (sleeve, collar, hat-brim, etc.); to raise (veil); (*c*) *Cards:* to turn up (card). **2.** (*a*) to open (door, etc.); **der Wind hat die Tür aufgeschlagen,** the wind blew the door open; (*b*) to open (book); **ein aufgeschlagenes Buch,** an open(ed) book; **das Buch lag aufgeschlagen auf dem Tisch,** the book lay open on the table; **eine bestimmte Stelle (in einem Buch) a.,** to open a book at a certain passage, to turn up a certain passage (in a book). **3.** to break (sth.) open; to break (egg); to crack (nut); **sich** *dat.* **den Kopf, usw., beim Fallen a.,** to cut one's head, etc., open in falling; **er hat sich** *dat.* **das Knie aufgeschlagen,** he (fell and) cut his knee open. **4.** to unlay (rope). **5.** to put up (bed, wardrobe, scaffolding, etc.); to erect (scaffolding, etc.); to pitch (tent, camp); to fix up (tent); to fix (camp); **seinen Wohnsitz auf dem Lande a.,** to take up one's abode in the country. **6.** *Com:* to raise (price); **etwas auf den Preis a.,** to put something on the price; **wenn wir die Waren ins Haus liefern, müssen wir etwas (auf den Preis) a.,** if we deliver the goods to the house we must make an additional charge. **7.** *Knitting:* **eine Masche a.,** to cast on a stitch; *abs.* **a.,** to cast on; **zwanzig a.,** to cast on twenty (stitches). **8. eine (gellende) Lache a.,** to burst into (shrill) laughter, into a (shrill) laugh; **einen Lärm a.,** to start making a (sudden) noise. **9.** *Ten:* **den Ball a.,** to serve the ball; *abs.* **a.,** to serve.

II. **aufschlagen,** *v.i.* **1.** (*sein*) (*of door, etc.*) to open; to spring open. **2.** (*a*) (*sein, haben*) (*of missile, etc.*) to strike; (*of aircraft*) to hit, strike, the ground; (*of ball*) to bounce; (*b*) (*sein*) **mit dem Kopf, usw., beim Fallen a.,** to hit, knock, strike, one's head, etc., in falling; **er schlug mit dem Kopf aufs Pflaster auf,** his head hit (against) the pavement; *Swim:* **mit dem Bauch (aufs Wasser) a.,** to do a belly-flop. **3.** (*haben, sein*) *Com: F:* (*of price*) to rise, to go up; **die Butter ist, hat, wieder etwas aufgeschlagen,** butter has gone up a little again.

III. *vbl s.* **Aufschlagen,** *n. in vbl senses; also:* erection (of scaffolding, etc.).

Aufschläger, *m. Ten:* server.

Aufschlagfeld, *n. Ten:* service-court.

Aufschlaggeschwindigkeit, *f.* striking velocity (of bomb).

Aufschlaggranate, *f. Artil:* percussion shell; shell with percussion fuze.

Aufschlag(s)linie, *f. Ten:* service-line.

Aufschlag(s)seitenlinie, *f. Ten:* service-side-line.

Aufschlagwasser, *n. Hyd.E:* water power.

Aufschlagzünder, *m. Artil:* percussion fuze; **empfindlicher A.,** graze fuze.

aufschlämmen, *v.tr. sep. Ch:* to suspend (particles) (in a solution).

aufschleppen, *v.tr. sep. Nau:* to haul up (ship) (on to beach, etc.).

Aufschlepphelling, *f. Nau:* slip(way).

aufschlicken, *v.sep.* **1.** *v.tr.* to silt up (canal, etc.). **2.** *v.i.* (*sein*) (*of canal, etc.*) to silt up.

aufschließen. I. *v.tr. sep.* (*strong*) **1.** (*a*) to open (door, box, room, etc.) (with key); to unlock (door, box, room, etc.); **ein Zimmer, ein Haus, a.,** to open, unlock, the door of a room, of a house; **j-m sein Herz a.,** to open one's heart to s.o., to unbosom oneself to s.o.; **ihr Herz schloß sich mir auf,** she opened her heart to me; *see also* **aufgeschlossen;** (*b*) to open up, open out, develop (mine, trade area); *Min:* to win (seam); (*c*) *Lit:* to throw light upon (sth.); to disclose the sense of (statement, etc.). **2.** (*a*) *Ch: etc:* to break down, break up (substance); to decompose, dissolve (silicates, phosphates, etc.); (*of gastric juices*) to break down, reduce (food); (*b*) *Min:* to break, crush (ore). **3.** *Mil: etc: abs.* **a.,** to close (up) the ranks; to close up.

II. *vbl s.* **Aufschließen** *n.*, **Aufschließung** *f. in vbl senses; also: Min: etc:* development (of mine, trade area); *Ch: etc:* decomposition (of phosphates, etc.).

aufschlitzen, *v.tr. sep.* to slit (sth.) open; to rip (sth.) open; **einen Sack a.,** to slit open a sack; **einem Tier den Bauch a.,** to slit open an animal's belly.

aufschluchzen, *v.i. sep.* (*haben*) to give a (sudden) sob.

aufschlürfen, *v.tr. sep.* to drink (sth.) up noisily, with relish; **er schlürfte die Suppe gierig auf,** he drank up the soup thirstily, greedily.

Aufschluß, *m.* **1.** *Geol:* (natural) section. **2.** information; enlightenment; **(j-m) A., Aufschlüsse, über etwas** *acc.* **geben, gewähren,** to give (s.o.) information about sth.; to enlighten (s.o.) on sth.; **A., Aufschlüsse, über etwas** *acc.* **erhalten, erlangen,** to receive, obtain, information about sth.; **die Urkunde gibt wichtige Aufschlüsse über die Baugeschichte der Kathedrale,** the document gives valuable information about, throws important light on, the history of the cathedral's construction; **sein Betragen hat mir interessante Aufschlüsse über seinen Charakter gegeben,** his behaviour threw interesting light on his character. **3.** *Min: etc:* development, opening up (of mine, trade area). **4.** *Ch: etc:* decomposition (of phosphates, etc.).

aufschlüsseln, *v.tr. sep.* to arrange, classify; **aufgeschlüsselt nach Größe, Typ, usw.,** classified, shown, according to size, type, etc.

aufschlußreich, *a.* informative; enlightening; revealing, illuminating.

aufschmeißen, *v.tr. sep.* (*strong*) to throw open (door, etc.) (violently). *See also* **aufgeschmissen.**

aufschmelzen, *v.sep.* **1.** *v.tr.* (*strong, occ. weak*) (*a*) to smelt (sth.) on; (*b*) to melt (sth.) (down); to smelt (ore); (*c*) to open (sth.) by melting, by smelting. **2.** *v.i.* (*strong*) (*sein*) (*a*) to melt; to be melted down; (*of ore*) to be smelted; (*b*) to be melted, smelted, open.

aufschmieden, *v.tr. sep.* to forge (sth.) on (**auf etwas** *acc.,* to sth.).

aufschmieren, *v.tr. sep.* to spread on (butter, etc.); **Butter aufs Brot a.,** to spread butter on bread; to butter bread; **Fett auf etwas** *acc.* **a.,** to smear grease on sth., to grease sth.

aufschminken, *v.tr. sep.* to paint, make up (one's face).

aufschnallen, *v.tr. sep.* **1. etwas (auf etwas** *acc.*) **a.,** to buckle sth. on (to sth.), to strap (sth.) on (to sth.). **2.** to unbuckle (sth.).

aufschnappen, *v.sep.* **1.** *v.tr.* (*a*) to catch (sth.) (as it falls, in mid-air); **der Hund schnappte den Knochen in der Luft auf,** the dog caught the bone (as it fell); (*b*) *F:* to pick up (news, word, etc.); **das Kind hat allerlei schlechte Ausdrücke aufgeschnappt,** the child has picked up all sorts of bad words. **2.** *v.i.* (*sein*) to snap open.

Aufschneidemaschine, *f.* cutting machine, slicing machine, slicer (for ham, etc.).

aufschneiden, *v.sep.* (*strong*) **1.** *v.tr.* (*a*) to cut (sth.) open; to slit (sth.) open; to split (rolls); *Surg:* to open (sth.); to open, lance (tumour, abscess, etc.); **j-m die Kehle a.,** to cut, slit, s.o.'s throat; **einen Knoten, die Schnur, a.,** to cut (through) a knot, the string; **ein neues Buch a.,** to cut the pages of a new book; (*b*) *Rail:* **eine Weiche a.,** to force open points. **2.** *v.tr.* (*a*) to cut up (meat, etc.); (*b*) to slice (meat, etc.). **3.** *v.i.* (*haben*) *F:* to talk big, to draw the long bow, to brag; **er schneidet wieder auf,** he's telling tall stories, drawing the long bow, again.

Aufschneider, *m.* **1.** cutter. **2.** *F:* teller of tall stories; braggart; show-off.

Aufschneiderei, *f. F:* big talk; bragging; **von seinen Aufschneidereien darf man sich nicht zu sehr beeindrucken lassen,** one shouldn't let oneself be over-impressed by his big talk.

aufschneiderisch, *a.* boastful; *adv.* boastingly.

aufschnellen, *v.i. sep.* (*sein*) (*a*) (*of ball, etc.*) to bounce up; (*of pers.*) to jump, spring, leap, bounce, up; (*of fish*) to leap; (*b*) (*of door, box, etc.*) to fly open, to spring open.

Aufschnitt, *m.* (**kalter**) **A.,** (slices of) cold meat, *U.S:* cold cuts.

Aufschnittmaschine, *f.* = **Aufschneidemaschine.**

aufschnüren, *v.tr. sep.* **1. etwas (auf etwas** *acc.*) **a.,** to tie sth. on (to sth.). **2.** to unlace (sth.); to untie (sth.); **sich a.,** to come unlaced; to come untied, undone; (*of woman*) to unlace one's corset. **3.** to thread (beads, etc.); to string (beads, onions, dried figs, etc.).

aufschrammen, *v.tr. sep.* to graze, scrape (skin, leg, etc.); **sich** *dat.* **das Bein a.,** to graze, scrape, one's leg, to scrape the skin off one's leg.

aufschrauben, *v.tr. sep.* **1. etwas (auf etwas** *acc.*) **a.,** to screw sth. on (to sth.). **2.** to unscrew (sth.); **einen Behälter a.,** to unscrew the lid of, to screw the lid off, a container. **3.** to screw (sth.) up, to screw (sth.) tight(er), to tighten (sth.); to intensify, force (one's interest, curiosity, etc.); to force up (estimates, etc.).

aufschrecken, *v.sep.* **1.** *v.tr.* (*weak*) to startle (s.o., game, etc.); to give (s.o.) a start, a jump; **j-n aus dem Schlafe a.,** to startle s.o. out of his sleep. **2.** *v.i.* (*strong*) (*sein*) to start, to jump, to give a start, a jump, to be startled; **aus seinem Schlafe a.,** to wake up with a start; to start from, out of, one's sleep.

Aufschrei, *m.* (*a*) shout, cry; yell; scream; shriek; (*b*) clamour; (public) outcry; **es ging ein A. durch die Presse,** there was an outcry in the press.

aufschreiben, *v.tr. sep.* (*strong*) **1.** (*a*) to write (sth.) down; to take (sth.) down; to make a note of (sth.), to note (sth.) down; **etwas in ein Buch, in einem Buch, a.,** to write, note, (sth.) down in a book; to enter, record, (sth.) in a book; (*of policeman, etc.*) **j-n a.,** to take s.o.'s name; (*b*) *Com:* = **anschreiben** I. 1 (*c*). **2.** to use up (paper, ink) (by writing).

Aufschreiber, *m. Games:* scorer.

aufschreien, *v.i. sep.* (*strong*) (*haben*) to give a shout, a cry; to cry out; to scream, shriek; **laut a.,** to give a loud cry.

Aufschrift, *f.* (*a*) address (on a letter, etc.); (*b*) inscription (on coin, monument, etc.); legend (on coin, stamp, etc.); lettering (on book, etc.); title (on book-cover, note-book, file, etc.); name, designation (of shop, etc.) (on fascia, window, door, etc.); (shop-)sign; **ein Laden mit der A. 'Confiserie',** a shop which calls itself 'Confiserie'.

aufschrumpfen, *v.tr. sep.* to shrink on (crank, etc.).

Aufschub, *m.* (*a*) postponing, postponement, putting off (of journey, visit, meeting, payment, etc.); deferring, deferment (of business, payment, etc.); delaying (of payment, etc.); holding

over (of decision); extension (of time-limit); (*b*) postponement, deferment, delay; **die Sache leidet, duldet, keinen A.,** the matter brooks, allows of, no delay; **ohne A.,** without delay; **einen A. erhalten,** to be granted an extension of time, more time; **um A. bitten,** to ask for an extension of time, for a postponement, for more time.

aufschultern, *v.tr. sep.* to shoulder (burden, etc.); **j-m etwas a.,** to put sth. on s.o.'s shoulders; *F:* to saddle s.o. with sth.; to put (responsibility) on s.o.'s shoulders; (**sich** *dat.*) **eine Verantwortung a.,** to shoulder, take on, a responsibility.

aufschüren, *v.tr. sep.* = **anschüren.**

aufschürfen, *v.tr. sep.* to graze, scrape (skin, leg, etc.); **sich** *dat.* **das Bein a.,** to graze, scrape, one's leg, to scrape the skin off one's leg.

aufschürzen, *v.tr. sep.* to tuck up (skirt, etc.); **sich a.,** to tuck up one's clothes.

aufschütteln, *v.tr. sep.* to shake up (pillows, etc.).

aufschütten. **I.** *v.tr. sep.* (*a*) to pile up, heap up (corn, stones, etc.); to heap up, bank up (earth); (*of river, etc.*) to deposit (earth, etc.); **etwas auf etwas** *acc.* **a.,** to pour sth. on to sth.; to spread sth. over sth.; to heap, pile, sth. up on sth.; **Stroh (im Stall) a.,** to scatter, strew, straw (in the stable); **Kohlen aufs Feuer a.,** to heap coal on the fire, to bank up the fire; (*b*) to brew (tea); to make (tea, coffee); (*c*) *Civ.E: etc:* **einen Damm, usw., a.,** to build a dam, etc., of loose earth, stones, etc.; (*d*) *Civ.E: etc:* to fill (up), pack (ditch, etc.) (with earth, etc.). **II.** *vbl s.* **1. Aufschütten,** *n.* in vbl senses. **2. Aufschüttung,** *f.* (*a*) = **II.** 1; *Geol:* deposition (of sediment); (*b*) heaped-up earth, stones, etc; *Geol:* mound of deposit.

Aufschüttungskegel, *m. Geol:* (*a*) alluvial cone; (*b*) accumulation cone (of volcano).

aufschwänzen, *v.tr. sep.* **1.** *St.Exch:* **die Baissiers a.,** to squeeze the bears. **2.** *F:* **j-n a.,** to chivvy s.o.; to put s.o. through it.

aufschwatzen, *v.tr. sep.* **j-m etwas a.,** to talk s.o. into taking sth., to persuade s.o. to take sth.; to talk s.o. into buying sth., to persuade s.o. to buy sth.

aufschweben, *v.i. sep.* (*sein*) to float up(wards).

aufschweißen, *v.tr. sep. Metalw:* to weld (sth.) on (**auf etwas** *acc.,* to sth.).

aufschwellen. **I.** *v.sep.* **1.** *v.i.* (*strong*) (*sein*) (*a*) to swell (up); to become inflated; to become distended; (*of river*) to swell; *Med:* to swell (up), to tumefy; (*b*) to grow puffy. **2.** *v.tr.* (*weak*) (*of wind*) **die Segel a.,** to fill the sails. **II.** *vbl s.* **1. Aufschwellen,** *n.* in vbl senses; *also:* inflation; distension; *Med:* tumefaction. **2. Aufschwellung,** *f.* (*a*) = **II.** 1; (*b*) swelling; protuberance; *F:* lump.

aufschwemmen. **I.** *v.tr. sep.* (*of foodstuffs*) to make (s.o.) flabby; **aufgeschwemmt,** flabby, puffy, bloated. **II.** *vbl s.* **Aufschwemmung,** *f.* (*a*) *Med:* swelling; (*b*) *Ch:* suspension.

aufschwindeln, *v.tr. sep.* **j-m etwas a.,** to trick s.o. into buying sth.

aufschwingen, *v.tr. sep.* (*strong*) **1.** to swing (sth.) up(wards). **2. sich aufschwingen,** (*a*) (*of pers., monkey, etc.*) to swing (oneself, itself) up(wards); (*of bird, etc.*) to fly up; to soar; (*b*) *F:* to rise; **sich vom Statisten zum Filmstar a.,** to rise from an extra to a film-star; **wir haben uns zu einem neuen Auto aufgeschwungen,** we have risen to a new car; (*c*) *F:* **sich zu etwas a., sich (dazu) a., etwas zu tun,** to force oneself, bring oneself, to do sth.; **er hat sich noch zu keinem Entschluß aufgeschwungen,** he hasn't brought himself to make any decision yet; **er hat sich endlich zu einem Brief aufgeschwungen,** he has at last brought himself to write a letter.

Aufschwung, *m.* (*a*) swing up, upward swing; *Gym:* upward circle; (*b*) rise; impetus, stimulus, impulse; upswing (of culture); **plötzlicher A. der Preise,** sudden advance, rise, in prices; **einen A. nehmen,** to improve; (*of prices*) to advance, to rise; (*of market*) to boom; **unser Geschäft nahm einen bedeutenden A.,** our affairs took a considerable turn for the better, improved considerably; (*of commerce, etc.*) **einen neuen A. nehmen,** to receive fresh impetus, to show renewed activity; **den Geschäften einen neuen A. geben,** to give a new stimulus, impulse, to trade; **j-m einen neuen A. geben,** to stimulate s.o.; to give s.o. fresh impetus; **der Vortrag hat ihm neuen geistigen A. gegeben,** the lecture gave him new inspiration, new mental stimulus; **religiöser A.,** increase in religious activity.

aufsehen. **I.** *v.i. sep.* (*strong*) (*haben*) to look up; **zum Himmel a.,** to look up at the sky; **von seiner**

Arbeit, von seinem Buch, a., to look up from one's work, from one's book; **zu j-m a.,** (i) to look up at s.o.; (ii) *F:* to look up to s.o. **II.** *vbl s.* **Aufsehen,** *n.* sensation, stir, notice; (*großes*) **A. erregen,** to create, make, cause, a (great) sensation, stir; to be a sensation; *F:* to make a splash; **wir wollen jedes A. vermeiden,** we must avoid attracting attention, notice, we don't want to create any kind of stir.

aufsehenerregend, *a.* sensational (happening, book, etc.).

Aufseher, *m.* overseer, supervisor; *Ind: Rail: etc:* inspector; (*in prison*) warder, *U.S:* guard; (*in store*) shop-walker, *U.S:* floor-walker; *Min:* (colliery) viewer; *Sch:* person in charge.

aufseilen, *v.tr. sep.* to pull, haul (sth., s.o.) up by a rope.

aufsein, *v.i. sep.* (*sein*) (*conj. like* **sein**) **1.** to be up; **bist du schon auf?** are you up, out of bed, yet, already? **2.** to be open.

aufsetzen, *v.tr. sep.* **1.** (*a*) **j-n a.,** to help s.o. to sit up, to help, raise, s.o. to a sitting position; **sich (im Bett) a.,** to sit up (in bed); (*b*) to stand, set, (sth.) up(right), on end; **die Kegel wieder a.,** to set up the (nine)pins again. **2.** to put (sth.) on; **etwas auf etwas** *acc.* **a.,** to put, place, sth. on sth.; **den Kessel a.,** to put on the kettle; **Wasser (zum Kochen) a.,** to put water on to boil; **das Essen a.,** to put the meal on to cook; **den Fuß a.,** to put one's foot on the ground; **er hat den Fuß falsch aufgesetzt,** he placed his foot in the wrong position; he placed, brought down, his foot awkwardly; **einen Flicken auf ein Kleid a.,** to put a patch on a dress, to patch a dress; **eine aufgesetzte Tasche,** a patch pocket; **ein neues Stockwerk auf ein Haus a.,** to add a new storey to a house; **j-m einen Hut, eine Krone a.,** to put, place, a hat, crown, on s.o.'s head; (**sich** *dat.*) **seinen Hut, seine Brille, usw., a.,** to put on one's hat, one's spectacles, etc; **eine ernste Miene a.,** to put on a grave expression; **sie hat heute einen Dickkopf aufgesetzt,** she is very obstinate, stubborn, today; **einem Ehemann Hörner a.,** to cuckold a husband; *F:* **das setzt allem die Krone auf!** that beats everything! that crowns all! that's the limit! **um allem die Krone aufzusetzen, hat er ..., to** crown all he ... ; **eine Statue mit aufgesetztem Kopf,** a statue with head worked separately and added; **den Ball a.,** *Golf:* to tee the ball, to tee up; *Rugby Fb:* to place the ball (on the ground); *Nau:* **die Schraube a.,** to ship the propeller; **ein Schiff a.,** to run a ship aground; *Art:* **eine Farbe a.,** to put on, add, a colour; **Glanzlichter, Lichter, a.,** to put in the highlights, light patches; *Ven:* (*of stag*) **Geweih a.,** *abs.* **a.,** to put forth, to grow, antlers; *see also* **Dämpfer. 3.** to draw up (document, contract, etc.); to draft (letter, etc.); to make a rough draft of (sth.); to make out (bill); **wichtige Briefe setze ich auf, ehe ich sie endgültig schreibe,** I make a (rough) draft of important letters before finally writing them out. **4.** *v.i.* (*haben*) (*a*) to land; **mit dem linken Fuß zuerst a.,** to put down, bring down, one's left foot first; (*b*) *Av:* to touch down. **5.** *v.i.* (*haben*) *Vet:* (*of horse*) to be a crib-biter.

aufseufzen, *v.i. sep.* (*haben*) to fetch, heave, a sigh; **er seufzte tief auf,** he sighed deeply, heavily, he fetched, heaved, a deep sigh, *F:* he sighed from his boots.

Aufsicht, *f.* **1.** top view (of machine, group of buildings, etc.); **etwas in A. zeichnen,** to draw the top view of sth. **2.** supervision; control; care; **die A. über j-n, etwas** *acc.,* **haben, führen,** to have charge of s.o., sth.; to keep a watch, an eye, on s.o., sth.; *Sch: etc:* (**die**) **A. haben, führen,** to be in charge (of class, etc.); to invigilate, *U.S:* to proctor (*at examination*); **die A. über j-n, etwas** *acc.,* **übernehmen,** to take charge of s.o., sth.; to take over control of s.o., sth.; **j-n unter (polizeiliche) A. stellen,** to put s.o. under (police) surveillance; **unter (polizeilicher) A. stehen,** to be under (police) surveillance; **er steht unter dauernder ärztlicher A.,** he is under constant medical supervision; **unter der A. von ...,** under the care, eye, of ... ; **under the supervision, control, of ..., supervised by ...; j-n, etwas, unter j-s A. stellen,** to put, place, s.o., sth., in, under, the care of s.o.; to commit s.o., sth., to the care of s.o.; **unter j-s A. sein,** to be under s.o.'s supervision, control, care; **j-n unter strenge A. nehmen,** to keep a strict eye on s.o.; **das Kind arbeitet nur unter A.,** the child will only work if supervised. **3.** person in charge; invigilator, *U.S:* proctor (*at examination*).

aufsichtführend, *a.* = **aufsichtsführend.**

Aufsichtsamt, *n.* supervisory committee, board; board of control.

Aufsichtsbeamte, *m.* supervisor; inspector; *Rail:* platform inspector, platform supervisor, assistant stationmaster.

Aufsichtsbehörde, *f.* supervisory body, supervisory committee; control commission; board of control, control board.

aufsichtsführend, *a.* supervisory (authority); supervising (teacher, etc.); invigilating, *U.S:* proctoring (teacher, etc.) (*at examination*).

Aufsichtsführung, *f.* supervision.

Aufsichtsrat, *m.* **1.** board of trustees, *approx.* = board of directors (of joint stock company, etc.). **2.** member of a board of trustees.

Aufsichtsucher, *m. Phot:* ground-glass viewfinder.

aufsieden, *v.sep.* (*conj. like* **sieden**) **1.** *v.tr.* to boil (sth.) up. **2.** *v.i.* (*sein, haben*) to boil up.

aufsingen, *v.i. sep.* (*strong*) (*haben*) to sing out.

Aufsitz, *m.* mounting; **zum A. bereit sein,** to be ready to mount (one's horse); to be ready to get on (one's motor-cycle, etc.).

aufsitzen, *v.i. sep.* (*strong*) **1.** (*haben*) (**auf etwas** *dat.*) **a.,** to be on top (of sth.); to be placed, fixed, on top (of sth.); to be detachable; **das Oberteil sitzt nur lose auf,** the upper part is not secured but just perched on top. **2.** (*sein*) (*a*) *Nau:* (*of ship*) to have run aground; to be aground; (*b*) (*of bird*) to be caught (in lime); (*c*) *F:* to be stuck (somewhere); **j-n a. lassen,** to let s.o. down (by not coming); *F:* to stand s.o. up; (*d*) *Austrian: F:* **j-m a.,** to be taken in, tricked, by s.o.; **du bist einem Schwindler aufgesessen,** you have been tricked by a swindler. **3.** (*haben*) (*a*) to sit up (in bed, etc.); (*b*) **die ganze Nacht a.,** to sit up all night. **4.** (*sein*) (*a*) to mount (one's horse); to get on (to) (bicycle, motor-cycle); **hinten a.,** to get up behind; **j-n hinten a. lassen,** to let s.o. ride behind; to take s.o. up behind; to take s.o. on the crupper; to let s.o. ride on the pillion (of motor-cycle); *Mil:* **aufgesessen!** (*to cavalry*) mount! (*of lorry-borne troops, etc.*) all aboard! **aufgesessene Abteilungen,** motorized units; (*b*) *F:* **j-m a.,** to drive s.o.: (*c*) to jump on to (horse, box, etc.) and land in a sitting position; (*d*) (*of bird*) to perch, to go to roost. **5.** *Sm.a:* **das Ziel a. lassen,** to aim just below the mark.

aufspalten. I. *v.tr. sep.* **1.** (*a*) to split (sth.); to cleave (sth.); to split (sth.) open; (*b*) *Ch: etc:* to break down, break up (substance); (*c*) **sich a.,** (i) to split; to cleave; to crack; to burst (open); (ii) (*of substance*) to be broken down, broken up. **2.** to divide up, split up (group, etc.); **eine Schulklasse in mehrere Gruppen a.,** to divide up, split up, a class into several groups; **sich a.,** to divide up, split up; **die Firma spaltet sich in mehrere Abteilungen auf,** the firm is divided into several departments; **die Partei spaltete sich in drei Gruppen auf,** the party split into three groups.

II. *vbl s.* **1. Aufspalten,** *n. in vbl senses; also:* division (into parts, groups, etc.); *Ch:* decomposition (of substance). **2. Aufspaltung,** *f.* (*a*) = II. 1; (*b*) cleavage; *Biol: etc:* fission.

aufspannen, *v.tr. sep.* to put (sth.) up; to stretch, spread (sth.); to open, put up (umbrella); **etwas auf etwas** *acc.* **a.,** to stretch sth. on sth.; to mount sth. on sth.; **ein Stück Stoff auf den Stickrahmen a.,** to put a piece of material in the embroidery frame; **Leinwand auf den Rahmen a.,** to stretch canvas on the frame; **die Segel a.,** to spread the sails; *Tex:* **die Kette a.,** to put in the warp.

Aufspannplatte *f.*, **Aufspanntisch** *m.* clamping-plate.

Aufspannvorrichtung, *f.* clamping device, holding device; (*on lathe*) chuck.

aufsparen, *v.tr. sep.* to save (sth.) up, to reserve (sth.), keep (sth.) in reserve (*for a particular purpose*); (*of God, fate, etc.*) to spare (s.o.); (**sich** *dat.*) **etwas für später a.,** to keep sth., save sth. (up), for later; **hat ihn das Schicksal nur deshalb aufgespart, um ihn jetzt zugrunde zu richten?** was he spared (by fate) only to be ruined now? **ich spare meine Kräfte lieber für etwas Besseres auf,** I'd rather save, reserve, my strength for something more worth-while; **sich für etwas a.,** to save oneself for sth.

aufspeichern. I. *v.tr. sep.* to store (sth.) (up); to lay up, hoard (up) (grain, supplies, treasure, etc.); to warehouse (goods); to store up, accumulate (electricity, heat, energy, etc.); *F:* **aufgespeicherte Energie,** accumulated, pent-up, energy.

II. *vbl s.* **Aufspeichern** *n.*, **Aufspeicherung** *f. in vbl senses; also:* accumulation (of energy, etc.); storage.

aufspeile(r)n, *v.tr. sep.* to skewer (meat, etc.).

aufsperren, *v.tr. sep.* (*a*) to open, unlock (door, etc.); (*b*) **eine Tür, die Augen, usw., (weit) a.,** to open a door, one's eyes, etc., wide; **den Mund a.,** to open one's mouth wide, to gape; *F:* **Mund und Nase (vor Erstaunen) a.,** to gape (with astonishment); *F:* **sperr doch die Augen auf!** look out! mind out! watch what you're doing! *F:* keep your eyes peeled! **sperr die Ohren auf!** listen carefully!

aufspielen, *v.sep.* **1.** (*a*) *v.tr.* to strike up (waltz, etc.); (*b*) *v.i.* (*haben*) to start playing, to strike up; **zum Tanz a.,** to strike up (music) for the dance. **2. sich aufspielen,** to give oneself airs, *F:* to put on side, to do the grand; **sich mit etwas a.,** to show sth. off; to brag about sth.; **sie spielt sich mit ihrer adligen Herkunft auf,** she brags about her noble descent; **sich mit seinen fortschrittlichen Ansichten a.,** to show off one's progressive views; **sich als Held, als Moralist, a.,** to set up for, to set oneself up as, a hero, a moralist.

aufspießen, *v.tr. sep.* to spear (sth.); to fork up (hay, etc.); to take (piece of meat, etc.) on one's fork; to impale (s.o., sth.); to run (s.o., sth.) through; *F:* to spit (s.o.); (*of horned animal*) to gore (s.o.).

aufspleißen, *v.tr. sep.* (*strong*) to split (wood, plank, etc.).

aufsplittern, *v.sep.* **1.** *v.tr.* (*a*) to splinter (sth.), to break (sth.) up into splinters; (*b*) to divide up, split up (group); **sich a.,** to divide up, split up; **die Partei hatte sich in mehrere kleine Gruppen aufgesplittert,** the party had split up into a number of small groups. **2.** *v.i.* (*sein*) to splinter, to break up into splinters.

aufspreizen, *v.tr. sep.* **1.** to spread, straddle (one's legs). **2. sich aufspreizen,** to show off ostentatiously, to make a pompous exhibition of oneself.

aufsprengen, *v.tr. sep.* **1.** to force (sth.) open; to open (safe, etc.) with an explosive, to blast (sth.) open. **2. Wasser, usw., auf etwas** *acc.* **a.,** to sprinkle water, etc., on sth.

aufsprießen, *v.i. sep.* (*strong*) (*sein*) (*of plant, friendship, etc.*) to spring up.

aufspringen, *v.i. sep.* (*strong*) (*sein*) **1.** (*of water, etc.*) to shoot up(wards); to gush, spout, forth; (*of pers., animal*) to jump, leap, spring, up; to jump, leap, spring, to one's, its, feet; **vom Sitz a.,** to jump up from one's seat. **2.** (*of ball, etc.*) to bounce; (*of pers., animal*) **hart, weich, a.,** to hit the ground hard, softly; **auf etwas** *acc.* **a.,** to land on sth. **3.** (*a*) (*of door, etc.*) to burst, fly, open; (*b*) (*of buds*) to burst; (*of skin, bark, etc.*) to crack, split; (*of skin*) to chap, become chapped; (*of seam*) to burst, split; **das Kleid ist (an den Nähten) aufgesprungen,** the dress has burst, split, at the seams; **aufgesprungene Hände,** chapped hands.

aufspritzen, *v.sep.* **1.** *v.tr.* to squirt, spurt, up (water, etc.). **2.** *v.i.* (*sein*) (*of water, etc.*) to squirt, spurt, up(wards).

aufsprossen, *v.i. sep.* (*sein*) = **aufsprießen.**

aufsprudeln, *v.i. sep.* (*sein*) (*of spring, boiling water, etc.*) to bubble (up).

aufsprühen, *v.sep.* **1.** *v.i.* (*sein*) (*of sparks, fountain, etc.*) to rise in a spray. **2.** *v.tr.* to emit (sparks, etc.) in a spray, to emit a shower of (sparks, etc.); to spray (sth.) on (to sth.).

Aufsprung, *m.* **1.** shooting up, gushing forth, spouting forth (of liquid); bound, leap, jump, spring (of pers., animal). **2.** bound, bounce, rebound (of ball, etc.). **3.** landing (after jump).

Aufsprungbahn, *f. Ski:* landing run.

aufspulen, *v.tr. sep.* to wind (cotton, ribbon, etc.) on to a reel, spool, etc.; to reel, spool (cotton, etc.).

aufspülen, *v.tr. sep.* (*a*) to wash up (dishes); *abs.* **a.,** to wash up, to do the washing-up, *U.S:* to do the dishes; (*b*) (*of sea, etc.*) to wash up (sand, wreckage, etc.).

aufspüren, *v.sep.* (*a*) *v.tr.* (*of dog*) to scent, smell (out), nose out (game); *F:* (*of pers.*) to track (sth.) down; to nose, ferret, (sth.) out; to unearth (sth.); (*b*) *v.i.* (*haben*) **j-m a.,** to track s.o. down.

aufstacheln, *v.tr. sep.* to rouse, incite, instigate (s.o.); to stir up, work up (feelings); **j-n zu etwas a., j-n (dazu) a., etwas zu tun,** to incite, rouse, instigate, s.o. to do sth., to spur s.o. on to do sth., to goad s.o. on to do, into doing, sth., *F:* to egg s.o. on to do sth.

aufstampfen, *v.sep.* **1.** *v.i.* (*haben*) to stamp; (**mit dem Fuß**) **a.,** to stamp (one's foot); (*of horse*) (**mit dem Huf**) **a.,** to paw the ground; **vor Wut (mit dem Fuß) a.,** to stamp with rage. **2.** *v.tr.* (*a*) to trample up (ground); (*b*) to ram (earth, etc.).

Aufstand, *m.* revolt, rebellion; (up)rising, insurrection; riot; *Hist:* mutiny; **einen A. erregen,** to stir up a revolt, rebellion, insurrection, to start a riot; **einen A. unterdrücken,** to suppress, put down, quell, a revolt, rebellion, (up)rising, riot; **das Land war im A.,** the country was in revolt, in a state of rebellion, insurrection, revolt.

aufständig, *a.* = **aufständisch.**

aufständisch, *a.* rebellious, insurgent; rioting; **die Aufständischen,** the rebels, insurgents; the rioters.

aufstapeln, *v.tr. sep.* to stack (up) (wood, planks, etc.); to pile (thgs) up; to store up, lay up (supplies, etc.).

Aufstau, *m.* head of water behind a dam.

aufstauen, *v.tr. sep.* **1.** to collect (water) (by damming). **2. sich aufstauen,** (*of water*) to collect, pile up (behind an obstruction *or* dam); (*of blood*) to collect (in a bruise); (*of emotions, energy*) to be pent up, bottled up; **der Haß, der sich seit Wochen in ihm aufgestaut hatte,** the hatred that had been pent up in him for weeks.

Aufstechbogen, *m. Print:* tympan-sheet.

aufstechen, *v.tr. sep.* (*strong*) **1.** to prick (sth.) open; *Surg:* to lance (abscess, etc.); **eine Blase a.,** to prick a blister. **2.** to take (sth.) up on a pointed instrument; to take (morsel) up on one's fork. **3.** *Ven:* to start (hare). **4.** to pin (sth.) on (**auf etwas** *acc.*, to sth.).

aufstecken, *v.tr. sep.* **1.** (*a*) to put up (hair, etc.); to pin up (hair, dress, etc.); **sie trägt ihr Haar aufgesteckt,** she puts up her hair; **sich** *dat.* **die Zöpfe a.,** to pin up one's plaits; (*b*) **etwas auf etwas** *acc.* **a.,** to pin sth. on to sth. **2.** (*a*) **etwas (auf etwas** *acc.*) **a.,** to put, fix, sth. on (sth.); **der Kopf des Verbrechers wurde auf einen Pfahl aufgesteckt,** the criminal's head was set up, impaled, on a stake; **eine Kerze a.,** to put, fix, a candle in a candlestick; **den Pferden Heu a.,** to put hay in the rack for the horses; **j-m ein Licht a.,** (i) to show s.o. a light; (ii) to enlighten s.o., to open s.o.'s eyes (*to facts*); to undeceive s.o.; **eine Fahne a.,** to set up a flag; *Nau:* **die Wache a.,** to set the watch; (*b*) **ein ernstes Gesicht a.,** to put on a grave expression; *see also* **Amtsmiene. 3.** *Dial:* to earn, gain (sth.). **4.** *F:* to give up (habit, activity, etc.); **ich habe das Radfahren aufgesteckt,** I have given up cycling; **die Sache a.,** to give up, *F:* throw up, in, the sponge; to turn it in, pack (it) in.

Aufstecker, *m. Turf:* (*horse*) stumer.

Aufsteckschlüssel, *m. Tls:* box-spanner, -wrench; *U.S:* socket-wrench.

aufstehen, *v.i. sep.* (*strong*) **1.** (*haben*) (*of door, etc.*) to stand open, to be open. **2.** (*haben*) to touch the ground; to stand; **das eine Tischbein steht nicht auf,** one of the table-legs doesn't touch the ground; **der Tisch stand nur mit drei Beinen auf,** the table stood on only three legs, had only three legs touching the ground. **3.** (*haben*) (**hoch**) **a.,** to rise, tower. **4.** (*sein*) to rise; to get up; (*a*) to stand up, to rise to one's feet, to get on one's feet, legs; (*after fall*) to get up (again), to get to one's feet; **für j-n in der Straßenbahn a.,** to get up for s.o., to give one's seat to s.o., in the tram; **vor j-m a.,** to stand up, rise, for, in deference to, s.o.; **vom Stuhl a.,** to get up from one's chair; **von, vom, Tisch, vom Essen, a.,** to get up, rise, from the table, to leave the table; (*b*) **vom Krankenlager a.,** to get up from, rise from, leave, one's sick-bed; **er darf jeden Tag für eine Stunde a.,** he is allowed to get up each day for an hour; *Lit:* **vom Tod a.,** to rise from the dead; (*c*) to get out of bed, to get up (in the morning); **früh a.,** to get up, rise, early; **aufgestanden sein,** to be up; *F:* **mit dem linken Fuß (zuerst) a.,** to get out of bed on the wrong side. **5.** (*sein*) *Ven:* (*of hare, etc.*) to break cover; (*of birds*) to rise; (*of fish*) to rise (to the surface), to come up for air. **6.** (*sein*) (*of prophet, etc.*) to (a)rise, to appear. **7.** (*sein*) (*of populace, etc.*) to rise (in revolt), to revolt; **gegen die Bedrücker a.,** to rise against the oppressors; **gegen eine Maßnahme a.,** to rise in revolt, to stand out, against a measure.

aufsteigen. I. *v.i. sep.* (*strong*) (*sein*) **1.** to climb on, to get on; to mount; **auf etwas a.,** to climb (up) on to sth.; to mount sth.; (**aufs Fahrrad**) **a.,** to get on (to) (one's bicycle); (**aufs Pferd**) **a.,** to mount (one's horse); **hinten a.,** to get up behind. **2.** (*a*) to rise, ascend; to climb up; to come up; to go up; (*of road*) to

climb; (*of smoke, balloon, sound, etc.*) to rise, ascend; (*of mist*) to rise from the ground; *Fb:* (*of team*) to go, move, up (to next division); **die Sonne steigt am Himmel auf,** the sun is rising in the sky; **der Saft steigt auf,** the sap rises; **eine Röte stieg in ihren Wangen auf,** the blood rushed, a blush rose, to her cheeks; **aufsteigende Tränen,** rising tears; **seltsame Bilder stiegen vor ihm, vor seinem geistigen Auge, auf,** strange images arose in his mind; **das Gebirge stieg vor uns auf,** the mountains rose (up) before us; **aufsteigende Linie,** ascending line; **Verwandte (in) aufsteigender Linie,** ascendants; *Mth:* **aufsteigende Potenz,** ascending power; *Mus:* **aufsteigende Tonleiter,** ascending scale; *Astrol:* **aufsteigende Zeichen,** ascending, ascendant, signs; *F:* **er ist ein aufsteigender Stern am politischen Horizont,** he is a rising star on the political horizon; (*b*) **zur Macht, zu hohen Würden, a.,** to rise to power, to high honours; (*c*) (*of feeling, wish, etc.*) to rise; **ihm stieg der Wunsch auf, sie wiederzusehen,** the desire rose in him to see her again; **mir stieg plötzlich ein Gedanke auf,** a thought suddenly occurred to, struck, me; **uns stieg sofort der Verdacht auf, daß . . . ,** the suspicion was immediately aroused in us that . . . .

II. *vbl s.* **1. Aufsteigen,** *n. in vbl senses; also:* ascent (of balloon, etc.); **im A. (begriffen) sein,** *Astrol. & F:* to be in the ascendant; *F:* **sein Stern ist im A.,** his star is in the ascendant. **2. Aufsteigung,** *f. Astr:* ascension (of star); **gerade A.,** right ascension; **schiefe A.,** oblique ascension.

aufstellen. I. *v.tr. sep.* **1.** to stand (sth.) (up, upright, on end); to set (sth.) up(right), on end; to put up (ladder, etc.); to set up, put up, erect (monument, etc.); to set up, fit up, erect (apparatus, etc.); to assemble, erect, mount (machine). **2.** (*a*) to stand, place (thgs); to arrange (thgs); **Flaschen in Reihen a.,** to stand, arrange, bottles, in rows; **Fallen a.,** to put down traps; **Tische, Stühle, irgendwo a.,** to stand tables, chairs, somewhere; **das Bett war in der Ecke des Zimmers aufgestellt,** the bed stood, *F:* was fixed up, in the corner of the room; **Truppen (in Schlachtordnung) a.,** to draw up, array, marshal, troops; **Wachen a.,** to post sentries; *Sp:* **j-n als Torhüter a.,** to choose s.o. as goalkeeper; **sich a.,** to place, station, oneself, to take up one's position; (*of troops*) to draw up; **er stellte sich vor der Tür auf,** he placed stationed, himself, took up his position, in front of the door; **sich in einer Reihe a.,** to form a line, to form into line, to stand in a line, to line up, form up; **sie stellten sich in zwei Reihen vor der Kirchtür auf,** they arranged themselves in, formed, two lines, in front of the church door; (*b*) to set up, put forward (candidate, etc.); **j-n als Kandidaten a.,** to set s.o. up, put s.o. forward, as candidate; **sich als Kandidat a. lassen,** to stand, offer oneself, as candidate; *U.S:* to run for office; **ein Heer a.,** to form, raise, an army; *Jur:* **j-n als Zeugen a.,** to call s.o. as a witness; (*c*) to set up, advance (theory); to lay down (principle, doctrine, rule); **eine Behauptung a.,** to make an assertion; **etwas als Norm a.,** to set sth. up as the norm; *Sp:* **einen Rekord a.,** to establish, set up, a record; (*d*) **eine Rechnung a.,** to draw up an account, to make out a bill; **eine Bilanz a.,** to make up a balance-sheet; **einen Fahrplan, eine Liste, a.,** to make (out), draw up, a time-table, a list. **3.** to keep, prop, (window, etc.) open. **4.** *F:* to contrive (to do) (sth.); to manage (to do) (sth.); **wir haben allerlei aufgestellt, um dieses zu erreichen,** we did all sorts of things to attain this end; **was haben die Kinder jetzt wieder aufgestellt?** what (tricks) have the children got up to now?

II. *vbl s.* **1. Aufstellen,** *n. in vbl senses.* **2. Aufstellung,** *f.* (*a*)=II. 1; *also:* erection (of scaffolding, monument, etc.); assembly (of machine, etc.); **A. einer Bilanz, usw.,** preparation of a balance-sheet, etc.; (*b*) arrangement; position; *Mil:* formation, disposition; *Sp:* arrangement, placing, disposition (of players); team composition; **die A. der Stühle überprüfen,** to check the arrangement of the chairs; **die A. des Denkmals ist ungünstig,** the monument is placed in an unfavourable position; (*c*) list, schedule; table, tabulation; statement; survey; report; specification, *U.S:* itemization; inventory; **eine A. aller notwendigen Ausgaben machen,** to make a list, a statement, of all necessary expenses.

Aufstellgleis, Aufstellungsgleis, *n. Rail:* siding, side-track.

aufstemmen, *v.tr. sep.* **1. die Arme a.,** to brace oneself with one's arms; to lean, rest, on one's elbows; **die Arme, sich mit den Armen, auf den Tisch a.,** to brace oneself with one's arms on the table; to put, lean, rest, one's elbows on the table. **2.** to prize open (box, etc.).

aufstempeln, *v.tr. sep.* to stamp (sth.) on; **etwas auf etwas** *acc.* **a.,** to stamp sth. on to sth.

aufsteppen, *v.tr. sep.* to stitch on (pocket, etc.) (with visible outside seam); **eine Tasche auf einen Rock a.,** to stitch a pocket on to a skirt.

aufsticken, *v.tr. sep.* to embroider (sth.) on (**auf etwas** *acc.*, to sth.).

aufstieben, *v.i. sep.* (*strong*) (*sein*) (*of birds*) to fly off, shoot up; (*of dust*) to rise in a cloud; (*of snow*) to spray up.

Aufstieg, *m.* **-s/-e. 1.** (*a*) ascent; climb; mounting (of bicycle); **A. auf den Berg,** ascent of the mountain, climb up the mountain; **ein beschwerlicher A.,** a difficult ascent; (*b*) rise (to power, etc.); social, economic, advancement; **im A. (begriffen) sein,** (*of pers., firm, nation*) to be on the up-grade; (*of ideology, etc.*) to be gaining ground; (*c*) promotion; *Fb:* (*of team*) promotion, move up (to the next division). **2.** way up, upward path; **ein steiler A.,** a steep path. *See also* **Abstieg.**

Aufstiegsmöglichkeiten, *f. pl.* possibilities of advancement.

aufstöbern, *v.tr. sep.* (*a*) *Ven:* to unearth (animal), to run (animal) to earth; (*b*) to unearth, turn up, discover (old manuscript, etc.).

aufstocken, *v.tr. sep.* **ein Haus a.,** to put a storey, *U.S:* story, on a house; to add a storey to a house; *abs.* **a.,** to put on a storey; to add a storey.

aufstöhnen, *v.i. sep.* (*haben*) to groan aloud; **tief, laut, a.,** to give, utter, a deep, loud, groan.

aufstöpseln, *v.tr. sep.* to take the stopper, plug, out of (sth.); to uncork (bottle); to unstopper (bottle).

aufstören, *v.tr. sep.* to disturb, stir up (wasps' nest, etc.); to disturb, rouse, startle (s.o., game); **j-n aus dem Schlaf a.,** to rouse s.o. from sleep, to awaken, disturb, s.o.; **Erinnerungen a.,** to stir up, awaken, memories.

Aufstoß, *m.* **1.** impact. **2.** *F:* (*of thieves*) **A. bekommen,** to be discovered.

aufstoßen. I. *v.sep.* (*strong*) **1.** *v.tr.* (*a*) to push (sth.) open; **etwas mit dem Fuß a.,** to kick sth. open; (*b*) **sich** *dat.* **die Hand, usw., a.,** to cut one's hand, etc., open (by knocking it). **2.** *v.i.* (*haben, sein*) (*a*) **auf etwas** *acc.* **a.,** to knock, strike, against sth.; *Nau:* **a.,** (*of ship, boat*) to strike, to touch, bottom; to strike, touch, bump. **3.** *v.i.* (*sein*) (*a*) (*of idea, etc.*) **j-m a.,** to strike s.o., occur to s.o., cross s.o.'s mind; **es ist mir plötzlich aufgestoßen, daß . . . ,** it suddenly occurred to me, struck me, crossed my mind, that . . . ; (*b*) (*of food*) to repeat; **j-m a.,** to repeat on s.o.; to make s.o. eruct, belch; **das Essen stößt mir auf,** my food repeats; **j-m sauer a.,** to give s.o. heartburn; *F:* **das könnte ihm noch sauer, übel, a.,** he may have to pay dearly for that. **4.** *v.i.* (*haben*) (*of pers.*) to eruct, eructate, *F:* belch; (*of baby*) to burp.

II. *vbl s.* **Aufstoßen,** *n. in vbl senses; also:* (*a*) eructation; (*b*) **saures A.,** heartburn.

aufstrahlen, *v.i. sep.* (*sein, haben*) (*of light, star, etc.*) to (begin to) shine, beam; **eine Hoffnung strahlt auf,** hope begins to dawn.

aufstreben, *v.i. sep.* (*haben*) (*a*) (*of pers., community*) to aspire, to strive; **eine aufstrebende kleine Stadt,** a rising little town; (*b*) (*of building, etc.*) to rise, to tower up(wards); to soar up; **aufstrebende Pfeiler,** soaring pillars.

aufstrecken, *v.tr. sep.* to raise, stretch out (one's hands, etc.); **die Arme zum Himmel a.,** to stretch out one's arms towards Heaven.

Aufstreich, *m.* knocking down (*at auction*).

aufstreichen, *v.tr. sep.* (*strong*) to spread on (butter, jam, etc.); **Butter aufs Brot a.,** to spread butter on bread, to butter bread.

aufstreifen, *v.tr. sep.* **den Ärmel a.,** to push up one's sleeve.

aufstreuen, *v.tr. sep.* **etwas auf etwas** *acc.* **a.,** to scatter (straw, etc.) on sth.; to sprinkle (sugar, etc.) on sth.

Aufstrich, *m.* **1.** (*a*) (*in writing*) up-stroke; (*b*) *Mus:* up-stroke, up-bow; **fangen Sie mit (dem) A. an, setzen Sie mit (dem) A. ein,** start with the up-bow. **2.** spread (for bread).

Aufstrom, *m.* up-current.

aufstuhlen, *v.tr. sep. Rail:* to chair (sleeper).

aufstülpen, *v.tr. sep.* **1.** to turn up (brim of hat, etc.); **eine aufgestülpte Nase,** snub nose, turned-up nose. **2.** to clap on (hat).

aufstützen, *v.tr. sep.* (*a*) to prop up, support (sth.); *N.Arch:* to shore up (vessel); (*b*) **die Arme, die Ellbogen, sich mit den Armen, Ellbogen, a.,** to prop oneself, to lean, rest, on one's elbows; **die Arme, Ellbogen, sich mit den Armen, Ellbogen, auf den Tisch a.,** to put, lean, rest, one's elbows on the table.

aufsuchen, *v.tr. sep.* to look (sth.) up; to seek (s.o.) out; to visit (s.o.), to call on (s.o.), *F:* to look (s.o.) up; **den Arzt a.,** to go to, to visit, to consult, the doctor; **j-n in seiner Wohnung a.,** to go to see s.o. at his home; **ich habe die Stätten meiner Kindheit aufgesucht,** I visited, went back to, the places of my childhood; **er hat alle Orte aufgesucht, in denen Goethe gelebt hat,** he sought out, visited, all the places where Goethe lived; **eine Stelle in einem Buch a.,** to look up a passage in a book.

aufsummen, aufsummieren, *v.tr. sep.* **1.** to add up (items). **2. sich aufsummen, sich aufsummieren,** to add up, mount up; **es summt sich auf,** it all mounts up.

auftakeln, *v.tr. sep.* (*a*) *Nau:* to rig (ship); (*b*) *F:* **sich a.,** to rig oneself out, to tog oneself up, to titivate (oneself); **mächtig aufgetakelt sein,** to be all rigged out, togged up, to be dressed up to the nines, to be dressed to kill.

Auftakt, *m.* **1.** *Pros: Mus:* anacrusis; *Mus:* upbeat; **mit dem A. einsetzen,** to start on the upbeat. **2.** *F:* prologue, introduction; prelude; preliminaries; **diese Besprechungen bildeten den A. zur Konferenz,** these discussions formed the prelude to the conference.

auftaljen, *v.tr. sep. Nau:* to bowse, bouse (crates, chain, etc.).

auftanken, *v.tr. sep.* to fill up, tank up (vehicle); to fuel *or* refuel (aircraft, rocket); **aufgetankt,** (*of vehicle*) filled up, with full fuel tanks.

auftauchen. I. *v.i. sep.* (*sein*) **1.** (*a*) to emerge (from water, etc.); *F:* to pop up; (*of fish, etc.*) to rise to the surface; *Navy:* (*of submarine*) to surface, to break surface; (*b*) to appear, to come into view; to loom (up); **plötzlich a.,** to appear suddenly; *F:* to bob up; **ein Segel tauchte am Horizont auf,** a sail appeared, came into view, on the horizon; **eine Gestalt tauchte aus dem Nebel auf,** a figure loomed out of the fog. **2.** to appear, to turn up; (*of difficulties, fears, doubts, etc.*) to arise, to crop up; (*of rumour*) to arise; **wieder a.,** to reappear, turn up again; **er tauchte nach Jahren wieder in Paris auf,** he reappeared, turned up again, years later in Paris; **diese Ideen tauchen immer wieder in seinen Büchern auf,** these ideas appear, turn up, emerge, again and again in his books; **es tauchte ein Gedanke in ihm auf,** a thought occurred to him, struck him, crossed his mind.

II. *vbl s.* **Auftauchen,** *n. in vbl senses; also:* emergence; appearance.

auftauen, *v.sep.* **1.** *v.tr.* to thaw (snow, etc.); **die Wasserleitung a.,** to thaw the water-pipes; *Aut:* **den Kühler a.,** to thaw out the radiator. **2.** *v.i.* (*sein*) (*a*) (*of snow, ice*) to thaw; (*b*) *F:* (*of pers.*) to thaw; to open out; to talk without reserve; **nach dem Essen taute er allmählich auf, fing er an aufzutauen,** after dinner he gradually began to thaw.

aufteilen. I. *v.tr. sep.* (*a*) to divide (sth.) (up); to share (sth.) out; **der Arzt mußte seine Zeit zwischen der Privatpraxis und dem Krankenhaus a.,** the doctor had to divide his time between his private practice and the hospital; **das Land wurde in drei Gebiete aufgeteilt,** the country was divided up, parcelled (out), into three districts; **das Land ist zwischen den vier Großmächten aufgeteilt worden,** the country has been divided, shared (out) among the four great powers; (*b*) to divide out, share out, distribute (thgs) (**unter mehrere,** amongst several people, etc.); **wir teilten die Vorräte gleichmäßig unter die Kunden auf,** we shared out, divided (out), the provisions evenly amongst the customers.

II. *vbl s.* **Aufteilen** *n.*, **Aufteilung** *f. in vbl senses; also:* division; distribution.

auftischen, *v.tr. sep.* to serve (up) (meals, dishes); **sie hat uns eine herrliche Mahlzeit aufgetischt,** she served us a magnificent meal, set a magnificent meal before us; *F:* **er tischt immer wieder dieselben Geschichten auf,** he serves up the same old stories again and again; *abs.* **j-m reichlich a.,** to serve s.o. up an ample meal, to regale s.o. with an ample meal.

auftönen, *v.i. sep.* (*haben*) to (begin to) sound.

auftoppen, *v.tr. sep. Nau:* to top, peak, cockbill (yard, etc.).

Auftrag, *m.* **-(e)s/⸚e. 1.** order; orders, instructions, directions; commission; (research) assignment; *Jur:* (barrister's) brief; **öffentlicher A.,**

official order; official contract; public works contract; **j-m einen A. geben, erteilen,** to entrust, charge, s.o. with sth.; to ask, request, s.o. to do sth.; to instruct s.o., to give s.o. instructions, to do sth.; to direct s.o., to give s.o. directions, to do sth.; *Adm:* to appoint s.o. to do sth., to charge s.o. with a commission; *Com:* to give s.o. an order, to place an order with s.o.; **j-m den A. erteilen, geben, etwas zu tun,** to entrust, charge, s.o. with doing sth.; to ask, request, s.o. to do sth.; to commission s.o. to do sth.; *Adm:* to appoint s.o. to do sth.; **einem Rechtsanwalt einen A. erteilen,** to brief a barrister; **einen A. ausführen,** to carry out, execute, an order; **Ihrem A. gemäß,** in accordance with your instructions, directions; **im A. und für Rechnung des Herrn X,** by order and for account of Mr X; **im A. von Herrn X (handeln),** (to act) on behalf of Mr X; **einer Firma einen A. auf 2000 Bücher geben,** to place an order for 2000 books with a firm, to order 2000 books from a firm; **wir haben in diesem Jahr verschiedene Aufträge aus Deutschland bekommen,** we have received a number of orders from Germany this year; **etwas (bei j-m) in A. geben,** to order sth. (from s.o.); to place an order (with s.o.) for sth.; to commission (statue, symphony, etc.); to commission s.o. to make (statue, etc.), write (symphony, etc.); *Mil:* 'A. erfüllt', 'mission accomplished'; **im Auftrage,** on s.o.'s behalf, in s.o.'s name; *Jur:* by attorney; by procuration, per pro., p.p.; *U.S:* per power of attorney, p.p.a.; *(signature at end of letter)* **im A. des Direktors, usw., im A.,** *abbr.* i.A., E. Braun, E. Braun (for the Director, etc.). **2.** *(a)* application, laying on of (paint, etc.); *(b)* layer (of paint, etc.). **3.** *Civ.E:* (earth used for) embankment. **Auftragdraht,** *m. Welding:* build-up wire.
auftragen. I. *v.sep. (strong)* **1.** *v.tr.* to spread (sth.) on; to smear (sth.) on; to lay on, apply (paint, etc.); to put on, apply (make-up); **die Farbe dick a.,** to lay the paint on thickly; *F: abs.* **dick, stark, a.,** to exaggerate, *F:* to lay it on thick, with a trowel. **2.** *v.tr.* to serve up, bring in (meal); **es ist aufgetragen,** dinner, supper, etc., is on the table, is served. **3.** *v.tr.* **j-m etwas a.,** to entrust, charge, s.o. with sth.; to put sth. in s.o.'s hands; to appoint s.o. to do sth.; **j-m a., etwas zu tun,** to entrust, charge, s.o. with doing sth.; to ask, request, s.o. to do sth.; to appoint s.o. to do sth.; to commission s.o. to do sth.; **j-m eine Arbeit a.,** to entrust s.o. with a job, to give s.o. a job; **er hat mir Grüße an Sie aufgetragen,** he asked me to give you his kindest regards. **4.** *v.tr.* to wear out, use up (garment, shoes, etc.). **5.** *v.i. (haben) (of clothes, etc.)* to be bulky; **auftragende Kleider,** bulky clothes.
II. *vbl s.* **Auftragen** *n.,* **Auftragung** *f. in vbl senses; also:* application (of paint, etc.).
Auftraggeber, *m.* person who places an order; person who gives a commission; patron (of an artist, etc.); *Com: Jur:* principal; **A. und Beauftragter,** principal and agent; **A. ist die Stadtverwaltung,** the work has been commissioned by the town council; **Michelangelos verschiedene Auftraggeber,** Michelangelo's various patrons.
Auftraglage, *f. Welding:* build-up layer.
Auftragnehmer, *m.* acceptor of an order *or* commission; contractor; *Jur:* authorized agent.
Auftragsbestand, *m. Com:* (number of) orders on hand; orders (still) to be executed, *U.S:* unfilled orders.
Auftrag(s)buch, *n. Com:* order-book.
Auftragseingang, *m. Com:* *(a)* receipt of (an) order; **innerhalb drei Wochen nach A.,** within three weeks of receipt of order; *(b)* intake of orders.
auftragsgemäß, auftrag(s)mäßig, *adv.* as ordered, as per order; according to instructions, directions.
Auftragsüberhang, *m. Com:* backlog of orders on hand.
auftrag(s)widrig, *a.* contrary to the order; contrary to instructions, directions.
Auftragwalze, *f. Print:* inking roller, colour roller.
Auftragswerk, *n. (painting, symphony, etc.)* commissioned work.
aufträufe(l)n, auftraufen, *v.sep.* **1.** *v.tr.* to apply (sth.) drop by drop. **2.** *v.i. (sein)* to fall drop by drop **(auf etwas acc.,** on to sth.).
auftreffen, *v.i. sep. (strong) (sein) (of bullet, etc.)* to strike.
Auftreffgeschwindigkeit, *f. Ball:* velocity on impact, impact velocity.
Auftreffpunkt, *m. Ball:* point of impact.
Auftreffwinkel, *m. Ball:* angle of impact.

auftreiben. I. *v.tr. sep. (strong)* **1.** to drive on (barrel-hoop, etc.). **2.** to open out (hole). **3.** to drive (cattle) to the mountain pasture. **4.** *(a) (of wind, etc.)* to drive (dust, waves, etc.) upwards; *(b)* to swell, blow up, blow out, bloat, distend (sth.); **die Hefe treibt den Teig auf,** yeast makes dough rise; **ein aufgetriebener Bauch,** a distended stomach. **5.** *(a) Ven: (of dog)* to start (game); *(b)* **j-n a.,** to force s.o. to get up; to drive, rout, s.o. out of bed; to drive s.o. off (his chair, etc.). **6.** to find, obtain, get (hold of) (sth.); to find (s.o.); **wo hat er das Geld für die Reise aufgetrieben?** where did he find, raise, get hold of, the money for the journey? **Whisky ist hier schwer aufzutreiben,** whisky is difficult to come by here, it is difficult to obtain, get hold of, whisky here.
II. **auftreiben,** *v.i. (sein)* **1.** *(of plants)* to come up. **2.** to swell, to become blown up, blown out, bloated, distended. **3.** *(of ship)* to run aground; **auf eine Sandbank a.,** to run on to a sand-bank.
auftrennen, *v.tr. sep.* to undo, unpick, *U.S:* rip (seam); to take (dress, etc.) to pieces.
auftreten, *v.sep. (strong)* I. *v.i. (sein).* **1.** to put one's foot, feet, on the ground; to tread; to walk; **er kann mit dem wunden Fuß nicht a.,** he can't stand, walk, on his sore foot; **leise a.,** to tread softly, to walk quietly; **fest a.,** to walk with a firm step. **2.** *(a)* (i) *Th: (of actor)* to enter; (ii) to appear (on the stage, in society); *(stage direction)* **Macbeth tritt auf,** enter Macbeth; **als Schauspieler, als Sänger, a.,** to appear as an actor, a singer; to appear on the stage; **zum ersten Male auf der Bühne, in der Gesellschaft, als Redner, a.,** to make one's début, one's first appearance, on the stage, in society, as an orator; **öffentlich a.,** to appear in public; **als Zeuge a.,** to appear as a witness; **als Kläger gegen j-n a.,** to bring an action, to appear, against s.o.; **als Wahlkandidat a.,** to stand as candidate; *F:* **sie treten immer zu dritt auf,** the three of them always appear, go around, together; *(b) (of thg)* to appear, make its appearance; *(of event, etc.)* to occur; **diese Krankheiten traten erst nach dem ersten Weltkrieg auf,** these diseases only made their appearance after the first world war; **solche Verbrechen treten nicht oft bei uns auf,** crimes of this sort do not occur frequently in our country. **3.** to behave, act; **sicher a.,** to have a confident, self-assured, manner; **energisch gegen etwas a.,** to oppose sth. firmly.
II. **auftreten,** *v.tr.* to kick open (door, etc.); to crack (nut) with one's foot.
III. *vbl s.* **Auftreten,** *n.* **1.** *in vbl senses; also:* *(a)* appearance (on stage, in society, as actor, etc.); **erstes A. auf der Bühne, in der Gesellschaft, als Redner, usw.,** début on the stage, in society, as an orator, etc.; *(b)* appearance (of phenomena, etc.); occurrence (of events, etc.). **2.** manner, way; behaviour; demeanour; **ein forsches A. haben,** to be brisk, to have a brisk manner; **er hat ein sicheres A.,** he has a confident, self-assured, manner.
Auftrieb, *m.* **1.** *(a)* **A. auf die Alm,** driving of cattle to mountain pasture; *(b)* driving of cattle to market; *(c)* cattle, pigs, etc., brought to market; **großer A. an Kälbern,** large number of calves (in the market). **2.** *Hydrostatics:* buoyancy (force); *Aer:* lift. **3.** impetus, stimulus; **unsere Geschäfte haben dadurch neuen A. bekommen,** it has given our business fresh impetus, stimulus; **die Ferien geben einem einen neuen A.,** holidays give one new impetus, new life; **er hat im Augenblick keinen A.,** he has no drive, go, at the moment.
auftriebserhöhend, *a. Av:* high-lift (device, etc.).
Auftriebsmittelpunkt, *m. Aer:* centre of pressure.
Auftriebwasser, *n. Oc:* upwelling deep water.
auftrinken, *v.tr. sep. (strong)* to drink up (milk, etc.).
Auftritt, *m.* **1.** *Th:* entrance (of actor). **2.** *(a) Th:* scene; appearance; **sie wartet auf ihren A.,** she is waiting for her scene; **er hat nur einen A.,** he has only one scene, he only appears (on the stage) once; he makes only one appearance; *(b) Th: (sub-division of play)* scene; **der zweite A. des dritten Aktes,** the second scene of Act III; **dritter Akt, zweiter A.,** Act III, scene 2; *(c)* scene; row; **ein peinlicher A.,** an embarrassing scene; **einen A. machen,** to make a scene; **jedesmal, wenn seine Schwiegermutter ihn besuchte, gab es einen häßlichen A.,** every time his mother-in-law visited him there was a nasty scene, a row. **3.** tread(-board) (of stair); *Fort:* banquette; *Equit:* mounting-block, horse-block.

auftrocknen, *v.sep.* **1.** *v.tr.* to dry (sth.); to mop up (liquid); *(of sun, etc.)* to evaporate (liquid); **den Fußboden mit einem Lappen a.,** to dry the floor with a cloth; **der Wind hat die Straßen aufgetrocknet,** the wind has dried (up) the roads. **2.** *v.i. (sein, haben)* to dry (up), to become dry; *(of liquid)* to evaporate; **alle Pfützen sind in der Sonne aufgetrocknet,** all the puddles have dried (up), evaporated, in the sun; **die Straßen sind wieder aufgetrocknet,** the streets have dried (up).
auftrumpfen, *v.i. sep. (haben)* to protest vehemently, to make a strong protest; to bring forward a crushing argument; to shout one's opponent down; **sie trumpfte damit auf, daß ihr Vater noch reicher sei als seiner,** she crushed him by saying that her father was even richer than his.
auftuchen, *v.tr. sep. Nau:* to roll up (sail).
auftun, *v.tr. sep. (strong)* **1.** *(a)* to open (door, mouth, etc.); **du hättest deinen Mund a. sollen,** you should have said something; *B:* **klopfet an, so wird euch aufgetan,** knock, and it shall be opened unto you; *(b)* to open (up) (business); to open, start (club, etc.). **2.** **sich auftun,** to open (up); *(a)* **die Erde tat sich vor unseren Füßen auf,** the earth opened before our feet; **eine herrliche Aussicht tat sich vor ihnen auf,** a magnificent prospect, view, opened up, out, unfolded, before their eyes; **bessere Aussichten tun sich jetzt für ihn auf,** better prospects are opening up, out, for him now; *(b)* **ein neuer Verein hat sich in unserer Stadt aufgetan,** a new society has opened, been formed, in our town. **3.** to put on (hat, etc.). **4.** *Ven: (of dog)* to start (hare).
auftunken, *v.tr. sep.* to sop up (remnants of gravy, etc.) with a piece of bread; to mop up, sop up (liquid) (with a piece of cloth, etc.); to sop pieces of bread in (one's soup, etc.).
auftupfen, *v.tr. sep.* **1.** to absorb (moisture, etc.) by dabbing it (lightly). **2.** to dab on (colour, etc.) (lightly).
auftürmen, *v.tr. sep.* **1.** to pile, heap, stack, (thgs) up, to pile (thgs) high; to accumulate (thgs); **seine Bücher lagen aufgetürmt auf dem Fußboden,** his books were piled, heaped, stacked up, were piled high, on the floor. **2. sich auftürmen,** to pile up; to gather, collect; to accumulate; *(of rocks, etc.)* to tower up; **die Wolken türmen sich auf,** the clouds are piling up, banking up; **das schmutzige Geschirr türmt sich in der Küche auf,** the washing-up is, *U.S:* the dirty dishes are, piling up, accumulating, in the kitchen; **Schwierigkeiten über Schwierigkeiten türmten sich vor ihm auf,** difficulties piled up in his path.
Auf-und-ab-Werk, *n. Clockm:* up-and-down work.
aufwachen, *v.i. sep. (sein)* **1.** to awake(n), to wake (up); **vom Schlaf a.,** to awaken from sleep; **er wachte endlich aus seiner Gleichgültigkeit auf,** he awoke at last from his apathy. **2.** *(of senses, memories, etc.)* to awaken.
aufwachsen, *v.i. sep. (strong) (sein)* **1.** to grow up; **er ist bei seinem Onkel aufgewachsen,** he grew up in his uncle's house; **sie sind ganz in Indien aufgewachsen,** they spent all their childhood and adolescence in India, they grew up in India; **sie ist zu einem schönen Mädchen aufgewachsen,** she has grown into a beautiful girl. **2.** to grow on (to sth.).
aufwägen, *v.tr. sep. (strong)* = **aufwiegen.**
Aufwall, *m.* = **Aufwallung,** *q.v.* under **aufwallen** II. 2.
aufwallen. I. *v.i. sep. (sein).* **1.** *(of liquid)* to boil up, to seethe, to bubble (up); *Cu:* **einmal a. lassen,** allow to boil up, come to the boil, once; **kurz a. lassen,** boil hard for a short time. **2.** *(of sea, waters, fog, etc.)* to surge, to swell, to seethe; *F: (of blood)* (i) to surge; (ii) to boil; *(of feeling, passion)* to surge (up), to rise (up); **Zorn wallte in ihm auf,** anger rose, surged (up), within him; **Liebe wallte in ihrem Busen auf,** love swelled, surged, in her bosom.
II. *vbl s.* **1. Aufwallen,** *n. in vbl senses.* **2. Aufwallung** *f. (a)* = II. 1; *(b)* surge, swell (of sea, etc.); surge, ebullition (of emotion, anger); **in der ersten A. der Freude,** in the first surge of joy.
Aufwand, *m.* **-s/.** expenditure; expense; cost; extravagance, luxury; **großen A. treiben,** to spend a great deal, to be very extravagant; **er hat seine Familie durch zu großen A. arm gemacht,** he has impoverished his family by his extravagance; **er treibt unnützen A.,** he wastes, squanders, money, he throws money away; **A. an Kraft,** expenditure of energy; **es wäre ein unnützer A. an Zeit,** it would be a waste of time; **das würde einen großen A. an Geld, Zeit, Mühe,**

bedeuten, that would mean a great expenditure of money, time, that would cost a great deal of money, time, effort; **diese Arbeit erfordert einen großen A. an Konzentration,** this work demands a great deal of concentration.

Aufwandgesetz, *n.* sumptuary law, luxury law.

Aufwandsentschädigung, *f.* repayment of expenses, *esp.* representation allowance; **Gehalt einschließlich A.,** salary including representation allowance.

Aufwandsteuer, *f.* luxury tax.

aufwärmen, *v.tr. sep.* to warm up, reheat, heat up (food, drink); *F:* to rehash (literary work, etc.); to unearth, revive, drag up (old scandal); **das ist alles aufgewärmter Nietzsche,** it's all a rehash of Nietzsche; **warum wärmst du diese alte Geschichte wieder auf?** why do you drag up that old story?

Aufwartefrau, *f.* charwoman, cleaner, *F:* daily, *U.S:* cleaning woman.

aufwarten. I. *v.i. sep.* (*haben*) **1.** (*a*) **j-m a.,** to attend s.o.; to attend on, upon, s.o.; to wait on s.o. (*at meal*); **j-m mit einem Glas Wein, usw., a.,** to bring s.o. a glass of wine, etc.; **bei Tisch a.,** to wait at table; (*b*) **mit etwas a.,** to oblige with sth.; **er weiß immer mit irgendeiner Neuigkeit aufzuwarten,** he always brings some piece of news; **Herr X wartete mit einem Gedicht auf,** Mr X obliged with a recitation; **womit können wir Ihnen a.?** what can we do for you? **2. j-m a.,** to wait upon s.o.; to pay one's respects to s.o., to call on s.o. **3.** (*of dog*) to (sit up and) beg.

II. *vbl s.* **1. Aufwarten,** *n. in vbl senses.* **2. Aufwartung,** *f.* (*a*)=II. 1; *also:* attendance; service (at table, etc.); (*b*) visit, call; **j-m seine A. machen,** to wait upon s.o.; to pay one's respects to s.o., to call on s.o.; (*c*) charwoman, cleaner, *F:* daily, *U.S:* cleaning woman.

Aufwärterin, *f.* (*a*) charwoman, cleaner, *F:* daily, *U.S:* cleaning woman; (*b*) *Nau:* stewardess.

Aufwartestelle, *f.* position, job, as charwoman, cleaner.

aufwärts, *adv.*, **aufwärts-,** *comb.fm.* upward(s), up; uphill; (*in relation to river*) upstream; **der Weg führt a.,** the road runs upwards, uphill; **ein aufwärtsführender Weg,** an upward, uphill, path; **nach einer Weile ging es wieder a.,** after a while the road began to climb again, the road went uphill; *see also* **aufwärtsgehen; a. steigen,** to ascend; **sich a. bewegen,** to move up(wards); (*of prices*) to rise.

Aufwärtsbewegung, *f.* upward movement (*esp. Com: Fin:* of prices).

aufwärtsgebogen, *a. Her:* arched.

aufwärtsgehen, *v.i. sep.* (*strong*) (*sein*) to improve; **es geht wieder aufwärts mit ihm,** his fortunes are improving, *F:* things are looking up with him; **es geht mit ihrer Gesundheit wieder aufwärts,** her health is improving; **mit seinem Geschäft geht's aufwärts,** his business is improving, *F:* looking up.

Aufwärtshaken, *m. Box:* upper-cut.

aufwärtsstreben, *v.i. sep.* (*haben*) (*a*) (*of pers.*) to aspire, to strive; (*b*) (*of pillars, spire, etc.*) to soar (up); (*of plant*) to climb.

Aufwärtstransformator, *m. El.E:* step-up transformer.

Aufwartung, *f. see* **aufwarten** II.

Aufwasch, *m.* (*a*) dirty crockery, etc.; washing-up, *U.S:* dirty dishes; (*b*) washing-up, *U.S:* dish washing; *F:* **es geht in einem A.,** it can all be done at (one and) the same time, at once.

Aufwäsche, *f.*=**Aufwasch.**

aufwaschen. I. *v.tr. sep.* (*strong*) **1.** to wash (floor); to wash up (dirty crockery, etc.); *abs.* **a.,** to wash up, to do the washing-up, *U.S:* to do the dishes. **2. sich** *dat.* **die Hände a.,** to make one's hands sore, to take the skin off one's hands, by doing the washing.

II. *vbl s.* **Aufwaschen,** *n. in vbl senses; F:* **es geht in einem A.,** it can all be done at (one and) the same time, at once.

Aufwäscher, *m.* **-s/-,** washer-up, dish-washer.

Aufwaschlappen, *m.* dish-cloth.

Aufwaschschüssel, *f.* washing-up bowl, *U.S:* dishpan.

Aufwaschtuch, *n.* dish-cloth.

Aufwaschwasser, *n.* washing-up water, dishwater.

aufwecken, *v.tr. sep.* to awake(n) (s.o.), to wake (s.o.) (up); to (a)rouse (s.o.) (from sleep). *See also* **aufgeweckt.**

aufweichen, *v.sep.* (*weak*) **1.** *v.tr.* to soften (sth.); to soak (sth.); **der Regen hat den Boden aufgeweicht,** the rain has softened the ground, has made the ground sodden. **2.** *v.i.* (*sein*) to soften, become soft; (*of ground, etc.*) to become sodden.

aufweinen, *v.i. sep.* (*haben*) to start to cry (audibly).

aufweisen, *v.tr. sep.* (*strong*) **1.** to produce, show, exhibit (document, etc.). **2.** to show (results, traces, etc.); **der Topf weist keine Brandspuren auf,** there are no traces of burning on the pan; **die Leiche wies keine Wunden auf,** there were no wounds on the corpse; **Beschädigungen a.,** to show signs of damage; **er hat keinen Erfolg aufzuweisen,** he can show no results, he has no results to show.

aufweiten, *v.tr. sep.* to stretch, expand (sth.); *Nau:* **eine Naht (mit dem Scharfeisen) a.,** to ream a seam.

aufwenden. I. *v.tr. sep.* (*conj. like* **wenden**) to spend, expend (money, time, care) (**für etwas,** on sth.); to use (money, energy, strength, means); to employ (time, means); **Mühe a.,** to take pains; **sie haben alles aufgewendet, aufgewandt, uns zu helfen,** they did everything possible to help us; **seine Kräfte dafür a., etwas zu tun,** to devote one's energies to doing sth.; **alle Mittel dafür a., sein Ziel zu erreichen,** to use, employ, every (possible) means to attain one's ends; **er hat viel Fleiß dafür aufgewendet, aufgewandt,** he put a lot of energy into it; **wir haben viel Zeit, viel Mühe, umsonst, unnütz, dafür aufgewendet, aufgewandt,** we wasted a lot of time, pains, on it.

II. *vbl s.* **1. Aufwenden,** *n. in vbl senses.* **2. Aufwendung,** *f.* (*a*)=II. 1; *also:* expenditure (of money, time); use (of money, energy, strength, means); employment (of time, means); (*b*) *pl.* **Aufwendungen,** expenditure, disbursements, expenses; **Aufwendungen für Bürobedarf,** expenditure on office requirements.

aufwendig, *a.* (project, building, etc.) involving great expense; (*of presentation of book*) expensive; lavish; extravagant; sumptuous.

aufwerfen, *v.tr. sep.* (*strong*) **1.** (*a*) to throw up, toss up (ball, etc.), to throw, toss (ball, etc.) into the air; (*b*) **den Kopf a.,** to toss one's head; **die Lippen a.,** to pout one's lips; **aufgeworfene Lippen,** protruding lips, thick lips; (*c*) to throw up, cast up, excavate (earth, etc.); (*d*) to build, raise (dam, embankment, etc.); to dig (trench, etc.); (*e*) to send up, form (bubbles, foam, etc.); **das Meer warf hohe Wellen auf,** the sea rose in high waves; (*f*) to raise (question, doubt, etc.); to bring up (question); **eine Vermutung a.,** to throw out a suggestion. **2.** (*a*) *A:* **j-n zu etwas a.,** to set s.o. up as sth.; to appoint s.o. as sth.; (*b*) **sich zu etwas a.,** to set oneself up as sth.; **sich zum Richter a.,** to set onself up as judge; **sich zum Kläger a.,** to assume the rôle of accuser; (*c*) **sich a.,** to be arrogant, to behave in an arrogant manner. **3.** to throw on (coal, etc.); *Cards:* to lay down, put down (card), to put (card) on the table. **4.** (*a*) to throw open, fling open (door, window, etc.); (*b*) *A:* to open (sth.) by throwing stones, etc., at it.

Aufwerfhammer, *m. Metalw:* tilt-hammer, trip-hammer.

aufwerten, *v.tr. sep. Fin:* to revalue (debt, mortgage, etc.) (*on account of inflation*); **Staatsanleihen werden zu** x **Prozent aufgewertet,** national loans are being revalued at x per cent; **Aufwertung** *f,* revaluation (of debt, mortgage, etc.).

Aufwickelkassette, *f. Cin:* take-up magazine.

aufwickeln. I. *v.tr. sep.* **1.** (*a*) to roll, wind, coil, (sth.) up; **sich** *dat.* **die Haare a.,** to curl one's hair, to put one's hair in curlers; **sich a.,** to roll up; *cp.* 2 (*a*); (*b*) to reel, spool (thread, etc.), to wind (thread, etc.) on to a reel, spool; *Cin:* **den Film a.,** to take up the film. **2.** (*a*) to unroll, unwind (sth.); **sich a.,** to unroll; to come unwound, uncoiled; (*b*) to unwind, unreel, wind off (thread, etc.); (*c*) to unwrap (parcel, etc.); to unswaddle (baby).

II. *vbl s.* **Aufwickeln** *n.*, **Aufwicklung** *f. in vbl senses; also:* **A. des Films,** take-up.

Aufwickelspule, *f. Cin:* take-up spool.

Aufwiegelei, *f.* **-/-en,** incitement, instigation.

aufwiegeln. I. *v.tr. sep.* to rouse (s.o.), to stir (s.o.) up; **j-n zu etwas a.,** to incite, instigate, s.o., urge s.o. on, to sth., to do sth.; *F:* to egg s.o. on to do sth.; **das Volk a.,** to stir up the people; **das Volk zum Aufruhr, Seeleute zur Meuterei, a.,** to incite the people to revolt, sailors to mutiny.

II. *vbl s.* **Aufwiegeln** *n.*, **Aufwiegelung** *f. in vbl senses; also:* incitement, instigation.

aufwiegen, *v.tr. sep.* (*strong*) to (counter)balance (sth.); to counterpoise, compensate, equilibrate (sth.); to offset (sth.); **j-s Gewicht mit Gold a.,** to measure s.o.'s weight in gold; *F:* **sie ist nicht mit Gold aufzuwiegen,** she is worth her weight in gold, she is invaluable; **die Vorteile wiegen die Nachteile auf,** the advantages balance, offset, the disadvantages; **seine Tugenden wiegen seine Laster nicht auf,** his virtues do not make up for, compensate for, cancel out, his vices.

Aufwiegler, *m.* **-s/-,** agitator; inciter, instigator; rabble-rouser.

aufwieglerisch, *a.* seditious, incendiary (speech, activities, etc.).

aufwiehern, *v.i. sep.* (*haben*) (*of horse*) to neigh (suddenly); *F:* (*of pers.*) to burst out laughing.

Aufwind, *m. Meteor:* anabatic wind; up-current.

Aufwindedraht, *m. Tex:* faller(-wire).

aufwinden, *v.tr. sep.* (*strong*) **1.** to wind (up) (rope, etc.), to wind (thread, etc.), to reel, spool (thread, etc.). **2. sich aufwinden,** (*a*) to coil up; to wind on (to reel, etc.); (*b*) to wind, coil, spiral, upwards; to rise in a spiral. **3.** to hoist (sth.) by means of a winch; *Nau:* to weigh, heave (up) (anchor).

Aufwinder, *m.* **1.** *Tex: etc:* (*pers.*) winder. **2.** *Tex:*=**Aufwindedraht.**

Aufwindevorrichtung, *f. Mec.E:* hoisting device *or* gear.

aufwirbeln, *v.sep.* **1.** *v.tr.* to unbolt (window). **2.** *v.tr.* (*of wind*) to whirl (dust, etc.) upwards, into the air, to send (dust, etc.) whirling upwards, into the air; *F:* **Staub a.,** to create, make, cause, a sensation, a stir; to set (people's) tongues wagging; **sein Buch hat viel Staub aufgewirbelt,** his book made a great stir; **der Fall hat seinerzeit viel Staub aufgewirbelt,** the case made a great sensation, was greatly talked of, at the time. **3.** *v.i.* (*sein*) to whirl, fly up(wards).

aufwischen, *v.tr. sep.* to wipe up (dust, etc.), to mop up (water, etc.); to clean (room); *Nau:* to swab (deck).

Aufwischer, *m.* wiper, person wiping up; swabber (of deck).

Aufwischlappen, *m.* cloth; wiper; floor-cloth; swab.

aufwogen, *v.i. sep.* (*sein*) (*of sea*) to surge, swell, billow.

aufwölben, *v.tr. sep.* to arch, vault (roof, etc.); (*of cupola, mountain, etc.*) **sich a.,** to rise.

aufworfe(l)n, *v.tr. sep.* to winnow (grain).

aufwuchern, *v.i. sep.* (*sein*) (*of vegetation*) to grow luxuriantly, exuberantly, to luxuriate.

Aufwuchs, *m.* **1.** growing, growth (of plants). **2.** (plant) growth, young growth (of plants, trees).

aufwühlen, *v.tr. sep.* **1.** (*a*) to turn up, turn over (soil); to churn up (water, etc.); to plough up, churn up (the ground); to rut (the ground); **die Schweine haben den Boden (mit dem Rüssel) aufgewühlt,** the pigs have (rooted and) churned up the ground; (*b*) to stir (s.o., s.o.'s soul, etc.); **ein Film, der die Menschen aufwühlt,** a film that stirs people to the depths (of their souls); **aufwühlende Musik,** music that stirs up the emotions. **2.** to turn (sth.) up; to grub (sth.) up; **etwas mit dem Pflug a.,** to turn sth. up with the plough; (*of pig*) **etwas mit dem Rüssel a.,** to root sth. up; *F:* **längst begrabenen Kummer wieder a.,** to stir up long-buried grief.

aufzählen. I. *v.tr. sep.* (*a*) to enumerate (reasons, events, s.o.'s virtues, etc.); to recite, detail (facts, etc.); **sie kann die römischen Kaiser der Reihe nach a.,** she can give, *F:* reel off, the names of all the Roman emperors in order; (*b*) **j-m das Geld auf den Tisch a.,** to count money out on the table for s.o.; *F:* **zwanzig aufgezählt bekommen,** to get twenty lashes.

II. *vbl s.* **1. Aufzählen,** *n. in vbl senses; also:* enumeration (of reasons, etc.). **2. Aufzählung,** *f.* (*a*)=II. 1; (*b*) enumeration; list; series; **das Buch besteht zur Hälfte aus langweiligen Aufzählungen von Ereignissen,** half of the book consists of boring lists of events.

aufzäumen, *v.tr. sep.* to bridle (horse); *F:* **das Pferd, den Esel, beim Schwanze a.,** to put the cart before the horse, to start sth. at the wrong end.

aufzehren, *v.tr. sep.* to consume, eat up, devour (sth.); (*a*) **wir haben alle unsere Vorräte aufgezehrt,** we have consumed, eaten (up), all our supplies; (*b*) **die schwere Arbeit hat seine Kräfte völlig aufgezehrt,** hard work has consumed, sapped, used up, all his energies; **nach einigen Monaten war sein ganzes Vermögen aufgezehrt,** after a few months his entire fortune was consumed, spent, exhausted.

aufzeichnen. I. *v.tr. sep.* **1.** to draw, sketch (sth.), to make a sketch, diagram (of sth.); **den Plan eines Hauses a.,** to draw the plan of a house; to make a sketch to show the plan of a

house; **ich werde dir a., wie man dahin kommt,** I'll make a diagram to show you how to get there. **2.** to write, note, (sth.) down, to make a note of (sth.); to record (sth.).

II. *vbl s.* **1. Aufzeichnen,** *n. in vbl senses.* **2. Aufzeichnung,** *f.* (*a*)=II. 1; (*b*) *usu. pl.* **Aufzeichnungen,** notes; record; **sich** *dat.* **(über etwas** *acc.***) Aufzeichnungen machen,** to make, take, notes (about sth.); to keep a record of sth.; **er macht sich genaue Aufzeichnungen über alles, was er tut,** he keeps an exact record of everything he does.

Aufzeichnungslichtbündel, *n. Cin:* spot; recording light beam.

Aufzeichnungsnadel, *f. Gramophones:* recording needle.

Aufzeichnungsplatte, *f. Gramophones:* recording disc, wax record.

Aufzeichnungsraum, *m. Cin:* recording-room.

aufzeigen, *v.sep.* **1.** *v.tr.*=**aufweisen** 2. **2.** *v.i.* (*haben*) *Sch:* to put up one's hand.

aufzerren, *v.tr. sep.* **1.** to tear, pull, tug, (sth.) open. **2.** to tear up, pull up (sth.).

Aufziehbrücke, *f.* drawbridge (of castle, etc.).

aufziehen, *v. sep.* (*strong*) I. *v.tr.* **1.** (*a*) to pull, draw, (sth.) up; to hoist (sth.); **die Zugbrücke, den Schlagbaum, a.,** to raise the drawbridge, the barrier; **den Vorhang a.,** to draw the curtain; *Th:* to raise the curtain; **sie zog die Vorhänge auf,** she drew, opened, the curtains; **die Rolläden a.,** to pull up, draw, the blinds; **eine Schleuse a.,** to open, draw up, a sluice-gate; **Segel, eine Fahne, a.,** to hoist sails, a flag; *Hist:* **j-n a.,** to subject s.o. to the strappado; (*b*) *F:* **j-n a.,** to tease, make fun of, poke fun at, s.o., to pull s.o.'s leg; **j-n mit etwas a.,** to tease, chaff, s.o. about sth.; **sie ziehen ihn damit auf, daß er immer einen Regenschirm mitnimmt,** they tease, chaff, make fun of, poke fun at, him, they pull his leg, for always carrying an umbrella. **2.** to wind (up) (clock, etc.). **3.** to stretch (sth.) (on sth.); to mount (photograph, etc.); **eine Stickerei auf den Rahmen a.,** to put a piece of embroidery in the frame; **Saiten auf eine Violine a.,** to string a violin; *F:* **wir werden andere, strengere, Saiten a. müssen,** we shall have to take a firmer line; *Tex:* **die Kette a.,** to put in the warp, to warp. **4.** *Med:* **eine Spritze a.,** to draw up an injection. **5.** to rear, raise (child, animal, plant); to bring up (child); to cultivate, grow (plant); **sie wurde von ihrer Tante aufgezogen,** she was brought up by her aunt. **6.** to pull open (drawer, etc.); to uncork, pull the cork out of (bottle); **eine Schleife a.,** to pull a bow undone. **7.** to set about (sth.); to start (enterprise); to plan, arrange, organize, get up (festivities, etc.); **der Karneval wurde dieses Jahr besonders groß aufgezogen,** the carnival was planned, was got up, in particularly grand style this year; **etwas falsch a.,** to go, set, about sth. the wrong way; **etwas politisch a.,** to make a political issue of sth., to use sth. to political ends.

II. **aufziehen,** *v.i.* (*sein*) **1.** (*a*) to approach, draw near; **ein Gewitter zieht auf,** a storm is coming, brewing; **Wolken ziehen am Himmel auf,** clouds are coming up; (*b*) *A:* to appear; **in seinem schönsten Putz a.,** to appear in one's finest clothes. **2.** (*of troops*) to march up; to parade; (*of oncoming guard*) to come on duty, to march up; **das Aufziehen der Wache,** the changing of the guard.

Aufzieherei, *f.* -/-en. *F:* teasing, chaff, banter.

Aufziehkrone, *f. Clockm:* = **Aufzugskrone.**

Aufziehleine, *f. Av:* rip-cord (of parachute).

Aufziehrechen, *m. Clockm:* repeater rack, winding rack (of repeater watch).

Aufziehschlitten, *m. N.Arch:* cradle.

Aufziehvorrichtung, *f.* winder (of clock, etc.).

Aufziehzapfen, *m. Clockm:* winding square.

Aufzins, *m. Fin:* interest upon interest.

aufzinsen, *v.tr. sep. Fin:* to pay interest on (capital).

Aufzucht, *f.* rearing, raising (of children, poultry, livestock).

aufzucken, *v.i. sep.* (*haben*) (*of pers.*) to start; to make a convulsive movement; (*of flame, etc.*) to leap up, shoot up (convulsively).

Aufzug, *m.* **1.** (*a*) hoist; elevator; goods *or* service lift, *U.S:* freight *or* service elevator; (*b*) lift, *U.S:* elevator; (*c*) *Gym:* heave. **2.** winder (of clock, etc.). **3.** *Tex:* warp. **4.** (*a*) marching up (of troops); parade; **A. der Wache,** changing of the guard; (*b*) procession; **in feierlichem Aufzuge,** in solemn procession. **5.** *Th:* (*division of play*) act. **6.** attire, get-up; **er kam in einem sonderbaren A. zu uns,** he came to us in strange attire, wearing a strange get-up.

Aufzugsschacht, *m.* lift-shaft, *U.S:* elevator shaft.

Aufzugsführer, *m.* lift-attendant, lift-man, *U.S:* elevator operator.

Aufzugskrone, *f. Clockm:* winder, button (of keyless watch).

aufzupfen, *v.tr. sep.* **1.** to pull up (plant). **2.** to pluck (small packet) open; to pluck (bow, etc.) undone.

aufzwängen, *v.tr. sep.* **1. etwas auf etwas** *acc.* **a.,** to force sth. on to sth. **2.** to force (sth.) open.

aufzwingen, *v.tr. sep.* (*strong*) **1.** (*a*) **etwas auf etwas** *acc.* **a.,** to force sth. on to sth.; (*b*) **j-m etwas a.,** to press, force, urge, sth. (up)on s.o.; to obtrude sth. on s.o. **2.** to force (sth.) open.

Augapfel, *m. Anat:* eye-ball, globe of the eye; *F:* apple of the eye; *F:* **er hütet es wie seinen A.,** it is the apple of his eye; **sie ist des Vaters A.,** she is the apple of her father's eye.

Augapfelgefäßhaut, *f.,* **Augapfelhäutchen,** *n. Anat:* choroid.

Augapfelhöhle, *f.*=**Augenhöhle.**

Augapfelvorfall, *m. Med:* exophthalmus.

Augbändsel, *n. Nau:* throat seizing.

Augbolzen, *m.* eye-bolt; ring-bolt.

Auge, *n.* **-s/-n. 1.** eye; **mit großen Augen,** with large, big, eyes; big-eyed; **mit trüben Augen,** with dull, bleary, eyes; blear-eyed; **mit blauen Augen,** with blue eyes; blue-eyed; **blaue Augen haben,** to have blue eyes, to be blue-eyed; *B:* **A. um A., Zahn um Zahn,** an eye for an eye, a tooth for a tooth; **j-m die Augen ausstechen,** to put out s.o.'s eyes; **ein A. verlieren,** to lose an eye; **auf einem A. blind, kurzsichtig, sein,** to be blind, short-sighted, *U.S:* near-sighted, in one eye; **ich kann auf, mit, dem linken A. besser sehen als auf, mit, dem rechten,** I can see better with my left eye than with my right; **künstliches A.,** artificial eye, *F:* glass eye; **sein A. brach,** his eyes grew dim (*in death*); **die Augen öffnen, aufmachen, auftun,** to open one's eyes; **mit offenen Augen,** with open eyes, with one's eyes open; **die Augen schließen, zumachen, zutun,** (i) to shut, close, one's eyes; (ii) to close one's eyes in death; **mit geschlossenen Augen,** with one's eyes shut, closed; **j-m die Augen schließen, zudrücken,** to close s.o.'s eyes (*as a last duty*); **seine Augen zum Himmel erheben,** to lift up, cast up, one's eyes to Heaven; **die Augen aufreißen,** to open one's eyes wide, to stare; **(große) Augen machen,** to open one's eyes wide, to stare (in astonishment); to be surprised; **Augen machen,** to look wistful; to look longingly; **nach etwas Augen machen,** to cast longing eyes on sth., to look longingly at sth.; **j-m Augen machen,** to make eyes at s.o., *F:* to give s.o. the glad eye; **die Augen gingen ihm über,** (i) *A. & Lit:* his eyes filled, brimmed (over), with tears; (ii) *F:* he stared (with astonishment); *F:* **die Augen werden ihm übergehen,** that will make him open his eyes, make him stare; **die Augen zusammenkneifen,** to screw up one's eyes; **ich habe die ganze Nacht kein A. zugetan,** I did not sleep a wink all night; **ich kann vor Schnupfen nicht aus den Augen schauen,** I have a bad cold in the head and can hardly see anything, *F:* my eyes are bunged up (with a cold); *F:* **ich kann vor (lauter) Müdigkeit nicht aus den Augen sehen, schauen,** I just can't see for tiredness; **etwas mit sehenden Augen, sehenden Auges, tun,** to do sth. with one's eyes open; **die Augen offen halten,** to keep one's eyes open, *F:* peeled, skinned; **er war so müde, daß er die Augen kaum offen halten konnte,** he was so tired that he could hardly keep his eyes open; **seine Augen überall haben,** to have all one's eyes about one; to keep an eye on everything; **j-m die Augen über etwas** *acc.* **öffnen,** to open s.o.'s eyes to sth.; to undeceive s.o. about sth.; **endlich gingen ihm die Augen auf,** at last his eyes were opened; **seine Augen gegen die Wahrheit verschließen,** to shut one's eyes to the truth; **wir wollen ein A. zudrücken und die Sache durchgehen lassen,** let's take a lenient view, let's stretch a point, and let it go at that; **diesmal drücken wir ein A. zu,** this time we'll pretend not to notice; this time we'll stretch a point; **dabei hat er beide Augen zugedrückt,** he turned a blind eye; **j-m in die Augen, ins A., sehen, schauen,** to look s.o. straight in the eye; to look s.o. (straight) in the face; **den Tatsachen ins A. sehen,** to look facts in the face, to face up to facts; **er hat dem Tod ins A. gesehen, geschaut,** he has looked death in the face; **A. in A.,** face to face; **er wagte es nicht, mir unter die Augen zu kommen,** he dared not face me; **komm mir nicht wieder vor die Augen!** keep out of my sight, out of my way, in future! **geh mir aus den Augen!** get out of my sight! **man sieht es ihm an den Augen an, daß er lügt,** you can see by his face that he is lying; **unter vier Augen,** confidentially, tête-à-tête; between you and me, between ourselves; **Gespräch unter vier Augen,** confidential conversation, tête-à-tête; **ich werde es dir unter vier Augen sagen,** I will tell you when we are alone, on our own, by ourselves; **j-m zu tief in die Augen sehen,** to fall in love with s.o.; **er ist seinem Vater wie aus den Augen geschnitten,** he is the very image, the living image, *F:* the very spit, the dead spit, of his father; **vier Augen sehen besser als zwei,** two heads are better than one; **die Familie ruht auf zwei Augen,** there is only one male survivor of the family; **gute, schlechte, Augen haben,** to have good, poor, eyes, (eye)sight; **Nähen strengt die Augen an,** sewing strains, taxes, the eyes, the (eye)sight; **sich** *dat.* **die Augen verderben,** to spoil, ruin, one's eyes, one's (eye)sight; **vor meinen Augen,** before my eyes, in front of my eyes; in my sight, before my face; **es geschah vor meinen Augen,** it happened before my eyes, in front of my eyes; it was done in my sight, before my face; I saw it happen with my own eyes; **etwas vor aller Augen tun,** to do sth. in sight of everybody; to do sth. in public; **etwas mit bloßem, unbewaffnetem, A. sehen,** to see sth. with the naked eye; **die Entfernung mit dem A., mit den Augen, messen,** to judge distance by eye; **etwas mit eigenen Augen sehen,** to see, witness, sth. with one's own eyes; **etwas mit dem geistigen A. sehen,** to see sth. in one's mind's eye; **seine Augen waren größer als sein Magen, sein Bauch,** his eyes were bigger than his belly; **ganz A. sein,** to be all eyes; **hast du keine Augen im Kopfe?** have you no eyes in your head? where are your eyes? *F:* **er hat vorn und hinten Augen,** he has eyes at the back of his head; **ich sehe die Frage mit anderen Augen an,** I look upon the problem with a different eye; **sie sieht die Dinge mit anderen Augen an als ich,** she sees things differently from me; she does not see eye to eye with me; **er ist in aller Augen schuldig,** in the eyes of all he is guilty; **vor den Augen Gottes und der Menschen,** in the eyes, in the sight, of God and man; **gleich vor dem A. des Gesetzes,** equal in the eye(s) of the law; *Hum:* **das A. des Gesetzes,** the policeman, *Hum:* the eye of the law; (*of thg*) **ins A. fallen, die Augen auf sich ziehen,** to draw the eye, to attract attention; to be conspicuous; **j-m ins A. fallen,** to catch s.o.'s eye; **es springt, sticht, in die Augen,** it leaps to the eye; **j-n ins A. fassen,** (i) to fix one's eye(s) on s.o.; (ii) to have s.o. in mind; **etwas ins A. fassen,** (i) to fix one's eye(s) on sth.; (ii) to contemplate sth., doing sth.; **etwas ins A. gefaßt haben,** to have sth. in view; **um das Ziel zu erreichen, das wir ins A. gefaßt haben,** to attain the end that we have in view; **seine Augen auf etwas** *acc.* **richten,** to turn one's eyes on sth.; to direct one's gaze towards sth.; **ein A. auf etwas** *acc.,* **auf j-n, haben,** to have an eye on sth., on s.o.; **auf j-n ein A. geworfen haben,** to have one's eye on s.o.; **ein wachsames A. auf j-n haben,** to keep a watchful, sharp, close, strict, eye on s.o.; **etwas, j-n, im A. behalten,** to keep sth., s.o., in sight, in mind; to keep an eye on sth., on s.o.; **behalte ihn im A.!** keep your eye on him! keep him in sight, in view! **er ließ sie nicht aus den Augen,** he didn't let her out of his sight; **laß ihn nicht aus den Augen!** keep your eye on him! don't let him out of your sight! **er arbeitete weiter, ohne den Fremden aus dem A., aus den Augen, zu lassen,** he went on working with one eye on the stranger; **j-n aus den Augen verlieren,** to lose sight of s.o.; **wir verloren ihn bald aus den Augen,** we soon lost sight, were out of sight, of him; **j-n im A. haben,** to have s.o. in mind; **etwas im A. haben,** to have sth. in mind, in view; **ich habe (es) im A., zu . . .,** I have it in mind to . . ., I intend to . . .; **er hat immer seinen eigenen Vorteil im A.,** he always has an eye to his own interest; **j-m etwas vor Augen führen,** to demonstrate sth. to s.o.; **j-m etwas vor Augen halten,** to impress sth. upon s.o.'s mind; to remonstrate with s.o. about sth.; **sich** *dat.* **etwas vor Augen halten,** to be mindful of sth., to bear sth. in mind; **ein A. für Farben, für Pferde, haben,** to have an eye for colour, for a horse; **ein geübtes A. haben,** to have a practised eye; *Sp: etc:* to have one's eye well in; *Poet:* **das A. des Tages,** the eye of day; the sun; *Mil:* **Augen rechts, links!** eyes right, left! **Augen geradeaus!** eyes front! *Prov:* **aus den Augen, aus dem Sinn,** out of sight, out of mind; *F:* **j-m Sand in die Augen streuen, j-m die**

Augen auswischen, to throw dust in s.o.'s eyes; *see also* **aufgehen I. 5, blau I. 1, Dorn 1, weiden. 2.** *TV: etc:* **magisches A.,** magic eye. **3.** (*a*) bird's eye (in mahogany, etc.); **Augen am Pfauenschwanz,** eyes in a peacock's tail; (*b*) *Hort:* (i) eye, bud (of plant); eye (of potato); (ii) (*in grafting*) eye; shield-bud; (*c*) hole (in bread, gruyère cheese, etc.); (*d*) speck of fat (on soup); (*e*) pip (on playing-card), spot (on dice, domino); **seine Augen zählen,** to count up the value of one's cards; (*f*) eye (of crane, hammer, anchor-shank, etc.); eye, eye-splice (on rope, cable); eyelet, eyelet-hole (of sail, etc.); *Tchn:* lug; lifting-ring (of turbine, etc.); *Mch:* gab (of eccentric rod); (*g*) eye (of cyclone). **4.** lustre, gloss, sheen (of stuffs, precious stones, etc.). **5.** *Print:* face (of letter).

Äugelchen, *n.* **-s/-,** (*dim. of* **Auge**) little eye; *F:* **j-m Ä. machen,** to make eyes at s.o., to give s.o. the glad eye.

äugeln. 1. *v.i.* (*haben*) (*a*) *esp. Ven:* to look; (*b*) **auf j-n ä.,** to eye s.o.; to glance meaningly at s.o.; (*c*) **mit j-m ä.,** to ogle s.o.; to exchange tender glances with s.o.; to wink at s.o. **2.** *v.tr. Hort:* to graft a shield-bud on (fruit-tree).

Augen-, *comb.fm.* **1.** (*a*) . . . of the eye(s); eye-; (pain, etc.) in the eye(s); *Anat: etc:* optic . . . ; ophthalmic . . . ; visual . . . ; ocular . . . ; **Augenfarbe** *f*, colour of the eyes; **Augensprache** *f*, language of the eyes; *Anat:* **Augenarterie** *f*, ophthalmic artery; **Augenkammer** *f*, chamber of the eye; **Augenmuskel** *m*, ocular muscle, eye-muscle; **Augennerv** *m*, optic nerve, visual nerve; (*b*) . . . round the eye; *Anat:* orbital . . . ; **Augenring** *m*, ring round the eye; *Anat:* **Augenhöhle** *f*, orbital cavity, eye-socket; (*c*) . . . situated near the eye; **Augenzahn** *m*, eye-tooth; **Augensprosse** *f*, brow antler (of stag). **2.** . . . for the eyes, . . . to aid the eyes; *Med:* ophthalmic . . . ; **Augendusche** *f*, eye-bath; **Augenglas** *n*, eye-glass; **Augenklinik** *f*, ophthalmic hospital, eye-hospital; **Augenmittel** *n*, ophthalmic remedy; **Augentropfen** *m pl*, drops for the eyes. **3.** . . . by the eye; . . . with (the aid of) the eye(s); visual . . . ; optical . . . ; ocular . . . ; **Augentäuschung** *f*, optical illusion; **Augenverbindung** *f*, visual communication; **Augenzeuge** *m*, eyewitness. **4.** *Nat. Hist: etc:* . . . with eye-like markings; eyespotted . . . , ocellate(d) . . . ; **Augenachat** *m*, eye-agate; **Augenmarmor** *m*, eyespotted marble. **5.** *Bot: Hort:* . . . of a bud; **Augenbildung** *f*, formation of a bud; **Augenpfropfen** *n*, budding, grafting of a bud.

äugen, *v.i.* (*haben*) *esp. Ven:* to look; **nach j-m, etwas, ä.,** to look out for s.o., sth.

Augenabstand, *m.* distance between the eyes, *Opt:* interocular distance.

Augenachat, *m. Miner:* eye-agate.

Augenachse, *f. Anat:* axis of the eye.

Augenaderhaut, *f. Anat:* choroid.

Augenanlage, *f.* **1.** *Biol:* primordium of an eye. **2.** *Bot:* primordium, first beginnings, of a bud.

Augenarzt, *m.* ophthalmologist, oculist, eye-specialist.

augenärztlich, *a.* (treatment, etc.) by an oculist; eye(-treatment); ophthalmologic(al) (instruments, etc.).

Augenaufschlag, *m.* raising of the eyes; upcast eyes; inviting, beseeching, *or* despairing glance (with upturned eyes); **einen A. haben,** to have an upward gaze; **mit schüchternem A.,** with shyly upcast eyes.

Augenbad, *n. Med:* bathing of the eye(s).

Augenbader, *m.* = **Augenbadewanne.**

Augenbadewanne, *f. Med:* eye-bath, eye-cup.

Augenbesichtigung, *f. Med:* ophthalmoscopy.

Augenbinde, *f.* bandage over the eyes; **j-m eine A. anlegen,** to blindfold s.o.

Augenbindehaut, *f. Anat:* conjunctiva.

Augenblende, *f.* **1.** eye-shade. **2.** = **Augenleder.**

Augenblick, *m.* **-(e)s/-e,** moment, instant; **der A. der Entscheidung,** the moment of decision, the decisive moment; the critical moment; *see also* **entscheiden III, kritisch; einen günstigen A. abwarten,** to wait for a favourable, an opportune, moment; **den rechten, richtigen, günstigen, A. abwarten,** to wait for the right moment; to bide one's time; **er schwieg einen A. (lang),** he was silent for a moment; **ich blieb stehen und horchte einen A. (lang),** I stood listening (for) a moment; **warten Sie einen A.!** wait a moment! **einen A., bitte!** one moment, just a minute, please! *F:* **Augenblick!** one moment! *F:* half a moment! half a tick! *V:* half a mo! **A. mal!** just a moment! just a minute! **er kam keinen A. zu früh,** he came not a moment, not an instant, too soon; **das haben wir keinen A. erwartet,** we didn't expect it for a moment, for an instant, for a minute; **wir hatten keinen A. Ruhe,** we didn't get a moment's peace; **von einem A. zum anderen,** from one moment to the next, from moment to moment; momentarily; **alle Augenblicke,** continually, constantly, at every moment; at every turn; **jeden A.,** any minute, at any moment; **ich erwarte ihn jeden A.,** I expect him any minute, at any moment, every instant; **er kann jeden A. zurückkommen,** he may return any minute, at any moment; **auf einen A.,** for a moment; **er verschwand auf einen A.,** he disappeared for a moment; **kannst du auf einen A. hereinkommen?** can you come in for a moment, for a minute? **für den A.,** for the moment, for the present, for the time being; **für den A. brauche ich nichts,** I don't want anything for the moment; **in einem A.,** in a moment, an instant, immediately; **es war alles in einem A. geschehen,** it was all over, it all happened, in a moment, in an instant; **komm diesen A.!** come this instant! **(gerade) in diesem, jenem, A.,** at this, that, very moment, instant; **im ersten A.,** at the first moment; at the very start; **(gerade) im letzten A.,** at the (very) last moment; **sie erreichte den Zug (gerade) im letzten A.,** she caught the train just in the nick of time, she only just caught the train; **im richtigen A.,** at the right moment; **das Buch erschien (gerade) im richtigen A.,** the book appeared just at the right moment; **Sie sind (gerade) im richtigen A. gekommen,** you have come just at the right moment, in the very nick of time; **im A.,** (i) at the moment, for the time being, at present, just now; (ii) in a moment, in an instant, immediately, directly; **ich kann es im A. nicht finden,** I can't find it at the moment; **ich bin im A. beschäftigt,** I am busy at the moment, just now; **ich habe im A. vergessen . . . ,** at, for, the moment I forget . . . ; **ich werde im A. kommen,** I'll come in a moment; **in dem A., als, wo, . . . ,** at the moment, when . . . ; **im A., als, wo, ich ihn erblickte, erkannte ich ihn,** the moment, the instant, I saw him I recognized him; **in dem A., im A., als er kam, wo er kommt,** the moment, the instant, he came, he comes; **von dem A., vom A., an, als, wo . . . ,** from the moment when . . . ; *Med:* **lichter A.,** lucid interval; *F:* **er hat seine lichten Augenblicke,** he has his (brighter) moments; **in einem lichten A.,** in one of his, her, brighter, more intelligent, moments.

Augenblickchen, *n.* **-s/-.** *F:* (brief) moment; **ein A., bitte!** one moment, just a minute, please! **Augenblickchen!** one moment! *F:* half a moment! half a tick! *V:* half a mo! **A. mal!** just a moment! just a minute!

augenblicklich. 1. *a.* (*a*) instantaneous; immediate (readiness, etc.); (*b*) momentary; **die augenblickliche Lage,** the situation at the moment; the present, immediate, situation. **2.** *adv.* (*a*) instantaneously; instantly, immediately, directly, in a moment; **komm a. her!** come here this instant! **ich werde a. gehen,** I'm going this instant, this very moment; (*b*) at the moment, at present, just now; for the time being; **ich kann es a. nicht finden,** I can't find it at, for, the moment; **ich bin a. beschäftigt,** I am busy at, for, the moment, just now; **a. brauche ich nichts,** I don't want anything for the moment.

augenblicks, *adv.* instantly, immediately, directly; in a moment.

Augenblicksdauer, *f.* momentary duration; instantaneousness, instantaneity.

Augenblickserfolg, *m.* momentary, brief, short-lived, success.

Augenblicksmensch, *m.* **1.** person who lives entirely in and for the moment; *Psy:* present-dweller. **2.** person who acts on the spur of the moment; impulsive person; creature of impulse.

Augenblicksstimmung, *f.* passing, fleeting, mood.

Augenblickswert, *m.* momentary value; *Mth:* magnitude at an instant.

Augenblickswirkung, *f.* instantaneous effect.

Augenblicksziel, *n. Mil: Navy:* fleeting target.

Augenblickszünder, *m. Artil:* instantaneous fuze.

Augenblickszündung, *f. Exp:* instantaneous ignition.

Augenblinzeln, *n.* blink(ing); flicker(-ing), of the eyelids.

Augenbogen, *m. Anat:* iris.

Augenbraue, *f.* eyebrow; **die Augenbrauen zusammenziehen,** to knit one's eyebrows, to frown, to scowl.

Augenbrauenbögen, *m.pl. Anat:* superciliary arches, superciliary ridges, brow-ridges.

Augenbrauenrunzler, *m.* **-s/-.** *Anat:* corrugator (muscle).

Augenbrauenstift, *m. Toil:* eyebrow pencil.

Augendecke, *f. Z:* nictitating membrane.

Augendeckel, *m.* **1.** *Anat: Z:* eyelid; *F:* **mit den Augendeckeln klappern,** to flutter one's eyelids. **2.** eye-cap (of optical instrument).

Augendiagnose, *f. Med:* iridiagnosis.

Augendiener, *m.* sycophant, toady; lick-spittle.

Augendienerei, *f.* **-/., Augendienst,** *m.* sycophancy, toadying, toadyism.

Augendusche, *f. Med:* **1.** eye-bath, eye-cup. **2.** bathing of the eyes.

Augenentzündung, *f.* inflammation of the eye(s), *Med:* ophthalmia; *see also* **ägyptisch.**

Augenerkundung, *f. Mil:* visual reconnaissance.

augenfällig, *a.* conspicuous; obvious; evident. manifest; **a. sein,** to draw the eye, to attract attention, to be conspicuous.

Augenfalter, *m. Ent:* satyr (butterfly).

Augenfehler, *m.* **1.** defect of the eye(s); defect of the sight. **2.** visual error.

Augenfell, *n. Med:* pterygium.

Augenfenster, *n.* eyepiece (of gas-mask, diver's helmet).

Augenfleck, *m.* **1.** *Nat.Hist:* eye, ocellus (on peacock's feather, etc.); eyespot (on butterfly's wing, etc.). **2.** fleck in the eye.

augenfleckig, *a. Nat.Hist:* ocellate, ocellated, eyespotted.

Augenflimmern, *n.* flickering of the visual image; **A. haben,** to get a flickering effect in one's vision.

Augenflüssigkeit, *f. Biol:* **glasartige A., wasserartige A.,** vitreous humour, aqueous humour (of the eye).

augenförmig, *a. Biol: etc:* oculiform, eye-shaped.

Augenglas, *n.* (*a*) eye-glass; **Augengläser,** (pair of) eye-glasses; pince-nez; (*b*) lens; (*c*) telescope; (*d*) eyepiece (of optical instrument, gas-mask, diver's helmet, etc.).

Augengrübchen, *n.* = **Augenhöhle.**

Augengymnastik, *f. Med:* eye exercises.

Augenhaut, *f. Anat:* **harte, weiße, A.,** sclerotica, sclera.

Augenheilanstalt, *f.* eye-hospital, ophthalmic hospital.

Augenheilkunde, *f.* ophthalmology.

Augenhintergrund, *m. Anat:* back, fundus, of the eye.

Augenhöhe, *f.* **in A.,** at eye-level.

Augenhöhle, *f. Anat:* eye-socket, orbital cavity, orbit (of the eye).

Augenhöhlenbögen, *m.pl.* = **Augenbrauenbögen.**

Augenhornhaut, *f. Anat:* cornea.

Augenkammer, *f. Anat:* chamber of the eye.

Augenkammerwasser, *n. Anat:* aqueous humour (of the eye).

Augenkeil, *m. Z:* ommatidium (of compound eye).

Augenklappe, *f.* **1.** *Z:* eyelid. **2.** = **Augenleder. 3.** eye patch.

Augenklinik, *f.* eye-hospital, ophthalmic hospital.

augenkrank, *a.* suffering from an eye-disease.

Augenkrankheit, *f.* eye-disease.

Augenkugel, *f. Anat:* eye-ball, globe of the eye.

Augenlampe, *f.* ophthalmic lamp.

Augenleder, *n. Harn:* blinker, eye-flap, *U.S:* blind(er).

Augenlederhaut, *f. Anat:* sclerotic, sclera.

Augenlehre, *f.* ophthalmology.

Augenleiden, *n.* affection of the eyes, eye-complaint; eye-disease.

Augenlicht, *n. Lit:* (eye)sight; **sein A. verlieren,** to lose one's (eye)sight, to go blind; *Poet:* **sie ist mein A.,** she is the light of my life.

Augenlid, *n.* eyelid.

Augenlid-, *comb.fm.* . . . of the eyelid; *Anat:* palpebral (artery, membrane, etc.).

Augenlid(er)entzündung, *f. Med:* blepharitis.

Augenlidwinkel, *m. Anat:* canthus.

Augenlinse, *f.* **1.** *Anat:* crystalline lens (of eye). **2.** *Opt:* eye-lens.

Augenloch, *n.* **1.** = **Augenhöhle. 2.** pupil (of eye).

augenlos, *a.* eyeless, without eyes; sightless, blind.

Augenlust, *f.* = **Augenweide.**

Augenmarmor, *m. Miner:* eyespotted, ocellated, marble.

Augenmaß, *n.* visual estimate; measure taken with the eye; judgment by the eye; **Länge nach dem A.** length (as) judged by the eye; **nach dem A., zeichnen,** to draw by eye; to draw freehand; **ein gutes A. haben,** (i) to have an eye for proportion; to have an accurate eye; to be sure-sighted; (ii) to have a sound, clear, good, judgment **(für,** of); **ihnen fehlt jedes A.,** they have no sense of proportion; they have no judgment; *Surv:* **Aufnahme nach dem A.,** eye-sketching.

Augenmensch, *m.* person sensitive to visual

impressions; **er ist ein A.,** he thinks in visual terms, *Psy:* he is eye-minded.
Augenmerk, *n.* (*usu. only in the phr.*) **sein A. auf etwas** *acc.* **richten,** to turn one's attention to sth.; to fix, focus, one's attention on sth.; to have sth. in view.
Augenmesser, *m. Opt:* ophthalmometer.
Augenmittel, *n. Med:* medicament for the eyes; ophthalmic remedy.
Augenmuschel, *f.* (*a*) *Opt:* eye-glass shade (of telescope, etc.); (*b*) eye-guard, eye-shield (on spectacles, goggles).
Augenmuskel, *m. Anat:* ocular muscle, eye-muscle.
Augennagel, *m. Anat:* unguis; lachrymal bone.
Augennerv, *m. Anat:* optic nerve, visual nerve.
Augennichts, *n.* sublimated zinc oxide, *Pharm: etc:* zinc dust, zinc powder.
Augenpaar, *n.* pair of eyes; **zwei neugierige Augenpaare blickten ihn an,** two pairs of curious eyes gazed at him.
Augenpfropfen, *n. Hort:* budding.
Augenpinsel, *m.* fine camel-hair brush (for use on the eye).
Augenprothese, *f. Surg:* ocular prosthesis; artificial eye.
Augenpulver, *n.* **1.** *Pharm:* medicament for the eyes (in powder form). **2.** *F:* tiny print (that tries the eyes).
Augenpunkt, *m. Opt: etc:* (*a*) visual, station, point; (*b*) point of sight, principal point.
Augenreim, *m. Pros:* eye-rhyme, rhyme only to the eye.
Augenreizstoff, *m. Mil:* lachrymator; tear-gas.
Augenrollmuskel, *m. Anat:* trochlear muscle.
Augensalbe, *f.* eyesalve, eye-ointment.
Augenscheibe, *f.* eyepiece (of gas-mask, diver's helmet).
Augenschein, *m.* **1.** inspection, examination; **etwas in A. nehmen,** to inspect sth.; to examine sth. closely, to subject sth. to a close inspection; *F:* to have a good look at sth.; **sich durch den A. (von etwas) überzeugen,** to convince oneself (of sth.) by actual inspection. **2.** appearance(s); **dem A. nach,** to, by, all appearance(s); **der A. trügt,** appearances are deceptive; things are not always what they seem.
augenscheinlich. 1. *a.* (*a*) (self-)evident, (self-)apparent; manifest; obvious, clear, plain, unmistakable; (*b*) apparent, seeming. **2.** *adv.* (*a*) evidently, manifestly; obviously, unmistakably; (*b*) apparently, seemingly; to, by, all appearance(s).
Augenscheinseinnahme, *f. Jur:* judicial inspection; visit to the scene (of a crime, etc.).
Augenschere, *f.* **1.** *Metalw:* block shears, tinman's shears. **2.** *Surg:* iridectomy scissors.
Augenschirm, *m.* eye-shade, eye-shield.
Augenschleim, *m.* **1.** *Physiol:* mucus (of the eyes). **2.**=**Augenschmalz.**
Augenschmalz, *n.* rheum, matter, gum (in the eyes).
Augenschmaus, *m. F:* **das war ein (richtiger) A.,** it was a feast for the eyes, it was something to feast one's eyes on.
Augenschützer, *m.* eye-guard, eye-shield, eye-protector; *Aut: etc:* goggles.
Augenschwäche, *f.* weakness of the eyes; weak sight, defective vision.
Augenspalte, *f. Anat:* sphenoidal fissure.
Augenspiegel, *m. Med:* ophthalmoscope; **Untersuchung des Auges mit dem A.,** ophthalmoscopy.
Augenspinner, *m. Ent:* Saturnian, Saturniid (moth).
Augensproß, *m.*, **Augensprosse,** *f.* brow antler (of stag).
Augenstechen, *n.* smarting of the eyes; shooting pains in the eyes.
Augensteckling, *m. Vit:* budded layer.
Augenstein, *m. Com:* zinc sulphate, white vitriol.
Augenstern, *m. Lit:* (*a*) eye; (*b*) pupil *or* iris (of the eye); (*c*) (*pers.*) dearest, beloved.
Augenstiel, *m. Crust:* eye-stalk.
Augenstreifgoldhähnchen, *n. Orn:* firecrest.
Augentäuschung, *f.* optical illusion.
Augentierchen, *n.pl. Prot:* ocellata.
Augentripper, *m. Med:* gonorrhoeal ophthalmia.
Augentropfen, *m.pl. Med: Pharm:* drops for the eyes, eye-drops.
Augentrost, *m.* **1.** (*a*) solace for the eyes; (*b*)=**Augenweide. 2.** *Bot:* (*a*) euphrasy, eye-bright; (*b*) *F:* **blauer A.,** (i) forget-me-not, (ii) skull-cap; **weißer A.,** stitchwort.
Augenverbindung, *f. Mil: etc:* visual communication.
Augenverdreher, *m. F:* sanctimonious hypocrite.
Augenwasser, *n.* **1.** water of the eye; *Biol:* aqueous humour. **2.** *Pharm:* eye-wash; collyrium.
Augenweide, *f.* (source of) delight to the eye(s); **es war eine A.,** it was a pleasure to look at, a delight to the eye(s), a feast for the eyes, something to feast one's eyes on, *F:* it was a sight for sore eyes, it was a treat to see it; *Lit:* **sie war ihm eine A.,** she was the delight of his eyes.
Augenweiß, *n.* white of the eye; *Anat:* sclerotic, sclera.
Augenweite, *f.* range of vision.
Augenwimper, *f.* eyelash.
Augenwink, *m.* meaning glance; wink.
Augenwinkel, *m.* corner of the eye; *Anat:* canthus; **aus dem A. blicken,** to look out of the corner of one's eye.
Augenwurz, *f. Bot:* **1.** (*in Alpine areas*) athamanta (cretensis). **2.** *F:* (*a*) wood anemone; (*b*) (any) plant used as a medicament for the eyes, *esp.* valerian.
Augenzahl, *f. Cards: etc:* number of pips (on cards), number of spots (on dice, etc.); value (of cards, throw of dice, etc.).
Augenzahn, *m.* eye-tooth, upper canine (tooth).
Augenzeuge, *m.* eyewitness.
Augenzeugenbericht, *m.* eyewitness account; **nach einem A.,** according to an eyewitness.
Augenzeugnis, *n.* testimony, evidence, of an eye-witness.
Augenzinke, *f.*=**Augensproß.**
Augenzittern, *n. Med:* nystagmus.
Augenzwinkern, *n.* wink.
Augias [auˈgiːas]. *Pr.n.m.* **-'.** *Gr.Myth:* Augeas.
Augiasstall, *m.* **den A. reinigen,** to cleanse the Augean stables.
-äugig, *comb.fm.* (*a*) -eyed; **ein braunäugiger Junge,** a brown-eyed boy, a boy with brown eyes; **großäugig,** big-eyed; **helläugig,** bright-eyed; **einäugig,** one-eyed; **zweiäugig,** two-eyed; (*b*) *Opt:* **einäugig,** monocular; **beidäugig,** binocular.
Augit [auˈgiːt], *m.* **-(e)s/-e.** *Miner:* augite.
Äuglein, *n.* **-s/-,** (*dim. of* **Auge**) **1.** little eye. **2.** *Bot:* (small) bud.
Äugler, *m.* **-s/-. 1.** ogler. **2.**=**Augendiener. 3.** *Ent:* satyr (butterfly).
Augling, Äugling, *m.* **-s/-e.** *Ent:* satyr (butterfly).
Augment [augˈmɛnt], *n.* **-(e)s/-e.** *Gram:* augment.
Augmentation [augmɛntaˑtsĭˈoːn], *f.* **-/-en.** *Gram: Mus:* augmentation.
Augmentativum [augmɛntaˑˈtiːvum], *n.* **-s/-va.** *Gram:* augmentative.
augmentieren [augmɛnˈtiːrən], *v.tr.* to augment (word, *Mus:* theme in fugue, etc.); **Augmentierung** *f*, augmentation.
Augsburger. 1. *m.* **-s/-.** *Geog:* inhabitant, native, of Augsburg. **2.** *inv.a. Geog:* of Augsburg; *Rel.Hist:* **der A. Religionsfriede,** the Religious Peace of Augsburg; **das A. Bekenntnis,** the Confession of Augsburg, the Augustan Confession.
augsburgisch, *a. Geog:* of Augsburg; *Rel.Hist:* **die Augsburgische Konfession**=**das Augsburger Bekenntnis,** *q.v. under* **Augsburger 2.**
Augspleiß, *m.*, **Augsplissung,** *f. Nau:* eye-splice.
Augsproß, *m.*, **Augsprosse,** *f.*=**Augensproß.**
Augur [ˈaugʊr], *m.* **-s & -(e)n/-en** [-ˈguːrən]. *Rom.Ant:* augur.
Augurenlächeln, *n. F:* knowing smile.
augurieren [auguˑˈriːrən], *v.tr.* to augur, prognosticate, forecast; to foresee.
Augurium [auˈguːrium], *n.* **-s/-rien,** augury, omen; prognostication.
August[1] [auˈgust], *m.* **-(e)s & -/-e.** August; **im (Monat) A.,** in (the month of) August; **der erste A.,** the first of August; *for other phrases cp.* **April.**
August[2] [ˈaugust]. *Pr.n.m.* **-s.** Augustus; **der dumme A.,** the auguste (clown) (*at circus*).
Augusta [auˈgustaː]. *Pr.n.f.* **-s** & *Lit:* **-tens.** Augusta.
Augustana, die [auguˈstaːnaː], *f.* **-.** *Rel.Hist:* the Augustan Confession, the Confession of Augsburg.
Auguste [auˈgustə]. *Pr.n.f.* **-s** & *Lit:* **-ns.** Augusta.
Augusteisch [auguˈsteːiʃ], *a.* Augustan (art, style, etc.); (art, style, etc.) of the Augustan age; **das Augusteische Zeitalter,** the Augustan age.
Augustin [ˈaugustiːn, auguˈstiːn]. *Pr.n.m.* **-s.** Augustine.
Augustiner [auguˈstiːnər]. *Ecc:* **1.** *m.* **-s/-.** Augustinian (monk); **die Augustiner,** the Augustinians, *Hist:* the Austin Friars. **2.** *inv.a.* Augustinian; **die A. Chorherren,** the Augustinian Canons.
Augustinerkloster, *n.* Augustinian monastery.
Augustinermönch, *m. Ecc:* Augustinian monk.
augustinisch [auguˈstiːniʃ], *a. Ecc:* Augustinian (doctrine, etc.).
Augustinus [auguˈstiːnus]. *Pr.n.m.* **-'.** Augustine.
Augustsaft, [auˈgust-] *m. Arb:* sappiness (of wood) in August.
Augustus [auˈgustus]. *Pr.n.m.* **-'.** Augustus; *Rom. Hist:* **der Kaiser A.,** the Emperor Augustus; **das Zeitalter des A.,** the Augustan age.
Augzahn, *m.*=**Augenzahn.**
Augzinke, *f.*=**Augensproß.**
Auken, *m.* **-s/-.** *North G.Dial:* loft.
Auktion [auktsĭˈoːn], *f.* **-/-en,** (sale by) auction, auction-sale; **etwas zur, in die, A. geben,** to put sth. up for, to, auction; to auction sth.; *Jur:* **gerichtliche A.,** sale by order of the court, compulsory sale.
Auktionator [auktsĭoˑˈnaːtor], *m.* **-s/-en** [-naˑˈtoːrən], auctioneer (and valuer, *U.S:* appraiser.).
auktionieren [auktsĭoˑˈniːrən], *v.tr.* to sell (sth.) by auction, *U.S:* at auction; to put (sth.) up to, for, auction; to auction (sth.).
Auktionskommissar, *m.* auctioneer (and valuer, *U.S:* appraiser).
Auktionslokal, *n.*, **Auktionssaal,** *m.* auction-room; auction-mart; sale-room.
Aula [ˈaulaː], *f.* **-/-len** [ˈaulən] **& -s,** hall (of university, college, etc.), *U.S:* auditorium; (*of school, etc.*) assembly hall.
Aulebäcker, *m.*, **Aulner,** *m.* **-s/-.** *Dial:* potter.
au pair [oː ˈpɛːr], *a. & adv.* au pair; **auf au pair Basis,** on an au pair basis; **au pair arbeiten,** to work au pair.
Aura [ˈauraː], *f.* **-/.** *Med: etc:* aura; **epileptische A.,** epileptic aura.
Auramin [auraˑˈmiːn], *n.* **-s/.** *Ch: Dy:* auramine.
Aurangseb [auraŋˈzeːp]. *Pr.n.m.* **-s.** *Hist:* Aurangzebe, Aurungzebe.
Aurat [auˈraːt], *n.* **-(e)s/-e.** *Ch:* aurate.
Aurel [auˈreːl]. *Pr.n.m.* **-s.** Aurelius; *Rom.Hist:* **Mark A.,** Marcus Aurelius.
Aurelia [auˈreːlĭaː]. *Pr.n.f.* **-s** & *Lit:* **-liens.** Aurelia.
Aurelian [aureˑlĭˈaːn]. *Pr.n.m.* **-s.** *Rom.Hist:* Aurelian.
aurelianisch [aureˑlĭˈaːniʃ], *a. Rom.Hist:* of Aurelian; **die Aurelianische Mauer,** Aurelian's Wall.
Aurelie [auˈreːlĭə]. *Pr.n.f.* **-s** & *Lit:* **-liens** [-liːəns]. Aurelia.
Aureole [aureˑˈoːlə], *f.* **-/-n. 1.** glory, aureole (around whole figure). **2.** *Meteor:* halo, nimbus, ring (round sun, moon). **3.** *El:* blue glow (round high-tension conductor). **4.** *Min:* gas cap, blue cap (in miner's lamp).
Aureomycin [aureˑoˑmyˑˈtsiːn], *n.* **-s/.** (*R.t.m.*) *Pharm:* aureomycin.
Aurichalzit [auriˑkalˈtsiːt], *m.* **-(e)s/.** *Miner:* aurichalcite.
Aurichlorid [auriˑkloˑˈriːt] -(e)s/. [-s, -ˈriːdəs]. *Ch:* auric chloride.
Auriga [auˈriːgaː]. *Br. n. m.* **-(s).** *Astr:* Auriga, the Waggoner, the Charioteer.
Aurignacien, das [oˑrinĭasĭˈɛ̃ː], **- & -s.** *Prehist:* the Aurignacian era.
Aurignacrasse [oˑrinˈĭak-], *f.* Aurignacian race.
Aurikel [auˈriːkəl], *f.* **-/-n.** *Bot:* auricula, bear's-ear.
aurikular [auriˑkuˑˈlaːr], *a.* auricular.
Aurikularbeichte, Aurikularkonfession, *f. Ecc:* auricular confession.
Aurin [auˈriːn], *m.* **-s/.** *Bot:* **1. (roter) A.,** lesser centaury, common centaury. **2. weißer, wilder, A.,** hedge hyssop.
Auripigment [auriˑpigˈmɛnt], *n.* **-(e)s/.** *Miner:* orpiment, yellow arsenic.
Aurizyanid [auriˑtsyˑaˑˈniːt], *n.* **-(e)s/.** [-s, -ˈniːdəs]. *Ch:* auric cyanide, auricyanide.
Aurochlorid [auroˑkloˑˈriːt], *n.* **-(e)s/.** [-s, -ˈriːdəs]. *Ch:* aurous chloride.
Aurora [auˈroːraː]. **1.** *Pr.n.f.* **-s.** *Myth:* Aurora. **2.** *f.* **-/-s,** aurora, polar lights. **3.** *f.* **-/-s.** *Ent:*=**Aurorafalter.**
Aurorafalter, *m. Ent:* orange-tip (butterfly).
Aurozyanid [auroˑtsyˑaˑˈniːt], *n.* **-(e)s/.** [-s, -ˈniːdəs]. *Ch:* aurous cyanide, aurocyanide.
aus. I. *prep.* (+*dat.*) **1.** out of; from; (*a*) **sie kam aus der Kirche,** she came out of (the) church; **er trank aus der Flasche,** he drank out of, from, the bottle; **wir nahmen die Zigaretten aus der Schachtel,** we took the cigarettes out of the box; (*b*) *Breed:* **Gladiator nach Monarch aus Gladia,** Gladiator by Monarch out of Gladia; (*c*) **er erwachte aus einem Traum (heraus),** he awoke from a dream; **da redet die Eifersucht aus ihr,** it's jealousy makes her say that; **das will mir nicht aus dem Sinn,** I can't get that out of, off, my mind; **sie hat mir aus der Seele gesprochen,** she expressed my feelings exactly; **er seufzte aus der Tiefe seines Herzens (heraus),**

he sighed deeply, from the very depths of his being; **das hast du nicht aus dir,** you didn't think of that yourself; **das sagt er nicht aus sich (heraus),** someone put the words into his mouth; **das Kind hat es ganz aus sich selbst (heraus) getan,** the child did it entirely of its own accord, all by itself; (*d*) **etwas aus zuverlässiger Quelle haben,** to have sth. from a dependable source; **aus erster Hand,** first-hand; at first hand; **etwas aus einem Buch lernen,** to learn sth. from a book; (*e*) (*denoting selection*) **lies mir eine Stelle aus deinem Buche vor,** read me a passage out of, from, your book; **eine Auswahl aus Goethe,** selections from Goethe; **einer aus ihrer Mitte,** one of their number; (*f*) *Sch: Austrian:* **Prüfung, Doktor, aus Englisch, Chemie, usw.,** examination, doctor's degree, in English, chemistry, etc. **2.** (*a*) from; **sie kommt aus weiter Ferne,** she comes from far away; **wir kommen eben aus Köln,** we have just come from Cologne; **meine Freundin aus England,** my friend from England; (*b*) **er ist, stammt, aus Hamburg,** he comes, hails, from Hamburg; **aus Sachsen gebürtig,** born in Saxony, a native of Saxony, a Saxon by birth; **aus guter Familie sein,** to be of good family; **er war ein Mann aus dem Volke,** he was a man of the people, a man of humble birth; **diese Uhr stammt noch aus meiner Jugend,** this watch dates back to my youth; **ein Tisch aus der Biedermeierzeit,** a table of the Biedermeier period; **eine Handschrift aus dem achten Jahrhundert,** an eighth-century manuscript. **3.** (*away*) (*a*) **er ging mir aus dem Wege,** (i) he got out of my way; (ii) he kept out of my way, he avoided me; **sie läßt ihn nicht aus den Augen,** she doesn't let him out of her sight; **es ist mir aus dem Gedächtnis entschwunden,** it has quite gone from my memory; (*b*) **aus der Mode,** out of fashion; **aus dem Gebrauch kommen,** to fall out of use. **4.** (*a*) made of; **ein Kleid aus Kunstseide,** a dress made of artificial silk; **der Krug ist aus feinstem Porzellan,** the jug is made of the finest china; **eine Statuette aus Ton,** a clay statuette; **eine Tasche aus Leder,** a leather bag; **sie nähte sich ein Kleid aus einer alten Gardine,** she made herself a dress (out) of an old curtain; **er machte ein Boot aus einem Baumstamm,** he made a boat from a tree-trunk; (*b*) **das beste aus einer Lage machen,** to make the best of a situation; **etwas aus seinem Leben machen,** to make something of one's life; **etwas aus sich machen,** (i) to make something of oneself; (ii) not to hide one's light under a bushel, to be proud of one's achievements; **aus dem Thema läßt sich etwas machen,** one could do something with that subject, something could be made of that subject; **aus dem Jungen werden wir nie einen Gelehrten machen können,** we shall never make a scholar of that boy, we shall never turn that boy into a scholar; (*c*) **aus diesem Plan wird nichts werden,** nothing will come of this plan, this plan won't come to anything; **aus dem Jungen wird nichts werden,** that boy will never make good, will never come to anything; *F:* will never get anywhere; **was ist aus ihm geworden?** what has become of him? **5.** for; from; because of; **aus diesem Grunde kann ich nicht mitkommen,** for this reason, that's why, I can't come with you; **aus Mangel an Geld mußte er zu Hause bleiben,** because he had no money he had to stay at home; **sie mußten das Bauprojekt aus Mangel an Geld aufgeben,** they had to give up the building programme for lack of money; **das hat er aus Unachtsamkeit getan,** he did that out of carelessness; **aus Liebe zu seiner Mutter,** out of, for, love of his mother; **so etwas tut man nur aus Freundschaft,** such things are done only out of friendship.

II. **aus,** *adv.* **1.** (*a*) (*space*) out; **aus und ein,** in and out; **die Leute gehen aus und ein,** the people go in and out; (*b*) **ich weiß nicht, wo aus noch ein, ich weiß weder aus noch ein,** I don't know what to do, which way to turn, I'm at my wits' end. **2.** (*a*) (*space*) **von . . . aus,** from . . . ; **von da aus fuhren wir nach Paris,** from there we went to Paris; **von hier aus kann man den Rhein sehen,** from here one can see the Rhine; **sie sahen den Unfall vom Fenster aus,** they saw the accident from the window, out of the window; (*b*) **er hat von Haus aus viel Geld,** he was born with a lot of money, he has a lot of money from his parents; **sie haben von Haus aus gute Manieren,** they were brought up to have good manners; **sie ist von Haus aus freigebig,** she is generous by nature; **er ist von Haus aus kein Physiker,** he's not a physicist by training; he wasn't originally, didn't start as, a physicist; **von Grund aus,** thoroughly; **er versteht sein Handwerk von Grund aus,** he knows his trade inside out; **er ist ein von Grund aus guter Kerl,** he is a thoroughly good fellow; **von mir aus,** (i) as far as I'm concerned; it's all the same to me, I don't mind, *F:* it's all right by me; I couldn't care less; (ii) on my own initiative, *F:* off my own bat; **er ist von sich aus zu mir gekommen,** he came to me of his own accord, on his own initiative, without being requested, *F:* off his own bat. **3. auf etwas** *acc.* **aus sein,** to be out to get sth., to be out for sth., to be after sth.; **auf Geld aus sein,** to be out for, to be after, money; **er ist auf Beförderung aus,** he is out for promotion, he is bent on getting promoted. **4.** out; away from home; **aus essen (gehen),** to eat out; **jeden Sonntag essen wir aus, gehen wir aus essen,** we eat out every Sunday. **5.** finished, over; **die Schule ist aus,** school is over, out; **wann ist das Theater aus?** what time does the play finish, is the play over? **alles ist aus,** all is lost; **mit mir ist's aus,** it's all over with me, *F:* I've had it, I'm finished; **es ist aus mit der Freude,** that's the end of our fun; *see also* **aussein. 6.** *subst. phr.* **das Aus und Ein,** coming and going. **7.** *Sp:* **ins Aus, im Aus,** *Fb:* out of play, *Golf:* out of bounds.

III. **aus.** (*ellipt. use, verbal or nominal element understood*) **1.** (*a*) **'Aus' — 'Ein'** (=**Ausfahrt — Einfahrt**), **'Out'—'In'; 'aus' — 'ein'** (=**ausatmen — einatmen**), **'in'—'out'; sie ist aus** (=**ausgegangen**), she is out, she has gone out; she is not in, not at home; (*b*) *Sp:* **aus!** out! **2. das Feuer ist aus** (=**ausgegangen**), the fire is out, has gone out; **Licht aus** (=**ausmachen**)! turn off, put out, the light! lights out! *El.E:* **'aus'** (=**ausgeschaltet**), 'out', 'out of circuit'; **'off'. 3. haben Sie das Buch aus** (=**ausgelesen**)? have you finished the book? **er hatte das Glas aus** (=**ausgetrunken**), he had emptied the glass; **das Lied ist aus** (=**ausgesungen**), the song is finished, ended.

aus-, *pref.* I. *vbl pref. sep.* (*cp. Note to* **ab-**) **1.** (*denoting removal from object or subject; motion from or out of sth. or s.o.*) (*Note: in older German the pref.* **aus-** *is frequently used in some of the meanings of this section where* **heraus-** *or* **hinaus-** *are now more usual*) (*a*) (*forming transitive verbs*) **ausbrechen,** to break (sth.) off; **aushauen,** to hew (sth.) out; (*with pers. or object affected in dat.*) **j-m einen Zahn ausschlagen,** to knock out one of s.o.'s teeth; **j-m die Augen ausstechen,** to put out s.o.'s eyes; **einem Faß den Boden ausstoßen,** to knock the bottom out of a barrel; (*b*) (*forming tr. verbs*) (*acc. may indicate either object removed or object from which sth. is removed*) **(Staub, eine Lade) ausbürsten,** to brush out (dust, a drawer); **(Wasser, einen Krug) ausschütten,** to pour out (water), to pour the water out of (a jug); **(Knoten, Haar) auskämmen,** to comb out (knots, hair); **(Gift, eine Wunde) aussaugen,** to suck out (poison); to suck (a wound) clean; (*c*) (*forming tr. verbs*) (*with sense of exclusion or expulsion*) **ausschließen,** to shut (s.o.) out; **aussetzen,** to expose (s.o., sth.); **ausräuchern,** to smoke out (bees, etc.); **ausbomben,** to bomb (s.o.) out; *A:* **j-n auswerfen,** to throw s.o. out; (*d*) (*forming tr. verbs*) (*with sense of selection*) **aussuchen,** to select (s.o., sth.); **auserlesen,** to choose, select, pick (sth., s.o.); **auslesen,** to select (fruit, etc.); **j-n auszeichnen,** to honour s.o., give s.o. an award; (*e*) (*forming tr. verbs*) (*with sense of allocating, apportioning or awarding sth.*) **auskegeln,** to play skittles for (sth.); **auslosen,** to draw lots for (sth.); (*f*) (*forming tr. verbs*) (*emission from subject*) **ausatmen,** to breathe out (carbon dioxide, etc.); **ausspeien,** to vomit (smoke, etc.); **ausstrahlen,** to radiate (heat, light, etc.); **ausrufen,** to shout (sth.); to exclaim; **ausposaunen, austrompeten,** to blazon (sth.) abroad; **ausströmen,** to pour (sth.) out, forth; (*g*) (*giving or sending away*) **ausgeben,** to hand (sth.) out; **aussenden, ausschicken,** to send (s.o.) out; (*h*) (*forming intr. verbs*) **ausgehen,** to go out; **ausschlüpfen,** to hatch (out); **aus etwas ausströmen,** to stream out from, of, sth.; (*i*) (*forming intr. verbs*) **ausbleiben,** to stay out; (*j*) (*forming intr. verbs*) (*deviation, evasion*) **ausbiegen, ausweichen,** to make way, to get out of the way; **ausgleiten, ausrutschen,** to slip, slide. **2.** (*a*) (*extension outwards*) (*forming intr. verbs*) **ausladen,** to project; **ausbiegen,** to curve (outwards); **ausbuchten,** to bulge (outwards); (*forming tr. verbs*) **ausbiegen,** to bend (sth.) (outwards); **ausbauschen,** to puff (sth.) out; (*b*) (*expansion*) (*forming tr. & refl. verbs*) **ausweiten,** to widen (sth.); **ausdehnen,** to stretch (sth.); **ausbreiten,** to spread (sth.) out; **sich ausweiten,** to extend, expand; **sich ausdehnen,** to stretch; to expand, dilate; **sich ausbreiten,** to spread. **3.** (*shaping of object in a form implied in the simplex*) **aushöhlen,** to hollow (sth.) out; **auszacken,** to jag (sth.); **ausbuchten,** to scallop (sth.); **ausfransen,** to fringe (sth.). **4.** (*obliteration of object*) **ausradieren,** to rub out (word, etc.); **auswetzen,** to whet out (notch); **auslöschen,** to put out (fire, etc.); **ausblasen,** to blow out (light, etc.); **ausstampfen,** to stamp out (fire). **5.** (*expressing deprivation or reversal of thg or state denoted in the simplex*) (*a*) **(seine Sachen, einen Koffer) auspacken,** to unpack (one's things, a case); **(Möbel, ein Zimmer) ausräumen,** to clear out (furniture, a room); **(Waren, einen Lastwagen) ausladen,** to unload (goods, a lorry); (*b*) **auskernen,** to stone (cherries, etc.); **ausbeinen,** to bone (meat, etc.); **ausfädeln,** to unthread (needle); **ausfleischen,** to flesh (hides). **6.** (*arrangement of objects*) (*forming tr. & intr. verbs*) **auslegen,** to display (wares, etc.); **ausliegen,** to be on display; **ausstellen,** to exhibit (works of art, etc.); **auspflanzen,** to plant out (seedlings, etc.). **7.** (*completion of action or state expressed in simplex*) (*a*) (*forming tr. verbs*) **auserzählen,** to tell (story) to the end, to finish telling (story); **austrinken,** to drink up (wine); to empty (glass); **ausrauchen,** to finish smoking (cigarette, etc.); **auskosten,** to taste (sth.) to the full; **(seine Wut) austoben,** to spend (one's rage); (*b*) (*forming intr. & refl. verbs*) **ausläuten,** to finish, cease, ringing; **auslärmen,** to stop making a noise; **ausharren,** to persevere; to hold out; to stand fast; **ausreifen,** to come to full maturity; **(sich) ausschlafen,** to have one's sleep out, to get enough sleep. **8.** (*denoting ending, resulting*) **(in eine Spitze) auslaufen,** to end in a point; (*of affair*) **schlecht ausgehen,** to end badly; **in etwas ausarten,** to degenerate into sth.; **sich zu etwas auswachsen,** to develop into sth. **9.** (*a*) (*provision of object with sth.*) (*from verbs*) **ausrüsten,** to equip (s.o., sth.); **ausstatten,** to provide, equip (s.o., sth.) (with sth.); (*from nouns*) **ausbuchsen,** to box (wheel); (*b*) (*treatment of interior, hollow object, etc., implying thoroughness*) **ausschmücken,** to decorate (room, etc.); **ausschmieren,** to grease (baking-tin, etc.); **ausmalen,** to paint (church, etc.) in fresco; **auskleiden,** to line (sth.); **(ein Gefäß) austrocknen,** to dry the inside of (a vessel); **ausfüllen,** to fill (sth.) in, up; (*c*) (*development of object*) **ausarbeiten,** to elaborate, fill in the details of (sth.); **ausschmücken,** to embellish sth.; **ausspinnen,** to elaborate, develop (sth.); (*d*) (*compensation*) **ausbalancieren,** to counterbalance (sth.); **ausgleichen,** to adjust (differences). **10.** (*intensifying meaning of simplex; forming tr. & intr. verbs*) **austrocknen, ausdörren,** to dry (sth.) up, to parch (sth.); **ausleeren,** to empty (sth.); **auspeitschen,** to whip, flog (s.o.); **ausschelten,** to scold (s.o.); **ausbacken,** to bake (bread, etc.) through; (*of bread, etc.*) to bake through.

II. **aus-, Aus-.** (*prefixed to nouns, adjs, advs*) **1.** (*forming verbal nouns & verbal adjs corresponding in meaning to the verbs from which they are derived*) (*a*) (*retaining verbal sense*) **Ausmarsch** *m*, marching out; **Auswanderung** *f*, emigration; **Ausführung** *f*, execution; **Auszahlung** *f*, payment; **ausfallend, ausfällig,** offensive, insulting; (*b*) **Ausgang** *m*, exit, way out; **Ausruf** *m*, shout; exclamation; **Auslese** *f*, selection; **Ausrüstung** *f*, equipment; gear, tackle; **Auswurf** *m*, ejected matter, expectoration; **Auspuff** *m*, exhaust. **2.** (*a*) (*implying outward motion*) **Ausweg** *m*, way out; **auswärts,** outwards; **auseinander,** apart; (*b*) (*position outside*) **Ausland** *n*, foreign countries; **auswärtig,** foreign; **Ausgebäude** *npl*, outhouses.

-aus, *suff.* out; **heraus, hinaus,** out (here, there); **geradeaus,** straight on, straight ahead; **jahraus, jahrein,** year in, year out.

ausapern, *v.i. sep.* (*haben*) *South G.Dial:* (*of snow on glacier, etc.*) to thaw.

ausarbeiten. I. *v.sep.* **1.** *v.tr.* to elaborate, to fill in the details of (plan, work of art, etc.); to elaborate (ornamentation, theory, etc.); to work (plan, etc.) out in detail; to finish (off), perfect, complete (piece of work, etc.); **an dieser Skulptur sind nur die Arme und Beine ausgearbeitet,** only the arms and legs of this piece of sculpture have been worked; **die Rückseite der Figur ist nicht ausgearbeitet,** the back of the figure has been left in the rough; **als er starb, war das Bild in der Anlage vollendet, aber er hat es nicht mehr selbst ausgearbeitet,** when he died

he had roughed out the composition of the picture, but not yet elaborated the details; **eine fein ausgearbeitete Schnitzerei,** a carving with delicate detail; **etwas bis ins kleinste a.,** to work sth. out to the last detail; **er hat seinen Aufsatz sorgfältig ausgearbeitet,** he has worked his essay out carefully; **der Autor hat seine Charaktere nicht gründlich genug ausgearbeitet,** the author has not developed his characters thoroughly enough. **2.** *v.i.* (*haben*) (*of wine*) to finish fermenting, working.

II. *vbl s.* **1. Ausarbeiten,** *n. in vbl senses.* **2. Ausarbeitung,** *f.* (*a*)=II. 1; *also:* elaboration (of work of art, plan, etc.); completion (of piece of work, etc.); development (of characters in drama, etc.); **an die A. eines Plans, eines Kunstwerks, usw., gehen,** to start elaborating a plan, to start work on the detail of a work of art, etc.; **er hatte den Plan seines Romans fertig und ging nun an die A.,** he had finished the plan of his novel and had now started writing it; (*b*) detail, finish (of work of art, etc.); (*c*) perfected, completed, elaborated, version (of essay, etc.).

ausarten, *v.i.* (*sein*) **1.** to deteriorate; to degenerate; **ein Zank, der in Rauferei ausartete,** a quarrel that degenerated into a brawl; **solche Versammlungen arten leicht aus,** such meetings are apt to get out of hand. **2.** *vbl s.* **Ausartung,** *f.* deterioration; degeneration; degeneracy.

ausästen, *v.tr. sep.* **1.** to prune (tree); to lop branches off (tree); to head (down) (tree). **2.** (*of tree*) **sich ausästen,** to put out branches, to branch forth; to ramify.

ausatmen. I. *v.sep.* **1.** *v.i.* (*haben*) to breathe out. **2.** *v.tr.* to breathe out (carbon dioxide, etc.); to exhale (vapour, smoke, etc.).

II. *vbl s.* **Ausatmen** *n.*, **Ausatmung** *f. in vbl senses; also:* exhalation (of vapour, etc.).

Ausatmungsluft, *f.* expired air.

ausätzen, *v.tr. sep.* **1.** to etch (pattern, etc.). **2.** (*a*) to etch off (blemish); (*b*) to cauterize (wound).

ausbacken, *v.sep.* (*conj. like* **backen**) **1.** *v.tr.* to bake (bread, etc.) through, thoroughly; **gut ausgebackenes Brot,** well-baked bread. **2.** *v.i.* (*sein*) (*a*) (*of bread, etc.*) to bake through; **der Kuchen, das Brot, ist nicht ausgebacken,** the cake is not properly cooked, the bread is not baked right through; (*b*) *F:* **nicht ganz ausgebacken,** (*of pers.*) not fully developed, immature, *F:* half-baked; (*of idea, scheme, etc.*) not properly thought out, *F:* half-baked. **3.** *v.i.* (*haben*) (*of pers.*) to finish baking.

ausbaden, *v.tr.* **1.** to bathe (wound, etc.). **2.** *F:* **etwas a.,** to pay for, to take the consequences for, sth., *U.S: F:* to hold the bag (for sth.); **er hat den Fehler gemacht, und wir müssen es a.,** he made the mistake and we have to take the consequences, have to pay for it, *F:* we have to carry the can; **das mußt du selber a.!** *F:* that's your funeral!

ausbaggern, *v.tr.* to dredge (river, harbour, etc.); to clear away (silt) (from river, etc.) by means of a dredge; to excavate (trench, ground on building site, etc.).

ausbähen, *v.tr. sep.* to bathe, foment (wound, etc.).

ausbaken, *v.tr.* *Nau:* to beacon, mark out (channel).

ausbalancieren, *v.tr. sep.* (*a*) to balance (sth.); to distribute the weight of (sth.) evenly; **ausbalanciert sein,** to be (well-)balanced; (*b*) **etwas (durch ein Gegengewicht) a.,** to counterbalance, to counterweight, sth.; **das eine wird durch das andere ausbalanciert,** the one is (counter)balanced by the other, the one (counter)balances the other; **ausbalancierter Schieber,** balanced slide-valve.

ausbaldowern, *v.tr. sep. F:* to find (sth.) out; to spy (sth.) out.

ausbalgen, ausbälgen, *v.tr.* to skin (animal).

Ausball, *m. Games:* ball that is out of bounds, that has crossed the touch-line *or* goal-line; *Fb:* ball out of play.

ausballotieren [ˈausbaloˑˌtiːrən], *v.tr. sep.* to exclude (s.o.) by adverse votes, to blackball (s.o.).

Ausbau, *m.* **-(e)s/.** **1.** (*a*) completion of the interior (of building, ship, etc.); **A. des Dachgeschosses,** (i) building of an attic with habitable rooms; (ii) conversion of the attic into habitable rooms; (*b*) *Civ.E: Min:* supporting *or* lining *or* timbering (of tunnel, shaft, etc.). **2.** (*a*) development, expansion, elaboration (of railway network, etc.); enlargement, extension, expansion (of university, hospital, etc.); (*b*) extension, expansion (of plans, policy, knowledge, etc.), elaboration (of plan, theory, etc.); strengthening, expansion, development (of trade relations, etc.); strengthening, consolidation (of position of power); *Mil:* consolidation (of position). **3.** *Wine-m:* seasoning(of wine). **4.** *pl.* **Ausbauten,** projecting parts (of building); attached outbuildings.

ausbauchen. I. *v.sep.* **1.** *v.tr.* (*a*) to cause (sth.) to bulge, to belly; (*b*) to dish (metal plate); (*c*) to curve, arch (sth.); (*d*) to widen (out) the opening of (vessel); to bell-mouth (vessel); to open out (pipe, etc.). **2. sich ausbauchen,** (*a*) (*of vessel*) to widen out at the mouth; (*b*) to become convex; to swell out; (*of sail*) to belly (out); *Dressm:* to flare out; *Arch:* (*of wall*) to bulge (out).

II. *vbl s.* **1. Ausbauchen,** *n. in vbl senses.* **2. Ausbauchung,** *f.* (*a*)=II. 1; (*b*) bulge, paunch (of vase, bottle, etc.); entasis (of column, etc.); bulge (of wall, etc.).

ausbauen. I. *v.tr. sep.* **1.** (*a*) to finish, complete, the interior of (house, etc.); to finish, complete (railway line, etc.); to convert (shed, etc.) into a habitable room *or* habitable rooms; **das Dachgeschoß, den Keller, a.,** to build a room *or* rooms into the loft, cellar; **ausgebaute Mansardenwohnung,** attic flat; **ein Zimmer im Dachgeschoß a.,** to build a room in the attic; (*b*) *Civ.E: Min:* to support *or* line *or* timber (walls of tunnel, shaft, etc.); (*c*) to enlarge (house, university, hospital, etc.); to develop, expand, elaborate (railway network, etc.); to develop (machine, etc.); to develop (institution, etc.); to extend, expand (policy, knowledge, etc.); to elaborate (theory); to cultivate (friendship, relations, etc.); to strengthen, expand, develop (trade relations, etc.); to strengthen, consolidate (position of power); *Mil:* to consolidate (position); **die Stelle ist jetzt nicht sehr gut, aber sie läßt sich a.,** the position, post, isn't a very good one now but it could be developed, but one could make something of it; *Rail:* **eine (eingleisige) Strecke zweigleisig a.,** to double an existing (single-line) track. **2.** to build (storey, etc.) so that it juts out; **3.** to remove (part of machine, etc.); to dismantle (machine). **4.** *Wine-m:* to season (wine); **ausgebauter Wein,** seasoned wine, wine ready for bottling.

II. *vbl s.* **Ausbauen** *n.*, **Ausbauung** *f.*=**Ausbau** 1, 2.

ausbaufähig, *a.* (*a*) (shed, attic, etc.) that can be converted into a habitable room *or* into habitable rooms; (*b*) (shaft walls, etc.) that can be supported, lined, timbered; (*c*) (house, etc.) capable of being enlarged; (railway network, etc.) that can be developed, expanded, elaborated; (machine, institution, trade relations, etc.) capable of development; (policy, etc.) capable of extension, expansion; (position) with good prospects.

ausbauschen, *v.tr. sep.* to puff (sth.) out, to swell (sth.) out; to cause (sth.) to bulge (out).

ausbedingen, *v.tr. sep.* (*p.t.* **bedang aus, bedingte aus;** *p.p.* **ausbedungen**). **1.** *A:* to except (sth., s.o.). **2. (sich** *dat.***) etwas a.,** to make sth. a condition, to stipulate for sth.; **sich** *dat.* **ein Recht a.,** to reserve a right; **sich** *dat.* **hundert Pfund als Belohnung a.,** to stipulate for a reward of one hundred pounds; **ich werde den Auftrag übernehmen, aber ich muß mir völlige Handlungsfreiheit a.,** I will undertake the commission on condition that I am given an entirely free hand; **ich bedinge mir das Recht aus, meine Arbeitszeit selbst zu bestimmen,** I reserve the right to fix my own hours of work; **sich** *dat.* **a., daß etwas getan wird,** to make it a condition, to stipulate, that sth. is done; **ich verlange nicht viel, aber ich bedinge mir aus, daß das wenige ordentlich getan wird,** I don't ask much, but I do expect, insist, that the little I do want is done well.

ausbehalten, *v.tr. sep.* (*strong*)=**ausbedingen.**

ausbeinen, *v.tr. sep.* **1.** to bone (meat, fish). **2.** to inlay (sth.) with bone.

ausbeißen, *v.sep.* (*strong*) **1.** *v.tr.* to bite (sth.) out; **sich** *dat.* **einen Zahn (an einem Kirschstein, usw.) a.,** to break a tooth (on a cherry-stone, etc.); *F:* **sich** *dat.* **die Zähne an etwas** *dat.* **a.,** to find sth. extremely difficult, *F:* to find sth. a tough nut to crack. **2.** *v.tr. A:* (*of animal*) to drive (animal) away by biting it; (*of pers.*) to frighten (s.o.) off; to oust (rival). **3.** *v.i.* (*haben*) *Geol: Min:* (*of seam, stratum, etc.*) to crop out, to outcrop.

ausbeizen, *v.tr. sep.* (*a*) to remove (stain, etc.) with caustic; (*b*) *Med:* to cauterize (wound) with caustic.

Ausbesserer, *m.* **-s/-,** mender, repairer, *U.S: F:* fixer.

ausbessern. I. *v.tr. sep.* **1.** to repair (building, boat, machine, clothes, shoes, etc.); to put (boat, machine, etc.) in repair; to mend (clothes, shoes, etc.); to darn (socks, clothes, etc.); to touch up (old picture, etc.); *U.S:* to fix (sth.) up. **2.** to correct (mistake, piece of work, etc.); to rectify (mistake), to put (mistake) right; to make up for (piece of stupidity, tactlessness, etc.).

II. *vbl s.* **1. Ausbessern,** *n. in vbl senses; also:* (*a*) repair; (*b*) correction; rectification. **2. Ausbesserung,** *f.* (*a*)=II. 1; (*b*) *pl.* **Ausbesserungen,** repairs; corrections.

Ausbesserungsarbeit, *f.* repair work; **Ausbesserungsarbeiten** *pl*, repairs.

ausbesserungsbedürftig, *a.* in need of repair; needing repair.

ausbesserungsfähig, *a.* reparable; repairable, mendable.

Ausbesserungswerk, *n. Rail:* repair shop.

Ausbesserungswerkstatt, *f. Ind:* repair shop, repair workshop.

Ausbeßrung, *f.*=**Ausbesserung,** *q.v. under* **ausbessern** II.

ausbeuchen, *v.tr. sep.*=**beuchen.**

ausbeugen, *v.sep.*=**ausbiegen.**

ausbeulen, *v.tr. sep.* **1.** to flatten out the bumps in (metal article, etc.); to remove bruises, dents, in (metal article, etc.); *Metalw:* to planish (metal). **2. sich ausbeulen,** (*of metal, etc.*) to become bumpy; to curve outwards; to bulge; (*of hat*) to become dented; to lose its shape; (*of trouser-legs, etc.*) to become baggy, to bag; **ausgebeult sein,** (*of metal, hat, etc.*) to be dented; (*of trouser-legs, etc.*) to bag, to be baggy.

Ausbeulwerkzeug, *n. Metalw:* dent-removing tool.

ausbeutbar, *a.* exploitable.

Ausbeute, *f.* (*a*) product, produce, yield; output (of mine); profit; returns; **A. liefern,** to be productive; to yield profits, to bring returns; (*b*) *F:* spoils, haul (from expedition, etc.); results (of research, etc.); **nach einem vollen Tag auf der Jagd bestand ihre ganze A. aus drei Hasen,** after a whole day's hunting all they brought back were, their entire bag consisted of, three hares; **das Kind kam vom Botanisieren nach Hause und zeigte stolz seine A.,** the child came home from a nature ramble and proudly displayed its spoils, what it had found; **wissenschaftliche A.,** scholarly results; scientific results; **des Gelehrten jahrelange Forschungen brachten ihm nur eine geringe A.,** the scholar's years of research brought, yielded, him small results, small profit; **die A. für die Wissenschaft steht in keinem Verhältnis zu dem Aufwand an Kraft und Zeit,** the scholarly *or* scientific results achieved bear no relation to the time and energy expended.

ausbeuteln, *v.tr. sep.* **1.** *Mill:* to bolt (flour). **2.** *F:* **j-n a.,** *F:* to fleece s.o., to clean s.o. out. **3.** (*of trouser-legs, etc.*) **sich ausbeuteln,** to bag, to be baggy, to become baggy; **ausgebeutelt sein,** to bag, to be baggy.

ausbeuten. I. *v.tr. sep.* (*a*) to make use of, to utilize (invention, etc.); to exploit, work (mine); to exploit (land, natural resources, etc.); (*b*) to take fullest advantage of, to make the most of, to make capital out of (success, popularity, etc.); to trade on (s.o.'s ignorance, etc.); to exploit, to take (unfair) advantage of (s.o.); to borrow from, to exploit, to make use of, *F:* to crib from (other people's work); **seine Arbeiter, Angestellten, usw., a.,** to exploit one's employees; **die Arbeiter a.,** to sweat labour.

II. *vbl s.* **Ausbeuten** *n.*, **Ausbeutung** *f. in vbl senses; also:* utilization (of invention, etc.); exploitation (of mine, land, natural resources, people, etc.).

Ausbeuter, *m.* **-s/-,** exploiter; **A. der Arbeiter,** sweater of labour.

Ausbeuterei, *f.* **-/-en,** exploitation (of people).

Ausbeutungstheorie, *f. Pol.Ec:* (doctrine of) surplus value.

ausbezahlen, *v.tr. sep.* to pay (salary, etc.) (in full); to pay (s.o.) off; **er hat mir mein Gehalt voll, ganz, ausbezahlt,** he paid me my salary in full; **er bekommt 500 Mark im Monat, davon 400 ausbezahlt,** he gets 500 marks a month, that is to say 400 net; **ich habe den Bäcker heute ausbezahlt,** I settled up with the baker today, I paid off the baker today; **einen Partner, einen**

Mitbesitzer, a., to buy out a partner, a part-owner.

ausbiegen, *v.sep.* (*strong*) **1.** *v.tr.* to bend (sth.) outwards. **2.** *v.i.* (*sein*) (*a*) (*of road, etc.*) to curve (outwards); (*b*) to make way, to get out of the way; **(vor) j-m, (vor) einem Fahrzeug, a.**, to make way for s.o., for a vehicle (to pass), to get out of s.o.'s, a vehicle's, way; to swerve to avoid s.o., a vehicle.

ausbieten, *v.sep.* (*strong*) **1.** *A:* (*a*) *v.i.* (*haben*) **j-m a.**, to challenge s.o.; (*b*) *v.i.* (*haben*) *& v.tr.* **j-m, j-n, a.**, to evict s.o. **2.** *v.tr.* to offer (wares, etc.) for sale.

ausbilden. I. *v.tr. sep.* **1.** to develop (ability, etc.). **2.** (*of thg*) **sich (zu etwas) ausbilden,** to develop (into sth.). **3.** to instruct (personnel, apprentices, troops, etc.); to train (troops, personnel, guide-dog, etc.); (*of higher educational institution*) to educate (s.o.); **j-n in etwas** *dat.* **a.**, to train s.o. in sth.; **j-n für etwas** *acc.* **a.**, to train s.o. for, to, sth.; **j-n als, zu, etwas a.**, to train s.o. to be sth.; **einen jungen Mann für die Marine a.**, to train a youth for the navy; **j-n im Gebrauch einer Waffe a.**, to train s.o. in the use of a weapon; **j-n für das Geschäftsleben a.**, to train s.o. to business; **ein in allen Richtungen gründlich ausgebildeter Geist,** a mind thoroughly educated, trained, in all fields; **ein vielseitig ausgebildeter Mensch,** a person educated in many different fields, with a thorough knowledge of many different subjects; **sich in einem Fach a. (lassen),** to train, to take a training, in a subject; **sich als Jurist, zum Juristen, a. (lassen),** to train as a lawyer, to undergo legal training; **sich in der Medizin a.**, to take a medical training; **sich im Gesang a. lassen, seine Stimme a. lassen,** to have one's voice trained; **sich musikalisch a. (lassen),** to learn music, to be trained in music.

II. *vbl s.* **1. Ausbilden,** *n. in vbl senses.* **2. Ausbildung,** *f.* (*a*)=II. 1; *also:* (i) development (of ability, etc.); (ii) instruction (of personnel, troops, etc.); education (of s.o.) (for sth.); (*b*) education; training; **eine gute, gründliche, A. haben,** to have a good, thorough, education, training; **vielseitige A.**, many-sided education; **seine A. als Jurist, als Arzt,** his training as a lawyer, as a doctor, his lawyer's doctor's, training; **körperliche A.**, physical training; **militärische A.**, military training; **eine A. in einem Beruf haben,** to be trained in a profession *or* trade; **die A. dauert drei Jahre,** the training takes three years.

Ausbilder, *m.* **-s/-**, instructor; trainer (of guide-dogs, etc.); *Mil:* instructor.

Ausbildling, *m.* **-(e)s/-e**, trainee.

Ausbildung, *f. see* **ausbilden** II. 2.

Ausbildungs-, *comb.fm.* training . . . ; instructional . . . ; . . . of training; . . . of instruction; **Ausbildungslager** *n*, training camp; **Ausbildungsmethoden** *fpl*, instructional methods, methods of instruction; *Mil:* training methods, methods of training; **Ausbildungsmöglichkeiten** *fpl*, training facilities, facilities for training.

Ausbildungseinheit, *f. Mil:* training unit.

Ausbildungsbeihilfe, *f.* education grant; training grant.

Ausbildungslehrgang, *m.* course of instruction; instructional course; course of training; *Mil: etc:* training course.

Ausbildungsleiter, *m. Ind: etc:* director *or* supervisor of training; head of a, the, training organization; *Mil:* officer *or* non-commissioned officer in charge of training.

Ausbildungsoffizier, *m. Mil:* (officer-)instructor.

ausbinden, *v.tr. sep.* (*strong*) *Print:* to tie up (page).

Ausbiß, *m. Geol: Min:* outcrop.

ausbitten, *v.tr. sep.* (*strong*) **1. sich** *dat.* **etwas a.**, (*a*) to request sth., to ask, beg, for sth.; to demand sth.; to insist on sth.; **sich** *dat.* **Bedenkzeit a.**, to ask for time to think it over; **ich bitte mir Ruhe aus! ich möchte mir Ruhe a.!** (can I have) silence, please! **ich muß mir völliges Schweigen a.**, I demand complete silence, I must insist on complete silence; **ihr dürft gerne baden gehen, aber ich bitte mir aus, ich muß mir a., daß ihr nicht zu weit hinausschwimmt,** you may go bathing but I must insist that you don't swim too far out; (*b*) to ask for sth.; **sich** *dat.* **von j-m etwas a.**, to ask s.o. to give, lend, one sth.; **ich möchte mir das Buch gerne auf zwei Wochen von Ihnen a.**, I wonder if you would lend me, if I might borrow, the book for a fortnight; **sie baten sich einen seiner Knechte zum Führer aus,** they asked for one of his servants as a guide. **2.** to ask (s.o.) out.

Ausblasehahn, *m. Mch:* blow-off gear; pet-cock.

ausblasen, *v.tr. sep.* (*strong*) **1.** to blow out, to puff out (smoke, etc.); *Mch:* **Dampf a.**, to let off, to blow off, steam. **2.** (*a*) **etwas (aus etwas) a.**, to blow sth. out (of sth.); (*b*) to clear (pipe, etc.) by blowing, to blow (pipe, etc.), to blow the obstruction from (pipe, etc.); to blow out (cylinder); *Metall:* to draw, to blow out (blast furnace); **ein Ei a.**, to blow an egg. **3.** to blow out, to extinguish (candle, etc.); *Lit:* **j-m das Lebenslicht a.**, to kill s.o. **4.** *A:* to publish, proclaim (news, etc.) by trumpet; to blazon (sth.) abroad. **5.** *v.i.* (*sein*) *Min:* (*of shot*) to blow out.

Ausbläser, *m. Artil:* weak charge; *Min:* blow, blown-out shot.

Ausblaserohr, *n. Mch:* exhaust-pipe.

Ausblaseventil, *n. Mch:* blow-off valve, pet-cock; blow-down valve.

ausbleiben. I. *v.i. sep.* (*strong*) (*sein*) (*a*) (*of pers.*) (i) to stay out; (ii) to stay away; to fail to appear; **wie lange ist er gestern ausgeblieben?** how long did he stay out yesterday? **die ganze Nacht a.**, to stay out all night; **wir bleiben nicht lange aus,** we shan't be gone, away, we shan't stay out, long; **da sie so lange ausblieb, fürchteten wir, sie sei verunglückt,** (i) as she didn't come, appear, turn up, (ii) as she didn't return, for such a long time, we were afraid she had had an accident; **er besuchte sie immer seltener, und schließlich blieb er ganz aus,** he visited her less and less till at last he stayed away altogether; (*b*) (*of thg*) to fail to appear; (*of breathing, pulse, etc.*) to stop, to cease; (*of menstrual period, etc.*) not to occur; (*of help, etc.*) not to be forthcoming; **gestern ist die Post ausgeblieben,** there was no post, no post came, yesterday; **die Überschwemmungen sind in diesem Jahr ausgeblieben,** the floods haven't come this year, there have been no floods this year; **die Anfälle sind bei ihr seit zwei Monaten ausgeblieben,** she has had no fits for two months; **er wurde mit dem neuen Mittel behandelt, aber der erwartete Erfolg, die erwartete Wirkung, blieb aus,** he was treated with the new drug, but it did not have the expected results; **er hat sich lange um diese Sache bemüht, aber der Erfolg blieb aus, und der Erfolg blieb auch nicht aus,** he had worked on it for a long time, but he was denied success, and success was not denied him; **das erhoffte Interesse an dem Unternehmen blieb leider aus,** the hoped-for interest in the undertaking was unfortunately not forthcoming; **die Nachrichten wurden immer spärlicher, bis sie schließlich ganz ausblieben,** news became scarcer and scarcer till at last there was none at all; (*c*) (*of punishment, revenge, success, etc.*) **nicht a. können,** to be inevitable; **die Wirkung konnte nicht a.**, there could only be one result; **es kann nicht a., daß . . .**, it is inevitable that . . . ; **es konnte nicht a., daß wir etwas vergaßen,** we couldn't fail to forget something, it was inevitable that we should forget something.

II. *vbl s.* **Ausbleiben,** *n. in vbl senses; also:* failure to appear; non-arrival, non-appearance; absence; **ihr langes A. hat uns Sorgen gemacht,** the fact that she was (gone, away, out) so long caused us anxiety; **man beunruhigte sich über sein A.**, (i) alarm was felt at his failure to appear again, because he did not return, (ii) alarm was felt at his absence, at his failure to appear; **das A. der Post,** the fact that there is, was, no post; **über das A. der Post, von Nachrichten, braucht man sich keine Gedanken zu machen,** there is no need to get worried because there is no post, no news; **das A. der Überschwemmungen,** the absence of the customary floods; **A. der Atmung, des Pulses,** cessation of breathing, failure of the pulse; **A. des Fiebers, der Periode,** absence of fever, of the period.

ausbleichen, *v.sep.* **1.** *v.tr.* (*a*) to bleach (sth.); (*of sun, etc.*) to fade (material, etc.); **von der Sonne ausgebleicht,** faded by the sun; (*b*) to wipe out, efface (memories, etc.). **2.** *v.i.* (*weak & strong, p.p. usu.* **ausgeblichen**) (*sein*) to fade; to bleach.

Ausbleichverfahren, *n. Phot:* bleaching-out process.

Ausblick, *m.* (*a*) view; outlook, prospect; **ein Haus mit herrlichem A.**, a house with a superb view, outlook, prospect; **das Haus hat einen wunderschönen A. auf den Hafen,** the house has a wonderful view of, over, a wonderful outlook over, the harbour; **von diesem Zimmer hat man einen A. auf den Park, dieses Zimmer gewährt einen A. auf den Park,** from this room one has a view of the park, this room overlooks the park; **von hier aus hat man einen schönen A. auf das Schloß, in das Tal,** (from) here you have a good view of the castle, a good view of, over, the valley; (*b*) **der A. in die Zukunft ist trübe,** the prospects are, the outlook is, the future looks, gloomy.

ausblicken, *v.i. sep.* (*haben*) **nach j-m, etwas, a.**, to look out, to be on the look-out, for s.o., sth.

ausblitzen, *v.impers. sep.* **es hat ausgeblitzt,** the lightning has finished.

ausblühen, *v.i. sep.* (*haben*) **1.** (*of flowers*) to fade, wither. **2.** *Ch:* to effloresce; **Ausblühung** *f*, efflorescence; **ausblühend,** efflorescent.

ausbluten, *v.sep.* **1.** *v.i.* (*haben*) (*a*) (*of wound, etc.*) to stop bleeding; (*b*) to lose all one's blood; **ein geschlachtetes Tier a. lassen,** to drain the blood from a carcass; (*c*) (*of dye, of dyed material*) to bleed. **2.** *v.tr. Poet:* **sein Leben a.**, (i) to die; (ii) to be gradually drained of one's energy.

ausbogen, *v.tr. sep.* to cut (sth.) out in curves, bays; to channel (sth.); *see also* **ausgebogt.**

ausbohlen, *v.tr. sep.* to plank, board over (deck, floor, etc.).

ausbohren, *v.tr. sep.* **1.** to bore (out) (cylinder, etc.); to drill (tooth); to bore, drill (hole). **2. etwas (aus etwas) a.**, to bore sth. out (of sth.); **j-m die Augen a.**, to gouge out s.o.'s eyes.

Ausbohrmaschine, *f. Mec.E:* boring-machine (for cylinders, etc.).

ausbojen, *v.tr. sep. Nau:* to buoy (channel).

ausbomben, *v.tr. sep.* to bomb (people, building) out; **wir sind zweimal ausgebombt worden,** we were bombed out twice.

ausbooten, *v.tr. sep.* (*a*) to take off (passengers, etc.) (from ship) in boats; (*b*) *F:* **j-n a.**, to get rid of s.o., *F:* to chuck s.o. out; to get s.o. chucked out.

ausborgen, *v.tr. sep.* **1.** to lend (sth.). **2. (sich** *dat.***) etwas a.**, to borrow sth.

ausbracken, *v.tr. sep. Husb.:* to cull (inferior animals) (from herd, flock, etc.).

ausbraten, *v.sep.* (*strong*) **1.** *v.tr.* (*a*) to roast *or* fry (meat) thoroughly; (*b*) **Speck, usw., a.**, to fry the fat out of bacon, etc. **2.** *v.i.* (*sein*) (*a*) (*of meat, etc.*) to roast *or* fry through; (*b*) (*of fat*) to be fried out.

ausbrausen, *v.i. sep.* (*haben*) *&* **sich ausbrausen,** (*of storm, gale*) to spend itself, to abate, to subside.

ausbrechen, *v. sep.* (*strong*) I. *v.tr.* **1.** (*a*) to break (sth.) off; **Äste (aus einem Baum) a.**, to lop branches (off a tree); **sich** *dat.* **einen Zahn a.**, to knock a tooth out; **j-m einen Zahn a.**, to knock out one of s.o.'s teeth; **er hat sich einen Zahn am Kirschstein ausgebrochen,** he broke a tooth on the cherry-stone; (*b*) to bore out (passage, hollow, etc.); to drive (gallery); (*c*) *Nau:* **den Anker a.**, to heave up, trip, weigh, the anchor. **2. das Essen wieder a.**, to bring up one's food.

II. **ausbrechen,** *v.i.* (*sein*) **1.** (*a*) (*of volcano, anger, passion, etc.*) to erupt; (*of fire, war, epidemic, etc.*) to break out; (*of storm*) to break; **plötzlich ausbrechende Wut,** sudden (outbreak of) fury; **der Schweiß brach ihm aus,** he broke out into a sweat; **(der) Schweiß brach auf seiner Stirn aus,** sweat broke out on his brow; (*b*) (*of pers.*) **in Schweiß a.**, to break out into a sweat; **in Lachen, Gelächter, a.**, to break (out) into a laugh, to burst out laughing; **in lautes Lachen, Gelächter, a.**, to burst into a loud laugh; **in Tränen, Weinen, a.**, to burst, break, into tears, to burst out crying; **in lautes Schluchzen a.**, to break (out) into loud sobs, into loud sobbing; **in Klagen a.**, to break into lamentation, to start lamenting; **in Wut a.**, to fly into a rage, *F:* explode with fury; **in Lobpreisungen a.**, to break into praises; **in Drohungen a.**, to burst out into threats; **in Beschimpfungen a.**, to break out into abuse, to start hurling abuse; **in (lautes) Geschrei a.**, to start shouting (loudly); **gegen j-n a.**, to attack, to revile, s.o.; **'ich hasse dich!' brach sie plötzlich aus,** 'I hate you!' she broke out. **2.** (*a*) (*of pers., animal, etc.*) to break out (of prison, cage, etc.); to escape (from prison, cage, etc.); (*of pers.*) to break away (from traditions, etc.); **aus dem Gefängnis a.**, to break out of prison, to break gaol; **zwei Gefangene sind gestern ausgebrochen,** two prisoners escaped yesterday; **wenn du das Kind zu streng behandelst, wird es eines Tages a.**, the child will cut loose some day if you treat it too severely; (*b*) *Equit:* (*of horse*) **(vor einer Hürde) a.**, to run out (at a fence).

III. *vbl s.* **Ausbrechen,** *n. in vbl senses; also:* (*a*) eruption (of volcano, anger, passion, etc.); outbreak (of volcano, anger, fire, war, epidemic, etc.); outburst (of laughter, anger, etc.); (*b*) **A.**

aus dem Gefängnis, prison-breaking; (c) *Equit:* refusal (of horse) (at a fence). *Cp.* **Ausbruch.**

ausbreiten, *v.tr. sep.* **1.** (a) to spread (sth.) (out); to unfold, open out (handkerchief, newspaper, etc.); to spread (out), to stretch (out) (wings); to spread out, stretch out (one's arms, etc.); *A:* to stretch out (one's hands, etc.) (towards s.o., sth.); to spread (sails); **(Adler, usw.) mit ausgebreiteten Flügeln,** (eagle, etc.) with outstretched wings, *Her:* (eagle, etc.) displayed; **die Bäume breiten ihre Äste aus,** the trees spread (out) their branches; **ein Tuch (über etwas) a.,** to spread a cloth (over sth.); **Papiere auf dem Tisch a.,** to spread papers out on the table; **seine Waren a.,** to display, set out, one's wares, to spread out one's goods for sale; **Heu a.,** to spread out hay; **die Wäsche auf dem Rasen a.,** to spread out the linen on the grass; (b) to flatten (metal). **2. sich ausbreiten,** (a) to spread, to extend, to stretch; **die Ebene breitete sich vor uns aus,** the plain stretched, spread, lay spread out, before us; (b) (of town, etc.) to grow, to spread; *F:* (of pers.) to spread oneself (out), to take up (a lot of) room; **breite dich mit deinen Büchern nicht so aus!** don't take up so much room with your books! (c) (of disease, fire, etc.) to spread; *Ph:* (of light, sound, etc.) to be propagated. **3.** to spread (rumours, fame, etc.); to diffuse (warmth, light, etc.).

Ausbreiteprobe, *f. Metalw:* hammering test.

Ausbreiter, *m.* **-s/-, Ausbreitmaschine,** *f. Tex:* spreading-, tentering-machine, tenter.

ausbrennen. I. *v.sep.* (conj. like **brennen**) **1.** *v.tr.* (a) **j-m die Augen a.,** (of pers., acid, etc.) to burn s.o.'s eyes out; (b) (of pers., acid, etc.) to burn (sth.) out; *Med:* to cauterize, sear (wound, etc.); (c) (of sun, etc.) to burn, parch, scorch (earth, etc.); **die Kehle war ihm, seine Kehle war, wie ausgebrannt,** his throat was parched. **2.** *v.i.* (sein) (a) (of fire, etc.) to burn (itself) out, to go out; **die Kerze ist ausgebrannt,** the candle has burned itself out, is spent; *El:* **die Birne ist ausgebrannt,** the bulb is spent; (b) (of building, etc.) to be burnt out, gutted; **zwei Räume waren (völlig) ausgebrannt,** two rooms were (completely) burnt out, were (completely) gutted; *F:* **wir sind zweimal ausgebrannt,** our house has been burnt out twice, we have been burnt out twice. **II.** *vbl s.* **Ausbrennen,** *n. in vbl senses; also:* cauterization (of wound).

ausbringen. I. *v.tr. sep.* (conj. like **bringen**) **1.** (a) *Nau:* to hoist (boat) out; to lay out, run out (cable, anchor); (b) to extract (metal) (from ore); (c) (of hen, etc.) to hatch out (chickens, etc.); (d) to get (sth.) out, off; (e) to divulge (secret), to spread (rumour), to break (news). **2.** *Print:* to drive out (matter), to drive (matter) over; *abs.* to drive out. **3. einen Trinkspruch a.,** to propose a toast; **ein Hoch, ein dreifaches Hoch, auf j-n a.,** to cheer s.o., to give three cheers for s.o.; **j-s Gesundheit a.,** to drink s.o.'s health. **4.** *F:* **sich nicht a. können vor Freude, Glück,** to be beside oneself with joy, happiness; **man kann sich hier nicht a. vor Lärm, vor Rauch,** the noise, smoke, in this place is unbearable. **II.** *vbl s.* **Ausbringen,** *n. in vbl senses; also:* (a) extraction (of metal) (from ore); (b) output; **das A. an Koks,** the output of coke.

Ausbruch, *m.* **1.** boring out (of passage, hollow, etc.); driving (of gallery, etc.). **2.** breaking out (of prison, cage, etc.), escape (from prison, cage, etc.); break (from prison); break-away (from tradition, etc.); **einen A. aus dem Gefängnis machen,** to make a break from, to break out of, to escape from, prison; **wir hatten drei Ausbrüche im vorigen Jahr,** we had three escapes last year. **3.** eruption (of volcano, anger, passion, etc.); outbreak (of volcano, fire, war, epidemic, anger, etc.); breaking (of storm); breaking out (of sweat); outburst (of laughter, joy, anger, etc.); burst (of laughter, anger, tears); **vor, bei, A. des Krieges,** before, at, the outbreak of war; **zum A. kommen,** (of disease) to develop, to become apparent; (of storm) to break, to burst forth; (of feelings) to burst forth; (of passions) to break out, to erupt; (of fury) to break out, to break loose; (of war, etc.) to break out; **das Gewitter kam nicht zum A.,** the storm did not break; **eine Sache nicht zum A. kommen lassen,** to prevent a matter from coming to a head; **nach diesem A. schwieg sie den ganzen Abend,** after this outburst she was silent for the rest of the evening. **4.** (a) wine from grapes already ripe enough to ooze juice; (b) virgin oil; (c) virgin honey.

Ausbruchsbeben, *n. Geol:* volcanic earthquake.

Ausbruchwein, *m.* wine from grapes already ripe enough to ooze juice.

ausbrühen, *v.tr. sep.* to scald (pan, etc.).

ausbrüllen, *v.sep.* **1.** *v.tr.* to roar, bellow (sth.) out. **2.** *v.i.* (haben) to stop roaring, bellowing.

ausbrunften, *v.i. sep.* (haben) (of deer, etc.) to cease rutting.

ausbrüten, *v.tr. sep.* to hatch out, to incubate (eggs), to hatch (chickens, etc.); **ausgebrütet werden,** to hatch (out); *F:* **etwas a.,** to be making schemes; **sie brüten wohl etwas aus,** I think they are hatching something up; **Ausbrüten** *n,* **Ausbrütung** *f,* hatching out, incubation (of eggs), hatching (of chickens); *Husb:* **künstliche Ausbrütung,** artificial incubation.

ausbuchsen, *v.tr. sep.Tchn:* to bush; to box (wheel).

ausbuchten. I. *v.sep.* **1.** *v.tr.* (i) to cut curves in (the edge of sth.), to scallop (sth.); (ii) to make indentations, an indentation, in (sth.); **ausgebuchtete Küste,** indented coast-line. **2.** *v.i.* (sein) to curve, bulge, outwards; **ausbuchtend,** curved; projecting. **II.** *vbl s.* **1. Ausbuchten,** *n. in vbl senses.* **2. Ausbuchtung,** *f.* (a)=II. 1; (b) indentation (of coast-line, etc.); (c) (curved) projection, projecting part; bay; (outward) curve.

ausbuddeln, *v.tr. sep. F:* to dig (sth.) up; to dig (sth., s.o.) out.

ausbügeln, *v.tr. sep.* to iron out (creases) (in a frock, etc.), to iron (out) (creased clothes, etc.); to press (down) (seam).

Ausbund, *m.* **ein (wahrer) A. von . . . . sein,** (a) (to be the very best . . .) to be a paragon, prodigy, model, *F:* pattern, of . . . ; **ein A. von Gelehrsamkeit, von Klugheit,** a prodigy of learning, of intelligence; **ein A. von Schönheit und Tugend,** a paragon, a model, of beauty and virtue; (b) (to be the very worst . . .) to be a monster of . . . , to be . . . personified; **ein A. von Grausamkeit, von Undankbarkeit,** a monster of cruelty, of ingratitude; **ein A. von Geiz sein,** to be avarice personified; **ein A. von Frechheit,** impudence personified; **ein A. von Dummheit,** a complete (and utter), an arrant, fool.

ausbündig, *a.* exceptional; excellent.

Ausbürger, *m. Hist:* citizen domiciled outside a town but retaining citizen's rights.

ausbürgern, *v.tr. sep.* to deprive (s.o.) of citizenship; to expatriate (s.o.); **Ausbürgerung** *f,* expatriation.

ausbürsten, *v.tr. sep.* (a) to brush (hair, coat, etc.); to give (hair, coat, etc.) a brushing; to brush out (hair); to brush out (container, etc.); (b) to brush out (dust, etc.).

ausbüxen, *v.i. sep.* (sein) *North G. Dial:* to make off, to slip away.

ausdampfen, *v.sep.* **1.** *v.tr.* to emit (sth.) as steam. **2.** *v.i.* (sein) to be emitted as steam; **die Feuchtigkeit, die aus den Wiesen ausdampfte,** the moisture which rose as vapour, like steam, from the meadows. **3.** *v.i.* (haben) (a) to steam; (b) to finish steaming. **4.** *v.i.* (sein) (of train, ship, etc.) to steam out (of station, port, etc.).

Ausdauer, *f.* tenacity, perseverance; endurance, staying power; **mit A. arbeiten,** to work perseveringly; **keine A. haben,** to have no staying power.

ausdauern. I. *v.sep.* **1.** *v.i.* (haben) to persevere; to hold out; *Rac:* (of horse) to stay. **2.** *v.tr.* to bear, to endure (sth.); to put up with (sth.). **II.** *pr.p. & a.* **ausdauernd,** *in vbl senses, esp.* (a) tenacious, persevering; **a. bei der Arbeit,** persevering in one's work; *Rac:* **ein ausdauerndes Pferd,** a horse with staying-power, a (good) stayer; (b) *Bot:* perennial.

ausdehnbar, *a.* (town, etc.) capable of expansion, extension, enlargement; (of material, etc.) elastic; extensible; (of metals, etc.) tensile, ductile; (of solids, gases, etc.) expansible, dilatable.

Ausdehnbarkeit, *f.* elasticity (of material, etc.); extensibility (of material, etc.); tensility, ductility (of metals, etc.); expansibility, dilatability (of solids, gases, etc.).

ausdehnen. I. *v.tr. sep.* **1.** (a) to stretch (sth.); to extend (sth.); to expand, dilate (sth.); **Gummiband a.,** to stretch elastic; **Wärme dehnt die Körper, die Gase, aus,** heat expands, dilates, solids, gases; (b) **etwas auf etwas** *acc.* **a.,** to extend sth. to sth.; **ich würde gern meine Ferien bis in den August a.,** I should like to extend my holidays into August; **seine Reise bis nach X a.,** to extend one's journey to X; **Handelsbeziehungen, den Außenhandel, a.,** to extend, expand, trade relations, one's foreign trade; **seinen Außenhandel auf Südamerika a.,** to extend one's foreign trade to South America; **seine Interessen auf etwas a.,** to extend one's

interest to (include) sth.; **er hat seine Freundschaft mit dem Vater auf den Sohn ausgedehnt,** he has extended the friendship he felt for the father to include the son. **2. sich ausdehnen,** to stretch; to expand, to dilate; to extend; (a) **die Wolljacke hat sich beim Waschen ausgedehnt,** the cardigan stretched in the wash; **die Wärme verursacht, daß die Körper sich ausdehnen,** heat causes solids to expand; (b) **die Stadt hat sich in den letzten Jahren sehr ausgedehnt,** the town has spread, grown, greatly during the last few years; **die Sitzung dehnte sich bis zwei Uhr morgens aus,** the session lasted till two o'clock in the morning; **unser Außenhandel hat sich weiter ausgedehnt, hat sich auf Südamerika ausgedehnt,** our foreign trade has expanded still more, has extended to South America; (c) **die Stadt dehnt sich sehr weit aus,** the town covers a wide area; **ein Besitz, der sich bis zum Meer ausdehnt,** an estate that extends, stretches, to the sea; **unser Außenhandel dehnt sich über ein großes Gebiet aus,** our foreign trade is very extensive. **II.** *vbl s.* **1. Ausdehnen,** *n. in vbl senses.* **2. Ausdehnung,** *f.* (a)=II. 1; (b) expansion (of solid, gas, etc.); dilation, dilatation (of solid, gas, etc.); extension; **lineare A.,** linear expansion (cp. (d)); (c) extent; range, compass; size; **an A. gewinnen,** to expand, to extend; to increase in size; **eine Stadt von großer A.,** an extensive town; (d) dimension; **der Raum hat drei Ausdehnungen,** space has three dimensions; **lineare A.,** linear dimension. **III.** *p.p. & a.* **ausgedehnt,** *in vbl senses; esp.* extensive (woods, practice, trade, etc.); prolonged (conversation, etc.); **ausgedehnte Besitzungen,** extensive property; **ausgedehnte Kenntnisse,** extensive knowledge.

ausdehnungsfähig, *a.* (of material, muscles, etc.) elastic; (of material, etc.) extensible, extensile; (of metals, etc.) tensile, ductile; (of solids, gases, etc.) expansible, expansive, dilatable; (town, etc.) capable of expansion, extension, enlargement.

Ausdehnungsfähigkeit, *f.* elasticity (of material, muscles, etc.); extensibility (of material, etc.); tensility, ductility (of metals, etc.); expansibility, expansiveness, dilatability (of solids, gases, etc.).

Ausdehnungsfuge, *f. Civ. E:* expansion joint.

Ausdehnungshub, *m. Mch: I.C.E:* power-stroke.

Ausdehnungskoeffizient, *m. Ph:* coefficient of expansion.

Ausdehnungskraft, *f.* expansive force.

Ausdehnungsrohr, *n. Mec.E:* expansion pipe.

Ausdehnungsstoß, *m.* expansion joint.

Ausdehnungsvermögen, *n.* elasticity; expansibility; expansiveness.

Ausdehnungszahl, *f. Ph:* coefficient of expansion.

ausdenkbar, *a.* imaginable, conceivable; **die Folgen sind nicht a.,** it is impossible to imagine the consequences; **es ist schwer a., was er in diesem Falle tun soll,** it is difficult to imagine what he should do in this case.

ausdenken, *v.tr. sep.* (conj. like **denken**) (a) to think (sth.) out, to work (sth.) out, to plan (sth.) (carefully, in detail); to contrive, devise (sth.); to imagine (sth.) in detail, to have a clear mental picture of (sth.); (sich *dat.*) **einen Plan a.,** to contrive, devise, think out, work out, a plan; **er hat sich etwas Gescheites ausgedacht,** he has thought out something clever, had a clever idea; **den Plan haben sie nur halb ausgedacht,** they have only half thought out, worked out, the plan; **er hat seine Rede schon in allen Einzelheiten ausgedacht,** he has already thought out, worked out, planned, all the details of his speech; **ich kann mir gar nicht a., was ich ihr zu Weihnachten schenken soll,** I just can't think what to give her for Christmas; **die Folgen sind, die Wirkung ist, nicht auszudenken,** the consequences are, the effect is, unimaginable; **es läßt sich gar nicht a., was hätte geschehen können,** what might have happened doesn't bear thinking of; (b) (sich *dat.*) **etwas a.,** to invent sth.; **das hat sie sich bloß ausgedacht,** she just invented, imagined, it; **jeder mußte sich eine Geschichte a.,** each one had to make up, invent, a story; **an dieser Sache ist kein wahres Wort, er hat sich die ganze Geschichte nur ausgedacht,** there's not a word of truth in this whole business, he invented, fabricated, the whole story.

ausdeuten. I. *v.tr. sep.* to interpret, to explain (sth.); (a) **er hat mir den Traum ausgedeutet,** he interpreted the dream for me; **können Sie mir ihr Benehmen a.?** can you explain the meaning of her behaviour, what her behaviour

means? **etwas falsch a.**, to misinterpret sth.; to misconstrue sth., to put a false construction on sth.; (*b*) **man hat ihm diesen Schritt als eine Feigheit ausgedeutet,** his action was interpreted as being a piece of cowardice; **j-m etwas übel a.**, to put a bad construction on s.o.'s actions *or* words; **j-m etwas falsch a.**, to misinterpret, to misconstrue, s.o.'s actions *or* words; **alles, was er tut, deutet man ihm ungünstig aus,** an unfavourable construction is put on everything he does; **sie hat es ihm übel ausgedeutet, daß er so lange ausblieb,** she put a bad construction on his staying out so long.

II. *vbl s.* 1. **Ausdeuten** *n. in vbl senses.* 2. **Ausdeutung,** *f.* (*a*)=II. 1; (*b*) interpretation, explanation (of dreams, etc.); **eine A. geben,** to give an interpretation, explanation; **eine falsche A.,** a misinterpretation; a misconstruction.

ausdichten, *v.tr. sep.* to think out, to invent (sth.).

ausdielen, *v.tr. sep.* to floor (room, etc.).

ausdienen, *v.i. sep.* (*haben*) (*a*) (*of pers.*) to finish, complete, one's (period of) service, to do one's time; **ein ausgedienter Soldat, Beamter,** a time-expired soldier, a retired civil servant; (*b*) (*of clothing, etc.*) **ausgedient haben,** to be worn out, *F:* to have had its day, to have done its time.

ausdingen, *v.tr. sep.* (*conj. like* **dingen**) 1. to hire (sth.) out. 2.=**ausbedingen.**

ausdobben, *v.tr. sep.* to clean out (ditch, etc.), to clean mud, etc., out of (ditch, etc.).

ausdocken, *v.tr. sep.* to undock (ship).

ausdonnern, *v.i. sep.* (*haben*) to stop thundering.

ausdornen, *v.tr. sep.* to drift (rivet-holes).

ausdorren, *v.i. sep.* (*sein*) to dry up; (*of soil, etc.*) to become parched; (*of plants*) to wither.

ausdörren, *v.tr. sep.* to dry (sth.) up, to parch (sth.); to wither (sth.); **die Hitze hat alles ausgedörrt,** the heat has dried everything up, has parched everything; **seine Kehle war (wie) ausgedörrt,** his throat was parched; **mein Gehirn war (wie) ausgedörrt,** my mind was a complete blank.

ausdrechseln, *v.tr. sep.* (*a*) to hollow (sth.) out on the lathe; (*b*) to work (sth.) (finely) on the lathe; (*c*) *F:* to polish (speech, literary work, etc.).

ausdrehen, *v.tr. sep.* 1. to twist (electric bulb, etc.) out (of its socket). 2. to turn, swing (sth.) outwards. 3. to turn off (gas, wireless, etc.); to turn out (light); to switch off (electric light); **dreh aus!** turn it off! switch (it) off! 4. (*a*)=**ausdrechseln;** (*b*) to bore (out) (cylinder, etc.).

ausdreschen, *v.tr. sep.* (*strong*) (*a*) to thresh (corn); (*b*) to thresh (corn) out; (*c*) *F:* to thrash (s.o.).

Ausdruck, *m.* -(e)s/⸚e. I. 1. expression; **etwas** *dat.* **A. geben, verleihen, etwas zum A. bringen,** to express sth.; to give expression, utterance, to one's feelings, etc.; to voice one's indignation, etc.; **seinem Dank A. geben, verleihen, seinen Dank zum A. bringen,** to give expression to, to express, one's gratitude; **seine Meinung zum A. bringen,** to express one's opinion; to express oneself; **die allgemeine Meinung zum A. bringen,** to voice, to give voice to, the general opinion; **seiner Liebe leidenschaftlichen A. verleihen,** to give passionate expression to one's love, to express one's love in passionate terms; **ich weiß nicht, wie ich meine Gefühle ihm gegenüber zum A. bringen soll,** I don't know how to express what I feel about him; (*of feeling, etc.*) **zum A. kommen, (seinen) A. finden,** to find expression; to be expressed; **ihre Gefühle fanden ihren A. in Tränen,** her feelings found expression in tears; **in diesem Artikel wird die Stimmung der Bevölkerung deutlich zum A. gebracht, kommt die Stimmung der Bevölkerung deutlich zum A., findet die Stimmung der Bevölkerung deutlichen A.,** this article expresses, voices, clearly the country's mood; **in dieser Handlung kam seine Großzügigkeit zum A.,** this action showed his generosity; **nehmen Sie den A. meines tiefempfundenen Dankes entgegen,** please accept (this expression of) my profound gratitude; **erlauben Sie den A. meiner vorzüglichen Hochachtung,** allow me to express my respectful regard; *Corr:* **mit dem A. vorzüglicher Hochachtung verbleibe ich . . .,** I remain yours respectfully . . . 2. expression (of face, eyes, voice, etc.); **sein Gesicht hat viel A.,** his face is full of expression, is very expressive; **ihr Gesicht hatte einen leidenschaftlichen A., einen A. tiefsten Ernstes,** her face had a passionate, a deeply serious, expression; **sein Gesicht blieb ohne A.,** his face remained expressionless, without expression; *Mus:* **mit, ohne, A. singen, spielen,** to sing, play, with, without, expression. 3. (*a*) expression, term; phrase, idiom; **wissenschaftlicher, technischer, A.,** scientific, technical, term; **der passende A.,** the appropriate term; the right expression; **ein vulgärer A.,** a vulgar expression, a vulgarism; **ein veralteter A.,** an obsolete expression, an archaic expression, an archaism; **er gebraucht manchmal merkwürdige Ausdrücke,** he sometimes uses strange expressions; **ich verbiete dir, solche Ausdrücke in meiner Gegenwart zu gebrauchen,** I forbid you to use such expressions, language, in my presence; **grobe Ausdrücke,** coarse language; **seine Ausdrücke wählen,** to choose, pick, one's words carefully; **nach Ausdrücken suchen,** to grope for the right words; *F:* **gebrauch keine Ausdrücke!** don't use bad language! (*b*) *Mth:* expression. 4.=**Ausdrucksweise;** *F:* **der hat einen A. am Leibe!** he uses shocking language.

II. **Ausdruck,** *m.* -(e)s/. (*a*) printing off, machining (of book); (*b*) printing (of word, etc.) in full.

ausdrückbar, *a.* expressible.

ausdrucken, *v.sep.* 1. *v.tr.* (*a*) to work all the copies off (form); to print off, machine (book); **das Buch ist ausgedruckt,** the book is printed off, has been machined; (*b*) to print (word, etc.) in full; (*c*) to wear out (type) (by printing). 2. *v.i.* (*haben*) (*of form*) **gut, schlecht, a.,** to print well, badly.

ausdrücken, *v.tr. sep.* 1. to squeeze out (liquid, etc.); to squeeze (out) the liquid from (sth.); **eine Zitrone a.,** to squeeze a lemon; **den Saft aus einer Zitrone a.,** to squeeze (out) the juice from a lemon; **einen Schwamm a.,** to squeeze out a sponge; **das Wasser aus einem Schwamm a.,** to squeeze out the water from a sponge; **ein Pickel a.,** to squeeze a pimple; **einen Pullover nach dem Waschen leicht a.,** to squeeze a jumper gently after washing. 2. to stub out (cigarette); to snuff out (candle) with one's fingers. 3. (*a*) to express, to voice, give voice to, utterance to (one's feelings, thoughts, etc.), to put (one's feelings, thoughts, etc.) into words; **ein so feines Gefühl vermag man nicht in Worten auszudrücken,** one cannot express such a delicate sentiment in words; **seine Dankbarket, sein Beileid, a.,** to express one's gratitude, one's condolences; **den Wunsch a., etwas zu tun,** to express the desire to do sth.; **seine Meinung a.,** to express one's opinion; to express oneself; **die allgemeine Meinung a.,** to voice, to give voice to, the general opinion; (*b*) (*of looks, gestures, etc.*) to express, show, manifest (pain, pleasure, etc.); **seine Miene drückte den tiefsten Haß aus,** the deepest hatred showed in his face, the expression of his face was one of deepest hatred; **ihre Augen drückten ihre Liebe aus,** her eyes spoke her love; **seine Haltung drückte Verachtung aus,** his attitude expressed, was expressive of, disdain; (*c*) **eine Menge in Kilogramm, eine Summe in Mark, a.,** to express a quantity in (terms of) kilograms, a sum in (terms of) marks; **etwas anders, in anderen Worten, a.,** to express, say, put, sth. differently, in another way; **um es anders auszudrücken . . ., anders ausgedrückt . . .,** to put it differently . . ., put (in) another way . . ., in other words . . .; **ganz einfach ausgedrückt,** (put) quite simply. 4. **sich ausdrücken,** (*a*) (*of pers.*) to express oneself; to speak; **sich durch Gesten a.,** to express one's meaning by gestures; **sie drückt sich sehr geschwollen aus,** she has a very pompous way of talking; **er hat sich ziemlich plump ausgedrückt,** he expressed himself rather clumsily; **sie drückte sich recht ungeschminkt aus,** she put it rather bluntly; **wenn ich mich so a. darf,** if I may so express myself, if I may put it that way; (*b*) (*of feeling, etc.*) to be expressed, shown; **in dieser Handlung drückte sich seine Großzügigkeit aus,** this action showed his generosity; **sein Haß drückte sich in seinem Gesicht aus,** his hatred showed in his face, his face betrayed his hatred; **in ihrem Gesicht drückt sich Willenskraft aus,** her face expresses strength of will, strength of will is reflected in her face.

ausdrücklich. 1. *a.* express, distinct, explicit, clear, emphatic (wish, order, etc.); **es war ihr ausdrücklicher Wunsch, daß . . .,** it was her express wish that . . .; **sie haben es auf ausdrücklichen Befehl der Behörde getan,** they did it at the express command of the authorities; **wir haben die ausdrückliche Erlaubnis dazu bekommen,** we were given express permission to do so; **es geschah gegen sein ausdrückliches Verbot,** it was done although he had expressly, distinctly, clearly, forbidden it. 2. *adv.* expressly, distinctly, explicitly, clearly, emphatically; **er hat es uns a. gesagt,** he told us so distinctly, explicitly, clearly; **er hat es nicht a. gesagt,** he didn't say so in so many words; **sie hat uns a. (darum) gebeten, es zu tun,** she expressly asked us to do so; **er hat sich a. dafür erklärt,** he declared himself emphatically in its favour.

Ausdrücklichkeit, *f.* distinctness, explicitness, clearness (of wish, order, etc.).

Ausdrückmaschine, *f. Ind:* (coke-)ram.

Ausdrucksart, *f.*=**Ausdrucksweise.**

Ausdrucksbewegung, *f.* movement expressing thought *or* feeling; (*on face*) (facial) expression; (*with body or limbs*) gesture.

Ausdrucksfülle, *f.* expressiveness (of face, etc.).

Ausdrucksgymnastik, *f.* rhythmic gymnastics.

Ausdruckskraft, *f.* expressiveness (of language, word, etc.).

Ausdruckskunst, *f.* art of expression; expressiveness (of actor, etc.).

ausdrucksleer, *a.* expressionless (face, etc.); blank, vacant (look); (face, look, etc.) devoid of (all) expression.

ausdruckslos, *a.* (*of face, voice, etc.*) expressionless, without expression; **ausdrucksloser Blick,** blank expression, blank look; **mit ausdrucksloser Stimme,** in an expressionless voice; **eine ausdruckslose Miene aufsetzen,** to put on a vacant look; **er sah mich a. an,** he looked at me blankly; *Mus:* **a. spielen,** to play without expression.

Ausdruckslosigkeit, *f.* expressionlessness (of face voice, etc.), lack of expression (in face, voice, etc.); blankness (of look).

Ausdruckstanz, *m.* (*a*) interpretative dancing; (*b*) interpretative dance.

ausdrucksvoll, *a.* expressive (face, eyes, movement, voice, etc.); (face, eyes, movement, voice, etc.) full of expression; **j-m einen ausdrucksvollen Blick zuwerfen,** to give s.o. an expressive, a significant, an eloquent, look; *adv.* expressively, with expression.

Ausdrucksweise, *f.* way of speaking; style of talking; (i) manner of, mode of, expression; (turn of) speech; style; choice of words; terminology; (ii) (manner of) speech; **eine gewählte A. haben,** to have an elegant way of speaking, turn of speech; **sie hat eine sehr gekünstelte A.,** her speech is very affected, she has a very affected way of speaking; **seine A. gefällt mir nicht,** I don't like his style of talking, the way he talks.

Ausdrusch, *m.* 1. threshing. 2. yield of corn from threshing.

ausduften, *v.sep.* 1. *v.tr.* to exhale, transpire (perfume); *abs.* **a.,** to exhale perfume, to be fragrant. 2. *v.i.* (*haben*) to lose its scent.

ausdulden, *v.sep.* 1. *v.tr.* to bear (pain, etc.) to the end. 2. *v.i.* (*haben*) (*a*) to come to the end of one's sufferings; (*b*) **ausgeduldet haben,** to have died, to have passed away; **sie hat ausgeduldet,** her sufferings are over.

ausdunsten, *v.sep.* 1. *v.i.* (*haben*) (*of liquid*) to evaporate, to exhale. 2. *v.tr.*=**ausdünsten** 1.

ausdünsten. I. *v.sep.* 1. *v.tr.* (*a*) to exhale (vapour); to give off (moisture) in the form of vapour; (*b*) *abs.* to steam; to exhale vapour; to give off fumes; (*of animal, human being*) to perspire, sweat. 2. *v.i.* (*haben*)=**ausdunsten** 1.

II. *vbl s.* 1. **Ausdünsten,** *n. in vbl senses; also:* exhalation (of vapour). 2. **Ausdünstung,** *f.* (*a*)=II. 1; (*b*) exhaled vapour, exhalation; **menschliche, tierische, Ausdünstungen,** human, animal, perspiration; **die Ausdünstungen der Haut,** insensible perspiration; **der Geruch menschlicher Ausdünstungen,** the odour of human beings, *F:* of humanity.

auseinander [aus^ʔai'nandər], *pron. adv.* (*also* **auseinander-,** *comb. fm.*) 1. (*a*) apart, asunder; **er stand mit den Füßen weit a.,** he stood with his feet wide apart; **sie wohnen weit a.,** they live far apart, at a distance from one another; **der Lehrer mußte die zwei Brüder weit a. setzen,** the teacher had to place the two brothers far apart; *see also* **auseinandersetzen; zwei Sachen auseinanderbringen,** to get two things apart; **man kann sie kaum auseinanderhalten,** one can scarcely tell them apart, one can scarcely distinguish between them; **eine Maschine auseinandernehmen,** to take a machine apart, to pieces; **sie waren früher Freunde, aber jetzt sind sie ganz a.,** they used to be friends, but now they have completely drifted apart; (*b*) **er und sein Bruder sind beinahe zehn Jahre a.,** there is a difference of nearly ten years between him and his brother; **unsere Geburtstage liegen zwei Monate a.,** there is a difference of two months between our birthdays; (*c*) away from one another; in different directions; in all directions; **auseinandersprengen,** to gallop away in all directions; **Leute, Tiere, usw., auseinandertreiben,** to

disperse, scatter, people, animals, etc. **2.** (*elliptical use*) **wollt ihr wohl a.** (=**auseinandergehen**)! break it up! **die Verlobung ist a.** (=**auseinandergegangen**), the engagement is off.

auseinanderbrechen, *v.sep.* (*strong*) **1.** *v.tr.* to break (sth.) apart, asunder. **2.** *v.i.* (*sein*) to break apart, asunder.

auseinanderbreiten, *v.tr. sep.* to unfold, open out, spread out (newspaper, handkerchief, etc.).

auseinanderbringen, *v.tr. sep.* (*conj. like* **bringen**) to separate, part (people, thgs); to get (thgs) apart; **zwei Streitende a.,** to separate, part, two combatants.

auseinanderfallen, *v.i. sep.* (*strong*) (*sein*) (*a*) to fall apart; to fall to pieces; to disintegrate, to crumble; (*b*) (*of family circle, political party, etc.*) to break up, to disintegrate; (*c*) to diverge; **Traumvorstellungen und Wirklichkeit fallen oft weit auseinander,** the world of one's dreams is often far removed from reality.

auseinanderfliegen, *v.i. sep.* (*strong*) (*sein*) to fly apart; (*of birds*) to fly off in different directions; to scatter; (*of crowd, etc.*) to scatter.

auseinandergehen, *v.i. sep.* (*strong*) (*sein*) **1.** (*of people*) to part, to separate; (*of party, meeting, crowd*) to break up; (*of crowd, etc.*) to disperse; **als gute Freunde a.,** to part good friends. **2.** (*a*) (*of roads, lines, etc.*) to diverge; (*b*) (*of opinions, statements, etc.*) to diverge, to differ. **3.** (*a*) (*of composite thg, of parts*) to come apart; to come unstuck; to break, to fall to pieces; (*b*) **es will nicht a., es geht nicht a.,** it won't come apart, it's impossible to get it apart; (*c*) (*of engagement*) to be broken off; (*d*) *F:* (*of mayonnaise, etc.*) to curdle, to separate. **4.** to spread; (*of knitted garment, etc.*) to stretch; (*of metal, etc.*) to expand; *F:* (*of pers.*) to spread, to grow fat.

auseinanderhalten, *v.tr. sep.* (*strong*) (*a*) to keep (persons, thgs) apart; (*b*) to tell (persons, thgs) apart, to distinguish between (persons, thgs); **sie sehen sich so ähnlich, daß man sie nicht a. kann,** they are so alike that it's impossible to tell them apart.

auseinanderjagen, *v.tr. sep.* to chase (animals, etc.) away from each other; to scatter, disperse, break up (crowd, etc.).

auseinanderkommen, *v.i. sep.* (*strong*) (*sein*) (*a*) to separate, to be separated, to become separated; **sie kamen im Gedränge auseinander,** they got separated, they lost (sight of) each other, in the crowd; (*b*) to drift apart, to cease being friends; to become estranged.

auseinanderlaufen, *v.i. sep.* (*strong*) (*sein*) **1.** (*a*) (*of crowd, etc.*) to disperse; to run in different directions, to scatter; (*b*) (*of persons*) to part, to separate. **2.** (*of roads, lines, etc.*) to diverge; *Mth:* (*of lines*) to diverge. **3.** (*of mixture, etc.*) to spread; to be too liquid; (*of biscuits, etc.*) to lose their shape (in the oven).

auseinanderlegen, *v.tr. sep.* **1.** (*a*) to unfold, open out, spread out (newspaper, handkerchief, etc.); (*b*) to take (machine, etc.) to pieces, apart. **2.** (*a*) to place (thgs, troops, etc.) at a distance from one another; (*b*) to put (patients, etc.) in different rooms; to put (children) in different beds. **3.** =**auseinandersetzen** I. 1.

auseinanderliegen, *v.i. sep.* (*strong*) (*haben*) to lie at a distance from one another, to lie apart; to be at a distance from one another; **ihre Güter liegen weit auseinander,** their estates lie, are, far apart, at a great distance from one another; **unsere Interessen liegen weit auseinander,** we have widely divergent interests.

auseinandermachen, *v.tr. sep.* (*a*) to separate, part (thgs); *F:* **die Beine a.,** (i) to place one's legs apart; to part one's legs; (ii) to uncross one's legs; (*b*) to undo (parcel, etc.).

auseinandernehmen, *v.tr. sep.* (*strong*) to take (sth.) apart, to pieces, *F:* to bits; to disassemble, dismantle, take down (machine).

auseinanderreißen, *v.sep.* (*strong*) **1.** *v.tr.* (*a*) to tear, force (thgs) apart; to separate (thgs) by force; (*b*) to tear (composite thg) apart, asunder; to separate, break up (family, etc.) (forcibly); **durch den Krieg sind viele Familien auseinandergerissen worden, der Krieg hat viele Familien auseinandergerissen,** many families were forcibly broken up by the war, the war separated, broke up, many families. **2.** *v.i.* (*sein*) to be torn apart, to break apart.

auseinandersetzen. I. *v.tr. sep.* **1. j-m etwas a.,** to set forth, explain, unfold (plan, reasons, etc.) to s.o., to lay (a plan) before s.o.; to explain (situation, etc.) to s.o.; to state, declare, expound (views), to explain, expound, (theories) to s.o.; to make sth. plain, clear, to s.o.; to elucidate sth. for s.o. **2. sich mit j-m a.,** to have it out with s.o.; to make an arrangement, to come to an agreement, an understanding, with s.o.; **sich mit j-m wegen einer Sache a.,** to argue, thrash, a matter out with s.o.; **sich mit seinen Gläubigern a.,** to compound, to come to an agreement, to terms, with one's creditors; **sich mit einer Situation a.,** to come to grips with, to face up to, a situation; **sich mit einem Problem a.,** to grapple with a problem; **sich mit dem Leben a.,** to battle with life. *See also* **auseinander** 1 (*a*).

II. *vbl s.* **1. Auseinandersetzen,** *n. in vbl senses.* **2. Auseinandersetzung,** *f.* (*a*)=II. 1; *also:* explanation, exposition (of views, theories, reasons, etc.); elucidation (of sth.); (*b*) settlement (with creditors, etc.); (*c*) argument; discussion; (*between countries*) differences; exchanges (of opinion); **eine heftige A. mit j-m haben,** to have a fierce argument with s.o.; **sie hatten eine A.,** they had words, words passed between them; **eine blutige A. haben,** to come to blows.

auseinanderstehen, *v.i. sep.* (*strong*) (*haben*) to stand, be, apart, at a distance, from one another; **die Pfeiler stehen weit auseinander,** the pillars stand, are, far apart.

auseinanderstellen. 1. *v.tr. sep.* to place (thgs, people) apart, at a distance, from each other; to separate (thgs, people). **2.** *vbl s.* **Auseinanderstellung,** *f. Ling:* disjunction.

auseisen, *v.tr. sep.* (*a*) to cut (sth.) clear of the ice, to free (sth.) from the ice; *F:* to extricate (s.o.) from a difficult situation; to get (s.o.) out of a difficulty; (*b*) to clear, rid (sth.) of ice.

auserkiesen, *v.tr. sep.* (*strong*) (*used mainly in p.t. & p.p.*) *Lit:* to choose, select; **Gott, der ihn zum Priester auserkor, . . . ,** God who chose him for, called him to be, a priest . . . ; **er hat sie zu seiner Frau auserkoren,** he chose her for his wife; *see also* **auserkoren.**

auserkoren, *p.p. & a. Lit:* chosen; (pre)destined; **zur Erlösung der Menschheit a. sein,** to be called to redeem mankind; *see also* **auserkiesen.**

auserlesen. 1. *v.tr. sep.* (*strong*) to choose, pick, select (s.o., sth.). **2.** *p.p. & a.* **auserlesen,** excellent, choice (food, etc.); choice, selected (fruit); select (company); **das Auserlesenste,** the flower, the pick, the cream.

Auserlesenheit, *f.* selectness (of company, goods, etc.); choiceness, excellence (of food); choiceness, selectness (of fruit).

ausersehen, *v.tr. sep.* (*strong*) to choose, select, destine (s.o., sth.); **das Schicksal hatte ihn zum Führer ausersehen,** fate had (pre)destined him to be a leader, for leadership; **zu Großem ausersehen sein,** to be (pre)destined for great things; **Ausersehung** *f,* selection; destiny (to higher thgs, etc.).

auserwählen, *v.tr. sep.* to choose, select (s.o., sth.); **das auserwählte Volk,** the chosen people; **die, die Gott auserwählt,** those whom God elects; *see also* **berufen** I. 2 (*a*).

Auserwählte, *m., f.* (*decl. as adj.*) one chosen (by God, etc.); **die Auserwählten, einige wenige Auserwählte,** *Theol:* the elect, the chosen; *F:* the favoured few; *Lit:* **sie ist die A. seines Herzens,** she is his chosen bride.

ausfachen, *v.tr. sep.* to divide (cupboard, etc.) into compartments.

ausfädeln, *v.tr. sep.* to unthread (needle).

ausfahren, *v.sep.* (*strong*) I. *v.i.* (*sein*) **1.** (*a*) to go for a drive, to drive out; (*of baby*) to be taken out, to go out; (*b*) (*of vehicle*) to leave; (*of train*) **(aus dem Bahnhof) a.,** to leave (the station), to draw out (of the station); (*of ship*) **(aus dem Hafen) a.,** to put (out) to sea, to leave port. **2.** *Min:* (*of miners*) to come up, to leave the pit. **3.** (*in biblical language; esp. of spirits, etc.*) to go forth, to go out, to come out.

II. **ausfahren,** *v.tr.* **1.** to take (s.o.) for a drive; to take (s.o.) for a ride; to take (baby) out (in pram); to take (invalid) out (in bath-chair, etc.). **2.** to open (pontoon bridge); *Av:* to extend (flaps); to lower (the undercarriage); *Nau:* to run out, lay out (cable); *Typewr:* **den Wagen nach rechts a.,** to move, run, push, slide, the carriage along to the right. **3.** to rut (road, path, etc.); **eine ausgefahrene Straße,** a road with a worn surface; a road full of ruts; *F:* **die ausgefahrenen Gleise verlassen,** to leave the beaten track. **4.** *Aut: etc:* **die Kurven a.,** to keep to the outside of the bends.

Ausfahrgleis, *n. Rail:* departure track.

Ausfahrgruppe, *f. Rail:* departure yard.

Ausfahrsignal, *n. Rail:* starting signal.

Ausfahrt, *f.* **1.** (*a*) (*of car, ship, train, etc.*) departure (from garage, port, station, etc.); **bei der A. aus dem Bahnhof . . . ,** as the train, we, etc., drew out of, left, the station . . . ; **wir werden die A. des Schiffes sehen,** we shall see the ship leave the harbour; (*b*) *Folkl:* setting out for the first day's work in the fields; (*c*) *Min:* ascent (from the mine). **2.** drive; outing; excursion; trip; **eine A. machen,** to take an outing; to go for a drive; to go for a ride; **das Kind hatte heute seine erste A.,** the child was taken out (in the pram) for the first time today. **3.** way out, exit (of garage, etc.); (exit) gateway; (exit) drive; exit (road) (from motorway); *P.N:* **'A.',** 'out'; **'Achtung, A.!'** 'caution, concealed drive'; *cp.* **Einfahrt.**

Ausfall, *m.* **1.** (*a*) falling out (of hair, teeth, etc.); **mit sechs Jahren erwartet man den A. der ersten Milchzähne,** one may expect the first milk-teeth to fall out at the age of six; **er ist bekümmert wegen des Ausfalls seiner Haare,** he is worried because his hair is falling out; (*b*) *Ch:* precipitation; (*c*) *Atom.Ph:* falling out (of radioactive matter). **2.** (*a*) dropping out (of competitors, etc.); dropping away, dropping off (of customers, etc.); (*b*) non-payment (of income, revenue, etc.); (*c*) breakdown, failure (of machine, engine, etc.); stoppage (of machine); *Med:* failure, collapse (of an organ); non-functioning (of machine, *Med:* of organ, etc.); **nach dem A. der Maschine, des Organs,** after the machine, the organ, had (i) failed, (ii) had been put out of action; (*d*) cancellation (of performance, train, etc.); (*e*) dropping (out) (of letter, word, etc.); omission (of passage, etc.). **3.** result, outcome, issue (of examination, election, etc.); **der A. der Ernte,** (the result of) the harvest. **4.** (*a*) *Com: etc:* loss (*caused by absence of expected custom, etc.*); deficiency, loss (in revenue); shortage; deficit; loss (of weight); **einen A. erleiden, haben,** to suffer a loss; **das schlechte Wetter bedeutete einen großen A. für die Hotelbesitzer,** the bad weather meant great losses to the hotel proprietors; (*b*) *Mil: etc: pl.* **Ausfälle,** casualties, losses (in men *or* materials). **5.** (*a*) *Ind:* waste; scrap; (*b*) *Ch:* precipitate; (*c*) *Atom.Ph:* (radioactive) fallout. **6.** (*a*) *Mil:* sortie, sally; **einen A. machen,** to make a sortie, a sally, to sally (out), to sortie; (*b*) *Fenc:* lunge, thrust, pass; *Gym:* lunge (with arms stretched above head); **einen A. auf den Gegner machen,** to lunge, thrust, make a pass, at one's opponent; (*c*) (rude) attack; **er hat in seinem Buch einen groben A. gegen die Regierung gemacht,** he made a violent attack on the government, he attacked the government violently, in his book; **seine Ausfälle gegen seine Mutter werden täglich schlimmer,** the abuse he showers on his mother grows worse every day. **7.** *Fort:* =**Ausfalltor.**

ausfällbar, *a. Ch:* precipitable.

Ausfällbarkeit, *f. Ch:* precipitability.

Ausfallbürgschaft, *f. Jur:* (contract of) guarantee (*imposing secondary liability*).

ausfallen. I. *v.i. sep.* (*strong*) (*sein*) **1.** (*a*) (*of hair, teeth, feathers, etc.*) to fall out, to drop out; to come out; **die Haare fallen ihr aus,** her hair is falling out; **dem Kind sind gestern zwei Zähne ausgefallen,** two of the child's teeth came out yesterday; (*b*) *Ch:* to precipitate, to be precipitated; (*c*) *Atom.Ph:* (*of radioactive matter*) to fall out. **2.** *South G.Dial:* (*of birds*) to hatch out. **3.** (*a*) (*of pers.*) to (have to) be counted out; to be unavailable; (*of competitor, etc.*) to drop out (of contest, etc.); *Mil: etc:* to be incapacitated; to become a casualty; (*b*) (*of income, revenue, etc.*) to fail to be paid, not to be forthcoming; (*c*) (*of machine, engine*) to become unserviceable, to fail, to be out of action, to go dead, *F:* to pack up; *Med:* (*of organ*) to fail, to collapse; to be put out of action; *Av:* **der linke Motor ist ausgefallen,** the port engine is out of action, is unserviceable, *F:* has packed up; **ausgefallener Motor,** dead engine; (*d*) (*of lecture, etc.*) to be cancelled, to be off; not to take place; (*of train, etc.*) to be cancelled; **den Unterricht, eine Vorstellung, a. lassen,** to cancel a lesson, a performance; **die Schule fällt heute aus,** there will be no school today; **die gestrige Vorstellung fiel aus,** yesterday's performance was cancelled; (*e*) to be omitted; to drop out; (*of vowel*) to be elided; **der Buchstabe s ist ausgefallen,** the letter s has dropped out; **diese Stelle werden wir a. lassen,** we will omit, leave out, this passage; **an dieser Stelle muß ein ganzer Satz ausgefallen sein,** a whole sentence must be missing from, must have been left out of, this passage. **4.** (*a*) *Mil:*

to make a sortie, sally; to sally (out), to sortie; (b) gegen j-n, etwas, a., to attack, make an attack on, s.o., sth.; to become offensive towards s.o.; (c) Fenc: to lunge, to thrust, to make a thrust. 5. gut, schlecht, a., to turn out well, badly; die Arbeiten sind im allgemeinen gut ausgefallen, the exercises were good on the whole; die Ernte ist in diesem Jahre schlecht ausgefallen, the harvest was bad, turned out badly, this year; wie ist deine Prüfung ausgefallen? what was the result of your examination? das Unternehmen fiel gut aus, the enterprise was, turned out, a success; die Entscheidung fiel zu unseren Gunsten aus, the decision was in our favour; die Dinge sind nicht so ausgefallen, wie er es erwartet hat, things haven't turned out, fallen out, as he expected. 6. v.tr. sich dat. einen Zahn a., to knock out one of one's teeth by a fall.
II. vbl s. Ausfallen, n. in vbl senses; also:= Ausfall 2, 3.
III. pr.p. & a. ausfallend, in vbl senses; esp. offensive, rude, abusive, insulting; er wird leicht a., wenn man ihn angreift, he quickly becomes abusive, F: turns nasty, if you attack him.
IV. p.p. & a. ausgefallen, in vbl senses; esp. extraordinary, strange, unusual, queer, curious; out of the ordinary, out of the way; striking; er hat immer die ausgefallensten Ideen, he always has the most extraordinary ideas; ein ausgefallenes Kleid, a striking (and unusual) dress; ich möchte nichts Ausgefallenes haben, I don't want anything markedly out of the ordinary, F: anything startling.
ausfällen, v.tr. sep. Ch: (of pers.) to precipitate (out) (a solid); Ausfällung f, precipitation.
ausfällig, a. offensive, rude, abusive, insulting; a. werden, to become offensive, F: to turn nasty.
Ausfälligkeit, f. 1. insulting behaviour, offensive behaviour, offensiveness. 2. insult: Ausfälligkeiten pl, insults, abuse.
Ausfällmittel, n. Ch: precipitant.
Ausfallmuster, n. Ind: out-turn sample; sample of the actual work.
Ausfallschwung, m. Ski: telemark.
Ausfallserscheinung, f. Med: Bot: deficiency symptom; Med: symptom of a pathological deficiency.
Ausfallstellung, f. Fenc: Gym: lunge (position).
Ausfallstraße, f. exit road.
Ausfall(s)winkel, m. Opt: angle of reflection.
Ausfalltor, n. Fort: sallyport.
ausfärben, v.tr. sep. Ind: to give the last dye to (material).
ausfasern, v.sep. 1. v.tr. to ravel out, to tease out (woven material); to fray out (edges of woven material). 2. v.i. (haben) & sich ausfasern, (of material) to ravel out; to fray (out) (at the edges).
ausfaulen, v.i. sep. (sein) (of seed) to rot.
ausfechten, v.tr. sep. (strong) to fight (sth.) out; to hold (contest); einen Streit a., (i) to settle a difference by fighting, with a duel; (ii) (with words) to fight it out; to have it out; sie haben die Sache unter sich ausgefochten, they fought the matter out between themselves.
ausfegen, v.tr. sep. to sweep (room) (out); to sweep (dirt, etc.) out (of room, etc.); to brush out (cupboard, etc.); F: to purge (government, official, etc.).
Ausfeger, m. 1. broom; brush. 2. last dance (before party breaks up).
ausfeilen, v.tr. sep. (a) to hollow (sth.) out with a file; (b) to file notches, etc., in (sth.); (c) to smooth (sth.) down, to polish (sth.), with a file, to file (sth.); F: to polish, file (sentence, verses, etc.).
ausfertigen. I. v.tr. sep. 1. to finish, give the finishing touch to (piece of work). 2. to draw up, to draft, Jur: to engross (document); to make out (document, cheque, bill, etc.); to write (out) (cheque); to issue (passport, etc.); eine Urkunde doppelt a., to draw up, make out, a document in duplicate.
II. vbl s. 1. Ausfertigen, n. in vbl senses. 2. Ausfertigung, f. (a)=II. 1; also: Jur: engrossment (of document); (b) draft; copy; erste A., original (of document); master copy, Jur: script; eine Urkunde in einfacher A. ausstellen, to make (only) a single draft of a document; in doppelter, dreifacher, vierfacher, A., in duplicate, triplicate, quadruplicate; eine Urkunde in zehnfacher A., a document of which ten copies have been made; jeder Teilnehmer sollte seine Arbeit In fünffacher A. einsenden, each competitor should submit five copies of his work.
ausfetten, v.tr. sep. to grease (baking-tin, etc.).
ausfeuern, v.i. sep. (haben) (of horse) to lash out.

ausfinden, v.sep. (strong) 1. v.tr.=ausfindig machen, q.v. under ausfindig. 2. sich ausfinden, to find one's way; to know one's way about, F: to be at home in (field of knowledge, etc.); ich finde mich in der Gegend gut aus, I know my way about, know how to get about, the district; das ist so kompliziert, da finde ich mich nicht mehr aus, it's so complicated I can't make it out, F: I can't make head or tail of it; sich in j-s Gedankengängen a., to follow s.o.'s train of thought.
ausfindig, a. (j-n, etwas) a. machen, to try to find (s.o., sth.); to find (s.o., sth.), to trace (s.o.); to find out (a fact); ich habe bis jetzt noch keinen Arzt a. gemacht, der mir wirklich helfen kann, I haven't yet found a doctor who can really help me; wir konnten den Eigentümer nicht a. machen, we were unable to trace the owner; we were unable to find out who the owner was; ich muß a. machen, warum er so plötzlich abgereist ist, I must find out why he went away so suddenly.
ausfischen, v.tr. sep. Pisc: to unstock, draw (pond).
ausflaggen, v.tr. sep. 1. Nau: to dress (ship) over all; abs. a., to dress ship over all, rainbow fashion. 2. Sp: to mark out (course) with flags; to flag out (course).
Ausfleischeisen, n. Tls: fleshing-iron, -knife.
ausfleischen, v.tr. sep. Leath: to flesh (hides).
Ausfleischmesser, n. Tls: fleshing-knife.
ausflicken, v.tr. sep. to mend (clothes, shoes), to repair (shoes); to patch up (clothes, shoes, wall, etc.).
ausfliegen, v.sep. (strong). I. v.i. (sein) 1. to fly out; (of bird) to fly away; to leave the nest; (of bee) to leave the hive; F: der Vogel ist ausgeflogen, the bird has flown. 2. to make an excursion, to go for a trip, to make, take, a trip. II. ausfliegen, v.tr. Av: to fly (people) out; to evacuate (casualties, etc.) by air.
ausfließen. I. v.i. sep. (strong) (sein) (aus etwas) a., (of liquid) to flow out, run out (of sth.), to issue (out of sth.), to be discharged (from sth.); (of spirit) to issue forth (from sth.), to emanate (from sth.). II. vbl s. Ausfließen, n.=Ausfluß 1.
ausflocken, v.sep. Ch: 1. v.tr. to flocculate (colloidal substance). 2. v.i. (sein) (of colloidal substance) to form a flocculent precipitate. 3. vbl s. Ausflockung f, flocculation.
Ausflucht, f. 1. -/-en, (way of) escape. 2. -/=e, excuse, pretext, subterfuge, shift, evasion; Ausflüchte machen, suchen, to make excuses; to use shifts, evasions; to prevaricate; to hedge; to seek excuses (so as not to do sth.); wenn man ihn darüber fragt, macht er Ausflüchte, if you ask him about it he becomes evasive, he gives evasive answers, F: he beats about the bush; mach keine Ausflüchte! don't prevaricate! F: don't beat about the bush! das sind leere Ausflüchte! those are mere excuses. 3. -/=e. A. & Dial:=Ausflug 2.
ausfluchten, v.tr. sep. 1. Surv: to extend (line, etc.). 2. to align (houses, etc.).
Ausflug, m. 1. flying out; flight (from the nest, the hive); F: es wird sein erster A. in die Welt sein, he will be going out into the world for the first time. 2. excursion; (i) tour, trip; (ii) jaunt, outing; (iii) ramble; (iv) F: excursion (into field of knowledge, etc.); einen A. machen, to go on, to make, an excursion; to make a trip, to go for a trip; to go for an outing, on a jaunt; wir machten einen A. aufs Land, we had an outing in the country.
Ausflügler, m. -s/-, tourist, tripper; excursionist.
Ausflugslokal, n. restaurant, café, etc., catering for excursionists; road-house.
Ausflugsort, m. (popular) resort for (day-)trippers.
Ausfluß, m. 1. (a) flowing out; outflow, outflowing, discharge, efflux (of water, gas, etc.); outfall, outflow, discharging (of sewer); outflow (of lava); (b) Med: discharge, flux (of blood, matter, etc.); (c) emanation (of happiness, etc.). 2. (a) water, etc., discharged; delivery, discharge, output (of pipe) (b) Med: discharge; flux. 3. product (of the imagination, etc.); emanation (of God, etc.); Ausflüsse einer überreizten Phantasie, products of an overwrought imagination; Glück und Tugend sind Ausflüsse von Gottes Reinheit, happiness and virtue are emanations of God's purity. 4. outlet; orifice, opening (through which water, etc., is discharged); outlet, outfall (of river, drain, etc.).
Ausflußkanal, m. Civ.E: outfall sewer.
Ausflußloch, n. Constr: drain-hole; weep-hole (in wall), F: weeper.
Ausflußmenge, f. amount (of water, etc.) discharged; delivery, discharge, output (of pipe).

Ausflußöffnung, f. orifice, opening, through which water, etc., is discharged; outlet.
Ausflußrohr, n., Ausflußröhre, f. (a) spout; (b) drain-pipe, outlet pipe, discharge pipe, escape pipe.
ausfolgen, v.tr. sep. Austrian: to hand (sth.) over, to hand (sth.) out.
ausforschen, v.tr. sep. (a) to find (sth.) out (by questioning); (b) to question (s.o.); to sound (s.o.) out; F: to pump (s.o.); j-n über etwas acc. a., to sound s.o. out about sth.; F: to pump s.o. about sth.; j-n über seine Absichten, seine Pläne, a., to sound s.o. out about his intentions, his plans; er versuchte, mich auszuforschen, he tried to get some information out of me, F: he tried to pump me.
Ausfracht, f. Nau: outward freight.
ausfragen, v.tr. sep. to question, interrogate (s.o.); j-n über etwas acc. a., to ask, question, interrogate, s.o. about sth.; to sound s.o. on, with regard to, sth.; to try to find sth. out from s.o.; sie fragten ihn über seine Herkunft aus, they questioned him, asked him questions, about his background; j-n über seine Ansichten a., to sound s.o. on his views; sie fragten den Gefangenen über die Namen seiner Helfershelfer aus, they tried to make the prisoner tell them the names of his accomplices, they questioned the prisoner about the names of his accomplices; man hat den Gefangenen drei Stunden lang ausgefragt, the prisoner was questioned, interrogated, for three hours; frag mich nicht so aus! stop asking questions!
ausfransen, v.sep. 1. v.tr. (a) to fringe (material); (b) to fray (material). 2. v.i. (sein) sich ausfransen, to fray (out); ausgefranste Hosen, Ärmel, frayed trousers, sleeves.
ausfräsen, v.tr. sep. Mec.E: Woodw: etc: to cut out (hole) (with a milling-machine, etc.); Metalw: Stonew: to mill out (hole); to sink (hole).
ausfressen, v.tr. sep. (strong) 1. (of animal) to eat up all the food in (trough, etc.); to eat (trough, etc.) clean; to eat (nut, etc.) out (of shell, etc.). 2. (of acid, etc.) to eat into, to corrode (metal, etc.); to erode (metal, rock, etc.); die Felsen sind vom Wasser ausgefressen, the rocks are worn away, hollowed out, eroded, by water. 3. F: (a) etwas a. müssen, to have to pay for sth.; a., was man eingebrockt hat, to take the consequences for one's actions; das mußt du selber a.! that's your funeral! (b) etwas ausgefressen haben, to have been up to some mischief; was hat er nun wieder ausgefressen? what (mischief) has he been up to now?
ausfrieren, v.i. sep. (strong) (sein) 1. (a) (of pond, etc.) to freeze right through; (b) (of pers.) F: ausgefroren sein, to be frozen (through). 2. (of seed) to be killed by frost.
ausfugen, v.tr. sep. Constr: to point, joint (wall, etc.).
Ausfuhr, f. -/-en. Com: 1. export, exportation, exporting (of goods, etc.); die A. von Gold ist nicht gestattet, the export of gold is prohibited. 2. export(s); Ausfuhren pl, exports (of a country); goods exported; wir müssen unsere A., unsere Ausfuhren, erhöhen, we must increase our export(s).
Ausfuhrartikel, m. Com: export; exported article; article for export; export article.
ausführbar, a. 1. Com: exportable (goods, etc.). 2. practicable, workable, feasible, executable (plan, etc.); sein Plan ist nicht a., his plan is not practicable, workable, it would be impossible to carry out his plan.
Ausführbarkeit, f. practicability, workability, workableness, feasibility (of plan, etc.).
Ausfuhrbestimmungen, f.pl. Adm: export regulations.
Ausfuhrbewilligung, f. Cust: (a) permission to export; (b) export certificate, export permit.
ausführen. I. v.tr. sep. 1. (a) A: to lead (people, animals) out; (b) to take (s.o.) out (to cinema, restaurant, etc.); (c) to take (dog) for a walk, a run, an airing; to exercise (horse, dog). 2. F: j-m etwas a., to take sth. away from s.o., to steal, purloin, sth. from s.o., F: to nick, pinch, sth. from s.o. 3. to export (goods). 4. (a) to carry (sth.) out; to execute (plan, command, commission); to follow up, act upon (orders); to carry (plan, command) into effect, to carry, put, (plan, command) into execution; to realize (plan); to fulfil (command, instructions, promise); to perform (promise); to put (thought, idea) into action; to perform (operation); to play (trick); to execute (complicated dance figure, etc.); Com: to fill (an order); die ausführende Gewalt, the executive power;

ausführende Organe, executives; executive authorities; einen Bau a., to carry out the construction of a building; er plante die gesamte Dekoration des Raumes, führte aber nur die Decke aus, he planned the decoration of the entire room, but all he actually completed was the ceiling; Pläne für ein neues Museumsgebäude waren seit langem vorhanden, es ist aber nie ausgeführt worden, plans for a new museum had existed for a long time, but it had never actually been built; sein Vorhaben a., to carry out, to effect, one's purpose; man hat den Befehl nicht in allen Einzelheiten ausgeführt, the order was not fully carried out; einen Überfall am hellen Tage a., to carry out a raid in broad daylight; die Skulptur ist nur im Groben ausgeführt, the statue has only been done in the rough; ein fein ausgeführtes Gemälde, a delicately executed painting; Mus: etc: der ausführende Künstler, the performer; the executant; (b) etwas in einem bestimmten Material, in einer bestimmten Art, a., to make something in a certain material, in a certain way; alle Holzarbeiten sind in Eiche ausgeführt, all the woodwork is in oak; die Sitze sind aufklappbar ausgeführt, the seats are made to fold up; die Gartenstühle sind in grünem Lack ausgeführt, the garden chairs have a green lacquer finish; der Kragen ist in Pikee ausgeführt, the collar is made of piqué; (c) eine Skizze weiter a., to elaborate a sketch; er hat dieses Thema in seinem zweiten Buche weiter ausgeführt, he elaborated, enlarged upon, dwelt at greater length on, this theme in his second book; (d) der Redner führte aus, daß . . ., the speaker said that . . .
II. vbl s. 1. Ausführen, n. in vbl senses. 2. Ausführung, f. (a)=II. 1; also: exportation (of goods); execution (of plan, command, dance, piece of work, etc.); realization (of plan); fulfilment (of command, promise, etc.); construction (of building); einen Plan zur A. bringen, to carry a plan into effect, into execution; zur A. kommen, (of plan) to be carried into effect, into execution, to be put into execution; (of building) to be constructed, erected; die A. des Baus wurde der Firma X übertragen, the contract for the building was placed with the firm of X; (b) method of making; workmanship; style, type; model; die A. des Schmuckkastens war in jeder Einzelheit tadellos, the casket was a faultless piece of workmanship; bei A. in Ölfarbe erhöht sich der Preis um . . ., if the work is done in oil-paint the price rises by . . .; Waren in billiger A., cheaply made goods; Koffer in den verschiedensten Ausführungen, cases of every varity, type; A. in Leder oder Kunststoff, (made in) leather or plastic; die größere A. wird etwas mehr kosten, the larger model is rather more expensive; Möbel, Sportgeräte, in hochwertiger A., high-quality furniture, sports equipment; wir liefern dieses Kleid in drei verschiedenen Ausführungen, we supply three different versions of this dress; (c) Rechnung, usw., in doppelter, usw., A., invoice, etc., in duplicate, etc., cp. ausfertigen II. 2(b); (d) pl. Ausführungen, talk, dissertation; speech; comments, remarks; lange Ausführungen über etwas acc. machen, to discourse at length on, to dwell at length upon, to hold forth on, sth.; to enlarge upon sth., to go into details, into detailed explanations, about sth.; in seinen Ausführungen sagte er unter anderem, daß . . ., in the course of his remarks (on this subject) he said amongst other things, inter alia, that . . .; ich bin Herrn Xs Ausführungen mit Interesse gefolgt, I listened with interest to what Mr X had to say; die Ausführungen des Redners waren sehr interessant, what the speaker said was very interesting; seine endlosen Ausführungen machen mich müde, his endless dissertations tire me.

Ausführer, m. Com: exporter.
Ausfuhrerlaubnis, f. Adm:=Ausfuhrgenehmigung.
Ausfuhrgang, m. Anat: duct.
Ausfuhrgenehmigung, f. Adm: (a) permission to export; (b) export licence, export permit.
Ausfuhrgut, n. Com: (commodity) export.
Ausfuhrhafen, m. port of exportation.
Ausfuhrhandel, m. export trade.
Ausfuhrhändler, m. Com: exporter.
Ausfuhrhändlervergütung, f. =Ausfuhrvergütung 2.
Ausfuhrkontingent, n. Adm: Com: export quota.
Ausfuhrland, n. Pol.Ec: Com: exporting country.
ausführlich, a. detailed, circumstantial, full (account, description); adv. in detail, fully, at

(some) length, circumstantially; er hat uns a. über die Ereignisse berichtet, er hat uns einen ausführlichen Bericht über die Ereignisse gegeben, he gave us a circumstantial account of the events, he went into every detail of the events for us; sie wird dir a., Ausführliches, von ihren Erlebnissen erzählen, she will give you details, a detailed, circumstantial, account, of her experiences; ich schreibe ihm morgen Ausführlicheres über unsere Pläne, I'll let him have further, fuller, details of our plans, I'll write to him at greater length, in greater, fuller, detail, more fully, about our plans, tomorrow; er hat a. über dieses Thema gesprochen, he spoke at some length on this subject; dieses Buch behandelt das Thema etwas ausführlicher, this book deals rather more fully with, is rather fuller on, the subject.
Ausführlichkeit, f. fullness (of account, description); etwas mit großer A. beschreiben, to describe sth. in great detail, at great length.
Ausfuhrliste, f. Adm: Com: export list.
Ausfuhrlizenz, f. Adm: export licence, export permit.
Ausfuhrmonopol, n. Pol.Ec: Com: export monopoly.
Ausfuhrprämie, f. Adm: export bounty, export premium; Cust: drawback.
Ausfuhrquota, Ausfuhrquote, f. 1. Pol.Ec: export rate. 2.=Ausfuhrkontingent.
Ausfuhrschein, m. Adm: A: preferential export licence (granted as a privilege, esp. to grain exporting firms).
Ausfuhrtarif, m. Rail: special transport rates, tariff, for certain exports.
Ausfuhrtaxe, f. Adm: levy on exports; export duty.
Ausfuhrüberschuß, m. Pol.Ec: export surplus.
Ausführung, f. see ausführen II.
Ausführungsbestimmungen, f.pl. directives for implementation (of law or order).
Ausführungsgang, m. Anat: duct; see also Drüse.
Ausführungsoffizier, m. Navy: executive officer.
Ausführungsorgan, n. executive; executive authority.
Ausfuhrverbot, n. Pol.Ec: export ban, export prohibition.
Ausfuhrvergütung, f. 1. Cust: drawback (on certain goods). 2. Adm: tax rebate (to exporters).
Ausfuhrware, f. Com: export; export commodity; exported article; article for export; pl. exports.
Ausfuhrzoll, m. export duty.
Ausfuhrzuschuß, m. Pol.Ec: export subsidy.
ausfüllen, v.tr. sep. to fill (sth.); to fill in, to fill up (hole, ditch, gap, space, etc.); (of employed pers.) to fill (position); (of thought, etc.) to fill, occupy (mind) (completely); (of work, etc.) to take up (time); Adm: etc: to fill in, to fill up, to complete (form); U.S: to fill out (a blank); ihre Backen haben sich ausgefüllt, her cheeks have filled out; sein Amt gut a., to fill one's post well; mit Herrn X war die Rolle vorzüglich ausgefüllt, the part was filled excellently by Mr X; er füllt dieses Amt nicht wirklich aus, he is not really adequate for, to, this position; der Gedanke, der seine Seele ausfüllte, the thought that filled, occupied, his mind; ihre Kinder füllen ihr Leben, füllen sie, ganz aus, her children are her whole life; der Durst nach Rache füllt ihre ganze Seele aus, lust for revenge is her one thought, fills her entire soul; seine Arbeit füllte alle seine Gedanken aus, füllte ihn ganz aus, he was completely absorbed in, engrossed in, preoccupied with, his work, his mind was completely taken up with his work; his work was his life; ich bin nicht unzufrieden in meiner Arbeit, aber sie füllt mich nicht aus, I'm not discontented with my job but it doesn't satisfy me, doesn't fill my life; meine Studien füllen alle meine freien Stunden aus, my studies fill (up), take up, occupy, all my spare time; das hat meine ganze Zeit ausgefüllt, it took up, occupied, all my time; unsere Tage sind sehr ausgefüllt, our days are very full; ihre Tage waren ausgefüllt mit Reiten und Schwimmen, her days were spent riding and swimming.
ausfuttern, v.tr. sep.=ausfüttern.
ausfüttern. I. v.tr. sep. to line (coat, cylinder, canal, etc.); ein Lager mit Weißmetall a., to line bearings with white metal.
II. vbl s. 1. Ausfüttern, n. in vbl senses. 2. Ausfütterung, f. (a)=II. 1; (b) lining (of coat, etc.); Mch: I.C.E: lining, liner (of cylinder, etc.).
Ausgabe, f. 1. (a) giving out, handing out; distribution; delivery (of post, etc.); issue, issuing (of tickets, passports, bank-notes, coins,

shares, etc.); emission (of paper currency, etc.); Mil: issue (of equipment, etc.); (b) Mil: etc: giving, telling (of password); issuing (of order). 2. (a) counter (for handing out luggage, etc.); hatch (for distribution of meals, etc.); window (for distribution of tickets, etc.); (b) Adm: etc: issuing office, office of issue; distribution centre; Mil: issuing centre; distribution centre. 3. expense; Ausgaben pl, expenses; expenditure; outlay; ein neues Auto wäre eine große A., a new car would be a great expense; Ausgaben machen, to spend; ich habe in diesem Jahre große Ausgaben gemacht, I have spent a great deal this year; große Ausgaben haben, to have big expenses; ich habe letzten Monat gar keine größeren Ausgaben gemacht, I didn't spend money on any big items last month; regelmäßig wiederkehrende Ausgaben, regular, recurrent, expenses; es wird große Ausgaben zur Folge haben, it will entail a large expenditure, a lot of expense: die Ausgaben decken, to meet, defray, expenses; die staatlichen Ausgaben für die Rüstung, the national outlay, expenditure, on armaments; kleine Ausgaben, petty expenses; Ausgaben außer der Reihe, extras; Adm: ordentliche, außerordentliche, Ausgaben, ordinary, extraordinary, expenses. 4. Publ: edition; kleine A., small edition; gekürzte A., abridged edition; A. letzter Hand, definitive edition.
Ausgabekurs, m. Fin: issue price (of securities).
Ausgabenbuch, n. expenses book; petty cash book; housekeeping-book.
Ausgabestelle, f. (a) Adm: etc: issuing office, office of issue; distribution centre; Mil: distribution centre; supply point; (b) counter (for handing out of luggage, etc.).
Ausgang, m. 1. (a) going out; egress, exit; departure; B: der Herr behüte deinen A. und Eingang . . ., the Lord shall preserve thy going out and thy coming in . . . ; (b) seinen A. von etwas nehmen, to take sth. as one's starting-point, one's point of departure; to start, work, from (a principle, etc,). 2. outing; time off; time to go out; es war mein erster A. nach dem Unfall, it was the first time I had been out (of doors) since my accident; das Dienstmädchen hat mittwochs A., the maid is free, is allowed to go out, has the, her, day off, afternoon off, on Wednesdays; Mil: A. haben, to be on pass. 3. (a) end, ending, termination (of word); end (of line); das Wort am A. der Zeile, the word at the end of the line; (b) Ling: off-glide; (c) end, close (of epoch, etc.); am A., gegen den A., des vorigen Jahrhunderts, at the end, close, towards the end, close, of the last century; (d) end, termination; issue; result, outcome, upshot (of election, battle, etc.); die Geschichte hatte einen glücklichen A., the affair ended happily; einen guten, schlechten, A. nehmen, haben, to end, to turn out, well, badly; einen gefährlichen A. nehmen, to have dangerous results; den A. der Ereignisse abwarten, to wait the issue of events; wir waren sehr neugierig auf den A. der Sache, we were very curious (to know) how the matter would end; alle haben sich über den A. des Prozesses gewundert, everyone was surprised at the outcome of the trial; diese Krankheit hat meistens einen tödlichen A., this disease generally proves fatal; ein Unfall mit tödlichem A., a fatal accident; der glückliche A. eines Unternehmens, the success, the good issue, of an undertaking; die Verhandlungen nähern sich ihrem A., the negotiations are drawing to a close. 4. exit, way out; egress; outlet (of tunnel, etc.); 'Ausgang' 'exit', 'way out'; 'kein Ausgang', 'no exit'; es gibt einen A. in die Gasse, there is an egress, an exit, into the lane; ich werde am A. auf dich warten, I'll wait for you at the exit; der Bahnhof hat vier Ausgänge, the station has four exits, there are four ways out of the station. 5. pl. Ausgänge, (a) Com: Fin: outgoings; die Ausgänge sind höher als die Eingänge, the outgoings exceed the incomings; (b) outgoing letters, etc.
Ausgangs-, comb.fm. 1. exit (road, etc.); (port, etc.) of exit; outlet (pipe, etc.); (line, point, etc.) of departure. 2. initial . . . ; starting . . . ; primary . . . ; original (material, position, etc.); parent (material, rock, etc,). 3. El.E: output (impedance, resistance, terminal, voltage, etc.)
Ausgangsbaumuster, n. Ind: original model; prototype.
Ausgangsfakturenbuch, n. Com: sales-book.
Ausgangsgestein, n. Geol: parent rock.
Ausgangskapital, n. Fin: original (invested) capital.
Ausgangsklaue, f. Watchm: exit pallet stone.

Ausgangskreis, *m. El.E:* output circuit.
Ausgangsleistung, *f. El.E:* (power) output.
Ausgangslinie, *f.* line of departure; *Mil:* base (-line), jumping-off line (for attack).
Ausgangsmaterial, *n. Ch: Ind: etc:* original, primary, material; initial, starting, material; raw material.
Ausgangspunkt, *m.* **1.** (*a*) starting-point; **dieser Platz ist der A. für drei Straßen,** three roads start at this square; **London war der A. unserer Reise,** our journey started from London, we started from London; **was für einen Weg man auch einschlägt, man kommt immer wieder am A. zurück,** whatever road you take, you always find yourself back where you started; (*b*) *Av: etc:* base; **die kleine Stadt war der A. von dem wir Ausflüge in die Umgebung machten,** the little town was the base from which we made excursions into the surrounding country. **2.** starting-point, point of departure; **am A. unserer Betrachtungen stand Botticellis Primavera,** Botticelli's Primavera was the point of departure for our discussion; **wir kommen nun auf unseren A. zurück,** we have now come full circle; we are back where we started.
Ausgangsspannung, *f. El.E:* output voltage.
Ausgangssperre, *f. Mil:* confinement to barracks, *F:* C.B.
Ausgangsstellung, *f.* initial position; *Sp: etc:* starting position; *Mec.E: El.E:* home position (of lever, switch, etc.); *Mil:* initial position, jumping-off position (for attack).
Ausgangsstoff, *m. Ch: Ind: etc:* initial substance; primary material; parent material.
Ausgangsstufe, *f.* **1.** initial stage. **2.** *El.E:* output stage.
Ausgangswahrscheinlichkeit, *f. Mth: etc:* initial probability.
Ausgangswiderstand, *m. El.E:* output resistance.
Ausgangszoll, *m.* export duty.
ausgären, *v.i. sep.* (*conj. like* **gären**) (*sein*) (*of wine, etc.*) to finish fermenting.
ausgasen, *v.tr. sep.* to fumigate (room, etc.).
ausgebacken, *p.p. & a. see* **ausbacken.**
ausgeben, *v.tr. sep.* (*strong*) **1.** (*a*) to hand out, give out, distribute (alms, prizes, forms, etc.); to distribute, issue (provisions, etc.); to issue (tickets, passports, bank-notes, coins, shares, etc.); *Mil:* to issue (equipment, etc.); to emit (paper currency, etc.); to deal (cards); *A:* (*of publisher, bookseller*) to issue, distribute, publish (book, etc.); (*b*) *Mil: etc:* **einen Befehl, die Parole, a.,** to issue an order, to give the password; (*c*) to spend (money); to expend, lay out (money); **er gibt wenig für Bücher aus,** he spends little on books; **viel für j-n a.,** to spend a lot on s.o.; **seinen Verdienst ganz a.,** to spend all one's earnings; to live up to one's income; **er gibt das Geld mit vollen Händen aus,** he is throwing money away right and left; **einen a.,** to buy, stand, s.o. a drink; **sich ganz a.,** to spend all one's energy; to expend one's strength; **er hat sich ganz ausgegeben im Dienste dieser Sache,** he has entirely spent himself in, he has spent all his energy in, this matter; (*d*) to yield; **Garben, die viel Korn a.,** sheaves which yield a lot of corn; *abs.* **gut a.,** to yield a lot, to have a good yield; (*e*) *abs.* (*of substance*) to go a long way; **die Gewürze sind teuer, aber sie geben sehr aus,** the spices are expensive, but a little goes a long way. **2.** *A:* to give (daughter, etc.) in marriage. **3.** *Ven: abs:* (*of hounds*) to give tongue. **4. sich für etwas, j-n, ausgeben,** to claim to be, to say one is, to give oneself out for, to give oneself out to be, to pretend to be, sth., s.o.; to set up for, to set oneself up as, sth., s.o.; to pose as sth., s.o.; **j-n für etwas, j-n, a.,** to say, declare, pretend, claim, that s.o. is sth., s.o.; **er gab sich für ihren Neffen aus,** he pretended to be, posed as, said he was, her nephew; **sich für einen Baron, als Baron, a.,** to give oneself out for, to give oneself out to be, to pose as, a baron; **sich für einen Sachverständigen a.,** to give oneself out for, to pretend to be, an expert; **er gab sich für einen Arzt, einen Franzosen, aus,** he pretended to be, posed as, a doctor, a Frenchman; **sie gibt sich für sehr musikliebend aus,** she claims to be, pretends to be, sets herself up as, a great lover of music; **seine Anhänger gaben ihn für den wahren Thronfolger aus,** his supporters declared him to be the true heir to the throne.
Ausgeber, *m.* (*a*) distributor (of alms, prizes, provisions, etc.); issuer (of provisions, tickets, passports, equipment, etc.); emitter (of paper currency, etc.); *Cards:* dealer; *A:* steward; (*b*) spender.

ausgebogt, *a. Her:* engrailed.
Ausgebot, *n.* (*a*) offering (of goods) for sale; (*b*) (*at auction*) first bid, opening bid.
ausgebrochen, *p.p. & a. Her:* voided; **ausgebrochenes Freiviertel,** canton charged with another. *See also* **ausbrechen.**
Ausgeburt, *f.* (i) product; offspring; creation, creature; (ii) monstrous product, monstrous creation; **die A. einer erhitzten Phantasie,** the product, creation, figment, of a fevered imagination; **A. der Hölle,** spawn of hell; **eine A. von Grausamkeit,** a monster of cruelty.
ausgedehnt, *p.p. & a. see* **ausdehnen.**
Ausgedinge, *n.*=**Altenteil.**
ausgefallen, *p.p. & a. see* **ausfallen.**
Ausgefallenheit, *f.* extraordinariness, singularity, eccentricity, queerness (of ideas, dress, etc.).
ausgeglichen, *p.p. & a. see* **ausgleichen.**
Ausgeglichenheit, *f.* (good) balance; (*a*) evenness (of temper); (*b*) uniformity; smoothness, evenness.
Ausgehanzug, *m.* (*a*) best suit; (*b*) *Mil: Navy:*= **Ausgehuniform.**
ausgehen. I. *v.i. sep.* (*strong*) (*sein*) **1.** (i) to go out, to leave the house; (ii) to go out (for a walk, to a restaurant, etc.); **er kann noch nicht a.,** (i) he can't go out yet; (ii) he is still confined to the house, he still can't get about; **bei j-m ein- und ausgehen,** to be in and out of s.o.'s house, to be a constant visitor at s.o.'s house; **wir gehen jeden Samstag Abend aus,** we go out every Saturday evening. **2. auf etwas** *acc.* **a.,** (*a*) to set out in search of sth; *see also* **Abenteuer** 1 (*a*), **Beute**[1], **Raub** ; (*b*) (*of pers.*) to aim at, to be bent on, sth.; **darauf a., etwas zu tun,** (*of pers.*) to set out to do sth., to aim to do sth., to aim at, to be bent on, doing sth.; (*of action, etc.*) to be calculated to do sth.; **sie geht darauf aus, Aufsehen zu erregen,** she sets out to create a sensation; **sein Plan ging darauf aus, die Aufmerksamkeit der Zuschauer abzulenken,** (the aim of) his plan was to distract the attention of the spectators; **jede seiner Handlungen geht darauf aus, mich zu demütigen,** everything he does is calculated to humiliate me. **3. leer a.,** to get nothing; to be left out; **wenn's ans Verteilen geht, geht der Kleinste immer leer aus,** when things are being handed out the smallest one never gets anything, is always left out. **4. von etwas, j-m, a.,** to come from sth., s.o.; (*a*) **drei Straßen gehen von diesem Platze aus,** three streets start at this square; three streets radiate from this square; **der Weg geht vom See aus,** the path starts at, comes from the lake; **unsere Reise ging von London aus,** we started from London; (*b*) to start, work, from a principle, etc.; **er geht immer von dem Standpunkt aus, daß . . . ,** he always works from the principle that . . . ; **wir gingen von der Annahme aus, daß . . . ,** we started from the assumption that . . . , we took the assumption that . . . as our starting-point, our point of departure; **ausgehend von dem Prinzip, daß . . . ,** starting, working, from the principle that . . . ; (*c*) *Theol: etc:* (*of spirit, etc.*) to emanate, proceed (from God, etc.); **der Heilige Geist geht vom Vater und vom Sohne aus,** the Holy Ghost proceeds from the Father and the Son; (*d*) to come from s.o., sth.; to emanate from s.o., sth.; **der Befehl ging vom König aus,** the order came from the King; **der Vorschlag ging von ihr aus,** the suggestion came from her, it was her suggestion; **die besten Gedanken gehen immer von dir aus,** the best ideas always start with, originate with, come from, you; **eine warme Menschlichkeit geht von ihm aus,** he spreads, radiates, a feeling of warmth and kindness; **eine wohltuende Ruhe geht von dem Bild aus,** an agreeable feeling of peace emanates from the picture; *B:* **. . . ein Gebot von dem Kaiser Augustus ausging,** . . . there went out a decree from Caesar Augustus. **5.** (*a*) *A:* (*of shoes, stockings, etc.*) to come off; (*b*) (*of hair*) to come out, to fall out; (*of colour*) to come out; to fade; (*of stain, spot*) to come out. **6.** (*a*) *A:* (*of year, etc.*) to come to an end, to a close; (*b*) (*of plant*) to die; **auf dieser Wiese waren früher immer Veilchen, aber jetzt sind sie alle ausgegangen,** there always used to be violets in this meadow but they have all died now; (*c*) (*of fire, light, etc.*) to go out; (*d*) to run out, to fail; **nach drei Wochen gingen uns die Vorräte aus,** after three weeks our provisions ran out, we ran out of provisions; **allmählich ging ihm die Geduld aus,** he was gradually losing patience; **der Atem ging ihr aus,** she was getting out of breath, becoming breathless; her breath was beginning to fail; **endlich ging mir der Gesprächstoff aus,** at last I ran out of conversation. **7.** to end; (*a*) **das Wort geht auf r, in r, aus,** the word ends in r; **in eine Spitze a.,** to end in a point, to taper off into a point; (*b*) **gut, schlecht, a.,** to end well, badly; **die Geschichte ist übel ausgegangen,** the affair ended badly.

II. *vbl s.* **Ausgehen,** *n. in vbl senses; also:* emanation (of spirit, etc.) (from God, etc.); *cp.* **Ausgang.**

III. *pr.p. & a.* **ausgehend,** *in vbl senses; esp.* (*a*) **ausgehende Post,** outgoing mail; **ausgehende Waren,** exports; *Nau:* **ausgehende Ladung,** outward cargo; (*b*) *Geol:* outcropping (seam); **Ausgehendes** *n,* outcrop(ping); (*c*) **im ausgehenden neunzehnten Jahrhundert,** in the closing years of, towards the close, end, of the nineteenth century.
Ausgehtag, *m.* day off; day on which servant, etc., has time off.
ausgehungert, *p.p. & a. see* **aushungern.**
Ausgehuniform, *f. Mil:* walking-out dress; *Navy:* shore kit; *U.S:* class A uniform.
Ausgehverbot, *n.* (*a*) curfew; **das A. über eine Stadt verhängen, ein A. in einer Stadt erlassen,** to impose a curfew on a town; (*b*) *Mil:* confinement to barracks, *F:* C.B.
ausgeizen, *v.tr. sep. Vit:* to prune (vines).
ausgekocht, *a.* arrant, unmitigated, utter (rogue). *See also* **auskochen.**
ausgelassen, *p.p. & a.* gay; boisterous, exuberant; wild, abandoned. *See also* **auslassen.**
Ausgelassenheit, *f.* exuberance, boisterousness; abandon(ment); wildness.
ausgelastet, *p.p. & a. see* **auslasten.**
ausgeleiert, *p.p. & a.* hackneyed, trite (theme, etc.). *See also* **ausleiern.**
ausgemacht, *p.p. & a. see* **ausmachen.**
ausgenommen. I. *p.p.* (*with preceding acc.*) except, excepting, with the exception of; **ich habe das ganze Haus abgesucht, den Keller a.,** I have searched the whole house except the cellar; **alle, deinen Vater nicht a., waren damit einverstanden,** everyone, your father not excepted, agreed to it; *see also* **ausnehmen.**

II. **ausgenommen,** *conj.* **1.** *co-ordinate conj.* except, but, with the exception of, *Lit:* save; (*a*) (+*following noun or pron.*) **er gab allen ein Geschenk, a. seinem Bruder, a. mir,** he gave everyone a present except his brother, except me; **ich habe nur noch 200 Mark für den Rest meines Urlaubs, a. einen eisernen Bestand von 50 Mark,** I have only got 200 marks left for the rest of my holiday, not counting the 50 marks I keep for an emergency; (*b*) (*with preceding or following nom.*) **alle haben einen Platz bekommen, ich a., a. ich,** everyone got a seat except me, with the exception of me, with the exception of myself everyone got a seat; (*c*) (+*prep. or adv.*) **an jedem Tag, a. am Sonntag, a. sonntags,** every day except (on) Sunday(s). **2.** *subordinate conj.* unless; **ich gehe jeden Abend spazieren, a. (, wenn) es regnet,** I go for a walk every evening except when, unless, it is raining; **die Polizei besaß keine Anhaltspunkte, a., daß sie einen anonymen Anruf erhielt,** the police had no clues except that they received an anonymous telephone call; **er ist überall, a. (da,) wo er sein sollte,** he is everywhere except, but, where he ought to be.
ausgepicht, *p.p. & a. F:* **ein ausgepichter Kerl,** a difficult, unapproachable, fellow; *see also* **auspichen.**
ausgeprägt, *p.p. & a. see* **ausprägen.**
Ausgeprägtheit, *f.* distinctness (of character, features); prominence (of cheek-bones, chin, etc.); pronounced nature (of contrasts, tendencies, etc.).
ausgerben, *v.tr. sep.* to tan (hides) thoroughly; *F:* **j-n a., j-m das Fell a.,** *F:* to tan s.o., s.o.'s hide.
ausgerechnet, *adv.* of all . . . ; just; **daß Sie, a. Sie, so was tun sollten!** that you, of all people, should do such a thing! **a. heute mußte sie kommen,** she had to come today of all days; **a. hier mußte das geschehen,** it had to happen here of all places, just here; **a. sie gewann das Los; dabei hat sie schon so viel Geld,** she of all people won the lottery, and she has so much money already; **es wundert mich, daß a. er, der doch so geizig ist, ihr das Geld gegeben habe,** I am surprised that of all people (just) he, who is so miserly, should have given her the money; **a. als er fortgehen wollte, kam sie zurück,** just at the moment when he was starting out she came back; of all times, she came back just as he was starting out. *See also* **ausrechnen.**
ausgereift, *p.p. & a. see* **ausreifen.**
Ausgereiftheit, *f.* ripeness, maturity.

ausgeschamt, *a. South G.Dial:* shameless (person).

ausgeschlossen, *a.* impossible, out of the question; **ausgeschlossen!** impossible! out of the question! **es ist nicht ganz a., daß er heute noch ankommt,** it is just possible that he may come today. *See also* **ausschließen.**

ausgesprochen, (*a*) *a.* distinct, pronounced; decided, marked; **eine ausgesprochene Ähnlichkeit mit j-m haben,** to bear a marked, decided, resemblance, an unmistakable resemblance, to s.o.; **er zeigt eine ausgesprochene Vorliebe für blonde Frauen,** he shows a marked preference, a distinct partiality, for fair women; **sie hat sehr ausgesprochene Ansichten über diese Sache,** she has very decided, pronounced, views on this matter; **ein ausgesprochener Erfolg,** a pronounced success; **eine ausgesprochene Abneigung gegen etwas haben,** to have a pronounced dislike of sth.; **er ist ein ausgesprochener Gegner dieser Partei,** he is a declared opponent of this party; **er ist ein ausgesprochener Gegner dieser Maßnahme,** he is distinctly opposed to this measure; **ein ausgesprochener Dummkopf,** an absolute, utter, fool; (*b*) *adv.* distinctly, pronouncedly, decidedly, markedly; **dieses Bild finde ich a. häßlich,** I find this picture decidedly ugly; **eine a. revolutionäre Zeitung,** a distinctly revolutionary paper; **das Mädchen ist a. hübsch, ist nicht a. hübsch,** the girl is decidedly pretty, is not exactly pretty; **a. slawische Gesichtszüge,** pronouncedly, markedly, Slav, *U.S:* Slavic, features. *See also* **aussprechen.**

ausgestalten. I. *v.tr. sep.* **1.** to arrange, to make the arrangements for (celebration, function, etc.). **2. etwas zu etwas a.,** to develop sth. into sth.; to turn sth. into sth.; **einen Aufsatz zu einem Buche a.,** to develop an essay into a book; **sie gestalteten das Treffen zu einer kleinen Feier aus,** they turned the meeting into a little celebration; **der Saal wurde zu einer Kapelle ausgestaltet,** the hall was turned into a chapel.

II. *vbl s.* **1. Ausgestalten,** *n. in vbl senses.* **2. Ausgestaltung,** *f. in vbl senses; also:* development (of sth., **zu etwas,** into sth.); **Herr X unternahm die A. der Feier,** Mr X undertook the arrangements for the celebration.

ausgesucht, *p.p. & a. see* **aussuchen.**

ausgewachsen, *p.p. & a.* full-grown; *F:* fully-fledged (artist, lawyer, etc.); complete, utter (coward, fool); arrant (fool); full-scale (rebellion, etc.); fully-developed (cold, etc.), *F:* nasty, beastly (cold, etc.). *See also* **auswachsen.**

ausgewogen, *p.p. & a.* (*a*) trim, well-trimmed (ship, airship); (*b*) (well-)balanced (arrangement, character, etc.). *See also* **auswiegen.**

Ausgewogenheit, *f.* (good) balance (of arrangement, character, etc.).

ausgezeichnet, *a.* excellent, *F:* first-rate; *adv.* extremely well; excellently; **das hat a. geschmeckt,** that tasted excellent, extremely good; **es hat ihm a. gefallen,** he liked it extremely; **das paßt mir a.,** that just suits me, that suits me all right, *F:* that suits me down to the ground, suits me to a T. *See also* **auszeichnen.**

ausgiebig, *a.* **1.** extensive; thorough; **ausgiebigen Gebrauch,** *adv.* **a. Gebrauch, von etwas machen,** to make extensive use of sth., use sth. extensively; *adv.* **sich a. mit etwas beschäftigen,** to make a thorough, an exhaustive, study of sth.; **ich habe mir die Stadt a. betrachtet,** I have made a thorough tour of the town; **a. frühstücken,** to do full justice to one's breakfast; to have, make, a really good breakfast. **2.** = **ergiebig.**

Ausgiebigkeit, *f.* **1.** extensiveness (of use); thoroughness, exhaustiveness (of study, etc.). **2.** = **Ergiebigkeit.**

ausgießen. I. *v.tr. sep.* (*strong*) **1.** to pour out (water, milk, wine, etc.); to pour away, throw away, throw out, empty out (water, etc.); to pour out, empty out, the contents of (pail, etc.); to empty (pail, jug, bowl, etc.). **2. etwas über, auf, j-n, etwas, a.,** (*a*) to pour (liquid) over s.o., sth.; (*of sun, etc.*) to pour forth (rays, light), to shed (light), upon s.o., sth.; *F:* to shower (presents, etc.) upon s.o.; to vent (one's rage) on s.o.; *Lit:* (*of God, etc.*) **die Schale des Zorns über die Menschen a.,** to pour out the vials of (His) wrath upon men; (*b*) (*of God, etc.*) to pour out (spirit, etc.) upon s.o., sth.; *B:* **ich will a. von meinem Geist auf alles Fleisch,** I will pour out of my spirit upon all flesh; (*c*) **sich a.** = **sich ergießen. 3.** to fill (cast, mould); **ein Loch mit Blei, usw., a.,** to fill a hole with (molten) lead, etc.; **eine Fläche mit Beton, usw., a.,** to lay a surface with concrete, etc.; *Mec.E:* to line (bearing).

II. *vbl s.* **1. Ausgießen,** *n. in vbl senses.* **2. Ausgießung,** *f. in vbl senses; also:* **die A. des Heiligen Geistes,** the effusion of the Holy Spirit.

ausglätten, *v.tr. sep.* to smooth out (folds, material).

Ausgleich, *m.* -(e)s/-e. **1.** = **ausgleichen** II. 1. **2.** (*a*) equilibrium; balance; counterpoise; **einen A. schaffen,** to create a balance; *cp.* 2 (*b*); *Fb: etc:* equalizing, equalization; **den A. schaffen,** to equalize (the score); (*b*) offset, set-off; counterweight; compensation; **zum A. meiner Ausgaben für die Firma bekam ich . . . ,** to balance my expenses, as compensation for my expenses, on the firm's behalf, I received . . . ; **dieser geringe Betrag ist kein A. für unsere Bemühungen,** this small fee is no compensation for the pains we have taken; **j-m einen A. schaffen,** to compensate s.o.; (*c*) *Com:* settlement (of account); **zum A. Ihres Kontos,** in settlement of your account. **3.** *Com:* (*esp. in Austria*) composition, legal settlement (between merchant and creditors); **in A. gehen,** to make a composition with one's creditors. **4.** compromise; settlement (*by way of mutual concessions*); **er hat zwischen den beiden Gegnern einen A. erreicht,** he has effected a compromise between the two contestants; **sie sind zu einem A. gekommen,** they have come to a compromise, have composed their differences; *Hist:* **der Österreichisch-Ungarische A.,** the Austro-Hungarian Compromise (*1867*); **der Böhmische A.,** the Bohemian Compromise (*1890*).

ausgleichbar, *a.* adjustable (differences, forces, weights, values); (loss) which can be compensated, made good.

ausgleichen. I. *v.tr. sep.* (*strong*) **1.** (*a*) to level away, smooth out (irregularities in surface); to adjust (differences of level, size); **die Trägerhöhe, Balkenhöhe, a.,** to bring girders, beams, to the same level; (*b*) to equalize, adjust, balance, equilibrate (forces, weights, values, etc.); *Mec:* to compensate (pendulum, etc.); to equalize (action); *El.E: W.Tel:* to compensate (circuit, etc.); to balance (circuits, modulator, etc.); (*c*) to adjust, level up (differences); to balance (exports and imports, income and expenditure, etc.); to even up (fortunes, etc.); to settle (debt); to compensate for, make good (a loss); *Book-k:* to balance, square (accounts); *Fb: abs.* **a.,** to equalize; **einen Nachteil durch einen Vorteil a.,** to balance a disadvantage by, with, an advantage; **einen Verlust durch einen Gewinn a.,** to set off a gain against a loss; **seine Fehler durch doppelte Aufmerksamkeit a.,** to make up, compensate, for one's errors by paying double the amount of attention; **seine Fehler werden durch seine guten Eigenschaften ausgeglichen,** his good qualities compensate for, make amends for, offset, his shortcomings; **die ausgleichende Gerechtigkeit,** poetic justice; a compensating gift of Providence; (*d*) to settle, adjust (quarrel, difference), to compose (quarrel). **2. sich ausgleichen,** (*of two thgs*) to cancel one another out; (*of differences*) to be adjusted, levelled up; (*of exports and imports, debit and credit, etc.*) to be balanced, to balance; *Mth:* (*of terms*) to cancel out; **seine Fehler gleichen sich durch seine guten Eigenschaften aus,** his good qualities compensate for, make amends for, offset, his shortcomings.

II. *vbl s.* **1. Ausgleichen,** *n. in vbl senses, also:* adjustment (of differences of level, size); equalization, equilibrium, adjustment, compensation (of forces, etc.); settlement (of debt, quarrel, etc.); adjustment (of differences, quarrels, etc.); equation (of supply and demand, etc.); *Mec: Clockm:* compensation (of pendulum, etc.), equalization (of action); *El.E: W.Tel:* compensation (of circuit, etc.). **2. Ausgleichung,** *f.* (*a*) = II. 1; (*b*) *Jur:* hotchpot; **eine Zuwendung zur A. bringen,** to bring a donation into hotchpot; (*c*) *Ling:* equalization, assimilative analogy.

III. *p.p. & a.* **ausgeglichen,** *in vbl senses; esp.* well-balanced (mind, pers., etc.); **er ist a., er hat eine ausgeglichene Natur,** he is (well-)balanced, he has an equable temperament; he has a well-balanced mind; **ausgeglichene Nahrung,** (well-) balanced diet.

Ausgleicher, *m.* -s/-. **1.** (*pers.*) equalizer; leveller; *Sp:* handicapper. **2.** *El.E: Mec.E:* equalizer.

Ausgleichfeder, *f.* compensating spring, equalizing spring, equalizer spring.

Ausgleichsantenne, *f. W.Tel:* balancing aerial; aerial screen.

Ausgleichsarbitrage, *f. Fin:* arbitration of exchange.

Ausgleichsdüse, *f. I.C.E:* compensator(-jet).

Ausgleichsfonds, *m. Adm:* equalization fund.

Ausgleichsforderung, *f. Fin: etc:* equalization claim.

Ausgleich(s)getriebe, *n. Aut:* differential gear, equalizing gear.

Ausgleichsgymnastik, *f.* remedial exercises for correction of asymmetry.

Ausgleichshebel, *m. Mch:* compensating beam, equalizer.

Ausgleichskapazität, *f. El.E:* balancing capacitance; neutrodyne capacitance.

Ausgleichskasse, *f. Adm:* equalization fund.

Ausgleichskonto, *n. Book-k:* suspense account; adjustments account.

Ausgleichsleitung, *f. Tg: Tp:* balancing network.

Ausgleichsmagnet, *m. El.E:* compensating magnet.

Ausgleichsrennen, *n. Sp:* handicap(-race).

Ausgleichsschaltung, *f. El.E:* balancing network.

Ausgleichsschuß, *m. Fb:* equalizing goal.

Ausgleichsspannung, *f. El.E:* compensating *or* balancing voltage.

Ausgleichsspule, *f. El.E:* compensating coil.

Ausgleichssteuer, *f. Adm:* equalization tax.

Ausgleichsstrom, *m. El.E:* equalizing current.

Ausgleichstreffer, *m. Fb: etc:* equalizing goal, equalizer.

Ausgleichsverfahren, *n.* **1.** procedure for settlement of international debts. **2.** partial satisfaction of creditors (to avoid bankruptcy proceedings).

Ausgleichswicklung, *f. El.E:* compensating winding.

Ausgleichswiderstand, *m. El.E:* balancing resistance.

Ausgleichszahlung, *f. Fin: etc:* equalization payment.

Ausgleichtransformator, *m. El.E:* balancing transformer.

Ausgleichung, *f. see* **ausgleichen** II.

Ausgleichungshaus, *n. Fin:* clearing-house.

Ausgleichungspflicht, *f. Jur:* obligation (of heir) to bring donations into hotchpot.

ausgleiten, *v.i. sep.* (*strong*) (*sein*) to slip, slide; **er glitt auf der vereisten Straße aus,** he slipped, slid, on the icy road; **ihr Fuß glitt aus, der Fuß glitt ihr aus,** her foot slipped, slid away (from under her).

ausgliedern, *v.tr. sep.* to separate out (part, etc.).

ausglühen, *v.tr. sep. Metall:* to reheat (steel, etc.); to anneal (steel, etc.).

Ausglühflammofen, *m. Metall:* annealing furnace.

Ausglühmetall, *n. Metall:* residue left after heating of amalgam.

ausgraben. I. *v.tr. sep.* (*strong*) (*a*) to dig up (plant, treasure); to uproot, root up, root out, grub up (plant); to lift (potatoes); to disinter, exhume (body); (*b*) *Archeol:* to excavate (ruins, etc.); *abs.* **a.,** to excavate, make excavations, to dig, to go digging; (*c*) *F:* to dig out, unearth (secrets, old manuscripts, ancient laws, etc.); to dig up, rake up (old grievances, etc.).

II. *vbl s.* **1. Ausgraben,** *n. in vbl senses.* **2. Ausgrabung,** *f.* (*a*) = II. 1; *also:* disinterment, exhumation (of body); excavation (of ruins, etc.); (*b*) excavation; dig; **die Ausgrabungen in Pompeji,** the excavations at Pompeii.

Ausgräber, *m.* (*pers.*) excavator; field worker.

ausgräten, *v.tr. sep.* to bone, to remove the bones from (fish).

ausgreifen, *v.t. sep.* (*strong*) (*haben*) (*a*) to step out; *F:* to step on it, to step on the gas; **mit weit ausgreifenden Schritten,** with long strides; (*b*) (*of policy, effect, etc.*) **weit a.,** to be far-reaching; **ein weit ausgreifender Plan,** a comprehensive scheme.

Ausguck, *m.* -(e)s/-e. *Mil: Nau: etc:* look-out (post); **der Mann am A.,** the look-out (man); **A. halten,** to keep a look-out.

ausgucken, *v.sep.* **1.** *v.i.* (*haben*) **nach j-m, etwas, a.,** to look out, to keep a look-out, to be on the look-out, for s.o., sth. **2.** *v.tr.* **sich** *dat.* **die Augen (nach j-m, etwas) a.,** to stare one's eyes out (looking for s.o., sth.).

Ausguß, *m.* **1.** pouring out; effusion (of feelings). **2.** (*a*) sink (for disposal of waste water); (*b*) spout; lip (of jug). **3.** (*a*) *Mec.E:* lining (of bearing); (*b*) *Art: A:* cast.

Ausgußventil, *n. Mch:* discharge valve.

Ausgußwasser, *n.* waste water.

aushaben, *v.tr. sep.* (*conj. like* **haben**) *F:* to have finished (sth.).

aushacken, *v.tr. sep.* (*a*) to hoe up (potatoes, etc.); (*b*) (*of birds*) to pick out (eyes); *F:* (*of pers.*) to scratch out (s.o.'s eyes). *See also* **Krähe.**

aushageln, *v.impers. sep.* **es hat ausgehagelt,** the hail has stopped, it has stopped hailing.

aushaken, *v.tr. sep.* to unhook (dress, etc.); to take (door, etc.) off its hook *or* hinges; to unhinge (door, etc.); **sich a.,** (*of door, dress, etc.*) to come unhooked; (*of door, etc.*) to come off its hinges.

aushalftern, *v.tr. sep.* to take the halter off (horse); (*of horse*) **sich a.,** to slip the halter.

aushalten. I. *v.tr. sep.* (*strong*) **1.** (*a*) to bear, stand, endure, *F:* to stick (pain, hardship, difficult situation, etc.); to sustain, stand up to (attack, etc.); *abs.* **a.,** to hold out, hang on, to bear it, stand it, endure it, *F:* stick it out; to persevere; **j-s Blick nicht a. können,** to be unable to sustain s.o.'s gaze, meet s.o.'s gaze firmly; **ich kann es hier nicht länger a.,** I can't bear, stand, it here any longer; **sie kann es nicht mehr mit ihm a.,** she cannot endure him any longer; she cannot bear being with him any more; **sie konnte es vor Schmerzen, vor Kälte, nicht a.,** she could not bear, stand, endure, the pain, the cold, any longer; **ich glaube kaum, daß er diese Arbeit länger als einen Monat aushält,** I don't think he'll stick (at) that job for more than a month; **wir haben manchen Schlag des Schicksals a. müssen,** we have had to sustain many a blow of fate; **wir müssen a., bis Verstärkungen herankommen,** we must hold out, hang on, until reinforcements come up; **er hält nirgends länger als zwei Wochen aus,** he doesn't stay anywhere for longer than a fortnight; (*b*) to bear, stand, stand up to (comparison); **als Schauspieler hält er den Vergleich mit seinem Bruder nicht aus,** as an actor he cannot be compared with his brother; **die Probe, die Prüfung, a.,** to bear, stand, the test; (*c*) *abs. Dial:* (*of garment, etc.*) to last indefinitely; (*d*) *Ven:* (*of game*) not to take flight (at hunter's approach). **2.** *Mus:* to sustain (note, etc.); to suspend (tone). **3.** to keep (mistress, lover). **4.** *Min:* to separate (ore).

II. *vbl s.* **Aushalten,** *n. in vbl senses; also:* endurance; perseverance; *Mus:* suspension (of tone); **es ist nicht zum A.,** it's beyond endurance, it's not to be borne, to be endured, it's unbearable.

aushämmern, *v.tr. sep.* to hammer out, beat out (metal).

aushändigen, *v.tr. sep.* (*a*) to hand out (leaflets, etc.); (*b*) to hand over (prisoner); to hand over, surrender, relinquish (sth.).

Aushang, *m.* **1.** notice-board. **2.** advertisement; notice.

Aushängebögen, *m.pl. Publ:* advance-proofs, -sheets.

aushängen, *v.sep.* (*conj. like* **hängen**) I. *v.tr.* **1.** (*a*) to hang out, put out (flags, etc.); (*b*) to put up (notice, etc.). **2.** (*a*) to take (door, window) off its hinges, to unhinge (door, window); (*b*) **den Hörer, das Telephon, a.,** to remove the receiver. **3. sich aushängen,** (*of clothes, etc.*) to lose creases, to become smooth (by hanging); *F:* to hang out; (*of creases*) to drop out.

II. **aushängen,** *occ.* **aushangen,** *v.i.* (*haben*) (*a*) (*of flags, etc.*) to have been hung out, put out; **überall in der Stadt hängen schon die Fahnen aus,** flags have been hung out, put out, already all over the town; (*b*) to be announced by a notice (on a notice-board); *F:* (*of couple to be married*) **sie hängen aus,** their banns have been published.

Aushängeschild, *n.* (*a*) sign(-board); shop-sign; (*b*) *F:* advertisement.

Aushängezettel, *m.* bill, poster, placard.

ausharren, *v.i. sep.* (*haben*) to persevere; to hold out; to stand fast, to stand one's ground; **bis zum Ende a.,** to hold out to the last, to stand fast to the end; **wer ausharrt, kommt zum Ziel,** he who perseveres wins through; **sie harrten in der Festung aus, bis die Verbündeten ihnen zu Hilfe kamen,** they held out in the fortress till their allies came to their aid.

aushaspen, *v.tr. sep.* to take (door, window) off its hinges, to unhinge (door, window).

Aushau, *m.* clearing, *Lit:* glade.

aushauchen, *v.tr. sep.* to breathe out, to exhale (sth.); (*of flowers*) to exhale (perfume); **die Seele, das Leben, a.,** to give up the ghost, to expire, to breathe one's last; **Aushauchung** *f,* exhalation.

aushauen, *v.tr. sep.* (*conj. like* **hauen**) **1.** to hew (sth.) out; **Stufen im Felsen, aus dem Felsen, a.,** to hew steps in the rock; **eine Statue in Marmor a.,** to hew a statue from marble; **einen Weg durch die Felsen a.,** to hew out a passage through the rocks. **2.** (*a*) to clear, thin (a wood); to thin out (trees); (*b*) to prune (trees); (*c*) to lop off, away, to prune (off, away) (branches, twigs). **3.** *F:* to give (child, etc.) a thorough hiding.

Aushauer, *m. Tls:* hollow punch.

Aushaumaschine, *f. Tchn:* nibbling machine.

aushäusig, *a. F:* out (of the house); **viel a. sein,** to be rarely at home, to go out a lot.

aushäuten, *v.tr. sep.* (*a*) to skin, flay (animal); (*b*) (*of snake*) **sich a.,** to cast its slough.

ausheben. I. *v.tr. sep.* (*strong*) **1.** (*a*) to dig up (stones, roots, etc.); to lift (potatoes); (*b*) to dig (trench); (*c*) to lift (door, etc.) off its hinges; (*d*) *Metall:* to lift off, withdraw (pattern); (*e*) *Wr:* to lift (opponent) off his feet; (*f*) to take (birds, eggs) out of (the nest); to rob (nest); **das Nest ist ausgehoben,** the nest has been robbed; (*of police, etc.*) **ein Verbrechernest a.,** to clean out a nest of criminals. **2.** (*a*) to recruit, levy, enlist, enrol, conscript (soldiers); (*b*) *A:* to select (passages, etc.) (as illustration).

II. *vbl s.* **1. Ausheben,** *n. in vbl senses.* **2. Aushebung,** *f.* (*a*)=II. 1; (*b*) *Mil:* recruitment, levy, enlistment, enrolment, conscription (of soldiers).

Ausheber, *m.* **1.** (*a*) *Mec.E:* lifting device; (*b*) garden trowel. **2.** recruiting officer.

aushebern, *v.tr. sep.* to siphon off (liquid); *Med:* to siphon (stomach).

aushecheln, *v.tr. sep. Tex:* to hackle (hemp); *F:* **ein ausgehechelter Plan,** a subtly contrived scheme.

aushecken, *v.tr. sep. F:* to hatch (plot); to devise (scheme); to think out (prank); **jeden Tag hecken sie einen neuen Streich aus,** they think out a new prank, they're up to a new prank, every day; **das hat nur er a. können,** only he could think of (doing) a thing like that; **sie hecken schon wieder was aus,** they're up to something again.

ausheilen, *v.sep.* **1.** *v.tr.* to heal (wound) (completely). **2.** *v.i.* (*sein*) (*of wound*) to heal (up); (*of disease*) to be cured; **seine Tuberkulose ist jetzt ausgeheilt,** his tuberculosis is now (completely) cured.

ausheimisch, *a.* (*a*) foreign; (*b*) exotic (plants, etc.).

aushelfen, *v.i. sep.* (*strong*) (*haben*) to help out; **j-m a.,** to help s.o. out; **ich bekomme erst morgen mein Gehalt, — könnten Sie mir inzwischen mit zehn Mark a.?** I don't get my salary till tomorrow, so could you help me out in the meantime by lending me ten marks, so could you lend me ten marks to tide me over? **könntest du mir heute Abend mit einem Kleid a.?** could you lend me a dress tonight? **wenn wir sehr viel zu tun haben, hilft sie uns immer aus,** whenever we have a lot to do she lends us a hand, helps us out; **mein Sohn hilft im Geschäft aus,** my son helps out in the shop.

Aushelfer, *m.* temporary assistant.

Aushieb, *m. For:* thinning, clearing (of trees).

Aushilfe, *f.* (*a*) (temporary) help, assistance, aid; **damals war sie zur A. bei uns, weil das Dienstmädchen krank war,** she was helping us out at the time as the maid had fallen ill; **abends arbeitet sie zur A. in einem Café,** in the evenings she helps out at a café; (*b*) (*pers.*) temporary helper, temporary assistant; substitute, *F:* stop-gap; **wenn der Chauffeur Ausgang hat, kommt sein Bruder als A.,** when the chauffeur has the afternoon off his brother comes to take his place, comes as a substitute, *F:* as a stop-gap; **sie hatten lange keinen Gärtner, aber jetzt haben sie wenigstens eine A., bis sie einen neuen finden,** they were without a gardener for a long time but now they at least have someone to help out till they find a new one; **ich möchte in die Ferien fahren, aber erst muß ich eine A. finden,** I want to go on holiday but first I must find someone to take my place.

aushilflich, *adv.*=**aushilfsweise.**

Aushilfsarbeit, *f.* temporary work; odd job(s); casual labour.

Aushilfsarbeiter, *m.* temporary worker; casual labourer; auxiliary worker.

Aushilfskraft, *f.* temporary worker; temporary assistant.

aushilfsweise, *adv.* by way of a substitute, *F:* a stop-gap; as a temporary worker; temporarily; **er hat keine feste Arbeit, aber er kommt manchmal a. zu uns,** he has no regular job but he sometimes comes to help us out, *F:* comes to us as a stop-gap; **wenn einer von den Angestellten in die Ferien fährt, arbeitet Herr X a. im Büro,** if one of the clerks goes on holiday Mr X takes his place temporarily in the office.

aushöhlen. I. *v.tr. sep.* (*a*) to hollow (sth.) out; (*of water*) to wear away, erode (river-bank, etc.); to undermine (river-bank, cliffs, etc.); (*b*) to scoop out (fruit, etc.); to scoop the pulp, etc., out of (fruit, etc.); (*of insect*) to eat the inside out of (fruit, etc.); **der Baumstamm war ganz ausgehöhlt,** the tree-trunk was completely hollow, a mere shell; (*c*) to undermine (a principle, the power of the state, etc.); to sap the foundations of (a principle, etc.); to render (a principle, etc.) meaningless.

II. *vbl s.* **1. Aushöhlen,** *n. in vbl senses.* **2. Aushöhlung,** *f.* (*a*)=II. 1; (*b*) erosion (of stone, etc.) (by water); (*c*) hollow, cavity.

ausholen, *v.sep.* **1.** *v.i.* (*haben*) (*a*) **(mit der Hand, mit dem Arm, mit einer Waffe, usw.) a.,** to raise one's hand, one's arm, a weapon, etc., to swing one's hand, one's arm, a weapon, etc., back (*before striking, throwing, etc.*); **er holte mit der Hand aus, als ob er schlagen wollte,** he raised his hand as if to strike; **er holte mit dem Speer aus,** he raised his spear (ready for the throw); **zum Wurf, zum Schlag, a.,** to raise the ball, weapon, etc., ready to throw, to strike; to make ready, get ready, to throw, to strike; (*b*) **weit a.,** to begin (one's story) right at the beginning; **2.** *v.tr.* (*a*) *Nau:* **ein Segel a.,** to haul a sail taut, to haul out a sail; (*b*) *F:* **j-n über etwas** *acc.* **a.,** to ask, to question, s.o., about sth.; to draw s.o. out about, on, sth.; to sound s.o. on, with regard to, sth.; *F:* to pump s.o. about sth.

Ausholer, *m.* **-s/-.** *Nau:* outhaul.

Ausholring, *m. Nau:* traveller(-ring) (of jib-boom, gaff, etc.).

ausholzen, *v.tr. sep.* to thin (forest).

aushorchen, *v.tr. sep.* **j-n (über etwas) a.,** to sound s.o. (on sth.); **j-n a.,** *F:* to pump s.o.

Aushub, *m. Civ.E: etc:* (*a*) excavation; (*b*) excavated material.

aushülsen, *v.tr. sep.*=**enthülsen.**

aushungern, *v.tr. sep.* (*a*) to starve, famish (s.o.); **ausgehungert aussehen,** to look starved, famished, ravenous; (*b*) to starve out (town, garrison, etc.).

aushusten, *v.sep.* **1.** *v.tr.* to cough up (blood, phlegm, etc.). **2.** *v.i.* (*haben*) to finish coughing. **3. sich aushusten,** (*a*) to have a good cough; (*b*) to finish coughing.

ausjäten, *v.tr. sep.* to take up, pull up, remove (weeds).

auskämmen, *v.tr. sep.* **1.** to comb out (hair, knots). **2.** *Tex:* to card, comb (wool, etc.). **3.** *Mil: etc: F:* to comb (area); to mop up (area).

auskämpfen, *v.sep.* **1.** *v.tr.* to fight out (battle, etc.); **wir haben die Sache unter uns ausgekämpft,** we fought the matter out, we fought it out, amongst ourselves. **2.** *v.i.* (*haben*) to cease fighting; **ausgekämpft haben,** (i) to have ceased, finished, fighting; (ii) to have died, passed away; **sie haben ausgekämpft,** their battles, struggles, are over.

Auskarde, *f. Tex:* finisher.

auskarren, *v.tr. sep.* to cart (sth.) away, out.

auskaufen, *v.tr. sep.* **1.** to buy up (shop, etc.). **2.** to buy (s.o.) off; to buy out (partner, etc.); **sich a.,** to buy oneself off; *Mil:* to buy oneself out (of the army). **3. die, seine, Zeit a.,** to make the best possible use of the, one's, time.

auskegeln, *v.sep.* **1.** *v.tr.* to play skittles, nine-pins, for (sth.). **2.** *v.i.* (*haben*) to finish playing skittles, ninepins. **3.** *v.tr.*=**auskugeln.**

auskehlen. I. *v.tr. sep.* to groove, channel (sth.); to make a hollow moulding in (architrave, etc.); **ausgekehlter Bilderrahmen,** grooved picture-frame.

II. *vbl.s.* **1. Auskehlen,** *n. in vbl senses.* **2. Auskehlung,** *f.* (*a*)=II. 1; (*b*) *Arch: etc:* channel, groove; hollow moulding; hollow (of moulding).

auskehren[1], *v.tr. sep.* to sweep (room) (out); to sweep (dirt, etc.) out of (room, etc.); *F:* to clean up (an organization, etc.); **das ganze Personal a.,** to make a clean sweep of the staff.

auskehren[2], *v.tr. sep.* **1.** to empty (sth.), to tip the contents out of (sth.). **2.** to distribute (dividends).

Auskehricht, *m. & n.* sweepings, refuse, rubbish.

auskeilen, *v.i. sep.* (*haben*) *Geol:* (*of lode etc.*) to pinch.

auskeimen, *v.sep.* **1.** *v.i.* (*haben*) to germinate; (*of potato, etc.*) to sprout. **2.** *v.tr.* to remove the eyes from (potato).

auskennen (sich), *v.refl. sep.* (*conj. like* **kennen**), to know one's way about; **sich in einem Orte a.,** to know one's way about a place; **kennst du dich in Hamburg aus?** do you know your way around Hamburg? **hier kenne ich mich nicht mehr aus,** I've lost my way, my bearings; I don't know the way from here; **sich in einem Fach a.,** to have a thorough knowledge of a subject to be well

versed, at home, in a subject; **sich in der Mathematik, in der Musik, a.,** to understand, know about, mathematics, music; **er kennt sich in Geschäftsangelegenheiten aus,** he is well versed in business matters, he understands business; **sich mit Pferden a.,** to understand horses; **sich bei, mit, j-m a.,** to know where one is with a person; **er kennt sich aus,** he knows what's what; he knows a trick or two; *F:* he knows his stuff; **er sagt, daß es etwas Gutes ist, und er kennt sich aus,** he says it's a good thing, and he knows; **ich kenne mich überhaupt nicht mehr aus,** I'm completely at a loss, I don't know where I am.

Ausker. *Pr.n. m.* **-s/-.** *Hist:* member of the Ausci tribe; **die Ausker,** the Ausci.

auskerben, *v.tr. sep.* to cut a notch, to cut notches, in (sth.); to notch (sth.).

auskernen, *v.tr. sep.*=**entkernen.**

auskesseln, *v.i. sep.* (*haben*) (*of ground*) to form a cauldron, a cauldron-shaped cavity; **Auskesselung** *f*, cauldron, cauldron-shaped cavity.

auskitten, *v.tr. sep.* to fill (cracks, etc.) with putty; to putty (up) (cracks, etc.).

ausklagen, *v.sep.* **1.** *v.tr.* **eine Schuld, usw., a.,** to sue for payment of a debt, etc. **2.** *v.i.* (*haben*) to cease complaining; to cease wailing; to cease moaning.

ausklammern, *v.tr. sep. Mth:* to remove the brackets from (word, *Mth:* expression, etc.); to take (word, etc.) out of the brackets; *Mth:* to extract (term, etc., from a bracket).

ausklamüsern, *v.tr. sep.* (*p.p.* **ausklamüsert**) *F:* to puzzle, worry, (sth.) out.

Ausklang, *m.* (*a*) final sound; (*b*) ending; end.

ausklarieren, *v.tr. sep.* (*p.p.* **ausklariert**) *Cust: Nau:* to clear (outward-bound ship); **Ausklarierung** *f*, clearance outwards, entry outwards.

ausklauben, *v.tr. sep.* to pick (sth.) out (of sth.); *Min:* to hand-sort (ore).

auskleben, *v.tr. sep.* **eine Schachtel, usw., mit Papier, usw., a.,** to paste a lining of paper, etc., inside a box, etc.

auskleiden. I. *v.tr. sep.* **1.** to undress (s.o.); **sich a.,** to undress (oneself); to take off one's clothes. **2.** to line (sth.); **einen Raum mit Holz a.,** to wainscot, panel, line, a room.

II. *vbl s.* **1. Auskleiden,** *n. in vbl senses.* **2. Auskleidung,** *f.* (*a*)=II. 1; (*b*) lining; wainscot, wainscotting, panelling (of room); **A. eines Zylinders,** lining, liner, of a cylinder.

ausklengen, *v.tr. sep.* to remove, extract, the seed from (pine-cones).

ausklingen, *v.i. sep.* (*strong*) (*sein*) **1.** (*of sounds*) to die away, to fade (away). **2.** to end; to culminate; **der so fröhliche Tag klang traurig aus,** the happy day ended sadly, on a sad note; **die Feier klang mit einem herrlichen Feuerwerk aus,** the celebrations ended with, culminated in, a magnificent firework display; **seine Ansprache klang mit einem Appell an die Gebefreudigkeit seiner Zuhörer aus,** his speech ended with an appeal to the generosity of his hearers; **der letzte Satz der Symphonie klingt in einen Jubelchor aus,** the last movement of the symphony enters on, passes into, a final triumphal chorus.

ausklinken, *v.tr. sep.* **1.** to notch (sth.), to cut notches in (sth.). **2.** (*a*) to unlatch (door); (*b*) *Mec.E:* to release (gear, catch, etc.), to disengage (catch); *Av:* **das Schleppseil a.,** to release the tow-rope (of glider).

Ausklinkvorrichtung, *f. Mec.E:* release gear, release device; trip-gear.

ausklopfen, *v.tr. sep.* (*a*) to beat the dust out of (sth.); to beat (carpet); *F:* **j-m den Rock (auf dem Leibe) a.,** to dust s.o.'s jacket, s.o.'s coat; to give s.o. a dusting; (*b*) to knock out (pipe); (*c*) to beat out (dust); to knock out (ashes); (*d*) *Mch:* to scale (off), to chip (boiler).

Ausklopfer, *m.* carpet-beater.

ausklügeln, *v.tr. sep.* to think (sth.) out (carefully); to work (sth.) out; to puzzle, worry, (sth.) out.

auskneifen, *v.i. sep.* (*strong*) (*sein*) *F:* to run away, make off, decamp.

ausknеten, *v.tr. sep.* **1.** to knead (dough, etc.) thoroughly. **2.** to knead (sth.) out (of sth.).

ausknipsen, *v.tr. sep. F:* to switch off (light, radio, etc.), *F:* to turn off, put off (light).

ausknobeln, *v.tr. sep. F:* (*a*) to throw dice for (sth.); to decide (sth.) by throwing dice; (*b*) to work (sth.) out; to puzzle, worry (sth.) out.

uskochen, *v.sep.* I. *v.tr.* **1.** (*a*) **etwas aus etwas a.,** to boil (fat, colour, stain, etc.) out of (meat, material, etc.); (*b*) to boil (bones) (*for making stock*); to boil down (meat); to boil all the goodness out of (meat, vegetable, etc.); *cp.* 2; (*c*) to clean (pan, etc.) by boiling water in it; to sterilize (instruments, etc.) (in boiling water); **Wäsche a.,** to boil linen (clean); (*d*) *Tex:* to boil (fibre). **2.** to boil (meat, etc.) thoroughly. **3.** *See also* **ausgekocht.**

II. **auskochen,** *v.i.* (*haben*) (*a*) (*of fat, vitamin, etc.*) to be boiled out (of meat, etc.); (*b*) (*of meat, vegetable, etc.*) to have all the goodness boiled out; (*of bones*) to be boiled (for stock); (*of meat*) to be boiled down.

Auskochtiegel, *m. Clockm:* boiling-out pan.

auskolken. I. *v.tr. sep.* (*of water*) to erode, excavate (river-bed); to scour, erode, undermine (river-bank, etc.); (*of glacier*) to erode, excavate (ground).

II. *vbl s.* **1. Auskolken,** *n. in vbl senses; also:* erosion, excavation (of river-bed, ground, etc.); underwashing (of river-bank). **2. Auskolkung,** *f.* (*a*)=II. 1. (*b*) pot-hole (in river); (glacial) pot-hole.

auskommen. I. *v.i. sep.* (*strong*) (*sein*) **1.** (*a*) to (manage to) get out (of doors); (*b*) to get out; to escape; (*c*) (*of chicken, etc.*) to hatch (out). **2.** (*a*) to manage (with), to get along (with), (sth.); **mit seinem Gehalt a.,** to manage on one's income, to make ends meet; **mit seinem Geld a.,** to manage on one's money, to get along with what money one has; **ich kann mit so wenig Geld nicht a.,** I can't manage with, get along with, so little money; **mit zehn Mark werde ich gut a.,** I can manage very well with ten marks, ten marks will be quite sufficient, will be adequate; **ohne etwas a.,** to manage, to do, without sth.; **sie kommt mit ganz wenigen Kleidern aus,** she manages with very few clothes; **wir haben nicht viel Geld, aber wir kommen gerade aus,** we haven't much money but we just manage, *F:* we manage to rub along; (*b*) **mit j-m (gut) a.,** to get on (well) with s.o., to hit it off (well) with s.o.; **mit j-m nicht a.,** not to get on, hit it off, with s.o.; **wir kommen recht gut miteinander aus,** we get on well together, we hit it off well, *F:* we rub along very well together; **sie kommen miteinander gar nicht aus,** they don't get on (with one another) at all; **mit ihm ist gut auszukommen,** he is an easy person to get on with.

II. *vbl s.* **Auskommen,** *n.* **1.** *in vbl senses.* **2.** (means of) subsistence; competence, competency; **er findet gerade sein A., er hat ein knappes A.,** he just has enough to live on, to make ends meet, he has a bare competency; **ein anständiges A. haben,** to have decent means, a decent competency. **3. es ist kein A. mit ihr,** it's impossible to get on, to hit it off, with her.

auskömmlich, *a.* sufficient, adequate (income, etc.); **er hat ein auskömmliches Gehalt,** he earns enough to live on.

Auskopierpapier, *n. Phot:* printing(-out) paper, *usu.* P.O.P.

auskoppeln, *v.tr. sep. Ven:* to slip, unleash, uncouple (hounds).

auskörnen, *v.tr. sep.* to remove the grain from (ear of corn); to remove the seed from, to seed (fruit).

auskosten, *v.tr. sep.* to taste (sth.) to the full; **er hat die Freuden des Lebens voll, bis zur Neige, ausgekostet,** he has tasted the joys of life to the full; **er hat die Leiden des Lebens bis zur Neige ausgekostet,** he has drained the cup of sorrow to the dregs.

auskragen, *v.sep. Constr:* **1.** *v.tr.* to make (cornice, etc.) project, jut out, overhang; **ausgekragt sein,** to project, to jut out; to overhang. **2.** *v.i.* (*haben*) (*of cornice, etc.*) to project, to jut out; to overhang. **3.** *vbl s.* **Auskragung,** *f.* projection; overhang.

auskramen, *v.tr. sep.* **1.** to take things out of, to empty (cupboard, etc.); to take (thgs) out (of cupboard, etc.); **das Kind hat sein ganzes Spielzeug wieder ausgekramt,** the child has pulled all his toys out again. **2.** to dig up, unearth (piece of information, news, old jokes, etc.); to bring up (subject) (again); to produce (piece of news, etc.); to display (one's knowledge).

auskratzen, *v.sep.* **1.** *v.tr.* **etwas aus etwas a.,** to scrape sth. out of sth. **2.** *v.tr.* (*a*) to scrape out (pan, etc.); *Surg:* to curette (womb); to scrape out (carious cavity); (*b*) **j-m die Augen a.,** to scratch s.o.'s eyes out; (*c*) to scratch out (word, etc.) (with penknife, etc.). **3.** *v.i.* (*sein*) *F:* to run away, make off, decamp.

auskreuzen, *v.tr. sep.* **1.** to chisel (sth.) off, to cut (sth.) off with a chisel. **2.** to cross out (word, etc.

auskriechen, *v.i. sep.* (*strong*) (*sein*) (*of birds, crocodiles, etc.*) to hatch (out); to emerge from the egg.

auskriegen, *v.tr. sep. F:* to get(jacket, shoes, etc.) off.

auskristallisieren, *v.i. sep.* (*sein*) to crystallize out.

auskugeln, *v.tr. sep.* to dislocate (shoulder, hip); **(sich,** *dat.***) den Arm, die Hüfte, a.,** to dislocate one's shoulder, hip.

auskühlen, *v.sep.* **1.** *v.i.* (*sein*) to cool (thoroughly), to become (thoroughly) cold; **etwas a. lassen,** to allow sth. to cool, to become (thoroughly) cold; **das Haus ist so ausgekühlt, daß es draußen wärmer ist als drinnen,** the house has become so thoroughly cold that it's warmer outside than in. **2.** *v.tr.* to cool (sth.) (thoroughly).

Auskultant [auskulˈtant], *m.* **-en/-en.** **1.** *Med:* auscultator. **2.** member (of committee, etc.) without power of voting.

Auskultation [auskulta·tsiˈoːn], *f.* **-/-en.** *Med:* auscultation; sounding.

Auskultator [auskulˈtaːtor], *m.* **-s/-oren** [-ta·ˈtoːrən]. *Med:* auscultator.

auskultieren [auskulˈtiːrən], *v.tr. sep. Med:* to sound (patient, patient's chest); to examine (s.o.) by auscultation.

auskundschaften. I. *v.sep.* **1.** *v.tr.* (*a*) to try to find, trace (sth.); (*b*) to trace, locate (sth.); to discover the whereabouts of (sth.). **2.** *v.tr.* to reconnoitre, explore, spy out (district); *abs.* **a. gehen,** to reconnoitre, to go reconnoitring.

II. *vbl s.* **1. Auskundschaften,** *n. in vbl senses; also:* exploration (of district, etc.). **2. Auskundschaftung,** *f.* (*a*)=II. 1; (*b*) reconnaissance, exploration.

Auskunft, *f.* **-/¨e.** **1.** information, intelligence; **falsche A.,** misinformation, incorrect information; **j-m falsche A., falsche Auskünfte, geben,** to misinform s.o.; **nähere A.,** further information; further particulars; **A., Auskünfte, über j-n, etwas** *acc.*, **einholen,** to seek information, to make enquiries, about s.o., sth.; **A., Auskünfte, über j-n, etwas, geben, erteilen,** to give, impart, information about s.o., sth., to give intelligence of sth.; **A., Auskünfte, über j-n, etwas, erhalten,** to receive, obtain, information about s.o., sth., to receive intelligence of sth.; **A. (bei j-m) einholen,** to seek information (from s.o.); **bei wem haben Sie A., Auskünfte, eingeholt?** from whom did you seek information? whom did you ask? **wir haben A. über seinen Verbleib erhalten,** we have received intelligence of, information regarding, his whereabouts; **um genaue A. bitten,** to ask for detailed information. **2.** (*enquiry office*) 'information', 'enquiries'; (*department of telephone exchange*) 'enquiries'; **ich werde bei der A. anfragen,** I'll ask at 'enquiries'.

Auskunftei, *f.* **-/-en.** **1.** *Rail: etc:* information office; enquiry office. **2.** confidential investigations office; private detective agency.

Auskunftsbeamte, *m.* enquiry clerk, enquiry official.

Auskunftsbüro, *n.* (*a*) information bureau, information centre; enquiry office, 'enquiries'; (*b*)=**Auskunftei.**

Auskunftspflicht, *f.* obligation to give information.

Auskunftsquelle, *f.* source of information.

Auskunftsstelle, *f.* enquiry office, 'enquiries'.

auskünsteln, *v.tr. sep.* to contrive (sth.); to work (sth.) out in detail.

auskuppeln, *v.tr. sep.* to disconnect (part, gear, etc.); to release (gear); *abs.* **a.,** *Aut: etc:* to declutch, to disengage the clutch.

auskurieren, *v.tr. sep.* to heal, cure (s.o., disease) (completely).

auskutten, *v.tr. sep. Austrian: Min:* to hand-sort (ore).

auslachen, *v.sep.* **1.** *v.tr.* **j-n a.,** to laugh at s.o.; to make fun of, to poke fun at, s.o.; to jeer at s.o.; **sie haben mich tüchtig, gründlich, ausgelacht,** they had a good laugh at my expense, they made great fun, great game, of me; **ich laß mich nicht a.,** I won't be laughed at; **er hat Angst, daß man ihn auslacht,** he's afraid of being laughed at; **sie lachen ihn aus, weil er einen Schirm trägt,** they laugh at him, make fun of him, poke fun at him, for carrying an umbrella; **laß dich nicht a.,** (i) don't be put off by people laughing at you; (ii) don't be ridiculous. **2.** *v.i.* (*haben*) & **sich auslachen,** to have one's laugh out, to laugh one's fill; to finish laughing.

ausladen[1], *v. sep.* (*strong*) I. *v.tr.* **1.** to unload (goods, etc.) (from vehicle, ship, etc.); to unload (ship, lorry, etc.); to unlade, discharge (ship, cargo); to unship (cargo). **2.** to make (cornice, etc.) project, jut out.

II. **ausladen,** *v.i.* (*haben*) (*of cornice, balcony, etc.*) to project, jut out; (*of upper storey, etc.*) to overhang; (*of tree, etc.*) **weit a.,** to have a broad overhang; **breit ausladend,** broad; **weit ausladend,** (*of balcony, etc.*) having a broad overhang; (*of gestures*) sweeping.

III. *vbl s.* **1. Ausladen,** *n. in vbl senses.* **2. Ausladung,** *f.* (*a*) *in vbl senses; also:* discharge (of ship, cargo); (*b*) projection (of cornice, etc.); overhang (of projecting part); (*c*) extent of projection; (extent of) overhang; projection; projecting part; overhang; **das obere Stockwerk hat vier Fuß A.,** the upper storey has a four foot overhang; **das Gesims hat anderthalb Fuß A.,** the ledge projects one and a half feet; (*d*) reach, radius, range (of crane); depth of throat (of punching-machine); gap (in lathe-bed).

ausladen[2], *v.tr. sep.* (*strong*) *F:* to cancel an invitation to (s.o.); to put off (guest); *F:* to uninvite (s.o.).

Ausladeplatz, *m.* unloading place; *Nau:* wharf, unloading dock.

Auslader, *m.* unloader.

Ausladestelle, *f.*=**Ausladeplatz.**

Auslage, *f.* **1.** (*a*) outlay, expenditure (of money); (*b*) outlay, expenditure, expense; **unsere Auslagen für Rohstoffe,** our outlay on raw materials; **j-m seine Auslagen ersetzen, erstatten,** to reimburse s.o. (for) his expenses, to repay, refund, s.o.'s expenses; **kleine Auslagen,** petty expenses, sundries. **2.** *Com:* display, show (of goods); window-display; **in der A.,** in the (shop-) window. **3.** *Fenc:* guard, on guard position; *Row:* starting position. **4.** *Ven:* span (between antlers). **5.** *Hyd.E:* outer dike. *Cp.* **auslegen** II.

Auslagekasten, *m. Com:* show-case.

auslagern, *v.tr. sep.* **1.** to place (goods, etc.) in a store-house away from the central office; to evacuate (art treasures, etc.) (*to a safe area*); **Auslagerung** *f* **der Kunstschätze,** evacuation of art treasures. **2.** to remove (goods) from a store-house.

Ausland, *n.* **das A.,** foreign countries; foreign parts; **das feindliche, neutrale, A.,** enemy countries, neutral countries; **ins A. gehen, fahren, reisen,** to go abroad, to travel abroad; **im A. reisen,** to travel abroad; **er ist viel im A. gereist,** he has travelled a lot abroad; **im A. leben,** to live abroad; **sie ist viel im A. gewesen,** she has been abroad, in foreign parts, a great deal; **Reisen ins A.,** (i) journeys abroad; (ii) going abroad, travelling abroad; foreign travel, travel abroad; **einen Bericht über seine Reisen im A. schreiben,** to write a report on one's foreign travels, one's travels abroad; **er ist gerade aus dem A. zurückgekehrt,** he has just returned from abroad; **Lieferungen nach dem A.,** deliveries abroad; shipments abroad; (*of ship*) **nach dem A. bestimmt sein,** to be bound for foreign parts; **unsere Beziehungen mit dem, zum, A.,** our relations with foreign countries; **Handel mit dem A.,** foreign trade, trade with foreign countries; **unser Ansehen im A.,** our prestige abroad.

Ausländer, *m.* **-s/-,** foreigner; *Adm:* alien; **unerwünschter A.,** *F:* **lästiger A.,** undesirable alien; **feindlicher A.,** enemy alien.

Ausländerpolizei, *f.* aliens' registration office.

ausländisch, *a.* foreign; *Adm:* alien.

Auslandsanleihe, *f.* foreign loan.

Auslandsaufenthalt, *m.* stay abroad, stay in a foreign country; time spent abroad.

Auslandsbeziehungen, *f.pl.* contacts in foreign countries, contacts abroad; relations with foreign countries, foreign relations.

Auslandsdebatte, *f.* foreign affairs debate.

Auslandsdeutsche, *m., f.* (*decl. as adj.*) German national living abroad; person of German extraction living abroad.

Auslandsdeutschtum, *n.* (*a*) German people living abroad; people of German extraction living abroad; (*b*) German national customs and culture preserved by groups of emigrants.

Auslandshandel, *m.* foreign trade.

Auslandshilfe, *f.* foreign aid.

Auslandskorrespondent, *m.* (*a*) *Com:* foreign correspondence translator, clerk; (*b*) *Journ:* foreign correspondent.

Auslandspaß, *m.* passport.

Auslandspostanweisung, *f.* foreign money order.

Auslandsreise, *f.* journey abroad; **von seinen Auslandsreisen erzählen,** to talk about one's travels abroad.

Auslandsschuld, *f.* foreign debt.

Auslandsstimmen, *f.pl. Journ:* extracts from foreign newspapers.

auslangen, *v.i. sep.* (*haben*) **1.** (*a*) **mit der Hand, usw., a.,** to raise one's hand, etc., to swing one's hand, etc., back (before striking, throwing, etc.); (*b*) **nach etwas a.,** to reach for, to stretch out one's hand for, sth. **2.** to be sufficient, adequate, to suffice; **das Geld hat nicht ausgelangt,** the money didn't last out; **glaubst du, daß drei Mark a. werden?** do you think three marks will be sufficient, adequate, enough?

auslängen, *v.i. sep.* (*haben*). *Min:* to push on the levels.

Auslaß, *m.* **-lasses/-lässe. 1.** outlet. **2.** discharge.

auslassen. I. *v.tr. sep.* (*strong*) **1.** (*a*) to let out (water, air); to let off (water, steam); to blow off (steam); to run off (water); (*b*) **seinen Zorn an j-m a.,** to vent one's temper, one's anger, on s.o.; to rail at s.o.; **seine schlechte Laune an j-m a.,** to vent, work off, one's bad temper on s.o. **2. sich über j-n, etwas** *acc.*, **a.,** to say sth. about s.o., sth., to mention s.o., sth.; to express one's opinion about s.o., sth.; **wie lange bleibt er weg?—darüber hat er sich nicht ausgelassen,** how long will he be away?—he didn't say; **sich des Längeren und Breiteren über j-n, etwas, a.,** to let oneself go on the subject of s.o., sth., to expatiate, dilate, on the subject of s.o., sth. **3.** *Dressm:* to let out (garment, seam, etc.); to let down (hem); **ein Kleid an den Ärmeln a.,** to let out the sleeves of a dress. **4.** (*a*) to leave out, miss out, to omit (word, letter, etc.); (*purposely*) to cut (sth.) out; **sonntags lassen wir das Mittagessen aus,** on Sundays we cut out, miss out, lunch; **sie hat keinen Tanz ausgelassen,** she didn't miss a dance; **er geht auf jeden Ball,—er läßt nichts aus,** he goes to every dance—he never misses anything; (*b*) *South G.Dial:* **laß mich aus!** leave me alone! **laß mich aus mit diesem Blödsinn!** don't bother me with such stupid things! **5.** to render down (fat); to melt (down) (butter, etc.). *See also* **ausgelassen.**

II. *vbl s.* **1. Auslassen,** *n. in vbl senses.* **2. Auslassung,** *f.* (*a*)=II. 1; *also:* omission (of letter, etc.); (*b*) omission; gap (in text); (*c*) *Ling:* ellipsis; elision; (*d*) **sich in längeren Auslassungen über etwas** *acc.* **ergehen, längere Auslassungen über etwas machen,** to talk at length about, to hold forth at length upon, sth.; **seine Auslassungen über . . . ,** what he said about . . . .

Auslaßklappen, *f.pl. Av:* cooling gills (of engine cowling).

Auslassungszeichen, *n. Gram:* apostrophe; *Print:* caret.

Auslaßventil, *n,* (*a*) exhaust valve, outlet valve, escape valve; (*b*) delivery valve.

auslasten, *v.tr. sep.* (*a*) *Tchn:* to balance, equalize (loads); (*b*) *Ind: Com: etc.:* to make (s.o., a firm) work to capacity, at full capacity; to employ (s.o.) fully; **ausgelastet sein,** to be working to capacity, at full, peak, maximum, capacity; (*of pers.*) to be fully employed, occupied.

auslatschen, *v.tr. sep.* to make (one's shoes) sloppy with wear; **ausgelatschte Schuhe,** sloppy (old) shoes.

Auslauf, *m.* **1.** sailing (of ship); **zum A. bereit sein,** to be ready to (set) sail. **2.** (*a*) *Sp:* (finishing) run (*to slow down gradually*); (*b*) *Av:* landing run. **3.** space, room, to move, to run, about in; **die Hühner haben hier einen guten A.,** the hens have plenty of room to run about in here. **4.** (*a*) (chicken-, etc.) run; (*b*) *Ten:* run-back. **5.** *Hyd.E:* (*a*) run-off; (*b*) outlet.

Auslaufbefehl, *m. Navy:* sailing orders.

auslaufen, *v.sep.* (*strong*) I. *v.i.* (*sein*) **1.** (*of ship*) to (set) sail, to leave port; to clear the harbour; to put (out) to sea; (*of train*) to leave (the station). **2.** (*a*) (*of liquid, sugar, sand, etc.*) to run out, flow out, leak out (**aus etwas,** of sth.); (*of grain, peas, etc.*) **aus dem Sack, usw., a.,** to run out of (the sack, etc.); to spill out (of the sack, etc.); (*b*) (*of fountain-pen, etc.*) to leak; **die Wärmflasche läuft aus,** the hot-water bottle is leaking; **der Tank ist ausgelaufen,** the tank is empty, has run dry; **die Sanduhr ist ausgelaufen,** the sand in the hour-glass has run out; (*c*) (*of colour*) to run; (*of ink, on soft paper, etc.*) to run. **3.** (*of streets, etc.*) **von einem Platz, usw., a.,** to start at, radiate from, a square, etc. **4.** (**in etwas,** *acc.*) **a.,** to end (in sth.); (*a*) **spitz, in eine Spitze, a.,** to end in a point; to taper off to a point; **das Hochgebirge läuft nach Norden (zu) in eine niedrige Hügelkette aus,** the mountains end towards the north in a chain of low hills; (*b*) **die Besprechung lief in Streit aus,** the discussion ended in a quarrel; **das wird schlecht a.,** that'll end badly. **5.** (*a*) to stop running, to finish running; (*of machine*) to run down; (*b*) **die Produktion dieses Artikels ist ausgelaufen,** production of this article has been discontinued: (*c*) (*of horse, etc.*) to slow down (past winning-post, etc.); (*of runner*) to run down.

II. **auslaufen,** *v.tr.* **1.** *Min:* to haul, wheel, tram, truck (coal). **2.** to run (course, etc.) to the end; **die Bahn nicht a. können,** to be unable to run the full course, stay the course. **3. sich auslaufen,** to run about, to walk about, to exercise; **in den Ferien haben wir uns tüchtig ausgelaufen,** we exercised our legs thoroughly, we did a lot of walking, in the holidays; **die Kinder können sich hier tüchtig a.,** the children can get plenty of exercise, have plenty of room to run about in, here; **der Hund kann sich in der Stadt nicht richtig a.,** the dog can't get enough exercise in the city; **auf der Wiese können die Hühner sich gut a.,** there's plenty of room in the meadow for the hens to run about in.

Ausläufer, *m.* **1.** (*pers.*) runner; (*in Switzerland*) errand-boy; *Min:* trammer, wheeler, drawer, roller, haulage-man. **2.** offshoot; branch (of lode, etc.); *Bot:* stolon, runner, sucker; *Ph. Geog:* spur, counterfort, buttress, branch (of mountain range); **die letzten Ausläufer der Alpen,** the last foothills of the Alps; **die A. der Haupstadt,** the fringes of the metropolis.

Auslaufhahn, *m.* waste-cock, drain-cock.

Auslaufmodell, *n. Com:* discontinued model; discontinued line.

auslaugen. I. *v.tr. sep.* (*a*) to wash, steep (linen, yarn, etc.) in lye; to soak (salted vegetables, etc.); **ausgelaugt sein,** (*of meat*) to have had all the goodness boiled out; *F:* (*of pers.*) to be washed out; *Agr: Glassm:* **ausgelaugte Asche,** buck-ashes, lye-ashes; *Sug-R:* **Rübenschnitzel a.,** to extract the sugar from beet slices; **ausgelaugte Rübenschnitzel,** spent slices, exhausted slices; (*b*) *Ch: etc:* to lixiviate (wood-ashes, etc.); (*c*) *Min: Ind:* to leach; *Ch:* to leach away, leach out (salts).

II. *vbl s.* **Auslaugen,** *n. in vbl senses; also: Ch: etc:* lixiviation (of wood-ashes, etc.).

auslausen, *v.tr. sep. Constr:* to plug (wall, etc.).

Auslaut, *m. Ling:* final sound (of word, syllable); **im A.,** at the end of the word.

auslauten, *v.i. sep.* (*haben*) (*of word, syllable*) to end, terminate; **in einem, einen, Vokal, a.,** to end, terminate, in a vowel; **auslautend,** final, ultimate (consonant, etc.).

ausläuten, *v.sep.* **1.** *v.tr.* to proclaim (sth., the end of sth.) by the ringing of bells; to ring out (old year). **2.** *v.i.* (*haben*) to finish, cease, ringing; **es hat, die Glocken haben, ausgeläutet,** the bells have finished ringing.

ausleben, *v.sep.* **1.** *v.tr.* (*a*) **sein Leben a.,** (i) to live (out) (one's life); (ii) to live one's life to the full; (*b*) **sich a.,** to live one's life to the full; to make the most of one's life; to have scope for one's abilities; **j-n sich a. lassen,** to give s.o. scope for his abilities; **sich nicht a. können,** to lack scope, to be frustrated; **sich gesellschaftlich a.,** to have a full, a satisfying, social life. **2.** *v.i.* (*haben*) to die, to pass away, to come to the end of one's days.

auslecken[1], *v.tr. sep.* to lick out (dish, etc.), to lick (dish, etc.) clean; to lap up (milk, etc.).

auslecken[2], *v.i. sep.* (*sein*) (*of liquid*) to run out, to leak (out).

ausleeren. I. *v.tr. sep.* **1.** to empty (bag, etc.); to empty, drain (glass, etc.); to eat (dish, etc.) clean; to empty water, rubbish, etc., out of (pail, basket, etc.); *Med:* to evacuate (bowels). **2. sich ausleeren,** (*of room, etc.*) to empty.

II. *vbl s.* **Ausleeren** *n.*, **Ausleerung** *f. in vbl senses; also:* evacuation (of bowels).

auslegen. I. *v.tr. sep.* **1.** (*a*) to lay (thgs) out (on table, etc.); to set out, lay out, display (wares), to expose (wares) for sale; (*b*) to put down (poison); to lay (mines). **2.** (*a*) **ein Zimmer mit Teppichen a.,** to cover the floor of a room with carpets, to carpet the floor of a room; **eine Schublade mit Papier a.,** to line a drawer with paper; **einen Korb mit Papier a.,** to put, lay, paper in a basket; **einen Boden, usw., mit Fliesen a.,** to tile a floor, etc.; to lay a floor, etc., with tiles; (*b*) to inlay (wood, etc.) (with ivory, etc.). **3.** to remove (sth.); (*a*) *Print:* (*of fly*) to deliver (sheets); (*b*) to pay out (cable). **4.** (*a*) *Row: abs.* to extend one's arms, to come forward; *Fenc:* to extend (weapon) (in on guard position); (*b*) *Motor-cycling: Bobsleighing:* **sich a.,** to lean out sideways (round corners). **5.** *Rail:* **einen Zug a.,** to cancel a train. **6.** (**j-m, für j-n**) **Geld a.,** to pay money (temporarily) (for s.o.); **können Sie mir den Betrag bis morgen a.?** can you pay this sum for me till tomorrow? **ich habe noch drei Mark von der Firma zu bekommen, die ich für Porto ausgelegt habe,** the firm still owes me three

marks which I spent on postage, three marks for postage. 7. (*a*) to interpret, explain (dream, prophecy, parable, passage, etc.); to expound (text); **einen Traum, usw., falsch a.,** to misinterpret a dream, etc.; (*b*) to interpret, construe (action, etc.); **etwas falsch a.,** to misinterpret sth., lo misconstrue sth., to put a false construction, a wrong interpretation, on sth.; **sie hat mir mein Schweigen falsch ausgelegt,** she put a wrong construction on, she misunderstood the reason for, my silence; **man legt ihm alles übel aus,** a bad, unfavourable, construction is put on everything he does; **wir haben seine Worte ganz anders ausgelegt,** we put quite another construction on his words, we understood his words to mean something quite different; **diese Handlung könnte man (ihm) falsch a.,** this action (of his) is open to misconstruction.

II. *vbl s.* 1. **Auslegen,** *n. in vbl senses; also: Print:* **A. der bedruckten Bogen,** delivery of the printed sheets (*from the press*). 2. **Auslegung,** *f.* (*a*)=II. 1; *also:* interpretation, explanation (of dream, prophecy, parable, passage, action, etc.); exposition (of text); commentary (on text); *Theol: etc:* exegesis; **falsche A.,** misinterpretation (of dream, etc.); misconstruction (of actions, words, etc.); (*b*) interpretation; explanation; construction (put on action, words, etc.); **falsche A.,** misinterpretation, wrong interpretation; misconstruction, wrong construction; **ich bin mit seiner A. dieser Stelle nicht einverstanden,** I do not agree with his interpretation of this passage; **es gäbe verschiedene Auslegungen seines Benehmens,** various different constructions might be put on his behaviour. *Cp.* **Auslage.**

Ausleger, *m.* **-s/-.** 1. interpreter, expositor (of texts, etc.); commentator; *Theol: etc:* exegetist, exegete. 2. (*a*) *Mec.E:* arm; bracket; jib (of crane); *Civ.E: Arch:* cantilever; (*b*) *Row:* outrigger; (*c*) *Print:* fly; flyer.

Auslegerarm, *m. Mec.E:* arm; bracket; jib (of crane).

Auslegerboot, *n. Row:* (*boat*) outrigger.

Auslegerbrücke, *f. Civ.E:* cantilever bridge.

Auslegerkran, *m. Mec.E:* jib-crane.

Auslegerstab, *m. Print:* flyer-finger.

Auslegerträger, *m. Civ.E:* cantilever girder, overhung girder.

Auslegetisch, *m. Print:* delivery table, delivery board.

ausleiden, *v.sep.* (*strong*) 1. *v.tr.* to bear, suffer (sth.) (to the end). 2. *v.i.* (*haben*) to come to the end of one's suffering; to die, to pass away; **sie hat ausgelitten,** her sufferings are over, are at an end.

ausleiern, *v.sep.* 1. *v.tr.* (*a*) to wear down (screw, wheel, etc.); (*b*) **eine Melodie a.,** to make a melody hackneyed, trite (by repetition). 2. *v.i.* (*sein*) *F:* (*of elastic*) to become stretched, to lose its elasticity. *See also* **ausgeleiert.**

ausleihbar, *a.* (books, etc.) that can be lent (out); **diese Bücher sind nicht a.,** these books are not borrowable, are not to be lent (out); **die Bücher im Lesesaal sind nicht a.,** books must not be taken out of the reading-room.

Ausleihbibliothek, *f.* lending library.

Ausleihbücherei, *f.* lending library; circulating library.

Ausleihe, *f.* 1. lending (out) (of books, etc.); handing out, distribution, issue, issuing (of books, etc.); (*in library*) **'A. von sechs bis acht',** 'books are issued between six and eight'. 2. issuing counter, department (of library, etc.).

ausleihen, *v.tr. sep.* (*strong*) (i) to lend (sth.); (*in library*) to lend (out) (books); (ii) to borrow (sth.); **Geld a.,** to lend money; **Geld auf Zinsen a.,** to lend money at interest, to put money out (at interest); **das Buch ist ausgeliehen,** the book is out; **sich** *dat.* **etwas a., (sich** *dat.*) **von j-m etwas a.,** to borrow sth., to borrow sth. from s.o.

Ausleiher, *m.* lender.

auslernen, *v.sep.* 1. *v.tr.* to learn all about (sth.); to finish (school-book, etc.). 2. *v.i.* (*haben*) to finish one's apprenticeship; **er hat jetzt ausgelernt,** he has served, finished, his apprenticeship now; *Prov:* **man lernt nie aus,** it's never too late to learn; (we) live and learn.

Auslese, *f.* 1. picking out, selection (of the best fruit, etc.); *Biol:* **natürliche A.,** natural selection. 2. (*a*) pick (of fruit, vegetables, etc.); (*tobacco*) selected leaf; *Wine-m:* wine made from specially selected grapes, finest grapes, choice grapes; (*b*) élite; flower, pick, cream (of society, etc.).

auslesen, *v.tr. sep.* (*strong*) 1. to choose (sth.); **Früchte, usw., a.,** to sort fruit, etc.; to pick out, select (the best) fruit, etc.; **ausgelesene Früchte,** selected fruit. 2. to finish reading (book, etc.), to read (book, etc.) to the end.

Ausleser, *m.* selector.

Auslesevorrichtung, *f. Ind: etc:* sorter; separator (for grain, etc.).

Auslesezylinder, *m. Ind:* sorting cylinder (for grain).

auslichten, *v.tr. sep.* to thin (a wood); to prune (trees).

Auslieferer, *m.* deliverer (of goods).

ausliefern. I. *v.tr. sep.* 1. to deliver (goods). 2. (**j-n**) (**j-m, an j-n**) **a.,** to hand (s.o.) over (to s.o.), to deliver (s.o.) (up, over) (to s.o.), to deliver (s.o.) (into s.o.'s hands); *Jur:* to extradite (criminal); **sein Land dem Feinde a.,** to deliver one's country into the hands of the enemy; **j-m ausgeliefert sein,** to be at s.o.'s mercy, to be in s.o.'s hands; **den Elementen hilflos ausgeliefert sein,** to be at the mercy of the elements; **sich j-m a.,** to put oneself in s.o.'s hands, to throw oneself on s.o.'s mercy.

II. *vbl s.* 1. **Ausliefern,** *n. in vbl senses.* 2. **Auslieferung,** *f.*=II. 1; *also:* delivery (of goods); *Jur:* extradition (of criminal).

Auslieferungslager, *n. Com:* warehouse; *Publ:* trade department.

Auslieferungsschein, *m. Com:* delivery note.

Auslieferungszettel, *m. Com:* delivery note.

ausliegen, *v.i. sep.* (*strong*) (*sein*) (*of wares*) to be on display, to be exposed for sale; (*of newspaper, etc.*) to be laid out (for reading); **alle größeren Tageszeitungen liegen in der Hotelhalle aus,** all the more important daily papers may be found in the hotel lobby; **Exemplare in Deutsch und Englisch liegen aus,** copies in both German and English are on show, are available.

Auslieger, *m.,* **Ausliegerstag,** *n. Nau:* bum(p)kin-stay.

ausloben, *v.tr. sep.* (*a*) to offer (reward) (for tracing criminal, etc.); (*b*) to offer (prize) (in competition); (*c*) **Auslobung** *f,* (i) offer of a reward; (ii) offer of a prize.

auslöffeln, *v.tr. sep.* to spoon (up) (one's soup, etc.); to spoon the food out of (plate, etc.); *see also* **einbrocken** (*b*).

auslogieren, *v.tr. sep.* to put (s.o.) up, to find accommodation for (s.o.), in a house other than one's own; to throw (s.o.) out.

auslöschen, *v.tr. sep.* (*a*) to extinguish, put out (fire, candle, etc.); to put out, switch off (electric light); *Lit:* to quench (fire); (*b*) to erase (words); to rub, wipe (word) off (blackboard); (*c*) to erase, efface, obliterate (memories); (*d*) to extinguish, annihilate, wipe out (race, people, etc.).

Auslösehebel, *m. Mec.E:* release lever.

Auslöseknopf, *m. Mec.E:* release button, release knob; *Mil: Av:* bomb-release button.

Auslösekontakt, *m. Rail:* releasing contact.

Auslösemagnet, *m. El.E:* release magnet.

auslosen, *v.tr. sep.* to draw lots for (sth.), to draw for (sth.); to draw (sth.) by lot; to draw (numbers); to toss (up) for (sth.).

auslösen. I. *v.tr. sep.* 1. to ransom (prisoner); to redeem (sth.) (from pawn). 2. **etwas aus etwas a.,** to remove sth. from sth.; **die Knochen (aus dem Fleisch) a.,** to take out the bones (from meat), to bone the meat. 3. (*a*) *Ch: etc:* (i) to dissolve out (substance); (ii) to release, liberate, set free (gas); (*b*) *Mec.E:* to release (part); to disconnect (part); to throw, put, (part) out of gear; to put (part) out of action; to ungear (part); *El.E:* (*of relay*) to release (mechanism); *Phot:* to release (shutter); *Aut: etc:* **die Kupplung a.,** to disengage the clutch, to declutch; *Mil. Av:* **Bomben a.,** to release bombs; *Mil:* **Feuer a.,** to deliver fire. 4. (*a*) to cause, set up (reaction); to set off (reaction); to set (reaction) going; **eine Kettenreaktion a.,** to start a chain reaction; (*b*) to start off (chain of events); to spark off (revolution, etc.); to call forth, elicit (reaction, etc.); to cause, bring about (war, etc.); to provoke, arouse (interest, indignation, etc.); to awaken (interest); to call forth, stir up (passion, feeling, etc.); to excite (interest, curiosity, passion, etc.); to give rise to (dissatisfaction, etc.); to call forth, evoke (memories); to have, produce (effect); to cause, provoke (mirth); to call forth (applause); **allgemeine Bewunderung a.,** to elicit universal admiration; *Mil:* **der Angriff wird durch das Wort 'Eidechse' ausgelöst,** the word 'Eidechse' will be the signal to begin the attack.

II. *vbl s.* 1. **Auslösen,** *n. in vbl senses.* 2. **Auslösung,** *f.* (*a*)=II. 1; *also:* redemption (of article in pawn); *Ch:* release, liberation (of gas); *Mec.E:* release (of part, etc.); *Mil.Av:* release (of bombs); (*b*) escapement (in piano).

Auslöser, *m.* **-s/-.** *Mec.E:* switch; release device; *Phot:* shutter-release; cable-release, wire-release.

Auslösestrom, *m. El.E:* releasing current.

Auslösevorrichtung, *f. Mec.E:* release gear, release device; *Mil.Av:* bomb-release (mechanism).

Auslösungshebel, *m.* (*a*)=**Auslösehebel;** (*b*) *Clockm:* lifting-piece.

Auslösungswiderstand, *m. Clockm:* unlocking resistance.

ausloten, *v.tr. sep.* to take (extensive) soundings of (lake, etc.); **der See war an dieser Stelle so tief, daß man ihn nicht a. konnte,** the lake was so deep here that the plumb-line did not reach the bottom.

auslotsen, *v.tr. sep.* to pilot (ship) out to sea.

auslüften, *v.tr. sep.* to air, ventilate (room, etc.); to air (clothes).

Auslug, *m.* **-(e)s/-e,** look-out (post).

auslugen, *v.i. sep.* (*haben*) to watch; to be on the look-out; **nach j-m a.,** to look out for, to be on the look-out for, s.o.

ausmachen, *v.tr. sep.* 1. **etwas aus etwas a.,** to remove sth. from sth., to get sth. out of sth.; **Kartoffeln a.,** to dig up, to lift, potatoes; **Flecken a.,** to remove stains. 2. to put out (fire, light); to switch off, turn off, turn out (light); to turn off (gas, primus stove, etc.); to put out, stub out (cigarette, cigar). 3. (*a*) to find, discover, trace, track down (sth.); to make (sth.) out, to discern (sth.); **ein Schiff am Horizont a.,** to make out, discern, a ship on the horizon; (*b*) **wir konnten nicht a., was er sagen wollte,** we couldn't make out what he meant. 4. (*a*) to constitute, make up, form (sth.); to total, to amount to, to come to (sth.); **sein Haus und seine Fabrik machen seinen ganzen Besitz aus,** his house and factory constitute, form, his entire estate; **die Mietzahlungen machen den größeren Teil meines Einkommens aus,** the money I get in rents constitutes, forms, the greater part of my income; **das Fahrgeld macht jede Woche eine beträchtliche Summe aus,** fares come to a considerable amount, fares amount to quite a lot of money, each week; **die Miete macht im Jahre tausend Mark aus,** the rent comes to, adds up to, a thousand marks a year; *F:* **es kann die Welt nicht a.,** it can't cost such an awful lot of money; (*b*) **etwas a.,** to matter, to make a difference; **das macht viel, wenig, aus,** it matters a lot, doesn't matter much; **das macht nichts aus,** it doesn't matter at all, it makes no difference, no odds, it's no odds; **was macht das aus?** what does it matter? what difference does it make? what's the odds? what of it? **als ob das was a. könnte!** as if it mattered! as if it made any difference! **es macht mir zwar nichts aus, nicht als ob es mir etwas ausmachte,** not that it makes any difference to me, not that it matters to me; **was kann dir das schon a.!** what can it possibly matter to you! what possible difference can it make to you! **macht es euch was aus, wenn . . . ?** is it all the same to you if . . . ? 5. (*a*) to arrange, decide, settle, agree on, come to an agreement on (sth.); **etwas mit j-m a.,** to arrange with s.o. about sth.; to arrange sth. with s.o.; **einen Treffpunkt a.,** to arrange a meeting-place; **einen Preis a.,** to settle, agree on, a price; **das müssen Sie miteinander a.,** you have to arrange, settle, that between, among, yourselves; **wir haben noch nicht ausgemacht, was wir morgen machen wollen,** we haven't yet arranged, decided, settled, agreed (on), what to do tomorrow; **sie haben ausgemacht, daß sie sich hier treffen wollen,** they have arranged, decided, agreed, to meet here; **wir haben ausgemacht, daß die Kinder mitkommen sollen,** we have decided, agreed, settled, that the children should come too; **es ist eine ausgemachte Sache,** it's a (dead) certainty, *F:* a sure thing, a safe thing, a dead cert; (*b*) **ausgemacht,** complete, absolute, thorough, thorough-paced; **ein ausgemachter Schwindel,** a downright, *F:* proper, regular, swindle; **ein ausgemachter Schuft,** a complete, an absolute, utter, a thorough-paced, rogue; **ein ausgemachter Narr,** an absolute, utter, arrant, fool.

ausmahlen, *v.tr. sep.* (*conj. like* **mahlen**) *Mill:* to mill (flour) with high extraction; **Mehl stark a.,** to extract a high percentage of flour; **Mehl bis zu 70% a.,** to extract 70%.

Ausmahlstuhl, *m. Mill:* reduction rolls.

ausmalen, *v.tr. sep.* 1. to paint (room, etc.); to paint (church, room, etc.) in fresco; **dieser Raum wurde von X ausgemalt,** the frescoes in this room were painted by X. 2. **sich** *dat.* **etwas a.,** (i) to think sth. out, to work sth. out; (ii) to picture

sth. (to oneself), to imagine sth.; **wir hatten uns den Plan in jeder Einzelheit ausgemalt,** we had thought, worked, out every detail of the plan; **ich kann mir sehr gut a., wie sie ausgesehen hat,** I can very well picture, imagine, what she must have looked like; **man male sich mein Erstaunen aus!** just picture, imagine, my astonishment!

ausmangeln, *v.tr. sep.* (*a*) to mangle (sth.), to put (sth.) through the mangle; (*b*) to flatten, extend, (sth.) by putting it through the mangle; (*c*) **Wasser, usw., aus etwas a.,** to squeeze out water, etc., from sth. by putting it through the mangle; (*d*) to mangle (sth.) thoroughly.

Ausmarsch, *m.* (*a*) marching out; **beim A. aus der Stadt hat die Kompanie . . . ,** when marching out of the town, as they marched out of the town, the company . . . ; (*b*) march out; departure (of army) (for the field).

ausmarschieren, *v.i. sep.* (*sein*) to march out; to set out.

Ausmaß, *n.* (*a*) measure, extent; scale; scope; **in großem A.,** in a large measure, in a high degree, to a large extent; on a large scale; **in gewissem A.,** to, in, some degree, to some extent, to a certain extent, in some measure; **in geringem A.,** to a slight degree, extent; **in größerem A.,** to a higher degree, extent; on a greater, wider, scale; **in geringerem A.,** to a lesser degree, extent; on a smaller scale; **das A. einer Katastrophe,** the extent, scale, of a disaster; **Reformen in großem A. durchführen,** to carry out wide, extensive, reforms, reforms on a wide scale; **Unternehmungen von großem A.,** undertakings on a wide scale, of wide scope; **ungeheure, ungeahnte, Ausmaße annehmen,** to take on vast, unthought of, proportions, dimensions; **das ganze A. seiner Güte,** the full extent of his kindness; **das volle A. seines Genies wurde nur nach und nach offenbar,** the full measure, extent, of his genius only revealed itself gradually; **das übersteigt das A. des Erträglichen,** that's beyond (the bounds of) endurance; (*b*) (*usu. pl.*) measurements; dimensions.

ausmauern, *v.tr. sep.* to nog (frame-work); to line (tunnel, shaft, cellar, etc.) with masonry; **ausgemauerter Keller, Tunnel,** brick-lined cellar, tunnel; **Ausmauerung** *f,* (brick) lining (of cellar, tunnel).

ausmausern, *v.i. sep.* (*haben*) (*of bird*) to finish moulting; (*of animal*) to finish shedding hair, fur.

ausmeißeln, *v.tr. sep.* to chisel (sth.); to carve (sth.) with a chisel; to hollow (sth.) out with a chisel; *F:* **(fein) ausgemeißelte Gesichtszüge,** (delicately) chiselled features; **ein Bildnis aus dem Block a.,** to chisel, carve, a likeness from the block.

ausmelken, *v.tr. sep.* (*conj. like* **melken**) to milk (cow, etc.) dry.

ausmergeln, *v.tr. sep.* **j-n a.,** to wear, tire, s.o. out; to exhaust s.o. (completely); to enervate s.o.; to drain s.o. of all strength, of all energy; to suck s.o. dry; to wear s.o. to a shadow, *F:* to reduce s.o. to a rag; **ausgemergelt sein, aussehen,** to be, look, haggard, emaciated; **ein ausgemergeltes Pferd,** an emaciated horse; **den Boden a.,** to exhaust the soil.

ausmerzen, *v.tr. sep.* (*a*) to destroy, wipe out (vermin); to eliminate (abuses, disease, etc.); (*b*) *Husb:* **minderwertige Tiere a.,** to cull inferior animals (from herd, flock, etc.); (*c*) to remove, weed out, eliminate (foreign words, mistakes, etc.); **die anstößigen Stellen aus einem Buch a.,** to cut out the objectionable passages in a book, to expurgate a book.

ausmessen, *v.tr. sep.* (*strong*) to measure (sth.); to take all the measurements of (room, etc.); to gauge, measure the capacity of (cask, etc.); to measure the tonnage of (ship); **ein Zimmer der Länge nach a.,** to measure the length of a room.

ausmieten[1], *v.tr. sep.* to hire (sth.) out.

ausmieten[2], *v.tr. sep. Agr:* to take (potatoes, etc.) out of the clamp *or* silo.

ausmisten, *v.tr. sep.* (*a*) to muck out (stable, etc.); *abs.* **a.,** to muck out; **den Augiasstall a.,** to cleanse the Augean stables; (*b*) *F:* to clear out (drawer, cupboard, desk, etc.); *abs.* **a.,** to have a good clear-out.

ausmöblieren, *v.tr. sep.* to furnish (house, etc.).

ausmünden, *v.i. sep.* (*haben*) **in etwas** *acc.* **a.,** (*of pipe-line, etc.*) to empty into sth.; (*of street, valley, etc.*) to open into (open space, plain, etc.).

ausmünzen, *v.tr. sep.* to mint money from (silver, etc.).

ausmustern, *v.tr. sep.* to discard (s.o., sth.); to reject (s.o., sth.) (as unsuitable); *Mil:* (i) to discharge (s.o.) (from the army); (ii) to exempt (s.o.) (from military service); **Ausmusterung** *f,* rejection (of sth.)(as unsuitable); *Mil:* discharge (of s.o.) (from army); exemption (of s.o.) (from military service).

ausnagen, *v.tr. sep.* (*a*) to gnaw (sth.) out (of sth.); (*b*) to gnaw (sth.) hollow; to gnaw the inside out of (sth.); to gnaw into (sth.); (*of river, etc.*) to erode (river bank, etc.).

Ausnahme, *f.* **-/-n,** exception; **die A. von der Regel,** the exception to the rule; **keine Regel ohne A.,** there's an exception to every rule; **die A. bestätigt die Regel,** the exception proves the rule; **ohne A.,** without exception; **alle ohne A. lehnten ab,** they all without exception declined, they one and all declined; **mit A. von . . . ,** with the exception of . . . , except . . . ; **mit einigen Ausnahmen,** with a few exceptions; **bei j-m eine A. machen,** to make an exception in s.o.'s case.

Ausnahmefall, *m.* special case; exceptional case; exception.

Ausnahmegericht, *n. Jur:* special court.

Ausnahmegesetz, *n.* (*a*) special law, exceptional law; (*b*) *Adm:* emergency regulation.

Ausnahmetarif, *m.* special tariff, exceptional tariff.

Ausnahmezustand, *m.* state of emergency; state of martial law; **den A. über eine Stadt verhängen,** to declare a state of emergency in a town.

ausnahmslos, *a. & adv.* without exception; **sie lehnten a. ab,** they all without exception, they one and all, declined.

ausnahmsweise, *adv.* by way of exception; exceptionally; for once in a way, in a while; **er hat es uns a. gezeigt,** he made (us) an exception and showed it to us; **das tun wir manchmal a.,** we do it once in a way, in a while.

ausnehmen. I. *v.tr. sep.* (*strong*) **1.** (*a*) **etwas aus etwas a.,** to take sth. out of, to remove sth. from, sth.; **Vögel, Eier, a.,** to take birds, eggs, out of the nest; **ein Nest a.,** to rob a nest; **Honig a.,** to remove honey (from the hive); (*b*) to dig up, lift (potatoes). **2.** (*a*) *Cu: etc:* to draw (fowl); to gut (rabbit, etc.); to gut, clean (fish); to disembowel, eviscerate (carcass); (*b*) *F:* **j-n a.,** to fleece s.o., to clean s.o. out. **3.** to make an exception of (s.o., sth.); *see also* **ausgenommen. 4. sich ausnehmen,** to look, appear; **sich traurig a.,** to cut a sorry figure; **er nimmt sich seltsam in dieser Mütze aus,** he cuts a queer figure in that cap; **es nähme sich nicht gut aus, es nähme sich seltsam aus, wenn . . . ,** it wouldn't look well if . . . , it would look odd if . . . .

II. *pr.p. & a.* **ausnehmend,** *in vbl senses; esp.* exceptional, outstanding; **eine a. schöne Frau,** an exceptionally, outstandingly, beautiful woman; **es hat mir a. gut dort gefallen,** I liked it there extremely.

Ausnehmer, *m. Austrian:* = **Altenteiler.**

ausnuten, *v.tr. sep.* to groove, slot (metal, wood).

ausnutzen. I. *v.tr. sep.* **1.** to use, utilize (sth.); to exploit (natural resources, etc.); to take advantage of (sth.); to make use of (sth.); **seine Zeit (gut) a.,** to make good use, the most, of one's time; **Gelegenheiten a.,** to make the most of opportunities; **den Raum gut a.,** to make the most of, best use of, the available space. **2.** to exploit (s.o., s.o.'s talents); to take (unfair) advantage of (s.o., s.o.'s weaknesses); **laß dich nicht von ihm a.!** don't let him take advantage of you! **j-s Unwissenheit a.,** to take advantage of, to trade upon, s.o.'s ignorance.

II. *vbl s.* **1. Ausnutzen,** *n. in vbl senses.* **2. Ausnutzung,** *f.* = II. 1; *also:* use, utilization, exploitation (of natural resources, etc.); exploitation (of s.o.).

ausnützen, *v.tr. sep.* = **ausnutzen** I. 1.

ausösen, *v.tr. sep. Nau:* to bail (water) (out).

auspacken, *v.tr. sep.* **1.** to unpack (goods, case, etc.); to take (thgs) out (of case, etc.); *abs.* **a.,** to unpack; *F:* **gründlich a.,** to speak one's mind, to let fly, to say one's say; **pack aus!** speak out! let's have it! **2.** to fill in, pack (sth. with sth.).

auspalen, *v.tr. sep.* to shell, hull, (un)husk (peas, etc.).

auspeilen, *v.tr. sep. Nau:* to take soundings in (harbour), along (coast).

auspeitschen, *v.tr. sep.* (*a*) to whip, flog (s.o.); (*b*) *A:* to whip (s.o.) out of town.

auspellen, *v.tr. sep.* (*a*) to shell, hull, (un)husk (peas, etc.); (*b*) *F:* (*of pers.*) **sich a.,** to take off a few layers (of clothing).

Auspendler, *m.* commuter who travels out of a town.

auspfänden, *v.tr. sep. Jur:* to distrain upon (s.o., s.o.'s belongings).

auspfeifen, *v.tr. sep.* (*strong*) to boo (at), hiss (at) (s.o., sth.); **einen Schauspieler, ein Stück, a.,** to boo, hiss, an actor (off the stage); *F:* to give an actor the bird; to boo, hiss, a play.

auspflanzen, *v.tr. sep.* to plant out (seedlings, etc.).

auspflastern, *v.tr. sep.* to pave (courtyard, etc.).

auspichen, *v.tr. sep.* to tar (barrel); *F:* **eine ausgepichte Kehle haben,** to be a hard drinker; *see also* **ausgepicht.**

auspissen, *v.sep. P:* **1.** *v.tr.* **das Feuer a.,** to piss out the fire. **2.** *v.i.* (*haben*) to finish pissing.

Auspizien [aus'pi:tsiən], *n.pl.* (*a*) *Rom.Ant:* auspices; (*b*) **unter günstigen A.,** under favourable auspices; **unter den A. des Oberbürgermeisters von X,** under the auspices, patronage, of the Lord Mayor of X.

ausplappern, *v.tr. sep.* to blab out, blurt out (secret).

ausplätten, *v.tr. sep.* to iron out (creases) (in a frock, etc.), to iron (out) (creased clothes, etc.); to press (down) (seam).

ausplatzen, *v.i. sep.* (*sein*) *F:* to burst out laughing.

ausplaudern, *v.tr. sep.* to let out, blab out, blurt out (secret); **sie plaudert immer alles aus,** she can't keep anything to herself; **j-m etwas a.,** to blurt sth. out to s.o., *F:* to let on about sth. to s.o.

ausplündern. I. *v.tr. sep.* to plunder (country, town, etc.); to pillage (town), to ransack (building); to rob (till); **j-n a.,** (i) to rob s.o.; (ii) *F:* to plunder s.o.; to suck s.o. dry, to bleed s.o. (white); to fleece s.o., to clean s.o. out; (iii) *F:* to pick s.o.'s brains; to plagiarize s.o.'s works; **nach dem Abzug des Feindes war das Land völlig ausgeplündert,** after the enemy withdrew the land was completely impoverished, was completely stripped of all its wealth.

II. *vbl s.* **Ausplündern** *n.,* **Ausplünderung** *f. in vbl senses; also:* plunder (of country, town); pillage (of town).

auspolstern. I. *v.tr. sep.* to pad (sth.); to pad (out) (one's figure); to pad (splint); to line (box, etc.) with padding; **einen Mantel, usw., a.,** to pad the shoulders of a coat, etc.; **ein Auto, usw., a.,** to upholster a car, etc.; *F:* (*of pers.*) **gut ausgepolstert,** well upholstered, well padded.

II. *vbl s.* **1. Auspolstern,** *n. in vbl senses.* **2. Auspolsterung,** *f.* (*a*) = II. 1; (*b*) upholstery (of car, etc.).

ausposaunen, *v.tr. sep.* (*a*) to proclaim (sth.) by trumpet; (*b*) *F:* to proclaim (sth.), to trumpet (sth.) forth, abroad, to blazon (sth.) forth, abroad, to noise (sth.) abroad, to broadcast (sth.), *F:* to proclaim, cry, (sth.) from the housetops; **du brauchst diese Sache nicht überall auszuposaunen,** there's no need for you to broadcast this business.

auspowern ['auspo:vərn], *v.tr. sep.* to impoverish (land, soil, people).

ausprägen. I. *v.tr. sep.* **in etwas** *dat.* **ausgeprägt sein, sich in etwas** *dat.* **a.,** to be stamped in, on, sth.; **die Grausamkeit ist in seinem Gesicht ausgeprägt, prägt sich in seinem Gesicht aus,** cruelty is stamped on his face; **Trübsinn prägt sich in ihrem Gesicht aus,** her face is marked, stamped, with melancholy; **Jahre des Leidens hatten sich in ihrem Gesicht ausgeprägt,** years of suffering had left their mark, impress, on her face; **ein Gesicht, in dem sich Entschlossenheit ausprägt,** a face that shows determination.

II. *vbl s.* **Ausprägung,** *f.* = **Ausgeprägtheit.**

III. *p.p. & a.* **ausgeprägt,** *in vbl senses, esp.* pronounced, strongly marked (features); (face) with strongly marked features; **stark a.,** (*of cheekbones, chin, etc.*) pronounced, prominent; (*of contrasts, tendencies, etc.*) pronounced, strongly marked; **ein ausgeprägter Gelehrtenkopf,** a typical scholar's head; **er ist ein ausgeprägter Gelehrtentyp, Schurke,** he has all the characteristics, marks, of a scholar, a scoundrel; *adv.* **a. slawische Gesichtszüge,** markedly, pronouncedly, Slav, *U.S:* Slavic, features.

auspressen, *v.tr. sep.* **1.** to squeeze out (liquid, etc.); to squeeze (out) the liquid from (sth.); to squeeze out (sponge, etc.), to squeeze out the water from (sponge, etc.); **eine Zitrone a.,** to squeeze a lemon; **den Saft aus einer Zitrone a.,** to squeeze (out) the juice from a lemon; *F:* **eine Träne a.,** to wring out, squeeze out, a tear. **2.** *Constr:* to grout (wall, etc.) under pressure.

Auspreßloch, *n. Constr:* grout hole.

Auspreßverfahren, *n. Constr:* pressure grouting, (grout) injection process.

ausprobieren, *v.tr. sep.* (*p.p.* **ausprobiert**) to try (sth.) out.

Auspuff, *m.* **-s/-e.** *Mch: I.C.E:* exhaust.

Auspuffdampfmaschine, *f. Mch:* non-condensing engine.

auspuffen, *v.i. sep.* (*haben*) (*of engine*) to let off exhaust.

Auspuffgas, *n. I.C.E:* exhaust gas.

Auspuffkanal, *m. I.C.E: etc:* exhaust port.

Auspuffkontrollhahn, *m. Mch:* fume-cock.

Auspuffkrümmer, *m. I.C.E:* exhaust manifold.

Auspuffleitung, *f. Mch: I.C.E:* exhaust-pipe; exhaust manifold.

Auspuffmaschine, *f. Mch:* non-condensing engine.

Auspuffring, *m. Av: I.C.E:* exhaust ring; circular exhaust manifold.

Auspuffrohr, *n. Mch: I.C.E:* exhaust-pipe; *Av:* exhaust branch-pipe.

Auspuffsammelleitung, *f.,* **Auspuffsammelrohr,** *n.,* **Auspuffsammler,** *m. Mch: I.C.E:* exhaust manifold.

Auspuffschlitz, *m. I.C.E: etc:* exhaust port.

Auspuffstutzen, *m. Av: I.C.E:* stub exhaust(-pipe).

Auspufftopf, *m. I.C.E:* silencer, *U.S:* muffler.

Auspuffventil, *n. I.C.E: etc:* exhaust valve, outlet valve, escape valve.

auspumpen, *v.tr. sep.* to pump (out) (water, etc.); to pump out (flooded mine, etc.); *Med:* **j-m den Magen a.,** to siphon s.o.'s stomach; *F:* **j-n a.,** to pump s.o., to pump a secret out of s.o.; *F:* **ausgepumpt sein,** to be worn out, exhausted, *F:* all in, *U.S:* pooped.

auspunkten, *v.tr. sep. Box:* to beat (s.o.) on points.

auspurren, *v.tr. sep. Nau:* **die Wache a.,** to rouse the watch.

auspusten, *v.tr. sep.* to blow out (candle, etc.).

Ausputz, *m.* 1. finishing; finish (of shoes, etc.). 2. adornment, decoration.

ausputzen, *v.tr. sep.* 1. to clean (out) (oven, etc.); to tidy up; to remove the dead wood from (trees, hedges, etc.); *Bootm:* to finish (shoes, etc.); *F:* **die Schüssel a.,** *F:* to lick the platter clean. 2. to decorate, adorn (sth., s.o.); **sich a.,** to dress up.

Ausputzerei, *f. Bootm:* finishing department.

Ausputzmaschine, *f. Bootm:* finishing machine.

ausquartieren, *v.tr. sep.* (*a*) *Mil:* to billet (soldier) out; (*b*) to throw (s.o.) out; (*c*) to put (s.o.) up, lodge (s.o.), elsewhere; **ich mußte das Kind für eine Nacht zur Großmutter a.,** I had to send the child round to sleep at his grandmother's for one night; **sich a.,** to find other quarters, another lodging; **der Lärm im Hotel war unerträglich; ich habe mich a. müssen,** the noise in the hotel was intolerable; I had to move out and find a room elsewhere.

ausquetschen, *v.tr. sep.* to squeeze out (liquid, etc.); to squeeze the moisture, etc., out of (sth.); **eine Zitrone a.,** to squeeze a lemon; **den Saft aus einer Zitrone a.,** to squeeze (out) the juice from a lemon; *F:* **j-n a.,** to pump s.o., to make s.o. talk; to drag things out of s.o. (by persistent questioning); **eine Träne a.,** to wring out, squeeze out, a tear.

ausradeln, *v.i. sep.* (*sein*) to go for a bicycle ride.

ausradieren, *v.tr. sep.* (*a*) to erase (writing, etc.), *esp.* to rub out (writing, etc.) (with rubber eraser); **ausradierte Stelle,** erased passage, erasion; (*b*) *F:* to obliterate, wipe out (town, etc.), to raze (town, etc.) to the ground.

ausrangieren, *v.tr. sep.* (*a*) to remove (sth.) from its place in a series *or* an activity; (*b*) *F:* to discard, throw away, throw out, scrap (sth.); to put (employee, etc.) on the shelf, to shelve (employee, etc.).

ausranken, *v.i. sep.* (*haben*) to send out shoots, tendrils.

ausrauben, *v.tr. sep.* to plunder (country, etc.); to rob (house, till, etc.); to ransack (building); to rob, plunder (s.o.).

ausrauchen, *v.sep.* 1. *v.tr.* (*a*) to finish (smoking) (one's cigarette, etc.); (*b*) *F:* **j-n sich a. lassen,** to give s.o. time to cool off. 2. *v.i.* (*haben*) (*a*) (*of pers.*) to finish smoking; to finish one's cigarette, etc.; (*b*) (*of chimney, burning material, etc.*) to stop smoking.

ausräuchern, *v.tr. sep.* (*a*) to fumigate (room, etc.); to match, fumigate (cask); (*b*) to smoke out (fox, wasps' nest, etc., *Mil:* enemy troops, dug-out, etc.); **Bienen (aus einem Bienenkorbe) a.,** to smoke out, unhive, bees.

ausraufen, *v.tr. sep.* to pull up, tear up (weeds); to pluck (ears of corn); **sich die Haare a.,** to tear one's hair; *F:* **ich könnte mir die Haare a.!** I could kick myself!

ausräumen, *v.tr. sep.* to clear (thgs) out of (room, cupboard, etc.); to empty, clear (out) (room, cupboard, grate, etc.); to clean out, dredge (ditch, etc.); *Med:* to clean out (womb, etc.); **die Möbel a.,** to remove, take out, clear out, the furniture; **ein Zimmer a.,** to clear the furniture out of a room, to empty, clear, a room (of furniture); **Schwierigkeiten a.,** to clear away difficulties; *F:* (*of thieves*) **j-m das Haus a.,** to clean out s.o.'s house.

ausrechnen. I. *v.tr. sep.* (*a*) to compute, calculate, reckon; to work, figure, (sth.) out; to reckon (sth.) up; **hast du schon ausgerechnet, wieviel ich dir schuldig bin?** have you worked out, reckoned up, calculated, how much I owe you? **er hat ausgerechnet, daß er vier Stunden am Tage arbeitet,** he has worked out, he calculates, reckons, that he does four hours' work a day; (*b*) *Mth:* to evaluate (expression). *See also* **ausgerechnet.**

II. *vbl s.* 1. **Ausrechnen,** *n. in vbl senses.* 2. **Ausrechnung,** *f.* (*a*)=II. 1; *also:* calculation; evaluation (of expression); (*b*) calculation, computation.

Ausreckeisen, *n. Leath:* slicker, sleeker, stretching-iron; **ein Fell mit dem A. bearbeiten,** to slick, sleek, a skin.

ausrecken, *v.tr. sep.* (*a*) (**sich** *dat.*) **den Hals (nach etwas) a.,** to crane one's neck (to see sth.); **sich (nach etwas) a.,** to stretch (in order to reach sth.); (*b*) to slick (hides); to draw (metal).

Ausrede, *f.* 1. excuse, pretext; **faule A.,** poor excuse, feeble excuse, lame excuse. 2. **A.:**= **Aussprache 1.**

ausreden, *v.sep.* I. *v.tr.* 1. **j-m etwas a.,** to dissuade s.o. from sth.; to put s.o. off sth., to talk s.o. out of sth. 2. **sich ausreden,** to make excuses, to excuse oneself. 3. *abs. A:* to speak. 4. *A:* to say (sth.); to pronounce (sth.).

II. **ausreden,** *v.i.* (*haben*) (*a*) to finish speaking; (*b*) to finish what one has to say; **j-n a. lassen,** to let s.o. finish (what he has to say); **laß ihn a.!** let him finish! hear him out! don't interrupt (him)!

ausregnen, *v. impers. sep.* **es hat (sich) ausgeregnet,** it has stopped raining, it has rained itself out; **die Wolken haben sich ausgeregnet,** the clouds have rained themselves out.

ausreiben, *v.tr. sep.* (*strong*) 1. to rub (sth.) out; **Schmutz a.,** to rub dirt out; **Kleider a.,** to rub the dirt out of clothes; **sich** *dat.* **die Augen a.,** to rub the sleep from one's eyes. 2. **ein Loch a.,** to broach, ream (out), a hole.

Ausreiber, *m. Tls:* broach, reamer(-bit).

ausreichen. I. *v.i. sep.* (*haben*) (*a*) to suffice; to be enough, sufficient, adequate; **das Brot reicht nicht für so viele Leute aus,** there is not enough, sufficient, bread for so many people; **der Stoff reicht gerade noch zu einem Kleid aus,** there is just enough material for a dress; **sein Einkommen reicht nicht für solche Dinge aus,** his income will not run to such things; (*b*) (*of pers.*) **mit etwas a.,** to have enough, sufficient, of sth.; **wir reichen mit dieser Summe nicht aus,** this amount won't be enough, sufficient, adequate, we shan't be able to manage with this amount of money.

II. *pr.p. & a.* **ausreichend,** enough, sufficient, adequate; *Sch:* (*on report*) **'ausreichend',** 'fair', 'fairly good'; *adv.* enough, sufficiently, adequately; **ausreichende Vorräte** adequate supplies; **nicht a.,** insufficient, inadequate; **haben wir a. Zucker?** have we enough, sufficient, sugar? **sie hatten nicht a. Geld,** they didn't have enough, sufficient, money, they had insufficient money.

ausreifen, *v.i. sep.* (*haben*) to ripen, to mature, to come to full maturity; **die Früchte am Baum a. lassen,** to leave the fruit to ripen on the tree; **ausgereift,** (*of fruit, cheese*) fully ripe, mature; (*of pers.*) mature; **ausgereifter Wein,** matured wine; **seine Pläne waren noch nicht ausgereift,** his plans were not yet matured.

ausreinigen, *v.tr. sep.* to clean the inside of (sth.), to clean (sth.); *Ecc:* to cleanse (chalice); **Ausreinigung** *f* **des Meßkelches,** ablution of the chalice.

Ausreise, *f.* departure, leaving; journey out, voyage out, outward journey, outward voyage; **bei der A. habe ich Schwierigkeiten mit meinem Paß gehabt,** on leaving the country, on my departure from the country, I had difficulty over my passport; **auf der A. nach Australien,** on the journey, voyage, out to Australia; *Adm:* **j-m die A. verweigern,** to prohibit s.o. from leaving the country.

Ausreiseerlaubnis, Ausreisegenehmigung, *f. Adm:* exit visa.

ausreisen, *v.i. sep* (*sein*) **(aus einem Lande) a.,** to leave a country.

ausreißen, *v.sep.* (*strong*) 1. *v.tr.* to tear out, pull out, pluck out (hair, etc.); to tear up, pull up (plants), to pull up, pull out (weeds); to root up, uproot (trees); **Fliegen die Beine a.,** to pull off flies' legs; **sich fühlen, als ob man Bäume a. könnte,** to feel strong enough for anything, to feel up to anything, *F:* to feel like a giant refreshed, to feel full of beans; **es geht ihm schon besser, aber er kann noch keine Bäume a.,** he's feeling better but he's still not overflowing with health and vigour, he's still not in the best of health; **Knöpfe a.,** to tear off buttons; *B:* **ärgert dich aber dein rechtes Auge, so reiß es aus,** but if thy right eye offend thee, pluck it out; *see also* **Bein** 2. 2. *v.i.* (*sein*) (*of seam*) to pull apart, to split; **der Ärmel ist ausgerissen,** the sleeve is pulling away from the armhole; **das Kleid ist an den Nähten ausgerissen,** the dress has pulled away at the seams; **die Knopflöcher sind ausgerissen,** the button-holes are torn. 3. *v.i.* (*sein*) to run away, run off, flee, *F:* to clear out; (*of horse, F: of pers.*) to bolt; **mit etwas a.,** to run away, abscond, make off, *F:* decamp, with sth.; **die Kinder rissen aus,** the children ran off, fled; **ausgerissener Sträfling,** escaped convict; **mit der Kasse a.,** to abscond, make off, with the cash. 4. *v.i.* (*sein*) (*of racing cyclist*) to get ahead by a sudden spurt.

Ausreißer, *m.* (*a*) runaway, fugitive; *Mil: F:* deserter; (*b*) *Mil: F:* (i) stray shell, (ii) wide shot.

ausreiten, *v.sep.* (*strong*) 1. *v.i.* (*sein*) (*a*) (*of cavalry*) to ride out; **aus der Stadt a.,** to ride out of the town; (*b*) to go for a ride; to ride out. 2. *v.tr.* (*a*) to take (horse) out; (*b*) **ein Pferd a.,** to ride a horse full out; (*c*) **die Reitbahn a.,** to ride the full course (without cutting the corners).

ausrenken. I. *v.tr. sep.* (*a*) (**sich** *dat.*) **ein Glied a.,** to dislocate a limb; **sich den Arm a.,** to dislocate one's arm, one's shoulder, to put one's arm, one's shoulder, out (of joint); **sich den Hals r., um etwas zu sehen,** to crane one's neck to see sth.; (*b*) (*of shoulder, etc.*) **sich a.,** to come out of joint, to become dislocated.

II. *vbl s.* **Ausrenken** *n.,* **Ausrenkung** *f. in vbl senses; also:* dislocation.

ausreuten, *v.tr. sep.*=**ausrotten.**

ausrichten. I. *v.tr. sep.* 1. to straighten (sth.); to adjust (sth.); to align (thgs); to bring (sth., thgs) into line, into alignment; (*a*) *Tchn:* **etwas (nach etwas) a.,** to adjust sth. (to sth.); to bring sth. into line (with sth.); to true sth. (up); to centre (piece of work) (on machine); (*b*) to bring (ideas, etc.) into line, into alignment; **seine Handlungsweise nach etwas a.,** to adjust one's behaviour to sth., to bring one's behaviour into line, alignment, with sth.; (*c*) *Mil: etc:* **die Glieder a.,** to dress the ranks; *abs. a.,* to dress; **nach vorne, nach dem Vordermann, a.,** to dress up. 2. *Min:* to win (seam). 3. (*a*) to do, accomplish (sth.); to get (sth.) done; **wir haben viel mehr ausgerichtet, als wir erwarteten,** we accomplished much more, got far more done, were far more successful, than we expected; **er hat die Sache gut ausgerichtet,** he managed very well; **damit wäre nichts ausgerichtet,** that would be no use, do no good, *F:* that wouldn't get us anywhere; **ich habe die verschiedensten Leute in dieser Sache angegangen, habe aber nirgendwo etwas ausgerichtet,** I approached all kinds of different people in this matter but had no success with any of them; **mit Zwang richtet man nichts bei ihm aus,** you'll get nowhere with him by force; **mit Schmeicheleien wirst du viel bei ihr a. können,** you'll get a long way with her by flattery; **was hast du ausgerichtet?** how did you get on? what did you get done? (*b*) **j-m eine Botschaft a.,** to give s.o. a message, to convey, pass on, a message to s.o.; **einen Gruß (an j-n) a.,** to pass on a greeting (to s.o.); **richte ihm von mir einen schönen Gruß aus,** remember me kindly to him, give him my (kind) regards; **j-m a. lassen, daß . . .,** to send s.o. a message, to leave s.o. a message, to let s.o. know, that . . . ; **j-m einen Auftrag a.,** to pass on instructions to s.o.; 4. (**seiner Tochter) die Hochzeit a.,** to arrange and pay for one's daughter's wedding.

II. *vbl s.* 1. **Ausrichten,** *n. in vbl senses.* 2. **Ausrichtung,** *f.* (*a*)=II. 1; *also:* adjustment, alignment (of sth., thgs); (*b*) alignment; **die A. prüfen,** to check the alignment.

ausringen[1]. *v.tr. sep.* (*strong*) to wring (out) (linen, etc.); to wring (the water) out (of linen, etc.).

ausringen[2], *v.i. sep.* (*strong*) (*haben*) to finish struggling; **er hat ausgerungen,** his struggles are over.

Ausringmaschine, *f. Ind:*=**Auswringmaschine.**

ausrinnen, *v.i. sep.* (*strong*) (*sein*) (*of water, sand, etc.*) to run, flow, leak, out; *F:* **die Zeit rinnt aus,** time is running out.

ausrippen, *v.tr. sep.* to stem, strip (tobacco leaves).

Ausritt, *m.* (*a*) riding out; **beim A. aus der Stadt,**

(on) riding out of the town; (b) outing on horseback, ride.

Ausrodemaschine, f. Agr: clearing-plough.

ausroden, v.tr. sep. to root up, uproot, grub up (tree, etc.); to tear up (tree, etc.) by the roots.

ausrollen, v.sep. **1.** v.tr. to pay out, run out (cable). **2.** v.tr. to roll (out) (dough, etc.). **3.** v.i. (haben) (of ball, etc.) to finish rolling, to roll to a standstill; Av: (of plane) to taxi to a standstill.

Ausrollstrecke, f. Av: landing-run.

ausrottbar, a. eradicable (vice, etc.).

ausrotten. **I.** v.tr. sep. **1.** A: to root up, uproot (tree, etc.), to tear up, pull up (tree, etc.) by the roots; to pull up (root). **2.** to exterminate, extirpate, destroy, wipe out (race, etc.); to extirpate, eradicate (vice, etc.), to eradicate (prejudice); **Mißbräuche, eine Rasse, mit Stumpf und Stiel a.,** to destroy abuses, a race, root and branch. **II.** vbl s. **1.** Ausrotten, n. in vbl senses. **2.** Ausrottung, f.=II. 1; also: extermination, extirpation; eradication.

Ausrotter, m. -s/-, exterminator; extirpator; destroyer; eradicator.

ausrücken, v.sep. **1.** v.i. (sein) (a) to set out; (of army, troops) to march out; (ins Feld) a., to go to the front; (b) F: to run off, abscond, make off, F: to decamp, (with the cash, etc.). **2.** v.tr. (a) to move (sth., thgs) out; **Kästen weiter a.,** to move boxes further apart, to space boxes out further; (b) Mec.E: to disengage, disconnect (part); to release (part); to disengage (clutch, gear).

Ausrücker, m. -s/-. Mec.E: disengaging lever.

Ausrückhebel, m. Mec.E: disengaging lever.

Ausrückkupplung, f. Mec.E: disengaging coupling.

Ausrückvorrichtung, f. Mec.E: disengaging gear.

Ausruf, m. **1.** cry, shout; exclamation, ejaculation; Gram: exclamation; A. der Freude, freudiger A., cry, exclamation, of joy; mit einem A. der Verwunderung, with a cry, an exclamation, of surprise; mit dem A. 'es lebe der Kaiser!' stürmten sie gegen den Feind an, crying, shouting, 'long live the Emperor!' they charged the enemy. **2.** proclamation; etwas durch öffentlichen A. bekanntmachen, to make something known by public proclamation.

ausrufen. **I.** v.tr. sep. (strong) **1.** (a) to call out (number, names, etc.); (of watchman) die Stunden a., to call the hours; (of auctioneer) die Lose a., to call out the lots; seine Waren a., to cry one's wares; einen verlorenen Gegenstand a., to publish the loss of an article (through loudspeaker, etc.); j-n a., to page s.o., to call out s.o.'s name (in restaurant, club, etc.); einen Streik a., to call a strike; A: Krieg a., to proclaim war; (b) j-n als Kaiser, zum Kaiser, a., to proclaim s.o. emperor; einen Tag als, zum, Feiertag a., to proclaim a day as a holyday. **2.** (in incidental clause) to cry, shout, exclaim, ejaculate; 'wie schade!' rief er aus, 'what a pity!' he cried, exclaimed, ejaculated. **II.** vbl s. **1.** Ausrufen, n. in vbl senses; also: etwas durch öffentliches A. bekanntmachen, to make sth. known by public proclamation. **2.** Ausrufung, f. (a)=II. 1; also: proclamation (of feast-day, etc.); (b) nach seiner A. zum Kaiser, after he had been proclaimed emperor; (c) exclamation.

Ausrufer, m. crier, barker, tout; (öffentlicher) A., town-crier; bellman.

Ausrufesatz, m. Gram: clause of exclamation.

Ausrufewort, n. -(e)s/-wörter, interjection.

Ausrufezeichen, n. Print: etc: exclamation mark, U.S: exclamation point.

Ausrufung, f. see ausrufen II.

Ausrufungszeichen, n. Print: etc: exclamation mark, U.S: exclamation point.

ausruhen, v. sep. **1.** v.i. (haben) & sich ausruhen, to rest (oneself); to take a rest; (sich) von den Anstrengungen des Tages a., to rest after the day's labours; hast du dich gut ausgeruht? did you have a good rest? are you really rested? F: (sich) auf seinen Lorbeeren a., to rest on one's laurels. **2.** v.tr. (a) to rest (limbs, eyes, etc.); (b) ausgeruht sein, to be rested; sich ausgeruht fühlen, to feel rested; nachdem sie drei Stunden geschlafen hatte, fühlte sie sich ausgeruht, after sleeping for three hours she felt rested.

ausrunden, v.tr. sep. to make (sth.) round, to round (sth.) (off); sich a., to become round; (of cheeks, etc.) to become round, full; das Innere eines Gefäßes a., to round the inside of a vessel.

ausrupfen, v.tr. sep. to pluck (out), tear out, pull out (hair, feathers, etc.).

ausrüsten. **I.** v.tr. sep. **1.** (a) to equip (s.o., sth.); to fit (s.o., sth.) out; to arm (s.o., sth.); to equip (troops, etc.); ein Schiff a., (i) to equip, fit out, (ii) to man, a vessel; j-n mit etwas a., to equip, provide, supply, furnish, s.o. with sth., to fit s.o. out with sth.; to arm s.o. with sth.; gut fürs Leben ausgerüstet sein, to be well equipped for life; (b) Tex: to dress, finish, stiffen (fabrics). **2.** Constr: to strike, remove, the centring of, to discentre (arch, etc.). **II.** vbl s. **1.** Ausrüsten, n. in vbl senses. **2.** Ausrüstung, f. (a)=II. 1; also: equipment (of troops, vessel, etc.); outfitting (of vessel); (b) (implements, etc.) equipment; gear, tackle; outfit; fittings; accoutrement(s) (of soldiers); in feldmarschmäßiger A., Mil. & F: in full marching order; (c) Tex: finish, stiffening (of fabrics).

Ausrüstungsgegenstand, m. piece of equipment; Mil: article of equipment.

ausrutschen, v.i. sep. (sein) (a) (of pers., thg) to slip, slide, skid; auf dem Eis, auf einer Bananenschale, a., to slip on the ice, on a banana-skin; die Feder ist mir ausgerutscht, (i) my pen slipped; (ii) F: I made a slip of the pen; F: beinahe wäre mir die Hand ausgerutscht, I could scarcely resist slapping him or her; (b) F: to make a gaffe, bloomer, faux pas, F: to drop a brick; to misbehave.

Aussaat, f. **1.** sowing, dissemination (of seed); natürliche A., natural dissemination, natural distribution of seeds; die Zeit der A., seed-time. **2.** (sown) seed. **3.** Med: secondary growth, metastasis.

aussäen, v.tr. sep. to sow, scatter (seed, etc.); F: to spread (happiness, discontent, etc.); to disseminate (ideas, etc.).

aussagbar, a. Log: etc: predicable.

Aussage, f. -/-n. **1.** statement; Jur: statement; evidence, testimony, deposition (of witness); eine A. machen, to make a statement; Jur: to give evidence, testimony; to make a deposition, to depose; A. vor Gericht, statement made, evidence given, in court; nach den Aussagen der beiden ersten Zeugen, according to the statements made by, the evidence given by, the testimony of, the first two witnesses; nach seiner A., according to what he said; nach seiner eignen A., on his own showing; according to his own statement; according to his own evidence. **2.** (a) Log: proposition; (b) Geom: proposition; (c) Gram: predicate.

aussagen. **I.** v.sep. **1.** v.tr. to state (sth.); etwas über j-n, etwas acc., a., to make a statement about s.o., sth. **2.** v.i. (haben) to make a statement, Jur: to make a statement; to give evidence, testimony; to depose; der Zeuge sagte aus, daß . . ., the witness said in evidence, stated, deposed, that . . . ; für, gegen, j-n a., to give evidence, to testify, in s.o.'s favour, to give evidence, to testify, against s.o. **II.** pr.p. & a. aussagend, in vbl senses; esp. Gram: predicative (adjective, etc.); aussagender Satz, clause of statement; adv. das Eigenschaftswort wird a. gebraucht, the adjective is used predicatively.

aussägen, v.tr. sep. to saw (sth.) out.

Aussagesatz, m. Gram: clause of statement.

Aussageweise, f. Gram: mood.

aussaigern, v.tr.=ausseigern.

aussalzen, v.tr. sep. Soapm: to salt out, to grain (out) (soap).

aussanden, v.tr. sep. to remove, dredge, the sand from (canal, etc.).

Aussatz, m. -es/. Med: leprosy.

aussätzig, a. leprous.

Aussätzige, m. & f. (decl. as adj.) leper; F: ein moralisch Aussätziger, a moral leper.

aussauern, v.i. sep. (sein) (of seedling) to rot below ground (on account of over-wet soil).

aussaufen, v.tr. sep. (strong) (of animal) to drink up (water, etc.); to empty (drinking-trough, etc.); P: (of pers.) to swill down (drink); to gulp down the contents of (cup, etc.).

aussaugen, v.tr. sep. (weak & strong) (a) to suck (sth.) out; den Saft aus einer Apfelsine a., eine Apfelsine a., to suck (the juice out of) an orange; eine Frucht völlig a., to suck a fruit dry; das Gift aus einer Wunde a., eine Wunde a., to suck the poison out of a wound; to suck a wound clean; (b) (usu. weak) to exhaust (land); F: j-n (bis aufs Blut) a., to suck s.o. dry; ein Land a., to drain the wealth of a country; die das Volk aussaugen, those who batten on the people.

Aussauger, m. F: leech, blood-sucker, extortioner.

ausschaben, v.tr. sep. to scrape (sth.) out; Surg: to curette (womb).

ausschachten. **I.** v.tr. sep. Civ.E: etc: to dig up,

throw up (earth); to excavate, dig (cellar, etc.); die Baugrube a., to dig, excavate, the foundations. **II.** vbl s. **1.** Ausschachten, n. in vbl senses; also: excavation (of cellar, foundations, etc.). **2.** Ausschachtung, f. (a)=II. 1; (b) excavation work.

Ausschachtungsarbeiten, f.pl. excavation work.

ausschäkeln, v.tr. sep. Nau: to unbend (cable).

ausschalen, v.tr. sep. Constr: (a) to line (walls, etc.) with timber; (b)=ausrüsten I. 2.

ausschälen, v.tr. sep. (a) die Knochen a., to take out the bones (from meat); (b) ein Schwein a., to cut away the fat under the skin of pork.

ausschalmen, v.tr. sep. For: to mark out (area, etc.) by blazing trees.

ausschalten, v.tr. sep. **1.** to exclude (s.o., sth.); to eliminate (s.o.) (from contest, etc.); to rule out, set aside, dismiss (possibility, objection, etc.); to eliminate (mistake, possibility, etc.); um Irrtümer auszuschalten, müssen wir . . ., to avoid, eliminate, (all chance of) mistakes we must . . . ; Herr X wurde aus den Verhandlungen ausgeschaltet, Mr X was excluded from the negotiations; den Zwischenhändler, den Zwischenhandel, a., to eliminate the middleman; ich möchte mich a., I should like to withdraw, to be excluded. **2.** El.E: (a) den Strom a., to switch off the current; abs. a., to open, break, the circuit; to switch off; (b) den Widerstand a., to cut out the resistance.

Ausschalter, m. El.E: circuit-breaker, cut-out; switch.

Ausschank, m. -(e)s/=e. **1.** sale of alcoholic drinks; verbotener A., illegal sale of alcoholic drinks; 'heute A.', 'beer on tap today'. **2.** (a) bar, counter (at which beer, etc., is sold); (b) public house, inn, tavern, F: pub.

ausscharren, v.tr. sep. to dig up (corpse, etc.); (of bird, etc.) to scratch up (worms, earth, etc.); to scratch (a hole); (of dog, etc.) to dig up, scrabble up (bone, etc.); to scrabble up (earth); to scrabble (a hole).

ausscharten, v.tr. sep. to pink (leather, cloth, etc.).

Ausschau, f. A. nach etwas, j-m, halten, to be on the look-out, watch, to keep a look-out, (a) watch, for sth., s.o., to look out, watch, for sth., s.o.; wir haben vergeblich nach ihm, nach seinem Wagen, A. gehalten, we watched for him, for his car, in vain; halt gut A.! keep a sharp look-out! watch out! die Kinder halten A., ob sie kommt, the children are on the look-out, are looking out, watching, for her arrival, to see if she is coming; auf der A. nach etwas, j-m, sein, to be on the look-out, to be looking out, watching, for sth., s.o.; to be looking for sth., s.o.; ich bin auf der A. nach einem billigen Hut, I am on the look-out, I am looking out, looking, for a cheap hat.

ausschauen. **I.** v.i. sep. (haben) **1.** nach etwas, j-m, a., to be on the look-out, watch, to keep a look-out, (a) watch, for sth., s.o., to look out, watch, for sth., s.o.; sie haben lange vergebens nach ihm ausgeschaut, they kept watch, they watched, for him for a long time in vain; hoffnungsvoll nach j-m a., to watch for s.o. hopefully, to keep (a) hopeful watch for s.o.; sie schaute den ganzen Tag nach einer Gelegenheit aus, ihn zu sprechen, she was on the look-out, she was looking out, watching, all day for an opportunity to speak to him. **2.** to look, seem; er schaut müde aus, he looks tired; es schaut so aus, als ob . . ., it looks as if . . . ; wie schaut's denn aus? how do things look, seem? wie schaut's bei ihm aus? how's he doing, getting on? **II.** pr.p. & a. ausschauend, in vbl senses; esp. (of plans) weit ausschauend, far-sighted.

ausschaufeln, v.tr. sep. to shovel (sth.) out; to bail out (water).

ausscheiden. **I.** v.sep. (strong) **1.** v.tr. (a) to exclude (s.o., sth.); j-n aus einem Rennen a., to eliminate s.o. from a race; sich a., to withdraw; (b) Physiol: to excrete (waste matter); to eliminate, expel (poison, foreign body, germs, etc.); to extrude (blood, etc.); to exude (sweat, etc.); Bot: to excrete (sap, etc.); die Lymphe wird durch die Wandung der Blutkapillare ausgeschieden, lymph is transferred through the (blood) capillary walls; sich a., (i) to be excreted; (ii) to be eliminated, expelled; (c) Ch: to precipitate, deposit (substance). **2.** v.i. (sein) (a) aus dem Amt, usw., a., to retire from, to leave, one's office; er ist vor drei Jahren aus der Firma ausgeschieden, he left the firm three years ago; he resigned from the firm three years ago; aus dem Geschäftsleben a., to retire from business; Herr X scheidet nächsten Monat aus dem Vorstand aus, Mr X leaves the board,

retires from the board, next month; (*of state, etc.*) **aus der Union, usw., a.,** to leave, to secede from, the Union, etc.; (*b*) to be excluded, not to take part; **aus einem Wettbewerb a.,** to retire from, to drop out of, a contest; to be eliminated from a contest; **er mußte wegen einer Verletzung aus dem Rennen a.,** he had to retire from the race on account of an injury; **er schied am Ende der dritten Runde aus,** he was eliminated *or* he dropped out at the end of the third round; (*c*) to be ruled out; not to be considered; to be left out of consideration; **sie scheidet bei der Verteilung der Preise aus,** she cannot be considered for a prize; **für diese Stelle scheidet er aus,** he cannot be considered for this post; **die Möglichkeit, daß sie mitkommt, scheidet aus,** it's out of the question that she should come too; **jede Möglichkeit unserer Beteiligung an diesem Unternehmen muß von vornherein a.,** any question of our taking part in this enterprise must be ruled out from the start.

II. *vbl s.* **1. Ausscheiden,** *n. in vbl senses; also:* (*a*)=II. 2 (*a*); (*b*) retirement (of s.o.) (from office, race, etc.); secession (of state, etc.) (from union, etc.). **2. Ausscheidung,** *f.* (*a*) *in vbl senses; also:* exclusion (of s.o., sth.); elimination (of s.o., sth.); excretion (of waste matter, sap, etc.); expulsion (of poison, etc.); extrusion (of blood, etc.); exudation (of sweat, etc.); *Ch:* precipitation, deposition (of substance); **die A. der Lymphe durch die Wandung der Blutkapillare,** the transference of lymph through the (blood) capillary walls; (*b*) excretion, excreted matter; excrement; *pl.* **Ausscheidungen,** excreted substances; eliminated substances; waste matter; *Physiol:* excreta, excrements.

Ausscheidungskampf, *m. Sp:* preliminary trial; preliminary, eliminating, qualifying, heat.

Ausscheidungsorgan, *n. Anat:* excretory organ.

Ausscheidungsrunde, *f. Sp: Rac:* qualifying heat; *Ten: etc:* qualifying round.

Ausscheidungsstoff, *m. Physiol:* excretion, excreted matter; *pl.* **Ausscheidungsstoffe,** excreta.

Ausscheidungssystem, *n. Anat: Physiol:* excretory system.

ausschelten, *v.tr. sep.* (*strong*) to scold (s.o.); to read (s.o.) a lecture; *F:* to tell, tick, (s.o.) off; to blow (s.o.) up; *U.S. & F:* to bawl (s.o.) out.

ausschenken, *v.tr. sep.* **1.** to pour out (drink). **2.** to sell (alcoholic drinks).

ausscheren[1], *v.tr. sep.* (*strong*) **1.** to cut out (hair, etc.); to shear out (wool). **2.** *Nau:* to unreeve (rope).

ausscheren[2], *v.i. sep.* (*weak*) (*sein*) to fall out of line; *Nau:* (*of ship*) to draw, haul, out of the line; *Av:* to leave formation.

ausscheuern, *v.tr. sep.* to scrub out (pan, bath, room, etc.); to scour out (pan, etc.).

ausschicken, *v.tr. sep.* (*a*) to send out (messenger, spy, etc.); to dispatch (messenger); **j-n auf Kundschaft a.,** to send s.o. out to reconnoitre; **die Magd a., etwas zu kaufen,** to send the maid out to buy sth.; (*b*) to send out (circulars, etc.).

ausschießen, *v.sep.* (*strong*) I. *v.tr.* **1.** (*a*) to shoot (sth.) out; **j-m ein Auge a.,** to shoot out one of s.o.'s eyes; (*b*) **einen Wald, usw., a.,** to shoot all the game in a wood, etc. **2.** (*a*) to throw out, discard, scrap (inferior products, etc.); *Nau:* **Ballast a.,** to discharge, throw out, ballast; (*b*) (*of baker*) **Brot aus dem Backofen a.,** to take bread out of the oven. **3.** *Print:* to impose (sheet, forme).

II. **ausschießen,** *v.i.* (*sein*) (*of wind*) to back.

III. *vbl s.* **Ausschießen,** *n. in vbl senses; also: Print:* imposition (of sheet, forme). *Cp.* **Ausschuß.**

Ausschießer, *m. Bookb:* gatherer, collator (of sheets).

ausschiffen. I. *v.sep.* **1.** *v.i.* (*sein*) (*a*) (*of ship, pers.*) to set sail, to sail, to leave the harbour; (*b*) (*of pers.*) to disembark, land. **2.** *v.tr.* to unship, unload, discharge (cargo); to disembark, land (passengers, troops); to bring (passengers, troops) ashore; *F:* to get rid of (minister, etc.).

II. *vbl s.* **1. Ausschiffen** *n.*, **Ausschiffung** *f. in vbl senses; also:* disembarkation.

ausschimpfen, *v.tr. sep.* to scold (s.o.); to read (s.o.) a lecture; *F:* to tell, tick, (s.o.) off; to blow (s.o.) up; *U.S. & F:* to bawl (s.o.) out.

ausschirren, *v.tr. sep.* to unharness (horse); to unyoke (oxen).

ausschlachten, *v.tr. sep.* **1.** (*a*) to cut up, dismember (carcass), to cut (carcass) into pieces; (*b*) to break up (machine, ship, etc.); to cannibalize (aircraft, car, etc.). **2.** to make use of (sth.), to turn (sth.) to advantage, to account, to make the most of (sth.), to exploit (sth.); to make capital out of (event, etc.); **ein Werk a.,** to draw heavily upon a work; **einen Fall politisch a.,** to make political capital out of a case.

Ausschlachter, *m. Nau:* ship-breaker.

ausschlafen, *v.sep.* (*strong*) **1.** *v.i.* (*haben*) & **sich ausschlafen,** to get enough sleep; to have one's sleep out; **ich habe heute Morgen nicht richtig a. können,** I had to get up too early this morning; **du kannst (dich) morgen früh a.,** you can sleep late tomorrow morning; **(sich) sonntags a.,** to sleep late, *F:* to have a good lie in, on Sundays; **die Nacht a.,** to sleep the night through; **ich habe keinen Morgen a. können,** I haven't been able to sleep late any morning. **2.** *v.tr.* **seinen Rausch a.,** to sleep off the effects of liquor, *F:* to sleep it off; **seine schlechte Laune a.,** to sleep off one's bad temper.

Ausschlag, *m.* **1.** (*a*) deflection (of pendulum, balance pointer, etc.); (*b*) **den A. geben,** to turn the scale, the balance, to tip the balance, to decide, to be decisive; **dieses Argument gab den A.,** this argument turned the scale; **seine Meinung gab den A.,** his opinion decided, settled, clinched, the matter; **seine Stimme gab den A.,** his was the casting vote; **ihre Meinung gab den A. bei der Entscheidung,** her opinion turned the scale in deciding the matter; **ihre Ansicht gibt immer den A. für mich,** her opinion always decides me, I am always swayed by her opinion, I always go by her opinion; **dieser Einwand gab den A. für unsere Entscheidung,** this objection decided us, was responsible for our decision. **2.** oscillation (of pendulum, etc.). **3.** (*a*) *Med:* rash, eruption; spots; **A. bekommen, entwickeln,** to come out in a rash, in spots; (*b*) (*on wall, etc.*) efflorescence.

Ausschlageisen, *n. Tls:* hollow punch.

ausschlägeln, *v.tr. sep. Lap:* to hollow out (gem).

ausschlagen, *v.sep.* (*strong*) I. *v.tr.* **1.** (*a*) to knock (sth.) out; **j-m einen Zahn a.,** to knock out one of s.o.'s teeth; *see also* **Boden** 3 (*a*); (*b*) to punch out (piece of material, etc.); (*c*) to beat out (flame, etc.). **2.** *Av:* to extend (flaps, etc.). **3.** to beat out, hammer out (metal, etc.). **4. einen Kasten, eine Schublade, usw., mit Papier, usw., a.,** to line a box, drawer, etc., with paper, etc. **5. ein Angebot, eine Stelle, a.,** to refuse, reject, an offer, the offer of a job; **einen Gedanken a.,** to dismiss an idea; **eine Erbschaft a.,** to renounce, relinquish, a succession, to refuse, turn down, an inheritance.

II. **ausschlagen,** *v.i.* **1.** (*haben*) (*of horse*) to kick (out), lash out, fling out; (*of pers.*) **mit den Händen a.,** to hit out, lash out, strike out (violently); **mit den Füßen a.,** to kick; **mit Händen und Füßen a.,** to lash out with one's hands and feet; **ausschlagendes Pferd,** kicking horse, kicker; *Her:* horse kicking. **2.** (*sein, haben*) (*of plant*) to bud, burgeon; to sprout; to put out shoots. **3.** (*sein, haben*) (*of pendulum, etc.*) to be deflected; **das Zünglein (an der Waage) schlägt (nach rechts, links) aus,** the pointer on the scales is deflected (to the right, left). **4.** (*haben*) to stop beating, hitting; (*of heart*) to stop beating; (*of clock*) to stop chiming. **5.** (*sein*) to turn out; **j-m zum Vorteil, Nachteil, a.,** to turn out to s.o.'s advantage, disadvantage; **es ist zu seinem Heil, Unheil, ausgeschlagen,** it had good, evil, consequences for him.

III. *vbl s.* **1. Ausschlagen,** *n. in vbl senses; also:* (*a*) refusal, rejection (of offer); *Jur:* renunciation, relinquishment (of succession); (*b*) deflection (of pendulum, balance pointer, etc.). **2. Ausschlagung,** *f.* (*a*)=III. 1; (*b*) oscillation (of pendulum, etc.).

ausschlaggebend, *a.* decisive; **dieses Argument war a.,** this argument turned, tipped, the scale, decided the matter; **seine Meinung ist immer a. für mich,** his opinion always decides me, has a decisive influence upon me; **ihre Meinung war a. bei der Entscheidung,** her opinion turned the scale in deciding the matter; **dieser Einwand war a. für unsere Entscheidung,** this objection decided us, was responsible for our decision; **von ausschlaggebender Bedeutung sein,** to be decisive, to tip the balance; to be of prime importance; **dieses Ereignis war von ausschlaggebender Bedeutung, war a., für seine Laufbahn,** this event determined his career, was of prime importance in deciding his career.

Ausschlagmaschine, *f.* punching machine.

Ausschlagpunzen, *m. Tls:* punch.

Ausschlagwinkel, *m.* angle of deflection.

ausschlämmen, *v.tr. sep.* to dredge (canal, etc.).

ausschleifen, *v.tr. sep.* (*strong*) **1.** to whet, grind, (knife, etc.)(thoroughly). **2.** to whet, grind, out (notch, etc.). **3.** to grind (sth.) hollow; to grind a hollow in (sth.).

Ausschleudermaschine, *f. Ind: etc:* drying-machine, centrifugal dryer, centrifugal extractor.

ausschleudern, *v.tr. sep.* to fling (sth.) out; to eject (sth.); (*of volcano, etc.*) to eject, vomit forth (stones, etc.).

ausschlichten, *v.tr. sep.* to planish (metal).

Ausschlichthammer, *m.* planishing hammer.

ausschließen. I. *v.tr. sep.* (*strong*) **1.** (*a*) to shut (s.o.) out; to lock (s.o.) out; to close one's door against (s.o.); *Ind:* to lock out (workers); **laß die Tür nicht zufallen, sonst bin ich ausgeschlossen,** don't let the door bang to or I shall be shut out; *Jur: etc:* **die Öffentlichkeit a.,** to exclude, not to admit, the public; (*b*) **j-n aus etwas a.,** to exclude s.o. from sth.; to expel s.o. from sth.; to disqualify s.o. from sth.; **j-n aus einer Gesellschaft a.,** to exclude, expel, s.o. from a society; **j-n aus der Gesellschaft a.,** to ostracize s.o., *F:* to send s.o. to Coventry; **aus der Gesellschaft ausgeschlossen sein,** to be shut off, shut out, excluded, from society; **er hat sich durch sein abstoßendes Benehmen aus der Gesellschaft ausgeschlossen,** he has cut himself off from society by, he has been ostracized because of, his disgusting behaviour; *Sch:* **ein Kind aus der Schule, einen Studenten aus der Universität, a.,** to expel a child from school; to send a student down (from the University); to rusticate a student; **ein Kind vom Schulbesuch a.,** (i) to refuse to admit a child to school; (ii) to expel a child from school; **j-n vom Universitätsstudium a.,** (i) to exclude s.o. from, to refuse s.o. entry to, *U.S:* to refuse s.o. admittance to, the University; (ii) to send s.o. down, *U.S:* dismiss s.o. (from the University); to rusticate, *U.S:* suspend, s.o.; *Mil:* **j-n aus der Armee a.,** to dismiss s.o. from the service; *Sp:* **j-n (von einem Wettkampf (a.,** to disqualify s.o. (from a contest); **sich durch Zuspätkommen, usw., von einem Wettkampf a.,** to be disqualified from a contest on account of lateness, etc.; **sich von einem Spiel a.,** to refuse to take part in a game; (*c*) to debar (s.o.) (from sth.); **Ausländer sind von der Bewerbung um diese Stellen ausgeschlossen,** aliens are debarred from applying for, aliens are excluded from, these posts; *Jur:* **einen Richter von der Ausübung des Richteramts a.,** to incapacitate, disqualify, a judge from officiating; (*d*) to except, exclude (s.o., sth.); **von diesem Vorwurf schließe ich niemanden aus,** I make this reproach to all without exception. **2.** to exclude, preclude, eliminate, rule out (sth.); to make (sth.) impossible; **das eine schließt das andere aus,** the one precludes, rules out, the other; **sein einmaliges Versagen schließt die Möglichkeit seiner zukünftigen Bewährung nicht aus,** the fact that he failed once in the past does not rule out the possibility of his proving himself in the future; **diese Maßnahme hat jede Möglichkeit eines Fehlers ausgeschlossen,** this measure has excluded, precluded, ruled out, eliminated, all possibility of a mistake, has made it impossible for there to be a mistake; **die Möglichkeit, daß . . . , kann nicht ausgeschlossen werden,** the possibility that . . . cannot be ruled out; **ich glaube, dieser Beweis wird jeden Einwand a.,** I think this piece of evidence will rule out, eliminate, all possibility of an objection; **ein Mißverständnis, usw., a.,** to preclude a misunderstanding, etc., to rule out, eliminate, exclude, all chance of a misunderstanding, etc.; **zwei Auffassungen, die sich gegenseitig a.,** two conceptions that are incompatible, that are mutually exclusive; *see also* **ausgeschlossen. 3.** *Print:* to justify, adjust (line of type).

II. *vbl s.* **1. Ausschließen,** *n. in vbl senses.* **2. Ausschließung,** *f.*=II. 1; *also:* (*a*)=**Ausschluß** 1; (*b*) exclusion (of one thg by another); (*c*) *Print:* justification, adjustment (of lines); (*d*) *Print:* space.

ausschließlich. 1. *a.* exclusive; sole, only; **das ausschließliche Recht auf etwas haben,** to have the exclusive right to, of, in, sth.; **das ausschließliche Recht darauf haben, etwas zu tun,** to have the exclusive right to do sth., to be the only person with the right to do sth.; **wir haben das ausschließliche Recht auf die Aufführung dieses Stücks,** we have the exclusive rights of, in, the production of this play, we have the exclusive right to produce this play; **im ausschließlichen Besitz von etwas sein,** to be the sole possessor of sth., the only person to possess sth.; **es ist seit zehn Jahren seine ausschließliche Beschäftigung gewesen,** it has been his exclusive, sole, occupation for ten years. **2.** *adv.* (*a*) exclusively; solely,

only; **er beschäftigt sich a. mit der spanischen Literatur,** he is studying Spanish literature and nothing else; **sie interessiert sich a. für ihre Katzen,** her cats are her sole, only, interest; (*b*) **bis Seite zwanzig a.,** to page nineteen inclusive, *U.S:* pages one through nineteen. **3.** *prep.*(+*gen.*) exclusive of . . . ; **der Preis des Abendessens a. des Weins,** the price of the dinner exclusive of wine.

Ausschließlichkeit, *f.* **1.** exclusiveness. **2.** exclusive interest; dedication; **die A., mit der er sich seiner Arbeit hingibt,** his complete dedication to his work.

Ausschließungsprinzip, das. *Atom.Ph:* the (Pauli) exclusion principle.

ausschlüpfen, *v.i. sep.* (*sein*) (*of birds, etc.*) to hatch (out); (*of caterpillar, butterfly*) to emerge (from the egg, from the chrysalis).

ausschlürfen, *v.tr. sep.* to drink up (soup, etc.) noisily, with relish; to empty (cup, etc.) noisily, with relish; *F:* to slurp (soup, etc.); **ein Ei a.,** to suck an egg; **er schlürfte gierig den Trank aus,** he swallowed the drink thirstily, greedily.

Ausschluß. *m.* **1.** (*a*) exclusion, non-admission (of public, etc.); *Ind:* lock-out; *Jur:* (*of case*) **unter A. der Öffentlichkeit stattfinden,** to be heard in camera; (*b*) exclusion (of s.o.); expulsion (of s.o.); disqualification (of s.o.); *Sp:* disqualification; **sein A. aus dem Verein hat ihn schwer getroffen,** his exclusion, expulsion, from the society hit him hard; *Sch:* **A. eines Kindes aus der Schule, eines Studenten aus der Universität,** expulsion of a child from school, sending down *or* rustication, *U.S:* dismissal *or* suspension, of a student; **dieser Streich hatte seinen A. aus der Universität auf ein Semester zur Folge,** this prank resulted in his being sent down, rusticated, for a term, *U.S:* suspended for a semester; **der A. eines Kindes vom Schulbesuch, eines Studenten vom Universitätsstudium,** (i) non-admission of a child to school, of a student to the University; (ii) expulsion of a child from school, sending down of a student; rustication of a student; (*c*) debarring (of s.o.) (from sth.); *Jur:* **der A. eines Richters von der Ausübung des Richteramts,** the incapacitation, disqualification, of a judge from officiating. **2.** exclusion, elimination, ruling out (of possibilities, etc.); **nach A. jeden Zweifels werden wir mit unseren Versuchen fortfahren können,** when all doubt has been eliminated we shall be able to continue with our experiments. **3.** *Print:* spaces, spacing material.

Ausschlußrecht, *n.* **1.** right to exclude; right to expel; right to disqualify. **2.** exclusive right; monopoly.

ausschmelzen, *v.sep.* **1.** *v.tr.* (*strong, occ. weak*) to melt out (fat, etc.); *Ind:* to try out (metal, whale fat, etc.); to melt (metal, fat, etc.); to fuse (metal) (**aus etwas,** from sth.). **2.** *v.i.* (*strong*) (*sein*) (*of fat, metal, etc.*) to melt; to be melted out (**aus etwas,** of sth.); (*of metal*) to fuse.

ausscnmieden, *v.tr. sep.* to forge, hammer out (metal).

ausschmieren, *v.tr. sep.* **ein Gefäß, usw., mit etwas a.,** to smear the inside of a vessel, etc., with sth.; **eine Tonne mit Teer a.,** to paint the inside of a barrel with tar, to tar the inside of a barrel; *Constr:* **Fugen a.,** to point joints; *Cu:* **eine Form a.,** to grease a baking-tin.

ausschmücken. I. *v.tr. sep.* (*a*) to adorn, decorate, deck out, ornament, embellish (sth.); **einen Saal mit Blumen a.,** to deck out, decorate, a room with flowers; (*b*) to embellish, embroider (a story, etc.); **er schmückte die Geschichte jedesmal mit neuen Einzelheiten aus,** he embellished, embroidered, the story every time with new details.

II. *vbl s.* **1. Ausschmücken,** *n. in vbl senses.* **2. Ausschmückung,** *f.* (*a*)=II. 1; *also:* adornment, decoration, ornamentation (of room, etc.); embellishment (of story, etc.); (*b*) adornment, decoration, ornamentation, embellishment; embroidery (in story, etc.); **er findet jedesmal neue Ausschmückungen für seine Erzählung,** he finds new embellishments, new embroidery, for his narrative every time.

Ausschneidekunst, *f.* cut-paper work, *esp.* silhouetting.

ausschneiden, *v.tr. sep.* (*strong*) (*a*) to cut (sth.) out; **Bilder aus einem Buch a.,** to cut pictures out of a book; **Figuren, usw., aus Papier a.,** to cut figures, etc., out of paper; **einen Baum, die Äste aus einem Baum, a.,** to prune a tree, to cut away the superfluous branches from a tree; *Mint:* **Münzplatten a.,** to cut blanks; *Surg:* **eine Geschwulst, usw., a.,** to cut out, excise, dissect out, a growth, etc.; (*b*) **ein Kleid, usw., tief a.,** to cut the neck of a dress, etc., low; **ein ausgeschnittenes Kleid,** a dress with a low neck, a low-cut, low-necked, décolleté, dress; **das Kleid war hinten tief ausgeschnitten,** the dress was cut low at the, *U.S:* in, back; **sie ging tief ausgeschnitten zum Fest,** she went to the party in a low-necked, a décolleté, evening dress, *U.S:* evening gown.

ausschneien, *v. impers. sep.* **es hat ausgeschneit,** it has stopped snowing.

Ausschnitt, *m.* **1.** cutting out (of sth.). **2.** *Com:* goods sold by the yard; **Tuch, usw., im A. verkaufen,** to sell cloth, etc., retail; to sell cloth, etc., by the yard. **3.** (*a*) piece cut out; **A. aus einer Zeitung,** cutting, clipping, from a newspaper; (*b*) *Geom:* sector (of sphere, circle); (*c*) extract, excerpt (from a work); **j-m einen A. aus 'Faust' vorlesen,** to read s.o. an extract from 'Faust'; (*d*) *Art:* detail; **A. aus Tafel IV,** detail from plate IV; (*e*) section; side, facet (of life, etc.); **hier hat sie einen charakteristischen A. des deutschen Lebens gesehen,** here she saw a characteristic side, facet, of German life. **4.** (*a*) neck (of dress, etc.); **viereckiger A.,** square neck; **runder A.,** round neck; **spitzer, spitziger, A.,** V neck; **ein Kleid mit tiefem A.,** a low-necked, décolleté, dress; (*b*) *Carp: etc:* notch; mortise.

Ausschnittarbeit, *f. Woodw:* fretwork.

Ausschnittmesser, *m. Phot:* iconometer, viewmeter.

ausschnüffeln, *v.tr. sep. F:* **etwas a.,** to nose for, after, sth., to try to nose sth. out; **ein Geheimnis a.,** to nose out a secret.

ausschöpfen, *v.tr. sep.* **1.** to scoop out (water); **Wasser aus einem Kahn a.,** to bail water out of a boat, to bail a boat (out); **einen Brunnen, das Wasser aus einem Brunnen, a.,** to draw all the water from, to exhaust, empty, a well; **ein Regenfaß a.,** to take, scoop, all the water out of, to empty, a rain-water barrel; **eine Baugrube a.,** to remove the water from excavations. **2.** to exhaust (possibilities, etc.).

ausschrägen, *v.tr. sep. Arch:* to splay (window).

ausschrämen, *v.tr. sep. Min:* to (under)cut, (under)hole (coal).

ausschrauben, *v.tr. sep.* to unscrew (plug, etc.); to screw out (tap, etc.).

ausschreiben. I. *v.tr. sep.* (*strong*) **1.** to finish (writing) (book, letter, etc.); to finish, cover (page, sheet); to finish, fill (exercise-book, etc.). **2.** (*a*) to write out (name, etc.) in full; to write out (number) in words; (*b*) to write out, make out (cheque); to make out (bill). **3.** to copy, write, (sth.) out; to copy, draw upon (author, author's works); to plagiarize (author, author's works); **seine Rolle, eine Stelle aus einem Buch, a.,** to write out, copy out, one's part, to copy (out) a passage from a book. **4.** to advertise (post, etc.); to announce (sth.) (in writing, by means of circulars, etc.); **einen Wettbewerb in der Zeitung a.,** to publish a competition in the newspaper; **500 Mark als Preis a.,** to offer a prize of 500 marks; *Com:* **einen Auftrag a.,** to invite tenders, *U.S:* bids, for supplies, etc. **5. sich ausschreiben,** to write oneself out; **ein Autor, der sich mit seinem ersten Roman ausschrieb,** an author who wrote himself out, exhausted his ideas, in his first novel. **6. eine ausgeschriebene Handschrift,** a developed, an individual, handwriting.

II. *vbl s.* **1. Ausschreiben,** *n. in vbl senses.* **2. Ausschreibung,** *f.*=II. 1; *also:* (*notice*) advertisement (of a vacancy); *Com:* invitation of tenders, *U.S:* bids (for supplies, etc.).

ausschreien, *v.tr. sep.* (*strong*) **1.** to shout (sth.) out; to proclaim (sth.); **seine Waren a.,** to cry one's wares. **2.** *F:* **sich** *dat.* **die Lunge a.,** to shout, scream, one's head off; **sich die Lunge nach j-m a.,** to shout one's head off trying to attract s.o.'s attention. **3. sich ausschreien,** (*of baby, etc.*) (*a*) to have a good scream, to exercise its lungs; (*b*) to finish screaming; to cry itself out.

ausschreiten. I. *v.sep.* (*strong*) **1.** *v.tr.* **ein Zimmer, usw., a.,** to pace off the length of a room, etc. **2.** *v.i.* (*sein*) to step out, *F:* to put one's best foot, foremost, forward; **wir müssen tüchtig a., wenn wir vor Abend ankommen wollen,** we shall have to step out, to put our best foot foremost, forward, *F:* to get a move on, if we want to arrive before evening. **3.** *v.i.* (*sein*) **gegen die Bevölkerung a.,** to commit offences, outrages, against the population, to commit excesses in the treatment of the population.

II. *vbl s.* **1. Ausschreiten,** *n. in vbl senses.* **2. Ausschreitung,** *f.* offence; outrage; **Ausschreitungen begehen,** to commit excesses; **die fremden Soldaten ließen sich Ausschreitungen gegen die Bevölkerung zuschulden kommen,** the foreign soldiers committed offences, outrages, against the population.

ausschroten, *v.tr. Austrian:* to cut (meat) into joints.

ausschuppen, *v.tr. sep.* to scallop (sth.); to engrail (sth.); *Her:* **ausgeschupptes Pfeileisen,** pheon, broad arrow(-head).

Ausschuß, *m.* **1.** *Com:* (i) sub-standard articles, sub-standard goods; rejects, *F:* throw-outs, wasters; *Paperm:* retree; casse-paper; (ii) rubbish, trash. **2.** committee; board; commission; panel; *Com:* Board of Directors; **ständiger A.,** permanent committee; standing committee; **gemeinsamer A.,** joint committee; **beratender A.,** advisory committee; **in einem A. sitzen, sein,** to sit on a committee, to be on a committee; to be on a board; to be a member of a commission; to be on a panel; **in einen A. gewählt werden,** to be elected to a committee, etc. **3.** point of exit (of bullet); exit wound.

Ausschußgeschirr, *n. Cer:* rejects.

Ausschußgetreide, *n.*=**Ausschußkorn.**

Ausschußholz, *n.* rejected timber, reject timber, *U.S:* culls, cull lumber.

Ausschußkorn, *n. Husb: Mill:* refuse grain; tailcorn, tailings, offal.

Ausschußmitglied, *n.* committee-member; member of a board, of a commission, of a panel.

Ausschußpapier, *n. Paperm:* retree; casse-paper.

Ausschußsitzung, *f.* committee meeting; board meeting.

Ausschußware, *f. Com:* (i) sub-standard article(s); sub-standard goods; reject(s), *F:* throw-out(s), waster(s); (ii) rubbish, trash.

ausschütteln, *v.tr. sep.* to shake out (dust, etc.); to shake the dust, etc., out of (sth.); **eine Matte, den Staub aus einer Matte, a.,** to shake (the dust out of) a door-mat.

ausschütten. I. *v.tr. sep.* **1.** (*a*) (i) to pour out, empty out (water, sand, etc.); to pour, empty, the contents out of (sth.), to empty (sth.); (ii) to spill (water, sand, grain, etc.); to spill the contents out of (sth.); **(etwas) Wasser aus einem Krug a.,** (i) to pour, (ii) to spill, some of the water out of a jug; **das Wasser aus einem Krug a.,** (i) to pour, empty, (ii) to spill, (all) the water out of a jug; **einen Sack Korn a.,** to empty a sack of corn; to spill a sack of corn; *see also* **Bad** 1 (*a*); (*b*) **(j-m) sein Herz a.,** to pour out, open, one's heart, to unbosom, unburden, oneself (to s.o.); (*c*) *F:* **sich vor Lachen a. wollen,** to be ready to burst with laughter, to be convulsed with laughter. **2.** *Com: Jur:* to distribute (dividends, etc.); **die Konkursmasse a.,** to distribute, divide, a bankrupt's property (among creditors).

II. *vbl s.* **1. Ausschütten,** *n. in vbl senses.* **2. Ausschüttung,** *f.* (*a*)=II. 1; *also:* distribution (of dividends, bankrupt's property, etc.); division (of bankrupt's property) (among creditors); (*b*) *Atom.Ph:* **radioaktive A.,** radioactive fall-out.

ausschwärmen, *v.i. sep.* (*sein*) (*of bees, etc.*) to swarm out; *Mil:* (*of troops*) to deploy.

ausschweben, *v.i. sep.* (*sein*) *Av:* to flatten out.

ausschwefeln, *v.tr. sep.* to sulphur (cask, etc.), to fumigate (cask, etc.) with burning sulphur.

ausschweifen. I. *v.sep.* **1.** *v.tr.* to curve (edge, etc.); to give (sth.) a curved outline. **2.** *v.tr.* to rinse (vessel, etc.). **3.** *v.i.* (*sein, haben*) (*a*) to wander; to digress; (*b*) to indulge in excess; to be dissolute; **im Essen, im Trinken, a.,** to eat, drink, excessively, to excess.

II. *vbl s.* **1. Ausschweifen,** *n. in vbl senses.* **2. Ausschweifung,** *f.* (*a*)=II. 1; (*b*) (outward) curve; (*c*) excess; dissoluteness, debauchery, loose living; **in A. leben,** to live a dissolute life; **er hat sich durch sein wüstes Treiben und seine Ausschweifungen zugrunde gerichtet,** he has brought about his own ruin by his wild life and his excesses; (*d*) *A:* digression (in speech, etc.).

III. *pr.p. & a.* **ausschweifend,** *in vbl senses; esp.* unbridled (imagination); dissolute, loose, debauched (life); **ein ausschweifendes Leben führen,** to lead a dissolute life.

ausschweigen (sich), *v.refl. sep.* (*strong*) *F:* to be, remain, silent; **er hat sich gründlich darüber ausgeschwiegen,** he never said a word about it, he was completely silent on the subject.

ausschwemmen, *v.tr. sep.* to rinse (sth.) out; to flush out (drain, etc.).

ausschwenken, *v.sep.* **1.** *v.tr.* (*a*) to rinse, swill, out (glass, etc.); (*b*) to extract (moisture) by centrifugal force; to dry (sth.) by the use of centrifugal force. **2.** *v.tr.* to swivel (machine part, etc.) (outwards); to traverse, turn, swivel

(gun). 3. *v.i.* (*sein*) to swivel (outwards); (*of gun*) to be traversed, turned.

Ausschwenkmaschine, *f. Ind:* centrifugal extractor, hydro-extractor.

ausschwingen, *v.sep.* (*strong*) **1.** *v.tr.* to swing (sth.) out. **2.** *v.i.* (*haben*) (*a*) *Gym: etc:* to swing out; *Ven:* (*of large birds*) to fly out (of tree); (*b*) (*of pendulum, etc.*) to cease swinging, oscillating.

Ausschwingungskurve, *f. N.Arch:* curve of extinction (of oscillations).

ausschwitzen. I. *v.sep.* **1.** *v.tr.* (*a*) to exude (moisture, sap, etc.); to sweat out (impurities, fever, etc.); (*b*) to sweat (moisture, etc.) out (of sth.). **2.** *v.i.* (*a*) (*sein*) (*of moisture, etc.*) to sweat out; to exude; to ooze out; (*b*) (*haben*) to cease sweating.

II. *vbl s.* **1. Ausschwitzen,** *n. in vbl senses; also:* exudation (of moisture, etc.). **2. Ausschwitzung,** *f.* (*a*) = II. 1; (*b*) exudation, exuded matter.

Ausschwung, *m.* swing out; outward swing; *Clockm:* overbanking.

Ausschwungstift, *m. Clockm:* banking-pin.

aussegeln, *v.i. sep.* (*sein*) to sail out, away, off.

aussegnen, *v.tr. sep.* (*of priest*) to church (woman); (*of woman after childbirth*) **ausgesegnet werden,** to be churched.

aussehen. I. *v.sep.* (*strong*) **1.** *v.i.* (*haben*) to look; **müde, krank, gesund, a.,** to look tired, ill, well; **älter, jünger, a., als man in Wirklichkeit ist,** to look older, younger, than one really is; **sie sieht nicht so alt aus, wie sie in Wirklichkeit ist,** she doesn't look her age; **für sein Alter jung a.,** to look young for one's age; **er ist erst dreißig Jahre alt, aber er sieht aus wie fünfzig,** he is only thirty, but he looks fifty; **er ist sehr gutmütig — so sieht er auch aus,** he is very good-natured—he looks it; **gut a.,** (*of pers.*) (i) to be good-looking; (ii) to look well, healthy; **er sieht gut in Uniform aus,** he looks well in uniform; **ein Kleid, das gut aussieht,** a dress that looks well, nice; **diese Speise sieht gut aus,** this dish looks good; **wie sieht er aus?** (i) what does he look like? (ii) how does he look? **wie siehst du denn aus!** you do look a sight! what a sight you are! **du siehst (so) aus, als ob du schlecht geschlafen hättest,** you look as if you had slept badly; **er hatte tagelang gehungert, und danach sah er auch aus,** he had been starving for days, and he looked like it; **er sieht aus, als ob er uns sprechen wollte,** he looks as if he wanted to speak to us; **sehe ich (so) aus, als ob ich spaßen wollte?** do I look as if I'm joking? **er sieht aus, als ob, wie wenn, er dazu fähig wäre,** he looks as if he would be capable of it; *F:* **das Kleid soll nach etwas a.,** the dress must look (quite) something; **er sieht nach nichts (Besonderem) aus,** he's nothing (much) to look at; *Iron: F:* **so siehst du aus!** *F:* (i) I bet! o(h) yeah! says you! (ii) you've got a hope! not likely! **du siehst mir danach aus!** I bet! o(h) yeah! **er sieht wie ein Matrose aus,** he looks like a sailor; **du siehst so sehr wie deine Mutter aus, daß . . .,** you look so (very much) like your mother that . . .; **er sieht wie ein Schurke, ein Dummkopf, aus,** he looks (like) a rogue, a fool; **die gefälschten Banknoten sahen ganz wie echte aus,** the forged banknotes looked just like real ones; **jetzt sieht es so aus, als ob wir's absichtlich getan hätten,** now it looks as if we had done it on purpose; **es sähe nicht gut aus, wenn wir so etwas täten,** it wouldn't look well for us to do a thing like that; **die Lage sieht günstig aus,** things look promising; **es sieht bös mit ihm aus,** things look bad, black, for him; he is in a bad way; **wie sieht's bei euch aus?** how are things with you? **es sieht so aus, als ob er gewönne,** it looks as if he were winning, he looks like winning; **es sieht nach Regen, wie Regen, aus,** it looks like rain; **es sieht nach schönem Wetter aus,** it looks like being fine, like fine weather, like a fine day. **2.** (*a*) *v.i.* (*haben*) **nach j-m, etwas, a.,** to be on the look-out, watch, to keep a look-out, (a) watch, for s.o., sth., to look out, watch, for s.o., sth.; (*b*) *v.tr.* **sich** *dat.* **die Augen nach j-m, etwas, a.,** to stare oneself blind looking for s.o., sth.

II. *vbl s.* **1. Aussehen,** *n.* appearance, exterior, look(s), aspect; **er hat ein angenehmes A.,** he has a pleasing appearance; **ein junger Mann von gutem A.,** a young man of good appearance; **ein Mann von furchterregendem, imposantem, A.,** a man of fearsome, impressive, aspect, appearance; **ein gutes A., aber kein Geld haben,** to have (good) looks but no money; **er hat nicht das A. eines reichen Mannes,** he doesn't look (like) a rich man; **man darf ihn nicht nach seinem A. beurteilen,** one must not judge him by his appearance, exterior; **seinem A. nach ist er . . .,** by the look(s) of him, to judge from his appearance, he is . . . **2.** *A:* = **Aussicht** 1.

III. *pr.p., adj. & comb.fm.* **aussehend,** -looking; **gutaussehend,** good-looking; **besser aussehend,** better-looking; **ernstaussehend,** serious-looking.

ausseigern, *v.tr. sep. Metall:* to liquate out (lead, etc.); **Ausseigern** *n,* **Ausseigerung** *f,* (i) liquation, (ii) segregation.

aussein, *v.i. sep.* (*sein*) (*conj. like* **sein**). **1.** (*a*) to be out; (*b*) **auf etwas** *acc.* **a.,** to be out for, to be after, sth.; **darauf a., etwas zu tun,** to be out to do sth. **2.** to be over, finished, ended; *see also* **aus** II. 5.

außen. 1. *adv.* outside; **der Kasten ist a. und innen schwarz,** the box is black inside and out(side); **a. an der Tür,** on the outside of the door; **die Tür geht nach a. auf,** the door opens outwards; **seine Füße nach a. setzen,** to turn one's feet out(wards); **der Lärm kommt von a.,** the noise is coming from outside; **von a. sieht das Haus wie neu aus,** from the outside the house looks like new; **nach a. hin schien alles in Ordnung zu sein,** outwardly everything seemed to be in order; **die Wirkung nach a. hin ist nicht das Wesentliche,** the outward, external, effect is not what counts. **2. außen-, Außen-,** *comb.fm.* (*a*) external . . .; outer . . .; outside . . .; exterior . . .; **Außenabmessungen** *fpl,* external, outside, dimensions; **Außendurchmesser** *m,* external, outside, diameter; **Außenfläche** *f,* external, outer, surface; **Außenkante** *f,* outer edge, outside edge; *Biol:* **Außendrüse** *f,* external gland; (*b*) outside . . .; outdoor . . .; external . . .; **Außenbeleuchtung** *f,* outdoor lighting; **Außentemperatur** *f,* outside, external, temperature; outdoor temperature; **außenbefindlich,** situated outside; *W.Tel:* **Außenantenne** *f,* outdoor aerial; outside aerial; (*c*) foreign . . ., external . . .; **Außenhandel** *m,* foreign trade, external trade; **Außenwert** *m,* foreign value (of currency, etc.).

Außenalster, die. *Geog:* the Outer Alster (in Hamburg).

Außenamt, *n.* (*in Austria*) = **Außenministerium.**

Außenaufnahme, *f. Phot:* outdoor photograph *or* exposure; *Cin:* exterior shot; *TV:* outdoor pick-up.

Außenbackenbremse, *f. Veh:* external-contracting shoe-brake.

Außenbahn, *f. Sp:* outside lane, outer lane (of track).

Außenbandbremse, *f. Veh:* external-contracting band-brake.

Außenbeleuchtung, *f.* outdoor lighting (on house, in street, etc.).

Außenbezirk, *m.* suburb (of a town); outlying district.

Außenbordmotor, *m. Nau: etc:* outboard motor.

außenbords, *adv. Nau:* outboard.

Außenbremse, *f. Veh:* outer brake.

außenbürtig, *a. Geol:* exogenous.

Außendeich, *m.* outer dike, fore-dike.

aussenden, *v.tr. sep.* (*conj. like* **senden**) (*a*) to send out (messenger, spy, etc.); to dispatch (messenger, etc.); **einen Boten, einen Spion, auf Kundschaft a.,** to send a messenger, a spy, out to get information; (*b*) **einen Befehl a.,** to issue, send out, an order; (*c*) to send out (rays, electric waves, etc.); (*d*) (*of plant*) to send out (shoots, etc.).

Außendienst, *m.* outside work, work as a representative (of firm, etc.); outdoor service.

außendienstlich, *a.* outside (work, etc.).

Außendruck, *m.* external pressure,

Außenfläche, *f.* outside surface, external surface (of a body); outer surface (of lens, dish, etc.); outside (of window, bowl, etc.).

Außenfront, *f. Arch:* façade.

Außengetriebe, *n. Mec.E:* external gearing.

Außengewinde, *n. Tchn:* male thread, external thread.

Außenhafen, *m.* outer harbour; outer port.

Außenhandel, *m.* foreign trade, external trade.

Außenhandelsbank, *f.* bank authorized to handle foreign exchange business.

Außenhandelskaufmann, *m.* **1.** exporter; importer. **2.** (*in firm*) export official *or* clerk; import official *or* clerk.

Außenhaut, *f.* **1.** outer skin (of fruit, etc.); *Anat:* epidermis; outer membrane (of organ). **2.** *N.Arch:* outside skin, case; shell-plating, outer plating.

Außenhautbeplankung, *f. N.Arch:* outside planking (of vessel).

Außenhautplattc, *f. N.Arch:* shell-plate.

Außeninstitut, *n.* experimental *or* research station (affiliated to university, etc.).

Außenkanzel, *f.* outdoor pulpit.

außenkeimig, *a. Bot:* exor(r)hizal; **außenkeimige Pflanze,** exor(r)hiza,

Außenkelch, *m. Bot:* calycle.

aussenken. I. *v.tr. sep. Carp: Metalw:* to countersink *or* counterbore (hole).

II. *vbl s.* **Aussenkung,** *f.* (*a*) *in vbl senses;* (*b*) countersunk hole, countersink; counterbore.

Außenklüver, *m. Nau:* main jib, outer jib.

Außenkreis, *m.* outer circle; *Sp:* (*in basketball*) restraining circle.

Außenlager, *n. Mec.E:* external, outer, bearing.

Außenlandung, *f. Av:* landing away from an air-field.

Außenläufer, *m. Fb: etc:* wing-half.

Außenleitung, *f.* **1.** *El.E: Civ.E: etc:* exterior wiring *or* piping; outside circuit. **2.** *El.E:* external leads.

Außenlenker, *m. Aut:* limousine with a partition.

außenliegend, *a.* (*a*) lying outside; on the outer side; outer; (*b*) outlying (district, village, etc.).

Außenlinie, *f. Fb: etc:* touch-line.

Außenmaße, *n.pl.* outside, external, measurements.

Außenmauer, *f.* outer wall; outside, external, wall.

Außenminister, *m.* Foreign Minister; (*British*) Secretary of State for Foreign Affairs, Foreign Secretary; *U.S:* Secretary of State; (*in Commonwealth countries*) Minister of External Affairs.

Außenministerium, *n.* Foreign Ministry; (*British*) Foreign Office; *U.S:* State Department; (*in Commonwealth countries*) Ministry of External Affairs.

Außenparasit, *m.* = **Außenschmarotzer.**

Außenplanken, Außenplatten, *f.pl. N.Arch:* shell-plates, outside plating (of vessel).

Außenpol, *m. El:* external pole.

Außenpolitik, *f.* (*a*) foreign policy; (*b*) foreign politics; foreign affairs.

außenpolitisch, *a.* pertaining to foreign affairs; **außenpolitische Debatte,** debate on foreign affairs, foreign affairs debate; **außenpolitische Probleme,** international problems.

Außenposten, *m. Mil:* advanced post.

Außenrand, *m.* outer edge; outer rim; outer margin.

Außenrinde, *f.* outer bark; *Bot:* periderm.

Außenriß, *m.* (*a*) outside crack (in house-wall, etc.); (*b*) *Arb:* external crack (on tree).

Außenrüttler, *m.* (*device*) external vibrator.

Außenschmarotzer, *m. Biol:* external parasite, ectoparasite.

Außenseite, *f.* outside (of window, bowl, etc.); outer side (of garment, etc.); outer surface (of dish, etc.); outer face (of wall).

Außenseiter, *m.* -s/-. **1.** (*pers.*) outsider. **2.** *Turf:* outsider.

Außenskelett, *n. Z:* ectoskeleton, exoskeleton.

Außensohle, *f. Bootm:* outsole.

Außenspiegel, *m.* outside mirror, side mirror, external driving mirror (of car).

Außenstände, *m.pl.* outstanding debts, accounts; **verlorene A.,** bad debts, doubtful debts.

außenstehend, *a.* outside; **Außenstehende** *pl,* outsiders; (mere) bystanders, persons not directly concerned; **ein Außenstehender kann das nicht beurteilen,** no mere bystander, mere onlooker, can judge that.

Außenstelle, *f.* branch. branch office (of firm).

Außenstürmer, *m. Fb: etc:* outside forward, *F:* winger; **linker, rechter, A.,** outside left, right.

Außentreppe, *f.* outside, external, staircase.

Außentür, *f.* outer door.

Außenversicherung, *f.* additional insurance covering articles housed elsewhere, taken on a journey, etc.

Außenviertel, *n.* outer part (of town); **in einem A. leben,** to live in the outer part of the town.

Außenwache, *f. Mil:* (*a*) outlying picket; (*b*) perimeter guard.

Außenwelt, *f.* outer world; outside world, world outside; **er hat jetzt so lange zurückgezogen gelebt, daß er nichts mehr von der A. weiß,** he has lived as a recluse for so long that he knows nothing about the outside world, the world outside; **die Beziehung des Ichs zur A.,** the relationship of the ego to the outer world.

Außenwerk, *n. Fort:* outwork.

Außenwinkel, *m. Geom:* exterior angle.

Außenwirtschaft, *f.* **1.** foreign sector of the, a, country's economy. **2.** international economic relations.

Außenzoll, *m.* external tariff (on goods originating from outside a customs union).

außer, *prep.* **1.** (+*dat., occ.*+*gen.*) outside; out of; **außer (dem) Hause sein,** to be out; **wir aßen**

gestern außer Hause, we ate out yesterday; **außer Landes sein,** to be abroad; **außer Landes gehen,** to leave the country, to go abroad. 2. out of; (a) (+dat.) **außer Gefahr, außer Atem, sein,** to be out of danger, out of breath; **j-n außer der Reihe bedienen,** to serve s.o. out of (his) turn; **außer sich sein,** to be beside oneself; **vor Freude, vor Wut, außer sich sein,** to be beside oneself with joy, rage; see also **Acht²**, **Dienst** 3 (a); (b) (+acc.) **eine Maschine außer Betrieb setzen,** to put a machine out of action; **eine Kanone, j-n, außer Gefecht setzen,** to put a gun out of action, to disable a person; see also **Kurs.** 3. (a) (+dat.) except, but, with the exception of, Lit: save; apart from; U.S: aside from; **außer meiner Schwester waren alle da,** everyone was present except my sister, everyone but my sister was present; **außer mir hat niemand es gehört,** nobody heard it except, apart from, myself; **er ist überall, außer da, wo er sein sollte,** he is everywhere except, but, where he ought to be; (b) conj. phr. **außer wenn ...,** except when ...; **außer daß ...,** except that ...; **er war unversehrt, außer daß er seinen Hut verloren hatte,** he suffered no damage except, all he suffered was, the loss of his hat. 4. (+dat.) in addition to, besides; **außer uns dreien waren zwanzig Leute zugegen,** besides, in addition to, apart from, us three there were twenty people present; **außer dem, was er mir schuldet,** in addition to, besides, over and above, what he owes me. 5. **außer-,** comb.fm. 'extra-; **außereuropäisch,** extra-European; **außerweltlich,** extramundane.

außerachselständig, a. Bot: extra-axillary.
Außerachtlassen, n., **Außerachtlassung,** f. failure to take (sth.) into consideration; ignoring, disregarding (of possibility, etc.); **die Außerachtlassung dieser Möglichkeit war ein großer Fehler,** it was a great mistake to ignore, disregard, this possibility.
außeramtlich, a. extra-official; unofficial; private.
außerdem, adv. (a) besides, in addition, as well, also, too, into the bargain; **nichts a.,** nothing besides, nothing else, nothing more; **ich habe a. zwei Neffen,** I have two nephews as well, I also have two nephews; **er kaufte uns ein Haus und a. noch eine Zimmereinrichtung,** he bought us a house and a suite of furniture besides, in addition, as well, too, into the bargain; (b) besides, moreover, furthermore; **es ist zu spät; a. bin ich müde,** it is too late; besides, and apart from that, I am tired.
außerdienstlich, a. extra-official; unofficial; private; adv. **ich muß ihn a. warnen, daß ...,** I must warn him unofficially, privately, F: off the record, that ...
außerehelich, a. extra-marital, extra-conjugal, irregular (relations, etc.); illegitimate (child)
äußere(r), äußere, äußere(s). 1. a. (used attributively only) outer; outside; exterior; external; outward; **äußere Bedeckung,** outer covering; **äußere Tür,** outer door; **das äußere Ohr,** the external ear, the outer ear; **eine äußere Verletzung,** an external injury; **äußere Umstände,** outward circumstances; external conditions; **die äußere Erscheinung eines Menschen,** a person's exterior, appearance; **äußerer Schein,** (outward, external) appearances; **man soll nicht nach dem äußeren Schein urteilen,** one should not judge by appearances, by externals; **der äußere Schein ist gegen ihn,** appearances are against him; **äußere Einflüsse,** outside influences. 2. (neuter) **das Äußere,** (a) the exterior, outside (of building, etc.); **das Haus hat ein imposantes Äußeres,** the house has an imposing exterior; (b) **das Äußere eines Menschen,** a person's appearance, exterior; **wenn man ihn nach seinem Äußer(e)n beurteilt,** if you judge him by his exterior, by his appearance, by his looks; **er urteilt immer nach dem Äußer(e)n eines Menschen,** he always judges people by their exterior, their appearance, by externals; **ein Mann von angenehmem Äußer(e)n,** a man of pleasant exterior, appearance; **viel auf das Äußere geben,** to be much concerned with outward things; to be much concerned with outward appearances; (c) **Minister des Äußer(e)n** =**Außenminister.**
außeretatmäßig, a. extra-budgetary.
außerfahrplanmäßig, a. Rail: etc: off-schedule, not as scheduled; unscheduled (train); special (train).
außergerichtlich, a. out of court; **zu einer außergerichtlichen Vereinbarung kommen,** adv. a. **zu einer Vereinbarung kommen,** to reach a settlement out of court.
außergeschäftlich, a. unofficial; private; adv.

was er a. tut, geht uns nichts an, his private affairs are none of our business.
außergesetzlich, a. outside the law; **eine außergesetzliche Erscheinung,** a phenomenon unexplained by natural laws.
außergewöhnlich, a. unusual, exceptional, remarkable; extraordinary; **ein außergewöhnlicher Mensch,** an exceptional, a remarkable, person; **außergewöhnliche Fähigkeiten,** exceptional, remarkable, extraordinary, powers; adv. **ein a. nervöser Mensch,** an unusually, exceptionally, extraordinarily, nervous person.
außerhalb. 1. prep. (+gen.) (a) outside; out of; exterior to; **ein Schiff, das a. des Hafens liegt,** a ship lying outside the harbour; **ein Tier, das man a. Europas nicht findet,** an animal that is not found outside, out of, Europe; **das liegt a. meines Bereichs, meiner Befugnisse,** that is outside, out of, not within, my province, that is beyond, outside, out of, my power; Geom: **ein Punkt a. der Kurve,** a point exterior to the curve; (b) **a. der Arbeitszeit, der Dienststunden,** out of (working, office) hours. 2. adv. outside the town; **a. wohnen,** to live outside the town, out of town; **Lieferungen nach a.,** deliveries to customers living outside the town; **unsere Milch kommt von a.,** our milk comes mostly from other areas.
außerirdisch, a. extramundane; extra-terrestrial.
außerkirchlich, a. non-ecclesiastical; **außerkirchliche Trauung,** civil marriage.
außerkontraktlich, a. not mentioned, not provided for, in the contract.
Außerkurssetzung, f. withdrawal (of money) from circulation; demonetization (of coins, etc.).
äußerlich. 1. a. external, outward; superficial (attitude, etc.); **man sollte sich nicht von seinem äußerlichen Gleichmut täuschen lassen,** one should not be deceived by his outward, apparent, equanimity; **er ist wohl etwas barsch, aber das ist nur ä.,** he is indeed somewhat gruff, but it's only on the surface, but he's different underneath; Pharm: **'äußerlich', 'nur zu äußerlichem Gebrauch',** 'for external application', 'for external use only', 'not to be taken'. 2. adv. on the outside; externally, outwardly; **ä. sieht das Radio wie neu aus, aber die Röhren sind durchgebrannt,** from the outside the radio looks like new, but the valves, U.S: tubes, have gone; **ä. war sie ganz ruhig,** outwardly she was quite calm; **ä. sah man ihm nichts an, aber er hatte fürchterliche Zahnschmerzen,** you wouldn't have known from his appearance, by looking at him, but he had terrible toothache; Pharm: **'äußerlich', 'ä. anzuwenden',** 'for external application', 'for external use only', 'not to be taken'.
Äußerlichkeit, f. 1. superficiality. 2. (a) external characteristic, superficial characteristic; **Äußerlichkeiten** pl, (outward) appearances, externals; **die Biographie befaßt sich nur mit Äußerlichkeiten,** the biography is taken up entirely with externals; **das sind bei ihm nur Äußerlichkeiten,** that is only his manner; **nichts auf Äußerlichkeiten geben,** to care nothing for (outward) appearances; (b) **das ist nur eine Ä.,** that is a mere formality, a mere matter of form.
außermittig, a. Mec.E: etc: eccentric; adv. eccentrically.
äußern. I. v.tr. 1. to express (opinions, doubt, feelings, etc.); **sie hat den Wunsch geäußert, dich noch einmal vor deiner Abreise zu sprechen,** she has expressed the wish to speak to you once more before you leave; **er äußerte seine Bedenken, ob diese Maßnahme die richtige Wirkung haben würde,** he expressed doubt as to whether this measure would have the right effect. 2. sich äußern, (a) to give one's opinion, one's views; **sich über etwas** acc., **zu etwas, ä.,** to give, express, put forward, an opinion, one's views, about sth.; **er hat sich begeistert darüber geäußert,** he was enthusiastic about it; **wie hat er sich über unseren Plan geäußert?** what did he say about, what opinion did he offer of, our plan? **sie haben sich gar nicht darüber geäußert,** they didn't express any opinion, they didn't give their views, about it; **sie hat sich ungünstig, abfällig, über ihre neuen Nachbaren geäußert,** she expressed an unfavourable opinion, she spoke unfavourably, of her new neighbours; **er äußerte sich dahin, daß ...,** he gave it as his opinion, his view, that ...; he said that ...; (b) sich in etwas dat. **ä.,** to be expressed, to find expression, in sth.; to be shown, manifested, in sth., to be apparent, to become apparent, in sth.; **sein unbewußtes Geltungsbedürfnis äußert sich in seiner Prahlerei,** his unconscious desire to assert

himself is apparent, is manifested, is betrayed, in his boasting; **das Leiden äußert sich anfänglich nur in geringfügigen Symptomen,** the first apparent symptoms of the disease are of a trivial nature.
II. vbl s. 1. **Äußern,** n. in vbl senses. 2. **Äußerung,** f. (a)=II. 1; also: expression (of wish, feeling, etc.); (b) observation, remark; utterance; **leichtfertige Äußerungen,** flippant remarks.
außernatürlich, a. outside nature; **außernatürliche Beziehungen,** relationships other than natural relationships, unnatural relationships.
außerordentlich, a. (a) extraordinary; **außerordentlicher Professor,** professor extraordinarius, approx.=reader, U.S: associate professor; **eine außerordentliche Versammlung der Aktionäre einberufen,** to call an extraordinary meeting of the shareholders; Adm: etc: **außerordentliche Ausgaben,** extra-budgetary expenses; see also **Etat;** (b) extraordinary; out of the ordinary; unusual, uncommon; exceptional; **außerordentliches Benehmen,** extraordinary conduct; **das Außerordentliche an der Sache ist, daß ...,** the extraordinary thing about it is that ...; **außerordentliche Fähigkeiten,** unusual, exceptional, abilities; abilities above the ordinary; **eine außerordentliche Leistung,** an unusual, uncommon, exceptional, achievement; **er hat Außerordentliches geleistet,** he has achieved something (quite) unusual, exceptional, (altogether) out of the ordinary; **er wird nichts Außerordentliches leisten,** he will not achieve anything (at all) unusual, uncommon, exceptional; (c) adv. extraordinarily; unusually, uncommonly; exceptionally; extremely; **ein a. anziehendes Mädchen,** an exceptionally, extremely, attractive girl.
Außerordentlichkeit, f. extraordinariness (of talents, conduct, etc.); unusual, uncommon, exceptional, nature (of talents, achievements, etc.); oddness, eccentricity (of conduct, etc.).
außerpersönlich, a. beyond personality; nonpersonal (relationships, etc.); (purely) formal or official (relationships).
außerplanmäßig, a. outside the schedule; Adm: Sch: supernumerary (post, official, professor, etc.); (post) additional to the normal establishment; Fin: etc: **außerplanmäßige Ausgaben,** expenditure not budgeted for, not covered by the budget; extraordinary expenditure; Rail: **außerplanmäßiger Halt,** unscheduled stop.
Außerrhoden. Pr.n.n. Geog: (Appenzell-)Außerrhoden, Outer Rhodes (of Appenzell).
äußerst. 1. a. (used attributively only) (a) farthest, farthermost, furthermost, uttermost, utmost; **bis zu den äußersten Grenzen der Erde,** to the farthermost, uttermost, utmost, ends of the earth; **im äußersten Sibirien,** in farthest Siberia; **im äußersten Norden,** in the extreme north; (b) maximum; minimum; latest; **der äußerste Preis,** (i) the highest, maximum, price; (ii) the lowest, minimum, price; **das ist der äußerste Preis, den man für diese Ware fordern kann,** that is the maximum price one can ask for this article; **das ist der äußerste Preis, zu dem ich mich herbeilassen kann,** that is the lowest price I can come down to; **die äußerste Belastung, die die Brücke ertragen kann,** the maximum load that the bridge can stand; **der äußerste Termin für die Bezahlung einer Schuld,** the latest (possible) date for the payment of a debt; (c) extreme, utmost; **von äußerster Wichtigkeit,** of extreme, utmost, importance; **das darf man nur im äußersten Notfall tun,** that should be done only in an extreme emergency; **in äußerster Gefahr sein,** to be in extreme peril; **in äußerster Armut leben,** to live in extreme poverty, in the utmost poverty; **im äußersten Fall,** (i) if the worst comes, came, to the worst; (ii) at the outside; **im äußersten Fall kann ich auf zehn Mark gehen,** the utmost I can manage is ten marks, the most I can afford is ten marks. 2. (a) adv. extremely, exceedingly, excessively, immensely; **ä. wichtig sein,** to be extremely important; **ä. gewissenhaft,** extremely conscientious, conscientious to a degree; (b) adv.phr. **aufs äußerste,** extremely, exceedingly, excessively, immensely; **wir waren aufs äußerste überrascht,** we were extremely, immensely, greatly, surprised. 3. (neuter) **das Äußerste,** (a) the maximum; the (extreme) limit; **vierzehn Mark wäre(n) das Äußerste, was ich dafür ausgeben würde,** fourteen marks would be the most I would pay for it; (b) the last extremity; the worst; **das Äußerste befürchten,** to fear the worst; **aufs, auf das, Äußerste, gefaßt sein,** to be prepared

for the worst; **wenn es zum Äußersten kommt,** if it comes to the worst, if the worst comes to the worst; **er hat es bis zum Äußersten getrieben,** he's gone to the last extreme; **wir wollen es nicht aufs Äußerste ankommen lassen,** we mustn't risk letting the worst come to the worst; **wir wollen es nicht zum Äußersten kommen lassen,** we mustn't let the worst come to the worst; **bis zum Äußersten gehen,** to go to the last extreme; **zum Äußersten gebracht sein,** to be reduced to the last extremity; to be desperate; **man hat ihn zum Äußersten gereizt, getrieben,** he was driven to extremities; **er wird sein Äußerstes, das Äußerste, wagen, um sein Ziel zu erreichen,** he will risk everything, anything, to attain his ends.

außerstand, außerstande, *a.* **j-n außerstand setzen, etwas zu tun,** to make it impossible for s.o. to do sth.; to put s.o. in a position where he cannot do sth.; **außerstande sein, etwas zu tun,** to be unable to do sth.; not to be in a position to do sth.; **wir sehen uns außerstande, dieses zu tun,** we find ourselves unable to do this; we do not find ourselves in a position to do this.

äußerstenfalls, *adv.* (*a*) if it comes to the worst, if the worst comes to the worst; (*b*) at the outside; **ä. kann ich auf zehn Mark gehen,** I can go to ten marks at the outside, the most I can afford is ten marks.

außerwärts, *adv.*=**auswärts.**

außerweltlich, *a.*=**außerirdisch.**

außerzeitlich, *a.* beyond time.

aussetzen, *v. sep.* I. *v.tr.* **1.** (*a*) **ein Boot a.,** to launch, to put out, a boat (from a ship); (*b*) **j-n auf einer Insel, in der Wildnis, auf hoher See, usw., a.,** to maroon s.o. on an island, to turn s.o. loose in the jungle, to cast s.o. adrift on the open sea; **ein neugeborenes Kind a.,** to expose a new-born infant; to abandon a new-born infant (secretly). **2.** (*a*) **etwas** *acc.* **der Luft, der Sonne, usw., a.,** to expose sth. to the air, to the sun, etc.; **sich dem Feuer des Feindes a.,** to expose oneself to the enemy fire; (*b*) **j-n, sich, der Gefahr a.,** to expose s.o., oneself, to danger; **er hat uns dem allgemeinen Spott ausgesetzt,** he has exposed us to universal ridicule; (*c*) *Ecc:* **das Sakrament a.,** to expose the Blessed Sacrament. **3.** to separate (thgs) out; to plant out (seedlings, etc.). **4.** to offer (prize, reward); **auf seinen Kopf ist eine Belohnung ausgesetzt,** there is a reward on his head. **5. etwas an etwas** *dat.*, **an j-m, a.,** to find fault with sth., s.o.; to object sth. against s.o.; to object to sth. in sth., s.o.; to make an objection to sth., s.o.; **ich habe nichts an ihm auszusetzen,** I have no fault to find with him; I have no objection (to make) to him; **an allem etwas auszusetzen haben,** to have an objection to make to everything; to find fault with everything; **an einem Vorschlag etwas a.,** to have an objection to a proposal; **hast du etwas an diesem Vorschlag auszusetzen?** have you any objection (to make) to this proposal? **6.** to suspend (payments, breathing, pulse, etc.); to interrupt (course of studies, etc.); *Jur:* **ein Verfahren a.,** to suspend proceedings; **die Strafvollziehung a.,** to suspend execution of sentence; **der Unterricht wurde wegen der Unruhen auf unbestimmte Zeit ausgesetzt,** the schools were closed down for an unspecified period on account of the riots.

II. **aussetzen,** *v.i.* (*haben*) (*a*) **mit etwas (auf einige Zeit) a.,** to interrupt sth. (for a time); to suspend sth. (for a time); **er mußte mit seinem Studium wegen des Krieges a.,** he had to interrupt, suspend, his studies on account of the war; (*b*) (*of payments, heart-beat, etc.*) to be interrupted, suspended; to stop; (*of engine*) to fail; to stop; **der Puls setzte einige Sekunden lang aus,** the pulse stopped, was suspended, for some seconds; **der Motor setzte alle fünf Minuten aus,** the engine stopped, failed, every five minutes; **seine Briefe wurden seltener, bis sie eines Tages ganz aussetzten,** his letters became more and more infrequent and finally stopped altogether.

III. *vbl s.* **1. Aussetzen,** *n. in vbl senses; also:* (*a*)=III. 2 (*a*); (*b*) suspension (of payments, etc.); (*c*) failure (of pulse, engine, etc.). **2. Aussetzung,** *f.* (*a*) *in vbl senses of* 1; *also:* (i) exposure, exposition (of child); *Ecc:* exposition (of Sacrament); (ii) suspension (of payments, proceedings, execution of sentence, etc.); (*b*) objection; **er hat verschiedene Aussetzungen an dem Vorschlag gemacht,** he raised various objections to the proposal.

Aussicht, *f.* -/-en. **1.** view; outlook, prospect; **ein Haus mit herrlicher A.,** a house with a superb view, outlook, prospect; **das Haus hat eine wunderschöne A. auf den Hafen,** the house has a wonderful view of, over, a wonderful outlook over, the harbour; **von diesem Zimmer hat man (eine) A. auf den Park, dieses Zimmer gewährt eine A. auf den Park,** from this room one has a view of the park, this room overlooks the park; **von hier aus hat man eine schöne A. auf das Schloß, in das Tal,** (from) here you have a good view of the castle, a good view of, over, the valley. **2.** (*a*) prospect; chance; **es besteht A., daß . . . ,** there is a likelihood that . . . ; **ich habe wenig A. auf Erfolg,** I have little prospect of success; the chances are against me; **er hat nicht die geringste A. auf Erfolg,** he hasn't the slightest chance, *F:* the ghost of a chance, an earthly chance, a dog's chance, of succeeding; **er hat keine A., gegen dich aufzukommen,** he stands no chance against you; **er hat gute Aussichten, gewählt zu werden,** he stands a good chance of being elected; **die Aussichten für ein Zustandekommen des Paktes sind nicht gut,** the prospects of achieving the pact are not good; (*b*) prospect; outlook; **er hat eine ausgezeichnete Stellung in A., eine ausgezeichnete Stellung steht für ihn in A.,** he has the prospect of an excellent job, he has an excellent job in prospect; **die für nächstes Jahr in A. genommenen Veränderungen,** the changes which have been planned for next year; **man hat uns verschiedene große Aufträge in A. gestellt,** we have been given the prospect of various large orders; **sie haben ihm eine neue Wohnung in A. gestellt,** they held out to him the prospect of a new flat; **die Aussichten sind nicht verlockend,** the outlook is not promising; **das sind trübe Aussichten,** that's a sad prospect, *F:* a bad look-out; (*in weather forecasts*) **(weitere) Aussichten,** further outlook; **die Aussichten für morgen,** the outlook for tomorrow; (*c*) *pl.* **Aussichten,** prospects; **er hat (gute) Aussichten in seinem Beruf,** his is a job with good prospects; **der Skandal hat seine Aussichten sehr beeinträchtigt,** the scandal has greatly injured his prospects.

Aussichtsaufnahme, *f. Cin:* distance shot, vista shot.

aussichtslos, *a.* (*a*) hopeless; **die Lage ist ziemlich a.,** the situation is pretty hopeless; **ein von vornherein aussichtsloser Versuch,** an experiment doomed to failure from the start; (*b*) (job, etc.) without prospects; **dieser Beruf ist zur Zeit völlig a.,** this profession offers no prospects whatsoever, *F:* is a dead end, at present.

Aussichtslosigkeit, *f.* hopelessness (of situation, etc.).

Aussichtspunkt, *m.* view-point, *U.S:* lookout.

aussichtsreich, *a.* (post, etc.) offering good prospects; **dieser Beruf ist sehr a.,** this is a profession in which one can go far; **die Lage ist nicht sehr a.,** the situation is not very hopeful, promising.

Aussichtsturm, *m.* observation tower, belvedere, gazebo.

aussichtsvoll, *a.*=**aussichtsreich.**

Aussichtswagen, *m. Rail:* observation car.

aussickern, *v.i. sep.* (*sein*) to seep out, ooze out.

aussieben, *v.tr. sep. Civ.E: Min: etc:* to screen; to sort, grade (gravel, etc.).

aussiedeln, *v.tr. sep.* to evacuate (inhabitants, etc.); **Aussiedeln** *n*, **Aussied(e)lung** *f.* evacuation.

aussieden, *v.tr. sep.* (*conj. like* **sieden**) to boil (sth.) out.

Aussiedler, *m.* evacuee; refugee.

aussingen, *v.sep.* (*strong*) **1.** *v.tr.* (*a* to sing (sth.) out; (*b*) to sing (song, etc.) out to the end; **das Lied ist ausgesungen,** the song is finished, ended; (*c*) (*of voice*) **ausgesungen sein,** to be tired, worn out, with singing, to have sung itself out; **eine ausgesungene Stimme,** a voice strained by too much singing. **2.** *v.i.* (*haben*) to finish singing; to sing one's song, etc., to the end.

aussinnen, *v.tr. sep.* (*strong*) **(sich** *dat.***) etwas a.,** to think sth. out; to work sth. out; to plan sth. (carefully, in detail); to contrive, devise (plan, etc.).

aussoggen, *v.tr. sep. Ch:* to precipitate (sth.) out in the form of crystals.

aussöhnen. I. *v.tr. sep.* (*a*) to reconcile **(j-n mit j-m,** s.o. with s.o.); **sich mit j-m a.,** to become reconciled with s.o.; **sie haben sich miteinander ausgesöhnt,** they have become reconciled, they have made their peace with one another; (*b*) **sich mit dem Schicksal usw., a.,** to reconcile oneself, to become reconciled, to one's fate, etc.

II. *vbl s.* **Aussöhnung,** *f.*, reconciliation, reconcilement.

aussondern. I. *v.tr. sep.* **1.** to pick out, choose, select, single out (sth.); to set (sth.) aside, apart (*for a special purpose*). **2.** *Physiol:* to excrete (waste matter); to eliminate, expel (poison, etc.).

II. *vbl s.* **1. Aussondern,** *n. in vbl senses.* **2. Aussonderung,** *f.*=II. 1; *also:* (*a*) selection; (*b*) *Physiol:* excretion (of waste matter); elimination, expulsion (of poison, etc.).

aussonderungsberechtigt, *a. Jur:* (creditor) who has a right to separate treatment (in distribution of bankrupt's property).

Aussonderungsrecht, *n. Jur:* (creditor's) right to separate treatment (in distribution of bankrupt's property).

aussortieren, *v.tr. sep.* to sort (thgs) out.

ausspähen, *v.sep.* **1.** *v.tr.* (*a*) to spy (sth.) out; to find out (secret, etc.) by spying; **die Lage des Feindes a.,** to spy out the position of the enemy; **a., wo das feindliche Lager liegt,** to spy out the whereabouts of the enemy camp; (*b*) **das feindliche Lager a.,** to find out, investigate, all details of the enemy camp. **2.** *v.i.* (*haben*) to keep a look-out, to watch **(nach etwas, j-m,** for sth., s.o.); **a., ob sich etwas im Gebüsch bewegt,** to watch for a movement in the undergrowth.

Ausspann, *m.* (*notice outside hotel*) 'stabling accommodation'.

ausspannen. I. *v.tr. sep.* **1.** (*a*) to unhitch, unharness, take out (horses); to unyoke (oxen); *abs.* **laß den Kutscher a.!** tell the coachman to unhitch, take out, the horses; (*b*) to take (embroidery, etc.) out of a frame; (*c*) *F:* **j-m etwas a.,** to steal sth. from s.o.; **er hat meinem Vetter die Freundin ausgespannt,** he has stolen my cousin's girl-friend. **2.** *abs.* to relax, *F:* to take it easy, to go easy; **du wirst eine Weile a. müssen,** you'll have to go easy for a bit. **3.** to stretch out, spread out (net, sheet, etc.).

II. *vbl s.* **1. Ausspannen,** *n. in vbl senses.* **2. Ausspannung,** *f.* (*a*)=II. 1; (*b*) relaxation, rest; recreation.

aussparen. I. *v.tr. sep.* (*a*) to reserve, leave, allow (space, etc.); to leave (figures, etc.) uncoloured; **wir haben zu viel Raum für die Bilder ausgespart,** we have left too much space for the pictures; **die Figuren sind (aus dem Grund) ausgespart,** the figures are reserved on the original ground, are reserved in the ground colour, are left uncoloured; (*b*) *Constr: Mec.E:* to recess; (*c*) *Mil: Av:* to leave (area, etc.) unbombed, unshelled, unattacked.

II. *vbl s.* **1. Aussparen,** *n. in vbl senses.* **2. Aussparung,** *f.* (*a*)=II. 1; (*b*) *Constr: etc:* recess.

Aussparungsloch, *n. Av:* lightening hole.

Ausspei, *m.* -s/. *Art:* **der A.,** the Whale Vomiting Out Jonah.

ausspeien, *v.tr. sep.* (*strong*) to spit (sth.) out; *Lit:* to spew (sth.) out, forth; (*of volcano*) **Feuer und Asche a.,** to vomit, belch forth, belch out, fire and ashes.

aussperren. I. *v.tr. sep.* to shut (s.o.) out; to lock (s.o.) out; to shut out (water, etc.); *Ind:* to lock out (workers).

II. *vbl s.* **1. Aussperren,** *n. in vbl senses.* **2. Aussperrung,** *f.*=II. 1; *also: Ind:* lock-out (of workers).

ausspielen. I. *v.sep.* **1.** *v.tr.* to play (game, piece of music, etc.) out, to the end; *F:* **er hat seine Rolle ausgespielt,** he's finished, done for; he has had his day. **2.** *v.tr.* (*a*) *Cards:* **eine Karte a.,** to play a card; *abs.* **a.,** to lead; **Sie spielen aus!** your lead! **den letzten Trumpf a.,** to play one's trump-card; *F:* **er mußte seinen letzten Trumpf a.,** he was put to his trumps; (*b*) **j-n gegen j-n a.,** to play s.o. off against s.o.; **sie spielt den einen Verehrer gegen den andern aus,** she plays off one admirer against the other. **3.** *v.tr.* to raffle (sth.). **4.** *v.tr.* (*a*) to improve the tone of (musical instrument) by use; (*b*) to wear out (musical instrument) by use. **5.** *v.i.* (*haben*) to finish playing; *F:* **er hat ausgespielt,** he's finished, done for; he has had his day.

II. *vbl s.* **1. Ausspielen,** *n. in vbl senses.* **2. Ausspielung,** *f.* (*a*)=II. 1; (*b*) lottery; raffle.

ausspinnen, *v.tr. sep.* (*strong*) **1.** (*of spider*) to spin out (thread). **2.** to spin (sth.) out, to prolong (sth.); to elaborate, develop (sth.); **eine Kurzgeschichte zu einem Roman a.,** to develop a short story into a novel, to spin a short story out into a novel; **eine Geschichte lang, breit, a.,** to spin out a story; **einen Gedanken (weiter) a.,** to elaborate, pursue, a train of thought.

ausspionieren, *v.tr. sep.* to find (sth.) out by spying; to spy out (position, etc.). *F:* **die Lage a.,** to spy out the lie of the land.

ausspitzen, *v.i. sep.* (*haben*) *Geol:* (*of lode, etc.*) to pinch.
ausspotten, *v.tr. sep.*=**verspotten.**
Aussprache, *f.* **1.** pronunciation; (*a*) pronouncing; **die A. des Russischen hat ihm Schwierigkeiten bereitet,** the pronunciation of Russian gave him difficulty; **falsche A. eines Wortes,** mispronunciation of a word; (*b*) **eine gute deutsche A. haben,** to have a good German pronunciation, a good German accent; **eine deutliche A. haben,** to articulate, enunciate, (one's words) clearly; **sie hat eine sehr verfeinerte A.,** she has a very refined way of speaking, her speech is very refined. **2.** talk; discussion; **die Außenminister hatten heute eine weitere A. über die Lage in X,** the Foreign Ministers had a further talk, discussion, on the situation in X today; **eine offene (und ehrliche) A. mit j-m haben,** to have a frank talk with s.o.
Aussprachebezeichnung, *f.* indication of pronunciation.
Aussprachewörterbuch, *n.* pronouncing dictionary.
aussprechbar, *n.* pronounceable (word, etc.); **ein schwer aussprechbares Wort,** a word that is hard to pronounce.
aussprechen, *v.sep.* (*strong*) **1.** *v.tr.* to pronounce (word, etc.); **das H wird am Anfang gewisser englischer Wörter nicht ausgesprochen,** the h is not pronounced at the beginning of certain English words; **er kann das deutsche R nicht richtig a.,** he can't pronounce, say, the German r correctly; **ein Wort falsch a.,** to pronounce a word wrongly, to mispronounce a word; *abs.* **gut a.,** to articulate, enunciate, well; **er spricht seine Worte nicht deutlich aus,** he doesn't articulate, enunciate, say, (his words) clearly. **2.** *v.tr.* (*a*) to utter, express (sth.); **er hat seine Meinung deutlich ausgesprochen,** he stated, expressed, his views clearly; **seinen Dank, einen Wunsch, a.,** to express one's thanks, a wish; **nicht alle Wahrheiten lassen sich a.,** not all truths will bear telling; (*b*) (*of emotion, etc.*) **sich a.,** to be expressed; **in seinem Gesicht sprach sich das höchste Erstaunen aus,** his face expressed the greatest amazement, the greatest amazement was expressed in his face; (*c*) **das Todesurteil (über j-n) a.,** to pronounce, pass, sentence of death (on s.o.). *See also* **ausgesprochen. 3. sich über etwas** *acc.* **aussprechen,** to give one's views, opinion, about sth.; to talk about sth.; **sich mit j-m über etwas** *acc.* **a.,** to discuss sth. with s.o.; **sich bei, mit, j-m a.,** to unburden oneself to s.o.; **wir müssen uns einmal gründlich a.,** we must have a heart-to-heart talk some time; **sich für j-n, etwas, a.,** to speak in support of, to speak for, s.o., sth.; to declare oneself for s.o., sth.; **sich gegen etwas a.,** to make objections to, to speak against, sth. **4.** *v.i.* (*haben*) to finish speaking; to finish what one has to say; **laß ihn a.!** let him finish (what he has to say)! hear him out!
auspreizen, *v.tr. sep.* to part (one's legs), to place (one's legs) apart; to spread (out) (one's legs, fingers, etc.); **mit weit ausgespreizten Armen,** with one's arms stretched out wide.
aussprengen, *v.tr. sep.* **1.** to blast (sth.) out; **ein Stück der Mauer wurde ausgesprengt,** a piece of the wall was blasted out. **2.** to spread, broadcast (rumour, etc.).
ausspringen, *v.i. sep.* (*strong*) (*sein*) **1.** (*a*) **aus der Tasse ist ein Stück ausgesprungen,** the cup is chipped, has a piece out; (*b*) to come out of place; **das Zahnrad ist ausgesprungen,** the cog has slipped, has come out of place. **2.** (*of pers.*) to turn renegade (from religious order, etc.); **ein ausgesprungener Mönch, ein ausgesprungener Sozialist,** a renegade monk, socialist; **aus einer Gruppe, einem Verein, einem Unternehmen, usw., a.,** to withdraw from a group, club, undertaking, etc., *F:* to drop out of a group, club, etc. **3.** to project, jut out; **ausspringender Winkel,** salient angle.
ausspritzen, *v.tr. sep.* **1.** to squirt out (water, etc.); to squirt water, etc., out of (sth.); (*of skunk, etc.*) to squirt, eject (secretion, etc.). **2.** *Med:* to syringe (out) (wound, ear, etc.); **3.** to put out, extinguish (fire) with a hose, etc.
Ausspritzungsgang, *m. Anat:* ejaculatory duct.
Ausspruch, *m.* (*a*) saying, dictum; utterance, words; statement; pronouncement; **nach einem A. des Heraklit,** according to Heraclitus; (*b*) *Jur:* finding, decision.
aussprühen, *v.tr. sep.* to send out, emit, a spray of (sparks, etc.); (*of volcano, etc.*) to belch forth (sparks, etc.).
ausspucken, *v.sep.* **1.** *v.tr.* to spit out (cherry-stone, food, etc.); *F:* to bring up (food); *F:* to give vent to (anger); *P:* to cough up (sum of money). **2.** *v.i.* (*haben*) to spit; **kräftig a.,** to spit vigorously; **vor j-m a.,** to spit in front of s.o. (to show one's contempt of him).
ausspülen, *v.tr. sep.* (*a*) to rinse out, wash out (bottle, glass, etc.); to flush out (drain, etc.); **sich** *dat.* **den Mund a.,** to rinse (out) one's mouth; (*b*) to rinse (washing); (*c*) to wash (sth.) out of (sth.); **die Reste aus einem Glas a.,** to rinse, wash, the residue out of a glass; (*d*) (*of river, etc.*) **das Ufer a.,** to wash away, erode, undermine, (part of) the bank.
ausspüren, *v.tr. sep. Ven:* (*of dog, etc.*) to track down (game).
ausstaffieren. I. *v.tr. sep.* to provide, equip, fit out (s.o., sth.) (with clothes, etc.); **er hat seine Kinder neu ausstaffiert,** he has fitted his children out with new clothes; **sie erschien prächtig ausstaffiert,** she appeared magnificently turned out.
II. *vbl s.* **1. Ausstaffieren,** *n. in vbl senses.* **2. Ausstaffierung,** *f.* (*a*)=II. 1; (*b*) outfit; set of clothes; **eine neue A. bekommen,** to get a new outfit (of clothes).
ausstampfen, *v.tr. sep.* **1.** to tread out (wheat, etc.). **2.** to stamp out (fire). **3. etwas mit Zement, usw., a.** to line sth. with rammed cement, etc.
Ausstand, *m.* **1.** (*a*) *Ind:* strike; **in den A. treten,** to strike, to come out on strike, to go on strike; **sich im A. befinden,** to be on strike; (*b*) *South G.Dial:* leaving of his job (by a worker). **2.** delay; **einem Schuldner einige Tage A. gewähren,** to give a debtor a few days' extension. **2.** *pl.* **Ausstände**=**Außenstände.**
Ausständer, *m. Ind:* striker.
ausständig, *a.* **1.** *Ind:* (worker) on strike. **2.** *Fin:* outstanding (debt).
ausstänkern, *v.tr. sep.* to stink out (enemy troops).
ausstanzen, *v.tr. sep. Metalw: etc:* to stamp (sth.) out, to punch (sth.) out.
Ausstanzmaschine, *f.* punching machine; *Bootm: etc:* cutting press.
Ausstanzmesser, *n. Tls:* punch.
ausstatten. I. *v.tr. sep.* **1.** (*a*) to provide, equip, furnish, fit out, set up, (s.o., sth.) (with sth.); **j-n mit Winterkleidern a.,** to provide s.o., to fit s.o. out, with winter clothing, to set s.o. up with, in, winter clothing; **dieses Tier ist mit scharfen Klauen ausgestattet,** this animal is equipped with sharp claws; **die Natur hat ihn mit reichen Gaben ausgestattet,** nature endowed him with great talents; **die Natur hat sie stiefmütterlich ausgestattet,** she was poorly endowed by nature; (*b*) to set up, establish (son, daughter) (in business, etc.); to provide (son, daughter) with equipment to establish himself, herself, in business, etc.; to dower (daughter), to give (daughter) her dowry, her marriage portion; (*c*) **j-n mit Rechten, Vollmacht, a.,** to vest s.o. with rights, with authority. **2.** (*a*) **etwas gut, reichlich, usw., a.,** to get sth. up well, richly, etc.; **ein gut ausgestattetes Buch,** a well-produced, well got up, book; **eine kostbar ausgestattete Handschrift,** a lavishly got up manuscript; (*b*) to fit out, equip (office, ship, etc.); **ein gut ausgestattetes Laboratorium,** a well-equipped laboratory; **eine Kirche a.,** to furnish a church; to provide the furnishings for a church.
II. *vbl s.* **1. Ausstatten,** *n. in vbl senses.* **2. Ausstattung,** *f.* (*a*)=II. 1; *also:* equipment (of s.o., house, office, etc.); (*b*) equipment; fixtures and fittings; appointments; furnishings, furniture (of church, etc.); **Wohnung mit moderner A.,** flat, *U.S:* apartment, with modern equipment and furnishings, with all modern conveniences; **er hat den Laden mit der gesamten A. gekauft,** he bought the shop with all fixtures and fittings; (*c*) outfit; kit; **A. für die Tropen,** tropical outfit, tropical kit; (*d*) get-up (of book, etc.); *Th:* décor and costumes; **eine Handschrift in kostbarer A.,** a lavishly got up manuscript; (*e*) provision (made to son, daughter) to set him, her, up in life; (bride's) dowry; marriage portion; marriage settlement in a daughter's favour; (*f*) (bride's) trousseau.
Ausstattungsstück[1], *n.* piece of equipment.
Ausstattungsstück[2], *n. Th:* play, revue, etc., in which the spectacle is the main attraction; spectacular revue, musical, *F:* spectacular.
ausstauben, *v.tr. sep.* to brush, wipe, the dust out of (sth.).
ausstäupen, *v.tr. sep.* to give (s.o.) a whipping.
ausstechen, *v.tr. sep.* (*strong*) **1.** (*a*) to poke (sth.) out; **j-m die Augen a.,** to put out s.o.'s eyes; (*b*) to cut (sth.) out; **Torf a.,** to dig, cut, peat; *Cu:* **Plätzchen a.,** to cut a biscuit mixture into shapes; **Plätzchen rund a.,** to cut a biscuit mixture into rounds; **Äpfel a.,** to core apples; (*c*) **ein Muster auf Papier, usw., a.,** to prick out a pattern on paper. **2.** to empty, drain (bottle, glass, etc.); **eine Flasche Wein mit j-m a.,** to drink a bottle of wine with s.o. **3.** *F:* **j-n bei j-m a.,** to oust s.o. in s.o.'s esteem, to cut s.o. out with s.o.; **er versucht, mich bei meinem Mädchen auszustechen,** he is trying to cut me out with my girl. **4.** *Nau:* **ein Reff a.,** to let out, shake out, a reef.
Ausstecher, *m. Dom.Ec:* (*a*) apple-corer; (*b*) pastry-cutter.
Ausstechform, *f. Dom.Ec:* pastry-cutter.
ausstecken, *v.tr. sep.* **1.** *Nau:* to pay out (rope, etc.). **2.**=**abstecken** 3 (*a*). **3.** *Austrian:* (*of vintner*) to hang out one's bush; (*notice outside inn, etc.*) **'ausgesteckt',** 'new wine on tap'.
ausstehen, *v.sep.* (*strong*) I. *v.i.* (*haben*) **1.** not to be forthcoming; (*a*) (*of money*) to be owing; (*of payment*) to be outstanding, overdue; **die Zahlung darf nicht länger a.,** payment must not be delayed any longer; **ausstehende Gelder,** outstanding debts; (*b*) **die Entscheidung stand noch aus,** the decision had not yet been made; **der Bericht stand noch aus,** the report had yet to come; **seine Antwort steht noch aus,** we are still awaiting his reply. **2.** (*of workers*) to strike, to be on strike.
II. **ausstehen,** *v.tr.* **1.** to stand through (lecture, concert, etc.). **2.** (*a*) to undergo, go through, come through, endure (sth.); **Hunger, Durst, Kälte, a.,** to endure hunger, thirst, cold; **Gefahren a.,** to come through danger; **sie hat furchtbare Schmerzen a. müssen,** she underwent terrible pain; **wir haben in jener Nacht große Angst ausgestanden,** we underwent, suffered, terrible anxiety that night; **du kannst dir nicht vorstellen, was ich dabei ausgestanden habe,** you can't imagine what I went through, what I endured; **sie hat viel bei ihrer Tante auszustehen,** she has to endure, bear, put up with, a lot from her aunt, at her aunt's; (*b*) *F:* to bear, stand, endure, *F:* to stick (sth., s.o.); **solche Bilder kann ich nicht a.,** I can't bear, stand, endure, pictures like that; **ich kann ihn nicht a.,** I can't bear him, bear the sight of him, I can't stand him, abide him, endure him, *F:* stick him; **sie kann ihn für den Tod nicht a.,** she can't stand him at any price; **er kann es nicht a., wenn man so etwas tut,** he can't bear it, stand it, if people do things like that, he can't bear people to do things like that.
aussteigen, *v.i. sep.* (*strong*) (*sein*) **1.** to climb out (of sth.). **2.** (*a*) to get out (of train, plane, car, etc.); to get off (train, plane, bus, ship); to alight (from train, carriage, bus, plane, etc.); to disembark (from ship, plane); *Mil: etc:* to detrain; to debus; to deplane; **hier müssen alle a.,** everyone must get out here; *Rail: etc:* **'alle(s) a.!'** 'all change!' (*b*) *Av: F:* to bale, *U.S:* bail, out.
Aussteigöffnung, *f.* trap-door (in roof).
aussteinen, *v.tr. sep.* to stone (plums, etc.).
ausstellen. I. *v.tr. sep.* **1.** to post (sentries); to lay (traps). **2.** to display, show, exhibit (goods, works of art, etc.); *abs.* **a.,** (*of painter, etc.*) to exhibit; **sein Bild ist im Museum zu X ausgestellt,** his picture is on view in the X museum; **die besten Muster waren im Schaufenster ausgestellt,** the best samples were on display, were displayed, exhibited, in the shop window, *U.S:* show window; **Waren im Schaufenster a.,** to show, put, goods in the window, to put goods on show; **die ausstellenden Firmen, Maler, die Ausstellenden,** the exhibiting firms, artists, the exhibitors. **3.** to make out (document, certificate, cheque, bill, etc.); to write (out) (cheque, certificate); to write (testimonial); to issue (passport, etc.); **eine Urkunde in dreifacher Ausfertigung a.,** to make out a document in triplicate; **die ausstellende Behörde,** the issuing authority. **4. etwas an j-m, an etwas** *dat.*, **a.,** to find fault with, to make objections to, s.o., sth.; **was hast du wieder an ihm auszustellen?** what fault have you to find with him now? what do you object to in him now? **5.** *occ.* **j-n, etwas, einer Gefahr, usw., a.,** to expose s.o., sth. to a danger, etc. **6.** *A:* to postpone (sth.).
II. *vbl s.* **1. Ausstellen,** *n. in vbl senses.* **2. Ausstellung,** *f.* (*a*)=II. 1; *also:* exhibition (of goods, works of art, etc.); display (of goods, etc.); (*b*) issue (of passport, etc.); (*c*) exhibition; (motor, etc.) show; *U.S:* exposition; **eine internationale A.,** an international exhibition; **in eine A. gehen,** to go to an exhibition; (*d*) objection; **er hatte viele Ausstellungen an dem**

Kandidaten, an dem Plan, zu machen, he had many faults to find with, many objections to make to, the candidate, the plan.

Aussteller, *m.* **1.** exhibitor. **2.** person who *or* authority that makes out (document, etc.); drawer, writer (of cheque, etc.); issuer (of passport, etc.); issuing authority.

Ausstellungsdatum, *n.* date of issue (of document, cheque, etc.).

Ausstellungsgegenstand, *m.* exhibit, thing exhibited; show-piece.

Ausstellungsgelände, *n.* exhibition site; exhibition grounds.

Ausstellungskasten, *m.* show-case.

Ausstellungsort, *m,* place of issue (of document, etc.).

Ausstellungsraum, *m.* exhibition room; showroom (of firm, etc.).

Ausstellungsstück, *n.* exhibit; **das ist kein A.,** it's not worth exhibiting; *F:* it's not much to look at, it's nothing beautiful; it's no show-piece.

ausstemmen, *v.tr. sep.* to chisel (sth.) out.

Aussterbeetat [-eˑ,ta:], *m.* **etwas auf den A. setzen,** to prepare to scrap, do away with, sth.; to destine sth. for abolition; **das Amt ist auf den A. gesetzt worden,** it has been decided to abolish this office (when the present occupant retires); **auf dem A. stehen,** to be about to be abolished.

aussterben. I. *v.i. sep.* (*strong*) (*sein*) (*a*) (*of race, family, custom, etc.*) to die out; (*of race, animals, plants, etc.*) to become extinct; **ausgestorben sein,** to have died out, to be extinct; **ein ausgestorbenes Geschlecht, eine ausgestorbene Pflanzengattung,** an extinct race, plant; (*b*) **die Straßen waren wie ausgestorben,** the streets were completely deserted, were as silent as the grave.

II. *vbl s.* **Aussterben,** *n. in vbl senses; also:* extinction; **das (allmähliche) A. eines Geschlechts,** the (gradual) extinction of a race.

Aussterbestand, *m.* state of threatened extinction (of race, animal, etc.).

Aussteuer, *f.* (bride's) trousseau and household goods; *F:* bottom drawer; **seiner Tochter eine angemessene A. gewähren,** to provide one's daughter with a suitable trousseau and the necessary articles to set up house.

aussteuern. I. *v.tr. sep.* **1.** to provide (daughter) with a trousseau and household goods. **2.** *Adm:* (*usu. in the phr.*) (*of pers.*) **ausgesteuert sein,** to have exhausted the right to statutory sickness *or* unemployment benefit; to have run out of benefit. **3.** (i) *W.Tel:* to modulate (carrier wave); (ii) **ein Meßgerät, ein Bandgerät, a.,** *abs.* **a.,** to set *or* adjust *or* control a measuring instrument, the recording *or* reproducing level of a tape-recorder.

II. *vbl s.* **1. Aussteuern,** *n. in vbl senses.* **2. Aussteuerung,** *f.*=II. 1; *also W.Tel:* modulation; level control (of tape-recording, etc.).

Aussteuerungsanzeiger, *m.* record(ing) level indicator.

Aussteuerungsregler, *m.* record(ing) level control.

Ausstich, *m.* **1.** *Civ.E:* (railway) cutting. **2.** *Com:* top-grade, choicest, goods, *esp.* wine of the finest quality.

Ausstieg, *m.* **-s/-e. 1.** (*a*) climbing out (of cellar, etc.); (*b*) disembarkation (from ship, plane); alighting (from train, carriage, bus, plane). **2.** (*a*) exit, way out; **A. aus dem Luftschutzkeller,** exit from, way out of, the air-raid shelter; (*b*) trap-door (in roof).

Ausstiegluke, *f.* escape-hatch (of rocket capsule).

ausstöbern, *v.tr. sep.* to ferret out, unearth (sth.).

ausstochern, *v.tr. sep.* **sich** *dat.* **die Zähne a.,** to pick one's teeth.

ausstocken, *v.tr. sep.* to stub up, grub up, the stumps of trees from (land).

ausstopfen, *v.tr. sep.* to stuff (animal, handbag, etc.); to pad out (shoulders, etc.); to fill in (hole); **die Schuhe mit Papier a.,** to stuff the toes of one's shoes with paper; **einen Koffer mit Papier a.,** to fill up the space in a suit-case with paper; **Ausstopfen** *n* **von Tieren,** stuffing of animals; taxidermy.

Ausstopfer, *m.* taxidermist.

Ausstoß, *m.* **1.** (*a*) ejection (of sth.); (*b*) *Navy:* discharging, launching (of torpedo); (*c*) expulsion (of s.o.) (from society, etc.); *cp.* **ausstoßen** III; (*d*) broaching, tapping, starting (of cask, barrel). **2.** *Navy:* torpedo-tube. **3.** *Ind:* output, production; **täglicher A. von zweihundert Stück,** daily output of two hundred units.

ausstoßen, *v.sep.* (*strong*) I. *v.tr.* **1.** to knock (sth.) out; **j-m einen Zahn a.,** to knock out one of s.o.'s teeth. **2.** (*a*) to eject (sth.); to emit (smoke, gas, etc.); to expel (waste matter, afterbirth, etc.); to eliminate (waste matter, etc.); (*of liquid*) to give off (bubbles); **der Vulkan stößt Rauchwolken aus,** the volcano ejects, emits, gives off, throws out, belches forth, clouds of smoke; (*b*) *Navy:* to discharge, launch (torpedo); (*c*) **einen Seufzer, einen Schrei, a.,** to utter, give, a sigh, a cry; to heave, fetch, a sigh; **einen Fluch a.,** to utter a curse. **3.** to expel (s.o.), to turn (s.o.) out, to throw (s.o.) out; **j-n aus einer Gesellschaft, einem Verein, a.,** to expel s.o. from, turn s.o. out of, a society, an association; **j-n aus der Gesellschaft a.,** to ostracize s.o.; **j-n aus der Kirche a.,** to expel s.o. from the church; to excommunicate s.o.; *Mil:* **einen Offizier (aus dem Heere) a.,** to cashier an officer. **4.** *Ling:* to suppress, drop (phoneme, syllable); to elide (vowel, syllable).

II. **ausstoßen,** *v.i.* (*haben*) **1.** (*a*) *Fenc:* to thrust, lunge; to make a pass; (*b*) *Swim:* to strike out. **2.** (*of liquid*) to burst out in froth; to froth over *or* out.

III. *vbl s.* **1. Ausstoßen,** *n. in vbl senses.* **2. Ausstoßung,** *f. in vbl senses; also:* ejection; emission (of smoke, gas, etc.); expulsion (of waste matter, afterbirth, etc.); elimination (of waste matter, etc.); expulsion (of s.o.) (from society, etc.); *Ecc:* excommunication; *Ling:* suppression (of phoneme, syllable); elision (of vowel, syllable)

Ausstoßer, *m.* (*device*) ejector.

Ausstoßfeile, *f. Comb-making:* grail.

Ausstoßrohr, *n.* ejector tube; *Navy:* torpedo-tube.

Ausstoßvorrichtung, *f.* ejector; *Navy:* (torpedo) launching apparatus.

Ausstoßzahlen, *f.pl. Ind:* output figures, production figures.

ausstrahlen. I. *v.sep.* **1.** *v.tr.* to radiate, emit (heat, light, etc.); **sie strahlt Heiterkeit aus,** she radiates gaiety. **2.** *v.tr. W.Tel:* (*of radio station*) to transmit (message, etc.). **3.** *v.i.* (*haben*) (*a*) (*of heat, light, happiness, etc.*) to radiate (from sth., s.o.); (*b*) (*of lines, streets, etc.*) **von einem Mittelpunkt, von einem Gebäude usw., a.,** to radiate from a central point, from a building, etc.

II. *vbl s.* **1. Ausstrahlen,** *n. in vbl senses.* **2. Ausstrahlung,** *f.* (*a*)=II. 1; *also:* radiation, emission (of heat, light, etc.); radiance; (*b*) radiation (from earth, etc.).

Ausstrahlungsvermögen, *n. Ph:* emissivity (of source of light, etc.).

ausstreben, *v.tr. sep. Constr: etc:* to strut, brace (framework, etc.).

ausstrecken, *v.tr. sep.* **1.** (*a*) to stretch (out) (one's legs, arms); to extend (one's legs, arms); to crane (one's neck); (*of snail*) **die Fühler a.,** to put out its horns; **die Arme nach etwas, j-m, a.,** to stretch out one's arms towards sth., s.o.; **die Arme nach seinen Helfern a.,** to stretch out one's arms towards one's rescuers; **mit ausgestreckten Armen,** with outstretched arms; **sich auf der Erde a.,** to stretch oneself out on the ground; **ausgestreckt auf der Erde liegen,** to lie stretched (out) on the ground; **lang ausgestreckt daliegen,** to lie stretched out full length; (*b*) **die Hand a.,** to put out, hold out, one's hand; to stretch out, reach out, one's hand; **die Hand nach etwas a.,** to stretch out to reach sth., to reach (out) for sth.; **der Bettler streckte die Hand aus in der Hoffnung, wir würden ihm etwas geben,** the beggar put out, held out, his hand, in the hope that we would give him something. **2.** (*of land, etc.*) **sich ausstrecken,,** to stretch (out), to extend; **die Ebene streckte sich vor uns aus,** the plain stretched, extended, lay stretched out, before us.

Ausstreicheisen, *n. Glassm:* flattening iron; *Sculp: Leath:* smoothing-stick.

ausstreichen, *v.sep.* (*strong*) I. *v.tr.* **1.** to smooth out (creases, creased material, etc.). **2.** (*a*) to fill (in) (hole, crack, etc.) (with putty, etc.); (*b*) to paint, smear, the inside of (sth.); **eine Backform (mit Fett) a.,** to grease a baking-tin. **3.** *Microscopy:* to spread (drop of blood, specimen, etc.) (on a slide for examination). **4.** to strike out, cross out, score out, delete, cancel (word, line, figure, etc.).

II. **ausstreichen,** *v.i.* (*haben*) **1.** (*of birds*) to fly out. **2.** *Geol:* (*of seam*) to outcrop.

III. *vbl s.* **1. Ausstreichen,** *n. in vbl senses.* **2. Ausstreichung** *f.* (*a*) *in vbl senses of* I; *also:* deletion, cancellation (of word, line, etc.); (*b*) (*deleted passage, etc.*) deletion.

Ausstreichfeile, *f. Tls:* equalizing file.

Ausstreichlineal, *n.*=**Ausstreicheisen.**

ausstreuen. I. *v.tr. sep.* **1.** to scatter (seed, etc.); to strew (rushes, etc.); to spread, diffuse, scatter (light); to spread, circulate (rumours, news); **Blumen vor j-m a.,** to strew, scatter, flowers in s.o.'s path; **Stroh in einem Stall a.,** to scatter, spread, straw in a stable.

II. *vbl s.* **1. Ausstreuen,** *n. in vbl senses.* **2. Ausstreuung,** *f.*=II. 1; *also:* diffusion (of light); circulation (of rumours, news, etc.).

Ausstrich, *m.* **1.** *Geol: Min:* outcrop. **2.** *Microscopy:* (blood, etc.) smear (on slide).

ausströmen, *v.sep.* **1.** *v.i.* (*sein*) (*a*) (*of water, etc.*) to stream out, to pour out, forth; to be discharged; (*of water, stream, etc.*) to gush forth, out; (*of light*) to stream out; (*of water, steam, gas*) to escape, issue forth; (*of heat*) to be radiated; **Wasser, Dampf, Gas, Öl, strömte von dem Loch in der Röhre aus,** water, steam, gas, oil, was pouring from, out of, escaping from, the hole in the pipe; (*b*) (*of happiness, peace, etc.*) to be radiated; **ruhige Zuversicht strömte von ihr aus,** she radiated quiet confidence, **die Gnade, die von Gott ausströmt,** the grace that emanates from God. **2.** *v.tr.* (*a*) to pour (water, blood, etc.); to stream (blood, etc.); to gush (water, oil, etc.); to pour out, emit (steam, etc.); **die Wunde strömte Blut aus,** the wound poured blood, streamed blood, blood was pouring, streaming, from the wound; (*b*) to radiate, shed (happiness, peace, etc.); **Segen auf j-n a.,** to pour, shower, blessings on s.o.; **eine Frau, die Zuversicht ausströmt,** a woman who radiates a feeling of confidence; **das Zimmer strömt Frieden aus,** the whole room breathes peace.

II. *vbl s.* **Ausströmen** *n.,* **Ausströmung** *f. in vbl senses; also:* discharge (of water, etc.); outflow (of water, gas, etc.); escape (of water, steam, gas, etc.); emanation (of divine grace, etc.).

ausstückeln, *v.tr. sep. Mint:* to cut (blanks).

ausstudieren, *v.sep.* (*p.p.* **ausstudiert**) **1.** *v.tr.* to study (sth.) thoroughly, exhaustively, to make a thorough, an exhaustive, study of (sth.); to think (sth.) out carefully. **2.** *v.i.* (*haben*) to finish studying, to finish one's studies.

ausstülpen. I. *v.tr. sep.* **1.** to push out (inverted finger of glove, etc.); *Surg: etc:* to evaginate, evert (bowel, etc.); (*of scolex of tapeworm, etc.*) **ausgestülpt werden,** to be evaginated, everted; **etwas in etwas** *acc.* **a.,** to push sth. into sth., to push sth. out so that it protrudes into sth. **2. sich ausstülpen,** (*of bag, sac, etc.*) to get pushed out; (*of bowel, scolex of tapeworm, etc.*) to become evaginated, everted.

II. *vbl s.* **1. Ausstülpen,** *n. in vbl senses.* **2. Ausstülpung,** *f.* (*a*)=II. 1; *also: Nat.Hist: Med: etc:* evagination, eversion (of bowel, scolex of tapeworm, etc.); (*b*) *Anat: Med:* diverticulum; *Med: etc:* protrusion; evagination.

ausstürzen, *v.tr. sep.* **1.** *Min: etc:* to empty (tub, skip, etc.); to tip (truck). **2.** *Min:* to stow (old workings).

aussuchen. I. *v.tr. sep.* **1.** to search (pockets, boxes, house, etc.) **(nach etwas,** for sth.). **2.** to choose, select, pick out (s.o., sth.); **sie sucht sich** *dat.* **immer die größten Eier aus,** she always selects, picks out, the biggest eggs; **ich werde mir etwas Schönes a.,** I shall choose myself something nice.

II. *vbl s.* **Aussuchen,** *n. in vbl senses; also:* choice (of clothes, etc.).

III. *p.p. & a.* **ausgesucht,** *in vbl senses; esp.* (*a*) choice, carefully chosen, selected (fruit, etc.); **Waren von ausgesuchter Qualität,** goods of the very best quality; (*b*) exquisite; **ausgesuchte Höflichkeit,** exquisite, extreme, politeness; **ausgesuchte Grausamkeit,** exquisite cruelty.

aussüßen, *v.tr. sep. Ch: etc:* to edulcorate; to wash out (precipitate).

Aust, *f.* **-/-en.** *North G.Dial:* **1.** August. **2.** swarm of may-flies.

austäfeln, *v.tr. sep.* to wainscot, panel (wall, room).

austanzen, *v.sep.* **1.** *v.tr.* (*a*) to dance (a dance) to the end; (*b*) **sich a.,** to dance to one's heart's content; to dance till one is tired. **2.** *v.i.* (*haben*) to finish dancing.

austapezieren, *v.tr. sep.* to paper (room, etc.); to hang, line, the walls of (room, etc.) with silk, etc.

austasten, *v.tr. sep.* **1.** to make a manual examination of (the inside of) (sth.), to examine (the inside of) (sth.) with one's hand(s). **2.** *TV:* to blank (electron beam); **Austastung** *f,* blanking.

Austastimpuls, *m. TV:* blanking pulse.

Austausch, *m.* exchange (of goods, students, prisoners, greetings, ideas, etc.); interchange (of

commodities, compliments, ideas, etc.); *Com:* exchange, barter; *Ch:* substitution; **ich habe das Buch im A. gegen ein anderes bekommen,** I got the book in exchange for, in return for, another one; **A. von Fertigprodukten gegen Rohstoffe,** exchange of finished products for raw materials; **einen A. vornehmen,** to make an exchange; **man plant einen A. zwischen den Studenten der beiden Universitäten,** an exchange is being planned between the students of the two universities; **A. unserer Lehrer mit Lehrern anderer Länder,** exchange, exchanging, of our teachers with teachers of other countries.

austauschbar, *a.* exchangeable (**gegen,** for); interchangeable (**mit, gegen,** with).

Austauschbarkeit, *f.* exchangeability; interchangeability.

Austauschdienst, *m.* **akademischer A.,** academic exchange service.

austauschen. I. *v.tr. sep.* (*a*) to exchange (goods, prisoners, ideas, etc.); to interchange (commodities, ideas, etc.); *Com:* to exchange, barter; **etwas gegen etwas a.,** to exchange one thing for another; **alte Erinnerungen a.,** to exchange reminiscences; **sie treffen sich, um ihre Gedanken, Meinungen, Erfahrungen, auszutauschen,** they meet to exchange, for an exchange of, ideas, views, to tell each other of their experiences, *F:* to compare notes; (*b*) **zwei Bücher, usw., a.,** to (ex)change, substitute, one book, etc., for another, to replace one book, etc., by another; **ohne mein Wissen hat sie die beiden Gläser ausgetauscht,** without my knowing it she exchanged the two glasses, changed the two glasses round.

II. *vbl s.* **Austauschen,** *n. in vbl senses; also:* exchange (of goods, prisoners, greetings, ideas, etc.); interchange (of commodities, compliments, ideas, etc.).

Austauschgefangene, *m., f.* (*decl. as adj.*) *Mil:* exchange prisoner.

Austauschoffizier, *m. Mil:* relief officer.

Austauschstoff, *m.* (*a*) (*foodstuff, etc.*) substitute; (*b*)=**Austauschwerkstoff.**

Austauschteil, *n. Mec.E: Aut: etc:* spare part, spare; duplicate.

Austauschstudent, *m.* exchange student.

Austauschwerkstoff, *m. Ind:* substitute (material); alternative, *U.S:* alternate, material.

austeilen. I. *v.tr. sep.* to distribute, deal out, hand out (thgs) (**an, unter, verschiedene Leute,** to various people); to divide, share, (thgs) out (**unter verschiedene Leute,** among various people); to deal (cards); **Almosen a.,** to distribute, deal out, dispense, alms; **Schläge a.,** to deal out blows, to lay about one; **Rollen a.,** to distribute parts; *Ecc:* **Kommunion a.,** to give Communion; **Weihwasser a.,** to sprinkle holy water.

II. *vbl s.* **Austeilen,** *n. in vbl senses.* **2. Austeilung,** *f.*=II. 1; *also:* distribution (of alms, etc.).

Auster¹, *f.* **-/-n.** *Moll:* oyster.

Auster². *Pr.n.m.* **-s.** *Myth: Poet:* Auster; the south wind.

Austerbaum, *m. Bot:* common mangrove.

Austernbank, *f.* oyster-bed, *U.S:* oyster-bank.

Austernbehälter, *m.* oyster-park.

Austerndieb, *m. Orn:*=**Austernfischer** 2.

Auster(n)fang, *m.* oyster-fishing.

Austernfisch, *m. Ich:* sea-wolf, sea-cat, wolf-fish.

Austernfischer, *m.* **1.** oyster-fisherman. **2.** *Orn:* oyster-catcher, sea-pie.

Austernfischerei, *f.* oyster-fishing

Austernhändler, *m.* oyster-dealer, oyster-man.

Austernhändlerin, *f.* oyster-dealer, oyster-woman.

Austernkultur, *f.* **1.**=**Austernzucht. 2.** *Archeol:* civilization characterized by the remnants of oysters found on excavation sites.

Austernmesser, *n.* oyster-knife.

Austernöffner, *m.* (*pers. or device*) oyster-opener, oyster-sheller.

Austernschale, *f.* oyster-shell, *U.S:* shuck.

Austernschwamm, Austernseitling, *m. Fung:* oyster mushroom.

Austernteich, *m.* oyster-farm.

Austernzucht, *f.* oyster-breeding, ostreiculture.

Austernzüchter, *m.* oyster-breeder.

austiefen. I. *v.tr. sep.* (*a*) to deepen (ditch, etc.); (*b*) to hollow (sth.) out.

II. *vbl s.* **1. Austiefen,** *n. in vbl senses.* **2. Austiefung,** *f.* (*a*)=II. 1; (*b*) hollow.

austifteln, *v.tr. sep.*=**austüfteln.**

austilgen. I. *v.tr. sep.* to extirpate, exterminate, extinguish, destroy, wipe out (race, etc.); to exterminate (vermin); to extirpate, eradicate (vice, etc.); to efface, obliterate, blot out (writing, memory of sth., etc.); to blot out (s.o.'s name, etc.); **etwas aus seinem Gedächtnis a.,** to blot sth. out of one's memory.

II. *vbl s.* **1. Austilgen,** *n. in vbl senses.* **2. Austilgung,** *f.*=II. 1; *also:* extirpation, extermination, extinction, destruction (of race, etc.); extirpation, eradication (of vice, etc.); obliteration (of memory, writing, etc.).

austoben, *v.sep.* **1.** *v.tr.* (*a*) to spend, work off (one's fury, etc.); (*b*) **sich a.,** (*of storm, rage, fever, etc.*) to spend itself, exhaust itself; (*of pers.*) to exhaust oneself; to have one's fling; *F:* to let off steam; **der Sturm hat sich ausgetobt,** the storm has ceased raging, is spent, has spent its fury, its force, has exhausted itself; **der Krieg hat sich nach drei Jahren ausgetobt,** the war has spent its fury after three years; **man muß die jungen Leute sich a. lassen,** young people must sow their wild oats, youth will, must, have its fling; *F:* young people must be allowed to let off steam. **2.** *v.i.* (*haben*) (*of storm, etc.*) to spend itself; (*of youth, etc.*) to have its fling.

austollen, *v.i. sep.* (*haben*) & **sich austollen,** to get rid of one's surplus energy; *F:* to let off steam; (*of children, etc.*) to romp.

austonnen, *v.tr. sep. Nau:* to beacon, buoy, mark out (channel).

Austrag, *m.* **-(e)s/⸗e. 1.** *Jur: etc:* settlement (of dispute, lawsuit, etc.); **eine Sache zum A. bringen,** to settle a matter; **bis zum A. der Sache,** pending settlement of the matter; *Jur: pendente lite,* while an action is pending; **bis zum gütlichen A. der Sache,** pending an amicable settlement of the matter; **diese wichtige Frage ist endlich zum A. gekommen,** this important question is at last being settled, being brought to an issue. **2.** *Hist:* (*a*) arbitration court, court of arbitration; (*b*) award (made by a court of arbitration). **3.**=**Altenteil** 1.

Austrägalgericht [austrɛˑˈgaːl-], *n. Hist:* arbitration court, court of arbitration.

Austrägalinstanz, *f.*=**Austrägalgericht.**

austragen, *v.tr. sep.* (*strong*) **1.** (*a*) to deliver (letters, newspapers, bread, etc.); **Zeitungen, Brot, usw., a.,** to do a newspaper round, a bread round, etc.; *U.S:* to have a (news)paper route; **bei uns wird die Milch nicht ausgetragen,** there is no delivery of milk where we live; (*b*) to spread, circulate (rumours, slander, etc.). **2.** *Ind:* (*a*) to remove (finished article) from the machine; (*b*) to take out, delete (item, name) (from list, etc.). **3.** (*a*) **ein Kind a.,** to carry a child for the full period of pregnancy; (*b*) to bear, put up with, endure, (sth.) to the end; (*c*) **Kleider a.,** to wear out clothes. **4.** (*a*) *Sp:* to play (match); (*of teams, participants*) **eine Meisterschaft a.,** to compete for a championship, to play a championship match; **die Tennismeisterschaften werden im Wimbledon ausgetragen,** the tennis tournaments are held at Wimbledon; **der Schwimmverein trägt seine diesjährige Meisterschaft aus,** the swimming club is holding its championship for this year; (*b*) **Meinungsverschiedenheiten a.,** to argue out differences of opinion, *F:* to have it out.

Austragende [ˈaustraˑkʔ,ɛndə], *n.* delivery end (of machine).

Austräger, *m.* (*a*) delivery-man, -boy; (baker's, etc.) roundsman; milkman; (news)paper-boy; (*b*) *F:* gossip(er), retailer of gossip, (tittle-)tattler.

Austrägerin, *f.* (*a*) delivery-woman, -girl; (news) paper-girl; (*b*) *F:* gossip(er), retailer of gossip, (tittle-)tattler.

Austrägler, *m.* **-s/-,** retired farmer who receives the 'Altenteil' (*q.v.*).

Austragrohr, *n.* discharge pipe.

austral [ausˈtraːl], *a.* austral; of the southern hemisphere.

australasiatisch [ausˈtraːlʔaˑzĭ,aːtiʃ], *a. Geog:* Australasian.

Australasien [austraːlʔˈaːzĭən]. *Pr.n.n.* **-s.** *Geog:* Australasia.

Australasier [austraːlʔˈaːzĭər], *m.* **-s/-.** Australasian.

Australien [ausˈtraːlĭən]. *Pr.n.n.* **-s.** *Geog:* Australia.

Australier [ausˈtraːlĭər], *m.* **-s/-.** Australian.

Australinseln, die. *Pr.n.f.pl. Geog:* the Austral Islands.

australisch [ausˈtraːliʃ], *a.* Australian.

Australlicht, *n.* aurora australis, southern lights.

Australneger, *m.* (Australian, Tasmanian) aboriginal.

Australtölpel, *m. Orn:* Australian gannet.

Austrasien [ausˈtraːzĭən]. *Pr.n.n.* **-s.** *A.Geog: Hist:* Austrasia.

austräumen, *v.sep.* (*a*) *v.tr.* to finish dreaming (dream), to dream (dream) to the end; *F:* **der Traum ist ausgeträumt,** that's the end of a beautiful dream; (*b*) *v.i.* (*haben*) to finish dreaming.

austreiben. I. *v.tr. sep.* (*strong*) **1.** (*a*) to drive (s.o.) out; to oust (s.o.); to eject (s.o.); to evict (tenant); (b) to drive (cattle) to graze; *abs.* **a.,** to drive cattle to graze; (*c*) to drive out, force out (nail, etc.); to punch (iron pin, etc.); (*d*) to drive out, expel (air, water, gas, etc.). **2.** (*a*) to cast out, exorcise (devil, evil spirit); **einen Teufel aus j-m a.,** to cast out, exorcise, a devil from, out of, s.o.; *F:* **den Teufel durch Beelzebub a.,** to cure one evil by a worse evil; (*b*) **j-m den Hochmut, den Dünkel, usw., a.,** to knock the arrogance, the conceit, etc., out of s.o.; **wir werden ihm diese Dummheiten a.,** we'll knock these silly ideas out of his head. **3.** *Print:* to drive out, to drive over (matter). **4.** *v.i.* (*haben*) (*of plants*) to run to seed, to sprout.

II. *vbl s.* **1. Austreiben,** *n. in vbl senses.* **2. Austreibung,** *f.*=II. 1; *also:* ejection (of s.o.); eviction (of tenant); expulsion (of air, water, gas, etc.); *Art:* **A. (der Händler) aus dem Tempel,** Christ driving the moneychangers out of the Temple.

Austreibungsperiode, Austreibungszeit, *f. Obst:* expulsive stage, second stage (of labour).

austreten, *v. sep.* (*strong*) I. *v.tr.* **1.** (*a*) to stamp, tread, (sth.) out (of sth.); to kick (sth.) out (of sth.); **j-m die Zähne a.,** to kick s.o.'s teeth out; (*b*) to tread out (wheat); **Trauben a.,** to tread (out) grapes, to tread the juice out of grapes. **2.** to tread out, stamp out (fire). **3.** (*a*) to wear down (steps, etc.); (*b*) **die Schuhe a.,** to stretch one's shoes (by wear); to break in (one's) new shoes; **sie hat meine neuen Schuhe zweimal getragen, um sie für mich auszutreten,** she has worn my new shoes twice so as to stretch them, break them in, for me; **ausgetretene Schuhe,** shoes stretched, broadened, by wear; shoes that have already been broken in; shoes that have become too big through wear; *F:* **die Kinderschuhe ausgetreten haben,** to have left one's childhood behind one, to be no longer a child.

II. **austreten,** *v.i.* (*sein*) **1.** (*a*) to step out; *Mil: etc:* **aus dem Glied a.,** to leave the ranks, to fall out; (*b*) *F:* to leave the room (to relieve nature), (*as euphemism*) to retire (for a moment), to go and wash one's hands. **2.** (**aus etwas**) **a.,** to leave (association, society, Church, federal union, etc.); to secede from (federal union); to withdraw, resign (from association, society, etc.); to resign membership (of association, society, etc.). **3.** (*of river*) to overflow its banks; **der Rhein ist ausgetreten,** the Rhine has overflowed its banks. **4.** (*a*) (*of thg*) to emerge (**aus etwas,** from sth.), to come out (**aus etwas,** of sth.); **wenn die Sonne aus dem Zeichen des Steinbocks austritt, . . . ,** when the sun passes out of the sign of Capricorn . . . ; **die Stelle, wo der Fluß aus dem Gebirge austritt,** the place where the river emerges from the mountains; *Opt:* **austretendes Strahlenbündel,** emergent beam; (*b*) (*of fluid*) to pass out (**aus etwas,** of sth.); (*of bile, sweat, etc.*) to be secreted (out); (*of blood, etc.*) (*from vessel*) to extravasate; (*c*) *Med:* (*of part of intestine, etc.*) to protrude; **die Augen traten ihm aus dem Kopf aus,** his eyes protruded; **durch den zerschmetterten Schädel trat das Gehirn aus,** through the shattered skull the brain protruded; (*d*) *Obst:* (*of child*) to be expelled (from mother's body), to be born.

III. *vbl s.* **Austreten,** *n. in vbl senses; also:* withdrawal, resignation (from association, society, etc.); *Med:* protrusion (of part of intestine, etc.); *Obst:* expulsion (of child from mother's body). *Cp.* **Austritt.**

Austriazismus [austrĭaˑˈtsismus], *m.* **-/-men.** *Ling:* Austrianism; Austrian word *or* turn of phrase

Austrien [ˈaustrĭən]. *Pr.n.n.* **-s.** *A.Geog: Hist:* Austrasia.

austrimmen, *v.tr. sep. Av:* to trim (the aircraft).

austrinken, *v.sep.* (*strong*) **1.** *v.tr.* (*a*) to drain, empty (glass, etc.); **seinen Wein, Tee, a.,** to drink up, to finish, one's wine, tea; **das Glas bis auf den letzten Tropfen a.,** to drain one's glass to the dregs, to the last drop; (*b*) *abs.* to finish one's drink, to drain one's glass; **trink aus, damit wir gehen können,** finish your drink, drink up, so that we can go; **trink aus! ich möchte anderen Wein einschenken,** finish your glass so that I can give you a different wine.

2. *v.i.* (*haben*) to finish drinking, to cease drinking.

austrisch [ˈaustriʃ], *a.* Austric (languages).

Austritt, *m.* **1. A.** (**aus etwas**), leaving (of association, society, federal union, Church, etc.); secession (from federal union); withdrawal, resignation, retirement (from association, society, etc.); **seinen A.** (**aus etwas**) **erklären,** to announce that one is leaving (association, etc.); **sein A. aus dem Verein hat uns sehr überrascht,** his resignation, retirement, from the society surprised us greatly. **2.** overflow, overflowing (of river, etc.). **3.** (*a*) **A.** (**eines Gegenstandes**) (**aus etwas**), emerging, emergence (of sth.) (from sth.); passing out, passage out (of fluid) (from sth.); egress, exit (of air, gas, steam, etc.); extravasation (of blood, etc., from vessel); *Opt:* emergence (of rays); *Astr:* emersion (of star, etc.); (*b*) protrusion (of part of intestine, etc.); (*c*) emergence, expulsion (of child from mother's body); **A. des Kopfes,** birth of the head. **4.** outlet, vent (for gas, steam, etc.); *Mch:* exhaust-port. **5.** (small) balcony. **6.** *F:* lavatory, w.c. *Cp.* **austreten** III.

Austrittsdüse, *f.* outlet nozzle; *Mch:* delivery jet (of injector).

Austrittserklärung, *f.* declaration of one's intention to leave (association, society, federal union, Church, etc.); declaration of intended withdrawal, resignation, retirement (from association, society, etc.).

Austrittskanal, *m. Mch:* exhaust port.

Austrittsmechanismus, *m. Obst:* mechanism of labour.

Austrittsöffnung, *f. Mch:* exhaust port.

Austrittsstufe, *f.* top step, top stair.

Austrittsventil, *n.* outlet valve; *Mch:* delivery valve (of injector).

austroasiatisch [ˌaustroˀaˑziˈaːtiʃ], *a. Geog: Ling:* Austro-asiatic.

austrocknen. I. *v.sep.* **1.** *v.tr.* (*a*) to dry (sth.) (up); to drain (land, bog, etc.); (*of sun, wind*) to dry up, parch (earth); to parch (mouth, throat); *Ch: Med:* to desiccate (substance, tissue, etc.); **die Hitze hat den Teich ausgetrocknet,** the heat has dried up the pond; **ein Wind, der die Haut austrocknet,** a wind that dries (up) the skin; (*b*) to dry (sth.) out; to dry the inside of (sth.); to season (wood); **die Schale ist nicht richtig ausgetrocknet,** the bowl has not been dried properly inside. **2.** *v.i.* (*sein*) (*of land, bog, pond, etc.*) to dry (up); (*of land*) to become parched; (*of skin*) to become dry; (*of substance*) to dry out, off; (*of wood*) to season; **meine Kehle ist wie ausgetrocknet,** my throat is dry, parched.

II. *pr.p. & a.* **austrocknend,** *in vbl senses; esp.* desiccative (properties); *Ch: Med:* **austrocknendes Mittel,** desiccative.

austrommeln, *v.tr. sep.* to announce (sth.) by beat of drums; *F:* **du brauchst es nicht gleich aus(zu)trommeln,** you need not tell everybody about it, there's no need to broadcast it, *F:* to shout it from the house-tops.

austrompeten, *v.tr. sep.* (*a*) to proclaim (sth.) by trumpet; (*b*) *F:* to proclaim (sth.), to trumpet (sth.) forth, abroad, to blazon (sth.) forth, abroad, to noise (sth.) abroad, to broadcast (sth.), *F:* to proclaim, cry, shout, (sth.) from the house-tops.

austronesisch [austroˑˈneːziʃ], *a. Geog: Ling:* Austronesian.

auströpfeln, austropfen, *v.i. sep.* (*sein*) to drip out; to trickle out.

austüfteln, *v.tr. sep.* to puzzle (sth.) out.

austun, *v.tr. sep.* (*strong*) *F:* to take off (piece of clothing, etc.).

austuschen, *v.tr. sep.* to colour (drawing, etc.).

ausüben. I. *v.tr. sep.* **1.** to practise, exercise (a profession); to follow, pursue, carry on (a trade, a profession); to ply (a trade); to be actively engaged in, to be an active participant in (a sport); **ein Amt a.,** to fulfil, carry out, exercise, an office; (*of pers., thg*) **eine Funktion a.,** to fulfil, exercise, a function; **er hat Forstwirtschaft studiert, aber er hat den Beruf nie ausgeübt,** he studied forestry, but he has never actually followed, practised, that profession; (*of doctor*) **eine Praxis a.,** to be in (private) practice; **eine Pflicht a.,** to fulfil, carry out, perform, a duty; **ein Verbrechen a.,** to commit, perpetrate (crime); **ein ausübender Arzt,** a practising doctor; **der ausübende Künstler,** the performer; the executant; **ein ausübender Pianist,** a professional pianist; *Pol:* **ausübende Gewalt,** executive power. **2.** to exert, make use of (force, etc.); to exercise (right, influence); **einen Einfluß auf j-n a.,** to have an influence on s.o.; **seinen Einfluß auf j-n a.,** to exert, use, exercise, one's influence on s.o., to bring one's influence to bear on s.o.; **einen Druck auf j-n a.,** to bring pressure to bear on s.o., to put pressure on s.o.; **eine starke Anziehungskraft auf j-n a.,** to have a great attraction, *F:* draw, for s.o.; **Wirkungen a.,** to have effects; **Aufsicht a.,** to exercise supervision.

II. *vbl s.* **1. Ausüben,** *n. in vbl senses.* **2. Ausübung,** *f. in vbl senses; also:* exercise (of function, duty, right, influence); exertion (of influence); practice (of profession); performance (of duty); **in A. seines Dienstes,** in performance of one's duty, *U.S:* in line of duty; **in A. seines Berufs sterben,** (i) to die at one's work, to die in harness; (ii) (*of fireman, etc.*) to die in the course of one's duty.

Ausverkauf, *m. Com:* (*a*) selling off, out (of stock); (*b*) sale; **Waren im A. kaufen,** to buy goods in the sale, at the sales.

ausverkaufen, *v.tr. sep. Com:* (*a*) to sell off, to clear (surplus stock); (*b*) to sell out, *U.S:* close out (article); **Eier sind ausverkauft,** eggs are sold out; we, they, etc., are sold out of eggs; *Th:* **ausverkauftes Haus,** full house, house filled to capacity; **vor ausverkauftem Hause spielen,** to play to a full house; **'ausverkauft',** 'sold out'; (*theatre notice*) 'house full'; (*c*) *abs.* to sell out, *U.S:* close out.

Ausverkaufspreis, *m.* sale price.

ausverschämt, *a. North G.Dial:* = **unverschämt.**

auswachsen, *v.sep.* (*strong*) I. *v.i.* (*sein*) **1.** (*of pers., plant, animal*) to attain full growth; **ein ausgewachsenes Tier,** a full-grown animal; **der Baum ist noch nicht ganz ausgewachsen,** the tree is not yet full-grown. *See also* **ausgewachsen. 2.** (*a*) (*of potatoes, wheat*) to sprout; (*b*) *occ.* (*of pers.*) **ausgewachsen sein,** to be hunchbacked, humpbacked. **3. in etwas** *acc.* **a.,** to end in sth.; **in Dornen auswachsende Zweige,** twigs ending in hard spines. **4. aus einem Kleidungsstück a.,** *v.tr.* **ein Kleidungsstück a.,** to grow out of, to outgrow, a garment.

II. **sich auswachsen. 1. sich zu etwas, in etwas** *acc.,* **a.,** to grow into, develop into, sth.; **sie hatte sich zu einem schönen Mädchen ausgewachsen,** she had grown into a fine girl; **die Lage könnte sich zu einer Katastrophe a.,** the situation could become a catastrophe; **der Grenzkonflikt könnte sich leicht zu einem größeren Krieg a.,** the border conflict could easily develop into a major war; **seine Magenschmerzen haben sich zu einer schweren Gastritis ausgewachsen,** his stomach-ache developed into a bad attack of gastritis. **2.** (*of flaw*) to become unnoticeable, to disappear; **die Narbe wird sich wohl mit der Zeit a.,** the scar will no doubt become invisible, unnoticeable, will disappear, in time; **seine O-Beine werden sich schon a.,** his bandy legs will grow straight, will right themselves, eventually; **er ist sehr unartig, aber das wird sich a.,** he is very naughty but he'll grow out of it.

III. *vbl s.* **Auswachsen,** *n. in vbl senses; also:* *F:* **das ist zum A.,** it's enough to drive you up the pole.

auswägen, *v.tr. sep.* (*strong*) to weigh (sth.) out; *see also* **ausgewogen.**

Auswahl, *f.* **1.** selection; (*a*) **j-m Muster, usw., zur A. senden,** to send s.o. patterns, etc., for selection, to choose from; **bei der Fülle wird die A. schwer,** such abundance makes choosing, a choice, difficult; (*b*) choice; assortment; **das Geschäft hat eine gute A. von, an, Weinsorten, in Weinen,** the shop has a good selection, wide choice, large assortment, of wines; **wir bieten eine sehr große A. von Hüten,** we have a very big selection of hats, we offer a wide range of hats; **eine A. aus den Werken eines Schriftstellers machen,** to make a selection of an author's works; **die Werke eines Dichters in A. herausgeben,** to publish a selection from a poet's works; **A. aus Goethe,** selections from Goethe; **A. aus den Werken Offenbachs,** selections from Offenbach; **eine A. treffen,** to make a selection. **2. die A.,** the choicest articles, specimens, etc.; the choicest wine, etc.; *F:* the pick of the bunch, basket; **die A. einer Nation, Gesellschaft, usw.,** the cream, élite, flower, *F:* pick, of a nation, society, etc.

auswählen, *v.tr. sep.* to choose, select (s.o., sth.), to pick out (sth.); **man hat sie aus Hunderten von Bewerbern ausgewählt,** she was chosen, selected, from hundreds of applicants; **nach langem Suchen hat sie sich** *dat.* **diesen Ring ausgewählt,** after much searching she selected, chose, picked out, this ring; **ausgewählte Gedichte aus der Barockzeit,** selections from baroque poets; **ausgewählte Stellen aus Goethes Werken,** selected passages, selections, from Goethe.

Auswahlmannschaft, *f. Sp:* team of picked players, competitors, 'select' team.

Auswahlregel, *f.* selection rule.

Auswahlsendung, *f. Com:* samples (sent for selection).

auswalzen, *v.tr. sep.* to roll (sth.) out (thin); *Cu:* to roll out (dough, paste); *Metall:* to laminate, flat(ten), roll (metal); *F:* to dwell on (sth.) excessively; to labour (a point) (in argument).

Auswanderer, *m.* emigrant.

Auswandererschiff, *n.* emigrant ship.

auswandern, *v.i. sep.* (*sein*) **1.** (*a*) (*of pers.*) to emigrate; **von, aus, England nach Australien a.,** to emigrate from England to Australia; **Auswanderung** *f,* emigration; (*b*) (*of a tribe, of birds, fishes, etc.*) to migrate; **Auswanderung** *f,* migration. **2.** *Anti-aircraft Artil:* (*of target*) to travel; **Auswanderung** *f,* (angular) travel.

Auswanderungsmesser, *m.* anti-aircraft range corrector.

Auswanderungsstrecke, *f. Anti-aircraft Artil:* linear travel, course, (of target) between present and future positions.

auswärtig, *a.* **1.** (people) from outside; (people) from another place; **auswärtige Kunden,** out-of-town customers; **auswärtige Gäste** (**auf einer Konferenz, usw.**), guests from outside, non-resident guests (at a conference, etc.); *Sch:* **die auswärtigen Schüler, die Auswärtigen,** the pupils (coming) from outside the town; the out-of-town pupils. **2.** foreign, external; **auswärtiger Handel,** foreign trade; **auswärtige Angelegenheiten,** foreign, external, affairs; **das Auswärtige Amt, das Ministerium des Auswärtigen,** the Foreign Ministry; (*British*) the Foreign Office; *U.S:* the State Department; (*in Commonwealth countries*) the Ministry for External Affairs; **Minister des Auswärtigen** = **Außenminister.**

auswärts, *adv.* **1.** (*a*) away from home, out; **a. essen, schlafen,** to eat out, to sleep out, to sleep away from home; (*b*) in another place, town; outside the town; **nach a. verziehen,** to move to another place, town; **von a. kommen,** to come from another town; to come from outside (the town); **sie hat jeden Abend eine lange Fahrt, denn sie wohnt a.,** she has a long journey every evening as she lives out of town. **2.** outwards; **die Füße a. stellen,** to turn one's feet outwards; to turn one's toes out; **das Fenster geht nach a. auf,** the window opens outwards.

auswärtsgehen, *v.i. sep.* (*strong*) (*sein*) to walk with one's feet, toes, turned out, to turn one's feet, one's toes, out as one walks.

Auswärtskehrung, *f. Med:* eversion (of eye-lid).

Auswärtsspiel, *n. Sp:* away match, away game.

auswaschbar, *a.* (stain, etc.) that can be washed out; washable (ink).

auswaschen, *v.tr. sep.* (*strong*) **1.** (*a*) to wash out (dirt, mark, soap, *Ch:* precipitate, etc.); to wash (stockings, clothes, etc.) out, through; **die Handtücher gut a.,** to wash the towels thoroughly; **die Farbe ist ganz ausgewaschen,** the colour is all washed out, has washed out; **ein ausgewaschenes Blau,** a washed-out blue; (*b*) to wash out (bottle, glass, etc.); **eine Wunde a.,** to wash out a wound. **2.** (*of river, sea, etc.*) to wash away, erode, undermine (part of river bank, seashore, etc.); **Auswaschung** *f,* erosion.

auswässern, *v.sep.* **1.** *v.tr.* (*a*) to soak, steep (rice, salt fish, etc.); to steep (stained fabric, etc.); (*b*) to wash out (dirt, stain, etc.). **2.** *v.i. Nau:* (*of upper part of hull*) to rise out of the water; **Auswässerung** *f,* freeboard.

Auswässerungslinie, *f. Nau:* load(-water-)line.

ausweben, *v.tr. sep. Nau:* **die Wanten a.,** to rattle down (*i.e.* put the ratlines on) the shrouds.

auswechselbar, *a.* exchangeable (**gegen,** for); replaceable (**gegen,** by); interchangeable (**gegen,** with); renewable (machine parts, etc.); detachable, removable (machine parts, etc.); interchangeable (machine parts, etc.).

Auswechselbarkeit, *f.* exchangeability (**gegen,** for); interchangeability (**gegen,** with); detachability, removability (of machine parts, etc.).

auswechseln, I. *v.sep.* **1.** *v.tr.* **etwas** (**gegen etwas**) **a.,** to change, exchange, sth. (for sth.); to replace sth. (by sth.); **ein Bild** (**in einer Ausstellung, usw.**) **gegen ein anderes a.,** to take out one picture (from an exhibition, etc.) and replace it by another, put in another (instead); **einen groben Ausdruck gegen einen feineren a.,** to remove a coarse expression and substitute something more refined; **eine Batterie, eine**

Glühbirne, usw., a., to change, replace, a battery, a bulb, etc.; **die Hölzer eines Tunnels a.,** to replace, renew, the timbering of a tunnel; **einen Schacht a.,** to retimber a shaft; **zwei Dinge a.,** to exchange, interchange, two things, to change two things round; **Maschinenteile, usw., a.,** (i) to replace, renew, machine parts, etc.; (ii) to exchange machine parts, etc., to change machine parts, etc., round (*to avoid uneven wear*); **Reifen halten länger, wenn sie von Zeit zu Zeit ausgewechselt werden,** tyres, *U.S:* tires, last longer if they are changed, *U.S:* shifted, round from time to time; **Maschinenteile, die ausgewechselt werden können,** detachable machine parts, machine parts that can be detached (and replaced); *F:* **wie ausgewechselt sein, sich wie ausgewechselt fühlen,** to be a different, new, man, woman, to feel a different, new, man, woman. **2.** *v.tr. Constr:* to trim (in) (joists, etc.). **3.** *v.i.* (*haben*) *Ven:* (*of game*) to go to new haunts.

II. *vbl s.* **Auswechseln** *n.*, **Auswechs(e)lung** *f. in vbl senses; also:* exchange, change (**von etwas gegen etwas,** of sth. for sth.); replacement (**von etwas gegen etwas,** of sth. by sth.); interchange (of two things); renewal (of timbering, machine part, etc.).

Auswechselrahmen, *m.* (picture-)frame in which various pictures can be inserted.

Ausweg, *m.* (*a*) way out; way of escape; **er sah keinen A. aus den Flammen,** he could find no escape from the flames; (*b*) **A. aus einer Verlegenheit, usw.,** way out of, escape from, an awkward situation, etc.; **er weiß (sich** *dat.*) **keinen A.,** he can see no way out; **ich sah keinen anderen A.,** I saw no other way out, no other way to get out of it; **als letzten A.,** as a last resort.

ausweglos, *a.* hopeless (situation, etc.).

Ausweglosigkeit, *f.* hopelessness (of situation, etc.).

Ausweich-, *comb. fm.* **1.** (*a*) avoiding . . . , evading . . . , evasive . . . ; **Ausweichbewegung** *f*, avoiding, evading, evasive, movement; **Ausweichschritt** *m*, evasive step; side-step; (*b*) passing-; **Ausweichstelle** *f*, passing-place; *Rail: etc:* passing-track, turn-out. **2.** alternative . . . , *U.S:* alternate . . . ; substitute . . . ; emergency . . . ; reserve . . . ; **Ausweichplan** *m*, alternative plan; **Ausweichtreibstoff** *m*, alternative fuel; **Ausweichkrankenhaus** *n*, reserve hospital, hospital for emergency use; **Ausweichlager** *n*, reserve store, emergency store; **Ausweichwohnungen** *fpl*, emergency accommodation (for the bombed-out, etc.).

Ausweiche, *f. Rail:* turn-out.

ausweichen. I. *v.i. sep.* (*strong*) (*sein*). **1.** to make way, to get out of the way; to keep out of the way; **(vor) j-m, (vor) einem Fahrzeug, a.,** to make way for s.o., for a vehicle (to pass), to get out of s.o.'s, a vehicle's, way; to give way to s.o., a vehicle; **einem anderen Schiffe a.,** to keep out of the way of another ship; to give way to another ship; **nach rechts, links, a.,** to swerve to the right, to the left; **ich habe dem Hund nicht mehr a. können,** I couldn't swerve in time to avoid the dog. **2.** (*a*) **einem Stoß a.,** to avoid, evade, dodge, a blow; *Fenc:* to parry a thrust; *abs.* **a.,** to dodge; *Box:* to duck *or* side-step a blow; **j-s Blicken a.,** to avoid (meeting) s.o.'s eyes, gaze; (*b*) **einer Gefahr, einer Frage, a.,** to elude, evade, a danger, a question; **seiner Pflicht a.,** to evade, shirk, one's duty; **einer Versuchung a.,** to avoid temptation; **der Frage a.,** to avoid, dodge, shirk, *F:* side-step, the issue; **er wich mir, meiner Frage, aus,** he evaded my question; **ausweichende Antwort,** evasive answer; non-commital answer; **seinen Verfolgern a.,** to elude one's pursuers, to give one's pursuers the slip; *Mil:* **(dem Feind) a.,** to avoid contact (with the enemy); (*c*) **j-m a.,** to avoid s.o.; **er weicht mir immer aus,** he always avoids me, avoids meeting me. **3.** *Mus:* **in eine andere Tonart a.,** to modulate into another key. **4.** (*of wall, etc.*) (*a*) to deflect; (*b*) to flow.

II. *vbl s.* **1. Ausweichen,** *n. in vbl senses; also:* (*a*) avoidance (**vor j-m, etwas,** of s.o., sth.); elusion (**vor j-m, etwas,** of s.o., sth.); evasion (**vor j-m, etwas,** of s.o., sth.); **ich sah den Hund erst, als ein A. nicht mehr möglich war,** I didn't see the dog till it was too late to avoid it; **das würde ein A. vor den Kernproblemen bedeuten,** that would be avoiding, that would be avoidance of, evasion of, the main problems; (*b*) deflection (of wall, etc.). **2. Ausweichung** *f.*, (*a*) *Mus:* transition, passing modulation; (*b*) plastic flow (of wall, etc.).

Ausweichflughafen, Ausweichflugplatz, *m. Av:* alternative airport, airfield.

Ausweichfrequenz, *f. W.Tel:* alternative frequency.

Ausweichgleis, *n. Rail:* passing-track, loop(-line), turn-out.

Ausweichhafen, *m.* alternative base (for ships, aircraft).

Ausweichklausel, *f.* escape clause (in contract, etc.).

Ausweichkurs, *m.* **1.** *Nau:* avoiding course. **2.** *St.Exch:* quotation intended merely to influence the market.

Ausweichlager, *n.* reserve store, emergency store.

Ausweichmanöver, *n. Mil: Navy: Mil.Av:* evading manoeuvre; **ein A. ausführen,** to take evasive action.

Ausweichmittel, *n. Ind: etc:* substitute.

Ausweichplatz, *m.* **1.** passing-place (in road). **2.** *Av:* = **Ausweichflugplatz.**

Ausweichstelle, *f.* **1.** passing-place (in road, trench, etc.); *Rail: etc:* passing-track, loop, turn-out. **2.** place to which an institution, etc., is evacuated (during wartime).

Ausweichstellung, *f. Mil:* alternative, *U.S:* alternate, position.

Ausweichstraße, *f.* by-pass.

Ausweichung, *f. see* **ausweichen** II.

Ausweichungsclivage [-kliˑˈvaːʒə], *f. Geol:* strain-slip cleavage.

Ausweichwelle, *f.* = **Ausweichfrequenz.**

Ausweichziel, *n. Mil.Av:* alternative, *U.S:* alternate, target.

ausweiden, *v.tr. sep.* (*of huntsman, bird of prey, etc.*) to gut (animal).

ausweinen, *v.sep.* **1.** *v.tr.* **seinen Schmerz, Jammer, a.,** to find relief for one's sorrow in tears; **seinen Schmerz an j-s Busen a.,** to weep out one's sorrows on s.o.'s breast; **sich** *dat.* **die Augen a.,** to weep, cry, one's eyes out. **2. sich ausweinen,** to find relief in tears, to have one's cry out; **sich an j-s Brust a.,** to weep out one's sorrows on s.o.'s breast. **3.** *v.i.* (*haben*) to stop weeping.

Ausweis, *m.* **-es/-e. 1. nach A.** + *gen.*, **nach A. von . . . ,** according to the evidence of . . . , as proved, shown, by . . . . **2.** certificate; **j-m einen A. über eine Leistung ausstellen,** to write s.o. a certificate testifying an achievement. **3.** (*document proving membership of a profession, club, etc., or showing rights to special privileges, etc.*) credentials; identification papers; (membership, admission, student's, etc.) card; (library, etc.) ticket; (traveller's) passport; *Mil: etc:* pass. **4.** *Bank:* statement, return.

ausweisen. I. *v.tr. sep.* (*strong*) **1.** to turn (s.o.) out; *Adm:* to expel (alien); **er wurde als unerwünschter Ausländer aus Deutschland ausgewiesen,** he was expelled from Germany as an undesirable alien. **2.** to prove, show, testify; **die Zeugnisse weisen seine Kenntnisse auf dem Gebiet . . . aus,** the testimonials are proof of his knowledge in the field of . . . . **3. sich ausweisen,** (*a*) to prove one's identity (by producing identification papers, etc.); **können Sie sich a.?** can you produce papers to prove your identity? **sich als Herr X a.,** to prove that, to produce papers, etc., proving that, one is Mr X; (*b*) **sich als guter Geschäftsmann, usw., a.,** to prove, show, oneself a good businessman, etc.; **er hat damit seine Tüchtigkeit ausgewiesen,** he proved his ability thereby; (*c*) **das wird sich a.,** it remains to be seen, we shall see.

II. *vbl s.* **1. Ausweisen,** *n. in vbl senses.* **2. Ausweisung,** *f.* = II. 1; *also:* expulsion (of alien).

Ausweiskarte, *f.* identification card; (membership, admission, student's, etc.) card; (library, etc.) ticket.

Ausweispapier, *n.* document of identification; **Ausweispapiere** *pl*, identification papers.

Ausweisungsbefehl, *m. Adm:* expulsion order.

ausweiten. I. *v.tr. sep.* (*a*) to widen (sth.); to expand, dilate (sth.); to enlarge (hole); to stretch (shoes, gloves, etc.); **seinen Horizont a.,** to broaden one's mind; **sich a.,** to widen, to grow wider; to expand, to dilate; to grow, become, larger; (*of shoes, gloves, etc.*) to stretch; (*b*) to extend (credit, interests, etc.); to extend, expand (trade relations, etc.); (*of trade relations, interests, etc.*) **sich a.,** to extend, expand.

II. *vbl s.* **1. Ausweiten,** *n. in vbl senses.* **2. Ausweitung,** *f.* (*a*) = II. 1; *also:* expansion, dilation (of sth.); enlargement (of hole, etc.); extension (of interests, trade relations, etc.); (*b*) *Carp: Metalw:* countersunk hole, countersink; (*c*) extension; enlargement.

auswendig. 1. (*a*) *a.* outer; outside; external; outward; **auf der auswendigen Seite,** on the outer side; (*b*) *adv.* outside, on the outside, externally; outwardly. **2.** *adv.* **etwas a. lernen,** to learn sth. by heart, to memorize sth.; **etwas a. können, wissen,** to know sth. by heart; **ein Stück a. spielen,** to play a piece without music, from memory; **etwas in- und a. können,** to know sth. inside out; **ein Gedicht a. aufsagen,** to recite a poem (by heart, from memory).

Auswendiglernen, *n.* learning (of poem, etc.) by heart; memorizing (of poem, etc.); **das A. fällt ihm schwer,** he finds learning by heart difficult; **eine Stelle zum A.,** a passage to learn by heart.

Auswendigspielen, *n. Mus:* playing (of a piece) from memory.

auswerfen. I. *v.tr. sep.* (*strong*). **1.** (*a*) to cast (nets, etc.); **die Angel a.,** to cast the line; to cast for fish; *see also* **Anker** 1; (*b*) *Nau: etc:* to discharge, throw out (ballast); to jettison (cargo); (*c*) *A:* **j-n a.,** to throw (s.o.) out; (*d*) to scatter (seed, etc,). **2. j-m ein Auge, einen Zahn, a.,** to knock out s.o.'s eye, one of s.o.'s teeth (by throwing a stone, etc.). **3.** (*a*) to throw up (earth, etc.); (*b*) to dig (trench, ditch, etc.). **4.** (*a*) to vomit (blood, etc.); to expectorate, cough up (phlegm, blood, etc.); (*of volcano*) to eject, belch forth, throw up, vomit (ashes, etc.); (*of sea*) to throw up, cast up (wreckage, etc.); (*b*) to eject (spent cartridge, etc.). **5.** *Ven:* to gut (hare). **6.** (*a*) to set aside, allow (sum of money) (**für etwas,** for sth.); to allocate (sum of money) (**für etwas, j-n,** to sth., s.o.); (*b*) to distribute (dividends); (*c*) to offer (prize).

II. *vbl s.* **Auswerfen,** *n. in vbl senses; also:* (*a*) discharge (of ballast); expectoration (of phlegm, blood, etc.); ejection (of ashes, etc.); (*b*) distribution (of dividends); allocation (of money). *Cp.* **Auswurf** 1.

Auswerfer, *m. Sm.a: etc:* ejector.

auswerten. I. *v.tr. sep.* (*a*) *Mth:* to evaluate (expression); (*b*) to use, utilize (sth.); to turn (sth.) to (good) account; to make (good) use of (sth.); to exploit (sth.); *Av: etc:* to interpret (photographs); *abs.* to plot; **die Ergebnisse seiner Untersuchungen a.,** to turn one's findings to account; **eine Statistik a.,** to interpret a set of statistics; **ein Experiment praktisch a.,** to make practical use of the results of an experiment; **die Erfindung wäre nicht kommerziell auszuwerten,** the invention could not be exploited commercially.

II. *vbl s.* **1. Auswerten,** *n. in vbl senses.* **2. Auswertung,** *f.* (*a*) = II. 1; *also:* use, utilization (of sth.); exploitation (of invention, etc.); interpretation (of statistics, *Av: etc:* of photographs); *Mth:* evaluation (of expression); (*b*) *Mil.Av:* = **Auswertestelle.**

Auswertestelle, *f. Mil: Av:* computing station; plotting station.

Auswerteverfahren, *n.* procedure for interpretation (of statistics, *Av: etc:* of photographs); *Av:* plotting method; *Mth:* method of evaluation (of expression).

auswettern, *v.tr. sep.* **1.** *Nau:* to weather out, ride out (gale). **2.** *v.i.* (*haben*) to exhaust one's ill-temper, *F:* to let off steam.

auswetzen, *v.tr. sep.* (*a*) **Scharten in einem Messer, usw., a.,** to whet, grind, out notches in a knife, etc.; (*b*) *F:* **eine Scharte a.,** to wipe out a stain on one's character; to repair, wipe out, a defeat, *F:* to even up the score; to redeem oneself.

auswickeln, *v.tr. sep.* to unwrap, undo (package, etc.); to unwrap (present, etc.); to extricate (sth.); to unswaddle, unswathe (infant).

auswiegen, *v.tr. sep.* (*strong*) (*a*) to weigh (whole piece, sackful, etc.); **soll ich Ihnen das ganze Stück a.?** shall I weigh the whole piece (for you)? (*b*) to balance (sth.) out; *Av:* to trim (airship); *see also* **ausgewogen;** (*c*) *abs. Turf:* to weigh in; **Auswiegen** *n*, weighing-in.

Auswindemaschine, *f. Ind:* = **Auswringmaschine.**

auswinden, *v.tr. sep.* (*strong*) to wring out (washing).

auswintern, *v.sep.* **1.** *v.tr.* to winter (animals, plants). **2.** *v.i.* (*haben*) *A:* to winter, to spend the winter (at a place). **3.** *v.i.* (*sein*) (*of seed*) to be killed by frost; (*of fish*) to die in winter (of suffocation due to ice).

Auswinterungsschäden, *m.pl.* winter killing (of plants, fish, etc.).

auswirken, *v. sep.* I. *v.tr.* **1.** to work, knead (dough, etc.). **2.** (*a*) *Farr:* to pare (horse's hoof); (*b*) *Ven:* to break up (deer, etc.). **3. etwas bei j-m a.,** to obtain, procure, sth. from s.o.; **j-m etwas a.,** to obtain, procure, sth. for s.o. **4.** (*of action, event, etc.*) **sich auswirken,** to have

consequences; to have its effects; **sich auf etwas** *acc.* **a.,** to affect sth.; to have an effect on sth.; **dieses Ereignis könnte sich schlimm für uns a.,** this event could have bad consequences for us; **eine Frage, die sich auf die Wohlfahrt des Landes auswirkt,** a question that affects, bears on, the welfare of the country; **sich günstig, ungünstig, auf etwas** *acc.* **a.,** to have a favourable, unfavourable, effect on sth.; **die Sache hat sich nicht zu unserem Vorteil ausgewirkt,** the business did not work out, turn out, to our advantage, in our favour; **sich als Vorteil, Nachteil, a.,** to turn out to be an advantage, a disadvantage.

II. **auswirken,** *v.i.* (*haben*) to take effect; **eine Arznei a. lassen,** to give a medicine time to take effect, to work.

III. *vbl s.* **Auswirkung,** *f.* result, consequence; effect; **ein an sich unbedeutendes Ereignis, das große Auswirkungen auf die Zukunft haben kann,** an event, in itself insignificant, which could affect the future greatly; **schlimme, günstige, Auswirkungen (auf etwas, für j-n) haben,** to have a bad, a good, effect (on sth., s.o.), to have bad, good, consequences (for sth., s.o.).

auswischen, *v.tr. sep.* **1.** (*a*) to wipe out (drawer, etc.); to clean out (gun barrel, etc.); to wipe (sth.) clean; **den Staub, den Schmutz, aus etwas a.,** to wipe the dust, dirt, out of sth.; **sich** *dat.* **die Augen a.,** to wipe, dry, one's eyes (after crying, laughing); to rub one's eyes; **sich** *dat.* **den Schlaf aus den Augen a.,** to rub (the sleep from) one's eyes; *Austrian: F:* **damit kannst du dir die Augen a.!** that's no use at all, no earthly use! (*b*) **Wörter, usw., (von der Tafel) a.,** to wipe off words, etc. (from the blackboard *or* slate). **2.** *F:* **j-m eins a.,** to give s.o. a jolt, *F:* to give s.o. something to think about; to play a (dirty) trick on s.o.

auswittern, *v.sep.* **1.** *v.tr.* (*of hound, etc., F: of pers.*) to scent out, smell out, nose out (game, etc.; *F:* secret, etc.). **2.** *v.tr.* (*a*) (*of air*) to corrode, wear away (metal, stone, etc.); (*b*) to cause (mineral, salt) to effloresce; (*c*) to season (wood). **3.** *v.i.* (*haben*) (*a*) *Ch:* (*of mineral, salt, etc.*) to effloresce; **Auswitterung** *f,* efflorescence; (*b*) (*of wood*) to season; (*c*) (*of rock, stone*) to weather; (*of wooden structure, etc.*) to suffer from exposure to the weather, to become weather-worn; (*of paint, colours*) to fade (through exposure to the air).

auswringen, *v.tr. sep.* (*strong*) to wring out (clothes, etc.); to wring (water) out (of clothes, etc.).

Auswringmaschine, *f. Ind: etc:* wringing-machine, wringer; drying-machine, dryer.

Auswuchs, *m.* **1.** excrescence, outgrowth, protuberance; *Med: etc:* tumo(u)r; *Bot:* apophysis; **krankhafter A.,** morbid growth, morbid excrescence; **knollenartiger A. an der Wurzel,** tuberous growth, tuberous excrescence, on the root. **2.** product, *esp.* unhealthy product; *usu. pl.* **Auswüchse,** extremist outgrowths (of an art, etc.); excesses; aberrations; **A. einer krankhaften Phantasie,** product, creation, figment, of a morbid imagination; **krankhafte Auswüchse der Phantasie,** morbid imaginings; **diese Erscheinungen sind Auswüchse eines korrupten Systems,** these things are products of a corrupt system.

auswuchten, *v.tr. sep.* to balance, counterbalance (weights); to balance (wheel, etc.).

Auswuchtmaschine, *f. Mec.E:* balancing machine.

auswühlen, *v.tr. sep.* to dig up, grub up (sth.); to throw out, excavate (earth); (*of swine, etc.*) to root up, root out (sth.); (*of rabbit, etc.*) to dig (burrow, etc.); (*of mole, etc.*) to burrow (passage underground).

Auswurf, *m.* **1.** vomiting (of blood, etc.); expectoration, coughing up (of phlegm, blood, etc.); ejection, throwing up (of rocks, etc.); throwing up, casting up (of wreckage); *cp.* **auswerfen II. 2.** (*a*) *pl.* **Auswürfe,** ejected matter, ejected material; *Geol:* ejecta, ejectamenta (of volcano); (*b*) expectoration; *Med:* sputum; **schleimiger A.,** phlegm; **starken, leichten, A. haben,** to cough up a lot of, a small amount of, matter; **blutiger A.,** expectorations mingled with blood; (*c*) *A:* excrement; (*d*) refuse, rubbish, rejects; *F:* scum, dregs (of society, etc.); **der A. der Menschheit,** the scum of the earth, the off-scourings of humanity.

auswürfeln, *v.tr. sep.* to throw dice, to dice, for (sth.).

Auswürfling, *m.* **-s/-e.** *Geol:* piece of ejected material; **(vulkanische) Auswürflinge,** ejecta, ejectamenta, ejected material.

Auswurfmassen, *f.pl.* ejected masses (of volcano).

Auswurfrohr, *n. Mch:* discharge-pipe.

auswüten, *v.i. sep.* (*haben*) (*of storm, etc.*) to spend itself, its fury, its force.

auszacken. I. *v.tr. sep.* to indent (sth.); to jag (sth.), to give (sth.) a zig-zag, jagged, edge; (*of edge, etc.*) **ausgezackt,** dentate, zig-zag, jagged.

II. *vbl s.* **1. Auszacken,** *n. in vbl senses.* **2. Auszackung,** *f.* (*a*) *in vbl senses; also:* indentation (of sth.); (*b*) indentation.

auszahlen. I. *v.tr. sep.* **1.** to pay (out) (sum of money, wages); to disburse (sum of money); **eine Geldsumme an j-n a.,** to pay s.o. a sum, to pay out a sum to s.o.; **j-m seinen Lohn, usw., a.,** to pay s.o. his wages, etc.; **j-m seinen Anteil, sein Erbteil, seinen Gewinn, a.,** to give s.o. his share, his inheritance, his winnings, to pay out his share, inheritance, winnings, to s.o.; **wir haben nur die Hälfte unseres Gehalts ausgezahlt bekommen,** we were paid only half our salary; **die Firma konnte mir letzte Woche mein Gehalt nicht voll a.,** the firm couldn't pay my salary in full last week; **er zahlt jede Woche Löhne in Höhe von 2000 Mark aus,** he pays out 2,000 marks in wages each week; **eine Postanweisung, einen Scheck, a.,** (*of official, etc.*) to cash, hand over cash in exchange for, a postal order, cheque. **2. einen Arbeiter a.,** (i) to pay a workman (his wages); (ii) to pay off a workman. **3. sich auszahlen,** (*a*) *F:* **es zahlt sich nicht aus,** it's not worth it; (*b*) *Dial:* (*of pers.*) to hurt, damage, oneself.

II. *vbl s.* **1. Auszahlen,** *n. in vbl senses.* **2. Auszahlung,** *f.* (*a*)=II. 1; *also:* payment (of money, wages, etc.); disbursement (of money); **volle A. eines Gehalts,** payment of a salary in full; (*b*) payment; disbursement; **die Firma hat Auszahlungen für verschiedene Zwecke gemacht,** the firm has paid out sums of money, made disbursements, for various purposes; *Bank:* **telegraphische A.,** telegraphic transfer, *U.S:* cable transfer (of money, etc.).

auszählen. I. *v.tr. sep.* **1.** (*a*) to count (thgs) out, over; **Stimmen a.,** to count votes; (*b*) to finish counting (sth., a number); (*c*) *abs. Rocketry: etc:* to count down. **2.** *Games:* to count out (players). **3.** *Box:* (*of boxer*) **ausgezählt werden,** to be counted out.

II. *vbl. s.* **1. Auszählen,** *n. in vbl senses.* **2. Auszählung,** *f. in vbl senses; also: Rocketry: etc:* count-down.

Auszählreim, *m. Games:* counting-out rhyme.

Auszahlungsschein, *m.* payment slip.

Auszahlungsstelle, *f.* paying office; office of payment.

auszanken, *v.sep.* **1.** *v.tr.* to scold (s.o.), to give (s.o.) a rating. **2.** *v.i.* (*haben*) to stop, cease (i) scolding, (ii) quarrelling.

auszehren, *v.tr. sep.* **1.** to consume; to emaciate, waste (body); to impoverish (country), to lay (country) waste, to ravage (country), to drain (country) of its strength; **ausgezehrter Körper,** wasted, emaciated, body; **von Krankheit ausgezehrt,** consumed, wasted, by disease; **auszehrende Krankheit,** consumptive disease. **2. Auszehrung** *f,* (*a*) wasting (away); *Med:* marasmus; (*b*) wasting disease; consumption; tabes; **sie starb an der A.,** she died of consumption.

Auszehrungskraut, *n. F:* medicinal infusion of herbs, *esp.* of lungwort.

auszeichnen. I. *v.tr. sep.* **1.** (*a*) to mark (sth.) out (for special attention); to blaze (trees); *A:* to mark, note, make a note of (passage in book, etc.); (*b*) *Com:* **Waren a.,** to put the price on articles, to mark (the price of) articles. **2.** (*a*) (*of pers.*) to mark (sth.); to emphasize (sth.); to make (sth.) stand out; to distinguish (sth.) (by sth.); *Print:* to display (words) in bold type; (*b*) to distinguish (s.o., sth.); **Höflichkeit und Hilfsbereitschaft zeichneten sie aus,** they were distinguished by, were outstanding for, their good manners and helpfulness; (*c*) **sich a.,** to distinguish oneself; **er wird sich (im Leben) a.,** he will distinguish himself, will make his mark (in life); **sie haben sich in mancher Schlacht ausgezeichnet,** they have distinguished themselves in many a battle; **sich durch seine Talente, seine Tapferkeit, usw., a.,** to distinguish oneself, be distinguished, by one's talents, courage, etc.; **sich (unter anderen, vor anderen) durch eine gewisse Eigenschaft a.,** to be outstanding, remarkable, for a certain quality; **sich im Klavierspielen, usw., a.,** to distinguish oneself at playing the piano, etc.; **seine Herrschaft zeichnete sich durch geschickte Handelspolitik aus,** his reign was distinguished, characterized, by a clever economic policy; **das Buch zeichnet sich durch eine besondere Ideenarmut aus,** the book is conspicuous for its singular paucity of ideas. **3. j-n a.,** to confer an honour on s.o.; to honour s.o.; to single s.o. out for distinction; **j-n mit einer Medaille a.,** to award a medal to s.o., to decorate s.o.; **j-n mit einem Preis a.,** to award a prize to s.o. **4.** to finish drawing (picture, etc.).

II. *vbl s.* **1. Auszeichnen,** *n. in vbl senses.* **2. Auszeichnung,** *f.* (*a*)=II. 1; *also: Com:* **verdeckte A.,** marking of price in code; (*b*) (mark of) distinction, honour; award; prize; decoration; *Sch:* **ein Examen mit A. bestehen,** to pass an examination with distinction; (*at university*) to obtain first class honours.

Auszeichnungsschrift, *f. Print:* bold type.

Auszeichnungszettel, *m. Com:* price ticket, price tag.

ausziehbar, *a.* (*a*) extractable; pull out (slide, tray, seat, etc.); (*b*) extensible; **ausziehbare Leiter, ausziehbares Stativ,** extension ladder, tripod, telescopic ladder, tripod.

ausziehen, *v.sep.* (*strong*) I. *v.tr.* **1.** (*a*) to pull out (hair, feathers, etc.); to draw, pull out, extract (tooth); to draw (nail); to remove, extract (thorn, splinter); to pull (turnips, etc.); to pull up (plants); *Ven:* **einen Vogel a.,** to draw a bird; (*b*) to extract (essence, chemical, etc.); (*of chemical, light, etc.*) to remove, take out (colour, etc.); (*c*) **ein Buch a., Stellen aus einem Buch a.,** to take, extract, passages from a book, to make extracts, excerpts, from a book; **aus einem Buche das Wesentliche a.,** to extract the essential passages from a book; *Com:* **ein Konto a.,** to make an abstract of an account; to draw up a statement of account; (*d*) *Mth:* to extract (root of number). **2.** (*a*) to take off (clothes); **er hat seinen Pullover ausgezogen,** he took off his pullover; **j-m die Schuhe, den Mantel, usw., a.,** to take off s.o.'s shoes, coat, etc.; *F:* **die Kinderschuhe a.,** to leave one's childhood behind, to grow up; *see also* **Adam 1;** (*b*) to undress (s.o.); **sich a.,** to undress (oneself), to get undressed, to take off one's clothes; **sich ganz a.,** to undress completely, to take off all one's clothes, to strip; **j-n (ganz, bis aufs Hemd) a.,** (i) to take off all s.o.'s clothes, to strip s.o.; (ii) *F:* to strip s.o. of all he has, to fleece s.o. **3.** (*a*) to pull out (drawer, extension piece, etc.); **ein Fernrohr a.,** to extend a telescope; **einen Tisch a.,** to pull out the draw-leaf of a table; (*b*) *Metall:* to draw (out) (metal); to draw (wire). **4.** to ink in (drawing); to draw in (line); **ausgezogene Linie,** unbroken line, continuous line (*not dotted*).

II. **ausziehen,** *v.i.* (*sein*) (*a*) to set out, set off; **in den Krieg a.,** to go off to war; **auf die Wanderschaft a.,** to set out, off, to start out, on one's travels (*usu. on foot*); to take the road; **zur Jagd a.,** to set out, off, to start out, for the hunt; (*b*) to move (out); to leave; **sie sind letzte Woche ausgezogen,** they moved out (of the house) last week; **aus einer Wohnung a.,** to move out of a flat, *U.S:* apartment.

III. *vbl s.* **Ausziehen,** *n. in vbl senses; also:* extraction (of tooth, splinter, essence, etc.); extension (of telescope, etc.). *Cp.* **Auszug.**

Auszieher, *m.* (*device*) extractor.

Ausziehfeder, *f. Draw:* drawing-pen, ruling-pen.

Ausziehgleis, *n. Rail:* turn-out track, draw-out track.

Ausziehleiter, *f.* extension ladder, extending ladder.

Ausziehplatte, *f.* draw-leaf (of table); pull-out leaf *or* slide (of desk, etc.).

Ausziehrohr, *n.* telescopic tube.

Ausziehschacht, *m. Min:* upcast (shaft).

Ausziehsitz, *m.* pull-out seat.

Ausziehtisch, *m. Furn:* draw-leaf table, draw table, pull-out table.

Ausziehtusche, *f.* drawing ink, Indian ink; waterproof ink.

auszieren, *v.tr. sep.* to adorn, decorate, deck out (room, etc.); **einen Saal mit Blumen a.,** to deck out, decorate, a room with flowers; **Auszierung** *f,* adornment, decoration, ornamentation (of room, etc.).

auszimmern, *v.tr. sep.* to timber, line (mine shaft, etc.).

auszirkeln, *v.tr. sep.* to measure (sth.) off with dividers; to mark (sth.) out with compasses.

auszischen, *v.tr. sep.* to hiss, boo, (at) (actor, play, etc.), *F:* to give (actor, play) the bird.

Auszug, *m.* **1.** (*a*) departure; **A. zur Jagd,** setting out for the hunt; **A. des Heeres in den Krieg,** taking of the field by the army; (*b*) *Swiss:* first

age-group of men liable for military service; (c) removal, move, moving out (from house); **A. aus einem Land,** emigration, *Lit:* exodus, from a country; **der A. der Kinder Israels, der Israeliten,** the Exodus. **2.** pulling out; drawing (out); extraction. **3.** (a) draw-leaf (of table); pull-out leaf *or* slide (of desk, etc.); (b) drawer; (c) *Bak:* draw-plate. **4.** *Ecc. Art:* superstructure of a Gothic carved altar. **5.** (a) *Ch: Ind: etc:* essence; extract; (b)=**Auszugmehl**; (c) excerpt, extract (from book, document, etc.); abstract, statement (of account); **er hat mir den Brief nur im A. mitgeteilt,** he told me only the gist of the letter; **Auszüge aus Cäsar,** extracts, excerpts, from Caesar; (d) *Mus:* arrangement (of orchestral *or* choral composition) (for piano); (e)=**Altenteil** 1.

Auszügler, *m.* -s/-. **1.** *Austrian: Swiss:* man in the first age-group of those liable for military service. **2.** *Swiss:*=**Altenteiler.**

Auszugmehl, *n.* superfine flour.

Auszugshieb, *m.*=**Aushieb.**

Auszugsofen, *m. Bak:* draw-plate oven.

auszugsweise, *a. & adv.* in extracts; **einen Artikel a. wiedergeben,** to reproduce an extract, extracts, from an article.

auszupfen, *v.tr. sep.* to pluck out (hair, etc.); to pluck (eyebrows); to pluck off (petals, etc.); to pull off (fly's leg, etc.); *Tex:* to pick (wool).

auszwicken, *v.tr. sep.* **1.** to pull (sth.) out with pincers *or* tweezers. **2.** *Constr:* to fill in the interstices in (rubble-work) with small stones.

Autarch [au'tarç], *m.* -en/-en, autarch, autocrat.

autark [au'tark], *a. Pol.Ec:* economically self-sufficient (state).

Autarkie [autar'kiː], *f.* -/-n [-'kiːən]. *Pol.Ec:* autarky; national, economic, self-sufficiency.

autarkisch [au'tarkiʃ], *a.*=**autark.**

auteln, *v.i.* (*haben*) *A:* to motor.

Authentie [autɛn'tiː], *f.* -/. authenticity, genuineness.

authentifizieren [autɛnti·fi·'tsiːrən], *v.tr.*=**authentisieren.**

authentisch [au'tɛntiʃ], *a.* (a) authentic, genuine; **authentischer Text,** authentic text (of document, etc.); authoritative text (of literary work, etc.); **ein Bild, ein Dokument, usw., als a. erweisen,** to authenticate, prove the authenticity of, a picture, a document, etc.; **authentisch,** *adv.* authentically, genuinely; **wir haben es von authentischer Seite,** we have it on reliable, good, authority; (b) *Ecc.Mus:* **authentische Tonart,** authentic mode; **authentische Kadenz, authentischer Schluß,** authentic cadence.

authentisieren [autɛnti·'ziːrən], *v.tr.* to authenticate; to certify, legalize (document, etc.).

Authentizität [autɛnti·tsi·'tɛːt], *f.* -/. authenticity, genuineness.

authigen [auti·'geːn], *a. Geol:* authigenic.

Autismus [au'tismus], *m.* -/. *Psy:* autism.

Autler, *m.* -s/-. *A:* motorist.

Auto ['auto:], *n.* -s/-s, (=**Automobil**) (motor-)car, *U.S:* automobile, *A. & U.S:* auto; **A. fahren,** to drive a car; to travel by car, by road; to motor; **sie fahren immer im A.,** they always travel, go, by car, by road; **im A. nach Paris fahren,** to drive, motor, to Paris; **wir werden mit dem A. kommen,** we'll come by car, by road; we'll drive over; **ich kam im A.,** I came by car, in the car, by road; **wir haben uns verspätet, wir müssen ein A. nehmen, in einem A. fahren,** we're late, we shall have to take a taxi, to go by taxi.

auto-, Auto-¹, *pref.* (a) auto-; **autogen,** autogenous; **autochthon,** autochthonous; **Autohypnose** *f*, autohypnosis; **Autokatalyse** *f*, autocatalysis; **autokephal,** autocephalous; **Automobil** *n*, automobile; (b) auto-, self-; **Autogamie** *f*, autogamy; self-fertilization; **automatisch,** automatic, self-acting; **Autotomie** *f*, autotomy, self-amputation.

Auto-², *comb.fm.* (=**Automobil-**) motor . . . ; motor-; car; motoring . . . ; **Autofahrer** *m*, motorist; car-driver; **Autoindustrie** *f*, motor industry, car industry; **Autoschule** *f*, motor-school, school of motoring; **Autostraße** *f*, motor-road; **Autounfall** *m*, motor(ing) accident, car accident.

Autoausstellung, *f.* motor show.

Autobahn, *f.* motorway, motor-road (for fast traffic); autobahn; *U.S:* freeway, throughway.

Autobesitzer, *m. F:* car-owner.

Autobiograph [auto·bi·o·'graf], *m.* -en/-en, autobiographer.

Autobiographie [auto·bi·o·gra·'fiː, 'auto·bi·o·gra·fiː], *f.* -/-n [-'fiːən], autobiography.

autobiographisch [auto·bi·o·'graːfiʃ], *a.* autobiographic(al).

Autobox ['auto·boks], *f.* lock-up (in a garage).

Autobrille, *f.* motoring goggles.

Autobus ['auto·bus], *m.* -busses/-busse, (motor-) bus; (motor) coach; **wir fuhren dorthin mit dem A., im A.,** we went there by bus *or* by coach.

Autobushaltestelle, *f.* bus stop; coach stop.

Autocar ['auto·kaːr], *m.* -s/-s. *Swiss:*=**Autobus.**

Autochrom [auto·'kroːm], *n.* -s/-e. *Phot:* autochrome.

Autochromie [auto·kro·'miː], *f.* -/. *Phot:* autochrome process.

Autochromplatte, *f. Phot:* autochrome plate.

Autochromverfahren, *n. Phot:* autochrome process.

autochthon [autox'toːn], *a.* autochthonous, autochthonal; aboriginal (race).

Autochthone [autox'toːnə], *m.* -n/-n, autochthon; **die Autochthonen,** the autochthons; the aborigines.

Autodafé [auto·da·'feː], *n.* -s/-s, auto-da-fé.

Autodidakt [auto·di·'dakt], *m.* -en/-en, autodidact, self-educated man.

Autodidaktentum [auto·di·'daktəntuːm], *n.* -s/. self-education.

autodidaktisch [auto·di·'daktiʃ], *a.* self-taught (knowledge, etc.).

Autodroschke, *f.* taxi(-cab), *U.S: & F:* cab.

Autodyn- [auto·'dyːn-], *comb.fm. W.Tel:* autodyne (reception, etc.).

Autodynempfänger, *m. W.Tel:* autodyne.

Autoempfänger, *m.* car radio (receiver).

Autoerotik [auto·ºe·'roːtik], *f. Psy:* auto-eroticism.

autoerotisch [auto·ºe·'roːtiʃ], *a. Psy:* auto-erotic.

Autofähre, *f.* (boat) car-ferry.

Autofahren, *n.* motoring; driving.

Autofahrer, *m.* motorist; car-driver.

Autofahrschule, *f.* motor-school, school of motoring, driving school.

Autofahrt, *f.* journey, trip, by car; drive; car ride, motor ride; **eine A. machen,** to go on a trip by car; to go for a drive.

Autofalle, *f. Aut:* speed-trap, police trap.

Autofriedhof, *m.* car dump.

Autoführer, *m.* taxi-driver, *U.S:* cabdriver; bus-driver; chauffeur (of private *or* hired car).

Autogamie [auto·ga·'miː], *f.* -/-n [-'miːən]. *Bot:* autogamy; *Biol: Bot:* self-fertilization.

autogamisch [auto·'gaːmiʃ], *a. Bot:* self-fertilizing (plant).

Autogarage, *f. Aut:* garage.

autogen [auto·'geːn], *a.* autogenous; **autogene Schweißung,** autogenous, (oxy-)acetylene, welding; *adv.* **a. schweißen,** to weld with acetylene.

Autogenapparat, *m.* (oxy-)acetylene welder.

Autogenese [auto·ge·'neːzə], *f.* -/. *Biol:* autogeny.

Autogiro [auto·'ʒiːro:], *n.* -s/-s. *Av:* autogyro, autogiro.

Autognosie [auto·gno·'ziː], *f.* -/. autognosis, self-knowledge.

Autogramm [auto·'gram], *n.* -(e)s/-e, autograph.

Autogrammjäger, *m.* autograph hunter.

Autograph [auto·'graf]. **1.** *m.* -en/-en, copying machine. **2.** *n.* -(e)s/-e & -e, autograph.

Autographie [auto·gra·'fiː], *f.* -/-n [-'fiːən]. **1.** *Lith:* autography, autolithography. **2.** *Med:* autographism; dermographia.

autographieren [auto·gra·'fiːrən], *v.tr. Lith:* to autograph (manuscript, etc.), to reproduce (manuscript, etc.) by autography.

autographisch [auto·'graːfiʃ], *a.* **1.** autographic (letter, etc.). **2.** (manuscript, etc.) reproduced by autography; autographic (ink, paper, etc.).

Autogravüre [auto·gra·'vyːrə], *f.* -/-n. *Phot.Engr:* autogravure.

Autogyro [auto·'ʒyːro:], *n.* -s/-s=**Autogiro.**

Autohalle, *f. Aut:* garage.

Autohaltestelle, *f.* (a) waiting-point (for cars); (b) taxi-rank, cab-rank, *U.S:* cabstand, taxi stand.

Autohändler, *m.* car dealer, *U.S:* automobile dealer.

Autoindustrie, *f.* motor industry, car industry, *U.S:* automotive industry.

Autoinfektion [auto·infɛktsi·'oːn], *f.* -/-en. *Med:* auto-infection.

Autointoxikation [auto·intoksi·ka·tsi·'oːn], *f.* -/-en. *Med:* auto-intoxication.

Autokarte, *m.* road map.

Autokartograph [auto·karto·'graf], *m.* -en/-en. *Surv:* stereoautograph.

autokephal [auto·ke·'faːl], *a.* autocephalous (church, etc.).

Autokino, *n.* drive-in cinema.

Autoklav [auto·'klaːf], *m.* -(e)s/-en [-s, -'klaːvəs/ 'klaːvən]. *Ch: Ind:* autoclave.

Autökologie [autºø·ko·lo·'giː], *f.* -/. *Bot:* autecology.

Autokrat [auto·'kraːt], *m.* -en/-en, autocrat.

Autokratie [auto·kra·'tiː], *f.* -/-n [-'tiːən], autocracy.

Autokratin [auto·'kraːtin], *f.* -/-innen, autocratrix.

autokratisch [auto·'kraːtiʃ], *a.* autocratic; *adv.* autocratically.

Autokrator [auto·'kraːtor], *m.* -s/-en [-kra·'toːrən], (esp. of Byzantine Emperor) autocrat(or).

Autolyse [auto·'lyːzə], *f.* -/. *Physiol:* autolysis.

autolytisch [auto·'lyːtiʃ], *a. Physiol:* autolytic.

Automat [auto·'maːt], *m.* -en/-en. **1.** automaton; mechanical figure. **2.** (a) *Mec.E: etc:* automatic, self-acting, machine *or* device; automatic mechanism; (b) *Com: etc:* (coin-in-the-)slot machine; automatic sales machine; vending machine; (c)=**Musikautomat;** (d)=**Spielautomat.**

Automatenrestaurant [auto·'maːtənresto·ˌrãː], *n.* self-service restaurant (with slot-machines); *U.S:* automat.

Automatenstahl, *m. Metall:* free cutting steel, free machining steel.

Automatie [auto·ma·'tiː], *f.* automatic action (of pers., *Physiol:* of organ).

Automatik [auto·'maːtik], *f.* -/-en. **1.** theory *or* science of automatic devices. **2.** *Mec.E:* automatic mechanism; automatic working.

Automation [auto·ma·tsi·'oːn], *f.* -/. *Ind:* automation.

automatisch [auto·'maːtiʃ], *a.* automatic (action, apparatus, etc.); self-acting (apparatus, etc.); mechanical (action by pers.); *adv.* automatically; (of pers.) **etwas a. tun,** to do sth. automatically, mechanically; **es geschieht a.,** it happens automatically.

automatisieren [auto·ma·ti·'ziːrən], *v.tr.* to automatize, mechanize (process, etc.); **Automatisierung** *f*, automatization, mechanization; *Ind:* automation.

Automatismus [auto·ma·'tismus], *m.* -/-men. *Med: Phil: Psychics:* automatism.

Automechaniker, *m.* car mechanic, *U.S:* automobile mechanic.

Automobil [auto·mo·'biːl], *n.* -(e)s/-e, (motor-)car, *esp. U.S:* automobile. *Cp.* **Auto.**

Automobilausstellung, *f.* motor show.

Automobilbau, *m. Ind:* car manufacturing, *U.S:* automobile manufacturing.

Automobilismus [auto·mo·bi·'lismus], *m.* -/. motoring.

Automobilist [auto·mo·bi·'list], *m.* -en/-en, motorist, *U.S: F:* autoist.

Automolit [auto·mo·'liːt], *m.* -(e)s/-e. *Miner:* automolite; gahnite.

automorph [auto·'morf], *a.*=**idiomorph.**

autonom [auto·'noːm], *a.* autonomous, self-governing; independent (state).

Autonomie [auto·no·'miː], *f.* -/-n [-'miːən], autonomy, self-government; independence.

Autonomist [auto·no·'mist], *m.* -en/-en, autonomist.

autonym [auto·'nyːm], *a.* (book) written by an author under his own name.

Autoparkplatz, *m. Aut:* car-park, *U.S:* parking lot.

Autopilot, *m. Av:* autopilot.

Autoplastik [auto·'plastik], *f.* -/-en. *Surg:* autoplasty.

autoplastisch [auto·'plastiʃ], *a. Surg:* autoplastic (graft, etc.).

Autopsie [auto·psiː], *f.* -/-n [-'psiːən], autopsy; *Med:* post-mortem (examination); autopsy.

Autor ['autor], *m.* -s/-en [au'toːrən], author; writer; maker (of a work of art).

Autoradio, *n.* car radio.

Autoreifen, *m.* car tyre.

Autoreiseführer, *m.* motoring guide, guide for motorists; road-book.

Autorenhonorar, *n. Publ:* (author's) royalty, royalties.

Autor(en)korrektur, *f. Print:* (a) correction (of proof) by the author; (b) (on proof) author's (i) correction, (ii) coll. corrections; (c) author's copy (of proof).

Autorennbahn, *f.* motor-racing track, car-racing track.

Autorennen, *n.* (a) motor-, car-racing; (b) motor-, car-race.

Autoreparatur, *f.* **1.** motor repairs, car repairs. **2.** motor, car, repair shop.

Autorisation [auto·ri·za·tsi·'oːn], *f.* -/-en, authorization.

autorisieren [auto·ri·'ziːrən], *v.tr.* to authorize (sth., s.o., to do sth.); **autorisierte Übersetzung,**

authorized translation; official translation; **Autorisierung** *f*, authorization.
autoritär [auto·ri·ˈtɛːr], *a.* authoritarian (state, régime, etc.).
Autorität [auto·ri·ˈtɛːt], *f.* **-/-en,** authority; (*a*) **die A. des Staates,** the authority of the State; **die A. der Eltern,** parental authority; **etwas aus eigener A. tun,** to do sth. on one's own authority, on one's own responsibility; **Körperschaft, die genügend A. genießt, um zu . . . ,** body with adequate authority to . . . , body competent to . . . ; **die A. wahren,** to maintain one's authority; to keep discipline; (*b*) **eine A. auf dem Gebiet des, der . . . sein,** to be an authority on . . . ; **er ist eine A. auf seinem Gebiet,** he is an authority in his field; **Autoritäten anführen,** to cite authorities; (*c*) **die Autoritäten (einer Stadt, usw.),** the authorities (of a town, etc.).
autoritativ [auto·ri·ta·ˈtiːf], *a.* authoritative.
Autorrecht, *n. Publ:* author's rights.
Autorschaft, *f.* -/. authorship.
Autosattler, *m.* car upholsterer.
Autosattlerei, *f.* **1.** (*trade*) car upholstery. **2.** car upholsterer's workshop.
Autoschau, *f.* motor show.
Autoschlepp, *m. Av:* catapulting (of glider) by towing vehicle and cable.
Autoschlosser, *m.* car mechanic, *U.S:* automobile mechanic.
Autoschuppen, *m.* car shed, *U.S:* automobile shed; shed used as a garage; carport.
Autosemantikon [auto·ze·ˈmanti·kon], *n.* **-s/-ka.** *Ling:* autosemanteme.
autosemantisch [auto·ze·ˈmantiʃ], *a. Ling:* autosemantic.
Autoskopie [auto·sko·ˈpiː], *f.* -/-n. *Med:* autoscopy.
Autosport, *m.* (*a*) motoring; (*b*) motor-, car-racing.
Autostopp, *m. F:* hitch-hiking; **mit, per, A. fahren,** to hitch-hike.
Autostraße, *f.* motor-road.
Autostunde, *f.* **zwei Autostunden entfernt,** two hours by car, two hours' drive away.
Autosuggestion [auto·zugɛstĭˈoːn], *f.* **-/-en,** autosuggestion.
autosuggestiv [auto·zugɛsˈtiːf], *a.* autosuggestive.
Autotaxe [ˈauto·taksə], *f.* **-/-n,** taxi, *U.S:* cab.
Autotechnik, *f.* automobile, motor, *U.S:* automotive, engineering.
Autotomie [auto·to·ˈmiː], *f.* **-/-n** [-ˈmiːən]. *Nat. Hist:* autotomy, self-amputation.
Autotoxin [auto·toˈksiːn], *n.* **-(e)s/-e.** *Med: Physiol:* autotoxin.
autotroph [auto·ˈtroːf], *a. Bot:* autotrophic (plant).
Autotypie [auto·ty·ˈpiː], *f.* **-/-n** [-ˈpiːən]. *Print:* autotype; half-tone reproduction.
Autounfall, *m.* motor(ing) accident, car accident.
Autovakzin [auto·vakˈtsiːn], *n. Med:* autovaccine.
Autovermietung, *f.* **1.** hiring (out), *U.S:* renting, of cars. **2.** car hire, *U.S:* car rental, service *or* firm.
autoxydabel [autˀoksy·ˈdaːbəl], *a. Ch:* autoxidizable.
autsch, *int.* (*indicating pain*) ouch!
autumnal [autumˈnaːl], *a.* autumnal.
Auwald, *m. Ph.Geog:* low-lying (deciduous) forest.
auweh [auˈveː], **auweih** [auˈvai], *int.* (*a*) (*indicating pain*) ouch! (*b*) (*dismay*) oh lord!
Auxanometer [auksa·no·ˈmeːtər], *n.* **-s/-.** *Bot:* auxanometer.
auxiliar [auksilĭˈaːr], *a.,* **Auxiliar-,** *comb.fm.* auxiliary (forces, troops, etc.); assistant (bishop, etc.).
Auxiliarbischof, *m. Ecc:* assistant bishop.
Auxiliartruppen, *f.pl. Mil:* auxiliary troops, auxiliaries.
Auxiliarverb, *n. Gram:* auxiliary verb.
Auxin [auˈksiːn], *n.* **-s/-e.** *Bot:* auxin.
auxochrom [aukso·ˈkroːm], *a. Bot:* auxochromic.
Auxospore [aukso·ˈʃpoːrə], *f. Algae:* auxospore.
Aval [aˈval], *m.* **-(e)s/-e.** *Fin:* guarantee, surety (for a bill); **A. geben,** to stand security, surety (for a bill, etc.).
Avalbürge, Avalgeber, *m.*=**Avalist.**
avalieren [avaˈliːrən], *v.tr. Fin:* to guarantee, back (a bill); to stand security, surety (for a bill, etc.).
Avalist [avaˈlist], *m.* **-en/-en.** *Fin:* guarantor, backer (of a bill); acceptor for honour, acceptor supra protest.
Avalkredit, *m. Fin:* credit secured by a bank guarantee.
Avance [aˈvãːsə], *f.* **-/-n. 1.** advance; lead; advantage. **2. j-m Avancen machen,** to make approaches, advances, to s.o.; to make up to s.o. **3.** *Fin: etc:* advance (of funds). **4.** gain(ing), going faster (of watch, clock); (*on regulator of watch*) **'Avance',** 'gain', 'fast'. **5.** *Agr:* differential per kilo live weight between buying price and selling price (of cattle).
Avancement [avã·səˈmãː], *n.* **-s/-s,** promotion, preferment, advancement; *Mil: A:* promotion.
avancieren [avã·ˈsiːrən]. **1.** *v.i.* (*sein*) (*a*) to advance; to move forward; (*b*) to advance, be promoted (in a service); **zum Hauptmann a.,** to be promoted captain. **2.** *v.tr.* **eine Taschenuhr a.,** (i) to make a watch go faster, (ii) to put a watch on, forward.
Avantage [avã·ˈtaːʒə], *f.* **-/-n,** advantage.
Avantageur [avã·ta·ˈʒøːr], *m.* **-s/-s & -e.** *Mil: A:* ensign.
Avantgarde [avã·ˈgardə], *f.* **-/-n.** *Mil: A:* advanced guard; *F:* vanguard.
Avantgardist [avã·garˈdist], *m.* **-en/-en,** person in the vanguard (of movement); avant-garde artist, avantgardist.
avantgardistisch [avã·garˈdistiʃ], *a.* avant-garde (artist, work, etc.).
Avanturin [avantu·ˈriːn], *m.* **-(e)s/-e=Aventurin.**
Avarie [a·va·ˈriː], *f.* **-/-n** [-ˈriːən]=**Havarie.**
Avatara [a·va·ˈtaːraː], *f,* **-/-.** *Hindu Rel:* avatar.
Ave [ˈaːveː], *n.* **-/- & -s/-s.** *Ecc: etc:* (*a*) Ave; (*b*)=**Ave-Maria;** (*c*)=**Ave-Läuten.**
avec, avek[1] [aˈvɛk], *adv. F:* **er war (mit) a.,** he had a lady, a girl, with him.
Avec, Avek[2], *m.* **-s/.** *F:* mettle, go, dash; **er hat A.,** he has plenty of go in him; he is game (for anything).
Ave-Läuten, *n. Ecc:* ave-bell; angelus.
Ave-Maria [ˈaːve·ma·ˈriːaː], *n.* **-/- & -s/-s.** *Ecc:* Ave Maria, Hail Mary; **drei Ave-Maria(s),** three Aves, three Ave Marias, three Hail Maries.
Aventin, der [a·vɛnˈtiːn], **-s.** *Geog:* the Aventine.
aventinisch [a·vɛnˈtiːniʃ], *a.* **der Aventinische Hügel,** the Aventine (Hill).
Aventiure [a·vɛnˈtyːrə], *f.* **-/-n.** *Mediev:* (*a*) adventure; **Frau A.,** the Muse of narrative poetry; (*b*) chapter, section (of epic, romance).
Aventüre [avã·ˈtyːrə], *f.* **-/-n,** adventure; venture.
Aventurin [aventu·ˈriːn], *m.* **-(e)s/-e.** *Miner:* aventurine.
Aventurinfeldspat, *m. Miner:* aventurine sunstone.
Aventuringlas, *n. Glassm:* aventurine (glass); gold flux.
Avenue [avəˈnyː], *f.* **-/-n** [-ˈnyːən], avenue.
Averbo [aˈvɛrboː], *n.* **-s/-s & -/-.** *Gram:* principal parts (of a verb); **das A. von** *fero* **sagen,** to give the principal parts of *fero*.
Averner [aˈvɛrnər], *inv.a. Geog:* **der A. See,** Lake Averno.
Avernus [aˈvɛrnus]. *Pr.n.m.* **-'.** *A.Geog: Myth:* Avernus.
Averroës [aˈvɛro·eːs]. *Pr.n.m.* **-'.** *Hist:* Aver-r(h)oes.
Averroismus [a·vɛro·ˈismus], *m.* -/. *Hist. of Phil:* Averr(h)oism.
Avers [a·ˈvɛrs], *m.* **-es/-e** [a·ˈvɛrzəs/a·ˈvɛrzə]. **1.** *Num:* obverse (of coin). **2.** *Fin:* settlement (of claim).
Aversalsumme [a·vɛrˈzaːl-], *f. Com: Fin:* lump sum paid in settlement (of a claim).
Aversion [a·vɛrzĭˈoːn], *f.* **-/-en,** aversion **(gegen,** to, for); dislike **(gegen,** for, of).
Aversionalkauf [a·vɛrzĭo·ˈnaːl-], *m. Com: Fin:* purchase for a lump sum.
Aversionalquantum, *n.,* **Aversionalsumme,** *f.,* **Aversum** [a·ˈvɛrzum], *n.* **-s/-sa=Aversalsumme.**
avertieren [avɛrˈtiːrən], *v.tr.* to advise, notify (s.o.); to warn (s.o.).
Avertissement [avɛrtisəˈmãː], *n.* **-s/-s,** advice, notification; warning.
Aviatik [avĭˈaːtik], *f.* -/. aviation.
Aviatiker [avĭˈaːtikər], *m.* **-s/-,** aviator.
Avidität [avi·di·ˈtɛt], *f.* **-/-en,** avidity, greed(iness).
avirulent [a·vi·ru·ˈlɛnt], *a. Med:* avirulent, non-pathogenic (disease).
Avis [aˈviː, aˈviːs], *m. & n.* **-es/-e** [aˈviːzəs/aˈviːzə]. *Com:* advice; notice; **laut A.,** as per advice; **bis auf weiteren A.,** till further notice; until you hear further.
Avisbrief, *m. Com:* advice-note, letter of advice.
avisieren [avi·ˈziːrən], *v.tr. Com: etc:* to advise, notify (s.o.); to give notice of (sth.); **eine Tratte a.,** to advise a draft.
Aviso[1] [aˈviːzoː], *n.* **-s/-s.** *Austrian:* **1.** *Com:*= **Avis. 2.** hint; warning.
Aviso[2] *m.* **-s/-s.** *Navy:* dispatch-boat, -vessel; advice-boat, aviso; sloop.
a vista [a ˈvistaː]. *Ital. adv.phr. Com:* at sight.
Avistawechsel, *m. Com:* sight bill.
Avitaminose [a·vi·ta·mi·ˈnoːzə], *f.* **-/-n.** *Med:* avitaminosis.
avivieren [avi·ˈviːrən], *v.tr.* to revive, brighten (colours, dyes).
Avocatobirne [avo·ˈkaːtoː-], *f. Bot:* avocado pear, alligator pear.
Avosette [avo·ˈzɛtə], *f.* **-/-n.** *Orn:* avocet, avoset.
avouieren [avu·ˈiːrən], *v.tr.* to confess, avow, admit; to acknowledge.
Avulsion [a·vulzĭ·ˈoːn], *f.* **-/-en.** *Jur:* avulsion (of land).
avunkular [a·vuŋku·ˈlaːr], *a. Breed:* avuncular (cross).
Avus, die [ˈaːvus], **-/.** (*abbr. of* **Auto-Verkehrs- und Übungsstraße)** the Avus speedway (outside Berlin).
Awaren [aˈvaːrən]. *Pr.n.pl. Ethn: Hist:* Avars.
Awesta, das [avɛˈstaː], **-.** *Ling:* the Avesta.
awestisch [aˈvɛstiʃ], *a. Ling:* Avestan, Avestic (language, etc.).
axial [aksĭˈaːl], *a.,* **Axial-,** *comb.fm.* axial; *adv.* axially; in the direction of the axis.
Axialbeanspruchung, *f.* axial stress.
Axialität [aksĭa·li·ˈtɛːt], *f.* **-/-en,** axiality.
Axialschub, *m. Mch: etc:* axial thrust.
Axialspiel, *n. Mec.E:* end-play.
Axialturbine, *f.* axial-flow turbine.
axillar [aksiˈlaːr], *a.,* **Axillar-,** *comb.fm. Biol: Nat.Hist:* axillary; *Biol:* **axillarer Strang,** notochord.
Axillarblüte, *f. Bot:* axillary flower.
Axinit [aksi·ˈniːt], *m.* **-(e)s/-e.** *Miner:* axinite.
Axiologie [aksĭo·lo·ˈgiː], *f.* **-/-n** [-ˈgiːən], science of values.
Axiolith [aksĭo·ˈliːt], *m.* **-(e)s/-e & -en/-en.** *Miner:* axiolite.
Axiom [aksĭˈoːm], *n.* **-(e)s/-e.** *Mth: Phil:* axiom.
Axiomatik [aksĭo·ˈmaːtik], *f.* -/. science *or* study of axioms.
axiomatisch [aksĭo·ˈmaːtiʃ], *a.* axiomatic(al).
Axiometer [aksĭo·ˈmeːtər], *n.* **-s/-.** *Nau:* helm indicator, steering indicator, tell-tale.
Axis [ˈaksis], *m.* **-/-, Axishirsch,** *m. Z:* axis, hog-deer.
Axolotl [akso·ˈloːtəl], *m.* **-s/-.** *Amph:* axolotl.
Axonometrie [akso·no·me·ˈtriː], *f.* **-/-n** [-ˈtriːən], axonometry.
axonometrisch [akso·no·ˈmeːtriʃ], *a. Mechanical Draw:* **axonometrische Projektion,** axonometric projection.
Axt, *f.* **-/⸚e,** axe; **die Axt an die Wurzel eines Übels legen,** to set the axe to the root of an evil; **die Axt im Haus erspart den Zimmermann,** do your own odd jobs and save money; do it yourself; **der Axt den Stiel nachwerfen,** to throw the helve after the hatchet.
Äxtchen, *n.* **-s/-,** (*dim. of* **Axt)** small axe; hatchet, chopper.
Axteisen, *n.* axe-head.
Axtgesicht, *n. F:* hatchet-face; **ein Mann mit einem A.,** a hatchet-faced man.
Axthammer, *m. Tls:* axe-hammer.
Axthelm, *m.*=**Axtstiel.**
Äxtlein, *n.* **-s/-,** (*dim. of* **Axt)=Äxtchen.**
Axtstiel, *m.* handle, helve (of axe).
Aye-Aye [ˈaiˈai], *m.* **-s/-s.** *Z:* aye-aye.
Azalee [a·tsa·ˈleːə], **Azalie** [a·ˈtsaːlĭə], *f.* **-/-n.** *Bot:* azalea.
Azarolapfel [a·tsa·ˈroːl-], *m. Bot:* azarole, (fruit of the) Neapolitan medlar.
Azarolbaum, *m.,* **Azarolmispel,** *f. Bot:* Neapolitan medlar.
azeotrop [a·tse·o·ˈtroːp], *a. Ph.Ch:* azeotrope (mixture); constant boiling-point (mixture).
Azephale [a·tse·ˈfaːlə], *m.,* **azephalisch** [a·tse·ˈfaːliʃ], *a.*=**Akephale, akephalisch.**
Azerazeen [a·tse·ra·ˈtseːən], *f.pl. Bot:* aceraceae.
azerb [aˈtsɛrp], *a.* tart, sour, bitter.
Azerbation [a·tsɛrba·tsĭˈoːn], *f.* **-/-en,** (*a*) acerbating; (*b*) *Med:* aggravation, worsening (of disease).
azerbieren [a·tsɛrˈbiːrən], *v.tr.* to acerbate.
Azetal [a·tse·ˈtaːl], *n.* **-s/.** *Ch:* acetal.
Azetaldehyd [a·ˌtseːtaˈlde·ˈhyːt], *m.* **-(e)s/.** *Ch:* acetaldehyde.
Azetat [a·tse·ˈtaːt], *n.* **-(e)s/-e.** *Ch:* acetate.
Azetatlack, *m. Ind: Aut:* cellulose varnish.
Azetatseide, *f. Tex:* cellulose acetate, acetate silk.
Azetessigester [a·ˈtseːt-], *m. Ch:* acetoacetic ester.
Azetessigsäure, *f. Ch:* acetoacetic acid.
Azetimeter [a·tse·ti·ˈmeːtər], *n.* **-s/-.** *Ind:* acetimeter.
Azetolyse [a·tse·to·ˈlyːzə], *f.* **-/-n.** *Ch:* acetolysis.
Azetometer [a·tse·to·ˈmeːtər], *n.* **-s/-.** *Ind:* acetimeter.
Azeton [a·tse·ˈtoːn], *n.* **-s/.** *Ch:* acetone.
Azetsäure, *f. Ch:* acetic acid.
Azetyl [a·tse·ˈtyːl], *n.* **-s/.** *Ch:* acetyl.
Azetylen [a·tse·ty·ˈleːn], *n.* **-s/.** *Ch:* acetylene.
Azetylengas, *n.* oxyacetylene.
Azetylengebläse, *n.* acetylene blowpipe.

Azetylenlampe, *f.* acetylene lamp.

Azetylensauerstoffbrenner, *m.* oxyacetylene burner.

Azetylenschweißung, *f.* (oxy)acetylene welding.

Azetylsalizylsäure, *f. Ch:* acetylsalicylic acid; aspirin.

Azetylsäure, *f. Ch:* acetic acid.

Azetylzahl, *f. Ch: (in analysis)* acetyl number.

Azetylzellulose, *f. Ch: Tex:* cellulose acetate.

Azid [aˑˈtsiːt], *n.* -(e)s/-e [-ˈtsiːts, -ˈtsiːdəs/-ˈtsiːdə]. *Ch:* azide.

Azidation [aˑtsiˑdaˑtsiˈoːn], *f.* -/-en. *Ch:* acidification.

azidieren [aˑtsiˑˈdiːrən], *v.tr. Ch:* to acidify.

Azidität [aˑtsiˑdiˑˈtɛːt], *f.* -/. *Ch:* acidity.

Azidite [aˑtsiˑˈdiːtə], *m.pl. Geol:* acidic rocks.

Azidose [aˑtsiˑˈdoːzə], *f.* -/-n. *Med:* acidosis.

Azidoverbindungen [aˑˈtsiːdoˑ-], *f.pl. Ch:* diazo-compounds.

Azilien, das [aˑziˑliˈɛː], *n.* -s. *Prehist:* the Azilian period.

Azimut [aˑtsiˑˈmuːt], *m. & n.* -(e)s/-e. *Astr: Surv:* azimuth.

azimutal [aˑtsiˑmuˑˈtaːl], *a.* azimuthal.

Azimutkompaß, *m.* azimuth compass.

azinös [aˑtsiˑˈnøːs], *a.* acinose, acinous (gland).

Azo- [ˈaːtsoˑ-], *pref. Ch:* azo-.

Azobenzol, *n. Ch:* azobenzene.

Azofarbe, *f.,* **Azofarbstoff,** *m. Ch: Ind:* azo dye.

Azoikum, das [aˑˈtsoːiˑkum], -s. *Geol:* the Azoic time.

azoisch [aˑˈtsoːiʃ], *a. Geol:* azoic.

Azolla [aˑˈtsolaː], *f.* -/-ollen. *Bot:* azolla.

Azoospermie [aˑtsoˑoˑspɛrˈmiː], *f.* -/. *Med: Physiol:* azoospermia, azoospermatism.

Azoren, die [aˑˈtsoːrən]. *Pr.n.f.pl. Geog:* the Azores.

Azot [aˑˈtsoːt], *n.* -(e)s/. *Ch: A:* nitrogen, *A:* azote.

Azotämie [aˑtsoˑtɛˈmiː], *f.* -/-n [-ˈmiːən]. *Med: Vet:* azotaemia.

azotisch [aˑˈtsoːtiʃ], *a. Ch: A:* nitrogenous, *A:* azotic.

Azotobakter [aˑtsoˑtoˑbakˈteːr], *m.* -s/-. *Bac:* azotobacter.

Azotogen [aˑtsoˑtoˑˈgeːn], *n.* -s/-e, nitrogenous fertilizer.

Azotometer [aˑtsoˑtoˑˈmeːtər], *n.* -s/-. *Ch:* azometer.

Azoxy- [aˑtsɔˈoksy-], *comb.fm. Ch:* azoxy-; **Azoxybenzol** *n,* azoxybenzene.

Azteke [atsˈteːkə], *m.* -n/-n. *Ethn: Hist:* Aztec.

Aztekenmöwe, *f. Orn:* laughing gull.

aztekisch [atsˈteːkiʃ], *a.* Aztecan, Aztec.

Azur [aˑˈtsuːr, ˈaːtsur], *m.* -s/-e. **1.** *(colour)* azure, sky-blue. **2.**=Azurstein.

azurblau. 1. *a.* azure. **2.** *s.* Azurblau, *n.* azure, sky-blue (colour).

Azureelinien [aˑtsuˑˈreː-], *f.pl.* blue lines (on ruled paper).

azur(e)n [aˑˈtsuːrn, ˈaːtsurn], *a.* azure.

azurieren [aˑtsuˑˈriːrən], *v.tr.* to blue; to tinge with blue; **azuriertes Papier,** blue-lined paper.

Azurit [aˑtsuˑˈriːt], *m.* -(e)s/-e. *Miner:* azurite, blue copper ore.

Azurstein, *m. Miner:* lapis-lazuli, azure-stone.

Azygospore [aˑˈtsyːgoˑ-], *f. Fung:* azygospore.

azyklisch [aˑˈtsyːkliʃ], *a. Ch: Opt: etc:* acyclic.

Azymon [ˈaːtsyˑmon], *n.* -s/-ma, azyme, unleavened bread.

B

B, b [beː], *n.* -/- (*in speech only* -s/-s [beːs]). **1.** (the letter) B, b; *Tp:* B wie Berta, B for Benjamin. **2.** *Mus:* (*a*) (the note) B flat, B♭; **B-dur, B-Dur, b-moll, b-Moll, (-Tonart),** (key of) B flat major, B flat minor; (*b*) ♭, flat, ♭; **ein ♭ vorschreiben, vorzeichnen,** to flatten (note), to mark (note) with a flat; **Tonart mit drei ♭s,** key with three flats. *See also List of Abbreviations.*

ba [ba], *int.* (i) (*expressing contempt*) bah, pooh; (ii) (*nursery language*) ugh! dirty!

bä [beː], *int.* (*bleat of sheep*) baa.

Baake, *f.* -/-n = Bake I.

Baal, *m.* -s/**Baalim.** *Rel.Hist:* Baal.

Baalsanbeter, *m.* Baalist; idolater.

Baalsdiener, *m.* Baalist; idolater.

Baalspriester, *m.* priest of Baal; *Pej:* false priest.

Baas, *m.* -es/-e. *Dial:* master, *F:* boss; *see also* **Heuerbaas, Schlafbaas.**

Baba, *f.* -/-s. *Cu:* baba.

Babakoto [ba·ba·'koːtoː], *m.* -s/-s. *Z:* babacoote, indri.

Babbelei, *f.* -/-en, babble, babbling.

babbelig, *a.* babbling; incoherent.

babbeln, *v.i.* (*haben*) to babble; to prattle.

Babbitmetall ['bɛbit-], *n. Metall:* white metal, Babbit metal, babbit; anti-friction metal.

Babbler, *m.* -s/-, babbler, chatterbox.

Babbser, *m.* -s/-. *Mil/F: A:* civilian, *F:* civvy.

Babe, Bäbe, *f.* -/-n. *Cu:* baba.

Babel ['baːbəl]. *Pr.n.n.* -s. *B.Hist:* Babel; **der Turm zu B.,** the Tower of Babel; *F:* **es war das reinste B.,** it was an absolute Babel.

Babette [ba·'bɛtə]. *Pr.n.f.* -s. Babs.

Babine [ba·'biːnə], *f.* -/-n, (*fur*) Russian cat-skin.

Babirussa [ba·bi·'rusaː], *m.* -s/-s. *Z:* babirussa, hog-deer, horned hog, Indian hog.

Babismus [ba·'bismus], *m.* -/. *Rel.Hist:* babism.

Babla(h) ['baːblaː], *m.* -/. *Bot: Dy:* babul, babool.

Babol ['baːbol], *m.* -/. = **Babul.**

Babu ['baːbuː, ba·'buː], *m.* -s/-s, baboo.

Babuin [ba·bu·'iːn], *m.* -s/-e. *Z:* cynocephalus, yellow baboon, dog-faced baboon.

Babul ['baːbul], *m.* -/. *Bot: Dy:* babul, babool.

Babulakazie, *f.,* **Babulbaum,** *m. Bot:* babul-tree, sant-tree.

Babulschote, *f. Bot: Dy:* sant-pod, garad.

Babusche [ba·'buʃə], *f.* -/-n. Turkish slipper, babouche.

Baby ['beːbiː & 'baːbiː], *n.* -s/-s & -bies, baby.

Babyausstattung, *f.* layette.

Babylon ['baːbyˌlon]. *Pr.n.n.* -s. Babylon.

Babylonien [ba·by·'loːnien]. *Pr.n.n.* -s. *A.Geog:* Babylonia.

Babylonier [ba·by·'loːniər], *m.* -s/-. Babylonian.

babylonisch [ba·by·'loːniʃ], *a.* Babylonian; **die Babylonische Gefangenschaft,** the Babylonian Captivity.

Babypuppe, *f.* baby doll.

Babysitter ['beːbiːˌsitər], *m.* -s/-, baby-sitter.

Baccarat [baka·'raː(t), 'baka·raː], *n.* -s/. = **Bakkarat.**

Bacchanal [baxa·'naːl, bakça·'naːl], *n.* -s/-ien & -e, (*a*) *Rom.Ant:* Bacchanal; **die Bacchanalien, the Bacchanalia;** (*b*) (*pl.* **Bacchanale**) Bacchanal, Bacchanalian feast, drunken revelry.

bacchanalisch [baxa·'naːliʃ, bakça·'naːliʃ], *a.* Bacchanalian.

Bacchant [ba·'xant, bak'çant], *m.* -en/-en. **1.** Bacchant; priest of Bacchus. **2.** *F: A:* wandering scholar.

Bacchantentanz, *m.* Bacchanal.

Bacchantin [ba·'xantin, bak'çantin], *f.* -/-innen. *Ant:* Bacchante, maenad.

bacchantisch [ba·'xantiʃ, bak'çantiʃ], *a.* Bacchic, Bacchanalian.

Baccheus [ba·'xeːus, bak'çeːus], *m.* -/-cheen [-'xeːən, -'çeːən] = **Bacchius.**

bacchisch ['baxiʃ, 'bakçiʃ], *a.* Bacchic, Bacchanalian.

Bacchius [ba·'xiːus, bak'çiːus], *m.* -/-chien [-'xiːən, -'çiːən]. *Pros:* bacchius.

Bacchus ['baxus, 'bakçus]. *Pr.n.m.* -'. *Myth:* Bacchus.

Bacchusdiener, *m.* son of Bacchus, Bacchant.

Bacchusdienerin, *f.* Bacchante, maenad.

Bacchusfest, *n.* Bacchanal.

Bach, *m.* -(e)s/⁼e, brook, (small) stream, streamlet; *Dial:* beck, burn; *F:* **es geht alles den B. hinunter,** it all goes down the drain; *F:* (*of child*) **einen B. machen,** to make water, *F:* to wee-wee: *Prov:* **viele Bäche machen einen Strom,** little streams make great rivers; many a little makes a mickle; *F:* many a mickle makes a muckle.

Bachamsel, *f. Orn:* water-ouzel, dipper.

Bachbunge, *f.,* **Bachbungenehrenpreis,** *m. Bot:* brooklime.

Bachburzel, *m.* -s/-. *Bot:* water purslane.

Bache, *f.* -/-n. *Ven:* (wild) sow.

Bacher, *m.* -s/-. *Ven:* young (wild) boar.

Bachforelle, *f. Ich:* brook trout.

Bachfrosch, *m. Amph:* common frog, grass-frog.

Bachfurche, *f.* = **Hohlweg.**

Bächlein, *n.* -s/-, brooklet, little brook, runnel; *F:* **ein B. machen,** (*of child*) to make water, to piddle, *F:* to wee-wee; (*of dog*) to make a puddle.

Bachminze, *f. Bot:* water mint.

Bachnelkenwurz, *f. Bot:* water avens.

Bachneunauge, *n. Ich:* brook-, creek-lamprey.

Bachsaibling, *m. Ich:* (i) common river trout, brook trout; (ii) **amerikanischer B.,** American brook trout, *U.S:* speckled trout.

Bachschisch ['bakʃiʃ], *n. & m.* -(es)/-e = **Bakschisch.**

Bachstelze, *f. Orn:* (white) wagtail; **gelbe B.,** blue-headed wagtail; **weiße B.,** white wagtail; **graue B.,** grey wagtail.

Bachulke [ba·'xulkə], *m.* -n/-n = **Pachulke.**

Bachweide, *f. Bot:* purple willow, rose-willow.

Bachweideneule, *f. Ent:* red underwing.

Back¹, *f.* -/-en & *n.* -(e)s/-e. **1.** *N.Arch:* forecastle, *F:* fo'c's'le; **halbe B.,** monkey forecastle, topgallant forecastle. **2.** mess-tin, -kettle; dixie, dixy. **3.** = **Backmannschaft. 4.** mess-table.

back², *adv. Nau:* (*of sail*) aback; **die Segel lagen b.,** the sails were aback; **die Segel b. bekommen,** to be caught, taken, aback; **alles b.,** all aback.

Bäck, *m.* -es/-e = **Bäcker.**

Backaroma, *n. Cu:* (aromatic) essence (for use in baking).

Backblech, *n. Cu:* baking-sheet; shallow baking-tin.

Backbord¹, *n. & m.* -(e)s/-e. *Nau: Av:* port (side), *A:* larboard.

backbord², *adv. Nau:* (to steer, etc.) to port.

Backbordbug, *m. Nau:* port bow; **über B. liegen,** to be on the port bow.

Backbordlaterne, *f. Nau:* port light.

Backbordwache, *f. Nau:* port watch.

backbrassen, *v.i.* (*haben*) & *tr.sep. Nau:* to brace aback.

Backbrett, *n. Cu:* pastry-board, paste-board.

Bäckchen, *n.* -s/-, (*dim. of* **Backe**) little cheek; **rote, rosige, Bäckchen,** rosy (little) cheeks (of child).

Backdeck, *n. Nau:* forecastle deck.

Backe, *f.* -/-n, *occ.* **Backen,** *m.* -s/-. **1.** (*a*) cheek; **mit dicken, runden, Backen,** with fat cheeks; **eine dicke, geschwollene, B. haben,** to have a swollen face; **er kaute auf beiden, mit vollen, Backen,** he munched (away) heartily; **mit vollen Backen blasen,** to blow with puffed-out cheeks; **ein Apfel mit roten Backen,** a rosy-cheeked apple; *F:* **au B.!** my eye! (*b*) *A:* jaw; (*c*) *pl.* **Backen,** buttocks; haunches (of animal). **2.** (*a*) side, wing (of arm-chair); *Sm.a:* cheek (of rifle-butt); (*b*) *Tchn:* (*usu.* **Backen** *m*) jaw (of vice, chuck, sliding callipers, etc.); shoe (of shoe-brake); cheek (of rail-chair); **Backen** *pl,* cheeks, side-pieces; *Nau:* cheeks, hounds (of mast); nose (of tongs, pliers, etc.); *Ski:* toe-irons (of binding).

Backen¹, *m.* -s/- *see* **Backe.**

backen², *v.* **1.** *v.tr.* (*p.t.* **buk & backte,** *p.p.* **gebacken**) (*a*) *Cu: etc:* to bake (bread, cake, soufflé, etc.); to cook (made-up dish, soufflé, etc.); to fry (fish, pancakes, doughnuts) (*usu. in deep fat*); to make (bread, cake, pancakes, etc.); **gebackener Fisch,** fried fish; **etwas bei mittlerer Hitze b.,** to bake, cook, sth. in a medium oven; **wir werden heute Brot, Kuchen, b.,** we are going to make, bake, bread, cakes *or* a cake, today; *abs.* **wir haben gestern gebacken,** we made cakes *or* a cake, etc., yesterday; (*in bakery*) we baked yesterday; (*b*) to burn, fire, bake, kiln (bricks, pottery, etc.). **2.** *v.i.* (*haben*) (*p.t.* **backte,** *p.p.* **gebacken**) (*of bread, cake, etc.*) to bake; to cook; **der Kuchen hat nicht lange genug gebacken,** the cake has not baked, cooked, long enough; **etwas eine halbe Stunde b. lassen,** to allow sth. to bake, cook, for half an hour. **3.** *v.i.* (*haben, sein*) (*p.t.* **backte,** *p.p.* **gebackt**) (*a*) (*of coal, snow, clay, etc.*) to cake; to stick (together); to form a mass; **backende Kohle,** caking coal; (*b*) **an etwas** *dat.* **b.,** to stick, cling, to sth.; **der Dreck backte an seinen Stiefeln,** the mud stuck to his boots.

Backenbart, *m.* (side-)whiskers, *U.S:* sideburns.

Backenbein, *n.* = **Backenknochen.**

Backenbindung, *f. Ski:* toe-iron binding.

Backenbohrer, *m. Mec.E:* hob(-tap), master-tap.

Backenbrecher, *m. Stonew:* jaw-breaker, jaw-crusher.

Backenbremse, *f. Veh:* shoe-brake; block brake.

Backenfeile, *f. Tls:* grooved file.

Backenfutter, *n. Mec.E:* jaw-chuck (of lathe, etc.).

Backenhobel, *m. Tls:* curved plane.

Backenhörnchen, *n. Z:* ground-squirrel, chipmunk.

Backenknochen, *m. Anat:* cheek-bone.

Backenquetscher, *m.* = **Backenbrecher.**

Backenriemen, *m. Harn:* cheek strap, cheek-piece (of bridle).

Backenschiene, *f. Rail:* main rail, line rail (at points); stock-rail.

Backensessel, *m. Furn:* grandfather chair, wing-chair, ear-chair.

Backenstein, *m.* cheek-stone (of a gutter).

Backenstreich, *m.* smack, slap, in the face.

Backenstück, *n. Harn:* = **Backenriemen.**

Backentasche, *f. Z:* cheek-pouch.

Backenzahn, *m. Anat:* molar (tooth), grinder; **kleiner, vorderer, B.,** premolar, bicuspid; **großer, hinterer, B.,** back tooth, molar.

Bäcker, *m.* -s/-, baker.

Bäckerbein, *n. Med:* baker's leg, knock-knee.

bäckerbeinig, *a. Med:* baker-legged, knock-kneed.

Bäckerbrot, *n.* bread baked at the baker's.

Bäckerbursche, *m.* = **Bäckerjunge.**

Bäckerei, *f.* -/-en. **1.** baker's trade, baking trade. **2.** bakery; (*a*) baker's shop; (*b*) bakehouse. **3.** *usu. pl.* **Bäckereien,** biscuits and cakes, etc.

Bäckerekzem, *n. Med:* baker's itch.

Bäckergeselle, *m.* journeyman baker.

Bäckergewerbe, *n.* = **Bäckerhandwerk.**

Bäckerhandwerk, *n.* baker's trade, bakery.

Bäckerjunge, *m.* baker's boy.

Bäckerkrätze, *f. Med:* baker's itch.

Bäckerladen, *m.* baker's shop.

Bäckermeister, *m.* master baker.

Bäckermützen, *f.pl. Nau: F:* white horses (on sea), skipper's daughters.

Backfett, *n. Cu:* cooking fat (*used for baking*).

Backfisch, *m.* **1.** *Cu:* fried fish. **2.** *F:* young girl; teenager.
Backfischalter, *n. F:* teens; age (of girls) between fourteen and seventeen years.
Backform, *f. Cu:* cake-tin, baking-tin.
Backgeld, *n.* price paid for having one's cake, etc., baked (at bakery).
Backgeschirr, *n. Nau:* mess kit, mess gear.
Backgeselle, *m. Nau:* messmate.
Backhähnchen, *n. Cu:* fried chicken.
Backhaube, *f. Dom.Ec:* Dutch oven (*for use on gas-stove*).
Backhaus, *n.* bakehouse.
Backhefe, *f.* baker's yeast.
backheiß, *a.* (tin, etc.) heated to baking temperature.
Backhendel, *n.* **-s/-(n).** *Austrian Dial:* fried chicken.
Backhitze, *f. Cu:* oven temperature, temperature required for baking.
Backhuhn, *n. Cu:* fried chicken.
-backig, -bäckig, *comb.fm. a.* -cheeked; **rotbackig,** red-, rosy-cheeked.
Backkohle, *f. Min:* soft, bituminous, coal; caking coal.
Backmannschaft, *f. Nau:* mess (party), group of sailors who mess together.
Backmulde, *f.* = **Backtrog.**
Backobst, *n.* dried fruit(s); *see also* **danken** I. 1(*a*).
Backöfel, *n.* **-s/-.** *Orn:* willow-warbler, -wren.
Backofen, *m.* (kitchen *or* baker's) oven; **dieses Zimmer ist wie ein B.,** this room is just like an oven.
Backofenstein, *m.* bakestone.
Backpfeife, *f.* smack, slap, in the face; **j-m eine B. geben, verabreichen,** to smack s.o.'s face.
Backpflaume, *f.* (dried) prune; dried plum.
Backprobe, *f.* sample of (s.o.'s) baking.
Backpulver, *n. Cu:* baking-powder.
Backpulverteig, *m. Cu:* baking-powder dough.
Backrädchen, *n. Cu:* pastry-wheel, pastry-cutter.
Backröhre, *f.* kitchen oven.
Backschaft, *f.* **-/-en** = **Backmannschaft.**
Backschafter, *m.* **-s/-.** *Nau:* (ship's) cook.
Backschisch [ˈbakʃiʃ], *n.* & *m.* **-(es)/-e** = **Bakschisch.**
Backschnee, *m. Ski:* caking snow.
Backsgast, *m.* **-es/-en.** *Nau:* forecastle hand.
Backsmaat, *m. Nau:* messmate.
Backspier, *f. Nau:* swinging boom, lower boom.
Backstag, *n. Nau:* guy, (back) stay.
Backstagsbrise, *f.,* **Backstagswind,** *m. Nau:* quarter(ing) wind, wind on the quarter.
Backstein, *m.* brick.
Backsteinbau, *m.* **1.** brickwork. **2.** (*pl.* **Backsteinbauten**) brick building.
Backsteinblattern, *f.pl. Vet:* salmonellosis.
backsteinern, *a.* of brick, brick-built.
Backsteinmaurer, *m.* bricklayer, brick-setter.
Backsteintee, *m. Com:* brick-tea, tile-tea.
Backstube, *f.* bakehouse, bakery.
Backtisch, *m. Nau:* mess-table.
Backtrog, *m.* kneading-trough.
Backvermögen, *n. Min:* caking quality (of coal).
Backwaren, *f.pl.* baker's produce; **feine B.,** fancy cakes, pastries, breads and biscuits.
backwarm, *a.* (bread, cake, etc.) still warm from the oven.
Backwerk, *n.* biscuits, small cakes, etc.; pastries.
backwinds, *adv. Nau:* with the wind on the quarter.
Backwunder, *n.* = **Backhaube.**
Backzahn, *m.* = **Backenzahn.**
Backzeit, *f.* baking time.
Bacon [ˈbeːkən], *m.* **-s/.** *Cu:* bacon, *esp.* gammon.
Baculagewebe [ˈbaːkuˑlaː-], *n. Constr:* wood lathing (*used as key in plastering*).
Bad, *n.* **-(e)s/¨-er. 1.** (*a*) bath; **kaltes Bad,** cold bath; **ein Bad nehmen,** to have, take, a bath; **das Bad einlaufen lassen,** to run the bath; *F:* **j-m ein Bad bereiten, richten,** to put a rod in pickle for s.o.; *F:* **das Kind mit dem Bade ausschütten,** to throw out the baby with the bath-water; *Art:* **Susanna im Bade,** Susanna and the Elders; *B:* **das Bad der Wiedergeburt,** the washing of regeneration; **türkisches Bad,** (i) Turkish bath; (ii) (*establishment*) Turkish baths, hammam; **medizinische Bäder,** medicinal baths; (*b*) (*in sea, river, etc.*) bathe; **ein Bad in den Wellen,** a bathe, swim, in the waves; **ein kurzes Bad,** a dip. **2.** (*a*) bathroom; **zwei Zimmer, Küche und Bad,** two rooms, kitchen and bath; (*b*) bath, (bath-)tub; (*c*) bathing establishment; bath(s); bathing-place (in river, etc.); **öffentliches Bad,** (i) public baths; (ii) public swimming pool. **3.** (*a*) watering-place, spa; baths; **nach X ins Bad gehen,** to go to take the waters at X; (*b*) *occ:* = **Seebad. 4.** *Ch: Phot: etc:* bath; dip, steep; *Tan: etc:* soak; **saures, alkalisches, Bad,** acid, alkaline, bath.
Badeanstalt, *f.* (*a*) (public) baths; (*b*) swimming-baths.
Badeanzug, *m.* bathing-costume, -suit.
Badearzt, *m.* spa-doctor, doctor at a spa.
Badebürste, *f.* back-brush.
Badediener, *m.* (*a*) (male) bath attendant; (*b*) (male) bathing attendant; *A:* bathing-man.
Badefrau, *f.* (*a*) (female) bath attendant; (*b*) (female) bathing attendant; *A:* bathing-woman.
Badegast, *m.* visitor, patient, at a spa; watering-place visitor.
Badegelegenheit, *f.* (*a*) bathing facilities; (*b*) bath(room).
Badehandschuh, *m.* washing-glove, bath-mitt.
Badehaube, *f.* bathing-cap.
Badehäuschen, *n.* bathing-hut.
Badehose, *f.* (pair of) bathing-trunks, -shorts, -drawers.
Badekabine, *f.* bathing-cabin, bathing-cubicle.
Badekappe, *f.* bathing-cap.
Badekarren, *m. A:* bathing-machine.
Badekraut, *n. Bot:* **1.** Italian lovage, garden lovage. **2.** pulicaria, (greater, common) fleabane. **3.** hedge woundwort.
Badekur, *f.* course of treatment at a spa, (the) cure; **eine B. in Baden-Baden nehmen, machen,** to take, drink, the waters, to take the cure, at Baden-Baden.
Badelaken, *n.* bath-sheet; bath-towel.
Bademantel, *m.* (i) bathing-wrap, bathing-gown; (ii) bath-wrap, bath-robe.
Bademeister, *m.* (*a*) bath attendant; (*b*) swimming instructor, superintendent at a public swimming-pool.
Bademütze, *f.* bathing-cap.
baden[1], *v.* **1.** *v.tr.* (*a*) to bath, *U.S:* bathe; **ein Kind b.,** to bath a child, to give a child a bath; *F:* **er ist als Kind zu heiß gebadet worden,** he was dropped on his head as a baby; (*b*) to bathe; to steep, dip; **sich** *dat.* **die Augen b.,** to bathe, rinse, one's eyes; **seine Wunden b.,** to bathe, wash, one's wounds; **seine Füße im Fluß b.,** to bathe one's feet in the river; **er war (wie) in Schweiß gebadet,** he was bathed in perspiration, he was in a bath of perspiration; **seine Hände waren in Blut gebadet,** his hands were bathed in blood; **in Sonnenlicht gebadet,** bathed, steeped, in sunlight. **2.** *v.i.* (*haben*) (*a*) to bath, to tub; to have, take, a bath; **kalt b.,** to have a cold bath; (*b*) (*out of doors*) to bathe; to have a bathe, a dip; **b. gehen,** to go bathing, swimming; to go for a bathe, a swim.
Baden[2]. *Pr.n.n.* **-s.** *Geog:* Baden; *A.Geog:* **das Großherzogtum B.,** the Grand Duchy of Baden.
Badende, *m., f.* (*decl. as adj.*) bather.
Badener, *m.* **-s/-** = **Badenser.**
Badenixe, *f.* bathing beauty.
Badenser [baˑˈdɛnzər], *m.* **-s/-.** *Geog:* inhabitant, native, of Baden, Badenese.
badensisch [baˑˈdɛnziʃ], *a. Geog: etc:* of Baden, Badenese.
Badeofen, *m.* bath-heater; geyser.
Badeort, *m.* (*a*) spa, watering place; (*b*) bathing resort; seaside resort.
Badeplatz, *m.* bathing-place.
Bader, *m.* **-s/-.** *A:* **1.** barber-surgeon. **2.** owner of a bathing establishment. **3.** = **Badende.**
Bäderbehandlung, Bäderheilkunde, *f.* balneotherapy.
Bäderkunde, *f.* balneology.
Badesalz, *n.* bath-salts, bath-crystals.
Badeschuh, *m.* bathing-shoe; (*for children*) paddling-shoe.
Badestelle, *f.* bathing place.
Badestrand, *m.* bathing-beach.
Badestube, *f.* bathroom.
Badetablette, *f.* bath tablet, bath-cube.
Badetuch, *n.* bath-towel; bath-sheet.
Badewanne, *f.* (i) bath, (bath-)tub; (ii) *Nau: F:* (*ship*) old tub; (iii) *Mil: F:* tin hat.
Badewasser, *n.* bath-water; **das B. einlaufen lassen,** to run the bath.
Badezelle, *f.* = **Badekabine.**
Badezeug, *n.* bathing gear, bathing things, *F:* bathing togs.
Badezimmer, *n.* bathroom.
Badezimmereinrichtung, *f.* bathroom fittings.
Badezimmermatte, *f.* bath-mat.
Badezuber, *m.* bath-tub.
Badian, *m.* **-s/-e.** *Bot:* star anise, Chinese anise.
Badin [baˑˈdɛ̃ː], *m.* **-s/-s,** wag, joker, banterer.
Badinage [baˑdiˑˈnaːʒə], *f.* **-/-n,** trifling, joking, jesting.
Badinerie [baˑdiˑnəˈriː], *f.* **-/-n** [-ˈriːən], (*a*) jest, piece of fun; (*b*) *Mus:* (*scherzo-like movement*) badinerie.
badinieren [baˑdiˑˈniːrən], *v.i.* (*haben*) to jest, joke, trifle.
badisch, *a. Geog: etc:* of Baden, Badenese.
Baedeker [ˈbɛːdəkər]. *Pr.n.* & *s.m.* **-s/-.** Baedeker('s Guide).
bäen, *v.i.* (*haben*) (*of sheep*) to bleat, baa.
Bafel, *m.* **-s/-. 1.** (*a*) *Tex:* silk waste; (*b*) *Ind:* waste, refuse; trash. **2.** *Yiddish:* chatter, gossip.
baff, *a.* dumbfounded, flabbergasted; **ich war völlig b.,** I was absolutely flabbergasted, you could have knocked me down with a feather.
Bäffchen, *n. pl.* = **Beffchen.**
bäffen, *v.i.* (*haben*) (*of dog*) to yap.
Bagage [baˑˈgaːʒə], *f.* **-/-n,** (*a*) *Mil:* baggage(-train); impedimenta; **die ganze B.,** the whole lot, bag and baggage; (*b*) *F:* rabble, rag-tag (and bobtail).
Bagagepferd, *n. Mil:* bat-horse.
Bagagewagen, *m. Mil:* baggage-wagon, -van.
Bagarre [baˑˈgarə], *f.* **-/-n,** affray, brawl; crowd, crush.
Bagasse [baˑˈgasə], *f.* **-/-n.** *Sug-R:* bagasse, megass.
Bagat [baˑˈgaːt], *m.* **-(e)s/-e** = **Pagat.**
Bagatelle [baˑgaˑˈtɛlə], *f.* **-/-n,** (*a*) bagatelle, trifle; (*b*) *Mus:* bagatelle; (*c*) *Jur:* petty law-case.
bagatellisieren [baˑgaˑtɛliˑˈziːrən], *v.tr.* to minimize (the importance of), make light of (an affair, etc.); to dismiss (affair, etc.) as trifling.
Bagatellprozeß, *m. Jur:* petty law-case.
Bagatellsache, *f.* (*a*) = **Bagatellprozeß;** (*b*) = **Bagatellschaden.**
Bagatellschaden, *m. Ins:* (case of) petty damage.
Bagdad [bakˈdaːt, ˈbakdat]. *Pr.n.n.* **-s.** *Geog:* Baghdad.
Bagger, *m.* **-s/-.** *Civ.E:* (*a*) dredger, dredge, drag; (*b*) excavator; mechanical navvy.
Baggerboot, *n.* dredge-boat, dredger.
Baggereimer, *m.* dredge-bucket.
Baggerer, *m.* **-s/-,** (*pers.*) dredger.
Baggergut, *n.* spoil(-earth).
Baggerloch, *n.* pot-hole (in river, etc.).
Baggermaschine, *f.* dredger, dredging-machine.
baggern, *v.tr.* & *i.* (*haben*) to dredge (river, harbour, etc.); to excavate (trench, ground on building site, etc.).
Baggerprahm, *m. Hyd.E:* (i) mud-barge, -lighter; hopper(-barge); (ii) mud-dredger.
Baggerschute, *f.* dredge-boat, dredger.
Baggertorf, *m.* machine-dug peat.
Baggertrommel, *f.* (dredging) tumbler.
Bagienrahe [ˈbaːgiən-], *f. Nau:* cross-jack yard.
Bagiensegel, *n. Nau:* cross-jack sail.
Bagno [ˈbanjoː], *n.* **-s/-s & -ni.** *Hist:* bagnio, convict prison.
Bagnokugel, *f. A:* (convict's) ball and chain.
Bagstall, *m.* **-s/-e.** *Austrian:* post (of fence).
Baguette [baˑˈgɛt], *f.* **-/-n** [-ˈgɛtən]. *Lap:* baguette.
bäh [bɛː], *int.* (i) (*bleat of sheep*) baa; (ii) (*mocking*) yah! boo to you!
Bahamaholz [baˑˈhaːmaː-], *n. Dy:* Bahama redwood.
Bahamainseln, die. *Pr.n.f.pl. Geog:* the Bahama Islands, the Bahamas.
bähen[1], *v.i.* (*haben*) (*of sheep*) to bleat, to baa.
bähen[2]. **I.** *v.tr.* (*a*) to bathe, foment (wound, etc.); (*b*) *occ:* to heat, warm (sth.); *South G. Dial:* to toast (bread).
II. *vbl s.* **Bähen** *n.,* **Bähung** *f. in vbl senses; also:* fomentation (of wound, etc.).
Bahiaholz [baˑˈhiːaː-], *n.* (kind of) red dye-wood.
Bähkissen, *n. Med:* small bag filled with herbs (*used for fomentation*).
Bählamm, *n.* (*nursery language*) baa-lamb.
Bahn, *f.* **-/-en. 1.** way, path, road; **eine B. brechen, machen,** to open (up), clear, a way, a path; to blaze a trail; **sich** *dat.* **B. brechen, machen,** to make, clear, a way, a path, for oneself; to make, force, push, one's way; **die B. für etwas frei machen,** to pave, prepare, the way, to clear the ground, for sth.; **B. frei!** out of the way! clear the way! **freie B. dem Tüchtigen,** *approx.* efficiency earns opportunity; **reine B. machen,** to clear the ground (for negotiation, etc.), *F:* to clear the decks; **in j-s B. wandeln,** to follow, tread, walk, in s.o.'s footsteps; **die B. der Pflicht, der Tugend, usw.,** the path of duty, of virtue, etc.; **j-n auf die rechte B. führen, bringen,** to lead s.o. into the right path, to put s.o. on the right track; **auf die schiefe B. kommen, geraten,** to get into evil ways; **j-n aus seiner B. reißen, werfen,** to throw s.o. off (his) balance, off (his) course; **ein Gespräch in die richtigen Bahnen lenken,** to turn, direct, a discussion into the right channels; **sich in ähnlichen Bahnen bewegen,**

(*of scholar, etc.*) to work on similar lines; (*of research, etc.*) to proceed on similar lines; (*of development, process, etc.*) **sich in ähnlichen Bahnen vollziehen,** to take a similar course, to develop in a similar way; *A:* (*of subject, etc.*) **auf die B. kommen,** to crop up, to come to the fore. **2.** (*a*) *Astr:* course (of star); orbit (of planet); path, track, orbit (of comet); **scheinbare B. der Sonne,** ecliptic; (*b*) *Ph:* trajectory, path (of moving body). **3.** (*a*) arena; *Rac:* (race-)course; *Sp:* (i) (running-, cinder-)track; (ii) (individual) lane; *Cy:* path; *Golf:* hole; **Golfplatz mit 18 Bahnen,** 18-hole course; **die kurzgeschnittene B.,** the fairway, the pretty; *Games:* (skittle-)alley; (bowling-)alley; (*b*) slide (on snow *or* ice); **eine B. schlagen,** to make a slide; *Sp:* (sleigh-, toboggan-)run, (toboggan-)slide; *Av:* runway; (*c*) carriage-road; (traffic) lane. **4.** (i) railway, *U.S:* railroad; (ii) tramways, *U.S:* streetcar line; (*a*) track, line; **eingleisige, zweigleisige, B.,** single-, double-track line; (*b*) train; rail; **mit der B. fahren,** to go, travel, by train, by rail; **in, auf, der B.,** in, on, the train; **mit der B., per B., senden, befördern,** to send, forward, by rail, per rail; *Com:* **frei B.,** free on rail, *abbr.* f.o.r.; *U.S:* free on board, *abbr.* f.o.b.; (*c*) (railway) station; **j-n an die B., zur B., bringen, begleiten,** to see s.o. off (at the station); to take s.o. to the station *or* the tram; **zur, auf die, B. gehen,** to go to the station *or* the tram stop. **5.** length (of paper, fabric, wallpaper, etc.); *Dressm:* panel; *Nau:* **Bahnen** *pl*, cloths (of a sail). **6.** (*a*) *Tls:* face (of hammer, plane, anvil); bit (of borer); edge (of chisel); (*b*) *Mec.E:* swan-neck (of loom); band, groove (of pulley, etc., for driving-belt); (*c*) *Tex:* race (board).

Bahnabzweigung, *f. Rail:* branch-line.

bahnamtlich, *a. Rail:* **bahnamtliche Mitteilungen,** official communications, notices (issued by the railway authorities); *adv.* **b. geöffnet, geprüft,** opened, examined, by the railway authorities.

Bahnanschluß, *m.* = **Eisenbahnanschluß.**

Bahnbeamte, *m.* (*decl. as adj.*) railway official.

Bahnblatt, *n. Artil:* bed-plate.

bahnbrechend, *a.* pioneering, epoch-making; **eine bahnbrechende Erfindung,** an epoch-making discovery; **er hat bahnbrechende Arbeit auf diesem Gebiet geleistet,** he has done pioneer work in this field.

Bahnbrecher, *m.* pioneer.

Bahnbreite, *f. Sp: etc:* width of the track; *Rail:* gauge of the track.

Bahnbrücke, *f.* railway bridge, viaduct.

Bahnbus, *m.* railway (company's) bus.

Bahndamm, *m. Rail:* (*a*) railway embankment; (*b*) = **Bahnkörper.**

bahneigen, *a.* belonging to the railway.

Bahneigentum, *n.* railway property.

bahnen, *v.tr.* **einen Weg b.,** to clear, prepare, a way; to open up, clear, a path; *F:* to blaze a trail; **sich** *dat.* **einen Weg b.,** to make a way for oneself; **sich** *dat.* **einen Weg durch eine Menschenmenge b.,** to make, work, force, push, one's way through a crowd; **j-m, etwas** *dat.*, **den Weg b.,** to clear, pave, prepare, the way for s.o., sth.

Bahnfahrt, *f.* train journey.

Bahnfeile, *f. Tls:* equalizing file.

bahnfrei, *a. Com:* free on rail, *abbr.* f.o.r.; *U.S:* free on board, *abbr.* f.o.b.

Bahngehen, *n. Sp:* walking-race.

Bahngelände, *n.* (*land*) railway property.

Bahngeleise, Bahngleis, *n.* railway track, line(s).

Bahnhobel, *m. Tls:* cooper's grooving plane.

Bahnhof, *m.* **1.** (*a*) (railway, *U.S:* railroad) station; (tramway, etc.) depot; **der Bonner B.,** the station at Bonn; **B. Schöneberg,** Schöneberg station; (*b*) *F:* **ich verstehe nur B.,** I can't understand a word, it's double Dutch to me; I can't make head or tail of it, it's Greek to me. **2.** *F:* **j-n mit großem B. empfangen,** to put out the red carpet for s.o., to receive s.o. with great ceremony; **j-n mit kleinem B. empfangen,** to give s.o. a modest reception (on his, her, arrival); **bitte, keinen B.,** please don't go to any trouble; please, no ceremony, no fuss.

Bahnhofseinfahrt, *f.* station-approach.

Bahnhofshalle, *f.* station hall; *U.S:* concourse.

Bahnhofshotel, *n.* station hotel.

Bahnhofskommandant, *m. Mil:* Railway Transport Officer (*abbr.* R.T.O.).

Bahnhofsmission, *f.* (*a*) Travellers' Aid Society; (*b*) Travellers' Aid (Society's) Office.

Bahnhofsrestaurant, *n.*, **Bahnhofsrestauration,** *f.* station restaurant.

Bahnhofsvorstand, Bahnhofsvorsteher, *m.* stationmaster.

Bahnhofswirtschaft, *f.* station restaurant.

-bahnig, *comb.fm. a.* -lane; **vierbahnige Straße,** four-lane street.

Bahnknoten(punkt), *m.* railway junction.

Bahnkörper, *m. Rail:* road-bed; permanent way.

Bahnkreuzung, *f. Rail:* railway crossing; crossover.

bahnlagernd, *a. Rail:* (parcel, etc.) to be collected from the station.

Bahnlinie, *f.* railway line; **eingleisige, zweigleisige, B.,** single-track, double-track, line.

bahnmäßig, *a.* (packing, etc.) (suitable) for railway transport; *adv.* (packed, etc.) for railway transport.

Bahnmeister, *m. Rail:* permanent way inspector.

Bahnmeisterwagen, *m. Rail:* (plate-layer's) trolley, lorry.

Bahnplanum, *n.* formation(-level), *U.S:* subgrade.

Bahnpolizei, *f.* railway police.

Bahnpost, *f.* railway postal service; *Rail:* **einen Brief per B. schicken,** to post a letter on the mail-train.

Bahnpostamt, *n. Rail:* station post-office.

Bahnpostwagen, *m. Rail:* mail-van, *U.S:* mail car.

Bahnräumer, *m. Rail:* guard-iron, life-, rail-guard, *U.S:* cowcatcher, pilot.

Bahnreiten, *n. Equit:* show-riding.

Bahnrennen, *n. Rac:* speedway racing; *Cy:* track-racing.

Bahnschwelle, *f. Rail:* sleeper, *U.S:* tie.

Bahnspediteur, *m.* rail orwarding agent.

Bahnspedition, *f.* **1.** forwarding (of goods) by rail. **2.** rail forwarding agency.

Bahnstation, *f.* railway station.

Bahnsteig, *m. Rail:* platform.

Bahnsteigbrücke, *f. Rail:* footbridge (leading from one platform to another).

Bahnsteigkarte, *f. Rail:* platform ticket.

Bahnsteigsperre, *f. Rail:* ticket barrier.

Bahnsteigtunnel, *m.* = **Bahnsteigunterführung.**

Bahnsteigüberführung, *f. Rail:* footbridge (leading from one platform to another).

Bahnsteigunterführung, *f. Rail:* subway (between platforms).

Bahnstrecke, *f.* = **Eisenbahnstrecke.**

Bahntransport, *m.* railway transport.

Bahnüberführung, *f. Rail:* over-bridge, overcrossing.

Bahnübergang, *m. Rail:* level crossing, *U.S:* grade crossing; **bewachter, beschrankter, B.,** guarded, gated, level crossing; **unbewachter, unbeschrankter, B.,** unguarded, ungated, level crossing.

Bahnunterführung, *f. Rail:* railway tunnel, railway arch.

Bahnwärter, *m. Rail:* (i) linesman, track-watchman; (ii) gate-keeper (at level crossing).

Bahnwärterhaus, Bahnwärterhäuschen, *n. Rail:* (i) linesman's box, cabin; (ii) gate-keeper's lodge.

Bahre, *f.* -/-n, (*a*) litter, stretcher; **fahrbare B.,** wheeled stretcher, (*in hospital*) (stretcher-) trolley; (*b*) bier (for coffin); **von der Wiege bis zur B.,** from the cradle to the grave; throughout one's life.

Bahrenträger, *m.* stretcher-bearer, -man.

Bahrgericht, Bahrrecht, *n. Hist:* Ordeal of the Bier, *A:* bier-right.

Bahrtuch, *n.* pall, hearse-cloth.

Bahrtuchhalter, *m.* pall-bearer.

Bähung *see* **bähen II.**

Bai, *f.* -/-en. *Geog:* bay; bight.

Baier, *m.* -n/-n, **Baiern,** *n.* -s = **Bayer, Bayern.**

Baigneuse [bɛnˈjøːzə], *f.* -/-n. **1.** (female) bather; *Art:* woman bathing. **2.** *A:* female bathing attendant.

Bainmarie [bɛ̃ˑmaˈriː], *n.* -s/-s. *Ch: Cu:* water-bath; *Cu:* bain-marie.

bairisch, *a.* = **bayrisch.**

Baisalz, *n.* bay-salt, sea-salt.

Baiser [bɛˈzeː], *m. & n.* -s/-s. *Cu:* meringue.

Baisse [ˈbɛːsə], *f.* -/-n. *St.Exch: etc:* decline, fall, drop, slump (in prices); depression (on the market); **auf B. spekulieren,** to speculate for a fall; to sell a bear, to go a bear, to bear, to sell short.

Baissegeschäft, *n. St.Exch:* bear transaction.

Baissespekulant, *m. St.Exch:* speculator for a fall; bear.

Baissespekulation, *f. St.Exch:* bear speculation, speculation for a fall.

Baissestimmung, Baisseströmung, *f.* = **Baissetendenz.**

Baissetendenz, *f. St. Exch:* bear tone, downward tendency (of prices); *F:* bearish tendency.

Baissier [bɛˈsĭeː], *m.* -s/-s. *St.Exch:* bear.

baissieren [bɛˈsiːrən]. **1.** *v.tr.* to lower. **2.** *v.i.* (*haben*) to sink, go down.

Bajä [ˈbaːjɛː]. *Pr.n.n.* -s. *A.Geog:* Baiae.

Bajadere [baˑjaˈdeːrə], *f.* -/-n, bayadere; (Indian) dancing-girl, nautch-girl.

Bajazzo [baˈjatsoː], *m.* -s/-s, clown; buffoon; *Th:* **der B.,** I Pagliacci.

Bajonett [baˑjoˈnɛt], *n.* -(e)s/-e. *Mil:* bayonet, side-arm; **das B. aufpflanzen,** to fix bayonet(s); **mit aufgepflanztem B.,** with fixed bayonet(s); **j-n mit dem B. durchbohren,** to bayonet s.o.

Bajonettangriff, *m.* bayonet charge.

Bajonettbaum, *m. Bot:* bayonet-plant; yucca, *F:* Adam's needle.

Bajonettfassung, *f. El:* bayonet(-joint) socket, bayonet holder (of bulb, etc.).

Bajonettfechten, *n.* fighting, fencing, with bayonets.

bajonettieren [baˑjoˑneˈtiːrən], *v.i.* (*haben*) *Mil:* to fight with bayonets.

Bajonettpflanze, *f. Bot:* moorva, bowstring hemp.

Bajonettsockel, *m. El:* bayonet(-joint) base (of bulb, etc.).

Bajonettstift, *m. El: etc:* pin (on base of electric bulb, etc.).

Bajonettverschluß, *m. Mec.E: etc:* bayonet-joint.

Bajonettwarze, *f.* = **Bajonettstift.**

Bajuvare, Bajuware [baˑjuˑˈvaːrə], *m.* -n/-n. *A. & Hum:* Bavarian.

bajuvarisch, bajuwarisch [baˑjuˑˈvaːriʃ], *a. A. & Hum:* Bavarian.

Bakauner [baˈkaunər], *m.* -s/- = **Bakonyer.**

Bakchos [ˈbakços]. *Pr.n.m.* -'. = **Bacchus.**

Bake, *f.* -/-n. **1.** *Nau: etc:* beacon; landmark. **2.** *Surv:* (range-)pole; staff, rod. **3.** *Rail:* warning signal-board.

Bakel, *m.* -s/-. *Sch:* cane; ruler, *A:* ferule.

Bakelit [baˑkəˈliːt], *n.* -s/-e. (*R.t.m.*) bakelite.

Bakenboje, *f. Nau:* beacon-buoy, leading buoy.

Bakengeld, *n.* beaconage.

Bakentonne, *f.* = **Bakenboje.**

Bakkalaureat [bakaˑlaureˑˈaːt], *n.* -(e)s/-e. *Sch:* baccalaureate, bachelor's degree.

Bakkalaureus [bakaˈlaureˑus], *m.* -/-rei [-reˑiː]. *Sch:* (*a*) bachelor; (*b*) = **Abiturient.**

Bakkarat [bakaˈraː(t), ˈbakaˑraː], *n.* -s/. *Cards:* baccara(t).

Bakken, *m.* -s/-. *Ski:* ski-jump.

Bakonyer [ˈbaːkonjər], *m.* -s/-, **Bakonyerschwein,** *n.* Bakony (pig), Hungarian variety of Bagun (pig).

Bakschisch [ˈbakʃiʃ], *n. & m.* -(es)/-e, ba(c)ksheesh, ba(c)kshish.

Bakteriämie [bakteˑrĭɛˑˈmiː], *f.* -/-n [-ˈmiːən]. *Med:* bacteriaemia.

Bakterie [bakˈteːrĭə], *f.* -/-n, bacterium; **Bakterien** *pl*, (i) bacteria; (ii) *F:* germs, bugs.

bakteriell [bakteˑrĭˈɛl], *a.* bacterial.

Bakterienbrand, *m. Agr: etc:* bacterial blight (*of various types, e.g. pseudomonas spongiosa*).

Bakterienfäule, *f. Bot:* potato rot (due to bacteria).

Bakterienfilter, *m.* filter (for removing bacteria from fruit juices, etc.).

Bakterienforscher, *m.* bacteriologist.

Bakterienforschung, *f.* bacteriology.

Bakteriengift, *n.* bacterial toxin.

Bakterienkrieg, *m.* bacterial warfare, germ warfare.

Bakterienkultur, *f.* (bacterial) culture.

Bakterienkunde, *f.* bacteriology.

Bakterienruhr, *f. Med:* bacillary dysentery.

bakterientötend, *a.* bactericidal; *F:* germ-killing; **bakterientötendes Mittel,** bactericide; *F:* germ-killer.

Bakteriologe [bakteˑrĭoˑˈloːgə], *m.* -n/-n, bacteriologist.

Bakteriologie [bakteˑrĭoˑloˑˈgiː], *f.* -/-n [-ˈgiːən], bacteriology.

bakteriologisch [bakteˑrĭoˑˈloːgiʃ], *a.* bacteriologic(al).

Bakteriolyse [bakteˑrĭoˑˈlyːzə], *f.* -/-n, bacteriolysis.

bakteriolytisch [bakteˑrĭoˑˈlyːtiʃ], *a.* bacteriolytic.

Bakteriophage [bakteˑrĭoˑˈfaːgə], *m.* -n/-n, bacteriophage.

Bakteriose [bakteˑrĭˈoːzə], *f.* -/-n. *Bot:* bacteriosis.

Bakteriotherapie, *f.* bacteriotherapy.

Bakterium [bakˈteːrĭum], *n.* -s/-rien, bacterium.

Bakteriurie [bakteˑriˑuˑˈriː], *f.* -/-n [-ˈriːən]. *Med:* bacteriuria.

bakterizid[1] [bakteˑriˑˈtsiːt], *a.* bactericidal.

Bakterizid[2] [bakteˑriˑˈtsiːt], *n.* -(e)s/-e [-s, -ˈtsiːdəs/-ˈtsiːdə], bactericide.

Baktra [ˈbaktraː]. *Pr.n.n.* -s. *A.Geog:* (town of) Bactria.

Baktrien [ˈbaktrĭən]. *Pr.n.n.* -s. *A.Geog:* (province of) Bactria.

Baktrier [ˈbaktrĭər], *m.* -s/-, (*pers.*) Bactrian.

baktrisch [ˈbaktriʃ], *a.* Bactrian.

Baku [ˈbaːkuː, baˈkuː]. *Pr.n.n.* -s. *Geog:* Baku.

Bakunerschwein [baˈˈkuːnər-], *n.*=**Bakonyer.**
Balaenoptera [baˈlɛˈˈnopteˑraː], *m.* **-s/-ren.** *Z:* balaenoptera; rorqual, fin-back.
Balaklawa [balaˑˈklaːvaː]. *Pr.n.n.* **-s.** *Geog:* Balaclava.
Balalaika [balaˑˈlaikaː], *f.* **-/-s.** *Mus:* balalaika.
Bälamm, *n.* (*nursery language*) baa-lamb.
Balance [baˈlɑ̃ːsə], *f.* **-/-n,** balance, equilibrium; **seine B. halten, verlieren,** to keep, lose, one's balance; *cp.* **Gleichgewicht.**
Balancé [balɑ̃ˑˈseː], *n.* **-s/-s.** *Danc:* set; balancing step.
Balanceakt, *m.* balancing act.
Balancement [balɑ̃ˑsəˈmɑ̃ː], *n.* **-s/-s.** *Mus:* tremolo.
Balanceruder, *n. Nau:* balanced rudder.
Balanceur [balɑ̃ˑˈsøːr], *m.* **-s/-e,** (*pers.*) balancer; tight-rope walker.
Balancier [balɑ̃ˑsiˈeː], *m.* **-s/-s,** (*a*) *Mch:* beam, walking-beam (of beam-engine); (*b*)=**Balancierpresse.**
Balancierdampfmaschine [balɑ̃ˑˈsiːr-], *f.*= **Balanciermaschine.**
balancieren [balɑ̃ˑˈsiːrən]. **1.** *v.tr.* to balance; **einen Stock auf der Nase b.,** to balance a stick on one's nose. **2.** *v.i.* (*haben, sein*) to balance, to poise; **auf einem Fuß b.,** to balance (oneself) on one foot.
Balanciermaschine, *f. Mch:* beam-engine, lever-engine.
Balancierpflug, *m. Agr:* balance plough, tipping plough.
Balancierpresse, *f.* fly-press, screw-press.
Balanciersäge, *f.* pendulum-saw.
Balancierstange, *f.* balancing-pole (of tight-rope walker).
Balander [baˑˈlandər], *m.* **-s/-.** *Nau:* canal barge.
Balane [baˑˈlaːnə], *f.* **-/-n.** *Crust:* balanus, acorn-barnacle, acorn-shell.
Balanitis [baˑlaˑˈniːtis], *f.* **-/.** *Med:* balanitis.
Balanze [baˈlantsə], *f.* **-/-n**=**Balance.**
Balasrubin [ˈbalasruˑˌbiːn], *m.* *Miner:* *Lap:* balas(-ruby).
Balata [baˑˈlaːtaː], *f.* **-/.** *Bot: Com:* balata.
Balatabaum, *m. Bot:* balata-tree, bully-tree.
Balatariemen, Balatatreibriemen, *m. Mec.E:* balata belt.
Balatum [baˑˈlaːtum], *n.* **-s/.** *Com:* rubber-impregnated felt floor-covering; (*R.t.m.*) congolium.
Balban [balˈbaːn], *m.* **-s/-e.** *Ven:* decoy black-cock.
Bälbaum, *m. Bot:* bael-, bel-fruit tree, Bengal quince.
Balbhahn, *m.*=**Balban.**
Balbier [balˈbiːr], *m.* **-s/-e.** *Dial:*=**Barbier.**
balbieren [balˈbiːrən], *v.tr. Dial:*=**barbieren.**
Balche, *f.* **-/-n, Balchen,** *m.* **-s/-**=**Blaufelchen.**
bald, *adv.* (**eher, ehest,** *occ.* **balder, bälder, baldest, bäldest,** *q.v.*) **1.** soon, before long, in a short time, in the near future; **b. darauf, b. danach,** soon after(wards), shortly after(wards); **wie b.?** how soon? **so b. wie möglich, möglichst b.,** as soon as possible, at the earliest possible moment; **ich komme b. wieder,** I shall be back soon; **allzu b.,** all too soon; **unsere Vorräte werden b. zu Ende sein,** our supplies will come to an end soon, will not last much longer; **es wird b. (wieder) Sonntag sein,** Sunday will soon come round (again); **es ist b. drei Monate her, es werden b. drei Monate (sein), seit wir Nachricht gehabt haben,** it is getting on for three months, it will soon be three months, since we had any news. **2.** quickly; easily; **den siehst du so b. nicht wieder,** *F:* you won't see him again in a hurry; **das ist b. gesagt,** that is easily explained, easy to explain; **b. gesagt, aber schwer getan,** sooner, easier, said than done. **3.** (*a*) *F:* almost, nearly; **als Fritz b. achtzehn Jahre alt war,** when Fritz was nearly eighteen; **ich warte b. seit drei Stunden,** I've been waiting for nearly three hours, for the best part of three hours; **ich wäre b. gestorben vor Angst,** I nearly died of fright; **b. hätte ich (et)was gesagt,** I pretty nearly said something; (*of second-hand article*) **b. neu,** in practically new condition, practically new; (*b*) *A:* near; **ich wohne b. am Ende der Straße,** I live near the end of the road; **das Haus ist b. an der Grenze,** the house is near the frontier, not far from the frontier. **4. bald . . ., bald . . .,** now . . ., now . . .; now . . ., and again . . .; sometimes . . ., sometimes . . .; **b. hier, b. da,** now here, now there; **er war b. traurig, b. wieder fröhlich,** he would be sad one moment and gay the next. **5.** *emotive particle* (*with nuance of impatience*) **kommst du wohl b. her!** ˈwill you come here! **hört ihr jetzt b. mit dem Geschrei auf!** ˈwill you stop that noise now! **hast du noch nicht b. genug?** haven't you had enough ˈyet?
Baldachin [ˈbaldaxiːn], *m.* **-s/-e,** baldachin; canopy; tester (of bed); *Av:* cabane.
Bälde, *f.* **-/.** (*used only in the phr.*) **in B.,** soon, in a short time, in the near future.
balde, *adv. Poet:*=**bald.**
Balder[1]. *Pr.n.m.* **-s.** *Myth:* Balder.
balder[2], **bälder,** *adv. occ.* sooner.
Balderich, *m.* **-(e)s/-e.** *A. Cost:* baldric.
baldest, bäldest, *adv. occ.* soonest; very soon; at the earliest possible moment, date; as soon as possible; **auf das, aufs, baldeste, bäldeste,** at the soonest, earliest (moment).
Baldewin. *Pr.n.m.* **-s.** Baldwin.
Baldgreis, *n. Bot:* (common) groundsel.
baldig, baldigst. 1. *a.* early; speedy; **wir wären für eine baldige Antwort dankbar,** we would appreciate, be grateful for, an early reply; **ich wünsche dir baldige Besserung,** I wish you a speedy recovery; **auf (ein) baldiges Wiedersehen!** see you again soon! **baldig(st)er Klimawechsel wäre zu empfehlen,** an early change of air would be advisable. **2. baldigst,** *adv.* (very) soon; at the earliest possible moment, date; as soon as possible; **ich werde mich baldigst zurückziehen,** I shall withdraw very soon, at the earliest possible moment.
baldmöglich, baldmöglichst, *a.* early, earliest; **um baldmöglich(st)e Rückgabe der Dokumente wird gebeten,** please return the documents as soon as possible, at your earliest convenience; *adv.* **ich werde Sie baldmöglichst aufsuchen,** I shall come to see you as soon as I can, at the earliest possible opportunity.
baldowern [balˈdoːvərn], *v.tr.*=**ausbaldowern.**
Baldr. *Pr.n.m.* **-s.** *Myth:* Balder.
Baldrian, *m.* **-s/-e.** *Bot:* valerian; **gemeiner B.,** common valerian, great wild valerian; **griechischer B.,** Greek valerian, Jacob's ladder, polemonium; **keltischer B.,** celtic nard, celtic spikenard.
Baldriangewächse, *n.pl. Bot:* valerianaceae.
baldriansauer, *a. Ch:* valeric; **baldriansaures Salz,** valerianate, valerate.
Baldriansäure, *f. Ch:* valeric acid.
Baldriantropfen, *m.pl. Pharm:* valerian (drops).
Balduin. *Pr.n.m.* **-s.** Baldwin.
Baldur. *Pr.n.m.* **-s.** *Myth:* Balder.
Baleare [baˑleˑˈaːrə], *m.* **-n/-n.** *Geog:* Balearean.
Balearen, die [baˑleˑˈaːrən]. *Pr.n.pl. Geog:* the Balearic Islands.
balearisch [baˑleˑˈaːriʃ], *a. Geog:* Balearean.
Balenit [baˑleˑˈniːt], *m.* **-(e)s/.** *Com:* artificial whalebone.
Balester [baˑˈlestər], *m.* **-s/-.** *A.Mil:* arbalest, arblast.
Balg[1], *m.* **-(e)s/⸚e. 1.** (*a*) coat, fur (of live vermin); pelt, skin (taken from dead vermin); skin with feathers (of bird); slough (of snake); **ausgestopfter B.,** stuffed skin (of fox, bird, etc.); **der Fuchs mußte seinen B. lassen,** the fox had to pay with his life; **einem Tier den B. abziehen,** to skin, flay, an animal; **einem Kaninchen den B. abziehen,** to skin a rabbit whole; *F:* **j-m den B. abziehen,** to fleece s.o. (of money), to bleed s.o. (for money); (*b*) *A. & P:* belly, paunch (of human being); (*c*) (cloth *or* leather) body (of doll); (stuffed) decoy-bird. **2.** (*a*) *Bot:* glume (of grasses); (*b*) *Dial:* shell, pod (of pea); husk, chaff (of corn); skin (of grape). **3.** (*a*) windbag (of bagpipes); *usu.pl.* **Bälge,** bellows (of organ, forge); **die Bälge treten,** (*in smithy*) **die Bälge ziehen,** to work the bellows; (*b*) *Phot:* (extension) bellows (of camera).
Balg[2], *n. & m.* **-(e)s/⸚e(r).** *F:* kid, urchin; brat; (*of adult*) *usu. Pej:* good-for-nothing, nuisance; pest; **ein süßes kleines B.,** a sweet little thing; **die frechen Bälger,** the naughty little beggars.
Balgauszug, *m. Phot:*=**Balgenauszug.**
Balgbrett, *n.* board *or* frame over which skins of smaller animals are stretched for drying.
Balgdrüse, *f. Anat:* lymphoid follicle, lymph-node (in tongue of mammals).
Balgdüse, *f. Metall:* tuyere, tue-iron (of forge).
Balge, *f.* **-/-n.** *North G.Dial:* (*a*) wash-tub; (*b*) channel in a tidal mud-flat.
balgen[1], **bälgen. 1.** *v.tr.*=**abbalgen 1** (*a*). **2.** (*a*) **sich balgen,** to scuffle, wrestle, have a tussle; **die Knaben balgten sich auf der Erde,** the boys were scuffling on the ground; (*b*) **sich balgen, bälgen,** (*of snake*) to slough its skin, to slough, to cast its slough.
Balgen[2], *m.* **-s/-.** *Phot:* (extension) bellows (of camera).
Balgenauszug, *m. Phot:* bellows extension.
Balgerei, *f.* **-/-en,** scuffle, tussle; hand-to-hand fight; **eine heftige B.,** a sharp tussle.
Bälgetreter, *m. Mus:* bellows-, organ-blower.
Balgfrucht, *f. Bot:* follicle, follicule.
Balggebläse, *n.* bellows (of forge, etc.).
Balggeschwulst, *f. Med:* atheroma; sebaceous cyst, wen.
Balghaare, *n.pl. Ven:* hair, wool, fur (of small ground-game); pelage.
Balgkamera, *f. Phot:* folding camera.
Balgkapsel, *f.*=**Balgfrucht.**
Balgkropf, *m. Med:* cystic goitre.
Balgmilbe, *f. Arach:* follicle mite, face-mite.
Balgschwengel, *m.* bellows-handle, rock-staff (of forge-bellows).
Balgtreter, *m.*=**Bälgetreter.**
balhornisieren [balhorniˑˈziːrən], *v.tr.* to corrupt (words, etc.).
Bali [ˈbaːliː]. *Pr.n.n.* **-s.** *Georg:* (the island of) Bali.
Balinese [baˑliˑˈneːzə], *m.* **-n/-n.** *Geog:* Balinese.
Balirind, *n. Z:* (domesticated variety of) banteng; Javanese ox.
Balistraße, die. *Pr.n. Geog:* the Bali Straits.
Balje, *f.* **-/-n**=**Balge.**
Balkan, der [ˈbalkaːn]. *Pr.n.* **-s.** *Geog:* **1.** the Balkan Mountains, the Balkans. **2.** the Balkan Peninsula; the Balkan States, the Balkans.
Balkanbund, der. *Hist:* the Balkan League.
Balkangebirge, das. *Pr.n. Geog:* the Balkan Mountains, the Balkans.
Balkanhalbinsel, die. *Pr.n. Geog:* the Balkan Peninsula.
balkanisch [balˈkaːniʃ], *a.* Balkan, Balkanic; *F:* Balkanized.
balkanisieren [balkaˑniˑˈziːrən], *v.tr.* *F:* to Balkanize.
Balkankriege, *m.pl. Hist:* Balkan Wars.
Balkanlachtaube, *f. Orn:* collared turtle-dove.
Balkanland, *n.*=**Balkanstaat.**
Balkanpakt, der=**Balkanbund, der.**
Balkanstaat, *m.* Balkan state; **die Balkanstaaten,** the Balkan States, the Balkans.
Bälkchen, *n.* **-s/-,** (*a*) small beam; (*b*) *Anat:* trabecula.
Balken, *m.* **-s/-. 1.** (*a*) *Constr:* beam, balk; girder; **Balken legen, einziehen,** to lay, put in, beams; **durchlaufender, kontinuierlicher, B.,** continuous beam, girder; **verstärkter B.,** reinforced beam, girder; **armierter, bewehrter, B.,** trussed, armed, beam *or* girder; truss-girder; **verdübelter B.,** dowelled beam; **verzahnter B.,** joggle-beam; **zusammengesetzter B.,** compound, built-up, beam *or* girder; **den B. im eigenen Auge nicht sehen,** not to see the beam in one's own eye; **Wasser hat keine Balken,** water's a bad floor to walk on; *F:* **lügen, daß die Balken brechen, krachen, daß sich die Balken biegen,** to lie like a trooper, like a gas-meter, like a lawyer; (*b*) beam, arm (of balance); beam (of plough); *Mus:* bass-bar (of violin, etc.). **2.** *Anat:* corpus callosum cerebri. **3.** *Her:* fess(e). **4.** *Agr:* (*a*) balk, baulk; **Balken pflügen,** to rafter (a field); (*b*) ridge of earth (formed by two plough furrows). **5.** corn-loft, granary. **6.** *Artil:* land (between rifling grooves of gun).
bälken, *v.tr.* (*a*) *Constr: Min:* to timber (a building, a shaft); (*b*) *Agr:* to rafter (a field).
Balkenanker, *m.* *Constr:* anchor-iron, -tie, cramp-iron, (beam-)anchor.
Balkenauflager, *n. Constr:* beam-bearing.
Balkenblase, *f. Med:* hypertrophy of the muscular fibres of the bladder.
Balkenbrücke, *f. Civ.E:* girder-bridge, beam-bridge.
Balkendecke, *f.* timbered ceiling.
Balkeneisen, *n. Miner:* kamacite.
Balkenfach, *n. Constr:* case-bay.
Balkenfachwerk, *n. Arch:* half-timbering (of building).
Balkenfeld, *n. Constr:* case-bay.
Balkengerüst, *n.* (*a*) (wooden) scaffolding; (*b*) beams and joists, timber-work (of building).
Balkengesims, *n. Arch:* (*type of eaves-moulding*) string-course.
Balkengleiche, *f. Constr:* last course, levelling course.
Balkengurt, *m.*=**Balkengesims.**
Balkenjoch, *n. Constr:* case-bay.
Balkenkiel, *m. N.Arch:* bar-keel.
Balkenknie, *n.* beam-knee.
Balkenkopf, *m. Arch:* (projecting) end of a beam, beam-head.
Balkenlage, *f. Constr:* (method of) timbering.
Balkenlager, *n. Constr:* beam-bearing.
Balkenlücke, *f. Arch:* panel.
Balkennetz, *n. Fish:* pole-trawl.

Balkenschleife, Balkenschleppe, *f. Agr:* drag, *U.S:* float; clod-breaker, -crusher.
Balkensperre, *f. Navy:* boom barrage.
Balkenspirale, *f. Astr:* barred spiral.
Balkenstein, *m. Arch:* corbel, bracket.
Balkenstich, *m.* **1.** *Surg:* piercing of the corpus callosum cerebri. **2.** timber-hitch.
Balkenträger, *m. Constr:* girder, beam.
Balkenträgerbrücke, *f. Civ.E:* girder-bridge.
Balkenüberschrift, *f. Print:* large head-line, banner head-line.
Balkenwaage, *f.* beam-scales.
Balkenweite, *f. Constr:* interjoist.
Balkenwerk, *n. Constr:* beams and joists, timber-work (of building).
Balkon [bal'koŋ, bal'ko:n], *m.* -s/-s *&* -e [bal'ko:nə]. **1.** *Arch:* balcony. **2.** *Th: etc:* dress-circle; balcony; (*in cinema*) circle.
Balkonkasten, *m.* flower-box (for balcony).
Balkweger, *m.* -s/-. *N.Arch:* beam-shelf; shelf (-piece).
Ball[1], *m.* -(e)s/⸗e, ball; (*a*) (tennis-, golf-, billiard-, hockey-, foot)ball; **B. spielen,** to play ball, to have a game of ball; *F:* **mit j-m B. spielen,** to use s.o. as a football; to kick s.o. around; *Ten:* **B. durch die Mitte,** shot going straight between (one's) opponents in doubles; **toter B.,** ball out of play, dead ball; *Bill:* **bespielter B.,** object-ball; **einen B. machen,** to pocket a ball; *see also* **fälschen I; der B. des Schicksals sein,** to be the ball, the sport, of fortune; to be at the mercy of fortune; **den B. ins Rollen bringen,** to set, start, the ball rolling; (*b*) ball, bulb (of rubber syringe, etc.); *Nau:* ball, globe (of buoy); (*c*) ball (of snow, paper, wool, string); clew (of wool, string); (*heavenly body*) globe, ball; **die Sonne stand wie ein feuriger B. am Himmel,** the sun hung in the sky like a ball of fire.
Ball[2], *m.* -(e)s/⸗e. *Danc:* ball; **auf einen, zu einem, B. gehen,** to go to a ball; **den B. eröffnen,** to open the ball, to lead the first dance.
Ball[3], *m.* -(e)s/. *Ven:* baying, barking, giving tongue (of hounds).
Ballabgabe, *f. Fb: etc:* pass; passing of the ball.
Ballade [ba'la:də], *f.* -/-n, ballad.
Balladendichter, *m.* ballad-maker, -writer.
balladenhaft, *a.* ballad-like.
Balladensänger, *m.* ballad-singer.
balladesk [bala·'dɛsk], *a.* ballad-like.
Ballarbeit, *f. Box:* practice with the punch-ball.
Ballasrubin ['balasru·,bi:n], *m. Miner: Lap:* balas(ruby).
Ballast ['balast, ba'last], *m.* -(e)s/-e, (*a*) *Nau: Aer:* ballast; ballast-fin (of yacht); **Schiff in B.,** ship in ballast(-trim); **fliegender B.,** shifting ballast; **der B. ist übergegangen,** the ballast has shifted; **B. einnehmen,** to take in ballast; **B. löschen, ausschießen,** to discharge, throw out, ballast; (*b*) *F:* lumber; (unnecessary) burden, impediment; (*in literary work, etc.*) padding.
Ballasteisen, *n. Nau:* kentledge.
ballasten ['balastən]. **1.** *v.tr.* to ballast (ship, balloon). **2.** *v.i.* (*haben*) to take in ballast.
Balläster [ba·'lɛstər], *m.* -s/-=**Balester.**
Ballastkleid, *n. Nau:* port-sail.
Ballastpforte, *f. N.Arch:* ballast-port, -hole.
Ballastpumpe, *f. Nau:* ballast-donkey, -pump.
Ballasttank, *m. N.Arch:* ballast-tank.
Ballastwiderstand, *m. El:* fixed, loading, resistance.
Ballawatsch, *m.* -/. *Austrian Dial:* muddle, mess; nonsense.
Ballbehandlung, *f. Fb: etc:* ball control.
Ballbohrer, *m. Coop: Tls:* pod-auger.
Balle, *f.* -/-n. *Swiss Dial:*=**Ball**[1].
Ballei [ba'lai], *f.* -/-en. *Hist:* commandery.
Balleisen, *n. Tls:* skew chisel.
Ballempfang, *m. W.Tel:* reception for rebroadcasting.
ballen[1]. **I.** *v.* **1.** *v.tr.* to make, shape, into a ball; to ball; **die (Hand zur) Faust b.,** to clench one's fist; **mit geballten Fäusten,** with clenched fists. **2. sich ballen,** to form into a ball, to conglobate; to agglutinate, to clump; (*of clouds*) to gather; (*of snow*) to cake; (*of hands*) to clench; *see also* **geballt. 3.** *v.i.* (*haben*) to play ball.
II. *vbl s.* **1. Ballen,** *n. in vbl senses.* **2. Ballung,** *f.* (*a*)=II. 1; (*b*) agglutination, agglutinated mass; cake; clump.
Ballen[2], *m.* -s/-. **1.** (*a*) *Anat:* ball (of foot, thumb); (*on hand*) thenar; (*in palmistry*) mount; pad (on foot of cat, dog, bear, etc.); bulb (on horse's hoof); tip (of nose); (*b*) *Med:* bunion. **2.** *Hort:* ball (of soil on roots of transplanted tree). **3.** *Com: etc:* bale; **ein B. Baumwolle,** a bale of cotton; **ein B. Papier,** a bale of (ten reams of) paper; **in, zu, B. verpacken,** to pack (goods) in bales, to bale (goods). **4.** (*a*) *Fenc:* button (of foil); (*b*) *Tls:* horn (of plane); (*c*) *A: Engr: etc:* dabber, ball; (*d*) bezel, basil (of cutting tool).
Ballenbinder, *m.* packer.
Ballenblume, *f. Arch:* ball-flower.
Ballenbrecher, *m. Tex:* bale-breaker, opener.
Balleneisen, *n.*=**Balleisen.**
Ballenentzündung, *f. Med:* bunion.
Ballengüter, *n.pl. Com:* bale goods.
Ballenpflanze, *f. Hort:* balled plant.
Ballenpflanzung, *f. Hort:* transplanting (of trees, etc.) retaining balls of soil on the roots.
Ballenpresse, *f.* baling-press, baler.
Ballenschnur, *f.* packing-cord.
Ballenstroh, *n.* straw in bales.
Ballenwaren, *f.pl. Com:* bale goods.
ballenweise, *adv. Com:* in bales, by the bale.
Baller, *m.* -s/-. *Cr: etc:* bowler.
Ballerbüchse, *f. Toys:* pop-gun.
Ballerina, Ballerine [balə'ri:na:, -'ri:nə], *f.* -/-nen, ballerina, ballet-dancer.
Ballerino [balə'ri:no:], *m.* -/-ni, (male) ballet-dancer.
ballern, *v.i.* (*haben*) (*of gun, etc.*) to boom, bang; *F:* (*of pers.*) **an, gegen, die Tür b.,** to bang against the door.
Ballester [ba·'lɛstər], *m.* -s/-=**Balester.**
Ballett [ba'lɛt], *n.* -(e)s/-e, ballet.
Ballettänzer, *m.* ballet-dancer.
Balletteuse [balɛ'tø:zə], *f.* -/-n, (female) ballet-dancer.
Ballettmeister, *m.* maître de ballet.
Ballettmusik, *f.* ballet-music.
Ballettrock, *m.,* **Ballettröckchen,** *n.* ballet-skirt; tutu.
Ballettschuh, *m.* ballet-slipper, -shoe.
Balletttruppe, *f.* corps de ballet.
ballförmig, *a.* ball-shaped, spherical, round.
Ballführen, *n. Fb: etc:* dribbling (of the ball).
Ballgang, *m. Ten:* exchange (of shots).
Ballhammer, *m. Metalw:* fuller.
Ballhaus, *n.* (*a*) *Hist:* (covered) tennis-court; *Fr.Hist:* **der Schwur im B.,** the Tennis-Court Oath; (*b*) assembly-room.
Ballhausplatz, der. *Pr.n.* (*a*) the Ballhausplatz (*in Vienna*); (*b*) *F:* the Ballhausplatz, the Austrian Foreign Office.
Ballhausschwur, der. *Fr.Hist:* the Tennis-Court Oath.
Ballholz, *n. Cr: etc:* bat.
ballhornisieren [balhorni·'zi:rən], *v.tr.*=**balhornisieren.**
Ballhülle, *f.* (leather) cover (of football, etc.).
Ballhupe, *f. Aut:* bulb-horn.
ballig, *a.* ball-shaped, spherical, round; outward-curved (rim of pulley-wheel).
Balliste [ba'listə], *f.* -/-n. *Rom.Ant:* bal(l)ista.
Ballistik [ba'listik], *f.* -/. ballistics; **innere, äußere, B.,** interior, exterior, ballistics.
ballistisch [ba'listiʃ], *a.* ballistic; **ballistisches Pendel,** ballistic pendulum; **ballistische Kurve,** trajectory (of a projectile); **ballistisches Geschoß,** ballistic missile; *see also* **Galvanometer.**
Ballistit [balis'ti:t], *n.* -(e)s/. *Exp:* ballistite.
Balljunge, *m. Ten:* ball-boy.
Ballkleid, *n.* ball dress, (lady's) evening dress.
Ballmann, *m.* -(e)s/-männer. *Cr: etc:* bowler.
Ballmutter, *f.* chaperon.
Ballnetz, *n. Ten: etc:* ball-bag (*made of string*).
Ballon [ba'loŋ, ba'lõ:, ba'lo:n], *m.* -s/-s *&* -e [ba'lo:nə]. **1.** balloon; **in einem B. aufsteigen,** to go up in a balloon. **2.** (*a*) *Ind:* carboy; (*b*) *Ch:* balloon(-flask), bulb. **3.** *F:* head; *F:* nut, *U.S:* bean; **eins auf den B. bekommen,** to get a crack on the nut.
Ballonett [balo·'nɛt], *n.* -(e)s/-e. *Aer:* (*a*) gas-bag, -cell, ballon(n)et (of dirigible); (*b*) small balloon.
Ballonettmaul, *n. Aer:* air-scoop of a ballonet.
Ballonfahrer, *m.* balloonist.
Ballonklüver, *m. Nau:* balloon fore-sail, balloon-jib (of yacht).
Ballonkorb, *m. Aer:* basket, nacelle, car, of a, the, balloon.
Ballonkröpfer, *m. Orn:* (kind of) pouter-pigeon.
Ballonmütze, *f. Cost:* (i) balloon-cap; (ii) chef's hat.
Ballonreifen, *m. Aut: etc:* balloon-tyre.
Ballonschiff, *n. Navy:* balloon-carrier.
Ballonsegel, *n. Nau:* spinnaker, balloon-sail (of yacht).
Ballonseide, *f. Tex:* balloon-silk; parachute-silk.
Ballonsperre, *f. Av:* balloon-barrage.
Ballonspiel, *n. Games:* pallone (*Italian national ball-game*).
Ballonstoff, *m.* balloon-cloth, -fabric.
Ballonwesen, *n.* ballooning, aerostation.
Ballot [ba'lo:], *n.* -s/-s. *Com:* ballot, small bale.
Ballota [ba'lo:ta:], *f.* -/-ten. *Bot:* **1.** ballota. **2.** fruit of the holm-oak.
Ballotage [balo·'ta:ʒə], *f.* -/-n, ballot, balloting (by white or black balls).
Ballote [ba'lo:tə], *f.* -/-n. *Bot:* ballota; **schwarze B.,** black horehound.
ballotieren [balo·'ti:rən], *v.i.* (*haben*) to ballot (by white or black balls).
Ballsaal, *m.* ballroom.
Ballschläger, *m. Games:* (*a*) (cricket-, rounders-) bat; (*b*) batsman.
Ballschöne, *f.* belle of the ball.
Ballschuh, *m.* evening shoe; dancing-shoe, dance-slipper.
Ballsendung, *f. W.Tel:* rebroadcasting.
Ballspiel, *n.* ball-game; game of ball.
Ballstaat, *m.* **in vollem B.,** in full evening-dress, *F:* in full regalia.
Ballung *see* **ballen**[1] II. 2.
Ballwechsel, *m. Ten:* exchange (of shots); **nach mehrmaligem B.,** after several exchanges.
Ballwerfer, *m.*=**Baller.**
Balme, *f.* -/-n. *Geol:* crag undercut by erosion.
Balmung. *Pr.n.m.* -s. *Myth:* (*Siegfried's sword*) Balmung.
Balneo- [balne·o·-], *comb.fm.* balneo-; **Balneographie** [balne·o·gra·'fi:] *f,* balneography.
Balneologie [balne·o·lo·'gi:], *f.* -/. balneology.
Balneotherapie [balne·o·te·ra·'pi:], *f.* -/. balneotherapy.
Balsa ['balza:], *f.* -/-s, balsa, (South American Indian) raft.
Balsabaum, *m. Bot:* balsa(-tree), corkwood.
Balsaholz, *n.* balsa-wood, corkwood.
Balsam ['balza(:)m], *m.* -(e)s/-e. *Pharm: etc:* balm, balsam; **kanadischer B.,** Canada balsam; **B. in ein wundes Herz gießen, träufeln,** to pour balsam into, upon, a wounded heart; **das war B. auf meine Wunden,** it was balm to my wounded soul.
Balsamapfel, *m. Bot:* balsam apple, balsam pear.
Balsambaum, *m. Bot:* balsam-tree; (*a*) amyris; Jamaica rosewood, sweetwood; (*b*) commiphora; bdellium; (*c*) balsam of Tolu, Tolu-tree.
Balsamfrüchte, *f.pl.* fruits of commiphora (*used as incense*).
Balsamgurke, *f.*=**Balsamapfel.**
Balsamholz, *n.* wood of commiphora (*used as incense*).
balsamieren [balza·'mi:rən], *v.tr.* (*a*) to anoint; (*b*) to embalm.
Balsaminazeen [balza·mi·na·'tse:ən], *f.pl. Bot:* balsaminaceae.
Balsamine [balza·'mi:nə], *f.* -/-n. *Bot:* balsum, balsamine, impatiens.
Balsaminengewächse, *n.pl. Bot:* balsaminaceae.
balsamisch [bal'za:miʃ], *a.* balsamic, balmy.
Balsamkörner, *n.pl.*=**Balsamfrüchte.**
Balsamkraut, *n. Bot:* costmary, balsam-herb.
Balsamkürbis, *m.*=**Balsamapfel.**
Balsampappel, *f. Bot:* balsam poplar, tacamahac.
Balsampflaume, *f. Bot:* spondias, hog-plum.
Balsamstaude, *f.,* **Balsamstrauch,** *m. Bot:* balm of Gilead tree.
Balsamtanne, *f. Bot:* balsam fir, silver fir of Canada; *U.S:* silver pine.
Balte, *m.* -n/-n. *Ethn:* Balt, Baltic person.
Balthasar ['balta·za:r]. *Pr.n.m.* -s. **1.** Balthasar. **2.** *B.Hist:* Belshazzar.
Baltikum, das ['balti·kum]. *Pr.n.* -s. *Geog:* the Baltic countries.
Baltimoretrupial, Baltimorevogel, ['balti·mo·r-], *m. Orn:* Baltimore bird, Baltimore oriole, golden robin, hangbird, hangnest.
baltisch, *a. Geog:* Baltic; **die Baltischen Länder, Staaten,** the Baltic countries; **das Baltische Meer,** the Baltic (Sea); **der Baltische Landrücken,** the Baltic ridge; *Geol:* **der Baltische Schild,** the Baltic Shield.
Baluster [ba·'lustər], *m.* -s/-. *Arch:* baluster; **mit Balustern,** balustered.
Balustersäule, *f. Arch:* baluster-column.
Balustrade [ba·lus'tra:də], *f.* -/-n. *Arch:* balustrade; **Balkon mit B.,** balustraded balcony.
balustriert [ba·lus'tri:rt], *a.* balustraded (balcony, etc.).
Balutschistan [ba·'lutʃista·n]. *Pr.n.n.* -s = **Belutschistan.**
Balz, *f.* -/-en, *occ. m.* -es/-e. *Ven:* (*a*) (i) courtship, play, display (by cock-bird); (ii) treading, coupling, pairing; (*b*) coupling-, pairing-season, pairing-time.
balzen, *v.i.* (*haben*) (*a*) *Ven:* (*of certain male game-birds*) (i) to court, woo, display; (ii) to tread, couple, pair; (*b*) (*of children*) to romp (about).

Balzplatz, *m. Ven:* display ground.

Balzruf, *m. Ven:* mating *or* display call (of bird).

Balzzeit, *f. Ven:* coupling-, pairing-season.

Bambino [bamˈbiːnoː], *m.* **-s/-ni.** *Art:* bambino, the infant Christ.

Bambola(h)schote [ˈbamboˑlaː-], *f.* = **Babulschote.**

Bambus [ˈbambus], *m.* **-/-** *&* **-ses/-se.** *Bot:* bamboo (-cane).

Bambusbär, *m. Z:* giant panda.

Bambuse [bamˈbuːzə], *m.* **-n/-n,** (African) native servant, boy.

Bambushut, *m.* hat made of bamboo fibre.

Bambuspalme, *f. Bot:* bamboo-palm.

Bambuspapier, *n. Paperm:* India, Chinese, paper; Bible paper.

Bambusratte, *f. Z:* bamboo rat.

Bambusrohr, *n.* bamboo-cane.

Bambusvorhang, der. *Pol:* the Bamboo Curtain.

Bambuszucker, *m.* bamboo sugar, bamboo manna, tabasheer.

Bammel, *m.* **-s/.** *F:* **einen mächtigen B. vor etwas haben,** to dread, be afraid of, sth.; *F:* to be in a blue funk about sth.

bammeln, *v.i.* (*haben*) *F:* to dangle, hang swaying.

bämmeln, *v.i.* (*haben*) *Dial:* to play (at) ducks and drakes.

bamsen, *v.tr. Dial:* to beat (hides, etc.); *F:* to give (s.o.) a beating.

Ban [baːn], *m.* **-s/-e,** (*pers.*) ban.

banal [baˑˈnaːl], *a.* commonplace, banal, trite.

banalisieren [baˑnaˑliˑˈziːrən], *v.tr.* to vulgarize; to render (sth.) commonplace.

Banalität [baˑnaˑliˑˈtɛːt], *f.* **-/-en. 1.** banality, triteness. **2.** *usu.pl.* **Banalitäten,** banalities.

Banane [baˑˈnaːnə], *f.* **-/-n.** *Bot:* (*a*) banana; (*b*) banana-tree.

Bananenfaser, *f.* abaca, Manilla hemp.

Bananenfresser, *m. Orn:* plantain-eater.

Bananenmehl, *n.* banana-meal, banana-flour.

Bananenpflanzung, *f.* banana-plantation.

Bananenpisang, *m. Bot:* banana-tree.

Bananenplantage, *f.* banana-plantation.

Bananenstecker, *m. El:* banana-plug.

Banat[1] [baˑˈnaːt], *n.* **-(e)s/-e.** Banat(e), Bannat.

Banat[2], **das** [baˑˈnaːt]. *Pr.n.* **-(e)s.** *Geog:* the Banat.

Banater [baˑˈnaːtər]. **1.** *m.* **-s/-.** *Ethn:* native, inhabitant, of the Banat. **2.** *inv.a.* of the Banat.

Banause [baˑˈnauzə], *m.* **-n/-n.** Philistine; low-brow; person of little or no imagination.

Banausentum, *n.* philistinism.

banausisch [baˑˈnauziʃ], *a.* Philistine; unimaginative.

Band[1]. I. *n.* **-(e)s/⸗er. 1.** (*a*) (silk, etc.) ribbon, riband; (*for non-decorative, esp. industrial, purposes*) tape; (*made of hemp*) webbing; *Tex:* sliver (of carded cotton, etc.); (*b*) (*round hair, sleeve, hat, etc.*) band; **Bänder,** strings, ties (of apron, etc.); (*on workman's apron*) tapes; (*c*) *Nau:* strain-band; *Bookb:* tape, band; **(Buch) auf Bänder geheftet,** (book) sewn on tapes; (*d*) **das Blaue B.,** (i) the (Blue) Ribbon of the Garter, (ii) the Blue Riband (of the Atlantic, in racing, etc.); **ein B. im Knopfloch tragen,** to wear a (medal-)ribbon in one's buttonhole; *Sp:* **das B. berühren,** to breast the tape; **das B. zerschneiden,** to cut the tape (in opening ceremony); (*e*) (recording-)tape; **auf B. sprechen,** to record one's voice; **eine Rede, usw., auf B. sprechen,** to record a speech, etc.; (*f*) *F:* ribbon (of road, etc.); line, stream (of traffic, etc.); **das Bächlein wand sich wie ein silbernes B. durch die Wiesen,** the stream wound like a silver ribbon across the meadows. **2.** (*a*) (metal) strip, band (used for packing, etc.); (*b*) *Carp: Constr:* iron strap; clamp; *Constr: N.Arch:* hoop (round beam, boom, mast); fish (round mast); *Tls:* bolster (of carving-tool); (*c*) *Veh:* (iron) tyre (of wheel); *Coop:* hoop (of cask); **außer Rand und B. sein, geraten,** (i) (*of cask*) to be in need of re-hooping; (ii) *F:* (*of children, crowd*) to be, get, out of hand. **3. endloses B.,** endless, continuous, band, belt; *Mec.E:* (i) (= **Treibriemen**) transmission band, belt; (ii) (= **Förderband**) conveyor-belt, -band; transport band; *Print: Bookb:* tape (on stop-cylinder press, on folding-machine); *Carp:* sand-belt, *Metalw:* abrasive belt (of grinding-machine); *Ind:* **laufendes B.,** conveyor-belt; **Produktion am laufenden B.,** moving-band production; *F:* **er schreibt Bücher am laufenden B.,** he turns out, *F:* churns out, books one after the other. **4.** *Carp: Constr: etc:* (*a*) tie, tie-piece; brace; strut; (*b*) hinge (of door, window, etc.). **5.** *Anat:* ligament; frenum, string (of tongue, etc.). **6.** *Moll:* hinge (of bivalve). **7.** (*a*) *Arch:* band, fascia; (*b*) *Geol:* seam, band, streak (of ore, mineral, etc.); *Mount:* (*on rock-face*) ledge (of grass, rubble, etc.). **8.** *W.Tel:* frequency-band, wave-band; *Ph: Opt:* spectrum-band.

II. **Band,** *m.* **-(e)s/⸗e,** (*a*) volume; **ein Werk in sechs Bänden,** a work in six volumes, a six-volume work; *F:* **das spricht Bände,** that speaks volumes; that is very revealing; **darüber ließen sich Bände reden, schreiben,** that would fill volumes; (*b*) *Bookb:* binding.

III. **Band,** *n.* **-(e)s/-e. 1.** bond, tie, link; **ein Band, Bande, der Freundschaft,** a bond, bonds, ties, of friendship; **Bande des Blutes,** ties of blood, kinship; **geistiges B.,** spiritual link; **B. der Ehe,** marriage tie, bonds of matrimony; **alle Bande mit seiner Heimat lösen, durchschneiden,** to cut all ties, to sever all links, with one's own country. **2.** *pl.* **Bande,** bonds, chains; shackles; trammels; **in (Ketten und) Banden liegen,** to be in chains, in irons; **j-n in Bande schlagen, legen,** to put, cast, s.o. into chains, irons; **die Bande des Aberglaubens,** the trammels of superstition.

band[2] *see* **binden.**

Bandachat, *m. Miner:* banded agate, ribbon agate.

Bandage [banˈdaːʒə], *f.* **-/-n. 1.** *Med: Box: Fenc: etc:* bandage; *Vet:* horse bandage. **2.** *Veh:* (steel) tyre.

bandagieren [bandaˑˈʒiːrən], *v.tr.* to bandage, to put a bandage on (s.o., sth.).

Bandagist [bandaˑˈʒist], *m.* **-en/-en,** bandagist; truss-maker.

Bandalge, *f. Algae:* desmid.

Bandanendruck [banˈdaːnən-], *m. Tex:* bandan(n)a.

Bandantenne, *f. W.Tel:* tape aerial.

Bandantrieb, *m. Mec.E:* **mit B.,** belt-driven.

bandartig, *a.* ribbon-like, like a ribbon.

Bandassel, *f. Myr:* scolopendra.

Bandaufnahme, *f.* tape-recording.

Bandaxt, *f. Tls:* carpenter's axe.

Bandblitz, *m.* ribbon lightning.

Bandblume, *f. Bot:* candytuft.

Bandbohrer, *m. Tls:* drill for making dowel-holes.

Bandbreite, *f.* (*a*) *W.Tel:* band-width; (*b*) *Fin:* range of variation (of exchange rates); (*c*) *Statistics:* spread (of figures, etc.).

Bandbremse, *f. Mec.E:* band-brake, ribbon-brake, belt-brake, strap-brake.

Bandbrille, *f. Tchn: Aut: etc:* (pair of) goggles.

Bändchenarbeit, *f.* point-lace.

Bändchenmikrophon, *n.* = **Bandmikrophon.**

Bande[1], *f.* **-/-n,** band (of robbers, bandits, brigands), gang (of thieves); *Mil:* (party of) guerillas; terrorist organization; *A:* band (of musicians), company (of actors); *F:* bunch, crowd (of people, etc.); **eine fröhliche B.,** a merry crowd, party; **die ganze B. zog los,** the whole crowd went off together; **ihr seid doch eine traurige B.!** you are a miserable lot, a sorry crew!

Bande[2], *f.* **-/-n,** (*a*) border, edge, rim; cushion (of billiard-table, skittle-alley); border (of riding-ring, playing-field); boards (of polo-field); *Bill:* **den Ball an die B. spielen,** to cushion the ball; (*b*) *Nau:* side (of ship).

Bande[3], *f.* **-/-n.** *Opt:* band (of spectrum), spectrum-band.

bände *see* **binden.**

Bandeau [bãˑˈdoː], *m.* **-s/-s. 1.** headband, bandeau, fillet. **2.** = **Bandgesims.**

Bandeisen, *n.* (*a*) hoop-iron; strip-iron, strap-iron; (*b*) *Meteor:* taenite.

Bändel, *n.* **-s/-,** string (of apron, etc.); (shoe-)lace; **j-n am B. haben,** *F:* (i) to have, keep, s.o. on a string, on a lead; (ii) to have s.o. hanging on one's skirts.

Bandelier [bandəˈliːr], *n.* **-s/-e.** *Mil: A:* bandoleer, bandolier, cross-belt.

Bandelwerk, *n. Art:* strapwork (of baroque period).

Bandendiebstahl, *m. Jur:* theft committed by a gang.

Bandenführer, *m.* (*a*) *Mil:* guerilla leader; (*b*) gang leader.

Bandenkrieg, *m. Mil:* guerilla war.

Bandenmitglied, *n.* (*a*) *Mil:* member of a terrorist organization, guerilla; (*b*) *F:* gangster; thug.

Bandenspektrum, *n. Ph:* band-spectrum.

Bandenstoß, *m. Bill:* stroke off the cushion; bricole.

Bandenwesen, *n.* (*a*) *Mil:* partisan organizations *or* activities; (*b*) *F:* gangsterism; thuggery.

Bander, *m.* **-s/-.** *Z:* bandar; rhesus monkey.

Bänder, *m.* **-s/-.** *Dial:* cooper.

bänderartig, *a. Anat:* ligamental, ligamentous.

Bänderentzündung, *f. Med:* desmitis.

Bändergneis, *m. Geol:* banded gneiss.

Banderilla [bandəˈriljaː], *f.* **-/-s.** *Bull-fighting:* banderilla.

Banderillero [bandərilˈjeːroː], *m.* **-s/-s.** *Bull-fighting:* banderillero.

Bänderlehre, *f. Med:* syndesmology.

bändern. I. *v.tr.* to band, stripe; to mark, decorate, with bands, stripes; *see also* **gebändert.**

II. *vbl s.* **Bänderung,** *f.* **1.** *in vbl senses.* **2.** *Nat.Hist: etc:* fasciation; stripes, bands; *Geol:* foliation, lamination.

Banderole [bandə-, bãˑdəˈroːlə], *f.* **-/-n. 1.** (*a*) banderole, streamer; *Mil:* lance-pennon; (*b*) (trumpet *or* bugle) cord; (*c*) *Art:* banderole, scroll. **2.** (*a*) revenue stamp (for tobacco); (*b*) band round a cigar.

Banderolensteuer, *f.* tobacco tax (collected through revenue stamps).

banderolieren [bandəroˑˈliːrən], *v.tr.* to affix a revenue stamp to (cigar, etc.).

Bänderriß, *m. Med:* torn ligament.

Bänderton, *m. Geog:* varve(d), laminated, clay.

Bandeule, *f. Ent:* underwing.

Bandfeder, *f.* flat coil spring.

Bandfilter, *m. & n.* (*a*) *W.Tel:* band-pass filter; (*b*) *Ind:* band filter.

Bandfink, *m. Orn:* cut-throat finch, ribbon finch.

Bandfisch, *m. Ich:* ribbon-fish; red snake-fish, red band-fish.

Bandflechte, *f. Moss:* evernia.

Bandförderer, *m. Ind:* belt-, band-conveyor, conveyor-belt.

Bandförderung, *f.* = **Bandtransport.**

bandförmig, *a.* ribbon-shaped, belt-shaped; *Bot:* ligulate; *Nat.Hist:* taeniate, taenioid.

Bandführung, *f. Typewr:* ribbon guide.

Bandgeflecht, *n. Art:* strapwork.

Bandgenerator, *m. El.E:* belt generator.

Bandgerät, *n.* tape-recorder.

Bandgeschwindigkeit, *f. Tape-recording:* tape speed.

Bandgesims, *n. Arch:* string-course, plain moulding.

Bandgras, *n. Bot:* ribbon-grass, lady's garters.

Bandhacke, *f.* = **Bandaxt.**

Bandhaken, *m.* (*a*) *Coop: etc:* hoop-cramp; dog-hook; (*b*) hinge-pin (of door, etc.).

Bandhobel, *m. Coop:* hoop-shave.

Bandholz, *n. Coop:* hoop-wood.

-bändig, *comb.fm. a.* -volumed; **sechsbändiges Werk,** six-volume(d) work.

bändigen, *v.tr.* to tame (wild animal), to break in (horse); to subdue, overcome, master (one's passions); to reduce (s.o.) to obedience, to discipline (s.o.); to keep (s.o., sth.) under control.

Bändiger, *m.* **-s/-,** tamer (of wild beasts), breaker (of horses); subduer, vanquisher (of people).

Bandikut [ˈbandiˑkuˑt], *m.* **-s/-s.** *Z:* **1.** (Australian) bandicoot, perameles, long-nosed bandicoot. **2.** Indian giant rat, bandicoot(-rat).

Bandiltis, *m. Z:* zoril, Cape polecat.

Bandit [banˈdiːt], *m.* **-en/-en,** bandit, brigand; gangster; *F:* ruffian, villain.

Banditenwesen, *n.* banditry, brigandage.

Bandjaspis, *m. Miner:* banded, striped, jasper; ribbon-jasper.

Bandkegel, *m.* hinge-pin (of door, etc.).

Bandkeramik, *f. Archeol:* band-ceramics, ribbon-ware.

Bandkeramiker, *m. Prehist:* one of the ribbon-ware folk.

Bandkette, *f.* sash-chain.

Bandkupplung, *f. Mec.E:* band-clutch, strap-clutch.

Bandlappen, *m.* flap, strap, of the hinge.

Bandlauf, *m. Artil:* strip-wound gun-barrel.

Bandmacher, *m.* ribbon-maker, ribbon-weaver.

Bandmacherstuhl, *m.* = **Bandstuhl.**

Bandmaß, *n.* tape-measure.

Bandmast, *m.* telescopic mast.

Bandmeißel, *m. Metalw: etc:* half-round cold chisel.

Bandmikrophon, *n. W.Tel:* ribbon microphone.

Bandmontage, *f. Ind:* belt assembly.

Bandmühle, *f.* = **Bandstuhl.**

Bandnagel, *m. Carp:* treenail; dowel.

Bandnudeln, *f.pl. Cu:* noodles.

Bandola [banˈdoːlaː], *f.* **-/-len** = **Bandura.**

Bandoline [bandoˑˈliːnə], *f.* **-/-n.** *Toil:* bandoline.

Bandoneon [banˈdoːneˑon], *n.* **-s/-s.** *Mus:* bandonion.

Bandonion, Bandonium [banˈdoːnĭon, -ˈdoːnĭum], *n.* **-s/-s** *&* **-nien.** *Mus:* bandonion.

Bandornament, *n. Art:* strap-ornament.

Bandpaß, *m. W.Tel:* band-pass filter.

Bandrippe, *f. Arch:* (built-up) rib.

Bandrolle, *f. Art:* banderole.

Bandrose, f. Bot: cabbage-rose, Provence rose.
Bandsäge, f. band-saw, belt-saw, ribbon-saw.
Bandsägerolle, f. band-saw pulley.
Bandschärmaschine, f. Tex: mill warping machine.
Bandschärverfahren, n. Tex: mill warping.
Bandscheibe, f. 1. (a) Anat: intervertebral disc; (b) F:=Bandscheibenvorfall. 2. Mec.E: band-, belt-pulley.
Bandscheibenvorfall, m. Med: prolapsed intervertebral disc, F: slipped disc.
Bandscheider, m. Min: etc: belt separator.
Bandschleifmaschine, f. Woodw: etc: belt-sander, belt-sanding machine.
Bandschneidemaschine, f. Stonew: stone-cutting saw, frame-saw.
Bandschütze, m. Tex: ribbon-loom shuttle.
Bandseeadler, m. Orn: Pallas's sea-eagle.
Bandseil, n. flat rope.
Bändsel, n. -s/-. Nau: lashing, seizing.
Bandsperre, f. W.Tel: band-stop filter.
Bandspitze, f. lace edging, ribbon-lace.
Bandspreizung, f. W.Tel: (a) bandspread(ing); (b) bandspread tuning.
Bandspule, f. Tape-recording: tape spool, tape reel.
Bandstahl, m. hoop-steel, strip-steel, steel-strip.
Bandstuhl, m. Tex: ribbon loom, small-ware loom.
Bandtransport, m. Ind: belt-transport, -conveying.
Bandura [ban'duːra:], f. -/-ren. Mus: mandore, bandora, pandore.
Bandurria [ban'duria:], f. -/-s. Mus: bandurria.
Bandwaren, f.pl. Com: small-ware(s), ribbons.
Bandweber, m. ribbon-weaver, ribbon-maker.
Bandweberei, f. 1. ribbon-weaving; ribbon-manufacture. 2. ribbon-factory.
Bandwebstuhl, m.=Bandstuhl.
Bandweide, f. Bot: common willow, common osier, basket-willow.
bandweise, a. & adv. Print: by (single) volumes.
Bandwerk, n. Art: strapwork.
Bandwurm, m. Ann: Med: tapeworm, taenia; bewaffneter, unbewaffneter, B., armed, unarmed, tapeworm; F: (of speech, essay, etc.) lang wie ein B., endless, interminable, F: a mile long.
Bandwurmmittel, n. Med: taeni(i)cide, taenifuge.
Bandwurmrede, f. F: endless, interminable, speech.
Bandzieher, m.=Bandhaken (a).
Bandzüngler, m.pl. Moll: taenioglossa.
Bang [baŋ], m. -s/-. b(h)ang, Indian hemp.
Bangbuxe, Bangbüxe, f. F: cowardly, F: chicken-hearted, person; poltroon, F: milksop, funk.
bang(e)[1], a. (banger, bänger; bangst, bängst) 1. afraid; anxious; worrying; (a) mir ist b., I am afraid; I feel frightened; j-m b. machen, to alarm, scare, s.o.; es wurde mir angst und b., mir wurde b. und bänger, I grew more and more alarmed, my anxiety mounted; (b) eine bange Nacht, an anxious night, a night full of anxiety; eine bange Ahnung, a premonition of evil; voll banger Ahnung, filled with, full of, apprehension. 2. (a) mir, ihr, ist b. um ihn, I am, she is, worried, uneasy, about him; es war ihm, ihr war, b. um ihre Gesundheit, he was anxious, concerned, worried, nervous, about her health; (b) ihm war b. nach seiner Mutter, he longed, was longing, for his mother. 3. timid, fearful; afraid, frightened; das Kind ist b., the child is (i) timid, (ii) afraid; j-n b. machen, to give s.o. a fright; Iron: du bist ja gar nicht b.! you have some cheek! you've got a nerve!
Bange[2], f. -/. anxiety; worry; hab nur keine B.! don't be afraid! don't worry!
Bangemachen, n. alarming, scaring; B. gilt nicht! you can't scare me!
bangen, I v.i. (haben) & sich bangen. 1. (sich) um j-n b., to be concerned, uneasy, to worry, about s.o. 2. (sich) nach j-m b., to long for s.o. 3. v.impers. es bangte ihr, ihr bangte, vor den Folgen, she was fearful of the outcome; es bangte ihm, ihm bangte, um, für, sein Leben, he was afraid for his life, he feared for his life. II. Bangen, n. anxiety; apprehension; mit, voller, B., filled with, full of, apprehension; see also hängen[1] II. 2.
Bangert, m. -(e)s/-e. Dial: orchard.
Bangheit, f. anxiety, anxiousness; uneasiness, nervousness; timidity, fearfulness.
Bangigkeit, f. anxiety; (mental) anguish; fear; apprehension.
bänglich, a. anxious, uneasy; timid, fearful; ihm wurde b. zumute, he began to get alarmed, to feel uneasy.

Bänglichkeit, f. timidity, fearfulness.
Bangnis, Bängnis, f. -/-nisse=Bangigkeit.
Bangsch, a. Med: Bangsche Krankheit, undulant fever.
Banian [ban'jaːn, 'banjan], m. -s/-en, banian, Hindu trader.
Baniane [ba'niːaːnə], f. -/-n. Bot: banyan(-tree).
Banianenbaum, m. Bot: banyan(-tree).
Banjan [ban'jaːn, 'banjan], m. -s/-en=Banian.
Banjo ['banjoː, 'bandʒoː], n. -s/-s. Mus: banjo.
Banjospieler, m. banjoist. banjo-player.
Bank[1], f. -/ːe. 1. bench, seat; (in school) form; (in church) pew; Sch: F: die Bänke drücken, to be at school; er predigt vor leeren Bänken, (i) he preaches to empty pews; he is addressing an empty hall; (ii) nobody listens to him; his advice, speech, etc., falls on deaf ears; Th: vor leeren Bänken spielen, to play to empty benches; F: durch die B., without exception, every single one, F: every man Jack of them; auf der B. der Spötter sitzen, to sit in the seat of the scornful; F: etwas auf die lange B. schieben, to put off, postpone, sth. 2. (a) (carpenter's, engineer's) bench; Mec.E: bed (of lathe); table (of drilling machine); Opt: optical bench; (b) A: money changer's table; (c) stall, counter (esp. of butcher). 3. (a) Geol: layer, bed (of stone, etc.); Min: seam (of coal, etc.); (b) (sand-, mud-) bank; shoal, shelf; (c) (coral-)shoal; (oyster-) bed; (d) bank (of clouds, of fog). 4. (a) Fort: banquette, firing-step (of trench); (for guns) barbette; über B. feuern, schießen, to fire in barbette, over the parapet; (b) Arch: bench-table. 5. Wr: crouch.
Bank[2], f. -/-en. 1. Com: Fin: bank, banking house, banking establishment; die großen Banken, the big banks, the big banking houses; die B. von England, the Bank of England; ein Sturm auf die Banken, a run on the banks; ein Konto bei einer führenden B. haben, to have an account with a leading bank; Geld auf der B. (stehen, liegen) haben, to have money in the bank; Kredit bei der B., bank credit; seine B. anweisen, beauftragen, to instruct one's bank; Adm: ein Scheck auf die B. von England, a cheque on the Bank of England. 2. Gaming: bank; die B. halten, B. machen, to hold the bank; die B. sprengen, to break the bank.
Bankaktie, f. Fin: bank share.
Bankakzept, n. Fin: bank acceptance.
Bankamboß, m. bench-anvil, hand-anvil; stake (-anvil).
Bankangestellte, m., f. (decl. as adj.) bank clerk.
Bankanweisung, f. Fin: order for payment (drawn on a bank).
Bankart, m. -s/-e=Bankert.
Bankausweis, m. Fin: bank return.
Bankauszug, m. Fin: statement of account.
Bankaxt, f. Tls: bench-axe, carpenter's axe.
Bankbeamte, m. (decl. as adj.) bank clerk; bank official.
Bankbericht, m.=Bankausweis.
Bankbohrer, m. Tls: auger.
Bankbote, m. bank-messenger.
Bankbruch, m.=Bank(e)rott[1].
Bankbuch, n. bank-book, pass-book.
Bänkchen, n. -s/-, small bench; footstool.
Bankdeckung, f. Fin: note cover in the form of bankable securities.
Bankdiskont, m. Fin: (a) bank discount; (b) bank rate, discount rate.
Bankdiskontsatz, m.Fin: bank rate, discount rate.
Bankdurchschlag, m. Tls: punch.
Bankeinlage, f. Fin: bank deposit.
Bankeisen, n. (a) Constr: cramp-iron, holdfast; (b) Tls: bench-stop; bench-holdfast, -hook.
Bänkelkind, n.=Bankert.
Bänkelsänger, m. (a) ballad-singer; (b) Pej: ballad-monger.
Bänkel(sänger)lied, n. (street-)ballad.
banken. 1. v.tr. Nau: to beach; to run (ship) aground. 2. v.i. (haben) Gaming: to hold the bank.
Bankerott[1] [baŋk'rot], m. -(e)s/-e=Bankrott[1].
bankerott[2], a.=bankrott[2].
Bankert, m. -s/-e, (a) A: bastard, natural child; (b) F: brat.
Bankett[1] [baŋ'kɛt], n. -(e)s/-e, banquet, feast.
Bankett[2], n. -(e)s/-e. 1. Constr: base-course (of foundation wall). 2. (a) Civ.E: side-path, bench, driftway (of road); (b) (raised) footway, banquette. 3. Civ.E: set-off, berm (of slope, etc.). 4. Fort: banquette, firing-step (of trench).
bankettieren [baŋkɛ'tiːrən], v.i. (haben) to banquet, to feast.

Bankfach, n. 1. banking; er arbeitet im B., he is in the banking line. 2. safe (at a bank).
bankfähig, a. bankable, negotiable (security, etc.).
Bankfähigkeit, f. Fin: negotiability (of security, etc.).
Bankfiliale, f. Fin: branch bank.
bankförmig, a. bench-shaped; Arch: bankförmiger Sockel, bench-table.
Bankgebäude, n. bank building.
Bankgebühren, n.pl. Fin: bank charges; banker's commission, commission charged by the bank.
Bankgeld, n. Fin: bank money.
Bankgeschäft, n. Fin: (a) banking business; (b) bank(ing) transaction; banking operation; Bankgeschäfte abwickeln, to carry out banking operations.
Bankguthaben, n. Fin: bank balance, sum at the bank; Book-k: cash at bank.
Bankhaken, m.=Bankeisen (b).
Bankhalter, m. 1.=Bankknecht. 2. Gaming: banker.
Bankhammer, m. Tls: riveting-hammer.
Bankhaus, n. Fin: banking house, bank.
Bankhobel, m. Tls: bench-plane; jointer, jointing-plane.
Bankhorn, n. Tls: beak-iron, stake.
Bankier [baŋkiˈeː], m. -s/-s, banker; financier.
Bankivahuhn [baŋˈkiːvaː-], n. Orn: red jungle-fowl.
Bankkapital, n. Fin: bank stock, capital of a bank.
Bankknecht, m. Tls: standing-vice, leg-vice, staple-vice.
Bankkohle, f. Min: bench-coal.
Bankkonto, n. Fin: bank(ing) account, U.S: checking account; ein B. haben bei . . ., to bank with . . ., to have a bank(ing) account with. . . .
Bankkrach, m. Fin: bank failure; crash, smash.
Bankkredit, m. Fin: bank credit, bank loan.
bankmäßig, a. Fin: bankmäßige Zahlung, payment by cheque, etc.; bankmäßige Deckung, note cover of bankable paper.
Bankmeißel, m. Tls: cold chisel.
Bankmesser, n. Tls: (meat-)chopper, cleaver.
Banknote, f. Fin: bank-note, U.S: bank bill.
Banknotenausgabe, f. Fin: issue of bank-notes.
Banknotenumlauf, m. Fin: circulation of bank-notes.
Banko ['baŋkoː], n. -s/-s. Fin: A: banco, bank value.
Bankpapier, n. 1. Fin: bank-paper, bank-stock. 2.=Bankpostpapier.
Bankpostpapier, n. Paperm: bank, bank post, bank-paper.
Bankprovision, f.=Bankgebühren.
Bankrate, f. Fin: bank rate, discount rate.
Bankrott[1] [baŋk'rot], m. -(e)s/-e, a (a) Com: bankruptcy; failure; B. machen, to go bankrupt; to fail; (b) Jur: bankruptcy; einfacher B., simple bankruptcy; betrügerischer B., fraudulent bankruptcy; (c) (political, etc.) failure; moralischer B., moral bankruptcy.
bankrott[2], a. (a) bankrupt (trader, firm, etc.); b. gehen, to go bankrupt; b. sein, to be bankrupt; j-n für b. erklären, to adjudge, adjudicate, s.o. bankrupt; F: ich bin b., I am dead broke; (b) moralisch b., morally bankrupt; geistig b. sein, to have exhausted one's intellectual resources.
Bankrotterklärung, f. declaration of bankruptcy.
Bankrotteur [baŋkro'tøːr], m. -s/-e, bankrupt.
bankrottieren [baŋkro'tiːrən], v.i. (haben) to go bankrupt.
Bankrottmasse, f. (a) Jur: bankrupt's estate, property, assets; insolvent company's assets; (b) F: die B., our, your, their, etc., few remaining pennies.
Banksatz, m.=Bankrate.
Bankscheck, m. Fin: banker's cheque, cheque on a bank.
Bankschneider, m. (pers.) flenser (of whales).
Bankschraubstock, m. Tls: bench-vice.
Banksie ['baŋksiə], f. -/-n. Bot: banksia.
Bankskiefer, f. Bot: Banks' pine, jack-pine.
Bankspesen, pl. bank charges; banker's commission, commission charged by the bank.
Banksrose, f. Bot: Banksia(n) rose.
Banktratte, f. Fin: banker's draft.
Bankul ['baŋkuˈl], m. -s/-s. Bot: candleberry-tree.
Bankulöl, n. candlenut oil.
Bankverbindung, f. Com: (on letter-head, etc.) 'Bankverbindungen . . .', 'bank(ing) accounts with . . .'.
Bankwagen, m. Veh: charabanc.
Bankwechsel, m. Fin: (a) banker's draft; (b) bank-bill.

Bankwerte, *m. pl. Fin:* bank shares, *U.S:* bank stock.
Bankwesen, *n. Fin:* banking; banking system.
Banlieue [bãli'ø:], *f.* -/-s = **Bannmeile** (*a*).
Bann, *m.* -(e)s/-e. **1.** *Hist:* (*a*) (king's, etc.) jurisdiction, soke; (*b*) soke; district under (s.o.'s) jurisdiction. **2.** *Hist:* (*a*) edict; (public) proclamation; (*b*) interdict, proscription; (proclamation of) banishment; ban; *Ecc:* anathema, (decree of) excommunication; **j-n in den B. tun, schlagen, j-n mit dem B. belegen,** (i) to banish, proscribe, s.o., (ii) *Ecc:* to excommunicate s.o.; **seinen B. brechen,** to break one's ban. **3.** spell; charm, enchantment; **in j-s B. geraten,** to come under s.o.'s influence, to be under s.o.'s spell; to fall a victim to s.o.'s charms; **der Redner hielt die Zuhörer in seinem B.,** the speaker held his audience spellbound; **den B. brechen,** to break the spell, the charm.
Bannbezirk, *m. Hist:* soke; district under (s.o.'s) jurisdiction.
Bannbrief, *m.* (*a*) (public) proclamation; (*b*) = **Bannbulle.**
Bannbruch, *m.* (*a*) *Hist:* breaking of (one's) ban; (*b*) *Jur:* infringement of the excise laws.
Bannbulle, *f. Ecc:* bull, decree, of excommunication.
Banndeich, *m. Dial: Hyd.E:* winter dike.
bannen, *v.tr.* **1.** *Hist:* **Wälder, einen Fluß, usw., b.,** to prohibit, ban, public use of woods, a river, etc. **2.** (*a*) *Hist:* to banish, proscribe (s.o.); *Ecc:* to excommunicate (s.o.); (*b*) **Geister b.,** (i) to exorcize, lay, spirits *or* ghosts; (ii) to conjure (up), raise, summon, invoke, call up, spirits *or* ghosts; **die Not b.,** to banish want; **Furcht b.,** to banish, cast out, dispel, fear. **3.** (*a*) to bewitch, charm, put a spell on (s.o., sth.), to transfix (s.o.); (*of fear, etc.*) to hold (animal) paralysed; **mit einem Blick bannte er sie an ihren Platz,** he transfixed her with a look; **wie gebannt starrte er auf das Bild,** he gazed spellbound at the picture; **er blieb wie gebannt stehen,** he stood (as though) spellbound; he seemed rooted to the ground; *adv.* **gebannt zuhören, lauschen,** to listen spellbound; (*b*) to capture (movement, voice, etc.) (on canvas, record, etc.); **der Künstler hat die Anmut ihrer Bewegungen auf die Leinwand gebannt,** the artist has captured their graceful movements on canvas.
Banner, *n.* -s/-, (*a*) banner, gonfalon; standard; *Ecc:* banner; **unter dem B. der Freiheit kämpfen,** to fight under the banner of freedom; (*b*) (advertising) banner; advertising streamer.
Banneret [banə'rɛ:], *m.* -s/-s. *Hist:* banneret.
Bannerherr, *m. Hist:* banneret.
Bannerträger, *m. Mil: Ecc:* standard-bearer.
Bannerwimpel, *m.* pennant, pennon.
Bannfluch, *m. Ecc:* anathema; ban; *Hist:* ban.
Bannforst, *m. Hist:* royal forest.
Banngebiet, *n.* = **Bannbezirk.**
Banngerechtigkeit, *f.* = **Bannrecht.**
Banngewalt, *f. Hist:* (power of) jurisdiction, soke.
Banngut, *n.* = **Bannware.**
Bannherr, *m. Hist:* feudal landlord.
bannig, *adv. North G.Dial:* very; tremendously, terribly, terrifically; **b. kalt,** terribly cold.
Bannkelter, *f. Hist:* bannal, communal, winepress.
Bannkreis, *m. Hist:* district under (s.o.'s) jurisdiction; *F:* **sie geriet ganz in seinen B.,** she came completely under his spell, his influence.
Bannmeile, *f.* (*a*) *Hist:* precincts of a town; (*b*) *Jur:* area around government buildings within which processions and meetings are prohibited.
Bannmühle, *f. Hist:* bannal, communal, mill.
Bannofen, *m. Hist:* bannal, communal, bakehouse.
Bannrecht, *n. Hist:* monopoly rights of the feudal landlord.
Bannspruch, *m.* ban; curse; *Ecc:* (decree of) excommunication.
Bannstein, *m.* boundary-stone, -mark.
Bannstrahl, *m.* **B. der Kirche, päpstlicher B.,** excommunication, anathema; the thunders of the Pope.
Bannvogt, *m. Hist:* soke-reeve.
Bannwald, *m.* (*a*) forest planted as protection *esp.* against avalanches; (*b*) = **Bannforst.**
Bannware, *f. Cust:* contraband goods.
Bannwart, *m. A. & Dial:* watchman, guard (over fields, etc.).
Banse, *f.* -/-n, **Bansen,** *m.* -/-. *Dial:* bay (in barn).
bansen, *v.tr. Dial:* to stack (sheaves).
Bantam ['bantam], *n.* -s/-s. *Husb:* bantam.
Bantamgewicht, *n. Box:* bantam-weight.
Bantamgewichtler, *m.* -s/-, (*boxer*) bantam-weight.
Bantamhuhn, *n. Husb:* bantam.
bantamisieren [banta·mi·'zi:rən], *v.tr. Husb:* to bantamize.
Banteng ['bantɛŋ], *m.* -s/-s. *Z:* banteng, banting.
Bantingkur, *f. Med:* banting (diet), reducing diet.
Bantu ['bantu:], *m.pl. Ethn:* Bantu.
Bantuneger, *m. Ethn:* Bantu.
Bantusprache, *f. Ling:* Bantu (language).
Banus ['ba:nus], *m.* -/- = **Ban.**
Banyan [ba·nĭ'a:n], *m.* -s/-en. *Bot:* banyan(-tree).
Baobab ['ba:o·bap], *m.* -s/-s. *Bot:* baobab(-tree), monkey-bread tree.
Baphie ['ba·fĭə], *f.* -/-n. *Bot:* baphia.
Bapst, *m.* -(e)s/⸗e. *A:* = **Papst.**
baptieren [bap'ti:rən], *v.tr.* (*a*) *A:* to baptize; (*b*) *Tchn:* to dip, immerse, (sth.) (in liquid, etc.).
Baptismus [bap'tismus], *m.* -/. *Ecc:* Baptist doctrine.
Baptist [bap'tist]. **1.** *Pr.n.m.* -s, (*a*) Baptist; (*b*) (St. John) the Baptist. **2.** *m.* -en/-en. *Ecc:* Baptist.
Baptisterium [baptis'te:rĭum], *n.* -s/-rien, baptist(e)ry.
Bar[1], *f.* -/-s. **1.** (*a*) bar (in public house, etc.); (*b*) public house, *esp.* night-club. **2.** *Furn:* drink-cabinet.
Bar[2], *n.* -s/-s. *Meteor.Meas:* bar.
Bar[3], *m.* -(e)s/-e. *Pros:* (*in the Middle High German lyric and the 'Meistergesang'*) strophe consisting of two 'Stollen' and the 'Abgesang'.
bar[4], *a.* **1.** bare, naked; **bar-,** *comb.fm.* bare-; **barfuß,** barefoot. **2.** *pred.* (+*gen.*) devoid of, lacking; without; **bar jeglicher Vernunft, jeglicher Vernunft bar,** devoid of, lacking, any sense; **aller Ehren bar,** stripped of all honours. **3.** pure, sheer; **bares Gold,** pure gold; **barer Unsinn,** sheer, downright, nonsense; **barer Leichtsinn,** sheer recklessness, sheer folly; **das ist die bare Wahrheit,** that is the plain, unadulterated, truth; **er nahm alles für bare Münze,** he took everything for gospel truth, he took it all in, *F:* he swallowed it whole. **4.** *Com: etc:* (*a*) **bares Geld,** cash, ready money; (*b*) *adv.* **(in) bar bezahlen,** to pay (in) cash, (in) ready money; **hundert Mark in bar bezahlen,** to pay a hundred marks in cash; **'Verkauf nur gegen bar',** 'cash sales only', 'no credit given'; **das Auto kostet £ 600 in bar,** the car costs £600 cash down.
Bar-, *comb.fm. Fin: Com:* cash . . . ; **Barpreis** *m,* cash price; **Bargeschäft** *n,* cash transaction; **Barverkauf** *m,* cash sale.
-bar, *a.suff.* **1.** (*appended to stem of verbs*) -able; -ible; that can be + *p.p.*; **erkennbar,** recognizable; **schiffbar,** navigable; **lesbar,** readable; **tanzbar,** danceable; **diskutierbar,** discussible; debatable; **wahrnehmbar,** perceptible; **absenkbar,** that can be lowered. **2.** (*appended to nouns*) -ful; **dankbar,** thankful, grateful; **wunderbar,** wonderful; **schandbar,** shameful; **furchtbar,** fearful, frightful.
Bär, *m.* -en/-en. **1.** (*a*) *Z:* bear; **gemeiner, brauner Bär,** brown bear; **schwarzer Bär,** American black bear; **australischer Bär,** Australian native bear, koala; *F:* **ungeleckter Bär,** unlicked cub; *F:* **hungrig wie ein Bär,** as hungry as a hunter; *F:* **j-m einen Bären aufbinden,** *F:* to tell s.o. a tall story, a whopping lie, a whopper; to pull s.o.'s leg; (*b*) *Com:* bearskin. **2.** *South G.Dial:* (*certain male animals, e.g.*) boar, male marmot, etc. **3.** *Ent:* tiger-moth; **Brauner Bär,** common tiger-moth; **Schwarzer Bär,** cream-spot tiger-moth. **4.** *Astr:* **der Große Bär,** the Great Bear, Ursa Major; **der Kleine Bär,** the Little Bear *or* Dipper, Ursa Minor. **5.** (*a*) *Civ.E: etc:* ram, monkey (of pile-driver); (*b*) *Metall:* bear, salamander, shadrach. **6.** *Fort:* batardeau.
Barabbas ['barabas]. *Pr.n.m.* -'. *B.Hist:* Barabbas.
Baracke [ba'rakə], *f.* -/-n, hut; **elende B.,** shanty; hovel; hole (of a place); *Mil: etc:* **in Baracken leben,** to live in huts, in hutments.
Barackenlager, *n. Mil: etc:* hutted camp; hutments.
Baranke [ba'raŋkə], *f.* -/-n. *Com:* Russian lambskin.
Baratterie [baratə'ri:], *f.* -/-n [-'ri:ən]. *Nau:* barratry.
Baratteur [bara'tø:r], *m.* -s/-s & -e. *Com:* defrauder; cheat, swindler.
Baratthandel [ba'rat-], *m. Com:* barter, truck.
barattieren [bara'ti:rən], *v.i.* (*haben*) *Com:* to exchange, truck, barter, goods, etc.
Baratt(o)geschäft [ba'rat(o:)-], *n.* = **Baratthandel.**
Barauslagen, *f.pl. Com:* out-of-pocket expenses; cash outlay, cash expenses.
Barbados ['barba·dos, bar'ba:dos]. *Pr.n.n.* -'. *Geog:* Barbado(e)s.
Barbadosaloe, *f. Bot: Pharm:* Barbados aloe.
Barbadosbein, *n. Med:* Barbados leg.
Barbadosstachelbeere, *f. Bot:* Barbados gooseberry.
Barbadoszeder, *f. Bot:* Barbados bastard cedar, Spanish cedar.
Barbakane [barba·'ka:nə], *f.* -/-n. *Fort: A:* barbican, outwork (of fortifications).
Barbar [bar'ba:r], *m.* -en/-en, barbarian.
Barbara ['barba·ra:]. *Pr.n.f.* -s. Barbara.
Barbarakraut, *n. Bot:* barbarea, winter-cress, yellow rocket.
Barbarei [barba·'rai], *f.* **1.** -/-en, barbarity, barbarism, barbarousness. **2.** *Pr.n.f.* -. *A.Geog:* **die B.,** Barbary, the Barbary States.
Barbareske [barba·'rɛskə], *m.* -n/-n. *Ethn: A:* Berber.
Barbareskenstaaten, die. *Pr.n.m.pl.* = **Barbarei 2.**
barbarisch [bar'ba:riʃ], *a.* (*a*) barbaric, primitive (people, art, etc.); uncouth; (*b*) barbarous, inhuman, brutal; (*c*) *F:* fearful, dreadful, frightful (cold, hunger, etc.).
barbarisieren [barba·ri·'zi:rən], *v.tr.* to barbarize (people, style, etc.).
Barbarismus [barba·'rismus], *m.* -/-men. **1.** *Ling:* barbarism. **2.** barbarity, rudeness, crudeness.
Barbarossa [barba·'rosa:]. *Pr.n.m.* -s. *Hist:* Barbarossa.
Barbe, *f.* -/-n. **1.** *Ich:* barbel. **2.** *Cost:* pinner (of coif). **3.** *Engr:* beard, barb, bur(r) (on engraved plate).
barbeinig, *a.* bare-legged.
bärbeißig, *a.* bearish, surly; like a bear with a sore head.
Bärbeißigkeit, *f.* bearishness, surliness.
Bärbel. *Pr.n.f. & n.* -s. (*dim. of* **Barbara**) Babs.
Bärbelkraut, Barbenkraut, *n.* = **Barbarakraut.**
Barbestand, *m.* (*a*) *Book-k:* cash in hand; (*b*) *Fin:* cash reserve; **B. der Zentralbank,** central bank gold, bullion, reserve.
Barbette [bar'bɛtə], *f.* -/-n. *Fort:* barbette.
Barbier [bar'bi:r], *m.* -s/-e, barber; *A:* **B. und Wundarzt,** barber-surgeon.
barbieren [bar'bi:rən], *v.tr.* to shave; *F:* **j-n über den Löffel b.,** to swindle, to fleece, s.o. (of money, etc.).
Barbierladen, *m.* barber's shop.
Barbiermesser, *n.* straight razor, *F:* cut-throat razor.
Barbierschild, *n.* barber's sign; (*in Germany*) barber's brass basin; (*in England*) barber's pole.
Barbiton [bar'bi·tɔn], *n.* -s/-s. *Mus:* barbiton.
Barbitursäure [barbi·'tu:r-], *f. Ch:* barbituric acid.
barbs, barbst, *pred.a. & adv. Dial:* = **barfuß.**
Barcarole [barka·'ro:lə], *f.* -/-n = **Barkarole.**
Barch, *m.* -(e)s/⸗e. *Dial:* castrated boar.
Barchan [bar'ça:n], *m.* -/-e, (*in desert*) barkhan.
barchen ['barçən], *a. Tex:* (of) fustian.
Bärchen, *n.* -s/-, young bear, bear cub.
Barchent ['barçənt], *m.* -s/-e. *Tex:* barchent.
Barches ['barçəs], *m.* -/-, (*bread*) challah.
Bardame, *f.* barmaid.
Barde[1] ['bardə], *m.* -n/-n, (Celtic) bard; poet.
Barde[2], *f.* -/-n. *Cu:* slice of bacon (*used to cover fowl, etc.*), *A:* bard.
Bardeckung, *f. Fin:* note cover of gold and foreign exchange; *Com:* cash cover.
Bardendichtung, *f.* bardic poetry.
bardieren [bar'di:rən], *v.tr. Cu:* (*a*) to bard (fowl, etc.) (with bacon); (*b*) to scale (fish).
bardisch ['bardiʃ], *a.* bardic (song, poetry, etc.).
Bare, *f.* -/-n = **Barfrost.**
Barège [ba'rɛ:ʒə], *m.* -/. *Tex:* barège; barrège.
Bareis ['ba·r⁹ais], *n.* ice without snow-cover.
Barelle [ba·'rɛlə], *f.* -/-n. *Dial:* apricot.
Bareme [ba·'rɛ:mə], *m.* -/-n. **1.** ready-reckoner, calculator. **2.** printed table, schedule (for prices).
Bärenbeißer, *m.* bear-hound (*used in bear-baiting*).
Bärenbeutler, *m. Z:* sarcophilus, Tasmanian devil.
Bärendienst, *m. F:* **j-m einen B. leisten,** to do s.o. a disservice.
Bärendill, *m. Bot:* spignel, baldmoney.
Bärendreck, *m. F:* liquorice.
Bärenfell, *n.* bearskin.
Bärenfellmütze, *f. Cost:* bearskin.
Bärenfenchel, *m. Bot:* spignel, baldmoney.
Bärenfett, *n. A:* bear's-grease (*used as pomade*).
Bärenführer, *m.* (*a*) bear-leader; (*b*) *F:* travelling tutor, *F:* bear-leader.
Bärenfuß, *m.* **1.** *Bot:* bear's-foot, stinking hellebore. **2.** *Vet:* acute development of (horse's) fetlock, causing the hoof to be pushed forward. **3.** *pl.* **Bärenfüße** = **Bärenklauen.**
bärenfüßig, *a. Vet:* (horse) having a weak fetlock causing the hoof to be pushed forward.

Bärengraben, *m.* bear-pit, *A:* bear-garden.
Bärengrube, *f.* **1.** = **Bärengraben. 2.** *Ven:* pitfall, trap.
Bärenhatz, *f.* bear-baiting.
Bärenhaut, *f.* bearskin; *F:* **auf der B. liegen**, to idle, to laze (about).
Bärenhäuter, *m.* **-s/-.** *F:* lazy-bones, idler.
Bärenhetze, *f.* bear-baiting.
Bärenhunger, *m. F:* **einen B. haben**, to be as hungry as a hunter.
Bärenhüter, **der.** *Pr.n. Astr:* the Bear Driver, the Bearwarden, Boötes.
Bäreninsel, **die.** *Pr.n. Geog:* Bear Island.
Bärenjagd, *f.* bear-hunt.
Bärenjunge, *n.* (*decl. as adj.*) young bear, bear cub.
Bärenklau, *m.* **-s/.** & *f.* **-/.** *Bot:* **1.** heracleum; **gemeine(r) B.**, cow-parsnip, hogweed, pigweed. **2.** acanthus; **echte(r) B.**, brank-ursine, bear's-breech.
Bärenklauen, *f.pl.* (*a*) *Cost:* round-toed shoes slashed at the toes, 'bear's paws'; (*b*) *Arm:* sollerets, steel-shoes.
Bärenklee, *m. Bot:* **1.** kidney-vetch, lady's-finger, woundwort. **2.** (common) melilot, yellow sweet clover.
Bärenlauch, *m. Bot:* ramson.
Bärenmaki, *m. Z:* awantibo.
Bärenmarder, *m. Z:* binturong.
Bärenmotte, *f. Ent:* tiger-moth.
Bärenmütze, *f. Mil.Cost:* bearskin.
Bärenohr, *n. Bot:* bear's-ear, auricula.
Bärenpavian, *m. Z:* chacma.
Bärenraupe, *f. Ent:* woolly bear (caterpillar).
Bärenrobbe, *f. Z:* fur-seal, ursine seal.
Bärenschote, *f. Bot:* milk-vetch.
Bärensee. *Pr.n.m. Geog:* **der Große B.**, Great Bear Lake.
Bärenspinner, *m. Ent:* tiger-moth.
bärenstark, *a.* (as) strong as an ox.
Bärentatze, *f.* **1.** bear's paw. **2.** *Fung:* clavaria botrytis.
Bärentraube, *f. Bot:* bearberry; *Bot: Pharm:* **immergrüne B.**, uva ursi.
Bärentreiber, *m.* (*a*) = **Bärenführer** (*a*); (*b*) = **Bärenhüter.**
Bärenwurz(el), *f. Bot:* **1.** spignel, baldmoney. **2.** = **Bärenklau 1.**
Bärenzwinger, *m.* bear-pit.
Barett [ba·'rɛt], *n.* **-(e)s/-e.** *Cost:* (*a*) (cleric's, German judge's, German university official's, etc.) biretta, cap; (*b*) (soft) cap; beret; (*in Scotland*) tam o' shanter (cap); (*c*) (*in England, etc.*) (square) academic cap; *F:* mortar-board, (*at Cambridge*) square.
Barettfeile, *f. Tls:* cant-file.
Barfreimachung, *f. Post:* bulk franking.
Barfrost, *m.* black frost.
barfuß, *pred.a.* & *adv.* barefoot, barefooted.
Barfüßer, *m.* **-s/-**, **Barfüßermönch**, *m. Ecc:* discalced Carmelite, Franciscan, etc.; barefooted (Carmelite, Franciscan, etc.) monk.
barfüßig, *a.* barefooted, barefoot.
barg, bärge *see* **bergen.**
Bargeld, *n. Com:* (*a*) cash, ready money; (*b*) *A:* coin, specie.
bargeldlos, *a. Bank: Fin:* **bargeldloser Zahlungsverkehr**, settlement by cheque, etc.; credit system.
barhaupt, *pred.a.* & *adv.* bare-headed.
barhäuptig, *a.* bare-headed; **b. vor dem König stehen**, to stand bare-headed before the king.
Barhocker, *m.* bar-stool.
Baribal ['ba:ri·bal], *m.* **-s/-s.** *Z:* American black bear.
Barilla [ba·'rilja:], *f.* **-/.**, **Barillasoda**, *n. Ind:* barilla.
Barille [ba·'rilə], *f.* **-/-n.** *Dial:* apricot.
Bärin, *f.* **-/-innen.** *Z:* she-bear.
Bariton ['ba:ri·ton], *m.* **-s/-e** [-to:nə]. *Mus:* **1.** (i) baritone (voice), (ii) (*pers.*) baritone; **lyrischer B.**, high baritone. **2.** *A:* barytone. **3.** = **Baritonhorn.**
Baritonhorn, *n. Mus:* barytone, euphonium.
Baritonist [ba·ri·to·'nist], *m.* **-en/-en.** *Mus:* baritone.
Baritonklarinette, *f. Mus:* alto clarinet.
Baritonsänger, *m.* baritone.
Barium ['ba:rium], *n.* **-s/.** *Ch:* barium; **kohlensaures B.**, barium carbonate; **chromsaures B.**, barium chromate; **schwefelsaures B.**, barium sulphate.
Barium-, *comb.fm. Ch:* barium-; **Bariumchlorid** *n*, barium chloride; **Bariumhydroxyd** *n*, barium hydroxide.
Bariumbrei, *m. Med:* barium meal.
Bariumchromat, *n. Ch:* barium chromate.
Bariumdioxyd, *n.* = **Bariumperoxyd.**
Bariumhydrat, *n. Ch:* barium hydrate.
Bariumhyperoxyd, *n.* = **Bariumperoxyd.**
Bariumkarbonat, *n. Ch:* barium carbonate.
Bariummonoxyd, *n. Ch:* barium monoxide, barium oxide.
Bariumoxyd, *n. Ch:* barium oxide.
Bariumperoxyd, *n. Ch:* barium peroxide, barium dioxide.
Bariumplatinzyanür, *n. Ch:* barium platinocyanide.
Bariumsalz, *n. Ch:* barium salt.
Bariumsulfat, *n. Ch:* barium sulphate.
Bariumsuperoxyd, *n.* = **Bariumperoxyd.**
Bark, *f.* **-/-en.** *Nau:* barque, bark.
Barkarole [barka·'ro:lə], *f.* **-/-n.** *Mus:* barcarol(l)e.
Barkasse [bar'kasə], *f.* **-/-n. 1.** *Navy:* launch, long-boat. **2.** *Nau:* small motor launch.
Barke [barkə], *f.* **-/-n**, small fishing-boat, sculling boat; bark.
-barkeit, *s.suff. f.* **1.** -ability; -ibility; **Schiffbarkeit**, navigability; **Heilbarkeit**, curability; **Hörbarkeit**, audibility; **Sichtbarkeit**, visibility. **2.** -fulness; **Dankbarkeit**, thankfulness; **Schandbarkeit**, shamefulness.
Barkerole [barkə'ro:lə], *f.* **-/-n** = **Barkarole.**
Barkholz, *n. N.Arch:* sheer-strake.
Barkschiff, *n. Nau:* barque, bark.
Barlaam ['barla:m]. *Pr.n.m.* **-s.** Barlaam; *Lit:* **B. und Josaphat**, Barlaam and Josaphat.
Bärlapp, *m.* **-s/.** *Bot:* lycopod(ium), club-moss.
Bärlappmehl, *n.*, **Bärlappsamen**, *m. Pharm: etc:* lycopodium powder, vegetable brimstone, vegetable sulphur.
Bärlatschen, *m.pl.* = **Bärenklauen.**
Barlauf, *m. Games:* prisoner's base.
Barlohn, *m.* wages (paid) in cash.
Barlowsch ['barlo:ʃ], *a. Med:* **Barlowsche Krankheit**, Barlow's disease; infantile scurvy.
Bärme, *f.* **-/.** *Dial:* barm; yeast.
Barmekide [barmə'ki:də], *m.* **-n/-n.** *Hist: Lit:* Barmecide.
Barmekidenmahlzeit, *f. Lit: F:* Barmecide Feast.
barmen, *v.i.* (*haben*) *Dial:* to moan; *Lit:* to wail, to lament.
Barmer. 1. *m.* **-s/-.** *Geog:* native, inhabitant, of Barmen. **2.** *inv.a.* of Barmen, Barmen ...; *Com:* **B. Artikel**, small-ware(s).
barmherzig [barm'hɛrtsiç], *a.* kind-hearted, kind; merciful (God, king, etc.); **der barmherzige** [barm'hɛrtsi·gə] **Samariter**, the good Samaritan; *B:* **der Herr ist b. und ein Erbarmer**, the Lord is very pitiful, and of tender mercy; *B:* **selig sind die Barmherzigen, denn sie werden Barmherzigkeit erlangen**, blessed are the merciful, for they shall obtain mercy; *Ecc:* **Barmherzige Brüder**, Brothers Hospitallers; **Barmherzige Schwestern**, Sisters of Mercy, Sisters of Charity.
Barmherzigkeit [barm'hɛrtsiçkait], *f.* mercy; kind-heartedness, mercifulness; **die Werke der B.**, the works of mercy; **B. üben**, to show mercy; *B:* **der Vater der B.**, the father of mercies; *B:* **mir ist B. widerfahren**, I obtained mercy; *B:* **und seine B. währet immer für und für bei denen, die ihn fürchten**, and his mercy is on them that fear him from generation to generation; *see also* **barmherzig.**
Barmittel, *n.pl.* (*a*) cash, ready money; (*b*) *Book-k:* cash in hand.
Bärmutter, *f. Anat: A:* uterus; womb, matrix.
Barnabas ['barna·bas]. *Pr.n.m.* **-'.** Barnabas, Barnaby.
Barnabit [barna·'bi:t], *m.* **-en/-en.** *Ecc:* Barnabite.
Barnaclesgans ['barnɛkəls-], *f. Orn:* barnacle (goose), bernacle-goose.
barock[1] [ba·'rok], *a.* (*a*) *Hist. of Art & Lit:* baroque; (*b*) quaint; exaggerated, extravagant (style, etc.).
Barock[2], *m.* & *n.* **-s/.** *Hist. of Art & Lit:* (i) baroque (style), (ii) baroque period.
barockisierend [ba·roki·'zi:rənt], *a.* in a baroque manner; slightly baroque (style, etc.).
Barockperle, *f.* irregularly shaped pearl, baroque pearl.
Barockstil, *m.* baroque style.
Barockzeit, *f.* baroque period.
Barograph [ba·ro·'gra:f], *m.* **-en/-en**, barograph, barometrograph; self-registering, recording, barometer.
Bärohr, *n. Bot:* bear's-ear, auricula.
Barometer [ba·ro·'me:tər], *n.* **-s/-**, barometer, weather-glass, *F:* glass; **das B. steigt**, the barometer rises, is rising; **das B. fällt**, the barometer falls, is falling; **das B. steht auf Regen**, the barometer points to, is set to, rain; *F:* **das B. steht auf Sturm**, there is a storm brewing, there is trouble brewing, there will be trouble before long.
Barometerstand, *m.* barometer reading.
Barometrie [ba·ro·me·'tri:], *f.* **-/.** barometry.
barometrisch [ba·ro·'me:triʃ], *a.* barometric(al); **barometrisches Gefälle**, barometric gradient.
Barometrograph [ba·ro·me·tro·'gra:f], *m.* **-en/-en** = **Barograph.**
Baron [ba·'ro:n], *m.* **-s/-e**, baron.
Baronat [ba·ro·'na:t], *n.* **-(e)s/-e**, barony.
Baronesse [ba·ro·'nɛsə], *f.* **-/-n**, baroness.
Baronie [ba·ro·'ni:], *f.* **-/-n** [-'ni:ən]. **1.** barony. **2.** baronage.
Baronin [ba·'ro:nin], *f.* **-/-innen**, baron's wife; baroness.
baronisieren [ba·ro·ni·'zi:rən], *v.* **1.** *v.tr.* to raise (s.o.) to the rank of baron. **2.** *v.i.* (*haben*) *Hum:* to be a gentleman of leisure.
Baronswürde, *f.* baronage.
Baroskop [ba·ro·'sko:p], *n.* **-s/-e.** *Ph: etc:* baroscope.
Barothermohygrograph [ˌba·ro·ˌtermo·ˌhy·gro·'gra:f], *m.* **-en/-en.** *Meteor:* barothermohygrograph, meteorograph.
Barozyklonometer [ˌba·ro·tsy·klo·no·'me:tər], *n.* **-s/-**, barocyclonometer.
Barrage [ba'ra:ʒə], *f.* **-/-n**, barrier, obstruction; *Hyd.E: etc:* barrage, dam.
Barras ['baras], *m.* **-/.** *Mil: F:* **1.** army; military life; military routine; **beim B.**, in the army. **2.** army bread.
Barre ['barə], *f.* **-/-n. 1.** (*a*) bar, rail (of metal, etc.); (*b*) railing, barrier. **2.** bar (in river *or* harbour); **durch eine B. versperrter Hafen**, barred harbour; *Nau:* **über die B. gehen, die B. passieren**, to cross the bar.
Barrebe ['bar'ʔre:bə], *f.* = **Bogrebe.**
Barreboje, *f. Nau:* bar buoy.
Barren, *m.* **-s/-. 1.** *Metall:* bar, ingot (of gold, tin, etc.); bullion (of gold, silver). **2.** *Gym:* parallel bars. **3.** *Husb:* crib, manger.
Barrenbeißen, *n. Vet:* crib-biting, cribbing (*by horse*).
Barrenbeißer, *m. Vet:* (*horse*) crib-biter, cribber.
Barreneisen, *n. Metalw:* bar-iron.
Barrenform, *f. Metalw: etc:* **1. in B.**, in bars. **2.** ingot-mould.
Barrengold, *n. Metalw: Fin:* bullion.
Barrenwetzen, *n. Vet:* rubbing of (its) teeth on the manger (*by horse*).
Barriere [bari'ɛ:rə], *f.* **-/-n**, barrier, gate; (*a*) *Rail:* (ticket) barrier; (*b*) *Rail:* level-crossing gate; (*c*) toll-gate.
Barrieretraktat, *n. Hist:* Barrier Treaty.
Barrierriff ['beriər-], *n. Ph.Geog:* barrier reef; *Geog:* **das Große B.**, the Great Barrier Reef.
Barrikade [bari·'ka:də], *f.* **-/-n**, barricade.
barrikadieren [bari·ka·'di:rən], *v.tr.* to barricade (street, etc.).
Barring ['bariŋ], *f.* **-/-en.** *Nau:* boat space (on upper deck).
Barsch[1], *m.* **-es/-̈e.** *Ich:* perch.
barsch[2], *a.* rough, harsh, curt; uncivil; surly; **j-n b. anfahren**, to speak to s.o. roughly, harshly; to snap at s.o.
Bärsch, *m.* **-es/-e**, **Bärsche**, *f.* **-/-n.** *Ich:* perch.
Barschaft, *f.* **-/-en**, cash, ready money; *F:* **das ist meine ganze B.**, that is all I have on me, that is all I have to my name.
Barscheck, *m. Com:* open cheque, uncrossed cheque.
Barschhechte, *m.pl. Ich:* percesoces.
Barschheit, *f.* roughness, harshness, curtness (of speech, manner, etc.).
Barschlaus, *f. Crust:* achtheres percarum.
Bärschling, *m.* **-(e)s/-e.** *Ich:* perch.
Barsoi [bar'zoy], *m.* **-s/-s**, borzoi (hound).
Barsortiment, *n.* book distributor *or* book distribution centre.
barst, bärste *see* **bersten.**
Barstuhl, *m.* bar-stool.
Bart, *m.* **-(e)s/-̈e. 1.** beard (of man, goat, etc.); whiskers (of cat); beard, wattles, gills (of bird); barb, barbels, wattles (of fish); beard, gills (of oyster); **sich einen B. wachsen lassen, stehen lassen**, to grow a beard; **er hat einen acht Tage alten B.**, he has a week's beard, a week's growth; **wallender B.**, flowing beard; *F:* **in seinen B. brummen, murmeln**, to mumble, mutter, into one's beard; *F:* **j-m um den B. gehen, streichen**, to flatter, coax, *F:* get round, s.o.; *F:* to butter s.o. up; **sich um des Kaisers B. streiten**, to quarrel over a mere trifle; **sich eins in den B. lachen**, to laugh up one's sleeve, in one's beard; **beim B. des Propheten!** by the beard of the prophet! *F:* **ein Witz mit B.**, a chestnut; **so ein B.!** Queen Anne is dead! that's got whiskers on it! **der B. ist ab**, (i) that's torn it, you've had it; (ii) all right, we know (and you needn't pretend

any more). **2.** *Bot:* barb, beard, awns, aristae (on ear of barley, etc.); vane, web, vexillum (of feather); *Astr:* beard (of comet). **3.** (*a*) bit, web (of key); (*b*) *Metalw: Engr: etc:* fin, beard, barb, bur(r) (on casting, engraved plate, etc.); fash (on bullet); *Print:* burr, beard (of letter); (*c*) *Mus:* beard (of organ-pipe). **4.** blob (on nib of pen); mildew, mould (on food, etc.); *Nau:* weed (on bottom of ship), foul bottom.

Bartaffe, *m. Z:* wanderoo.

Bartalk, *m. Orn:* whiskered auklet.

Barte[1], *f.* **-/-n.** *Tls:* broad axe, chip axe.

Barte[2], *f.* **-/-n.** *Z:* (plate of) whalebone.

Bartel[1], *f.* **-/-n.** *Ich:* barbel, barb, wattle (of fish).

Bartel[2]. *Pr.n.m.* **-s=Barthel.**

bärteln, *v.tr. Tex:* to hatchel, hackle (hemp).

Bartenwal, *m. Z:* whalebone whale, right whale.

Bartfaden, *m.* **1.** *Ich:* barbel, barb, wattle (of fish). **2.** *Bot:* pentstemon, beard-tongue.

Bartfinne, *f.*=**Bartflechte** 2.

Bartflechte, *f.* **1.** *Moss:* usnea, greybeard lichen. **2.** *Med:* sycosis, barber's itch.

Bartgeier, *m. Orn:* bearded lammergeyer, vulture.

Bartgras, *n. Bot:* andropogon, beard-grass.

Bartgrasmücke, *f. Orn:* subalpine warbler.

Bartgrind, *m. Med:* sycosis, barber's itch.

Bartgrundel, *f. Ich:* stone loach, common loach.

Barthaar, *n.* (*a*) hair of (s.o.'s, the) beard; (*b*) *coll.* beard and moustache.

Barthafer, *m. Bot:* wild oat.

Barthel. *Pr.n.m.* **-s.** (*dim. of* **Bartholomäus**) Bartholomew, Bart; *F:* **wissen, wo B. den Most holt,** to know what's what, to know the ropes, to know one's onions.

Bartholomäus [barto·lo·ˈmɛːus]. *Pr.n.m.* **-'.** Bartholomew.

Bartholomäusnacht, die. *Fr.Hist:* the Massacre of St Bartholomew.

Bartholomit [barto·lo·ˈmiːt], *m.* **-en/-en.** *Ecc:* Bartholomite.

Bärtierchen, *n. Arach:* tardigrade, water-bear; **die Bärtierchen,** the tardigrada.

bärtig, *a.* bearded; **ein bärtiger Mann,** a bearded man; *Vit:* **bärtige Trauben,** grapes attacked by dodder; **-bärtig,** *comb.fm.* -bearded; **rotbärtig,** red-bearded; **vollbärtig,** full-bearded.

Bärtigkeit, *f.* beardedness.

Bartkauz, *m. Orn:* Lapland owl, great grey owl.

Bartkluppe, *f. Tls:* (locksmith's) hand-vice.

Bartkomet, *m. Astr:* bearded comet.

Bartkuckuck, *m. Orn:* puff-bird, barbet.

Bartlappen, *m.pl. Orn:* wattles, gills (of fowl, etc.).

Bartlaubsänger, *m. Orn:* Radde's bush warbler.

Bartling, *m.* **-(e)s/-e.** *Bot:* male hemp (plant).

bartlos, *a.* beardless, clean-shaven; **bartloser Jüngling,** beardless youth; **bartlose Mode,** fashion of the beardless face.

Bartlosigkeit, *f.* beardlessness, lack of beard.

Bartmannskrug, *m. A:* greybeard, bellarmine.

Bartmeise, *f. Orn:* bearded tit, reedling.

Bartmesser, *n.*=**Barbiermesser.**

Bartmoos, *n.*=**Bartflechte** 1.

Bartnagel, *m.* barbed nail.

Bartnelke, *f. Bot:* sweet-william.

Bartnuß, *f. Bot:* (*a*) filbert, cob-nut; (*b*) filbert-tree.

Bartrams-Uferläufer, *m. Orn:* upland plover.

Bartrobbe, *f. Z:* bearded seal.

Bartscherer, *m. F:* barber.

Bartstoppeln, *f.pl.* stubble (on chin).

Bartstufe, *f.* notch (in web of key).

Barttasse, *f.* moustache-cup.

Barttracht, *f.* style of beard.

Bartvogel, *m. Orn:* barbet.

Bartweizen, *m. Bot:* beard-wheat; durum wheat, hard wheat.

Bartwichse, *f. Toil:* pomade, wax, for the moustache *or* beard.

Bartwisch, *m. Austrian:* hand-brush.

Bartwuchs, *m.* growth of beard; **starker B.,** strong beard.

Barutsche [ba·ˈrutʃə], *f.* **-/-n.** *Veh:* barouche.

Barutschel [ba·ˈrutʃəl], *n.* **-s/-.** *Ich:* crucian (carp).

Bärwurz(el), *f.*=**Bärenwurz(el).**

Barysphäre [ba·ry·ˈsfɛːrə], *f. Geol:* barysphere.

Baryt [ba·ˈryːt], *m.* **-(e)s/-e.** **1.** *Miner:* barytes, heavy spar. **2.** *Ch:* baryta, barium oxide; **schwefelsaurer B.,** barium sulphate; **kohlensaurer B.,** barium carbonate.

Baryterde, *f. Miner:* baryta, heavy-earth.

Barytgelb, *n. Ch: Ind:* barium yellow.

barythaltig, *a. Miner:* barytic, containing barytes; *Ch:* baric, containing barium.

Barytkreuzstein, *m. Miner:* harmotome.

Baryton [ˈbaːry·ton], *n.* **-s/-e** [-toːnə]. *Mus:* **1.** *A:* barytone. **2.**=**Baritonhorn.**

Barytonon [ba·ˈryːto·non], *n.* **-s/-tona.** *Ling:* barytone.

Barytpapier, *n.* baryta paper, art paper.

Barytsalpeter, *m. Ch:* barium nitrate.

Barytsalz, *n. Ch:* barium salt.

Barytwasser, *n. Ch:* baryta water.

Barytweiß, *n. Ch: Ind:* baryta white, permanent white.

Baryum [ˈbaːrĭum], *n.* **-s/.=Barium.**

baryzentrisch [ba·ry·ˈtsɛntriʃ], *a. Ph:* barycentric.

Baryzentrum [ba·ry·ˈtsɛntrum], *n. Ph:* barycentre.

Barzahlung, *f. Com:* cash payment; cash down, money down; **'nur gegen B.',** 'terms cash'.

Bärzeit, *f.* mating season of bears.

Barzoi [bar'zoy], *m.* **-s/-s,** borzoi (hound).

Bas, *m.* **-es/-e = Baas.**

basal [ba·ˈzaːl], *a.* (*a*) basic, fundamental; (*b*) *Geol: etc:* basal, basic.

Basalmembran, *f. Anat:* basement membrane.

Basalmeningitis, *f. Med:* tuberculous meningitis.

Basalmessung, *f. Med:* measurement of the basal body temperature.

Basalstoffwechsel, *m. Physiol:* basal metabolism.

Basalt [ba·ˈzalt], *m.* **-(e)s/-e.** *Geol: Miner:* basalt.

Basaltemperatur, *f. Med:* basal body temperature.

basalten [ba·ˈzaltən], *a.* basaltic.

Basaltglas, *n. Miner:* basaltic glass.

basaltig [ba·ˈzaltiç], **basaltisch** [ba·ˈzaltiʃ], *a.* basaltic; *Geol:* **basaltische Schichten,** trap-rock.

Basaltlava, *f.* basaltic lava.

Basaltsäulen, *f.pl. Geol:* basalt columns.

Basaltstein, *m.* basalt.

Basaltsteinbruch, *m.* basalt quarry.

Basalzelle, *f. Anat:* basal cell.

Basan [ba·ˈzaːn]. *Pr.n.n.* **-s.** *B.Geog:* Bashan.

Basane [ba·ˈzaːnə], *f.* **-/-n.** *Leath:* basan, basil.

Basanit [ba·za·ˈniːt], *m.* **-(e)s/-e.** *Miner:* basanite, touchstone.

Basar [ba·ˈzaːr], *m.* **-(e)s/-e.** **1.** (*a*) (oriental) bazaar; (*b*) bazaar, emporium, cheap stores. **2.** (charity) bazaar.

Bäschen, *n.* **-s/-,** (*dim. of* **Base**[1]) (*esp. as term of endearment*) cousin.

Baschi-Bosuk [ˌbaʃiː-bo·ˈzuk], *m.* **-s/-s.** *Turk.Hist:* bashi-bazouk.

Baschkire [baʃˈkiːrə], *m.* **-n/-n.** *Ethn:* Bashkir.

Baschlik [ˈbaʃlik], *m.* **-s/-s.** *Cost:* bashlyk, bashlik.

Base[1], *f.* **-/-n,** (*a*) (female) cousin: (*b*) *A:* aunt.

Base[2] [ˈbaːzə], *f.* **-/-n.** **1.** *Ch:* base. **2.=Basis.**

Basedow [ˈbaːzədoː]. *Pr.n.&s.m.* **-s.** *Med:* Graves's disease, ophthalmic goitre.

Basedowsch [ˈbaːzədoːʃ], *a. Med:* **Basedowsche Krankheit,** Graves's disease, ophthalmic goitre.

Basel. *Pr.n.n.* **-s.** *Geog:* Basle, Basel.

Baseler. 1. *m.* **-s/-.** *Geog:* native, inhabitant, of Basle. **2.** *inv.a.* of Basle, Basle . . .; *Hist:* **das B. Konzil,** the Council of Basle.

Baselkraut, *n.*=**Baselle.**

Baselle [ba·ˈzɛlə], *f.* **-/-n.** *Bot:* basella; **weiße B.,** Malabar nightshade, climbing nightshade.

Basidie [ba·ˈziːdĭə], *f.* **-/-n.** *Fung:* basidium.

Basidienpilze, *m.pl.,* **Basidiomyzeten** [ba·zi·dĭo·my·ˈtseːtən], *m.pl. Fung:* basidiomycetes.

Basidiospore [ba·zi·dĭo·ˈspoːrə], *f. Fung:* basidiospore, acrospore.

Basidium [ba·ˈziːdĭum], *n.* **-s/-dien.** *Fung:* basidium.

basieren [ba·ˈziːrən]. **1.** *v.tr.* to base, ground, found (opinion, etc.) (**auf**+*acc.*, on). **2.** *v.i.* (*haben*) **& sich basieren,** (*of argument, opinion, etc.*) **auf etwas** *dat.*, **sich auf etwas** *acc.*, **b.,** to be based, founded, on sth.; *occ.* (*of pers.*) to take sth. as a basis.

Basilianer [ba·zi·lĭ·ˈaːnər], *m.* **-s/-.** *Ecc:* Basilian (monk).

Basilie [ba·ˈziːlĭə], *f.* **-/-n, Basilienkraut,** *n. Bot:* common basil, sweet basil.

Basilika [ba·ˈziːli·kaː], *f.* **-/-ken.** *Rom.&Ecc.Arch:* basilica.

basilikal [ba·ziːli·ˈkaːl], *a.* basilican; **basilikaler Grundriß,** ground-plan of a basilica.

Basilikum [ba·ˈziːli·kum], *n.* **-s/-s & -ken=Basilie.**

Basilikumöl, *n.,* **Basilikumsalbe,** *f. Pharm:* basilicon (ointment).

Basilisk [ba·zi·ˈlisk], *m.* **-en/-en.** *Myth: Rept:* basilisk; *B:* cockatrice; *Art:* **Christus auf Löwen und Basilisken,** Christ trampling on the Evil Beasts.

Basiliskenblick, *m. Myth. & F:* basilisk glance, withering glance.

Basiliskenbrut, *f. F:* viper's brood.

Basiliskeneier, *n.pl. B:* cockatrice's eggs; *F:* viper's brood.

Basilius [ba·ˈziːlĭus]. *Pr.n.m.* **-'.** Basil; *Ecc.Hist:* **B. der Große,** St Basil the Great.

Basis [ˈbaːzis], *f.* **-/-sen** [ˈbaːzən]. **1.** (*a*) basis, foundation; *Arch: etc:* foot, base (of pillar, etc.); pedestal (of statue, etc.); *Surv:* base(-line), ground-line; *Geom:* base (of triangle, etc.); **ein Geschäft auf einer gesunden B. aufbauen,** to build up a business on a sound basis; (*b*) *Mil: etc:* base (of operations). **2.** base, basis (of system, etc.); *Mth:* base, radix (of system of notation); radix, root, basis (of logarithm); *Geol:* basis, base (of rock, etc.); *Cryst:* base, basal plane (of crystal); *Ch:*=**Base**[2] 1.

Basisapparat, *m.*=**Basismeßapparat.**

Basisbruch, *m. Surg:* fracture of the cranial base.

basisch [ˈbaːziʃ], *a. Ch:* basic (salt, etc.); *Metall:* **basischer Prozeß,** basic process; **basische Schlacke,** basic slag; **basisches Ofenfutter,** basic lining; *adv.* **b. zugestellt, ausgefüttert,** basic-lined.

Basismeßapparat, *m. Surv:* instrument for measuring the base-line (in triangulation).

Basiswinkel, *m. Geom:* angle at the base (of isosceles triangle).

Basizität [ba·zi·tsi·ˈtɛːt], *f.* **-/.** *Ch:* basicity.

Baske, *m.* **-n/-n.** *Ethn:* Basque.

Baskenmütze, *f. Cost:* beret.

Baskenwal, *m. Z:* southern right whale.

Basketball [ˈbaːskət-], *m. Games:* basket-ball.

Baskin, *f.* **-/-innen.** *Ethn:* Basque woman *or* girl.

baskisch. 1. *a. Geog:* Basque. **2.** *s.* **Baskisch,** *n. Ling:* Basque.

Basküle [bas'kyːlə], *f.* **-/-n.** *Tchn:* lever locking device (of window, etc.).

Basler, *m. & a.*=**Baseler.**

Basrelief [ba·re·lĭ·ˈɛf], *n. Art:* bas-relief, low relief.

baß[1], *adv.* **1.** *A:* better. **2.** *A. & Lit:* very, (very) much, most; **ich war baß erstaunt,** I was most, (very) much, highly, astonished.

Baß[2], *m.* **Basses/Bässe** *Mus:* **1.** (*a*) bass, bass-part; **begleitender, obligater, Baß,** thoroughbass, continued bass; **bezifferter, figurierter, Baß,** figured bass; (*b*) *F: usu.pl.* **Bässe,** bass-tones *or* -notes. **2.** bass (voice, singer); **hoher Baß,** singing bass, bass-baritone; **tiefer Baß,** (i) deep bass, (ii) (*speaking voice*) deep bass voice. **3.** (stringed) double-bass, contrabass.

Bassa [ˈbasaː], *m.* **-s/-s & -sen/-sen** [ˈbasən], pasha.

Bassangans [ba'saːn-], *f. Orn:* gannet, solan-goose.

Baßbalken, *m.* bass-bar (of violin, etc.).

Baßbariton, *m. Mus:* bass-baritone.

Basse, *m.* **-n/-n.** *Ven:* mature wild boar.

Basselissestuhl [ˌbas'lis-], *m. Tex:* low-warp loom.

Basset [ba'seː], *m.* **-s/-s,** basset hound, badger-dog.

Bassett [ba'sɛt], *m.* **-(e)s/-e.** *Mus:* bass viol.

Bassetthorn, *n. Mus:* basset-horn, tenor clarinet in F.

Baßfaser, *f. Com:* bass-fibre.

Baßgeige, *f. Mus:* double-bass, contrabass; *see also* **Himmel** 1 (*a*).

Baßgeiger, *m.* double-bass player.

Baßhorn, *n. Mus: A:* bass horn.

Bassin [ba'sɛ̃ː], *n.* **-s/-s.** **1.** reservoir, receptacle, tank (for liquid); (wash-)basin. **2.** basin (of fountain, etc.); ornamental lake; (swimming-)pool. **3.** *Nau:* dock, basin.

Bassist [ba'sist], *m.* **-en/-en.** *Mus:* (*a*) bass (singer); (*b*) player of a bass instrument, bass player.

Baßklarinette, *f. Mus:* bass clarinet.

Baßlaute, *f. Mus: A:* theorbo, archlute.

Bäßling, *m.* **-(e)s/-e.** *Bot:* female hemp (plant).

Baßnote, *f. Mus:* bass note.

Baßpartie, *f. Mus:* bass part.

Baßpfeife, *f. Mus:* (*on organ*) bass-pipe; (*on bagpipes*) drone.

Baßpommer, *m. Mus:* bombardon (stop) (of organ).

Baßposaune, *f. Mus:* bass trombone.

Baßregelung, *f. W: etc:* bass control.

Baßsaite, *f. Mus:* bass string (of instrument).

Baßsänger, *m. Mus:* bass (singer).

Baßsaxophon, *n. Mus:* bass saxophone.

Baßschlüssel, *m. Mus:* bass clef, F clef.

Baßstimme, *f.* (*a*) bass (voice); **tiefe B.,** (i) deep bass, (ii) (*speaking voice*) deep bass voice; (*b*)=**Baßpartie.**

Baßtölpel, *m. Orn:* gannet, solan-goose.

Baßton, *m.* bass tone.

Baßtuba, *f. Mus:* bass-tuba; **B. in B,** euphonium, barytone.

Baßviole, *f. Mus: A:* bass-viol.

Bast, *m.* **-(e)s/-e.** **1.** (*a*) *Bot:* inner bark, bast, phloem; gum (of raw silk, hemp, etc.); (*b*) *Com: etc:* bass, bast (for making baskets, etc.); **raffia** (for fancy-work, tying up plants, etc.); raffia matting. **2.** *Nat. Hist:* velvet (on stag's horns).

basta [ˈbastaː], *int.* enough of it; **und damit b.!** and that's that! and there's an end of it! **ich**

mache, was ich will, damit b.! I shall do as I like, so there!
Bastard ['bastart], *m.* -(e)s/-e [-s, -stardəs/-stardə]. **1.** bastard; natural, illegitimate, child. **2.** (*a*) (*pers.*) half-breed, half-caste, mestizo; (*b*) (*animal*) hybrid, half-breed, cross-breed; cross-bred, mongrel (dog); (*c*) *Bot:* hybrid (plant); **abgeleiteter B.**, derived hybrid.
Bastardbalken, *m.* **1.**=**Bastardfaden. 2.** *N.Arch:* half-beam; cross-beam, cross-carling.
Bastardeibisch, *m. Bot:* Indian mallow.
Bastardfaden, *m. Her:* scarpe, escarpe.
Bastardfeile, *f. Tls:* bastard file.
Bastardfenster, *n. Arch:* mezzanine window.
Bastardformat, *n.* bastard size (of paper, book, etc.).
Bastardhieb, *m.* bastard cut (of file).
bastardieren [bastar'di:rən], *v.i.* (*haben*) *Biol:* to hybridize; **Bastardierung** *f*, hybridization.
Bastardklee, *m. Bot:* Alsike clover, hybrid clover.
Bastardlorbeer, *m. Bot:* laurustine, laurustinus.
Bastardmahagoni, *m. Bot:* bastard mahogany.
Bastardmakrele, *f. Ich:* scad, horse-mackerel.
Bastardnachtigall, *f. Orn:* icterine warbler.
Bastardpflanze, *f. Bot:* hybrid (plant).
Bastardsafran, *m. Bot:* safflower, bastard saffron.
Bastardschrift, *f.* **1.** *Pal: Hist. of Print:* slanting writing (between round hand and running hand). **2.** *Print:* bastard type.
Bastardschwamm, *m. Com:* sponge of inferior quality.
Bastardstab, *m. Her:* baton; *F:* bar sinister.
Bastardwechsel, *m. Com:* bill drawn on a fictitious, non-existent, person; dummy bill.
Bastardwespe, *f. Ent:* bembex.
Bastardzeder, *f. Bot:* Barbados bastard cedar.
Bastei [bas'tai], *f.* -/-en. *Fort:* bastion.
Bastelarbeit, *f.* (*a*) handicraft (done as a hobby); (*b*) (piece of) handwork.
Bastelei, *f.* -/-en, (*a*)=**Basteln,** *q.v. under* **basteln;** (*b*) handicraft (done as a hobby); (*c*) (piece of) handwork.
basteln, *v.tr. & i.* (*haben*) to do handicrafts; to build (models, home-made radios, etc.); *F:* to rig up, to fix up (home-made furniture, etc.); **Basteln** *n*, (*hobby, primary school subject, etc.*) handicrafts, handwork.
basten, *a.* (made) of bast.
Basterzucker, *m. Sug-R:* bastard sugar.
Bastfaser, *f.* bast-fibre, bass-fibre.
Basthut, *m.* hat made of bast.
bastig, *a.* like bast, bast-like.
Bastille [bas'ti:jə, bas'tiljə], *f.* -/-n. *Fort:* small fortress; *Hist:* **die B.**, the Bastille.
Bastion [basti'o:n], *f.* -/-en. *Fort:* bastion.
bastionieren [bastio·'ni:rən], *v.tr.* to fortify with bastions; **bastioniert,** bastioned (front, etc.).
Bastkäfer, *m. Ent:* fig-wasp.
Bastkohle, *f. Miner:* fine lignite, brown coal.
Bastler, *m.* -s/-, handicraft worker, amateur craftsman.
Bästling, *m.* -(e)s/-e. *Bot:* female hemp (plant).
Bastmatte, *f.* (*for floor*) bass(-mat); (*for table*) raffia mat.
Baston(n)ade [basto(·)'na:də], *f.* -/-n, bastinado.
baston(n)ieren [basto(·)'ni:rən], *v.tr.* to bastinado (s.o.).
Bastseide, *f. Tex:* raw silk, gum silk.
Bastseife, *f. Ser:* degumming soap.
Bastseil, *n.* bass-rope.
Basuto [ba·'zu:to:], *m.* -s/-(s), *f.* -/-(s). Basuto.
Basutoland. *Pr.n.n.* -s. *Geog:* Basutoland.
bat *see* **bitten.**
Bataille [ba'ta·jə, ba'taljə], *f.* -/-n. *Mil:* battle, fight.
Bataillon [batal'jo:n], *n.* -s/-e. *Mil:* battalion. (*Note: the strength of a German* **'Bataillon'** *may vary greatly from that of an English* 'battalion' *and may in some cases be nearer the English concept of* 'regiment'.)
Batate [ba·'ta:tə], *f.* -/-n. *Bot:* batata, sweet potato, Spanish potato.
Bataver ['ba:ta·vər], *m.pl.* **1.** *Hist:* Batavi. **2.** *Poet:* Dutchmen.
Batavia [ba·'ta:via:]. *Pr.n.* **1.** *f.* -s. *A.Geog:* Batavia, the Netherlands. **2.** *n.* -s. *Geog:* Batavia, Jakarta.
Bataviafieber, *n. Med:* malaria.
batavisch [ba·'ta:viʃ], *a. Hist:* Batavian; *Ph:* **batavischer Tropfen,** Prince Rupert's drop, ball, tear.
bäte *see* **bitten.**
Bathmetall ['ba:θ-], *n. Metall:* Bath metal.
Batholith [ba·to·'li:t], *m.* -(e)s/-e & -en/-en. *Geol:* batholite.
Bathometer [ba·to·'me:tər], *n.* -s/-. *Oc:* bathometer, bathymeter.
Bathoolith [ba:θᵒo·o·'li:t], *m.* -(e)s & -en/. *Geol:* Bath oolite; Bath-stone.
Bathorden ['ba:θ-], *m.* Order of the Bath.
Bathseba ['batse·ba:]. *Pr.n.f.* -s. Bathsheba.
Bathybius [ba·'ty:bius], *m.* -/-bien. *Oc:* bathybius.
bathygraphisch [ba·ty·'gra:fiʃ], *a. Oc:* bathygraphic.
Bathymeter [ba·ty·'me:tər], *n.* -s/- =**Bathometer.**
Bathysphäre [ba·ty·'sfe:rə], *f. Oc:* area of greatest ocean depth.
Batik ['ba:tik], *m.* -s/-en. *Tex:* batik.
Batikdruck, *m. Tex:* batik (work).
batiken ['ba:tikən], *v.tr. Tex:* to ornament (silk, etc.) with batik work.
Batist [ba'tist], *m.* -es/-e. *Tex:* batiste, cambric.
batisten [ba'tistən], *a.* of batiste.
Batistmusselin, *m. Tex:* cambric-muslin.
batonnieren [ba·to·'ni:rən], *v.i.* (*haben*) to fence with quarterstaffs; **Batonnieren** *n*, quarterstaff fencing.
Batrachier [ba·'traxiər], *m.* -s/-. *Z:* batrachian; **die Batrachier,** the batrachia.
Batrachomyomachie [ba·traxo·my·o·ma'xi:], *f.* -/. *Gr.Lit:* batrachomyomachia, batrachomyomachy.
batschen, *v.tr. Tex:* to batch (jute); **Batschen** *n*, batching (of jute).
Battarismus [bata·'rismus], *m.* -/. inarticulateness of speech; stuttering, gabbling.
Battement [bat(ə)'mã:], *n.* -s/-s. **1.** *Mus:* ornament similar to mordent. **2.** *Danc:* high kick. **3.**=**Battuta** 2.
Batterie [batə'ri:], *f.* -/-n [-'ri:ən]. **1.** (*a*) *Mil:* battery; **reitende B.**, horse battery; (*b*) *Navy:* battery-deck. **2.** *El: etc:* **elektrische B.**, electric battery; **galvanische B.**, galvanic battery, galvanic pile; **erschöpfte B.**, run-down, worn out, battery; **die B. laden, aufladen,** to charge the battery; **die B. entladen,** to discharge the battery; **die B. überladen, die B. kochen lassen,** to milk the battery. **3.** *Plumb:* combination tap. **4.** set, collection; **eine B. Kochtöpfe,** a set of saucepans; *F:* **eine ganze B. Flaschen,** a whole regiment, army, of bottles. **5.** *Husb:* battery (for fowls). **6.** *Mus:* beat (of drum), roll (on side-drum).
Batteriedeck, *n. Navy:* battery deck.
batteriegespeist, *a.* battery-operated (radio, etc.).
Batteriehahn, *m. Plumb:* combination tap.
Batteriehaltung, *f. Husb:* battery system (of poultry-keeping).
Batteriekessel, *m.* battery-boiler.
Batteur [ba·'tø:r], *m.* -s/-e. *Tex:* cotton breaker, shaker.
battieren [ba'ti:rən], *v.tr. Fenc:* to knock the foil out of (one's opponent's) hand.
Battist [ba'tist], *m.* -es/-e =**Batist.**
Battologie [bato·lo·'gi:], *f.* -/. battology.
battologisieren [bato·lo·gi·'zi:rən], *v.i.* (*haben*) to battologize, to gabble.
Battuta [ba'tu:ta:], *f.* -/-ten. **1.** *Mus:* beat; *esp.* strong beat, down beat. **2.** *Fenc:* bind, beat.
Battute [ba'tu:tə], *f.* -/-n=**Battuta.**
Batum ['ba:tum]. *Pr.n.n.* -s. *Geog:* Bat(o)um.
Batzen, *m.* -s/-. **1.** *Num:* (*silver coin*) batz. **2.** lump, mass, heap; **ein B. Erde,** a lump, clod, of earth; **ein B. Gold,** a lump of gold; **er hat einen schönen B. Geld,** he has a nice pile, lot, of money; **das wird einen ganzen B. kosten,** that will cost a lot of money, *F:* a pretty penny.
Batzenware, *f.* cheap articles, goods of low quality.
Bau, *m.* I. -(e)s/. **1.** building, construction, erection; **das Haus ist im Bau,** the house is being built; the house is in course of construction; **Pläne zum Bau einer neuen Brücke,** plans for the construction of a new bridge. **2.** (*a*) structure, method of construction; **er studierte eingehend den Bau der Maschine,** he carefully studied the structure of the machine; (*b*) structure, composition; **der Bau eines Systems,** the structure of a system; **eine Symphonie von gutem Bau,** a well-constructed symphony; **der komplizierte Bau des menschlichen Auges,** the intricate structure of the human eye; (*c*) build; **sie ist von zartem Bau,** she is of slight build, she is slightly built. **3.** building-trade; **er arbeitet beim Bau,** he is in the building-trade, in the building line; *F:* **er ist vom Bau,** he is in the profession, he is in the racket; he is one of us. **4.** (*pl.* **Bauten**) (*a*) building, edifice, structure; **ein imposanter, stattlicher, Bau,** an imposing, a stately, an impressive, building; a noble pile; **ein leichter Bau,** a light structure; (*b*) house in course of construction; **er ist auf dem Bau,** he is on the site. **5.** *Mil: F:* **drei Tage Bau,** three days confined to barracks, *abbr.* C.B.
II. **Bau,** *m.* -(e)s/-e. **1.** *Ven:* burrow, hole (of rabbit); earth, kennel (of fox); set (of badger); lodge (of beaver); couch (of otter); *F:* **niemals aus seinem Bau kommen,** never to leave one's burrow. **2.** *Min:* mine, underground workings (of a mine); **verlassener Bau,** disused, abandoned, mine.
-bau, *comb.fm. m.* -(e)s/. **1.** (*a*) -construction, -building; **Straßenbau,** road-construction; **Schiffbau,** shipbuilding; (*b*) -mining; **Bergbau,** mining; **Kupferbau,** copper-mining. **2.** -culture; **Ackerbau,** agriculture; **Weinbau,** viticulture.
Bauabnahme, *f.* (*a*) examination of a new building by the Board of Surveyors; (*b*) taking over of a new building after an examination by the Board of Surveyors.
Bauabrechnung, *f.* builder's account, building account.
Bauabschnitt, *m.* stage, phase, in the construction (of church, road, etc.).
Bauabstand, *m.*=**Bauwich.**
Bauakademie, *f.* school of architecture.
Bauamt, *n. Adm:* (District) Surveyor's Office.
Bauanschlag, *m.* building estimate, builder's estimate.
Bauarbeiten, *f.pl.* building operations; construction work; road works; road repairs.
Bauarbeiter, *m.* builder's labourer; workman in the building-trade; construction worker.
Bauart, *f.* **1.** (*a*) method of construction (of engine, etc.); (*b*) type, model; **ein Auto modernster B.**, a car of the latest type, the latest model in cars. **2.**=**Bauweise** 1.
Bauaufseher, *m.* building inspector, district surveyor.
Bauaufsicht, *f.*=**Bauleitung.**
Bauauftrag, *m.* order for constructional work; building commission (*given to architect*).
Bauausschreibung, *f.* invitation to tender for building *or* constructional work.
Baubank, *f.* building society, *U.S:* building and loan association.
Baubassin, *n. Nau:* construction dock.
Baubedarf, *m.* building supplies.
Baubehörde, *f.* building authority.
Baublock, *m. Constr:* block (of buildings).
Baubuch, *n.* builder's journal, diary.
Baubude, *f.*=**Bauhütte** 1.
Bauch, *m.* -(e)s/⸗e. **1.** (*a*) *Anat:* abdomen, belly; **mein B. tut (mir) weh,** I have a pain in my abdomen, *F:* middle; I have a belly-, *F:* tummy-ache; **auf dem B. liegen,** to lie on one's belly, on one's stomach; **vor j-m auf dem B. liegen, kriechen,** to grovel before s.o., to cringe to, before, s.o.; **sich** *dat.* **vor Lachen den B. halten,** to laugh till one's sides ache, to split, burst, one's sides with laughter; *F:* **j-m Löcher in den B. fragen,** to plague s.o. with everlasting questions, to be for ever asking questions of s.o.; *B:* **auf deinem B. sollst du gehen,** upon thy belly shalt thou go; *B:* **böse Tiere, faule Bäuche,** evil beasts, slow bellies; *F:* **ein fauler B.**, a lazy-bones; (*b*) paunch, *F:* corporation, pot-belly; **einen B. bekommen,** to grow stout, to develop a corporation; **er hat einen stattlichen B.**, he is portly, corpulent, *F:* pot-bellied; (*c*) *F:* womb; (*d*)=**Bauchstück** 1. **2.** *Anat: F:* stomach, *F:* tummy; belly; **einen leeren B. haben,** to have an empty stomach; **ein hungriger B. läßt sich mit Worten nicht abspeisen,** words won't fill an empty belly; **einen vollen B. haben,** to have eaten one's fill, to be full up; *F:* **ein voller B. studiert nicht gern,** the well-fed have no use for books; **seine Augen waren größer als sein B.**, his eyes were bigger than his belly; **sich** *dat.* **den B. füllen,** *P:* **vollschlagen,** to eat one's fill, *P:* to fill one's belly; **sich** *dat.* **den B. pflegen, seinem B. dienen, frönen,** to make a god of one's belly; *B:* **welchen der B. ihr Gott ist,** whose god is their belly. **3.** belly (of ship); bowels (of earth); **Feuer schoß aus dem B. der Erde,** fire belched from the bowels of the earth. **4.** *Tchn:* belly, bulge, paunch, swell (of vase, bottle, etc.); belly, bilge, bulge (of cask, etc.); belly, body (of blast furnace); entasis (of column, etc.); barrel (of bell); belly (of violin, etc.); bulge (of wall, etc.); belly, bag, bunt (of sail).
Bauch-, *comb.fm. Anat: Med:* abdominal . . . ; **Bauchwand** *f*, abdominal wall; **Bauchwassersucht** *f*, abdominal dropsy.
Bauchaorta, *f. Anat:* abdominal, descending, aorta.
Bauchatmung, *f. Physiol:* abdominal, diaphragmatic, respiration.

Bauchaufschlitzen, Bauchaufschneiden, *n.* disembowelment.
Bauchband, *n. Nau:* belly-band (of a sail).
Bauchbeine, *n.pl.*=**Bauchfüße.**
Bauchbeschwerden, *f.pl.* abdominal complaints, bowel complaints; *F:* stomach trouble.
Bauchbinde, *f.* 1. (a) *Surg:* abdominal bandage; abdominal belt; (b) body-belt, flannel-belt (worn by men). 2. (a) (advertising) band (on book); (b) band round a cigar.
Bauchbruch, *m. Med:* ventral rupture, laparocele.
Bauchdecke, *f. Anat:* abdominal wall.
Bauchdiener, *m.* glutton, gormandizer.
Bauchdienerei, *f.* gluttony, gormandism; belly-worship.
bauchdienerisch, *a.* greedy, gluttonous.
Bäuche[1] see **Bauch.**
Bäuche[2], *f.* -/-n = **Beuche.**
Baucheisen, *n. Tls:* seaming stake; flange, flanging tool.
bauchen, *v.*=**ausbauchen;** *see also* **Bauchung; gebaucht.**
bäuchen, *v.tr.*=**beuchen.**
Bauchfell, *n. Anat:* peritoneum, peritonaeum.
Bauchfellentzündung, *f. Med:* peritonitis.
Bauchfinne, *f.*=**Bauchflosse.**
Bauchfleck, *m. Swim: F:* belly-flop, flatter.
Bauchflosse, *f. Ich:* ventral, abdominal, fin; belly fin; **ohne Bauchflossen,** apodal; **Fisch ohne Bauchflossen,** apodan.
Bauchflosser, *m.* -s/-. *Ich:* abdominal (fish).
Bauchfreiheit, *f. Aut:* bulge clearance, bulk clearance.
Bauchfüße, *m.pl. Nat.Hist:* abdominal feet; spurious legs, pseudo-legs; pleopods.
Bauchfüßler, *m.* -s/-.*Moll:* gast(e)ropod.
Bauchgegend, *f. Anat:* abdominal region; **obere B.,** epigastric region, epigastrium; **mittlere B.,** mesogastric region, mesogastrium; **untere B.,** hypogastric region, hypogastrium.
Bauchgording, *f. Nau:* buntline.
Bauchgrimmen, *n.* gripes, griping pains; colic.
Bauchgurt, *m. Harn:* belly-band; girth; surcingle.
Bauchhieb, *m.*=**Bauchquart.**
Bauchhöhle, *f. Anat:* abdominal cavity.
Bauchhöhlenschwangerschaft, *f. Med:* extra-uterine pregnancy.
Bauchhöhlenwassersucht, *f.*=**Bauchwassersucht.**
bauchig, *a.* bulbous, bulging; convex; **eine bauchige Flasche,** a big-bellied bottle.
bäuchig, *a.* (a)=**bauchig;** (b) -**bäuchig,** *comb.fm.* -bellied; **dickbäuchig,** big-bellied, *F:* pot-bellied.
Bauchkiemer, *m.* -s/-. *Ich:* hag(-fish), borer, slime-eel.
Bauchklatscher, *m. Swim:* belly-flop, flatter.
Bauchkneifen, Bauchkneipen, *n.* gripes, griping pains; colic.
Bauchladen, *m.* hawker's tray.
Bauchlage, *f. Gym: Swim: etc:* prone position.
Bauchlandung, *f. Av:* belly-landing, *F:* belly-flop.
Bauchlappen, *m. Cu:* belly (of pork).
Bäuchlein, *n.* -s/-, tummy; *Iron:* paunch, *F:* corporation.
bäuchlings, *adv.* on one's belly; **b. liegen,** to lie (flat) on one's belly, on one's stomach, on one's face.
Bauchlinie, *f. Anat:* **weiße B.,** linea alba.
Bauchmuskel, *f. Anat:* abdominal muscle, stomach-muscle, *F:* tummy-muscle.
Bauchnabel, *m. Anat:* navel, umbilicus.
Bauchpanzer, *m. Rept:* plastron (of turtle).
Bauchpilze, *m.pl. Fung:* gastromycetes.
bauchpinseln, *v.tr. see* **gebauchpinselt.**
Bauchplatte, *f. Ent:* sternum.
Bauchpresse, *f.* pressure produced by contraction of the abdominal muscles.
Bauchpunktion, *f. Surg:* puncture, tapping, of the abdomen.
Bauchquart, *f. Fenc:* cut in low quart.
Bauchredekunst, *f.* ventriloquism, ventriloquy; ventriloquistic art.
bauchreden, *v.i. insep.* (haben) to ventriloquize; **Bauchreden** *n,* ventriloquism, ventriloquy.
Bauchredner, *m.* ventriloquist.
bauchrednerisch, *a.* ventriloquistic, ventriloquial, ventriloquous.
Bauchrednernummer, *f.* (at *entertainment*) ventriloquist turn.
Bauchring, *m. Anat:* abdominal, inguinal, ring.
Bauchsäge, *f. Tls:* two-man crosscut saw (with curved breast).
Bauchsammler, *m. Ent:* bee that collects pollen by hairs on the under side of the abdomen.
Bauchschmerzen, *m.pl.* abdominal pains, belly-ache; stomach-ache, *F:* tummy-ache.
Bauchschnitt, *m. Surg:* laparotomy.

Bauchschuß, *m. Med:* abdominal gunshot wound *or* bullet wound.
Bauchschwangerschaft, *f.* = **Bauchhöhlen-schwangerschaft.**
Bauchseising, *n. Nau:* furling-gasket, bunt-gasket.
Bauchspeck, *m.* (a) belly-fat, excess fat below the waist; (b) *Cu:* streaky bacon.
Bauchspeichel, *m. Physiol:* pancreatic juice.
Bauchspeicheldrüse, *f. Anat:* pancreas.
Bauchstich, *m. Surg:* puncture, tapping, of the abdomen.
Bauchstück, *n.* 1. *Cu:* (a) belly (of pork); breast (of veal); breast, flank (of mutton); thin flank (of beef); (b) streaky bacon. 2. *N.Arch:* floor (-frame, -timber).
Bauchtanz, *m.* belly-dance.
Bauchtänzerin, *f.* belly-dancer.
Bauchtyphus, *m. Med:* typhoid (fever), enteric fever.
Bauchung, *f.* bulge, paunch (of vase, bottle, etc.); entasis (of column, etc.); bulge (of wall, etc.).
Bauchwand, *f. Anat:* abdominal wall.
Bauchwassersucht, *f. Med:* ascites, abdominal dropsy.
bauchwassersüchtig, *a. Med:* ascitic(al).
Bauchweh, *n.*=**Bauchschmerzen.**
Bauchwelle, *f. Gym:* hip-circle (on horizontal bar).
Bauchwolle, *f. Com: etc:* belly-wool, underlocks (of sheep, etc.).
Bauchzange, *f. Metall:* crucible tongs.
Baucis ['bautsis]. *Pr.n.f.* -'. *Gr. & Rom.Lit:* Baucis.
Baudarlehen, *n.* building loan.
Baude, *f.* -/-n, mountain inn; mountain hut.
Baudenkmal, *n.* monument of architecture; architectural monument; historical building; **mittelalterliche Baudenkmäler Englands,** English mediaeval buildings.
Baudock, *n. N.Arch:* (ship-building) stocks; slip-dock, building-slip.
Bauelement, *n. Constr:* constructional element, unit; *Tchn:* component (part).
bauen. I. *v.tr.* 1. (a) to build, construct (houses, roads, bridges, machines, etc.); to build (ships, organs, etc.); to erect (temples, monuments, etc.); to make (violins, etc.); **die Mauern waren aus Granit gebaut,** the walls were built of granite; **Vögel bauen Nester aus Heu und Moos,** birds build their nests with hay and moss; (b) **Luftschlösser b.,** to build castles in the air; *F:* **sich einen Anzug b. lassen,** to have a suit made; **ein Examen b.,** to take an examination; **seinen Doktor b.,** to take one's doctor's degree; *see also* **Haus** 1. 2. *Agr: etc:* (a) to cultivate (soil); (b) to grow; **Kartoffeln, Weizen, Wein, b.,** to grow potatoes, wheat, vines.
II. **bauen,** *v.i.* (haben) 1. (a) to build; **wir werden nächstes Jahr b.,** we are going to build next year; **auf Sand b.,** (i) *Constr:* to build on sand, on gravel, (ii) to build on sand, to be engaged in an undertaking that has no solid foundation; **an etwas** *acc.* **b.,** to build near sth.; **wir wollen nicht zu nahe an der Straße b.,** we don't want to build too near the road; (b) **an etwas** *dat.* **b.,** to work on sth.; **fünf Jahre lang wurde an der Brücke gebaut,** they were working on the bridge for five years; **an der Zukunft eines Staates b.,** to work for the future of a country. 2. **auf j-n, etwas** *acc.,* **b.,** to depend, count, rely, build, on s.o., sth.; to trust s.o., sth.; **auf ein Versprechen b.,** to build, rely, on a promise; **auf sein Glück b.,** to trust to luck, to one's lucky stars. 3. *Min:* **auf Kupfer, auf Gold, b.,** to mine (for) copper, gold.
Bauentwurf, *m.* architect's plan, drawing.
Bauer[1], *m.* -s & -n/-n. 1. (a) farmer, husbandman; **kleiner B.,** smallholder; (b) peasant, rustic, countryman, *F:* country bumpkin; *F:* **so fängt man Bauern,** I don't rise to that fly; you won't catch me that way; **ein B. bleibt ein B., B. bleibt B.,** once a rustic always a rustic; what's bred in the bone will come out in the flesh; you can't make a silk purse out of a sow's ear; *Prov:* **was der B. nicht kennt, das frißt er nicht,** some people won't trust anything they don't know. 2. (a) *Chess:* pawn; **zur Dame gekrönter B.,** ringed pawn; (b) *Cards:* knave, jack.
Bauer[2], *m.* -s/-, builder, constructor; -**bauer,** *comb.fm.* -builder, -maker; **Schiffsbauer,** ship-builder; **Modellbauer,** model-maker.
Bauer[3], *n. & m.* -s/-, bird-cage.
Bäuerchen, *n.* -s/-, (*dim.* of **Bauer**[1]) (a) small farmer; smallholder; **ein armes B.,** a poor peasant; (b) *F:* (baby's) burp; **ein B. machen,** to bring up wind, to burp.
Bäuerin, *f.* -/-innen, farmer's wife; (woman) farmer.

bäuerisch, *a.*=**bäurisch.**
Bäuerlein, *n.* -s/- =**Bäuerchen.**
bäuerlich, *a.* rural; **bäuerliche Kultur,** rural culture; **bäuerliche Verhältnisse,** rural conditions.
Bäuerling, *m.* -(e)s/-e. *Orn:* redwing.
Bauernadel, *m.* yeomanry.
Bauernaufstand, *m. Hist:* peasants' revolt.
Bauernbefreiung, *f. Hist:* rural emancipation.
Bauernbrot, *n.* farmhouse bread (with rye flour).
Bauernbrueghel [-ˌbrɔygəl]. *Pr.n.m.* -s. *Hist.* of *Art:* Pieter Brueghel the Elder.
Bauernbursche, *m.* country lad, farmer's boy.
Bauernbutter, *f.* farm butter.
Bauerndienst, *m.* forced *or* statute labour; corvee.
Bauerndirne, *f.* country girl, country wench.
Bauerndorf, *n.* farming village, country village.
Bauernemanzipation, *f. Hist:* rural emancipation.
Bauernfänger, *m.* trickster, confidence man; card-sharper.
Bauernfängerei, *f.* -/. trickery, confidence trick(s).
Bauernfrau, *f.* (a) countrywoman, peasant woman; (b) farmer's wife.
Bauernfrühstück, *n. Cu:* omelette filled with fried potatoes and bacon; *omelette parmentière.*
Bauerngarten, *m.* cottage garden.
Bauerngut, *n.* farm, holding.
Bauernhaus, *n.* farmhouse.
Bauernhochzeit, *f.* country wedding.
Bauernhof, *m.* farm; farmstead.
Bauernjunge, *m.* country lad, farmer's lad; *F:* **es regnet Bauernjungen,** it is raining cats and dogs.
Bauernkarpfen, *m. Ich:* crucian (carp).
Bauernkirsche, *f. Bot:* gean, sweet cherry.
Bauernkittel, *m. Cost:* smock.
Bauernknecht, *m.* farm-hand, farm-labourer.
Bauernkresse, *f. Bot:* (a) mithridate pepperwort, cow-cress; (b) penny-cress.
Bauernkrieg, *m. Hist:* peasants' war.
Bauernkunst, *f.* rural crafts.
Bauernlegen, *n. Hist:* expropriation of farmers.
Bauernleier, *f. Mus:* hurdy-gurdy.
Bauernmädchen, *n.* country girl; **ein dralles B.,** a buxom country wench.
Bauernmagd, *f.* farm-girl, farmer's maid.
Bauernmöbel, *n. pl.* farmhouse furniture.
Bauernomelett, *n.*=**Bauernfrühstück.**
Bauernregel, *f.* weather maxim.
Bauernrhabarber, *m. Bot:* (root of) cypress spurge.
Bauernrose, *f. Bot:* peony.
Bauernsame, *f.* -/. *Swiss Dial:*=**Bauernschaft.**
Bauernschaft, *f.* -/. *coll.* farmers, peasantry.
bauernschlau, *a.* artful, crafty, sly, cunning.
Bauernschminke, *f. Bot:*=**Ackersteinsame(n).**
Bauernschmuck, *m.* peasant jewellery.
Bauernschötchen, *n. Bot:* teesdalia.
Bauernschrank, *m.* farmhouse cupboard *or* wardrobe.
Bauernschwalbe, *f. Orn:* barn-swallow, house-swallow, chimney-swallow.
Bauernsenf, *m. Bot:* (a) candytuft; (b) mithridate pepperwort, cow-cress; (c) penny-cress; (d) (i) teesdalia; (ii) shepherd's-cress, pepper-cress; (e) wild radish, jointed, joint-podded, charlock; (f) shepherd's-purse; (g) charlock, wild mustard.
Bauernsohn, *m.* farmer's son.
Bauernspiel, *n.* peasant play *or* pageant.
Bauernstand, *m.* farmers, peasantry.
Bauernstube, *f.* farmhouse room.
Bauernstuhl, *m.* farmhouse chair; back-stool.
Bauerntanz, *m.* peasant dance; country dance.
Bauerntochter, *f.* farmer's daughter.
Bauerntölpel, *m.* country yokel, country bumpkin.
Bauerntum, *n.* -(e)s/. *coll.* farmers, peasantry.
Bauernverband, *m.* farmers' league, union.
Bauernverein, *m.* agricultural association.
Bauernvolk, *n.* 1. country-folk. 2. race of peasants; nation of farmers.
Bauernweib, *n.* countrywoman, peasant woman.
Bauernwetzel, *m.* -s/. *Med: F:* mumps.
Bauernzwang, *m. Hist:* right of feudal landowners to punish their tenants.
Bauersame, *f.* -/. *Swiss Dial:*=**Bauernschaft.**
Bauersfrau, *f.*=**Bauernfrau.**
Bauersleute, *pl.* country people, country-folk.
Bauersmann, *m.* -(e)s/-leute, peasant, country-man.
Baufach, *n.* architectural profession; building-trade, *F:* the building line.
baufähig, *a. Min:* workable, exploitable (seam, etc.); *Agr:* arable, tillable, cultivable (soil); **baufähiges Land,** plough-land.
baufällig, *a.* (of *building, etc.*) beyond repair, derelict; dilapidated, ramshackle, tumble-down.
Baufälligkeit, *f.* dilapidated, ruinous, state (of

building); state of being beyond repair, in decay; dilapidation.

Baufehler, *m.* structural fault (of building, machine, etc.).

Baufluchtlinie, *f.* building line (of street, etc.).

Baufuge, *f. Arch:* line where a, the, new building phase becomes discernible.

Bauführer, *m.* = **Bauleiter.**

Bauführung, *f.* = **Bauleitung.**

Baugelände, *n.* building ground, building land.

Baugeld, *n.* building capital.

Baugenehmigung, *f.* building licence.

Baugenossenschaft, *f.* (co-operative) building society.

Baugerippe, *n. Constr: N.Arch: etc:* framework, shell, skeleton (of house, ship, etc.); carcass, frame (of ship).

Baugerüst, *n. Constr: etc:* **1.** scaffold(ing), stage, staging. **2.** = **Baugerippe.**

Baugeschichte, *f.* structural history (of building).

Baugesellschaft, *f.* building society; housing association.

Baugesuch, *n.* application for a building licence.

Baugewerbe, *n.* building-trade(s), *F:* building line.

Baugewerkschule, *f. Sch:* school of architecture and civil engineering.

Bauglaser, *m.* glazier.

Bauglied, *n.* structural *or* architectural member.

Baugrube, *f. Civ.E: etc:* excavation, cavity, pit, trench.

Baugrund, *m. Constr:* **1.** foundation soil; foundation bed. **2.** building plot.

Baugrundstück, *n.* building site, building plot, ground-plot.

Bauhandwerk, *n.* building trade(s), *F:* building line.

Bauhandwerker, *m.* workman in the building trade.

Bauherr, *m.* **1.** building owner. **2.** (*in Bremen*) church councillor.

Bauhilfsarbeiter, *m.* bricklayer's labourer.

Bauholz, *n.* (building) timber.

Bauhütte, *f.* **1.** building shed. **2.** (*a*) masons' lodge, guild; (*b*) masonic, freemasons', lodge.

Bauhypothek, *f.* building mortgage.

Bauingenieur, *m.* constructional engineer; **B. für Tiefbau**, civil engineer; **B. für Hochbau**, structural engineer.

Bauinschrift, *f.* (commemorative) inscription on a building.

Bauinspektor, *m.* building inspector, district surveyor.

Baujahr, *n.* year in which (house, ship, etc.) was built; date (of a building) ; year of construction (of ship, machine, etc.); year of manufacture (of machine, car, etc.); year (of car); **'B. 1960'**, (*of car*) '1960 model'; (*on railway truck, etc.*) 'built 1960'.

Baukapital, *n.* building capital.

Baukasten, *m. Toys:* box of bricks; construction set; building set.

Baukastensystem, *n.* unit construction system (for buildings, machine-tools, etc.).

Baukeramik, *f.* architectural terra-cotta.

Baukis ['baukis]. *Pr.n.f.* **-'**. *Gr. & Rom. Lit:* Baucis.

Bauklotz, *m. Toys:* building block, brick; *F:* **da staunt man Bauklötze**, that makes one's eyes pop out.

Baukomplex, *m.* complex of buildings.

Baukonsens, *m.* building licence.

Baukontrakt, *m.* building contract.

Baukörper, *m.* main part, body, of a building.

Baukosten, *pl.* building expenses, building costs.

Baukostenanschlag, *m.* (detailed) building estimate, builder's (detailed) estimate; tender.

Baukostenüberschlag, *m.* (general) building estimate, builder's (general) estimate.

Baukostenzuschuß, *m.* contribution to the building costs (of rented house, etc.).

Baukunst, *f.* architecture.

Baukünstler, *m.* architect.

baukünstlerisch, *a.* architectural.

Bauland, *n.* (*a*) building land, building ground; (*b*) arable land.

Baulebung, *f. A.Jur:* heriot.

Bauleiter, *m.* overseer of building works, clerk of the works, works foreman.

Bauleitung, *f.* supervision of building works.

Bauleute, *pl.* **1.** builder's labourers; *B:* **der Stein, den die B. verworfen haben**, the stone which the builders rejected. **2.** *A:* farmers, husbandmen.

baulich, *a.* architectural; structural; **in baulicher Hinsicht**, from the architectural point of view; **bauliche Anordnung**, architectural arrangement; **bauliche Änderungen**, structural alterations; *adv.* **das Haus ist b. in gutem Zustand**, the house is in good repair.

Baulichkeit, *f. usu. pl.* **Baulichkeiten**, (ministry, hospital, farm, etc.) buildings; **die Baulichkeiten der Universität**, the university buildings.

Baulizenz, *f.* (*a*) building licence; (*b*) construction licence.

Baulücke, *f.* gap in a row of buildings (caused by demolition, etc.).

Baum, *m.* **-(e)s/⸚e. 1.** *Bot:* tree; **ein blühender B.**, a tree in blossom; **immergrüner B.**, evergreen (tree); **der B. ist eingegangen**, the tree has died; **Tag des Baumes**, (official) tree-planting day, *U.S:* Arbor Day; **er ist stark wie ein B.**, he is as strong as a horse; **der B. des Lebens**, the tree of life; **es ist dafür gesorgt, daß die Bäume nicht in den Himmel wachsen**, there is a limit to everything; *F:* **das ist, um auf die Bäume zu klettern**, it's enough to drive one up the wall, it's enough to drive one crazy, mad; *Bot:* **B. der Reisenden**, traveller's tree; *Prov:* **einen B. soll man biegen, solange er jung ist, das Bäumchen biegt sich, doch der B. nicht mehr**, as the twig is bent, the tree is inclined; *B:* **an der Frucht erkennt man den B.**, the tree is known by its fruit; *see also* **ausreißen** 1, **Erkenntnis** I. 1 (*b*), **Hieb**[2] 1 (*a*), **Wald. 2.** (*a*) *Mec.E:* shaft, spindle, axle (of turbine, etc.); *Tex:* beam (of loom); *Leath:* (currier's) tree, beam; *Fort:* beam (of cheval de frise); *Fish:* pole (of pole-trawl); *Agr:* pole (for holding down load of hay, etc.); *Nau:* spar, boom; mast; (*b*) (harbour) boom.

Baumachat, *m. Miner:* tree-agate, dendritic, arborescent, agate; moss-agate, Mocha stone.

Baumagame, *f. Rept:* iguana.

baumähnlich, *a.* tree-like; arborescent.

Baumallee, *f.* avenue (of trees).

Baumaloe, *f. Bot:* American aloe, century-plant.

Baumann, *m.* **-(e)s/-leute.** *A:* farmer, husbandman; *see also* **Bauleute.**

baumartig, *a.* like a tree, tree-like; arborescent; **baumartiger Strauch**, arborescent shrub.

Baumast, *m.* branch, bough, of a tree.

Baumaterial, *n.* building material.

Baumausputzer, Baumausschneider, *m.* pruning-hook, bill-hook.

Baumaxt, *f. Tls:* felling-axe.

Baumbart, *m. Moss:* greybeard lichen, usnea.

Baumbast, *m. Bot:* inner bark, bast, phloem.

Baumbeschnitt, *m.* = **Baumschnitt.**

Baumbestand, *m. For:* plantation; stand (of timber-trees); crop; stock.

Baumblüte, *f.* (*a*) blossom of a tree; (*b*) blossom-time (*esp.* of fruit trees); **zur B. fahren**, to go to see the blossom; **während der B.**, when the trees are blossoming.

Baumbürste, *f.* tree-brush, bark-brush.

Bäumchen, *n.* **-s/-**, small tree, sapling; little tree; *F:* **dein B. steht im Himmel noch**, just wait, you'll get your present in good time; *Games:* **verwechselt das B., B. wechsel dich, spielen**, to play (at) puss in the corner; *see also* **Baum** 1.

Baumégrad [bo'me:-], *m. Ph. Meas:* degree Baumé.

Baumeister, *m.* (*a*) master builder; building contractor, builder; (*b*) architect (of a cathedral, etc.).

baumeln, *v.i.* (*haben*) to dangle, to swing, to hang swaying; **mit den Beinen b., seine Beine b. lassen**, to dangle, swing, one's legs; **morgen muß er b.**, tomorrow he must hang, tomorrow he will swing.

Baumelschub, *m. Games:* devil among the tailors.

baumen. 1. = **bäumen** 1. **2.** *v.i.* (*haben*) (*of animal*) to tree, to seek refuge in a tree; (*of bird*) to take to a tree; to go to roost.

bäumen, *v.tr.* **1.** (*a*) *Tex:* to beam (the warp); (*b*) *Agr:* to fasten (a load of hay, etc.) with a pole. **2. sich bäumen**, (*of horse, etc.*) to rear; to buck; **sein Stolz bäumte sich dagegen**, his pride rose up, *F:* kicked, against it.

Baumente, *f. Orn:* tree-duck.

Baumethode, *f.* method of building.

Baumfalke, *m. Orn:* hobby.

Baumfalle, *f. Ven:* beam-trap.

Baumfarn, *m. Bot:* tree-fern.

Baumfeldwirtschaft, *f.* arboriculture in conjunction with farming.

Baumfraß, *m.* tree-blight.

Baumfreund, *m. Bot.* = **Fensterblatt.**

Baumfrevel, *m.* unlawful damaging of trees.

Baumfrosch, *m. Amph:* tree-frog, tree-toad.

Baumgang, *m.* avenue.

Baumgans, *f. Orn:* barnacle (goose), bernacle-goose.

Baumgarten, *m.* orchard.

Baumgärtner, *m. For: Hort:* nurseryman, nursery-gardener; arboriculturist.

Baumgärtnerei, *f. For: Hort:* **1.** nursery of young trees. **2.** arboriculture, tree-culture.

baumgerade, *a. & adv.* (as) straight as a post.

Baumgrenze, *f. Geog:* tree-line, -limit, timber-line.

Baumgruppe, *f.* clump, group, of trees.

Baumhaar, *n. Com:* vegetable horsehair, fibre.

Baumhacker, *m. Orn:* nuthatch.

Baumharz, *n.* resin.

Baumhasel, *f. Bot:* Constantinople hazel.

Baumhaus, *n. Ethn:* tree-house.

Baumheber, *m.* tree-heaver.

Baumhecke, *f.* hedge of trees.

Baumheide, *f. Bot:* tree heath, white heath, brier.

Baumhippe, *f.* pruning-knife, pruning-bill.

Baumhuhn, *n. Orn:* **1.** American partridge. **2.** curassow.

Baumkänguruh, *n. Z:* tree-kangaroo.

Baumkante, *f. Carp:* wane, waney edge.

baumkantig, *a.* rough-hewn, rough-squared (timber); waney (plank, etc.); **b. beschlagen,** to rough-hew, rough-square (timber).

Baumkauz, *m. Orn:* tawny owl, wood owl, hoot owl.

Baumkitt, *m. Hort:* putty used for treating damaged trees.

Baumkleber, *m. Amph:* tree-frog, tree-toad.

Baumkohl, *m. Bot:* kale, kail.

Baumkorb, *m.* tree-guard.

Baumkrätze, *f.* tree-lichen.

Baumkratzer, *m.* tree-scraper, bark-scraper.

Baumkreuz, *n. Ecc.Art:* tree-cross.

Baumkrone, *f.* top, crown, of a tree.

Baumkuchen, *m. Cu:* iced *or* chocolate covered cake in the shape of a fir-tree.

Baumkult, *m. Rel.Hist:* tree-cult; arborolatry, worship of trees.

Baumkunde, *f.* dendrology.

baumlang, *a.* (as) tall as a lamp-post, as a maypole.

Baumläufer, *m. Orn:* creeper; **langkralliger B.**, tree-creeper; **kurzkralliger B.**, short-toed tree-creeper.

Baumlaus, *f. Ent:* aphis, plant-louse, green-fly.

Baumleguan, *m. Rept:* iguana.

Baumlerche, *f. Orn:* wood lark.

Baumliest, *m. Orn:* wood kingfisher.

baumlos, *a.* treeless; **baumlose Hügel**, treeless hill-tops.

Baummalve, *f. Bot:* tree-mallow.

Baummarder, *m. Z:* pine-marten, tree-marten.

Bäummaschine, *f. Tex:* beaming machine.

Baummesser[1], *n.* pruning-knife, pruning-bill.

Baummesser[2], *m.* dendrometer.

Baummörder, *m. Bot:* celastrus, staff-tree; **kletternder B.**, climbing bittersweet, waxwork.

Baummörtel, *m.* = **Baumkitt.**

Baumnachtigall, *f. Orn:* hedge-warbler, hedge-sparrow, dunnock.

Baumnoddiseeschwalbe, *f. Orn:* white-capped noddy.

Baumnuß, *f. Bot:* walnut.

Baumnymphe, *f. Myth:* dryad, wood-nymph.

Baumöl, *n.* olive-oil.

Baumpfahl, *m.* tree-prop.

Baumpflanzung, *f.* (*a*) plantation; nursery; (*b*) tree-planting.

Baumpieper, *m. Orn:* tree pipit; **indischer B.**, Indian tree pipit.

Baumrinde, *f. Bot:* bark (of a tree).

Baumrose, *f. Bot:* **1.** water-elder, guelder rose, cranberry tree. **2.** = **Brandrose.**

Baumrute, *f. Tex:* beam-bar.

Baumrutscher, *m. Orn:* **1.** tree-creeper. **2.** nuthatch.

Baumsäge, *f.* pruning-saw.

Baumsarg, *m.* tree-coffin (*made of split tree-trunk*).

Baumschärmaschine, *f. Tex:* beam warping machine.

Baumschärverfahren, *n. Tex:* beam warping.

Baumscheibe, *f.* **1.** *Arb:* circular bed round a tree, *esp.* fruit-tree. **2.** *Tex:* warp-beam flange.

Baumschere, *f.* **1.** tree-pruner. **2.** pruning-scissors, pruning-shears.

Baumschilf, *n. Bot:* bamboo.

Baumschläfer, *m. Z:* loir, edible dormouse.

Baumschlag, *m.* **1.** (*a*) *Bot:* characteristics of the branching and foliage (of a tree); (*b*) *Art:* method of painting the foliage of trees. **2.** *For:* (*a*) tree-felling; (*b*) fell. **3.** *Arb:* anastomosis of the bark.

Baumschlange, *f. Rept:* tree-snake.

Baumschleppnetz, *n. Fish:* pole-trawl, beam-trawl.

Baumschliefer, *m. Z:* tree-cony, tree-hyrax.

Baumschlüpfer, *m. Orn:* wren.

Baumschnitt, *m.* (*a*) cutting back (of tree): trimming, lopping, cutting away (of branches); (*b*) pruning (of tree).

Baumschoner, *m.* tree-guard.
Baumschröter, *m. Ent:* stag-beetle, lucanus.
Baumschule, *f. For:* nursery (of young trees).
Baumschulgärtner, *m. For:* nurseryman, nursery-gardener; aboriculturist.
Baumschützer, *m.* tree-guard.
Baumschwälbchen, *n. Orn:* pied fly-catcher.
Baumschwamm, *m. Fung:* tree-fungus.
Baumsegel, *n. Nau:* boom-sail.
Baumsegler, *m. Orn:* tree-swift.
Baumseide, *f. Tex:* mercerized cotton.
Baumsperling, *m. Orn:* tree-sparrow, mountain-sparrow.
Baumsperre, *f.* obstacle of tree-trunks.
Baumstachelbeere, *f. Bot:* Coromandel gooseberry.
Baumstachelschwein, *n. Z:* tree-porcupine.
Baumstamm, *m.* **1.** tree-trunk. **2.** *Cu:* chocolate log.
Baumstammwerfen, *n. Sp:* tossing the caber.
baumstark, *a.* (as) strong as a horse.
Baumsteiger, *m.* **1.** *Amph:* dendrobates. **2.** *Orn:* tree-creeper.
Baumstein, *m.* = **Baumachat.**
Baumstraße, *f.* avenue; tree-lined road.
Baumstubben, *m.* = **Baumstumpf.**
Baumstück, *n.* **1.** *A:* orchard. **2.** *Art:* painting, study, of trees.
Bäumstuhl, *m. Tex:* beaming frame, warp-frame.
Baumstumpf, *m.* stump, stub, of a tree.
Baumstütze, *f.* tree-prop.
Baumtiere, *n.pl. Nat.Hist:* arboreal animals, tree-dwelling animals.
Baumtorte, *f.* = **Baumkuchen.**
Baumuster, *n. Ind: etc:* model; **ein neues B. entwickeln,** to develop a new model.
Baumvogel, *m. Orn:* passerine, percher; perching, roosting, bird; **die Lerche ist kein B.,** the lark is not a perching bird.
Baumwachs, *n. Arb:* grafting-wax, lute.
Baumwachtel, *f. Orn:* American partridge, bob-white.
Baumwanze, *f. Ent:* shield-bug.
Baumweichsel, *f. Bot:* wild, dwarf, cherry; sour cherry.
Baumweißling, *m. Ent:* black-veined white butterfly.
Baumwinde, *f.* tree-heaver.
Baumwipfel, *m.* tree-top.
Baumwollabfall, *m. Ind:* cotton waste.
Baumwollanbau, *m.* cotton growing, cotton cultivation.
Baumwollanbaugebiet, *n.* = **Baumwollgebiet.**
Baumwolländer, *n.pl.* cotton-growing countries.
Baumwollbaum, *m. Bot:* kapok-tree.
Baumwolldruck, *m. Tex:* cotton-printing, calico printing.
Baumwolldrucker, *m. Tex:* cotton-printer.
Baumwolle, *f.* **1.** *Bot: Ind:* cotton; **langstapelige B.,** long-staple cotton, black-seed cotton; **kurzstapelige B.,** short-staple cotton, green-seed cotton; **rohe B.,** raw cotton. **2.** (*a*) *Tex:* cotton (-cloth); (*b*) knitting cotton.
baumwollen, *a. Tex:* (of) cotton; **baumwollene Unterhosen,** cotton pants.
Baumwollernte, *f.* cotton harvest.
Baumwollerzeugnisse, *n.pl. Tex:* cotton goods, cotton stuffs.
Baumwollfaser, *f.* cotton fibre.
Baumwollflanell, *m. Tex:* cotton flannel; flannelette.
Baumwollgarn, *n. Tex:* cotton yarn.
Baumwollgebiet, *n.* cotton region, cotton belt, *U.S:* cotton-patch.
Baumwollgewebe, *n. Tex:* cotton(-cloth), cotton fabric.
Baumwollhandel, *m.* cotton trade.
Baumwollindustrie, *f.* cotton industry.
Baumwollkammgarn, *n. Tex:* combed cotton yarn.
Baumwollkapsel, *f. Bot:* cotton boll.
Baumwollkapselkäfer, *m. Ent:* boll-weevil.
Baumwollköper, *m. Tex:* cotton twill.
Baumwollpflanze, *f. Bot:* cotton-plant, gossypium.
Baumwollpflanzung, *f.* cotton-plantation.
Baumwollplantage, *f.* cotton-plantation.
Baumwollratte, *f. Z:* cotton rat.
Baumwollrüßler, *m. Ent:* boll-weevil.
Baumwollsamen, *m.* cotton-seed.
Baumwollsamenkuchen, *m. Husb:* cotton-cake.
Baumwollsamenöl, *n.* cotton-seed oil.
Baumwollsamt, *m. Tex:* cotton velvet, velveteen.
Baumwollspinner, *m.* cotton-spinner.
Baumwollspinnerei, *f.* **1.** cotton-spinning. **2.** cotton-mill.
Baumwollstaude, *f. Bot:* cotton-plant, gossypium.
Baumwollstoff, *m. Tex:* cotton(-cloth), cotton fabric; **bedruckter B.,** printed cotton, printed calico.
Baumwolltwist, *m.* darning cotton.
Baumwollwatte, *f. Surg: etc:* cotton-wool.
Baumwollzeug, *n. Tex:* cotton(-cloth); **grobes B.,** coarse cotton.
Baumwollzwirn, *m.* sewing cotton; cotton thread.
Baumwucherer, *m. Bot:* dendrobium.
Baumwürger, *m.* = **Baummörder.**
Baumzange, *f.* tree-pruner.
Baumzucht, *f.* arboriculture, tree-culture.
Baunzerl, *n.* **-s/-(n).** *Austrian: Bak:* (kind of) soft white roll.
Bauopfer, *n. Rel.Hist:* foundation sacrifice.
Bauordnung, *f.* building regulations, building bye-law.
Bauperiode, *f.* **1.** time allowed for building *or* construction. **2.** building period.
Bauplan, *m.* architect's plan, drawing, *F:* blueprint.
Bauplastik, *f.* architectural sculpture.
Bauplatte, *f. Constr:* building board.
Bauplatz, *m.* building-site, building plot, ground-plot.
Baupolizei, *f. Adm:* (Borough *or* Town) Surveyors; Surveyors' Office.
Bauprojekt, *n.* building scheme.
Baurat, *m.* government *or* municipal architect.
Baurecht, *n.* **1.** right to build. **2.** building law.
baureif, *a.* (site, etc.) suitable for building purposes.
Baureihe, *f. Ind:* (production) series.
bäurisch, *a.* rustic; unrefined, clumsy; **bäurische Manieren,** rustic, clumsy, manners, rustic ways.
Baurіß, *m.* architect's plan, drawing, *F:* blueprint.
Bausand, *m.* building sand.
Bausch, *m.* **-es/-e & ⸗e. 1.** (*a*) bulge, bagging part (of garment, sail, etc.); hanging fold, bosom (of garment); belly (of sail); **etwas in den B. stecken,** to put sth. into one's bosom; **das Kleid macht vorne einen B.,** the dress bulges, bags, at the front; (*b*) **in B. und Bogen,** wholesale, in bulk; without distinction; **Bücher in B. und Bogen kaufen,** to buy a job lot of books; **er verurteilt alles in B. und Bogen,** he condemns everything wholesale. **2.** ball, wad (of paper, etc.); *Surg: etc:* wad, pad, plug (of cotton-wool, etc.). **3.** = **Bauscht.**
Bauschäden, *m.pl.* structural damage.
Bauschein, *m.* building licence.
Bäuschel[1], *m. & n.* **-s/-.** *Tls:* miner's hammer.
Bäuschel[2], *n.* **-s/-** = **Beuschel.**
bauschen. 1. *v.tr.* to bulge, puff out; to swell; **der Wind bauscht die Segel,** the wind fills the sails, makes the sails swell; **mit gebauschten Segeln,** with full sails. **2. sich bauschen,** to bulge, to swell; (*of sail*) to belly, to fill; (*of dress, sail, etc.*) to billow (out); **die Gardinen b. sich im Wind,** the curtains billow (out) in the wind. **3.** *v.i.* (*haben*) to bulge; **das Kleid bauscht,** the dress bulges, bags, the dress is baggy.
bauschig, *a.* bulgy, baggy; puffed (out); **bauschige Ärmel,** full sleeves, (*short*) puff(ed) sleeves; **bauschige Segel,** full sails.
Bauschlosser, *m.* locksmith.
Bauschreiner, *m.* joiner.
Bauscht, *m.* **-(e)s/-e.** *Paperm:* post (of 180 sheets).
Bauschule, *f.* **1.** *Sch:* school of architecture and civil engineering. **2.** *Hist. of Arch:* regional style of architecture.
Bauschutt, *m.* debris (on building-site).
Bausohle, *f. Min:* working level.
bausparen, *v.i. insep.* (*haben*) (*p.p.* **baugespart**) (*usu. only as inf. & vbl s.*) to save through a building society.
Bausparer, *m.* member of a building society.
Bausparkasse, *f.* building society, *U.S:* building and loan association.
Bausparvertrag, *m.* building society savings agreement.
Bauspekulant, *m.* building speculator; **schwindelhafter B.,** jerry-builder.
Baustahl, *m.* structural steel.
Baustahlgewebe, *n.* reinforcing steel mesh (*for reinforced concrete*).
Baustatik, *f.* statics of structures.
Baustein, *m.* (*a*) *Constr:* building stone, brick; **einen B. kaufen,** to buy a brick (for a building fund); (*b*) component, element (of structure, system, etc.); (*c*) important contribution (to a science, etc.); (*d*) *Toys:* building brick, block.
Baustelle, *f.* building-site, building ground, building plot; site of road works, working site.
Baustil, *m.* style of building; architectural style; **gotischer B.,** Gothic style.
Baustoffe, *m.pl.* building materials.
Baustoffwechsel, *m. Physiol:* anabolism, assimilation.
Bausucht, *f. F:* building craze.
Baute, *f.* **-/-n,** building, structure.
Bautechnik, *f.* (*a*) construction technique; (*b*) constructional engineering.
Bautechniker, *m.* constructional engineer.
Bauteil, *n. Mec.E: Constr:* (structural) member; **tragende Bauteile,** *Constr:* supporting members (of building), *Av:* primary structure (of aircraft).
Bautischler, *m.* joiner.
Bauübernahme, *f.* = **Bauabnahme** (*b*).
Bauunternehmer, *m.* building contractor, builder; master-builder.
Bauunternehmung, *f.* building firm, (firm of) building contractors.
Bauvergebung, *f.* allocation of a building contract.
Bauvertrag, *m.* building contract.
Bauvorhaben, *n.* building scheme.
Bauweise, *f.* **1.** method of building, style of architecture; (*a*) **eine primitive B.,** a primitive method of building; **die gotische B.,** the Gothic style; (*b*) **offene B.,** detached building; **geschlossene B.,** terracing. **2.** = **Bauart** 1.
Bauwerk, *n.* building, edifice, structure.
Bauwesen, *n.* building (industry); **öffentliches B.,** public building.
Bauwich, *m.* **-(e)s/-e,** space between two adjacent houses.
Bauwinde, *f.* builder's winch, hoist.
bauwürdig, *a. Min:* workable, exploitable (seam, etc.); *Agr:* arable, cultivable, tillable (soil).
Bauwürdigkeit, *f.* profitableness (of mine, etc.).
Bauxit [bau'ksiːt], *m.* **-(e)s/.** *Miner:* bauxite.
bauz, *int.* (*nursery language*) bumps-a-daisy; **b. machen,** to take a tumble, to fall down.
Bauzaun, *m.* hoarding.
Bauzeichner, *m.* structural draughtsman, draftsman.
Bauzeichnung, *f.* construction drawing, *F:* blueprint.
Bavard [ba'vaːr], *m.* **-s/-s,** chatterer, chatterbox.
Bavardage [bavar'daːʒə], *f.* **-/-n,** chatter(ing), chit-chat; gossip.
Bavaria [ba·'vaːriaː]. *Pr.n.f.* **-s. 1.** *Geog:* Bavaria. **2.** (statue of a woman representing) Bavaria.
Bavella [ba·'vɛlaː], *f.* **-/.** *Tex:* silk waste.
bavochieren [bavo'ʃiːrən], *v.tr.* to blur, smear (engraving).
Bavochüre [bavo'ʃyːrə], *f.* **-/-n,** blurred, smeared, engraving.
Bayaweber ['baiaː-], *m. Orn:* baya.
Bayblätter ['beː-], *n.pl. Pharm: etc:* leaves of the bayberry.
Bayer, *m.* **-n/-n.** Bavarian.
bayerisch, *a.* = **bayrisch.**
Bayerland. *Pr.n. n. Geog:* Bavaria.
Bayern. *Pr.n.n.* **-s.** *Geog:* Bavaria.
Bayöl ['beː-], *n. Pharm:* bay-oil.
Bayreuth [bai'royt]. *Pr.n.n.* **-s.** *Geog:* Bayreuth.
bayrisch. 1. *a. Geog: etc:* Bavarian; **die Bayrischen Alpen,** the Bavarian Alps. **2.** *s.* **Bayrisch,** *n. Ling:* Bavarian (dialect).
Bayrum ['beːrum], *m. Toil:* bay-rum.
Bazar [ba·'zaːr], *m.* **-(e)s/-e** = **Basar.**
bazillär [ba·tsi'lɛːr], *a. Biol: etc:* bacillar(y).
Bazillarialen [ba·tsila·ri'aːlən], **Bazillariazeen** [ba·tsila·ria·'tseːən], **Bazillarien** [ba·tsi'laːriən], *f.pl. Algae:* bacillariales, bacillariaceae, bacillarieae.
Bazille [ba·'tsilə], *f.* **-/-n.** *Biol:* bacillus.
Bazillenausscheider, *m. Med:* chronic carrier.
bazillenförmig, *a.* bacilliform.
Bazillenkrieg, *m.* bacterial warfare, germ warfare.
Bazillenruhr, *f. Med:* bacillary dysentery.
Bazillenträger, *m. Med:* germ-carrier.
Bazillienkraut [ba·'tsiliən-], *n. Bot:* samphire.
Bazillus [ba·'tsilus], *m.* **-/-len.** *Biol:* bacillus.
Bdellium ['bdɛlium], *m.* **-s/-lien.** *Bot: etc:* bdellium, gum-resin.
B-dur, B-Dur, *n. Mus:* (key of) B flat major.
Be [beː], *n.* **-/- & -s/-s.** *Mus:* flat, ♭; **ein Be vorschreiben, vorzeichnen,** to flatten (note), to mark (note) with a flat; **Tonart mit drei Be(s),** key with three flats.
be-, *insep.pref.* **I.** *forming tr. vbs* **1.** (*with sense of all over, all round, in all directions*) (*a*) (*from verbs*) **bemalen,** to paint (all over); **beschmieren,** to smear; **bespritzen,** to bespatter, to splash all over; (*b*) (*from nouns*) **betauen,** to bedew; **benebeln,** to befog; to bedim; **be(weih)räuchern,** to perfume with incense. **2.** (*from intr. verbs*) (*a*) **beachten,** to pay attention to (sth.); **beherrschen,** to rule over, to dominate (s.o., sth.); **bejammern,** to bemoan; (*b*) (*with sense of*

contact) **betasten, berühren,** to touch; (*c*) (*with sense of inclusion and possession*) **besetzen,** to occupy, to take possession of (sth.); **besitzen,** to possess, to own; **belagern,** to beleaguer, besiege; (*d*) (*intensifying*) **bearbeiten,** (i) to belabour (s.o.); (ii) to work on (sth.); **bedenken,** to consider, to reflect on (sth.). **3.** (*from nouns*) (*a*) (*to provide with sth.*) **bemänteln,** to cloak; **bebildern,** to illustrate; **beurlauben,** to give (s.o.) leave; (*b*) (i) (*to act as s.o.*) **bemuttern,** to mother (s.o.); *Hum:* **beonkeln,** to play uncle to (s.o.); (ii) *Hum: & Pej:* (*to call, to dub*) **bejunkern,** to sir, to beknight (s.o.). **4.** (*to put oneself, s.o., into the state expressed in the simplex*) (*a*) (*from adjs*) **bereichern,** to enrich (s.o., oneself); **befähigen,** to enable (s.o.); **sich etwas** *gen.*, **j-s, bemächtigen,** to take possession of, to possess oneself of, sth., s.o.; (*b*) (*from nouns*) **befrieden,** to pacify; **befriedigen,** to satisfy; **beschädigen,** to damage.

II. *forming intr. vbs* (*with sense of persisting in one state or place*) **auf etwas** *dat.*, *occ.* **in etwas** *dat.* **beruhen,** to rest on, to be based on, sth.; **bei etwas beharren,** to stick to sth.; **auf etwas** *dat.* **beharren,** to stand by, to persist in, sth.

III. *forming adjs* **benachbart,** neighbouring; **beleibt,** stout, corpulent; **betagt,** aged, advanced in years; **behaart,** hairy; **bebrillt,** bespectacled.

IV. *forming* (*mainly vbl*) *nouns* **Begriff** *m*, notion, conception; **Behuf** *m*, purpose, object; **Belang** *m*, importance, consequence; **Besuch** *m*, visit; visitors.

beabsichtigen, *A:* **beabsichten,** *v.tr.* (*a*) **etwas b.,** to intend sth., to mean sth., to have sth. in mind, in view; **wir haben nichts Böses beabsichtigt,** we intended no harm, we did not mean any harm; **die beabsichtigte Wirkung,** the intended, desired, effect; **der beabsichtigte Zweck,** the object in view; (*b*) **b., etwas zu tun,** to intend to do sth., doing sth., to mean to do sth.; to propose to do sth.; **beabsichtigen Sie, lange zu bleiben?** do you intend, mean, to stay long? **der Gegenstand, den ich heute abend zu besprechen beabsichtige,** the subject I propose to discuss tonight.

beachtbar, *a.*= **beachtenswert.**

beachten. I. *v.tr.* **1. etwas b.,** to attend to sth., to pay attention to sth.; to regard sth., to have, pay, regard to sth.; to heed sth., to give, pay, heed to sth.; to observe (regulations, etc.); **j-s Ratschläge b.,** to attend to s.o.'s recommendations; **beachten Sie meine Worte,** attend to, pay heed to, my words; **etwas besonders, sorgfältig, b.,** to pay particular attention to sth.; **j-s Rat b.,** to regard, follow, s.o.'s advice; **'besonders zu b.',** 'please take note'; **es ist zu b., daß . . . ,** regard must be had, paid, to the fact that . . . **2. j-n, etwas, b.,** to notice, to take notice of, s.o., sth.; **j-n, etwas, nicht b.,** to take no notice of, to disregard, s.o., sth.; **j-n nicht b.,** to ignore s.o., s.o.'s existence; **einen Einwand nicht b.,** to take no notice of, to disregard, to ignore, an objection; **nicht wert, beachtet zu werden,** beneath notice, not worth notice.

II. *vbl s.* **1. Beachten,** *n. in vbl senses.* **2. Beachtung,** *f.* (*a*)=II. 1; (*b*) attention; regard; heed; notice; note; **etwas** *dat.* **B. schenken**=**etwas beachten,** *q.v. under* I. 1; **er schenkt Ihrer Kritik wenig B.,** he takes little heed of your criticisms; **etwas** *dat.* **keine B. schenken,** to pay no attention, regard, to sth.; to take no heed of sth.; **ohne der öffentlichen Meinung B. zu schenken,** heedless of public opinion; **einem Befehl keine B. schenken, einen Befehl der B. nicht würdigen,** to ignore, to take no notice of, to take no heed of, an order; **es verdient B.,** it is worth notice, worthy of notice, note; **es verdient keine B.,** it is not worth notice, beneath notice; **das Gerücht fand keine besondere B.,** the rumour received no particular notice; **'zur B.',** 'notice'; **wir bitten um B. folgender Vorschriften,** please observe the following regulations.

beachtenswert, *occ.* **beachtenswürdig,** *a.* (*of fact, etc.*) noteworthy, worthy of notice, of note, worth notice; (thg) deserving attention; remarkable (thg, pers.); considerable (sum, etc.).

beachtlich, *a.* remarkable; considerable (sum, etc.).

Beachtung, *f. see* **beachten II.**

beachtungswert, beachtungswürdig, *a.* = **beachtenswert.**

beackern, *v.tr.* (*a*) *Husb:* to till, to plough (field); (*b*) **dieses Gebiet ist schon von vielen Gelehrten beackert worden,** this field has already been worked through by many scholars.

Beamte, *m. decl. as adj. &* **-n/-n,** officer, official; civil servant; *Lit. & F:* functionary; **staatlicher Beamter,** government official; civil servant; **städtischer Beamter,** municipal officer; local government official; **Beamter bei der Eisenbahn,** railway official; **Beamter im öffentlichen Dienst,** civil servant; public servant; **Beamter auf Lebenszeit,** established civil servant; **er ist Beamter,** he is in the civil service; **er ist nur ein kleiner Beamter,** he is only a petty official.

beamten, *v.tr.* **1.** *A:* **j-n b.,** to establish s.o. in a post. **2.** (*a*) *p.p. & a.* **beamtet,** permanently employed, appointed (*usu. as civil servant*); **in beamteter Stellung sein,** to hold a permanent post (in the civil service, in a bank, etc.); (*b*) **Beamtete** *m, f. A:*=**Beamte.**

Beamtenapparat, *m. coll.* civil servants; machinery of the civil service, civil service machinery.

Beamtenbeleidigung, *f. Jur:* insult to, insulting of, an official while on duty.

Beamteneid, *m.* oath of office; **den B. ablegen,** to be sworn in.

Beamtenhaftung, *f. Jur:*=**Amtshaftung.**

Beamtenherrschaft, *f.* bureaucracy.

Beamtenkörper, *m.*=**Beamtenschaft.**

Beamtenlaufbahn, *f.* (the) civil service (*as a career*); **die B. einschlagen,** to become a civil servant, to enter the civil service.

Beamtenschaft, *f.* **-/.** *coll.* civil servants, civil service.

Beamtenstelle, *f.*=**Beamtenstellung** (*a*).

Beamtenstellung, *f.* (*a*) official position; post in the civil service; permanent post (in the civil service, in a bank, etc.); (*b*) capacity as a civil servant; official position.

Beamtenstolz, *m.* conceit of (petty) officials.

Beamtentum, *n.* **-(e)s/.** (*a*) officialdom, bureaucracy; (*b*)=**Beamtenschaft.**

Beamtenwesen, *n.*=**Beamtentum** (*a*).

Beamtenwirtschaft, *f. F:* officialdom, *F:* red tape.

Beamtenwürde, *f.* official dignity.

Beamtete, *m., f. see* **beamten.**

Beamtin, *f.* **-/-innen,** (woman) civil servant; *for other phrases cp.* **Beamte.**

beängstigen, *A:* **beängsten.** I. *v.tr.* to alarm (s.o.); to make (s.o.) (feel) uneasy, uncomfortable; to cause (s.o.) anxiety; to fill (s.o.) with anxiety; **lassen Sie sich nicht (davon) b.,** don't be alarmed (at it).

II. *vbl s.* **1. Beängstigen,** *n. in vbl senses.* **2. Beängstigung,** *f. in vbl senses; also:* uneasiness; anxiety, anguish.

III. *pr.p. & a.* **beängstigend,** (*a*) alarming (news, situation, appearance, person, etc.); disquieting (news, feeling, etc.); uneasy (feeling, thought, etc.); uncomfortable (feeling, thought, news, etc.); **es war ein beängstigender Gedanke,** it was a disquieting thought; (*b*) *adv.* **b. stark,** alarmingly strong; **b. blaß,** alarmingly pale; **ein b. hoher Prozentsatz von Fehlern,** a disquietingly high percentage of errors.

beanlagt, *a.*=**begabt,** *q.v. under* **begaben III.**

Beanlagung, *f.*=**Anlage** 8.

beanspruchen. I. *v.tr.* **1.** (*of pers.*) **etwas b.,** to claim (a right, an honour, etc.); to have a claim to sth., to lay claim to sth.; to pretend to (a right, title, etc.); **das Recht b., etwas zu tun,** to claim the right to do sth.; **ein Vorrecht b.,** to claim a privilege; **eine Tugend für sich b.,** to claim a virtue; **er hat eine Eigenschaft, die wenige von uns für sich b. können,** he has a quality that few of us can claim; **ein Kunstwerk, usw., für sich b.,** to claim, lay claim to, the authorship of a work of art, etc.; **wir fordern nicht mehr, als was wir b. dürfen,** we claim no more than (is) our due; *Jur:* **Schadenersatz b.,** to make, put in, a claim for damages. **2.** (*a*) (*of pers.*) **etwas b.,** to claim, call for (attention, etc.); to demand (help, etc.); (*b*) (*of situation, etc.*) **etwas b.,** to demand, claim, call for (attention, time, etc.); to take, require (time, etc.); **j-n b.,** to call for, to demand, to need, s.o.; **dieses Problem beansprucht meine ganze Aufmerksamkeit,** this question demands, claims, calls for, all my attention; **es beanspruchte seine ganze Kraft, sie zurückzuhalten,** it required all his strength to hold them back; **eine solche Arbeit beansprucht den ganzen Mann,** this kind of work calls for a man prepared to devote himself to it unconditionally. **3.** (*a*) (*of pers.*) **j-s Dienste b.,** to make use, *Lit:* to avail oneself, of s.o.'s services; **öffentliche Mittel b.,** to have recourse to public money; **ich brauche seine Hilfe nicht zu beanspruchen,** I don't need (to seek) his help; (*b*) **j-s Zeit zu sehr, über Gebühr, b., zu viel von j-s Zeit b.,** (*of pers.*) to encroach (up)on s.o.'s time, to trespass on s.o.'s time; (*of work, etc.*) to take (up) too much of s.o.'s time; **j-s Geduld zu sehr b.,** to try, tax, s.o.'s patience to the utmost, to the limit; to make too great demands on s.o.'s patience; to strain, put a strain on, s.o.'s patience; **meine Zeit ist stark beansprucht,** I have many demands (up)on, claims on, my time; *Mec: etc:* (*of parts of machinery, material, etc.*) **(stark) beansprucht werden,** to be stressed, to be subjected to (great) stress, strain; **bei Überlastung werden die Reifen zu stark beansprucht,** overloading puts too great a strain on the tyres. *Cp.* **Anspruch.**

II. *vbl s.* **1. Beanspruchen,** *n. in vbl senses.* **2. Beanspruchung,** *f.* (*a*)=II. 1; (*b*) recourse to, use of (services, public money, etc.); (*c*) claim on, demands (up)on (time); demands (up)on, strain on (patience, etc.); *Fin:* **starke B. des Geldmarktes,** strong demand on the money market; (*d*) *Mec: etc:* stress, strain (on parts of machinery, etc.); **zulässige B.,** allowable stress, working stress; safe load; **starker B. ausgesetzt,** under, subjected to, great stress, strain; *Av:* **B. des Flugzeugs,** stressing of the aircraft; **Maschine für normale B.,** machine for normal service; **Maschine für jede Art von B. geeignet,** machine suitable for all conditions.

beanstanden, *Austrian:* **beanständen.** I. *v.tr.* **1.** (*a*) **etwas b., etwas an etwas** *dat.* **b.,** to take exception to sth.; to find fault with sth.; to object to sth., to raise objections to sth.; to demur at, to, sth.; **sie hat immer etwas zu b.,** she is always finding fault, she is always carping at something; **das Problem wurde gelöst, ohne daß jemand die Entscheidung, etwas an der Entscheidung, beanstandete,** the question was solved without anyone taking exception to the decision; **ich finde, habe, nichts daran zu b.,** I have no fault to find with it, I see nothing wrong with it, I find nothing exceptionable in it; **ich beanstande (an ihm) nur seine Eitelkeit,** the only thing I dislike about him, I object to in him, is his vanity; (*b*) *Com: etc:* **Waren b.,** to register, make, a complaint about goods; *Com:* to reject goods delivered; **beanstandete Waren,** rejects; *Post:* **beanstandete Postsendungen,** mail, parcels, etc., rejected (by the postal authorities); (*c*) to contest, to question (a point, a right, the conduct of an election, etc.); to challenge (s.o.'s right); *Com:* **eine Rechnung b.,** to question, query, an invoice. **2.** *A:* **etwas b.,** to delay, postpone, sth.

II. *vbl s.* **1. Beanstanden,** *n. in vbl senses.* **2. Beanstandung,** *f.* (*a*)=II. 1; *also:* **B. einer Sache,** objection to sth.; contestation of sth.; *Com:* **B. von Waren,** rejection of goods delivered; (*b*) **B. (an etwas** *dat.***),** objection, exception, (to sth.); complaint (about sth.); **er machte keine weiteren Beanstandungen,** he made no further demur, objections; **Beanstandungen (an etwas) machen**=**(an etwas) beanstanden,** *q.v. under* I. 1 (*a*); *Com: etc:* **bei B. . . . ,** if dissatisfied . . . , in case of complaint . . . ; **Beanstandungen (bei j-m) geltend machen,** to bring a complaint to (s.o.'s) notice; (*c*) *A:* postponement, delay.

beantragen, I. *v.tr.* (*weak*) (*a*) **etwas (bei j-m) b.,** to apply to make an application, (to s.o.) for sth.; **Gelder (bei der Regierung, usw.) b.,** to make, put in, a claim, an application, for a (government, etc.) grant, an allocation; *Sch:* **Gebührenerlaß b.,** to apply for a grant; *Jur:* **Schadenersatz b.,** to make, put in, a claim for damages; (*b*) **etwas b.,** to propose sth.; to ask for sth.; (*in an assembly*) to bring forward, put, a motion for sth.; *Parl: etc:* to move (for) sth.; **b., daß etwas geschehe, etwas zu tun,** to propose, move, that sth. be done; *Pol:* **eine Abänderung b.,** to move an amendment; *Jur:* (*of counsel for the prosecution*) **eine Gefängnisstrafe b.,** to propose, to ask for, to demand, a prison sentence; **sein Anwalt beantragte die Vertagung der Verhandlung für eine Woche, die Verhandlung für eine Woche zu vertagen,** his counsel moved that the case be adjourned for a week. *Cp.* **Antrag.**

II. *vbl s.* **Beantragen** *n.*, **Beantragung** *f. in vbl senses; also:* application; request.

beantwortbar, *a.* (question, etc.) that can be answered; answerable (question, etc.).

Beantwortbarkeit, *f.* **die B. dieser Frage hängt davon ab . . . ,** whether this question can be answered depends on . . . .

beantworten. I. *v.tr.* **(j-s) Briefe, Fragen, b.,** to answer, to reply to, (s.o.'s) letters, questions; **können Sie mir diese Frage b.?** can you answer this question (for me)? **die Frage läßt sich nicht leicht b., ist nicht leicht zu b.,** the question is not easy to answer; **(j-m) etwas schriftlich b.,** to write (s.o.) an answer, to give (s.o.) a written reply, to answer (s.o.) in writing; **zu**

beantwortende Briefe, letters to be answered; **das beantwortet sich von selbst,** it answers itself; it is obvious; **er beantwortete ihre Freundlichkeit mit Beleidigungen,** he repaid her kindness with insults.
II. *vbl s.* **1. Beantworten,** *n. in vbl senses.* **2. Beantwortung,** *f. in vbl senses; also:* answer, reply; **die B. Ihrer Frage,** the answer to your question; **in B. Ihres Schreibens,** *Com:* **Ihrer geschätzten Zuschrift,** in reply, answer, to your letter, *Com:* to your favour; *Com:* **wir bitten höflichst um B.,** the favour of an answer is requested.

Beantwortungsschreiben, *n.* = **Antwort(s)schreiben.**

bearbeitbar, *a.* workable (wood, stone, clay, leather, etc.); *Metalw:* machinable; **leicht bearbeitbares Eisen,** easily wrought iron.

Bearbeitbarkeit, *f.* good working properties, workabilitity (of stone, metal, etc.); good machining properties, machinability (of metal).

bearbeiten. I. *v.tr.* **1.** (*a*) *Agr: etc:* to cultivate (the soil, a garden); **den Boden mit der Haue, mit dem Spaten, b.,** to hoe, dig, the ground; **bearbeiten Sie Ihren Garten selbst?** do you do your own gardening? (*b*) *Tchn:* to process (raw material); to work (wood, iron, clay, etc.); to dress (timber, leather, hides); to dress, hew (stone); *Metalw:* to tool, to machine (castings, etc.); *Stonew: Metalw:* **(die Oberfläche) b.,** to face, to dress; **bearbeitete Oberfläche,** faced surface; *Metalw:* **mit dem Hammer b.,** to hammer; **leicht zu bearbeitendes Eisen,** easily wrought iron; *Stonew: Sculp:* **im Groben, Rohen, b.,** to rough-hew (stone, statue); *Stonew:* **mit dem Scharriereisen b.,** to tool, to tooth; (*c*) to shape, form, fashion (clay, stone, soft metals, etc.); (*d*) **ein beschmutztes Kleidungsstück mit Fleckenwasser b.,** to treat a stained garment with stain remover; *Ch:* **ein Metall mit einer Säure b.,** to treat a metal with an acid; (*e*) **ein Musikinstrument b.,** (i) *A:* to play (on) a musical instrument; (ii) *F:* to play away on a musical instrument; to pound on, away at (the piano); to bang on (a drum); to scrape away at (the violin, etc.). **2.** (*a*) **ein Thema, eine Sache, b.,** to work on, to deal with, *Lit: Art:* to treat, a subject, a matter; **ein Wörterbuch b.,** to revise a dictionary; *Jur:* **einen Fall b.,** to handle a case, to deal with a case, to be on, in charge of, a case; *Adm:* **einen Antrag b.,** to handle, deal with, an application; *Com:* **einen Auftrag b.,** to deal with an order; (*b*) **ein Manuskript für die Drucklegung b.,** to prepare a manuscript for the printer, for publication; to edit a manuscript; *Library:* **ein Buch (für die Katalogisierung) b.,** to process a book; (*c*) to adapt (play, novel); **einen Roman für die Bühne b.,** to adapt a novel for the stage; **das Buch ist für Anfänger bearbeitet,** the book is adapted for beginners; **Stück nach dem Französischen bearbeitet,** play adapted from the French; *Mus:* **ein Stück, eine Partitur, für Klavier b.,** to arrange a piece, a score, for the piano; (*d*) **ein Buch neu b.,** to revise, re-edit, a book; **ein Buch vollkommen, gänzlich, neu b.,** to revise a book completely. **3. einen Wahlbezirk b.,** to canvass a constituency; *F:* to work a constituency; (*of commercial traveller*) **einen Bezirk b.,** to work a district. **4.** (*a*) **j-n (mit den Fäusten) b.,** to belabour s.o. (with one's fists), to thrash, trounce, s.o. soundly, to hammer away at s.o., to punch s.o., *F:* to beat s.o. up; (*b*) **j-n b.,** to influence s.o., to work on s.o., on s.o.'s mind; to try to persuade s.o.; **nachdem sie ihn zwei Stunden lang bearbeitet hatte, willigte er endlich ein,** after she had tried for two hours to persuade him he finally consented; **du brauchst ihn nur ein bißchen zu b., dann wird er schon mitkommen,** he only needs a little persuasion and he will come with you. **5. sich bearbeiten,** *A:* = **sich bemühen,** *q.v. under* **bemühen** II.
II. *vbl s.* **1. Bearbeiten,** *n. in vbl senses.* **2. Bearbeitung,** *f.* (*a*) = II. 1; *also:* cultivation (of the soil, a garden); treatment (of a subject, a matter); preparation (of a manuscript for the printer); compilation (of a dictionary); adaptation (of a play, a novel); revision (of a book); *Mus:* arrangement (of a piece for the piano, etc.); **j-m etwas zur B. übertragen, übergeben,** to place, put, sth. in s.o.'s hands, charge; to leave s.o. to deal with sth.; **Neuauflage in B. (begriffen),** new edition in preparation; **technische, chemische, B.,** mechanical, chemical, treatment; **Werkstatt für mechanische, maschinelle, B.,** machine shop; (*b*) (*adapted version*) **französische B. des lateinischen Urtextes,** French adaptation of the Latin original; **freie B.,** free adaptation; **neue B.,** revised edition; *Mus:* **B. für Klavier,** arrangement for piano.

Bearbeiter, *m.* **-s/-,** adapter (of novel, play); editor (of text, etc.); compiler (of dictionary); arranger (of piece of music, score); official in charge (of project, etc.); official responsible (for dealing with applications, etc.).

Bearbeitung, *f. see* **bearbeiten** II.

bearbeitungsfähig, *a.* = **bearbeitbar.**

Bearbeitungsfläche, *f. Metalw:* surface to be machined, surface ready for machining.

Bearbeitungsgrad, *m.* (degree of) workability (of stone, metal, etc.); (degree of) machinability (of metal).

Bearbeitungsmethode, *f.* = **Bearbeitungsverfahren.**

Bearbeitungsmöglichkeit, *f.* workability (of material).

Bearbeitungsplan, *m. Tchn: Ind:* operation plan.

Bearbeitungstechnik, *f. Tchn:* machining practice, tooling practice.

Bearbeitungsverfahren, *n. Tchn:* manufacturing method; *Metalw: etc:* machining method, tooling method; **spanabhebendes B.,** metal-cutting operation; **spanloses B.,** non-cutting operation.

Bearbeitungsvorgang, *m. Tchn:* mechanical operation.

Bearbeitungsweise, *f.* = **Bearbeitungsverfahren.**

Bearbeitungszugabe, *f. Tchn: Ind:* working allowance; machining allowance.

beargwohnen, beargwöhnen, *v.tr.* to be, feel, suspicious about, of, towards (s.o., sth.).

beästet, *a.* (*of tree*) branched, branching.

Beata [be·ˈaːtaː]. *Pr.n.f.* **-s** & *Lit:* **-tens.** Beatrice.

Beate [be·ˈaːtə]. *Pr.n.f.* **-s** & *Lit:* **-ns.** Beatrice.

Beatifikation [be·a·ti·fi·ka·tsĭˈoːn], *f.* **-/-en.** *Ecc:* beatification.

beatifizieren [be·a·ti·fi·ˈtsiːrən], *v.tr. Ecc:* to beatify.

beatmen, *v.tr. Med:* to apply artificial respiration to (s.o.) (by means of breathing apparatus); **(künstliche) Beatmung,** artificial respiration.

Beatrice [be·a·ˈtriːsə, be·a·ˈtriːtʃə], **-s** & *Lit:* **-ns, Beatrix** [ˈbe·a·triks, be·ˈaːtriks], **-'** & *Lit:* **-ens.** *Pr.n.f.* Beatrice, Beatrix.

Beau [boː], *m.* **-/-s,** beau, dandy.

beaufschlagen, *v.* (*weak*) *Turb:* **1.** *v.tr.* to subject (turbine, vane) to the impact of water, steam, etc.; (*of water, steam, etc.*) to impinge on (vanes of a turbine); **eine Turbine voll, partiell, b.,** to make the water, steam, etc., impinge fully, partially, on the vanes of a turbine; **eine durch Abgase beaufschlagte Turbine,** a turbine driven by exhaust gases. **2.** *vbl s.* **Beaufschlagung,** *f.* admission, inlet; supply, flow; **partielle B.,** partial admission.

beaufsichtigen. I. *v.tr.* to supervise (work, studies, a class, etc.); to superintend (work, workers, etc.); **die Arbeiten persönlich b.,** to superintend the work personally; **die Kinder b.,** to take charge, to be in charge, of the children; to look after, keep an eye on, the children; **j-n streng b.,** to keep a sharp eye, watch, on s.o.; *Sch:* **Examenskandidaten b.,** to invigilate, *U.S:* to proctor, at an examination, to supervise examination candidates.
II. *vbl s.* **Beaufsichtigen** *n.*, **Beaufsichtigung** *f. in vbl senses; also:* supervision (of work, studies, a class, etc.); superintendence (of work, etc.); *Sch:* invigilation, *U.S:* proctoring (*at an examination*). *Cp.* **Aufsicht.**

beauftragen, *v.tr.* (*weak*) (*a*) **j-n mit etwas b.,** to entrust, charge, s.o. with (doing) sth.; *Adm:* to appoint s.o. to sth.; **wir haben unseren Korrespondenten mit dieser Sache beauftragt,** we have entrusted this matter to our correspondent, we have entrusted our correspondent with this matter; *Adm:* **j-n mit einem Sonderdienst b.,** to appoint s.o. to a special office; to charge s.o. with a special commission; **j-n mit seiner Vertretung b.,** to make s.o. one's deputy; **mit etwas beauftragt sein,** to be entrusted with sth., with doing sth.; to have charge, be in charge, of sth.; *Adm:* **mit den Geschäften beauftragt,** (person, officer, official) in charge; *Sch:* **mit Vorlesungen beauftragt,** invited to deliver lectures; recognized as a lecturer (*on a temporary basis*); (*b*) **j-n b., etwas zu tun,** to instruct s.o. to do sth.; to direct s.o. to do sth.; to charge s.o. to do sth.; to commission s.o. to do sth.; *Adm:* to appoint s.o. to do sth.; **ich bin von der Direktion beauftragt, Ihnen mitzuteilen, daß . . . ,** I am instructed by the Board to inform you that . . . ; **ich war beauftragt, nach England zu reisen,** I was directed to proceed, to go, to England; **einen Künstler beauftragen, ein Porträt zu malen,** to commission an artist to paint a portrait; **eine Kommission b., zu . . . ,** to appoint a commission to . . . ; (*c*) *Jur:* **einen Rechtsanwalt b.,** to brief a barrister; **beauftragter Richter,** commissioner (appointed to conduct judicial investigation, etc.).

Beauftragte, *m., f.* (*decl. as adj.*) representative; *Jur: Com:* agent; **persönlicher Beauftragter des Präsidenten,** personal representative of the President.

beäuge(l)n, *occ.* **beaugen,** *v.tr.* to watch (sth., s.o.) closely, with curiosity; to eye (s.o.) (attentively).

beaugenscheinigen. I. *v.tr.* to inspect, to view (sth., s.o.); to look closely, to take a good look, at (sth., s.o.); to examine (sth.) closely.
II. *vbl s.* **Beaugenscheinigen** *n.*, **Beaugenscheinigung** *f. in vbl senses; also:* inspection, view.

beaugt, beäugt, *a. A:* (*a*) (*of peacock's feather, etc.*) eyed; (*b*) clear-sighted.

Beauté [bo·ˈteː], *f.* **-/-s,** beautiful woman, beauty.

bebaken, *v.tr. Nau:* to beacon, mark out (channel).

bebändern, *v.tr.* (*a*) to decorate, trim, (sth.) with ribbon(s); (*b*) **bebändert,** decorated, trimmed, with ribbon(s); *F:* beribboned; *Her:* stringed (hunting-horn, etc.); *Nat.Hist:* ribboned; *A:* (*of officer*) **bebändert und besternt,** beribboned and bemedalled.

bebauen. I. *v.tr.* **1. ein Gelände b.,** to build over, upon, a site, a piece of land; **bebaute Fläche, bebautes Land,** built-up area. **2.** *Agr:* **das Land b.,** to cultivate, farm, till, the land.
II. *vbl s.* **Bebauen** *n.*, **Bebauung** *f. in vbl senses; also:* cultivation (of land, etc.).

Bebauungsplan, *m.* (*a*) plan for building, housing plan; (*b*) building project; (*c*) lay-out (of a town, etc.).

bebbern, *v.i.* (*haben*) = **bibbern.**

Bebé [ˈbe·beː, be·ˈbeː], *n.* **-s/-s.** *Swiss:* (*a*) baby; (*b*) baby doll.

Bebe, *f.* **-/-n.** *Swiss Dial:* gourd, pumpkin.

beben. I. *v.i.* (*haben*) (*a*) (*of earth, building, etc.*) to tremble, quake, shake; (*of rock*) to tremble, shake; (*of air*) to vibrate (with sound); (*b*) *Poet:* **(leise) b.,** (*of leaves, strings*) to quiver; (*of light, torch*) to flicker; (*c*) (*of pers.*) **vor Kälte b.,** to shiver, shake, with cold; **am ganzen Leibe, an allen Gliedern, b.,** to tremble in all one's limbs, in every limb; **vor Angst b.,** to tremble, shake, quake, with fear; **der bloße Gedanke daran machte ihn, sein Herz, b.,** he trembled at the mere thought of it; **vor Zorn b.,** to shake, quiver, with anger; **mit bebender Stimme,** in a trembling voice; **mit bebenden Nüstern,** with quivering nostrils; **für j-n b.,** to tremble for s.o.; **vor j-m b.,** to stand in fear of s.o., to tremble before s.o.
II. *vbl s.* **1. Beben,** *n.* (*a*) *in vbl senses; also:* vibration (of air); tremble, shake (in voice, etc.); (*b*) earthquake. **2. Bebung,** *f.* vibration; *Mus:* (*on clavichord*) tremolo; (*on violin, etc.*) vibrato.

Bebenschwarm, *m.* earthquake cluster.

Beber, *m.* **-s/-.** *Mus:* tremolo stop (of organ).

Bebersche, *f. Bot:* aspen.

bebildern, *v.tr.* to illustrate (book, etc.); **Bebilderung** *f,* illustration (of book, etc.).

beblättern, *v.tr.* to cover (tree, etc.) with leaves; (*of tree, etc.*) **sich b.,** to come, break, into leaf, to put out leaves; **beblättert,** (tree, etc.) in leaf; leafy (bough, etc.); *Bot:* foliate (stalk, etc.); foliaged (tree, etc.).

beblümt, *a.* flowery (meadow, etc.); **bunt b.,** gay with flowers.

bebohlen, *v.tr.* to board over, plank over (deck, etc.); to floor (room, etc.).

bebrillt, *a.* wearing spectacles, bespectacled.

bebrüten, *v.tr.* (*a*) (*of hen, etc.*) to sit on (eggs); to incubate (eggs); (*b*) *F:* to brood on, over (suggestion, etc.).

Bebung, *f. see* **beben** II. 2.

bebuschen (sich), *v.refl.* to become overgrown, covered, with shrubs, bushes; **bebuscht,** bush-covered (hill, etc.), (hill, etc.) covered with bushes, shrubs.

Bechamelsauce [beːʃaˈmɛlzoːsə], *f. Cu:* bechamel sauce; white sauce.

Becher, *m.* **-s/-.** **1.** (*a*) cup; mug; (*of glass, without handle and foot*) tumbler; (*of plastic*) beaker; (*without handle*) goblet; (*for ice-cream*) cup; glass; tub (*made of cardboard*); **großer B.,** beaker; **silberner B.,** silver mug; **B. einer Thermosflasche,** screw-cap, beaker, of a vacuum flask; (*b*) **ein B. Milch,** a glass, beaker, of milk; **ein B. Wein(es),** a glass of wine; *Lit:* **die Becher kreisen lassen,** to circulate the wine; to keep the wine flowing; **den B. (bis zur Neige) leeren,**

to drain one's glass (to the last drop); (*c*) **den B. der Freude bis auf den Grund leeren, bis zum letzten Tropfen auskosten,** to drain the cup of pleasure to the dregs. **2.** *Tchn:* bucket (of elevator, conveyor). **3.** *Bot:* cupule; cup (of acorn); calyx (of flower); scyphus, cup (of lichen). **4.** *Astr:* **der B.,** Crater, the Cup, the Bowl.

becherartig, *a.* cup-like (shape, etc.).

Becherblume, *f. Bot:* burnet, blood-wort.

Bechereisen, *n. Tls:* beak-iron.

Becherfarn, *m. Bot:* bristle-fern.

Becherflechte, *f. Moss:* cladonia, reindeer-moss, cup-moss.

becherförmig, *a.* cup-shaped; cupped; *Bot:* cupular.

Becherfrucht, *f. Bot:* fruit of a cupuliferous plant.

Becherfrüchtler, *m.pl. Bot:* cupuliferae.

Becherglas, *n. Ch: etc:* beaker.

Becherglaskolben, *m. Ch:* conical flask, Erlenmeyer flask.

Becherheld, *m.* toper; roisterer; pot-valiant; swashbuckler.

Becherhülle, *f. Bot:* cupule.

Becherkeim, *m. Biol:* gastrula.

Becherkette, *f. Tchn:* chain of buckets, bucket-chain, conveyor-chain.

Becherkettenförderer, *m.*=**Becherwerk.**

Becherklang, *m.* chinking of (wine-)glasses.

Becherkolben, *m.*=**Becherglaskolben.**

Becherlarve, *f. Biol:*=**Becherkeim.**

Becherling, *m.* **-s/-e.** *Fung:* cup-fungus.

Bechermoos, *n.*=**Becherflechte.**

bechern, *v.i.* (*haben*) to drink hard, heavily, to tipple.

Becherpilz, *m.*=**Becherling.**

Becherprimel, *f. Bot:* Japanese primrose.

Becherqualle, *f. Coel:* stauromedusa.

Becherrost, *m. Fung:* cluster-cup.

Becherschwamm, *m.*=**Becherling.**

Becherspiel, *n.* thimble-rig.

Becherspieler, *m.* thimble-rigger.

Becherstrauch, *m.*=**Becherblume.**

bechertragend, *a. Bot:* cupuliferous.

Bechertraube, *f. Tls:* (potter's) bat.

Becherwerk, *n. Civ. E:* bucket-conveyor; bucket-elevator, paternoster(-elevator); **B. für schräge Förderung,** inclined elevator; **B. für senkrechte Förderung,** vertical elevator; **schaufelndes B.,** dipping bucket conveyor.

Becherzelle, *f. Anat:* gland cell.

Beck, *m.* **-(e)s/-e.** *A:*=**Bäcker.**

Becken, *n.* **-s/-. 1.** (*a*) basin; bowl; hand-basin, wash-basin; (kitchen-)sink; (lavatory) pan, bowl; *Med:* bed-pan; kidney-bowl; *Ecc:* piscina; font; (*b*) **(künstliches) B.,** (artificial) basin (*for lake, pond, etc.*); (*c*) *Ph. Geog:* drainage basin, catchment (of river); *Geol:* basin; **das Mainzer B.,** the Mainz basin; (*d*) nose (of tongs). **2.** *Mus: pl.* **Becken,** cymbals. **3.** *Anat:* pelvis; **oberes, großes, B.,** false pelvis; **unteres, kleines, B.,** true pelvis.

Becken-, *comb.fm. Anat:* pelvic ..., ... of the pelvis; **Beckenabweichung** *f,* abnormal structure of the pelvis; **Beckenboden** *m,* pelvic diaphragm; **Beckenknochen** *m,* pelvic bone, *F:* hip-bone; **Beckengürtel** *m,* pelvic arch, girdle, *F:* hip girdle.

Beckenarterie, *f. Anat:* hypogastric artery, interior iliac artery.

Beckenbruch, *m. Surg:* pelvic fracture, fracture of the pelvis; fractured, broken, pelvis.

Beckenendlage, *f. Obst:* breech presentation; footling presentation; knee presentation.

beckenförmig, *a.* (vessel, cavity, etc.) in the form of a basin; basin-shaped (cavity, etc.).

Beckenhaube, *f. Arm:* bas(i)net.

Beckenmesser, *m. Med:* (*instrument*) pelvimeter.

Beckenmessung, *f. Med:* pelvimetry.

Beckenschlag, *m. Mus:* clash of cymbals.

Beckenschlagader, *f.*=**Beckenarterie.**

Beckenschläger, *m. Mus:* cymbalist, cymbal-player.

Beckhammer, *m.* (*a*) clinch-hammer; (*b*) riveting hammer; (*c*) *Farr:* shoeing hammer.

Beckmesser, *m.* **-s/-,** (*character in Wagner's 'Meistersinger'*) *F:* captious person.

Beda. *Pr.n.m.* **-s.** *Hist:* **B. der Ehrwürdige, B. Venerabilis,** the Venerable Bede.

bedachen. 1. *v.tr.* to roof (a house, etc.). **2.** *vbl s.* **Bedachung,** *f.* (*a*) (*action*) roofing; (*b*) roof, roofing.

Bedacht[1], *m.* **-(e)s/.** (*used mainly in adv. and vbl phrases*) reflection, thought, deliberation, consideration; care; caution, circumspection, wariness; **ohne B. handeln,** (i) to act rashly, inconsiderately, without consideration, without thinking, without forethought, carelessly; (ii) to act heedlessly, incautiously; **er handelt ohne B.,** (i) he takes no thought over what he does; (ii) he has no care for what he does; **mit B.,** (i) thoughtfully, carefully, deliberately, with care, with deliberation; (ii) circumspectly, with circumspection, cautiously, warily, *Scot:* cannily; **sie hat diese Handschuhe mit B. ausgesucht,** she has chosen these gloves with great care; **der alte Mann stieg mit B. die Treppe hinunter,** the old man descended the stairs cautiously; **voll B.,** considerate, full of consideration, regardful; **auf etwas** *acc.* **B. nehmen, haben,** (i) to bear, keep, sth. in mind; to give some thought to sth.; (ii) to be wary, cautious, of sth.; **darauf B. nehmen, daß etwas geschieht,** to take care, to be careful, that sth. is done.

bedacht[2], *a.* **1.** (*a*) careful; deliberate; circumspect; cautious; *adv.* **b. handeln,** to act (i) deliberately, (ii) cautiously; (*b*) **auf etwas, j-n, b. sein,** to look after sth., s.o., to be attentive to sth., s.o.; to be concerned about sth., s.o.; **er ist darauf b., mir jede Mühe zu ersparen,** he is careful to spare me all trouble; **er ist nicht ein bißchen auf seine Mutter b.,** he has no thought for his mother; **er ist sehr darauf b., zu gefallen,** he is (very) anxious to please; **auf seinen Ruf b. sein,** to have a care for one's reputation, to be careful, mindful, of one's good name; **er ist sehr auf sich (selbst) b.,** he is very much concerned with himself; *F:* he takes great care of number one; **auf seinen (eigenen) Vorteil b. sein,** to have an eye to one's own interest; to look after one's own interest(s); **nur auf sich b. sein,** to think only of oneself, to care only for oneself, to be selfish; *Com:* **'stets auf prompte Erledigung Ihrer Aufträge b.', 'stets darauf b., Ihre Aufträge prompt zu erledigen',** 'assuring you of our prompt attention to your orders'. **2.** (*a*) provided (with), endowed (with); **vom Schicksal wohl b.,** favoured by fortune; **mit irdischen Gütern wohl b.,** well endowed with earthly goods; **übel, schlecht, b.,** ill provided for; badly, poorly, off; (*b*) **Bedachte** *m, f,* beneficiary, recipient; *Jur:* legatee. *See also* **bedenken.**

Bedachtheit, *f.*=**Bedacht**[1].

bedächtig, (*a*) *a.* reflective, thoughtful, serious-minded, deliberate (person); careful (person, walk); deliberate, slow (speech, walk); **mit bedächtigem Schritt gehen,** to pick one's way, one's steps, slowly, carefully; **er ist b. in all seinen Bewegungen,** he is deliberate in all his movements; (*b*) *adv.* **b. handeln, b. zu Werke gehen,** to act, to set about sth., with (careful) deliberation, deliberately, with (great) caution, cautiously; **b. reden,** to speak with deliberation, to speak deliberately, slowly; to weigh one's words.

Bedächtigkeit, *f.* reflectiveness, thoughtfulness, deliberateness; care, caution; slowness.

bedächtiglich, *adv. A. & Lit:* thoughtfully, with deliberation, deliberately.

bedächtlich, *a. A:*=**bedächtig.**

Bedächtlichkeit, *f. A:* caution; carefulness; deliberateness.

bedachtlos, *a.* thoughtless, careless, without consideration, deliberation; rash (act, words, etc.); *adv.* **b. handeln**=**ohne Bedacht handeln,** *q.v. under* **Bedacht**[1].

Bedachtlosigkeit, *f.* thoughtlessness, carelessness, lack of consideration, deliberation; rashness.

bedachtsam, *a.*=**bedacht**[2] 1 (*a*); **er ist viel zu b., ein viel zu bedachtsamer Mensch, um so etwas zu tun,** he is far too cautious, too wary, to do such a thing.

Bedachtsamkeit, *f.*=**Bedacht**[1].

bedachtvoll, *a.*=**voll Bedacht,** *q.v. under* **Bedacht**[1].

Bedachung, *f. see* **bedachen.**

bedanken. 1. *v.tr.* (*used in passive only*) *Lit:* **sei, seid, seien Sie, (bestens) bedankt, du sollst, Sie sollen, (bestens) bedankt sein,** (please) accept my, our, (sincere) thanks; *A:* (*of thg, pers.*) **bedankt werden,** to be rewarded with thanks, (*of pers.*) to receive thanks. **2.** (*a*) **sich bedanken,** to express one's thanks, to say thank you; **sich bei j-m (für etwas) b.,** to thank s.o., to give one's thanks to s.o. (for sth.); **sich überschwenglich bei j-m b.,** to thank s.o. effusively; (*b*) *Iron:* **sich (für etwas) b.,** to refuse (sth.) (emphatically). **sie würden, werden, sich schön dafür b.,** they 'would be, 'will be, pleased with it; **ich würde mich bestens b., wenn jemand mir so etwas anböte,** I should be most indignant if anyone offered me anything like that.

bedarf[1] *see* **bedürfen.**

Bedarf[2], *m.* **-(e)s/. 1.** want, need, requirement; (*a*) **j-s, seinen, B. decken,** to provide for s.o.'s, one's, wants, to meet s.o.'s, one's, requirements; **j-s, seinen, B. an Kleidungsstücken, usw., decken,** to make provisions for s.o.'s, one's, clothing, etc., requirements; **B. an etwas** *dat.* **haben,** to need, require, want, sth.; **mein persönlicher B. ist sehr gering,** my personal wants are very few; **B. an Menschen und Material,** need for men and materials; **bei, nach, B.,** if, when, required, as may be required, if need(s) be, on request; **die Güter können (je) nach B. geliefert werden,** the goods can be supplied as they are required, wanted; **wir sind über B. eingedeckt,** we have more than we want; **mein B. ist gedeckt,** (i) my needs are supplied; (ii) *F:* I've had about enough; *F:* **mein B. an Kino ist für die nächsten zwölf Monate gedeckt,** I've had enough of the pictures to last me for the next twelve months; *Pol.Ec:* **der öffentliche, der ordentliche, der außerordentliche, B.,** public, recurrent, non-recurrent, requirements; **der heimische B.,** home requirements (of a country); **Deckung des Bedarfs,** satisfying of wants, covering of requirements; **ein weit über den lokalen B. hinausgehendes Angebot,** a supply far in excess of local needs, requirements; (*of small farm, etc.*) **nur für den eigenen B. arbeiten, erzeugen,** to work, produce, only for (its) own requirements; (*b*)=**Bedarfsartikel** (*a*). **2.** *Pol.Ec: etc:* demand; **der B. nimmt von Jahr zu Jahr zu,** demand increases yearly; **die einheimische Produktion genügt nicht, den steigenden B. zu decken,** home production is insufficient to meet the increasing demand; **der B. für diesen Artikel ist groß,** there is a great demand for this line; *F:* **wir haben hier keinen B. für Leute wie dich,** people like you are not wanted here. **3.** supply; **sie kaufen ihren täglichen B. an Lebensmitteln auf dem Markt ein,** they buy their daily supply of food in the market; *Com:* **wir haben unseren B. für die kommende Saison auf der Frankfurter Messe bestellt,** we have ordered our supplies for the coming season at the Frankfurt fair.

Bedarfsartikel, *m.pl.* (*a*) *Com:* requisites, necessaries; **B. für Buchdruckereien,** printing, necessaries; **B. für Metzgereien,** butchers' requisites, supplies; **kaufmännische B.,** trade supplies; (*b*)=**Bedarfsgüter.**

Bedarfsdeckung, *f. Pol.Ec:* satisfaction of wants, needs; provision for needs.

Bedarfs(deckungs)wirtschaft, *f. Pol.Ec:* economy directed towards the satisfaction of wants.

Bedarfselastizität, *f. Pol.Ec:* elasticity of demand.

Bedarfsfall, *m.* **im B.,** if need(s) be, in case of need, if necessary, when required; **im B. würde ich es tun,** I should do it if the necessity arose.

Bedarfsfrage, *f. Adm:* **die B. prüfen,** to look into the state of demand, to examine the need (for granting a licence, etc.).

Bedarfsgegenstände, *m.pl.*=**Bedarfsartikel.**

Bedarfsgruppe, *f. Pol.Ec:* consumer group; **diese Fabrik versorgt drei Bedarfsgruppen,** this factory caters for three types of consumer.

Bedarfsgüter, *n.pl.* essential commodities.

Bedarfshaltestelle, *f.* request stop.

Bedarfslage, *f. Pol.Ec:* state of demand.

Bedarfsland, *n. Pol.Ec:* consuming country.

Bedarfsträger, *m. Pol.Ec:* consumer.

Bedarfswirtschaft, *f.*=**Bedarfsdeckungswirtschaft.**

bedarfswirtschaftlich, *a. Pol.Ec:* (planning, etc.) for the direct satisfaction of wants.

Bedarfszug, *m. Rail:* relief train.

bedauerlich, *a.* regrettable; unfortunate (mistake, etc.); lamentable (incident, etc.); **sehr b.,** deplorable; **es ist b., daß er allein blieb,** it is sad that he should have remained alone; *adv.* **die Zahl der Teilnehmer war b. klein,** there was a regrettably small attendance.

bedauerlicherweise, *adv.* unfortunately.

bedauern, 1. *v.tr.* **1.** (*a*) **etwas b.,** to regret sth.; **etwas tief, sehr, b.,** to regret sth. deeply, to deplore sth.; **b., etwas getan zu haben,** to regret, to be sorry for, having done sth., to be sorry to have done sth.; **ich bedauerte (es) nicht, zu Bett gegangen zu sein, daß ich zu Bett gegangen war,** I was not sorry to have gone to bed, that I had gone to bed; **ich bedaure, es sagen zu müssen,** I regret to have to say it; **ich bedaure, sagen zu müssen, daß ...,** I am sorry to say that ...; **ich bedaure, Ihnen mitteilen zu müssen ...,** I regret to have to inform you ...; **wir bedauern, Ihr Anerbieten nicht annehmen zu können,** we regret that we are unable to accept your offer; **mit bedauerndem Achselzucken,** with a shrug of apology; **es ist zu bedauern,** it is to be regretted, it is regrettable, unfortunate; (*b*) *abs.* **bedaure (sehr)!** sorry (I cannot oblige). **2. j-n b.,** to pity, to feel pity for, s.o., to feel sorry for

s.o.; **sich selbst b.,** to feel sorry for oneself; **er ist sehr zu b.,** he is greatly to be pitied; **er läßt sich gerne b., er ist gerne bedauert,** he likes to be pitied.

II. *vbl s.* **Bedauern,** *n. in vbl senses; also:* **1.** regret; **B. über den Verlust einer Sache,** regret for the loss of sth.; **ich habe ihnen mein B. darüber ausgedrückt, daß . . . ,** I expressed to them my regret that . . . ; **mit B. von etwas hören, mit B. hören, daß . . . ,** to hear with regret of sth., to hear with regret that . . . ; **zu meinem B. sehe ich mich gezwungen, zu . . . ,** (much) to my regret I find myself constrained to . . . . **2.** pity; sorrow; **ihr B. kannte keine Grenzen,** her pity was unbounded; **sein Anblick war zum B.,** it was pitiful, pitiable, to see him; **ein Blick voll B.,** a sorrowful, pitying, glance; **zu meinem B.,** to my sorrow; **j-n mehr mit B. als mit Zorn betrachten,** to look at s.o. more with sorrow than with anger.

Bedauernis, *f.* **-/-nisse.** *A:*=Bedauern, *q.v. under* **bedauern II.**

bedauernswert, bedauernswürdig, *a.* (*a*) pitiable (person, condition, etc.); pitiful (person, condition, etc.); piteous, lamentable (condition, etc.); **es war ein bedauernswerter Anblick,** it was pitiable to see (it), it was a pitiful sight; *adv.* **er sieht b. aus,** it is pitiful to see him, he looks wretched; (*b*)=**bedauerlich.**

Bede, *f.* **-/-n.** *Hist:* feudal tax on property.

bedecken. I. *v.tr.* to cover; (*a*) (*etwas*) **mit Erde b.,** to cover (sth.) with earth; **(ganz) mit Staub bedeckt sein,** to be covered, overlaid, with dust, *F:* to be all over dust; **ganz, über und über, mit Schlamm bedeckt,** bespattered with mud; **sie bedeckte ihr Gesicht mit den Händen,** she hid her face in her hands; she put her hands over her face; **seine Blöße b.,** to cover one's shame; **sich b.,** to put on one's hat; **bedeckt bleiben,** to remain covered, to keep one's hat on; **mit Schnee bedeckt,** covered with snow; **eine mit Efeu bedeckte Mauer,** a wall covered with ivy, an ivy-covered wall; **die Wiese war über und über mit Blumen bedeckt,** the meadow was carpeted with flowers; *Mil:* **bedecktes Gelände,** wooded country *or* inhabited area; (*b*) **j-n, sich, mit Schande b.,** to cover s.o., oneself, with shame; **j-s Namen mit Schande b.,** to besmirch s.o.'s good name; **sich mit Ruhm b.,** to cover oneself with glory; **er bedeckte sie mit Küssen,** he smothered her with kisses; *B:* **Finsternis bedeckt das Erdreich und Dunkel die Völker,** the darkness shall cover the earth, and gross darkness the people; (*c*) **der Himmel bedeckt sich (mit Wolken), es bedeckt sich,** the sky, it, is clouding over; **bedeckter Himmel, bedecktes Wetter,** overcast sky, weather; (*d*) *Astr:* to occult (a planet, a star); (*e*) *occ:* to shield, to screen, to protect; (*f*) *A: Breed:*=**decken I. 4.**

II. *vbl s.* **1. Bedecken,** *n. in vbl senses.* **2. Bedeckung,** *f.* (*a*)=II. 1; (*b*) *occ.* cover; (*c*) escort; *Mil:* escort; *Navy:* convoy; **er wurde unter polizeilicher B. abgeführt,** he was led away under police escort; **unter B. von zwei Polizisten,** escorted by two policemen; (*of ship*) **unter B. fahren,** to sail, proceed, under convoy; (*d*) *Astr:* occultation (of planet, star); (*e*) *occ.*= **Deckung** (*d*), (*g*), *q.v. under* **decken III.**

bedecktsamig, *a. Bot:* angiospermous; **bedecktsamige Pflanze,** angiosperm.

Bedeckung, *f. see* **bedecken II.**

Bedeckungsabteilung, Bedeckungsmannschaft, *f. Mil:* covering party.

Bedeckungsscheibe, *f. Mec.E:* cover-plate.

Bedeckungsschiff, *n.* convoy-ship.

Bedeckungstruppen, *f.pl. Mil:* covering forces.

Bedegar [beˑdeˑˈgaːr], *m.* **-s/-s.** *Bot:* bedeguar.

bedeichen, *v.tr.* to (em)bank (river, etc.); to dike (land).

Bedel, *m.* **-s/-.** *Ecc:* collection bag.

bedenken. I. *v.tr.* (*conj. like* **denken**) **1.** (*a*) **etwas b.,** to consider, weigh, ponder, sth.; to think sth. over, to turn sth. over in one's mind; **es ist zu b., man muß b., daß . . . ,** it must be borne in mind that . . . ; **wenn man all(es) das bedenkt,** taking all this into consideration, in view of all this; **wenn man es richtig, recht, bedenkt . . . ,** looking at it from the right angle . . . ; looking back at it . . . ; on second thoughts . . . , when you come to think of it . . . ; **wenn ich bedenke, was alles hätte passieren können!** when I think of what might have happened! **bedenke es wohl!** think it over carefully! **ich muß (mir) dies eine Weile b.,** I shall have to think it over for a while; **eine Sache, die man nicht bedacht hat,** a fact that has been left out of consideration; **du mußt immer b., daß . . . ,** bear in mind that . . . , don't forget that . . . ; **Sie hätten das vorher b. müssen,** you should have thought of that before; **die Folgen b.,** to consider the consequences; **j-m etwas zu b. geben, j-m zu b. geben, daß . . . ,** to draw s.o.'s attention to sth., to the fact that . . . ; to put sth. before s.o.; to urge s.o. to consider that . . . ; *B:* **was du tust, so bedenke das Ende,** whatever thou takest in hand, remember the end; (*b*) **sich b.,** to think (about it, etc.), to reflect (on it, etc.), to consider (it, etc.); to turn (sth.) over in one's mind; **sich eines anderen, Besseren, b.,** to change one's mind, to think better of it. **2. j-n b.,** to give s.o. presents, to remember s.o.; **reich (mit Geschenken) bedacht werden,** to receive many presents; to have gifts showered upon one; **j-n im Testament b.,** to remember s.o. in one's will, to leave s.o. something in one's will; **j-n mit etwas b.,** to confer, bestow, sth. (up)on s.o.; to provide s.o. with sth.; **die Natur hatte sie mit Reizen überreich bedacht,** Nature had endowed her richly with charms. *See also* **bedacht**[2].

II. *vbl s.* **Bedenken,** *n.* **1.** *in vbl senses; also:* reflection, thought; **er willigte ohne B. ein,** he did not think twice before he accepted; **j-n ohne B. empfehlen,** to recommend s.o. unhesitatingly; **da gibt es kein B.,** that does not need thinking about. **2.** *usu. pl.* **Bedenken,** (*a*) doubts; misgivings; **ich habe (so) meine B.,** I have my doubts; I have certain misgivings; **ich habe große B., ob er es je tun wird,** I am very much in doubt, I doubt very much, whether he will ever do it; (*b*) scruples; **moralische B.,** scruples of conscience; conscientious objections; **B. haben,** to have scruples, qualms (of conscience); **keine B. haben, tragen, etwas zu tun,** to have no scruples about doing sth., *F:* to make no bones about doing sth.; **Sie können meine Hilfe ohne B. annehmen,** you need have no scruples about accepting my help.

bedenkenlos. 1. *pred. a.* (*of pers.*) unscrupulous. **2.** *adv.* (*a*) without thinking, thought, without reflection; **er willigte b. ein,** he accepted without hesitation, without another thought; (*b*) without scruple; **er nimmt alles b. an, was sich ihm bietet,** he does not scruple to accept everything that comes his way.

Bedenkfrist, *f.*=**Bedenkzeit.**

bedenklich, *a.* **1.** *pred.* (*of pers.*) thoughtful, pensive; **dies stimmte ihn sehr b.,** this put him in a very thoughtful mood; this made him think. **2.** (*a*) (*of situation, position, etc.*) dangerous; critical, serious; delicate, precarious; risky; **seine Krankheit nahm einen bedenklichen Verlauf,** his illness took a dangerous course; **die Verhandlungen nahmen eine bedenkliche Wendung,** the negotiations took a serious turn; *adv.* **es sieht mir b. nach Masern aus,** it looks to me suspiciously like measles; **ein bedenklicher Zustand,** a critical situation, state; *F:* **sein Geisteszustand scheint mir etwas b.,** he seems to me a little unbalanced; **j-n in eine bedenkliche Lage bringen,** to put s.o. in a delicate, precarious, position; **sein neues Unternehmen scheint uns sehr b.,** his new enterprise strikes us as rather risky; (*b*) (*of action, character, etc.*) doubtful, dubious, questionable; **bedenkliche Handlungsweise,** questionable conduct, conduct open to question; (*of action, etc.*) **ein bedenkliches Licht auf j-n, j-s Charakter, werfen,** to reflect badly (up)on s.o., s.o.'s character.

Bedenklichkeit, *f.* **1.** (*a*) critical nature, seriousness (of illness, situation, etc.); precariousness (of state, situation, etc.); (*b*) doubtfulness, dubiousness, questionableness (of character, action, etc.). **2.** scruple; indecision, irresolution.

Bedenkzeit, *f.* time to think (sth.) over, time to consider; **ich gebe Ihnen achtundvierzig Stunden B.,** I will give you forty-eight hours to think it over.

bedeppert, *a. F:* abashed, crestfallen; downcast; sheepish; mazed, in a maze.

bedeuten. I. *v.tr.* **1.** (*a*) (*of word, phrase, etc.*) to mean, signify; **was bedeutet dieses Wort?** what does this word mean, signify? what is the meaning of this word? **was bedeutet . . . ?** what is meant by . . . ? what is . . . ? (*b*) to symbolize, stand for, mean, denote; **was bedeutet diese Zeremonie?** what is the import, significance, of this ceremony? what does this ceremony mean? **der Pfau bedeutet Unsterblichkeit,** the peacock is a symbol of, stands for, denotes, immortality; **Ph.D. bedeutet Doktor der Philosophie,** Ph.D. stands for Doctor of Philosophy; **vierblättrige Kleeblätter bedeuten Glück,** four-leafed clovers mean luck; (*c*) to portend, presage, bode; **sie glauben, daß Sonnen- und Mondfinsternisse Unglück bedeuten,** they believe that eclipses portend evil; **das bedeutet nichts Gutes,** that bodes no good; **mit einem Lächeln, das nichts Gutes bedeutete . . . ,** with an ominous smile . . . . **2.** (*a*) to mean, matter; to be of importance, consequence; **seine Weigerung bedeutet meinen Ruin,** his refusal means my ruin; **ich kann dir nicht sagen, was er für mich, mir, bedeutet hat,** I cannot tell you what he has meant to me; **wenn Sie wüßten, was es bedeutet, allein zu leben!** if you knew what it means to live alone! **es hat nichts zu b.,** it's of no consequence, it means nothing, it does not matter; **es bedeutet viel für mich,** it matters a great deal to me; **was kann ein Unterschied von zwei Tagen schon b.!** what can two days more or less matter! what difference can two days more or less make! **das eigene Glück bedeutet nicht alles,** personal happiness is not everything; **er bedeutet hier viel,** he is of some importance here; (*b*) (*denoting indignation*) **was soll das, dieses Benehmen, b.?** what is the meaning of this? what do you mean by such behaviour? **3.** (*a*) *A:* **j-n b., daß . . . , etwas zu tun,** to instruct s.o. that . . . , to do sth.; to advise s.o. that . . . , to do sth.; (*b*) *A:* **j-m etwas b.,** to notify s.o. of sth.; **j-m seine Absichten b.,** to notify s.o. of one's intentions; (*c*) *v.i.* (*haben*) **j-m b., etwas zu tun,** to intimate to s.o., to give s.o. to understand, that he must do sth.; **j-m durch Zeichen b.,** to make a sign, signs, to s.o.; **ich bedeutete ihm, daß er seine Schulden bezahlen müsse,** I intimated to him that he must meet his debts; **man bedeutete ihm, es wurde ihm bedeutet, sofort zu gehen,** he was notified that he must depart at once; **ich bedeutete ihm, daß es vorteilhaft sein würde, zu . . . ,** I put it, represented, to him that it would be advantageous to . . . .

II. *vbl s.* **Bedeutung,** *f.* **1.** meaning, signification, sense (of word, phrase); meaning (of symbol, notion, etc.); import, significance (of ceremony, omen); meaning, significance (of gesture, etc.); **allgemein anerkannte B. (eines Wortes),** (general) acceptation (of a word); **in des Wortes wahrster, tiefster, (ur)eigenster, B.,** in the full meaning, sense, acceptation, of the word; **wörtliche B.,** literal sense, meaning; **übertragene B.,** figurative meaning; **in der allgemeinen B. des Wortes,** in the ordinary sense, meaning, of the word; **Wörter von gleicher B.,** words of the same meaning; synonymous words; **Wörter von ähnlicher B.,** words of similar meaning; near-synonyms; **einem Wort eine falsche B. unterlegen,** to take a word in the wrong way, sense, meaning; to put a wrong interpretation on a word; **die B. des Pfaus als Symbol, die symbolische B. des Pfaus,** the symbolic(al) meaning of the peacock; **ein Vorzeichen von schlimmer B.,** a bad omen; **ein Blick voll tiefer B.,** a look of deep significance. **2.** importance, consequence; prominence; **ein Mann von B.,** a man of importance, consequence, an important, prominent, man; **eine Einzelheit ohne B.,** an unimportant detail, a detail without, of no, importance, consequence; **es ist von geringer B.,** it is of slight, of no great, importance, consequence, it is unimportant; **einer Sache B. beimessen, beilegen,** to attach importance to sth.; **einer Sache B. geben,** to give point to sth.; to give prominence to sth.; **an B. gewinnen,** (*of idea, etc.*) to gain in significance, to become more significant; (*of pers., idea*) to increase in importance; (*of thg, idea, pers.*) **B. erlangen, gewinnen,** to come into prominence; to become important; (*of argument, etc.*) **von ausschlaggebender B. sein,** to be decisive, to tip the balance; to be of prime importance.

III. *pr.p. & a.* **bedeutend,** *in vbl senses; esp.* **1.** (*a*) significant, meaning (look, gesture, event, etc.); (*b*) important, prominent (pers., idea, position, etc.); outstanding (pers.); eminent, distinguished, great (artist, etc.); remarkable (feat, etc.); considerable (sum, etc.); **eine ganz bedeutende Persönlichkeit,** an outstanding personality; **er sieht b. aus,** he looks an important person; (*of activity, science, etc.*) **eine bedeutende Stelle einnehmen,** to take a prominent place; **einer Sache einen bedeutenden Platz, eine bedeutende Stelle, einräumen,** to give sth. a prominent place; *see also* **Kopf. 2.** *adv.* (*a*) *A:* significantly, meaningly; **er sah ihn b. an,** he gave him a meaning look, he glanced meaningly at him; (*b*) (+*comp.*) considerably, much; **b. kleiner, größer, mehr, weniger,** considerably, much, smaller, bigger, more, less; **b. wichtiger,**

much more important; **es ist b. besser, zu . . .**, it is much better to . . . ; **es geht ihm b. besser heute,** he is considerably, much, better today.

Bedeuten(d)heit, *f.* importance, consequence; prominence.

bedeutsam, *a.* (*a*) significant (word, gesture, smile); meaning (glance); (word, look) full of meaning, of significance; **diese Begriffe sind in bedeutsamer Weise miteinander verknüpft,** these concepts are linked together in a significant way; **bedeutsame Worte,** words pregnant with, full of, meaning; **ein überaus bedeutsames Ereignis,** an event of great significance; *adv.* **er lächelte b.,** he smiled significantly; **j-n b. ansehen,** to glance meaningly at s.o.; (*b*) *occ:* important; prominent.

Bedeutsamkeit, *f.* significance.

Bedeutung, *f.* see **bedeuten** II.

Bedeutungsentwicklung, *f. Ling:* semantic, semasiological, development.

Bedeutungsfeld, *n. Ling:* semantic, semasiological, group.

Bedeutungsgehalt, *m. Ling:* lexical content (of word).

bedeutungsleer, *a.* (*of word, concept, etc.*) void of meaning, empty; shallow.

Bedeutungslehnwort, *n. Ling:* translation loan-word, calque.

Bedeutungslehre, *f. Ling:* semantics, semasiology.

bedeutungslos, *a.* (*a*) meaningless (word, etc.); insignificant (word, gesture); (*b*) (*of pers., action, position, etc.*) unimportant, of no importance, consequence.

Bedeutungslosigkeit, *f.* insignificance.

bedeutungsreich, *a.*=**bedeutungsvoll.**

bedeutungsschwanger, bedeutungsschwer, *a.* (word) full of, pregnant with, meaning; (event, act) fraught with significance; (moment) heavy with significance; **bedeutungsschwere Entscheidung,** momentous decision; **das Bedeutungsschwere an dieser Sache ist, daß . . .,** the really significant fact about this matter is that . . .

Bedeutungsschwere, *f.* pregnancy (of word, event, etc.); significance (of situation, action, etc.).

Bedeutungsumfang, *m. Ling:* range of meaning (of word).

bedeutungsvoll, *a.* meaning (look, word, etc.); significant (word, gesture, look, event, etc.); (word, look, etc.) full of meaning, significance; **ein bedeutungsvoller Blick,** a look of deep significance; a significant, meaningful, look; **er erwähnte diese Einzelheit mit bedeutungsvollem Unterton,** he mentioned this detail in a meaning way; *adv.* **er nickte b.,** he nodded meaningly.

Bedeutungswandel, Bedeutungswechsel, *m. Ling:* semantic, semasiological, change; change of meaning.

bedielen, *v.tr.* to floor, to lay a floor in (room, etc.).

bedienen. I. *v.tr.* **1. j-n b.,** (*a*) to wait on s.o.; to attend on, upon, s.o.; *A:* to be a servant to s.o., to serve s.o.; **er läßt sich gern b.,** he likes being waited on; *F:* **sich von vorne und hinten b. lassen,** to be waited on hand and foot; (*b*) *Breed:* (*of stallion*) to serve (mare); *P:* (*of man*) to sleep with (woman); (*c*) to serve, attend (to) (customer, etc.), to wait on (s.o. at table); **werden Sie (schon) bedient?** are you being served? are you being attended to? **wir wurden von drei Kellnern bedient,** we were served, attended, by three waiters; **in diesem Restaurant, Geschäft, wird man sehr gut bedient,** you get very good service in this restaurant, shop; *Swiss:* (*at table*) **sind Sie bedient?** have you finished? *see also* **reell. 2. etwas b.,** to operate, work (machine, etc.); *Artil:* to serve (gun); **die Feuerung b.,** to stoke the (boiler-)fire; **den Lift b.,** to operate the lift; **das Telephon b.,** to look after the switchboard; to take (telephone) calls. II. **sich bedienen. 1. sich etwas** *gen.* **b.,** to use sth.; to employ (force, method, etc.); to avail oneself of (opportunity, etc.); **sich einer List b.,** to use a stratagem; **er bediente sich aller Mittel, die ihm zu Gebote standen,** he used every means he could command; **sich j-s b.,** to make use of s.o. **2.** (*at table*) **bitte, bedienen Sie sich!** please serve, help, yourself! III. **bedienen,** *v.i.* (*haben*) **1.** to serve (in a shop); to wait, to serve (at table). **2.** *Cards:* to follow suit. IV. *vbl s.* **1. Bedienen,** *n. in vbl senses of* I, III. **2. Bedienung,** *f.* (*a*) *in vbl senses of* I, III. 1; *also:* operation (of machine, etc.); (*b*) attendance, service (in shop, hotel, etc.); *Com:* attention; **in diesem Restaurant, Geschäft, ist die B. ausgezeichnet,** the service in this restaurant, shop, is excellent; **zehn Prozent (für)**

B., ten per cent for service; (*c*) (domestic) staff (of hotel, restaurant); servant(s); shop assistant(s); *Artil:* (gun) crew. V. *p.p.* **bedient,** *in vbl senses; esp.* **1. gut, schlecht, mit etwas b. sein,** (i) to get good, poor, value in sth.; (ii) to be given sth. that is useful, no use; (iii) to get better, harsher, treatment, etc., than one deserves; **mit diesem Artikel sind Sie sehr gut b.,** this article is very good value; **ich bin b.,** (i) *F:* I have enough (food, work, etc.); (ii) *F:* I've had about enough; (iii) *Swiss:* (*in restaurant*) I've finished. **2.** *A:* **j-m b. sein,** to be in s.o.'s service, to be s.o.'s servant; to serve s.o.

Bedienerin, *f.* -/-**innen.** *Austrian:* domestic servant; charwoman, *U.S:* cleaning woman.

bedienstet, *a. Lit:* (*a*) **bei j-m b. sein,** to be in s.o.'s service, to be s.o.'s servant; (*b*) **Bedienstete** *m, f,* servant; *A:* civil servant; *coll.* **die Bediensteten,** the servants, the domestic staff.

bedient, *p.p. see* **bedienen** V.

Bediente, *m.* (*decl. as adj.*) *Lit:* man-servant, valet.

Bedienten-, *comb.fm. cp.* **Diener-, Gesinde-.**

Bedientenart, *f.* servile manner.

bedientenhaft, *a.* servile, cringing.

Bedientenhaftigkeit, *f.* servility.

Bedientenkleidung, *f.* livery.

Bedientenpack, *n. Pej:* lot, bunch, of menials.

Bedientenseele, *f.* servile, cringing, nature.

Bedienung, *f. see* **bedienen** IV.

Bedienungsanweisung, *f.* operating instructions.

Bedienungsbühne, *f. Ind: etc:* operating platform; starting platform.

Bedienungsfeld, *n. El.E:* control panel.

Bedienungsgeld, *n.* (charge for) service (*at hotel, etc.*).

Bedienungshebel, *m. Mec.E:* operating-lever; starting-lever; control lever.

Bedienungsmann, *m. Ind:* operator (of machine, etc.).

Bedienungsmannschaft, *f. Ind: etc:* personnel (operating machines, etc.); *Artil:* gun crew.

Bedienungsstand *m. Ind: Rail: etc:* control station (of machine); control cabin (of engine).

Bedienungstritt, *m. Mus:* treadle (on harmonium).

Bedienungsvorschriften, *f.pl. Ind: etc:* working instructions, operating instructions.

Beding, *m. & n.* -(e)s/-e=**Bedingung,** *q.v. under* **bedingen** II.

bedingen. I. *v.tr.* **1.** (*weak*) **etwas b.,** (*a*) to condition sth.; to determine sth.; to depend on sth.; **das Leben des Menschen ist durch Naturgesetze bedingt,** man's life is conditioned by natural laws; **das ganze menschliche Leben ist durch Zufälle bedingt,** the whole of human life depends on chance; **Faktoren, die einander, sich gegenseitig, bedingen,** factors that depend on each other, that condition each other; **die Kraft ist bedingt durch die Länge des Hebels,** the force is relative to, depends on, the length of the lever; **niedrige Preise sind durch Überfluß bedingt,** cheapness is conditional upon, is caused by, abundance; **der Preis ist durch das Angebot bedingt,** the price is determined by the supply; *Gram:* **bedingend,** conditional; (*b*) *A. & Lit:* to qualify sth.; to limit, to restrict, sth.; *cp.* III. **2.** (*a*) (*p.t.* **bedang,** *p.p.* **bedungen**)=**ausbedingen 2;** *cp.* II. 2; (*b*) (*conj. like* **dingen**)=**dingen.** II. *vbl s.* **Bedingung,** *f.* condition. **1.** (*a*) (pre)requisite; *Phil:* condition; **negative, positive, B.,** negative, positive, condition; **notwendige B.,** essential condition; **gesunder Schlaf ist die erste B. für gute Gesundheit,** sound sleep is the prerequisite, is a prime condition, of good health, is essential to good health; (*b*) qualification, reservation, restriction; **mit dieser B.,** with this reservation; **(gewisse) Bedingungen an etwas knüpfen,** to make reservations with respect to sth., to place, set, certain restrictions on sth.; to qualify sth.; **ich knüpfe nur eine B. an meine Zustimmung, mache meine Zustimmung von einer B. abhängig,** I agree with only one reservation, subject to one qualification, condition; **ich nehme unter jeder B. an,** I accept without qualification, reservation, I accept under any condition; **keiner B. unterworfen=bedingungslos;** (*c*) *Jur:* condition; **ausdrückliche, stillschweigend verstandene, B.,** express, implied, condition; *see also* **auflösen** I. 4 (*a*), **aufschieben** I. 2; (*d*) stipulation, proviso; **eine B. stellen,** to make a condition, stipulation, proviso, to stipulate sth.; **mit, unter, der B., daß . . .,** with the proviso that . . ., on the stipulation that . . ., on condition that . . .; **mit dieser B.,** subject to this proviso; **die einzige B., die ich**

stelle, ist, daß du um zehn Uhr zu Hause bist, the only stipulation, condition, I make is that you shall be in by ten o'clock; **Kurzschrift erwünscht, aber nicht B.,** shorthand desirable, an advantage, but not essential; (*e*) understanding; **unter, mit, der ausdrücklichen B., daß . . .,** on the distinct understanding that . . . ; with, on, the express condition that . . . ; (*f*) *Gram:* **Nebensatz der B.,** conditional clause; (*g*) circumstance; **unter guten, schwierigen, Bedingungen arbeiten,** to work under good, difficult, conditions; **etwas unter günstigen Bedingungen tun,** to do sth. under favourable conditions; **unter keiner B.,** in no circumstances, on no account, not on any account, in no case. **2.** *Com: etc: usu. pl.* **Bedingungen,** conditions, terms; **zufriedenstellende Bedingungen,** satisfactory terms; **unter ähnlichen Bedingungen,** on similar terms; **ich werde es Ihnen zu günstigen Bedingungen überlassen,** I will let you have it on easy terms; **was für Bedingungen können Sie uns bieten?** what terms can you offer us? **unter diesen Bedingungen kann ich annehmen,** I can accept on these terms; **auf diese Bedingungen wird er kaum eingehen,** he will hardly accept these terms; **Bedingungen eines Waffenstillstands,** terms of an armistice; **j-m (harte) Bedingungen auferlegen,** to impose (severe) conditions on s.o.

III. *p.p. & a.* **bedingt,** *in vbl senses; esp.* (*a*) conditional; qualified, limited, restricted, subject to qualification, restriction; relative; *Gram:* conditional (mood), conditioned (proposition, etc.); *Phil:* conditioned (existence, etc.); **bedingte Zustimmung,** qualified approval; **mein Versprechen war (nur) bedingt,** my promise was conditional; **bedingte Richtigkeit einer Behauptung,** relative truth, correctness, of a statement; **bedingtes Lob,** restricted, qualified, praise; **ein sehr bedingtes Übereinkommen,** an agreement subject to numerous qualifications, restrictions; *Ling:* **bedingter Lautwandel,** conditioned *or* heteronomous phonetic change; *Com:* **bedingte Annahme,** qualified acceptance; *Log:* **bedingte Behauptung,** modal proposition; *Jur:* **bedingte Strafaussetzung,** probation under suspended sentence; *see also* **Anwartschaft** 2, **Erbanspruch;** (*b*) *adv.* conditionally; relatively; **das trifft nur b. zu, ist nur b. richtig, wahr,** that is only relatively true, correct.

Bedingnis, *f.* -/-**nisse,** & *n.* -**nisses**/-**nisse.** *A:*=**Bedingung,** *q.v. under* **bedingen** II.

Bedingnisheft, *n. Constr: Ind: etc:* (i) specifications; (ii) articles and conditions (of sale, contract, etc.).

Bedingtgut, *n. Publ:* books on sale or return.

Bedingtheit, *f.* relative nature, character; relativeness, relativity, conditionality; *Phil:* mode.

Bedingtverkehr, *m. Publ:* distribution of books to retailers on sale or return.

Bedingung, *f. see* **bedingen** II.

bedingungsfeindlich, *a. Jur:* **bedingungsfeindliche Rechtsgeschäfte,** legal transactions to which no condition may be annexed.

Bedingungsform, *f. Gram:* conditional (mood).

Bedingungsgleichung, *f. Math:* equation of conditions.

bedingungslos, *a.* (*of approval, etc.*) unconditional, unreserved, without qualification, reservation; unquestioning (loyalty, etc); **bedingungsloses Festhalten an einer Entscheidung, einem Entschluß,** unreserved adherence to a decision; **bedingungslose Kapitulation,** unconditional surrender; *adv.* **etwas b. annehmen,** to accept sth. without reservation, qualification, unconditionally; **j-m b. vertrauen,** to trust s.o. unreservedly; **b. kapitulieren,** to surrender unconditionally.

Bedingungslosigkeit, *f.* unreserved, unconditional, nature; unquestioning nature (of loyalty, etc.).

Bedingungssatz, *m. Gram:* conditional clause.

bedingungsweise, *adv.* on certain conditions, conditionally.

bedrängen. I. *v.tr.* to press (s.o.) hard, closely, to beset (s.o.); to plague, harry, pester, badger (s.o.); **die Feinde bedrängten sie von allen Seiten,** they were hard, close, pressed on all sides by the enemy; they were constantly harried by the enemy; **aufs äußerste bedrängt, mußten sie sich ergeben,** pressed, harried, to the utmost they had to surrender; **von Hunger bedrängt,** beset by hunger; **seine Gläubiger bedrängen ihn,** his creditors are pressing him hard, are dunning him; **j-n mit Fragen b.,** to plague, pester, s.o. with questions; **ich kann ihn nicht in dieser bedrängten Lage lassen,** I cannot leave him in such a state of distress; **in bedrängten Verhältnissen leben,** (i) to live in cramped conditions;

(ii) to be in embarrassed, straitened, circumstances, in financial, pecuniary, difficulties; to be hard up.

II. *vbl s.* **Bedrängung,** *f.* **1.** *in vbl senses.* **2.** = **Bedrängnis.**

Bedrängnis, *f.* **-/-nisse,** affliction, tribulation, sorrow, anguish, distress; **finanzielle B.,** financial straits, embarrassments, difficulties; **in ärgster B.,** in dire straits; **in der B. meines Herzens,** in my (heart's) anguish, sorrow; **in meiner B. betete ich zu Gott,** in my distress I prayed to God; **in großer B. sein,** to be in straitened, embarrassed, circumstances, in great difficulties; *Lit:* to be in great extremity.

Bedrängtheit, *f.* = **Bedrängnis.**

bedräuen, *v.tr. A. & Lit:* = **bedrohen.**

bedrecken, *v.tr.* to (be)foul, to make filthy, dirty; **bedreckt,** filthy, dirty, mucky.

bedripst, *a. F:* = **bedeppert.**

bedrohen. I. *v.tr.* to threaten, menace (s.o.); **j-n mit etwas b.,** to threaten s.o. with sth.; **j-n mit dem Tode b.,** to threaten s.o. with death; **vom Tode bedroht,** threatened by death; **eine große Gefahr bedroht euch,** a great danger threatens you.

II. *vbl s.* **1. Bedrohen,** *n. in vbl senses.* **2. Bedrohung,** *f.* (*a*) = II. 1; *also: Jur:* intimidation; (*b*) threat, menace (**etwas** *gen.*, to sth.); **eine B. unserer Zivilisation,** a threat to our civilization.

bedrohlich, *a.* threatening, menacing; dangerous; **bedrohliches Schweigen,** ominous silence; **das Wetter sieht b. aus,** the weather looks threatening; **das Kind war in bedrohlicher Nähe des Feuers,** *adv.* **war dem Feuer b. nahe,** the child was dangerously near to the fire.

bedröppelt, *a. F:* = **bedeppert.**

bedrucken[1], *v.tr.* **etwas (mit etwas) b.,** to (im)print sth. (with sth.); **Stoff mit Mustern b.,** to print patterns on material; **bedrucktes Papier,** printed(-on) paper; **einseitig bedrucktes Papier,** paper printed on one side.

bedrücken (*A. & South G.Dial:* **bedrucken**[2]). I. *v.tr.* **j-n b.,** (*a*) (*of pers.*) to oppress, to press, s.o.; **die Armen b.,** to grind (down) the poor, to grind the faces of the poor; **das Volk war von Steuern (hart) bedrückt,** the people were (over)burdened with taxes, crushed by taxation; (*b*) (*of event, weather, etc.*) to depress, deject, s.o.; **bedrückende Landschaft,** depressing landscape; **bedrückende Hitze,** (i) depressing, (ii) oppressive, heat.

II. *vbl s.* **1. Bedrücken,** *n. in vbl senses.* **2. Bedrückung,** *f.* (*a*) *in vbl senses; also:* oppression; (*b*) = **Bedrücktheit.**

III. *p.p. & a.* **bedrückt,** (*a*) oppressed, downtrodden (nation, etc.); (*b*) depressed, dejected; **in bedrückter Stimmung sein,** to feel depressed; *adv.* **er ging b. davon,** he went away depressed, in dejection.

Bedrücker, *m.* **-s/-,** oppressor.

Bedrücktheit, *f.* (*a*) depression, dejection; (*b*) *occ:* oppression.

Beduine [bedu'iːnə], *m.* **-n/-n.** Bedouin.

beduinisch [bedu'iːniʃ], *a.* Bedouin.

bedungen, *p.p. see* **bedingen** I. 2.

bedünken. I. *v.tr. usu. v.impers.* (*conj. like* **dünken**) *A. & Lit:* **j-n,** *occ.* **j-m, b.,** to appear, seem, to s.o.; **es bedünkt mich, es will mich b.,** it appears, seems, to me, *Lit. & A:* methinks.

II. *vbl s.* **Bedünken,** *n. Lit:* opinion, view; **meines Bedünkens, nach meinem B.,** in my opinion, view.

bedürfen, *v.i.* (*haben*), *occ. v.tr.* (*conj. like* **dürfen**) **etwas** *gen.*, *occ. acc.*, **b.,** to need, require, want, sth., to be, stand, in need, want, of sth.; **j-s,** *occ.* **j-n, b.,** to need, want, s.o., to be, stand, in need of s.o.; *A: abs.* **b.** = **bedürftig sein,** *q.v. under* **bedürftig; ich bedarf dringend seiner Hilfe,** I am, stand, in great need of, I badly want, his assistance, help; **des Trostes b.,** to need consolation; **der Ruhe b.,** to want, need, rest; **diese Tatsachen bedürfen keiner Erklärung,** these facts need no comment, no explanation; **das bedarf keiner weiteren Worte,** that goes without saying; no more needs to be said about it; **ich bedarf deiner,** I need you; *impers.* **es bedurfte keiner besonderen Erinnerung für mich,** I did not need to be reminded of it, I required no reminding; **es bedurfte der Schrecken des Krieges, (um) euch die Augen zu öffnen,** it needed the horrors of war to open your eyes; *B:* **die Gesunden bedürfen des Arztes nicht,** they that are whole need not a physician.

Bedürfnis, *n.* **-nisses/-nisse. 1.** need, want, requirement; (*a*) **B. für etwas haben,** to have need, to stand, be, in need, of sth.; **es ist kein B. dafür vorhanden,** it is not needed, wanted, required; there is no need of it; **dieses Buch hilft einem lange, seit langem, fühlbaren B. ab,** this volume meets a long-felt want; (*b*) *pl.* **meine Bedürfnisse sind gering,** my needs, wants, are few; **j-s Bedürfnisse befriedigen,** (*of pers.*) to attend, minister, to s.o.'s needs, wants; to provide for s.o.'s wants, to supply s.o.'s needs; (*of thg, pers.*) to meet s.o.'s requirements. **2.** *A: n. & f.* **-/-nisse,** (*a*) need want; poverty; (*b*) necessity; (*c*) *pl.* **Bedürfnisse,** necessities, necessaries. **3.** (*a*) wish, desire; **dringendes B.,** urge, strong desire; **ein B. nach etwas** *dat.* **ausdrücken,** to express a wish, desire, for sth.; **(ein) B. nach Glück, Frieden, haben,** to wish for happiness, peace, to long for, to have a desire for, happiness, peace; **das dringende B. haben, etwas zu tun,** to have, feel, the urge, a strong desire, to do sth.; **ich habe kein großes B., ihn wiederzusehen,** I have no great wish, I feel, have, no great desire to see him again; **aus dem B. heraus, zu . . . ,** out of a desire to . . . ; **es ist mir ein tiefgefühltes B., Ihnen allen zu danken,** it is my heartfelt wish to thank you all; (*b*) **sein B. verrichten,** to relieve oneself.

Bedürfnisanstalt, *f.* **öffentliche B.,** public convenience, *U.S:* comfort station.

Bedürfnisfrage, *f. Adm:* = **Bedarfsfrage.**

bedürfnislos, *a.* (pers.) having few wants, needs, (pers.) who wants, needs, little; **ein bedürfnisloser Mensch,** a person of few wants, needs; an undemanding person; **b. sein,** to have few wants, needs, to be modest in one's requirements.

Bedürfnislosigkeit, *f.* absence of wants, needs; **seine B. ist bemerkenswert,** he has remarkably few wants, needs, he is very modest in his requirements.

bedürftig, *a.* **1.** *pred.* **etwas** *gen.* **b. sein,** to be, stand, in need of sth., to be in want of sth., to need, want, sth.; **der Ruhe b. sein,** to want, need, rest. **2.** *attrib. & pred.* needy, poor, indigent; **b. sein,** to be in need, want, to be poor; **die Bedürftigen,** the needy, the poor, those in need, in want.

Bedürftigkeit, *f.* neediness, indigence; need, want; **in B. leben,** to be living, to live, in want; **seine Familie lebt in größter B.,** his family is in dire want, distress, straits; **sie leben in großer B.,** they live in straitened circumstances, *F:* they can hardly keep body and soul together.

Bedürftigkeitsprüfung, *f. Adm:* means test.

beduseln (sich), *v.refl. F:* to get slightly drunk, tipsy, to get (be)fuddled; **beduselt,** (i) drowsy; (ii) tipsy, (be)fuddled.

Beefsteak ['biːfsteːk], *n.* **-s/-s.** *Cu:* steak; **deutsches B.,** Vienna steak; hamburger.

beehren, *v.tr.* (*a*) **j-n b.,** to honour, favour, s.o., to do honour to s.o.; **j-n mit seiner Anwesenheit, mit seinem Besuch, b.,** to honour, favour, s.o. with one's presence, visit; (*b*) **sich b., etwas zu tun,** to have the honour to do sth.; **ich beehre mich, Ihnen mitzuteilen, daß . . . ,** I have the honour to inform you that . . . , *Com:* I beg to inform you that . . . ; **wir beehren uns, unsere Verlobung bekanntzugeben,** we have the honour to announce our engagement; = (*in England*) the engagement is announced between . . . ; **wir beehren uns, Sie zum Abendessen einzuladen,** we request the favour of your company to dinner.

beeiden, beeidigen, *v.tr.* **1. etwas b.,** to declare sth. on oath; to take one's oath on, to, sth.; **b., etwas getan zu haben,** to swear to having done sth.; **können Sie b., daß Sie während der fraglichen Zeit zu Hause waren?** could you swear to it that you were at home at the time in question? **2. j-n b.,** to swear s.o. in, to administer, tender, the oath to s.o. **3.** *Adm: etc:* **beeidigt** = **vereidigt,** *q.v. under* **vereidigen.**

beeilen, *v.tr.* **1. etwas b.,** to hasten sth., to speed sth. up, to hurry sth. on; **seine Schritte b.,** to quicken one's pace. **2. sich beeilen,** to hasten, make haste, to hurry up; to be quick; **beeil(e) dich!** hurry up! look sharp! *F:* buck up! **bitte beeilen (Sie sich)!** hurry along, please! **sich bei einer Arbeit, usw., b.,** to hurry over a task, etc.; **etwas tun, ohne sich zu b.,** not to hurry over sth.; to do sth. leisurely; **sich b., nach Hause zu kommen,** to hurry home; **sich b., etwas zu tun,** to hasten, to make haste, to do sth., to lose no time in doing sth.; **wir beeilen uns, Ihnen zu versichern, daß . . . ,** we hasten to assure you that . . . .

beeindrucken, *v.tr.* to impress (s.o.); **es hat mich tief beeindruckt, ich war tief davon beeindruckt,** it impressed me deeply, I was deeply impressed by it.

beeinflussen. I. *v.tr.* to influence (s.o., sth.), to have an effect (up)on (s.o., sth.); to exercise, have, an influence over, on (s.o., sth.); (*of pers.*) to put pressure upon (s.o.); (*of thg*) to affect (result, event, etc.); **j-n dahin(gehend) b., daß . . . ,** to influence s.o. to . . . ; **von etwas, j-m, durch etwas, j-n, beeinflußt werden,** to be under the influence of s.o., sth., to be influenced by s.o., sth.; (*of thg*) to be affected by sth.; **j-n, etwas, günstig, stark, b.,** to have a good, great, effect on s.o., sth.; **j-s Geist b., j-n geistig b.,** to have, produce, an effect on s.o.'s mind; **die Zeitungen, die die öffentliche Meinung beeinflussen,** the papers that sway public opinion; *Jur:* **Zeugen b.,** to suborn, tamper with, interfere with, *F:* get at, witnesses; **j-n widerrechtlich b.,** to exert an undue influence on s.o.

II. *vbl s.* **1. Beeinflussen,** *n. in vbl senses.* **2. Beeinflussung,** *f.* (*a*) *in vbl senses; also:* **wechselseitige, gegenseitige, B.,** mutual influence; (*b*) **B. j-s durch j-n,** influence exercised by s.o. on s.o.; **ihre B. durch die Schule,** the influence of school upon her; **die B. eines Künstlers durch sein Publikum,** the public's influence on an artist.

beeinträchtigen. I. *v.tr.* to be detrimental, prejudicial, to, to detract from, to prejudice (s.o.'s interests, reputation, rights, etc.); to derogate from (s.o.'s dignity, etc.); to damage, to be injurious, hurtful, to (s.o.'s interests, reputation); to hurt, injure (s.o.'s interests, cause); to impair (s.o.'s health, authority, strength, etc.); **das wird seinen Ruf b.,** it will injure, detract from, his reputation; **Zweifel, die mein Vertrauen beeinträchtigen,** doubts that disturb my faith; **j-s Vergnügen ein wenig, sehr, b.,** to detract sth., much, from s.o.'s pleasure; **ohne meine Rechte, mich in meinen Rechten, zu b.,** without detriment, prejudice, to my rights; **den Wert einer Sache, eine Sache in ihrem Wert, b.,** to detract from the value of a thing.

II. *vbl s.* **Beeinträchtigung,** *f.* prejudice, detriment (**etwas** *gen.*, to sth.); (moral) injury (**etwas** *gen.*, to sth.); damage (**etwas** *gen.*, to sth.); derogation, detraction (**etwas** *gen.*, from sth.); impairment; **ohne B. meiner Rechte,** without detriment, prejudice, to my rights; **ohne B. meiner Würde,** without derogation from, impairing, my dignity; **B. der Gesundheit,** impairment of health; **B. des Wertes einer Sache,** detraction from, impairment of, the value of a thing.

beeisen, *v.tr.* to cover with ice.

Beelzebub [be'ɛl-, 'bɛltsəbuːp]. *Pr.n.m.* **-s. 1.** *B.Lit:* Beelzebub. **2.** *F:* the Devil.

beenden. I. *v.tr.* (*a*) to end (speech, quarrel, etc.); to finish (work, meal, etc.); to close, conclude (speech, etc.); to bring (war, etc.) to an end; **beendet sein, werden,** to be at, come to, an end; **eine Rede mit einem Zitat b.,** to end, conclude, close, a speech with a quotation; **ich hatte die Arbeit bald beendet,** I had soon finished, done, the work; **er beendete seine Laufbahn als General,** he ended his career as a general; (*b*) = **beendigen** I. (*a*).

II. *vbl s.* **Beendung,** *f.* = **Beendigung,** *q.v. under* **beendigen** II.

beendigen. I. *v.tr.* (*a*) to complete (work, etc.); to put an end to, terminate (war, quarrel, career, etc.); **beendigt sein,** (*of work, etc.*) to be completed, finished; (*of war, etc.*) to be at an end; **die Arbeit wird bald beendigt sein,** the work will soon be completed, finished; the work is near(ing) completion; **der Unfall beendigte seine Laufbahn als Tänzer,** the accident put an end to, ended, terminated, his career as a dancer; (*b*) *occ.* = **beenden** I. (*a*).

II. *vbl s.* **Beendigung,** *f. in vbl senses of* (i) **beendigen** I. (*a*), (ii) **beenden** I. (*a*); *also:* completion (of work, etc.); termination (of war, etc.); conclusion (of speech, etc.); **nach B. des Krieges,** after the end of the war; **die Arbeit steht kurz vor der B.,** the work is near(ing) completion.

beengen. 1. *v.tr.* (*of thg*) **j-n b.,** (*a*) to constrict, restrict, confine, s.o.'s movements, etc.; **das Kleid beengt mich,** the dress is too tight, cramps, restricts, my movements; **beengter Raum,** narrow, confined, space; **(im Raum) beengt sein,** to be cramped (for space); **in beengten Verhältnissen leben,** to live in cramped conditions; **beengt stehen, sitzen,** to stand, sit, crowded, *F:* crammed, together; (*b*) to oppress s.o.; **die Luft hier beengt mich,** the air here oppresses, stifles, me; **beengende Atmosphäre,** oppressive atmosphere; **sich auf der Brust beengt fühlen,** to feel a tightness across the chest; **sich beengt fühlen,** to feel (i) tight in the chest, (ii) oppressed, hemmed in, shut in, (iii) embarrassed, uneasy. **2.** *vbl s.* **Beengung,** *f.* = **Beengtheit.**

Beengtheit, *f.* (*a*) constriction, narrowness; cramped condition; (*b*) tightness; **Gefühl der B.,** feeling of oppression.

Beer-, *comb.fm. cp.* **Beeren-.**
beerben, *v.tr.* **j-n b.**, to inherit s.o.'s estate, to become s.o.'s heir.
Beerblume, *f. Bot:* basella, Malabar nightshade.
beerdigen. I. *v.tr.* to bury, inter (corpse).
II. *vbl s.* **1. Beerdigen**, *n. in vbl senses.* **2. Beerdigung**, *f.* (*a*) *in vbl senses; also:* burial, interment; (*b*) funeral; **die B. fand in aller Stille statt**, the funeral was very quiet; (*in announcement*) **'die B. findet in aller Stille statt'**, 'funeral private'.
Beerdigungsanstalt, *f.* = **Beerdigungsinstitut.**
Beerdigungsinstitut, *n.* (firm of) undertakers; undertaking, undertaker's, business, funeral directors, *U.S:* funeral parlor, funeral home.
Beerdigungskosten, *pl.* funeral expenses; funeral fees.
Beere, *f.* -/-n. *Bot:* berry; **B. einer Weintraube**, grape; **eine Weintraube mit großen Beeren**, a bunch of large grapes; (*of shrub*) **Beeren tragen**, to bear berries, to berry; **mit, voll(er), Beeren**, with berries; covered with berries; berried; **Beeren sammeln, pflücken, (gehen), in die Beeren gehen**, to go berrying.
beerenähnlich, *a.* like a berry.
Beerenangelika, *f. Bot:* = **Bergangelika.**
Beerenapfel, *m. Bot:* Siberian crab(-tree), cherry-apple (tree).
beerenartig, *a.* = **beerenähnlich.**
Beerenauslese, *f. Wine-m:* wine made from specially selected overripe single grapes.
Beerenbaum, *m. Bot:* **1.** American gooseberry (-tree). **2.** Ceylon cornel-tree.
Beerenblau, *n. Bio-Ch:* anthocyan(in).
Beerendill, Beerenfenchel, *m. Bot:* spignel.
beerenförmig, *a.* shaped like a berry, *Bot:* bacciform.
beerenfressend, *a. Z:* baccivorous, berry-eating.
Beerenfresser, *m. Z:* baccivorous animal *or* bird.
Beerenfrucht, *f.* berry.
Beerengelb, *n. Dy: etc:* buckthorn yellow, buckthorn brown.
Beerengrün, *n. Dy: etc:* Chinese green; sap-green.
Beerenheide, *f. Bot:* (black-berried) crowberry, heath-berry.
Beer(en)kraut, *n. Bot:* **1.** (common) agrimony. **2.** garden spinach.
Beerenmispel, *f. Bot:* (*a*) June-berry; (*b*) Savoy medlar.
Beerenobst, *n. Hort:* small fruits; *Com:* soft fruit.
Beerentang, *m. Algae:* sargasso, gulf-weed.
beerentragend, *a. Bot:* bacciferous, berry-producing.
Beerenwanze, *f. Ent:* berry-eating shieldbug.
Beerenwein, *m.* home-made wine, *esp.* red-currant *or* elderberry wine.
Beerenwinde, *f. Bot:* bearbind, (hooded) bindweed.
Beerenzapfen, *m. Bot:* berry-cone, *esp.* juniper-berry.
Beerenzwetsche, *f. Bot:* **1.** coco(a)-plum. **2.** coco(a)-plum (tree), icaco.
Beeresche, *f. Bot:* mountain-ash, rowan-tree, fowler's pear-tree.
Beergrün, *n.* **1.** *Bot: F:* periwinkle. **2.** = **Beerengrün.**
beerig, *a. Bot:* (*a*) berry-bearing; **beerige Salzpflanze**, (berry-bearing, prickly) glasswort; **beerige Taubnessel**, hedge nettle; (*b*) *comb.fm.* **-beerig**, -berried; **schwarzbeerig**, black-berried.
Beermelde, *f. Bot:* strawberry blite, strawberry spinach.
Beermutterwurz, *f. Bot:* spignel.
Beerschwamm, *m. Med:* framboesia, yaws, pian.
Beer-Seba [be:r'se:ba:]. *Pr.n.n.* **-s.** *B.Geog:* Beersheba.
Beerwurz, *n. Bot:* **1.** spignel. **2.** sulphurwort, hog's-, sow's-fennel.
Beet, *n.* **-es/-e**, (*a*) *Hort:* (flower-, vegetable-)bed; (vegetable-)patch; (*b*) *Agr:* land (*i.e. space between water-furrows*).
Beetbau, *m. Agr:* ploughing in lands.
Beete, *f.* -/-n. *Bot:* beet; **rote B.**, beetroot.
Beeteinfassung, *f. Hort:* edging, border.
Beetkultur, *f. Agr:* ploughing in lands.
Beetpflug, *m. Agr:* one-way plough.
Beetpflügen, *n. Agr:* ploughing in lands.
befächeln, *v.tr.* to fan (s.o., sth.).
befähigen. I. *v.tr.* (*of thg*) **j-n zu etwas b.**, to fit s.o. for sth.; to qualify s.o. for sth.; **j-n b., etwas zu tun**, to enable s.o. to do sth.; to put s.o. in a position to do sth.; to fit s.o. to do sth.; to qualify s.o. for doing sth., to do sth.; **nichts befähigt den Körper besser, Anstrengungen zu ertragen**, nothing fits the body better to stand effort; **seine Ausbildung befähigt ihn (dazu), verschiedene Berufe zu ergreifen**, his training enables, qualifies, him to take up various careers.
II. *vbl s.* **Befähigung**, *f.* (*a*) ability, fitness; aptitude; capability; competence; (*b*) qualification; **die nötigen Befähigungen für eine Stelle haben**, to have the necessary qualifications for a post.
III. *p.p. & a.* **befähigt**, able, apt, capable; qualified, fit; **einer meiner befähigtsten Schüler**, one of my aptest, ablest, most capable, pupils; **zu etwas b. sein**, to be fit, qualified, for sth.; **b. sein, etwas zu tun**, to be able to do sth., to be capable of doing sth.; to be fit, qualified, to do sth.; **er ist zu dieser Aufgabe wenig b.**, he is little qualified for this task.
Befähigungsnachweis, *m.*, **Befähigungszeugnis**, *n.* certificate of competency; qualifying certificate.
befahl *see* **befehlen.**
befahrbar, *a.* (road) passable, practicable, for vehicles; navigable (river); **die Straße ist nicht b.**, the road is impassable, impracticable, for vehicles.
befahren[1], *v.tr.* (*strong*) **1.** (*a*) **eine Strecke täglich, zum ersten Mal, b.**, (*of pers.*) to drive (over), travel (on), a route every day, for the first time; (*of bus, train, etc.*) to cover a route, (*o train*) to cover a stretch of line every day, for the first time; **ein Land mit dem, im, Auto b.**, to cover a country by car; **eine wenig befahrene Straße**, a little used road; **eine stark, lebhaft, befahrene Straße**, a busy, a much frequented, road; (*b*) *Nau:* **das Meer, die Meere, b.**, (*of pers., ship*) to sail the seas; (*of ship*) to plough the seas; **die Küste b.**, to coast; **einen Fluß b.**, to navigate a river; **befahrener Seemann**, able (-bodied) seaman; **befahrenes Volk**, experienced seamen, *F:* old salts, jack tars; (*c*) *Min:* **Gruben b.**, to inspect mines; *occ.* **die Grube b.**, to descend the pit; **die Grube wird befahren**, the mine is in operation; (*d*) *Ven:* **ein befahrener Bau**, an inhabited earth. **2. eine Straße mit Kies b.**, to gravel a road; **ein Feld mit Mist b.**, to manure a field.
befahren[2], *v.* (*weak*) *A:* **1.** *v.tr.* to fear (sth.); **b., (daß) etwas geschehe**, to fear (i) (that) sth. will happen, (ii) lest sth. should happen. **2. sich etwas** *gen.* **befahren**, (i) to fear sth., to be afraid of sth.; (ii) to beware of sth.
Befall, *m.* **-(e)s/.** attack (by disease, pest, etc.).
befallen, *v.tr.* (*strong*) (*of disease, etc.*) to attack (s.o., animal, plant); (*of fear, etc.*) to assail, seize (s.o.); **Krankheit, die gewöhnlich nur Kinder befällt**, disease that usually attacks only children; **von einer Krankheit befallen werden**, to be attacked by a disease, to catch a disease; **vom Fieber befallen**, stricken with fever; **die Übel, die uns b. könnten**, the evils that might assail us, to which we might be subject; **wenn Furcht uns befällt**, when fear assails us; **Furcht befiel ihn, es befiel ihn Furcht, er war von Furcht befallen**, he was seized, struck, smitten, with fear; **ein schweres Unglück hat uns befallen**, a grave misfortune befell us, came upon us; **eine schwere Müdigkeit befiel ihn**, deep fatigue came over him.
befangen. I. *A:* *v.tr.* (*strong*) **1.** (*a*) to comprise, embrace, encompass, contain (sth.); (*b*) to surround (s.o.); to hold (s.o., sth.); to hem (s.o.) in; to enclose (sth.). **2. sich befangen** = **sich befassen**, *q.v. under* **befassen** II.
II. *p.p. & a.* **befangen. 1.** *pred.* **in etwas b. sein**, (i) *A:* to be involved, engaged, in sth.; (ii) to be imprisoned, enmeshed, entangled, in sth.; **in Irrtum b. sein**, to be caught up in one's delusions; **in Vorurteilen b. sein**, to be bound, blinded, by prejudices; **in Schuld b. sein**, to be engulfed in sin. **2.** *attrib. & pred.* **b. sein**, to be embarrassed, self-conscious, ill at ease; to be shy, bashful, abashed; **befangenes Lächeln**, embarrassed smile; **j-n b. machen**, to embarrass, abash, s.o.; to make s.o. self-conscious, shy. **3.** *attrib. & pred.* prejudiced, biased; prepossessed; partial; **sich für b. erklären**, to state that one is prejudiced, *Jur: etc:* to plead partiality, prejudice.
Befangenheit, *f.* **1.** self-consciousness; shyness, bashfulness. **2.** prejudice, bias; prepossession; *Jur:* partiality; **einen Richter wegen Besorgnis der B. ablehnen**, to challenge a judge on the ground of partiality.
befassen. I. *v.tr.* **1.** *A:* to comprise, encompass (sth.); to comprehend (sth.). **2.** to touch, feel, finger (sth.).
II. **sich befassen**, (*a*) **sich mit etwas b.**, to engage in sth.; to occupy oneself with sth., to be occupied with sth.; to concern oneself with, about, in, sth.; to attend to sth.; to look into (problem, etc.); (*of book, author, etc.*) to deal with (a subject, etc.); **ich bin zu beschäftigt, ich kann mich damit jetzt nicht b.**, I am too busy, I can't be bothered with this now; (*b*) **sich mit j-m b.**, to attend, see, to s.o.; to be occupied with s.o.; **sich mit den Kindern b.**, to see to the children; to be occupied with the children.
befedert, *a.* feathered (front legs of dog).
befehden, *v.tr.* to be at feud, war, with (s.o.); to war against (s.o., sth.); to fight against, to contend, battle, with (enemy, opinion, etc.); to attack (opinion, theory, etc.); **einander, sich, b.**, to be at feud with one another.
Befehl, *m.* **-(e)s/-e. 1.** (word of) command; order, instruction; **schriftlicher B.**, written order, instructions; **auf B. von . . .**, by order of . . . ; under instructions from . . . ; **auf B. handeln**, to act on, under, orders, according to instructions; **etwas auf j-s B. tun**, to do sth. on s.o.'s orders, at, by, s.o.'s command; **bis auf weiteren B.**, until further orders; **Diensthandlung auf B.**, duty covered by orders; **(den) B. erteilen, geben, etwas zu tun, daß etwas getan werde**, to give orders for sth. to be done, that sth. should be done; **ich habe (den) B. gegeben, die Kisten zu packen**, I gave orders for the boxes to be packed; **ich habe den B., hier zu bleiben**, I have orders, I am ordered, to remain here; **einen B. ausführen**, to carry out, execute, an order; **einem B. Folge leisten, gehorchen**, to obey an order, to act according to instructions; **Befehle von j-m entgegennehmen, sich** *dat.* **von j-m Befehle erteilen lassen**, to take orders from s.o.; **Ihr Wunsch ist mir B.**, your wish is my command; **B. ist B.**, orders are orders; *Mil:* **'zu B., Herr Hauptmann!'** 'very good, sir!' 'yes, sir!' 'right, sir!' *Nau:* **'zu B.!'** 'aye, aye, sir!' **2.** *Mil:* (position of) command, authority; **unter dem B. von . . .**, under (the) command of . . . ; **den B. über etwas führen, haben, übernehmen**, to be in, to assume, take, command of sth.
befehlen, *v.tr.* (*strong*) **1.** (*a*) to command, order (sth.); **j-m etwas b., j-m b., etwas zu tun**, to command, order, s.o. to do sth.; **er tat, was, wie, ich ihm befohlen hatte**, he did what, as, I had commanded him (to do); he did as I had directed him; **er befahl ihm strengstes Stillschweigen**, he ordered him to maintain the strictest secrecy; **tu, was, wie, man dir befiehlt!** do as you are told! **sie befahlen, ihn zu erhängen**, they ordered him to be hanged; **ich lasse mir nichts b.**, I won't be dictated to; **(die) Klugheit befiehlt, abzuwarten**, common sense dictates a policy of wait and see; **tu, was, wie, die Pflicht befiehlt**, do as duty directs; **'wie das Gesetz es befahl'**, 'they did their duty (and died)'; **in befehlendem Ton sprechen**, to speak in a commanding, peremptory, in an imperious, tone; *Gram:* **befehlende Redeweise**, imperative mood; (*b*) **j-n zu sich b.**, to order s.o. to appear before one; **der König hatte die Offiziere zur Tafel befohlen**, the king had commanded the officers to dine with him; (*c*) (*form of politeness*) **der Herr befehlen?** your order, sir? **wie Sie befehlen, meine Dame!** as you wish, madam. **2. (j-m) etwas b.**, to entrust s.o. with sth., to put, place, sth. in s.o.'s care; **seine Seele Gott, Gottes Schutz, b.**, to commend one's soul to God; **Gott befohlen!** God be with you! God bless you! *B:* **befiehl dem Herrn deine Wege**, commit thy way unto the Lord; *see also* **Hand 1** (*c*).
befehlerisch, *a.* imperious; peremptory; fond of ordering people about, *F:* bossy.
befehligen, *v.tr. Mil:* to command, be in command of (army, fleet, etc.); to lead (troops, etc.).
Befehls-, *comb.fm. Mil: Navy:* **1.** command . . . ; **Befehlspanzer** *m*, command tank. **2.** . . . of orders; **Befehlsübermittlung** *f*, transmission of orders.
Befehlsausgabe, *f.* issue of orders; *Mil: Mil.Av: etc:* briefing.
Befehlsempfänger, *m.* **1.** recipient of an order. **2.** *Pej:* (i) person lacking initiative, slave to orders, mere agent; (ii) puppet.
Befehlsflagge, *f. Nau:* pennant.
Befehlsform, *f. Gram:* imperative (mood).
befehlsgemäß, *a. & adv.* according to instructions; according to orders; **b. handeln**, to act according to instructions, orders; **Auftrag b. ausgeführt**, order carried out according to instructions.
Befehlshaber, *m.* **-s/-.** *Mil:* commander; *Navy:* commander-in-chief; **oberster B.**, supreme commander.
befehlshaberisch, *a.* imperious, dictatorial, authoritative.
Befehlshaberstelle, *f. Mil:* commandership.
Befehlssatz, *m. Gram:* imperative clause *or* sentence.
Befehlsstab, *m. Rail:* station official's signalling-disc; = guard's flag.

Befehlsstand, *m. Mil:* command post.
Befehlsstelle, *f. Mil:* control post; command post.
Befehlston, *m.* commanding, imperious, peremptory, authoritative, tone (of voice).
Befehlsübermittler, *m. Mil:* **1.** signal transmitter. **2.** (*pers.*) messenger.
Befehlsübermittlungsanlage, *f. Mil:* signal distributor.
Befehlsverweigerung, *f. Mil:* refusal to obey an order.
befehlswidrig, *a. & adv.* contrary to instructions; contrary to orders.
Befehlswimpel, *m. Mil: Nau:* pennant; pennon.
Befehlszentrale, *f.* control room.
befenstern. I. *v.tr.* to put windows in (building); **befenstert,** windowed.
II. *vbl s.* **Befensterung,** *f.* (*a*) *in vbl sense; also: Arch:* fenestration; (*b*) *Arch:* windows, fenestration.
befesten, *v.tr. A:*=**befestigen.**
befestigen. I. *v.tr.* **1.** (*a*) **etwas an etwas** *dat., acc.,* **auf etwas** *dat.,* **b.,** to fasten, fix, sth. to, on, sth., to make sth. fast to sth.; **einen Anhänger an einem Paket b.,** to fasten, tie, a label on a parcel, to label a parcel; **eine Decke mit einem Riemen am Koffer b.,** to fasten a blanket to one's suitcase with a leather strap, to strap a blanket to one's suitcase; **ein Siegel an einer Akte b.,** to append a seal to an act; **einen Pfahl in der Erde b.,** to fix a stake into the ground; **etwas mit Dübeln (an etwas** *dat., acc.*) **b.,** to fasten sth. with dowels (to sth.), to dowel sth.; **ein Boot an einem Pfahl b.,** to fasten, tie up, a boat to a post; *Nau:* **ein Tau an der Klampe b.,** to cleat a rope; (*b*) **etwas (wieder) b.,** to secure, fasten, fix, sth., to make sth. secure; **eine Planke b.,** to secure a plank, to make a plank secure; **einen losen Dachziegel (wieder) b.,** to fix, secure, a loose tile. **2.** (*a*) *Mil:* to fortify (town, etc.); to entrench, retrench (position); **befestigtes Lager,** fortified camp; **befestigte Zone,** fortified area; (*b*) to consolidate (foundations, an empire, an alliance, etc.); to strengthen (power, faith, opinion, etc.); *Com:* to consolidate, stabilize (prices); *Dy:* to **fix** (dye); **die Straßendecke b.,** to consolidate the road surface; **befestigte Straße,** paved road; **die Bande der Freundschaft b.,** to draw the bonds of friendship closer; (*c*) **sich b.,** to grow firm, to strengthen; *Com:* (*of prices*) to firm up, to steady.
II. *vbl s.* **1. Befestigen,** *n. in vbl senses.* **2. Befestigung,** *f.* (*a*)=II. 1; *also:* consolidation (of foundations, an empire, an alliance, etc.); *Mil:* fortification (of town, etc.); entrenchment, retrenchment (of position); (*b*) *Com:* consolidation, stabilization (of prices); (*c*) (*device*) fastening(s); (*d*) *pl.* **Befestigungen**=**Befestigungsanlagen.**
Befestigungs-, *comb.fm.* **1.** *Mec.E:* fixing . . ., fastening . . . ; **Befestigungsklammer, Befestigungsklaue** *f,* fixing lug, fastening lug. **2.** *Mil:* . . . of fortification, fortification . . . ; **Befestigungsturm** *m,* fortification tower; *cp.* **Festungs-.**
Befestigungsanlagen, *f.pl. Mil:* fortifications, defences; **tief gestaffelte B.,** forts in depth.
Befestigungsarbeiten, *f.pl. Mil:* work on fortifications, defences.
Befestigungsbaukunst, *f.*=**Befestigungskunst.**
Befestigungsbauten, *m.pl. Mil:* fortifications, defences.
Befestigungsgürtel, *m. Mil:* ring of fortifications.
Befestigungskunst, *f. Mil:* art of fortification.
Befestigungsmittel, *n. Mec.E: etc:* fastening(s).
Befestigungsschraube, *f. Mec.E:* fixing screw; hold-down screw; set screw.
befeuchten, *v.tr.* to damp, to moisten (sth.).
befeuern. I. *v.tr.* **1.** (*of emotion, wine, etc.*) to stimulate, stir up (s.o., s.o.'s zeal, courage, spirit, etc.), to excite (passion, etc.), to spur (s.o.) on; **von Leidenschaft befeuert,** spurred on by passion. **2.** *Nav:* to mark (coast line, airfield, etc.) with lights; to beacon. **3.** *Mil:* to shoot, to fire, at, on, upon (s.o., sth.).
II. *vbl s.* **1. Befeuern,** *n. in vbl senses.* **2. Befeuerung,** *f.* (*a*)=II. 1; (*b*) *Nav:* lighting, lights (of coast line, airfield, etc.).
Beffchen, *n.pl.* (clergyman's, etc.) bands.
befiedern. I. *v.tr.* **1.** (*a*) to feather (arrow, etc.); (*b*) *Mus: A:* to quill (harpsichord); (*c*) (*of fowl*) **sich b.,** to grow feathers. **2.** *p.p. & a.* **befiedert,** feathered.
II. *vbl s.* **Befiederung,** *f.* **1.** *in vbl senses.* **2.** feathering; feathers, plumage.
befiehlst, befiehlt *see* **befehlen.**
befilzen, *v.tr.* to felt (piano hammer).
befinden. I. *v.* (*strong*) **1.** *v.tr.* (*a*) **etwas gut, richtig, falsch, b.,** to find, judge, sth. (to be) good, right, wrong; **nach eingehender Prüfung wurde es gut befunden,** after detailed examination it was pronounced, judged, good; **er wurde stets treu und redlich befunden,** he was always found to be loyal and honest; (*b*) **es (für) gut, richtig, b., etwas zu tun,** to think, consider, deem, it good, proper, to do sth.; **etwas (für) gut, richtig, b.,** to think, consider, deem, sth. good, proper; **ich befand es (für) richtig, abzureisen,** I thought it proper to depart; *Iron:* **er hat es für nötig befunden, mich zu besuchen,** he deemed it necessary to pay me a visit. **2.** *v.i.* (*haben*) **über etwas, in einer Sache, b.,** to judge, decide, sth.; to make, give, a decision on sth. **3. sich befinden,** to be; (*a*) **ihr Haus befindet sich am anderen Ende des Dorfes,** her house is at the other end of the village; **er befand sich zu dieser Zeit im Ausland,** he was abroad at the time; **sich auf Reisen b.,** to be away; **sich in Gefahr, in einer heiklen Situation, b.,** to be in danger, in a tricky situation; (*b*) **sich wohl, besser, b.,** to be, feel, well, better; **sich bei guter, bester, Gesundheit b.,** to be in good, in the best of, health; **wie befinden Sie sich heute?** how are you today?
II. *vbl s.* **Befinden,** *n.* **1.** judgment; opinion, view; **nach meinem B.,** in my judgment; in my opinion, view; **je nach B.,** according to taste, as one thinks fit. **2.** condition, (state of) health; **sich nach j-s B. erkundigen,** to inquire after s.o.'s health; **ihr B. verschlechterte sich von Tag zu Tag,** her condition, health, deteriorated daily.
befindlich, *a.* (*a*) *attrib.* **die im Hafen befindlichen Schiffe,** the ships (lying) in port; **alle im Hause befindlichen Personen,** all persons (present) in the house; **in einem in der Nähe befindlichen Wäldchen,** in a copse (lying) nearby; (*b*) *pred.* **b. sein,** to be; **er war gerade auf einer Reise b.,** he happened to be on a journey.
befingern, *v.tr.* to finger, feel (sth.), to touch (s.o., sth.) with one's fingers.
befirsten, *v.tr. Constr:* to ridge (roof); to finish off (roof) (with ridge-tiles, galvanized iron, etc.).
beflaggen. I. *v.tr.* to deck (house, etc.) with flags; to put out bunting; **alle Häuser sollen beflaggt werden,** all householders are asked to put out flags; **bunt beflaggte Straßen,** streets gay with bunting; *Navy:* **das Schiff b.,** to dress the ship; **beflaggtes Schiff,** ship dressed overall.
II. *vbl s.* **1. Beflaggen,** *n. in vbl senses.* **2. Beflaggung,** *f.* (*a*)=II. 1; (*b*) bunting; flags.
beflechten, *v.tr.* (*strong*) to cover (sth.) with wicker(work); to bottom *or* back (chair) (with straw, rushes, cane); *El:* to braid (wire); **den Sitz, die Lehne, eines Stuhles b.,** to bottom, back, a chair; **beflochtener Leitungsdraht,** braided conductor-wire.
beflecken. I. *v.tr.* **1.** (*a*) to stain, soil (garment, one's hands, etc.); (*b*) to pollute, defile, profane, (sacred place, institution, etc.); (*of sin, etc.*) to taint, stain (s.o., the soul); (*of objects, activities under taboo*) to defile (s.o.); **befleckt werden, sich b.,** to become defiled; **seine Hände mit Blut b.,** to stain one's hands with blood; **seine mit Märtyrerblut befleckten Hände,** his hands defiled, stained, with the blood of martyrs; (*c*) to sully, tarnish, blemish, (be)smirch, cast a slur, a stain, on (s.o.'s, one's, honour, reputation, etc.); **er ging durch diese Angelegenheit durch, ohne seinen Ruf zu b.,** he came out of this business without a stain on his character. **2.** *Bootm:* to heel *or* tip (shoes).
II. *vbl s.* **1. Beflecken,** *n. in vbl senses.* **2. Befleckung,** *f.* (*a*)=II. 1; *also:* pollution, defilement, profanation (of sacred place, etc.); (*b*) (*receiving of*) taint; stain; blemish; smirch; **frei von B. durch die Sünde,** free from the taint, stain, of sin; **sein Ruf blieb frei von B.,** his character remained free from blemish, unblemished, stainless.
beflegeln, *v.tr. Austrian:* to abuse (s.o.); to insult (s.o.).
befleißen (sich), *v.refl.* (*strong*)=**befleißigen (sich);** *see also* **beflissen.**
befleißigen (sich), *v.refl.* **sich etwas** *gen.* **b.,** to apply oneself (industriously) to sth., to apply one's mind to sth.; to strive for, after, sth.; to be solicitous of sth.; **sich b., etwas zu tun,** to apply oneself to doing sth.; to be eager to do sth.; to put, lay, oneself out to do sth.; to take, be at, (great) pains to do sth.; to endeavour, strive, set oneself, to do sth.; to make it one's study to do sth.; **sich des Studiums b.,** to bend one's mind to study; **sich des Studiums der Rechte b.,** to study law, (*in England*) to study for the bar; **sich der Höflichkelt b.** to be at pains, to take pains, to be polite; **sich b., (j-m) zu Gefallen zu sein,** to endeavour, to put, lay, oneself out, to make it one's study, to be eager, to please (s.o.).
befliegen, *v.tr.* (*strong*) (*of bees, etc.*) to visit (flowers); *Av:* to fly, cover (route).
befliß, beflisse *see* **befleißen.**
beflissen, *a.* **1.** (*a*) *attrib.* **etwas** *gen.* **b.,** intent on sth., solicitous of sth.; **ein der Kunst beflissener junger Mann,** a young man keenly interested in art; a young man zealous in the pursuit of art; *cp.* 2; (*b*) *pred.* **etwas** *gen.* **b. sein, b. sein, etwas zu tun**=**sich etwas befleißigen, sich befleißigen, etwas zu tun,** *q.v. under* **befleißigen. 2. Beflissene** *m, f,* (eager) student (of sth.); **ein des Rechtsstudiums Beflissener,** a law-student; **ein der Kunst Beflissener,** an eager student of art; a votary of art.
Beflissenheit, *f.* eagerness, solicitousness, studiousness, intentness.
beflissentlich, *adv.*=**geflissentlich** (*b.*)
beflochten, *p.p. & a. see* **beflechten.**
beflоren, *v.tr.* (*a*) to cover, decorate (sth.) with crape; (*of pers.*) **(den Arm, den Hut) beflort,** wearing a mourning band (round one's arm, one's hat); (*b*) to veil (sth.); to darken (sth.); to shroud (sth.).
beflügeln, *v.tr.* to quicken, accelerate (s.o.'s steps, course, etc.); *Lit:* **die Angst, die Erwartung, beflügelte seine Schritte, ihn,** fear, expectation, lent him wings, winged his steps; **beflügelten Schrittes,** swift of foot.
befluten, *v.tr.* (*of river, sea*) to wash (against) (bank, shore, etc.); **vom Meer beflutet,** washed by the sea.
befőhle, befohlen *see* **befehlen.**
befolgen, *v.tr.* to follow, act upon (advice, instruction, rule); to obey (instruction); to comply with (rule); to abide by (rule, principle); **ich habe Ihre Anweisungen befolgt,** I followed, acted upon, obeyed, your instructions.
Beförderer, *m. A:*=**Förderer** 1.
beförderlich, *a.* **1.** *A:*=**förderlich. 2.** *Swiss:* accelerated (delivery, etc).
befördern. I. *v.tr.* **1.** (*a*) *A:* to promote, further (the arts, a cause, etc.); (*b*) *A:* to accelerate, hasten (sth.); (*c*) (*of thg*) to aid, stimulate, promote (digestion, circulation, etc.). *Cp.* **fördern. 2. j-n (im Amt) b.,** to promote s.o.; **befördert werden,** to be promoted, to advance; **zum Hauptmann befördert werden,** to be promoted (to be) captain; **in einen höheren Dienstgrad befördert werden,** to be promoted, to advance, to a higher rank. **3.** (*a*) *Trans: Com: etc:* (*of pers.*) to dispatch, despatch, forward (goods); (*of pers., vehicle*) to convey, transport, carry (goods, persons); **Güter per Schiff, auf dem Wasserwege, b.,** to ship goods; **Güter per Post, mit der Post, per Bahn, mit der Bahn, b.,** to send, dispatch, forward, goods by post, by rail; to rail goods; **Güter zur Bahn b.,** to carry, transport, goods to the station; **Pakete zur Post b.,** to take, carry, parcels to the post(-office), to post, *U.S:* to mail, parcels; **die Eisenbahn befördert Güter und Personen,** the railway carries, conveys, goods and persons; **sie wurden in einem Omnibus zum Bahnhof befördert,** they were conveyed, taken, to the station in a bus; (*b*) *F:* **j-n aus dem Zimmer b.,** to throw, *F:* pitch, s.o. out of the room; **j-n an die Luft b.,** to chuck s.o. out; **j-n ins Jenseits, in die andere Welt, b.,** to dispatch, kill, s.o., *F:* to launch s.o. into eternity.
II. *vbl s.* **1. Befördern,** *n. in vbl senses.* **2. Beförderung,** *f.* (*a*)=II. 1; *also:* dispatch, despatch (of goods); carriage (of goods), conveyance, transport (of goods, persons); **B. auf dem Wasserweg,** waterborne transport; **wir behalten uns das Recht vor, die B. von sperrigen Gütern abzulehnen,** we reserve the right to refuse to carry, convey, bulky goods; (*b*) promotion (to higher rank, etc.); **er hat gestern seine B. zum Hauptmann gefeiert,** he celebrated his promotion to captain yesterday.
Beförderungsanweisungen, *f.pl.* forwarding instructions.
Beförderungsbedingungen, *f.pl.* forwarding conditions; conditions of conveyance.
Beförderungsbestimmungen, *f.pl. Rail: etc:* regulations governing passenger and goods traffic.
Beförderungsgebühr(en), *f.(pl.),* **Beförderungskosten,** *pl.* transport charges.
Beförderungsmittel, *n.* (means of) transport, conveyance; **öffentliche Beförderungsmittel,** (i) public means of conveyance; (ii) public service vehicles.

Beförderungsvorschriften, *f.pl.* forwarding instructions.

beforsten. I. *v.tr. For:* to (af)forest; to put (district) under timber.

II. *vbl s.* **Beforsten** *n.*, **Beforstung** *f.* timbering, afforestation.

Beförsterung, *f.* administration of a (privately owned) forest (*by forestry authority*).

befrachten. I. *v.tr. Com: etc:* to load (vehicle); *esp.* to freight, to charter and load (ship).

II. *vbl s.* **Befrachten** *n.*, **Befrachtung** *f. in vbl senses; also:* freightage, affreightment (of ship).

Befrachter, *m. Com:* freighter, charterer (of ship), shipper.

Befrachtungsvertrag, *m. Nau: Com:* freightage-contract, *esp.* charter-party.

befrackt, *a.* (*of waiter, etc.*) tail-coated, in tails.

befragen. I. *v.tr.* (*conj. like* **fragen**) **1.** (*a*) to question (s.o.), to ask (s.o.) questions; to interrogate (witness, etc.); **j-n über etwas** *acc.* **b.,** to question, ask, s.o. about sth.; (*b*) to consult (s.o., history, a dictionary, an oracle, etc.); **j-n in einer Sache, über etwas** *acc.*, **wegen etwas** *gen.*, **b.,** to consult s.o. on, about, sth.; **sein Gewissen b.,** to consult, to sound, one's conscience; **die Sterne b.,** to consult, *F:* to question, the stars; (*c*) *occ.* **j-n um etwas b.,** to ask s.o. for sth. **2.** *A:* **sich befragen,** (*a*) **sich (bei j-m) b.,** to ask (s.o.) (about sth.); (*b*) **sich mit j-m b.,** to take counsel with s.o.; **sich (miteinander) b.,** to take counsel, to consult, together.

II. *vbl s.* **Befragen** *n.*, **Befragung** *f. in vbl senses; also:* interrogation (of witness, etc.); consultation (of s.o., a dictionary, etc.).

befransen, *v.tr.* to fringe, to put a fringe on (sth.); **befranst,** with a fringe, fringed.

befreien. I. *v.tr.* to free. **1.** (*a*) to liberate (a nation, trade, etc.) **(von Unterdrückung, usw.,** from oppression, etc.); to deliver (s.o.) **(von, aus,** from); to rescue (captive, etc.); to release (s.o.) **(aus dem Gefängnis, usw.,** from prison, etc.); to set (s.o.) free; **j-n aus der Gefangenschaft b.,** to deliver s.o. from, out of, captivity; **j-n aus der Hand seiner Feinde, von seinen Feinden, b.,** to deliver s.o. from his enemies; **j-n von seinen Banden b.,** to loose s.o. from his bonds; **j-n von, aus, einem Leben der Knechtschaft b.,** to free s.o. from a life of servitude; **j-n von Furcht b.,** to free s.o. from fear; **den Geist von Vorurteilen b.,** to free, liberate, the mind from prejudice; **ein befreites Gefühl,** a feeling of release; (*b*) **j-n, einen Ort, von etwas, j-m, b.,** to rid s.o., a place, of sth., s.o.; to clear a place of sth., s.o.; **sich (von etwas) b.,** to get clear, rid, free (of sth.); **ein Land von Banditen, von der Banditenplage, b.,** to rid, clear, a country of bandits; **j-n von seinen Feinden b.,** to rid s.o. of his enemies; **er war von einem lästigen Rivalen befreit,** he was rid of a troublesome rival; **endlich bin ich von ihm befreit,** at last I am free, rid, of him; **j-n von einer Last, einer Sorge, b.,** to free s.o. of a burden, a worry; **sich von einer schweren Last befreit fühlen,** to feel relieved of a great weight; **befreit aufatmen,** to heave a sigh of relief; *Lit:* **vom Eise befreit,** freed from ice; *Hum:* **j-n von seinem Geld b.,** to lighten s.o.'s purse; (*c*) to extricate, disentangle (s.o., oneself) **(aus, von,** from); **j-n aus einer unangenehmen Lage b.,** to extricate s.o. from a critical position; **sie versuchte, ihre Hand aus seinem Griff zu b.,** she tried to withdraw, release, her hand from his grasp; **sie versuchte, sich aus seiner Umarmung zu b.,** she tried to free herself, to shake herself free, from his embrace; **er befreite sich mit einem, durch einen, heftigen Ruck,** he wrenched himself free; **sich von einem Einfluß b.,** to break free from an influence. **2.** to exempt, excuse, dispense (s.o. from sth.); **j-n vom Militärdienst b.,** to exempt s.o. from military service; **j-n von einer Aufgabe b.,** to excuse s.o. from, let s.o. off, a task; **j-n von der Teilnahme b.,** to excuse s.o. from attendance; *Mil:* **vom Arbeitseinsatz befreit,** dispensed, exempt, from fatigues.

II. *vbl s.* **1. Befreien,** *n. in vbl senses.* **2. Befreiung,** *f.* (*a*)=II. 1; *also:* (*action of*) (i) liberation (of a nation, of trade, etc.); (ii) extrication, disentanglement; (*b*) liberation; **der Tag unserer B. ist nahe,** the day of our liberation draws near; **B. vom Joche der Sklaverei,** liberation from the yoke of slavery; (*c*) exemption, dispensation (from a service, etc.); **ich bitte um B. von der Teilnahme am Turnunterricht,** I ask to be excused from (attending) gymnastics.

III. *pr.p. & a.* **befreiend,** *in vbl senses; esp.* **befreiendes Lachen, Wort, usw.,** laughter, word, etc., that breaks, loosens, the tension.

Befreier, *m.* **-s/-**, liberator, deliverer; rescuer.

Befreiungskampf, *m.* struggle for independence *or* liberation.

Befreiungskrieg, *m.* war of independence *or* liberation; *G.Hist:* **die Befreiungskriege,** the Wars of Liberation (1813–15).

befremden. I. *v.tr.* to surprise (s.o.); to astonish (s.o.); to appear, seem, strange, odd, queer (to s.o.), to strike (s.o.) as odd, queer; **Ihr Benehmen befremdet mich,** I am surprised, amazed, at your behaviour; **es befremdete mich, ich war befremdet, ihn hier zu sehen,** I was surprised, amazed, at seeing, to see, him here, I thought it strange that he should be here; **befremdend= befremdlich.**

II. *vbl s.* **Befremden,** *n.* surprise; astonishment, amazement; **zu meinem B. habe ich gehört, daß . . . ,** I have heard to my amazement, astonishment, that . . . ; **mein B., ihn hier zu sehen,** my surprise, astonishment, amazement, at seeing him here; **er drückte sein B. darüber aus,** he showed marked surprise at it.

befremdlich, *a.* strange; odd, queer; surprising; **befremdliches Benehmen,** strange behaviour; **ich finde sein Verhalten sehr b.,** I am very much surprised at his behaviour, (in the circumstances) I find his behaviour rather strange, odd, queer, surprising; **es ist b., daß er noch nicht angekommen ist,** it is odd, strange, that he has not come yet, that he should not have arrived yet; **das Befremdliche an der Sache, daran, ist, daß . . . ,** the odd thing about the matter, about it, is that . . . .

Befremdlichkeit, *f.* strangeness; queerness.

befreunden (sich). I. *v.refl.* **1. sich mit j-m b.,** to form a friendship, to make friends, with s.o. **2. sich mit etwas b.,** to get used to, accustomed to, sth.; to come to like sth.; **er kann sich nicht mit unseren neuen Vorhängen b.,** he cannot get used to our new curtains, he cannot bring himself to like our new curtains; **ich kann mich nicht mit dem Gedanken b., morgen schon fort zu müssen,** I cannot get accustomed, used to the idea that I shall have to go tomorrow.

II. *p.p. & a.* **befreundet.** **1.** *pred.* **mit j-m b. sein,** to be friendly, friends, with s.o.; **wir sind mit seiner Familie seit Jahren b.,** we are old friends of his family, we have been friends with his family for years; **ich bin mit niemandem hier b.,** I have no friends here; **sehr, eng, gut, mit j-m b. sein,** to be very intimate with s.o., to be great friends with s.o., to be intimately acquainted with s.o.; **eng, sehr, gut, (miteinander) b. sein,** to be great, intimate, close, friends; **sie sind nicht mehr (miteinander) b.,** they are no longer friends. **2.** *attrib.* **eine uns befreundete Familie,** friends of ours; **ein ihm befreundeter Soldat,** a soldier friend of his; **ein mir befreundeter Schauspieler,** an actor friend of mine; **befreundete Macht,** friendly power; **befreundete Stämme,** friendly tribes; **(miteinander) befreundete Stämme,** tribes living in friendship, in harmony.

befrieden. I. *v.tr.* **1.** *A:* to close in, fence in (piece of ground, etc.). **2.** to pacify, to restore (the) peace in (country).

II. *vbl s.* **Befriedung,** *f.* pacification; **nach der B. Galliens,** when peace was restored in Gaul.

befriedigen. I. *v.tr.* **1.** *A:*=**befrieden.** **2.** to satisfy; (*a*) (*of pers.*) to please (s.o.); (*of pers., thg*) to meet (s.o.'s needs, etc.); (*of thg*) to give satisfaction to (s.o.); **j-s Ansprüche, j-n, b.,** to meet, to comply with, s.o.'s requests; **die Ansprüche seiner Gläubiger, seine Gläubiger, b.,** to satisfy the claims of one's creditors, to satisfy one's creditors; **ein Leben der Untätigkeit kann ihn nicht b.,** a life of leisure cannot give him satisfaction; **eine solche Arbeit könnte mich nie b.,** I could never find satisfaction in this kind of work, I could never get any satisfaction out of this kind of work, this kind of work could never give me satisfaction; **etwas, das jeden Geschmack befriedigt,** sth. that suits, meets, every taste; *see also* **Bedürfnis** 1 (*b*); (*b*) to gratify (curiosity, whims, etc.); to satiate, sate (passions, etc.); **eine persönliche Rache b.,** to gratify a private spite; **j-s Verlangen b.,** to satisfy, gratify, s.o.'s desire; **seine Begierden b.,** to gratify one's appetites; **seine Lust b.,** to satiate, sate, one's passions; to gratify one's lust. **3. sich befriedigen,** (*a*) *A:* to content oneself, to be content (with sth.); (*b*) to gratify one's sexual desires; **sich selbst b.,** to masturbate.

II. *vbl s.* **1. Befriedigen,** *n. in vbl senses.* **2. Befriedigung,** *f.* (*a*)—II. 1; *also:* satisfaction (of creditor, s.o.'s requests, needs, etc.); gratification (of passions, one's appetites, curiosity, whims, etc.); *see also* **absondern I.** 4 (*a*); (*b*) satisfaction; contentment; gratification; **seine B. über etwas ausdrücken,** to express (one's) satisfaction at, with, contentment with, sth.; **die B. haben, etwas getan zu haben,** to have the satisfaction of having done sth.; **die B. haben zu wissen, daß man sein Bestes getan hat,** to have the satisfaction, gratification, of knowing one has done one's best; **(volle) B. in seinem Beruf finden,** to find (complete) satisfaction in one's work; **ich stelle mit B. fest, daß . . . ,** I note with satisfaction that . . . ; **mit einem, dem, Gefühl innerer B.,** with a feeling of inward satisfaction.

III. *pr.p. & a.* **befriedigend,** *in vbl senses; esp.* (*a*) satisfactory; satisfying; **in befriedigender Weise,** in a satisfactory manner, satisfactorily; **das Ergebnis ist vollauf, nicht sehr, b.,** the result is entirely, not very, satisfactory; **das befriedigende Gefühl haben, etwas getan zu haben,** to have the satisfaction, the gratifying feeling, of having done sth.; (*b*) *Sch:* (*on report*) satisfactory; **ein Examen (mit) 'b.' bestehen,** to get a pass in an examination, to satisfy the examiners.

IV. *p.p. & a.* **befriedigt,** *in vbl senses; esp.* satisfied; content; *adv.* with satisfaction; **bist du endlich b.?** are you satisfied, content, now? **du hast keinen Grund, b. zu sein,** you have no cause for satisfaction; **mit befriedigtem Lächeln,** with a satisfied smile, *F:* with a smug look; **etwas b. betrachten,** to regard, look at, sth. with satisfaction; **dann kann ich ja b. gehen,** now I can leave in peace.

Befriedung, *f. see* **befrieden.**

befristen. I. *v.tr. Com: Jur: etc:* to set a date for the beginning *or* ending of (contract, etc.); to limit the duration of (contract, etc.); *esp.* (*a*) **eine Zahlungsforderung b.,** to grant a respite for payment; **befristete Forderung,** deferred claim; (*b*) to set a time-limit, to set, put, a term, to (sth.); **die Ablieferung der Waren ist bis zum 1. Mai befristet,** delivery of the goods must be effected not later than May 1st; **befristeter Anspruch,** claim subject to a time-limit; *Bank:* **befristete Einlage,** time deposit.

II. *vbl s.* **Befristen** *n.*, **Befristung** *f. in vbl senses; also:* postponement; deferment.

befruchten. I. *v.tr.* **1.** (*a*) *Biol: etc:* to fertilize (ovum, ovule, female); to impregnate (female); **künstlich b.,** to inseminate (ewe, etc.) artificially; **das befruchtete Ei,** the fertilized egg; (*b*) (*of pers., ideas, influences, etc.*) to render (s.o., s.o.'s mind, etc.) productive, fertile, to fertilize (s.o., s.o.'s mind, etc.); **die mannigfachen Eindrücke, die Italien bot, befruchteten den Künstler, des Künstlers Seele,** the rich variety of impressions that Italy offered had a productive effect on the artist's mind. **2.** (*of rain, sun, etc.*) to make (land, etc.) fertile, to bring fertility to (land, etc.); **die befruchtende Kraft des Regenwassers, der Sonnenstrahlen,** the fertilizing, life-giving, power, the fecundity, of the rain, the sun; **befruchtender Regen,** fertile rain.

II. *vbl s.* **1. Befruchten,** *n. in vbl senses.* **2. Befruchtung,** *f. Biol: etc:* fertilization; impregnation; fecundation; **künstliche B.,** artificial insemination.

Befruchtungshaar, *n. Bot:* trichogyne.

befugen, *v.tr.* **1.** to authorize, empower (s.o. to do sth.), to give (s.o.) authority (to do sth.); **ich habe Sie nicht dazu befugt, dies zu tun, zu sagen,** I did not authorize you to do, to say, that. **2. befugt sein, etwas zu tun,** to be authorized, empowered, to have authority, authorization, to do sth.; to be entitled, to have the right, to do sth.; **ich bin nicht befugt, darüber Auskunft zu geben,** I am not authorized, I am not in a position, to give information on the matter; **er hält sich (für) befugt, Befehle zu erteilen,** he considers himself authorized, he assumes the authority, to give orders; **etwas tun, ohne (dazu) befugt zu sein,** to do sth. without authority, to act *ultra vires.*

Befugnis, *f.* **-/-nisse,** authority, authorization, power; warrant; right; **seine Befugnisse überschreiten,** to exceed, go beyond, one's powers, one's authority; **das überschreitet meine B.,** this does not lie, is not within, this lies beyond, my competence, power, sphere; **in Überschreitung seiner Befugnisse handeln,** to act *ultra vires.*

befühlen, *v.tr.* to feel (sth., s.o.), to examine (s.o., sth.), test (sth.) (by feeling); **einen Stoff b.,** to feel, test, a material.

befummeln, *v.tr. F:* **1.=befühlen.** **2. eine Sache b.,** to look a matter over.

Befund, *m.* **-(e)s/-e,** (*a*) result (of test, of medical examination, etc.); findings; (scientifically

established) fact, facts; (architectural, etc.) set-up; *Com:* stock-taking; 'ohne B.', *abbr.* 'o.B.', (i) 'no evidence;' (ii) 'negative (reaction)'; (*b*) (expert's, medical, official, etc.) report.

Befundbericht, *m.*=Befund (*b*).

befürchten. I. *v.tr.* etwas b., to fear sth., to be afraid of sth.; b., daß etwas geschieht, to be afraid that sth. will happen, to be afraid of sth. happening; du hast nichts zu b., you have nothing to fear, to be afraid of; ich habe das seit langem befürchtet, I have been afraid of that for some time, I have long feared that this would happen; das Schlimmste b., to fear the worst; es ist zu b., daß . . . , it is to be feared that . . . ; es ist nicht zu b., daß er wiederkommt, there is no fear that he will come back, of his coming back; man befürchtet allgemein, daß er blind wird, it is generally feared that he may become, go, blind.

II. *vbl s.* **Befürchtung,** *f.* apprehension, fear; Grund zu Befürchtungen geben, to give cause for apprehension; ich habe keine Befürchtungen für seine Sicherheit, I entertain no apprehension, no fears, for his safety; ich habe (so) meine Befürchtungen, I have certain apprehensions.

befürsorgen, *v.tr. Austrian:* (*official language*) to look after (s.o.); to have care of (s.o.).

befürworten. I. *v.tr.* to support, *F:* back up (s.o.'s application, petition, a cause, etc.); to advocate (a cause, etc.).

II. *vbl s.* **Befürwortung,** *f.* 1. *in vbl senses.* 2. recommendation, reference; j-m eine B. schreiben, to write s.o. a recommendation, reference, to write on s.o.'s behalf.

Befürworter, *m.* -s/-, supporter, advocate (of a cause, etc.).

Befürwortungsschreiben, *n.* letter of recommendation, recommendatory letter.

Beg [bɛk, beːk], *m.* -s/-s. *Turk.Adm:* bey.

begaben. I. *v.tr. A. & Lit:* to give (s.o.) presents; to confer, bestow (sth.) (upon s.o.); to endow (s.o.) (with qualities, etc.).

II. *vbl s.* **Begabung,** *f.* 1. *A. & Lit: in vbl senses; also:* endowment. 2. natural gift, talent; genius; capacity, aptitude; künstlerische B., artistic talent; intellektuelle, verstandesmäßige, geistige, B., intellectual capacity; musikalische, schauspielerische, B. haben, to have a natural gift, bent, for music, for acting; (eine) B. für Sprachen haben, to have a talent for languages; ein Mann von ungewöhnlicher B., a man of exceptional talent, an exceptionally talented, gifted, man; eine B. (dafür) haben, (immer) das Richtige, das Falsche zu tun, to have a talent, a genius, for doing the right, wrong, thing. 3. talented person, talent; er ist eine B. auf dem Gebiete der Mathematik, he is gifted in the field of mathematics.

III. *p.p. & a.* **begabt,** *in vbl senses; esp.* gifted, talented; able; apt; intelligent, bright; künstlerisch b., artistically endowed; geistig, verstandesmäßig, intellektuell, b., intellectually endowed; ein begabter Schüler, a gifted, an apt, pupil; einer meiner begabtesten Schüler, one of my brightest, aptest, pupils; die Begabtesten, the most gifted, the best brains; Auslese der Begabten, selecting, selection, of the most gifted, the most intelligent, individuals; ein sehr begabter junger Mann, a young man of talent, a very talented, gifted, young man; eine begabte Schauspielerin, a talented actress; für Sprachen b. sein, to have a talent for languages; er ist für Mathematik, Musik, b., he has a natural gift for mathematics, music; *Iron:* das war sehr b. von dir, that 'was clever, bright, of you.

Begabtenauslese, *f. Psy: etc:* selecting, selection, of the most gifted individuals.

Begabtenförderung, *f.* (official) financial assistance to gifted pupils *or* students.

Begabtheit, *f.*=Begabung, *q.v. under* begaben II. 2.

Begabungsprüfung, *f. Psy:* intelligence test.

begaffen, *v.tr.* to gape at (s.o., sth.); to stare at (s.o., sth.) open-mouthed.

Begam ['beːgam], *f.* -/-en=Begum.

Begängnis, *n.* -nisses/-nisse. *A:* celebration (of wedding, etc.); holding of a memorial service; *esp.* funeral (service).

begann, begänne *see* beginnen.

Begard [beˑ'gart], *m.* -en/-en [-'gardən]. *Ecc.Hist:* Beghard.

Begasse [beˑ'gasə], *f.* -/-n=Bagasse.

begatten. I. *v.tr. Physiol: etc:* 1. (*of male*) to mate, copulate, with (female); (*of male mammal*) to serve, cover (female). 2. sich begatten, (*of animals*) to mate, pair, couple, copulate; (*of birds*) to mate, pair; (*of persons*) to mate, copulate; *Lit:* (*of ideas, etc.*) to marry.

II. *vb s.* 1. **Begatten,** *n. in vbl senses.* 2. **Begattung,** *f.* (*a*)=II. 1; *also:* service (of female by male); (*b*) mating, pairing, copulation (of animals); mating, sexual union, coitus, coition (of pers.).

Begattungsorgan, *n.* sexual organ.

Begattungstrieb, *m.* sexual instinct.

Begattungswerkzeug, *n.* sexual organ.

Begattungszeit, *f.* mating season, pairing season.

begaukeln, *v.tr.* to charm, bewitch (s.o.).

begaunern, *v.tr.* to swindle, cheat (s.o.).

begebbar, *a. Fin: Com:* negotiable; transferable; nicht b., not negotiable; begebbares Wertpapier, negotiable instrument; begebbare Wertpapiere, Effekten, transferable, negotiable, securities.

Begebbarkeit, *f. Fin: Com:* negotiability; transferability.

begeben. I. *v.tr.* (*strong*) 1. *A:* to give (sth.) up, to yield (sth.) (up). 2. *Fin:* (*a*) to issue (bill, loan, etc.); to float, place (loan); (*b*) to negotiate (loan, bill); to endorse (bill of exchange) (in s.o.'s favour); to dispose of, sell (securities, etc.).

II. **sich begeben.** 1. sich etwas *gen.* b., to renounce, give up, forgo, sth.; to relinquish sth.; sich seiner Rechte b., to forgo, renounce, one's rights; sich eines Anspruchs b., to relinquish, waive, a claim; sich der Welt b., to renounce the world; sich seines Amtes b., to resign office, one's post; to demit office. 2. (*a*) sich nach einem, an einen, Ort b., to proceed, repair, *Lit:* to betake oneself, to a place; to make one's way to, towards, a place; to make for a place; sich in aller Eile nach einem, an einen, Ort b., to make all speed to a place; morgen wird er sich nach London b., tomorrow he will proceed to London; sich nach Hause b., to make for home; sich nach Frankreich b., to make for France; begebt euch an eure Plätze! (i) take (up) your position! (ii) go to your places! *Mil:* sich zu seiner Einheit b., to join one's unit; *Nau:* sich nach dem Ankerplatz b., to make for the anchorage; (*b*) sich zur Ruhe b., to go to bed; sich in j-s Dienste b., to enter s.o.'s service; sich an die Arbeit b., to begin work; to set, fall, to work; sich wieder an die Arbeit b., to return, to go back, to work; sie begaben sich ans Essen, sie begaben sich daran, zu essen, they began to eat; they fell to (eating); sich ins Bad b., to go and have one's bath; sich in, unter, j-s Schutz b., to place oneself under s.o.'s protection; to take refuge with s.o.; sich auf Reisen b., to travel (abroad); sich in Gefahr b., to expose oneself to danger; to run into danger; to court danger; *Prov:* wer sich in (die) Gefahr begibt, kommt darin um, he who looks for trouble finds it. 3. (*of event, occurrence, etc.*) to happen, to take place, to come about; (*impers.*) es begab sich, it came about, it (so) happened; *B:* es begab sich aber zu der Zeit . . . , and it came to pass in those days . . . .

III. *vbl s.* **Begebung,** *f. Fin:* (*a*) issue (of bill, loan, etc.); floating, flo(a)tation (of loan); (*b*) negotiation (of bill of exchange, etc.); disposal, sale (of securities, etc.).

Begebenheit, *f.* occurrence, incident, happening, event; eine lustige B., an amusing incident; eine seltsame B., a strange happening; eine wichtige B., an important event.

Begebnis, *n.* -nisses/-nisse=Begebenheit.

Begebungs-, *comb.fm. cp.* Emissions-.

Begebungskonsortium, *n. Fin:* issuing syndicate.

Begebungsvertrag, *m. Fin:* deed of transfer, instrument of transfer.

begegnen. I. *v.i.* (*sein, A: sein, haben*) 1. (*a*) (*of pers.*) to meet (s.o., sth.); to come across (s.o., sth.); to come upon, light upon (sth.); (*of thg*) to be found, to be met with; j-m, etwas *dat.*, zufällig b., to meet, come across, s.o., sth., by chance, to chance upon s.o., sth.; to stumble upon sth.; dem Feinde b., to encounter the enemy; j-m auf seinem Wege b., to run across s.o.; to run into s.o.; sich, einander, b., to meet; (*of hostile armies*) to come into contact, to clash; j-s Blick b., to meet s.o.'s glance; ihre Blicke begegneten sich, their eyes met; solchen Männern begegnet man nicht oft, such men are not often found, met with, to be met; ich bin diesem Ausdruck, dieser Ausdruck ist mir, bei einer Reihe von Schriftstellern begegnet, I met, came across, happened upon, this expression in the works of a number of authors; dieses Wort begegnet einige Male bei Schiller, this word is found, occurs, several times in Schiller; ein immer wieder begegnendes Wort, a word found, met with, again and again; diesem Fehler begegnet man überall, this mistake is met with everywhere; (*b*) to meet (a wish, etc.); ich werde mein Bestes tun, Ihren Wünschen zu b., I will do my best to meet your wishes; wird das Ihren Ansprüchen b.? will this meet your requirements? unsere Wünsche begegnen sich, our wishes conform; unsere Absichten begegnen sich, our plans agree; in diesem Wunsch begegnen wir uns, in this desire we are at one; (*c*) to meet with (difficulties, approval, etc.); to encounter (obstacles, difficulties, etc.); (*d*) (*of thg*) to happen (to s.o.); to befall (s.o.); eine Begebenheit, die mir vor kurzem begegnete, an incident that happened to me a short while ago; das ist ihm noch nie begegnet, it never happened to him; das soll mir nicht wieder b., I'll take care that it will not happen to me again; ein Unglück ist ihm begegnet, he has met with a disaster, a disaster has befallen him; (*e*) *abs.* to occur, to happen; was mag wohl begegnet sein? what can have happened? 2. j-m freundlich b., to receive s.o. in a friendly manner, with friendliness; j-m übel, feindlich, b., to give s.o. a bad, hostile, reception, to treat s.o. badly, with hostility; man begegnete ihm herzlich, he was cordially received, he was given a cordial welcome, he met with a cordial reception; j-m mit Höflichkeit, höflich, b., to treat s.o. with politeness; begegnest du mir so? is that how you treat me? wenn man mir mit Arroganz begegnet, werde ich mich entsprechend verhalten, if I am treated with arrogance, I shall respond accordingly. 3. to meet (danger, difficulty, etc.); to obviate (difficulty, danger, etc.); to provide against (accident, etc.); to take precautions against (illness, accident, etc.); to take preventive measures against (sth.); to counter, counteract (plan, etc.); to take action against (sth.); to fight (s.o., sth.); einer Gefahr mit Umsicht b., to meet a danger with circumspection; Gewalt mit Gewalt b., to meet force with force; er begegnete ihrer Widerspenstigkeit mit Güte, he met her obstinacy with kindness; einer Krankheit beizeiten b., to take timely precautions against an illness; der Kriegsgefahr b., to take preventive measures against the danger of war; er begegnete ihrer Auffassung mit guten Gründen, he countered her opinion with sound reasons; alles ist versucht worden, diesem Mißstand zu b., everything has been tried to counteract this abuse.

II. *vbl s.* **Begegnung,** *f.* 1. meeting; encounter; B. mit dem Feind, encounter with the enemy; bei unserer ersten B., at our first meeting; eine flüchtige B., a brief encounter; B. mit Gott, encounter with God; gestern hatte ich eine seltsame B., I had an unusual encounter yesterday; unsere B. wird immer zu meinen schönsten Erinnerungen gehören, our meeting, our encounter, will always be one of my most cherished memories. 2. *A:* treatment; behaviour.

Begegnis, *f.* -/-nisse, & *n.* -nisses/-nisse. *A:* 1. meeting; encounter. 2. treatment. 3.=Begebenheit.

Begegnungsgefecht. *n. Mil:* encounter-battle.

begehen. I. *v.tr.* (*strong*) 1. (*a*) to walk, go, along (road) (for the first time, frequently, etc.); ein kaum begangener Pfad, a little used path; ein viel begangener Pfad, a much trodden path; (*b*) to inspect (field, etc.); *esp. Rel:* die Flur, die Felder, b., to go in procession round the fields (*on Rogation days, etc.*). 2. (*of stallion*) to serve, cover (mare); (*of animals*) sich b., to mate. 3. to celebrate (feast, etc.); to keep (day, etc.) (as a holiday, as a festival); das Weihnachtsfest in alter Weise b., to keep Christmas in the old style; heute begehen wir das Fest des hl. Johannes, today we celebrate the Feast of St John; wir wollen diesen Tag festlich b., we will keep this day as a holiday, celebrate this day in a festive way; das Osterfest wurde mit Prunk begangen, Easter was celebrated with splendour. 4. to commit, perpetrate (crime, sin, blunder); to make (mistake, etc.); Selbstmord, Ehebruch, b., to commit suicide, adultery; ein Verbrechen an j-m b., to commit a crime *or* offence against s.o.; einen Diebstahl an j-m b., to steal (sth.) from s.o.; einen Diebstahl an öffentlichem Eigentum b., to steal (from) public property; einen Mord an j-m b., to murder s.o.; er beging einen unverzeihlichen Irrtum, he made, committed, an unforgivable error; diesen Fehler begeht man oft, this mistake is often, frequently, made; this is a common mistake.

II. *vbl s.* 1. **Begehen,** *n. in vbl senses; also:* (*a*) celebration (of feast, etc.); (*b*) perpetration (of crime, etc.). 2. **Begehung,** *f. in vbl senses; also:* inspection (of field, etc.); *esp. Rel:*

procession (round the fields) (*on Rogation days, etc.*).

Begehr, *m. & n.* **-(e)s/-e,** desire, wish; request; *Pol.Ec:* demand; **er fragte nach ihrem B.,** he asked what they desired.

begehren. I. *v.tr. & i.* (*haben*) (*a*) **etwas, nach etwas,** *A:* **etwas** *gen.*, **b.,** to covet, desire, want (sth.), to wish for (sth.); **heftig, inbrünstig, b.,** to yearn, long, for (sth.); to crave for, after (sth.); **b., etwas zu tun,** to desire, to have a desire, to do sth.; **alles was das Herz begehrt,** everything one can wish for, everything the heart could desire; **sein Herz begehrte nach Zärtlichkeit,** his soul craved, yearned, for affection; *B:* **du sollst nicht b. deines Nächsten Haus,** neither shalt thou covet thy neighbour's house; (*b*) **j-n, nach j-m,** *A:* **j-s, b.,** to desire s.o., *Lit:* to lust after s.o.; *Lit:* **j-n zur Ehe, zur Frau, b.,** to seek s.o., s.o.'s hand, in marriage; *B:* **wer ein Weib ansiehet, ihrer zu b. . . . ,** whosoever looketh on a woman to lust after her . . . ; (*c*) *Ven:* (*of animal*) to be in rut; to be on heat.

II. *vbl s.* **Begehren,** *n.* (*a*) *in vbl senses;* (*b*) desire, wish (**nach,** for); **heißes B.,** eager, ardent, desire; (*c*)=**Begierde** 2.

III. *p.p. & a.* **begehrt,** (*of thg*) desired, wished for, *Com:* in demand, in request; (*of pers., thg*) sought after; **ein viel, sehr, begehrter Mann,** a man much sought after; *Com:* **dies ist ein sehr begehrter Artikel,** this is a very popular article, line, there is a great demand for this article, line.

begehrenswert, *a.* desirable, to be wished for.

begehrlich, *a.* **1.** covetous, longing, wistful (eyes, glances); lustful (eyes); **etwas, j-n, mit begehrlichen Augen, Blicken, betrachten,** *adv.* **b. nach, auf, etwas, j-n, blicken, schauen,** to cast covetous, longing, wistful, eyes, glances, on sth., to look covetously, longingly, wistfully, at sth.; to look at s.o. with lust in one's eyes, to cast lustful eyes on s.o.; **das Kind sah, schielte, mit begehrlichen Augen,** *adv.* **b., nach dem Kuchen,** the child looked with wistful, covetous, hungry, eyes at the cake, looked wistfully at the cake. **2.** *A:*=**begehrenswert.**

Begehrlichkeit, *f.* covetousness; wistfulness; lustfulness.

Begehung, *f. see* **begehen** II.

Begehungssünde, *f. Theol:* sin of commission.

begeifern, *v.tr.* to slobber, dribble, on (sth., s.o.); **j-s guten Namen, j-n, b.,** to (be)smirch, smudge, cast a slur on, cast aspersions on, s.o.'s good name; to slander, libel, s.o.

begeisten, *v.tr. A: Poet:*=**begeistern I. 1.**

begeistern. I. *v.tr.* **1.** (*of god, muse, etc.*) to inspire (s.o.); to breathe inspiration into (s.o.); **ein von Gott begeisterter Prophet,** a prophet inspired by, *Lit:* of, God; **ein von der Muse begeisterter Dichter,** a poet inspired by the muse. **2.** to fire (s.o.) with, to rouse (s.o.) to, enthusiasm; to enrapture; **j-n für etwas, j-n, b.,** to make s.o. enthusiastic, to fire, fill, s.o. with enthusiasm, for sth., s.o.; **j-n zur Tat b.,** to inspire s.o. to action; **sich b.,** to become, grow, get, to be, enthusiastic, excited; **sich für j-n, etwas, b.,** to become, grow, wax, to be, enthusiastic, to go into raptures, over s.o., sth.; to become keen on s.o., sth.; *F:* to enthuse over, about, sth.; **er begeistert sich leicht, läßt sich leicht b., ist leicht begeistert,** he is easily moved to enthusiasm, easily fired; **sich an etwas b.,** to be moved to enthusiasm by sth.; to be fired by sth.; **begeistert sein,** to be enchanted, delighted; **(über etwas) begeistert sein,** to be enraptured, to be in raptures (with sth.); **(hingerissen) in begeisterter Bewunderung, in begeistertem Entzücken,** in raptures of admiration, of delight; **sich für Musik und Kunst b., für Musik und Kunst begeistert sein,** to be an enthusiast for, a devotee of, music and art; **für Musik begeistert sein,** to be a music enthusiast; **ein begeisterter Wagneranhänger, Anhänger Wagners, Wagnerianer,** a Wagner enthusiast; **für die Garbo begeistert sein, ein begeisterter Verehrer, Anhänger, der Garbo sein,** to be a Garbo fan; **ein begeisterter Angler,** an enthusiastic, a keen, angler; **begeisterte Rede,** impassioned speech; **begeisternde Rede,** rousing speech; *adv.* **begeistert annehmen,** to accept enthusiastically, with enthusiasm; **begeistert über etwas sprechen,** to speak enthusiastically, with enthusiasm, of sth.

II. *vbl s.* **1. Begeistern,** *n. in vbl senses.* **2. Begeisterung,** *f.* (*a*) (sacred) inspiration, fire; afflatus; **von heiliger B. erfüllt sein,** to be filled with the sacred fire; (*b*) enthusiasm, rapture; fire; **die B. der Jugend, die jugendliche B.,** the fire, enthusiasm, of youth; **Buch, das B. hervorruft,** book that arouses enthusiasm; **j-n in B. versetzen, zu B. hinreißen,** to throw s.o. into raptures; **j-s B. entfachen, entzünden,** to arouse, excite, s.o.'s enthusiasm (for sth.); **j-s B. dämpfen,** to damp s.o.'s enthusiasm, ardour; **in B. (über etwas) geraten,** to go into raptures (over sth.); *F:* to enthuse over, about (sth.); **von B. für etwas erfüllt sein,** to be fired with enthusiasm for sth.; **B. erfüllte alle Herzen,** enthusiasm fired all hearts; **er ist leicht zu B. hingerissen, läßt sich leicht zu B. hinreißen,** he is easily moved to enthusiasm; **seine B. ging auf mich über, er steckte mich an mit seiner B.,** he fired me with his enthusiasm; **voll B. über etwas, j-n, sprechen,** to speak with enthusiasm of sth., s.o.; **mit B. sprechen,** to speak with warmth, with feeling; **etwas mit B. annehmen,** to accept sth. with enthusiasm, enthusiastically; **etwas ohne B. tun,** to do sth. without any enthusiasm, unenthusiastically, to do sth. half-heartedly, in a half-hearted way; *F:* **etwas mit B. tun,** to love, adore, doing sth.

begeisterungsfähig, *a.* capable of enthusiasm; easily moved to enthusiasm.

Begeisterungsfähigkeit, *f.* capacity for enthusiasm.

begichten, *v.tr. Metall:* to charge (shaft furnace).

Begichtungskübel, *m. Metall:* charging bucket.

Begier, *f.* **-/.** *Lit:*=**Begierde.**

Begierde, *f.* **-/-n. 1.** (ardent) desire, wish (**nach,** for); longing, craving, hunger (**nach,** for); **B. nach Lob,** desire, craving, eagerness, for praise; **B. nach Erfolg,** eagerness to succeed, craving for success; **er hatte eine (starke) B. nach Macht,** he had a craving for power; **er empfand eine heftige B., sie zu sehen,** he felt a craving, an eager desire, to see her; **das machte meine B., ihn zu sehen, nur noch größer,** this only heightened, increased, my desire, eagerness, to see him. **2.** (covetous, fleshly) desire; appetite, lust; *Phil:* appetite; **geschlechtliche B.,** sexual desire, appetite; **von B. verzehrt,** consumed with desire; **Begierden erwecken,** to arouse covetous desires; **fleischliche Begierden,** lusts of the flesh, fleshly lusts; **die (fleischlichen) Begierden abtöten,** to mortify the carnal lusts, the lusts of the flesh; **böse, sündhafte, Begierden in j-m entfachen, erwecken,** to kindle unholy desires, lusts, in s.o.

-begierde, *comb.fm. f.* **-/.** desire for . . . , eagerness for . . . ; **Wißbegierde,** thirst for knowledge; **Ruhmbegierde,** desire for, eagerness for, fame; **Machtbegierde,** desire for power.

begierig, *a.* desirous, eager, anxious, keen, hungry; **b. auf etwas** *acc.*, **nach etwas,** *Lit:* **etwas** *gen.*, **sein,** to be desirous of, eager for, hungry for, sth; to hunger after, for, sth.; **(darauf) b. sein, etwas zu tun,** to be eager, anxious, keen, to do sth., desirous of doing sth.; **b., anzufangen,** eager, anxious, to start; **ich bin b. (darauf), ihn zu sehen,** I am eager, anxious, to see him; **er ist nicht sehr b., sie zu treffen,** he is not very anxious to meet her; **j-n auf etwas b. machen,** to arouse s.o.'s appetite for sth., to set s.o. (all) agog for sth.; *adv.* eagerly, anxiously, keenly; **b. zuhören,** to listen eagerly, keenly.

-begierig, *comb.fm. a.* eager, hungry, for . . . ; **wißbegierig,** eager, hungry, for knowledge; **ruhmbegierig,** eager, hungry, for fame.

begierlich, *a.*, **Begierlichkeit,** *f. A:*=**begehrlich, Begehrlichkeit.**

begießen, *v.tr.* (*strong*) (*a*) to pour (liquid) on, over (sth., s.o.); to water (plants, etc.); *Poet:* **etwas mit seinen Tränen b.,** to water sth. with one's tears; *Cu:* **den Braten b.,** to baste the meat; *F:* **dastehen wie ein begossener Pudel,** to stand bewildered; to stand abashed; to stand looking sheepish; (*b*) *F:* to celebrate (sth.) (with a drink); **das müssen wir b.!** this calls for a drink! **einen Handel b.,** to wet a bargain, a deal.

Begine [be'gi:nə], *f.* **-/-n. 1.** *Ecc:* Beguin(e). **2.** *Cost:* hood (of Beguine nun); (baby's) bonnet.

Beginenhof, *m.* Beguine convent.

Beginn, *m.* **-(e)s/.** beginning, start, commencement, outset; **zu B.,** at the start; at first; to start with; **bei, zu, B.**+*gen.*, at the beginning of . . . ; **zu B. des Semesters,** at the beginning of term; *Th: etc:* **'B. der Vorstellung 8 Uhr',** 'performance begins, commences, at 8 o'clock'; **bei B. der Vorstellung,** at the beginning of the performance, when the performance begins, commences; when the curtain rises; **5 Minuten vor, nach, B. der Vorstellung,** 5 minutes before, after, the performance begins. *Cp.* **Anfang.**

beginnen. I. *v.* (*strong*) **1.** *v.tr.* (*a*) to begin, start, commence; to undertake; to open (conversation, debate, etc.); **seine Arbeit b.,** to begin start, one's work; **eine Rede mit einem Zitat b.,** to begin a speech, to open, with a quotation; **ein neues Leben b.,** to start afresh, to turn over a new leaf; (*b*) to take (sth.) in hand; to set **one's** hand to, address oneself to (task); to set about (task); **ich weiß nicht, wie ich es b. soll,** I don't know how to set about it, how to do it; (*c*) to manage, contrive, to do (sth.); to do (sth.); **was soll ich damit b.?** what am I to do with it? **ich weiß nicht, was ich b. soll,** I don't know what to do; I don't know which way, where, to turn. **2.** *v.i.* (*haben*) (*a*) to begin, start, commence; **die Vorstellung beginnt um 7 Uhr,** the performance starts, begins, commences, at 7 o'clock; **das Stück beginnt mit einem Prolog,** the play begins, starts, commences, opens, with a prologue; **die Heide beginnt am Ende dieser Straße,** the heath starts, begins, at the end of this road; **der Regen hat gerade begonnen,** it has just started to rain; **morgen beginnt die Schule,** school, term, starts tomorrow; **er hatte als Arzt begonnen,** he had begun as a doctor; *Prov:* **wohl, gut, begonnen, halb gewonnen,** well begun is half done; (*b*) **b., etwas zu tun,** to begin, start, to do sth.; to begin, start, doing sth.; **zu lachen, weinen, zu singen, b.,** to begin, start, to laugh, to cry, to sing; to begin, start, laughing, crying, singing; **es beginnt zu regnen,** it is beginning, starting, to rain; it is coming on to rain; **damit b., etwas zu tun, daß man etwas tut,** to begin, start, by doing sth.; (*c*) *Lit:* (*introduction of, or insertion in, direct speech*) **er, sie, begann; begann er, sie,** he, she, said, began; said he, she. *Cp.* **anfangen.**

II. *vbl s.* **Beginnen,** *n.* **1.** *in vbl senses.* **2.** activity, doings; undertaking; enterprise; **vergebliches, nutzloses, B.,** fruitless effort(s); **seltsames, wunderliches, B.,** strange doings; **kühnes B.,** bold undertaking; bold enterprise; **ein großes B.,** a mighty undertaking.

Beginner, *m.* **-s/-**=**Anfänger.**

begipsen, *v.tr.* to plaster (over) (sth.).

beglänzen, *v.tr. Poet:* to shine on, upon (sth.); **der volle Mond beglänzte den See,** the full moon shone upon the lake.

beglasen, *v.tr.* to glaze (window, etc.).

beglauben, *v.tr. A:*=**beglaubigen.**

beglaubigen. I. *v.tr. Adm: Jur: etc:* **1.** to attest, certify, authenticate (document, copy, signature); **amtlich b.,** to legalize, exemplify (document, copy, signature); **eine Unterschrift amtlich b. lassen,** to have a signature legalized; **beglaubigte Abschrift,** attested, certified, exemplified, copy; **die Richtigkeit der Abschrift wird hiermit beglaubigt . . . ,** I certify this a true copy . . . , 'certified true copy'. **2. einen Gesandten bei einer Regierung b.,** to accredit an ambassador to a government.

II. *vbl s.* **1. Beglaubigen,** *n. in vbl senses.* **2. Beglaubigung,** *f. in vbl senses; also:* (*a*) attestation, authentication (of document, copy, signature); **amtliche B.,** legalization (of document, copy, signature); **öffentliche B. einer Erklärung,** declaration authenticated by a notary public; (*b*) accreditation (of ambassador) (to a government).

Beglaubiger, *m.* **-s/-.** *Jur: etc:* attestor; certifier.

Beglaubigungsschreiben, *n. Com: Dipl: etc:* credentials.

begleichen. I. *v.tr.* (*strong*) *Com: etc:* to settle, discharge, pay (off) (bill, debt); **ich werde meine Schulden bei Ihnen im kommenden Monat b.,** I shall settle (up) with you next month; **wir möchten Sie höflichst bitten, die Rechnung vollständig zu b.,** we should be glad if you would settle the bill in full.

II. *vbl s.* **1. Begleichen,** *n. in vbl senses.* **2. Begleichung,** *f. in vbl senses; also:* settlement, discharge, payment (of bill, debt); **vollständige, restlose, B.,** payment, settlement, in full; **zur (vollständigen, restlosen) B. . . . ,** in (full) settlement . . . ; **zur teilweisen B. des noch ausstehenden Betrages . . . ,** in part payment of the outstanding balance.

begleißen, *v.tr.*=**beglänzen.**

Begleit, *n.* **-(e)s/.** *A:*=**Begleitung,** *q.v. under* **begleiten II.**

Begleitadresse, *f. Post:* despatch note.

Begleitbrief, *m.*=**Begleitschreiben.**

begleiten. I. *v.tr.* (*weak*) to accompany. **1.** (*a*) to go, come, with (s.o.); **begleiten Sie mich?** are you coming with me? **j-n zur Tür b.,** to see s.o. to the door; **j-n nach Hause b.,** to see, take, s.o. home; **j-n zum Bahnhof, zur Bahn, b.,** to accompany s.o. to the station, to see s.o. off; **j-n ein Stück (Weges) b.,** to go part of the way with

s.o.; *Corr:* **begleitender Brief,** covering letter; (*b*) to escort, attend (on) (s.o. as a retinue, etc.); **von seinem Sekretär, von einem General, begleitet,** accompanied by his secretary, by a general; **von seinen Leuten begleitet sein,** to be attended by one's servants; **j-n zu Pferde b.,** to escort s.o. on horseback; **Priester, von zwei Chorknaben begleitet,** priest attended by two choir boys; **eine Reisegesellschaft b.,** to escort a party of tourists; **darf ich Sie nach Hause b?** may I escort you home, see you home? (*c*) **unsere besten Wünsche begleiten Sie,** our best wishes go with you, attend you; **das Alter und die Übel, die es begleiten,** old age and its attendant ills; **meine Bestrebungen waren von Erfolg begleitet,** success attended my efforts; **Schönheit ist oft von Hochmut begleitet,** beauty is often accompanied by arrogance; **er begleitete seine Worte mit lebhaften Gebärden,** he accompanied his words with lively gestures; **Lungenentzündung von hohem Fieber begleitet,** pneumonia accompanied by a high temperature; **begleitender Umstand**=**Begleitumstand.** 2. *Mus:* (i) to accompany (s.o.) (on an instrument); (ii) to play, take, the second part; (iii) to sing the descant; **j-n auf dem Klavier, auf, mit, der Geige, b.,** to accompany s.o. on the piano, on, with, the violin; **sein Lied mit der Gitarre b.,** to sing to the guitar; **sie begleitet sich selbst,** she plays her own accompaniments; **begleitende Stimme**=**Begleitstimme.**

II. *vbl s.* 1. **Begleiten,** *n. in vbl senses.* 2. **Begleitung,** *f.* (*a*) company; **in j-s B. sein,** to be accompanied by s.o., to be in s.o.'s company; to be attended by s.o.; to be escorted by s.o.; **sind Sie allein oder in B.?** are you alone or is there anyone with you? **darf ich Ihnen meine B. anbieten, gnädige Frau?** may I escort you, madam? **er kam in B. einer reizenden jungen Dame,** he was accompanied by, he was in the company of, a charming young lady; **in B. seines Sekretärs, eines Generals,** accompanied by his secretary, by a general; **in B. seiner Leute,** attended by his servants; **sie machten einen Spaziergang in B. einer Gouvernante,** they went for a walk escorted by a governess; (*b*) train, retinue, suite, attendants (of sovereign, etc.); **in j-s B. sein,** to be in s.o.'s train, suite, retinue (*cp.* (*a*)); **der Prinz und seine B.,** the prince and his attendants; (*c*) *Mus:* accompaniment; **ohne B. singen,** to sing unaccompanied.

Begleiter, *m.* **-s/-.** 1. (*a*) companion; **sein treuer, steter, B.,** his faithful, his constant, companion; (*b*) attendant (of sovereign, etc.); escort (to a lady); **der Prinz und seine Begleiter,** the prince and his attendants, and his train, retinue, suite. 2. *Mus:* accompanist.

Begleiterin, *f.* **-/-innen.** 1. (i) (lady) companion; (ii) chaperon. 2. *Mus:* (lady) accompanist.

Begleiterscheinung, *f.* accompanying, attendant, concomitant, symptom *or* phenomenon; concomitant; **diese Gebrechen sind die Begleiterscheinungen des Alters,** these infirmities are attendant on, are the concomitants of, come with, old age; **das Alter und seine üblen Begleiterscheinungen,** old age and its attendant ills, old age and the discomforts that come with it; **die unangenehmen Begleiterscheinungen der Grippe,** the discomforts accompanying, attached to, attendant on, 'flu; **erhöhte Kriminalität ist eine B. der Wohlstandsgesellschaft,** increased criminality accompanies the affluent society.

Begleitjäger, *m. Av:* escort fighter.

Begleitkommando, *n. Mil:* escort (detachment).

Begleitmannschaft, *f. Mil:* escort.

Begleitmusik, *f.* background music; incidental music.

Begleitpapier, *n.* accompanying document.

Begleitschein, *m. Com:* way-bill; *Cust:* permit; bond-note.

Begleitschiff, *n. Navy:* escort vessel.

Begleitschreiben, *n.* covering letter; *Com:* letter of advice, advice-note.

Begleitstern, *m. Astr:* satellite.

Begleitstimme, *f. Mus:* (i) (*in part-singing*) supporting voice; (ii) secondary part.

Begleitumstand, *m. usu. pl.* **Begleitumstände,** accompanying, attendant, concomitant, circumstances; incidental circumstances.

Begleitung, *f. see* **begleiten II.**

begleitungsweise, *adv.* by way of accompaniment.

Begleitzettel, *m. Cust: Rail:* customs clearance certificate.

Beglik [ˈbɛklik], *n.* **-s/-s.** *Turk.Adm:* beylic.

beglotzen, *v.tr.* to gaze open-eyed at (s.o., sth.); to stare round-eyed at (s.o., sth.); to goggle at (s.o., sth.).

beglücken. I. *v.tr.* 1. (*of thg*) **j-n b.,** to make s.o. happy, feel happy; **ihre Nähe, ihre Liebe, beglückte ihn,** her presence, her love, made him happy, gave him a feeling of happiness; **das beglückende Gefühl seiner Liebe,** the warm feeling of his love; **es beglückt mich, mein Herz, ihn zu hören,** it rejoices my heart to hear him, it makes me happy to hear him; **deine Zustimmung hat mich tief beglückt,** your consent has made me most happy; **über etwas beglückt sein,** to be happy about, over, sth., to feel happiness about, over, sth.; **sie lächelte beglückt,** she smiled happily. 2. *usu. Iron:* **j-n mit etwas b.,** to present s.o. with sth.; **j-n (mit seinem Besuch) b.,** to treat s.o. to a visit, to favour s.o. with a visit, to give s.o. the pleasure of a visit; **j-n mit seiner Gegenwart b.,** to treat s.o. to one's company; **meine Tante wird uns nächste Woche schon wieder (mit ihrem Besuch) b., wir werden nächste Woche schon wieder von meiner Tante beglückt,** we shall have the pleasure of my aunt's company, we shall be blessed with my aunt, again next week.

II. *vbl s.* **Beglückung,** *f.*=**Beglücktheit.**

Beglücker, *m.* **-s/-,** benefactor (of mankind, etc.).

beglückseligen, *v.tr. A:*=**beglücken.**

Beglücktheit, *f.* happiness; felicity; **ein Gefühl tiefinnerer B.,** a feeling of deep happiness.

beglückwünschen. I. *v.tr.* **j-n zu etwas b.,** to congratulate s.o. on sth., on having done sth.; to compliment s.o. (on success, etc.); **erlauben Sie mir, Sie zu b.,** allow me to congratulate you; **sie sind beide zu b.,** they are both to be congratulated.

II. *vbl s.* **Beglückwünschung,** *f.* congratulation; **darf ich Ihnen meine herzlichste B. aussprechen?** may I offer you my warmest congratulations?

begnaden, *v.tr.* 1. (*of God, etc.*) to endow (s.o.) (with talents, virtues, etc.); **begnadeter Künstler,** inspired artist; highly gifted artist. 2. *A:*=**begnadigen.**

begnadigen. I. *v.tr. Jur:* to pardon (s.o.); to reprieve (s.o.); to grant (s.o.) a free pardon; **j-n durch Amnestie(erlaß) b.,** to amnesty s.o.; **j-n zu lebenslänglichem Zuchthaus b.,** to commute the death sentence on s.o. (in)to one of penal servitude for life.

II. *vbl s.* 1. **Begnadigen,** *n. in vbl senses.* 2. **Begnadigung,** *f. in vbl senses; also:* pardon; free pardon; mercy; reprieve; **allgemeine B.,** general pardon, amnesty; **Recht der B.,** right of pardon; **B. zu lebenslänglichem Zuchthaus,** commutation of the death sentence (in)to one of penal servitude for life.

Begnadigungsbrief, *m. Jur:* pardon; reprieve.

Begnadigungsgesuch, *n. Jur:* petition for reprieve, mercy; appeal for mercy; **ein B. machen,** to petition for mercy; to appeal for mercy.

Begnadigungsrecht, *n. Jur:* right of pardon.

begnügen (sich), *v.refl.* **sich mit etwas b.,** *A:* **sich** *acc., occ. dat.,* **etwas b. lassen, sich mit, an, etwas** *dat.,* **b. lassen,** to be content, satisfied, with sth., to content oneself with sth.; to make shift, to make do, with sth.; **sich damit b., etwas zu tun,** to be content, satisfied, to content oneself, with doing sth.; **sich mit Wenigem b.,** to be content with little, to have only few wants, needs, requirements; **Pflanze, die sich mit wenig Wasser begnügt,** plant that requires only a little water; **mit bloßen Worten begnüge ich mich nicht,** I am not satisfied with mere words, mere words do not satisfy me; **ich kann mich mit einer solchen Erklärung nicht b.,** I cannot be satisfied with such an explanation; **ich werde mich mit der Hälfte b.,** I shall make shift, make do, with half the amount; **du wirst dich damit b. müssen,** you will have to make shift, make do, with that; **ich kann mich damit nicht b.,** that's not enough, that won't do, for me; **ich möchte mich damit b. zu bemerken, daß . . . ,** I will merely point out that . . . .

begnüglich, begnügsam, *a. A:* content, satisfied (**mit, an**+*dat.*, with); (pers.) of few wants.

Begoniazeen [be·goːnĭa·ˈtseːən], *f.pl. Bot:* begoniaceae.

Begonie [be·ˈgoːnĭə], *f.* **-/-n.** *Bot:* begonia, *F:* elephant's ear.

begönne, begonnen *see* **beginnen.**

begönnern, *v.tr.* to treat (s.o.) condescendingly, patronizingly, in a patronizing manner; **ich lasse mich nicht von ihr b.,** I won't allow her to patronize me.

begoß, begossen *see* **begießen.**

begraben, *v.tr.* (*strong*) to bury (corpse, animal, object); to inter (corpse); to entomb (corpse); **j-n auf hoher See b.,** to bury s.o. at sea; **j-n mit militärischen Ehren b.,** to bury s.o. with military honours, to give s.o. a military funeral; **j-n lebendig b.,** to bury s.o. alive; *F:* **das hieße, sich lebendig b.,** that would mean burying oneself alive (*in a remote place*); **auf dem Friedhof zu X begraben liegen,** to be buried, to lie, in the cemetery at X; **die See begrub ihre Opfer,** the sea swallowed up its victims; **unter dem Schutt begraben,** buried in the ruins; *F:* **das Kriegsbeil b.,** to bury the hatchet; **ich fand es unter meinen Papieren begraben,** I found it buried under my papers; **etwas in Vergessenheit b.,** to consign sth. to oblivion; **einen Plan b.,** to bury a plan in oblivion; **sie möchte die ganze Sache begraben und vergessen sein lassen,** she wishes the whole thing buried and forgotten; **alle Hoffnungen b.,** to bury all one's hopes; **seine Meinungsverschiedenheiten b.,** to sink one's differences; **ein Geheimnis in seinem Herzen b.,** to hide away a secret in one's heart; *F:* **da möchte ich nicht begraben sein,** I wouldn't live there if you paid me; *F:* **wenn ich das tun soll, dann kann ich mich auch gleich b. lassen,** if I have to do that I might as well give up; *F:* **du kannst dich b. lassen,** go and boil your head; *F:* **da liegt der Hund begraben,** that's why; that's the point; that's where the trouble lies.

Begräbnis, *n.* **-nisses/-nisse.** 1. (*a*) burial, interment; entombment; **kirchliches B.,** Christian burial; **j-m ein christliches B. verweigern,** to refuse Christian burial to s.o.; (*b*) funeral; **feierliches B.,** funeral with full ceremonial; obsequies; **militärisches B.,** military funeral; **B. erster Klasse,** (i) expensive funeral; (ii) *F:* adroit disposal (of s.o.); **beim B.,** at the funeral; **an j-s B. teilnehmen, j-s B. beiwohnen,** to attend s.o.'s funeral. 2. burial-place; (last) resting-place.

Begräbnisfeier, *f.* funeral (ceremony).

Begräbnisfeierlichkeiten, *f.pl.* funeral ceremonies; obsequies.

Begräbnisgebühren, *f.pl.* funeral fees.

Begräbniskasse, *f.* burial society.

Begräbniskosten, *pl.* funeral expenses; funeral fees.

Begräbnisort, *m.* (*a*)=**Begräbnisstätte;** (*b*)=**Begräbnisplatz.**

Begräbnisplatz, *m.* burial-ground, cemetery.

Begräbnisriten, *m.pl.* funeral rites, burial rites.

Begräbnissitten, *f.pl.* burial customs; funeral rites, burial rites.

Begräbnisstätte, *f.* burial-place; (last) resting-place; **die B. der deutschen Kaiser,** the resting-place of the German emperors.

begradigen, *v.tr.* to straighten (alignment of a road, frontier, course of a river); *Mil:* to shorten (the front).

begrannt, *a. Bot:* bearded, aristate.

begrasen, *v.tr.* 1. (*of cattle*) to graze (on) (pasture). 2. to put (land) under grass; **begrast,** grass-covered.

begreifbar, *a.*=**begreiflich.**

begreifen, *v.tr.* (*strong*) 1. *A:* to touch (sth.); to handle (sth.). 2. **etwas in sich b.,** *occ.* **etwas b.,** to contain, comprise, include, embrace, cover, sth.; *Lit:* to comprehend sth.; **dieser eine Satz begreift alle unsere Probleme in sich, in diesem einen Satz sind alle unsere Probleme begriffen,** this sentence embraces all our problems, sums up all our problems in a nutshell, all our problems are summed up in this sentence; **in etwas** *dat.* **begriffen sein,** to be included in sth. (*cp.* 4). 3. to understand, comprehend; **der Junge begreift schwer, leicht,** the boy is slow-minded, slow in, on, the uptake; the boy is nimble-minded, quick in, on, the uptake; **ich habe seine Beweisführung nicht begriffen,** I did not grasp, get, his point; **die Bedeutung einer Sache b.,** to grasp the importance of a matter; **ich fange an zu b., langsam, allmählich, begreife ich,** I am beginning to understand; **ich kann es nicht b.,** I can't understand it, it is beyond me; **es ist nicht zu b.,** I am, we are, at a loss to understand it; it is impossible to understand; **es ist schwer zu b., es läßt sich schwer b., wie er so etwas tun konnte,** it is hard to understand, it is difficult to understand, how he could do such a thing; **ich kann nicht b., wie du mit diesem Menschen verkehren kannst,** it is beyond me how you can associate with that person, I fail to understand your association with that person; **das läßt sich leicht b.,** that's easily understood, that is easy to see. 4. **in etwas** *dat.* **begriffen sein,** (*of pers.*) to be engaged in, busy, doing sth.; to be in the act of doing sth.; (*of thg*) to be in (the) process of sth.; **sie waren in Unterhandlung(en) begriffen,** they were engaged

in negotiations; **er war im Aufbruch begriffen,** he was just leaving, he was on the point of leaving; **auf einer Reise begriffen sein,** to be on a journey; **auf dem Wege zum Erfolg begriffen sein,** to be on the road to success; **in der Entwicklung begriffen,** in process of (i) formation, (ii) development; **in Ausdehnung begriffen,** in process of extension; **in der Ausführung begriffen,** (work) in process of being carried out, (work) under way, in progress; **in Reparatur begriffen,** under repair; **im Umbau begriffen,** (building, etc.) in process of (constructional) alteration; **im Bau begriffen,** (building, etc.) in process of construction; **die Wunde ist in (der) Heilung begriffen,** the wound is healing up; **mitten in der Arbeit begriffen sein,** to be in the midst of one's work.

begreiflich, *a.* (*a*) understandable; comprehensible; **das ist leicht b.,** that is easily understood; **leicht begreifliche Tatsache,** (i) easily understood, grasped, fact; (ii) fact easily accounted for; **begreifliche Angst, Aufregung,** understandable fear, excitement; **sein Beweggrund war die begreifliche Sorge um sein Geld,** his motive was the understandable fear for his money; **es ist mir durchaus b., daß du wütend bist,** I can well understand your being furious, I find your anger quite natural; **es ist mir absolut nicht b., wieso ich schuld sein soll,** I entirely fail to see, I cannot see at all, why I should be to blame; **sein merkwürdiges Verhalten wird mir allmählich b.,** I am gradually coming to understand his strange conduct; (*b*) **j-m etwas b. machen,** to make s.o. understand, see, sth.; to bring sth. home to s.o., to make sth. clear to s.o.; **j-m den Vorteil eines Unternehmens b. machen,** to point out clearly the advantage of a project to s.o.; **j-m b. machen, was er verloren hat,** to bring it home to s.o. what he has lost; **ich werde (es) ihm schon b. machen, daß er mit mir nicht zu rechnen braucht,** I shall make it clear to him, bring it home to him, that he needn't count on me.

begreiflicherweise, *adv.* understandably; naturally; **man griff ihn an; b. wehrte er sich,** he was attacked; naturally he hit back; **er war b. ärgerlich,** naturally, understandably, he was annoyed.

begrenzen. I. *v.tr.* **1.** (*a*) to bound, to form the boundary of (country, etc.); *Mth:* to bound (surface, solid); to intercept (surface, space); **Italien ist im Norden von den Alpen begrenzt, die Alpen begrenzen Italien im Norden,** Italy is bounded to the north by the Alps, the Alps form the northern boundary of Italy; (*b*) to define (concepts, etc.). **2.** (*of knowledge, mental faculties, etc.*) **begrenzt sein,** to be limited, to be restricted; **sein Wissen ist sehr begrenzt, er hat ein sehr begrenztes Wissen,** his knowledge is very limited; **meine Zeit ist begrenzt,** my time is restricted; **die Rededauer ist auf 15 Minuten begrenzt,** the time-limit for speeches is 15 minutes.

II. *vbl s.* **1. Begrenzen,** *n. in vbl senses.* **2. Begrenzung,** *f.* (*a*) *in vbl senses; also: Clockm:* **B. (der Unruhe),** banking; (*b*)= **Begrenztheit**; (*c*) boundary; limit; *Mth:* surface (of solid), side, face, surface (of polyhedron), limiting line (of surface); **obere, untere, B.,** top, bottom (of object); **seitliche B.,** side (limit); lateral surface.

Begrenztheit, *f.* limitation (of knowledge, etc.); **enge B.,** narrowness (of mental outlook, etc.).

Begrenzungsfläche, *f. Mth: etc:* (bounding) surface (of solid); periphery (of rounded body); side, face (of polyhedron); **obere, untere, seitliche, B.=obere, untere, seitliche, Begrenzung,** *q.v. under* **begrenzen II.**

Begrenzungslicht, *n. Veh:* side-lamp; **Begrenzungslichter** *pl,* side-lamps; side-lights.

Begrenzungslinie, *f.* boundary (line), bounding line; *Mth:* limiting line; periphery (of curvilinear figure).

Begrenzungsschicht, *f.* limiting layer.

Begriff, *m.* **-(e)s/-e. 1.** *A:* sum; summary; compendium. **2. im B. sein, stehen, etwas zu tun,** to be on the point of doing sth., to be about, to be going, to do sth.; **ich war im B., etwas zu sagen,** I was about, going, to say something, I was on the point of saying something; **gerade als er im B. war zu gehen,** just as he was about to leave, on the point of leaving; *Hum:* **ich bin im Begriff(e) des Begreifens,** I am just about to do it. **3.** understanding, apprehension, comprehension; **schwer von B. sein,** to be slow in understanding, slow of apprehension, comprehension, dull-witted, slow-witted, slow in, on, the uptake; **das geht über meine Begriffe, meinen B.,** that is beyond my understanding, comprehension, that passes my comprehension, *F:* that is beyond, above, me. **4.** (*a*) imagination; conception, idea, notion; **sich** *dat.* **einen B. von etwas machen,** to imagine sth., to form an idea, a notion, of sth., to conceive of sth.; **du kannst dir keinen B. davon machen,** you can't imagine (it); **du machst dir keinen B. davon, wie beunruhigt ich war,** you have no idea how anxious I was; **Sie haben sich einen falschen B. von meiner Vermögenslage gemacht,** you have formed a wrong idea, notion, a wrong estimate, of my financial position; **einen klaren B. von etwas haben,** to have a clear conception, idea, notion, of sth.; **einen hohen B. von der, von seiner, Pflicht haben,** to have a high conception, idea, of one's duty; **er hat einen merkwürdigen B. von (der) Pflicht,** he has a curious idea, notion, of duty; **j-m einen allgemeinen B. von etwas geben,** to give s.o. a general idea of sth.; **um Ihnen einen B. zu geben . . . ,** to give you an idea . . . ; **nach meinen Begriffen ist das kein Glück,** that is not my idea of happiness, I wouldn't call that happiness; **über alle Begriffe,** inconceivably, indescribably; **ihre Schönheit übersteigt alle Begriffe,** she is inconceivably beautiful, she is indescribably beautiful; her beauty is beyond description; (*b*) *Gram: etc:* term; **gleichbedeutender, bedeutungsgleicher, B.,** synonym; **bedeutungsähnlicher B.,** near-synonym; **entgegengesetzter B.,** opposite, antonym; **grammatikalischer B.,** grammatical term; **geographischer B.,** (i) geographical term; (ii) geographical concept; (*c*) *Phil: Log:* concept; conception, notion; *Log:* term (of syllogism); **historischer B.,** historical concept; **allgemeiner B.,** (universal) concept, universal; **die fünf logischen Begriffe,** the five predicables, the universals; **abstrakter B.,** abstract concept, abstraction; **der B. 'Pferd', der B. des Pferdes,** the concept 'horse'; **klarer, fest umrissener, scharf abgegrenzter, B.,** clearly defined concept; **Umfang eines Begriff(e)s,** extent, extension, of a concept; **Inhalt eines Begriff(e)s,** content of a concept, connotation; **der B. des Guten bei Plato,** Plato's concept, conception, of (the) good; (*d*) **das, es, ist mir ein, kein, B.,** that, it, means something to me, does not mean anything to me; **er ist mir kein B.,** his name does not mean anything to me; **Bruckner ist mir kein B.,** Bruckner is a mere name to me; Bruckner does not mean anything to me; **ist Ihnen das ein B.?** does that mean, convey, anything to you?

begriffen, *p.p. & a. see* **begreifen.**

begrifflich, *a. Phil: Log:* conceptual; abstract; **begriffliche Synthese,** conceptual synthesis; **begriffliche Bestimmung eines Wortes,** (conceptual) definition of a word; **begriffliches Denken,** thinking in concepts; thinking in the abstract; **begriffliche Bedeutung eines Wortes,** abstract meaning of a word; *adv.* **etwas b. bestimmen,** to give a (conceptual) definition of sth., to define sth. (conceptually); **etwas b. erfassen,** to form a (precise) concept of sth.

Begriffsbestimmung, *f. Phil: etc:* definition (of concepts).

Begriffsbildung, *f. Phil: etc:* conception, forming of concepts.

Begriffsform, *f. Phil:* conceptual category, predicament.

Begriffsinhalt, *m. Phil: Log:* content of a concept; connotation.

Begriffsklasse, *f.*=**Begriffsform.**

begriffsmäßig, *a.*=**begrifflich.**

Begriffsschrift, *f.* **1.** *Log: etc:* pasigraphy. **2.** ideogram, ideograph.

begriffsstutzig, *a.* (*of pers.*) dull, obtuse, dull-witted, slow-witted, slow in, on, the uptake, *F:* thick-headed.

Begriffsstutzigkeit, *f.* dullness, slowness (of wit), obtuseness, stupidity.

Begriffssynthese, *f. Phil:* conceptual synthesis.

Begriffsumfang, *m. Phil: Log:* extent, extension, of a concept.

Begriffsvermögen, *n.* (*a*) understanding, apprehension, comprehension; **Rede, die das B. der Zuhörer übersteigt,** speech above the heads of the audience; **in den Grenzen des kindlichen Begriffsvermögens,** within the comprehension of a child; (*b*) *Phil: Log:* (faculty of) conception.

Begriffsverwechslung, *f. Phil: etc:* confusion of concepts.

Begriffsverwirrung, *f. Phil: etc:* confusion of concepts; *F:* **er leidet an B.,** he is a little confused.

Begriffswort, *n.* **-(e)s/-wörter.** *Gram:* notional term.

begründen. I. *v.tr.* **1.** to found (empire, business, college, newspaper, etc.); to set up, establish (business, etc.); to float (company, etc.); to start (business, newspaper, etc.); (*in art, philosophy, etc.*) **eine Schule, Richtung, b.,** to found, to be the founder of, a school; **eine Dynastie b.,** to be the founder of a dynasty; **einen eigenen Hausstand b.,** to set up house; **er hat diese Industrie, diesen Industriezweig, begründet,** he founded, was the founder of, this industry; **seine Macht b.,** to establish one's power. **2.** (*a*) to substantiate (claim, charge, statement, etc.); to establish (claim, charge); to give arguments in support of (statement); **können Sie das näher b.?** could you substantiate that a little further? could you give a little more evidence to support that? (*b*) to state, give, the reason, the grounds, for (sth.); **eine Entscheidung b.,** to state one's reasons for a decision; **sein Tun b., b., warum man etwas tut,** to give one's reasons for doing sth.; **er begründete seine Weigerung damit, daß . . . ,** he gave as the reason for his refusal the fact that . . . ; **womit begründet er seine Leugnung dieser Tatsache?** what are his grounds for denying this fact? **womit begründest du deine Abneigung gegen ihn?** what is your reason for disliking him? *Jur:* **ein Urteil b.,** to give the grounds for a judgment; (*c*) *Gram:* **begründend,** causal (conjunction, etc.).

II. *vbl s.* **1. Begründen,** *n. in vbl senses.* **2. Begründung,** *f.* (*a*)=II. 1; *also:* foundation (of empire, business, college, newspaper, school, dynasty, etc.); (*b*) substantiation, establishment (of claim, charge, etc.); **B. einer Behauptung,** substantiation of a statement; foundation for a statement; (*c*) reason, ground; **er gab mir keine B. für sein Verhalten,** he gave me no reasons for his conduct; **er hatte eine sehr gute B. bereit,** he had a very good reason ready; **er entschuldigte sich mit der B., krank zu sein,** he excused himself on the grounds of illness; *Jur:* **B. eines Urteils,** grounds for a judgment.

III. *p.p. & a.* **begründet,** *in vbl senses; esp.* well-founded, well-grounded, reasonable, justified (hope, suspicions, etc.); **(wohl) begründeter Verdacht,** well-founded, well-grounded, fully justified, suspicions; **mein Verdacht war nicht b.,** my suspicions were unfounded, groundless, unjustified.

Begründer, *m.* founder (of business, school, race, dynasty, etc.).

begrünen, *v.tr.* (*of spring, etc.*) to make (fields, etc.) green, *Lit:* verdant; (*of tree, field, etc.*) **sich b.,** to grow, become, green; **mit, von, Efeu begrünte Mauer,** wall green with ivy.

begrüßen. I. *v.tr.* **1.** to greet, welcome (s.o.); to receive (s.o.) (at one's home); to say hullo, good morning, good day, etc., to (s.o.); **sie begrüßte ihre Gäste,** she greeted, welcomed, received, her guests; **die Kinder begrüßten den Onkel mit lautem Freudengeschrei,** the children gave their uncle a noisy welcome; **j-n mit Beifallsrufen b.,** to greet, receive, s.o. with cheers; **sein Erscheinen wurde mit lang anhaltendem Beifall begrüßt,** his appearance was hailed, greeted, with prolonged applause; **j-n mit einer Ansprache b.,** to address a welcome to s.o.; **ich freue mich, Herrn X in unserer Mitte b. zu können,** I am pleased to welcome Mr X among(st) us; **j-n mit Handschlag b.,** to shake hands with s.o.; **hast du Frau X heute morgen schon begrüßt?** have you said good morning to Mrs X? **ich habe sie schon auf der Straße begrüßt,** I have already met her in the street; (*in letter of invitation*) **wir würden uns freuen, Sie Sonntag abend bei uns b. zu dürfen,** we should like to have the pleasure of your company on Sunday evening. **2.** to welcome (step, decision, opportunity, etc.); **eine Diskussion b.,** to welcome a discussion; **die Entscheidung wurde allseitig wärmstens begrüßt,** the decision was warmly welcomed by all. **3.** *A:* **j-n um etwas b.,** to petition s.o. for sth., to ask s.o. for sth.

II. *vbl s.* **1. Begrüßen,** *n. in vbl senses.* **2. Begrüßung,** *f.* (*a*) salutation, greeting; (*at end of letter*) **mit freundlicher B. (verbleibe ich) Ihr(e) . . . ,** (I remain) yours truly . . . , yours sincerely . . . ; (*b*) welcome; **der Präsident sprach einige Worte der B.,** the president spoke a few words of welcome; **nach einigen Worten der B.,** after a few words of welcome.

Begrüßungsansprache, *f.* address of welcome.

Begrüßungsformel, *f.* salutation.

Begrüßungswort, *n.* (*a*) (*pl,* **-wörter**) word of greeting; salutation; (*b*) word(s) of welcome; **Begrüßungsworte** *pl.* words of welcome.

begucken, *v.tr.* to look at (s.o., sth.).

Beguine [beˈgiːnə], *f.* -/-n = Begine.

Begum [ˈbeːgum], *f.* -/-en, (*in India*) begum, queen, princess.

begünstigen. I. *v.tr.* **1.** to favour (s.o.), to show favour towards, partiality for (s.o.); **von j-m begünstigt werden,** to be favoured by s.o.; to be s.o.'s favourite; **vom Glück begünstigt,** favoured by fortune. **2.** (*a*) to favour, to be in favour of (s.o.'s plans, interests, etc.); to encourage, foster (s.o.'s plans, actions, vices); (*of circumstances, etc.*) to facilitate, to be favourable to (s.o.'s plans, etc.), to promote, foster (progress, etc.); (*of success, action, etc.*) **von den Umständen begünstigt sein,** to be favoured by circumstances; **Regen begünstigt das Wachstum,** rain promotes growth; **das feuchte Klima begünstigte die Ausbreitung der Seuche,** the damp climate helped to spread, favoured the spread of, the epidemic; *Lit:* **von der Nacht begünstigt,** under favour of the night; (*b*) *Jur:* to be (an) accessory after the fact to (s.o.'s crime).
II. *vbl s.* **1. Begünstigen,** *n. in vbl senses.* **2. Begünstigung,** *f.* (*a*) = II. 1; *also:* encouragement, facilitation (of plan, etc.); promotion (of progress, etc.); (*b*) encouragement (for sth.); favour; *Lit:* **unter der B. der Nacht,** under favour of the night; *Jur:* **j-m B. gewähren,** to be an accessory after the fact to s.o.'s crime.

Begünstiger, *m.* -s/-. *Jur:* accessory after the fact.

begürten, *v.tr.* to gird (s.o.) (with sth.); **sich mit dem Schwert b.,** to gird (on) one's sword; **seine Lenden b.,** to gird up one's loins.

begutachten. I. *v.tr.* to give an expert opinion on (sth.); to appraise, evaluate (damage); **etwas b. lassen,** to have an expert's report made on sth.; **eine Arbeit b.,** to value, evaluate, work done, *Constr:* to survey a building, etc., for work done.
II. *vbl s.* **1. Begutachten,** *n. in vbl senses.* **2. Begutachtung,** *f.* (*a*) = II. 1; *also:* expert valuation; expert appraisement; (*b*) expert opinion, expert's report.

Begutachter, *m.* -s/-, expert; valuer.

begüten, *v.tr. A:* = **begütigen.**

begütert, *a.* wealthy, rich, well-to-do; **er war ein begüterter Mann,** he was a wealthy man, a man of wealth; he was a man of property.

Begüterung, *f. A:* wealth.

begütigen, *v.tr.* to soothe (s.o.), to calm (s.o.) (down); to appease (s.o.).

behaaren (sich), *v.refl.* (*of animal, plant, etc.*) to grow hair; (*of part of human body*) to become covered with hair; **die kahle Stelle wird sich wieder b.,** hair will grow again on the bald patch.

behaart, *a.* (*a*) (*of human body, animals, plants*) hairy; **rauh b.,** hirsute; **stark behaarte Beine,** legs covered with a strong growth of hair, (very) hairy legs; (*b*) *Nat.Hist:* crinite; pilose, pilous; **seidig b.,** sericeous, with silky hair; **dicht, wollig, b.,** woolly, tomentose, tomentous; (*c*) *Bot:* downy, villous, villose; pubescent; comose, comate (seed); (*of plant*) **rauh b.,** hirsute; **mit behaartem Stengel,** hairy-stemmed.

Behaartheit, *f.* hairiness; *Nat.Hist:* pilosity; *Bot:* villosity; pubescence.

Behaarung, *f.* **1.** (*a*) growth of hair; (*b*) = **Behaartheit;** *Med:* **übermäßige B.,** excessive growth of hair, hypertrichosis, pilosis. **2.** hair (of human body, animals, plants); *Bot:* down, pubescence.

behaben (sich). I. *v.refl.* **1.** *A:* to behave (oneself). **2.** *Swiss Dial:* (*a*) to restrain oneself; (*b*) to occupy, busy, oneself (with sth.); (*c*) to complain (about sth., s.o.).
II. *vbl s.* **Behaben,** *n.* behaviour; deportment.

behäbig, *a.* easy-going (pers.); (pers.) who likes his ease, his comforts; (pers.) who is not easily put out; unworried, unperturbed (pers.); **ein dicker, behäbiger Wirt,** a fat, comfortable-looking innkeeper; **eine behäbige alte Frau,** *F:* a comfortable old body; **im überfüllten Abteil saß eine Bauersfrau behäbig auf ihrem Platz,** in the overcrowded compartment a peasant woman sat at ease, placidly, unperturbed, in her seat; **er saß b. in seiner Ecke,** he sat there in his corner at his ease, taking his ease; *Pej:* **feiste, behäbige Bürger, die an nichts denken als an ihr Bier und ihr Geld,** fat, stodgy townsmen who think only of their beer and their money.

Behäbigkeit, *f.* easy-going character; comfortable appearance *or* nature; placidness; **sie saß da in breiter B.,** she sat there at her ease, placidly, unperturbed.

behacken, *v.tr. Agr:* to hoe (root-crops, vineyard, etc.).

behaftet, *a.* afflicted, cursed (with disease, etc.); burdened (with debts, etc.); **mit Fehlern b.,** full of defects, faults; **er wird sein Leben lang mit Schulden b. sein,** he will be burdened with debts, he will be in debt, he will have debts, all his life; **mit einer entstellenden Narbe b. sein,** to be afflicted with, to have, a disfiguring scar; *F:* **mit einer Brille b. sein,** to be cursed with spectacles; *Hum:* **sie ist mit fünf Kindern b.,** she is saddled, afflicted, with five children.

behagen. I. *v.i.* (*haben*) (*of thg*) **j-m b.,** to please s.o., to be to s.o.'s taste; **eine Arbeit, die ihm wenig behagt,** work which he finds rather unpleasant, disagreeable, which is not to his taste, his liking; **nichts behagt ihm, nichts will ihm b.,** nothing pleases, suits, him; **ein solches Leben behagt mir nicht,** such a life is not to my taste, does not appeal to me; I care little for such a life; **unsere Kost behagt ihm wohl nicht mehr,** he does not seem to like our food any more, our food does not seem to suit him any more; *impers.* **es behagt mir hier nicht,** I do not like it here, it does not suit me here; **tu, wie es dir behagt,** do as you please, please yourself, suit yourself; **sich's bei etwas b. lassen,** to enjoy sth. at leisure; **sie ließen's sich beim Wein b.,** they enjoyed their wine at leisure, in comfort, they relished their wine; **sich's bei j-m b. lassen,** to enjoy s.o.'s company, to feel at home in s.o.'s house; **er ließ es sich dort b.,** he felt at home there, he liked it there.
II. *vbl s.* **Behagen,** *n.* pleasure; enjoyment, relish; content(ment), contentedness; **(sein) B. an etwas** *dat.* **finden, (sein) B. daran finden, etwas zu tun,** to find (one's) pleasure in sth., in doing sth.; **nach seinem B. tun, handeln,** to do as one pleases; **er zog mit sichtlichem B. an seiner Zigarre,** he puffed at his cigar with visible enjoyment, relish; **er trank seinen Wein mit, in, stillem B.,** he drank his wine with quiet enjoyment; **die Katze rieb (sich) mit B. ihren Kopf an seiner Schulter,** the cat rubbed its head on his shoulder luxuriously; **er erzählte die Geschichte immer mit großem B.,** he always told the story with great relish; **in stillem häuslichem B. leben,** to live in the quiet contentment of one's home.

behaglich, *a.* **1.** *A:* pleasant, agreeable; sweet; **dem Auge b.,** pleasant, pleasing, to the eye; **ein behaglicher Mensch,** a pleasant, an agreeable, person; **behagliches Lächeln,** sweet smile. **2.** comfortable; cosy, snug (room, etc.); **ein behagliches Leben führen,** to lead a calm, tranquil life; to lead an easy life; **in behaglicher Ruhe,** in quiet comfort; **sein behagliches Auskommen haben,** to have a comfortable income, to be comfortably off; **ein behagliches Stübchen,** a cosy, snug, little room; **es ist warm und b. hier,** it is warm and cosy, comfortable, here; *adv.* **sich b. fühlen,** to feel, be, comfortable, cosy; to feel, be, at (one's) ease; to feel at home; **machen Sie es sich b.,** make yourself comfortable; **b. im Sessel sitzen,** to sit snugly in one's armchair; **b. im Bett liegen,** to lie snug in bed; **sie saßen b. beim Feuer,** they were sitting comfortably by the fire, they had made themselves snug by the fire; **etwas b. genießen,** to enjoy sth. at leisure.

Behaglichkeit, *f.* **1.** *A:* pleasure; relish; satisfaction. **2.** ease, easiness, comfort; (feeling of) well-being; **seine B. lieben,** to like one's comfort, one's ease; **in der B. seines häuslichen Lebens,** in the cosy comfort of his family life.

behalsbandet, *a. Her:* (*of hound, etc.*) collared.

behalten, *v.tr.* (*strong*) to keep. **1.** (*a*) **den Hut auf dem Kopf b.,** to keep one's hat on; **den Ring am Finger b.,** to keep one's ring on (one's finger); **ein Bonbon lange im Mund b.,** to keep a sweet in one's mouth for a long time; **bitte behalten Sie Platz!** please remain seated! please don't get up! (*b*) **darf ich das Geld b.?** may I keep the money? **du kannst das Buch, das ich dir geliehen habe, b.,** you may keep the book I lent you; **ich möchte das Buch noch eine Weile b.,** I should like to keep the book a little longer; **etwas für sich b.,** to keep sth. for oneself; (*cp.* 1 (*c*)); **er hat einen Teil davon weggegeben und einen Teil (für sich) behalten,** he gave some of it away and some of it he kept (for himself); **vom letzten Wurf haben wir zwei Kätzchen behalten,** we kept two kittens from the last litter; (*c*) **etwas für sich b.,** to keep sth. to oneself; **ich habe meine Eindrücke für mich behalten,** I kept my impressions to myself; **seine Gedanken für sich b.,** to keep one's thoughts to oneself, to keep one's own counsel; **behalt es für dich!** keep it to yourself, *F:* keep it under your hat! **deine dummen Bemerkungen kannst du für dich b.,** you may keep your silly remarks to yourself; **etwas bei sich b.,** to hold one's tongue, to keep sth. to oneself; **er kann nichts bei sich b.,** (i) he can't keep anything to himself, he can't keep a secret; (ii) he can't keep any food, anything, down; (*d*) **die Oberhand b.,** to keep the upper hand; **recht b.,** to be right in the end; **j-n im Auge b.,** (i) to keep s.o. under one's eye; not to let s.o. out of (one's) sight; (ii) to bear s.o. in mind; **etwas im Auge b.,** not to lose sight of sth.; to bear sth. in mind; **j-n lieb b.,** not to lose one's affection for s.o.; **j-n in liebendem Andenken b.,** to keep s.o.'s memory green; **j-n in ehrendem Andenken b.,** to honour s.o.'s memory; **etwas im Griff b.,** to retain hold of sth.; **die Gewalt, Kontrolle, über sein Auto b.,** to retain control of one's car, to keep one's car under control; (*e*) **etwas für später b.,** to keep sth. for later (on); **etwas übrig b.,** to have sth. left (over); **von allem, was er besaß, behielt er nur noch ein Haus,** he was left with only one house out of all his property; **er ist fast ganz wiederhergestellt, nur den Husten hat er behalten,** he has almost completely recovered, but he still has a cough; **seinen englischen Akzent b.,** not to lose one's English accent; *B:* **und welchen ihr sie (= die Sünden) b. werdet, denen sind sie behalten,** and whose soever sins ye retain they are retained; *Ar:* **zwei hinschreiben, fünf b.,** put down two and carry five; (*f*) **j-n zu Hause b.,** to keep s.o. at home; **j-n bei sich b.,** to keep s.o. (with one); **j-n zu Tisch b.,** to make s.o. stay for dinner; **j-n als Geisel b.,** to hold, keep, detain, s.o. as a hostage; **j-n im Dienst b.,** to retain s.o.'s services; to keep s.o. on; **j-n im Amt b.,** to maintain s.o. in office. **2.** to retain (sth.) (in one's mind); **ich kann es nicht b.,** I can't (manage to) remember it; **etwas im Kopf b.,** to keep, retain, sth. in one's head; **das Kind kann nichts (im Kopf) b.,** the child can't keep a thing in his head; **etwas im Gedächtnis b.,** to retain sth. in one's memory, to keep sth. in remembrance, to keep sth. in mind; **etwas klar im Gedächtnis b.,** to retain a clear memory of sth.; **ich habe diesen Vorfall gut (im Gedächtnis) behalten,** this incident has stuck in my memory; **ich werde es, ihn, stets in angenehmer Erinnerung b.,** I shall always retain, have, an agreeable memory of it; I shall always like to remember it, him; **etwas im Sinn b.,** to keep sth. in mind; **etwas im Herzen b.,** to treasure sth. in one's mind; *B:* **die das Wort hören und behalten in einem feinen, guten Herzen,** they, which in an honest and good heart, having heard the word, keep it. **3. seine Fassung b.,** to keep, maintain, one's composure, to keep one's countenance; to keep one's head, to keep cool; **seine Ehre b.,** to preserve one's honour; **seinen guten Ruf b.,** to keep, maintain, one's good reputation; **seine Illusionen, seine Unschuld, b.,** to keep one's illusions, one's innocence; **seine gute Figur b.,** to keep one's figure; **sein jugendliches Aussehen b.,** to keep one's looks; (*of thg*) **seine Form, seine Farbe, b.,** to keep its shape, colour; *B:* **denn wer sein Leben will b., der wird's verlieren,** for whosoever will save his life shall lose it.

Behälter, *m.* -s/-, container; receptacle; (*for water oil, etc.*) tank; (coal-)bunker; *Ind:* (gas-, oil-, etc.) holder; (vacuum, ice-, etc.) chamber; *Ch: Ind:* receiver; *El:* (accumulator, etc.) tank; *Rail: Com:* container.

Behälterverkehr, *m. Rail: etc:* container traffic.

Behälterwagen, *m. Rail:* **1.** tank-wagon, *U.S:* tank car. **2.** container-wagon.

Behältnis, *n.* -nisses/-nisse. **1.** container; receptacle. **2.** store-room; (storage) closet; (store) cupboard.

behämmern, *v.tr.* to hammer (metal, etc.).

behandeln. I. *v.tr.* to treat (s.o., sth.). **1.** (*a*) **j-n gut, schlecht, b.,** to treat s.o. well, badly; **sie wird von ihrer Tante schlecht, nicht gut, behandelt,** she is badly treated by her aunt, her aunt treats her badly; her aunt is unkind to her; **j-n milde, mit Milde, b.,** to deal leniently with s.o.; **j-n anständig b.,** to deal civilly with s.o.; to treat s.o. civilly; **ich weiß, wie man ihn b. muß,** I know how to deal with him, how to handle him; **j-n von oben herab b.,** to behave patronizingly to s.o., to put on airs with s.o.; **die Art, wie er, mit der er, seine Freunde behandelt,** the way he treats his friends, his treatment of his friends; **ich habe ihn ziemlich rauh, unsanft, behandelt,** I treated him rather roughly; **stiefmütterlich behandelt werden,** to get a raw deal; **die Natur hat sie etwas stiefmütterlich behandelt,** nature has been unkind to her; **j-n wie einen Freund, als Freund, b.,** to treat s.o. like, as, a friend; **j-n wie ein Kind b.,** to treat s.o. like a child;

j-n wie seinesgleichen b., to treat s.o. as an equal; j-n wie Dreck b., to treat s.o. like dirt; to look on s.o. as so much dirt; etwas als Witz b., to treat sth. as a joke; (*b*) Werkzeuge, Maschinen, usw., mit Sorgfalt b., to treat tools, machines, etc., with care; zerbrechliche Waren müssen beim Transport vorsichtig, mit Vorsicht, behandelt werden, breakable goods should be handled with care in carriage; seine Bücher mit Sorgfalt, sorgfältig, b., to treat one's books with care; die Manuskripte sind beim Benutzen mit Sorgfalt zu b., the manuscripts should be handled with care. 2. (*a*) to treat (patient, disease); to attend (patient); einen Kranken, eine Krankheit, mit Chinin b., to treat a patient, a disease, with quinine; sich wegen Krebs b. lassen, wegen Krebs behandelt werden, to be treated for cancer, to undergo treatment for cancer; er wurde durch ein Versehen auf Rheumatismus behandelt, he was treated for rheumatism by mistake; Sie müssen sich ärztlich b. lassen, you must have medical attention; wer, welcher Arzt, behandelt Sie? which doctor is treating, attending, you? who is your doctor? der behandelnde Arzt, the doctor in attendance; (*b*) *Ch: Ind: etc:* ein Metall mit einer Säure b., to treat a metal with an acid; Quartz mit Quecksilber b., to treat quartz with mercury; hartnäckige Flecken sind beim Waschen besonders zu b., obstinate stains must be treated with special care in washing. 3. to discuss, handle, treat, deal with (subject); (*of book, etc.*) to treat of, deal with (subject); einen Gegenstand erschöpfend b., to treat a subject exhaustively, to make an exhaustive study of a subject; to exhaust a subject; die Dinge leichtfertig b., to make light of things.

II. *vbl s.* 1. Behandeln, *n. in vbl senses.* 2. Behandlung, *f.* (*a*) *in vbl senses; also:* treatment (of pers., thg, patient, subject, etc.); attendance on (patient); (*b*) treatment; schlechte B., maltreatment, ill-treatment; ich habe eine solche B. nicht von dir erwartet, I did not expect such treatment from you; eine solche B. bin ich nicht gewöhnt, I am not accustomed to such treatment; noch nie war ihm eine so gerechte B. widerfahren, never had he been treated with such fairness; das Thema hat eine erschöpfende B. erfahren, the subject has been treated exhaustively; (*c*) nach dreimaliger B., nach drei Behandlungen, mit der Salbe wird der Ausschlag verschwinden, the eczema will disappear after three applications of the ointment; (*d*) (medical) treatment; (medical) attention; sich in ärztliche B. begeben, to put oneself under a doctor, to have medical treatment; Kranke in B., patients under treatment; wegen Krebs in B. sein, sich einer B. wegen Krebs unterziehen, to undergo treatment for cancer, to be treated for cancer; sie ist bei Dr. X wegen Rheumatismus in B., she is having treatment from Dr X, she is being treated by Dr X, for rheumatism; Sie müssen in ärztliche B. gehen, you must have medical attention; er wird sich zur B. in ein Krankenhaus begeben, he is going to have treatment in a hospital.

behändigen, *v.tr.* to hand (sth.) (over), to deliver (sth.); Behändigung *f,* delivery.

Behandler, *m.* -s/-, treater (of subject, etc.).

Behandlungsart, Behandlungsmethode, *f.* (method of) treatment.

Behandlungsstuhl, *m.* patient's chair, *esp.* (i) examination chair; (ii) dentist's chair.

Behandlungsweise, *f.* (way of) treatment; eine solche B. bin ich nicht gewöhnt, I am not accustomed to such treatment.

behandschuht, *a.* gloved.

Behang, *m.* -(e)s/⸗e. 1. (*a*) hangings, tapestry; *A:* arras; (*b*) (*any pendant ornament, e.g.*) tassels, fringes. 2. fruit hanging on a tree, crop; unsere Apfelbäume haben guten B. dieses Jahr, our apple-trees have a good crop this year. 3. *Ven:* lop-ears, pendulous ears (of hunting dog). 4. fetlock (of horse).

behängen, *v.tr.* (*conj. like* hängen[2]) 1. to hang, drape (room, wall, etc.) (with tapestries, etc.); to adorn, deck (out), decorate (sth.) (with pendant ornaments, chains, studs, etc.); ein Tor mit Girlanden b., to hang a gate with garlands, festoons, to festoon, garland, a gate; schwarz behangene, behängte, Kirche, church hung, draped, with black; Standbild mit Blütengirlanden behängt, behangen, statue garlanded with flowers; der Weihnachtsbaum war ganz mit Sternen und Lametta behängt, behangen, the Christmas-tree was loaded with stars and tinsel; sich mit Schmuck b., to cover, load, oneself with jewellery; sie war von oben bis unten (mit Schmuck) behangen, behängt, she was bejewelled from head to toe; seine ganze Brust war mit Orden behängt, behangen, he was beribboned and bemedalled; die Bäume waren voll behangen (mit Früchten), the trees were laden (with fruit). 2. *Ven:* to train (dog) on the leash.

beharken, *v.tr.* to rake (path, etc.); *Mil: Av:* to rake (position, etc.) with gun-fire.

beharren. I. *v.i.* (*haben*) 1. (*a*) *Phil: etc:* (*of substance, etc.*) to remain unchanged, constant, to remain, to persist; das beharrende Sein, the permanent being, the unchangeable substance; die Substanz beharrt, substance remains identical, remains unchanged, constant, substance persists; (*b*) *Ph: etc:* (*of body, etc.*) to remain in a state of inertia, to remain inert; to remain motionless. 2. (*of pers.*) (*a*) *A. & B:* to persevere; to continue; to endure; *B:* wer aber beharret bis ans Ende, der wird selig, he that shall endure to the end, the same shall be saved; (*b*) in etwas *dat.* b., to persevere in sth.; in der Sünde b., to continue in sin; im Guten b., to live in righteousness; im Glauben b., to be steadfast in one's faith, to continue, persevere, in one's faith; bei seiner Arbeit b., to keep, stick, to one's work; (*c*) auf etwas *dat.* b., to persist in sth.; auf seiner Meinung b., to persist in, to stand by, to stick to, one's opinion; auf seinem Entschluß b., etwas zu tun, to persist in, to adhere to, one's decision to do sth.; er beharrt darauf, he persists in it; he sticks to it; sie beharrte auf dieser Lüge, she persisted in this lie.

II. *vbl s.* 1. Beharren, *n. in vbl senses.* 2. Beharrung, *f. in vbl senses; also:* (*a*) perseverance (in sth.); persistence (in one's opinion, etc.); adherence (to one's decision to do sth.); (*b*) *Phil: etc:* constancy, permanence, permanency (of substance, etc.); *Ph: etc:* (i) inertness (of body); (ii) inertia; *Biol:* epistasis; *Ph:* das Gesetz der B. = Beharrungsgesetz, das.

III. *pr.p. & a.* beharrend, *in vbl senses; esp. Phil: etc:* permanent; unchanged, unaltered; persistent; das Beharrende, the persistent; the unchangeable substance.

beharrlich, *a.* (*a*) (*of pers.*) steady, steadfast, persevering, assiduous (in doing sth., in one's work, etc.); b. im Glauben sein, to be steadfast in one's faith, to continue, persevere, in one's faith; *adv.* b. an seiner Arbeit sitzen, to do one's work assiduously, steadfastly; (*b*) constant (work, fidelity, etc.); untiring, unceasing (effort, etc); dogged (work, etc.).

Beharrlichkeit, *f.* perseverance; assiduity; doggedness; mit B., perseveringly; doggedly; B. beim Studium, close application to study, perseverance in study; er erreicht alles durch B. allein, he achieves everything solely by dint of perseverance.

Beharrung, *f. see* beharren II.

Beharrungsfutter, *n. Husb:* maintenance ration (of fodder).

Beharrungsgesetz, das. *Ph: etc:* the law of inertia.

Beharrungsmoment, *n. Ph: etc:* moment of inertia.

Beharrungsvermögen, *n. Ph: etc:* inertia, *vis inertiae;* das Gesetz des Beharrungsvermögens = Beharrungsgesetz, das.

beharzen, *v.tr.* to resin (sth.); to dip (firewood, etc.) in resin; to impregnate (laminated plastic, etc.) with resin.

Beharzungsmaschine, *f. Ind:* Beharzungs- und Imprägniermaschine, impregnating machine (for laminated plastic, etc.).

behauben, *v.tr.* to hood (hawk, etc.).

behauchen, *v.tr.* (*a*) to breathe (up)on (s.o., sth.); einen Spiegel b., to breathe upon a mirror; (*b*) *Ling:* to aspirate (consonant).

behauen, *v.tr.* (*conj. like* hauen) (*a*) to hew, dress (up), square (stone); to trim, dress (piece of wood); to rough-hew (statue); roh behauene Steinblöcke, rough-hewn blocks of stone; *Constr:* (vierkant) behauenes Holz, scantling(s), squared timber; (*b*) *Arb:* to prune, trim (trees).

behäufeln, *v.tr. Hort: Agr:* to earth (up), ridge, hill (plants, *esp.* potatoes).

behaupten. I. *v.tr.* 1. to keep, retain, possession of (sth.); to maintain, retain (position, etc.); sich b., (i) to hold one's own, to stand one's ground; (ii) *Com: Fin:* (*of prices, etc.*) to remain firm, steady; to be maintained; sich b., sich in seiner Stelle b., to retain, hold on to, one's position; eine Festung, sich in einer Festung, b., to retain control of a fortress; seine Rechte b., to assert one's rights; seinen Thron, sich auf seinem Thron, b., to keep, retain, one's throne, to remain (up)on the throne; sich gegen j-n, etwas, b., to stand up against s.o., sth.; er wird sich hier, bei uns, nicht b. können, he won't be able to hold out, last out, here for very long. 2. to claim (to know sth., to be sth., etc.); to declare, assert, affirm, maintain (that ...); etwas b., to make an assertion; man soll nie etwas b., was man nicht beweisen kann, one should never assert anything that one cannot prove; er behauptet, daß er unschuldig sei, er sei unschuldig, he declares, maintains, that he is innocent, he declares, asserts, his innocence; ich behaupte das Gegenteil, I maintain the opposite; ich behaupte, daß es nicht wahr ist, I maintain that it is not true; der Zeuge behauptete, daß er den Angeklagten gesehen habe, den Angeklagten gesehen zu haben, the witness claimed to have seen the accused; ich habe immer behauptet, daß ..., I have always contended that ...; ich würde das nicht so leichtsinnig b., I shouldn't be so quick to assert that; *F:* das kann der stärkste Mann nicht b., 'nobody can claim that. 3. man behauptet, daß ..., es wird behauptet, daß ..., die Leute behaupten, daß ..., it is said that ..., they say that ...; man behauptete, er sei tot, he was said, alleged, to be dead; man behauptet allgemein, er habe zwei Frauen, es wird von ihm behauptet, er habe zwei Frauen, he is said to have two wives, they say he has two wives; von niemandem läßt sich b., er habe ihn verstanden, nobody can be said to have understood him; das kann man von ihm nicht b., you cannot say that of him.

II. *vbl s.* 1. Behaupten, *n. in vbl senses; also:* maintenance (of position, opinion, etc.); declaration, affirmation, assertion (of opinion, etc.); *Gram:* Verben des Behauptens, verbs of statement. 2. Behauptung, *f.* (*a*) = II. 1; (*b*) declaration, assertion, affirmation; allegation; *Log: Geom:* proposition; eine B. aufstellen, machen, to make a declaration, an assertion, an affirmation; to make a contention; seine Behauptungen beweisen, to prove one's assertions; nach seiner eigenen B., according to his own statement; das ist eine kühne B., that is a bold statement.

Behauptungssatz, *m. Gram:* clause of statement.

behausen. I. *A: v.tr.* to lodge, accommodate, house (s.o.); *occ.* sich b., to settle (in town, etc.); behaust, (pers.) with a home; (pers.) resident, domiciled (in a place).

II. *vbl s.* Behausung, *f.* 1. *in vbl senses; also:* accommodation (of s.o.). 2. lodgings, accommodation; dwelling(-place); home; seine ärmliche B., his humble dwelling; menschliche Behausungen, human habitations.

Behaviorismus [bi·he·vio'rismus], *m.* -/. *Psy:* behaviourism.

beheben. I. *v.tr.* (*strong*) 1. to remove (difficulty, etc.); to put an end to (abuse, etc.); to redress, remedy (abuse, damage, etc.); to repair (damage); to rectify (fault); to relieve (traffic jam, etc.); der Schaden war schnell behoben, the damage was soon mended. 2. *Austrian:* Geld b., to draw out, withdraw, money (from the bank, etc.).

II. *vbl s.* Beheben *n.,* Behebung *f. in vbl senses; also:* (*a*) removal (of difficulty, etc.); relief (of traffic jam, etc.); (*b*) *Austrian:* withdrawal (of money) (from the bank).

beheimatet, *a.* (in einem Land, usw.) b. sein, (i) (*of pers.*) to be resident, domiciled (in a country, etc.), to have one's home, to live (in a country, etc.); (ii) (*of pers., animal, etc.*) to be a native (of a country, etc.), to come (from a country, etc.); (*of pers.*) to hail (from a country, etc.); (*of work of art, custom, religion, etc.*) to come (from a country, etc.); (*of ship*) in Bremen, Hamburg, b. sein, to hail from Bremen, Hamburg; in London beheimatetes Schiff, ship hailing from London, ship whose home port is London.

Beheimatung, *f.* (*a*) permanent home, address; (*b*) place of origin.

beheizen, *v.tr.* to heat, warm (room, etc.); Beheizung *f,* heating.

Behelf, *m.* -(e)s/-e. 1. *A:* (*a*) help, resource; (*b*) *Austrian:* = Hilfsmittel 1 (*a*); (*c*) *Jur:* (i) adminicle, corroboratory evidence; (ii) excuse, subterfuge. 2. makeshift; die Baracke ist nur ein B., bis das Haus fertig ist, the hut is only a makeshift till the house is ready.

behelfen (sich), *v.refl.* (*strong*). 1. *A:* to help oneself; sich mit etwas b., to know how to use sth., to make use of sth. 2. to make do, to make shift; sich mit wenig b., to make do with little; er wird sich schon irgendwie b., he will make do, manage, somehow; wir müssen uns in dieser kleinen Wohnung noch eine Weile b., we must make do in this small flat for a little while

longer; **haben Sie etwas, womit Sie sich vorläufig b. können?** have you anything you can make do with, improvise with, for the time being?

Behelfsbrücke, *f.* temporary bridge; improvised bridge.

Behelfshaus, Behelfsheim, *n.* temporary house, home.

behelfsmäßig, *a.* temporary, makeshift, rough and ready (apparatus, accommodation, etc.); *adv.* **etwas b. reparieren,** to repair sth. temporarily; to patch sth. up.

Behelfsmaßnahme, *f.* temporary measure; emergency measure.

behelligen. I. *v.tr.* to worry, trouble, bother, pester (s.o.); to disturb (s.o.); **darf ich Sie mit einer Frage b.?** may I trouble you with a question? do you mind if I ask you a question? **er gelangte an sein Ziel, ohne von jemandem behelligt zu werden,** he reached his goal without being disturbed by anyone.

II. *vbl s.* **Behelligung,** *f.* **1.** *in vbl senses.* **2.** trouble; disturbance; **ohne weitere B.,** without further trouble, without being bothered any further.

behelmt[1], *a.* (*a*) helmeted; (*b*) *Nat.Hist:* galeate(d).

behelmt[2], *a.* handled (tool, etc.).

Behemoth [ˈbeːheˑmoːt], *m.* **-(e)s/-e & -s.** *B:* behemoth.

Behen [ˈbeːən], *n.* **-s/-.** *Bot:* **1.** behen; **weißes B.,** white behen. **2.**=**Behennuß.**

behend(e) [bəˈhɛnt, bəˈhɛndə], *a.* (*of pers.*) nimble, agile, sharp, quick; (*of movement, etc.*) nimble, light, dexterous; *adv.* nimbly, with agility, quickly; **b. die Treppe hinaufspringen,** to spring nimbly up the stairs.

behendig [bəˈhɛndiç], *a.*=**behend(e).**

Behendigkeit [bəˈhɛndiçkait], *f.* agility, nimbleness, quickness.

behenkelt, *a.* (*of jug, etc.*) with a handle, with handles.

Behennuß, *f. Bot:* ben-nut.

Behennußbaum, *m. Bot:* horse-radish tree.

Behennußöl, *n.*=**Behenöl.**

Behenöl, *n. Pharm:* oil of ben.

Behenwurzel, *f.* (*a*) *Bot: Pharm:* behen (root); (*b*) *Bot:* **echte B.,** (root of) white behen.

beherbergen. I. *v.tr.* (*a*) to give (s.o.) hospitality; to take (s.o.) in (as one's guest); to put (s.o.) up; to give (s.o.) shelter; to harbour (criminal, etc.); **die Obdachlosen b.,** to harbour the harbourless; *B:* **ich bin ein Gast gewesen, und ihr habt mich beherberget,** I was a stranger and ye took me in; (*b*) to take in, lodge (paying guest, etc.).

II. *vbl s.* **1. Beherbergen,** *n. in vbl senses.* **2. Beherbergung,** *f.* (*a*)=II. 1; (*b*) accommodation; lodgings.

Beherbergungsgewerbe, *n.* hotel trade.

Beherbergungssteuer, *f.* hotel and lodging tax.

beherrschen. I. *v.tr.* **1.** (*a*) to rule (country); to rule, be ruler, over (country, people); to hold, have, sway, dominion, over (people, country); **Alexander beherrschte alle Völker bis zum Indus,** Alexander held sway over all the peoples, the nations, as far as the Indus; **Rom beherrschte die damals bekannte Welt,** Rome held dominion over the then known world; **Gott beherrscht das Weltall,** God is the ruler of the universe; (*b*) to dominate (a person, one's children, etc.); to hold (s.o.) in one's power, in one's grip; to have dominion over (s.o.); (*of influence, etc.*) to dominate (an age, s.o.); *Mil:* **die See, den Luftraum, b.,** to have naval supremacy, air supremacy; *Sp:* **seinen Gegner b.,** to have the mastery over one's opponent; **von Furcht beherrscht sein,** to be dominated, ridden, by fear; **seine Leidenschaften beherrschten ihn,** he was ruled by his passions. **2.** to control (oneself, one's passions, etc.); to have control over (oneself, one's passions, etc.); to keep (one's feelings, etc.) in check; to have (one's passions, etc.) under control; **seine Zunge b.,** to be careful (of) what one says; **seine Gefühle b.,** to master one's feelings; to keep one's feelings in check; **er konnte seine Gefühle nicht länger b.,** he could not contain his feelings any longer; **man muß sich b. können,** one must (be able to) exercise self-control; **es ist manchmal schwer, sich (selbst) zu b.,** it is sometimes difficult to control oneself; self-control is sometimes a difficult thing; *F:* **danke, ich kann mich b.,** no thank you, I can resist the temptation. **3.** to be master of (subject); to have a command of (language, etc.); **mehrere Sprachen b.,** to have a command of several languages; **eine Situation b.,** to be master of, in control of, a situation. **4.** (*of mountains, etc.*) to tower over, dominate (a place); **die Festung beherrscht die Stadt,** the fort dominates, commands, the town; **die Burg beherrscht das Tal,** the castle overlooks, looks down on, dominates, the valley.

II. *vbl s.* **1. Beherrschen,** *n. in vbl senses.* **2. Beherrschung,** *f. in vbl senses; also:* (*a*) domination, rule (of people, country); (*b*) control (of horse, passions, etc.); mastery (of feelings, etc.); command (of subject, etc.); (*c*) self-control; **die B. verlieren,** to lose one's self-control.

Beherrscher, *m.* ruler (of, over, people); dominator (of people); (*of caliph*) **B. der Gläubigen,** Commander of the Faithful.

Beherrschtheit, *f.* self-control.

beherzen, *v.tr. A:* **1.** to encourage (s.o.); to instil courage into (s.o.); *see also* **beherzt. 2.**= **beherzigen** I. 2.

beherzigen. I. *v.tr.* **1.** *A:*=**beherzen** 1. **2.** to take (sth.) to heart; to mark (sth.) well; to take good heed of (sth.).

II. *vbl s.* **Beherzigung,** *f.* (*a*) *in vbl senses;* (*b*) **zur B.!** mark well! take good heed!

beherzigenswert, beherzigungswürdig, *a.* worth taking to heart.

beherzt, *a.* courageous, brave, valiant (person, action, etc.); spirited (person).

Beherztheit, *f.* courage, bravery, valiance; spirit.

behexen, *v.tr.* (*a*) to bewitch (s.o., sth.); to cast a spell, put a spell, (up)on (s.o., sth.); (*b*) *F:* to bewitch, captivate (s.o.); to turn (s.o.'s) head.

behilflich, *pred.a.* helpful, willing to help; **j-m (bei etwas) b. sein,** to help s.o. (in sth.); to be helpful to s.o. (in sth.); **kann ich Ihnen b. sein?** can I help, assist, you? can I be of assistance to you?

behindern. I. *v.tr.* to hinder, impede, hamper (s.o., s.o.'s plans, etc.); to block, obstruct (traffic, opponent, etc.); **Schwierigkeit, die unsere Pläne behindert,** difficulty that impedes our plans; **in der Ausübung seiner Pflicht behindert werden,** to be obstructed in the execution of one's duty; **seine Blindheit behinderte ihn in der Ausübung seines Berufes,** his blindness was a hindrance to him in the carrying out of his profession; **Kurzsichtigkeit behindert beim Schwimmen,** short-sightedness is a handicap in swimming; **der Flugverkehr wurde durch den Nebel stark behindert,** air traffic was badly affected, disrupted, by the fog; **ihr langer Rock behindert sie, behindert sie in ihrer Bewegung,** her long skirt hampers her, hampers her movements; **das enge Kleid behindert mich beim Atmen,** the tight dress restricts my breathing; **die hohen Bäume behindern unseren Blick,** the tall trees impede our view.

II. *vbl s.* **1. Behindern,** *n. in vbl senses.* **2. Behinderung,** *f.* (*a*) *in vbl senses; also:* obstruction; (*b*) hindrance; obstacle, impediment, obstruction (to sth.); (*c*) restriction (in breathing); (physical) disability; **er hat eine leichte B. beim Gehen,** he has a slight difficulty in walking.

III. *p.p. & a.* **behindert,** *in vbl senses; esp.* **körperlich b.,** with a physical disability; physically disabled, handicapped.

Behle, *f.* **-/-n.** *Dial:* **1.** child. **2.** old woman.

Behmlot, *n. Ph:* absolute altimeter.

behobeln, *v.tr.* to plane, smooth (wood); to planish (metal).

beholzen, *v.tr.* **1.** to cover (sth.) with wood; to reinforce (dike, etc.) with wooden stakes. **2.** (*a*) *For:* to afforest; to put (region) under timber; (*b*)=**abholzen. 3.** *Arb:* **sich beholzen,** to run to wood.

Beholzungsgerechtigkeit, *f.*, **Beholzungsrecht,** *n.* right of felling wood in a forest belonging to another person.

behorchen, *v.tr.* to listen secretly to (s.o.); to eavesdrop on (s.o.'s conversation); **wir werden behorcht,** someone is listening to us.

Behörde, *f.* **-/-n.** *Adm:* (public) authority; board; (town, etc.) council; **die Behörden,** the authorities; **die örtlichen Behörden,** the local authorities.

behördlich, *a. Adm:* official (report, seal, etc.).

behören, *v.tr. Swiss:* (*a*) to examine, test (orally); (*b*)=**behorchen.**

behörig, *a. A:*=**gehörig.**

behost, *a.* (*a*) (pers.) wearing trousers, in trousers; (*b*) feathered (legs of bird); (*c*) feathered (hind legs of dog).

Behringstraße, die=**Beringstraße, die.**

Behuf, *m.* **-(e)s/-e,** purpose, aim, object; **zum B.+** *gen.*, for the purpose of . . . ; **zu welchem B.?** for what purpose, object, to what end? **zu diesem B.,** for this purpose; *A:* **zu j-s B.,** on s.o.'s behalf.

behufs, *adv.* (+*gen.*)=**zum Behuf,** *q.v. under* **Behuf.**

behuft, *a. Z:* hoofed, ungulate (animal); **behufte Tiere,** ungulata, ungulates.

behummsen, behumpsen, *v.tr. F: Dial:* to cheat, *F:* diddle (s.o.); **sie haben dich behummst, behumpst,** *F:* you've been had.

behüten, *v.tr.* **1.** to protect, shield, guard (s.o.) (**vor etwas** *dat.*, from sth.); (*of guardian angel, etc.*) to watch over (s.o.); **j-n vor einer Gefahr b.,** to keep s.o. safe from a danger, to shield s.o. from a danger; **j-n vor Übel b.,** to keep, protect, s.o. from evil; **ein Geheimnis b.,** to keep a secret; **Gott behüte dich, euch!** God keep you! God be with you! **Gott wird uns b.,** God will keep, protect, us; **die Engel mögen dich b.!** angels guard thee! **ein behütetes junges Mädchen,** a young girl who has led a sheltered life; a carefully brought-up young girl; **behüt Gott!** God bless you! good-bye! **Gott behüte!** God forbid! heaven forbid! **behüte!** certainly not! good heavens, no! God forbid! *Hum:* **behütet sein,** to be wearing a hat. **2.** *Husb:* **eine Wiese b.,** to graze cattle on a meadow.

Behüter, *m.* **-s/-,** protector; guardian, keeper.

behutsam, *a.* careful, cautious (person, behaviour, movement, etc.); gentle (movement); **b. sein,** to be careful, to take care; *adv.* **etwas b. behandeln,** to treat sth. gently, with care; **etwas sehr b. tun,** to do sth. with great care, very carefully, with great caution, very cautiously; **sie ging b. die Treppe hinauf, um niemanden zu wecken,** she went upstairs carefully in order not to wake anyone.

Behutsamkeit, *f.* carefulness, cautiousness; gentleness.

bei[1]. I. *prep.* (+*dat.*) (*Note:* **bei dem** *is frequently contracted to* **beim,** *q.v.*) (*the uses of* **bei** *as a general link between verb or adj. and its complements are shown under the respective words that take this construction, e.g.* **j-n anschwärzen bei, sich beliebt machen bei,** *etc.*) **1.** (*denoting proximity in space*) (*a*) by, next to (sth.); near (sth.); **bei der Tür,** by the door; next to the door; at the door; **er saß bei ihr,** he sat by her, next to her; **der Vater stand bei dem weinenden Kind,** the father was standing by the crying child; **dicht bei dicht,** closely packed; **Seite bei Seite,** side by side; **ich kenne den Rhein nur bei Mainz,** I only know the Rhine at *or* near Mainz; **der Fluß fließt dicht bei unserem Haus vorbei,** the river flows right past our house; **die Schlacht bei Belle-Alliance,** the Battle of Waterloo; (*with place names*) **Altenberg bei Köln,** Altenberg near Cologne; *Hist:* **der Pfalzgraf bei Rhein,** the Count Palatine of the Rhine; (*b*) at; with; **bei uns (zu Hause),** at home, (i) at our house, (ii) in our country; **er wohnt bei Schmidts, bei uns,** he lives with the Schmidts, with us; **ich werde eine Woche bei meiner Tante bleiben,** I am going to stay with my aunt, at my aunt's, for a week; **du warst lange nicht bei mir,** it's a long time since you came to see me; **sind wir heute Abend bei ˈdir?** are we meeting at ˈyour house, place, to-night? **seine Visitenkarte bei j-m hinterlassen,** to leave one's card with s.o., at s.o.'s house; **Dokumente bei einer Bank einreichen,** to hand in documents to, at, a bank; **bei j-m anklopfen,** to knock at s.o.'s door; to give s.o. a knock (when passing); *F:* to sound s.o.; (*address on letter*) **Herrn Müller bei Schmidt,** Mr Müller, care of, c/o, Schmidt; *F:* **es ist bei uns nicht wie bei armen Leuten,** we are not rationed here, we don't stint ourselves in this house; **bei Hofe,** at court; **etwas bei Woolworth kaufen,** to buy sth. at Woolworth's; **ein Konto bei der Bank haben,** to have an account at, with, the bank; **erschienen, verlegt, bei N.,** published by N.; (*c*) **bei j-m arbeiten,** to work at, with (a firm), for (a pers.), at (s.o.'s house); **bei der Marine, bei der Luftwaffe, dienen,** to serve in the navy, in the airforce; **er arbeitet bei der Frankfurter Zeitung, bei den Olympia-Werken,** he works on the Frankfurter Zeitung, at the Olympia Works; **sie arbeitet als Dienstmädchen bei Frau Müller, bei Müllers,** she works as a maid for Mrs Müller, at the Müllers; **bei wem hast du Stunde?** with, from, whom do you take lessons? **bei wem hörst du?** whose lectures are you going to? under whom are you studying? (*d*) **es kommt bei Lessing vor,** it occurs in Lessing; **wie es bei Goethe heißt,** as Goethe says; **es steht bei Schiller,** the quotation comes from Schiller; (*e*) on, with; **hast du das Buch, die Schlüssel, bei dir?** have you (got) the book, the keys, with you? **ich habe kein Geld bei mir,** I have no money on me, about me; **das Dokument wurde bei ihm**

gefunden, the document was found on his person; *A:* **der Abbé, der schon sehr viel Wein bei sich hatte,** the Abbot, who was already well loaded with wine; (*f*) **bei sich denken,** to think to oneself; (*g*) **sei bei der Sache!** put your mind to it! concentrate! **er ist nicht bei der Sache,** his thoughts are wandering; **bei der Stange bleiben,** to keep, *F:* stick, to the point, to business; **j-n bei der Stange halten,** to keep s.o. to his, her, job, duty, course, etc.; (*h*) **es bleibt bei unserer Verabredung,** our arrangement stands, our arrangement stays just as before. **2.** (*a*) **bei den Tieren,** with animals, in the animal kingdom; **bei den Menschen,** with humans, in the human race; **bei gewöhnlichen Leuten,** with ordinary people; (*b*) **bei ihr ist alles möglich,** she is capable of anything; **bei solchen Leuten kannst du das nicht erwarten,** you cannot expect that from such people; **die Entscheidung steht bei ihm,** the decision rests with him; *B:* **bei Gott ist kein Ding unmöglich,** with God nothing shall be impossible. **3.** (*a*) (*A. & Dial:*+*acc.*) **j-n bei der Hand nehmen,** to take s.o. by the hand; **j-n bei den Haaren packen,** to seize s.o. by the hair; (*b*) **bei der Hand sein,** (*of pers., thg*) to be at hand, (*of thg*) to be handy; **zu flink bei der Hand,** over-eager, too rash; (*c*) **j-n bei seinem, beim, Namen nennen,** to call s.o. by (his) name; *occ.* **j-n bei seinen roten Haaren kennen,** to know s.o. by his red hair. **4.** (*expressing state, mood, etc.*) **nicht bei Kräften,** not in possession of one's full strength; **j-n bei guter Gesundheit treffen,** to find s.o. in good health; **bei Geld sein,** to be in funds, to be flush with money; *F:* **knapp bei Kasse,** low in funds; **(nicht) bei Sinnen,** (not) in one's right mind; **nicht bei Laune,** out of humour; **nicht ganz ˈbei sich,** not all there; **du bist wohl nicht ganz ˈbei dir,** I don't think you are quite in your right mind; **nicht bei Trost,** out of one's senses, off one's head. **5.** (*a*) (*time*) by, in, during; **bei Tag,** by day, in day-time; **bei Ebbe,** at low tide; **bei Nacht und Nebel,** under cover of night; **bei der Arbeit,** at work, while working; **bei Tisch(e),** at table; **bei einem Glas(e) Wein,** over a glass of wine; (*b*) (*point in time*) **bei dieser Nachricht,** on receiving this news; **schon bei dem ersten Versuch gelang es,** at the very first attempt it was successful; **bei seiner Ankunft,** on his arrival; **bei Gelegenheit,** when convenient; *Com:* **zahlbar bei Sicht,** payable at, on, sight; (*c*) **bei der Zubereitung ist darauf zu achten...,** during preparation care should be taken...; **bei der Bewerbung sind einzureichen...,** with application submit...; (*d*) (i) (present) at; (ii) at, during; **warst du bei der Beerdigung?** were you at the funeral? **bei der Krönung,** (i) (present) at the coronation, (ii) during the coronation (ceremony), (iii) in the coronation. **6.** (*a*) (*conditional*) **bei Verfall des Schecks,** if the cheque lapses; **bei einem Rabatt von zehn Prozent können wir die Ware abnehmen,** we can take the goods at a discount of ten per cent; **bei einer Miete von 900 Mark kann ich die Wohnung nicht nehmen,** I cannot take, afford, the flat at a rent of 900 marks; **bei günstiger Witterung,** weather permitting; **bei reiflicher Überlegung,** (up)on careful consideration; **bei näherer Bekanntschaft,** on closer acquaintance; **bei näherem Zusehen,** *F:* **bei Licht besehen,** on close examination; **bei hohem Fieber kann dieses Mittel nicht verabreicht werden,** this drug is not to be administered if the patient has a high temperature; **bei Abnahme von größeren Mengen wird ein Preisnachlaß gewährt,** discount is allowed for larger quantities; **bei steigender Produktion,** when *or* where production is rising; in conditions of rising production; **bei abnehmender Geschwindigkeit,** when *or* where speed is decreasing; with decreasing speed; (*b*) **bei Tageslicht,** by daylight; **bei Kerzenlicht,** by candle-light; **bei jedem Wetter,** in all weathers; *Phot:* **nur bei rotem Licht zu entwickeln,** develop in, by, red light; *Cu:* **bei mittlerer Hitze (zu) backen,** bake in a moderate, moderately hot, oven; (*c*) **bei dieser Hitze,** in this heat; **bei diesem schönen Wetter,** on a fine day like this; (*d*) **bei dieser Unordnung kann man nichts finden,** you can't find anything in this muddle; **j-n bei Brot und Wasser einsperren,** to lock s.o. up on bread and water; (*in weather forecast*) **bei westlichen Winden Temperaturen auf 10° ansteigend,** westerly winds, temperatures rising to 10°; (*e*) (*in spite of*) **bei all(en) seinen Fehlern ist er ein guter Arbeiter,** with, for, all his faults he is a good worker; **bei alledem,** for all that; (*emphatic phrase*) **bei aller Liebe, das geht wirklich nicht,** with all goodwill, making every possible allowance, it just won't do. **7.** (*a*) (*in oaths, affirmations*) **bei Gott schwören,** to swear by God; **bei meiner Ehre,** on my honour; *A:* **bei meinem Eid,** upon my oath; (*in exclamations*) **bei Gott,** by God! by Jove! (*b*) **bei Todesstrafe,** on pain of death; **das Betreten (des Grundstücks) ist bei Strafe verboten,** trespassers will be prosecuted. **8.** (*a*) *A:* (*approximate number*) **es waren bei 2000 Mann,** there were about 2000 men; **bei sieben Fuß lang,** about seven feet long; (*b*) *A. & South G.Dial:* **bei Pfunden einkaufen,** to buy by the pound; (*c*) *occ.* **j-n bei Heller und Pfennig bezahlen,** to pay s.o. the last farthing; (*d*) (*approximate time*) *North G.Dial:* **es ist bei fünfe,** it is about five; **nun wird es bei kleinem Zeit,** it's very nearly time (to go to bed, etc.); (*e*) **er war bei weitem der Fähigste,** he was by far the most efficient. **9.** *A. & Dial:* (+*acc.*) to; **komm bei mich,** come to me; **er setzt sich bei das Feuer,** he sits down by the fire; **bei die Hühner sehen,** to see to the chickens.

II. **bei,** *adv.* (*a*) (*emphasized by other particles*) **dicht bei, nahe bei,** near by, hard by, close by; **er wohnt nahe bei,** he lives near by; (*b*) *Nau:* **alles bei (haben),** (to be) under full sail. **2.** (*colloquially abbreviated from* **dabei, wobei, herbei, hierbei,** *q.v.*) **da ist kein Vorteil bei,** there is no profit in it; **da will ich auch bei sein,** I want to be there too.

bei- *comb.fm.* **1.** (*with nouns*) (*a*) (*denoting pers., object, of parallel status* = **mit-**) joint...; co-; **Beivormund** *m,* co-guardian; **Beierbe** *m,* co-heir, joint heir; *Mth:* **Beiwert** *m,* coefficient; (*b*) (*denoting sth. ancillary* = **neben-**) accessory...; secondary...; subsidiary...; subordinate...; side-; **Beistrom** *m,* secondary stream, current; **Beiwagen** *m,* side-car; **Beiknecht** *m,* under servant; **Beiklang** *m,* overtone; **Beiblatt** *n,* supplement; (*c*) (*denoting sth. added*) supplementary..., extra...; **Beifutter** *n,* supplementary, extra, auxiliary, fodder; **Beilast** *f,* auxiliary, extra, cargo; **Beizoll** *m,* extra duty. **2.** (*with intr. verbs*) (*a*) *A:* near, by; up; **beistehen,** to stand by; **beikriechen,** to creep up; (*b*) with; **j-m beiliegen,** to lie with s.o.; **etwas** *dat.* **beiliegen,** to be enclosed with sth.; **j-m beistimmen,** to agree with s.o. **3.** (*with tr. verbs*) (*denoting addition of sth. to sth.*=**an-, dazu-, hinzu-, zu-**) (i) to; on to; (ii) with; into; **etwas etwas** *dat.* **beikleben,** to stick sth. (on) to sth.; **etwas etwas** *dat.* **beigießen,** to pour sth. on to sth.; **etwas etwas** *dat.* **beifalten,** to fold sth. in with sth.; **etwas beischmieren,** to scrawl sth. in; (*e*) *A:* (*denoting approach*=**herbei-, herein-,** *etc.*) **j-n beirufen,** to call s.o. in; to call for s.o. to come; **j-n beilassen,** to let s.o. in. **4.** (*with adverbs, adjectives*) (*denoting proximity*) **beieinander,** next to each other; *A:* **beiher,** by the side, alongside.

Bei[2] [bai, beː], *m.* **-s/-e & -s.** *Turk.Adm:* bey.

beiab [baiˀˈap], *adv. A:*=**seitab.**

beian [baiˀˈan], *adv. A:*=**nebenan.**

Beianker, *m. Nau:* kedge-anchor.

beiankern, *v.i. sep.* (*haben*) *Nau:* to kedge.

beibehalten. I. *v.tr. sep.* (*strong*) to keep up, on, to continue (custom, tradition, law); to maintain (speed, pace, etc.); to retain (military unit, institution, etc.); to adhere to, keep to, *F:* stick to (scheme, etc.); *Nau:* **den Kurs b.,** to keep course.

II. *vbl s.* **Beibehalten** *n.,* **Beibehaltung** *f. in vbl senses; also:* continuation (of tradition, custom, etc.); retention (of military unit, etc.); adherence (to a plan); *Com:* **unter Beibehaltung unseres Firmennamens,** while continuing the name of our firm, under the old name.

beibiegen, *v.tr. sep.* (*strong*) **1.** *Com: A:* to add, attach (rider, etc.) (to document). **2.** *F:* **j-m etwas b.,** to make sth. perfectly clear to s.o.; to make s.o. understand sth.

Beiblatt, *n.* supplement (to newspaper, etc.).

beibleiben, *v.i. sep.* (*strong*) *North G.Dial:* =**dabeibleiben.**

Beiboot, *n. Nau:* (*a*) dinghy, cock-boat, tender; long-boat (*carried on sailing-ship*); (*b*) (*usually with sails*) pinnace, jolly-boat.

beibringen. I. *v.tr. sep.* (*conj. like* **bringen**) **1.** (*a*) **j-m etwas b.,** to impose sth. on s.o.; to inflict sth. on s.o.; **dem Gegner eine Wunde b.,** to inflict a wound on an adversary; *Mil:* **dem Feind(e) eine Niederlage b.,** to inflict defeat upon the enemy; (*b*) *Med: A:* to give (s.o. sth.); to administer, apply (sth. to s.o.); **j-m ein Klistier b.,** to give s.o. an enema. **2.** (*a*) to produce, bring forward; **Beweise b.,** to produce, adduce, evidence; **Zeugen b.,** to produce, bring forward, witnesses; **einen Bericht b.,** to furnish, provide, a piece of information; **einen Beweisgrund b.,** to bring forward, put forward, an argument; (*b*) *A. & B:* =**beweisen** (*a*). **3.** (*a*) **j-m etwas b.,** to teach s.o. sth.; to drill, drum, drub, sth. into s.o.; to try to make s.o. understand sth.; **sich selbst etwas b.,** to teach oneself sth.; **j-m Gehorsam b.,** to teach s.o. to obey; *F:* **ich werde dir Lebensart, die Flötentöne, b.,** *F:* I'll teach you what's what; (*b*) **j-m eine schlechte Meinung von etwas, von j-m, b.,** to speak ill of sth., s.o., to s.o.; to give s.o. a bad opinion of sth., s.o.; **j-m eine Nachricht schonend b.,** to break a piece of news gently to s.o.

II. *vbl s.* **Beibringen** *n.,* **Beibringung** *f. in vbl senses; also:* infliction (of wound, etc.); production, adduction (of evidence, etc.).

Beichtandacht, *f. Ecc:* prayers before confession.

Beichtbrief, *m. Ecc:* dimissory letter.

Beichte, *f.* **-/-n.** *Ecc:* confession; **B. ablegen,** to confess; **zur B. gehen,** to go to confession; **j-m die B. abnehmen, hören,** to hear s.o.'s confession, to confess s.o.

beichten, *v.tr.* (*a*) *Ecc:* **(seine Sünden) b.,** to confess (one's sins) **(j-m, bei j-m,** to s.o.); **bei wem beichtest du?** who is your confessor? *Prov:* **wohl gebeichtet ist halb gebüßt,** confession is half way to atonement; (*b*) to confess, own up to (sth.); *F:* **ich muß dir was b.,** I have something to tell you, I have a confession to make.

Beichtformel, *f. Ecc:* order of confession.

Beichtgänger, *m.*=**Beichtkind.**

Beichtgebot, *n. Ecc:* obligation to go to confession.

Beichtgeheimnis, *n. Ecc:* secret of the confessional; seal of the confession; confessional secret.

Beichtgroschen, *m.*=**Beichtopfer.**

Beichtiger, *m.* **-s/-**=**Beichtvater.**

Beichtkind, *n. Ecc:* penitent, confessant.

Beichtopfer, *n.,* **Beichtpfennig,** *m.* confession-money.

Beichtschein, *m.*=**Beichtzeugnis.**

Beichtsiegel, *n.*=**Beichtgeheimnis.**

Beichtspiegel, *m. R.C.Ch:* penitential (book); guide to the examination of conscience.

Beichtstuhl, *m. Ecc:* confessional (box, stall).

Beichtvater, *m. Ecc:* (father) confessor; director of conscience.

Beichtzettel, *m. R.C.Ch:* (*a*) (child's) list of sins; *F: Austrian:* **wie ein B.,** as thin as a rake; (*b*)=**Beichtzeugnis.**

Beichtzeugnis, *n. Ecc:* certificate of confession.

beidarmig, *a. & adv. Sp:* two-armed, two-handed (throw, etc.).

beidäugig, *a. Opt:* binocular; **beidäugiges Sehen,** binocular vision.

beide. 1. *a.* (*a*) (*stressed*) both; **b. Beine,** both legs; **b. Herren suchen ein Einzelzimmer,** both (of the) gentlemen are looking for a single room; **unsere beiden Väter,** both our fathers; **seine beiden Schwestern, b. Schwestern,** both his sisters, both sisters; (*b*) (*unstressed*) two; **die beiden Hügel,** the two hills; **die beiden Kinder,** the two children; **seine beiden Schwestern,** his two sisters; **ihr beiden jungen Leute,** you two young people; (*c*) both, either; **in beiden Fällen,** in both cases, in either case; **auf beiden Seiten,** on both sides, on either side. **2.** *pron.* **beide, beides,** both; (*a*) **die beiden,** the two (of them); **wir b.,** both of us; **nur wir b. (allein),** just the two of us; **alle b. sind wieder da,** they are both back; **wir kochen b. gern,** we both like cooking; **wir haben es b. gesehen,** both of us saw it; **kommt ihr b.?** are you both coming? **wir haben an sie b. geschrieben,** we wrote, have written, to them both; **sie kommen b. nicht,** neither of them is coming; *Ten:* **dreißig b.,** thirty all; **nehmen Sie Milch und Zucker? — beides,** do you take milk and sugar?—both; **beides ist mir recht,** it is all the same to me, I don't mind either way; (*b*) **einer, keiner, von beiden,** either, neither, of them; **welcher von beiden?** which of the two? **ich habe keinen von beiden gesehen,** I have not seen either of them.

beidemal, *adv.* both times; in both cases.

beidenthalben, *adv.* **1.** from both sides. **2.** for both reasons.

beidentwegen, *adv.* for both reasons.

beiderlei, *indef. a. inv.* of both kinds, sorts; **Kinder b. Geschlechts,** children of either sex, of both sexes; **auf b. Art,** (in)both ways, either way; *Ecc:* **Abendmahl in, unter, b. Gestalt,** communion in both kinds.

beiderseitig. 1. *a.* (*a*) on both sides; **beiderseitige Lähmung,** bilateral paralysis, paralysis on both sides, paraplegia; (*b*) mutual (agreement, etc.);

zu beiderseitigem Vorteil, to mutual advantage. 2. *adv.*=**beiderseits** (*b*).

beiderseits, *prep. & adv.* (*a*) on both sides; at both ends; **b. gelähmt**, paralysed (on) both sides; **b. der Grenze**, on both sides of the boundary; *Her:* **b. gespitzt**, pointed at each end, at both ends; *Mil:* on both flanks; (*b*) *adv.* mutually, reciprocally; **der Vorschlag wurde b. angenommen**, the proposal was accepted by both parties, sides, men, etc.

Beiderwand, *f. Tex:* linsey-woolsey.

Beidhänder, *m.* -s/-, ambidexter; ambidextrous person.

beidhändig, *a.* ambidextrous.

Beidhändigkeit, *f.* ambidexterity, ambidextrousness.

Beidleber, *m.* -s/-. *Nat.Hist:* amphibian.

beidlebig, *a. Nat.Hist:* amphibious.

beidrecht, *a. Tex:* reversible (cloth).

beidrehen, *v.tr. & i. sep.* (*haben*) 1. to heave to, to bring to; **ein Schiff b.**, to bring a ship to; **beigedreht liegen**, to be hove to. 2. **das Schiff dreht bei**, the ship is coming to a standstill; the ship is stopping her, its, engines.

beidrücken, *v.tr. sep.* to affix (seal) to (document).

beidseitig, *a.*=**beiderseitig**.

beieinander, *pron. adv.* (*a*) together; next to one another; **dicht b.**, close together; **sie saßen b.**, they sat together, next to each other; (*b*) *F:* **gut b. sein**, to be in good form; *F:* **er ist nicht ganz b.**, he is not all there.

beiern, *v.i.* (*haben*) to play on bells (by striking them on the outside).

Beiessen, *n. Cu:* side-dish.

Beifahrer, *m.* 1. *Motor-cycling:* (*a*) side-car passenger; (*b*) pillion-rider. 2. *Aut:* passenger (next to the driver), *esp.* (*in lorry, etc.*) driver's mate.

Beifall, *m.* -(e)s/. (*a*) approval, approbation; commendation; **B. finden, haben**, to meet with approval, to be approved of; **B. zeigen**, to show approval; **B. nicken**, to nod approval; **der Plan findet seinen B.**, the plan meets with his approval; **das findet keinen B. bei mir**, I do not, cannot, approve of that; **seine Handlung fand den B. des Publikums**, his action earned the approbation of the public; **ich hoffe, daß es Ihren vollen, uneingeschränkten, B. finden wird**, I hope that it will meet with your entire approval; (*b*) acclamation, (i) applause, clapping, (ii) cheers, cheering; **großer B.**, (i) loud applause, (ii) loud cheers; **stürmischer B.**, thundering applause; **stürmischen B. hervorrufen**, to bring the house down; **B. klatschen, spenden**, to applaud, to clap (heartily); **B. ernten**, to win applause, to be applauded; **B. rufen**, to cheer; **er wurde mit lautem B. begrüßt**, he was greeted with loud (i) applause, (ii) cheers; **mit B. aufgenommene Rede**, speech greeted with (i) applause, (ii) cheers.

beifallen, *v.i. sep.* (*strong*) (*sein*) *A:* 1. **j-m b.**, to stand by s.o., to support s.o.; to approve of s.o. 2. *impers.* to come to mind; **es fällt mir bei**, it occurs to me.

beifällig, *a.* approving (gesture, etc.), (gesture, look) of approval; favourable (report, etc.); *adv.* approvingly, in approval; favourably.

Beifallklatschen, *n.* applause, clapping.

Beifallklatscher, *m.* applauder.

Beifallsäußerung, *f.* acclamation, (i) applause, (ii) cheers, cheering.

Beifallsbezeugung, *f.* sign, mark, evidence, of approval.

Beifallsdonner, *m.* thunder of applause.

Beifallsgemurmel, *n.* murmur of approbation, of approval.

Beifallsgeschrei, *n.* loud cheering.

Beifallsgetöse, *n.* thunder of applause; burst of cheering; loud cheering.

beifallsgierig, *a.* eager for approbation; eager for applause.

Beifallsruf, *m.* cheer; **laute, kräftige, Beifallsrufe**, loud, hearty, cheers.

Beifallssturm, *m.* storm of applause.

Beifang, *m.* 1. land (*i.e.* space between water-furrows) four to eight furrows wide. 2. fenced-in piece of land.

Beifilm, *m. Cin:* supporting film, second feature.

beiflicken, *v.tr. sep.*=**anflicken**.

beifolgend, *a.* enclosed; **b. ein Scheck**, enclosed herewith a cheque; **b. senden wir Ihnen . . .**, we send you herewith . . . ; **b. sende ich . . .**, I enclose . . . , enclosed please find . . .

Beifracht, *f. Nau:* mariner's venture *or* portage; private cargo.

beifügen. I. *v.tr. sep.* 1. to add (sth.); to enclose (cheque, invoice, etc.); to annex, join, append, attach (notes, etc.); to subjoin (list, etc.); **einem Bericht ein Dokument b.**, to annex a document to a report; **das Ihrem Briefe beigefügte Muster**, the sample attached to, enclosed with, your letter. 2. *Gram:* **beifügend**, attributive (adjective, etc.).

II. *vbl s.* 1. **Beifügen**, *n. in vbl senses; also:* addition. 2. **Beifügung**, *f.* (*a*)=II. 1; *also:* **unter B. eines Schecks**, enclosing a cheque; (*b*) addition; enclosure (with letter); (*c*) *Gram:* (i) adjunct; (ii) attribute.

Beifuß, *m.* 1. *Bot:* (*a*) wormwood; (*b*) mugwort. 2. *Nau:* truss.

Beifußhuhn, *n. Orn:* sage-grouse.

Beigabe, *f.* (*a*) addition; (*b*) *Cu:* side-dish; (*c*)=**Grabbeigabe**.

Beige[1] [ˈbaigə], *f.* -/-n=**Holzbeige**.

beige[2] [beːʒ, ˈbeːʒə, beːʃ]. 1. *inv.a.* beige. 2. *s.* **Beige**, *n.* -s/-s, (the colour) beige.

Beige[3] [ˈbeːʒə, ˈbeːʃə], *f.* -/-s. *Tex:* unbleached cloth; cloth in natural colour.

beigeben, *v.tr. sep.* (*strong*) 1. to add (sth.) (to sth.); to give, assign (s.o.) (to s.o.) (*as companion, for assistance*); **einer Warensendung ein Begleitschreiben b.**, to send a covering letter with goods; **ich muß ihm einen Gehilfen b.**, I must give him an assistant; **er wurde ihr als Begleitung beigegeben**, he was assigned, delegated, to her as an escort. 2. **klein b.**, to yield, submit, give in; *F:* to knuckle under; to climb down; **j-m klein b.**, to yield, submit, give way, to s.o.

beigebunden, *p.p. & a.* bound together; in the same volume; **'Die Wahlverwandtschaften', b. diverse Flugblätter**, 'The Elective Affinities', bound together with various pamphlets.

beigehen, *v.i. sep.* (*strong*) (*sein*) *A:* 1. (*of document, etc.*) to be enclosed (in letter, etc.). 2. (*a*) *impers.* **es geht mir bei**, it occurs to me, it comes into my mind; (*b*) **sich b. lassen, etwas zu tun**, to allow oneself to do sth.; to venture, to dare, to do sth.

beigen, *v.tr.* to stack, pile (wood, etc.).

beigeordnet, *p.p. & a. see* **beiordnen**.

Beigeordnete, *m., f.* (*decl. as adj.*) assistant; deputy; second in command; deputy mayor.

Beigericht, *n. Cu:* side-dish.

beigeschlossen, *p.p. & a.* enclosed, subjoined, hereto annexed (documents, etc.).

Beigeschmack, *m.* slight flavour; smack, savour; tang (of vinegar, etc.); **Speise mit einem unangenehmen B.**, food with an unpleasant taste; **eine Pille mit einem guten B.**, a pill with a nice taste; **der Kuchen hat einen B. von faulen Eiern**, the cake has a taste of rotten eggs; *F:* **sein Lob hatte einen B. von Ironie**, there was a tang, a suggestion, of irony in his praise; **das Wort hat einen etwas altertümlichen B.**, the word sounds slightly old-fashioned, the word has a slightly old-fashioned flavour; **die Angelegenheit hatte einen bitteren B.**, the occasion was tinged with bitterness.

beigesellen, *v.tr. sep.* **j-n j-m, einer Gruppe, b.**, to put s.o. together with s.o., to put s.o. into a group; **er wurde dem Ausschuß als Berater beigesellt**, he was attached to the committee as adviser; **sich j-m b.**, to join s.o., to attach oneself to s.o.; **er gesellte sich der Gruppe bei**, he joined, attached himself to, the group.

Beignet [bɛnˈjeː], *m.* -s/-s. *Cu:* fritter.

Beiguß, *m. Cu:* sauce; gravy.

beihaben, *v.tr. sep.* (*conj. like* **haben**) *A. & F:* to have (sth.) at hand; to have (sth.) with, on, one.

Beihälterin, *f.*=**Beischläferin**.

Beihau, *m. Dial:* make-weight of bone (thrown in with meat).

Beiheft, *n.* supplement, supplementary number (of periodical, etc.).

beiheften, *v.tr. sep.* **etwas** *dat.* **etwas b.**, to attach, affix, fasten sth. on to sth., to fix sth. on to sth.; to clip sth. on to sth.; to pin (document, etc.) on to (report, etc.); to stitch (new pages) into (unbound book, pamphlet).

beiher [baiˈheːr], *adv. A:* alongside; by the side.

Beihilfe, *f.* 1. assistance, help, aid; *esp. Jur:* aiding and abetting; **j-m B. leisten, gewähren**, to aid and abet s.o.; **j-m B. zu einem Verbrechen leisten**, to abet s.o. in a crime. 2. (*sum of money*) *Adm: etc:* grant (in aid); (*for project, etc.*) subsidy, subvention; **staatliche B. zum Studium**, government grant for study; **eine B. von 50 Mark bekommen, erhalten**, to receive a grant of 50 marks.

Beihirsch, *m. Ven:* rascal, unwarrantable stag.

beiholen, *v.tr. sep. Nau:* **das Segel b.**, to take in the sail.

beikommen, *v.i. sep.* (*strong*) (*sein*) 1. (*a*) **j-m b.**, to get at, near, s.o.; to reach through to s.o.; **Menschen, denen mit Vernunft nicht beizukommen ist, denen man mit Vernunft nicht b. kann**, people who cannot be reached by reason, people who do not respond to reason; **man kann ihm nicht so leicht b., ihm ist nicht so leicht beizukommen**, he is not so easy to deal with; **dem Kind kann man mit nichts b.**, you just can't do anything with the child, the child is completely unmanageable; **mit Gewalt kann man ihm auch nicht b.**, he does not even react to force; (*b*) **etwas** *dat.* **b.**, to get by, round, sth.; to overcome sth.; **einer Schwierigkeit b.**, to overcome, get the better of, a difficulty; **eine Krankheit, der man mit Hausmitteln nicht b. kann**, an illness which does not respond to home treatment. 2. *A:* to approach s.o., to come near s.o. (in intelligence, etc.); **j-m nicht b.**, not to compare with s.o. 3. *A:*=**beiliegen** 2 (*a*). 4. *impers.* **es kommt mir bei**, it occurs to me, it comes into my mind.

Beikost, *f.* (*a*) supplementary feeding (for babies); (*b*) *Cu:* side-dish.

Beil, *n.* -(e)s/-e. *Tls:* (*a*) hatchet; chopper; *Arb:* trimming axe; *Butchery:* cleaver, chopper; (*b*) (*larger*) axe; **Hinrichtung durch das B.**, (execution by) beheading, decapitation (with the axe).

beiladen. I. *v.tr. sep. Com: etc:* to add (sth.) to a consignment.

II. *vbl s.* 1. **Beiladen**, *n. in vbl senses.* 2. **Beiladung**, *f.* (*a*)=II. 1; (*b*) *Com: etc:* extra freight; *Nau:* extra cargo; (*c*) *Sm.a:* priming charge, ignition charge.

Beilage, *f.* 1. addition, supplement; (*a*) supplement (to newspaper, etc.); appendix (to report, etc.); (*b*) enclosure (with letter); relevant papers, documents (forwarded with application, etc.); (*c*) *Cu:* (i) food served with main item, *e.g.* vegetables; (ii) garnish(ing), trimmings (of dish). 2. *Tchn:* shim, packing-strip.

Beilageheft, *n.*=**Beiheft**.

Beilager, *n. Lit. & A:* nuptials, *esp.* consummation of marriage; **das B. vollziehen**, to consummate the marriage.

Beilagscheibe, *f. Mec.E:* washer.

Beilander, *m.* -s/-, canal barge.

Beilast, *f. Nau:* (*a*) mariner's venture, mariner's portage; private cargo; (*b*) ballast.

beiläufig, *a.* 1. incidental (circumstance, question, etc.); **beiläufige Bemerkung**, casual, passing, remark; *adv.* incidentally; by way of parenthesis, parenthetically; **etwas b. erwähnen**, to mention sth. in passing; **b. sei erwähnt . . .**, be it said by the way, parenthetically, incidentally . . . . 2. *Dial:* approximate; *adv.* approximately, about.

Beilbrief, *m.* 1. *Nau:* ship's register. 2. (*in Switzerland*) deed of a land mortgage.

beilegen. I. *v.tr. sep.* 1. (*a*) **etwas etwas** *dat.* **b.**, to add sth. to sth.; to annex, join (document, etc.) to (report, etc.); **etwas einem Brief b.**, to enclose sth. in a letter; (*b*) *A:* to give (woman) as mistress *or* wife. 2. (*a*) **j-m einen Titel b.**, to confer, bestow, a title upon s.o.; **sich** *dat.* **etwas b.**, to assume, claim, lay claim to, sth.; (*b*) to attribute, ascribe (quality, etc.) (to s.o.); **einem Wort eine Bedeutung b.**, to assign a meaning to a word; **einer Sache Wichtigkeit, Bedeutung, b.**, to attach importance, significance, to a thing. 3. to settle, compose (quarrel); to reconcile (difference of opinion). 4. *A:* to put, set, lay, (sth.) aide; to lay (sth.) in store, to lay (sth.) up. 5. *v.i.* (*haben*) *A:*=**beidrehen**.

II. *vbl s.* **Beilegen** *n.*, **Beilegung** *f. in vbl senses; also:* 1. (*a*) bestowal, conferment (of title); (*b*) attribution (of quality); assignment (of meaning). 2. settlement (of quarrel); reconciliation (of difference of opinion).

Beileger, *m.* -s/-. 1. peace-maker (in quarrel, dispute). 2. *Tex:* warp-beam rod.

beileibe [baiˈlaibə], *adv.* (*in negative phrases*) **b. nicht**, by no means; not in the least, not at all; **sie ist b. nicht häßlich**, she is by no means ugly; **er ist b. nicht dumm**, he is by no means, not at all, stupid; **er ist b. kein Feigling**, he is by no means a coward, he is certainly no coward.

Beileid, *n.* condolence; **herzliches, inniges, B.**, heartfelt, deep(est), sympathy; **j-m sein B. aussprechen, bezeigen**, to offer s.o. one's condolences; to express one's sympathy to s.o.

Beileidsbesuch, *m.* visit of condolence.

Beileidsbezeugung, *f.* expression of sympathy, condolence.

Beileidsbrief, *m.*, **Beileidsschreiben**, *n.* letter of condolence.

Beileidskarte, *f.* condolences card.

beilen, *v.tr.* 1. *Ven:* **einen Hirsch b.**, to bring a

stag to bay. 2. *Woodw:* to trim with a hatchet. 3. *A. & Dial:* to gauge, measure (liquor in barrel).

beilförmig, *a.* hatchet-shaped; axe-shaped.

Beilhammer, *m. Tls:* axe-hammer.

Beilhieb, *m.* blow, stroke, with the axe; **mit einem B.**, with a stroke of the axe.

beiliegen, *v.i. sep. (strong)* 1. *A:* **einem Mann, einer Frau, b.**, to sleep, *Lit:* to lie, with a man, a woman. 2. *(a) (of thg)* **etwas** *dat.* **b.**, to be added to sth.; to be enclosed with sth.; to be subjoined annexed, to sth.; **beiliegend**, enclosed, annexed, subjoined (document, etc.); **beiliegend sende ich . . .**, I enclose . . . ; *(b) A: (of houses, etc.)* to be adjoining, neighbouring. 3. *Nau:* to lie to, to be hove to.

Beilke, *f.* -/. *Games:* shovelboard, shuffleboard.

beilken, *v.i. (haben)* to play shovelboard.

Beilkespiel, *n.*=**Beilke.**

Beilklinge, *f. Her:* doloire; adze.

Beilkraut, *n. Bot:* 1. buaze fibre plant. 2. hatchet vetch; crown vetch; scorpion-senna.

Beilstein, *m. Miner:* nephrite; jade; greenstone.

Beilwicke, *f. Bot:* hatchet vetch.

beim, *prep. (contraction of* **bei dem**; *cp.* **bei**) *(for usage of* **beim** *and* **bei dem** *compare notes to* **am**) 1. *(in adv. phrases) (resolution into* **bei dem** *is sometimes possible) (a) (time)* **beim Frühstück**, at breakfast; **beim Tode meines Großvaters**, at the death of my grandfather, when my grandfather died; *(b) (space)* **ein Haus beim See**, a house by the lake; **beim Feuer sitzen**, to sit by the fire(side); *(c) (with pers.)* (i) **sein Einfluß beim König**, his influence with the king; (ii) **sie war beim Bäcker**, she was at the baker's; *(d) (with superlative+noun) (resolution into* **bei dem** *is rare)* **beim ersten Anblick**, at first sight; **beim besten Willen**, with the best will in the world; *(e) (with verbs and verbal phrases) (resolution into* **bei dem** *would sound stilted)* (i) **j-n beim Kragen packen**, to seize s.o. by the collar; **j-n beim Wort nehmen**, to take s.o. at his word; **ein Ding beim rechten Namen nennen**, to call a thing by its right name, to call a spade a spade; **es bleibt alles beim alten**, things will not change, will remain the same; (ii) *(in oaths, affirmations)* **beim Himmel schwören**, to swear by Heaven; **beim Zeus!** by Jove! 2. *(with neuter vbl s.* **beim** *can never be resolved into* **bei dem**) **beim Lesen**, whilst reading, in the course of reading; **beim Singen**, whilst, when, singing; **Vorsicht beim Überschreiten der Fahrbahn!** take care when crossing the road.

beimengen, *v.tr. sep.*=**beimischen.**

beimessen, *v.tr. sep. (strong)* **j-m, etwas** *dat.*, **etwas b.**, to attribute, ascribe, sth. to s.o., sth.; **einer Sache eine übermäßige Bedeutung b.**, to attach excessive, undue, importance to a matter; **einer Nachricht Glauben b.**, to credit, believe, give credence to, a piece of news; **etwas einer bestimmten Ursache b.**, to put sth. down, set sth. down, ascribe sth., to a certain cause.

beimischen. I. *v.tr. sep.* **etwas** *dat.* **etwas b.**, *(a)* to (ad)mix, mingle, sth. with sth.; **dem Wein Wasser b.**, to mix wine with water; *(b) Cu: etc:* to add sth. to sth.; to stir (liquid, etc.) into sth.

II. *vbl s.* 1. **Beimischen**, *n. in vbl senses.* 2. **Beimischung**, *f.* *(a)*=II. 1; *(b)* admixture.

Bein, *n.* -(e)s/-e. 1. bone; *B:* **B. von meinem B.**, bone of my bones; *see also* **Mark**² *(b)*, **Stein.** 2. leg (of pers., animal, etc.); *A. & F:* shank; **künstliches B.**, artificial leg; **ohne Beine**, legless; **dünne, dürre, Beine**, thin, skinny, legs; legs like matchsticks; **dicke Beine**, fat legs; **stramme Beine haben**, to have a stout pair of legs; **Beine weg!** mind your legs! **auf einem B. stehen**, to stand on one leg; *F:* **auf einem B. kann man nicht stehen**, you can't stop at one (drink); **auf den Beinen sein**, to be on one's feet, legs; to be up and about, to be on the go; **früh auf den Beinen sein**, to be up early; **das ganze Dorf war auf den Beinen**, the whole village was afoot, astir; **wieder auf die Beine kommen**, to get on to one's feet again; **sich auf die Beine machen**, to set out, off; to be off; to get moving; **j-m auf die Beine helfen**, (i) to help s.o. to his feet, (ii) to set s.o. on his feet, legs, again; **etwas auf die Beine bringen**, (i) to set sth. going, to launch, start, sth., (ii) to get, scrape, sth., things, together; to (manage to) produce sth., things; *F:* **ein Klotz am B.**, a drag, *F:* a bind; **sie ist mir ein Klotz am B.**, she is a millstone round my neck; *F:* **ich habe zur Zeit viel am B.**, I have a great deal to do at the moment, I have a lot on my hands just now; **etwas ans B. binden, streichen**, to give sth. up for lost, to write sth. off as a bad debt; **j-m etwas ans B. binden, streichen**, to tell s.o. a tall story; **du hast noch junge Beine**, your legs are younger than mine; *F:* **alles, was Beine hat**, all the world and his wife; **mit einem B. im Grabe stehen**, to have one foot in the grave; **er war immer mit einem B. im Gefängnis**, he was on the shady side of the law; **j-m ein B. stellen**, to trip s.o. up; **j-m Beine machen**, to make s.o. run; *F:* **er reißt sich kein B. aus**, he won't break his back working; he takes it easy; **ich werde mir deswegen kein B. ausreißen**, I'm not going to break my neck for that, I'm not going to kill myself for that; **sich** *dat.* **die Beine vertreten**, to stretch one's legs; **sich** *dat.* **die Beine in den Leib stehen**, to be kept standing (a long time); **die, seine, Beine gebrauchen**, to run fast, *F:* to leg it; **seine Beine (lang) ausstrecken**, to stretch out one's legs; **die Beine in die Hand, unter den Arm, nehmen**, to pick up one's heels, to put on a spurt; to put one's best foot forward; **j-m einen Knüppel zwischen die Beine werfen**, to put a spoke in s.o.'s wheel; **kein B.!** (i) nobody! (ii) certainly not! *Prov:* **Lügen haben kurze Beine**, lies are short-lived; *see also* **ablaufen** II. 2, **brechen** I. 1, **Hals** 1 *(a)*. 3. *(a)* leg (of chair, table, etc.); *(b) pl.* **Beine**, legs (of trousers); *(c) Min:* rib; post.

Bein-, *comb.fm. cp.* **Knochen-.**

beinah ['baiːnaː], **beinahe** [bai'naːhə], *adv.* nearly, almost; *(a) (time)* **ich bin b. fertig**, I am nearly, almost, ready; I have nearly finished; **das Werk ist b. vollendet**, the work is almost completed, all but completed; **jetzt sind wir b. da**, we are nearly there now; **es ist b. Zeit**, it is nearly time; *(b)* almost, roughly, approximately; **ich glaube es b.**, I almost think so; **es, das, ist ja b. dasselbe**, it is very much, pretty much, pretty nearly, the same thing; *(c)* **b. hätte ihr die Stimme versagt**, her voice almost, nearly, failed her; **die Ärzte hätten mich b. umgebracht**, the doctors nearly killed me; **b. hätte ich Lust dahinzugehen**, I almost feel like going (there), I've half a mind to go (there); *Prov:* **'beinah' haben die Hasen gern**, if ifs and ans were pots and pans, there'd be no trade for tinkers.

beinähnlich *a.* *(a)* bone-like; bony, osseous; *(b)* shaped like a leg, leg-like.

Beiname, *m.* 1. *(a)* appellation, designation; **Robert II. verdiente kaum den Beinamen 'der Fromme'**, Robert II hardly deserved his appellation of the Pious; *(b)* nickname. 2. *(a) occ.* surname; *(b) Rom.Ant:* cognomen.

Beinarbeit, *f. Sp:* foot-work (of boxer, tennis-player, etc.); leg-action (of swimmer, etc.).

Beinarbeiter, *m.* worker in bone.

beinartig, *a.*=**beinähnlich.**

Beinasche, *f.* bone-ash, bone-earth.

Beinberge, *f.*=**Beinschiene.**

Beinblume, *f. Bot:* marsh marigold.

Beinbrech, *m.* -s/. 1. *Bot:* bog asphodel, Lancashire asphodel. 2. *Miner:* calcareous tubes.

Beinbrecher, *m. Orn:* sea-eagle, osprey, erne.

Beinbrechgras, *n.*=**Beinbrech** 1.

Beinbruch, *m.* 1. *Surg:* fracture of the leg; fractured, broken, leg; *see also* **Hals- und Beinbruch.** 2.=**Beinbrech.**

Beinchen, *n.* -s/-, *(dim. of* **Bein**) small, little, leg.

Beinerde, *f.* bone-earth.

Beinfäule, *f. Med:* caries.

Beinfessel, *f. Wr:* leg-lock.

Beinfolter, *die. Hist:* (the torture of) the boot.

Beingeige, *f.*=**Gambe.**

Beingeschwür, *n. Med:* ulcer on the leg, *esp.* varicose ulcer.

Beingewächs, *n. Farr:* osselet (on fetlock, etc.).

Beinglas, *n. Glassm:* bone-glass.

Beinhai, *m. Ich:* basking shark.

beinhalten [bəˀ'inhaltən], *v.tr. (weak)* to contain (idea, etc.); **b., daß . . .**, to contain the idea that . . . .

Beinharnisch, *m. Arm:* leg armour; *(for thighs)* cuisses *pl*; *(for shins)* greaves *pl.*

Beinhauer, *m. A. & Dial:* butcher.

Beinhaus, *n.* charnel-house, ossuary.

Beinheil, *n. Bot:* *(a)* bog asphodel, Lancashire asphodel; *(b)* comfrey.

Beinholz, *n. Bot:* 1. *(a)* dogwood, prickwood; *(b)* common privet. 2. honeysuckle.

-beinig, *comb.fm. a. (with adj. or numeral prefixed)* -legged; **kurzbeinig**, short-legged; **zweibeinig**, two-legged.

Beinkehle, *f. Anat:* hollow of the knee.

Beinkleider, *n.pl. Cost: A. & Com:* (pair of) trousers; (women's) knickers; *A:* breeches.

Beinkreisen, *n. Gym:* rotation of the leg *or* legs.

Beinling, *m.* -s/-e. 1. leg (of stocking, *occ.* of pants, trousers). 2. *Her:* gaiter, legging. 3. hide from an animal's leg.

Beinmuskulatur, *f. Anat:* leg muscles.

Beinprothese, *f. Surg:* artificial leg.

Beinring, *m.* 1. anklet. 2. *Orn:* ring.

Beinröhre, *f.* 1. *Anat:* *(a)* tibia; *(b) Z:* cannon-bone (of horse). 2. *Arm:* greave.

Beinschellen, *f.pl.* fetters, shackles (for legs).

Beinschere, *f. Wr:* scissor(s) hold.

Beinschiene, *f.* 1. *Arm:* leg armour; *(for lower leg)* greave; *(for thigh)* cuisse. 2. *Surg:* leg-splint; **eiserne Beinschienen**, (leg-)irons. 3. *Sp:* (hockey-)pad.

Beinschlag, *m. Swim:* leg kick; leg beat.

Beinschnitzerei, *f.* bone-carving.

Beinschrauben, *die, f.pl. Hist:* (the torture of) the boot.

Beinschützer, *m.* *(a) Sp: etc:* leg-guard; *Cr:* pad, leg-guard; *Fb:* shin-guard; *(b) pl.* **Beinschützer**, (mackintosh) leggings (of cyclist, etc.).

Beinschwarz, *n.* bone black, bone char.

Beinspat, *m. Vet:* bone-spavin.

Beinsperren, *n. Wr:* leg-lock.

Beinstäbe, *m.pl. Coop:* barrel staves.

Beinstellen, *n. Box: Wr:* tripping.

Beinstumpf, *m.* stump of a leg.

Beintasche, *f. Arm:* tasses *pl*, tassets *pl.*

Beintürkis, *m. Lap:* fossil turquoise.

Beinwaren, *f.pl.* objects made of bone, bone goods.

Beinweide, *f.*=**Beinholz.**

Beinwell, *m.* -s/. 1. *Bot:* comfrey. 2. *Miner:* calcareous tubes.

Beinwurz(el), *f. Bot:* comfrey.

Beinzeug, *n. Arm:* leg armour.

beiordnen. I. *v.tr. sep.* 1. *Adm:* to give (s.o.) as assistant, etc., (to s.o.); **beigeordneter Bürgermeister**, deputy mayor; *cp.* **Beigeordnete.** 2. **etwas etwas** *dat.* **b.**, to set, place, sth. at the side of sth.; to place sth. on a level with sth.; *Gram:* **beiordnendes Bindewort**, co-ordinating conjunction; **beiordnende Konstruktion**, paratactic construction; **beigeordnete Glieder**, paratactic members; co-ordinate members.

II. *vbl s.* **Beiordnen** *n.*, **Beiordnung** *f. in vb senses; also: Gram:* parataxis; co-ordination.

Beiorgel, *f. Mus:* small church-organ.

Beipaß, *m. Mch: etc:* by-pass.

beipflichten, *v.i. sep. (haben)* **j-m (in etwas** *dat.*) **b.**, to agree, concur, with s.o. (on, in, sth.); **einem Vorschlag b.**, to consent, agree, to a proposal; to approve a proposal; to give one's adhesion to a proposal; to endorse a proposal; **ich pflichte Ihnen, Ihrer Meinung, bei**, I concur in your opinion; I concur with you; I am of the same opinion, mind, as you.

Beiprodukt, *n. Ind:* by-product.

Beiprogramm, *n. Cin:* supporting programme.

Beiram ['bairam], *m. & n.* -s/-s. *Moham.Rel:* Bairam.

Beirat, *m.* 1. *A:* advice, counsel. 2. *Adm: etc:* *(a)* adviser, counsellor; **juristischer B.**, legal adviser; *(b)* advisory board, commission, committee.

beiraten, *v.i. sep. (strong) (haben) A:* to advise, counsel; to give advice.

beirechnen, *v.tr. sep.* *(a)* to add (sth.) (**etwas** *dat.*, to sth.); *(b)* to include, reckon, count (s.o., sth.) (**etwas** *dat.*, in sth.); **den Großen beigerechnet werden**, to be numbered with, among, the great.

beirren, *v.tr.* **sich nicht (in einem Vorhaben) b. lassen**, not to be diverted, dissuaded (from a plan); **laß dich nicht b.**, don't be put off, don't let them put you off.

Beirut [bai'ruːt]. *Pr.n.n.* -s. *Geog:* Beirut.

Beisa ['baizaː], *f.* -/-s, **Beisaantilope**, *f. Z:* beisa (antilope).

beisammen [bai'zamən], *adv.* together; **dicht b.**, close together; **b. sein**, to be together; **die ganze Familie b. haben**, to have the whole family (gathered) together; **seine Gedanken b. haben**, to concentrate, to pay attention; **ich hatte meine Gedanken nicht b.**, my mind was wandering; *F:* **er hat (sie) nicht alle b., er hat seine fünf Sinne, seinen Verstand, nicht ganz b.**, he is not all there, he is a little weak in the head.

beisammenbleiben, *v.i. sep. (strong) (sein)* to stay, remain, together.

beisammenhalten, *v.tr. sep. (strong)* to keep (things, persons) together; **die Gedanken b.**, to concentrate, to pay attention.

Beisammensein, *n.* *(a)* being together; *(b)* gathering, reunion (of friends, family, etc.); **geselliges B.**, (i) friendly gathering, social, (ii) informal reception.

beisammensitzen, *v.i. sep. (strong) (haben)* to sit together.

beisammenstehen, *v.i. sep. (strong) (haben)* to stand together.

Beisaß, Beisasse, *m.* -sassen/-sassen. **1.** (*a*) *Hist:* inhabitant without full civil rights; *approx.*= denizen; (*b*) *A:* (landless) cottager; tenant farmer. 3. *A:*=**Beisitzer.**

Beisatz, *m.* **1.** (*a*) addition; (*b*) admixture, alloy (of inferior metal in gold, etc.). **2.** *Gram:* (*a*) adjunct; (*b*) apposition; appositive.

beischaffen, *v.tr. sep.* (*weak*) **1.** to procure, obtain; **Geld b.,** to raise, obtain, find, money; *F:* **kannst du ihr einen Tanzpartner b.?** can you get hold of a dancing partner for her? **2.** *A:* (*a*) (i) to put (sth.) aside, to put (sth.), on one side (ii) to dispose of (sth.); (*b*) to misappropriate, embezzle (funds, etc.).

beischießen, *v.tr. sep.* (*strong*) *occ.* to contribute (sum of money).

Beischiff, *n. Nau:* (ship's) tender.

Beischilddrüsen, *f.pl. Anat:* parathyroid glands.

Beischlaf, *m.* sexual intercourse; coitus, coition; **außerehelicher B.,** adulterous intercourse; extramarital relations.

beischlafen, *v.i. sep.* (*strong*) (*haben*) **einer Frau b.,** to sleep with, *Lit:* to lie with, a woman; to have intercourse with a woman.

Beischläfer, *m.* (*a*) *A:* bed-fellow; (*b*) lover, paramour, gallant.

Beischläferin, *f.* mistress, concubine.

Beischlag, *m.* **1.** terrace (in front of house with steps leading down to street). **2.** *Num:* (i) imitation; counterfeiting; (ii) imitated coin, imitation; counterfeit (coin).

beischließen, *v.tr. sep.* (*strong*) **1.** to enclose (document in letter, etc.). **2.** *A:* to lock (sth.) away, up.

Beischluß, *m.* enclosure (in letter, parcel, etc.).

Beischmack, *m.* **-s/.** *A:*=**Beigeschmack.**

beischreiben[1], *v.tr. sep.* (*strong*) to write, note, (sth.) in the margin; **ein paar Worte b.,** to add a few words *or* comments to (s.o. else's letter, etc.).

Beischreiben[2], *n.* enclosed letter; covering letter.

Beischrift, *f.* (*a*) inscription, caption (to picture, etc.); (*b*) *A:* (i) postscript; (ii) side-note (to document, etc.).

Beisegel, *m. Nau:* light sail, *esp.* staysail *or* studding sail.

beisegeln, *v.i. sep.* (*sein*) *Nau:* (*a*) to lower the sails; (*b*) to sail close-hauled, close to the wind.

beisein. I. *v.i. sep.* (*conj. like* **sein**) *F:*=**dabeisein.**

II. *vbl s.* **Beisein,** *n.* (*a*) presence; **in meinem B.,** in my presence; (*b*) *A:*=**Beischlaf.**

beiseite [bai'zaitə], *adv.* aside. **1.** on one side; apart; **Spaß, Scherz, b.,** joking apart; *Th:* **b. gesprochene Worte,** words spoken aside. **2.** to one side; to the side; aside; **b. treten,** to step, stand, aside, to draw to one side; **j-n b. nehmen,** to take, draw, s.o. aside; **j-n, etwas, b. schieben,** to push, shove, s.o., sth., aside; **etwas, j-n, b. schaffen,** (i) to move sth. aside, to one side; (ii) to get rid of sth., s.o.; to get sth., s.o., out of the way; (iii) to put sth. aside, on one side (for one's own use); **etwas b. bringen,** (i) to move sth. aside, to one side; (ii) to get rid of sth.; to get sth. out of the way; (iii) to put sth. aside, on one side (for one's own use); **etwas b. legen,** to lay, put, sth. aside; **Geld b. legen,** to put money by, aside; to save money for the future; **etwas b. setzen,** to set, put, sth. aside; **j-n b. setzen,** to neglect s.o.; to pay no attention to s.o.; **b. stehen,** to stand back; to stand in the background; **wenn alle helfen, dann möchte ich nicht b. stehen,** if everyone is helping, I should not like to stand in the background, just to stand by; **etwas b. stellen,** (i) to put sth. aside; (ii) to leave, shelve, (point, problem, etc.) for the time being.

Beisel, *n.* **-s/-.** *Austrian Dial:* tavern, *F:* pub.

beisetzen. I. *v.tr. sep.* **1.** (*a*) **etwas etwas** *dat.* **b.,** to add sth. to sth.; to set, place, sth. by (the side of) sth., alongside sth.; (*b*) *A:* to put (kettle, etc.) on the fire. **2.** to bury, entomb, inter (corpse); to lay (ashes) in the grave; to inter (ashes); **in der Familiengruft beigesetzt werden,** to be laid in the family vault; **auf hoher See beigesetzt werden,** to be buried at sea. **3.** *Nau:* to let out, loose out, unfurl (sail); to set (sail); **alle Segel b.,** to carry a press of sail, to cram on sail, to crowd on (all) sail.

II. *vbl s.* **1. Beisetzen,** *n. in vbl senses.* **2. Beisetzung,** *f.* (*a*) *in vbl senses; also:* burial, interment; entombment; (*b*) funeral; obsequies; (*c*) burial; **die letzten Beisetzungen auf dem kürzlich ausgegrabenen Friedhof datieren aus dem 5. Jahrhundert n.Chr.,** the last burials at the recently excavated cemetry date from the 5th century A.D.

beisitzen, *v.i. sep.* (*strong*) (*haben*) to sit (in court of law, etc.) as assessor (to magistrate, etc.).

Beisitzer, *m.* **-s/-.** **1.** *Jur:* assessor (to magistrate, etc.); associate judge. **2.** voting member (of body, association, etc.).

beispannen, *v.tr. sep.* to harness (horse, etc.) together with another, others.

Beispiel, *n.* **1.** example; (*a*) **ein gutes B. geben, setzen,** to set a good example; **j-n als B. anführen, aufstellen,** to hold s.o. up as an example; **sich** *dat.* **ein B. an j-m nehmen,** to take an example from s.o., to take a leaf from s.o.'s book; **nimm dir ein B. daran,** let that be an example to you; **j-s B. folgen,** to follow s.o.'s example; *Prov:* **böse Beispiele verderben gute Sitten,** bad examples corrupt good manners; (*b*) instance, precedent; **warnendes B.,** warning, caution; **abschreckendes B.,** deterrent; **ohne B.=beispiellos. 2.** example, illustration; instance; **zum B.,** *abbr.* z.B., for example, for instance, by way of example, *abbr.* e.g.; **große Städte, wie zum B. London,** large towns, as for example, London; **Beispiele aus Livius,** examples, illustrations, from Livy; **ein praktisches, konkretes, B.,** a practical, concrete, example; **ein isoliertes B.,** an isolated instance; **als B. seiner Redlichkeit,** as an instance of his honesty; **ein B. für eine Regel geben,** to give an example of a rule, to exemplify a rule; *see also* **anführen** 2.

beispielhaft, *a.* exemplary.

beispiellos, *a.* unexampled, without example, unparalleled, without parallel; unequalled (monument, beauty, etc.); unprecedented (action); **beispiellose Grausamkeit,** cruelty without parallel, unparalleled cruelty.

beispielshalber, *adv.*=**beispielsweise.**

beispielsweise, *adv.* for example, by way of example, for instance.

beispringen, *v.i. sep.* (*strong*) (*sein*) **j-m b.,** to come to s.o.'s aid, assistance, relief; to help s.o. out (in an emergency).

Beißbeere, *f. Bot:* capsicum; chilli; Guinea-pepper, Guinea-grains.

beißen, *v.tr. & i.* (*strong*) (*haben*) **1.** (*a*) to bite; **beißt der Hund?** does the dog bite? **der Hund biß ihn, ihm, ins Bein,** the dog bit him in the leg; **der Hund biß nach mir,** the dog snapped at me; **auf etwas Hartes b.,** to bite on sth. hard; **sich** *dat.* **auf die Zunge, auf die Lippen, b.,** to bite one's tongue, one's lips (*esp. in order not to laugh, to hold back an unfortunate remark*); **in einen Apfel b.,** to bite into an apple; *F:* **in den sauren Apfel b.,** to swallow the (bitter) pill, to take one's medicine; *F:* **nichts zu b. haben,** to have nothing to eat; **sich** *dat.* **die Nägel b.,** to bite one's nails; *F:* **ins Gras b.,** to die, *F:* to bite the dust; **der Ring beißt mir ins Fleisch,** the ring cuts, bites, into my flesh; *see also* **bellen**; (*b*) (*of fleas, mosquitoes, etc.*) to bite; **von Flöhen gebissen werden,** to be bitten by fleas; (*c*) *F:* **sich mit j-m b.,** to quarrel, squabble, bicker, with s.o.; (*of two colours*) **sich b.,** to clash (with each other). **2.** (*a*) to sting, smart; to bite, cut; **Pfeffer beißt auf der Zunge,** pepper bites the tongue, burns on the tongue; **der Rauch beißt die Augen, beißt in die Augen, beißt in den Augen,** smoke makes the eyes smart; **es beißt,** (i) it stings, smarts; (ii) it itches; **der Wind beißt,** the wind is biting; **der beißende Schmerz (einer Wunde),** the smarting (of a wound); (*b*) **beißende Ironie,** biting irony; **beißender Spott,** sarcasm; **eine beißende Bemerkung,** a cutting, an acid, a caustic, remark; **beißende Reue,** biting, bitter, remorse.

Beißer, *m.* **-s/-.** **1.** (*animal*) biter. **2.** (*a*) *Anat:* incisor; (*b*) *F:* tooth. **3.** *Austrian Dial: Tls:* lever. **4.**=**Beitzker.**

Beißerchen, *n.* **-s/-,** (*dim. of* **Beißer**) (*nursery language*) toothy-peg.

beißig, *a.*=**bissig.**

Beißker, *m.* **-s/-=Beitzker.**

Beißkohl, *m. Bot: Cu:* (Swiss) chard.

Beißkorb, *m.* muzzle (for horse, dog, etc.).

Beißring, *m.* teething ring (for baby).

Beißrübe, *f. Agr:* mangel-wurzel.

Beißwerkzeuge, *n.pl.* (*a*) teeth (of mammals, etc.); (*b*) masticatory organs (of insects, etc.).

Beißwurz, *f. Bot:* pasque-flower, pulsatilla.

Beißzahn, *m. Anat:* incisor.

Beißzange, *f. Tls:* (*a*) pincers; (*b*) cutting-pliers; wire-nippers, -cutters.

Beistand, *m.* **1.** help, assistance, aid; support; **j-m B. leisten,** to help s.o.; to come to s.o.'s aid; to give, lend, render, s.o. assistance; **j-s B. anrufen,** to call in s.o.'s aid, help. **2.** (*pers.*) assistant, helper; help; support; *Jur:* (i) mother's legally appointed adviser exercising parental control; (ii) (lay) person acting in support of defendant (in court); **ärztlicher B.,** medical adviser.

Beistandsvertrag, *m.* pact for mutual assistance.

beistechen, *v.i. sep.* (*strong*) (*haben*) *Nau:* to sail close-hauled, close to the wind.

beistehen, *v.i. sep.* (*strong*) (*haben*) **1. j-m b.** to help, assist, aid, s.o.; to support s.o., to back s.o. up (in an undertaking); **j-m mit Trost b.,** to comfort s.o.; **j-m mit Rat b.,** to help, assist, s.o. with (one's) advice, to give s.o. the benefit of one's advice. **2.** to stand by, near; **die Beistehenden,** the bystanders, onlookers. **3.** *Nau:* **alle Segel b. lassen,** to carry a press of sail, to cram on sail, to crowd on (all) sail.

Beisteher, *m.* **-s/-.** **1.** helper, assistant. **2.** *Nau:* consort (ship).

Beisteuer, *f.* (voluntary) contribution, share (*esp.* of money); **eine B. geben,** to make a contribution; **um eine kleine B. bitten,** to ask for a small contribution.

Beisteuerer, *m.* **-s/-,** contributor (to expenses, newspaper, etc.).

beisteuern, *v.tr. & i. sep.* (*haben*) to contribute, to make a contribution (**zu etwas,** to sth., towards sth.); **Geld b.,** to contribute money; **einen Artikel zu einer Festschrift b.,** to contribute an article to a commemorative volume.

Beistich, *m. Nau:* half-hitch.

beistimmen. I. *v.i. sep.* (*haben*) **j-m (in etwas** *dat.*) **b.,** to agree, concur, with s.o. (on, in, sth.); **einem Vorschlag b.,** to consent, agree, to a proposal; to approve a proposal; **ich stimme Ihnen, Ihrer Meinung, bei,** I agree, concur, with you; I am of the same opinion, mind, as you.

II. *vbl s.* **1. Beistimmen,** *n. in vbl senses.* **2. Beistimmung,** *f. in vbl senses; also:* agreement, concurrence (with s.o.); consent, agreement (to a proposal); approval (of a proposal).

Beistrich, *m. Print: etc:* comma.

Beitel, *m.* **-s/-.** *Tls:* chisel.

Beitöne, *m.pl. Mus:* overtones.

Beitrag, *m.* **-(e)s/⸗e,** (*a*) contribution; share, quota (paid into fund, etc.); **B. an Geld,** contribution of money; **einen B. geben, leisten,** to make a contribution; **wir haben einen großen B. dazu geleistet,** we made a handsome contribution to it; (*b*) (membership) subscription (to club, party, etc.); *U.S:* (membership) dues; *Fin: Ins:* premium; **regelmäßiger B. zu einer mildtätigen Stiftung,** regular subscription to a charity; **seinen B. zahlen,** to pay one's subscription; (*c*) contribution (to learning, etc.); contribution, article (in newspaper, etc.); **sein Werk stellt einen wichtigen B. zur modernen Wissenschaft dar,** his work has made an important contribution to modern science; **Beiträge für eine Zeitung schreiben, liefern,** to write articles for a newspaper, to contribute articles to a newspaper; **historische, kritische, Beiträge,** historical, critical, essays.

beitragen, *v.tr. & i. sep.* (*strong*) (*haben*) **1.** (*a*) to contribute; **zu etwas b.,** to contribute to, to give towards, sth.; **sein, seinen, Teil b.,** to contribute one's share; to pay one's share; **zu einer mildtätigen Stiftung b.,** to subscribe, contribute, to a charity; (*b*) **zu einer Zeitung b.,** to contribute to a newspaper, to write for a newspaper. **2.** to contribute, conduce; **zum Erfolg eines Unternehmens b.,** to contribute, be conducive, conduce, to the success of an enterprise; **alles trug dazu bei, ihn glücklich zu machen,** everything contributed to make him happy; **das trägt viel dazu bei, ihren Verlust zu ersetzen,** that goes a long way to compensate for her loss; **das trägt nur dazu bei, ihn zu ärgern,** it only irritates him, it only serves to irritate him; **dies trägt nichts zu unserem Zwecke bei,** this does nothing to further our object.

Beiträger, *m.* contributor (to expenses, newspaper, etc.).

beitragspflichtig, *a.* (member of club, etc.) liable to subscription.

Beitragszahlung, *f.* payment of subscription, contribution.

beitragzahlend, *a.* **beitragzahlendes Mitglied,** subscribing member (of club, party, etc.).

beitreiben. I. *v.tr. sep.* (*strong*) to exact (sum of money); to recover, collect, get in (debts, taxes, etc.) (by force); *Mil: etc:* to requisition, commandeer (provisions, troops, etc.); to impress (men of fighting age); *A:* to bring in, drive in (sheep, etc.).

II. *vbl s.* **Beitreiben** *n.*, **Beitreibung** *f. in vbl*

senses; also: exaction (of sum of money); enforced collection (of taxes, etc.); requisition (of provisions, troops, etc.).

beitreten, *v.i. sep.* (*strong*) (*sein*) (*a*) **einem Verein, einer Partei, b.,** to join a club, a party, to become a member of a club, a party; **einem Bündnis b.,** to accede to a treaty (already in existence); **der protestantischen Lehre b.,** to adopt the protestant faith, to become a Protestant; (*b*) **j-s Meinung b.,** to fall in with, come over to, come round to, s.o.'s opinion; to concur in s.o.'s opinion.

Beitritt, *m.* **1.** (*a*) joining (of club, party, etc.); **B. zu einem Bündnis,** accession to a treaty; **B. zu der protestantischen Lehre,** adoption of the protestant faith; **seinen B. zu einem Verein erklären,** to declare one's membership of a club; **j-m den B. zu einem Verein, usw., gestatten,** to grant s.o. admittance, admission, to a club, etc.; (*b*) concurrence (**zu etwas,** in sth.). **2.** *Ven:* slot of a stag (*with marks of hind feet next to those of fore-feet*).

Beitrittserklärung, *f.* declaration of membership (of club, party, etc.); declaration of accession (to treaty).

Beitzker, *m.* **-s/-.** *Ich:* weatherfish, thunderfish.

Beiurteil, *n. Jur: A:* interlocutory decree *or* judgment.

beiurteilen, *v.i. sep.* (*haben*) *Jur: A:* to award an interlocutory decree.

Beiwache, Beiwacht, *f. Mil: A:* bivouac.

beiwachten, *v.i. insep.* (*haben*) *Mil: A:* to bivouac.

Beiwagen, *m.* **1.** side-car (on motor-cycle). **2.** trailer (on tram-car, etc.).

Beiwart, *m.*=**Beisitzer** 1.

Beiweib, *n. A:* concubine.

Beiwerk, *n.* accessory; accessories *pl*; decoration; trimmings; accessory figures, objects (in picture); embellishments, *F:* frills (to a story, an account); **ohne das überflüssige B. wäre der Aufsatz gut,** without the padding it would be a good composition.

beiwohnen. I. *v.i. sep.* (*haben*) **1.** (*a*) (*of pers.*) **etwas** *dat.* **b.,** to be (present) at sth., to attend sth.; **einem Ereignis b.,** to witness an event; **einer Feier b.,** to attend a ceremony; (*b*) *A:* (*of quality, etc.*) **j-m b.,** to be (present) in s.o. **2. j-m b.,** to cohabit with s.o.; to sleep, *Lit:* to lie, with s.o.; to have sexual intercourse with s.o.

II. *vbl s.* **1. Beiwohnen,** *n. in vbl senses; also:* presence (at an event). **2. Beiwohnung,** *f.* (*a*)=II. 1; (*b*) cohabitation; sexual intercourse, coitus, coition; **außereheliche B.,** adulterous intercourse; extramarital relations.

Beiwort, *n.* **-(e)s/-wörter,** epithet; *Gram:* adjective.

Beizahl, *f. Mth:* coefficient.

beizählen, *v.tr. sep.* to include, reckon, count (s.o., sth.) (*dat.,* in sth.); **den Großen beigezählt werden,** to be numbered with, among, the great.

beizäumen, *v.tr. sep. Equit:* **ein Pferd b.,** *abs.* **b.,** to hold a horse's head in an upright position.

Beizbrüchigkeit, *f.* acid-shortness (of wire, etc.).

Beizbrühe, *f.* (*a*) *Dy: etc:* mordant; (*b*) *Leath:* sour-water, bate.

Beizbütte, *f.* pickling tank; *Leath:* maceration tub, vat.

Beize, *f.* **-/-n. 1.** mordant chemical; sharp acid *or* saline; corrosive; (*a*) *Med: Pharm:* caustic; (*b*) *Dy: etc:* mordant; (*c*) *Gilding:* gold-size, mordant, mixtion; (*d*) *Art:* aqua fortis, nitric acid (for etching); (*e*) *Leath:* (i) sour-water, bate; (ii) tan(ning)-liquor, ooze, pickle; (iii) carroting agent; (*f*) *Tobacco Ind:* sauce; (*g*) *Agr: Hort:* chemical used to protect seeds from parasites; (*h*) *Cu:* marinade; pickle. **2.** (wood-)stain. **3.** *Ven:* hawking; falconry.

Beizeichen, *n.* **1.** attribute. **2.** *Her:* difference, mark of cadency; bisure.

Beizeisen, *n. Tls:* chasing-chisel.

beizeiten [bai'tsaitən], *adv.* in good time, early, *Lit:* betimes.

beizen. I. *v.tr.* **1.** (*a*) (*of acid*) to corrode; to eat into, bite into (metal); **beizende Flüssigkeit,** mordant, caustic, corrosive, liquid; (*b*) (*of smoke, etc.*) to sting (the eyes), to make (the eyes) smart; (*of sun*) to brown (sth.). **2.** (*of pers.*) to treat (sth.) with chemicals, acids, saline liquids; (*a*) *Ind:* to scour (surface) (with acid); to etch (metal); to pickle (metal sheets, etc.); (*b*) *Med:* to cauterize (wound, etc.) (with caustic); (*c*) *Dy:* to mordant (fabric, leather); (*d*) *Leath:* (i) to dip, soak (skins); (ii) to pure, bate (skins); (iii) to carrot (pelts); (*e*) *Agr: Hort:* to treat (seeds) with protective agent; (*f*) *Cu:* to marinade; to pickle. **3.** to stain (wood, etc.). **4.** *Ven:* to go hawking; **Hasen b.,** to hunt hares with a hawk *or* falcon.

II. *vbl s.* **Beizen** *n.,* **Beizung** *f. in vbl senses; also:* (*a*) corrosion; (*b*) maceration (of leather, etc.); (*c*) *Med:* cauterization (of wound, etc.) (with caustic); (*d*) hawking; falconry.

Beizenfarbstoff, *m.* mordant dye, acid dye.

Beizer, *m.* **-s/-. 1.** stainer. **2.** *Ven:* falconer.

Beizfalke, *m. Ven:* falcon.

Beizflüssigkeit, *f.* **1.** mordant, corrosive, liquor; (*a*) *Cu: etc:* pickling liquor, pickle; (*b*) *Leath:* tan(ning)-liquor; ooze, pickle. **2.** (wood-)stain.

Beizhund, *m.* hound (used in game-hawking).

beiziehen, *v.tr. sep.* (*strong*) to call in (doctor, expert, etc.) (for a second opinion).

Beizjagd, *f. Ven:* hawking; falconry.

Beizker, *m.* **-s/-**=**Beitzker.**

Beizkraft, *f.* (*a*) corrosive power; causticity; (*b*) staining power.

Beizkufe, *f.*=**Beizbütte.**

Beizmeister, *m. Ven:* falconer.

Beizmittel, *n.* (*a*) caustic; mordant; corrosive; (*b*) stain.

Beizofen, *m.* (*a*) *Metalw:* scaling furnace; (*b*) furnace used in wood-staining.

Beizung, *f. see* **beizen II.**

Beizvogel, *m. Ven:* bird used in falconry, *esp.* falcon *or* hawk.

bejahen. I. *v.tr.* (*a*) to say 'yes' to (sth.); to affirm (sth.); to give an affirmative answer to (sth.); to assert (sth.); **er gab eine bejahende Antwort,** he gave an answer in the affirmative; he said 'yes'; *Gram:* **bejahender Satz,** affirmative sentence; (*b*) **das Leben b., eine bejahende Haltung dem Leben gegenüber einnehmen,** to have a positive, an affirmative, attitude to life.

II. *vbl s.* **1. Bejahen,** *n. in vbl senses.* **2. Bejahung,** *f.* (*a*)=II. 1; *also:* affirmation, assurance; assertion; **die B. des Lebens,** the positive attitude to life; (*b*) affirmative answer.

bejahendenfalls, *adv.* in the event of an affirmative answer; if the answer is 'yes'.

bejahrt, *a.* aged, old; **b. sterben,** to die full of years; **ein bejahrter Greis,** a venerable old man.

Bejahrtheit, *f.* old age.

Bejahungsfall, *m.* **im B.**=**bejahendenfalls.**

Bejahungssatz, *m. Gram:* affirmative sentence.

Bejahungswort, *n.* **-(e)s/-wörter.** *Gram:* affirmative adverb.

bejammern, *v.tr.* to lament (s.o., sth.); to wail over (misfortune, s.o.'s fate, etc.).

bejammernswert, bejammernswürdig, *a.* lamentable (condition, etc.); wretched, pitiable (pers., condition, etc.).

bejubeln, *v.tr.* to shout for joy about (sth.); to acclaim (sovereign, etc.); to give an ovation to (actress, etc.); to give (s.o.) a rousing welcome.

bekacken, *v.tr. P:* to (be)foul (sth.); to dirty, soil (sth.) (with excrement).

bekalken, *v.tr.* to whitewash, to lime-wash (wall, etc.); *Agr:* to sprinkle (the ground, etc.) with lime, to lime (the ground, etc.); to lime-wash (fruit-trees, etc.).

bekalmen, *v.tr. Nau:* to becalm (a ship).

bekämpfen. I. *v.tr.* to combat, to fight (against) (opponent, etc.); to contend, to battle, with; to fight against (epidemics, temptation, opinion, etc.); to curb (desires, etc.); to oppose (plan, s.o., etc.); **ein Feuer b.,** to fight a fire; **Schädlinge b.,** to take action, measures, against pests; **einen Mißbrauch b.,** to make a stand against an abuse; **er bekämpfte es mit allen Mitteln,** he opposed it tooth and nail, he opposed it with all the means at his command; **sich (gegenseitig) b.,** to oppose one another; **Parteien, die sich bekämpfen, sich bekämpfende Parteien,** contending parties.

II. *vbl s.* **1. Bekämpfen,** *n. in vbl senses.* **2. Bekämpfung,** *f.*=II. 1; *also:* opposition to (plan, etc.); fight against (s.o., sth.); battle against (sth.); **B. von Schädlingen, usw.,** pest, etc., control.

bekannt[1], *p.p. see* **bekennen.**

bekannt[2], *a.* (*a*) known; **es ist allgemein b.,** it is well known, generally known; **eine (allgemein) bekannte Sache, etwas allgemein Bekanntes,** a well-known matter; a matter of common knowledge; *Pej:* a notorious affair; **etwas als b. vorraussetzen, annehmen,** to assume sth. as already known; **dies ist sein bekanntestes Buch, das bekannteste seiner Bücher,** this is the best-known of his books; **ein bekannter Schriftsteller,** a well-known writer, a writer of note; **er ist hier allen b.,** *F:* **er ist hier b. wie ein bunter Hund,** he is known here to everybody; **b. werden, sich b. machen,** to become well known, to make a name for oneself; **er ist als Lügner b.,** he is known to be a liar; **er ist b. für seine Grausamkeit,** he is notoriously cruel, he is known, notorious, for his cruelty; **ein Hotel b. für seine gute Küche, von b. guter Küche,** a hotel noted for, renowned for, its good cuisine; **er ist in Bonn b.,** he is well known in Bonn; *cp.* (*d*); (*b*) (*of pers., thg*) known (to s.o.); (*of pers.*) **sich mit einer Sache b. machen,** to make oneself familiar, acquainted, with a subject, to acquaint, familiarize, oneself with a subject; *see also* **bekanntmachen; mit j-m b. werden,** to become acquainted with s.o.; *see also* **bekanntwerden; sie ist mir gut, nicht näher, nur flüchtig, b.,** I know her well, I don't know her very well, I know her only slightly; **wenn ich besser mit ihm b. bin, sein werde,** when I know him better, when I have become better acquainted with him; **er ist mir vom Sehen b.,** I know him by sight; **er ist mit mir b.,** he is an acquaintance of mine; **wir sind miteinander b.,** we are acquainted; **j-n mit j-m b. machen,** to introduce s.o. to s.o.; **j-n mit etwas b. machen,** to acquaint s.o. with sth., to acquaint s.o. of a fact; **sie wurde bald mit ihm b.,** she soon got to know him; (*c*) (*of thg*) familiar; **es kommt einem b. vor,** it strikes one as familiar; **seine Stimme kam mir b. vor,** his voice sounded, seemed, familiar to me; (*d*) **er ist in Bonn b.,** he knows Bonn well, he is familiar with Bonn; *F:* **(mit etwas, j-m) b. tun,** to be overfamiliar (with sth., s.o.).

Bekannte, *m., f.* (*decl. as adj.*) (*a*) acquaintance; friend; **wir sind alte Bekannte,** we are old acquaintances; we have known each other for a long time; **ich war gestern bei Bekannten,** I went to see some friends (of mine) yesterday; **ein guter Bekannter, eine gute B., von mir,** a good friend of mine; **ein Bekannter,** an acquaintance; **er ist nicht mein Freund, er ist nur ein Bekannter von mir,** he is not a friend of mine, merely an acquaintance; (*b*) **meine B.,** my girl-friend, *F:* my girl; **mein Bekannter,** my boy-friend, *F:* my young man.

Bekanntenkreis, *m.* circle of acquaintances; **einen ausgedehnten, großen, B. haben,** to have a wide, large, circle of acquaintances.

bekanntermaßen, *adv.* as is generally, well, known.

Bekanntgabe, *f.* **-/-n,** (public) announcement; publication (of decree, etc.); **feierliche B.,** promulgation, proclamation (of law, etc.).

bekanntgeben, *v.tr. sep.* (*strong*) to announce; to make (sth.) known; to disclose (sth.); **wir gestatten uns, hiermit die Verlobung unserer Tochter mit Herrn X bekanntzugeben,** we beg to announce the engagement of our daughter to Mr X; **etwas (öffentlich) b.,** to make sth. public, to publish (decree, etc.); **das Wahlresultat b.,** to declare the poll; **feierlich b.,** to proclaim, promulgate (law); **j-m etwas b.,** to make sth. known to s.o.; to notify s.o. about sth.

bekanntlich, *adv.* as is generally, well, known; **b. sind die Frauen . . . ,** everyone knows that women are . . . .

bekanntmachen. I. *v.tr. sep.* to make public, to announce (news, plans, etc.); to publish (scientific discoveries, decrees, etc.); to make (sth.) known; to give notice of (sth.); **j-m etwas b.,** to make sth. known to s.o.; to notify s.o. about sth.; **etwas amtlich b.,** to announce sth. officially, to make an official announcement; **etwas durch Anschlag b.,** to post up sth.; to advertise (sale, etc.); **hiermit wird bekanntgemacht, daß . . . ,** notice is hereby given that . . . ; *see also* **Anschlag** 3; **etwas durch Ausrufen b. lassen,** to have sth. cried by the town-crier; **in diesem Buch werden verschiedene wichtige Funde erstmalig bekanntgemacht,** in this book several important finds are published for the first time; **diese Veröffentlichung hat den Zweck, sein Werk einer breiteren Öffentlichkeit bekanntzumachen,** this publication is intended to make his work known to a wider public; *see also* **bekannt**[2].

II. *vbl s.* **1. Bekanntmachen,** *n. in vbl senses.* **2. Bekanntmachung,** *f.* (*a*)=II. 1; *also:* publication (of scientific discovery, decree, etc.); (*b*) announcement; **amtliche B.,** official announcement; official notice; (*of town-crier, announcer, etc.*) **eine amtliche B. verlesen,** to proclaim, read out, an official announcement.

Bekanntschaft, *f.* **-/-en. 1.** (*a*) acquaintance; **j-s B. machen,** to make s.o.'s acquaintance; to meet s.o. (socially); **es hat mich gefreut, Ihre B. gemacht zu haben,** I am pleased to have met you; **er gewinnt bei näherer B.,** he improves upon closer acquaintance; **langjährige B. mit j-m,** long-standing acquaintance with s.o.; **er hat auf der Reise die B. einer netten jungen Dame, eine nette B., gemacht,** he has met a nice young lady on the journey; (*b*) **B. mit etwas,** acquaintance, familiarity, with sth.; knowledge of sth. **2.** *Coll:* acquaintance(s), acquaintanceship; **ich**

habe meine ganze B. eingeladen, I have invited everyone I know; **in meiner ganzen B.,** among all my acquaintances. 3. (*pers.*) acquaintance; friend; **er hat seltsame Bekanntschaften,** he has strange friends, acquaintances. **4. -bekanntschaft,** *comb.fm.* . . . acquaintance; **Wirtshausbekanntschaft,** pub acquaintance; **sie ist eine Ferienbekanntschaft, Reisebekanntschaft, von mir,** I met her on holiday, I met her on the journey.

bekanntwerden, *v.i. sep.* (*sein*) (*conj. like* **werden**) (*of thg*) to come to (s.o.'s) knowledge, notice; to become known; to become public; to become public knowledge; to transpire; **es ist mir bekanntgeworden, daß . . . ,** it has come to my notice, knowledge, that . . . ; **wie ist dir das bekanntgeworden?** how did you come to know that? **drei Repliken dieser Statue sind bis jetzt bekanntgeworden,** there are three known replicas of this statue; **zehn Fälle dieser Krankheit sind bekanntgeworden,** there have been ten known cases of this disease; **es wurde bekannt, daß . . . ,** it became public, known, that . . . , it transpired that . . . ; **es soll nicht b.,** it must not be known, be spread, get around; **mit der Zeit wird alles bekannt,** everything will be known, will come out, in time; *see also* **bekannt**².

bekappen, *v.tr.* **1.** (*a*) to hood (hawk, etc.); **bekappt,** hooded; (*b*) to top (shoe). **2.** to pollard, top, lop (tree).

Bekasse [be·'kasə], *f.* -/-n. *Orn:* woodcock.

Bekassine [be·ka'siːnə], *f.* -/-n. *Orn:* common snipe; Wilson's snipe; **große B.,** great snipe; **Nordische B.,** Faeroe snipe; **nadelschwänzige B.,** pintail snipe.

bekehrbar, *a.* (*of pers.*) convertible.

bekehren. I. *v.tr.* (*a*) to convert (s.o.) (to a creed); **j-n zum Christentum b.,** to convert s.o. to Christianity; **j-n zu Gott b.,** to turn s.o.'s heart to God; to convert s.o.; **zu Gott bekehrt werden, sich (zu Gott) b.,** to have one's heart turned to God, to be converted; **(zum Christentum) bekehrt werden, sich (zum Christentum) b.,** to become converted (to Christianity); to turn Christian; to become a convert (to Christianity); (*b*) **j-n zu einer Meinung b.,** to convert s.o., bring s.o. round, to an opinion; **sich zu j-s Ansicht b.,** to come round to s.o.'s point of view, opinion; *F:* **sich b.,** to change one's opinion, point of view.

II. *vbl s.* **1. Bekehren,** *n. in vbl senses.* **2. Bekehrung,** *f.* (*a*)=II. 1; *also:* conversion (of s.o.); (*b*) conversion; **nach seiner B. zum Christentum,** after his conversion to Christianity, after he had become a Christian; **B. Pauli,** conversion of St. Paul.

III. *p.p. & a.* **bekehrt,** *in vbl senses; esp.* **Bekehrte** *m, f,* convert; proselyte.

Bekehrer, *m.* -s/-, missionary; converter; *B.Lit:* **B. der Heiden,** converter of the Gentiles.

Bekehrungseifer, *m.* proselytism; missionary zeal.

bekehrungseifrig, *a.* zealous to make converts.

Bekehrungsreise, *f. Rel:* missionary journey.

Bekehrungssucht, *f.* proselytism.

bekennen. I. *v.tr.* (*conj. like* **kennen**) **1.** (*a*) to confess (sin, etc.); to avow; to admit; to acknowledge; *abs.* **b.,** to admit one's guilt, to confess; **er bekannte seine Schuld,** he confessed, admitted, his guilt; **b., daß man etwas getan hat,** to own up to having done sth., to confess that one has done sth.; **ich muß b., ich bekenne, daß ich unrecht hatte,** I confess, I own, I admit, (that) I was wrong; **ich muß b., es hat mich überrascht,** I was surprised, I must say; (*b*) to declare one's belief (in God, etc.); to confess, profess (one's faith); *Ecc:* **Bekennende Kirche,** Confessional Church; *see also* **Farbe** 2 (*b*). **2.** (*a*) **sich zu etwas bekennen,** to profess (a religion, doctrine, etc.); to confess to (a crime, etc.); to acknowledge, own, to own (up) to (deed); **sich zu j-m b.,** to stand by, to believe in, s.o.; to stand up openly for s.o.; to declare oneself a follower of (leader, etc.); to proclaim one's loyalty to s.o.; **sich zum Christentum b.,** to profess Christianity, to profess oneself a Christian; **sich zum Kommunismus b.,** to profess communism; to avow oneself a communist; to be an (avowed) adherent of communism; **sich zu j-s Meinung b.,** to pronounce oneself in agreement with s.o.'s opinion; **sich nicht zu seiner Meinung b.,** not to stand up for one's opinion; **sich zu Christus b.,** to declare oneself for Christ, to testify to Christ; **sich zu einem Kinde b.,** to own, acknowledge, a child; (*b*) **sich (für) schuldig b.,** to acknowledge one's guilt, to admit one's guilt; to confess to one's guilt, to being guilty; to plead guilty; **sich als j-s Anhänger b.,** to declare oneself s.o.'s follower; **sich als Verfasser b.,** to avow, acknowledge, oneself (as) author.

II. *vbl s.* **Bekennen,** *n. in vbl senses; also:* confession, admission (of sin, etc.); avowal (of creed, etc.); profession (of faith, etc.); acknowledgement (of error, crime, etc.).

Bekenner, *m.* -s/-, confessor (of religion, faith); **heilige Bekenner** *pl,* holy confessors; *Eng.Hist:* **Eduard der B.,** Edward the Confessor.

Bekennermut, *m.* unshakeable faith; (the) courage of one's (religious) convictions.

Bekenntnis, *n.* -nisses/-nisse. **1.** (*a*) confession (of sin, etc.); **ein vollständiges B. ablegen,** to make a full confession, to confess fully; (*b*) profession (of faith, etc.); avowal (of creed, etc.); declaration (for, against, sth.); **B. zu etwas,** declaration of loyalty (to one's country, a leader, etc.); affirmation of the value of (beauty, life, etc.); **ein B. zu Christus ablegen,** (i) to make an avowal of Christ; (ii) to testify to Christ. **2.** (*a*) confession (of faith), creed; **Augsburger B.,** Confession of Augsburg; (*b*) (religious) persuasion; denomination; creed; **Schule für Kinder aller Bekenntnisse,** school open to (children of) every creed, denomination; **Mitglieder aller christlichen Bekenntnisse,** members of all Christian denominations.

Bekenntnisbücher, *n.pl. Lutheran Theol:* dogmatic symbols contained in the Book of Concord.

Bekenntnischrist, *m. Ecc:* professing Christian.

bekenntnisfrei, *a.* **bekenntnisfreie Schule,** non-denominational school.

Bekenntnisfreiheit, *f.* religious freedom.

bekenntnisgläubig, *a. Rel:* conformable to the creed.

Bekenntniskirche, *f.* **1.** Lutheran church emphasizing the predominance of doctrinal adherence. **2.** *Ecc:* Confessional Church.

bekenntnismäßig, *a.* comformable to the creed.

Bekenntnisschrift, *f. Theol:* (*a*) confession of faith; creed; (*b*) *pl.* **Bekenntnisschriften**= **Bekenntnisbücher.**

Bekenntnisschule, *f.* denominational school.

bekenntnistreu, *a.* adhering to the creed.

Bekenntnistreue, *f.* devotion, faithful adherence, to the creed (of a church).

Bekenntniszwang, *m. Ecc:* stipulation for Lutheran clergy to conform to the dogmatic symbols in the Book of Concord.

bekichern, *v.tr.* to laugh, giggle, at (sth., s.o.).

bekiesen, *v.tr.* to gravel (road).

beklagen. I. *v.tr.* **1.** (*a*) to mourn (for) (s.o.); to grieve over, lament (the loss, death, of s.o.); **sein Tod wurde von allen, allgemein, beklagt,** his death was universally mourned; **seine Toten b.,** to mourn one's dead; **Menschenleben waren nicht zu b.,** there was no loss of life; (*b*) to lament, bewail (sth.); **sein Unglück b.,** to lament one's misfortune; **sein Schicksal b.,** to lament, bewail, one's fate; **seine Sünden b.,** to bewail one's sins; (*c*) to deplore, regret (fact, etc.); **diese Entscheidung ist zu b.,** this decision is regrettable; *impers.* **es ist zu b., daß...,** it is regrettable, to be regretted, that.... **2. sich beklagen,** to complain (**bei j-m über etwas** *acc.,* to s.o. about sth.); **sie hat sich bei mir über diese Ungerechtigkeit beklagt,** she complained to me about this injustice; **er beklagte sich (darüber), daß er nicht pünktlich bezahlt würde,** he complained that he was not paid on time; **er hat sich über alles beklagt,** he complained about everything, he found fault with everything. **3.** *Jur: A:* to accuse (s.o.).

II. *p.p. & a.* **beklagt,** *in vbl senses; esp. Jur:* (*in civil case*) **der, die, Beklagte, die beklagte Partei,** the defendant, the accused.

beklagenswert, beklagenswürdig, *a.* pitiable (pers., condition, etc.); lamentable (fate, condition, etc.); deplorable (condition); **es ist beklagenswert, daß . . . ,** it is deplorable that . . . .

beklatschen, *v.tr.* to applaud (s.o., sth.).

bekleben. I. *v.tr.* **etwas mit etwas b.,** to paste sth. with sth., to glue, stick, sth. over, on, sth.; **etwas mit Etiketten b.,** to label sth., to stick labels on sth.; **eine Mauer mit Plakaten b.,** to placard a wall, to paste posters on a wall.

II. *vbl s.* **Bekleben,** *n. in vbl senses; also:* **das B. der Wand ist verboten,** stick, *U.S:* post, no bills.

Beklebepapier, *n.* gummed paper; (self-)adhesive paper.

Beklebezettel, *m.* label; gummed label; stick-on label; *Bookb:* paste-on label.

bekleckern, *v.tr. F:* to stain, to spot (garment, etc.); **sich b.,** to soil one's clothes; **sich mit Suppe b.,** to spill soup over one's clothes.

beklecksen, *v.tr.* to daub, to smear, to blot, to stain (with ink, etc.).

Bekleidekeule, *f. Nau:* serving mallet.

bekleiden. I. *v.tr.* **1.** (*a*) to clothe, dress (s.o.); **j-n mit einem Gewand b.,** to dress, clothe, *Lit:* attire, s.o. in a garment; *B:* **ich bin nackt gewesen, und ihr habt mich bekleidet,** I was naked, and ye clothed me; (*b*) to invest (s.o.) (with insignia); **der Bischof wurde mit Ring und Stab bekleidet,** the bishop was invested with ring and staff; **j-n mit einem Amt, einer Würde, b.,** to invest s.o. with an office, a dignity; *Her:* **ein bekleideter Arm,** an arm vested. **2. ein Amt, eine Stelle, b.,** to hold an office, to fill a position. **3.** *Constr:* to cover, face (wall, etc.) (with stones, etc.); *Fort:* to revet.

II. *vbl s.* **1. Bekleiden,** *n. in vbl senses; also:* investiture (with insignia, etc.); tenure (of office). **2. Bekleidung** *f.* (*a*)=II. 1; (*b*) dress, clothes; (*c*) *Fort:* revetment.

Bekleidungsamt, *n. Mil:* clothing depot.

Bekleidungsgegenstände, *m.pl.* (articles of) clothing.

Bekleidungsgewerbe, *n.* clothing trade.

Bekleidungsindustrie, *f.* clothing industry.

Bekleidungskissen, *n. Nau:* chess-tree mat.

Bekleidungsmauer, *f. Fort:* revetment wall.

Bekleidungsstück, *n.* (article of) clothing.

Bekleidungsvorschriften, *f.pl. Mil: etc:* dress regulations.

bekleistern, *v.tr.* to paste (sth.) over; to stain (sth.) with paste.

beklemmen. I. *v.tr.* (*weak: p.p. also* **beklommen**) (*of air, anxiety, etc.*) to stifle; to oppress (breath, chest, etc.); **das beklemmt mein Herz,** that fills my heart with anguish; **es beklemmt mir den Atem,** it stifles my breath; **beklemmende Luft,** suffocating, stifling, air; **in beklemmter Lage sein,** to be in an awkward corner, in a tight spot; **beklommen,** uneasy, anxious; oppressed (by fear); **ihm war beklommen zumute,** he was feeling uneasy, he was uneasy in his mind.

II. *vbl s.* **Beklemmung,** *f.* (*a*) oppressed feeling; **B. der Brust,** tightness of the chest; **B. des Atems,** breathlessness; (*b*) feeling of constriction.

Beklemmtheit, *f.* oppressed feeling; tightness (of chest).

beklexen, *v.tr.*=**beklecksen.**

beklommen, *p.p. & a. see* **beklemmen.**

Beklommenheit, *f.* uneasiness; apprehension; (mental) anguish.

beklopfen, *v.tr.* to knock, to tap (wall, etc.) (*to test thickness, etc.*); to sound (rails, etc.); *Med:* to sound (chest, etc.) by percussion; to percuss.

bekloppt, *a. F:* cracked, barmy, crazy.

beknabbern, beknappern, *v.tr.* (*of rodent, etc.*) to gnaw, nibble, at (sth.).

bekneifen (sich), *v.refl.* (*strong*) *Nau:* **die Schläge des Ankertaues bekneifen sich auf dem Bratspill,** the cable runs foul upon the windlass.

bekneipen (sich), *v.refl. F:* to get drunk, tipsy.

beknie(e)n, *v.tr. F:* **j-n b.,** to work on s.o., to work on s.o.'s mind; to try to make s.o. do sth.

bekochen, *v.tr. F:* to feed, to cook for (s.o.).

beködern, *v.tr. Fish:* **eine Angel b.,** to bait a line.

bekohlen, *v.tr.* **1.** (*a*) *Nau:* to coal (ship), to bunker (ship) (with coal); (*b*) *Rail:* to coal (engine); (*c*) *Metall:* to feed (furnace, etc.). **2.** *Min:* to staff (mine). **3.** *F:* to lie to (s.o.); *F:* to tell fibs to (s.o.).

Bekohlungsanlage, *f.* coaling plant.

Bekohlungskran, *m.* coaling crane.

bekommen, *v.* (*strong*) I. *v.tr.* **1.** to get, to obtain; (*a*) **wo haben Sie das bekommen?** where did you get it? **etwas für j-n b.,** to get sth. for s.o., to get s.o. sth.; **man kann die Sache nirgendwo b.,** you can't get the thing anywhere; the thing is not to be had anywhere; **ich bekomme meinen Wein von X,** I get my wine from X; **ich habe das Pferd billig bekommen,** I got the horse cheap; **kann ich hier ein Zimmer b.?** can I get, have, a room here? **einen Preis b.,** to get, win, a prize; **er hat 500 Pfund im Jahr bekommen,** he got £500 a year; **ich habe noch zehn Mark zu b.,** I still have ten marks to come; **ich will sehen, was ich dafür b. kann,** I will see what I can get for it; **sein Teil b.,** to get what is due to one; to get one's share; **Arbeit b.,** to get work, to get a job; **Resultate b.,** to get, obtain, results; **mit diesem Buch hat er einen Namen bekommen,** he made a name for himself with this book; **auf diese Weise wird er nie eine Frau b.,** he will never get

a wife that way; (von j-m) (die) Erlaubnis b., etwas zu tun, to get, obtain, leave, permission (from s.o.) to do sth.; seinen eigenen Willen b., to get one's own way; (*b*) sie bekommt ein Kind, she is going to have a child, a baby; sie hat ein Kind bekommen, she has had a baby; der Baum wird viele Äpfel b., there will be a good crop of apples on this tree; das Bäumchen bekommt schon Blätter, the little tree is already putting out leaves; er bekommt schon einen Bart, he is already getting a beard; (*of baby*) Zähne b., to teethe; die zweiten Zähne b., to get one's second teeth; graue Haare b., to get grey hairs; (*c*) *W.Tel:* einen Sender b., to get a station; *Tp:* ich hatte einige Schwierigkeiten, deine Nummer, dich, zu b., I had some difficulty in getting your number, you. 2. to get, to receive (present, letter, etc.); ich habe seine Antwort heute morgen bekommen, I received his answer this morning; Bescheid b., to be informed (of sth.); ein Zimmer, das keine Sonne bekommt, a room that gets no sun; wir werden Regen b., we shall have rain; etwas zu essen, zu trinken, b., to get, to have, sth. to eat, to drink; du wirst eine Erkältung b., you will get, catch, a cold; einen Schlag b., (i) to get a blow; (ii) *Med: F:* to have a stroke; Prügel b., to get a thrashing; einen Schreck b., to get a fright, a shock; *F:* er hat zehn Jahre bekommen, he got ten years, he got ten years' imprisonment. 3. (*a*) etwas an eine bestimmte Stelle b., to get sth. somewhere; wie soll ich dieses Paket nach Hause b.? how am I to get this parcel home? (*b*) j-n dazu b., etwas zu tun, to get s.o. to do sth.; ich kann ihn nicht dazu b., früh aufzustehen, I can't get him to get up early; ich möchte ihn gerne in unseren Verein b., I would like to persuade him to join our club. 4. (*a*) etwas gemacht, getan, b., to get sth. done (by s.o.); kann ich das Kleid geändert b.? can I get, have, this dress altered? ich bekomme die Schuhe bis morgen repariert, the shoes will be (repaired) ready for me by tomorrow; (*b*) etwas getan b., to get sth. done, finished; ich bekomme heute gar nichts getan, I am not getting anything done today; ich werde das Kleid heute nicht mehr fertiggenäht b., I shall not be able to finish sewing the dress today after all, *cp.* fertigbekommen. 5. (*a*) etwas zu hören b., to get a lecture; etwas zu sehen, zu Gesicht, b., to get to see sth.; etwas zu tun b., (i) to get sth. to do; (ii) to get work, a job; du wirst etwas Schönes zu hören b., wenn du nach Hause kommst, you'll get a good talking-to when you get home; von dem Kuchen werden wir nichts zu sehen b., we shall see nothing of the cake; hast du auf der Reise viel zu sehen bekommen? did you see a great deal on your journey? ich wünschte, ich bekäme bald wieder etwas zu tun, I only wish I could get something to do again soon; ich habe ein Kleid zu nähen bekommen, I have been given a dress to sew; (*b*) *F:* es mit der Angst zu tun b., to get scared, to get the wind up; wenn er dich beleidigt, wird er es mit mir zu tun b., if he insults you he'll have me to deal with; (*c*) (*used to form personal passive*) etwas geschenkt, geliehen, b., to get, to be given, sth. as a present, on loan; etwas erzählt b., to be told sth.; ich weiß nicht, ob es wahr ist; ich habe es so erzählt bekommen, I don't know if it's true, but that's the way I heard it; wir bekamen ausgezeichneten Fisch vorgesetzt, we were served with, had, excellent fish; etwas vorgespielt b., to have sth. played for one. 6. (*a*) Hunger, Durst, b., to get, become, hungry, thirsty; Mut b., to become, grow, courageous; Lust zu etwas b., Lust b., etwas zu tun, to develop a desire for sth., to do sth.; etwas satt b., to get sick, tired, of sth.; es satt b., etwas zu tun, to grow tired of doing sth.; Heimweh b., to become, grow, get, homesick; *see also* Angst; (*b*) seine Augen bekamen einen glasigen Ausdruck, his eyes took on a glazed expression; seine Stimme bekam einen zärtlichen Ton, his voice took on a tender tone; (*c*) (*of wall, etc.*) Risse b., to crack, to develop cracks; (*of dress, etc.*) Flecke(n) b., to get stained; Löcher b., to get holes. 7. -bekommen, *comb.fm.* (*prefixed by adv.*), to get (sth.) (off, out, in, etc.); etwas herunterbekommen, to get sth. down; etwas hineinbekommen, to get sth. in (to sth.); *see also* abbekommen, aufbekommen.

II. bekommen, *v.i.* (*sein*) 1. (*of food, medicine, treatment, etc.*) j-m b., to agree with s.o.; to do s.o. good; unsere Kost scheint dem Kind gut zu b., our food seems to be good for the child; der Wein ist ihm nicht bekommen, the wine did not agree with him; Schweinefleisch bekommt ihr nicht, pork does not agree with her; wohl bekomm's! (i) enjoy your food! (ii) your health! (iii) *Iron:* good luck to you!; sie, der Umgang mit ihr, ist ihm nicht gut bekommen, she was not good for him; die Behandlung ist mir nicht bekommen, the treatment did not agree with me; das Klima bekommt ihm nicht, the climate does not agree with him; *F:* das viele Arbeiten bekommt mir nicht, hard work does not agree with me; die Reise ist ihr gut bekommen, the journey has done her good. 2. das wird euch schlecht, übel, b., this won't do you any good; you'll regret it; es wird dir schlecht b., wenn du heute abend nicht zur Zeit zu Hause bist, if you don't come home on time tonight it will be the worse for you; das soll ihm übel, schlecht, b., he'll have to pay for that.

bekömmlich, *a.* easily digestible (food, etc.); beneficial (climate, etc.); Gebratenes ist nicht sehr, nicht leicht, b., fried foods are not very, not easily, digestible; Kochen macht Nahrungsmittel bekömmlicher, leichter b., cooking makes foods more easily digestible; *cp.* leichtbekömmlich.

Bekömmlichkeit, *f.* digestibility (of food, etc.); beneficial effect (of climate, etc.).

bekomplimentieren, *v.tr.* to compliment (s.o.).

beköstigen. I. *v.tr.* j-n b., to board, feed, s.o.; sich selbst b., to cook for oneself, to do one's own cooking; meine Wirtin beköstigt mich nur mittags, abends beköstige ich mich selbst, my landlady gives me lunch, in the evening I cook for myself.

II. *vbl s.* 1. Beköstigen, *n. in vbl senses.* 2. Beköstigung, *f.* (*a*)=II. 1; (*b*) board; volle B., full board.

bekotzen, *v.tr. P:* to vomit on (sth.); to be sick on (sth.); er hat sich von oben bis unten bekotzt, he was sick all over himself.

bekräftigen. I. *v.tr.* 1. (*a*) j-n in seinem Glauben, in seiner Meinung, b., to strengthen, confirm, s.o. in his belief, opinion, to strengthen, confirm, s.o.'s belief, opinion; seine Antwort bekräftigte mich in meiner Annahme, his answer strengthened my assumption; dieses Ereignis bekräftigte ihn in seinem Vorhaben, this event strengthened him in his intention; (*b*) etwas b., to reinforce, strengthen, reaffirm, sth.; etwas mit einem Eid, Schwur, b., to reinforce sth. by an oath; er bekräftigte seine Aussage mit der Versicherung, daß . . . , he reinforced his statement with the assurance that . . . ; seine Behauptung wurde durch Augenzeugenaussagen bekräftigt, his statement was supported by the testimony of eye-witnesses; er bekräftigte sein Versprechen mit einem Kuß, he sealed his promise with a kiss; *see also* eidlich. 2. *A:* to strengthen (s.o., s.o.'s health, power, etc.); *B:* und Salomo ward in seinem Reich bekräftiget, and Solomon was strengthened in his kingdom.

II. *vbl s.* Bekräftigen *n.*, Bekräftigung *f. in vbl senses, also:* reinforcement; reaffirmation; zur Bekräftigung, in, as a, confirmation; in support; as a solemn affirmation.

bekränzen, *v.tr.* to wreathe, garland, bedeck (s.o., sth.) (with flowers); to crown (s.o.) (with laurels, etc.) (as sign of victory); mit Rosen bekränzt, crowned with roses.

bekreuzen, *v.tr.*=bekreuzigen.

bekreuzigen, *v.tr. Ecc:* to make the sign of the cross over (s.o.); sich b., to cross oneself.

bekriegen[1], *v.tr.* to fight, war, combat, against (s.o., sth.).

bekriegen[2] **(sich),** *v.refl. F:* to collect oneself; to settle down (*after upsetting experience, etc.*).

bekritteln, *v.tr.* to criticize (s.o., sth.); to cavil at (sth.); to find fault with (s.o., sth.); alles b., to find fault with everything.

bekritzeln, *v.tr.* to scrawl, scribble, on (sth.); to doodle on (sth.).

bekrönen. I. *v.tr.* 1. *Lit:* to crown (s.o., s.o.'s head); to wreathe (s.o., s.o.'s head) (with laurels). 2. (*of success, glory, etc.*) to crown (s.o., old age, youth, etc.); mit Ruhm bekrönt kehrte er zurück, he returned crowned with fame. 3. to head, surmount, crown (column, etc.); to cap (pier, etc.); to cope, crown (wall, etc.); (*of castle, etc.*) to cap, crown (mountain, etc.); Gebäude, mit Statuen bekrönt, building crowned with statues; eine Säule, von einer Figur bekrönt, a column crowned with a figure.

II. *vbl s.* 1. Bekrönen, *n. in vbl senses.* 2. Bekrönung, *f.* (*a*)=II. 1; (*b*) crowning piece (of building, etc.).

bekrusten, *v.tr.* to cover (sth.) with a crust, to encrust (sth.) (with rust, etc.); sich b., to become encrusted, crusted over.

bekümmern, *v.tr.* 1. (*a*) to trouble, worry (s.o.); to disturb (s.o.); über etwas *acc.*, um j-n, bekümmert sein, to feel concerned, to worry, about sth., s.o.; sein Aussehen bekümmert mich, I am very concerned, anxious, about him, he doesn't look at all well to me; dein Entschluß bekümmert mich, your decision troubles me; er schien darüber sehr bekümmert, he seemed to be very troubled, concerned, about it; mit bekümmertem Gesicht, with a troubled, worried, face; (*b*) *impers.* es bekümmert mich, daß . . . , it worries, troubles, me that . . . ; es bekümmert mich, daß das Kind gar keine Fortschritte macht, it worries me that the child makes no progress, does not get on at all. 2. sich um etwas *acc.*, j-n, bekümmern, to concern oneself with sth., s.o., to trouble oneself about sth., s.o.; warum soll ich mich um ihre Angelegenheiten b.? why should I trouble myself, bother, about her affairs? du brauchst dich nicht um mich zu b., (i) you need not trouble yourself, bother, about me; (ii) you can leave me alone.

Bekümmernis, *f.* -/-nisse, grief, sorrow, worry, trouble; zu meiner großen B., to my great grief.

bekunden. I. *v.tr.* 1. *Jur:* eine Aussage eidlich b., to make a statement on oath; der Zeuge bekundete eidlich, daß . . . , the witness deposed that . . . . 2. (*a*) to manifest, declare (sth.); to show openly, to evince (sth.); to make (sth.) known; er hat seine Zuneigung zu ihr öffentlich bekundet, he showed his liking for her openly, he made his liking for her known to all; seine Freude, sein Leid, b., to display one's joy, grief; (*b*) to reveal, to betray; to show; (*of thg*) sich b., to reveal itself, to become apparent; mit jedem Wort, das er sagte, bekundete er seine Unkenntnis, he betrayed, revealed, his ignorance with every word he spoke; hier bekundet sich ihre Klugheit, here her intelligence becomes evident, apparent; das bekundet seinen Mangel an Geist, that shows, reveals, his lack of intellect.

II. *vbl s.* 1. Bekunden, *n. in vbl senses.* 2. Bekundung, *f.* manifestation, display (of joy, grief, knowledge, etc.); revelation (of ignorance, etc.); zur B. seiner Freude, as a sign of his joy.

bekupfern, *v.tr.* to cover (sth.) with copper, to copper.

Bel[1] [beːl], *m.* -s/Bealim ['beːaˑlim]. *Rel.Hist:* Baal.

Bel[2] [bɛl], *n.* -s/-. *Ph. Meas:* (*unit of sound*) bel.

belächeln, *v.tr.* to smile in a superior manner at (remark, scheme, behaviour, etc.); to make light of (suggestion, scheme, etc.); to smile pityingly at (s.o.); to be amused at (sth.).

beladen, *v.tr.* (*strong*) to load (s.o., sth.); einen Wagen mit Heu b., to load (up) a waggon with hay; ein Schiff mit Korn b., to load a ship with grain; ein mit Korn beladenes Schiff, ein Schiff, mit Korn beladen, a ship laden with grain; der Tisch war mit Speisen beladen, the table was loaded, laden, with food; schwer beladen sein, to be heavily laden, loaded; sie kam schwer beladen vom Markt zurück, she returned from the market heavily laden; seinen Geist mit zu viel Wissen b., to overburden one's mind with too much knowledge; sich mit etwas b., to burden oneself with sth.; *B:* alle, die ihr mühselig und beladen seid, all ye that labour and are heavy laden.

Belag, *m.* -(e)s/=e. 1. (*a*) covering (of floor, bridge, etc.); flooring, planking, chesses (of bridge); surface (of road); (*b*) coat, coating (of plaster); (enamel, etc.) coating; (silver) plating; covering, foil (of mirror); lining (of brake); *El:* coating (of Leyden jar); plate (of condenser); (*c*) layer (of dust, mould, etc.); *Miner: Ch: etc:* incrustation, efflorescence; film (of verdigris, etc.); bloom (of sulphur on rubber); *Med:* fur (on tongue). 2. *Cu:* filling, topping (of open sandwich); filling (of roll).

Belagerer, *m.* -s/-, besieger, beleaguerer.

belagern. I. *v.tr.* 1. to besiege, beleaguer, invest (town, etc.); to lay siege to (town, etc.); eine Festung von allen Seiten b., to besiege a fortress from all sides; die Stadt wurde drei Monate lang belagert, the town was beleaguered, under siege, invested, for three months; Cäsar, Cäsars Armee, war von allen Seiten belagert, Caesar, Caesar's army, was surrounded; the enemy closed in upon Caesar, upon Caesar's army. 2. to beset, to beleaguer (s.o.); (*of crowd*) to throng (round), to crowd round (s.o., sth.); die Tür ist von Bettlern belagert, Bettler belagern die Tür, beggars throng round the door; sein Haus war von Zeitungsreportern belagert, Zeitungsreporter belagerten sein Haus, his house was besieged by newspaper reporters, newspaper reporters thronged round, laid siege to, his house.

II. *vbl s.* 1. **Belagern,** *n. in vbl senses.* 2. **Belagerung,** *f.* (*a*)=II. 1; (*b*) *Mil:* siege; **förmliche B.,** regular siege; **die B. eröffnen,** to begin the siege; **die B. aufheben, abbrechen,** to raise the siege; **der B. standhalten,** to withstand the siege.

Belagerungsartillerie, *f.* siege-artillery.

Belagerungsgeschütz, *n.* siege-gun, siege-piece.

Belagerungsheer, *n. Mil:* besieging army.

Belagerungskrone, *f. Rom. Ant:* obsidional crown.

Belagerungsmaschine, *f. A.Mil:* siege-machine.

Belagerungsmünze, *f. Num:* obsidional coin, siege-coin, siege-piece.

Belagerungspark, Belagerungstrain, *m. Artil: A:* siege-train.

Belagerungsturm, *m. A.Mil:* siege-tower.

Belagerungswerke, *n.pl.* siege-works.

Belagerungszustand, *m.* state of emergency; state of siege; **den B. über eine Stadt verhängen,** to declare a town to be in a state of siege.

Bel-Ami, Belami [bɛla·ˈmiː], *m.* -(s)/-s. *F:* lady's man; lady-killer.

Belang, *m.* -(e)s/-e. 1. (*of fact, event, etc.*) **von B.,** of importance, consequence, moment; **Sache ohne B.,** unimportant, trifling, trivial, matter; matter of no importance, consequence, import; **eine Frage von B.,** a question of importance, of consequence, a momentous, weighty, question. 2. *pl.* **Belange,** interests; **die britischen Belange im mittleren Osten,** the British interests, spheres of interest, in the Middle East; **ich werde Ihre Belange vertreten,** I will represent your interests; **er vertritt die kulturellen Belange der Stadt,** he is concerned with the cultural affairs of the town.

belangbar, *a. Jur:* indictable, suable.

belangen. I. *v.tr.* 1. *Jur:* **j-n (gerichtlich) b.,** to sue, prosecute, indict, arraign (s.o.) (**wegen,** for); **dafür können Sie gerichtlich belangt werden,** you can be prosecuted for this. 2. *impers.* **was mich, ihn, belangt,** as far as I am, he is, concerned.

II. *vbl s.* **Belangen** *n.*, **Belangung** *f. Jur:* prosecution, arraignment (**wegen,** for).

belanglos, *a.* unimportant, trifling, trivial, insignificant (matter), (matter) of no importance, consequence, import; **es ist völlig b., ob . . . ,** it does not matter whether . . . , it is of no importance whether . . . .

Belanglosigkeit, *f.* (*a*) unimportance, insignificance; (*b*) trifle, trifling matter, matter of no importance; **er redet nichts als Belanglosigkeiten,** his talk consists of nothing but trivialities.

belangvoll, *a.* (*of fact, event, etc.*) important, of consequence.

belassen, *v.tr.* (*strong*) (*a*) **etwas bei etwas b.,** to leave sth. at sth., to let sth. rest at sth.; (*b*) **j-n (im Amt, usw.) b.,** to keep, retain, s.o. (in office, etc.).

belasten. I. *v.tr.* 1. (*a*) to load (sth.); to make (sth.) heavy; to put a, the, weight, load, on (sth.); **etwas mit Steinen b.,** to weigh sth. down with stones; **das Auto war zu sehr, zu stark, belastet,** the car was overloaded; **sein Gedächtnis mit unnützen Zahlen b.,** to burden one's memory with unnecessary dates; **man soll abends seinen Magen nicht zu sehr b.,** one should not overburden one's stomach at night; (*b*) (*of pers.*) to be in (s.o.'s) way, to be a burden to (s.o.); *F:* to be a dead weight on (s.o.); (*c*) to make demands on (electricity, etc., supply, railway lines, etc.); to subject (electricity, etc., supply, railway lines, etc.) to strain; to put (motor, etc.) under load; **die öffentlichen Verkehrsmittel sind morgens und abends am stärksten, vormittags am wenigsten, belastet,** public transport has its peak hours in the mornings and evenings; the demand is lowest before noon; **elektrische Leitungen dürfen nur bis zu einer bestimmten Grenze belastet werden,** electrical wiring may only be loaded to a certain limit; **das Telephonnetz, das elektrische Leitungsnetz, ist zu stark belastet,** the telephone, electricity, network is overloaded; **das Telephonnetz ist nachts weniger belastet,** the telephone network is less busy at night. 2. (*a*) to weigh (s.o.) down, to weigh heavily upon (s.o.), to burden (s.o.); **ein Volk mit Steuern b.,** to burden a people with taxes; **er war mit Sorgen belastet,** his worries weighed heavily upon him, weighed him down; **es belastet mein Gewissen,** it weighs on my conscience; **mit Schulden belastet sein,** to be encumbered, burdened, with debts; (*b*) *Com: etc:* to charge, debit (s.o.'s account) (with a sum); **ein belastetes Grundstück,** an encumbered, a burdened, estate; **ein mit einer Hypothek belastetes Grundstück, Haus,** an estate, a house, encumbered with a mortgage; *see also* **Hypothek, hypothekarisch;** (*c*) *Jur:* to incriminate (s.o.); **belastende Zeugenaussage,** incriminating evidence; *see also* **erblich** [2].

II. *vbl s.* 1. **Belasten,** *n. in vbl senses.* 2. **Belastung,** *f.* (*a*)=II. 1; *also: Jur:* incrimination (of accused); (*b*) weight, load; burden; *F:* (*of pers.*) encumbrance, dead weight; **steuerliche B.,** (i) tax-contribution of the individual, (ii) incidence of taxation, (iii) burden of taxation; **es ist eine große B. für ihn, daß er seine Schwiegermutter zu erhalten hat,** it is a great strain for him to have to keep his mother-in-law; **wir wollen das Kind nicht mitnehmen, es wird nur eine B. sein,** we won't take the child with us, he will only be a burden, be in the way; (*c*) *Tchn: Constr: El.E: etc:* load; **zulässige B.,** safe, working, load; **höchste B.,** maximum, peak, load; **geringste B.,** minimum load; *Mch: El.E:* base load; **gleichbleibende B.,** constant load; *Constr:* **ruhende B.,** dead load; **bewegliche B.,** live load; **Maschine, die mit voller B. arbeitet,** machine working (at) full load; **Maschine, die ohne B. läuft,** machine running with, on, no load, machine running light; *Rail:* **betriebliche B.,** engagement; *Rail: El.E: Tp:* **die Zeiten größter B.,** peak hours, peak periods; **Zeiten geringer B.,** off-peak hours, quiet periods; *Hyd.E:* **B. des Überfalles,** head of water over the spillway; (*d*) *Com: etc:* debit (of account); encumbrance (of estate); (*e*) *Jur:* incrimination (by witness, etc.); *see also* **erblich** [2].

belästigen. I. *v.tr.* (*a*) (*of condition, etc.*) to inconvenience, incommode (s.o.); to disturb (s.o.); **mein Rauchen belästigt Sie hoffentlich nicht,** I hope you don't mind my smoking, my smoking doesn't bother you; (*b*) to bother, pester, annoy (s.o.); *F:* to badger (s.o.); to obtrude oneself on (s.o.); to importune, molest (s.o.); **darf ich Sie damit noch einmal b.?** may I trouble you with it once more? **j-n mit Fragen b.,** to pester s.o. with questions; **von Mücken belästigt werden,** to be bothered by mosquitoes; **das Mädchen wurde von Männern belästigt,** the girl was molested by men.

II. *vbl s.* 1. **Belästigen,** *n. in vbl senses.* 2. **Belästigung,** *f.* (*a*)=II. 1; *also:* obtrusion (on s.o.); disturbance (of s.o.); molestation (of s.o.); (*b*) molestation; annoyance; disturbance; inconvenience; **die dauernden Belästigungen fallen mir auf die Nerven,** the constant molestations get on my nerves; **ich hoffe, daß mein Besuch keine B. ist,** I hope my visit is not inconvenient.

Belastung, *f. see* **belasten II.**

Belastungsanzeige, *f. Com:* debit note.

Belastungsfähigkeit, *f.* load capacity; carrying capacity.

Belastungsgebirge, *n. El: Rail: etc:* load curve for the year, season, etc.

Belastungsgrenze, *f. El:* limit of carrying capacity; limit of load.

Belastungskurve, *f. El.E: etc:* load curve.

Belastungslinie, *f. Constr:* load line.

Belastungsprobe, *f. Mec.E: Constr: etc:* load test; *F:* **unsere Freundschaft wird jeder B. standhalten,** our friendship will stand every test.

Belastungsraum, *m. Nau:* hold.

Belastungsschwankung, *f. El.E:* fluctuation of load.

Belastungsspitze, *f. El: Rail: etc:* load peak.

Belastungstal, *n. El: Rail: etc:* lowest point of load curve.

Belastungszahl, *f. Constr:* load coefficient.

Belastungszeuge, *m. Jur:* witness for the prosecution.

belatscht, *a. Orn:* muffed (pigeon).

belauben. I. *v.tr.* (*of spring, etc.*) to cover (tree, etc.) in leaves; **sich b.,** (*of tree, etc.*) to leaf, to break, come, into leaf, to put out leaves; **belaubt,** in leaf; **der Baum ist dicht belaubt,** the tree is thickly, densely, covered in leaves; **grün belaubt,** green with leaves.

II. *vbl s.* **Belaubung,** *f.* (*a*) *in vbl senses;* (*b*) foliage, leaves.

Belaubtheit, *f.* leafiness.

belauern, *v.tr.* to watch, observe, (s.o.) secretly; to spy upon (s.o.).

Belauf, *m.* -(e)s/. 1. *Com:* amount (of bill, etc.); sum; **der ganze B.,** the total. 2. forester's district. 3. *N.Arch:* run; rising of a ship's floor.

belaufen, *v.* (*strong*) 1. *v.tr.* (*a*) *A:* to run over, inspect (land, etc.); (*b*) to cover (sth.) (with sth.); (*of smoke, etc.*) to penetrate, pervade (sth.); (*c*) *Breed:* (*of male animal*) to cover (female); **sich b.,** to mate. 2. *v.i.* (*sein*) (*of window-pane, etc.*) to cloud, mist, over. 3. **sich belaufen,** (*a*) (*of window-pane, etc.*)=**belaufen** 2; (*b*) (*of sum, etc.*) **auf . . . +acc.,** to amount, to come, run, to; **die Spesen belaufen sich auf mehrere tausend Mark,** the expenses mount up to several thousand marks; **ich weiß nicht, auf wieviel sich meine Schulden belaufen,** I don't know what my debts amount to.

belauschen, *v.tr.* to overhear (s.o., sth.); to listen secretly to (s.o., sth.); to eavesdrop on (s.o.); *Lit:* **die Nachtigall b.,** to listen to, *Lit:* to hearken unto, the nightingale.

Belbaum [ˈbɛl-], *m. Bot:* bael-, bel-fruit tree, Bengal quince.

Belche, *f.* -/-n. 1. *Orn:* coot. 2. *Ich:*=**Blaufelchen.**

Belchen, *m.* -s/. *Geog:* rounded mountain top, *ballon;* **Sulzer B.,** Sulzer *ballon.*

beleben. I. *v.tr.* 1. (*a*) (*of God, sun, etc.*) to endue (s.o., sth.) with life; to animate, give life to (s.o., sth.); **die Sonne belebt alle Pflanzen,** the sun gives life to, enlivens, all plants; **ich war wie neu belebt,** I was given a new lease of life; I was a new man, woman; I was revived; **wieder b.,** to restore (s.o.) to life, to revive (s.o.); (*b*) to invigorate (s.o.); to enliven, quicken, animate, stimulate (conversation, etc.); (*of success, pleasant events, etc.*) to give new life to, to encourage (s.o.); **die Seeluft wird Sie b.,** the sea air will invigorate you, set you up; **die grünen Pflanzen beleben das Zimmer ein wenig,** the green plants brighten the room a little; **wenn ich ganz besonders müde bin, kann mich nur noch Kaffee b.,** when I am especially tired only coffee can restore me; **ein belebendes Getränk,** a stimulating, revivifying, drink; **belebende Wirkung,** reviving, stimulating, effect (of drug, coffee, tea, etc.); restorative effect (of medicine); stimulating effect (of climate); **belebende Wärme,** life-giving warmth. 2. **sich beleben,** to revive, reanimate, oneself; to come to life; (*of nature, hope, etc.*) to quicken; (*of road, etc.*) to become lively, busy; **seine Hoffnungen belebten sich (wieder),** his hopes quickened, revived (again); **plötzlich belebte sich die Straße mit Menschen,** all of a sudden the street came alive (with people), came to life.

II. *vbl s.* 1. **Beleben,** *n. in vbl senses.* 2. **Belebung,** *f.* (*a*) *in vbl senses; also:* vivification; animation; invigoration; revival; stimulation (of conversation, etc.); **die B. der Totengebeine,** the resurrection of the dry bones; **die B. Adams,** God('s) breathing life into Adam; (*b*) revival.

III. *p.p. & a.* **belebt,** *in vbl senses; esp.* 1. animate (creature, etc.); *Ling:* **belebtes Genus,** animate gender. 2. lively, animated (conversation, etc.); lively, busy (road, etc.); much frequented (road, etc.); *St.Exch:* **belebte Börse,** brisk market; **sie wohnen in einer der belebtesten Straßen,** they live in one of the busiest streets.

Beleber, *m.* -s/-, giver of life.

Belebtheit, *f.* 1. state of being animate, animation. 2. animation, liveliness (of conversation, etc.); liveliness (of street, town, etc.); *St.Exch:* briskness (of market).

Belebungsmittel, *n.* stimulant, restorative.

Belebungsversuch, *m.* attempt to bring (s.o.) back to life, to restore life (to s.o.).

belecken, *v.tr.* to lick (at) (s.o., sth.); **der Hund beleckt seine Pfote,** the dog licks its paw; *F:* **von der Kultur beleckt,** (*of nation, pers.*) with a veneer of culture.

beledern, *v.tr.* to cover (sth.) with leather; *Mec.E: Mch:* to pack (piston).

Beleg, *m.* -(e)s/-e. 1. (documentary) proof (of sth.); evidence, *Jur:* supporting evidence (for sth.); voucher; receipt (used to support claims *or* to account for expenses); *Book-k: etc:* document; **Unkostenabrechnung mit Belegen,** statement of expenses incurred accompanied by vouchers; **Belege beibringen,** to furnish evidence. 2. evidence (adduced to verify statement, to prove use of word, etc.); instance, example (of use of word, etc.); illustration, illustrative quotation, authority, reference (for word, etc.); **als B. für das Vorkommen des Wortes kann ich drei Stellen in Plautus zitieren,** as evidence for the occurrence of the word I can quote three passages in Plautus; **als B. für seine These gibt er Plato an,** he cites Plato as authority for his thesis; **er gibt keinerlei Belege in diesem Buch,** in this book he gives no references at all; **für den Gebrauch dieses Wortes könnte ich zahllose Belege beibringen,** I could cite innumerable instances of the use of this word. 3.=**Belegexemplar.**

Belegbank, *f. Nau:* cross-piece.
Belegbogen, *m. Sch:* form recording the lectures and classes for which a student registers.
Belegbuch, *n. Sch:* book recording the lectures and classes for which a student registers; students' record book.
Belegbuchhaltung, *f. Book-k:* slip-system.
belegen[1]. I. *v.tr.* **1.** (*a*) to cover (sth.) (with sth.); **etwas mit Brettern b.,** to board sth.; **ein Zimmer mit Dielen b.,** to floor a room; **etwas mit Planken b.,** to plank (over) sth.; **den Fußboden mit Fliesen b.,** to tile the floor; **den Boden mit Teppichen b.,** to cover the floor with carpets; **Brötchen b.,** to fill rolls (with meat, etc.); **ein Brötchen mit Schinken b.,** to put (some) ham on a roll; *Mil:* **eine Stellung mit Schnellfeuer b.,** to cover a position with rapid fire; **eine Stadt mit Bomben b.,** to bomb a town; to plaster a town with bombs; *Her:* **ein Stück mit einem anderen b.,** to charge one piece with another; **mit . . . belegt,** charged with . . . ; *see also* **wiederbelegt;** (*b*) *Aut: etc:* to line (brake); *El:* to coat (Leyden jar); (*c*) (*of queen-bee*) **Zellen mit Eiern b.,** to lay eggs in cells; (*of bird*) **das Nest mit Eiern b.,** to lay eggs in the nest. **2.** (*a*) to put sth. on (a seat, etc.) in order to reserve it; to reserve, secure, *F:* to bag (seat, place, etc.); to fill (beds, wards, in hospital); **dieser Platz ist belegt,** this seat is taken; **alle Plätze sind belegt,** all the seats are taken; **alle Betten sind belegt,** (*in hotel*) all the rooms are booked, taken, *U.S:* all the rooms are reserved; (*in hospital*) all the beds are occupied, full; *Rail:* **belegtes Gleis,** occupied track; (*b*) *Sch:* **eine Vorlesung b.,** to enrol, register, for a course of lectures, *U.S:* to sign up for a course; *abs.* **b.,** to register (for a term); (*c*) to man, staff (factory, etc.); **eine Grube (mit Arbeitern) b.,** to employ workmen in a mine, to man a mine; *Mil:* **einen Posten b.,** to man a post. **3.** (*a*) to impose (sth.) on (s.o., sth.); **j-n mit einer Geldstrafe b.,** to impose a fine on s.o.; **ein Land mit Steuern b.,** to impose a tax on a country, to tax a country; **etwas mit Abgaben b.,** to impose taxes on sth.; to levy duties on sth.; **einen Ort mit Einquartierung b.,** to quarter, billet, soldiers on a place; *see also* **Bann 2** (*b*), **Beschlag 4, Gefängnis 2;** (*b*) **er wurde mit dem Beinamen 'der Gerechte' belegt,** he received, was given, the appellation 'the Just'. **4.** *Breed:* (*of male animal*) to cover (female). **5.** (*a*) to furnish evidence (for sth.); **eine Abrechnung mit Quittungen b.,** to accompany an account with receipts, vouchers; (*b*) to prove, substantiate (statement, etc.); to adduce evidence, examples (for occurrence of word, etc.); **er konnte seine Aussage urkundlich b.,** he was able to substantiate his statement with documents; **etwas mit Beispielen b.,** to illustrate, substantiate, sth. with examples; **können Sie dieses Wort b.,** can you give an instance of the occurrence of this word? **das Wort ist mehrfach in Plautus belegt,** the word occurs several times in Plautus; **das Wort ist nicht sicher belegt,** there is no definite evidence for this word; **sie hat jede ihrer Behauptungen vorzüglich belegt,** she has documented each of her assertions with excellent effect. **6.** (*a*) *Fenc:* **die Klinge b.,** to bind one's adversary's blade; (*b*) *Nau:* **ein Boot b.,** to belay a boat. **7. sich belegen,** (*of thg*) to become covered, coated (with dust, mould, etc.); (*of tongue, throat*) to become coated, furred; (*of voice*) to become thick, husky, throaty; **belegte Zunge,** coated, furred, tongue; **eine belegte Stimme,** a thick, husky, throaty, voice.
II. *vbl s.* **1. Belegen,** *n. in vbl senses.* **2. Belegung,** *f.* (*a*)=II. 1; (*b*) *El:* coating (of Leyden jar, etc.); plate (of condenser); *cp.* **Belag.**
belegen[2], *a. A:* situated.
Belegexemplar, *n.* specimen (of advertisement, etc.); file copy; *Publ:* (i) voucher copy; (ii) author's copy.
Belegholz, *n. Carp:* veneer.
Beleghölzer, *n.pl. Nau:* bitts.
Belegklampe, *f. Nau:* belaying cleat.
Belegknochen, *m. Anat:* membrane bone.
Belegnagel, *m. Nau:* belaying pin.
Belegschaft, *f.* **-/-en.** *coll.* workers and staff, labour force (of factory, etc.).
Belegschaftsaktie, *f.* worker's *or* employee's (single) share (in a company).
Belegschein, *m.* **1.** voucher. **2.** *Sch:* (i) copy (*for official record*) of the entries made in the student's record book; (ii) *Austrian:* attendance form for a lecture-course.
Belegstelle, *f.* reference (for word, etc.); instance, example (of use of word, etc.), illustration, illustrative quotation; **für das Vorkommen des Wortes kann ich drei Belegstellen bei Plautus zitieren,** I can quote three passages in Plautus in which the word occurs, I can quote three instances of this word from Plautus; **leider gibt er keine Belegstellen,** unfortunately he gives no references.
Belegstück, *n.* **1.** voucher; receipt. **2.**=**Belegexemplar.**
Belegzelle, *f. Anat:* cell of the fundus gland.
Belegzettel, *m.*=**Belegschein.**
belehnen. I. *v.tr.* **1.** *Hist:* to enfeoff (s.o.) (with land, etc.); to invest (s.o.) (with a fief, an honour, etc.); to invest (bishop, etc.) (with insignia). **2.** *Swiss Dial:* **ein Grundstück b.,** to lend money on property.
II. *vbl s.* **Belehnen** *n.,* **Belehnung** *f. Hist:* enfeoffment; investiture, investment (with a fief, an honour, insignia).
Belehnungsurkunde, *f. Hist:* deed of enfeoffment.
belehrbar, *a.* open to reason; teachable.
belehren. I. *v.tr.* to teach, to instruct (s.o.); **j-n über etwas** *acc., Lit:* **etwas** *gen.,* **von etwas, b.,** to advise s.o. on sth.; to make sth. clear to s.o.; to give s.o. to understand (sth.), to warn s.o. about sth.; **j-n über den wahren Sachverhalt b.,** to inform s.o. of the true facts (of the matter, case); **sich b. lassen,** to take advice; to be open to reason; to be ready to learn; to be willing to listen; **ich habe mich darüber b. lassen, daß . . . ,** I am, have been, advised that . . . ; **sich durch Erfahrung b. lassen,** to draw lessons from experience; **er läßt sich nicht b.,** he is intractable; he won't listen to reason, he won't take advice; **j-n eines Besseren b.,** to enlighten s.o. about sth.; to correct s.o.'s misconception; **j-n eines anderen b.,** to undeceive s.o.
II. *vbl s.* **1. Belehren,** *n. in vbl senses.* **2. Belehrung,** *f.* (*a*)=II. 1; *also:* instruction; (*b*) **zu Ihrer B.,** for your information, instruction; **lassen Sie sich das eine B. sein,** let this be a lesson to you; **dieses möge Ihnen zur B. dienen,** may this serve to instruct you; may this be a lesson to you.
III. *pr.p. & a.* **belehrend,** *in vbl senses; esp.* instructive; **eine belehrende Unterhaltung,** an instructive conversation; **belehrende Literatur,** educational literature; informative literature; **belehrendes Gedicht,** didactic poem.
Belehrungseifer, *m.* pedagogical zeal.
Belehrungssucht, *f.* mania for teaching.
beleibt, *a.* stout, corpulent, bulky, portly; **b. werden,** to grow stout.
Beleibtheit, *f.* stoutness; corpulence.
beleidigen. I. *v.tr.* **1.** to offend (s.o.), to give offence to (s.o.); to affront (s.o.); to insult, abuse (s.o.) (with words); **sie fühlt sich, ist, leicht beleidigt,** she easily takes offence; she is touchy, thin-skinned; **wenn ich das sagen darf, ohne Sie zu b.,** if I may say so without giving offence; **beleidigende Worte,** abusive, offensive, words; **beleidigter Stolz,** offended pride; *Jur:* **j-n (schriftlich) b.,** to libel s.o.; **j-n tätlich b.,** to assault s.o.; *B:* **bittet für die, so euch beleidigen,** pray for them which despitefully use you. **2.** (*of thg*) **das Ohr, das Auge, den Gaumen, b.,** to offend the ear, the eye, the palate.
II. *vbl s.* **1. Beleidigen,** *n. in vbl senses.* **2. Beleidigung,** *f.* (*a*)=II. 1; (*b*) offence (*gen.,* to); abuse (*gen.,* of); insult (*gen.,* to); **B. des guten Geschmacks,** offence against good taste; **B. des Ohrs, für das Ohr, für das Auge, des Auges,** offence to the ear, eye; **das stellt eine B. meiner Person dar,** this constitutes an affront to my person; **eine B. einstecken,** to swallow an affront; (*c*) *Jur:* **grobe B.,** gross insult; **schriftliche B.,** libel; **verleumderische B.,** libel *or* slander; **einfache B.,** (i) insult, (ii) slander, (iii) assault; **tätliche B.,** assault and battery; **B. durch Schimpfworte,** use of insulting language.
Beleidiger, *m.* **-s/-,** offender, insulter, abuser; *Jur:* offending party.
Beleidigte, *m., f.* (*decl. as adj.*) one who is offended, abused, insulted; *Jur:* offended party.
Beleidigungsklage, *f. Jur:* (minor) action for (i) slander, (ii) insult, (iii) petty assault.
beleihbar, *a.* pledgeable (security, etc.); (house, etc.) that can be mortgaged.
beleihen, *v.tr.* (*strong*) (i) to raise, (ii) to grant, a loan on (house, securities, etc.); **ein Haus, ein Grundstück, b.,** to raise a mortgage on a house, an estate.
Beleihungsgrenze, *f. Com:* limit to which money can be loaned (on securities, etc.).
Beleihungswert, *m. Com:* value placed upon property, security, etc., for purposes of a loan.
belemmern, *v.tr.* **1.** *F:* to cheat (s.o.); to confuse (s.o.) **2.** *F:* **das ist belemmert,** that's a sorry business, a wretched business; **er stand ganz belemmert da,** he stood there sheepishly. **3.** *Nau:* to encumber (ship).
Belemnit [be·lɛmˈniːt], *m.* **-en/-en.** *Paleont:* belemnite, fingerstone.
belesen, *a.* well-read; **er ist auf diesem Gebiet sehr b.,** he has read a great deal about this subject.
Belesenheit, *f.* familiarity, acquaintance, with literature; wide reading.
Belesprit [bɛlɛˈspriː], *m.* **-s/.** bel esprit; pretty wit.
Beletage [bɛle·ˈtaːʒə], *f.* **-/-n,** first floor.
beleuchten. I. *v.tr.* **1.** (*of lamp, pers., etc.*) to light, illuminate (sth.); (*of lamp, sun, etc.*) to give light to (sth.), to shine on (s.o., sth.); *Th:* to light (the stage); to throw a spotlight on, to spotlight (actor, etc.); **ein Auto, usw., b.,** to put, switch, on car, etc. lights; **das Auto war beleuchtet,** the car had its lights on, was lit; **er beleuchtete die Treppe mit seiner Taschenlampe,** he lit up the stairs with his torch, *U.S:* flashlight; **das Zimmer ist mit Gas beleuchtet,** the room is lit by gas; **das Zimmer ist indirekt beleuchtet,** the room has indirect lighting; **die Sonne beleuchtet die Bergspitzen,** the sun shines on (to) the mountain-tops; **eine beleuchtete Straße,** a lighted road; **eine mangelhaft beleuchtete Straße,** a poorly lit road; **der Vollmond beleuchtete die Straße,** the full moon illuminated, shone upon, the road; **das Fahrzeug muß bei Nacht vorschriftsmäßig beleuchtet sein,** the vehicle must be lit at night according to the regulations. **2.** to illuminate, shed, throw, light (up)on (sth.), to elucidate (sth.); **einen unklaren Punkt b.,** to shed, throw, light on an obscure point; **der Redner beleuchtete seinen Gegenstand von verschiedenen Seiten,** the speaker shed light upon, elucidated, his subject from various angles.
II. *vbl s.* **1. Beleuchten,** *n. in vbl senses.* **2. Beleuchtung,** *f.* (*a*)=II. 1; *also:* illumination (of room, road, train, etc.); elucidation (of subject); (*b*) light, lighting; illumination; **elektrische B.,** electric lighting; **B. mit Gas,** gas lighting; **indirekte, mittelbare, B.,** indirect lighting; **B. durch Röhrenlampen,** tubular lighting; **künstliche B.,** artificial light; **festliche B.,** festive illumination; *Th:* **B. der Bühne,** stage-lighting; *Aut: etc:* **B. der Fahrzeuge,** vehicle lighting; **vorschriftsmäßige B.,** lighting according to regulations; **ein Zimmer mit kümmerlicher B.,** a poorly-lit room; *see also* **bengalisch;** (*c*) exposure to light; illumination; **ein Gemälde kann durch zu starke B. leiden,** a painting can be damaged by excessive exposure to light; **einem Gegenstand die rechte B. geben,** to put a matter in its true light, into perspective; (*d*) *Opt:* illumination; **geometrische B.,** geometric illumination.
Beleuchter, *m.* **1.** *Th:* stage-lighter; *Cin:* lighter. **2.** *Mil. Av:* flare-dropper, marker; pathfinder.
Beleuchtungsanhänger, *m. Mil:* searchlight trailer.
Beleuchtungsanlage, *f.* lighting installation; lighting fitting(s); light-fitting(s).
Beleuchtungsapparat, *m.* illuminating apparatus.
Beleuchtungsarmaturen, *f.pl. El:* light fittings.
Beleuchtungseinrichtung, *f.* = **Beleuchtungsanlage.**
Beleuchtungsgerät, *n.* illuminating apparatus.
Beleuchtungsingenieur, *m.* illuminating engineer; lighting engineer.
Beleuchtungskabel, *n. El:* light cable.
Beleuchtungskonstruktionen, *f.pl. Ph:* graphic representation of isophotic areas.
Beleuchtungskörper, *m. El:* lighting appliance.
Beleuchtungskran, *m. Cin:* light crane.
Beleuchtungsmesser, *m. Opt:* illuminometer, luxmeter.
Beleuchtungsmikroskop, *n.* lucernal microscope.
Beleuchtungsmittel, *n.* illuminant.
Beleuchtungsschirm, *m.* reflector.
Beleuchtungsspiegel, *m.* illuminating mirror.
Beleuchtungsstärke, *f. Opt:* illumination.
Beleuchtungstechnik, *f.* illuminating engineering.
Beleuchtungstrupp, *m. Mil:* searchlight section.
Beleuchtungsverband, *m. Mil. Av:* flare-dropping unit, marker unit.
Beleuchtungsvorrichtung, *f.* = **Beleuchtungsanlage.**
Beleuchtungsvorschriften, *f.pl. Aut: etc:* lighting regulations.
Beleuchtungszweck, *m. El:* lighting purpose; **Strom zu Beleuchtungszwecken,** current for lighting purposes.
beleumdet, *a.*=**beleumundet.**
beleumundet, *a.* **gut, schlecht, b.,** held in good, bad, repute.
belfern, *v.i.* (*haben*) (*of dog, etc.*) to yelp, to yap; *F:* (*of pers.*) to cry out, bawl, shout.

Belfried, *m.* -(e)s/-e, belfry.
Belga, *m.* -(s)/-(s), (*Belgian unit of exchange*) belga.
Belgen, *m.pl. Ethn:* Belgae.
Belgien [ˈbɛlgiən]. *Pr.n.n.* **-s.** *Geog:* Belgium.
Belgier [ˈbɛlgiər], *m.* **-s/-.** 1. *Geog:* Belgian. 2. heavy (Belgian) draught-horse.
belgisch, *a.* Belgian; *Ethn:* Belgic.
Belgisch-Kongo. *Pr.n.n.* **-s.** *Geog:* the Belgian Congo.
Belgrad [ˈbelgraːt]. *Pr.n.n.* **-s.** *Geog:* Belgrade.
Belial [ˈbeːliaˑl]. *Pr.n.m.* **-s.** *B:* Belial, the Devil.
belichten. I. *v.tr. Phot:* to expose; **einen Film eine fünfzigstel Sekunde b.,** to expose a film for a fiftieth of a second; **belichtete Platte,** exposed plate; **zu lange b.,** to overexpose; **zu kurz b.,** to underexpose.
II. *vbl s.* 1. **Belichten,** *n. in vbl senses.* 2. **Belichtung,** *f.* (*a*)=II. 1; (*b*) *Phot:* exposure.
Belichtungsapparat, *m. Phot:* fadeometer.
Belichtungsdauer, *f. Phot:* time of exposure.
Belichtungsmesser, *m. Phot:* exposure meter.
Belichtungsschaltuhr, *f. Phot:* exposure switch timer.
Belichtungstabelle, *f. Phot:* exposure table.
Belichtungsuhr, *f. Phot:* clockwork exposure timer.
Belichtungszeit, *f. Phot:* time of exposure.
beliebäugeln, *v.tr.* to have an eye on, to covet, cast a covetous, wistful, eye on (sth.); to look covetously, wistfully, at (sth.).
belieben. I. *v.* 1. *v.tr.* (*a*) *A:* (*of pers.*) to like, to favour (sth.); (*b*) to wish; **was belieben der Herr?** what would you like, sir? what would the gentleman like? **gnädige Frau belieben?** madam wishes? **sich etwas b. lassen,** to choose to do sth.; **wie Sie belieben,** as you please, as you wish; (*with* **zu**+*inf.*) **belieben Sie einzutreten,** enter, if you please, please enter; **Sie belieben wohl zu scherzen,** surely you are joking, I take it you are joking. 2. *impers.* (*with dat. of pers.*) **es beliebt,** it pleases (s.o.), it is agreeable to (s.o.); **wenn es Gott beliebt,** please God, if God pleases; **wie es Ihnen beliebt,** as you like, as you choose; **meine Herren, wenn's beliebt,** (i) gentlemen, if you please; (ii) time, gentlemen, please; **kommen Sie, wenn es Ihnen beliebt,** come if you like, if you so choose; **wie beliebt?** I beg your pardon?
II. *vbl s.* **Belieben,** *n.* 1. choice; convenience; **nach B.,** according to one's choice, liking; as much as one pleases; *F:* ad lib.; *Mus:* ad lib(itum); *Cu:* to taste; **Gewürz nach B.,** seasoning to taste; **tun Sie bitte ganz nach (Ihrem) B.,** please do exactly as you wish, like; **er fand ein Zimmer nach seinem B.,** he found a room that suited him, a room to his mind, his liking; **es steht in Ihrem B.,** do as you think best, as you think fit; I leave it to you; **ich stelle es Ihrem B. anheim,** I leave it to your convenience. 2. *A:* pleasure; **B. an etwas haben, finden,** to find pleasure in sth.; to take a liking to sth.
beliebig, (*a*) *a.* optional, arbitrary; ad libitum, *F:* ad lib.; **eine beliebige Zahl,** any number, an optional, arbitrary, number; **zu jeder beliebigen Zeit,** at any time (you please); **jede beliebige Person, jeder Beliebige,** anyone you please, any person whatever, no matter who; **von jeder beliebigen Menge,** of any quantity (whatever); (*b*) *adv.* **b. viel, b. viele,** as much, as many, as you like; ad lib.; **etwas in b. große Stücke schneiden,** to cut sth. (up) into pieces of any desired size. *See also* **x-beliebig.**
beliebt, *a.* (*of pers.*) popular, liked; (*of thg*) popular; *Com:* in demand; **ein beliebter Schauspieler,** a popular actor; **eine beliebte Redensart,** a popular expression; **diese Handtaschen sind bei unseren Kunden sehr b.,** these handbags are very popular, in great demand, with our customers; **Kartenspielen ist hier eine sehr beliebte Unterhaltung,** playing cards is a very popular pastime here; **sich (bei j-m) b. machen,** to make oneself popular (with s.o.); to curry favour, to ingratiate oneself, (with s.o.).
Beliebtheit, *f.* popularity; **sich großer B. erfreuen,** to enjoy great popularity, high favour.
beliefern, *v.tr.* to supply, furnish (s.o.) (with sth.); **wir können Sie zu der angegebenen Zeit nicht b.,** we cannot supply you (with the goods) at the specified time; **manche Geschäfte sind während des Streiks schlecht beliefert worden,** some shops were badly supplied during the strike.
Belisar [ˈbeːliˑzaˑr]. *Pr.n.m.* **-s.** Belisarius.
Belkanto [bɛlˈkantoː], *m.* **-s/-s.** *Mus:* bel canto.
Bella. *Pr.n.f.* **-s.** (*dim. of* **Arabella** *or* **Isabella**) Bella.
Belladonna [bɛlaˑˈdonaː], *f.* **-/-nen.** *Bot:* belladonna, *F:* deadly nightshade, great morel; *Pharm:* belladonna.
Belladonnalilie, *f. Bot:* belladonna lily, amaryllis (belladonna).
Bellatrix [bɛˈlaːtriks], *f.* **-/.** *Astr:* bellatrix.
Belle [bɛl], *f.* **-/-s.** *Cards:* rubber game.
Belle-Alliance [bɛlaliˈɑ̃s]. *Pr.n.n.* **-.** *Hist:* **die Schlacht bei B.-A.,** the Battle of Waterloo.
bellen, *v.i.* (*haben*) (*of dog*) to bark, to yelp, to yap; to give tongue, to give mouth; (*of hound*) to bay; *F:* (*of pers.*) to cough loudly; **bellender Husten,** barking, hacking, cough; **bellende Stimme,** yapping voice; **mein Magen bellt vor Hunger,** my stomach is rumbling with hunger; *Prov:* **Hunde, die viel bellen, beißen nicht,** barking dogs seldom bite.
Bellenholz, *n. Bot:*=**Schwarzpappel.**
Beller, *m.* **-s/-,** barking dog, barker.
Belles Lettres [bɛlˈlɛtrə], *f.pl.* belles-lettres.
Belletrist [bɛleˑˈtrist], *m.* **-en/-en,** (*a*) *A:* belletrist; (*b*) author of light literature; *Pej:* author of tasteful but unscholarly works.
Belletristik [bɛleˑˈtristik], *f.* **-/.** (*a*) *A:* belles-lettres; (*b*) light literature; fiction.
belletristisch [bɛleˑˈtristiʃ], *a.* (*a*) *A:* belletristic, concerned with belles-lettres; (*b*) **belletristische Literatur,** light literature; **belletristische Zeitschrift,** (literary) magazine.
Bellevue [bel(ə)ˈvyː], *n.* **-/-n** [-ˈvyːən], vantage-point; (*as name for castle, hotel, etc.*) Bellevue.
Bellhammel, *m. Husb:* bellwether.
Bellhenne, *f. Orn:* coot.
bellikos [bɛliˑˈkoːs], *a.* warlike, bellicose.
Bellit [bɛˈliːt], *n.* **-s/.** *Exp:* bellite.
beloben, *v.tr.* I. *A:* to praise, laud (s.o., sth.).
II. *vbl s.* 1. **Beloben,** *n. in vbl senses.* 2. **Belobung,** *f.* (*a*)=II. 1; (*b*) praise; *Mil:* **eine B. erhalten,** to be mentioned in dispatches, *U.S:* to receive a citation.
belobigen. I. *v.tr.* to commend (s.o.), to praise (s.o.) (for sth.); *Mil:* to cite (s.o.); **j-n für seine Tapferkeit b.,** to commend s.o. for his bravery.
II. *vbl s.* 1. **Belobigen,** *n. in vbl senses.* 2. **Belobigung,** *f.* (*a*)=II. 1; (*b*) commendation; **schriftliche B.,** letter of commendation; **eine B. erhalten,** to receive a commendation.
belohnen. I. *v.tr.* to reward (s.o., sth.); **wir werden ihn b., wie er es verdient,** we will reward him as he deserves; **seine Treue wurde belohnt,** his loyalty was rewarded; **j-n mit Undank b.,** to repay s.o. with ingratitude.
II. *vbl s.* 1. **Belohnen,** *n. in vbl senses.* 2. **Belohnung,** *f.* (*a*)=II. 1; (*b*) reward; **hohe B.,** high reward; **eine B. aussetzen,** to offer a reward; **brauner Dachshund verloren — 50 Mark B.,** lost, (a) brown dachshund; 50 marks reward; **als B. für Ihre Dienste,** as a reward for your services, in return for your services.
Belohner, *m.* **-s/-,** rewarder.
Belonit [beˑloˑˈniːt], *m.* **-(e)s/-e.** *Miner:* acicular bismuth.
Belorusse [ˈbeˑloˑrusə], *m.* **-n/-n.** *Geog:* Byelorussian, White Russian.
belorussisch [ˈbeˑloˑrusiʃ], *a. Geog:* Byelorussian, White Russian.
Belsazar, Belsazer [bɛlˈzaːtsaˑr, -tsər]. *Pr.n.m.* **-s.** *B.Hist:* Belshazzar; **Belsazars Gastmahl,** Belshazzar's Feast.
Belt, *m.* **-(e)s/-e.** *Geog:* **der Große, Kleine, B.,** the Great Belt, the Little Belt (*of the Baltic*).
beludern (sich), *v.refl. Ven:* (*of deer*) to cram itself (with food).
belüften. I. *v.tr.* to air, to ventilate, to air-condition (room, etc.); *Av:* to ventilate (cabin, etc.); *Constr:* **belüfteter Beton,** air-entrained concrete; *Hyd.E:* **belüfteter Überfall,** aerated sheet of water.
II. *vbl s.* 1. **Belüften,** *n. in vbl senses.* 2. **Belüftung,** *f.* (*a*)=II. 1; *also:* ventilation; *Av:* aeration, ventilation; (*b*) ventilation; *Hyd.E:* air-intake (of valve); *Av:* aeration, ventilation.
Belüftungsanlage, *f.* air conditioning plant; ventilation system, plant.
Belüftungshaube, *f. Av:* air-scoop.
Belüftungskanal, *m. Constr:* air-channel, flue.
Belüftungsklappe, *f. Aut:* etc: ventilator.
Belüftungsleitung, *f. Av:* etc: air-inlet, air-intake; vent-line, vent; air-valve (for furnace door).
Belüftungsmesser, *m. Constr:* air (entrainment) meter (for concrete).
Belüftungsmittel, *n. Constr:* air-entraining agent (for concrete).
Beluga [beˑˈluːgaː], *f.* **-/-s.** 1. *Ich:* beluga. 2. *Z:* beluga, white whale.
belugen, *v.tr. Lit:* to look at (s.o., sth.); **j-n, etwas, neugierig b.,** to eye, watch, s.o., sth., inquisitively.
belügen, *v.tr.* (*strong*) to lie to (s.o.), to tell (s.o.) lies; to deceive (s.o.) by lies; **sich selbst b.,** to deceive oneself.
belustigen. I. *v.tr.* to amuse, entertain (s.o.); to divert (s.o.); **dieses Schauspiel hat mich sehr belustigt,** this play greatly amused me, I was greatly amused by this play; **der Zauberer belustigte die Kinder,** the conjurer entertained, amused, the children; **das Kind belustigte sich den ganzen Nachmittag damit, Steinchen ins Wasser zu werfen,** the child amused himself all afternoon by throwing pebbles into the water; **ihre Aufregung belustigte ihn,** her excitement amused him; **ein belustigtes Lächeln,** an amused smile.
II. *vbl s.* 1. **Belustigen,** *n. in vbl senses.* 2. **Belustigung,** *f.* (*a*)=II. 1; *also:* amusement; entertainment; diversion; **zu ihrer B.,** for their entertainment, amusement, (in order) to amuse them; (*b*) **zur großen B. der Volksmenge,** much to the entertainment of the crowd; **zur allgemeinen B. fiel er ins Wasser,** to everybody's amusement he fell into the water; (*c*) entertainment, amusement, diversion; **es gab allerlei Belustigungen für die Kinder,** there were all sorts of amusements, diversions, for the children.
Belustiger, *m.* **-s/-,** entertainer.
Belustigungsort, *m.* place of amusement; amusement ground; place for popular entertainment.
Belutsche [beˑˈlutʃə], *m.* **-n/-n.** *Ethn:* Baluchi.
belutschen, *v.tr.* to lick, suck at (sth.).
belutschisch [beˑˈlutʃiʃ], *a.* Baluchi.
Belutschistan [beˑˈlutʃistaˑn]. *Pr.n.n.* **-s.** *Geog:* Baluchistan.
Belvedere [bɛlveˑˈdeːrə], *n.* **-(s)/-s.** *Arch:* belvedere, gazebo.
Bema [ˈbeːmaː], *n.* **-/-ta.** 1. *Gr.Ant:* bema. 2. *Ecc.Arch:* bema, sanctuary (of a church).
bemachen, *v.tr. P:* to (be)foul (sth.), to dirty, to soil (sth.) (with excrement).
bemächtigen (sich), *v.refl.* (*a*) **sich einer Sache b.,** to lay, take, hold of sth., to seize (upon) sth.; to secure, possess oneself of, sth., to take possession of sth.; **sich des Thrones b.,** to usurp, seize, the throne; **die Feinde bemächtigten sich der Burg,** the enemy seized, occupied, took possession of, the castle; (*b*) **sich j-s b.,** (*of pers.*) to lay hands on s.o., to seize s.o.; (*of emotion*) to overcome s.o., to take possession of s.o.; **eine große Angst bemächtigte sich ihrer,** she was seized with a great fear; **ein wilder Zorn bemächtigte sich seiner,** a flaming rage took possession of him, possessed him.
bemähnt, *a.* (*of horse, lion*) maned; *Her:* crined.
bemäkeln, *v.tr.*=**bemängeln.**
bemalen, *v.tr.* to cover (sth.) with paint, crayon, chalk, etc.; to paint (sth.) (with sth.); to daub (sth.) (with sth.); **Porzellan mit Blumen b.,** to decorate china with flowers; **die Kinder haben die Wände bemalt,** the children daubed the walls with paint, covered the walls with crayon, chalk; **bemalte Keramik,** hand-painted pottery; **sich** *dat.* **das Gesicht schwarz b.,** to paint one's face black; *F:* **sich b.,** to paint one's face.
bemallen, *v.tr. N.Arch:* to mould (timber).
bemängeln, *v.tr.* to criticize (s.o., sth.); to cavil at (sth.); to find fault with (s.o., sth.).
bemannen. I. *v.tr.* 1. to man (trench, fort, gun, etc.); *Nau:* to man (a vessel); to equip, commission (a vessel); *Navy:* **bemannter Torpedo,** manned, human, torpedo. 2. *A. & Hum:* **eine bemannte Frau,** a woman who has a man.
II. *vbl s.* 1. **Bemannen** *n. in vbl senses.* 2. **Bemannung,** *f.* (*a*)=II. 1; (*b*) *Nau:* crew, ship's company; *F:* hands; *Av:* crew (of aircraft); **ein Schiff mit voller B.,** a ship with a full complement.
bemänteln. I. *v.tr.* to cloak, to cover (over), to disguise (fault, etc.); to put a gloss on, to varnish (over) (facts, etc.); to palliate (vice, etc.); **er hat es immer verstanden, seine Fehler zu b.,** he always knew how to disguise his faults; **er bemäntelt seine Unwissenheit mit dem Anschein der Gleichgültigkeit,** he puts on an air of indifference to cover, disguise, his ignorance.
II. *vbl s.* 1. **Bemänteln,** *n. in vbl senses.* 2. **Bemäntelung,** *f.* (*a*)=II. 1; (*b*) cover, cloak, disguise; gloss.
bemaßen, *v.tr.* to mark (the) measurement on a plan, etc.; to provide a plan, etc., with (the) measurements.
bemasten. I. *v.tr. Nau:* to mast (ship); **to set up** the lower mast of (ship).
II. *vbl s.* 1. **Bemasten,** *n. in vbl senses.*

2. Bemastung, *f.* (*a*)=II. 1; (*b*) *Coll:* masts (of a ship).

Bembex, *n.* -/. *Ent:* bembex.

bemeiern, *v.tr.* **1.** *A:* **ein Gut b.,** to lease land to a tenant-farmer. **2.** *F:* to cheat (s.o.); to get the better of (s.o.).

bemeistern, *v.tr.* **1.** *A:* to subdue (animal, etc.); to overcome, conquer, control (sth.). **2.** (*of pers.*) to curb, bridle, control (passion, etc.); to master (emotion, etc.); (*of emotion*) to take possession of (s.o.); **er konnte seine Ungeduld nicht länger b.,** he could curb, control, his impatience no longer; **seine Angst b.,** to get the better of, to overcome, to master, one's fear(s); **der Zorn bemeisterte ihn,** he was seized with fury; **sich (selbst) b.,** to control oneself, to control one's feelings. **3.** *A:* **sich j-s bemeistern =sich j-s bemächtigen,** *q.v. under* **bemächtigen.**

bemengen (sich), *v.refl. F:* **sich mit etwas b.,** to busy oneself with sth.; to concern oneself with sth.; *F:* to poke one's nose into sth.

bemerkbar, *a.* noticeable, perceptible, sensible; apparent; **sich b. machen,** (*of pers.*) to bring oneself into notice, to draw attention to oneself; (*of thg*) to make itself felt; to become noticeable, apparent; **sich unangenehm b. machen,** (*of pers.*) to make one's presence unpleasantly felt; (*of thg*) to become painfully apparent; **meine Leber macht sich b.,** my liver is giving me trouble; **der Mangel an Nahrungsmitteln machte sich b.,** the scarcity of food became apparent, noticeable.

bemerken. I. *v.tr.* **1.** to notice, observe (s.o., sth.); to become aware of (s.o., sth.); to note (fact, etc.); **zufällig bemerkte ich ihn unter der Menschenmenge,** by chance I noticed, observed, him in the crowd; **ich habe es nie bemerkt,** I have never noticed it; **er bemerkte einen brenzlichen Geruch,** he became aware of a smell of burning; **Sie werden b., daß ein Fehler in der Abrechnung ist,** you will note, observe, that there is a mistake in the account; **ein Irrtum, der sogleich bemerkt wurde,** a mistake that was noticed, noted, *F:* spotted, at once. **2.** (*a*) to observe, to remark; **sie bemerkte, es sei spät,** she remarked, said, that it was getting late; **'Sie haben unrecht', bemerkte er,** 'you are wrong', he remarked, observed; (*b*) to remark, comment; **ich habe mancherlei zu den Worten des Redners zu b.,** I have several comments to make in connection with what the speaker said; **wie er so treffend bemerkte,** as he so aptly remarked, commented; **es darf bemerkt werden, daß . . . ,** it may be remarked that . . . , it may be mentioned that . . . ; **wie oben bemerkt,** as stated above; **nebenbei bemerkt,** incidentally, by the way; in parenthesis.

II. *vbl s.* **1. Bemerken,** *n. in vbl senses.* **2. Bemerkung,** *f.* (*a*)=II. 1; *also:* observation; (*b*) (*written or spoken*) remark, observation, comment; **spöttische, unfreundliche, Bemerkungen,** sarcastic, unfriendly, remarks; **ich habe noch einige Bemerkungen zu machen,** I have a few remarks, comments, to add; **er machte eine treffende B.,** he made an apt remark; **eine kritische B. über etwas,** a critical remark, comment, about sth.; **Bemerkungen an den Rand schreiben,** to make marginal notes; **er lehnte das Angebot mit der B. ab, daß . . . ,** he declined the offer by saying that . . . .

bemerkenswert, *a.* (*of fact, etc.*) remarkable; notable; deserving notice, noteworthy, worthy of note; (*of pers.*) remarkable; striking; **ein bemerkenswerter Unterschied,** a noteworthy, notable, difference; **ein Mann mit bemerkenswertem Mut,** a man with remarkable courage; **eine bemerkenswerte Persönlichkeit,** a striking personality; **es ist b., daß...,** it is worthy of note that..., it is noteworthy that...; *adv.* **sie spricht b. gut Französisch,** she speaks French remarkably well.

bemerklich, *a.*=**bemerkbar.**

bemessen. I. *v.tr.* (*strong*) **1. etwas nach etwas b.,** (*a*) to measure sth. by sth.; to evaluate sth. according to sth.; **ich bemesse seine Leistung nach seinen beschränkten Kräften,** I measure, rate, his achievement in the light of his limited powers; (*b*) to proportion, adjust, adapt, sth. to sth.; to conform sth. to sth.; **die Ausgaben nach den Einnahmen b.,** to proportion one's expenditure to one's takings; **den Lohn nach der Leistung b.,** to pay according to the quality of the work; **eine Zuteilung, usw., knapp b.,** to cut an allocation, etc., as fine as possible. **2.** *Mec.E:* to rate; *El.E:* to determine (resistance).

II. *vbl s.* **1. Bemessen,** *n. in vbl senses.* **2. Bemessung,** *f.* (*a*)=II. 1; (*b*) *Mec.E:* **B. eines Motors,** rating of a motor.

III. *p.p. & a.* **bemessen. 1.** *in vbl senses.* **2.** (*a*) limited; restricted; **meine Zeit, meine Geduld, ist b.,** my time, my patience, is limited; (*b*) *Mec.E: El.E:* **bemessene Leistung,** rated load.

Bemessungsformel, *f. Mec.E:* rating formula.

bemisten, *v.tr.* to dung, manure (land, etc.).

bemitleiden, *v.tr.* to commiserate with (s.o.); to pity (s.o.), to take pity on (s.o.); to be sorry for (s.o.); **er ist zu b.,** he is to be pitied.

bemitleidenswert, bemitleidenswürdig, *a.* pitiable; **er ist b.,** he is to be pitied.

bemittelt, *a.* (*of pers.*) well-to-do, well off, wealthy; in easy circumstances; of (independent) means; **ein bemittelter Mann,** a man of means.

Bemitteltheit, *f.* wealth; easy circumstances.

Bemme, *f.* -/-n. *Saxon Dial:* (i) sandwich; (ii) open sandwich; (*thick slice of bread covered with butter, dripping, etc.*) *F:* doorstep.

bemogeln, *v.tr. F:* to cheat, to swindle (s.o.); *F:* to do, diddle (s.o.).

bemoosen (sich), *v.refl.* to become covered with moss; **ein bemooster Baum, Felsen,** a mossy tree, rock; *Sch: F:* **bemoostes Haupt, bemooster Bursche,** old student, veteran; **ein bemooster Herr,** an old gentleman; *F:* an old boy.

bemopsen, *v.tr.*=**bemogeln.**

bemühen. I. *v.tr.* **1.** to trouble (s.o.) (**in etwas** *dat.*, **wegen etwas,** about sth.); **es tut mir leid, Sie b. zu müssen,** I am sorry to have to trouble you; **es tut mir leid, daß ich Sie vergebens bemüht habe,** I am sorry to have troubled you for nothing; **ich will Sie nicht in, wegen, dieser Sache b.,** I do not wish to trouble you about this matter; **ich werde Sie nicht mit Einzelheiten b.,** I shall not trouble you with details. **2.** (*a*) **um j-n bemüht sein=sich um j-n b.,** *q.v. under* II. 1 (*b*); (*b*) **bemüht sein, etwas zu tun,** to be at pains to do sth.; **er war eifrig bemüht, ihr zu gefallen,** he was eager to please her; **ich werde bemüht sein, bleiben, alles zu Ihrer Befriedigung auszuführen,** I shall endeavour, I shall continue to endeavour, to carry everything out to your satisfaction; *Com. Corr:* **stets bemüht, Ihre Wünsche aufs beste zufriedenzustellen,** we shall always endeavour to fulfil your orders to your complete satisfaction.

II. **sich bemühen. 1.** (*a*) to trouble oneself (**in etwas** *dat.*, **wegen etwas,** about sth.); **Sie brauchen sich in dieser Sache nicht weiter zu b.,** you need not trouble yourself about it any more; **sich bei j-m für j-n b.,** to use one's influence with s.o. for s.o.; to put in a good word for s.o.; **in dieser Angelegenheit werde ich mich gerne für Sie b.,** I shall gladly be of service to you in this matter; **bitte bemühen Sie sich nicht, heraufzukommen,** please don't trouble, *F:* bother, to come up(stairs); (*in polite speech*) **bitte bemühen Sie sich nicht!** please do not trouble; *F:* please don't bother; (*b*) **sich um j-n b.,** to busy oneself about s.o.; to concern oneself about s.o.; to attend to s.o.; (*cp.* 2 (*a*)); **alle bemühten sich um das ohnmächtige Mädchen,** everyone went to the aid of the unconscious girl; **vergeblich hatten die Ärzte sich um sie bemüht,** the doctors had tried in vain to help her; **du brauchst dich nicht weiter um mich zu b.,** you need not trouble, concern, yourself, *F:* bother, about me any longer, any further. **2.** (*a*) **sich um etwas b.,** to go to great pains, to make an effort, to obtain sth.; to strive after sth.; **wenn du dich darum nicht bemühst, wird es dir nie gelingen,** if you don't make an effort, you'll never succeed; **er hat sich eifrig um diese Stelle bemüht,** he made every effort to get this job; **Sie bemühen sich vergeblich,** you are wasting your time (on it), it is a waste of time for you, it is a waste of effort; **man erreicht nichts, ohne sich zu b.,** one achieves nothing without pains, without working for it; **sich um j-s Aufmerksamkeit b.,** to solicit s.o.'s attention, to try to attract, gain, s.o.'s attention; **die Firma bemüht sich um Ihre Kundschaft,** the firm solicits your custom; **sich um j-s Gunst b.,** to court s.o.'s favour; **er bemüht sich schon lange um das Mädchen, um des Mädchens Gunst,** he has been trying for a long while to win the girl's favour, he has been courting the girl for a long time; (*b*) **sich (darum) b., etwas zu tun,** to take trouble, pains, to do sth.; to endeavour to do sth.; **sich (darum) b., etwas zu erlangen,** to go to great pains, to try (hard), to endeavour, to obtain sth.; **bemühe dich, zur rechten Zeit nach Hause zu kommen,** try to get, come, home at the right time; **sie bemühte sich zu lächeln,** she tried, endeavoured, made an effort, to smile; **wenn du dich ein bißchen bemühst, wirst du es schaffen,** with a little effort you will succeed, you will manage it; **er bemühte sich, ihre Zuneigung zu gewinnen,** he was striving to win her affection; **sie bemühte sich mit all ihren Kräften, den Anforderungen ihres Berufes gerecht zu werden,** she made every effort to do her job adequately.

III. *vbl s.* **1. Bemühen,** *n.* effort, endeavour; **ein eifriges B.,** a zealous effort, endeavour; **ein vergebliches B.,** a vain, useless, wasted, effort, endeavour; **mein ganzes B. ist, Ihnen zu dienen,** my constant aim is, it is my constant endeavour, to serve you. **2. Bemühung,** *f.* trouble, effort; pains; **nach vielen vergeblichen Bemühungen,** after many vain endeavours; **alle Bemühungen der Ärzte, sie zu retten, waren vergeblich,** all the doctors' efforts to save her were in vain; **was darf ich Ihnen für Ihre Bemühungen geben?** what may I give you for your trouble, pains, for the trouble you have taken? **Honorar für ärztliche Bemühungen,** fee for medical attention.

bemüßigen, *v.tr.* (*usu. only in*) **sich bemüßigt fühlen, sehen, finden, etwas zu tun,** to feel obliged, to consider it one's business, to do sth.; **er fühlte sich nicht bemüßigt, ihm zu antworten,** he did not feel obliged, he did not find it necessary, to answer him; **er fühlte sich bemüßigt, sich in alle meine Angelegenheiten einzumischen,** he felt obliged to meddle in all my affairs.

bemustern, *v.tr.* **1.** to figure, pattern (sth.). **2.** (*a*) **ein Angebot b.,** to attach a sample to an offer; (*b*) to sample (material, etc.).

bemuttern, *v.tr.* to mother, to act as a mother to (s.o.); **er läßt sich gerne b.,** he likes to be mothered.

bemützt, *a.* wearing a cap, with a cap.

benachbart, *a.* neighbouring; adjoining; **die uns benachbarte Familie,** neighbours of ours; the family next-door; **er wohnt im benachbarten Haus,** he lives (in the house) next door; **im benachbarten Städtchen,** in the little town nearby; **die benachbarten Gärten,** the neighbouring, adjoining, gardens; **benachbarte Fachgebiete,** allied, related, fields (of study).

benachrichtigen. I. *v.tr.* to inform, notify (s.o.); to give notice (to s.o. of sth.); *Com:* to apprise, advise (s.o.); **sie wurde von seinem Tod benachrichtigt,** she was informed of his death; **er war nicht rechtzeitig von unserer Ankunft benachrichtigt worden,** he was not notified in time of, about, our arrival; **ich möchte Sie hiermit b., daß Herr X morgen nachmittag eintreffen wird,** I beg to inform you herewith that Mr X will arrive tomorrow afternoon; **sie kam gestern, ohne uns vorher zu b.,** she came, arrived, yesterday without giving us any previous notice; **er wurde benachrichtigt, daß man sein Paket gefunden hatte,** he was informed, notified, that his parcel had been found; **Sie hätten mich b. sollen,** you ought to have let me know; **Sie werden von dem Ergebnis benachrichtigt werden,** you will be notified of, about, the result; **die Behörden b.,** to give notice to, to notify, the authorities; *Com:* **wir haben das Vergnügen, Sie zu b., daß . . . ,** we have pleasure in advising you that . . . .

II. *vbl s.* **1. Benachrichtigen,** *n. in vbl senses.* **2. Benachrichtigung,** *f.* (*a*)=II. 1; *also:* information; notification; (*b*) (i) notice; notification; information; *Com:* advice; **ich habe keine B. darüber erhalten,** I have received no notification about it; **um B. bitten,** to ask to be informed, notified; (ii) *Sch:*=**Benachrichtigungsschreiben.**

Benachrichtigungsschreiben, *n.* (i) letter of notification; *Com:* letter of advice, advice note; (ii) *Sch:* letter warning a parent that his child will not be moved up next term.

benachteiligen. I. *v.tr.* (*of pers.*) to place (s.o.) at a disadvantage; to deal unfairly with (s.o.); to discriminate against (s.o.); (*of thg*) to handicap (s.o.); to affect (s.o.) unfavourably; to disadvantage (s.o.); **sich benachteiligt fühlen,** to feel at a disadvantage; to feel (oneself) handicapped; to feel oneself to be unfairly treated; **durch etwas benachteiligt sein,** to be at a disadvantage owing to sth.; **j-n zugunsten eines anderen b.,** to discriminate against s.o. in favour of s.o. else; **bei einer Erbschaft benachteiligt werden,** to be unfairly treated in a will, *F:* to come off badly in a will; **durch seine Kurzsichtigkeit ist er benachteiligt,** he is handicapped by his short sight.

II. *vbl s.* **1. Benachteiligen,** *n. in vbl senses; also:* discrimination against (s.o.). **2. Benachteiligung,** *f.* (*a*)=II. 1; (*b*) discrimination; (*c*) disadvantage; handicap.

III. *p.p. & a.* **benachteiligt,** *in vbl senses; esp.* **die benachteiligte Person, der, die, Benachteiligte,** the injured party; the person who has been unfairly treated, *F:* who has come off badly.

benageln, *v.tr.* to provide (sth.) with nails; to

hobnail (shoes); *Nau:* to spike down (sth.); **benagelte Schuhe,** hob-nailed shoes.

benagen, *v.tr.* (*of rodent, etc.*) to gnaw at (sth.); to nibble at (sth.); **einen Knochen b.,** (*of dog, etc.*) to gnaw a bone; (*of pers.*) to pick a bone; **die Rehe benagen die Rinde,** the deer nibble at the bark.

benamen, *v.tr.* to name, to give a name to (s.o., sth.); **. . . benamt,** by the name of . . . .

benamsen, *v.tr. A. & F:* = **benamen.**

benannt *see* **benennen.**

benarben, *v.tr.* to mark with scars, to scar (s.o., sth.); (*of wound*) **sich b.,** to heal (up), to skin over, scar over; **ein benarbtes Gesicht,** a face marked with scars.

benässen, *v.tr.* to moisten, wet (sth.), to make (sth.) wet; **ihre Wangen waren ganz mit Tränen benäßt,** her cheeks were bedewed with tears.

Bendix [ˈbɛndiks]. *Pr.n.m.* -ˈ & **-ens.** Benedict.

Bendixanlasser, *m. Aut:* Bendix starter.

bene[1] [ˈbeːneː]. *Lt.adv. F:* **sich** *dat.* **b. tun,** to do oneself well.

Bene[2], *n.* **-s/.** *F:* **j-m ein B. antun,** to do s.o. a good turn.

benebeln, *v.tr.* (*a*) *A:* (*of fog*) to cover, to cloud (over) (sth.); **benebelt,** covered in mist; (*b*) *Lit:* (*of emotion, darkness, etc.*) to befog, cloud, bedim (mind, the vision, etc.); (*c*) (*of wine, etc.*) to befog, fuddle (s.o.); (*of pers.*) **sich b.,** to get tipsy, *F:* fuddled; **benebelt sein,** *F:* to be fuddled, to be tipsy, slightly drunk.

benedeien [beˑneˑˈdaiən], *v.tr.* **1.** *Rel:* (*of God*) to bless (s.o.); *B:* (*of Mary*) **gebenedeiet bist du unter den Weibern,** blessed art thou amongst women; *B:* **gebenedeiet ist die Frucht deines Leibes,** blessed is the fruit of thy womb. **2.** to bless, to praise (God); to glorify (God); **Gott loben und b.,** to praise and glorify God.

Benedikt [ˈbeːneˑdikt]. **1.** *Pr.n.m.* **-s.** Benedict. **2.** *m.* **-s/-e(n).** *Bot:* holy thistle, blessed thistle.

Benedikte [beˑneˑˈdiktə], *f.***-/-n** = **Benediktenkraut.**

Benediktenkarde, *f. Bot:* = **Benediktenkraut** 1.

Benediktenkraut, *n. Bot:* **1.** holy thistle, blessed thistle. **2.** herb bennet, common, mountain, avens.

Benediktenrose, *f. Bot:* (common) peony.

Benediktiner [beˑneˑdikˈtiːnər], *m.* **-s/-.** **1.** *Ecc:* Benedictine (monk). **2.** Benedictine (liqueur).

Benediktiner-, *comb.fm. Ecc:* Benedictine . . . ; **Benediktinerkloster** *n,* Benedictine monastery; **Benediktinermönch** *m,* Benedictine monk.

Benediktinerdistel, *f. Bot:* holy thistle, blessed thistle.

Benediktinerin [beˑneˑdikˈtiːnərin], *f.* **-/-innen.** *Ecc:* Benedictine (nun).

Benediktinerorden, *m. Ecc:* Benedictine order, order of St. Benedict.

benediktinisch [beˑneˑdikˈtiːniʃ] *a. Ecc:* Benedictine (piety, etc.).

Benediktion [beˑneˑdiktsĭˈoːn], *f.* **-/-en,** benediction.

Benediktionale [beˑneˑdiktsĭoˑˈnaːleː, -ˈnaːlə], *n.* **-(s)/-n.** *Ecc:* benedictional.

benedizieren [beˑneˑdiˑˈtsiːrən], *v.tr.* to bless (sth.); to consecrate (church, etc.).

Benefaktion [beˑneˑfaktsĭˈoːn], *f.* **-/-en,** benefaction.

Benefaktor [beˑneˑˈfaktor], *m.* **-s/-en** [-ˈtoːrən], benefactor.

Benefiz [beˑneˑˈfiːts], *n.* **-es/-e.** **1.** benefit; profit. **2.** *Ecc:* benefice, living. **3.** *Th: etc:* = **Benefizvorstellung.**

Benefiziant [beˑneˑfiˑtsĭˈant], *m.* **-en/-en.** **1.** *A:* benefactor. **2.** *Th: etc:* (*a*) artist for whom a benefit (performance) is given; (*b*) artist in whose honour a performance is given.

Benefiziar [beˑneˑfiˑtsĭˈaːr], *m.* **-s/-e.** *Ecc: Jur:* beneficiary.

Benefiziat [beˑneˑfiˑtsĭˈaːt], *m.* **-en/-en.** *Ecc: Jur:* beneficiary.

Benefizium [beˑneˑˈfiːtsĭum], *n.* **-s/-zien.** *Ecc: Jur:* benefice, living.

Benefizvorstellung, *f. Th: etc:* (*a*) benefit (performance); (*b*) performance given in honour of an artist.

benehmen. I. *v.tr.* (*strong*) **1.** *A. & Lit:* **j-m etwas b.,** *occ.* **j-n etwas** *gen.* **b.,** to take sth. away from s.o., to remove sth. from s.o.; **um ihn alles Zweifels zu b.,** in order to take away, dispel, all doubt from his mind; **der Schreck benahm ihm die Sprache,** the shock struck him dumb; **die unerwartete Freude benahm ihr den Atem,** the unexpected joy took her breath away, made her breathless; *cp.* **benommen. 2. sich benehmen,** to behave (oneself); **sich zu b. wissen,** to know how to behave; **benimm dich!** behave yourself! (*to child, etc.*) be good! **sich gut b.,** to behave (oneself) well; **sich schlecht,** *F:* **daneben, b.,** to behave badly, to misbehave. **3. sich mit j-m benehmen** = **sich mit j-m ins Benehmen setzen,** *q.v. under* II. 2. **4.** *Dial:* **sich mit etwas benehmen,** to busy oneself with sth.

II. *vbl s.* **Benehmen,** *n.* **1.** conduct, behaviour; manners; **gutes B.,** good conduct, behaviour; good manners; **das ist kein B.,** that's no way to behave; **er hat kein B.,** he's got no manners; **ihr B. gefällt mir nicht,** I don't like her behaviour; *F:* I don't like the way she carries on. **2. sich mit j-m ins B. setzen,** to communicate with s.o., to get in touch with s.o.; to try to reach an agreement with s.o.; **mit j-m ins B. kommen,** to come to an agreement with s.o.

beneiden, *v.tr.* to envy (s.o.); **j-n um etwas b.,** *A:* **j-m etwas b.,** to envy s.o. (for) sth.; **j-n um sein Glück b.,** to envy s.o. (for) his good fortune; **wegen einer solchen Sammlung könnte er von einem Fachmann beneidet werden,** his collection might be envied by an expert; **du wirst darum beneidet, man beneidet dich darum,** you are envied for that, for that reason, on that account.

beneidenswert, *a.* enviable; **er ist ein beneidenswerter Mensch,** he is a person much to be envied; **er hat ein beneidenswertes Glück,** he is to be envied for his good luck; *adv.* **b. glücklich sein,** to be enviably happy; **sie ist eine b. schöne Frau,** she is a woman of enviable beauty.

Beneluxstaaten [ˈbeːneˑluks-], *m.pl. Pol:* Benelux countries.

benennen. I. *v.tr.* (*conj. like* **nennen**) **1.** (*a*) to name, to give a name to (sth., s.o.); *Ar:* to denominate (sth.); *Jur:* to name (true owner of property); **diese Nelkenart ist von Professor X neu benannt worden,** this variety of carnation has been newly named, has been given a new name, by Professor X; **man hat die Straße neu benannt,** the street has been given a new name; **das Kind nach dem Vater b.,** to name, call, the child after the father; **etwas recht, mit dem rechten Namen, b.,** to call sth. by, to give sth., its right name, to designate sth. correctly; *F:* to call a spade a spade; (*b*) to define (sth.); to find a term for (sth.); **können Sie dieses Phänomen genauer b.?** can you define this phenomenon more precisely? *Jur:* **Benannte** *m, f,* person named as the true owner. **2.** *A. & Lit:* to appoint, set, fix (date, etc.); to nominate, suggest (s.o.) (for an appointment, employment, etc.). **3.** *Ar:* **benannte Zahl,** denominate, concrete, number; **zusammengesetzte benannte Zahl,** compound number.

II. *vbl s.* **1. Benennen,** *n. in vbl senses.* **2. Benennung,** *f.* = II. 1; *also:* nomenclature; designation; appellation; definition (of concept, etc.); *Mth:* denomination (of number, etc.).

benept, *a. Nau:* neaped, beneaped.

benetzen, *v.tr.* to moisten, dampen, sprinkle, wet (sth.); *Ch:* to wet; **Wangen mit Tränen benetzt,** cheeks bedewed with tears; **das Gras war vom Tau benetzt,** the grass was wet, besprinkled, with dew.

Benetzer, *m.* **-s/-.** *Ch:* wetting agent.

Benetzungsmittel, *n. Ch:* wetting agent.

Benevent [beˑneˑˈvɛnt]. *Pr.n.n.* **-s.** *Geog:* Beneventum.

beneventanisch [beˑneˑvɛnˈtaːniʃ], *a.* Beneventan.

benevolent [beˑneˑvoˑˈlɛnt], *a.* benevolent.

Benevolenz [beˑneˑvoˑˈlɛnts], *f.* **-/.** benevolence.

Bengal [ˈbɛŋgaːl]. **1.** *Pr.n.m.* **-s.** *Geog:* Bengal. **2.** *m.* **-s/.** *Tex:* bengaline.

Bengale [bɛŋˈgaːlə], *m.* **-n/-n.** Bengali, Bengalese.

Bengalen [bɛŋˈgaːlən]. *Pr.n.n.* **-s.** *Geog:* Bengal.

Bengalese [bɛŋgaˑˈleːzə], *m.* **-n/-n.** Bengali, Bengalese.

Bengali [bɛŋˈgaːliː], *n.* **-(s).** *Ling:* Bengali.

Bengaline [bɛŋgaˑˈliːnə] *f.,* **-/.** *Tex:* bengaline.

bengalisch [bɛŋˈgaːliʃ], *a.* Bengali, Bengalese; **bengalischer Tiger,** Bengal tiger; **bengalisches Feuer,** Bengal light; **bengalische Beleuchtung,** Bengal lights; *F:* brilliant illumination; *Geog:* **der Bengalische Meerbusen,** the Bay of Bengal.

Bengel, *m.* **-s/-.** **1.** (*a*) heavy wooden stick; club, cudgel; bludgeon; *Hist:* (*weapon*) morning star, holy water sprinkler; (*b*) *Print:* impression handle. **2.** (i) youth, lad; urchin; (ii) callow youth; rascal, scamp; rogue; **ein großer B.,** (i) a great lout; (ii) a big lad; **ein kleiner B.,** an urchin, *F:* a little chap; **ein ungeschliffener B.,** a boor, churl; **ein fauler B.,** a lazy beggar; **ein frecher B.,** a cheeky blighter.

Bengelchen, *n.* **-s/-,** urchin; little rogue, rascal.

Bengelei, *f.* **-/.** rude behaviour; boorishness, churlishness.

bengelhaft, *a.* boorish, churlish; **(ein) bengelhaftes Benehmen,** boorish behaviour; rude behaviour.

Bengelkraut, *m. Bot:* (*a*) copperleaf, three-seeded mercury; (*b*) = **Bingelkraut.**

beniesen, *v.tr.* to sneeze at (sth.); *F:* **etwas b.,** to prove the truth of a statement by an accidental sneeze.

benigne [beˈniːgnə], *a. Med: etc:* benign, non-malignant (disease, tumour, etc.).

Benignität [beˑnigniˑˈtɛːt], *f.* **-/-en.** *Med: etc:* benignity (of tumour, fever, etc.).

Benimm, *m.* **-s/.** *Hum:* manners; **er hat keinen B.,** he has no manners.

Benit [beˑˈniːt], *m.* **-(e)s/., Benitzucker,** *m.* barley sugar.

Benjamin [ˈbɛnjaˑmiːn]. *Pr.n.m.* **-s.** Benjamin, *F:* Ben.

Benjaminbaum, *m. Bot:* benjamin bush *or* tree, benzoin(-laurel); spice-bush, spice-laurel; wild allspice.

Benkulen [ˈbɛnkuˑlən]. *Pr.n.n.* **-s.** *Geog:* Bencooleen.

Benne, *f.* **-/-n.** *Swiss Dial:* push-cart; wheelbarrow.

Bennuß [ˈbeːn-], *f.* = **Behennuß.**

Benöl, *n.* = **Behenöl.**

benommen, *a.* bemused, dazed; **b. sein,** to be in a daze, *F:* to be dopey; **ein benommenes Gefühl,** a dazed, *F:* dopey, feeling; **er ist durch die Hitze ganz b.,** he is dazed by the heat; **sie war von der übergroßen Freude wie b.,** she was overwhelmed with joy.

Benommenheit, *f.* numbness; dullness (of mind, etc.); dazed, *F:* dopey, feeling.

benötigen, *v.tr.* **etwas b.,** *A:* **etwas** *gen.* **benötigt sein,** to need, require, want, sth.; to be, stand, in need, to be in want, of sth.; **ich benötige dringend seine Hilfe,** I am in great need of, I urgently want, his help, assistance; **2000 Mark werden noch benötigt,** 2000 marks are still needed; **hast du alles, was du zur Reise benötigst, hast du alle zur Reise benötigten Dinge?** have you everything you need, everything necessary, for the journey? **er rüstete ihn mit allem Benötigten aus,** he equipped him with everything he needed.

Bensäure [ˈbeːn-], *f. Ch:* benic acid.

benschen, *v.tr. Yiddish:* to say a blessing, to bensh.

Benthos [ˈbɛntos], *n.* **-/.** fauna and flora of the sea bottom, benthos.

Bentonit [bɛntoˑˈniːt], *m.* **-(e)s/-e.** *Geol:* bentonite.

benutzbar, *a.* usable; **die Schreibmaschine ist nicht mehr b.,** the typewriter is no longer usable; **das Buch ist schwer b., weil es keinen Index hat,** this book is difficult to use because it has no index.

Benutzbarkeit, *f.* usability; use.

benutzen. I. *v.tr.* (*a*) to use (sth.); **ich habe das Handtuch erst einmal benutzt,** I have only used the towel once; **ist die Bettwäsche schon benutzt?** has the bed-linen already been used? **wir benutzen dieses Zimmer im Winter nicht,** we don't use, live in, this room in the winter; **die beiden Mietparteien müssen die Küche gemeinsam b.,** the two tenants must share the (use of) the kitchen; **ich habe die Rückfahrkarte nicht benutzt,** I did not use the return ticket; **Fahrkarten als nicht benutzt bescheinigen,** to certify tickets as 'not used'; (*b*) to use, to make use of (sth.), to use, to consult (books, etc.); to use, to read at (library); **ich benutzte das Geld, um mein Haus neu zu bauen, ich benutzte das Geld zum Wiederaufbau meines Hauses,** I used the money to rebuild my house; **dazu benutzt man besser einen kleineren Hammer,** one should use a smaller hammer for this; **welche Zahnpasta benutzen Sie?** what make of toothpaste do you use? **ein Alpenpaß, der schon bekannt und benutzt ist,** an alpine pass already known and used; **ich benutze die Straßenbahn jeden Morgen,** I take, use, the tram every morning; **Leute, die die Eisenbahn regelmäßig benutzen,** people who use the railway regularly; **er benutzt jede Gelegenheit, sie schlecht zu machen,** he takes every opportunity to blacken her character; **ich möchte die Gelegenheit dazu b., . . .,** I should like to take, avail myself of, this opportunity to . . .; **ich habe die Zeit dazu benutzt, (um) mir die Stadt anzusehen,** I used, took advantage of, the time to look round the town; **ich habe bei meiner Arbeit das neue Lexikon viel benutzt,** in my work I have made great use of, often consulted, the new dictionary; **'benutzte Literatur',** 'books consulted', 'bibliography'; **etwas zu einem (besonderen) Zweck b.,** to use sth. for a (special) purpose; **etwas als etwas b.,** to use sth. as, for, sth.; **sie benutzten eine Zeitung als Tischtuch,** they used a newspaper as a tablecloth; **er hat meinen Namen dort benutzt, um sich eine Stellung zu verschaffen,** he utilized, made use of, my name there in order to get

himself a position; **er hat ihn als Werkzeug benutzt, um seine Pläne zu verwirklichen,** he used him as a tool in order to accomplish his plans.

II. *vbl s.* **Benutzen** *n.*, **Benutzung** *f. in vbl senses; also:* use; use, consultation (of books); **die Benutzung dieses Fußweges ist nur Anliegern gestattet,** only residents may use this footpath; **das Schwimmbad wurde zur öffentlichen Benutzung freigegeben,** the swimming pool was opened to the public; **zur allgemeinen, öffentlichen, Benutzung,** for general, public, use; **die Benutzung des Badezimmers ist nach 10 Uhr abends nicht gestattet,** the bathroom is not to be used after 10 p.m., the use of the bathroom is not permitted after 10 p.m.; **die Benutzung der Institutsbibliothek ist nur Mitgliedern gestattet,** the library of the institute is only open to members.

benützen, *v.tr.* = **benutzen.**

Benutzer, *m.* -s/-, user; *Library:* reader, borrower.

Benutzerkarte, *f. Library:* reader's ticket; borrower's ticket; library ticket, *U.S.:* card.

Benutzungsgebühr, *n.* charge, fee (for the use of sth.); toll (for the use of road, etc.).

Benutzungsordnung, *f. Library:* rules, conditions, for the use of a, the, library.

Benutzungszwang, *m. Adm:* enforced use of a public utility (*e.g.* slaughter-house, etc.).

Benz-, *comb.fm. Ch:* benz(o)-; **Benzanalid** *n*, benzanilide; **Benzonitril** *n*, benzonitrile.

Benzaldehyd [bɛntsaˑldeˑˈhyːt], *m.* **-s** & **-es/-e** [-s, ˈhyːdəs/-ˈhyːdə]. *Ch:* benzaldehyde.

Benzarsinigsäure [bɛntsarziˑˈniːk-], *f. Ch:* benzarsinous acid.

Benzarsinsäure [bɛntsaˑrˈziːn-], *f. Ch:* benzarsinic acid.

Benzidin [bɛntsiˑˈdiːn], *n.* -s/. *Ch:* benzidine.

Benzin [bɛnˈtsiːn], *n.* -s/-e. **1.** *Ch: Ind:* benzine. **2.** *Aut: etc:* petrol, *U.S.* gasoline.

Benzin-, *comb.fm.* **1.** *Ch: etc:* benzine . . . . **2.** *Aut: etc:* petrol . . . , *U.S:* gasoline . . . , *F:* gas . . . ; **Benzinkocher** *m*, petrol stove, *U.S:* gasoline stove; **Benzintank** *n*, petrol tank, *U.S:* gas(oline) tank.

Benzinabscheider, *m.* petrol separator, petrol trap.

Benzinabsperrventil, *n.* petrol stop-valve.

Benzinabstellhahn, *m. Aut: etc:* petrol stopcock.

Benzinausgabestelle, *f. Mil: etc:* petrol point.

Benzinbehälter, *m.* petrol tank.

Benzin-Benzol-Gemisch, *n. Aut: etc:* benzine-benzol mixture.

benzinbetrieben, *a.* petrol-driven.

Benzindampf, *m. Aut: etc:* benzine vapour; petrol vapour.

Benzindruckmesser, *m. Aut: etc:* petrol pressure gauge.

Benzinfallzuleitung, *f.* gravity petrol feed.

Benzinfilter, *m.* & *n. Aut: etc:* petrol filter, petrol separator, petrol strainer.

Benzinhahn, *m.* petrol tap.

Benzinkanister, *m. Aut: etc:* petrol can; *Mil: F:* jerrycan.

Benzinlager, *n.* petrol store, petrol dump.

Benzinlampe, *f. Min:* Davy-lamp, safety-lamp.

Benzinlötlampe, *f.* benzine blow-lamp.

Benzinmanometer, *n. Av:* petrol pressure gauge.

Benzinmotor, *m. Aut: etc:* petrol engine.

Benzinofen, *m.* petrol heater; petrol stove.

Benzinpumpe, *f.* **1.** *Aut: etc:* petrol pump, fuel pump. **2.** (*at petrol station*) petrol pump, *U.S:* gas(oline) pump.

Benzinreiniger, *m. Aut: etc:* petrol filter.

Benzinseife, *f.* benzine soap.

Benzinseiher, *m.* petrol filter.

Benzinstand, *m. Aut: etc:* petrol level.

Benzinstandanzeiger, *m.* petrol gauge.

Benzinsteig(e)rohr, *n.* petrol delivery pipe.

Benzintankuhr, *f.* delivery meter (on petrol pump).

Benzintrichter, *m.* petrol funnel.

Benzinuhr, *f. Aut: etc:* (*dial-type*) petrol gauge.

Benzinverbrauch, *m. Aut: etc:* petrol consumption, fuel consumption.

Benzinvergaser, *m. I.C.E:* carburetter.

Benzinwagen, *m.* petrol-driven car.

Benzinzapfsäule, *f.* (wayside) petrol pump.

Benzoat [bɛntsoˑˈaːt], *n.* -s/-e. *Ch:* benzoate.

Benzoäther [ˌbɛntsoˑˈɛːtər], *m. Ch:* benzoic ether.

Benzochinon [ˌbɛntsoˑçiˑˈnoːn], *n. Ch:* benzoquinone.

Benzoe [ˈbɛntsoˑeː], *n.* -s/. & *f.* -/. *Ch: etc:* (gum-) benzoin.

Benzoebaum, *m. Bot:* (styrax) benzoin, benzoin (-laurel), benjamin tree.

Benzoeharz, *n.* = **Benzoe.**

Benzoelorbeer, *m. Bot:* spice-bush.

Benzoesalz, *n. Ch:* benzoate.

benzoesauer, *a. Ch:* combined with benzoic acid, benzoate of . . . ; **benzoesaures Natrium,** sodium benzoate, benzoate of soda.

Benzoesäure, *f. Ch:* benzoic acid.

Benzoester [ˌbɛntsoˑˈɛstər], *m. Ch:* benzoic ester.

Benzoin [bɛntsoˑˈiːn], *m.* -s/-e. **1.** *Ch:* (gum-) benzoin. **2.** *Bot:* benzoin tree, benjamin tree.

benzoiniert [bɛntsoˑiˑˈniːrt], *a. Ch:* benzoinated, benzoated.

Benzol [bɛnˈtsoːl], *n.* -s/-e. *Ch: Com:* benzol, benzene.

Benzolbindung, *f. Ch:* benzene linkage.

Benzoleinsäure [bɛntsoˑleˑˈiːn-], *f. Ch:* benzoleic acid.

Benzyl [bɛnˈtsyːl], *n.* -s/. *Ch:* benzyl.

Benzylalkohol *m. Ch:* benzyl(ic) alcohol.

Benzyläther, *m. Ch:* benzyl ether.

Beo [ˈbeːoː], *m.* -s/-s. *Orn:* Indian grackle.

beobachten. I. *v.tr.* **1.** (*a*) to observe (sth.); to watch (s.o., sth.) (*for medical, scientific, etc., purpose*); to keep (s.o., sth.) under observation; **den Zug der Wolken, das Wachstum der Pflanzen, b.,** to observe, to study, the movement of clouds, the growth of plants; **den Lauf der Sterne b., die Sterne b.,** to observe, study, the stars; **eine Substanz auf ihre Reaktion hin b.,** to study, watch, a substance for its reaction, the reaction of a substance; **die nach einem besonderen Verfahren behandelte Lösung wurde (für) längere Zeit beobachtet,** the specially treated solution was watched, kept under observation, for some time; **den Gang der Zeitereignisse b.,** to watch, follow, the course of current events; **den Feind b.,** to observe the enemy; **man beobachtet uns,** we are being watched; **ich habe ihn dabei beobachtet,** I watched him at it; **dein Betragen wird ständig beobachtet,** your behaviour is under constant observation; **die Polizei beobachtete das Haus,** the police watched, kept a watch on, the house, kept the house under observation; **ich habe die Kinder eine ganze Weile beobachtet,** I watched the children for some time; (*b*) to notice, to observe; **drei Flugzeuge unbekannter Herkunft wurden beobachtet,** three unidentified aircraft were observed, spotted, sighted; **er beobachtete alles, was um ihn herum vorging,** he took stock of, had his eye on, everything around him; **das habe ich an ihm nie beobachtet,** I have never noticed that with him; *abs:* **er beobachtet ungeheuer scharf,** he is a man who observes very keenly, he is a very keen observer. **2.** to observe, to keep to, to comply with, to adhere to (rules, laws, etc.); **die Regeln des Anstands b.,** to observe the proprieties; **Schweigen, Stillschweigen, b.,** to keep, observe, preserve, silence; **strenge Diät b.,** to keep to, to follow, a strict diet; **die ärztlichen Vorschriften b.,** to observe, follow, the doctor's instructions.

II. *vbl s.* **1. Beobachten,** *n. in vbl senses.* **2. Beobachtung,** *f.* (*a*) *in vbl senses; also:* (i) observation (of s.o., sth.); **bei näherer B.,** on closer observation; *Mil:* **B. am Geschütz,** observation at the piece; (ii) observance (of law, etc.); (b) observation; (*of police, etc.*) **ein Haus unter B. halten,** to keep a house under observation, to keep a watch on a house; **j-n zur B. ins Krankenhaus bringen,** to take s.o. to hospital for observation; **einen Kranken unter B. halten,** to keep a patient under observation; **er war unter ständiger B.,** he was under constant observation; **sich der B. entziehen,** to escape observation; (*c*) observation; **astronomische B.,** astronomical observation; **eine B. machen,** to make an observation; **seine Beobachtungen über . . . veröffentlichen,** to publish one's observations on . . . ; **Beobachtungen über die Lebensgewohnheiten der Ameisen machen,** to make observations on the habits of ants; **Beobachtungen niederlegen, niederschreiben,** to record observations; **ich habe eine interessante B. an dem Kind gemacht,** I have observed an interesting trait in the child; **beim Studium der Bienen hat er eine sehr gute B. gemacht,** in his study of bees he achieved a very good piece of observation.

Beobachter, *m.* -s/-. **1.** observer; watcher; spectator; *Mil.Av:* observer; navigator-observer; *Mil:* observer; **er ist ein äußerst scharfer B.,** he is a very keen observer, a man of very keen observation; **er stand als belustigter B. dabei,** he was an amused onlooker, spectator; *Pol:* **politischer B.,** political observer. **2.** observer; **ein pedantischer B. der Umgangsformen** a strict observer of etiquette, a man who adheres meticulously to the proprieties.

Beobachterdelegation, *f.* (team of) observers.

Beobachterkompaß, *m. Av: Nau:* navigator's compass.

Beobachterposten, *m.* = **Beobachtungsposten** 1.

Beobachterraum, *m. Av:* observer's, navigator's, cockpit.

Beobachtersitz, *m. Av:* observer's, navigator's, seat.

Beobachterstand, *m.* **1.** *Av:* observer's position (in aircraft). **2.** = **Beobachtungsstand.**

Beobachtung, *f. see* **beobachten** II.

Beobachtungsabschnitt, *m. Mil:* sector under observation.

Beobachtungsabteilung, *f. Mil:* (artillery) survey unit.

Beobachtungsbatterie, *f. Mil:* (artillery) survey troop.

Beobachtungsdeck, *n. Nau: Aer:* observation platform.

Beobachtungsentfernung, *f. Mil: etc:* observation range.

Beobachtungsfähigkeit, *f.* = **Beobachtungsgabe.**

Beobachtungsfenster, *n.* observation-window.

Beobachtungsfernrohr, *n. Mil: etc:* observation telescope, sighting telescope.

Beobachtungsflugzeug, *n. Mil.Av:* observation plane.

Beobachtungsgabe, *f.* gift, talent, faculty, for observation; **ein Mensch ohne B.,** a person with no powers of observation.

Beobachtungsgerät, *n.* observation instrument.

Beobachtungsmine, *f. Navy:* controlled mine; observed mine.

Beobachtungsposten, *m. Mil: etc:* **1.** look-out (post), observation post. **2.** (*pers.*) look-out, observer.

Beobachtungsraum, *m. Mil: etc:* zone of observation.

Beobachtungsrohr, *n. Mil:* **1.** (*a*) observation telescope; (*b*) *A. Mil:* trench periscope. **2.** *Radar:* presentation tube.

Beobachtungsscharte, *f. Mil:* vision slit, loophole (on tank, etc.).

Beobachtungsschlitz, *m.* sight-hole, peep-hole; *Opt:* observation-slit, observation-aperture (on scientific apparatus).

Beobachtungsspiegel, *m.* observation-mirror; periscope.

Beobachtungsstand, *m. Mil:* observation post.

Beobachtungsstation, *f.* observation station; *Meteor: etc:* observatory; *Med:* observation ward.

Beobachtungstrupp, *m. Mil:* observation section.

Beobachtungsturm, *m. Mil: etc:* observation tower.

Beobachtungswagen, *m.* **1.** *Mil:* reconnaissance car. **2.** *Rail:* observation car.

Beobachtungswarte, *f. Mil: etc:* observation tower.

beohrt, *a.* with ears; **-beohrt,** *comb.fm.* -eared; **langbeohrt,** long-eared, with long ears.

beordern, *v.tr. Mil: etc:* to order, command (s.o.) (to a place, etc.); **er wurde nach Berlin beordert,** he was ordered (to go) to Berlin; **er wurde vom Arzt in ein Bad beordert,** the doctor ordered him to a spa.

bepacken, *v.tr.* to load (s.o., sth.) (with parcels, bundles, etc.); **schwer bepackt nach Hause kommen,** to come home heavily laden; **er war mit Geschenken bepackt,** he was laden with gifts.

bepanzern. I. *v.tr.* (*a*) *A:* to put a cuirass on (s.o.); **sich b.,** to put one's cuirass on; **bepanzert,** in a cuirass, wearing a cuirass; *Nat.Hist:* loricate, loricated; (*b*) to coat (ship, car, etc.) with armour-plate; **bepanzertes Schiff,** armoured ship, *A:* iron-clad.

II. *vbl s.* **1. Bepanzern,** *n. in vbl senses.* **2. Bepanzerung,** *f.* (*a*) = II. 1; (*b*) armour (-plating) (of ship, car, etc.).

bepelzt, *a.* furred, furry; *Nat.Hist:* tomentose.

beperlen, *v.tr.* (*of dew, etc.*) to pearl (grass, etc.); **vom Tau beperlt,** dew-pearled, bedewed.

bepfählen, *v.tr.* (*a*) to provide (sth.) with stakes; to palisade (sth.); (*b*) to prop, stake (vine, etc.); to prop up (young tree).

bepflanzen, *v.tr.* to plant (sth.) (with sth.); **ein Feld mit Kohl b.,** to plant a field with cabbages, to plant cabbages in a field; **eine Straße mit Pappeln b.,** to line a road with poplar-trees.

bepflastern. I. *v.tr.* **1.** to pave (street, courtyard, etc.) (with stone, wood, etc.); **mit Holz bepflasterte Straße,** wood-paved street; *Mil.F:* to cover, *F:* plaster, (sth.) with shell-fire. **2.** to put a plaster on (wound, etc.).

II. *vbl s.* **1. Bepflastern,** *n. in vbl senses.* **2. Bepflasterung,** *f.* (*a*) = II. 1; (*b*) pavement, paving.

bepflügen, *v.tr. Agr:* to till, to plough (up) (land).

bepichen, *v.tr.* to pitch (sth.).

bepinkeln, *v.tr.* to make water, *F:* to piddle, on (sth.).

bepinseln, *v.tr. F:* to paint (sth.) (with sth.); to daub (sth.) (with sth.); to brush over (pastry, etc.) (with sth.); *Med:* to paint (throat, etc.) (with iodine, etc.); *F:* **sich, sein Gesicht, b.,** to paint one's face.

bepissen, *v.tr.* (*not in polite use*) to make water, *V:* to piss, on (sth.).

beplanken, *v.tr.* to plank, to board over, to plank over (deck, etc.).

beplan(t)schen, *v.tr.* to splash (sth., s.o., oneself) with water.

bepudern, *v.tr.* to dust (sth.) over with powder; to powder (sth., s.o., oneself).

bequem, *a.* & *adv.* **1.** *A:* apt; *adv:* aptly. **2.** (*a*) (*of thg*) comfortable; **ein bequemer Sessel,** a comfortable armchair; **diese Schuhe sind sehr b.,** these shoes are very comfortable; **eine bequeme, b. sitzende, Jacke,** a comfortable, an easy-fitting, jacket, coat; **eine sehr bequeme Wohnung,** a very comfortable flat; **machen Sie sich's b.,** make yourself comfortable; make yourself at home; *Com:* **bequeme Raten,** easy terms; *adv.* **b. wohnen,** (i) to live comfortably; (ii) to live in a convenient place; (*b*) (*of way of life, etc.*) convenient, easy; **eine sehr bequeme Lösung,** a very convenient, simple, easy, solution; **eine bequeme Moral,** a convenient set of morals; **sein Gewissen ist b.,** he is a man with a lax conscience; **sich das Leben b. machen,** to make life easy for oneself; **er hat es sich, wie immer, b. gemacht,** as usual, he took the easy way out; **wann ist es Ihnen am bequemsten?** when will it be most convenient to you? **du könntest es bequemer haben, ein bequemeres Leben haben,** you could be better off, could live more easily, comfortably; *Nau: A:* **bequemer Wind,** fair wind; *adv.* **in diesem Sessel wirst du bequemer sitzen,** you will be more comfortable in this armchair; **in diesem Wagen können sechs Personen b. Platz finden,** the car will seat six people comfortably; **das hättest du bequemer haben, bekommen, können,** you could have got it with less trouble; **man kann diese Strecke b. in einem Tag zurücklegen,** one can cover this distance easily, comfortably, in one day. **3.** (*a*) (*of pers.*) *occ:* easy-going, good-natured, easy to get on with; (*b*) (*of pers.*) indolent, lazy; (*of life, etc.*) easy; **sie kommt in das Alter, wo man b. wird,** she has reached the age when one likes to take things quietly, comfortably; **er ist zu b. zum Arbeiten,** he is too lazy to work; **er hat ein bequemes Leben,** he has an easy life.

bequemen (sich), *v.refl.* **1.** *A:* (*a*) (*of pers.*) to accommodate oneself, to settle down (somewhere); (*b*) (i) to adapt, accommodate, oneself (to sth.), (ii) (*of thg*) to suit (sth.). **2. sich zu etwas b., sich (dazu) b., etwas zu tun,** to bring oneself, to trouble oneself, to do sth.; to take the trouble, to make an effort, to do sth.; to consent to sth., to do sth.; **er sträubte sich lange dagegen, Flüchtlinge in sein Haus aufzunehmen, aber er mußte sich schließlich doch dazu b.,** for a long while he refused to take refugees into his house, but in the end he had to consent to it; **endlich bequemte er sich, herzukommen,** at long last he deigned, troubled, he had the grace, to come here; **endlich bequemte sie sich zu einem Geständnis,** at last she deigned, she consented, to make a confession; **ich fürchte, Sie werden sich (dazu) b. müssen, aufzustehen,** I am afraid you will have to condescend (to take the trouble) to get up.

bequemlich, *a.* & *adv.* (*of pers.*) indolent, lazy; **ein bequemlicher alter Herr,** an easy-going old gentleman; **sie ist gleichgültig und b.,** she is indifferent and lazy.

Bequemlichkeit, *f.* **1.** (*a*) comfort, ease; **er liebt die B.,** he likes comfort; **zur größeren B. unserer Gäste,** for the greater comfort, convenience, of our guests, patrons; (*b*) indolence; idleness; laziness; **wegen seiner Gleichgültigkeit und B. macht er keine Fortschritte,** he makes no progress because he is indifferent and lazy; **das tut er aus lauter B.,** he does it because he is lazy, out of sheer laziness. **2.** (*a*) comfort(s); **mit allen Bequemlichkeiten,** with all comforts, conveniences; **er vermißt seine gewohnte B.,** he misses the comforts to which he is accustomed; (*b*) *A:* (public) convenience.

Beracha [be'ˈraxaː], *n.* **-/.** *Jew.Rel:* berakah.

berankt, *a.* covered with creeper; **eine berankte Mauer,** a wall covered with creeper, a creeper-covered wall.

Berapp, *m.* **-(e)s/.** *Constr:* rough coat (of plaster).

berappen[1], *v.tr.* **1.** *Constr:* to rough-cast, rough-coat, plaster (wall). **2.** to rough-hew, rough-square (timber).

berappen[2], *v.tr. F:* to pay, *F:* to fork out, stump up, shell out (money); *F:* **ich habe die Schulden dieses jungen Mannes immer wieder b. müssen,** I have had to stump up again and again for this young man's debts.

beraten. I. *v.* (*strong*) **1.** *v.tr. A:* to endow, provide (s.o.) (with sth.); to provide for (s.o.). **2.** *v.tr.* (*a*) to advise (s.o.); to give (s.o.) advice; **j-n gut b.,** to give s.o. good advice, a sound piece of advice; to advise s.o. well; **wohl beraten sein,** to be well, soundly, advised; **schlecht, übel, beraten sein,** to be badly advised; to be ill-advised; **du solltest dich b. lassen,** you should get, take, seek, advice; (*b*) **etwas b.** = **über etwas b.,** *q.v. under* 3. **3.** *v.i.* (*haben*) to confer; to be in conference; **sie berieten drei Stunden,** they conferred for three hours; **über etwas** *acc.* **b.,** to consider, debate, discuss, sth.; to deliberate on, over, sth.; **über einen Gesetzentwurf b.,** to consider, debate, a bill; **(sich) mit j-m (über etwas** *acc.*) **b.,** to confer with s.o. (on, about, sth.); to deliberate with s.o. (on sth.); to take counsel with s.o. (about sth.); to consult with s.o. (about sth.); **sie berieten (sich) miteinander, untereinander,** they conferred (together).

II. *vbl s.* **1. Beraten,** *n. in vbl senses.* **2. Beratung,** *f.* (*a*) = II. 1; *also:* deliberation, consideration; (*b*) (technical, etc.) advice; *Jur: Med:* consultation; (*c*) deliberation, consideration; debate; consultation; (*of pers.*) **in B. sein,** to be in conference; **im Laufe der parlamentarischen B. des Gesetzes,** in the course of the parliamentary debate on the bill; (*d*) consideration; (*of thg*) **in B. sein,** to be under consideration; (*e*) consultation, conference; **Beratungen** *pl, Pol:* consultations, *F:* talks; **nach einer zweistündigen B.,** after a consultation lasting two hours; **eine geheime B. abhalten,** to hold a secret consultation; *Jur:* to sit in camera; **im Laufe der Tagung wurden mehrere Beratungen abgehalten,** there were several special discussions in the course of the conference.

III. *pr.p.* & *a.* **beratend,** *in vbl senses; esp:* advisory; consultative; in an advisory capacity; **beratender Ausschuß,** advisory committee; **beratende Körperschaft,** (i) advisory body; (ii) deliberative body; **beratende Funktion,** advisory capacity; **nur eine beratende Stimme haben,** to be present in an advisory (but non-voting) capacity; *Pol:* **Beratende Versammlung des Europarates,** Consultative Assembly of the Council of Europe; *Ind: etc:* **beratender Ingenieur, Chemiker,** consulting engineer, chemist.

Berater, *m.* **-s/-,** adviser; counsellor; *Ind: etc:* **technischer B.,** technical adviser, consultant; **wirtschaftlicher B.,** economic adviser; **außenpolitischer B.,** adviser on foreign policy, political adviser; *Ecc:* **geistlicher B.,** spiritual adviser.

beratschlagen. I. *v.i.* (*haben*) **über etwas** *acc.* **b.,** to consider, debate, discuss, sth.; to deliberate on, over, sth.; to talk sth. over; **(sich) mit j-m (über etwas** *acc.*) **b.,** to confer with s.o. (on, about, sth.); to concert with s.o. (about sth.); to take counsel with s.o. (about sth.); **sie beratschlagten (untereinander, miteinander), sie beratschlagten sich (untereinander, miteinander), wie ...,** they talked over, debated, concerted, how ....

II. *vbl s.* **1. Beratschlagen,** *n. in vbl senses.* **2. Beratschlagung,** *f.* (*a*) = II. 1; *also:* consideration; deliberation; **nach längerer B.,** after due deliberation, consideration, reflection; (*b*) discussion; consultation; conference; *F:* confab, pow-wow, get-together.

beratschlagend, *a. Ling:* deliberative.

Beratung, *f. see* **beraten** II. 2.

Beratungsdienst, *m. Com: Ind: etc:* advisory service.

Beratungsgegenstand, *m.* subject under consideration; item for discussion (on agenda).

Beratungskosten, *pl. Jur:* consultation fee(s).

Beratungssaal, *m.* council chamber; conference room.

Beratungsstelle, *f.* advisory bureau, advice bureau; *Med:* medical health centre.

Beratungszimmer, *n.* conference room.

berauben. I. *v.tr.* (*a*) **j-n etwas** *gen.* **b.,** to rob, strip, s.o. of sth.; to deprive s.o. of sth.; **sich etwas** *gen.* **b.,** to deprive oneself of sth.; **j-n der Ehre b.,** to strip s.o. of honour; to take away s.o.'s good name; **j-n seiner Hoffnung b.,** to deprive s.o. of hope, to take away s.o.'s hope; **der Tod beraubte sie ihres Kindes,** death robbed her of her child; **ein Unfall beraubte ihn seines Vaters,** an accident bereaved him of his father; **er wurde aller seiner Wertsachen beraubt,** he was robbed, stripped, *F:* he was relieved, of all his valuables; **ich bin beraubt worden!** I have been robbed! **einen Garten der Blumen b.,** to strip a garden of flowers; **ich beraube Sie doch nicht?** can you spare it, them? I am not depriving, robbing, you (of it, them), am I? **der König wurde seiner Macht beraubt,** the king was deprived, divested, of his power, his authority; **die Empörung hatte ihn der Sprache beraubt,** indignation had deprived, bereft, him of speech; **die Kleinlichkeit ihres Vorgesetzten beraubte sie aller Freude an ihrer Arbeit,** the pettiness of her superior took all the pleasure out of her work; **aller Hoffnung beraubt,** bereft of (all) hope; **aller Hilfe beraubt,** deprived of all help; **der Sinne beraubt,** bereft of reason; *Lit:* **des Augenlichts beraubt,** bereft of sight; (*b*) to pillage, plunder, loot (town).

II. *vbl s.* **Beraubung,** *f.* robbing; robbery; theft.

beräuchern, *v.tr.* = **beweihräuchern** (*a*), (*b*).

beraumen, beräumen, *v.tr. Min:* = **abräumen** I. (*b*).

berauschen, *v.tr.* to intoxicate (s.o.), to make (s.o.) drunk, *F:* tipsy, fuddled; **der Wein hat ihn berauscht,** the wine has gone to his head; **sich b.,** to become intoxicated, inebriated, to get drunk, *F:* tipsy, fuddled, tight; **sich an Schlagwörtern b.,** to be carried away by slogans; **er war von seiner eigenen Beredsamkeit (wie) berauscht,** he was drunk with his own eloquence; **von seiner Macht berauscht,** drunk with power; **von Erfolg berauscht,** drunk, intoxicated, with success; **von Freude berauscht,** wild with joy; **berauschend,** intoxicating; enthralling; **berauschende Getränke,** intoxicating liquors, drinks, intoxicants; **berauschende Mittel,** narcotics; anaesthetics; intoxicants; sedatives; **berauschender Duft,** intoxicating, heady, perfume.

Berber [ˈbɛrbər], *m.* **-s/-,** (*a*) *Ethn:* Berber, Kabyle; (*b*) = **Berberpferd.**

Berberaffe, *m. Z:* Barbary ape, pygmy ape, magot.

Berberei, die [bɛrbəˈrai]. *Pr.n.* **-.** *A.Geog:* Barbary, the Barbary States.

Berberin [bɛrbəˈriːn], *n.* **-s/.** *Ch: Pharm:* berberin(e).

Berberis [ˈbɛrbəris], *f.* **-/-** = **Berberitze.**

berberisch [ˈbɛrbəriʃ], *a. Ethn:* Berber.

Berberitze [bɛrbəˈritsə], *f.* **-/-n.** *Bot:* berberis; **gemeine B.,** barberry, berberry.

Berberlöwe, *m. Z:* Barbary lion.

Berberpferd, *n.* (*breed of horse*) Barb, Barbary horse.

Berbersprache, *f. Ling:* Berber.

Berbesbeere [ˈbɛrbəzbeːrə], *f. Bot: F:* barberry, berberry.

Berceuse [bɛrˈsøːzə], *f.* **-/-n.** *Mus:* lullaby, cradle-song.

Berches [ˈbɛrçɛs], *m.* **-/-** = **Barches.**

Berchtold. *Pr.n.m.* **-s** = **Bertold.**

berechenbar, *a.* calculable, computable; **der Schaden ist nicht leicht b.,** the damage cannot easily be estimated, is not easily computable.

Berechenbarkeit, *f.* calculability, computability.

berechnen. I. *v.tr.* **1.** (*a*) to calculate, work out, reckon (price, cost, etc.); to estimate, assess, compute, appraise (damage); **einen Verlust b.,** to estimate, assess, (the extent of) a loss; **den Verkaufspreis b.,** to calculate, work out, the selling price; **etwas falsch b.,** to miscalculate sth.; *Mth:* **den Inhalt eines Rechtecks b.,** to calculate the area of a rectangle; **berechne $x(x-3)$ für $x=7$,** find the value of $x(x-3)$ when $x=7$; **berechne $3\frac{1}{7}$ auf vier Dezimalstellen,** evaluate $3\frac{1}{7}$ to four decimal places; *Ph: etc:* **berechnetes Gefälle,** theoretical height of fall; *Nau:* **das Besteck b.,** to work out the ship's reckoning; *Mec.E:* **für eine Dauerleistung von 10 PS berechneter Motor,** motor rated at 10 h.p.; **berechnete Leistung,** rated load; *Print:* **den Satzpreis b.,** to calculate the cost of setting; **ein Manuskript b.,** to cast off a manuscript; (*b*) **die Wirkung einer Rede, usw., b.,** to calculate, estimate, gauge, the effect of a speech, etc.; **es ist schwer, den Wert seiner Arbeit in Zahlen zu b.,** it is difficult to evaluate his work in material terms; **die Folgen lassen sich nicht b.,** the consequences are incalculable; **alles wohl berechnet,** everything taken into account, all things considered; **bei ihr ist alles auf Effekt berechnet,** she does everything for effect, for show; she aims entirely at effect; **etwas für etwas b.,** to intend, mean, design, devise, sth. for

sth.; **die Rede war nur für Schüler berechnet,** the talk was only intended, meant, for schoolboys; **Worte, die dazu berechnet sind, uns wieder in Sicherheit zu wiegen,** words calculated to reassure us. **2.** *Com: Fin:* **j-m einen Betrag b.,** to charge s.o. a sum; to charge a sum up to s.o., to debit s.o. with a sum, to enter a sum, put a sum down, to s.o.'s account; **j-m 20 Mark für einen Artikel b.,** to charge s.o. 20 marks for an article; **j-m zuviel b.,** to overcharge s.o.; **j-m etwas zum Selbstkostenpreis b.,** to charge s.o. cost price for sth., to let s.o. have sth. at cost price; **dem Kunden das Porto b.,** to charge (up) the postage to the customer; **jedes telegraphierte Wort wird berechnet,** every word telegraphed is charged for; **Verpackung wird nicht berechnet,** no charge is made for packing; **der Spitzenbesatz ist zu 9 Mark das Meter berechnet,** the lace trimming is priced, charged for, at 9 marks a metre; **sich** *dat.* **etwas b.,** to allow oneself sth.; **ich habe mir 10 Mark für das berechnet,** I have allowed myself 10 marks for that; **der Verkäufer kann sich keinen großen Gewinn b.,** the seller cannot allow himself much profit.

II. *vbl s.* **1. Berechnen,** *n.* (*a*) *in vbl senses; also:* calculation; (*b*) *Print:* (*of compositor*) **im B. stehen,** to work on piece-rates. **2. Berechnung,** *f.* (*a*) *in vbl senses;* (*b*) calculation, computation, estimate (of price, weight, etc.); **falsche B.,** miscalculation, miscomputation; **annähernde B.,** approximation; **nach meiner ungefähren B.,** according to my rough estimate; **meiner B. nach,** by my reckoning; **nach untenstehender B.,** according to the statement below; **eine genaue B. anstellen,** to make an exact calculation, a precise estimate; **die B. des Wertes der Möbel,** the valuation of the furniture; **seine Berechnungen wurden über den Haufen geworfen,** his calculations were upset, thrown out; *Print:* **B. des Manuskriptumfangs,** (i) casting off (of the) copy, (ii) cast-off; (*c*) *Com:* **bei billigster B.,** at the lowest price; **wir bitten Sie, dieses Paket unter B. Ihrer Auslagen an uns weiterzubefördern,** please send the packet on to us and note your expenses in this connection; (*d*) calculation; deliberation; **mit kühler B. vorgehen,** to act, proceed, in a cool, calculating, manner, with cool deliberation; **bei ihm ist alles B.,** everything is a matter of calculation with him; *U.S:* he has everything figured out in advance; **das ist alles nur B. bei ihr,** it is entirely calculated on her part; **etwas aus B. tun,** to do sth. from motives of self-interest; **etwas mit B. tun,** to do sth. in a calculating, calculated, manner.

III. *pr.p. & a.* **berechnend,** *in vbl senses; esp.* calculating, long-headed (pers., policy).

Berechner, *m.* **-s/-,** (*a*) estimator, assessor; (*b*) reckoner, computer, calculator.

Berechnungstafel, *f. Mth: Mec.E: etc:* table of calculations; calculating chart; diagram, nomograph.

berechtigen. I. *v.tr.* **j-n zu etwas b.,** to give s.o. the right to sth.; to entitle s.o. to sth.; **j-n (dazu) b. etwas zu tun,** (*of pers.,* *thg*) to authorize, empower, s.o. to do sth.; (*of thg*) to justify, warrant, s.o.'s doing sth.; **zu etwas berechtigt sein,** to be entitled, to have the right, to sth.; **berechtigt sein, etwas zu tun,** (i) to be authorized to do sth.; (ii) to have the right to do sth.; (iii) to be justified in doing sth.; **das Gesetz berechtigte sie dazu, ihre Kinder zu behalten,** the law gave her the right to her children; **diese Entdeckungen berechtigen uns zu glauben, daß . . .,** these discoveries entitle us to believe that . . .; **nach dem Testament des Vaters ist sie berechtigt, das Haus zu bewohnen,** the father's will entitles her to live in, gives her the right to occupy, the house; **der Grad seiner Verletzung berechtigt ihn zum Empfang einer Unterstützung,** the degree of his injury qualifies him for assistance; **ich bin (dazu) berechtigt, das zu fordern,** I am entitled to claim that; **diese Karte berechtigt zum Eintritt,** this card authorizes admission; **er berechtigte seine Sekretärin, den Brief zu unterschreiben,** he authorized his secretary to sign the letter; **der Ausschuß hat ihn (dazu) berechtigt, die Veränderungen durchzuführen,** the committee has empowered him to make the changes; **wir sind nicht (dazu) berechtigt, Tabak zu verkaufen,** we are not licensed to sell tobacco; **sein Zorn war nicht berechtigt,** his anger was unjustified, not justified; **sind Sie berechtigt, das zu verweigern?** are you justified in refusing it? **es gibt nichts, was diese Hoffnungen b. könnte, nichts berechtigt zu solchen Hoffnungen,** there is nothing to warrant, justify, such hopes; **die Bedingungen berechtigen uns, vollen Schadenersatz zu verlangen,** the terms justify our claiming full compensation; **seine Rede berechtigte zu der Annahme, daß . . .,** his speech justified the supposition that . . .; **dieses berechtigt uns zu der Annahme, daß er hier nicht lange bleiben wird,** that justifies our assumption that he will not remain here for long; **was berechtigt Sie zu glauben, daß . . .?** what right have you to think, suppose, that . . .? what justification have you for supposing that . . .? **sich für berechtigt halten,** to consider, hold, oneself justified; to consider oneself qualified, competent; **er hält sich nicht für berechtigt, seine Hilfe anzubieten,** he does not feel justified in offering his services; **ich hielt mich nicht für berechtigt, über die Sache ein Urteil abzugeben,** I did not consider myself qualified, competent, to express an opinion on the matter; **j-n für berechtigt halten,** to declare, hold, s.o. to be in the right; **berechtigte Bemerkung,** just remark; **berechtigter Einwand,** justifiable objection; **berechtigte Hoffnung,** just, legitimate, hope; **berechtigte Kritik,** justified criticism; **berechtigter Vorwurf,** just reproach; **berechtigtes Interesse,** legitimate interest; *Publ:* **berechtigte Übertragung,** authorized translation; *Jur:* **Berechtigte** *m, f,* legitimate claimant, rightful claimant *or* owner; person (who is) entitled to (alimony, etc.).

II. *vbl s.* **Berechtigung,** *f.* **1.** (*a*) rightness, correctness, validity (of claim, argument, etc.); justness (of reproach, anger, demand, etc.); **das Gerücht hat keine B.,** the rumour has no, is without, foundation; (*b*) right; justification; warrant; authority, authorization; **volle B. haben, etwas zu tun,** to be fully entitled to do sth.; **sie hatten keine B., so zu handeln, zu dieser Handlungsweise,** they had no warrant for doing, no authority to do, what they did; **sie sprachen ihm jede B. ab, darüber zu urteilen,** they disputed his right, his competence, to pass judgment on it; **etwas mit voller B. tun, sagen,** to be entirely justified in doing, saying, sth.; to do, say, sth. with every justification; **dies würde ihnen die moralische B. geben, es für sich zu fordern,** this would give them the moral right to claim it for themselves. **2.** right(s), title (to sth.); **B. zum Bergwerksbetrieb,** title to work a mine; **durch das Abiturzeugnis erwirbt man die B. zum Besuch der Universität,** the 'Abitur' certificate qualifies the holder, serves as a qualification, for admission to the university; **B. zu lehren,** qualification for teaching; **B., einen Titel zu führen,** right to bear a title; **B. zum Empfang einer Unterstützung nachweisen,** to establish one's right, title, to assistance; **B. zu freiem Eintritt,** right to free admission.

Berechtigungsnachweis, *m.* licence; certificate; **den B. erbringen,** to show title to sth.; to produce documents to prove one's right to sth.

Berechtigungsschein, *m.* document entitling the holder to receive, obtain, articles, etc., specified therein; permit; voucher; (written) authorization, *F:* chit; *Fin:* scrip.

Berechtigungswesen, *n.* system of (educational) qualification.

Berechtsame, *f.pl. Min:* exploitation rights.

bereden, *v.tr.* **1.** (*a*) **etwas b.,** to talk sth. over; **wir haben Ihre Angelegenheit beredet,** we have talked your business over; **etwas mit j-m b.,** to discuss sth., to talk sth. over, with s.o.; to debate sth. with s.o.; (*b*) **j-n b.,** to talk, gossip, about s.o.; **j-m etwas b.,** (i) to criticize s.o.'s actions, etc.; (ii) to meddle in s.o.'s affairs; **er beredet alles, was ich tue,** he finds fault with, criticizes, comments on, everything I do. **2. j-n (dazu) b., etwas zu tun,** to persuade, induce, prevail upon, s.o. to do sth., to talk, wheedle, s.o. into doing sth.; **sie hat ihn (dazu) beredet, mitzukommen,** she has talked him into coming along; **seine Freunde haben ihn beredet, zu . . .,** he has been prevailed upon, persuaded, by his friends to . . .; **sie war nicht dazu zu b.,** she was not to be talked into it; **sich b.,** to persuade oneself (into sth.); **er hat sich beredet, das zu glauben,** he has persuaded, talked, himself into believing it. **3. sich (mit j-m) über etwas** *acc.* **bereden,** to confer (with s.o.) about sth.; to talk sth. over (with s.o.); **wir haben uns mit ihm darüber beredet,** we have conferred with him about it, we have talked it over with him.

beredsam, *a.* eloquent, fluent, gifted (orator, etc.).

Beredsamkeit, *f.* eloquence; fluency of speech; persuasiveness; **die Kunst der B.,** oratory, rhetoric; **er suchte, sie mit großer B. von seiner Unschuld zu überzeugen,** he sought, tried, with great persuasiveness to convince her of his innocence.

beredt, *a.* eloquent, fluent, gifted (orator, etc.); **er ist sehr b.,** he is a very fluent speaker, he has a ready flow of talk, a ready tongue; *Pej:* **er hat eine beredte Zunge,** he has a glib tongue; **der Wein hat ihn b. gemacht,** the wine has loosened his tongue, has made him eloquent; **beredtes Schweigen,** eloquent, expressive, significant, meaningful, silence; **ihre Kleider sind beredte Zeugen ihrer Armut,** her clothes bear eloquent witness to, of, her poverty; **ihre Augen waren beredter als ihr Mund,** her eyes were more expressive than her mouth; *adv.* eloquently; **b. stellte er seinen Zuhörern die Not dieser Menschen vor Augen,** he represented the plight of these people in eloquent and persuasive terms to his listeners.

Beredtheit, *f.* eloquence; fluency of speech.

beregnen. I. *v.* (*a*) *v.tr.* to spray (sth.); **beregnet werden,** (*of land, etc.*) to be watered (by rain *or* artificial means); (*of pers.*) to get wet, *Hum:* to get rained on; *Lit:* **j-n mit etwas b.,** to shower, rain, sth. on s.o.; **sich b. lassen,** to let oneself get wet, to get oneself wet, in the rain; (*b*) *v.i.* (*sein*) to get wet (with rain).

II. *vbl s.* **Beregnung,** *f.* **1. (künstliche) B.,** overhead irrigation, watering, (of garden, etc.) by a (pipe-)sprinkler. **2.** rain, precipitation.

Beregnungsanlage, *f.* overhead irrigation plant, line irrigator, pipe-sprinkler.

Bereich, *m. & n.* **-(e)s/-e,** (*a*) region; district; domain; *Mil:* zone, area; range (of telescope, gun); sweep (of gun, searchlight); *Mth:* domain (of a function); *W.Tel: etc:* band, range (of frequencies); *Opt:* region (of spectrum); *Meteor:* region (of a front, etc.); **die Ruinen liegen im B. der Stadt, des Schlosses,** the ruins lie in the region, area, neighbourhood, of the town, within the domains, purlieus, precincts, of the castle; **dieses Zimmer ist ihr B.,** this room is her domain, sanctum, *F:* territory; *Meteor:* **Deutschland bleibt im B. einer Hochdruckzone,** Germany continues to be influenced by an anticyclone; (*b*) domain (of science, art, literature); province (of an expert, of science); department (of an expert, of science, etc.); field (of science, art); scope (of work, research, an inquiry); sphere, orbit (of influence, control); compass, range, extent (of knowledge, duty); range (of products, *Mth:* derivatives); purview (of an authority, an inquiry); realm(s) (of fancy); world (of reality); **es gehört in seinen B.,** that is his province, *F:* department; *F:* that's right up his street; **es gehört nicht in seinen B., es ist nicht innerhalb seines Bereichs,** that is not (within) his province, *F:* (in) his department; that is not in his line (of country), not within his scope, sphere; that is not within his ken; **eine Frage im B. der Astronomie,** a question within the domain of astronomy; **es fällt in den B. der Naturwissenschaft,** it belongs to, comes within, the province of natural science; **im zivilen, militärischen, B.,** in the civil, military, sphere, sector; **eine maßvolle körperliche Bestrafung liegt im B. verantwortlichen erzieherischen Handelns,** moderate corporal punishment comes within the scope, compass, of responsible training and teaching; **ein Gegenstand, der außerhalb des Bereichs der Wissenschaft liegt,** a subject that lies outside the province of science; **außerhalb des Bereichs des menschlichen Verstandes,** beyond the compass of the human mind; **Kentnisse, die innerhalb, außerhalb, meines Bereichs liegen,** knowledge, within, beyond, my compass, my ken; **im B. der Wirtschaft,** in the economic sphere; **in weiten Bereichen der Wirtschaft sind die Preise weiter stabil,** in broad sectors of the economy prices remain stable; **im B. der Industrie, im industriellen B.,** in the industrial sector; **es liegt im B. des Verkehrsministeriums,** it comes, lies, within the purview of the Ministry of Transport; **es liegt im B. des Möglichen, der Möglichkeit, daß . . .,** it is within the bounds, range, of possibility, that . . .; **ein offener Angriff liegt im B. der Möglichkeit, des Möglichen,** it is possible that there may be an open attack; **es liegt nicht im B. des Unmöglichen, der Unmöglichkeit, daß . . .,** it is not impossible, it is not beyond the bounds of possibility, that . . .; **das Ereignis wurde in den B. der Fabel verwiesen,** the incident was relegated to the realms of fiction; **der Regisseur lenkt die Kamera in jene Bereiche, wo die Individualität des einzelnen nichts gilt,** the director turns the camera into worlds where the individual counts for nothing: **die tieferen Bereiche der menschlichen**

Seele, the profound depths, the deeper levels, the lower reaches, of the human soul.

bereichern. I. *v.tr.* to enrich (s.o., sth.); to make (s.o.) wealthy; **eine Sprache b.,** to enrich, add to, a language; **seine Kenntnisse, seinen Wortschatz, b.,** to enlarge, extend one's knowledge, one's vocabulary; **sein Leben wurde durch ihre Liebe bereichert,** he was made richer, enriched, by her love; **eine Biographie, bereichert mit unbekannten Tatsachen,** a biography enriched with new facts; **sich b.,** to enrich oneself, to acquire wealth, riches, to make money; *F:* to line one's pockets; *F:* to make one's pile; **sich auf Kosten anderer b.,** to enrich oneself, to grow wealthy, to prosper, at the expense of others; to batten on others; **die Steuerpächter bereicherten sich an den Steuereinnahmen,** the tax-farmers enriched themselves from the taxes they levied.

II. *vbl s.* **1. Bereichern,** *n. in vbl senses.* **2. Bereicherung,** *f.* = II. 1; *also:* (*a*) enrichment (of s.o., language, etc.); extension (of knowledge); enlargement (of vocabulary); (*b*) extension (of knowledge); gain (to knowledge); *F:* **er ist eine bedeutende B. unserer Partei,** he is an important, a great, acquisition to our party; **durch diese Entwicklungen hat die Landwirtschaft eine wesentliche B. erfahren,** these developments have constituted a real gain for agriculture; (*c*) *Jur:* **ungerechtfertigte B.,** conversion of funds to one's own use; improper conversion, misappropriation, of funds; fraudulent misuse (of funds, etc.).

Bereicherungsklage, *f. Jur:* action for (improper) conversion; *A:* action of trover.

bereifen[1]. I. *v.tr.* (*a*) to hoop (barrel, gun); **ein Faß neu b.,** to re-hoop a barrel; (*b*) *Aut: etc:* to put, fit, a tyre on, to tyre (wheel); (*with metal*) to shoe (wheel); **ein Auto neu b.,** to equip a car with a new set of tyres, to fit a new set of tyres on, to, a car; **neu bereift,** (having) new tyres, re-tyred.

II. *vbl s.* **Bereifen,** *n. in vbl senses; also:* fitting (on) of a tyre, of (a set of) tyres. **2. Bereifung,** *f.* (*a*) = II. 1; (*b*) (set of) tyres; **ein Auto mit neuer B.,** a car with new tyres.

bereifen[2], *v.tr.* (*of winter, etc.*) to cover (field, bushes, etc.) with hoar(-frost), with rime; **bereift,** (i) hoar-covered, frosted; (*of beard, hair*) white with frost; (ii) *Bot:* pruinose; covered with bloom; velvety; (iii) *Poet:* hoary (head, beard); **die bereiften Äste der Bäume,** the rime-encrusted branches of the trees; **bereifte Dächer,** frosted, rime-covered, roofs; **der Wald war bereift,** the forest lay under a white hoar-frost.

bereinen, *v.tr.* = **bereinigen.**

bereinigen. I. *v.tr.* to settle (matter, dispute, account); to compose (dispute); to adjust (account, dispute, legislation, boundary, frontier); to correct, adjust (statistics); to clear up (misunderstanding); to resolve, clear up, straighten out, *F:* to iron out (initial difficulties, etc.); *Fin:* to re-assess (securities, etc.); to validate (securities).

II. *vbl s.* **Bereinigen** *n.*, **Bereinigung** *f. in vbl senses; also:* settlement (of dispute, account); adjustment (of account, dispute, legislation, boundary, frontier); correction, adjustment (of statistics); *Fin:* re-assessment (of securities, etc.); validation (of securities).

bereisen, *v.tr.* **ein Land b.,** to tour (in), to travel (over), a country; to visit a country; **eine Gegend zu Fuß, im Auto, b.,** to cover, tour, an area on foot, by car; **er hat die ganze Welt bereist,** he has travelled (all over) the world; **die Delegation bereiste Deutschland auf Einladung der Regierung,** the delegation toured Germany at the invitation of the government; **er bereiste Deutschland zwei Monate lang,** he toured Germany, travelled in Germany, for two months; **die Messen b.,** to tour, frequent, the fairs; (*of commercial traveller*) **einen Bezirk b.,** to travel in a district; to work, cover, a district; **Italien ist ein viel bereistes Land,** Italy is a country greatly favoured by travellers, tourists, Italy is a much-visited country; **ein bereister Mann,** a widely-, much-travelled, man; *Lit:* **die Meere b.,** (*of pers.*) to sail the seas.

bereit, *a.* **1.** (*of pers.*) willing, prepared, ready; **b. sein, etwas zu tun,** to be willing, prepared, ready, to do sth.; **ich bin b., Ihr Angebot anzunehmen,** I am willing to accept your offer; **er ist b., das Amt des Präsidenten zu übernehmen,** he is willing, ready, to take over the office of President; **sie sind nicht b., diese Frage mit uns zu untersuchen,** they are not prepared, willing, to discuss this question with us; **sind Sie b. zu schweigen?** are you prepared, willing, to keep silent? **es war der einzige Vorschlag, den er anzunehmen b. war,** it was the only proposal which he was prepared to accept; **falls er b. ist, Ihnen das Geld zu leihen,** if he is prepared, willing, to lend you the money; **er ist b., an Wunder zu glauben,** he is a ready believer in miracles; **er ist zu allem b.,** (i) *F:* he is quite willing to fall in with any arrangement; he doesn't mind what he does; *F:* he is game for anything; (ii) he sticks at nothing; **er ist zu schnell b., andere zu verdächtigen,** he is too ready to suspect others; **wir sind jederzeit b., Ihnen nähere Auskünfte zu geben,** we are always ready, we shall always be glad, to supply you with further information; **zu Gegendiensten sind wir gern b.,** we shall be glad to render you a similar service; **sich b. erklären, etwas zu tun,** to express oneself willing, prepared, ready, to do sth.; **die Regierung hat sich wiederholt b. erklärt, über die Sache zu verhandeln,** the government has repeatedly expressed its willingness to discuss the matter; **sich b. finden, etwas zu tun,** to be prepared to do sth.; **können Sie sich b. finden, ihr zu verzeihen?** are you prepared to forgive her? can you see your way to forgiving her? **ich kann mich nicht b. finden, Ihnen eine Einladung zu verschaffen,** I am not prepared to get you an invitation. **2. b. sein,** to be ready, prepared; **das Essen ist b.,** dinner is ready; **b. sein ist alles,** readiness is everything, *A:* readiness is all; **für alle Fälle b. sein,** to be prepared, ready, for anything, for all contingencies; **die Rettungsboote müssen b. zum Zuwasserlassen sein,** the life-boats must be ready for lowering; **etwas b. haben,** to have sth. ready, to be ready with sth.; **seine Antwort b. haben,** to be ready with one's answer, to have one's answer pat; **er hat für alles eine Antwort b.,** he has an answer ready for everything; **sie haben einen herzlichen Empfang für ihn b.,** there is a hearty welcome in store for him; **der Führer hatte schon eine Taschenlampe b.,** the guide had a torch ready; **etwas b. halten,** to hold sth. ready, in readiness, for s.o.; **ein Zimmer für j-n b. halten,** to hold a room ready, in readiness, for s.o.; **sich b. halten,** to hold oneself ready, in readiness; to stand by; **das Bataillon hielt sich b., einem Angriff zu begegnen,** the battalion held itself in readiness to meet an attack; **die Ambulanz hielt sich b., um die Verwundeten ins Krankenhaus zu bringen,** the ambulance stood by to take the injured to hospital; *see also* **bereithalten**; **etwas b. machen,** to make, get, sth. ready; **j-n zu etwas b. machen,** to prepare s.o. for sth.; **machen Sie bitte das Auto b.,** please get the car ready; **sich b. machen,** to get ready; *see also* **bereitmachen**; **zum Kampf, Angriff, b. stehen,** to be ready to fight, to attack; *see also* **bereitstehen.**

bereiten[1]. I. *v.tr.* **1.** (*a*) *Lit:* to prepare, get ready (meal, dish); to make (tea, coffee), to brew (punch); to prepare (medicine); to mix (concrete); **j-m etwas b.,** to prepare sth. for s.o., to make sth. ready for s.o.; **j-m ein Bad b.,** (i) to prepare a bath for s.o.; (ii) *F:* to put a rod in pickle for s.o.; **sie bereiteten ihm ein Lager auf dem Fußboden,** they made up a bed for him on the floor; *B:* **bereitet dem Herrn den Weg!** prepare ye the way of the Lord! *B:* **ich gehe hin, euch die Stätte zu b.,** I go to prepare a place for you; *A:* **sich b.,** to prepare oneself; (*b*) to curry, dress (leather); **den Boden b.,** (i) *Agr:* to prepare the ground, soil; (ii) to prepare the ground (for negotiations, etc.). **2.** (*a*) (*of pers.*) **j-m etwas b.,** to give s.o. sth.; **j-m eine Überraschung b.,** to give s.o. a surprise; **j-m eine Freude b.,** to give s.o. a present, a treat; to do something nice for s.o.; **Sie haben mir mit Ihrem Besuch eine große Freude bereitet,** your visit has given me great pleasure, you have given me a great deal of pleasure with your visit; **die Kinder haben mir mit diesem Geschenk eine große Freude bereitet,** the children have given me a great deal of happiness with their present; **ich möchte ihr eine kleine Freude b.,** I should like to give her a treat, do something nice for her; **ich muß dir eine Enttäuschung b.,** I have a disappointment in store for you, I must give you a disappointment; **sie haben der Delegation einen begeisterten Empfang bereitet,** they gave, accorded, the delegation an enthusiastic reception; (*b*) (*of thg, pers.*) to cause (s.o.) (trouble, etc.); **j-m Schmerz, Sorge, Verlegenheit, b.,** to cause s.o. pain, concern, embarrassment; **es hat ihm großen Kummer bereitet,** it has caused him much grief; **das wird mir viel Unannehmlichkeit b.,** that will cause me a great deal of inconvenience, of bother; **dieser Verleumdungsprozeß hat uns viel Verdruß bereitet,** this libel suit has made a great deal of trouble for us; **der Wettbewerb wird seinem Geschäft den Untergang b.,** the competition will ruin his business; **j-m Schande b.,** to bring disgrace, shame, on s.o.; **j-m Freude b.,** to give s.o. pleasure, happiness, joy, to make s.o. happy; **es würde mir große Freude b.,** it would give me much, great, pleasure; **meine Kinder haben mir nichts als Freude bereitet,** my children have given, brought, me nothing but happiness; **es bereitet mir Genugtuung,** it gives, affords, me satisfaction; **es bereitete dem Alten viel Vergnügen, die Kinder singen zu hören,** it gave the old man much pleasure to hear the children sing; **das Buch hat mir großes Vergnügen bereitet,** the book has given me much, a great deal of, pleasure, has provided me with a great deal of enjoyment; **es würde mir das größte Vergnügen b., wenn Sie mich besuchen würden,** it would give me great pleasure if you would visit me; **Japan bereitet dem deutschen Export ernsthafte Konkurrenz,** Japan offers serious competition to German exports.

II. *vbl s.* **Bereiten** *n.*, **Bereitung** *f. in vbl senses; also:* preparation (of meal, food, etc.).

bereiten[2], *v.tr.* (*strong*) **1.** to ride through, across, (a country) on horseback; to visit, patrol, cover, (a district) on horseback; to ride over (an area). **2. ein Pferd b.,** to break in a horse. **3.** *see* **beritten.**

Bereiter[1], *m.* -s/- = **Lederbereiter; Tuchbereiter.**

Bereiter[2], *m.* -s/-. *Equit:* horse-breaker; rough-rider; horse-trainer.

bereithalten, *v.tr. sep.* (*strong*) **etwas b.,** to hold sth. ready, in readiness; to keep sth. at, on, hand; **die notwendigen Geräte werden in der Feuerwache bereitgehalten,** the essential equipment is kept on hand at the fire-station; **das Buch hält auf jede Frage eine Antwort bereit,** the book has an answer, a ready answer, to every question; **ein Auto wurde für die Ankunft des Präsidenten bereitgehalten,** a car was held in readiness for the arrival of the President; **bitte, die Pässe b.!** have your passports ready, please! *see also* **bereit** 2.

bereitlegen, *v.tr. sep.* to lay, put, (sth.) out in readiness, to place (sth.) ready; **die Kleider waren auf dem Bett bereitgelegt,** the clothes were laid out, put out, on the bed; **würden Sie bitte die zu der Besprechung nötigen Papiere für mich b.,** will you please put out the necessary papers for the meeting for me.

bereitliegen, *v.i. sep.* (*strong*) (*haben*) to be, to lie, ready; **es liegt alles bereit,** everything is ready; **das Schiff lag zur Abfahrt bereit,** the ship lay ready to depart; (*of goods, etc.*) **zur Abholung b.,** to be ready for collection, to be ready to be collected; (*of cargo*) **zur Verladung b.,** to be, lie, ready for shipment.

bereitmachen, *v.tr. sep.* to make, get, (sth.) ready; **einen Wagen b.,** to get a car ready; **ein Lager b.,** to make up a bed; **sich b.,** to get ready; *see also* **bereit** 2.

bereits, *adv.* (*a*) already; **es war b. zu spät,** it was already too late; **es dämmerte b.,** it was already growing, getting, dark; **er war b. tot,** he was already dead; **sie wartet b. auf Sie,** she is already waiting for you; **eine bereits eingereichte Resolution,** a resolution that has already been presented; **b. um 3000 v. Chr. wurde in China Astronomie getrieben,** astronomy was studied as a science in China as early as the third millenium B.C.; **er beabsichtigt, b. am Sonntag zu kommen,** he intends to come as early as Sunday; (*b*) *Swiss & South G.Dial:* almost, nearly; (*of second-hand book, etc.*) **b. neu,** in practically new condition.

Bereitschaft, *f.* -/-en. **1.** (*a*) readiness; preparedness; *Mil:* stand-to, alert; **alles war in B.,** (i) everything was in readiness, ready; everything was in a state of preparedness; (ii) everyone was in readiness, ready; **etwas in B. halten,** to hold, keep, sth. ready, in readiness; **sich in B. halten,** to hold, keep, oneself in readiness; **etwas für j-n in B. haben,** to have sth. in readiness, ready, for s.o.; to have sth. prepared for s.o.; **er hat immer ein paar Bosheiten in B.,** he is always ready with a gibe or a sneer; he always has a few nasty tricks up his sleeve; **in ständiger B. sein,** to be always ready, permanently on the alert; to be in a permanent state of readiness; **die Feuerwehr ist, hält sich, in ständiger B., für den Fall eines Alarms,** the fire-brigade is always on call; **in B. liegen,** to lie ready; **die feindlichen Streitkräfte lagen südlich der Grenzlinie in B.,** the enemy forces lay ready, in readiness, south of the

border; **in B. stehen,** to be ready and waiting; to stand by; (*b*) willingness; **(seine) B. zeigen,** to show (one's) willingness; **(seine) B. erklären,** to indicate, express, (one's) willingness; **B. zur Diskussion zeigen,** to show willingness to discuss matters; **B. zur Zusammenarbeit,** willingness to co-operate; **Dänemark erklärte seine B. zur, für die, Aufnahme deutscher Waren,** Denmark expressed her willingness, readiness, to take German goods; **seine schnelle B. zu helfen,** his immediate readiness, willingness, to help; **mit aller, voller, B.,** with a good will; with a willing spirit. **2.** (*a*)=**Bereitschaftsdienst;** (*b*) squad, team (of rescue workers, etc.); **B. der Schutzpolizei,** company of the civil, rural, police; **Bereitschaften** *pl, Mil:* supports, reserves; (*c*) *Av:* duty flight.

Bereitschaftsanlage, *f. Ind:* stand-by plant.

Bereitschaftsbataillon, *n. Mil:* stand-to battalion.

Bereitschaftsbüchse, *f.* gas-mask container.

Bereitschaftsdienst, *m.* (*a*) stand-by duty; *Mil:* stand-to duty; **im B. sein, B. haben,** to be on stand-by, *Mil:* stand-to, duty; (*of doctor, etc.*) to be on call; (*of pharmacy*) to operate a dispensing service, to be open for dispensing, out of hours; (*b*) auxiliary, emergency, police force.

Bereitschaftsgraben, *m. Mil:* support trench.

Bereitschaftskosten, *pl. Ind: etc:* financial allocation for possible increases in staff, etc.

Bereitschaftspolizei, *f.* mobile police.

Bereitschaftsraum, *m.* **1.** *Mil:* stand-to area. **2.** *Mil.Av:* operations room; briefing room.

Bereitschaftsstellung, *f.* starting position; *Mil:* position of readiness.

Bereitschaftstasche, *f.* carrying case (for camera, first-aid kit, etc.), ever ready case (for camera).

bereitstehen, *v.i. sep.* (*strong*) (*haben*) (*of pers.*) to be ready; (*of thg*) to be ready, available; *Mil:* to stand-to; *Nau:* to stand by; (*of cargo*) **zur Verschiffung b.,** to be ready for shipment; **die notwendigen Mittel stehen bereit,** the necessary means, funds, are available, to hand; **zur Abholung b.,** to be ready for collection; **am Bahnhof stand schon ein Auto für mich bereit,** a car stood ready, was waiting, for me at the station; **er bestieg das bereitstehende Flugzeug,** he boarded the waiting plane; *Fin:* **bereitstehende Mittel,** available funds; *see also* **bereit 2.**

bereitstellen. I. *v.tr. sep.* (*a*) to place (sth.) ready; *Mil:* to assemble (troops); **die Gläser waren auf dem Tisch bereitgestellt,** the glasses stood, were placed, ready on the table; **Stühle b.,** to put out, arrange, chairs; **der Zug wird in X bereitgestellt,** the train (i) is made up at X, (ii) starts from X; (*b*) to provide, supply (sth.); to make (sth.) available, to allocate (sth.); **der Bürgermeister wird die notwendigen Transportmittel b.,** the mayor will provide the necessary transport; **zwanzig Betten sind für die Verletzten bereitgestellt worden,** twenty beds have been provided for, allotted to, allocated to, the injured; **die notwendigen Mittel b.,** to make the necessary funds available.

II. *vbl s.* **1. Bereitstellen,** *n. in vbl senses.* **2. Bereitstellung,** *f.* (*a*)=II. 1; *also:* provision (of money, etc.); earmarking, appropriation, allocation (of funds); allotment, allocation (of theatre seats, etc.); (*b*) *Mil:* (i) assembly; (ii) action stations, battle stations.

Bereitstellungsfonds, *m. Pol:* appropriation.

Bereitstellungsraum, *m. Mil:* assembly area.

Bereitung, *f. see* **bereiten**[1] II.

Bereitungsvorschrift, *f. Cu: Pharm: etc:* recipe.

bereitwillig, (*a*) *a.* ready; willing; obliging; **b. sein, etwas zu tun,** to be willing, ready, to do sth.; **er ist immer b.,** he is always obliging, ready to oblige; **die Erzählung fand bereitwillige Aufnahme,** the story found ready acceptance; (*b*) *adv.* readily; willingly; **j-m b. dienen,** to serve s.o. willingly; **er antwortete b.,** he answered readily; **er gab b. seine Zustimmung,** he gave a ready consent, he consented readily; **sie erteilte mir b. Auskunft über ihn,** she readily gave me information about him; **das Volk nahm b. alle Schwierigkeiten auf sich,** the population accepted all the difficulties readily.

Bereitwilligkeit, *f.* willingness; readiness; readiness to oblige; **B. zeigen,** to show willingness; **er hat immer große B. gezeigt,** *F:* he has always shown readiness to oblige, he has always shown himself willing, *F:* shown willing; **sie haben keine B. gezeigt, auf den Vergleich einzugehen,** they have shown no willingness to accept the compromise; **B. zu Gegendiensten,** readiness to reciprocate; **etwas mit der größten B. tun,** to do sth. most readily, with the utmost willingness; **mit der größten B. ging er mit,** he came most readily; **seine B. erklären, etwas zu tun,** to indicate, express, one's willingness to do sth.; **mit verdächtiger B.,** with suspicious readiness; **übergroße B. zeigen,** to show over-eagerness; **er zeigte keine übergroße B.,** *F:* he was not too eager, none too keen.

Berengar ['be:rɛŋgar]. *Pr.n.m.* **-s.** *Hist:* Berengarius.

Berenice, Berenike [be·re·'ni:tsə, -'ni:kə]. *Pr.n.f.* **-s.** Berenice; *Astr:* **Haar der Berenike, Berenikes Haupthaar,** (*the constellation*) Coma Berenices.

berennen. I. *v.tr.* (*conj. like* **rennen**) to rush, charge, assault (walls of fortress, etc.); to attack, storm (fortress, etc.); *Mil:* **eine Stellung b.,** to rush a position; **die Barrikaden b.,** to charge the barricades; **eine Stadt b.,** to assail, make an assault on, a town.

II. *vbl s.* **Berennung,** *f. in vbl senses; also:* **die B. einer Stadt, usw.,** the assault on a town, etc.

bereuen, *v.tr.* (*a*) to repent (of) (one's sins, misdeeds, etc.); **etwas tief b.,** to repent sth. sincerely; **er bereute, diese Grausamkeit begangen zu haben,** he repented of his cruel action; (*b*) to regret, to repent (of), *Lit:* to rue (course of action, etc.); **etwas sehr b.,** to regret sth. deeply, very much; **sie bereute bitter, gesprochen zu haben,** she bitterly regretted, repented, having spoken; **er hat seine Entscheidung nie bereut,** he has never regretted, repented, his decision; **wenn du seine Hilfe zurückweist, wirst du es später b.,** if you refuse his help you will be sorry, you will regret it, later on; **das wirst du bitter b.!** you will be sorry for it, regret it! **ich habe nichts zu b.,** I have no regrets; **Sie werden es nicht zu b. haben,** you will not regret it, *F:* you won't be sorry; **jetzt bereue ich meine (frühere) Voreiligkeit,** I have come to rue my past rashness; **ich bereue es nicht, die Ausstellung besucht zu haben,** I am not sorry to have been to the exhibition.

Berg, *m.* **-(e)s/-e. 1.** (*a*) mountain, (*in S. Africa*) berg; hill; peak (of mountain range); (*in proper name*) Mount; *Anat:* mount; **die Berge,** the mountains, *esp.* the Alps; **feuerspeiender B.,** volcano; *Geol:* **wurzelloser B.,** klippe; **der B. Horeb,** the peak Horeb, Mount Horeb; **B. und Tal,** mountain and valley; **über B. und Tal,** over hill and dale; far away; **über alle Berge sein,** to be beyond reach, to be far away, miles away; **jetzt ist er schon über alle Berge,** he is miles away (by) now; **auf einen B. steigen, einen B. besteigen,** to climb (up) a mountain, a hill; *Lit:* to make the ascent of a mountain; to ascend, scale, a peak; *Lit:* to ascend, mount, a hill; **in die Berge gehen, fahren,** to go (up) into the mountains, hills; to take a holiday, to holiday, in the mountains; **den B. hinauf,** *Lit:* **hinan,** uphill; **den B. hinunter, hinab,** down, downhill; **zu Berg(e) fahren,** (i) to go (up) into the mountains, hills; (ii) to move to mountain pastures; (iii) (*of pers., boat*) to go, to journey, up-stream, to go up-river, to go up a river; **ein Mann wie ein B.,** a mountain of a man; **am, vor einem, B. stehen,** to stand at the foot of a mountain; *F:* to be confronted with, to come up against, insuperable, insurmountable, difficulties, to come to a standstill (before an obstacle); to reach an impasse; *F:* **sie steht da wie der Ochs am, vorm, B.,** she's at a loss, nonplussed; she doesn't know which way, where, to turn; **hinter den Bergen,** beyond the mountains, the hills; *F:* **hinterm Berge wohnen auch (noch) Leute,** you're not the only clever one; you're not the only pebble on the beach; you're not the only person in this world; **mit etwas hinter dem Berge halten,** to keep quiet, dark, about sth.; to hold, keep, sth. back; to hide, conceal, sth.; to keep sth. dark; **ich werde mit meiner Meinung nicht hinter dem Berge halten,** I will not conceal my opinion; I shall not hesitate to give my opinion; *F:* **über den B. sein,** to be over the worst of one's difficulties; to have broken the back of the work; (*of invalid*) to have turned the corner, to have passed the crisis, to be over the worst; **wir sind noch nicht über den B.,** we are not yet out of the wood; our troubles are not yet over; we have not come to the end of it yet; **jetzt sind wir über den B.,** the worst is behind us now; *F:* now we are over the worst hurdles; *F:* now we can see daylight; **der Glaube, der Berge versetzt,** the faith that moves mountains; **der B. kreißte und gebar eine Maus,** the mountain laboured and brought forth a mouse; **wenn der B. nicht zum Propheten, zu Mohammed, kommt, muß der Prophet, Mohammed, zum B. kommen,** if the mountain won't come to Mahomet, Mahomet must go to the mountain; *B:* **ich hebe meine Augen auf zu den Bergen,** I will lift up mine eyes unto the hills; (*b*) *F:* pile, mountain (of food, etc.); **Berge von Obst, Büchern, Leichen,** piles of fruit, books, corpses; **Berge von schmutziger Wäsche,** piles of dirty washing; **Berge von Sorgen, Schulden,** a load of cares, debts; (*c*) *F:* **j-m die Haare zu Berge stehen lassen,** to make s.o.'s hair stand on end; **eine Geschichte, die einem die Haare zu Berge stehen läßt,** a hair-raising story; **die Haare standen ihm zu Berge,** his hair stood on end; **die Haare konnten einem dabei zu Berge stehen,** it was enough to make your hair stand on end; (*d*) *Ph: Statistics:* peak (of wave, curve, etc.). **2.** *Min:* (*a*) *pl.* **Berge,** deads, attle, refuse, slates; gangue; (*for stowing*) gob, waste; **grobe Berge,** big shale; **eigene Berge,** waste from the mine; **fremde Berge,** waste from outside the mine; *F:* **goldene Berge versprechen,** to promise miracles, to promise the moon (and the stars), to make extravagant promises; (*b*) steep roadway. **3.** *Fr.Hist:*=**Bergpartei.**

Berg-, *comb.fm.* **1.** mountain . . ., mountain-; climbing . . .; **Bergbach** *m,* mountain stream; **Bergschuh** *m,* climbing boot. **2.** mining . . ., mining-; mine . . ., mine-; miner's . . .; **Bergfach** *n,* mining profession; **Berginspektor** *m,* mine surveyor, mine inspector; **Berghaue** *f.* miner's pick. *Cp.* **Gebirgs-.**

bergab [bɛrk'ᵓap], *adv.* **1.** (*a*) downhill, down the mountain(-side); **der Weg führte b.,** the way led, went, downhill; *see also* **bergauf;** (*b*) downstream. **2.** (i) **es geht b. mit ihm,** he, his business, is going downhill, his business is on the downgrade; (ii) *Med:* he is going downhill, down the hill; he is sinking; his sands are running out; **Nation, mit der es b. geht,** nation on the downgrade.

Bergabhang, *m.*=**Berghang.**

bergabwärts, *adv.* down, downhill.

Bergacker, *m.* field on a mountainside.

Bergahorn, *m. Bot:* sycamore (maple), great maple.

Bergakademie, *f.* mining academy, college of mining.

Bergalant, *n. Bot:* mountain inula.

Bergalaun, *n. Miner:* rock-alum.

Bergalraun, *m. Bot:* allium victoriale, *F:* long-rooted garlic.

Bergamaske[1] [bɛrga·'maskə], *m.* **-n/-n.** *Geog:* inhabitant, native, of Bergamo, Bergamask.

Bergamaske[2], *f.* **-/-n.** *Danc: A:* Bergamask.

Bergamasker, *inv. a.,* **bergamaskisch** [bɛrga·'maskər, -'maskiʃ], *a.* Bergamask.

Bergamotapete ['bɛrga·mo:ta·pe·tə], *f. Tex:* bergamot tapestry.

Bergamottbaum [bɛrga·'mot-], *m. Bot:* bergamot (-tree).

Bergamotte [bɛrga·'motə], *f.* **-/n,** (*a*) bergamot (orange, lime, lemon); (*b*) bergamot (pear).

Bergamottöl, *n.* bergamot oil.

Bergamottzitrone, *f. Hort:* bergamot (lemon).

Bergamsel, *f. Orn:* ring-ouzel.

Bergamt, *n. Adm:* mining office.

bergan [bɛrk'ᵓan], *adv.*=**bergauf.**

Bergangelika, *f. Bot:* aralia.

Berganteil, *m. Fin:* mining share.

Bergarbeiter, *m.* miner, mine-worker; pitman; mine-digger.

Bergarbeiterkolonie, *f.* mining community; miner's housing estate.

Bergart, *f. Miner:* matrix, gangue, mother rock, parent rock.

Bergasche, *f.*=**Bergblau.**

Bergaster, *f. Bot:* purple Italian starwort.

bergauf [bɛrk'ᵓauf], *adv.* uphill; up the mountain; **b. und bergab,** up and down, *Lit:* up hill and down dale; **b. steigen,** to go uphill; **sie fingen an, wieder b. zu steigen,** they began to climb, they began climbing, upwards again.

Bergbach, *m.* mountain stream.

Bergbahn, *f.* mountain railway.

Bergbarte, *f. Min: Tls:* miner's axe, miner's hatchet.

Bergbau, *m.* mining; mining industry; working of mines.

Bergbauberechtigung, *f.* mining licence.

Bergbaufreiheit, *f. Min:* freedom to prospect.

Bergbauingenieur, *m.* mining engineer.

Bergbaukunde, *f. Min:* science of mining.

Bergbaukunst, Bergbaulehre, *f.*=**Bergbaukunde.**

Bergbauschule, *f.* school of mines.

Bergbauverein, *m.* mining association, mining company.

Bergbeamte, *m.* (*decl. as adj.*) mining official.

Bergbehörde, *f.*=**Bergamt.**

bergbeschreibend, *a.* orographic(al).
Bergbeschreiber, *m.* orographer.
Bergbeschreibung, *f.* orography.
Bergbewohner, *m.* mountain-dweller, highlander; hill-man.
Bergblau, *n. Miner:* blue copper ore, azurite.
Bergbock, *m. Z:* = **Steinbock.**
Bergbohrer, *m. Min: Tls:* miner's bar, plain chisel, drill(-bit), cutting-bit, borer, jumper.
Bergbraunelle, *f. Orn:* mountain accentor.
Bergbruch, *m.* = **Bergsturz.**
Bergbuch, *n. Adm:* register of mining licences.
Bergbutter, *f. Miner:* mountain butter, rock-, stone-butter.
Bergdohle, *f. Orn:* alpine chough.
Bergdorf, *n.* mountain village, (*in India and Africa*) hill village; **einsames B.,** remote, lonely, mountain village; mountain retreat.
Bergdrossel, *f. Orn:* White's thrush, golden mountain-thrush.
Berge-, *comb.fm. cp.* **Bergungs-.**
Bergedamm, *m. Min:* bulkhead.
bergehoch, *a.* = **berghoch.**
Bergeidechse, *f. Rept:* common lizard.
Bergeisen, *n. Min: Tls:* small pick; dresser.
Bergelohn, *m.* salvage, payment for salvage-work.
bergen. I. *v.tr.* (*strong*) **1.** (*a*) to recover (shipwrecked cargo, shipwrecked goods, dead body, damaged vehicle, etc.); to salvage, make salvage of (shipwrecked cargo); to salvage, salve (vessel, submarine, cargo); to save (cargo); to rescue, save (shipwrecked person); to bring (trapped miners, etc.) to safety; to rescue, recover (wounded); **einen Ertrunkenen b.,** to recover the body of a drowned man; **die Rettungsboote haben zwanzig Menschen aus Seenot geborgen,** the lifeboats have saved, rescued, twenty people from the sea; **zehn Kinder konnten lebend geborgen werden,** ten children were saved, rescued (alive); **die Insassen konnten nur als Leichen geborgen werden,** only the bodies of the passengers could be recovered; (*b*) **die Ernte b.,** to get in, gather in, house, the crop; **wir müssen die Ernte noch vor dem Regen b.,** we must get the crop in, we must secure the crop, before it rains. **2.** to shelter, shield, protect, s.o. (**vor,** from); **j-n vor seinen Feinden b.,** to protect, shield, s.o. from his enemies; **sich b.,** to take shelter, get under cover, retire to a place of safety; **geborgen sein,** to be safe; **hier bist du sicher und geborgen,** you are safe here; **das Gefühl, geborgen zu sein,** the feeling of being safe, of security, of safeness. **3. etwas (in sich) b.,** to hold sth., to hide sth.; **die Höhle birgt viele Geheimnisse (in sich),** the cave holds many secrets; **dieses Unternehmen birgt gewisse Gefahren in sich,** this enterprise involves, holds, certain dangers; **dieser eine Satz birgt alle unsere Probleme in sich,** all our problems are summed up, contained, in this one sentence; **die Erde birgt noch viele Schätze,** the earth still holds much treasure; **sie barg ihr Gesicht in ihren Händen,** she hid, buried, her face in her hands. **4.** *Nau:* **die Segel b.,** to shorten, take in, sail.
II. *vbl s.* **1. Bergen,** *n., in vbl senses.* **2. Bergung,** *f.* = II. 1; *also:* salvage (of ship, cargo); rescue (of shipwrecked person); recovery (of wounded, dead body, shipwrecked goods, etc.).
Bergenge, *f.* defile, gorge.
Bergente, *f. Orn:* scaup-duck.
Bergeppich, *m. Bot:* mountain-parsley.
Berger[1], *inv.a. Geog:* of, from, Bergen.
Berger[2], *m.* -s/-, salvor, salvager, saver.
Bergère [bɛrˈʒɛːrə], *f.* -/-n. **1.** shepherdess. **2.** easy-chair.
Bergerecht, *n.* right to salvage.
Bergerfisch, *m. Com:* dried ling.
Bergerippe, *f. Min:* stone pack.
Bergesche, *f. Bot:* = **Beeresche.**
Bergeschlämme, *m.pl. Min:* tailings.
Bergeshöhe, *f.* (*a*) height of a mountain; (*b*) *Poet:* peak, mountain top.
Bergeversatz, *m. Min:* gob; stowing (of old workings, etc.).
Bergeversetzer, *m. Min:* packer.
Bergezug, *m. Mil:* recovery platoon.
Bergfach, *n.* (science of) mining; mining profession.
Bergfahrt, *f.* **1.** (*a*) uphill journey; *Aut:* hill climb; (*b*) = **Almfahrt;** (*c*) trip into the mountains; *Aut:* driving in the mountains. **2.** *Nau:* (*of ship*) passage up-stream.
Bergfäustel, *m. Min: Tls:* miner's hammer, miner's mallet, sledge(-hammer).
Bergfenchel, *m. Bot:* seseli, meadow saxifrage.
bergfertig, *a.* (*of miner*) no longer fit for work underground.
Bergfeste, . **1.** *Min:* pillar (that is left permanently). **2.** mountain fortress, mountain stronghold.
Bergfett, *n.* = **Bergtalg.**
Bergfeuer, *n.* (*a*) *Folkl:* mountain bonfire (lit on Midsummer day, etc.); (*b*) *occ. Myth:* ignis fatuus (on mountains).
Bergfex, *m. F: A:* enthusiastic alpinist.
Bergfink, *m. Orn:* brambling, bramble finch.
Bergflachs, *m.* **1.** *Bot:* mountain flax; toad-flax. **2.** *Miner:* mountain flax, fossil flax, amiant(h)us.
Bergfleisch, *n. Miner:* = **Bergflachs** 2.
Bergflockenblume, *f. Bot:* greater knapweed.
Bergfreiheit, *f.* = **Bergbaufreiheit.**
Bergfried, *m.* -(e)s/-e, (*a*) *Arch:* keep, stronghold, donjon (of castle); (*b*) belfry; tower; (*c*) *A.Mil:* belfry, turret.
Bergführer, *m.* mountain guide.
Bergfußebene, *f. Ph.Geog:* pediment.
Berggeist, *m. Folkl:* mountain-spirit, gnome.
Berggelb, *n. Miner:* yellow ochre.
Berggeologe, *m.* mining geologist.
Berggeum, *n. Bot:* mountain-avens.
Berggipfel, *m.* mountain peak; mountain top; summit of a mountain.
Bergglas, *n.* = **Bergkristall.**
Berggold, *n.* vein-gold, reef gold.
Berggorilla, *m. Z:* mountain gorilla.
Berggott, *m. Myth:* mountain god; god of the hills.
Berggras, *n. Bot:* sheep's fescue.
Berggrat, *m.* crest, ridge, of a mountain.
Berggrün, *n. Miner:* green copper ore; green verditer, malachite.
Berghaarstrang, *m. Bot:* mountain-parsley.
Berghafer, *m. Bot:* (meadow) oat grass, perennial oat.
Berghäher, *m. Orn:* nut-cracker.
Berghalde, *f.* (*a*) mountain slope; hill-side; (*b*) *Min:* spoil-bank, -heap, -dump; tip.
Berghänfling, *m. Orn:* twite, mountain-linnet.
Berghang, *m.* slope, incline, mild declivity; hill-side; **steiler B.,** declivity.
Berghaue, *f. Min: Tls:* miner's pick, pickaxe, miner's hoe.
Berghauer, Berghäuer, *m. Min:* cutter, hewer.
Bergheimat, *f.* mountain home.
berghoch, *a.* as high as mountains, mountain(s)-high; **die Wellen türmten sich b.,** the waves rose mountains-high; **der Schmutz liegt b.,** the dirt lies thick.
Berghöhe, *f.* height of a mountain.
Bergholder, Bergholunder, *m. Bot:* red-berried elder.
Bergholz, *n.* (*a*) *Miner:* mountain wood; (*b*) *Nau:* wale.
Berghopfen, *m. Bot:* common, white, horehound.
bergicht, *a. A:* = **bergig.**
bergig, *a.* mountainous, hilly (country, etc.).
Bergingenieur, *m.* mining engineer.
berginisieren [bɛrgi·ni·ˈziːrən], *v.tr. Ind:* to berginize (coal, etc.); **Berginisierung** *f,* berginization.
Berginspektor, *m.* mine surveyor, mine inspector.
Berginverfahren [bɛrˈgiːn-], *n. Ind:* Bergius process.
Bergiusverfahren [ˈbɛrgĭus-], *n. Ind:* Bergius process.
Bergkamm, *m.* crest, ridge, of a mountain.
Bergkegel, *m.* (*a*) (mountain) peak; (*b*) sugar-loaf mountain.
Bergkessel, *m. Geol:* cirque, corrie, basin-shaped valley.
Bergkette, *f.* chain, range, ridge, of hills *or* mountains; mountain chain, mountain range.
Bergkiefer, *f. Bot:* mountain pine.
Bergkiesel, *m. Miner:* rock flint, chert, hornstone, felsite, petrosilex.
bergkieselartig, *a. Miner:* petrosilicous.
Bergkluft, *f.* chasm; ravine; gully.
Bergknappe, *m. Min:* miner, pitman.
Bergkork, *m. Miner:* mountain cork, fossil cork, rock-cork.
bergkrank, *a.* (*a*) = **bergfertig;** (*b*) affected by mountain sickness, height sickness.
Bergkrankheit, *f.* mountain sickness, height sickness.
Bergkresse, *f. Bot:* shepherd's-cress, pepper-cress.
Bergkristall, *m. Miner:* rock-crystal, quartz.
Bergkult, *m. Rel.Hist:* mountain cult.
Bergkümmel, *m. Bot:* spignel.
Bergkunde, *f.* (*a*) orography, orology; (*b*) = **Bergbaukunde.**
bergkundig, *a.* orographic(al).
Bergkuppe, *f.* round(ed) mountain top, dome-shaped mountain top.
Bergland, *n.* mountain country; hill-country; highland region; highland.
Berglandschaft, *f.* mountain scenery.
Berglattich, *m. Bot:* = **Alpenlattich.**
Berglaubsänger, *m. Orn:* Bonelli's warbler.
Bergleder, *n.* **1.** *Min.Cost:* breech-leather **2.** *Miner:* rock-leather, mountain leather.
Berglehne, *f.* slope, incline, hillside.
Berglehrling, *m. Min:* pit-boy.
Bergleite, *f.* = **Berglehne.**
Bergleute, *pl. see* **Bergmann.**
Berglinse, *f. Bot:* alpine milk-vetch.
Bergmann, *m.* -(e)s/-leute, miner, mine-worker; pitman; mine-digger; *Mch:* **Eiserner B.,** continuous miner.
bergmännisch, *a.* (*a*) miner's; in miner's fashion; (*b*) mining.
Bergmannsbauer, *m.* miner who owns a small farm *or* works a small farm in his spare time.
Bergmannsdorf, *n.* mining village.
Bergmannsgruß, *m.* miners' greeting.
Bergmassiv, *n. Geog:* mountain mass, main group of mountains; massif.
Bergmehl, *n. Miner:* kieselguhr, infusorial earth, fossil farina.
Bergmilch, *f. Miner:* agaric mineral.
Bergminze, *f. Bot:* **1.** wild marjoram. **2.** calamint.
Bergmispel, *f. Bot:* common cotoneaster.
Bergmittel, *n. Min:* attle, deads, gang(ue).
Bergmolch, *m. Rept:* = **Alpenmolch.**
Bergnaphta, *f. Miner:* naphtha, bitumen.
Bergnelke, *f. Bot:* maiden pink.
Bergnelkenwurz, *f. Bot:* mountain-avens.
Bergnest, *n.* mountain fastness (of brigands, etc.); mountain village.
Bergnot, *f.* (*of climber*) **in B. sein,** to be in difficulties, to be in need of help; **einen Bergsteiger aus B. retten,** to rescue a climber who has got into difficulties.
Bergnymphe, *f. Myth:* mountain nymph, oread.
Bergöl, *n. Miner:* rock-oil, petroleum, mineral oil.
Bergordnung, *f.* mining regulations.
Bergpanorama, *n.* mountain view(s).
Bergpapier, *n. Miner:* mountain paper.
Bergpartei, die. *Fr.Hist:* the Mountain.
Bergpaß, *m.* mountain pass; defile.
Bergpech, *n. Miner:* mineral pitch, Jew's pitch, asphalt.
Bergpetersilie, *f. Bot:* mountain-parsley.
Bergpfeffer, *m. Bot:* = **Seidelbast.**
Bergpferd, *n. Z:* = **Bergzebra.**
Bergpieper, *m. Orn:* water pipit, alpine pipit.
Bergpolizei, *f. Adm:* mine security police.
Bergpredigt, *f. B:* **die B.,** the Sermon on the Mount.
Bergprüfung, *f. Aut:* mountain trial.
Bergquitte, *f. Bot:* common cotoneaster.
Bergrecht, *n. Adm:* mining law(s).
bergrechtlich, *a.* according to mining law.
Bergrennen, *n. Aut:* (i) hill climb; (ii) hill climbing.
Bergrettungsdienst, *m.* mountain rescue service.
Bergrettungsmannschaft, *f.* mountain rescue team.
Bergrohrgras, *n. Bot:* purple melic-grass.
Bergrücken, *m.* crest, ridge, of a mountain.
Bergrüster, *f. Bot:* = **Bergulme.**
Bergrutsch, *m.* (*a*) = **Bergsturz;** (*b*) *Pol:* landslide.
Bergsalbei, *f. Bot:* lantana.
Bergsattel, *m. Ph.Geog:* saddle, col.
Bergschaden, *m.* damage caused by mining operations, *esp.* damage through subsidence.
Bergschaf, *n. Z:* = **Bighorn.**
Bergschi, *m. Ski:* upper ski.
Bergschierling, *m. Bot:* laserpitium, laser-wort.
Bergschiffahrt, *f. Nau:* up-stream traffic.
Bergschilf, *n. Bot:* bushgrass.
Bergschlägel, *m. Min: Tls:* miner's hammer, miner's mallet, sledge(-hammer).
Bergschlipf, *m.* = **Bergsturz.**
Bergschrund, *m. Ph.Geog:* bergschrund.
Bergschuh, *m.* climbing boot.
Bergschule, *f.* school of mines.
Bergsee, *m.* mountain-lake; **kleiner B.,** tarn.
Bergseife, *f. Miner:* mountain-soap, rock-soap.
Bergspalte, *f.* cleft, crevice, fissure, in a rock.
Bergspitze, *f.* mountain top; mountain peak; summit of a mountain.
Bergstamm, *m.* mountain tribe.
Bergstart, *m. Aut:* hill-start.
Bergsteigefähigkeit, *f.* hill climbing ability (of car).
Bergsteigen, *n.* mountaineering, (mountain-) climbing; **Bergsteigen in den Alpen,** alpinism, alpine climbing.
Bergsteiger, *m.* mountaineer, climber; alpinist.

Bergstelze, *f. Orn:* grey wagtail.
Bergsternkraut, *n. Bot:* mountain inula.
Bergstiefel, *m.* climbing boot.
Bergstock, *m.* **1.** mountain mass, main group of mountains, massif. **2.** alpenstock.
Bergstraße, *f.* **1.** mountain road. **2.** *Geog:* **die B.,** the hilly orchard district lying between Darmstadt and Heidelberg.
Bergstriche, *m.pl. Mapm:* hachure; hachure lines.
Bergsturz, *m.* land-slide, landslip; rock-fall, rockslide; fall, slip, slide (of land, rock, etc.).
Bergsucht, *f. Med:* miners' disease, miners' anaemia; ankylostomiasis.
bergsüchtig, *a.*=**bergfertig.**
Bergtalg, *m. Miner:* ozocerite, ozokerite, mineral wax, fossil wax, mineral tallow, mountain tallow, hatchettite.
Bergtäschelkraut, *n. Bot:* candytuft.
Bergtee, *m. Bot:* gaultheria, partridge-berry, checker-berry, wintergreen.
Bergteer, *m. Miner:* maltha, pissasphalt, mineral tar.
Bergthymian, *m. Bot:* calamint.
Bergtour, *f.* trip into the mountains; climbing holiday; climbing tour; climbing expedition.
Bergtracht, *f.* miner's costume.
bergüber [ˌbɛrkˀˈyːbər], *adv.* above, over, a mountain.
Bergulme, *f. Bot:* Scotch elm, wych-elm, witch-elm.
Berg- und Talbahn, *f.* switchback; scenic railway.
Bergunfall, *m.* climbing accident.
Bergung, *f. see* **bergen** II. 2.
Bergungs-, *comb.fm.* salvage . . .; rescue . . .; **Bergungsarbeiten** *f pl,* salvage operations; rescue work; **Bergungskran** *m,* salvage crane; **Bergungsversuch** *m,* salvage attempt; rescue bid.
Bergungsarbeiter, *m.* salvage worker.
Bergungsfahrzeug, *n.* salvage vehicle; *Nau:* salvage tug.
Bergungskontrakt, *m.*=**Bergungsvertrag.**
Bergungslohn, *m.*=**Bergelohn.**
Bergungsschiff, *n. Nau:* salvage vessel.
Bergungsvertrag, *m. Jur: Nau:* salvage agreement, salvage bond.
Bergunschlitt, *m.*=**Bergbutter.**
Bergversatz, *m. Min:* gob, gobbing.
Bergverwaltung, *f. Adm:* administration of mines.
Bergvolk, *n.* mountain tribe, mountain race, hill-folk, hill-people.
Bergvorsprung, *m. Ph.Geog:* (*a*) spur, ledge (of mountain); (*b*) spur, counterfort, buttress, branch, foot-hills, of a mountain range.
Bergwaage, *f. Surv:* clinometer.
Bergwachs, *n. Min:* fossil wax, mineral wax, ozocerite, ozokerite.
Bergwacht, *f.* mountain rescue service.
Bergwand, *f.* wall, face, of a cliff *or* mountain; bluff.
Bergwegerich, *m.*=**Bergwohlverleih.**
Bergweide, *f.* (*a*) mountain pasture; (*b*) *Bot:* goat-willow.
Bergwelt, *f.* **die B.,** the mountains; **die herbe B.,** the wild, rugged, mountain country.
Bergwerk, *n. Min:* mine.
Bergwerksabgaben, *f.pl. Min:* mining royalties.
Bergwerksaktie, *f.* mining share.
Bergwerksanteil, *m. Fin:* mining share.
Bergwerksaufseher, *m.* mine superintendent, colliery viewer.
Bergwerkseigentümer, *m.* mine-owner.
Bergwerksgesellschaft, *f.* mining company.
Bergwerksindustrie, *f.* mining industry.
Bergwerksinspektor, *m.* mine surveyor, mine inspector.
Bergwerksschacht, *m.* mine-shaft.
Bergwerksunglück, *n.* mining accident.
Bergwicht, *m.,* **Bergwichtel,** *n.*=**Berggeist.**
Bergwirtschaft, *f.* mining; mining industry; working of mines.
Bergwissenschaft, *f. Min:* science of mining.
Bergwohlverleih, *m. Bot:* mountain tobacco.
Bergysop, *m. Bot:* helianthemum, rock-rose.
Bergzebra, *n. Z:* mountain zebra.
Bergzeichnung, *f. Mapm:* hachure.
Bergziege, *f. Z:* Rocky Mountain goat, mountain-goat.
Bergziest, *m. Bot:* hedge woundwort.
Beriberi [ˌbeːriːˈbeːriː], *f.* -/. *Med:* beriberi.
Bericht, *m.* **-es/-e,** report (**über etwas** *acc.,* on proceeding, etc.; **über etwas** *acc.,* **von etwas,** of proceeding, speech, investigation, etc.); account (of voyage, experience, historical event, etc.); survey (of situation); commentary (on news, political situation, etc.); (official) bulletin; summary (of news, information); minutes (of meeting); record (of meeting, telephone conversation); report, paper, on (excavation work, scientific research); (examiner's) report; **umfassender B.,** comprehensive report; **genauer B.,** exact report, exact account; **günstiger B.,** favourable report; **falscher B.,** false report, misreport; **B. des Schriftführers,** secretary's report; **B. zur Lage,** report, commentary, on the situation; **B. aus, von, Berlin,** report, dispatch, from Berlin; **B. aus dem Ausland,** report from abroad; **wie Berichte aus Marokko vermuten lassen . . .,** as reports from Morocco indicate . . .; **j-m einen B. geben,** to give s.o. a report, to make a report to s.o., to report to s.o.; **Herr X gab einen B. über seine neuesten Forschungen,** Mr X gave a report on his latest investigations; **ein B. über die neuesten Ausgrabungen wird demnächst veröffentlicht werden,** a report on the latest excavations will be published shortly; **einen B. abfassen,** to draw up, to compose, a report; **einen B. anfertigen,** to write a report; **einen B. für j-n anfertigen,** to make a report for s.o.; **B. erstatten,** to report, to produce, make, give, a report; **j-m einen B. über eine Versammlung erstatten,** to give s.o. a report on a meeting; **der Innenminister hat einen B. über die Situation erstattet,** the Home Secretary has made a statement on the situation; **einen B. über einen Plan vorlegen,** to present a report on a plan; **der B. macht die Hoffnungen auf eine Belebung des Handels zunichte,** the report destroys any hope of a revival of trade; **der B. beruht auf Wahrheit,** the report is true; **wir haben zwei Berichte über diese Firma erhalten,** we have received two reports on this firm; **er gab uns einen ausführlichen B. über seine Abenteuer,** he gave us a full, detailed, account of his adventures; **der Regierung liegt vorerst nur ein B. ihres Botschafters vor,** at present, only the ambassador's dispatch, the report of the ambassador, is available to the government; **wir haben Berichte aus dem Ausland, daß dieser Artikel schwer abzusetzen ist,** we have advices from abroad that this article is selling badly; *Com:* **laut B.,** as per advice; *Adm:* **'zum B.',** 'for information'; 'please report'; *Adm:* **statistischer B. über Geburten, Todesfälle und Eheschließungen,** returns of births, deaths, and marriages.
Berichtabstatter, *m.* **-s/-,** *occ.*=**Berichterstatter.**
berichten, *v.tr. & i.*(*haben*) (*of pers., newspaper, etc.*) to report (sth.); to record (historical event); **j-m (von) etwas b.,** *A:* **j-n etwas** *gen.* **b.,** to report sth. to s.o.; to inform, apprise, s.o. of sth.; to tell s.o. about sth.; **j-m ausführlich b.,** to give s.o. full particulars; to tell s.o. in detail; **über etwas** *acc.* **b.,** to report on sth.; **j-m über etwas b.,** to report sth. to s.o.; to make a report on sth. to s.o.; **über etwas ausführlich b.,** to report (on) sth. in detail; to make a detailed report on sth.; **über eine Versammlung b.,** to report, to give an account of, a meeting; to cover a meeting; **über einen Plan b.,** to report on, to make a report on, a plan; **j-m über den Stand der Arbeit b.,** to report progress to s.o.; to report to s.o. on the state of the work; *Journ:* **er wird unseren Lesern über die Genfer Konferenz b.,** he will cover the Geneva Conference for our readers; **unsere Berliner Zweigstelle berichtet (über) eine bedeutende Verbesserung der Geschäftslage,** our Berlin branch reports a marked improvement in business; **einem Vorgesetzten b.** to (make a) report to a superior; **er berichtet für die Abendzeitung,** he reports for the evening paper; **es wird berichtet, daß . . ., man berichtet, daß . . .,** it is reported that . . .; *Journ:* **aus Paris wird berichtet, daß . . .,** it is reported from Paris that . . .; **wie die Agenturen b.,** as agencies report; *W.Tel:* **wir werden unseren Hörern laufend über die Reise des Ministers b.,** we shall give the listener(s) frequent reports on the minister's journey; **man berichtet Gutes, Schlechtes, über ihn,** he is well, badly, reported on; **es wird in der Bibel berichtet . . .,** it says in the Bible . . .; **Livius berichtet, wie . . .,** Livy records how . . .; **der Historiker, der diese Tatsachen berichtet,** the historian who relates these facts; **er hat dem Kanzler über die politische Entwicklung in den Vereinigten Staaten berichtet,** he has made a report to the Chancellor on (the) political developments in the United States; **haben Sie ihnen von der Versammlung in Lübeck berichtet?** have you told them of the meeting in Lübeck? have you reported the meeting in Lübeck to them? **seine Worte wurden dem König berichtet,** his words were reported to the king; **er hat mir über seine Abenteuer berichtet,** he has given me an account of his adventures; **man hat mir anders berichtet,** I have been told, informed, advised, otherwise, differently; **er berichtete von einem Gespräch mit dem Komponisten,** he told of, related, a conversation with the composer; **wie berichtet,** as reported; **die Sache ist mir falsch berichtet worden,** I have been misinformed.
Berichterstatter, *m.* **-s/-,** (*a*) (newspaper, etc.) reporter; correspondent; (radio) commentator; rapporteur (of a conference); recorder (of historical event); **B. einer Zeitung,** reporter for a (news)paper; **unser Pariser B.,** our Paris correspondent; **auswärtiger B.,** foreign correspondent; (*b*) *Jur: approx.*=clerk of the court, *A:* recorder.
Berichterstatterin, *f.* **-/-innen.** *Journ:* woman reporter.
Berichterstattung, *f.* reporting; **zuverlässige B.,** reliable reporting; reliable reports; **der Botschafter wurde zur B. zurückbeordert,** the ambassador was recalled to make a report; **laufende B.,** running commentary; **B. geschichtlicher Ereignisse,** account of historical events.
berichtigen. I. *v.tr.* (*a*) to correct, rectify, right (mistake, error, etc.); to correct (misconception, statement, official register); to put, set (a mistake) right; to amend (corrupt text, inaccurate plan); to make emendations to (text); *Pol:* to rectify, adjust (frontier); **j-n b.,** to put, set, s.o. right; to correct s.o.; **ein Fehler, der berichtigt werden kann,** a mistake that can be corrected, put right, rectified; *Book-k:* **einen Eintrag b.,** to rectify an entry; **ein Versehen b.,** to rectify an oversight; **einen verderbten Text b.,** to amend, emend, a corrupt text; **diese Preisliste ist zu b.,** this price list will have to be revised, corrected; **berichtigte Zahl,** revised, corrected, figure; **wir sind gebeten worden, eine berichtigende Mitteilung zu veröffentlichen,** we have been asked to publish a correction (to the report); **die Grenzen sind zu b.,** the frontiers will have to be rectified; *Opt:* **einen Sehfehler b.,** to correct a defect in vision; *Artil:* **die Schußweite b.,** to correct the range; *Com:* **berichtigte Rechnung,** corrected invoice; (*b*) to pay, settle, *F:* square (account, debt, bill, claim); **aus dem Gesamtgute sind zunächst die Verbindlichkeiten zu b.,** the liabilities must first be met from the joint estate.
II. *vbl s.* **1. Berichtigen,** *n. in vbl senses.* **2. Berichtigung,** *f.* (*a*)=II. 1; *also:* correction (of mistake, error, inaccuracy, *Adm:* of official register, *Tchn:* of instrument); rectification (of error); amendment, emendation (of corrupt text); adjustment (of frontier); payment (of debt, etc.); settlement (of account, claim, etc.); (*b*) correction (to report, statement, etc.); adjustment (in, to, frontier); amendment, emendation; rectification; *Sch:* 'corrections'; (*on fly-leaf of book*) **'Berichtigungen', 'errata'.**
Berichtigungsanspruch, *m. Adm: etc:* claim for rectification of entry in a register, etc.
Berichtigungskonto, *n. Book-k:* suspense account; adjustments account.
Berichtigungspflicht, *f. Publ:* obligation of a newspaper editor to publish a correction to an inaccurate report.
Berichtigungsveranlagung, *f. Adm:* reassessment of taxes.
Berichtsjahr, *n.* year under report.
beriechen, *v.tr.* (*strong*) (*of pers.*) to smell, sniff at (sth.); *F:* to poke one's nose into (sth.); (*of dog, rabbit, cat, etc.*) to smell, sniff, nose, at (s.o., sth.); **der Hund beroch meine Hand,** the dog sniffed (at), snuffed, my hand; (*of dogs*) **einander b.,** to sniff at one another; (*of pers.*) *F:* **j-n b., einander b.,** *F:* to size s.o., one another, up; *F:* to give s.o., each other, the once-over.
berieselbar, *a.* irrigable, irrigatable (land).
berieseln. I. *v.tr.* (*a*) (*of stream, etc.*) to trickle over (sth.); to wet (sth.); *Agr:* to irrigate (meadow, etc.); to water (field, etc.) with spraying apparatus; to irrigate with sewage; (*b*) *Min:* to water (roadway, etc.); to spray (working, gallery) with water; (*c*) *Gasm: Ind:* to scrub (gas).
II. *vbl s.* **1. Berieseln,** *n. in vbl senses.* **2. Berieselung,** *f.*=II. 1; *also: Agr:* irrigation (of meadow, etc.); overhead irrigation (of field, etc.); irrigation with sewage; *Tex:* spraying (of bobbins).
Berieselungsfeld, *n.* sewage farm.
Berieselungskühler, *m. Ind:* surface cooler.
Berieselungsturm, *m. Ch: Gasm: Ind:* scrubber; scrubbing plant, apparatus.
Berill [beˈril], *m.* **-s/-e** =**Beryll.**
berindet, *a.* (*of tree, etc.*) covered with bark.

Bering, *m.* **im Bering(e) der Stadt,** within the boundaries of the town; **im Bering(e) eines Schlosses,** within, in, the precincts of a castle.

beringen, *v.tr.* **1.** (*a*) to adorn (finger) with a ring; **beringt,** ringed, covered with rings; **beringter Finger,** ringed finger; **beringte Hände,** hands covered with rings; (*b*) to ring (bird); (*c*) *Arb:* to grease-band (tree). **2.** *vbl s.* **Beringung,** *f.* (*a*) ringing (of birds); (*b*) *Arb:* grease-banding (of tree).

Beringmeer, das [ˈbeːriŋ-]. *Pr.n. Geog:* the Bering Sea.

Beringsmöwe, *f. Orn:* glaucous-winged gull.

Beringstraße, die. *Pr.n. Geog:* the Bering Straits.

Beritt, *m.* **-(e)s/-e. 1.** area covered by a mounted patrol. **2.** *Mil.A:* cavalry section (of four troopers).

beritten, *a.* mounted; **berittene Abteilung,** (i) mounted unit; (ii) cavalry unit; **berittene Polizei,** mounted police.

Berkan [bɛrˈkaːn], *m.* **-s/-e.** *Cost:* barracan, barragan.

Berkelium [bɛrˈkeːlium], *n.* **-s/.** *Ch:* berkelium.

Berle, *f.* **-/-n.** *Bot:* **(schmalblättrige) B.,** water-parsnip.

Berlin [bɛrˈliːn]. *Pr.n.n.* **-s.** *Geog:* Berlin.

Berline [bɛrˈliːnə], *f.* **-/-n.** *Veh: A:* berline, berlin.

Berliner [bɛrˈliːnər]. **1.** *m.* **-s/-,** (*a*) *Geog:* Berliner; (*b*) *Cu:* doughnut. **2.** *inv.a.* of Berlin, Berlin . . . ; **B. Blau,** Berlin blue; **B. Braun,** Prussian brown; **B. Ofen,** large tiled stove; **B. Weißbier, B. Weiße,** Berlin light ale (brewed from wheat malt); *Cu:* **B. Pfannkuchen,** doughnut; *Cer:* **B. Porzellan,** Berlin ware; *Ch:* **B. Blausäure,** Prussic acid, hydro-cyanic acid.

Berlinerblau, *n.* Berlin blue.

berlinerisch [bɛrˈliːnəriʃ]. **1.** *a.* of Berlin; Berlin (dialect, etc.). **2.** *s.* **Berlinerisch,** *n.,* Berlin dialect.

berlinern [bɛrˈliːnərn], *v.i.* (*haben*) to speak with a Berlin accent; to speak Berlin dialect.

Berlingot [bɛrlɛ̃ˈgoː], *m.* **-s/-s.** *Veh: A:* two-seated berline.

berlinisch [bɛrˈliːniʃ], *a.* of Berlin, Berlin . . . .

Berlocke [bɛrˈlɔkə], *f.* **-/-n,** watch-charm.

Berlweide, *f. Bot:* golden willow.

Berme, *f.* **-/-n. 1.** *Fort:* berm, foreland. **2.** *Civ.E:* set-off; bench (with footpath); berm.

Bermudagras [bɛrˈmuːdaː-], *n. Bot:* dog's-tooth grass.

Bermudainseln, die, *f.pl.,* **Bermudas, die** [bɛrˈmuːdaˑs], *pl. Pr.n. Geog:* the Bermudas.

bermudisch [bɛrˈmuːdiʃ], *a. Geog:* Bermudian.

Bern. *Pr.n.n.* **-s.** *Geog:* Berne, Bern.

Bernakelgans [bɛrˈnaˑkəl-], *f.* = **Bernikelgans.**

Berner. 1. *m.* **-s/-.** *Geog:* Bernese, inhabitant of Berne. **2.** *inv.a.* Bernese; **die B. Alpen,** the Bernese Alps; **das B. Oberland,** the Bernese Oberland, the Bernese Uplands; **die B. Konvention, Übereinkunft,** the Berne Convention.

Bernhard. *Pr.n.m.* **-s.** Bernard; **Sankt B.,** St Bernard; *Geog:* **der Große St. B.,** the Great St Bernard; **der kleine St. B.,** the Little St Bernard.

Bernhardiner [bɛrnharˈdiːnər]. **1.** *m.* **-s/-,** (*a*) *Ecc.Hist:* Bernardine; **die Bernhardiner,** the Bernardines; (*b*) St Bernard (dog). **2.** *inv.a. Ecc.Hist:* Bernardine.

Bernhardinerhund, *m.* St Bernard (dog).

Bernhardinerkraut, *n. Bot:* holy thistle, blessed thistle.

Bernhardinerkrebs, *m. Crust:* hermit-crab, pagurian.

Bernhardskraut, *n.* = **Bernhardinerkraut.**

Bernhardskrebs, *m.* = **Bernhardinerkrebs.**

Bernikelgans [bɛrˈniːkəl-], *f. Orn:* brent-goose, *U.S:* brant-goose.

Bernina, die [bɛrˈniːnaː]. *Pr.n. f.* **-.** *Geog:* the Bernina Alps.

bernisch, *a.* Bernese.

Bernstein, *m.* **-(e)s/.** (yellow) amber, succin, succinite; **schwarzer B.,** jet; **grauer B.,** ambergris.

Bernsteinarbeit, *f.* amber-work; article made of amber.

Bernsteinarbeiter, *m.* worker in amber.

Bernsteinbaggerei, *f.* amber-fishing.

Bernsteinbaum, *m.* (*fossil*) amber tree.

Bernsteindrechsler, *m.* amber turner.

Bernsteinelektrizität, *f. Ph:* negative electricity.

bernsteinen, *a.* = **bernsteinern.**

bernsteinern, *a.* amber.

Bernsteinfarbe, *f.* amber(-colour).

bernsteinfarben, bernsteinfarbig, *a.* amber (-coloured).

Bernsteinfauna, *f.* amber fauna.

Bernsteinfett, *n. Ch:* ambrein(e).

Bernsteinfischerei, *f.* = **Bernsteinbaggerei.**

Bernsteinflora, *f.* amber flora.

bernsteinhaltig, *a. Ch:* succinic.

bernsteinhell, *a.* = **bernsteinfarben.**

Bernsteinknochen, *m.* bony amber.

Bernsteinkolophonium, *n.* amber colophony, amber pitch.

Bernsteinküste, die. *Pr.n.f. Geog:* the coast of Samland.

Bernsteinlack, *m.* amber varnish.

Bernsteinmundstück, *n.* amber mouthpiece; **Pfeife mit Bernsteinmundstück,** amber-tipped pipe.

Bernsteinöl, *n.* oil of amber.

Bernsteinperle, *f.* amber bead.

Bernsteinsalz, *n. Ch:* succinic salt.

bernsteinsauer, *a. Ch:* succinate of . . . ; . . . combined with succinic acid.

Bernsteinsäure, *f. Ch:* succinic acid.

Bernsteinschnecke, *f. Z:* amber snail.

Bernsteinspitze, *f.* amber cigar(ette)-holder.

Bernsteinwald, *m.* amber forest.

berohren, *v.tr.* **1.** to provide, supply (cold-storage chamber, etc.) with pipes. **2.** to cover (wall) with reeds. **3.** *vbl s.* **Berohrung,** *f.* piping, (set of) pipes (in cold-storage chamber, etc.).

Bersagliere [bɛrsalˈjeːreː], *m.* **-(s)/-ri.** *Mil:* (*in Italy*) bersagliere, sharpshooter, light-infantry-man.

Bersching, *m.* **-s/-e** = **Barsch**[1].

Berserker [bɛrˈzɛrkər, ˈbɛrzɛrkər], *m.* **-s/-,** berserker; **rasend wie ein B.,** raging like a lunatic.

berserkerhaft, *a.* berserk.

Berserkerwut, *f.* berserk rage; **in eine B. geraten,** to go berserk.

bersten. I. *v.i.* (*strong, but occ. weak in present sg. and in imp.*) (*sein*) (*a*) (*of boiler, etc.*) to burst; (*of pipe*) to burst, to spring a leak; (*of bubble*) to burst, break; (*of ice*) to crack, break, split, splinter; (*of ground*) to crack; (*of wall*) to crack, to develop a gaping crack, gaping cracks; *Lit:* (*of cloud*) to burst; **in Stücke b.,** to burst into pieces; **das Faß barst mitten entzwei,** the cask burst asunder; **das Schiff barst in zwei Teile,** the ship broke in two; (*b*) *F:* **vor Zorn, Wut, Ungeduld, b.,** to be bursting with anger, fury, impatience; **vor Lachen b.,** to split one's sides (with) laughing, to explode with mirth; **er barst beinahe vor Lachen,** (i) he was laughing fit to burst, *F:* to bust; he split his sides with laughing, he nearly died of, with, laughing; (ii) he was bursting with (suppressed) laughter.

II. *vbl s.* **Bersten,** *n. in vbl senses; also:* **zum B. voll,** full to bursting; ready to burst; **der Zug war zum B. voll,** the train was full to bursting; **die Säcke waren zum B. voll,** the sacks were bursting; **die zum B. gefüllten Speicher,** the bursting, *Lit:* groaning, storehouses; **ihr Herz war zum B. voll,** her heart was ready to burst.

Berstenkraut, *n. Bot:* **1.** = **Berstgras** 1. **2.** (*a*) poison hemlock, common hemlock; (*b*) water-hemlock, cow-bane.

Berstgras, *n. Bot:* **1.** carex acuta. **2.** reed meadow-grass.

Berstkraut, *n.* = **Berstenkraut.**

Berta. *Pr.n.f.* **-s** = **Bertha** 1.

Berte, *f.* **-/-n.** *Cost:* bertha (collar).

Bertha. *Pr.n.f.* **1. -s** & *Lit:* **-ens.** Bertha. **2. -s.** *Hist:* (*1914-1918*) **die dicke B.,** Big Bertha (*German giant gun*).

Berthe, *f.* **-/-n.** *Cost:* = **Berte.**

Berthold. *Pr.n.m.* **-s** = **Bertold.**

Bertholletia [bɛrtoˈleːtsiaː], *f.* **-/-tien.** *Bot:* Brazil-nut tree.

Bertold. *Pr.n.m.* **-s.** Bert(h)old.

Bertram[1]. *Pr.n.m.* **-s.** Bertram, Bertrand.

Bertram[2], *m.* **-s/-e.** *Bot:* (*a*) feverfew; (*b*) pellitory of Spain; (*c*) sneezewort.

Bertramsgarbe, *f. Bot:* sneezewort.

Bertram(s)wurzel, *f. Bot:* **echte, Römische, B.,** pellitory of Spain; **deutsche B.,** German pellitory.

Bertramwurz, *f.* = **Bertram**[2] (*a*).

berüchtigt, *a.* notorious (criminal, etc.); disreputable (house, locality); **berüchtigter Mörder,** notorious murderer; **berüchtigter Mädchenjäger,** notorious lady-killer; **berüchtigtes Hafenviertel,** disreputable, notorious, ill-famed, dock area; **er ist wegen seiner Grausamkeit, Hartherzigkeit, b.,** he is notorious for his cruelty, known for his hardheartedness; **die Straße ist für Unfälle b.,** the street is notorious for accidents; *see also* **berühmt.**

berücken. I. *v.tr.* **1.** *A:* to (en)snare (birds); to net, catch (fish); to trap, catch (animals). **2.** to take (s.o.) in; to beguile (s.o.); to captivate, charm, enchant (s.o.); (*of beauty, etc.*) to enchant, enthrall (s.o.); **sich b. lassen,** to allow oneself to be taken in, to allow oneself to be beguiled; **j-n mit Worten, mit Blicken, b.,** to beguile s.o. with words, glances; **j-s Herz b.,** to win, steal, s.o.'s heart; to capture s.o.'s affections; **sie berückt alle mit ihrer Schönheit,** her beauty entrances everybody, everybody is entranced by her beauty.

II. *vbl s.* **Berückung,** *f. in vbl senses; also:* **1.** *A:* snare. **2.** enchantment; charm; spell.

III. *pr.p. & a.* **berückend,** captivating, charming; bewitching, enchanting; entrancing; **mit berückender Anmut,** with bewitching grace; **berückendes Lächeln,** bewitching, captivating, enchanting, charming, smile; **b. schöne Augen,** lovely eyes, compellingly beautiful eyes; **von berückender Schönheit, b. schön,** of entrancing beauty, entrancingly beautiful.

berücksichtigen. I. *v.tr.* **etwas b.,** (i) to take sth. into consideration, into account; to consider sth.; to pay regard to sth.; to bear sth. in mind; (ii) to allow for sth., to make allowance(s) for sth.; **j-n b.,** (i) to bear s.o. in mind; to consider s.o.; to take s.o. into account; (ii) to have consideration for, to consider, s.o.; **Umstände, Bedingungen, Tatsachen, b.,** to take circumstances, conditions, facts, into consideration, into account; **Einzelheiten, Besonderheiten, b.,** to pay regard to details; to take details, peculiarities, into account, to allow for peculiarities; **wir müssen b., daß . . . ,** we must take into consideration that . . . ; **bei den Zuteilungen für den Winter ist nicht berücksichtigt worden, daß . . . ,** in making the winter allocations it has not been taken into account that . . . ; **wir müssen die Jugend des Angeklagten b.,** we must allow, make allowance, for the youth of the accused; **du mußt b., daß er krank ist,** you must allow for his being ill; **die Auslage, das Risiko, b.,** to consider the expense, the risk; **j-s Gefühle b.,** to consider s.o.'s feelings; **Sie müssen b., daß das Kind erst zehn Jahre alt ist,** note, bear in mind, consider, that the child is only ten years old; **Sie brauchen ihn nicht zu b.,** you need not consider, bother about, him; **später eintreffende Anträge können nicht berücksichtigt werden,** late applications cannot be considered; **ich wäre dankbar, wenn Sie bei der Besetzung der Stelle mich, meinen Antrag, b. würden,** I would be grateful if you would consider me, my application, for the position; **die Botanik ist von vornherein immer sehr berücksichtigt worden,** botany has always received, been given, special attention.

II. *vbl s.* **Berücksichtigung,** *f.* consideration; regard; (*of proposal, application, etc.*) **B. finden,** to be considered; to be given, taken into, consideration; **besondere B. finden,** to be specially taken into consideration; to be given special notice; **die B. seines Antrags ist ausgeschlossen,** consideration of his application is out of the question; his application cannot be given consideration; **bei, unter, B. der Abnutzung,** taking into account, allowing for, depreciation, wear and tear; **bei, unter, B. des ganzen Sachverhalts,** taking all things into consideration, account; **bei, unter, B. aller den Wert beeinflussenden Punkte,** taking into consideration, account, all points affecting the value; **bei, unter, voller B. der wirtschaftlichen Interessen,** full consideration being given to, full account being taken of, (the) economic interests; **unter B. der Umstände,** in view of the circumstances; **unter B. seiner tadellosen Vergangenheit,** in consideration of, in view of, his blameless past, his unblemished record; **der Stundenplan wurde unter, mit, besonderer B. der wissenschaftlichen Fächer gemacht,** in planning the syllabus special attention was given to scientific subjects; **in B. dieses Umstandes,** in view of this; **ohne B. der Umstände,** without regard to the circumstances.

Berückung, *f. see* **berücken** II.

Beruf, *m.* **-(e)s/-e,** (i) vocation, (divine) call, calling; (ii) profession; vocation; career; trade; craft; (regular) occupation, work, job; **den B. zum Priesteramt haben, in sich fühlen,** to have, feel, a vocation for, a call to, the Church; **seinen B. verfehlt haben** to have missed, mistaken, one's vocation; **die bürgerlichen Berufe,** (i) the middle-class callings; (ii) the stable, respectable, occupations; (iii) the civilian occupations; **die handwerklichen Berufe,** the crafts; **Angehörige der handwerklichen Berufe,** craftsmen, artisans; **die landwirtschaftlichen Berufe,** the agricultural occupations; **kaufmännische Berufe,** careers in commerce; **technische Berufe,** technical professions and skilled trades; **soziale Berufe,** professions associated with social work; **die freien Berufe,** the professions: **Angehörige der freien Berufe,**

members of the professions; **der B. des Künstlers,** (i) the artist's mission; (ii) the artist's profession, vocation; **er ist Arzt von B.,** he is a doctor by profession; **er ist Elektriker von B.,** he is an electrician by trade; **im freien B. arbeiten,** (*of journalist, writer, etc.*) to work as a free-lance; (*in legal profession, medicine, etc.*) to work in *or* have a private practice; to practise privately; **in den freien B. gehen,** to take up a profession; to take up free-lance work (as a journalist, etc.); to go into private practice; **einen B. ergreifen,** to take up a profession; to take up a career; **einen B. ausüben,** to follow a profession; to follow, carry on, ply, a trade; **seinem B. nachgehen,** to pursue one's work; to carry on with one's work; to stick to one's job; **in einem B. ausgebildet sein,** to have professional, vocational, training; to have been trained in a profession; to have learnt a trade; **einen B. erlernen,** to learn a trade; **j-n einen B. erlernen lassen,** to put s.o. to a trade; **sich auf einen B. vorbereiten,** to train for a career; **einen B. wählen,** to choose a career; **ohne B.,** without profession; without a trade; (*on official form*) without occupation, no occupation; **er ist ohne festen B., übt keinen B. aus, hat keinen B.,** he has no fixed, settled, profession *or* trade; he is a person without any particular profession *or* trade; **im B. stehen,** to work, to be working; to have a job; (*of woman*) to go out to work; to be a working woman; **seinem B. leben,** to live for one's work, one's job; **in seinem B. aufgehen,** to be completely absorbed by one's work, one's job; **seinem Mann im B. helfen,** to help one's husband in his work; **glücklich in seinem B. sein,** to be happy in one's work, job; **dieser B. hat keine Aussichten,** there are no prospects in this line, in this trade; **alle Berufe sind überfüllt,** all professions, all vocations, are overcrowded; **er kann in seinem (wirklichen) B. keine Arbeit finden,** he cannot find work in his own line; **diese Arbeit ist nicht jedermanns B.,** this trade is not every man's job; **aus einer Liebhaberei einen B. machen,** to make a career out of a hobby; **etwas zum B. erheben,** to turn sth. into a profession; **einen Sport zum B. erheben,** to professionalize a sport; **der B., in dem man ausgebildet ist, entspricht nicht immer dem inneren B.,** the profession in which one is trained, the trade one has learnt, does not always correspond to one's true vocation, calling; **welchen B. haben Sie im Auge?** what profession do you intend to follow? *B:* **ein jeglicher bleibe in dem B., darinnen er berufen ist,** let every man abide in the same calling wherein he was called.

berufen. I. *v.tr.* (*strong*) **1.** to summon, call together, convoke (assembly); to call, convene (meeting); **j-n zu sich b.,** to summon s.o., to send for (subordinate, etc.); **Gott hat ihn zu sich berufen,** God has called him home. **2.** (*a*) (*of the Deity*) to call (s.o.) (to the ministry, monastic life, etc.); **Jesus beruft die ersten Jünger,** Jesus calls the first disciples; **viele sind berufen, aber wenige sind auserwählt,** many are called but few chosen; **zum Lehramt, Priesteramt, usw., berufen sein,** to be called to, to feel a vocation for, a call to, the teaching profession, the Church, etc.; **sich (als Priester, usw.) berufen fühlen,** to feel a vocation, call (for, to, the Church, etc.); **er wurde Mönch, ohne berufen zu sein,** he became a monk without having the call; **von Gott (dazu) berufen, Richter zu sein,** ordained of God to be judge; **auf den Thron berufen werden, sein,** to be called to the throne; **der Künstler ist dazu berufen, zu . . .,** the artist's mission is to . . ., the artist is called upon to . . .; **er war dazu berufen, Zwietracht zu stiften,** he was destined to cause discord; *cp.* III; (*b*) to appoint (s.o.) (to an office, to a committee, board, etc.); to ask (s.o.) to join (a committee, board, etc.); *esp. Sch:* (i) to offer a chair to (a professor); (ii) to appoint (lecturer, etc.) to a professorship; **er wurde auf den Lehrstuhl für Klassische Philologie berufen,** (i) he was offered the chair of classics; (ii) he was appointed professor, to the professorship, of classics, he obtained the chair of classics; **an die Universität X berufen werden,** (i) to be offered a professorship, chair, at X University; (ii) to be appointed professor, to a professorship, at X University, to obtain, get, a chair, professorship, at X University. **3.** (*a*) **etwas b.,** to tempt providence by praising sth.; **wir wollen es nicht b.!** touch wood! (*b*) *A:* **j-n b.,** to reproach s.o. **4. sich berufen,** (*a*) *Jur: A:* **sich auf j-n, an j-n, auf, an, ein höheres Gericht, b.,** to appeal to s.o., to a higher court; *cp.* II; (*b*) **sich auf etwas, j-n, b.,** to quote, cite, sth., s.o., as one's authority (for a statement, etc.); to call, take, sth., s.o., to witness; to plead sth.; to take one's stand on sth.; **sich auf j-n, j-s Zeugnis, b.,** to refer to, rely on, put one's faith in, s.o., s.o.'s evidence; **er beruft sich auf Ihr Vorbild,** he quotes, cites, your example as his authority; **ich kann mich hier auf meinen Kollegen, auf andere ähnliche Fälle, b.,** in this matter, here, I can quote, cite, refer to, my colleague, other similar cases; **sich auf sein Recht b.,** to take one's stand on one's legal rights; **sich auf ein Gesetz, eine Bestimmung, b.,** to quote, cite, a law, a regulation; **du kannst dich nicht auf deine Unwissenheit in dieser Sache b., du kannst dich nicht darauf b., daß du nichts davon gewußt hast,** you can't plead (your) ignorance of this fact; **sich auf jugendliche Unerfahrenheit b.,** to plead the inexperience of youth; **sich auf die Verzögerung der Postzustellung b.,** to plead postal delays; **die Angeklagten berufen sich auf Befehle,** the accused plead that they had to obey orders; **Sie können sich auf mich b.,** you may mention, use, my name (as a reference); **wenn Sie Herrn X aufsuchen, berufen Sie sich auf mich,** if you call on Mr X you may mention my name.

II. *vbl s.* **1. Berufen,** *n. in vbl senses.* **2. Berufung,** *f.* (*a*)=II. 1; *also:* convocation (of assembly, etc.); appointment (of s.o.) (to an office, professorship, committee, etc.); (*b*) **die B. der Heiden,** the vocation of the gentiles; **die B. der ersten Jünger,** Jesus calling his first disciples; (*c*) reference; **unter B. auf . . .,** with reference, referring, to . . .; on the authority of . . .; **eine Aussage unter B. auf j-n machen,** to advance a statement on the authority of s.o.; **unter B. auf mein Recht,** taking my stand on my legal rights; (*d*) *Jur:* **B. zum Erben,** entitlement, to inherit under a will; **B. zur Vormundschaft,** legal qualification to be a guardian; **mehrfache B. haben,** to be a beneficiary under several provisions in a will; (*e*) vocation, (divine) call, calling; **die B. zum Priesteramt haben,** to feel a vocation for, call to, calling for, the Church; **die B. der Kunst zur Transzendenz,** the transcendental mission of art; **die B. des Künstlers,** the artist's mission; **er wurde Mönch, ohne (wirkliche) B. zu haben,** he became a monk without any true calling, vocation; (*f*) (i) offer of appointment; (ii) appointment (to an office, a committee, etc.); *esp. Sch:* (i) offer of a chair, professorship; (ii) appointment (to a chair, professorship); **die B. auf einen Lehrstuhl erhalten,** (i) to be offered a chair; (ii) to be appointed professor, to a professorship, to obtain, get, a chair; **nach seiner B. an die Universität Köln,** after his appointment as professor at Cologne University; **auf seine B. warten,** to wait for one's appointment as professor, to a professorship; to wait for the offer of a chair; **eine B. annehmen, ablehnen,** to accept, refuse, a professorship, a chair; **Professor X hatte zwei Berufungen zur gleichen Zeit,** Professor X was offered two chairs simultaneously; *cp.* **Ruf;** (*g*) *Jur:* appeal against conviction *or* judgment; **B. gegen ein Urteil,** appeal against a conviction *or* judgment; **B. einlegen,** to lodge, set down, an appeal (**bei einem höheren Gericht, an ein höheres Gericht,** with a higher court), to appeal (**bei einem höheren Gericht, an ein höheres Gericht,** to a higher court); **B. gegen ein Urteil einlegen,** to appeal against a conviction *or* judgment; **seine Absicht, B. einzulegen, erklären,** to give notice of appeal; **gegen eine Entscheidung des Gerichts B. einlegen,** to appeal against a decision of the court; **gegen das Urteil eines niedrigeren Gerichts bei einem höheren B. einlegen,** to appeal from a lower court to a higher court; **eine B. verwerfen, zurückweisen,** to dismiss an appeal; **die Urteile dieses Gerichts sind nicht mit der B. anfechtbar,** there is no appeal from this court, no appeal lies from (judgments of) this court; **eine B. direkt an das Berufungsgericht ist zulässig,** an appeal lies direct to the court of appeal; **eine B. gegen den Entscheid ist nicht zulässig,** no appeal lies against the decision; **der B. stattgeben,** to allow the appeal.

III. *p.p. & a.* **berufen,** *in vbl senses; esp.* **1.** competent; qualified; (pers.) in a position (to judge, etc.); **ein berufener Kritiker,** a competent critic; **von berufener Seite,** from a competent source; **aus berufenem Munde,** (judgment, opinion, etc.) from a competent authority, from one qualified, competent, to speak; **er ist dazu b., er ist der berufene Mann, den Streit zu schlichten,** he is the (right) man to settle the dispute; **niemand könnte mehr b., könnte berufener sein, das zu beurteilen,** nobody could be more competent, could be in a better position, to judge this; **Sie sind eher b., das zu beurteilen,** you are in a better position, more competent, better qualified, to judge in this matter; **ich fühle mich nicht b., darüber zu urteilen,** I am not, I do not feel, competent, qualified, I am not in a position, to judge in this matter. **2.** *Jur:* **zum Erben b. sein,** to be entitled to inherit (under a will); **zur Vormundschaft b. sein,** to be legally qualified to act as a guardian; **Berufene** *m, f,* (i) person entitled (under a will) to inherit; (ii) person legally qualified to act as guardian. **3.** *A:* (*a*) famous; (*b*) notorious (criminal, etc.).

Berufenheit, *f.* **1.** vocation (to the ministry, etc.). **2.** competence (to judge in a matter, etc.).

Berufkraut, *n. Bot:* **1.**=**Beschreikraut. 2.** sneezewort.

beruflich, *a. & adv.* professional; vocational; *adv.* professionally; vocationally; **berufliche Ausbildung,** vocational training; professional training; **berufliche Tüchtigkeit,** efficiency in one's work; **berufliche Weiterbildung,** extended vocational training; **j-n b. in Anspruch nehmen,** to consult s.o. professionally; to take professional advice from s.o.; **b. in einer Sache beschäftigt sein,** to be professionally engaged in sth.; **b. verhindert sein,** to be detained by work; **b. tätig sein**=**berufstätig sein,** *q.v. under* **berufstätig; ich habe b. hier zu tun,** I am here on business; **seine Heirat hat ihn b. geschädigt, hat ihm beruflichen Schaden zugefügt,** his marriage harmed his career, did him harm in his job.

Berufsabteilung, *f.* class, category, of occupation.

Berufsanwärter, *m.* person intending to enter a profession *or* trade; aspirant to a profession *or* trade.

Berufsarbeit, *f.* work, occupation, job; (professional) duties.

Berufsausbildung, *f.* (professional) training; vocational training; **eine (abgeschlossene) B. haben,** to have a professional training; to have had vocational training; to be trained (in a profession *or* trade); **die B. dauert drei Jahre,** training takes three years; **die Universität soll nicht nur der B. dienen,** the university should not only provide for vocational training.

Berufsaussichten, *f.pl.* professional prospects; **die B. für Lehrer sind augenblicklich günstig,** the prospects in the teaching profession are favourable at present.

Berufsbeamte, *m.* (*decl. as adj.*) (permanent) civil servant, official.

Berufsbeamtentum, *n.* (permanent) officialdom; (the) tradition of the irremovable official.

Berufsberater, *m.* vocational adviser.

Berufsberatung, *f.* vocational guidance.

Berufsberatungsstelle, *f.* vocational guidance centre.

Berufsbezeichnung, *f.* description (of occupation); style, designation, title (of pers.).

Berufsdiplomat, *m.* professional diplomat, *U.S:* career diplomat.

Berufsehre, *f.* professional honour.

Berufseignung, *f.* suitability for a type of career.

Berufseignungsprüfung, *f.* vocational suitability test.

Berufsethik, *f.* professional code (of ethics).

Berufsfachschule, *f.* technical school, college.

Berufsfahrer, *m.* **1.** professional cyclist. **2.** *Aut:* (i) professional driver; (ii) professional racing driver.

Berufsförderung, *f. Sch: etc:* vocational advisory service; appointments board facilities; *Mil:* preparation *or* training for civilian employment.

Berufsfreiheit, *f.* freedom to take up any profession *or* trade.

Berufsgeheimnis, *n.* **1.** professional secret. **2.** professional secrecy.

Berufsgenosse, *m.* colleague.

Berufsgenossenschaft, *f.* professional association; *esp.* employers' association (with liability for industrial insurance).

Berufsgruppe, *f.* occupational group; type of occupation.

Berufsheer, *n.* professional, regular, army.

Berufskamerad, *m.* colleague; fellow-worker; workmate.

Berufskleidung, *f.* work(ing) clothes.

Berufskollege, *m.* colleague.

Berufskrankheit, *f.* occupational disease.

Berufskraut, *n.*=**Berufkraut.**

Berufskunde, *f.* knowledge of careers.

Berufsleben, *n.* professional life; work; profession; occupation; **im B. stehen,** to work, to be working; (*of woman*) to be a working woman.

berufslos, *a.* without profession; without occupation.
Berufsmantel, *m.* overall (coat); smock; (doctor's) coat.
berufsmäßig, *a.* professional; **er ist ein berufsmäßiger Spion,** he is a professional spy; *adv.* **etwas b. tun,** to do sth. professionally; to do sth. as a regular occupation.
Berufsoffizier, *m.* regular officer.
Berufsorganisation, *f.* professional association, *e.g.* medical association, etc.
Berufsparlamentarier, *m.* professional parliamentarian.
Berufspolitiker, *m.* professional politician.
Berufsrisiko, *n.* occupational hazard, risk.
Berufsschicht, *f.* professional category; profession; trade.
Berufsschule, *f.* school for (compulsory) vocational training; vocational school.
Berufssoldat, *m.* professional, regular, soldier.
Berufsspieler, *m. Sp:* professional player.
Berufsspielertum, *n.* **-(e)s/.** *Sp:* professionalism.
Berufssport, *m.* professional sport(s).
Berufssportler, *m.* professional (sportsman); **B. werden,** to turn professional.
Berufssportlertum, *n.* -(e)s/. *Sp:* professionalism.
Berufssprache, *f.* professional jargon; jargon of a, the, trade.
Berufsstand, *m.* profession; trade; **der B. der Einzelhändler,** the retail trade; **die freien Berufsstände,** the professional classes.
Berufsstatistik, *f.* labour statistics.
Berufsstraßenfahrer, *m. Sp:* professional cyclist.
berufstätig, *a.* working; having employment, a job, an occupation; **b. sein,** to work; to have a job; **berufstätige Frauen,** women who go out to work; working women, career women; **seit mein Mann tot ist, bin ich wieder b.,** since the death of my husband I have taken a job again; **Berufstätige** *pl*, working people.
Berufstätigkeit, *f.* **1.** employment (of women, etc.). **2.** work, occupation, job; (professional) duties.
Berufstreue, *f.* loyalty to one's profession *or* trade.
berufsunfähig, *a. Adm:* disabled.
Berufsunfähigkeit, *f. Adm:* disability, disablement.
Berufsverbände, *m.pl.* professional *or* workers' associations.
Berufsverbrecher, *m.* professional criminal.
Berufsverbrechertum, *n.* professional crime; **der Kampf gegen das B.,** the fight against professional crime.
Berufsvereine, *m.pl.* professional *or* workers' associations.
Berufsvertretung, *f.* professional association; *esp.* state-sponsored trade *or* agricultural association.
Berufsvormund, *m.* public guardian (of illegitimate children).
Berufsvormundschaft, *f.* public guardianship (of illegitimate children).
Berufswahl, *f.* choice of one's career.
berufswidrig, *a.* unprofessional; **berufswidriges Verhalten,** unprofessional conduct.
Berufszählung, *f.* employment census.
Berufszweig, *m.* branch of a profession *or* trade.
Berufung, *f. see* **berufen II.**
Berufungsbegründung, *f. Jur:* (statement of) grounds of appeal.
Berufungsbeklagte, *m., f.* (*decl. as adj.*) *Jur:* defendant, respondent (before the court of appeal).
Berufungseinlegung, *f. Jur:* (lodging of) appeal.
berufungsfähig, *a. Jur:* appealable; **die Urteile dieses Gerichts sind nicht b.,** there is no appeal from this court, no appeal lies from (judgments of) this court.
Berufungsfrist, *f. Jur:* (prescribed) period within which an appeal has to be lodged.
Berufungsgericht, *n. Jur:* court of appeal.
Berufungsgerichtsbarkeit, *f. Jur:* appellate jurisdiction.
Berufungsgrund, *m. Jur:* **1.** entitlement to inherit (under a will); **mehrere Berufungsgründe haben,** to be a beneficiary under several provisions in a will. **2.** *pl.* **Berufungsgründe,** grounds of appeal.
Berufungsinstanz, *f. Jur:* higher court; court of appeal; **B. in Strafsachen,** court of criminal appeal; **oberste, höchste, B.,** supreme court of appeal; **in der B. freigesprochen werden,** to be acquitted on appeal; **ein Urteil in der B. annullieren,** to quash a sentence on appeal.
Berufungsklage, *f. Jur:* appeal.
Berufungskläger, *m. Jur:* appellant, appealing party.
Berufungsrecht, *n.* **1.** *Jur:* right of appeal. **2.** right to appoint s.o. *or* to offer an appointment to s.o.
Berufungsrichter, *m. Jur:* judge of appeal.
Berufungsschreiben, *n. Sch:* (written) offer of a professorship, letter inviting s.o. to accept appointment to a chair.
Berufungsschrift, *f. Jur:* notice of appeal.
Berufungssumme, *f. Jur:* value (of article, etc.) involved in a case carried to appeal.
Berufungsverfahren, *n. Jur:* procedure on appeal.
Berufungsverhandlung, *f.* **1.** *Jur:* hearing of an appeal. **2.** *pl.* **Berufungsverhandlungen,** *Sch:* preliminary correspondence in connection with the offer of a professorship.
beruhen, *v.i.* (*haben*) **1.** (*of thg*) **auf,** *occ.* **in, etwas** *dat.* **b.,** to be founded, based, on sth.; to have its cause, its root, in sth.; to be due to sth.; to rest in sth.; to rest on sth.; **seine Aussagen beruhen auf Tatsachen,** his statements are founded, based, on facts; **auf Tatsachen beruhend,** founded on facts; **sein Verdacht beruht auf einer schlechten Erfahrung,** his suspicion is founded, based on, has its root, its cause, in, an unpleasant experience; **diese Regel beruht auf mathematischen Gesetzen,** this rule is based on mathematical laws; **seine falschen Resultate beruhen auf einem methodischen Irrtum,** his wrong results are caused by, due to, an error of method; **worauf beruht die Popularität des Kinos?** what are the causes of the popularity of the cinema? **die Überlegenheit dieser Maschine beruht darauf, daß man sie vielseitig verwenden kann, beruht auf der Vielseitigkeit ihrer Verwendungsmöglichkeiten,** the superiority of this machine is due to the variety of its uses; **der Ruf dieser Zigarette beruht auf der überlegenen Güte der Tabakmischung,** the reputation of this cigarette is due to, is based on, the superior quality of the mixture; **die ganze Schwierigkeit beruht auf der Tatsache, beruht darauf, daß . . . ,** all the difficulty rests in, is due to, the fact that . . . , rests in, is due to, this, that . . . ; **seine Theorie beruht auf falschen Voraussetzungen,** his theory is based on, rests on, false tenets; **unsere Abneigung beruht auf Gegenseitigkeit,** the dislike is mutual; **Herr X kann dich nicht leiden — das beruht auf Gegenseitigkeit,** Mr X doesn't like you—the feeling is mutual; **2. eine Sache auf sich b. lassen,** to let a matter rest, lie; not to proceed further with a matter; **wir wollen die Sache (vorläufig) auf sich b. lassen,** let us let the matter rest (for the time being); let us leave it at that; let us not pursue the matter further; **ich kann diese Beleidigung nicht auf sich b. lassen,** I can't let this insult pass (unnoticed); I'm not going to take this insult lying down; **ich werde das nicht auf sich b. lassen,** I shall not let it rest at that; I'm going to do something about it; **wir können das nicht auf sich b. lassen,** we shall have to do something about it; **da dieser Diebstahl sein erstes Vergehen ist, wollen wir die Sache auf sich b. lassen,** as this theft is his first offence we shall overlook it, we won't take proceedings against him.
beruhigen. I. *v.tr.* **1. j-n b.,** to appease, pacify, s.o.; to calm, soothe, s.o.; to quiet s.o., to calm s.o. down; to allay s.o.'s excitement; to set s.o.'s mind at rest; to compose, calm, allay, s.o.'s fears; to reassure s.o.; **den Sturm, die Wellen, b.,** to calm, quiet, still, the tempest, the waves, to allay the tempest; **ein weinendes Kind b.,** to quiet, hush, a crying child; **j-s Nerven b.,** to soothe s.o.'s nerves; **er versuchte, die erregte Frau zu b.,** he tried to calm (down), soothe, quiet, the excited woman, he tried to allay the woman's excitement; **sein Gewissen b.,** to quiet(en), soothe, calm, one's conscience; to pacify one's conscience; **ich tat es, um mein Gewissen zu b.,** I did it for conscience sake; **ich hoffe, das wird die Gemüter b.,** I hope this will set people's minds at rest; I hope this will satisfy them, *F:* shut them up; **j-n über etwas** *acc.* **b.,** to reassure s.o. about sth.; **j-n darüber b., daß . . . ,** to reassure s.o. that . . . ; **Sie können darüber beruhigt sein,** you may feel reassured about this, you may set your mind at rest about this, on this account; **darüber sei ganz beruhigt,** set your mind, heart, at rest about it; make yourself easy about it; don't be uneasy about it; **einen beruhigenden Einfluß auf j-n ausüben,** to exercise a calming, soothing, influence on s.o.; **er sprach ihr beruhigend zu,** he spoke soothingly to her; **ein beruhigender Gedanke,** a reassuring thought; **beruhigende Nachrichten,** reassuring, heartening, news; **die Gerüchte sind nicht sehr beruhigend,** the rumours are rather disquieting; *Med:* **beruhigende Mittel,** soothing, sedative, drugs, sedatives; **diese Medizin wirkt beruhigend,** this medicine acts as a sedative. **2. sich beruhigen,** (*a*) (*of pers.*) to become appeased, pacified; (*of pers., mind, etc.*) to calm down, to grow quiet; (*of pers.*) to compose one's mind, oneself, to recover one's composure; to feel reassured; (*of storm, excitement, etc.*) to subdue, to abate; (*of wind, etc.*) to die down, die away, to drop; (*of political situation, etc.*) to become stable, to quieten (*after unrest, etc.*); **der Sturm hatte sich beruhigt,** the storm had spent itself, had blown over; **beruhigen Sie sich!** (i) steady! compose yourself! pull yourself together! (ii) calm down! don't get excited! (iii) set your mind at rest; **Sie können sich darüber b.,** you may feel reassured about this; you may set your mind, heart, at rest about it; **die Gemüter werden sich schon wieder b.,** people will stop worrying, talking, about it; it will all blow over; **ich kann mich gar nicht darüber b., daß er der Täter ist,** I can't get over it that he has done it; **sie konnte sich nicht darüber b., daß man ihre Handtasche gestohlen hatte,** she couldn't get over someone's having stolen her handbag; (*b*) **sich bei etwas b.,** to be contented, satisfied, with sth.; to take sth. complacently, with complacency; **ich würde mich nicht dabei b., daß er sich entschuldigt hat, ich würde mich nicht bei seiner Entschuldigung b.,** I would not be satisfied with the fact that he has apologized; **sich dabei, bei dem Gedanken, b., daß . . .** to console, comfort, oneself with the thought that . . . ; **sie beruhigte sich dabei, bei dem Gedanken, daß sie das Unglück doch nicht hätte verhindern können,** she consoled herself with the thought that she could not have prevented the accident; **er beruhigte sich dabei, bei dem Gedanken, daß er für die Arbeit nicht kräftig genug sei,** he comforted, consoled, himself with the thought that he was not strong enough for the work.
II. *vbl s.* **1. Beruhigen,** *n. in vbl senses.* **2. Beruhigung,** *f.* (*a*) = II. 1; *also:* appeasement, pacification; **zur B.,** (in order) to appease, pacify, calm; for appeasement; **ich tat es zur B. meines Gewissens,** I did it for conscience sake; **nimm dies zur B. deiner Nerven,** take this to soothe your nerves; **zur B. der Gemüter,** to set people's minds at rest; to stop people talking; (*b*) reassurance; comfort; **es würde mir eine große B. sein, wenn Sie das Kind begleiten würden,** it would greatly reassure me, it would be a load off my mind, if you would accompany the child; **er hat ihr das nur zur B. gesagt,** he said this only to reassure her; **ihre Anwesenheit, sie, war mir eine große B.,** her presence, she, was a great comfort to me, was very reassuring to me; **das ist mir keine B.,** that is no comfort to me, that doesn't reassure me; **diese Tatsache sollte den Nachbarn Deutschlands eine B. sein,** this fact ought to be a reassurance to Germany's neighbours, ought to allay the fears of Germany's neighbours; (*c*) calm; peace; **eine Zeit der B.,** a period of calm; **nach dem gestrigen Aufruhr ist heute eine gewisse B. eingetreten,** after yesterday's rioting comparative calm has been restored, a comparative calm has set in.
Beruhigungsmittel, *n.* means to soothe, calm, the mind; *Med:* sedative.
Beruhigungspille, *f. Med:* sedative; *F:* **j-m eine B. geben, verabreichen,** to give s.o. sth. *or* say sth. to s.o. to keep him quiet; *F:* to give s.o. a sop.
berühmen (sich), *v.refl. A:* = **sich rühmen,** *q.v. under* **rühmen.**
berühmt, *a.* **1.** famous, celebrated, renowned, famed; illustrious; well-known, noted; **in der Geschichte b.,** famous, celebrated, renowned, in history; **berühmte Männer der Geschichte,** men famous in history, history's illustrious, famous, men; **ein berühmtes Orchester,** a famous orchestra; **eine Stadt b. für ihren Wein, ihre Kunstdenkmäler,** a town famous, famed, noted, for its wine, for its monuments; **berühmte Kunststätten,** famous centres of art; **sie war eine berühmte Schönheit, eine b. schöne Frau,** she was a famous beauty, a woman famous, celebrated, for her beauty; **j-n b. machen,** to make s.o. famous; **b. werden,** to become, grow, famous, to win fame, renown; **früh b. werden,** (*of pers.*) to become famous at an early age, (*of pers., thg*) to win early fame; **schnell b. werden,** (*of thg, pers.*) to become famous in a short time, quickly, (*of pers.*) to rise to fame quickly; **von heute auf morgen, über Nacht, b. werden,** to become famous in a day, to awake to find oneself famous; **b. und berüchtigt,** (famous and) notorious; notoriously famous (pers., spot, etc.). **2.** *F:* (*used only in the negative*) **nicht b.,** not very,

particularly, good, nothing particular, special; not up to much; *F:* nothing to write home about; **der Wein, das Essen, ist nicht so b. hier,** the wine, the food, here is nothing special, not up to much, *F:* nothing to write home about; **das Wetter war nicht b.,** the weather wasn't very good; **die Aufführung war nicht b.,** the performance wasn't particularly, very, good; **die Schauspieler hier sind nicht b.,** the actors here are not very good.

Berühmtheit, *f.* **1.** fame, renown, celebrity; **B. erlangen,** to win fame, renown, to become, grow, famous; **zweifelhafte B.,** doubtful fame; **eine traurige B. erlangen,** to attain a regrettable fame. **2.** famous, celebrated, person, celebrity; person of note; **in dieser kleinen Stadt wohnen einige Berühmtheiten,** a few celebrities live in this small town; **er ist eine B. in seinem Fach,** he is a great name in his own field.

berührbar, *a.* touchable, that can be touched.

berühren. I. *v.tr.* **1.** to touch; (*a*) **etwas mit dem Finger, mit einem Stock, usw., b.,** to touch sth. with one's finger, with a stick, etc.; **j-n an der Schulter, am Arm, b.,** to touch, tap, s.o. on the shoulder, on the arm; **j-n leicht b.,** to touch s.o. lightly; **(bitte) nicht b.!** (please) do not touch! **er berührte ihre Lippen mit einem flüchtigen Kuß,** he kissed her lightly on the lips; **ich stand so nahe, daß ich sie mit der Hand hätte b. können,** I stood so close that I could have touched her with my hand; **sowie der Gegenstand von der Luft berührt wurde, zerfiel er zu Staub,** as soon as the object was exposed to, came out into, the air it fell to dust; **ein kalter Luftzug berührte ihn,** he felt a cold breath of air; **die letzten Sonnenstrahlen berührten die Bergesgipfel,** the last rays of the sun touched the mountain tops; **er hat das Essen nicht berührt,** he did not touch the food, he left the food untouched; (*b*) (*be in contact with*) **der Punkt, wo die Tangente den Kreis berührt,** the point where the tangent touches the circle; **die Gerade berührt den Kreis,** the straight line is tangent to, touches, the circle; **an dieser Stelle berührt die Straße die Bahnlinie,** here the road touches, comes close to, the railway line; **er stand dicht neben ihr, so daß sein Arm den ihren berührte,** he stood so close to her that his arm touched hers; (*c*) to reach; **der Weihnachtsbaum war so groß, daß er die Decke berührte,** the Christmas-tree was so high that it touched, reached, the ceiling; **das Kind saß auf einem hohen Stuhl, so daß seine Beinchen den Fußboden kaum b. konnten,** the child was sitting on a high chair so that its little legs could hardly touch, reach, the floor; **ich kann die Decke eben b.,** I can just touch the ceiling; **das Zimmer war so niedrig, daß sein ausgestreckter Arm die Decke b. konnte,** the room was so low that he could touch the ceiling with his outstretched arm; (*d*) (*of railway line, road, train, etc.*) to touch, to go, lead, through, to pass (town, etc.); (*of pers.*) to pass, come through, *F:* to touch (town, etc.) (*on a journey*); *Nau:* (*of ship*) to touch, call, at (a port); **berührt der Zug Mailand?** does the train touch, go through, Milan? **wir haben auf unserer Reise Köln nur berührt,** we only went through, passed, Cologne on our journey; **wir haben die Reiseroute so gewählt, daß wir die wichtigsten Städte des Landes b. werden,** we chose our route with a view to being able to see, take in, the most important towns of the country; **wir haben Heidelberg gar nicht berührt,** we did not come through Heidelberg at all, we did not go near Heidelberg; **er wird auf der Reise nach Edinburg Durham kurz b.,** he will make a short stop, stay, at Durham on his way to Edinburgh; **die Hauptstraße berührt diesen Ort nicht,** the main road does not lead, go, through this place, does not touch this place; **die Straße führt nicht durch den Ort durch, sondern berührt ihn nur,** the road does not go right through the place but merely by-passes it; **das Schiff wird die folgenden Orte b.,** the ship will touch at, call at, the following ports; (*e*) to touch on, allude to, mention (subject, etc.); **ich habe diese Fragen schon berührt,** I have already touched on these questions; **wir wollen dieses Thema lieber gar nicht mehr b.,** we'd rather not mention this subject any more, we'd better leave this subject alone, keep off this subject; **er hat diese Themen kurz in seiner Rede berührt,** he briefly mentioned, touched (on), alluded to, these subjects in his speech; **er berührte die Frage, ohne näher darauf einzugehen,** he touched on the question without going into detail. **2.** (*a*) to have an effect on (s.o.), to touch (s.o.); **die Verderbtheit ihrer Umgebung hatte sie nicht berührt,** the depravity of her surroundings had left her untouched, had not touched, affected, tainted, her; **ein Land, das die moderne Zivilisation noch nicht berührt hat, das von der modernen Zivilisation noch nicht berührt ist,** a country untouched, not yet spoiled, by modern civilisation; **nicht berührt von der Sünde,** untouched, untainted, by sin; (*b*) **eine Frau b.,** to interfere with, lay hands on, touch, a woman; **er hat noch nie eine Frau berührt,** he has never touched a woman; *B:* **es ist dem Menschen gut, daß er kein Weib berühre,** it is good for a man not to touch a woman. **3.** to touch, concern, affect; to impress (in some way), make an impression (of some kind) on (s.o.); **die Frage berührt Sie sehr nahe,** the question touches you nearly, concerns you closely; **eine Frage, die die ganze Welt berührt,** a question in which the whole world is concerned, which concerns the whole world; **das berührt mich nicht,** that does not concern, affect, me; **du bist am nächsten berührt,** you are the most closely concerned, affected; **die Angelegenheit berührt dich in keiner Weise,** you are in no way concerned in the business, the business in no way touches you, does not concern, affect, you in any way; **er tat so, als ob er von der ganzen Sache überhaupt nicht berührt wäre,** he behaved as if he had no concern in the matter, as if the matter did not concern him at all; **sein Benehmen hat mich unangenehm berührt, ich war von seinem Benehmen unangenehm berührt,** his behaviour made an unpleasant impression on me, impressed me unpleasantly; **seine Worte haben mich peinlich berührt, ich war von seinen Worten peinlich berührt,** his words made me feel embarrassed, caused me embarrassment, I felt embarrassment at his words; **ich war von seinen Worten seltsam berührt,** his words gave me a strange feeling, I was strangely affected, impressed, by his words; **alle waren von seiner Höflichkeit angenehm berührt, seine Höflichkeit berührte alle angenehm,** everybody was pleasantly impressed by his politeness, his politeness made a pleasant impression on everybody; **es berührt mich schmerzlich, daß . . .,** it pains me, it gives me pain, that . . .; **es hat mich sehr seltsam, merkwürdig, berührt, daß . . .,** it struck me as very odd that . . ., it seemed very odd to me that . . . . **4. sich, einander, b.,** to touch; to be in contact; to come into contact; *Geom: etc:* to touch, to be tangent; **sich mit etwas b.,** to be, come, near to sth.; to be in contact with sth.; to come into contact with sth.; to approximate to sth.; to touch sth.; **jetzt waren sie so dicht aneinander, daß sie sich fast berührten,** now they were so close to each other that they almost touched; **ihre Lippen berührten sich,** their lips met; **unsere Wege werden sich kaum b.,** our ways are not likely to meet; **die beiden Drähte dürfen sich nicht b.,** the two wires must not touch, must not come into contact; **der Punkt, in dem Kreis und Tangente sich berühren,** the point where the tangent touches the circle; **die Kreise berühren sich in einem Punkt,** the circles touch at one point; **zwei Kurven, die sich berühren, zwei sich berührende Kurven,** two curves that touch; **unsere Gedankengänge berühren sich kaum,** our ways of thinking have hardly anything in common; **unsere Arbeitsgebiete berühren sich nur wenig, in einigen Punkten, häufig,** there are few, several, many, points at which our fields touch; **unsere Arbeitsgebiete berühren sich, aber sie überschneiden sich nicht,** our fields are close to one another, are allied, but they do not overlap; **in diesem einen Punkt berühren sich unsere Anschauungen,** our views approximate to, approach, come close to, one another, meet, on this one point; **Plan, der sich mit einem anderen berührt,** plan that approximates to, is not unlike, another, plan that bears a resemblance to another; **seine Ideen berühren sich mit meinen,** his ideas approximate to, come close to, near to, mine.

II. *vbl s.* **1. Berühren,** *n. in vbl senses;* **B. verboten!** (please) do not touch! **2. Berührung,** *f.* (*a*)=II. 1; (*b*) contact; touch; *Geom: etc:* contact, tangency; contingence; *El:* contact; **mit etwas, j-m, in B. kommen,** (*of pers., thg*) to come into contact with sth., s.o.; to touch sth., s.o.; (*of pers.*) to get into (direct) touch with s.o.; **mit etwas, j-m, in B. sein,** (*of pers., thg*) to be in contact with sth., s.o.; to touch sth., s.o.; (*of pers.*) to be in (direct) touch with s.o.; **(miteinander) in B. kommen, sein,** (*of two thgs, persons*) to touch; to come into contact; to be in contact; **j-n mit etwas, etwas mit etwas, in B. bringen,** to bring s.o., sth., into contact with sth.; **zwei Dinge, Personen, (miteinander) in B. bringen,** to bring two things, persons, into contact, to establish contact between two things, persons; **die beiden Drähte dürfen nicht (miteinander) in B. kommen,** the two wires must not touch, must not come into contact; **ich bin mit dem Kranken nicht direkt in B. gekommen, gewesen,** I have not come into, have not been in, direct contact with the patient; **Krankheiten, die durch unmittelbare B. übertragen werden,** diseases that are transferred by immediate contact; (*c*) touch; (light) tap; **bei der ersten, leisesten, B.,** at the first, slightest, touch; **jede B. tut mir weh,** every touch hurts me; **ich fühlte eine leichte B. am Arm,** I felt a touch, a light tap, on my arm; **B. mit dem Zauberstab,** touch of, with, the wand.

Berührungsebene, *f. Geom: etc:* tangent plane.

Berührungselektrizität, *f.* contact electricity.

Berührungsfläche, *f.* surface of contact; *Geom: etc:* tangent plane.

Berührungskompositum, *n. Ling:* close compound.

Berührungslinie, line of contact; *Geom:* tangent.

Berührungspunkt, *m.* point of contact; *Geom: etc:* tangential point.

Berührungsschutz, *m. El: etc:* protection against accidental contact (of wires, cables, etc.).

Berührungsstelle, *f.* point, place, of contact; *Geom: etc:* tangential point.

Berührungswinkel, *m. Geom:* angle of contingence.

berußen, *v.tr.* to cover (sth.) with soot, to soot (sth.); to blacken (one's face, etc.) (with soot); **berußte Mauern,** sooty walls; **berußte Hände, berußtes Gesicht,** sooty hands, face; hands, face, black with soot; (*as disguise*) blackened hands, face.

Berut [be'ruːt]. *Pr.n.n.* **-s.** *Geog:* Beirut.

Beryll [be'ryl], *m.* **-s/-e.** *Miner:* beryl; **edler B.,** transparent beryl; aquamarine.

Beryllerde, *f. Ch: Miner:* glucina, beryllia.

Beryllium [be'rylium], *n.* **-s/.** *Ch:* beryllium, glucin(i)um.

Berylliumerde, *f.*=**Beryllerde.**

Berzel, *m.* **-s/-** =**Bürzel.**

besabbern, *v.tr.* (*of child, etc.*) to dribble, slobber, on, over (s.o., sth.); **das Kind hat sich besabbert,** the child has dribbled on, over, himself.

besäen, *v.tr.* (*a*) *Agr: etc:* to sow (a field); (*b*) to strew, to cover; **mit Blumen, mit Sternen, besät,** (be)studded with flowers, with stars; **der Pfad war besät mit Blütenblättern,** the path was strewn with flower petals; **der Himmel ist mit Sternen besät,** the sky is spangled with stars; **Wiesen mit Blumen (wie) besät,** meadows covered, gay, with flowers; *Her:* **mit Lilien besäter Schild,** shield semée of, with, powdered with, fleurs-de-lis.

besagen. I. *v.tr.* (*a*) to say; **der Wortlaut des Vertrages besagt . . .,** the text of the treaty says . . .; (*b*) to mean, signify; **das besagt nicht viel, das hat nicht viel zu b.,** that means very little, that does not mean much, that amounts to very little.

II. *p.p. & a.* **besagt,** (afore-)said, previously cited; above(-mentioned); **besagter Brief,** the said letter; **in besagtem Schreiben,** in the above document; *Hum:* **um auf besagten Hammel zurückzukommen,** let us return to our subject, *Hum:* to our muttons.

Besahn [be'zaːn, 'beːzaːn], *m.* **-s/-e** =**Besan.**

besaiten, *v.tr.* to string (violin, piano, etc.); *F:* (*of pers.*) **zart besaitet,** sensitive; touchy, thin-skinned, easily offended.

besamen. I. *v.tr. Biol:* to inseminate, impregnate (female animal, etc.); to pollinate (plant); *F:* **besamt sein,** to have pots of, heaps of, money.

II. *vbl s.* **Besamen** *n.*, **Besamung** *f.* insemination, impregnation (of female animal, etc.); pollination (of plant); **künstliche Besamung,** artificial insemination.

Besan [be'zaːn, 'beːzaːn], *m.* **-s/-e.** *Nau:* mizzen (-sail).

Besanbramstenge, *f. Nau:* mizzen-topgallant mast.

besanden, *v.tr.* to sand, gravel (path, etc.).

Besandirk, *m. Nau:* spanker-boom topping-lift.

besänftigen, *v.tr.* **1.** to appease, calm, soothe, pacify (s.o.); **besänftigendes Mittel,** soothing draught; **eine erregte Menge b.,** to calm, pacify, an excited crowd; **j-s Zorn b.,** to calm, soothe, s.o.'s temper. **2. sich besänftigen,** to calm down, to grow quiet; (*of storm, waves, excitement, etc.*) to subside, abate, calm (down).

Besanmars, *m. Nau:* mizzen-top.

Besanmast, *m. Nau:* mizzen-mast (of barque); jigger-mast (of four- *or* five-master).

Besansegel, *n. Nau:* mizzen(-sail).

Besanstenge, *f. Nau:* mizzen-topmast.
Besatz, *m.* **-es/⸚e.** **1.** trimming, decoration (of dress, hat, etc.); **ein weißes Kleid mit rotem B.,** a white dress trimmed with red, a white dress with red trimming. **2.** *Bootm:* vamp, upper (of shoe). **3.** *Min: etc:* tamping (of blast-hole). **4.** *Pisc:* stocking (of water) with young fish.
Besatzband, *n. Needlew:* edging, ribbon (used for trimming).
Besatzlitze, *f. Needlew:* braid(ing).
Besatzschnur, *f. Needlew:* cord (used for trimming).
Besatzstreifen, *m. Needlew:* edging.
Besatzteich, *m. Pisc:* breeding-pond, nursery.
Besatzung, *f.* **1.** *Mil: etc:* occupation (of defeated country, conquered town, etc.); **einem Land B. auferlegen,** to keep occupation troops in a country, to keep a country occupied, **2.** *Mil: etc:* (*a*) garrison (of stronghold, etc.); **B. in eine Stadt legen,** to garrison a town; (*b*) crew (of aircraft, ship, tank); complement (of ship), (ship's) company; **volle B.,** full complement; **Schiff mit voller B. von Offizieren und Leuten,** ship with a full complement of officers and men; (*c*) army of occupation, occupation troops (in defeated country). **3.** *Locksm:* ward, snap (of lock).
Besatzungsamt, *n.* administrative office of the military government.
Besatzungsarmee, *f. Mil:* army of occupation, occupation troops.
Besatzungsbehörde, *f. Mil:* military authority in occupation; military government.
Besatzungsmacht, *f. Mil:* (*a*) occupying power; (*b*) military authority in occupation.
Besatzungsmitglied, *n.* member of the crew.
Besatzungstruppen, *f.pl. Mil:* occupation troops, occupation forces.
besaufen (sich), *v.refl.* (*strong*) *F:* to get drunk; **besoffen sein,** to be drunk; **total besoffen, besoffen wie ein Schwein,** dead, blind, drunk; as drunk as a lord, as a fiddler; **du bist wohl total besoffen,** you must be completely mad; **in seinem besoffenen Kopf,** in his drunken state, in his drunkenness.
besäumen, *v.tr.* (*a*) to edge, fringe, border (field, road, etc.); **von Pappeln besäumte Straße,** road edged with poplars; **die Eichen, die den Wald besäumen,** the oaks that fringe the forest; **mit Buchsbaum besäumter Pfad,** path bordered with box; (*b*) *Carp:* to square, to slab (beam, plank).
beschädigen. I. *v.tr.* to damage, injure (sth.); to do damage, injury, to (sth.); **die Möbel b.,** to damage, to do damage to, the furniture; **beim Transport beschädigt,** damaged in transit; **das Bild ist beim Transport beschädigt worden,** the picture was damaged, suffered damage, in transit; **das Haus ist schwer beschädigt worden,** the house has suffered extensive damage, was seriously damaged; **leicht beschädigt,** (i) (*of goods, etc.*) slightly damaged, injured; slightly soiled; (ii) *Hum:* (*of pers.*) slightly unbalanced, *F:* dotty; *Print:* **beschädigter Buchstabe, beschädigte Type,** broken letter, battered letter, *F:* batter.
II. *vbl s.* **1. Beschädigen,** *n. in vbl senses.* **2. Beschädigung,** *f.* (*a*)=II. 1; *also:* damage, injury; *Jur:* **absichtliche B.,** wilful damage; **böswillige B.,** malicious damage; (*b*) damage, injury; **die Beschädigungen der Maschine,** the damage to the engine; **nach dem Transport wurde(n) erhebliche Beschädigung(en) an den Waren festgestellt,** the goods were found to have suffered extensive damage in transit; **Beschädigungen eines Hauses verursacht durch Feuchtigkeit,** damage to a building due to dampness.
beschaffen[1]. I. *v.tr.* (*weak*) to procure (sth.); to provide (sth.); to raise (money); **bis heute abend muß ich das Geld b.,** I must procure, find, raise, the money by tonight; **er versuchte, ihm Arbeit zu b.,** he tried to find, get, him employment, a job; **ich muß Brot für die ganze Familie b.,** I have to provide bread for the whole family; **dieses Buch ist schwer zu b.,** this book is difficult to procure, to get; **ich kann dir das Material leicht b.,** I can easily procure, get, the material for you.
II. *vbl s.* **1. Beschaffen,** *n. in vbl senses.* **2 Beschaffung,** *f. in vbl senses; also:* procurement; provision; **die B. des Materials wird keine Schwierigkeiten bereiten,** it will not be difficult to procure, get, the material; **die B. der nötigen Geldmittel,** the raising of the necessary funds; **B. von Lebensmitteln,** provision of food supplies.
beschaffen[2], *a.* (*of thg*) **b. sein,** to be in (good, bad) condition, state; **wie b.?** of what nature? of what sort? **wie ist es mit seiner Gesundheit b.?** what is the state of his health? how is his health? **wie ist es damit b.?** what is the situation as far as that is concerned? what about that? **wie ist es mit dem Wohnen b.?** what about the living conditions? **es ist nicht gut, es ist übel, damit b.,** it is bad, it is in a bad way; **ich möchte wissen, wie die Dinge wirklich b. sind,** I want to know the real state of things; **wie auch immer die Angelegenheit b. sein mag,** whatever the state of the case may be; **ich bin eben so b.,** I'm just made that way.
Beschaffenheit, *f.* (*a*) peculiar quality, property; **die B. der Materie,** the properties of matter; **die natürliche B. der Kohle,** the natural properties of coal; **die eigenartige B. dieser Flüssigkeit,** the singular qualities, properties, of this liquid; **ein Sekret von wässeriger B.,** a secretion of a watery consistency, quality; (*b*) state, condition; **die B. der Waren ist ausgezeichnet,** the condition of the goods is excellent; **hervorragende B. der Straßen,** first-class state, condition, of the roads; *Agr:* **B. des Bodens,** condition, state, of the soil.
Beschaffung, *f. see* **beschaffen**[1] II.
Beschaffungsamt, *n.*, **Beschaffungsstelle,** *f. Com: etc:* supply office; *Mil:* directorate of procurement.
beschäftigen. I. *v.tr.* **1.** (*of pers.*) to employ, to occupy (s.o.); to keep (s.o.) occupied; **sich (mit etwas) b.,** to occupy, busy, oneself (with sth.); **zwanzig Arbeiter b.,** to employ twenty workmen; **als . . . beschäftigt,** employed as . . .; **die Kinder müssen nützlich beschäftigt werden,** the children must be kept usefully occupied; **ich werde ihn schon beschäftigt halten,** I shall keep him busy, occupied; **ich bin augenblicklich beschäftigt,** I am occupied, busy, at the moment, at present; **ein stark beschäftigter Mann,** a very busy man; **er beschäftigte sich meist mit seinen Briefmarken,** he usually occupied, busied, himself with his stamps; he was usually busy with his stamps. **2.** (*a*) **sich mit einem Problem, usw., b.,** to concern oneself, to be concerned, with a problem, etc.; **er beschäftigte sich ernsthaft mit dieser Frage,** he concerned himself seriously with, he put his mind seriously to, this question; **er beschäftigte sich mit diesem Problem sein ganzes Leben lang,** he was concerned, he concerned himself, with this problem all his life; (*b*) (*of matter, incident, etc.*) to occupy, fill (s.o.'s) mind; **der Vorfall beschäftigte ihn,** the incident occupied, filled, his mind, his mind dwelt on the incident; **dieses Problem beschäftigte ihn sein ganzes Leben lang,** he was concerned, he concerned himself, with this problem all his life.
II. *vbl s.* **1. Beschäftigen,** *n. in vbl senses.* **2. Beschäftigung,** *f.* (*a*)=II. 1; (*b*) employment, job; occupation; **regelmäßige B. haben,** to have regular employment, a regular job; **j-m eine B. verschaffen,** to find employment for s.o.; **seiner B. nachgehen,** to go to work, to work, to do one's job; **ohne B. sein,** to be unemployed, to be out of a job; **Malen ist eine angenehme B.,** painting is a pleasant occupation; **ich werde ihm schon B. geben, schaffen,** I shall give him something to keep him occupied, busy; I shall give him something to do.
Beschäftiger, *m.* **-s/-,** employer.
Beschäftigungsbehandlung, *f. Med:* occupational therapy.
Beschäftigungsgenehmigung, *f. Adm:* labour permit.
beschäftigungslos, *a.* unemployed, without employment; **b. sein,** to be unemployed, to be out of work, out of a job.
Beschäftigungslosigkeit, *f.* unemployment.
Beschäftigungsneurose, *f. Med:* occupational neurosis.
Beschäftigungsspiele, *n.pl.* creative games (in kindergarten).
Beschäftigungstherapie, *f.* **-/.** *Med:* occupational therapy.
beschälen[1], *v.tr.* to strip the bark off (tree).
beschälen[2], *v.tr. Breed:* (*of stallion*) to serve, cover (mare); **Beschälung** *f,* serving, service, covering (by stallion).
Beschäler, *m.* **-s/-.** *Breed:* stallion, stud-horse.
Beschälgeld, *n.* stud-fee.
Beschälhengst, *m. Breed:* stallion, stud-horse.
Beschälkrankheit, *f. Vet:* dourine.
beschallen, *v.tr.* (*a*) to fill (room, etc.) with sound; (*b*) *Med:* to give VHF treatment, supersonic frequency treatment, to (s.o.); to treat (s.o.) with supersonic vibrations.
Beschälseuche, *f. Vet:* dourine.
Beschälstation, *f. Breed:* stud-farm.
beschämen. I. *v.tr.* to put (s.o.) to shame, to confusion; to shame (s.o.); **j-n tief b.,** to make s.o. feel deeply ashamed; to humiliate s.o.; **er war tief beschämt,** he was deeply ashamed, overwhelmed with shame; **ich will mich nicht von dir b. lassen,** I won't allow you to shame me, you shall not put me to shame; **er beschämte mich durch seine Freundlichkeit,** he overwhelmed me with his kindness; his kindness made me feel ashamed; **es war ein beschämender Augenblick,** it was a humiliating moment; **mit beschämtem Blick,** shame-faced, abashed; **er schlich beschämt davon,** he slunk away in shame.
II. *vbl s.* **1. Beschämen,** *n. in vbl senses.* **2. Beschämung,** *f.* (*a*)=II. 1; (*b*) shame, humiliation; **zu meiner B. muß ich gestehen, daß . . .,** to my shame I must confess that . . ., I am ashamed to have to confess that . . .; **es war eine B. für mich,** it was a humiliation for me, it was humiliating for me.
beschatten, *v.tr.* (*a*) to shade; to protect (sth.) against the sun; *Hort:* **junge Pflanzen b.,** to shade young plants; **Bäume, die das Haus beschatten,** trees shading the house; **von Pappeln beschattete Straße,** road shaded by poplars; **der Hut beschattete sein Gesicht,** the hat shaded his face, the hat protected his face against the sun; **seine Augen mit der Hand b.,** to shade one's eyes with one's hand, to shield one's eyes from the sun with one's hand; (*b*) **vom heiligen Geist beschattet,** overshadowed by the Holy Ghost; (*c*) (*of detective, etc.*) to shadow (s.o.); (*d*) *Art:* to shade (drawing, etc.).
Beschau, *f.* **-/.** **1.** (*a*) inspection (of animals, goods, etc.); (customs) examination; (*b*) (official) inspection of meat; (*c*) testing, assaying (of gold, silver). **2.** *Dial:* = **Brautschau.**
Beschaubefund, *m.* result of the inspection (of meat, goods, etc.).
beschauen. I. *v.tr.* **1.** to look at (picture, scenery, etc.); **sich im Spiegel b.,** to look at oneself in the mirror; **er beschaute (sich) das Denkmal von allen Seiten,** he looked at, viewed, the monument from all sides. **2.** to examine, inspect (goods, etc.); to inspect (meat).
II. *vbl s.* **1. Beschauen,** *n. in vbl senses.* **2. Beschauung,** *f.* (*a*) inspection, examination (of goods, etc.); (*b*) = **Beschaulichkeit.**
Beschauer, *m.* **-s/-.** **1.** beholder (of picture, etc.); observer, onlooker. **2.** (*a*) (official) inspector of meat; (*b*) inspector (of goods, etc.).
beschaufeln, *v.tr. Mch:* to blade (turbine, etc.); to provide (turbine, etc.) with blades; **Beschaufelung** *f,* blades, blading (of turbine, etc.).
beschaulich, *a.* contemplative, meditative, introspective (pers., frame of mind); **das beschauliche Leben,** the contemplative life; **ein beschauliches Leben führen,** (i) to lead a contemplative life, to lead a life of contemplation; (ii) *F:* to lead a leisurely, carefree, life, *F:* to take it easy; **beschaulicher Orden,** contemplative, closed, order; **ein beschauliches Gemüt,** a meditative, an introspective, mind.
Beschaulichkeit, *f.* contemplation, meditation; introversion; **ein Leben der B. führen,** to lead a life of contemplation, meditation; to lead a contemplative life.
Beschaustempel, *m.* (meat, etc.) inspector's stamp.
Beschauzeichen, *n.* **1.** hall-mark (on gold, silver). **2.** inspector's stamp (on meat, etc.).
Bescheid, *m.* **-(e)s/-e.** **1.** (*a*) answer, decision; information; **vorläufiger B.,** provisional decision; **endgültiger B.,** final decision; **abschlägiger B.,** refusal; rebuff; **Sie werden so bald wie möglich B. bekommen, erhalten,** you will be informed, notified, as soon as possible; (*b*) *Jur:* ruling, decision, award; judgment; (*c*) **(j-m) B. tun, trinken,** to drink to s.o. (in return); to reply to, answer, s.o.'s toast. **2.** information, instruction; **j-m B. sagen, geben,** to give s.o. information, to inform, instruct, s.o.; **ich werde dir später noch B. sagen, wann du kommen kannst,** I will tell you later, let you know later, when you can come; *F:* **j-m gehörig B. sagen,** to give s.o. a good dressing-down; **B. wissen,** to be informed; **er weiß genau B.,** he knows all about it; he knows exactly what he has to do; **in einem Hause B. wissen,** to know one's way about a house; **er weiß gut B. in seinem Fach,** he knows his subject, *F:* his stuff, well; he is well up in his subject.
bescheiden[1], *v.tr.* (*strong*) **1.** (*a*) to inform (s.o.) (of a decision, etc.); *see also* **abfällig 7, abschlägig;** (*b*) to summon; **er wurde vors Gericht beschieden,** he was summoned to appear in court; **ich habe ihn zu mir beschieden,** I summoned him to me; I sent for him. **2.** to grant;

ihm war kein langes Leben beschieden, it was not granted to him to live long; **Gott hat es beschieden,** it was God's will; **es war ihm nicht beschieden, seine Heimat wiederzusehen,** the gods did not grant him, he was not destined, to see his country again. **3. sich bescheiden,** to be satisfied, content(ed); **mit dieser Antwort mußte sie sich b.,** she had to be satisfied with this answer; **man muß sich oft mit wenigem b.,** one must often be content with little; **er wird sich damit b. müssen,** he will have to resign himself to it.

bescheiden², *a.* (*a*) modest; unassuming; **bescheidenes Benehmen,** modest behaviour; **ein bescheidener Mann,** a modest, an unassuming, man; **nach meiner bescheidenen Meinung,** in my humble opinion; **er trat sehr b. auf,** he behaved very modestly, with great modesty; (*b*) moderate, modest (price, means, desire, etc.); **bescheidenes Vermögen,** modest fortune; **bescheidene Ansprüche haben,** to be modest in one's requirements; **b. in seinen Wünschen,** moderate, reasonable, in one's desires; **mit bescheidenem Gehalt auskommen,** to manage on a modest salary; **in bescheidenem Maße,** in a small way; (*c*) simple; humble; **in einer bescheidenen Hütte leben,** to live in a humble cottage; **er verzehrte sein bescheidenes Mahl,** he partook of his simple, frugal, meal; **unter meinem bescheidenen Dach,** under my humble roof; **b. leben,** to live humbly.

Bescheidenheit, *f.* modesty (of pers., behaviour, etc.); unpretentiousness, simplicity (of house, display, etc.); **falsche B.,** false modesty; **bei aller B. muß gesagt werden,** be it said with all due modesty; **die B. ihres Heims,** the modesty, simplicity, of their home; *Prov:* **B. ist eine Zier, doch weiter kommt man ohne ihr,** you won't get far with modesty, however becoming it may be.

bescheidentlich, *adv.* modestly, humbly; unpretentiously.

bescheinen¹, *v.tr.* (*strong*) to shine (up)on; **der Vollmond beschien die Straße,** the full moon shone upon the road; **ein Platz, der nie von der Sonne beschienen wird,** a place never visited, reached, by the sun.

bescheinen², *v.tr.* (*weak*) *A:* = **bescheinigen.**

bescheinigen. I. *v.tr.* to certify, to confirm in writing; **wir bescheinigen hiermit, hiermit wird bescheinigt, daß . . .,** we hereby certify that . . .; **können Sie mir das b.?** can you give me a certificate for that? **den Empfang von Waren b.,** to acknowledge receipt of goods, to confirm receipt of goods (in writing); to give a receipt for goods; **die bescheinigende Behörde,** the certifying authority.

II. *vbl s.* **1. Bescheinigen,** *n. in vbl senses.* **2. Bescheinigung,** *f.* (*a*) *in vbl senses; also:* acknowledgement (of receipt of goods, etc.); certification; (*b*) certificate; **eine B. ausstellen,** to write, issue, a certificate; **ärztliche B.,** doctor's certificate, medical certificate; **amtliche B.,** official certificate; **B. über die Teilnahme am Unterricht, usw.,** certificate of attendance at lessons, etc.

Bescheiniger, *m.* **-s/-,** certifier; confirmer.

bescheißen. I. *v.tr.* (*strong*) *P:* (*a*) to foul (sth.) with excrement; (*b*) **j-n b.,** to cheat s.o.; *F:* to do, have, s.o.; **laß dich nicht b.,** don't let them do you, chisel you; **die haben mich schön beschissen,** I've been properly had.

II. *p.p. & a.* **beschissen,** *in vbl senses; esp.* dirty; lousy; **der beschissene Kerl,** the lousy fellow, the dirty rat; **das ist äußerst b., das ist ein beschissener Kram,** that's a lousy mess.

Bescheißer, *m.* **-s/-.** *P:* swindler, cheater.

beschelten, *v.tr.* (*strong*) *A:* to scold (s.o.); to tell (s.o.) off; **j-s guten Ruf b.,** to ruin s.o.'s reputation; *see also* **bescholten.**

beschenken, *v.tr.* **j-n b.,** to give a present to s.o.; to give, make, s.o. a present; **er beschenkte ihn mit einem Auto,** he presented him with a car; he made him a present of a car; **meine Frau hat mich mit einem Töchterchen beschenkt,** my wife has presented me with a baby daughter; **wir wurden reich, reichlich, beschenkt,** we were showered with gifts, with presents.

Beschenkte, *m., f.* (*decl. as adj.*) recipient (of a present).

bescheren¹, *v.tr.* (*strong*) to trim (beard, hair, etc.).

bescheren². I. *v.tr.* (*weak*) (*a*) **(j-n) b.,** to give (s.o.) presents (*esp.* for Christmas); **die Kinder zu Weihnachten b.,** to give the children Christmas presents; **bei uns wird am Weihnachtsabend beschert,** we get our presents on Christmas Eve; (*b*) **j-m etwas b.,** to bless s.o. with sth.; **Gott bescherte ihnen Kinder,** God blessed them with children; **möge ihm viel Glück beschert sein,** may he be blessed with much good fortune; **uns waren viele glückliche Jahre beschert,** we were blessed with many years of happiness.

II. *vbl s.* **1. Bescheren,** *n. in vbl senses.* **2. Bescherung,** *f.* (*a*) = II. 1; (*b*) presentation of gifts (*esp.* at Christmas); **bei uns ist B. am Weihnachtsabend,** we get our presents on Christmas Eve; (*c*) *Iron:* mess; **da haben wir die B.! das ist ja eine schöne, nette, reizende, B.!** that's a nice mess! here's a pretty, a fine, kettle of fish!

beschicken. I. *v.tr.* **1.** to send exhibits to, to exhibit at (fair, exhibition, etc.); to send a representative to (meeting, etc.), a competitor to (tournament, etc.). **2.** (*a*) to attend to, see to, look after (affairs, animals, etc.); to till (soil); to feed, make up, stoke (fire); to charge (furnace, etc.); to fire (boiler); **einen Ofen b.,** to put (i) bread, etc. in an oven, (ii) pottery, bricks, in a kiln; **sein Haus b.,** to put, set, one's affairs in order; (*b*) to alloy, mix (metal).

II. *vbl s.* **1. Beschicken,** *n. in vbl senses; also:* tillage (of soil); alloyage (of metal). **2. Beschickung,** *f.* (*a*) = II. 1; (*b*) charge (of furnace); (*c*) alloy.

Beschickungsanlage, *f.* charging *or* bunkering installation.

Beschickungsapparat, *m.* = **Beschickungsmaschine.**

Beschickungsmaschine, *f. Ind:* charging machine, charger, feeder.

beschiefern, *v.tr.* to slate (roof, etc.).

beschienen, *v.tr.* (*a*) to lay rails on (sleepers, etc.); (*b*) to tyre, shoe (wheel), to put a (metal) tyre on (wheel).

beschießen. I. *v.tr.* (*strong*) **1.** (*a*) *Mil: etc:* to fire on, at, shoot at (sth.); **eine Stadt mit Artillerie b.,** to bombard, shell, a town; **eine Festung b.,** to fire on a fort, to bombard, batter, a fort; **feindliche Stellungen b.,** to fire on the enemy's positions; **ein Schiff b.,** to fire at, on, to cannonade, a ship; **beschossen werden,** to be under fire; **vom Feind beschossene Stellungen,** positions under the enemy's fire; (*b*) *Ven:* to shoot at (herd of deer, flock of birds, etc.) (*to flush them*); (*c*) *Ph:* **einen Atomkern mit Neutronen b.,** to bombard an atomic nucleus with neutrons; *Med:* **einen Krebsherd mit Ultraschall b.,** to bombard the seat of a cancer infection with supersonic vibrations. **2.** (*a*) to test-fire (gun, etc.); (*b*) **beschossen sein,** to be supplied with ammunition. **3.** (*a*) *A:* to board, plank (wall, partition, etc.); (*b*) to coat, spray (wall, etc.) (with paint, etc.).

II. *vbl s.* **Beschießen** *n.*, **Beschießung** *f. in vbl senses; also:* cannonade, bombardment (of ship, fort, etc.); *cp.* **Beschuß.**

beschiffen, *v.tr.* **1.** to sail, plough (the sea). **2.** *F:* to urinate, *F:* to piddle, on (sth.).

beschildern. I. *v.tr.* to label (luggage, etc.); to ticket (goods, etc.); to mark (street) with street-plates; to provide (road) with road signs, to signpost (road); **ungenügend beschilderte Straße,** road inadequately signposted.

II. *vbl s.* **1. Beschildern,** *n. in vbl senses.* **2. Beschilderung,** *f.* (*a*) = II. 1; (*b*) **die Straße hat keine gute B.,** the road is inadequately signposted.

beschilft, *a.* (pond, etc.) full of reeds; reedy.

beschimmeln, *v.i.* (*sein*) to go mouldy; **beschimmeltes Brot,** mouldy, mildewed, bread.

beschimpfen. I. *v.tr.* **j-n b.,** to abuse, slander, vilify, s.o.; to speak ill of s.o., *F:* to run s.o. down; to insult, affront, s.o.; **er hat mich auf offener Straße beschimpft,** he insulted, abused, me publicly, before everyone; **sie beschimpften sich gegenseitig,** they abused each other, they called each other names; **j-s guten Namen b.,** to drag s.o.'s name in the mud; to cast a slur on s.o.'s reputation; to stain s.o.'s reputation, s.o.'s good name; **j-s Ehre b.,** to cast aspersions on s.o.'s honour, to tarnish, blemish, s.o.'s honour.

II. *vbl s.* **1. Beschimpfen,** *n. in vbl senses; also:* abuse, slander. **2. Beschimpfung,** *f.* (*a*) = II. 1; (*b*) abuse, slander; insult, affront; **es war eine grobe, gröbliche, B.,** it was a gross insult; **er hat mich mit Beschimpfungen überhäuft,** he heaped insults on my head.

beschindeln, *v.tr.* to shingle (roof, etc.).

beschinden, *v.tr.* (*strong*) to scrape, scratch (wall, furniture, etc.); **sich** *dat.* **den Ellbogen, das Schienbein, b.,** to graze, bark, one's elbow, one's shin.

beschirmen, *v.tr. Lit:* to shelter, shield, protect, guard (s.o.) (vor, from); *B:* **er läßt's den Aufrichtigen gelingen, und beschirmet die Frommen,** he layeth up sound wisdom for the righteous: he is a buckler to them that walk uprightly.

Beschirmer, *m.* **-s/-,** protector, guardian, shield, *B:* buckler.

Beschirmerin, *f.* **-/-innen,** protectress, guardian.

beschirren. I. *v.tr.* to harness (horse, etc.); **mit vier Pferden beschirrte Kutsche,** coach drawn by four horses.

II. *vbl s.* **1. Beschirren,** *n. in vbl senses.* **2. Beschirrung,** *f.* (*a*) = II. 1; (*b*) harness.

Beschiß, *m.* **-schisses/-schisse.** *P:* swindle; **das ist ja B.,** that is cheating.

beschissen *see* **bescheißen.**

beschlabbern, *v.tr.* to slobber on, over (sth., s.o., oneself).

Beschlächt, *f.* **-/-en.** *Civ.E:* sheet-piling.

beschlafen, *v.tr.* (*strong*) **1. eine Sache b.,** to sleep on a matter, a question; to take counsel of one's pillow. **2. eine Frau b.,** to sleep, *A:* to lie, with a woman.

Beschlag, *m.* **-(e)s/⸗e. 1.** (*a*) covering, fitting (sth.) with iron; providing (sth.) with iron fittings; shoeing (of horse, wheel, etc.); (*b*) *Ven:* (*used of deer*) covering, serving (of female by male); copulation, mating (of male with female). **2.** (*a*) metal fitting(s), mount(s), furnishing(s) (of door, chest of drawers, etc.); plated parts, mountings (of car, etc.); mountings (of rifle); *N.Arch:* sheathing, skin (of ship); *Constr: N.Arch:* (metal) hoop (round beam, mast, etc.); (steel) tyre, shoe (of wheel, etc.); shoe (of sledge); ferrule (of umbrella, walking-stick, etc.); shoe, band, cap (of pile, wooden beam, etc.); clasp, hasp, catch, fastener (of book, lady's bag, etc.); (*b*) *Farr:* horseshoe; (*c*) *Tex:* card-clothing (for carding-machine); (*d*) *Locksm:* ward(s) (of lock). **3.** (*a*) thin coating, thin surface layer; *Miner: Ch: etc:* incrustation; efflorescence; film (of verdigris, etc.); bloom (of sulphur on rubber); (*b*) steam, mist, film, vapour (on window-pane, etc.); blur, film (of breath on mirror); dew (on plants, etc.); bloom (on fruit); (*c*) (protective) layer; coating (of Leyden jar, etc.); lagging (of boiler); *Ch: Cer:* lute, luting (of retort, etc.); *Metall:* brasque, lute, luting (of crucible). **4.** seizure, confiscation; **in B. nehmen, mit B. belegen,** to seize, attach (real estate), to distrain upon, to confiscate (goods, etc.), to lay an embargo on, to embargo, to attach (ship); **Schmuggelwaren in B. nehmen, mit B. belegen, auf Schmuggelwaren B. legen,** to seize, confiscate, contraband goods; **j-n mit B. belegen, j-n ganz in B. nehmen,** to monopolize s.o., s.o.'s attention; **die besten Plätze mit B. belegen,** to reserve, *F:* to bag, the best seats.

Beschlagbändsel, *n. Nau:* furling-line; furling-gasket.

Beschlagbrille, *f.* semi-rimless spectacles.

beschlagen. I. *v.tr.* (*strong*) **1.** to square (beam, plank, etc.); to hew (stone); **Balken, usw., grob b.,** to rough-square beams, etc.; **grob beschlagene Steine,** rough-hewn stones. **2.** (*a*) to provide (sth.) with iron fittings; to fit, mount, (sth.) with iron; to shoe, cap (wooden beam, etc.); to shoe (walking-stick, etc.); to tyre, shoe (wheel); to hoop (cask); *N.Arch:* to sheathe, copper, skin (ship); **einen Schiffsboden b.,** to sheathe a ship's bottom; **ein Dach mit Kupfer, usw., b.,** to cover, line, a roof with copper, etc.; *Farr:* **ein Pferd b.,** to shoe a horse; **ein Pferd scharf b.,** to rough-shoe, to calk, a horse; **scharf beschlagenes Pferd,** rough-shod, roughed, frost-nailed, sharped, horse; **Schuhe mit (groben) Nägeln b.,** to hobnail shoes; **mit Nägeln beschlagene Schuhe,** hobnailed shoes, shoes studded with hobnails; (*b*) to cover, hang (wall, etc.) (with cloth, etc.); (*c*) to coat (Leyden jar, etc.); to lag (boiler); *Ch: etc:* to lute (retort, etc.); *Metall:* to lute, brasque (crucible); (*d*) (*of steam, etc.*) to dim, cloud (glass, etc.). **3.** *Nau:* to furl (sail). **4.** *Ven:* (*of male deer*) to cover, serve (female); **beschlagene Ricke,** doe in fawn. **5.** *v.i.* (*sein*) & **sich beschlagen,** (*of window-pane, wall, etc.*) to steam up; (*of mirror, etc.*) to cloud over, film over, to become blurred; **die Fensterscheiben sind beschlagen,** the window-panes are steamed up, the window is steamed up.

II. *p.p. & a.* **beschlagen,** *in vbl senses; esp:* **1.** (*of pers.*) knowledgeable, well-informed; well versed; proficient; **in einem Fach, einem Gebiet, gut b. sein,** to have a thorough knowledge of a subject, to be perfectly at home with, to know all about, a subject; **in Botanik gut, sehr, b. sein,** to know a lot about botany; **ich bin in Geschichte nicht sehr gut b.,** I am not very well up in, not very well versed in, history; **er ist in Geschäfts-**

sachen gut b., he is a man well up in, well versed in, business matters. **2.** *A. & Dial:* (pers.) of ready wit.

Beschlagenheit, *f.* (thorough, sound) knowledge; **seine B. in diesen Dingen,** his knowledge in these matters; **seine juristische, sprachliche, B.,** his (sound) legal, linguistic, knowledge.

Beschlaghammer, *m. Farr:* shoeing-hammer.

Beschlagkitt, *m. Ch: Cer:* lute (of retort, etc.); *Metall:* brasque, lute (of crucible).

Beschlagleine, *f. Nau:* furling-line.

Beschlagmetall, *n.* sheathing metal (for ship's bottom, roof, etc.).

Beschlagnahme, *f.* **-/-n.** *Adm: etc:* seizure, seizing (of goods, of neutral vessel, etc.); confiscation, impounding (of contraband goods, documents, etc.); seizure, attachment, forfeiture, *Jur:* sequestration (of property, etc.); requisition (of houses, etc.); *Nau:* embargo, detention (of ship); **B. von Immobilien,** seizure, attachment, of real property; *Jur:* **gerichtliche Anordnung der B.,** writ of sequestration; **B. der Ernte,** seizure of crops; **die B. eines Schiffes anordnen, verfügen,** to order the detention of a ship, to lay an embargo on a ship; **die B. eines Schiffes aufheben,** to take off, to raise, the embargo on a ship; **unter B.,** (ship, goods, etc.) under an embargo, requisitioned (house, etc.), confiscated (contraband goods, etc.).

Beschlagnahmeanordnung, *f. Jur:* writ of sequestration.

beschlagnahmefrei, *a.* not liable to confiscation *or* seizure.

beschlagnahmen. I. *v.tr. Adm: etc:* to seize, attach (real estate); to seize, distrain upon, confiscate, impound, *Jur:* to sequester, sequestrate (property, goods, etc.); to requisition (houses, etc.); to commandeer (provisions, etc.); to lay an embargo on, to embargo, to attach (ship); **die Waren wurden beschlagnahmt,** the goods were seized, confiscated; **die Polizei beschlagnahmte die in der Wohnung vorgefundenen Opiumbestände,** the police seized the opium found in the flat; (*of police*) **die Leiche, die Mordwaffe, b.,** to take charge of the body, of the murder weapon; **viele Häuser wurden von der Regierung beschlagnahmt,** many houses were requisitioned by the government; *Jur:* **j-s Eigentum b.,** to distrain upon, to confiscate, s.o.'s belongings; **ein Schiff b.,** to lay an embargo on, to embargo, to attach, a ship; **beschlagnahmt sein,** (*of ship, goods, etc.*) to be under an embargo, (*of house, etc*) to be requisitioned; **j-n b.,** to monopolize s.o., s.o.'s attention; **die besten Plätze b.,** to reserve, *F:* to bag, the best seats.

II. *vbl s.* **1. Beschlagnahmen,** *n. in vbl senses.* **2. Beschlagnahmung,** *f.* = **Beschlagnahme.**

Beschlagnahmeverfügung, *f. Jur:* writ of sequestration.

Beschlagnahmeversicherung, *f.* insurance against confiscation.

Beschlagschmied, *m. Farr:* shoeing-smith, farrier.

Beschlagseising, *f. Nau:* furling-gasket.

Beschlagteile, *m.pl.* (metal) fittings (of door, car, etc.).

Beschlagwerk, *n. Art:* strapwork (of late Renaissance period).

beschleichen, *v.tr.* (*strong*) (*a*) to stalk (animal, pers.); to creep up on (animal, pers.) stealthily; to spy upon (s.o.); (*b*) (*of fear, etc.*) to overcome (s.o.); **ein Gefühl der Angst beschlich ihn,** a sense of fear crept over him, took hold of him.

beschleifen[1], *v.tr.* (*weak*) to adorn (s.o., sth.) with bows.

beschleifen[2], *v.tr.* (*strong*) to grind, set an edge on (knife, etc.).

beschleunigen. I. *v.tr.* **1.** (*a*) **die Geschwindigkeit b.,** to accelerate, quicken, the speed, *Aut:* to accelerate, (*of train, etc.*) to gather, pick up speed, (*of ship*) to increase speed; **gleichförmig beschleunigte Bewegung,** uniform acceleration; **eine beschleunigende Kraft,** a quickening force; **seine Schritte b.,** to quicken, hasten, one's steps, to quicken one's pace; **die Angst beschleunigte seine Schritte,** fear lent wings to his flight, fear lent him wings; **das Tempo b.,** (i) *Mus:* to quicken the tempo, (ii) *Rac:* to quicken the pace; *Med:* **beschleunigter Puls,** quick(ened) pulse; (*b*) to hasten, speed up, expedite (undertaking, etc.); **j-s Abreise b.,** to hasten, hurry, precipitate, s.o.'s departure; **die Lieferung b.,** to speed up delivery; **die Arbeit b.,** to speed (up) the work; **ein Verfahren b.,** to accelerate, speed up, expedite, proceedings; **die Entwicklung b.,** to speed up developments; **diese Aktion beschleunigte seinen Zusammenbruch,** this action hastened his collapse; *Hort:* **das Wachstum einer Pflanze b.,** to speed up the growth of a plant, to force a plant. **2. sich beschleunigen,** (*a*) (*of movement, pulse, etc.*) to quicken, to become faster; **ihre Schritte beschleunigten sich,** her steps quickened; (*b*) **durch diesen Vorfall beschleunigte sich ihre Abreise,** this incident hastened her departure.

II. *vbl s.* **1. Beschleunigen,** *n. in vbl senses; also:* acceleration. **2. Beschleunigung,** *f.* (*a*)=II. 1; (*b*) *Astr: Ph: etc:* acceleration; *Med:* quickening (of pulse); **konstante B.,** constant acceleration.

Beschleuniger, *m.* **-s/-.** *Ch: Atom.Ph: etc:* accelerator.

Beschleunigungsabnahme, *f.* deceleration, negative acceleration; retardation.

Beschleunigungsapparat, *m. Atom.Ph:* accelerating apparatus (for particles).

Beschleunigungshebel, *m. Aut: etc:* accelerator.

Beschleunigungsmesser, *m. Mec:* accelerometer.

Beschleunigungspumpe, *f. I.C.E:* accelerator pump.

Beschleunigungszunahme, *f.* increase of acceleration.

beschleusen, *v.tr. Hyd.E:* to lock (canal, river).

beschließen, *v.tr.* (*strong*) **1.** (*a*) *A:* to enclose, shut in; **die Mauern, welche die Stadt beschließen,** the walls that girdle, encompass, the town; **von Felsen beschlossen,** shut in, enclosed, by rocks; (*b*) **etwas in sich b.,** to contain, comprise, include, embrace, sth.; **dieser eine Satz beschließt alle unsere Probleme in sich, in diesem einen Satz sind, liegen, alle unsere Probleme beschlossen,** this sentence embraces all our problems, sums up all our problems in a nutshell, all our problems are summed up in this one sentence; (*c*) *A. & Dial:* to lock up, to close. **2.** to end, to conclude; to close; **eine Rede mit einem Zitat b.,** to end off, up, to wind up, a speech with a quotation; **er beschloß seine Rede mit einer Würdigung der Verdienste seines Vorgängers,** he closed, concluded, wound up, his speech with an appreciation of the services of his predecessor; **die Feuerwehr beschloß den Zug,** the fire-brigade closed the procession, the fire-brigade brought up the rear in the procession; **seine Tage in Frieden b.,** to end, close, one's days in peace. **3.** (*a*) to resolve, determine (upon), to decide (sth.); **wir haben beschlossen, daß . . .,** we have resolved, decided, that . . ., we have come to the conclusion that . . .; **was ist beschlossen worden?** what has been decided? what has been resolved? **einstimmig beschlossen,** decided unanimously; **die Sache ist beschlossen, es ist beschlossene Sache,** the matter is settled, *F:* fixed up; (*b*) to make up one's mind (to do sth.); to decide (after deliberation) (to do sth.); **ich habe noch nicht beschlossen, was ich tun werde, wie ich antworten werde, ob ich gehen werde,** I have not yet decided what I shall do, what answer I shall give, whether I shall go; **es wurde beschlossen, seine Antwort abzuwarten,** it was decided to await his reply; **der Ausschuß beschloß, diesen Schritt zu autorisieren,** the committee resolved to authorize this step.

Beschließer, *m.* **-s/-,** custodian, keeper, caretaker (of castle, museum, etc.); warder, *A:* turnkey (of prison).

Beschließerin, *f.* **-/-innen,** (woman) keeper, caretaker (of castle, etc.).

beschlossenermaßen, *adv.* as agreed upon, as decided.

Beschluß, *m.* **-schlusses/-schlüsse. 1. unter B.,** (*of thg*) under lock and key, (*of pers.*) in custody. **2. zum, als, B.,** in conclusion; **zum B. möchte ich Sie bitten, dieses nützliche Gerät auch Ihren Freunden zu empfehlen,** to conclude, I would like to ask you to recommend this useful gadget to your friends; **den B. machen,** (i) to conclude (sth.), to bring (sth.) to an end, (ii) to bring up the rear; **die Feuerwehr machte den B. des Zuges,** the fire-brigade closed the procession, the fire-brigade brought up the rear. **3.** resolution, decision; *Jur:* decree, order; act (of parliament); **einen B. fassen,** to come to, arrive at, to make, a decision; to pass, make, a resolution; **den B. fassen, etwas zu tun,** to make a resolution to do sth., to resolve, determine, to do sth.; to make up one's mind to do sth.; **sie konnten zu keinem B. kommen,** they could not come to, arrive at, any decision; **durch B.,** by resolution; by vote; **einstimmiger B.,** unanimous decision; **laut B. des Ausschusses,** in accordance with the committee's decision, resolution.

beschlußfähig, *a.* **b. sein,** to form, have, a quorum; **nicht b. sein,** not to have a quorum.

Beschlußfähigkeit, *f.* presence of a quorum (at meeting); **zur B. erforderliche Zahl anwesender Mitglieder,** quorum.

Beschlußfassung, *f.* passing of a resolution.

beschlußreif, *a.* (*of motion, etc.*) ready to be voted on.

beschlußunfähig, *a.* **b. sein,** not to have a quorum.

Beschlußunfähigkeit, *f.* lack of a quorum (at meeting).

beschmaddern, *v.tr. F:* to dirty, smear (one's hands, book, wall, etc.).

beschmeißen, *v.tr.* (*strong*) *P:* = **bewerfen.**

beschmieren, *v.tr.* **1.** (*a*) to smear, coat, cover; **mit Öl b.,** to grease, oil, lubricate; **Brot mit Butter b.,** to butter bread; **mit Teer b.,** to tar, *Nau:* to pay; **mit Pech b.,** to pitch; (*b*) to smear, dirty (one's face, wall, etc.); to soil (one's clothes, etc.) with grease; to scribble, scrawl on (piece of paper, etc.); **mit Dreck beschmiert,** plastered with mud, overlaid with mud; **beschmierte Hände,** dirty, smeary, messy, hands; **mit Tinte beschmierter Tisch,** ink-stained table; (*c*) *Dial. & F:* to diddle, swindle (s.o.). **2. sich beschmieren,** to smear, dirty, oneself, one's clothes, etc.; **er hat sich ganz mit Marmelade beschmiert,** he has smeared himself all over with jam.

beschminken, *v.tr. F:* = **schminken.**

beschmuddeln, *v.tr.* to get (oneself, one's hands, one's clothes, etc.) grubby.

beschmunzeln, *v.tr.* to smile, smirk, at (s.o., sth.).

beschmutzen, *v.tr.* to dirty, soil (oneself, linen, wall, etc.); to dirty (one's hands, plate, book, etc.); to stain, spot (garment, etc.); to splash, bespatter (shoes, etc.) (with mud, etc.); to make (floor, clothes, etc.) dirty; **beschmutztes Kleid,** dirty, bespattered, dress; **sich die Hände b.,** (i) to dirty one's hands, to get one's hands dirty, (ii) to soil one's hands, to lower oneself (by doing sth. degrading); **er beschmutzt sich nicht gern die Hände,** he doesn't like to get his fingers dirty, he doesn't like to work; **ich werde mir damit die Hände nicht b.,** I shall not soil my hands with that, by doing that, I shall have nothing to do with that; **sich b.,** (i) to dirty, soil, oneself, to get oneself dirty, (ii) to soil one's hands, to lower oneself (by doing sth. degrading); **damit, dadurch, wirst du dich nicht b.,** you won't lower, degrade, yourself by doing it, it won't do you any harm to do it; **j-s guten Namen b.,** to drag s.o.'s name in the mud, to stain s.o.'s good name, s.o.'s reputation; **j-s Ehre b.,** to cast aspersions on s.o.'s honour, to tarnish, blemish, s.o.'s honour; *see also* **Nest.**

beschnapsen (sich), *v.refl. F:* to get drunk, tipsy.

beschnarchen, *v.tr. V:* **1. etwas b.,** to meddle with, interfere in (sth.); to poke one's nose into sth.; **alles b., anderer Leute Sachen b.,** to poke one's nose into everything, into other people's business. **2.** = **beschlafen 1.**

beschnattern, *v.tr. F:* (*of pers.*) to gabble, chatter, prattle, about (sth.).

Beschneidehobel, *m.* = **Beschneidemesser.**

Beschneid(e)maschine, *f. Bookb: Paperm: etc:* trimming machine, trimmer; cutting press, guillotine, plough; *Metalw:* shearing machine, shearer, cropper.

Beschneidemesser, *n. Tls:* cutter; clipper; trimmer; plough.

beschneiden. I. *v.tr.* (*strong*) **1.** to cut (down), trim, clip; (*a*) to trim, clip (hair, beard, etc.); to crop (dog's ears, etc.); to crop, dock (horse's tail, etc.); **j-m die Haare b.,** to cut, clip, trim, s.o.'s hair; **sich** *dat.* **die Nägel b.,** to cut, trim, one's nails; **einem Vogel die Flügel b.,** to clip the wings of a bird; *F:* **j-m die Flügel, die Krallen, b.,** to clip s.o.'s wings, s.o.'s claws; **einem Pferd, einem Hund, den Schwanz b.,** to dock a horse, a dog, a horse's tail, a dog's tail; (*b*) *Hort: etc:* to cut back, to prune (tree, plant); to cut back, lop (off, away), trim (branches); to cut back, cut down, dress (tree, vinestock, leaving only the stump); to prune (tree-roots); to trim (edges of lawn, etc.); **einen Baum an der Krone b.,** to pollard, poll, top, a tree; **eine Hecke b.,** to clip, trim, a hedge; (*c*) to cut down, trim (paper, etc.); *Print:* to trim, dress (type); *Carp: etc:* to chamfer, trim (piece of wood, block of stone, etc.); *Metalw:* to shear, crop (metal); **eine Münze b.,** to clip a coin; *Bookb:* **ein Buch b.,** to cut, trim (down), the edges of a book; **ein Buch zu sehr, zu stark, b.,** to bleed a book; **die (Seiten-)Ränder b.,** to cut down, trim, crop, the margins of the sheets; **die Buchdeckel b.,** to cut, trim, the boards. **2.** (*a*) to cut down, reduce (salary, expenses, rations, etc.); **die Ausgaben b.,** to curtail, cut down, reduce, expenses; *F:* to axe

expenditure; **j-s Monatswechsel b.**, to cut down, curtail, s.o.'s monthly allowance; (*b*) to restrict (s.o.'s freedom, s.o.'s power, etc.); **j-s Macht b.**, **j-n in seiner Macht b.**, to restrict, limit, lessen, s.o.'s authority. **3.** *Wine-m:* = **verschneiden. 4.** to circumcise (pers.).

II. *vbl s.* **1. Beschneiden,** *n. in vbl senses; also:* (*a*) reduction, curtailment (of expenses, etc.); restriction, limitation (of s.o.'s freedom, s.o.'s authority, etc.); (*b*) circumcision. **2. Beschneidung,** *f.* (*a*)=II. 1; (*b*) circumcision; *Ecc:* **(das Fest der) B. Jesu,** the Circumcision; *B:* **denn wir sind die B.,** for we are the circumcision.

III. *p.p. & a.* **beschnitten,** *in vbl senses; esp.* circumcised (pers.); **die Beschnittenen,** the circumcised.

Beschneidepresse, *f.* = **Beschneid(e)maschine.**

Beschneider, *m.* **-s/-. 1.** trimmer, cutter (of paper, books, sheet iron, etc.); clipper (of coins); shearer (of metal); pruner (of trees, etc.). **2.** circumciser.

Beschneidungsfest, das. *Ecc:* the Circumcision.

beschneien, *v.i.* (*sein*) to become covered with snow; **beschneit,** snow-capped, snow-covered; **beschneites Dach,** snow-covered roof.

beschnippeln, *v.tr.* to cut, snip, bits off (piece of paper, etc.).

Beschnitt, *m.* **-(e)s/.** (*a*) *Paperm: Bookb: etc:* cutting down, trimming (of book, edges, etc.); *Metalw:* shearing, cropping (of metal); (*b*) *Hort: etc:* pruning, cutting back, cutting low (of tree, etc.); trimming, lopping (of branches, etc.); trimming, clipping (of hedge).

beschnitten *see* **beschneiden.**

beschnitzen, *v.tr.* to carve (piece of wood).

beschnüffeln, *v.tr.* (*of dog, etc.*) to sniff at (s.o., sth.); (*of pig, etc.*) to snuffle, snort, at (s.o., sth.); *F:* (*of pers.*) to poke one's nose into (sth.); **sich gegenseitig, einander, b.,** *F:* to size one another up, to give each other the once-over.

beschnuppern, *v.tr.* (*of rabbit, dog, cat, etc.*) to smell, sniff, nose, at (s.o., sth.); **der Hund beschnupperte meine Hand,** the dog sniffed (at) my hand.

bescholten, *p.p. & a.* blemished, tarnished, sullied (reputation, honour, etc.); unsavoury, bad (reputation, character); (pers.) of evil repute.

Bescholtenheit, *f.* bad repute (of s.o., s.o.'s character, etc.).

beschönen, *v.tr.* = **beschönigen.**

beschönigen. I. *v.tr.* to make (sth.) appear less ugly; to put (sth.) in a favourable light; **seine Handlungen b.,** to varnish, gloss over, put a good face on, one's actions; **die Wahrheit b.,** to gloss, camouflage, disguise, the truth; to put a gloss on the truth; **j-s Fehler zu b. suchen,** to try to cover up, to gloss over, s.o.'s faults; **die Tatsachen b.,** to gloss (over), disguise, the facts.

II. *vbl s.* **1. Beschönigen,** *n. in vbl senses.* **2. Beschönigung,** *f.* (*a*)=II. 1; **ohne B.,** without glossing over anything, without any regard for Mrs Grundy; (*b*) gloss, cover, disguise, varnish; **komme mir nicht mit Beschönigungen,** don't try to gloss over anything, don't try to put a gloss on anything.

Beschores [bəˈʃoːrəs], *m.* **-/.** *Yiddish:* illegal profit.

beschottern. I. *v.tr. Civ.E:* to metal, macadamize (road); *Rail:* to ballast (track).

II. *vbl s.* **1. Beschottern,** *n. in vbl senses; also:* macadamization (of road). **2. Beschotterung,** *f.* (*a*)=II. 1; (*b*) macadam, (road) metal; *Rail:* ballast.

beschränkbar, *a.* restrictable, limitable.

beschranken, *v.tr.* to provide (level crossing, etc.) with gates; **beschrankter Bahnübergang,** guarded, gated, level crossing.

beschränken. I. *v.tr.* to limit; to restrict, to confine; to set bounds, limits, to (s.o.'s power, rights, etc.); **seine Ansprüche b.,** to limit one's requirements; **seine Ausgaben auf das Notwendigste b.,** to limit one's expenses to the essential; **ihr Wirkungskreis ist beschränkt auf . . .,** their sphere of activity is limited to . . .; **sich auf . . . b.,** to limit, confine, oneself to . . .; **sich auf das Notwendigste b.,** to limit oneself to the essential necessities, to the essentials; **sich darauf b., etwas zu tun,** to confine oneself to doing sth.; **sich in seinem Studium auf ein Gebiet b.,** to confine one's studies to one field; **ich muß mich darauf b., Ratschläge zu erteilen,** I am restricted to advising; **ein Dichter, der sich darauf beschränkt, die Alten nachzuahmen,** a poet who confines himself to imitation of the ancients; **nur beschränkte Mittel zur Verfügung haben,** to have only limited resources; **in beschränkten Verhältnissen leben,** to live in straitened circumstances; *Com:* **Gesellschaft mit beschränkter Haftung,** limited (liability) company; **beschränkte Absatzmöglichkeiten,** limited market; **beschränkte Anzahl von Plätzen, Personen, usw.,** limited number of seats, persons, etc.; **der Saal faßt nur eine beschränkte Anzahl von Personen,** the hall holds only a limited number of people, the hall has only a limited seating capacity; *Publ:* **beschränkte Auflage,** limited edition; **beschränktes Fassungsvermögen,** limited capacity; **beschränkte Intelligenz,** limited intelligence; **beschränkter Horizont,** limited horizon.

II. *vbl s.* **1. Beschränken,** *n. in vbl senses; also:* limitation, restriction (of expenses, resources, s.o.'s power, etc.). **2. Beschränkung,** *f.* (*a*)=II. 1; **B. der Ausgaben,** restriction of expenditure; (*b*) limitation, restriction; **j-m gewisse Beschränkungen auferlegen,** to set, impose, certain restrictions on s.o.

III. *p.p. & a.* **beschränkt,** *in vbl senses; esp.* (*of pers.*) (i) of limited intelligence, (ii) of restricted outlook, of limited views; narrow-minded; **er ist außerordentlich b., er ist ein außerordentlich beschränkter Mensch,** he is (i) of very limited intelligence, (ii) of very restricted outlook; **beschränkte Leute,** people of limited views, narrow-minded people.

Beschränktheit, *f.* (*a*) mental restriction, limitation; limited intelligence; obtuseness, stupidity; (*b*) narrowness of outlook; **die B. seiner Ansichten,** his narrow-mindedness.

beschreibbar, *a.* describable.

beschreiben. I. *v.tr.* (*strong*) **1.** to write on (piece of paper, etc.); **das Papier ist ganz beschrieben,** the paper is covered with writing, is written all over. **2.** to describe, to give a description, an account; **j-n, etwas, ausführlich b.,** to describe s.o., sth., in detail, to give a detailed description of s.o., sth.; **die Szene läßt sich mit Worten nicht b., ist mit Worten nicht zu b., Worte können die Szene nicht b.,** words cannot describe the scene; **seine Reise b.,** to give an account of one's journey; **beschreibende Geometrie, Botanik, usw.,** descriptive geometry, botany, etc.; **beschreibendes Verzeichnis,** descriptive catalogue. **3.** to describe (circle, curve, etc.); (*a*) *Geom: etc:* **einen Kreis um ein Vieleck b.,** to describe, draw, a circle about a polygon; (*b*) **der Weg beschreibt einen Bogen um das Schloß,** the road curves, sweeps, round the castle; **im dichten Nebel hatten wir einen Kreis beschrieben,** in the dense fog we had gone round in, described, a circle; **die Flugzeuge beschrieben Kreise über uns,** the planes circled overhead; **die Planeten beschreiben ihre bestimmten Bahnen,** the planets describe, follow, their ordained, set, paths.

II. *vbl s.* **1. Beschreiben,** *n. in vbl senses; also:* description. **2. Beschreibung,** *f.* (*a*)=II. 1; (*b*) description (of pers., building, lost article, etc.); account (of incident, journey, etc.); **eine lebenswahre B. von j-m geben,** to give a true description of s.o.; **eine genaue B. des Verbrechers wurde veröffentlicht,** an exact description of the criminal was circulated; **B. eines Autos,** description of a car, particulars of a car; **B. der Erde,** description of the earth, (descriptive) geography; **B. einer Reise,** account, report, of a journey; **es war über alle B. schön,** it was beautiful beyond description; **nach seiner eigenen B.,** by his own account; **seiner B. nach, war es ein schwerer Unfall,** by his account of it, the accident was serious; **der B. entsprechen,** to answer to the description; **es spottet jeder B.,** it is beyond all description, it defies, *F:* beggars, all description; (*c*) description (of circle, curve, etc.).

Beschreiber, *m.* **-s/-,** describer.

Beschreibungstalent, *n.* descriptive talent.

beschreien, *v.tr.* (*strong*) **1.** *A:* = **verschreien. 2. etwas b.,** to tempt providence by praising sth.; **bisher haben wir noch keinen einzigen Unfall gehabt, — man soll es nicht b.!** so far we haven't had a single accident,—touch wood!

Beschreikraut, *n. Bot:* **1.** (*a*) erigeron, flea-bane; **echtes B.,** blue flea-bane; **kanadisches B.,** Canadian flea-bane, butter-weed; (*b*) spikenard, flea-bane; (*c*) ploughman's spikenard; (*d*) greater flea-bane, common flea-bane; (*e*) groundsel. **2.** baneberry, herb Christopher. **3.** dead-nettle. **4.** (*a*) pale annual woundwort; (*b*) hedge-woundwort.

beschreiten, *v.tr.* (*strong*) (*a*) to walk on, go along (road, etc.); **ein kaum beschrittener Pfad,** a little-used path; **ein viel beschrittener Weg,** a much-trodden path; **in seiner Arbeit hat er ganz neue Wege beschritten,** he has trodden new paths in his work; **den Rechtsweg b.,** to take, begin, legal proceedings, to go to court, to law; (*b*) *Lit:* **das Ehebett b.,** to ascend the nuptial couch.

beschriebenermaßen, *adv.* as described.

beschriften. I. *v.tr.* to mark (sth.) with letters, to letter, inscribe (sth.); to caption (illustration, etc.); *Com: Jur: etc:* to classify, number, letter (documents, etc.); to cut (wax stencils); **Lichtbilder b.,** to inscribe photographs.

II. *vbl s.* **1. Beschriften,** *n. in vbl senses; also:* inscription (of photographs, etc.); classification (of documents, etc.). **2. Beschriftung,** *f.* (*a*)=II. 1; (*b*) inscription (on photograph, etc.); classification, number, letter (on document, etc.); caption (of illustration).

beschroten, *v.tr. Carp: Metalw: etc:* to trim, cut down; to remove rough edges from (sth.).

beschuhen. I. *v.tr. Tchn:* to tip (sth.) with metal; to shoe (pile, etc.); *Farr:* **ein Pferd b.,** to shoe a horse; **beschuht,** (pers.) wearing shoes; ferruled, iron-shod (stake, etc.).

II. *vbl s.* **1. Beschuhen,** *n. in vbl senses.* **2. Beschuhung,** *f.* (*a*)=II. 1; (*b*) footwear, shoes; *Tchn:* shoe (of pile, etc.).

beschuldbar, *a.* accusable (of), chargeable (with) (crime, etc.).

beschuldigen. I. *v.tr.* to accuse (s.o. of sth., of doing sth.); **j-n eines Verbrechens, eines Vergehens, b.,** to accuse s.o. of a crime, of an offence; to indict s.o. for a crime; to charge s.o. with a crime, with an offence; to (in)criminate, inculpate, s.o.; to tax s.o. with an offence; **j-n der Feigheit b.,** to accuse s.o. of cowardice; **j-n fälschlich b.,** to accuse s.o. wrongfully; **sie beschuldigten sich gegenseitig,** they accused each other; **des Diebstahls beschuldigt,** accused of, charged with, theft; under a charge of theft; **er leugnet die Taten ab, deren man ihn beschuldigt,** he denies the actions of which he is accused; **der, die, Beschuldigte,** the accused.

II. *vbl s.* **1. Beschuldigen,** *n. in vbl senses; also:* accusation; (in)crimination; inculpation. **2. Beschuldigung,** *f.* (*a*)=II. 1; (*b*) accusation; indictment, charge; inculpation; imputation; **eine B. gegen j-n vorbringen, erheben,** to raise, bring, an accusation, to make, bring, a charge, against s.o.; **Beschuldigungen gegen j-n schleudern,** to hurl accusations against s.o.; **falsche B.,** false accusation; *Jur:* malicious prosecution.

Beschuldiger, *m.* **-s/-,** accuser, indicter.

beschulen, *v.tr.* to provide (village, etc.) with a school.

beschummeln, *v.tr. F:* to diddle, cheat, bamboozle (s.o.); **da kann man leicht beschummelt werden,** one can easily be cheated, *F:* had, there.

Beschummler, *m.* **-s/-.** *F:* diddler, cheater, cheat; twister.

beschuppt, *a. Nat.Hist: etc:* covered with scales; scaly.

Beschuß, *m.* **-schusses/. 1.** test-firing (of gun, etc.). **2.** *Mil: etc:* fire; shelling, bombardment, cannonade (of ship, fort, etc.); **unter B. sein,** to be under fire; **unter feindlichem B.,** under the enemy's fire. **3.** *Ven:* bag.

Beschußanstalt, *f.* gun testing station.

beschütten, *v.tr.* to throw (sand, water, etc.) on, over (s.o., sth.); **einen Deich mit Erde b.,** to cover a dike with earth; **j-n, etwas, mit Wasser b.,** to pour, throw, water over s.o., sth.

beschützen, *v.tr.* to protect, shelter, guard, shield (gegen, vor, against, from); **j-n vor einer, gegen eine, Gefahr b.,** to guard s.o. from, against, a danger; **j-n mit seinem eigenen Körper b.,** to shield s.o. with one's own body; **seine Heimat b.,** to defend one's country; **mögen die Engel dich b.!** angels guard thee!

Beschützer, *m.* **-s/-,** (*a*) protector, guardian, shield; defender; **B. des Glaubens,** defender of the faith; (*b*) patron.

Beschützerin, *f.* **-/-innen,** (*a*) protectress; (*b*) patroness.

beschwänzt, *a.* having a tail; *Nat.Hist:* caudate, tailed.

beschwatzen, beschwätzen, *v.tr.* **1.** to talk, gossip, about (sth., s.o.). **2. j-n b.,** to talk s.o. into (sth., doing sth.); to talk s.o. round to (sth.); **sie werden ihn nicht dazu b. können, er wird sich von ihnen nicht dazu b. lassen, es anzunehmen,** they will not persuade him into accepting; **laß dich nicht von ihnen b.,** don't let them talk you into it, don't let them persuade you; **endlich habe ich sie doch b. können,** I talked them round at last.

beschwefeln, *v.tr. Hort: etc:* to spray, treat (trees, etc.) with sulphur.

beschweißen, *v.tr.* **1.** to make (sth.) wet with sweat. **2.** *Ven:* (*of wounded animal*) to leave blood on (track, etc.); **beschweißte Fährte,** track with blood.

Beschwer, *n.* **-(e)s/.** & *f.* **-/.** = **Beschwerde** 1.

Beschwerde, *f.* **-/-n. 1.** burden, inconvenience; difficulty; *Med:* complaint; **die Beschwerden des täglichen Lebens,** the difficulties of daily life; **es tut mir leid, daß ich dir so viele Beschwerden machen muß,** I am sorry to cause you so much inconvenience, I am sorry to be such a burden to you; **Beschwerden des Alters,** inconveniences of old age; **es macht mir Beschwerden, die Treppe hinaufzugehen,** I have difficulty in climbing the stairs; **in letzter Zeit habe ich gar keine Beschwerden mehr gehabt,** I have not had any trouble at all lately; **beim Atmen Beschwerden haben,** to have difficulty in breathing; **mit dem Magen Beschwerden haben,** to have, suffer from, a stomach complaint, *F:* to have stomach trouble. **2.** (*a*) complaint; **gegen, über, j-n, etwas, B. führen,** to lodge, make, a complaint against, about, s.o., sth., to complain against, about, s.o., sth.; **bei j-m B. einlegen,** to lodge a complaint with s.o.; **ich habe keinen Grund zur B.,** I have no cause for complaint, I have nothing to complain of; **in letzter Zeit sind mehrere Beschwerden eingelaufen,** several complaints have reached us recently, there have been several complaints recently; (*b*) *Jur:* objection (to court order, procedure, etc.).

Beschwerdeamt, *n. Adm: Com:* Complaints Office.

Beschwerdebuch, *n.* complaints book.

Beschwerdebüro, *n. Adm: Com:* Complaints Office.

beschwerdeführend, *a.* **beschwerdeführende Partei,** complaining party, complainant; *adv.* **sich b. an j-n wenden,** to lodge a complaint with s.o.

Beschwerdeführer, *m.* person who lodges a complaint; complainer, *Jur:* complainant.

Beschwerdeführung, *f.* lodging of a complaint, complaining.

Beschwerdegegenstand, *m.* subject, matter, of complaint.

Beschwerdegrund, *m.* reason, ground(s), for (a, the) complaint.

Beschwerdeheft, *n. Sch:* book for complaints about a pupil's conduct.

beschwerdelos, *a.* free from illness *or* pain; **in den letzten drei Monaten war er völlig b.,** in the last three months he has had no pain, no trouble, at all.

Beschwerdelosigkeit, *f.* freedom, relief, from pain, etc.; **vollständige B.,** complete freedom from all pain.

Beschwerdepunkt, *m.* point of complaint.

Beschwerdeschrift, *f.* (written) complaint.

Beschwerdesumme, *f. Jur:* value of the subject of complaint.

Beschwerdeweg, *m. Jur: etc:* **den B. beschreiten, einschlagen,** to lodge a (formal) complaint.

beschweren. I. *v.* **1.** *v.tr.* (*a*) to weight, load (sth.); to make (sth.) heavy; to weight (fishing-net, etc.); to lead (fishing-line, etc.); to ballast (balloon, ship, etc.); *Paperm:* to load, weight (paper pulp); *Ser:* to weight (silk); *Tex:* to dress, finish, stiffen (fabrics); **lose Blätter, Briefe, b.,** to weight (down) loose sheets, letters (with a paper-weight); **ein Dach mit Steinen b.,** to weight a roof with stones; **ein Lot mit Blei b.,** to lead a plumb-line; *Paperm:* **beschwertes Papier,** loaded, weighted, paper; (*b*) to burden (s.o., one's memory, etc.); **sein Gedächtnis mit nutzlosen Tatsachen b.,** to burden, clog, one's memory with useless facts; **j-m das Herz b.,** to make s.o.'s heart heavy; **das beschwert sein Gewissen nicht,** that won't weigh, lie, on his conscience, he won't have a bad, guilty, burdened, conscience because of that. **2. sich beschweren,** to complain, to lodge a complaint; **sich über etwas b.,** to complain against, about, sth., to protest against sth., to grumble about sth.; **sich darüber b., daß . . .,** to complain that . . .; **er beschwerte sich darüber, daß er nicht pünktlich bezahlt würde,** he complained that he was not paid on time; **sich über das Essen b.,** to grumble about, over, to complain about, the food; **ich kann mich nicht b.,** I cannot complain, grumble, I have nothing to complain of, I have no cause for complaint; **sich über j-n b.,** to complain about, against, s.o., to lodge, make, a complaint against s.o.; **sich bei j-m b.,** to lodge a complaint with s.o.

II. *vbl s.* **1. Beschweren,** *n. in vbl senses.* **2. Beschwerung,** *f.* (*a*) = II. 1; (*b*) weight, sinker (of fishing-net, etc.); lead (of fishing-line, plumb-line, etc.); ballast (of balloon, ship, etc.); (*c*) = **Beschwerde.**

III. *p.p. & a.* **beschwert,** *in vbl senses; esp. Jur:* **Beschwerte** *m, f,* trustee (under a will).

Beschwerer, *m.* **-s/-,** paper-weight; weight, sinker (of fishing-net, etc.).

beschwerlich, *a.* wearisome, tedious, tiring, tiresome; trying; arduous; **eine beschwerliche Reise,** a tedious, tiring, wearisome, trying, journey; **beschwerlicher Aufstieg,** arduous, tiring, ascent; **eine beschwerliche Arbeit,** a wearisome, tiresome, tiring, task; (*of pers.*) **j-m b. fallen,** to be a burden, an inconvenience, *F:* a nuisance, to s.o.; to inconvenience s.o.; **das Gehen ist mir sehr b.,** I find walking very tiring.

Beschwerlichkeit, *f.* (*a*) wearisomeness, tediousness, tiresomeness; arduousness; **die B. der Reise,** the tediousness of the journey; (*b*) burden; inconvenience; **j-m Beschwerlichkeiten machen, verursachen,** to be a burden, *F:* a nuisance, to s.o., to cause inconvenience, to be an inconvenience, to s.o.; **ich verursache Ihnen viele Beschwerlichkeiten,** I am putting you to a lot of inconvenience; **Beschwerlichkeiten bereitwillig auf sich nehmen,** to accept inconveniences willingly, cheerfully.

Beschwernis, *n.* **s-nises/-nisse** = **Beschwerde** 1.

beschwichtigen. I. *v.* **1.** *v.tr.* to appease, calm, soothe, pacify (s.o.); **er versuchte, die erregte Frau zu b.,** he tried to calm (down), soothe, quiet, the excited woman, he tried to allay the woman's excitement; **eine aufständische Volksmenge b.,** to calm, pacify, a rebellious crowd, a crowd in revolt; **ein weinendes Kind b.,** to quiet, hush, a crying child; **j-s Zorn, j-s Ärger, b.,** to calm, soothe, s.o.'s temper, s.o.'s anger; **seinen Hunger b.,** to appease one's hunger; **j-s Sorgen, j-s Angst, b.,** to still, allay, s.o.'s sorrows, s.o.'s fears; **sein Gewissen b.,** to quiet(en), soothe, calm, one's conscience; **ich tat es, um mein Gewissen zu b.,** I did it for conscience sake; **sein beschwichtigender Einfluß,** his calming, soothing, influence; **er sprach ihr beschwichtigend zu,** he spoke soothingly to her. **2. sich beschwichtigen,** to calm down, to grow quiet; (*of storm, waves, excitement, etc.*) to subdue, abate, calm (down).

II. *vbl s.* **1. Beschwichtigen,** *n. in vbl senses.* **2. Beschwichtigung,** *f.* (*a*) = II. 1; *also:* appeasement, pacification; **ich tat es zur B. meines Gewissens,** I did it for conscience sake; (*b*) soothing, calming, word *or* gesture; **seine Beschwichtigungen waren erfolglos,** his soothing words had no effect.

Beschwichtigungspolitik, *f.* appeasement policy.

beschwindeln, *v.tr.* (*a*) to tell (s.o.) a tall story, a fib, a lie; **er beschwindelt uns,** he's telling us fibs; (*b*) to diddle, bamboozle, cheat (s.o.); **j-n um zwanzig Mark b.,** to diddle, do, s.o. out of, *F:* to sting s.o. for, twenty marks; **du bist beschwindelt worden,** you've been bamboozled, cheated, done, *F:* stung; **mich könnt ihr nicht b.,** you can't diddle, bamboozle, me.

beschwingen, *v.tr.* (*weak*) (*a*) to quicken (s.o.'s steps, etc.) *Lit:* **die Erwartung, die Sehnsucht, beschwingte seine Schritte,** expectation, longing, lent him wings, winged his steps; **beschwingten Schrittes, beschwingten Fußes,** swift of foot; (*b*) to elate, elevate, exhilarate (s.o., s.o.'s spirit, etc.); **große Gedanken beschwingten seine Seele,** great thoughts raised, elevated, ennobled, his soul; **beschwingt sein,** to be, feel, elevated, elated, exhilarated; to walk on air; **beschwingten Geistes,** elevated in mind; **beschwingte Gedanken,** elated, elevated, thoughts.

beschwipsen (sich), *v.refl. F:* to get tipsy, fuddled; **beschwipst sein,** to be slightly drunk, tipsy, fuddled.

beschwören. I. *v.tr.* (*conj. like* **schwören**) **1.** to swear to (sth.); to take an oath on, to (sth.); *Jur:* **seine Aussage (vor Gericht) b.,** to take the oath on one's evidence; **ein Bündnis b.,** to swear to an alliance; **ich würde es b.,** I would swear to it, I would take my oath on it, to it; **wir hätten (es) b. können, daß wir Schreie hörten,** we could have sworn (to it that) we heard cries; **ich könnte (es) nicht b., daß er es war,** I could not swear to it that it was he, *F:* him. **2.** (*p.t. usu.* **beschwor**) to command (spirits, etc.); to charm (snake, etc.); **Geister b.,** (i) to conjure (up), raise, summon, invoke, call up, (ii) to lay, spirits; **die Seelen der Toten b.,** to call up the souls of the dead; **den Sturm b.,** to dispel the storm; **ein Platz, der alte Erinnerungen beschwört,** a spot that conjures up old memories. **3.** (*p.t. usu.* **beschwor**) **j-n b., etwas zu tun,** to implore, entreat, beseech, *Lit:* adjure, conjure, s.o. to do sth.; **sie beschworen ihn zu bleiben,** they implored, entreated, begged, him to stay; **laß mich allein, ich beschwöre dich!** leave me alone I implore, beseech, you! **sie beschwor ihn, ihr zu helfen,** she implored, begged, him to help her; **er sah sie beschwörend, mit einem beschwörenden Blick, an,** he gave her an imploring, a beseeching, look, he gave her a look of entreaty.

II. *vbl s.* **1. Beschwören,** *n. in vbl senses; also:* conjuration (of spirits, etc.). **2. Beschwörung,** *f.* (*a*) = II. 1; (*b*) incantation, conjuration, magic formula, charm; **Beschwörungen murmeln,** to mumble incantations; **wilde Beschwörungen,** wild incantations; (*c*) *usu. pl.* **Beschwörungen,** entreaties, beseeching; **er war taub gegen alle ihre Beschwörungen, alle ihre Beschwörungen rührten ihn nicht,** he was deaf to all her entreaties; **auf seine dringenden Beschwörungen,** at his urgent entreaty.

Beschwörer, *m.* **-s/-,** (*a*) incantator, enchanter, *A. & Lit:* conjurer (of spirits, etc.); (*b*) snake-charmer.

Beschwörungsformel, *f.* incantation, conjuration; magic formula, charm.

Beschwörungskunst, *f.* incantation, conjuration, magic.

beseelen. I. *v.* **1.** *v.tr.* (*a*) (*of God, etc.*) to breathe life into (body); to endow (man) with a living soul; to quicken (s.o.); **beseelte Wesen,** beings with a living soul; **Völkerstämme, die sich alle Dinge in der Natur beseelt vorstellen,** tribes who attribute a living soul to all things in nature; **die beseelte Natur,** sentient nature; **beseelende Kraft, beseelendes Prinzip,** animating, quickening, life-giving, power, principle; (*b*) to inspire, animate (s.o., sth.); **von etwas beseelt sein,** to be inspired with sth.; **von neuer Hoffnung beseelt,** inspired with new hope, buoyed up with new hope; **nur von einem Wunsch, von einem Verlangen, beseelt sein,** to be filled, inspired, inflamed, with only one desire; **ihr beseeltes Spiel,** her inspired playing; her playing, imbued with deep feeling; **der Geist, der sein Werk beseelt,** the spirit that breathes through his work; **ihr beseeltes Antlitz,** the warm humanity reflected in her face. **2. sich beseelen,** to come to life, to quicken; **selbst die Natur scheint sich zu b.,** even nature seems to become sentient.

II. *vbl s.* **1. Beseelen,** *n. in vbl senses.* **2. Beseelung,** *f.* (*a*) = II. 1; *also:* inspiration, animation; (*b*) = **Beseeltheit.**

Beseeler, *m.* **-s/-,** giver, instiller, of life; quickener; animator; **Gott, der B. und Beleber,** God, in whom we live and move and have our being.

Beseeltheit, *f.* (*a*) possession of a (living) soul; **B. der Natur,** sentient quality of nature; (*b*) **die B. ihres Spiels,** the feeling in her playing; **die B. der Figuren dieses Künstlers,** the living human quality in the figures of this artist.

besegeln. I. *v.tr. Nau:* **1.** to rig (ship) with sails. **2. die Meere b.,** to sail (on, over) the seas.

II. *vbl s.* **1. Besegeln,** *n. in vbl senses.* **2. Besegelung,** *f.* (*a*) = II. 1; (*b*) sails (of ship); **neue B.,** new suit of sails.

besehen, *v.tr.* (*strong*) **1.** (*a*) to look at (picture, scenery, etc.); (**sich** *dat.*) **etwas genau(er) b.,** to look at, examine, inspect, sth. closely, carefully; **genau(er) besehen,** looked at, inspected, closely; on close(r) inspection; **etwas bei Licht, bei Tage, b.,** to look at, view, sth. in daylight; **sich im Spiegel b.,** to look at oneself in the mirror, in the glass; **ein Stück Stoff, ein Ei, gegen das Licht b.,** to look at a piece of material, an egg, against the light; **von außen besehen, ist das Haus . . .,** looked at from the outside, the house is . . .; **er besah (sich) das Denkmal von allen Seiten,** he looked at, viewed, the monument from all sides; (*b*) *F:* **ich kann ihn nicht b.,** I can't bear the sight of him. **2.** *F:* **etwas b., Prügel b.,** to get a hiding, a licking.

beseichen, *v.tr. V:* to urinate, *P:* to piss, on (sth.).

beseilen. 1. *v.tr. Nau:* to rig (ship) with ropes. **2.** *vbl s.* **Beseilung** *f. Nau:* (*a*) rigging (of ship) with ropes; (*b*) cordage, ropes; gear.

beseitet, *a. Her:* accosted.

beseitigen. I. *v.tr.* (*a*) to remove, clear away (sth.); to remove (dandruff, wrinkles, etc.); to destroy, kill, get rid of (vermin, etc.); to do away with (rule, etc.); to put right, correct (mistake, etc.); to eliminate, remove (source of trouble, mistakes, etc.); **Schutt, Trümmer, b.,** to clear away, remove, rubble, debris; **Hindernisse b.,** to remove, clear away, brush aside, obstacles; **Schwierigkeiten b.,** to smooth away, remove, difficulties; **Schönheitsfehler b.,** to smooth out imperfections; **Fehler in einem verderbten Text b.,** to make emendations in, to emend, amend, a corrupt text; **üble Gerüche b.,** to

dispel, kill, unpleasant odours; **die Ursache eines Streites b.,** to remove the cause of a quarrel; **einen Mißstand, ein Übel, b.,** to cure, remedy, an abuse, an evil; to put a trouble right; (b) **j-n b.,** to make away with s.o., to get rid of s.o., to kill, dispatch, murder, s.o.
II. *vbl s.* **Beseitigen** *n.,* **Beseitigung** *f. in vbl senses; also:* removal (of rubble, obstacle, difficulty, wrinkles, etc.); destruction (of vermin, etc.); correction (of mistake, etc.); elimination (of source of trouble, mistakes, etc.); dispatch, murder (of rival, enemy, etc.); **Haarwasser zur Beseitigung von Schuppen,** hair lotion for the removal of dandruff; **Beseitigung von unangenehmen Gerüchen,** deodorization.
beseligen. I. *v.tr.* to make happy, blissful; **die beseligende Gewißheit, daß . . .,** the blissful certainty that . . .; **beseligt in der Erwartung eines Wiedersehens,** happy, overjoyed, in the expectation of a reunion; **beseligt lächeln,** to wear a beatific smile; to smile blissfully.
II. *vbl s.* **1. Beseligen,** *n. in vbl senses.* **2. Beseligung,** *f.* (a)=II. 1; (b) blissfulness, bliss; happiness.
Besemer ['be:zəmər], *m.* -s/-, **Besemerwaage,** *f.* steelyard.
Besen, *m.* -s/-. **1.** (a) broom, (sweeping) brush; (*made of rush, etc.*) besom; **grober B.,** hard broom, yard broom; **mit eisernem B. kehren,** to rule with a rod of iron; *F:* **ich fresse einen B., wenn das was wird,** I'll eat my hat if it comes off; *Prov:* **neue B. kehren gut,** a new broom sweeps clean; (b) *Paint:* brush (for plastering); (c) *Dom.Ec:* (i) brush whisk; egg-beater, egg-whisk; (ii) saucepan brush, pot-scourer. **2.** *F:* (*woman*) (a) girl; woman; **ein patenter B.,** a good sort; a good sport; (b) battle-axe; dragon; **ein alter B.,** an old battle-axe; **sie ist ein richtiger B.,** she is a real battle-axe, she is a holy terror; (c) (house-)maid; (d) (girl) dancing partner.
Besenbinder, *m.* broom-maker; *A:* **laufen wie ein B.,** to run like a lamplighter, to run like mad.
Besenbinderei, *f.* **1.** broom-making. **2.** broom-maker's workshop.
Besenginster, *m. Bot:* broom.
Besengras, *n. Bot:* purple melic-grass.
Besenheide, *f. Bot:* heather, heath.
Besenkraut, *n. Bot:* **1.** broom. **2.** heather, heath. **3.** Guinea corn, Indian millet, Turkey millet.
Besenpfriem(en), *m. Bot:* broom.
Besenputz, *m. Constr:* rough-cast(ing), rough-coating, rough-rendering; rough coat (of plaster).
besenrein, *a.* swept clean.
Besenreisig, *n.* birch-twigs (for making brooms).
Besenstiel, *m.* broomstick; *F:* **steif wie ein B.,** stiff as a poker; **er geht, als ob er einen B. verschluckt hätte,** he holds himself as straight as a ramrod.
Besenstrauch, *m. Bot:* broom.
Besenwinde, *f. Bot:* broom-bindweed.
besessen, *a.* (a) possessed, dominated (by an evil spirit, etc.); mad; (**vom Teufel) b. sein,** to be possessed with the devil; **ein Besessener,** (i) a man possessed with the devil, a demoniac; (ii) a sufferer from an obsession; **sich wie ein Besessener gebärden,** to behave like one possessed; **wie ein Besessener schreien,** to scream like one possessed; **die Heilung des Besessenen,** the healing of the man possessed with a devil, the healing of the demoniac; (b) infatuated, obsessed, possessed (with an idea, etc.); **von einer Idee (wie) b. sein,** to be obsessed, possessed, with an idea; **von Angst b.,** possessed with fear; **von Zweifeln b.,** possessed with doubts; **er rannte wie b.,** he ran like mad; **du bist wohl b.,** you are surely possessed, you must be mad. *See also* **besitzen.**
Besessenheit, *f.* (a) possession (by, of, the devil, an evil spirit, etc.); madness; (b) obsession (with an idea, etc.); **seine B. geht so weit, daß . . .,** he is obsessed to such an extent that . . .; **man kann ihn von dieser B. nicht heilen, seine B. ist unheilbar,** one can't cure him of this obsession, this obsession of his is incurable.
besetzen. I. *v.tr.* **1.** (a) to occupy (seat, table, car, etc.); **einen Platz im Zug, usw., b.,** to take a seat in the train, etc.; **alle Plätze sind besetzt,** all seats are taken; **dieser Platz ist leider besetzt,** I'm afraid this seat is taken; **ist dieser Platz besetzt?** is this seat taken? **ein mit vier Personen besetztes Auto,** a car with four occupants, with four people in it; **der Autobus ist voll besetzt,** the bus is full up; '**besetzt',** (i) (*of seat, table, etc.*) 'taken', 'engaged', (*of lavatory, etc.*) 'engaged', 'occupied', (*of bus, etc.*) 'full up', (*of hotel*) 'full', (ii) *Tp:* '(line) engaged'; **die Telephonleitung zehn Minuten lang besetzt halten,** to

engage the line for ten minutes; *Th: etc:* **gut besetzte Vorstellung, gut besetztes Theater, voll besetztes Haus,** full, crowded, house, crowded audience; **eine mit köstlichen Speisen besetzte Tafel,** a table laden with delicious things, with good things; (b) to fill (up) (post, etc.); to man (orchestra, etc.); *Mil:* to man, occupy (position, etc.); **ein Amt, eine offene Stelle, b.,** to fill (up) a post, a vacancy; **zwei Stellen sind noch zu b.,** two places remain to be filled; **sie wollen diese Stelle mit einer jüngeren Kraft b.,** they wish to appoint a younger person to this post; *Sch:* **einen Lehrstuhl b.,** to fill a chair; **die Stelle ist schon besetzt,** the post has already been filled; **ein vollständig besetztes Orchester,** a fully-manned orchestra; **voll besetzter Stundenplan,** full, crowded, time-table; *Th:* **eine Rolle b.,** to fill a part; **die Rollen eines Stückes b.,** to cast a play; **das Stück ist sehr gut besetzt,** the play has a very good cast; *Sp:* **ein stark besetztes Rennen, eine stark besetzte Regatta,** a race, a regatta, with many entries, with many competitors; **international besetzte Regatta,** international regatta; *Mil:* **einen (Schützen-)Graben b.,** to man a trench; **eine Festung b.,** to man a fort, to garrison a stronghold, a fort; **ein Geschütz b.,** to man a gun; (c) *Pisc:* to stock (fish-pond); **einen Teich b.,** to stock, fill, a pond (with fry); (d) *Min: etc:* to stem, tamp (blast-hole); *Metall:* to charge (furnace). **2.** *Mil: etc:* to occupy, take possession of (town, fort, heights, etc.); **ein Land besetzt halten,** to keep a country occupied, to keep occupation troops in a country; **vom Feind besetzte Gebiete,** enemy-occupied territory. **3.** to trim, decorate (hat, dress, etc.); to stud (crown, etc.) (with jewels, etc.); **ein Kleid mit einer Borte b.,** to trim, edge, a dress with braid, to braid a dress; **mit Pelz besetzte Jacke,** fur-trimmed jacket; **mit Rubinen besetzter Ring,** ring set with rubies; **mit Diamanten besetzter Schwertgriff,** sword-handle set, studded, with diamonds. **4.** *Civ.E: etc:* to ram down, tamp (paving-stones).
II. *vbl s.* **1. Besetzen,** *n. in vbl senses; also:* (a) engagement (of table, etc.); (b) decoration (of hat, dress, etc.) (with braid, jewels, etc.). **2. Besetzung,** *f.* (a)=II. 1; *also: Mil:* occupation (of town, fort, heights, etc.); **B. feindlichen Gebietes,** occupation of enemy territory; (b) *Th: etc:* cast (of a play); players (of orchestra, etc.); **das Stück wird in erstklassiger B. gegeben,** the play has an excellent cast; *Sp:* **Rennen, Regatta, mit internationaler B.,** international race, regatta; *Fb: etc:* **B. des Angriffs und der Verteidigung,** selection of attackers and defenders; (c) *Locksm:* ward, snap (of lock). *Cp.* **Besatz, Besatzung.**
Besetzplatte, *f. Civ.E: etc:* (paving-)flag; paving-tile.
Besetzramme, *f. Civ.E: etc:* (paving-)beetle, rammer, punner.
Besetzschlegel, Besetzstößel, *m. Civ.E: etc:* (paving-)beetle, rammer, punner.
Besetzteich, *m. Pisc:* breeding-pond, nursery.
Besetztzeichen, *n. Tp:* 'engaged' signal.
beseufzen, *v.tr.* to sigh over, to bemoan (sth., s.o.'s fate, etc.); **sein Geschick, sein Schicksal, b.,** to bemoan one's fate; **sie beseufzte und beweinte den Tod ihres einzigen Sohnes,** she moaned and cried over the death of her only son, she bemoaned the loss of her only son.
Besicht, *m.* -(e)s/-. *A:*=**Besichtigung,** *q.v. under* **besichtigen** II; *see also* **Kauf** 1 (a).
besichtigen. I. *v.tr.* (a) to look round (town, castle, etc.); to visit, look round, go round (museum, factory, etc.); to inspect, look round, go round (school, etc.); **wir wollen morgen Schloß X b.,** we intend to visit, see, the castle of X tomorrow; **London b.,** to go sight-seeing in London, to see the sights of London; **ich würde es gern näher b.,** I should like to inspect it more closely, I should like to get a nearer view of it; **diese Räume können nur an Wochentagen besichtigt werden,** these rooms are on view, are open to the public, on week-days only; *Jur:* **den Tatort eines Verbrechens b.,** to inspect the scene of a crime; (b) to look over (house to be let, articles for auction, etc.); to examine, inspect (goods, etc.); *Nau:* to survey (ship); *Ins: etc:* to inspect (extent of) (damage); to survey, assess (damage); **die Gemälde können in den letzten drei Tagen vor der Auktion besichtigt werden,** the paintings will be on view, will be open to inspection, during the three days preceding the auction; (c) (*of official, etc.*) to inspect (sth.); *Mil:* to inspect, review (troops, etc.); to hold an inspection, a review, of (troops,

etc.); **ein Regiment b.,** to inspect, review, a regiment; **die Truppen, die Flotte, b.,** to review the troops, the fleet.
II. *vbl s.* **1. Besichtigen,** *n. in vbl senses.* **2. Besichtigung,** *f.* (a)=II. 1; *also:* inspection (of school, factory, house to be let, goods, etc.); visit (to castle, museum, etc.); sightseeing (in town, etc.); *Com: etc:* examination (of goods, etc.); *Nau:* survey (of ship); **bei näherer B.,** on close, closer, inspection, examination; **B. eines Museums, usw.,** (i) visit to, (ii) looking round, a museum, etc.; **das Schloß wird dem Publikum zur B. geöffnet werden,** the castle will be open to the public; **eine Stadtrundfahrt in London mit B. der wichtigsten Denkmäler,** a sightseeing tour of London taking in the most important monuments; **drei Tage vor der Auktion werden die Gegenstände zur B. freigegeben,** the articles will be on view, will be open to inspection, during the three days preceding the auction; *Com: etc:* **bei B. der gelieferten Waren wurden erhebliche Beschädigungen festgestellt,** an examination of the goods delivered revealed extensive damage; *Nau:* **eine B. ausführen,** to carry through a survey; *Jur:* **B. des Tatortes eines Verbrechens,** inspection of the scene of a crime; (b) *Mil:* inspection, review (of troops, etc.); **eine B. abhalten,** to hold an inspection, a review; **Befehl zur B.,** inspecting order.
Besichtiger, *m.* -s/-, inspector (of factory, school, goods, etc.); examiner (of goods); *Nau:* surveyor (of ship).
Besichtigungsbericht, *m.* inspector's report.
Besichtigungsfahrt, *f.* sight-seeing excursion.
Besichtigungsoffizier, *m. Mil:* inspecting officer.
Besichtigungsreise, *f.* tour of inspection.
Besichtigungsrunde, *f.* tour of inspection; round, tour (of official, etc.); **der Inspektor macht seine B.,** the inspector is on his round.
Besichtigungstour, *f.* sightseeing excursion.
Besichtigungszertifikat, *n. Nau:* certificate of survey.
Besichtigungszeugnis, *n.* certificate of inspection.
besiedeln. I. *v.tr.* to colonize; to settle; to people, populate; **dicht, stark, besiedelte Gegend,** thickly, densely, populated district; **dünn besiedelt,** thinly populated, thinly peopled.
II. *vbl s.* **1. Besiedeln,** *n. in vbl senses.* **2. Besiedelung,** *f.* (a)=II. 1; *also:* colonization, settlement (of region); (b) (*being populated*) **dichte, dünne, B.,** dense, sparse, settlement of population; **auf B. wartendes Land,** land awaiting settlement.
Besied(e)lungsplan, *m.* settlement project.
Besiedlung, *f.*=**Besiedelung,** *q.v. under* **besiedeln** II.
besiegbar, *a.* conquerable, vanquishable.
besiegeln. I. *v.tr.* to seal (pact, alliance, etc.); to set one's seal on (contract, etc.); to confirm (friendship, etc.); **ein Versprechen mit einem Kuß, mit einem Handschlag, b.,** to confirm, seal, a promise with a kiss, with a handshake; **sein Schicksal, sein Geschick, ist besiegelt,** his fate is sealed; **sein Untergang ist besiegelt,** his doom is sealed.
II. *vbl s.* **1. Besiegeln,** *n. in vbl senses; also:* confirmation (of friendship, etc.). **2. Besiegelung,** *f.* (a)=II. 1; (b) **ein Kuß als B. eines Versprechens,** a kiss as the seal of a promise.
besiegen. I. *v.tr.* (a) to defeat, conquer, vanquish, worst (adversary); to get the better of (s.o.); to defeat, rout, overthrow (army, etc.); to outdo, beat (rival); *Sp: etc:* to beat, defeat, *F:* lick (s.o., team, etc.); **den Feind b.,** to beat, defeat, the enemy; **j-n im Schach(spiel) b.,** to beat s.o. at chess; **j-n haushoch b.,** to beat s.o. hollow; **sich für besiegt erklären,** to admit oneself beaten, *F:* to throw up the sponge, to throw in one's hand; **besiegt werden,** to be beaten, defeated, conquered, vanquished, (*in a fight, etc.*) to be worsted, to get the worst of it; **der Besiegte,** the defeated, conquered, vanquished, *Sp: etc:* the loser; **die Sieger und die Besiegten,** the conquerors and the conquered, *Sp: etc:* the winners and the losers; (b) to overcome, master, conquer, fight down, vanquish, get the better of (feelings, passions, etc.); to conquer, master (one's, s.o.'s, will, etc.); to overcome (prejudices, etc.); **seine Gefühle, seine Leidenschaften, b.,** to master one's feelings, one's passions; **j-s Widerstand b.,** to overcome s.o.'s resistance; **seine Großmut hat mich besiegt,** I was won over by his generosity.
II. *vbl s.* **Besiegen** *n.,* **Besiegung** *f. in vbl senses; also:* defeat.
Besieger, *m.* -s/-, conqueror, vanquisher; *Sp: etc:* winner.

Besieglung, *f.*=Besiegelung, *q.v. under* besiegeln II.

Besigue, Besik [bə-, beˑˈziːk], *n.* -/s. *Cards:* bezique.

Besing, *m.* -s/-e. *Bot:* bilberry, whortleberry.

besingen, *v.tr.* (*strong*) (*a*) to write a song about, to (s.o., sth.); to sing of (s.o., sth.); (*b*) to sing, sound, the praises of, to extol (s.o., sth.); **j-s Vorzüge b.,** to praise, extol, the merits of s.o.; **die Schönheit eines Landes b.,** to extol the beauty of a country; **das viel besungene Venedig,** Venice, much praised, much honoured, in song; **der viel besungene Held,** the much lauded hero.

besinnen (sich). I. *v.refl.* (*strong*) **1.** to think about, consider (sth.); **ich muß mich erst ein wenig b.,** I shall have to think about it, consider it, first; I shall have to give some thought to it; **sie besann sich eine Weile, dann folgte sie ihm,** she thought for a moment, she considered a moment, then she followed him; **bevor er sich b. konnte, bevor er sich recht besonnen hatte,** before he had time to think, before he had time to collect his thoughts; **sich anders, sich eines anderen, b.,** to change one's mind, one's opinion; **sich eines Besseren b.,** to think better of sth.; **er hat sich eines Besseren besonnen,** he has thought better of it, he has come round; **ohne sich lange zu b., lief sie ihm nach,** without thinking twice, without a moment's thought, she ran after him. **2.** to remember, think of (s.o., sth.); **ich kann mich nicht auf seine Adresse b.,** I cannot remember, think of, his address; **besinne dich doch!** try to remember! try and think! **ich besinne mich (darauf), es gesehen zu haben,** I remember seeing it; **ich besinne mich darauf, ich kann mich darauf b., daß Peter sagte . . .,** I remember Peter saying that . . .; **ich besinne mich, ich kann mich b., daß er eines Tages fortging,** I remember his going away one day, I remember that he went away one day; **ich kann mich im Moment nicht auf seinen Namen b.,** I can't remember, think of, his name for the moment; **wenn ich mich recht besinne,** if I remember correctly; **jetzt besinne ich mich,** I (can) remember now, it's coming back to me now: **sich auf sich selbst b., sich auf seinen Wert b.,** to remember what one owes to oneself, to remember one's dignity; **sich auf seine Pflichten b.,** to remember one's duty; *see also* besonnen[1].

II. *vbl s.* **1. Besinnen,** *n.* consideration (of sth.); reflection (on sth.); **nach längerem B.,** after long consideration, after considerable reflection; **ohne B. sprang er ihr ins Wasser nach,** without thinking, without pausing, he dived into the water after her; **nachdem er ihr die Lage klargemacht hatte, nahm sie seinen Vorschlag ohne langes B. an,** after he had explained the situation to her, she accepted his proposal without hesitating, without hesitation. **2. Besinnung,** *f.* (*a*) **Stunden der B.,** hours of contemplation, meditation; (*b*) consciousness; **bei voller B. sein,** to be fully conscious; **die B. verlieren,** to lose consciousness, to faint; **ohne B.,** unconscious; **die B. wiedererlangen,** to regain consciousness; **trotz der furchtbaren Schmerzen war er immer bei B.,** despite the terrible pains he never lost consciousness, he was always fully conscious; **du bist wohl nicht ganz bei B.,** you must be out of your mind.

besinnlich, *a.* thoughtful, contemplative, meditative (pers., frame of mind, etc.); **besinnliche Stunden,** hours of contemplation, meditation, hours spent in thought; **allerlei Besinnliches über einen Spaziergang im Frühling,** various reflections on taking a walk in spring.

Besinnlichkeit, *f.* thoughtfulness; contemplation, meditation.

besinnungslos, *a.* **1.** unconscious; **b. sein,** to be unconscious, to have lost consciousness. **2.** thoughtless (action, etc.); *adv.* thoughtlessly, without thinking.

Besinnungslosigkeit, *f.* **1.** unconsciousness, loss of consciousness; **sie tranken bis zur B.,** they drank themselves unconscious. **2.** thoughtlessness.

Besitz, *m.* -es/-e. **1.** possession; ownership; *Jur:* possession, occupancy (of land, house, etc.) (*as opposed to ownership*); *Jur:* **tatsächlicher B.,** actual possession; **angenommener, fingierter, B.,** constructive possession; **juristischer B.,** juristical possession, possession in law; **Recht des Besitzes,** right of possession, possessory right; **der B. von Häusern führt viele Verpflichtungen mit sich,** house-property involves many responsibilities; **unerlaubter B. von Feuerwaffen,** illegal possession of firearms; *Fin:* **B. von Aktien,** holding of shares, shareholding; **der B. von Geld allein macht nicht glücklich,** money doesn't always make for happiness; money isn't everything; **im B. einer Sache sein, sich im B. einer Sache befinden,** to own, possess, sth., to be in possession of sth., to have sth. in one's possession; **von etwas B. ergreifen, etwas in B. nehmen,** to take possession of sth.; **in den B. einer Sache kommen,** to get possession of sth.; to come by sth.; **wieder in den B. einer Sache kommen,** to regain, resume, possession of sth.; **im B. einer Sache bleiben,** to remain in possession of sth., to retain possession of, (the) ownership of, sth.; **j-m den B. entziehen,** to dispossess, expropriate, *Jur:* to eject, evict, disseise, s.o.; **j-m den B. einer Sache, an einer Sache, streitig machen,** to dispute s.o.'s ownership of sth.; **die gestohlenen Gegenstände befanden sich in seinem B.,** the stolen articles were (found) in his possession; **wie sind Sie in den B. dieser Uhr gekommen?** how did you come by this watch? **das Gemälde ging aus dem B. des Herrn X in den B. des Herrn Y über,** the painting, formerly owned by Mr X, passed into the possession of Mr Y; **das Schloß wird in seinen B. übergehen,** the castle will come, pass, into his possession; **im B. eines Reisepasses,** in possession of a passport; **wir sind bereits im B. von Angaben über . . .,** we are already in possession of data regarding . . .; **dieses geschickte Manöver brachte ihn in den B. des Gutes,** this clever, cunning, move put him in possession of the estate; **im vollen B. seiner Vernunft,** in full possession of his faculties; **sei im Besitze, und du wohnst im Recht,** possession is nine points of the law. **2.** (*a*) property; possessions; belongings; effects; **sein persönlicher B.,** his personal possessions, belongings, effects; **all unser irdischer B.,** all our worldly goods, our worldly possessions; **mein B. an Geld und Gut,** my worldly possessions; **privater, öffentlicher, B.,** private, public, property; **(Gemälde, usw.) aus dem B. des Grafen X, aus privatem B.,** (painting, etc.) formerly the property of Count X, previously owned by Count X; (painting, etc.) formerly in private ownership; **in privatem B.,** privately owned; **diese Uhr stammt aus dem B. meines Vaters,** this watch used to belong to my father, was one of my father's possessions; **B. an Siemens-Aktien,** holdings in Siemens; (*b*) possession; property; **dieser Sessel ist mein persönlicher B.,** this armchair is my personal property, belongs to me, is my own; **sein stolzester B. ist ein Fahrrad,** his most precious possession is a bicycle; (*c*) (landed) property; estate; **er hat einen kleinen B. auf dem Lande,** he has a small property in the country; **ein ansehnlicher B.,** a large estate; (*d*)=Besitzrecht. *Cp.* besitzen II.

Besitzanspruch, *m.* claim for possession; claim of ownership.

besitzanzeigend, *a. Gram:* possessive (pronoun, adjective).

Besitzdauer, *f.* term (of possession).

Besitzeinweisung, *f.* putting (of new owner) into possession.

besitzen. I. *v.tr.* (*strong*) **1.** (*of hen, etc.*) to sit on (eggs, etc.). **2.** (*a*) to possess, own; to be in possession of (sth.); **damals, als ich noch ein Boot besaß,** in the days when I owned a boat; **alles, was ich besitze,** all I possess, all my belongings, all my possessions; **ein großes Vermögen b.,** to be in possession of a large fortune, to be the possessor of a large fortune; **gewisse Rechte b.,** to possess certain rights; **sie hat immer einen großen Garten besessen,** she has always owned a big garden; **er besitzt zwei Autos,** he possesses, owns, has, two cars; **er besitzt Aktien mehrerer Unternehmungen,** he has holdings in several companies; **die besitzenden Klassen, die Besitzenden,** the propertied classes, the wealthy; (*b*) to possess, have (quality, gift, etc.); **sie besitzt die Gabe, schnell Freunde zu gewinnen,** she has the gift of making friends quickly; **wenn Sie die Freundlichkeit b. würden,** if you would have the kindness, if you would be so kind; **j-s unbedingtes Vertrauen b.,** to have s.o.'s complete confidence; **sie besitzt mein volles Vertrauen,** I trust her implicitly, I have complete confidence in her; **Hunde besitzen einen guten Geruchssinn,** dogs have a keen sense of smell; *F:* (*of pers.*) **eine gute Nase für etwas b.,** to have a good nose for sth.; (*c*) **eine Frau b.,** to possess a woman, to have one's will of a woman. *See also* **besessen.**

II. *vbl s.* **1. Besitzen,** *n. in vbl senses; also:* possession. **2. Besitzung,** *f.* (landed) property; holding, estate; **sein Vater hatte eine große B. in Friesland,** his father had a big estate in Frisia; **seine Besitzungen in Afrika,** his estates in Africa; **er hatte mehrere kleinere Besitzungen in der Normandie,** he had several small holdings in Normandy. *Cp.* **Besitz.**

Besitzentziehung, *f.* dispossession; expropriation; *Jur:* disseizin.

Besitzentziehungsklage, *f. Jur:* action of ejectment.

Besitzer, *m.* -s/-, possessor, owner; proprietor; *Jur:* possessor, occupant, occupier (of land, house, etc.) (*as opposed to proprietor*); **der B. des Hundes,** the owner of the dog; **die Besitzer eines Schiffes,** the owners of a ship; **B. eines Hotels, eines Ladens,** proprietor of an hotel, of a shop; **der B. dieses Gemäldes,** the owner of this painting; **er ist der stolze B. eines Autos,** he is the proud possessor, owner, of a motor-car; **den B. wechseln,** to change hands; **wer ist der B. dieses Grundstücks?** who owns this land?

Besitzergreifer, *m.* occupier, occupant; **widerrechtlicher B.,** usurper.

Besitzergreifung, *f.* taking possession; occupation, occupancy; seizure; *Jur:* entry; **widerrechtlicher B.,** unauthorized assumption of possession; usurpation.

Besitzerrecht, *n.* possessor's, owner's, right *or* privilege.

Besitzerwechsel, *m.* change of ownership; **nach mehrmaligem B. . . .,** after changing hands several times . . .

Besitzerwerb, *m.*=Besitznahme.

Besitzfall, *m. Gram:* genitive, possessive, case.

Besitzfürwort, *n. Gram:* possessive pronoun *or* adjective.

Besitzklage, *f.* -/. *Jur:* action for possession, possessory action.

Besitzkonto, *n. Book-k:* property account.

besitzlos, *a.* without possessions; unpropertied; poor; **die Besitzlosen,** the unpropertied (classes); the poor; **der Neid der Besitzlosen,** the envy of the have-nots.

Besitzlosigkeit, *f.* (situation of) not having any possessions; poverty.

besitzmäßig, *a.* possessory.

Besitznahme, *f.* -/. taking possession, coming into possession.

Besitzrecht, *n.* right of possession, possessory right; (right of) ownership; *Jur:* title; **das B. an einer Sache erwerben,** to gain possession of sth.; **das B. an seinem Gut behalten,** to retain the property in, the ownership of, one's estate.

Besitzsteuern, *f.pl. Adm:* taxes on earned and unearned income.

Besitzstörer, *m. Jur:* trespasser.

Besitzstörung, *f. Jur:* disturbance; molestation; nuisance; *Jur:* trespass.

Besitzstörungsklage, *f. Jur:* action to cease disturbance of possession; action for trespass.

Besitztitel, *m. Jur:* title-deed.

Besitztum, *n.* -(e)s/=er, (*a*) possession; **das wertvollste B. meines Vaters,** my father's most valued possession; (*b*) (landed) property; **die bischöflichen Besitztümer,** the bishop's lands; **königliche Besitztümer,** crown lands, crown estates.

Besitzübernahme, *f.* taking (over) possession.

Besitzübertragung, *f.* transfer (of property).

Besitzung, *f. see* **besitzen II.**

Besitzurkunde, *f. Jur:* title-deed.

Besitzveränderung, *f.* transfer (of property).

Besitzveränderungsabgaben, *f.pl.* transfer duty (on property).

Besitzwechsel, *m.* transfer (of property).

Besitzwechselsteuer, *f.* transfer duty (on property).

Besmer, *m.* -s/-, steelyard.

besoden, *v.tr.* to cover with sods *or* turf; to turf; **besodeter Abhang,** turfed slope, swarded slope.

besoffen *see* **besaufen.**

Besoffenheit, *f. F:* drunkenness, intoxication.

besohlen, *v.tr.* to sole (shoe, etc.); **Stiefel neu b. lassen,** to have boots re-soled; to have new soles put on boots; **-besohlt,** -soled; **dick-, dünn-, gummibesohlt,** thick-, thin-, rubber-soled.

besolden. I. *v.tr.* to pay a salary to (civil servant, etc.); to pay a stipend to (magistrate, clergyman, etc.); to pay (soldier); **besoldete Regierungsstelle,** paid government post.

II. *vbl s.* **1. Besolden,** *n. in vbl senses.* **2. Besoldung,** *f.* (*a*)=II. 1; *also:* payment (of soldiers, civil servants, etc.); (*b*) pay (of soldiers, etc.); salary (of civil servants, etc.); stipend (of magistrate, clergyman, etc.); **die B. im Heer war sehr schlecht,** pay in the army, the soldiers' pay, was very bad.

Besoldungsgruppe, *f.* salary class.

Besoldungsordnung, *f. Mil: Adm:* pay regulations, scales of pay.

Besoldungsstufe, *f.* salary grade.

besömmern, *v.tr. Agr:* to plant (land) with root-crops, clover, etc., in summer only; *see also* **Brache** 1.

besondere(r), besondere, besondere(s), *attrib.a.* **1.** separate; **diese Abteilung ist in einem besonderen Gebäude untergebracht,** this department is housed in a separate building; **der kranke Löwe ist in einem besonderen Käfig,** the sick lion is in a separate cage; **ich habe mir deine Wünsche auf einem besonderen Zettel notiert,** I wrote down your requests on a separate slip of paper. **2.** (*a*) special, particular; **auf besonderen Wunsch,** by, at, special request; *Adm:* (*on passport*) **besondere Kennzeichen,** special peculiarities; **besondere Eigenart,** special feature (of character, etc.); **besonderer Auftrag,** special mission; **besondere Erlaubnis haben,** to have special permission; **das Besondere daran ist . . .,** the special thing about it is . . ., the special feature of it is . . .; (*b*) special, particular, especial; peculiar; **sein besonderer Wunsch war . . .,** his particular wish, his special request, was . . .; **er hat einen besonderen Grund,** he has a special, a particular, reason, he has his own peculiar reason; **besondere Sorgfalt bei etwas anwenden,** to take special, particular, extra, care over sth.; **mein besonderer Freund,** my special, particular, friend; **zu einem besonderen Zweck,** for a special purpose; **ein Kleid für besondere Gelegenheiten,** a dress for special occasions; **Anzug für ganz besondere Gelegenheiten,** suit for extra-special occasions; **ich hege eine besondere Abneigung gegen ihn,** I have a particular dislike for him; **von besonderer Bedeutung,** of (e)special, particular, importance; **von besonderem Interesse,** of special, particular, peculiar, interest; **eine besondere Anstrengung machen,** to make an extra effort; **das ist etwas ganz Besonderes,** that is something very, extra-, special; **etwas ganz Besonderes zum Abendessen haben,** to have something extra-special for dinner; (*c*) out of the ordinary, unusual; special; **mit diesem Ring hat es eine besondere Bewandtnis, hat es etwas Besonderes auf sich,** there are unusual, special, circumstances attached to, there is something special about, this ring; there is a special story about this ring, this ring has a story; **ich habe dir nichts Besonderes zu erzählen,** I have nothing special to tell you; **ich habe nichts Besonderes bemerkt, mir ist nichts Besonderes aufgefallen,** I didn't notice anything unusual, anything out of the ordinary, anything peculiar; **es ist nichts Besonderes,** it is (i) nothing special, particular, (ii) nothing much, nothing serious, (iii) nothing unusual, *F:* nothing to write home about. **3.** *adv.phr.* **im besonderen,** in particular, particularly, (e)specially; **der Einfluß des Klimas und im besonderen der Feuchtigkeit,** the influence of climate and in particular of moisture; *cp.* **besonders.**

Besonderheit, *f.* peculiarity (of s.o., sth.); peculiar nature (of sth.); characteristic; special feature (of a belief, a character, etc.).

besonderlich. 1. *a.*=**sonderlich. 2.** *adv.*= **besonders.**

besonders. 1. *adv.* separately; **Wein wird b. berechnet,** wine is extra. **2.** *adv.* (*a*) in particular, particularly; **beachten Sie b., daß . . .,** notice particularly, in particular, that . . .; **achte b. darauf, zu . . .,** be especially careful to . . .; **er freute sich b. darüber, daß . . .,** he was particularly pleased that . . .; **es war b. sein Humor, der ihn so beliebt machte,** it was above all his sense of humour which made him so popular; **der Einfluß des Klimas und b. der Feuchtigkeit,** the influence of climate and in particular of moisture; **ganz b.,** in particular, above all (*cp.* (*b*)); (*b*) (e)specially, particularly; **b. sorgfältig mit etwas umgehen,** to be especially careful with sth., to take special care of sth.; **(ganz) b. niedriges Auto,** extra-low car; **er ist ein b. freundlicher Mensch,** he is a particularly kind person; **er ist nicht b. reich,** he is not particularly rich; **sie ist nicht b. intelligent,** she is not particularly, outstandingly, intelligent; **etwas b. Gutes zum Abendessen haben,** to have something extra-special for dinner; **es ist nicht b. gut,** *F:* **es ist nicht b.,** it is not particularly, specially, good, it is not outstanding; **ich finde das Haus nicht so b. schön,** *F:* **nicht so b.,** I don't think, find, the house particularly beautiful; I don't think the house is anything special; **b. gern gehe ich nicht,** I don't particularly want to go. **3.** *a. F:* **er ist heute so b.,** he is so strange, so queer, today.

besonnen[1], *a.* circumspect, prudent; deliberate; calm; **ein besonnener Mann,** a man who always keeps his head, his presence of mind, who always keeps calm; **selbst in bedrängter Lage war er immer b.,** he kept calm, he never lost his head, even in an emergency; **ruhig und b.,** calm and collected; **b. handeln,** to act with thought, with care, with deliberation, circumspectly, with circumspection; *see also* **besinnen.**

besonnen[2], *v.tr.* **sich b. lassen,** to lie in the sun, to sun oneself, to sun-bathe; **die besonnte Seite eines Tales,** the sunny side of a valley; **besonnte Terrasse,** terrace steeped in sunshine; **besonnte Hügel,** hills bathed in sunshine; **die besonnte Vergangenheit,** the happy days of long ago.

Besonnenheit, *f.* circumspection, circumspectness; deliberation; prudence; **mit B. handeln**= **besonnen handeln,** *q.v. under* **besonnen**[1]; **seine B. in schwierigen Lagen,** his calmness, his presence of mind, in difficult situations.

besorgen. I. *v.tr.* **1.** to look after, care for (s.o., animals, etc.); to see to (affairs, business, etc.); to execute, carry out (order, etc.); to carry out, do (duty, etc.); **während du fort bist, werde ich die Kinder b.,** I'll look after the children while you are away; **die Tiere müssen auch besorgt werden,** the animals must be looked after, cared for, too; **während seiner Krankheit besorgte sie das Füttern der Tiere,** during his illness she saw to the feeding of the animals; **ich werde die Sache, es, b.,** I shall see to the matter, to it; **es wird alles zu Ihrer Zufriedenheit besorgt werden,** everything will be done to your satisfaction; **wir werden das alles b.,** we shall see to, attend to, do, all that; **es ist alles besorgt,** everything has been done; **er will die Angelegenheit für mich b.,** he will attend to, see to, the matter for me; **die Firma wird auch das Abladen b.,** the firm will also do the unloading; **ich werde das Gepäck b.,** I'll see to the luggage; **ich werde heute das Abwaschen b.,** I will do the washing-up today; **j-m den Haushalt, die Wirtschaft, b.,** to keep house for s.o., *F:* to do for s.o.; **seine Pflichten, die Hausfrauenpflichten, b.,** to attend to one's duties, to the household duties; **sein Geschäft b.,** to attend to, see to, one's business; *F:* **ich werde es ihm schon noch gründlich b.,** I'll pay him back, I'll get my own back on him, I'll get even with him. **2.** to procure, to get; to buy; **j-m etwas b.,** to get, procure, sth. for s.o.; **er hat uns zwei Plätze besorgt,** he got, procured, two seats for us; **ich kann Ihnen ein Zimmer b.,** I can find you, get you, a room; **er wird versuchen, uns Theaterkarten zu b.,** he is going to try to get theatre tickets for us; **die nötigen Mittel müssen wir (uns) irgendwie b.,** we must procure the necessary funds somehow; **der Mann besorgte uns ein Taxi,** the man got us a taxi, got a taxi for us; **die Schuhe habe ich mir in X besorgt,** I bought, got, the shoes in X; **Butter und Eier b.,** to buy butter and eggs; **ich habe heute viel in der Stadt zu b.,** I have a lot to do in (the) town today; **hast du noch etwas zu b.?** have you any more errands to do? is there anything else you have to do? **die Äpfel haben wir uns von einem Bauern besorgt,** we bought the apples from a farmer. **3.** (*a*) *A:* to fear (sth.); **b., daß etwas geschieht, geschehe,** to be afraid, to fear, that sth. might happen; (*b*) *v.impers.* **es ist zu b., daß die gesamte Besatzung des verunglückten Flugzeuges das Leben verloren hat,** it is to be feared that all members of the crew of the crashed plane have lost their lives.

II. *vbl s.* **1. Besorgen,** *n. in vbl senses; also:* execution (of order, etc.); procurement (of tickets, etc.). **2. Besorgung,** *f.* (*a*)=II. 1; *also:* **ich werde es dir zur B. überlassen,** I shall leave you to attend to it, I shall leave the matter to you; (*b*) **eine B. machen,** to do an errand, to go on an errand; to buy sth.; **ich muß einige Besorgungen machen, ich habe einige Besorgungen zu machen,** there are some things I have to do, I have some errands to do; I have some shopping to do.

III. *p.p. & a.* **besorgt,** *in vbl senses; esp.* (*a*) anxious, concerned, worried, apprehensive, uneasy (**um j-n, etwas,** about s.o., sth.); **ein besorgter Blick,** an anxious look; **Baby hat Husten, und das macht mich etwas b.,** baby has a cough and it rather worries me; **du hast keinen Grund, b. zu sein,** you have no cause to worry, no cause for concern; **seid meinetwegen nicht b., ihr braucht meinetwegen nicht b. zu sein,** don't (you) worry about me, you needn't worry about me; **ich bin um seine Gesundheit b.,** I am concerned, anxious, worried, about his health; **er fragte b., ob . . .,** he inquired anxiously, with concern, whether . . .; **um, für, j-n, j-s Sicherheit, b. sein,** to be anxious, afraid, concerned, for s.o., for s.o.'s safety, to fear for s.o., for s.o.'s safety; **er ist immer am meisten um, für, seine persönliche Sicherheit b.,** he is always most afraid, concerned, for his own safety; (*b*) concerned (about s.o., s.o.'s welfare, sth., etc.); solicitous (for s.o., s.o.'s comfort, etc.); **ängstlich darum b. sein, das Rechte zu tun,** to be anxious, to be at great pains, to do the right thing; **er ist darum, dafür, b., mir jede Mühe zu ersparen,** he is careful, anxious, to spare me all trouble; **er war immer zärtlich b. um seine Frau,** he was always full of tender concern for his wife; **ein besorgter Vater,** an anxious father; **er ist sehr b. um seine Mutter,** he has much thought for his mother; **um j-s Wohlergehen b. sein,** to be solicitous for s.o.'s well-being; **seine Wirtin ist sehr b. um, für, sein leibliches Wohl,** his landlady is very, most, concerned for his physical welfare.

Besorger, *m.* -s/-, (*a*) person entrusted with a commission (to provide sth., distribute sth., deliver a message etc.); messenger; (*b*) *Austrian:* caretaker.

besorglich, *a.* disturbing, disquieting, perturbing, alarming (news, situation, etc.).

Besorgnis, *f.* -/-nisse, anxiety, worry; concern; alarm; apprehension, fear; **der Zustand des Kranken gibt Anlaß zur B.,** the patient's condition gives cause for alarm, rise to anxiety; **kein Grund zur B.,** no cause to worry, no cause for alarm, for concern; **die Besorgnisse der Regierung für die Sicherheit des Landes,** the government's fears for the security of the country.

besorgniserregend, *a.* alarming, worrying; **der Zustand des Kranken ist b.,** the patient's condition gives cause for alarm, rise to anxiety.

Besorgtheit, *f.* (*a*) anxiety, worry; alarm; (*b*) solicitude; concern; (tender) care.

Besorgungszettel, *m.* list (of errands, shopping).

bespannen. I. *v.tr.* **1. einen Wagen (mit Pferden) b.,** to harness horses to, to put horses to, a carriage; **einen Ochsenwagen b.,** to yoke oxen to a cart; **mit vier Pferden bespannte Kutsche,** coach drawn by four horses, coach and four; **bespannt,** horse-drawn. **2.** (*a*) to string (violin, tennis-racket, etc.); to hair (violin-bow); *Tex:* to warp (loom); **einen Tennisschläger neu b.,** to re-string a tennis-racket; (*b*) to cover (frame, etc.) (with paper, cloth, etc.); *Av: etc:* to cover (fuselage, etc.) with canvas *or* fabric; **einen Wandschirm mit Leinen b.,** to cover a screen with linen; **die Wände mit Seide b.,** to cover, hang, the walls with silk; **einen Lampenschirm (mit Stoff) b.,** to cover a lampshade; **eine Trommel b.,** to cover the frame of a drum with vellum, to stretch vellum over the frame of a drum. **3.** *Pisc:* to fill (fish-pond) with water.

II. *vbl s.* **1. Bespannen,** *n. in vbl senses.* **2. Bespannung,** *f.* (*a*)=II. 1; (*b*) team (of horses, oxen, etc.); (*c*) strings, stringing (of violin, racket, etc.); *Tex:* warp (of loom); covering (of screen, wall, etc.); lining (of baby's basket, pram, etc.); covering (stretched across sides and ends of cot, brass bed, etc.); (wire-)mesh (of sieve, etc.); *Av: etc:* (fabric) skin, covering (of fuselage, etc.); **B. einer Trommel,** (i) drum parchment, (ii) drum-head.

bespeien, *v.tr.* (*strong*) (*a*) to spit (up)on (s.o., sth.); (*b*) to abuse (s.o.).

bespicken, *v.tr.* (*a*) *Cu:* to lard (piece of meat); (*b*) to stud, spike (sth. with sth.); **mit spitzen Nägeln bespicktes Brett,** board studded with sharp nails, spiked board.

bespiegeln. 1. *v.tr.* (*a*) *occ.*=**spiegeln;** (*b*) to dazzle (s.o.) with a mirror. **2. sich bespiegeln,** (*a*) (*of pers., thg*) to be reflected (as) in a mirror; (*b*) (*of pers.*) **sich (selbst) b.,** to preen oneself, to be full of self-complacency, *F:* to be always slapping oneself on the back.

bespielen, *v.tr.* (*a*) (*of theatre company, etc.*) to perform in, *F:* to play (town, etc.); (*b*) *Mus:* (*of orchestra, pianist, etc.*) **eine Schallplatte b.,** to make a record, a recording; **ein Tonband b.,** to record on a tape; to make a tape-recording; **bespieltes Band,** recorded tape; (*c*) *Bill:* **bespielter Ball,** object ball.

bespinnen, *v.tr.* (*strong*) (*a*) to cover, lap, wrap (wire, etc.) (with silk, cotton, etc.); *El.E: etc:* **mit Baumwolle besponnenes Kabel,** cotton-covered, cotton-lapped, cable; (*b*) **im Herbst sind die Wiesen oft mit feinen Fäden besponnen,** in autumn the meadows are often covered with gossamer.

bespitzeln, *v.tr.* to watch (s.o.), to spy on (s.o.); to have (s.o.) shadowed, watched.

bespötteln. I. *v.tr.* to mock (at), make fun of, ridicule (s.o., sth.); to deride, scoff at, jeer at (s.o., sth.); to make derisive remarks about

(s.o., sth.); to hold (s.o., sth.) up to ridicule; **sie bespöttelten jede seiner Äußerungen,** they ridiculed, jeered at, everything he said.

II. *vbl s.* **1. Bespötteln,** *n. in vbl senses; also:* derision. **2. Bespöttelung,** *f.* (*a*)=II. 1; (*b*) derision, ridicule; mockery; **er hatte sich der B. ausgesetzt,** he had made himself an object of ridicule, of derision, he had laid himself open to ridicule; (*c*) derisive remark.

besprechen. I. *v.tr.* (*strong*) **1.** to cure (disease, etc.) by incantations; **krankes Vieh b.,** to cure sick cattle by magic formulas. **2. eine Schallplatte b.,** to make a recording, a record, of one's voice; to record one's voice; to make a personal recording; **ein Tonband b.,** to record speech, spoken words, on a tape; **besprochenes Band,** recorded tape. **3.** (*a*) to discuss (sth.); to talk (sth.) over; to debate (sth.); **ein Thema b.,** to discuss a subject; **etwas mit j-m b.,** to discuss sth. with s.o., to talk sth. over with s.o.; to have a talk, a discussion, with s.o. on sth.; **wir wollen die Sache b.,** let us discuss the matter, let us talk the matter over; **wir wollen es in Ruhe b.,** let's talk it over quietly; **besprechen Sie die Angelegenheit mit ihm,** discuss the matter with him; **die Frage ist erneut besprochen worden, wurde erneut besprochen,** the question has been debated anew; **viel besprochene Frage,** much discussed, much debated, question; **wir besprechen gerade, wer eingeladen werden sollte,** we are discussing who should be invited; **nähere Einzelheiten werden wir später noch b.,** we will discuss further details later, further details will be discussed later; **ehe wir zum nächsten Punkt übergehen, wollen wir doch diese Angelegenheit zu Ende b.,** before going on to the next item, let us finish discussing this matter; (*b*) to review (book, play, etc.); **das Buch ist mehrmals besprochen worden,** the book has had several reviews. **4. sich mit j-m besprechen,** to confer with s.o., to consult s.o. (**über etwas,** on, about, sth.); **ich möchte mich mit dir gründlich darüber b.,** I want to talk things out with you; **wir haben uns über die Sache besprochen,** we consulted about the matter, we discussed the matter; **die Ärzte besprachen sich miteinander,** the doctors held a consultation. **5.** *F:* **wie der Arzt sagt, kannst du das Krankenhaus nächste Woche verlassen; aber besprich es nicht,** the doctor says you will be able to leave hospital next week—but keep your fingers crossed.

II. *vbl s.* **1. Besprechen,** *n. in vbl senses.* **2. Besprechung,** *f.* (*a*)=II. 1; *also:* discussion (of sth.); **B. einer Frage,** discussion of a question; **nach längerer B. einer Sache,** after much discussion of sth.; (*b*) discussion, talk; debate; conference, consultation; **eine B. abhalten,** to hold a conference; **die Frage wird morgen zur B. kommen,** the question will come up for discussion tomorrow; **B. über eine Frage,** discussion, debate, on a question; **nach einer mehrstündigen B.,** after a discussion, after talks, lasting several hours; **die Minister trafen zu neuen Besprechungen zusammen,** the ministers met for new talks; **Besprechungen auf hoher Ebene,** high-level talks; (*c*) (book-)review; review, criticism (of play, etc.); **das Buch hatte eine sehr gute B.,** the book had a very good review; **Besprechungen schreiben,** to write reviews.

Besprecher, *m.* **-s/-,** reviewer, critic (of books, plays, etc.).

Besprechungsexemplar, Besprechungsstück, *n. Publ:* review copy; press-copy.

besprengen, *v.tr.* (*a*) to sprinkle (linen, floor, etc.) (with water); to water (streets, plants, etc.); to sprinkle, spray (lawn, seedlings, etc.); (*b*) *R.C.Ch:* **j-n, sich, etwas, (mit Weihwasser) b.,** to sprinkle s.o., oneself, sth., with holy water.

bespringen. **1.** *v.tr.* (*strong*) *Breed:* (*of male animal*) to cover, serve (female). **2.** *vbl s.* **Bespringen** *n.*, **Bespringung** *f.* covering, serving, service (of female by male animal).

bespritzen, *v.tr.* to splash (s.o., oneself, sth.) (with water, mud, etc.); to (be)spatter (s.o., sth.) (with mud, etc.); *Hort:* to spray (tree, etc.) (with insecticide, etc.); **j-n von oben bis unten mit Wasser b.,** to splash s.o. all over, to drench, douse, s.o., with water; **etwas mit Tinte b.,** to splash sth. with ink, to splash ink over sth.; **mit Tinte bespritzte Seite,** page spattered, splashed, with ink; **das Tischtuch mit Sauce b.,** to splash the table-cloth with gravy, to splash gravy over the table-cloth; **j-n mit Schmutz b.,** to spatter, splash, s.o. with mud; **mit Schmutz bespritzte Stiefel,** mud-splashed boots, boots bespattered with mud; **seine Hände waren mit Blut bespritzt,** his hands were (be)spattered, splashed, with blood; **sich b.,** (i) to splash oneself with water, etc.; (ii) to get one's stockings, coat, etc., splashed, to get splashes on one's stockings, coat, etc.; **meine Strümpfe sind bespritzt,** my stockings are splashed; **sich gegenseitig (mit Wasser) b.,** to splash water at one another.

besprühen, *v.tr.* to spray (s.o., sth.) (with foam, etc.); to shower (s.o., sth.) (with sparks, etc.); **das Dach wurde mit Funken besprüht,** the roof was showered with sparks.

bespucken, *v.tr.* to spit (up)on (s.o., sth.).

bespülen, *v.tr.* (*of sea, river, etc.*) to wash (against), *Lit:* to lave (shore, cliff, etc.); **der Fels(en) wird vom Meer bespült,** the rock is washed by the sea; **Wellen, die das Ufer bespülen,** waves washing, *Lit:* laving, the shore.

Bessarabien [bɛsa·ˈraːbĭən]. *Pr.n.n.* **-s.** *Geog:* Bessarabia.

Bessarabier [bɛsa·ˈraːbĭər], *m.* **-s/-.** *Ethn:* Bessarabian.

bessarabisch [bɛsa·ˈraːbiʃ], *a. Geog:* Bessarabian.

Bessemerbirne [ˈbɛsəmər-], *f. Metall:* Bessemer converter.

bessemern [ˈbɛsəmərn], *v.tr. Metall:* to bessemerize.

Bessemerprozeß, *m. Metall:* Bessemer process, bessemerizing.

Bessemerstahl, *m. Metall:* Bessemer (steel).

Bessemerverfahren, *n. Metall:* Bessemer process, bessemerizing.

besser. I. *a.* **1.** (*a*) better; **b. werden,** to get, become, better, to improve, to change for the better; (*of pers.*) to grow better, to improve; **das Wetter ist b.,** the weather is better, has improved; **dieser Tabak ist b., dieses ist ein besserer Tabak,** this is a better tobacco, this tobacco is better; **Sie werden kein besseres Hotel finden als dieses,** you will find no better hotel than this, you will not find a better hotel than this; **dieser Stoff ist viel b. in der Qualität,** this material is far better, far superior, in quality, this material is of a much better quality; **bessere Zeiten, bessere Tage,** better days; **sie haben bessere Tage gesehen, gekannt,** they have seen better days; **er ist ein besserer Mensch als du,** he is a better man than you; *F:* **meine bessere Hälfte,** my better half, my wife; (*at games, etc.*) **du bist b. als ich,** you are better than I (am); **er ist nicht b., nicht viel b., als ein Bauer,** he is no better, little better, than a peasant; **ich habe ein bessere Meinung von ihm,** I have a better opinion of him; **ich hatte bessere Dinge erhofft, ich hatte auf bessere Dinge gehofft,** I had hoped for better things; **ich habe Besseres zu tun, als stundenlang auf ihn zu warten,** I have something better to do than wait hours for him; **weißt du vielleicht etwas Besseres?** do you know of anything better? do you know of a better way? **in Ermangelung eines Besseren,** for lack of, want of, something better; **er könnte Besseres leisten,** he could do, he ought to do, better; **Wendung zum Besseren,** change for the better; improvement; **die Dinge wenden sich zum Besseren,** things are taking a turn for the better, things are improving, *F:* are looking up; **j-n eines Besseren belehren,** to correct s.o., to set s.o.'s (mistaken) opinion right; to enlighten s.o.; *F:* **ich werde dich eines Besseren belehren, als so mit mir zu sprechen!** I'll teach you to speak to me like that! *see also* **besinnen** I. 1; (*b*) (*impers.*) better; **es ist b. so,** it is better (that it should be) so, it is better that way; **es könnte nicht b. sein,** it couldn't be better, nothing could be better; **immer b.,** better and better; **umso b.,** so much the better, all the better; **noch b.,** better still; **so ist es b.,** that's better; **oder b. . . . ,** or rather . . . , or perhaps I should say . . . ; **es ist b. als nichts,** it is better than nothing; **ich werde meinen Regenmantel doch mitnehmen, — b. ist b.,** I shall take my raincoat with me after all,—it is better to be on the safe side; **es wäre b., fortzugehen als zu bleiben,** it would be better, *Lit:* it were better, to go away than to stay; **es wäre b., wenn wir jetzt gingen, wir gingen jetzt b.,** we had better go now. **2.** better; better-class, superior; respectable; **ein besseres Hotel,** a better-class hotel; **die besseren Klassen,** the better classes; **eine Straße mit besseren Häusern,** a street of better-class, of respectable, houses; **dieses ist eine bessere Gegend,** this is a better-class, a respectable, district; this is a genteel neighbourhood; **bessere Leute,** better-class people, *Iron:* superior people; **sie ist besserer Leute Kind,** she comes from a respectable family, *Iron:* she comes from a superior, genteel, family; **aus besserer Familie,** from a better-class family; *F:* **ein besserer Herr,** a (respectable) gentleman, *F:* a toff; *Com:* **besserer Artikel,** superior article; (*in shop, etc.*) **darf es etwas Besseres sein?** may I show you something rather better? may I show you something in a higher price range?

II. **besser,** *adv.* better; **sie kocht viel b. als ich,** she cooks much better than I (do), she is a much better cook than I (am); **ich weiß das b. als du,** I know that better than you; **er will immer alles b. wissen, er weiß immer alles b.,** he thinks he knows better about everything, *F:* he is a know-all; **ich kann es umso b. verstehen, weil . . . ,** I can understand it all the better because . . . ; **so geht es b.,** that's better, it works better that way; **es geht ihm etwas b., es geht etwas b. mit ihm,** he is a little better, his health is improving a little; **sein Geschäft geht b., es geht b. mit seinem Geschäft,** his business is improving; **die Geschäfte gehen b.,** business is improving, *F:* things are improving, are taking a turn for the better, are looking up; **b. gekleidet,** better dressed; **du siehst heute viel b. aus,** you look much, ever so much, better today; **du siehst viel b. aus in dem Hut,** you look ever so much nicer in that hat; **ich verdiene hier b. als in meiner vorigen Stellung,** I earn more money here, I am better paid here, than in my previous job; **sich b. stehen,** to be better off (than before); **er ist finanziell jetzt viel b. gestellt,** he is much better off financially now, his financial position is much better now; **die Kinder der finanziell b. gestellten Eltern,** the children of the better-off parents; **b. daran sein als zuvor,** to be better off than before; **er ist deshalb nicht b. daran,** he is none the better for it; **du tätest b. daran zu bleiben,** you had better stay.

bessergestellt, *a.* **1.** better-off (pers.); *see also* **besser** II. **2. Bessergestellte,** *m., f.* person enjoying more favourable conditions; better-off person; **finanziell Bessergestellte** *pl*, people in a better financial position, people who are financially better off, better-off people.

bessern. I. *v.* **1.** *v.tr.* to make (sth.) better; to improve (situation, health, soil, etc.); to better (conditions, etc.); to reform, edify (character, etc.); **ich fand ihn, seinen Zustand, sehr gebessert,** I found him much improved (in health); **wir können ihre Wohnverhältnisse etwas b., aber wir können keine durchgreifende Hilfe geben,** we can improve their living conditions to some extent, but we cannot give any decisive help; **die Disziplin in der Schule wird dazu beitragen, seinen Charakter zu b.,** the discipline at school will help to improve his character; **ihre Lage wurde durch diese Streitigkeiten nicht gebessert,** their position was not bettered, improved, by these quarrels; *Agr:* **den Boden b.,** to improve, fertilize, the soil. **2. sich bessern,** (*a*) to get, become, better, to improve, to change for the better; (*of health, etc.*) to improve, to mend, to be on the mend; (*of pers.*) to improve, to mend one's ways, to reform, *F:* to turn over a new leaf; **sein Zustand hat sich seitdem wenig gebessert,** his condition, his health, has improved little, has got little better, since then; **in letzter Zeit hat er, sein Benehmen, sich sehr gebessert,** he, his behaviour, has much, greatly, improved lately; **er hat sich sehr gebessert,** he has greatly, vastly, improved; **sich in Latein b.,** to improve, get better, in (one's) Latin; **die Lage hat sich gebessert,** the situation has improved; **seine finanzielle Lage hat sich gebessert,** his financial position has improved; **die Geschäfte bessern sich,** business is improving, *F:* things are improving, things are taking a turn for the better, things are looking up; (*b*) *Com:* (*of prices, markets, etc.*) to improve; (*of prices, etc.*) to rise, to go up; **die Preise bessern sich,** prices are rising, advancing, going up.

II. *vbl s.* **1. Bessern,** *n. in vbl senses.* **2. Besserung,** *f.* (*a*) *in vbl senses; also:* improvement (of situation, soil, character, etc.); betterment (of conditions, etc.); reform, edification (of character, etc.); **Vorschläge zur B. der Wirtschaftslage,** proposals for the improvement of the economic situation; **die moralische B. des Volkes,** the moral improvement, edification, of the people; *Agr:* **B. des Bodens durch Düngen,** improvement of the soil by manuring; (*b*) improvement (of health, situation, character, etc.); change for the better (in health, character, etc.); **auf dem Wege der B.,** on the road to recovery, on the mend; **(ich wünsche dir) gute B.,** I hope you will be better soon, I wish you a speedy recovery; **sein Zustand zeigt weiterhin eine B.,** his condition continues to show improvement; **es ist eine B. eingetreten,** there has been a change for the better, there has been an improvement;

man kann eine B. seines Charakters kaum noch erwarten, one can hardly expect him to reform now; *Pol: etc:* **es ist eine B. der Lage eingetreten,** there is an improvement in the situation; (*c*) improvement; **alle diese sogenannten Besserungen,** all these so-called improvements.

Besserstellung, *f.* **finanzielle, soziale, B.,** improvement in, betterment of, (s.o.'s) financial position, social conditions.

Besserungsanstalt, *f.* house of correction; approved school, reform school, reformatory (for young delinquents, etc.); reformatory prison; *U.S:* workhouse; **einen Jungen in eine B. schicken,** to send a boy to a reformatory.

besserungsfähig, *a.* capable of being improved, open to improvement; (*of pers.*) capable of being reformed.

Besserwisser, *m.* **-s/-,** overbearing person; wiseacre, *F:* know-all, *U.S:* know-it-all; **er ist ein B.,** he is a know-all, he always knows better.

Besserwisserei, *f.* **-/.** overbearing, *F:* know-all, manner.

besserwisserisch, *a.* overbearing, *F:* know-all (pers., etc.); **sein besserwisserisches Gehabe,** his know-all manner.

beßre(r), beßre, beßre(s), Beßre(s)=**bessere(r), bessere, bessere(s), Bessere(s),** *q.v. under* **besser I.**

Beßrung, *f.*=**Besserung,** *q.v. under* **bessern II.**

Best, *n.* **-(e)s/-e.** *Dial:* prize, reward.

best-, *comb.fm.* (*pref. to participles*) (*a*) best . . .; best-; **bestgekleidet,** best dressed; **bestaussehend,** best looking; **die bestsitzende Jacke,** the best-fitting jacket; (*b*) most . . .; **bestgehaßt,** most hated; **die bestbesuchte Ausstellung,** the most visited exhibition, the exhibition that attracts, attracted, (the) most visitors.

Bestäder, *m.* **-s/-** =**Besteder.**

bestallen. I. *v.tr.* to appoint, nominate, name, (s.o.) to an office *or* post; to appoint (guardian, trustee, etc.); *Adm:* to give (formal) state approval to (newly qualified doctor); **j-n als Kammerdiener b.,** to appoint s.o. valet; *cp.* **bestellen I. 5.**

II. *vbl s.* **1. Bestallen,** *n. in vbl senses.* **2. Bestallung,** *f.* (*a*) *in vbl senses; also:* appointment, nomination, (of s.o.) to an office *or* post; *Adm:* (formal) state approval (of newly qualified doctor); (*b*)=**Bestallungsurkunde.**

Bestallungsurkunde, *f.* certificate of appointment (to an office *or* post); (certificate of) (formal) state approval (of newly qualified doctor).

Bestand, *m.* **-(e)s/=e. 1.** (*a*) permanence, (continued) existence; **B. einer Rasse,** continued existence of a race; **Einrichtung von dauerndem B.,** permanent institution; (*b*) duration, continuance (of reign, war, peace, etc.); stability (of weather, etc.); **von B. sein, B. haben,** (*of friendship, peace, etc.*) to be lasting, enduring; (*of peace, etc.*) to be settled, abiding; **von kurzem B.,** of short duration, of short continuance; **der Frieden war von kurzem B., der Frieden war nicht von B.,** the peace was of short duration; the peace did not last long; **Glück von kurzem B.,** short-lived happiness; **das gute Wetter hatte keinen B.,** the good weather did not last, continue. **2.** (*a*) stock(s); stores, supply; number (of things in one's possession, etc.); holdings (of library, museum, etc.); *Com: etc:* stock (in hand); stock-in-trade; **B. an Holz,** stock, supply, of wood; **einen guten B., gute Bestände, an Wein haben,** to have a good stock, a good supply, good stores, good supplies, of wine; **mein B. an Wein ist erschöpft,** I am at the end, I have come to the end, of my stock of wine; **unsere Bestände an Nahrungsmitteln sind sehr gering,** our stocks, supplies, of food are very low; **seine Bestände auffüllen, erneuern,** to replenish one's stocks; **mit diesem Zuschuß wird die Bücherei ihre Bestände ergänzen,** with this grant the library is going to increase its holdings; **unerschöpfliche Bestände,** inexhaustible supplies (of wine, money, etc.); **alte Bestände,** old stocks (in shop etc.); primary, original, collection (of library, museum); original nucleus (of a collection); **unverkäufliche Bestände,** dead stock; **Überprüfung der Bestände,** overhauling of stock; **den B. aufnehmen,** to take stock, *U.S:* to take inventory; **eiserner B.,** emergency ration, *F:* iron ration; **Stück, das zum eisernen B. des Spielplans gehört,** stock play; **toter B.,** dead stock, implements (on a farm, etc.); **B. an lebendem Vieh,** live stock, grazing stock; cattle; **der B. an Rotwild in diesem Park ist nicht sehr groß,** the number of red deer in this park is not very large; (*b*) *Mil:* (number of) effectives; **B. an kampffähigen Truppen,** effective force; effective strength; (*c*) *Com: Fin:* **B. (an Geld),** (cash) reserves; cash-balance; assets; *Fin:* **B. (an Effekten),** securities in hand, holdings; **B. der Kasse,** cash (in hand); (*in shop, etc.*) till money; takings; **B. eines Landes an Gold und Silber,** gold and silver holding, reserve, of a country; **mein ganzer B. ist auf fünfzehn Mark zusammengeschmolzen,** my resources have shrunk to fifteen marks; **wir haben alle unsere Bestände zusammengelegt,** we have pooled our resources. **3.** *For:* (*a*) plantation; stand (of timber-trees); crop; stock; (*b*) **(un)gleichmäßiger B.,** (un)even growth (of trees). **4.** *Austrian Jur:* lease; tenure.

Bestandbuch, *n. Com: etc:* stock-book; inventory book.

bestandfähig, *a.* (*of race, genus, etc.*) capable of continued existence.

Bestandgeber, *m. Austrian Jur:* lessor; landlord.

beständig, *a.* **1.** (*a*) (*of weather, etc.*) stable, settled; (*of temperature, pressure, etc.*) constant, uniform, invariable; (*of peace, friendship, etc.*) lasting, enduring; (*of policy, etc.*) unwavering; *Ch: etc:* (*of substance, etc.*) stable; **wir hoffen alle, daß dieser Frieden b. sein wird,** we all hope that this will be a lasting, an enduring, peace; (*b*) (*of pers.*) constant; steadfast; **b. in seiner Freundschaft sein,** to be a constant friend; **ein Mann soll in der Gefahr b. sein,** a man should be steadfast in danger; **in der Liebe, im Unglück, b. sein,** to be steadfast in love, in adversity. **2.** (*a*) constant, persistent, perpetual (rain, headaches, etc.); continual (complaints, etc.); **beständiger Regen, beständiges Regenwetter,** constant, persistent, continual, rain; **seine beständige Nörgelei macht mich wütend,** his constant, continual, perpetual, nagging makes me furious; **es herrschte beständiger Streit zwischen ihnen,** they were constantly, continually, quarrelling; (*b*) constant, permanent, perpetual, continual (fear, etc.); constant, perpetual (danger, etc.); **sie lebt in beständiger Furcht,** she lives in constant, perpetual, fear, she lives in a permanent state of fear. **3.** *adv.* constantly, perpetually; persistently; permanently; always; **in den letzten Tagen hat es b. geschneit,** it has been snowing constantly, persistently, these last few days; **hier regnet es b.,** it rains constantly, permanently, continually, here; **er leidet b. an Kopfschmerzen,** he suffers constantly, perpetually, from headaches; **man muß b. auf sie aufpassen,** one has to watch her constantly, continually; **er lebt b. in der Angst, daß er krank werden könnte,** he lives in constant, perpetual, fear that he might become ill; **es herrschte b. Streit zwischen ihnen,** they were constantly, continually, quarrelling; **er ist b. betrunken,** he is constantly, always, drunk.

Beständigkeit, *f.* (*a*) lastingness, enduringness (of peace, friendship, etc.); stability (of weather, etc.); constancy, uniformity, invariability (of temperature, pressure, etc.); **man kann mit gutem Grund die B. dieses Friedens bezweifeln,** one has good reason to doubt whether this peace will last, endure; **man kann sich sehr selten auf die B. des Wetters verlassen,** one can very rarely count on the weather's remaining stable, settled; (*b*) constancy, steadfastness (of pers., character, etc.); **die B. ihrer Freunde half ihr durch diese schwere Zeit,** the steadfastness, the unfailing support, of her friends helped her through this difficult time; **B. in Zeiten der Prüfung,** steadfastness in times of trial; **seine B. im Dienste des Volkes,** his constancy, steadfastness, in the service of the people.

Bestandnehmer, *m.* **-s/-.** *Austrian Jur:* lessee, lease-holder; tenant.

Bestandsaufnahme, *f.* (*in shop, hospital, etc.*) stocktaking; (*in library, etc.*) inspection, stock-check; **B. machen,** to take stock, *U.S:* to take inventory; (*in library, etc.*) to check (the books, etc.).

Bestandsdichte, *f. For:* crop density.

Bestandsgründung, *f. For:* planting of a new stand of trees.

Bestandskarte, *f. For:* coloured map showing distribution and age of trees in a plantation.

Bestand(s)liste, *f.* stock-list; inventory.

Bestandslockerung, *f. For:* thinning (out), clearing (of forest).

Bestandsmasse, *f. For:* total volume of the timber contained in a stand.

Bestand(s)nachweis, *m.* stock-list; inventory.

Bestandteil, *m.* part (of a whole); component; (constituent) unit, member, (standardized) part, element (of sectional structure, etc.); *Ch: etc:* element, constituent, ingredient (of substance, etc.); **die Bestandteile von Luft, Milch, Wasser,** the elements of air, milk, water; **fetthaltiger, bitterer, aktiver, B. einer Substanz,** fatty, bitter, active, principle *or* constituent of a substance; **wesentlicher, integrierender, B.,** essential, integral, part; **ein wesentlicher B. von etwas sein, einen wesentlichen B. von etwas bilden,** to be an essential, integral, part of sth.; *Constr:* **die Bestandteile eines Baugerippes,** the elements, the parts, of a framework; **etwas in seine Bestandteile zerlegen,** to reduce sth. to its elements; to take sth. to pieces; **Bestandteile einer Maschine, einer Uhr,** parts of a machine, of a clock; **um die Maschine gründlich zu reinigen, muß man sie in ihre Bestandteile zerlegen,** in order to clean the machine thoroughly it must be taken to pieces; **wesentliche Bestandteile einer griechischen Tragödie,** essential parts of a Greek tragedy.

Bestandverfahren, *n. Austrian Jur:* action concerning a lease dispute.

Bestandvertrag, *m. Austrian Jur:* lease (by landlord to tenant); (real) agreement.

Bestandverzeichnis, *n.* stock-list; inventory.

bestärken. I. *v.tr.* to strengthen, fortify (s.o.) (in his belief, opinion, etc.); to encourage (s.o.) (in his vices, etc.); to strengthen (suspicion, belief, opinion, etc.); **j-n in einem Vorsatz b.,** to strengthen, fortify, s.o. in a resolution; **bestärkt in ihrem Vorsatz, mit ihm zu sprechen, machte sie sich auf den Weg,** strengthened, fortified, in her resolution to speak to him, she set out on her way; **j-n in seinem Glauben, in seiner Überzeugung, b.,** to strengthen s.o. in his beliefs, in his convictions; **von neuer Hoffnung bestärkt,** strengthened, fortified, by new hope; **dieser Vorfall bestärkte sie in ihrer irrigen Annahme, in ihrem Irrtum,** this incident strengthened her in her mistaken belief; **seine Antwort bestärkte mich nur noch in meiner früheren Meinung, seine Antwort bestärkte nur noch meine frühere Meinung,** his answer only strengthened my former opinion; **eine Entdeckung, die mich in meinem Verdacht bestärkte, eine Entdeckung, die meinen Verdacht bestärkte,** a discovery that strengthened my suspicions; **j-n in seinen Untugenden b.,** to encourage s.o. in his faults; **j-n in seiner Faulheit b.,** to encourage s.o. to be lazy, to encourage s.o. in his laziness; **du bestärkst das Kind nur noch in seinem Trotz,** you only encourage the child in its obstinacy.

II. *vbl s.* **Bestärken** *n.*, **Bestärkung** *f. in vbl senses; also:* encouragement (of s.o.) (in his vices, etc.).

bestätigen. I. *v.tr.* **1.** (*a*) to confirm (news, appointment, rumour, suspicion, etc.); to confirm, corroborate, bear out (evidence, statement, etc.); to verify, prove (statement, etc.); to confirm, approve, sanction (nomination, decision, etc.); *Jur:* to confirm, ratify, validate, *Scot:* homologate (deed, contract, etc.); *Com:* to acknowledge (receipt) (of sth.); to confirm (order, etc.); **das Gerücht wurde heute von amtlicher Seite bestätigt,** the rumour was officially confirmed today; **spätere Ereignisse bestätigten seinen Verdacht, seine Voraussage,** subsequent events verified, confirmed, his suspicions, his prediction; **er bestätigte meine Befürchtungen,** he confirmed my fears; **seine Antwort bestätigte meine Meinung von ihm,** his answer confirmed my opinion of him; **die Erfahrung hat seine Theorie, hat die Richtigkeit seiner Theorie, bestätigt,** experience has confirmed, proved, his theory; **dadurch wird meine Behauptung bestätigt, das bestätigt meine Behauptung,** that proves, bears out, my assertion; **nicht bestätigte Nachrichten,** unconfirmed reports; **das Berufungsgericht hat das Urteil bestätigt,** the court of appeal has confirmed the judgment; **die Tatsachen bestätigen seine Aussage,** the facts corroborate his statement; **der Präsident hat die Ernennung des Herrn X bestätigt, hat Herrn X bestätigt,** the president has confirmed, approved, the appointment of Mr X; **in der jährlichen Mitgliederversammlung wurde der bisherige Schatzmeister (in seinem Amt) bestätigt,** at the members' annual meeting the retiring treasurer was reappointed; **den Empfang eines Briefes b.,** to acknowledge receipt of a letter; **bitte, bestätigen Sie den Empfang der Sendung,** please acknowledge receipt of the consignment; **ich bestätige hiermit meinen telephonischen Auftrag für zehn Ballen Baumwolle,** I herewith confirm my telephone order for ten bales of cotton; **ich bestätige dankend Ihren Auftrag,** I confirm with thanks your order; **bestätigend,** confirmative (judgment),

corroborative (statement), confirmatory (declaration); **er nickte bestätigend,** he nodded in confirmation; (*b*) **b., daß . . .,** to confirm that . . .; **ich bestätige hiermit, daß ich bereit bin, den Schaden zu bezahlen,** I herewith confirm that I am willing to pay for the damage; **er bestätigte mir, daß der Mann das Haus verlassen hatte,** he confirmed (to me) that the man had left the house; **es wird hierdurch bestätigt, daß . . .,** this is to confirm that . . .; this is to certify that . . .; **ich werde Ihnen gern b., daß Sie drei Monate bei mir gearbeitet haben,** I shall be pleased to certify, to give you a certificate stating, that you have worked for me for three months; **er wird dir b., daß ich die Wahrheit gesagt habe,** he will confirm, tell you, that I have spoken the truth; **ich konnte ihr nur b., was sie schon gehört hatte,** I could only confirm, tell her again, what she already knew; **dieser Brief bestätigt, daß er noch lebt,** this letter confirms, proves, that he is still alive. **2.** *Ven:* to locate, establish the presence of (game). **3. sich bestätigen,** (*of news, etc.*) to prove (to be) true, correct; (*of prophecy, etc.*) to come true, to turn out to be true; **seine Voraussage bestätigte sich,** his prediction proved true, came true, proved correct; **die Nachricht bestätigte sich nicht,** the news did not prove (to be) true, the news proved false; **falls sich das Gerücht b. sollte,** should the rumour prove (to be) true.

II. *vbl s.* **1. Bestätigen,** *n. in vbl senses.* **2. Bestätigung,** *f.* (*a*) *in vbl senses; also:* confirmation (of report, appointment, judgment, evidence, rumour, etc.); corroboration (of evidence, statement, etc.); verification (of statement, etc.); approval (of nomination, decision, etc.); *Jur:* confirmation, ratification, validation, *Scot:* homologation (of deed, contract, etc.); *Com:* acknowledgement (of receipt) (of sth.); **nach der offiziellen B. des Gerüchtes,** after the official confirmation of the rumour; **zur B.,** in confirmation of (statement, decision, etc.), in corroboration of (statement, evidence, etc.); **zur B. dessen werde ich Ihnen den offiziellen Bericht zeigen,** in confirmation of this, to confirm this, I will show you the official report; **um B. des Empfangs wird gebeten,** please acknowledge receipt; (*b*) (*report, certificate, etc.*) confirmation (of news, appointment, judgment, rumour, etc.); approval (of nomination, decision, etc.); *Jur:* **(formale) B.,** confirmation, *Scot:* homologation (of deed, contract, etc.); *Com:* acknowledgement (of receipt) (of sth.); receipt; **diese Tatsache ist nur eine B. seiner Lehre,** this fact is only a confirmation of his doctrine; **heute wurde eine offizielle B. der Meldung veröffentlicht,** an official confirmation of the report was published today; **können Sie mir bitte eine schriftliche B. schicken,** would you please send me a written confirmation, would you please confirm in writing; **dieser Brief gilt als B. meines telephonischen Auftrages,** this letter is confirmation of my telephone order, this letter confirms my telephone order; **als B. nickte er,** he nodded in confirmation; **B. finden,** (*of news, rumour, etc.*) to be confirmed, to prove true, correct, (*of prophecy, etc.*) to come true, to turn out to be true.

Bestätigungsrecht, *n.* right of approval (of nominations, etc.).

bestatten. I. *v.tr.* (i) to bury, inter, entomb (corpse), (ii) to cremate (corpse); **j-n zur letzten Ruhe b.,** to lay s.o. to rest, to lay s.o. in the grave; **j-n auf hoher See b.,** to bury s.o. at sea; **er wurde auf dem Friedhof zu X bestattet,** he was buried, he was laid to rest, in the cemetery at X.

II. *vbl s.* **1. Bestatten,** *n. in vbl senses.* **2. Bestattung,** *f.* (*a*) *in vbl senses; also:* burial, interment, entombment; **B. durch Verbrennung,** cremation; **B. auf hoher See,** burial at sea; (*b*) funeral; **feierliche B.,** funeral with full ceremonial; obsequies; **bei der B.,** at the funeral; (*c*) burial; **die letzten Bestattungen auf dem kürzlich ausgegrabenen Friedhof datieren aus dem 5. Jahrhundert n. Chr.,** the last burials in the recently excavated cemetery date from the 5th century A.D.

bestätten, *v.tr.* to convey, cart (goods, etc.).

Bestatter, *m.* **-s/-,** undertaker.

Bestätter, Bestätterer, *m.* **-s/-,** conveyor, carter, carrier (of goods, etc.).

Bestattung, *f. see* **bestatten** II. 2.

Bestattungsanstalt, *f.*=**Bestattungsinstitut.**

Bestattungsfeierlichkeiten, *f.pl.* funeral ceremonies; obsequies.

Bestattungsgebühren, *f.pl.* funeral fees.

Bestattungsinstitut, *n.* (firm of) undertakers; undertaking, undertaker's, business; funeral directors, *U.S:* funeral parlor, funeral home.

Bestattungskosten, *pl.* funeral expenses; funeral fees.

Bestattungsort, *m.* burial-place; resting-place.

Bestattungsriten, *m.pl.* funeral rites, burial rites.

Bestattungssitten, *f.pl.* burial customs; funeral rites, burial rites.

bestauben (*occ.***bestäuben**). **1.** *v.tr.* to make (sth.) dusty; to cover (sth.) with dust; **beim Fegen bestaubt man die Möbel,** when sweeping one makes the furniture dusty; **auf dem trockenen Feldweg bestaubt man seine Schuhe, bestaubt man sich** *dat.* **die Schuhe,** on the dry footpath one gets one's shoes covered with dust. **2.** *v.i.* (*sein*) (*of furniture, shoes, road, etc.*) to get dusty; **bestaubt,** dusty, covered with dust; **weiß bestaubt,** white with dust; **bestaubte alte Bücher,** dusty old books, old books covered with dust.

bestäuben (*occ.* **bestauben**). I. *v.tr.* **1.** *Nat.Hist:* to pollinate (stigma); **sich (selbst) b.,** to self-pollinate; **bestäubte Narbe,** pollinated, fertilized, stigma. **2.** (*a*) to sprinkle, powder, dust (sth.); **mit Mehl b.,** to flour (baking-tin, etc.), to dust (baking-tin, etc.) with flour; **einen Kuchen mit Puderzucker b.,** to dust, sprinkle, a cake with icing sugar; **mit feinem Schnee bestäubt,** covered, sprayed, with fine snow; (*b*) *Hort: etc:* to spray (plant, etc.) (with water, insecticide, etc.); to dust (plant, etc.) (with insecticide, etc.).

II. *vbl s.* **1. Bestäuben,** *n. in vbl senses.* **2. Bestäubung,** *f. Nat.Hist:* pollination, pollinization; fertilization; **B. durch den Wind,** wind pollination; **B. durch Insekten,** insect pollination.

Bestäuber, *m.* **-s/-.** **1.** *Nat.Hist:* pollinator, agent of pollination. **2.** *Hort: etc:* sprayer, duster.

bestauden (sich), *v.refl.*=**bestocken** 2.

bestaunen, *v.tr.* to look at, gaze at (s.o., sth.) in astonishment, in amazement, in surprise, in wonder; to admire (s.o., sth.); **j-n, etwas, mit offenem Munde b.,** to stand in open-mouthed astonishment before s.o., sth.; to gape at s.o., sth., in astonishment; to stare open-mouthed at s.o., sth.; **die Kinder bestaunten die Wache in ihrer schmucken Uniform,** the children admired the guard in his smart uniform; **die Zuschauer bestaunten die Geschicklichkeit des Jongleurs,** the audience admired, marvelled at, the skill, the dexterity, of the juggler; **von allen Seiten bestaunt werden,** to be looked at, stared at, gaped at, from all sides.

bestaunenswert, *a.* amazing, astonishing; **bestaunenswerte Geschicklichkeit,** amazing skill; **eine wahrhaft bestaunenswerte Leistung,** a truly amazing, astonishing, achievement.

bestbietend, *a. Com: etc:* making the highest bid.

beste, *a. see* **beste(r).**

bestechen. I. *v.tr.* (*strong*) **1.** to stitch (sth.); to decorate (sth.) with stitching; to oversew, *U.S:* overhand (seam, etc.); to thong (edge of) (shoe, leather bag, etc.); **eine Tasche mit buntem Bast b.,** to stitch a bag with coloured raffia. **2.** (*a*) to bribe (s.o., institution, etc.); *Jur:* to bribe, to buy (over), to corrupt, to suborn (witness, etc.); **j-n b.,** to bribe s.o., *F:* to oil, grease, s.o.'s palm; to square s.o.; **j-n b., etwas zu tun,** to bribe s.o. to do sth.; **man hatte ihn dazu bestochen zu schweigen,** he had been bribed to keep quiet; **j-n zu b. versuchen,** to try to bribe s.o., to offer a bribe, bribes, to s.o.; **Beamten b.,** to bribe, to offer bribes to, officials; **sich b. lassen,** to take, accept, a bribe, bribes; **bestochene Zeugen,** bribed, corrupted, suborned, witnesses; (*b*) (*of pers., manner, etc.*) to captivate, charm, fascinate (s.o.); to take (s.o.) in; *abs.* **b.,** to charm, to be captivating, fascinating, attractive; **seine schönen Worte können mich nicht b., mit seinen schönen Worten kann er mich nicht b., ich lasse mich von seinen schönen Worten nicht b.,** he cannot captivate me, charm me, take me in, with his fine words; I will not be taken in by his fine words; **er besticht alle durch seine Liebenswürdigkeit,** he captivates, fascinates, everybody with his charm; he takes everybody in with his charm; **er besticht durch sein feines Benehmen,** he charms by his beautiful manners; **sie besticht überall durch ihre Schönheit,** her beauty charms, captivates, everyone.

II. *vbl s.* **1. Bestechen,** *n. in vbl senses.* **2. Bestechung,** *f.* (*a*) *in vbl senses; also:* bribery (of s.o., institution, etc.); subornation (of witness, etc.); **B. von Zeugen,** bribery, bribing, subornation, corruption, of witnesses; (*b*) bribery; corruption; *U.S:* graft; **der B. zugänglich,** open to bribery, bribable; corruptible; *Jur:* **aktive B.,** bribery; **passive B.,** accepting, acceptance, of a bribe, of bribes; **er wurde wegen passiver B. angeklagt,** he was accused of having accepted a bribe, bribes; (*c*) act, case, of bribery; **häufige Bestechungen,** frequent cases of bribery; **Bestechungen waren an der Tagesordnung,** bribery and corruption were the order of the day (*d*) bribe; *U.S:* graft; **eine B., Bestechungen, annehmen,** to accept a bribe, bribes; **er nimmt jede B. an,** he will accept any bribe; **er bot mir fünfzig Mark als B. an,** he offered me fifty marks as a bribe.

III. *pr.p. & a.* **bestechend,** *in vbl senses; esp.* captivating, fascinating, attractive, charming, winning, taking, engaging (pers., manner, etc.); attractive, tempting (offer, prospect, etc.); **bestechendes Lächeln,** captivating, charming, winning, engaging, smile; **bestechende Liebenswürdigkeit,** captivating charm; **er hat bestechende Manieren,** he has charming, engaging, manners; **seine Theorie ist sehr b.,** his theory is most attractive; **das Angebot ist sehr b.,** the offer is most attractive, most tempting; **sie hat etwas Bestechendes an sich,** there is something captivating, fascinating, charming, engaging, about her, she has a charming, an engaging, manner; *adv.* **b. lächeln,** to smile captivatingly, engagingly; **sie hat ihre Gründe b. dargelegt,** she has presented her reasons most persuasively; *F:* **ein b. schöner Hund,** a most beautiful dog.

Bestecher, *m.* **-s/-.** *Jur:* briber; suborner (of witness, etc.).

bestechlich, *a.* bribable, open to bribery; corruptible; venal; corrupt; **bestechliche Presse,** corrupt press.

Bestechlichkeit, *f.* corruptibility; venality; corruption; **allgemeine B.,** general corruption.

Bestechungsgeld, *n.* bribe (of money).

Bestechungsversuch, *m.* attempt to bribe; **wegen Bestechungsversuches angeklagt,** accused of attempted bribery.

Besteck, *n.* **-(e)s/-e.** **1.** (*a*) case, kit, set (of instruments, etc.); **(chirurgisches) B.,** (case of) surgical instruments; (*b*) (i) (single set of) knife, fork, and spoon, etc., (ii) (complete set of) cutlery; service; **er gab mir ein silbernes B.,** he gave me a silver knife, fork, and spoon (set); **wir besitzen ein vollständiges silbernes B. mit diesem Muster,** we have a complete set of silver cutlery, a complete set of silver, with this pattern; **das B., die Bestecke, putzen,** to clean the cutlery, to clean, polish, the silver; (*c*) place (at table); **bitte, legen Sie noch ein B. auf,** please lay one more place; **wie viele Bestecke soll ich auflegen?** how many places shall I lay? for how many people shall I lay (the table)? **drei Bestecke auflegen,** to set the table, to lay (the table), for three; (*d*) *F:* (*of pers.*) **er ist ein komisches B.,** he is an odd, a peculiar, fellow, he is an oddity; **ein freches kleines B.,** a naughty little thing. **2.** *Nau: Av:* reckoning, position; **geschätztes, gegißtes, B.,** dead reckoning; estimated position; fix; **observiertes, astronomisches, B.,** position by observation; astronomical fix; **das B. (auf)nehmen,** to work out the ship's, the aircraft's, reckoning, to determine the ship's, the aircraft's, position; to fix one's position; to take the ship's, the aircraft's, bearings; to take a fix; **mit dem B. voraus, zurück, sein,** to be ahead, astern, of one's reckoning. **3.** (*a*) *Civ.E: etc:* (determination of, working out of) profile (of dam, etc.); (*b*) low criss-cross fencing of short sticks used to retain the loose sand (of dunes).

Besteckaufnahme, *f.*=**Besteсknahme.**

Besteckbreite, *f. Nau: Av:* latitude of fix; **gegißte B.,** latitude by dead reckoning.

bestecken, *v.tr.* (*a*) *Hort:* to stick, prop, stake (beans, peas, etc.); (*b*) *Civ.E: Surv: etc:* to mark out, stake out (road, ground, etc.); (*c*) *Min:* to fix handle to, to haft, to helve (tool); (*d*) **etwas mit etwas b.,** to stick sth. on sth.; to decorate sth. with sth.; **den Weihnachtsbaum mit Kerzen b.,** to put candles on the Christmas-tree; **sich** *dat.* **den Hut mit Blumen, mit Federn, b.,** to stick flowers, feathers in one's hat, to decorate one's hat with flowers, with feathers; **seine Uniform war mit vielen Schleifen und Orden besteckt,** his uniform was decorated with many ribbons and medals, his uniform, he, was beribboned and bemedalled.

Besteckfabrik, *f.* cutlery works.

Besteckkasten, *m.* (*a*) cutlery-box; cutlery-basket; (*b*) canteen of cutlery, *U.S:* cutlery chest.

Bestecklänge, *f. Nau: Av:* longitude of fix; **gegißte B.,** longitude by dead reckoning.

Bestecknahme, f. -/. Nau: Av: working out of (ship's, aircraft's) reckoning; determination of (ship's, aircraft's) position; fix.

Besteckort, m. Nau: Av: (position of) fix.

Besteckrechnung, f. Nau: Av: reckoning; gegißte B., dead reckoning.

Besteckschrank, m. cutlery-cabinet.

Besteckversetzung, f. Nau: Av: difference between dead and observed reckoning.

Besteder, m. -s/-, person or authority commissioning the building of a ship.

Besteg, m. -(e)s/-e. Min: Geol: selvage, selvedge, gouge (of vein).

bestehen. I. v.i. (strong) (haben) 1. to have one's being in (s.o., sth.); B: es bestehet alles in ihm, by him all things consist. 2. (a) to exist, to be; to have a continued existence; solange die Welt besteht, hat es so etwas noch nie gegeben, there has not been anything like it since the beginning of the world; in diesem Teil des Landes bestehen noch einige alte Gebräuche, a few old customs still exist, subsist, endure, in this part of the country; die Gesellschaft besteht noch, the company is still in being, the company still exists; die Firma besteht seit fünfzig Jahren, the firm has been in existence for fifty years; das Gesetz bestand schon, als es noch keine Autos gab, the law already existed before there were any cars; die größte Schule für Blinde besteht in M, the largest school for the blind is in M; britische Botschaften bestehen in fast allen anderen Ländern, there are British embassies in nearly all other countries; (of claim, opinion, etc.) zu Recht b., to be justified; seine Forderung besteht zu Recht, zu Unrecht, his claim is justified, is not justified; die Tatsache besteht, daß . . ., the fact remains that . . .; dieses Problem besteht schon seit Jahren, this problem has existed for years; alles Bestehende, everything existing, everything in existence; am Bestehenden festhalten, to adhere to tradition; see also bestehenbleiben; (b) to be; es bestehen zwei Möglichkeiten, there are two ways, two possibilities; es besteht leider keine Möglichkeit, ihnen zu helfen, there is unfortunately no possibility of helping them; es besteht keine Aussicht, keine Hoffnung, auf Besserung, there is no hope of recovery; es besteht kein Zweifel, es scheint kein Zweifel zu b., daß . . ., there is no doubt, there seems to be no doubt, that . . .; natürlich besteht dabei immer die große Gefahr, daß . . ., of course there is always (the) great danger that . . .; es besteht keine Gefahr, there is no danger. 3. to stand, to hold one's own (in fight, etc.); gegen j-n, etwas, b., to hold one's own, to hold out, to stand, hold, one's ground, against s.o., sth.; to stand up to s.o., sth.; gegen die Besten b., to hold one's own with the best; was die Schönheit anbetraf, konnte sie gegen alle ihre Gegnerinnen b., she held her own in beauty with all her rivals; in einem Kampf, in einer Gefahr, b., to stand, hold, one's ground, to prove oneself, in a battle, in danger; in einer Prüfung b., (i) to stand firm in a time of trial; to stand a test, to stand up to a test; (ii) Sch: to pass (in) an examination; cp. II; in seiner letzten Prüfung hat er in Latein nicht bestanden, in his last examination he did not pass, he failed, in Latin; vor Gott b., to be justified before God, in the sight of God; wie kann ich vor ihr b.? how shall I be able to face her? how can I justify myself to her? B: o Herr, wer wird b.? O Lord, who shall stand? B: so bestehet nun in der Freiheit, damit uns Christus befreiet hat, stand fast therefore in the liberty wherewith Christ hath made us free. 4. auf etwas dat. b., to insist on sth.; to persist in sth.; auf etwas acc. b., to insist on sth.; darauf b., etwas zu tun, to insist on doing sth.; darauf b., daß etwas geschieht, to insist that sth. should be done; darauf b., daß j-d etwas tut, to insist that s.o. shall do sth., to insist on s.o.'s doing sth.; auf einem Punkt b., to insist (up)on a point; auf seiner Meinung b., to persist in one's opinion, to stick to one's opinion; sie bestand hartnäckig auf dieser Lüge, she persisted in this lie, she stuck to this lie; auf seiner Unschuld b., to insist upon one's innocence, to insist (upon it) that one is innocent; auf seinen Rechten b., auf seine Rechte b., to insist on one's rights; auf seinen Forderungen b., to stand out for, insist on, persist in, one's claims; auf einer sofortigen Antwort b., auf eine sofortige Antwort b., to insist on, press for, an immediate answer; auf Bezahlung b., to insist on, press for, payment; er bestand darauf, sofort bezahlt zu werden, er bestand auf seiner sofortigen Bezahlung, he insisted on being paid at once;

er besteht darauf, he insists on it; ich muß darauf b., I must insist (on it); ich werde nicht darauf b., I won't insist (on it); ich bestehe darauf, daß mir gehorcht wird, I insist on obedience, I insist on being obeyed; er besteht darauf, es gesehen zu haben, he insists that he saw it; er besteht darauf, daß du kommst, he insists on your coming. 5. aus etwas b., (a) to consist of sth.; to be composed of sth.; sein Mahl bestand aus Brot und Käse, his meal consisted of bread and cheese; der einfache Satz besteht aus Subjekt, Prädikat und Objekt, the simple sentence consists of subject, predicate and object; eine Maschine besteht aus vielen Teilen, a machine is composed of many parts; die Personen, aus denen unsere Familie besteht, the persons of whom our family consists, is composed; sein Vermögen besteht im wesentlichen aus Aktien, his fortune consists mainly of shares; Gut, das aus Wald und Wiesenland besteht, aus Wald und Wiesenland bestehendes Gut, estate composed of woods and meadowland; Erbteil, das aus zwei Häusern besteht, aus zwei Häusern bestehendes Erbteil, inheritance consisting of two houses; (b) to be made of sth.; der Schrank besteht ganz aus Rosenholz, the cupboard is made entirely of rosewood. 6. b. in, to consist, lie, in (sth.); die Schwierigkeit besteht darin, daß . . ., the difficulty consists, lies, in the fact that . . .; der einzige Unterschied besteht darin, daß der Rahmen aus Holz anstatt aus Metall gemacht ist, the only difference is, lies in the fact, that the frame is made of wood instead of metal; wahres Glück besteht darin, andere glücklich zu machen, true happiness consists, lies, in making others happy; seine ganze Arbeit bestand darin, die Blumen zu begießen, his whole work consisted in watering the flowers; die Gefahr besteht darin, daß durch Überbeanspruchung wichtige Metallteile abgenutzt werden können, the danger lies in the fact, the danger is, that vital metal parts might be worn out by excessive stress.

II. bestehen, v.tr. (a) to fight (battle, etc.); to go through (danger, trial, etc.); to meet, encounter, have (adventures); Prüfungen b., to go go through times of trial; er hatte einen schweren Kampf zu b., he had a hard, difficult, battle to fight; der Ritter wird manchen Kampf zu b. haben, the knight will have to fight many a battle; er hatte auch diesen Kampf glücklich bestanden, he had won, come out victorious from, this fight too; nach glücklich bestandener Gefahr, having come safely through, having survived, this danger; (b) Sch: etc: to pass (test, examination, etc.); die schriftliche Prüfung b., to pass (in) the written examination; die mündliche Prüfung b., to pass (in) the oral (examination); eine Prüfung mit Auszeichnung b., to pass an examination with distinction; er hat sein Examen nicht bestanden, he has not passed his examination, he has failed (in) his examination; 'bestanden', 'pass'; nach bestandener Prüfung, having passed, having got through, the examination.

III. vbl s. Bestehen, n. in vbl senses; also: 1. existence; seit dem B. der Welt, since the beginning of the world; das B. eines solchen Gesetzes ist durchaus gerechtfertigt, the existence of such a law is completely justified; heute sind seit dem B. der Firma fünfzig Jahre vergangen, heute kann die Firma auf ein fünfzigjähriges B. zurückblicken, today the firm has been in existence for fifty years, today is the fiftieth anniversary of the firm's foundation; seit dem B. der Firma, since the firm was founded; die Firma feiert in diesem Jahr ihr hundertjähriges B., the firm celebrates its centenary this year; der Verein feiert sein fünfundzwanzigjähriges B., the society is celebrating its twenty-fifth anniversary. 2. insistence; persistence; sein B. auf seiner Unschuld, his insistence upon his innocence; sein hartnäckiges B. darauf, his obdurate, stubborn, insistence (upon it); ihr hartnäckiges B. auf dieser Lüge, her persistence in this lie. 3. Sch: etc: das B. der Prüfung befähigt zum Eintritt in die Universität, passing the examination, a pass in the examination, qualifies for entrance to the university; nach (erfolgreichem) B. der Prüfung, having passed the examination.

IV. p.p. & a. bestanden, in vbl senses; esp. mit Bäumen und Büschen bestandener Abhang, slope on which trees and shrubs grow; slope covered with trees and shrubs; mit hohen Pappeln bestandene Allee, avenue of, avenue set with, tall poplars; mit dichtem Wald bestandener Hügel, densely wooded hill.

bestehenbleiben, v.i. sep. (strong) (sein) to continue to exist; to stand; to subsist; to endure; to last; der Einspruch bleibt bestehen, the objection stands, holds; die Abmachung, die Wette, bleibt bestehen, the bargain, the bet, stands, holds good; mein Angebot bleibt bestehen, my offer stands; die Tatsache bleibt bestehen, daß . . ., the fact remains that . . .; ein Brauch, der bestehengeblieben ist, a custom that still exists, subsists, endures; wieviel wird von seiner Philosophie b.? how much of his philosophy will last, will endure?

bestehlen, v.tr. (strong) to steal from (s.o., institution, etc.); to rob (s.o., institution, etc.); j-n um etwas b., to steal sth. from s.o.; to rob, strip, F: relieve, s.o. of sth.; er wurde um sechzig Mark bestohlen, he was robbed of sixty marks, sixty marks were stolen from him; ich bin bestohlen worden, man hat mich bestohlen, I have been robbed; den Staat b., to rob the state.

besteigen. I. v.tr. (strong) to climb (up) (mountain, tree, ladder, etc.); to go up, climb (tower, etc.); to mount (horse, etc.); einen Berg b., to climb (up), Lit: to ascend, a mountain; das Flugzeug, den Zug, b., to board, to enter, get into, the plane, the train; to take the plane, the train; die Kanzel b., to mount the pulpit; den Thron b., to mount the throne; to ascend the throne; to succeed to the throne; das Schafott b., to mount the scaffold; ein Pferd, ein Fahrrad, b., to mount, get on, a horse, a bicycle; Pferd, das sich nicht leicht b. läßt, horse hard, difficult, to mount; eine Leiter b., to climb (up), mount, a ladder; nachdem wir, als wir, den Gipfel bestiegen hatten, when we had climbed the peak, after the ascent of the peak; ein Berg, der noch nie bestiegen worden ist, an unconquered mountain.

II. vbl s. 1. Besteigen, n. in vbl senses. 2. Besteigung, f. (a)=II. 1; also: ascent (of mountain, etc.); B. des Thrones, accession to the throne; (b) ascent (of mountain, etc.); sie machten mehrere Besteigungen, they made several ascents.

bestellbar, a. 1. arable, cultivable, tillable (land, etc.). 2. bookable, U.S: reservable (seats, etc.).

Bestellbuch, n. Com: order-book.

bestellen. I. v.tr. 1. etwas mit etwas b., to put, place, sth. on sth.; (mit Speisen) reich bestellter Tisch, richly laden table, table richly laden, set, with food. 2. (a) to cultivate, farm, till (soil, etc.); bestellter Acker, bestelltes Feld, cultivated field, field in, under, cultivation; schlecht bestellte Felder, badly cultivated fields; (b) sein Haus b., to settle one's affairs, to put, set, one's affairs in order, to set one's house in order. 3. (a) Post: to deliver (letter, parcel, etc.); die Post wird dreimal am Tage bestellt, the mail is delivered three times a day, there are three postal deliveries a day; (b) to deliver, give (message, greetings, etc.); j-m etwas b., to give s.o. a message, to give, deliver, a message to s.o.; kann ich etwas b.? can I take a message? kann ich ihm etwas b.? can I give him a message? can I take a message for him? bestelle deiner Mutter einen schönen Gruß, schöne Grüße, von mir, give your mother my kindest regards, give my kindest regards to your mother; bitte, bestellen Sie ihm, daß ich morgen nicht kommen kann, please tell him that I shall not be able to come tomorrow; F: du kannst ihm das von mir b.! you can tell him that from me! 4. (a) to order (goods, taxi, tickets, etc.); to place, give, an order for (goods, etc.); to commission (picture, work of art, etc.); to book, U.S: reserve (room, seat, etc.); abs. b., (in restaurant) to order; Waren b., to order goods, to put goods on order; Waren aus Paris b., to order goods from Paris; bei j-m etwas b., to order sth. from s.o., to place an order with s.o. for sth., to give s.o. an order for sth.; einen Anzug b., to order a suit (of clothes); er hat bei uns fünf Tonnen Zement bestellt, he has ordered five tons of cement from us, he has given us an order for five tons of cement; der Artikel ist bestellt, wir haben den Artikel bestellt, the article is on order; ich habe zwei Theaterkarten für nächsten Mittwoch bestellt, I have ordered two theatre tickets, I have booked two seats for the theatre, for next Wednesday; Theaterplätze telephonisch b., to book seats for the theatre by telephone; ich habe den Wagen auf, für, vier Uhr bestellt, I have ordered the car for four o'clock; ein Zimmer im voraus b., to book a room in advance; (in restaurant) haben Sie schon bestellt? have you given your order? have you ordered (yet)? have you already ordered? er bestellte eine Flasche Wein, he ordered, he asked for, a bottle of wine; (b) j-n b., to make,

fix, an appointment with s.o.; to ask s.o. to come (to see one, to a meeting-place, etc.); to make s.o. come (to see one, to a meeting-place, etc.); **j-n zu sich b.,** to summon, to send for, s.o.; **ich habe ihn zu mir bestellt,** I asked him to come to see me; I summoned him to me; **j-n zu einem Interview b.,** to ask s.o., to invite s.o., to come for an interview; **sie hatte ihn in das Restaurant am Bahnhof bestellt,** she had asked him, told him, to meet her in the restaurant near the station; **ich werde sie für sechs Uhr b.,** I shall make an appointment with her for six o'clock, I shall tell her to come at six o'clock; **ich bin bestellt,** I am here by appointment; **sind Sie bestellt?** have you an appointment? *F:* **sie sitzt, steht, wie bestellt und nicht abgeholt,** there she is—all dressed up and nowhere to go. **5.** to appoint (s.o.) (to an office *or* post); **j-n zum Bürgermeister b.,** to appoint s.o. (as) mayor; **j-n zum Richter b.,** (i) to appoint s.o. as a court judge; (ii) to make s.o. judge (in an argument, etc.); **j-n zu seinem Erben b.,** to appoint s.o. (as) one's heir, to make s.o. one's heir; **er wurde zum Vormund, zum Treuhänder, bestellt,** he was appointed, made, a guardian, a trustee; **der Direktor bestellte Herrn X zu seinem Vertreter,** the director appointed Mr X as his deputy, the director made Mr X his deputy.

II. *vbl s.* **1. Bestellen,** *n.* in *vbl senses.* **2. Bestellung,** *f.* (*a*) in *vbl senses; also:* cultivation (of soil, etc.); delivery (of message, letter, parcel, etc.); (*b*) appointment (of s.o.) (to an office *or* post); **die B. von Herrn X zum Vertreter des Direktors,** Mr X's appointment as deputy to the director; (*c*) (postal) delivery; **sonntags gibt es keine B.,** there is no delivery on Sundays; (*d*) message; **j-m eine B. ausrichten,** to give, deliver, a message to s.o.; **eine B. an deine Mutter,** a message to your mother; (*e*) order (for goods, etc.); booking, *U.S:* reservation (for room, seat, etc.); **er hat uns eine B. auf, für, fünf Tonnen Zement gegeben,** he has given us an order for five tons of cement; **Bestellungen aus aller Welt laufen ein,** orders come in from all over the world; **Bestellungen werden hier entgegengenommen,** orders are, will be, accepted here; **auf B.,** to order; **auf B. gemacht, gefertigt,** made to order, *U.S:* custom-made, -built.

III. *p.p. & a.* **bestellt,** *in vbl senses; esp.* **es ist schlecht, nicht gut, um ihn b.,** he is in a bad way, (i) he is in bad health, he is not well, (ii) he is badly off, he is in a bad position, in difficulties, in a predicament; **es ist nicht gut um sein Geschäft b.,** his business is in a bad way; **es ist schlecht b. um das Land,** the country is in a bad way; **jetzt ist es besser um das Land b. als je zuvor,** the country is better off now, is in a better way now, than ever before; **es scheint schlecht um die Dinge b. zu sein,** things seem (to be) in a bad way, things are looking bad; **es ist schlecht um die Ernte b.,** the crops are in a bad way, are in danger.

Besteller, *m.* **-s/-.** **1.** person *or* firm ordering (goods, etc.); person *or* society commissioning (picture, work of art, etc.). **2.** messenger; deliverer (of letters, etc.).

Bestellgebühr, *f.* = Bestellgeld.

Bestellgeld, *n.* delivery charge; charge for delivery (of newspapers, etc.).

Bestelliste, *f. Com: etc:* order-list.

Bestellschein, *m. Com: etc:* order-form; *Library:* order-slip, order-form.

Bestellungsbrief, *m.* letter of appointment.

Bestellungszeiten, *f.pl. Post:* times of delivery.

Bestellzettel, *m.* order-slip, order-form (in libraries, etc.); *Com: etc:* order-form.

bestempeln, *v.tr.* to stamp (sth.); to put a stamp on (sth.).

bestenfalls, *adv.* at (the) best; **er wird b. die Note 'gut' erhalten,** the best mark he can hope for will be 'good'; **b. wird es Ihnen fünfzig Mark einbringen,** at (the) best it will bring you in fifty marks; **b. können wir morgen ankommen,** at best, at the earliest, we shall arrive tomorrow.

Bestenliste, *f. Sp: etc:* **die B. anführen,** to head the list (of top players, athletes, riders, etc.); to be the best in the championship class.

bestens, *adv.* **1. es ist alles b. besorgt,** everything has been done most satisfactorily; **es geht ihm b.,** (i) he is in the best of health, (ii) he is doing very well; **sein Geschäft, mit seinem Geschäft, geht es b.,** his business is going very, extremely, well. **2.** *St.Exch:* **eine Order b. ausführen,** to execute an order at best.

Bestensorder, *f. St.Exch:* order to execute at the best possible, most favourable, rates, order to execute at best.

---

beste(r), beste, beste(s), *a.* **1.** best; (*a*) **der beste Mensch auf der Welt,** the best man on earth; **er ist der beste Mensch, der beste aller Menschen,** he is the best of men, the best man alive; **er ist der beste Schüler, der Beste, in seiner Klasse,** he is the best (pupil) in his class, he is top of his class; **er war einer von unseren Besten, einer unserer Besten,** he was one of our best; **im Singen kann er sich mit den Besten messen, kann er es mit den Besten aufnehmen,** he can sing with the best; **er ist mein bester Freund,** he is my best friend; **bester Freund,** dearest friend; (*as patronizing form of address*) **mein Bester,** my dear fellow; **meine Beste,** my dear, my dear woman, (*to young woman*) my dear child; **du bist doch mein Bester, meine Beste,** you are the best (of them all), you are my pet, my darling; **beste Frau Müller, wie geht es Ihnen?** my dear Mrs Müller, how are you? **mein bestes Kleid,** my best dress; **seine besten Kleider anziehen,** to dress in one's best clothes, to put on, don, one's best clothes; **der Wein war nicht vom besten,** the wine was not of the best; **wir tranken vom, von seinem, besten Wein, wir tranken vom, von seinem, Besten,** we drank of the best, of his best (wine); **das ist bester Dickens,** that is Dickens at his best; **die besten Familien in der Stadt,** the best families of the town; *F:* **das kommt in den besten Familien vor,** it can happen in the best families; **in den besten Kreisen verkehren,** to move in the best circles; **in der besten Verfassung sein,** to be at one's best; **ein Mann in den besten Jahren, im besten Alter,** a man in his prime, in the prime of life; **sich von seiner besten Seite zeigen,** (i) (*of pers.*) to show the best side of one's character; to be on one's best behaviour; (ii) (*of town, landscape, etc.*) to present itself in its most attractive aspect; **diese Handlung zeigt seine Persönlichkeit im besten Licht, läßt seine Persönlichkeit im besten Licht erscheinen,** this action shows, puts, his personality in the most favourable light; **unter (den) besten Bedingungen arbeiten,** to work under the best conditions; **zum besten Preise verkaufen,** to sell at the highest, best, price; **der beste Plan wäre zu . . . ,** the best plan, the best thing, would be to . . . ; **im besten Fall(e),** at (the) best; **selbst im besten Fall(e) können wir erst morgen ankommen,** at best, at the earliest, we shall arrive tomorrow; **wir werden in das erste beste, in das nächste beste, Hotel gehen,** we shall go into the first hotel we come to, we come across; **wir werden den Wagen in die erste beste, nächste beste, Werkstatt bringen,** we shall take the car to the first garage we come to; **der erste beste,** (just) anybody, *F:* any Tom, Dick or Harry; **der beste Weg dahin ist dieser,** the best way to get there is this; **auf dem besten Wege sein zu . . . ,** to be well on the way to . . . , to be in a fair way to . . . ; **er ist auf dem besten Wege, ein Verbrecher zu werden,** he is well on the way to becoming a criminal; **ich kann ihm beim besten Willen nicht helfen,** with the best will in the world I can't help him; **ich kann hier beim besten Willen nichts finden,** I have looked, searched, everywhere, but I cannot find anything here; **ich konnte ihn beim besten Willen nicht verstehen,** I could not understand him however hard I tried; **etwas in der besten Absicht, in bester Absicht, tun,** to do sth. with the best (of) intentions; **ich tat es in der besten Absicht,** I did it with the best (of) intentions, I did it for the best; **nach besten Kräften, nach bestem Vermögen,** to the best of one's ability *or* abilities; **nach bestem Wissen,** to the best of one's knowledge; in all good faith; **nach meinem besten Wissen,** to the best of my knowledge, belief; **nach bestem Wissen und Gewissen handeln,** to act in all good faith; **im besten Zuge sein,** to be in the middle, in the midst, of (doing) sth.; to be in full swing; **er war mit seiner Erzählung im besten Zuge, als . . . ,** he was in full swing with his story when . . . ; **ich war im besten Lesen, als . . . ,** I was in the middle of reading when . . . ; (*b*) **wir sind die besten Freunde,** we are the best of friends; **in bestem Zustand,** in first-class condition; **ich befinde mich bei bester Gesundheit,** I am in the best of health; **in bester Stimmung sein,** to be in an excellent, in a very good, mood; **aus bester Familie kommen, stammen,** to come of a very good family; **besten Dank,** many thanks, thank you very much; **mit bestem Dank,** with many thanks; **mit bestem Gruß, mit besten Grüßen,** with kindest regards; **mit j-m in bestem Einvernehmen sein,** to be in perfect harmony with s.o.; to be on very good terms with s.o.; **sie schieden im besten Einvernehmen,** they parted on the best

---

of terms. **2.** (*neuter*) (*in certain contexts spelt with a capital B*) (*a*) **es wäre das beste, das beste wäre es, nichts zu sagen,** the best thing, the best way, would be to say nothing; **das beste wäre (es), zu . . . ,** the best plan, the best thing, would be to . . . ; **das Beste, was du tun kannst, ist . . . ,** the best thing you can do is . . . ; **das beste an der Sache, das beste daran, ist, daß . . . ,** the best part of it, the best of it, is that . . . ; **das Beste aus der Sache, daraus, machen,** to make the best of the matter, of it; **etwas für das beste halten,** to think, consider, sth. best; **tu, was du für das beste hältst,** do as you think best; **ich hielt es für das beste zu bleiben,** I thought it best to stay; **wissen, was das beste für j-n ist,** to know what is best for s.o.; **das Beste hoffen,** to hope for the best; **hoffen wir das Beste,** let us hope for the best; (*b*) **das Beste auslesen,** to pick, choose, the best; **das Beste bis zuletzt aufheben, aufsparen,** to keep the best till the end, to the last; **das Beste ist mir gerade gut genug,** the best is just about good enough for me; **das Beste vom Besten,** the very best, *F:* the best, the pick, of the bunch, the pick of the basket; (*c*) **es wird sich alles zum Besten wenden,** everything will turn out well, for the best; **es ist alles nur zum Besten, für das Beste,** it is all for the best; **zum Besten, für das Beste, handeln,** to act for the best; **zum Besten, für das Beste, des Volkes,** for the public welfare, for the welfare of the people; **ich handle nur zu deinem Besten, ich habe nur dein Bestes im Auge,** I am acting in your best interests; **ich tat es zu deinem Besten,** I did it for your benefit; **Aufführung zum Besten der Armen,** performance for the benefit of the poor, charity performance; (*d*) **das Beste in j-m erwecken,** to bring out the best in s.o.; **das Beste aus j-m herausholen,** to get the best out of s.o.; **sein Bestes tun,** to do one's best, the best one can, everything in one's power; **ich tat mein Bestes, sie zu trösten,** I did my best to comfort her; **ich tue mein Bestes für dich,** I am doing my (level) best, the best I can, for you; **ich werde mein Bestes tun,** I shall do my best; **tue dein Bestes,** do your best, do the best you can; **sie taten ihr Bestes für die Verwundeten,** they did their best for the wounded; (*of pianist, actor, etc.*) **sein Bestes geben,** to give of one's best; **die Darsteller gaben alle ihr Bestes,** all the actors gave of their best. **3.** *adv.phr.* (*a*) **am besten,** best; best of all; (i) (*adj. use*) (= **das beste,** *q.v. under* **2** (*a*)) **es wäre am besten, zu . . . ,** it would be best to . . . ; **es wäre am besten, zu Haus zu bleiben, wir blieben am besten zu Hause,** it would be best to stay at home; **es wird am besten sein, mit dem Auto zu fahren, wir werden am besten mit dem Auto fahren,** we had best go by car, it would be best for us to go by car; (ii) (*adj. use*) **am besten war er immer in Latein,** he was always best at Latin; **er ist am besten als Landschaftsmaler,** he is best at landscape painting; (iii) (*adv. use*) **sie tanzt am besten,** she dances best of all, she is the best dancer; **dieser Hut gefällt mir am besten,** I like this hat best (of all); **du weißt es am besten,** you know best; **er sah am besten in Uniform aus,** he looked his best in uniform; **von den drei Schwestern sah sie am besten aus,** she was the best looking of the three sisters; **die am besten aussehenden Frauen,** the best looking women; **der am besten gekleidete Mann,** the best dressed man; **am besten abschneiden,** to come off best, to get, have, the best of it, of the bargain; **du hast am besten abgeschnitten,** you have come off, come out, best; (*b*) **der Kuchen ist nicht zum besten gelungen,** the cake has not turned out very well, the cake has not turned out (to be) a success; **mit seinem Geschäft steht es augenblicklich nicht zum besten,** his business is not going too well at the moment; **es steht nicht zum besten mit der Ernte,** the harvest does not look too promising; **es ist alles aufs, auf das, beste besorgt,** everything has been done most satisfactorily; **wir wurden aufs, auf das, beste bewirtet,** we were handsomely, lavishly, entertained, we had the best of everything; (*c*) **etwas zum besten geben,** to entertain an audience, etc., with sth.; **ein Gedicht zum besten geben,** to recite a poem (to an audience); **Herr Schmidt gab mehrere Lieder zum besten,** Mr Smith sang several songs, Mr Smith obliged with several songs; **er hat wahrscheinlich wieder seine dummen Witze zum besten gegeben,** he has probably been telling his silly jokes again; **j-n zum besten halten, haben,** to make fun of s.o., to make a fool of s.o., *F:* to pull s.o.'s leg; **da hat dich jemand zum besten gehalten, gehabt,** somebody's been pulling your leg.

besternt, *a.* star-spangled, starry, star-lit (sky, etc.); (sky, etc.) studded with stars; *F:* bemedalled (uniform); *Her:* **besternter Schild,** shield semée of, powdered with, mullets.

besteuern. I. *v.tr.* to tax, impose a tax on (s.o., goods, luxuries, motor cars, etc.); to lay a rate on (building, real estate, etc.); **das Einkommen b.,** to tax income; **alles ist besteuert,** everything is taxed; **hoch besteuert sein,** to be heavily taxed; **hoch besteuertes Gebäude,** heavily rated building.

II. *vbl s.* **1. Besteuern,** *n. in vbl senses.* **2. Besteuerung,** *f.* (*a*)=II. 1; *also:* taxation; **eine Reform der B.,** a reform in taxation; (*b*) **direkte, indirekte, B.,** direct, indirect, taxation; **die B. ist zu hoch,** taxation is too heavy; (*on building, etc.*) the rates are too high.

Bestfall, *m.* **im B.,** at (the) best.

bestgehend, *a.* best-selling (article, book, etc.).

bestgemeint, *a.* best-intentioned; **er weist selbst den bestgemeinten Rat zurück,** he refuses even the best-intentioned advice.

Besthaupt, *n. A.Jur:* heriot.

bestialisch [bɛstĭ'aːlɪʃ], *a.* bestial; brutal; inhuman; *F:* beastly (weather, etc.); **eine bestialische Tat,** a bestial, brutal, deed; *adv.* **er wurde b. ermordet,** he was brutally murdered; *F:* **es herrscht eine bestialische Kälte,** it is beastly cold.

Bestialität [bɛstĭa·li·'tɛːt], *f.* -/-en. **1.** (*a*) bestiality; brutality; (*b*) bestial, brutal, act. **2.** sodomy.

Bestiar [bɛstĭ'aːr], *n.* -s/-e, **Bestiarium** [bɛstĭ'aːrĭum], *n.* -s/-rien. *Lit.Hist:* bestiary, book of beasts.

Bestich, *m.* -(e)s/. *Constr:* rough-coat, rough-cast(ing).

Bestick, *n.* -(e)s/.=**Besteck** 3 (*a*).

besticken. I. *v.tr.* **1.** to embroider (sth.); **ein Taschentuch b.,** to embroider a handkerchief; **einen Stoff mit Blumen b.,** to embroider a material with flowers, to embroider flowers on a material; **mit Perlen besticktes Kleid,** dress embroidered, stitched, with beads. **2.** *Civ.E:* to cover (dike) with a protective layer of straw.

II. *vbl s.* **1. Besticken,** *n. in vbl senses.* **2. Bestickung,** *f.* (*a*)=II. 1; (*b*) *Civ.E:* protective layer of straw (on dike).

Bestie ['bɛstĭə], *f.* -/-n, (i) brute beast, (wild) animal; brute; (ii) bestial, brutal, inhuman, person; brute; *F:* beast; **ein gereizter Tiger ist eine gefährliche B.,** an angry tiger is a dangerous beast; **er war eine B. in Menschengestalt,** he was a beast in human form; **die B. in uns,** the beast in us; **der Alkohol macht Menschen zu Bestien,** alcohol turns men into beasts; **die kleine B.,** (*of child, pet, etc.*) the little brute, devil, beast.

bestielen, *v.tr.* **1.** to fix a handle to, to helve, to haft (tool). **2.** *Nat.Hist:* **bestielt,** stemmed, stalked (flower, fruit, leaf, etc.).

Bestiensäule, *f. Arch:* pillar *or* column carved with monsters and human figures.

bestiften, *v.tr. Ap:* (*of queen bee*) **die Zellen mit Eiern b.,** to lay eggs in the cells.

bestimmbar, *a.* determinable (conditions, quantity, etc.); (plant, etc.) that can be determined; definable (concept, etc.), (concept, etc.) that can be defined.

bestimmen. I. *v.tr.* **1.** (*a*) to determine, fix, settle, decide (up)on (date, time, place, price, conditions, etc.); to set (time, date, etc.); to appoint (date, time, place, etc.); to determine, fix (value, etc.); **einen Tag, einen Treffpunkt, b.,** to determine, fix, settle, a day, a meeting-place; **den Tag und den Ort b.,** to arrange, fix, appoint, settle, the day and the place; **an dem bestimmten Tage,** on the set, stated, day, on the day fixed; **zur bestimmten Zeit,** at the fixed, appointed, time; **ich möchte die Bedingungen selbst b.,** I want to lay down my own conditions; **Bedingungen, die noch (näher) bestimmt werden müssen,** conditions still to be determined; **es ist noch nichts bestimmt worden,** nothing has been decided, fixed, settled, yet; **die Erbfolge b.,** to settle the succession; **bestimmte Formeln,** set formulas; **genau bestimmte Grenzen,** well-defined, precisely defined, limits; **die von den Herstellern bestimmten Preise,** the prices laid down by the manufacturers; (*b*) to order (sth.); to lay down (conditions, etc.); **Gott bestimmt alles nach seinem Willen,** God disposes all things according to His will; **Gott hat es so bestimmt,** it was God's will; **du hast in dieser Angelegenheit nichts zu b.,** you have no say, you have no voice, in this matter. **2.** (*a*) to destine; **ihm war kein langes Leben bestimmt,** he was not destined, it was not granted to him, to live long; **es war ihm nicht bestimmt, seine Heimat wiederzusehen,** the gods did not grant him, he was not destined, to see his country again; **es war ihm bestimmt, auf dem Schafott zu sterben,** he was destined, fated, doomed, to die on the scaffold; (*b*) **j-s Schicksal b.,** to determine, decide, s.o.'s fate; **sein Geschick wird jetzt bestimmt,** his fate is now being decided; **dieser Vorfall bestimmte seine ganze Laufbahn, war bestimmend für seine ganze Laufbahn,** this incident determined, decided, his whole career, this incident was decisive for his whole career; (*c*) to determine (sth.); **der Radius bestimmt den Kreisumfang, der Kreisumfang wird durch den Radius bestimmt,** the circumference of a circle is determined by the radius; **die Güte des Weines wird von der Qualität der Trauben bestimmt, die Qualität der Trauben bestimmt die Güte des Weines,** the quality of the wine is determined by, depends on, the quality of the grapes; **der Preis wird von Angebot und Nachfrage bestimmt,** the price is determined by, depends on, supply and demand; **der bestimmende Faktor hierbei ist . . .,** the determining, decisive, factor here is . . .; **die den Preis bestimmenden Faktoren,** the factors which determine the price, the factors on which the price depends. **3.** (*a*) to intend (s.o.) (for office, etc.); to designate, nominate, appoint (s.o.) (for post, etc.); **er hatte seinen Sohn zum Juristen bestimmt,** he had intended his son for the legal profession, for the bar; **wir bestimmten unseren Sohn für die Kirche,** we intended our son for the Church, to enter the Church; **j-n zu seinem Vertreter, zu seinem Erben, b.,** to appoint s.o. one's deputy, one's heir, to make s.o. one's deputy, one's heir; **j-n zu seinem Nachfolger b.,** to designate, nominate, s.o. as one's successor; (*b*) to intend (sth.) (for s.o., sth.); to assign (sth.) (to sth.); to intend, appropriate, set apart, earmark, allocate (sth.) (for a certain use); **ich hatte diesen Geldbeutel dir, für dich, bestimmt,** I intended, meant, this purse for you; **der Kunde, für den dieses Auto bestimmt war, hat seinen Auftrag zurückgezogen,** the customer for whom this car was intended has cancelled his order; **dieses Bild ist für mein Schlafzimmer bestimmt,** this picture is intended for my bedroom; **diese Geschichte ist nicht für Kinderohren bestimmt,** this story is not (meant) for children to hear; **das Buch war nicht für dich bestimmt,** the book was not (meant) for you; **das für Nichtschwimmer bestimmte Becken ist nicht sehr tief,** the pool (intended, provided) for non-swimmers is not very deep; **diese Bemerkung war für dich bestimmt,** this remark was meant, intended, for you; **die Kugel war dir, für dich, bestimmt,** the bullet was intended for you; **dieses Geld ist für einen neuen Teppich bestimmt,** this money is intended for, is (to be used) for, a new carpet; **Schiffe, die für den Flußverkehr, für eine Geschwindigkeit von 20 Knoten, bestimmt sind,** boats designed, intended, for river traffic, for a speed of 20 knots; **das Schiff war nach Indien bestimmt,** the ship was bound for, was making for, India; **die zur Vernichtung bestimmten Dokumente,** the documents to be destroyed. **4.** to give the definition of (sth.); to define, determine (species, word, etc.); to parse (word); to define (concept, etc.); *Mth: etc:* to find, determine, work out (value, quantity, etc.); **eine Pflanze b.,** to define a plant; **einen Satz, einen Satzteil, b.,** to define a sentence, a part, a member, of a sentence; **den Inhalt eines Zylinders b.,** to find, work out, the capacity of a cylinder; **eine unbekannte Größe b.,** to determine an unknown quantity; **etwas näher, genauer, b.,** to define sth. more clearly, more accurately; to specify sth.; **sofern nicht anderweitig bestimmt,** unless otherwise specified. **5.** *Gram: etc:* to qualify, modify (verb); **das Adverb bestimmt das Verb näher,** the adverb modifies, qualifies, the verb; **das Adjektiv bestimmt das Substantiv,** the adjective serves to qualify, define, the noun; **bestimmendes Fürwort,** determinative pronoun. **6. j-n zu etwas b.,** to induce, impel, move, s.o. to do sth.; **nichts wird ihn dazu b., seine Meinung zu ändern,** nothing will induce him to change his mind, nothing will make him change his mind; **ich ließ mich von meiner Abneigung gegen ihn b.,** I let myself be moved, influenced, guided, by my dislike of him; **Umstände, die j-n in seinem Urteil bestimmen, die j-s Urteil bestimmen,** circumstances which guide, influence, s.o.'s judgment; **von geheimen Beweggründen bestimmt,** impelled, moved, by secret motives.

II. **bestimmen,** *v.i.* (*haben*) **1.** (*a*) **über etwas** *acc.* **b.,** to dispose of sth.; **über seine Zeit frei b.,** to dispose of one's time freely, to be master of one's time; **ich kann über meine Güter b., wie ich will,** I can dispose of my possessions as I wish, I can do what I like with my possessions; **Sie können nach Belieben darüber b.,** it is entirely at your disposal, you can, may, do what you like with it; **Sie können über mich b.,** I am at your disposal, at your service; **ich kann über meinen Mann nicht b.,** I cannot anticipate my husband's decisions, I cannot answer for my husband; (*b*) **über etwas** *acc.* **b.,** to give orders, instructions, directions, in respect of sth.; to give a decision on sth.; **hast du über das Haus schon bestimmt?** have you given any instructions, directions, as to what should be done with the house? have you decided what should be done with the house? **über j-s Geschick b.,** to dispose of s.o.'s fate, to decide on s.o.'s fate. **2.** to order, to give orders; to decree; to ordain, to rule; **b., daß etwas getan werden soll,** to order, give orders, direct, that sth. should be done; **in dieser Angelegenheit hat keiner von euch zu b.,** none of you has any say, has any voice, in this matter; **hier bestimme ich!** I am the boss here! I am in charge here! **wenn ich zu b. hätte, würde ich . . .,** if I were the boss, if I had my way, if it were for me to decide, I would . . .; **das Gesetz bestimmt, daß . . .,** the law says that . . ., the law provides that . . .; **das Gericht bestimmte, daß der Präsident seiner Pflichten enthoben werden sollte,** the court ordained, ruled, that the president should be suspended; **in seinem Testament bestimmte er, daß das Geld zum Bau einer Schule verwendet werden sollte,** he provided, directed, in his will that the money should be used to build a school.

III. *vbl s.* **1. Bestimmen,** *n. in vbl senses.* **2. Bestimmung,** *f.* (*a*) *in vbl senses; also:* determination, settlement, appointment (of date, time, place, etc.); determination (of value, of s.o.'s fate, etc.); destination (of s.o.) (for the church, etc.); designation, nomination, appointment (of s.o.) (as deputy, successor, etc.); assignation, appropriation, allocation (of money, etc.) (for a certain use); definition, determination (of species, word, etc.); definition (of concept, etc.); *Gram:* qualification, modification (of verb); (*b*) definition (of species, word, object, concept, etc.); **Totschlag, der unter die B. Mord fällt,** homicide which falls under the definition, category, of murder; (*c*) intended purpose (of building, sum of money, etc.); **ein Gebäude seiner B. übergeben,** to inaugurate a building; **das Schiff wurde feierlich seiner B. als Schulschiff übergeben,** with all due ceremony the ship was handed over for its function as a training-ship; (*d*) destination; **am Ort seiner B. ankommen,** to arrive at, to reach, one's destination; **die Waren haben den Ort ihrer B. nicht erreicht,** the goods failed to arrive at their destination; (*e*) fate; destiny; **man kann nicht gegen seine B. ankämpfen,** there is no striving against fate; (*f*) *Gram:* **adverbiale, umstandswörtliche, B.,** adverbial element; adverbial phrase; adverbial modifier; **adverbiale B. der Zeit, des Ortes, des Grundes, der Art und Weise,** adverbial element of time, of place, of cause, of manner; (*g*) regulation, rule; provision (of law, treaty, etc.); decree; order; **eine B. erlassen,** to issue, set up, lay down, a regulation, a rule; to issue an order, a decree; **gegen die Bestimmungen, entgegen den Bestimmungen, den Bestimmungen zuwider,** contrary to, against, the regulations, the rules; **gemäß den Bestimmungen handeln,** to act in accordance with, according to, the regulations, the rules; **die Bestimmungen im Zollverkehr,** the customs regulations; **polizeiliche Bestimmungen,** police regulations; police ordinances; **amtliche Bestimmungen,** official regulations; **gesetzliche B.,** legislative enactment; **ausführende Bestimmungen,** regulations for enactment; enacting clauses (of an act); **die neuen Bestimmungen für den Autoexport,** the new regulations for the export of cars.

IV. *p.p. & a.* **bestimmt,** *in vbl senses; esp.* **1.** determined, resolute, firm, decided (pers., manner, voice, etc.); definite, firm, decided, positive (answer, judgment, etc.); **in bestimmtem Ton,** in a resolute, firm, definite, decided, tone; **ich muß eine bestimmte Antwort haben,** I must have a definite, firm, positive, answer; **er war nicht sehr b. in seinem Urteil,** he was not very definite in his judgment; **bestimmte Absichten,** definite intentions; **j-m bestimmte Information über seine Absichten geben,** to give s.o. definite information as to one's intentions; **eine bestimmte Weigerung, ein bestimmtes 'Nein',** a decided, definite, firm, refusal, a decided,

definite, firm, 'no'; **mit bestimmten Schritten ging er auf sie zu,** with firm, resolute, steps he went towards her. **2.** (*a*) determined, definite, well-defined (area, purpose, etc.); particular, specific, special (aim, reason, etc.); given, fixed, certain (point, number, date, etc.); **in einer bestimmten Richtung,** in a given, certain, direction; **bei einer bestimmten Anzahl von Umdrehungen,** at a given, certain, number of revolutions; **Wort, das in einem ganz bestimmten Sinn gebraucht ist,** word used in a very special sense; **zu bestimmten Zwecken,** for special purposes; for certain purposes; **verfolgst du damit einen bestimmten Zweck, eine bestimmte Absicht?** are you doing it for a special purpose, with a special purpose in mind? **ich ging aus keinem bestimmten Grunde fort,** I left for no particular, special, specific, reason; **ich habe meine ganz bestimmten Gründe dafür,** I have my own particular reasons for it; **er schrieb immer an einem bestimmten Tage,** he used to write on a certain day; **ich komme in einer bestimmten Angelegenheit,** I have called on particular business; **keine bestimmten Pläne haben,** to have no fixed, definite, particular, plans; **nichts Bestimmtes zu tun haben,** to have nothing particular, nothing special, to do; **hast du heute etwas Bestimmtes vor?** are you doing anything particular, anything special, today? have you any particular, special, plans for today? (*b*) (*undetermined*) certain; **es gibt bestimmte Dinge, die . . .,** there are certain things that . . .; **bestimmte Bedingungen in dem Vertrage sind überflüssig,** certain conditions in the contract are superfluous; **bis zu einem bestimmten Grade,** to a certain degree; **das Museum ist nur an bestimmten Tagen geöffnet,** the museum is open only on certain days; **mit Frauen in einem bestimmten Alter, mit Frauen eines bestimmten Alters,** with women of a certain age; (*c*) *Gram:* **bestimmter Artikel, bestimmtes Geschlechtswort,** definite article; *Mth: etc:* **bestimmte Zahlen, bestimmte Größen,** given, fixed, numbers, given, fixed, quantities. **3.** *adv.* (*a*) for certain; definitely; certainly; **etwas b. wissen,** to know sth. for certain, to know sth. definitely; **ich weiß ganz b. daß . . .,** I know for certain, for a certainty, I know quite definitely, that . . .; **er wird b. kommen,** he is certain, sure, to come; he will come for certain, he will definitely come; **ich gehe ganz b. nicht hin,** I most definitely, most certainly, won't go there; **ich kann nicht b. sagen, wann er abfahren wird,** I cannot say for certain, I cannot say definitely, when he will start; **der Direktor sagte ihm freundlich, aber b., daß man ihm keine Arbeit geben könnte,** the director told him kindly but firmly that they could not give him a job; **sie weigerte sich höflich, aber b., mit ihm zu gehen,** she refused politely but firmly to go with him; **das ist (ganz) b. wahr,** it is definitely true; **ich habe es ihm b. versprochen,** I gave him a definite promise; **ich rechne b. darauf,** I am definitely counting on it; **er wird b. Erfolg haben,** he is sure, certain, to succeed; **auf das, aufs, bestimmteste,** most definitely; **ich habe die Einladung auf das, aufs, bestimmteste abgelehnt,** I refused the invitation most firmly, most definitely; **der Vater hatte seinem Sohn auf das bestimmteste verboten, auf diesen Baum zu steigen,** the father had most strictly, most definitely, forbidden his son to climb this tree; (*b*) certainly; surely; **ich wäre b. gekommen, wenn . . .,** I would certainly have come if . . .; **es wird dir b. gefallen,** I'm sure you will like it, you are sure to like it; **ich kann das Buch nicht finden, er hat es b. mitgenommen,** I can't find the book; he must have taken it with him; **ist das b. wahr?** are you sure it is true? **wir haben uns b. schon einmal gesehen,** surely we have met before, I'm sure we have met before; **das habe ich ganz b. nie gesagt,** I am quite sure, certain, absolutely sure, certain, I never said that; **ich habe es b. nicht mit Absicht getan,** I definitely didn't do it on purpose; honestly, I didn't do it on purpose; **er hat es b. gut gemeint,** I am sure, certain, he meant well; **b. hat er das gewußt,** he must have known it, I'm certain, sure, he knew it; he certainly knew it; **hast du es b. nicht vergessen?** are you sure you haven't forgotten it? **du hast das doch b. auch gelesen,** you must have read that too; **er ist b. verrückt, sonst . . .,** he must (surely) be mad, otherwise . . .; **komm aber b. früh,** be sure to come early, *F:* be sure and come early; **meinst du, daß er kommen wird? — b.!** do you think he will come?—I'm sure he will! I'm sure of it! **certainly! darf ich Ihnen noch etwas auflegen? —**

nein, danke. — **b. nicht?** may I give you some more?—no, thank you.—are you sure? really not? **ist dir hier warm genug? — ja, danke. — b.?** are you warm enough here?—yes, thank you.—(are you) sure? are you, really?

Bestimmtheit, *f.* **1.** definiteness (of concept, etc.). **2.** (*a*) definiteness, resoluteness, firmness (of pers., manner, voice, etc.); **die B. ihres Tones,** the firmness of her voice; (*b*) *adv.phr.* **mit B.,** for certain, definitely; certainly; **etwas mit B. wissen,** to know sth. for a certainty, for certain; **ich kann nicht mit B. sagen, wann er abfahren wird,** I cannot say for certain, I cannot say definitely, when he will leave.
Bestimmung, *f.* see **bestimmen** III.
Bestimmungsbuch, *n. Bot:* book containing tables for identification of plants.
Bestimmungsfürwort, *n. Gram:* determinative (pronoun).
bestimmungsgemäß, *a. & adv.* according to, in accordance with, the regulations, the rules.
Bestimmungsgleichung, *f. Mth:* conditional equation, equation of condition.
Bestimmungshafen, *m. Nau:* port of destination.
Bestimmungsland, *n.* country of destination.
Bestimmungsmensur, *f.* students' fencing encounter (*not as affair of honour*).
Bestimmungsort, *m.* destination; **an seinem B. ankommen, seinen B. erreichen,** to arrive at, to reach, one's destination; **die Waren haben ihren B. nicht erreicht,** the goods failed to arrive at their destination; **der B. des Schiffes ist Bordeaux,** the ship is bound for, is making for, Bordeaux.
Bestimmungssatz, *m. Gram:* defining clause, determinative clause, restrictive, limitative, limiting, clause.
Bestimmungsstück, *n. Mth: etc:* datum; given value; one of the data (required for determination of quantity, etc.); *Phil:* determinative element, characteristic element (of thg).
bestimmungswidrig, *a.* contrary to, against, the regulations, against the rule(s); **bestimmungswidrige Handlung,** action that is against the rules; *adv.* in contravention of the regulations.
Bestimmungswort, *n.* -(e)s/-wörter. *Ling:* determinative element (of compound).
Bestleistung, *f. Sp: etc:* best performance; record, record performance; **eine neue B. aufstellen,** to set up a new record; **seine alte B. überbieten,** to beat one's previous best, one's previous record, to better one's previous best performance.
Bestmann, *m.* -(e)s/-leute. *Nau:* (*a*) *A:* experienced able seaman; (*b*) mate (of small coaster).
bestmöglich, *attrib.a.* best possible; most favourable (conditions, price, rate, etc.); **der bestmögliche Preis,** the best price possible; **die bestmögliche Lösung,** the best possible solution; **mit der bestmöglichen Sorgfalt,** with the utmost care; **sein Bestmögliches tun, das Bestmögliche tun,** to do one's utmost, to do everything in one's power.
bestmöglichst, *adv. Fin:* at the most favourable price(s), rate(s), at best; *St.Exch:* **eine Order b. ausführen,** to execute an order at best.
bestocken, *v.tr.* **1.** *Arb: etc:* to plant (land) (with trees, vines, etc.); **mit Bäumen gut bestocktes Land,** well-wooded, well-timbered, country. **2.** *Agr: Hort:* **sich bestocken,** to tiller, to stool; **Getreide, das sich gut bestockt,** corn that tillers well; **Bestockung** *f,* tillering, stooling.
bestöhnen, *v.tr.* to bemoan, to moan about (sth., s.o.'s fate, etc.).
bestoßen, *v.tr.* (*strong*) **1.** to knock a piece off (sth.); to chip (china, glass, etc.); to knock, mark (piece of furniture, wall, etc.); **einen Teller, eine Tasse, b.,** to chip (off a piece from) a plate, a cup; **die Wand b.,** to chip, scrape, (the plaster off) the wall; **sich** *dat.* **den Ärmel b.,** to chafe, fray, one's sleeve; **die Ecken dieses Buches sind leider ziemlich bestoßen,** the corners of this book are unfortunately somewhat damaged, rather worn; **eine an vielen Stellen bestoßene Statue der Diana,** a statue of Diana chipped, damaged, in many places. **2.** to rough-plane (wood); to dress, trim, chamfer (piece of wood, block of stone, etc.); to file (metal) with a coarse file; *Print:* to plane (down) (forme).
Bestoßfeile, *f. Tls:* rough file, coarse file, straw file.
Bestoßhobel, *m. Tls:* rough plane; jack-plane.
Bestoßmaschine, *f. Tls:* (rough-)planing machine.
Bestoßzeug, *n. Tls:* planing or bevelling device.
Bestpreis, *m. Com: etc:* highest price, best price; **zum B. verkaufen,** to sell at the highest price, to sell at best.

bestrafen. **I.** *v.* **1.** *v.tr.* to punish (offender, offence); to punish, chastise (child, etc.); **j-n für etwas, wegen etwas, b.,** to punish s.o. for sth.; **für seine Frechheit bestraft werden,** to be punished for one's impudence; **für seinen Leichtsinn bestraft werden,** to be punished for one's recklessness; **er wird für meine Schwäche bestraft,** he is punished for my weakness; **j-n für ein Verbrechen, für eine Lüge, b.,** to punish s.o. for a crime, for a lie; to inflict a punishment on s.o. for a crime, for a lie; **diese Frechheit muß bestraft werden,** this impudence must be punished; **ein Verbrechen mit dem Tode b.,** to punish a crime by death. **2.** (*of irresponsible action, etc.*) **sich bestraft machen,** to be punished; **sein Leichtsinn wird sich bestraft machen,** his recklessness will be punished, he will be punished for his recklessness.
II. *vbl s.* **1. Bestrafen,** *n.* in vbl senses. **2. Bestrafung,** *f.* (*a*)=II. 1; *also:* punishment (of offender, offence); chastisement (of child, etc.); **körperliche B.,** corporal punishment; **die B. eines Kindes,** the punishment, punishing, chastisement, of a child; **B. von unbefugtem Waffenbesitz,** punishment of, for, illegal possession of firearms; (*b*) punishment, being punished; **der B. entgehen,** to escape punishment, to go unpunished; (*c*) punishment; penalty; **Gesetz, das B. vorsieht für . .,** law providing punishment, penalties, for . . . .
Bestrafer, *m.* -s/-, punisher.
bestrahlen. **I.** *v.tr.* (*a*) (*of sun, etc.*) to shine (up)on, to irradiate (earth, etc.); (*of light, heat, etc.*) to irradiate (earth, surface, etc.); (*of light rays, etc.*) to irradiate, illuminate (sth.); **sich von der Sonne b. lassen,** to take a sun-bath, to lie in the sun; to expose oneself to the sun; **bestrahlt von Gottes Gnade,** irradiated by God's grace; (*b*) *Med:* to irradiate (s.o., part of body, etc.); to give (s.o.) ray treatment, radiation treatment; (*c*) *Atom.Ph:* to irradiate (fuel slug, etc.).
II. *vbl s.* **1. Bestrahlen,** *n.* in vbl senses. **2. Bestrahlung,** *f.* (*a*)=II. 1; *also:* irradiation (of earth, etc.); illumination (of surface, etc.); *Med:* irradiation (of s.o., part of body, etc.); (*b*) *Med:* ray treatment, radiation treatment, irradiation; radiotherapy; **B. durch Höhensonne,** sun-ray treatment; **viele Hautkrankheiten können durch B. geheilt werden,** many skin diseases can be cured by ray treatment, by radiotherapy; **schon nach wenigen Bestrahlungen hatte sich ihr Leiden gebessert,** after only a few ray treatments, a few radiations, her condition had improved; (*c*) *Atom.Ph:* irradiation.
Bestrahlungsfeld, *n. Med:* irradiation field.
Bestrahlungslampe, *f. Med:* radiation lamp.
bestreben (sich). **I.** *v.refl.* **sich b., bestrebt sein,** etwas zu tun, etwas zu sein, to endeavour, strive, try, to be anxious, to do sth., to be sth.; **sie bestrebte sich, sie war bestrebt, ihren Eltern Freude zu machen,** she endeavoured, strove, she was always anxious, to please her parents; **er war eifrig bestrebt, ihr zu gefallen,** he was eager, anxious, to please her; **ich werde mich b., ich werde bestrebt sein, alles zu Ihrer Befriedigung auszuführen,** it will be my endeavour, I shall endeavour, to carry out everything to your satisfaction, to give every satisfaction; *Com. Corr:* **stets bestrebt, Ihre Wünsche aufs beste zu erfüllen,** we shall always endeavour, it will be our constant endeavour, to fulfil your orders to your complete satisfaction.
II. *vbl s.* **1. Bestreben,** *n.* endeavour; effort; aim; desire; **stetes B.,** constant endeavour; **eifriges B.,** zealous endeavour; zealous effort; **mein ganzes B., mein heißes B., geht dahin, ist, dir zu dienen,** I endeavour always to serve you, my only aim, my ardent desire, is to serve you; **es wird stets mein B. sein, es wird mein stetes B. sein, Sie zufriedenzustellen,** it will be my constant endeavour to satisfy you. **2. Bestrebung,** *f.* endeavour; effort; tendency; **alle meine Bestrebungen gehen dahin, zu . . .,** all my endeavours, all my efforts, are aimed at . . .; **es sind Bestrebungen im Gange, strengere Kontrollen einzuführen,** efforts are being made to introduce tighter controls.
bestreichen, *v.tr.* (*strong*) **1.** (*a*) to stroke, pass one's hand over (sth.); (*b*) *A:* **j-n mit Ruten b.,** to birch s.o.; to flog s.o. with birch-rods. **2.** to coat, cover (sth.) (with paint, tar, etc.); to spread (bread, etc.) (with butter, jam, etc.); to cover (skin, wound, etc.) (with ointment, etc.); **eine Tür mit grüner Farbe b.,** to give a door a coat of green paint, to paint a door green; **die Wand war mit Farbe bestrichen,** the wall was coated with paint; **einen Zaun mit Kreosot b.,** to

coat a fence with creosote, to creosote a fence; **ein Stück Brot mit Butter b.,** to spread a slice of bread with butter, to spread butter on a slice of bread, to butter a slice of bread; **ein Stück Brot mit Honig, mit Marmelade, b.,** to spread honey, jam, on a slice of bread; **einen Kuchen mit Eigelb b.,** to paint, brush, a cake with egg; *Med:* **mit Jod b.,** to paint with iodine; **eine Brandwunde mit Öl b.,** to spread oil on a burn. **3.** (*a*) *Artil:* to rake, sweep, (area) with fire; **der Länge nach b., durch Flankenfeuer b.,** to enfilade, rake, flank (trench, etc.); **bestrichenes Gelände, bestrichener Raum,** area under fire; beaten zone; danger-zone; (*b*) (*of bird, etc.*) to fly over, to pass through (district); (*of wind, rain, etc.*) to beat (house, window, etc.).

Bestreichungswinkel, *m. Ball:* arc of fire, of traverse; balayage (of gun, machine-gun).

bestreiken, *v.tr. Ind: etc:* to strike against (firm, etc.); **die Transportarbeiter bestreikten sämtliche Autobuslinien,** the transport workers struck on all bus routes, all bus routes were affected by the transport workers' strike; **bestreikte Werften,** shipyards affected by the strike(s).

bestreitbar, *a.* **1.** contestable, disputable, challengeable (point, right, etc.); controversial (statement, etc.); deniable (facts, guilt, etc.). **2.** payable, defrayable (costs, etc.).

bestreiten. I. *v.tr.* (*strong*) **1.** (*a*) *A:* to fight (against), to battle against (s.o., sth.); to beleaguer, attack (town, etc.); (*b*) *Sp:* **einen Wettlauf b.,** to contest a race. **2.** to contest, dispute, challenge (point, right, etc.); to deny (facts, guilt, etc.); **j-s Recht b., j-m das Recht b., etwas zu tun,** to challenge s.o.'s right to do sth.; **ich bestreite sein Recht,** I dispute, question, challenge, his right; **eine Behauptung b.,** to deny a statement; **die Tatsache läßt sich nicht b., man kann die Tatsache nicht b.,** there is no denying the fact; **b., daß man etwas getan hat,** to deny having done sth.; **der Angeklagte bestritt, daß er die Worte gesagt hätte,** the accused denied (having said) the words; **ich bestreite gar nicht, daß er klug ist,** I don't dispute, deny, that he is clever; **ich kann (es) nicht b., daß Sie recht haben,** I cannot deny that you are right; **es läßt sich nicht b.,** there is no denying it, one cannot deny it, *F:* there is no getting away from it; **man kann kaum b., es läßt sich kaum b., daß diese Zugeständnisse gefährlich sind,** one can hardly deny that these concessions are dangerous. **3.** (*a*) to pay, defray, bear, meet (expenses, cost, etc.); to pay, settle (debt, etc.); **die Kosten von etwas b.,** to pay, bear, meet, defray, the cost of sth.; **ich kann selbst alle Unkosten b.,** I can meet, defray, all the expenses myself, I myself am equal to all the expenses; **er hat immer seine eigenen Ausgaben bestritten,** he has always supported himself, paid his way; **er kann unmöglich alle Kosten selbst b., aus eigener Tasche b.,** he cannot possibly pay, meet, all the costs himself, from his own pocket; **kannst du das Essen, die Kosten des Essens, b.?** can you (afford to) pay for the food? can you foot the bill for the food? **die Transportkosten werden von uns bestritten,** the cost of transport is borne, paid, defrayed, by us; (*b*) **einen großen Teil der Unterhaltung b.,** to contribute a large share of the talk, to do most of the talking; **eine Unterhaltung allein b.,** to do all the talking; **der berühmte Pianist, der das ganze Programm mit eigenen Werken bestritt,** the famous pianist who filled the whole programme with, who devoted the whole programme to, his own works; **X bestritt die ganze erste Hälfte des Programms,** X carried the whole of the first half of the programme.

II. *vbl s.* **Bestreiten** *n.*, **Bestreitung** *f. in vbl senses; also:* **1.** contestation (of point, right, etc.); denial (of facts, guilt, etc.). **2.** payment, defrayal (of costs, etc.); settlement (of debts, etc.); **zur Bestreitung seiner Unkosten,** (in order) to cover, pay (for), one's expenses; **die Bestreitung auswärtiger Schulden durch den Export,** the payment, settlement, of foreign debts by (means of) export.

bestreuen. I. *v.tr.* **etwas mit etwas b.,** to strew, sprinkle, sth. with sth.; **mit Mehl b.,** to flour (baking-tin, etc.), to dust (baking-tin, etc.) with flour; **einen Kuchen mit Puderzucker b.,** to sprinkle, dust, dredge, a cake with icing sugar; **Fleisch, usw., mit Mehl b.,** to dredge meat, etc. with flour; to dredge flour over meat, etc.; **den Fußboden mit Sand b.,** to strew, sprinkle, the floor with sand, to sand the floor; **einen Fußweg mit Sand, mit Kies., b.,** to sand, gravel, a footpath; **mit Kies bestreuter Weg,** gravelled path; **den Boden mit Blumen b.,** to strew the floor with flowers; **der Pfad war mit Blütenblättern bestreut,** the path was strewn with flower petals.

II. *vbl s.* **1. Bestreuen,** *n. in vbl senses.* **2. Bestreuung,** *f.* (*a*)=II. 1; (*b*) sand, gravel, etc. (on road, footpath, etc.).

bestricken, *v.tr.* **1.** (*a*) to cover (ball, button, etc.) with knitted fabric; (*b*) *F:* to provide (s.o.) with knitted garments; **sie bestrickt die ganze Familie,** she knits for the whole family, she supplies the whole family with knitted garments. **2.** (*of pers., manner, etc.*) to captivate, charm, fascinate (s.o.); **er bestrickt alle durch seine Liebenswürdigkeit,** he captivates, wins, everybody with his charm; he takes everybody in with his charm; **ihr bestrickendes Lächeln,** her captivating, winning, charming, smile.

bestrumpft, *a.* (pers.) wearing stockings *or* socks.

Bestseller [ˈbɛstsɛlər], *m.* **-s/-,** best-seller, best-selling book.

bestücken. I. *v.tr.* (*a*) *Navy:* to arm (ship); to provide (ship) with guns; **mit schweren Kanonen bestücktes Schiff,** ship armed with heavy guns; **ein Schiff, das mit fünfzehn Geschützen bestückt ist,** a ship carrying fifteen guns; (*b*) *F:* to provide (sth.) (with sth.); **mit Orden reich bestückte Uniform,** uniform glittering with medals, bemedalled uniform.

II. *vbl s.* **1. Bestücken,** *n. in vbl senses.* **2. Bestückung,** *f.* (*a*)=II. 1; (*b*) (naval) armament; guns, ordnance (of ship); **Schiff mit schwerer B.,** ship with heavy ordnance, ship carrying heavy guns.

bestuhlen, *v.tr.* to provide (church, hall, etc.) with seating, with seats; **Bestuhlung** *f*, seating, seats, benches, chairs (in church, hall, etc.).

bestürmen. I. *v.tr.* **1.** (*a*) *Mil:* to make an assault on, to charge, storm, attack, rush (enemy, stronghold, etc.); **den Feind b.,** to charge, attack, the enemy; **eine Stellung b.,** to storm, rush, attack, a position, to make an assault on a position; (*b*) *F:* to rush, make a rush on (speaker's platform, shop, etc.); **einen Laden b.,** to make a rush on a shop, to rush a shop; **die Zuschauer bestürmten die Bühne,** the audience rushed the platform. **2.** to pester, plague, worry, press, *F:* badger (s.o.) (with questions, requests, etc.); **j-n mit Fragen b.,** to bombard, pester, press, ply, plague, s.o. with questions; **j-n mit Bitten um Geld b.,** to pester, plague, s.o. (with requests) for money; **j-n b., etwas zu tun,** to pester, press, *F:* badger, s.o. to do sth.; **sie bestürmten ihn, noch länger zu bleiben,** they pressed, urged, *F:* badgered, him to stay longer; **der Vater wurde von allen Seiten bestürmt, seine Erlaubnis zu geben,** the father was pressed, plagued, *F:* badgered, from all sides to give his permission.

II. *vbl s.* **1. Bestürmen,** *n. in vbl senses.* **2. Bestürmung,** *f.* (*a*) *in vbl senses; also:* attack (of stronghold, etc.); (*b*) attack, assault, charge (on enemy, stronghold, etc.); *F:* rush (on shop, etc.); (*c*) urgent, pressing, request *or* entreaty; **er konnte ihren Bestürmungen nicht standhalten,** he could not stand up to, he had to give in to, their entreaties, their badgering.

Bestürmer, *m.* attacker (of enemy, stronghold, etc.).

bestürzen. I. *v.tr.* **1.** *Tchn:* to charge (furnace, etc.). **2.** to dismay (s.o.), to strike (s.o.) with consternation, with dismay; **die Nachricht bestürzte ihn,** the news dismayed him, the news struck him with consternation, with dismay; **bestürzt,** dismayed, in dismay; consternated, struck with consternation, with dismay; **j-n bestürzt machen,** to dismay s.o., to strike s.o. with consternation, with dismay; to cause consternation to s.o.; **wir waren bestürzt über die Nachricht, die Nachricht machte uns bestürzt,** we were dismayed, struck with consternation, with dismay, at the news; **sie sah ihn bestürzt an,** she looked at him in consternation, in dismay; she gave him a look of consternation, of dismay; **sie sahen sich bestürzt an,** they looked at each other in consternation, in dismay; **sie machte ein ganz bestürztes Gesicht,** she looked quite dismayed, her face showed great consternation, great, blank, dismay.

II. *vbl s.* **1. Bestürzen,** *n. in vbl senses.* **2. Bestürzung,** *f.* consternation, dismay; **in B. geraten,** to be seized, struck, with consternation, with dismay; **auf ihrem Gesicht malte sich, zeigte sich, große B.,** her face showed great consternation, great, blank, dismay; **diese Worte lösten größte B. aus,** these words caused the greatest consternation, these words struck everyone with the greatest consternation, the greatest dismay; **mit großer B. las er ihren Brief,** he read her letter with great consternation, with great dismay.

Bestürztheit, *f.* consternation, dismay; **seine B. war echt,** his consternation, his dismay, was genuine.

Bestwirkungsgrad, *m. Mec.E:* optimum efficiency.

Bestzeit, *f. Sp: etc:* record, record time; **eine neue B. erreichen,** to set up a new record; **seine alte B. verbessern, unterbieten,** to beat one's previous best, one's previous record.

Bestzustand, *m.* first-class condition.

Besuch, *m.* **-(e)s/-e. 1.** (*a*) visiting (of exhibition, museum, etc.); visit to (exhibition, museum, etc.); **beim B. des Museums,** when visiting the museum; **ein B. der Ausstellung lohnt sich sehr,** a visit to the exhibition is well worth while; (*b*) attendance (at lecture, meeting, church, cinema, etc.); **starker B. der Vorstellungen,** good attendances at the performances; **der B. der Ausstellung hat nachgelassen,** the number of visitors to the exhibition has fallen. **2.** (*a*) (social) visit, call; **B. des Bischofs, bischöflicher B.,** pastoral visitation (by bishop); **j-m einen B. machen, abstatten,** to pay s.o. a visit, a call, to visit s.o., to call on s.o.; **einen B. machen, auf B. gehen,** to go on a visit; **j-m einen kurzen B. machen,** to pay s.o. a short visit, *F:* to drop in on s.o.; **j-s B. erwidern,** to return s.o.'s visit, s.o.'s call; **formeller B.,** formal visit, formal call; ceremonial call; **offizieller B.,** official visit, official call; **wir bitten um die Ehre Ihres Besuches,** we shall be honoured to receive a visit from you; (*b*) visit, call, attendance (by doctor, etc.); **B. eines Vertreters, eines Reisenden,** visit from, by, a representative; (*c*) attendance (at lecture, meeting, school, church, etc.); visit (to exhibition, museum, theatre, etc.); **bei jedem meiner Besuche des Museums,** on every one of my visits to the museum, every time I visited the museum. **3.** visit, stay; sojourn; **ein vierzehntägiger B.,** a fortnight's visit, a fortnight's stay; **wir entschlossen uns, unseren B. in Rom zu verlängern,** we decided to prolong our visit to Rome, our stay in Rome; **sein B. war nur kurz,** his visit, his stay, was only short, was only a short one; **er traf zu einem privaten B. in England ein,** he arrived in England for a private visit; **bei Freunden auf, zu, B. sein,** to be on a visit to friends; **ich bin hier nur zu, auf, B.,** I am only here on a visit; **Onkel Walter kommt morgen zu, auf, B.,** Uncle Walter is coming for a visit, is coming to stay, tomorrow. **4.** visitor(s), caller(s); company; **sie hat B.,** she has (i) a visitor, (ii) visitors; she has company; **wir erwarten B.,** we are expecting visitors, we are expecting company; **B. empfangen,** to receive visitors; **der Kranke darf noch keinen B. empfangen, haben,** the patient is not yet allowed to receive, have, any visitors; **seinen B. herzlich empfangen,** to give a warm welcome to one's visitors; **hoher B.,** important visitor(s), important guest(s); **ein willkommener B.,** a welcome visitor, a welcome guest; **unser B. muß morgen wieder abfahren,** (i) our visitor, our guest, has to, (ii) our visitors, our guests, have to, leave again tomorrow.

besuchen. I. *v.tr.* (*a*) **j-n b.,** to visit s.o., to call on s.o., to pay s.o. a visit, a call; to go to see, go and see, s.o.; **j-n kurz b.,** to pay s.o. a short visit, *F:* to drop in on s.o.; **von j-m besucht werden,** to be visited by, receive, have, a visit from, s.o.; **ich werde sie nächste Woche b. (gehen),** I shall visit her next week, I shall go and see her next week; **ich besuchte ihn gestern,** I called on him, visited him, looked him up, dropped in on him, yesterday; **der Bischof besucht seine Diözese,** the bishop visits his diocese; **die Armen b.,** to visit the poor; (*of doctor*) **einen Patienten b.,** to visit, attend, a patient; **einen Kunden b.,** to visit, call on, a client; *Com:* **unser Vertreter, unser Reisender, wird Sie b.,** our representative will call on you; *Freemasonry:* **besuchender Bruder,** brother visitor, visiting brother; (*b*) *Nat.Hist:* (*of bee, etc.*) to visit (and pollinate) (flower, etc.); (*c*) to visit, to go to (museum, exhibition, theatre, foreign country, etc.); to attend, to go to (school, church, lecture, meeting, etc.); **ich besuchte die Schule in M,** I went to school in M; **regelmäßig Vorträge b.,** to attend, go to, lectures regularly; **wir besuchten die Museen,** we visited the museums; we went round the museums; **ein Restaurant, ein Theater, häufig b.,** to frequent, to patronize, a restaurant, a theatre; **letztes Jahr besuchten wir Italien,** last year we visited, we went to, Italy; **ein Ort, der von wenigen besucht wird, ein wenig**

besuchter Ort, a place visited by few; an unfrequented spot; **bitte, besuchen Sie unsere Ausstellungsräume,** please visit, come and see, look round, our showrooms; **die Versammlung war gut besucht,** there was a good attendance at the meeting, the meeting was well attended; **gut besuchte Vorstellungen,** well-attended performances, performances with good attendance; **eine stark, gut, besuchte Ausstellung,** an exhibition which attracts many visitors; **sehr stark besuchte Ferienorte,** crowded holiday resorts.
II. *vbl s.* **Besuchen,** *n.*=**Besuch** 1 (*a*).

Besucher, *m.* **-s/-.** **1.** visitor; caller; guest; **der Kranke darf noch keine Besucher haben, empfangen,** the patient is not yet allowed to have, receive, any visitors; **ein willkommener B.,** a welcome visitor, a welcome guest; **alle Besucher müssen sich beim Empfang melden,** all visitors, callers, have to report to reception; **ein häufiger B. bei j-m sein,** to be a frequent visitor, caller, at s.o.'s house; **häufiger B. eines Restaurants, eines Theaters,** frequent visitor to a restaurant, to a theatre, frequenter, (regular) patron, of a restaurant, of a theatre, (regular) theatre-goer; **Besucher des Museums,** visitors to the museum; **ein B. vom Mars,** a visitor from Mars; **ein unheimlicher B.,** an uncanny, a ghostly, visitor, an uncanny guest; **ausländische Besucher,** foreign visitors. **2.** *Nat.Hist:* insect, etc., which visits (and pollinates) (flower, etc.).

Besuchsameise, *f. Ent:* leaf-cutting ant, leaf-cutter (ant); visiting ant.

Besuchskarte, *f.* visiting-card, *U.S:* calling card.

Besuchskartenpappe, *f. Paperm:* Bristol board.

Besuchsreise, *f.* journey to visit s.o. *or* a place; **eine B. nach Amerika,** a visit to America.

Besuchsritze, *f. F:* (*of overnight guest*) **auf der B. schlafen,** to sleep on the join between two beds.

Besuchstage, *m.pl.* visiting days (at hospital, etc.).

Besuchszeit, *f.* visiting hours (at hospital, etc.).

Besuchszimmer, *n.* **1.** visitors' room, visiting room (at convent, prison, etc.). **2.** spare room, guest room.

besudeln, *v.tr.* to soil (one's hands, s.o.'s honour, etc.); **den Fußboden b.,** to defile, befoul, the floor; **j-s guten Namen b.,** to drag s.o.'s name in the mud, in the mire; to stain s.o.'s good name, s.o.'s reputation; **j-s Ehre b.,** to cast aspersions on s.o's honour, to tarnish, blemish, s.o.'s honour; **ich werde mir damit die Hände nicht b.,** I shall not soil my hands with that, by doing that; **sie haben sich die Hände mit dem Blute Unschuldiger besudelt,** they have soiled, stained, their hands with innocent blood, their hands are dripping, are stained, with innocent blood; **mit Blut besudelte Hände,** hands bathed in blood, blood-stained hands.

Beta ['be:ta:], *n.* **-(s)/-s.** *Gr.Alph:* beta.

betäfeln, *v.tr.*=**täfeln.**

betagt, *a.* **1.** (*of pers.*) aged, old, advanced in years. **2.** *Com:* (*of bill, etc.*) due.

Betagtheit, *f.* old age.

Betain [beˑtaˑ'i:n], *n.* **-s/.** *Ch:* betaïne.

betakeln. I. *v.tr. Nau:* **1.** to rig (vessel, mast). **2.** to whip (rope, etc.).
II. *vbl s.* **1. Betakeln,** *n. in vbl senses.* **2. Betakelung,** *f.* (*a*)=II. 1; (*b*) rig, rigging (of vessel).

betanken, *v.tr.* to fill up, to tank (up) (car, aircraft, etc.) with petrol; to fuel (rocket); to (re)fuel (aircraft).

betasten. I. *v.tr.* to feel, touch (s.o., sth.); to finger, handle (material, etc.); to examine (s.o., sth.) by feeling; *Med:* to palpate; **Blinde erkennen Gegenstände, indem sie sie betasten,** the blind recognize objects by feeling them, by touch; **er betastete vorsichtig seinen Fuß,** he felt, touched, examined, his foot cautiously, gingerly.
II. *vbl s.* **Betasten** *n.*, **Betastung** *f. in vbl senses; also: Med:* palpation.

Betastrahlen, *m.pl. Ph:* beta rays.

betätigen. I. *v.* **1.** *v.tr.* to set (sth.) in operation, in action; to operate, work (machine, etc.); to practise (virtue, etc.); **die Bremsen b.,** to put on, apply, operate, work, the brakes; **bei zu hoher Temperatur wird eine Sicherheitsvorrichtung automatisch betätigt,** when the temperature is too high a safety device is automatically set in action; **mechanisch betätigtes Ventil,** mechanically operated, worked, valve. **2. sich betätigen,** to do sth., to do a job; to take (a) part in, to help with (piece of work, etc.); **sich politisch b.,** to be in politics; to dabble in politics; **sich künstlerisch b.,** to dabble in art; **er hat sich bei den Vorbereitungen für die Veranstaltung betätigt,** he helped with the preparations for the show; **mein Bruder hat sich in den Sommerferien als Eisverkäufer betätigt,** in the summer holidays my brother worked as, had a job as, an ice-cream seller; **sich nützlich b.,** to make oneself useful; **du kannst dich hier nützlich b.,** you can make yourself useful here, you can do something useful, a useful job, here; **er könnte sich zur Abwechslung auch einmal b.,** he might even do some work for a change.
II. *vbl s.* **1. Betätigen,** *n. in vbl senses.* **2. Betätigung,** *f.* (*a*)=II. 1; *also:* operation, application (of brakes, etc.); (*b*) job; work; occupation; **nützliche B.,** useful job; useful work.

Betätiger, *m.* **-s/-,** operator (of machine, etc.).

Betätigungshebel, *m. Mec.E:* operating arm, lever; actuating lever.

Betätigungskolben, *m. Mec.E:* operating piston.

Betätigungsschalter, *m. El: etc:* actuating switch; trip-switch.

Betätigungsspindel, *f. Mec.E:* operating screw.

Betätigungszylinder, *m. Mec.E:* operating cylinder.

Betatron ['be:taˑtron], *n.* **-s/-e** [be:taˑ'tro:nə]. *Atom.Ph:* betatron.

betatschen, *v.tr. F:* to finger, feel (sth.).

betäuben. I. *v.tr.* **1.** (*a*) to stun, daze (s.o.) (by blow, noise, etc.); to deafen (s.o.) (by noise, etc.); (*in slaughtering*) to stun (animal); **j-n durch einen Schlag b.,** to knock s.o. senseless, to stun, daze, s.o. by a blow; to knock s.o. out; **betäubender Schlag,** stunning blow; *F:* knock-out blow; **betäubender Lärm,** deafening, ear-splitting, noise; **wir waren wie betäubt von der Nachricht,** we were stunned, dazed, by the news; **wie betäubt vor Schreck,** stunned, dazed, numb(ed), with shock; in a stupor of dismay; **er war wie betäubt,** he seemed to be dazed, stunned, he seemed to be in a daze; **vor Kummer (wie) betäubt,** stupefied with grief; (*b*) to deaden, kill, numb (pain, etc.); to dull, deaden, stupefy (the senses); to allay, assuage (grief, etc.); to appease, take the edge off (hunger, etc.); to quiet(en), silence (one's conscience, etc.); **seine Sinne, sich, durch Rauschgift b.,** to drug, dope, oneself; **sich mit Opium b.,** to drug oneself with opium; **den Schmerz betäubendes Mittel,** analgesic, anodyne; pain-killer; palliative; **er suchte, sich, seinen Kummer, im Wein zu b.,** he sought to drown his sorrows in drink. **2.** *Med:* to anaesthetize (s.o.), to give (s.o.) an anaesthetic; **j-n mit, durch, Chloroform b.,** to chloroform s.o.; to give s.o. chloroform; **j-n mit, durch, Äther b.,** to etherize s.o.; *Dent:* **j-n mit Lachgas,** *F:* **mit Gas, b.,** to give s.o. gas; **j-n örtlich b.,** to give s.o. a local anaesthetic; **betäubendes Mittel,** anaesthetic; narcotic.
II. *vbl s.* **1. Betäuben,** *n. in vbl senses.* **2. Betäubung,** *f.* (*a*)=II. 1; *also: Med:* anaesthetization (of pers.); **B. durch Chloroform,** chloroforming; (*b*) insensibility; daze; stupor; oblivion; **als er aus seiner B. erwachte,** when he woke from his daze; when he came back to reality, when he came to; **er suchte B. im Wein,** he sought to drown, to forget, his sorrows in drink; **sie fand B. in ihrer Arbeit,** her work dulled, eased, her grief, her work made her forget her grief; **in dumpfer B.,** in numb oblivion; (*c*) *Med:* anaesthesia; **allgemeine B., B. des Bewußtseins,** general anaesthesia; narcosis; **örtliche, lokale, B.,** local anaesthesia; **eine Operation unter B. ausführen,** to perform, carry out, an operation under an anaesthetic; **aus der B. erwachen,** to come round from the anaesthetic.

Betäubtheit, *f.* insensibility; daze, dazed state; stupor; oblivion.

Betäubungsmittel, *n.* (i) *Med:* anaesthetic; narcotic; drug; (ii) (*for existing pain*) analgesic, anodyne; pain-killer; palliative; **sie hatten ein B. in seinen Wein getan,** they had drugged his wine.

betaut, *a.* (grass, etc.) covered with dew; dewy, *Lit:* bedewed (grass, etc.).

Betbruder, *m.* zealous church-goer; (religious) bigot.

Bete[1] ['be:tə], *f.* **-/-n.** *Bot:* beet; **rote B.,** beetroot.

Bete[2] ['bɛ:tə], *f.* **-/-n.** *Cards:* stake; **B. sein, B. machen,** to lose (the game).

beteeren, *v.tr.* to coat (sth.) with tar, to tar (sth.).

beteiligen. I. *v.* **1.** *v.tr.* **j-n an etwas** *dat.* **b.,** to give s.o. a share in sth.; **j-n an einem Unternehmen b.,** to make s.o. a party to an undertaking; **j-n an einem Geschäft b.,** to give s.o. a financial interest, a partnership, in a business; **j-n am Gewinn b.,** to give s.o. a share in the profits; **am Gewinn beteiligt sein,** to have a share, an interest, in the profits, to share, participate, in the profits. **2. sich an etwas** *dat.* **beteiligen,** (*a*) to participate in, share in, take (a) part in (work to be done, etc.); to participate, take part in (competition, race, etc.); to join in (conversation, etc.); to compete in (race, etc.); to take a hand in, to be, become, a party to (plot, etc.); to contribute to (present, collective work, etc.); **sich an einem Werk b.,** to participate, share, in a work; to collaborate in a work; to contribute to a work; **das Kind beteiligt sich eifrig am Unterricht,** the child takes an active part in lessons; **zweihundert Leute beteiligten sich an dem Wettbewerb,** two hundred people took part in the competition; **alle beteiligten sich an dem Wiederaufbau der Kirche,** everybody helped, everybody gave, lent, a hand, with the rebuilding of the church; **Feuerwehrleute und Freiwillige beteiligten sich an den Rettungsarbeiten,** firemen and volunteers took part in the rescue work; **die an dem Unfall beteiligten Fahrzeuge,** the vehicles involved in the accident; **sich geldlich an etwas b.,** to contribute financially to sth.; **willst du dich an einem Geschenk für sie b.?** would you like to contribute, to make a contribution, to a present for her? **ich war an der Sache nicht beteiligt,** I had no share, no part, in the business, I had nothing to do with the business; **ich will an so einer Sache nicht beteiligt sein,** I don't wish to have any share, any part, in, be a party to, any such thing, I don't wish to have anything to do with any such thing; (*b*) *Com: Fin:* to become (financially) interested, to become a partner, to have a share, in (business, venture, etc.); **(finanziell) an einem Unternehmen beteiligt sein,** to be financially interested in, to have a money interest in, a venture; to be a partner in a venture; **ich bin an dem Unternehmen nicht (finanziell) beteiligt,** I have no financial interest, no money interest, in the concern.
II. *vbl s.* **1. Beteiligen,** *n. in vbl senses.* **2. Beteiligung,** *f.* (*a*) *in vbl senses; also:* **ein System zur B. der Arbeiter am Gewinn einführen,** to initiate a profit-sharing scheme; (*b*) participation (in work to be done, conversation, competition, crime, plot, etc.); collaboration (on book, etc.); contribution (to collective work, etc.); attendance (at lecture, meeting, etc.); **rege, eifrige, B. am Unterricht,** active participation in lessons; **die B. an der Versammlung war gut,** there was a good attendance at the meeting, the meeting was well attended, well supported; **gute B. an der Wahl,** heavy polling, heavy poll; **schlechte B. an der Wahl,** small poll; **die Beerdigung fand unter lebhafter B. der ganzen Bevölkerung statt,** the funeral was accompanied by demonstrations of public sympathy; (*c*) *Com: Fin:* interest, share, participation (in business, etc.); partnership, holding (in company, etc.); **stille B.,** sleeping partnership; **tätige B.,** active partnership; **j-m eine B. in seinem Geschäft anbieten,** to offer s.o. an interest in one's business; to offer s.o. a partnership in one's business.
III. *p.p. & a.* **beteiligt,** *in vbl senses; esp.* **die beteiligten Parteien, Personen, die Beteiligten,** the interested parties, the persons, parties, concerned; **Handlung, die allen beteiligten Personen, allen Beteiligten, zur Schande gereicht,** action disgraceful to all concerned; **es wird für alle Beteiligten von Vorteil sein,** it will be of advantage to all (parties, people) concerned; **nach der Vorstellung wurde allen Beteiligten herzlicher Beifall gespendet,** after the performance there was hearty applause for all the participants, for all those who had taken part, for all concerned.

Beteiligungsgesellschaft, *f. Fin:* holding company.

Betel, *m.* **-s/-.** *Bot:* betel.

Betelkauen, *n.* betel chewing.

Betelnuß, *f. Bot:* betel-nut, areca-nut.

Betelnußpalme, *f. Bot:* areca palm, betel palm, areca catechu.

Betelöl, *n.* betel oil.

Betelpalme, *f.*=**Betelnußpalme.**

Betelpfeffer(strauch), *m. Bot:* betel vine; pan.

beten. **1.** *v.tr.* to say, recite (prayer); **das Vaterunser b.,** to say the Lord's Prayer; **den Rosenkranz b.,** to go through the rosary, to tell one's beads. **2.** *v.i.* (*haben*) to pray, to say one's prayer(s); **inbrünstig b.,** to pray fervently; **zu Gott b.,** to pray to God; **für j-n b.,** to pray for s.o.; **für j-s Seele b.,** to pray for s.o.'s soul; **für die Toten, für die Verstorbenen, b.,** to pray for the dead, to say a prayer, prayers, for the dead; **bete für mich,** pray for me, remember me in your prayers; **vor der Mahlzeit, vor dem Essen, b.,** to say grace before the meal; **lasset uns b.,** let us

pray; **um etwas b.,** to pray for sth.; **um Frieden b.,** to pray for peace; **um Regen b.,** to pray for rain; **ich bete darum, daß er in Sicherheit sein möge,** I pray that he may be safe.

Beter, *m.* **-s/-,** praying man; man at his prayers.

Beterei, *f.* **-/.** (endless) praying.

Beterin, *f.* **-/-innen,** praying woman; woman at her prayers.

beteuern. I. *v.tr.* to protest, asseverate (sth.); to declare (sth.) solemnly; **seine Unschuld b.,** to protest, asseverate, one's innocence, to make a protestation, protestations, of one's innocence; **ernsthaft b., daß . . .,** to make a solemn protestation that . . ., to declare solemnly that . . .; **er beteuert, daß er nichts dergleichen getan hat,** he protests, vows, swears, that he did no such thing.
II. *vbl s.* **1. Beteuern,** *n. in vbl senses.* **2. Beteuerung,** *f.* (*a*)=II. 1; *also:* protestation, asseveration (of one's innocence, good faith, etc.); (*b*) protestation, asseveration; solemn declaration; **eidesgleiche B.,** solemn affirmation (instead of oath); **laute Beteuerungen seiner Unschuld,** loud protestations of his innocence; **Beteuerungen seiner Freundschaft,** his protestations of friendship.

Beteuerungsformel, *f.* solemn affirmation (instead of oath).

Betfahrt, *f.* pilgrimage.

Bethalle, *f.*=**Betsaal.**

Bethanien [beˈtaːniən]. *Pr.n.n.* **-s.** *B.Hist:* Bethany.

Bethel. *Pr.n.n.* **-s.** *B.Hist:* Bethel.

Bethesda [beˈtesdaː]. *Pr.n.m.* **-(s).** *B.Hist:* **(der Teich) B.,** (the Pool of) Bethesda.

Bethlehem [ˈbeːt-, ˈbetleˑhem]. *Pr.n.n.* **-s.** *Geog:* Bethlehem.

Bethlehemit [beˑtleˑheˈmiːt], *m.* **-en/-en.** **1.** inhabitant of Bethlehem, Bethlehemite. **2.** *Rel. Hist:* Bethlehemite.

bethlehemitisch [beˑtleˑheˑˈmiːtiʃ], *a.* of Bethlehem; **der Bethlehemitische Kindermord,** the Massacre, the Slaughter, of the Innocents.

Beting, *m.* **-s/-e** & *f.* **-/-e.** *Nau:* (wooden) bitt; bollard (on ship).

Betingschlag, *m. Nau:* bitter.

betippen, *v.tr.* **1.** to touch (sth.) lightly. **2.** *F:* to write on (piece of paper, etc.) with a typewriter, to type on (piece of paper, etc.).

Betise [beˈtiːzə], *f.* **-/-n,** (*a*) stupidity, folly; silliness; (*b*) stupid, silly, thing; **Betisen sagen,** to say stupid things.

betiteln. I. *v.tr.* **1.** (*a*) to entitle, give a title to (book, document, etc.); to head, give a heading to (article, chapter, etc.); **Artikel betitelt . . .,** article entitled . . ., article headed . . .; (*b*) (*of book, etc.*) **sich b.,** to be entitled; **der Aufsatz betitelt sich . . .,** the paper is entitled . . ., has the title . . . . **2.** to give (s.o.) a title; to address (s.o.) (by a title); **j-n 'Baron' b.,** to style s.o. 'baron'; to call, address, s.o. by the title of 'baron'; **er betitelte mich 'Oberst',** he called me, addressed me as, 'Colonel'; **ich liebe es nicht, 'Fräulein' betitelt zu werden,** I don't like being called, addressed as, 'Fräulein'.
II. *vbl s.* **1. Betiteln,** *n. in vbl senses.* **2. Betitelung,** *f.* (*a*)=II. 1; (*b*) title (of book, document, etc.); heading (of article, chapter, etc.); (*c*) title; form of address.

Betnuß, *f.* (rosary) bead.

Beton [beˈtõː, beˑˈtoːn, beˑˈtoŋ], *m.* **-s/-s.** *Civ.E: Constr: etc:* concrete, beton; **B. ohne Bewehrung,** plain concrete; **armierter, bewehrter, B.,** reinforced concrete, ferro-concrete; **fetter B.,** rich concrete; **in B. einbetten,** to embed, set, in concrete; **in B. eingebettet,** embedded in concrete; **B. schütten,** to deposit concrete; **eine Wand, Mauer, mit B. verkleiden,** to face a wall with concrete.

Betonautomat, *m.* concrete mixer.

Betonbalken, *m.* concrete beam.

Betonbau, *m.* **-(e)s/.** **1.** (method of) building with concrete. **2.** (*pl.* **Betonbauten**) concrete building.

Betonbereitung, *f.* concrete mixing.

Betonbett, *n.*, **Betonbettung,** *f.* concrete bed, base.

Betonblock, *m.* concrete block.

Betonbrücke, *f.* concrete bridge.

Betondachstein, *m.* concrete roofing slab.

Betondecke, *f.* concrete ceiling; concrete cover; concrete surface, concrete layer (of road); concrete roof (of shelter).

Betondichtungsstoff, *m.* concrete densifying agent.

Betondrahtgewebe, *n.* mesh reinforcement (for concrete).

betonen. I. *v.tr.* to stress (syllable); to lay stress on (syllable, word); to emphasize, to lay emphasis on (word, fact); to accentuate (syllable, detail, *Mus:* note); **eine Tatsache (besonders) b.,** to lay stress, particular stress, particular emphasis, on a fact; **das letzte Wort im Satz ist betont,** the stress is on the last word in the sentence; **wie in Regierungskreisen betont wird . . .,** as is emphasized in government circles; **seine Kleider betonten seine Armut,** his clothes emphasized his poverty; **Kleid, das die Figur betont,** dress that emphasizes the figure; **das dunkle Kleid betonte ihre Magerkeit, ihre Blässe,** the dark dress emphasized her thinness, accentuated her pallor; *Dressm:* **Paris betont in dieser Saison die Hüftlinie,** Paris emphasizes, accents, the hip-line this season; **durch diese Maßnahme wurde die Arbeitslosigkeit noch stärker betont,** this measure underlined the degree of unemployment; **die Schule betont die praktischen Fächer,** the school puts, places, emphasis on practical subjects; **ich betone, möchte betonen, daß . . .,** I must stress (the fact) that . . .; **er betonte, daß . . .,** he stressed (the point) that . . .; **der Bericht betont, daß . . .,** the report emphasizes that . . .; **ich möchte die Tatsache nicht zu sehr b.,** I do not want to stress the fact too much; **betone es nicht zu sehr!** don't stress it too much; don't press it too far!
II. *vbl s.* **1. Betonen,** *n. in vbl senses.* **2. Betonung,** *f.* (*a*)=II. 1; *also:* accentuation (of vowel, detail, characteristic, *Mus:* note, etc.); **die starke B. der Religionsfrage,** the strong emphasis placed on the religious question; (*b*) stress, accent (on word, etc.); emphasis (on fact); **zur B.,** for emphasis; in order to emphasize; *Ling:* **fallende B.,** falling stress; **germanische B.,** Germanic accentuation; **B. im Satz,** stress within the sentence; intonation; **die B. liegt auf . . .,** (i) the stress falls (up)on . . .; (ii) the emphasis is on . . .; **die erste Silbe hat die B.,** the stress is on the first syllable, the first syllable takes the stress; *see also* **anschwellen** I.
III. *p.p.* & *a.* **betont,** *in vbl senses; esp.* (*a*) accentuated; *Ling:* **betonte Silbe,** stressed, accented, syllable; (*b*) marked, striking (simplicity, etc.); emphatic (declaration, etc.); **betonter Optimismus,** marked optimism; **er benahm sich b. höflich,** he was pointedly, markedly, polite.

Betonfarbe, *f.* concrete paint.

Betonfußboden, *m.* concrete floor.

Betonglas, *n.* thick pressed glass (for glass bricks, etc.); glass brick; glass block.

Betongranate, *f. Artil:* anti-concrete shell.

Betongründung, *f.* concreting; foundation in concrete.

Betonguß, *m. Constr: Sculp: etc:* (*a*) concrete casting; (*b*) concrete cast.

Betonhartstoff, *m.* concrete hardening agent.

Betonie [beˈtoːniə], *f.* **-/-n.** *Bot:* (*a*) betony; (*b*) stachys, *F:* woundwort; **rote B.,** wood-betony.

betonieren [beˑtoˑˈniːrən]. **1.** *v.tr.* to concrete (road, etc.); to construct (road) with concrete; **die Straße ist frisch betoniert worden,** the road has been newly concreted; **betonierte Straße,** concrete road; **betonierter Keller,** concrete cellar; *Av:* **betonierte Start- und Landebahnen,** concrete runways. **2.** *vbl s.* **Betonierung,** *f.* concreting; concrete (work).

Betonierungseinrichtungen, *f.pl.* equipment for handling concrete.

Betonkasten, *m. Hyd.E:* concrete caisson.

Betonkern, *m. Constr:* concrete core, *esp. Hyd.E:* concrete core-wall (of dam).

Betonmasse, *f.* concrete (mixture).

Betonmischer, *m.*, **Betonmischmaschine,** *f.* concrete mixer.

betonnen. *Nau:* **1.** *v.tr.* to buoy (channel). **2.** *vbl s.* **Betonnung,** *f.* buoyage.

Betonpfahl, *m. Constr: Civ.E:* concrete pile.

Betonpfosten, *m.* concrete post *or* pile.

Betonplatte, *f.* concrete slab.

Betonrohr, *n.*, **Betonröhre,** *f.* concrete pipe.

Betonschiff, *n. Nau:* concrete ship.

Betonschüttung, *f. Civ.E: Constr:* laying, depositing, of concrete.

Betonsperre, *f.* concrete road-block.

Betonstein, *m.* pre-cast concrete block.

Betonstraße, *f.* concrete road.

betont, *p.p.* & *a. see* **betonen** III.

Betonträger, *m.* concrete beam.

Betonung, *f. see* **betonen** II.

Betonungsgesetze, *n.pl. Ling:* laws of stress, laws of accentuation.

Betonungsregeln, *f.pl. Ling:* rules for accentuation.

Betonungszeichen, *n. Ling:* stress-mark; *Mus:* accent mark.

Betonversenkung, *f. Civ.E: Constr:* depositing of concrete (under water).

Betonware, *f.* concrete products.

Betonwerk, *n.* **1.** concrete works. **2.** *Mil:* concrete fortifications.

Betonzusatzmittel, *n.* concrete aggregate.

betören. I. *v.tr.* (i) to dazzle s.o.; to bewitch (s.o.); (ii) to take (s.o.) in; **sich b. lassen,** (i) to allow oneself to be dazzled; (ii) to allow oneself to be taken in; **sie, ihre Schönheit, hat ihn ganz und gar betört,** she, her beauty, has quite bewitched him; **er ließ sich von ihrer Schönheit b.,** he fell under the spell of her beauty, he was bewitched by her beauty; he was dazzled by her beauty; **sie ließ sich von seinen schmeichlerischen Reden b.,** she was taken in by his flattering words; **er hat das Volk mit seinen Versprechungen betört,** he dazzled the people with his promises; he has taken in the people with his promises; **betörend,** dazzling (beauty, etc.); bewitching (smile, beauty, etc.); seductive (words, etc.); **eine betörend schöne Frau,** a woman of dazzling beauty, a dazzlingly beautiful woman; **betörend lächeln,** to smile bewitchingly.
II. *vbl s.* **Betörung,** *f.* **1.** *in vbl senses.* **2.** bewitched, bemused, state.

Betpult, *n.* praying-desk, prie-dieu.

Betracht, *m.* **-(e)s/.** (*a*) (*used only in vbl phrases*) **in B. ziehen,** (i) to consider (s.o., sth.); to contemplate (sth.); (ii) to take (sth.) into account, into consideration, to make allowance for (sth.), to allow for (sth.); **in B. ziehen, daß . . .,** to consider, to bear in mind, that . . .; **in B. ziehen, etwas zu tun,** to consider, contemplate, doing sth.; **nicht in B. ziehen,** (i) not to consider (s.o., sth.); (ii) to disregard (sth.), not to take (sth.) into account, into consideration; to make no allowance for (sth.); to leave (sth.) out of consideration, aside; **in B. kommen,** (*of pers.*) to be a possible candidate, etc. (for promotion, a post, etc.); (*of thg*) to be a possibility, to be possible; **nicht in B. kommen,** (*of pers.*) to be unsuitable (for a post, etc.); to have to be ruled out (as a suspect, etc.); (*of thg*) to be out of the question; **außer B. lassen,** to leave (sth., s.o.) out of consideration, out of account; to disregard (sth., s.o.); to rule out (sth., s.o.); **außer B. bleiben,** to be left out of consideration, out of account; to be disregarded; to be ruled out; **dieses Projekt kommt nicht in B.,** this scheme is out of the question; **es kommt nicht in B., daß wir . . .,** it is out of the question for us to . . .; **wenn man alles in B. zieht,** taking all things into consideration, all things considered, taking everything into account; **eine Möglichkeit in B. ziehen,** to consider a possibility; **unter den Maßnahmen, die bis jetzt in B. gezogen wurden, . . .,** among the measures considered so far . . .; **eine Tatsache, die außer B. geblieben ist,** a fact that has been left out of consideration, out of account; **wenn man Einzelheiten außer B. läßt, . . .,** disregarding details . . ., leaving details aside . . .; **er kommt für diese Stelle nicht in B.,** he cannot be considered as a candidate for this job; he is quite unsuitable for this job; **du mußt in B. ziehen, daß er krank ist, du mußt seine Krankheit in B. ziehen,** you must allow for his being ill; you must make allowance for his illness; (*b*) *A: adv.phr.* **in jedem, keinem, gewissem, B.,** in every, no, respect, in certain respects; *prep. phr.* **in B.+*gen.*, in B. (dessen), daß . . .**=**in Anbetracht,** *q.v. under* **Anbetracht.**

betrachten. I. *v.tr.* **1.** (*a*) to look at (s.o., sth.); **etwas, j-n, nachdenklich b.,** to look at sth., s.o., thoughtfully; **etwas näher b.,** to look closely at sth.; to inspect sth.; **ein Bild aufmerksam b.,** to examine a picture carefully; **sich im Spiegel b.,** to look at oneself in the glass, in the mirror; **wenn man ihn betrachtet, könnte man sagen . . .,** to look at him one would say . . .; **von außen betrachtet, ist das Haus nicht schlecht,** the house, looked at from the outside, is not bad; **sein Werk wohlgefällig, mit Wohlgefallen, b.,** to regard one's work with satisfaction; to be proud of one's work; (*b*) to see (sth.) (mentally); to look at, consider, contemplate (a matter, etc.); **die Geschehnisse anders b.,** to take a different view of events; **ich betrachte das Problem mit anderen Augen,** I look upon the problem with a different eye, I see the problem in quite another light; **wie man es auch b. mag,** however, whichever way, one looks at it; in whatever light one regards it; whichever way you may take it; **wie ich die Sache betrachte . . .,** in my view . . ., to my mind . . ., to my way of thinking . . . as I

see the matter . . .; **etwas von der falschen Seite b.**, to see sth. in a false light; to take a wrong view of sth.; (*c*) to watch (events, developments, etc.) (anxiously, carefully, etc.); **j-n, etwas, wohlwollend, mit Wohlgefallen, b.**, to be kindly disposed towards s.o.; to be favourably disposed towards sth.; (*d*) **j-n, etwas, als etwas b.**, to regard, consider, s.o., sth., as, to be, sth.; to look upon s.o., sth., as sth.; to deem s.o., sth., to be sth.; to take s.o., sth., for, to be, sth.; **sich als etwas b.**, to regard, consider, oneself as, to be, sth.; to look upon oneself as sth.; **ich betrachte es als eine Ehre, Ihnen dienen zu dürfen**, I (ac)count it, deem it, an honour to serve you; **etwas als ein Verbrechen, als gesetzwidrig, b.**, to regard, look (up)on, sth. as a crime, as illegal; **ich betrachte es als meine Pflicht zu . . .**, I regard it as my duty to . . .; **er betrachtete das Haus als sein eigenes**, he regarded, looked upon, the house as his own; **früher betrachtete ich ihn als meinen treuesten Freund**, I used to consider him, look upon him, as my most faithful friend; **er betrachtet sich als mein Freund**, he considers himself to be my friend, he regards himself as my friend; **du kannst dich als eingeladen b.**, you may consider yourself invited. **2.** (*a*) to meditate (up)on (sth.); *abs.* **b.**, to meditate, to contemplate; **das Leiden Christi b.**, to meditate on the Passion; **seine Sünden b.**, to meditate, reflect, on one's sins; (*b*) to look at (problem, subject, etc.); to examine (question, subject); **ein Problem eingehend b.**, to examine a question thoroughly.

II. *vbl s.* **1. Betrachten**, *n. in vbl senses.* **2. Betrachtung**, *f.* (*a*)=II. 1; *also:* consideration; examination (of subject, problem, etc.); reflection, meditation (on, upon, sth.); contemplation; **bei der B. des Bildes**, when looking at the picture; **bei näherer B.**, (i) on closer inspection, on closer examination; (ii) upon further consideration; on reflection; **in B. versunken**, lost, deep, (i) in contemplation, (ii) in contemplation, meditation; **wenn wir die Ergebnisse unserer B. überblicken**, surveying the results of our examination, our inquiry; **sie widmen ihr Leben ganz der B.**, they devote their lives entirely to meditation, they lead a contemplative life; (*b*) reflection; meditation; contemplation; **Betrachtungen über etwas anstellen**, to meditate (up)on sth.; to reflect on sth.; **Betrachtungen zur Geschichte der Nachkriegszeit**, reflections on, upon, the history of the post-war period; **Betrachtungen über die Unsterblichkeit der Seele**, meditations on the immortality of the soul; (*c*) *A:*=**Betracht.**

III. *pr.p. & a.* **betrachtend**, *in vbl senses; esp.* meditative, contemplative.

Betrachter, *m.* **-s/-**, beholder, viewer (of picture); spectator (of film, etc.); observer; onlooker; **ein unbeteiligter B. (der Situation)**, a passive, an impartial, observer (of the situation); **ein aufmerksamer B.**, an attentive observer.

beträchtlich. **1.** *a.* considerable, important, large (sum, etc.); considerable, large (quantity); handsome (sum, fortune, dowry, etc.); substantial (increase, etc.); considerable, extensive (damage); *Lit:* goodly (fortune, etc.); *F:* sizeable (sum, fortune, etc.); **Schäden von beträchtlichem Ausmaß, beträchtliche Schäden**, considerable, extensive, damage; **beträchtliche Schulden**, considerable debts. **2.** *adv.* **b.**, *adv.phr.* **um ein beträchtliches**, considerably; **die Unfallsziffer ist b., um ein beträchtliches, gestiegen**, the accident rate has risen considerably; **die Bibliothek ist b., um ein beträchtliches, vermehrt worden**, the library has been considerably added to.

Beträchtlichkeit, *f.* importance, considerable size (of sum, damage, etc.).

betrachtsam, *a.* contemplative, meditative.

Betrachtsamkeit, *f.* contemplation, meditation; **in tiefer B.**, deep, plunged, in meditation.

Betrachtungsart, *f.*=**Betrachtungsweise.**

Betrachtungsbuch, *n.* devotional work.

Betrachtungsweise, *f.* kind of vision; mental outlook; attitude of mind; point of view; method (of research); approach (to a subject); *F:* way of looking at things.

Betrag, *m.* **-(e)s/=e**, amount; sum; sum of money; **bis zum Betrag(e) von . . .**, (up) to the amount of . . .; **Rechnung im Betrag(e) von . . .**, invoice, bill, for the amount of . . .; **wir bitten, den B. unserem Konto gutzuschreiben**, please credit the amount, the sum, to our account; **einen Scheck über den B. von . . . ausstellen**, to write out a cheque for the amount of . . .; **ich kann den B. zur Zeit nicht flüssig machen**, I cannot realize the sum at present, for the moment; **ich könnte den ganzen B. nächsten Monat bezahlen**, I could pay the total (amount) next month; **er hat ihm einen größeren B. geliehen**, he has lent him a considerable sum; **größere Beträge**, larger sums (of money), larger amounts; **auch kleinste Beträge sind willkommen**, even the smallest amount is welcome; **wir nehmen Spenden in jedem B. entgegen**, we accept gifts, contributions, of any size; (*on invoice, bill*) **'B. (dankend) erhalten'**, 'received with thanks'.

betragen. I. *v.* (*strong*) **1.** *v.i.* (*haben*) (*of sum, etc.*) to amount to; to come to; **sein Vermögen betrug zehntausend Pfund**, his fortune amounted to ten thousand pounds; **die Differenz beträgt 20**, the difference is 20; **die Gesamtsumme beträgt 250**, the total amounts to, comes to, is, 250; **wieviel beträgt es?** how much does it amount to, come to? how much is it? **2. sich betragen**, to behave, to conduct oneself; **sich schlecht b.**, to misbehave; **sich gut, schlecht, gegen j-n b.**, to behave well, badly, towards s.o.; **er hat sich immer tadellos betragen**, his conduct has always been faultless.

II. *vbl s.* **Betragen**, *n.* conduct; behaviour; *Sch:* conduct; **sein B. läßt viel zu wünschen übrig**, his conduct leaves much to be desired; **B. gegen j-n**, conduct, behaviour, towards s.o.; **freches B.**, insolent conduct, insolence; *Sch:* **das Kind hat im B. 'gut' bekommen**, the child got 'good' for conduct.

Betragensnote, *f. Sch:* mark for conduct.

betränt, *a.* (face, etc.) wet with tears.

betrauen, *v.tr.* **j-n mit etwas b.**, to entrust s.o. with sth.; to charge s.o. with sth.; to commit, consign, sth. to s.o.'s care, to place sth. in s.o.'s charge; to put a matter into s.o.'s hands; **j-n damit b., etwas zu tun**, to entrust s.o. with doing sth.; to charge s.o. with the task of doing sth.; **j-n mit der Sorge für etwas b.**, to entrust s.o. with the care of sth., to entrust the care of sth. to s.o., to leave s.o. in charge of sth.; **j-n mit einer besonderen Aufgabe b.**, to entrust s.o. with a special task; **mit etwas betraut sein**, to be in charge of sth., to have the care of sth.

betrauern, *v.tr.* to mourn (for, over) (s.o., sth.); **sein Tod wurde im ganzen Lande betrauert**, his death was mourned throughout the country; **den Verlust eines wertvollen Besitzes b.**, to mourn the loss of a valued possession.

beträufeln, *v.tr.* **etwas mit einer Flüssigkeit b.**, to let a liquid drip on to sth.; to put a few drops of a liquid on sth.

Betreff, *m.* **-(e)s/.** **1.** *Com: Adm:* (*abbr.* **Betr.:**) (*at head of letter*) reference (*abbr.* Ref.). **2.** (*a*) **in dem B.**, in this respect; (*b*) *prep. phr.* (*also spelt with small b*) **in B., in b.+gen.=betreffs.**

betreffen. I. *v.tr.* (*strong*) **1.** *A:* **j-n bei etwas b., j-n dabei b., etwas zu tun**, to catch s.o. at sth., doing sth.; to catch s.o. in (a lie, the act, etc.); to find s.o. at sth., doing sth. **2.** (*of disease, etc.*) to attack (s.o.); (*of evil, etc.*) to assail, come upon (s.o.); **ein schweres Unglück hat die Stadt betroffen**, a grave misfortune has befallen the town. **3.** (*a*) (*of disease, misfortune, etc.*) to affect (s.o.); to touch (s.o.); (*of measure, etc.*) to affect, concern (s.o., sth.); (*of catastrophe, etc.*) to hit (s.o., town, country, etc.); (*of detail, etc.*) to be relevant to (a matter); **der Krieg hat uns schwer, hart, betroffen, wir waren vom Krieg schwer, hart, betroffen**, we were hard hit by the war; **er war besonders hart betroffen, es hat ihn besonders hart betroffen**, he was especially hard hit; **die von dem Brand am schwersten betroffenen Stadtteile**, the districts worst affected, hit, by the fire; **das betrifft dich nicht**, that does not affect, concern, you; **sein Schicksal betrifft uns alle (mit), wir sind alle von seinem Schicksal (mit) betroffen**, his fate affects all of us; we are all concerned in his fate; **diejenigen, die persönlich betroffen sind, die persönlich Betroffenen**, those personally affected, those concerned personally; **Gesetz, das Bayern betrifft**, law concerning, affecting, Bavaria; **Lebensmittel sind durch diese Anordnung nicht betroffen**, articles of food are not affected by this order; (*b*) to concern, regard, (s.o., sth.); **was . . . betrifft**, as concerns . . ., as regards . . ., as far as . . . is concerned, as far as regards . . ., as to . . ., as for . . ., for . . . part, regarding . . .; **was mich betrifft**, as far as I am concerned, for my part; **was diese Frage betrifft**, as concerns this question, as far as this question is concerned, as to, as for, regarding, this question; **sie ist streng, was Disziplin betrifft**, she is strict as regards discipline; *Com: Adm:* (*at head of letter*) **Betrifft:** (*abbr.* **Betr.:**) reference: (*abbr.* Ref.).

II. *pr.p. & a.* **betreffend**, *in vbl senses; esp.* **1.** (*abbr.* **betr.**) regarding, concerning; concerned with; **Akten, Herrn X b., Akten b. Herrn X**, files concerning, relating to, Mr X; **eine Anfrage, das Schulgeld b., eine das Schulgeld betreffende Anfrage**, an enquiry regarding, concerned with, the school fees; **den Vorfall betreffende Einzelheit, Einzelheit, den Vorfall b.**, detail relevant to the event; **er hat einen Brief b. diese Angelegenheit, diese Angelegenheit b., einen diese Angelegenheit betreffenden Brief, geschrieben**, he has written a letter concerning, regarding, this matter, he has written in this matter. **2.** (matter, pers., thg) in question; referred to; concerned; **zu der betreffenden Zeit**, at the time in question; at the material time; **der betreffende Fall**, the case in question; the case referred to; **Bewerber werden gebeten, die Anträge an die betreffende Behörde einzureichen**, applicants are requested to send their applications to the relevant authority; **die betreffenden Personen, die Betreffenden**, the persons, parties, in question, concerned.

III. *p.p. & a.* **betroffen**, *in vbl senses; esp.* disconcerted; dismayed, in dismay; **er hielt b. in seiner Erzählung inne**, disconcerted he broke off his story, he broke off his story in dismay.

betreffs, *prep.* (+*gen.*) (*abbr.* **betr.**) concerning, about, regarding, respecting, with respect, regard, to, as to; **b. Ihrer Anfrage**, regarding your enquiry.

betreiben. I. *v.tr.* (*strong*) **1.** *A:* **Wiesen mit Vieh b.**, to put cattle to pasture on meadows. **2.** to operate (railway line, etc.); to work (mine, etc.); to run (machine, plant, train, etc.) (on oil, steam, etc.); to work (machine, etc.) (by steam, etc.); **einen Kran elektrisch b.**, to work, operate, a crane electrically; **mit Dampf, Elektrizität, betrieben werden**, to be worked by, to run on, steam, electricity; **diese Bahn(linie) wird elektrisch, mit Dampf, betrieben**, the trains on this line are electrically driven, steam-driven. **3.** (*a*) to pursue, follow, carry on (trade, business, etc.); to pursue (one's studies); **sie betreibt einen kleinen Handel in X**, she has a small business in X; **er betreibt seine Studien mit großem Eifer**, he devotes himself to his studies, he applies himself industriously to his studies; (*b*) to work for the fulfilment of (plan, etc.); to push (sth.) on; to hurry on (affair, work, etc.); to urge forward (piece of work, etc.); **ich habe die Sache nicht weiter betrieben**, I did not pursue the matter further; I did not push the matter any further; **j-s Wahl, Ernennung, b.**, to work for s.o.'s election, appointment; to root for a candidate for election; **etwas mit Nachdruck b.**, to push on, press on, with sth.

II. *vbl s.* **1. Betreiben**, *n.* (*a*) *in vbl senses;* (*b*) **auf j-s B., auf B. von . . .**, at, by, s.o.'s instigation, at, by, the instigation of . . .; at s.o.'s prompting, at the prompting of . . .; **es geschah auf B. seiner Anhänger**, it was done at the instigation, prompting, of his followers. **2. Betreibung**, *f. in vbl senses. Cp.* **Betrieb** 1.

betressen, *v.tr.* to trim, ornament, (sth.) with braid, to braid (sth.); **mit Gold betreßter Mantel**, coat braided with gold, gold-braided coat; **ein (mit Gold) betreßter Offizier**, a gold-braided officer.

betretbar, *a.* (*of path, etc.*) walkable; passable; (*of house, etc.*) enterable.

betreten. I. *v.tr.* (*strong*) **1.** to walk on (path etc.); to step on (ladder, fresh paint, flower-bed, etc.); to go into, step into, enter (house room, etc.); to set foot in (house, etc.); to set foot on (territory, land, etc.); to step over, cross (threshold); to mount (pulpit); to enter (career) **ein Grundstück, usw., unbefugt b.**, to trespass on property, etc., *abs.* to trespass; **bitte den Rasen nicht (zu) b.!** please keep off the grass, please do not walk on the grass; **englischen Boden zum ersten Mal b.**, to set foot on English soil for the first time; **ich habe sein Haus nie betreten**, I have never set foot inside his house; **ich werde sein Haus nie wieder b.**, I shall never set foot in his house again; **die Kinder dürfen sein Arbeitszimmer nicht b.**, the children are not allowed (to go) into his study, are forbidden to go into his study, the study is forbidden to the children **die Arena, den Kampfplatz, b.**, to enter the arena to come on to the field *or* track; *Lit. & F:* to enter the fray, the lists; **ein viel betretener Pfad** a well-trodden path. **2.** (*of cock*) to tread (hen) **3.** *A:* to catch (s.o.) (at a crime, etc.).

II. *vbl s.* **Betreten**, *n. in vbl senses; also* **unbefugtes B.**, trespass (on property, etc.); *P.N*

das B. des Rasens ist verboten, (please) keep off the grass, do not walk on the grass; **Unbefugten ist das B. der Bahnanlagen verboten,** no trespassing on railway property; **das (unbefugte) B. des Grundstücks ist bei Strafe verboten,** trespassers will be prosecuted.
III. *p.p. & a.* **betreten,** *in vbl senses; esp.* abashed; embarrassed; **b. aussehen, ein betretenes Gesicht machen,** to look embarrassed; to look sheepish; **ein betretenes Schweigen,** an embarrassed silence; *adv.* **b. schweigen,** (i) to keep an, (ii) to subside into, embarrassed silence.
Betretenheit, *f.* embarrassment; abashment.
betreuen. I. *v.tr.* to look after (s.o., sth.); to tend (s.o., sth.); to have care of (s.o.); **von j-m betreut werden,** to be in, under, s.o.'s care; to be committed to the care of s.o.; **das Kind wird hier gut betreut werden,** the child will be well looked after here.
II. *vbl s.* **Betreuen** *n.,* **Betreuung** *f. in vbl senses; also:* care, welfare (of animals, children, old people, the sick, etc.); **B. entlassener Gefangener,** prisoners' after-care.
Betrieb, *m.* -(e)s/-e. **1.** (*a*) operating, operation (of railway line, etc.); working (of mine, etc.); running (of machine, plant, train, etc.) (on oil, steam, etc.); working (of machine, etc.) (by steam, etc.); **den B. aufnehmen,** to begin work(ing); (*of business, etc.*) to open; **den B. wieder aufnehmen,** to resume work; **den B. einstellen,** to cease work(ing); to close (down); **das neue Restaurant wird am Montag den B. aufnehmen,** the new restaurant will open on Monday; **unsere Firma wird den B. nächste Woche wieder aufnehmen,** our firm will resume work next week; **die Fabrik hat den B. vorübergehend einstellen müssen,** the factory had to close down temporarily; *Rail:* **der B. auf dieser Strecke wird demnächst aufgenommen werden,** trains will be running on this line shortly, this line will be opened shortly; **wir sehen uns gezwungen, den B. dieser, auf dieser, Strecke einzustellen,** we see ourselves compelled to close this line; (*b*) service; **aus dem B. ziehen,** to take (obsolete vehicle, machinery, aircraft, etc.) out of service; to take (bus) off the road; to ground (aircraft) (*temporarily*); **im B. sein,** (*of railway coach, aircraft, machinery, etc.*) to be in service; (*of bus*) to be on the road; (*c*) (*adv. phrases*) **in B. sein,** (*of machine, etc.*) to work, to be in operation, in action, in gear; (*of furnace*) to be in blast; (*of factory, etc.*) to work, to be in operation; (*of railway line, etc.*) to be in operation; to be running; **in vollem B.,** in full operation, in full action; (*of furnace*) in full blast; **das Werk ist in vollem B.,** the factory is, the works are, going at full blast; **in B. setzen,** to set (machine, etc.) working, going, to throw (machine, etc.) into gear; to put, set (machine, plant, etc.) in operation, in action; **in B. nehmen,** to bring, put (new machinery, plant, etc.) into service; to put (bus) on the road; to open (railway line); to open (road, etc.) to, for, traffic; to begin work in (new pit, etc.); **in B. genommen werden,** (*of machine, plant, etc.*) to go into operation; (*of railway coach, bus, machine, plant, etc.*) to be brought, put, into service; (*of road, railway line, etc.*) to open, to be opened to, for, traffic; **außer B. setzen,** to put (sth.) out of action; to put (machine, etc.) out of order; to throw (machine, etc.) out of gear; **außer B.,** out of action; (*of machine*) out of gear, not working; out of order; (*notice on slot-machine, etc.*) 'out of order'; **der Fahrstuhl ist außer B.,** the lift is not working, is out of order; **in B. halten,** to keep (machine, etc.) working, running, going, in gear; to keep (furnace) going. **2.** (*a*) (teaching, scientific, etc.) activity (of university, institution, etc.); (*b*) traffic (on road, etc.); bustle, stir, commotion (in streets, restaurant, etc.); rush (in streets, shop, railway station, etc.); **es herrschte reger B. in der Stadt, es war viel B. in der Stadt,** the town was very busy; there was a terrific rush in town; **samstags ist der B. in der Stadt unerträglich,** on Saturdays the rush in town is unbearable; **der B. auf den Bahnhöfen ist vor Weihnachten besonders groß,** the rush at the stations is particularly heavy before Christmas; **in diesem Restaurant ist immer viel B.,** this restaurant is always busy; (*c*) *F:* merry-making, goings-on; *F:* high jinks; **B. machen,** to make merry; to liven up the party; **unsere Nachbarn hatten großen B.,** our neighbours had a noisy party, had a high time; **auf der Hochzeit war großer B.,** it was a very lively wedding party; we had a gay, high, time at the wedding party.

3. (*industrial, etc., establishment; branch of business, etc., undertaking under separate management*) (gewerblicher) B., business; (business) concern, undertaking; firm; **(industrieller) B.,** industrial undertaking; industrial concern; industrial establishment; works; (*as part of large undertaking*) workshop(s), shop(s); *Min:* workings; **landwirtschaftlicher B.,** agricultural undertaking; *e.g.* farm; market-garden; dairy; **große, mittlere, kleine, Betriebe,** large, medium, small, concerns, businesses, enterprises; **lebenswichtige Betriebe,** vital industries; **die Gesellschaft hat mehrere ihrer Betriebe stillegen müssen,** the company has had to close, shut, down several of its works; **er arbeitet im B. seines Vaters,** he works in his father's firm, in his father's business; **der B. macht jedes Jahr einen gemeinsamen Ausflug,** our firm has an annual outing.
betriebsam, *a.* bustling; active; industrious; busy; energetic; **b. sein,** to be bustling about; **eine betriebsame Stadt,** a bustling town, *F:* a hive of industry.
Betriebsamkeit, *f.* bustle; business; activity.
Betriebsangehörige, *m., f.,* (*decl. as adj.*) worker; employee; member of a firm.
Betriebsanlagen, *f.pl. Ind: etc:* plant; *Rail:* working stock.
Betriebsanleitung, Betriebsanweisung, *f. Ind: etc:* operating instructions (for machine, etc.).
Betriebsaufnahme, *f. Adm:* industrial and business census.
Betriebsausflug, *m.* firm's outing; works outing.
Betriebsausgaben, *f.pl.* working expenses.
Betriebsausstattung, *f.* furniture and fittings (in firm, etc.).
Betriebsbeamte, *m. Ind: etc:* supervising or managing official.
Betriebsbuchführung, *f.* = **Betriebsbuchhaltung** (*a*).
Betriebsbuchhaltung, *f. Com:* (*a*) internal accounting; (*b*) internal accounts department.
Betriebsdruck, *m. Mch:* working pressure.
Betriebseinnahmen, *f.pl.* working receipts, operating receipts; *Rail:* traffic receipts.
betriebsfähig, *a.* (*of machine, etc.*) in working order.
Betriebsferien, *pl.* (firm's, works) holiday; staff holiday; (*of firm*) **B. machen,** to close, shut down, for the holidays.
betriebsfertig, *a.* ready for use; ready for service; in working order.
Betriebsführer, *m. Ind: etc:* manager; managing director; works manager.
Betriebsführung, *f.* **1.** management (of business, factory, etc.); **schlechte B.,** bad management, mismanagement. **2.** *Coll:* management; board of managers.
Betriebsgas, *n.* gas fuel (for vehicle, etc.).
Betriebsgeheimnis, *n. Jur:* trade secret.
Betriebsgemeinschaft, *f.* staff and management.
Betriebsgewicht, *n. Mec.E: etc:* dead weight (of vehicle).
Betriebsingenieur, *m.* operating engineer; production engineer; manufacturing engineer.
Betriebskapital, *n.* working capital.
Betriebsklima, *n.* climate of relationships (in office, factory, etc.); **gutes B.,** congenial atmosphere.
Betriebskosten, *pl.* = **Betriebsunkosten.**
Betriebsleiter, *m.* = **Betriebsführer.**
Betriebsleitung, *f.* = **Betriebsführung.**
Betriebsmaterial, *n. Ind: etc:* working materials; *Rail:* rolling stock.
Betriebsmittel, *n.pl. Ind: etc:* **1.** working capital. **2.** capital goods. **3.** working materials.
Betriebsordnung, *f.* regulations governing the conditions of work (in a firm, etc.).
Betriebspersonal, *n. Rail: etc:* operating staff.
Betriebsprüfer, *m.* auditor.
Betriebsprüfung, *f.* auditing (of the accounts of a firm); (*of firm, etc.*) **B. haben,** to have the auditors in.
Betriebsrat, *m. Ind: etc:* **1.** works committee; staff committee. **2.** member of the works or staff committee.
Betriebsratmitglied, *n.* member of the works or staff committee.
Betriebsruhe, *f.* (*notice in shops, hotels, etc.*) **heute B.,** no business today; closed today.
betriebssicher, *a.* (*of machine, etc.*) safe to operate; reliable in operation; dependable (in service); (*of machine, aircraft, etc.*) foolproof.
Betriebssicherheit, *f. Ind: Rail: etc:* safety in operation, in service; reliability in operation, in service; dependability (of machine).
Betriebsspannung, *f. El:* working voltage; *Mch:* working pressure.

Betriebsstatistik, *f.* industrial or agricultural statistics.
Betriebsstätte, *f.* (business, etc.) premises.
Betriebsstillegung, *f.* shut-down, shutting down, closing down (of a works, etc.).
Betriebsstockung, *f.* interruption of work; *Rail: etc:* dislocation of service; hold-up.
Betriebsstoff, *m.* (*a*) *I.C.E:* (motor-)fuel; (*b*) *Ind: etc:* **Betriebsstoffe** *pl,* working materials.
Betriebsstoffwechsel, *m. Physiol:* catabolism, dissimilation.
Betriebsstörung, *f.* interruption of work (in factory, etc.); dislocation (of industry, train-service, etc.); hold-up (on railway); breakdown (of machine, railway, etc.).
Betriebsunfall, *m.* accident suffered while at work; industrial accident.
Betriebsunkosten, *pl.* (working) expenses; running costs; maintenance costs; overhead expenses, *F:* overhead(s).
Betriebsverfassung, *f.* industrial relations code.
Betriebsversammlung, *f. Ind:* (*a*) (the) working body (including salaried staff); (*b*) meeting of the working body.
Betriebswirt, *m.* business administrator.
Betriebswirtschaft, *f.* business administration.
betriebswirtschaftlich, *a.* . . . with regard to the economic efficiency (of undertaking, industrial unit, etc.); (problems, etc.) of business management, of practical economics; (factors, etc.) affecting the operational efficiency (of factory, etc.); **betriebswirtschaftliche Technik,** business management.
Betriebswirtschaftslehre, *f. Sch:* business administration; science of industrial management.
Betriebszustand, *m.* working condition (of machine, etc.).
Betriebszweig, *m. Ind:* branch of manufacturing; branch of industry.
betrinken (sich), *v.refl.* (*strong*) to get (oneself) drunk, to get intoxicated, *F:* tight; **betrunken sein,** to be drunk, to be intoxicated, *F:* tight; **j-n betrunken machen,** to make s.o. drunk; **schwer betrunken, sinnlos betrunken,** dead drunk, blind drunk; **betrunken wie ein Schwein,** as drunk as a lord; **Betrunkene** *m, f,* drunk.
betroffen, *p.p. & a. see* **betreffen** III.
Betroffenheit, *f.* bewilderment; dismay; disconcertedness, disconcertment.
betrog, betröge. betrogen *see* **betrügen.**
Betrogene, *m., f.* (*decl. as adj.*) one who is deceived, deceived person; (the) deceived; dupe, gull.
betröpfeln, *v.tr.* etwas (mit einer Flüssigkeit) b., to let a liquid drip on to sth.; to sprinkle sth. with a liquid; (*of liquid*) etwas b., to drip on to sth.
betropfen, *v.tr.* to make (sth., s.o.) wet; to moisten (sth., s.o.), (*of liquid, candle*) to drip on to (sth.), (on s.o.'s head, etc.); **betropft,** wet, moistened; spotted (with wax).
betrüben. I. *v.tr.* **1.** to make (s.o.) sad, to sadden (s.o.); to distress (s.o.); to grieve (s.o.); **es betrübt mich zu hören . . .,** I am distressed to hear . . .; **es betrübt mich sehr, ihn verlassen zu müssen,** I am very sorry to have to leave him, I am unhappy at having to leave him; **die Nachricht hat mich tief betrübt,** the news made me very sad, grieved me deeply, I was very sad about, deeply grieved at, the news; **es betrübt mich, ihn so verändert zu sehen,** it grieves me, makes me sad, to see him so changed; **betrübend** = **betrüblich. 2. sich betrüben,** to grieve; to grow sad, to sadden.
II. *p.p. & a.* **betrübt. 1.** sad; miserable; grieved; sorrowful (look, etc.); **mit betrübtem Gesicht,** with a sad face, with a woebegone expression; **b. aussehen, ein betrübtes Gesicht machen,** to look sad; **b. sein,** to be sad; to be, feel, miserable; **j-n b. machen,** to make s.o. sad, to sadden s.o.; to distress s.o.; to grieve s.o.; **über etwas b. sein,** to be sad about sth., to be grieved at sth.; to be distressed about sth.; **zu Tode b.,** sad at heart; extremely sad; down at heart; *B:* **meine Seele ist b. bis an den Tod,** my soul is exceeding sorrowful even unto death; *adv.* sadly, with sadness; **j-n b. anschauen,** to look, gaze, sadly at s.o.; to give s.o. a look of sorrow. **2. die Betrübten,** the sad; the afflicted; the distressed; **Tröster der Betrübten,** comforter of the afflicted; **die Betrübten trösten,** to comfort the afflicted.
betrüblich, *a.* (*of news, etc.*) sad, saddening; distressing; grieving, grievous.
Betrübnis, *f.* -/-nisse, (*a*) sorrow; grief; (*b*) sadness; distress; misery.
betrübt, *p.p. & a. see* **betrüben** II.

Betrübtheit, *f.* sadness; distress; misery.

Betrug, *m.* -(e)s/. **1.** deceit, deception; cheating; fraud; trickery; trick; swindle; imposture, imposition; defrauding (of s.o., of the tax authorities, etc.); (*at games*) cheating; *Jur:* fraud; cheating; **er ist ein Meister des Betrugs,** he is a master of deception, of deceit, he is an arch-deceiver; **er ist keines Betruges fähig,** he is incapable of deception, of cheating; **er lebt vom B.,** he lives by fraud; **sich des Betruges schuldig machen,** to be guilty of fraud; **sich Geld durch B. verschaffen,** to obtain money by fraud, by, on, under, false pretences; **sich etwas durch einen geschickten B. verschaffen,** to obtain sth. by a clever trick; **B. begehen,** to commit fraud; **einen B. an j-m begehen**=**j-n betrügen,** *q.v. under* **betrügen; es steckt ein B. dahinter,** there is a swindle in this somewhere; **ein frommer B.,** a pious fraud; **ein gemeiner B.,** (i) a mean piece of trickery; (ii) plain cheating; a common swindle, trick; **ein B., der schwerwiegende Folgen hatte,** a piece of deceit with grave consequences. **2.** fraudulence; deceit; guile; **er kennt keinen B., er kennt den B. nicht, in ihm ist kein B.,** he is without deceit, in him is no guile; *B:* **so leget nun ab . . . allen B.,** wherefore laying aside . . . all guile; **. . . noch B. in seinem Munde gewesen ist,** neither was any deceit in his mouth.

betrügbar, *a.* deceivable.

betrügen. I. *v.tr.* (*strong*) (*a*) to deceive; to cheat; to trick; to swindle; to defraud (s.o., the tax authorities, etc.); to impose on, upon (s.o.); (*at games*) to cheat; **j-n um etwas b.,** to defraud s.o. of sth., to cheat s.o. (out) of sth., to swindle s.o. out of sth., to swindle sth. out of s.o., to trick s.o. out of sth.; **sich (selbst) b.,** to deceive oneself; **den Tod, das Schicksal, b.,** to cheat death, fate; **den Zoll b.,** to cheat the customs; **mit, in, der Absicht, j-n zu b.,** with (the) intent to defraud s.o., *Jur:* in fraud of s.o., to the fraud of s.o.; **ich lasse mich nicht so leicht b.,** I am not so easily swindled, cheated; **man hat mich betrogen, ich bin betrogen worden,** I have been deceived, tricked, cheated, swindled; **wir sind um unsere besten Jahre betrogen worden,** we have been cheated of our best years; **beim Wiegen b.,** to give short weight; *B:* **die Schlange betrog mich,** the serpent beguiled me; (*b*) to deceive (one's husband, one's wife); **der betrogene Ehemann,** the deceived husband.

II. *vbl s.* **Betrügen,** *n. in vbl senses; also:* deception, deceit; cheat; fraud; *cp.* **Betrug.**

Betrüger, *m.* -s/-, deceiver; swindler; cheat; trickster; impostor; defrauder (of s.o., of the tax authorities, etc.); (*at games*) cheat; (*at cards*) sharper; **der betrogene B.,** the deceiver (being) deceived, *F:* the biter bit.

Betrügerei, *f.* -/-en. **1.** (persistent) cheating; deception, deceit; swindling, swindle. **2.** (piece of) deceit; (piece of) trickery, trick; swindle; dishonest acts; fraud; **sich** *dat.* **Betrügereien zuschulden kommen lassen,** to commit a number of frauds; **mit allerhand kleinen Betrügereien hat er allmählich eine hübsche Summe Geld zusammengebracht,** he amassed a tidy sum by all kinds of small frauds; **durch seine Betrügereien ist sie um ihr Vermögen gekommen,** she has lost her fortune through his frauds; **er fürchtete eine B. von meiner Seite,** he feared a trick on my part.

betrügerisch, *a.* **1.** (*of pers.*) deceitful; swindling; *Jur:* fraudulent; **in betrügerischer Absicht,** with fraudulent intent, with (the) intent to defraud; **der betrügerische Charakter, das Betrügerische, einer Handlung,** the fraudulent nature, the fraudulence, of an action; **in betrügerischer Weise,** fraudulently; *adv.* deceitfully; fraudulently. **2.** *A. & occ:* deceptive; treacherous.

betrüglich, *a. A:* deceptive; treacherous.

betrunken, *p.p. & a. see* **betrinken.**

Betrunkenheit, *f.* drunkenness, intoxication; drunken state.

Betsaal, *m.* prayer-hall; meeting-hall, -house.

Betschemel, *m.* prayer-stool, praying-desk.

Betschuanaland [bɛtʃuˑ'aːnaˑ-]. *Pr.n.n.* -s. *Geog:* Bechuanaland.

Betschuane [bɛtʃuˑ'aːnə], *m.* -n/-n. *Ethn:* Bechuana.

Betschwester, *f.* (over-)devout, *F:* churchy, woman; *F:* **eine alte B.,** an old church-hen.

Betstuhl, *m.* prayer-stool, praying-desk, kneeling-chair, prie-dieu.

Betstunde, *f.* (*a*) hour of prayer; (*b*) prayer-meeting.

Bett, *n.* -(e)s/-en. **1.** (*a*) bed; *Av: Nau: Rail:* berth, *F:* bunk; **einschläfriges B.,** single bed; **zweischläfriges B.,** double bed; **anderthalbschläfriges B.,** three foot six bed; **Zimmer mit einem B., mit zwei Betten,** single, double, room; single-, double-bedded, room; **ihr Schlafraum war eine Dachkammer mit drei Betten,** their dormitory was an attic with three beds, was a three-bed attic; **in getrennten Betten schlafen,** to sleep in separate beds; **ins B. steigen,** to get, climb, into bed; **aus dem B. steigen,** to get out of bed; **aus dem B. springen,** to leap, jump, out of bed; **im B. sein, liegen,** (i) to be, lie, in bed, (ii) to be (lying) ill in bed; **ins, zu, B. gehen,** *F:* **in die Betten gehen,** to go to bed, *F:* to turn in; **sich ins B. legen,** (i) to go to bed, (ii) to get into bed, *F:* to get between the sheets, (iii) (*through illness*) to take to one's bed; **sich auf das B. legen,** to lie down on the bed; **das B. hüten,** to keep to one's bed, to be confined to one's bed, to be laid up; **ans B. gefesselt sein,** to be bed-ridden; **drei Tage im B.,** three days in bed; **das B. aufschlagen,** to turn back the bed-clothes; **die Betten machen.** to make the beds; **ein Kind ins, zu, B. bringen,** to put a child to bed; **die Kinder ins, zu, B. schicken,** to send, *F:* pack, the children off to bed; (*b*) **das eheliche B.,** the marriage bed; **Kind aus dem zweiten B.,** child of the second bed, of the second marriage; *Jur:* **Scheidung von Tisch und B.,** separation from bed and board, judicial separation; *see also* **entehren** I. (*b*); (*c*) bedstead; **eisernes B.,** iron bedstead; (*d*) feather-bed; **die Betten lüften,** to air the beds, the bedding. **2.** *Ven:* (stag's) harbour, lair. **3.** bed, bottom (of river, etc.). **4.** (*a*) *Rail:* bed (of rails, etc.); (*b*) *Mec.E: etc:* seating, bed, cradle foundation; bed (of lathe, planing-machine, etc.); table (of drilling-machine); bed(-plate), base-plate, seating (of engine etc.). **5.** (*a*) *Geol:* layer, bed, deposit, stratum (of ore, sand, etc.); *Min:* bed, seam (of coal, etc.); (*b*) *Constr: etc:* bed, layer (of mortar, clay, planks, etc.).

Bettag, *m.* day of prayer; *see also* **Bußtag.**

Bettbank, *f. Austrian:* bed-settee.

Bettbecken, *n. Hyg:* bed-pan.

Bettbehang, *m.* bed hangings; valance.

Bettbezug, *m. plumeau* case.

Bettchen, *n.* -s/-, small bed; (child's) cot, crib.

Bettcouch, *f.* bed-couch, studio-couch; divan bed.

Bettdecke, *f.* (*a*) bedspread, bed-cover; counterpane; (*b*) bed-cover, coverlet; **wollene B.,** blanket.

Bettdrell, Bettdrillich, *m. Tex:* drill.

Bettel, *m.* -s/. (*a*) begging; beggary; mendicity, mendicancy; **sich vom B. ernähren, vom B. leben,** to live by begging; (*b*) *F:* **der ganze B. hängt mir zum Halse heraus,** I'm sick of the whole wretched business; **ich habe ihm den ganzen B. vor die Füße geworfen,** I threw the whole thing back at him.

bettelarm, *a.* desperately poor, destitute.

Bettelbrief, *m.* **1.** begging letter. **2.** licence to beg.

Bettelbrot, *n.* **das B. essen,** to live by begging; to live on charity.

Bettelbruder, *m.* **1.**=**Bettelmönch. 2.** beggar.

Bettelei, *f.* -/-en, (*a*) begging; beggary; mendicity, mendicancy; (*b*) *F:* pleading, begging; pestering.

Bettelfrau, *f.* beggar-woman.

Bettelgeld, *n.* (*a*) alms; (*b*) *F:* **etwas für ein B. bekommen,** to get sth. for very little money, for next to nothing.

bettelhaft, *a.* beggarly.

Bettelhaftigkeit, *f.* beggarliness.

Bettelhandwerk, *n.* begging; **sich auf das B. (ver)legen, das B. treiben,** to live by begging.

Betteljunge, *m.* beggar-boy.

Bettelkram, *m.*=**Bettel** (*b*).

Bettelleute, *pl.* beggars; mendicants.

Bettelmann, *m.* -(e)s/-leute. **1.** beggar(-man); mendicant. **2.** *Cards:* beggar-my-neighbour.

Bettelmönch, *m. Ecc:* mendicant (friar), begging friar.

betteln. I. *v.i.* (*haben*) (*a*) to beg; **um Almosen b.,** to beg for alms; **um sein Brot b.,** to beg (for) one's bread; **b. gehen,** to go begging; to live by begging; **auf den Straßen b.,** to beg in the streets; **er hat sich durch das ganze Land gebettelt,** he has begged his way through, over, the whole country; (*b*) to plead, entreat, beg; (*of dog, etc.*) to beg; **die Kinder bettelten darum, in den Zoo gehen zu dürfen,** the children pleaded, begged, to be allowed to go to the zoo; **sie bettelten, er möge noch bleiben, daß er noch bleiben möge,** they begged, entreated, him to stay; **er sah sie bettelnd an,** he looked at her pleadingly.

II. *vbl s.* **Betteln,** *n.* (*a*) begging; beggary; mendicity, mendicancy; **sich durch B. ernähren,** to live by begging; **'B. und Hausieren verboten',** 'no beggars, no hawkers'; (*b*) *F:* pleading, begging; **all ihr B. war vergebens,** all her pleading was in vain, all her entreaties were in vain.

Bettelnonne, *f. Ecc:* nun of a mendicant order.

Bettelorden, *m. Ecc:* mendicant order, begging order; **Angehöriger eines Bettelordens,** mendicant (friar), begging friar.

Bettelordenskirchen, *f.pl. Ecc.Arch:* friars' churches.

Bettelpack, *n.* (pack, crowd, of) beggars.

Bettelsack, *m.* beggar's sack, *A:* scrip.

Bettelstab, *m.* beggar's staff; **j-n an den B. bringen,** to reduce s.o. to beggary, to make a beggar of s.o.; **an den B. kommen,** to be reduced to beggary; to be forced to live by begging.

Bettelvogt, *m. A:* beadle.

Bettelvolk, *n.* (pack, crowd, of) beggars.

Bettelweib, *n.* beggar-woman.

Bettelwesen, *n.* begging; mendicity, mendicancy.

Bettelzinken, *m.* tramp's (code-)sign (on doors).

betten. I. *v.tr.* **1.** (*a*) to bed; **j-n auf Kissen, auf Stroh, b.,** to lay, bed, put, s.o. on cushions, on straw; **in, auf, weiche Kissen gebettet,** lying, resting, on soft cushions; **auf Stroh gebettet,** bedded, lying, on straw; **j-n weich b.,** to make s.o. a soft bed; *F:* to find s.o. a comfortable situation, *F:* a cushy job; **j-n zur letzten Ruhe b.,** to lay s.o. to rest, to lay s.o. in the grave; (*b*) *I.C.E:* to seat (valve). **2. sich betten,** to make a bed for oneself; to lie down on a bed, etc.; *F:* **durch diese Heirat hat er sich weich gebettet,** he has feathered his nest properly by this marriage, he has done well for himself with this marriage; *Prov:* **wie man sich bettet, so liegt man,** as you make your bed, so you must lie on it.

II. *vbl s.* **1. Betten,** *n. in vbl senses.* **2. Bettung,** *f.* (*a*) *Rail:* ballast; *Civ.E:* (ballast-) bed, foundation, bottom (of road, etc.); **die B. feststampfen, stopfen,** to ram, tamp, the ballast; (*b*) *Mch:* seating, bed, cradle, foundation; bed(-plate), base-plate, seating (of engine, etc.); *I.C.E:* seat(ing) (of valve); *Artil:* **B. eines Geschützes,** mounting of a gun, gun-platform; (*c*) *Constr: etc:* bed, layer, foundation (of mortar, clay, planks, etc.); **B. von Beton,** bed of concrete; **B. von Steinen,** bed of stones.

Bettfedern, *f.pl.* **1.** bed-feathers. **2.** bed-springs.

bettfest, *a. A:*=**bettlägerig.**

Bettflasche, *f.* hot-water bottle.

Bettgenosse, *m.* bedfellow.

Bettgeschirr, *n. Hyg:* chamber(-pot), pot; bed-pan.

Bettgeselle, *m.* bedfellow.

Bettgestell, *n.* bedstead, bed-frame.

Betthäschen, *n.,* **Betthase,** *m. F:* (*girl*) bedmate; **sein Betthäschen,** his little bit of fluff.

Betthimmel, *m.* canopy, tester (of bed).

Bettina [bɛ'tiːnaː]. *Pr.n.f.* **-s** *& Lit:* **-nens.** (*dim. of* **Elisabeth**) Betty.

Bettjacke, *f.* bed-jacket.

Bettkammer, *f.* bedroom, *A:* bedchamber.

Bettkasten, *m.* (*a*) (wooden) bed-frame; (*b*) bedding box (in settee-bed, etc.).

Bettlade, *f.* (wooden) bedstead, bed-frame.

bettlägerig, *a.* confined to bed, laid up; bed-ridden, *U.S:* bedfast; **er ist schon lange b.,** he has been bed-ridden for a long time; *adv.* **b. krank sein,** to be laid up, confined to bed.

Bettlägerigkeit, *f.* confinement to bed; being bed-ridden; **jahrelange B.,** years of lying in a sick-bed.

Bettlaken, *n.* (bed-)sheet.

Bettlampe, *f.* wall lamp (above bed).

Bettleiter, *f.* bed-steps.

Bettlektüre, *f.* bedside books.

Bettler, *m.* -s/-, beggar; mendicant; **j-n zum B. machen,** to reduce s.o. to beggary, to make a beggar of s.o.

Bettlergesindel, *n.* (pack, crowd, of) beggars.

bettlerhaft, *a.* beggarly.

Bettlerherberge, *f.* doss-house.

Bettlerin, *f.* -/-innen, beggar-woman.

Bettlerjunge, *m.* beggar-boy.

Bettlerleier, *f. A:* hurdy-gurdy.

Bettlermädchen, *n.* beggar-girl, beggar-maid.

Bettleroper, die. *Mus:* the Beggar's Opera.

Bettlerpack, *n.* (pack, crowd, of) beggars.

Bettlerschaft, *f.* -/. (community of) beggars.

Bettlerstand, *m.* (community of) beggars; beggardom.

Bettlertum, *n.* -(e)s/. **1.** mendicity, mendicancy; begging. **2.** (community of) beggars; beggardom.

Bettlinnen, *n.* bed-linen; sheeting.

Bettnässen, *n. Med:* bed-wetting, (nocturnal) enuresis.

Bettnässer, *m.* -s/-, bed-wetter.

Bettnische, *f.* alcove, bed-recess, bed-closet.

Bettpfanne, *f.* (*a*) warming-pan; (*b*) *Hyg:* bed-pan.

Bettpfosten, *m.* bed-post.

Bettrolle, *f.* (*a*) (French) bolster; (*b*) roll of bedding.

Bettruhe, *f.* staying in bed (when ill); *U.S:* bed rest; **der Arzt verordnete B.,** the doctor ordered him to stay in bed, to keep to his bed.

Bettsack, *m.* bag in which to keep a *plumeau.*

Bettschere, *f.* bed-guard.

Bettschieber, *m. Hyg:* bed-pan.

Bettschuh, *m.* bed-sock.

Bettschüssel, *f. Hyg:* bed-pan.

Bettschwere, *f. F:* **die nötige B. haben,** to be (quite) ready for a sleep.

Bettsessel, *m.* bed-chair.

Bettsocken, *m.pl.* bed-socks.

Bettsofa, *n.* settee-bed, bed-sofa; sofa-bed(stead).

Bettstatt, *f.* = **Bettstelle.**

Bettstelle, *f.* bedstead, bed-frame.

Bettstütze, *f.* bed-rest.

Bettüberzug, *m. plumeau* case.

Bet-Tuch, *m.* (Jewish) prayer-shawl.

Bettuch, *n.* (bed-)sheet.

Bettung, *f. see* **betten II.**

Bettungskörper, *m. Rail: Civ.E:* ballast-bed (of track, road, etc.).

bettungslos, *a. Rail: etc:* unballasted (track, etc.).

Bettungsmaterial, *n. Rail: Civ.E:* ballast(ing); **das B. feststampfen,** to ram, tamp, the ballast.

Bettungsstoff, *m.* = **Bettungsmaterial.**

Bettunterlage, *f.* under-blanket; mattress pad.

Bettvorhänge, *m.pl.* bed-curtains.

Bettvorleger, *m.* bedside rug.

Bettwanze, *f. Ent:* bed-bug.

Bettwärme, *f.* warmth in bed.

Bettwärmer, *m.* bed-warmer, (*a*) hot-water bottle, (*b*) warming-pan, (*c*) (electric) bed-warmer, (electric) warming pad; electric blanket.

Bettwäsche, *f.* bed-linen; **frische B.,** clean sheets (and pillow-case).

Betty. *Pr.n.f.* **-s.** (*dim. of* **Elisabeth**) Betty.

Bettzeug, *n.* **1.** bedding. **2.** *Tex:* ticking.

Bettzipfel, *m.* corner of the feather-bed; *F:* **nach dem B. schnappen,** to yawn.

betüdeln, *v.tr.* to fuss over (s.o.).

betulich, *a.* fussing, (over-)attentive; solicitous (for s.o.'s comfort, etc.).

Betulichkeit, *f.* fussing (about), (over-)attentiveness; solicitude.

Betulin [beˈtuˑliːn], *n.* **-s/.** *Ch:* betulinol, betulin.

betümpeln (sich), *v.refl. F:* to get tipsy, fuddled.

betun (sich), *v.refl.* (*strong*) to fuss, make a fuss (about s.o., sth.).

betupfen, *v.tr.* **1.** to mark (sth.) with dots, with spots; to dot, speckle, fleck (sth.) **2.** to touch (sth.) lightly; to dab (at) (sth.); to dab (wound, etc.) (with lint); **etwas mit dem Finger b.,** to dab at sth. with one's finger; **er betupfte sich die Stirn mit dem Taschentuch,** he dabbed his forehead with his handkerchief, he mopped his forehead, his brow, with his handkerchief.

betüpfeln, *v.tr.* to mark (sth.) with dots; to dot, speckle, fleck (sth.); **das Gefieder dieses Vogels ist mit Weiß betüpfelt,** this bird's feathers are speckled with white.

beturbant [bəˈturbaːnt], *a. F:* turbaned, wearing a turban.

Beuche, *f.* **-/-n.** **1.** lye, buck, bucking lye. **2.** bucking, boiling *or* steeping (linen, etc.) in lye; *Tex:* boiling (linen, etc.) in alkaline lye before bleaching.

beuchen, *v.tr.* to buck (linen, etc.), to boil *or* steep (linen, etc.) in lye; *Tex:* to boil (linen, etc.) in alkaline lye before bleaching.

Beuchfaß, *n.* bucking-tub.

Beuchkessel, *m.* (bucking-)kier, (bleaching-)kier.

Beuchlauge, *f.* = **Beuche 1.**

beugbar, *a.* **1.** bendable. **2.** = **beugungsfähig.**

Beuchwasser, *n.* = **Beuche 1.**

Beugbarkeit, *f.* **1.** capability of being bent. **2.** *Gram:* = **Beugungsfähigkeit.**

Beuge, *f.* **-/-n.** **1.** (*a*) *Gym:* bent position; knees-bend; **in der B. bleiben!** keep your knees bent; **Arme in der B. halten!** keep your arms bent; **aus der B. heraus die Arme zurückschnellen!** from the bent position swing the arms back sharply; **in die B. gehen!** knees bend! (*b*) *occ.* bend, curve (of river, road, etc.). **2.** bend (of knee, arm); crook (of arm). **3.** *Tls: Coop:* cramp.

Beugefall, *m.* = **Beugungsfall.**

Beugehaft, *f. Jur:* imprisonment to force a witness to give evidence, a debtor to make a sworn statement as to his seizable effects.

Beugel, *n.* **-s/-.** *Austrian: Cu:* roll of short pastry filled with nuts *or* poppy-seed.

Beugemuskel, *m. Anat:* flexor.

beugen. **I.** *v.tr.* **1.** (*a*) to bend (knee, elbow, neck, etc.); to bow (head, knee, back, etc.); *Gym:* to bend (knees, etc.); **den Oberkörper nach vorne, nach hinten, b.,** to bend one's body forward, backward; **seine Knie vor dem Altar b.,** to bend, bow, the knee before the altar, to genuflect before the altar; **j-s Stolz b.,** to bring down, to break, s.o.'s pride; **j-s Nacken unter das Joch b.,** to bend s.o.'s neck under the yoke; **Sorgen und Alter haben ihn tief gebeugt,** care and age have bowed him (down); **tief gebeugt von Sorgen,** bowed down with care; **gebeugt vom Alter,** bent with age, bowed down by age; **gebeugt gehen,** to walk with a stoop; **das Recht b.,** to bend, stretch, the law; to warp justice; (*b*) *Gram:* to inflect (word), to decline (noun, adjective); (*c*) *Ph:* to diffract, bend (light, rays, etc.); **beugend,** diffractory, diffractive. **2. sich beugen,** (*of pers.*) to bend; to bow; (*of neck, back, etc.*) to bend; **er beugte sich über das Geländer,** he leant over the railing; **er beugte sich aus dem Fenster,** he leant out of the window; **er beugte sich über das bewußtlose Kind,** he bent over the unconscious child; **sich nach vorne b.,** to bend forward; **sich unter einer Last b.,** to bend under a burden; **sich der höheren Gewalt b.,** to bow to superior power.

II. *vbl s.* **1. Beugen,** *n. in vbl senses.* **2. Beugung,** *f.* (*a*) = II. 1; (*b*) *Gram:* inflection (of word), declension (of noun, adjective); *Ph:* diffraction (of light, rays, etc.).

Beuger, *m.* **-s/-.** *Anat:* flexor.

Beugestellung, *f.* bent position.

beugsam, *a. occ.* = **biegsam.**

Beugungsbild, *n. Ph:* diffraction image.

Beugungsendung, *f. Gram:* flexional ending.

Beugungserscheinungen, *f.pl. Ph:* diffraction phenomena.

beugungsfähig, *a. Gram:* (word) that can be inflected; (noun, adjective) that can be declined; (verb) that can be conjugated.

Beugungsfähigkeit, *f. Gram:* ability (of word) to inflect; ability (of noun, adjective) to decline.

Beugungsfall, *m. Gram:* case (of word).

Beugungsfigur, *f. Ph:* diffraction pattern.

Beugungsgitter, *n. Ph:* diffraction grating.

Beugungslinie, *f. Ph:* diffraction line.

Beugungsscheibchen, *n. Ph:* diffraction disk.

Beugungssilbe, *f. Gram:* inflexional syllable.

Beugungsspektrum, *n. Ph:* diffraction spectrum.

Beugungsstrahl, *m. Ph:* diffracted ray.

Beugungswinkel, *m. Ph:* diffraction angle.

Beule, *f.* **-/-n,** protuberance, bulge. **1.** (*on body*) bump, lump, swelling; bruise; (*caused by inflammation*) boil; *Vet:* warble; **er war am ganzen Körper mit Beulen bedeckt,** his whole body was covered with boils. **2.** (*on metal, etc.*) bulge; bruise, dent; (*of tin, hat, etc.*) **voller Beulen sein,** to be badly battered, dented.

beulen, *v.tr.* **1.** to buckle (metal, etc.). **2.** (*of metal, etc.*) **sich beulen,** to buckle (up).

beulenartig, *a.* like a bulge; like a bump; like a boil; **eine beulenartige Geschwulst,** a swelling like a boil.

Beulenbrand, *m. Agr:* (*disease*) maize, boil, smut.

Beulenfieber, *n.* = **Beulenseuche.**

Beulenkrankheit, *f. Med:* Aleppo boil, Aleppo button, Biskra button.

Beulenpest, *f. Med:* bubonic plague.

Beulenseuche, *f. Vet: Med:* **(Sibirische) B.,** anthrax, malignant pustule, splenic fever, *Med:* wool-sorters' disease.

beulig, *a.* **1.** (*of body*) covered with bumps, lumps; bruised. **2.** (*of metal, etc.*) bruised, dented; (*of hat, tin, etc.*) battered, dented.

Beunde, *f.* **-/-n.** *Dial:* fenced-in piece of ground.

beunruhigen. **I.** *v.tr.* to make (s.o.) anxious, uneasy; to disquiet, trouble, disturb (s.o.); *F:* to worry (s.o.); **sich b.,** to become anxious, to worry, to get uneasy; **beunruhigen Sie sich seinetwegen nicht,** don't worry about him, over him; **beunruhigen Sie sich darüber, deswegen, nicht,** don't trouble, *F:* don't bother your head, about that; **es beunruhigt mich wenig, was sie darüber denken,** I don't mind, I don't much care, *Lit:* I care little, what they think about it; I am not concerned about what they think about it; **das beunruhigt mich wenig,** I am little disturbed by that; **lassen Sie sich dadurch nicht b.,** don't be disturbed by that, don't let that worry you; **sein Gesundheitszustand beunruhigt mich, ich beunruhige mich wegen seines Gesundheitszustandes, ich bin wegen seines Gesundheitszustandes, über seinen Gesundheitszustand, beunruhigt,** I am anxious, worried, about his health; I am concerned about his health; **beunruhigt sein,** to be anxious, uneasy; **sie war seinetwegen ußerst beunruhigt,** she was extremely anxious, worried, about him; **ich war beunruhigt über sein langes Ausbleiben,** I was worried by his long absence; **ich fühle mich in keiner Weise beunruhigt,** I have no misgivings; my mind is easy; **ich war einigermaßen, ziemlich, beunruhigt,** I was rather worried; **nicht beunruhigt sein über etwas,** to be unconcerned regarding sth.; **beunruhigt sah er nach der Tür,** he looked at the door uneasily, anxiously; **er sah sehr beunruhigt aus,** he looked very much concerned; **er ist über das Ausbleiben einer Antwort beunruhigt,** he is worried at getting no answer; **ich bin über sein Verhalten beunruhigt, sein Verhalten beunruhigt mich,** I am concerned over his conduct; **sich über etwas beunruhigt fühlen,** to feel ill at ease, to feel concerned about sth.; **es beunruhigte mich, nicht mehr von ihm zu hören,** I was uneasy at hearing nothing more of him; **beunruhigend,** disquieting, alarming, disturbing, upsetting (news, etc.); **eine beunruhigende Vorahnung,** a disquieting premonition; **es war ein beunruhigender Gedanke,** it was a disquieting, an uneasy, thought; **eine beunruhigende Wendung,** an alarming turn (of events); **sein Zustand ist höchst beunruhigend,** his condition is extremely worrying; *Mil:* **den Feind b.,** to harass, worry, the enemy.

II. *vbl s.* **1. Beunruhigen,** *n. in vbl senses.* **2. Beunruhigung,** *f.* (*a*) = II. 1; (*b*) anxiety, uneasiness, misgivings, disquietude, disturbance; **Zustand der B.,** state of anxiety; anxious state of mind; **kein Grund zur B.,** no cause for anxiety, uneasiness; **er lebte in dauernder B.,** he lived in constant anxiety.

Beunruhigungsfeuer, *n. Mil:* harassing fire.

Beunte, *f.* **-/-n** = **Beunde.**

beurgrunzen, *v.tr.* *F:* **1.** = **beaugenscheinigen.** **2. etwas b.,** to give one's opinion on sth., *F:* to put in one's spoke.

beurkunden. *Jur:* **I.** *v.tr.* **1.** to produce legal documents in support of (sth.), to prove (sth.) by legal documents. **2.** to attest, certify, authenticate (statement, contract, etc.); *Adm:* to register (birth, death, marriage); **der Kaufvertrag muß vom Notar, notariell, beurkundet werden,** the contract of sale must be authenticated by a notary public.

II. *vbl s.* **1. Beurkunden,** *n. in vbl senses.* **2. Beurkundung,** *f.* (*a*) = II. 1; *also:* attestation, certification, authentication (of statement, contract, etc.); *Adm:* registration (of birth, death, marriage); **notarielle, öffentliche, B.,** authentication (of contract, etc.) by a notary public; **zur B. dieses,** in witness whereof; (*b*) documentary proof.

beurlauben. **I.** *v.tr.* (i) to give, grant (s.o.) leave (of absence); to give (s.o.) time off; *U.S: Mil: Adm:* to furlough (s.o.), *Mil:* to discharge (troops, etc.) conditionally; (ii) *Adm:* to suspend (civil servant, officer, member of parliament, etc.); **sich (bei j-m) b.,** to take one's leave (of s.o.); **sich b. lassen,** (i) to ask for leave; to ask for time off; (*of students, etc.*) to apply for leave of absence; (ii) *Adm:* to apply for suspension; **j-n auf unbestimmte Zeit vom Dienst b.,** to suspend s.o. indefinitely; **er beurlaubte die Dienerschaft für diesen Abend,** he sent his servants away for the evening; **man beurlaubte ihn für mehrere Wochen von seiner Truppe,** he was given leave from his unit for several weeks; **für ein halbes Jahr beurlaubt,** on six month's leave; **wegen Krankheit, krankheitshalber, beurlaubt sein,** to be on sick-leave; **er ist für einige Zeit, vorübergehend, zeitweilig, beurlaubt,** (i) he is on temporary leave; (ii) *Adm:* he is temporarily suspended.

II. *vbl s.* **1. Beurlauben,** *n. in vbl senses.* **2. Beurlaubung,** *f.* (*a*) = II. 1; *also:* (i) *Mil:* (conditional) discharge (of troops, etc.); (ii) *Adm:* suspension (of civil servant, etc.); (*b*) (i) leave (of absence); *Mil:* furlough; *Mil:* (conditional) discharge (of troops, etc.); (ii) *Adm:* suspension (of civil servant, etc.); **einen Antrag auf B. stellen,** (i) to apply for leave; (ii) *Adm:* to apply for suspension; **j-s zeitweilige B. (vom Dienst) anordnen,** to order s.o. to be temporarily suspended.

Beurlaubtenstand, *m.* **1.** reserve status. **2.** reserve.

beurteilen. **I.** *v.tr.* to judge (s.o., sth.); to pass judgment on (s.o., sth.), to give one's opinion on (subject); **soweit ich das b. kann,** as far as I can judge, as far as I can see; **wie ich die Sache beurteile,** in my view, to my mind, as I see the matter; **wie man den Fall auch b. mag,** however, whichever way, one looks at the case, in whatever light one regards the case; **ich kann nicht b.**

wie lange das noch dauern wird, I can't judge how much longer that will last; **es ist deine Sache, das zu b., das mußt du selbst b.**, it is for you to judge; **ich kann nicht b., wer hier im Unrecht ist**, I can't judge which party is in the wrong; **ich kann das nicht b.**, I am not competent to judge; **die Geschehnisse anders b.**, to take a different view of the events; **ich beurteile die Sache anders**, I see, view, the matter differently; I do not look on, do not view, the matter in that light; **ich beurteile das völlig anders**, I look upon it, see it, from quite a different angle; **j-n, etwas, falsch b.**, to see s.o., sth., in a false light; to be mistaken in one's judgment of s.o., sth.; to misjudge s.o., sth.; **die Lage falsch b.**, to take a wrong view of the situation; **j-n, etwas, richtig b.**, to judge s.o., sth., correctly, rightly; **er besitzt die Fähigkeit, Menschen und Dinge richtig zu b.**, he is capable of sizing up persons and things; **wir beurteilen die Lage sehr ernst**, we take a grave view of the situation, we regard the situation as serious; **ich beurteile die Aussichten in diesem Beruf sehr günstig**, I think the prospects in this profession are very good; **das Stück wurde günstig, ungünstig, beurteilt**, the play received favourable, unfavourable, criticism; **beurteilen Sie dieses Versehen nicht zu streng**, don't be too hard on this mistake, don't take too harsh a view of this mistake; **etwas nach etwas anderem b.**, to judge sth. by sth. else; **beurteilen Sie ihn nicht nach seinem Äußeren, sondern nach seinen Taten**, don't judge him by his appearance, but by his actions; **j-n, etwas, nach dem äußeren Schein b.**, to judge s.o., sth., by appearances; **andere nach sich selbst b.**, to judge others by oneself.

II. *vbl s.* **1. Beurteilen**, *n. in vbl senses.* **2. Beurteilung**, *f.* (*a*)=II. 1; (*b*) opinion (of s.o.; of, on, sth.), view (of sth.), views (on a matter, etc.); judgment (of s.o., sth.); **nach meiner B.**, in my judgment, in my view, to my mind, as I see the matter; **seine B. der Lage erwies sich als richtig**, his view of the situation proved to be right; **j-m etwas zur B. vorlegen**, to submit sth. to s.o. for an opinion; **ich glaube, man kann seiner B. des Sachverhalts Glauben schenken**, I think one can trust his opinion on the facts of the case; **die Zeitungen waren sich in der B. seiner sportlichen Leistung einig**, the newspapers were unanimous in their judgment of his performance in the field of sport; **eine falsche B. könnte sich in diesem Fall verhängnisvoll auswirken**, an error of judgment could have disastrous consequences in this case.

Beurteiler, *m.* -s/-, judge.

Beuschel, *n.* -s/-. *Austrian:* pluck (of animal); *Cu:* dish of heart and lung.

beut. *A: see* **bieten.**

Beute[1], *f.* -/. booty, spoil(s), plunder, *F:* loot; prey; capture; *F:* (*of thief*) haul; *Mil:* captured material; *Navy:* prize; *Ven:* quarry, game; bag; **B. machen**, to loot, plunder, pillage; **sie zogen den ganzen Tag herum, machten B. und zerstörten alles**, they roamed about the whole day looting and destroying everything; **sie beschlossen, die B. zu teilen**, they decided to share the booty; **auf B. ausgehen, B. suchen**, to go plundering; (*of animal*) to go in search of prey, *Lit:* to raven; **seinen Anteil an der B. verlangen**, to claim one's share of the spoil(s); **Bienen, die ihre B. suchen**, bees gathering their spoil; **der Löwe verfolgte seine B.**, the lion pursued his prey, quarry; **das Lager fiel plündernden Banden zur B.**, the encampment fell a prey to maurauding bands; **eine B. der Furcht sein**, to be a prey to fear; **einer Krankheit zur B. fallen**, to fall a prey, a victim, to a disease; **die feindlichen Schiffe wurden als rechtmäßige B. erklärt**, the enemy ships were declared a lawful prize; **das Piratenschiff schleppte seine B. in eine kleine Bucht**, the pirate ship towed its capture into a small bay; **die Einbrecher machten keine große B.**, the burglars did not get much of a haul; **der Dieb machte sich mit seiner B. davon**, the thief made off with his booty, *F:* haul, with the swag; **er ist (eine) leichte B. für Gauner und Spitzbuben**, he is fair game for rogues and swindlers; **eine reiche, willkommene, B.**, a rich, welcome, booty; **die Jäger verfolgten ihre B.**, the hunters pursued their quarry, game; **sie kamen mit reicher B. von der Jagd zurück**, they returned from the hunt with a good bag; *B:* **und so nahmen sie es von den Ägyptern zur B.**, and they spoiled the Egyptians.

Beute[2], *f.* -/-n, (*a*) beehive; (*b*) kneading-trough.

beutebeladen, *a.* (pers., ship, etc.) laden with spoils, booty.

Beutegeschütz, *n. Mil:* captured gun.

Beutegier, *f.* lust for booty; **in ihrer B. schraken sie vor nichts zurück**, in their lust for booty they stopped at nothing.

beutegierig, *a.* eager for booty.

Beutegut, *n. Coll.* captured goods, booty, spoil(s), plunder, *F:* loot.

Beutel, *m.* -s/-, (*a*) bag (for flour; for toilet, sewing, shoe-cleaning, articles, etc.); (pouch-shaped) handbag; pochette, Dorothy bag; (dust-)bag (in vacuum-cleaner); (tobacco) pouch; satchel (*with shoulder-strap*); *A:* (*beggar's*) wallet; **ein B. zum Zuziehen**, a draw-string bag; (*b*) purse; *F:* **das geht an den B.**, that costs a lot; **ein voller B.**, a long, heavy, well-lined, purse; **ein leerer B.**, an empty, a light, purse; **tief in den B. greifen**, to dive into one's purse, pocket; **das hat ein Loch in meinen B. gerissen**, that made quite a hole in my pocket; **ich muß mich nach meinem B. richten**, I have to consider my pocket; I must cut my coat according to my cloth; **mein B. ist leer**, my purse is empty; **Sie werden sich dazu bequemen müssen, den B. zu ziehen, aufzumachen**, I am afraid you will have to pay up, *P:* cough up; (*c*) (*in Turkey*) *A:* purse of gold (=10,000 *piastres*); purse of silver (=500 *piastres*); (*d*) *Bill:* pocket; (*e*) *Anat:* bursa; (*f*) *Z:* pouch (of marsupial); (*g*) *Mill:* bolter(-sieve); (*h*) *El:* sack (of sack battery).

Beutelanlage, *f. Mill:* bolting apparatus.

beutelartig, *a.* like a bag, bag-like; like a pouch, pouch-like.

Beutelbär, *m. Z:* koala (bear), koolah, Australian native bear.

Beutelbilch, *m. Z:* pouched mouse, phascogale.

Beutelbisam, *n.*=**Beutelmoschus.**

Beutelblattlaus, *f. Ent:* aphis bursaria.

Beuteldachs, *m. Z:* marsupial badger, (Australian) bandicoot, perameles.

Beuteleichhorn, *n. Z:* petaurist, flying phalanger, flying squirrel, flying opossum.

Beutelelement, *n. El:* sack-type Leclanché battery.

Beutelfalte, *f. Z: Anat:* pouch-fold.

Beutelfilter, *m. Tchn:* bag filter.

Beutelfledermaus, *f. Z:* pouched bat, taphien.

beutelförmig, *a.* bag-shaped; pouch-shaped.

Beutelgalle, *f. Bot:* pocket gall.

Beutelgarn, *n. Fish:* bag-net.

Beutelgaze, *f. Mill:* bolting-cloth.

Beutelgazelle, *f. Z:* springer, springbock.

Beutelhase, *m. Z:* hare-kangaroo, hare-wallaby, kangaroo-hare.

Beutelhund, *m. Z:*=**Beutelwolf.**

beutelig, *a.* (*of garment, etc.*) baggy.

Beutelkammer, *f. Mill:* bolting-room *or* -house.

Beutelkasten, *m. Mill:* (*a*) bolter(-sieve), flour-box, flour-dredger; (*b*) flour-bin, meal-tub, meal-chest.

Beutelkiste, *f. Mill:*=**Beutelkasten.**

Beutelknochen, *m.pl. Z: Anat:* marsupial, epipubic, bones.

Beutelkrabbe, *f.*, **Beutelkrebs**, *m. Crust:* robber-crab, coconut crab, purse-crab.

Beutelmagen, *m. Med:* hour-glass stomach.

Beutelmarder, *m. Z:* dasyure.

Beutelmaschine, *f.* **1.** *Mill:* bolting-machine, bolter. **2.** bag-making machine.

Beutelmaulwurf, *m. Z:* marsupial mole.

Beutelmaus, *f. Z:* **1.** wombat. **2.** opossum-mouse, flying-mouse, pygmy petaurist.

Beutelmeise, *f. Orn:* penduline tit.

Beutelmelone, *f. Hort:* cantaloup, musk-melon.

Beutelmoschus, *n. Com:* musk in pod, musk in bag.

Beutelmühle, *f.* bolting-mill, bolting-reel.

Beutelmull, *m. Z:* marsupial mole.

Beutelmurmeltier, *n. Z:* wombat.

beuteln. **1.** *v.tr.* (*a*) *Mill:* to bolt (flour); (*b*) *F:* **j-n b.**, (i) to give s.o. a good shaking, to shake s.o. like a rat; (ii) (*at cards, etc.*) to clean s.o. out. **2.** *v.i.* (*haben*) & **sich beuteln**, (*of garment, etc.*) to bag, to be baggy; **der Rock beutelt (sich)**, the skirt bags, is baggy; (*at the front, at the back*) the skirt sticks out; (*at the back*) the skirt has seated.

Beutelnager, *m. Z:* wombat.

Beutelnest, *n.* hanging, pensile, pendulous, nest; hangnest.

Beutelnetz, *n.* (*a*) *Ven:* purse-net; (*b*) *Fish:*=**Beutelgarn.**

Beutelperücke, *f.* bag-wig.

Beutelquallen, *f.pl. Coel:* cubomedusae.

Beutelratte, *f. Z:* opossum, sarigue, quica, marmose; **Surinamische Beutelratte**, mouse-opossum, murine opossum.

Beutelschneiden, *f. F:* (*a*) purse-snatching; (*b*) swindling.

Beutelschneider, *m. F:* (*a*) pickpocket, *A:* cut-purse; (*b*) swindler.

Beutelschneiderei, *f. F:* (*a*) purse-snatching; (*b*) swindling.

Beutelsieb, *n. Mill:* bolter, bolter-sieve.

Beutelspringmaus, *f. Z:* jerboa pouched mouse.

Beutelstar, *m. Orn:* cacique, cassicus, mocking-bird.

Beutelstäubling, *m. Fung:* calvatia saccata.

Beutelstrahler, *m.* -s/-. *Paleont:* cyst(o)id, cyst(o)idean; **die Beutelstrahler**, the cyst(o)idea.

Beutelteufel, *m. Z:* sarcophilus, Tasmanian devil.

Beuteltier, *n. Z:* marsupial; pouched mammal.

Beuteltuch, *n. Mill:* bolting-cloth.

beutelustig, *a.* eager for booty; **b. sein**, to be out for booty.

Beutelvorrichtung, *f. Mill:* bolter, sifter.

Beutelwerk, *n. Mill:* bolter, bolting-machine, bolting-mill.

Beutelwolf, *m. Z:* Tasmanian wolf, Tasmanian tiger, thylacine, zebra-opossum, zebra-wolf, pouched dog.

Beutenleim, *m.*=**Bienenharz.**

Beutesammelstelle, *f. Mil:* dump for captured material.

beuteschwer, *a.* loaded with spoils, booty.

Beutestück, *n. Ven: etc:* trophy; prize; **Beutestücke**, spoils; trophies; gains, *F:* winnings.

Beutetier, *n. Ven: etc:* quarry.

Beutetrupp, *m.* party for carrying away captured material.

Beutevieh, *n.* cattle taken as spoil, captured cattle.

Beutezug, *m.* plundering expedition.

Beutler, *m.* -s/-. **1.** *Z:* marsupial, pouched mammal. **2.** *Mill:* (*pers.*) bolter, sifter. **3.** bag-maker.

Beutlerei, *f.* -/-en. *Mill:* (*a*) bolting; (*b*) bolting-mill, bolting-reel.

beutst. *A: see* **bieten.**

bevölkern. **I.** *v.tr.* (i) (*of pers., animal*) to people, populate, inhabit (district, etc.); (ii) (*of government, etc.*) to settle, populate, people (district, etc.), to fill (district, etc.) with inhabitants; **eine dicht, stark, bevölkerte Gegend**, a thickly, densely, populated district; a thickly, densely, peopled district; a populous district; **schwach, dünn, spärlich, bevölkert**, sparsely, thinly, populated; sparsely, thinly, peopled; **der Wald ist von allen Arten von Singvögeln bevölkert**, the wood is full of all kinds of song-birds; **die Regierung bemüht sich, die unbewohnten Gegenden zu b. und urbar zu machen**, the government is trying to settle and cultivate the uninhabited areas; **sich b.**, to become peopled; **am Morgen b. sich die Straßen mit Leuten, die zur Arbeit gehen**, in the morning the streets become alive with people going to work; **der Spielplatz war mit Kindern bevölkert**, the playground was full of children.

II. *vbl s.* **1. Bevölkern**, *n. in vbl senses.* **2. Bevölkerung**, *f.* (*a*)=II. 1; *also:* population; (*b*) (*body of inhabitants*) population; **die ansässige, einheimische, B.**, the indigenous, native, population; **die ganze B. Londons war in Aufregung**, the whole population of London was in a ferment; **eine zahlreiche B.**, a large population; **Leute aus allen Schichten der B.**, people from all classes of society, from all walks of life, from all classes of the community; (*c*) (*number of people in a country, district, etc.*) **die B. wächst ständig an, nimmt ständig zu**, the population increases steadily; **absolute B.**, total population (of country, district, etc.); **relative B.**, density of population per square kilometre *or* square mile; (*d*) (*density of population*) **dichte B.**, dense population.

Bevölkerungsabnahme, *f.* fall in population, decrease in population.

Bevölkerungsdichte, *f.* density of population; **hohe B.**, high population density; **die schwankende B.**, the varying density of population; **geringe B.**, low density of population, sparseness of population.

Bevölkerungsdichtigkeit, *f.*=**Bevölkerungsdichte.**

Bevölkerungsdruck, *m.* population pressure.

Bevölkerungspolitik, *f.* population policy.

Bevölkerungsschichten, *f.pl.* strata of the population; classes of society; **Leute aller B.**, people from all classes of society, from all walks of life, from all classes of the community.

Bevölkerungsschutz, *m.* **ziviler B.**, civil defence (service); protection of the civil population.

Bevölkerungsstand, *m.* level of population.

Bevölkerungsüberschuß, *m.* surplus population.

Bevölkerungsverschiebung, *f.* population change, population movement.

Bevölkerungszahl, *f.* number of the population; population figure; **geringe B.,** small population.

Bevölkerungszunahme, *f.* increase in population.

bevollmächtigen. I. *v.tr.* **j-n zu etwas b., j-n b., etwas zu tun,** to authorize s.o., to give s.o. authority, to do sth.; *Jur:* to confer powers of attorney on s.o., to give s.o. a power of attorney, to do sth.; **j-n uneingeschränkt, generell, b.,** to give s.o. full authority; *Jur:* to furnish, invest, s.o. with full powers; **bevollmächtigt sein zu etwas, etwas zu tun,** to be authorized to do sth.; to have authority to do sth.; **ich bevollmächtige hiermit Herrn X, den Vertrag für mich zu unterzeichnen,** I herewith authorize Mr X to sign the contract on my behalf; **zum Handeln bevollmächtigt sein,** to be authorized to act, to have authority to act.

II. *vbl s.* **1. Bevollmächtigen,** *n. in vbl senses.* **2. Bevollmächtigung,** *f.* (*a*)=II. 1; *also:* authorization (of s.o. to do sth.); (*b*) authorization, authority (to do sth.); *Jur:* power of attorney; **schriftliche B.,** written authorization; **er hat keine B., den Vertrag zu unterzeichnen,** he has no authority, is not authorized, to sign the contract.

III. *p.p. & a.* **bevollmächtigt,** authorized; **nicht b.,** unauthorized, not authorized; piratical (printer); **bevollmächtigte Person, Bevollmächtigte** *m, f,* authorized person; authorized agent; **bevollmächtigter Vertreter, Bevollmächtigter,** authorized representative; *Jur:* attorney; *Dipl:* **bevollmächtigter Botschafter,** minister plenipotentiary; *Dipl: etc:* **Bevollmächtigter,** plenipotentiary; **j-n zum Bevollmächtigten einsetzen,** to appoint s.o. as one's authorized representative; *Jur:* to give s.o. (a) power of attorney; **er ist der Bevollmächtigte von . . .,** he is the authorized representative of . . .; *Jur:* he holds a power of attorney for . . . .

Bevollmächtigungsschreiben, *n.* letter of authorization; *Jur:* letter, power, of attorney.

Bevollmächtigungsurkunde, *f. Jur:* letter, power, of attorney.

Bevollmächtigungsvertrag, *m. Jur:* letter, power, of attorney.

bevor. 1. *conj.* (*a*) before; **kurz b.,** shortly before; **unmittelbar b.,** immediately before; **lange b.,** long before; **kommen Sie bei mir vorbei, b. Sie abreisen,** come and see me before you leave; **noch b. die Nacht hereingebrochen war, hatte ihn die Unglücksbotschaft erreicht,** before nightfall he had received the bad news; **noch b. ich mich von meiner Überraschung erholen konnte, fuhr er in seinem Bericht fort,** before I got over my surprise he went on with his report; **b. ich abreiste, mußte ich den Konsul aufsuchen,** previous to my departure I had to see the consul; **b. er zum Außenminister ernannt wurde, war er Botschafter,** prior to his appointment as foreign minister he was an ambassador; **nicht aussteigen, b. der Zug hält,** do not alight before the train stops, while the train is in motion, do not alight from moving train; (*b*) (*with expletive* **nicht**) until; **wir können keine weiteren Schritte unternehmen, b. wir nicht seine Meinung haben,** we cannot make any further move until we have his opinion; **ich werde kein Urteil über das Buch abgeben, b. ich es nicht gründlich studiert habe,** I shall not pass judgment on the book until I have studied it thoroughly. **2.** *adv. A. & Dial:* **den Tag b.,** the day before, the previous day.

bevormunden. 1. *v.tr. insep.* to treat (s.o.) as if he were a child; to patronize (s.o.), to treat (s.o.) in a patronizing manner, patronizingly; to keep (s.o.) in tutelage; *F:* to (try to) do s.o.'s job for (him); **unser Volk wird sich nicht länger durch fremde Mächte b. lassen,** our people will no longer be kept in tutelage by foreign powers. **2.** *vbl s.* **Bevormundung,** *f.* patronizing; **ich werde mir seine dauernde B. nicht länger gefallen lassen,** I won't be kept in leading-strings any longer.

bevorraten, *v.tr.* (*weak*) *insep.* **j-n mit etwas b.,** to stock s.o. up with sth.

bevorrechten. 1. *v.tr. insep.* (*used mainly in passive*) **bevorrechtet sein,** to be privileged; **die bevorrechteten Stände,** the privileged classes; **einige wenige Bevorrechtete,** a privileged few. **2.** *vbl s.* **Bevorrechtung** *f.* privilege; **die B., die gewisse Leute genießen, stellt eine Ungerechtigkeit gegen die anderen dar,** the privileges enjoyed by a certain few constitute an injustice towards the others.

bevorrechtigen. 1. *v.tr. insep. Com: Jur:* to give (s.o.) a prior claim; **bevorrechtigter Gläubiger,** preferential creditor; **bevorrechtigte Forderung,** preferential, preferred, privileged, claim; **bevorrechtigte Schuld,** preferential, preferred, privileged, debt. **2.** *vbl s.* **Bevorrechtigung,** *f.* preferential right, preference.

bevorschussen. 1. *v.tr. insep.* to advance (s.o.) money, to make an advance (of money) to (s.o.); *Com:* to advance money on (outstanding debt, etc.). **2.** *vbl s.* **Bevorschussung,** *f.* (*a*) *in vbl senses;* (*b*) advance (on outstanding debt, etc.).

bevorstehen, *v.i. sep.* (*strong*) (*haben*) **1.** (*a*) (*of event, etc.*) to be approaching; **(nahe) b.,** to be near, close, to be impending; (*of hour, day, etc.*) to be at hand; to be near, close, at hand; (*of crisis, etc.*) to be imminent; **seine Ankunft steht unmittelbar bevor,** he will be arriving immediately; **der Tag steht bevor, an dem wir über unsere Handlungen Rechenschaft ablegen müssen,** the day is upon us when we shall have to justify our actions; **Weihnachten stand bevor,** Christmas was near, approaching; it was near to Christmas; **der Friede steht unmittelbar bevor,** peace is very near; **die Stunde steht bevor, da . . .,** the hour is at hand, when . . .; **seine Ernennung zum Direktor stand bevor,** he was about to be appointed as director, his appointment as director was impending; **sein Ende steht nahe bevor,** he is nearing his end, his end is imminent; **unsere Befreiung steht nahe bevor,** liberation is near, close, at hand; **bevorstehend,** approaching; forthcoming; impending; **sein bevorstehender Tod,** his approaching death; **die bevorstehende Konferenz,** the forthcoming conference; **ihre bevorstehende Ankunft,** her impending arrival; **der drohend bevorstehende Krieg,** the imminent war; (*b*) **die Auszählung der Stimmen für die übrigen Wahlkreise steht noch bevor,** the votes of the other constituencies are still waiting to be counted. **2.** (*a*) **j-m b.,** (*of surprise, joy, etc.*) to be in store for s.o.; to await s.o.; (*of danger, etc.*) to hang over s.o., over s.o.'s head; to be impending, threatening; **eine große Freude, eine unangenehme Überraschung, steht ihm bevor,** a great joy, an unpleasant surprise, is in store for him, awaits him; **ein schrecklicher Tod steht ihm bevor,** a horrible death awaits him; **ein Prozeß steht mir bevor,** I am faced with a lawsuit; **eine große Gefahr steht ihnen bevor,** a great danger hangs over them, over their heads; **das Examen stand ihm (drohend) bevor,** the examination hung over him; **die ihm (drohend) bevorstehende Gefahr,** the danger that hung over his head; **das Gespräch mit dem Minister steht mir (sehr) bevor,** I dread the thought of the interview with the Minister; (*b*) **die noch bevorstehenden Überraschungen,** the surprises yet to come; **in Erwartung der noch bevorstehenden Freuden,** in anticipation of the joys to come; **dieses Vergnügen steht mir noch bevor,** that is a pleasure I have yet to enjoy; that pleasure is still to come; **das schriftliche Examen habe ich bestanden, das mündliche steht mir noch bevor,** I have passed the written examination, but I still have to take the oral.

bevorteilen, *v.tr. insep. A:* =**übervorteilen.**

bevorworten, *v.tr. insep.* to write a preface to, to preface (book, etc.).

bevorzugen. I. *v.tr. insep.* **1.** to prefer (s.o., sth.); **etwas vor etwas, etwas gegenüber, b.,** to prefer sth. to sth.; **ich bevorzuge ihn seinem Bruder gegenüber,** I prefer him to his brother; **Bewerber mit akademischer Ausbildung bevorzugt,** applicants with university education preferred; **von den drei Bewerbern würde ich den ersten b.,** I should choose the first of the three applicants in preference to the others, rather than the others; **ich bevorzuge kaltes, trockenes Wetter,** I prefer cold and dry weather; **ich bevorzuge gut durchgebratenes Fleisch,** I prefer well-done meat; **welche von diesen Farben bevorzugen Sie?** which colour do you prefer, favour? **2.** to favour (s.o.); to allow (s.o.) special privileges; **bevorzugt werden,** to be favoured (by s.o.), to be (s.o.'s) favourite; to get privileges, favours; **Eltern sollten keines ihrer Kinder b.,** parents should not show partiality for any one of their children; **er bevorzugt gerne diejenigen, die ihm schmeicheln,** he is likely to favour those who flatter him; **kein Kunde wird von uns bevorzugt,** no special favours are granted to any one customer; **er wird immer ungerecht bevorzugt,** he is always favoured unduly; he is always getting privileges; he is always treated differently; **die Natur hat ihn bevorzugt,** nature has favoured him.

II. *vbl s.* **1. Bevorzugen,** *n. in vbl senses.* **2. Bevorzugung,** *f.* (*a*)=II. 1; (*b*) preference; preferential treatment; **die ungerechte B., die man seinem Bruder zuteil werden ließ, machte ihn eifersüchtig,** the undue preference given to his brother, the undue favour shown towards his brother, the partiality shown to his brother, made him jealous.

III. *p.p. & a.* **bevorzugt,** *in vbl senses; esp.* **1.** preferential; privileged; **j-n b. behandeln,** to treat s.o. differently, to allow s.o. special privileges; **eine Angelegenheit b. behandeln,** to give priority to a matter; **Kriegsbeschädigte werden b. abgefertigt,** war-disabled persons have priority; **im Falle einer Lebensmittelknappheit werden Krankenhäuser b. beliefert,** in the case of a food shortage supplies to hospitals will be given priority; **eine bevorzugte Behandlung erfahren,** to be given preferential treatment; **eine bevorzugte Stellung einnehmen,** (*of pers.*) to have a privileged position; (*of task, etc.*) to have priority; **im Werk dieses Gelehrten nimmt die Vererbungslehre eine bevorzugte Stellung ein,** the theory of heredity plays a prominent part in the work of this scholar; **einige Bevorzugte durften die Bilder sehen,** a privileged few were allowed to see the pictures; *F:* **das ist wohl nur für einige Bevorzugte?** I suppose this is only for a favoured few? *Adm:* **bevorzugte Zuweisung,** priority allocation; *Post:* (*of perishable goods, telegrams, etc.*) **b. abgefertigt werden,** to receive priority, to be given priority; *Jur:* **bevorzugter Gläubiger,** preferential creditor. **2.** favourite; **meine bevorzugte Oper,** my favourite opera; **meine bevorzugte Marke,** my favourite brand.

bewachen. I. *v.tr.* (*a*) to guard (prisoner, house, gate, etc.); to set a guard on (gates, bridge, etc.); (*of shepherd, watchman, etc.*) to watch over, keep watch over (flock, property, etc.); **mehrere Soldaten bewachten den Gefangenen,** several soldiers guarded the prisoner; **der Gefangene wurde scharf bewacht,** the prisoner was closely guarded; they kept a close watch on the prisoner; **um einen Überfall zu verhindern, wurden die Stadttore bewacht,** in order to prevent a surprise attack a guard was set on the gates of the town; **sie ließen die Brücke b., um zu verhindern, daß sie gesprengt wurde,** they set a guard on the bridge to prevent its being blown up; **während unserer Abwesenheit werden wir das Haus nachts b. lassen,** we shall arrange to have our house guarded at night during our absence; **die Firma stellt einen Nachtwächter ein, der ihr Gebäude von Einbruch der Dunkelheit bis zum Morgen bewacht,** the firm employs a night-watchman to guard its building from dusk till morning; **der Bauer hielt sich einen Hund, der ihm das Haus bewachte,** the farmer kept a dog which guarded the house for him; **bewachter Parkplatz,** car park with an attendant; (*b*) to watch (s.o., sth.); **sie bewachten jeden meiner Schritte,** they watched my every move; **sie ließen ihn unauffällig b.,** they had him watched discreetly, they set a discreet watch on him; **man bewacht uns die ganze Zeit,** we are being watched all the time; **zu dieser Zeit wurden alle Ausländer schärfstens bewacht,** at this time a sharp watch was kept on all foreigners.

II. *vbl s.* **1. Bewachen,** *n. in vbl senses.* **2. Bewachung,** *f.* (*a*)=II. 1; (*b*) guard; escort; **sie ließen das Lager unter sicherer B. zurück,** they left the camp under a heavy guard; **einen Gefangenen unter B. zurücklassen,** to leave a prisoner under guard; **die Kriegsgefangenen wurden unter B. ins Lager geschickt,** the prisoners of war were sent to the camp under escort.

bewachsen. 1. *v.tr.* (*strong*) (*of plants, etc.*) to cover; **der Waldboden war mit dichtem Moos bewachsen, dichtes Moos bewuchs den Waldboden,** the forest floor was covered, carpeted, with moss; **die Mauern sind mit Efeu bewachsen,** the walls are overgrown, covered, with ivy; *see also* **Gelände. 2.** *vbl s.* **Bewachsung,** *f.* (i) flora; (ii) ground vegetation (in forest, etc.).

Bewachung, *f. see* **bewachen II.**

Bewachungsfahrzeug, *n. Navy:* escort, escort-vessel.

bewaffnen. I. *v.tr.* (*a*) to arm (s.o., regiment, country, etc.); to equip (regiment, country, etc.) with arms; **sich (gegen j-n, gegen einen Angriff, usw.) b.,** to arm oneself (against s.o., an attack, etc.); **sich mit einem Stein b.,** to arm oneself with a stone; **bewaffnet,** armed, in arms; **mit einem Gewehr bewaffnet,** armed with a gun; **eine bewaffnete Demonstration,** an armed demonstration; **bewaffneten Wiederstand leisten,** to offer armed resistance; **bewaffnete Neutralität,** armed neutrality; **bewaffneter Friede,** armed

peace; **bewaffneter Überfall,** armed raid; armed attack; **bewaffnete Macht,** armed force; (*of country*) military power; **es wurde als Frevel angesehen, das Heiligtum mit bewaffneter Hand zu betreten,** it was considered a crime to enter the sanctuary armed; **bewaffnete Männer, Bewaffnete** *pl*, armed men; (*of animal*) **mit Zähnen bewaffnet,** armed with teeth; **bis an die Zähne bewaffnet,** armed to the teeth; **von Kopf bis Fuß bewaffnet,** (i) armed to the teeth; (ii) *A. & F:* armed at all points; **leicht bewaffnet,** lightly armed; *see also* **Bandwurm; leichtbewaffnet;** (*b*) **sich mit etwas b.,** to arm oneself with sth.; **er war mit allen nur möglichen Werkzeugen bewaffnet,** he was armed with every conceivable tool; **sich mit Geduld b.,** to arm oneself with patience; **mit bewaffnetem Auge,** (i) with an artificial aid to vision; with spectacles; with a microscope, a telescope, etc.; (ii) with protection for the eyes; *F:* **sich mit einem Regenschirm b.,** to arm oneself with an umbrella.

II. *vbl s.* **1. Bewaffnen,** *n. in vbl senses.* **2. Bewaffnung,** *f.* (*a*)=II. 1; (*b*) armament; **die B. der Truppe ist nicht ausreichend,** the armament of the troops is not sufficient; **mit schwerer B.,** heavily armed; **mit leichter B.,** lightly armed; *Hist:* **ein Ritter mit schwerer B.,** a heavily armed knight.

Bewahranstalt, *f.* (*a*) day-nursery; (*b*) children's home.

bewahren. I. *v.tr.* **1.** to guard, keep (s.o., sth.); to look after, mind (a child, s.o.'s house, etc.); to keep, store (food, etc.); to lock up (house, etc.); **Engel mögen dich b.,** may angels guard, keep, you; **bewahrt das Feuer und das Licht!** look to your fires and your lights! **seine Zunge b.,** to guard one's tongue, to keep a watch on one's tongue; **Geld an einem sicheren Ort b.,** to keep money in a safe place; *B:* **bewahre meine Lippen,** keep the door of my lips. **2. j-n (vor etwas) b.,** to keep s.o. (from trouble, misfortune, evil influence, etc.); to preserve, save, s.o. (from danger, death, etc.); **etwas (vor etwas) b.,** to keep sth. (from sth.); **Gott bewahre mich vor falschen Freunden,** may God preserve, save, keep, me from false friends; **Gott möge mich davor b., diesem Menschen in die Hände zu fallen,** may God keep, save, me from falling into the hands of this man; **er hat mich vor dem Ertrinken bewahrt,** he has saved me from drowning; **j-n vor einer Torheit b.,** to save s.o. from a foolish action; **ich möchte Sie davor b., Dummheiten zu begehen,** I should like to keep you from acting foolishly; **nur ein glücklicher Zufall bewahrte ihn vor dem Tode,** only a lucky coincidence saved him from death; **die tapferen Verteidiger der Stadt bewahrten Frauen und Kinder vor der Grausamkeit des Feindes,** the courageous defenders of the town saved, preserved, the women and children from the cruelty of the enemy; **j-n vor seiner eigenen Unbesonnenheit b.,** to protect s.o. against his own rashness; **er blieb sein Leben lang vor Krankheit bewahrt,** he was spared (from) illness all his life; **mögest du vor Unglück bewahrt bleiben,** may misfortune never cross your path, come your way; **sie errichteten Deiche, um das Land vor Überschwemmung zu b.,** they put up dikes to protect the land from being flooded; **die Ernte vor dem Verderb b.,** to keep the crops from being ruined; **(Gott) bewahre!** *F:* **i bewahre!** God forbid! heaven forbid! good heavens, no! **Frau X wird dich morgen besuchen kommen. — Gott bewahre!** Mrs X is going to pay you a visit tomorrow.—God forbid! heaven forbid! **gehst du in diesen Vortrag? — Gott bewahre (nein)!** are you going to this lecture?—God forbid! heaven forbid! good heavens, no! **3.** (*a*) to keep (up), preserve (tradition, etc.); to keep, guard (a secret); to keep, preserve (silence); to keep (one's looks, one's figure, etc.); **die Fassung b.,** to keep, preserve, maintain, one's composure; to keep one's countenance; **den Gleichmut, kaltes Blut, ruhig Blut, die Ruhe, b.,** to keep cool and collected, calm and collected; to keep cool; to keep one's temper; to keep one's head, to keep a cool head; **das (seelische) Gleichgewicht b.,** to keep one's equilibrium; **die Ehre rein b., rein bewahrt erhalten,** to preserve one's honour; to keep one's honour untarnished; **seinen guten Ruf b.,** to keep, maintain, one's good reputation; **seine Illusionen, seine Unschuld, b.,** to keep one's illusions, one's innocence; **sich (von Sünde rein) b.,** to keep oneself pure (from sin); **den (äußeren) Schein b.,** to keep up, preserve, appearances; **sein Gesicht b.,** to save one's face; **j-m die Treue b.,** to keep faith with s.o.; to remain faithful to s.o.; **etwas im Herzen b.,** to treasure sth. in one's heart; **ich werde diese Worte im Herzen b.,** I shall treasure these words, I shall cherish these words in my heart; **er konnte kaum den Ernst b.,** he could scarcely keep a straight face, his countenance; (*of thg*) **seine Form, seine Farbe, b.,** to keep its shape, colour; (*b*) **j-n im Gedächtnis b.,** to keep s.o. in one's memory, thoughts; to keep s.o.'s memory green; **etwas im Gedächtnis b.,** to retain sth. in one's memory, to keep sth. in remembrance, to keep sth. in mind; **ich werde diese deine Worte stets im Gedächtnis b.,** I shall always bear, keep, your words in mind; *see also* **andenken** II. 1.

II. *vbl s.* **Bewahren** *n.*, **Bewahrung** *f. in vbl senses; also:* preservation.

bewähren. I. *v.tr.* **1.** to prove (one's loyalty, friendship, courage, etc.); *A:* to prove (sth.) (to be true); to try (s.o., sth.); *B:* **und welcherlei eines jeglichen Werk sei, wird das Feuer b.,** and the fire shall try every man's work of what sort it is. **2. sich bewähren** (*of pers.*) to prove oneself efficient (in one's profession, etc.); to prove one's worth (in adversity, etc.); to give a good account of oneself, to prove oneself, to prove one's mettle (in battle, etc.); *Jur:* to maintain good conduct (during period of probation); (*of remedy, etc.*) to prove effective; to prove a success; (*of principle, theory, invention, etc.*) to prove its worth; to stand the test; (*of system*) to work well; (*of principle*) to hold good; (*of machine, material, etc.*) to stand (up to) the test; to prove a success; (*of loyalty, etc.*) to stand the test; **sich (als etwas) b.,** (*of pers.*) to prove oneself (as), to prove to be (a reliable friend, a good worker, etc.); to prove one's worth (as a friend, a soldier); to prove one's mettle (as a soldier, etc.); to prove one's ability (as a business man, etc.); to prove efficient (as a clerk, etc.); **er hat sich in allen Lebenslagen bewährt,** he has proved his worth in all situations; he has shown his mettle in all situations; **er hat sich als ausgezeichneter Arzt bewährt,** he has proved himself an excellent doctor; **er hat sich als Arzt nicht bewährt,** he has not proved to be a good doctor; he has proved a failure, has failed, as a doctor; **der Schäferhund hat sich als Blindenhund gut bewährt,** the Alsatian has proved to be a very good guide-dog for the blind, has proved successful, a success, as a guide-dog for the blind; **seine Treue hat sich im Unglück glänzend bewährt,** his loyalty has fully stood the test of adversity, has proved unshaken in adversity; **unsere Vorsichtsmaßnahmen haben sich bewährt,** our precautions have proved effective; **das Mittel hat sich gegen Erkältungskrankheiten bestens bewährt,** the remedy has proved highly effective against colds; **das neue Flugzeug hat sich als Transportmaschine bewährt,** the new aircraft has proved excellent for transport work; **die neue Maschine hat sich nicht bewährt,** the new machine has not stood up to the test; the new machine has proved a failure, has failed; **das Buch hat sich als Einführung in das Englische bewährt,** the book has proved its worth as an introduction to the English language, has proved (to be), has proved itself, a good introduction to the English language.

II. *vbl s.* **Bewährung,** *f.* **1.** *in vbl senses; also: Jur:* **Strafaussetzung zur B.,** probation under suspended sentence. **2.** trial; **er hat mir in Zeiten der B. die Treue gehalten,** he remained loyal to me in times of trial. **3.** (*a*) rehabilitation; (*b*)=**Bewährungsfrist.**

III. *p.p. & a.* **bewährt,** *in vbl senses; esp.* tried (friend, etc.); experienced (solicitor, etc.); well-established, long-standing (friendship, etc.); (friendship, etc.) of long standing; well-tried, well-established, proved, proven (remedy, etc.); **dieser Stoff ist ein bewährtes Material für Regenmäntel,** this cloth has proved to be a reliable material for raincoats; **ein bewährtes Mittel gegen Grippe,** an established, a well-tried, proved, proven, remedy for influenza; **die alten, bewährten Methoden,** the old approved methods, the methods that have stood the test of time; the good old methods; **in bewährter Hilfsbereitschaft bot er uns sofort eine Summe Geldes an,** with his usual willingness to help he immediately offered us a sum of money; **er ist eine bewährte Kraft in unserer Firma,** he is an old and trusted member of our firm.

Bewahrer, *m.* **-s/-,** keeper; **Gott ist mein B. und Erhalter,** God keeps me and supports me.

bewahrheiten. 1. *A: v.tr.* **etwas b.,** to prove sth. **2. sich bewahrheiten,** (*of news, etc.*) to prove (to be) true; (*of prophecy, etc.*) to come true; **wenn sich deine Worte bewahrheiten,** if what you say proves (to be) true; **die Nachricht bewahrheitete sich nicht,** the news did not prove (to be) true; the news proved false; **falls sich das Gerücht b. sollte,** if the rumour (should) prove (to be) true; **seine Voraussage bewahrheitete sich,** his prediction came true; **das Sprichwort wird sich an dir b.,** you will experience the truth of the proverb, find that the proverb proves true; you will be a living illustration of the proverb.

Bewährtheit, *f.* reliability (of pers., method, etc.); efficiency (of civil servant, etc.); efficacy (of medicine, etc.).

Bewährung, *f. see* **bewähren II.**

Bewährungsauflagen, *f.pl. Jur:* terms, conditions, of probation; **den Bewährungsauflagen zuwiderhandeln,** to break the terms of probation.

Bewährungsbataillon, *n. Mil:* rehabilitation battalion.

Bewährungsfrist, *f. Jur:* probation; **j-m B. zubilligen,** to put s.o. on probation; to bind s.o. over; **acht Monate Gefängnis mit zwei Jahren B.,** two years' probation under suspended sentence of eight months.

Bewährungshelfer, *m. Jur:* probation officer.

Bewährungsprobe, *f.* test; **die B. bestehen,** to stand the test; **die Methode hat die B. der Zeit bestanden,** the method has stood the test of time; **seine Freundschaft hat die B. des Unglücks bestanden,** his friendship has stood the test of the adversity; **die Maschine hat ihre B. bestanden,** machine has passed the test, stood (up to) the test.

Bewährungszeit, *f. Jur:* (time, period, of) probation.

bewalden (sich). I. **1.** *v.refl.* (*of countryside, hill, etc.*) to become covered with woods, forest. **2.** *p.p. & a.* **bewaldet,** wooded, woody (country, hill, etc.); (country, hill, etc.) clothed with forest; (area, etc.) under timber; **bewaldete Hänge,** wooded slopes.

II. *vbl s.* **Bewaldung,** *f.* (*a*) *in vbl senses;* (*b*) woods, forests; **eine ausreichende B. schützt die Dörfer vor Lawinen,** sufficient woods, forests, protect the villages from avalanches.

bewaldrechten, *v.tr.* to rough-hew, rough-square (timber).

bewältigen. I. *v.tr.* to overcome, surmount (obstacle); to conquer, master, surmount (difficulty); to accomplish (task); to bring, get, (sth.) under control; *A:* to overcome (s.o.); **eine Arbeit b.,** to manage a piece of work; **sie bewältigten die Aufgabe spielend,** they accomplished the task effortlessly; **das letzte Stück des Weges konnten sie nur mit Mühe b.,** they could only manage the last part of the way with difficulty; **er konnte den schweren Baumstamm kaum b.,** he could scarcely manage to carry the heavy tree-trunk; **das Pferd bewältigte die Hindernisse spielend,** the horse easily cleared, took, the obstacles; **ein Fach b.,** to master a subject; **der Verkehr ist an Sonntagen kaum zu b.,** on Sundays the traffic can hardly be controlled; **sie bewältigten den Berg in neun Stunden,** they climbed the mountain in nine hours; *F:* **können Sie noch ein Stück Kuchen b.?** can you manage a piece of cake?

II. *vbl s.* **Bewältigen** *n.*, **Bewältigung** *f. in vbl senses; also:* accomplishment; **die Bewältigung dieser Aufgabe wird uns noch manche Schwierigkeiten bereiten,** we shall still have a great deal of difficulty in accomplishing this task; **die Bewältigung dieser Schwierigkeit hat uns mit großer Genugtuung erfüllt,** overcoming, surmounting, this difficulty has given us great satisfaction; **die Bewältigung dieses Hindernisses ist ein großer Fortschritt,** the overcoming of this obstacle is a great step forward; **die Bewältigung des Verkehrs ist unter den gegebenen Umständen sehr schwierig,** it is very difficult to control the traffic under the given circumstances; **die Bewältigung des Berges in neun Stunden stellt eine große Leistung dar,** the climbing of the mountain in nine hours constitutes a great achievement.

bewandern. I. *v.tr.* to walk through (district, etc.); to hike through (country, etc.); to travel (through) (area, etc.); **er hat ganz Europa bewandert,** he has travelled all over Europe; **er hat den ganzen Schwarzwald bewandert,** he has walked all through the Black Forest; **der Lake District wird viel bewandert,** the Lake District is a popular area for walking.

II. *p.p. & a.* **bewandert,** *in vbl senses; esp.* (*of pers.*) knowledgeable, well-informed; well versed; proficient; **in einem Fach, einem Gebiet, wohl, gut, b. sein,** to have a thorough knowledge

of a subject, to be perfectly at home with, to know all about, a subject; **ich bin in Geschichte nur wenig, schlecht, nicht sehr gut, b.,** I am not very well up, not very well versed, in history; **er ist in Geschäftssachen gut b.,** he is a man well up, well versed, in business matters; **ich bin in Latein nicht sehr b.,** I am not very proficient in Latin, I don't know much Latin.

Bewandertheit, *f.* knowledge; **seine B. in diesen Dingen,** his knowledge in these matters; **seine juristische, sprachliche, B.,** his legal, linguistic, attainments.

bewandt, *pred.a. Lit:* **damit ist es folgendermaßen b.,** (i) it has this peculiarity; (ii) the story behind it is as follows; **ich weiß nicht, wie es damit, darum, b. ist,** I don't know (i) what the real case is, (ii) the story behind it; **wie es auch damit, darum, b. sein möge,** whatever the reason for it is; **ich möchte wissen, wie es um die Dinge wirklich b. ist,** I want to know the real state of affairs.

Bewandtnis, *f.* **-/-nisse,** (i) peculiar quality (of sth.); (ii) (special) circumstances; **mit diesem Ring hat es seine eigene, besondere, B.,** there is (i) something special about this ring, (ii) a special story about this ring; **was für eine B. hat es damit?** what is special, peculiar, about it? **es hat damit folgende B.,** (i) it has this peculiarity; (ii) the story behind it is as follows; **ich weiß nicht, was für eine B. es damit hat,** I don't know (i) what the real case is, (ii) the story behind it; **damit hat es eine ganz andere B.,** (i) that's something quite different; (ii) that's quite another, a different, story.

bewangen, *v.tr.* to strengthen (sth.) by means of cheeks *or* side-pieces; to fish (mast, beam, etc.).

bewässern. I. *v.tr.* (*of pers.*) to irrigate (fields, etc.); (*of river, etc.*) to water, irrigate (country, etc.); **das Gebiet wird mit Hilfe kleiner Kanäle bewässert,** the region is irrigated by means of small canals; **eine künstlich bewässerte Gegend,** an artificially irrigated area; **ein von vielen Bächen bewässertes Land,** a country watered by many streams; **Ägypten wird vom Nil bewässert,** Egypt is watered, irrigated, by the Nile; **ein gut bewässertes Land,** a well-watered country.

II. *vbl s.* **1. Bewässern,** *n. in vbl senses.* **2. Bewässerung,** *f.* (*a*)=II. 1; *also:* irrigation; (*b*) irrigation; water supply; **künstliche B.,** (artificial) irrigation; **natürliche B.,** natural irrigation, water supply.

Bewässerungsanlage, *f.* irrigation plant; irrigation works; **ausgedehnte Bewässerungsanlagen,** extensive irrigation works; an extensive irrigation system.

Bewässerungsgruben, *m.* irrigation ditch; water-trench.

Bewässerungskanal, *m.* irrigation canal.

Bewässerungspumpe, *f.* irrigation pump.

Bewässerungssystem, *n.* irrigation system.

bewegbar, *a.* that can be moved, movable.

bewegen¹. I. *v.tr.* (*weak*) **1.** (*a*) to move (sth.); to stir (the surface of the water, etc.); to agitate (the surface of the water, etc.); **etwas hin und her b.,** to move sth. to and fro; **etwas von der Stelle b.,** to move sth. from the spot, its place; **j-n von der Stelle b.,** to move s.o. from the spot, to make s.o. move; **er konnte seinen Arm nicht b.,** he could not move his arm; **das Wasser bewegt das Mühlrad,** the water moves the mill-wheel; **kein Windhauch bewegt die Blätter, den See,** not a breath of wind stirs the leaves, the lake; **von einer Feder, Elektrizität, bewegt,** moved by a spring, by electricity; **die bewegende Kraft im Universum,** the motive force in the universe; **die bewegende Kraft ist in diesem Fall Elektrizität,** in this case the motive power is electricity; **ein bewegter Wellengang, eine bewegte See,** a troubled, rough, sea; **bewegte Luft,** moving air; **ein Pferd b.,** to exercise a horse; *Mil:* **Truppen b.,** to move troops; *Mus:* **bewegt,** con moto; (*b*) **etwas im Herzen b.,** to ponder over sth.; *B:* **Maria aber behielt alle diese Worte und bewegte sie in ihrem Herzen,** but Mary kept all these things, and pondered them in her heart. **2.** (*a*) to stir (s.o.'s mind, etc.); to occupy (s.o.'s mind, etc.); to move (s.o.) (to sth.); **große Ideen bewegten dieses Zeitalter, die Menschen dieses Zeitalters,** great ideas stirred the people of that age; **soziale Gerechtigkeit war eine der Ideen, die das neunzehnte Jahrhundert bewegten,** social justice was one of the moving ideas of the nineteenth century; **dieser Mord bewegte die Gemüter lange Zeit,** this murder occupied people's minds for a long time; **von Leidenschaften bewegt,** stirred by passions; **von Haß, Angst, bewegt,** moved by hatred, fear; **ein bewegtes Leben führen,** to lead a colourful, an eventful, life; to lead a gay life; **ein bewegtes Leben hinter sich haben,** to have led an adventurous life; (*of woman*) to have a (colourful) past; **bewegte Zeiten,** stirring, eventful, times; stormy times; **bewegte Diskussion,** lively, animated, discussion; *F:* stormy discussion; **bewegte Periode (der Geschichte),** troubled period (of history); **das Stück hat eine bewegte Handlung,** the action of the play is lively; **j-n zum Mitleid b.,** to move s.o. to pity; **hie und da wird er vom Mitleid bewegt,** now and again he is moved to pity; **Tränen werden ihn nicht (zum Mitleid) b.,** tears will not move him (to pity); **sich (zum Mitleid) b. lassen,** to (allow oneself to) be moved (to pity); (*b*) to move, touch, affect (s.o.); **von einem Anblick bewegt werden,** to be affected at a sight; **j-s Herz b.,** to move someone's heart; **die Seele b.,** to move the soul; **er war von dieser Nachricht sehr bewegt,** he was much moved by this news; **eine bewegende Erzählung, Ansprache,** a moving tale, speech; **(tief) bewegt,** (deeply) moved, touched; **es bewegte mich tief,** it touched me to the heart; **mit bewegter Stimme,** in a voice touched with emotion; **etwas mit bewegten Worten schildern,** to describe sth. vividly.

II. **sich bewegen,** to move; to take exercise; to stir (in one's sleep, etc.); (*of air, water, etc.*) to stir; *Mec.E:* (*of part*) to move, travel; *Ph: etc:* (*of light, train, etc.*) **sich mit einer Geschwindigkeit von . . . b.,** to travel at a speed of . . .; **sich von der Stelle, vom Fleck, b.,** to move; **sich vorwärts, rückwärts, seitwärts, auf und ab, b.,** to move forwards, backwards, sidewards, up and down; **bewegen Sie sich nicht!** don't move! *F:* **beweg dich!** get a move on! stir your stumps! **er bewegte sich mit Würde,** he moved with dignity; **die Prozession bewegte sich durch die Straßen,** the procession moved through the streets; **wir sahen hinab auf die Menge, die sich auf der Straße bewegte,** we looked down on the crowd moving in the street; **er bewegte sich nicht aus dem Hause,** he did not stir out of the house; **dort drüben bewegt sich etwas,** something is moving over there; **Lichter bewegten sich in der Dunkelheit,** lights were moving about in the darkness; **kein Lufthauch, Lüftchen, bewegte sich,** there was not a breath of air stirring; **die Zweige bewegten sich im Wind,** the branches were moving, stirring, in the wind; **das Spielzeug bewegt sich,** the toy moves; **die Erde bewegt sich um die Sonne,** the earth moves, revolves, round the sun; **die Erde bewegt sich um ihre eigene Achse,** the earth rotates, revolves, about, on, its own axis; **ein Körper, der sich mit einer hohen Geschwindigkeit bewegt,** a body moving at a high speed; **sich in der besten Gesellschaft b.,** to move in high society; **er bewegt sich immer in höheren Sphären,** he lives in an unreal world; **das wirkliche Leben bewegt sich nicht auf der politischen Ebene,** real life does not move on the political plane; **die Diskussion bewegte sich auf einer hohen Ebene,** the discussion moved on an elevated plane; **die Fragen bewegten sich alle in der gleichen Richtung,** the questions all tended in the same direction; **er bewegte sich in Zweideutigkeiten,** he dealt in ambiguities; **das Leben des alten Mannes bewegte sich dem Ende zu,** the old man's life was moving to its end; **der Kongreß bewegte sich dem Höhepunkt zu,** the congress was nearing the climax; **die Temperatur bewegte sich zwischen zwanzig und dreißig Grad,** the temperature ranged from twenty to thirty degrees, fluctuated between twenty and thirty degrees; **die Preise bewegen sich zwischen fünfzig und sechzig Mark,** prices range from fifty to sixty marks; *Typewr:* **der Wagen bewegt sich von rechts nach links,** the carriage travels from right to left.

III. *vbl s.* **1. Bewegen,** *n. in vbl senses; also:* movement; **das B. des Armes verursacht ihm große Schmerzen,** it gives him great pain to move his arm; **das B. eines gebrochenen Gliedes ist sehr schmerzhaft,** the moving, movement, of a broken limb is very painful. **2. Bewegung,** *f.* (*a*)=II. 1; (*b*) motion (of vehicle, etc.); motion, revolution (of heavenly body, etc.); movement (of earth, moon, etc.); *Ph: Mus:* motion; **relative, absolute, B.,** relative, absolute, motion; **beschleunigte B.,** accelerated motion; **dauernde B.,** perpetual, continuous, motion; **gleichmäßige B.,** regular motion (of machine, etc.); smooth motion (of carriage, etc.); **schwingende B.,** vibration; oscillation; **zwangsläufige B.,** positive movement; *Astr:* **rückläufige B.,** retrogradation; **einem Körper B. mitteilen,** to impart motion to a body; **(etwas) in B. setzen,** to set, put, (sth.) in motion; to bring, call, (sth.) into action; to put, set, (sth.) in action; to set (machinery) going; to start (engine, etc.); to actuate (machine, etc.); *F:* **j-n in B. setzen,** to make s.o. get a move on; **sich in B. setzen,** (*of pers.*) to start to move; to move off; *F:* to make a move; (*of thg*) to start to move; to start off, set off; (*of machine*) to begin working, come into action; **in B. sein** (*of pers.*) to be in a state of activity; to be on the go; (*of thg*) to be moving, in motion; (*of water, lake, etc.*) to be troubled; **j-n in B. halten,** to keep s.o. on the go; **in B. geraten,** to begin to move; **eine B. zwangsläufig mitmachen,** to move through linkage with another moving body; **B. der Erde um die Sonne,** motion of the earth round the sun, revolution of the earth about the sun; **B. der Erde um ihren Mittelpunkt,** rotation of the earth about its centre; **Fortpflanzung der B.,** communication of motion; **der Zug setzte sich in B.,** the train started (to move); **eine allgemeine B. ging durch den Saal,** there was a general movement in the hall, a stir throughout the hall; **die ganze Stadt war in B.,** the whole town was out and about, astir; **der Ameisenhaufen geriet in B.,** the ant-hill became alive; **er ist immer in B.,** he is always on the go; **er setzte Himmel und Erde in B., um ihn zu retten,** he moved heaven and earth to save him; **wir müssen alles in B. setzen, ihm zu helfen,** we must use every means, we must do all we can, to help him; *see also* **Hebel;** (*c*) (physical) exercise; **ich muß mir ein wenig B. verschaffen,** I must take some exercise; *Med:* (*in massage*) **passive B.,** passive movements; (*d*) movement; move; gesture, motion (of hand, etc.); (*in gymnastics, swimming, etc.*) **Bewegungen,** motions; **jede B. des Armes tat ihm weh,** every movement of his arm caused him pain; **der Dieb machte eine B. zur Türe,** the thief made a move, movement, towards the door; **ein Gedicht mit B., Bewegungen, aufsagen,** to recite a poem with actions; **eine B. der Ungeduld machen,** to make a movement of impatience; **er deutete mit einer vielsagenden B. zur Türe,** he pointed at the door with a significant gesture, motion; (*e*) (*of police, etc.*) **j-s Bewegungen beobachten,** to study s.o.'s movements; *Mil:* **Bewegungen der feindlichen Truppen,** movements of the enemy troops; (*f*) **soziale, religiöse, politische, B.,** social, religious, political, movement; (*g*) emotion; **ohne die geringste B. zu verraten,** without showing the least emotion; **er konnte seine B. kaum verbergen,** he could scarcely hide his emotion, feelings; **seine B. teilte sich den anderen mit,** his emotion was communicated to, spread to, the others; **in tiefer B.,** deeply moved; (*h*) (*in poem, painting, etc.*) movement; action; **seine Landschaftsbilder sind voller B.,** his landscapes are full of movement; **das Stück ist voll dramatischer B.,** the play is full of dramatic action.

bewegen², *v.tr.* (*strong*) (*a*) **j-n zu etwas b., j-n dazu b., etwas zu tun,** (*of pers., thg*) to move s.o. to do sth.; to prompt s.o. to do sth.; to get, bring, s.o. to do sth.; to induce s.o. to do sth.; to make s.o. do sth.; (*of pers.*) to prevail upon s.o. to do sth.; **nichts wird ihn dazu b., das zu tun,** he is not to be moved, nothing will move, induce, him, to do that, **weder Drohungen noch Versprechungen werden mich dazu b., meine Freunde zu verraten,** neither threats nor promises will induce, get, me to betray my friends; **ich habe ihn dazu bewogen, uns zu begleiten,** I have induced him to accompany us; **nichts wird ihn dazu b., seine Meinung zu ändern,** nothing will induce him to change his mind; **seine Gutmütigkeit bewog ihn dazu, unsere Bitte anzuhören,** his kind nature induced him to listen to our request; **j-n zur Zustimmung b.,** to get s.o. to consent; to prevail upon s.o. to consent; **was bewog dich zu kommen?** what prompted you to come? what made you come? **er wurde von einem Gefühl des Mitleids bewogen, die Sache auf sich beruhen zu lassen,** he was prompted by a feeling of pity to let the matter rest; **ich bewog ihn dazu, mir zu helfen,** I got him to help me; **er läßt sich nicht dazu bewegen, ist nicht (dazu) zu b., die Sache ernst zu nehmen,** he can't be got, brought, to take the matter seriously; (*b*) **sich zu etwas bewogen fühlen, sich bewogen fühlen, etwas zu tun,** to be, feel, inclined to do sth.; to feel prompted to do sth.; to feel like doing sth.; **nach seinem beleidigenden Verhalten fühle ich mich nicht zum Nachgeben bewogen,** after his offensive behaviour I don't feel inclined, prompted, to give way, I

don't feel like giving way; **er fühlte sich immer noch nicht bewogen aufzustehen,** he still did not feel inclined to get up.

Beweger, *m.* -s/-, mover; **Gott, der erste B. der Natur,** God, the sovereign mover of nature.

Beweggrund, *m.* motive (*gen.*, **für,** for); **einen B. haben, etwas zu tun,** to have a motive in, for, doing sth.; **aus einem bestimmten B. handeln,** to act from, for, a definite motive; **der hauptsächliche B.,** the prime motive; **der wahre, tiefere, B.,** the true motive; **der verborgene, geheime, tiefere, B.,** the hidden, ulterior, motive; **die letzten Beweggründe,** the basic motives; **seine Beweggründe waren religiöser Art,** his motives were of a religious nature; **er muß einen B. (dafür) gehabt haben, das zu tun,** he must have had a motive in, for, doing that; **der Angeklagte weigerte sich, die Beweggründe seiner Handlung, für seine Handlung, anzugeben,** the accused refused to give the motives for his action.

Bewegkraft, *f.* = **Bewegungskraft.**

beweglich, *a.* **1.** (*a*) capable of movement; mobile; *Biol:* motile (cell, etc.); **in sechs Wochen wird sein Arm wieder b. sein,** in six weeks he will be able to move his arm again; (*b*) **bewegliche Feste,** movable feasts; (*c*) **bewegliche Sandbank,** shifting sand. **2.** (*a*) that can be moved, movable; that can move; mobile; *Mec.E:* moving (parts of a machine, etc.); sliding (parts of a machine, etc.); **die Glieder der Puppe sind b.,** the limbs of the doll move, are movable; **ein bewegliches Spielzeug,** a mobile toy; **wir werden diese Teile der Maschine b. konstruieren,** we shall make these parts of the machine movable; **ein Pendel frei b. aufhängen,** to suspend a pendulum to allow free movement; (*b*) (re)movable; mobile; *Tch:* portable (plant, etc.); **bewegliches Eigentum, bewegliche Habe, bewegliches Gut, bewegliche Güter, bewegliche Effekten,** movable effects, movables, movable property, personal estate, chattels, personalty; *F:* goods and chattels; *Print:* **bewegliche Typen,** movable types; *Mil:* **bewegliche Truppenteile,** mobile units; **bewegliche Sanitätskolonne,** mobile medical column; **bewegliches Maschinengewehr,** free gun, movable gun; (*c*) moving (target). **3.** mobile (features, etc.); agile (hands, pers., mind, etc.); manœuvrable (ship, aircraft, etc.); flexible, pliable, supple (policy, strategy, etc.); nimble (pers., mind, etc.); versatile (pers., mind, etc.); *Nat.Hist: Bot: Orn: etc:* versatile (organ, limb, etc.); **für sein Alter ist er noch sehr b.,** for his age he is still very active, he gets around very well for his age; **ein beweglicher Geist,** a versatile mind; **er ist geistig b.,** he has an active mind; **sie hat eine bewegliche Zunge,** she talks a lot, her tongue does wag; **frei b. sein,** to be free to move; **wenn ich allein reise, bin ich beweglicher,** I have more freedom of movement if I travel alone; **wenn ich mit dem Auto reise, bin ich beweglicher,** I am more mobile if I go by car; **unsere Truppen sind nicht b. genug,** our troops are not sufficiently mobile; **bewegliche Preise,** flexible prices; *Mil:* **bewegliches Feuer,** shifting fire; fire at various ranges. **4.** moving, touching; **ihren beweglichen Bitten konnte man nicht widerstehen,** one could not resist her moving, touching, pleas, entreaties.

Beweglichkeit, *f.* **1.** power of movement, ability to move; mobility; *Biol:* motility (of cell, etc.); **der Gipsverband sollte die freie B. des Unterarms nicht behindern,** the plaster should not restrict the free movement of the forearm; **B. in einer bestimmten Richtung,** ability to move in a certain direction. **2.** mobility (of features, etc.); agility (of s.o.'s hands, of pers., mind, etc.); manœuvrability (of ship, aircraft, car, etc.); flexibility, pliability, suppleness (of policy, strategy, etc.); nimbleness (of pers., mind, etc.); versatility (of pers., mind, etc.); *Nat. Hist: Bot: Orn: etc:* versatility (of organ, limb, etc.); **für sein Alter besitzt er noch eine erstaunliche B.,** for his age he is still very active, he gets around astonishingly well for his age; **er ist noch im Besitz seiner geistigen B.,** he still has an active mind; **die außerordentliche B. unserer Truppen hat uns den Sieg gebracht,** the exceptional mobility of our troops brought us victory; **der Vorzug dieses Wagens ist seine außergewöhnliche B.,** the advantage of this car is its extreme manœuvrability.

Bewegung, *f. see* **bewegen**[1] III.

Bewegungsantrieb, *m.* **1.** *Mec:* impulse; impulsion; impulsive, impelling, force; propulsion; propulsive, propelling, force. **2.** *Mec.E:* drive; driving gear.

Bewegungsaufnahmen, *f.pl.* animated photography: *Cin:* action shots.

Bewegungsbehandlung, *f. Med:* kinesitherapy, movement cure.

Bewegungsdrang, *m.* urge to move; urge to be active; **Kinder haben einen natürlichen B.,** children have a natural urge to be active; **wir müssen seinen B. eindämmen,** we must restrain his urge to be active.

Bewegungsempfindung, *f.* sensation of movement; *Physiol:* kin(a)esthesia, kin(a)esthesis.

Bewegungsenergie, *f. Mec:* kinetic energy, motive energy, motivity.

bewegungsfähig, *a.* capable of movement, able to move; mobile; *Z: Bot:* motile (cells, etc.); **der Verletzte war kaum b.,** the injured man was scarcely able to move.

Bewegungsfähigkeit, *f.* power of movement, mobility; *Biol:* motility.

Bewegungsfreiheit, *f.* (*a*) freedom of movement; room to move; **volle, uneingeschränkte, B.,** full, unrestricted, freedom of movement; **B. im Umkreis von zehn Kilometern,** freedom of movement within the radius of ten kilometres; **die Internierten litten unter der Einschränkung ihrer B.,** the internees suffered under the restriction of their freedom of movement; **die Tiere im Zoo haben viel B.,** the animals in the zoo have plenty of room to move about; **ihr langer Rock behindert sie in ihrer B.,** her long skirt restricts, hampers, her movements; (*b*) liberty of action; **ich kann den Fall nicht untersuchen, wenn ich nicht volle, uneingeschränkte, B. habe,** I cannot investigate the case unless I have full liberty of action.

Bewegungsgröße, *f. Mec: Ph:* quantity of motion; momentum, impulse (*mv*).

Bewegungshaufen, *m. Astr:* moving cluster (of stars).

Bewegungskraft, *f.* motive power; motive force.

Bewegungskrieg, *m. Mil:* field warfare, open warfare, war of movement, war of manœuvre.

Bewegungslehre, *f.* **1.** theory of motion; *Mth: Ph: etc:* mechanics; dynamics; kinematics; kinetics. **2.** *Mil:* tactics of manœuvre.

bewegungslos, *a.* motionless; immobile; still; **er stand b.,** he stood motionless; **völlig b. dastehen,** to stand quite still, stock-still; **das Meer war b.,** the sea was motionless; **sein Gesicht blieb völlig b.,** his face remained quite impassive.

Bewegungslosigkeit, *f.* motionlessness; stillness; **das Tier lag in völliger B.,** the animal lay motionless, *F:* as still as still.

Bewegungsmechanismus, *m.* actuating mechanism; action (of piano, etc.).

Bewegungsmöglichkeit, *f.* (*a*) possibility of movement; (*b*) scope, room, for action.

Bewegungsmuskel, *m.* motor, motory, muscle.

Bewegungsnerv, *m. Anat:* motor, motory, nerve.

Bewegungsorgan, *n. Physiol:* motory organ.

Bewegungsphotographie, *f.* cinematography; motion-picture photography.

Bewegungsrichtung, *f.* direction of motion; **die B. eines Körpers bestimmen,** to define the direction in which a body is moving, the direction of a moving body.

Bewegungssitz, *m. Mec.E:* clearance fit.

Bewegungsspiel, *n.* (*a*) game involving bodily exercise, active game; (*b*) movement (of the muscles, etc.).

Bewegungsstörung, *f.* impediment in movement; *Med:* ataxy.

Bewegungsstudie, *f.* **1.** *Art: Phot:* study in, of, movement. **2.** *Ind:* motion study; *Art: Phot:* study of movements; **Bewegungsstudien an Pferden machen,** to study the movements of horses.

Bewegungstemperatur, *f.* body temperature after vigorous exercise.

Bewegungstrieb, *m.* = **Bewegungsdrang.**

bewegungsunfähig, *a.* incapable of movement, unable to move.

Bewegungsvermögen, *n.* power of movement, mobility; *Biol:* motility.

Bewegungswahrnehmung, *f.* perception of movement; *Physiol:* kin(a)esthesia, kin(a)esthesis.

Bewegungswiderstand, *m.* resistance (to motion).

Bewegungszustand, *m.* (state of) motion; **im B.,** in motion.

bewehren. I. *v.tr.* (*a*) to arm (s.o.); to fortify (town, etc.); **sich mit einem Stein b.,** to arm oneself with a stone; **mit einer Lanze bewehrt,** armed with a lance; **eine mit Zinnen bewehrte Mauer,** a crenellated wall; (*b*) *El.E: etc:* to armour (cable); *Civ.E: Constr:* to reinforce; **bewehrter Beton,** reinforced, armoured, concrete; *see also* **Balken** 1; (*c*) *Her:* **bewehrt,** armed; **bewehrter Löwe,** lion armed, lion with claws; **bewehrter Bock,** goat armed, goat horned; **bewehrter Hirsch,** stag attired; **bewehrter Elefant,** elephant tusked.

II. *vbl s.* **1. Bewehren,** *n. in vbl senses; also:* fortification (of town, etc.); *Civ.E: Constr:* reinforcement (of concrete). **2. Bewehrung,** *f.* (*a*) = II. 1; (*b*) *El.E:* armouring (of cable).

beweiben, *v. A. & Hum:* **1.** *v.tr.* to find a wife for, *A:* to wive (a man); **beweibt,** married. **2. sich beweiben,** to take a wife, to marry, *A:* to wive.

beweiden, *v.tr.* (*of cattle, etc.*) to graze (on) (a meadow, etc.); to pasture (a meadow, etc.); (*of shepherd, etc.*) to graze a flock on (a meadow, etc.).

beweihräuchern, *v.tr.* (*a*) to perfume (sth.) with incense; *Ecc:* to cense (altar, priest, etc.); (*b*) *F:* **j-n b.,** to adulate s.o.; **Beweihräucherung** *f,* adulation, excessive flattery.

beweinen, *v.tr.* to weep, to shed tears, to cry, over (s.o., sth.); to lament (for, over) (s.o., sth.); to mourn (for, over) (s.o., sth.); to bewail (one's sins, one's lot, the loss of s.o., etc.); **sein Tod wurde von allen beweint,** his death was universally mourned; **die Beweinung (Christi),** the Mourning of Christ.

beweinenswert, beweinenswürdig, *a.* pitiable, deplorable (pers., sight, etc.).

Beweinung, *f. see* **beweinen.**

Beweis, *m.* -es/-e. **1.** (action of) proving; substantiation (of statement, claim, etc.); demonstration (of fact, theorem, etc.); **der B. seiner Unschuld wird schwierig sein,** it will be difficult to prove his innocence; **zum B. meiner Behauptung,** to prove my assertion, in proof of my assertion; **zum B. erwähnte er, daß . . .,** by way of proof he mentioned that . . . . **2.** (*a*) proof (**für,** of); **als B.,** as proof; **klarer B.,** clear, positive, proof; **eindeutiger, schlüssiger, stichhaltiger, schlagender, B.,** conclusive, striking, proof; *F:* cast-iron proof; **urkundlicher, dokumentarischer, B.,** proof by documentary evidence; **etwas unter B. stellen,** to provide proof of sth.; **den B. liefern, erbringen, daß . . .,** to prove that . . .; **den B. führen,** to prove (one's argument); **den B. antreten, daß . . .,** to offer proof that . . .; **das ist der B. dafür, daß er lügt,** this is proof that he is lying; **wenn diese Aussagen eines Beweises bedürfen,** if proof is needed for these statements; **er zögerte; ein B., daß er sich nicht sehr sicher fühlte,** he hesitated, a clear sign, a proof, that he was not very sure of himself; **die Beweise für die Existenz Gottes,** the proofs of the existence of God; (*b*) (piece of) evidence; proof; argument; **ein zwingender, schlüssiger, B.,** a conclusive argument; **direkte, indirekte, Beweise,** direct, indirect, evidence; **schriftliche Beweise,** written evidence, evidence in writing; **einen B., Beweise, liefern,** to furnish evidence; to tender evidence; **einen B., Beweise, beibringen,** to produce, adduce, evidence; **Beweise sammeln,** to collect evidence; **als B. anführen, daß . . .,** to put in as evidence that . . .; to submit as evidence that . . .; **ich habe keinen B., keine Beweise, dafür,** I have no evidence for, proof of, it; **die Beweise sprachen sehr gegen ihn,** the evidence was strongly against him; **Klatschgeschichten sind keine Beweise,** common gossip is not evidence; *Jur:* **urkundliche Beweise,** documentary evidence, documentary proof; **B. des ersten Anscheins,** prima facie evidence; **zulässiger B.,** admissible evidence; **etwas als B. zulassen,** to admit sth. as evidence; **den B., die Beweise, aufnehmen, erheben,** to take, hear, evidence; **aus Mangel an Beweisen freigesprochen werden,** to be acquitted on the grounds of insufficient evidence; **Sicherung des Beweises,** perpetuating of evidence; (*c*) proof, evidence (of goodwill, gratitude, intelligence, etc.); mark (of goodwill, esteem, resentment, etc.); proof, sign, token (of one's friendship, etc.); **(etwas) unter B. stellen,** to give, show, proof of, give evidence of (one's goodwill, gratitude, intelligence, etc.); (*of action, etc.*) **ein B. für etwas sein,** to give evidence of (s.o.'s goodwill, gratitude, intelligence, etc.); **als einen B. meiner Hochachtung,** as a mark of my esteem; **Beweise seiner Freundschaft, für seine Freundschaft, geben,** to give proofs, signs, tokens, of one's friendship; **er hat uns viele Beweise seiner Anhänglichkeit, für seine Anhänglichkeit, gegeben,** he has given us many proofs, signs, tokens, of his loyalty, he has proved his loyalty over and over again.

Beweisartikel, *m.* **1.** = **Beweissatz. 2.** = **Beweisstück.**

Beweisaufnahme, *f. Jur:* (taking, hearing, of) evidence; **zur B. schreiten,** to begin with the hearing of the evidence.

Beweisaufnahmetermin, *m.* = **Beweistermin.**

beweisbar, *a.* (proposition, etc.) that can be proved, capable of being proved; provable.
Beweisbarkeit, *f.* provableness.
Beweisbeschluß, *m. Jur:* decision (of the court) regarding the procedure to be followed in the hearing of evidence.
Beweisdokument, *n.* document in proof.
Beweiseinrede, *f. Jur:* objection to the admissibility of evidence.
beweisen, *v.tr.* (*strong*) (*a*) to prove (fact, the truth of sth., etc.); to establish, prove (s.o.'s innocence, etc.); to demonstrate, establish, the truth of (proposition, etc.); to substantiate (statement, claim, etc.); to prove, make good (assertion, etc.); **beweisen, daß . . .,** to prove that . . .; **eindeutig, unwiderlegbar, schlagend, b.,** to prove beyond doubt, conclusively; **seine Handlungsweise beweist, daß er ein Feigling ist.** his action proves him to be a coward; (*b*) (*of pers.*) to show, display (intelligence, courage, etc.); to prove, show, to give, show, proof of, to give, show, evidence of (one's goodwill, one's gratitude, etc.); to show proof of (one's cowardice, etc.); (*of action, etc.*) to prove, show, (s.o.'s good heart, good taste, bad taste, etc.); to be a sign, mark, of (s.o.'s good character, etc.); to evidence (s.o.'s impatience, genius, etc.); to give evidence of (s.o.'s intelligence, etc.); **Anteilnahme an j-m, an etwas** *dat.*, **b.,** to show interest in s.o., sth.; **Eifer in einer Angelegenheit b.,** to show zeal in doing sth.; **er hat uns mehr als einmal seine Treue bewiesen,** he has more than once shown, given, us proof of his loyalty; **eine Auswahl, die j-s Geschmack beweist,** selection that proves, shows, s.o.'s taste; (*c*) **sich als etwas b.,** (*of pers.*) to prove oneself (as), to prove (to be) (a reliable friend, etc.); to prove (to be) (loyal, reliable, etc.); (*of thg*) to prove (to be) (useful, etc.).
Beweiserhebung, *f.*=**Beweisaufnahme.**
Beweisfähigkeit, *f. Jur:* validity (as evidence).
Beweisfrist, *f. Jur:* time granted to produce evidence.
Beweisführung, *f.* argumentation; (line of) argument; *Jur:* marshalling of the evidence; **ich konnte seiner B. nicht folgen,** I could not follow his (line of) argument; **seine B. ist geschickt angelegt,** he has marshalled his arguments well.
Beweisgrund, *m.* argument; **der entscheidende B.,** the clinching argument; **er führte verschiedene Beweisgründe an,** he produced several arguments, reasons.
Beweiskraft, *f.* (*a*) cogency (of argument, etc.); **die B. seiner Argumente läßt zu wünschen übrig,** his arguments lack conclusive force; **das Experiment hat keine B.,** the experiment is not conclusive; (*b*) *Jur:* probative weight (of evidence); **über die gesetzliche B. einer Urkunde entscheiden,** to decide whether a document is admissible as evidence.
beweiskräftig, *a.* (*of argument*) cogent; forceful; (*of experiment, etc.*) conclusive.
Beweislast, *f. Jur:* burden of proof, onus of proof; **die B. trifft den Kläger,** the onus of proof lies with, is on, the plaintiff.
Beweismaterial, *n. Jur: etc:* (probative) evidence; **urkundliches, dokumentarisches B.,** documentary evidence; **schriftliches B.,** written evidence, evidence in writing, written proof; **B. sammeln,** to collect evidence.
Beweismittel, *n. Jur: etc:* (piece of) evidence; **Zulässigkeit von Beweismitteln,** admissibility of evidence.
Beweisnachholung, *f. Jur:* introduction of new evidence (during proceedings).
Beweisrecht, *n. Jur:* law of evidence.
Beweissatz, *m. Jur:* fact, etc., to be proved.
Beweissicherung, *f. Jur:* perpetuating of evidence.
Beweisstelle, *f.* illustrative quotation.
Beweisstück, *n.* (piece of) evidence, document in proof; *Jur:* exhibit.
Beweistermin, *m. Jur:* (date fixed for the) hearing of evidence.
Beweisthema, *n. Jur:* fact, etc., to be proved.
Beweisurkunde, *f.* document in proof.
Beweisverfahren, *n. Jur:* (procedure of) taking, hearing, evidence; **das B. aufnehmen,** to begin with the hearing of the evidence.
Beweiswürdigung, *f. Jur:* assessment of evidence.
bewenden. I. *v.* (*used only in the inf. with* **lassen**) **eine Angelegenheit, eine Sache, dabei, damit, b. lassen, es dabei, damit, b. lassen,** to let a matter, let it, rest at that; to leave a matter as it is; to leave it at that; **damit, dabei, wollen wir es für heute b. lassen,** that will be enough for to-day; **diesmal kann ich es nicht dabei b. lassen, ihn nur zu verwarnen,** I cannot let him off this time with just a warning; **wir müssen es beim Notwendigsten b. lassen,** we must be content with bare necessities.
II. *vbl s.* **Bewenden,** *n.* **1. ich werde dir diesen Betrag leihen, aber dabei, damit, muß es sein B. haben,** I shall lend you this amount, but I can do no more for you; **diesmal mag es mit einer Warnung sein B. haben,** let a caution suffice this time; **damit mag es für heute sein B. haben,** let that be enough for to-day. **2.**=**Bewandtnis.**
bewerben (sich). I. *v.refl.* (*strong*) **sich um etwas b.,** to apply for sth.; to compete for (a prize); to court (s.o.'s favour); **sich bei j-m um etwas b.,** to apply to s.o. for sth.; **sich um eine Stelle b.,** to apply for a post; *F:* to put in for a post; **mehrere Firmen haben sich um den Auftrag beworben,** several firms have made, put in, sent in, their tenders; **sich um ein Mädchen, um die Hand eines Mädchens, b.,** to propose to a girl; to ask for a girl's hand in marriage, to sue for a girl's hand.
II. *vbl s.* **Bewerbung,** *f.* application (for a post, etc.); **eine B. einreichen,** to send in an application.
Bewerber, *m.* **-s/-,** applicant (for a post); suitor, wooer; admirer; *Sp: etc:* competitor (for a prize).
Bewerbungsformular, *n.* application form, *U.S:* application blank.
Bewerbungsschreiben, *n.* (written) application.
bewerfen, *v.tr.* (*strong*) **1. j-n, etwas, mit etwas b.,** to throw sth. at s.o., sth.; to fling sth. at s.o., sth.; to pelt s.o., sth., with (stones, snowballs, etc.); **j-n mit Schmutz b.,** to throw dirt, mud, at s.o.; to sling mud at s.o. **2.** *Constr:* (*a*) to rough-cast (wall); to rough-render (wall); to parget (wall); **mit Kieseln b.,** to give a pebble-dash finish to (wall); (*b*) to plaster (wall).
bewerkstelligen, *v.tr.* to manage (sth.); to effect (sth.); **ich werde das, die Sache, schon b.,** I shall manage it, the affair; **ich weiß nicht, wie sie das bewerkstelligt haben,** I do not know how they managed it; **ich weiß, wie das zu b. ist,** I know how to manage it; **der Rückzug wurde in guter Ordnung bewerkstelligt,** the retreat was effected in good order; *F:* **da hast du etwas Schönes bewerkstelligt,** now you've done it.
bewerten. I. *v.tr.* to rate (sth., s.o.); to appraise (achievement, etc.); **ein Grundstück, usw., auf eine bestimmte Summe b.,** to value, estimate, assess, property, etc., at a certain amount; **hoch b.,** to rate (sth., s.o.) high; to set a high value on (sth.); to have a high opinion of (sth., s.o.); **niedrig, gering, b.,** to set a low value on (sth.); to have a low opinion of (sth., s.o.); **zu hoch b.,** to overrate (sth., s.o.); to overestimate (sth., s.o.); to set too high a value on (sth.); to overvalue (goods); **zu niedrig, gering, b.,** to underrate (sth., s.o.); to underestimate (sth., s.o.); to set too low a value on (sth.); to undervalue (goods); **j-n nach seinen Fähigkeiten b.,** to rate, assess, s.o. by his abilities; **sie bewerteten ihre Freiheit höher, geringer, als ihr Leben,** they priced their freedom higher, lower, than their lives; *Sp:* **j-s Leistung nach Punkten b.,** to assess s.o.'s performance on points.
II. *vbl s.* **Bewerten** *n.*, **Bewertung** *f. in vbl senses; also:* valuation; estimation; assessment; appraisal.
bewettern, *v.tr. Min:* to ventilate (coal-mine, etc.); **Bewetterung** *f*, ventilation (of coal-mine, etc.).
bewickeln, *v.tr.* **etwas mit etwas b.,** to wind (ribbon, etc.) round sth.; to wind (cotton, etc.) on to (reel, etc.); to wrap (insulating tape, etc.) round (wire, etc.); to wrap (wire, etc.) in (insulating tape, etc.).
bewilligen. I. *v.tr.* to grant (sum of money, etc.) (to s.o.); to grant (s.o.'s application); to allow (s.o.) (sum of money, etc.); *Com:* to allow (s.o.) (discount, etc.); *Parl:* to sanction (tax, etc.); to vote (sum of money, etc.); **eine Sonderausgabe b.,** to pass, allow, a special item of expenditure; **er bewilligte ihm eine Unterredung,** he granted him an interview; **sein Gesuch wurde anstandslos bewilligt,** his application was granted without any objections being made.
II. *vbl s.* **Bewilligen** *n.*, **Bewilligung** *f. in vbl senses; also:* grant (of sum, etc.); allowance (of sum, etc.); **ich warte auf die B. meiner Pension,** I am waiting for my pension to be granted.
Bewilligungsrecht, *n. Parl:* right to sanction taxes; right to vote a sum.
bewillkomm(n)en. I. *v.tr.* (*a*) to welcome (s.o.); to greet, salute (s.o.); **j-n herzlich b.,** to welcome s.o. heartily; **j-n mit einem Lächeln, einem Kuß, b.,** to greet s.o. with a smile, a kiss; **er wurde mit Hochrufen bewillkommt,** he was greeted, received, with cheers; (*b*) to welcome (a suggestion, etc.); **eine Gelegenheit, etwas zu tun, b.,** to welcome an opportunity to do sth.
II. *vbl s.* **1. Bewillkomm(n)en,** *n. in vbl senses.* **2. Bewillkomm(n)ung,** *f.* (*a*)=II. 1; (*b*) welcome; **j-m eine herzliche B. zuteil werden lassen,** to give s.o. a hearty welcome.
bewimpeln, *v.tr.* to put a pennant on (bicycle, etc.); to put a pennon on (boat, etc.); to dress (ship); **ein bunt bewimpeltes Schiff,** a gaily dressed ship.
bewimpert, *a.* (*a*) having eye-lashes; *comb.fm.* **-bewimpert,** -lashed; **langbewimperte Augen,** long-lashed eyes; (*b*) *Biol: Nat.Hist:* ciliate, ciliated.
bewinden, *v.tr.* (*strong*) to entwine (wire frame, etc.) with (flowers, etc.).
bewinkelt, *a. Her:* cantoned.
bewirken, *v.tr.* to cause (sth.); to bring about (sth.); to occasion (excitement, despondency, etc.); to effect (change, cure, etc.); to work (cure, etc.); to produce (sensation, etc.); **die Pillen bewirken einen Rückgang der Temperatur,** the pills induce, cause, a fall in temperature; **die Hefe bewirkt, daß ein Gärungsprozeß stattfindet,** the yeast causes, brings about, a process of fermentation; **die schlechte Behandlung bewirkte, daß das Kind halsstarrig wurde,** bad treatment caused the child to become stubborn.
bewirten. I. *v.tr.* to entertain (s.o.) (with food, etc.); to regale (s.o.) (with food, etc.); to give (s.o.) hospitality; **seine Gäste mit Speise und Trank b.,** to entertain, regale, one's guests with food and drink; **sie wurden festlich, königlich, bewirtet,** they were lavishly, regally, entertained; **wir wurden freundlich bewirtet,** we were received with real hospitality; **ich muß heute zwanzig Leute b.,** I have to entertain, feed, twenty people today; **bist du gut bewirtet worden?** were you well looked after?
II. *vbl s.* **1. Bewirten,** *n. in vbl senses.* **2. Bewirtung,** *f.* (*a*)=II. 1; (*b*) hospitality; **ich möchte mich für Ihre freundliche B. bedanken,** I should like to thank you for your kind hospitality; **die Zimmer in diesem Hotel sind klein, aber die Bewirtung ist ausgezeichnet,** the rooms in this hotel are small, but the food and service are excellent.
bewirtschaften. I. *v.tr.* **1.** to farm (land); to cultivate (field); to manage (farm, etc.); to run (hotel, farm, etc.); **ein schlecht bewirtschaftetes Feld,** a badly cultivated field; **die Berghütte ist im Winter nicht bewirtschaftet,** there is no service in the mountain hut in winter. **2.** *Adm:* to ration (food, etc.); to control (foreign exchange, housing, etc.); **Güter b.,** to control (production and distribution of) goods; **die Preise für bewirtschaftete Güter sind festgesetzt,** prices of controlled goods are fixed.
II. *vbl s.* **Bewirtschaften** *n.*, **Bewirtschaftung** *f. in vbl senses; also:* **1.** cultivation (of land); management (of farm, etc.); **schlechte Bewirtschaftung des Bodens führt zu großen Verlusten,** poor cultivation of the soil leads to considerable loss. **2.** control (of goods, foreign exchange, housing, etc.).
Bewirtschaftungssystem, *n. Adm:* rationing system; system of control.
bewitzeln, *v.tr.* to deride, scoff at, jeer at (s.o., sth.); to make derisive remarks about (s.o., sth.); to mock (at), make fun of, ridicule (s.o., sth.); to hold (s.o., sth.) up to ridicule; **sie bewitzelten jede seiner Äußerungen,** they ridiculed, jeered at, everything he said.
bewog, bewöge, bewogen *see* **bewegen**[2].
bewohnbar, *a.* (*of country, etc.*) (in)habitable; (*of house, etc.*) fit to live in; (in)habitable.
Bewohnbarkeit, *f.* habitableness.
bewohnen, *v.tr.* (*of group of people, etc.*) to inhabit, live in (country, house, etc.); (*of pers.*) to live in (house, etc.); to occupy (house, etc.); **er bewohnt eine ganze Zimmerflucht,** he occupies a whole suite of rooms; **das Schloß ist schon lange nicht mehr bewohnt,** the castle has not been lived in, inhabited, occupied, for a long time; **vorwiegend von Arbeitern bewohnte Häuser,** houses mainly inhabited, occupied, by workers; **ein bewohntes Haus,** an inhabited house; **bewohnte Gegenden,** inhabited areas.
Bewohner, *m.* **-s/-,** inhabitant (of country, town, house, etc.); occupant, occupier (of house); resident (of district, etc.); **die Bewohner des Landes waren gastfreundlich,** the inhabitants of the country were hospitable; **die Bewohner des Waldes, der Luft,** the inhabitants, *Poet:* the denizens, of the forest, of the air.

-bewohner, *comb.fm. m.* (a) -dweller; inhabitant of . . .; **Landbewohner** *pl*, country-dwellers; **Höhlenbewohner** *pl*, cave-dwellers; **Schloß-bewohner**, inhabitant of a, of the, castle; (b) *Nat.Hist:* (animal) that lives in . . .; (plant) that grows in . . .; **Holzbewohner**, (i) animal that lives in the woods; (ii) plant that grows in the woods; (iii) insect that lives in wood; fungus that lives on wood; xylophilous insect, fungus; lignicolous moss, fungus.

bewölken. I. *v.tr.* 1. *Lit:* to cloud (sky, mind, etc.). 2. **sich bewölken**, (of sky) to cloud (up, over), to become overcast, to darken; (of mind) to become clouded; (of brow) to cloud (over), to darken; **der Himmel bewölkte sich**, the sky was clouding over; **seine Stirne bewölkte sich**, his brow clouded (over), darkened; **der politische Horizont hat sich drohend bewölkt**, the political horizon has darkened ominously. II. *vbl s.* **Bewölkung**, *f.* clouds; **leichte, starke, B.**, light, heavy, clouds; **von Westen aufkommende B.**, clouds coming up from the west; **anfänglich leichte B., später sonnig**, slight cloud giving way to fine weather. III. *p.p. & a.* **bewölkt**, clouded, cloudy, overcast (sky); clouded, darkened (brow); **der Himmel war leicht, stark, b.**, there were light, heavy, clouds in the sky.

Bewölktheit, *f.* cloudiness.

bewollen (sich), *v.refl.* (of sheep, etc.) to grow wool; **bewollt**, woolly.

Bewuchs, *m.* **-es/.** vegetation (on ground, rock, etc.).

bewulstet, *a.* *Her:* **bewulsteter Mohrenkopf**, moor's head wreathed.

Bewunderer, *m.* **-s/-,** admirer.

bewundern. I. *v.tr.* to admire (s.o., sth.); **j-n wegen seines Mutes, für seinen Mut, b.**, to admire s.o. for his courage; **sich im Spiegel b.**, to admire oneself in the glass; **er ist ein bewunderter Schauspieler**, he is a much-admired actor. II. *vbl s.* 1. **Bewundern**, *n. in vbl senses.* 2. **Bewunderung**, *f.* (a) = II. 1; *also:* admiration (of sth., s.o.); (b) admiration (for sth., s.o.); **j-n mit B. erfüllen**, to fill s.o. with admiration; **j-s B. erregen**, to excite the admiration of s.o.; **voller B. für j-n, etwas, sein**, to be full of admiration for s.o., sth.; **mit B. auf j-n, etwas, sehen**, to look at s.o., sth., with admiration, admiringly; **in B. vor j-m, etwas, stehen**, to stand in admiration before s.o., sth.; **to be full of, filled with, admiration for s.o., sth.

bewundernswert, *a.* admirable; **er hat bewundernswerte Erfolge errungen**, he has achieved admirable success, has succeeded to admiration.

Bewunderungssucht, *f.* (a) yearning for admiration; (b) **die B. der Massen**, the masses' hankering for the hero.

bewunderungswürdig, *a.* = bewundernswert.

Bewurf, *m.* **-(e)s/⁻e.** *Constr:* (a) rough coat (of plaster); parget; **grober, rauher, B.**, rough-cast; (b) (wall-)plaster.

bewurzeln (sich), *v.refl.* (of plant) to grow roots; *Her:* **bewurzelte Eiche**, oak-tree eradicated.

bewußt, *a.* 1. (a) *Phil: etc:* conscious; **der Mensch als bewußtes Lebewesen**, man as a conscious being; (b) conscious; deliberate, intentional; **eine bewußte Bewegung**, a conscious movement; **bewußte Absicht**, conscious, deliberate, intention; **eine bewußte Beleidigung**, a deliberate, an intentional, insult; *adv.* consciously, deliberately, intentionally, knowingly; **ich habe ihn niemals b. beleidigt**, I have never consciously, deliberately, intentionally, knowingly, insulted him; **seine b. zur Schau getragene Überlegenheit**, his conscious air of superiority; (c) **sich** *dat.* **etwas** *gen.* **b. sein, werden**, to be, become, conscious of sth.; to be, become, aware of sth.; to be, become, sensible of sth.; **sich** *dat.* **etwas** *gen.* **b. machen**, to make oneself (fully) aware of sth.; to make oneself clear about sth.; (of fact, etc.) **j-m b. sein**, to be known to s.o.; **sich seiner Schuld b. sein**, to be conscious, aware, of one's guilt; **sich keiner Schuld b. sein**, to have a good, easy, clean, clear, conscience; **sich der Folgen seiner Handlungsweise nicht b. sein**, not to be aware, to be ignorant, of the consequences of one's action; **sich der Schwere seines Verbrechens voll, völlig, b. sein**, to be fully aware of the gravity of one's crime; **ich bin mir vollkommen, völlig, b., es ist mir vollkommen, völlig, b., daß . . .**, I am well, fully, aware that . . .; **ohne mir dessen b. zu sein, hatte ich . . .**, without being aware of it, I had . . .; **ich wurde mir b., es wurde mir b.**, it dawned on me; it occurred to me, to my mind; **er ist sich seiner Fehler b.**, he is conscious of, aware of, sensible of, alive to,

his defects; **ich bin mir der Ehre b., in diesem Kreise sprechen zu dürfen**, I am aware of the honour of being allowed to address this company; **ich bin mir der Einzelheiten nicht mehr b., die Einzelheiten sind mir nicht mehr b.**, I no longer remember the particulars; **er war sich der Sensation, die er verursachte, nicht b.**, he was unconscious, unaware, of the sensation he was causing; **ich war mir seiner Anwesenheit nicht b.**, I was not conscious of his presence; **er hat sich die Gefahr nicht b. gemacht**, he has not made himself (fully) aware of the danger. 2. (matter, person, etc.) in question; fixed, agreed (hour, etc.); afore-mentioned (hour, etc.); **die bewußten Personen werden wissen, was sie zu tun haben**, the persons in question will know what they have to do; **die bewußte Dame ist eben weggegangen**, the lady in question, *F:* you know who, has just left; **finde dich zur bewußten Zeit am Bahnhof ein**, come to the station at the time fixed, agreed; **zur bewußten Stunde machten sie sich auf den Weg**, they set out at the time mentioned; **unter den bewußten Bedingungen werde ich den Vertrag unterzeichnen**, I shall sign the contract under the conditions we mentioned.

Bewußtheit, *f.* *Phil: etc:* consciousness, awareness (of an idea, etc.); consciousness (of conscious being).

bewußtlos, *a.* unconscious; insensible, senseless; **b. werden**, to become unconscious; to swoon, faint; **b. sein**, to be unconscious, insensible; to be in a (dead) faint; **b. zu Boden fallen**, to fall senseless, insensible; **j-n b. schlagen**, to knock s.o. unconscious, senseless; **man fand ihn b.**, he was found unconscious, in an unconscious state.

Bewußtlosigkeit, *f.* (a) unconsciousness; **nach mehreren Stunden der B.**, after several hours of unconsciousness; (b) *F:* **er schikaniert seine Angestellten bis zur B.**, he drives his staff mad with his petty tyranny; **ich habe an diesem Buch bis zur B. gearbeitet**, I have worked myself silly on that book; **ich habe das Stück bis zur B. geübt**, I have practised this piece endlessly.

Bewußtsein, *n.* **-s/.** 1. *Phil: etc:* consciousness (of conscious being); **das moralische B.**, moral consciousness. 2. (a) consciousness; awareness; **j-m etwas zum B. bringen**, to make s.o. conscious, aware, sensible, of sth.; **j-m zum B. bringen, daß . . .**, to make s.o. aware that . . ., conscious of the fact that . . .; **sich etwas zum B. bringen**, to make oneself (fully) aware of sth., to make oneself clear about sth.; **j-m zum B. kommen**, to dawn on s.o.; to occur to s.o., to s.o.'s mind; **im vollen B. der Folgen handeln**, to act in full consciousness, awareness, of the consequences; **im B. meiner Unschuld**, having a clear conscience; conscious of my innocence; (b) consciousness; **bei B. sein**, to be conscious; **zu B. kommen**, to become conscious; **wieder zu B. kommen**, to regain consciousness; to recover one's senses, one's wits, *F:* to come to, to come round; **das B. verlieren**, to lose consciousness; to swoon, faint; **j-n wieder zum B. bringen**, to bring s.o. round; **er war bis zuletzt bei B.**, he was conscious to the end.

Bewußtseinsgrad, *m.* *Psy:* degree of consciousness.

Bewußtseinsinhalt, *m.* *Phil: etc:* conscious experience; **j-m zum B. werden**, to become a conscious experience to s.o.

Bewußtseinskunst, *f.* *Lit:* stream-of-consciousness technique.

Bewußtseinsschwelle, *f.* *Psy:* threshold of consciousness.

Bewußtseinsspaltung, *f.* *Psy:* dividing of consciousness; divided consciousness; dissociation.

Bewußtseinsstörung, *f.* disturbance of consciousness.

Bewußtseinsstrom, *m.* stream of consciousness.

Bewußtseinsstufe, *f.* level of consciousness.

Bewußtseinstrübung, *f.* clouding of consciousness; clouded consciousness; *Med:* somnolence.

Bewußtseinszustand, *m.* (state of) consciousness.

Bey [bai, beː], *m.* **-s/-e & -s.** *Turk.Adm:* bey.

bezahlbar, *a.* payable.

bezahlen. I. *v.tr. & i.* (*haben*) 1. (a) to pay (money); to pay, discharge, settle (debt, fine, bill, etc.); to pay off (debt); *Fin:* to honour (bill of exchange); **bar b.**, to pay (in) cash, (in) ready money; **sofort, auf der Stelle, b.**, to pay forthwith, *F:* on the nail; **voll, vollständig, restlos, b.**, to pay in full; **teilweise b.**, to pay in part; (on receipted bill) **'bezahlt', 'paid'**; **was, wieviel, haben Sie dafür bezahlt?** how much did you pay for it, them? **zuviel für etwas b.**, to pay too much for sth.; **einen Betrag in voller Höhe b.**, to pay

an amount in full; **Kinder im Alter von 10 Jahren und darüber müssen voll, den vollen Fahrpreis, b.**, children of 10 years and over must pay the full fare; **einen Teil der Summe auf Abschlag, den Rest in Monatsraten b.**, to pay a part of the sum on account and the rest in monthly instalments; **die Zeche b.**, to pay the bill; *F:* to foot the bill; **eine Schuld auf Heller und Pfennig b.**, to pay a debt to the last penny; **ich werde meine Schulden bei Ihnen nächsten Monat b.**, I'll settle up with you next month; **j-m, an j-n, etwas b.**, to pay s.o. sth.; **ich habe ihm 100 Mark dafür bezahlt**, I paid him 100 marks for it, them; **für j-n b.**, to pay for s.o. (in a restaurant, at the theatre, etc.); **soll ich für alle b.?** shall I settle for everybody? **wieviel hast du für mich bezahlt?** how much did you pay for me, on my account? **er hat im Kino für mich bezahlt**, he paid for me at the pictures; (b) *St.Exch:* (on list of dealings) **'bezahlt'**, *abbr.* **'b.', 'bez.'**, 'bargains done'. 2. (a) **etwas b., für etwas b.**, to pay for sth.; **das Fleisch ist schon bezahlt**, the meat has been paid for; **etwas im Voraus b.**, to pay for sth. in advance; to prepay (carriage, etc.); **bezahlte Arbeit**, paid work, employment, work against payment; **gut, schlecht, bezahlte Stelle**, well-paid, badly paid, job, situation; **eine Runde b.**, to stand a round (of drinks); **ich bezahle, I'll pay, let me pay, I'll treat you; bitte bezahlen Sie das Taxi**, will you please pay the taxi? **er läßt sich jede Handreichung b.**, he expects to be paid for every little thing he does; **das ist teuer bezahlt**, (i) that's a stiff price, (ii) that's dearly paid for; **das kann man mit Geld nicht b.**, it is invaluable, money cannot buy it; **er hat seine Gutmütigkeit teuer bezahlt, b. müssen**, he paid dearly for his kind-heartedness; **er hat seine Verwegenheit mit dem Leben bezahlt**, he paid for his rashness with his life; **seine Dummheit b. (müssen)**, to pay for one's folly; **dafür, das, soll er mir b.!** he shall pay for this! I'll make him pay for this! (b) **j-n b.**, to pay s.o.; **j-n für seine Dienste b.**, to pay, remunerate, s.o. for his services; **monatlich bezahlt werden**, to be paid monthly; **ich würde es nicht noch einmal tun, selbst wenn ich dafür bezahlt würde**, I wouldn't do it again, even if I was paid (for it); **sich b. lassen**, to take payment; **er läßt sich für alles, was er tut, schwer b.**, he charges highly for everything he does; **bezahlte Arbeitskräfte**, paid labour; **bezahlte Mörder**, paid, hired, assassins; **bezahlte Zeugen**, bribed witnesses; **bezahlte Dirne**, prostitute, *P:* pro. 3. (of thg) **sich bezahlt machen**, to pay; **es macht sich nicht bezahlt**, it does not pay; **diese Arbeit macht sich nicht bezahlt**, this work does not pay; **Ehrlichkeit macht sich bezahlt**, honesty pays; **ich bekomme kein Geld für diese Arbeit, aber sie wird sich mir schon auf andere Weise bezahlt machen**, I am not being paid any money for this work but it will pay for itself in another way, other ways. II. *vbl s.* 1. **Bezahlen**, *n. in vbl senses.* 2. **Bezahlung**, *f.* (a) = II. 1; *also:* payment (of money, debt, etc.); discharge, settlement (of debt, bill, etc.); payment (of employee, etc.); **volle, vollständige, restlose, B.**, payment, settlement, in full; **teilweise B.**, part payment, settlement; **bei B.**, on payment; (b) payment; remuneration; pay; **gegen B.**, against payment; **ohne B.**, without payment; **als B. für Ihre Dienste**, as payment, in remuneration, for your services; **B. annehmen**, to accept payment; **die B. bei dieser Firma ist schlecht**, the pay at, in, this firm is bad, this firm pays badly.

Bezahler, *m.* **-s/-,** payer.

bezähmbar, *a.* (of anger, curiosity, etc.) controllable, capable of being controlled, restrained.

bezähmen, *v.tr.* (a) *A. & Lit:* to tame (animal); to break in (horse); to subdue (the elements, etc.); (b) to master, control (one's passions, feelings); to subdue, curb, overcome (one's passions); to restrain, suppress (one's anger, curiosity, desire, etc.); to control (one's hunger, thirst, desire); **sich b.**, to control, restrain, oneself; **seine Zunge b.**, to curb, bridle, one's tongue; to put a curb, bridle, on one's tongue.

bezahnen. I. *v.tr.* 1. *Mec.E:* to tooth, cog, ratch (wheel, etc.). 2. *Nat.Hist:* **sich bezahnen**, to develop teeth; **bezahnt**, having teeth, with teeth. II. *vbl s.* **Bezahnung**, *f.* 1. *in vbl senses.* 2. *Coll.* (a) *Mec.E:* toothing, teeth (of wheel, etc.); (b) *Nat.Hist:* teeth (of animal, human being); dentition (of animal).

bezaubern. I. *v.tr.* (a) *A:* to bewitch (s.o.); to cast, put, a spell (up)on (s.o.), to lay (s.o.) under a spell; *B:* **und bezauberte das samaritische Volk**, and bewitched the people of Samaria;

(*b*) to captivate, charm (s.o.); to bewitch (s.o.), to turn (s.o.'s head); to enchant (s.o.); (*of beauty, etc.*) to entrance (s.o.); **ihre Schönheit bezaubert alle, sie bezaubert alle mit ihrer Schönheit,** her beauty turns everyone's head, entrances everybody, everybody is entranced by her beauty; **Musik, die das Ohr bezaubert,** music that charms the ear.

II. *vbl s.* **Bezauberung,** *f.* **1.** *in vbl senses; also:* enchantment. **2.** charm; spell.

III. *pr.p. & a.* **bezaubernd,** captivating, charming, delightful; bewitching; enchanting; entrancing; **mit bezaubernder Anmut,** with bewitching grace; **sie war von bezaubernder Anmut,** she was bewitchingly graceful; **bezauberndes Lächeln,** bewitching, captivating, enchanting, charming, smile; **bezaubernde Augen,** bewitching, arresting, eyes; **sie ist ein bezauberndes Kind,** she is an enchanting child; **bezaubernde Landschaft,** entrancing, enchanting, landscape; **der Frühling ist in dieser Gegend b.,** spring is enchanting in this area; **sie hatte ein bezauberndes Kleid an,** she was wearing a charming dress; **bezaubernde Schönheit,** entrancing beauty; **b. schön,** (*of pers., scenery, etc.*) bewitchingly beautiful; (*of picture, etc.*) entrancing, enchanting; **sie sieht heute b. aus,** she looks charming today; **er spielt b., sein Spiel ist b.,** his playing is enchanting; **sie singt b.,** she sings delightfully; **sie hat eine bezaubernde Stimme,** she has a delightful, charming, voice; **das Bezaubernde,** the charm (of a pers., scenery, voice, s.o.'s beauty, etc.).

bezeichnen. I. *v.tr.* (*a*) to mark, put a mark on (sth.), to sign, put a sign on (sth.); *For:* to mark, notch, blaze (trees); **einen Weg b.,** to mark out a path; to signpost a path; **bezeichneter Wanderweg,** marked-out walk; **schlecht bezeichnete Straße,** inadequately signposted road; **Wörter mit Akzenten b.,** to put the accents on words; **einen Ort auf der Karte b.,** to mark a place on the map; **sich mit dem Kreuz, mit dem Zeichen des Kreuzes, b.,** *abs.* **sich b.,** to sign oneself with the sign of the cross, to make the sign of the cross, to cross, sign, oneself; (*b*) to mark, indicate (sth.); *Mus: Pros:* to indicate (tempo, metre); **die Lücken sind durch Punkte, mit Punkten, bezeichnet,** the gaps are marked, indicated, shown, by dots; **die Ausgänge müssen deutlich durch Leuchtbuchstaben bezeichnet sein,** the exits must be clearly indicated by illuminated lettering; **Pfähle, die die Route bezeichnen,** posts marking the course; **Bach, der die Grenze eines Grundstücks bezeichnet,** stream that marks the boundary, bounds, of an estate; (*c*) **das bezeichnet seine Gesinnung,** that illustrates, is indicative of, significant of, his attitude of mind; *cp.* III; (*d*) to indicate (sth.); to appoint, name, fix (date, day, meeting-place, etc.); to set (a date, day); **auf die bezeichnete Weise,** in the manner indicated; **ich traf ihn an der bezeichneten Stelle,** I joined him at the appointed place; **zur bezeichneten Stunde,** at the hour indicated; **an dem bezeichneten Tag,** on the appointed day; **ich habe ihm das Haus, vor dem wir uns treffen wollen, genau bezeichnet,** I gave him precise details of the house in front of which we intend to meet; (*e*) to denominate, name, designate, give a name to (sth., s.o.); to describe (sth., s.o.); *Com:* to label (goods); **die unbekannte Größe mit (dem Buchstaben)** *x* **b.,** to call the unknown quantity *x*, to designate the unknown quantity by the letter *x*; **j-n mit dem Namen . . . b.,** to call s.o., refer to s.o., by the name of . . .; **j-n als Lügner b.,** to describe s.o. as a liar, to call s.o. a liar; **er ist als der großzügigste Mann seiner Zeit bezeichnet worden,** he has been described as, designated (as), the most generous man of his age; **Sie sind mir als fähiger Mann bezeichnet worden,** you have been described, pointed out, to me as a capable man; **er bezeichnet sich als Oberst, Philosoph,** he calls himself a colonel, a philosopher; **Regeln, die als willkürlich bezeichnet werden,** rules described, designated, as arbitrary; **man kann diese Erscheinungen auch anders b.,** one can give other names to these phenomena; **wie immer Sie es auch b. wollen,** by whatever name you call it; **etwas genau b.,** to state sth. in detail, precisely; to specify sth.; **die auf beiliegender Liste näher bezeichneten Gegenstände,** the objects specified in the enclosed list; (*f*) **Zahlen durch Buchstaben, Laute durch Symbole, b.,** to indicate, represent, numbers by letters, sounds by symbols; (*g*) to denote, signify, mean (sth.); **(der Buchstabe)** *x* **bezeichnet eine unbekannte Größe,** (the letter) *x* denotes, signifies, an unknown quantity; **das Wort bezeichnet in diesem Zusammenhang etwas ganz anderes,** the word denotes, means, something completely different in this context, in this context the word assumes, has, a completely different meaning.

II. *vbl s.* **1. Bezeichnen,** *n. in vbl senses.* **2. Bezeichnung,** *f.* (*a*)=II. 1; *also:* indication (of direction, tempo, metre, etc.); denotation (of sth. by sth.); **B. eines Lautes durch ein Symbol, einer Zahl durch einen Buchstaben,** representation, notation, of a sound by a symbol, a number by a letter; **genaue, nähere, B.,** detailed description, specification; (*b*) mark; sign; symbol; *Pros:* (accent, etc.) mark; *Mus:* indication (of tempo, etc.); **dynamische Bezeichnungen,** accent marks; (*c*) name, appellation, denomination; designation; term, expression; description, title, style (of pers., office); *Com:* name (of a firm); (trade) name; *Mth:* term, notation; **Bezeichnungen der verschiedenen Teile, für die verschiedenen Teile, einer Sache,** names of, for, the different parts of sth.; **eine andere B. für . . .,** another name for . . .; **ich kenne den Gegenstand nur unter der B. . . .,** I know the thing only as . . ., by, under, the name, designation, of . . .; **unter verschiedenen Bezeichnungen bekannt,** known by, under, several names, designations; **einer Pflanze eine neue B. geben,** to give a new name to a plant; **die B. 'der Gute' ist für ihn kaum gerechtfertigt,** the appellation 'the good' is hardly justified for him; **falsche B.,** wrong term, expression, designation; misnomer; **irreführende B.,** misleading term, name, description; **treffende B.,** apt term, description; (*d*)=**Bezeichnungsweise.**

III. *pr.p. & a.* **bezeichnend,** *in vbl senses; esp.* significant, indicative (**für,** of); typical, characteristic (**für,** of); **dieses Symptom ist b. für diese Krankheit,** this symptom is characteristic of this disease; **das ist b. für seine Gesinnung,** that is indicative, significant, of his attitude; **nichts ist bezeichnender für eines Menschen Charakter, als was er lächerlich findet,** nothing is more indicative, significant, of a man's character than what he finds laughable; **Handlung, die für den Mann b. ist,** action that is typical, characteristic, of the man, that characterizes the man; **das ist b. für ihn,** that is typical of him, that is just like him; **das war (ein)mal wieder b.!** that was just typical!

Bezeichnungsschild, *n.* label; (tie-on) tag.

Bezeichnungssystem, *n.*=**Bezeichnungsweise.**

Bezeichnungsweise, *f.* nomenclature; *Mth: Mus: etc:* notation.

bezeigen. I. *v.tr.* (*a*) to show, display, exhibit, manifest (a quality, an emotion); **seine Freude, seinen Kummer, b.,** to show one's joy, one's grief; **j-m seine Dankbarkeit b.,** to show, express, give expression to, one's gratitude to s.o.; **j-m seine Teilnahme b.,** to show one's sympathy to s.o.; **seine Hochachtung, Bewunderung, für j-n b.,** to profess, show, one's high regard, admiration, for s.o.; (*b*) **j-m Ehre b.,** to pay, do, honour to s.o., to honour s.o.; (*c*) **sich freundlich, gefällig, b.,** to show oneself friendly, obliging.

II. *vbl s.* **1. Bezeigen,** *n.* (*a*) *in vbl senses;* (*b*) *A:* behaviour, conduct; attitude. **2. Bezeigung,** *f.* (*a*) *in vbl senses; also:* manifestation, display, exhibition (of a quality, an emotion); expression (of gratitude, sympathy, etc.); (*b*) sign, manifestation, expression, demonstration (of gratitude, etc.).

Bezette [be·'tsɛtə], *f.* -/-n. *Dy:* bezetta.

bezeugen. I. *v.tr.* **1.** (*a*) (*of pers.*) to attest (sth.), to bear testimony, to bear witness, to testify, to (sth.); **b., daß etwas wahr ist,** to attest, testify, that sth. is true; *B:* **und der das gesehen hat, der hat es bezeuget,** and he that saw it bare record; (*b*) (*of document, etc.*) to attest (sth.); to provide evidence of (sth.); **die Urkunde bezeugt (die Tatsache), daß . . .,** the document attests the fact that . . .; **seine Großmut ist in vielen zeitgenössischen Quellen bezeugt,** his magnanimity is attested by many contemporary sources, there is evidence of his magnanimity in many contemporary sources; **das Wort ist für das 6. Jahrhundert v. Chr. inschriftlich bezeugt,** there is epigraphical evidence of, inscriptions prove, the occurrence of the word in the 6th century B.C.; **diese Darstellung ist nur literarisch bezeugt,** we know this iconography from literary sources only, there is only literary evidence of this iconography; **ein Volksbrauch, der schon für das Altertum bezeugt ist,** a custom known to have existed in antiquity; **seine Autorschaft ist sicher bezeugt, nicht sicher bezeugt,** his authorship is definitely attested, not definitely attested, there is definite evidence for, proof of, no definite evidence for, proof of, his authorship; (*c*) (*of thg*) to show (sth.), to attest (sth.), to bear witness, to bear testimony, to testify, to (sth.); **eine Arbeit, die seine gründliche Kenntnis des Gegenstandes bezeugt,** a work that testifies to his deep knowledge of the subject; **Antwort, die einen urteilsfähigen Geist bezeugt,** answer that shows a judicious mind; **seine Schriften bezeugen seinen Fleiß,** his writings attest, bear witness to, his industry; **Auswahl, die seinen guten Geschmack bezeugt,** selection that shows his good taste. **2.** *occ.*=**bezeigen.**

II. *vbl s.* **1. Bezeugen,** *n. in vbl senses.* **2. Bezeugung,** *f.* (*a*)=II. 1; *also:* attestation; (*b*)=**Bezeigung,** *q.v. under* **bezeigen II.**

bezichtigen. I. *v.tr.* **j-n etwas** *gen.* **b.,** to accuse s.o. of sth.; to charge, tax, s.o. with sth.; **j-n der Feigheit b.,** to accuse s.o. of, charge s.o. with, cowardice; **j-n des Hochverrats b.,** to accuse s.o. of, charge s.o. with, high treason; **er leugnet die Handlungen, deren er bezichtigt wird, deren man ihn bezichtigt,** he denies the actions of which he is accused; **er bezichtigte mich der Undankbarkeit,** he taxed me with ingratitude; **er wurde bezichtigt, mit den Aufständischen im Bunde zu sein,** he was accused of, charged, taxed, with, being in league with the rebels.

II. *vbl s.* **1. Bezichtigen,** *n. in vbl senses.* **2. Bezichtigung,** *f.* (*a*)=II. 1; *also:* accusation; (*b*) charge, accusation.

beziehbar, *a.* **1.** (*of goods, etc.*) obtainable. **2.** (*of house, flat, etc.*) ready for occupation, ready to move into. **3.** (subject, etc.) that can be related, referred; referable (**auf**+*acc.*, to).

beziehen. I. *v.tr.* (*strong*) **1.** (*a*) to cover (upholstered furniture, eiderdown, etc.) (with material); to put cover on (soft chair, cushion, eiderdown, etc.); **einen Sessel mit Plüsch b.,** to cover an armchair with plush; **ein Kissen mit Seide b.,** to cover a cushion with silk; **eine Steppdecke b.,** (i) to cover an eiderdown (with material); (ii) to put a linen cover on an eiderdown; **Polstermöbel, eine Steppdecke, neu b.,** to re-cover upholstered furniture, an eiderdown; **ein Kopfkissen (frisch) b.,** to put a clean case, slip, on a pillow; **das Bett (frisch) b.,** to put clean linen on the bed, to change the (bed-)linen; **ein frisch bezogenes Bett,** a bed with clean linen; **Knöpfe b.,** to cover buttons (with material, leather); **bezogene Knöpfe,** (self-)covered buttons; (*b*) to string (violin, etc.); (*c*) (*of deity, etc.*) to cover (the sky) (with clouds); (*of clouds*) to cover, overcast, obscure (the sky); **der Himmel ist (mit Wolken) bezogen,** the sky is dark with clouds, has clouded over, is cloudy. **2.** (*a*) to move into, to occupy (house, flat); **das Haus kann Anfang nächsten Jahres bezogen werden,** the house will be ready to move into, for occupation, at the beginning of next year; **die neuen Mieter haben die Wohnung soeben erst bezogen,** the new tenants have only just moved into the flat; **eine Wohnung, ein Haus, wieder b.,** to reoccupy, to resume occupation of, to reinstall oneself in, a flat, a house; (*b*) *Mil:* (*of troops*) **ein Lager b.,** to go into camp; **die Winterquartiere b.,** to go into winter quarters; **eine Stellung b.,** to occupy, move into, a position; **sie bezogen vorbereitete Stellungen,** they moved into prepared positions; **sie bezogen ihre alten Stellungen wieder,** they reinstalled themselves in, they reoccupied, their old positions; **die Wache b.,** to mount guard; to go on guard; (*c*) *Sch:* **eine Universität b.,** to enter, go to, a university; **1930 bezog er die Universität Oxford, Cambridge,** in 1930 he went up to Oxford, Cambridge; **nach dem Abgang von der Schule bezog er die Universität Heidelberg,** on leaving school he went to Heidelberg University, he began his studies at Heidelberg (University). **3.** to buy, get (goods, supplies), to be supplied with (goods); to take, get (newspaper); to subscribe to, to be a subscriber to (periodical, etc.); to draw, receive (salary, pension, pay); **seine Waren von, bei, j-m b.,** to get one's supplies from, to be supplied with one's goods by, s.o.; **wir beziehen alle unsere Lebensmittel aus, von, London,** we get all our groceries from London; **Waren aus dem Ausland b.,** to get, be supplied with, goods from abroad; **ich beziehe meine Zigarren immer von, bei, der gleichen Firma,** I always get, buy, my cigars from the same firm; **einen bestimmten Artikel regelmäßig b.,** to have a standing order for a certain article; **durch den Einzelhandel, durch alle Buchhandlungen, zu b.,** stocked by all

retailers, booksellers, obtainable at, from, can be bought from, all retailers, booksellers; **direkt vom Verlag, durch die Post, zu b.**, obtainable direct from the publishers, obtainable (by order) through the post; **regelmäßige Einkünfte von, aus, etwas b.**, to draw, get, a regular income from, out of, sth.; **er bezieht sein Wissen nur aus Enzyklopädien**, he gets all his knowledge from encyclopedias; *F:* **Prügel, Schläge, b.**, to get a hiding; *Fin:* **neue Aktien b.**, (to exercise the right) to buy new shares. **4.** *Fin:* **j-n b.**, to draw a bill, *abs.* to draw, (up)on s.o.; **j-s Konto b.**, to draw on s.o.'s account. **5. etwas auf etwas** *acc.* **b.**, to relate sth. to sth.; to connect sth. with sth., to link sth. up with sth.; **alles auf sich b.**, to view everything in terms of self; to take everything personally; **verschiedene Tätigkeiten eng aufeinander b.**, to bring different activities into close relationship; **ein Ereignis auf eine bestimmte Periode b.**, to assign, refer, an event to a certain period; **wenn man diesen Satz auf das Vorhergehende bezieht, . . .**, if one takes this sentence in relation to, connection with, what goes before . . .; *Gram:* if you relate this sentence to the preceding one . . .; **etwas falsch, richtig, b.**, to draw the wrong, right, inference; *Gram:* to put sth. in a false, correct, relation; **diese Stelle kann auch anders bezogen werden**, this passage can stand in a quite different relationship; **(zwei) Tatsachen aufeinander b.**, to relate (two) facts to one another, to correlate (two) facts; **man könnte diese Bemerkung auf ihn b.**, one could take this remark as referring, relating, to him; **das war nicht auf dich bezogen**, that was not aimed at, intended for, meant for, you, *F:* that was not a hit, dig, at you.

II. **sich beziehen. 1.** (*of sky*) to cloud over, to become cloudy; *impers.* **es bezieht sich**, it is getting cloudy, overcast, it is clouding over. **2.** (*a*) (*of pers.*) **sich auf etwas** *acc.* **b.**, to refer to sth.; **sich auf j-n, auf j-s Aussage, b.**, to refer to s.o., s.o.'s evidence; **sich auf eine Autorität b.**, to refer to an authority; **sich auf eine Urkunde b.**, to refer to a document; (*b*) (*of thg*) **sich auf etwas** *acc.* **b.**, to relate, refer, to sth., to bear a relation to sth., to be related to sth., to have reference to sth.; **eine Stelle, die sich auf eine andere bezieht**, passage relating, related, that relates, refers, has reference, to another; **Fragen, die sich auf einen Gegenstand beziehen**, questions relating, referring, to a subject; **Auskunft, die sich auf eine Sache, Person, bezieht**, information relating, referring, to a matter, a person; **die Anschuldigung bezieht sich auf schwerwiegende Handlungen**, the charge relates to serious acts; **das bezieht sich in keiner Weise auf die gegenwärtige Lage**, that bears, has, no relation, that is in no way related, to the present situation; **die Dokumente, die sich auf diese Angelegenheit beziehen**, the documents relating to this matter, the relevant documents; **diese Beschreibung kann sich nur auf die Schlacht bei X b.**, this description can only refer to the battle of X; **diese Bemerkung bezieht sich auf dich**, this remark refers to you; this remark is aimed at you, intended for, meant for, you, *F:* is a hit, dig, at you; **das Relativpronomen bezieht sich auf das Subjekt des Hauptsatzes**, the relative pronoun refers to the subject of the main clause.

III. *vbl s.* **1. Beziehen,** *n. in vbl senses; also: Mil:* occupation (of position); *cp.* **Bezug** 1, 2. **2. Beziehung,** *f.* (*a*)=III. 1; (*b*) relation, connection; *Phil: Mth:* relation; **B. zwischen Ursache und Wirkung**, relation, connection, between cause and effect; **des Menschen B. zur Umwelt**, man's relation(ship) to his environment; **enge B. zwischen zwei Tatsachen, zweier Tatsachen zueinander**, close connection between two facts; **wechselseitige B.**, correlation; interrelation; **B. zu etwas haben, in B. zu etwas stehen**, to be related to sth., to bear a relation to sth., to have reference to sth.; **keine B. zu etwas haben, in keiner B. zu etwas stehen**, to bear no relation, to be out of all relation, to sth.; **die beiden Ereignisse haben keine B., stehen in keiner B., zueinander**, the two events are totally, entirely, unconnected, unrelated; **Tatsachen, die in direkter B. zueinander stehen**, facts closely bound up with one another, closely connected facts; **Tatsachen ohne B. zueinander**, unrelated facts; **verschiedene Tätigkeiten in enge B. zueinander setzen, bringen**, to bring different activities into close relationship; **ohne B. zum Gegenstand**, irrelevant (to the subject); without any, having no, bearing on the subject; without reference to the subject; **die Frage steht in enger B. zu . . .**, the question bears closely upon . . ., the question is intimately connected, bound up, linked up, with . . .; **ich habe keine innere B. zu meinem Bruder**, my brother and I have no real understanding for one another; **ich habe keine (innere) B. zu Wagner**, Wagner does not mean anything to me; (*c*) respect, regard; connection; **in B. auf . . .**, with respect, regard, to . . .; **in dieser B.**, in this respect, in this connection; **in jeder B.**, in all respects, in every respect, in every way; **in vieler B.**, in many respects; **in mancher B., in gewisser B.**, in some, in certain, respects; **in anderer B.**, in other respects, otherwise; **in keiner B.**, in no respect; **die Gemeinde ist in religiöser B. sehr rege**, the community has a very active religious life; **in künstlerischer B. läßt das Gebäude viel zu wünschen übrig**, artistically, from the artistic point of view, the building leaves much to be desired; **der Hafen ist in strategischer B. von besonderer Bedeutung**, strategically, from a strategic point of view, the port is especially important; **überlegen in B. auf Intelligenz**, superior in respect, in point, of intelligence; **es gibt Schwierigkeiten in B. auf den Wortlaut**, there are difficulties in connection with, with respect to, regarding, about, the wording; *Gram:* **Akkusativ der B.**, accusative of respect; *cp.* **Bezug** 3; (*d*) *pl.* **Beziehungen**, (*between persons*) relations; intercourse; connection; (*between thgs*) connections, links; affinities; similarities, corresponding features; (*between persons and thgs*) connections; **menschliche Beziehungen**, human relations, intercourse; **die Beziehungen zwischen der französischen und der deutschen Literatur des Mittelalters**, the connections, links, affinities, between French and German mediaeval literature; **die Beziehungen zwischen den verschiedenen Legenden von der Sintflut**, the similarities, affinities, between, the corresponding features in, the common features of, the various legends of the Flood; **die Beziehungen Goethes zur Deutschen Romantik**, Goethe's connections with, Goethe and, the German Romantic School; **wechselseitige Beziehungen zwischen zwei Ländern**, mutual relations between two countries; **in Beziehungen zu j-m treten, Beziehungen zu j-m aufnehmen**, to enter into, to establish, relations with s.o.; **Beziehungen zu j-m haben, unterhalten**, to have relations, dealings, with s.o.; **zu j-m in guten Beziehungen stehen**, to be on good terms with s.o.; **freundschaftliche Beziehungen**, friendly relations; **gute Beziehungen zu Frankreich**, good relations, good understanding, with France; **geschäftliche Beziehungen**, business connections; **in geschäftliche Beziehungen zu einer Firma treten**, to open up a business connection with a firm; **alle Beziehungen zu j-m abbrechen**, to break off all relations, all connections, all dealings, with s.o., *F:* to drop s.o.; **gespannte Beziehungen**, strained relations; **diplomatische Beziehungen aufnehmen, abbrechen, wieder aufnehmen**, to establish, break off, re-establish, diplomatic relations; (*e*) **(gute) Beziehungen haben**, to have influential friends, to have good connections, to have influence; **seine Beziehungen spielen lassen**, to make use of one's connections, to pull strings; **er hat alle seine Beziehungen spielen lassen**, he pulled every string; **mit Beziehungen kann man alles erreichen**, you can do anything with a little string-pulling; **er verdankt seine Stellung nur seinen Beziehungen**, he owes his position to influence; **ein Mann mit Beziehungen**, a man with good connections, with influence; **er hat keine Beziehungen im Außenministerium**, he does not know anybody with influence at the Foreign Office; **er hat überall (gute) Beziehungen**, he has influential friends, he has contacts, everywhere.

IV. *p.p. & a.* **bezogen**, *in vbl senses; esp.* **1.** relative; related; **wechselseitig, aufeinander, b.**, interrelated; correlative; **wechselseitig, aufeinander, b. sein**, to be interrelated; to be in correlation, to correlate; *Gram:* **bezogene Zeit**, relative tense. **2.** *Ph:* specific (weight). **3.** *Fin:* **Bezogene** *m, f*, acceptor (of bill), drawee.

beziehentlich, *adv.*=**beziehungsweise** 2.

Bezieher, *m.* **-s/-**, subscriber (to newspaper, etc.); *Fin:* **B. neuer Aktien**, buyer of, subscriber to, new shares.

Beziehung, *f. see* **beziehen** III.

Beziehungsfürwort, *n. Gram:* relative pronoun.

beziehungslos, *a.* (*of events, facts, etc.*) unrelated; unconnected; **b. zu etwas**, without relation, connection, to sth.; irrelative to sth.; irrelevant to sth.; *adv.* **Kinder setzen oft Wörter b. nebeneinander**, children often put words together without connecting them; **die beiden Sätze stehen b. nebeneinander**, the two sentences stand unconnected side by side.

Beziehungslosigkeit, *f.* unconnectedness, unrelatedness.

Beziehungssatz, *m. Gram:* (*a*) relative clause; (*b*) antecedent.

beziehungsweise, *adv.* **1.** relatively; in certain respects; with (certain) qualifications; in a qualified sense. **2.** (*abbr.* **bzw.**) respectively; or; or . . . as the case may be; **die Löhne der ungelernten und gelernten Arbeiter werden um 3 b. 5 Mark wöchentlich erhöht**, the wages of unskilled and skilled workers will be raised by 3 and 5 marks respectively; **der Betrag ist auf ein Bank- b. Sparkassenkonto einzuzahlen**, the amount should be paid in to a bank or savings bank account (as the case may be). **3.** *F:* or rather; **ich b. mein Mann**, I, or rather my husband.

Beziehungswort, *n.* **-(e)s/-wörter.** *Gram:* (*a*) antecedent; (*b*) relational word.

Beziehungswortsatz, *m. Gram:* relative clause.

Beziehungszahl, *f. Statistics:* relative number.

beziffern. I. *v.tr.* **1.** (*a*) to number (lines in book, etc.); (*b*) *Mus:* to figure (bass); **bezifferter Baß**, figured bass. **2.** (*a*) to estimate, put (sth.) (**auf**+*acc.*, at); **die Geschäftsleitung beziffert den Verlust auf zehntausend Mark**, the management estimates, puts, the loss at ten thousand marks; (*b*) **sich beziffern**, to amount (to), to work out (at); to number; **Transaktionen, die sich auf mehrere Millionen Pfund beziffern**, transactions amounting to several million pounds; **die Gesamtsumme beziffert sich auf sechs Pfund**, the total works out at, amounts to, six pounds; **sie beziffern sich auf mehrere tausend**, they number several thousand.

II. *vbl s.* **1. Beziffern,** *n. in vbl senses.* **2. Bezifferung,** *f.* (*a*)=II. 1; (*b*) numbers; numbering; (*c*) *Mus:* figuring (of thorough-bass).

Bézigue [beˈziːk], *f.* **-s/.** *Cards:* bezique.

bezinnen, *v.tr.* to crenel(l)ate, embattle (wall); **bezinnte Mauer**, crenel(l)ated wall, embattled wall.

Bezirk, *m.* **-(e)s/-e. 1.** district; region; *esp.* administrative district of German and Austrian provinces (*in former Prussian territory comprising several sub-districts, in Bavaria approx.*= county); division, administrative *or* postal district of large town (*esp. in Vienna approx.*= borough *in London*); *Mil:*=**Wehrbezirk**; *Jur:*= **Amtsbezirk**; *cp.* **Wahlbezirk. 2.** field, scope, domain, sphere (of science, activity, etc.); **das gehört in den B. der Literargeschichte**, it falls within the domain, department, of literary history; **das liegt nicht in meinem B.**, it does not come within my domain, province, sphere.

Bezirks-, *comb.fm.* regional . . .; area . . .; **Bezirksleitung** *f*, regional administration (of association, etc.); **Bezirksdirektor** *m*, area manager (of insurance firm, etc.).

Bezirksamt, *n. Adm:* (*esp. in Bavaria*) **1.** district, *approx.*=county. **2.** regional local authority, *approx.*=county council. **3.** headquarters of regional local government, *approx.*=county offices.

Bezirksarzt, *m.* medical officer (of administrative district).

Bezirkshauptmann, *m. Adm:* (*in Austria*) chief officer of the district administration.

Bezirkshauptmannschaft, *f. Adm:* (*in Austria*) administrative district (*subdivision of a* 'Land').

Bezirkskommando, *n. Mil:*=**Wehrbezirkskommando.**

Bezirkspostamt, *n.* district post office.

Bezirksregierung, *f.* regional local authority, district administration.

bezirksweise, *a. & adv.* by districts; (division, etc.) into districts.

bezirzen, *v.tr. F:* (*of woman*) to allure, bewitch (man); to ensnare (man).

Bezoar [beˈtsoːˈaːr], *m.* **-s/-e**, bezoar, bezoar stone.

Bezoarwurzel, *f. Bot: Pharm:* contrayerva(-root).

Bezoarziege, *f. Z:* pasan(g), bezoar-goat.

bezog, bezöge, bezogen *see* **beziehen.**

Bezogenheit, *f.* relatedness; relativity.

Bezug, *m.* **-(e)s/-̈e. 1.** moving in (to house, flat), occupation (of house, flat, *Mil:* position); (*of house, etc.*) **fertig zum B.**, ready to move into, ready for occupation. **2.** buying, purchase (of goods, supplies); being supplied (with goods); subscribing, subscription (to newspaper, etc.); drawing (of salary, income, pension); **dieser Gutschein berechtigt zum B. von . . .**, this coupon entitles the holder to purchase . . .;

bei B. durch die Post, if delivered by post; B. von Waren aus dem Ausland, purchase of goods from abroad; drawing of supplies from abroad; bei regelmäßigem B., with, for, a standing order; bei B. von 20 Stück wird ein Diskont von 10% gewährt, a discount of 10% is given with orders of 20; berechtigt zum B. einer Rente, entitled to draw a pension; *Fin:* B. von neuen Aktien, buying of new shares. 3. (*a*) reference; B. auf etwas nehmen, (*of pers.*) to refer to sth.; (*of thg*) to relate, refer, to sth., to bear a relation, to be related, to have reference, to sth.; mit B. auf . . ., with reference to . . . , referring to . . .; B. nehmend, mit B., auf mein Schreiben vom 20. d.M., with reference, referring to, my letter of the 20th inst.; die Dokumente, die auf diese Angelegenheit B. nehmen, haben, the documents relating to this matter, the relevant documents; (*b*) *prep. phr.* (*spelt with small b*) in b. auf . . ., with respect, regard, to . . . , as regards . . ., regarding . . . , respecting . . . , about . . . , as to . . . , as concerns . . . , concerning . . . , with reference to . . .; in connection with . . .; in respect of . . .; überlegen in b. auf Intelligenz, superior in respect of, in point of, intelligence; es gibt Schwierigkeiten in b. auf den Wortlaut, there are difficulties in connection with, with respect to, regarding, about, the wording; Verhandlungen in b. auf ein Bündnis, negotiations regarding, relative to, an alliance; in b. auf das Wetter hatten wir Glück, we were lucky as far as the weather was concerned, regarding, concerning, with respect to, the weather, with the weather; in b. auf Ihre Anfrage, regarding your enquiry; was sind seine Absichten in b. auf dich? what are his intentions regarding you? ich habe nichts Neues in b. auf diese Sache erfahren, I have learnt nothing new regarding this matter. *Cp.* beziehen III. 4. *pl.* Bezüge, (*a*) earnings (including allowances, fees, etc.); emoluments; (*b*) *occ. Com:* purchases; orders. 5. (*a*) covering, cover (of upholstered furniture, eiderdown, etc.); loose cover; dust-cover; (cushion) cover; (pillow-, bolster-)case; pillow-slip; (*b*) (set of) strings (of violin, etc.).

bezüglich. 1. *a.* relating, referring; relative; relevant; (auf+*acc.*, to); alle auf diese Angelegenheit, darauf, bezüglichen Dokumente, all documents relating to this matter, to it, all relevant documents; *Gram:* bezügliches Fürwort, relative pronoun *or* adjective. 2. *prep.* (+*gen.*) (*abbr.* bez.) concerning, about, regarding, respecting; with respect, regard, to; as to; es gibt Schwierigkeiten b. des Wortlauts, there are difficulties in connection with, with respect to, regarding, about, the wording; Verhandlungen b. eines Bündnisses, negotiations regarding, relative to, an alliance; b. des Wetters hatten wir Glück, we were lucky as far as the weather was concerned, regarding, concerning, with respect to, the weather, with the weather; b. Ihrer Anfrage, regarding your enquiry; ich habe nichts Neues b. dieser Sache erfahren, I have learnt nothing new regarding this matter.

Bezugnahme, *f.* -/. *Com:* unter B. auf mein Schreiben vom 20. d.M., with reference, referring, to my letter of the 20th inst.

Bezugsaktien, *f.pl.* shares of a new issue.

Bezugsanweisung, *f. Com:* order to deliver goods; authorisation to collect goods.

Bezugsbedingungen, *f.pl. Com:* terms of supply.

bezugsberechtigt, *a.* entitled to draw (pension, etc.); entitled to receive (supplementary rations, etc.); Bezugsberechtigte *m, f,* person entitled to a pension, to supplementary rations, etc.; *Ins:* beneficiary.

Bezugsdauer, *f. Com:* period elapsing between the dispatch and delivery (of goods).

Bezugsebene, *f. Surv: etc:* reference plane; datum level.

Bezugsgenossenschaft, *f.* agricultural co-operative purchasing association.

Bezugskosten, *pl. Com:* delivery costs.

Bezugslinie, *f. Surv: etc:* reference line; datum line.

Bezugsmarke, *f.* (food-)coupon.

Bezugspreis, *m.* price (for newspaper, etc.); subscription (price) (for periodical, etc.); *Com:* price delivered.

Bezugspunkt, *m. Surv: etc:* point of reference; datum point.

Bezugsquelle, *f.* source of supply; supplier; können Sie mir eine B. für diesen Artikel nennen? can you give me the name of a supplier for this article?

Bezugsrecht, *n. Fin:* (application) right(s); ohne B., ex rights; mit B., cum rights.

Bezugssatz, *m. Gram:* relative clause.

Bezug(s)schein, *m.* 1. (ration, etc.) coupon; permit (entitling holder to purchase supplementary rations, etc.); *Mil:* indent form. 2. *Fin:* scrip. 3.=Bezugsanweisung.

bezug(s)scheinpflichtig, *a.* (*of goods*) rationed.

Bezugstag, *m. Fin:* 1. day of issue (of new shares). 2. day from which the right to buy new shares may be exercised.

Bezugsweise, *f. Com:* method of obtaining (goods, periodicals, etc.).

bezwecken, *v.tr.* etwas b., (*of pers.*) to aim at sth., to intend sth., to have sth. in view, in mind; (*of thg*) to aim at sth., to have sth. for, as, an object; was bezwecken Sie mit Ihrer Reise? what is the object of your journey? wir haben nichts Böses damit bezweckt, we intended no harm, we did not mean any harm; ohne etwas Böses zu b., with no ill intent, without intending any harm; was bezweckst du damit? what is your objective? what are you aiming at? er bezweckt damit, zu . . ., his aim is to . . .; was bezweckt das alles? what is the object of all this? what is the end in view? was bezwecken diese Fragen? what is the aim, purpose, object, of these questions? Maßnahme, die bezweckt, Mißstände zu beheben, measure intended to remove abuses; dieses Gesetz bezweckt zwei Dinge, this law has two objects, aims, in view; Erlaß, der bezweckt, bestehende Ungerechtigkeiten zu mildern, decree that aims at, aiming at, alleviating existing injustices; dieser Brief bezweckt, Sie darüber in Kenntnis zu setzen, daß . . ., the object of this letter is to inform you that . . . .

bezweifelbar, *a.* questionable, open to doubt, doubtful.

bezweifeln, *v.tr.* etwas b., to doubt, to question, to have (one's) doubts about, sth., to be doubtful of, as to, about, sth.; to call, bring, sth. into question; sein Mut konnte nicht bezweifelt werden, war nicht zu b., ließ sich nicht b., his courage was beyond all question; Tatsachen, die nicht bezweifelt werden können, facts beyond doubt, unquestionable facts; das kann nicht mehr bezweifelt werden, läßt sich nicht mehr b., there is no longer any doubt about it; die Aufrichtigkeit ihres Empfangs ließ sich nicht b., konnte nicht bezweifelt werden, there was no doubting the sincerity of their welcome; den Wert einer Sache b., to question the value of sth.; seine Ehrlichkeit ist nie bezweifelt worden, his honesty has never been in question, never been doubted; ich bezweifle es, I doubt it; ich bezweifle, daß ich das gesagt habe, I doubt whether I said that; ich bezweifle sehr, möchte sehr b., daß er stark genug ist, I doubt, have my doubts, whether he is strong enough; ich habe nie bezweifelt, daß er arbeiten kann, wenn er will, I have never doubted that he can work if he wants to, wishes to; ich bezweifle nicht, daß er dir helfen wird, I do not doubt (but) that he will help you; I am confident, *Lit:* I doubt not, that he will help you; ich bezweifle (sehr), daß das wahr ist, I have my doubts as to, about, this being true, I am (very) doubtful whether this is true; es ist nicht zu b., daß . . ., it is not to be questioned, doubted, that . . . .

bezwingbar, *a.* conquerable; controllable (passion, etc.).

bezwingen. I. *v.tr.* (*strong*) to vanquish, conquer, overcome, worst (enemy, etc.); to conquer (town, fortress, etc.); to overcome, master, fight down, get the better of (feelings, difficulties, etc.); to master, control (passions, one's feelings); to conquer (mountain); sich b., to command oneself, to keep oneself under control, to restrain oneself; to keep one's feelings in check, under control, to control, restrain, one's feelings; to keep down one's anger, one's impatience, etc.; seine Angst b., to get the better of, to conquer, to overcome, one's fears; seinen Zorn b., to master, keep down, get the better of, one's anger; ich habe mich bezwungen und nichts gesagt, I restrained my feelings and said nothing; seine Heiterkeit b., to restrain one's mirth.

II. *vbl s.* Bezwingen *n.*, Bezwingung *f. in vbl senses; also:* conquest (of fortress, mountain, etc.).

Bezwinger, *m.* -s/-, vanquisher; conqueror.

Bhang [baŋ], *m.* -s/. *Bot: etc:* b(h)ang, Indian hemp, hashish.

Bi-, bi-, *pref.* (*a*) (*having two*) bi-; bimanisch, bimanous; (*b*) (*double, doubly, of two*) bi-, di-; bikonkav, biconcave; Bichromat *n*, bichromate, dichromate; Biduum *n*, space of two days; (*c*) (*occurring every two . . .*) bi-; biennal, biennial.

bibbern, *v.i.* (*haben*) *F:* (*of pers.*) to shake, tremble (with fear), to shiver (with cold); er bibberte am ganzen Leib, *F:* he was all of a tremble.

Bibel, *f.* -/-n, Bible; die Bibel, the Bible, the Scriptures; *F:* Marx' 'Kapital' ist seine B., Marx's 'Capital' is his bible.

Bibelanstalt, *f.* Bible Society.

Bibelausleger, *m.* commentator on the Bible, Bible commentator, exegete (of the Bible).

Bibelauslegung, *f.* interpretation of the Bible, biblical commentary, exegesis (of the Bible).

Bibelchrist, *m.* Bible Christian.

Bibeldruck, *m.* (*esp. early*) edition of the Bible.

Bibeldruckpapier, *n.* Bible paper, India paper.

Bibeleid, *m.* Bible oath; oath sworn upon the Bible.

Bibelerklärer, *m.*=Bibelausleger.

Bibelerklärung, *f.*=Bibelauslegung.

bibelfest, *a.* well versed, deeply versed, in the Bible, in the Scriptures, in Scripture.

Bibelforscher, *m.* student of the Bible; *esp. Rel:* Ernste Bibelforscher *pl*, Jehovah's Witnesses.

bibelgemäß, *a.* scriptural; in accordance with, in conformity to, with, the Bible, the Scriptures.

Bibelgemäßheit, *f.* conformity to, with, the Bible, the Scriptures, Scripture.

Bibelgesellschaft, *f.*=Bibelanstalt.

bibelgläubig, *a.* believing in the Bible; adhering to the letter of the Bible.

Bibelgläubigkeit, *f.* adherence to the letter of the Bible, literal adherence to the Scriptures; biblicism, scripturalism.

Bibelinstitut, *n.* Päpstliches B., Pontifical Biblical Institute.

Bibelkanon, der, the (sacred) canon, the canonical books.

Bibelkenner, *m.* man well versed in Scripture, the Scriptures; scripturalist; biblical critic.

Bibelkommission, *f.* Päpstliche B., Pontifical Biblical Commission.

Bibelkonkordanz, *f.* concordance of, to, the Bible.

Bibelkritik, *f.* biblical criticism; textual criticism (of the Bible).

bibelkundig, *a.*=bibelfest.

Bibelleser, *m.* (*a*) Bible-reader, reader of the Bible; (*b*) Scripture reader; *A:* Bible-reader (amongst the poor and sick).

bibelmäßig, *a.*=bibelgemäß.

Bibelmäßigkeit, *f.* Bibelgemäßheit.

Bibelpapier, *n.*=Bibeldruckpapier.

Bibelregal, *n. Mus:* regal.

Bibelspruch, *m.* verse, text, from the Bible, (Scripture, biblical) text.

Bibelstelle, *f.* passage, text, in, from, the Bible.

Bibelstunde, *f.* Bible-class; *Sch:* scripture lesson.

Bibelübersetzung, *f.* translation of the Bible; die Luther(i)sche B., Luthers B., Luther's translation of the Bible.

Bibelverbot, *n. Hist:* prohibition (by the Catholic Church) of Bible-reading in the vernacular.

Bibelvers, *m.* verse of, from, the Bible.

Biber, *m.* -s/-. 1. (*a*) *Z:* beaver; (*b*) *F:* man with a beard, *F:* beaver. 2. beaver fur. 3. *Tex:* beaver (cloth); beaverette.

Biberbau, *m.* beaver's lodge.

Biberbaum, *m. Bot:* magnolia(-tree), beaver-tree.

Biberburg, *f.* beaver's lodge.

Biberente, *f. Orn:* goosander, merganser, dundiver.

Biberette [biːbəˈrɛtə], *f.* -/-n. *Com:* imitation beaver (fur), beaverette.

Biberfell, *n. Leath:* castor; (*fur*) beaver(-skin); fettes B., beaver in season; gerupftes B., plucked (unhaired) beaver; tiefgeschorenes B., sheared beaver.

Bibergeil, *n.* -(e)s/. *Pharm:* castor(eum).

Bibergeildrüse, *f.* castor gland.

Bibergeilen, *f.pl.* beaver-stones.

Bibergeilkampfer, *m.* castorin.

Biberhahn, *m.* turkey-cock.

Biberhödchen, Biberhödlein, *n.* -s/. *Bot:* pilewort.

Biberhut, *m. A:* beaver (hat), *F: A:* castor.

Biberin, *f.* -/-innen, female beaver, she-beaver.

Biberklee, *m. Bot:*=Bitterklee.

Biberkraut, *f. Bot:* skull-cap.

Bibernelle [biːbɐˈnɛlə], *f.* -/-n. *Bot:* burnet, blood-wort; pimpernel.

Biberpelz, *m.* beaver (fur).

Biberratte, *f. Z:* myopotamus, coyp(o)u, nutria.

Bibersack, *m.* castor sac.

Biberschwanz, *m.* (*a*) beaver's tail; (*b*) flat (roof-)tile, plain tile; (*c*) *Tls:* pad-saw.

Biberseehund, *m.* fur-seal.

Biberstoff, *m. Tex:* beaver (cloth).

Bibertaucher, Bibervogel, *m.*=Biberente.

Bibi, *m.* - *&* **-s/-s,** (man's) hat, *F:* titfer.
biblio- [biˑbliˑoˑ-], *comb.fm.* biblio-; **Bibliomane** *m,* bibliomaniac; **Bibliographie** *f,* bibliography.
Bibliograph [biˑbliˑoˑˈgraːf], *m.* **-en/-en,** bibliographer.
Bibliographie [biˑbliˑoˑgraˑˈfiː], *f.* **-/-n** [-ˈfiːən], bibliography.
Bibliographin, *f.* **-/-innen,** bibliographer.
bibliographisch [biˑbliˑoˑˈgraːfiʃ], *a.* bibliographic(al).
Bibliomane [biˑbliˑoˑˈmaːnə], *m., f.* **-n/-n,** bibliomaniac; *F:* bookworm.
Bibliomanie [biˑbliˑoˑmaˑˈniː], *f.* **-/.** bibliomania.
Bibliophile [biˑbliˑoˑˈfiːlə], *m., f.* **-n/-n** *& decl. as adj.* bibliophile, book-lover.
Bibliophilie [biˑbliˑoˑfiˑˈliː], *f.* **-/.** love of books.
Bibliothek [biˑbliˑoˑˈteːk], *f.* **-/-en,** library; **öffentliche B.,** lending library, public (lending) library.
Bibliothekar [biˑbliˑoˑteˑˈkaːr], *m.* **-s/-e,** librarian.
bibliothekarisch [biˑbliˑoˑteˑˈkaːriʃ], *a.* concerning libraries *or* librarians; library (purposes, etc.); librarian's (career, etc.).
Bibliotheksausgabe, *f.* library edition.
Bibliotheksdirektor, *m.* librarian (of University Library, etc.); director of a library.
Bibliothekseinband, *m.* library binding.
Bibliotheksgebäude, *n.* library (building).
Bibliothekssignatur, *f.* library mark, sign, stamp.
Bibliotheksverwaltung, *f.* library management, library administration.
Bibliothekswesen, *n.* librarianship; library affairs.
Bibliothekswissenschaft, *f.* (study of) librarianship; library science.
Bibliothekszeichen, *n.* = **Bibliothekssignatur.**
biblisch, *a.* biblical, scriptural; **die biblischen Geschichten, Erzählungen,** the Bible stories, the stories from the Bible; *Sch:* **biblische Geschichte,** scripture; *see also* **Alter**[2] 1 (*c*).
Biblizismus [biˑbliˑˈtsismus], *m.* **-/.** biblicism.
Bichlorid [biˑkloˑˈriːt], *n.* **-(e)s/-e** [-s, -ˈriːdəs/ -ˈriːdə]. *Ch:* bichlorid(e), dichlorid(e).
Bichromat [biˑkroˑˈmaːt], *n.* **-(e)s/-e.** *Ch:* bichromate, dichromate.
Bichromatelement, *n. El:* bichromate cell.
bichromatisch [biˑkroˑˈmaːtiʃ], *a.* bichrome, bichromatic.
Bicinie [biˑˈtsiːniə], *f.* **-/-n.** *Mus: A:* two-part song.
Bickbeere, *f. Bot: North G.Dial:* whortleberry, bilberry.
Bicksand, *m.* scouring sand.
biderb [biˑˈdɛrp], *a.* **1.** = **bieder. 2.** (*of pers.*) coarse, uncouth, unrefined.
Bidet [biˑˈdeː], *n.* **-s/-s.** *Hyg:* bidet.
Bi-de-Winder, *m.* **-s/-.** *Dial: Coel:* physalia, *F:* Portuguese man-of-war.
bidmen, *v.i.* (*haben*) *A:* = **beben.**
Biduum [ˈbiːduˑum], *n.* **-s/-duen,** space of two days.
Bieberit [biˑbəˈriːt], *m.* **-s/.** *Miner:* bieberite, red vitriol.
bieder, *a.* (*a*) honest, trustworthy, upright, reliable; ingenuous; **ein biederer Charakter,** an honest, straightforward character; (*b*) gullible, easily deceived; simple-minded; **biedere Bürger,** simple-minded bourgeois; (*c*) *F. & Hum:* worthy, honest; **ein biederes Bäuerlein,** a worthy rustic.
Biederkeit, *f.* (*a*) honesty, trustworthiness, integrity (of pers.); ingenuousness (of pers., character); (*b*) gullibility, simple-mindedness (of bourgeois); (*c*) *F. & Hum:* worthiness (of rustic, etc.).
Biederleute, *pl.* good, upright, honest, folk.
Biedermann, *m.* **-(e)s/-männer,** honest, honourable, upright, man.
Biedermeier[1], *m.* **-s/-,** honest but narrow-minded bourgeois type; *Pej:* philistine.
Biedermeier[2], **das, -s.** (*style of art, interior decoration and furniture current in Germany from 1815 to 1848*) Biedermeier.
Biedermeierei, *f.* **-/.** *Pej:* philistinism.
Biedermeierstil, *m.* = **Biedermeier**[2].
Biedermeiertum, *n.* **-s/.** = **Biedermeierei.**
biegbar, *a.* **1.** flexible, pliable (wood, wire, etc.); ductile, malleable (metal). **2.** = **beugungsfähig.**
Biegbarkeit, *f.* **1.** flexibility, pliability (of wood, etc.); ductility, malleability (of metal). **2.** = **Beugungsfähigkeit.**
Biege, *f.* **-/-n,** bend, curve, curvature; *cp.* **biegen** II. 2 (*b*).
Biege-, *comb.fm.* bending . . .; *Mec: etc:* **Biegebeanspruchung** *f,* bending stress, bending strain; **Biegemaschine** *f,* bending machine, bender.
Biegebacke, *f. Metalw:* bending jaw.
Biegedorn, *m. Mec:* bending mandrel.
Biegeeisen, *n.* (*a*) bending tool; (*b*) tyre-lever (*for putting on tyres*)
Biegefestigkeit, *f. Mec:* bending strength.
Biegegröße, *f. Tchn:* bending coefficient.
biegen. I. *v.* (*strong*) **1.** *v.tr.* (*a*) to bend (metal, bamboo, etc.); to curve (sth.); to crook (one's finger, etc.); *Anat:* to flex (a limb); **etwas krumm b.,** to bend sth. crooked; **etwas seitwärts, nach unten, nach oben, b.,** to bend sth. to one side, down, up; **etwas gerade b.,** to bend sth. straight, to straighten sth.; **etwas einwärts b.,** to bend, turn, sth. in; to curve sth. inwards; **aus freier Hand b.,** to bend (sth.) freehand; **gebogen,** *Nat. Hist:* flexuous (form, etc.); *Bot:* flexuose (stem, etc.); (*b*) **das Recht b.,** to stretch the law; **die Wahrheit b.,** to twist, wrench, strain, the truth; **das kann man wieder gerade b.,** that can be put, set, right, that can be set to rights; (*c*) *Gram:* = **beugen** I. 1 (*b*). **2. sich biegen** *& v.i.* (*sein*) (*a*) to bend, to curve; (*of river, path, etc.*) to wind; (*of static object*) to be curved, bent; (*of arch*) to curve, to be curved; (*of wood*) to warp; (*of wall*) to bulge (out); (*of metal, rails, etc.*) to buckle (*from heat, under pressure, etc.*); **um eine Straßenecke b.,** to turn round a street corner; **die Straße biegt (sich) nach links,** the road bends, curves, to the left; **sich unter einer Last b.,** to bend, sag, give, under a load; (*of tree, etc.*) **sich im Winde b.,** to sway in the wind; *F:* **sich vor Lachen b.,** to double up with laughter, to split one's sides with laughter; **sich vor Höflichkeit b.,** to bow and scrape, to be obsequious; **ich werde hingehen, mag es b. oder brechen,** I shall go there whatever happens, *F:* by hook or by crook; *F:* **er lügt, daß sich die Balken biegen,** he lies like a trooper, like a gas-meter, like a lawyer; (*b*) *Gram:* (*of word*) to inflect; (*of noun, etc.*) to decline.

II. *vbl s.* **1. Biegen,** *n. in vbl senses; also: Anat:* flexion (of limb); *F:* **es geht auf B. oder Brechen,** *F:* it is neck or nothing; **die Auseinandersetzung mit dem Gegner geht auf B. und Brechen,** the dispute with the opponent has come to a crisis. **2. Biegung,** *f.* (*a*) = II. 1; (*b*) bend, wind (of road, river); curve (of arch); curvature (of the earth's surface); *Geol:* flexure (of strata, etc.); **nach der nächsten B.,** round the next bend; (*c*) *Gram:* = **Beugung,** *q.v. under* **beugen** II. 2.
Biegepresse, *f. Metalw:* bending press.
Biegeprobe, *f. Mec.E:* (*a*) bending test; (*b*) specimen of bending (work).
Bieger, *m.* **-s/-.** *Metalw: etc:* bender.
Biegeschritt, *m. Danc:* coupee.
Biegespannung, *f. Mec:* bending stress.
Biegestanze, *f. Metalw:* bending die (set).
Biegesteifigkeit, *f. Mec: etc:* stiffness in flexure.
Biegewange, *f.* = **Biegebacke.**
Biegewelle, *f. Mec.E:* flexible shaft.
Biegezange, *f. Metalw:* bending pliers; *El.E:* (conduit-)bender.
biegsam, *a.* (*a*) pliant (willow, etc.); flexible, pliable (wire, wood); ductile (metal); lithe, supple (body, figure); **biegsame Platte,** pliable sheet(ing); *Bookb:* **biegsamer Einband,** limp binding; (*b*) docile, pliant, tractable (nature).
Biegsamkeit, *f.* (*a*) pliancy, pliability, flexibility (of branch, etc.); ductility (of metal); suppleness, litheness (of body, figure); *Bookb:* limpness (of binding); (*b*) docility; pliability (of character).
Biegungs-, *comb.fm.* bending . . .; *Mec:* **Biegungsmoment** *n,* bending moment; **Biegungsvorrichtung** *f,* bending device.
Biegungsapparat, *n. Metalw:* bending machine, bender.
Biegungselastizität, *f. Mec:* elasticity of flexure.
biegungsfähig, *a. Gram:* = **beugungsfähig.**
Biegungsfall, *m. Gram:* = **Beugungsfall.**
Biegungsfestigkeit, *f.* = **Biegefestigkeit.**
Biegungslinie, *f. Mec:* curve of deflection.
Biegungsmesser, *m. Mec:* deflectometer.
Biegungspfeil, *m. Mec:* amount of, direction of, deflection.
Biegungspolygon, *n.* = **Biegungslinie.**
Biegungssilbe, *f.* = **Beugungssilbe.**
Biegungsvermögen, *n. Mec.E: etc:* flexibility, pliability.
Biel. *Pr.n.n.* **-s.** *Geog:* Bienne, Biel.
Bielbrief, *m.* = **Beilbrief.**
Biele, *f.* **-/-n.** *Dial:* child.
Bieler, 1. *m.* **-s/-.** *Geog:* inhabitant, native, of Bienne. **2.** *inv.a.* (of, from) Bienne; **der B. See,** the Lake of Bienne.
Bien, *m.* **-s/.** *Dial:* = **Bienenvolk.**
Biene, *f.* **-/-n. 1.** bee, *esp.* hive-, honey-bee; **wilde B.,** wild bee; **fleißig wie eine B.,** (as) busy as a bee; *Ap:* **Bienen züchten, halten,** to keep bees; *see also* **gesellig, schmarotzend, solitär, stachellos. 2.** *Astr:* **die Biene,** Apis, the Bee. **3.** *P:* louse, bug.
Bienenameise, *f. Ent:* bee-ant.
bienenartig, *a.* bee-like (type, industry, etc.).
Bienenbeute, *f.* hive (of forest bees).
Bienenblume, *f. Bot:* bee-orchis.
Bienenbrot, *n. Ap:* beebread.
Bienenbrut, *f. Ap:* brood (of bees).
Bienenfalter, *m. Ent:* = **Bienenmotte.**
Bienenfang, *m. Bot:* dead-nettle; archangel.
bienenfressend, *a.* apivorous.
Bienenfresser, *m.* **1.** *Orn:* bee-eater. **2.** *Ent:* bee-beetle.
Bienenfutter, *n. Ap:* bee-forage.
bienenhaft, *a.* = **bienenartig.**
Bienenharz, *n.* propolis, bee-glue.
Bienenhaus, *n.* apiary.
Bienenheide, *f. Bot:* (*a*) heath; (*b*) Dutch myrtle, bog myrtle.
Bienenhonig, *m.* natural (bees') honey.
Bienenkäfer, *m. Ent:* bee-beetle.
Bienenkasten, *m.* (movable-)frame hive, movable-comb hive.
Bienenkitt, *m.* = **Bienenharz.**
Bienenkenner, *m.* apiologist.
Bienenklee, *m. Bot:* white clover, Dutch clover.
Bienenkönigin, *f.* queen bee.
Bienenkorb, *m.* (bee-)hive; **B. aus Stroh,** bee-skep; *Ap:* **(Bienen) in einen B. setzen,** to hive (bees).
Bienenkraut, *n. Bot:* (*a*) garden thyme; (*b*) = **Bienenheide.**
Bienenlaus, *f. Ent:* braula, *F:* bee-louse.
Bienenmeise, *f. Orn:* blue tit(mouse).
Bienenmeister, *m.* = **Bienenzüchter.**
Bienenmörder, *m. Bot:* white water-lily.
Bienenmotte, *f. Ent:* bee-moth.
Bienenmutter, *f.* queen-bee.
Bienenorche, Bienenorchis, *f. Bot:* bee-orchis.
Bienenpest, *f. Ap:* foul brood.
Bienenräuber, *m. Orn:* drongo(-shrike).
Bienenraubwespe, *f. Ent:* robber-wasp.
Bienenrecht, *n. Adm: Jur:* law concerning bee-keeping.
Bienensaug, *m. Bot:* (*a*) melittis, bastard balm; (*b*) = **Bienenfang;** (*c*) hedge woundwort.
Bienenschwarm, *m.* (*a*) swarm of bees; (*b*) *Pyr:* fire-ball.
Bienenstaat, *m.* bee society.
Bienenstachel, *m.* (*organ*) bee's sting, sting of a bee.
Bienenstand, *m.* apiary.
Bienenstich, *m.* (*a*) bee-sting, sting of, from, a bee; (*b*) *Cu:* (kind of) cake with cream filling and sugar and almonds on top.
Bienenstock, *m. Ap:* stock.
Bienenvater, *m.* = **Bienenzüchter.**
Bienenvolk, *n. Ap:* colony of bees.
Bienenwabe, *f. Ap:* honeycomb.
Bienenwachs, *n.* beeswax.
Bienenweisel, *m.* queen-bee.
Bienenwespe, *f.* = **Bienenraubwespe.**
Bienenwolf, *F:* 'bee-hunter' (*popular name for various apivorous creatures, e.g.* bee-eater, bee-beetle, digger-wasp).
Bienenzelle, *f. Ap:* cell, alveole.
bienenzellenförmig, bienenzellig, *a.* honey-combed, cellular; *Nat.Hist:* faveolate, alveolate, alveolar.
Bienenzucht, *f.* apiculture, bee-keeping, bee-rearing, bee-culture; **Bienenzucht-,** *comb.fm.* apicultural . . . .
Bienenzüchter, *m.* bee-keeper, apiculturist, apiarist.
Bienenzünsler, *m. Ent:* bee-moth.
bienn [biˑˈɛn], *a. Bot:* biennial.
biennal [biˑɛˈnaːl], *a.* biennial; **die Biennale,** the Biennale, the Biennial (Film and Art) Festival.
Biennium [biˑˈɛnĭum], *n.* **-s/-nien,** period, space, of two years.
Bier, *n.* **-s/-e,** beer; **helles B.,** (i) lager(-type) beer; (ii) light beer; **dunkles B.,** (i) dark beer; (ii) (German) malt beer; **beim B. sitzen,** to sit over a glass of beer; **ein B. trinken gehen,** to go and have a beer; *see also* **Faß** 1.
Bierakzise, *f.* = **Biersteuer.**
Bieramsel, *f.* = **Pirol.**
Bieranzapfgerät, *n. Brew:* broaching appliance.
Bierapparat, *m.* beer-engine.
Bierausschank, *m.* (*a*) licence to sell beer; (*b*) sale of beer; (*c*) bar; beer-shop, ale-house.
Bierbank, *f.* bench in a public house.
Bierbankpolitik, *f. F:* pot-house politics.
Bierbankpolitiker, *m. F:* one who holds forth on politics in a public house; *F:* pot-house politician.
Bierbankstratege, *m. F:* pot-house strategist.
Bierbann, *m.* brewer's monopoly (in a certain district); system of tied houses.

Bierbar, *f.* tavern; public bar.
Bierbauch, *m. F:* pot-belly, corporation.
Bierbecher, *m.* beer-glass, beer-mug.
Bierbottich, *m. Brew:* beer vat, tun.
Bierbrauen, *n.* brewing (of beer).
Bierbrauer, *m.* brewer.
Bierbrauerei, *f.* **1.** brewery. **2.** brewing (of beer).
Bierbruder, *m.* habitual beer-drinker; (convivial) tippler, *F:* pot-companion, boon companion.
Bierchen, *n.* **-s/-.** *F:* **das heißt ein B!** *F:* that's a nice drop (of beer)! **wir gehen schnell noch ein B. holen,** we're going to have a quick one.
Biercomment, *m.* (beer-)drinking code (*in German student circles*).
Biercouleur, *f.* caramel (*used for darkening beer*).
Bierdeckel, *m.* (*a*) beer-mat; (*b*) *F:* (student's) cap.
Bierdruckapparat, *m.* beer-engine, beer-pump.
Biereifer, *m. F:* excessive zeal.
biereifrig, *a. F:* over-zealous.
Bieressig, *m.* malt vinegar, beer vinegar.
Bierfahrer, *m.*=**Bierkutscher.**
Bierfaß, *n.* beer-barrel.
Bierfilz, *m.* beer-mat.
Bierflasche, *f.* beer-bottle.
Bierflaschenfüllapparat, *m.* beer-bottling machine.
Bierflaschenfüllmaschine, *f.* beer-bottling machine.
Biergarten, *m.* beer-garden; open-air café.
Biergeld, *n.* (*a*) beer-money; (*b*)=**Trinkgeld;** (*c*)=**Biersteuer.**
Bierglas, *n.* beer-glass.
Bierhahn, *m.* **1.** (stop-)cock; spigot, tap, faucet. **2.** *Orn:*=**Pirol.**
Bierhaken, *m.* can-hook.
Bierhebegerät, *n.* beer-pump; beer-engine.
Bierheber, *m.*=**Bierhebegerät.**
Bierhefe, *f.* brewer's yeast; barm.
Bierhefentrübung, *f.* yeast turbidity in beer.
Bierherz, *n. Path:* enlarged heart due to excessive beer-drinking.
Bieridee, *f. F:* crazy notion.
Bierkaltschale, *f.* cold sweet soup made with beer.
Bierkarren, *m.* (brewer's) dray.
Bierkasten, *m.* beer(-bottle) crate.
Bierkeller, *m.* (*a*) beer-cellar; (*b*) underground drinking den, *F:* dive.
Bierkessel, *m.* (brewer's) copper.
Bierkneipe, *f. F:* pub.
Bierkran, *m.*=**Bierhahn 1.**
Bierkrücke, *f. Brew:* oar (for stirring mash).
Bierkrug, *m.* **1.** beer-mug, beer-pot, *U.S:* stein. **2.** *North G.Dial:* public house, *F:* pub.
Bierkühlapparat, *m. Brew:* refrigerator.
Bierkühler, *m.* beer-cooler.
Bierkutscher, *m.* (brewer's) drayman.
Bierland, *n.* district where mainly beer (rather than wine) is drunk; beer country.
Bierleiche, *f. F:* person who is dead drunk, who has passed out, who is dead to the world.
Bierlokal, *n.*=**Bierstube.**
Biermärte, *f.*=**Bierkaltschale.**
Biermaß, *n.* beer-mug, *U.S:* stein; measure of beer.
Biermeile, *f.* square mile in which brewer's monopoly functions.
Biermersch, *a. Med:* **Biermersche Krankheit, Biermersche Anämie,** pernicious anaemia.
Biermusik, *f.* **1.** music played in a public house. **2.** bad music.
Bierniederlage, *f.*=**Bierverlag.**
Bieroberhefe, *f.* top fermentation yeast.
Bierpech, *n.* brewer's pitch.
Bierpfahl, *m.* sign (outside a tavern).
Bierpfennig, *m.*=**Biersteuer.**
Bierpolitik, *f.*=**Bierbankpolitik.**
Bierpolitiker, *m.*=**Bierbankpolitiker.**
Bierprobe, *f.* (*a*) beer test; (*b*)=**Bierwaage;** (*c*) sample of beer.
Bierprob(ier)er, *m.* beer-taster, beer-tester.
Bierpumpe, *f.* beer-pump, beer-pull, beer-engine.
Bierquelle, *f.* bar-room, tap-room; beer-shop.
Bierrecht, *n.* (*a*)=**Braugerechtigkeit;** (*b*)=**Biersteuer.**
Bierreise, *f. F:* pub-crawl.
Bierreste, *m.pl.* dregs of beer.
Bierruhe, *f.* imperturbable, unshakable, calm; **er hat eine B.,** nothing can shake him, he never loses his equanimity.
Biersäufer, *m.* beer-drinker; toper.
Bierschlauch, *m.* (*a*) beer hose; (*b*) *F:* heavy beer-drinker, *F:* boozer.
Bierschöne, *f.* **-/.** *Brew:* finings.
Bierschönen, *n.*, **Bierschönung,** *f. Brew:* fining (of beer).
Bierschragen, *m.* trestle, stand, for beer-barrels.
Bierschröter, *m.* **-s/-,** drayman; beer loader.
Bierschwengel, *m.* beer-pull.
Bierseidel, *n.* (squat) beer-mug, beer-glass.
bierselig, *a.* beery; pleasantly intoxicated, *F:* happy.
Bierstein, *m. Brew:* beer stone, beer scale.
Biersteuer, *f.* duty on beer, beer duty.
Bierstube, *f.* public house, tavern, *F:* pub; tap-room.
Biersuppe, *f.* sweet soup made with beer.
Biertisch, *m.* table in a, the, public house.
Biertonne, *f.* (*a*) beer tun, beer barrel; (*b*) *F:* pot-bellied beer drinker; man full of beer.
Biertreber, *m.pl. Brew:* draff, grain.
Biertrinker, *m.* beer drinker; **ich bin kein B.,** I do not drink beer, I am not a beer drinker.
Biertripper, *m. Med: P:* urethritis.
Biertrübung, *f.* turbidity in beer.
Bierverlag, *m.* beer depot, beer store.
Bierverleger, *m.* retailer of beer; brewer's sales agent.
Bierwaage, *f. Brew:* hydrometer; saccharometer.
Bierwagen, *m.* **1.** (brewer's) dray. **2.** *Rail:* beer wagon (for transporting beer).
Bierwärmer, *m.* beer-warmer (*metal tube filled with hot water for warming beer in the glass*).
Bierwirt, *m.* publican, *U.S:* saloonkeeper.
Bierwirtschaft, *f.*=**Bierstube.**
Bierwürgel, *m.* rotary beer-pump, hand pump for filling beer-barrels.
Bierwürze, *f.* wort (of beer).
Bierzapfer, *m.* **1.** tapster; publican. **2.** *Brew:* racker, cask filler.
Bierzeche, *f.* **1.** (beer-)drinking bout, carouse. **2.** bill, account, for beer (in public house).
Bierzeitung, *f. Sch:* comic paper (composed for and read at a convivial party).
Bierzeug, *n.*=**Bierhefe.**
Bierzipfel, *m. Sch:* ribbon worn on the watch-chain displaying the colours of a student club.
Bierzwang, *m.*=**Bierbann.**
Biese[1], *f.* **-/-n,** (*a*) piping (on uniform, etc.); (*b*) *Dressm:* tuck; (*c*) *Bootm:* backstay.
Biese[2], *f.* **-/-n**=**Biesfliege.**
Biese[3], *f.* **-/-n**=**Bise.**
biesen, *v.i.* (*haben*) (*of cattle*) to run with (the) fly.
Biesfliege, *f. Ent: Vet:* oestrus, gad-fly, bot(t)-fly; warble(-fly).
Biest[1], *m.* **-es/.** *Vet:* beestings.
Biest[2], *n.* **-es/-er,** beast; creature; animal; *F:* **ein reizendes kleines B.,** a sweet little thing; **sie ist ein B.,** she is a bitch; **du B.!** you beast! you brute! (*of children, animals, etc.*) **die kleinen Biester,** the little devils; the little brutes.
biester, *a. North G.Dial:* dark; miserable; confused.
Biesterei, *f.* **-/-en.** *North G.Dial:* muddle; *F:* mess-up.
biestern, *v.i.* (*haben*) *North G.Dial:* to be gloomy; to be muddled.
Biestmilch, *f. Vet:* beestings.
Bieswurm, *m. Ent: Vet:* bot(t).
bieten. I. *v.tr.* (*strong*) **1.** to offer; to tender; to give; (*a*) **j-m die Hand b.,** (i) to hold out one's hand to s.o.; (ii) to hold out the olive-branch to s.o.; **die Hand zur Freundschaft, zur Hilfe, b.,** to offer one's hand in friendship, to offer, lend, a helping hand; **einer Frau die Hand b.,** to propose (marriage) to a woman; **einer Dame den Arm b.,** to offer one's arm to a lady; **den Mund (zum Kusse) b.,** to offer one's lips (for a kiss); (*b*) **j-m einen guten Morgen b.,** to wish s.o. good morning; **j-m die Tageszeit b.,** to greet s.o., to wish, bid, *A:* give, s.o. good-day; (*c*) **sich** *dat.* **alles b. lassen,** to submit, give way, to everything; to put up with everything; **das lasse ich mir von niemand(em) b.,** I won't take, stand, tolerate, that from anyone; **j-m etwas b.,** (i) *F:* to give s.o. a whale of a time; (ii) to insult s.o.; to ask too much of s.o., to impose upon s.o.; *F:* **mir ist heute allerhand geboten worden,** I ˈhave had a time of it today, I've had a very trying day today; (*d*) **j-m Trotz, die Stirn, b.,** to defy s.o., to bid defiance to s.o.; **j-m die Stirn b.,** to hold one's own against s.o., to stand up to s.o.; *Chess:* **dem König Schach b.,** to check the king. **2.** *Com:* to offer, to give; (*at auction sale*) to bid; (*a*) **was, wieviel, bieten Sie (mir) dafür?** what will you give me for it? **etwas zum Kaufe b.,** to offer sth. for sale; **500 Mark auf etwas b.,** to bid 500 marks for sth.; *B:* **sie boten ihm dreißig Silberlinge,** they covenanted with him for thirty pieces of silver; (*b*) *v.i.* (*haben*) **auf ein Haus b.,** to bid for a house; **hoch, gering, b.,** to bid high, low; **zuerst b.,** to make the first bid. **3.** to offer; to provide, to furnish; to present; **dieses Buch bietet gute Unterhaltung,** this is an entertaining book; this book makes good reading; **ein Studium, das keine Schwierigkeiten bietet,** a subject that presents no difficulties; **die Geschichte bietet dafür mehrere Beispiele,** history affords several examples of it. **4.** to show; to display; **wo die Mauer eine Lücke bietet,** where there is a gap in the wall; **etwas zur Schau b.,** to put sth. on show; **keine Angriffsfläche b.,** (i) *F:* (*of pers.*) to have no chink in one's armour; (ii) *F:* (*of argument, etc.*) to have no weak points, *F:* to be watertight. **5.** *A:* to announce; to grant; **der König bietet uns Gnade,** the king grants us grace; **Rache b.,** to announce, proclaim, revenge. **6.** (*a*) *A:* to order, to command; **biet allen, sie sollen sich bereit halten!** order everyone to stand prepared! (*b*) *Lit:* **j-n zu Gaste b.,** to invite s.o. **7.** *Cards:*=**ansagen 2.**
II. **sich bieten,** (*of thg*) to offer itself, to present itself; **wenn sich die Möglichkeit bietet,** when the possibility offers, occurs, arises; **bei der nächsten Gelegenheit, die sich mir bietet, . . ., bei der nächsten sich bietenden Gelegenheit,** at the first opportunity, . . .; **der Anblick, der sich meinem Auge bot,** the view that met, greeted, my eyes; *see also* **Bild 2.**
III. *vbl s.* **Bieten,** *n.* (*at auction sale*) bidding.
Bieter, *m.* **-s/-,** person making an offer; (*at sale*) bidder.
Biewitz, *m.* **-es/-e.** *East G.Dial: Bot:* rape, (i) summer-rape, colza; (ii) winter-rape, rape-seed, coleseed.
Bifang, *m.* **1.** *Hist:* newly acquired land of a village farming community. **2.** *Agr:*=**Beifang.**
biferisch [biˈfeːriʃ], *a. Bot:* bifarious.
bifilar [biˑfiˑˈlaːr], *a.* bifilar (suspension, etc.); two-wire (system, etc.).
Bifilarmagnetometer [-magneˑtoˑˌmeːtər], *n. Ph:* bifilar magnetometer.
Bifilarwicklung, *f. El.E:* bifilar winding, two-wire winding.
bifokal [biˑfoˑˈkaːl], *a. Opt:* bifocal.
Bifokalgläser, *n.pl. Opt:* bifocal lenses.
bifolisch [biˑˈfoːliʃ], *a. Bot:* bifoliate.
Bifolium [biˑˈfoːlium], *n.* **-s/-lia & -lien.** *Bot:* bifoliate leaf.
biform [biˑˈfɔrm], *a.* biform, biformed.
Biformität [biˑfɔrmiˑˈtɛːt], *f.* **-/-en,** biformity.
Bifröst, der, -s. *Old Norse Myth:* Bifrost.
Bifurkation [biˑfurkaˑtsiˈoːn], *f.* **-/-en,** bifurcation, fork, branching (of river, etc.).
Biga [ˈbiːgaː], *f.* **-/-gen.** *Classical Ant:* biga, two-horsed chariot.
Bigamie [biˑgaˑˈmiː], *f.* **-/-n** [-ˈmiːən], bigamy.
bigamisch [biˑˈgaːmiʃ], *a.* bigamous.
Bigamist [biˑgaˑˈmist], *m.* **-en/-en,** bigamist.
Bigaradenbaum [biˑgaˑˈraːdən-], *m.* Seville orange tree, bitter orange tree.
Bigaradie [biˑgaˑˈraːdiə], *f.* **-/-n,** bitter orange, Seville orange.
Bigarelle [biˑgaˑˈrɛlə], *f.* **-/-n.** *Hort:* bigarreau, bigaroon (cherry).
bigenerisch [biˑgeˑˈneːriʃ], *a. Bot: Z:* bisexual, bisexed.
Bighorn [ˈbighorn], *n. Z:* bighorn, Rocky Mountain sheep.
Bignoniazeen [bignoˑniaˑˈtseːən], *f.pl. Bot:* bignoniaceae.
Bignonie [biˈgnoːniə], *f.* **-/-n.** *Bot:* bignonia.
bigott [biˑˈgɔt], *a.* (*a*) (over-)devout, *F:* churchy; bigoted (in religious belief); superstitious; (*b*) hypocritically pious, sanctimonious.
Bigotterie [biˑgɔtəˈriː], *f.* **-/-n** [-ˈriːən], (*a*) religious bigotry, *F:* churchiness; (*b*) religious hypocrisy.
Bijouterie [biˑʒuˑtəˈriː], *f.* **-/-n** [-ˈriːən], trinkets, trinketry; jewel(le)ry, *esp.* costume jewel(le)ry.
Bijouteriehandel, *m.* jeweller's trade, business.
Bijouteriehandlung, *f.* jeweller's shop.
Bijouteriewaren, *f.pl.* trinketry, bijouterie; jewel(le)ry.
Bikarbonat [biˑkarboˑˈnaːt], *n.* **-(e)s/-e.** *Ch:* bicarbonate.
bikephalisch [biˑkeˑˈfaːliʃ], *a.* bicephalous, double-headed.
Bikini [biˑˈkiːniː], *m.* **-s/-s.** *Cost:* bikini.
bikonkav [biˑkonˈkaːf], *a.* biconcave.
bikonvex [biˑkonˈvɛks], *a.* biconvex.
Bikornen [biˑˈkɔrnən], *n. pl. Bot:* ericales.
Bikuspidalklappe [biˑkuspiˑˈdaːl-], *f. Anat:* bicuspid valve, mitral valve.
bilabial [biˑlaˑbiˈaːl], (*a*) *Ling:* bilabial (consonant); (*b*) *Bot:* bilabiate.
Bilander [ˈbiːlandər, biˑˈlandər], *m.* **-s/-.** *Nau:* bilander.
Bilanz [biˑˈlants], *f.* **-/-en.** *Book-k:* **1.** (i) balance; (ii) net result (of negotiations, conference, etc.); assessment (of year, life, etc.); **die B. ziehen,** (i) to strike the balance; (ii) to take stock (of one's

life, etc.). 2. balance-sheet; **eine B. aufstellen,** to draw up a balance-sheet; **eine B. prüfen,** to audit a balance-sheet; **die B. frisieren, verschleiern,** to fiddle, doctor, the accounts; to cook the books.

Bilanzauszug, *m. Book-k:* (*a*) extract from a balance-sheet; (*b*) abstract of a balance-sheet.

Bilanzbogen, *m. Book-k:* cash-ruled columnar paper.

Bilanzbuch, *n. Book-k:* balance ledger.

Bilanzbuchhalter, *m.* book-keeper capable of handling a complete set of books; *approx.* = accountant.

Bilanzgliederung, *f. Book-k:* arrangement of the balance-sheet.

bilanzieren [biˑlanˈtsiːrən], *v.i.* (*haben*) *Book-k:* (*a*) to strike a balance; (*b*) to balance (the accounts); (*c*) to show in the balance-sheet.

Bilanzjahr, *n. Com: Fin:* financial year (of firm, etc.).

Bilanzkonto, *n. Book-k:* balance-sheet.

Bilanzlesen, *n. Book-k:* reading the balance-sheet.

bilanzmäßig, *a.* as shown by the balance-sheet.

Bilanzperiode, *f. Book-k:* accounting period.

bilanzsicher, *a. Book-k:* **bilanzsicherer Buchhalter,** book-keeper capable of handling a complete set of books; *approx.* = accountant.

Bilanzstichtag, *m. Book-k:* date of balance-sheet.

Bilanzsumme, *f. Book-k:* total of balance-sheet.

Bilanztabelle, *f.* = **Bilanzbogen.**

Bilanzwert, *m. Com:* book value.

bilateral [biˑlaˑteˑˈraːl], *a.* bilateral; two-sided.

Bilboquet [bilboˑˈkɛː], *n.* **-s/-s.** *Toys:* (*a*) cup-and-ball; (*b*) (*weighted figure*) tumbler.

Bilch, *m.* **-(e)s/-e.** *Z:* dormouse.

Bilchmaki, *m. Z:* dwarf lemur.

Bilchmaus, *f. Z:* dormouse.

Bild, *n.* **-(e)s/-er. 1.** (*a*) picture; image; likeness, representation, effigy; *B:* **Gott schuf den Menschen Ihm zum Bilde,** God created man in His own image; **ein sprechend ähnliches B.,** a speaking likeness; **j-n im Bilde verbrennen, hängen,** to burn, hang, s.o. in effigy; **ein B. der Gesundheit,** a, the very, picture of health; *F:* **sie ist ein B. von einem Mädchen,** she is a lovely girl, a perfect picture, *F:* a peach of a girl; **ein anschauliches B.,** a vivid picture, a graphic description; **ein B. von etwas entwerfen,** to draw, paint, a picture of sth., to describe, depict, sth., to give a description of sth.; (*b*) (i) painting; drawing; engraving; print; figure; (ii) portrait; **zu einem Bilde sitzen,** to sit for a portrait; (iii) (= **Standbild**) statue; figure; (iv) (*in books*) illustration; figure; *Mth:* graph: **das B. der Gleichung** $x = y$, the graph of the equation $x = y$; (v) *Num:* head; face; image, effigy; **B. oder Wappen?** heads or tails? (*c*) *Cards: pl.* **Bilder,** court cards, picture-cards, *U.S:* face cards; **Karten ohne Bilder,** low cards; (*d*) *Phot:* photograph; exposure (on roll of film); *TV:* image, picture; *Cin: TV:* frame; *TV:* **Sendung von 25 Bildern je sec,** transmission at 25 frames per second. **2.** scene, spectacle, sight; *Th:* tableau; **lebende Bilder,** tableaux vivants, living pictures; **es bietet sich ein anderes B.,** the scene changes, there is a change of scene. **3.** idea, conception, notion; **sich ein wahres, rechtes, B. von etwas verschaffen, machen,** to form a true notion of sth.; **ich habe, mache mir, kein klares B. davon,** I have no clear idea, conception, of it; **im Bilde sein,** to be informed, to know about something, *F:* to be in the picture; **j-n ins B. setzen,** to inform, brief, s.o., *F:* to put s.o. in the picture, *U.S:* to put s.o. wise. **4.** metaphor, simile; imagery; **in Bildern reden,** to speak figuratively, metaphorically.

Bildabtaster, *m. TV:* scanner, scanning device.

Bildabtastung, *f. TV:* scanning.

Bildabzug, *m.* photographic copy, photostat.

Bildaufbau, *m. TV:* build-up (of the picture).

Bildaufklärung, *f. Mil.Av:* photographic reconnaissance.

Bildauflösung, *f. TV:* resolution, definition (of the picture).

Bildaufnahmegerät, *n.* **1.** *Cin:* cine-camera. **2.** *TV:* vision pick-up apparatus.

Bildaufrichtung, *f. Microscopy: etc:* erection of the image; *Cin:* inversion of the image.

Bildausschnitt, *m.* **1.** detail (of picture). **2.** *Phot:* trimmed print. **3.** *Cin:* framing of the image; frame.

Bildauswertung, *f. Mil:* interpretation of (air) photographs.

Bildband, *n.* **1.** *Cin:* film; *TV:* video tape. **2.** *Publ:* book, volume, of plates.

Bildbandgerät, *n. TV:* video tape recorder.

bildbar, *a.* = **bildsam.**

Bildbarkeit, *f.* = **Bildsamkeit.**

Bildbericht, *m. Journ:* photographic report; report with photographs; picture story; *Cin:* photographic report.

Bildberichterstatter, *m. Journ:* press photographer; *Cin:* news cameraman.

Bildbeschreiber, *m.* iconographer.

Bildbeschreibung, *f.* iconography.

Bildbetrachter, *m. Phot:* viewer, *esp.* slide viewer.

Bildbrief, *m. Tg:* telautogram.

Bildchen, *n.* **-s/-,** small, little, picture; tiny image; *Cin:* single picture; frame.

Bildchronik, *f.* picture-chronicle; illustrated history.

Bilddienst, *m. Journ: Advertising:* picture service.

Bilddruckstock, *m. Print:* block.

Bildebene, *f. Geom:* (i) picture plane, perspective plane; (ii) projection plane; *Phot:* focal plane; *Art:* picture plane.

Bildeinstellhebel, *m. Cin:* framing lever.

Bildeinstellung, *f. Phot: Cin:* focusing.

Bildempfänger, *m. TV:* television receiver.

bilden. I. *v.tr.* **1.** (*a*) to form, shape, fashion, mould, create, make (**aus,** out of, from); **seinen Stil an j-m, etwas, b.,** to model one's style on s.o., sth.; **den Charakter eines Kindes b.,** to form a child's mind, to shape, mould, a child's character; **etwas nach einem Muster, Modell, b.,** to form, make, sth. after, from, (up)on, a model; **der Regen hatte große Pfützen auf der Straße gebildet,** the rain had formed large puddles in the street; **neue Wörter b.,** to coin (new) words, to neologize; **Beispiele b.,** to make up, invent, examples; **einen Satz b.,** to construct, make (up), a sentence; (*b*) *Gram:* **den Plural eines Substantivs, die Zeiten eines Verbums, b.,** to form the plural of a noun, the tenses of a verb; **einige Wörter bilden den Plural auf -er und -e,** some words form the plural in -er and -e; (*c*) (*of liquids*) **Blasen b.,** to form bubbles; (*of blood*) **Klumpen b.,** to form clots; *see also* II. 1 (*a*). **2.** to form, set up (committee, business company, political party, etc.); **j-n beauftragen, eine Regierung zu b.,** to invite s.o. to form a government; **eine Allianz, einen Bund, b.,** to form an alliance. **3.** to form, compose, make (up), be; **die Teile, die das Ganze bilden,** the parts that compose, constitute, the whole; **das Kind bildet ihr ganzes Glück,** the child constitutes her whole happiness; **der Mord bildete das Hauptthema unseres Gespräches,** the murder was, constituted, our main topic of conversation; **graue Wände bilden den besten Hintergrund für Gemälde,** grey walls make the best background for paintings; **die Nachhut b.,** to bring up the rear, to form the rearguard; **die Spitze (einer Prozession, eines Zuges) b.,** to head (a procession); *Mil:* **die Vorhut (einer Armee) b.,** to form the vanguard (of an army); **ein Hindernis b.,** to form, be, constitute, an obstacle; **die Grenze b.,** to form the frontier, boundary. **4.** to educate train (pers., mind, etc.); to develop (mind, etc.); **sich** *dat.* **eine Meinung bilden,** to form an opinion; **man kann den Geschmack b.,** taste can be formed, developed; **Reisen bildet,** travel broadens the mind; *see also* **gebildet.**

II. **sich bilden,** (*a*) (*of clouds, bubbles, blisters, crystals, buds, etc.*) to form, to be formed; **es bildet sich Dampf,** steam is given off, produced, generated; *Lit:* **es bildet ein Talent sich in der Stille,** talent develops best in solitude; (*of feelings, etc.*) to arise, to be created; (*b*) to educate oneself; to cultivate, improve, one's mind.

III. *vbl s.* **1. Bilden,** *n. in vbl senses.* **2. Bildung,** *f.* (*a*) formation, creation; invention; production; coining, coinage (of new word, expression, etc.); *Gram:* forming, formation (of plural, etc.); *Ch: etc:* generation (of gas, steam); **B. einer Regierung, einer Gesellschaft, usw.,** forming, formation, of a government, a business company, etc.; (*b*) education, (i) (formal) education; (ii) culture; (good) breeding; **höhere B.,** secondary education; **humanistische B.,** classical education; **eine allgemeine, universale, B.,** a liberal education; **ohne B.,** without education, uneducated, uncultured, uncultivated; ill-bred, ill-mannered; *see also* **akademisch;** (*c*) (*thg formed*) form, shape, formation; *Geol:* formation; *Lit:* stature, features; **seine B. erinnerte an beide Eltern,** his features had something of both his parents, he reminded one of both his parents.

IV. *pr.p. & a.* **bildend,** *in vbl senses; esp.* **die bildenden Künste, die bildende Kunst,** the fine arts, the arts of design; *esp.* the plastic, sculptural, arts.

Bild(er)achat, *m. Miner:* figured agate.

Bilderabziehen, *n. Cer: etc:* decalcomania; transferring of pictures.

Bild(er)anbeter, *m. Rel.Hist:* iconolater.

Bild(er)anbetung, *f.* iconolatry, image-worship.

Bilderbibel, *f.* illustrated Bible, picture Bible.

Bilderbogen, *m.* (*a*) sheet of pictures; **B. zur deutschen Geschichte,** a pictorial history of Germany; (*b*) *Art:* (pictorial) broadsheet.

Bilderbuch, *n.* picture-book.

Bilderchronik, *f.* picture-chronicle.

Bilderdienst, *m.* **1.** *Rel.Hist:* iconolatry, image-worship. **2.** = **Bilddienst.**

Bildererklärung, *f.* iconology.

Bilderfibel, *f.* illustrated primer, picture primer.

Bildergalerie, *f.* picture-gallery.

Bild(er)geräusch, *n. Cin:* frame noise.

Bildergeschichte, *f.* story told in pictures; picture-story.

Bilderglaser, *m.* picture-framer.

Bilderhaken, *m.* picture-hook.

Bild(er)kunde, *f.* iconology.

Bilderkundung, *f.* = **Bildaufklärung.**

Bilderleiste, *f.* picture-moulding, picture-rail.

Bilderrätsel, *n.* picture-puzzle; rebus.

bilderreich, *a.* (*a*) rich in pictures; richly illustrated (book); (*b*) rich in images, metaphors; picturesque (language, style, etc.); flowery, florid (speech, style, etc.); ornate (style, etc.).

Bilderreihe, *f. Cin:* shot.

Bildersaal, *m.* picture-gallery.

Bilderschrift, *f.* pictography, picture-writing; hieroglyphics.

Bildersprache, *f. Lit:* imagery.

Bilderstreit, *m. Rel.Hist:* (*Byzantine*) iconoclasm.

Bildersturm, *m. Rel.Hist:* breaking of images.

Bilderstürmer, *m.* iconoclast; image-breaker.

Bilderstürmerei, *f.* **-/.** iconoclasm.

bilderstürmerisch, *a.* iconoclastic.

Bilderteppich, *m.* = **Bildteppich.**

Bilderverehrer, *m.*, **Bilderverehrung,** *f.* = **Bild(er)anbeter, Bild(er)anbetung.**

Bilderwand, *f. Ecc.Arch:* (*in Eastern Church*) iconostasis.

Bildfänger, *m. Cin:* cine-camera.

Bildfängerröhre, *f. TV:* pick-up tube.

Bildfehler, *m. Opt: etc:* distortion (of the image).

Bildfeld, *n.* (*a*) = **Bildfläche;** (*b*) *Opt: Phot: etc:* (i) field of vision, of view; (ii) **(brauchbares) B.,** useful field.

Bildfeldmaske, *f. Phot:* (printing-)mask.

Bildfeldwölbung, *f. Opt:* curvature of the field.

Bildfenster, *n. Cin:* picture gate (of projector).

Bildfläche, *f. Art:* (surface of, surface area of) painting, canvas, relief; picture plane; **die B. ist durch rote Farbflecke belebt,** the canvas is enlivened by touches of red; *F:* **auf der B. erscheinen,** to appear (on the scene); **von der B. verschwinden,** to disappear (from the scene, from sight).

Bildformat, *n.* size of picture; *Cin:* frame size.

Bildfrequenz, *f. Cin:* camera speed; *TV:* frame frequency, picture frequency.

Bildfunk, *m.* (*a*) radio picture transmission, phototelegraphy; (*b*) television; **durch B. übertragen,** to televise.

Bildgewebe, *n. Tex:* figured stuff.

Bildgießer, *m.* statue-founder, bronze-founder; caster of bronzes, of statues.

Bildgießerei, *f.* **1.** (art of) casting, founding, statues. **2.** bronze-foundry.

Bildguß, *m.* = **Bildgießerei 1.**

bildhaft, *a.* pictorial. **1.** like a picture. **2.** visual (imagination, etc.). **3.** graphic, vivid (description, etc.); pictorial (style, etc.).

Bildhauer, *m.* sculptor; *Astr:* **der B.,** the Sculptor.

Bildhauerarbeit, *f.* sculpture; carving; **halberhabene B.,** low relief, bas(s)-relief.

Bildhauerei, *f.* = **Bildhauerkunst.**

Bildhauerin, *f.* **-/-innen,** sculptress.

bildhauerisch, *a.* sculptural (ornamentation, etc.).

Bildhauerkitt, *m.* badigeon.

Bildhauerkunst, *f.* (art of) sculpture, statuary, carving.

Bildhauerleim, *m.* = **Bildhauerkitt.**

Bildhauermarmor, *m.* statuary marble.

bildhübsch, *a.* (as) pretty as a picture; lovely.

Bildkamera, *f. Cin:* film camera.

Bildkarte, *f.* **1.** picture postcard. **2.** *Cards:* court card, picture-card, *U.S:* face-card. **3.** pictorial map.

Bildkippgerät, *n. TV:* frame time-base.

Bildkombinationsaufnahme, *f. Cin:* composite shot.

Bildkraft, *f.* creative power; plasticity; *Biol:* plastic force.

Bildkunst, *f.* imagery.

bildlich, *a.* pictorial; *Mth: etc:* graphic; (*of*

language, style, etc.) figurative, metaphoric(al), allegoric(al), symbolic(al); **bildlicher Ausdruck**, metaphorical expression, metaphor; *adv.* **etwas b. darstellen**, (i) to picture sth.; (ii) to express sth. figuratively, graphically; **b. auslegen**, to allegorize, to symbolize.
Bildlichkeit, *f.* figurativeness.
bildlos, *a.* (*a*) (*of temple, etc.*) without figural representation (in its decoration); (*of race, etc.*) without figural art; (*b*) *Cards:* **bildlose Karten**, number cards; (*c*) *Ch: etc:* amorphous.
Bildmarmor, *m. Miner:* figured marble.
bildmäßig, *a.* pictorial.
Bildmesser, *m. Phot:* iconometer, view-meter.
Bildmeßkunst, *f.*, **Bildmeßverfahren**, *n.*, **Bildmeßwesen**, *n. Surv:* photogrammetry.
Bildmonitor, *m. TV:* picture monitor.
Bildner, *m.* **-s/-**. **1.** (*a*) former, creator, maker; **der B. der Natur, der Welt, des Alls, der himmlische B.**, the Maker, our Maker, the Maker of the universe, of all; (*b*) artist (in one of the sculptural arts); sculptor. **2.** *Ch:* component.
Bildnerei, *f.* **-/.** sculpture, carving.
bildnerisch, *a.* sculptural, sculpturesque.
Bildnis, *n.* **-nisses/-nisse**, picture, image, likeness, portrait; (*on coins*) head, effigy.
Bildnismaler, *m.* portrait-painter.
Bildnismalerei, *f.* portraiture.
Bildplan, *m. Artil: Surv:* mosaic.
Bildpostkarte, *f.* picture postcard.
Bildpunkt, *m.* **1.** *Ph:* image point. **2.** *TV:* picture element, *F:* spot; **helle Bildpunkte**, high lights.
Bildraum, *m. Opt: etc:* field of vision.
Bildröhre, *f. TV:* cathode ray tube, picture tube; television tube.
Bildrolle, *f. Art:* illuminated roll.
bildsam, *a.* (*a*)=**biegsam**; (*b*) capable of being formed, moulded; plastic; (*c*) improvable, cultivable, educable.
Bildsamkeit, *f.* (*a*)=**Biegsamkeit**; (*b*) capacity for being formed, moulded: plasticity; (*c*) capacity for improvement, educability.
Bildsäule, *f.* statue; **eine mit Bildsäulen geschmückte Halle**, a statued hall.
Bildschärfe, *f. Opt: etc:* definition (of the image).
Bildschirm, *m. TV:* (television) screen.
Bildschnitt, *m. Cin:* cutting of the picture track.
Bildschnitzer, *m.* carver (in wood, ivory).
Bildschnitzerei, Bildschnitzerkunst, *f.* carving (in wood, ivory).
bildschön, *a.* very beautiful; **eine bildschöne Frau**, a very, most, beautiful woman, a woman of great, of outstanding, beauty.
Bildschreiber, *m.* **1.** *Tg:* phototelegraph. **2.** *Draw:* eidograph.
Bildschriftzeichen, *n.* hieroglyph.
Bildschritt, *m. Cin:* frame gauge.
Bildseite, *f. Num:* obverse, face, head (of coin).
Bildsender, *m. TV:* picture transmitter.
Bildsignal, *n. TV:* picture signal, vision signal, *esp. U.S:* video signal.
Bildstecher, *m.* engraver.
Bildstein, *m. Miner:* agalmatolite, figure-stone.
Bildstelle, *f.* **1.** photographic service; **Staatliche B.**, *approx.*=National Buildings Record. **2.** *Mil.Av:* photographic interpretation post.
Bildstock, *m.* **1.** (*in Catholic areas*) wayside shrine. **2.** *Print:* block (of illustration).
Bildstreifen, *m.* (*a*) *Cin:* picture strip, film strip; *Phot:* roll of film, (roll) film; (*b*) *Journ:* strip cartoon, comic strip.
Bildstrich, *m. Cin:* frame line.
Bildstricheinstellung, *f. Cin:* framing.
Bildsucher, *m. Phot:* viewfinder.
Bildtelegramm, *n.* phototelegram.
Bildtelegraph, *m. Tg:* phototelegraph.
Bildtelegraphie, *f.* phototelegraphy.
Bildteppich, *m.* tapestry; tapestry-carpet; **eine Wand mit Bildteppichen schmücken**, to hang a wall with tapestry.
Bildton, *m. Phot:* (general) tone of a photographic print.
Bildtonkamera, *f. Cin:* sound-film camera.
Bildtonmaschine, *f. Cin:* sound-projector.
Bildträger, *m.* **1.** *Art:* material on which a picture is painted; base; canvas; panel. **2.** *TV:* picture carrier.
Bildtreiberei, *f.* embossing.
Bildübergang, *m. Cin:* lap dissolve, mix.
Bildübertrager, *m.* **1.** *TV:*=**Bildsender**. **2.** *Tg:*=**Bildschreiber, Bildtelegraph.**
Bildübertragung, *f.* (*a*) picture telegraphy, phototelegraphy; (*b*) *TV:* picture transmission.
Bildumkehrprisma, *n. Opt:* inverting prism (*in binoculars, etc.*).
Bildumschlag, *m.* illustrated jacket.
Bildung, *f. see* **bilden** III. 2.
Bildungsanstalt, *f.* school; educational establishment, institution.
Bildungsarbeit, *f.* educational work.
bildungsbeflissen, *a.* eager to learn, studious, zealous for learning, eager for knowledge; **ein Bildungsbeflissener**, an anxious seeker after culture.
Bildungsdrang, *m.* desire for education, culture, self-improvement.
Bildungselement, *n.* (*a*) constituent (element); (*b*) *Gram:* formative (element).
Bildungsendung, *f. Gram:* formative suffix.
bildungsfähig, *a.* (*of pers., etc.*) educ(at)able, civilizable; (*of faculties*) cultivable.
Bildungsfeind, *m.* opponent of culture, enemy of education.
bildungsfeindlich, *a.* opposed, hostile, to culture, to education.
Bildungsgang, *m.* (course of) education.
Bildungsgewebe, *n. Bot:* meristem; formative tissue.
Bildungsgrad, *m.* standard of education.
Bildungsideal, *n.* educational ideal, concept of education.
Bildungskraft, *f. Biol:* plastic force.
bildungslos, *a.* (*of pers.*) uneducated, uncultured, uncultivated.
Bildungslücke, *f.* gap in (s.o.'s) education.
Bildungsprozeß, *m.* process of formation, formative process.
Bildungsreife, *f.* intellectual maturity.
Bildungsroman, *m. Lit:* 'novel of education' (*tracing formation and development of individual character*).
Bildungssilbe, *f. Ling:* formative syllable, derivative syllable; affix.
Bildungstrieb, *m.*=**Bildungsdrang.**
Bildungswesen, *n.* educational and cultural matters.
Bildunterschrift, *f.* caption.
Bildverstellungshebel, *m. Cin:* framing lever.
Bildverzerrung, *f. Opt:* distortion, deformation, of the image.
Bildwand, *f. Phot:* (projection) screen.
Bildwandler, *m.* image converter tube (of electron telescope, etc.); *TV:* image section.
Bildweber, *m.*, **Bildweberei**, *f.*=**Bildwirker, Bildwirkerei.**
Bildwechselfrequenz, Bildwechselzahl, *f. Cin: TV:* picture frequency.
Bildwechselzeit, *f. Cin:* feeding time.
Bildweite, *f.* image distance.
Bildwerfer, *m.* (*a*) projection lantern, (picture-) projector; *A:* magic lantern; (*b*) epidiascope.
Bildwerk, *n.* **1.** image, sculpture, carving. **2.** needlework, tapestry(-work). **3.** book of plates; picture-book.
Bildwirker, *m.* tapestry-weaver, -worker; damask weaver.
Bildwirkerei, *f.* tapestry-making, -weaving, -work; damask-work.
bildwirksam, *a.* photogenic (pers., face, etc.).
Bildwirkung, *f.* (visual) effect (of a picture); *see also* **plastisch.**
Bildwölbung, *f. Opt: Phot:* (*a*) curvature of the image; (*b*)=**Bildfeldwölbung.**
Bildzähler, *m. Cin:* frame counter.
Bildzauber, *m.* sympathetic magic (using images).
Bildzeichen, *n.* **1.** (picture) symbol. **2.** *TV:* picture signal.
Bildzeile, *f. TV:* (scanning) line.
Bildzeitung, *f.* illustrated (news)paper.
Bildzerleger, *m. TV:* analyser; scanner, scanning device.
Bildzerrung, *f.*=**Bildverzerrung.**
Bildzuschrift, *f.* letter (of application, etc.) enclosing a photograph.
Bileam [ˈbiːleˑam]. *Pr.n.m.* **-s.** *B.Hist:* Balaam.
Bileamit [biˑleˑaˑˈmiːt], *m.* **-en/-en.** *B.Hist:* Balaamite.
Bilge, *f.* **-/-n.** *Nau:* bilge.
Bilgeladung, *f. Nau:* cargo in ballast.
Bilgepumpe, *f.* bilge-pump.
Bilgewasser, *n. Nau:* bilge-water.
Bilharzia [bilˈhartsiaː], *f.* **-/-zien.** *Ann:* bilharzia.
Bilharziakrankheit, *f.*, **Bilharziosis** [bilhartsiˈoːzis], *f.* **-/.** *Med:* bilharziosis, bilharziasis.
biliar [biˑliˈaːr], **biliär** [biˑliˈɛːr], *a. Anat:* biliary (system, etc.).
Bilimbibaum [biˑˈlimbiː-], *m. Bot:* bilimbi; cucumber-tree.
bilinear [biˑliˑneˑˈaːr], *a. Mth:* bilinear.
biliös [biˑliˈøːs], *a.* bilious.
Bilirubin [biˑliˑruˑˈbiːn], *n.* **-s/.** *Bio-Ch:* bilirubin.
Biliverdin [biˑliˑverˈdiːn], *n.* **-s/.** *Bio-Ch:* biliverdin.
Billard [ˈbiljart, bilˈjart], *n.* **-s/-s & -e [-s/-jardə].** **1.** (game of) billiards; **B. spielen**, to play billiards; **eine Partie B. spielen**, to have a game of billiards. **2.** billiard-table.
Billardball, *m.* billiard-ball.
billardieren [biljarˈdiːrən], *v.tr. Bill:* to hit the ball twice (unintentionally).
Billardkugel, *f.* billiard-ball.
Billardqueue [ˈbiljart,køː], *n.* billiard cue.
Billardsaal, *m.* billiard-room; billiard-hall.
Billardspiel, *n.* (game of) billiards.
Billardspieler, *m.* billiard-player.
Billardstab, Billardstock, *m.* billiard cue.
Billardüberzug, *m.* billiard cloth.
Billardzimmer, *n.* billiard-room.
Bille, *f.* **-/-n.** **1.** *Tls:* stone-dressing pick. **2.** *N.Arch:* **Billen** *pl* **eines Schiffes**, buttocks of a ship.
Billetdoux [biˑjɛˑˈduː], *n.* **-/-**, love-letter.
Billeteur [biljɛˈtøːr], *m.* **-s/-e**=**Billet(t)eur.**
Billett [bilˈjɛt], *n.* **-(e)s/-e**, (*a*) *A:* note, short letter; card; notice; (*b*) *Th: etc:* ticket, admission card; *Rail: esp. Swiss:* ticket. *Cp.* **Fahrkarte.**
Billett-, *comb.fm. cp.* **Fahrkarten-.**
Billettausgabe, *f.* (*a*) booking (of tickets); (*b*) *Rail:* booking-office; *Th:* box-office.
Billet(t)eur [biljɛˈtøːr], *m.* **-s/-e.** *A. & Swiss Dial:* (*a*) *Rail:* booking-clerk; *Th: etc:* box-office man; (*b*) conductor (of bus *or* tram).
Billetteuse [biljɛˈtøːzə], *f.* **-/-n.** *A. & Swiss Dial:* (*a*) *Rail:* (female) booking-clerk; *Th: etc:* box-office girl *or* woman; (*b*) conductress (of bus *or* tram), *F:* clippie.
billettieren [biljɛˈtiːrən], *v.tr.* to label, to ticket.
Billettmaschine, *f.* slot-machine for tickets, ticket-machine.
Billiarde [biliˈardə], *f.* **-/-n**, a thousand billions, 10^{15}; *U.S:* quadrillion.
billig, *a.* **1.** just, equitable (conduct, law, etc.); fair (decision, etc.); **das ist nicht mehr als b.**, that is only fair; **ein billiges Verlangen**, a reasonable demand; **ein billiger Zorn**, a legitimate, righteous, anger; **recht und b.**, right and proper; *Jur:* **billiges Ermessen**, discretion; *Prov:* **was dem einen recht ist, ist dem andern b.**, what is right for the one is right for the other, *Prov:* what is sauce for the goose is sauce for the gander; *adv.* **sie nimmt meine Geduld mehr als b. in Anspruch**, she tries, taxes, my patience unduly, more than is justifiable. **2.** reasonable, moderate (prices); cheap, inexpensive, low-priced (goods, etc.); *Pej:* cheap, shoddy (goods, etc.); low, common (public house, etc.); (*of girl*) cheap, common; **billige Preise**, low prices; **ein billiger Mantel**, an inexpensive coat; **das Kleid sieht b. aus**, it looks a cheap dress; **billige Witze, Komplimente**, cheap jokes, flattery; *F:* **billiger Jakob**, dealer in cheap merchandise, *F:* cheapjack; *F:* **eine billige Ausrede**, a feeble, weak, poor, excuse; *adv.* **b. einkaufen**, to buy cheaply; to spend moderately; (*in advertisement*) **b. zu verkaufen, b. abzugeben**, offered for sale at a reasonable, moderate, price; **ich habe es b. bekommen**, (i) I got it at a low price, (ii) *F:* I got it cheap, on the cheap; **etwas möglichst b. machen**, to do sth. on the cheap; *see also* **davonkommen, Flagge.**
billigdenkend, *a.* fair-minded; right-thinking; just.
billigen. I. *v.tr.* to approve of (action, etc.); to sanction, countenance; to approve (suggestion, etc.); **eine Rechnung b.**, to pass an invoice; **ich billige sein Verlangen**, I admit, acknowledge, the justice of his demand; **ich kann es nicht b., daß du dorthin gehst**, I cannot approve of your going there.
II. *vbl s.* **1. Billigen**, *n. in vbl senses.* **2. Billigung**, *f.* (*a*) *in vbl senses; also:* approval, approbation, sanction (of action, etc.); (*b*) approval; approbation; **sein Benehmen hat meine B. nicht, findet keine B. bei mir**, his behaviour does not meet with my approval, I cannot approve of his behaviour.
billigermaßen, billigerweise, *adv.* justly, equitably, with justice, in equity; fairly; **Sie können ihm seine Bitte billigerweise nicht abschlagen**, you cannot in fairness reject his plea.
Billigkeit, *f.* **1.** justice, equity, equitableness (of law, conduct, etc.); fairness (of decision, etc.); **der B. gemäß**, in accordance with justice; **er hat wider Recht und B. gehandelt**, he (has) acted in defiance of truth and justice; **aus Gründen der B.**, for reasons of equity. **2.** reasonableness (of prices); cheapness, low price, low rate (of goods, etc.); *Pej:* cheapness, shoddiness.
Billigkeitsanspruch, *m. Jur:* claim in equity.
Billigkeitsgefühl, *n.* sense of justice.
Billigkeitsrecht, *n. Jur:* equity.
Billigung, *f. see* **billigen** II.

Billion [bili'oːn], *f.* -/-en, billion; 10^{12}; *U.S:* trillion.

Billon [bil'jõː, bi·'jõː], *m. & n.* -s/. *Num:* (*a*) alloy (of gold *or* silver with copper); (*b*) coin of little value, base coin.

Billrothbatist ['bilroːtba·,tist], *m. Surg:* waterproof woollen bandage.

Bilrost, der, -s. *Old Norse Myth:* Bifrost.

Bilse, *f.* -/-n. *Bot:* bullace.

Bilsenkraut, *n. Bot:* henbane.

Bilsenschnitt, *m. G.Myth:* patch in a cornfield where the corn appears to have been cut by a sickle.

Biluxlampe ['biːluks-], *f. El:* two-filament lamp.

Bilwiß, *m.* **-wisses/.**=**Bilwißschneider.**

Bilwißschneider, *m. G.Myth:* evil spirit who cuts the corn with sickles attached to his toes.

bim, *int.* (*sound of small bell*) ding.

Bimane [bi·'maːnə], *m.* -n/-n. *Z:* bimane.

bimanisch [bi·'maːniʃ], *a. Z: etc:* bimanous, two-handed.

bimanuell [bi·ma·nu·'ɛl], *a.* bimanual.

bimbam, (*a*) *int.* ding-dong; (*b*) *s.* **Bimbam,** *m.* **-s/., heiliger B!** good gracious! good Heavens!

bimbambum, *int.* ding-dong-dell.

bimembrisch [bi·'mɛmbriʃ], *a.* two-limbed.

Bimester [bi·'mɛstər], *n.* **-s/-,** period of two months.

Bimetall ['biːme·tal], *n.* bimetal.

Bimetallismus [bi·me·ta'lismus], *m.* -/. *Pol.Ec:* bimetallism.

Bimetallist [bi·me·ta'list], *m.* **-en/-en,** bimetallist.

bimetallistisch [bi·me·ta'listiʃ], *a. Pol.Ec:* bimetallic (currency, etc.); bimetallist (policy, etc.).

Bimetallstreifen, *m. El.E: etc:* bimetallic strip.

Bimmel, *f.* **-/-n,** small bell.

Bimmelbahn, *f.*, **Bimmelbähnchen,** *n.* **-s/-.** *F:* small local train with a warning bell.

bimmeln. **1.** *v.i.* (*haben*) (*of small bell*) to tinkle; *F:* (*of pers.*) to ring the doorbell. **2.** *vbl s.* **Bimmeln,** *n.* tinkling, tinkle.

Bims, *m.* **-es/-e.** **1.** (*a*) pumice(-stone); (*b*) *F:* army bread; (*c*) *F: Dial:* money. **2.** *pl.* **Bimse,** (*a*) *F: Mil:* hard drilling; (*b*) *F:* blows; beating, thrashing; **Bimse bekommen,** to get a beating, a thrashing.

Bimsbeton, *m. Constr:* (i) pumice concrete; (ii) foamed slag concrete.

Bimsbetonhohlblockstein, *m. Constr:* hollow pumice-concrete block.

Bimsbetonstein, *m. Constr:* (i) pumice-concrete brick *or* block; (ii) foamed slag concrete brick *or* block.

bimsen, *v.tr.* **1.** to pumice; to polish, clean (metal, etc.) with pumice-stone. **2.** (*a*) *F: Mil:* to drill (men) hard; (*b*) *F:* to give (s.o.) a beating, a thrashing.

Bimshohlblockstein, *m.*=**Bimsbetonhohlblockstein.**

Bimskies, *m.* ground pumice-stone; coarse pumice powder.

Bimskreisel, *m. Bootm:* cylinder on the scouring-machine.

Bimsmaschine, *f. Carp:* sand-papering machine.

Bimssand, *m.*=**Bimskies.**

Bimsstein, *m.* **1.** (*a*) pumice-stone; **etwas mit B. abreiben,** to polish, clean *or* rub, sth. with pumice-stone; (*b*) *Leath:* stock-stone; (*c*) *Nau:* holy-stone. **2.** *Constr:* breeze block.

bimssteinartig, *a.* pumiceous (rock, etc.).

Bimssteinbruch, *m.* pumice-stone quarry.

Bimssteinpulver, *n.* pumice powder.

Bimssteinseife, *f.* pumice soap.

bin *see* **sein**[2].

binär, binar(isch) [bi·'nɛːr, bi·'naːr(iʃ)], *a. Ch: Astr: etc:* binary.

Binarkies, *m. Miner:* marcasite.

binaural [bi·nʔau'raːl], *a.* binaural (stethoscope).

Bindahle, *f. Tls:* (saddler's) drawing-awl.

Bindaxt, *f. Tls:* (cooper's) axe.

Bindbast, *m.* (common) elm(-tree).

Bindbaum, *m.* bar (on hay-waggon) for holding down hay.

Binde, *f.* **-/-n.** **1.** band; tie; (*a*) (i) arm-band, armlet; (ii) head-band, *Ant:* fillet; (iii) *Cost:* **weiße B.,** white (bow-)tie; *F:* **sich eins hinter die B. gießen,** to have a drink, *F:* to wet one's whistle; (*b*) *pl.* **Binden,** (*round ankles*) straps, bands; *Mil:* gaiters; *Egypt.Ant:* wrappings (of mummies); (*c*) bandage (for blindfolding); **eine B. vor den Augen,** a bandage over the eyes; **die B. fiel mir von den Augen,** the scales fell from my eyes; **mir ist die B. von den Augen genommen,** my eyes have been opened; I have been disillusioned, disabused. **2.** (*a*) *Surg:* (roller) bandage; **elastische B.** elastic bandage; (*b*) (arm-)sling; **den Arm in der B. tragen,** to have, carry, one's arm in a sling; (*c*) *Hyg:* (*woman's*) sanitary towel, *U.S:* sanitary napkin. **3.** (*a*) *Anat:* fascia; aponeurosis; (*b*) *Nat.Hist:* fascia, band of colour (on butterfly's wing, etc.). **4.** *Her:* fess(e). **5.** *Publ:*=**Buchbinde.**

Bindebalken, *m. Constr:* tie-beam.

Bindeband, *n.* tape, ribbon (for tying); *Cost:* bonnet-string.

Bindeblech, *n. Tchn:* cover-plate, tie-plate.

Bindebogen, *m. Mus:* slur, tie, bind.

Bindebücher, *n.pl. Paperm:* outside, cording, quires, outsides (of a ream).

Bindebuchstabe, *f.* letter used in forming compounds (*e.g. the medial s in* Sicherheitsnadel).

Bindedraht, *m.* binding wire.

Bindefähigkeit, *f.* bonding property, bonding strength.

Bindegarn, *n.* string, twine; packthread.

Bindegerte, *f.*=**Bindeweide** 2.

Bindegesperre, *n. Constr:* principal rafters.

Bindegewebe, *n. Anat:* connective tissue.

Bindegewebsentzündung, *f. Med:* inflammation of the connective tissue; phlegmon.

Bindeglied, *n.* (connecting) link; bond, tie.

Bind(e)gras, *n. Bot:* naked cupped canary grass.

Bindegrün, *n.* greenery used in wreath- and bouquet-making.

Bindehaut, *f. Anat:* conjunctiva.

Bindehautentzündung, *f. Med:* conjunctivitis.

Bindekalk, *m.* quick-setting lime; Roman cement.

Bindekette, *f.* **1.** *Rail:* attachment chain. **2.** *Tex:* stitching *or* binding warp.

Bindeklammer, *f. Tls:* (joiner's) cramp.

Bindekraft, *f.* binding power; bonding power (of mortar, synthetic resin, etc.).

Bindelattich, *m. Hort:*=**Bind(e)salat** 2.

Bindemäher, *m.*, **Bindemähmaschine,** *f.* reaper and binder (machine).

Bindemittel, *n.* binding agent; binding, sticking, substance; vehicle, medium (in paint); *Constr:* binding material (for stones, etc); *Civ.E: etc:* binding material, binder (of road); *Ind:* bonding agent; *Paperm:* adhesive; agglutinant; *Cu:* thickening (for sauce, etc.).

binden. I. *v.tr.* (*strong*) to tie; to bind. **1.** (*a*) to tie up (**mit,** with); **Besen b.,** to make brooms; **Korn (in Garben) b.,** to bind corn (into sheaves), to sheave corn; **einen Kranz b.,** to make a garland *or* wreath; **Rosen zum, in einen, Kranz b.,** to make (up) roses into a garland *or* wreath; (*b*) *Bookb:* to bind (books); **in Pappe gebunden,** bound in boards *or* stiff paper; **in Leinen gebunden,** bound in cloth, cloth-bound; **in Franzband gebunden,** (full-)bound in calf; **in Halbfranz gebunden,** half-bound in calf; (*c*) *Coop:* to hoop (barrel). **2.** (*a*) to tie (together); to join (up) (two letters, etc.); **eine Schleife b.,** to tie a bow; **eine Krawatte b.,** to knot a tie; (*b*) *Mus:* (i) to tie, (ii) to slur (two or more notes), (iii) to play (sth.) legato; **gebunden spielen,** to play legato; **gebundene Noten,** tied notes; (*c*) *Ling:* to link (two words) (in pronunciation), to sound the liaison; **falsch b.,** to make an incorrect liaison. **3.** (*a*) to fasten (up); *Vit:* to tie up (vine); **einen Hund an die Kette b.,** to chain up, tie up, a dog; **ein Pferd an einen Baum b.,** to tie, tether, a horse to a tree; **den Kahn ans Ufer b.,** to moor, fasten, the boat to the shore; (*b*) to tie (sth.) round (sth.); **ein Seil um etwas b.,** to tie a rope round sth., to rope sth. up; **(sich** *dat.***) ein Tuch um den Hals b.,** to put, tie, a scarf round one's neck; **j-m ein Tuch vor, um, die Augen b.,** to tie a scarf over, round, s.o.'s eyes; to blindfold s.o.; **etwas um den Finger b.,** to tie sth. round one's finger, to bind up one's finger (with sth.); (*c*) *Fenc:* **die Klinge b.,** to bind one's adversary's blade; **die Klingen b.,** to engage foils; (*d*) **etwas auf etwas** *acc.* **b.,** to tie sth. on to sth.; **j-m etwas auf die Seele b.,** to impress sth. upon s.o.; to lay sth. upon s.o.'s conscience; **j-m auf die Seele b., etwas zu tun,** (solemnly) to charge, instruct, s.o. to do sth., to beg, urge, s.o. to do sth.; *F:* **j-m etwas auf die Nase b.,** (i) to tell s.o. a tall story, to take s.o. in, (ii) *F:* to hold sth. under s.o.'s nose; **ich brauche es doch nicht jedem auf die Nase zu b.,** I've no need to go round telling everyone, to broadcast the fact. **4.** to fetter, bind; (*a*) **Gefangene b.,** to bind, chain, fetter, prisoners; **gebunden liegen,** to lie bound, enchained, in chains; **an Händen und Füßen gebunden sein,** to be bound hand and foot; (*b*) **die Hände sind mir, mir sind die Hände, mir sind Hände und Füße, gebunden,** my hands are tied; **ans Haus gebunden,** tied to the house; *see also* **Scholle.** **5.** (*a*) to compel, oblige; to tie down; **durch einen Eid gebunden sein,** to be bound by an oath; **wir binden Sie nicht an diese Preise,** we do not bind, limit, you to these prices; **j-n an etwas gebunden halten,** to hold s.o. (down) to sth., to keep s.o. to, sth.; **sich an etwas** *acc.* **b.,** to bind oneself, pledge one's word, commit oneself, to sth.; **sich an die Zeit b.,** to keep to time; **sich an die Regel b.,** to keep, *F:* stick, to the rules; **sich an etwas gebunden fühlen,** to feel bound, pledged, committed, to sth.; **eine bindende Abmachung,** a binding agreement; **er betrachtet unsere Abmachung nicht als bindend,** he does not regard our agreement as binding; (*b*) *Pros:* **gebundene Rede,** metrical speech; verse; poetry; **in gebundener Form,** in metrical form, in verse. **6.** (*a*) *Ch:* (*of element*) **etwas b.,** to combine with sth., to enter into combination with sth., to form a compound with sth.; **Wärme b.,** to absorb latent heat; **gebundene Wärme,** latent heat; *Ph:* **gebundene Elektrizität,** latent electricity; (*b*) *Constr:* to bond (stones, bricks); (*c*) *Cu:* to thicken, give body to (sauce, etc.); to bind (mixture) (with eggs, flour, etc.); **sich b. lassen,** to thicken; (*d*) to join, unite; **die Ehe bindet zwei Menschen,** marriage unites two people; **die bindende Kraft der Liebe,** the binding power of love.

II. **binden,** *v.i.* (*haben*) **1.** (*a*) to have binding power; to unite; **die Ehe bindet,** marriage unites; *Theol:* **die Kraft zu b. und zu lösen,** the power to bind and to loose; (*b*) **b., bindend sein,** to be binding (**für j-n,** on s.o.); **ein Versprechen bindet, ist bindend,** a promise is binding; **Entscheidung, die für alle Parteien bindend ist,** decision binding on all parties. **2.** (*of cement, etc.*) to set; to harden; **langsam, schnell, bindender Zement,** slow-, quick-setting cement. **3.** *Tex:* (*of thread*) to bind, to be bound; **die Noppe bindet um einen Schuß,** the kink binds, is bound, round one weft-thread.

III. *vbl s.* **1. Binden,** *n. in vbl senses; also:* **Ihr Buch ist beim B.,** your book is being bound. **2. Bindung,** *f.* (*a*) *in vbl senses of* I. 6 (*a*); (*b*) (i) (way, method of) binding, tying, fastening; (ii) fastening; tie; *Bookb:* binding; *Ski:* binding (*fastening ski to boot*); (*c*) *Mus:* bind, binding note, tie slur, ligature; *Ling:* liaison, linking (of words); (*d*) *Ch:* linkage (of atoms in molecule, etc.); (*e*) *Tex:* weave (of fabric); interweaving (of threads); (*f*) *Fenc:* (i) engagement; (ii) bind; (*g*) commitment, obligation (to agreement, duty, etc.); (religious, social, etc.) tie(s); limitation, restriction (to prices); **B. an das Gesetz,** subjection, subordination, to the law; **Goethes B. an seine Zeit,** the bonds which unite Goethe to his time; **ein Mensch ohne Bindungen,** (i) a person without, free of, obligations, without attachments (to other people), (ii) a person without roots; *Pol:* **parteiliche Bindungen,** party labels.

-bindend, *comb. fm. a. Ch:* combining with . . .; **ammoniakbindend,** combining with ammonia.

Bindenfregattvogel, *m. Orn:* great frigate bird.

Bindenkreuzschnabel, *m. Orn:* two-barred cross-bill.

Bindensandlerche, *f. Orn:* bar-tailed desert lark.

Bindenschwein, *n. Z:* Sumatra pig.

Binder, *m.* **-s/-,** binder; *Agr:* (mechanical) sheaf-binder; reaper and binder; *Cost:* (neck-)tie; *Constr:* (*a*) header; bonder; bond-stone; (*b*) truss (of roof, bridge, etc.); girder.

Binderabstand, *m.* space, distance, between trusses.

Binderbalken, *m. Constr:* (*a*) tie-beam; (*b*) main girder, main beam.

Binderbarte, *f. Tls:* (cooper's) broad axe.

Binderei, *f.* **-/-en.** **1.** *Bookb:* bindery. **2.** (*a*) (art of) wreath- and bouquet-making, *esp.* with artificial flowers; (*b*) (florist's) wreath- and bouquet-making department.

Bindereis, *n.*=**Bindeweide.**

Bindermesser, *n.* cooper's hacking-knife.

bindern, *v.tr.* to bind (books).

Binderschicht, *f.* **1.** *Constr:* course of headers, heading(-course). **2.** *Civ.E:* macadam foundation layer.

Bindersparren, *m. Constr:* principal rafter (of roof).

Binderverband, *m. Constr:* heading bond.

Binderwurzel, *f. Pharm:* (yellow) gentian root.

Bind(e)salat, *m. Hort:* **1.** (garden-)endive. **2.** cos lettuce, Roman lettuce; long-leaved lettuce.

Bindeschäfte, *m.pl. Tex:* front heddles, front healds.

Bindeschlüssel, der. *Theol:* the keys.

Bindeschuh, *m.* (light, *esp.* child's) lace-up shoe.

Bindestein, *m. Constr:* bond-stone; header bonder.

Bindestrich, *m.* (*a*) hyphen; (*b*) *Calligraphy:* upstroke.
Bindestrich-Amerikaner, *m.* foreigner naturalized in the U.S.A., *esp.* German-American; *U.S: F:* hyphenated American.
Bindeton, *m. Cer:* ball-clay.
Bindevermögen, *n.*=**Bindekraft.**
Bindevokal, *m. Gram:* (i) connecting vowel, (ii) thematic vowel.
Bindeweide, *f.* **1.** *Bot:* (*a*) white willow; (*b*) violet willow; (*c*) purple, rose, willow; (*d*) common willow, common osier, basket-willow. **2.** osier tie, withe, withy.
Bindewerk, *n.* lathing, lath-work.
Bindewort, *n.* **-(e)s/-wörter.** *Gram:* conjunction.
Bindezange, *f. Tls:* pliers.
Bindezeichen, *n.* hyphen.
Bindezeit, *f.* setting time (of cement, etc.).
Bindfaden, *m.* string, twine; binding thread; packthread; *F:* **es regnet Bindfäden,** it is raining cats and dogs.
Bindfadenrolle, *f.* (*a*) coil, roll, of string; (*b*) string-reel.
Bindgras, *n. Bot:* esparto (grass), hooded matweed.
Bindholz, *n.* (*a*) *Coop:* cask wood, stave-wood; wood for cooperage; (*b*) *Constr:* framing wood.
bindig, *a.* **1.** (*a*) joined, connected; *Constr:* bonded; (*b*)=**bündig 1. 2.** heavy, sticky (soil).
-bindig, *comb.fm. Tex:* **vierbindiges Gewebe,** four-thread cloth.
Bindling, *m.* **-s/.** *Bot:* bindweed, convolvulus.
Bindloch, *n. Needlew: etc:* eyelet.
Bindlochstickerei, *f. Needlew:* broderie anglaise.
Bindriegel, *m. Constr: etc:* tie-rod, tie-bolt; intertie.
Bindriemen, *m.* (*a*) strap; thong; (*b*) **Bindriemen** *pl,* purse-strings.
Bindseil, *n. Nau:* (mooring-)rope.
Bindsel, *n.* **-s/-.** *Nau:*=**Bändsel.**
Bindung, *f. see* **binden III.**
Bindungsbogen, *m.*=**Bindebogen.**
Bindungsenergie, *f. Atom.Ph:* binding energy.
Bindungsquadrat, *n. Tex:* square on design paper.
Bindungstype, *f. Tex:* mark on design paper.
Bindungswärme, *f. Ch:* heat of formation.
Bindwand, *f. Constr:* framed partition.
Bindweide, *f. Bot:* golden osier, yellow willow, golden willow.
Bindwerk, *n.* lathing, lath-work.
Binge, *f.* **-/-n.** *Min:* surface dip; funnel-shaped hollow on surface (*caused by collapse of shaft*).
Bingelkraut, *n. Bot:* mercury; **einjähriges B.,** garden mercury.
Bingenbau, *m. Min:* opencast (working).
binieren [biˑˈniːrən], *v.i.* (*haben*) *R.C.Ch:* to say mass twice on the same day.
binnen, *prep.* (+*dat. or gen.*) (*a*) (*time*) within; **b. drei Tagen,** within three days; **b. einer Stunde,** within an hour; **b. zwölf Monaten,** within twelve months; **b. kurzem,** shortly; in, within, a short time; before long; (*b*) *A:* (*space*) within, inside; **b. den Stadtmauern,** within, inside, the city walls.
Binnen-, *comb.fm.* (*a*) inner (harbour, etc.); internal (part, etc.); **Binnenkammer** *f,* inner chamber; (*b*) inland; domestic (administration, etc.); home (trade, etc.); **Binnenwasserstraßen** *f.pl,* inland waterways; **Binnenmarkt** *m,* home market.
Binnenachtersteven, *m. N. Arch:* false, inner, stern-post.
Binnenalster, die. *Geog:* the Inner Alster (in Hamburg).
Binnenasseln, *f.pl. Crust:* entoniscidae.
Binnenberme, *f. Hyd.E:* set-off on the inner side (of large dam).
binnenbords, *adv. Nau:* inboard.
Binnendeich, *m. Hyd.E:* inner dike.
Binneneis, *n. Geol:* inland ice.
Binnenfischerei, *f.* freshwater fishing.
Binnenfleet, *n.*=**Binnentief.**
Binnengeräusche, *n.pl. Med:* head-noises, noises in the head; buzzing in the ears.
Binnengewässer, *n.* inland body of water.
Binnenhafen, *m.* (*a*) close port; river port; (*b*) (*in port*) inner harbour.
Binnenhandel, *m.* domestic trade, home trade.
Binnenhaut, *f. N.Arch:* ceiling.
Binnenhintersteven, *m. N.Arch:* inner, false, stern-post.
Binnenkanal, *m. Hyd.E:* junction canal.
Binnenklasse, *f.* class of non-seagoing yachts.
Binnenklima, *n.* continental climate.
Binnenland, *n.* (*a*) inland; interior (of a country); **im B.,** inland; (*b*) (*in North Germany*) land protected by dikes, diked land.
Binnenländer, *m.* **-s/-. 1.** (*pers.*) inlander. **2.** canal barge.
binnenländisch, *a.* inland.
binnenlaufen, *v.i. sep.* (*sein*) *Nau:* to enter harbour.
Binnenlotse, *m.* river pilot.
Binnenmeer, *n. Ph.Geog:* inland sea, enclosed sea, landlocked sea.
Binnenreim, *m. Pros:* internal rhyme.
Binnenmauer, *f. Constr:* party wall.
Binnenschiff, *n.* river *or* canal vessel; barge.
Binnenschiffahrt, *f.* inland navigation.
Binnenschläge, *m.pl. Agr:* strict rotation of crops (*on fields nearest farmhouse*).
Binnenschmarotzer, *m. Biol:* internal parasite, endoparasite.
Binnensieltief, *n.*=**Binnentief.**
Binnensohle, *f. Bootm:* middle-sole.
Binnenstaat, *m.* country, state, enclosed by land; inland state, country.
Binnenstich, *m. Nau:* inner clinch.
Binnentief, *n. Hyd.E:* catchwater drain (behind dike).
Binnenverkehr, *m.* inland traffic *or* transport.
Binnenvordersteven, *m. N.Arch:* apron.
Binnenwanderung, *f.* migration within a country.
Binnenwandung, *f. N.Arch:* ceiling-plates, inner planks.
binnenwärts, *adv. A:* inwards.
Binnenwasser, *n.* rain- and spring-water collecting in the lowland behind dikes.
Binnenzeichnung, *f. Art:* lines (*within outlines*); details (of drapery folds, etc.); features (of face).
Binnenzoll, *m.* internal tariff (on goods traded in a customs union).
Binode [biˑˈnoːdə], *f.* **-/-n.** *El.E:* binode.
binokular [biˑnoˑkuˑˈlaːr], *a. Opt:* binocular.
Binokularmikroskop, *n.* binocular microscope.
Binom [biˑˈnoːm], *n.* **-s/e.** *Mth:* binomial.
binomial [biˑnoˑmiˈaːl], *a.*=**binomisch.**
Binomialreihe, *f. Mth:* binomial series.
Binomialsatz, *m. Mth:* binomial theorem.
binomisch [biˑˈnoːmiʃ], *a. Mth:* binomial (factor, etc.); **der binomische Satz,** the binomial theorem.
Binse, *f.* **-/-n.** *Bot:* (*a*) rush, *esp.* bulrush, club-rush; **graue B.,** hard rush; **die Binsen,** the rush family, the juncaceae; (*b*) *F:* **in die Binsen gehen,** to go to rack and ruin; **etwas in die Binsen gehen lassen,** to let sth. go by the board.
Binsenastrild, *m. Orn:* ruficauda finch.
Binsenblume, *f. Bot:* flowering rush, water-gladiole.
Binsenbohne, *f. Bot:* henbane.
Binsenbusch, *m.*=**Binsengebüsch.**
Binsendecke, *f.* rush-mat; rush matting.
binsenförmig, *a.* rushlike.
Binsengebüsch, *n.* plantation, cluster, of rushes; rush-bed.
Binsengeflecht, *n.* rush plaiting.
Binsengras, *n. Bot:* **1.** (*a*) rush; (*b*) shining-fruited rush; (*c*) spike-rush. **2. die Binsengräser,** the sedge family.
Binsenhalm, *m. Bot:* **1.** calamus; rattan(-palm). **2.** purple melic-grass.
Binsenklapperhülse, *f. Bot:* Bengal hemp, sunn(-hemp).
Binsenknopf, *m. Bot:* echinops, globe-thistle.
Binsenkorb, *m.* (*a*) frail; plaited shopping basket; *B:* **Moses im B.,**=Moses in the bulrushes; (*b*) frail (for packing figs, etc.).
Binsenkraut, *n.*=**Bilsenkraut.**
Binsenlauch, *m.* (*a*) *Bot:* Welsh onion, stone-leek; (*b*) *Bot: Cu:* (garden) chives.
Binsenlicht, *n.* rushlight, rush-candle, rush-dip.
Binsenmatte, *f.* rush mat.
Binsenmesser, *m.* long-handled scythe (for clearing ponds, rivers, etc., of rushes).
Binsennuß, *f. Bot:* tiger-nut, chufa.
Binsenpfeffer, *m.* cubeb pepper.
Binsenpfrieme, *f.,* **Binsenpfriemenkraut,** *m. Bot:* Spanish broom.
Binsenpulver, *n. Ch: Pharm:* veratrine, veratria.
Binsenpuppe, *f. Fish:* float (for lines).
Binsenquecke, *f. Bot:* bent(-grass); sea wheat (-grass).
Binsenralle, *f. Orn:* water-rail.
binsenreich, *a.* full of rushes, rushy.
Binsenrohrsänger, *m. Orn:* aquatic warbler.
Binsenschnitter, *m.*=**Bilwißschneider.**
Binsenschwertel, *m. Bot:* flowering rush, water-gladiole.
Binsenstuhl, *m.* rush-bottomed chair.
Binsenwahrheit, Binsenweisheit, *f.* self-evident truth; truism.
Binsenwolle, *f. Bot:* cotton-grass.
Binsicht, *n.* **-(e)s/-e,** plantation of rushes; rush-bed.
Binturong [ˈbintuˑroŋ], *m.* **-(e)s/-s.** *Z:* binturong.
Bio-, bio- [biˑoˑ-], *pref.* bio-; **Biochemie** *f,* biochemistry; **biographisch,** biographical.
Bioblast [biˑoˑˈblast], *m.* **-en/-en,** bioblast.
Biochemie [biˑoˑçeˑˈmiː], *f.* biochemistry.
Biochemiker [biˑoˑˈçeːmikər], *m.* biochemist.
biochemisch [biˑoˑˈçeːmiʃ], *a.* biochemical.
Biodynamik [biˑoˑdyˑˈnaːmik], *f.* biokinetics.
biodynamisch [biˑoˑdyˑˈnaːmiʃ], *a.* biokinetic.
biogen[1] [biˑoˑˈgeːn], *a.* biogenous; biogenic.
Biogen[2] [biˑoˑˈgeːn], *n.* **-s/-e.** *Biol:* biogen.
Biogenese [biˑoˑgeˑˈneːzə], *f.* **-/.** *Biol:* biogenesis.
biogenetisch [biˑoˑgeˑˈneːtiʃ], *a.* biogenetic.
Biogenie [biˑoˑgeˑˈniː], *f.* **-/.** biogenetics.
Biograph [biˑoˑˈgraːf], *m.* **-en/-en,** biographer.
Biographie [biˑoˑgraˑˈfiː], *f.* **-/-n** [-ˈfiːən], biography.
biographisch [biˑoˑˈgraːfiʃ], *a.* biographic(al).
Biolith [biˑoˑˈliːt], *m.* **-(e)s/-e.** *Geol:* biolith, biolite.
Biologe [biˑoˑˈloːgə], *m.* **-n/-n,** biologist.
Biologie [biˑoˑloˑˈgiː], *f.* **-/.** biology.
biologisch [biˑoˑˈloːgiʃ], *a.* biological.
Biometrie [biˑoˑmeˑˈtriː], *f.* **-/.** biometry.
Biometrik [biˑoˑˈmeːtrik], *f.* **-/.** biometry.
Bionomie [biˑoˑnoˑˈmiː], *f.* **-/.** bionomics.
Biophysik [biˑoˑfyˑˈziːk], *f.* biophysics.
Biose [biˑˈoːzə], *f.* **-/-n.** *Ch:* biose.
Bioskop [biˑoˑˈskoːp], *n.* **-s/-e.** *A:* biograph, bioscope; (early form of) cinema.
Biosphäre [biˑoˑˈsfɛːrə], *f.* **-/.** biosphere.
biotisch [biˑˈoːtiʃ], *a. Nat.Hist:* biotic.
Biotit [biˑoˑˈtiːt], *m.* **-s/.** *Miner:* biotite.
Biotop [biˑoˑˈtoːp], *m.* **-s/-e.** *Nat.Hist:* biotope.
Biozönose [biˑoˑtsøˑˈnoːzə], *f.* **-/.** *Nat.Hist:* biocoenosis.
Bipede [biˑˈpeːdə], *m.* **-n/-n,** biped.
bipedisch [biˑˈpeːdiʃ], *a.* biped(al).
bipolar [biˑpoˑˈlaːr], *a. El: Ph:* bipolar, two-pole.
Bipontiner [biˑponˈtiːnər], *m.* **-s/-.** *Hist. of Print:* Bipont(ine) (edition) (*printed at Zweibrücken*).
Biprisma [biˑˈprismaː], *n. Opt:* biprism.
Biquadrat [biˑkvaˑˈdraːt, ˈbiːkvaˑdraˑt], *n. Mth:* biquadratic; fourth power (of a number).
biquadratisch [biˑkvaˑˈdraːtiʃ, ˈbiːkvaˑdraˑtiʃ], *a. Mth:* biquadratic (equation, etc.).
Biquet [biˑˈkɛː], *m.* **-s/-s,** precision balance for weighing coins.
birchen, *v.i.* (*haben*) (*of cattle*) to have a prolapse (of the womb).
Bircher-Benner, *m. see* **Müsli.**
Bircht, *m. & n.* **-(e)s/.** *Swiss:* hoar-frost.
Bireme [biˑˈreːmə], *f.* **-/-n.** *A.Hist:* bireme.
Birett [biˑˈrɛt], *n.* **-(e)s/-e.** *Ecc.Cost:* biretta.
birg, birgst, birgt *see* **bergen.**
Birke, *f.* **-/-n,** (*a*) *Bot:* birch(-tree); **niedrige B.,** shrubby birch; (*b*) birch(-wood).
birken, *a.* made of birch(-wood).
Birkenbaum, *m. Bot:* birch-tree.
Birkenbesen, *m.* birch-broom.
Birkenblättling, *m.* **-s/-e.** *Fung:* birch leather-gills.
Birkenfreund, *m. Ent:* rhynchites.
Birkengehölz, *n.*=**Birkenhain.**
Birkengewächse, *n.pl. Bot:* (the) birch family, betulaceae.
Birkengretchen, *n. F:* birch-rod.
Birkenhaarwasser, *n.* alcoholic hair-lotion made from birch-water.
Birkenhain, *m.* birch grove.
Birkenholz, *n.* birch(-wood).
Birkenknopfhornwespe, *f. Ent:* saw-fly of the birch-tree, birch saw-fly.
Birkenkohle, *f.* birch charcoal.
Birkenlaubsänger, *m. Orn:* willow-warbler, willow-wren.
Birkenlöcherschwamm, *m. Fung:* birch bracket.
Birkenmeier, *m. Dial:* birch-bark cup.
Birkenmesser, *m. Ent:* geometrid moth of the birch-tree.
Birkenmet, *m.* birch wine.
Birkenöl, *n. Pharm:* birch oil.
Birkenpilz, *m. Fung:* boletus scaber.
Birkenporling, *m. Fung:* birch bracket.
Birkenreis, *n.* **1.** (*a*) birch sprig; birch twig; (*b*) birch-rod. **2.** *Bot:* shrubby birch.
Birkenreizker, *m. Fung:* gripping toadstool.
Birkenrindöl, *n. Pharm:* birch oil.
Birkenritterling, *m. Fung:* tricholoma flavobrunneum.
Birkenröhrling, *m. Fung:* trachypus scaber.
Birkenrute, *f.* birch-rod, birch.
Birkensaft, *m.* sap of the birch-tree.
Birkenschwamm, *m.*=**Birkenpilz.**
Birkenspanner, *m. Ent:* peppered moth.
Birkenstecher, *m. Ent:* birch borer.
Birkentee, *m. Bot:* tormentil.
Birkenteer, *m. Pharm: Leath:* birch oil.
Birkentochter, *f. F:* birch-rod, birch.

Birkenvogel, *m.* = **Birkenspanner.**
Birkenwald, *m.* birch wood, birch forest.
Birkenwäldchen, *n.* birch-coppice, -grove.
Birkenwasser, *n.* **1.** birch-water; sap of the birch-tree. **2.** = **Birkenhaarwasser.**
Birkenwein, *m.* birch wine.
Birkenwickler, *m. Ent:* birch leaf roller.
Birkenzeisig, *m. Orn:* redpoll; **Grönländischer B.,** greater redpoll; **Nordischer B.,** mealy redpoll.
Birkfuchs, *m. Z:* light-bellied fox.
Birkhahn, *m. Orn:* black-cock.
Birkhenne, *f. Orn:* grey-hen.
Birkhuhn, *n. Orn:* black grouse.
Birkicht, *n.* **-s/-e,** birch-coppice, -grove.
Birkling, *m.* **-s/-e.** *Fung:* birch boletus, birch fungus.
Birkwild, *n. Orn: Coll:* black grouse, black game; heath-fowl.
Birkwurz, *f. Bot:* tormentil, shepherd's knot.
Birkwurzel, *f. Bot:* giant fennel, ferula.
Birlig, *m.* **-(e)s/-e.** *Swiss:* small haystack.
Birma ['birmaː]. *Pr.n.n.* **-s.** *Geog:* Burma(h).
Birmane [bir'maːnə], *m.* **-n/-n.** Burmese.
birmanisch [bir'maːniʃ], *a.* Burmese.
Birn-, *comb.fm. Cp.* **Birnen-.**
Birnball, *m. Box:* punch-ball.
Birnbaum, *m.* (*a*) *Bot:* pear-tree; (*b*) pear-wood.
Birnblattwespe, *f. Ent:* pear slug, pear saw-fly.
Birnblütenstecher, *m. Ent:* apple-blossom weevil.
Birne, *f.* **-/-n. 1.** (*a*) (*fruit*) pear; **eine mehlige B.,** a mealy pear; a sleepy pear; (*b*) pear-tree. **2.** pear-shaped object; (*a*) (electric light) bulb; (*b*) *Metall:* converter; (*c*) *Box:* punch-ball; (*d*) *Mus:* birn (on clarinet, etc.); (*e*) (pear-shaped) gag. **3.** *F:* head, *F:* nut, loaf, *U.S:* bean; **er hat eine weiche B.,** he's weak in the head, in the upper storey, he's a bit touched; **j-m eins auf die B. geben,** to give s.o. a crack on the nut.
birnenartig, *a.* pear-like.
Birnenäther, *m. Ch:* synthetic pear oil.
Birnenessenz, *f. Ch:* synthetic pear oil.
birnenförmig, *a.* pear-shaped; pyriform.
Birnenschnitzel, *n. & m.* slice of dried pear.
Birnenstäubling, *m. Fung:* lycoperdon pyriforme.
Birngallmücke, *f. Ent:* pear-midge.
Birnholz, *n.* pear(-wood).
Birnkopfschiene, *f. Rail:* pear-shaped rail-head.
Birnkraut, *n.* **1.** *Bot:* pyrola, wintergreen. **2.** *Cu:* condensed pear-pulp (*of treacly consistency*).
Birnmoos, *n. Bot:* thread-moss.
Birnmost, *m.* (*a*) (*alcoholic*) perry; (*b*) (*non-alcoholic*) pear-juice.
Birnmotte, *f. Ent:* ermine moth.
Birnöl, *n. Ch.* amyl acetate.
Birnquitte, *f. Bot:* pear-quince.
Birnsauger, *m. Ent:* pear-louse, pear-sucker, pear-tree psylla.
Birnschalter, *m.* pear-switch (of electric light); pear-push (of bell).
Birnschnecke, *f. Moll:* pear-shell.
Birnstab, *m. Arch:* ogee moulding, keel moulding.
Birnstern, *m. Z:* apiocrinite, pear-encrinite.
Birnwalze, *f. Moll:* pear-shell.
Birnwein, *m.* perry.
Birsch, *f.* **-/.** = **Pirsch.**
birschen, *v.* = **pirschen.**
birst *see* **bersten.**
Birutsche [bi·'rutʃə], *f.* **-/-n.** *Veh:* barouche.
Birzstrauch, *m. Bot:* German tamarisk.
bis[1]. I. *prep.* (+*acc.*) **1.** (*space*) up to, as far as, to; (*a*) **von London bis Paris,** from London to Paris; **ich reise bis Wien,** I am travelling as far as Vienna; **wir kommen heute noch bis Prag,** we shall get as far as Prague today; **(von) Seite fünf bis (Seite) zehn,** (from) page five to page ten, pages five to ten; **von Kopf bis Fuß,** from head to foot; **von vorne bis hinten,** from one end to the other; **bis hierher und nicht weiter,** this far and no farther; **bis dahin,** that far; **bis wohin?** how far? (*b*) (+*second prep.*) **bis an den Rhein,** up to, as far as, the Rhine; **ich begleite dich bis an die Grenze,** I shall accompany you as far as the border; **das Wasser reicht mir bis an die Schultern,** the water reaches up to my shoulders; **der Rock reicht bis ans, zum, Knie,** the skirt reaches to the knee; **ich kann bis zum obersten Ast des Baumes reichen,** I can reach (up to) the highest branch of the tree; **bis nach München,** as far as Munich; **der Brocken ist bis nach Erfurt sichtbar,** the Brocken is visible as far as Erfurt; **wir kamen bis vor das Tor,** we came up to the gate; **er folgte mir bis ins Zimmer,** he followed me right into the room; **die Landschaft ist hügelig bis kurz vor Köln,** the country is hilly nearly as far as Cologne. **2.** (*denoting duration in time*) till, until; to; (*a*) **von Montag bis Freitag,** from Monday till, to, Friday; *U.S:* Monday through Friday; **ich bleibe noch bis zum Abend,** I shall stay for the afternoon; **ich bleibe noch bis heute abend,** I shall stay till this evening; **der Laden bleibt bis sechs Uhr offen,** the shop stays open till six o'clock; **Sprechstunden von neun bis zwölf Uhr,** consulting hours from nine to twelve; **von morgens bis abends,** from morning till, to, night; **bis heute,** until today; **bis jetzt,** till now, until now; so far; hitherto; **bis morgen!** see you tomorrow! (*b*) (+*second prep.*) **vom Morgen bis zum Abend,** from morning till, to, night; **bis gegen sieben Uhr,** till nearly seven o'clock; **ich arbeite bis in die Nacht hinein,** I work late into the night, *F:* I burn the midnight oil; **bis vor einem Jahr,** until a year ago; **bis zum bitteren Ende,** to the bitter end; **er hat sie bis zum Ende treu gepflegt,** he cared for her faithfully to the end; **bis auf weiteres,** (i) for the meantime, (ii) until further orders. **3.** (*denoting time limit*) by; (*a*) **der Regen wird bis morgen aufgehört haben,** the rain will have stopped by tomorrow; **er wird mir das Geld bis Ostern schicken,** he will send me the money by Easter; **bis wann kannst du fertig sein?** by what time can you be ready? (*b*) (+*second prep.*) **das Buch wird bis zum nächsten Jahr fertig sein,** the book will be finished by next year; **ich erwarte eine Antwort bis in vierzehn Tagen,** I await a reply within fourteen days. **4.** (*denoting limitation in degree or number*) (*a*) **naß bis auf die Haut,** wet to the skin; **streng bis zur Grausamkeit,** severe to the point of cruelty; **bis ins Letzte (hinein),** to the last detail; **verliebt bis über beide Ohren,** head over heels in love; **bis zum Sterben müde,** tired, wearied, to death; **Kampf bis zum Tode,** fight to the death; **treu bis in den Tod,** true till death, faithful unto death; *B:* **meine Seele ist betrübt bis an den Tod,** my soul is exceeding sorrowful, even unto death; (*b*) **bis auf,** (i) up to but not including, (ii) up to and including; **alle starben bis auf den Feldwebel,** they all died except the sergeant; **ihre Truppe war bis auf die Hälfte reduziert,** their troop was reduced to half its number; **er muß alles bis auf den letzten Heller bezahlen,** he must pay up to the last farthing; **sie fielen bis auf den letzten Mann,** they fell, died, to a man; **bis (und) mit,** up to and including; **bis (und) mit Zeile zehn,** up to line ten inclusive; (*c*) **bis zehn zählen,** to count up to ten; **die englischen Könige von Wilhelm dem Eroberer bis Heinrich VII.,** the English kings from William the Conqueror to Henry VII; **alle sächsischen Könige bis herunter zu Alfred,** all the Saxon kings down to Alfred; **vom Prinzen bis herunter zum Bettelmann,** from prince down to beggar; **vom sechsten bis (zum) achten Jahrhundert,** from the sixth to the eighth centuries; (*d*) (*in approximate figures*) to; (*between consecutive numbers*) or, to; **acht bis zehn Mark,** eight to ten Marks; **sechs bis sieben Meter,** six or, to, seven metres; **die Handschrift stammt aus dem neunten bis zehnten Jahrhundert,** the manuscript dates from the ninth to the tenth century, from the ninth or the tenth century; **bis an tausend Männer,** close on, up to, a thousand men.

II. **bis,** *conj.* **1.** till, until; **ich warte, bis du gesprochen hast,** I shall wait until you have spoken; **nicht eher ... (als) bis ...,** not ... until ...; **das Kind hörte nicht eher zu weinen auf, als bis es vor Müdigkeit einschlief,** the child did not stop crying until it fell asleep, the child only stopped crying when it fell asleep; **du gehst mir nicht aus dem Haus, bis (daß) du (nicht) deine Aufgaben fertig hast,** you're not going out of the house till you've finished your homework; **getraue dich ja nicht, nach Hause zu kommen, bis du nicht dein Armband gefunden hast,** don't you dare come home till you've found your bracelet. **2.** *Austrian:* when; **bis er fertig ist, wird er nachkommen,** he will follow when he is ready.
bis[2]. *Lt.adv. Mus: etc:* bis; twice.
Bisam ['biːzam], *m.* **-s/-e. 1.** (*a*) *Z:* musk. (*b*) *Bot:* musk. **2.** musquash (fur); musk-rat skin.
bisamartig, *a.* musky.
Bisambeutel, *m.* musk-bag.
Bisambirne, *f. Bot:* musk-pear.
Bisamblume, *f. Bot:* sweet sultan.
Bisambock, *m. Ent:* = **Moschusbock.**
Bisamcentaurea, *f. Bot:* sweet sultan.
Bisamdistel, *f. Bot:* musk-thistle.
Bisameibisch, *m. Bot:* abel-musk, musk-mallow.
Bisamente, *f. Orn:* Muscovy duck, Barbary duck, musk duck.
bisamfarben, *a.* musk-coloured.
Bisamfell, *n.* musquash (fur); musk-rat skin.
Bisamflockenblume, *f. Bot:* sweet sultan.
Bisamgarbe, *f. Bot:* musk milfoil, alpine yarrow.
Bisamgeruch, *m.* (*a*) smell, scent, of musk; (*b*) musky smell.
Bisamgünsel, *m. Bot:* iva, ground-pine, herb-ivy.
Bisamhahnenfuß, *m. Bot:* musk crowfoot, moschatel.
Bisamhibiskus, *m. Bot:* abel-musk, musk-mallow.
Bisamhirsch, *m. Z:* (male) musk-deer.
Bisamhyazinthe, *f. Bot:* muscari; grape hyacinth.
Bisamkäfer, *m. Ent:* musk-beetle.
Bisamkatze, *f. Z:* civet(-cat).
Bisamknabenkraut, *n. Bot:* (*a*) butterfly orchis; (*b*) musk orchis.
Bisamkörner, *n.pl. Toil:* musk-seed; ambrette.
Bisamkraut, *n. Bot:* (*a*) (tuberous) moschatel; (*b*) musk stork's-bill; (*c*) = **Bisamknabenkraut;** (*d*) musk milfoil; (*e*) **echtes B.,** musk crowfoot, moschatel.
Bisamkugel, *m.* musk-ball.
Bisamkürbis, *m.* musky gourd, musk-melon.
Bisammalve, *f. Bot:* musk-mallow.
Bisamochse, *m. Z:* musk-ox; ovibos.
Bisampappel, *f. Bot:* abel-musk, musk-mallow.
Bisamratte, *f. Z:* musk-rat, musquash.
Bisamreiherschnabel, *m. Bot:* musk stork's-bill.
Bisamrose, *f. Bot:* musk-rose.
Bisamrüßler, *m. Z:* desman.
Bisamschafgarbe, *f. Bot:* musk milfoil, alpine yarrow.
Bisamschwein, *n. Z:* peccary.
Bisamspitzmaus, *f. Z:* desman.
Bisamstier, *m. Z:* musk-ox; ovibos.
Bisamstorchschnabelkraut, *n. Bot:* musk stork's bill.
Bisamstrauch, *m. Bot:* musk, abel-musk.
Bisamtier, *n. Z:* musk-deer.
Bisan [bi·'zaːn, 'biːza·n], *m.* **-s/-e.** *A:* = **Besan.**
bischen, *v.tr. Dial:* to calm, quiet.
Bischof, *m.* **-s/⸗e. 1.** *Ecc:* bishop. **2.** mulled wine, bishop.
Bischofit [biʃo·'fiːt], *m.* **-s/.** *Miner:* bischofite.
bischöflich, *a.* (*a*) episcopal; belonging to a bishop; **die bischöfliche Residenz,** the bishop's residence, the episcopal residence; **die bischöfliche Würde,** (i) the dignity of a bishop, (ii) the office of a bishop, the episcopal office; **mit der bischöflichen Würde bekleidet werden,** to be made a bishop; *Hist: etc:* **die Bischöflichen,** (i) the bishop's supporters, men, (ii) the bishop's party; *see also* **Palais; Gnade;** (*b*) *R.C.Ch:* pontifical (mass, etc.); (*c*) **die Bischöfliche Kirche,** the Episcopal Church.
Bischofsamt, *n. Ecc:* episcopate, office of bishop.
Bischofshut, *m.* **1.** *Ecc.Cost: Her:* bishop's hat. **2.** *Bot:* (*a*) alpine barrenwort; (*b*) mitre-wort, bishop's cap.
Bischofskleidung, *f. Ecc:* pontificals.
Bischofskreuz, *n. Ecc:* (bishop's) pectoral cross.
Bischofskrokus, *m. Bot:* purple crocus.
Bischofsmantel, *m. Ecc:* pall; pallium.
Bischofsmeise, *f. Orn:* crested titmouse.
Bischofsmütze, *f.* **1.** *Ecc:* mitre. **2.** *Bot:* (*a*) alpine barrenwort; (*b*) mitre-wort, bishop's cap. **3.** *Hort: F:* pumpkin; squash-melon. **4.** *Fung:* (*a*) edible turban-top; (*b*) bishop's mitre mushroom. **5.** *Moll:* mitra; mitre shell.
bischofsmützenförmig, *a. Nat.Hist:* mitriform.
Bischofsornat, *m. Ecc:* pontificals.
Bischofspalast, *m.* bishop's palace.
Bischofspfennig, *m. Paleont:* trochite, entrochite.
Bischofsring, *m. Ecc:* episcopal ring; (bishop's) pastoral ring.
Bischofssitz, *m. Ecc:* **1.** see; **Trier ist ein B.,** Trier is a cathedral town. **2.** bishop's palace.
Bischof(s)stab, *m.* **1.** *Ecc:* bishop's crook; crosier, crozier, pastoral staff. **2.** *Paleont:* lituite.
Bischof(s)stuhl, Bischofsthron, *m.* episcopal throne.
Bischofstracht, *f. Ecc:* pontificals.
Bischofswürde, *f.* (*a*) dignity of a bishop; (*b*) office of bishop, bishopric, episcopate.
Bise, *f.* **-/-n,** north(-east) wind.
biseautieren [bi·zo·'tiːrən], *v.tr.* to mark, nick (cards).
Bisektion [bi·zɛktsi'oːn], *f.* **-/-en,** bisection.
Bisektrix [bi·'zɛktriks], *f.* **-/-trizes** [-tri·'tse·s]. *Geom: Opt:* bisectrix.
Biserta [bi·'zɛrtaː]. *Pr.n.n.* **-s.** *Geog:* Bizerta.
bisextil [bi·zɛks'tiːl], *a.* bissextile.
bisexuell [bi·zɛksu·'ɛl], *a.* bisexual, bisexed.
bisher [bis'heːr], *adv.* up to now; hitherto; so far; **wie b.,** as hitherto, as before; **b. erschienen drei**

Bände der Ausgabe, three volumes of the edition have appeared so far; **der b. erschienene Teil des Romans,** the part of the novel published to date, so far; (*of serial story*) the story so far **die b. kälteste Nacht des Winters,** the coldest night yet this winter.

bisherig, *a.* as up to the present; **mein bisheriger Lehrer,** the teacher I have had till now; **unsere bisherige Wohnung,** the flat we have had till now; **der bisherige Rekord,** the previous record; **in meinem bisherigen Leben,** in my life so far; **die bisherigen Verhandlungen haben zu keinem Ergebnis geführt,** the negotiations hitherto, so far, to date, have not led to any result; **der bisherige Außenminister,** the former foreign minister; **der bisherige Präsident,** the retiring, outgoing, president; **der bisherige Präsident wurde wiedergewählt,** the sitting president was re-elected.

Biskaya [bisˈkaːjaː]. *Pr.n.f.* -. *Geog:* Biscay; **der Golf von B.,** the Bay of Biscay.

Biskayer [bisˈkaːjər], *m.* -s/-. *Geog:* Biscayan.

biskayisch [bisˈkaːjiʃ], *a. Geog:* Biscayan; **der Biskayische Meerbusen,** the Bay of Biscay.

Biskotte [bisˈkotə], *f.* -/-n. *Cu:* dry sponge-finger.

Biskuit [bisˈkviːt], *m. & n.* -(e)s/-e. **1.** *Cu:* (*a*) dry sweet biscuit; (*b*) = **Biskuitteig. 2.** *Cer:* unglazed porcelain, biscuit ware, bisque.

Biskuitgut, *n. Cer:* biscuit ware.

Biskuitporzellan, *n.* = **Biskuit** 2.

Biskuitrolle, Biskuitroulade, *f. Cu:* Swiss roll.

Biskuitteig, *m. Cu:* sponge mixture.

bislang [bisˈlaŋ], *adv.* = **bisher.**

Bismarckarchipel, der. *Pr.n. Geog:* the Bismarck archipelago.

Bismarckbraun, *n. Dy:* Bismarck brown.

Bismarckhering, *m. Com:* (kind of) marinaded herring.

Bismut [ˈbismuːt], *m.* -(e)s/. *Ch: Miner:* bismuth.

Bismutin [bismu·ˈtiːn], *n.* -s/-e. *Miner:* bismuthin, bismuthinite, bismuth glance.

Bismutit [bismu·ˈtiːt], *m.* -(e)s/-e. *Miner:* bismutite.

Bison [ˈbiːzon], *m.* -s/-e. *Z:* bison.

biß[1] *see* **beißen.**

Biß[2], *m.* **Bisses/Bisse,** bite; **der B. einer Schlange,** the bite of a snake, a snake-bite.

Bissa, *f.* -/-. *Rept:* hawk's-bill (turtle).

Bißchen. I. *n.* -s/-, small piece; small bite; morsel.

II. **bißchen,** *n.* (*also used as inv.a. & adv.*) (*a*) bit; little bit; **ein kleines b.,** a wee bit, a tiny bit; **ein ganz kleines b.,** a tiny little bit; **noch ein b.,** a little more; *Int.* **du liebes b.!** good Heavens! my goodness! **ich muß jetzt mal ein b. essen,** I must have something to eat now; **gib mir ein b. von deinem Kuchen,** give me a little of your cake; **das b., das ihnen von ihrer Freiheit übrigbleibt,** the little that remains of their freedom; (*time*) **bleib noch ein b.,** stay a little (while) longer; (*b*) a little, a (little) bit of; **ein b. Wein,** a little wine; **ein b. Brot,** a little bit of bread; **mein b. Geld,** my little bit of money; what little money I have; **ein b. Glück,** (i) a spot of luck, (ii) a little happiness; **er kann ein b. Englisch,** he knows a little, a bit of, English, he has a smattering of English; **ich habe ein b. Kopfweh,** I have a bit of a headache, I have a slight headache; (*c*) a little, a bit, slightly; **ein b. dumm,** a bit silly; **du mußt ihm ein b. vertrauen,** you must trust him a little: **ein b. besser,** a little better, slightly better; **ich habe mich ein b. verbrannt,** I have burned myself slightly; **sie ist ein b. verschnupft,** (i) she has a slight cold, a bit of a cold, (ii) she is a bit sulky; **das ist ein b. viel verlangt,** that's asking rather a lot, that's rather a tall order; **kein b.,** not at all, not in the least; **ich bin kein b. müde,** I am not at all, not a bit, not in the least, tired.

bisse *see* **beißen.**

bissel, *n. Dial:* = **bißchen.**

Bisselachse, *f. Rail:* pony-track (of engine).

Bissen, *m.* -s/-, (*a*) mouthful; **der B. blieb mir im Halse stecken,** the food stuck in my throat; (*b*) morsel, small piece (of bread, etc.); **ich habe heute keinen B. gegessen,** I haven't had a bite all day; **er gönnt mir nicht einmal einen B. Brot,** he begrudges me the prime necessities of life; *F:* **ein fetter B.,** a piece of good luck (bringing financial gain); a lucrative business; (*c*) snack, small meal; **iß doch einen B. mit mir,** do have a snack, a bite, with me; **einen warmen B. haben,** to have, eat, sth. hot; (*d*) = **Bolus** (*b*).

bissenweise, *adv.* in mouthfuls; mouthful by mouthful.

bissextil [biseksˈtiːl], *a.* bissextile.

bissig, *a.* (*a*) biting (horse, etc.); **ein bissiger Hund,** a dog that bites; **'Achtung, bissiger Hund!'** 'beware of the dog'; **dieser Hund ist b.,** this dog bites; (*b*) cross, snappy, cantankerous (person); (*c*) biting, mordant, caustic, pungent (wit, speech, etc.); cutting (remark); *adv.* **sie antwortete b.,** she replied bitingly.

Bissigkeit, *f.* (*a*) viciousness (of dog, horse, etc.); (*b*) crossness, cantankerousness (of person); (*c*) mordancy, pungency, causticity (of wit, etc.); bite (of remark).

Bißkraut, *n. Bot:* pasque-flower.

Bißwunde, *f.* bite.

bist *see* **sein**[2].

bisten, *v.i.* (*haben*) (*of hazel-hen*) to call.

Bister [ˈbiːstər], *m. & n.* -s/. bistre.

Bisterbraun, *n.* **1.** bistre. **2.** *a.* **bisterbraun,** bistre; blackish-brown.

Bistouri [bisˈtuːriː], *m. & n.* -s/-s. *Surg:* bistoury.

Bistum, *n.* -s/⸗er. *Ecc:* **1.** bishopric, diocese. **2.** *occ:* office of bishop, bishopric, episcopate.

Bisulfit [biːzulˈfiːt], *n.* -s/-e. *Ch:* bisulphite.

bisweilen [bisˈvailən], *adv.* sometimes, at times, now and then; off and on; occasionally.

Biswind, *m.* = **Bise.**

bisyllabisch [bi·zy'laːbiʃ], *a.* dis(s)yllabic.

Bithynien [bi·ˈtyːniən]. *Pr.n.n.* -s. *A.Geog:* Bithynia.

Bithynier [bi·ˈtyːniər], -s/-. Bithynian.

bithynisch [bi·ˈtyːniʃ], *a.* Bithinian.

Bittabend, *m.* wedding eve.

Bittag, *m. Rel:* **die Bittage,** the Rogation days.

Bittamt, *n. Ecc:* rogation mass.

Bittbrief, *m.* letter of request; (written) petition; begging letter.

Bitte, *f.* -/-n, (*a*) request (**um,** for); wish (**um,** for); (formal) petition; **dringende B.,** entreaty; **B. um Geld,** request for money; **auf Ihre B. (hin),** at your request; **auf meine dringende B. (hin),** at my urgent request; **eine B. aussprechen,** to make a request; to ask for sth.; **eine B. an j-n richten, tun,** to ask s.o. a favour, a favour of s.o.; **j-m eine B. vortragen,** to make a request to s.o.; **eine B. gewähren, erfüllen,** to grant a request, wish; **ich habe eine (große) B. an dich,** I have a (great) favour to ask of you; **ich habe ˈeine B. an euch,** I have just ˈone thing to ask you; **er blieb taub gegen alle meine Bitten,** he remained deaf to all my entreaties; *Rel:* **die sieben Bitten des Vaterunsers,** the seven petitions of the Lord's Prayer; (*b*) prayer, supplication; **Herr, erhöre meine B.,** (O) Lord, hear my prayer.

bitten. I. *v.tr.* (*strong*) **1.** (*a*) **j-n um etwas b., j-n etwas b.,** to ask s.o. for sth.; to request sth. of s.o.; to beg s.o. for sth.; **j-n b., etwas zu tun,** to ask, request, s.o. to do sth.; **j-n (um Erlaubnis) b., etwas tun zu dürfen,** to ask s.o.'s permission, leave, to do sth.; **um Brot b.,** to ask for bread; **um Geld b.,** to ask for money; **um Gnade b.,** to beg for mercy; **um Gehör b.,** to request a hearing, to ask to be heard; (*at meeting, etc.*) **darf ich um Gehör b.?** may I have your attention? **j-n um Entschuldigung b.,** to beg s.o.'s pardon; **um Antwort wird gebeten, (u.A.w.g.),** an answer is requested, (R.S.V.P.); **um Überweisung per Scheck wird gebeten,** kindly remit by cheque; **darf ich um Ihren Namen b.?** may I ask your name? **man bat uns um unsere Pässe, wir wurden um unsere Pässe gebeten,** we were asked for our passports; **eine Frau um ihre Hand b.,** to ask a lady for her hand (in marriage), to propose (marriage) to a lady; **dürfte ich Sie um Feuer b.?** might I trouble you for a light? **ich bat sie um Verzeihung,** I asked, begged, her forgiveness; I asked her to forgive me; **ich möchte Sie um etwas b., um eine Gefälligkeit b.,** I should like to ask you a favour, I have a favour to ask of you; *Com:* **wir bitten um Ihre werte Kundschaft,** we solicit your custom; *B:* **bittet, so wird euch gegeben,** ask, and it shall be given you; **ich bat, ihn sehen zu dürfen,** I asked to see him; **er bat, ein paar Worte sagen zu dürfen,** he asked to be allowed to say a few words; **es wird gebeten, die Türe zu schließen,** you are requested to close the door; **darf ich Sie b., Ihren Hut abzunehmen?** would you be kind enough to take off, remove, your hat? (*b*) **j-n zu etwas b.,** to ask, invite, s.o. to sth.; **j-n zum Tee b.,** to ask, invite, s.o. to tea; **j-n zu einem Glas Wein b.,** to invite s.o. to (have) a glass of wine; **j-n zu Tisch b.,** (i) to invite s.o. to a meal; (ii) to ask s.o. to come to table; **j-n auf einen Abend zu sich b.,** to ask s.o. round for the evening. **2.** (*a*) **bei j-m für j-n b.,** to plead with s.o. for s.o.; to intercede with s.o. on s.o.'s behalf; (*b*) *Rel:* to pray, intercede (for s.o.); **bitte für uns!** pray for us! **zu Gott und allen Heiligen b.,** to pray to God and all the saints. **3.** (*expressing indignation, surprise, etc.*) **da muß ich doch sehr b.!** how could you say such a thing! I really must protest; please be careful what you say; **ich bitte dich!** (i) I ask you! would you believe it! (ii) (*slightly irritated*) really! I ask you! **4. bitte;** (*a*) please; **bitte, weinen Sie nicht,** please don't cry; **bitte, sei mir nicht böse,** please don't be cross with me; **bitte, sagen Sie mir,** please tell me, tell me, please; **bitte, bleiben Sie ein bißchen,** do stay a little; **sei bitte so freundlich und hilf mir,** please be so kind as to help me; **bitte wenden!** *abbr.* **b.w.,** please turn over, *abbr.* P.T.O.; **bitte nicht stören!** please do not disturb; **bitte Türe schließen!** please close the door; **hierher, bitte!** this way, (if you) please! **das Kind kann schon 'bitte, bitte' machen,** the baby can already clap its hands (*meaning 'please'*); (*reply to knock on door*) **bitte!** come in! **darf ich Ihren Bleistift benutzen? — bitte!** (*more formal*) **ich bitte Sie darum!** may I use your pencil? certainly! with pleasure! (*b*) (*as reply often not translated*) **danke (schön) — bitte (sehr)!** thank you—don't mention it, *F:* that's all right, you're welcome; **Entschuldigung! — bitte!** sorry, (I beg your) pardon—don't mention it, *F:* that's all right; **könnten Sie mir das Salz reichen?** — bitte! could you pass me the salt?—certainly; (*offering sth.*) **bitte!** help yourself, do take some, one; (*c*) **bitte? wie bitte?** pardon? I beg your pardon? *F:* I didn't quite catch that; (*indignant*) **wie bitte?** I ˈbeg your pardon! *See also* **gebeten.**

II. *vbl s.* **Bitten,** *n. in vbl senses; also:* (*a*) solicitation; (*b*) prayers, entreaties; **nach langem Bitten,** after long pleading; by dint of long entreaty; **all mein B. und Flehen half mir nichts,** all my prayers and entreaties were of no avail.

III. **bittend,** *pr.p. & a. in vbl senses; esp.* **1.** pleading, beseeching; **er fragte sie in bittendem Ton,** he asked her beseechingly. **2. Bittende,** *m. f.* supplicant, suppliant.

bitter[1], *a.* **1.** (*a*) bitter (taste); **bittere Galle,** bitter gall; **bitterer Wein, bitteres Bier,** bitter wine, beer; **ich habe einen bitteren Geschmack auf der Zunge,** I have a bitter taste in my mouth; **das Bittere,** the bitter principle (of substance); *see also* **Pille;** (*b*) bitter (cold); biting, bitter, raw (wind); sharp (frost); (*c*) bitter (person); **ein bitteres Lächeln,** a bitter smile; **das Leiden hat ihn b. gemacht, er ist durch Leiden b. geworden,** suffering has embittered him, he has grown bitter through suffering; (*d*) **eine bittere Erfahrung,** a bitter, galling, experience; **eine bittere Enttäuschung,** a bitter disappointment; **bittere Reue,** bitter remorse; **bittere Schmerzen,** (i) grievous pains, (ii) dire grief; **der bittere Tod,** cruel death; **sie weinte bittere Tränen,** she wept bitter tears; **das ist b.,** that is hard to bear; (*e*) bitter (attack, scorn); biting (irony); biting, bitter, stinging (criticism); **er hat eine bittere Ausdrucksweise,** he has a caustic way of expressing himself; *Lit:* **des Todes bittere Pfeile,** the cruel arrows of death; (*f*) (*intensive*) **bittere Armut,** abject poverty; **bittere Not,** desperate need, dire distress; **bitterer Haß,** bitter, fierce, hatred; **bittere Feinde,** bitter enemies; **bitteres Unrecht,** grievous wrong; **bitterer Hunger,** gnawing, raging, hunger; **die bitterste Verzweiflung,** the depths of despair; **in bitterer Verlegenheit,** in dire straits; **bis zum bitteren Ende,** to the bitter end. **2.** *adv.* **b. kalt,** bitterly cold; **b. weinen,** to weep bitterly; **er ist mir b. feind,** he is my bitter enemy; **Sparsamkeit ist b. nötig,** economy is of the utmost, of the direst, necessity; **sie tun uns b. Unrecht,** they do us grievous wrong; *see also* **Ernst**[3] (*b*).

Bitter[2], *m.* -s/-. *Dist:* bitters.

Bitter[3], *m.* -s/-, supplicant, suppliant.

Bitter[4], *m.* -s/-. *Orn:* redwing.

Bitterapfel, *m. Bot:* bitter-apple, colocynth.

Bitterbier, *n.* bitter beer, bitter.

Bitterblatt, *n. Bot:* (*a*) gentianella, *esp.* (i) slender cicendia, (ii) least cicendia; (*b*) buck-bean, bog bean, marsh trefoil.

Bitterbohne, *f. Bot:* white lupin.

bitterböse, *a.* (*a*) furious, livid (with anger); (*b*) very wicked, very evil; **ein bitterböser Mann,** a villainous character.

Bitterbrunnen, *m.* = **Bitterwasser.**

Bitterdistel, *f. Bot:* holy thistle, blessed thistle.

Bitterende, *n. Nau: F:* salt beef, (salt) junk.

Bittererde, *f. Ch: Pharm:* magnesia, magnesium oxide.

bitterernst, *a.* dead serious (matter, words, etc.); **es ist mir b. (damit),** I am dead serious (about it).

Bitteresche, *f. Bot:* quassia(-tree); (*a*) bitter

damson, mountain damson; (*b*) bitter-wood, bitter ash.
Bitterfäule, *f.* bitter rot (of fruit).
Bitterfisch, *m.* = **Bitterling.**
Bittergurke, *f.* = **Bitterapfel.**
Bitterholz, *n. Bot:* **1.** = **Bitteresche.** **2.** quassia (wood).
Bitterholzbaum, *m.* = **Bitteresche.**
Bitterkalk, *m. Miner:* dolomite (marble); magnesian limestone.
bitterkalt, *a.* bitterly cold; bitter, raw.
Bitterkeit, *f.* (*a*) bitterness (of fruit, etc., of sorrow); (*b*) sharpness (of frost, etc.); asperity (of tone); (*c*) grievousness (of pain).
Bitterklee, *m. Bot:* menyanthes, buck-bean, bog bean, bog trefoil, marsh trefoil, water trefoil.
Bitterkleesalz, *n.* = **Sauerkleesalz.**
Bitterknöterich, *m. Bot:* water-pepper, smart-weed.
Bitterkraut, *n. Bot:* (any) bitter-tasting herb, *esp.* (i) erythraea, (lesser *or* common) centaury, (ii) picris.
Bitterkresse, *f. Bot:* (*a*) cuckoo-flower, lady's-smock, mayflower; (*b*) scurvy-grass.
Bitterkürbis, *m.* = **Bitterapfel.**
Bitterlattich, *m. Bot:* (*a*) ox-tongue; (*b*) dandelion.
bitterlich, *a.* (*a*) rather, slightly bitter (taste); (*b*) *adv.* bitterly; grievously, deeply; **b. weinen,** to weep bitterly.
Bitterling, *m.* **-s/-e.** **1.** *Bot:* (*a*) **(durchwachsener) B.,** yellow centaury; (*b*) = **Bitterlattich;** (*c*) = **Bitterknöterich.** **2.** *Fung:* peppery toadstool. **3.** *Ich:* bitterling. **4.** = **Bitterwasser.**
Bittermandel, *f.* bitter almond.
Bittermandelöl, *n.* oil of bitter almonds; *Ch:* benzaldehyde.
Bittermandelölkampfer, *m. Com:* gum benzoin; *F:* benjamin.
Bittermittel, *n. Pharm: etc:* bitter(s).
Bitternis, *f.* **-/-nisse,** (*a*) = **Bitterkeit;** (*b*) painful event; distress.
Bitterrinde, *f. Bot:* quassia (bark).
Bittersalz, *n. Pharm:* Epsom salts.
Bitterschwamm, *m. Fung:* peppery toadstool.
Bitterspat, *m. Miner:* (*a*) magnesite; (*b*) dolomite.
Bitterstein, *m. Miner:* (*a*) jade; (*b*) nephrite; (*c*) jadeite; (*d*) saussurite.
Bitterstoff, *m. Ch:* bitter principle, bitter constituent.
bittersüß[1], *a.* bitter-sweet.
Bittersüß[2], *n.* **-/.** *Bot:* woody nightshade, bitter-sweet.
Bitterwasser, *n.* bitter mineral water (containing magnesium sulphate).
Bitterweide, *f. Bot:* crack-willow.
Bitterwein, *m.* bittered wine; vermouth.
Bitterwurz(el), *f. Bot:* **1.** (*a*) yellow gentian, bitterwort; (*b*) yellow centaury; (*c*) American centaury. **2.** common sorrel; patience-dock.
Bittessen, *n.* supper on the wedding eve.
Bittfahrt, *f.* (*a*) pilgrimage; (*b*) (religious) procession.
Bittflehende, *m., f.* (*decl. as adj.*) supplicant, suppliant.
Bittgang, *m.* (*a*) approach (to s.o. for sth.); **einen B. tun, machen,** to approach s.o. for sth.; **ihr B. war vergeblich,** her mission was fruitless; (*b*) *Rel:* pilgrimage; (*c*) *Rel:* procession, *esp.* during rogation week.
Bittgebet, *n. Rel:* petitionary prayer.
Bittgesuch, *n.* petition (**um,** for); formal, solemn, request (**um,** for).
Bittgottesdienst, *m.* rogation service.
Bittleihen, *n. Austrian Jur:* precarium.
Bittling, *m.* **-s/-e.** *Husb:* weaned calf (*under one year of age*).
Bittprozession, *f. Rel:* procession round the fields, *esp.* on rogation days.
Bittschreiben, *n.* = **Bittschrift.**
Bittschrift, *f.* (written) petition; **eine B. an j-n richten,** to petition s.o.
Bittsteller, *m.* **-s/-,** petitioner.
bittweise, *adv.* through, by way of, by means of, prayers, entreaty.
Bittwoche, *f. Rel:* rogation week, procession week.
Bitumen [biˑˈtuːmən], *n.* **-s/.** *Ch: Miner:* bitumen; asphalt.
Bitumenpackpapier, *n. Com:* pitch-paper, tarred paper.
Bitumenpappe, *f.* tar-board, tarred felt, roofing felt.
Bitumenverputz, *m. Constr:* bituminous coating.
bituminieren [biˑtuˑmiˑˈniːrən], *v.tr.* to bituminize; to cover (road, etc.) with bitumen.
Bituminit [biˑtuˑmiˑˈniːt], *m.* **-s/.** *Miner:* boghead (coal).
bituminös [biˑtuˑmiˑˈnøːs], *a.* bituminous; **bituminöser Schiefer,** bituminous shale, oil-shale.
Bitz, *m.* **-es/.** **1.** *Dial:* = **Bißchen.** **2.** sharp flavour, tang (of cheese, etc.).
bitzeln, *v. Dial:* **1.** *v.i.* (*haben*) (*a*) (*of taste*) to be sharp, to burn; (*b*) (*of pers.*) to tingle (with anger, etc.). **2.** *v.tr.* to cut (sth.) into small pieces.
Bitzl, Bitzli, *n.* **-s/-.** *Dial:* = **Bißchen.**
bivalent [biˑvaˑˈlɛnt], *a. Ch:* bivalent, divalent.
Bivalve [biˈvalvə], *m.* **-n/-n.** *Moll:* bivalve.
Biwak [ˈbiːvak], *n.* **-s/-e** & **-s.** *Mil: etc:* bivouac.
biwakieren [biˑvaˈkiːrən], *v.i.* (*haben*) *Mil: etc:* to bivouac.
Bixazeen [biksaˑˈtseːən], *f.pl. Bot:* bixaceae.
Bizarde [biˑˈtsardə], *f.* **-/-n** = **Bizarre.**
bizarr [biˑˈtsar], *a.* peculiar, eccentric, queer, odd, outlandish, bizarre.
Bizarre [biˑˈtsarə], *f.* **-/-n.** *Hort:* bizarre.
Bizarrerie [biˑtsarəˈriː], *f.* **-/-n** [-ˈriːən], deliberate eccentricity.
bizentrisch [biˑˈtsɛntriʃ], *a. Geom:* bicentral.
bizephalisch [biˑtseˑˈfaːliʃ], *a.* = **bikephalisch.**
Bizeps [ˈbiːtsɛps], *m.* **-es/-e.** *Anat:* biceps (muscle).
bizonal [biˑtsoˑˈnaːl], *a. Hist:* (*in Occupied Germany*) bizonal (administration, etc.).
Bizone, die [ˈbiˑtsoˑnə]. *Hist:* (*in Occupied Germany*) the British-American Zone, *F:* Bizonia.
blach, *a. A. & Lit:* flat, level, even.
Blache, *f.* **-/-n.** **1.** *A. & Lit:* = **Blachfeld.** **2.** *Dial:* = **Blahe.**
Blachfeld, *n. A. & Lit:* plain, champaign; (battle-)field.
Blachfrost, *m.* black frost.
Blackfisch [ˈblakfiʃ], *m. Moll:* cuttle(-fish), sepia.
Blackfischbein, *n.* cuttle-bone, cuttle-fish bone.
blaff, *int.* (*a*) pop! bang! whack! (*b*) (*dog's bark*) woof!
blaffen, bläffen, *v.i.* (*haben*) (*of dog*) to bark.
Blaffert, *m.* **-(e)s/-e.** *Swiss: Num:* blaffert.
Blag, *n.* **-s/-en, Blage,** *f.* **-/-n.** *F:* brat.
blagieren [blaˑˈgiːrən], *v.i.* (*haben*) to boast, to brag.
Blahe, *f.* **-/-n,** canvas; tarpaulin.
blähen. I. *v.tr.* **1.** (*a*) to inflate, distend; to puff out, blow out, bulge (one's cheeks); to dilate (nostrils); (*of wind*) **die Segel b.,** to fill, to belly (out), the sails; (*b*) *Med:* to distend; to make (abdomen) flatulent; *Vet:* to hove, to blow, (sheep, cattle). **2. sich blähen,** (*a*) to become inflated; (*of abdomen*) to become distended; *Vet:* (*of sheep, etc.*) to become hoven, blown, blasted; (*of skirt, etc.*) to balloon out; *Nau:* (*of sails*) to belly; (*b*) to puff oneself up; to give oneself airs; *B:* **die Liebe blähet sich nicht,** charity is not puffed up.
II. *vbl s.* **1. Blähen,** *n. in vbl senses; also:* inflation; distension (of abdomen); dilation (of nostrils). **2. Blähung,** *f.* (*a*) = II. 1; (*b*) *pl.* **Blähungen,** *Med:* flatulence, flatulency, *F:* wind; **Blähungen haben,** (*of person*) to suffer from flatulence, wind; (*of animal*) to be hoven, blown, blasted; *Pharm:* **Mittel gegen Blähungen,** carminative; **Blähungen vertreibend,** carminative.
Blähhals, *m. Med:* goitre.
Blähsucht, *f.* **1.** *Med:* flatulence, flatulency, *F:* wind. **2.** *Vet:* (*a*) bloat, blast, hoove; (*b*) grain-founder, grain-sick.
Blak, *m.* **-(e)s/.** *North G.Dial:* black smoke (from oil lamps).
blaken, *v.i.* (*haben*) (*of lamp*) to smoke.
blamabel [blaˑˈmaːbəl], *a.* embarrassing, humiliating; shameful; **eine blamable Geschichte,** (i) an embarrassing, a humiliating, business; (ii) a shameful, disgraceful, business.
Blamage [blaˑˈmaːʒə], *f.* **-/-n,** (*a*) fiasco; disgrace; scandal; (*b*) humiliation; **es war eine furchtbare B.,** (i) it was dreadfully embarrassing; (ii) it was a complete fiasco; it was an absolute disgrace.
blamieren [blaˑˈmiːrən], *v.tr.* **1.** to make a fool of (s.o.); to let (s.o.) down, to disgrace, to compromise (s.o.); **das Kind hat mich schrecklich blamiert,** the child disgraced me, let me down. **2. sich blamieren,** to make a fool of oneself; to lose face; to make a blunder, *F:* to put one's foot in it, to make a gaffe, to make a bloomer.
Blanc fixe [ˈblãː ˈfiːks], *n.* **-/.** *Ch:* permanent white.
Blanchiereisen [blãˑˈʃiːr-], *n. Tls:* fleshing-iron.
blanchieren [blãˑˈʃiːrən], *v.tr. Cu:* to blanch (vegetables, etc.); *Leath:* to flesh (hides).
Blanchierspäne, *m.pl. Leath:* fleshings.
Blanchisseuse [blãˑʃiˑˈsøːzə], *f.* **-/-n,** washer-woman, laundress.
Blancmanger [blãˑmãˑˈʒeː], *f.* **-/-.** *Cu:* blanc-mange.
blank, *a.* **1.** shining, shiny, bright; (*of animal*) sleek; **blanke Augen,** (i) bright, shining, eyes; (ii) feverish eyes; **blanke Taler,** shining thalers; **etwas b. scheuern, putzen, machen,** to polish sth., to rub sth. till it shines; *see also* **Hans** 1 (*b*). **2.** bare, uncovered, naked; **blankes Schwert,** bare, naked, drawn, sword; **blanke Waffen,** side-arms; **b. ziehen,** to draw one's sword; **blankes Eis,** smooth ice, ice not covered by snow; **blanke Fäuste,** bare, naked, fists; **blanker Hintern,** bare bottom; **die blanke Wahrheit,** the naked, unvarnished, truth; *F:* **ich bin völlig b.,** I am quite penniless, *F:* stony broke.
Blankett [blaŋˈkɛt], *n.* **-(e)s/-e,** blank form, blank cheque.
Blankglühen, *n. Metall:* bright annealing.
Blankleder, *n.* sleeked leather, harness leather.
blanko [ˈblaŋkoː], *inv.a.* (*of form, etc.*) blank, not filled in; *Com:* uncovered, unsecured; **in b.,** in blank; **in b. trassieren,** to draw in blank; *St.Exch:* **b. abgeben, verkaufen,** to sell short, *F:* to sell, to go, a bear.
Blankoakzept [ˈblaŋkoˑˀaktsɛpt], *n. Com: Fin:* blank acceptance.
Blankogiro, *n.* **-s/-s.** *Fin: etc:* blank endorsement.
Blankokredit, *m. Com: Fin:* blank credit, open credit.
Blankoscheck, *m.* blank cheque.
Blankounterschrift, *f. Com: Jur:* paper signed in blank; blank signature.
Blankoverkauf, *m. St.Exch:* short sale.
Blankoverkäufer, *m. St.Exch:* bear.
Blankovollmacht, *f. Com: Jur:* full power of attorney; 'carte blanche'.
Blankowechsel, *m. Com: Fin:* blank bill.
Blankscheit, *n. Cost:* busk.
Blankvers, *m. Pros:* blank verse.
blankziehen, *v.i. sep.* (*strong*) (*haben*) to draw one's sword.
blarren, *v.i.* (*haben*) *F:* to cry, howl; *P:* to blub, blubber.
Bläschen, *n.* **-s/-,** small blister; small bubble; *Anat: Med:* vesicle; **Bläschen auf der Zunge,** blisters on the tongue.
Bläschenausschlag, *m.,* **Bläschenflechte,** *f. Med:* herpes.
bläschenförmig, *a. Anat:* vesicular, aveolar (gland).
Blase, *f.* **-/-n.** **1.** (*a*) *Anat:* bladder; air-bladder (of fish); (*b*) bladder (of football, etc.); (*c*) (*in strip cartoon*) balloon. **2.** (*a*) blister (on skin, metal, paint, on surface of plastics); (*of paint*) **Blasen werfen,** to blister; *Med:* **Blasen ziehen,** to blister; **ein Finger voller Blasen,** a blistered finger; **sich** *dat.* **eine B. laufen,** to get a blister on one's foot; (*b*) bubble (of water, soap, etc.); (*in glass*) bleb; (*in dough, etc.*) air bubble; *Plastics:* (i) (*trapped within material*) bubble; (ii) (*breaking through surface*) open bubble; **Blasen machen,** to blow bubbles; (*of water*) to bubble; (*of dough*) **Blasen werfen,** to become aerated. **3.** *Dist:* still; (*in resin production*) (condensing and distilling) kettle. **4.** *Pej:* gang, crew.
Blasebalg, *m.* **1.** (*for fire*) bellows (in forge, etc.), pair of bellows (in house). **2.** (*in organ, etc.*) bellows; **den B. treten, ziehen,** to work the bellows.
Blasemaschine, *f.* blowing-machine.
Blasemeister, *m.* (*person*) blower.
blasen, *v.* (*strong*) (*p.t. occ.* **blus**). **1.** *v.tr.* (*a*) to blow; **der Wind bläst ihm den Staub ins Gesicht,** the wind blows dust in his face; **die Suppe, die Finger, b.,** to blow on one's soup, on one's fingers; (*b*) *Mus:* to blow, sound, play (wind instruments); **Flöte b.,** to play the flute; **ein Horn, eine Trompete, b.,** to sound a horn, trumpet; **ein Lied b.,** to play a tune (*on flute, horn, etc.*); *F:* **Trübsal b.,** to be miserable; *F:* **du kannst mir eins b.,** *F:* go hang yourself! *see also* **Horn** 3 (*a*), **Marsch**[2] 3; (*c*) *Glassm:* **Glas b.,** to blow glass. **2.** *v.i.* (*haben*) (*a*) to blow; **es bläst draußen,** it is blowing, there's a wind, outside; **der Wind bläst,** the wind is blowing; (*b*) (*of person*) to play (on a wind-instrument); (*of wind-instrument*) to sound; **zum Angriff b.,** to sound the charge; **zum Rückzug b.,** to sound the retreat; **die Trompeten blasen zum Aufbruch,** the trumpets are sounding the departure.
Blasenausschlag, *m. Med:* pemphigus.
Blasenbaum, *m. Bot:* bladder-senna.
Blasenbinse, *f. Bot:* scheuchzeria.
Blasenbruch, *m. Med:* rupture of the bladder, cystocele.
Blasenentzündung, *f.* = **Blasenkatarrh.**
Blasenfarn, *m. Bot:* cyspopteris, *F:* bladder-fern.
Blasenfuß, *m. Ent:* thrips, thysanopter.
blasenfüßig, *a. Ent:* thysanopterous.
Blasenfüß(l)er, *m. Ent:* thysanopter.

Blasengestein, n. Geol: amygdaloid.
Blasengrind, m. Med: impetigo.
Blasengrün, n. Dy: etc: sap-green.
Blasenkäfer, m. Ent: cantharis, Spanish fly, blister fly.
Blasenkatarrh, m. Med: cystitis, inflammation of the bladder.
Blasenkeim, m. Biol: blastula.
Blasenkirsche, f. Bot: (Franchet's) winter cherry, bladder-herb.
Blasenkrankheit, f. 1. Med: disease of the bladder, bladder disease. 2. Vet: fowl pox. 3. Bot: leaf blister.
Blasenkraut, n. Bot: bladder campion.
Blasenleiden, n. Med: bladder complaint; affection of the bladder.
blasenleidend, a. b. sein, to be suffering from a bladder complaint.
Blasenmole, f. Obst: hydatid, cystic, mole.
Blasennuß, f. Bot: (a) bladder-nut (tree); (b) bladder-nut.
Blasenpflaster, n. Med: Pharm: blistering plaster; vesicant, vesicatory.
Blasenqualle, f. Coel: physalia, F: Portuguese man-of-war.
Blasenraum, m. Geol: vesicle.
Blasenrobbe, f. Z: hooded seal.
Blasenrohr, n. Med: cystoscope.
Blasenrost, m. Fung: peridermium.
Blasenschnitt, m. Med: cystotomy.
Blasenschötchen, n. Bot: vesicaria.
Blasenschote, f. Bot:=Blasenstrauch.
Blasenschwindel, m. Vet: (blind) staggers.
Blasensegge, f. Bot: bladder-sedge.
Blasensenne, f. Bot:=Blasenstrauch.
Blasenspiegel, m. Med: cystoscope.
Blasensprengung, f. Obst:=Blasenstich.
Blasensprung, m. Obst: rupture of the amnion.
Blasenspülung, f. Med: bladder irrigation.
Blasenstahl, m. blister-steel.
Blasenstein, m. Med: vesical calculus; stone in the bladder.
Blasenstich, m. Obst: perforation of the membrane.
Blasenstrauch, m. Bot: bladder-senna.
Blasentang, m. Algae: bladder-wrack.
Blasenvorfall, m. Med: cystocele.
Blasenwurm, m. Ann: bladder-worm, cysticercus.
Blasenwurmkrankheit, f. Med: brain disease caused by echinococcus.
blasenziehend, a. Med: epispastic; **blasenziehendes Mittel,** epispastic, vesicant.
Blaseofen, m.=Blasofen.
Bläser, m. -s/-. 1. Mus: blower, player (of wind-instrument); (in orchestra) **die Bläser,** (the players of) the wind-instruments, the wind. 2. Min: blower, gas-vent.
Bläserchor, m. chorus of wind instruments.
Blasewerk, n. bellows.
Blasform, f. Metall: tuyere.
blasiert [bla·'zi:rt], a. blasé.
Blasiertheit [bla·'zi:rt,hait], f. blasé attitude.
blasig, a. (of skin, etc.) blistered; (of dough) aerated.
Blasinstrument, n. Mus: wind-instrument
Blasius ['bla:zïus]. Pr.n. m. -'. Blaise.
Blaskapelle, f. Mus: brass band; silver band.
Blaskopf, m. bellows.
Blasloch, n. Mus: blow-hole (of flute, etc.); mouth-hole (of horn, etc.).
Blasmaschine, f. Glassm: blowing-machine.
Blasmusik, f. (a) music for wind instruments; music for brass instruments; (b) music, playing, of wind instruments; music, playing, of a brass band.
Blasofen, m. blast-furnace.
Blason [bla·'zõ:, -'zo:n], m. -s/-e & -s. 1. blazon, coat of arms. 2. blazonry.
Blasoneur [bla·zo·'nø:r], m. -s/-e=Blasonist.
blasonieren [bla·zo·'ni:rən], v.tr. Her: to blazon.
Blasonist [bla·zo·'nist], m. -en/-en, blazoner, armorist.
Blasorchester, n. Mus: (a) orchestra of wind instruments; (b) brass band.
Blasphemie [blasfe·'mi:], f. -/-n [-'mi:ən], blasphemy.
blasphemieren [blasfe·'mi:rən], v.i. (haben) to blaspheme.
blasphemisch [blas'fe:miʃ], a. blasphemous (remark, etc.).
Blasphemist [blasfe·'mist], m. -en/-en, blasphemer.
blasphemistisch [blasfe·'mistiʃ], a. blasphemous.
Blasrohr, n. 1. (a) blow-tube, -pipe (for killing birds, etc.); (Malay's) sumpitan; (child's) pea-shooter. 2. (a) Mch: exhaust-pipe; (b) blast-pipe. 3. Mus: (on bagpipe) blow-pipe, mouth-tube.

blaß, a. (blasser, blässer; blassest, blässest) pale; pallid, colourless, wan; **blasse Wangen,** pallid, pale, wan, cheeks; **blasse Lippen,** pale, colourless, lips; **blasses Licht,** pale, wan, light; **b. machen,** to make pale, to pale; **die Krankheit hatte ihn b. gemacht,** sickness had made him pale, had paled him; **b. werden,** to become, to grow, pale; **(vor Angst) b. werden,** to pale, to turn pale (with fear).
Bläßbock, m. Z: blesbock.
Blässe, f. 1. -/. paleness; pallor, wanness, colourlessness. 2. -/-n, blaze (on animal's face). 3. -/-n. Orn:=Bläßhuhn.
blaßfarbig, a. light-coloured.
Blaßfußsturmtaucher, m. Orn: pale-footed shearwater.
Bläßgans, f. Orn: white-fronted goose; **Grönländische B.,** white-fronted Greenland goose; **kleine B.,** lesser white-fronted goose.
blaßgelb, a. pale yellow.
Blaßgesicht, n. paleface.
Bläßhuhn, n. Orn: coot.
bläßlich, a. palish.
blaßrot, a. pale red.
Blaßsegler, m. Orn: pallid swift.
Blaßspötter, m. Orn: olivaceous warbler.
Blastem [blas'te:m], n. -s/-e. Biol: blastema.
Blasto- [blasto·-], comb.fm. Biol: blasto-.
Blastoderm [blasto·'dɛrm], n. -(e)s/-e. Biol: blastoderm.
Blastogenese [blasto·ge·'ne:zə], f. blastogenesis.
Blastom [blas'to:m], n. -s/-e. Med: blastoma.
Blasverfahren, n. Ind: blowing.
Blatt, n. -(e)s/=er. 1. Bot: leaf (of plant, tree); petal (of flower); **Blätter treiben,** to put out leaves, to grow leaves; to be in leaf; see also **abwerfen** I. 1 (b), gefiedert; Ven: (of stag) **auf das B. laufen, springen,** to be decoyed (by huntsman imitating call of doe); F: **kein B. vor den Mund nehmen,** to speak one's mind, not to mince matters; Ent: **wandelndes B.,** leaf insect. 2. (a) leaf, sheet (of paper); Art: drawing, engraving, print, etc.; **ein B. Papier,** a piece of paper; **fliegende, lose, Blätter,** loose leaves, sheets; F: (of pers.) **ein unbeschriebenes B. sein,** to be (i) inexperienced, (ii) a dark horse, (iii) a nonentity; (b) leaf, page (of book); folio (of manuscript); F: **das steht auf einem anderen B.,** that's quite a different matter; **das B. hat sich gewendet,** (i) (my) luck has changed; (ii) the tables are turned; (c) Mus: sheet; **vom B. spielen, singen,** to sight-read; to play, sing, at sight; (d) (news)paper; **ein Londoner B.,** a London paper. 3. (a) sheet, lamina (of metal, etc.); (b) blade (of oar, saw, air-screw, etc.); head (of axe, etc.); reed (of wood-wind instrument); Tex: reed, slay (of loom). 4. Cards: (a) hand; **ein gutes B.,** a good hand; (b) card. 5. Ven: breast, brisket (of deer). 6. Carp: joint, scarf(-joint). 7. Geom: folium; **Kartesisches B.,** folium of Descartes.
blattabwerfend, a.=blätterabwerfend.
Blattachsel, f. Bot: (leaf-)axil.
Blattang, m. -s/-e. Algae: laminaria, sea-tangle; kelp.
Blattanordnung, f. Bot: phyllotaxis.
Blattauge, n. Bot:=Blattknospe.
Blattbeulen, f.pl. Bot: (disease) leaf blister.
Blattbleiche, f. Bot: chlorosis.
Blattbrand, m. Hort: etc: leaf-blight, leaf-rust, brown rot.
Blattbräune, f. Hort: etc: leaf-blight.
Blättchen, n. -s/- & occ. **Blätterchen.** (dim. of **Blatt**) 1. Bot: (a) small leaf; leaflet, foliole; (b) small petal; (c) lamella (of fungus, etc.). 2. (a) **ein B. Papier,** a slip, a small piece, of paper; (b) small page, leaf, (of book). 3. (a) **das B. hat sich gewendet,** (i) (my) luck has changed; (ii) the tables are turned; (b) (local) (news)paper; **es hat gestern im B. gestanden,** it was in yesterday's paper; (c) (metal-)foil. 4. flake; Metall: Geol: etc: lamina.
Blätterchenpulver, n. Mil: flake powder.
Blattdorn, m. Bot: (leaf-)spine.
Blattdürre, f. Hort: etc: leaf-blight.
blatten, v. 1. v.tr. to strip (a plant) of its leaves. 2. v.i. (haben) Ven: to imitate the call of a doe (in order to decoy a roebuck). Cp. **Blattung.**
Blatter[1], f. -/-n. Med: pock; pustule; **die Blattern,** smallpox.
Blatter[2], m. -s/-. Ven: instrument for imitating the call of a roe-)doe.
blätterabwerfend, a. Bot: deciduous.
Blätterchen[1], n. -s/-, small pock(-mark).
Blätterchen[2], n.pl. see **Blättchen.**
Blättererz, n.=Blättertellur.
Blätterfisch, m. Ich: ophiocephalida.
blätterförmig, a. leaf-shaped; foliated, laminated.

blätterfressend, a. Ent: phyllophagous.
Blätterfresser, m. Ent: phyllophagan.
blatt(e)rig, a. pock-marked, -pitted.
blätterig, a.=blättrig 1.
Blätterkohle, f. Geol: foliated, slaty, coal.
Blätterkrone, f. trefoiled crown.
Blättermagen, m. Z: third stomach (of ruminant), Dial: manyplies.
blättern. I. v. 1. v.i. (haben) **in einem Buch b.,** to leaf, U.S: page, through a book; to glance, skim, through a book. 2. (a) v.i. (haben) & **sich blättern,** (of minerals, etc.) to flake, to foliate, to laminate; to cleave, to split up; (b) **sich b.,** A: (of flower) to drop its petals. II. vbl s. 1. **Blättern,** n. in vbl senses. 2. **Blätterung,** f. in vbl senses of I. 2 (a); also: lamination, foliation.
Blatternarbe, f. pock-mark.
blatternarbig, a. pock-marked, -pitted.
Blätterpilz, m. Fung: agaric.
blätterreich, a. leafy.
Blättersandstein, m. Geol: foliated sandstone.
Blätterschwamm, m. Fung:=Blätterpilz.
Blatterstein, m. Geol: variolite.
Blätterteig, m. Cu: puff-paste, puff-pastry.
Blättertellur, n. Miner: nagyagite.
Blätterwald, der. F: (the products of) the press.
Blätterz, n. Miner:=Blättertellur.
Blätterzeolith [-tse·o·'li:t], m. Geol: heulandite, foliated zeolite.
Blattfall, m. Bot: (a) fall of the leaf; (b) (disease) leaf-drop.
Blattfallkrankheit, f. Bot: leaf-scorch.
Blattfeder, f. laminated spring, leaf-spring, plate-spring.
Blattfederchen, n. Bot: plumule.
Blattfinger, m. Rept: Corsican gecko.
Blattfisch, m. Ich: cichlid (of the Amazon).
Blattfläche, f. Bot: leaf-blade, lamina.
Blattflechte, f. Bot: leaf-lichen.
Blattfleck, m. Bot: leaf-spot.
Blattfleckenkrankheit, f. Bot: leaf-spot; **eckige B.,** angular leaf-spot.
Blattfloh, m. Ent: (a) psylla; (b) flea-beetle.
blattfüßig, a. Crust: phyllopodous.
Blattfüß(l)er, m. -s/-. Crust: phyllopod; **die Blattfüß(l)er,** the phyllopoda.
Blattgelb, n. Ch: Bot: xanthophyll.
Blattgold, n. gold-foil; gold-leaf.
Blattgolddruck, m. gold-leaf gilding.
Blattgrün, n. 1. Ch: Bot: chlorophyll, F: leaf-green. 2. Dy: etc: leaf-green.
Blattgrund, m. Bot: leaf-base.
Blatthäutchen, n. Bot: ligula, ligule (of graminaceae).
Blatthonig, m. (a) honey-dew; (b) honey-dew honey.
Blatthörner, m. -s/-=Blatthornkäfer.
Blatthornkäfer, m. Ent: lamellicorn.
Blatthühnchen, n. Orn: jacana.
Blattkäfer, m. Ent: leaf-beetle, plant-beetle.
Blattkaktus, m. Bot: epiphyllum.
Blattkapitell, n. Arch: foliated capital.
Blattkeil, m. Mec.E: flat cotter.
Blattkeim, m. Bot: plumule.
Blattkeimer, m. -s/-. Bot: dicotyledon.
Blattkiemer, m. -s/-. Moll: lamellibranch.
Blattknospe, f. Bot: leaf-bud.
Blattknospenanlage, f. Bot: vernation, prefoliation.
Blattkohl, m. Hort: kale, kail.
Blattkrebs, m. Crust: phyllosoma.
Blattkyma, n. Arch: leaf moulding.
Blattlaus, f. Ent: aphis, plant-louse, green-fly.
Blattlausfliege, f. Ent: green lace-wing fly.
Blattlaushonig, m. honey-dew honey.
Blattlauskäfer, m. Ent: coccinella; ladybird, U.S: lady-bug.
Blattlauslöwe, m. Ent: larva of the lace-wing fly.
blattlos, a. Bot: aphyllous, leafless.
Blattlose, f. -n/-n. Bot: lily pink.
Blattlücke, f. Bot: leaf-gap, foliar gap.
Blattmark, n. Bot: mesophyll(um).
Blattmaske, f. Art: foliated head.
Blattmetall, n. leaf metal; foil.
Blattmittelgewebe, n. Bot: mesophyll(um).
Blattnarbe, f. Bot: leaf-scar.
Blattnase, f. Z: leaf-nosed bat.
Blattornament, n. foliage ornament.
Blattpflanze, f. foliage plant.
Blattrand, m. Bot: edge, margin, of the leaf; limb, limbus.
Blattranke, f. Bot: leaf-tendril; Art: foliage scroll; tendril.
blättrig, a. 1. (a) foliated, lamellar, laminated; (b) flaky, scaly. 2. -blättrig, comb.fm. -leaved,

with . . . leaves; **vierblättriges Kleeblatt,** four-leaved clover; **kleinblättrig,** small-leaved, with small leaves.
Blattroller, *m. Ent:* = **Blattwickler.**
Blattrollkrankheit, *f. Bot: Hort:* leaf-roll, leaf-curl.
Blattrot, *n. Ch: Bot:* carotin.
Blattsäge, *f. Carp:* pad-saw.
Blattsauger, *m. Ent:* psylla.
Blattscheide, *f. Bot:* (leaf-)sheath.
Blattschlauch, *m. Bot:* ascidium, vasculum, *F:* pitcher.
Blattschmetterling, *m. Ent:* leaf-butterfly.
Blattschneider, *m. Ent:* **1.** leaf-cutter (ant). **2.** leaf-cutter (bee), upholsterer bee.
Blattschneiderameise, *f. Ent:* leaf-cutting ant, leaf-cutter (ant).
Blattschneiderbiene, *f. Ent:* leaf-cutting bee, leaf-cutter (bee).
Blattschorf, *m. Bot:* black-spot.
Blattschuß, *m. Ven:* shot in region of breast.
Blattseuche, *f. Bot:* = **Blattbräune.**
Blattsilber, *n.* silver-foil; silver-leaf.
Blattspindel, *f. Bot:* = **Blattspreite.**
Blattspreite, *f. Bot:* leaf-blade, lamina.
Blattstachel, *m. Bot:* = **Blattdorn.**
Blattstellung, *f. Bot:* phyllotaxis.
Blattstiel, *m. Bot:* leaf-stalk, petiole.
Blattstoß, *m. Carp:* scarf(-joint).
Blattung, *f. Carp:* (*a*) halved joint; (*b*) halving and lapping; scarfing. *Cp.* **blatten.**
Blattvergoldung, *f.* gilding (with gold-leaf).
Blattwelle, *f. Arch:* leaf moulding.
Blattwerk, *n.* foliage; *Arch: etc:* foliage-work, leaf-work, ornamental foliage.
Blattwespe, *f. Ent:* saw-fly.
Blattwickler, *m. Ent:* tortrix, leaf-roller moth.
Blattwurzel, *f. Av:* blade shank (of airscrew).
Blattzeit, *f. Ven:* rutting season (of deer).
Blattzinn, *n. Metalw:* sheet tin; tinfoil.
Blatz, *m.*-**es**/⸗**e,** sweet white loaf; **B. mit Rosinen,** currant loaf.
blau. I. *a.* **1.** (*a*) blue; *Her:* azure; **etwas b. färben, machen,** to colour *or* dye sth. blue; to make sth. blue; *cp.* **blaumachen;** *Nau:* **der Blaue Peter,** the Blue Peter; **blauer Heinrich,** (i) viper's bugloss; (ii) *Cu: F:* thin rice *or* barley soup; *Her:* **im blauen Felde,** in a field azure; *see also* **Band**[1] I. 1 (*d*); (*b*) **Metall b. anlaufen lassen,** to blue metal; (*of pers.*) **b. im Gesicht anlaufen,** to go black in the face; **b. vor Wut,** purple with rage; **b. vor Kälte,** blue with cold; **blaue Flecken,** bruises; **blauer Fleck,** Mongolian spot; **j-n braun und b. schlagen,** to beat s.o. black and blue; **blaues Auge,** black eye; **j-m ein blaues Auge schlagen,** to give s.o. a black eye; *F:* **mit einem blauen Auge davonkommen,** to escape, to get off, with a few scratches, a few scars; to get off lightly; to have a lucky escape; *F:* **unsere blauen Jungs,** our sailors, *F:* the boys in blue; *Med:* **blaues Baby,** blue baby; *Cu:* **Fisch b. kochen,** to boil fish; *see also* **Bohne** 2; (*c*) **blaues Blut,** blue blood; *A. & F:* **blauer Brief,** official letter; *F:* **den blauen Brief bekommen,** (i) *Mil: A:* to be discharged; (ii) *Sch:* to receive a letter of warning, of complaint; *F:* **j-m (einen) blauen Dunst vormachen,** to dupe s.o., *F:* to pull the wool over s.o.'s eyes; *F:* **da kannst du dein blaues Wunder erleben,** you'll get the surprise of your life; (*threat*) I'll show you! **blauen Montag machen,** to take Monday off (unofficially), *A:* to keep Saint Monday; *F:* **b. sein,** to be drunk, *F:* to be tight, blotto. **2.** *s.* **Blaue** (*decl. as adj.*) (*a*) *n.* **das Blaue,** the blue; **Fahrt ins Blaue,** trip into the blue, mystery tour; *F:* **das Blaue vom Himmel (herunter)reden, lügen,** to lie like a trooper, like a gas-meter, like a lawyer; *F:* **das Blaue vom Himmel herunterschwatzen,** *F:* to talk the hind leg off a donkey, to talk nineteen to the dozen; **ins Blaue hineinreden,** to talk wildly; (*b*) *m. F:* **ein Blauer,** a policeman, *F:* a copper, a cop; (*c*) *m.pl. F:* **die Blauen,** (i) the Prussians, (ii) the Protestants.
II. **Blau,** *n.* -(**s**)/-**s,** blue; blue colour; blueness; *Her:* azure; **Berliner B.,** Prussian blue; **in B. gekleidet,** dressed in blue; **das B. (des Himmels),** the blue (of the sky).
Blaualgen, *f.pl.* blue-green algae, cyanophyceae.
Blauamsel, *f. Orn:* = **Blaumerle.**
Blauanilin, *n. Ch: Dy:* pure aniline.
Blauanlassen, *n. Metalw:* blu(e)ing.
Blauaugenkormoran, *m. Orn:* blue-eyed cormorant.
blauäugig, *a.* blue-eyed.
Blaubart. *Pr.n.m.* Bluebeard.
Blaubeere, *f. Bot:* bilberry, whortleberry.
blaublind, *a. Med:* blue-blind.
Blaublindheit, *f. Med:* blue-blindness.
blaublütig, *a.* blue-blooded.
Blaublütigkeit, *f.* blue-bloodedness.
Blaubock, *m. Z:* roan antelope.
Blaubruch, *m. Metall:* blue shortness.
blaubrüchig, *a. Metall:* blue short.
Blaubuch, *n. Adm:* blue book.
Blaubulle, *m. Z:* nylghau, nilgau, nilgai; blue bull.
Blaudrossel, *f. Orn:* blue rock thrush.
Blaudruck, *m. Tex:* blue and white printed calico.
Bläue, *f.* -/. blue(ness); **die B. des Himmels,** the blue(ness) of the sky; the blue (sky); azure, sky-blue.
Blaueisenerde, *f. Miner:* = **Blaueisenerz.**
Blaueisenerz, *n. Miner:* vivianite.
Bläuel, *n.* -**s**/. *Laund:* bluc-bag.
Blauelster, *f. Orn:* azure-winged magpie.
Bläuemesser, *m. Meteor:* cyanometer.
blauen, *v.* **1.** *v.i.* (*haben*) *Lit:* (*of sky, etc.*) to be blue; **über uns blaute der Himmel,** above us was the blue sky; **in der Ferne blauen die Berge des Apennins,** in the distance are the blue mountains of the Apennine range. **2.** *v.tr.* to blue (linen, etc.).
bläuen, *v.tr.* to blue (sth.), to tint (sth.) blue; *Laund:* to blue (linen).
Blauerz, *n. Miner:* vivianite.
Blaufarbe, *f.* blue colour(ing), blue dye; *Glassm:* smalt.
Blaufäule, *f. Fung:* blue mould.
Blaufelchen, *m. Ich:* powan; gwyniad.
Blaufisch, *m. Ich:* coal-fish, green pollack.
Blauflügelente, *f. Orn:* blue-winged teal.
Blaufuchs, *m. Z:* arctic fox; *Com:* blue fox(-fur).
Blaufuß, *m. Orn:* **1.** saker. **2.** young woodcock.
Blaufußtölpel, *m. Orn:* blue-footed booby.
Blaugas, *n.* Blau oil-gas.
blaugrau, *a.* bluey-grey, bluish-grey, blue-grey.
Blaugrund, *m. Miner:* blue ground.
Blaugummibaum, *m. Bot:* blue gum-tree.
Blauhäher, *m. Orn:* blue jay.
Blauhai, *m. Ich:* blue shark.
Blauholz, *n. Bot: Com:* campeachy wood; logwood.
Blaujacke, *f. F:* sailor, blue-jacket.
Blaukehlchen, *n.* -**s**/-. *Orn:* blue-throat; **rotsterniges B.,** red-spotted blue-throat; **weißsterniges B.,** white-spotted blue-throat.
Blaukohl, *m.* red cabbage.
Blaukopf, *m. Ent:* diloba caeruleocephala.
Blaukreuz, *n.* temperance organisation, *approx.* = the blue ribbon.
Blaukreuzler, *m.* -**s**/-, teetotaller (*member of the 'Blaukreuz' organization*).
Blaukrone, *f. Bot:* aristea.
Blaukropf, *m. Orn:* = **Blaukehlchen.**
bläulich, *a.* bluish.
bläulichgrün, *a.* bluish-green.
bläulichweiß, *a.* bluish-white.
Bläuling, *m.* -**s**/-**e. 1.** *Ent:* lycaenid (butterfly); large blue (butterfly). **2.** *Fung:* amethyst (toadstool).
blaumachen, *v.i. sep.* (*haben*) *F:* to take time off (unofficially).
Blaumann, *m.* -(**e**)**s**/-**männer.** *Com:* skin of a young seal.
Blaumeise, *f. Orn:* blue tit.
Blaumerle, *f. Orn:* blue rock-thrush.
Blaumütze, *f. Bot: F:* monk's-hood, wolf's-bane, blue rocket.
Blauofen, *m. Metall:* closed-hearth furnace.
Blauöl, *n. Ch: Dy:* = **Blauanilin.**
Blaupapier, *n.* (*a*) blue carbon paper; (*b*) = **Blaupauspapier.**
Blaupause, *f.* blueprint, cyanotype.
Blaupauspapier, *n.* blueprint paper.
Blauracke, *f. Orn:* roller (*coracias garrulus*).
Blausäure, *f. Ch:* hydrocyanic acid, cyanhydric acid, *F:* prussic acid.
Blauschaf, *n. Z:* bharal, nahoor, blue (wild) sheep.
Blauschimmel, *m.* **1.** dapple-grey (horse). **2.** *Fung:* blue mould.
Blauschnabelente, *f. Orn:* white-headed duck.
Blauschwanz, *m. Orn:* red-flanked bluetail.
blauschwarz, *a.* blue-black.
Blausieb, *n. Ent:* leopard-moth.
Blauspat, *m. Miner:* blue-spar, lazulite.
Blauspecht, *m. Orn:* nuthatch.
Blaustein, *m.* **1.** *Ch:* blue-stone, blue vitriol. **2.** *Miner:* lazulite.
Blaustern, *m. Bot:* scilla.
Blaustift, *m.* (*a*) indelible pencil; (*b*) blue crayon, blue pencil.
Blaustrumpf, *m.* (*woman*) blue-stocking.
Blausucht, *f. Med:* cyanosis, *F:* blue disease, blue jaundice.
Blauwal, *m. Z:* blue whale.
Blauwangenbienenfresser, *m. Orn:* blue-cheeked bee-eater.
Blauzwecke, *f.* tintack.
Blech, *n.* -(**e**)**s**/-**e. 1.** (*a*) *Metalw:* (i) sheet metal; (ii) (metal) sheet, plate; (*b*) cheap metal, tin; (*c*) *Cu:* = **Backblech. 2.** *F:* (*money*) brass, *P:* dibs, dough. **3.** *F:* (*nonsense*) balderdash, rubbish, piffle, *P:* bosh, tripe.
Blecharbeit, *f.* (*a*) tin-working, tinwork; (*b*) tin-work, tin(-plate) ware.
Blechbalkenbrücke, *f.* = **Blechträgerbrücke.**
Blechbearbeitungswerkstatt, *f. Metall:* plate-works.
Blechbiegemaschine, *f. Metalw:* plate-bending machine.
Blechbläser, *m. Mus:* player of a brass instrument; (*in orchestra*) **die Blechbläser,** the brass (section).
Blechblasinstrument, *n. Mus:* = **Blechinstrument.**
Blechbordelpresse, *f. Metalw:* jointing-press.
Blechbüchse, *f.* tin(-box, -container); *U.S:* can.
Blechdose, *f.* tin, *U.S:* can; (biscuit, cake, etc.) tin, metal (cigarette) box.
Blechdruck, *m. Print:* plate-printing.
Blechdruckmaschine, *f. Print:* plate press.
blechen, *v.i.* (*haben*) *F:* to pay out money, *F:* to fork out, to stump up, to cough up.
blechern, *a.* (*a*) metal . . ., of metal-plate; (*b*) (*of sound*) brassy; (*of sound, voice*) tinny.
Blechgefäß, *n.* tin *or* aluminium vessel, container.
Blechinstrument, *n. Mus:* brass instrument.
Blechkalotte, *f.* = **Buckelplatte.**
Blechklinke, *f.* = **Blechlehre.**
Blechlehre, *f. Mec.E: etc:* sheet-metal gauge.
Blechmusik, *f.* music from brass instruments; brass-band music.
Blechnapf, *m.* billy(-can), pannikin; *Mil: F:* dixie, dixy.
Blechphotographie, *f.* **1.** (*process*) ferrotype (photography). **2.** (*picture*) ferrotype, tin-type.
Blechplatte, *f.* (metal) plate.
Blechrohr, *n.* sheet-metal tube.
Blechschere, *f.* tinman's shears, block shears; plate-shears.
Blechschmied, *m.* tinman, tinsmith.
Blechstärke, *f. Metalw:* thickness of plate.
Blechtafel, *f.* (metal) plate, sheet.
Blechträger, *m. Constr:* plate-girder, web-girder.
Blechträgerbrücke, *f.* plate-girder bridge.
Blechwalze, *f.* sheet-metal roller.
Blechwalzwerk, *n.* plate-mill, metal rolling mill, flatting-mill.
Blechwanne, *f.* tin bath.
Blechwaren, *f.pl.* tin(-plate) ware.
blecken, *v.tr.* **die Zähne b.,** to bare one's teeth.
Blei[1], *m.* -(**e**)**s**/-**e.** *Ich:* bream.
Blei[2], *n.* -(**e**)**s**/-**e,** (*a*) lead; **aus B.,** lead . . ., leaden; **(etwas) mit B. beschweren,** to weight (sth.) with lead, to lead (sth.), to load (cane, die); **(etwas) mit B. überziehen,** to lead (sth.), to coat, to cover (sth.) with lead; **mit B. überzogen,** leaded, lead-covered, lead-coated; **B. gießen,** (i) *Metall:* to cast lead; (ii) to tell fortunes from molten lead poured into water; **meine Füße sind wie B.,** my feet are like lead, are as heavy as lead; **es liegt mir wie B. in den Gliedern,** my limbs are like lead, are leaden, I feel as heavy as lead; (*b*) = **Bleilot;** (*c*) *Fish:* sinker; (*d*) *F:* pencil; **mit B. schreiben,** to write in pencil; (*e*) *Sm.a:* lead shot; *Poet:* **Pulver und B.,** powder and shot.
Bleiantimonat, *n. Ch:* lead antimoniate.
Bleiantimonglanz, *m. Miner:* zinkenite.
Bleiasche, *f. Ch:* lead ashes.
Bleibad, *n.* lead bath.
Bleibaum, *m. A.Ch:* arborescent lead.
Bleibe, *f.* -/-**n,** accommodation; home; **ich habe keine B.,** I have nowhere to stay, nowhere to live.
bleiben. I. *v.i.* (*strong*) (*sein*) **1.** (*a*) to remain, stay; **(eine Woche) in Köln b.,** to stay (a week) at Cologne; **zu Hause b.,** to stay, remain, at home; **ich darf nicht lange b.,** I must not stay long; **länger b., als den Gastgebern lieb ist,** to outstay one's welcome; **soll ich noch etwas b.?** should I stay a little longer? **an Ort und Stelle b.,** to stay, remain, where one is, to stay put; **an der Arbeit b.,** to go on, to continue, working; *Tp:* **bitte, bleiben Sie am Apparat,** hold the line, please; **das bleibt unter uns,** that's strictly between ourselves, between you and me, *F:* that's between you, me and the gate-post, bed-post; **(immer) bei j-m b.,** to remain, stay, (for ever) with s.o., at s.o.'s side; *B:* **bleibe bei uns, denn es will Abend werden,** abide with us; for it is toward evening; **(auf dem Schlachtfelde, Platze) b.,** to be killed (on the battlefield); (*b*) **bei etwas b.,** to abide by, to keep to, to adhere to, to stick to, sth.; **bei der**

Wahrheit b., to stick to the truth; **er bleibt bei seinem Entschluß,** he sticks to, keeps to, adheres to, abides by, his decision, resolve; **bei seiner Aussage b.,** to adhere, stick, to one's statement; **bei der Stange b.,** to stick it out; **bei der Sache b.,** (i) to concentrate; (ii) to keep, stick, to the subject; **es bleibt dabei,** that's agreed, that's final; **bleiben wir dabei,** let's stick, keep, to that (arrangement); **er bleibt immer auf dem Boden des Gesetzes,** he always abides by the law, he is law-abiding; **es bleibt alles beim alten,** everything goes on as before, nothing changes; (*c*) **im Gange, in Bewegung, b.,** to keep going; **in der Schwebe b.,** to be still in the balance; **ohne Wirkung b.,** to be to no effect; **am Leben b.,** to be (still) alive, to survive; (*d*) **bleib mir vom Leibe!** keep off! keep away from me! don't touch me! **bleib davon!** keep away from it! don't touch! **bleiben Sie aus dem Spiel!** don't meddle! don't get mixed up in it! *F:* don't stick your nose in! **2.** (*a*) **im Amt b.,** to remain, continue, in office; **Soldat b.,** (i) to be still a soldier, still in the army; (ii) to act as if one were still in the army; (iii) to remain in the army, to become a regular soldier; **derselbe, sich** *dat.* **gleich, b.,** to remain, to stay, the same, as one is; not to change; **sie bleibt doch immer meine Schwester,** all the same, she's still my sister; (*b*) **ernst b.,** to remain serious, to keep a straight face; **ruhig b.,** to keep calm; **gesund b.,** to keep well, fit; **bleiben Sie gesund!** keep well! look after yourself! **kräftig b.,** to keep (up), to maintain, one's strength; **geschlossen b.,** to stay, remain, closed, to be kept closed; **ledig b.,** to remain, stay, single; **nüchtern b.,** (i) to go without food, (ii) to stay sober; **unbestraft, unbeachtet, b.,** to go unpunished, unnoticed; (*c*) **leben b.,** to be (still) alive, to remain, to be left, alive; to survive; *cp.* **hängenbleiben, klebenbleiben, liegenbleiben, sitzenbleiben, steckenbleiben, stehenbleiben;** (*d*) to last, endure; *B:* **der Herr aber bleibt ewiglich,** but the Lord shall endure for ever. **3.** (*a*) **von seinem ganzen Vermögen blieb ihm nur sein Haus,** of his whole estate only his house was left, he was left with only his house; **ihm bleibt nichts, als sich aufzuhängen,** there's nothing left to him but to hang himself; **es blieb ihm keine Wahl,** he had no choice; **alle gingen, er allein blieb,** everyone went and he alone remained; **drei von sieben bleibt vier,** three from seven leaves four; *cp.* **übrigbleiben;** (*b*) to stay out; to be a long time coming, to be late; **sie bleibt aber lange,** (i) she's (been gone) a long while; (ii) she is a long time coming, she is late; (*c*) **ich weiß nicht, wo er geblieben ist,** I don't know where he's got to, what's happened to him; **wo bleibt er denn?** where has he got to? **wo ist das Geld geblieben?** what's happened to the money? where has the money gone, got, to? **er kann sehen, wo er bleibt,** let him fend for, look after, himself.

II. *vbl s.* **Bleiben,** *n. in vbl senses; also:* stay, *Lit:* sojourn; **hier ist meines Bleibens nicht (mehr), nicht länger,** I can remain here no longer.

III. *pr.p. & a.* **bleibend,** *in vbl senses; esp.* lasting, permanent, fixed; **keine bleibende Stätte haben,** to have no fixed abode; *B:* **denn wir haben hier keine bleibende Stadt,** for here we have no continuing city; **bleibende Eindrücke,** lasting impressions; **bleibender Wert,** lasting, permanent, value.

bleibenlassen, *v.tr. sep.* (*strong*) to leave, let, (sth.) alone; **laß diesen Unsinn bleiben,** (i) stop that nonsense! (ii) don't bother with that rubbish! **wir wollen das lieber b.,** it would be better not to do it, don't let's do it; **wenn du nicht willst, laß es bleiben,** if you don't want to, then don't; if you don't want to, forget it.

Bleiblech, *n.* sheet lead.

bleich, *a.* pale, white; pallid, wan (cheeks, etc.); pale, light (colour); **b. wie der Tod,** deathly pale, as pale as death, ashen; **der bleiche Mond,** the pale moon; **b. werden,** (*of pers.*) to grow, turn, pale, white; **b. vor Furcht werden,** to turn pale, white, to blanch, with fear.

Bleichart, *m.* light-red wine; (German) rosé.

Bleiche, *f.* **-/-n. 1.** paleness; pallor, wanness. **2.** bleaching-field, -green, -ground.

bleichen, *v.* **1.** *v.tr.* (*weak*) (*a*) to make (sth., s.o.) pale, white; (*of fear*) to blanch (the face), (*of age, etc.*) to blanch (hair); (*b*) to bleach (washing, hair, etc.). **2.** *v.i.* (*weak, occ. strong*) (*a*) to turn pale, white; (*of face, person*) to blanch (with fear, etc.); (*of hair*) to blanch (with age, etc.); (*b*) (*of washing, hair*) to bleach.

Bleicher, *m.* **-s/-. 1.** *Tex:* (*pers.*) bleacher. **2.** = **Bleichart.**

Bleicherde, *f. Tex:* fuller's earth; bleaching earth.

Bleicherei, *f.* **-/-en, Bleichereianlage,** *f. Tex:* bleachery, bleaching-house, bleaching-works.

Bleichert, *m.* **-s/-e** = **Bleichart.**

Bleichflüssigkeit, *f.* bleaching-liquid, -water.

Bleichgesicht, *n.* paleface.

Bleichholländer, *m. Paperm:* Hollander, rag-engine.

Bleichkalk, *m.* bleaching-powder; chloride of lime.

Bleichkessel, *m. Tex:* kier, keir.

Bleichmittel, *n.* bleach, bleaching agent.

Bleichsand, *m.* = **Bleicherde.**

Bleichsellerie, *f. & m. Hort: Cu:* celery.

Bleichsucht, *f. Med:* chlorosis, green-sickness; **ägyptische B.,** ankylostomiasis, hookworm disease, miners' anaemia, tunnel disease.

bleichsüchtig, *a. Med:* chlorotic.

Bleichwand, *f.* wattle-and-daub wall.

Bleichwasser, *n.* bleaching-liquid, -water.

Bleidach, *n.* (*a*) lead roof; (*b*) = **Bleikammer** 2.

Bleide, *f.* **-/-n.** *Mil.Hist:* trebuchet.

Bleidraht, *m.* lead wire.

Bleie, *f.* **-/-n.** *Ich:* bream.

bleien, *v.tr.* **1.** to lead; (*a*) to cover, to coat, with lead; (*b*) to weight with lead; (*c*) *I.C.E:* **gebleiter Kraftstoff,** leaded fuel. **2.** = **loten** 1.

Bleier, *m.* **-s/-.** *Ich:* roach.

Bleierde, *f. Geol:* lead earth.

bleiern, *a.* of lead, leaden; **bleierne Glieder,** leaden limbs, limbs as heavy as lead; *F:* **wie eine bleierne Ente,** *F:* (to dance, etc.) like a sack of potatoes; (to swim) like a stone.

Bleierz, *n. Min:* lead ore.

Bleiessig, *m. Pharm:* Goulard water, Goulard's extract.

Bleifarbe, *f.* **1.** (*a*) *Ind: Paint: etc:* lead colour; (*b*) *Paint:* lead paint. **2.** leaden colour; lividness, ashy pallor (of face).

bleifarben, bleifarbig, *a.* lead-coloured, leaden; livid, ashen.

Bleifeder, *f.* (lead) pencil.

Bleifolie, *f.* lead-foil.

Bleigelb, *n. Ch: Ind:* (*a*) massicot, yellow lead; (*b*) lead chromate.

Bleigießen, *n.* molybdomancy; fortune-telling from molten lead poured into water.

Bleigießer, *m.* worker in lead.

Bleigießerei, *f.* lead-works.

Bleiglanz, *m. Miner:* lead glance, galena, sulphide of lead.

Bleiglas, *n.* lead-glass.

Bleiglasur, *f. Cer:* lead-glaze.

Bleiglätte, *f. Ch: Ind:* litharge, yellow lead oxide.

bleigrau. 1. *a.* lead grey, leaden, livid. **2.** *s.* **Bleigrau,** *n.* lead grey.

bleihaltig, *a.* plumbiferous, lead-bearing.

Bleihe, *f.* **-/-n.** *Ich:* bream.

Bleihütte, *f.* lead-works.

Bleikabel, *n. El.E:* lead-covered cable, leaded cable.

Bleikammer, *f.* **1.** *Ind:* lead chamber. **2.** *Hist:* **die Bleikammern,** the Piombi (at Venice), the Leads (of Venice).

Bleikammerverfahren, *n. Ind:* chamber process (for producing sulphuric acid).

Bleikehlchen, *n. Orn:* = **Braunelle** 2.

Bleikolik, *f. Med:* lead-colic.

Bleikönig, *m. Metall:* lead regulus.

Bleikrankheit, *f.* = **Bleivergiftung.**

Bleikristall, *n.* lead-crystal.

Bleikugel, *f.* lead bullet.

Bleilasur, *f. Miner:* linarite.

Bleilot, *n. Constr: Nau:* plumb-line, plummet; *Nau:* lead line.

Bleimennige, *f. Ch:* minium, red oxide of lead; *Com:* red lead.

Bleimine, *f.* (i) (black) lead, graphite, plumbago; (ii) (pencil) refill.

Bleiminium, *n. Ch:* = **Bleimennige.**

Bleimulde, *f. Metall:* pig-lead.

Bleimulm, *m. Miner:* earthy galena.

Bleiniere, *f.* **1.** *Miner:* bindheimite. **2.** *Med:* = **Bleischrumpfniere.**

Bleioxyd, *n. Ch:* lead oxide; **gelbes B.,** litharge; **rotes B.,** minium, *Com:* red lead.

Bleipapier, *n.* paper-thin sheet lead.

Bleipflaster, *n. Pharm:* diachylum plaster, lead plaster.

Bleipflastersalbe, *f. Pharm:* diachylon ointment.

Bleiplatte, *f.* lead plate, lead sheet.

bleirecht, *a.* = **lotrecht.**

Bleiröhre, *f.* lead pipe.

Bleirot, *n.* = **Bleimennige.**

Bleisammler, *m. El:* lead accumulator, lead storage battery.

bleisauer, *a. Ch:* plumbate of . . .; combined with plumbic acid.

Bleisaum, *m. Med:* blue line round the gums (*due to lead-poisoning*).

Bleisäure, *f. Ch:* plumbic acid.

Bleischaum, *m.* = **Bleiasche.**

Bleischnur, *f.* = **Bleilot.**

Bleischrot, *n. Sm.a:* lead shot, small shot.

Bleischrumpfniere, *f. Med:* granular kidney (*caused by lead-poisoning*).

Bleischwamm, *m. Ch:* lead sponge.

Bleischweif, *m. Ch: Miner:* lead glance, galena.

bleischwer, *a.* as heavy as lead; leaden.

Bleisicherung, *f. El.E:* lead fuse.

Bleisiegel, *n. Com: etc:* lead(en) seal.

Bleisoldat, *m. Toys:* lead soldier.

Bleispat, *m. Miner:* cerusite; **roter B.,** crocoite, crocoisite.

Bleistift, *m.* (lead) pencil; **mit B. schreiben,** to write in pencil; **etwas mit B. in ein Buch schreiben,** to write sth. in pencil, to pencil sth., in a book.

Bleistiftspitzer, *m.* **-s/-,** pencil-sharpener.

Bleistiftzeder, *f. Bot:* Virginian juniper, (common red) cedar(-tree), pencil cedar.

Bleisulfat, *n. Ch:* lead sulphate.

Bleisulfid, *n. Ch:* lead sulphide.

Bleivergiftung, *f. Med:* lead-poisoning, plumbism, saturnism.

Bleivitriol, *n. Miner:* anglesite, lead vitriol.

Bleiwaage, *f. Constr:* vertical level, plumb-level, plumb-line.

Bleiwasser, *n. Pharm:* Goulard water; lead wash, lead water.

Bleiweiß, *n. Ch: etc:* white lead.

Bleiweißfarbe, *f.* white-lead paint.

Bleiwurz, *f. Bot:* plumbago, leadwort.

Bleizinn, *n.* pewter.

Bleizinnober, *m. Ch:* = **Bleimennige.**

Bleizucker, *m. Ch:* lead acetate, sugar of lead.

Blendanstrich, *m. Mil: Navy:* dazzle (paint).

Blendarkade, *f.* blind arcade, blind arcading.

Blendboden, *m.* = **Blindboden.**

Blendbogen, *m. Arch:* blind arch, blind arcade, wall arcade; **Blendbogen** *pl,* blind arcade, blind arcading.

Blende, *f.* **-/-n. 1.** (*a*) *Phot:* diaphragm, stop; (*b*) (window) blind; shutter; (*c*) *Miner:* (i) blende; (ii) (= **Zinkblende**) zinc blende, false galena, sphalerite, *F:* black jack; (*d*) *Min:* (i) = **Wetterblende;** (ii) lamp, light; (*e*) *Mil: Fort:* blind, screen; blindage; *Arch:* facing; blind arch, blind niche; (*f*) *A:* blinker, eye-flap (of horse); (*g*) *Dressm:* (contrasting) facing, trimming. **2.** *Bot:* = **Buchweizen.**

blenden. I. *v.tr.* **1.** (*a*) to blind (s.o.), to put out (s.o.'s) eyes; (*b*) to blind, dazzle (s.o.); **der Schnee, das Licht, blendet,** the snow, the light, is dazzling; (*c*) to delude, deceive (s.o.), to take (s.o.) in; **sie wurde von seinen schmeichelhaften Reden geblendet,** she was deceived, taken in, by his flattering words. **2.** *occ. Constr:* = **verblenden.**

II. *vbl s.* **1. Blenden,** *n. in vbl senses.* **2. Blendung,** *f.* (*a*) = II. 1; (*b*) *A:* = **Blende** 1 (*e*); (*c*) *A:* delusion, deception.

III. *pr.p. & a.* **blendend,** *in vbl senses; esp* (*a*) dazzling, resplendent, radiant (beauty, etc.); glaring (light); brilliant (attainment, etc.); **blendende Erscheinung,** dazzling, brilliant, magnificent, appearance; (*b*) *F:* wonderful, magnificent, *F:* super, grand, smashing; **es geht ihr b.,** she's wonderfully well, *F:* she's in the pink.

Blendeneinstellung, *f. Phot:* diaphragm setting.

Blendenöffnung, *f. Phot:* diaphragm aperture.

Blendenscheibe, *f. Phot: Cin:* revolving shutter.

Blender, *m.* **-s/-,** superficially brilliant person, *F:* dazzler.

Blendfassade, *f.* blind wall, dead wall.

Blendfeuer, *n. Mil:* flare(s).

Blendglas, *n.* tinted glass, smoked glass.

blendieren [blɛn'diːrən], *v.tr. Constr:* = **verblenden.**

Blendlampe, *f.* anti-dazzle lamp.

Blendlaterne, *f.* dark lantern, bull's-eye lantern.

Blendleder, *n.* blinker, eye-flap (of horse).

Blendleiste, *f. Constr: etc:* cover strip.

Blendling, *m.* **-s/-e. 1.** *A:* (*dog, etc.*) mongrel, cross-breed; *Bot:* hybrid plant, mongrel plant; (*pers.*) hybrid, mongrel, half-breed, *F:* cross-breed. **2.** (*a*) gull, gullible person; (*b*) dazzler.

Blendmauer, *f.* blind wall.

Blendnische, *f.* blind niche.

Blendrahmen, *m.* **1.** *Arch:* (outer) frame, case, casing (of door, window). **2.** *Art:* canvas-stretcher.

Blendscheibe, *f.* (*a*) *Aut:* anti-dazzle shield, *U.S:* sun visor; **B. für Nebel,** fog disc for a head-lamp; (*b*) (*on electric torch*) diaphragm; (*c*) *Metalw:* welder's shield; (*d*) *Sp:* eye-shade.

Blendschirm, *m.* **1.** *Ven:* hide, *U.S:* blind. **2.** *Sp:* eye-shade.

Blendschutzanstrich, *m. Navy: etc:* dazzle (paint).

Blendschutzfarbe, *f. Navy: etc:* dazzle (paint).

Blendschutzscheibe, *f. Aut:* anti-dazzle shield, *U.S:* sun visor.

Blendschutzvorrichtung, *f. Aut:* dimmer.

Blendstein, *m. Constr:* (*a*) facing stone; (*b*) facing brick.

Blendung, *f. see* **blenden II.**

blendungsfrei, *a.* non-glare.

Blendwand, *f. Constr:* timbered wall with stone facing.

Blendwerk, *n.* deception, delusion; illusion; mirage; **B. des Teufels,** snares of the Devil.

Blendziegel, *m. Constr:* facing brick.

Blenheim [ˈblɛnɛm], *m.* **-s/-s.** *Breed:* Blenheim spaniel.

Blenker, *m.* **-s/-** = **Blinker** 3.

blenkern, *v.i.* (*haben*) *Fish:* to spoon.

Blennorrhagie [blɛnoraˑˈgiː], *f.* **-/.** *Med:* blennorrhagia, gonorrhoea.

Blennorrhö, Blennorrhöe [blɛnoˈrøː], *f.* **-/-rhöen** [-ˈrøːən]. *Med:* blennorrhoea.

Blepharadenitis [bleˑfaˑraˑdeˈniːtis], *f.* **-/.** *Med:* ciliary blepharitis.

Blepharitis [bleˑfaˑˈriːtis], *f.* **-/.** *Med:* blepharitis.

Bleßbock, *m. Z:* blesbock.

Blesse, *f.* **-/-n. 1.** blaze (on face of horse, cow, etc.). **2.** animal with a blaze on its face.

Bleßhuhn, *n. Orn:* coot.

blessieren [blɛˈsiːrən], *v.tr.* to wound.

Blessur [blɛˈsuːr], *f.* **-/-en,** wound.

bleu [bløː], *inv. a.* (pale) blue.

bleuen, *v.tr.* to beat, thrash (s.o.).

Blick, *m.* **-(e)s/-e,** (*a*) glance, look; **auf den ersten B.,** at first glance, at first sight; **Liebe auf den ersten B.,** love at first sight; **etwas mit einem B. übersehen,** to see sth., to take sth. in, at a glance; **sprechender B.,** telling glance, look; **ein böser B.,** an evil, angry, look; *F:* a dirty look; **der böse B.,** the evil eye; **finsterer B.,** scowl, black look; **j-m einen finsteren B., finstere Blicke, zuwerfen,** to give s.o. a black look, black looks, to frown, to scowl, at s.o.; **einen B. auf etwas werfen,** to take a look at sth., to glance at sth., to run, to cast, one's eye over sth.; **einen neidischen B. auf etwas werfen,** to cast a covetous eye on sth.; **ein schräger B., ein B. von der Seite,** a side-glance, a sidelong glance; **j-m verliebte Blicke zuwerfen,** to send s.o. amorous glances; **flüchtiger B.,** glimpse, fleeting glance, cursory glance; **ich habe nur einen flüchtigen B. darauf geworfen,** I only glimpsed at it, I only gave it a cursory glance; **einen B. (in ein Buch) werfen,** to glance, dip (into a book); **die Blicke auf sich lenken,** to draw the eye, to attract attention, to be conspicuous; **den B. heben, senken,** to raise, lower, one's eyes; **den B. gen Himmel richten,** to cast one's eyes up to Heaven; **den B. ins Leere gerichtet,** gazing into the distance, into space, gazing vacantly ahead; **j-n mit dem B. verfolgen,** to follow s.o. with one's eyes; **er wandte den B. nicht von ihr,** his eyes never left her, he never took his eyes off her; **ihre Blicke trafen sich,** their eyes met; **den Blicken entschwinden,** to disappear from view, from sight; (*b*) insight; eye; **einen B. für etwas haben,** to have an eye for sth.; **er hat einen sicheren B.,** he has a sure eye; **innerer B.,** inner eye; **sich den B. nicht trüben lassen,** not to be taken in, not to be deceived, to keep a clear head; (*c*) view; **Zimmer mit einem B. auf die Berge,** room with a view of the mountains; (*d*) fulguration (of silver, etc.).

Blicke, *f.* **-/-n.** *Ich:* white bream.

blicken, *v.i.* (*haben*) **1.** (*a*) to look; **auf j-n, etwas, nach j-m, etwas, b.,** to look at s.o., sth.; **er blickte schnell zur Seite,** he looked away quickly; **der Mond blickte (verstohlen) aus den Wolken,** the moon was looking, shining, peeping, from between the clouds; **Zorn, Verachtung, blickte aus seinen Augen,** his eyes flashed anger, his eyes spoke his contempt; **finster, freundlich, b.,** to wear an angry, friendly, expression, look; (*b*) *v.tr. Lit:* **ihre Augen blicken Liebe,** her eyes express, speak, her love; (*c*) **sich, etwas, b. lassen,** to show oneself, sth., to let oneself, sth., be seen; **er hat sich lange nicht mehr b. lassen,** he hasn't been seen for a long time; **sie wagt es nicht, sich b. zu lassen,** she dare not show her face, *F:* she's making herself scarce; **lassen Sie sich nie wieder in meinem Hause b.!** never show yourself in my house again! never darken my doors again! **das läßt tief b.!** that's revealing; that opens vistas; *F:* it makes you think; **2.** (*of metals*) to brighten, to fulgurate.

Blickfang, *m. Com:* eye-catcher.

Blickfeld, *n. Opt: etc:* field of vision, of view, visual field (*esp.* of the moving eye).

Blickfeuer, *n.* = **Blinkfeuer.**

Blickkrampf, *m. Med:* conjugate deviation of the eyes.

Blicklinie, *f. Opt:* line of vision, line of sight.

Blickpunkt, *m.* (*a*) *Opt: etc:* vision; visual focus; *F:* **im B. sein,** to be in the centre of things; to be in the limelight; (*b*) point of view.

Blickrichtung, *f.* direction in which one is looking; line of vision, line of sight.

Blicksilber, *n. Metall:* refined silver.

Blickwinkel, *m. Opt: etc:* visual angle.

blieb, bliebe *see* **bleiben.**

blies, bliese *see* **blasen.**

blind. 1. *a.* blind; (*a*) *Anat:* **blinder Fleck,** blind spot (of the eye); **b. geboren,** blind from birth; **b. werden,** to go blind; **auf einem Auge b. sein,** to be blind in one eye; **b. machen,** to blind, to make blind; **von Tränen b.,** blinded by tears; **sich b. lesen,** to read oneself blind; **wenn du nicht ganz b. wärest . . .,** if you weren't quite blind . . ., *F:* if you had half an eye . . .; *F:* **ein blindes Huhn findet auch mal ein Korn,** a fool's bolt may sometimes hit the mark, a fool must now and then be right by chance; (*b*) **blinde Wut,** blind rage; **blinder Eifer, Glaube, Gehorsam,** blind enthusiasm, faith, obedience; **die Liebe hat ihn für ihre Fehler b. gemacht,** love has blinded him, made him blind, to her faults; **blinder Zufall,** pure chance; **b. gegen die Gefahr sein,** to be blind to danger; **blinde Heiden,** unenlightened heathens; (*c*) (*of mirror, glass, etc.*) clouded; (*of metal*) mat, dull, tarnished; (*of window*) opaque (with age *or* dirt); **b. werden,** (*of glass*) to cloud, to become clouded, (*of metal*) to become mat, dull, tarnished, to tarnish; (*d*) (*of window*) blind, blank; fixed, dead; (*of wall, door*) blind, blank; **blinde Patrone,** blank cartridge; *Min:* **blinder Schacht,** staple, blind shaft; *Print:* **blinde Zeile,** blank line; **blinder Kauf,** fictitious purchase; *A:* **blinder Soldat,** dummy soldier, false muster, faggot; **blinder Passagier,** stowaway; *see also* **Alarm, Lärm** 3; (*e*) (*hidden*) **blinde Klippe,** blind rock; **blindes Loch,** blind hole, dead hole, *Golf:* blind hole. **2.** *adv.* (*a*) **j-m b. vertrauen,** to trust s.o. blindly, implicitly; **b. zugreifen,** to grab blindly, wildly, to make a wild grab; **b. spielen,** to play (chess) without seeing the board, blindfold; *Av:* **b. fliegen,** to fly blind; *Typewr:* **b. schreiben,** to touch-type; (*b*) **b. schießen,** (i) to fire (off) blank cartridges, (ii) to shoot into the air; (iii) to shoot wildly, at random; **b. laden,** to load a gun with a blank cartridge; *Mil.Av:* **Bomben b. abwerfen,** to drop bombs 'safe'. **3. Blinde,** *m., f.* (*decl. as adj.*) blind man, woman; **die Blinden,** the blind; **es ist, wie wenn ein Blinder einen Blinden führt,** it is a case of the blind leading the blind; *F:* **das sieht doch ein Blinder mit dem Krückstock, im Finstern,** you can see that with half an eye, that's as plain as a pike-staff; **er redet davon wie der Blinde von der Farbe,** he talks about it without knowing the first thing about it, *F:* he's talking through his hat; *Prov:* **unter Blinden ist der Einäugige König,** in the country of, among, the blind the one-eyed man is king.

Blindaal, *m. Ich:* hag(-fish), borer, slime-eel.

Blindabwurf, *m. Mil.Av:* dropping bombs 'safe'.

Blindband, *m. Publ:* dummy.

Blindbaum, *m. Bot:* excoecaria.

Blindboden, *m.* rough floor, sub-floor (under parquet, etc.).

Blindbremse, *f. Ent:* = **Blindfliege.**

Blindbuchen, *n. Cin:* blind booking (of films).

Blinddarm, *m. Anat:* (*a*) caecum; (*b*) *F:* appendix.

Blinddarmentzündung, *f. Med:* (*a*) typhlitis; (*b*) *F:* appendicitis.

Blinddruck, *m. Bookb:* blind blocking, blind tooling.

blinddrucken, *v.tr. sep. Bookb:* to blind-tool.

Blindekuh, *f. Games:* blind-man's-buff.

Blindenanstalt, *f.* institute for the blind; blind institution.

Blindendruck, *m.* (embossed) printing for the blind, braille.

Blindenführ(er)hund, *m.* guide dog, blind man's dog, *U.S:* seeing-eye dog.

Blindenfürsorge, *f.* welfare of the blind, blind welfare.

Blindenheim, *n.* home for the blind.

Blindenhund, *m.* guide dog, blind man's dog, *U.S:* seeing-eye dog.

Blindenleiter, *m.* leader of the blind; *B:* **sie sind blinde B.,** they be blind leaders of the blind.

Blindenschrift, *f.* braille (type *or* writing).

Blindenschriftmaschine, *f.* braille typewriter.

Blindenuhr, *f.* braille watch.

Blindfenster, *n.* blind, blank, window; fixed, dead, light.

Blindfisch, *m. Ich:* hag(-fish), borer, slime-eel.

Blindflansch, *m.* blind, blank, flange.

Blindfliege, *f. Ent:* chrysops, small horse-fly.

Blindflug, *m. Av:* (*a*) blind flying; (*b*) blind flight.

Blindgänger, *m.* **-s/-.** *Artil: etc:* blind shell, dud (shell); unexploded bomb *or* shell.

blindgeboren, *a.* born blind, blind from birth; **der Blindgeborene,** the man blind from birth.

Blindheit, *f.* blindness, *Lit:* cecity.

Blindholz, *n.* **1.** *Woodw:* inferior wood (under veneer); core, ground (of plywood). **2.** *Vit:* cut canes (for propagating).

blindieren [blinˈdiːrən], *v.tr. Constr:* = **verblenden.**

Blindlandung, *f. Av:* blind landing.

Blindleistung, *f. El:* reactive volt-amperes, wattless power.

Blindling, *m.* **-(e)s/-e** = **Blendling.**

blindlings, *adv.* blindly, wildly, at random, headlong; **b. drauflosschlagen,** to hit out at random, to lash out wildly; **er rannte b. die Straße entlang,** he ran headlong down the street.

Blindlingsspiel, *n.* blindfold chess.

Blindlingsspieler, *m.* = **Blindspieler.**

Blindmaterial, *n. Print:* spacing material.

Blindmaus, *f.,* **Blindmoll,** *m. Z:* mole-rat.

Blindmuster, *n. Publ:* dummy.

Blindmutter, *f. Mec.E:* blind nut.

Blindprägung, Blindpressung, *f.* = **Blinddruck.**

Blindrahmen, *m.* = **Blendrahmen.**

Blindrebe, *f. Vit:* cut cane (for propagating).

Blindschacht, *m. Min:* staple, blind shaft.

Blindscheibe, *f. Paperm:* loose pulley (in rag-engine).

blindschlagen, *v.tr. sep.* (*strong*) *Print:* to leave blank.

Blindschlange, *f. Rept:* typhlops; blind-snake.

Blindschleiche, *f. Rept:* slow-worm, blind-worm.

Blindschloß, *n.* mortise-lock.

Blindspieler, *m. Chess:* blindfold player.

Blindstrom, *m. El:* idle current, wattless current.

Blindtram, *m.* = **Fehltram.**

Blindwanze, *f. Ent:* capsid leaf-bug.

Blindwiderstand, *m. El:* reactance.

Blindwühle, *f.,* **Blindwühler,** *m. Amph:* caecilian.

blindwütig, *a.* raving; blind with rage.

Blink, *m.* **-(e)s/-e,** flash.

blinken, *v.i.* (*haben*) **1.** (*a*) (*of stars, lights*) to twinkle, wink; (*of light*) to flash, blink; (*of sun, moon, light*) to shine; (*b*) (*of metal, leather, glass, water, etc.*) to shine; (*of material*) to be bright. **2. nach etwas b.,** to look, glance, at sth.; **mit den Augen b.,** to blink (one's eyes). **3.** *Mil: etc:* to signal (with lamps).

Blinker, *m.* **-s/-. 1.** *Mil: etc:* (lamp) signal operator, signaller. **2.** *Aut:* flashing indicator. **3.** *Fish:* spoon-bait.

blinkern, *v.i.* (*haben*) **1.** = **blinken** 1, 2. **2.** *Fish:* to spoon.

Blinkfeuer, *n. Nau:* flashing light.

Blinkgerät, *n. Mil: etc:* (lamp) signalling apparatus.

Blinklampe, *f. Mil: etc:* signalling-lantern, -light.

Blinkleuchte, *f. Aut:* flashing indicator.

Blinklicht, *n.* **1.** *Nau:* = **Blinkfeuer. 2.** *Aut:* = **Blinkleuchte.**

Blinkvorrichtung, *f.* flash-light; **Taschenlampe mit B.,** flash-light, -lamp.

blinzeln, *v.i.* (*haben*) (*a*) to blink (at light, etc.); (*b*) to wink (at s.o.); (*c*) to screw up one's eyes (to see better, etc.); (*d*) to half-close one's eyes (with tiredness).

Blinzelreflex, *m. Anat:* conjunctival reflex.

blinzen, *v.i.* (*haben*) *A:* = **blinzeln.**

Blinzhaut, *f.* = **Nickhaut.**

Blitz, *m.* **-es/-e,** (*a*) lightning; *Myth:* (Jupiter's) thunderbolt; **ein B.,** a flash of lightning; **der B. schlug ein,** the lightning struck; **der B. schlug in das Haus ein,** the lightning struck the house, the house was struck by lightning; **wie vom B. getroffen, gerührt,** thunderstruck; **rennen wie ein B.,** to run like lightning; *F:* **wie ein geölter B.,** like greased lightning, like a streak of lightning; **wie ein B. aus heiterm Himmel,** like a bolt from the blue; **Blitz! Potz B.! Gotts B.!** good heavens! phew! (*b*) flash; **B. des Zornes,** flash of anger, flashing anger, fury of rage; **Blitze des Witzes,** flashes of wit, flashing wit; **der B. deines Auges,** the flash, sparkle, of your eyes; (*c*) *Phot:* flash(-light); **eine Aufnahme mit B. machen,** to take a photo with a flash.

Blitzableiter, *m.* lightning-conductor.

Blitzableiterstange, *f.* lightning-rod.

blitzartig, *a.* like lightning.

blitz(e)blank, *a.* spick and span, as bright as a new pin.

blitzen. **I.** *v.* **1.** *v.impers.* **es blitzt,** it lightens, it is lightening; *F:* **es blitzt bei dir, bei ihr,** your, her, slip is showing. **2.** *v.i.* (*haben*) (*a*) to flash; (*of light, sun, moon, etc.*) to shine; (*of light*) to flash, sparkle; (*of sword, water, etc.*) to gleam, flash, sparkle; (*of gun*) to flash; (*of eyes*) to flash, shine; (*b*) to flash, to move like lightning. **3.** *v.tr. Poet:* **ihre Augen blitzten Feuer,** her eyes flashed fire.

II. *vbl s.* **Blitzen,** *n. in vbl senses; also:* flash.

Blitzer, *m.* **-s/-.** *Phot:* flash-gun.

Blitzesschnelle, *f.* lightning speed; **mit B.,** at lightning speed, like a flash (of lightning), in a (lightning) flash.

Blitzfänger, *m.* lightning-conductor.

Blitzfeuer, *n. Nau:* flashing light; **B. mit Gruppen,** group flashing light.

Blitzfigur, *f. Med:* keraunograph.

Blitzfunktelegramm, *n.* priority radiotelegram.

Blitzgerät, *n.* = **Blitzlichtgerät.**

Blitzgespräch, *n. Tp:* special priority call.

Blitzjunge, *m. F:* stunning, ripping, boy, chap.

Blitzkerl, *m. F:* stunning, ripping, fellow.

Blitzkrieg, *m.* lightning war.

Blitzlampe, *f.* = **Blitzlichtlampe.**

Blitzlicht, *n. Phot:* flash-light; magnesium light.

Blitzlichtaufnahme, *f.* flash(-light) photograph.

Blitzlichtbirne, *f. Phot:* flash-bulb.

Blitzlichtgerät, *n. Phot:* flash-gun.

Blitzlichtlampe, *f. Phot: F:* flash-gun.

Blitzlichtphotographie, *f.* (*a*) flash(-light) photography; (*b*) flash(-light) photograph.

Blitzlichtpulver, *n. Phot:* flash-light powder.

Blitzlichtröhre, *f. Phot:* (electronic) flash(-tube) (in flash gun).

Blitzmädel, *n.* **1.** *F:* smart, smashing, girl; smasher. **2.** *Mil: F:* (German) woman signals auxiliary.

Blitzpfeil, *m.* (*warning sign on high-voltage apparatus, pylon, etc.*) danger arrow.

Blitzphotographie, *f.* photography of lightning.

Blitzpulver, *n.* **1.** = **Bärlappmehl. 2.** = **Blitzlichtpulver.**

Blitzröhre, *f.* **1.** *Geol:* fulgurite. **2.** = **Blitzlichtröhre.**

blitzsauber, *a.* = **blitz(e)blank.**

Blitzschaden, *m.* damage by lightning.

Blitzschlag, *m.* stroke of lightning; **vom B. getroffen,** struck by lightning; **ein Haus gegen B. versichern,** to insure a house against damage by lightning.

blitzschnell, *a.* as quick as lightning.

Blitzschutz, *m. El.E:* (*a*) protection against lightning; (*b*) = **Blitzschutzvorrichtung.**

Blitzschutzvorrichtung, *f. El.E:* lightning-arrester, lightning-protector (for electrical apparatus).

Blitzsinter, *m. Geol:* fulgurite.

Blitzstein, *m. A:* meteorite, *A:* thunderbolt.

Blitzstrahl, *m.* flash of lightning; thunderbolt.

Blitztelegramm, *n.* (*in Germany*) special priority telegram (*costing ten times as much as ordinary telegram*).

blitzvergnügt, *a. F:* as happy as a king, as a sandboy.

Blitzvisite, *f. F:* flying visit.

Blitzvogel, *m. Orn:* great crested grebe.

Blitzzug, *m. F:* express train.

Blizzard [ˈblizǝrt], *m.* **-s/-s,** blizzard.

Bloch, *m.* **-(e)s/-e & ⸗er.** *South G. & Swiss Dial:* stem, trunk; stump; log.

Blöchelhobel, *m. Tls: Coop:* jointer.

blochen, *v.tr. Swiss Dial:* = **blocken 1** (*c*).

Block, *m.* **-s/⸗e,** block. **1.** cake, bar, block (of soap, etc.); slab (of chocolate, etc.); trunk, stump (of tree); block, log (of wood); *Metall:* ingot, bar (of gold, silver, steel); bloom, slab, sow (of iron); pig (of iron, lead); *Atom.Ph:* (fuel) slug; *Geol:* boulder, rock; **erratischer B.,** erratic (block). **2.** (*pl.* **-s & ⸗e**) (*a*) pad, block (of paper, etc.); book (of tickets, etc.); (*b*) *Constr:* block (of houses, etc.); (*c*) *Pol:* coalition (of parties); bloc; (*d*) *Cards:* pool (of stakes). **3.** (*a*) *Hist:* (i) (executioner's) block; (ii) stocks; **j-n in den B. legen,** to put s.o. in the stocks; (*b*) *Nau: etc:* (pulley-)block; **einscheibiger, zweischeibiger, B.,** single, double, (pulley-) block. **4.** *Rail:* block (section). **5.** *F:* blockhead, idiot, fool.

Blockabschnitt, *m. Rail:* block (section).

Blockade [bloˈkaːdǝ], *f.* **-/-n. 1.** *Mil: Nau:* blockade; **wirksame B.,** effective blockade; **eine B. (über ein Land) verhängen,** to impose a blockade (on a country); **die B. aufheben,** to raise the blockade; **die B. brechen,** to run the blockade. **2.** *Print:* (space marked by) turned letter(s). **3.** *Med:* obstruction.

Blockadebrecher, *m.* blockade-runner.

Blockadebruch, *m.* blockade-running.

Blockbandsäge, *f. Tls:* band-saw for cutting logs.

Blockbau, *m.* = **Blockhaus.**

Blockbild, *n. Geol:* = **Blockdiagramm.**

Blockblei, *n. Metall:* pig-lead.

Blockbruchbau, *m. Min:* block-caving.

Blockbuch, *n. Print:* block-book.

Blockbuchen, *n. Cin:* block-booking (of films).

Blockbude, *f. Rail:* = **Blockstation.**

Blockdecke, *f. Mil:* blindage.

Blockdiagramm, *n. Geol:* relief diagram.

Blockdruck, *m. Print: Tex:* block-printing.

blocken, *v.* **1.** *v.tr.* (*a*) *Rail:* to block (line) (by signal); (*b*) *Sp:* to block (opponent); (*c*) *South German:* to polish (floor). **2.** *v.i.* (*haben*) (*of birds of prey*) to perch.

blöcken, *v.tr.* to block (hat, shoe).

Blocker, *m.* **-s/-.** *Bio-Ch:* inhibitor.

Blockfeld, *n.* **1.** *Geol:* residual boulders, rock rubble. **2.** *Rail:* block instrument.

Blockflöte, *f. Mus:* recorder (*instrument or organ stop*).

blockfrei, *a. Pol:* **blockfreie Staaten,** uncommitted, non-aligned, nations.

Blockguß, *m. Metall:* ingot casting.

blockhaft, *a.* (*of sculpture, etc.*) compact, massive, solid; block-like.

Blockhalde, *f. Geol:* = **Blockfeld.**

Blockhaus, *n.* log-cabin, -house, -hut; *Mil:* blockhouse.

Blockhütte, *f.* log-cabin, -hut.

blockieren [bloˈkiːrǝn]. **I.** *v.tr.* **1.** to block (sth.) (up), to obstruct (sth.); to jam, lock (brakes, controls, etc.); *Mil: Nau:* to blockade (town, harbour, etc.); *Rail:* to block (line) (by signal); *Bio-Ch:* to inhibit (passage of an impulse, action of an enzyme); *Sp:* to block (opponent); *Fin:* to lock up (capital); (*of authority*) to block (funds). **2.** *Print:* to turn (letters), to mark (a space) by turning letters.

II. *pr.p. & a.* **blockierend,** *in vbl senses; esp.* **die blockierende Macht, der Blockierende,** the blockader.

blockig, *a.* blockish, lumpish, clumsy.

Blockkalender, *m.* block-calendar; tear-off calendar.

Blockkarren, *m.* = **Blockwagen** (*b*).

Blockkette, *f. Mec.E:* block-chain.

Blockkondensator, *m. W.Tel:* blocking condenser.

Blockkreissäge, *f. Tls:* circular saw for cutting logs.

Blocklehm, *m. Geol:* boulder-clay, till

Blockmeer, *n. Geol:* = **Blockfeld.**

Blockmeißel, *m. Metalw:* hardy, anvil chisel.

Blockmotor, *m. I.C.E:* block, monobloc(k) (engine).

Blockpartei, *f. Pol:* coalition.

Blocksberg, der. *Pr.n. Geog:* the Blocksberg, the Brocken; *Myth:* the Witches' Mountain.

Blockschiff, *n.* **1.** *Navy:* blockship. **2.** raft.

Blockschlitten, *m.* wood-sledge, *U.S:* dray.

Blockschokolade, *f.* slab chocolate; cooking chocolate.

Blockschrift, *f.* block capitals, block letters; *Print:* block letters; **fette B.,** Egyptian (type); **halbfette B.,** clarendon.

Blocksignal, *n. Rail:* block signal.

Blockstation, *f. Rail:* (block) signal-box, *U.S:* (block) switch tower.

Blockstein, *m. Constr:* bond-stone, bonder.

Blockstelle, *f. Rail:* = **Blockstation.**

Blockstrecke, *f. Rail:* block (section).

Blockstufe, *f.* solid wood step (of stairs).

Blocksystem, *n. Rail:* block system.

Blockverband, *m. Constr:* Old English bond.

Blockverschluss, *m. Artil:* breech-block mechanism.

Blockwagen, *m.* truck; (*a*) hand-cart; trolley; (*b*) *For:* logging-wheels, bar-wheels (for moving logs), *U.S:* dray; (*c*) *Rail:* box-wagon, *U.S:* boxcar; (*d*) *Metall:* ingot car, *U.S:* ingot buggy.

Blockwalzwerk, *n. Metall:* blooming-mill, -rolls.

Blockwand, *f.* log wall.

Blockwart, *m.* (*in Nazi period*) Party warden (in charge of block of flats).

Blockwärter, *m. Rail:* signalman.

Blockwerk, *n. Rail:* block.

Blockzentrale, *f.* (electric) main (for a block of houses).

Blockzinn, *n.* block-tin.

Blockzucker, *m.* glucose.

blödäugig, *a. A:* weak-sighted.

blöd(e), *a.* (*a*) *A. & Lit:* weak; (*b*) imbecile, mentally deficient, cretinous; (*c*) timid, shy, bashful; *Prov:* **ein blöder Hund wird selten fett,** faint heart ne'er won fair lady; (*d*) *F:* silly, stupid, foolish, *F:* daft; **sei nicht so b.!** don't be so silly! **ich stand ganz b. da,** (i) I stood there foolishly, I stood there without knowing what to do, (ii) I stood there feeling bashful.

blödeln, *v.i.* (*haben*) *F:* to fool about, around.

Blödheit, *f.* = **Blödigkeit.**

Blödian, *m.* **-(e)s/-e.** *F:* fool, blockhead, idiot.

Blödigkeit, *f.* (*a*) shyness, timidity; (*b*) foolishness, stupidity; (*c*) *A. & Lit:* weakness; **B. der Augen,** weak-sightedness.

Blödling, *m.* **-s/-e.** *F:* = **Blödian.**

Blödmann, *m. F:* = **Blödian.**

blödsichtig, *a. A:* weak-sighted.

Blödsinn, *m.* **1.** idiocy, imbecility, mental deficiency. **2.** *F:* rubbish, nonsense; **laß den B.!** (i) stop fooling about! stop messing about! (ii) don't be silly, stupid, ridiculous, idiotic! **rede keinen B.!** don't talk rubbish, nonsense! *P:* stop blathering! don't talk tripe! (*b*) **B. machen, treiben,** to fool around, about, *F:* to mess about.

blödsinnig. 1. *a.* (*a*) imbecile, mentally deficient, cretinous; **ein Blödsinniger,** an imbecile, a mental defective, a cretin, a moron; (*b*) ridiculous, idiotic, stupid, foolish; **blödsinniges Geschwätz,** foolish, ridiculous, talk; **das ist total b.,** that's absolutely ridiculous, idiotic. **2.** *adv.* (*a*) like an imbecile; (*b*) stupidly, foolishly, ridiculously, idiotically; (*c*) *F:* enormously, immensely; **sich b. freuen,** to be immensely pleased; **b. kalt,** terribly cold.

blöken, *v.i.* (*haben*) (*of sheep, calf*) to bleat; (*o, cattle*) to low.

blond, *a.* (*a*) fair, fair-haired; **blondes Haar,** fair hair; **eine blonde Frau,** a fair-haired woman, a blonde; *Hum:* (*of woman*) **blondes Gift,** peroxide blonde; (*b*) (*of light, etc.*) pale; **blonder Schein,** pale light; *F:* **blondes Bier,** frothy light ale.

Blonde[1] [ˈblɔndǝ], *m., f., n.* (*decl. as adj.*) (*a*) fair-haired man, woman; (*b*) *F:* **eine (kühle) Blonde, ein (kühles) Blondes,** a glass of light ale.

Blonde[2] [ˈblõːdǝ, ˈblɔndǝ], *f.* **-/-n.** Blonde (lace).

blondgelockt, *a.* = **blondlockig.**

Blondhaar, *n.* fair hair.

blondieren [blɔnˈdiːrǝn], *v.tr.* to bleach (hair).

Blondine [blɔnˈdiːnǝ], *f.* **-/-n,** (*a*) fair-haired woman; (*b*) blonde (woman).

Blondinette [blɔndiˑˈnɛtǝ], *f.* **-/-n.** *Orn:* (breed of) frilled pigeon.

Blondkopf, *m.* fair-haired person.

blondlockig, *a.* with fair curls.

bloß. **I.** *a.* **1.** (*a*) naked, bare; **nackt und b.,** (i) naked, (ii) impoverished; **mit bloßen Händen,** with (one's) bare hands; **mit bloßen Füßen gehen,** to go barefoot; **mit bloßem Kopfe,** bare-headed; **mit bloßen Schultern,** with bare shoulders; **der bloße Hintern,** *F:* **der Bloße,** the bare bottom; **(mit) dem bloßen Auge wahrnehmbar,** visible to the naked eye; **bloßes Schwert,** bare, naked, sword; **bloße Erde,** bare ground; **auf dem bloßen Fußboden schlafen,** to sleep on the bare boards; **sich b. machen,** to undress; (*of baby*) **sich b. strampeln,** to kick off the coverings, bedclothes; *Lit:* **von Bäumen b.,** bare of trees; **aller Sorgen b.,** free of all cares; (*b*) poor, *B:* naked; (*c*) *Lit:* exposed; **jedem Zufall, der Sünde, b.,** exposed, a prey, to chance, to sin. **2.** mere; **bloße Worte,** mere words; **ein bloßer Hilfsarbeiter,** a mere labourer; **im bloßen Hemde,** in nothing but one's shirt; **mir wird schwach bei dem bloßen Gedanken,** the very, the mere, the bare, thought makes me feel weak; **auf bloßen Verdacht (hin) verhaftet werden,** to be arrested on mere, bare, suspicion.

II. **bloß,** *adv.* **1.** only, merely, simply, solely, just; **b. er konnte so was machen,** only he, he alone, could do a thing like that; **ich habe b. ein Kleid,** I only have, I have just, one dress; **das sagt er b., weil . . .,** he only, just, says that, he says that merely, simply, solely, because . . . . **2.** (*a*) **was mache ich b.?** whatever, what on earth, shall I do? **wo ist sie b. geblieben?** wherever, where on earth, has she got to? (*b*) (*threat*) **sag das ˈb. nicht deiner Mutter,** don't (you) dare tell your mother that; **faß ihn ˈb. nicht an,** don't (you) dare touch him; (*c*) *Dial:* just; **er ist b. weggegangen,** he's only just gone, he's just this minute gone.

Blöße, *f.* **-/-n,** (*a*) nakedness; **seine B. bedecken,** (i) to cover one's nakedness, to cover one's shame; (ii) to put some clothes on; (*b*) weak

spot; unguarded spot; *Fenc:* (section of) target; **sich** *dat.* **eine B. geben,** (i) *Fenc:* to expose oneself; (ii) to lay oneself open to attack; (iii) to compromise oneself; **sich** *dat.* **keine B. geben,** to show no weakness; to offer no grounds for attack; **keine B. bieten,** to have no chinks in one's armour; to be invulnerable; (*c*) *A. & Lit:* poverty; (*d*) (*in wood*) clearing; (*e*) *Leath:* skin prepared for tanning.

blößen, *v.tr. A:* to uncover.

bloßerdings, *adv. A:* only, merely, just.

bloßfüßig. **1.** *a.* barefoot(ed) (child, etc.). **2.** *adv.* barefoot.

bloßgeben, *v.tr. sep.* to expose (s.o., oneself); to give (s.o., oneself) away.

bloßlegen, *v.tr. sep.* to lay bare, uncover, expose (roots, secrets, plans, etc.).

bloßliegen, *v.i. sep.* (*strong*) (*haben*) to be uncovered.

bloßstellen, *v.tr. sep.* to expose (s.o., oneself); to compromise (s.o., oneself); to unmask (s.o.); to give (s.o., oneself) away; **bloßgestellt,** exposed, compromised, unmasked; (*of secret, plan, etc.*) compromised.

blubbern, *v.i.* (*haben*) *North G.Dial:* (*a*) (*of water*) to bubble; (*b*) (*of pers.*) to gabble.

Blücher. *Pr.n.m.* **-s.** *Hist:* Blücher; *F:* **'rangehen wie B.,** (i) to go straight into the attack; (ii) to set to with a will.

Blues [blu:s], *m.* **-/-.** *Mus: Danc:* blues.

Bluest [blu:st], *f. & n.* **-(s)/.** *Dial: Poet:* = **Blüte** 1 (*a*), (*b*).

Bluff [bluf, blœf], *m.* **-s/-e & -s,** bluff.

bluffen [ˈblufən], *v.i.* (*haben*) & *v.tr.* to bluff.

blühen. I. *v.i.* (*haben*) **1.** (*a*) (*of plant*) to flower, to blossom, to bloom, to be in flower, in blossom, in bloom; (*of field, garden, etc.*) to be gay with flowers; *F:* **jetzt blüht sein Weizen,** *F:* his ship has come home; (*b*) (*of country, business, person, etc.*) to flourish, thrive, prosper; (*of business*) to boom; (*of art, science, etc.*) to flourish, to thrive; **sein Geschäft blühte, war blühend,** his trade, business, was flourishing, thriving, prospering, booming; (*c*) (*of pers.*) to flourish, to thrive; (*d*) **wer weiß, wo mir mein Glück blüht, was mir noch blüht,** who knows what is in store for me; **das kann dir auch noch b.,** that can happen to you too; *F:* **dir blüht heute noch was!** you've got something coming to you today! **2.** (*of face*) to be covered in spots, etc.; (*of face, cheeks*) to be rosy.

II. *pr.p. & a.* **blühend,** *in vbl senses; esp.* flowery, radiant, prosperous; **eine blühende Wiese,** a flowery meadow, a meadow gay with flowers; **ein blühendes Mädchen,** a girl glowing, radiant, with health, a girl in the full bloom of youth; **sie sieht blühend aus,** she looks flourishing, blooming; **wie das blühende Leben aussehen,** to look the picture of health; **blühende Schönheit,** radiant beauty; **blühende Jugend,** radiant, blooming, youth; **blühende Gesundheit,** glowing, radiant, health; **blühender Unsinn, Blödsinn,** arrant nonsense; *see also* **Alter** 1 (*a*).

blühweiß, *a.* snow-white, snowy white.

Blümchen, *n.* **-s/-,** (*a*) little flower, small flower, *Poet:* floweret; (*b*) star (on animal's forehead).

Blümchenkaffee, *m. F:* weak coffee.

Blume, *f.* **-/-n.** **1.** (*a*) flower; **wilde Blumen,** wild flowers; **Blumen züchten,** to grow flowers; **mit Blumen schmücken,** to decorate (sth.) with flowers, to deck (s.o., sth.) (out) with flowers; **j-m Blumen auf den Weg streuen,** to strew s.o.'s path with flowers; **laßt Blumen sprechen!** say it with flowers; *F:* **durch die B. sprechen,** to speak in a veiled manner; **j-m etwas durch die B. sagen,** to tell s.o. sth. in veiled language, to convey sth. to s.o. in a roundabout way; *B:* **eine B. zu Saron,** the Rose of Sharon; (*b*) flower (of speech, of rhetoric); (*c*) *A. & Lit:* maidenhead, virginity; (*d*) *A:* menstruation, *A:* flowers; (*e*) bouquet, bloom (of wine); froth, head (on beer, etc.); **prosit B.!** your health! **2.** tail, scut (of rabbit, hare); tip of fox's tail, tag; star (on forehead of horse, etc.). **3.** *Cu:* silverside.

blümen, **1.** *v.i.* (*haben*) *A:* to bloom, blossom. **2.** *v.tr.* to decorate, deck, with flowers; *see also* **geblümt.**

Blumenampel, *f.* hanging flower-pot.

blumenartig, *a.* flower-like.

Blumenbalg, *m. Bot:* glume.

Blumenbeet, *n.* flower-bed.

Blumenbild, *n. Art:* flower-piece.

Blumenbinderei, *f.* = **Binderei** 2.

Blumenbinse, *f. Bot:* flowering rush, water-gladiole.

Blumenblatt, *n. Bot:* petal.

blumenblattartig, *a. Nat.Hist:* petaloid.

blumenblattlos, *a. Bot:* apetalous.

Blumenblau, *n. Bot:* anthocyanin.

Blumenbrett, *n.* shelf for pot plants.

Blumenbrueghel [-ˌbroygəl]. *Pr.n.m.* **-s.** *Hist. of Art:* Velvet Brueghel.

Blumendeckblatt, *n. Bot:* sepal; involucral leaf.

Blumendecke, *f. Bot:* perianth.

Blumendraht, *m.* fine wire for arranging flowers, flower-wire.

Blumenduft, *m.* fragrance, scent, of flowers.

Blumendünger, *m. Hort:* fertilizer for flowers.

Blumenerde, *f.* garden mould.

Blumenesche, *f. Bot:* flowering ash, manna ash.

Blumenfenster, *n.* large window with a wide sill for pot plants.

Blumenfliegen, *f.pl. Ent:* anthomyidae; anthopilous flies.

Blumenflor, *m.* luxuriant flowers; **der Garten stand im schönsten B.,** the garden was a mass of flowers.

Blumengarten, *m.* flower-garden.

Blumengärtner, *m.* nurseryman, nursery-gardener, florist.

Blumengärtnerei, *f.* **1.** nursery-garden. **2.** floriculture, flower growing.

Blumengehänge, *n.* festoon of flowers.

Blumengeschäft, *n.* = **Blumenhandlung.**

Blumengewinde, *n.* garland.

Blumengirlande, *f.* garland, festoon of flowers.

Blumengöttin, *f. Myth:* goddess of flowers.

blumenhaft, *a.* flower-like.

Blumenhandel, *m.* flower-trade, flower-selling.

Blumenhändler, *m.* florist.

Blumenhandlung, *f.* flower-shop, florist's (shop).

Blumenhülle, *f. Bot:* perianth.

Blumenkäfer, *m. Ent:* flower-beetle.

Blumenkasten, *m.* flower-box, *esp.* window-box.

Blumenkelch, *m.* flower-cup, *Bot:* calyx.

Blumenkenner, *m.* flower expert, expert on flowers.

Blumenkerze, *f.* flower candle.

Blumenkohl, *m. Hort:* cauliflower.

Blumenkohlgewächs, *n. Med:* papilloma.

Blumenkohlschwamm, *m. Fung:* clavaria botritis.

Blumenkorb, *m.* flower-basket.

Blumenkorso, *m.* battle of flowers.

Blumenkresse, *f. Hort:* dwarf nasturtium, Tom Thumb nasturtium.

Blumenkrone, *f. Bot:* corolla.

Blumenlese, *f. Lit:* anthology (of verse); florilegium.

Blumenmädchen, *n.* flower-girl.

Blumenmalerei, *f. Art:* flower-painting.

Blumenmarkt, *m.* flower market.

Blumenphase, *f.* = **Blütenperiode.**

Blumenrohr, *n. Bot:* canna, Indian-shot.

Blumensauger, *m. Orn:* humming-bird.

Blumenscherbe, *f.,* **Blumenscherben,** *m. A. & Dial:* flower-pot.

Blumenschlaf, *m.* closing of flowers (at night-time, etc.).

Blumensimse, *f. Bot:* (*a*) scheuchzeria; (*b*) = **Blumenbinse.**

Blumenspiele, *n.pl.* floral games (*literary competitions held yearly at Toulouse*).

Blumensprache, *f.* language of flowers.

Blumenspritze, *f. Hort:* sprayer, spray-diffuser, sprinkler.

Blumenständer, *m.* flower-stand.

Blumenstengel, *m.* (flower) stem, stalk.

Blumenstiel, *m.* = **Blumenstengel.**

Blumenstrauß, *m.* bouquet, bunch of flowers.

Blumenstück, *n.* **1.** *Art:* flower-piece. **2.** *Cu:* (*meat*) silverside.

Blumentiere, *n.pl. Coel:* anthozoa.

Blumentopf, *m.* flower-pot; *F:* **damit kannst du ˈauch keinen B. gewinnen,** that won't win you any prizes.

Blumenwerk, *n. Art:* festoon, floral work.

Blumenwespe, *f. Ent:* bee.

Blumenzucht, *f.* floriculture, flower-growing.

Blumenzüchter, *m.* nurseryman, nursery-gardener, florist; floriculturist.

Blumenzwiebel, *f. Hort:* flower bulb.

Blumenzwiebelzucht, *f.* bulb-growing.

Blumenzwiebelzüchter, *m.* bulb-grower.

blümerant [blyˑmaˈrant], *adv. F:* **es ist mir b. zumute,** I feel dizzy, giddy; my head begins to turn, to swim.

blumicht, *a. A:* = **blumig.**

blumig, *a.* **1.** (*a*) **blumiges Feld,** flowering field, field studded with flowers; (*b*) **blumiges Kleid,** flowered, *F:* flowery, dress, dress with floral design; (*c*) **blumige Redensarten,** flowery, florid, speech; (*d*) (*of wine*) flowery, of great bouquet. **2.** **-blumig,** *comb.fm.* -flowered; **großblumig,** large-flowered.

Blümtlerche, *f. Orn:* mountain-accentor, alpine accentor.

Blunderbüchse, *f. Sm.a: A:* blunderbuss.

blus *see* **blasen.**

Bluse, *f.* **-/-n.** *Cost:* blouse; (peasant's, etc.) smock.

blusig, *a. Dressm:* bloused (top of dress); **blusiger Schnitt,** bloused style; *adv.* **b. geschnitten,** cut to give a bloused effect.

Blust, *m. & n.* **-es/.** & *f.* **-/.** *Dial: Poet:* = **Blüte** 1 (*a*), (*b*).

Blut, *n.* **-(e)s/.** **1.** blood; (*a*) **B. spucken,** to spit blood; **B. stillen,** to sta(u)nch, stop, blood; **B. spenden,** to give, donate, blood; **B. übertragen,** to transfuse blood; to make a blood transfusion; **B. vergießen,** to shed, spill, blood; **viel B. ist geflossen,** much blood has been spilt, there has been much bloodshed; **nach B. dürsten,** to thirst for blood; **mit B. befleckt,** blood-stained; **er lag in seinem Blute,** he was lying in his own blood; **mit B. bedeckt,** covered, steeped, in blood; **in B. baden,** to steep oneself, to bathe, in blood; **das B. schoß ihr ins Gesicht,** the blood rushed to her face; **alles B. wich aus ihrem Gesicht,** all the blood (was) drained from her face; **B. schwitzen,** (i) to sweat blood, (ii) to be terrified; **j-n bis aufs B. peitschen,** to flog s.o. till blood is drawn; **j-n bis zum letzten Tropfen B. verteidigen,** to defend s.o. to the very end, to the last ditch; **mir stockte das B. in den Adern,** the blood curdled in my veins, my blood ran cold; **ihm wallte das B.,** (i) (*passion*) his blood raced, (ii) (*anger*) his blood boiled, his blood was up; **j-n bis aufs B. peinigen,** to torture s.o. to the utmost, *F:* to give s.o. hell; **j-n bis aufs B. hassen,** to loathe s.o., to hate s.o., like poison, like the plague; **j-n bis aufs B. aussaugen,** to bleed s.o. white; *B:* **Sein B. komme über uns,** His blood be on us; **sein B. sei auf meinem Haupt,** his blood be on my head; **er hat sein B. fürs Vaterland gelassen, hingegeben,** he laid down his life for his country; **heißes, leichtes, schweres, B. haben,** to be hot-blooded, light-hearted, morose; **das gibt böses B.,** that will make bad blood, mischief; **kaltes B. in der Gefahr bewahren,** to remain calm, to keep a cool head, to maintain one's sang-froid, in the face of danger; **ruhig B.!** keep calm! **das B. der Reben,** the juice, blood, of the grape; (*b*) (*kindred*) **Bande des Blutes,** ties of blood, of kinship; **Kinder eines Blutes,** children of the same blood; **sie sind unseres Blutes, von unserem Blute,** they are of the same blood as we; **B. ist dicker als Wasser,** blood is thicker than water; **das liegt, steckt, sitzt, ihm im B.,** it's in his blood; **die Stimme des Blutes,** the call of blood; *see also* **Band III.** 1; (*c*) (*birth, race*) **blaues B.,** blue blood; **von bürgerlichem B.,** of middle-class family, stock; **von adligem, königlichem, B.,** of noble, royal, blood; **das B. spricht in ihm,** blood tells in him; **einer Unternehmung neues B. zuführen,** to infuse new blood into an undertaking; **B. und Boden** (*as Nazi concept*), 'blood and soil'. **2.** (*of people*) **junges B.,** (i) young blood, (ii) youth, young people; **ein junges Blut,** a young man, young woman; **ein wildes, lustiges, B.,** a wild, gay, young man, young woman.

Blutacker, der. *B:* the field of blood.

Blutader, *f. Anat:* vein.

Blutalge, *f. popular name for various algae, esp.* **1.** chlamydomonas. **2.** sea blossom, sea bloom. **3.** red alga.

Blutampfer, *m. Bot:* bloody(-veined) dock.

Blutandrang, *m. Med:* congestion.

Blutapfelsine, *f.* blood-orange.

blutarm[1] [ˈblu:tˀarm], *a.* anaemic.

blutarm[2] [ˈblu:tˈarm], *a.* very poor, as poor as a church mouse.

Blutarmut, *f. Med:* anaemia.

Blutauge, *n.* **1.** *Med:* bloodshot eye. **2.** *Bot:* marsh cinquefoil.

Blutausstrich, *m. Med:* blood smear.

Blutbad, *n.* blood-bath, carnage, massacre, slaughter.

Blutbahn, *f. Physiol:* blood stream.

Blutbank, *f. Med:* blood bank.

Blutbann, *m. Hist:* jurisdiction with capital powers.

Blutbaum, *m. Bot:* dracaena, dragon-tree.

blutbedeckt, *a.* covered, steeped, in blood.

blutbefleckt, *a.* blood-stained.

Blutbeule, *f. Med:* blood blister.

Blutbild, *n. Med:* blood-picture; haemogram; blood-count; **ein B. machen,** to take a blood-picture; to make an analysis of a blood sample.

Blutbildung, *f.* (*a*) forming, formation, of blood; (*b*) composition of the blood.

Blutblase, *f. Med:* blood blister.

Blutblume, *f. Bot:* haemanthus, blood-flower.

Blutbrechen, *n. Med:* vomiting of blood, haematemesis.

Blutbruch, *m. Med:* haematocele.
Blutbruder, *m.* blood-brother.
Blutbuche, *f. Bot:* copper beech.
Blutbühne, *f.* scaffold.
Blutchampignon, *m. Fung:* **großer B.,** bleeding brown mushroom; **echter, kleiner, B.,** wood mushroom, brown wood mushroom.
Blütchen, *n.* **-s/-.** *Bot:* floret.
Blutdruck, *m. Med:* blood pressure; **hoher, niedriger, B.,** high, low, blood pressure.
Blutdruckmesser, *m.* blood pressure gauge, sphygmomanometer.
Blutdruckmessung, *f.* measuring of the blood pressure.
Blutdrüse, *f. Anat:* endocrine gland, ductless gland.
Blutdünger, *m.* (dried) blood manure.
Blutdurst, *m.* thirst, lust, for blood; blood-lust.
blutdürstig, *a.* thirsty, athirst, for blood; blood-thirsty.
Blüte, *f.* **-/-n. 1.** (*a*) flowering, blossom(ing), blooming, (in)florescence; **in B.,** in bloom, flower; in blossom; **in voller B. stehen, sein,** to be in full bloom, in full flower; (*b*) flowering period, time (of plant); blossom-time (of tree, etc.). **2.** (*a*) blossom, bloom, flower; **duftende Blüten,** fragrant blossom(s), flowers, blooms; **Blüten treiben,** to blossom, bloom, flower; **am Birnbaum sind die Blüten aufgebrochen,** the pear-tree has burst into bloom, into flower; *F:* **er sucht aus jeder B. Honig zu saugen,** he tries to turn everything to his own advantage; (*b*) **seine Unternehmungen trugen seltsame Blüten,** his efforts had strange offshoots; (*c*) *Iron:* striking example of badness (in art, style, etc.); howler; **von den vielen schlechten Bildern hier ist das die B.,** of all these bad pictures this one is the worst, *F:* this one takes the cake. **3.** (*a*) prime; flowering period, time (of art, literature, science, etc.); **die Wissenschaft ist, steht, in voller, höchster, B.,** science has reached its peak, its prime; **seine B. erreichen,** to reach one's peak, prime; **er hatte seine B. um die Mitte des achtzehnten Jahrhunderts,** he flourished in the middle of the eighteenth century; **sie war in der B. ihrer Jahre, ihrer Schönheit,** she was in her prime, in the full bloom, in the prime, of her beauty; **er fiel in der B. der Jugend,** he fell, was killed, in the prime, bloom, of youth; **in der B. des Lebens sein,** to be in the prime, heyday, of life, in the flower of one's age; (*b*) best part, cream, flower; **die B. des Staates, des Adels, usw.,** the cream, the flower, of the nation, of the nobility, etc.; **die B. der deutschen Jugend,** the flower of Germany's youth. **4.** *F:* forged money, *F:* dud money; **Blüten,** *F:* duds, *U.S:* green goods. **5.** (*on body*) rash, eruption; **sein Gesicht ist voller Blüten,** his face is covered in a rash, in pimples, in spots.
Blutegel, *m.* **-s/-.** *Ann:* leech; **j-m Blutegel ansetzen,** to apply leeches to s.o.
Blutegelzucht, *f.* hirudiniculture, leech-breeding.
bluten. I. *v.i.* (*haben*) (*a*) to bleed; **seine Nase blutet,** he is bleeding at the nose, his nose is bleeding; **seine Wunden bluten,** his wounds are bleeding; **heftig b.,** to bleed freely, heavily, to pour blood; **b. wie ein Schwein,** to bleed like a pig; **fürs Vaterland b.,** to give one's blood for one's country; **das Herz blutete ihm bei diesem Anblick,** his heart bled, he was filled with sorrow, at the sight; **ich gebe dir etwas ab, damit dir das Herz(chen) nicht blutet,** I'll give you some, so that you don't feel left out; **mein Herz blutet für sie,** my heart bleeds for her; **blutenden Herzens,** with an aching, heavy, heart; *Bot:* **blutendes Herz,** bleeding heart; (*b*) *F:* to stump up, to fork out, to cough up (money); **er mußte tüchtig b.,** he had to stump up a lot of money, he had to pay through the nose; **j-n b. lassen,** to make s.o. pay through the nose.
II. *vbl s.* **1. Bluten,** *n. in vbl senses.* **2. Blutung,** *f. Med:* discharge of blood, haemorrhage; **bei starker Blutung, bei starken Blutungen,** in the event of serious haemorrhage.
Blütenachse, *f. Bot:* floral axis.
blütenarm, *a. Bot:* pauciflorous.
Blütenart, *f. Bot:* flower family.
Blütenauge, *n.* flower-bud.
Blütenbau, *m.* flower structure.
Blütenbecher, *m. Bot:* cupule.
Blütenbefruchter, *m. Bot:* pollinator.
Blütenbestäubung, *f. Bot:* pollin(iz)ation.
blütenbildend, *a.* flower-forming.
Blütenbildung, *f.* flower-formation.
Blütenblatt, *n. Bot:* petal.
blütenblattlos, *a. Bot:* apetalous.
Blütenboden, *m. Bot:* receptacle, torus, thalmus.
Blütenbüschel, *m. & n.* tuft (of flowers).
Blütendecke, *f. Bot:* involucre, involucrum.
Blütendiagramm, *n.* floral diagram.
Blütendolde, *f. Bot:* umbel.
Blütendürre, *f. Bot:* (*disease*) blossom wilt.
Blütenesche, *f.* = **Blumenesche.**
Blütenfarbe, *f.* flower colour, *Bot:* flower pigment.
Blütenfarbstoff, *m.* flower colour, *Bot:* flower pigment.
Blütenfäule, *f. Bot:* (*disease*) flower-rot.
Blütengehänge, *n. Art:* flower-chain, festoon of flowers.
Blütenhülle, *f. Bot:* perianth.
Blütenhüllenblatt, *n. Bot:* sepal.
Blütenkätzchen, *n. Bot:* catkin.
Blütenkelch, *m. Bot:* calyx.
Blütenknäuel, *m. & n.* cluster of flowers, *Bot:* glomerule.
Blütenknospe, *f.* flower-bud.
Blütenknospenanlage, *f. Bot:* aestivation, prefloration.
Blütenkolben, *m. Bot:* spadix.
Blütenköpfchen, *n. Bot:* capitulum.
Blütenkörbchen, *n. Bot:* capitulum (of compositae), anthodium.
Blütenkrone, *f. Bot:* corolla.
Blütenkuchen, *m. Bot:* coenanthium.
Blütenlager, *n. Bot:* receptacle, torus.
Blütenlese, *f. Lit:* anthology, florilegium.
blütenlos, *a.* without flowers; *Bot:* cryptogamous; **blütenlose Pflanzen, Blütenlose** *pl,* cryptogamia.
Blütenöl, *n.* essential oil of flowers.
Blütenperiode, *f. Bot:* flowering period.
Blütenpflanze, *f.* flowering plant; *Bot:* phanerogam; **die Blütenpflanzen,** the phanerogamia.
Blütenpolster, *n. Bot:* torus.
Blütenschaft, *m. Bot:* (*a*) (flower-)stalk; (*b*) flower-shoot.
Blütenscheibe, *f. Bot:* thalamus.
Blütenscheide, *f. Bot:* spathe.
blütenscheidig, *a. Bot:* spathaceous.
Blütenschraube, *f. Bot:* lady's tresses.
Blütenspelze, *f. Bot:* glume.
Blütensproß, *m. Bot:* flower shoot.
Blütenstand, *m. Bot:* inflorescence.
Blütenstandstiel, *m. Bot:* peduncle.
Blütenstaub, *m. Bot:* pollen.
Blütenstecher, *m. Ent:* anthonomus.
Blütenstiel, *m. Bot:* pedicle.
blütenstielständig, *a. Bot:* pediculate, pedicellate.
Blütenstrauch, *m.* flowering shrub.
Blütentang, *m.* red seaweed.
Blutentnahme, *f. Med:* removal of blood, *esp.* blood sample.
blütentragend, *a.* flower-bearing; *Bot:* floriferous.
Blütentraube, *f. Bot:* raceme.
Blutentziehung, *f. Med:* blood-letting, venesection.
blütenweiß, *a.* snow-white, snowy white.
Blütenzweig, *m.* flower spray; spray of flowers, of blossom.
Bluter, *m.* **-s/-.** *Med:* haemophiliac, haemophile; *F:* bleeder.
Bluterbrechen, *n. Med:* = **Blutbrechen.**
Bluterguß, *m. Med:* (*a*) extravasation, effusion; haemorrhage; (*b*) contusion; bruise; haematoma.
Bluterkrankheit, *f. Med:* haemorrhagic diathesis; haemophilia.
Blütezeit, *f.* (*a*) flowering period, time (of plant); blossom-time (of tree, etc.); (*b*) prime; flowering period, time (of art, literature, science, etc.); (*c*) heyday (of youth, of life, etc.); **in der B. des Lebens,** in the springtime of life, in life's heyday.
Blutfarbe, *f.* **1.** (*a*) colour of the blood; (*b*) *Physiol:* blood pigment. **2.** blood colour, crimson.
blutfarbig, *a.* blood-coloured, crimson.
Blutfarbstoff, *m. Physiol:* haemoglobin.
Blutfaserstoff, *m. Ch: Physiol:* fibrin.
Blutfennich, *m.,* **Blutfingergras,** *n.* = **Bluthirse** (*b*).
Blutfink, *m. Orn:* bullfinch.
Blutfleck(en), *m.* blood-stain.
Blutfleckenkrankheit, *f. Med:* purpura, *F:* purples.
Blutfluß, *m.* (*a*) *A. & B:* discharge of blood, haemorrhage; (*b*) *B:* (*menstruation*) flowers; (*c*) *Med: A:* menorrhagia.
blutflüssig, *a. A. & B:* (pers.) suffering from a discharge of blood, a haemorrhage; *B.Lit:* **das blutflüssige Weib,** the woman with the issue of blood.
Blutflüssigkeit, *f. Physiol:* blood plasma.
Blutführung, *f. Breed:* pedigree.
Blutgarbe, *f. Bot:* knot-grass.
Blutgefäß, *n. Physiol:* blood-vessel.
Blutgefäßmal, *n. Med:* vascular naevus.
Blutgeld, *n.* blood-money.
Blutgeräusch, *n.* haemic murmurs.
Blutgericht, *n. Hist:* **1.** assize. **2.** scaffold.
Blutgerinnsel, *n. Med:* clot of blood, blood-clot.
Blutgerinnung, *f.* clotting, coagulation, congealing, of the blood.
Blutgerüst, *n.* scaffold.
Blutgeschwulst, *n. Med:* bruise, swelling; haematoma.
Blutgeschwür, *n. Med:* furuncle, *F:* boil.
Blutgier, *f.* thirst, lust, for blood.
blutgierig, *a.* bloodthirsty; thirsty, athirst, for blood.
Blutgruppe, *f.* blood group.
Bluthänfling, *m. Orn:* linnet.
Blutharnen, *n.* **1.** *Med:* haematuria. **2.** *Vet:* red-water (disease).
Bluthasel, *f. Bot:* = **Blutnuß.**
Blutheil, *n. Bot:* tutsan.
Bluthelmling, *m. Fung:* **purpurschneidiger B.,** mycena sanguinolenta.
Bluthirse, *f. Bot:* (*a*) glabrous finger-grass; creeping panic grass; (*b*) crab grass, hairy finger-grass.
Bluthochzeit, *f. Fr.Hist:* **die Pariser B.,** the Massacre of St. Bartholomew.
Blutholz, *n. Bot: Com:* Campeachy wood; logwood.
Blutholzbaum, *m.* = **Blutbaum.**
Bluthund, *m.* **1.** (type of) bloodhound. **2.** bloodthirsty person, man of blood.
Bluthusten, *n. Med:* haemoptysis, spitting of blood.
bluthustend, *a. Med:* haemoptysical.
blutig, *a.* **1.** blood-stained; bloody, covered in blood; sanguinary; gory; **blutige Schlacht,** bloody, sanguinary, battle; **blutige Tat,** bloody, sanguinary, deed; **blutige Zwischenfälle,** incidents involving bloodshed; **sich** *dat.* **die Hände b. machen,** to get blood on one's hands; **j-n b. schlagen,** to beat s.o. raw; **j-m die Nase b. schlagen,** to hit s.o. on the nose so that it bleeds; to give s.o. a bloody nose; **blutige Tränen weinen,** to weep bitter tears. **2. es ist mein blutiger Ernst,** I am dead serious; **blutiger Dilettant, Laie,** complete dilettante, layman; **ein blutiger Anfänger,** a mere beginner, an utter novice, *F:* a greenhorn, Johnny Raw.
-blütig[1], *comb.fm.* -blooded; **vollblütig,** full-blooded; **heißblütig,** hot-blooded.
-blütig[2], *comb.fm.* -blossomed, -bloomed, with . . . blossoms; **eine rotblütige Pflanze,** a plant bearing red blossoms.
Blutikterus, *m. Med:* haemolytic jaundice.
Blutindianer, *m. Ethn:* Blood Indian.
Blutjaspis, *m. Miner:* heliotrope, blood-stone.
blutjung, *a.* very young; green; **als wir noch b. waren,** in our salad days, in our tender youth.
Blutkapillar, *n. Anat:* (blood) capillary.
Blutkieme, *f. Ich: etc:* blood-gill.
Blutkonserve, *f. Med:* blood preserved by mixing it with an anti-coagulant.
Blutkörperchen, *n.* blood corpuscle; **rotes B., red** corpuscle, erythrocyte; **weißes B.,** white corpuscle, leucocyte.
Blutkraut, *n. Bot: F:* (*a*) herb Robert, bloodwort; (*b*) blood geranium, bloody crane's bill; (*c*) = **Gelbwurz** 2; (*d*) bloody dock; (*e*) **kanadisches B.,** blood root, red puccoon.
Blutkreislauf, *m.* blood circulation, circulation (of the blood); *Med:* **mangelhafter B.,** defective circulation.
Blutkristall, *m. Physiol:* blood crystal.
Blutkuchen, *m. Physiol:* clot (of blood).
Blutlache, *f.* pool of blood.
Blutlauf, *m. Physiol:* = **Blutkreislauf.**
Blutlaugensalz, *n. Ch:* (*a*) **gelbes B.,** potassium ferrocyanide; (*b*) **rotes B.,** potassium ferricyanide.
Blutlaus, *f. Ent:* woolly plant-louse, American blight.
blutleer, *a.* bloodless; **er ist ein blutleerer Charakter,** he has no blood in his veins.
Blutleere, *f. Med:* anaemia (*caused by shock, etc.*); ischaemia; **künstliche B.,** constriction of a limb by the application of a tourniquet; ischaemia.
Blutleiter, *m. Anat:* sinus (of the brain).
Blutlinie, *f. Breed:* pedigree (of dog, etc.).
blutlos, *a.* bloodless.
Blutmangel, *m. Med:* anaemia.
Blutmehl, *n. Agr:* blood meal.
Blutmole, *f. Obst:* blood mole.
Blutnachweis, *m.* blood-test (for purposes of identification).
Blutnelke, *f. Bot:* maiden pink; Carthusian pink.
Blutnessel, *f. Bot:* figwort.
Blutnetzen, *n. Vet:* = **Blutharnen** 2.

Blutnuß, *f. Bot:* red filbert.

Blutopfer, *n.* (blood) sacrifice.

Blutorange, *f.* blood-orange.

Blutparasit, *m.* blood parasite.

Blutpilz, *m. Fung:* boletus satanas.

Blutplasma, *n.* blood plasma.

Blutplättchen, *n. Physiol:* blood platelet; thrombocyte.

Blutprobe, *f.* **1.** *Med:* blood test. **2.** *Hist:* ordeal of the bier, *A:* bier-right.

Blutpfropf, *m. Med:* clot (of blood), thrombus.

Blutrache, *f.* blood-vengeance, blood revenge.

Bluträcher, *m.* avenger of blood.

Blutrausch, *m.* orgy of blood.

Blutregen, *m.* blood rain.

blutreinigend, *a. Med:* depurative, blood-cleansing; **blutreinigendes Mittel,** depurative, blood-cleanser.

Blutreinigungsmittel, *n. Med:* depurative, blood-cleanser.

Blutreinigungstee, *m. Pharm:* blood-cleansing decoction.

Blutreizker, *m. Fung:* saffron milk cap.

Blutröschen, *n. Bot:* blood-red geranium.

blutrot, *a.* blood-red; crimson.

blutrünstig, *a.* **1.** bloodthirsty. **2.** bleeding, bloody.

Blutrute, *f. Bot:* red dogwood.

Blutsauger, *m.* **1.** *Rept:* blood-sucker. **2.** *Surg:* instrument for blood-letting. **3.** *F:* blood-sucker, leech, extortioner.

Blutsbrüderschaft, *f.* blood brotherhood; **sie haben B. getrunken,** (i) they have become blood brothers by drinking each other's blood; (ii) *F:* they are as thick as thieves.

Blutschande, *f.* incest.

Blutschänder, *m.* incestuous person.

blutschänderisch, *a.* incestuous.

Blutscheibe, *f.* = **Blutkörperchen.**

Blutscheu, *f.* haem(at)ophobia; fear of the sight of blood.

Blutschierling, *m. Bot:* hemlock.

Blutschmarotzer, *m.* blood parasite.

Blutschnabelmöwe, *f. Orn:* Magellan gull.

Blutschnabelweber, *m. Orn:* red-billed weaver.

Blutschnee, *m.* red snow.

Blutschuld, *f.* blood-guilt(iness); murder.

Blutschwamm, *m.* **1.** *Fung:* (*a*) = **Bovist;** (*b*) beef-steak fungus. **2.** *Med:* haemangioma.

Blutschwäre, *f. Med:* furuncle, *F:* boil.

Blutsenkung, *f. Med:* **1.** hypostasis. **2.** sedimentation of the blood; **eine B. machen,** to test the sedimentation-rate of the blood.

Blutsenkungsgeschwindigkeit, *f. Med:* sedimentation-rate of the blood.

Blutserum, *n.* blood serum.

Blutspat, *m. Vet:* bog-spavin, blood-spavin.

Blutspecht, *m. Orn:* Syrian woodpecker.

Blutspeien, *n. Med:* = **Bluthusten.**

Blutspender, *m. Surg:* blood-donor, -giver.

Blutspucken, *n.,* **blutspuckend,** *a.* = **Bluthusten bluthustend.**

Blutspur, *f.* trace of blood.

Blutstatus [ˈbluːtˌstaːtus], *m. Med:* = **Blutbild.**

Blutstauung, *f. Med:* passive, venous, hyperaemia.

Blutstein, *m. Miner:* red haematite.

blutstillend, *a. Med:* (*a*) haemostatic; (*b*) styptic; **blutstillendes Mittel,** styptic; haemostat.

Blutstillung, *f. Med:* sta(u)nching, stopping, of the blood.

Blutstockung, *f.* **1.** *Physiol:* haemostasia. **2.** *Med: F:* amenorrhoea.

Blutstorchschnabel, *m. Bot:* bloody crane's-bill, blood geranium.

Blutstrom, *m.* **1.** *Physiol:* blood stream. **2.** stream of blood.

Blutströpfchen, *n.* **1.** spot, speck, of blood. **2.** *Bot: F:* (*a*) adonis, pheasant's eye; (*b*) maiden pink; (*c*) sweet william; (*d*) great burnet, blood-wort. **3.** *Ent:* burnet-moth.

Blutstropfen, *m.* drop of blood.

Blutsturz, *m. Med:* haemorrhage; bleeding.

Blutsucht, *f.* = **Bluterkrankheit.**

Blutsverwandte, *m., f.* blood relation.

Blutsverwandtschaft, *f.* blood relationship, consanguinity.

Bluttat, *f.* bloody deed; murder.

Bluttau, *m.* blood rain (caused by red-coloured algae).

Bluttäubling, *m. Fung:* blood-red russule.

Bluttaufe, *f. Theol:* baptism of blood; *F:* martyrdom.

Bluttransfusion [ˈbluːttransfu·zi̯oːn], *f. Surg:* blood transfusion.

bluttriefend, *a.* dripping with blood.

Blutübertragung, *f. Surg:* blood transfusion.

Blutumlauf, *m.* = **Blutkreislauf.**

Blutung, *f. see* **bluten II.**

blutunterlaufen, *a.* suffused with blood; bloodshot (eye).

Blutuntersuchung, *f.* blood test.

Blutvergießen, *n.* bloodshed.

Blutvergiftung, *f.* blood-poisoning; sepsis; septicaemia.

Blutverlust, *m.* loss of blood.

blutvoll, *a.* full of life, lively; racy, vivid (personality, picture, description, etc.).

Blutwallung, *f. Med:* = **Blutandrang.**

Blutwärme, *f.* blood heat.

Blutwarze, *f. Med:* angioma.

Blutwasser, *n. Physiol:* blood serum.

Blutweide, *f.* = **Blutrute.**

Blutweiderich, *m. Bot:* purple loosestrife.

blutwenig, *inv.a.* extremely little.

Blutwurst, *f.* black pudding, blood pudding, *U.S:* blood sausage.

Blutwurz(el), *f. Bot:* **1.** = **Blutkraut** (*b*), (*e*). **2.** = **Blutwurzfingerkraut.**

Blutwurzfingerkraut, *n. Bot:* tormentil, septfoil, shepherd's knot.

Blutzelle, *f. Physiol:* blood cell, blood corpuscle.

Blutzeuge, *m.* martyr.

Blutzirkulation, *f.* = **Blutkreislauf.**

Blutzucker, *m. Physiol:* blood sugar.

Blutzufuhr, *m.* supply of blood (*to the heart, etc.*).

b-moll, b-Moll, *n. Mus:* (key of) B flat minor; **b-moll-Arie,** aria in B flat minor.

Bnehargem [bne·ˈha·rgɛm]. *Pr.n.m.pl. B:* Boanerges (the sons of thunder).

Bö, *f.* -/-en. *Av: Nau:* squall, gust; *Nau:* flaw; **weiße Bö,** white squall; **trockene Bö,** dry squall.

Boa [ˈboːaː], *f.* -/-s. **1.** *Rept:* boa; boa-constrictor. **2.** *Cost:* (fur *or* feather) boa.

Boas [ˈboːas]. *Pr.n.m.* -ʼ. *B.Hist:* Boaz.

Bob [bɔp], *m.* -s/-s. *Sp:* bob-sled, bob-sleigh; *F:* bob.

Bobaum, *m. Bot:* bo-tree, peepul-tree.

Boberelle [bo·bəˈrɛlə], *f.* -/-n = **Blasenkirsche.**

Bobine [bo·ˈbiːnə], *f.* -/-n, (*a*) *Tex:* bobbin, spool; (*b*) *Min:* winding reel; flat rope winding drum.

Bobinenpapier, *n. Paperm:* coils.

Bobinet [bo·bi·ˈnɛt], *m.* -s/-s. *Tex:* bobbinet, bobbin-net.

Bobinetstreifen, *f.pl.* quilling, trimming lace.

bobinieren [bo·bi·ˈniːrən], *v.tr.* to spool, reel (thread, etc.); to wind a bobbin.

Bobinoir [bo·bi·no·ˈaːr], *m.* -s/-s. *Tex:* winding-machine, roving-frame, bobbin-frame.

Boblink, Bobolink, *m.* -s/-e. *Orn:* bobolink.

Bobsleigh [ˈbɔpsleː], *m.* -s/-s = **Bob.**

Boccia [ˈbɔtʃaː], *f.* -/-s, **Bocciaspiel,** *n.* (game of) bowls.

Bochara [bo·ˈxaːraː]. *Pr.n.n.* -s. *Geog:* = **Buchara.**

Bock, *m.* -(e)s/¨e. **1.** (*male of deer, antelope, chamois, hare, rabbit*) buck; (*of goat*) he-goat, *F:* billy-goat; (*of sheep*) ram; **nach (dem) B. riechen, wie ein B. stinken,** to smell, stink, like a goat; to smell rank; *F:* **den B. zum Gärtner machen,** to put an unsuitable person in charge of sth.; *F:* to set the fox to keep the geese; **die Schafe von den Böcken scheiden,** to separate the sheep from the goats; *see also* **melken** 1. **2.** (*a*) *F:* pigheaded person, *F:* mule; awkward customer; **einen B. haben,** to be as stubborn, obstinate, as a mule; *F:* **ihn stößt der B.,** he is (being) stubborn, difficult; **den B. wegschicken,** to take, knock, the nonsense out of a child; (*b*) *F:* tailor, *F:* snip; (*c*) *P:* (*of man*) **(alter) geiler B.,** (insatiable) old goat, old lecher. **3.** (*a*) *F:* **einen B. schießen,** to make a mistake, *F:* a bloomer; to (make a) blunder; (*b*) *Gym:* buck; **B. springen,** (i) *Gym:* to vault over the buck; (ii) *Games:* to leap-frog; *Games:* **j-m B. stehen,** to make a back for s.o. (*at leap-frog*); (*c*) *Veh:* box; **auf dem B. mitfahren,** to sit with the driver, to ride on the box. **4.** (*a*) stool; (*b*) stand; rest; trestle; bench; block; *Carp:* = **Sägebock;** (*c*) prop, stay, strut; *Constr:* truss (of roof, bridge); **einsäuliger B.,** king-post truss; (*d*) *Mec.E: Mch:* bracket, bearer, support (of machine parts, etc.); pedestal (of bearing); overhung support (on bed-plate); bed (of machine); engine-bed; standard (of machine); *Mec.E: Constr: etc:* gin, crab, derrick, sheers, sheer-legs; *Nau:* (i) mast-crane, derrick (crane), masting sheers; (ii) 'A' bracket; (*e*) = **Furnierbock; Rammbär, Sturmbock. 5.** (*a*) flat-bottomed boat; *F:* pitching aeroplane; (*b*) *Dial:* hay-rack; (*c*) fire-dog, andiron; (*d*) *Bill:* (billiard-cue) rest, *F:* jigger; (*e*) *Hist:* **spanischer, polnischer, B.,** (the torture of) the boot. **6.** *Mus:* (i) tremolo stop (of organ); (ii) bagpipe. **7.** *Anat:* **B. des Ohrs,** tragus. **8.** *Ent: F:* = **Bockkäfer. 9.** *Brew:* = **Bockbier.**

bockbeinig, *a.* (*a*) stiff, awkward; (*b*) stubborn, mulish, intractable; (*c*) crooked-legged.

Bockbeinigkeit, *f. F:* mulishness, pigheadedness.

Bockbier, *n.* bock(-beer); double beer.

Bockbrett, *n. Veh:* footboard (in front of driver).

Bockbrücke, *f.* trestle-bridge.

Bockbücksflinte, *f. Sm.a:* over-and-under rifle-shotgun.

Böckchen, *n.* -s/-, (*dim. of* **Bock**) (*a*) (i) = **Bockkalb;** (ii) male kid, young male goat; male lamb; (*b*) stool; *Tchn:* support.

Bockdecke, *f. Veh:* hammer-cloth.

bocken, *v.i.* (*haben*) **1.** (*a*) (*of female sheep, goat, hare, rabbit*) to be on, in, heat; to be in season; (*b*) to smell of goat; to smell rammish. **2.** (*a*) (*of horse*) to buck(-jump), to leap; to rear; to jib; (*b*) (*of child*) to sulk, to be sulky; (*of pers.*) to be obstinate, stubborn, recalcitrant, refractory; to be obstinately sulky. **3.** (*of ship*) to pitch (and toss), to heave; (*of gun*) to jump; *Aut:* (*of engine*) to misfire, *U.S:* to buck; *Av:* **bockendes Flugzeug,** pitching aeroplane. **4.** (*of ram*) to butt.

Bockerl, *n.* -s/-n. *Austrian:* fir-cone, pine-cone.

Bockfell, *n.* goatskin; buckskin.

Bockfellschlauch, *m.* goatskin bottle, goatskin.

Bockformmaschine, *f.* upright moulding machine.

Bockfräse, *f. Woodw: Tls:* single spindle vertical shaper.

Bockgerüst, *n.* (*a*) *Agr:* cradle (of scythe); (*b*) base (of post-mill, etc.).

Bockgestell, *n. Veh:* under-body, -carriage; *Rail:* trestle frame (of truck); *Mch:* bed (for vertical engine); *El.E:* trestle stand.

Bockhirsch, *m. Gr.Myth:* tragelaph(us).

Bockholz, *n.* (*a*) *Bot:* guaiacum wood, lignum vitae; (*b*) *Bootm:* boot-stretcher.

Bockhuf, *m. Vet:* club-foot (of horse).

bockig, *a.* **1.** hircine, goaty; rammish; (*of female sheep, goat*) in, on, heat; **bockiger Geruch,** goatish smell. **2.** (*a*) stubborn, obstinate, mulish, *F:* pigheaded; refractory; (*b*) **bockiges Pferd,** jibber, jibbing horse. **3.** *Av:* (*of air*) bumpy, turbulent.

Bockigkeit, *f.* (*a*) stubbornness, *F:* pigheadedness; (*b*) *Meteor: Av:* turbulence (of air).

Bockkäfer, *m. Ent:* capricorn beetle; longicorn.

Bockkalb, *n. Ven:* (*male fallow deer of the first year*) fawn; roe-buck *or* chamois-buck of the first year.

Bockkasten, *m. Veh:* boot (of coach).

Bockkitz, *n. Ven:* roe-buck *or* chamois-buck of the first year.

Bockkonstruktion, *f.* trestle-work, trestle structure.

Bockkran, *m. Mec.E:* gantry(-crane).

Bocklager, *n. Mec.E:* pillow-, plummer-block bearing, pedestal bearing.

Bocklamm, *n.* male lamb; male kid, young male goat.

bockledern, *a.* (*a*) goatskin (rug, etc.); **bockledern Hose,** buckskin breeches, buckskins; (*b*) (*of pers., speech, book*) dull, uninteresting; (*of lecture, subject*) dry(-as-dust), boring.

Böcklein, *n.* -s/-, (*dim. of* **Bock**) = **Böckchen** (*a*).

Bockleiter, *f.* step-ladder, (pair, set, of) steps.

Bockmelkerei, *f. Hum:* useless labour, wasted effort.

Bockmotor, *m.* vertical engine (with cylinder below crank-shaft).

Bockmühle, *f.* German mill, post-mill.

Bocknuß, *f. Bot:* butter-nut, souari nut.

Bockpfeife, *f. Mus:* bagpipe(s).

Bockprahm, *m. Nau:* sheer-hulk, shear-hulk.

Bocksattel, *m.* hussar saddle, light cavalry saddle.

Bocksauge, *n.* **1.** (*a*) *Moll:* patella, limpet, goose-mussel; (*b*) *Lap:* cat's-eye, tiger-eye. **2.** (*a*) goat's eye; (*b*) person with small eyes, with pig's eyes.

Bocksbart, *m.* **1.** goat's beard; (*on pers.*) goatee. **2.** *Bot:* (*a*) tragopogon, *F:* goat's-beard; (*b*) **kleiner B.,** sheep's fescue; (*c*) = **Borstengras; Geißbart 2; Pulsatille; Ziegenbart.**

Bocksbeutel, *m.* **1.** (i) flat wine flask; (ii) white wine from the Würzburg area, in a flat flask. **2.** *A:* (i) bag used for carrying hymn-book, statute-book, etc.; (ii) old-fashioned, outdated, customs, ideas; monotonous routine, *F:* jog-trot; **j-m den B. anhängen,** to hold s.o. up to ridicule, to poke fun at s.o.

bocksbeut(e)lig, *a. F:* pedantic; behind the times; pettifogging.

Bocksbohne, *f.* = **Bitterklee.**

Bockschere, *f. Metalw: etc:* bench shears.

Bockschiff, *n.* = **Bockprahm.**

Bockschnurbund, *m. Nau: etc:* square lashing, transom lashing.

Bocksdorn, *m. Bot:* (*a*) lycium, *F:* box-thorn; (*b*) tragacanth, astragalus, milk-vetch.

Bockseiche, *f. P:* bad beer.

Bockseife, *f. Miner:* mountain soap, rock soap.

Böckser, *m.* **-s/-, Böcksern,** *n.* **-s/.** *Vit:* goatish smell *or* taste (*of wine made from wrongly-manured vines*).

Bocksetzen, *n.* pile-driving.

Bocksfeige, *f. Bot:* wild fig(-tree), goat fig(-tree).

Bocksfuß, *m.* (*a*) goat's foot; cloven hoof; (*b*) *Myth:* satyr, goat-foot.

bock(s)füßig, *a.* goat-footed, cloven-footed, cloven-hoofed.

Bocksgeile, *f. Bot:* (i) satyrion, (ii) lizard orchis.

Bock(s)geruch, *m.* goatish smell; **einen B. haben,** to smell goatish.

Bockshorn, *n.* (*a*) buck's horn, buck-horn; *F:* **j-n ins B. jagen,** (i) to intimidate, *F:* browbeat, bully, s.o.; (ii) to fool s.o.; to lead s.o. up the garden-path; **ich lasse mich nicht ins B. jagen,** (i) I won't be intimidated; (ii) I won't allow myself to be fooled, *F:* led up the garden-path; (*b*) *Mus: A:* buckhorn; **ins B. blasen,** to sound an alarm; (*c*) = **Bockshornklee; Johannisbrot** 1; (*d*) = **Bockshornband.**

Bockshornband, *n.* curved ornamental fitting (for a door *or* window).

Bockshornklee, *m. Bot:* trigonella; **echter B.,** fenugreek.

Bockshornkraut, *n. Bot:* fenugreek.

Bocksitz, *m.* (*on coach*) driver's seat.

Bocksknie, *n. Farr:* **Pferd mit B.,** knee-sprung horse.

Bockskraut, *n. Bot:* (*a*) goat's rue; (*b*) lungwort.

Bocksmelde, *f. Bot:* stinking goose-foot.

Bocksorche, *f. Bot:* lizard orchis.

Bockspetersilie, *f. Bot:* burnet saxifrage.

Bockspringen, *n. Games:* leap-frog; *Gym:* vaulting over the buck.

Bocksprung, *m.* leap-frog; caper; *Equit:* capriole, goat's leap; buck-jump; **einen B. (über j-n, etwas) machen,** to leap-frog, do a leap-frog (over s.o., sth.); to cut a caper; **Bocksprünge machen,** (i) to caper, leap, about; to cut capers; (*of young animal*) to frolic, gambol, frisk (about); (*of horse*) to capriole; (ii) (*of pers.*) to cut capers, play one's pranks, be up to one's tricks.

Bocksriemenzunge, *f. Bot:* lizard orchis.

Bockständer, *m. Constr:* roof standard, roof pole.

bocksteif, *a.* = **bockbeinig** (*a*), (*b*).

Bockverstellung, *f. Constr:* centring (of an arch).

Bockwinde, *f. Mec.E: Ind: etc:* windlass; crab; winch.

Bockwindmühle, *f.* = **Bockmühle.**

Bockwurst, *f.* thick sausage (for boiling).

Bockzaun, *m. Rail:* (portable) snow fence.

Bodden, *m.* **-s/-.** *Geog:* sea-inlet (on the Baltic coast).

Bodega [bo·'de:ga:], *f.* **-/-s & -gen. 1.** bodega, wine-cellar, wine-shop. **2.** warehouse (at seaport).

Bödeli, das. *Pr.n.* **-s.** *Swiss: Geog:* the flat plain between the lakes of Brienz and Thun.

Boden, *m.* **-s/- & ⸗. 1.** soil, earth, ground, land; (*a*) *Agr:* **gesunder B.,** healthy, sweet, soil, soil which is in good heart; **ausgesogener B.,** impoverished, exhausted, soil; **fruchtbarer B.,** fertile soil; **unfruchtbarer B.,** poor soil, infertile land; **frisch gepflügter B.,** newly-ploughed land; **je fetter der B., um so fetter das Unkraut,** the better the soil, the bigger the weeds; (*of pers.*) **(mit) dem B. verbunden sein,** to be bound to the soil; (*b*) **gewachsener B.,** natural ground; **schwerer B.,** heavy soil, ground, earth; **fester B.,** firm ground; hard ground; **steiniger B.,** stony ground; **primärer B.,** sedentary soil; **rutschender B.,** falling, crumbling, earth; **aufgeschütteter B.,** embankment, mound, bank; made ground. **2.** (*a*) bottom, bed (of lake, sea, ocean, etc.); bottom, floor (of valley, ocean, etc.); (*b*) floor, flooring (of a room); **einen B. legen,** to lay a floor; (*c*) *A:* = **Stockwerk;** (*d*) loft; **auf dem B.,** in the loft; (*e*) storehouse. **3.** (*a*) bottom (of box, bag, bottle, etc.); *Coop:* bottom, head (of a cask); **(Koffer) mit doppeltem B.,** (case) with a false, double, bottom; double-bottomed (case); **am, auf dem, B. des Beutels,** at, in, on, the bottom of the bag; **einen B. in etwas,** *Coop:* **in ein Faß, setzen,** to put a bottom in, on, to, sth.; *Coop:* to bottom a cask, a barrel, to head (up) a barrel; *F:* **das schlägt dem Faß den B. aus!** that's the limit! that puts the lid on it! **ohne B.,** bottomless; *F:* **sein Magen ist wie ein Faß ohne B.,** his stomach is like a bottomless pit; (*b*) seat (of trousers); **einen neuen B. in eine Hose einsetzen,** to put a new seat in, to reseat, a pair of trousers; (*c*) *Nau:* (i) bottom, (underwater) hull (of ship); (ii) floor (of ship); *Sm.a:* base (of shell case, cartridge); *Mch:* head, bottom, end(-plate) (of boiler); *Metall:* plug, bottom (of converter); **(Schiff) mit flachem, kupfernem, B.,** flat-bottomed, copper-bottomed (boat); **lösbarer B.,** drop bottom (of cupola furnace); **scheitrechter B.,** level plate (of blast furnace); (*d*) back (of watch); base-board (of folding camera); *Mus:* back (of violin, etc.); (*e*) *Bot:* receptacle; bottom (of artichoke); (*f*) *Cu:* undercrust, bottom (of pie); **B. (mit Rand),** case (for flan, tart, pie, etc.). **4. auf dem B.,** (i) on the ground, floor; (ii) on the land; **auf deutschem B.,** on German soil; **in fremdem B., begraben sein,** to be buried in foreign soil, in a foreign land; **heiliger B.,** sacred soil, holy ground; **am,** *A:* **zu, B. liegen,** (i) to lie prostrate; (ii) to lie on the ground; **auf dem B. liegen,** to lie on the floor; *Av:* **vom B. freikommen, loskommen,** to leave the ground, to become airborne, to lift, to take off; **auf den B. fallen,** to fall on, to, the floor, ground; **auf festem B. stehen, festen B. unter den Füßen haben,** (i) to stand on firm ground, to be on terra firma, dry land; (ii) *F:* to be on sure, firm, ground; to be sure of one's ground; **B. fassen,** (*of pers.*) to put down roots; (*of idea, etc.*) to take root; **ihm brannte, es brannte ihm, der B. unter den Füßen,** he was impatient to be off, away, *F:* he was itching to be off; *see also* **heiß**[1] 1 (*b*); (*of ideas, etc.*) **an B. gewinnen,** to gain ground, to spread; **j-m B. abgewinnen,** to gain (ground) on s.o.; **den B. (unter den Füßen) verlieren,** (i) to be swept, carried, off one's feet; to lose one's footing; to get out of one's depth (while bathing, etc.); (ii) *F:* to get, be, out of one's depth; to be all at sea; **den B. verlieren,** to lose one's grip; **der B. schwankte unter seinen Füßen,** the ground rocked under his feet, under him; **sich auf schwankendem B. bewegen,** *F:* to get out of one's depth, element; **zu B. fallen, stürzen,** to fall down, to the ground; to fall off (horse); **zu B. sinken,** to sink, fall, drop, to the ground; (*o*) *bird, snow, etc.*) to sink to earth; **er wäre am liebsten vor Scham in den B. gesunken,** he could have sunk through the floor, ground, with shame; *Box:* **zu B. gehen,** to hit the canvas, to go down; **j-n zu B. drücken,** to weigh, crush, press, bear, s.o. down; **j-n zu B. schlagen, strecken,** to knock, strike, s.o. down, to floor s.o.; to send s.o. sprawling, to stretch s.o. out (on the ground); **j-s Hoffnungen zu B. schlagen,** to floor, shatter, *F:* dash, s.o.'s hopes; *Lit:* **sie schlug die Augen zu B.,** she cast down her eyes; **j-n zu B. werfen, schleudern,** to throw s.o. (down); to fling s.o. to the ground, down; **den Feind zu. B. werfen,** to crush the enemy; **sich anbetend (vor j-m) zu, auf den, B. werfen,** to prostrate oneself (before s.o.); *F:* **etwas aus dem B. stampfen,** to conjure up sth.; to produce sth. out of a hat; **auf dem B. der Tatsachen,** on the basis of (the) facts, on a factual basis; **stelle dich auf den B. der Wirklichkeit, der Tatsachen!** be realistic! face facts! **sich auf den B. des Gesetzes stellen,** to act, be, within the law; to keep within (the bounds of) the law; to have the law behind one; **festen B. gewinnen,** to get, gain, a footing, a foothold; **festen B. finden,** (*of pers.*) to find one's feet; (*of financial undertaking, etc.*) to get on its feet; **etwas auf festen, sicheren, B. stellen,** to place sth. on a firm foundation, firm footing; **gemeinsamen B. für Verhandlungen finden,** to find common ground, a basis, for negotiations; *Prov:* **Handwerk hat (einen) goldenen B.,** a useful trade pays dividends, is a valuable, a profitable, asset.

Bodenabstand, *m. Veh: esp. Aut:* ground clearance.

Bodenabtragung, *f. Geol:* soil-erosion; denudation.

Bodenabwehr, *f. Mil:* ground defences.

Bodenaffe, *m. Z:* terrestrial monkey.

Bodenamboß, *m. Metalw:* bottom fuller.

Bodenanalyse, *f.* soil analysis.

Bodenanschwemmung, *f. Geol:* accretion through alluvion; aggradation.

Bodenart, *f.* type of soil, soil type.

Bodenauflockerung, *f. Agr:* loosening, breaking up, of the soil.

Bodenbearbeitung, *f.* cultivation of the land, tilling of the soil, tillage.

Bodenbelag, *m.* flooring; floor covering.

Bodenbeleuchtung, *f. Av:* ground lighting.

Bodenbeschaffenheit, *f.* (*a*) topographical features; nature of the ground; (*b*) *Agr:* condition, state, of the soil.

Bodenbeschlag, *m. N.Arch:* sheathing.

Bodenbesitz, *m.* landed property.

Bodenbewegung, *f.* (*a*) shifting of earth (*in excavation*); (*b*) *Geol:* soil creep; (*c*) *Meteor:* seism; **mikroseismische B.,** microseism.

Boden-Boden-Rakete, *f.* surface-to-surface missile.

Boden-Bord-Verkehr, *m. W.Tel: Av:* ground-to-air communication.

Bodenbrett, *n.* base-board.

Bodenbrüter, *m.* ground-nesting bird.

Bodenchemie, *f.* soil chemistry.

Bodendecke, *f.* covering of soil, soil-cover.

Bodendraht, *m. Paperm:* **B. der Form,** (laid) wire of the mould (*for laid paper*).

Bodendruck, *m.* **1.** *Ph:* **B. einer Flüssigkeit,** pressure of a liquid on the bottom of a container. **2.** *Mec.E: Constr:* load on ground; *Constr: etc:* pressure of the earth; **zulässiger B.,** safe load on ground. **3.** *Meteor:* ground pressure.

Bodeneinsatzwagen, *m. Metall:* truck, *U.S:* car, with a converter bottom.

Bodeneis, *n.* (*a*) = **Grundeis;** (*b*) (*in tundra*) ground ice, fossil ice.

Bodeneisen, *n. Glassm:* battledore; flattening-iron.

Bodenentwässerung, *f.* land drainage, draining of the soil.

Bodenerhebung, *f.* rise in the ground, elevation, eminence.

Bodenerosion, *f.* soil erosion.

Bodenertrag, *m.* produce, yield, of a piece of ground; *Pol.Ec:* **das Gesetz vom abnehmenden B.,** the law of diminishing returns (in relation to agriculture).

Bodenerzeugnis, *n.* product of the soil.

Bodenfenster, *n.* attic, garret, window; dormer (-window).

Bodenfeuer, *n. Av:* ground light; beacon.

Bodenfläche, *f.* (*a*) *Agr:* acreage; (*b*) ground-space (of building); floor-space (of room).

Bodenfliese, *f.* floor-tile.

Bodenfräse, *f. Agr:* rotary hoe, rotary cultivator.

Bodenfreiheit, *f. Veh: esp. Aut:* ground-clearance; *Av:* **B. der Luftschraube,** airscrew clearance.

Bodenfront, *f. Meteor:* front on the surface, on the ground.

Bodenfrost, *m.* ground frost.

Bodenfund, *m.* archaeological find (from an excavation).

Bodenfunkstelle, *f. W.Tel:* ground wireless, *U.S:* radio, station.

Bodengare, *f. Agr:* favourable soil conditions (for cultivation).

Bodengeschoß, *n.* top storey (of house).

Bodengestalt, *f. Surv:* topography.

Bodenhaftung, *f. Aut:* road-holding (qualities).

Bodenhöhe, *f.* ground level.

Bodenholz, *n. Coop:* (wood for) heading (of cask).

Bodenkamm, *m. Tls: Coop:* croze.

Bodenkammer, *f.* **1.** garret, attic; box-room, store-room. **2.** *Artil:* cup (of shrapnel shell); shell-base.

Bodenkapital, *n.* capital invested in landed property.

Bodenkappe, *f. Sm.a: Artil:* (percussion) cap (of cartridge); base-plate (of shell).

Bodenkennung, *f. Av:* route-marking light.

Bodenklappe, *f.* (*a*) trap-door (in loft, etc.); (*b*) hinged bottom (of dipper dredger); *Metall:* drop-bottom (of cupola-furnace).

Bodenkohlrabi, *m. Agr:* Swedish turnip, swede.

Bodenkredit, *m.* loan on landed property.

Bodenkreditanstalt, *f.,* **Bodenkreditbank,** *f.,* **Bodenkreditinstitut,** *n. Fin:* land-mortgage bank, land-bank.

Bodenkrepierer, *m.* **-s/-.** *Artil:* dud (shell).

Bodenkruste, *f.* soil mantle; *Miner:* **verkalkte B.,** caliche.

Bodenkunde, *f.* soil science, pedology.

Bodenleder, *n. Bootm:* sole leather.

Bodenlockerung, *f. Agr:* loosening, breaking up, of the soil.

bodenlos. 1. *a.* (*a*) bottomless, fathomless (sea, etc.); **bodenlose Tiefe,** (i) abyss, chasm, unfathomable depth(s), (ii) *Lit:* (*of ocean*) the unfathomed deep; (*b*) abysmal (stupidity, ignorance); (*c*) **bodenlose Frechheit,** unbounded cheek; **bodenlose Lüge,** colossal lie, *F:* thumping, whacking, lie, whopper. **2.** *adv.* exceedingly, excessively, abysmally, crassly (ignorant, stupid).

Bodenluft, *f.* soil air.

Bodenluftdruck, *m. Meteor:* air pressure at ground level.

Boden-Luft-Rakete, *f.* surface-to-air missile.
Bodenlüftung, *f.* aeration of the soil, soil ventilation.
Bodenluke, *f.* (*a*) dormer-window; skylight; (*b*) trap-door in a loft; (*c*) *Av:* escape hatch.
Bodenmannschaft, *f. Av:* ground crew.
Bodenmechanik, *f. Agr: Civ.E:* soil mechanics.
Bodenmehl, *n.* = **Bodensatzmehl.**
Bodenmelioration, *f. Agr:* improvement of the soil.
Bodenmüdigkeit, *f. Agr:* soil exhaustion.
Bodennagel, *m.* floor brad.
Bodennähe, *f.* ground level; *Av:* low, zero, altitude; **in B.,** near the ground, at ground level.
Bodennebel, *m. Meteor:* ground fog, ground mist.
Bodennutzung, *f. Agr:* cultivation of (the) land, the soil.
Bodenpeilstelle, *f. W.Tel:* ground direction-finding station.
Bodenpersonal, *n. Av:* ground personnel, ground staff; ground maintenance crew.
Bodenpfahl, Bodenpflock, *m. Surv:* levelling stake.
Bodenphysik, *f.* soil science.
Bodenplanke, *f. N.Arch:* garboard-plank.
Bodenplatte, *f.* base-board (of typewriter, etc.); *Mch:* bed-plate, base-plate (of machine); *Metall:* bed-plate (of furnace); *El.E:* ground-plate; *Artil:* base-plate (of mortar).
Bodenpunkt, *m. Surv:* surveyed point, spot-height; trig(onometrical) point.
Bodenrad, *n. Clockm:* third wheel.
Bodenrand, *m. Sm.a:* flange, rim (of cartridge case).
Bodenraum, *m.* (*a*) storage space; (*b*) = **Bodenkammer** 1.
Bodenreform, *f. Pol.Ec:* agrarian, land, reform.
Bodenrente, *f.* = **Grundrente.**
Bodensaite, *f. Mus:* snare (of drum).
Bodensatz, *m.* (*a*) *Ind: etc:* sediment, deposit; settlings (of liquid); lees (of wine); foot (of oil, sugar); mother (of vinegar); *Ch:* residuum, precipitate; **einen B. ablagern,** to deposit a sediment; **einen B. haben, enthalten,** to contain sediment, to be feculent; (*b*) *Med:* (*in fever*) sordes.
Bodensatzmehl, *n.* fecula, farina, starch.
Bodensäure, *f. Ch: Agr:* soil acid; geic acid.
Bodenschätze, *m.pl.* mineral resources, wealth underground.
Bodenschicht, *f.* layer of soil, earth, soil layer; *Geol:* **älteste Bodenschichten,** primary formations.
Bodenschnelle, *f. Gym:* push-up.
Bodenschraube, *f. Sm.a:* (percussion) cap, primer (of cartridge); *Artil:* base plug (of shell).
Bodenschwankung, *f. Astr:* nutation.
Bodenschwelle, *f.* **1.** (*a*) *Constr: Min: etc:* = **Grundschwelle;** (*b*) *Rail:* floor joist (of wagon). **2.** swell of ground; *Ph.Geog:* shelf (of ocean bed).
Bodensee, der. *Pr.n. Geog:* Lake Constance, the Lake of Constance.
Bodensenke, *f.* depression, hollow, dip (in the ground).
Bodensenkung, *f.* (*a*) sinking, subsidence (of ground, soil); (*b*) = **Bodensenke.**
Bodensicht, *f. Meteor: Av:* ground visibility.
Bodenskelett, *n. Geol:* (group of) gravels.
Bodenspalte, *f.* fissure in the ground.
Bodenspeicher, *m.* granary, *U.S:* (grain) elevator.
Bodenspekulation, *f.* land-jobbing; speculation in land (*esp. in building-sites*).
Bodenspieker, *m.* floor brad.
Bodenstampfmaschine, *f. Metall:* plug ramming machine (*for converter*).
bodenständig, *a.* (*a*) *Bot:* **bodenständige Blätter,** radical leaves, root-leaves; (*b*) indigenous, native, sedentary; **bodenständige Kultur,** indigenous culture; **bodenständige Bevölkerung,** (i) indigenous, autochthonous, native, population, (ii) sedentary, settled, population; **bodenständiges Brauchtum,** local custom(s).
Bodenständigkeit, *f.* sedentariness.
Bodenstation, *f. W.Tel: Av:* ground station.
Bodenstein, *m. Mill:* lower, *A:* nether, millstone, bedder, bed-stone; *Metall:* sole (of furnace).
Bodenstück, *n.* **1.** *Constr: etc:* ground-sill. **2.** *N.Arch:* floor(-frame, -timber). **3.** *Coop:* heading. **4.** *Artil:* breech-ring (of gun); *Sm.a:* butt-end (of machine-gun).
Bodentemperatur, *f.* (*a*) soil temperature; (*b*) *Meteor:* ground temperature.
Bodenteppich, *m.* (floor) carpet.
Bodenturnen, *n. Gym:* free-standing gymnastics.
Bodenunebenheit, *f.* (*a*) unevenness, roughness, of the ground; (*b*) bump *or* hollow in the ground.
Bodenunruhe, *f. Meteor:* seism; **mikroseismische B.,** microseism.
Bodenuntersuchung, *f.* (*a*) testing (of) the soil, soil testing; soil analysis; (*b*) *Min:* prospecting.
Bodenventil, *n.* (*a*) foot-valve (of air-pump); (*b*) *Nau:* Kingston valve.
Bodenverarmung, *f.* impoverishment of the soil.
Bodenverbesserung, *f.* (long-term) improvement of the land, soil.
Bodenverfestigung, *f. Agr:* fixation of sandy soil; binding of the soil.
Bodenverlagerung, *f.* displacement of (the) soil.
Bodenvertiefung, *f.* = **Bodensenke.**
Bodenwaage, *f.* weigh-bridge.
Bodenwärme, *f.* (*a*) soil temperature, heat in the ground; (*b*) *Meteor:* ground temperature.
Bodenwasser, *n.* water in the soil, ground.
Bodenwelle, *f.* (*a*) swell of ground; bump in the ground; (*b*) *W.Tel:* ground wave.
Bodenwert, *m. Pol.Ec:* land-value.
Bodenwichse, *f.* floor-polish.
Bodenwind, *m. Av: etc:* ground wind, surface wind.
Bodenwrange, *f. N.Arch:* floor; floor-frame; floor-plate; (*of wooden ship*) floor-timber; **B. des Hauptspants,** main floor, midship floor.
Bodenzins, *m.* ground-rent.
Bodenzünder, *m. Artil:* base-fuse.
Bodhibaum [ˈboːdiː-], *m.* = **Bobaum.**
bodmen, *v.tr.* **1.** *A:* to floor (a room); *Coop:* to bottom, head (a cask). **2.** *Nau:* to raise money (on a ship) by a bottomry bond.
Bodmerei [boˑdməˈrai], *f.* -/-en. *Nau:* bottomry; (*on cargo*) respondentia.
Bodmereibrief, *m. Nau:* bottomry bond.
Bodmereiprämie, *f. Nau:* bottomry interest.
Bodmereischuld, *f. Nau:* bottomry loan.
Bodmerist [boˑdməˈrist], *m.* -en/-en. *Nau:* lender on bottomry.
Bodonischrift [boˑˈdoːniː-], *f. Print:* Bodoni type.
Böe, *f.* -/-n = **Bö.**
Böenband, *n. Meteor:* squall belt.
Böenfront, *f. Meteor:* (secondary) squall front.
Böengefühl, *n. Meteor: Av:* bumpiness.
Böenlinie, *f. Meteor:* squall line, cold front.
Böenschreiber, *m. Meteor:* gust recorder.
Bofist [ˈboːfist, boˑˈfist], *m.* -es/-e = **Bovist.**
bog, böge *see* **biegen.**
Bogen, *m.* -s/- & ⸗. **1.** curve, arc; sweep; *Geom: etc:* arc (of a circle); *Ski:* turn; *Skating:* curve; **einen B. (mit dem Zirkel) schlagen,** to draw, trace, a curve, to describe an arc (with compasses); **flacher B.,** flat curve; **der Fluß fließt in großem B. um die Stadt,** the river flows in a wide sweep round the town; **die Straße macht hier einen B.,** the road bends, makes a bend, here; **die Straße macht einen B. um das Schloß,** the street curves round, skirts, the castle; (*of pers.*) **einen B. machen, schlagen,** to make a detour; **einen großen B. um j-n machen,** to give s.o. a wide berth; *F:* **er flog in großem, hohem, B. aus dem Haus hinaus,** he was pitched, slung, out of the house; *F:* **er spuckte im großen B.,** he spat in a neat arc; *F:* **den B. (he)raushaben,** (i) to have, get, the hang, the way, of sth.; (ii) to be astute, artful; *Artil:* **in höchstem B. schießen,** to fire at maximum elevation. **2.** (*a*) *Arch: Constr:* arch; **gestelzter B.,** raised, stilted, arch; **gedrückter B.,** depressed, drop, arch; **flacher B.,** segmental arch; **steigender, einhüftiger, B.,** rampant arch; **scheitrechter B.,** flat, straight, square-headed, arch; **ausgeschrägter B.,** splayed arch; **eingehender B.,** recessed arch; **eingespannter B.,** non-articulated arch; **einfacher B.,** single arch; **durchlaufende Bögen,** series of arches, continuous arches; (*b*) = **Regenbogen;** (*c*) *El:* (voltaic, electric) arc; (*d*) bridge (of spectacles); *Harn:* (saddle-)bow. arch (of saddle); (*e*) *Mus:* (*sign*) slur; (*f*) arch (of the eyebrows); *Anat:* superciliary arch *or* ridge, the brow ridge; (*e*) *Games:* hoop (at croquet, pall-mall); *A:* port (at billiards). **3.** (*a*) (archer's) bow; **eingespannter B.,** single stave bow; **den B. spannen,** to draw, bend, the bow; **den B. zu straff spannen, überspannen,** to overbend the bow; (*b*) *F:* **der B. der Erwartung war aufs äußerste gespannt,** expectation had reached its highest pitch; **allzu straff gespannt, zerspringt der B.,** everything has its breaking-point; **den B. überspannen,** (i) to carry things too far, *F:* to overdo it; (ii) to overtax oneself, to drive s.o., oneself, to breaking-point; (*c*) wing, quadrantal arc (of compasses); bend (of pipe); *Tls:* frame (of bow-saw); *Tex:* (felter's) bow. **4.** *Mus:* (*a*) bow (of violin, etc.); (*b*) crook (of horn, trumpet, etc.). **5.** sheet of paper; *Print:* (= **Druckbogen**) (printed) sheet; **Bücher in ungebundenen Bogen,** books in sheets, in quires.
Bogenableger, *m. Print:* lay-boy, laying-machine.
Bogenachter, *m. Skating:* figure of eight.
Bogenanfall, Bogenanfang, *m. Arch:* impost, spring, springing (of arch).
Bogenanfänger, *m. Arch:* springer.
Bogenanleger, *m. Print:* layer-on, stroker-in, feeder.
Bogenanlegerapparat, *m. Print:* (automatic) feeder.
Bogenauswerfer, *m. Print:* shoo-fly.
Bogenblende, *f. Arch:* blind arch.
Bogenbohrer, *m. Tls:* bow-drill, fiddle-drill.
Bogenbrücke, *f.* arched bridge.
Bogendüne, *f.* (*in desert*) barkhan.
Bogenelement, *n. Geom: etc:* linear element of a curve.
Bog(e)ner, *m.* -s/-. *A:* = **Bogenmacher.**
Bogenfachwerk, *n. Constr:* arch truss.
Bogenfeder, *f. Mec.E:* bow-spring.
Bogenfeile, *f. Tls:* bow-file.
Bogenfeld, *n. Arch:* tympanum (of door); lunette (of arch).
Bogenfenster, *n.* arched window.
Bogenfibel, *f. Prehist:* fibula with a high arch.
Bogenflanke, *f. Her:* flanch; flasque; voider.
Bogenform, *f.* form, shape, of an arch, arched form; curved shape.
bogenförmig, *a.* arched, arch-like, arch-shaped, arcuate(d); curved; bow-shaped.
Bogenfries, *m. Arch:* arched corbel-table; arched moulding.
Bogenführung, *f.* **1.** *Mus:* bowing; **eine gute B. haben,** to bow well; **seine B. ist ausgezeichnet,** his bowing is perfect. **2.** line (of arched bridge, etc.). **3.** *Print:* feeding (of sheets into machine).
Bogengang, *m.* **1.** *Arch:* arcade; colonnade. **2.** *pl.* **Bogengänge,** *Anat:* semicircular canals (of the ear).
Bogengerüst, *n. Constr:* centring, centre, truss, template. for an arch; **das B. entfernen,** to strike, remove, the centring of, to discentre (arch, etc.).
Bogengrab, *n.* arched tomb.
Bogengröße, *f.* size of sheet (of paper).
Bogenhaare, *n.pl. Mus:* bow hair.
Bogenhalter, *m. Print:* (blanket) pin.
Bogenhanf, *m. Bot:* sansevieria, bowstring hemp; **indischer B.,** Indian bowstring hemp.
Bogenhöhe, *f.* = **Bogenstich.**
Bogenholz, *n.* **1.** bow-wood. **2.** *Constr:* block (of a centre).
Bogenkalander, *m. Paperm:* calender; **mit B. geglättet,** sheet-calendered.
Bogenkante, *f.* edge of a sheet (of paper).
Bogenkrümmung, *f. Arch:* curving, curvature.
Bogenlaibung, *f. Arch:* intrados.
Bogenlampe, *f. El:* arc-lamp.
Bogenlaufen, *n. Skating:* figure-skating.
Bogenlehre, *f.* **1.** *Mth:* science of curves. **2.** *Constr:* = **Bogengerüst.**
Bogenleier, *f. Constr:* rotating template.
Bogenlicht, *n. El:* arc-light.
Bogenlied, das. *B.Hist:* David's lament for Saul and Jonathan.
Bogenlinie, *f. Geom: etc:* curve, curved line; curvature.
Bogenmacher, *m.* bowyer, bow-maker.
Bogenmaß, *n. Mth:* radian measure.
Bogenmauer, *f. Hyd.E:* arch dam.
Bogenminute, *f. Geom: Astr:* minute of arc.
Bogenöffnung, *f.* **1.** *Arch:* span, width, of an arch; opening of an arch. **2.** *Geom: Constr:* angular measurement of an arc.
Bogenpfeilermauer, *f. Hyd.E:* multiple-arch dam.
Bogenradius, *m.* radius of curvature.
Bogenrippe, *f. Constr:* rib (of centring).
Bogenrohr, *n.* angle-pipe.
Bogenrücken, *m. Arch:* extrados.
Bogensäge, *f. Tls:* (i) scribing, coping, saw; (ii) = **Bügelsäge;** (iii) = **Bauchsäge.**
Bogenschärfe, *f.* curved dress (of mill-stone).
Bogenschenkel, *m. Arch:* side, haunch (of an arch).
Bogenschere, *f. Ind:* shearing-machine; crocodile shears.
Bogenschießen, *n.* archery.
Bogenschiffchen, *n. Tex:* curved shuttle.
Bogenschluß, *m. Arch:* keystone, crown, centre voussoir.
Bogenschub, *m. Constr:* horizontal thrust.
Bogenschuß, *m.* (*a*) bowshot; (*b*) *Ball:* high angle fire.
Bogenschütze, *m.* (*a*) archer, bowman; (*b*) *occ. Astr:* **der B.,** Sagittarius.

Bogensehne, *f.* **1.** bowstring. **2.** *Geom:* chord of a segment.

Bogensekunde, *f. Geom: Astr:* second of arc.

Bogensprung, *m.* leap, bound, jump, spring; *Equit:* curvet; (*of small animal*) **in Bogensprüngen dahinhüpfen,** to travel, move, in leaps *or* bounds.

Bogenstein, *m. Arch:* voussoir, arch-stone.

Bogenstellung, *f. Arch:* arcade, row, series, of arches; arching; arcature.

Bogenstich, *m. Arch:* pitch, rise, height, of an arch.

Bogenstrebe, *f. Arch:* arch-brace, -buttress.

Bogenstrich, *m. Mus:* (*a*) stroke of the bow; **mit ganzem B. (zu spielen),** (to be played) with the full (length of the) bow; (*b*) bowing technique.

Bogenstück, *n.* **1.** *Arch:* tierceron (rib). **2.** curved piece; *Constr:* block (of a centre).

Bogenträger, *m. Constr:* bowstring-, arch-girder.

bogenverzahnt, *a. Mec.E:* (gear) with curved teeth; helical, spiral (gear).

Bogenverzahnung, *f. Mec.E:* curved, *esp.* helical, spiral, toothing *or* teeth.

bogenweise, *adv.* (*a*) by the sheet; in sheets; (*b*) *Arch:* in arches.

Bogenweite, *f.* span of an arch.

Bogenwinde, *f. A:* moulinet, windlass (of cross-bow).

Bogenwirkung, *f. Constr:* lateral thrust of an arch.

Bogenzeichen, *n. Print:* signature.

Bogenzirkel, *m.* bow-compass; quadrant compasses; wing-compass(es).

bogig, *a.* arched; **-bogig,** *comb.fm. Arch:* **rundbogig,** round-arched; **spitzbogig,** pointed, ogival.

Bogomilen [bo·go·ˈmiːlən], *m.pl. Rel.Hist:* Bogomils.

Bogrebe, *f. Vit:* vine trained in a curve.

Böheim. *Pr.n.n.* **-s.** *A:*=**Böhmen.**

Boheme [bo·ˈhɛːmə, bo·ˈheːmə, bo·ˈɛːm]. *f.* **-/.** Bohemia (of the artistic world).

Bohemer [bo·ˈheːmər], *m.* **-s/-.** *Orn:*=**Böhmer**[2].

Bohemien [bo·(h)e·miˈɛ̃ː], *m.* **-(s)/-s.** Bohemian, unconventional person.

Bohle, *f.* **-/-n,** thick plank; chess (of bridge).

bohlen, *v.tr.* to plank, board over (deck, floor, etc.).

böhlen, *v.tr.*=**abhaaren** 1.

Bohlenbahn, *f.* (*a*) planking; (*b*) corduroy road; (*c*) *Games:* skittle alley.

Bohlenbelag, *m.* planking, plank covering.

Bohlenbrücke, *f.* plank-bridge.

Bohlendach, *n. Constr:* curved plank roof.

Bohlenrost, *m. Constr:* grillage, foundation, of planks, plank bottom.

Bohlensäge, *f. Tls:* rip-saw.

Bohlenwand, *f. Civ.E:* row of piles; sheet-piling.

Bohlenweg, *m. F:* corduroy road, path; *U.S:* boardwalk.

Bohlenzwinge, *f. Constr:* wedge-key.

Bohlstamm, *m.* timber trunk.

Böhme, *m.* **-n/-n,** (*a*) *Ethn: Geog:* Bohemian; (*b*) *occ.* gipsy.

Böhmen. *Pr.n.n.* **-s.** *Geog:* Bohemia.

Böhmer[1], *inv.a.* Bohemian; *Geog:* **der Böhmer Wald,** the Bohemian Forest.

Böhmer[2], *m.* **-s/-.** *Orn:* (*a*) brambling, mountain finch; (b) ampelis, waxwing, chatterer.

böhmisch, *a.* **1.** *Geog: etc:* Bohemian; **böhmisches Kristallglas,** Bohemian glass. **2. Böhmisch,** *n.* Bohemian language, dialect; Bohemian. **3.** *F:* **es klingt mir b.,** it sounds strange, odd, queer, peculiar, suspect, to me; *see also* **Dorf.**

Böhnchen, *n.* **-s/-,** (*dim. of* **Bohne**) small bean; **kleine grüne Böhnchen,** French beans.

Bohne, *f.* **-/-n.** **1.** bean; (*a*) **dicke B.,** broad bean; **kleine weiße B.,** kidney bean, haricot bean, *U.S:* bush bean; **grüne B.,** (i) French bean, string-bean; (ii) runner-bean; **türkische B.,** scarlet runner; **Bohnen legen,** to sow beans; (*b*) (coffee-) bean, (coffee-)berry; (cocoa-)bean; **japanische B.,** soya-bean, soy; **springende B.,** jumping-bean; (*c*) *F:* **nicht die B.,** not at all, not in the least; nothing whatever; **ich mache mir nicht die B. draus,** I don't care a bean; **er versteht nicht die B. davon,** he doesn't understand the first thing about it; **das hat nicht die B. damit zu tun,** that has nothing whatever to do with it. **2.** (*a*) *Mil: F:* **blaue B.,** (rifle-)bullet; (*b*) *pl.* **Bohnen,** droppings (of sheep, etc.); (*c*) *Vet:* mark (on horse's tooth), mark of mouth; (*d*) *Vet:* lampas.

bohnen, *v.tr.*=**bohnern.**

Bohnenbaum, *m. Bot:* (*a*) *popular name for several varieties of* cytisus, *esp.* laburnum; white Spanish broom; yellow-flowered broom; (*b*) **indischer B.,** pigeon pea; (*c*) ringworm-shrub.

Bohnenfest, *n.* Twelfth-night.

bohnenförmig, *a.* bean-shaped.

Bohnengans, *f. Orn:* bean-goose.

Bohnenjochblatt, *n. Bot:* bean-caper.

Bohnenkaffee, *m.* pure coffee.

Bohnenkaper, *f. Bot:* bean-caper.

Bohnenkönig, *m.* king (of Twelfth-night festivities).

Bohnenkraut, *n. Bot: Cu:* savory.

Bohnenkuchen, *m.* Twelfth-cake.

Bohnenlied, *n. F:* **das geht übers B.,** it really is too bad, that's really too much.

Bohnenmehl, *n. Cu:* bean meal; bean flour.

Bohnenranke, *f.* bean-stalk.

Bohnenschneidemaschine, *f. Cu:* bean slicer.

Bohnenstange, *f.* bean-stick; *F:* (*pers.*) bean-pole, maypole; **lang wie eine B.,** as tall as a lamp-post; *see also* **dürr** 1 (*b*).

Bohnenstrauch *m.*=**Bohnenbaum.**

Bohnenstroh, *n.* bean-straw; *F:* **dumm wie B.,** as stupid as an ox, an ass.

Bohnensuppe, *f. Cu:* haricot (bean) soup; **grüne B.,** soup with French beans.

Bohner, *m.* **-s/-.** *F:*=**Bohnerbesen.**

Bohnerbesen, *m. Dom.Ec:* floor-polisher, polishing block.

Bohnerbürste, *f.* polishing brush.

Bohnerlappen, *m.* polishing cloth.

Bohnermasse, *f.* polish.

bohnern, *v.tr.* to polish (floor, etc.), to (bees)wax (floor).

Bohnerwachs, *n.* floor-polish, *F:* (bees)wax.

Bohnerz, *n. Min:* pea-ore.

Böhnhase, *m. North G.Dial:* **1.** *F:* botcher, bungler. **2.** (*a*) *F:* spoil-trade; (*b*) outside, unlicensed, broker, *F:* outsider.

Bohr-, *comb.fm.* boring . . ., boring-; drilling . . ., drilling-; drill-, drill . . .; bore-; **Bohrgerät** *n,* boring-, drilling-tool; set of boring tools; **Bohrprogramm** *n,* drilling programme; **Bohrhülse** *f,* drill sleeve; **Bohrkrone** *f,* bore-crown.

Bohrarbeit, *f.* boring, drilling.

Bohrassel, *f. Crust:* gribble.

Bohrautomat, *m. Mec.E:* automatic boring *or* drilling machine.

Bohrbank, *f. Mec.E:* boring-mill.

Bohrbirne, *f. Min:* swage.

Bohrbogen, *m. Tls:* drill-bow.

Bohrbüchse, *f.* **1.** drill bush(ing). **2.** *Tls:* reaming auger.

Bohrbügel, *m. Tls:* ratchet clamp; drill post, drill stand.

Bohrdiamant, *m. Min: Ind:* diamond (in diamond-drill).

Bohregge, *f. Agr:* drill-harrow.

Bohreisen, *n. Tls:* boring bit; drill; *Min:* boring-bar.

bohren. I. *v.* **1.** *v.tr.* (*a*) to bore *or* drill (hole); **ein Loch in, durch, etwas** *acc.* **b.,** to bore *or* drill a hole in, through, sth.; (*b*) **einen Brunnen, Schacht, b.,** to sink, bore, a well, a shaft; **einen Tunnel b.,** to cut, drive, a tunnel; *Sculp:* **gebohrte Augen,** pupils indicated by a drill-hole; (*c*) **eine Schraube in etwas** *acc.* **b.,** to put, sink, a screw in sth.; **einen Stock in die Erde b.,** to work, dig, a stick into the ground; **j-m das Schwert durch den Leib b.,** to run s.o. through with one's sword, to pass one's sword through s.o.; *Lit:* **ein Schiff in den Grund b.,** to sink a ship, to send a ship to the bottom; (*d*) (*of worm*) **sich in das Holz b.,** to bore, burrow, into (the) wood; **das Wasser bohrt sich durch die Felsen,** the water bores (its way) through the rocks; **sein scharfer Blick bohrte sich in ihre Augen,** his keen eyes bored into hers; (*e*) **sich** *dat.* **die Nase bohren,** to pick one's nose; *A:* **j-m ein Eselsohr, einen Esel, b.,** to ridicule s.o. **2.** *v.i.* (*haben*) (*a*) *Mec. E: etc:* (*in solid material*) to drill; (*to enlarge hole*) to bore; *Dent:* to drill; (*b*) **in etwas** *dat.* **b.,** to bore into, to poke (away) at, sth.; **er bohrte immer in der gleichen Wunde,** he continually turned his knife in the wound; **sich** *dat.* **(mit dem Finger) in der Nase, in den Ohren, b.,** to pick one's nose, to poke one's ears; (*c*) **an j-m b.,** to pester, worry, bother, plague, torment, s.o.; (*d*) *Equit:* (*of horse*) to bore; (*e*) *Min:* **auf, nach, Wasser, Mineralien, usw., b.,** to bore for water, minerals, etc.; (*f*) **bohrend,** *Ent:* boring, terebrant (insect); boring, *Med:* terebrating (pain); *Lit:* gnawing (grief, jealousy).

II. *vbl s.* **1. Bohren,** *n. in vbl senses; also:* (*a*) *Min:* **chinesisches B.,** rope-boring, -drilling; (*b*) *Equit:* boring (movement) (of horse). **2. Bohrung,** *f.* (*a*)=II. 1; (*b*) bore (of cylinder, etc.); *Carp: etc:* hole, drill-hole; *Min:* bore-hole, bore.

Bohrer, *m.* **-s/-.** **1.** (*pers.*) borer; driller. **2.** *Tls:* (*bit or entire tool*) borer; drill; *Woodw:* boring bit; auger; *Mec.E: Min:* boring-, drilling-machine; **laufender B.,** running drill; **der B. dreht sich, läuft. leicht,** the drill revolves, turns, easily. **3.** *Moll:*=**Bohrmuschel;** *Ent:* borer. **4.** *Astr:* **der B.,** Terebellum. **5.** *Swim:* screw dive.

Bohrer-, *comb.fm. cp.* **Bohr-.**

Bohrerabstand, *m. Mec.E:* pitch of drills.

Bohrerangel, *f. Tls:* tang of a bit *or* drill.

Bohrerdurchmesser, *m.* (drilling *or* boring) capacity; diameter of drill *or* bit.

Bohrerlehre, *f. Tls:* drill gauge.

Bohrerzapfen, *m. Tls:* drill shank; drill tang.

Bohrfäustel, *m. Min: Tls:* hammer.

Bohrfutter, *n. Mec.E:* drill-chuck; tap-holder.

Bohrgang, *m.* (*a*) *Sculp:* groove (made by the drill); path of the drill; (*b*) gallery (bored by an insect, etc.).

Bohrgestänge, *n. Min:* boring-rod; set of (drill-) rods.

Bohrgrat, *m. Metalw:* burr.

Bohrhalter, *m.*=**Bohrspindel.**

Bohrhammer, *m. Civ.E: Min:* hammer-drill.

Bohrkäfer, *m. Ent:* anobium, death-watch (beetle).

Bohrkern, *m. Min:* drill-core; core-sample.

Bohrknarre, *f.*=**Bohrratsche.**

Bohrkopf, *m. Tls:* drill(ing) head; drill-holder boring head.

Bohrkurbel, *f. Tls:* brace (and bit).

Bohrladung, *f. Exp: Min:* blasting charge.

Bohrlänge, *f. Mec.E: etc:* depth of bore.

Bohrlehre, *f. Mec.E:* (*a*) drill *or* boring jig; (*b*) drill gauge.

Bohrloch, *n.* **1.** (*a*) *Civ.E: Mec.E: etc:* bore-hole, drill-hole, bore; (*b*) *Min: etc:* blast-hole, shot-hole. **2.** burrow (of worm).

Bohrlöffel, *m. Min: Tls:* bailer, sludger.

Bohrmaschine, *f.* **1.** *Tls:* drill; hand-drill; *Dent:* (dentist's) drill. **2.** (*a*) *Mec.E:* (i) boring-, drilling-machine; **mehrspindelige B.,** multiple-spindle drilling-machine, gang-driller; (ii) drill-press; drilling-mill; (*b*) *Civ.E:* rock-drill, driller, borer.

Bohrmehl, *n.* bore-dust, borings.

Bohrmeißel, *m. Mec.E:* boring tool, cutter; *Min:* drill(-bit), cutting-bit; borer; jumper.

Bohrmesser, *n.* boring-cutter.

Bohrmuschel, *f. Moll:* (*a*) pholas, piddock, stone-borer; (*b*)=**Bohrwurm** (*a*).

Bohrpatrone, *f.* blasting cartridge.

Bohrpflug, *m. Agr:* drill-plough.

Bohrpresse, *f.* drill-press.

Bohrprobe, *f. Min:* core-sample.

Bohrratsche, *f. Tls:* ratchet (drill-)brace.

Bohrsäule, *f. Mec.E:* drilling-pillar.

Bohrschablone, *f. Mec.E:* drilling template.

Bohrscheibe, *f. Tls:* drill-plate.

Bohrschlamm, *m. Min:* sludge.

Bohrschmand, *m. Min:* sludge; detritus, debris.

Bohrschmied, *m.* auger-smith.

Bohrschmiedehandwerk, *n.* auger-smithery.

Bohrschnecke, *f. Moll:* terebellum.

Bohrschwämme, *m.pl. Spong:* boring-sponges.

Bohrschwengel, *m. Min:* walking-beam (of drilling apparatus).

Bohrseil, *n. Min:* drilling rope.

Bohrspäne, *m.pl. Metalw: Carp:* borings, bore-chips.

Bohrspindel, *f. Tls:* (*a*) drilling-spindle; drill stock; drill-holder, -chuck, bit-holder; (*b*) *Mec. E:* cutter-bar; boring-bar.

Bohrstahl, *m. Mec.E:* boring tool.

Bohrstange, *f. Mec.E:* boring-bar; *Min:* drill-rod.

Bohrtiefe, *f. Mec.E: etc:* depth of bore.

Bohrturm, *m. Min:* drilling derrick.

Bohrversuch, *m.* trial boring.

Bohrwerk, *n. Mec.E:* drilling-machine; boring-machine; boring-mill.

Bohrwerkzeug, *n. Tls:* boring-tool.

Bohrwinde, *f. Tls:* (bit-)brace; brace and bit.

Bohrwinkel, *m. Tls:* drill post.

Bohrwurm, *m.* (*a*) *Moll:* teredo; ship-worm; borer; (*b*) *F:* (*of pers.*) pest.

Boi [boy], *m.* **-(e)s/-.** *Tex:* baize.

böig, *a. Meteor:* squally, gusty; *Av:* (*of air*) bumpy, turbulent; **böiger Wind,** gust of wind.

Böigkeit, *f. Meteor: Av:* turbulence.

Boiler [ˈbɔylər], *m.* **-s/-.** *Dom.Ec: Ind:* boiler.

boisieren [bo·a·ˈziːrən], *v.tr.* to panel, wainscot (wall, room).

Bojar [bo·ˈjaːr], *m.* **-en/-en,** boyar.

Boje, *f.* **-/-n.** **1.** (*a*) *Nau:* buoy; **Bojen** *pl,* buoyage; **stumpfe B.,** can-buoy; **spitze B.,** conical buoy; nun-buoy; **an einer B. vertäuen, festmachen,** to make fast to a buoy; **an einer B. vertäut,** secured to a buoy; **an die B. gehen,** to pick up one's buoy; **eine B. verankern,** to put down a buoy;

Bojen auslegen, to put down, lay, buoys; **ohne B.,** unbuoyed; **die Fahrrinne durch Bojen kennzeichnen,** to beacon, buoy (out), mark out, a channel; (*b*) *Fish:* float (of net). **2.** *pl.* **Bojen,** *A:* (*esp. Nau:*) bilboes.

Bojenlegen, *n. Nau:* setting of buoys, buoying.

Bojensystem, *n. Nau:* buoyage system (of channel, etc.).

Bojer, *m.* -s/-. *Nau:* boat that puts down buoys; (*in England*) Trinity House vessel.

Bojereep, *n.* buoy-rope.

boken, *v.tr. Tex:* (i) to break, brake (flax); (ii) to soften (hemp) by beating.

Bokmühle, *f. Tex:* (i) breaking mill; breaking machine, brake (for flax); (ii) softening machine (for hemp).

Bol, *m.* -s/.=**Bolus.**

Bola ['bo:la:], *f.* -/-s, (cowboy's) bolas.

-bold, *s.suff. m.* -(e)s/-e. **Raufbold,** brawler; **Trunkenbold,** drunkard; **Witzbold,** wag.

Bolero [bo·'le:ro:], *m.* -s/-s. *Danc: Cost:* bolero.

Boletus [bo·'le:tus], *m.* -/-ti. *Fung:* boletus.

Bolid [bo·'li:t], *m.* -s/-e [-'li:ts/-'li:də] & **-en/-en** [-'li:dən]. *Astr:* bolide, fire-ball.

Bolivianer [bo·li·vi'a:nər], *m.* -s/-. Bolivian.

bolivianisch [bo·li·vi'a:niʃ], *a. Geog:* Bolivian.

Bolivien [bo·'li:viən]. *Pr.n.n.* -s. *Geog:* Bolivia.

bölken. I. *v.i.* (*haben*) *Dial:* (*of cow*) to low, *F:* to moo; (*of pers.*) to shout, to bellow.

II. *vbl s.* **Bölken,** *n. in vbl senses; also: Vet:* gulping (of horse).

Bollandist [bolan'dist], *m.* **-en/-en.** *Ecc.Hist:* Bollandist.

Bolle, *f.* -/-n. *Dial: Bot:* **1.** (*a*)=**Zwiebel;** (*b*) =**Knolle. 2.** boll (of flax).

Boller, *m.* -s/-. *Nau:* (small) bitt, kevel-head, mooring-post, bollard.

Böller, *m.* -s/-. *Artil:* **1.** mortar. **2.** (*a*) saluting gun; (*b*)=**Böllerschuß.**

bollern, *v.i.* (*haben*) to kick up a row, rumpus; *F:* to boom, to roar, to thunder.

böllern, *v.i.* (*haben*) *Artil:* to fire (with) a mortar, mortars.

Böllerschuß, *m. Artil:* (*a*) mortar-shot; (*b*) gun-salute; **die Böllerschüsse der Neujahrsnacht,** the gun-salutes on New Year's Eve; **er wurde mit 21 Böllerschüssen empfangen,** he was received with a 21-gun salute, with a salute of 21 guns.

Bollerwagen, *m.* hand-cart, -truck.

Böllhuhn, *n. Orn:* European coot.

Bollmehl, *n. Mill:* middlings, sharps, pollard.

Bollwerk, *n.* **1.** (*a*) *A.Fort:* bulwark; bastion; stronghold; **mit Bollwerken,** bastioned; **halbes B.,** half-, demi-bastion; **das letzte B. des Feindes,** the last stronghold of the enemy; (*b*) *F:* bulwark, stronghold (of liberty, etc.); **das B. des Christentums,** the bulwark of Christianity; **ein B. gegen etwas errichten,** to build up, establish, a bulwark against sth. **2.** (*a*)=**Bohlenwand;** (*b*) dam; (*c*) quay; wharf. **3.** *Nau:* bulwark (of ship).

Bollwerksohr, *n. Fort: A:* orrill(i)on.

Bollwerksschild, *m.*, **Bollwerkswehr,** *n. Fort:* counterguard.

Bollwurm, *m. Ent:* boll-weevil.

Bologna [bo·'lonja:]. *Pr.n.n.* -s. *Geog:* Bologna.

Bolognese [bo·lon'je:zə], *m.* -n/-n. *Geog:* Bolognese, Bolognian.

Bologneser [bo·lon'je:zər]. **1.** *inv.a.* Bolognese, Bolognian; of Bologna. **2.** *s.m.* -s/-, Bologna dog.

bolognesisch [bo·lon'je:ziʃ], *a.*=**Bologneser** 1.

Bolometer [bo·lo·'me:tər], *n.* -s/-. *Ph:* bolometer.

Bolschewik [bolʃe·'vik, bolʃə'vik], *m.* **-en/-en & -i** [-'viki:]. Bolshevik, Bolshevist.

bolschewisieren [bolʃe·-, bolʃəvi·'zi:rən], *v.tr.* to bolshevize; **Bolschewisierung** *f,* Bolshevization.

Bolschewismus [bolʃe·'vismus, bolʃə'vismus], *m.* -/. Bolshevism.

Bolschewist [bolʃe·'vist, bolʃə'vist], *m.* **-en/-en.** Bolshevik, Bolshevist.

bolschewistisch [bolʃe·'vistiʃ, bolʃə'vistiʃ], *a.* Bolshevist.

Bolte, *f.* -/-n=**Bolten**[1].

Bolten,[1] *m.* -s/-. *Nau: usu. pl.* **Bolten,** patches (of a sail).

Bolten[2], *m.* -s/-. *North G.Dial: Meas:*=*approx.* bolt (of canvas, etc.).

Bolus ['bo:lus], *m.* -/. (*a*) *Miner:* bole; **roter B.,** reddle, ruddle, red ochre; **armenischer B.,** bole armeniac; **weißer B.,** kaolin; (*b*) *Pharm: Vet:* bolus.

Bolz, *m.* -es/-e=**Bolzen**[1].

Bolzen[1], *m.* -s/-. **1.** (*a*) *Mec.E:* (i) bolt, pin; (ii) pin, pintle (of hinge); (iii) pulley-pin; *Carp:* peg, plug, dowel; treenail; *Constr:* gudgeon, joggle; *Mec.E: etc:* **durchgehender B.,** through-bolt; **etwas mit einem B., mit Bolzen** *pl,* befestigen, to bolt sth., to secure sth. with a bolt; **Befestigung mit einem B., mit Bolzen** *pl,* bolting; **einen B. anziehen, sichern,** to do up, secure, a bolt; (*b*) *Mec.E: etc:* key, chock, gib, quoin. **2.** (*a*) heater (in box-iron); (*b*) *Tls: Metalw:* soldering-iron, bolt; (*c*) *Constr: Min:* studdle, post, prop, stay, shore. **3.** (air rifle) dart; *A:* bolt, quarrel (shot from cross-bow); *Her:* bird-bolt; **gerade wie ein B.,** bolt-upright, straight as a poker, ramrod; **alle seine Bolzen verschießen,** (i) to empty one's quiver; (ii) *F:* to have nothing left to fall back on; **einen B. auf j-n abschießen,** to fire, shoot, discharge, a bolt at s.o.; *F:* to have a dig, sly hit, at s.o.; **alles zu Bolzen drehen,** to use every means to attain an end; to leave no stone unturned.

bolzen[2], *v.i.* (*haben*) *Fb:* to play a rough game, to play rough.

Bolzenabschneider, *m.*=**Bolzenschere.**

Bolzenbüchse, *f.* (i) air rifle (*firing darts*); (ii) *Toys:* pop-gun.

Bolzenbügeleisen, *n. Dom.Ec:* box-iron.

Bolzeneisen, *n. Dom.Ec:* box-iron.

Bolzengelenk, *n. Mec.E:* pin-joint.

bolzengerade, *adv.* bolt upright.

Bolzengewehr, *n.*=**Bolzenbüchse.**

Bolzengewinde, *n. Mec.E:* (external, male) thread on a bolt.

Bolzenhammer, *m. Butchery:* humane killer.

Bolzenkette, *f. Tchn:* roller-chain; pintle-chain; block-chain.

Bolzenkopf, *m.* bolt-head.

Bolzenkupplung, *f. Mec.E:* pin coupling.

Bolzenloch, *n. Mec.E: etc:* bolt-hole.

Bolzenscheibe, *f.* bolt washer.

Bolzenschere, *f. Tls:* bolt-clipper, -cropper, -cutter.

Bolzenschloß, *n.* padlock.

Bolzenschneidemaschine, *f. Mec.E:* screw-cutting machine for bolts.

Bolzenschrotzimmerung, *f. Min: etc:* shaft-timbering.

Bolzensetzapparat, *m.* (cartridge-operated) stud-driver.

Bolzenverbindung, *f. Mec.E:* (i) join(t)ing by means of a pin; (ii) pin-joint.

Bolzenzange, *f. Tls:* bolt-cutting pliers.

Bölzung, *f. Civ.E:* timbering.

Bombage [bõ·'ba:ʒə, bom'ba:ʒə], *f.* -/. (*a*) *Tchn:* bending (of glass, etc.) into convex shape; dishing (of metal plate); (*b*) *Metalw:* flanging, dishing (of a sheet).

Bombarde [bom'bardə], *f.* -/-n. **1.** *A.Artil:* bombard. **2.** *Mus:* (*a*)=**Bomhart;** (*b*) bombardon (stop) (of organ).

Bombardement [bombardə'mã:], *n.* -s/-s, (*a*) *Mil: etc:* bombardment; shelling; bombing; (*b*) *Ph:* bombardment (with water particles, etc.).

bombardieren [bombar'di:rən]. I. *v.tr.* (*a*) *Mil:* to bomb (town, etc.); *A:* to bombard (town, port, fort); *F:* **j-n mit Fragen b.,** to bombard s.o. with questions; (*b*) *Ph:* =**beschießen** I. 1 (*c*).

II. *vbl s.* **Bombardierung,** *f.*=**Bombardement.**

Bombardierkäfer [bombar'di:r-], *m. Ent:* bombardier beetle.

Bombardist [bombar'dist], *m.* **-en/-en**=**Bombardierkäfer.**

Bombardon [bombar'dõ:], *n.* -s/-s. *Mus:* bombardon; bass-tuba.

Bombasin [bõ·ba'zɛ̃:, bomba'zi:n], *m.* -s/-s & -e [-'zi:nə]. *Tex:* bombasine.

Bombast [bom'bast, 'bombast], *m.* **-es/.** **1.** *Tex: A:* bombast. **2.** bombast, turgidity, fustian; grandiloquence, magniloquence, pomposity; rodomontade.

bombastisch [bom'bastiʃ], *a.* pompous, high-faluting (speech); bombastic (style).

Bombe, *f.* -/-n. **1.** (*a*) *Mil:* bomb; *A:* bomb-shell; **Bomben im Reihenwurf,** stick of bombs; **fliegende B.,** flying-bomb, *F:* doodle-bug; **Bomben (ab)werfen,** to throw bombs; (*of aircraft*) to drop, release, bombs, to bomb; **den Feind durch Bomben aus seiner Stellung vertreiben,** to bomb out the enemy; **die Bomben im Notwurf abwerfen,** to jettison one's bombs; *see also* **belegen**[1] I. 1; (*b*) *F:* **die Bekanntmachung schlug wie eine B. ein,** the announcement came, struck, like a bomb-shell; **die B. ist geplatzt,** (i) the expected has happened; (ii) *F:* the balloon has gone up; **wie eine B. hereinplatzen,** to come bursting in; (*c*) *F:* (*performer, play, song, etc.*) smash-hit, *P:* wow; *Com:* (*article*) outstanding attraction; *F: Fb: etc:* (*shot*) sizzler. **2.** (*a*) *Ph:* bomb (of bomb calorimeter); (*b*) *Ind:* gas-cylinder; oxygen bottle, cylinder; (*c*) *Geol:* **vulkanische B.,** volcanic bomb; (*d*) *Cu:* ice-pudding, *bombe glacée.*

Bomben-, *comb.fm.* **1.** *Mil.Av:* bomb . . .; bombing . . .; **Bombenlast** *f,* bomb load; **Bomben(ziel)anflug** *m,* bombing run. **2.** *F:* super . . .; *Th: etc:* **Bombenattraktion** *f,* super attraction; big draw; **Bombengehalt** *n,* enormous, colossal, salary; *Com:* **Bombenauftrag** *m,* huge order.

Bombenabwurf, *m.* bombing; **gezielter B.,** target, precision, bombing; **ungezielter B.,** random bombing; **B. aus großer Höhe,** high-level bombing.

Bombenabwurfgerät, *n. Mil.Av:* bomb-release gear.

Bombenabwurfschacht, *m. Mil.Av:* bomb-chute.

Bombenabwurfzielgerät, *n. Mil.Av:* bomb-sight.

Bombenangriff, *m.* bombing raid, attack, bomb attack; air raid.

Bombenanschlag, *m.*, **Bombenattentat,** *n.* (*with political motive*) bomb attempt (on s.o.'s life); bomb attack (on building, group of persons); bomb outrage.

Bombenauslöser, *m.*, **Bombenauslösung,** *f. Mil. Av:* bomb-release (gear).

Bombeneinschlag, *m.* **1.** bomb-explosion. **2.** bomb-hole.

Bombenerfolg, *m. Th: etc: F:* huge, striking, success, *F:* smash hit; **einen B. haben,** to score a hit, to be a huge success; **das Stück war ein B.,** the play was a great hit.

Bombenfallkurve, *f. Mil.Av:* flight-path, trajectory (of bomb).

bombenfest, *a.* (*a*) *Mil: etc:* bomb-proof (shelter, etc.); shell-proof (tank, etc.); bomb-resistant (building materials, buildings, etc.); (*b*) *F:* **das steht b.,** it's a certainty, *F:* a sure thing, a dead cert.

Bombenflüchtling, *m.* evacuee, refugee from bombing.

Bombenflugzeug, *n. Mil.Av:* bomber, bombing plane, bomb-carrier.

bombengeschädigt, *a.* **1.** *a.* bomb-damaged, blitzed (house, etc.). **2. Bombengeschädigte** *m,* sufferer from bomb-damage; bomb-damage claimant.

Bombenkalorimeter, *n. Ph:* bomb calorimeter.

Bombenkeller, *m.* underground air raid shelter (*esp. under house*).

Bombenklappe, *f. Mil.Av:* bomb-door.

Bombenkopf, *m.* nose of a bomb.

Bombenkrater, *m.* bomb-crater.

Bombenlast, *f. Mil.Av:* bomb-load.

Bombenloch, *n.* bomb-crater, -hole.

Bombenlücke, *f.* bomb(ed) site.

Bombenofen, *m. Ch:* Carius furnace.

Bombenpunktzielwurf, *m. Mil.Av:* precision bombing, pin point bombing.

Bombenräumtrupp, *m.* bomb disposal squad.

Bombenreihenwurf, *m. Mil.Av:* pattern bombing; stick bombing.

Bombenrohr, *n. Ch:* bomb tube, Carius tube.

Bombensache, *f. F:* smasher, stunner; **es war eine B.,** (i) (*of entertainment, etc.*) it was smashing, super, (ii) (*of thg*) it was a smasher.

Bombenschacht, *m. Mil.Av:* bomb bay.

Bombenschaden, *m.* bomb damage; **Bombenschäden** *pl,* (claim for) bomb damage.

Bombenschütze, *m. Mil.Av:* bomb-aimer, *U.S:* bombardier.

bombensicher, *a.* (*a*) bomb-proof; **bombensicherer Unterstand,** bomb-proof shelter, *Mil:* dug-out; **bombensicheres Gewölbe,** bomb-proof vault; (*b*) *F:* as sure as death, as fate, as a gun, *F:* as sure as eggs is eggs; **es ist b.,** it is as safe as the Bank of England.

Bombensplitter, *m.* bomb splinter.

Bombensprengkommando, *n.* bomb disposal squad.

Bombenteppich, *m. Mil.Av:* (*a*) screen target for bombing-practice; (*b*) carpet of bombs.

Bombenteppichwurf, *m. Mil.Av:* carpet-bombing.

Bombentiefangriff, *m. Mil.Av:* low-level bombing (attack).

Bombenträger, *m. Mil.Av:* bomb-carrier, bomb-rack.

Bombentragfähigkeit, *f. Mil.Av:* bomb capacity.

Bombentreffer, *m.* bomb hit; (*of house, etc.*) **einen B. erhalten, bekommen,** to be hit by a bomb, to get a hit.

Bombentrichter, *m.* bomb-crater, bomb-hole.

Bombenvisier, *n. Mil.Av:* bomb-sight.

Bombenvolltreffer, *m.* direct bomb hit.

Bombenwerfer, *m.* bomb-thrower.

Bombenwurf, *m.* bombing; *cp.* **Bombenabwurf.**

Bombenziel, *n. Mil:* bomb(ing) target.

Bombenzielgerät, *n. Mil.Av:* bomb-sight.

Bombenzünder, *m.* bomb detonator; bomb fuse.

Bomber ['bombər], *m.* -s/-. *Mil.Av:* bomber;

leichter B., light bomber; **schwerer B.**, heavy bomber.

Bombergeschwader, *n. Mil.Av:* bomber wing, *U.S:* bomber group.

Bombergruppe, *f. Mil.Av:* bomber wing, *U.S:* bomber group.

Bomberstaffel, *f. Mil.Av:* bomber squadron.

Bomberverband, *m. Mil.Av:* bomber formation.

bombieren [bɔmˈbiːrən], *v.tr.* **1.** *Tchn:* to dish (metal plate, etc.); **bombierter Boden**, dished end (of boiler, etc.); **bombiertes Blech**, corrugated iron; *Ind:* **bombierte Dose**, blown tin. **2.** *vbl s.* **Bombierung** *f*, camber, cambering (of road).

bombig, *a. F:* super, smashing, stunning.

Bombykometer [bɔmbi·ko·ˈmeːtər], *n.* **-s/-.** *Tex:* table for sizing, numbering, yarn.

Bombyx [ˈbɔmbyks], *m.* **-(es)/-e.** *Ent:* bombyx.

Bomhart, *m.* **-s/-s.** *Mus: A:* bombard.

Bommel, *f.* **-/-n** *& m.* **-s/-(s).** *Cost: etc:* pompon.

Bommert, *m.* **-s/-s.** *Mus: A:*=**Bomhart.**

Bon [bõː, bɔŋ], *m.* **-s/-s.** *Com: etc:* receipt; chit; voucher; credit note; ticket.

bona fide [ˈboːnaː ˈfiːdeː], *a. & adv.* bona fide.

Bonaparte-Möwe [bo·na·ˈpartə-], *f. Orn:* Bonaparte's gull.

Bonapartist [bo·na·parˈtist], *m.* **-en/-en**, Bonapartist.

bonapartistisch [bo·na·parˈtistiʃ], *a.* Bonapartist.

Bonbon [bõ·ˈbõː, bɔŋˈbɔŋ], *m. & n.* **-s/-s**, sweet, bonbon, sweetmeat, comfit, *U.S:* piece of candy.

Bonbonniere [bõ·boniˈɛːrə], *f.* **-/-n**, fancy sweet box; decorated box of sweets; *A:* sweetmeat box, comfit box.

Bonbontüte, *f.* bag of sweets, *U.S:* of candy.

Bond[1] [bõː], *m.* **-s/-s**, bound, leap (of horse).

Bond[2] [bɔnt], *m.* **-s/-s.** *Fin:* bond.

Bonde, *m.* **-n/-n.** *Dial:* (*in Schleswig-Holstein*) freeholder; peasant proprietor, peasant landowner.

Bondengut, *n. Jur:* indivisible landed property; estate that cannot be broken up.

bondern, *v.tr. Metall:* to bonderize.

bondieren [bɔnˈdiːrən, bõ·ˈdiːrən], *v.i.* (*haben*) (*of horse, etc.*) to leap, bound.

Bonducbaum [bõ·ˈdyk-], *m. Bot:* bonduc(-tree).

Bonducnuß, *f. Bot:* bonduc seed, nicker-nut.

Bönhase, *m.*=**Böhnhase.**

Bonhomie [bono·ˈmiː], *f.* **-/-n** [-ˈmiːən]. **1.** simple good-heartedness; good nature, bonhomie. **2.** simplicity, guilelessness. **3.** simpleness, simple mindedness.

Bonhomme [boˈnɔm], *m.* **-/-s.** **1.** simple, good-natured, man. **2.** honest, honourable, upright, worthy, man.

Bonifatius [bo·ni·ˈfaːtsius]. *Pr.n.m.* **-'.** Boniface.

Bonifatiuspfennig, *m. Paleont:*=**Bischofspfennig.**

Bonifaz [ˈboniˑfaːts]. *Pr.n.m.* **-'.** =**Bonifatius.**

Bonifikation [bo·ni·fi·ka·tsiˈoːn], *f.* **-/-en.** *Com:* allowance, rebate, reduction, reimbursement; compensation; *Fin:* commission; *Cust:* rebate on duty paid on bonded goods when exported (from Germany); **j-m eine B. von 10 Prozent gewähren**, to make s.o. an allowance, to give s.o. a reduction, rebate, of 10 per cent, to allow s.o. 10 per cent compensation.

bonifizieren [bo·ni·fi·ˈtsiːrən], *v.tr. Com:* to make (s.o.) an allowance, to allow (s.o.) a rebate, to compensate, indemnify, reimburse (s.o.).

Bonität [bo·ni·ˈtɛːt], *f.* **-/-en.** *Com:* solvency, soundness, good standing, reliability (of firm); credit (of firm, customer); validity, soundness (of draft, claim); (good, high, superior) quality (of article); *Agr:* quality, grade of fertility (of soil).

Bonite [bo·ˈniːtə], *m.* **-n/-n.** *Ich:* bonito.

Boniteur [bo·ni·ˈtøːr], *m.* **-s/-e**, valuer, assessor, appraiser.

bonitieren [bo·ni·ˈtiːrən]. **I.** *v.tr.* to value, estimate, assess, appraise, determine the quality of (sth.)

II. *vbl s.* **Bonitierung**, *f.* valuation, classification (of land, etc.).

Bonito [bo·ˈniːtoː], *m.* **-s/-s.** *Ich:* bonito.

Bonitur [bo·ni·ˈtuːr], *f.* **-/.** *Husb:* grading of lambs according to the fleece; *Tex:* grading of wool.

Bonmot [bõ·ˈmoː], *n.* **-s/-s**, witty remark, witticism.

Bonne [ˈbɔnə], *f.* **-/-n**, nursemaid; governess.

Bonneterie [bɔnɛtəˈriː], *f.* **-/-n** [-ˈriːən], hosiery trade; *Swiss:* haberdashery.

Bonus [ˈboːnus], *m.* **-/-** *&* **-ses/-se.** *Com: Fin:* bonus; extra dividend.

Bonvivant [bõ·vi·ˈvãː], *m.* **-s/-s**, man who likes to do himself well; man who enjoys life.

Bönzchen, *n.* **-s/-.** *F:* lesser light.

Bonze [ˈbɔntsə], *m.* **-n/-n.** (*a*) bonze, Buddhist priest; (*b*) *Pej: F:* high priest, bigwig, *F:* big bug, big pot, big shot, boss, *U.S:* big wheel (of political party, etc.).

Bonzentum, *n.*, **Bonzenwirtschaft**, *f.* corrupt rule; *U.S:* boss rule.

Boogie-Woogie [bugi·ˈvugiː], *m.* **-s/-s.** *Danc:* boogie-woogie.

Boom [buːm], *m.* **-s/-s.** *Com: Fin:* boom.

Boort, *m. & n.* **-(e)s/.**=**Bort.**

Boot, *n.* **-(e)s/-e**, (*a*) boat; row(ing)-boat; dinghy; dory; *Nau:* ship's boat; launch; **leichtes B.**, light craft; skiff; *Nau:* gig; *Navy:* whaler (of destroyer); **kleines B.**, jolly-boat; **gedecktes B.**, decked boat; **offenes B.**, open, undecked boat; *Nau:* **ein B. aussetzen**, to lower, launch, hoist out, a boat; **die Boote einsetzen**, to hoist in, take in, the boats; **ein B. voll von Matrosen**, a boatload, boatful, of sailors; **ein B. bemannt von . . .**, a boat manned by . . .; **ein B. mit voller Bemannung**, a fully manned boat; **alle Mann an die Boote!** man the boats! **in die Boote!** take to the boats! **etwas in Booten an Land bringen**, to carry sth. ashore by boat, in boats; **in einem Boot(e) fahren**, to go in a, by, boat, to boat; **B. fahren**, to go boating; **ein B. auf einem Teich schwimmen lassen**, to sail, float, a (toy) boat on a pond; (*b*) *Av:* hull (of flying-boat); body (of glider).

Bootaxt, *f. Prehist:* boat-axe.

Bootbauerei, *f.* boat-building.

Bootes [bo·ˈoːtɛs]. *Pr.n.m.* **-'.** *Astr:* Boötes, the Bear Driver, the Bearwarden.

Bootfahren, *n.* boating.

bootförmig, *a.* boat-shaped; *Bot: etc:* cymbiform.

Bootführer, *m.* waterman, boatman.

Böotien [bøˈoːtsiən]. *Pr.n.* **-s.** *A.Geog:* Bœotia.

Böotier [bøˈoːtsiər], *m.* **-s/-.** **1.** *A.Geog:* Bœotian. **2.** *F:* bumpkin, clod.

böotisch [bøˈoːtiʃ], *a.* **1.** *A.Geog:* Bœotian. **2.** *F:* unintelligent, ignorant, dull-witted.

Bootsanker, *m. Nau:* boat's anchor; grapnel.

Bootsaußenhaut, *f.* outer skin of a boat.

Bootsbau, *m.* boat-building.

Boot(s)bauer, *m.* boat-builder, boat-wright.

Bootsbesatzung, *f.* boat's crew.

Bootsbreite, *f. Nau:* (breadth of) beam (of boat); *Av:* beam (of flying-boat).

Bootsdavit, *m. Nau:* davit.

Bootsdeck, *n. Nau:* boat-deck.

Bootsdolle, *f. Nau:* thole-pin (of boat).

Bootseigentümer, *m.* owner of a boat.

Bootsfahrt, *f.* row; sail; boat trip.

Bootsfierapparat, *m. Nau:* boat-lowering apparatus.

Bootsführer, *m. Nau: Row:* coxswain, *F:* cox.

Bootsgalgen, *m. Nau:* skid-beams; (boat-)skids.

Bootsgast, *m.* **-es/-en.** *Nau:* sailor; member of a boat's crew.

Bootshaken, *m. Nau: etc:* boat-hook; grapnel, grappling-iron; setting-pole, punt-pole.

Bootshaus, *n.* boat-house; club-house.

Bootsheißmaschine, *f. Nau:* boat-hoist engine.

Bootshütte, *f.* boat-house.

Bootsklampe, *f. Nau:* boat chock, cradle, crutch.

Bootsklauer, *m.pl. Nau:* (boat-)gripes.

Bootskleid, *n.* boat cover.

Bootskörper, *m.* boat; hull, body (of boat, submarine, flying-boat).

Bootskrabber, *m.pl. Nau:* (boat-)gripes.

Bootskran, *m. Nau:* davit crane.

Bootslack, *m.* boat varnish.

Bootsladung, *f.* boatload.

Bootsläufer, *m. Nau:* cable of davit crane.

Bootsleine, *f.* tow-line, tow-rope, tow.

Bootsmann, *m.* **-(e)s/-leute.** **1.** *Nau:* boatswain, *F:* bos'n, bosun. **2.** *Navy:* petty officer.

Bootsmannsbrief, *m. Nau:* boatswain's certificate.

Bootsmannschaft, *f.* boat's crew.

Bootsmannskammer, *f. Nau:* boatswain's room.

Bootsmannsmaat, *m. Nau:* boatswain's mate.

Bootsmannspfeife, *f. Navy:* boatswain's pipe.

Bootsmannsstuhl, *m. Nau: Constr: etc:* bosun's chair, seat, cradle.

Bootsmanöver, *n. Nau:* boat-drill.

Bootsnagel, *m. N.Arch:* treenail.

Bootspersonal, *n.* crew (of launch, etc.).

Bootspflicht, *f. Nau:* cuddy (of half-decked boat).

Bootspflock, **Bootspfropfen**, *m.* boat-plug.

Bootsrennen, *n.* boat-race.

Bootsriemen, *m.* oar.

Bootsrippe, *f.* rib of a boat.

Bootsruder, *n. Nau:* rudder (of boat).

Bootsruderpinne, *f. Nau:* bar, tiller (of boat).

Bootsrumpf, *m.*=**Bootskörper.**

Bootsschleppe, *f.* boat-slide.

Bootsschuppen, *m.* boat-shed.

Bootssteg, *m.* landing-stage, -place.

Bootssteuer, *n. Nau:* rudder (of boat).

Bootssteuerer, *m.*=**Bootssteuermann.**

Bootssteuermann, *m. Nau:* coxswain (of boat crew); *Row:* coxswain, *F:* cox.

Bootsstoßkissen, *n.pl. Nau:* boat-pads, puddening, pudding (fender).

Bootsstummel, *m. Av:* (i) float, (ii) stabilizing sponson (on flying-boat).

Bootstau, *n. Nau:* painter (of boat).

Bootsüberzug, *m.* boat cover.

Bootsvermieter, *m.* person who hires out boats.

Bootsvermietung, *f.* letting out on hire of boats, boat-hire.

Bootswächter, *m. Nau: etc:* boat-keeper.

Bootswagen, *m.* boat trailer.

Bootwanze, *f. Ent:* boat-fly, water-boatman, boatman, *U.S:* boat bug.

Bootswerft, *f.* boat-yard.

Bootswinde, *f.* boat-hoist.

Bootszelt, *n. Nau:* awning, tilt, canopy (of boat's stern).

Bootszieher, *m.* tow-rope, tow-line; *Nau:* hauling-rope; guess-rope.

Bor [boːr], *n.* **-s/.** *Ch:* boron.

borartig, *a. Ch:* boric, *F:* boracic (acid).

Borassus [bo·ˈrasus], *m.* **-/.**, **Borassuspalme**, *f. Bot:* palmyra.

Borat [bo·ˈraːt], *n.* **-s/-e.** *Ch:* borate.

Boräthyl [bo·ˈr], *n. Ch:* borethyl.

Borax [ˈboːraks], *m.* **-/.** *Ch: etc:* borax; **natürlicher B.**, tincal.

Boraxblei, *n. Ch:* lead borate.

Boraxfirnis, *m.* borax varnish.

Boraxglas, *n. Glassm:* borax glass.

Boraxhonig, *m. Pharm:* borax honey.

Boraxperle, *f. Ch:* borax bead.

Boraxseife, *f. Pharm: etc:* boracic soap.

Borazit [bo·ra·ˈtsiːt], *m.* **-s/.** *Miner:* boracite.

Borborygmus [bɔrbo·ˈrygmus], *m.* **-/.** *Med:* rumbling(s) (in the bowels).

Borch, *m.* **-(e)s/⸗e.** *Dial:*=**Barch.**

Bord[1], *m.* **-(e)s/-e.** **1.** edge, border, side (of road, etc.); edge, end (of gable roof); *Poet:* rim (of cup, etc.), brim (of river), margin (of fountain). **2.** *Nau:* (i) board, side (of ship); (ii) gunwale, gunnel (of boat); **an B.**, on board (ship, aircraft, etc.); **alle Mann an B.!** all aboard! **an B. meines Schiffes**, on board, aboard, my ship; **an B. gehen**, to go aboard, on board, to board (a) ship; **an B. kommen**, to come aboard, on board; **Passagiere, eine Ladung, Wasser, an B. nehmen**, to take on passengers, to take on, in, to ship, a cargo, to take in (a supply of) water; **etwas an B. bringen**, to load, take, sth. aboard; **das Leben an B. eines Schiffes**, life aboard (ship); *Com:* **frei an B.**, free on board; *Nau:* **einem Schiffe an B. treiben**, to fall aboard (of) a ship, to run aboard a ship; *Row:* **ein Bord-an-Bord-Kampf**, *F:* a neck-and-neck struggle; **von B. zu B.**, from side to side; **von B. gehen**, to leave the ship, to go ashore; **über B.**, overboard; **Mann über B.!** man overboard! **über B. gehen, fallen**, (*of mast, cargo, etc.*) to go overboard, to go by the board, (*of pers.*) to go, fall, overboard; **etwas, j-n, über B. werfen**, to heave, throw, sth., s.o., overboard, to jettison (cargo, ballast); **über B. gespült werden**, to be washed overboard; **das Schiff bekam eine schwere See über B.**, the vessel shipped a heavy sea, was washed by a heavy sea; *F:* **(die Vorsicht, alle Sorgen, eine Theorie) über B. werfen**, to abandon, forsake (caution, one's cares), to dismiss (a theory).

Bord[2], **Börd**, *n.* **-(e)s/-e**, shelf; (set of) shelves; rack, stand (for books).

Bordanker, *m. Nau:* bower(-anchor).

Bordanlage, *f. Av:* electrical *or* wireless equipment aboard aircraft; airborne equipment; *Nau:* marine installation; ship's (electrical, etc.) installation; *Navy:* shipborne equipment.

Bordanlasser, *m. Av:* cockpit starter.

Bordaufklärer, *m. Navy:* shipborne reconnaissance plane.

Bordbuch, *n. Av:* flight log, log-book; *Nau:* ship's log(-book).

borddienstunfähig, *a. Av:* unfit for flying duty; *Nau:* unfit for service afloat.

Borde, *f.* **-/-n.** *Dial:*=**Borte.**

Börde, *f.* **-/-n.** *Geog:* (*in North Germany*) fertile plain (bounded by hills).

Bordeaux [bɔrˈdoː], *m.* **-/-.** Bordeaux (wine); **roter B.**, claret.

Bordeauxbrühe, *f. Vit:* Bordeaux mixture.

bordeauxrot [bɔrˈdoːroːt], *a. Dy:* Bordeaux (red), claret.

Bordeauxwein, *m.*=**Bordeaux.**

Bordelaiser [bɔrdəˈlɛːzər], *inv.a.* **B. Brühe**=**Bordeauxbrühe.**

Bördelblech, *n.* flanged plate.

Bördeleisen, *n. Tls:* flange, flanging tool; seaming stake.

Bordelese [bordəˈleːzə], *m.* **-n/-n**, native, inhabitant, of Bordeaux.

Bordeleser [bordəˈleːzər], *inv.a.* of Bordeaux.

Bordell [borˈdɛl], *n.* **-s/-e**, (licensed) brothel.

Bördelmaschine, *f. Metalw:* flanging machine.

bördeln. I. *v.tr. Metalw:* to flange, edge, fold, crease (plate, sheet); to curl (plate), to wire (edge of plate); to bead (tube end).
II. *vbl s.* **1. Bördeln**, *n. in vbl senses.* **2. Bördelung**, *f.* flange.

Bördelpresse, *f. Metalw:* flanging press.

Bordereau [bordəˈroː], *m. & n.* **-s/-s.** *Com: etc:* memorandum, (detailed) statement; invoice; delivery note; *Bank:* list of bills for discount.

Bordflugzeug, *n. Navy:* ship's aircraft, ship-plane, carrier-borne aircraft.

Bordfrack, *m. Navy: Cost:* mess-jacket.

bordfrei, *a. Com:* free on board.

Bordfunkanlage, *f. W.Tel: Av: Space:* airborne wireless equipment; *Av:* aircraft's wireless; *Nau:* ship's wireless.

Bordfunker, *m. Nau: Av:* wireless operator, radio operator (aboard ship, aircraft).

Bordfunkgerät, *n. W.Tel: Av:* aircraft wireless equipment; *Space:* rocket wireless equipment; *Nau:* ship's wireless (equipment).

Bordfunkstelle, *f. W.Tel: Av:* aircraft wireless post; *Nau:* ship's wireless post, wireless room.

Bordgerät, *n. Av: Space:* airborne equipment, *esp.* intercommunication telephone; **Bordgeräte** *pl*, flight instruments.

Bordiamant, *m. Ch: Ind:* (i) diamond boron, adamantine boron; (ii) boron diamond.

bordieren [borˈdiːrən]. I. *v.tr.* **1.** *Dressm: etc:* to edge (sth.) with braid, etc.; *Art:* to put a border on (picture). **2.** *Metalw:*=**bördeln.**
II. *vbl s.* **Bordierung**, *f.* (*a*) *in vbl senses;* (*b*)=**Borte.**

Bording, *m.* **-s/-e.** *Nau:* lighter, barge.

Bordinstrumente, *n.pl. Av:* (flying) instruments; *Space:* rocket(-borne) instruments; **nach Bordinstrumenten fliegen**, to fly on instruments.

Bordinstrumentenbrett, *n. Av:* instrument-board, -panel.

Bordjäger, *m. Av:* fleet fighter.

Bordkanone, *f. Mil.Av:* aircraft cannon.

Bordkante, *f.* edge of the kerb (on pavement); *Mec.E:* edge of a flange.

Bordkino, *n. Nau:* ship's cinema.

Bordkonnossement, *n. Nau:* 'shipped' bill of lading.

Bordküche, *f. Av:* galley, pantry (on aircraft).

Bordlandefackel, *f. Av:* landing light (on aircraft).

bordlos, *a. Rail:* **bordloser Wagen**, flat goods-truck, *U.S:* flatcar.

Bordmechaniker, *m. Av:* flight engineer.

Bordmonteur, Bordmontör, *m. Av:* flight mechanic.

Bordnetz, *n. Av:* aircraft wiring system.

Bordpeiler, *m. W.Tel: Nau: Av:* **1.** ship's, aircraft's, direction-finder; radio-compass. **2.** D/F operator.

Bordpeilgerät, *n. W.Tel: Nau: Av:* D/F equipment.

Bordplanken, *f.pl. N.Arch:* planking; sheathing.

Bordrakete, *f. Mil.Av:* airborne rocket; *Mil:* rocket carried by a missile.

Bordscheinwerfer, *m. Av:* landing lamp.

Bordschicht, *f. Arch: Constr:* barge-course.

Bordschütze, *m. Mil.Av:* air-gunner.

Bordschwelle, *f.* kerb, *U.S:* curb (of pavement).

Bordseite, *f. Nau:* side (of a vessel); *A:* wall (of wooden vessel).

Bordsprechanlage, *f. Tp: Nau: Av: Mil:* intercommunication telephone, *F:* intercom (of ship, aircraft, tank).

Bordstein, *m.* kerb-stone; kerb, *U.S:* curb.

Bordsuchgerät, *n. W.Tel:* airborne search apparatus.

Bordtelephonanlage, *f. Tp: Nau: Av:* intercommunication telephone, *F:* intercom.

Borduhr, *f. Av: Nau:* chronometer.

Bordun [borˈduːn], *m.* **-s/-e.** *Mus:* (*a*) drone bass; (*b*) drone (of bagpipes, etc.); (*c*) *A:* (sound of) bass string (of theorbo, etc.); (*d*) bourdon stop (of organ).

Bordüre [borˈdyːrə], *f.* **-/-n. 1.** border (of picture, etc.); (ornamental) border(-strip) (in book, manuscript, etc.). **2.** *Dressm:* edging, trimming; border.

Bordürenband, *n.* trimming-ribbon.

Bordürenleiste, *f. Tex:* list (of cloth).

Bordwache, *f. Nau:* (the) watch on deck.

Bordwaffen, *f.pl. Mil.Av:* aircraft armament, aircraft cannon *or* machine-guns.

Bordwagen, *m. Rail:* open goods-truck; *U.S:* gondola car.

Bordwand, *f.* (*a*) *Nau:* side (of a vessel); *A:* wall (of wooden vessel); (*b*) *Rail:* side planking (of goods-truck).

Bordzeit, *f. Nau:* ship's time.

Bordzeitung, *f. Nau:* ship's newspaper.

Bordziegel, *m.* edge tile (on a gable roof).

Bord-zu-Bord-Verkehr, *m. W.Tel:* (*a*) *Nau:* ship-to-ship traffic; (*b*) *Av:* air-to-air traffic.

boreal [boreˑˈaːl], *a.* boreal, north(ern).

Boreas [ˈboːreˑas]. *Pr.n.m.* **-'**. *Myth:* Boreas; *Poet:* the North Wind.

Boretsch, *m.* **-es/.** *Bot:* borage.

Borg[1], *m.* **-(e)s/.** *F:* borrowing; *F:* tick; **auf B. leben**, to live by borrowing, *F:* to live on tick; **(von j-m) etwas auf B. nehmen**, to borrow sth. (from s.o.); to get, have, sth. (from s.o.) on credit, *F:* on tick; **etwas auf B. kaufen**, to buy sth. on credit, *F:* on tick; **etwas auf B. geben**, to give sth. on loan; **j-m etwas auf B. geben**, to lend, *U.S:* loan, sth. to s.o.; to let s.o. have sth. on (i) loan, (ii) credit.

Borg[2], *m.* **-(e)s/-s**=**Barch.**

borgen. I. *v.tr.* **1.** to borrow (money, etc.) **(von**, **bei**, from, of); *Mth:* **eins b.**, to borrow one; **ich habe mir ein Buch von, bei, ihm geborgt**, I have borrowed a book from him; **er borgt gern, aber gibt nicht zurück**, he is good at borrowing, but bad at giving back; **fremde Gedanken b.**, to borrow, *F:* crib, ideas from someone else. **2.** to lend, *U.S:* to loan (sth. to s.o.); **kannst du mir 10 Mark b.?** can you lend me 10 marks? **man hatte es mir geborgt**, it had been lent to me.
II. *vbl s.* **Borgen**, *n. in vbl senses; also: Prov:* **B. macht Sorgen**, he who goes a-borrowing goes a-sorrowing.

Borger, *m.* **-s/-. 1.** borrower. **2.** lender.

Borgerei, *f.* **-/.** (habit, custom, of) borrowing.

Borgis [ˈborgis], *f.* **-/., Borgisschrift**, *f. Print:* bourgeois; nine-point type.

Borgkauf, *m. Fin:* hire-purchase.

Borid [boˑˈriːt], *n.* **-(e)s/-e** [-s, -ˈriːdəs/-ˈriːdə]. *Ch:* boride.

Borium [ˈboːrĭum], *n.* **-s/.**=**Bor.**

Borkarbid, *n. Ch: Ind:* boron carbide.

Borke, *f.* **-/-n. 1.** (*a*) bark (of tree); (*b*) *Tan:* spent bark, tan. **2.** *Dial:* scab, crust (on wound).

Borkenflechte, *f. Vet:* ringworm.

Borkenkäfer, *m. Ent:* bark-beetle, shot-hole borer.

Borkenkrätze, *f. Med:* Boeck's scabies, Norwegian itch.

Borkenkrepp, *m. Tex:* crépon.

Borkenratte, *f. Z:* Philippine bushy-tailed rat.

Borkentier, *n. Z:* Steller's sea-cow.

borkig, *a.* **1.** covered with bark; resembling bark. **2.** *Med:* herpetic.

Born, *m.* **-(e)s/-e.** *A. & Poet:* source; spring; fountain; well; *Lit:* fount; **der B. der Weisheit**, the fount of (all) wisdom, of (all) knowledge; **unsere Kinder sind für uns ein rechter B. der Freude**, our children are a great source of happiness to us; **aus dem B. seiner Erfahrung schöpfen**, to draw on one's fund of experience; *cp.* **Brunnen** 1 (*a*).

Born-, *comb.fm. Cp.* **Brunnen-.**

borneisch [borˈneːiʃ], *a. Geog:* Bornean.

bornen, börnen, *v.tr. Dial:* to water (cattle).

Borneo [ˈborneˑoː]. *Pr.n.* **-s.** *Geog:* Borneo.

Borneol [borneˑˈoːl], *n.* **-s/-e.** *Ch: Pharm:* borneene; borneol; Borneo camphor.

bornieren [borˈniːrən], *v.tr.* **1.** to limit, restrict (thought, etc.). **2.** *p.p. & a.* **borniert**, (pers.) of limited outlook, of restricted intelligence; obtuse, stupid (pers.); **sie sind borniert, sie sind bornierte Leute**, they are people of limited views, limited understanding.

Borniertheit [borˈniːrthait], *f.* **-/.** narrow-mindedness, narrowness of outlook; obtuseness, stupidity; **seine B. ist unvorstellbar**, his stupidity defies description, he is incredibly stupid.

Bornit [borˈniːt], *m.* **-(e)s/.** *Miner:* bornite.

Borokalzit [boˑroˑkalˈtsiːt], *m. Miner:* borocalcite.

Borpulver, *n. Pharm:* boracic powder.

Borraginazee [boraˑgiˑnaˑˈtseːə], *f.* **-/-n** [-ˈtseːən]. *Bot:* (any) one of the borraginaceae; **die Borraginazeen**, the borraginaceae, *F:* the borageworts.

Borrago [boˈraːgoː], *m.* **-s/.**=**Borretsch.**

Borretsch, *m.* **-es/.** *Bot:* borage.

Borromäerin [boroˑˈmɛːərin], *f.* **-/-innen.** *Ecc:* Sister of St Carlo Borromeo.

Borromäus [boroˑˈmɛːus]. *Pr.n.m.* **-'. (Karl) B.**, St Carlo Borromeo.

Borromäusverein, der, the Roman Catholic book-club and lending-library (in Germany).

Borromeisch [boroˑˈmeːiʃ], *a. Geog:* **die Borromeischen Inseln**, the Borromean Isles.

Borsalbe, *f. Pharm:* boracic ointment.

borsauer, *a. Ch:* borated; borate of . . .; **borsaures Salz**, borate; **borsaures Natron**, borax.

Borsäure, *f. Ch:* boric, *F:* boracic, acid.

Borsäurelösung, *f. Pharm:* boracic solution.

Börsch, *m.* **-s/-e**=**Börskohl.**

Borscht(sch) [borʃt(ʃ)], *m.* **-s/.** *Cu:* borsch.

Börse, *f.* **-/-n. 1.** (*a*) purse; money-bag; (*b*) *Sp:* purse; **eine B. einrichten**, to give, to put up, a purse. **2.** *Fin:* stock exchange; stock-market; money-market; commodity market; **die Berliner B.**, the Berlin Bourse; **die Londoner B.**, the Stock Exchange, *F:* the House; **die Pariser B.**, the (Paris) Bourse; **die B. war heute sehr lebhaft, belebt**, the market was very active to-day; **auf die B. gehen**, to go to, to visit, the Stock Exchange; **an der B.**, on the Stock Exchange; *F:* on 'Change; in the money-market; **an der B. kaufen, verkaufen, handeln**, to buy, sell, deal, on the Stock Exchange; **an der B. spielen, spekulieren**, to dabble, speculate, gamble, on the Stock Exchange, *U.S:* to play the market, the stock market; **an der B. gehandelte Wertpapiere**, securities dealt in on the Stock Exchange; **an der B. notierte Aktien**, officially quoted shares, listed stock; **diese Aktien sind an der B. nicht notiert worden**, these shares are not quoted on 'Change; (*of share, bond, etc.*) **zum Handel und zur amtlichen Notierung an der B. zugelassen werden**, to be admitted to quotation; **die Zulassung der neuen Stammaktien zum Handel und zur amtlichen Notierung an der B. wird alsbald beantragt werden**, application will shortly be made to the Council of the Stock Exchange for permission to deal in and for quotation of these new ordinary shares.

Börsenauftrag, *m. St.Exch:* order to buy, sell, (shares, etc.) on the Stock Exchange.

Börsenbeginn, *m. St.Exch:* **bei B.**, when trading starts, when the market opens.

Börsenbericht, *m. Fin:* market report.

Börsenbesuch, *m.* attendance on, admission to, the Stock Exchange; **vom B. ausgeschlossen werden**, to be excluded from attendance on, from membership of, the Stock Exchange; **die Zulassung zum B.**, admission to, permission to attend on, the Stock Exchange.

Börsenbesucher, *m.* member of the Stock Exchange; person authorized to enter the Stock Exchange; visitor to the Stock Exchange.

Börsenblatt, *n.* (*a*)=**Börsenzeitung**; (*b*) *Publ:* trade paper for the German book-trade.

Börsendiener, *m.* Stock Exchange Attendant; (*on London Stock Exchange*) waiter.

Börseneinführung, *f. Fin:* admission (of shares, etc.) to official quotation; **Bekanntmachung über B.**, (notice of) official quotation.

börsenfähig, *a. Fin:* (*a*) (person) qualified (i) to enter, (ii) to trade on, an exchange; (*b*) **börsenfähige Aktien**, stock negotiable on the Stock Exchange.

Börsenfähigkeit, *f. Fin:* (*a*) qualification for trading (on an Exchange); (*b*) negotiability (of stock, etc.) on the Stock Exchange.

börsengängig, *a.*=**börsenfähig** (*b*).

Börsengeschäft, *n.* (*a*) business on the Stock Exchange; (*b*) Stock Exchange transaction, deal; **Börsengeschäfte machen**, to speculate on the Stock Exchange; to deal on the Stock Exchange.

Börsengesetz, *n.* law relating to stock exchanges and commodity markets.

Börsenhalle, *f. St.Exch:* the hall of the Exchange.

Börsenhandel, *m. Fin:* dealing on the Stock Exchange; **die Zulassung von Wertpapieren zum B.**, the admission of securities to quotation.

Börsenindex, *m. St.Exch:* stock index, stock price average.

Börsenjobber, *m. St.Exch:* stock-jobber.

Börsenkommissionsgeschäft, *n. Fin:* **1.** firm of stockbrokers; stockbroking business. **2.** stock-broking transaction.

Börsenkrach, *m. Fin:* collapse of the market.

Börsenkurs, *m. St.Exch:* quotation; market-price, -rate; **zum B. kaufen**, to buy at the price quoted.

Börsenmakler, *m. Fin:* stockbroker on the Exchange, broker-member of the Stock Exchange.

Börsenmanöver, *n. Pej: Fin:* market-rigging, -jobbery, stock-jobbing; agiotage.

Börsenmarkt, *m. Fin:* stock market.
börsenmäßig, *a. St.Exch:* according to Stock Exchange procedure; **der börsenmäßige An- und Verkauf von Bezugsrechten,** the buying and selling of subscription rights according to Stock Exchange procedure.
Börsenname, *m. Fin:* Stock Exchange abbreviation.
Börsennotierung, *f. Fin:* (Stock Exchange) quotation.
Börsenordnung, *f.* Stock Exchange *or* commodity market regulations.
Börsenpapiere, *n.pl. Fin:* listed stock, shares, securities.
Börsenplatz, *m.* Stock Exchange centre.
Börsenpreis, *m. St.Exch:* market price.
Börsensaal, *m. St.Exch:* **im B.,** on the floor of the Stock Exchange.
Börsenscheinverkauf, *m. St.Exch:* fictitious sale of a security, *U.S:* wash sale.
Börsenschluß, *m. St.Exch:* **1.** minimum trading unit, *U.S:* board lot, full lot. **2.** close of the market; **bei B.,** when the market closed.
Börsenschwindel, *m. Pej: Fin:* stock-jobbing, market-jobbery.
Börsenschwindler, *m. Fin: St.Exch:* market-rigger.
Börsenspekulant, *m. St.Exch:* stock-jobber; premium-hunter, 'stag'; dabbler on the Stock Exchange, *U.S:* stock market speculator.
Börsenspekulation, *f. Fin:* (i) speculation on the Stock Exchange; jobbery; (ii) deal on the Stock Exchange.
Börsenspieler, *m. Pej:* manipulator, operator, gambler (on the Stock Exchange).
Börsensprache, *f. Fin:* Stock Exchange parlance.
Börsenstimmung, *f. St.Exch:* tone of the market.
Börsentag, *m. St.Exch:* market-day.
Börsentermingeschäft, *n.* (*a*) forward dealing, trading in futures, on an exchange; (*b*) account dealing; transaction for the account.
Börsentip, *m. Fin:* tip (to investors).
Börsenumsatzsteuer, *f.* tax on Stock Exchange dealings; stamp-duty.
Börsenverein, *m. see* **Buchhändler.**
Börsenvertreter, *m.* representative (of a bank, etc.) on the Stock Exchange.
Börsenvorstand, *m.* Committee of the Exchange; Stock Exchange Committee; (*in London*) Council of the Stock Exchange; *U.S:* Board of Governors of the Stock Exchange.
Börsenwert, *m. Fin:* market value.
Börsenzeit, *f.* official hours of a Stock Exchange.
Börsenzeitung, *f.* Stock Exchange journal, gazette; financial newspaper.
Börsenzettel, *m. Fin:* official (Stock Exchange) price-list; stock-list; (*in London*) Stock Exchange Daily Official List.
Börsianer [bø(ˑ)rzīˈaːnər], *m.* **-s/-** = **Börsenspekulant.**
Börskohl, *m. Dial: Hort:* savoy (cabbage).
Borste, *f.* **-/-n. 1.** (*a*) bristle (of hog, etc.); quill, spine (of hedgehog); vibrissa (of bird); *Nat.Hist:* seta; (*b*) *Hum:* (i) bristle (on man's chin); (ii) hair (on head); **seine Haare sind wie Borsten,** his hair is like bristle; (*c*) bristle (of broom, brush); *Com:* **reine Borste,** pure bristle; **ist das gute Borste?** is it a good bristle? **2.** *Bot: pl.* **Borsten,** strigæ; **hakenförmige Borsten,** glochidiate hairs; **mit Borsten bedeckt,** strigose.
börste, *occ. see* **bersten.**
borsten, *v.i.* (*haben*) & **sich borsten,** (*of hair*) to bristle (up), to rise, to stand on end.
borstenartig, *a. Nat.Hist:* bristly, setaceous; bristle-like.
Borstenbesen, *m.* bristle broom, hair broom, soft broom.
Borstendolde, *f. Bot:* torilis, *F:* hedge-parsley.
Borstenfäule, *f. Vet:* bristle-rot.
Borstenfedergras, *n. Bot:* pennisetum.
Borstenferkel, *n. Z:* ground-pig, cane-rat.
Borstenfisch, *m. Ich:* chaetodon.
borstenförmig, *a. Bot:* bristle-shaped; setiform.
Borstengras, *n. Bot:* **1.** mat-grass, nard. **2.** setaria, bristle-grass; millet.
Borstengürteltier, *n. Z:* hairy armadillo.
Borstenhirse, *f. Bot:* setaria, bristle-grass; Italian millet.
Borstenigel, *m. Z:* tanrec, tenrec, tendrac.
Borstenkraut, *n. Bot:* safflower, bastard saffron.
Borstenlilie, *f. Bot:* aristea.
Borstenpinsel, *m.* bristle brush.
Borstenscheibe, *f. Tchn:* buffing brush.
Borstentier, *n. Nat.Hist:* setiferous animal; *Hum:* pig, hog.
borstentragend, *a. Nat.Hist:* setiferous, setigerous, *Bot:* bristle-bearing.
Borstenträger, *m. Nat.Hist:* setiferous animal.
Borstenvieh, *n. Z:* domestic hog; *coll.* swine.
Borstenwurm, *m. Ann:* chaetopod, bristle-worm; nereid.
borstig, *a.* **1.** (*a*) bristly, bristled (boar); spiny (hedgehog); *Nat.Hist:* setose, setaceous (hair, etc.); (*b*) bristly, *F:* stubbly (beard, hair, etc.); (*c*) *Bot:* bristly, strigose, hispid (leaf, etc.); **borstige Grundfeste,** (i) small, rough hawk's-beard; (ii) bristly hawk's-beard. **2.** *F:* crabby, cross-grained, crusty; rough, uncouth; **b. werden,** to fly into a rage, temper.
Borstigkeit, *f.* **1.** bristliness. **2.** *F:* crabbiness.
Bort, *m. & n.* **-(e)s/.** *Lap:* bort.
Borte, *f.* **-/-n,** (*a*) border (of picture, carpet, etc.); (wall-paper) border, frieze; (*b*) *Tex:* trimming, edging, braid, braiding; **(etwas) mit Borten besetzen,** to trim, edge, (sth.) with braid, to braid (sth.); **ein mit Borten besetztes Kleid,** a braided garment; **Besetzen mit Borten,** braiding.
Bortenmacher, *m. Tex:* maker of braid, of passementerie.
Bortennäher, *m. Needlew:* binder (of sewing machine).
Bortenweberei, *f. Tex:* weaving of trimmings.
bortieren [bɔrˈtiːrən], *v.tr.* = **bordieren** 1.
Bortrioxyd, *n. Ch:* boron trioxide.
Borusse [boˑˈrusə], *m.* **-n/-n.** Prussian.
Borussia [boˑˈrusiaː]. *Pr.n.f.* **-s.** Prussia.
Borverbindung, *f. Ch:* boride.
Borwasser, *n. Pharm:* boracic lotion.
Borwatte, *f. Surg:* boracic lint.
Borwolframsäure, *f. Ch:* borotungstic acid.
bös, *a.* = **böse.**
bösartig, *a.* **1.** malicious, vicious, ill-natured (pers.); vicious (animal); **er ist von Natur b.,** he is vicious by nature; **sie hat einen bösartigen Charakter,** she has a nasty, vicious, nature; *adv.* **j-n b. anschauen,** to eye s.o. malignantly, evilly. **2.** *Med:* malignant; virulent; **bösartige Geschwulst,** malignant tumour, *F:* malignant; **bösartiges Fieber,** virulent fever; **bösartige Erkrankung,** virulent disease.
Bösartigkeit, *f.* **1.** malignity; viciousness; spitefulness; ill-nature; **die B. seines Charakters,** the viciousness of his nature; **2.** *Med:* malignancy, malignity (of disease); virulence (of disease, fever).
böschen. I. *v.tr.* to slope (ditch, embankment, etc.); to embank (track); to batter (wall); *Fort:* to escarp (glacis, etc.); **das Flußufer steil b.,** to cut the bank of a river into a steep slope.
II. *vbl s.* **1. Böschen,** *n. in vbl senses; also: Fort:* escarpment. **2. Böschung,** *f.* (*a*) = II. 1; (*b*) slope; *Civ.E:* batter; ramp; embankment (of railway); **natürliche B.,** slope of the ground; bank (of river); (*c*) *Fort:* escarpment, (e)scarp, talus; **innere B.,** escarp; **äußere B.,** counterscarp.
Boschhorn, *n. Aut: etc:* (electric) klaxon.
Böschungsanlage, *f.* slope, embankment.
Böschungsarbeiten, *f.pl. Civ.E: etc:* construction of embankments; embanking.
Böschungsfläche, *f.* face of a slope.
Böschungsflügel, *m. Civ.E:* retaining wing, wing-wall (of abutment).
Böschungsfluß, *m. Geog:* consequent (river).
Böschungsfuß, *f.* base of an embankment.
Böschungsmauer, *f. Civ.E:* revetment wall, embankment wall; toe wall.
Böschungsmesser, *m. Surv:* clinometer.
Böschungspflaster, *n. Civ.E:* stone pitching, facing (of embankment).
Böschungswinkel, *m. Civ.E:* angle of inclination; **natürlicher B.,** (natural) angle of repose.
böse. I. *a.* **1.** (*a*) evil, wicked, bad; malevolent; malicious; **wissen, was gut und b. ist,** to know good and evil; **ein böser Mensch,** a wicked, an evil, person; *F:* a bad lot, a bad hat; **böse Taten, Gedanken,** evil deeds, thoughts; **böse Lust, Begierde,** evil, unholy, desires; lust; **böse Gewohnheit,** evil, bad, habit; evil, pernicious, practice; **sein böser Geist, Engel,** his evil genius; **der böse Feind,** the Evil One, the Devil; **böse Gesellschaft,** bad company; **er hat ein böses Auge,** he has an evil eye; **der böse Nachbar,** one's unfriendly neighbour; **böse Zeiten,** evil times; **Macht an sich ist b.,** power in itself is evil; absolute power corrupts; **er wird noch ein böses Ende nehmen,** he will come to a bad end (yet); *see also* **Blick** (*a*); **Bube** 3; (*b*) bad, unpleasant; unfortunate; nasty; hard; **es sieht b. mit ihm aus,** things look bad, black, for him; he is in a bad way; **böse Zeiten,** hard times; **in guten und bösen Tagen,** through good and evil; **böse Nachrichten,** bad news; **böser Traum,** bad, unpleasant, dream; nightmare; **böses Wetter,** (i) bad, nasty, weather; (ii) *Min:* choke-damp; **böses Gewitter,** bad thunder-storm; **böser Zufall,** unfortunate coincidence; **gute Miene zum bösen Spiel machen,** to make the best of a bad job, of a bad bargain; to put a brave face on things; **das ist eine böse Sache, eine böse Geschichte,** that's a bad business; *Iron:* this is a nice state of affairs; **die böse Sieben,** unlucky seven; (*c*) wicked, malicious, vicious; **eine böse Zunge,** a wicked, malicious, spiteful, venomous, an evil, tongue; **böse Zungen zum Schweigen bringen,** to silence evil, wagging, tongues; **ein böses Weib,** a malicious woman; *F:* **eine böse Sieben,** a shrew (of a woman), a scold, a termagant, a virago; **ein böser Hund,** a vicious dog; **es ist kein böser Wille dabei,** there's no malice in it, attached to it; *Jur:* **in böser Absicht,** with malice aforethought, with, of, through, malice prepense; maliciously; with malicious intent; (*in nursery language*) **der böse Tisch,** the naughty table; *adv.* **(es ist) nicht b. gemeint,** no harm (is) intended; **ihm wurde b. mitgespielt,** he was shabbily, scurvily, treated. **2.** angry; annoyed, cross, *F:* mad; offended; **b. werden,** to become, get, angry; **j-n b. machen,** to make, get, s.o. angry, *F:* mad; **man hört nie ein böses Wort,** one never hears a cross word; **j-m böse Worte geben,** to say hard things to s.o.; **er war b., daß sie ihnen nicht geholfen hatte;** he was angry, annoyed, that she had not helped them; **er sieht sehr b. aus,** he looks very angry; **der Vorfall hat viel böses Blut gemacht,** the incident has caused, created, much ill-feeling, bad blood; **j-m b. sein,** to be angry, cross, with s.o.; **(mit) j-m b. sein,** to be offended with s.o.; *F:* to be out, *U.S:* at outs, with s.o.; **sei mir nicht b.!** don't be cross with me, *F:* mad at me; **auf j-n b. sein,** to be annoyed, cross, with s.o.; **er ist b. auf mich, weil ich zu spät gekommen bin,** he is cross with me for being late; **sie sind sich b.,** they are on bad terms, at loggerheads, with one another. **3.** bad, nasty, sore; **böser Husten,** bad, nasty, cough; **eine böse Erkältung haben,** to have a bad cold; **sie hat einen bösen Finger,** she has a bad, sore, poisoned, finger; **böse Wunde,** bad, nasty, wound; **böse Geschwulst,** malignant tumour; **böses Fieber,** virulent fever; **das sieht b. aus,** that looks bad, nasty, angry; *Med: A:* **böser Kopf,** favus, scald-head, crusted ringworm, honey-comb ringworm; *A:* **das böse Wesen, Weh, Übel,** epilepsy, *A:* the falling sickness; *A:* **böse Säfte,** peccant humours.
II. **Böse,** *m., f.* (*decl. as adj.*) (*a*) wicked, evil, person; evil-doer; impious, ungodly, person; (*of child*) **das ist ein ganzer Böser,** he is a wicked, nasty, little devil; (*b*) **der Böse,** the Evil One, the Devil.
III. **Böse,** *n.* (*decl. as adj.*) evil; harm; ill; **das B. in der Welt,** the evil in the world; **er denkt sich nichts Böses dabei,** (i) he means no harm by it; he means nothing nasty by it; (ii) he sees nothing wrong in it; **Böses tun,** to do evil; **j-m Böses tun,** to do s.o. harm; **j-m alles Böse wünschen,** to wish s.o. ill, evil, harm; **ich wünsche ihm nichts Böses,** I wish him no harm; **diese Rede wird nur Böses verursachen,** this speech will only cause harm; **j-m Böses nachreden,** to speak ill of s.o., to run s.o. down; **Böses muß man mit Bösem bekämpfen,** desperate cases require desperate remedies.
Bösewicht, *m.* rogue, rascal, scoundrel, villain; evil-doer; wicked, evil, person; *Th: etc:* villain (of the piece); *F:* **du kleiner B.!** you little scamp, you little rascal!
bösgläubig, *a. Jur:* (purchaser, etc.) in bad faith; mala fide (purchaser, etc.).
Bösgläubigkeit, *f. Jur:* bad faith, mala fides.
boshaft, *a.* **1.** wicked, evil. **2.** spiteful, ill-natured, unkind; malicious; **eine boshafte Bemerkung,** a malicious, unkind, spiteful, nasty, remark; **boshaftes Vergnügen,** malicious pleasure.
Boshaftigkeit, *f.* **1.** spite, spitefulness; unkindness; **alle, seine ganze, B. an j-m auslassen,** to vent one's spite, spleen, on s.o. **2.** = **Bosheit** 2.
Bosheit, *f.* **1.** wickedness, depravity, evilness, badness; malignity; malignance; spite, spitefulness; unkindness; ill-nature; **voller B. sein,** to be full of wickedness; **aus reiner B.,** out of pure, sheer, spite, malice. **2.** (piece of) malice; malicious act; **er hat mir allerlei Bosheiten gesagt,** he said all manner of unkind things to me; **er hat immer ein paar Bosheiten bereit,** he is always ready with a gibe or a sneer; he always has a few nasty tricks up his sleeve.
Boskett [bosˈkɛt], *n.* **-(e)s/-e,** thicket, shrubbery, grove; bosk(et).

böslich, *a. & adv.* (*a*) *A:*=böse; (*b*) *Jur:* j-n b. verlassen, to desert s.o. wilfully, without cause.

Bösling, *m.* -(e)s/-e. *Austrian Dial:* female hemp (plant).

bösmeinend, *a.* ill-meaning, -intentioned; *adv.* maliciously.

Bosnickel, *m.* -s/-. *Austrian Dial:* malicious, spiteful, devil.

Bosnien ['bosniən]. *Pr.n.n.* -s. *Geog:* Bosnia.

Bosnier ['bosniər], *m.* -s/-. Bosnian.

bosnisch ['bosniʃ], *a.* Bosnian, Bosniac.

Boson ['bo:zon], *n.* -s/-en [bo·'zo:nən]. *Atom.Ph:* boson.

Bosporus, der ['bospo·rus]. *Pr.n.* -. *Geog:* the Bosp(h)orus.

Bossage [bo'sa:ʒə], *f.* -/-n. *Arch:* rustication, rustic-work; bossage (of building-stone).

Bossageeckstein, *m.* *Arch:* rusticated quoin.

Bosse, *f.* -/-n. 1. (*a*) *Sculp:* roughed-out, blocked-out figure; **in Bossen stehen lassen**, to leave (sth.) blocked out, in sketch; (*b*)=**Bossenquader**. 2. (*a*) *Arch:* boss; (*b*) *Arm:* umbo (of shield); boss (on shield).

Boße, *m.* -n/-n & *f.* -/-n. *Dial:* bundle of flax, of straw.

Bossel, *f.* -/-n. *Games:* (*form of*) bowl.

Bosselei, *f.* -/-en, small job; fiddling job.

bosselieren [bosə'li:rən], *v.tr. Sculp: etc:* to shape, to mould; to emboss.

Bosselkugel, *f.*=**Bossel**.

bosseln[1], *v.i.* (*haben*) *Games: North G.Dial:* (i) to play (at) bowls; (ii) *approx.*=to curl.

bosseln[2], *v.i.* (*haben*) to do small, odd, jobs.

bosseln[3], *v.tr.*=**bossieren**.

boßeln. 1. *v.tr.* to bundle (flax). 2. *v.i.* (*haben*)=**bosseln**[1].

Bossenquader, Bossenstein, *m.* rusticated stone; hammer-dressed, rock faced, pitch-faced, building-stone.

Bossenwerk, *n.* *Arch:* rustication, rustic work; bossage (of building-stone).

Boßhammer, *m.* *Tls:*=**Bossierhammer** (*a*).

Bossierarbeit [bo'si:r-], *f.* (*a*) moulding; modelling; embossing; (*b*) embossed work; (*c*) *Sculp:* embossment; relief, relievo.

Bossiereisen, *n.* (*a*) *Sculp:* embossing-iron, boaster, roughing-chisel; (*b*) *Stonew:* point(er).

bossieren [bo'si:rən]. I. *v.tr.* (*a*) *Sculp:* (**etwas in Wachs**) **b.**, to shape, mould (sth. in wax); to rough-hew, block-out, rough-in (statue); (*b*) *Stonew:* to dress, shape, square (building-stone); to rusticate (stonework); **bossiert**, hammer-dressed, rock-faced, pitch-faced; rusticated. II. *vbl s.* **Bossieren** *n.*, **Bossierung** *f.* *in vbl senses; also: Arch:* bossage (of building-stone); rustication.

Bossierhammer, *m.* *Tls:* (*a*) stonemason's hammer; (*b*) bush-hammer.

Bossierholz, *n.* *Tls: Sculp:* (wooden) modelling tool.

Bossierwachs, *n.* *Sculp:* moulding wax.

Böst[1], *f.* -/-e. *Dial:*=**Zorn**.

Böst[2], *n.* -/. *Dial:*=**Verlust**.

Boston ['bostən]. 1. *m.* -s/-s. *Danc:* Boston. 2. *n.* -s/-s. *Cards:* boston.

böswillig, *a.* malevolent, ill-willed; malicious; vicious; *Jur:* **böswillige Beschädigung**, malicious damage; **böswillige Absicht**, malice aforethought, malice prepense; **böswilliges Verlassen**, wilful, malicious, desertion, desertion without cause.

Böswilligkeit, *f.* malevolence, ill-will; maliciousness, malice (of debtor); viciousness.

bot *see* **bieten**.

Botanik [bo'ta:nik], *f.* -/. botany; **beschreibende B.**, descriptive botany, phytography.

Botaniker [bo'ta:nikər], *m.* -s/-, botanist, *A:* herbalist.

botanisch [bo'ta:niʃ], *a.* botanic(al); **botanische Exkursion**, botanizing excursion; *see also* **Garten**.

Botanisierausflug [bo·ta·ni·'zi:r-], *m.* botanizing excursion.

botanisieren [bo·ta·ni·'zi:rən], *v.i.* (*haben*) to botanize; **b. gehen**, to go botanizing; *Sch:* to go on a nature ramble.

Botanisiertrommel, *f.* (botanist's) vasculum.

Botanybai ['botəni·bai]. *Pr.n.f.* -. *Geog:* Botany Bay.

Botanybaigummi, *m.*=**Akaroidharz**.

Botarga [bo'targa], *f.* -/. *Cu:* botargo.

Bötchen, *n.* -s/-. (*dim. of* **Boot**) *F:* small pleasure steamer; motor boat.

Bote, *m.* -n/-n. 1. (*a*) messenger; courier; bearer; *Dial:* postman; commissionaire; carrier, carter (of goods); *A:* apparitor; *A:* **reitender B.**, estafette, courier, mounted messenger; **einen Brief durch Boten schicken**, to send a letter by

hand; *Journ:* (*as name of newspaper*) (the) Messenger; **der hinkende B.**, (i) bearer, bringer, of evil tidings, ill news; (ii) bad news; trouble; **alles ist richtig, aber der hinkende B. kommt nach**, everything is as it should be, but trouble is on the way; (*b*) *A. & Lit:* ambassador; emissary; deputy; apostle; angel; *B:* **die Boten des Friedens**, the ambassadors of peace; **ein B. Gottes**, a messenger from God; an angel of the Lord; **die Boten Christi**, (i) the Apostles (of Christ); (ii) the missionaries of Christ; **Amalie, B. des Himmels**; Amalia, angel of Heaven; **j-n als B. schicken**, to send s.o. as (an) emissary, as a deputy. 2. *Lit:* herald; **die Lerche, der B. des Morgens**, the lark, the herald of the morn; **die Boten des Todes**, the signs of death.

böte *see* **bieten**.

Bötel, *m.* -s/-. *North G.Dial:* *Husb:* wether.

Botendienst, *m.* (*a*) messenger service; (*b*) j-m **Botendienste leisten**, to carry messages for s.o.

Botenfrau, *f.* messenger(-woman).

Botengang, *m.* errand; message; **Botengänge besorgen, machen**, to run errands, messages.

Botengänger, *m.* messenger.

Botenlohn, *m.* (*a*) messenger's fee; delivery fee; porterage; (*b*) reward for bringing good news.

Botenmädchen, *n.* messenger girl; errand-girl.

Botenstab, *m.* (*a*) messenger's sign of office; (*b*)=**Botschaftstab**.

Botin, *f.* -/-innen, (female) messenger; **Iris, die B. der Götter**, Iris, the messenger of the gods; *cp.* **Bote**.

Botkude [bo·to·'ku:də], *m.* -n/-n. *Ethn:* Botocudo.

Botmäßig, *a.* in subjection; tributary; **j-m b. sein**, to be in subjection to s.o., to be under s.o.'s dominion; **die Juden wurden den Römern b. gemacht**, the Jews were made tributaries of the Romans.

Botmäßigkeit, *f.* (imperial) rule; dominion; sway; **unter der B. eines Tyrannen**, under the rule, sway, of a tyrant; **ein Volk unter seine B. bringen**, to bring a people under one's sway; to gain dominion over a people; **die Völker unter Roms B.**, peoples under the sway of Rome.

Botschaft, *f.* -/-en. 1. message; **frohe B.**, glad tidings; gospel; message; **B. ausrichten, bestellen**, to deliver, give, a message. 2. embassy; **die deutsche B. in London**, the German Embassy in London; **eine B. errichten**, to create, establish, an embassy.

Botschafter, *m.* -s/-, ambassador; (*within the British Commonwealth*) High Commissioner; **zum B. ernannt werden**, to be appointed ambassador; **der deutsche B. in Paris, in Frankreich**, the German Ambassador in Paris, to France; **der britische B. in Indien**, the British High Commissioner in India; *see also* **bevollmächtigen** III. (*a*).

Botschafterin, *f.* -/-innen, ambassadress.

Botschafterposten, *m.* ambassadorship; ambassadorial post, appointment.

Botschaftsrat, *m.* *Dipl:* counsellor.

Botschaftssekretär, *m.* *Dipl:* (first, second, third) secretary at an embassy.

Botschaftstab, *m.* (aborigines') message-stick

Böttcher, *m.* -s/-, cooper.

Böttcherarbeit, *f.* cooperage; coopery.

Böttcherbeil, *n.* *Tls:* cooper's adze.

Böttcherei, *f.* -/-en. 1. cooperage; coopery. 2. cooper's shop.

Böttcherhandwerk, *n.* cooperage.

Böttcherholz, *n.* wood for cooperage, cooper's wood.

Böttchermeister, *m.* master cooper.

Böttcherwerkstätte, *f.* cooper's workshop.

Böttcherzange, *f.* *Tchn:* cooper's dog.

Botte[1], *f.* -/-n=**Bütte** 1.

Botte[2], *f.* -/-n. *Dial:* boot.

Bottega [bo'te:ga], *f.* -/-s & -gen=**Bodega**.

Bottelier [botə'li:r], *m.* -s/-s. *Nau:* steward.

Botten[1] ['botən]. *Pr.n.n.* -s. *Geog:* Bothnia.

botten[2], *v.tr. Tex:* to brake (flax).

Böttgerporzellan, Böttgersteinzeug, *n.* *Cer:* Böttger ware.

Botthammer, *m.* *Tls:* bott-hammer.

Bottich, *m.* -s/-e, tub; wash-tub; *Brew: Wine-m:* tun, vat (for fermentation); *Ind:* tank, cistern; **ein B. voll**, a tubful, vatful.

Bötticher, *m.* -s/-,=**Böttcher**.

Bottichgeläger, *n.* *Brew:* tun sediment.

Bottichmantel, *m.* tun casing.

Bottine [bo'ti:nə], *f.* -/-n, (lady's) ankle-boot, bootee.

Bottler, *m.* -s/- =**Bottelier**.

Bottlerei, *f.* -/-en. *Nau:* steward's room, store-room; *Navy: A:* issuing room.

bottnisch, *a.* *Geog:* Bothnian; **der Bottnische Meerbusen**, the Gulf of Bothnia.

Botulismus [bo·tu·'lismus], *m.* -/. *Med: Vet:* botulism; *Vet:* **B. der Enten**, limber-neck.

Bouclé [bu·'kle:], *n.* -s/-s. *Tex:* knop-wool, bouclé wool.

Boudoir [bu·do·'a:r], *n.* -s/-s, boudoir, (lady's) sanctum.

Bouffon [bu'fõ:], *m.* -s/-s, buffoon.

Bouffonnerie [bufonə'ri:], *f.* -/-n [-'ri:ən], buffoonery.

Bougainvillee [bu·gẽ·vi·'le:ə], *f.* -/-n. *Bot:* bougainvillea.

Bougie [bu·'ʒi:], *f.* -/-s. *Surg:* bougie.

bougieren [bu·'ʒi:rən]. 1. *v.i.* (*haben*) *Surg:* to insert, introduce. a bougie into a passage of the body. 2. *vbl s.* **Bougieren**, *n.* bouginage.

Bouillabaisse [bu·ja'bɛs], *f.* -/-n [-sən]. *Cu:* Provençal fish-soup, bouillabaisse.

Bouilleur [bu·'jø:r], *m.* -s/-e, boiler.

Bouilleurkessel, *m.* *Mch:* French boiler.

Bouillon[1] [bu·'jõ:, bul'jõ:], *f.* -/-s. *Cu:* meat broth, clear (meat) soup.

Bouillon[2], *m.* -s/. *Tex:* bullion.

Bouillonkultur, *f.* *Biol:* culture medium; gelatine meat-broth.

Bouillontafel, *f.* *Cu:* soup tablet.

Bouillonwürfel, *m.* *Cu:* bouillon cube.

boukanieren [bu·ka·'ni:rən], *v.tr.* to smoke-dry, cure (meat).

Boulette [bu·'lɛta], *f.* -/-n=**Bulette**.

Boulevard [bu·lə'va:r], *m.* -s/-s, boulevard.

Boulevardpresse, *f. Pej:* gutter press.

Boulevardstück, *n. Pej:* low-life play.

Boullearbeit ['bu:l-], *f. Furn:* buhl, boulle, work.

Boullemöbel, *n. pl. Furn:* buhl, boulle, furniture.

Boulleschrank, *m. Furn:* buhl, boulle, cabinet.

Bouquet [bu·'kɛ], *n.* -s/-s =**Bukett**.

Bourbone [bu·r'bo:nə], *m.* -n/-n. *Hist:* Bourbon; **das Haus der Bourbonen**, the House of Bourbon.

bourbonisch [bu·r'bo:niʃ], *a.* Bourbonian (party, etc.); **bourbonische Nase**, Bourbon nose.

Bourbonist [bu·rbo·'nist], *m.* -en/-en. *Hist:* Bourbonist.

Bourdon [bu·r'dõ:], *m.* -s/-s. 1. palm-wine. 2.=**Bordun**.

Bourgeois[1] [burʒo·'a:], *m.* -/-, (*a*) middle-class person; (*b*) *F:* Philistine, bourgeois.

Bourgeois[2], *f.* -/.=**Borgis**.

Bourgeoisie [burʒo·a·'zi:], *f.* -/-n [-'zi:ən], middle-class; bourgeoisie.

Bourrette [bu·'rɛtə], *f.* -/. *Tex:* silk waste, floss silk.

Boussole [bu'so:lə], *f.* -/-n =**Bussole** (*a*).

Boutade [bu·'ta:də], *f.* -/-n. 1. whim, caprice. 2. (*a*) *A:* improvised ballet; (*b*) musical fantasy.

Bouterolle [bu·tə'rol], *f.* -/-n, slaughtering mask.

Boutique [bu·'ti:k], *f.* -/-n [-kəh], (fashion, etc.) boutique.

Bouton [bu·'tõ:], *m.* -s/-s, (*a*) *Bot:* bud; (*b*) (paste) button; button-shaped earring.

Boutonnière [bu·toni'ɛ:rə], *f.* -/-n. 1. buttonhole. 2. *Surg:* external urethrotomy.

Boviden [bo·'vi:dən], **Bovinen** [bo·'vi:nən], *pl.* *Z:* Bovidae, bovines.

Bovist ['bo:vist, bo·'vist], *m.* -(e)s/-e. *Fung:* puff-ball, fuzz-ball.

Bovovakzin [bo·vo·vak'tsi:n], *n.* *Vet:* bovo-vaccine.

Bowdenzug ['baudən-], *m.* *Mec.E:* Bowden cable.

Bowdenzugbremse, *f.* cable brake.

Bowiemesser ['bo:vi:-], *n.* *U.S:* bowie(-knife).

Bowle ['bo:lə], *f.* -/-n, (*a*) (*vessel*) bowl; (*b*) cold drink consisting of fruit *or* herbs, hock and champagne *or* soda-water, *U.S:* bowl; *see also* **ansetzen**.

Bowlengefäß, *n.* bowl.

Bowlenlöffel, *m.* ladle.

Bowlenterrine, *f.*=**Bowlengefäß**.

Bowstringhanf ['bo:striŋ-], *m.* *Bot:* afrikanischer B., African bowstring hemp.

Box [boks], *f.* -/-en, (*a*) *Phot:* box-camera; (*b*)=**Boxe**.

Boxball, *m.* punch-ball, *U.S:* punching bag.

Boxbeutel, *m.*=**Bocksbeutel**.

Boxbirne, *f.*=**Boxball**.

Boxcalf ['bokskalf], *n.* -s/-. *Leath:* boxcalf.

Boxe ['boksə], *f.* -/-n, (*a*) *Av:* blast-bay (for aircraft); *Navy:* submarine pen; *Aut:* lock-up (in a garage); (*in motor-racing*) pit; (*b*) loose box (in stable).

boxen ['boksən], (*a*) *v.i.* (*haben*) *Sp:* to box; **mit j-m b.**, to box, spar, with s.o.; (*b*) *v.tr.* to punch (s.o.).

Boxer[1] 'boksər, *m.* -s/-. 1. boxer; pugilist.

2. *Breed:* boxer (dog). 3. *Min:* (compressed air) rock-drill.
Boxer[2], *m.pl. Hist:* Boxers.
Boxerei [boksə'rai], *f.* -/-en, fight; brawl; *F:* set-to; fisticuffs.
Boxergage, *f. Box:* purse.
Boxermotor, *m. Mec. E:* engine with horizontally opposed cylinders.
Boxerohr, *n. Med:* cauliflower ear.
Boxfreund, *m.* boxing fan, patron of boxing.
Boxhandschuh, *m.* boxing-glove.
Boxkalf ['bokskalf], *n.* -s/- =**Boxcalf.**
Box-Kamera, *f. Phot:* box-camera.
Boxkampf, *m. Sp:* boxing-match, bout; **ein B. von fünfzehn Runden,** a fifteen-round contest.
Boxkunst, *f.* art, science, of boxing, the (noble) art of self-defence.
Boxmeisterschaften, *f.pl. Sp:* boxing championships.
Boxring, *m.* boxing-ring.
Boxschuh, *m.* boxing shoe.
Boxsport, *m. Sp:* boxing.
Boxstaffel, *f. Sp:* boxing team.
Boxverband, *m. Sp:* Boxing Association.
Boy[1] [boy], *m.* -s/-s, (*a*) hotel messenger, page-boy; *U.S:* bellboy, *F:* bellhop; (*b*) *Furn:* dumb-waiter; tea trolley, dinner-wagon.
Boy[2], *m.* -(e)s/-s =**Boi.**
Boykott [boy'kot], *m.* -s/-e, boycott.
boykottieren [boyko'ti:rən], *v.tr.* (*p.p.* **boykottiert**) to boycott (s.o., sth.).
Bozen ['bo:tsən]. *Pr.n.n.* -s. *Geog:* Bolzano.
Boz(z)etto [bo(·)'tsɛto:], *m.* -s/-ti. *Sculp:* sketch.
Brabant [bra·'bant]. *Pr.n.n.* -s. *Geog:* Brabant.
Brabanter [bra·'bantər]. 1. *m.* -s/-, (*a*) Brabantine; (*b*) *Hist:* mercenary (soldier), Brabanter; (*c*) *Breed:* Brabant horse. 2. *inv.a.* (*a*) *Geog:* Brabantine; (*b*) **B. Spitze,** Mechlin lace; *Bot:* **B. Myrte,** bog myrtle, sweet gale; *Lap:* **B. Rose,** Brabant rose.
brabantisch [bra·'bantiʃ], *a.* Brabantine.
brabbeln, *v.i.* (*haben*) to mumble.
brach[1] *see* **brechen.**
brach[2], *pred. a. Agr:* fallow, uncultivated, unploughed, untilled, waste; **b. liegen**=**brachliegen.**
Brachacker, *m.* fallow field, fallow; fallow-break.
Brachdistel, *f. Bot:* eryngium, field eringo.
Brache, *f.* -/-n. *Agr:* 1. fallow; (*a*) fallowing; **grüne B.** summer fallow; **schwarze B.,** bare fallow; **besömmerte B.,** green, cropped, fallow; (*b*) fallow field. 2.=**Brachzeit.**
Brachebearbeitung, *f. Agr:* fallowing, fallow.
brachen, *v.tr. Agr:* to plough up (fallow land), to fallow (land).
Brachet, *m.* -s/-e. *A. & Poet:* June.
Brachfeld, *n.*=**Brachacker.**
Brachflur, *f.* fallow land.
Brachhühnchen, *n. Orn:* golden plover.
brachial [bra·xi'a:l], *a.*, **Brachial-,** *comb.fm. Anat:* brachial.
Brachialgewalt, *f.* muscular strength, brute force.
Brachiopode [bra·xio·'po:də], *m.* -n/-n. *Moll:* brachiopod; **die Brachiopoden,** the brachiopoda, brachiopods.
Brachistochrone [bra·xi·sto·'kro:nə], *f.* -/-n. *Mth:* brachistochrone.
Brachjahr, *n.* 1. *Jew. Hist:* sabbatical year. 2. *Agr:* year in which the land lies fallow.
Brachkäfer, *m. Ent:* midsummer cockchafer.
Brachland, *n.* fallow land.
Brachläufer, *m. Orn:* meadow-lark, meadow-pipit.
Brachlerche, *f. Orn:* 1. skylark. 2.=**Brachpieper.**
brachliegen, *v.i. sep.* (*strong*) (*haben*) *Agr:* to lie fallow; **ein Feld b. lassen,** to let a field lie, rest, fallow, to leave a field uncultivated; to lay a field fallow; *F:* **brachliegende Geisteskräfte,** unexerted intellectual powers; mind that lies fallow.
Brachling, *m.* -s/-e=**Brachpilz.**
Brachmane [brax'ma:nə], *m.* -n/-n=**Brahmane.**
Brachmännchen, *n.*=**Brachpilz.**
Brachmonat, *m. A. & Poet:* June.
brachpflügen, *v.tr.sep. Agr:* to plough up, to fallow (land).
Brachpieper, *m. Orn:* tawny pipit.
Brachpilz, *m. Fung:* field mushroom.
Brachschwalbe, *f. Orn:* collared pratincole; **schwarzflügelige B.,** black-winged pratincole.
Brachse, *f.* -/-n, **Brachsen,** *m.* -s/-. *Ich:* bream.
brachte, brächte *see* **bringen.**
Brachvogel, *m. Orn:* curlew; **großer B.,** common curlew, *Scot:* (great) whaup; **kleiner B.,** lesser curlew, whimbrel; **dünnschnäbliger B.,** slender-billed curlew.
brachy-, Brachy- [braxy·-]. *comb.fm.* brachy-; **brachypodisch** [braxy·'po:diʃ], brachypodous; **Brachygraphie** [braxy·gra·'fi:] *f*, brachygraphy.
brachykephal [braxy·ke·'fa:l], *a.* =**brachyzephal.**
Brachylogie [braxy·lo·'gi:], *f.* -/. brachylogy.
brachyzephal [braxy·tse·'fa:l], *a. Anthr:* brachycephalic, brachycephalous.
Brachyzephale [braxy·tse·'fa:lə], *m., f.* -n/-n. *Anthr:* brachycephal.
Brachyzephalie [braxy·tse·fa·'li:], *f.* -/. brachycephaly, brachycephalism.
Brachzeit, *f.* fallowing season.
Brack[1], *n.* -(e)s/-e & -en. 1. *Com:* reject; *coll.* refuse, waste. 2. impure amber.
Brack[2], *n.* -(e)s/-en, young predatory animal.
brack[3], *a.*=**brackig.**
Bracke[1], *m.* -n/-n & *f.* -/-n, (*a*) *Breed:* hound; (*b*)=**Brack**[2].
Bracke[2], *f.* -/-n. *Veh:* splinter-bar.
bracken, *v.tr.* 1. *Com:* *etc:*=**ausbracken.** 2. *Husb:* to brake (flax).
Bracker, *m.* -s/-. *Com:* sorter (of goods), bracker.
Brackgut, *n. Com:* refuse, rubbish, rejects; *esp.* sub-standard (fur) skins.
Brackholz, *n.* decayed wood.
brackig, *a.* brackish (water).
brackisch, *a.* brackish (water); *Geol:* **brackische Bildung,** sedimentary rock *or* bed formed by brackish water.
Brackschafe, *n.pl. Husb:* sheep that have been rejected; culls.
Brackvieh, *n. Husb:* cattle that have been rejected; culls.
Brackwasser, *n.* brackish water.
Bradykardie [brady·kar'di:], *f.* -/. *Med:* bradycardia.
Brahma ['bra:ma:]. *Pr.n.m. & n.* -s. Brahma.
Brahmahuhn, *n. Husb:* brahma(pootra).
Brahmaismus [bra·ma·'ismus], *m.* -/. brahmanism.
Brahman ['bra:man]. *Pr.n.n.* -s. Brahma.
Brahmane [bra·'ma:nə], *m.* -n/-n, brahman.
brahmanisch [bra·'ma:niʃ], *a.* brahminic(al), brahmanee.
Brahmanismus [bra·ma·'nismus], *m.* -/. brahmanism.
Brahmaputra [bra·ma·'pu:tra:]. 1. *Pr.n.m.* -(s). *Geog:* Brahmaputra. 2. *n.* -(s)/-(s). *Husb:* brahma(pootra).
Brahmaputrahuhn, *n. Husb:* brahma(pootra).
Brailleschrift ['bra:jə-], *f.* braille.
Brakteat [brakte·'a:t], *m.* -en/-en. *Num:* bracteate coin.
Braktee [brak'te:ə], *f.* -/-n. *Bot:* bract.
Bram[1], *f.* -/-en & *m.* -s/-e. *Nau:* topgallant mast; **Bram-,** *comb.fm.* topgallant . . .; **Bramschote** *f,* topgallant sheet; **Bramstag** *n,* topgallant stay.
Bram[2], *m.* -s/. *Bot:* broom.
Bram[3], **Bräm,** *m.* -(e)s/-e =**Brame, Bräme.**
Bramarbas [bra·'marbas], *m.* -/-se, braggart.
bramarbasieren [bra·marba·'zi:rən], *v.i.* (*haben*) to brag.
Brame, Bräme, *f.* -/-n. 1. (*a*) hedge *or* bushes surrounding a field, etc.; brushwood on the edge of a forest; (*b*) fur trimming. 2. soot-mark.
Bramgut, *n. Nau:* topgallant gear.
Braminenweih [bra·'mi:nən-], *m. Orn:* brahminy kite.
Bramme, *f.* -/-n. *Metall:* slab (of iron).
Brammenschere, *f. Tls:* slab shears.
Bramrahe, *f. Nau:* topgallant yard.
Bramrahgast, *m. Nau:* topgallant yardman.
Bramsaling, *f. Nau:* topgallant cross-trees, topmast cross-trees.
Bramsegel, *m. Nau:* topgallant sail.
Bram(segel)tuch, *n. Nau:* duck (canvas), harding.
Bramstagsegel, *n. Nau:* topgallant staysail.
Bramstenge, *f. Nau:* topgallant mast.
Branche ['brã:ʃə], *f.* -/-n. 1. line (of business), trade; **in welcher B. ist er?** what is his line (of business)? **er ist in der chemischen B.,** he is in the chemical business. 2. *Com:* branch (of store, company, bank, etc.).
Branchenverzeichnis, *n. Tp:* classified directory.
Branchiaten [brançi'a:tən], *m.pl. Ich:* branchiata.
Branchien ['brançiən], *f.pl. Biol: Ich:* branchia, branchiae.
Branchiopoda [brançio·'po:da:], *pl. Crust:* branchiopoda.
Brand, *m.* -(e)s/=e. 1. (*a*) burning, fire, blaze; **ausgedehnter B.,** widespread fire; conflagration; **der B. der Sonne,** the burning of the sun, the scorching heat of the sun; **in B. geraten,** to catch fire; **in B. sein,** to be on fire, to be ablaze; **einen B. entfachen,** to kindle a fire; **ein Haus in B. stecken, setzen,** to set a house on fire, to set fire to a house; **nach B. riechen, schmecken,** to smell, taste, of burning; **ein Land, Dorf, mi Mord und B. verwüsten,** to lay a country, village, waste with fire and sword; *Mil:* **in B. schießen,** to set fire to (house, etc.) by gunfire; (*b*) fire; **der B. griff um sich,** the fire spread; (*c*) *Lit:* ardour (of love), fervour, flame (of love, wrath, etc.); **von einem inneren B. verzehrt,** consumed by a burning passion; (*d*) *F:* raging, unquenchable, thirst; **einen B. haben,** to be extremely thirsty, *F:* to be parched. 2. *Brickm: Cer:* (*a*) baking (of bricks); firing, kiln-drying, burning (of pottery, bricks); (*b*) baking, batch (of bricks, pots, etc.); **Töpfe von einem B.,** pots from one batch. 3. (*a*) *Metall:* refining (of gold, silver); (*b*) *Dist:* distilling, distillation (of fruit, etc.). 4. (*a*)=**Brandfackel;** (*b*) fuel. 5. *occ.* brand (on cattle, sheep, etc.); mark made by branding. 6. *Med:* gangrene; necrosis; mortification; sphacelation; **kalter, trockener, B.,** cold, dry, gangrene; **heißer, feuchter, B.,** hot, humid, gangrene. 7. *Agr: etc:* blight (of cereals, etc.), smut (of cereals); **von B. befallen,** blighted, (*of cereals*) smutted. 8. *Poet:* sword, *Poet:* brand.
Brand-, *comb.fm. cp.* **Feuer-.**
Brandbalsam, *m.*=**Brandsalbe.**
Brandbinde, *f. Surg:* special bandage for burns.
Brandblase, *f.* blister (caused by a burn).
Brandblättchen, *n.pl. Mil.Av:* incendiary leaves.
Brandbock, *m.* fire-dog, andiron.
Brandbombe, *f.* incendiary bomb, fire-bomb.
Brandbrief, *m.* 1. *A:* letter threatening arson. 2. (i) letter urgently demanding money; *F:* S.O.S. (for money); (ii) urgent demand for payment of a debt.
Branddirektor, *m. approx.*=chief fire officer, *U.S:* fire chief.
Brandeisen, *n.* branding iron.
branden. I. *v.i.* (*haben*) (*of waves, sea, etc.*) to foam, to break, to surge, to roar; **die Wellen branden schäumend ans Ufer,** the foaming waves break against the shore; **die brandende See,** the foaming sea; **der Beifall brandete um ihn,** roaring applause surrounded him; **die Angriffe des Feindes brandeten gegen unsere Stellung,** the enemy's attacks surged against our lines.
II. *vbl s.* 1. **Branden,** *n. in vbl senses.* 2. **Brandung,** *f.* (*a*)=II. 1; (*b*) surf; breakers; **tosende B.,** foaming surge, tumult, of the sea; **durch die B. schwimmen,** to swim through the breakers; **die B. der Begeisterung,** the waves of enthusiasm; (*c*) roar(ing) (of sea, organ music, etc.).
Brandenburg. *Pr.n.n.* -s. *Geog:* Brandenburg.
Brandenburger. 1. *m.* -s/-, native, inhabitant, of Brandenburg. 2. *inv.a.* of Brandenburg, Brandenburg . . .; **das B. Tor,** the Brandenburg Gate (in Berlin).
brandenburgisch, *a.* of Brandenburg, Brandenburg . . .; *Mus:* **die Brandenburgischen Konzerte,** the Brandenburg concertos.
Brandente, *f. Orn:* sheldrake, shelduck, shell-duck, sheld-duck.
Brander, *m.* -s/-. 1. *Naval Hist:* fire-ship. 2. *Ven:*=**Brandfuchs.**
Branderz, *n. Miner:* bituminous shale, idrialite.
Brandfackel, *f.* fire-brand, torch; **eine B. schleudern,** to hurl a fire-brand, *F:* **die B. des Krieges,** the torch of war.
Brandfleck(en), *m.* burn, mark of burning; scald; flaw (in china, pottery, etc.).
Brandfuchs, *m.* 1. *Z:* black fox. 2. burnt chestnut (horse).
Brandgans, *f. Orn:* (*a*)=**Brandente;** (*b*) **Neuseeländische B.,** paradise-duck.
Brandgasse, *f.* narrow lane between houses to prevent the spreading of fire.
brandgelb, *a.* reddish yellow.
Brandgeschoß, *n.* incendiary projectile, shell.
Brandgeschwür, *n. Med:* gangrenous ulcer.
Brandgetreide, *n. Agr:* blighted corn.
Brandglocke, *f.* fire-bell, tocsin.
Brandgold, *n.* refined gold.
Brandgrab, *n. Prehist: Archeol:* grave containing burial urn(s).
Brandgranate, *f. Artil:* incendiary shell.
Brandgutachten, *n. Ins:* expert's report on damage by fire.
Brandharz, *m.* empyreumatic resin.
Brandheide, *f. Bot:* heather, ling.
Brandherd, *m.* 1. source of fire. 2. (*in figurative usage*) storm-centre; source of all the trouble.
Brandhorn, *n. Moll:* murex.
brandig, *a.* 1. (smelling, tasting) of burning. 2. (*a*) *Med:* gangrenous, gangrened; sphacelated; mortified; **b. werden,** to sphacelate; to become gangrenous *or* mortified; (*b*) *Agr:* blighted, smutted.

Brandkasse, *f.* fire insurance association.
Brandkraut, *n. Bot:* phlomis, Jerusalem sage.
Brandkugel, *f. A.Mil:* carcass, fire-ball.
Brandlattich, *m. Bot:* coltsfoot.
Brandleder, *n. Bootm:* leather for insoles.
Brandlegung, *f. esp. Austrian Jur:* = **Brandstiftung.**
Brändlein, *n.* -s/. *Bot:* black nigritella, black orchis, satyrion.
Brandloch, *n.* **1.** hole made by burning. **2.** *Artil:* priming-hole, vent (of gun).
Brandmal, *n.* **1.** *(a)* = **Brandfleck**; *(b)* brand. **2.** (moral, etc.) stigma, blemish.
Brandmalerei, *f.* pyrography, pyrogravure, poker-work.
brandmarken. I. *v.tr. insep.* **1.** to brand (animal, slave). **2.** to brand (s.o.); to stigmatize (s.o., sth.); **als Schwindler gebrandmarkt sein,** to be branded as a swindler.
II. *vbl s.* **Brandmarken** *n.*, **Brandmarkung** *f. in vbl senses; also:* stigmatization.
Brandmauer, *f. Constr:* fire wall.
Brandmaus, *f. Z:* field-mouse.
Brandmeise, *f. Orn:* coal-titmouse.
Brandmeister, *m.* *(in fire service) approx.* = (i) sub-officer, *U.S:* lieutenant; (ii) station officer (in voluntary brigade).
Brandnarbe, *f.* scar from a burn.
Brandöl, *n.* empyreumatic oil.
Brandopfer, *n.* burnt-offering; holocaust.
Brandopferaltar, *m.* altar of the burnt-offering.
Brandpappe, *f. Paperm:* press-board, pressing board.
Brandpfeil, *m.* fire-arrow.
Brandpflaster, *n.* special plaster for burns.
Brandpilz, *m. Fung:* smut (fungus).
Brandprobe, *f.* fire test.
Brandrakete, *f.* incendiary rocket.
Brandrose, *f. Bot:* hollyhock, rose-mallow.
brandrot, *a.* fiery red.
Brandsalbe, *f. Pharm:* salve, ointment for burns.
Brandsatz, *m. Exp:* powder train.
Brandschaden, *m.* damage caused *or* loss suffered by fire.
brandschatzen. I. *v.tr. insep. Mil: Hist:* to lay (s.o., sth.) under contribution; to plunder, pillage.
II. *vbl s.* **1. Brandschatzen,** *n. in vbl senses.* **2. Brandschatzung,** *f.* *(a)* = II. 1; *(b)* forced contribution by the inhabitants of occupied territory.
Brandschiefer, *m. Geol:* bituminous shale, oil shale.
Brandschimmel, *m.* red-roan (horse).
Brandschlag, *m. Artil: A:* quick-match.
Brandschneise, *f. For:* fire-line, fire-break.
Brandschopf, *m. Bot:* celosia.
Brandschott, *n.* fire-proof bulkhead. fire-wall.
Brandschutt, *m.* charred ruins (of buildings, etc.).
Brandseeschwalbe, *f. Orn:* Sandwich tern; *(in N. & Central America)* Cabot's tern.
Brandsilber, *n.* refined silver.
Brandsohle, *f.* insole, inner sole (of shoe).
Brandstatt, Brandstätte, *f.* **1.** *(a)* scene of a fire; *(b)* charred ground (in wood, etc.); burnt-out ruins. **2.** *A:* hearth.
Brandstelle, *f.* *(a)* burnt patch, spot; burn; *(b)* = **Brandstätte.**
Brandstifter, *m.* incendiary, fire-raiser; *U.S:* fire-bug.
brandstifterisch, *a.* incendiary.
Brandstiftung, *f.* arson, incendiarism, fire-raising.
Brandteig, *m. Cu:* choux pastry.
Brandtür, *f.* fire-proof door (in fire-wall).
Brandung, *f. see* **branden** II.
Brandungsboot, *n. Nau:* surf-boat.
Brandungsreiten, *n.* surf-riding.
Brandwache, *f.* *(a)* fire-watch; fire-watching (duty); *(b)* fire-watcher(s).
Brandwirtschaft, *f. Agr:* burn-baiting, burn-beating.
brannte *see* **brennen.**
Branntwein, *m.* spirit(s), brandy.
Branntweinbrenner, *m.* distiller.
Branntweinbrennerei, *f.* **1.** distilling, distillation. **2.** distillery.
Branntweinwaage, *f.* alcoholometer.
Brasil [bra·ˈziːl], *f.* -/-. Brazil cigar.
Brasilettoholz [bra·zi·ˈlɛtoː-], *n. Com: Dy:* braziletto, Jamaica wood.
Brasilianer [bra·zi·li·ˈaːnər], *m.* -s/-. Brazilian.
brasilianisch [bra·zi·li·ˈaːniʃ], *a. Geog:* Brazilian.
Brasilien [bra·ˈziːliən]. *Pr.n.n.* -s. *Geog:* Brazil.
Brasilienholz, *n.* Brazil wood.
Brasilier [bra·ˈziːliər], *m.* -s/-. Brazilian.
brasilisch [bra·ˈziːliʃ], *a. Geog:* Brazilian.
Brasilkastanie, Brasilnuß, *f.* *(a)* Brazil-nut (tree); *(b)* Brazil nut.

Brasse[1], *f.* -/-n. *Nau:* brace.
Brasse[2], *f.* -/-n, **Brassen,** *m.* -s/-. *Ich:* bream.
brassen, *v.tr. Nau:* to brace; **beim Wind b.,** to haul, hug, the wind.
Bratapfel, *m. Cu:* baked apple.
braten[1], *v.tr.* *(strong, occ. weak)* **1.** *(in oven)* to roast, *(on fire or gridiron)* to broil; *(with water, etc.)* to braise; **auf dem Rost b.,** to grill; **am Spieß b.,** to roast on a spit; *U.S:* to barbecue; **in der Pfanne b.,** to fry in a frying-pan; **Äpfel b.,** to bake apples; **gar b.,** to roast, cook (meat) until tender; **gar gebraten,** well done; **Gebratenes** *n*, roast, fried. meat; **gebratenes Huhn,** roast chicken; *Prov:* **gebratene Tauben fliegen, eine gebratene Taube fliegt, keinem ins Maul,** nothing comes to you on a plate; *F:* **da brat' mir einer einen Storch!** well, I never! **2.** *v.i.* *(haben)* *(a)* to be cooked; to be roasted; to be grilled; *(of meat, potatoes, etc.)* to be fried; *(b)* *(of pers.)* **in der Sonne b.,** to sunbathe; to roast in the sun; **sich in der, von der, Sonne b. lassen,** to roast, tan, oneself, in the sun; **in der Hölle b.,** to roast in hell.
Braten[2], *m.* -s/-, roast; joint; **den B. begießen,** to baste the meat; *F:* **den B. riechen,** (i) to sense sth. in the air; (ii) to smell a rat; *see also* **fett**[1].
Bratenfett, *n.* dripping.
Bratensaft, *m. Cu:* juice (of roast meat).
Bratensoße, *f.* gravy.
Bratenwender, *m.* roasting-jack.
Bräter, *m.* -s/-, iron casserole.
Bratfett, *n.* cooking fat.
Bratfisch, *m. Cu:* fried fish.
Bratfrischarbeit, *f. Metalw:* roasting, refining.
Brathering, *m. Cu:* (i) grilled herring preserved in vinegar; (ii) fried *or* grilled herring; (iii) fresh herring (for grilling).
Brathuhn, *n. Cu:* roaster, roasting fowl; broiler, broiling fowl.
Bratkartoffeln, *f.pl. Cu:* (i) fried potatoes; (ii) *(done in the oven or in a casserole)* roast potatoes; (iii) *(in their jackets)* baked potatoes.
Bratling, *m.* -s/-e. *Cu:* (made-up) cutlet; rissole.
Brätling, *m.* -s/-e. **1.** *Fung:* agaric; **grüner B.,** green agaric. **2.** *Ich:* sprat.
Bratofen, *m.* (kitchen) oven.
Bratpfanne, *f.* frying-pan.
Bratrost, *m.* broiler; grid(iron); grill.
Bratsche [ˈbraːtʃə], *f.* -/-n. *Mus:* viola, tenor violin.
Bratschist [bra·ˈtʃist], *m.* -en/-en, viola player.
Bratspieß, *m. Cu:* spit, broach.
Bratspill, *n. Nau:* winch, windlass.
Bratwurst, *f. Cu:* sausage (for frying); bratwurst; **geräucherte B.,** smoked cooking sausage.
Bratwürstchen, *n. Cu:* sausage (for frying).
Bräu, *m. & n.* -(e)s/. **1.** *(a)* gyle, brew; *(b)* beer. **2.** brewery.
Brauch, *m.* -(e)s/⸚e. **1.** *(a)* usage, custom; **nach altem B.,** (i) according to an old custom; (ii) as usual; *(b)* practice. **2.** *A:* use.
brauchbar, *a.* **1.** useful (pers., thg); *(of pers.)* capable, able; suitable. **2.** *(of thg)* serviceable; *(of clothes)* fit for use, wearable.
Brauchbarkeit, *f.* usefulness; suitability.
brauchen, *v.tr.* **1.** = **gebrauchen. 2. er brauchte drei Jahre, um es zu schreiben,** he took three years to write it; **er wird zwei Stunden (dazu) b.,** it will take him two hours; **wie lange braucht man, um . . .?** how long does it take to . . .? **hast du aber lange gebraucht!** what a time you have been! **3.** *(a)* to need, to want (sth., s.o.); **er braucht dringend Geld,** he needs money urgently; **ich brauche dich,** I want, need, you; **ich brauche die Schuhe sehr nötig,** I need the shoes very badly; **der Boden braucht Regen,** the soil needs rain; **unser Land braucht mehr Bergarbeiter,** our country needs more miners; **ich brauche dringend Hilfe,** I am in great need of help; **wir brauchen Zeit,** we need time; *(b)* *v. impers.* (+*gen.*) **es braucht keiner weiteren Beweise,** there is no need for further proof. **4.** (+*inf. with* **zu**) *(a)* to need, to have (to do sth.); **Sie brauchen es nur zu sagen,** you only have to say so, you need only say so; **das braucht niemand zu wissen,** no one need know this; **du brauchst nicht zu schreiben,** you don't have to write, don't trouble to write; **ich gäbe viel darum, wenn ich nicht hinzugehen brauchte,** I would give a lot not to have to go; *(b)* *(used as negation of* **müssen)** **darauf braucht man nicht stolz zu sein,** this is nothing to be proud of; **ich brauchte nicht daran erinnert zu werden,** I did not need to be reminded of it; **wir brauchen das nicht erst zu überlegen,** we need not think about it at all.

brauchgemäß, *a.* according to custom.
Brauchtum, *n.* -s/. custom; tradition; folklore.
brauen, *v.* **1.** *v.tr.* *(a)* to brew (beer, etc.); *(b)* *F:* **Unheil b.,** to brew mischief; **die Wiesen, die Berge, brauen Nebel,** mist is hanging over the meadows, the mountains. **2.** *v.i.* *(haben)* *(of haze, etc.)* to rise; **der Nebel braut,** the mist is rising, thickening.
Brauer, *m.* -s/-, brewer.
Brauerei, *f.* -/-en. **1.** brewery. **2.** brewing, beer-making, brewery.
Brauereibetrieb, *m.* brewery.
Brauereifach, *n.* brewing business; **er ist im B.,** he is in the brewing business.
Brauereigenossenschaft, *f.* = **Braugenossenschaft.**
Brauereigewerbe, *n.* brewing industry.
Brauereipferd, *n.* dray-horse.
Brauergilde, *f.* brewers' guild.
Brauerinnung, *f.* brewers' guild.
Braugenossenschaft, *f.* brewers' co-operative.
Braugerechtigkeit, *f. Hist:* right, privilege, of brewing.
Braugerste, *f.* barley (used for brewing).
Brauhaus, *n.* brewery.
Braumeister, *m.* master brewer.
braun. 1. *a.* brown; **(von der Sonne) b. werden,** to get tanned; **ein Brauner,** (i) a bay (horse); (ii) *Austrian:* a cup of coffee with a dash of milk. **2.** *s.* **Braun,** *n.* -(s), *(a)* (the colour) brown; *(b)* *Lit: & F:* **(Meister) Braun,** Bruin; Mr Bear.
Braunalgen, *f.pl.* fission algae.
braunäugig, *a.* brown-eyed.
Braunbär, *m. Z:* brown bear.
Braunbleierz, *n. Miner:* pyromorphite.
Braunbleioxyd, *n.* plattnerite.
Braunbrustschilffink, *m. Orn:* chestnut-breasted finch.
Bräune, *f.* -/. **1.** brown colour; (sun) tan. **2.** *Med: F:* *(a)* diphtheria; *(b)* angina pectoris.
Brauneisenerz, *n.*, **Brauneisenstein,** *m. Miner:* brown iron ore, brown hematite, limonite.
Braunelle [brauˈnɛlə], *f.* -/-n. **1.** *Bot:* *(a)* prunella, self-heal; *(b)* burnet, bloodwort; *(c)* common bugle. **2.** *Orn:* accentor; hedge accentor, hedge-sparrow, shuffle-wing, dunnock; **Sibirische B.,** mountain accentor.
bräunen, *v.* **1.** *v.tr.* *(a)* to make brown; to darken; to dye brown; to bronze; *(of sun)* to tan; *(b)* *Cu:* to brown (flour, onions, etc.); **Zucker b.,** to make caramel. **2.** *v.i.* *(haben)* to brown, to become brown; **sich (von der Sonne) b. lassen,** to get oneself tanned; to sunbathe.
Braunfäule, *f. Agr:* brown rot.
Braunfisch, *m. Z:* porpoise; *F:* sea-hog.
braungefleckt, *a.* speckled, mottled, with brown; brindled (cow).
Braunheil, *n. Bot:* prunella, self-heal.
Braunheu, *n. Agr:* brown hay.
Braunholz, *n.* **1.** = **Brasilienholz. 2.** Japan wood.
Braunholzpapier, *n. Paperm:* nature-brown(s).
Braunholzschliff, *m. Paperm:* leather board pulp, brown mechanical pulp.
Braunit [brauˈniːt], *m.* -(e)s/-e. *Miner:* braunite.
Braunkehlammer, *f. & m. Orn:* red-headed bunting.
Braunkehlchen, *n. Orn:* whinchat.
Braunkohl, *m. Hort: Cu:* curly kale, green kale; Scotch kale; borecole.
Braunkohle, *f. Miner:* brown coal, lignite.
Braunkohlenbrikett, *n.* brown-coal briquette.
Braunkohlenfeld, *n.* field of lignite.
Braunkohlenformation, *f. Geol:* tertiary system containing lignite.
Braunkohlengrube, *f. Min:* brown-coal quarry.
Braunkohlenlager, *n.* lignite bed, deposit.
Braunkohlenschicht, *f.* band of lignite.
Braunkohlenteer, *m.* lignite tar.
Braunkopfammer, *f., occ. m. Orn:* red-headed bunting.
bräunlich, *a.* brownish.
Braunmaina, *m. Orn:* jungle mynah.
braunrot, *a.* brownish-red; *(of horse)* bay.
Braunsch, *a. Radar: TV:* **Braunsche Röhre,** cathode ray tube.
braunscheckig, *a.* brown mottled, brown flecked; brown piebald (horse); brindled (cow).
Braunschliff, *m. Paperm:* = **Braunholzschliff.**
Braunschnäpper, *m.* -s/-. *Orn:* brown fly-catcher.
Braunschweig. *Pr.n.n.* -s. *Geog:* Brunswick.
Braunschweiger. 1. *m.* -s/-, native, inhabitant, of Brunswick. **2.** *inv.a.* of Brunswick; **B. Grün,** Brunswick green.
braunschweigisch, *a.* (of) Brunswick.
Braunsilge, *f. Bot:* basil, sweet basil.
Braunspat, *m. Miner:* brown spar.
Braunstein, *m. Miner:* pyrolusite.

Braunsteinkiesel, *m. Miner:* spessartite, spessartine.
Braunsteinrahm, *m. Miner:* bog manganese.
Braunwurz, *f. Bot:* **1.** scrophularia, figwort. **2.** = **Braunelle** 1 (*a*).
Braus, *m.* **-es/.** *see* **Saus.**
Brausche, *f.* **-/-n,** bruise, swelling.
brauschen, *v.i.* (*haben*) to neigh, to snort.
Brause, *f.* **-/-n. 1.** (*a*) rose, sprinkler, spray-, sprinkling-nozzle (of watering can, etc.); shower (in bathroom); (*b*) shower-bath; shower. **2.** *F:* mineral water; fizzy lemonade, etc., *F:* pop.
Brausebad, *n.* shower(-bath).
Brausehahn, *m. Orn:* sandpiper.
Brausekopf, *m.* **1.** = **Brause** 1 (*a*). **2.** *F:* impetuous person.
brausen. I. *v.* **1.** *v.i.* (*haben*) (*of liquid*) to bubble, to effervesce; **brausende Flüssigkeit,** effervescent liquid. **2.** *v.i.* (*a*) (*haben*) (*of wind, water, etc.*) to roar; **die Orgel brauste,** the organ thundered; **es braust mir in den Ohren,** there is a buzzing in my ears; **mit brausendem Beifall,** with roaring applause; (*b*) (*sein*) (*of car, train, motor-cycle, etc.*) to roar; **der Zug brauste durch die Nacht,** the train roared, thundered, through the night. **3.** (*a*) *v.tr.* to spray, to water; (*b*) *v.i.* (*haben*) to have a shower(-bath).
II. *vbl s.* **Brausen,** *n. in vbl senses; also:* (*a*) effervescence; (*b*) **das mächtige B. der Orgel,** the mighty swell of the organ; *B:* **ein B. vom Himmel,** (a sound from heaven, as of) a rushing, mighty wind.
Brausepulver, *n.* sherbet powder; *Pharm:* **(abführendes, englisches) B.,** Seidlitz powder.
Brausewind, *m.* **1.** blast, violent wind. **2.** *F:* reckless, unruly, young person.
Braut, *f.* **-/⸗e. 1.** fiancée, bride-to-be; *A. & Lit:* betrothed. **2.** (*on wedding-day*) bride; **B. und Bräutigam,** bride and bridegroom; **B. Christi,** bride of Christ. **3.** *Bot:* **B. in Haaren,** fennel-flower, love-in-the-mist, devil-in-the-bush.
Brautbett, *n.* wedding bed, marriage bed; bridal bed; *Lit:* nuptial couch.
Brautente, *f. Orn:* summer-duck.
Brautexamen, *n. R.C.Ch:* (priest's) interview with a couple about to be married.
Brautführer, *m.* bride's (male) attendant.
Brautgabe, *f.* young man's present to his fiancée.
Brautgemach, *n.* bridal chamber.
Brautgeschenk, *n.* fiancé's *or* fiancée's present; *usu.pl.* **Brautgeschenke,** presents exchanged by an engaged couple.
Bräutigam, *m.* **-s/-e. 1.** fiancé; *A. & Lit:* betrothed. **2.** (*on wedding-day*) bridegroom; **himmlischer B.,** heavenly bridegroom.
Brautjungfer, *f.* bridesmaid; **erste B.,** chief bridesmaid.
Brautkind, *n. Jur:* child born to an engaged couple.
Brautkleid, *n.* wedding-dress.
Brautkranz, *m.* bridal wreath (*in Germany, myrtle; in England, orange blossom*).
Brautkrone, *f.* bridal crown.
Brautleute, *pl.* **1.** engaged couple. **2.** bride and bridegroom (at wedding).
bräutlich, *a.* bridal; nuptial.
Brautmädchen, *n.* = **Brautjungfer.**
Brautmesse, *f. Ecc:* nuptial mass.
Brautnacht, *f.* wedding night.
Brautpaar, *n.* bridal pair, newly married couple.
Brautraub, *m.* abduction of the bride.
Brautring, *m.* (*a*) engagement ring; (*b*) wedding-ring.
Brautschatz, *m. A:* dowry, dower.
Brautschau, *f.* **auf (die) B. gehen,** to look out for, go in quest of, a wife.
Brautschleier, *m.* bridal veil.
Brautschmuck, *m.* **1.** bridal array. **2.** bride's jewellery.
Brautstaat, *m.* bridal array.
Brautstand, *m.* state of betrothal; state of being engaged.
Brautsuche, *f.* **ein junger Mann auf B.,** a young man looking for, in search of, a wife.
Brautunterricht, *m. R.C.Ch:* instruction of those about to marry.
Brautwerber, *m.* match-maker; go-between; (*professional*) marriage-broker.
Brautwerbung, *f.* (*a*) courting, wooing; (*b*) matchmaking.
Brautzeit, *f.* (time of) engagement.
Brautzug, *m.* bridal procession.
brav. 1. *a.* (*a*) brave; **der brave Soldat,** the brave soldier; *Nau:* **brave Westwinde,** brave westerlies; (*b*) worthy, honest, good; **ein braver Mann,** an honest man; **er hat eine brave Frau,** he has a good, loyal, wife; **das Mädchen sieht so b. aus,** she looks such a good little girl; (*c*) good, well-behaved; **ein braves Kind,** a well-behaved child; **sei hübsch b.,** be good; **das war b. von dir!** well done! there's a good child. **2.** *adv.* (*a*) bravely; **er hat sich b. gehalten,** he acted bravely, showed courage; (*b*) **geht b. spielen,** go and play like good children; **nun mußt du b. ins Bett gehen,** be a good child and go to bed.
bravo[1] ['bra:vo:], *int.* **1.** bravo! well done! **b. rufen,** to shout bravo; to cheer. **2.** *s.* **Bravo,** *n.* **-s/-s,** loud cheer; bravo.
Bravo[2], *m.* **-s/-s & -vi,** bravo, assassin.
Bravoruf, *m.* cheer.
Bravour [bra·'vu:r], *f.* **-/.** (*a*) bravado, courage, gusto; (*b*) brilliance.
Bravourarie [bra·'vu:rˀ,a:riə], *f.* bravura aria.
Bravourstück, *n.* **1.** act of daring. **2.** piece of music played, sung, with bravura.
Breccie ['brɛtʃə, 'brɛktsiə], *f.* **-/-n** = **Brekzie.**
Brechanlage, *f. Cokem: etc:* crushing-plant.
Brecharznei, *f. Pharm:* emetic.
brechbar, *a.* breakable; *Ph: Opt:* refrangible.
Brechbarkeit, *f.* breakability; *Ph: Opt:* refrangibility.
Brechbohne, *f. Cu:* French bean.
Brechdurchfall, *m. Med:* cholera nostras.
Breche, *f.* **-/-n.** *Tex:* brake, breaker (for flax, hemp).
Brecheisen, *n.* = **Brechstange.**
brechen. I. *v.tr.* (*strong*) to break. **1.** (*a*) to break (sth.) (into pieces); to crush (coke, stones); to quarry (stones); to cut (coal); **Brot b.,** to break bread into pieces, *B:* to break bread; (*b*) **sich** *dat.* **das Bein, den Arm, einen Knochen, b.,** to break, fracture, one's leg, one's arm, a bone; **sich, j-m, den Hals, das Genick, b.,** to break one's, s.o.'s, neck; (*c*) to pick, pluck, *Lit:* to cull (flowers, fruit, etc.); to break (off) (branches); (*d*) **für j-n, etwas, eine Lanze b.,** to defend s.o., sth., to champion s.o.'s cause, the cause of sth.; **den Stab über j-n b.,** (i) *Hist:* (*of judge*) to pass sentence of death on s.o.; to put on the black cap; (ii) to condemn s.o. utterly; **eine Sache übers Knie b.,** to rush a thing, to do sth. hastily; **einen Streit vom Zaun b.,** to pick a quarrel. **2.** (*a*) to break (open) (seal); (*b*) to fold (sheet of paper); (*c*) *Agr:* to break (the soil), to turn (the earth); (*d*) (*occ. weak*) *Tex:* to break (flax, hemp). **3.** (*a*) **seine Ketten b.,** to break one's chains; (*of waves, etc.*) **den Damm b.,** to damage, break, breach, the dike; **das Eis b.,** to break the ice; *Prov:* **Not bricht Eisen,** needs must when the devil drives; *see also* **Blockade 1;** (*b*) **j-s Widerstand b.,** to break (down) s.o.'s resistance; **j-s Stolz b.,** to break s.o.'s pride; (*c*) (*of age, illness, etc.*) to break (s.o.); **sie sah ganz gebrochen aus,** she looked completely broken; (*of pers., grief, etc.*) **j-m das Herz b.,** to break s.o.'s heart; (*d*) to break (the law, the peace, a promise, the silence, rules, etc.); **die Ehe b.,** to commit adultery; **der Bann war gebrochen,** the spell was broken; (*e*) **den Rekord b.,** to beat, break, the record. **4.** (*a*) *Ph: Opt:* to refract, bend (rays, etc.); **gebrochen werden,** to be refracted, to suffer refraction; (*b*) to break (the force of) sth.; (*of dike, etc.*) **die Gewalt der Wellen b.,** to break the force of the waves. **5.** to break, make (a path); *see also* **Bahn 1. 6.** to vomit (blood, gall, etc.).
II. **brechen,** *v.i.* (*strong*) **1.** (*sein*) (*a*) to break, get broken; (*of bones*) to break, to fracture; **in Stücke b.,** to break into pieces; *Prov:* **der Krug geht so lange zu Wasser, bis er bricht,** the pitcher goes so often to the well that it is broken at last; the pitcher goes once too often to the well; **Glück und Glas, wie bald bricht das,** happiness is brittle stuff; (*b*) (*of voice*) (i) to break; (ii) to break, falter (with emotion); (*of eyes*) to become glazed (in death); **mit gebrochener Stimme,** with a broken voice; **sein brechendes Auge,** his dying eye; **das Herz bricht mir vor Kummer,** my heart is breaking with sorrow, sorrow is breaking my heart; (*c*) **das Wetter bricht,** the weather is breaking, is changing; **die Kälte ist gebrochen,** the frost has broken; (*d*) **die Geduld bricht mir,** my patience is exhausted; **ihr Widerstand brach,** her resistance broke down. **2.** (*sein*) (*of silk, etc.*) to split; (*of leather, plaster, etc.*) to crack. **3.** (*haben*) (*a*) **mit j-m b.,** to break (off), to fall out, with s.o.; **mit der Tradition b.,** to break the, with, tradition; **mit seinem früheren Leben b.,** to break away from one's old life; **mit einer Gewohnheit b.,** to break oneself of a habit; **mit dem Herkömmlichen b.,** to break with, away from, tradition; (*b*) *Box:* to break (away); **brechen!** break! **4.** (*sein*) (*a*) (*of pers., animal, etc.*) **durch etwas b.,** to break through sth.; **durch die feindlichen Scharen b.,** to break through the enemy's ranks; **die Sonne bricht durch die Wolken, durch die Zweige,** the sun breaks through the clouds, shines through the branches; (*b*) **in ein Haus b.,** to break into a house. **5.** (*haben*) *F:* to be sick, to vomit.
III. **sich brechen. 1.** (*a*) *Ph: Opt:* (*of rays, etc.*) to be refracted; (*b*) (*of echo, etc.*) to be broken; **die Wellen brachen sich an den Felsen,** the force of the waves was broken by the rocks; **der Wind brach sich an der hohen Mauer,** the high wall broke the force of the wind. **2.** *F:* to be sick, to vomit.
IV. *vbl s.* **1. Brechen,** *n. in vbl senses; also:* **zum B. voll,** full to bursting point; *see also* **biegen** II. 1. **2. Brechung,** *f.* (*a*) *Ph: Opt:* refraction (of rays, etc.); **doppelte B.,** double refraction; (*b*) *Ling:* fracture (of vowel). *Cp.* **Bruch.**
V. *pr.p. & a.* **brechend,** *in vbl senses; esp.* **der Saal war b. voll,** the hall was bursting, was full to capacity; *F:* was packed out; **es war b. voll gestern abend,** there was a tremendous crowd last night.
VI. *p.p. & a.* **gebrochen,** *in vbl senses; esp.* (*a*) *Mth: etc:* broken (line, etc.); fractional (number, etc.); *Geol:* faulted (fault); *Ch:* **gebrochene Destillation,** fractional distillation; *Mus:* **gebrochener Akkord,** broken chord, arpeggio; *Pal: Print:* **gebrochene Schrift** = **Bruchschrift;** (*b*) **in gebrochenem Deutsch,** in broken German; *adv.* **g. Englisch sprechen,** to speak broken English; (*c*) stricken (by fate, grief, etc.); **vom Alter g.,** broken down with age; **ein gebrochener Mann,** a broken man; **gebrochenen Herzens, mit gebrochenem Herzen,** broken-hearted, heartbroken; **an gebrochenem Herzen sterben,** to die of a broken heart, to die broken-hearted.
Brecher, *m.* **-s/-. 1.** *Nau:* breaker. **2.** = **Wellenbrecher. 3.** breaking machine, breaker; crushing machine, crusher. **4.** child who is teething.
-brecher, *comb.fm. m.* **-s/-. 1.** breaker of . . ., violator of . . .; **Friedensbrecher,** breaker of the peace. **2.** -breaker; **Eisbrecher,** ice-breaker.
Brecherbse, *f. Hort:* edible-podded pea, sugar pea.
Brechhammer, *m. Tls:* (stoneworker's) sledge-hammer.
Brechhaselkraut, *n. Bot:* asarabacca, hazelwort.
Brechklaue, *f. Tls:* claw; crowbar.
Brechkoks, *m.* cut coke, crushed coke.
Brechkörner, *n.pl. Pharm:* castor beans.
Brechmaschine, *f.* breaking-machine.
Brechmittel, *n. Pharm:* emetic; *F:* **er ist ein richtiges B.,** he is enough to make one sick.
Brechnuß, *f. Bot: Pharm:* **1.** nux vomica, vomit-nut. **2.** physic-nut.
Brechnußbaum, *m. Bot:* nux vomica tree, vomit-nut tree.
Brechpulver, *n. Pharm:* emetic.
Brechreiz, *m. Med:* nausea.
Brechrollen, *f.pl. Cokem: etc:* crushing rolls.
Brechstange, *f. Tls:* **1.** crowbar; case-opener. **2.** (burglar's) jemmy, *U.S:* jimmy.
Brechung, *f. see* **brechen IV.**
Brechungsebene, *f. Ph: Opt:* plane of refraction.
Brechungsexponent, *m.* = **Brechungsindex.**
Brechungsgesetz, *n. Ph: Opt:* law of refraction.
Brechungsindex, *m.,* **Brechungsverhältnis,** *n. Ph: Opt:* refractive index, index of refraction.
Brechungswinkel, *m. Ph: Opt:* angle of refraction.
Brechwalzwerk, *n. Min: etc:* crusher (for ore, etc.); crushing mill.
Brechwein, *m. Pharm:* antimonial wine; wine of antimony.
Brechweinstein, *m. Ch: Pharm:* tartar emetic; tartarated antimony.
Brechwurz, *m. Bot:* **1.** (*a*) ipecacuanha; (*b*) fever-root, bastard ipecac, horse-gentian. **2.** false, green, white, hellebore. **3.** = **Brechhaselkraut.**
Brechwurzel, *f. Bot:* **1.** ipecacuanha, wild ipecac. **2.** (*a*) ionidium, green violet; (*b*) white ipecacuanha, new ipecac. **3.** = **Brechwurz. 4.** black bryony, lady's seal.
Brechzahl, *f.* = **Brechungsindex.**
Bredouille [bre·'duljə], *f.* **-/.** *F:* **in der B. sein,** to be in a scrape.
Bregen, *m.* **-s/-,** brain; *esp. Cu:* brains.
Brei, *m.* **-(e)s/-e,** paste; pulp; mash; (*of snow*) slush; *Cu:* pap (for babies); (invalids') gruel; purée; (*made of oatmeal*) porridge; (semolina, rice, etc.) pudding; **Wasser und Mehl zu einem glatten B. anrühren,** to mix flour and water to a smooth paste; **zu B. kochen,** to overcook, to pulp (potatoes, etc.); *F:* **wie die Katze um den heißen B. gehen,** to beat about the bush; *Prov:* **viele Köche verderben den B.,** too many cooks

spoil the broth; *P:* **j-n zu B. schlagen,** to beat s.o. to a pulp, to pound s.o. to a jelly.

Breiapfel, *m. Bot:* (*a*) naseberry, sapodilla; (*b*) marmalade-tree, -plum.

Breiapfelbaum, *m. Bot:* (*a*) naseberry, sapodilla; (*b*) marmalade-tree.

breiartig, *a.*=**breiig.**

Breifaß, *n. Paperm:* pulp-vat.

breiig, *a.* pulpy, pasty, pulpous; semiliquid; (*of snow*) slushy; **breiige Nahrung,** food in purée form; strained food.

breit. 1. *a.* (*a*) broad, wide; **einen Finger, eine Hand, b.,** a finger's, a hand's, breadth; **die Straße ist zehn Meter b.,** the road is ten metres wide; **vier Meter lang und zwei Meter b.,** four metres long and two metres wide, broad, four metres by two; **der Stoff liegt 90 Zentimeter b.,** the material is 90 centimetres wide; **eine breite Feder,** a broad nib; **der breite Fluß,** the wide river; **der Fluß ist 100 Meter b.,** the river is a 100 meters wide, across; **mit breitem Gesicht,** broad-faced; **eine breite Stirn,** a broad forehead; **ein breites Lachen,** a fat laugh; **er ist so b. wie lang,** he is as broad as he is tall; **er hat einen breiten Rücken, Buckel,** (i) he has a broad back, (ii) *F:* he can take it; **eine Untersuchung auf breiter Grundlage durchführen,** to make a broadly-based investigation; **die Schuhe b. treten,** to make one's shoes sloppy with wear; **Metall b. schlagen,** to flatten metal; **das Brett einen halben Meter b. machen,** to make the board half a metre wide; **etwas breiter machen,** to widen, to broaden, sth.; *see also* **breitmachen, breitschlagen, breittreten;** (*b*) **eine breite Darstellung,** a long-winded description; **einen breiten Stil haben,** to have a prolix style; (*c*) **die breite Masse des Volkes,** the broad, great, mass of the people; the general public; **breite Schichten der Bevölkerung, des Volkes,** large sections of the population, of the people; the bulk of the population; (*d*) **ein breiter Dialekt,** (a) broad dialect. **2.** *adv.* (*a*) **groß und b.,** clearly; **da steht es groß und b.,** there it is for all to see; (*b*) **weit und b.,** far and wide; **sie ist weit und b. bekannt,** she is known everywhere; (*c*) **etwas b. erzählen,** to tell a story in great detail, to spin out a tale; **j-m etwas lang und b. erklären,** to explain sth. to s.o. at great length; (*d*) **b. grinsen,** to grin broadly.

Breitbeil, *n. Tls:* broad axe; chip-axe.

breitbeinig, *a. & adv.* with legs apart; **b. dastehen,** to stand sturdily; **b. gehen,** to straddle, to roll; **er stellte sich b. vor mich hin,** he came and stood squarely before me.

breitblättrig, *a.* broad-leaved; *Bot:* latifoliate.

Breite, *f.* **-/-n. 1.** (*a*) breadth, width; *Tls:* width (of cutting tool, etc.); **die Tür hat eine B. von einem Meter,** the door is one metre wide; **das Feld mißt 20 Meter der B. nach, in der B.,** the field measures 20 metres across; **etwas der B. nach legen, ausmessen,** to lay, measure, sth. breadthways, breadthwise, broadwise; **der Fußweg hat eine B. von 2 Metern,** the footpath is 2 metres in width; **die B. eines Zimmers,** the width of a room; **zu dem Rock brauche ich zwei-mal die B. (des Stoffes),** I need two widths of the material for the skirt; **die B. der Schultern,** the breadth of the shoulders; **um eines Fingers B.,** by a finger's breadth; *see also* **Haar** 1; *F:* **in die B. gehen, wachsen,** to put on weight, to grow broad; *Hort:* **einen Baum in die B. ziehen,** to train the branches of a tree horizontally; **die B. der Grundlage,** the broadness of the basis (of an investigation, etc.); (*b*) *N.Arch:* breadth, beam (of a ship); **größte B.,** extreme breadth, extreme beam; (*c*) longwindedness, prolixity (of speech, style, etc.); **epische B.,** epic breadth; (*d*) *A. & Lit:* expanse; breadth (of outlook, etc.). **2.** (*a*) *Geog: Nau:* latitude; **in nördlichen Breiten,** in northern latitudes; **30° nördlicher B.,** latitude 30° north; (*b*) *Astr:* (celestial) latitude.

Breiteisen, *n. Tls:* (mason's) broad tool; brick chisel, drove (chisel); boaster.

Breitengrad, *m. Geog:* degree of latitude; parallel; **der dreißigste B.,** the thirtieth parallel.

Breitenkreis, *m. Geog:* parallel (of latitude).

breitflossig, *a. Ich:* broad-finned.

breitfüßig, *a.* broad-, splay-footed.

Breitfußschiene, *f. Rail:* flat-bottom rail.

breitgestirnt, *a.* with a broad brow.

breitgetakelt, *a. Nau:* square-rigged.

Breithacke, *f. Tls:* mattock, grubbing-hoe.

Breithalter, *m. Tex:* temple, tenter, tension-frame.

Breithammer, *m. Tls:* (blacksmith's) sledge (-hammer).

Breithaue, *f.*=**Breithacke.**

breithörnig, *a. Z:* broad-horned.

breithufig, *a. Z:* broad-hoofed.

breithüftig, *a.* broad-hipped.

breitkrempig, *a.* broad-brimmed (hat).

Breitleinwand, *f. Cin:* wide screen.

Breitling, *m.* **-s/-e. 1.** *Ich:* sprat. **2.** *Fung:*=**Brätling.**

breitmachen (sich), *v.refl. sep.* (i) to spread oneself, to take up room; (ii) to intrude and make oneself at home; **mach dich nicht so breit mit deinen Büchern,** don't take up so much room with your books.

Breitnasen, die. *Z:* the platy(r)rhina, the platy(r)-rhines.

breitnasig, *a.* (*a*) broad-, flat-nosed; (*b*) *Z:* platy(r)rhine (ape, monkey).

Breitsaat, *f. Agr:* **1.** broadcast-sowing, broad-casting. **2.** broadcast-seed(s).

Breitsämaschine, *f. Agr:* broadcast sowing-machine.

Breitsame, *m. Bot:* **1.** orlaya. **2.** daucus grandi-florus.

breitschlagen, *v.tr. sep.* (*strong*) *F:* **j-n b.,** to persuade s.o.; **j-n b., etwas zu tun,** to persuade s.o. to do sth., to talk s.o. into doing sth.; **ich ließ mich (dazu) b., mit ihnen zu gehen,** I let my-self be talked into going with them.

Breitschnabel, *m. Orn:* shoveller (duck).

Breitschnabelfliegenschnäpper, *m. Orn:* brown fly-catcher.

breitschultrig, *a.* broad-shouldered.

Breitschwanz, *m.* **1.** *Z:* broadtail, astrak(h)an. **2.** *Orn:*=**Breitschwanzlori.**

Breitschwanzlori, *m. Orn:* broadtail (parrot).

Breitschwanzmöwe, *f. Orn:* pomarine skua.

Breitseite, *f.* long side, broad side; *Nau:* broad-side.

Breitspur, *f. Rail:* broad gauge.

breitspurig, *a.* (*a*) *Rail:* broad-gauge (line, etc.); (*b*) *F:* pompous; imperious.

breitstirnig, *a.* with a broad forehead, broad-browed.

breittreten, *v.tr. sep.* (*strong*) **etwas b.,** (i) to dwell on sth. excessively, to labour a point (in argument); (ii) to spread sth. abroad; **breit-getreten sein,** (i) (*of subject, etc.*) to be hackneyed, to be discussed ad infinitum; (ii) (*of rumour, etc.*) to be in everybody's mouth.

Breitwand, *f. Cin:* wide screen.

Breitwandfilm, *m. Cin:* wide-screen film.

Breitwandprojektion, *f. Cin:* wide-screen projec-tion.

Breitwandverfahren, *n. Cin:* wide-screen process.

Breitwandvorsatz, *m. Cin:* anamorphic lens attachment.

breitzehig, *a. Z:* platydactylous.

breitzinnenförmig, *a. Her:* dovetailed (dividing line, etc.).

Breiumschlag, *m. Med:* cataplasm, poultice.

Brekzie [ˈbrɛktsĭə], *f.* **-/-n.** *Geol:* breccia.

Breme, *f.* **-/-n** =**Bremse**[1].

Bremen. *Pr.n.n.* **-s.** *Geog:* Bremen.

Bremer. 1. *m.* **-s/-.** *Geog:* inhabitant, native, of Bremen. **2.** *inv.a.* of Bremen, Bremen . . .; (*title of fairy-tale*) **die Bremer Stadtmusikanten,** the town band of Bremen.

Bremerblau, *n.* Bremen blue, water blue.

Bremergrün, *n.* Bremen green, malachite green.

bremisch, *a.* of Bremen, Bremen . . .

Brems-, *comb.fm. Aut: Rail: etc:* brake-, brake . . .; **Bremsfutter** *n,* brake-lining; **Bremskette** *f,* brake-chain; *Atom.Ph:* slowing-down . . ., moderating . . .; **Bremsfläche** *f,* slowing-down area.

Bremsausgleich. *m. Aut:* (brake) compensator.

Bremsbacken, *m. Veh:* brake-shoe.

Bremsband, *n. Aut: etc:* brake-band.

Bremsbelag, *m. Aut: etc:* brake-lining; **den B. erneuern,** to re-line the brakes.

Bremsberg, *m. Rail:* braking incline.

Bremsdichte, *f. Atom.Ph:* slowing-down density.

Bremse[1], *f.* **-/-n.** *Ent:* (*a*) gad-fly; breeze; horse-fly; cleg; (*b*) oestrus; bot(t)-fly, warble-fly.

Bremse[2], *f.* **-/-n. 1.** brake; *Aut:* **die B. anziehen,** to set, put on, apply, the (hand-)brake; **die B. lösen,** to take off the (hand-)brake. **2.** *Vet:* barnacles.

bremsen. I. **1.** *v.i.* (*haben*) *Aut: etc:* to brake, to put on the brakes. **2.** *v.tr.* (*a*) *Aut: etc:* to stop, halt (vehicle); (*b*) *Atom.Ph:* to slow down, moderate (particles); (*c*) **j-s Übermut b.,** to curb s.o.'s exuberance; (*d*) **glaubst du, daß er hingeht? — er wird sich b.,** do you think he'll go?—no fear! not likely! there's no fear of that!

II. *vbl s.* **1. Bremsen,** *n. in vbl senses.* **2. Bremsung,** *f.*=II. 1; *also: Atom.Ph:* modera-tion (of particles).

Bremsen(larven)schwindel, *m. Vet:* staggers.

Bremser, *m.* **-s/-.** *Rail:* brakesman, *U.S:* brake-man.

Bremserhaus, Bremserhäuschen, *n. Rail:* brakes-man's compartment (in goods wagon).

Bremsfallschirm, *m. Av:* braking parachute.

Bremsfliege, *f.*=**Bremse**[1].

Bremsfußhebel, *m. Aut:* brake pedal.

Bremsgestänge, *n. Veh:* (system of) brake-rods.

Bremsgitter, *n. El:* suppressor grid.

Bremshebel, *m.* brake lever.

Bremskern, *m. Atom.Ph:* slowing-down kernel.

Bremsklappe, *f. Av:* brake-flap.

Bremsklotz, *m. Veh: Rail: etc:* brake-block; *Av:* wheel chock.

Bremslänge, *f. Rail: etc:* braking distance; *Atom.Ph:* slowing-down length.

Bremsleistung, *f. Aut:* brake horse-power; *Rail:* braking efficiency.

Bremsleuchte, *f.,* **Bremslicht,** *n. Aut:* brake light, stop light.

Bremslüfter, *m.* brake magnet.

Bremsmittel, *n. Atom.Ph:* moderator, moderating material.

Bremsnutzung, *f. Atom.Ph:* resonance escape probability.

Bremspedal, *n. Aut:* brake pedal.

Bremspfeiler, *m. Hyd.E:* baffle pier.

Bremspferdestärke, *f. Mec:* brake horse-power.

Bremsprüfung, *f. Rail: Aut:* brake test.

Bremsrad, *n.* braking-wheel.

Bremsrakete, *f. Rocketry:* brake rocket.

Bremsschuh, *m. Veh: Aut:* brake-shoe.

bremssicher, *a. Rail: etc:* with reliable braking; *Aut:* skid-proof (tyre).

Bremssicherheit, *f.* brake-efficiency; *Aut:* skid resistance (of tyre).

Bremsspindel, *f.* brake-spindle, brake-screw.

Bremsspur, *f. Aut: etc:* skid mark (due to heavy braking).

Bremsstrahlung, *f. Ph: Atom.Ph:* bremsstrahlung.

Bremsträger, *m. Veh:* brake back-plate.

Bremstrommel, *f.* brake-drum.

Bremsverhältnis, *n. Atom.Ph:* moderating ratio.

Bremsvermögen, *n. Atom.Ph:* moderating power, slowing-down power.

Bremswagen, *m. Rail:* brake-van; guard's van; *U.S:* caboose.

Bremsweg, *m. Aut: etc:* braking distance.

Brenke, *f.* **-/-n.** *Brew:* yeast-tub.

Brennapparat, *m.* **1.** *Ch: Ind:* distilling appara-tus, still. **2.** instrument for cauterization. **3.** burner used for poker-work.

brennbar, *a.* burnable; *Ch: etc:* combustible; (in)flammable; burnable.

Brennbarkeit, *f.* combustibility; (in)flammability; (in)flammableness.

Brennblase, *f.*=**Brennkolben.**

Brennbock, *m. Tex:* small crabbing machine.

Brenndauer, *f.* burning time (*El:* of lamp, bulb; *Exp:* of fuse); *El:* **Birne mit langer B.,** long-burning bulb.

Brennebene, *f. Opt:* focal plane.

Brenneisen, *n.* **1.** branding iron; *Surg:* (i) (actual) cautery; (ii) thermo-cautery. **2.** curling-tongs, curling-irons.

brennen. (*p.t.* **brannte,** *p.p.* **gebrannt**) I. *v.i.* (*haben*) **1.** to burn; (*a*) **das Feuer brennt im Ofen,** the fire is burning in the hearth; **das ganze Dorf brannte,** the whole village was burning, was on fire, was in flames; **es brennt,** there is a fire; *F:* **wo brennt's denn?** what's your hurry? what's the matter? *F:* where's the fire? **der Himmel brennt von der untergehenden Sonne,** the sky is aglow with the setting sun; (*b*) **das Holz, der Ofen, brennt gut,** the wood, the stove, burns well; **die Zigarette, das Streichholz, brennt nicht,** the cigarette isn't alight, the match won't strike; **die neue Pfeife brennt gut,** the new pipe smokes nicely; (*c*) **die Kerzen brennen,** the candles are burning, are lit; **die Straßenlampen brannten schon,** the street lamps were already lit; **eine hell brennende Lampe,** a bright light; **im Haus brannten alle Lichter,** all the lights were on in the house; **bitte, laß das Licht nicht b.,** please do not leave the light on; (*d*) **die Liebe brannte in ihm, er brannte vor Liebe,** he was aflame with love; **vor Neid und Haß b.,** to burn with envy and hate; **mein Herz brennt,** my heart is burning; **darauf b., etwas zu tun,** to burn to do sth., to be burning to do sth.; to be all agog to do sth.; (*e*) (*of wound, etc.*) to smart, burn; (*of extremities*) to tingle; **meine Fingerspitzen b. (vor Kälte),** my finger-tips are tingling with cold; *F:* **es brennt mir auf den Nägeln,** I just can't wait; I can hardly contain myself; I am all agog; (*f*) **Pfeffer brennt auf**

der Zunge, pepper burns, bites, the tongue. **2.** (*a*) **die Sonne brennt,** the sun is burning; *F:* **die Sonne brennt ihm auf den Pelz,** the sun is scorching him; (*b*) **die feindlichen Scharen brennen und morden,** the enemy hosts are burning and murdering.

II. **brennen,** *v.tr.* **1.** (*a*) to burn (coal, wood, peat, etc.); (*b*) to use, burn (gas, electricity); **viel Licht b.,** to use a lot of electricity; (*c*) **Kohlen (aus Holz) b.,** to burn charcoal. **2.** to distil (fruit, pitch, tar, etc.); **Wein b.,** to make, distil, brandy; **gebrannte Wasser,** distilled liquors; spirits. **3.** *Metall:* (*a*) to anneal (metal); (*b*) to refine (silver, etc.); *F:* **j-n weiß b.,** to purify s.o. (of sins); to clear s.o. (of suspicion). **4.** to roast (coffee, etc.); **gebrannte Mandeln,** sugared roasted almonds. **5.** to burn (bricks, lime, etc.); to bake (bricks, pottery, etc.); to kiln (pottery); to fire (pots, etc.); to burn, calcine (gypsum, ore); **gebrannte Erde,** terra-cotta. **6. das Haar b.,** to curl one's hair with curling tongs. **7.** (*a*) to brand (animals, cork, etc.); (*b*) *F:* **j-m eins auf den Pelz, aufs Fell, b.,** to singe s.o.'s hide. **8.** *Med:* to cauterize (wound). **9.** *Nau:* to bream (ship). **10.** (*a*) (*of reproach, contempt, etc.*) **j-n b.,** to rankle in s.o.'s mind, in s.o.'s heart; **der Vorwurf brannte sie,** the reproach rankled with her; (*b*) **es brennt mich auf den Nägeln** = **es brennt mir auf den Nägeln,** *q.v. under* I. 1 (*d*). **11.** *A:* **sich brennen,** to burn, scald, oneself; *Prov:* **(ein) gebranntes Kind scheut das Feuer,** a burnt child dreads the fire; once bitten, twice shy.

III. *vbl s.* **Brennen,** *n. in vbl senses; also:* (*a*) distillation; (*b*) *Ch: Ind:* calcination; (*c*) *Med:* cauterization. *Cp.* **Brand.**

IV. *pr.p. & a.* **brennend,** *in vbl senses; esp.* **1. ein brennender Wunsch,** a fervent desire; **brennende Liebe,** (i) ardent love, (ii) *Bot:* scarlet lychnis; *B:* **der brennende Busch,** the burning bush; *Bot:* **brennender Busch,** (i) burning bush; (ii) evergreen thorn, pyracanth, Egyptian thorn; **brennender Durst,** parching thirst; **eine brennende Frage,** an urgent, a burning, question. **2.** *adv.* **etwas b. wünschen,** to desire sth. passionately, to have a burning desire for sth.; **etwas b. nötig haben,** to be in dire need of sth.; **er tut das b. gern,** he is always eager to do this; he loves doing this.

Brenner[1], *m.* **-s/-.** **1.** (*pers.*) distiller. **2.** (*a*) (*fixture*) burner; (*b*) (*apparatus*) burner; (*c*) *Tls:* (cutting *or* welding) blowpipe *or* torch. **3.** *Vit:* blight; **schwarzer B.,** anthracnose; black spot. **4.** *Ent:* anthonomus.

Brenner[2], **der.** *Pr.n.* **-s.** *Geog:* the Brenner (Pass).

Brennerei, *f.* **-/-en.** **1.** distillery. **2.** distilling.

Brennereianlage, *f.* distilling plant.

Brennessel, *f. Bot:* stinging nettle.

Brennfläche, *f. Opt: Geom:* caustic surface.

Brennfleck, *m. X Rays:* focal spot.

Brenngas, *n.* burnable, combustible, gas; *I.C.E: etc:* fuel gas, gas-fuel.

Brenngemisch, *n. I.C.E:* combustible mixture.

Brenngerste, *f.* barley for distilling purposes.

Brennglas, *n.* burning glass.

Brenngut, *n.* **1.** burning material; fuel. **2.** distilling materials.

Brennhaar, *n.* stinging hair, sting (on stinging nettle, etc.).

Brennherd, *m.* **1.** hearth. **2.** *Metall:* furnace, *esp.* refining furnace.

Brennheu, *n.* = **Braunheu.**

Brennholz, *n.* firewood.

Brennkapsel, *f. Cer: Metall:* saggar.

Brennkegel, *m. Cer: etc:* pyrometric cone; sentinel pyrometer; Seger cone.

Brennkolben, *m. Ch:* still; *A:* alembic.

Brennkraft, *f.* heating power; calorific power.

Brennkraftmaschine, *f.* internal combustion engine.

Brennkraut, *n. Bot:* crowfoot; virgin's bower.

Brennlinie, *f. Opt:* caustic (curve).

Brennlinse, *f.* (*a*) convex lens; (*b*) = **Brennglas.**

Brennmalerei, *f.* = **Brandmalerei.**

Brennmaterial, *n.* fuel.

Brennmeister, *m.* **1.** chief distiller. **2.** foreman (brick-, lime-)burner.

Brennmittel, *n.* burning agent; corrosive (agent); *Ch: Med:* caustic.

Brennofen, *m. Ind: Metall: etc:* furnace; *Ind:* calciner; roasting furnace; *Brickm: Cer:* kiln.

Brennöl, *n.* fuel oil, oil-fuel.

Brennpalme, *f. Bot:* toddy palm; caryota palm.

Brennpflanzen, *f.pl.* stinging plants.

Brennprobe, *f. Tex:* burning test.

Brennpunkt, *m.* **1.** (*a*) *Geom: Ph:* focus, focal point; (*b*) *Aer:* aerodynamic centre. **2. im B. der Ereignisse, des Interesses, stehen,** to be the focal point of events, the focus of interest; **B. des Verkehrs,** converging point of traffic. **3.** *Ph:* fire point (of combustible matter).

Brennreizker, *m. Fung:* edible agaric.

Brennschere, *f.* curling-tongs, curling-irons.

Brennschluß, *m. Rocketry:* burn-out.

Brennschlußgeschwindigkeit, *f. Rocketry:* burn-out velocity, burnt velocity.

Brennschneiden, *n. Ind:* flame cutting, gas cutting.

Brennschwindung, *f. Cer:* shrinkage (during firing process).

Brennspannung, *f. Rad.-A:* trigger voltage (in radiation detector).

Brennspiegel, *m. Ph: etc:* concave mirror, burning mirror.

Brennspiritus, *m.* methylated spirit; denatured alcohol.

Brennstahl, *m.* blister steel.

Brennstoff, *m.* **1.** fuel; **fester, flüssiger, B.,** solid, liquid, fuel. **2.** *A.Ch:* phlogiston.

Brennstoffverbrauch, *m.* fuel consumption.

Brennstrahl, *m. Opt:* focal ray.

Brennstunde, *f. El.Meas:* lamp-hour.

Brennweite, *f. Opt:* focal length, focal distance.

Brennwert, *m.* calorific value, heat value.

Brennwurz, *f. Bot:* **1.** (*a*) spurge laurel; (*b*) mezereon, spurge olive. **2.** (*a*) creeping climber, (sweet) virgin's bower; (*b*) white climber, upright virgin's bower. **3.** devil-in-the-bush, fennel flower; black cumin.

Brennzeit, *f.* burning time; *cp.* **Brenndauer.**

Brennziegel, *m.* **1.** fire-brick. **2.** *Fuel:* briquette.

Brennzone, *f.* firing zone (of furnace, kiln).

Brennzünder, *m. Exp: Mil:* combustion time-fuse.

Brennzylinder, *m. Pharm:* moxa (cylinder).

Brenz, *m.* **-es/-e.** **1.** empyreuma, 'burnt' smell (*of certain organic substances*). **2.** *pl.* **Brenze,** inflammable minerals; inflammables; combustibles.

Brenz-, *comb.fm.* (*in chemical and pharmaceutical nomenclature usu.*) pyro-.

Brenzapfelsäure, *f. Ch:* maleic acid.

brenzeln, *v.i.* (*haben*) to smell, taste, of burning.

Brenzessiggeist, *m. Ch:* acetone.

Brenzgallussäure, *f. Ch:* pyrogallic acid; *Phot: F:* pyro.

Brenzharz, *n.* empyreumatic resin.

brenzholzsauer, *a. Ch:* combined with pyroligneous acid.

Brenzholzsäure, *f. Ch:* pyroligneous acid.

Brenzkatechin, *n. Ch: Phot:* pyrocatechin.

brenzlich, brenzlig, *a.* (*a*) burnt (smell, taste); **brenzlicher, brenzliger, Geruch,** (i) burnt smell, (ii) smell of burning; *adv.* **es riecht b.,** it smells of burning; (*b*) dangerous (matter); precarious (situation); **eine brenzliche, brenzlige, Angelegenheit,** a dangerous matter; a matter of touch-and-go; (*c*) *Ch:* empyreumatic.

Brenzöl, *n.* empyreumatic oil.

Brenzsäure, *f. Ch:* pyro-acid.

Brenzweinsäure, *f. Ch:* pyrotartaric acid.

Bresche, *f.* **-/-n,** breach, gap; **eine B. legen, schlagen, schießen,** to make a breach (in sth.); **eine B. in die feindlichen Linien schlagen,** to make a breach in the enemy's lines; **für j-n in die B. springen, treten,** to fill the breach for s.o., to help s.o. out of a tight corner.

bresthaft, *a. A. & Lit:* frail, weak, feeble.

Bretagne, die [breˈtanjə]. *Pr.n.f.* **-.** *Geog:* Brittany.

Bretone [breˈtoːnə], *m.* **-n/-n.** *Ethn: Geog:* Breton.

bretonisch [breˈtoːnɪʃ]. **1.** *a. Ethn: Geog:* Breton. **2.** *s.* **Bretonisch,** *n. Ling:* Breton.

Brett, *n.* **-(e)s/-er.** **1.** board; (*more than 2 in. thick*) plank; **Bretter schneiden, sägen,** to cut, saw, boards; (*a*) **(Waren, usw.) mit Brettern verschlagen,** to crate (goods, etc.); **ein Fenster, usw., mit Brettern vernageln,** to board up a window, etc.; **etwas aus Brettern roh zusammenschlagen,** to knock sth. together out of wood; **der Fußboden bestand nur aus rohen Brettern,** the floor consisted merely of rough boards; *F:* **sechs Bretter und zwei Brettchen,** the coffin, *F:* the long box; **das B. bohren, wo es am dünnsten ist,** to take the easy way out; (*b*) *F:* **hier ist die Welt mit Brettern vernagelt,** this is the end of the world; this is a great obstacle; **er hat ein B. vorm Kopf,** he is slow on the uptake; he is a bit dim, thick; (*of girl*) **flach wie ein B.,** flat-chested, *F:* flat as a board. **2.** (*a*) (wooden) shelf; (bread-, pastry-, etc.) board; (diving-, etc.) board; *A:* **aufs B. bezahlen,** to pay cash down; (*b*) **Schwarzes B.,** notice-board, *U.S:* bulletin board. **3.** *F: pl.* **Bretter,** skis. **4.** *Games:* (chess-, draught-, etc.) board. **5.** *Th: F:* **die Bretter,** the stage, *F:* the boards; **ein Stück über die Bretter gehen lassen,** to put on a play; **das Stück ist in allen Provinzstädten über die Bretter gegangen,** the play has run in all the provincial towns; **auf den Brettern, die die Welt bedeuten,** on the stage, *F:* on the boards. **6.** *Box: F:* **j-n auf die Bretter schicken,** to knock s.o. down; **er mußte bis acht auf die Bretter,** he went down to a count of eight.

Brett- *cp.* **Bretter-.**

Brettchen, *n.* **-s/-,** (*dim. of* **Brett**) (*a*) small (thin) board; *Dom.Ec:* = **Frühstücksbrett;** (*b*) *Tex:* hole-board.

Brettchenweberei, *f. Tex:* tablet-weaving.

Brettdecke, *f. Constr:* panelled ceiling; board-ceiling.

Brett(e)l, *n.* **-s/-(n).** *South G.Dial:* ski.

Bretterbude, *f.* wooden hut; shack; (market) stall.

Bretterschalung, *f. Constr:* boarding.

Brettertür, *f.* door made out of plain wooden boards, plank door.

Bretterverkleidung, *f.* boarding; casing; wooden lining.

Bretterverschalung, *f.* = **Bretterschalung.**

Bretterverschlag, *m.* (*a*) wooden partition; (*b*) wooden shed; (*c*) crate (for goods); **einen Speicher in Bretterverschläge abteilen,** to partition off a loft.

Bretterwand, *f.* hoarding; (*indoors*) wooden partition; outer wall (of hut) made of wood.

Bretterzaun, *m.* hoarding; wooden fence; *U.S:* board-fence.

Brettmühle, *f.* saw-mill.

Brettnagel, *m.* floor brad.

Brettsäge, *f. Tls:* pit-saw; rip-saw.

Brettspiel, *n.* game played on a board, board-game.

Breve [ˈbreːveː, ˈbreːvə], *n.* **-s/-s,** (papal) breve, brief.

Brevet [breˈveː, brəˈvɛː], *n.* **-s/-s,** brevet.

brevetieren [breveˈtiːrən], *v.tr.* to brevet.

Brevier [breˈviːr], *n.* **-s/-e.** **1.** *Ecc:* breviary; **sein B. beten,** to say one's breviary. **2.** *Print:* brevier.

Brevis [ˈbreːvɪs], *f.* **-/-ves.** *Mus:* breve.

Brezel, *f.* **-/-n.** *Bak:* pretzel.

brich, brichst, bricht *see* **brechen.**

Bricke, *f.* **-/-n.** *Ich:* lamprey.

Bridge [ˈbrɪdʒ], *n.* **-/.** *Cards:* bridge; **eine Partie B.,** a game of bridge.

Bridgespieler, *m.* bridge player.

Brief, *m.* **-(e)s/-e.** **1.** letter; *B:* epistle; **Briefe wechseln,** to correspond; **einen B. an j-n, j-m einen B., schreiben,** to write a letter to s.o., to write s.o. a letter; **einen B. auf die Post geben, bringen, einen B. aufgeben,** to post, mail, a letter; **Briefe austragen,** to deliver letters; **offener B.,** open letter; **eingeschriebener B.,** registered letter; **geschäftlicher B.,** business letter; **er gab mir B. und Siegel darauf,** he gave me his word on it. **2.** = **Briefchen** (*b*). **3.** *St.Exch:* (*in quotation: usu. abbreviated* **B**) offered, sellers; **Siemens 150 B.,** Siemens, sellers only at 50% above par.

Briefabfertigung, *f. Post: etc:* dispatch of mail.

Briefabholung, *f.* collection of letters.

Briefablegekasten, Briefablegekorb, *m.* letter-tray.

Briefadel, *m.* patent of nobility.

Briefannahme, *f. Post:* receiving counter for letters.

Briefaufgabe, *f.* posting of letters.

Briefaufschrift, *f.* address on a letter.

Briefausgabe, *f.* (*a*) distribution, handing out, of letters; (*b*) *Post:* (i) handing out of letters; (ii) poste-restante counter.

Briefbeschwerer, *m.* **-s/-,** paper-weight, letter-weight.

Briefblock, *m.* writing-pad, letter-pad.

Briefbogen, *m.* (sheet of) notepaper; letter-paper.

Briefbote, *m.* postman, *U.S:* mailman.

Briefbuch, *n. Com:* letter-book.

Briefchen, *n.* **-s/-,** (*a*) short note; (*b*) **ein B. Streichhölzer,** a book of matches; **ein B. Nähnadeln,** a packet of needles.

Briefeinwurf, *m.* (i) slot of a letter-box; (ii) *Post:* posting-box, *U.S:* mailbox.

Briefeschreiber, *m.* **ein eifriger B.,** a great letter-writer.

Brieffach, *n.* (*a*) pigeon-hole; (*b*) *Post:* post-office box.

Brieffrankiermaschine, *f.* franking machine.

Briefgeheimnis, *n. Jur: etc:* secrecy of correspondence.

Briefhülle, *f. A:* envelope.

Briefhypothek, *f.* certified mortgage.

Briefkarte, *f.* correspondence card (with envelope).

Briefkassette, *f.* writing-case.
Briefkasten, *m.* (*a*) letter-box, post-box, *Post:* posting-box, *U.S:* mailbox; (*b*) (*in door, etc.*) letter-box; letter-cage; *U.S:* mailbox.
Briefklammer, *f.* letter-clip; paper-clip.
Briefkopf, *m.* letter-head.
Briefkopierpresse, *f.* letter-press, copying-press.
Briefkorb, *m.* letter-tray, letter-basket.
Briefkurs, *m. St.Exch:* selling-price.
Briefkuvert, *n.* envelope.
brieflich, *a. & adv.* by letter; in writing.
Briefmappe, *f.* portfolio, writing-case.
Briefmarke, *f.* (postage) stamp.
Briefmarkenalbum, *n.* stamp-album.
Briefmarkenautomat, *m.* stamp-machine.
Briefmarkenheftchen, *n.* book of stamps.
Briefmarkenkunde, *f.* philately.
Briefmarkenpapier, *n.* stamp-paper.
Briefmarkensammler, *m.* stamp-collector, philatelist.
Briefmarkensammlung, *f.* stamp-collection.
Briefnadeln, *f.pl.* paper pins.
Brieföffner, *m.* letter-opener.
Briefordner, *m.* letter-file.
Briefpapier, *n.* note paper; letter-paper.
Briefporto, *n.* postage for, on, letters.
Briefpost, *f.* letter post.
Briefpresse, *f.* letter-press.
Briefroman, *m.* epistolary novel.
Briefschaften, *f.pl.* letters; correspondence; papers.
Briefschreibekunst, *f.* epistolography; (the) art of letter-writing.
Briefschreiber, *m.* writer of a letter, letter-writer; correspondent.
Briefschulden, *f.pl.* outstanding correspondence, arrears of correspondence.
Briefsendung, *f. Post:* light piece of mail (*not parcel*).
Briefsortierer, *m.* letter sorter.
Briefständer, *m.* letter-rack.
Briefsteller, *m.* -s/-. **1.** (*pers.*) letter-writer, -composer. **2.** (*book*) (model) letter-writer.
Briefstempel, *m.* **1.** *Post:* post-mark. **2.** *Post: etc:* letter-stamp, cancellation (mark).
Briefstil, *m.* style of a letter; epistolary style.
Brieftasche, *f.* wallet (for bank-notes, papers, etc.); pocket-book; letter-case; *U.S:* billfold.
Brieftaube, *f. Orn:* carrier pigeon, homing pigeon, homer.
Brieftelegramm, *n.* letter telegram, *U.S:* letter-gram.
Briefträger, *m.* postman, *U.S:* mailman.
Briefumschlag, *m.* envelope.
Briefwaage, *f.* letter-balance, -weight, -scales, -weigher.
Briefwahl, *f. Adm: Pol:* postal vote, voting by post.
Briefwechsel, *m.* correspondence.
briet *see* **braten.**
Brigade [briˈgaːdə], *f.* -/-n, brigade.
Brigadegeneral, *m.* -s/-e. **1.** *Mil:* brigadier. **2.** *Mil.Av:* air commodore.
Brigadier [briˑgaˑˈdiːr], *m.* -s/-s, brigadier.
Brigant [briˑˈgant], *m.* -en/-en, brigand.
Brigantine [briˑganˈtiːnə], *f.* -/-n. *Nau:* brigantine.
Brigg, *f.* -/-s. *Nau:* brig.
Briggschoner, *m. Nau:* brigantine; hermaphrodite (brig).
Briggsegel, *n. Nau:* spanker.
Brigitta, Brigitte [briˑˈgitaː, -tə]. *Pr.n.f.* -s & *Lit:* **Brigittens.** Bridget.
Brikett [briˑˈkɛt], *n.* -s/-s, briquette.
Brikettfabrik, *f.* briquette works, briquetting plant.
Brikettieranlage [briˑkɛˈtiːr-], *f.* briquette works, briquetting plant.
Brikettiermaschine, *f.* briquette machine.
Brikole [briˑˈkoːlə], *f.* -/-n. *Billiards:* bricole.
Brill, *m.* -s/-s. *Ich:* brill.
Brillant[1] [brilˈjant], *m.* -en/-en, brilliant, brilliant-cut diamond.
brillant[2], *a.* brilliant (pers., idea, performance, etc.).
Brillant[3], *f.* -/. *Print:* four to pica.
brillanten [brilˈjantən], *a.* made of brilliants.
Brillantfeuer(werk), *n. Pyr:* cascade.
Brillantgelb, *n. Dy:* brilliant yellow.
brillantieren [briljanˈtiːrən], *v.tr.* **1.** to treat metal (with saltpetre). **2.** to cut (diamond) into brilliants.
Brillantine [briljanˈtiːnə], *f.* -/-n. **1.** brilliantine. **2.** (*a*) metal-polish; (*b*) black-lead. **3.** shoe-polish. **4.** *Tex:* brilliantine, figured stuff.
Brillantring, *m.* ring set with brilliants.
Brillantschliff, *m. Lap:* brilliant cut.
Brillantschmuck, *m.* brilliant jewellery, brilliants.
Brillantschrift, *f.* = **Brillant**[3].
Brillanstoff, *m. Tex:* figured stuff.
Brillantsucher, *m. Phot:* brilliant (view)finder.
Brille, *f.* -/-n. **1.** (*a*) (pair of) glasses, spectacles; **randlose B.,** rimless spectacles; **dunkle B.,** dark glasses; **goldene B.,** gold-rimmed spectacles. **eine B. tragen,** to wear spectacles; **etwas durch eine rosige B. betrachten,** to see sth. through rose-coloured spectacles; (*b*) (*marking of animals*) spectacles; (*c*) *Harn:* blinkers. **2.** (*a*) lavatory seat; (*b*) *Mec.E: Mch:* (stuffing box) gland, follower; (*c*) *Tls:* back-rest (of lathe).
Brillenachse, *f. Opt:* spectacle-axis.
Brillenbär, *m. Z:* spectacled bear.
Brillenbehälter, *m.* spectacle-case, glasses-case.
Brillenbügel, *m.* bow, earpiece, of spectacles.
Brilleneinfassung, *f.* spectacle-frame.
Brillenente, *f. Orn:* surf-scoter.
Brilleneutui, *n.* spectacle-case, glasses-case.
Brillenfassung, *f.* spectacle-frame.
Brillenferngläser, *n.pl.* spectacle-type binoculars.
brillenförmig, *a.* spectacle-shaped; *Nat.Hist:* **mit brillenförmiger Zeichnung,** spectacled.
Brillenfutteral, *n.* spectacle-case, glasses-case.
Brillengestell, *n.* spectacle-frame.
Brillenglas, *n.* spectacle-glass, spectacle-lens; **Brillengläser schleifen,** to grind lenses.
Brillengrasmücke, *f. Orn:* spectacled warbler.
Brillengrauschlüpfer, *m. Orn:* spectacled warbler.
Brillenlupe, *f.* spectacle-type magnifying glass.
Brillenmacher, *m.* -s/-, optician, spectacle-maker.
Brillennase, *f. Orn:* goatsucker.
Brillenofen, *m. Metall:* spectacle-furnace, furnace with two tap-holes.
Brillenpelikan, *m. Orn:* Australian pelican.
Brillenpinguin, *m. Orn:* jackass penguin.
Brillensalamander, *m. Rept:* black salamander.
Brillenscheide, *f.* spectacle-case, glasses-case.
Brillenschlange, *f. Rept:* spectacled cobra, Indian cobra.
Brillenschötchen, *n.* -s/-. *Bot:* biscutella.
Brillenstein, *m. Geol:* concretionary nodule.
Brillentaucher, *m. Orn:* spectacled penguin.
Brillenteiste, *f. Orn:* spectacled guillemot.
Brillenträger, *m.* person who wears spectacles.
Brillenvogel, *m.* **1.** *Ent:* = **Blaukopf. 2.** *Orn:* white-eye.
brillieren [brilˈjiːrən], *v.i.* (*haben*) (*mainly of pers.*) to sparkle, to shine.
Brillonetten [briljoˑˈnɛtən], *f.pl. Jewel:* half-brilliants.
Brimborium [brimˈboːrium], *n.* -s/. *F:* fuss; **B machen,** to fuss.
Brinellhärte [briˑˈnɛl-], *f. Ph:* Brinell hardness.
bringen. *v.tr.* (*p.t.* **brachte,** *p.p.* **gebracht**) **1.** to bring *or* take (sth., s.o.); (*Note: if the speaker sees the action from the standpoint of the grammatical subject,* **bringen** *usually corresponds to the English* '*take*'; *but if he sees it from the standpoint of the destination of the object in transit, or of the dative object in the grammatical structure, then the appropriate translation is* '*bring*'.) (*a*) **j-m ein Geschenk b.,** to bring *or* take s.o. a present; **j-m ein Glas Wasser b.,** to bring, fetch, take, s.o. a glass of water; **hat der Briefträger die Post schon gebracht?** has the postman brought the letters yet? **der Wind hat den Regen gebracht,** the wind has brought the rain; **j-n ins Haus b.,** to bring *or* take s.o. to one's home; **j-n vor den Richter b.,** to bring *or* take s.o. before the judge; **der Storch hat ein Kind gebracht,** the stork has brought a baby; **was bringt dich zu mir?** what has brought you to me? (*b*) (*of pers.*) **j-m Grüße von j-m b.,** to bring s.o. greetings from s.o.; **j-m eine Nachricht b.,** to bring *or* take news to s.o.; **j-m Hilfe b.,** to bring s.o. help, to aid s.o.; **j-m Trost b.,** to bring comfort to s.o., to console s.o.; **j-m ein Ständchen b.,** to serenade s.o.; (*c*) **den Göttern ein Opfer b.,** to sacrifice, make a sacrifice, to the gods; **etwas zum Opfer b.,** to offer (up) sth. as a sacrifice; **er hat sein Leben lang Opfer gebracht, um das zu erreichen,** he made sacrifices throughout his life in order to achieve this; (*d*) (*of pers., thg, action*) **j-m Glück, Unglück, b.,** to bring s.o. good, bad, luck; **Unglück über j-n b.,** to bring misfortune (up)on s.o.; **j-m Ärger b.,** to annoy s.o.; **das Haus hat uns nichts als Ärger gebracht,** the house has caused us nothing but annoyance; **'du hast uns diesen Verdruß gebracht,** 'you have brought this trouble on us; **Zwietracht in eine Familie b.,** to bring discord into a family; *Prov:* **Scherben bringen Glück,** broken dishes bring good luck; **sich regen bringt Segen,** it is the busy bee that makes the honey. **2.** to take, carry (sth., s.o.); **etwas zu j-m, an einen Ort, b.,** to take sth. to s.o., to a place; **die Schuhe zum Schuster, die Kleider zur Reinigung, b.,** to take the shoes to the shoe repairer, the clothes to the cleaner(s); **einen Brief auf die, zur, Post b.,** to take a letter to the post, to post a letter; **das Geschirr in die Küche b.,** to take, carry, the dishes to the kitchen; **wir bringen Ihnen die Waren ins Haus,** we deliver the goods to your address; **seine Koffer zum Bahnhof b. lassen,** to have one's bags taken to the station; **die Kohlen in den Keller b.,** to carry the coal to the cellar; **j-n zu, ins, Bett b.,** to put s.o. to bed; **j-n ins Krankenhaus b.,** to take s.o. to hospital; **man brachte ihn ins Gefängnis, auf die Polizei,** he was taken to prison, to the police-station; **ich bringe dich noch ein Stück (des Weges),** I'll come along with you part of the way; **der Omnibus wird dich in zwei Stunden nach X b.,** the bus will take you to X in two hours; **er brachte mich an die, zur, Bahn,** he came to the station with me, he saw me off at the station; he saw me to the train; **sie brachten die Damen nach Hause,** they saw the ladies home; **er brachte mich zu sich nach Hause,** he took me to his home; **keine zehn Pferde brächten mich wieder dahin,** wild horses would not drag me there again. **3.** (*a*) (*of newspaper, etc.*) to carry, print (news); **die 'Times' bringt heute einen Bericht über . . .,** today the 'Times' prints a report about . . .; **alle Zeitungen brachten es auf der Titelseite,** all the newspapers had it on the front page; **was bringen die Zeitungen?** what is in the papers? (*b*) *W.Tel:* to broadcast, to present (sth.); *Th:* to present, to put on (a play); **die Skala bringt jeden Monat eine neue Revue,** the Scala puts on a new revue every month. **4.** to bring forth, to produce; to yield; (*a*) (*of animals*) **Junge b.,** to bring forth young; **ein Kind zur Welt b.,** *A:* **ein Kind b.,** to give birth to a child; **sie brachte ihm zwei gesunde Knaben,** she bore him two healthy boys; (*b*) (*of trees, etc.*) to bear (fruit); (*of soil, etc.*) to yield (crop, etc.); *B:* **ein jeglicher Baum, der nicht gute Früchte bringet . . .,** every tree that bringeth not forth good fruit . . .; (*c*) **Zinsen b.,** to yield, produce, interest; **das Geschäft bringt nicht viel,** the business does not yield much profit. **5.** (*a*) **j-n in eine Lage b.,** to put s.o. into a position; **j-n, etwas, in Sicherheit b.,** to bring, remove, s.o., to remove sth., to safety; **sich in Sicherheit b.,** to get to a place of safety; to find safety; **j-n in Schwierigkeiten, in Gefahr, b.,** to lead s.o. into difficulties, into danger; to put s.o. in a difficult, a dangerous, position; **j-n in Verlegenheit b.,** to embarrass s.o.; **j-n ins Verderben b.,** to bring about s.o.'s downfall, ruin; to bring s.o. to perdition; **j-n, sich, ins Unglück b.,** to ruin s.o., oneself; **j-n in eine gute, schlechte, Laune b.,** to put, get, s.o. into a good, bad, mood; **j-n auf den rechten Weg b.,** to put s.o. on (to) the right path; (*b*) **j-n an den Bettelstab b.,** to bring s.o. to beggary; **j-n an den Galgen b.,** to bring s.o. to the gallows; **j-n ans Gericht b.,** to bring s.o. before the law, into court; (*c*) **j-n aus einer Lage b.,** to change, alter, s.o.'s position, condition; **j-n aus der Fassung b.,** to disconcert s.o. **6.** (*a*) **etwas ans Licht b.,** to bring sth. to light; **etwas an den Tag b.,** to lay sth. bare, to expose sth. **etwas an die Öffentlichkeit b.,** to make sth. pnblic, **eine Nachricht unter die Leute b.,** to spread the news; (*b*) **etwas auf die Seite b.,** to appropriate sth.; to embezzle sth.; *F:* **j-n um die Ecke b.,** to kill s.o., *F:* to do s.o. in. **7.** (*a*) **etwas zuwege, zustande,** *F:* **vom Fleck, b.,** to accomplish, achieve, sth.; to get sth. done; **etwas hinter sich** *acc.* **b.,** to get sth. over and done with; (*b*) **es zu etwas b.,** to achieve sth.; **es dahin b., daß . . .,** to get so far that . . .; **du wirst es noch weit b.,** you'll go far; **er hat es bis zum Major gebracht,** he rose to be a major; (*c*) **etwas in seinen Besitz b.,** to acquire sth.; to get sth. into one's possession; **etwas an sich** *acc.* **b.,** to take possession, get possession, of sth.; (*d*) **j-n um etwas b.,** to do s.o. out of sth.; **j-n um den Verstand b.,** to drive s.o. mad; **j-n um seinen guten Ruf b.,** to damage s.o.'s reputation; **j-n ums Leben b.,** (*of pers.*) to kill, murder, s.o.; (*of grief, etc.*) to cause s.o.'s death, to kill s.o.; **sich um etwas b.,** to rob oneself of sth.; **er brachte sich um seinen Sieg, um sein Vermögen,** he cheated himself of victory, he threw away his fortune. **8. j-n auf etwas** *acc.* **b.,** to put s.o. on to sth.; to put sth. into s.o.'s head, mind; **j-n darauf b., etwas zu tun,** to lead, influence, s.o. to do sth.; **j-n auf dumme Gedanken b.,** to put foolish ideas, thoughts, into s.o.'s head; **das bringt mich darauf . . .,** that reminds me . . .; **du hast mich selbst darauf gebracht,** you suggested it yourself. **9. j-n dazu b., etwas zu tun,** to make s.o. do sth., to get s.o.

to do sth.; to bring s.o. to do sth.; **sich dazu b., etwas zu tun,** to bring oneself to do sth.; **j-n (bis) zum Mord, Wahnsinn, b.,** to drive s.o. to murder, to madness; **er ist nicht dazu zu b., uns zu helfen,** we cannot get him to help us; **ich habe sie dazu, soweit, gebracht, daß sie . . .,** I have persuaded her to . . .; **er kann sich nicht dazu b., darüber zu reden,** he cannot bring himself to talk about it; (*b*) **etwas über sich, übers Herz, b.,** to be able to bear sth.; **ich bringe es nicht über mich, übers Herz, zu . . .,** I can't bear to . . ., I can't bring myself to . . . **10.** (*of thg, action, etc.*) **etwas mit sich b.,** to produce sth. as a consequence; to be followed, attended, by sth.; to involve sth., to entail sth.; **es mit sich b., daß . . .,** to bring it about, to have the consequence, that . . .; **die Schwierigkeiten, welche das mit sich b. würde,** the difficulties which this would involve, entail; **die Vorteile, die diese Stelle mit sich bringt,** the advantages attaching to the position; **mein Beruf bringt es mit sich, daß ich viel auf Reisen bin,** my work involves a great deal of travelling. **11.** (*a*) **j-n zur Ruhe b.,** (i) to calm s.o. down; to quieten s.o.; to pacify s.o.; (ii) to send s.o. off to sleep; **etwas zu Ende b.,** to finish, complete, sth.; **etwas zu einem guten Ende, Schluß, b.,** to bring sth. to a successful conclusion; *see also* **Ende** 2 (b), **Fall**[1] 1 (*a*); (*b*) **j-n zum Fallen b.,** to make s.o. fall down; **j-n zum Lachen b.,** to make s.o. laugh; **j-n zum Weinen b.,** to make s.o. cry, to bring tears to s.o.'s eyes; *Cu:* **etwas zum, ans, Kochen b.,** to bring sth. to the boil; (*c*) **etwas in Gang b.,** to start sth., to get sth. going; **Geld, usw., in Umlauf b.,** to bring money, etc., into circulation; **etwas in Mode b.,** to make sth. fashionable; to bring sth. into fashion; (*d*) **etwas in Ordnung b.,** to put sth. in order; to tidy sth. (up); **etwas in Erfahrung b.,** to find out, discover, get to know, sth.; **ich habe in Erfahrung gebracht, daß . . .,** it has come to my knowledge that . . .; (*e*) **j-m etwas zum Bewußtsein b.,** to make sth. clear to s.o.; to put s.o. in mind of sth.; **j-m etwas zur Kenntnis b.,** to bring sth. to s.o.'s knowledge; (*f*) **j-n (wieder) zur Vernunft b.,** to bring s.o. (back) to reason; to bring s.o. to his senses; **j-n wieder zu sich, zum Bewußtsein, b.,** to bring s.o. round (*after a faint*); (*g*) **etwas zu Papier b.,** to write sth. down; to commit sth. to writing; to get sth. down (on paper); to set sth. down in black and white. (*Note: there are many periphrastic phrases using* **bringen** *with the verbal noun, which are virtually identical in meaning with the verb, e.g.* **in Anrechnung bringen = anrechnen; in Anwendung bringen = anwenden; zur Durchführung bringen = durchführen;** *such phrases may be found listed under the relevant verbal substantive*).

Bringer, *m.* **-s/-, -bringer,** *comb.fm. Lit:* bringer, one who brings; **B. der Freuden, Freudenbringer,** bringer of joys.

Bringschuld, *f. Jur:* debt to be discharged at the domicile of the creditor.

Brink, *m.* **-(e)s/-e,** grassy hill, embankment.

Brio [ˈbriːoː], *n.* **-s/.** *Mus:* brio.

Brioche [briˈoʃ], *f.* **-/-s,** brioche, sweet roll.

brisant [briˈzãː, briˈzant], *a. Exp:* shattering, disruptive.

Brisanz [briˈzants], *f.* **-/-en.** *Exp:* fragmentation (effect).

Brisanzgranate, *f. Artil:* fragmentation shell.

Brise, *f.* **-/-n,** breeze.

Brisling, *m.* **-s/-e.** *Ich:* brisling.

Brissago [briˈsaːgoː], *f.* **-/-(s)** *Swiss:* long, thin cheroot (with an inserted straw).

Bristolkanal, der [ˈbristəl-]. *Pr.n. Geog:* the Bristol Channel.

Bristolpapier, *n.,* **Bristolkarton,** *m. Paperm:* Bristol paper, Bristol board.

Britanniametall [briˈtaniă-], *n.* Britannia metal, *F:* britannia.

Britannien [bri-, briˈtaniən]. *Pr.n.n.* **-s.** *Geog:* Britain.

Brite [ˈbriːtə, ˈbritə], *m.* **-n/-n.** *Hist: Geog:* Briton.

Britin [ˈbriːtin, ˈbritin], *f.* **-/-innen.** *Hist: Geog:* (female) Briton, British woman.

britisch [ˈbriːtiʃ, ˈbritiʃ], *a.* British; **das Britische Museum,** the British Museum; **die Britischen Inseln,** the British Isles.

Britschka, *f.* **-/-s.** *Veh:* britzka.

Broccoli [ˈbrokoˑliː], *pl. Hort: Cu:* broc(c)oli.

Broché [broˈʃeː], *n.* **-(s)/.** *Tex:* broché; (*a*) brocaded fabric; (*b*) figure, pattern (on brocaded fabric).

Bröckchen, *n.* **-s/-,** (*dim. of* **Brocken**[2]) bit, small piece; morsel; crumb; fragment.

Bröckel, *m.* **-s/- = Bröckchen.**

Brockelerbse, *f. Hort:* garden pea.

bröck(e)lig, *a.* crumby, crumbly; brittle; friable.

Bröckelkohl, *m. Hort: Cu:* (*a*) broc(c)oli; (*b*) *F:* Brussels sprouts.

bröckeln. **1.** *v.tr.* to break into pieces; to crumble. **2.** *v.i.* (*haben*) to crumble; to become brittle.

Brocken[1], **der.** *Pr.n.* **-s.** *Geog:* the Brocken.

Brocken[2], *m.* **-s/-.** **1.** (*a*) piece; bit; lump (of earth, stone, etc.); morsel (of food); mouthful; *F:* **ein harter B.,** a hard task; **j-n mit ein paar Brocken abspeisen,** to give s.o. short shrift; (*b*) *Mil: F:* bomb, shell, *F:* cookie; *Atom.Ph:* fuel slug; (*c*) *F:* (*of pers.*) **ein schwerer B.,** a great lump. **2.** *pl.* scraps; odds and ends; bits and pieces; (*a*) **meine paar Brocken,** my bits and pieces; (*b*) **einige Brocken Französisch,** a few scraps of French.

brocken[3], *v.tr.* **1. Brot in die Milch, in die Suppe, b.,** to break bread into milk, soup. **2.** *South G.Dial:* to pluck (flowers).

Brockenanemone, *f. Bot:* pulsatilla, pasque-flower.

Brockenbesen, *m. Bot:* cotton-grass.

Brockenblume, *f.* = **Brockenanemone.**

Brockengespenst, *n. Meteor:* spectre of the Brocken; mountain spectre.

Brockengestein, *n. Geol:* breccia.

Brockenglas, *n.* broken glass; cullet.

Brockenmoos, *n. Moss:* Iceland lichen, moss.

Brockenmyrte, *f. Bot:* crowberry, heath-berry; *Dial:* crake-berry.

Brockensammlung, *f.* (*a*) junk-heap; (*b*) collecting *or* collection of old clothes, jumble.

Brockenstärke, *f.* lump starch.

brockenweise, *a. & adv.* bit by bit; little by little; gradually; piecemeal; **einen Bericht b. aus j-m herausbekommen,** to drag a piece of news out of s.o. bit by bit.

Bröcklein, *n.* **-s/- = Bröckchen.**

brodeln, *v.i.* (*haben*) (*of liquid matter*) to bubble; to seethe; to effervesce; to boil fiercely.

Brodem, *m.* **-s/.** vapour, steam; foul air; fumes.

Broderie [broˑdəˈriː], *f.* **-/-n** [-ˈriːən], (piece of) embroidery.

brodieren [broˑˈdiːrən], *v.tr.* to embroider.

Brokat [broˑˈkaːt], *m.* **-(e)s/-e.** **1.** *Tex:* brocade; **Brokat-,** *comb.fm.* brocade . . ., brocaded; **Brokatgewand** *n,* brocade gown; **Brokatseide** *f,* brocade silk. **2.** *Paint:* (coarse-flaked) bronze pigment.

Brokatell [broˑkaˑˈtɛl], *m.* **-s/-e, Brokatelle** [broˑkaˑˈtɛlə], *f.* **-/-.** *Tex:* brocatelle.

Brokatello [broˑkaˑˈtɛloː], *m.* **-(s)/.** = **Brokatmarmor.**

Brokatfarbe, *f.* (coarse-flaked) bronze paint.

Brokatmarmor, *m. Miner:* brocatello, brocatelle, clouded marble.

Brokatpapier, *n. Paperm:* brocade paper.

Brokatstoff, *m. Tex:* brocade fabric, brocade.

Brokkoli [ˈbrokoˑliː], *pl. Hort: Cu:* broc(c)oli.

Brom [broːm], *n.* **-s/.** *Ch:* bromine.

Bromalhydrat [broˑˈmaːl-], *n. Ch:* bromal hydrate.

Bromalin [broˑmaˑˈliːn], *n.* **-s/.** *Ch:* bromal(ine).

Bromäther, *m. Ch:* ethyl bromide.

Bromazetylen, *n. Ch:* acetylene bromide.

Brombeere, *f. Bot:* blackberry, bramble(berry).

Brombeerfalter, *m. Ent:* green hairstreak.

Brombeerpflanze, *f. Bot:* blackberry (plant).

Brombeerstrauch, *m.* blackberry, bramble, bush.

Bromdampf, *m. Ch:* bromine vapour.

Bromeisen, *n. Ch:* iron bromide, ferrous bromide.

Bromeliazeen, die [broˑmeˑliaˑˈtseːən], *f.pl. Bot:* the bromeliaceae, the bromeliads.

Bromelie [broˑˈmeːliə], *f.* **-/-n.** *Bot:* bromelia.

Bromessigsäure, *f. Ch:* bromoacetic acid.

Bromgoldkalium, *n. Ch:* potassium bromaurate.

Bromhydrat, *n. Ch:* hydrobromide.

Bromid [broˑˈmiːt], *n.* **-(e)s/-e** [-s, -ˈmiːdəs/-ˈmiːdə]. *Ch:* bromide.

Bromidpapier, *n. Phot:* bromide paper.

bromieren [broˑˈmiːrən], *v.tr. Ch:* to bromize.

Bromismus [broˑˈmismus], *m.* **-/.** *Med:* bromism.

Bromit [broˑˈmiːt], *m.* **-(e)s/.** *Miner:* bromyrite.

Bromkalium, *n. Ch:* potassium bromide.

Bromoformium [broˑmoˑˈformium], *n.* **-s/.** *Ch:* bromoform.

Bromsalz, *n. Ch:* bromine salt.

Bromsäure, *f. Ch:* bromic acid.

Bromsilber, *n. Ch:* silver bromide.

Bromspat, *m. Miner:* bromyrite.

Bromür [broˑˈmyːr], *n.* **-s/-e.** *Ch:* (ferrous, cupreous, etc.) bromide.

Bromwasser, *n. Ch:* bromine water.

Bronche [ˈbronçə], *f.* **-/-n = Bronchie.**

bronchial [bronçiˈaːl], *a.* bronchial.

Bronchialasthma, *n. Med:* bronchial asthma.

Bronchialkatarrh, *m. Med:* bronchial catarrh, bronchitis.

Bronchie [ˈbronçĭə], *f.* **-/-n.** *Anat:* bronchium; **Bronchien** *pl,* bronchia.

Bronchitis [bronˈçiːtis], *f.* **-/.** *Med:* bronchitis.

Bronchopneumonie [bronçoˑpnoymoˑˈniː], *f. Med:* bronch(i)o-pneumonia; catarrhal, lobular, pneumonia.

Bronchoskopie [bronçoˑskoˑˈpiː], *f.* **-/.** *Med:* bronchoscopy.

Bronchotomie [bronçoˑtoˑˈmiː], *f.* **-/-n** [-ˈmiːən]. *Surg:* bronchotomy.

Bronchus [ˈbronçus], *m.* **-/-chen.** *Anat:* bronchus.

Bronn, *m.* **-s/-en, Bronnen,** *m.* **-s/-.** *Poet:* (i) well; (ii) spring.

Brontosaurus [brontoˑˈzaurus], *m.* **-/-rier** [-rĭər]. *Paleont:* brontosaurus.

Bronze [ˈbrõːsə, ˈbrõːzə], *f.* **-/-n.** **1.** *Metall:* bronze; *Art:* bronze (object); **eine Sammlung von Bronzen,** a collection of bronzes. **2. Bronze-, -bronze,** *comb.fm.* bronze . . ., (-)bronze; **Bronzestatue** *f,* bronze statue; **Bronzedraht** *m,* bronze wire; **Bronzefarbe** *f,* bronze paint; **Phosphorbronze** *f,* phosphor-bronze.

Bronzearbeiter, *m.* maker of bronzes.

bronzeartig, *a.* bronze-like.

Bronzeblau, *n.* bronze blue.

Bronzediabetes, *f. Med:* bronze diabetes, bronzed diabetes.

Bronzedruck, *m. Print:* bronze printing.

Bronzefarbe, *f.* (*a*) bronze colour; (*b*) bronze paint.

bronzefarben, *a.* bronze-coloured.

Bronzefruchttaube, *f. Orn:* green imperial pigeon.

Bronzegießer, *m.* bronze-founder.

Bronzegießerei, *f.* (*a*) bronze foundry; (*b*) bronze casting.

Bronzegrün, *n.* bronze green.

Bronzeguß, *m.* (*a*) bronze casting; (*b*) bronze cast.

Bronzekrankheit, *f. Med:* Addison's disease.

Bronzekunst, *f.* the art of working in bronze.

Bronzelack, *m.* bronze varnish; bronze lacquer.

Bronzemedaille, *f. Sp: etc:* bronze medal.

bronzen [ˈbrõːsən], *a.* (*a*) bronze (object); (*b*) bronze colour; **bronzene Haut,** bronzed, tanned, skin.

Bronzepulver, *n.* bronze powder.

Bronzetinktur, *f.* bronzing liquid.

Bronzevergoldung, *f.* bronze gilding.

Bronzewaren, *f.pl.* bronzes; **falsche B.,** imitation bronzes.

Bronzezeit, die. *Prehist:* the Bronze Age.

bronzieren [brõˑˈsiːrən], *v.tr.* to bronze (metal, etc.).

Bronzierpulver, *n.* bronzing powder.

Bronziersalz, *n.* bronzing salt.

Bronzit [brõˑˈsiːt], *m.* **-(e)s/.** *Miner:* bronzite.

Brookgeitau, *n. Nau:* throat-brail.

Brookit [bruˈkiːt], *m.* **-(e)s/.** *Miner:* brookite.

Brosame, *f.* **-/-n,** *usu. pl.* **Brosamen,** crumbs (of bread, etc.).

Brosche, *f.* **-/-n,** brooch; large pin.

Bröschen [ˈbrøːsçən], *n.* **-s/-.** *Cu:* sweetbread.

broschieren [broˈʃiːrən]. **I.** *v.tr.* **1.** *Bookb:* to sew, stitch (book); **broschiertes Buch,** paper-bound, paper-backed, book. **2.** *Tex:* to brocade, to figure; **broschiertes Gewebe,** figured fabric. **3.** *Leath:* to whitewash (glove-leather) (before dying it).

II. *vbl s.* **1. Broschieren,** *n. in vbl senses.* **2. Broschierung,** *f.* (*a*) = II. 1; (*b*) *Bookb:* = **Broschur.**

Broschierlade, *f. Tex:* weaving lathe.

Broschur [broˈʃuːr], *f.* **-/-en.** *Bookb:* **1.** stitching, sewing (of books); binding (of books) in paper-covers. **2.** paper-cover (of book).

Broschüre [broˈʃyːrə], *f.* **-/-n,** booklet; pamphlet; brochure.

Brösel, *m. & n.* **-s/-.** *Cu:* (*a*) *usu. pl.* **Brösel,** bread-crumbs; *Austrian:* **Karfiol mit Brösel** *pl,* cauliflower au gratin, with breadcrumbs; (*b*) croûton.

Brosme, *m.* **-n/-n.** *Ich:* torsk.

Brossage [broˈsaːʒə], *f.* **-/.** *Tex:* carding.

brossieren [broˈsiːrən], *v.tr. Tex:* to card (pile, etc.).

Brot, *n.* **-(e)s/-e.** **1.** (*a*) bread; **frisches, frisch gebackenes, B.,** fresh, new, bread; **trockenes B.,** (i) old, stale, bread; (ii) dry bread; **B. backen,** to bake bread; **B. schneiden,** to cut, slice, bread; **B. anschneiden,** to cut a loaf; **ein Stück, eine Scheibe, B.,** a piece, slice, of bread; **ein Laib B., ein B.,** a loaf (of bread); **ein halbes B.,** half a loaf; **geweihtes B.,** consecrated bread; **um B. betteln,** to beg for bread; (*b*) (a slice of) bread and butter; **Brote streichen, machen,** to cut bread and butter, to make sandwiches; **ein B. mit Käse, Schinken,** (i) a slice of bread with cheese, ham, an open cheese-, ham-sandwich; (ii) a cheese-, ham-sandwich; *see also* **brechen** I.

1 (*a*). **2.** nourishment, sustenance; living; **das tägliche B.,** the daily bread; *B:* **unser täglich B. gib uns heute,** give us this day our daily bread; **sich selbst sein B. verdienen,** to earn one's own living; *F:* to earn one's bread and butter; **sein gesichertes B. haben,** to have a (steady) income; **ein hartes B. haben,** to work hard for one's living; **j-m das, sein, B. nehmen,** to deprive s.o. of his living; *B:* **im Schweiße deines Angesichts sollst du dein B. essen,** in the sweat of thy face shalt thou eat bread; **der Mensch lebet nicht vom B. allein,** man shall not live by bread alone; *Prov:* **wes B. ich ess', des Lied ich sing',** I believe in supporting my benefactor; **er sah aus, als hätten die Hühner ihm das B. weggenommen,** he looked completely taken aback, quite dumbfounded. *See also* **Butter, Wasser.**

Brotaufstrich, *m.* spread (for bread).

Brotbäcker, *m.* baker (of bread).

Brotbäckerei, *f.* bakery.

Brotbaum, *m.* = **Brotfruchtbaum.**

Brotbereitung, *f.* manufacture of bread; making, baking, of bread.

Brotberuf, *m.* utilitarian profession; bread-and-butter job.

Brotbeutel, *m.* haversack; bread bag.

Brotbohrer, *m. Ent:* meal beetle.

Brotbrechen, *n. Ecc:* breaking of bread.

Brotbrett, *n.* bread-board.

Brötchen, *n.* -s/-, (*a*) (bread) roll; **belegtes B.,** roll with meat, cheese, etc.; (*b*) small loaf.

Broterwerb, *m.* (means of) living; livelihood; **die Kunst ist sein B.,** art is his livelihood.

Brotfabrik, *f.* bread-factory.

Brotform, *f.* (*a*) baking-tin for bread, *U.S:* bread pan; (*b*) shape of loaf.

Brotfrucht, *f. Bot:* bread-fruit.

Brotfruchtbaum, *m. Bot:* bread-fruit tree; jack-tree.

Brotgeber, *m.* = **Brotherr.**

Brotgetreide, *n.* bread-cereals, bread-stuffs.

Brotherr, *m.* employer, boss; master.

Brothobel, *m.* bread-cutter.

Brotkäfer, *m. Ent:* meal beetle.

Brotkammer, *f.* bread-store; *Nau:* bread-room; bread-locker.

Brotkapsel, *f.* bread-bin, *U.S:* bread box.

Brotkarte, *f. Adm:* bread (ration-)card.

Brotkasten *m.* bread-bin, *U.S:* bread box.

Brotkorb, *m.* bread-basket; *F:* **j-m den B. höher hängen,** to put s.o. on short allowance, on short rations, commons.

Brotkrankheit, *f.* mould (disease) (in bread).

Brotkrume, *f.* bread-crumb.

Brotkruste, *f.* (*a*) bread-crust; (*b*) crust (of bread), end of a loaf.

Brotlaib, *n.* loaf of bread.

brotlos, *a.* without means of living; unemployed; **eine brotlose Kunst,** an unremunerative art *or* trade; **er ist b. geworden,** he has lost his livelihood, his job; **j-n b. machen,** to deprive s.o. of his living.

Brotmarke, *f. Adm:* bread (ration-)coupon.

Brotmaschine, *f.* bread-cutter, bread-slicer.

Brotmehl *n.* flour for bread.

Brotmesser, *n.* bread-knife.

Brotneid, *m.* professional jealousy.

Brotnußbaum, *m. Bot:* bread-nut tree.

Brotpflaster, *n. Med:* bread-poultice.

Brotpilz, *m. Fung:* pore-fungus.

Brotpudding, *m. Cu:* bread-pudding.

Brotraffinade, *f.* loaf-sugar.

Brotrinde, *f.* bread-crust.

Brotröster, *m.* (electric) toaster.

Brotsäge, *f.* bread-saw.

Brotsauce, *f. Cu:* bread-sauce.

Brotscheibe, *f.* slice of bread; **geröstete B.,** piece of toast.

brötscheln, *v.i.* (*haben*) & *tr. Dial:* (*a*) to fry (sth.); (*b*) = **brutzeln.**

Brotschieber, *m.* (oven-)peel.

Brotschimmel, *m. Fung:* blue, green, mould.

Brotschneidemaschine, *f.* bread-cutter, bread-slicer.

Brotschnitte, *f.* slice of bread.

Brotschrift, *f. Print:* body-type.

Brotsonntag, *m.* laetare Sunday.

Brotstudium, *n.* utilitarian study.

Brotsuppe, *f. Cu:* bread-soup, panada.

Brotteig, *m.* bread dough.

Brotteller, *m.* round bread-board.

Brottorte, *f. Cu:* (kind of) cake with breadcrumbs and almonds.

Brottrommel, *f.* bread-bin, *U.S:* bread box.

Brotverdiener, *m.* breadwinner.

Brotwürfel, *m. Cu:* bread-cube; **gerösteter B.,** croûton.

Brotwurzel, *f. Bot:* Chinese yam, Chinese potato, cinnamon vine.

Brotzeit, *f. South German:* (*a*) (mid-morning *or* afternoon) break for a snack; **B. machen,** to break off for a snack; to have a snack; (*b*) (substantial) mid-morning *or* afternoon snack.

Brotzeit, *f. Dial:* **1.** = tea-break. **2.** (afternoon) snack.

Brotzucker, *m.* loaf-sugar.

brouillieren [bruˑ'ji:rən, brul'ji:rən], *v.tr.* **1.** to mix up, to jumble; to throw sth. into confusion. **2.** to set (people) at variance; to cause misunderstanding between people.

Brouillon [brul'jõ:], *n.* -s/-s, (*a*) rough draft; (*b*) rough-book, waste-book.

Browning ['brauniŋ], *m.* -s/-s, automatic (pistol), Browning.

Brownsch [braunʃ], *a. Ph:* **Brownsche Bewegung,** Brownian motion.

Browns-Sittich ['brauns], *m. Orn:* Brown's parakeet.

Bruch[1] [brux], *m.* -(e)s/⸚e. **1.** (*a*) breaking, bursting (of dyke, etc.); breakage, rupture (of metal, parts of machinery, etc.); (*b*) breaking away from, renunciation of (tradition, one's old way of life, etc.); rupture (of relations, between persons, etc.); **es kam zwischen ihnen zum B.,** they broke off their friendship, broke off friendly relations; **trotz aller Bemühungen kam es zu einem öffentlichen B.,** in spite of all efforts formal relations were broken off; (*c*) breaking, violation (of the law); infringement (of treaty); **B. des Friedens,** breach of the peace; (*d*) breaking (of voice) (*at manhood*). **2.** (*a*) crack, fissure, chink (in china, glass); crack (in metal); fissure (in stone, etc.); burst, leak (in pipe); breach (in dyke, etc.); fracture (in china, metal, wood, stone); **glatter B.,** clean break (in china, etc.); **faseriger B.,** fibrous fracture (in metal, wood); **splitteriger B.,** splintery fracture (in stone, wood, metal, china); (*b*) *Geol:* fault, break; (*c*) break, interruption (in development, etc.); **der B. in seiner künstlerischen Entwicklung zeigt sich deutlich in . . .,** the break in his artistic development is clearly visible in . . .; (*d*) fold (in paper); split (in silk, etc.); crack (in leather, etc.). **3.** (*a*) things broken, breakages; (*b*) scrap (metal, etc.); *F:* rubbish; (*c*) *Av:* crash; **B. machen,** to crash; (*d*) green twigs used for (i) marking trail left by deer, (ii) covering wound on deer, (iii) decorating hunter's hat after killing deer; (*e*) **zu B. gehen,** *F:* **in die Brüche gehen,** (*of china, etc.*) to break, to get broken; *F:* (*of friendship, etc.*) to break up; (*of pers.*) to fail, to come to naught. **4.** cheese-curd. **5.** *Min:* quarry; stone-pit. **6.** (*a*) *Surg:* fracture; **einfacher B.,** simple fracture; **komplizierter B.,** compound fracture; **einen B. einrichten,** to set a fracture; (*b*) *Med:* hernia, rupture; **irreponibler B.,** irreducible hernia; **eingeklemmter B.,** incarcerated *or* strangulated hernia; **einen B. haben,** to suffer from a hernia, to be ruptured; **einen B. einbringen,** to reduce a hernia; **sich einen B. heben,** (i) to contract a hernia by lifting a heavy object; (ii) *F:* to overstrain oneself (by lifting). **7.** *Mth:* fraction; **echter, unechter, B.,** proper, improper, fraction; **einfacher B.,** simple fraction; **einen B. erweitern,** to reduce a fraction to higher terms; **einen B. kürzen,** to reduce a fraction (by a factor).

Bruch[2] [brux], *m.* -(e)s/⸚e & *n.* -(e)s/⸚e(r), bog, marsh; morass, swamp.

Bruchband, *n. Med:* truss.

Bruchbau, *m. Min:* caving system.

Bruchbeanspruchung, *f. Mec:* breaking-strain, breaking-stress.

Bruchbeere, *f. Bot:* (*a*) great bilberry, bog bilberry, bog whortleberry; (*b*) red whortleberry, cowberry.

Bruchbelastung, *f. Mec:* breaking load.

Bruchbildung, *f. Med:* herniation.

Bruchblei, *n.* scrap lead.

Bruchboden, *m.* boggy, marshy, ground.

Bruchbude, *f. F:* **1.** tumbledown, ramshackle, building. **2.** precarious, ramshackle, business.

Bruchdecke, *f. Constr:* ridge-plate.

Bruchdehnung, *f. Mec:* (breaking) elongation.

Bruchebene, *f. Geol:* fault-plane.

Brucheinklemmung, *f. Med:* incarceration *or* strangulation of a hernia.

bruchfest, *a. Mec: etc:* fracture-resisting.

Bruchfestigkeit, *f. Mec:* breaking strength, ultimate strength.

Bruchfläche, *f.* fracture-surface, surface of fracture; fracture; *Geol:* (i) fracture plane; (ii) fault-plane.

Bruchfuge, *f. Geol:* fracture.

Bruchgebirge, *n. Geol:* fault scarp.

Bruchglas, *n.* cullet, broken glass.

Bruchgleichung, *f. Mth:* fractional equation.

Bruchhasenohr, *n. Bot:* hare's ear, thorough-wax, thoroughwort.

Bruchheide, *f. Bot:* (*a*) grey, black, heath; purple, red, Scotch, heather; (*b*) bell-heather, crow-ling, honey-bottle; (*c*) Cornish heath, moor-heath.

bruchig ['bru:xiç], *a.* boggy, marshy.

brüchig ['bryçiç], *a.* (*a*) brittle; friable; (*of metal, clay*) short; (*b*) cracked (voice); (*of leather, etc.*) liable to crack; flawy, weak (metal, etc.); weak (pact, union, etc.); **brüchige Seide,** silk that splits (where it is creased); **brüchige Stelle,** flaw, weak spot (in metal, china, etc.).

-brüchig, *comb.fm. a.* **1.** *Metall:* -short; **rotbrüchig,** red-short. **2.** (pers.) who has broken, violated (a promise, treaty, etc.); **eidbrüchig,** perjurious; **ehebrüchig,** adulterous.

Brüchigkeit, *f.* brittleness; friability; liability to become cracked, split, etc.; *Metall:* shortness (of iron).

-brüchigkeit, *comb.fm. f.* **1.** *Metall:* -shortness; **Rotbrüchigkeit** *f,* red-shortness. **2.** (repeated) breaking, violation (of promise, treaty); **Eidbrüchigkeit,** perjury; **Treubrüchigkeit,** perfidiousness.

Bruchinhalt, *m. Med:* contents of a hernia.

Bruchknabenkraut, *n. Bot:* marsh orchis, marsh orchid; meadow rocket; dead man's fingers; male satyrion.

Bruchkraut, *n. Bot:* **1.** rupture-wort, burst-wort. **2.** French, golden, lung-wort; wall hawkweed. **3.** agrimony. **4.** hare's ear; thorough-wax; thoroughwort.

Bruchlager, *n. Stonew:* natural bed of stone.

bruchlanden, *v.i. insep.* (*sein*) (*p.p.* **bruchgelandet)** *Av:* (*of aircraft, pilot*) to make a crash-landing, to crash-land; **Bruchlandung** *f,* crash-landing.

Bruchlast, *f. Mec.E: Constr: etc:* breaking load; *Av:* failing load.

Bruchlinie, *f. Geol: etc:* (i) fracture (in rock); (ii) faultline; (iii) split (in wall, rock, etc.); (line of the) break (in china, etc.).

Bruchmetall, *n.* scrap metal.

Bruchprobe, *f. Mec:* breaking test.

Bruchrechnung, *f.* fractional arithmetic; *F:* fractions.

Bruchreis, *m.* broken rice.

Bruchrohrsänger, *m. Orn:* Cetti's warbler.

Bruchsack, *m. Med:* sack of a hernia.

Bruchschaden, *m. Com:* (damage by) breakage.

Bruchschiene, *f. Surg:* splint.

Bruchschlange, Bruchschleiche, *f. Rept:* slow-worm, blind-worm.

Bruchschrift, *f. Print:* Gothic type, letter; *Pal:* Gothic script.

Bruchspalte, *f. Geol:* fault cleft, fault fissure.

Bruchspannung, *f. Mec:* breaking-stress, breaking-strain; breaking load.

Bruchstein, *m.* quarry stone; rough stone; rubble.

Bruchsteinmauerwerk, *n.* quarry-stone bond; quarry-stone masonry.

Bruchstelle, *f.* (*a*) break; fracture; crack; broken place; (*b*) breaking point.

Bruchstrich, *m. Mth:* line between two parts of a fraction; fraction bar.

Bruchstück, *n.* fragment; part; splinter (of wood, etc.); chip (of stone, etc.); **kleines B.,** small fragment; particle; **etwas aus Bruchstücken wieder zusammensetzen,** to piece fragments of sth. together; **Bruchstücke von Mauerwerk,** broken pieces of masonry; **Bruchstücke einer Unterhaltung, eines Liedes,** scraps of a conversation, snatches of a song.

bruchstückhaft, *a.* fragmentary; *adv.* (*of text*) **b. überliefert,** transmitted, handed down, as a fragment, as fragments, in fragmentary form; (*of work of art, text, etc.*) **b. erhalten,** preserved, surviving, as a fragment, as fragments, in fragments, in fragmentary form.

bruchstückweise, *adv.* in fragments; (*of work of art, text, etc.*) **b. erhalten sein,** to be preserved in fragments; **ich habe das Gespräch nur b. verstehen können,** I could only understand scraps of the conversation.

Bruchstufe, *f. Geol:* step fault.

Bruchteil, *m.* fraction.

Bruchwasserläufer, *m. Orn:* wood sandpiper.

Bruchweide, *f. Bot:* crack-willow.

Bruchweißkehlchen, *n. Orn:* sedge-warbler.

Bruchwurz, *f. Bot:* agrimony.

Bruchzahl, *f. Mth:* fraction(al) number.

Brücke, *f.* -/-n. **1.** bridge; **hölzerne, eiserne, B.,** wooden, iron, bridge; **bewegliche B.,** movable,

opening, bridge; **gerade, schiefe, B.,** straight, skew, bridge; **zweigeschossige B.,** double-level bridge; **fliegende B.,** flying-bridge (*on suspension cable*); trail-bridge; **die B. senken,** to lower the bridge; **die B. heben,** to lift, raise, the bridge; **eine B. bauen,** to build a bridge; **eine B. über den Fluß schlagen,** to build, throw a bridge across the river; **eine B. abbrechen,** to dismantle a bridge; **die B. ausfahren, einfahren,** to open, close, the bridge; **eine B. führt über, überspannt, den Strom,** a bridge crosses, spans, the river; **B. zur Vergangenheit,** link with the past; *F:* **alle Brücken hinter sich abbrechen,** to burn one's boats; *F:* **j-m goldene Brücken bauen,** to give s.o. an easy way out, an easy retreat. **2.** *Nau:* (*a*) (captain's) bridge; (*b*) landing-stage; jetty, pier; wharf; (landing) gangway. **3.** (*a*) *Dent:* bridge; (*b*) bridge (of spectacles); (*c*) (floor) rug; (*d*) *Geol:* bridge, connecting ridge. **4.** *Anat:* **B. des Varolius,** pons Varolii. **5.** *El:* bridge; **Wheatstonesche B.,** Wheatstone's bridge. **6.** *Gym:* back-bend (position).

Brückenarbeit, *f. Dent:* bridgework.

Brückenbahn, *f.* floor of a bridge; carriageway, roadway, road, of a bridge.

Brückenbalken, *m.* bridge girder.

Brückenbau, *m.* bridge construction, bridge-building.

Brückenbauer, *m.* builder of bridges.

Brückenbaukommando, *n. Mil:* bridging-party.

Brückenbock, *m.* trestle of a bridge.

Brückenbogen, *m.* arch of a bridge.

Brückenboot, *n.* pontoon.

Brückendeck, *n. Nau:* bridge-deck.

Brückenechse, *f. Rept:* tuatara.

Brückenfigur, *f.* (sculptured) figure on a bridge.

Brückengeländer, *n.* (*a*) parapet, balustrade; (*b*) railing, side-rail, hand-rail (of bridge).

Brückengeld, *n.* bridge-toll; bridge-money.

Brückenhaus, *n.* **1.** toll-house (on bridge). **2.** *Nau:* bridge-house.

Brückenhöhe, *f.* breast-height; breast level.

Brückenjoch, *n.* **1.** bay of a bridge. **2.** *Civ.E:* (wooden) pier of a bridge.

Brückenkanal, *m.* aqueduct bridge, aqueduct.

Brückenkopf, *m.* **1.** end, head, of a bridge. **2.** *Mil:* bridge-head.

Brückenkran, *m.* bridge-crane.

Brückenlappen, *m. Surg:* pedicled graft (of skin).

Brückenoberbau, *m.* superstructure of a bridge.

Brückenöffnung, *f.* opening of a bridge.

Brückenpfahl, *m.* bridge pile.

Brückenpfeiler, *m.* pier of a bridge; *Civ.E: etc:* gantry pier (of distributing machinery).

Brückenplastik, *f. Surg:* pedicled transplantation (of skin).

Brückenrampe, *f.* approach to a bridge.

Brückenschaltung, *f. El:* bridge connection.

Brückenschanze, *f. Mil:* bridge-head.

Brückenschiff, *n.* pontoon.

Brückenschwelle, *f. Rail:* bridge-sleeper.

Brückensicherung, *f. El:* bridge fuse.

Brückensteg, *m.* footbridge.

Brückensyndrom, *n. Med:* Foville's syndrome.

Brückenträger, *m.* bridge girder.

Brückenüberbau, *m.* superstructure of a bridge.

Brückenwaage, *f.* weigh-bridge.

Brückenwärter, *m.* bridge-keeper.

Brückenwiderstand, *m. El:* bridge resistance.

Brückenzoll, *m.* bridge-toll.

Brückner, *m.* **-s/-,** bridge-keeper.

Brüden, *m.* **-s/.** *North G.Dial:* =**Brodem.**

brüden, *v.tr. North G.Dial:* to tease (s.o.).

Bruder, *m.* **-s/¨-,** brother. **1. leiblicher B.,** own, full, brother, brother-german; **älterer, jüngerer, B.,** elder, younger, brother; **die Brüder Schmitt,** the brothers Schmitt, the Schmitt brothers; **Joseph und seine Brüder,** Joseph and his brethren; *B:* **soll ich meines Bruders Hüter sein?** am I my brother's keeper? *Lit:* **das Motiv der feindlichen Brüder,** the theme of the hostile brothers. **2.** (*a*) friend, companion; fellow; **alle Menschen sind Brüder,** all men are brothers; **und willst du nicht mein B. sein, so schlag' ich dir den Schädel ein,** you be my friend, or I'll knock your block off; **ein lustiger B.,** a jolly fellow, a merry chap; *F:* a boon companion; *F:* **B. Jonathan,** Brother Jonathan; *F:* **unter Brüdern ist es zehn Mark wert,** (i) between friends it costs, would be, ten marks; (ii) even between friends it's only worth ten marks; *Prov:* **gleiche Brüder, gleiche Kappen,** (i) what one does, the others must do too; we must all hang together; we're all in the same boat; (ii) share and share alike; *B:* **was ihr getan habt einem unter meinen geringsten Brüdern, das habt ihr mir getan,** inasmuch as ye have done it unto one of the least of these my brethren, ye have done it unto me; *Ecc:* **meine lieben Brüder,** dearly beloved brethren; **Brüder in Christo,** brothers in Christ; (*b*) colleague; **B. in Apoll,** fellow poet; **Brüder im Geiste,** spiritual brothers; (*c*) *Pej:* fellow; **ein böser, fauler, B.** *F:* a bad egg, a bad lot, an unpleasant type; a bad fellow; *see also* **warm. 3.** (*in monastic order*) lay brother; **Brüder vom gemeinsamen Leben,** Brothers of the Common Life; **die Böhmischen Brüder,** the Moravian Brethren, the United Brothers; **die Barmherzigen Brüder,** the Brothers Hospitallers; **'B. Franz,'** 'Brother Francis'. **4. -bruder,** *comb.fm.* brother . . . , fellow . . . , fellow-; **Amtsbruder,** colleague, *esp.* fellow-clergyman; **Waffenbruder,** brother, fellow, soldier, brother-in-arms; **Blutsbruder,** blood brother.

Bruderart, *f.* **nach B.,** in a brotherly manner.

Bruderbund, *m.* fraternity; brotherhood; close alliance.

Brüderchen, *n.* **-s/-,** (*dim. of* **Bruder**) little brother.

Bruderfehde, *f.* fraternal feud.

Brüdergemeinde, *f.* **1.** fraternity. **2.** *Rel.Hist:* **die B.,** the religious society of Herrnhut, the Moravian Brethren.

Bruderhand, *f.* **j-m die B. reichen,** to hold out, extend, a friendly hand to s.o.; **er fiel durch B.,** he fell by his brother's hand.

Bruderhaß, *m.* fraternal hate.

Brüderhaus, *n. Ecc:* institute for the training of Protestant deacons.

Bruderherz, *n. Lit:* brother's heart; *Lit. & Hum:* (*esp. as form of address*) dear brother.

Bruderkrieg, *m.* fraternal, civil, war.

Brüderlein, *n.* **-s/-,** (*dim. of* **Bruder**) little brother.

brüderlich, *a.* brotherly, brother-like, fraternal; *adv.* in a brotherly manner; **b. teilen,** to share and share alike.

Brüderlichkeit, *f.* brotherliness; fraternity.

Bruderliebe, *f.* brotherly, fraternal, love; love of one's fellow men.

Brudermord, *m.* fratricide.

Brudermörder, *m.* (*pers.*) fratricide.

brudermörderisch, *a.* fratricidal.

Bruderpaar, *n.* pair of brothers.

Bruderpflicht, *f.* brotherly duty.

Brüdersaal, *m. Ecc:* fratry.

Bruderschaft, *f.* **-/-en. 1.** brotherhood. **2.** (religious, etc.) society; fraternity; brotherhood; confraternity.

Brüderschaft, *f.* **-/-en. 1. B. mit j-m trinken,** to drink (the pledge of) 'brotherhood' with s.o. (*subsequently addressing each other as* '*du*'); **B. mit j-m schließen,** to make close friends with s.o. **2.** confraternity.

Brudersfrau, *f. A:* sister-in-law.

Brudersinn, *m.* brotherliness.

Bruderskind, *n.* brother's child; nephew *or* niece.

Brüderunität, *f.*=**Brüdergemeinde 1.**

Brudervolk, *n.* nation of a kindred race.

Bruderzunft, *f.* confraternity.

Bruderzwist, *m.* fraternal feud, strife.

Brügge. *Pr.n.n.* **-s.** *Geog:* Bruges.

Brühe, *f.* **-/-n. 1.** *Cu:* (*a*) broth; stock; **klare B.,** clear (meat-)soup; (*b*) gravy; (*c*) vegetable water; decoction (of herbs). **2.** (*a*) *F:* dirty water; (*of drink*) dishwater; hogwash; (*b*) *F:* **in der B. stecken,** to be in the soup; **j-n in der B. sitzen lassen,** to leave s.o. in the lurch. **3.** *Dy:* dyeing liquor; *Leath:* liquor, solution; extract; *Tex:* solution; *Tobacco Ind:* sauce.

brühen, *v.tr.* (*a*) *Cu:* to boil; to immerse (sth.) in boiling water; to pour boiling water over (sth.); **brühend heiß**=**brühheiß;** (*b*) *Tex: Leath: etc:* to scour, to liquor (material); to treat (material) with hot water.

Brühengärbung, *f. Tan:* paddle-method tanning.

Brühfutter, *n.* scalded fodder.

brühheiß, *a.* scalding hot, piping hot.

Brühkartoffeln, *f.pl. Cu:* potatoes in broth.

brühwarm, *a.* scalding hot; **brühwarme Neuigkeit,** hot news; *adv.* **j-m etwas b. erzählen,** to repeat sth. straight away to s.o.; to bring s.o. hot news of sth.

Brühwürfel, *m.* bouillon cube, *esp.* beef cube.

Brühwurst, *f.,* **Brühwürstchen,** *n. Cu:* sausage for boiling; *esp.* Frankfurter.

Brüllaffe, *m. Z:* howling monkey, howler.

brüllen, *v.i.* (*haben*) & *v.tr.* (*of pers.*) to roar, to shout; (*of babies*) to bellow, to howl, *F:* to holler; (*of lion, gun, etc.*) to roar; (*of cattle*) to low; (*of bull*) to bellow; **b. vor Lachen,** to roar with laughter; **sich heiser b.,** to roar oneself hoarse; **vor Schmerz, Wut, b.,** to cry out, roar, with pain, in anger; **ein Lied b.,** to roar out a song; **brüllend,** roaring; **brüllendes Gelächter,** roar(s) of laughter; *B:* **der Teufel geht umher wie ein brüllender Löwe,** the devil, as a roaring lion, walketh about.

Brüller, *m.* **-s/-,** one who roars, shouts; (*baby*) howler.

Brüllerkrankheit, *f. Vet:* nymphomania (of cow).

Brüllfrosch, *m. Amph:* bullfrog.

Brüllhusten, *m.* barking cough.

Brüllstimme, *f.* stentorian voice.

Brummbär, Brummbart, *m. F:* grumbler, growler.

Brummbaß, *m. Hum:* (*a*) (growling) bass (voice); (*b*) double-bass.

Brummeisen, *n. Mus:* Jew's harp.

brummen. I. *v.tr. & i.* (*haben*) **1.** (*of pers.*) to speak in a deep voice; to speak indistinctly; to mumble; to growl; to grumble; to sing (i) in a deep bass voice, (ii) tunelessly; (*of double bass*) to growl; (*of organ*) to boom; (*of insect*) to buzz, to drone; (*of engine*) to buzz, to boom; (*of a top*) to spin, to hum; *W.Tel: etc:* (*of valve, etc.*) to hum; *F:* **mir brummt der Schädel,** (i) my head aches, I have a bad head; (ii) my head is buzzing; *see also* **Bart** 1. **2.** *F:* to do time; to do a stretch; to be locked up.

II. *vbl s.* **Brummen,** *n. in vbl senses; also:* growl; buzz; boom; hum; drone.

Brummer, *m.* **-s/-. 1.** *F:* (*a*) grumbler, growler; (*b*) *El: Tp:* buzzer; (*c*) (*of aircraft*) *F:* buzzer; (*d*) *Mil: F:* heavy shot. **2.** *Ent:* bluebottle.

Brummfliege, *f. Ent:* bluebottle.

Brummhahn, *m.*=**Birkhahn.**

brummig, *a.* grumbling, growling; bad-tempered; sulky; surly.

Brummkäfer, *m.* (any) buzzing beetle.

Brummkreisel, *m.* humming top.

Brummochs(e), *m. F:* (*a*) bull; (*b*) fool, block-head.

Brummschädel, *m. F:* headache; hangover; **einen B. haben,** to have a bad head(ache); to have a hangover.

Brummstimme, *f.* deep bass (voice).

Brummton, *m.* buzz, buzzing noise (of bell, organ, etc.); droning tone, drone (of bag-pipes, etc.) growl, growling noise; *W.Tel: etc:* humming noise (of radio, etc.).

Brunelle [bru'nɛlə], *f.* **-/-n. 1.** *Bot:*=**Braunelle** 1. **2.**=**Brünelle.**

Brünelle [bry'nɛlə], *f.* **-/-n. 1.** (dried) prune. **2.** *Hort:* nectarine.

brünett [bry'nɛt], *a.* (*of woman*) brunette.

Brünette [bry'nɛtə], *f.* **-/-n,** brunette.

Brunft, *f.* **-/.** *Ven:* rut, rutting (time); **in der B. sein,** to rut.

Brunftfeige, *f. Ven:* head scent gland (of chamois buck).

brunftig, brünftig, *a. Ven:* rutting (deer, etc.); **b. sein,** to rut.

Brunftplatz, *m.* place of rutting (of deer).

Brunftzeit, *f. Ven:* rutting season.

Brunhild, Brünhild. *Pr.n.f.* **-s.** Brunhild.

brünieren [bry'niːrən], *v.tr. Metalw:* to brown. to burnish; to blue.

Brünierstein. *m.* burnishing stone.

Brunn, *m.* **-(e)s/-en.** *Poet:* (i) spring; (ii) well.

Brünnchen, *n.* **-s/-,** (*dim. of* **Brunnen**) *esp.* (*a*) drinking-fountain; (*b*)=**Brunnen 4.**

Brünne, *f.* **-/-n.** *Arm: Her:* shirt of mail.

Brunnen, *m.* **-s/-. 1.** (*a*) spring; *Lit:* fountain; **klarer,** *Poet:* **lauterer, B.,** clear spring; **der B. des Lebens,** the fount of life; **der B. der Weisheit,** the fount(ain) of wisdom; (*b*) *A. & Lit:* water (from a spring); (*c*) mineral spring, waters from mineral springs, medicinal water; **B. trinken,** to take the waters (at a spa); (*d*) *A:* spa. **2.** (*a*) well; draw-well; fountain; drinking fountain; **offener B.,** open well; **artesischer B.,** artesian well; **abessinischer B.,** driven well, drive-well; tube-well; **einen B. senken,** to drive, sink, a well; **einen B. graben, bohren,** to dig, bore, a well; **die Brunnen plätschern, rauschen,** the fountains splash; *Lit:* the fountains are plashing; *B:* **der B. des Abgrunds,** the bottomless pit; (*b*) pump; water-tap; water-cock. **3.** (*a*) shaft, pit (of mine); (*b*) *Constr:* pit (for concrete pier, etc.); (*c*) *Nau:* well; space between bridge and forecastle. **4.** *A. & F:* water, urine; **einen B. machen,** to pass water.

Brunnenanlage, *f.* **1.** construction, installation, of a well, a fountain. **2.** installations of a watering establishment.

Brunnenanstalt, *f.* watering establishment.

Brunnenarzt, *m.* physician attached to a watering establishment.

Brunnenbau, *m.* construction of a well, a fountain.

Brunnenbauer, *m.* (*pers.*) well-sinker, -digger, -borer.

Brunnenbohrer, *m.,* **Brunnenbohrgerät,** *n.* well-borer.

Brunnenbrüstung, *f.* curb, parapet, rim, of a well.
Brunnendeck, *n. Nau:* after-deck.
Brunneneimer, *m.* well-bucket.
Brunneneinfassung, *f.* curb, rim, lip, of a well.
Brunnenfaden, *m. Bac:* crenothrix polyspora.
Brunnenfigur, *f.* sculptured figure on a fountain.
Brunnenfundierung, *f.* 1. well-foundation. 2. *Constr:* foundation-shafting.
Brunnengeländer, *n.* railing of a well.
Brunnengründung, *f. Constr:* foundation-shaft.
Brunnenhaus, *n.* (*a*) well-house; (*b*) pavilion (at mineral spring); pump-room.
Brunnenkammer, *f.* pump-room.
Brunnenkranz, *m.* construction shell of a well *or* pit.
Brunnenkraut, *n. Bot:* (*a*) brook liverwort, stone liverwort; (*b*) black crottles, stone-crottles, -rag, -raw.
Brunnenkresse, *f. Bot:* (*a*) water-cress; lady's smock; bitter cress; (*b*) winter cress; London rocket.
Brunnenkur, *f.* course of medicinal waters; spa cure.
Brunnenlattich, *m. Bot:* coltsfoot.
Brunnenloch, *n.* well-hole; well-pit.
Brunnenmacher, *m.* = **Brunnenbauer.**
Brunnenmantel, *m. Constr:* lining of a well.
Brunnenmeister, *m.* inspector of wells.
Brunnenmoos, *n. Moss:* **1.** philonotis. **2.** (greater) water moss.
Brunnenmund, *m.* lip of a well.
Brunnenpest, *f. Bac:* crenothrix polyspora.
Brunnenschacht, *m.* pit, shaft, of a well.
Brunnenschlinge, *f.* = **Brunnenkranz.**
Brunnenständer, *m.* (*a*) water-crane; stand-pipe (for water); (*b*) drinking fountain.
Brunnenstange, *f.* pole of a draw-well.
Brunnenstock[1], *m.* = **Brunnenständer.**
Brunnenstock[2], *m. Bot:* great bindweed.
Brunnenstube, *f.* (*a*) pump-room; (*b*) well-chamber; *F:* **die B. der deutschen Dichtung,** the well-springs of German poetry.
Brunnentrog, *m.* trough of a fountain.
Brunnenvergiftung, *f.* poisoning, infection, of a well; **moralische B.,** wholesale calumny.
Brunnenwasser, *n.* well-water, fountain-water.
Brunnenzoll, *m. Hyd:* water-inch.
Brünnlein, *n.* -s/- = **Brünnchen.**
Brunnquell, *m. Poet:* well-spring; **der B. des Lebens,** the well-spring, the fount, of life.
Brunst, *f.* -/⸗e, (*a*) heat (of animals); (*b*) (i) sexual passion, excitement; (ii) *Lit:* ardour, passion, fervency; (*c*) *A:* = **Brand 1.**
brunsten, *v.i.* (*haben*) (*of animals*) to be on, in, heat.
brünstig, *a.* (*a*) (animal) on, in, heat; (*of animals*) **b. sein,** to be on, in, heat; (*b*) *Lit:* ardent, fiery; **brünstiges Flehen,** ardent supplication; *B:* **brünstige Liebe,** fervent charity.
Brunstzeit, *f.* period of sexual excitement; season of heat.
brunzen, *v.i.* (*haben*) *P:* to urinate.
Brüsch, *f.* -/. *Dial: Bot:* heather, ling.
brüsk, *a.* brusque, abrupt; rough; rude; *adv.* **sie fertigte ihn b. ab,** she was very short with him.
brüskieren [brys'kiːrən]. **I.** *v.tr.* to be sharp, abrupt (with s.o.); to treat (s.o.) with scant courtesy; to snub (s.o.); *F:* to brush (s.o.) off.
II. *vbl s.* **Brüskierung,** *f.* (*a*) *in vbl senses;* (*b*) affront, snub, insult.
Brussa ['brusaː]. *Pr.n.n.* -s. *Geog:* Brusa.
Brüssel. *Pr.n.n.* -s. *Geog:* Brussels.
Brüsseler, Brüßler. 1. *m.* -s/-. *Geog:* native, inhabitant, of Brussels. **2.** *inv.a.* of Brussels, Brussels . . .; **Brüsseler Kohl,** Brussels sprouts; **Brüsseler Spitze,** Brussels lace; *see also* **Teppich.**
brüßlerisch, *a.* of Brussels, Brussels. . . .
Brust, *f.* -/⸗e. **1.** (*a*) chest; breast (of pers., animal); thorax (of insect); **eine breite B.,** a broad chest; **eine breite B. haben,** to be broad-chested; **eine schmale B.,** a narrow chest; (*b*) *Cu:* breast (of veal, chicken, etc.); brisket (of beef); (*c*) **j-n an die B. drücken,** to press s.o. to one's breast; **j-n an seine B. ziehen,** to clasp s.o. to one's breast; **seine B. entblößen,** to bare one's breast; **j-m die Pistole auf die B. setzen,** (i) to stick a gun in s.o.'s ribs; (ii) *F:* to hold a pistol at s.o.'s head; **sich** *dat. & acc.* **an die B. schlagen, an seine B. klopfen,** (i) to beat one's breast (as a sign of contrition); (ii) to be sorry; **du mußt an deine eigene B. klopfen, dir selber an die B. schlagen,** it is your own fault; **sich in die B. werfen,** to pose, to strut; **B. 'raus!,** chest out! **B. an B. stehen,** to stand shoulder to shoulder. **2.** chest; **eine schwache B. haben,** to have a weak chest; **er hat es auf der B.,** (i) he is short of breath; (ii) he has a touch of bronchitis; **er ist schwach auf der B.,** (i) he has a weak chest; (ii) *F:* he is short of money; **aus voller B. singen,** to sing lustily; **aus voller, tiefer, B. stöhnen,** to sigh from the depths of one's soul; **tief in seiner B. wußte er, daß . . .,** he knew in his inmost heart that . . . **3.** (woman's) breast; **die Brüste,** the breasts, the bosom; **ein Kind an der B. haben,** to have a child at the breast; **einem Kind die B. geben,** to give a child the breast, to suckle a child. **4.** *Cost:* front, breast (of shirt, etc.); bodice; *Arm:* breast-plate. **5.** *Min:* working-face, breast; face (of quarry). **6.** *Tchn: etc:* front, front-part (of apparatus, etc.). **7.** *Nau:* breast (of ship's bow).
Brustatmung, *f. Physiol:* costal respiration; deep breathing.
Brustband, *n.* = **Brustbinde.**
Brustbandsturmschwalbe, *f. Orn:* white-winged petrel, collared petrel.
Brustbandsturmvogel, *m. Orn:* Gould's petrel.
Brustbaum, *m. Tex:* breast-beam.
Brustbeere, *f. Bot:* **1.** jujube (fruit). **2.** *F:* sebesten (plum).
Brustbein, *n. Anat:* breastbone, sternum.
Brustbeklemmung, *f. Med:* tightness of the chest.
Brustbeschwerde, *f.* chest-complaint.
Brustbeule, *f. Vet:* swelling on a horse's chest.
Brustbeutel, *m. Mil: etc:* money-bag (worn round neck).
Brustbild, *n.* (*a*) portrait (of head and shoulders); half-length portrait; (*b*) *Sculp:* bust.
Brustbinde, *f.* (*a*) *Surg:* breast bandage; plastron; (*b*) *Cost:* breast-band.
Brustblatt, *n.* **1.** *Harn:* breast-band. **2.** *Anat:* sternum, marsupial plate.
Brustbohrer, *m. Tls:* breast-drill; brace (and bit).
Brustbonbon, *m.* cough-sweet, cough-drop.
Brustbräune, *f. Med: F:* angina pectoris.
Brustbreite, *f. Sp:* **um B. gewinnen,** to win by a (mere) foot.
Brüstchen, *n.* -s/-, (*dim. of* **Brust**) (*a*) small breast; (*b*) bodice.
Brustdrüse, *f. Anat:* mammary gland; **innere B.,** thymus (gland); **die Brustdrüsen,** the mammaries.
Brustdrüsenentzündung, *f. Med:* mastitis.
Brustdrüsenkrebs, *m. Med:* cancer of the breast.
Brustelixir, *n.* cough-mixture.
brüsten (sich), *v.refl.* to boast, to brag (**mit,** about).
Brustentzündung, *f. Med: F:* (*a*) mastitis; (*b*) pleurisy; (*c*) pneumonia.
Brustfell, *n. Anat:* pleura.
Brustfellentzündung, *f. Med:* pleurisy; **trockene B.,** dry pleurisy; **feuchte B.,** wet pleurisy.
Brustfernsprecher, *m.* portable telephone.
Brustfinne, *f.* = **Brustflosse.**
Brustfläche, *f. Tls:* top face (of cutting tool).
Brustflosse, *f. Ich:* pectoral fin, breast-fin.
Brustflosser, *m.* -s/-. *Ich:* thoracic (fish).
Brustgang, *m. Anat:* thoracic duct.
Brustgurt, *m.* **1.** *Harn:* breast-band. **2.** *Swim:* harness (for learner).
Brustgürtel, *m. Anat:* pectoral girdle.
Brustharnisch, *m. Arm:* (i) cuirass; (ii) breast-plate; plastron.
Brusthieb, *m. Fenc:* inside flank-cut.
brusthoch, *a. & adv.* breast-high.
Brusthöhle, *f. Anat:* thoracic cavity.
Brustholz, *n. Nau:* cutwater.
Brustjunge, *n.* (*decl. as adj.*) *Z:* suckling.
Brustkasten, *m. Anat: F:* thorax.
Brustkind, *n.* breast-fed baby.
Brustkorb, *m. Anat:* thorax.
Brustkrampf, *m. Med: A:* asthma.
brustkrank, *a.* suffering from a weak chest.
Brustkrankheit, *f.* chest-disease; chest trouble.
Brustkrause, *f. A.Cost:* shirt-frill, ruffle, jabot.
Brustkrebs, *m. Med:* cancer of the breast.
Brustkreuz, *n. Ecc:* (bishop's, etc.) pectoral cross.
Brustlattich, *m. Bot:* coltsfoot.
Brustlatz, *m. A.Cost:* (*a*) (woman's) modesty-vest; (*b*) (man's) plastron.
Brustlehne, *f.* parapet; balustrade; window-rail; railing, rail.
Brustleiden, *n. Med:* chest complaint.
Brustleier, *f. Tls:* brace (and bit).
Brüstlein, *n.* -s/- = **Brüstchen** (*a*).
Brustmauer, *f. Arch: Constr:* parapet (wall) (of bridge, etc.); breast-wall (of window).
Brustmesser, *m. Med:* stethometer.
Brustmikrophon, *n.* chest microphone.
Brustmilch, *f.* breast-milk.
Brustmuskel, *m. Anat:* pectoral muscle; **großer, kleiner, B.,** pectoralis major, minor; **die Brustmuskeln,** the pectoral muscles; the chest-muscles.
Brustnadel, *f.* breast-pin; *U.S:* stickpin.
Brustnerv, *m. Anat:* thoracic nerve.
Brustpanzer, *m.* **1.** *Arm:* cuirass. **2.** plastron (of tortoise, etc.).
Brustplatte, *f. Tls:* breast-plate.
Brustpulver, *n. Pharm:* Kurella's powder (used to relieve chest and bowels).
Brustquart, *f. Fenc:* inside flank-cut.
Brustriemen, *m. Harn:* breast-harness, breast-strap.
Brustring, *m. Ent:* segment of the thorax; **mittlerer B.,** mesothorax.
Brustschild, *n. Ecc:* pectoral.
Brustschutz, *m.* (*a*) *Fenc: etc:* plastron; breast-protector; (*b*) chest-protector.
Brustschwimmen, *n.* breast-stroke.
Brustschwimmer, *m.* breast-stroke swimmer.
Brustseuche, *f. Vet:* contagious pleuropneumonia.
Bruststärker, *m. Gym:* chest expander.
Bruststich, *m.* **1.** stabbing pain in the chest. **2.** *Surg:* puncture of the thorax.
Bruststimme, *f. Mus:* chest-voice.
Bruststück, *n.* (*a*) *Art:* = **Brustbild;** (*b*) *Arm:* breast-plate; *Cost:* front, breast (of shirt, etc.); (*c*) *Ent: Arach: Crust:* thorax; (*d*) *Cu:* = **Brust 1** (*b*).
Brusttasche, *f.* breast-pocket.
Brusttee, *m. Pharm:* (infusion of) pectoral herbs; pectoral tea.
Brustterz, *f. Fenc:* outside flank-cut.
brusttief, *a. & adv.* breast-deep; *adv.* **b. im Wasser stehen,** to stand up to one's chest in water.
Brustton, *m. Mus:* chest-tone; *F:* **im B. der Überzeugung (sprechen),** (to speak) with overriding conviction.
Brusttuch, *n. Cost:* kerchief (worn round neck); neckerchief; jabot.
Brustumfang, *m.* (*of man*) chest-measurement; (*of woman*) bust-measurement.
Brüstung, *f. Arch:* balustrade, parapet (of bridge, etc.); parapet (of window).
Brüstungsgitter, *n.* (iron, etc.) balustrade, railing (of French window, balcony).
Brüstungsmauer, *f. Arch: Constr:* parapet-wall.
Brustwalze, *f. Paperm:* breast-roll.
Brustwams, *n. A.Cost:* doublet.
Brustwarze, *f. Anat:* nipple, papilla.
Brustwasser, *n.* **1.** *Med:* serous fluid of the pleural cavity. **2.** *Pharm:* spirit of peppermint.
Brustwassersucht, *f. Med:* dropsy of the chest, hydrothorax.
Brustwehr, *f. Fort: etc:* breastwork, parapet.
Brustwerk, *n. Mus:* breast (of an organ).
Brustwinkel, *m. Tls:* cutting-angle; cutting-face.
Brustwirbel, *m. Anat:* thoracic vertebra.
Brustwurz, *f. Bot:* **1.** angelica, lung wort. **2.** sweet flag. **3.** butcher's broom, knee holly.
Brut, *f.* -/-en. **1.** brooding, sitting; (*of hen*) **in der B. sein,** to sit (on eggs). **2.** (*a*) brood; hatch; fry, spawn (of fish); nest (of insect eggs); brood (of bees); young (of oviparous animal); (*b*) progeny, *F:* brood; **mit seiner ganzen B.,** with all his brood; **eine häßliche B.,** an ugly brood; an ugly set; a bad lot; (*c*) *Bot:* shoot; gemma.
brutal [bru·'taːl], *a.* brutal, bestial; cruel; **brutaler Mensch,** brute, beast; **brutale Gewalt,** brute force; **b. machen,** to make brutal, to brutalize; **b. werden,** to become brutal, brutalized.
Brutalität [bru·ta·li·'tɛːt], *f.* -/-en, brutality, bestiality; cruelty.
Brutamme, *f. Ent:* (*of bees, ants*) nurse.
Brutanstalt, *f. Husb: Pisc:* hatchery.
Brutapparat, *m. Husb: Med:* incubator.
Brutbecher, *m. Bot:* gemma-cup (of liverworts).
Brutbiene, *f. Ap: A:* drone.
Brutblatt, *n. Bot:* bryophyllum.
Brutei, *n.* (*a*) egg for hatching; (*b*) addled, rotten, egg.
brüten. I. *v.* **1.** *v.i.* (*haben*) (*a*) to brood, to incubate; (*of hen*) to sit; **die Henne brütet auf den Eiern,** the hen sits on the eggs; (*b*) *F:* to brood (over sth.); to ponder, to reflect (about sth.); to meditate; **er sitzt da und brütet vor sich hin,** he sits there brooding; **er brütet über seinem Unglück,** he is brooding over his misfortune; (*c*) to brood, to weigh heavily; **die brütende Hitze der Sonne,** the oppressive heat of the sun; **brütend heiße Luft,** stifling, oppressively hot, air; *Lit:* **Nacht, Stille, brütet auf der Szene,** night, silence, broods over the scene. **2.** *v.tr.* (*a*) (i) = **ausbrüten;** (ii) = **bebrüten;** (*b*) *F:* to hatch, to plan; to brood (over mischief, etc.); **Rache b.,** to plan revenge, to brood over schemes of revenge.
II. *vbl s.* **Brüten** *n. in vbl senses; also:* incubation; **künstliches B.,** artificial incubation.
Brüter, *m.* -s/-, (*a*) broody hen, etc., brooder; (*b*) incubator, hatcher; *U.S:* brooder.
Brutflecken, *m.pl. Orn:* brooding-spots.
Bruthenne, *f.* sitting hen, brood-hen.

Bruthitze, *f.* incubation heat; *F:* scorching, tropical, heat.

brütig, *a.* (*a*) broody (hen); addled (egg); (*of hen*) **b. werden,** to go broody: **brütige Henne,** broody hen, brooder; (*b*) *South G.Dial:* sultry, oppressive (weather).

Brutkasten, *m. Husb: Med:* incubator.

Brutknolle, *f. Bot:* tuber.

Brutknospe, *f. Bot:* **1.** (*a*) brood-bud; (*b*) bulbil, bulblet. **2.** *Biol:* gemma.

Brutkorn, *n. Bot:* gemma.

Brutmaschine, *f. Husb: Med:* incubator.

Brutofen, *m. Husb: Med:* incubator.

Brutpflege, *f. Nat. Hist:* brood care, care of the brood, of the young.

Brutraum, *m. Ap:* brood-chamber.

Brutschrank, *m. Husb: Bac:* incubator; *Pisc:* hatching apparatus.

Brutstätte, *f.* **1.** breeding-ground, breeding-place; spawning-ground. **2.** *F:* breeding-ground, hothouse, hotbed (of corruption, intrigue, etc.).

Bruttasche, *f. Z:* marsupium, marsupial pouch.

Brutteich, *m. Pisc:* spawning pond.

brutto [ˈbruto:], *a. Com:* (*of weight, receipts, etc.*) gross.

Bruttobilanz, *f. Com:* gross balance; *Book-k:* **eine B. aufstellen,** to make, take out, a trial balance.

Bruttoeinkommen, *n.* gross income.

Bruttoeinnahmen, *f.pl. Com:* gross takings; *Book-k:* gross receipts.

Bruttoertrag, *m. Com:* gross receipts; *Com: Agr: etc:* gross yield.

Bruttogehalt, *n,* gross salary.

Bruttogewicht, *n. Com:* gross weight.

Bruttogewinn, *m. Com:* gross profit.

Bruttolohn, *m.* gross wage(s).

Bruttoregistertonne, *f. Nau:* (gross) register ton (100 *cubic feet*).

Bruttosozialprodukt, *n. Pol.Ec:* gross national product.

Bruttotonnengehalt, *m. Nau:* gross tonnage.

Bruttowert, *m. Com:* gross value.

Bruttrog, *m. Pisc:* hatching-box.

Brutus [ˈbru:tus]. *Pr.n.m.* -'. Brutus; **auch du, mein (Sohn) Brutus!** et tu Brute!

Brutwabe, *f. Ap:* brood-comb.

Brutwärme, *f.* incubation temperature.

Brutzeit, *f.* brooding time, sitting time (of bird); spawning time (of fish).

Brutzelle, *f.* **1.** *Ap:* brood-cell. **2.** *Bot:* gonidium.

brutzeln, *v.i.* (*haben*) (*a*) to fry, to be frying; (*b*) to sizzle, to crackle, to sputter.

Brutzwiebel, *f. Bot:* (*a*) offset-bulb; (*b*) bulblet, bulbil.

Bruyèreholz [bry·ˈjɛ:r-], *n.* brier-root.

Bruyèreholzpfeife, *f.* briar pipe.

Bruzin [bru·ˈtsi:n], *n.* -s/. *Ch:* brucine.

Bruzit [bru·ˈtsi:t], *m.* -(e)s/. *Min:* brucite.

Bryologe [bry·o·ˈlo:gə], *m.* -n/-n, bryologist.

Bryologie [bry·o·lo·ˈgi:], *f.* -/-n [-ˈgi:ən], bryology.

Bryonie [bry·ˈo:niə], *f.* -/-n. *Bot:* bryony.

Bryozoen [bry·o·ˈtso:ən], *n.pl. Biol:* bryozoa, polyzoa, sea-mosses.

bu, *int.* boo!

Bub, *m.* -en/-en. *South G.Dial:*=**Bube** 1.

bubbeln, *v.i.* (*haben*) to bubble.

Bübchen, *n.* -s/-, (*dim. of* **Bube**) little boy.

Bube, *m.* -n/-n. **1.** (*a*) (little) boy; **sie haben drei Buben und ein Mädel,** they have three boys and a girl; (*b*) *South G.Dial:* boy; son (*esp.* young son), young man, lad, youth; apprentice. **2.** *Hist:* servant, baggage-boy, pot-boy, page, etc. **3.** (*a*) (i) **böse Buben,** naughty boys; rascals; (ii) *B:* **wenn dich die bösen Buben locken, so folge nicht,** if sinners entice thee, consent thou not; (*b*) *North G.Dial:* rogue, scoundrel, knave, blackguard, coward; **j-n einen Buben schelten,** to call s.o. a scoundrel. **4.** *Cards:* jack, knave.

bübeln, *v.i.* (*haben*) **1.** to play boyish pranks. **2.** to behave in a loose, lascivious, manner; *A:* to wanton.

Buben-, *comb.fm. cp.* **Knaben-.**

buben, *v.i.* (*haben*) *A:* **1.** to behave in a rascally manner. **2.** to lead a debauched life; **huren und b.,** to fornicate, to whore.

Bubenfist, *m.* -(e)s/-e=**Bovist.**

Bubenkopf, *m.*=**Bubikopf.**

Bubenkragen, *m.*=**Bubikragen.**

Bubenstreich, *m.* **1.** boyish prank, lark. **2.** rascally, knavish, trick; foul play.

Bubenstück, *n.*=**Bubenstreich** 2.

Büberei, *f.* -/-en=**Bubenstreich** 2.

Bubi, *m.* -s/-s. *F:* (*pet name*) sonny.

Bubikopf, *m.* (woman's) short hair-cut; bob; shingled hair; Eton crop.

Bubikragen, *m.* Peter Pan collar.

bübisch, *a.* treacherous, knavish, rascally, foul, villainous.

Büblein, *n.* -s/- =**Bübchen.**

Bubo[1] [ˈbu:bo:], *m.* -s/-s. *Orn:* eagle-owl.

Bubo[2] [ˈbu:bo:], *m.* -s/-nen [bu·ˈbo:nən], **Bubon** [ˈbu:bo·n], *m.* -s/-en [bu·ˈbo:nən]. *Med:* bubo.

Bubonenpest, *f. Med:* bubonic plague.

Buc- *cp.* **Buk-.**

Buccinator [buki·ˈna:tor], *m.* -is/. [-na·ˈto:ris]. *Anat:* buccinator (muscle).

Buccoblätter [ˈbuko:-], *n.pl. Pharm:* buchu, buka, leaves.

Buch, *n.* -(e)s/=er. **1.** book, volume; work; (*a*) **gebundenes Buch,** bound book, bound volume; **ungebundenes Buch,** unbound book, book in sheets; **broschiertes Buch,** paper-backed, -bound, book; **ein dünnes Buch,** a slim volume; **in all seinen Büchern . . .,** in all his books, works, writings . . .; **etwas aus einem Buch lesen,** to read sth. (aloud) from a book; **ein Buch, an einem Buch, schreiben,** to write, to be writing, a book; **das Buch der Bücher,** the book of books, the Book, the Bible; *B:* **ein Buch versiegelt mit sieben Siegeln,** a book sealed with seven seals; *F:* **ein Buch mit sieben Siegeln,** a sealed book, a complete mystery; *F:* **er ist gelehrt wie ein Buch,** he is extremely knowledgeable, he's a walking encyclopaedia, a mine of information; **er spricht wie aus dem, aus einem, Buch,** he speaks like a book, in formal phrases; **er redet wie ein Buch,** he keeps up a continuous flow of talk; **wie es im Buch(e) steht,** (i) in accordance with the book; (ii) *F:* typical, perfect, complete; **er ist ein Geizhals, wie er im Buch(e) steht,** he is the sort of miser who might have come straight out of a book; *see also* **hocken**[1] 1 (*b*), **vergriffen, vertiefen;** (*b*) book, main division (of literary work); **ein Roman in vier Büchern,** a novel in four books; **die Bücher des Alten Testaments,** the books of the Old Testament; (*c*) notebook; exercise book; *Sch:* **einen Schüler ins Buch schreiben,** to give a pupil a black mark, an order-mark; *F:* **in j-s schwarzem Buch(e) stehen,** to be in s.o.'s bad, black, books. **2.** *Com: etc:* **Bücher,** books, accounts; **Buch, die Bücher, führen,** to keep accounts; **etwas ins Buch, in die Bücher, eintragen, etwas zu Buch bringen,** to enter sth. in the books, to book sth.; **Bücher auf den neuesten Stand bringen,** to bring books, accounts, up to date; **zu Buch stehen (mit) . . .,** to be valued (at) . . .; **über etwas** *acc.* **Buch und Rechnung führen,** (i) to keep an exact account of sth.; (ii) *F:* to make a (mental) note of everything concerning sth. **3. das Buch des Lebens, der Natur, des Schicksals,** the book of life, of nature, of fate; **das Buch, die Bücher, der Geschichte,** the annals of history. **4.** *Cards:* full suit; (*at whist*) the book. **5.** *Turf:* (betting-) book; **ein Buch machen,** to make a book. **6.** (*pl.* **Buch**) book (of gold-leaf); *Com:* quire (of paper). **7.** *Z:*=**Blättermagen.**

Buch-, *comb.fm. cp.* **Bücher-, Buchdrucker-, Buchungs-.**

Buchadel, *m.*=**Briefadel.**

Buchampfer, *m. Bot:* wood-sorrel.

Buchara [bu·ˈxa:ra:]. *Pr.n.n.* -s. *Geog:* Bokhara, Bukhara.

Buchare [bu·ˈxa:rə], *m.* -n/-n. *Geog:* Bokharian.

Bucharei, die [bu·xa·ˈrai]. *Pr.n.* -. *Geog:* the Khanate of Bokhara; Bukharia.

bucharisch [bu·ˈxa:riʃ], *a.* Bokharian.

Buchausstattung, *f.* get-up of a book.

Buchbeschneidemaschine, *f. Bookb:* trimmer, guillotine.

Buchbesprechung, *f.* book review.

Buchbeutel, *m.*=**Bocksbeutel** 2 (i).

Buchbinde, *f. Publ:* (advertising) band (of book).

Buchbinden, *n.* bookbinding.

Buchbinder, *m.* (book-)binder.

Buchbinderbeschneidehobel, *m. Bookb:* plough (-knife).

Buchbinderei, *f.* **1.** (book-)bindery, bookbinder's workshop *or* establishment. **2.** bookbinding, bookbinding trade.

Buchbindergold, *n.* gold-leaf.

Buchbinderhandwerk, *n.* bookbinding, bookbinder's craft.

Buchbinderhobel, *m. Bookb:* plough(-knife).

Buchbinderkattun, *m.* embossed calico.

Buchbinderleinen, *n.,* **Buchbinderleinwand,** *f.* book cloth, bookbinder's cloth; book linen, bookbinder's calico; buckram.

Buchbindermarke, *f.* (book)binder's mark.

Buchbinderspan, *m. Bookb:* scaleboard.

Buchbinderwerkstatt, *f.* bindery, binder's workshop.

Buchblock, *m. Bookb:* inner book, (unbound) text, folded and collated sheets.

Buchbock, *m.*=**Bockkäfer.**

Buchbörse, *f.* Book Exchange; (*in London*) Stationers' Hall.

Buchbrot, *n.*=**Buchampfer.**

Buchdecke, *f. Bookb:* cover, binding.

Buchdeckel, *m. Bookb:* (book-)cover.

Buchdrama, *n.* play intended for reading only; *A:* closet play.

Buchdruck, *m.* printing, letterpress printing, typography.

Buchdruck-, *comb.fm. see* **Buchdrucker-.**

Buchdrucker, *m.* **1.** printer; letterpress printer; **B. und Verleger,** printer and publisher. **2.** *Ent:* typographer beetle.

Buchdruckerei, *f.* **1.** [ˈbu:xdrukərai] printing. **2.** [bu:xdrukəˈrai] printing-office, printer's press.

Buchdruckerfarbe, *f.* printer's ink, printing ink.

Buchdruckerkreuz, *n.* printer's peel.

Buchdruckerkunst, *f.* typography; art of printing; **die Erfindung der B.,** the invention of the printing-press.

Buchdruckerleiste, *f. Print:* border; head-piece; tail-piece.

Buchdruckermarke, *f. Print:* printer's device, printer's mark.

Buchdruckerpresse, *f.* printing-press.

Buchdruckerwalze, *f. Print:* impression roller.

Buchdruckerwerkstätte, *f.*=**Buchdruckerei** 2.

Buchdruckerzeichen, *n.*=**Buchdruckermarke.**

Buche, *f.* -/-n. *Bot:* beech.

Buchecker, *f. Bot:* beech-nut; *Husb:* **Bucheckern** *pl,* beech-mast.

Bucheckernöl, *n.* beech-oil.

Bucheichel, *f.*=**Buchecker.**

Bucheignerzeichen, *n.* book-plate, ex-libris.

Bucheinband, *m.* binding, book-cover.

Bucheinhängemaschine, *f. Bookb:* casing-in machine.

Buchel, Büchel[1], *f.* -/-n =**Buchecker.**

Büchel[2], *n.* -s/-. (*dim. of* **Buch**) *South G.Dial:* little book, booklet.

Büchelchen, *n.* -s/- =**Büchlein** 1.

buchen[1], *occ.* **büchen,** *a.* beech(-wood) (furniture, etc.); *A. & Lit:* beechen.

buchen[2]. I. *v.tr.* **1.** (*a*) *Book-k:* to book (item, sum), to enter (transaction) in the books; to place (amount) to an account; (*b*) **etwas als Gewinn, Erfolg, Verlust, usw., b.,** to count sth. as a gain, success, loss, etc. **2.** to book, reserve (passage, flight, etc.).

II. *vbl s.* **1. Buchen,** *n. in vbl senses.* **2. Buchung,** *f.* (*a*)=II. 1; (*b*) booking, reservation; **'Buchungen hier',** 'bookings here'; (*c*) *Book-k:* entry; **eine B. machen,** to make an entry (in the books); **eine gleichlautende B. vornehmen,** to effect a corresponding entry; **falsche B.,** misentry.

Buchenbaum, *m.*=**Buche.**

Buchenfarn, *m. Bot:* beech-fern.

Buchengallapfel, *m. Bot:* beech-apple, beech-gall.

Buchengallwespe, *f. Ent:* gall-fly, gall-wasp.

Buchengewächse, *n.pl. Bot:* fagaceae.

Buchenholz, *n.* beech(-wood, -timber).

Buchenholzkohle, *f.*=**Buchenkohle.**

Buchenholzteer, *m.* beech-tar.

Buchenkeimlingskrankheit, *f. Arb:* beech-saddling mildew.

Buchenkernöl, *n.*=**Bucheckernöl.**

Buchenkohle, *f.* beech-coal.

Buchenland, das. *Pr.n. Geog:* Bukovina.

Buchenmast, *f. Husb:* beech-mast.

Buchenöl, *n.*=**Bucheckernöl.**

Buchenpech, *n.* beech-wood creosote.

Buchenpilz, *m. Fung:* (*a*) oyster mushroom; (*b*) *fomes fomentarius.*

Buchenrüßler, *m. Ent:* beech-weevil.

Buchenschwamm, *m.*=**Buchenpilz.**

Buchenspinner, *m. Ent:* beech-moth.

Buchenteer, *m.*=**Buchenholzteer.**

Buchenwürger, *m. Bot:* beech-drops, cancer-drops.

Bücher-, *comb.fm. cp.* **Buch-.**

Bücherabgabe, *f.*=**Bücherrückgabe.**

Bücherabschluß, *m. Com:* closing, balancing, of books, of accounts.

Bücherauktion, *f.* trade-sale (of books).

Bücherausgabe, *f. Library:* (*a*) issuing of books; (*b*) counter at which books are issued; issuing counter.

Bücherbeschreibung, *f.* bibliography.

Bücherbestellzettel, *m.* (*a*) *Library:* application *or* request slip; application form; (*b*)=**Bücherzettel.**

Bücherbohrer, *m.*=**Bücherwurm** 1.

Bücherbord, Bücherbrett, *n.* bookshelf.
Bücherei, *f.* -/-en, library.
Bücherfreund, *m.* book-lover, bibliophile.
Büchergestell, *n.* (open) bookcase.
Bücherkenner, *m.* bibliologist; bibliographer.
Bücherkommission, *f. Hist:* **Kaiserliche B.,** imperial commission dealing with censorship and copyright.
Bücherkunde, *f.* bibliology; bibliography.
bücherkundig, *a.* well versed in books.
Bücherlaus, *f. Ent:* book-louse, atropos, death-watch.
Bücherlehre, *f.=***Bücherkunde.**
Bücherleidenschaft, *f.* bibliomania.
Bücherliebhaber, *m.* book-lover, bibliophile.
Bücherliebhaberei, *f.* love of books, biblio-philism.
Büchermacher, *m. F:* hack writer.
Büchermappe, *f.* briefcase, brief-bag, *Sch: etc:* satchel.
Büchermarder, *m. F:* book-thief.
Büchermarke, *f.=***Buchdruckermarke.**
Büchermensch, *m.* bookman, scholar; bookish person; **er ist ein reiner B.,** he lives only for books.
Büchermilbe, *f.=***Bücherlaus.**
Büchernachweis, *m.* (a) bibliography; (b) *Library:* location list (of books).
Büchernarr, *m.* bibliomaniac.
Bücherprivilegium, *n. Hist:* privilege of printing a book.
Bücherregal, *n.* (open) bookcase; (set of) book-shelves.
Bücherregister, *n.* (a) book-catalogue; (b) biblio-graphy.
Bücherrevision, *f. Com:* audit.
Bücherrevisor, *m. Com:* auditor; accountant.
Bücherrückgabe, *f.* (a) returning of books; (b) counter at which books are handed in, handing-in counter.
Bücherschatz, *m.* collection of (precious) books.
Bücherschrank, *m.* bookcase.
Bücherskorpion, *m. Arach:* book-scorpion.
Büchersprache, *f.* book language.
Bücherständer, *m.* bookcase; **drehbarer B.,** revolving bookcase.
Bücherstaub, *m.* dust from books; the dust of the library.
Bücherstube, *f.* (a) book-room; (b) bookshop.
Bücherstudium, *n.* study, book-work.
Büchertasche, *f. Sch:* satchel.
Bücherverbot, *n.* banning, prohibition, of books.
Bücherverehrer, *m.* bibliolater.
Bücherverehrung, *f.* bibliolatry.
Bücherverzeichnis, *n.* (a) *Library:* book cata-logue; list of books; (b) bibliography.
Bücherwagen, *m.* 1. vehicle used for transporting books. 2. *Library:* book truck, trolley.
Bücherwissen, *n.* book-learning.
Bücherwurm, *m.* 1. *Ent:* book-worm. 2. *F:* inveterate reader, *F:* bookworm.
Bücherwut, *f.* bibliomania.
bücherwütig, *a.* bibliomaniac.
Bücherzensur, *f.* censorship of the press; *R.C.Ch:* **kirchliche B.,** Index (librorum prohibitorum).
Bücherzettel, *m.* (in book trade) printed card for ordering books.
Buchesche, *f. Bot:* (i) hornbeam; (ii) maple.
Buchfälschung, *f.* 1. forgery of books. 2. *Com:* falsification of the books.
Buchfink, *m. Orn:* chaffinch.
Buchforderung, *f. Book-k: etc:* book-claim, ledger-claim; book-debt.
Buchform, *f.* shape of a, the, book; **in B.,** in (printed) book form.
Buchformat, *n.* size (of a book).
Buchführer, *m.=***Buchhalter.**
Buchführung, *f.* book-keeping; accountancy; **einfache B.,** single-entry book-keeping; **doppelte B.,** double-entry book-keeping; **amerikanische B.,** tabular book-keeping.
Buchgelehrsamkeit, *f.* book knowledge, book-learning; bookishness.
buchgelehrt, *a.* book-learned; bookish; **Buch-gelehrte** *m,f,* book-learned, bookish, person.
Buchgemeinschaft, *f.* book-club.
Buchgewerbe, *n.* book-trade, -craft.
Buchgold, *n.=***Buchbindergold.**
Buchhalter, *m.* -s/-, book-keeper.
Buchhalterei, *f.* -/-en. 1. book-keeping; account-ancy. 2. counting-house, accounts department.
Buchhalterknie, *n.=***Buchhalternase.**
Buchhalternase, *f. Book-k:* oblique stroke (used to bridge gap between entries).
Buchhaltung, *f. Com:* 1. book-keeping; account-ancy. 2. counting-house, accounts department.
Buchhaltungswesen, *n.* book-keeping.

Buchhandel, *m.* book-trade, bookselling.
Buchhändler, *m.* bookseller, *U.S:* bookdealer; **fliegender B.,** book-hawker, colporteur; **Börsen-verein der Deutschen Buchhändler,** Association of German Booksellers; (in England) approx.= Stationers' Company.
Buchhändlerblatt, *n.* bookseller's circular.
Buchhändlerbörse, *f.=***Buchbörse.**
Buchhändlerbörsenverein, *m.=***Börsenverein der Deutschen Buchhändler,** *q.v. under* **Buchhändler.**
Buchhändlerhaus, *n.* **das Deutsche B.,** head-quarters of the Association of German Book-sellers (in Leipzig); approx.=Stationer's Hall (in London).
Buchhandlung, *f.* bookshop, *U.S:* bookstore; (kiosk, etc.) bookstall.
Buchheftmaschine, *f. Bookb:* book-sewing machine.
Buchhülle, *f.* (a) book wrapper (made of cloth, leather, etc.); (b) occ. dust-cover.
Buchhypothek, *f.* inscribed, uncertified, mortgage.
Buchillustration, *f.* book illustration.
Buchkarte, *f. Library:* book-card.
Buchklee, *m. Bot:=***Buchampfer.**
Buchkredit, *m. Book-k: etc:* book-credit.
Buchkunst, *f.* art, craft, of making books.
Buchladen, *m.* bookshop.
Büchlein, *n.* -s/-. (dim. of **Buch**) 1. (a) little book, booklet; **ein schmales B.,** a slim volume; (b) notebook, diary. 2. *Z:=***Blättermagen.**
Buchleinen, *n.=***Buchbinderleinen.**
Buchmacher, *m.* -s/-. *Turf:* bookmaker, *F:* bookie.
Buchmacherei, *f.* -/. *Turf:* bookmaking.
Buchmachergehilfe, *m. Turf:* tick-tack man.
Buchmagen, *m. Z:=***Blättermagen.**
Buchmaler, *m.* illuminator (of manuscripts).
Buchmalerei, *f.* illumination of manuscripts, book illumination.
Buchmarder, *m. Z:=***Edelmarder.**
buchmäßig, *a. Com:* according to, as shown by, the books.
Buchmast, *f.=***Buchenmast.**
Buchnuß, *f. Bot:* beech-nut.
Buchnußöl, Buchöl, *n.=***Bucheckernöl.**
Buchornament, *n.* book ornament, ornament in manuscript.
Buchornamentik, *f.=***Buchschmuck.**
Buchprämie, *f. Sch:* book (presented as a) prize.
Buchprüfer, *m. Com:* auditor; accountant.
Buchrolle, *f. Hist:* roll; scroll.
Buchrücken, *m.* back, spine, of a book.
Buchs-, *comb.fm. cp.* **Buchsbaum-.**
Buchs, *m.* -es/-e. *Bot:* 1.=**Buchsbaum.** 2. (i) cow-berry, red whortleberry; (ii) **wilder B.,** box-leafed milkwort, bastard box (milkwort).
Buchsachverständige, *m.* (decl. as adj.)=**Buch-prüfer.**
Buchsbaum, *m. Bot:* (a) box(-tree); **kleinblättriger B.,** ground box, dwarf box; (b) **deutscher B.,** spindle-tree, prickwood.
Buchsbaumeinfassung, *f. Hort:* box edging.
buchsbaumen, buchsbäumen, *a.* (of) boxwood.
Buchsbaumgewächse, *n.pl. Bot:* buxaceae.
Buchsbaumhecke, *f. Hort:* box hedge.
Buchsbaumholz, *n.* boxwood.
Buchsbaumrand, *m. Hort:* box edging.
buchsblättrig, *a. Bot:* box-leafed; **buchsblättrige Kreuzblume=Buchs** 2 (ii).
Buchschenkkarte, *f.* book token.
Buchschließe, *f.* book-clasp.
Buchschloß, *n.* book-clasp.
Buchschmuck, *m.* book-ornamentation, book decoration; ornaments of books, manuscripts.
Buchschnitt, *m.* book edge.
Buchschrein, *m.* book-casket.
Buchschuld, *f. Book-k: etc:* book-debt.
Buchse, *f.* -/-n. 1. *Mec.E:* bush(ing) (of bearing, etc.); sleeve (of shaft, etc.); liner (of cylinder, etc.); *El.E:* socket; bushing. 2.=**Buxe.**
Büchse, *f.* -/-n. 1. tin; (for preserving food) (sealed) tin, can; (of wood, cardboard, precious metal) box; (of china, etc., for ointment, etc.) pot, jar; (for needles, etc.) case; *Ecc: etc:* (of ivory, precious metal) pyx; **in Büchsen ein-machen,** to tin, to can (meat, fruit, etc.); **Fleisch, Obst, usw., in Büchsen,** tinned, canned, meat, fruit, etc. 2. (a) *Mec.E:* box (of axle, etc.); (b)=**Buchse** 1. 3. (a) *A:* gun, firearm, musket; (b) *Sm.a:* sporting rifle, sporting gun (with rifled barrel).
büchsen¹, *v.tr.* 1. *A:* to shoot. 2. *F:* to steal, filch (sth.).
büchsen², *v.i.* (haben) *F:* 1. to pay. 2. to drink too much.
Büchsenatmer, *m. Mil: etc:* box respirator.
Büchsenbier, *n.* canned beer.

Büchsenfleisch, *n.* tinned meat, canned meat.
büchsenförmig, *a.* box-shaped.
Büchsenfrucht, *f. Bot:* pyxidium.
Büchsenfutteral, *n.* gun-case.
Büchsengemüse, *n.* tinned vegetables, canned vegetables.
Büchsenkartätsche, *f. Artil: A:* case-shot, canister-shot.
Büchsenknall, *m.* report, sound, of a rifle shot.
Büchsenkonserven, *f.pl.* tinned, canned, food.
Büchsenkugel, *f.* rifle bullet.
Büchsenkunst, *f.* (art of) gun-making.
Büchsenlauf, *m.* rifle barrel.
Büchsenlicht, *n. Ven: Mil: Mil.Av:* state of visibility that makes aiming possible; **bei B.,** at first light.
Büchsenmacher, *m.* -s/-. 1. *Mil: A:* armourer. 2. gunsmith.
Büchsenmacherei, *f.* -/-en. 1.=**Büchsenmacher-handwerk.** 2. gunsmith's shop.
Büchsenmacherhandwerk, *n.* gunsmith's trade, gun-making.
Büchsenmeister, *m. Mil: A:* artilleryman; rifle-man; musketeer.
Büchsenmeisterei, *f. Mil: A:* artillery, gunnery.
Büchsenmetall, *n.* Babbit metal, babbit.
Büchsenmilch, *f.* tinned, *U.S:* canned, milk; evaporated milk; condensed milk.
Büchsenmoos, *n.=***Becherflechte.**
Büchsenöffner, *m.* tin-opener, *U.S:* can-opener.
Büchsenrohr, *n.=***Büchsenlauf.**
Büchsenschaft, *m.* stock of a rifle *or* musket.
Büchsenschäfter, *m.* -s/-, (gun-)stocker.
Buchsenschleifmaschine, *f. Mec.E:* bush grind-ing machine.
Büchsenschloß, *n.* lock (of rifle).
Büchsenschmied, *m.=***Büchsenmacher.**
Büchsenschuß, *m.* rifle-shot.
Büchsenschußweite, *f.* **auf B.,** at rifle range.
Büchsenschütze, *m. Mil. Hist:* rifleman, arque-busier; *F:* **rennen wie die Büchsenschützen,** to be off like a shot.
Büchsenstein, *m. Miner:* iron pyrites.
Büchsenwaren, *f.pl.* tinned, canned, goods.
Büchsflinte, *f. Sm.a:* double-barrelled (sporting) gun with one rifled and one smooth-bore barrel.
Buchskreuzblume, *f. Bot:* box-leaved milkwort, bastard box (milkwort).
Büchsner, *m.* -s/- =**Büchsenmeister.**
Buchspange, *f.=***Buchschließe.**
Buchsring, *m.* axle-ring; packing-ring.
Buchstabe, *m.* -ns & -n/-n, letter, character; (a) **großer B.,** capital letter; **kleiner B.,** small letter; **angehängter, vorgesetzter, B.,** suffixed, prefixed, letter; **aus zwei, drei, Buchstaben bestehend,** (word) of two, three, letters; biliteral, triliteral (word); **(etwas) mit Buchstaben versehen,** be-zeichnen, to letter (sth.); **B. für B.,** letter by letter, literatim; **in Buchstaben,** in words, in full; **lateinische Buchstaben,** roman type, roman characters; **verzierter B.,** ornamented letter, *Print:* swash letter; *Print:* **den Buchstaben greifen,** to pick up the type; (b) **sich an den Buchstaben halten,** to keep, adhere, to the letter; **etwas nach dem Buchstaben auslegen,** to take sth. literally; **etwas bis auf den letzten Buchstaben erfüllen,** to carry sth. out to the letter; **der B. des Gesetzes,** the letter of the law; **auf den Buch-staben genau,** exact, punctilious; *B:* **der B. tötet, aber der Geist macht lebendig,** the letter killeth but the spirit giveth life; *F:* **die vier Buchstaben,** *F:* bottom, b.t.m.; **setz dich auf deine vier Buch-staben!** (to child) sit down! (c) *Jur: etc:* (in document) sub-paragraph.
Buchstabenbezeichnung, *f. Alg:* literal notation.
Buchstabenbild, *n. Print:* face.
Buchstabenchiffre, *f.* substitution cipher.
Buchstabenform, *f.* (a) type, shape, of letter; (b) *Print:* type-mould.
Buchstabenglaube, *m.* strict adherence to the letter (of sacred writings, law, etc.); literalism.
buchstabengläubig, *a.* keeping strictly to the letter (of sacred writings, law, etc.); literalistic; **er ist b.,** he is a literalist.
Buchstabengleichklang, *m.* alliteration.
Buchstabengleichung, *f. Mth:* literal equation.
Buchstabengröße, *f.* literal number.
Buchstabenholz, *n. Bot:* leopard-wood, letter-wood.
Buchstabenklauber, *m.* -s/-, quibbler, one who quibbles about the meaning of words.
Buchstabenkoeffizient, *m. Mth:* literal coeffi-cient.
Buchstabenkrämer, *m.=***Buchstabenmensch** 2.
Buchstabenmensch, *m.* 1. *A:* man of letters. 2. *Pej:* literal-minded person, literalist.
Buchstabenpinsel, *m.* lettering brush.

Buchstabenpunze, *f.* letter-punch, -stamp.

Buchstabenrätsel, *n.* anagram, logogriph.

Buchstabenrechnung, *f. Mth:* use of letter symbols; algebra.

Buchstabenreim, *m.* alliteration.

Buchstabenschloß, *n.* combination-lock, letter-lock, puzzle-lock.

Buchstabenschrift, *f.* alphabetic script; alphabet.

Buchstabenspiel, *n.* word game (using cards, etc.).

Buchstabentafel, *f.* table of letters, alphabet.

Buchstabenversetzung, *f. Ling:* metathesis, transposition (of letters).

Buchstabenvertauschung, *f. Ling:* permutation.

buchstabenweise, *adv.* letter by letter, literatim.

Buchstabierbank [bu·xʃta·ˈbiːr-], *f.* = **Abc-Bank.**

buchstabieren [bu·xʃta·ˈbiːrən], *v.tr.* to spell (word, name, etc.).

Buchstabierer, *m.* **-s/-,** speller.

Buchstabiertafel, *f.* spelling table.

Buchstabierverfahren, *n.* spelling system.

Buchstabier(wett)spiel, *n.* spelling-bee.

buchstäblich, *a.* (*a*) literal; **der buchstäbliche Sinn eines Wortes,** the literal meaning, sense, of a word; *adv.* **etwas b. auslegen,** to take sth. literally, in a literal sense; (*b*) *adv.* **wir hatten b. keinen Pfennig mehr,** we literally had not a single penny left; **er ist b. verhungert,** he literally starved to death; **es ist b. wahr,** it is literally true.

Buchstand, *m.* bookstall.

Buchsteindruck, *m. Print:* lithotypy, typolithography.

Buchstützen, *f.pl.* book-ends.

Bucht, *f.* **-/-en. 1.** bay, recess; *Geog:* bay, bight; **die Große Australische B.,** the Great Australian Bight; **in eine B. eingeschlossen,** embayed; **kleine B.,** creek, cove, inlet. **2.** *Nau:* (*a*) camber (of deck, keel); (*b*) loop, bight (of rope, etc.). **3.** (*a*) pen, pigsty, sheepfold, etc.; (*b*) *North G.Dial:* bed.

Buchtel, *f.* **-/-n.** *Cu:* (baked) yeast dumpling.

buchten. I. *v.tr.* **1.** to indent (sth.), to hollow (sth.) out. **2. sich buchten,** to have bays, recesses; to be indented. **3. gebuchtet** = **buchtig.**
II. *vbl s.* **1. Buchten,** *n. in vbl senses.* **2. Buchtung,** *f.* (*a*) = II. 1; (*b*) indentation; bay.

buchtenreich, *a.* (coastline) having many bays.

buchtig, *a.* (*a*) indented; **eine buchtige Küstenlinie,** an indented coastline; (*b*) *Bot:* sinuate.

Buchung, *f. see* **buchen**[2] II.

Buchungsfehler, *m. Book-k:* misentry, error in the books.

Buchungsmaschine, *f.* book-keeping machine.

Buchungsnummer, *f. Book-k:* number of entry.

Buchungsstelle, *f.* accountancy department.

Buchverleih, *m.* (*a*) lending of books; (*b*) lending library, circulating library.

Buchweizen, *m. Bot: Agr:* (*a*) buckwheat, saracen corn; (*b*) **wilder B.,** black bindweed, corn bindweed, running buckwheat.

Buchweizenknöterich, *m. Bot:* common buckwheat.

Buchweizenmehl, *n.* buckwheat flour.

Buchwert, *m. Book-k:* book-value.

Buchwinde, *f. Bot:* = **wilder Buchweizen,** *q.v. under* **Buchweizen.**

Buchzeichen, *n.* (i) book-mark(er); (ii) = **Bucheignerzeichen.**

Buchzwang, *m.* legal obligation to keep (account) books.

Buckel, *m.* **-s/-,** bulge, hump. **1.** (*a*) hump (of hunchback), humped back; **einen B. haben,** to have a humpback, to be a humpback, hunchback; (*b*) *F:* back; **ein krummer B.,** a round back; **die Katze machte einen B.,** the cat arched its back; **einen breiten B. haben,** to be able to stand a lot, a good deal; *F:* **du kannst mir den B. (he)runterrutschen,** nothing doing! go and take a running jump at yourself! go to hell! **j-m den B. voll prügeln, schlagen, den B. schmieren,** to give s.o. a good hiding, leathering, thrashing, drubbing, dressing-down, lathering, licking; **einem den B. voll lügen,** to tell s.o. a pack of lies. **2.** (*occ. f.* **-/-n**) (*a*) boss, stud, knob; (*on shield*) umbo, boss; *Harn:* boss (on bit); **etwas mit Buckeln beschlagen,** to stud sth.; **mit Buckeln beschlagen (sein),** (to be) studded, bossed; (*b*) buckle; (*c*) curl. **3.** (*a*) *Nat.Hist:* protuberance, boss, knob, umbo; *Bot:* knot, gnarl; (*b*) *Geol:* mound; hump; boss; hummock, knoll.

Buckelblech, *n. Metalw:* buckled, dished, plate *or* sheet-metal.

Buckelbrut, *f. Ap: A:* brood of drones.

Buckeleisen, *n.* **1.** *Haird:* curling-irons, -tongs. **2.** *Ind:* = **Buckelblech. 3.** *Ind:* steel rod with a knob for making dents in sheet-metal.

Buckelfliege, *f. Ent:* bee-fly.

buck(e)lig, *a.* (*a*) (*of pers.*) hunchbacked, humpbacked; (*of pers., moon*) gibbose, gibbous; **Buck(e)lige** *m, f,* hunchback; *Bot:* **buck(e)lige Wasserlinse,** gibbous duckweed; **sich b. lachen,** to double up with laughter, split one's sides with laughing; (*b*) bumpy (road, etc.); hilly (country); (*c*) studded, bossed, bossy.

Buckelkäfer, *m. Ent:* pea-weevil, -beetle, -bug.

Buckelkeramik, *f. Prehist:* embossed pottery.

Buckellocke, *f.* (tight) curl.

Buckelmeißel, *m. Tls:* = **Buckeleisen** 3.

buckeln. I. *v.i.* (*haben*) (*a*) to hump, arch, one's back; *F:* to cringe, to bow and scrape; **vor j-m b.,** to bow and scrape, to crawl, to s.o.; **gebuckelt,** humpbacked, hunchbacked; (*b*) to drudge, to slave.
II. **buckeln,** *v.tr.* **1.** to take (sth.) on one's back. **2.** to boss (metal); **gebuckelt,** (*of metal pottery*) bossed.
III. *vbl s.* **1. Buckeln,** *n. in vbl senses.* **2. Buckelung,** *f.* (*a*) = III. 1; (*b*) embossment.

Buckelochse, *m. Z:* zebu.

Buckelplatte, *f. Constr:* buckle plate; buckled, dished, plate.

Buckelquader, *m. Arch:* rustic(a).

Buckelquaderwerk, *n. Arch:* rustication, rustic work.

Buckelrind, *n. Z:* zebu.

Buckelschild, *m. Arm:* buckler.

Buckelstein, *m. Arch:* = **Buckelquader.**

Buckeltier, *n. F:* camel.

Buckelurne, *f. Prehist:* embossed urn.

Buckelwal, *m. Z:* humpback whale.

Buckelzirpen, *f.pl. Ent:* tree hoppers, membracidae.

Bucken, *m.* **-s/-.** *Bot:* common mugwort.

bücken. 1. *v.tr.* (*a*) *A:* **das Haupt, die Schultern, b.,** to bow one's head, shoulders; (*b*) **gebückt sein,** to be bent, bowed; **er war von Gram und Alter gebückt,** he was bowed (down) with, by, grief and age; **gebückt, in gebückter Haltung, gehen,** to walk with a stoop. **2. sich bücken,** to bend (down), to stoop; **er bückte sich nach dem Ball,** he bent, stooped, to pick up the ball.

Buckerl, *n.* **-s/-.** *F:* **ein B. machen,** to bow (obsequiously), to make a bow.

Bücking, *m.* **-s/-e** = **Bückling** 1.

Buckler, *m.* **-s/-.** *Arm:* buckler.

bucklicht, *a. A:* = **buck(e)lig.**

Bückling, *m.* **-s/-e. 1.** *Com:* buckling; bloater. **2.** *F:* bow; **einen tiefen B. machen,** to make a low bow, to bow low; *F:* **(j-m) seinen B. machen,** to pay one's respects (to s.o.).

Buckoblätter [ˈbukoː-], *n.pl.* = **Buccoblätter.**

Buckram [ˈbakrɛm], *m.* **-s/.** *Tex:* buckram.

Buda [ˈbuːdaː]. *Pr.n.n.* **-s.** *Geog:* Buda.

Budapest [ˈbuːda·pɛst, bu·da·ˈpɛst]. *Pr.n.n.* **-s.** *Geog:* Budapest.

Büdchen, *n.* **-s/-,** (*dim. of* **Bude**) (*a*) (confectionery, cigarette, etc.) kiosk; (*b*) *F:* little room.

Buddel, *f.* **-/-n.** *Dial:* bottle.

buddeln, *v. F:* (*a*) *v.tr.* to dig (hole); (*b*) *v.i.* (*haben*) to dig (in the ground).

Buddha [ˈbudaː]. *Pr.n.m.* **-s.** Buddha.

Buddhismus [buˈdismus], *occ.* **Buddhaismus** [buda·ˈismus], *m.* **-/.** Buddhism.

Buddhist [buˈdist], *m.* **-en/-en.** Buddhist.

buddhistisch [buˈdistiʃ], *a.* Buddhist, Buddhistic(al); Buddhic.

Bude, *f.* **-/-n. 1.** (*a*) (wooden) hut, cabin, *U.S:* shack; **eine alte verfallene B.,** an old shack; a ramshackle, dilapidated, house; (*b*) *F:* lodgings, room; *F:* place; den; (student's, etc.) digs; **sturmfreie B. haben,** (i) to have a room with independent access; (ii) to be able to have guests, visitors; to have got the place to oneself; **wir können auf meine B. gehen,** we can go to my place, digs; **die B. auf den Kopf stellen,** to turn the place upside down; **Leben in die B. bringen,** to liven the place, the company, up; **j-m auf die B. rücken,** to call on s.o. unexpectedly, to pay s.o. a surprise visit. **2.** (*at market, fair, etc.*) stall, stand, booth; (newspaper, cigarette) kiosk; *A:* shop; *F:* **die B. zumachen,** to shut up shop, to pack up; to knock off.

Budenangst, *f. F:* claustrophobia.

Budenbesitzer, *m.* owner, proprietor, of a stall, stand, booth; stall-keeper.

Budengeld, *n.* stall-rent.

Budenzauber, *m.* lively party (in s.o.'s lodgings).

Budget [bydˈʒɛː, bydˈʒɛː], *n.* **-s/-s.** *Fin: Parl:* budget; **das B. vorlegen,** to present the budget.

Budgetberatung, *f. Parl:* debate on the budget

budgetieren [bydʒe·ˈtiːrən], *v.i.* (*haben*) **(für eine gewisse Ausgabe) b.,** to budget (for a certain expenditure).

Budgetperiode, *f.* period covered by the budget.

Budgetrecht, *n. Parl:* right to prove *or* contest the budget.

Budike [bu·ˈdi·kə], *f.* **-/-n,** (*a*) (small) general store; stall, booth; (*b*) small (low) tavern.

Budiker [bu·ˈdi·kər], *m.* **-s/-,** (*a*) stall-keeper; keeper of a small general store; (*b*) keeper of a small (low) tavern.

Büdner, *m.* **-s/-. 1.** *A:* = **Budenbesitzer. 2.** *North G.Dial:* small landholder, cottager, crofter.

Büdnerrecht, *n.* heritable lease (of smallholding, cottage).

Büfett [by·ˈfɛt, by·ˈfeː], *n.* **-(e)s/-e,** (*a*) sideboard, buffet, cupboard; (*b*) (i) buffet, refreshment-bar, room; (ii) (snack-)counter, bar; (*c*) **kaltes B.,** cold buffet, buffet meal.

Büfettier [by·fɛti·ˈeː], *m.* **-s/-s,** barman, *U.S:* bartender.

Büfettière [by·fɛti·ˈɛːrə], *f.* **-/-n,** barmaid.

Büfettkellner, *m.* barman, *U.S:* bartender.

Büfettmamsell, *f.* barmaid.

Buffalo [ˈbufa·loː], *m.* **-s/-s.** *Z:* American bison, *F:* buffalo.

Buffalogras, *n.* = **Büffelgras.**

Buffbohne, *f. Bot: Cu:* broad bean.

Büffel, *m.* **-s/-. 1.** *Z:* buffalo; **indischer B.,** Indian buffalo; **amerikanischer B.,** American bison; **eine Herde von fünfzig Büffeln,** a herd of fifty buffaloes, of fifty buffalo. **2.** *F:* boor, lout, blockhead, clumsy person. **3.** *Tex:* buffalo cloth.

Büffelbeere, *f. Bot:* buffalo berry.

Büffelei, *f.* **-/-en,** hard work; *F:* sweat, grind; *Sch:* swot.

Büffelgras, *n. Bot:* buffalo grass.

Büffelhaut, *f.* buffalo hide, buff(-leather).

Büffelhorn, *n.* (*a*) buffalo horn; (*b*) *Her:* (elephant's) trunk.

Büffelkäfer, *m. Ent:* carpet-beetle, *U.S:* buffalo bug.

Büffelkalb, *n. Z:* buffalo calf.

Büffelkopf, *m.* (*a*) buffalo's head; (*b*) = **Büffel** 2.

Büffelkopfente, *f. Orn:* buffle-headed duck, bufflehead.

Büffelkuh, *f. Z:* cow-buffalo.

Büffelleder, *n.* buff(-leather).

büffelledern, *a.* buff, of buff-leather.

Büffelmücke, *f. Ent:* buffalo gnat.

büffeln, *v.tr. F:* to work hard at, *F:* to grind, slog, (away) at, to sweat (away) at, over (subject, etc.); *Sch:* to swot, mug, (up) (subject, etc.); *abs.* **b.,** to work hard, *F:* to swot; **Mathematik b.,** to swot, mug up, maths.

Büffelrock, *m. Mil: A:* buff-coat.

Büffelseuche, *f. Vet:* buffalo cholera.

Büffelwams, *n. Mil: A:* buff-jerkin.

Büffelweber, *m. Orn:* buffalo bird.

Buffer, *m.* **-s/-** = **Puffer.**

Buffet [by·ˈfeː, by·ˈfɛː, by·ˈfɛt], *n.* **-s/-s** = **Büfett.**

Buffjacke, *f. Mil: A:* buff-jerkin.

Büffler, *m.* **-s/-.** *F:* plodder, hard worker; *Sch:* swot; *U.S:* grind.

Bufonit [bu·fo·ˈniːt], *m.* **-en/-en.** *Miner:* bufonite, toadstone.

Bug[1], *m.* **-(e)s/-e. 1.** (*a*) *Nau:* bow(s), head (of ship); **scharfer B.,** clipper bow; **völliger B.,** bluff bow; **(den) B. gegen die See halten,** to keep head on to the sea, to head the sea; **über den verkehrten B. fallen,** to cast the wrong way; **von einem B. auf den anderen gehen,** to tack; **über dem anderen B. liegen,** to be on the opposite tack; (*b*) *Av: Mil:* nose (of aeroplane, tank); bow (of flying-boat, airship, tank). **2.** *Constr: Carp:* = **Büge. 3.** (*a*) joint; *Z:* shoulder, shoulder-blade, blade-bone (of horse, ox, etc.); withers (of horse); hock, hough (of horse); chest, brisket; (*b*) *Cu:* shoulder (of beef), shoulder (of mutton); chuck rib. **4.** *A. & Lit:* bend, curve. **5.** (sharp) fold, crease.

Bug[2], **der.** *Pr.n.* **-s.** *Geog:* the (river) Bug.

Bugader, *f.* cephalic vein (of horse).

Buganker, *m. Nau:* bower(-anchor).

Bugband, *n. N.Arch:* breast-hook.

Bugbeule, *f. Vet:* = **Brustbeule.**

Büge, *f.* **-/-n.** *Constr: Carp:* brace; strut.

Bügel, *m.* **-s/-,** bent piece (of metal, wood, etc.); curved handle (of basket, pail, etc.); bow (of spectacles, watch, brooch); earpiece (of spectacles); hoop (of net, etc.); frame (of bag, purse, fret-saw); bow, guard (of sword hilt); (*in machinery*) stirrup; *Dom.Ec:* coat-, dress-hanger; *Sm.a:* trigger-guard; *El.E:* pantograph, bow(-shaped) collector; *Aut:* tightening band; *Equit:* stirrup; **fest in den Bügeln sitzen,** to be firm in one's stirrups; **mit langen, kurzen, Bügeln reiten,** to ride with long, with short, stirrups.

Bügelaufzug, *m. Clockm:* stem winding; **Uhr mit B.,** stem-winder.

Bügelautomat, *m.* electric iron with automatic heat control, heat-controlled iron, thermostatic iron.
Bügelblech, *n. Av:* trimming tab.
Bügelbrett, *n. Dom.Ec:* ironing-board.
Bügeldohne, *f.* springe (for birds).
bügelecht, *a.* (material, etc.) that cannot be spoilt by ironing.
Bügeleisen, *n.* **1.** *Dom.Ec:* (flat-)iron, laundry iron; box-iron; *Tail:* goose; **elektrisches B.**, electric iron. **2.** *Mil: etc: F:* (i) shrapnel; (ii) ship.
Bügeleisenbolzen, *m. Dom.Ec:* heater (for box-iron).
Bügelfalte, *f.* crease (in trousers).
bügelfest, *a.* **1.** firm in one's stirrups. **2.** (material) that cannot be spoilt by ironing.
Bügelfibel, *f. Prehist:* fibula with an arched bow.
bügelförmig, *a.* hooped, stirrup-shaped, bow-shaped.
bügelfrei, *a.* not requiring ironing; non-iron (fabric, etc.); drip-dry (shirt, etc.).
Bügelgatter, *n. Tls:* bow-saw frame.
Bügelhelm, *m. Arm: Her:* grilled helm.
Bügelhorn, *n. Mil: Mus:* bugle; *Mus:* **B. mit Ventilen**, cornet, saxhorn.
Bügelknopf, *m. Clockm:* pendant; **drehbarer B.**, turning pendant.
Bügelkrone, *f.* crown with arches.
bügellos, *a.* **b. werden**, to lose one's stirrups.
Bügelmaschine, *f. Dom. Ec:* ironing machine.
bügeln, *v.tr.* to iron (clothes, etc.); to press (trousers, etc.); **eine Naht b.**, to press down a seam.
Bügelnadel, *f. Prehist:* safety-pin type brooch; fibula.
Bügelpumpe, *f.* stirrup-pump.
Bügelriemen, *m.* stirrup-leather, -strap.
Bügelrock, *m. A.Cost:* farthingale, hooped petticoat.
Bügelsäge, *f. Tls:* crosscut saw with frame; hack-saw.
Bügelschraube, *f.* strap-bolt.
Bügelstahl, *m.*=**Bügeleisenbolzen.**
Bügelstromabnehmer, *m. El.E:* bow collector.
Bügeltisch, *m.* ironing table.
Bügelverschluß, *m.* snap-top closure (of bottle).
Bugfeuer, *n. Navy:* bow fire.
Bugfigur, *f. N.Arch:* figure-head.
Bugflagge, *f. Nau:* ship's flag; jack.
Bugflaggenstock, *m. Nau:* jack-staff.
Buggeschütz, *n. Navy:* bow-chaser.
Bugholz, *n.* **1.** bentwood. **2.** *N.Arch:* hawse piece.
Bugholzmöbel, *n.pl.* bentwood furniture.
Bugkanzel, *f. Av:* bow cockpit, forward cockpit.
Bugklappe, *f. Navy:* bow ramp.
buglahm, *a. Vet:* shoulder-shot.
Buglahmheit, *f. Vet:* shoulder-strain.
buglastig, *a. Av:* nose-heavy.
Buglastigkeit, *f. Av:* nose-heaviness.
Bugleine, *f. Nau:* bowline.
Büglerin, *f.* **-/-innen**, (woman) ironer.
Buglicht, *n. Av:* head-, front-light.
Bugmann, *m.* **-(e)s/-männer.** *Row:* bow(-oar), bowman.
Bugpanzer, *m. Mil:* front, bow, armour (of tank).
Bugpforte, *f. N.Arch:* raft-port.
Bugrad, *n. Av:* front wheel, nosewheel.
Bugradfahrgestell, *n. Av:* tricycle undercarriage.
Bugradfahrwerk, *n.*=**Bugradfahrgestell.**
Bugraum, *m.* forward, bow, compartment.
Bugriemen, *m. Row:* bow-oar.
Bugrohr, *n. Navy:* bow torpedo-tube.
Bugruder, *n. Row:* bow-oar.
Bugschütze, *m. Mil: Av:* forward, bow, gunner.
Bugschützgerät, *n. Navy:* paravane.
Bugsieranker [buk'siːr-, bug'ziːr-], *m. Nau:* kedge(-anchor).
Bugsierboot, *n.*=**Bugsierdampfer.**
Bugsierdampfer, *m.* tug(-boat), tow-boat.
bugsieren [buk'siːrən, bug'ziːrən], *v.tr.* to tow (ship, car), to take (ship, car) in tow; to haul, tug, (ship); to trail, tow, (trailer); to pull, draw, (train); *F:* to pull, drag, push, lead (s.o., sth.).
Bugsierer [buk'siːrər, bug'ziːrər], *m.* **-s/-**, (*a*) tug-boatman, (boat-)tower; (*b*) tug(-boat), tow-boat.
Bugsiertau, *n. Nau:* tow-line, -rope, towing-line, -rope.
Bugsiertrosse, *f. Nau:*=**Bugsiertau.**
Bugspriet, *n. Nau:* bowsprit.
Bugstagen, *n.pl. Nau:* bowsprit-shrouds.
Bugstand, *m. Mil: Av:* forward gunner's position (in aeroplane, tank).
Bugstück, *n.* **1.** *N.Arch:*=**Bugholz. 2.** *Navy:*=**Buggeschütz. 3.** *Cu:* brisket (of beef), shoulder (of mutton).
Bugverzierung, *f. N.Arch:* trail-boards.
Bugwelle, *f. Nau. & Av:* bow-wave (of ship, flying-boat).
buh, *int.* boo!
Bühel, *m.* **-s/-**, **Bühl**, *m.* **-s/-e.** *South G.Dial:* hill.
buhen, *v.i.* (*haben*) to boo.
Buhldirne, *f. A. & Lit:* whore, bawd.
Buhle. *A. & Poet:* **1.** *m.* **-n/-n**, lover, swain, love, sweetheart. **2.** *f.* **-/-n**, mistress, lover, love, sweetheart.
buhlen, *v.i.* (*haben*) **1.** *A:* (*a*) **mit j-m b.**, to have illicit relations, to wanton, to toy, with s.o.; *Poet:* (*of wind*) **mit j-m, etwas, b.**, to caress, toy with, s.o., sth.; (*b*) **um j-n b.**, to court, woo, s.o. **2.** *Lit:* **um etwas b.**, to strive after sth.; **sie buhlten um die Gunst des Kardinals**, they courted the cardinal's favour.
Buhler, *m.* **-s/-. 1.** *A:* suitor. **2.** *A. & Lit:* lecher, fornicator.
Buhlerei, *f.* **-/-en.** *A:* (*a*) (love) affair; flirtation; (*b*) fornication, lechery.
Buhlerin, *f.* **-/-innen.** *A:* lover; *A. & Lit:* concubine, courtesan, paramour; prostitute.
buhlerisch, *a. Lit:* lascivious, lecherous; (*of wind*) playful, caressing.
Buhlin, *f.* **-/-innen**=**Buhle** 2.
Buhlkraut, *n. Bot:* stinking goosefoot.
Buhlschaft, *f.* **-/-en.** *A:* (love) affair.
Buhlteufel, *m. Myth:* incubus.
Buhne, *f.* **-/-n. 1.** breakwater, mole, jetty; groyne. **2.** *Nau: etc:* wharf. **3.** *Pisc:* crawl.
Bühne, *f.* **-/-n**, stage, platform, dais. **1.** (*a*) *Th:* stage, *F:* the boards; **drehbare B.**, revolving stage; **die B. betreten, auf die B. gehen**, to appear on, come, go, on to, the stage; **zur, auf die, B. gehen**, to go on the stage, to become an actor *or* actress; (*of play*) **über die B. gehen**, to be produced; **ein Stück auf die B. bringen**, to stage, produce, put on, a play; **im Vordergrund, im Hintergrund, der B.**, down-stage, up-stage; **für die B. schreiben**, to write for the stage, theatre; **die deutsche, englische, B.**, the German, English, stage, drama; *see also* **abgehen, abtreten, auftreten**; (*b*) theatre; **die Londoner Bühnen**, the London theatres; **Städtische Bühnen X**, X Municipal Theatre; (*c*) **die politische B.**, the political scene. **2.** (*a*) *Constr: etc:* platform, cradle; *Min:* sollar; **fliegende, schwebende, B.**, hanging stage, flying scaffold, travelling cradle; (*b*) *Glassm:* siege (of melting furnace). **3.** *South G.Dial:* ceiling; loft. **4.** *Poet:* vault (of heaven).
Bühneisen, *n. Glassm:* pontil, ponty, punty.
Bühnenangaben, *f.pl. Th:* stage directions.
Bühnenangehörige, *m., f.* (*decl. as adj.*) member of the theatrical profession.
Bühnenanweisungen, *f.pl. Th:* stage directions.
Bühnenarbeiter, *m. Th:* stage-hand, scene-shifter.
Bühnenaufführung, *f. Th:* performance (on the stage), stage performance.
Bühnenaussprache, *f.* standard pronunciation.
Bühnenausstattung, *f. Th:* stage properties; scenery.
Bühnenbearbeitung, *f. Th:* (*a*) adaptation (of play) for the stage, dramatization; (*b*) play adapted for the stage, dramatization.
Bühnenbeleuchtung, *f.* stage lighting.
Bühnenbild, *n. Th:* scene, scenery, setting; décor; stage design.
Bühnenbildner, *m.* **-s/-.** *Th:* stage designer.
Bühnendekoration, *f. Th:* stage decoration, stage-setting, décor.
Bühnendeutsch, *n.* standard German; standard (German) pronunciation.
Bühnendichter, *m.* playwright, dramatist.
Bühnendichtung, *f.* play, drama.
Bühneneffekt, *m. Th:* stage-effect.
Bühneneffekten, *pl. Th:* stage-properties.
Bühnenfestspiele, *n.pl.* drama festival.
Bühnengebäude, *n.*=**Bühnenhaus.**
bühnengerecht, *a.* suitable, adapted, for the stage, actable; **b. machen**, to adapt, to arrange, for the stage.
bühnenhaft, *a.*=**bühnenmäßig.**
Bühnenhaus, *n.* **1.** *Th:* stage and backstage. **2.** theatre.
Bühnenheld, *m.* stage hero; *Pej:* idol of the gods.
Bühnenhimmel, *m. Th:* cyclorama.
Bühnenhintergrund, *m. Th:* back of the stage; **im B.**, up-stage.
Bühnenkenntnis, *f.* (*a*) experience of the stage; (*b*) stagecraft.
Buhnenkrone, *f.* surface of a groyne.
Bühnenkunst, *f.* dramatic art.
Bühnenkünstler, *m. Th:* actor, performer, artiste.
Bühnenlaube, *f. Th:* stage-box.
Bühnenlichtregulator, *m.*=**Bühnenregulator.**
Bühnenmaler, *m. Th:* scene-painter.
bühnenmäßig, *a.* (i) suitable for the stage, (ii) theatrical.
Bühnenmusik, *f.* incidental music.
Bühnenöffnung, *f. Th:* proscenium arch.
Bühnenrahmen, *m. Th:* frame of the stage, proscenium.
Bühnenrechte, *n.pl. Th:* stage-rights.
Bühnenregulator, *m. Th:* (stage-)dimmer.
Bühnenrequisiten, *n.pl. Th:*=**Bühnenzubehör.**
Bühnenschriftsteller, *m.* playwright, dramatist.
Bühnenspiel, *n.* (*a*)=**Bühnenstück**; (*b*) theatrical performance.
Bühnensprache, *f.* **1.**=**Bühnenaussprache. 2.** language of the theatre.
Bühnenstück, *n. Th:* stage play.
Bühnentechniker, *m. Th:* stage mechanic.
Bühnenverein, *m.* **Deutscher B.**, Union of German Theatre Directors.
Bühnenvertrieb, *m.* theatrical agency (for plays).
Bühnenvorgang, *m. Th:* action.
Bühnenwerk, *n. Th:* play, drama, dramatic work.
Bühnenwirkung, *f. Th:* stage-effect.
Buhnenwurzel, *f.* land end of a groyne.
Bühnenzubehör, *n. Th:* stage equipment, stage-properties.
Bühnloch, *n. Min:* holing.
Buhu, *m.* **-s/-e & -s.** *Dial:* eagle-owl.
buk, büke *see* **backen.**
Bukanier [buˑ'kaːnïər, buˑkaˑ'niːr], *m.* **-s/-.** *Hist:* buccaneer.
bukanieren [buˑkaˑ'niːrən], *v.tr.* to buccan (meat).
Bukarest ['buːkaˑrɛst]. *Pr.n.n.* **-s.** *Geog:* Bucharest.
Bukentaur [buˑkɛn'tauər], *m.* **-en/-en** [-'taurən]. *Myth:* bucentaur.
Bukephalos, Bukephalus [buˑ'keːfaˑlos, -lus]. *Pr.n.m.* **-'.** *A.Hist:* Bucephalus.
Bukett [buˑ'kɛt], *n.* **-s/-e. 1.** bouquet, bunch (of flowers). **2.** bouquet (of wine, perfume).
bukettreich, *a.* (wine) of great bouquet.
Bukettzweig, *m. Bot:* compound fruit spur.
Bukgording, *m. Nau:* bandline.
Bukhara [buˑ'kaːraː]. *Pr.n.n.* **-s.** *Geog:*=**Buchara.**
Bukharei [buˑka'rai]. *Pr.n.f.* **-.** *Geog:*=**Bucharei.**
Bukkoblätter ['bukoː-], *n.pl.*=**Buccoblätter.**
bukolisch [buˑ'koːliʃ], *a.* bucolic, pastoral; **bukolische Dichtung**, bucolic poetry; **bukolisches Gedicht**, bucolic.
Bulbeisen, *n. Com: Nau:* bulb-iron.
bulbförmig, *a.* bulbiform, bulbous; *N.Arch:* **bulbförmiger Bug**, bulbous bow.
Bulbille [bul'bilə], *f.* **-/-n.** *Bot:* bulbil, bulblet.
bulbös [bul'bøːs], *a.* bulbiform, bulbous.
Bülbül ['bylbyl], *m.* **-s/-s.** *Orn:* bulbul, Persian nightingale.
Bulbus ['bulbus], *m.* **-/-bi. 1.** *Bot:* bulb, tuber, corm. **2.** *Anat:* bulb; eye-ball, bulb of the eye.
Bulette [buˑ'lɛtə], *f.* **-n/-n.** *Cu:* (meat) rissole, meat-ball.
Bulgare [bul'gaːrə], *m.* **-n/-n.** *Ethn: Geog:* Bulgarian.
Bulgarien [bul'gaːriən]. *Pr.n.n.* **-s.** *Geog:* Bulgaria.
bulgarisch [bul'gaːriʃ]. **1.** *a.* Bulgarian. **2.** *s.* **Bulgarisch**, *n. Ling:* Bulgarian; the Bulgarian language.
Bulge, Bülge, *f.* **-/-n. 1.** *Nau: North G.Dial:* wave, billow, breaker. **2.** metal flask. **3.** *A:* leather bucket.
Bulimie [buˑliˑ'miː], *f.* **-/.** bulimia, bulimy, morbid hunger.
Bulin [buˑ'liːn], *f.* **-/-n**, **Buline** [buˑ'liːnə], *f.* **-/-n.** *Nau:* bowline.
Bulinstich, *m. Nau:* bowline-knot, -hitch.
Bullarium [bu'laːrïum], *n.* **-s/-rien**, collection of papal bulls, bullary.
Bullauge, *n. Nau:* port-hole, bull's eye.
Bulldog, *m.* **-s/-s.** *Metalw:* bulldozer.
Bulldogg, *m.* **-s & -en/-en**=**Bulldogge.**
Bulldogge, *f. Breed:* bulldog.
Bulldoggfledermaus, *f. Z:* mastiff-bat, bulldog-bat, molossus.
Bulle[1], *m.* **-n/-n**, (*a*) *Z:* (i) bull; (ii) bull-dog; (*b*) *F:* (i) boor, lout, clumsy person; (ii) strong, tough, person; (iii) policeman, *F:* copper.
Bulle[2], *f.* **-/-n. 1.** *Rom.Ant:* bulla, locket (of Roman children). **2.** *Hist:* *esp. Ecc.Hist:* (*a*) (*seal of official document*) bull, bulla; (*b*) (*document*) bull; **päpstliche B.**, papal bull; **die Goldene B.**, the Golden Bull.
bullen, *v.i.* (*haben*) (*of cow*) to be on, in, heat; to bull, to take the bull.
Bullenbeißer, *m.* bulldog; *F:* ferocious-looking person, dragon.
Bullenhetze, *f.* bull-baiting.

Bullenhitze, *f. F:* extreme heat; **es war eine B.,** it was baking, boiling, hot.
Bullenkalb, *n.* bull-calf.
Bullenochse, *m.* castrated, gelded, bull; ox, bullock.
Bullenring, *m. Husb:* nose-ring (for bull).
Bullensammlung, *f.* = **Bullarium.**
Bullentau, *n. Nau:* boom-guy.
Bullenwiese, *f. F:* rich pastureland.
bullerig, *a.* banging, rumbling, thundering, booming.
Bullerjahn, *m.* -s/-e. *North G.Dial:* rowdy.
bullern, *v.i.* (*haben*) **1.** (*of water*) to boil, bubble, seethe; (*of fire in stove*) to roar. **2.** (*a*) (*of pers., weather, etc.*) to rage, storm; (*b*) **gegen etwas b.,** to knock loudly on, thunder at, sth., to fling (sth.) at sth.
Bulletin [bʏlə'tẽː], *n.* -s/-s, bulletin.
Bullfinch ['bʊlfɪntʃ], *m.* -/-es. *Equit:* bullfinch.
Bullfrosch, *m. Amph:* bull-frog.
Bulli ['buliː], *n. & m.* -s/-s = **Bully.**
Bullion ['buliən], *n.* -s/. bullion.
Bullkater, *m.* bogey(-man).
Bullrichsalz, *n. Com:* bicarbonate of soda.
Bullterrier, *m. Breed:* bull-terrier.
Bully ['buliː], *n. & m.* -s/-s. *Hockey:* bully.
Bülow ['byːloː], *m.* -s/-s. *Orn: F:* **der Vogel B.,** the oriole.
bulstern, *v.tr. North G.Dial:* to shell, pod, hull (peas).
Bult, *m.* -s/-en. *North G.Dial:* = **Bülte.**
Bultbeere, *f. Bot: F:* cranberry, moorberry.
Bülte, *f.* -/-n. *North G.Dial:* hillock, tussock, grassy mound.
Bultenbett, *n. Prehist:* dolmen, cromlech.
Bultsack, *m.* (sailor's) straw mattress.
Bulwersturmschwalbe ['bulvər-], *f. Orn:* Bulwer's petrel.
Bulwersturmvogel, *m. Orn:* Bulwer's petrel; **großer B.,** Macgellivray's petrel.
bum, *int.* boom! bang!
Bumann, *m.* (*nursery language*) bogey-man.
Bumboot ['bum-], *n. Nau:* bumboat.
Bumerang ['buːməraŋ], *m. & n.* -s/-e, boomerang, throw-stick.
bumfiedeln, *v.tr. F:* to flatter; **j-n b.,** to flatter, try to get round, s.o.
Bummel[1], *m.* -s/-, stroll; **einen B. machen,** (i) to go for a stroll, (ii) to go out; to pub-crawl; **auf den B. gehen,** to go on the spree; to pub-crawl.
Bummel[2], *f.* -/-n. *Cost: etc: F:* pom-pom.
Bummelant [bumə'lant], *m.* -en/-en = **Bummler.**
Bummelantentum, *n.* -s/. *Ind: F:* absenteeism.
Bummelei, *f.* -/-en, (*a*) extreme slowness; dawdling; (*b*) sluggishness, negligence, slovenliness, sloppiness.
Bummelfritz, *m.* = **Bummler.**
bumm(e)lig, *a.* (*a*) slow; (*b*) untidy, slovenly, slack, sloppy.
Bummelleben, *n.* dissipated life; **ein B. führen,** to lead an idle, a dissolute, a dissipated, life.
bummeln, *v.i.* (*a*) (*sein*) to stroll, saunter; to loaf; *U.S:* to bum; **ich bin zwei Stunden durch die Stadt gebummelt,** I strolled through the town for two hours; (*b*) (*haben*) (*of vehicle*) to crawl; (*of pers.*) to dawdle (on one's way, at one's work); to work slowly; to slack at one's work, to waste time; (*c*) (*haben*) to gad about, to knock about; **b. gehen,** to go on the spree.
Bummelstreik, *m.* go-slow (strike), *U.S:* slow-down.
Bummelzug, *m. F:* slow train.
bummern, *v.i.* (*haben*) *Dial:* to knock repeatedly; to bang, crash, boom, thunder.
Bummler, *m.* -s/-, (*a*) saunterer, stroller; idler, loafer, lounger, *U.S:* bummer, bum; (*b*) dawdler, slowcoach, sluggard; slovenly, sloppy, person; *U.S:* slowpoke; (*c*) gadabout.
Bums[1], *int.* thud! bang! (*nursery language*) **b. machen,** to make a bang.
Bums[2], *m.* -es/-e. **1.** thud; thump; bump; bang. **2.** = **Bumslokal. 3.** *South G.Dial:* = **Bimsstein.**
bumsen, *v.i.* (*haben*) (*of falling object, etc.*) to thud, thump, bump; **gegen etwas b.,** to bang, bump, against sth.
Bumslandung, *f. Av: F:* heavy, pancake, landing.
Bumslokal, *n.* dive, low-class night-club.
Buna ['buːnaː], *n.* -/. *Plastics:* (*R.t.m.*) buna.
Bund[1], *m.* -(e)s/=e. **1.** (*a*) bond; agreement, compact, *Lit. & B:* covenant; **der Alte, der Neue, B.,** the Old, the New, Testament; **die Propheten des Alten Bundes,** the Old Testament prophets; (*b*) *Pol:* (i) alliance, coalition; (ii) union, (con)federation, confederacy; *Com: etc:* federation; *Com: Sch: etc:* association, union; **einen B. schließen,** to enter into an agreement, to form an alliance; **der B. der Ehe,** the bond of marriage; **den B. fürs Leben schließen,** to take the marriage vows; **im Bunde mit,** in conjunction with, with the co-operation of; (in alliance) with; **mit j-m im Bunde sein,** (i) to be associated with s.o.; to be in league with s.o.; (ii) to collaborate with s.o.; **der Dritte im Bunde sein,** to be the third party in an agreement; to be one of three friends; **B. Deutscher Architekten,** Association of German Architects; *Hist:* **der Deutsche, Norddeutsche, B.,** the German, North German, Confederation; **der Hanseatische B.,** the Hanseatic League; (*c*) *Pol:* **der B.,** the administrative organization(s) of the Federal Government; **die Gesetzgebung des Bundes und der Länder,** (*in Germany*) Federal and 'Land' legislation; **dem B. zufließende Steuern,** taxes going to the Federal Government; **vom B. zur Verfügung gestellte Mittel,** funds provided by the Federal Government. **2.** (*a*) *Cost:* band; waistband (of skirt, trousers); neckband (of shirt, etc.); (*b*) *Mus:* fret (of guitar, etc.); (*c*) *Mec.E:* collar, flange; (*d*) *Bookb:* rib, raised band (on back of book); (*e*) *Arch:* band; *Constr:* (roof) truss.
Bund[2], *n.* -(e)s/- & -e, (*a*) bundle (of faggots); bunch (of radishes, etc.); skein, hank (of wool); bundle, truss (of hay, straw); *Metall:* faggot (of iron); (*b*) (*also m.* -(e)s/-e) bunch (of keys).
Bundauge, *n. Tex:* small square.
Bundaxt, *f. Tls: Carp:* mortise-axe, mortising axe.
Bundbalken, *m. Constr:* tie-beam.
bundbrüchig, *a.* perjured, treacherous; **b. werden,** to break, violate, a treaty, an alliance, to turn traitor; to break a contract.
Bündchen, *n.* -s/-. (*dim. of* **Bund**) *Dressm:* neckband; (sleeve-, wrist-, etc.) band.
Bundeisen, *n. Metall:* faggot-iron.
Bündel, *n.* -s/-, bundle, parcel, packet, package; bundle (of faggots, clothes, straw, wires, etc.); bunch (of keys); bundle, truss (of straw); bunch, bundle (of asparagus, etc.); bundle (of thread, wool); *Ph:* beam (of rays, electrons, etc.); *El:* tube (of lines of force); *Mth:* sheaf; *F:* (*of pers.*) **ein B. Knochen,** a bag of bones; *F:* (*of pers.*) **ein B. Nerven,** a bundle of nerves; **sein B. schnüren,** (i) to pack one's belongings, (ii) *F:* to pack up (one's traps), to sling one's hook, to hook it; **etwas in ein B. packen,** to make a bundle, parcel, of sth.
bündelförmig, *a. Bot: Z:* (*of hairs, etc.*) fascicular, fasciculate, growing in bunches, in clusters.
Bündelholz, *n.* = **Bundholz** 1.
bündeln, *v.tr.* to make, to tie, (sth.) up into a bundle, into bundles, to make a bundle, bundles, of (sth.); to bundle up (articles); *Metall:* to faggot (iron, steel); *Ph:* to concentrate (rays of light, sound waves) into a beam; to focus (electron beam); **Wäsche b.,** to bundle up washing; **Holz b.,** to bundle wood, *Arch:* **gebündelt,** clustered.
Bündelpfeiler, *m. Arch:* clustered pier, clustered pillar, compound pier.
Bündelpresse, *f. Ind:* bundling-press; baling-press.
bündelweise, *adv.* in bundles.
Bunder, *m.* -s/-. *Z:* = **Bander.**
Bundes-, *comb.fm. Pol: Adm:* federal . . .; **Bundesinnenminister** *m,* Federal Minister of the Interior; **Bundesverwaltung** *f,* Federal Administration; **Bundesmittel** *npl,* federal funds.
Bundesakte, *f. Hist:* Act of the German Confederation.
Bundesanwalt, *m.* attorney of the Federal Supreme Court.
Bundesanzeiger, der, (*official organ of the German Federal Republic*) the Federal Gazette.
Bundesauszug, *m. Swiss:* first age-group of men liable for military service.
Bundesbahn, *f.* Federal Railway(s).
Bundesbank, *f.* Federal Bank.
Bundesbeschluß, *m. Hist:* decree of the Federal Government.
Bundesbruder, *m. Sch:* fellow-member of a students' association.
Bundesebene, *f.* Federal level; **auf B.,** at (the) Federal level.
Bundesexekution, *f. Hist:* federal execution.
Bundesfinanzhof, *m.* (*in Germany*) Federal Finance Court.
bundesflüchtig, *a.* = **bundbrüchig.**
Bundesfürst, *m. Hist:* ruler of a state belonging to the German Confederation.
Bundesgenosse, *m.* ally, confederate.
Bundesgenossenkriege, *m.pl. Rom. & Gr.Hist:* Social Wars.
Bundesgenossenschaft, *f.* (*a*) confederation, confederacy; (*b*) alliance.
bundesgenössisch, *a.* federal.
Bundesgericht, *n.* Federal Court; (*in Switzerland*) Federal Tribunal.
Bundesgerichtshof, *m.* (*in Germany*) Federal Supreme Court.
Bundesgesetz, *n.* Federal Law.
Bundesgesetzblatt, *n.* (*in Germany, Austria*) Federal Law Gazette.
Bundeshaus, *n.* headquarters of the German Federal Parliament (in Bonn).
Bundesheer, *n.* Federal Army.
Bundeshymne, die, the Austrian national anthem.
Bundeskanzlei, *f.* (*in Switzerland*) headquarters of the Federal Council.
Bundeskanzler, *m.* Federal Chancellor.
Bundeskanzleramt, *n.* Federal Chancellery.
Bundeskasse, *f.* Federal Treasury.
Bundeslade, die. *B.Hist:* the Ark of the Covenant.
Bundesland, *n.* (*in Austria*) federal province.
Bundesluftwaffe, *f.* German Federal Air Force.
Bundesmarine, *f.* German Federal Navy.
bundesmäßig, *a.* in accordance with the agreement, treaty.
Bundesministerium, *n.* Federal Ministry; **B. für Wirtschaft,** Federal Ministry for Economic Affairs; **B. der Finanzen,** Federal Ministry of Finance.
Bundespflicht, *f.* duty to the Federal Government.
Bundespost, *f.* Federal Post Office; Federal Postal Administration *or* Services.
Bundespräsident, *m.* Federal President; (*in Germany*) President of the Federal Republic; (*in Austria*) President of the Republic; (*in Switzerland*) President of the Confederation.
Bundespräsidialamt, *n.* = **Bundespräsidium** 2.
Bundespräsidium, *n.* **1.** Federal Presidency. **2.** headquarters of the German Federal President.
Bundesrat, *m.* Federal Council; (*in German Federal Republic*) Federal Council, Upper House of Parliament.
Bundesregierung, *f.* Federal Government.
Bundesrepublik, *f.* Federal Republic; **die B. Deutschland,** the Federal Republic of Germany.
Bundesschiedsgericht, *n. Hist:* tribunal of the German Confederation.
Bundesstaat, *m.* (*a*) federal state, federation, federal union; (*b*) member state of a federation.
bundesstaatlich, *a.* federal, of the federal state; **bundesstaatliche Verfassung,** federal constitution.
Bundesstelle, *f.* department of the Federal Government.
Bundesstraße, *f.* Federal Highway; *approx.* = 'A' road.
Bundestag, *m.* Lower House of the German Parliament; *Hist:* Diet of the German Confederation.
Bundesverfassung, *f.* Federal Constitution.
Bundesverfassungsgericht, *n.* (German) Federal Constitutional Court.
Bundesversammlung, *f.* Federal Assembly; *Hist:* Diet of the German Confederation.
Bundesvertrag, *m. Swiss Hist:* Confederate Pact.
Bundeswehr, *f.* German Federal Armed Forces.
Bundeszwang, *m. Pol:* federal execution.
bundförmig, *a.* = **bündelförmig.**
bundfrei, *a. Mus:* unfretted (clavichord).
Bundgarn, *n.* **1.** thread in hanks, in skeins. **2.** *Fish:* stake-net.
Bundgatter, *n. Tls:* multiple-blade saw-frame; gang saw.
Bundgesparre, Bundgesperre, *n. Constr:* principal rafters.
Bundholz, *n.* **1.** faggots, wood in bundles, bundle-wood. **2.** *Constr:* timbers (of roof truss).
bündig, *a.* **1.** (*a*) binding, valid; (*b*) concise, succinct, to the point; (*of argument*) valid, conclusive; *see also* **kurz. 2.** *Constr:* on a level, flush; **b. machen,** to level (sth.), to make (sth.) level, to make (sth.) flush.
Bündigkeit, *f.* precision, brevity, conciseness; validity, conclusiveness (of argument).
bündisch, *a.* belonging to a confederation, league, association, union, etc.; **bündische Jugend,** young people belonging to youth organisations.
Bündler, *m.* -s/-. *Iron:* member of a league, association, etc.
Bundmutter, *f. Mec.E:* collar nut.
Bündner, *m.* -s/-. **1.** = **Bundesgenosse. 2.** = **Graubündner.**
Bündnerfleisch, *n. Swiss Cu:* raw dried beef (in paper-thin slices).
bündnerisch, *a.* = **graubündnerisch.**
Bündnis, *n.* -nisses/-nisse, agreement, compact; alliance; **ein B. eingehen,** to enter into an

agreement, alliance; **mit j-m im B. stehen,** to be in league, have an alliance, with s.o.

Bundpfosten, *m. Constr:* = **Bundsäule.**

Bundrad, *n. Tex:* = **Bundscheibe.**

Bundriegel, *m. Constr:* inter-tie.

Bundring, *m. Mec.E:* collar.

Bundsäule, *f. Constr:* principal post (in timber-work).

Bundscheibe, *f. Tex:* tappet-wheel.

Bundschnur, *f. Tex:* ridge band.

Bundschuh, *m.* **1.** *Cost:* sports shoe (with leather strap round top); *A:* peasant's shoe (tied at ankle with leather strap). **2.** *Hist:* **der B.,** (name assumed by rebels in the Peasants' Insurrections, 1492–1514) the *Bundschuh.*

Bundschwelle, *f. Constr:* ground-plate, ground-sill, groundsel.

Bundseite, *f. Constr:* exterior face (of beam, etc.).

Bundsparren, *m. Constr:* principal rafter.

Bundstab, *m. Tex:* reed.

Bundstahl, *m. Metall:* faggot-steel.

Bundständer, *m. Constr:* = **Bundsäule.**

Bundsteg, *m. Print: Bookb:* back (in a forme of type *or* in a printed sheet *or* of folded pages).

Bundstiel, *m. Constr:* = **Bundsäule.**

Bundwand, *f. Constr:* (wall) timbers.

Bundweite, *f.* **1.** *Constr:* distance between roof trusses. **2.** waist measurement (of skirt, trousers).

Bundzeichen, *n. Constr:* jointing mark (on timbers).

Bungalow [ˈbuŋgaˑloː], *m.* **-s/-s,** bungalow.

Bunge, *f.* **-/-n. 1.** *Bot:* = **Bachbunge. 2.** *Pisc:* net for catching fish.

Bunker[1], *m.* **-s/-,** (*a*) *Nau: Ind:* (coal, fuel oil, etc.) bunker; *Ind:* (storage) bin; hopper; *Min:* (ore) bunker; *Agr:* (grain) silo; (*b*) *Golf:* bunker; (*c*) *Mil:* bunker, pill-box, concrete dugout; air-raid shelter; *Navy:* (submarine) pen.

Bunker[2], *m.* **-s/-.** *Ich: U.S:* menhaden.

Bunkerde, *f. Agr:* top stratum of a peatbog.

Bunkerkohle, *f.* bunker coal

bunkern, *v.tr.* to bunker (coal, etc.).

Bunkeröl, *n.* bunker oil, bunker fuel.

Bunsenbrenner, *m. Ch:* bunsen burner.

Bunsenelement, *n. El:* bunsen cell.

bunt, *a.* **1.** (*a*) coloured; colourful; *Opt:* **die bunten Farben,** the chromatic colours (of the spectrum); *Laund:* **bunte Wäsche, das Bunte,** coloured washing, *F:* coloureds, *U.S:* colors; (*b*) multi-coloured; parti-coloured; pied, dappled, speckled, mottled; (*of birds, flowers, insects*) variegated; bright, gay; **bunter Marmor,** brocatelle; **bunte Farben,** bright, gay, colours; **ein buntes Kleid,** a brightly coloured, gay, dress; **der bunte Rock,** (i) *B:* the coat of many colours, (ii) *A:* military uniform, 'the red coat'; **bunte Wiese,** meadow gay with, pied with, flowers; **bunte Kuh,** *F:* **Bunte,** skewbald cow; *F:* **ein bunter Vogel,** a rare bird; *F:* **er ist bekannt wie ein bunter Hund,** he is known all over the place, everyone knows him. **2.** (*a*) varied; motley; **bunte Platte,** plate of varied, attractively garnished open sandwiches; **bunter Teller,** plate filled with a variety of good things; **bunte Unterhaltungsmusik,** musical medley; **eine bunte Menge,** a motley crowd; **bunte Reihe,** alternate (*esp.* seating) arrangement of ladies and gentlemen; **laßt uns bunte Reihe machen,** let's arrange ourselves (men and women) alternately; **ein buntes Leben,** a life full of variety; *see also* **Abend** 2; (*b*) confused; **etwas b. durcheinander werfen,** to throw sth. topsy-turvy, higgledy-piggledy; **ein buntes Durcheinander,** a confusion, a complete muddle; **hier sieht's b. aus,** this place is all at sixes and sevens, upside-down; **die Sache wird immer bunter,** the matter is getting more and more complicated, confused, out of hand; **das wird mir zu b.,** that's too much, that's going too far, for my liking; *F:* **es zu b. treiben,** to go too far; to overdo things, it.

Buntbild, *n.* coloured picture, *esp.* coloured photograph, coloured lantern slide.

buntblättrig, *a. Bot:* variegated.

Buntblättrigkeit, *f. Bot:* variegation.

Buntbleierz, *n. Miner:* pyromorphite; green lead ore.

Buntbock, *m. Z:* bontebok.

Buntdruck, *m.* colour-printing; chromotypography, chromotype; **lithographischer B.,** chromolithography.

Buntfalke, *m. Orn:* American sparrow-hawk; American kestrel.

Buntfarbenanstrich, *m. Mil:* camouflage.

buntfarbig, *a.* brightly coloured, gay; motley.

Buntfeuer, *n. Pyr:* Bengal light; light signal, flare.

Buntfütterer, *m.* **-s/-.** *A:* furrier.

buntgesprenkelt, *a.* dappled, speckled, mottled.

Buntheit, *f.* (*a*) colour, colourfulness, vividness, brightness; (*b*) variety, diversity.

Bunting [ˈbøn-, bantiŋ], *n.* **-s/.** *Tex:* bunting.

Buntkäfer, *m. Ent:* variegated beetle.

buntkariert, *a.* checked (in colour); tartan; *F:* **mir ist b. zumute,** my head is swimming, going round.

Buntkormoran, *m. Orn:* red-legged cormorant.

Buntkuckuck, *m. Orn:* brain-fever bird, common hawk-cuckoo.

Buntkupfererz, *n. Miner:* bornite; erubescite, variegated copper ore, horseflesh ore.

Buntkupferkies, *m. Miner:* = **Buntkupfererz.**

Buntmarmor, *m. Miner:* brocatelle.

Buntmetall, *n.* (common) heavy non-ferrous metal.

Buntpapier, *n.* coloured, stained, paper.

Buntprachtkäfer, *m. Ent:* buprestis (beetle).

Buntsandstein, *m. Geol:* Bunter sandstone, new red sandstone, mottled sandstone.

buntscheckig, *a.* skewbald (cow); *F:* motley (crowd); gaudy (dress, etc.).

buntschillernd, *a.* iridescent, chatoyant, opalescent.

Buntsittich, *m. Orn:* Rosella parakeet.

Buntspecht, *m. Orn:* **(großer) B.,** great(er) spotted woodpecker; **kleiner B.,** lesser spotted woodpecker.

Buntstickerei, *f.* coloured embroidery.

Buntstift, *m.* coloured pencil, crayon.

Buntstreusel, *m. Cu:* hundreds and thousands.

Buntwaren, *f.pl. Tex:* printed cotton goods.

Buntwäsche, *f. Laund:* coloured washing, *F:* coloureds, *U.S:* colors.

Buntweberei, *f.* coloured weaving.

Buntwerk, *n. A:* furriery.

Buntwerker, *m.* **-s/-.** *A:* furrier.

Bürde, *f.* **-/-n,** burden; load.

Bure, *m.* **-n/-n.** Boer.

Bureau [byˑˈroː, ˈbyːroː], *n.* **-s/-s** = **Büro.**

Burenkrieg, der. *Hist:* the Boer War.

Büretsch, *m.* **-/.** *Dial:* = **Spinat.**

Bürette [byˑˈrɛtə], *f.* **-/-n.** *Ch:* burette.

Burg, *f.* **-/-en. 1.** (*a*) (i) stronghold, fortress, fort; (ii) refuge; **feste B.,** (i) strong fortress, firm stronghold; (ii) safe refuge; **ein' feste B. ist unser Gott,** a safe stronghold our God is still; *B:* **meine Zuversicht und meine B.,** my refuge and my fortress; (*b*) castle; citadel; *Gr.Ant:* acropolis. **2.** *Z:* (beaver's) lodge, burrow.

Burgbann, *m. Hist:* castellany; (i) district under castellan's jurisdiction, (ii) office, position, of castellan.

Burgberg, *m.* castle mountain, mound; *Gr.Ant:* acropolis; **auf den B. gehen,** to go up to the castle.

Burgbesatzung, *f. Hist:* castle guard, garrison.

Burgding, *n. Hist:* castellan's jurisdiction, castellany.

bürge[1] *see* (i) **bergen,** (ii) **bürgen.**

Bürge[2], *m.* **-n/-n.** *Jur: Com:* guarantor, security, surety, bondsman; **einen Bürgen stellen,** to find surety, security; **B. für j-n sein, werden, als B. für j-n haften,** to be s.o.'s guarantor, to stand guarantee for s.o., to become, to stand, surety, security, for s.o.; (*for prisoner*) to go, stand, bail for s.o.; **B. für etwas sein, werden, als B. für etwas haften,** (i) *Jur: Com:* to stand security for sth.; (ii) to guarantee sth., to vouch, answer, for sth.; **ich bin B. dafür! dafür möchte ich B. sein!** I'll vouch, answer, for that! *F:* I'll go bail for that!

bürgen, *v.i.* (*haben*) (*a*) **für j-n b.,** (i) *Jur: Com:* to be s.o.'s guarantor, to stand guarantee for s.o., to become, to stand, surety, security, for s.o.; (*for prisoner*) to go, stand, bail for s.o.; (ii) to vouch, answer, for s.o., *F:* to go bail for s.o.; (*b*) **für etwas b.,** (i) *Jur: Com:* to stand security for sth.; (ii) to guarantee sth.; to vouch, to answer, for sth., *F:* to go bail for sth.; **wer bürgt mir dafür, daß er es tut?** how do I know he will do it?

Bürger, *m.* **-s/-. 1.** *A:* (*a*) townsman, burgess, burgher; **die Bürger,** the citizenry; (*b*) civilian. **2.** (*a*) (= **Stadtbürger**) resident; citizen; *A:* freeman; (*b*) (= **Staatsbürger**) citizen; **deutscher B.,** German citizen; (*c*) **akademischer B.,** student, gownsman. **3.** member of the middle classes; (*a*) solid middle-class citizen; *F:* member of the 'white collar' classes; (*b*) (*as opposed to aristocracy*) commoner; *Lit:* **der B. als Edelmann,** the Cit turned Gentleman, le Bourgeois gentilhomme, the Would-be Gentleman.

Bürgeradel, *m.* patriciate, (*a*) patrician order, aristocracy; (*b*) patrician rank.

Bürgeramt, *n. Hist:* (*in Bremen*) committee of citizens.

Bürgerausschuß, *m. Hist:* committee of citizens.

Bürgerball, *m.* (*esp. in Vienna*) annual citizens' ball.

Bürgerbauten, *m.pl.* civic architecture.

Bürgerbrief, *m. Hist:* patent of citizenship.

Bürgerbuch, *n. Hist:* = **Bürgerrolle.**

Bürgerbund, *m. Hist:* = **Bürgergarde.**

Bürgereid, *m. Hist:* citizen's, freeman's, oath.

Bürgergarde, *f. Hist:* civic guard, militia.

Bürgergeld, *n. Hist:* fee paid for citizenship.

Bürgerglocke, *f. Hist:* alarm-bell, tocsin.

Bürgerhauptmann, *m. Hist:* captain of the militia.

Bürgerhaus, *n.* town house.

Bürgerklasse, *f.* = **Bürgerstand.**

Bürgerkönig, *m. Fr.Hist:* **der B.,** the Citizen King.

Bürgerkranz, *m. Rom.Hist:* = **Bürgerkrone.**

Bürgerkrieg, *m.* civil war.

Bürgerkrone, *f. Rom.Hist:* civic crown.

Bürgerkunde, *f.* civics.

bürgerkundlich, *a.* **bürgerkundlicher Unterricht,** (instruction in) civics.

Bürgerlehre, *f.* civics.

bürgerlich, *a.* **1.** (*a*) *Adm: Jur: etc:* civic, civil; **die bürgerlichen Tugenden,** the civic virtues; **bürgerliche Gesellschaft,** community; **bürgerliche Rechte,** civic rights; **bürgerliches Jahr,** civil year; *Jur:* **bürgerliches Recht,** civil law; **Bürgerliches Gesetzbuch** (*abbr.* **BGB**), German Civil Code; **bürgerliche Eheschließung,** civil marriage; **bürgerlicher Tod,** civil death; *see also* **aberkennen I, II, Ehrenrecht;** (*b*) civil, civilian; **im bürgerlichen Leben,** in civil, civilian, life. **2.** (*a*) middle-class; **bürgerlicher Haushalt,** middle-class family; *Pol:* **bürgerliche Parteien,** non-socialist parties; *Lit:* **bürgerliches Trauerspiel,** domestic tragedy; (*b*) **Bürgerliche** *m, f,* commoner; **die Gräfin hat einen Bürgerlichen geheiratet,** the countess has married a commoner. **3.** (*a*) homely, simple, plain; **bürgerliche Küche,** plain cooking; **bürgerlicher Mittagstisch,** (eating-place with) home cooking; *adv.* **b. gekleidet,** plainly, simply, dressed; (*b*) conventional; *Pej:* plebeian; bourgeois; (*in art circles*) philistine.

Bürgerlichkeit, *f.* homeliness, simplicity, plainness; conventionality.

Bürgermädchen, *n.* middle-class girl.

Bürgermeister, *m.* mayor; burgomaster; (*in Scotland*) provost; **Regierender B.,** Governing Mayor (of Berlin).

Bürgermeisteramt, *n.* **1.** mayor's office, department. **2.** mayoralty.

Bürgermeisterei, *f.* **-/-en** = **Bürgermeisteramt** 1.

Bürgermeistermöwe, *f. Orn:* glaucous gull, burgomaster gull.

Bürgermiliz, *f.* = **Bürgergarde.**

Bürgerpflicht, *f.* civic duty, citizen's duty, duty as a citizen.

Bürgerquartier, *n. Mil: A:* billet; **im B. liegen,** to be billeted on a householder.

Bürgerrat, *m. Hist:* = **Bürgerausschuß.**

Bürgerrecht, *n.* civic rights, privileges of a citizen; citizenship; *Hist:* **Römisches B.,** Roman franchise.

Bürgerrechtsgeld, *n. Hist:* = **Bürgergeld.**

Bürgerrock, *m. A:* (*a*) *Cost:* (plain) townsman's coat; (*b*) **der B.,** civilian clothes, mufti.

Bürgerrolle, *f. Hist:* official list, register, of citizens.

Bürgerschaft, *f.* **-/-en,** (*a*) (all the) citizens, inhabitants, (of a town); (*b*) (*in Bremen, Hamburg*) (i) *Hist:* (the) House of Burgesses; (ii) *Pol:* (the) City Parliament.

Bürgerschule, *f. A:* higher-grade elementary school (for middle-class children).

Bürgersfrau, *f.* middle-class woman.

Bürgersinn, *m.* sense of good citizenship, public spirit; civism; **er hat B. gezeigt,** he showed public spirit, he showed himself a good citizen.

Bürgersmann, *m.* **-(e)s/-leute,** (*a*) member of the middle classes, *pl.* middle-class people; **ihr Vater war ein einfacher B.,** she comes from a simple middle-class family; (*b*) (*as opposed to aristocracy*) commoner.

Bürgerstand, *m.* the middle class, the bourgeoisie.

Bürgersteig, *m.* pavement, *U.S:* sidewalk.

Bürgersteuer, *f.* poll-tax.

Bürgerstolz, *m.* (*a*) (complacent) pride in middle-class achievement; (*b*) civic pride.

Bürgertugend, *f.* civic virtue.

Bürgertum, *n.* **-s/.** (the) middle class, (the) bourgeoisie.

Bürgervolk, *n. A:* citizens, townspeople.

Bürgerwache, Bürgerwehr, *f. Hist:* = **Bürgergarde.**

Burgfrau, *f. Hist:* lady of the castle; chatelaine.

Burgfräulein, *n. Hist:* young lady of the castle.

Burgfreiheit, *f. Hist:*=**Burgbann.**

Burgfriede, *m. Hist:* **1.** (right of) jurisdiction over a town, over the precincts of a fortress. **2.** area under a castellan's jurisdiction, castellany. **3.** *Pol: etc: F:* truce.

Burgfriedensbruch, *m. Hist:* infringement of a castellan's right of jurisdiction.

Burggericht, *n. Hist: approx.*= manorial court.

Burggraben, *m.* castle moat.

Burggraf, *m. Hist:* burgrave.

Burggrafenamt, *n.* office of burgrave, burgraviate.

Burggräfin, *f. Hist:* chatelaine.

Burggrafschaft, *f.* burgraviate.

Burghauptmann, *m. Hist:* commander of the castle guard.

Burgherr, *m. Hist:* lord, knight, of the castle; castellan.

Burgherrin, *f. Hist:* lady of the castle; chatelaine.

Burghof, *m.* bailey, castle court(yard); **innerer B.**, inner bailey; **äußerer B.**, outer bailey, base-court.

Burgmann, *m.* **-(e)s/-leute.** *Hist:* member of the castle guard.

Burgsaß, *m.* **-sassen/-sassen.** *Hist:* inhabitant of a castle, person under a burgrave's jurisdiction.

Bürgschaft, *f.* **-/-en.** *Jur: Com:* surety, security, guarantee, *Lit:* bond; (*for release of prisoner*) bail; **(für j-n, etwas) B. leisten, die B. übernehmen**, to stand surety, security (for s.o., sth.); **j-n gegen eine B. freilassen**, to release s.o. on bail.

Bürgschaftserklärung, *f. Jur: Com:* guarantee, declaration of surety; **schriftliche B.**, surety-bond, written guarantee; (*for release of prisoner*) bail-bond.

bürgschaftsfähig, *a. Jur: Com:* bailable.

Bürgschaftsleistung, *f. Jur: Com:* suretyship.

Bürgschaftsschein, *m. Jur: Com:* surety-bond; (*for release of prisoner*) bail-bond.

Bürgschaftsvertrag, *m. Jur: Com:* contract of suretyship.

Burgund [bur'gunt]. *Pr.n.n.* **-s.** *Geog:* Burgundy.

Burgunder [bur'gundər]. **1.** *inv.a. & comb.fm.* **Burgunder-**, Burgundian; of Burgundy. **2.** *m.* **-s/-**, (*a*) Burgundian; (*b*) burgundy (wine).

Burgundereiche, *f. Bot:* Turkey oak.

Burgunderharz, *n.* Burgundy pitch.

Burgundernase, *f. F:* red inflamed nose; nose covered with grog-blossoms, grog-blossomed nose.

Burgunderpech, *n.*=**Burgunderharz.**

Burgunderwein, *m.*=**Burgunder** 2 (*b*).

burgundisch [bur'gundiʃ], *a.* Burgundian; of Burgundy; *Geog:* **die Burgundische Pforte**, the Belfort Gap.

Burgverlies, *n.* dungeon, oubliette.

Burgvogt, *m. Hist:* castellan, castle governor.

Burgwache, *f. Hist:*=**Burgbesatzung.**

Burgwarte, *f.* watchtower (of castle).

Burin [by·'rɛ̃:], *m.* **-s/-s.** *Tls:* graver, graving tool, etcher's needle, burin.

burisch, *a.* Boer.

Burjäte [bur'jɛ:tə], *m.* **-n/-n.** *Ethn:* Buriat, Buryat.

burlesk [bur'lɛsk], *a.* farcical.

Burleske [bur'lɛskə], *f.* **-/-n.** *Th:* farce.

Burma ['burma:]. *Pr.n.n.* **-s.** *Geog:* Burma(h).

Burmese [bur'me:zə], *m.* **-n/-n.** *Ethn: Geog:* Burman, Burmese.

burmesisch [bur'me:ziʃ], *a.* Burman, Burmese.

Burnus ['burnus], *m.* **-/-se.** Arab cloak, burnous(e).

Büro [by·'ro:, 'byro:], *n.* **-s/-s.** **1.** *Furn: A:* bureau. **2.** office.

Büroarbeit, *f.* office-work.

Bürobeamte, *m.* clerk.

Bürobedarf, *m.* office supplies, requirements.

Bürochef, *m.*=**Bürovorsteher.**

Bürodiener, *m.* (office) commissionaire.

Bürohaus, *n.* block of offices, office block.

Bürojunge, *m.* office-boy.

Büroklammer, *f.* paper-clip.

Bürokraft, *f.* office worker; **Bürokräfte** *pl*, office personnel.

Bürokrat [by·ro·'kra:t], *m.* **-en/-en**, bureaucrat.

Bürokratie [by·ro·kra·'ti:], *f.* **-/-n** [-'ti:ən], (*a*) bureaucracy, officialdom; (*b*) *F:* red tape, bumbledom.

bürokratisch [by·ro·'kra:tiʃ], *a.* bureaucratic; *adv.* bureaucratically.

Bürokratismus [by·ro·kra·'tismus], *m.* **-/.** bureaucracy, officialdom; *F:* red tape, bumbledom.

Bürokratius [by·ro·'kra:tsius], *m.* **-/.** *Hum:* **der heilige B.**, red tape, red-tapedom, -tapism.

Büroleim, *m.* office paste.

Bürovorsteher, *m.* chief clerk, head clerk, senior clerk.

Bürozeit, *f.* office hours.

burren, *v.i.* (*haben*) *Dial:* (*a*) to buzz; (*b*) to growl.

Burrhahn, *m. Orn:* ruff.

Burrstein, *m. Geol:* burr(-stone).

Bürschchen, *n.* **-s/-**, (*dim. of* **Bursche**) little fellow, little chap; **ein naseweises B.**, a whipper-snapper; *F:* **ein sauberes B.**, a bad lot.

Bursche, *m.* **-n/-n.** **1.** *Sch: A:* full member of a 'Burschenschaft'. **2.** (*a*) boy, lad, youth, young man; (*b*) *A:* apprentice; journeyman; (*c*) *Mil:* batman, orderly; (*d*) sweetheart, young man; (*e*) fellow; **kleiner B.**, little boy, little fellow; **ein übler B.**, a bad lot, *F:* a bad egg, a bad hat.

Burschenschaft, *f.* **-/-en.** *Sch:* 'Burschenschaft', (German) students' association.

Burschenschafter, *m.* **-s/-.** *Sch:* member of a 'Burschenschaft'.

Burschenschaftler, *m.* **-s/-**=**Burschenschafter.**

burschikos [burʃi·'ko:s], *a.* (*a*) *A:* carefree (life, etc.); (*b*) boyish (girl, type, appearance, etc.); hearty (woman, manner, etc.).

Burschikosität [burʃi·ko·zi·'tɛ:t], *f.* **-/.** boyishness (of girl, appearance, etc.); heartiness (of woman, manner, etc.).

Bürschlein, *n.* **-s/-** =**Bürschchen.**

Burse, *f.* **-/-n.** **1.** *Sch:* (*a*) students' hostel, *A:* college; (*b*) grant, scholarship. **2.** *R.C.Ch:* burse.

Bürste, *f.* **-/-n.** **1.** brush. **2.** *El.E:* brush (of commutator). **3.** *F:* bristly hair; crew cut.

Bürstel, *n.* **-s/-.** *Ich:*=**Bürstling.**

bürsten, *v.* **1.** *v.tr. & i.* (*haben*) to brush. **2.** *v.tr. F:* (i) to scold (s.o.), *F:* to tell (s.o.) off, to blow (s.o.) up, to haul (s.o.) over the coals; (ii) to beat (s.o.), to give (s.o.) a hiding. **3.** *v.i.* (*haben*) *A: F:* (*a*) to drink; (*b*) to run, to dash about.

Bürstenabzug, *m. Print:* brush-proof.

Bürstenbinder, *m.* **1.** brush-maker; *F:* **trinken wie ein B.**, to drink like a fish; **laufen wie ein B.**, to run like a hare, *F:* to hare, to run like mad. **2.** *Ent:*=**Bürstenraupe.**

Bürstenbinderei, *f.* (*a*) brushmaking; (*b*) brushmaker's workshop.

Bürstenbinderwaren, *f.pl.* brush-ware.

Bürstenentladung, *f. El:* brush discharge.

Bürstenhalter, *m.* (*a*) *Dom.Ec:* brush-holder; (*b*) *El.E:* brush-holder, -carrier.

Bürstenholz, *n.* (wood for the) back of a brush.

Bürstenkraut, *n. Bot:* safflower, bastard saffron.

Bürstenmacher, *m.* brush-maker.

Bürstenmaschine, *f.* brush-making machine.

Bürstenraupe, *f. Ent:* hairy caterpillar, larva of the tussock-moth.

Bürstenscheibe, *f. Ind:* brush-wheel.

Bürstenschnitt, *m.* (*hair style*) crew cut.

Bürstenspinner, *m. Ent:* tussock(-moth).

Bürstenwalze, *f.* rotary brush.

Bürstling, *m.* **-s/-e.** *Ich:* perch.

Bürstmaschine, *f. Ind:* brushing machine.

bürtig, *a. A:*=**gebürtig.**

Bürzel, *m.* **-s/-**, (*a*) rump, uropygium (of bird); *Cu: F:* parson's, pope's, nose; (*b*) *Ven:* tail (of wild boar, badger, etc.).

Bürzeldrüse, *f.*=**Bürzelöldrüse.**

Burzelkraut, *n. Bot:* purslane.

Bürzelöldrüse, *f.* (*in birds*) preen gland, uropygial gland, oil gland.

Bus, *m.* **-ses/-se**, bus; coach.

Busch, *m.* **-es/-e.** **1.** (*a*) bush, shrub; (*b*) branch (with foliage); (*used as tavern sign*) bush; (*c*) bunch of flowers. **2.** (*sg. only*) bushes, scrub; (brush)wood; **der (afrikanische, usw.) B.**, the (African, etc.) bush. **3.** *F:* **(bei) j-m auf den B. klopfen**, to sound s.o. (about sth.), to feel s.o.'s pulse; **hinter dem B. halten**, to be reticent, to beat about the bush; **sich (seitwärts) in die Büsche schlagen**, (i) to slink off into the bushes; to disappear; (ii) *F:* to go behind a bush. **4.** crest, tuft (of bird); *Cost:* aigrette; plume (of helmet).

Buschaffe, *m. Z:* orang-(o)utang.

Buschammer, *f., occ. m. Orn:* bunting.

Buschbaum, *m. Hort:* dwarf-tree.

Buschbock, *m. Z:* bush-buck.

Buschbohne, *f. Hort:* dwarf bean, *U.S:* bush bean.

Buschegge, *f. Agr:* bush-, brush-harrow.

Büschel, *n. & m.* **-s/-**, clump, cluster, bunch; wisp (of straw, etc.); tuft, handful (of hair); *Nat.Hist:* fascicle; *Ph: Mth:* pencil (of rays, lines); *El:* brush.

Büschelentladung, *f. El:* brush discharge.

büschelförmig, *a.* clustered, bunched, tufted.

Büschelkiemer, *m.* **-s/-.** *Ich:* lophobranch, lophobranchiate.

büschelkiemig, *a. Ich:* lophobranch, lophobranchiate.

Büschelkraut, *n. Bot:* tick trefoil.

Büschelnelke, *f. Bot:* sweet-william.

Büschelrose, *f. Bot:* cluster-rose.

Büschelschwamm, *m. Fung:* tufted yellow mushroom.

Buschen, *m.* **-s/-.** *South G.Dial:*=**Busch 1** (*c*).

Buschhemd, *n.* (i) bush-shirt; (ii) play-shirt; beach-shirt; jacket-shirt.

Buschholz, *n.* (*a*) undergrowth, brushwood; (*b*) sticks, faggots, branches.

Buschhorn(blatt)wespe, *f. Ent:* (Scotch fir) saw-fly.

Buschhuhn, *n. Orn:* brush-turkey.

Buschhund, *m. Z:* bush-dog.

buschig, *a.* **1.** (*of hair, eyebrows, etc.*) bushy. **2.** (*of ground*) covered with bushes, with scrub, bushy.

Buschkatze, *f. Z:* serval, bush-cat, tiger-cat.

Buschklepper, *m.* bandit, highwayman; *A:* cut-purse, footpad.

Buschkohle, *f.* charcoal.

Buschkrieg, *m.* bush-fighting.

Buschmann, *m.* **-(e)s/-männer.** *Ethn:* (*in S. Africa*) bushman.

Buschmannkerze, *f. Bot:* bushman's candle.

Buschmeister, *m. Rept:* bush-master.

Buschmesser, *n.* bush-knife; (*in S. America*) machete.

Buschneger, *m.* maroon, runaway negro slave.

Buschobst, *n.* (*a*) dwarf fruit-trees; (*b*) fruit from dwarf fruit-trees.

Buschratte, *f. Z:* kangaroo-rat.

Buschrohrsänger, *m. Orn:* Blyth's reed-warbler.

Buschschnepfe, *f. Orn:* woodcock.

Buschspinne, *f. Arach:* mygale, trap-door spider; bird-eating spider, bird-spider.

Buschspötter, *m. Orn:* booted warbler.

Buscht, *m.* **-(e)s/-e**=**Bauscht.**

Buschteufel, *m. Z:* sarcophilus, *F:* Tasmanian devil.

Buschtiger, *m. Z:*=**Beutelwolf.**

Buschtruthuhn, *n. Orn:*=**Buschhuhn.**

Buschwald, *m.* scrub, bushes.

Buschwerk, *n.* bushes, shrubbery; undergrowth, underwood.

Buschwindröschen, *n. Bot:* wood-anemone.

Büse, *f.* **-/-n.** *Nau:* herring-boat.

Busen, *m.* **-s/-.** **1.** (*a*) bosom, breast (*esp.* of woman); **ihr B. hob sich**, her bosom, breast, heaved; **üppiger B.**, ample, full, bosom; *F:* **angriffslustiger B.**, prominent, pointed, aggressive, bosom; (*b*) bosom, breast, heart; **ein Gefühl im B. hegen**, to harbour a feeling in one's bosom, breast, heart; **Haß im B. nähren**, to nourish hatred in one's bosom, breast, heart; **ein Geheimnis, usw., im B. verschließen**, to keep a secret, etc., locked in one's heart; **eine Schlange am B. nähren, hegen**, to cherish, nourish, a snake, a viper, in one's bosom; (*c*) bosom (of dress); **sie steckte den Brief in ihren B.**, she put the letter in her bosom. **2.** *Geog:* gulf, bay.

Busenfreund, *m.* bosom friend.

Busennadel, *f.* scarf-pin.

Busentuch, *n.*=**Brusttuch.**

Bushido [bu·'ʃi:do:], *n.* **-(s)/.** *Japanese Civil:* Bushido.

busper, *a. South G.Dial:* fresh, bright.

Bußaar, *m.*, **Bussard**, *m.* **-s/-e.** *Orn:* buzzard.

Bußbruder, *m. Ecc:* penitent; **Bußbrüder Jesu Christi**, Penitent Brothers, Penitentes.

Bußbuch, *n. Ecc:* penitential.

Buße, *f.* **-/-n.** **1.** expiation (of fault, etc.); *Theol:* (i) atonement (for sins), penance; (ii) satisfaction; *B:* repentance; **B. tun**, to do penance, *B:* to repent; *Ecc: etc:* **j-m eine B. auferlegen**, to impose a penance on, to penance, s.o.; *Theol:* **das Sakrament der B.**, the sacrament of penance. **2.** fine; **5 Mark B.**, a fine of 5 marks.

büßen. I. *v.tr. & i.* (*haben*) **1.** (*a*) **(für) seine Sünden, usw., b.**, to expiate, atone for, pay the penalty of (sin, etc.); **etwas mit seinem Leben b.**, to pay for sth. with one's life; **ein Vergehen mit Geld b.**, to pay a fine for an offence; *F:* **er hat es schwer b. müssen**, he paid heavily for it, *F:* he paid for it up to the hilt; *F:* **das sollst du mir b.!** you'll pay for that! (*b*) *A. & Lit:* **seine Lust b.**, to satisfy one's desires. **2.** *A. & Dial:* **j-n b.**, to fine s.o.

II. *vbl s.* **Büßen** *n.*, *occ.* **Büßung** *f. in vbl senses; also:* expiation, atonement.

Büßer, *m.* **-s/-**, penitent.

Büßerbank, **die.** *Ecc:* the penitent bench.

Büßerhemd, *n.* penitential robe; cilice, hair shirt, shirt of hair.

Busserl, *n.* **-s/-(n).** *South G.Dial:* (little) kiss; peck.

Büßerorden, *m. Theol:* order of penitents.

bußfällig, *a. Jur:* punishable, finable (offence).

bußfertig, *a.* penitent, repentant, contrite.

Bußgang, *m. Ecc:* (penitential) pilgrimage *or* procession.

Bußgewand, *n.* penitential robe.

Bußkleid, *n.* penitential robe; **härenes B.,** cilice, hair-shirt, shirt of hair.

Büßling, *m.* -(e)s/-e. *Bot:* (female) hemp plant.

Bussole [bu'soːlə], *f.* -/-n, (*a*) compass; (*b*) *Surv:* transit theodolite, transit compass; (*c*) *El:* galvanometer.

Bussoleninstrument, *n. Surv: Astr:* transit instrument.

Bussolenrichtkreis, *m. Mil: Surv:* azimuth circle.

Bussolentheodolit, *m. Surv:* transit theodolite, transit compass.

Bußpredigt, *f.* (*a*) exhortation to repentance; (*b*) lenten sermon.

Bußpsalmen, *m.pl.* penitential psalms.

Bußsakrament, *n. Theol:* sacrament of penance.

Bußschwester, *f. Ecc:* penitent.

Bußtag, *m. Ecc:* (*a*) day of repentance; (*b*) **B., Buß- und Bettag,** day of prayer and repentance.

Bußübung, *f.* penance; **Bußübungen** *pl,* works of penance; penitential good works.

Bußwerke, *n.pl.* penitential good works, works of penance.

Büste, *f.* -/-n. **1.** *Sculp: etc:* bust. **2.** (*woman's*) bust.

Büstenformer, *m. Cost:* pre-shaped brassière.

Büstenhalter, *m. Cost:* brassière, *F:* bra.

Büstenhebe, *f.* -/-n. *Cost:* uplift brassière.

Butadien [buˑtaˑdiˈeːn], *n.* -s/. *Ch:* butadiene.

Butan [buˈtaːn], *n.* -s/-e. *Ch:* butane.

Butanol [buˑtaˈnoːl], *n.* -s/. *Ch:* butanol, butyl alcohol.

Butanon [buˑtaˈnoːn], *n.* -s/. *Ch:* butanone.

buten. *North G.Dial:* (*a*) *adv.* outside; beyond; (*b*) **Buten-,** *comb.fm.* outer...; **Butendeich** *m,* outer dike.

Butike [buˈtiˑkə], *f.* -/-n = **Budike.**

Butiker [buˈtiˑkər], *m.* -s/- = **Budiker.**

Butluv, *m.* -s/-e. *Nau:* bum(p)kin.

Butt, *m.* -(e)s/-e. *Ich:* (*a*) die **Butte,** the bothidae; (*b*) flatfish, *esp.* flounder.

Buttdarm, *m.* blind gut, caecum (of cattle, pigs).

Butte, *f.* -/-n. **1.** *Bot:* hip (of wild rose); haw (of hawthorn). **2.** = **Bütte.**

Bütte, *f.* -/-n. **1.** (*a*) butt, tub; *Paperm: etc:* vat; (*b*) portable vat (for grape-gathering). **2.** (*in Rhenish carnival*) platform.

Butteil, *m. A.Jur:* heriot.

Buttel, *f.* -/-n = **Buddel.**

Büttel, *m.* -s/-. *A:* beadle.

Bütten, *n.* -s/- = **Büttenpapier.**

Büttengeselle, *m. Paperm:* vatman, dipper.

Büttenmacher, *m.* cooper.

Büttenpapier, *n.* hand-made paper.

Büttenrede, *f.* (*in Rhenish towns*) carnival oration.

Butter, *f.* -/. butter; **gesalzene B.,** salt(ed) butter; **frische B.,** new, fresh, butter; **ein Stück Brot mit** **B. bestreichen,** (be)schmieren, to butter a piece of bread, to spread a piece of bread with butter; *F:* **mir fiel die B. vom Brot, als er es mir sagte,** when he told me I was absolutely knocked into a cocked hat, you could have knocked me down with a feather; **ein Gesicht machen, wie wenn einem die B. vom Brot gefallen wäre,** to make a face as long as a fiddle; **alles ist in Butter,** everything's in order, going fine; **er läßt sich nicht die B. vom Brot nehmen,** he won't let himself be done out of his rights; **er ist weich wie B.,** (i) he is very soft-hearted; (ii) *Pej:* he's as weak as water.

butterartig, *a.* like butter; *Ch:* butyraceous.

Butterbaum, *m. Bot:* butter-tree, shea(-tree).

Butterbereitung, *f.* butter-making.

Butterbirne, *f.* butter-pear.

Butterblume, *f. Bot:* **1.** buttercup. **2.** *F:* dandelion.

Butterbrot *n.* -(e)s/-e, (*Dial: occ.* -bröte) piece, slice, of bread and butter; **Butterbrote,** bread and butter; **B. mit Wurst, Käse, usw.,** bread and butter spread with sausage, cheese, etc.; **belegtes B.,** open sandwich; **ein B. schmieren, machen,** to cut a piece, a slice, of bread and butter, a sandwich; *F:* **etwas für ein B. bekommen,** to get sth. for an old song, for a (mere) song; *F:* **er schmiert mir dauernd aufs B., daß ich seinen Geburtstag vergessen habe,** he keeps rubbing in the fact that I forgot his birthday; **er schmierte ihm seinen Fehler aufs B.,** he rammed his mistake down his throat; **du brauchst es mir nicht aufs B. zu schmieren,** you needn't rub it in.

Butterbrotpapier, *n.* grease-proof paper.

Butterdose, *f.* (screw-top) butter jar.

Butterfaß, *n.* (*a*) butter-churn; (*b*) butter-tub.

Butterfett, *n.* butter-fat, *Ch:* butyrine.

Butterfisch, *m. Ich:* butter-fish, gunnel.

Butterform, *f.* butter-stamp, butter print.

butterhaltig, *a.* containing butter; *Ch:* butyraceous, butyrous.

butterig, *a.* **1.** buttery. **2.** *Ch:* butyrous.

Butterkelle, *f. Dom.Ec:* butter paddle.

Butterknetmaschine, *f.* butter-worker.

Butterkrebs, *m. Crust:* fresh-water crayfish that has just cast its shell.

Butterkuchen, *m.* sugar-coated yeast cake.

Butterkugel, *f.* **1.** butter-pat. **2.** *Bot: F:* globe-flower.

Butterland, *n. Nau:* illusion of land created by a cloud formation.

Buttermaschine, *f.* butter-churn.

Buttermesser¹, *n. Dom.Ec:* butter-knife.

Buttermesser², *m. Ch:* butyrometer.

Buttermilch, *f.* buttermilk.

buttern, *v.* **1.** *v.tr.* to butter (bread). **2.** *v.i.* (*haben*) (*a*) to make butter, to churn; (*b*) (*of cream*) to thicken, to turn to butter; **der Rahm will nicht b.,** the cream won't thicken.

Butternapf, *m.* butter-dish.

Butternuß, *f. Bot:* butter-nut.

Butterpilz, *m. Fung:* boletus luteus; *F:* butter-fungus.

Butterraps, *m. Bot:* gold-of-pleasure.

Butterröhrling, *m. Fung:* = **Butterpilz.**

Buttersame, *m. Bot: F:* = **Butterraps.**

Buttersäure, *f. Ch:* butyric acid.

Butterschmalz, *n. Cu:* run butter, clarified butter; ghee.

Butterstempel, *m.* butter-stamp, butter print.

Butterstulle, *f.* piece, slice, of bread and butter.

Butterteig, *m. Cu:* = **Blätterteig.**

Buttervogel, *m. Ent: F:* (white) butterfly.

butterweich, *a.* as soft as butter.

Büttner, *m.* -s/-. *Dial:* cooper.

Büttnerschilf, *n. Bot:* typha, cat('s)-tail.

buttrig, *a.* = **butterig.**

Butyl [buˈtyːl], *n.* -s/. *Ch:* butyl.

Butylalkohol, *m. Ch:* butyl alcohol.

Butylen [buˑtyˈleːn], *n.* -s/. *Ch:* butylene.

Butylenglykol, *n. Ch:* butylene glycol.

Butyrat [buˑtyˈraːt], *n.* -s/-e. *Ch:* butyrate.

butz¹, *int.* wallop! smack!

Butz², *m.* -en/-en = (i) **Butze¹,** (ii) **Butzen.**

Butze¹, *m.* -n/-n, (*a*) gnome; (*b*) dwarf.

Butze², *f.* -/-n. *North G.Dial:* **1.** (*a*) wall bed; (*b*) partition. **2.** lump, irregularity (in glass, metal, etc.).

Bütze, *f.* -/-n. *Dial:* = **Beuche.**

Butzen, *m.* -s/-. *Dial:* **1.** core (of apple, etc.). **2.** *Anat:* secretion. **3.** lump, irregularity (in glass, metal, etc.).

Butzenmann, *m.* -(e)s/-männer, bogey-man.

Butzenscheibe, *f. Glassm:* bottle-glass, bull's-eye (pane).

butzig, *a.* **1.** (glass, etc.) that has lumps, irregularities. **2.** = **rotzig.**

Butzkopf, *m. Z:* grampus.

Buxazeen [buksaˈtseːən], *f.pl. Bot:* buxaceae.

Buxbaum, *m. Bot:* = **Buchsbaum.**

Büxe, Buxe, *f.* -/-n. *F:* (pair of) trousers.

buxen, *v.tr. F:* to steal, *F:* to pinch (sth.).

Buzentaur [buˈtsɛnˈtauər], *m.* -en/-en [-ˈtauərn] = **Bukentaur.**

Buzephalus [buˈtseːfaˑlus]. *Pr.n.m.* -'. = **Buke-phalos.**

Byssus ['bysus], *m.* -/. *Archeol: Biol:* byssus.

Byzantiner [byˈtsanˈtiːnər], *m.* -s/-. **1.** Byzantine. **2.** *Hist: Num:* bezant. **3.** toady, toad-eater, flatterer.

byzantinisch [byˈtsanˈtiːniʃ], *a.* **1.** *Hist:* Byzantine; **das Byzantinische Reich,** the Byzantine Empire. **2.** obsequious.

Byzantinismus [byˈtsantiˈnismus], *m.* -/. **1.** Byzantinism. **2.** obsequiousness.

Byzantinist [byˈtsantiˈnist], *m.* -en/-en. Byzantine scholar.

Byzanz [byˈtsants]. *Pr.n.n.* -'. *Geog:* Byzantium.

C

C, c [tseː], *n.* -/- (*in speech only* -s/-s [tseːs]).
1. (the letter) C, c; *Tp:* **C wie Cäsar,** C for
Charlie; **Ch** [tseːˈhaː] **wie Charlotte,** C for
Charlie, H for Harry. **2.** *Mus:* (the note) C;
C-dur, C-Dur, c-moll, c-Moll, (-Tonart), (key of)
C major, C minor. *See also List of Abbrevia-*
tions.
Cabalministerium, das [kaˈbaːl-]. *Eng.Hist:* the
Cabal.
Cabanholz [kaˈbaːn-], *n. Bot:* camwood.
Cabaret [kabaˈreː, -ˈrɛː], *n.* -s/-s = **Kabarett** 1.
Cabochon [kaboˈʃõː], *m.* -s/-s. *Lap:* cabochon.
Cabochonsmaragd, *m. Lap:* emerald en *cabochon,*
tallow-drop emerald.
Cabriolet [kabriˈoˈleː], *n.* -s/-s = **Kabriolett.**
Cacao [kaˈkau, kaˈkaoː], *m.* -s/-s = **Kakao.**
Cachenez [kaʃ(ə)ˈneː], *n.* -/- [-ˈneː(s)/-ˈneːs], silk
scarf; muffler.
Cachet [kaˈʃeː], *n.* -s/-s. **1.** cachet, seal. **2.** *Cin:*
keyhole view.
Cachot [kaˈʃoː], *m.* -s/-s. **1.** prison, gaol. **2.** close
arrest.
Cachou [kaˈʃuː], *n.* -s/-s. **1.** *Pharm:* cachou.
2. = **Katechu** 1.
Cachoubraun, *n.* (*colour*) catechu brown.
cachoutieren [kaʃuˈtiːrən], *v.tr.* to dye (material)
with catechu.
Cäcilia, Cäcilie [tseˈtsiːliːa, -liːə]. *Pr.n. f.* -s & *Lit:*
-liens. Cecilia, Cicely; **die heilige C.,** Saint
Cecilia.
Cadeau [kaˈdoː], *n.* -(s)/-s, present, gift.
Cadeöl [ˈkaːdə-], **Cadieöl** [ˈkaːdiːə-], *n. Bot: Com:*
cade-oil.
Cadinen [kaˈdiːnen], *n.* -s/. *Ch:* cadinene.
Cadmium [ˈkatmĭum], *n.* -s/. *Ch:* cadmium; *for*
compounds see **Kadmium-.**
Caduceus [kaˈduːtseˈus], *m.* -/. *Gr. & Rom. Ant:*
caduceus.
Caelius, der [ˈtseːliˈus], -, the Caelian (Hill).
Caesarea [tseˈzaˈreːaː]. *Pr.n.n.* -s. *Geog:* Caesarea.
Caesur [tseˈzuːr], *f.* -/-en. *Pros: Mus:* caesura.
Café [kaˈfeː], *n.* -s/-s, coffee-house; café.
Cafetier [kafəˈtiːeː], *m.* -s/-s, proprietor of a coffee-
house.
Cafetière [kafətiˈɛːrə], *f.* -/-n. **1.** proprietress of a
coffee-house. **2.** coffee-pot.
Caguare [kaˈgŭaˈreː], *m.* -s/-s. *Z:* tamandua;
small ant-eater.
Cairn [kɛrn], *m.* -s/-s. *Prehist:* cairn.
Caisson [kɛˈsõː], *m.* -s/-s. *Civ.E:* caisson.
Caisson(arbeiter)krankheit, *f. Med:* = **Taucher-**
krankheit.
Calababalsam [kaˈlaːbaˈ-], *m.* calababalsam.
Calais [kaˈlɛː]. *Pr.n.n.* -'. *Geog:* Calais; **die Straße**
von C., the Straits of Dover.
Calamus [ˈkaːlaˈmus], *m.* -/-mi. **1.** *Ant:* calamus;
reed pen. **2.** *Bot:* calamus, rattan(-palm).
3. *Orn:* calamus (of feather).
calcificieren [kaltsiˈfiˈtsiːrən], *v.tr.,* **calcinieren**
[kaltsiˈniːrən], *v.tr.* = **kalzifizieren, kalzinieren.**
Calcium [ˈkaltsĭum], *n.* -s/. *Ch:* calcium; *for com-*
pounds see **Kalzium-.**
Caldera [kalˈdeːraː], *f.* -/-ren & -s. *Geol:* caldera.
Calembour(g) [kaˈlãˈbuːr], *m.* -s/-s, pun.
Calendula [kaˈlɛnduˈlaː], *f.* -/. *Bot:* calendula.
Caliche [kaˈˈliːtʃə], *f. & m.* -/. *Miner:* caliche, Chile
saltpetre.
Calla [ˈkalaː], *f.* -/-s = **Kalla.**
Calvaria [kalˈvaːriaː], *f.* **1.** *Pr.n.f.* -s. *B.Lit:*
Calvary. **2.** *f. Anat:* calvaria, calvarium.
Calvin [kalˈviːn]. *Pr.n.m.* -s. *Rel.Hist:* Calvin.
calvinisch [kalˈviːniʃ], *a.* = **calvinistisch.**
Calvinismus [kalviˈnismus], *m.* -/. *Rel:* Calvinism.
Calvinist [kalviˈnist], *m.* -en/-en. *Rel:* Calvinist.
calvinistisch [kalviˈnistiʃ], *a.* Calvinistic(al).

Camaïeu [kamaˈˈjøː], *f.* -s/-s. **1.** cameo. **2.**
camaieu, monochrome painting.
Cambalholz [kamˈbaːl-], *n.* = **Camholz.**
Cambridgewalze [ˈkeːmbridʒ-], *f. Agr:* Cam-
bridge roller.
Camembert [kamãˈbɛːr, ˈkamãˈbɛːr], *m.* -s/-s.
Camembert (cheese).
Camera [ˈkamɵraː], *f.* -/-s. *Phot:* camera.
Camholz [ˈkam-], *n. Bot:* camwood, barwood.
Camion [kamĭˈõː], *m.* -s/-s. *Swiss:* lorry.
Camionnage [kamĭoˈnaːʒə], *f.* -/. *Swiss:* (fee for)
carriage, haulage.
Camouflage [kamuˈˈflaːʒə], *f.* -/-n. **1.** disguise.
2. *Mil:* camouflage.
camouflieren [kamuˈˈfliːrən], *v.tr.* to camouflage.
Camp [kɛmp], *n.* -s/-s, camp.
Campagna, die [kamˈpanjaː]. *Pr.n.f.* -. *Geog:* the
Campagna.
Campanile [kampaˈniːlə], *m.* -s/-s. *Arch:* cam-
panile.
Campeche [kamˈpɛːtʃeː]. *Pr.n.n.* -s. *Geog:*
Campeachy.
Campecheholz, *n. Com:* Campeachy wood.
Camper [ˈkɛmpər], *m.* -s/-, camper.
Campher [ˈkamfər], *m.* -s/. *A:* = **Kampfer.**
Campignien, das, [kãmpinjĭˈɛː], -s/. *Prehist:*
the Campignian culture.
Campinerhuhn [kamˈpiːnər-], *n. Husb:* Silver
Campine fowl.
Camping [ˈkɛmpiŋ], *n.* -s/-s, camping.
Campingplatz, *m.* camping-ground, *U.S:* camp-
ground.
Campylometer [kampyˈloˈˈmeɪtər], *n.* -s/-. *Surv:*
campylometer.
Canaille [kaˈnaljə], *f.* -/-n. *P:* (*a*) scoundrel,
blackguard; (*b*) *coll.* scoundrels, blackguards.
Canasta [kaˈnastaː], *n.* -s/. *Cards:* canasta.
Cancan [kãˈkãː], *m.* -s/-s. *Danc:* cancan.
Candela [kanˈdeːlaː], *f.* -/- (*abbr.* **cd**). *Ph.*
Meas: candela, *esp. U.S:* (new) candle.
candidatus [kandiˈdaːtus], *m.* -/. *Sch:* student
preparing for final examination; *esp.* **c. medi-**
cinae (*abbr.* **cand. med.**), medical student in fifth
or later term.
Candlekohle [ˈkandəl-], *f.* = **Cannelkohle.**
Cannä [ˈkaneː]. *Pr.n.n.* -s. *Rom.Hist:* Cannae; **die**
Schlacht bei C., the battle of Cannae.
Cannelé [kanəˈleː], *n.* -s/-s. *Tex:* rep(p), reps.
Cannelkohle [ˈkanəl-], *f. Min:* cannel(-coal),
candle-coal.
Cañon [kanˈjon, ˈkanjon], *m.* -s/-s. *Geog:* canyon.
Cant [kɛnt, kant], *m.* -s/. cant; (*a*) hypocrisy;
(*b*) jargon; slang.
cantabile [kanˈtaːbiˈleː]. *Mus:* **1.** *adv.* cantabile.
2. Cantabile *n.* -s/-s, cantabile.
Canticumcanticorum [ˈkantiˈkumkantiˈˈkoːrum],
n. -s -, the Song of Songs, the Song of Solomon.
Cantus [ˈkantus], *m.* -/-, song, melody; *Sch: F:*
einen C. steigen lassen, to sing a song; *Mus:*
C. firmus, *cantus firmus,* canto fermo; **C.**
planus, *cantus planus,* plainsong, Gregorian
chant.
Cape [keːp], *n.* -s/-s. *Cost:* cape.
Capella [kaˈpɛlaː]. *Pr.n.f.* -s. *Astr:* Capella.
Capitulare [kapituˈlaːrə], *n.* -/-ria. *Jur: Hist:*
capitulary.
Cappa [ˈkapaː], *f.* -/-s. *Ecc. Cost:* cappa, cope;
R.C.Ch: pluvial.
Caprese [kaˈpreːzeː], *m.* -n/-n, **Capresin,** *f.*
-/-innen. *Geog:* inhabitant, native, of Capri;
man, woman, of Capri.
capresisch [kaˈpreːziʃ], *a. Geog:* of Capri.
Capri [ˈkaːpriː]. *Pr.n.n.* -s. *Geog:* **(die Insel) C.,**
(the island of) Capri.
Caprice [kaˈpriːs(ə), kaˈpriːtsə], *f.* -/-n, caprice.

Capricornus [kaˈpriˈkornus]. *Pr.n.m.* -'. *Astr:*
Capricorn, the Goat.
Caprinsäure [kaˈpriːn-], *f. Ch:* capric acid.
Caprivizipfel, der [kaˈpriːviː-]. *Pr.n. Geog:*
Caprivi's Finger.
Capronsäure [kaˈproːn-], *f. Ch:* caproic acid.
Caprylsäure [kaˈpryːl-], *f. Ch:* caprylic acid.
Capsien, das [kapsiˈɛː], -s. *Prehist:* the Capsian
culture.
Capuchon [kapyˈˈʃõː], *m.* -s/-s. *Cost:* **1.** (*a*)
hood; (*b*) cowl. **2.** (lady's) coat with a hood.
Carbamid-, Carbid-, Carbol-, Carbon-, *etc. see*
Karbamid-, Karbid-, Karbol-, Karbon-, *etc.*
Carbonado [karboˈnaːdoː], *m.* -s/-s = **Karbonat**[2].
Carbonyl [karboˈnyːl], *n.* -s/-e, **Carbonyl-,**
comb.fm. Ch: carbonyl; **Carbonylchlorid** *n,*
carbonyl chloride; **Carbonylgruppe** *f,* carbonyl
group; **Carbonylsauerstoff** *m,* carbonyl oxygen;
Carbonylverbindung *f,* carbonyl compound.
Carborundum [karboˈrundum], *n.* -s/. (*R.t.m.*)
carborundum.
Carcel [karˈtsɛl], *m.* -(s)/-. *Ph.Meas: A:* carcel.
Carcellampe, *f.* Carcel lamp.
Cariama [kaˈriˈaːmaː], *f.* -/-s. *Orn:* cariama.
Caries [ˈkaːriˈes], *f.* -/. *Med:* caries.
Carillon [kariˈˈjõː], *n.* -s/-s. *Mus:* carillon.
Carina [kaˈriːnaː], *f.* -/. *Orn: Bot:* carina.
Caritas [ˈkaːriˈtas], *f.* -/. (*a*) charity; (*b*) (Roman
Catholic) charitable organizations.
Caritasverband, *m.* (Roman Catholic) charit-
able organization.
caritativ [kaˈriˈtaˈtiːf], *a.* charitable; **caritative**
[kaˈriˈtaˈtiːve] **Verbände,** charitable organiza-
tions; *adv.* **sich c. betätigen,** to do charitable
works, works of charity.
Carl. *Pr.n.m.* -s. Charles.
Carneval [ˈkarneval], *m.* -s/-s & -e = **Karneval.**
Carolina, die [kaˈroˈliːnaː], -. *Hist. of Law:* the
'Constitutio Criminalis Carolina' of 1532.
Carotin [kaˈroˈtiːn], *n.* -s/-e = **Karotin.**
Carotis [kaˈroːtis], *f.* -/-tiden [-roˈtiːdən]. *Anat:*
carotid artery.
Carpentariagolf, der [karpənˈtaːriaː-]. *Pr.n.*
Geog: the Gulf of Carpentaria.
Carrara [kaˈraːraː]. *Pr.n.n.* -s. *Geog:* Carrara.
Cartagena [kartaˈgeːnaː]. *Pr.n.n.* -s. *Geog:*
Carthagena.
Cartesianismus [karteˈziaˈnismus], *m.* -/. Carte-
sianism.
cartesisch [karˈteːziʃ], *a.* = **kartesisch.**
Cartesius [karˈteːzius]. *Pr.n.m.* -'. Descartes.
Casaca [kaˈsakaː], *m.* -s/-s. *Z:* quica; South
American opossum.
Casanova [kazaˈnoːvaː]. *Pr.n.m.* -s & *s.m.* -/-s.
Casanova; **er ist ein (richtiger) C.,** he is a
proper, regular, Casanova.
Cäsar [ˈtseːzaːr]. **1.** *Pr.n.m.* -s. Caesar. **2.** *m.*
-en/-en [tseˈzaːrən]. *Rom.Hist: etc:* Caesar.
Cäsarentum [tseˈzaːrəntuːm], *n.* -s/. *Hist: Pol:*
Caesarism.
Cäsarenwahn, *f.* (*a*) madness caused by too much
power; (*b*) megalomania.
Cäsar(e)opapismus [tseˈzaˈr(e)oˈpaˈpismus], *m.*
-/. *Ecc.Hist:* Caesaro-papism.
Cäsarewitsch [tseˈzaˈreːvitʃ], *m.* -(es)/-e =
Zarewitsch.
cäsarisch [tseˈzaːriʃ], *a. Hist: Pol:* Caesarean,
Caesarian.
Cäsarismus [tseˈzaˈrismus], *m.* -/. *Hist: Pol:*
Caesarism.
Cäsium [ˈtseːziuːm], *n.* -s/. *Ch:* caesium.
Cassa [ˈkasaː], *f.* -/. = **Kasse; per cassa,** in cash.
Cassata [kaˈsaːtaː], *f.* -/-(s) = **Kassata.**
Cassinensisch [kasiˈnɛnziʃ], *a.* Cassinese (script,
etc.)

Cassinisch [ka'si:niʃ], *a.* Cassinian; **Cassinische Linien, Kurven, Ovale,** Cassinian ovals.

Cassiodor [kasio'do:r]. *Pr.n.m.* -s. *Lt.Lit:* Cassiodorus.

Cassiopeia [kasio'paia:]. *Pr.n.f.* -s & *Lit:* -peiens. *Gr.Mth: Astr:* Cassiopeia.

Cassis [ka'si:], *n.* -/. cassis; black-currant liqueur.

Cassonade [kaso'na:də], *f.* -/. *Sug-R:* cassonade.

Castor[1] ['kastor], *m.* -(s)/-e = **Kastor**[1].

Castor[2] ['kastor]. *Pr.n.m.* -s. *Gr.Myth: Astr: etc:* Castor.

Cäsur [tsɛ'zu:r], *f.* -/-en. *Pros: Mus:* caesura.

Casus ['ka:zus], *m.* -/-. *Gram:* case; **casus obliquus,** oblique case.

Cathedra ['kate·dra:], *f.* -/-drae [-drɛ:], (bishop's, etc.) throne; **ex cathedra,** ex cathedra.

Catilina [ka·ti·'li:na:]. *Pr.n.m.* -s. *Rom.Hist:* Catiline.

catilinarisch [ka·ti·li·'na:riʃ], *a. Rom.Hist:* Catiline; *Lit:* **die Catilinarischen Reden,** the Catiline orations; (*pers.*) **catilinarische Existenz,** revolutionary; profligate.

Cato ['ka:to]. *Pr.n.m.* -s. *Rom.Hist:* Cato.

catonisch [ka·'to:niʃ], *a.* Catonian; stern, austere.

Catullus ['ka'tulus]. *Pr.n.m.* -'. *Lt.Lit:* Catullus.

Causerie [ko·zə'ri:], *f.* -/-n [-'ri:ən]. *A:* chat.

Causeur [ko'zø:r], *m.* -s/-e. *A:* (*a*) talker, conversationalist; (*b*) *F:* tattler, blab(ber).

Causeuse [ko'zø:zə], *f.* -/-n. *A:* 1. gossip, *F:* tattler. 2. *Furn:* small sofa *or* settee for two people.

Cayenne [ka'jɛn]. *Pr.n.n.* -s. 1. (*town*) Cayenne. 2. **(die Insel) C.,** (the Island of) Cayenne.

Cayennepfeffer, *m.* Cayenne pepper, red pepper.

C-Barren, *m. Metall:* foundry ingot.

C-dur, C-Dur, *n. Mus:* (key of) C major.

Cecilie [tse·'tsi:liə]. *Pr.n.f.* -s & *Lit:* -ns. Cecilia, Cicely.

Cedille [se'diljə, se'di:jə], *f.* -/-n. *Print:* cedilla.

Celanese [selə'ni:z], *f.* -/-n. *Tex:* celanese.

Celaster [tse'lastər], *m.* -s/-. *Bot:* celastrus, stafftree.

Celebes ['tse:le·bɛs]. *Pr.n.n.* -'. *Geog:* (**die Insel**) **C.,** (the Island of) Celebes; **von C.,** Celebesian.

Celebrant [tse·le·'brant], *m.* -en/-en. *Ecc:* celebrant, officiant, officiating priest.

celebrieren [tse·le·'bri:rən], *v.tr. Ecc:* **die Messe c.,** to say mass.

Celebrität [tse·le·bri·'tɛt], *f.* -/-en, celebrity.

Celesta [tʃe·'lɛsta:], *f.* -/-s & -ten. *Mus:* celesta.

Cella ['tsɛla:], *f.* -/-lae [-lɛ:]. *Gr. & Rom. Arch:* cella.

Cellerar [tsɛlə'ra:r], *m.* -s/-e, **Cellerarius** [tsɛlə'ra:rius], *m.* -/-rii. *Ecc:* cellarer.

Cellist [tʃɛ'list], *m.* -en/-en. *Mus:* violoncellist, 'cellist, 'celloist.

Cello ['tʃɛlo:], *n.* -s/-s & -li. *Mus:* violoncello, 'cello.

Cellophan [tsɛlo'fa:n], *n.* -s/. (*R.t.m.*) cellophane.

Cellophanhülle, *f.* cellophane wrapping, envelope; **Brot in C.,** cellophane-wrapped bread.

Celosie [tse·'lo:ziə], *f.* -/-n. *Bot:* celosia.

Celsius ['tsɛlzius]. *Pr.n.m.* -'. Celsius; *Ph.Meas:* −10° C., −10° centigrade.

Celsiusskala, *f. Ph:* Celsius (thermometer) scale.

Celsiusthermometer, *n. Ph:* centigrade thermometer, Celsius thermometer.

Celt [tsɛlt], *m.* -s/-e. *Prehist:* celt.

Cembalist [tʃɛmba·'list], *m.* -en/-en, harpsichord, cembalo, player.

Cembalo ['tʃɛmba·lo:], *n.* -s/-s. *Mus:* harpsichord, cembalo.

Centaurea [tsɛntau're:a:], *f.* -/-reen, **Centauree** [tsɛntau·'re:ə], *f.*-/-reen [-'re:ən]. *Bot:* centaurea, centaury.

Cento ['tʃɛnto:], *m.* -s/-s & -nes [tʃɛn'to:nɛs]. *Lit:* cento; pastiche.

-cephal [-,tse·'fa:l], *comb.fm. a.*=**-zephal.**

cephalo-, Cephalo- ['tse·fa·lo·-], *comb.fm.* = **kephalo-, Kephalo-.**

Cepheide [tse·fe·'i:də], *m.* -n/-n. *Astr:* cepheid variable.

Cepheus ['tse:-, 'ke:foys]. *Pr.n.m.* -'. *Gr.Myth: Astr:* Cepheus.

Cercle ['sɛrkl], *m.* -s/-s. 1. reception, social gathering; **C. halten,** to have an at-home. 2. *Th: Austrian:* orchestra stalls.

Cerclesitz, *m. Th: Austrian:* (seat in the) orchestra stalls.

Cerealien [tse·re·'a:liən], *f.pl. Rom.Ant:* Cerealia.

Cer(er)it [tse·(re·)'ri:t], *n.* -(e)s/-e. *Miner:* cerite.

Ceres ['tse:rɛs, 'tse:rɛs]. *Pr.n.f.* -'. *Myth:* Ceres.

Cerevis [tse·re·'vi:s], *n.* -/-, student's small cap.

Ceri- ['tse:ri-], *comb.fm. Ch:* ceric . . .; cerium . . .; **Cerichlorid** *n,* ceric, cerium, chloride.

cerise [sə'ri:z], *inv. a.* cerise, cherry-red.

Cerium ['tse:rium], *n.* -s/. *Ch:* cerium.

Cero- ['tse:ro:-], *comb.fm. Ch:* cerous . . .; cerium . . .; **Cerosalz** *n,* cerous salt, cerium salt.

Certosa [tʃɛr'to:za:], *f.* -/. Carthusian monastery (*in Italy*).

Cerumen [tse·'ru:mən], *n.* -s/. *Physiol:* cerumen.

Cerviden, die [tsɛr'vi:dən], *m.pl. Z:* the cervidae, the deer tribe.

ces, Ces [tsɛs], *n.* -/-. *Mus:* (the note) C flat, C♭; **Ces-dur, Ces-Dur, ces-moll, ces-Moll,** (-Tonart), (key of) C flat major, C flat minor.

Cestoden [tsɛs'to:dən], *m.pl. Med:* tapeworms.

Cetan [tse·'ta:n], *m.* -s/. *Ch:* cetane.

Cetanzahl, *f. I.C.E:* cetane number (*of fuel*).

Ceten [tse·'te:n], *m.* -s/. *Ch:* cetene.

Ceterach ['tse:tərax], *n.* -/. *Bot:* ceterach, fingerfern, scale-fern.

Cettisänger ['tsɛti:-], *m. Orn:* Cetti's warbler.

Cevennen, die [se·'venən]. *Pr.n.pl. Geog:* the Cevennes Mountains.

Ceylon ['tsailon]. *Pr.n.n.* -s. *Geog:* Ceylon.

ceylonisch [tsai'lo:niʃ], *a.* Ceylonese; of Ceylon; *see also* **Opal** 1.

Ch. *Tp: see* **C.** *Words not listed under Ch may be found under Sch-, Tsch-.*

Chabasit [kaba·'zi:t], *m.* -(e)s/-e. *Miner:* chabazite.

Cha-cha(-cha) [tʃatʃa(tʃa)], *m.* -/-s. *Danc:* cha-cha(-cha).

Chaconne [ʃa'kon], *f.* -/-s & -n [-nən]. *Danc: Mus:* chacon(n)e.

Chagrin [ʃa·'grɛ̃], *m.* -s/-s. *Leath:* shagreen, grained leather, grain-leather; shark-skin.

chagrinieren [ʃa·gri·'ni:rən], *v.tr. Leath:* to shagreen (leather).

Chagrinleder, *n.*=**Chagrin.**

Chairleder ['ʃɛ:r-], *n.*=**Dänischleder.**

Chaise ['ʃɛ:zə], *f.* -/-n. 1. *Veh:* (*a*) chaise; (*b*) sedan-chair. 2. *Furn:*=**Chaiselongue.**

Chaiselongue [ʃɛ:z(ə)'lõ:(g), -'lon], *f.* -/-s, *occ. n.* -s/-s. *Furn:* chaise-longue, lounge-chair; *F:* couch.

Chalaze [ça·'la:tsə], *f.* -/-n. *Biol:* chalaza.

Chalazion [ça·'la:tsion], *n.* -s/-zien. *Med:* chalazion.

Chalcedon. 1. *Pr.n.n.* [çaltse·'do:n, çalke·'do:n], -s. *A.Geog:* Chalcedon. 2. *m.* [kaltse·'do:n], -s/-e = **Chalzedon.**

Chalcedonier [çaltse·'do:niər], *m.* -s/-. Chalcedonian.

chalcedonisch [çaltse·'do:niʃ], *a.* Chalcedonian.

Chalcidice, die [çal'tsi:di·tse:, çal'ki:di·ke:]. *Pr.n.* -. *A.Geog:* Chalcidice, Chalcidike.

Chaldäa [çal'dɛ:a:, kal'dɛ:a:]. *Pr.n.n.* -s. *A.Geog:* Chaldea.

Chaldäer [çal'dɛ:ər, kal'dɛ:ər], *m.* -s/-. Chaldean, Chaldee.

chaldäisch [çal'dɛ:iʃ, kal'dɛ:iʃ]. 1. *a.* Chaldean, Chaldaic, Chaldee. 2. *s.* **Chaldäisch,** *n. Ling:* Chaldean, Chaldee.

Chalet [ʃa'lɛ:, ʃa'le:], *n.* -s/-s, (*a*) (Swiss) chalet; (*b*) country cottage.

Chalkedon [kalke·'do:n], *m.* -s/-e. *Lap:* = **Chalzedon.**

Chalkidike, die [çal'ki:dike:]. *Pr.n.* -.=**Chalcidice.**

Chalkograph [çalko·'gra:f], *m.* -en/-en, chalcographer.

Chalkographie [çalko·gra·'fi:], *f.* -/-n [-'fi:ən]. *Engr:* 1. chalcography. 2. chalcograph.

Chalkolith [çalko·'li:t], *m.*-(e)s/-e & -en/-en. *Miner:* chalcolite, torbenite, copper uranite.

Chalkolithikum, das [çalko·'li:ti·kum], -s/. *Prehist:* the Chalcolithic age, period.

Chalkopyrit [çalko·py·'ri:t], *m. Miner:* chalcopyrite, copper pyrites, *F:* yellow ore.

Chalkosin [çalko·'zi:n], *m.* -s/-e. *Miner:* chalcocite, glance-copper.

Chalzedon [kaltse·'do:n], *m.* -s/-e. *Lap:* chalcedony.

Chalzidize, die [çal'tsi:di·tse:].*Pr.n.*-.=**Chalcidice.**

Cham [kam]. *Pr.n.m.* -s. *B.Hist:* Ham.

Chamäleon [ka'mɛ:le·on], *n.* -s/-s. *Rept:* chameleon.

Chamäleonfisch, *m. Ich:* chanchito.

chamäleontisch [kamɛ·le·'ontiʃ], *a.* chameleonlike, chameleonic.

Chammurabi [çamu·'rabi:]. *Pr.n.m.* -s. *Hist:* Hammurabi.

Chamois[1] [ʃamo·'a], *n.* -/-. 1. chamois-leather. 2. (*colour*) chamois.

chamois[2], *inv. a.* chamois (colour).

Chamoisleder, *n.* chamois-leather.

Champagner [ʃam'panjər], *m.* -s/-, (*wine*) (French) champagne.

Champignon [ʃampin'jõ:, 'ʃampinjon], *m.* -s/-s. *Fung:* agaric; (common *or* field) mushroom, *U.S:* meadow mushroom; *Cu:* mushroom; (*small*) button mushroom.

Champion ['tʃɛmpiən], *m.* -s/-s, champion.

Champlevé [ʃã·iə'veː], *n.* -s/. champlevé (enamel).

Chamsin [kam'si:n], *m.* -s/-s, khamsin.

Chan [ka:n], *m.* -s/-e=**Khan.**

Chance ['ʃã:sə], *f.* -/-n, chance; **es ist deine letzte C.,** it's your last chance; **keine C. haben,** not to stand a chance; **bei j-m Chancen haben,** to stand a chance (of success) with s.o.; **die Chancen sind gut,** the prospects are good; **seine Chancen ausnutzen,** to seize one's opportunities; **sich** *dat.* **eine C. entgehen lassen,** to miss a chance, an opportunity; **die C. vorübergehen lassen,** to miss one's chance, one's opportunity; **die Chancen sind gleich,** the chances are even.

Change ['ʃã:ʒə], *m. &f.* -/. exchange.

changeant[1] [ʃã·'ʒã:], *a. Tex:* (*of material*) shot; (*of tints*) shimmering.

Changeant[2], *m.* -s/-s, **Changeantstoff,** *m. Tex:* shot material.

changieren [ʃã·'ʒi:rən], *v.i.* (*haben*). 1. (*a*) to change; (*b*) to exchange. 2. to shimmer, to be iridescent. 3. *Equit:* (*of pers.*) to change hand, to change a horse; (*of horse*) to change the leg. 4. *Ven:* (*of hounds*) to take fresh scent.

Chanson [ʃã·'sõ:], *n.* -s/-s, (French) song; chanson.

Chansonette [ʃã·so·'netə], *f.* -/-n, (*a*) comic song; (*b*) (female) singer of chansons.

Chansonnier [ʃã·soni'e:], *m.* -s/-s, chansonnier (*who sings his own songs in cabaret*).

Chanukka ['xanuka:], *n.* -s/. *Jew:* Hanukkah.

Chaos ['ka:os], *n.* -/. chaos.

chaotisch [ka·'o:tiʃ], *a.* chaotic.

Chapeau [ʃa'po:], *m.* -s/-s. 1. hat, *Hum:* chapeau; **c. claque** [ʃapo·'klak], opera-hat, crush-hat. 2. *A:* dance-partner.

Chaperon [ʃap(ə)'rõ:], *m.* -s/-s. 1. (*pers.*) chaperon. 2. *Cost: A:* chaperon.

chaperonieren [ʃapəro·'ni:rən], *v.tr.* to chaperon (s.o.).

chaptalisieren [ʃapta·li·'zi:rən], *v.tr. Wine-m:* to chaptalize; **Chaptalisierung** *f,* chaptalization.

Charaban [ʃara·'bã:], *m.* -(e)s/-e. *Veh:* (horse-) charabanc.

Charakter [ka·'raktər], *m.* -s/-e [ka·rak'te:rə]. 1. *Print: etc:* character. 2. (*a*) character; nature; **einen guten, schlechten, weichen, starken, C. haben,** to have a good, bad, weak, strong, character; **seinen wahren C. zeigen,** to reveal one's true character, nature; **es liegt in seinem C.,** it is in his character; it is part of his character, nature; **die Charaktere sind verschieden,** people differ; (*b*) character; **den C. bilden,** to build, form, the character; **C. zeigen,** to show strength of character; **er hat C., er ist ein Mann von C.,** he has strength of character, he is a man of (strong) character; **er hat keinen C.,** he lacks strength of character; he has no backbone; (*c*) (*pers.*) character; **er ist ein schwieriger C.,** he is a difficult person; **er ist ein interessanter, merkwürdiger, übler, C.,** he is an interesting, an odd, a nasty, character. 3. (*a*) **eine Gegend (ganz) eigenen Charakters, mit einem (ganz) eigenen C.,** a region with a character of its own; **das Haus paßt nicht zum C. der Landschaft,** the house is not in keeping with the character of the landscape; (*b*) quality, nature; **die Besprechung trug vertraulichen C.,** the discussion was of a confidential nature; **das Interview nahm fast den C. eines Verhörs an,** the interview acquired, took on, almost the nature of a cross-examination; **der Raum hat intimen C.,** the room has an intimate quality, there is an intimate quality about the room. 4. **die Charaktere eines Theaterstücks,** the characters in a play; *Gr.Lit:* **die Charaktere des Theophrast,** the characters of Theophrastus. 5. capacity, status, *Mil:* honorary rank, brevet rank; **Dozent mit Titel und C. eines Professors,** lecturer with the title and capacity, status of a professor; *Mil:* **Major mit C. als Oberstleutnant,** honorary lieutenant-colonel; **Hauptmann mit C. eines Majors,** brevet major. 6. *Alg:* character (of group element).

Charakteranlage, *f.* disposition; **seine Charakteranlagen haben ihn zum Verbrecher bestimmt,** his natural tendencies destined him to be a criminal; **seine edleren Charakteranlagen haben ihn davor bewahrt,** the nobler side of his character saved him.

Charakterbild, *n.* 1. character-sketch; characterstudy. 2. character, disposition.

charakterbildend, *a.* character-building, -moulding.

Charakterbildung, *f.* (*a*) character-building, -moulding; (*b*) formation, development, of character.

Charakterdarsteller, *m. Th:* actor specializing in 'Charakterrollen' (*q.v*).

Charakterdrama, *n.*=**Charakterstück**.
charakterfest, *a.* (pers.) of firm character.
charakterisieren [ka·raktəri·'ziːrən]. I. *v.tr.*
 1. (*a*) to characterize, to be characteristic of (pers., style, etc.); (*b*) **j-n c.**, to characterize s.o., to portray, depict, delineate, s.o.'s character, to give a character-sketch of s.o. 2. *Mil:* to grant honorary rank to (s.o.); **Major charakterisiert (als) Oberstleutnant**, major with honorary rank as lieutenant-colonel.
 II. *vbl s.* **Charakterisieren** *n*, **Charakterisierung** *f. in vbl senses; also:* characterization; delineation, depiction, portrayal, of character.
Charakteristik [ka·rakte'ristik], *f.* -/-en.
 1. characterization; portrait; delineation, depiction, portrayal, of character. 2. *Mth:* characteristic (of logarithm, surface, etc.).
Charakteristikum [ka·rakta'risti·kum], *n.* -s/-ka.
 1. characteristic; **dieses ist ein C. unseres Staates, seines Stils**, this is a characteristic, a distinguishing feature, of our state, of his style. 2. *Mth:* characteristic; parameter.
charakteristisch [ka·raktə'ristiʃ], *a.* characteristic, typical; **charakteristische Merkmale**, characteristics, characteristic features, characteristic traits; **c. für etwas, j-n, sein**, to be characteristic, typical, of sth., s.o.; **in charakteristischer Weise**, in a characteristic manner, characteristically.
Charakterkomödie, *f. Lit:* comedy of character.
Charakterkopf, *m.* (*a*) distinctive head; head full of character, full of individuality; (*b*) person of strikingly individual aspect, of distinctive appearance.
Charakterkunde, *f.* the study of character; characterology.
charakterlich, *a.* of, concerning, (the) character, the personality; **charakterliche Ausbildung**, development, formation, moulding, of character; **c. zurückgeblieben**, retarded in the development of character, of personality.
charakterlos, *a.* (*a*) characterless; without, lacking (in), character; insipid, colourless; **charakterlose Landschaft**, characterless landscape; **charakterloses Bild**, characterless, insipid, picture; **charakterlose Farbe**, insipid colour, *F:* wishy-washy colour; *F:* **charakterloser Kaffee**, insipid, tasteless, coffee, *F:* wishy-washy coffee; (*b*) (pers.) lacking strength of character; **ein charakterloser Mensch**, a person without strength of character, who lacks strength of character; a spineless creature.
Charakterlosigkeit, *f.* (*a*) characterlessness, lack of character; colourlessness, insipidness; (*b*) lack of strength of character; spinelessness.
Charaktermaske, *f.* character mask.
Charakterologie [ka·raktəro·lo·'giː], *f.* -/. characterology.
Charakterrolle, *f. Th:* rôle with a strongly marked development of character.
Charakterschilderung, *f.* characterization (of person), delineation, depiction, portrayal, of (person's) character; character-study.
Charakterschulung, *f.* character-building, -moulding, -training.
charakterschwach, *a.* of weak character; **er ist c.**, he is weak, he lacks strength of character.
Charakterschwäche, *f.* weakness of character.
Charakterskizze, *f.* character-sketch.
Charakterstärke, *f.* strength of character.
Charakterstück, *n.* 1. *Lit:* play portraying (the development of) a central character *or* central characters. 2. *Mus:* character piece, mood picture.
Charakterstudie, *f.* character-study.
Charakterveränderung, *f.* change of character.
charaktervoll, *a.* (pers.) of strong (moral) character.
Charakterzeichnung, *f.*=**Charakterschilderung**.
Charakterzug, *m.* characteristic; distinguishing feature, trait, mark.
Charazeen [ça·ra·'tseːən], *f.pl. Bot:* stoneworts.
Charbin [çar'biːn]. *Pr.n.n.* -s. *Geog:* Harbin, Kharbin.
Charcuterie [ʃarky·tə'riː], *f.* -/-n [-'riːən]. *South G. Dial:* (*a*) (pork-)butchery, (pork-)butcher's trade; (*b*) (pork-)butcher's business, shop.
Charcutier [ʃarky·ti'eː], *m.* -s/-s. *South G. Dial:* (pork-)butcher.
Chardonnetseide [ʃardo·'neː-], *f. Tex:* Chardonnet rayon, nitrocellulose rayon
Charge ['ʃarʒə], *f.* -/-n. 1. *Mil: Adm:* rank; **eine C. bekleiden, innehaben**, to hold a (certain) rank; **j-m eine C. verleihen**, to confer a (certain) rank on s.o., to invest s.o. with a (certain) rank. 2. (*a*) *Mil:* officer; **Chargen und Mannschaften**, officers and other ranks; (*b*) *Sch:* representative

of a students' association. 3. *Mil: A:* (*a*) (cavalry) charge; (*b*) salvo. 4. *Metall:* charge (of a furnace). 5. *Th:* character part.
Chargenpferd, *n.* charger.
Chargenspieler, *m. Th:* character-actor.
chargieren [ʃar'ʒiːrən]. 1. *v.tr. A:* (*a*) to charge (s.o.) (with sth., with doing sth.); (*b*) to load and fire (gun). 2. *v.tr. A) Metall:* to charge (furnace); (*b*) *Tex:* to weight (silk); (*c*) *Th:* to overact, overdo, guy (a part). 3. *v.i.* (*haben*) *Sch:* to represent a students' association; (*of students' association*) to send representatives (to official functions).
Chargierte [ʃar'ʒiːrtə], *m.* (*decl. as adj.*) representative of a students' association.
Charier- [ʃa·'riːr-], *comb.fm. see* **Scharrier-**.
Charisma ['ça·risma:], *n.* -s/-rismen [ça·'rismən] & -rismata [ça·'risma·taː]. *Theol:* charism.
charismatisch [çaris'ma:tiʃ], *a.* charismatic.
charitativ [ka·ri·ta·'tiːf], *a.*=**caritativ**.
Charité, die [ʃari·'teː]. *Pr.n.* -. the Charité Hospital (in Berlin).
Chariten, die [ça·'riːtən], *f.pl. Gr.Myth:* the Charites, the (three) Graces.
Charitin [ça·'riːtin], *f.* -/-innen. *Gr.Myth:* Charis; **die Charitinnen**, the Charites, the (three) Graces.
Charivari [ʃa·ri·'va·riː], *n. & m.* -s/-s. tin-kettle music, mock serenade.
Charkow ['çarkof]. *Pr.n.n.* -s. *Geog:* Kharkov.
Charleston ['tʃarlstən], *m.* -/-s. *Danc:* charleston.
Charlotte [ʃar'lotə]. 1. *Pr.n.f.* -s & *Lit:* -ns. Charlotte. 2. *f.* -/-n. *Cu:* (*a*) apple charlotte; (*b*) trifle; **C. nach russischer Art, russische C.**, charlotte russe.
charmant [ʃar'mant], *a.* charming.
Charme ['ʃarm], *m.* -s/. charm.
Charmeur [ʃar'møːr], *m.* -s/-e, charmer.
Charmeuse [ʃar'møːzə], *f.* -/. *Tex:* charmeuse.
charmieren [ʃar'miːrən]. 1. *v.tr.* to charm (s.o.). 2. *v.i.* (*haben*) to lay on the, one's, charm.
Charon ['ça:ron]. *Pr.n.m. Gr.Myth:* Charon.
Chäronea [çε·ro·'neːa]. *Pr.n.n.* -s. *A.Geog:* Chaeronea.
Charonsnachen, der ['ça:rons-]. *Gr.Myth:* Charon's bark, boat, ferry.
Charta ['karta:, 'çarta:], *f.* -/-s. *Pol: Hist:* charter (of the Constitution); deed; **die C. der Vereinten Nationen**, the United Nations Charter; *Eng.Hist:* **die Magna C.**, Magna C(h)arta.
Charte ['ʃarta], *f.* -/-n. *Hist:* (*a*) document, record; (*b*) charter (of the Constitution).
Chartepartie [ʃartpar'tiː], *f. Nau: Com:* charter-party.
Charter ['(t)ʃartər], *m.* -s/-s, charter.
Charterer ['(t)ʃartərər], *m.* -s/-. *Nau: Com:* charterer.
chartern ['(t)ʃartərn], *v.tr. Com:* to charter (ship, etc.); *F:* to hire, to get hold of (sth.).
Chartervertrag, *m. Nau: Com:* charter-party.
Chartismus [ʃar'tismus], *m.* -/. *Eng.Hist:* chartism.
Chartist [ʃar'tist], *m.* -en/-en. *Eng.Hist:* Chartist.
Chartreuse [ʃar'trøːzə]. 1. *f.* -/. **die (Grande) C.**, the Grande Chartreuse. 2. *m.* -/. (*R.t.m.*) Chartreuse (liqueur). 3. *f.* -/-n. *Cu:* Chartreuse.
Chartum [kar'tum]. *Pr.n.n.* -s. *Geog:* Khartum.
Charybdis [ça·'rypdis, ka·'rypdis]. *Pr.n.f.* -'. *Gr.Myth:* Charybdis.
Chasan [xa'saːn], *m.* -s/-e. *Jew.Rel:* hazzan, cantor.
Chasma ['çasma:], *n.* -s/-men. *Med:* (attack of) spasmodic yawning.
Chasmodie [çasmo·'diː], *f.* -/-n [-'diːən], yawning.
Chasmogamie [çasmo·ga·'miː], *f.* -/-n [-'miːən]. *Bot:* chasmogamy.
Chassé [ʃa'seː], *n.* -/-s. *Danc:* chassé.
chassen ['ʃasən], *v.tr. F:* to give (s.o.) the sack; to expel (s.o.) (from school).
Chassepotgewehr [ʃas'po:-], *n. A:* chassepot rifle.
Chassidim [xasi·'diːm], *pl. Jew.Rel:* Hasidim.
Chassidismus [xasi·'dismus], *m.* -/. *Jew.Rel:* Hasidism.
chassieren [ʃa'siːrən], *v.i.* (*haben*) *Danc:* to chassé.
Chassis [ʃa'siː], *n.* -/- [-'siː(s)/-'siːs]. *Aut: etc:* frame, chassis.
Château [ʃa'toː], *n.* -/-s, château.
Chatelain [ʃat(ə)'lɛ̃], *m.* -s/-s. *A:* castellan.
Chatelaine [ʃat(ə)'lɛːnə], *f.* -/-s. 1. (pers.) chatelaine. 2. (*also n.* -s/-s) chatelaine (for keys, etc.).
Chatelet [ʃatə'leː], *m.* -s/-s, small castle.
Chatham-Kormoran ['tʃɛtəmkormo·raːn], *m. Orn:* Chatham cormorant.
Chaton [ʃa'tõː], *m.* -/-s, **Chatonfassung**, *f. Jewel:* box-mount.

Chatte ['çatə, 'katə]. *Pr.n.m.* -n/-n. *Hist:* one of the C(h)atti; **die Chatten**, the C(h)atti.
Chaudeau [ʃo·'doː], *m.* -s/-s. *Cu:* thick frothy mixture of wine, eggs and sugar (*used as dessert or sauce*).
Chauffeur [ʃo·'føːr], *m.* -s/-e, chauffeur.
chauffieren [ʃo·'fiːrən], *v.i.* (*haben*) to drive (a car); to act as chauffeur.
Chauken ['çaukən]. *Pr.n.m.pl. Hist:* Chauci (a Teutonic tribe).
Chaussee [ʃo·'seː], *f.* -/-n [-'seːən], high road, *U.S:* highway.
chaussieren [ʃo·'siːrən], *v.tr. A:* to macadamize (road); **chaussierter Weg**, macadamized road; **Chaussierung** *f*, macadamization, macadamizing.
Chauvinismus [ʃo·vi·'nismus], *m.* -/. chauvinism.
Chauvinist [ʃo·vi·'nist], *m.* -en/-en, chauvinist.
chauvinistisch [ʃo·vi·'nistiʃ], *a.* chauvinist(ic).
Check[1] [ʃɛk], *m.* -s/-s. *Swiss:* cheque, *U.S:* check.
Check[2] [tʃɛk], *m.* -s/-s. *Ice-Hockey:* check.
Cheddit [çɛ'diːt], *m.* -s/. *Exp:* cheddite.
Chef [ʃɛf], *m.* -s/-s, (*a*) head (of firm, department, etc.), *F:* boss, chief; *Adm:* director; *F:* head, principal (of school, etc.); (*b*) superior; (*c*) *Mil:* commander (of unit), head (of section, branch, etc.); **C. des Generalstabs**, chief of general staff; **Chef des Heeresjustizwesens**, Judge Advocate General; *Dipl.* **C. des Protokolls**, Chief of Protocol.
Chefarzt, *m.* medical superintendent (of hospital); head doctor; *Mil:* senior medical officer.
Chefeuse [ʃɛ'føːzə], *f.* -/-n. *Hum:*=**Chefin**.
Chefin ['ʃɛfin], *f.* -/-innen, (*a*) (woman) head (of firm, etc.); (woman) principal (of school, etc.): (*b*) *F:* boss's wife.
Chefpilot, *m. Av:* chief pilot.
Chefredakteur, *m.* (chief) editor (of newspaper, periodical, etc.).
Cheiloschisis [çailo·'sçiːzis], *f.* -/. *Med:* hare-lip.
Cheiro- ['çairo-], *comb.fm. see* **Chiro-**.
Chelifer ['çeːlifər], *m.* -s/-e(n) [çe·li·'feːrə(n)]. *Arach:* chelifer.
Chelléen, das [çɛle·'ɛ̃ː], -(s). *Prehist: A:* the Chellean culture.
Chelone [çe·'loːnə], *f.* -/-n. *Rept:* chelone.
Chemie [çe·'miː], *f.* -/. chemistry; **analytische C.**, analytical chemistry; **angewandte C.**, applied, practical, chemistry; **organische, anorganische, C.**, organic, inorganic, chemistry; **physikalische C.**, physical chemistry; **technische C.**, technical chemistry; **gerichtliche C.**, forensic chemistry.
Chemiefaser, *f. Tex:* chemical fibre; man-made fibre.
Chemigraphie [çe·mi·gra·'fiː], *f.* -/. *Engr:* chemigraphy.
Chemikalien [çe·mi·'ka:liən], *f.pl.* chemicals.
chemikalienbeständig, *a.* chemical-resistant.
Chemiker ['çe:mikər], *m.* -s/-, (analytical, professional) chemist; student of chemistry.
chemisch ['çe:miʃ], *a.* 1. chemical; **chemische Produkte**, chemicals; **chemische Fabrik**, chemical works; **chemische Industrie**, chemical industry; **chemisches Gleichgewicht**, chemical equilibrium; **chemischer Vorgang**, chemical process; **chemische Umsetzung**, chemical change; **chemischer Krieg**, chemical warfare; **chemische Reinigung**, dry cleaning; *adv.* **c. rein**, chemically pure. 2. **chemisch-**, *comb.fm.* chemico-; **chemisch-physisch**, chemico-physical; **chemisch-technisch**, techno-chemical; **chemisch-technischer Assistent**=**Chemotechniker**.
Chemischblau, *n. Dy:* chemic blue.
Chemischgelb, *n. Dy:* patent yellow, Cassel yellow.
Chemischgrün, *n. Dy:* sap green.
Chemischrot, *n. Dy:* Venetian red.
Chemise [ʃə'miːzə], *f.* -/-n. *Cost:* (*a*) shirt; (*b*) dressing-gown, *U.S:* robe.
Chemisett [ʃe·mi·'zɛt], *n.* -(e)s/-s & -e, **Chemisette** [ʃemi·'zɛtə], *f.* -/-n. *Cost:* (*a*) (man's) false shirt-front, *F:* dicky; (*b*) (woman's) chemisette, modesty-front, -vest.
Chemismus [çe·'mismus], *m.* -/. chemism.
Chemist [çe·'mist], *m.* -en/-en=**Chemiker**.
Chemitypie [çe·mi·ty·'piː], *f.* -/. *Engr:* chemitype.
Chemosorption [çe·mo·zorptsi'oːn], *f.* -/-en. *Ph.Ch:* chemisorption.
chemotaktisch [çe·mo·'taktiʃ], *a.* chemotactic.
Chemotaxe [çe·mo·'taksə], *f.* -/-n, **Chemotaxis** [çe·mo·'taksis], *f.* -/-xen, chemotaxis; chemotropism.
Chemotechniker [çe·mo·'tεçnikər], *m.* chemist (*with a technical college diploma*); technician (in chemical laboratory).
Chemotherapie [çe·mo·te·ra·'piː], *f.* -/. *Med:* chemotherapy.

Chemotropismus [çe·mo·tro·ˈpismus], *m.* **-/-men,** chemotropism.
-chen, *s.suff.* **-s/-** (*forming diminutives, often implying affection, & always rendering noun neuter*) **Bürschchen,** little fellow; **Blümchen,** little flower; **Entchen,** little duck, duckling; **Schweinchen,** little pig, piglet, pigling; **Blättchen,** little leaf, leaflet; *pl.* **Blättchen, Blätterchen,** little leaves, leaflets; **Lämmchen,** little lamb, lambkin; **Männchen,** little man, mannikin; **Kätzchen,** little cat, kitten; (*in nursery language*) -y, -ie; **Schweinchen,** piggy; **Pferdchen,** horsie.
Chenille [ʃəˈniljə, ʃəˈniːjə], *f.* **-/-n.** *Tex:* chenille.
Chersones [çɛrzo·ˈneːs]. *Pr.n.m.* -/-e [ˈneːzə]. *A.Geog:* **der Taurische, der Thrakische, C.,** the Tauric, Thracian, Chersonese.
Cherub [ˈçeːrup, ˈkeːrup], *m.* **-s/-im** & **-inen** [ˈçeː-, ˈkeːru·biːm & çe·-, ke·ru·ˈbiːnən], cherub.
Cherubikon [çe·ˈruːbi·kon], *n.* **-s/-ka.** *Ecc:* cherubikon, cherubic hymn.
cherubinisch [çe·ru·ˈbiːniʃ, ke·ru·ˈbiːniʃ], *a.* cherubic.
Cherubshymne, *f. Ecc:* cherubikon, cherubic hymn.
Cherusker [çe·ˈruskər], *m.* **-s/-.** *Hist:* Cheruscan; **Hermann der C.,** Arminius.
Chesterkäse [ˈtʃɛstər-], *m. Com:* (*a*) Cheshire cheese; (*b*) processed cheddar (cheese).
Chetiter [xe·ˈtiːtər], *m.* **-s/-.** *A.Hist:* = **Hethiter.**
chevaleresk [ʃəvaləˈrɛsk], *a.* chivalrous; gallant.
Chevalier [ʃəvaliˈeː], *m.* **-s/-s,** knight.
Cheviot [ˈçɛvïot, ˈtʃɛviot], *m.* **-s/-s.** *Tex:* Cheviot (cloth).
Chevreau [ˈʃɛvroː], *n.* **-s/-., Chevreauleder,** *n.* kid(-skin).
Chevron [ʃəˈvrõː], *m.* **-s/-s,** (*a*) *Her:* chevron; (*b*) *Mil:* chevron; long-service stripe; (*c*) *Tex:* cloth with herring-bone pattern.
Chi [çiː], *n.* **-(s)/-s.** *Gr.Alph:* chi.
Chianti [kiˈantiː], *m.* **-(s)/.** (*wine*) chianti.
Chiaroscuro [kïa·rosˈkuːroː], *n.* **-(s)/.** *Art:* chiaroscuro.
Chiasmus [çi·ˈasmus], *m.* **-/.** *Rh:* chiasmus.
chiastisch [çi·ˈastiʃ], *a.* chiastic.
Chiastolith [çi·asto·ˈliːt], *m.* **-(e)s/-e** & **-en/-en.** *Miner:* chiastolite, cross-stone, macle.
Chibouharz [ʃi·ˈbuː-], *n.* cachibou.
chic [ʃik], *a.* = **schick.**
Chiclegummi [ˈtʃik(ə)l-], *m.* chicle(-gum).
Chicorée [ˈʃiko·reː], *f.* **-/.** *Cu: Bot:* (broad-leaved) chicory.
Chid(h)er [ˈkiːdər]. *Pr.n.m.* **-s.** *Hist:* Khidr.
Chiffon [ʃiˈfõː, ʃiˈfoŋ, *Austrian:* ʃiˈfoːn], *m.* **-s/-s** & *Austrian:* -e [-ˈfoːnə]. *Tex:* chiffon.
Chiffonier [ʃifoniˈeː], *m.* **-s/-s.** *Furn:* chiffonier.
Chiffonnière [ʃifoniˈɛːrə, -ˈɛːrə], *f.* **-/-n. 1.** sewing-table; sewing-box. **2.** *Austrian: Swiss:* wardrobe.
Chiffre [ˈʃifrə, ˈʃifər], *f.* **-/-n. 1.** number. **2.** code; cipher; (*in advertisement*) box number.
Chiffreschrift, *f.* code; cipher.
Chiffreur [ʃiˈfrøːr], *m.* **-s/-e,** (i) coder, cipherer; (ii) decoder, decipherer.
chiffrieren [ʃiˈfriːrən], *v.tr.* to code (message, etc.), to write (message, etc.) in code; to encipher (message, etc.); **chiffrierter Brief,** letter in code.
Chiffrierkunst, *f.* (art of) coding, cipher(ing).
Chiffrieroffizier, *m.* cipher officer.
Chigger [ˈtʃigər], *m.* **-s/-.** *Ent:* chigoe, jigger.
Chignon [ʃinˈjõː], *m.* **-s/-s,** chignon; coil of hair; knot of hair; *F:* bun.
Chikago [ʃi·ˈkaːgoː]. *Pr.n.n.* **-s.** *Geog:* Chicago.
Chile [ˈtʃiːleː, ˈçiːleː]. *Pr.n.n.* **-s.** *Geog:* Chile.
Chileerdbeere, *f. Bot: Hort:* Chilean strawberry; pine-strawberry.
Chilene [tʃi·ˈleːnə, çi·ˈleːnə], *m.* **-n/-n, Chilenin,** *f.* **-/-innen,** Chilean, Chilian.
chilenisch [tʃi·ˈleːniʃ, çi·ˈleːniʃ], *a.* Chilean, Chilian.
Chile-Pelikan, *m. Orn:* Chilean pelican.
Chilesalpeter, *m.* Chile saltpetre; sodium nitrate.
Chili [ˈtʃi(ː)liː], *n.* **-s/. 1.** *Bot:* chil(li), chilly. **2.** *Cu:* chil(l)i sauce, chilly sauce.
Chiliade [çi·liˈaːdə], *f.* **-/-n,** chiliad.
Chiliasmus [çi·liˈasmus], *m.* **-/.** *Rel.Hist:* chiliasm, millenarianism.
Chiliast [çi·liˈast], *m.* **-en/-en.** *Rel.Hist:* chiliast, millenarian.
chiliastisch [çi·liˈastiʃ], *a.* millenarian.
Chilifichte [ˈçiːliː-], *f. Bot:* Chile pine, *F:* monkey puzzle.
Chilisalpeter, *n.* = **Chilesalpeter.**
Chil(l)y [ˈtʃiliː], *m.* **-s/-s** & **Chil(l)ies.** *Bot: Cu:* chil(l)i, chilly.
Chilopode [çi·lo·ˈpoːdə], *m.* **-n/-n.** *Ent:* chilopod; **die Chilopoden,** the chilopoda, chilopods.
Chimära [çi·ˈmɛːraː], *f.* **-/.** *Gr.Myth:* chimera.
Chimäre [çi·ˈmɛːrə], *f.* **-/-n. 1.** (*a*) *Gr.Myth:* chimera; (*b*) chimera, bogy. **2.** *Bot:* chimera. **3.** *Ich:* chimaera.
chimärisch [çi·ˈmɛːriʃ], *a.* chimerical, imaginary.
China [ˈçiːnaː]. *Pr.n.n.* **-s.** *Geog:* China.
Chinaalkaloide, *f. Ch: Bot:* cinchona alkaloid.
Chinaapfel, *m.* orange.
Chinaaster, *f. Bot:* China aster.
Chinabase, *f. Ch: Bot:* cinchona alkaloid.
Chinabaum, *m.* = **Chinarindenbaum.**
Chinafahrer, *m. Nau:* ship engaged in the China trade, *F:* Chinaman.
Chinagerbsäure, *f. Ch:* quinotannic acid.
Chinagras, *n. Bot:* China-grass, ramee, ramie, grass-cloth plant.
Chinakrepp, *m. Tex:* crêpe de Chine.
Chinaldin [çi·nalˈdiːn], *n.* **-(e)s/.** *Ch:* quinaldine.
Chinaldingelb, *n. Dy:* = **Chinolingelb.**
Chinarinde, *f. Pharm:* cinchona (bark), quinquina (bark), Peruvian bark.
Chinarindenbaum, *m. Bot:* quinquina, cinchona.
Chinarot, *n. Dy:* cinchona red.
Chinasalz, *n. Ch: A:* calcium nitrate, wall-saltpetre.
Chinasäure, *f. Ch:* quinic acid.
Chinasee, die. *Pr.n. Geog:* the China Sea.
Chinasilber, *n.* German silver, nickel silver.
Chinastechwinde, *f. Bot:* smilax china, China-root.
Chinatinktur, *f.* tincture of cinchona.
Chinawein, *m.* quinine wine.
Chinawurzel, *f. Bot: Pharm:* China-root.
Chinchilla [tʃinˈtʃiljaː, tʃinˈtʃilaː], *f.* **-/-s,** & *n.* **-s/-s.** *Z: Tex:* chinchilla.
Chiné [ʃi·ˈneː], *m.* **-(s)/.** *Tex:* shadow(ed) cretonne, chiné.
Chinese [çi·ˈneːzə], *m.* **-n/-n.** Chinese, Chinaman.
Chinesernelke, *f. Bot:* China pink, Indian pink.
Chinesin [çi·ˈneːzin], *f.* **-/-innen.** Chinese (woman *or* girl).
chinesisch [çi·ˈneːziʃ]. **1.** *a.* Chinese; **die Chinesische Mauer,** the Great Wall of China; **das Chinesische Meer,** the China Sea; **chinesisches Papier,** Chinese India, Bible, paper; **chinesische Tusche,** Indian ink, Chinese ink; **chinesisches Gras, chinesischer Hanf,** China-grass, ramee, ramie, grass-cloth plant; **chinesischer Talg,** vegetable tallow; **chinesisches Feuer,** Bengal lights; **chinesisches Wachs,** Chinese wax; **chinesisch-japanisch,** Chino-Japanese, Sino-Japanese; *see also* **bohren** II. 1 (*a*). **2.** *s.* **Chinesisch,** *n. Ling:* Chinese.
Chinesischweiß, *n. Com:* Chinese white, zinc white.
Chinidin [çi·ni·ˈdiːn], *n.* **-s/.** *Ch:* quinidine.
chinieren [çi·ˈniːrən], *v.tr. Tex:* to cloud, shadow, mottle (fabric); **chiniert,** clouded, shadowed (fabric); watered, moiré (silk); **Chinierung** *f,* clouding, mottling (of fabric).
Chinin [çi·ˈniːn], *n.* **-s/.** *Ch:* quinine.
Chininrausch, *m. Med:* cinchonism, quininism.
Chininsäure, *f. Ch:* quininic acid.
Chininsulfat, *n. Pharm:* (sulphate of) quinine.
Chininvergiftung, *f. Med:* cinchonism, quinism.
Chininwein, *m.* quinine wine.
Chinoiserie [çino·azə·ˈriː], *f.* **-/-n** [-ˈriːən], chinoiserie; (i) decoration, (ii) curio, in Chinese style.
Chinol [çi·ˈnoːl], *n.* **-s/.** *Ch:* quinol, hydroquinone.
Chinolin [çi·no·ˈliːn], *n.* **-s/.** *Ch:* quinoline.
Chinolinblau, *n. Ch: Dy:* quinoline blue; cyanine.
Chinolingelb, *n. Dy:* quinoline yellow.
Chinolinsäure, *f. Ch:* quinolinic acid.
Chinon [çi·ˈnoːn], *n.* **-s/-e.** *Ch:* quinone.
Chintz [tʃints], *m.* **-es/-e.** *Tex:* chintz.
Chios [ˈçiːos]. *Pr.n.n.* **-'.** *Geog:* (the Island of) Scio, Chios.
Chippendale [ˈtʃipəndeːl], *n.* **-(s)/.** Chippendale (furniture).
Chiragra [çi·ˈraːgraː], *n.* **-s/.** *Med:* gout in the hand, chiragra.
chiro-, Chiro- [çi·ro·ˈ-]. *comb.fm.* chiro-, cheiro-; **Chirognomie** *f,* chirognomy; **chirographisch,** chirographal; **Chiromantie** *f,* chiromancy.
Chirograph [çi·ro·ˈgraːf], *m.* **-en/-en,** chirograph.
chirographarisch [çi·ro·gra·ˈfaːriʃ], *a. Jur: A:* chirographary.
Chirologie [çi·ro·lo·ˈgiː], *f.* **-/.** = **Chiromantie.**
Chiromant [çi·ro·ˈmant], *m.* **-en/-en,** palmist.
Chiromantie [çi·ro·manˈtiː], *f.* **-/.** chiromancy, palmistry.
Chiromantin [çi·ro·ˈmantin], *f.* **-/-innen,** (lady) palmist.
Chiropraktik [çi·ro·ˈpraktik], *f.* chiropractic.
Chiroptera [çi·ˈroptəraː], *f.pl.,* **Chiropteren** [çi·ropˈteːrən], *n.pl. Z:* chiroptera, bats.
Chirospasmus [çi·ro·ˈspasmus], *m.* **-/-men.** *Med:* chirospasm, writer's cramp.
Chirurg [çi·ˈrurk], *m.* **-en/-en** [-ˈrurgən]. **1.** surgeon. **2.** *Ich:* surgeon-fish.
Chirurgie [çi·rurˈgiː], *f.* **-/.** surgery.
chirurgisch [çi·ˈrurgiʃ], *a.* surgical.
Chitin [çi·ˈtiːn], *n.* **-s/.** *Ch: Z:* chitin.
chitinig [çi·ˈtiːniç], *a. Ch: Z:* chitinous.
Chiton [çi·ˈtoːn], *m.* **-s/-e.** *Gr.Ant:* chiton.
Chlamys [[çla·ˈmyːs], *f.* **-/-.** *Gr.Ant:* chlamys.
Chlodwig [ˈkloːtviç]. *Pr.n.m.* **-s.** *Hist:* Clovis, C(h)lodowig.
Chloe [ˈkloːeː]. *Pr.n.f.* **-s.** Chloe.
Chlor [kloːr], *n.* **-s/.** *Ch:* chlorine.
Chloral [klo·ˈraːl], *n.* **-s/.** *Ch:* chloral.
Chloralhydrat, *n. Pharm:* chloral (hydrate).
Chloral(hydrat)vergiftung, *f.,* **Chloralismus** [klo·ra·ˈlismus], *m.* **-/.** *Med:* chloralism.
Chlorammonium, *n. Ch:* ammonium chloride, sal ammoniac.
Chlorat [klo·ˈraːt], *n.* **-s/-e.** *Ch:* chlorate.
Chlorbleispat, *m. Miner:* phosgenite.
Chlorbrompapier, *n. Phot:* chlorobromide paper.
Chlorbromsilber, *n. Ch: Phot:* silver chlorobromide.
Chlorbromsilberpapier, *n. Phot:* (silver) chlorobromide paper.
chloren [ˈkloːrən]. I. *v.tr.* **1.** *Hyg:* to chlorinate (water). **2.** *Ind:* to chlore, chlorinate (wool, etc.).
II. *vbl s.* **Chloren** *n.,* **Chlorung** *f.* chlorination, chlorinating; chloring.
Chloressigsäure, *f. Ch:* chloroacetic acid.
Chlorhydrin [klo·rhy·ˈdriːn], *n.* **-s/-e.** *Ch:* chlorohydrin.
Chlorid [klo·ˈriːt], *n.* **-(e)s/-e** [-s, -ˈriːdəs/-ˈriːdə]. *Ch:* chloride.
chlorieren [klo·ˈriːrən]. I. *v.tr. Ch:* to chlorinate, chlorinize.
II. *vbl s.* **Chlorieren** *n.,* **Chlorierung** *f.* chlorination, chlorinating.
chlorig [ˈkloːriç], *a. Ch:* chlorous.
chlorigsauer, *a. Ch:* combined with chlorous acid; chlorite of . . .; **chlorigsaures Salz,** chlorite.
Chlorigsäure, *f. Ch:* chlorous acid.
Chlorit[1] [klo·ˈriːt], *m.* **-(e)s/-e.** *Miner:* chlorite.
Chlorit[2], *n.* **-(e)s/-e.** *Ch:* chlorite.
Chlorkali, Chlorkalium, *n. Ch:* potassium chloride.
Chlorkalk, *m.* (*a*) *Ch:* = **Chlorkalzium;** (*b*) *Com: etc:* bleaching-powder.
Chlorkalksalbe, *f. Pharm:* bleach ointment.
Chlorkalzium, *n. Ch:* calcium chloride, chloride of lime.
Chlorkohlenoxyd, *n. Ch:* carbonyl chloride; phosgene.
Chlornatrium, *n. Ch:* sodium chloride.
Chloroform [klo·ro·ˈform], *n.* **-s/.** *Med:* chloroform; **j-n mit C. betäuben,** to chloroform s.o., to give chloroform to s.o., to put s.o. under chloroform.
chloroformieren [klo·ro·forˈmiːren], *v.tr.* to chloroform (s.o.), to give chloroform to (s.o.), to put (s.o.) under chloroform.
Chlorohydrat, *n. Ch:* chlorhydrate, hydrochloride.
Chlorophyll [klo·ro·ˈfyl], *n.* **-s/.** *Ch: Bot:* chlorophyll, *F:* leaf-green.
Chloroplatinat [klo·r·o·pla·ti·ˈnaːt], *n.* **-s/-e.** *Ch:* chloroplatinate.
Chlorose [klo·ˈroːzə], *f.* **-/-n. 1.** *Med:* chlorosis, *F:* green-sickness. **2.** *Bot:* chlorosis.
Chlorpikrin [ˈkloːrpi·kriːn], *n.* **-s/.** *Ch:* chloropicrine.
chlorsauer, *a. Ch:* combined with chloric acid; chlorate of . . .; **chlorsaures Salz,** chlorate.
Chlorsäure, *f. Ch:* chloric acid.
Chlorsäureanhydrid, *n. Ch:* chloric anhydride.
Chlorsilber, *n. Miner:* horn-silver, cerargyrite.
Chlorür [klo·ˈryːr], *n.* **-s/-e.** *Ch:* chloride.
Chlorwasser, *n. Ch:* chlorine water.
Chlorwasserstoff, *m. Ch:* hydrogen chloride, hydrochloric acid.
Chlotachar, Chlothar [ˈkloːta·xaːr, ˈkloːtaːr]. *Pr.n.m.* **-s.** *Hist:* Chlothar, Clotaire, Lothair.
Choc [ʃok], *m.* **-s/-s** = **Schock**[2].
Chok [ʃok], *m.* **-s/-s,** shock, percussion, impact (of two bodies).
chokant [ʃoˈkant], *a.* shocking.
chokieren [ʃoˈkiːren], *v.tr.* **1.** to strike, knock (sth.), to bump against (sth.). **2.** = **schockieren.**
Cholagogum [ço·la·ˈgoːgum], *n.* **-s/-ga.** *Med:* cholagogue.
Chol(al)säure [ˈçoːl-, ço·ˈlaːl-], *f. Ch:* cholic acid.
Cholämie [ço·lɛ·ˈmiː], *f.* **-/-n** [-ˈmiːən]. *Med:* chol(a)emia.
Cholansäure [ço·ˈlaːn-], *f. Ch:* cholanic acid.
Choledochotomie [ço·le·doxo·to·ˈmiː], *f.* **-/.** *Surg:* choledochotomy.

choledochus [ço·le·'doxus], *a. Anat:* **(ductus) c., choledoch** (duct).

Cholein [ço·le·'i:n], *n. -s/. Ch:* cholein.

Choleinsäure, *f. Ch:* choleic acid.

Cholera ['ko:ləra:, 'koləra:], *f. -/. Med: Vet:* cholera; *Med:* **asiatische C.,** Asiatic, malignant, epidemic, cholera.

Choleraanfall, *m.* fit, attack, of cholera.

Choleradistel, *f. Bot:* xanthium spinosum, thorny clotbur.

Choleratropfen, *m.pl. Pharm:* cholera-drops.

Choleriker [ko·'le:rikər], *m. -s/-,* choleric person; *F:* irascible person.

Cholerine [ko·lə·'ri:nə], *f. -/. Med:* cholerine, summer cholera, bilious cholera.

cholerisch [ko·'le:rif], *a.* choleric (humour); *F:* irascible.

Cholesterin [ço·lɛstə·'ri:n], *n. -s/. Ch:* cholesterol.

Cholezystitis [ço·le·tsys'ti:tis], *f. -/. Med:* cholecystitis.

Cholezystostomie [ço·le·tsystosto·'mi:], *f. -/. Med:* cholecystostomy.

Cholezystotomie [ço·le·tsystoto·'mi:], *f. -/. Med:* cholecystotomy.

choliambisch [ço·li·'ambif], *a. Pros:* choliambic.

Choliambus [ço·li·'ambus], *m. -/-ben. Pros:* choliamb.

Cholin [ço·'li:n], *n. -s/. Ch:* cholein.

chondral [çon-, xon-, kon'dra:l], *a. Anat:* chondroid.

Chondren ['çon-, 'xon-, 'kondrən], *m.pl. Miner:* chondrules, chondri.

Chondrin [çon-, xon-, kon'dri:n], *n. -s/. Ch:* chondrin.

Chondrit [çon-, xon-, kon'dri:t], *m. -(e)s/-e. Miner:* chondrite.

Chondrom [çon-, xon-, kon'dro:m], *n. -s/-e. Med:* chondroma.

Chopper ['tfopər], *m. -s/-s. Ph:* chopper.

Chor [ko:r], *m. & n. -s/-e & =e.* **1.** *m.* (*a*) *Gr.Ant:* chorus (in drama); (*b*) choir, chorus (of singers); **Stück für C. und Orchester,** composition for choir and orchestra; **C. der Engel, der Vögel,** choir of angels, of birds; **gemischter C.,** mixed choir; **im C. singen,** (i) to sing in chorus, to chorus; (ii) to sing in, to be a member of, the choir; **sie riefen im C.,** they all shouted together, in chorus; **alle im C.!** all together (now)! *B:* **Lied im höhern C.,** song of degrees; (*c*) (*piece of music*) chorus; (*d*) section (of orchestra); **C. der Blasinstrumente,** wind section; (*e*) group of piano strings (tuned in unison). **2.** (*occ.n.*) (*a*) host; crowd; group; **die neun Chöre der Engel,** the nine choirs of angels; **C. der Musen,** the nine Muses; **sie fielen wie ein C. der Rache über ihn her,** they attacked him like a host of avenging spirits; (*b*) *Pej:* crew, lot, tribe; (*esp. of children*) **ein gräßliches C.,** a dreadful crowd, a ghastly tribe, lot. **3.** *m. & n. Ecc.Arch:* (*a*) choir; chancel; (*b*) (organ) gallery, loft. **4.** *Tex:* division, group, of threads (in harness).

Chorabschluß, *m. Ecc.Arch:* termination of the choir.

Chorage [ko·'ragə, ço·'ra:gə], *m. -n/-n. Gr.Ant:* choragus, leader of the chorus.

choragisch [ko·'ra:gif, ço·'ra:gif], *a.* choragic.

Choral [ko·'ra:l], *m. -s/=e. Mus:* (*a*) choral(e); (*b*) (Gregorian) chant; plainsong; (*c*) hymn.

Choralbuch, *n.* choir-book.

Choralnotation, *f. A.Mus:* neum(e)s.

Choralnoten, *f.pl. A.Mus:* neum(e)s.

Choralsingen, *n. Mus:* (*a*) (practice of) singing Gregorian chant; (*b*) singing of choral(e)s *or* hymns.

Choranlage, *f. Ecc.Arch:* choir.

chorartig, *a. Arch:* in the form of a choir.

Chorbischof, *m. Ecc.Hist:* chorepiscopus.

Chorbrett, *n. Tex:* comber board, harness board.

Chorbuch, *n. A.Mus:* part-book.

Chorbühne, *f. Ecc.Arch:* choir loft.

Chörchen ['kœrçən], *n. -s/-. Ecc.Arch:*=**Chörlein.**

Chorda ['çorda:, 'korda:], *f. -/-den. Anat:* (*a*) cord; (*b*) spinal cord.

Chordaten [kor'da:tən], *pl. Nat.Hist:* chordata.

Chordatiere, *n.pl. Nat.Hist:* chordata.

Chorde ['çordə, 'kordə], *f. -/-n* = **Chorda.**

Chordirektor, *m.* = **Chorleiter.**

Chordonier [çor'do:niər], *m.pl.* = **Chordatiere.**

Chordotonalorgan [cordo·to·'na:lɔr,gа:n], *n. Ent:* chordotonal organ.

Chorea [ço·'re:a:], *f. -/. Med:* chorea, *F:* Saint Vitus's dance.

choreatisch [ço·re·'a:tif], *a. Med:* choreic.

Chorege [ko·'re:gə, ço·'re:gə], *m. -n/-n. Gr.Ant:* choragus, leader of the chorus.

choregisch [ko·'re:gif, ço·'re:gif], *a.* choragic.

Choreograph [ko·re·o·'gra:f], *m. -en/-en,* choreographer.

Choreographie [ko·re·o·gra·'fi:], *f. -/-n* [-'fi:ən], choreography.

choreographisch [ko·re·o·'gra:fif], *a.* choreographic.

Choreus [ço·'re:us, ko·'re:us], *m. -/-reen. Pros:* choree, trochee.

Choreut [ko·'royt], *m. -en/-en. Gr.Ant:* choral dancer, choreutes.

Choreutik [ko·'roytik], *f. -/. Gr.Ant:* (art of) choral dancing.

choreutisch [ko·'roytif], *a.* choreutic.

Chorfenster, *n. Ecc.Arch:* choir-window.

Chorfrau, *f. Ecc:* **(regulierte) C.,** (regular) canoness.

Chorführer, *m.* **1.** *Gr.Ant:* choragus, leader of the chorus. **2.** choirmaster.

Chorgebet, *n. Ecc:* Divine Office (recited in choir).

Chorgesang, *m.* **1.** (*a*) *Gr.Ant:* choral singing, choral song; (*b*) choral singing, singing in chorus. **2.** (*a*) *Gr.Ant:* = **Chorlied** 1; (*b*) choral song, chorus.

Chorgestühl, *n.* choir-stalls.

Chorhaupt, *n. Ecc.Arch:* chevet.

Chorhemd, *n. Ecc.Cost:* surplice.

Chorherr, *m. Ecc:* **(regulierter) C.,** (regular) canon.

Choriambus [ço·ri·'ambus, ko·ri·'ambus], *m. -/-ben. Pros:* choriamb(us).

-chörig [-'kø:riç], *comb.fm.* **1.** *Arch:* having ... choirs; **doppelchörig,** having two choirs. **2.** *Mus:* -chord; **dreichöriges Klavier,** trichord piano.

Chorioidea [ço·ri·o·ʔi·'de:a:], **Chorioides** [ço·ri·o·'i:dɛs], *f. -/. Anat:* choroid (coat) (of the eye).

Chorion ['ço:rion], *n. -s/. Biol: Obst:* chor on.

choripetal [ço·ri·pe·'ta:l], *a. Bot:* choripetalous; **die Choripetalen,** the choripetalous plants, the choripetalae.

chorisch ['ko:rif], *a. Mus: Th:* choral.

Chorist [ko·'rist], *m. -en/-en,* member of a choir.

Chorkantate, *f. Mus:* choral cantata.

Chorkapelle, *f. Ecc.Arch:* chevet chapel.

Chorknabe, *m.* chorister, choirboy.

Chörlein ['kø:rlain], *n. -s/-. Arch:* oriel(-window).

Chorleiter, *m.* choir-master.

Chorlied, *n.* **1.** *Gr.Ant:* choral ode, chorus. **2.** choral song, chorus.

Chorlyrik, *f. Gr.Lit:* choral lyric (poetry).

Chormantel, *m. Ecc.Cost:* cope.

Chormusik, *f.* choral music.

Chornische, *f. Ecc.Arch:* apse.

Chorographie [ço·ro·gra·'fi:], *f. -/-n* [-'fi:ən], chorography.

Chorologie [ço·ro·lo·'gi:], *f. -/. Biol:* chorology.

Chororgel, *f. Mus:* small church-organ.

Chorregent, *m.* = **Chorleiter.**

Chorrock, *m.* = **Chorhemd.**

Chorsänger, *m.* member of a choir; *Ecc:* chorister.

Chorschranken, *f.pl. Ecc:* choir-screen, chancel-screen.

Chorschwester, *f. R.C.Ch:* choir-sister.

Chorstuhl, *m.* choir-stall.

Chorton, *m. Mus:* choir-pitch.

Chorturm, *m. Ecc.Arch:* tower over the choir of a church.

Chorumgang, *m.* ambulatory (of the choir).

Chose ['ʃo:zə], *f. -/-n. F:* matter, business.

Chrestomathie [kresto·-, çresto·ma·'ti:], *f. -/-en* [-'ti:ən], chrestomathy.

Chrisam ['çri:-, 'kri:zam], *m. -s/.,* **Chrisma** ['çrisma:], *n. -s/. Ecc:* chrism, holy oil.

Chrismale [kris-, çris'ma:lə], *n. -/-n,* chrisom-cloth, -robe, chrismal.

Chrismarium [kris-, çris'ma:rïum], **Chrismatorium** [kris-, çrisma·'to:rïum], *n. -s/-ria,* chrismal.

Chrismon ['kri:smon], *n. -s/-men. Pal:* chrismon.

Christ [krist]. **1.** *Pr.n.m. -s. Christ:* **der Heilige C.,** (i) Jesus, Christ; the Christ-child; (ii) Christmas(-time); *F:* **ein heiliger C.,** a Christmas present. **2.** *m. -en/-en. Christian:* **ein katholischer C.,** a Catholic; **ein evangelischer C.,** a Protestant; **ein koptischer C.,** a Copt; **die alten Christen,** the Early Christians; **C. werden,** to become (a) Christian; **als guter C. sterben,** to die a good Christian; *F:* **ein toller, wunderlicher, C.,** an extraordinary person, an eccentric character.

Christ- *cp.* **Weihnachts-.**

Christabend, *m.* Christmas Eve.

Christbaum, *m.* Christmas-tree.

Christbaumschmuck, *m.* Christmas-tree decoration(s).

Christbeere, *f. Bot:* gooseberry(-bush).

Christblume, *f. Bot:* = **Christrose.**

Christdorn, *m. Bot:* **1.** (*a*) Christ's thorn (jujube);

(*b*) Christ's thorn, paliurus. **2.** holly. **3.** (*a*) hawthorn, whitethorn, may(-bush, -tree); (*b*) sweet briar, eglantine. **4.** gooseberry(-bush).

Christdornbrustbeere, *f.* = **Christdorn** 1 (*a*).

Christenfeind, *m.* enemy of Christianity.

christenfeindlich, *a.* antichristian.

Christengemeinde, *f.* Christian community.

Christenglaube, *m.* Christian belief, Christian faith.

Christenheit, die. Christendom.

Christenlehre, *f.* catechism class; *approx.* = Sunday school.

Christenpflicht, *f.* Christian duty, duty as a Christian.

Christenseele, *f.* Christian.

Christentum, *n. -s/.* Christianity; **das C. annehmen,** (i) to adopt the Christian faith, to turn Christian; (ii) (*of nation*) to be christianized; **das C. verkünden, verbreiten,** to preach, spread, Christianity, to evangelize; **sich zum C. bekennen,** to profess the Christian faith; **j-n zum C. bekehren,** to convert s.o. to Christianity; **es ist nicht sehr weit her mit seinem C.,** he's not much of a Christian; **im Geist des Christentums handeln,** to behave, act, in a Christian manner, in a Christian spirit.

Christenverfolger, *m.* persecutor of the Christians.

Christenverfolgung, *f.* persecution of the Christians.

Christfest, *n.* Christmas.

Christgang, *m.* carol-singing.

Christiania [kristi·'a:nïa:], *m. -s/-s. Ski:* = **Kristiania** 2.

christianisieren [kristïa·ni·'zi:rən], *v.tr.* to convert (a nation, etc.) to Christianity, to christianize (a nation, etc.); **Christianisierung** *f,* conversion to Christianity, christianization.

Christianswurz ['kristïa:ns-], *f. Bot:* = **Christrose.**

Christin ['kristin], *f. -/-innen.* Christian (woman).

Christina, Christine [kris'ti:na:, -nə]. *Pr.n.f. -s & Lit:* -nens. Christina, Christine.

Christinenkraut, *n. Bot:* lesser fleabane.

christkatholisch, *a.* **1.** strictly Catholic; **ein christkatholisches Leben,** a good Christian life. **2.** *Ecc:* (Swiss) Old Catholic; **die Christkatholische Kirche,** the (Swiss) Old Catholic Church.

Christkind, das. *Pr.n.* the Christ-child; the infant Jesus.

Christkindchen, *n.* (*a*) **das C.,** the Christ-child; the infant Jesus; (*b*) *F:* Christmas present.

Christkönigsfest, das. *R.C.Ch:* the Feast of Christ the King.

christlich, *a.* Christian; Christlike; christianlike; **christliche Nächstenliebe,** Christian charity, love for one's neighbour; **christliche Lehre, christlicher Glaube,** Christian doctrine, faith; **Christliche Wissenschaft,** Christian Science; **Christlicher Verein Junger Männer,** Young Men's Christian Association; **christliche Geduld,** Christlike patience; **christliches Benehmen,** Christian, christianlike, behaviour; *adv.* **c. leben,** to live a Christian life; **c. handeln,** to act in a Christian manner.

christlich-demokratisch, *a.* Christian Democrat (party, etc.).

Christmesse, *f.* = **Christmette.**

Christmette, *f. Ecc:* Christmas matins, Christmas mass, *esp.* midnight mass.

Christmonat, Christmond, *m. A. & Poet:* December.

Christnacht, *f.* night of Christmas Eve, night before Christmas (Day).

Christoflemetall [kri'stofəlme·,tal], *n.* German silver, nickel silver.

Christogramm [kristo·'gram], *n. -s/-e,* monogram of Christ.

Christologie [kristo·lo·'gi:], *f. -/-n* [-'gi:ən], Christology.

christologisch [kristo·'lo:gif], *a.* Christological.

Christoph ['kristof]. *Pr.n.m. -s.* Christopher.

Christophorus [kri'stofo·rus]. *Pr.n.m. -'.* Christophorus, Christopher.

Christophskraut, *n. Bot:* baneberry, herb Christopher.

Christpalme, *f. Bot:* Palma Christi, ricinus, castor-oil plant.

Christrose, *f. Bot:* Christmas rose, black hellebore.

Christstolle, *f.,* **Christstollen,** *m. Cu:* yule loaf.

Christtag, *m.* Christmas Day.

Christus ['kristus]. *Pr.n.m. inv. or gen.* Christi, *dat. occ.* Christo, *acc. occ.* Christum, *voc. occ.* Christe. Christ; Jesus C., Jesus Christ; **die Geburt Christi,** the birth of Christ, *esp. Art:* the Nativity; **nach C., nach Christi Geburt,** (*abbr.* **n.Chr.**), after Christ, (*abbr.* A.D.); **vor**

C., vor Christi Geburt, (*abbr.* v.Chr.), before Christ, (*abbr.* B.C.); 300 v.Chr., in 300 B.C.; 300 n.Chr., in A.D. 300; *see also* **Himmelfahrt.**
Christusakazie, *f. Bot:* honey locust.
Christusauge, *n. Bot:* 1. Christ's eye. 2. rose campion. 3. yellow garden hawkweed.
Christusbild, *n.* image of Christ.
Christusdorn, *m. Bot:*=**Christdorn.**
Christusfisch, *m. Ich:* (John) Dory.
Christuskind, das=**Christkind.**
Christuskopf, *m.* (*a*) *Art: etc:* head of Christ; (*b*) **er hat einen C.,** his head resembles that of Christ; he looks like someone out of the Bible.
Christusmonogramm, *n.* monogram of Christ.
Christusorden, der. *Rel.Hist:* the Supreme Order of Christ.
Christusträne, *f. Bot:* Job's tears.
Christvogel, *m. Orn:* F: crossbill.
Christwurz(el), *f. Bot:* 1. baneberry, herb Christopher. 2. spring adonis. 3. winter aconite. 4. Christmas rose.
Chrom [kro:m], *n. -s/.* 1. *Ch:* chromium. 2. *Com:* chrome.
Chromalaun, *m.* chrome alum.
Chromasie [kro·ma·'zi:], *f. -/.* chromatism.
Chromat [kro·'ma:t], *n. -s/-e. Ch:* chromate.
Chromatdruck, *m.* chromatic print(ing).
Chromatide [kro·ma·'ti:də], *f. -/-n. Biol:* chromatid.
Chromatik [kro·'ma:tik], *f. -/. Mus: Opt:* chromatics.
Chromatin [kro·ma·'ti:n], *n. -s/-e. Biol:* chromatin.
chromatisch [kro·'ma:tiʃ], *a. Mus:* chromatic (scale); *Opt:* **chromatische Abweichung, Aberration,** chromatic aberration; *Ling:* **chromatischer Akzent,** chromatic accent.
Chromatismus [kro·ma·'tismus], *m. -/-men. Psy:* chromatism, photism.
Chromatographie [kro·ma·to·gra·'fi:], *f. -/. Ch:* process of chromatographic adsorption, chromatography.
chromatographisch [kro·ma·to·'gra:fiʃ], *a. Ch:* chromatographic (adsorption).
Chromatometer [kro·ma·to·'me:tər], *n. -s/-,* chromatometer.
Chromatophor [kro·ma·to·'fo:r], *n. -s/-en. Biol:* chromatophore.
Chromatoskop [kro·ma·to·'sko:p], *n. -s/-e. Opt:* chromatoscope.
Chromatropie [kro·ma·tro·'pi:], *f. -/-n* [-'pi:ən]. *Ch:* chromotropism.
Chrombeize, *f. Dy:* chromium mordant.
Chromchlorid, *n. Ch:* chromic chloride.
Chromeisen, *n. Metall:* chrome iron, ferrochrome.
Chromeisenerz, *n.,* **Chromeisenstein,** *m. Miner:* chromite.
chromen ['kro:mən], *v.tr. Dy:* to chrome.
Chromfarbe, *f.* chromium dye; chrome colour.
chromgegerbt, *a.* chrome-tanned (leather).
Chromgelatine, *f. Phot:* gum bichromate.
Chromgelatinepapier, *n. Phot:* gelatine paper.
Chromgelb, *n.* chrome-yellow.
Chromgerbung, *f. Leath:* chrome-tanning.
chromi-, Chromi- [kro·mi·-], *comb.fm. Ch:* chromic...; **Chromichlorid** *n,* chromic chloride.
Chromichromat [kro·mi·kro·'ma:t], *n. Ch:* chromic chromate.
chromieren [kro·'mi:rən], *v.tr. Dy:* to chrome.
Chromierfarbstoff [kro·'mi:r-], *m.* chrome dye.
Chromioxyd [kro·mi·'ꝺ'ksy:t], *n. Ch:* chromic oxide.
Chromit¹ [kro·'mi:t], *m. -(e)s/-e. Miner:* chromite, chrome iron ore.
Chromit² [kro·'mi:t], *n. -(e)s/-e. Ch:* chromite.
Chromkali, *n. Ch:* potassium bichromate.
Chromleder, *n.* chrome leather.
Chromleim, *m.*=**Chromgelatine.**
Chromnickel, *n. Metall:* chrome nickel, nickel-chrome.
Chromnickelstahl, *m.* chrome-nickel steel.
chromo-, Chromo- [kro·mo·-], *comb.fm.* 1. chromo-; **chromophor, chromophoric; Chromophor** *m,* chromophore. 2. *Ch:* chromous...; **Chromochlorid** *n,* chromous chloride; **Chromosulfat** *n,* chromous sulphate.
chromogen [kro·mo·'ge:n], *a. Biol: etc:* chromogenic; chromogenous.
Chromokollotypie [kro·mo·kolo·ty·'pi:], *f. -/. Phot.Engr:* chromocollotypy.
Chromolithographie [kro·mo·li·to·gra·'fi:], *f. -/-n* [-'fi:ən]. 1. (*process*) chromolithography. 2. (*print*) chromolithograph, F: chromo.
Chromooxyd [kro·mo·'ꝺ'ksy:t], *n. Ch:* chromous oxide.
Chromoplast [kro·mo·'plast], *m. -en/-en. Biol:* chromoplast.

Chromoskop [kro·mo·'sko:p], *n. -s/-e,* (*a*) *Opt:* chromoscope; (*b*) *Phot:* kromoskop.
Chromosom [kro·mo·'zo:m], *n. -s/-en. Biol:* chromosome.
Chromosphäre [kro·mo·'sfɛrə], *f. -/. Astr:* chrom(at)osphere, colour sphere (round the sun).
Chromotherapie [kro·mo·te·ra·'pi:], *f. -/-n* [-'pi:ən], chromotherapy.
chromotrop [kro·mo·'tro:p], *a. Ch:* chromotropic.
Chromotropsäure, *f. Ch:* chromotropic acid.
Chromotypie [kro·mo·ty·'pi:], *f. -/-n* [-'pi:ən]. *Print:* 1. (*process*) chromotype, chromotypography. 2. (*print*) chromotype.
Chromotypographie [kro·mo·ty·po·gra·'fi:], *f.* chromotypography, chromotypography.
Chromoxyd, *n. Ch:* chromium oxide.
Chromrot, *n. Dy:* chrome red.
Chromsalz, *n. Ch:* chromic salt.
chromsauer, *a. Ch:* combined with chromic acid; chromate of...; **chromsaures Kali,** potassium chromate.
Chromsäure, *f. Ch:* chromic acid.
Chromsäureanhydrid, *n. Ch:* chromic anhydride.
Chromstahl, *m.* chrome steel.
Chronik ['kro:nik], *f. -/-en,* chronicle; *B:* **die Bücher der C.,** the Chronicles; *F:* **eine wandelnde C. sein,** to know all the latest gossip.
Chronika ['kro:ni·ka:]. 1. *n.pl. B:* **die C.,** the Chronicles; **das erste, zweite, Buch der C.,** the First, Second, Book of Chronicles. 2. *f. -/. A:*=**Chronik.**
chronikalisch [kro·ni·'ka:liʃ], *a.* in chronicle form.
chronisch ['kro:niʃ], *a.* chronic (disease, *F:* financial difficulties, etc.).
Chronist [kro·'nist], *m. -en/-en,* chronicler; recorder (of contemporary events).
chrono-, Chrono- [kro·no·-], *comb.fm.* chrono-; **chronometrisch,** chronometric(al); **Chronometrie** *f,* chronometry.
Chronogramm [kro·no·'gram], *n. -(e)s/-e,* chronogram.
Chronograph [kro·no·'gra:f], *m.-en/-en.* 1. chronograph. 2. (*pers.*) chronographer, annalist. 3. **der C. von 354,** the Calendar of (A.D.) 354.
Chronographie [kro·no·gra·'fi:], *f. -/-n* [-'fi:ən], chronography.
chronographisch [kro·no·'gra:fiʃ], *a.* chronographic.
Chronologe [kro·no·'lo:gə], *m. -n/-n,* chronologer, chronologist.
Chronologie [kro·no·lo·'gi:], *f. -/-n* [-'gi:ən], chronology.
chronologisch [kro·no·'lo:giʃ], *a.* chronological.
Chronometer [kro·no·'me:tər], *n. -s/-,* chronometer.
Chronometerhemmung, *f. Clockm:* chronometer escapement.
Chronometrie [kro·no·me·'tri:], *f. -/.* chronometry.
chronometrisch [kro·no·'me:triʃ], *a.* chronometric(al).
Chronoskop [kro·no·'sko:p], *n. -s/-e,* chronoscope.
Chronostichon [kro·'nostiçon], *n. -s/-chen & -cha,* chronosticon.
Chrotta ['krota:], *f. -/-s. A.Mus:* crowd.
Chrysalide [cry·za·'li:də], *f. -n/-n. Ent:* chrysalis, pupa (*esp.* of butterfly).
Chrysantheme [kry·zan'te:mə, çry·zan'te:mə], *f. -/-n. Bot: Hort:* chrysanthemum.
Chrysanthemum [çry·-, kry·'zante·mum], *n. -s/-themen* [-zan'te:mən]. *Bot:* chrysanthemum; **eigentliches C.,** garden chrysanthemum.
chryselephantin [çry·ze·le·fan'ti:n], *a. Art:* chryselephantine.
chrys(o)-, Chrys(o)- [çry·z(o·)-], *comb.fm. Ch: Miner: etc:* chrys(o)-; **chryselephantin,** chryselephantine; **Chrysokoll** *m,* chrysocolla.
Chrysoberyll [çry·zo·be·'ryl], *m. -s/-e. Miner:* chrysoberyl; cymophane.
Chrysokoll [çry·zo·'kol], *m. -s/. Miner:* chrysocolla.
Chrysolith [çry·zo·'li:t], *m. -(e)s/-e & -en/-en. Miner:* chrysolite; **grüner C.,** olivine.
Chrysopras [çry·zo·'pra:s], *m. -es/-e. Lap: Miner:* chrysoprase.
Chrysostomos, Chrysostomus [çry·'zosto·mos, -mus]. *Pr.n.m. -'.* Chrysostom.
chthonisch ['çto·niʃ], *a.* chthonian; of the underworld; **chthonische Gottheiten,** chthonian deities; gods of the underworld.
Chthonisotherme [çto·nꝺi·zo·'tɛrmə], *f. Geol:* geo-isotherm.
Churfürst ['ku:r-], *m.*=**Kurfürst.**
Chuzpe ['xutspə], *f. -/. Yiddish: F:* insolence, *F:* cheek.
chylopoetisch [çy·lo·po·'e:tiʃ], *a. Physiol:* chylopoietic.

chylös [çy·'lø:s], *a. Physiol:* chylaceous, chylous.
Chylurie [çy·lu·'ri:], *f. -/. Med:* chyluria.
Chylus ['çy:lus], *m. -/. Physiol:* chyle.
Chylusgefäß, *n. Physiol:* chyliferous vessel.
Chymifikation [çy·mi·fi·ka·tsi'o:n], *f. -/. Physiol:* chymification.
Chymus ['çy:mus], *m. -/. Physiol:* chyme.
Ciacona [tʃa·'ko:na:], *f. -/-s. Danc: Mus:* chacon(n)e.
Ciborium [tsi·'bo:rïum], *n. -s/-rien. Ecc: Ecc.Arch:* ciborium.
Cicero¹ ['tsi(:)tsəro:]. *Pr.n.m. -s. Cl.Lit:* Cicero.
Cicero², *f. -/. Print:* pica; twelve-point type; **anderthalb C.,** 1½ C., great primer; 18-point type; **3 C.,** two-line great primer, three-line pica; 36-point type; **5 C., 6 C., 7 C., 8 C.,** five-line, six-line, seven-line, eight-line, pica.
Cicerone [tʃi·tʃə'ro:nə, -'ro:ne:], *m. -s/-ni,* guide, cicerone.
Ciceronianer [tsi(·)tsəro·ni'a:nər], *m. -s/-. Hist. of Lit:* Ciceronian.
ciceronianisch [tsi(·)tsəro·ni'a:niʃ], *a.* Ciceronian.
Ciceronianismus [tsi(·)tsəro·nï a'nismus], *m. -/. Hist. of Lit:* ciceronianism.
ciceronisch [tsi(·)tsə'ro:niʃ], *a.* Ciceronian, Ciceronic (style, etc.); **die Ciceronischen Reden,** Cicero's speeches.
Ciceroschrift, *f. Print:*=**Cicero².**
Cicisbeo [tʃi·tʃis'be:o:], *m. -/-s,* cicisbeo, attendant gallant (to a woman).
Cilicien [tsi·'li:tsïən]. *Pr.n.n. -s. Geog:* Cilicia.
Cilicier [tsi·'li:tsïər], *m. -s/-.* Cilician.
cilicisch [tsi·'li:tsïʃ], *a.* Cilician.
Cilicium [tsi·'li:tsïum], *n. -s/-cien,* cilice, hairshirt.
Cilli ['tsili:]. *Pr.n.f. -s.* (*dim. of* **Cäcilie**) Cissie.
Cimber ['tsimbər], *m. -s/-n*=**Kimber.**
cimbrisch ['tsimbriʃ], *a.*=**kimbrisch.**
Cimelie [tsi·'me:lïə], *f. -/-n,* precious object, *esp.* manuscript, from a church treasure.
Cinchone [tsin'ço:nə], *f. -/-n. Bot:* cinchona.
Cinchonin [tsinço·'ni:n], *n. -s/. Ch:* cinchonine.
Cinnabarit [tsina·ba·'ri:t], *m. -(e)s/. Miner:* cinnabar.
Cinquecentist [tʃiŋkve·tʃen'tist], *m. -en/-en,* cinquecentist.
Cinquecento, das [tʃiŋkve·'tʃento:], -s, the cinquecento.
Cipollin [tʃipo·'li:n], *m. -s/. Miner:* cipolin.
Cippus ['tsipus], *m. -/-. Rom.Ant:* cippus.
circa ['tsirka:], *adv.* about, approximately.
Circe ['tsirtse:]. *Pr.n.f. -s. Gr.Myth:* Circe.
circensisch [tsir'tsɛnzif], *a. Rom.Ant:* circensian (games, etc.).
Circulus vitiosus ['tsirku·lus vi·tsi'o:zus], *m. - -/-li -si,* vicious circle.
cis, Cis [tsis], *n. -/-. Mus:* (the note) C sharp, C♯; **Cis-dur, Cis-Dur, cis-moll, cis-Moll,** (-Tonart), (key of) C sharp major, C sharp minor.
cisis, Cisis ['tsisis], *n. -/-. Mus:* (the note) C double sharp.
Cistensänger ['tsistən-], *m. Orn:* fan-tailed warbler.
Citrin¹ [tsi·'tri:n], *n. -s/. Ch:* citrin.
Citrin² [tsi·'tri:n], *m. -s/-e. Miner:* citrine.
Civette [tsi·'vetə], *f. -/-n. Z:* (African) civet-cat.
civis academicus ['tsirvis a·ka'de:mi·kus], *m.*=**akademischer Bürger,** *q.v. under* **akademisch** 1.
Claire¹ ['klɛ:r], *m. -s/-. Ost:* fattening pond, claire.
Claire². *Pr.n.f. -s & Lit: -ns.* Clara, Clare.
Clairon [klɛ·'rõ:], *n. -s/-s. Mus:* bugle, *A:* clarion.
Claque ['klakə], *f. -/. Th:* hired applauders; claque.
Claqueur [kla·'kø:r], *m. -s/-e. Th:* hired applauder.
Cläre ['klɛ:rə]. *Pr.n.f. -s & Lit: -ns.* Clara, Clare.
Claudia ['klaudïa:]. *Pr.n.f. -s & Lit: -diens. Rom. Hist:* Claudia.
Claudian [klaudi'a:n]. *Pr.n.m. -s. Lt.Lit:* Claudian, Claudianus.
Claudisch ['klaudiʃ], *a. Rom.Hist:* Claudian.
Claudius ['klaudïus]. *Pr.n.m. -'.* Claudius, Claud; *Rom.Hist:* Claudius.
Clearing ['kli:riŋ], *n. -s/-s. Fin:* clearing.
Clearingverkehr, *m. Fin:* clearing.
Cleve ['kle:və]. *Pr.n.n. -s. Geog:* Cleve(s).
Cliché [kli·'ʃe:], *n. -s/-s* = **Klischee.**
Clinch [klintʃ], *m. -es/. Box:* clinch; **einen C. öffnen,** to break a clinch.
Clique ['klikə], *f. -/-n,* clique, set; coterie.
Cliquenwesen, *n.,* **Cliquenwirtschaft,** *f.* cliquism.
Clivage [kli·'va:ʒə], *f. -/-n. Geol:* cleavage.
Clivia ['kli:vïa:], *f. -/-vien,* **Clivie** ['kli:vïə], *f. -/-n. Bot:* clivia.

Cloisonné [klo·azo'neː], *n.* **-s/-s.** *Art:* cloisonné (enamel).
Clölia ['kløːlĭaː]. *Pr.n.f.* **-s** & *Lit:* **-liens.** Cloelia.
Cloqué [klo'keː], *m.* **-s/.** *Tex:* cloque.
Clothilde [klo·'tildə]. *Pr.n.f.* **-s** & *Lit:* **-ns.** Clothilda; *Hist:* Clot(h)ilde.
Clou [kluː], *m.* **-s/-s,** (important) point; (*a*) **der C. dabei ist . . .,** the whole point is . . .; (*b*) *F:* **der C. des Festes, der Aufführung,** the highlight, high spot, of the fête, of the performance.
Clown [klaun, kloːn], *m.* **-s/-s,** clown.
Clownerie [klaunə'riː, klo·nə'riː], *f.* **-/-n** [-'riːən], clownery.
Club [klup], *m.* **-s/-s,** club; *for compounds see* **Klub-.**
c-moll, c-Moll, *n. Mus:* (key of) C minor.
Cobbler ['koblər], *m.* **-s/-,** (*drink*) cobbler.
Coca ['koːkaː], *f.* **-/-(s)=Koka.**
Cocain [ko·ka·'iːn], *n.* **-s/.=Kokain.**
Coccidiose [koktsi·dĭ'oːzə], *f.* **-/-n=Kokzidiose.**
Coccus ['kokus], *m.* **-/-cen = Kokkus.**
Coccygeum [kok'tsyːge·um], *n.* **-s/-geen.** *Anat:* coccyx.
Cochenille [koʃe·'niljə, -'niːjə], *f.* **-/-n.** *Com:* cochineal; *Ent:* cochineal(-insect).
Cochenillelaus, *f.* cochineal-insect.
Cochinchina [kotʃin'çiːnaː]. *Pr.n.n.* **-s.** *Geog:*= **Kotschinchina.**
Cochlea ['koxle·aː], *f.* **-/-leae** [-le·ɛː]. *Anat:* cochlea (of the ear).
Cochon [ko'ʃõː], *m.* **-s/-s,** dirty pig, swine (of a man).
Cochonnerie [koʃonə'riː], *f.* **-/-n** [-'riːən], obscenity; filth; *F:* smut.
Cockpit ['kokpit], *n.* **-s/-s.** *Nau: Av:* cockpit (of yacht, motor-boat, aircraft).
Cocktail ['kokteːl], *m.* **-s/-s,** cocktail.
Cocktailkleid, *n. Cost:* cocktail dress.
Cocytus [ko·'tsyːtus, ko·'kyːtus]. *Pr.n.m.* **-'.** *Cl. Myth:* Cocytus.
Coda ['koːdaː], *f.* **-/-s.** *Mus:* coda.
Code [koːd], *m.* **1. -/-s,** code; **der Code Napoléon,** the Code Napoléon. **2. -s/-s.** *Telecom:* code; **ein Telegramm in C.,** a telegram in code.
Codebuch, *n.* code-book.
Codein [ko·de·'iːn], *n.* **-s/.** *Pharm:* codeine.
Codeschlüssel, *m.* key to a code.
Codex ['koːdɛks], *m.* **-/-dices** ['koːdi·tseːs] (*abbr.* **Cod.**) manuscript; codex; *cp.* **Kodex.**
Coeur [køːr], *n.* **-(s)/-(s).** *Cards:* hearts.
Coffein [kofe·'iːn], *n.* **-s/.=Koffein.**
Coiffeur [ko·a'føːr], *m.* **-s/-e,** hairdresser.
Coiffeuse [ko·a'føːzə], *f.* **-/-n,** (female) hairdresser.
Coiffüre [ko·a'fyːrə], *f.* **-/-n.** *Haird:* coiffure, hair-style.
Coir [ko·'iːr], *n.* **-/.** coir, coconut fibre.
Cojote [ko'joːtə], *m.* **-n/-n.** *Z:* coyote.
Col [kol], *m.* **-s/-s.** *Geog:* col.
Cola ['koːlaː], *f.* **-/.** *Bot:* kola, cola.
Colanuß, *f. Bot:* kola-nut.
Colaschokolade, *f.* kola chocolate.
Cölestiner [tsølɛs'tiːnər], *m.* **-s/-, Cölestinerin,** *f.* **-/-innen.** *Ecc:* Celestine (monk *or* nun).
Colinhuhn ['koːlin-], *n. Orn:* American partridge, bob-white.
Colitis [ko·'liːtis], *f.* **-/.** *Med:* colitis.
Colleg [ko'leːk], *n.* **-(e)s/-s=Kolleg.**
College ['kolidʒ], *n.* **- & -s/-s,** college.
Collie ['koliː], *m.* **-s/-s,** collie(-dog).
Collier [kol'jeː], *n.* **-s/-s,** necklace.
Colocasie [kolo·'kaːziə], *f.* **-/-n.** *Bot:* colocasia.
Colonel [ko·lo·'nɛl], *m.* **-s/-s.** *Mil: A:* colonel.
Coloradokäfer[ko·lo'raːdoː-], *m.*=**Kartoffelkäfer.**
Colt [kolt], *m.* **-s/-s.** *Sm.a:* Colt (revolver).
Columnist [kolum'nist], *m.* **-en/-en.** *Journ:* columnist.
Colzaöl ['koltsa·ᵓøːl], *n.* colza oil.
Comer ['koːmər], *inv.a. Geog:* **der C. See,** Lake Como, the Lake of Como.
Comment [ko'maŋ, ko'mãː], *m.* **-s/.** *Sch:* students' code, *esp.* as relating to drinking ceremonial.
Communiqué [komy·ni·'keː], *n.* **-s/-s,** communiqué.
Compagnon ['kompanjoŋ, kompan'jõː], *m.* **-s/-s,** (business) partner; associate.
Complet[1] [kom'pleː], *n.* **-(s)/-s.** *Cost:* dress *or* skirt with matching (three-quarter length) coat.
Complet[2] [kom'pleːt], *f.* **-/-e.** *Ecc:* compline.
Compoundmaschine ['kompaund-], *f. Mch:* compound engine.
Compoundmotor, *m. El.E:* compound(-wound) motor.
Compoundwicklung, *f. El.E:* compound winding.
Comptoir [kõ·to·'aːr], *n.* **-s/-s=Kontor.**
Concha ['konçaː], *f.* **-/-chen.** **1.** *Moll:* conch. **2.** *Anat:* conch(a) (of the nose, ear). **3.** *Ecc.Arch:* (*roof or apse*) conch(a).
Conche ['konçə], *f.* **-/-n.** **1.** *Ecc. Arch:* (*roof or apse*) conch(a). **2.** conche, conching machine (*in chocolate manufacture*).
Conditio sine qua non [kon'diːtsĭoː 'ziːnə kvaː 'noːn], *f.* **- - - -/.** sine qua non.
Conférencier [kõ·fe·rã·si'eː], *m.* **-s/-s,** (*a*) *Th:* compère (*of variety performance*); (*b*) (*at party, etc.*) Master of Ceremonies, *F:* M.C.
Confessio [kon'fesĭoː], *f.* **-/.** *Ecc.Arch:* confession (of a martyr).
Confiserie [konfi·zə'riː], *f.* **-/-n** [-'riːən]= **Konfiserie.**
Confiteor [kon'fi(·)te·or], *n.* **-/.** *R.C.Ch:* confiteor.
Confucius [kon'fuːtsĭus]. *Pr.n.m.* **-' = Konfuzius.**
Coniin [koni·'iːn], *n.* **-s/.** *Ch:* coni(i)ne.
Cönobit [tsøːno·'biːt], *m.* **-en/-en,** coenobite.
Conrad ['konraːt]. *Pr.n.m.* **-s.** Conrad.
Consecutio temporum [konze·'kuːtsĭoː 'tɛmpo·rum], *f.* **- -/.** *Gram:* sequence of tenses.
Consol [kon'zoːl], *m.* **-s/-s.** *Fin:* consol.
Consommé [kõ·so'meː], *f.* & *n.* **-/-s.** *Cu:* consommé, clear meat soup.
Consulardiptychon [konzu·'laːrdipty·çon], *n. Rom.Ant:* consular diptych.
Contre-billet ['kontrəbi·'jeː], *n.* **-s/-s.** **1.** *Jur:* counter-deed, pocket-agreement, defeasance. **2.=Kontermarke.**
Conus ['koːnus], *m.* **-/-ni.** **1.** *Geom: Bot: etc:* cone. **2.** *Anat: Med:* conus.
Convoi, Convoy ['konvoy], *m.* **-s/-s,** convoy.
Copyright ['kopi·rait], *n.* **-s/-s.** *Publ:* copyright.
coram publico ['koːram 'puːbli·koː]. *Lt.adv.phr.* in public; publicly.
Cord [kort], *m.* **-(e)s/-e** [korts, 'kordəs/'kordə]. *Tex:* (*a*) corduroy, cord; (*b*) cord tyre-fabric.
Cordelier [kordəl'jeː], *m.* **-s/-s.** *Ecc: Fr.Hist:* Cordelier.
Cordhose ['kort-], *f.* corduroy trousers.
Cordläufer, *m. Tex:* rep carpet.
Cordonnet [kordo'neː], *n.* **-s/-s.** *Tex:* cordonnet yarn.
Cordsamt, *m. Tex:* corduroy.
Corduan ['kordu·aːn], *n.* **-s/-e=Korduan.**
Cordzwirn, *m. Tex:* cordonnet yarn.
Corium ['koːrĭum], *n.* **-s/.** *Anat:* corium (of the skin).
Corlißdampfmaschine ['korlis-], *f. Mch:* Corliss engine.
Corlißhahn, *m. Mch:* Corliss valve.
Cornea ['korne·aː], *f.* **-/.** *Anat:* cornea (of the eye).
Corneal-Schale [korne·'aːl-], *f. Opt:* corneal contact lens.
Cornichon [korni·'ʃõː], *n.* **-s/-s.** *Hort:* gherkin.
cornisch ['korniʃ], *a.* Cornish.
Corona [ko·'roːnaː], *f* **-/-nae** [-nɛː]=**Korona.**
coronar [ko·ro·'naːr], *a. Anat: etc:* coronary.
Corporale [korpo·'raːlə], *n.* **-/.** *Ecc:* corporal(-cloth).
Corps [koːr], *n.* **-/-** [koːrs/koːrs], corps.
Corpsstudent, *m.* member of a students' duelling association.
Corpus ['korpus]. **1.** *n.* **-/-pora,** (*a*) *Anat:* corpus; **C. vitreum,** vitreous body (of the eye), corpus vitreum; (*b*) *Jur:* **C. delicti,** corpus delicti; exhibit; material proof; (*c*) corpus, collection (of writings, works of art, etc.); **das C. der mittelalterlichen Glasmalereien,** the corpus of medieval stained glass; *Jur:* **C. juris,** corpus juris. **2.** *m.* **-/-se.** *Hum:* (human) body. **3.** *m.* **-/.** (*a*) main part, body (*esp.* of piece of furniture); (*b*) *Mus:* resonance box (*esp.* of string instrument). **4.** *f.* **-/.** *Print:* long primer, ten-point type.
corriger la fortune [kori·'ʒeː la for'tyːn]. *Fr.vbl phr.* to help one's luck; to cheat; **das ist ein Fall von c.,** that's a case of helping one's luck; that's (a case of) cheating.
Corsage [kor'saːʒə], *f.* **-/-n.** *Cost:* (boned strapless) bodice (of dress); suntop; *Hist. of Cost:* corsage.
Cortisch ['korti·ʃ], *a. Anat:* **Cortisches Organ,** organ of Corti.
Cortison [korti·'zoːn], *n.* **-s/.** *Pharm:* cortisone.
Cöruleum [tsø·'ruːle·um], *n.* **-s/.** **1.** *Ch:* ceruleum. **2.** *Dy:* ceruleum, cerulean blue.
Cosinus ['koːzi·nus], *m.* **-/-.** *Trig:* cosine; **C. versus,** versed cosine.
Cosinuslinie, *f. Trig:* cosine curve.
Cosinussatz, *m. Trig:* cosine formula.
Cosmaten, die [kos'maːtən], *m.pl. Hist. of Art:* the Cosmati.
Costa Rica [ˌkosta·'riːkaː]. *Pr.n.n.* **-s.** *Geog:* Costa Rica.
costaricensisch [kosta·ri·'kɛnziʃ], *a.* Costa-Rican.
Cotangens ['koːtaŋgɛns], *m.* **-/-.** *Trig:* cotangent.
Cotelé [ko·t(ə)'leː], *n.* **-(s)/.** *Tex:* corduroy; corded material.
Coton [ko·'tõː, co·'toŋ], *m.* **-s/.** *Tex:* cotton.
Cottage ['kotidʒ], *n.* **-/-s.** **1.** cottage. **2.** *Austrian:* select residential area.
Cottisch ['kotiʃ], *a. Geog:* **die Cottischen Alpen,** the Cottian Alps.
Cotton ['kot(ə)n], *m.* & *s.* **-s/.** *Tex:* cotton.
Cottonade [koto·'naːdə], *f.* **-/-n.** *Tex:* cottonade.
cottonisieren [koto·ni·'ziːrən], *v.tr.*=**kotonisieren.**
Cottonmaschine ['kot(ə)n-], *f. Tex:* Cotton's (hosiery-knitting) machine.
Cottonöl, *n.* cotton-seed oil.
Cottonstrumpf, *m.* fully-fashioned stocking.
Cottonstrumpfwaren, *f.pl.* fully-fashioned hosiery.
Cottonstuhl, *m.*=**Cottonmaschine.**
cou-, Cou- [ku·-], *cp.* **ku-, Ku-.**
Couch [kautʃ], *f.* **-/-es** & **-en.** *Furn:* couch.
couéieren [ku·e·'iːrən], *v.i.* (*haben*) *F:* to practise Couéism.
Couéismus [ku·e·'ismus], *m.* **-/.** *Med:* Couéism.
coulant [ku·'lant], *a.* (*esp. of firm, etc.*) obliging.
Couleur [ku·'løːr], *f.* **-/-en** & **-s.** **1.** colour. **2.** *Sch:* colours (of a students' association). **3.** *Cards:* trump. **4.=Zuckercouleur.**
Couleurstudent, *m.* member of a students' association wearing colours.
Couloir [ku·lo·'aːr], *m.* **-s/-s.** **1.** corridor, passage. **2.** gully, couloir (on mountain side).
Coulomb [ku·'lõː], *n.* **-s/-s.** *El.Meas:* coulomb.
Coup [kuː], *m.* **-s/-s,** stroke; coup; **C., c., d'état** [ku·de·'ta], coup d'état; **einen (großen) C. machen, landen,** to bring off a (grand) coup.
Coupage [ku·'paːʒə], *f.* **-/.** *Dist: Wine-m:* blending, mixing.
Coupé [ku·'peː], *n.* **-s/-s.** **1.** *Veh.* & *Aut:* brougham, coupé. **2.** (*a*) *A:* front compartment (of stage-coach); (*b*) *Rail:* compartment.
coupieren [ku·'piːrən], *v.tr.*=**kupieren.**
Couplet [ku·'pleː], *n.* **-s/-s.** **1.** *Pros:* couplet. **2.** (music-hall) song.
Coupon [ku·'põː, ku·'poŋ], *m.* **-s/-s.** **1.** (*a*) pattern (cut off material); (*b*) *Com:* length (of material), *esp.* suit-length. **2.** (*a*) *Fin:* coupon, dividend-warrant; (*b*) counterfoil.
Cour [kuːr], *f.* **-/.** (*a*) court (of prince, etc.); (*b*) **einer Dame die C. machen, schneiden,** to court, to pay court to, one's addresses to, one's attentions to, a lady.
Courage [ku·'raːʒə], *f.* **-/.** courage; spirit; *F:* pluck, go; *F:* **Angst vor der eignen C. kriegen,** *F:* to feel one has stuck one's neck out.
couragiert [ku·ra·'ʒiːrt], *a.* (*a*) courageous; *F:* plucky; (*b*) tough.
Courante [ku·'rãːt(ə)], *f.* **-/-n** [-tən]. *Mus: Danc:* courante.
Courbarilholz [kurba·'riːl-], *n. Com:* locust-wood.
Courmacher, *m.* **-s/-, Courschneider,** *m.* (*a*) suitor, admirer, beau; (*b*) lady's-man, beau, *F:* lady-killer.
Courtage [kur'taːʒə], *f.* **-/-n.** *St.Exch:* brokerage.
Courtier [kurti'eː], *m.* **-s/-s.** *Com: Fin:* broker.
Courtoisie [kurto·a·'ziː], *f.* **-/-n** [-'ziːən], (*a*) courtesy, courteousness; gallantry; (*b*) (act of) courtesy.
Cousin [ku·'zɛ̃ː, ku·'zɛŋ], *m.* **-s/-s,** cousin.
Cousine [ku·'ziːnə], *f.* **-/-n,** (female) cousin.
Couvade [ku·'vaːdə], *f.* **-/.** *Anthr:* couvade, man-childbed.
Couvert [ku·'veːr, ku·'vɛːr], *n.* **-s/-s = Kuvert.**
Couveuse [ku·'vøːzə], *f.* **-/-n.** *Husb: Med:* incubator.
Covercoat ['kavərkoːt], *m.* **-(s)/-s.** **1.** *Tex:* covert-coating. **2.** *Tail:* covert-coat.
Cowboy ['kauboy], *m.* **-s/-s,** cowboy.
Cowper ['kaupər, 'kuːpər], *m.* **-s/-s.** *Ind:* Cowper stove.
Coxa ['koksaː], *f.* **-/-xae** [-ksɛː]. *Anat:* coxa, hip.
Coxalgie [koksal'giː], *f.* **-/-n** [-'giːən]. *Med:*= **Koxalgie.**
Coyote [ko'joːtə], *m.* **-n/-n.** *Z:* coyote.
Cozymase [koːtsy·'maːzə], *f.* **-/.** *Bio-Ch:* cozymase.
Crack [krɛk], *m.* **-s/-s.** *Turf: Sp:* crack.
Crackanlage ['krɛk-], *f. Oil Technology:* cracking plant.
Cracker ['krɛkər], *m.* **-s/-s.** **1.** dry biscuit, (cream) cracker. **2.** (Christmas) cracker.
Cracovienne [kra·ko·vi'ɛn], *f.* **-/-s.** *Danc:*= **Krakowiak.**
Cranium ['kraːnĭum], *n.* **-s/-nia.** *Anat:* cranium.
Craquelée [krak(ə)'leː], *f.* **-/-s,** & *n.* **-s/-s.** *Cer: etc:* **1.** (*finish*) crackle. **2.** *occ.* crackle-ware.
Craquelure [kra·kə'lyːrə], *f.* **-/-n,** (*on painting, etc.*) (i) fine crack; (ii) *coll.* craquelure, fine cracks.
Crawl [kroːl], *n.* **-(s)/.** *Swim:*=**Kraul.**

Crayon [krɛˈjõː], *m.* -s/-s. **1.** crayon, coloured pencil. **2.** pencil sketch, drawing.

Creas [ˈkreːas], *n.* -/. *Tex:* creas.

Credo [ˈkreːdoː], *n.* -s/-s. **1.** *Theol:* creed (*esp. as part of the mass*). **2.** profession of faith, creed; sein politisches C., his political creed.

Cremaillere [kreˈmalˈjeːrə], *n.* -s/-s. *Clockm:*=**Aufziehrechen.**

Creme[1] [ˈkreːm(ə), ˈkrɛːm(ə)], *f.* -/-s. **1.** *Cu:* custard; cream (pudding, filling, etc.). **2.** (*a*) *Toil:* cream; (*b*) shoe-polish, shoe-cream. **3.** *F:* die C. der Gesellschaft, the cream of society, the élite.

creme[2] [krɛːm, kreːm]. **1.** *inv. a.* cream (-coloured). **2.** *s.* **Creme,** *n.* -s/. cream (colour).

Cremefarbe, *f.* cream (colour).

cremefarben, cremefarbig, *a.* cream(-coloured).

Cremeschnittchen, *n. Cu:* cream slice.

Cremetorte, *f.* cake with butter icing; cream cake.

Cremona [kreˈmoːnaː]. *Pr.n.n.* -s. *Geog:* Cremona.

Cremoneser [kremoˈneːzər], *inv.a. Mus:* C. Geige, Cremona (violin).

Crêpe [krɛːp], *m.* -/-s. *Tex:* crêpe; C. de Chine [krɛːpdəˈʃiːn], crêpe de Chine; C. Georgette [krɛːpʒɔrˈʒɛt], georgette; C. Satin [krɛːpzaˈtɛ̃ː], satin crêpe; *cp.* **Krepp.**

Crepeline [krɛːpˈliːn(ə)], *f.* -/-n [-nən]. *Tex:* crêpeline, crêpoline.

Crepon [krɛːˈpõː], *m.* -s/-s. *Tex:* crépon.

crescendo [krɛˈʃɛndoː], *adv.,* **Crescendo,** *n.* -s/-s & -di. *Mus:* crescendo.

Cretonne [kreˈton], *f.* -/-s. *Tex:* cretonne.

Crew [kruː], *f. & m.* -/-s. **1.** *Nau:* crew. **2.** *Navy:* cadets of the same year, of the same age-group.

Crochets [kroˈʃeː], *pl. Com:* crochet goods.

Croisé [kroaˈzeː], *n.* -s/-s. **1.** *Tex:* twill. **2.** *Danc:* croisé.

croisiert [kroaˈziːrt], *a. Tex:* twilled (cloth).

Cromagnonrasse [kroˈmanˈjõː-], *f. Anthr:* Cro-Magnon race.

Cromlech [ˈkromlɛç, -lɛk], *m.* -(s)/-e & -s. *Prehist:* stone circle, (*in Brittany*) cromlech.

Crookessch [kruksʃ], *a. Ph:* **Crookessche Röhre,** Crookes tube.

Croquet [kroˈkeː], *n.* -s/-s=**Krocket.**

Croquette [kroˈkɛtə], *f.* -/-n. *Cu:* croquette.

Croquis [kroˈkiː], *n.* -/- [-ˈkiː(s)/-ˈkiːs]=**Kroki.**

Crosne [ˈkroːn], *m.* -/-s. *Hort:* Chinese artichoke.

Cross-Country [krosˈkantriː], *n.* -s/. (*a*) *Turf:* point-to-point race; (*b*) *Motor-Cy:* scramble; (*c*) *Sp:* cross-country race.

Crossing-over [krosiŋˈouvər], *n.* -/. *Biol:* crossing-over (*of chromosomes*).

Croton [ˈkroːton], *m.* -s/-e. *Bot:* croton.

Croupade [kruˈpaːdə], *f.* -/-n=**Kruppade.**

Croupier [kruˈpiˈeː], *m.* -s/-s, croupier.

Croupon [kruˈpõː], *m.* -s/-s. *Leath:* butt.

Croustade [kruˈstaːdə], *f.* -/-n. *Cu:*=**Krustade.**

Crouton [kruˈtõː], *m.* -s/-s. *Cu:* croûton.

Crux [kruːks], *f.* -/. **1.** crux, difficult matter, puzzle. **2.** *Astr:* Crux, the Southern Cross.

Csardas [ˈtʃardas, ˈtʃardaʃ], *m.* -/-. *Danc:* csardas.

C-Schlüssel, *m. Mus:* C clef.

Csikos [ˈtʃikoːʃ], *m.* -(es)/-e. Hungarian horse-boy; gipsy.

Cuba [ˈkuːbaː]. *Pr.n.n.* -s. *Geog:*=**Kuba.**

Cuiteseide [ˈkviːt-], *f. Tex:* boiled-off silk.

Cul de Paris [kyː də paˈriː], *m.* - - -/-s - -. *Cost: A:* bustle.

Culiciden [kuliˈtsiːdən], *f.pl. Ent:* culicidae; mosquitoes and gnats.

Cumarin [kumaˈriːn], *n.* -s/. *Ch:* coumarin.

Cumaron [kumaˈroːn], *n.* -s/. *Ch:* coumarone.

Cumaronharz, *n.* coumarone resin.

cum grano salis [kum ˈgraːnoː ˈzaːlis]. *Lt.adv.phr.* with a pinch of salt, cum grano salis.

cum laude [kum ˈlaudə]. *Sch:* with honours, *U.S:* with distinction; *approx.*=lower second class.

cum tempore [kum ˈtɛmporeː], (*abbr.* c.t.) (*after time named for lecture, etc.*) with a few minutes' grace; *Sch:* fifteen minutes after the time stated.

Cup [køp, kap], *m.* -s/-s. *Sp:* (challenge-)cup.

Cupido [kuˈpiːdoː]. *Pr.n.m.* -s. Cupid.

Cuprein [kuˈpreˈiːn], *n.* -s/. *Ch:* cupreine.

Cupren [kuˈpreːn], *n.* -s/. *Ch:* cuprene.

Curaçao [kyraˈsaoː], *m.* -s/-, curaçao (liqueur).

Cura posterior [ˈkuraː poˈsteːrioːr], *f.* - -/. secondary worry.

Curée [kyˈreː], *f.* -/. *Ven:* (*a*) parts of the stag given to the hounds; curée; *A:* quarry; (*b*) breaking up (of the deer).

Curettage [kyrɛˈtaːʒə], *f.* -/-n. *Surg:* curettage.

Curette [kyˈrɛtə], *f.* -/-n. *Surg:* curette.

curettieren [kyrɛˈtiːrən], *v.tr. Surg:* to curette (womb).

Curiatier, die [kuˈriˈaːtsïər]. *Pr.n.m.pl. Rom.Hist:* the Curiatii.

Curie[1] [kyˈriː], *n.* -/-. *Rad.-A. Meas:* curie.

Curie[2] [ˈkuːriə], *f.* -/-n. *Rom.Hist: Ecc:* curia.

Curium [ˈkuːrium], *n.* -s/. *Ch:* curium.

Curling [ˈkørliŋ], *n.* -s/. *Games:* curling.

Curriculum vitae [kuˈriːkuˈlum ˈviːtɛː], *n.* - -/-la -, brief statement of previous career; curriculum vitae.

Curry [ˈkøri, ˈkariː], *m. & n.* -s/-s, curry-powder.

Cut [køt], **Cutaway** [ˈkøtəveː], *m.* -(s)/-s. *Cost:* cutaway (coat), morning coat.

Cutber(ch)t [ˈkutbər(ç)t]. *Pr.n.m.* -s. (St) Cuthbert.

Cutter [ˈkøtər, ˈkatər], *m.* -s/-. *Cin:* cutter.

Cyan [tsyˈaːn], **Cyanid** [tsyaˈniːt], *etc. see* **Zyan, Zyanid,** *etc.*

Cybele [ˈtsyːbeˈleː, ˈkyːbeˈleː]. *Pr.n.f.* -s. *Myth:* Cybele.

cyci-, Cycl- [tsyˈkl-] *cp.* zykl-, Zykl-.

Cyclops [ˈtsyːkloˈps], *m.* -/-piden [tsyˈkloˈpiːdən]. *Crust:* cyclops, water-flea.

Cyclotron [tsyˈkloˈtron], *n.* -s/-e [ˈtsyˈkloˈtroːnə]. *Atom.Ph:* cyclotron.

Cymbal [ˈtsymbaˈl], *n.* -s/-e. *Mus:* **1.** *A:* cymbal. **2.** dulcimer; *A:* cymbalo.

Cymbelkraut [ˈtsymbaˈl-], *n. Bot:* cymbalaria.

Cymophan [tsymoˈfaːn], *m.* -s/-e. *Miner:* cymophane.

Cypern [ˈtsyːpərn], **cyprisch** [ˈtsyːpriʃ], *etc. see* **Zypern, zyprisch,** *etc.*

Cyperschwertel [ˈtsyːpər-], *m. Bot:* flowering rush, water-gladiole.

Cyrenaika, die [tsyreˈnaːiˈkaː]. *Pr.n.* -. *Geog:* Cyrenaica.

cyrillisch [tsyˈriliʃ], *a.* Cyrillic (script, alphabet, etc.).

Cyropädie, die [tsyroˈpɛˈdiː, kyˈroˈpɛˈdiː], -. *Gr.Lit:* the Cyropaedia.

cyst-, Cyst- [tsyst-] *see* zyst-, Zyst-.

Cythere [tsyˈteːrə, kyˈteːrə]. *Pr.n.n.* -s. *A.Geog:* Cythera.

Cytherenapfel, *m. Bot:* (fruit of the) hog-plum.

cyto-, Cyto- [tsyˈtoˈ-] *see* zyto-, Zyto-.

Czimbal [ˈtsimbaˈl], *n.* -s/-e = **Cymbal 2.**

D

D, d [de:], *n.* -/- (*in speech only* -s/-s [de:s]). **1.** (the letter) D, d; *Tp:* **D wie Dora,** D for David. **2.** *Mus:* (the note) D; **D-dur, D-Dur, d-moll, d-Moll, (-Tonart),** (key of) D major, D minor. *See also List of Abbreviations.*

da. **I.** *adv.* **1.** (*space*) (*demonstrative*) (*a*) there; **warst du schon da?** have you been there already? **da ist er!** there he is! **da geht er ja!** ah, there he goes! **wir haben ihn da gesehen,** we saw him here; **darf ich da sitzen, stehen?** may I sit, stand, there? *cp.* **dasitzen, dastehen; da ist viel zu sehen,** there's a lot to be seen (there); **Platz da!** make way there! **der da, dieser da, der Mann da,** that man (over) there; **Sie da!** you (over) there! **der Baum da,** that tree (over) there; **das Ding da,** that thing (over) there; **wo er ist, da ist sie auch,** wherever he is, she is (there) too; **von da (aus) fahren wir nach Berlin,** from there, *Lit:* (from) thence, we shall go to Berlin; **von da ab, von da an,** from there on, *Lit:* (from) thence; **da und dort, hie(r) und da,** here and there; now and then; **da und da,** in such and such a place; **da draußen,** outside, out there; **da herum,** round there; **da oben,** up there; **da vorn(e),** in front, ahead; **da unten,** down there, down below; (*b*) (*when offering sth.*) **da hast du einen Groschen!** there's, here's, tuppence for you! **da (nimm es) here,** take it! (*c*) **da hast du's!** there you are! **da haben wir's!** there we are! that proves it! **da stimme ich nicht bei,** I don't agree there; **da hast du etwas Dummes gemacht,** that was a stupid thing to do, you acted stupidly there; **na, da kann er lange warten,** well, he'll have to wait a long time then, *F:* he's got a hope! **da liegt die Schwierigkeit,** that's, there's, the difficulty; **sieh da!** (i) look (there)! (ii) well, well! **siehe da!** *Lit:* behold! lo! *F:* lo and behold! *F:* **nichts da!** nothing doing! it's no good! (*d*) *F:* (*emphasis*) **in** London, **da gibt es viele Museen,** in London there are many museums; **da hast du aber eine Menge Blumen!** what a lot of flowers you have! you ¹have got a lot of flowers! (*e*) there, here, present; in existence; **bist du da?** are you here, there? **ist er da gewesen?** (i) was he there? was he present? (ii) has he been here? was he here? **sie sind schon da,** they're here already, they've already arrived; **da bin ich!** here I am! **da bist du ja!** ah, there you are! **da kommt er ja!** ah, here he comes! **vor einer Minute war sie noch da,** she was still here, there, a moment ago; **wer da?** who's there? *Mil:* who goes there? **ist ein Brief für mich da?** is there a letter for me? **ist noch etwas da?** is there any left? **ist noch jemand da?** is anyone still here? **bleib da!** stay where you are! *F:* stay put! **wozu sind wir da?** why are we here (on earth)? what are we here for? why do we exist? **wozu ist der Tisch da?** what purpose does the table serve? what is the table (there) for? *see also* **dableiben, dasein;** (*f*) *A. & Lit:* (*after relative pronouns, not translated in English*) **alles, was da lebt,** everything which is alive, all living things; *B:* **wer da suchet, der findet,** he that seeketh, findeth; *B:* **wer da hat, dem wird gegeben,** whosoever hath, to him shall be given. **2.** (*a*) then; in that case; in which case; so, for which reason; **wenn ich es überhaupt tun muß, da tue ich's lieber gleich,** if I've got to do it at all, (then) I'd rather do it straight away; **er hat viel leiden müssen, da kann man es ihm nicht verdenken, daß er bitter geworden ist,** he has had much to suffer, so, for which reason, in which case, one cannot blame him for becoming embittered; **du kennst ihn nicht?** nun, **da hast du etwas verpaßt!** don't you know him? well you've missed something then! **was macht man da?** now what does one do? **da bleibt einem gar nichts anderes übrig (als . . ., als zu . . .),** there's nothing else for it (but. . ., but to . . .); (*b*) yet,

nevertheless; **er hat seine Examen bestanden, und da sagen Sie, er sei dumm!** he has passed his examinations and yet you say he is stupid! **und da überlegst du noch lange!** and yet you still hesitate! **3.** (*time*) (*a*) then, at that time; in those days; **da war er noch blutjung,** then, at that time, in those days, he was still very young; **da erst, erst da,** only then, not till then; **von da ab, von da an,** from that time forward, from then on, from that time on, thenceforward, thenceforth; **von da ab, von da an, war er wie besessen,** from that time on, from then on, he seemed as though possessed; (*b*) (*introducing main clause in paratactic sentence*) and, then, and then, so, and so, and so then, and then there; **sie beleidigte ihn, da ging er weg,** she insulted him (and) so he went away; **ich gab ihm das Geld, da schien er sich sehr zu freuen,** I gave him the money and he seemed very pleased; **während sie marschierten, da erschien in der Ferne ein Heer von zehntausend Mann,** while they were marching there appeared in the distance an army of ten thousand men; **ich ging nichtsahnend spazieren, da sprang ein toller Hund auf mich los!** I went for a walk unsuspectingly, and was attacked by a mad dog! (*c*) *F:* **und da . . ., und da . . .,** and then . . ., and then . . .; (*d*) (*denoting surprise, indignation, etc.*) **da fügen die Bildhauer ein paar Drähte zusammen und nennen es 'der Unbekannte Gefangene',** sculptors just put a few pieces of wire together and call it 'the Unknown Prisoner'; **da sitzen sie und halten Reden, und dabei sind es Taten, die not tun,** they just sit and talk, while it's actions that ʼare needed; *F:* **da schlag' (mir) einer lang hin!** you could knock me down with a feather!

II. da, *rel. use A. & Lit:* **1.** where; *B:* **da ich bin, könnet ihr nicht hinkommen,** where I am, thither ye cannot come. **2.** when, that; **das letzte Mal, da ich euch sah,** (the) last time (that) I saw you; **zu der Zeit, da . . .,** at the time when . . .; **in dem Augenblick, da . . .,** at the moment when, the moment that . . . .

III. da, *conj.* **1.** (*causal*) as, since, because; **da ich kein Geld habe, kann ich mir nichts kaufen,** as, since, I have no money I cannot buy myself anything; **er darf nicht schwimmen, da er sich erkältet hat,** he must not go swimming because he has a cold; **da du nicht fertig bist, können wir nicht gehen,** as you are not ready we cannot go. **2.** *Lit:* (*a*) when; **da ich noch jung war, (da) reiste ich viel,** when I was young I did a lot of travelling; *B:* **da ich ein Kind war, da redete ich wie ein Kind,** when I was a child, I spake as a child; (*b*) **nun da . . ., da . . . nun,** now that . . .; **nun da ich es zum zweiten Mal sehe, da ich es nun zum zweiten Mal sehe,** now that I see it for the second time; (*c*) while, as; *B:* **da die Engel von ihnen gen Himmel fuhren, sprachen die Hirten untereinander,** as the angels were gone away from them into heaven, the shepherds said one to another . . . . **3.** (*concessive*) **da . . . doch,** when, although; **wie kannst du ihr bloß so etwas sagen, da du doch weißt, wie empfindlich sie ist?** how could you say such a thing to her, when you know how sensitive she is?

IV. da-, *comb.fm.* **1.** (*prefixed to preps; where the prep. begins with a vowel the 'r' of the older form 'dar' is retained*) (*a*) (*forming pron. adverbs referring to things only*) . . . it, . . . them, . . . that, . . . those; **darauf,** on it, on them; **darüber,** over, about, it, them; **darum,** round it, them; **was mache ich damit?** what shall I do with it, them? **er legte ein Tuch darauf,** he spread a cloth over it, them; **ich weiß nichts davon,** I know nothing about it; (**da** *is sometimes separated from the prep. in archaic and colloquial*

German) *F:* **da weiß ich nichts von,** I know nothing about that; **da behüte mich Gott vor!** God forbid! (*b*) *Lit:* (*rel. use*) . . . which; **der Teich, darin Seerosen blühten,** the pool in which water-lilies bloomed; **der Boden, darauf er stand,** the ground on which he stood. **2.** (*prefixed to advs or preps*) (*a*) (*forming advs*) (. . .)there, . . . that place; **dahin,** (i) there, to that place, thither; (ii) away; **daher,** (i) from there, from that place, thence; (ii) along; (*b*) (*forming conjs*) **daher,** therefore, for this reason; **damit,** in order that, so that. **3.** (*prefixed to verbs*) here, there; **dableiben,** to stay here, there, to stay where one is; **dastehen,** to stand here, there.

dabei [da-ˈbai, *when emphatic* ˈdaːbai, *in compounds* daːˈbai-], *pron. adv.* **1.** (*a*) by, near, it, them; with . . . attached (to it, to them); **ein Haus mit einem Garten d.,** a house with a garden (attached) (to it); (*b*) **d. bleiben,** to stick to one's point; **das habe ich gesagt, und ich bleibe d.,** that's what I said and I stick to it; **nun gut, es bleibt d.,** all right, that's settled; (*emphatic*) **d. bleibt es,** that's final, that's that; *see also* **dabeibleiben;** (*c*) **es ist nichts d.,** (i) there's no harm in it; (ii) it's nothing extraordinary; **was ist schon d.?** (i) what does it matter? what harm can it do? (ii) what is so remarkable about it? (*emphatic*) **d. kann man nichts finden,** one can find nothing wrong in that; **d. kann man nichts machen,** in a case like that, one can do nothing; (*d*) **er hat sich nichts d. gedacht,** he didn't mean anything by it; (*emphatic*) **d. hat er sich wirklich nichts gedacht,** he meant absolutely nothing by that; **wir haben nichts d. gewonnen,** we gained nothing by it; (*emphatic*) **d. haben wir nichts gewonnen,** we gained nothing by that; (*e*) *F:* with one, on one; **ich habe kein Geld d.,** I have no money on me; **er hat kein Badezeug d.,** he hasn't his bathing things with him. **2.** in the act; **j-n d. ertappen, erwischen,** to catch s.o. at it, in the act, *F:* red-handed; **d. sein, etwas zu tun,** to be (in the act of) doing sth.; **er war gerade d., seine Sachen auszupacken,** he was just unpacking his things; **nahe d. sein, etwas zu tun,** to be on the point, the verge, of doing sth.; **da sind sie schon wieder d.!** they're at it again! *see also* **dabeisein.** **3.** (*a*) at the same time; while doing so; **er spielte Klavier und sang d.,** he played the piano and sang at the same time; (*b*) **d. sitzen, stehen,** to sit, stand, to remain sitting, seated, standing, (while doing sth.); (*emphatic*) **d. darfst du sitzen,** you can remain seated, you can sit, while doing that; *see also* **dabeisitzen, dabeistehen;** (*c*) moreover, in addition, at the same time, into the bargain, withal; **das Kleid ist alt und d. schmutzig,** the dress is old, and dirty as well, into the bargain; (*d*) yet, (yet) at the same time; **und d. ist er doch ein sehr netter Mann,** and yet at the same time he is a very nice man; (*emphatic*) **d. darf man nicht vergessen, daß . . .,** (i) at the same time, (ii) in this connexion, one must not forget that . . .; (*emphatic*) **sie haben sich ein elegantes Auto gekauft, und d. haben sie nicht einmal das Geld für die Miete,** they have bought themselves a smart car when, and yet, they haven't even the money to pay the rent.

dabeibleiben, *v.i. sep.* (*strong*) (*sein*) to stay with it, with them.

dabeisein, *v.i. sep.* (*sein*) (*conj. like* sein) to be present, there; **sie war dabei, als es geschah,** she was there, present, when it happened; **sein Herz war nicht dabei,** his heart was not in it; **ich bin dabei!** I'm with you! I'm game! **mit Eifer d.,** to take part eagerly; *F:* **der muß aber auch überall mit d.,** he always wants to join in, he always wants to be there.

dabeisitzen, *v.i. sep.* (*strong*) (*haben*) to sit there, by; **er sitzt bloß dabei und sagt nichts,** he just sits there and says nothing.
dabeistehen, *v.i. sep.* (*strong*) (*haben*) to stand by, near; to be standing near; **er stand teilnahmslos dabei,** he stood by indifferently.
dableiben, *v.i. sep.* (*strong*) (*sein*) to remain, stay, here, to remain, stay, where one is; **er kann nicht länger d.,** he cannot stay (here) any longer; **bleiben Sie doch noch ein wenig da!** stay (here) a little longer!
Dacapo [da·ˈka:po:], *n.* **-s/-s.** **1.** *Mus:* repeat. **2.** (*at opera, concert, etc.*) encore.
da capo, *adv.* (*a*) *Mus:* da capo; (*b*) (*at opera, concert, etc.*) encore; **da c. rufen,** to shout encore, to encore, to call for an encore.
Dacapoarie, *f. Mus:* aria (with da capo part).
d'accord [daˈko:r], (*a*) *pred. a.* in agreement; (*b*) *int.* agreed! granted! quite so!
Dach, *n.* **-(e)s/⸗er.** **1.** (*a*) roof (of building, *Min:* of gallery, *Veh:* of car, etc.); *Poet:* roof, vault, canopy (of heaven, trees); **ohne D.,** roofless; **einhängiges D.,** pent roof, lean-to roof; **flaches D.,** flat roof; **holländisches D.,** hip-roof; **schräges D.,** slanting roof; **ein Haus unter D. bringen,** to put the roof on a house, to roof a house; **das D. der Welt,** the roof of the world (*the plateau of the Pamirs*); *F:* **j-m aufs D. steigen,** *F:* to blow s.o. up, to haul s.o. over the coals, to give it s.o. hot; *F:* **j-m auf dem D. sein, sitzen,** *F:* to be after s.o.; to watch s.o. closely; *F:* **bei dem ist gleich Feuer im D.,** he's hot-headed, he flies into a passion readily, *F:* he goes off the deep end, flies off the handle, instantly; *F:* **j-m eins aufs D. geben,** (i) to box s.o.'s ears, to hit s.o. over the head; *F:* to clip s.o. over the ear, to give s.o. a crack on the nut; (ii) *F:* to give s.o. a good dressing-down, to give it s.o. hot; *F:* **eins aufs D. bekommen, kriegen,** *F:* (i) to get a clip over the ear, a crack on the nut; (ii) to get a good ticking-off, a good dressing-down; (*b*) roof, house; **mit j-m unter einem Dache wohnen,** to live under the same roof as s.o.; **mein bescheidenes D.,** my humble dwelling, my humble abode; *B:* **Herr, ich bin nicht wert, daß du unter mein D. gehest,** Lord, I am not worthy that thou shouldst come under my roof; (*c*) shelter; **unter D. (und Fach) sein,** to have found shelter, to be under cover; **die Ernte unter D. (und Fach) bringen,** to bring in the harvest; **(ein Projekt, usw.) unter D. und Fach bringen,** to settle, to find backing for (a project, etc.); (*d*) *Ten: A:* penthouse. **2.** *North G.Dial:* thatching materials. **3.** *Nat. Hist:* (*a*) (snail-)shell; (*b*) back and wings (of bird). **4.** *Gram: F:* (*diacritical sign*) circumflex.
Dachabfall, *m.* = **Dachneigung.**
Dachbinder, *m. Constr:* roof truss.
Dachbinderbalken, *m. Constr:* tie-beam.
Dachboden, *m.* loft.
Dachbrücke, *f. Tls:* slater's anvil.
Dachbund, *m. Constr:* roof truss.
Dachdecker, *m.* roofer; (*of tile roofs*) tiler; (*of slate roofs*) slater; (*of thatched roofs*) thatcher.
Dachdeckerarbeiten, *f. pl.* roofing; slating; tiling; thatching.
Dachdeckerhammer, *m. Tls:* slater's hammer.
Dachdeckerstift, *m.* slater's peg.
Dachdeckung, *f.* **1.** (action of) roofing. **2.** roofing (materials), roofage, roof covering.
Dachdeckungsarbeiten, *f.pl.* = **Dachdeckerarbeiten.**
Dachdeckungsmaterial, *n.* roofing (material).
dachen, *v.tr.* to roof (building); **Dachung** *f,* roofing.
Dachfahne, *f.* wind-vane, weather-vane.
Dachfenster, *n.* roof light, skylight; dormer window, attic window.
Dachfilz, *m.* roofing felt.
Dachfirst, *m.* roof ridge.
Dachfläche, *f.* **1.** *Constr:* roof surface. **2.** *Geol:* surface stratum.
Dachform, *f.* style, shape, of roof.
dachförmig, *a.* in the shape of a roof; triangular.
Dachfuß, *m. Constr:* eaves.
Dachgarten, *m.* roof-garden.
Dachgaupe, *f. Arch:* dormer window.
Dachgerüst, *n. Constr:* roof framework; roof timbers.
Dachgeschoß, *n.* (*a*) attic storey; (*b*) loft.
Dachgesellschaft, *f. Fin:* holding company.
Dachgesims, *n. Constr:* eaves moulding.
Dachgespärre, *n. Constr:* rafters.
Dachgleiche, *f. Austrian:* **1.** erection of the roof timbers. **2.** celebration to mark the erection of the roof timbers.
Dachgleichenfeier, *f. Austrian:* = **Dachgleiche 2.**
Dachhaken, *m.* roof hook.
Dachhammer, *m.* = **Dachdeckerhammer.**
Dachhase, *m. F:* cat.
Dachhaube, *f. Constr:* cap (of building).
Dachhaut, *f.* roofing, roofage, roof covering.
Dachholz, *n. Constr:* roof member.
Dachjuchhe [ˈdaxjuxhe:], *n. F:* **unterm, im, D. wohnen,** to live under the roof.
Dachkammer, *f.* attic, garret.
Dachkappe, *f. Constr:* = **Dachhaube.**
Dachkehle, *f. Constr:* valley(-channel, -gutter).
Dachklappe, *f. Constr:* folding window (in roof).
Dachknappe, *m.* = **Dachhaken.**
Dachlatte, *f. Constr:* roof-batten.
Dachlattung, *f. Constr:* roof-battens.
Dachlauch, *m. Bot:* houseleek, Jupiter's beard.
Dachluke, *f.* roof light, skylight.
Dachnase, *f. Arch:* dormer-window with a gablet.
Dachneigung, *f. Arch:* pitch, slope, of roof.
Dachöhre, *f.* loft (for storing grain, etc.).
Dachorganisation, *f. Fin: etc:* umbrella organization; holding organization.
Dachpappe, *f.* roofing board, roofing felt; tarred felt; tar-board.
Dachpfanne, *f.* pantile; *F:* tile.
Dachpfette, *f. Constr:* purlin.
Dachplatte, *f.* flat tile, plain tile.
Dachrahm, *m. Constr:* purlin.
Dachraum, *m.* **1.** loft (space). **2.** attic, garret.
Dachreiter, *m. Arch:* ridge turret.
Dachrinne, *f.* (eaves-)gutter.
Dachrinnenschnauze, *f. Arch:* gargoyle.
Dachrohr, *n.* **1.** reed for thatching. **2.** = **Dachröhre.**
Dachröhre, *f. Constr:* gutter-pipe, rain-water pipe, down pipe.
Dachs [daks], *m.* **-es/-e.** **1.** *Z:* badger; **amerikanischer D.,** carcajou, American badger; **australischer D.,** (i) (Tasmanian) wombat; (ii) bandicoot; *F:* **schlafen wie ein D.,** to sleep like a log, like a top. **2.** *F:* **ein frecher D.,** a (young) whipper-snapper, puppy; **ein junger D.,** a young fellow.
Dachsattel, *m.* saddle (of roof).
Dachsbau, *m.* badger's set.
Dachsbeil, *n. Tls:* adze.
dachsbeinig, *a.* bandy-legged.
Dachschalung, *f.* roof boarding.
Dachschiefer, *m.* (roofing) slate.
Dachschifter, *m. Constr:* jack-rafter.
Dachschilf, *n.* (reeds for) thatch.
Dachschindel, *f. Constr:* roof-shingle, shingle (-board).
Dachschütze, *m. Mil:* sniper.
Dachschwelle, *f. Constr:* pole-plate.
Dächsel, *m.* **-s/-.** **1.** dachshund. **2.** *Tls:* = **Dechsel.**
Dachshund, *m.* dachshund; **langhaariger, kurzhaariger, D.,** long-haired, short-haired, dachshund.
Dachsilhouette, *f.* roof line.
Dächsin, *f.* **-/-innen.** *Z:* female badger.
Dachsparren, *m. Constr:* rafter, spar.
Dachstein. **1.** *Pr.n. Geog:* **der D.,** the Dachstein (Mountain). **2.** *m. Constr:* roofing slab.
Dachstock, *m.* **1.** *South G.Dial:* loft. **2.** wooden peg (for thatching).
Dachstroh, *n.* thatch.
Dachstube, *f.* attic, garret.
Dachstuhl, *m.* roof framework; roof timbers.
Dachstuhlsäule, *f. Constr:* post (among roof timbers).
dachte, dächte *see* **denken.**
Dachtel, *m.* **-s/-.** *Dial:* box on the ears.
dachteln, *v.tr. Dial:* to give (s.o.) a box on the ears.
Dachtraufe, *f. Constr:* eaves.
Dachüberhang, *m. Constr:* eaves.
Dachung, *f. see* **dachen.**
Dachverband, *m.* **1.** *Constr:* roof truss. **2.** *Adm:* umbrella association.
Dachwand, *f. Constr:* wall against which a pent roof is built.
Dachwerk, *n. Constr:* roof.
Dachwurzel, *f. Bot:* = **Dachlauch.**
Dachziegel, *m.* (roofing) tile.
Dacien [ˈda:tsiən]. *Pr.n.n.* **-s** = **Dazien.**
Dacier [ˈda:tsiər], *m.* **-s/-** = **Dazier.**
Dackel, *m.* **-s/-,** dachshund.
dackelbeinig, *a.* bandy-legged.
Dadaismus [da·da·ˈismus], *m.* **-/.** *Art: Lit:* dadaism.
Dadaist [da·da·ˈist], *m.* **-en/-en.** *Art: Lit:* member of the Dada School; **die Dadaisten,** the Dada School.
dädalisch [dɛ·ˈda:liʃ], *a.* Daedalian; of Daedalus; *Lit:* inventive.
Dädalos, Dädalus [ˈdɛ:da·los, -lus]. *Pr.n.m.* **-'.** *Gr.Myth:* Daedalus.
dadran, *pron. adv. F:* = **daran.**
dadrauf, *pron. adv. F:* = **darauf.**
dadrin, *pron. adv. F:* = **darin.**
dadrüber, *pron. adv. F:* = **darüber.**
dadrum, *pron. adv. F:* = **darum.**
dadrunter, *pron. adv. F:* = **darunter.**
dadurch, *pron. adv.* **1.** [da·ˈdurç] (*a*) (*also* **dadurch-,** *comb.fm.*) through it, them; **das Tor war offen, d. sah man das Haus,** the gate was open and through it you could see the house; **in der Mauer waren Löcher, d. strömte das Wasser,** there were holes in the wall and water came pouring through (them); (*b*) by it; **was hat er d. gewonnen?** what has he gained by it? (*c*) *rel. use A:* by which, through which. **2.** [ˈda:durç] (*a*) for this reason, in this way, thus; **d. geschah es, daß wir keine Zeit hatten,** that was (the reason) why we had no time, for this, for which, reason we had no time, thus, in this way, it came about that we had no time; (*b*) **d., daß . . .,** (i) because; **d., daß die Preise gestiegen sind, ist das Leben teurer geworden,** because prices have risen the cost of living has gone up; **es geschah d., daß . . .,** it happened because . . .; (ii) **d., daß er jede Woche etwas spart, bringt er allmählich eine Menge Geld zusammen,** by saving a little every week he is gradually amassing a lot of money.
dafern [da·ˈfɛrn], *conj. Lit:* inasmuch as.
dafür, *pron. adv.* **1.** [da·ˈfy:r] (*a*) for it, for them; **er bekam zwanzig Mark d.,** he got twenty marks for it, for them; (*b*) **er ist bekannt d., daß er alles verliert,** he has a reputation for losing everything; **sie gibt alles d. auf,** she is giving up everything for it; **sie gibt alles d. auf, ans Theater zu kommen,** she is giving everything up to become an actress; (*cp.* 2 (*a*)); (*c*) in its place, instead; **wenn du mir das schwarze Kleid nicht geben kannst, so nehme ich das braune d.,** if you cannot give me the black dress I'll take the brown one instead; *Austrian Dial:* **es steht nicht d.,** it's not worth it; (*d*) **ich habe keinen Beweis d.,** I have no proof (of it, that it is so); **er kann keinen Grund d. angeben,** he can give no reason for it; **das ist ein Beispiel d.,** that's an example of it; (*e*) **etwas, nichts, d. tun können,** to be able to do something about it, to be unable to do anything about it; **was können wir d. tun?** what can we do about it? (*f*) **es gibt kein Mittel d.,** there's no remedy for it; (*g*) (*also* **dafür-,** *comb.fm.*) **d. sein,** to be for it, in favour of it, to think it right; **bist du d.?** are you for it, in favour of it? do you think it the right thing to do? **ich bin d., wir gehen jetzt gleich,** I am for, in favour of, going immediately, I think we should go immediately; **d. spricht, daß . . ., d. läßt sich sagen, daß . . .,** a point in (its) favour is that . . .; **er hat in der Versammlung d. gesprochen,** he spoke in its favour, in favour of it, at the meeting; **d. und dagegen, d. und dawider,** for and against (it, them); (*cp.* 2 (*a*)). **2.** [ˈda:fy·r] (*a*) (*emphatic*) for that, for those; **d. muß er büßen,** he must pay for that; **d. gibt es keine Erklärung,** that cannot be explained, there is no way of explaining that; **d. kann er nichts,** he cannot help, is not to blame for, that; *see also* **dafürkönnen; er sagt, sein Bruder sei ein Dieb, aber d. halte ich ihn eigentlich nicht,** he says his brother is a thief, but I don't actually think he is one; *see also* **dafürhalten; sie ist eine große Schwätzerin, — d. ist sie allgemein bekannt,** she is a great gossip, and is known everywhere for it, as such; **d. läßt sich manches sagen,** there's a lot to be said for that; (*b*) therefore, for that reason, that's why; **d. bin ich hierher gekommen,** that's why I came here, that's what I came here for; **er soll die Meinung des Volks zum Ausdruck bringen, d. ist er ein Volksvertreter,** he ought to represent the opinion of the people, that's what he's a Member of Parliament for, that's his job as a Member of Parliament, as an M.P.; **laß ihn doch sein Geld ausgeben, d. hat er's ja!** let him spend his money, that's what he has it for, that's what it's for. **3.** [da·ˈfy:r] (but) on the other hand, as a compensation; **sie ist nicht hübsch, d. hat sie eine tolle Figur,** she is not pretty, but on the other hand, to make up for it, she has a marvellous figure; **wir haben nicht viel Geld, d. sind wir aber gesund,** we haven't much money, but at least we are healthy.
dafürhalten [da·ˈfy:r-]. **I.** *v.i. sep.* (*strong*) (*haben*) **d., daß . . .,** to think, to be of the opinion, that . . .; **ich halte dafür, daß wir den Plan aufgeben (sollen),** I think that, I am of the opinion that, we should give up the plan.
II. *vbl s.* **Dafürhalten,** *n.* opinion; **nach meinem D.,** in my opinion, in my estimation.

dafürkönnen [da·'fy:r-], *v.i. sep.* (*haben*) (*conj. like* **können**) to be to blame; **er kann nichts dafür**, he can't help it, he's not to blame (for it), it's not his fault; **he can't stop it; was können 'wir dafür?** is it 'our fault? how are 'we to blame (for it)? **sie kann nichts dafür, daß sie alles fallen läßt**, she can't help dropping everything, it's not her fault, she's not to blame, if she drops everything.

dagegen. I. *pron. adv.* [da·'ge:gən, *when emphatic* 'da:ge:gən] 1. (*a*) against it, them; **am Straßenrand lag ein Ziegelhaufen; er rannte im Dunkeln d.**, a pile of bricks was standing at the side of the road, and he ran against it in the dark; (*b*) instead (of it, of them), in exchange (for it, for them); **ich habe es d. bekommen, eingetauscht**, I got it in exchange (for it, them); **wir haben nichts d. zu geben**, we have nothing to give in exchange; (*c*) **es gibt kein Mittel d.**, there's no remedy for it; (*emphatic*) **d. ist kein Kraut gewachsen**, (i) there's no remedy for that, (ii) *F:* there's no way of dealing with that; (*d*) to the contrary; **ich habe keinen Beweis d.**, I have no proof to the contrary; (*e*) **etwas d. haben**, to have an objection; **wenn Sie nichts d. haben**, if you don't mind, if you have nothing against it, if you have no objection; **was hat er denn d.?** what has he (got) against it then? what objection has he then? **hast du etwas dagegen, wenn ich die Tür schließe?** do you mind, would you mind, my shutting, if I shut, the door? (*emphatic*) **d. haben wir nichts**, we have no objection to that. 2. (*also* dagegen-, *comb.fm.*) (*a*) **d. sein**, to be against, opposed to, it, them; **sollen wir's tun? — ich bin d.**, should we do it? — I'm against it; **d. sein, etwas zu tun**, to be against, opposed to, doing sth.; **d. sein, daß etwas geschieht**, to be against, opposed to, sth.'s happening; **ich bin d., daß die Kinder allein bleiben**, I am against the children's remaining, being left, alone; (*b*) against, in contradiction of, in opposition to, it; **dagegensprechen**, to speak against it; **er hat in der Versammlung dagegen gesprochen**, he spoke against it at the meeting; **d. spricht, d. läßt sich sagen, einwenden, daß . . .**, one may object on the grounds that . . .; (*emphatic*) **d. läßt sich nichts sagen, einwenden**, no one can object to that; **d. steht die Tatsache, daß . . .**, opposed to that, against that, there is the fact that . . . . 3. by comparison; **sie ist so schön, daß ihre Schwester ganz häßlich d. scheint**, she is so beautiful that her sister seems quite ugly by comparison; **das tut so weh — Zahnschmerzen sind nichts d.**, that hurts so much that toothache is nothing by comparison; **wir haben so viel dabei gewonnen, daß die Mühe gering d. scheint**, we have gained so much by it that the trouble seems small by comparison; *see also* **dagegenhalten.**
II. **dagegen** [da·'ge:gən], *conj.* however, but; on the other hand; (*a*) **er spricht nicht viel, d. handelt er**, he doesn't say much, but he does get things done; **mein Partner möchte das Geschäft aufgeben, d. halte ich es für richtig es zu behalten**, my partner would like to give up the business; I however, on the other hand, think we should keep it; (*b*) **sie ist groß und schlank, er d. klein und untersetzt**, she is tall and slim, he however, on the other hand, is short and stocky.

dagegenhalten, *v.tr. sep.* (*strong*) 1. (*a*) to hold (sth.) against it, them; (*b*) (*in comparison*) to set (sth.) against it, them. 2. **etwas, nichts, d.**, to raise an objection, no objection (to it, them).

dagewesen, *p.p. & a. see* **dasein.**

Dagg, *m. & n.* -s/-en. *Nau: A:* rope's end; colt; **durch die Daggen laufen**, to run the gauntlet.

Daguerreotyp [da·gɛ(·)ro·'ty:p], *n.* -s/-e. *A.Phot:* daguerreotype.

Daguerreotypie [da·gɛ(·)ro·ty·'pi:], *f.* -/-n [-'pi:ən]. *A.Phot:* 1. daguerreotypy. 2. daguerreotype.

daguerreotypieren [da·gɛ(·)ro·ty·'pi:rən], *v.tr. A.Phot:* to daguerreotype.

Dahabieh, Dahabije [da·ha·'bi:je:], *f.* -/-n, dahabeeyah, dahabiah (*Nile sailing-ship*).

daheim[1] [da·'haim], *adv.* at home; **d. sein**, to be (i) at home, (ii) in one's own (part of the) country; **d. bleiben, sitzen**, to stay at home.

Daheim[2], *n.* -s/. home.

Daheimgebliebene, *m., f.* (*decl. as adj.*) one who has remained at home.

daher, *adv.* 1. [da·'he:r] (*also* daher-, *comb.fm. prefixed to verbs*) (*a*) from there, *Lit:* (from) thence; **sie kam gestern d.**, she came from there yesterday; **er stammt, kommt, auch d.**, he comes, hails, from there too; (*b*) (*prefixed to verbs of motion*) along; **dahergehen**, to be walking along; **daherkommen**, to be coming along, to approach; **daherlaufen**, to be running along; **daherfliegen**, to be flying along; **dahersausen**, to be dashing along; **daherfahren**, (i) to be driving along; (ii) to be travelling, going, along; (iii) to be moving (along); (*prefixed to verbs of activity, denotes aimlessness*) **ein Lied dahersingen**, to hum, drone, a song; *cp.* **daherreden;** (*c*) *A. & F:* here; **stell den Stuhl d.**, put the chair down here. 2. [da·'he:r] *rel. use A. & Lit:* whence. 3. ['da:he:r] (*emphatic*) from there, *Lit:* (from) thence; **ja, d. kommt er**, yes, that's where he comes from; *F:* **d. weht der Wind**, *F:* so that's the way the wind's blowing. 4. ['da:he:r] (*a*) that's why; for this reason, therefore; hence, thence; **d. kommt es, daß wir ihn nicht gesehen haben**, so that's (the reason) why we didn't see him; **d. kam es, daß sie sehr müde waren**, that's why, it was for this reason that, they were so tired; **d. sein verdächtiges Benehmen**, hence his suspicious behaviour; **d. glaubte man, daß . . .**, hence, therefore, for this reason, that's why, it was thought that . . .; (*b*) *conj.* **er geht immer spät schlafen, d. kann er morgens nie aufstehen**, he always goes to bed late, that's why he can never get up in the morning. 5. ['da:he:r] (*time*) *A. & Lit:* **bis d.**, until then.

dahermachen, *v.tr. sep.* **viel d.**, to make a lot of fuss; **mach nicht soviel daher!** don't make so much fuss!

daherreden, *v.i. sep.* (*haben*) *F:* **red nicht so dumm daher!** don't talk rubbish! **geschwollen d.**, to speak pompously, to mouth it.

daherum, *adv.* thereabouts, approximately; **zweihundert Leute, oder d.**, two hundred people or thereabouts; *see also* **da.**

dahier [da·'hi:r], *adv. Lit:* here.

dahin, *adv.* 1. [da·'hin] (*also* dahin-, *comb.fm. prefixed to verbs*) (*a*) there, to that place, *Lit:* thither; **ich fahre morgen d.**, I'm going there tomorrow; **was gehört d., das Bild oder die Vase?** which belongs there, the picture or the vase? **er ist endlich dahin gekommen, wo er hinkommen wollte**, at last he has got where he wanted to be; (*b*) along; past, by; **der majestätisch dahinströmende Fluß**, the river flowing majestically by, past; **im Tanz dahinschweben**, to glide over the dance-floor; **er ging eilenden Schrittes dahin**, (i) he walked along, (ii) he passed by, went past, with hasty step; **die Tage gehen, eilen, dahin**, the days go, hurry, by; **der Sturm brauste dahin**, the storm raged past; *F:* **dahintrudeln**, to tootle along; (*c*) **er hat es nur so dahingesagt**, he just said it without meaning anything; **seine Tage dahinträumen, dahinschlummern**, to dream one's days away; (*d*) *Lit:* **er rannte dahin**, he ran away; **er schoß dahin wie ein Pfeil**, he was off like a shot (from the bow); (*e*) *Lit:* away; **dahinschwinden, dahinwelken**, (i) to fade away, (ii) to die; **dahinsein**, to have gone; **dahinsiechen**, to waste away; **dahinraffen**, to snatch away, carry off; (*f*) *Lit:* down; **dahinsinken**, to sink down. 2. [da·'hin] *rel. use A. & Lit:* to which, whither. 3. ['da:hin] (*emphatic*) (*a*) to that place, there; **ich reise gern, aber d. möchte ich nicht fahren**, I like travelling, but I shouldn't like to go 'there, to 'that place; (*b*) **bis d.**, (i) as far as there, that far, up to there, up till then; (ii) till then, till that time; (iii) by then, by that time; **bis d. war der Weg chaussiert**, as far as there, up to there, up till then, it was a made road; *F:* **es steht mir bis d.**, I'm fed up with it, I'm sick and tired of it; **bis d. gefiel er mir ganz gut**, until then, up to that moment, I liked him quite well; **die Frage wird vielleicht bis d. geklärt sein**, the question will perhaps have been clarified by then; (*c*) to that point, so far; **sein barsches Benehmen hat ihn d. gebracht, daß er keine Freunde mehr hat**, his surly behaviour has reached such a point that he has no friends left; **ist es wirklich d. gekommen?** has it really come to this, to that? **es ist d. gekommen, daß wir das große Haus nicht mehr unterhalten können**, it has come to the point when we can no longer run this big house; (*d*) to that effect; **er hat es d. ausgelegt, daß . . .**, he interpreted it as meaning that . . .; **hat sie sich wirklich d. ausgesprochen?** did she really speak to that effect? is that what she really implied? **sie äußerten sich d. (gehend), daß . . .**, they spoke to the effect that . . .; **seine Meinung geht d., daß . . .**, it is his opinion that . . .; (*e*) to that end; **sie arbeiten, wirken, d., die Regierung umzustürzen**, they are working for the overthrow of the government, their aim is to overthrow the government; (*f*) **dahin-**, *comb.fm.* (*prefixed to preps forming advs denoting aim of motion*) there; **dahinab, dahinunter**, down there; **dahinauf**, up there; **dahinaus**, out there; **dahinein**, in(to) there.

dahinaus ['da:hin-], *adv.* out there; **bis d.**, to the last degree, completely, utterly; immensely, enormously; **sie ist eitel bis d.**, she is immensely vain, vain to the last degree; **er ist verwöhnt bis d.**, he is utterly, completely, spoilt.

dahinfahren, *v.i. sep.* (*strong*) (*sein*) 1. to drive, travel, go (along, by, past). 2. (*a*) to go away, to depart; (*of time, joys, etc.*) to pass; (*b*) to die, to pass away; *B:* **. . . daß er dahinfährt, . . .** and he passeth.

dahinfliegen, *v.i. sep.* (*strong*) (*sein*) 1. to fly (along); (*of aircraft, bird, etc.*) **d. wie ein Pfeil**, to shoot past, by, to pass, like a shot (from the bow); *B:* **wie ein Vogel dahinfleugt, der aus dem Nest getrieben wird**, as a wandering bird cast out of the nest. 2. (*of time*) to fly by; **die Zeit fliegt nur so dahin**, time simply flies by; *B:* **meine Tage sind leichter dahingeflogen denn eine Weberspule**, my days are swifter than a weaver's shuttle.

dahingeben, *v.tr. sep.* (*strong*) *Lit:* (*a*) to give (sth.) away; to give (sth.) up, to sacrifice (sth.); (*b*) to hand (s.o.) over, to deliver (s.o.) up (to enemies, etc.); *B:* **welcher ist um unsrer Sünden willen dahingegeben**, who was delivered for our offences.

dahingegen [da·hin'ge:gən], *pron. adv.* (*a*) in opposition to it; **er war für sofortiges Handeln, d. war ich der Meinung, daß . . .**, he wanted immediate action, but I thought that . . .; (*b*) = **dagegen II.** (*a*).

dahingehen, *v.i. sep.* (*strong*) (*sein*) 1. to go, to move (along). 2. (*a*) to pass, to disappear; **das Leben geht schnell dahin**, life passes, goes by, quickly; **die Jahre gehen dahin**, the years pass, are passing; (*b*) *Lit:* to die, to pass away; *B:* **des Menschen Sohn gehet zwar dahin**, the Son of Man goeth.

dahingehend. 1. [da·'hin-] *pr.p. of* **dahingehen.** 2. ['da·'hin] *adv.* (*incorrect*) = **dahin gehend**, *q.v. under* **dahin** 3 (*d*).

dahingestellt [da·'hin-], *a.* **es d. sein lassen**, (**ob . . .**), to leave it undecided (whether . . .), to form no opinion as to (whether . . .); **wir wollen es d. sein lassen, ob seine Handlungsweise richtig oder falsch war, aber . . .**, leaving aside the question of whether his action was right or not . . .; **es bleibt d., ob . . .**, (i) it remains to be seen whether . . ., (ii) it's impossible to judge, say, whether . . . .

dahinleben, *v.i. sep.* (*haben*) to live, to go on existing, from day to day; **gedankenlos d.**, to live, go on existing, from day to day with no thought for the future; **sie haben nun fünfzehn Jahre lang nebeneinander dahingelebt**, they've been living alongside each other now for fifteen years.

dahinscheiden, *v.i. sep.* (*strong*) (*sein*) to pass away, to depart this life; **der Dahingeschiedene**, the departed.

dahinsein, *v.i. sep.* (*sein*) (*conj. like* **sein**) 1. to have gone, to have disappeared; (*a*) **die Träume der Jugend sind dahin**, the dreams of youth have passed, are no more; **der Sommer ist dahin**, summer is past, is over; (*b*) to be dead, to have passed away, to be no more. 2. to be spoilt, ruined, destroyed; **die ganze Ernte ist dahin**, all the crops are ruined; **die ganze Stadt ist dahin**, the whole city has gone, has disappeared, has been destroyed; *B:* **mein Volk ist dahin**, my people are destroyed.

dahinsiechen, *v.i. sep.* (*sein*) (*of pers.*) to waste away.

dahinstehen, *v.i. sep.* (*strong*) (*haben*) to be undecided, uncertain; **es steht noch dahin, ob wir morgen kommen können**, it is still uncertain, it is still a matter of doubt, whether we shall be able to come tomorrow.

dahinten [da·'hintən], *adv.* behind, back there; **d. ist es**, it's back there.

dahintenbleiben, *v.i. sep.* (*strong*) (*sein*) *A:* to remain behind.

dahinter [da·'hintər], *pron. adv.* 1. behind (it, them); **ein Haus mit einem Garten d.**, a house with a garden behind (it), at the back (of it); **die Alpen und die Ebenen d.**, the Alps and the plains behind, beyond; **ein schönes Gesicht, aber nichts d.**, a beautiful face, but nothing behind it; **zuerst kamen Soldaten zu Pferde, d. kam die Musik**, first came soldiers on horseback and behind them the band; **in der Mitte war ein Tisch, und d. stand, war, ein Stuhl**, in the centre there was a table, and behind it stood a chair; **im Vorzimmer stand ein Schreibtisch; d. saß eine Sekretärin**, in the ante-room was a desk and behind it sat a secretary; **er öffnete die Tür und verbarg sich d.**, he opened the door and hid behind it; **es ist nichts d.**, (i) there is nothing

behind it; (ii) it's of no value; (iii) there's nothing, no mystery, behind it; *see also* **dahinterkommen, dahintersein, dahintersetzen, dahintersitzen, dahinterstecken, dahinterstehen. 2.** *rel. use A. & Lit:* behind which.

dahinterher [da·hintər'heːr], *adv.* (*a*) behind; (*b*) **d. sein, etwas zu tun,** to be very keen on, at pains to do, sth.; **sie sind tüchtig d.,** they are taking great pains over it; **sie war sehr d., uns zu überzeugen,** she was very keen, dead set, on convincing us, she was at great pains to convince us.

dahinterkommen, *v.i. sep.* (*strong*) (*sein*) to find out about it; to get at the truth about sth.; **er wird schon bald d.,** he'll find out about it soon, it won't take him long to find out about it.

dahintermachen (sich), *v.refl. sep.* to go hard at it.

dahintersein, *v.i. sep.* (*sein*) (*conj. like* **sein**) **bei j-m d.,** (i) to chivvy s.o. up; (ii) to keep an eye on s.o.; **man muß ständig d., sonst machen einem die Leute nichts fertig,** one has to keep on chivvying, otherwise nothing gets done.

dahintersetzen, *v.sep.* **1.** *v.tr.* to put (s.o.) on to it; **wir haben unseren Anwalt dahintergesetzt,** we have put our solicitor on to it. **2. sich dahintersetzen,** to put one's back into it, to go hard at it; **du wirst dich ordentlich d. müssen,** you'll have to put your back into it, *F:* you'll have to pull up your socks, to buckle to.

dahintersitzen, *v.i. sep.* (*strong*) (*haben*) to go hard at it; **jetzt sitzt er tüchtig dahinter,** now he's going really hard at it.

dahinterstecken, *v.i. sep.* (*haben*) (*a*) to be behind it; **es steckt etwas dahinter,** there's something behind it, there's more to it than meets the eye; **ich will wissen, was dahintersteckt,** I want to know what's behind it; **es steckt nichts dahinter,** there's nothing, no mystery, behind it; (*b*) to be at the bottom of it; **dieser verdächtig aussehende Mann steckt wohl dahinter,** I think that suspicious-looking man is behind it, at the bottom of it.

dahinterstehen, *v.i. sep.* (*strong*) (*haben*) to be behind it (*i.e. an enterprise, etc.*); **die reichsten Leute des Landes stehen dahinter,** the richest people in the country are behind, backing, it.

Dahlie ['daːliə], *f.* **-/-n.** *Bot:* dahlia.

Dahome [da·ho·'meː]. **1.** *Pr.n.n.* **-s.** *Geog:* Dahomey. **2.** *m. & f. inv.* Dahoman.

dahomisch [da·'hoːmiʃ], *a.* Dahoman.

Daidalos ['daida·los]. *Pr.n.m.* **-'.=Dädalos.**

Daimyo, Daimio ['daimioː], *m.* **-/-s.** *Hist:* daimio (*feudal prince in Japan*).

Dajak ['daːjak], *m.* **-(s)/-s.** *Ethn:* Dyak.

Dajaldrossel ['daːjal-], *f.* *Orn:* dayal-bird, magpie-robin.

Dakapo [da·'kaːpoː], *n.* **-s/-s=Dacapo.**

Daker ['daːkər], *m.* **-s/-=Dazier.**

Dakien ['daːkiən]. *Pr.n.n.* **-s=Dazien.**

dakish ['daːkiʃ], *a.*=**dazisch.**

Dakryolith [dakry·o·'liːt], *m.* **-en/-en.** *Med:* dacryolith.

Dakryon ['dakry·on], *n.* **-s/.** *Anat:* dacryon.

daktylisch [dak'tyːliʃ], *a. Pros:* dactylic (verse).

Daktylograph [dakty·lo·'graːf], *m.* **-en/-en.** *Swiss:* typist.

Daktylologie [dakty·lo·lo·'giː], *f.* **-/.** dactylography, dactylology.

Daktyloskopie [dakty·lo·sko·'piː], *f.* **-/-n** [-'piːən], finger-print identification, dactyloscopy.

Daktylus ['dakty·lus], *m.* **-/-len** [-'tyːlən]. *Pros:* dactyl.

Dalai-Lama, der ['daːlai 'laːmaː], *m.* **-s/.** *Buddhist Rel:* the Dalai Lama, the Grand Lama.

dalassen, *v.tr. sep.* (*strong*) to leave (sth.) behind; **er hat seinen Mantel dagelassen,** he left his coat behind.

Dalbe, *f.* **-/-n,** *usu.pl.* **Dalben,** *Nau:* (*group of mooring posts*) dolphin.

daliegen, *v.i. sep.* (*strong*) (*haben*) to lie (there); **hingestreckt d.,** to lie (there) stretched out; **ich sah ihn krank, tot, d.,** I saw him lying (there) ill, dead.

Dalila [da·'liːlaː]. *Pr.n.f.* **-s** *& Lit:* **-lens.** Delilah.

Dalk, *m.* **-(e)s/-e.** *Austrian Dial:* simpleton, fool.

dalket, *a. Austrian Dial:* clumsy.

Dalle, *f.* **-/-n=Dalbe.**

Dalles ['daləs], *m.* **-/.** *F:* **im D. sein, den D. haben, an D. leiden,** *F:* to be hard up, to be (stony) broke.

dalli, *int. F:* **(mach) d.! ein bißchen d.!** hurry up! *F:* get a move on! step on it! get cracking!

Dalmatien [dal'maːtsiən]. *Pr.n.n.* **-s.** *Geog:* Dalmatia.

Dalmatika [dal'maːti·kaː], *f.* **-/-ken.** *Ecc.Cost:* dalmatic.

Dalmatiner [dalma·'tiːnər], *m.* **-s/-. 1.** native of Dalmatia, Dalmatian. **2.** Dalmatian (dog).

dalmatinisch [dalma·'tiːniʃ], *a.* Dalmatian.

dalmatisch [dal'maːtiʃ], *a.* Dalmatian.

dalo-nordisch, *a. Ethn:* Dalo-Nordic.

Daltonismus [dalto·'nismus], *m.* **-/.** *Med:* daltonism.

Dam, *m.* **-(e)s/-e.** *Z:* fallow deer; buck.

damalig ['daːmaːliç], *a.* then, of that time; **der damalige Präsident,** the then president, the president at that time; **meine damalige Lage,** my situation at that time; **die damaligen Gesetze, Menschen,** the laws, people, of that time, of that day, of those days; **in der damaligen Zeit,** at that time, in those days.

damals, *adv.* then, at that time; in those days; **d. gab es noch keine Eisenbahn,** in those days there were no railways; **die Leute (von) d.,** the people of that time; **d., als . . . ,** (in the days, at the time) when . . .; **bis d., als . . . ,** (up) till the time when . . .; **erst d.,** only then, not till then; **seit d.,** since then, since that time; **schon d.,** even then, even in those days, even at that time.

Damaskus [da·'maskus]. *Pr.n.n.* **-'.** *Geog:* Damascus; **sein D. erleben, finden,** to be converted, to become a new man.

Damassé [dama'seː], *m.* **-s/-s.** *Tex:* damask silk.

damassieren [dama'siːrən], *v.i.* (*haben*) *Tex:* to damask.

Damassin [dama'sɛ̃ː], *m.* **-(s)/-s.** *Tex:* light cotton damask, damassin.

Damast [da·'mast, 'damast], *m.* **-es/-e. 1.** *Tex:* damask. **2.** *Metall:* damask steel.

Damastarbeit, *f.* damask-work.

damasten [da·'mastən, 'damastən], *a. Tex:* damask.

Damastpapier, *n.* damask paper.

Damastweber, *m.* damask weaver.

Damastweberei, *f.* damask-work.

Damaszene [da·mas'tseːnə], *f.* **-/-n.** *Hort:* damson.

Damaszener [da·mas'tseːnər]. **1.** *m.* **-s/-,** (*a*) *Geog:* Damascene; (*b*) Damascene sword-blade. **2.** *inv.a.* Damascene; **D. Stahl,** damask steel; *Bot:* **D. Rose,** damask rose; **D. Pflaume,** (i) satin-leaf; (ii) damson; **kleine D. (Pflaume),** bullace.

damaszenisch [da·mas'tseːniʃ], *a.* Damascene.

damaszieren [da·mas'tsiːrən], *v.tr. Metalw:* to inlay, damascene, damaskeen (blade, etc.); **damaszierter Stahl,** damask steel; **Damaszierung** *f,* damascening, damaskeening.

Damaszierer [da·mas'tsiːrər], *m.* **-s/-.** *Metalw:* damascener, damaskeener.

Dambock, *m. Z:* fallow deer; buck.

Dambose [dam'boːzə], *f.* **-/.** *Ch:* inosite, inosin.

Dambrett, *n.*=**Damebrett.**

Dämchen, *n.* **-s/-.** *Pej:* (*a*) spoilt, fine, lady; (*b*) lady of easy virtue, loose woman.

Dame, *f.* **-/-n. 1.** lady; (*a*) **junge, alte, D.,** young, old, lady; (*spoken form of address*) **meine D.,** madam; **meine Damen (und Herren)!** ladies (and gentlemen)! **treten Sie doch herein, meine Damen!** won't you come in, ladies? (*in shop*) **die D. wünschen?** what does madam require? can I help madam? *F:* **meine alte D.,** my mother, *F:* the mater; (*on door of public convenience, etc.*) **'Damen',** 'Ladies'; *Bot:* **D. in Trauer,** iris; (*b*) **adlige D.,** lady of the nobility, noble lady; **der Ritter und seine D.,** the knight and his lady; **eine feine, große, vornehme, D.,** a fine, great, lady; **die (vornehme) D. spielen,** to play the fine lady; to set up for a lady; **wie eine D. aussehen,** to look a lady; **ganz D. sein,** to be a perfect lady; **dazu ist sie zu sehr D.,** she's too much the lady to do that; **D. der Gesellschaft,** society lady; **D. von Welt,** lady of poise and experience; (*c*) *Pej:*=**Dämchen. 2.** (*a*) *Cards:* queen; (*b*) *Draughts:* (i) (the game of) draughts, *U.S:* checkers; **D. spielen,** to have a game of, to play, draughts; (ii) king; (*c*) *Chess:* queen; (*of pawn*) **zur D. gehen,** to queen, to go to queen; **sich** *dat.* **eine D. machen, die D. ziehen, in die D. gehen,** to queen a pawn.

Damebrett, *n.* draught-board, *U.S:* checker-board.

Dämel, *m.* **-s/-,** fool, *F:* ass, blockhead, fathead.

Däm(e)lack, *m.* **-s/-e** *&* **-s.** *F:* (*a*) fool, *F:* ass, blockhead, fathead; (*b*) dreamer.

Dämelei, *f.* **-/-en.** *F:* foolishness, tomfoolery.

dämelich, *a.*=**dämlich.**

dämeln, *v.i.* (*haben*) *F:* (*a*) to talk nonsense; (*b*) to fool about; (*c*) to be dizzy, *F:* dopey.

Damenabteil, *n. Rail:* compartment for ladies only; 'ladies only' compartment.

Damenartikel, *m. Com:* article for the use of ladies; *pl.* **Damenartikel,** ladies' articles, ladies' requisites.

Damenbad, *n.* ladies' (public) bath(s).

Damenbart, *m.* superfluous facial hair (on women).

Damenbekleidung, *f. Com:* ladies' wear.

Damenbesuch, *m.* (*a*) visit from a lady, woman, *or* from ladies, women; (*b*) lady, woman, visitor *or* lady, women, visitors.

Damenbinde, *f.* (*woman's*) sanitary towel, *U.S:* sanitary napkin.

Damendoppel, *n. Ten:* women's doubles.

Dameneinzel, *n. Ten:* women's singles.

Damenfahrrad, *n.* lady's bicycle.

Damenfriede, der. *Hist:* the treaty of Cambrai, the *paix des dames.*

Damenfriseur, *m.* ladies' hairdresser.

Damengesellschaft, *f.* **1.** company of ladies *or* of a lady, female company; **in D.,** in the company of ladies *or* of a lady. **2.** company, group, party, of ladies. **3.** party for ladies, *F:* hen-party.

damenhaft, *a.* (*a*) ladylike; (*b*) (*of small girl*) grown-up.

Damenhandschuh, *m.* lady's, woman's, glove.

Damenheld, *m. F:* (*a*) lady-killer; (*b*) carpet-knight.

Damenhemd, *n.* lady's, woman's, vest.

Damenhose, *f.* (pair of) ladies', women's, slacks.

Damenhut, *m.* lady's, woman's, hat.

Damenkleid, *n.* (lady's, woman's) dress; *pl.* **Damenkleider,** ladies' dresses; ladies' clothes.

Damenkleiderstoff, *m. Tex:*=**Damenstoff.**

Damenkleidung, *f.* ladies' clothes; *Com:* ladies' wear.

Damenkonfektion, *f.* ladies' ready-to-wear, ready-made, clothes.

Damenlandung, *f. Av: F:* upside-down landing.

Damenmantel, *m.* lady's, woman's, (over)coat.

Damennachthemd, *n.* night-dress, *U.S:* -gown.

Damenpartie, *f.* **1.** company, group, party, of ladies. **2.** excursion, party, for ladies only.

Damenpferd, *n.* lady's horse.

Damenrad, *n.* lady's bicycle.

Damensattel, *m.* side-saddle.

Damenschlüpfer, *m.* (pair of) ladies', womens' (i) knickers, (ii) panties.

Damenschneider, *m.* ladies' tailor.

Damenschneiderei, *f.* **1.** dressmaking; ladies' tailoring. **2.** tailor's shop, dressmaker's.

Damenschneiderin, *f.* dressmaker.

Damenschuh, *m.* lady's, woman's, shoe; *pl.* **Damenschuhe,** ladies' shoes.

Damensitz, *m.* side-saddle; **(im) D. reiten,** to ride side-saddle.

Damenslip, *m.* (pair of) ladies', women's, briefs.

Damenspiel, *n.*=**Damespiel.**

Damenspringer, *m. Chess:* queen's knight.

Damenstift, *n.* home for gentlewomen; community of gentlewomen.

Damenstoff, *m. Tex:* material for ladies' clothes, ladies' material.

Damenstrümpfe, *m.pl.* ladies', women's, stockings; *Com:* ladies' hose.

Damenuhr, *f.* lady's watch.

Damenwahl, *f. Danc:* lady's choice.

Damenwäsche, *f.* ladies' underwear; lingerie.

Damenweg, der. *Geog:* the Chemin-des-dames.

Damenwelt, die, (the) ladies; **beliebt bei der D.,** popular with the ladies.

Damenzigarre, *f.* lady's cigar; whiff.

Damenzimmer, *n.* **1.** (*in private house*) lady's sitting-room; lady's sanctum; lady's boudoir. **2.** (*in hotel, etc.*) ladies' lounge.

Damespiel, *n.* **1.** (the game of) draughts, *U.S:* checkers. **2.** draught-board and pieces, *U.S:* checker-board and checkers.

Damestein, *m. Draughts:* piece, (draughts)-man.

Damgeiß, *f. Z:* doe (of fallow deer).

Damhirsch, *m. Z:* fallow deer; buck.

Damiette [da·mi'ɛt(ə)]. *Pr.n.n.* **-s.** *Geog:* Damietta.

damisch, *a. South G.Dial:*=**dämlich.**

dämisch, *a. A:*=**dämlich.**

damit. I. *pron. adv.* [da·'mit, *when emphatic* 'daːmit.] **1.** (*a*) with it, with them; **was macht man d.?** what does one do with it, them, (*emphatic*) that, those? **die Katze fraß die Maus nicht, sondern spielte nur d.,** the cat didn't eat the mouse, but just played with it; **Sie haben die Papiere, also heraus d.!** you've got the papers, so hand them over! (*emphatic*) **d. ist nichts anzufangen,** there's nothing to be done with that, those; **siehst du das rote Auto dort drüben? d. bin ich gestern gefahren,** do you see that red car over there? I went for a drive in it yesterday; (*b*) with it; by it; thereby; **hör auf d.!** stop it, that! **was hat er denn d. zu tun?** what has he to do with it, (*emphatic*) with that? **was meint sie d.? was will sie d. sagen?** what does she mean by it,

(*emphatic*) by that? (*emphatic*) **d. hilft man nicht**, one does no good by that, like that, that doesn't help; (*emphatic*) **d. wollen wir gar nicht sagen, daß . . .,** we don't in the least mean by that that . . .; (*emphatic*) **d. will ich nichts zu tun haben**, I don't want to have anything to do with that; **damit bewies er seine Schuld**, he thereby proved himself guilty; (*c*) **es ist nichts d.**, it's no good; **es hat nichts d. auf sich**, it's of no importance, significance; (*emphatic*) **d. hat's noch Zeit**, that can wait; (*d*) (*emphatic*) with that, thereupon; **und d. verließ er das Zimmer**, whereupon he left the room, and thereupon, and with that, he left the room; **und d. hatte die Sache ein Ende**, and there the matter rested, ended; *see also* **basta**. **2.** (*a*) **d. einverstanden sein, daß etwas geschieht**, to agree to sth.'s happening; **ich bin d. einverstanden, daß er zwei Tage hier bleibt**, I agree to his staying here for two days; (*b*) **d., daß . . .,** by (+*gerund*); **du machst die Sache nicht besser d., daß du jetzt heulst**, you don't improve matters by crying; **d., daß du ihn ins Haus genommen hast, hast du ihm nichts Gutes getan**, you haven't helped him by taking him into your house. **3.** *rel. use A. & Lit:* with which; by which; wherewith; whereby.

II. **damit** [daˑˈmit], *conj.* so that, in order that, in order to, so as to; (*a*) (*verb in main clause in past, verb in subsidiary clause in past subjunctive*) **ich nahm die Medizin, d. ich nicht krank würde**, I took the medicine so as not to, in order not to, so that I should not, get ill; **wir gaben ihm eine Liste, d. er nichts vergäße**, we gave him a list so that he wouldn't forget anything; (*b*) (*verb in main clause in primary tense, verb in subsidiary clause in indicative*) **man muß taktvoll mit ihm umgehen, d. er sich nicht ärgert**, one has to be tactful with him, so that he doesn't get angry, so as not to anger him.

Damkalb, Damkitz, *n. Z:* fawn (of fallow deer).

damledern, *a.* buckskin.

dämlich, *a. F:* (*a*) silly, stupid, foolish, *F:* asinine; (*b*) dizzy, *F:* dopey; **mir war ganz d. im Kopf davon**, it made my head go round, swim; *see also* **dumm** 1; (*c*) huge, enormous, terrific; **ich habe dämliches Glück gehabt**, I had terrific good luck.

Dämlichkeit, *f. F:* foolishness, silliness.

Dämling, *m.* -(e)s/-e. **1.** *Z:* (little) fallow deer. **2.**=**Dämel.**

Damm, *m.* -(e)s/-̈e. **1.** (*a*) dike; causeway; bank, embankment, *U.S:* levee (of waterway); (*in river, etc.*) dam; weir; *Hyd.E:* dam, barrage; *Min:* dam; *Metall:* (i) dam(-stone) (of furnace); (ii) casting pit; **einen D. bauen, aufführen, aufwerfen**, to build a dike, an embankment, a dam; **nach der Sturmflut war der D. an mehreren Stellen durchbrochen, gerissen**, after the high tide the dike had burst in several places; **die Insel ist durch einen D. mit dem Festland verbunden**, the island is connected to the mainland by a causeway; (*b*) *Nau: etc:* (i) pier; jetty; (ii) breakwater; (*c*) *F:* barrier; check; **j-m einen D. entgegensetzen**, to check s.o.'s advance, to put an obstacle in s.o.'s way, path. **2.** (*a*) *Rail: etc:* embankment; (*b*) roadway; (*c*) *F:* **auf dem D. sein**, to be alert, *F:* to be on one's toes; **nicht recht auf dem D. sein**, *F:* to be out of sorts, to be under the weather, to feel seedy, not to be up to the mark; **wieder auf dem D. sein**, (i) to be well again; (ii) *F:* to be on one's feet, afloat, again; **j-n auf den D. bringen**, (i) *F:* to put s.o. on his feet, to give s.o. a leg up; (ii) to chase s.o. off. **3.** *Anat:* perineum.

Dammar [ˈdamaːr], *n.* -s/. *Com:* dammar(-resin).

Dammarafichte [daˈmaːraː-], *f. Bot:*=**Dammarfichte.**

Dammarfichte [ˈdamaːr-], *f. Bot:* dammara, dammar pine; **australische D.**, kauri pine.

Dammarharz, *n. Com:* dammar (resin).

Dämmatte, *f. Constr:* insulating mat *or* pad (*for thermal or sound insulation*).

Dammbalken, *m. Hyd.E:* stop log.

Dämmbrett, *n. Tls:* smoother.

Dammbruch, *m.* **1.** breach in a dam, in a dike, *U.S:* crevasse. **2.** *Med:* perineal hernia.

Dammel, *m.* -s/-. *North G.Dial:*=**Dämel.**

dämmen. I. *v.tr.* to dike (land against sea); to embank (river, etc.); to dam (river, etc.); *F:* to check (s.o., sth.); to stem the tide of (s.o.'s anger, etc.); to dam up the tide of (s.o.'s eloquence).

II. *vbl s.* **Dämmen** *n.*, **Dämmung** *f. in vbl senses; also:* embankment.

Dämmer, *m.* -s/. *Poet:* (morning and evening) half-light, twilight, dusk; (*at evening*) gloaming.

Dammerde, *f.* (*a*) *Hort:* humus, (vegetable-)mould; (*b*) *Metall:* foundry sand.

dämmerhaft, *a.* (*a*) dim, (rather) dark; (*b*) half-awake, dazed (condition); (*c*) uncertain, vague, shadowy (forms, etc.).

dämm(e)rig, *a.* **1.** (*a*) dim, (rather) dark; **es ist noch d.**, it is still rather dark, it is still dusk, it is not yet light; **es wird d.**, (i) it is growing dark, the light is fading, dusk is falling; (ii) it is growing light; **der dämmrige Schein der Kerzen, der Lampen**, the dim, faint, light of the candles, of the lamps; (*b*) gloomy, dull (day). **2.** vague, uncertain, indefinite, shadowy (forms, etc.).

Dämmerlicht, *n.* half-light, twilight, dusk; **beim, im, D.**, in the half-light, twilight, (i) in the dusk (of evening), in the gloaming; (ii) in the morning twilight; **im D. des sinkenden Abends**, in the approaching twilight, in the falling dusk; **im D. des Krankenzimmers**, in the half-darkness of the sick-room.

dämmern. I. *v.i.* (*haben*) **1.** to dawn, to grow light; (*of hope, etc.*) to dawn; **der Tag, der Morgen, dämmert**, *v.impers.* **es dämmert**, day is breaking, dawning, the dawn is coming, it is growing light; **in dämmernder Frühe**, at the crack of dawn, in the early dawn; *F:* **jetzt dämmert's bei mir**, now it dawns on me, now I begin to realize; **es dämmert mir ganz schwach, daß . . .,** I have a vague idea that . . ., I remember dimly that . . . . **2.** (*a*) to grow dark, to become twilight; **es dämmert, der Abend dämmert**, it is growing dark, dusk; twilight, dusk, is falling; **im dämmernden Schein des Abends**, in the fading light of evening; (*b*) to be dark, dim; **es dämmerte im Saal**, it was dark, the light was dim, in the hall; **im dämmernden Saal**, in the dim light of the hall; (*c*) (*of light, candle, etc.*) to shine faintly, feebly; to diffuse a feeble light; **der dämmernde Schein der Kerzen**, the faint, feeble, light of the candles.

II. *vbl s.* **Dämmern** *n. in vbl senses; also:* dawn; *cp.* **Dämmerung.**

Dämmerschein, *m.* (i) first light, half-light, early dawn; (ii) twilight, dusk (of evening); **beim ersten D.**, at first light, at early dawn, in the half-light; **beim D. der Kerzen**, in the faint, feeble, light of the candles.

Dämmerschlaf, *m.* **1.** half-sleep, light sleep. **2.** *Obst:* twilight sleep.

Dämmerstunde, *f.* (evening) twilight, dusk (of evening); **in der D.**, at twilight, at dusk; **'Musik zur D.'**, 'Music at Twilight', 'Twilight Hour'.

Dämmerung, *f.* half-light, twilight, dusk; (*in the morning*) dawn; **astronomische, bürgerliche, D.**, astronomical, civil, twilight; **in der D.**, (i) at dusk, at twilight, in the dusk of evening, in the gloaming; (ii) at dawn, in the morning twilight; **beim ersten Schein der D.**, at first light; **in der D. Geschichten erzählen**, to tell stories in the (evening) twilight.

Dämmerungsfalter, *m. Ent:*=**Nachtfalter.**

Dämmerungssehen, *n.* twilight vision, scotopic vision.

Dämmerzustand, *m.* dazed, half-awake, condition; twilight state (following epileptic fit, etc.).

Dammfluß, *m.* river flowing on a higher level than the surrounding land.

Dammgrube, *f. Metall:* casting-pit.

Dämmplatte, *f. Constr:* insulating board (*for thermal or sound insulation*).

Dammriff, *n. Ph.Geog:* barrier reef.

dämmrig, *a. see* **dämm(e)rig.**

Dammriß, *m. Med:* perineal tear.

Dämmstoff, *m. Constr:* insulating material (*for thermal or sound insulation*).

Dämmung, *f. see* **dämmen II.**

Dammweg, *m.* causeway.

damnabel [damˈnaːbəl], *a.* damnable.

damnifizieren [damniˑfiˑˈtsiːrən], *v.tr. Jur: A:* to damnify.

Damno [ˈdamnoː], *m. & n.* -s/. *Com:* loss, discount (on mortgages, security, etc.).

Damokles [ˈdaːmoˑkles]. *Pr.n.m.* -ˈ. *A.Hist:* Damocles.

Damoklesschwert, das, the sword of Damocles.

Dämon [ˈdɛːmon], *m.* -s/-en [dɛˑˈmoːnən], (*a*) *Myth:* demon, (good, evil) genius; spirit; *F:* **mein guter D.**, my good genius; (*b*) **(böser) D.**, evil spirit, evil genius; demon, devil, fiend; **er ist ihr böser D.**, he is her evil genius.

Dämonenglaube, *m.* demonism.

dämonenhaft, *a.*=**dämonisch** 1.

Dämonie [dɛˑmoˑˈniː], *f.* -/-n [-ˈniːən], demonic nature; **die D. Nietzsches**, the demonic, the demonic element, in Nietzsche, Nietzsche's demonic nature.

dämonisch [dɛˑˈmoːniʃ] *a.* **1.** (*a*) of the nature of a demon; demoniac, demoniacal, demonic; (*b*) demonic, diabolical (force, attraction, etc.); demoniac (glance, appearance); (person) possessed (of a devil); demoniac(al) (person). **2. das Dämonische**, (i) the demonic (element); (ii) the demoniac, the demoniacal (element); **das Dämonische bei Goethe**, the demonic in Goethe, in Goethe's works; **das Dämonische in Goethe**, the demonic element in Goethe's nature.

Dämonismus [dɛˑmoˑˈnismus], *m.* -/. *Hist. of Rel:* demonism.

Dämonologie [dɛˑmoˑnoˑloˑˈgiː], *f.* -/-n [-ˈgiːən], demonology.

Dampf, *m.* -(e)s/-̈e. **1.** *Ph: Mch:* steam; **nasser, feuchter, D.**, wet steam; **trockener, getrockneter, D.**, dry steam; **gesättigter D.**, saturated steam; **ungesättigter, überhitzter, D.**, superheated steam; **mit D. betrieben, angetrieben, werden**, to work by steam; **durch D. erwärmt**, heated by steam; **D. aufmachen**, to get up steam, to raise steam; **D. aufhaben**, to have steam up; **D. erzeugen**, to generate steam; **den D. ablassen, abblasen, ausblasen, auslassen**, to let off, blow off, steam; **den D. abschneiden, absperren**, to cut off the steam; **den D. anlassen**, to put steam on; **den vollen D. anlassen**, to put on full steam, to make all steam; **mit vollem D.**, at full steam, with all steam on; **unter D. sein**, to be under steam; *F:* **mit vollem D. an die Arbeit gehen**, to set to work with a will; *F:* **D. dahintermachen, dahintersetzen**, (i) to go at it with a will; (ii) to give things a push, to chivvy things along; *F:* **D. geben**, (i) *Aut:* to accelerate; *F:* to step, tread, on the gas; (ii) to make haste; *F:* to step, tread, on the gas. **2.** (*pl.* **Dämpfe**) (*a*) mist, haze, vapour (over meadow, etc.); steam (from hot food, hot body, etc.); (visible) breath; *B:* **denn was ist euer Leben? ein D. ist's . . .,** for what is your life? it is even as a vapour . . .; *Ind: etc:* **Dämpfe**, fumes, *U.S:* vapors (of ammonia, alcohol, etc.); (*b*) **(ein) Hans D. (in allen Gassen)**, (i) a busybody, one who has a finger in every pie; (ii) a jack-of-all-trades. **3.** smoke (from gunpowder, etc.). **4.** (*a*) *A:* annoyance, vexation; **j-m (den) D. antun**, to annoy s.o.; (*b*) intoxication; (*c*) *F:* fear; *F:* **D. kriegen, haben**, *F:* to have, get, the wind up. **5.** *Vet:* broken wind (in horses); **den D. haben**, to be broken-winded.

Dampfabblaserohr, *n. Mch:* waste-steam pipe; exhaust-pipe.

Dampfabscheider, *m.* steam-separator.

Dampfabsperrschieber, *m. Mch:* gate-valve.

Dampfakkumulator, *m. Ind:* steam-accumulator.

Dampfantrieb, *m. Mec.E:* steam drive; **Maschine mit D.**, steam-driven machine, machine working by steam.

Dampfarbeit, *f. Mch:* work done by steam.

Dampfaustritt, *m. Mch:* escape of steam.

Dampfaustrittskanal, *m.*, **Dampfaustrittsöffnung**, *f. Mch:* exhaust port.

Dampfbad, *n.* Russian bath; steam-bath; *Med:* vapour-bath; *Ind: Dom.Ec:* steam-bath.

Dampfbarkasse, *f. Nau:* steam-launch.

Dampfboot, *n.* steamboat, (small) steamer.

Dampfbremse, *f. Rail:* steam brake.

dampfdicht, *a.* steam-tight.

Dampfdom, *m. Mch:* steam-dome.

Dampfdreschmaschine, *f. Husb:* steam-thresher.

Dampfdruck, *m.* **1.** steam-pressure. **2.** vapour-pressure.

Dampfdruckmesser, *m.* steam (pressure-)gauge.

Dampfdruckregelventil, *n. Mch:* reducing-valve.

Dampfdüse, *f.* steam-nozzle.

Dampfeinlaß, *m. Mch: etc:* steam-inlet.

Dampfeinströmungsrohr, *n. Mch: etc:* steam-inlet.

Dampfeintrittsflansch, *m. Mch: etc:* steam-inlet (of cylinder).

Dampfeintrittsöffnung, *f. Mch:* steam-port, induction-port.

dampfen, *v.* **1.** *v.i.* (*a*) (*haben*) to steam; **die Wiese dampfte nach dem Regen**, the meadow was steaming after the rain; **ihre Pferde dampften**, their horses were steaming; **dampfend heiße Suppe**, steaming hot soup; (*b*) (*sein*) (*of ship, train*) to steam (along, away, off); *F:* (*of pers.*) to go (to a place), to leave (for a place), by steamship *or* train; **das Schiff dampfte aus dem Hafen**, the ship steamed out of the harbour; *F:* **er dampfte nach Amerika**, he went to America (by steamship). **2.** *v.tr.* to smoke (pipe).

dämpfen. I. *v.tr.* **1.** (*a*) to deaden, muffle, *Cin:* to damp (sound); to muffle (drum, bell. oars); to mute (bowed instrument, brass instrument); to soften (colour, light); *F:* to suppress, curb (emotion); to damp (enthusiasm); **gedämpfte**

Musik, (i) soft music, (ii) far-away music; **gedämpfte Stimmen,** muffled voices; **sie sprachen mit gedämpfter Stimme,** they spoke in, with, hushed, lowered, voices; **gedämpftes Licht,** soft, shaded, subdued, light; **ihre Freude war gedämpft,** her joy was muted; (*b*) to bank, damp down (furnace). **2.** (*a*) *Ph: Mec: etc:* to damp (out) (oscillations); *El:* to damp (a magnetic needle); (*b*) *Av:* to stabilize (aircraft); (*c*) *W.Tel: etc:* to attenuate (wave). **3.** *Cu:* to stew, braise (meat); to steam (fish, potatoes, etc.); to stew (fruit).

II. *vbl s.* **1. Dämpfen,** *n. in vbl senses.* **2. Dämpfung,** *f.*=II. 1; *also: Av:* stabilization (of aircraft); *Cin:* (sound-)deadening, (sound-) damping; *W.Tel: etc:* attenuation (of wave).

Dampfentweichung, *f. Ph: Mch: etc:* escape of steam.

Dampfer, *m.* **-s/-,** steamer, steamship.

Dämpfer, *m.* **-s/-. 1.** *Mch: etc:* damper; *Mus:* damper (of piano); mute (for bowed, brass, instrument); *F:* **j-s Begeisterung, j-m, einen D. aufsetzen,** to damp s.o.'s enthusiasm; to put a damper on s.o.'s enthusiasm. **2.** *Ind: Agr: etc:* steamer.

Dampferlinie, *f.* steamship line.

Dampfgummi, *n. Ch: Ind:* dextrin(e).

Dampfhahn, *m.* steam-cock.

Dampfhammer, *m.* steam-hammer.

Dampfheizung, *f.* steam-heating, (central) heating by steam.

dampfig, *a.* steamy; vaporous.

dämpfig, *a. Vet:* broken-winded (horse).

Dämpfigkeit, *f. Vet:* broken wind.

Dampfjacht, *f.* steam-yacht.

Dampfjacke, *f. Mch:*=**Dampfmantel.**

Dampfkammer, *f. Ind:* steam-chest; steam-chamber.

Dampfkasten, *m. Mch:* steam-box, -chest, -chamber.

Dampfkessel, *m.* **1.** steam-boiler. **2.** *Med:* steam-kettle.

Dampfkesselwärter, *m.* boilerman, stoker.

dampfklar, *a. Nau:* **d. sein,** to be under steam, in steam, to have steam up.

Dampfkocher, *m.* **1.** *Cu:* pressure-cooker. **2.** *Surg: etc:* sterilizer.

Dampfkochtopf, *m. Cu:*=**Dampfkocher 1.**

Dampfkochung, *f. Ind:* heating (of liquids) by steam.

Dampfkohle, *f.* steam-coal.

Dampfkolben, *m.* (steam-engine) piston.

Dampfkompresse, *f. Med:* fomentation, hot wet compress.

Dampfkraft, *f.* steam power.

Dampfkran, *m.* steam-crane.

Dampflastwagen, *m.* steam-lorry.

Dampflöffelbagger, *m. Civ.E:* steam-shovel, steam-navvy.

Dampfmantel, *m. Mch:* steam-jacket, cylinder-casing, -jacket.

Dampfmaschine, *f.* steam-engine.

Dampfnudel, *f. Cu:* (sweet yeast) dumpling.

Dampfpfeife, *f.* steam-whistle; (ship's, factory) siren.

Dampfpflug, *m. Agr:* steam plough, tractor plough, *U.S:* steam plow.

Dampfrohr, *n.* steam-pipe.

Dampfroß, *n. Hum:* railway engine, *U.S:* locomotive, *Hum:* iron horse.

Dampfsack, *m. I.C.E:* vapour-lock.

Dampfsammler, *m. Mch: etc:* steam-collector.

Dampfsättiger, *m. Mch:* (steam-)saturator.

Dampfschiff, *n.* steamer, steamship, steam-vessel.

Dampfschiffahrt, *f.* steam navigation.

Dampfschiffahrtsgesellschaft, *f.* steamship company.

Dampfschlange, *f.* steam-coil.

Dampfspeicher, *m. Ind:* steam accumulator.

Dampfspill, *n. Nau:* steam capstan(-engine); steam-winch.

Dampfstrahler, *m. Mch:* (steam-engine) ejector.

Dampfstraßenwalze, *f. Civ.E:*=**Dampfwalze.**

Dampftopf, *m. Dom.Ec:* steamer; *Ch: Pharm: Cu: etc:* digester.

Dampftrockner, *m.* **1.** *Ind:* steam dryer; apparatus for drying by means of steam. **2.** *Mch:* steam separator.

Dampfturbine, *f.* steam turbine.

Dampfumformer, *m. Mch:* desuperheater.

Dämpfung, *f. see* **dämpfen II.**

Dämpfungsentzerrer, *m. W.Tel: Tp: Tg:* attenuation equalizer; equalizing network.

Dämpfungsfläche, *f. Av:* stabilizer.

Dämpfungsflosse, *f. Av:* tailplane.

Dämpfungsglied, *n. El:* attenuator; attenuator pad.

Dämpfungsvorrichtung, *f. Mec.E:* damping device.

Dampfverbrauch, *m. Mch:* steam consumption.

Dampfwagen, *m.* **1.** steam-lorry. **2.** *A:* (railway) train.

Dampfwalze, *f. Civ.E:* steam-roller; *P.N:* **'Achtung D.!'** 'steam-roller at work'; **wie eine D. herankommen,** to crush, *F:* steam-roller, everything in one's path; *Hist: F:* **die russische D.,** the Russian steam-roller.

Dampfwäscherei, *f.* steam laundry.

Dampfweg, *m.* steam-way.

Dampfwinde, *f. Nau: etc:* steam-winch.

Dampfzuteilung, *f. Mch: etc:* steam supply.

Damtier, *n. Z:*=**Damgeiß.**

Damwild, *n. Z: Coll.* fallow deer.

Dan. *Pr.n.n.* **-s.** *B.Geog:* Dan.

danach [da·ˈnaːx, *when emphatic* ˈdaːnaːx], *pron. adv.* **1.** (*a*) behind, after (it, them); (*emphatic*) behind, after, that, those; **voran fuhren die Panzer, d. kamen die Lastwagen,** first came the tanks and behind them, after them, the lorries; (*b*) after (it, them), afterwards, after that; (*emphatic*) after that, after those; **sie aßen Gemüsesuppe und d. Obstsalat,** they ate vegetable soup followed by fruit salad; (*emphatic*) **und d. fuhren wir nach Hause,** and after that we drove home; **bald d.,** soon after(wards), soon after that; **d. lebte er noch zwei Wochen,** he lived for another two weeks after that; **um die Jahrhundertwende und danach,** at the turn of the century and after; **ich habe den Brief zweimal gelesen, d. wußte ich, wie er gemeint war,** I read the letter twice, then I understood how it was meant; (*c*) according to, in accordance with, it, them, (*emphatic*) that, those; accordingly; like that, so; **so lautet die Verordnung, nun richtet euch, handelt, d.!** that is the decree, now act according to, in accordance with, it, now act accordingly! **dieses war sein Glaube, d. hat er gelebt,** this was his creed, and he lived in accordance with it; (*emphatic*) **ich habe seine Lebensbeschreibung gelesen; d. war er ein bedeutender Mann,** I have read his biography; according to, judging by, that he was a man of importance; **sie ist sehr krank, aber sie sieht nicht d. aus,** she is very ill, but she does not look it; **die Kleider sind billig, und sie sind auch d.,** the clothes are cheap and are of correspondingly bad quality; **er hat einen ungeheuren Ehrgeiz, aber seine Begabung ist nicht d.,** he is immensely ambitious, but he is not correspondingly gifted; **er ist nicht der Mann d.,** he is not the man for it, he isn't equal to it; he is not the right type of man; (*emphatic*) **d. sieht er auch aus,** that's just the way he looks, that's just what he looks like, that's just what one would expect judging by his appearance; **er sieht vorzeitig gealtert aus, aber er treibt es auch d.,** he looks prematurely aged, which is hardly surprising considering the life he leads; (*d*) to, for, about, it, them; **hast du dich d. erkundigt?** have you asked, found out, about it, them? **mein Sinn steht nicht d.,** I don't feel like it, I'm not in the mood for it; **ich frage nichts d.,** I don't care about, for, it, them; it means, they mean, nothing to me; **d. streben,** to strive for it, them; **sich d. sehnen,** to long for it, them; **unser Ziel ist Friede; d. streben wir,** our goal is peace; that is what we are striving for; **ein ruhiges Leben bedeutete für sie Glück; sie sehnte sich, es verlangte sie, ihr ganzes Leben lang d.,** a quiet life was her idea of happiness; she longed for it all her life; (*e*) **d.**+*inf.*, **d., daß . . ., d., ob . . .,** (**danach** *in all cases untranslated*); **hast du dich d. erkundigt, hast du d. gefragt, ob der Zug fährt?** have you enquired whether the train is running? **mein Sinn steht nicht d., heute ins Kino zu gehen,** I don't feel like going to the pictures today, I'm not in the mood for going to the cinema today; **trachtet d., daß ihr in Frieden lebt,** strive to live together in peace. **2.** [da·ˈnaːx] *rel. use A:* behind which; after which; for which; about which; according to which.

Danae [ˈdaːna·eː]. *Pr.n.f.* **-s.** *Gr.Myth:* Danae.

Danaer, die [ˈdaːna·ər], *m.pl.* the Danai, the Greeks.

Danaergeschenk, *n.* harmful, treacherous, gift.

Danaide [da·na·ˈiːdə], (*a*) *f.* **-/-n.** *Gr.Myth:* Danaid; **das Faß der Danaiden,** a hopeless, endless, task, a Sisyphean labour; (*b*) *m.* **-n/-n.** *Ent:* Danaid.

Danaidenfaß, *n.* hopeless, endless, task, Sisyphean labour.

Dandytum [ˈdɛndi·-], *n.* **-(e)s/.** dandyism.

Dandywalze, *f. Paperm:* dandy-roll(er).

Däne, *m.* **-n/-n.** *Ethn: Geog:* Dane.

daneben. 1. *pron. adv.* (*a*) [da·ˈneːbən, *when emphatic* ˈdaːneːbən] next to, beside, it, them, (*emphatic*) that, those; alongside; **dicht, gleich, d.,** close beside, close to, it, them, close by, hard by, near by; **ein Haus mit einer Garage d.,** a house with a garage next to, beside, it; **im Haus d.,** next door, in the house next door; (*b*) [da·ˈneːbən] in addition, as well, besides; **er hat ein schönes Landhaus und d. eine Wohnung in der Stadt,** he has a beautiful country house and a flat in the town as well, besides, in addition. **2. daneben-** [da·ˈneːbən], *comb.fm. sep.* (*a*) next to, near, by, it, them; **danebenstehen,** to stand near, by; **sich danebensetzen,** to sit down beside (s.o., sth.); (*cp.* 2 (*b*)); **danebenliegen,** to lie near (s.o., sth.); (*b*) beside it, them; wide of the mark; **danebenschießen,** to shoot wide of the mark, to miss; **danebenfallen,** to miss, to fall beside it; **sich danebensetzen,** to miss (the seat); (*cp.* 2 (*a*)).

danebengehen, *v.i. sep.* (*strong*) (*sein*) (*a*) (*of bullet, etc.*) to miss (the target), to go wide of the mark; *F:* **die Bemerkung ist danebengegangen,** the remark misfired, missed its effect; (*b*) *F:* to go wrong, to misfire; **der Plan ist ihm danebengegangen,** his plan misfired.

danebenhauen. 1. *v.i. sep.* (*haben*) (*conj. like* **hauen**) *F:* (*a*) to miss; **er wollte einen Nagel in die Wand schlagen, aber er haute immer wieder daneben,** he tried to knock a nail into the wall, but he missed it again and again; (*while playing the piano*) **andauernd d.,** to keep hitting the wrong note; (*b*) to make a mistake *or* mistakes; to be wide of the mark; **in der Geschichtsklausur hat er gründlich danebengehauen,** he made a frightful hash of the history paper. **2.** *v.tr. sep.* **eine Klassenarbeit (gründlich) d.,** to make a (complete) mess of a test.

Dänemark. *Pr.n.n.* **-s.** *Geog:* Denmark.

dang, dänge *see* **dingen.**

danieder [da·ˈniːdər], *adv.*=**darnieder.**

Daniel [ˈdaːnie·l, ˈdaːniɛl]. *Pr.n.m.* **-s.** Daniel.

Daniellelement, *n. El:* Daniell cell.

Daniellsch [ˈdaːniɛlʃ], *a. Ph:* **Daniellsches (Kondensations-)Hygrometer,** Daniell hydrometer.

Dänin, *f.* **-/-innen.** *Ethn: Geog:* Dane, Danish woman.

dänisch. 1. *a.* Danish. **2.** *s.* **Dänisch,** *n. Ling:* Danish.

Dänischleder, *n.* suède.

danisieren [da·ni·ˈziːrən], *v.tr.* to make (s.o., sth.) Danish in character, in outlook.

Dank¹, *m.* **-(e)s/.** (*a*) thanks; gratitude; **Gott sei D.!** thank God! *F:* thank goodness! **vielen, besten, schönen, herzlichen, D.!** thank you very, so, much! (very) many thanks! *F:* thanks very much! thanks a lot! thanks awfully! **vielen herzlichen D.! tausend D.! haben Sie vielen D.!** thank you very much (indeed)! **sein D. ist dir gewiß,** you can be sure of his gratitude, you can count on his gratitude; **j-m (seinen) D. (für etwas) sagen, abstatten, aussprechen,** to thank s.o. (for sth.), to give, render, thanks, to extend, offer, express, one's thanks, to s.o. (for sth.); *Ecc:* **wir sagen Dir D. für Deine große Güte,** we give thanks to Thee for thy great mercy; *cp.* **danksagen; j-s D. ernten,** to earn s.o.'s gratitude; **j-m D. schulden,** to owe s.o. thanks, gratitude, to be indebted to s.o.; **ich schulde Ihnen D. für Ihre Bemühungen, ich bin Ihnen für Ihre Bemühungen zu D. verpflichtet,** I am greatly indebted to you for your efforts; **j-m (für etwas,** *A:* **etwas** *gen.*) **D. wissen,** to be grateful to s.o. (for sth.); **man wird dir dafür keinen D. zollen, du wirst dir keinen D. damit ernten,** they won't thank you for that; **das ist der Dank dafür, daß man ihm beisteht,** that's all the thanks, gratitude, one gets for standing by him; *F:* **das ist der ganze D. dafür!** *F:* that's all the thanks one gets! **etwas mit D. annehmen, zurückgeben,** to accept, return, sth. with thanks; **j-s D. entgegennehmen,** to accept s.o.'s thanks; **j-n zu D. verpflichten,** to earn s.o.'s thanks; *Lit:* to oblige s.o.; **er hat uns dadurch zu (großem) D. verpflichtet, daß er die Sache unternommen hat,** he has earned our (grateful) thanks, he has greatly obliged us, by undertaking the business; **j-m etwas als, zum, D. geben,** to give s.o. sth. by way of thanks, as a reward for his services; **etwas als, zum, D. erhalten,** to be given sth. by way of thanks, as a reward for one's services; **wir können ihm nichts zu Danke machen,** we can do nothing to please him, nothing we do is right in his eyes; (*b*) *A:* **wider seinen D.,** against his will.

dank², *prep.* (+*gen. or dat.*) thanks to; **d. seiner Bemühungen, seinen Bemühungen,** thanks to his efforts; **d. ihres großen Vermögens, ihrem**

großen Vermögen, thanks to their great wealth.

dankbar, *a.* **1.** thankful, grateful; **wir können d. sein, daß wir heil durchgekommen sind,** we can be thankful to have come through it unscathed; **j-m (für etwas) ewig d. sein,** to be eternally grateful, thankful, to s.o. (for sth.); **sich j-m (für etwas) d. zeigen, beweisen,** to show oneself grateful to s.o. (for sth.). **2.** rewarding, profitable, worth-while; **eine dankbare Arbeit, Aufgabe,** a rewarding, worth-while, task; **ein dankbarer Stoff,** (*a*) *Tex:* a hard-wearing material; (*b*) a rewarding subject (*for a novel, play, etc.*); *Th:* **ein dankbares Publikum,** an appreciative audience; **eine dankbare Rolle,** a rewarding part, a part offering scope to the actor.

Dankbarkeit, *f.* **1.** gratitude, thankfulness; **D. gegen j-n,** gratitude to s.o.; **etwas aus (reiner, bloßer) D. tun,** to do sth. out of, from, (pure) gratitude; **in aufrichtiger D.,** with sincere gratitude; **seine D. (be)zeigen,** to show one's gratitude; **D. an den Tag legen,** to show gratitude, to show oneself grateful. **2.** profitableness (of task, etc.).

dankbarlich, *a. A:*=**dankbar 1.**

danken. I. *v.i.* (*haben*) (*a*) to thank; **-m für etwas d.,** to thank s.o. for sth.; **er dankte mir, daß ich gekommen war,** he thanked me for coming; **j-m herzlich, von Herzen, d.,** to thank s.o. sincerely, heartily; **j-m d. lassen,** to send one's thanks to s.o.; **sie läßt sehr d.,** she asked me to thank you very much; **bitte, bitte, nichts zu d.!** please don't mention it! the pleasure was mine! **er grüßte, sie dankte,** he greeted her, and she acknowledged his greeting; **etwas dankend annehmen,** to accept sth. with thanks; **etwas dankend ablehnen,** to decline sth. with thanks; *Iron:* **(na,) ich danke! (ich) danke für Backobst!** no thanks! no thanks, I'm not having any! *Com:* **dankend erhalten,** received with thanks; (*b*) to praise, to give thanks (to God, etc.); to say grace (after a meal); **Gott sei gedankt!** the Lord be praised! thank the Lord! thank Heaven(s)! thank goodness! *B:* **da sie aber aßen, nahm Jesus das Brot, dankte, und brach's,** and as they were eating, Jesus took bread, and blessed it, and brake it; *B:* **und da er (Paulus) das gesaget, nahm er das Brot, dankte Gott vor ihnen allen . . . ,** and when he (Paul) had thus spoken, he took bread, and gave thanks to God in presence of them all . . . ; *B:* **danket dem Herrn; denn er ist freundlich, O,** give thanks unto the Lord; for he is good; (*c*) to refuse (sth.); **sie bot noch Kuchen an, aber er dankte,** she offered more cake, but he refused; **ich danke,** no, thank you; (*d*) **danke!** (i) thank you! *F:* thanks; (ii) no, thank you! *F:* no thanks! **danke sagen,** to say thank you; **möchten Sie noch ein Stück Kuchen? — (nein) danke! — danke nein!** would you like another piece of cake?—no, thank you! **danke schön, sehr, bestens,** (i) thank you very much: (ii) no, thank you very much; **wie geht es Ihnen? — danke (der freundlichen Nachfrage), gut,** how are you?—very well, thank you.

II. *vbl s.* **Danken,** *n.* thanking, saying thank you; **das D. fällt ihm schwer,** he finds it difficult to say thank you; **D. kostet nichts,** thanks cost nothing; **(das) D. will gelernt sein,** one has to learn how to say thank you gracefully; **beim D.,** in saying thank you; while expressing one's thanks.

dankenswert, *a.* (*a*) (thing) one can be grateful for; kind (efforts, etc.); (*b*) rewarding, profitable, worth-while (task, etc.).

dankerfüllt, *a.* full of gratitude.

Dankesbezeigung, *f.* (expression of) thanks.

Dankesbrief, *m.* letter of thanks, *F:* thank-you letter.

Dankesschreiben, *n.* letter of thanks.

Dankeswort, *n.* -(e)s/-e, (expression, word, of) thanks.

Dankgottesdienst, *m.* thanksgiving service.

Dankopfer, *n.* thank-offering.

danksagen. I. *v.i. insep.* (*haben*) *esp. Ecc:* to give, return, thanks; *B:* **und danksaget dem Vater,** giving thanks unto the Father.

II. *vbl s.* **1. Danksagen,** *n. in vbl senses.* **2. Danksagung,** *f.* thanksgiving.

Dankschreiben, *n.* letter of thanks.

dann. **1.** *adv.* (*a*) then; **d. und d.,** at such and such a time; **d. und wann,** (every) now and then, from time to time; **erst d.,** only then, not till then; **selbst d.,** even then; **selbst d. verstand er's nicht,** even then he didn't understand; (*b*) then, next, after that, afterwards; **erst besuchte uns die Mutter, d. die Tochter,** first the mother visited us, then the daughter; **er hat es mir zweimal erklärt, d. wußte ich, wie es gemeint war,** he explained it twice to me, then I knew how it was meant; **und wenn er keine Lust dazu hat, was (machen wir) d.?** and if he is not interested in doing it, what then? *A. & Lit:* **dann . . . dann . . . ,** now . . . now . . . ; *Prov:* **erst wägen, d. wagen,** look before you leap; (*c*) then, furthermore, besides; **und d. muß man (noch) bedenken, daß . . . ,** and then, besides, furthermore, one must consider that . . . ; **d. hat er auch noch zwei große Autos,** and (then) he has two big cars; (*d*) (*sometimes not translated*) then, in that case; **was soll 'd. aus dir werden?** what will become of you then? **wenn die Sache so steht, d. können wir nichts dafür,** if that's the state of affairs (then) we can do nothing about it; **selbst d., wenn . . . ,** even if; **selbst d., wenn wir Zeit hätten, würden wir's nicht tun,** even if we had time we shouldn't do it; **wenn du nicht kommst, d. gehe ich auch nicht,** if you don't come (then) I shan't go either; **d. (eben) nicht!** all right then, don't! **2.** *A:*= **denn I. 1, 2, 3.** **3.** *emotive particle* (*a*) (*denoting impatience*) well then; all right then; **(na) d. komm schon!** well, come along then! all right, come along then! **d. geh doch!** well, go then! all right then, go! **d. sag mir schon, was du willst!** well, tell me what you want then! (*b*) (*affirmative*) **es bleibt d. (also) dabei,** well, that's final, that's settled, then! **das ist d. genug,** well that's enough then! **sag ihm d., er kann kommen,** all right (then), well (then), tell him he can come; (*c*) *A. & Dial:* (*stressed question*) **was ist d. das?** what's that? **wie d.?** why? how? **wer sind Sie d.?** who are you?

dannen, *adv. Lit:* **1. von d.,** (i) (from) hence; (ii) (from) thence; **von d. gehen, ziehen,** to depart, to go away; **von d. reiten,** to ride away, off. **2.** *rel. use* **von d.,** (from) whence.

dannzumal, *adv. Swiss:* (*referring to future*) then.

Dante, *m.* -/-s. *Games, esp. Cards:* counter.

dantesk [dan'tesk], *a. Lit: etc:* Dantesque.

dantisch, Dantisch, *a. Lit:* Dantean; of Dante; Dantesque.

Danzig. *Pr.n.n.* **-s.** *Geog:* Danzig.

Danziger. **1.** *m.* -s/-, inhabitant, native, of Danzig. **2.** *inv.a.* of Danzig, Danzig . . . ; **die D. Bucht,** the Gulf of Danzig.

Daphne ['dafne:]. **1.** *Pr.n.f.* **-s.** *Myth:* Daphne. **2.** *f.* -/-n. *Bot:* daphne.

dar. **1.** *adv. A:* **auf mich, ihn, dar,** attacking me, him; **auf ihn dar!** at him. **2. dar-,** *comb.fm.* (*a*) (*prefixed to prep. with initial vowel*) it, them; **darauf, daran,** on it, them; **darin,** in it, them; **darüber,** over, above, about, it, them; **darum,** round it, them; **darunter,** under, amongst, it, them; *A. & Dial:* (*prefixed to any prep.*) **darnach, darzu**=**danach, dazu;** (*b*) (*prefixed to verbs, implies open presentation or display*) **darbieten,** to offer; **darstellen,** to represent.

daran [da'ran, *when emphatic* 'da:ran, *in compounds* da'ran-], *pron. adv.* (*F:* **dran,** *q.v.*) **1.** (*a*) on it, on them, (*emphatic*) on that, on those; **sie hatten einen Weihnachtsbaum mit viel Schmuck d.,** they had a Christmas-tree with a lot of decorations on it; (*b*) on (to) it, them; **halt dich d. fest!** hold on tight to it! **das ist ein schöner alter Brauch; d. sollte man festhalten,** this is a nice old custom, and people should stick to it; **man kann sich nicht d. halten, was er verspricht,** one cannot depend on his promises; *see also* **dranhalten;** (*c*) (on) to it, (on) to them; **wir haben Bilder d. geklebt,** we stuck pictures (on) to it, them; **hat er das Tau d. befestigt?** has he fastened the rope to it? **die Tür ist frisch gestrichen; paß auf, daß du nicht d. kommst!** the door has been newly painted, so take care you don't touch it; *see also* **drankommen;** (*d*) against it, them; **das Geländer ist sehr schwach; lehne dich nicht d.!** the banisters are very weak; don't lean on, against, them; (*e*) **etwas d. tun,** to add sth. to it, them; **tu, gieß, noch etwas Milch d.,** pour some more milk into it, add some more milk to it; **ich werde eine Sauce d. machen,** I will put a sauce with it; (*f*) at it, at them; **ein Tisch mit zwölf Personen d.,** a table with twelve people sitting at it; **sie fanden einen einladend gedeckten Tisch und setzten sich sogleich d.,** they found a table laid invitingly and sat down at it immediately; *see also* **daransetzen;** **es war eine große Aufgabe, aber er arbeitete jeden Abend d.,** it was a big task but he worked on, at, it every evening; (*g*) **die Pralinenschachtel ist halb leer, — wer ist d. gewesen?** the chocolate box is half empty—who has been at it? **die Schranktür ist offen, — wer war d.?** the cupboard is open — who has been at it? *cp.* **dran 2;** (*h*) **nahe d.,** near to, close to, it, them; **nahe d. sein, etwas zu tun,** to be on the point, on the verge, of doing sth.; **er war nahe d., seine Stellung aufzugeben,** he was on the point, on the verge, of giving up his job, he nearly gave up his job. **2.** (*translation of constructions with* **daran** *depends on the translation of* **an** *in connection with the verb, etc., in question; the uses of* **an & daran** *are illustrated under the respective verbs, etc., taking* **an.**) **es ist etwas d.,** there's something in it; **es ist kein wahres Wort d.,** there's not a word of truth in it; **ich bin nicht schuld d.,** I'm not to blame for it, it is not my fault; **sie taten gut d., das Haus zu verkaufen,** they did well, they were wise, to sell the house, it was a good idea of theirs to sell the house; **denke d.!** don't forget (it)! think of that! **ich denke nicht d. (, es zu tun),** I wouldn' tthink of it, of doing so, I have no intention of doing so; (*emphatic*) **d. mag ich nicht denken,** I don't like to, I daren't, think of, about, that; **d. zweifeln,** to doubt it, to have (one's) doubts about it; (*emphatic*) **d. darfst du nicht zweifeln,** you mustn't doubt that, you must have no doubts about that; **d. leiden,** to suffer from it; **d. sterben,** to die of it; (*emphatic*) **d. erkennt man ihn,** you can see by that, from that, what he's like; **es liegt viel d.,** a great deal depends on it, it matters a great deal, it's of great importance; (*emphatic*) **d. liegt's,** that's what it is, that's the reason for it; *see also* **erinnern, gewöhnen, glauben.** **3.** *rel. use A. & Lit:* on which, of which, in which, at which; whereon; whereof; wherein; whereat; *B:* **Elisa ward krank, d. er auch starb,** now Elisha was fallen sick of a sickness whereof he died.

darangeben, *v.tr. sep.* (*strong*) **1.**=**daransetzen 1.** **2. sich darangeben,** to set to work, to start; **sie gab sich daran, Kartoffeln zu schälen,** she set to work, she started, to peel, peeling, potatoes.

darangehen, *v.i. sep.* (*strong*) (*sein*) (*a*) to set to work (on it, them); **er ging mit Eifer daran, sein Fahrrad zu putzen,** he set eagerly to work cleaning his bicycle; **sie ging sofort daran, ihre Hausaufgaben zu machen,** she set to work on her homework at once; (*b*) to set about it; **er ging vorsichtig daran, die äußere Hülle abzunehmen,** he cautiously set about taking off the outer covering.

daranhalten (sich), *v.refl. sep.* (*strong*) =**dranhalten.**

darankommen, *v.i. sep.* (*strong*) (*sein*) =**drankommen.**

daranmachen (sich), *v.refl. sep.* to set to work (on it), to go at it; **sich d., etwas zu tun,** to set about, *F:* to get down to, doing sth.; **wir müssen uns jetzt d.,** we must set to work on it, *F:* we must get down to it, set about it, now; *see also* **daran.**

darannehmen, *v.tr. sep.* (*strong*) =**drannehmen.**

daransetzen, *v.tr. sep.* **1. alles, sein Letztes, d.,** etwas zu erreichen, to do one's utmost, *F:* one's level best, to attain sth.; *F:* to go at it baldheaded; **einen Tag d.,** to give up a whole day to it, to make a day of it. **2. sich daransetzen, etwas zu tun,** to set to work to do sth., to set about doing sth. *Cp.* **daran 1** (*f*).

darauf [da'rauf, *when emphatic* 'da:rauf]. (*F:* **drauf**) *pron. adv.* **1.** (*a*) (up)on it, them, (*emphatic*) that, those, there; **ich füllte den Topf und tat den Deckel d.,** I filled the pan and put the lid on it; (*emphatic*) **d. darf man nicht gehen,** one's not allowed to walk on that, those, there; **eine Straße mit einer Menge Leute d.,** a street with a lot of people in it; **schau das Bild genau an und sag mir, was du d. siehst,** look closely at the picture and tell me what you see in it; (*b*) **d. zugehen, losgehen,** to go towards it, them; **als unser Hund die Hühner sah, ging er gleich d. los,** when our dog saw the hens it went straight towards, for, them; *see also* **drauflosgehen;** (*c*) **sie kaufte immer wieder neue Kleider, — ihr ganzes Geld ging d.,** she was always buying herself new clothes—all her money went on them; *see also* **draufgehen;** **wir hätten das Wichtigste übersehen, wenn er unsere Aufmerksamkeit nicht d. gelenkt hätte,** we should have missed the most important thing, had he not drawn our attention to it. **2.** (*translation of constructions with* **darauf** *depends on the translation of* **auf** *in connection with the verb or adj. in question; the uses of* **auf** *and* **darauf** *are illustrated under the respective verbs and adjs taking* **auf.**) (*a*) **obgleich die Frage dringend war, bekamen wir keine Antwort d.,** although the question was urgent we received no reply (to it); **ich freue mich jetzt schon d.,** I am looking forward to it already; **d. hinweisen,** to point it out; **d. hinweisen, daß . . . ,** to indicate that . . . ; **alles**

deutet d. hin, everything points to it; *cp.* **daraufhin; sich d. besinnen,** to remember it; **d. kommen,** (i) to remember it; (ii) to think of it; (iii) to come to it; **ich kenne seinen Namen gut, aber ich kann im Augenblick nicht d. kommen,** I know his name well, but I can't remember, I can't think of, it, for the moment; **wie kommt er bloß d.?** however did he get that idea? whatever made him think (of) that? **das brauchen wir noch nicht zu besprechen; wir kommen später d.,** we don't need to discuss that now; we'll come to it later; **er kennt meine Gefühle, aber er nimmt keine Rücksicht, er achtet nicht, d.,** he knows my feelings, yet he does not take them into consideration; **sich d. verlassen,** to rely, depend, on it; (*emphatic*) **er wird bestimmt kommen; d. kannst du dich verlassen,** he is sure to come; you can depend on that; **stolz d. sein,** to be proud of it, them; **d. schwören,** (i) to swear to it; (ii) to swear by, to be very keen on, it, them; **d. wetten,** to bet, to lay a wager, on it; **morgen wird es regnen, d. wette ich,** it will rain tomorrow, I'll bet on it, I'll be bound; **j-m die Hand d. geben,** to give s.o. one's hand on it; **d. trinken,** to drink to it; **d. bestehen, dringen,** to insist on, to urge, it; **d. versessen sein,** to be determined, very keen, on it; (*emphatic*) **d. wäre ich nie reingefallen,** I should never have fallen for, been taken in by, that; **d. steht der Tod,** the penalty for that is death; *see also* **ankommen** I. 5, **aussein** 1 (*b*); (*b*) **wir freuen uns sehr d., Sie zu sehen,** we are very much looking forward to seeing you; **alles deutet d. (hin), daß die Sache schief gehen wird,** everything points to the business's going wrong; **alles war d. angelegt, den Gegner zu täuschen,** everything was calculated to deceive the opponent; **er besann sich d., daß er den Mann dort gesehen hatte,** he remembered having seen the man there, that he had seen the man there; **wie kommt er d., daß wir ihm helfen können?** how has he got the idea, what makes him think, that we can help him? **Sie müssen d. gefaßt sein, daß er den Vorschlag abweist,** you must be prepared to see him turn down the proposal; **du mußt d. achten, sehen, daß sie sich nicht treffen,** you must make sure, take care, you must see to it, that they do not meet; **Sie müssen Rücksicht d. nehmen, daß er nicht mehr jung ist,** you must take into consideration, you must have regard for, the fact that he is no longer young; **du kannst dich d. verlassen, daß er kommt,** you can depend on his coming, you can depend on it that he will come; **sie legt großen Wert d., daß wir sie besuchen,** she is very anxious that we should visit her, for us to visit her, she sets great store by our visiting her; **er ist stolz d., reich zu sein, daß er reich ist,** he is proud of being, proud that he is, rich; **ich kann d. schwören, daß ich es hier gelassen habe,** I can swear that I left it here; **ich wette d., daß du ihn nie wiedersiehst,** I'm ready to bet that you'll never see him again; **er gab mir die Hand d., daß er mich nie im Stich lassen würde,** he swore he would never let me down and gave me his hand on it; **er richtet seine Bemühungen d., den Lebensstandard der Eingeborenen zu heben,** he devotes his energies to raising the natives' standard of living; **d. ausgehen, aussein, etwas zu tun, daß etwas getan wird,** to insist on doing sth., on sth.'s being done; **d. bestehen, dringen, daß etwas getan wird,** to insist on sth.'s being done; **d. versessen sein, daß etwas geschieht,** to be determined on sth.'s being done, that sth. should be done; **d. eingehen, daß etwas geschieht,** to agree to sth.'s happening; **sich d. einlassen, etwas zu tun,** to agree to do sth., to let oneself in for doing sth.; (*c*) **d. und daran sein, etwas zu tun,** to be on the point, on the verge, of doing sth. **3.** *adv.* (*a*) after that; **den Tag d., am Tag d.,** (on) the day after (that); **im Frühjahr d.,** (in) the next spring; **zwei Jahre d.,** two years later; **bald, gleich, kurz, d.,** soon, immediately, shortly, after (that), afterwards; (*b*) (*emphatic*) on that, thereupon; **d. gestand er, daß er das Geld gestohlen habe,** and thereupon he confessed that he had stolen the money; **d. beschlossen wir, das Land zu verlassen,** and on that, thereupon, we decided to leave the country. **4.** *rel. use A. & Lit:* (*a*) on which, towards which, to which, for which; whereon; whereto; wherefore; (*b*) whereupon.

daraufhin [da·rauf'hin], *adv.* as a result, consequently, so; on the strength of it; **ich sehe eben, daß ich morgen frei habe, d. kann ich später aufstehen,** I see I have tomorrow off, so I can get up later in the morning; **sein Vater versprach ihm fünfhundert Pfund, d. kaufte er sich ein neues Auto,** his father promised him five hundred pounds, on the strength of which he bought himself a new car.

darauflosgehen [da·rauf'loːs-], *v.i. sep.* (*strong*) (*sein*) = **drauflosgehen.**

daraus [da·'raus, *when emphatic* 'daːraus], (*F:* **draus**) *pron. adv.* **1.** (*a*) out of, from, it, them, (*emphatic*) out of that, those; **gib mir die bunte Tasse! — ich trinke so gerne d.,** give me the coloured cup—I like drinking out of, from, it; (*emphatic*) **d. darfst du nicht trinken,** you mustn't drink out of, from, that (one); (*b*) (out) of, with, from, it, them; **sie kaufte einen schönen Stoff und machte sich ein Kleid d.,** she bought a nice piece of material and made a dress of, with, it; **der Bildhauer nahm den Lehm und formte einen Kopf d.,** the sculptor took the clay and fashioned a head (out) of, from, it; (*emphatic*) **d. kann man nichts machen,** one can make nothing with, out of, from, that, those; **er macht sich viel d.,** he cares a lot about it; it means a lot to him; **wir machen uns nichts d.,** we don't care, we don't mind (about it); it means nothing to us; **er hat eine große Sache d. gemacht,** (i) he made a big thing of it, he turned it into something big; (ii) *F:* he made a mountain out of a molehill; (*c*) of it, them; **was wird d.?** what will become of it, them? what will happen to it, them? **ich weiß nicht, was d. geworden ist,** I don't know what has come of it, them; **es wird nichts d.,** nothing will come of it; (*emphatic*) **d. wird nichts,** nothing will come of that; **es wird nichts Gutes d. werden,** no good will come of it; **als ich das Hündchen kaufte, wußte ich nicht, daß so eine große Dogge d. werden sollte,** when I bought the puppy I didn't know that it would become such a large mastiff, I did not know it would turn into, grow into, such a large mastiff; **ich werde nicht klug d.,** I can't understand it, *F:* I can't make head or tail of it; (*d*) from it; (*emphatic at beginning of sentence*) from this, from that; hence, thence; **wenn dieses die Wahrheit ist, so folgt d., daß . . . ,** if this is the truth, then it follows that . . . ; **d. folgt, daß . . . ,** it follows (from this) that . . . , hence, thence, it follows that . . . ; **d. schließen wir, daß . . . ,** from this we conclude, we infer, that . . . . **2.** *rel. use A. & Lit:* out of, with, from, of, which; *B:* **ich will wieder umkehren in mein Haus, d. ich gegangen bin,** I will return into my house from whence I came out.

darben. I. *v.* **1.** *v.i.* (*haben*) to want, to live in poverty, in want, to be needy; to go without, to go short; to famish. **2.** *v.tr. A:* to do without (sth.), to go short of (sth.).

II. *vbl s.* **Darben,** *n. in vbl senses; also:* poverty, need.

darbieten. I. *v.tr. sep.* (*strong*) **1.** to offer, to present (sth.); **die Wange (zum Kuß) d.,** to offer one's cheek (to be kissed); **etwas als Opfer d.,** to offer sth. as a sacrifice, to sacrifice sth.; **im Konzert heute abend werden Werke von Mozart dargeboten,** works by Mozart will be played at tonight's concert; *B:* **so dir jemand einen Streich gibt auf deinen rechten Backen, dem biete den andern auch dar,** whosoever shall smite thee on thy right cheek, turn to him the other also. **2. sich darbieten,** to offer oneself; **sich zum Opfer d.,** to sacrifice oneself, to offer oneself as a sacrifice; **ein wundervoller Anblick bot sich unserem Auge dar,** a magnificent sight met our eyes.

II. *vbl s.* **1. Darbieten,** *n. in vbl senses.* **2. Darbietung,** *f.* (*a*) = II. 1; *also:* presentation; (*b*) *Th: etc:* performance; (musical, sports, etc.) item; (variety) act; **alle Darbietungen des Abends zeichneten sich durch besondere Güte aus,** all the performances of the evening were distinguished by their excellence; **sportliche und musikalische Darbietungen verschönerten die Feier,** sports and musical items lent added enjoyment to the festivities.

Darbisten [dar'bistən]. *Pr.n.m.pl. Rel.Hist:* Plymouth Brethren.

darbringen. I. *v.tr. sep.* (*conj. like* **bringen**) to offer (sth.); **Gott ein Opfer d.,** to sacrifice (sth.) to God, to make a sacrifice to God; **etwas zum Opfer d.,** to give, offer, sth. as a sacrifice; **j-m seine Huldigung d.,** to pay homage to s.o.; **j-m eine Ovation d.,** to give s.o. an ovation.

II. *vbl s.* **1. Darbringen,** *n. in vbl senses.* **2. Darbringung,** *f.* = II, 1; **die D. (Christi) im Tempel,** the Presentation of Christ in the Temple.

Dardanellen, die [darda·'nɛlən]. *Pr.n.pl. Geog:* the Dardanelles.

Dardschiling [da·r'dʒiːliŋ]. *Pr.n.n.* **-s.** *Geog:* Darjeeling.

darein [da·'rain, *when emphatic* 'daːrain, *in compounds* da·'rain] (*F:* **drein**), *pron. adv.* **1.** (*also* **darein-**, *comb.fm.*) (*a*) in(to) it, them; **ich goß Wasser d.,** I poured water into it, them; (*b*) **sich dareinmischen, dareinmengen,** to interfere (in it); **sich d. fügen,** to agree to it, to fit in (with it); **sich d. finden,** to become resigned to it, to get used to it, to put up with it; **sich d. ergeben,** to resign oneself (to it); **er hat sich d. ergeben, daß er sich nicht durchsetzen kann,** he has become resigned to the fact that he cannot get his way; **dareinwilligen, seinen Willen dareingeben,** to agree (to it). **2.** *rel. use A:* in which, wherein; *B:* **Kanaan, d. ich euch führen will,** Canaan, whither I bring you.

dareinreden, *v.i. sep.* (*haben*) = **dreinreden.**

darf, darfst *see* **dürfen.**

Darg, *m.* **-s/-e,** (sandy) peat.

darin [da·'rin, *when emphatic* 'daːrin] (*F:* **drin,** *q.v.*) *pron. adv.* **1.** (*a*) in it; in them; (*emphatic*) in that; in those; **ich sah in alle Kisten hinein, aber es war nichts d.,** I looked into all the boxes, but there was nothing in them, inside (them); (*emphatic*) **nein, d. wirst du nichts finden,** no, you'll find nothing in that, in those, (in) there; (*b*) (*emphatic*) there, in that; **d. sind wir uns ähnlich,** there, in that, we resemble one another; **ich kann ihr d. nicht beistimmen,** I cannot agree with her there; **d. hat er sich geirrt, getäuscht,** he was wrong, mistaken, there, in that; (*c*) **d., daß . . . ,** in, by (+ *gerund*); in that . . . ; **wir haben uns d. geirrt, daß wir annahmen, er käme erst morgen,** we made a mistake in, by, thinking he wouldn't come till tomorrow; **der Grund des Mißlingens liegt d., daß die Anordnungen nicht genau beachtet wurden,** the reason for the failure lies in the fact that the instructions were not properly carried out; **seine Anschauung unterscheidet sich von der meinen d., daß er die Freiheit des menschlichen Willens abstreitet,** his outlook differs from mine in that he denies free will; **der Wert dieses Gegenstandes besteht d., daß man ihn zu verschiedenen Zwecken gebrauchen kann,** the value of this article lies in the fact that it can be used for various purposes; **meine ganze Hoffnung liegt d., daß er die Sache vergißt,** my whole hope lies in his forgetting the matter. **2.** *rel. use A. & Lit:* in which, wherein; *B:* **das Land, d. sie Fremdlinge waren,** the land wherein they were strangers.

darinnen [da·'rinən, *when emphatic* 'daːrinən], *pron. adv. A. & Lit:* = **darin;** *cp.* **drinnen.**

Dariole [da·ri'oːlə], *f.* **-/-n.** *Cu:* dariole; (sort of) cream tartlet.

darlegen. I. *v.tr. sep.* **1.** *A:* to give, to present (sth.); to spend, offer (money); to offer (oneself, etc.) as payment, as a sacrifice; *B:* **und legt dar alles Gut in seinem Hause,** he shall give all the substance of his house. **2.** to set forth, explain, unfold (plan, reasons), to lay (plan) before (s.o.); to state, declare, expound (views); to explain, expound (theories); **etwas umständlich, mit vielen Worten, d.,** to explain sth. in detail, at great length; **er hat mir seine Gründe im einzelnen dargelegt,** he explained his reasons to me in detail.

II. *vbl s.* **1. Darlegen,** *n. in vbl senses.* **2. Darlegung,** *f.* (*a*) = II. 1; *also:* explanation, exposition (of views, theories, reasons); (*b*) exposé, explanation, exposition, argument; **seine Darlegungen waren sehr interessant,** his speech was, his words were, very interesting; **er gab uns eine knappe D. seiner Pläne,** he gave us a brief exposition, exposé, of his plans, he explained his plans to us briefly.

Darlehen, Darlehn, *n.* **-s/-.** *Fin:* loan; **j-m ein D. geben, gewähren,** to make, grant, s.o. a loan; **ein D. aufnehmen,** to raise a loan; **D. gegen Sicherheiten,** loan against security; **kündbares D.,** loan at notice, at call; **unkündbares D.,** time loan; **befristetes D.,** loan for a fixed term; **unbefristetes D.,** undated loan; **kurzfristiges D.,** short loan; **gesichertes D.,** secured loan; **ungesichertes D.,** loan on trust, unsecured loan.

Darlehnsgeber, *m. Fin:* loaner; loan-holder.

Darlehnskasse, *f.* loan bank (*esp. for farmers*).

Darlehnskassenschein, *m.* loan certificate.

Darlehnskassenverein, *m.* loan-society.

Darlehnskonto, *n. Fin:* loan account.

Darlehnsnehmer, *m.* borrower, loanee.

Darlehnsschuld, *f. Fin:* nominal amount of loan.

Darlehnsverein, *m.* loan-society.

Darleihen, *n.* **-s/-.** *Swiss:* = **Darlehen.**

Darleiher, *m.* **-s/-.** *Fin: Jur:* loaner, *U.S:* lender.

Darm, *m.* **-(e)s/⸗e. 1.** *Anat:* intestine, bowel, gut. **2.** *Com:* (*a*) gut; (*b*) (sausage-)skin. **3. Darm-,** *comb.fm.* intestinal . . . , . . . of the intestine(s);

Darmgeschwür *n*, intestinal ulcer; **Darmleiden** *n*, intestinal affection, affection of the intestines.

Darmausleerung, *f.* = **Darmentleerung.**

Darmbad, *n.* colonic irrigation, colonic lavage.

Darmbandwurm, *m. Med:* tapeworm.

Darmbein, *n. Anat:* ilium, iliac bone; **Darmbein-,** *comb.fm.* iliac . . . ; **Darmbeingrube** *f*, iliac fossa.

Darmbewegung, *f. Physiol:* peristaltic movement.

Darmblatt, *n. Biol:* entoderm.

Darmblutung, *f. Med:* enterorrhagia, intestinal hæmorrhage.

Darmbruch, *m. Med:* enterocele.

Darmeinklemmung, *f. Med:* strangulation of the intestines.

Darmeinlauf, *m. Med:* enema.

Darmeinspritzung, *f. Med:* rectal injection.

Darmentleerung, *f.* evacuation (of the bowels).

Darmentzündung, *f. Med:* enteritis.

Darmerkrankung, *f. Med:* intestinal affection, affection of the intestines.

Darmfäule, *f. Med:* dysentery.

Darmfell, *n. Anat:* peritoneum.

Darmfistel, *f. Med:* stercoraceous fistula, stercoral fistula.

Darmgang, *m. Anat:* intestinal tract.

Darmgicht, *f. Med:* ileus.

Darmgrimmen, *n. Med:* colic, *F:* stomach-ache, gripes.

Darmgrippe, *f. Med:* gastric influenza.

Darmkanal, *m. Anat:* intestinal tract.

Darmkatarrh, *m.* enteritis.

Darmknochen, *m. Anat:* ilium, iliac bone.

Darmkot, *m. Physiol:* faeces.

Darmlarve, *f. Biol:* gastrula.

Darmleiden, *n. Med:* = **Darmerkrankung.**

Darmnetz, *n. Anat:* omentum, epiploon.

Darmrohr, *n. Anat:* intestinal tube.

Darmsaite, *f. Mus:* catgut string.

Darmschlinge, *f. Anat:* intestinal loop, loop of the intestine.

Darmschnitt, *m. Surg:* enterotomy.

Darmspülung, *f.* (*a*) *Med:* enema; (*b*) = **Darmbad.**

Darmstein, *n. Med:* enterolith.

Darmstiel, *m. Biol:* vitelline duct.

Darmtätigkeit, *f. Physiol:* function of the bowels; *Med:* **die D. fördern, regulieren,** to promote, regulate, the function of the bowels.

Darmtier, *n. Biol:* metazoon.

Darmübel, *n.* = **Darmerkrankung.**

Darmverschließung, *f.* = **Darmverschluß.**

Darmverschlingung, *f. Med:* twisting, kinking, of the bowel, of the intestine; volvulus.

Darmverschluß, *m. Med:* obstruction, stoppage, of the bowels; intestinal stoppage.

Darmverstopfung, *f. Med:* constipation, costiveness.

Darmwurm, *m.* intestinal worm.

Darmzotten, *f.pl. Anat:* intestinal villi.

darnach [dar'naːx], *pron. adv. A:* = **danach.**

darneben [dar'neːbən], *pron. adv. A:* = **daneben.**

darnieder [dar'niːdər], *adv. Lit:* down; on the ground.

darniederliegen, *v.i. sep.* (*strong*) (*haben*) *Lit:* (*a*) to be lying down; (**krank**) **d.,** to lie ill, to be laid up; **an Lungenentzündung d.,** to lie ill with, to be laid up with, to be confined to one's bed with, pneumonia; **rettungslos d.,** to be hopelessly ill; (*b*) (*of trade*) to be depressed.

darob [da·'rop], *pron. adv.* = **darüber.**

daroben [da·'roːbən], *adv.* = **droben.**

Darre, *f.* **-/-n. 1.** (kiln-)drying, desiccation (of fruit, etc.); kilning (of malt); *Metall:* liquation. **2.** (*a*) (drying-)kiln; (malt-)kiln; (*for hops*) oast; *Metall:* liquation hearth; (*b*) grid. **3.** = **Darrsucht.**

darreichen, *v.tr. sep.* to hand, give (sth.); to offer, hold out (one's hand, etc.).

darren. I. *v.tr.* (*a*) to (kiln-)dry, to kiln (hops, etc.); to cure (flax, etc.) (by drying); to torrefy (maize, etc.); to desiccate (fruit, etc.); (*b*) *Ch: Metall:* to liquate.

II. *vbl s.* **Darren** *n.*, **Darrung** *f. in vbl senses; also:* (*a*) torrefaction; desiccation; (*b*) liquation.

Darrgras, *n. Bot:* hierochloe.

Darrmalz, *n.* kiln-dried malt.

Darrofen, *m.* = Darre 2 (*a*).

Darrsucht, *f.* (*generic term for*) *Vet:* consumption; atrophy; *Bot:* withering.

darstellbar, *a.* (*a*) representable (subject), (subject) capable of being represented; **ihre Schönheit ist nicht d.,** her beauty cannot be portrayed (in words, on canvas, etc.); (*b*) (play) suitable for presentation; actable (part); **schwer d.,** (play) difficult to present; (part) difficult to act; (*c*) *Mth:* **graphisch d.,** (curve, etc.) that can be plotted, graphed; (equation, etc.) that can be illustrated by means of a graph; (*d*) *Ch:* (element) that can be prepared, disengaged.

darstellen. I. *v.tr. sep.* **1.** (*a*) *A:* to present, bring, produce, place (sth.); *B:* **und sollst . . . den Leuchter d.,** and thou shalt bring in the candlestick; (*b*) *A:* to present, bring, produce (s.o.); *B:* **laßt sie ihre Zeugen d.,** let them bring forth their witnesses; **daß sie ihn darstellten dem Herrn,** to present him to the Lord; (*c*) *F:* to afford, manage; **sie möchte gern Champagner für ihren Ball haben, aber das können wir wohl nicht d.,** she would like to have champagne at her ball, but I don't think we can afford, manage, it; (*d*) *Ch:* to prepare, disengage (oxygen, etc.). **2. sich darstellen,** (*a*) *A:* (*of pers.*) to present oneself (to s.o.), to appear (before s.o.); *B:* **der Philister . . . stellte sich dar vierzig Tage,** the Philistine . . . presented himself forty days; (*b*) (*of pers., thg*) to show oneself, itself, to appear (to s.o.) (as . . .); **so hat sich mir die Sache dargestellt,** that's how the matter appeared to me; **er hat sich hier in all seinen Schwächen dargestellt,** he revealed, betrayed, all his weak points here; (*c*) to be; **Ohnmacht stellt sich physiologisch als Blutleere im Gehirn dar,** physiologically syncope is anaemia of the brain; (*d*) **es stellt sich (deutlich) dar, (daß . . .),** it is clear, apparent, obvious (that . . .). **3.** (*a*) (*of artist, poet, work of art, poem*) to represent, depict, portray (s.o., sth.); (*of poet, poem*) to describe (s.o., sth.); **der Künstler stellt einen traurigen Aspekt des Lebens auf seinem Bild dar,** the artist depicts, portrays, presents, a sad aspect of life in his picture; **was stellt das Bild denn dar?** what does the picture represent, depict, portray? **der Dichter, das Gedicht, stellte das Leben des Menschen dar,** the poet, the poem, depicted, portrayed, described, the life of man; **dieses Bild stellt Rembrandts Frau als Flora dar,** this picture (re)presents, portrays, Rembrandt's wife as Flora; (*b*) (*of actor*) to interpret (character, part), to represent (character); **der Schauspieler stellte den Hamlet zu heroisch dar,** the actor (re)presented, interpreted, Hamlet as too heroic a character; (*c*) *Mth:* **(eine Kurve, usw.) graphisch d.,** to graph, plot (a curve, etc.); **eine Gleichung graphisch d.,** to draw a diagram of an equation, to illustrate an equation by means of a graph; **einen Körper im Aufriß d.,** to draw the front view of an object. **4.** to represent, describe (s.o., sth.); **etwas, j-n, falsch d.,** to misrepresent s.o., sth.; **er stellt seinen Vater als ein Ungetüm dar,** he represents his father as (being) a monster; **wie hat sie mich dargestellt?** how did she describe me? **sie stellten die Sache so dar, als sei ich an allem schuld,** they represented the matter as though I were to blame for everything. **5.** (*of thg*) to be, to represent, to constitute; **seine Arbeit stellt einen wichtigen Beitrag zu unserer Wissenschaft dar,** his work constitutes, represents, an important contribution to our field of study.

II. *vbl s.* **1. Darstellen,** *n. in vbl senses.* **2. Darstellung,** *f.* (*a*) representation (of subject, pers.) (in art, etc.); depiction, portrayal (of subject, character); description (of character, thg); *Th:* (i) (re)presentation, interpretation (of part, character); (ii) (re)presentation, performance (of play); *Mth:* **graphische D.,** illustration (of an equation) by means of a graph (*cp.* (*d*)); **dieser Dichter zeichnet sich durch seine D. der Natur, der Charaktere, aus,** this poet excels in the description of nature, in the description, depiction, portrayal, presentation, delineation, of character; **ihre D. der Kleopatra war höchst originell,** her interpretation of the part of Cleopatra was extremely original; (*b*) *Ch:* preparation (of oxygen, etc.); (*c*) **die D. (Christi) im Tempel,** the Presentation of Christ in the Temple; (*d*) **bildliche D.,** picture; presentation in pictorial, graphic, form; **symbolische, sinnbildliche, D.,** symbolic representation, symbolization; **es gibt eine große Zahl von bildlichen Darstellungen des trojanischen Krieges,** there are a great number of pictures, pictorial representations, of the Trojan war; *Mth:* **graphische D.,** graph; **D. im Aufriß,** front view (of solid); **ein Problem durch graphische D. erläutern,** to explain a problem by means of a graph; (*e*) representation, statement, account; version; **nach seiner eigenen D.,** according to his own words, account, representation, version, story; **eine genaue D. der Tatsachen,** an exact account, statement, of the facts; **ich glaube, er wird ihnen eine wahrheitsgemäße D. meiner Ansichten geben,** I think he will give them a truthful account of my views; **falsche D.,** misrepresentation.

III. *pr.p. & a.* **darstellend,** *in vbl senses, esp.* **darstellende Künste,** interpretative arts; **darstellende Geometrie,** descriptive geometry; **Darstellende** *m, f* = **Darsteller.**

Darsteller, *m.* **-s/-, Darstellerin,** *f.* **-/-innen,** (*a*) *Th:* interpreter (of a part); actor; (*female*) actress; (*b*) portrayer, depicter, depictor; interpreter (of a subject).

darstellerisch, *a.* acting, of acting; **eine glänzende darstellerische Leistung,** a triumph of acting; **d. ausgezeichnet,** excellent as regards the acting.

Darstellung, *f. see* **darstellen II.**

Darstellungsart, *f.* manner of representation.

Darstellungsgabe, *f.* gift, power, of (i) graphic (re)presentation, (ii) dramatic (re)presentation.

Darstellungskunst, *f.* art of (graphic, artistic, dramatic, etc.) (re)presentation, interpretation.

Darstellungsweise, *f.* (*a*) = **Darstellungsart;** (*b*) *Ch:* method of preparation (of oxygen, etc.).

darstrecken, *v.tr. sep. A:* (*a*) to extend, offer, hold out (one's hand, etc.); **das Haupt, den Hals, d.,** to lay one's head on the block; (*b*) to give (up), to lay down (one's life); **Geld d.,** (i) to lend money; (ii) to give (up) one's money.

Dartfordsänger, *m. Orn:* Dartford warbler, *sylvia undata dartfordiensis.*

dartun, *v.tr. sep.* (*strong*) **1.** *A:* (*a*) to spend (money); *B:* **und so du was mehr wirst d.,** and whatsoever thou spendest more; (*b*) to lend (money, etc.); (*c*) to sacrifice (oneself, etc.). **2.** = **darlegen** I. 2.

darüber [da·'ryːbər, *when emphatic* 'daːryːbər, *in compounds* da·'ryːbər-] (*F:* **drüber**), *pron. adv.* (*also* **darüber-,** *comb.fm.*) **1.** (*a*) over, across, it, them; (*emphatic*) over, across, that, those, over there, across there; **wenn niemand deine Sachen sehen soll, so leg ein Tuch d.,** if no one is to see your things, put a cloth over them; **der Rasen ist frisch gemäht; Kinder, lauft nicht d.!** the lawn is newly mown, so don't run over, across, it, children! **die Mauer stand ihm im Wege, aber er stieg schnell d.,** the wall blocked his way, but he climbed quickly over it; **der Fluß war zu tief, um durchzuwaten, also mußte man eine Brücke d. bauen,** the river was too deep to wade through, so they had to build a bridge over, across, it; (*emphatic*) **d. wird man keine Brücke bauen können,** they won't be able to build a bridge over, across, that, there; (*b*) over, above, it, them, (*emphatic*) that, those; **an der Wand hing eine Uhr und d. ein Bild,** on the wall hung a clock and over it, above it, a picture; **der Priester sprach einen Segen d.,** the priest said a blessing over it, them; **eine Tür mit einer Inschrift d.,** a door with an inscription over, above, it; (*c*) at, over, it, them; **er hatte viele Bücher gekauft und saß jeden Abend d.,** he had bought a lot of books and sat at them, pored over them, every evening; **diese Arbeit muß am Ende der Woche fertig sein, also werde ich täglich d. sitzen müssen,** this piece of work must be finished by the end of the week, so I shall have to sit at it daily; (*d*) over it, them; **der Geizhals hatte solche Angst, daß jemand sein Geld stehlen könnte, daß er Tag und Nacht d. wachte,** the miser was so afraid that somebody might steal his money that he watched, stood guard, over it day and night; **dieses ist mein Reich, — eines Tages wirst du Herr d. sein,** this is my kingdom—some day you will be lord of, over, it; **er hat ein hitziges Temperament, aber er ist Herr d.,** he has a quick temper, but he is master of it, he masters it; (*e*) **d. hinaus,** beyond it; **d. hinaus sein,** to be beyond, to have passed, it, them; **meines Bruders Klasse ist immer noch beim ersten Buch Cäsar; d. sind wir längst hinaus,** my brother's class is still reading the first book of Caesar, but we got beyond, past, that long ago; **es gab eine Zeit, wo ich mir große Sorgen ums Leben machte, aber jetzt bin ich d. hinaus,** there was a time when I worried greatly about life, but now I've got past that stage; **sie hat lange unter seiner Treulosigkeit gelitten, aber jetzt ist sie d. hinaus,** for a long time she was greatly distressed by his infidelity, but now she has got over it; (*f*) **d. hinaus,** in addition, moreover; **d. hinaus besaß er mehrere Häuser,** in addition (to this), moreover, he owned several houses; (*g*) **d. hinweggehen,** to pass it over, to take no notice of it, to ignore it; **er ging (leicht) d. hinweg,** he only touched lightly on it, he scarcely mentioned it; **er hatte große Fehler, aber weil er so begabt war, sah man d. hinweg,** he had great faults, but because he was so gifted they were ignored; **es gibt Hindernisse auf unsrem Wege,**

aber wir kommen schon d. hinweg, there are obstacles in our way, but we shall get over them; **jetzt trauert sie noch über ihren Verlust, aber sie wird schon d. hinwegkommen,** she is still mourning her loss, but she will get over it; (*h*) **es geht nichts d.,** there's nothing better, *F:* there's nothing to beat it; **es geht ihm nichts d.,** he likes nothing better, it's the thing he likes best; (*i*) more; **es sollte nur zwanzig Mark kosten, aber sie forderten noch drei Mark d.,** it ought to have cost only twenty marks, but they demanded three marks more; **fünfzig Jahre und d.,** fifty years and more; **eher d. als darunter,** rather more than less. **2.** (*translation of constructions with* **darüber** *depends on the translation of* **über** *in connection with the verb, etc., in question; the uses of* **über** *&* **darüber** *are illustrated under the respective verbs, etc., taking* **über.**) **sich d. freuen,** to be pleased about it; **er freut sich sehr d., daß er seine Examen bestanden hat,** he is very pleased that he has passed his examinations; **d. weinen, jammern, klagen,** to weep, wail, complain, about it; **d. staunen, erstaunt sein,** to be amazed at it, about it; **sich d. wundern,** to be surprised at, about, it; **sich d. ärgern,** to be angry about it; **d. sinnen, denken, reden, sprechen,** to think, speak, about it; **d. lesen,** to read about it; **ein Buch, eine Abhandlung, d. schreiben,** to write a book, a dissertation, about, on, it, them; **Rechnung d. ablegen,** to account for it; **Auskunft d. erhalten,** to obtain information about it; **eine Liste d. führen,** to keep a list of them. **3.** in the process; in the meantime; **er hat zwei Jahre lang um sein Recht gestritten und ist d. zum armen Mann geworden,** he has been fighting for his rights for two years and has become a poor man in the process; **sie war so in den Roman vertieft, daß sie d. die Zeit vergaß,** she was so absorbed in the novel that she forgot the time; **sie hat so lange gezögert, daß er schließlich d. weggegangen ist,** she hesitated so long that in the end he went away before hearing her decision; **er schrieb jahrelang an dem Buch und ist schließlich d. gestorben,** he worked on the book for years and in the end died while still engaged on it; **er konnte sich nicht entschließen, wohin er fahren sollte, und d. sind die Sommerferien hingegangen,** he couldn't decide where to go and in the meantime, and while he was still trying to decide, the summer holidays were over. **4.** *rel. use A. & Lit:* over which, above which, across which, about which.

darübermachen (sich), *v.refl. sep.* to go at, fall upon, attack, set to work on, it, them; **als er das Essen auf dem Tisch sah, machte er sich sofort darüber,** when he saw the food on the table he fell upon it, attacked it, pitched in, immediately; **wenn du so viele Aufgaben aufhast, mach dich lieber gleich darüber,** if you have so much homework to do you'd better set to work on it, pitch in, straight away.

darum [da·ˈrum, *when emphatic* ˈdaːrum, *in compounds* da·ˈrum-]. (*F:* **drum**) I. *pron. adv.* **1.** (a)round it, them, (*emphatic*) that, those, there; **ein Garten mit einem Zaun d.,** a garden with a fence round it; (*emphatic*) **d. sollst du das Band nicht tun,** you shouldn't tie the ribbon round that, those, there; **d. herumkommen,** to get out of it; **er wollte uns dazu zwingen, aber wir sind d. herumgekommen,** he wanted to force us to do it, but we got out of it. **2.** (*translation of constructions with* **darum** *depends on the translation of* **um** *in connection with the verb, etc., in question; the uses of* **um** *and* **darum** *are illustrated under the respective verbs, etc., taking* **um**) (*a*) for it, them; **d. bitten, beten, betteln,** to ask, pray, beg, for it, them; **geh nicht hin! ich bitte dich d.,** don't go! I beg you not to; don't go, I beg of you! **sie flehte mich d. an, ich sollte ihren Mann freigeben,** she implored me to set her husband free; **d. kämpfen,** to fight for, strive after, it; **d. losen,** to cast lots for it, them; **wir losten d., wer es ihm sagen sollte,** we cast lots (for) who should tell him; *see also* **geben** I. 1 (*d*), **tun;** (*b*) about it, them; **d. wissen,** to know about it; **d. zürnen,** to be angry about it; **es sei d.!** (i) so be it! (ii) what does it matter? who cares? (*c*) **es handelt sich d., . . . ,** it's a matter, a question, of . . .; **es handelt sich d., ob er einwilligen wird,** the question is, whether he will agree to it; *see also* **handeln** I. 4; (*d*) **j-n d. betrügen,** to cheat s.o. out of it; **jetzt hat er kein Geld mehr; man hat ihn d. betrogen, gebracht,** he has no money left now; he was cheated, done, out of it; *see also* **darumkommen. 3.** *rel. use A. & Lit:* (a)round which, for which, about which; wherefore; *B:* **was ist die Sache, d. ihr hie seid?** what is the cause, wherefore ye are come?

II. **darum** (*emphatic*). **1.** *conj.* therefore, for this (that) reason, that's (the reason) why; **ich hörte, du seist krank; d. bin ich hierher gekommen,** I heard you were ill; that's why I came. **2.** *adv.* (*a*) **d., (. . .) weil,** *A:* **d. daß,** because; **er tat es d., weil er uns zu helfen gedachte,** he did it because he thought he could help us; **hatte sie d. recht, weil niemand ihr zu widersprechen wagte?** was she right, simply because no one dared to contradict her? **so, darum!** so that's (the reason) why! *B:* **und da es aufging, verdorrte es, d. daß es nicht Saft hatte,** and as soon as it was sprung up, it withered away, because it lacked moisture; (*b*) (*official language*) *A:* **von d.,** for this, that, reason; **wir taten es von d.,** we did it for this, that, reason.

darumkommen, *v.i. sep.* (*strong*) (*sein*) (i) to lose it, them; to be deprived of it, them; (ii) to get out of it; (iii) to be left out (of it); **er hatte mal Geld, ist aber im Krieg darumgekommen,** he had money once, but he lost it in the war; **er wird nicht d., zu dem Empfang zu gehen,** he won't get out of going to the reception; **alle bekamen Geschenke, nur ich bin darumgekommen,** everyone received presents—I was the only one left out; *cp.* **darum** I, II.

darumlegen, *v.tr. sep.* **(etwas) d.,** to put (sth.) (a)round it, them.

darunter [da·ˈruntər, *when emphatic* ˈdaːruntər] (*F:* **drunter**), *pron. adv.* **1.** (*a*) under(neath), beneath, below, it, them, (*emphatic*) that, those; underneath; **ich hob den Stein auf und fand einen Beutel Geld d.,** I lifted the stone and found a purse full of money under(neath), beneath, it, underneath; **an der Wand hing eine Ikone, und d. brannte eine Kerze,** on the wall hung an icon and under, beneath, below, it burned a candle; **der Baum ist morsch; stell dich bloß nicht d.!** the tree is rotten; whatever you do don't stand under, beneath, it; (*b*) less, under; **die Waren kosten zwanzig Mark; wir können sie nicht d. verkaufen,** the goods cost twenty marks; we cannot sell them for less, we cannot sell them under, below, that price; **zehn Grad und d.,** ten degrees or under, or less; **eher d. als darüber,** rather less than more; (*c*) among(st) them, in it; **wenn man von ihm Kohlen kauft, so findet man immer Steine d.,** if you buy coal from him you always find stones amongst it; **er nahm echte Perlen und mischte synthetische d.,** he took real pearls and mixed synthetic ones amongst, with, them. **2.** (*a*) **d. leiden,** to suffer from it, them; **es gab unzählige Mücken auf dem Strand, und die Feriengäste litten sehr d.,** the beach was infested with flies and the holiday visitors suffered greatly from them; **seine Arbeit ist so schwer, daß seine Gesundheit d. leidet,** his work is so heavy that his health is suffering (from it); **er leidet sehr d., daß sie so unfreundlich zu ihm ist,** he suffers greatly from her unkindness, from her being so unkind, to him; (*b*) **(etwas) d. verstehen, sich** *dat.* **(etwas) d. vorstellen,** to understand (sth.) by it, them; **was verstehst du d.?** what do you understand by it? what does it mean to you? **er kann sich nichts d. vorstellen,** he has no idea what it means; (*c*) **einen Unterschied d. machen,** to distinguish, to make a distinction, between them. **3.** *rel. use A. & Lit:* under(neath) which, beneath which, below which; from which; by which; between which.

Darwinismus [darvi·ˈnismus], *m.* **-/.** Darwinism.

Darwinist [darvi·ˈnist], *m.* **-en/-en.** Darwinist.

darwinistisch [darvi·ˈnistiʃ], *a.* Darwinian.

Darwinsch [ˈdarviːnʃ], *a.* Darwin's, Darwinian; *Anthr:* **Darwinscher Höcker, Ohrhöcker,** Darwin's, Darwinian, tubercle.

das *see* **der.**

Dase, *f.* **-/-n. 1.** *Ent:* = **Dasselfliege. 2.** *Ich:* = **Döbel.**

dasein[1], *v.i. sep.* (*sein*) (*conj. like* **sein**) (*see also* **da** I. 1 (*a*), (*e*)) **1.** to be there, present; **ich kann dir die Szene genau beschreiben, denn ich bin dagewesen,** I can describe the scene to you exactly because I was there, present; **bei diesem Feste wird er auch d.,** he'll be (present) at the celebration too. **2.** (*a*) to be (there, in existence), to exist; **das ist das größte Gebäude, das je dagewesen ist,** that's the biggest building (there has) ever (been), that has ever existed; **es ist alles schon mal dagewesen,** all this has happened before; there's nothing new under the sun; **wärst du nicht dagewesen, so wären wir alle ums Leben gekommen,** if you hadn't been there, had it not been for you, we should all have lost our lives; **noch nicht, noch nie, dagewesen,** unheard-of, unprecedented; **so ein Krieg ist noch nie dagewesen,** there has never been such a war (before); *F:* **so was ist auch noch nicht dagewesen!** that beats the band! it beats everything! **ein noch nie dagewesener Erfolg,** an unprecedented, unheard-of, success; **alles bisher Dagewesene in den Schatten stellen,** to break all records, to put all previous achievements in the shade; (*b*) to be there, at hand, available; **es sind fünf Flaschen Wein da,** there are five bottles of wine.

Dasein[2], *n.* **-s/. 1.** *A:* presence; **im D. so vieler Gäste,** in the presence of so many guests. **2.** existence, life; being; *Phil:* existence; **ins D. treten,** to come into being, into existence; **einem Kinde zum D. verhelfen,** to bring a child into the world; **etwas ins D. rufen,** to call sth. into being, existence; **der Kampf ums D.,** the struggle for existence, life; **im künftigen D.,** in the next life, in the next world, in the after-life; **ein trauriges, elendes, D. (führen),** (to lead) a sad, miserable, life, existence; *see also* **fristen.**

Daseinsberechtigung, *f.* reason for existing; reason for (sth.'s) existence; raison d'être.

daseinshungrig, *a.* hungry for life.

Daseinskampf, *m.* struggle for existence, for life.

daseinsmüde, *a.* tired, weary, of life.

daselbst [da·ˈzɛlpst], *adv.* there; in that (very) place.

dasig, *a. A. & Austrian:* = **dortig.**

dasitzen, *v.i. sep.* (*strong*) (*haben*) (*a*) to sit there, by; **es ist so langweilig, wenn die Leute nur d. und nichts tun,** it's so boring when people just sit there and do nothing; *cp.* **da** 1 (*a*); (*b*) *F:* to be left in the lurch.

dasjenige *see* **derjenige.**

dasmal, *adv. A:* = **diesmal.**

daß, *conj.* that. **1.** (*statement*) (*a*) (*verb in main clause in primary tense, verb in subordinate clause in ind.; verb in main clause in past, verb in subordinate clause in sub.*) **er behauptet, daß es falsch ist,** he declares that it is wrong; **ich nehme an, daß es heute regnen wird,** I suppose it will rain today; **sie sagte, daß er sehr krank sei,** she said (that) he was very ill; **sie wußten, daß es nicht wahr sein könne,** they knew (that) it couldn't be true; (*b*) **es ist noch nicht sicher, daß er tot ist,** it is not yet certain that he is dead; **ein Glück, daß wir nicht ausgingen!** how fortunate that we didn't go out! **es ist merkwürdig, daß . . . ,** it is strange that . . .; **ich bin überrascht, erstaunt, enttäuscht, daß . . . ,** I am surprised, amazed, disappointed, that . . . ; (*c*) (*time*) (i) that; (ii) since; **es war im Jahre 1910, daß er nach England reiste,** it was in the year 1910 that he went to England; **es ist schon zehn Jahre her, daß ich zum letzten Mal bei ihr war,** it is ten years since I was at her house; **es sind vier Tage, daß er uns nicht angerufen hat,** he hasn't rung us up for four days; (*d*) **die Tatsache, daß . . . ,** the fact that . . .; **die Tatsache, daß sie es nicht tun dürfen, wird sie keineswegs daran hindern,** the fact that they are not allowed to do it will in no way stop them; **außer, nur, daß . . . ,** except that . . .; **mir geht's gut, außer, nur, daß ich im Augenblick Kopfschmerzen habe,** I'm very well except that just at the moment I have a headache; **außerdem, daß . . . ,** besides (the fact that . . .); **außerdem, daß er keine Lust dazu hat, (so) fehlt ihm auch die Zeit,** besides, apart from, the fact that he is not keen on doing it, besides, apart from, his not being keen on doing it, he has no time; **bis daß . . . ,** until (the time when . . . , such time as . . .); **wir müssen warten, bis daß die Gelegenheit sich bietet,** we must wait till (the time when, such time as) the opportunity arises; **(an)statt daß . . . ,** instead of . . .; **(an)statt, daß er sich uns dankbar erwies, schien er uns sehr böse zu sein,** instead of being grateful to us he seemed very angry with us; **ohne daß . . . ,** (i) without . . .; (ii) *A:* except that . . .; **er trat ins Zimmer herein, ohne daß ich ihn hörte,** he entered the room without my hearing him; **nicht daß . . . ,** not that . . .; **nicht daß ich ihm nicht glaube,** not that I don't believe him; *Lit:* **sie wird nicht genesen, es sei denn, daß ein Wunder geschehe,** she will not recover unless a miracle happens; *A. & Lit:* **. . . daß . . . nicht . . . ,** without . . .; **ich sehe sie nie, daß ich nicht entzückt bin,** I never see her without being delighted; *A:* **um daß . . . ,** because . . . . **2.** (*a*) (*after verbs of direct perception*) **wir bemerkten, daß sie müde war,** we noticed (that) she was tired; **er sah, daß es nutzlos war,** he saw (that) it was useless; **sie hörten, daß der Wagen abfuhr,** they heard the car drive away; **ich kann mir denken, vorstellen, daß sie sich darüber freut,** I can imagine that

she's happy about it; **daß es ihm nicht gefällt, das leuchtet mir ein, das verstehe ich,** I can well believe, I can quite understand, that he doesn't like it; (*b*) (*after verbs of indirect perception*) (*verb in main clause in primary tense, verb in subordinate clause in ind.; verb in main clause in past, verb in subordinate clause in sub.*) **sie hörten, daß der Wagen abgefahren sei,** they heard, were told, that the car had driven away; (*c*) (*implication of possibility; verb in subordinate clause in past sub.*) **ich kann mir denken, vorstellen, daß es wahr sein könnte,** I can imagine that it could, might, be true; **ich kann mir vorstellen, daß es ihm nicht gefiele, gefallen könnte,** I can well believe that he might not like it; (*d*) (*verb in main clause in primary tense, verb in subordinate clause in ind.; verb in main clause in past, verb in subordinate clause in sub.*) **das dürfen Sie tun unter der Bedingung, daß Sie mir die Hälfte des Gewinns abgeben,** you can do that on condition that you give me half the profits; **für den Fall, im Falle, daß ich spät nach Hause komme,** in case I come home late, in the event of my coming home late. **3.** (*a*) **sie erlaubte, daß das Kind allein in die Stadt ging,** she allowed the child to go into the town alone; **ihm ist es recht, daß wir hier bleiben,** he is willing for us to remain here; **er bewirkte, daß das Gesetz geändert wurde,** he brought about the alteration of the law; **es ergab sich, daß wir recht hatten,** it turned out, transpired, that we were right; (*b*) (*result, reason*) **daraus folgt, ergibt sich, daß das Ganze ein Irrtum war,** it turns out, transpires, from this that the whole thing was a mistake; **wie kommt es, daß du das nicht weißt?** how is it that you don't know that? **daher geschah es, daß wir uns nicht trafen,** thus it came about that we didn't meet, that's why we didn't meet; **was hat er denn getan, daß du ihm so böse bist?** what did he do that you are so angry with him? what did he do to make you so angry? **was können wir dafür, daß die Sache schief gegangen ist?** is it our fault that the business went wrong? **4.** (*verb in main clause in primary tense, verb in subordinate clause in ind.; verb in main clause in past, verb in subordinate clause in sub.*) (*a*) (*after verbs of wishing, command*) **sie hoffte, wünschte, wollte, daß es geschähe, geschehen sollte,** she hoped, wished, (that) it would happen, she wanted it to happen; **er befahl, daß wir das Holz holten, holen sollten,** he gave orders that we should, he ordered us to, fetch the wood; (*b*) (*after verbs of fear*) **wir fürchten, daß er den Zug verpaßt,** we are afraid (that) he will miss his train; **ich hatte Angst, daß er fallen könnte,** I was afraid (that) he might fall, lest he should fall; (*c*) (*after verbs of precaution*) **du sollst dafür sorgen, daß alle genug zu essen bekommen,** you must see (to it) that everyone has enough to eat; **gib acht, daß er nicht wegläuft!** take care (that) he doesn't escape, lest he escape! **sie gaben sich große Mühe, daß alles gut ablaufen sollte,** they took great pains to see that all went well. **5.** (*a*) **so ... daß,** (i) so ... that; (ii) in such a way ... that; **er war so dumm, daß er nicht einmal das erste Examen bestehen konnte,** he was so stupid (that) he couldn't even pass his first examination; **ich bin so müde, daß ich zu nichts Lust habe,** I am so tired (that) I don't feel like doing anything; **sie benahm sich so, daß niemand mit ihr Mitleid hatte,** she behaved in such a way that no one was sorry for her; **die Sache steht so, daß man nur Verderben voraussehen kann,** the situation is such that one can only foresee disaster; *see also* **so**; (*b*) **als daß ...,** than that ...; **er ist zu rücksichtsvoll, als daß er das tun könnte,** he is too thoughtful to do that; **sie ist zu unzuverlässig, als daß man ihr trauen kann,** she is too unreliable to be depended upon; **ich bin schon zu alt, als daß ich noch heiraten könnte,** I am too old to marry now; (*c*) **auf daß ...,** so that, (in order) that, (in order) to; **iß tüchtig, auf daß du kräftig werdest!** eat a lot so that you get strong, so as to get strong! (*d*) **nicht daß ich wüßte,** not that I know of, not as far as I know; (*e*) lest, in case; **daß ich's nicht vergesse, sie hat abgesagt,** lest, before, in case, I forget (it), she said she couldn't come. **6.** (*exclamatory*) (i) may ..., o that ..., if only ..., would that ...; (ii) (*implying impatience or surprise*) fancy ..., how surprising that ...; (iii) see to it that ..., take care that ...; (iv) (*implying indignation*) that ...; **daß Gott erbarm!** (may) God have mercy! (good) Heavens! **daß ihn der Teufel, der Kuckuck, hole!** (may the) devil take him! (o) **daß ich (doch) wieder nach Hause könnte!** if only, would that, o that, I could go home! **daß ich dich doch nie kennengelernt hätte!** would that, if only, I had never met you! **daß er immer noch so naiv ist!** fancy his still being so naive! **daß du es nicht vergißt!** and (mind you) don't forget it! **daß wir dich nie wieder in diesem Hause sehen!** (i) may we never see you in this house again! (ii) take care, see to it, that we never see you in this house again! **daß ihre Mutter doch immer dabeisein muß!** what a nuisance that her mother has always to be there! **daß so etwas geschehen kann!** (how dreadful) that such a thing can happen!

dasselbe *see* **derselbe.**

Dasselbeule, *f. Vet:* warble.

Dasselfliege, *f. Ent: Vet:* oestrus, gad-fly, bot(t)-fly; warble(-fly); **Larve der D.,** bot(t).

Dasselplage, *f. Vet:* warbles.

dastehen, *v.i. sep.* (*strong*) (*haben*) (*a*) to stand (there); **er stand unentschlossen da,** he stood (there) undecided; **verlegen d.,** to stand (there) looking embarrassed; (*b*) **wie stehe ich nun da!** (i) what a fool I've made of myself! what a fool I've been made to look! what an awkward position I'm in! (ii) what do you think of that! what do you think of me now! **ohne Mittel d.,** to be without means; **allein d.,** to be (all) alone (in the world); **unerreicht, einmalig, d.,** to be unrivalled, unequalled; **eine einzig dastehende Leistung,** an unprecedented achievement; **gut, schlecht, d.,** to be in a good, a bad, position; **er steht schlecht da,** he is in a bad way; **jetzt steht er nicht mehr so gut da,** he's not so well off, he's not doing so well, now.

Data, *n.pl. see* **Datum** 2.

Datar [da·ˈtaːr], *m.* **-s/-e.** *R.C.Ch:* datary.

Datarie [da·ta·ˈriː], *f.* **-/.** *R.C.Ch:* datary, dataria.

Datenverarbeitung, *f. Electronics:* data processing.

datieren [da·ˈtiːrən], *v.* **1.** *v.tr.* (*a*) to date (letter, etc.); **der Brief ist vom 2. August datiert,** the letter is dated, is under (the) date of, August 2nd; **einen Scheck falsch d.,** to misdate a cheque; (*b*) to date, to assign a date to (work of art, etc.); **das Bild ist nicht genau datiert,** the exact date of the picture is not known; **das Manuskript ist durch seine Subskription datiert,** we know the correct date of the manuscript from its colophon, the manuscript can be dated exactly by its colophon; **können Sie diese Skulptur d.?** can you give the date of this piece of sculpture? **2.** *v.i.* (*haben*) (**aus ..., von ...**) **d.,** to date (from ...); **dieser Aberglaube datiert aus uralter Zeit,** this superstition dates from the earliest times; **der Brief datiert vom 2. August,** the letter is dated August 2nd.

Dativ [ˈdaːtiːf, da·ˈtiːf], *m.* **-s/-e** [-tiːvə]. *Gram:* dative (case).

Dativobjekt, *n. Gram:* indirect object.

Dativus [da·ˈtiːvus], *m.* **-/-ve.** *Gram:* dative (case).

dato [ˈdaːtoː], *adv. Com:* **a dato, de dato,** after date, from today; **sie müssen sechs Monate dato, a dato, bezahlen,** they must pay six months after date, at six months' date; **bis dato,** to date, up to now.

Datowechsel, *m. Com:* time-bill.

Datscha [ˈdatʃaː], **Datsche** [ˈdatʃə], *f.* **-/-schen,** dacha.

Dattel, *f.* **-/-n.** *Bot:* date; **chinesische D.,** jujube (fruit).

Dattelbaum, *m. Bot:* date-palm.

Dattelfieber, *n. Med:* dengue-fever, *F:* dandy-fever, *U.S:* breakbone fever.

Dattelmuschel, *f. Moll:* common piddock.

Dattelpalme, *f. Bot:* date-palm.

Dattelpflaume, *f. Bot:* (*a*) **(virginische) D.,** persimmon, date-plum; (*b*) **chinesische D.,** Chinese persimmon, keg fig.

Datterich, *m.* **-(e)s/.** *Dial:*=**Tatterich.**

Datum [ˈdaːtum], *n.* **-s/-ten. 1.** date; **was für ein D. haben wir heute?** what is today's date, the date today? **von welchem D. ist diese Zeitung?** what is the date of this paper? **dieser Brief ist ohne D.,** this letter is undated, dateless; **der Brief trägt das D. 1812,** the letter is dated 1812; **sein Schreiben heutigen, gestrigen, Datums,** his letter of today, yesterday; **ein Schreiben heutigen, gestrigen, Datums,** a letter bearing today's, yesterday's, date; **unter dem D. des 12. Juni,** under (the) date of June 12th; **ich kann Ihnen die genauen Daten meiner Reise nicht angeben,** I can't tell, give, you the exact dates for my journey; **neuesten, jungen, Datums sein,** to be new, recent; **das Geschichtsbuch ist nicht gerade neuesten Datums,** (i) the history book is not altogether a new, a recent, one; (ii) the history book is not altogether up-to-date; **die wichtigsten Daten der Geschichte,** the most important dates in history. **2.** (*pl.* **Daten** *&* **Data**) datum; **Daten, Data,** data, facts; **die technischen Daten eines Motors,** the technical data of a motor.

Datumei, *n.* date-stamped egg.

Datumgrenze, *f. Geog:* date-line (*meridian of* 180°).

Datumstempel, *m.* date-marker, date-stamp.

Dature [da·ˈtuːrə], *f.* **-/-n.** *Bot:* datura, *esp.* thorn-apple, stramony, *U.S:* jimson weed.

Dau, *f.* **-/-en.** *Nau:* d(h)ow.

Daube, *f.* **-/-n.** *Coop:* (barrel) stave; *Games:* (*curling*) tee.

Daubenholz, *n. Coop:* stave-wood.

Dauer, *f.* **-/.** (*a*) length, duration (of stay, etc.); duration (of life); duration, continuance (of reign, war, etc.); *Ph:* time, period (of oscillation); **für die, eine, D. von zwei Wochen,** for (a period of) two weeks; (*b*) **auf die D.,** (i) in (the course of) time, with time; in the long run; (ii) for a length of time; permanently; **man wird diese Arbeit auf die D. leid,** with time, in the long run, one grows tired of this work; **auf die D. möchte ich hier nicht wohnen,** I shouldn't care to live here for any length of time, permanently; **diese Atmosphäre kann man auf die D. nicht aushalten,** one cannot bear this atmosphere for any length of time, this atmosphere becomes too much for one in the long run; (*c*) permanence, lastingness; **keine D. haben, nicht von D. sein,** to have no permanence, no durability; **seine Dankbarkeit hatte keine D., war nicht von D.,** his gratitude didn't last; **diese Einrichtung ist nicht für die D.,** this arrangement is not (intended to be) permanent, lasting; **wir wollen hoffen, daß die Besserung von D. sein wird,** let's hope the improvement will last, will prove permanent; **unser Glück war von kurzer D.,** our happiness was of short duration, was short-lived; **von langer D. sein,** to last a long time; **wir hoffen, daß dieser Friede von langer D. sein wird,** we hope that this peace will last a long time, will be, prove, lasting; **ihre Freundschaft wird wohl nicht von langer D. sein,** I don't suppose their friendship will last long; (*d*) (i) *A:*=**Dauerhaftigkeit**; (ii) **auf D. gearbeitet,** made to last.

Dauerangestellte, *m., f.* permanent employee; **Dauerangestellte** *pl,* established personnel.

Dauerauftrag, *m. Com: Bank:* standing order.

Dauerausscheider, *m.* **-s/-.** *Med:* chronic carrier (of disease).

Dauerbackwaren, *f. pl.* cakes, biscuits, that keep.

Dauerbefehl, *m. Mil:* standing order.

Dauerbelastung, *f. Ph: etc:* permanent load, *U.S:* constant load.

Dauerbetrieb, *m.* continuous working, continuous operation; **hier wird im D. gearbeitet,** work continues here (day and night) without stopping.

Dauerbier, *n.* lager beer.

Dauerbrandlampe, *f.* enclosed arc lamp.

Dauerbrandofen, *m.* slow-combustion stove, slow-burning stove.

Dauerbrenner, *m.* **1.** slow-combustion stove, slow-burning stove. **2.** *P:* long, burning kiss.

Dauerbruch, *m. Mec.E: Med:* fatigue fracture.

Dauerbutter, *f.* preserved butter.

Dauerdrehmoment, *n. El.E:* continuous torque.

Dauerei, *n. Crust: etc:* resting egg, winter egg.

Dauererhitzung, *f.* prolonged heating.

Dauererhitzungswanne, *f. Ind:* sterilization apparatus, *esp.* pasteurization apparatus.

Dauererlaß, *m. Adm:* standing order.

Dauerfahrt, *f. Cy:* endurance run.

Dauerfarbe, *f.* fast dye; fast colour, fast paint.

Dauerfestigkeit, *f. Mec.E: etc:* fatigue limit, *U.S:* fatigue strength (of materials.)

Dauerfestigkeitsprüfung, *f. Mec.E:* endurance test.

Dauerfeuer, *n. Mil:* sustained fire.

Dauerflämmchen, *n.,* **Dauerflamme,** *f.* pilot-burner, -flame, -jet (of gas-lamp, heater, etc.).

Dauerfleisch, *n.* preserved meat, *esp.* smoked *or* pickled meat.

Dauerflug, *m. Av:* duration flight; endurance flight.

Dauergast, *m.* (*a*) permanent resident (at hotel, etc.); (*b*) guest who outstays the time for which he was invited, *F:* permanent fixture.

Dauergewebe, *n. Bot:* permanent tissue.

dauergewellt, *a.* (*of hair*) permanently waved.

dauerhaft, (*a*) *a.* lasting, enduring (peace, pleasures, etc.); durable, hard-wearing (material, etc.); solid (building); fast (colour, dye); (*b*) *adv.* durably, solidly; **d. gemacht,** (material, etc.) made to last, made to be durable, made to wear well; (dye) made to be fast; **d. gebaut,** solidly built (building).

Dauerhaftigkeit, *f.* lastingness, enduringness (of

peace, pleasures, etc.); durability, durableness (of material, etc.); solidity (of building); fastness (of dye).

Dauerhefe, *f.* permanent yeast.

Dauerkarte, *f. Th: Rail: etc:* season ticket.

Dauerlager, *n. Mil:* permanent camp.

Dauerlauf, *m.* (i) *Gym:* jog-trot; (ii) *Sp:* endurance-run; **D. machen,** to jog-trot, to jog; *F:* **er lief im D. zum Bahnhof,** he ran all the way to the station.

Dauerlaut, *m. Ling:* continuant.

Dauerleistung, *f.* continuous output; *El.E:* continuous rating.

Dauerlolch, *m. Bot:* perennial rye-grass, English meadow-grass.

Dauerlutscher, *m. F:* (*a*) lollipop; (*b*) gob-stopper.

Dauermagnet, *m. Ph:* permanent magnet.

Dauermarsch, *m. Mil:* forced march.

Dauermiete, *f.* permanent tenancy.

Dauermieter, *m.* permanent tenant.

Dauermilch, *f.* sterilized milk.

Dauermoment, *n.* = **Dauerdrehmoment.**

dauern[1]. I. *v.* **1.** *v.tr. A:* to bear, endure, put up with (sth.); **ich kann es nicht länger d.,** I can't bear, endure, it any longer. **2.** *v.i.* (*haben*) (*a*) (*of thg*) to last, continue, go on; to take (time); **unsere Liebe wird ewig d.,** our love will last, endure, for ever; **wie lange hat der Vortrag gedauert?** how long did the lecture last? **seine Rede dauerte noch eine halbe Stunde,** his speech lasted, continued, went on, for, his speech took, another half hour; **das wird lange d.,** that will take a long time; **diese Dinge dauern ihre Zeit,** these things take time; **das dauert ihm zu lange,** it takes too long for his liking; (*b*) (*impers.*) **es wird noch zwei Stunden d., bis ich in London bin,** it will take me another two hours to reach London; **es dauerte ein halbes Jahr, bis sie sich eingelebt hatte,** it was six months before she became acclimatized, it took her six months to become acclimatized; **es dauerte lange, bis er das Ufer erreichte,** he was a long time reaching the shore; **es wird nicht lange d., so werden wir abreisen können,** it won't be long before we can leave; **es dauerte nicht lange, so hatte er schon genug davon,** it wasn't long before he had had enough of it.

II. *pr.p. & a.* **dauernd,** *in vbl senses; esp.* **1.** *a.* (*a*) lasting, enduring; permanent; **ewig d.,** everlasting, perennial; **ewig dauernde Jugend,** perennial youth; **eine dauernde Stellung,** a permanent position, post; **dauernder Friede,** permanent, lasting, peace; **ein dauernder Wohnsitz,** a permanent residence; **dauernde Liebe,** lasting, enduring, love; (*b*) constant, perpetual; **dauerndes Gelächter,** constant, continual, laughter; **in dauernder Sorge,** in (a state of) constant, perpetual, anxiety; **dauernde Gefahr,** constant, perpetual, danger. **2.** *adv.* continually, constantly, always; **er fragt mich d., wie es dir geht,** he is always, continually, constantly, asking me how you are; **sie ist d. unterwegs,** she is always travelling, she travels continually, she is always on the move.

dauern[2], *v.tr.* to make (s.o.) sorry; (*a*) **er dauert mich,** I am sorry for him; **mich dauert sein Unglück, mich dauert, daß er so unglücklich ist,** I am sorry that he is so unhappy; (*b*) **die Zeit, das Geld, die Mühe, dauert mich,** I begrudge the time, the money, the effort; **mich dauert das Geld, das ich dafür ausgegeben habe,** I regret, begrudge, the money I spent on it; **laß dich dein Geld nicht d.!** don't begrudge the money! **es dauert sie jeder Augenblick, den sie dabei verbringt,** she regrets, begrudges, every moment she has to spend on it.

Dauerniere, *f. Anat:* metanephros.

Dauerplissé, *n. Tex:* durably *or* permanently pleated material.

Dauerprobe, *f. Mec.E: etc:* endurance test.

Dauerprüfmaschine, *f. Ind:* endurance tester.

Dauerredner, *m. F:* marathon speaker.

Dauerriß, *m. Mec.E: etc:* fatigue crack (in material).

Dauerritt, *m. Sp:* endurance-ride (on horseback).

Dauerrudern, *n. Row:* endurance-run.

Dauerschlaf, *m. Med:* cataphora.

Dauerspore, *f. Bot:* resting spore.

Dauerstellung, *f.* permanent position, permanent post.

Dauerstrom, *m. El:* constant current, closed-circuit current.

Dauerton, *m. Tg:* prolonged tone.

Dauertypus, *m. Biol:* permanent type.

Dauerversuch, *m. Mec.E:* endurance test.

Dauerwald, *m. For:* permanent forest.

Dauerwäsche, *f.* long-wearing linen.

Dauerweide, *f.* permanent pasture.

Dauerwelle, *f. Haird:* permanent wave, *F:* perm; **sie hat Dauerwellen,** her hair is permanently waved, *F:* permed; **j-m eine D. machen,** to give s.o. a permanent wave, *F:* to give s.o. a perm, to perm s.o.'s hair.

Dauerwirkung, *f.* lasting effect, permanent effect.

Dauerwurst, *f.* hard smoked sausage (*e.g.* salami).

Daumeisen, *n.* small anvil.

Daumen, *m.* **-s/-. 1.** (*a*) thumb; **zwischen Finger und D.,** between finger and thumb; **(die) Daumen drehen,** to twiddle one's thumbs; *F:* **j-n über den D. drehen,** to cheat s.o.; **etwas über den D. peilen, schätzen,** to judge sth. roughly, to give a rough estimate of sth.; **unter j-s D. sein,** to be under s.o.'s thumb; **j-n unter dem D. halten,** to keep s.o. under one's thumb; **j-m den D. aufs Auge setzen, halten, drücken,** to force s.o. to do sth.; *F:* to put the screws on s.o., to put on the screw; to clamp down on s.o.; **j-m den D. halten,** to cross one's fingers, to keep one's fingers crossed, for s.o.; **D. halten!** keep your fingers crossed! cross fingers! (*b*) *A:* big toe. **2.** *A. & Dial: Meas:* inch. **3.** *Mec.E:* cam, lifter, wiper, tappet.

Daumenabdruck, *m.* thumb-mark.

Daumenabzieher, *m. Anat:* abductor pollicis.

Daumenballen, *m. Anat:* thenar eminence, thenar prominence, ball of the thumb.

Daumenbeuger, *m. Anat:* flexor pollicis.

Daumenbreite, *f.* thumb's width; **um eine D.,** by about an inch.

Daumendreher, *m. F:* lazy-bones, loafer.

Daumendrücker, *m. Locksm:* thumb-piece.

Daumenkappe, *f.* thumb-stall.

Daumennagel, *m.* thumb-nail.

Daumenrad, *n. Mec. E:* sprocket(-wheel).

Daumenregister, *n.* thumb-index.

Daumenscheibe, *f. Mec.E:* cam plate, cam disc.

Daumenschraube, *f.* **1.** thumb-screw, wing-bolt. **2.** *Hist:* = **Daumschrauben.**

Daumenschützer, *m.* thumb-stall.

Daumensteuerung, *f. I.C.E:* cam-gear.

Daumenwelle, *f. Mec.E:* cam-shaft.

daumesdick. 1. *a.* as thick as one's thumb; the size of one's thumb. **2.** *Pr.n.m.* **-s. Daumesdick** = **Däumling** 3.

Daumkraft, *f.* (screw-)jack, *U.S:* jackscrew.

Däumling, *m.* **-s/-e. 1.** *Mec.E:* cam, lifter, wiper, tappet. **2.** (*a*) thumb (of glove); (*b*) thumb-stall. **3.** *Pr.n.m.* **-s.** Tom Thumb.

Daumschrauben, *f.pl. Hist:* (*instrument of torture*) thumb-screws; *F:* **j-m D. anlegen,** to put on, tighten, the screw; to put the screws on s.o.

Daun, *m.* **-(e)s/.** *Bot:* hemp-nettle, stinking nettle.

Daune, *f.* **-/-n,** downy feather; **Daunen** *pl,* down.

Daunenbett, *n.* feather-bed.

Daunendruckpapier, *n. Paperm:* featherweight paper.

Daunen(stepp)decke, *f.* eiderdown (quilt).

Dauphin [do·ˈfɛ̃ː], *m.* **-s/-s.** *Fr.Hist:* Dauphin.

Dauphine [do·ˈfiːnə], *f.* **-/-n.** *Fr.Hist:* Dauphiness.

Dauphiné, die [do·fi·ˈneː]. *Pr.n.* **-.** *Geog:* the Dauphiny.

Daus[1], *m.* **-es/-e,** devil (*only used in certain phrases*); (*a*) *A:* **ein Junge wie ein D.,** a stunning, ripping, boy, chap; **er tanzt wie ein D., er ist ein D. im Tanzen,** he dances wonderfully, he's a wonderful dancer; (*b*) **ei der D.! was der D.! Potz D.!** (i) what the deuce! what the devil! (ii) good Lord! how wonderful!

Daus[2], *n.* **-es/-e & ⸗er,** (*a*) (*dice*) deuce; (*b*) *Cards:* ace.

David [ˈdaːvi(·)t, ˈdaːfi(·)t]. *Pr.n.m.* **-s.** David.

Davidshirsch, *m. Z:* Père David's deer.

David(s)stern, *m.* star, shield, of David.

Davit [ˈdeːvit], *n.* **-s/-s.** *Nau:* davit.

Davitgeie, *f.pl. Nau:* davit-guys.

Davitspur, *f. Nau:* davit socket.

davon [da·ˈfon, *when emphatic* ˈdaːfon, *in compounds* da·ˈfon-], *pron. adv.* **1.** (*also* **davon-** *comb.fm.*) (away) from it, them, (*emphatic*) that, those; away; (*a*) **der Hund ist bissig; halte dich fern d.,** the dog is fierce, so keep well away from it; **ich kenne den Ort, den Sie meinen, denn ich wohne nicht weit d. (entfernt),** I know the place you mean as I live not far away (from it); **bleib d.!** keep away from it, don't touch it, them! leave it, them, alone! **er war nicht weit d. (entfernt), es zu tun,** he wasn't far from doing it, he almost did it; (*b*) away, off; **davongehen, auf und d. gehen,** to go away; **davonkommen,** to get away, to escape; **(etwas) davonnehmen,** to take (sth.) away; **das Bild war so schön, daß er die Augen nicht d. abwenden konnte,** the picture was so beautiful that he couldn't take his eyes off it; **sich d. trennen,** to part with it, them; (*c*) off it, them; **der Teller ist mir zu schmutzig; d. kann ich nicht essen,** the plate is too dirty for me to eat off (it). **2.** (*a*) from it, them, (*emphatic*) that, those; **was hat er denn d.?** what does he get from, out of, it? what does he gain by it? what good will it do him? **was werden sie d. haben, wenn sie ihr ganzes Geld anlegen?** what will they get from, gain by, investing all their money? (*emphatic*) **d. werden wir wenig Nutzen haben,** we shan't get, gain, much by that; **das kommt d.!** that's what happens when you do things like that! it serves you right! **das kommt d., wenn man unvorsichtig ist,** that comes of being careless! it serves one right for being careless! **das kommt d., daß . . . ,** that's because . . . ; (*emphatic*) **d. kommt es, daß wir diesen Irrtum machten,** that's why we made, that's how we came to make, this mistake; (*b*) **d. sterben,** to die of it; **iß die Beeren nicht, du könntest d. sterben,** don't eat those berries, they might kill you; (*c*) **d. abhängen,** to depend on it, them; **es hängt d. ab, ob wir die Zeit dazu haben,** it all depends on whether we have the time for it; **d. leben,** to live on it, them; **sein Gehalt ist zu klein; er kann nicht d. leben,** his salary is too small; he can't live on it; **er lebt d., daß er Zeitungen verkauft,** he lives by selling newspapers. **3.** of it, them, (*emphatic*) that, those; **sie kaufte zwölf Eier, aber zwei d. waren faul,** she bought twelve eggs, but two of them were bad; **ein Teil d.,** part of it, some of them; **hier ist ein schöner Obstsalat; iß d.,** here is a nice fruit salad; eat some (of it); **ich habe genug d.,** I've had enough (of it, them); **er hat mich jahrelang belästigt; jetzt habe ich genug d.,** he has been molesting me for years; now I've had enough of it; **wenn man d. zehn Prozent abzieht,** if you take away, deduct, ten per cent; **zwei d. ab, weg, bleibt sechs,** take away, subtract, two, and six remain. **4.** of, about, it, them, (*emphatic*) that, those; **d. sprechen, reden,** to speak, talk, about it, them; **d. schweigen,** to keep quiet, to say nothing, about it, them; **d. hören,** to hear about it, them; **er sagte nichts d., daß er seine Mutter verloren hatte,** he did not mention that he had lost his mother; **sie sprachen, redeten, d., daß er große Aussichten habe,** they were talking about his having great prospects; **sie sprach, redete, d., ihr Haus zu verkaufen,** she talked of selling her house; **nichts mehr d.!** say no more about it! let's hear no more about it! **ein andermal mehr d.!** we'll discuss it further another time; **was hält, denkt, er d.?** what does he think of it, them? (*emphatic*) **d. ist nicht die Rede,** that's not the question. **5.** *rel. use A. & Lit:* (away) from which; off which; of which; on which; by which.

davonfahren, *v.i. sep.* (*strong*) (*sein*) (*of pers., vehicle*) to drive away, to drive off, to leave.

davongehen, *v.i. sep.* (*strong*) (*sein*) to go away, to leave.

davonkommen, *v.i. sep.* (*strong*) (*sein*) to escape, to get off; **er ist mit dem Schrecken davongekommen,** he escaped with a fright; **glimpflich d.,** to get off lightly; **billig d.,** to get off cheaply, lightly; **er ist noch mal davongekommen,** he got off lightly; **wir sind gerade noch so davongekommen,** we had a narrow escape, it was a near thing, *F:* a near go; *P:* we had a narrow squeak; *see also* **blau** I. 1 (*b*), **davon** 2 (*b*), **knapp**[1], **ungeschoren.**

davonlaufen, *v.i. sep.* (*strong*) (*sein*) to run away; **es ist zum Davonlaufen,** it's unbearable.

davonmachen (sich), *v.refl. sep.* to make off; **sich eilends d.,** to take to one's heels; **sich heimlich d.,** to steal away.

davontragen, *v.tr. sep.* (*strong*) to carry off (sth.); to receive, get (sth.); **den ersten Preis d.,** to carry off, get, (the) first prize; **Verletzungen d.,** to receive injuries; **von etwas dauernden Schaden d.,** to suffer permanent damage from sth.; *see also* **Sieg.**

davor [da·ˈfoːr, *when emphatic* ˈdaːfoːr, *in compounds* da·ˈfoːr], *pron.adv.* **1.** (*a*) (*also* **davor-,** *comb.fm.*) (*place*) before, in front of, it, them, (*emphatic*) that, those; **er ging auf das Bild zu und blieb dicht d. stehen,** he went up to the picture and stopped close in front of it; (*b*) (*time*) before it; (*emphatic*) before that; **ich gehe heute abend ins Theater; d. muß ich aber zum Friseur,** I am going to the theatre tonight, but first, but before that, I must go to the hairdresser's; **gestern hatte er Examen; er war schon viele Tage d. aufgeregt,** he sat his examinations yesterday; he had been worrying about them for days beforehand. **2.** (*a*) of it, of them; **sich d. fürchten, Angst d. haben,** to be afraid of it, them; (*emphatic*) **d. habe ich keine Angst,** I'm not afraid

of that, of ˈthem; **sich d. hüten, sich d. in acht nehmen,** to beware of it, them; **du mußt dich d. hüten, es zu tun,** you must beware of doing it, you must take care not to do it; (*b*) from it, them; **j-n d. schützen, bewahren,** to protect, save, s.o. from it, them; **sie hat ihn d. bewahrt, in die Fremdenlegion einzutreten,** she saved him from joining the Foreign Legion; **d. sei Gott! Gott bewahre uns d.!** God forbid! God preserve us (from it)! **3.** *rel. use A. & Lit:* in front of which; before which; of which; from which; for which.

davorstehen, *v.i. sep.* (*strong*) (*haben*) to stand before, in front of, it, them; **das Feuer ist zu heiß, — du sollst nicht d.,** the fire is too hot—you shouldn't stand in front of it.

dawider [da·ˈviːdər], *adv.* = **dagegen; dafür und d.,** for and against (it, them).

dawiderreden, *v.i. sep.* (*haben*) to speak against it; to object, to make objections (to it, them).

Dayak [ˈdaːjak], *m.* **-s/-s.** *Ethn:* Dyak.

Dazien [ˈdaːtsiən]. *Pr.n.n.* **-s.** *A.Geog:* Dacia.

Dazier [ˈdaːtsiər], *m.* **-s/-.** *A.Hist:* Dacian.

dazisch [ˈdaːtsiʃ], *a. A.Geog:* Dacian.

dazu [da·ˈtsuː, *when emphatic* ˈdaːtsuː, *in compounds* da·ˈtsuː], *pron. adv.* (*also* **dazu-**, *comb.fm.*) **1.** (*a*) to it, to them; (*emphatic*) to that, to those; **als er die Menschenansammlung vor dem brennenden Hause sah, stellte er sich d.,** when he saw the crowd in front of the burning house he joined them; (*b*) **hier sind die Geschenke; lege deins d.!** here are the presents; add yours to them, put yours with them; **er gab ihr nicht nur Bonbons, sondern auch noch Blumen und Zigaretten d.,** he gave her not only sweets but flowers and cigarettes into the bargain, as well, in addition; **er ist arm und krank d.,** he is poor and ill into the bargain; **hast du die Fahrkarten dazugerechnet?** have you added in the cost of the tickets? (*c*) for it, them; **d. geschaffen, gemacht, sein,** to be born, made, for it; **er war nicht d. gemacht, eine so schwere Aufgabe zu übernehmen,** he wasn't made to undertake such a difficult task; **sie ist d. geschaffen, alle Leute aus der Fassung zu bringen,** she was born to upset everyone; **du mußt einen neuen Hut haben, — hier ist das Geld d.,** you must have a new hat—here is the money for it; **ich muß ein neues Kleid haben, aber diesen Stoff kann ich nicht d. gebrauchen,** I must have a new dress, but I can't use this material for it; (*emphatic*) **d. ist kein Grund vorhanden,** there is no reason for that; **er muß die Klasse in Ordnung halten;** (*emphatic*) **d. ist er da,** he must keep the class in order; that's what he's there for; (*d*) with it, with them; **wir werden Fleisch zum Mittagessen haben, aber ich weiß noch nicht, welches Gemüse wir d. essen werden,** we shall have meat for lunch but I don't yet know what vegetable we shall have with it; **sie tanzte, und er spielte Klavier d.,** she danced and he accompanied her on the piano; **sie sang und spielte Gitarre d.,** she sang and accompanied herself on the guitar; (*e*) about it, to it; **was sagt er d.?** what does he say about it, to it? (*emphatic*) **d. wird er nichts sagen können,** he won't be able to say anything to that; **sie machte einen gutgemeinten Vorschlag, d. schwieg er aber,** she made a well-meant suggestion, but he made no reply; **ich habe die Berichte über diese Angelegenheit in den meisten Zeitungen gelesen, — was schreibt der Guardian d.?** I've read the reports on this business in most of the newspapers—what has the Guardian to say about it? what comment does the Guardian make? (*emphatic*) **d. gehört Mut,** that takes courage; *see also* **dazugehören;** (*f*) **etwas d. tun,** to do sth. about it; **was kann ich d. tun?** what can I do about it? *see also* **dazutun. 2.** *adv.* (*translation of constructions with* **dazu** *depends on the translation of* **zu** *in connection with the verb, etc., in question; the uses of* **zu** *and* **dazu** *are illustrated under the respective verbs, etc., taking* **zu**) **er bringt es nicht d., seinen Vater zu überreden,** he won't succeed in persuading his father; (*emphatic*) **er wollte Rechtsanwalt werden, aber d. kam es nie,** he wanted to be a lawyer, but he never got that far; **wir haben sie dazu gebracht, sich ein neues Kleid zu kaufen,** we persuaded, induced, her to buy herself a new dress; (*emphatic*) **ich sollte den Rasen mähen, aber d. komme ich heute nicht mehr,** I ought to mow the lawn, but I shan't get round to it today; (*emphatic*) **d. wird es wohl nicht kommen,** I don't think it will come to that; **wie kam sie d., ihn für einen Franzosen zu halten?** how did she come to take him for a Frenchman? **es ist d. gekommen, daß sie keine Freunde mehr haben,** it has got to the point where they have no friends left; *see also* **dazukommen; d. bereit, fähig, sein,** to be ready to do it, to be capable of (doing) it; **d. bereit, fähig, sein, etwas zu tun,** to be ready to do sth., to be capable of doing sth.; (*emphatic*) **d. bin ich zu müde, zu faul,** I'm too tired, too lazy, for that; **er hat keine Lust, keine Zeit, d.,** he doesn't feel like (doing) it, he has no time for it; **ich habe keine Lust d., stundenlang auf sie zu warten,** I don't feel like waiting hours for her; **ist er religiös? — eigentlich nicht, aber er hat eine Neigung d.,** is he religious?—not really, but he has a tendency in that direction; **Anlaß, Gelegenheit, ein Recht, d. haben,** to have reason, an opportunity, for it, to have a right to it. **3.** *rel.use A. & Lit:* to which; with which; for which.

dazugehören, *v.i. sep.* (*haben*) (*a*) to belong to it, to them; **er ist Mitglied unseres Klubs; er gehört schon seit Jahren dazu,** he is a member of our club; he has belonged to it for years; **sie fand in der Sammlung ein Buch, das nicht dazugehörte,** she found among the collection a book which did not belong (to, in, it); (*b*) to go with it; **sie wird bestimmt Erfolg in der Gesellschaft haben, denn sie hat alles, was dazugehört,** she will certainly be a success in society, for she is perfectly equipped for it, *F:* she's got what it takes; **eine gute Stellung und alles, was dazugehört,** a good position and everything that goes with it; *F:* **das gehört so mit dazu,** it's all in the day's work; *cp.* **dazu 1** (*e*).

dazugehörig, *a.* belonging to it, them; proper, appropriate; **ein Haus des sechzehnten Jahrhunderts mit der dazugehörigen Ausstattung,** a sixteenth-century house with the furnishings that go with it, with the appropriate furnishings; **um ein guter Diplomat zu werden, muß man den dazugehörigen Takt haben,** to become a good diplomat one must have the proper, appropriate, gift of tact.

dazuhalten (sich), *v.refl.* (*strong*) to stick close (to it, them); to keep at it, to keep going; **halt dich dazu, sonst essen die anderen alles auf!** (i) stick close, or the others will eat it all up! (ii) eat up, or the others will finish the lot!

dazukommen. I. *v.i.sep.* (*strong*) (*sein*) (*a*) (*of pers.*) to appear (on the scene); to come; to join (group of people, etc.); **es stand schon eine große Menge auf der Straße, und es kamen immer mehr Leute dazu,** there was already a big crowd in the street and all the time more and more people kept appearing, joining it; **er kam gerade dazu, als . . . ,** he appeared (on the scene) just as . . . , just (at the moment) when . . . ; (*b*) (*of thg*) to be added; **immer neue Mißgeschicke kamen dazu,** misfortune followed upon misfortune; **ich finde sie nicht besonders hübsch; dazu kommt noch, daß . . . ,** I don't find her particularly good-looking, (and) moreover . . . . *Cp.* **dazu 2.**

II. *vbl s.* **Dazukommen,** *n. in vbl senses; also:* (sudden, unexpected) arrival (of s.o.); **sein D. rettete die Situation,** the situation was saved by his arrival.

Dazukunft, *f.* = **dazukommen II.**

dazumal [ˈdaːtsu·maːl], *adv.* then, at that time; *see also* **Anno**[1].

dazuschreiben, *v.tr. sep.* (*strong*) to add (sth. in writing); **er las den Brief noch einmal durch, dann schrieb er eine Nachschrift dazu,** he read his letter through once more, then added a postscript.

dazusetzen, *v.tr.sep.* **1.** to add (sth.); **er setzte seine Unterschrift dazu,** he added, appended, his signature. **2. sich dazusetzen,** to sit down with, to join (group of people, etc.); **die Familie saß im Garten; nach einer Weile setzte er sich dazu,** the family was sitting in the garden, and after a while he joined them.

dazutun, *v.tr. sep.* (*strong*) to add (sth. to sth.); **tu noch etwas Wasser dazu!** add a little more water (to it)! **das Seine d.,** to do one's share, *F:* to do one's bit, to pull one's weight; *cp.* **dazu 1** (*f*).

dazwischen [da·ˈtsviʃən], *pron.adv.* (*also* **dazwischen-**, *comb.fm.*). **1.** (*a*) between them; (in) between; **auf beiden Seiten ragten Felswände auf, und d. floß der Strom,** walls of rock towered on either side and the river flowed between them; **zwei Wiesen mit einer Hecke d.,** two meadows with a hedge between (them); **man darf weder die eine noch die andere Erklärung völlig glauben; die Wahrheit liegt wohl irgendwo d.,** one should not believe either explanation fully; presumably the truth lies somewhere between the two; (*b*) **man konnte nicht richtig verstehen, was sie sagte, denn sie lachte immer d.,** one couldn't properly understand what she said, for she kept laughing while she spoke. **2.** among(st) them; **in diesem Beet sind fast nur Astern, aber es gibt auch einige Dahlien d.,** nearly all the flowers in this bed are asters, but there are a few dahlias among(st) them. **3.** *A:* = **inzwischen.**

dazwischenfahren, *v.i. sep.* (*strong*) (*sein*) to intervene (in a quarrel, fight, etc.).

dazwischenfunken, *v.i. sep.* (*haben*) *F:* to butt in (during a discussion, etc.).

dazwischenkommen. I. *v.i. sep.* (*strong*) (*sein*) (*of pers., thg*) to intervene; to interfere; (*of pers.*) to interpose; **ich wollte gerade die Privatbriefe lesen, als mein Vater dazwischenkam,** I was just going to read the private letters when my father appeared, interposed; **wenn wir ausgehen wollen, kommt immer etwas dazwischen,** whenever we want to go out something always happens to stop us, something always interferes with our plans; **ich hatte die beste Absicht zu schreiben, aber im letzten Moment ist mir etwas dazwischengekommen,** I had every intention of writing, but at the last moment something prevented me.

II. *vbl s.* **Dazwischenkommen,** *n. in vbl senses; also:* intervention; interference.

Dazwischenkunft, *f.* = **dazwischenkommen II.**

dazwischenrufen, *v.sep.* (*strong*) (*a*) *v.i.* (*haben*) to interrupt (by shouting), to shout interruptions; **während der Abgeordnete sprach, riefen seine Gegner fortwährend dazwischen,** while the delegate was speaking his opponents kept interrupting him, kept shouting interruptions; (*b*) *v.tr.* **ich konnte nicht weiterreden, denn die Zuhörer riefen dauernd dumme Bemerkungen dazwischen,** I couldn't go on speaking because the audience kept shouting stupid remarks, kept interrupting me with stupid remarks.

dazwischensetzen, *v.tr. sep.* **1.** (*a*) to put, place (sth.) between them (*i.e. two pillars, chairs, etc.*); (*b*) to interpose (sth.). **2. sich dazwischensetzen,** (*a*) (*of pers.*) to sit down between them (*i.e. two people, chairs, etc.*); (*b*) to interpose, intervene.

dazwischentreten. I. *v.i. sep.* (*strong*) (*sein*) (*of pers.*) to intervene; **wenn er nicht dazwischengetreten wäre, hätten die beiden Gegner sich noch schwerere Verletzungen zugefügt,** had he not intervened the two combatants would have been still more seriously injured.

II. *vbl s.* **Dazwischentreten,** *n.* intervention; **durch sein D. wurde das Schlimmste abgewendet,** by his intervention he averted more serious consequences.

dazwischenwerfen, *v.tr. sep.* (*strong*) to throw (sth.) between them; to interpose, interject (remark).

D-dur, D-Dur, *n. Mus:* (key of) D major.

de-, De-, *pref.* (*privative*) **1.** de-; **dekortizieren,** to decorticate; **demobilisieren,** to demobilize; **Depilation** *f*, depilation. **2.** dis-; **deplazieren,** to displace; **Decharge** *f*, discharge.

Debakel [de·ˈbaːkəl], *n.* **-s/-,** collapse, breakdown; *débâcle.*

debankieren [de·baŋˈkiːrən], *v.i.* (*haben*) *Gaming:* to break the bank.

Debardeur [de·barˈdøːr], *m.* **-s/-e,** docker, stevedore, *U.S:* longshoreman.

debardieren [de·barˈdiːrən], *v.tr. Nau:* to unload.

debarkieren [de·barˈkiːrən], *v.tr.* to unship, unload, discharge (cargo); to disembark, land (passengers).

Debatte [de·ˈbatə], *f.* **-/-n,** (*a*) (oral) discussion; debate; *Parl:* debate; **etwas zur D. stellen,** to put sth. to the debate; **etwas in die D. werfen,** to throw in a suggestion; to make a suggestion.

Debattenschrift, *f. A:* contracted shorthand (*used in reporting parliamentary debates, etc.*).

Debatter [de·ˈbatər], *m.* **-s/-.** *F:* debater.

debattieren [de·baˈtiːrən], *v.tr. & i.* (*haben*) to discuss, debate (sth.); **mit j-m über etwas** *acc.* **d.,** to debate with s.o. on sth.

Debattierklub, *m.* (*a*) debating society; (*b*) discussion group.

Debauche [de·ˈboːʃ(ə)], *f.* **-/-n[-ʃən],** debauchery.

debauchieren [de·bo(·)ˈʃiːrən]. **1.** *v.i.* (*sein*) to become debauched; to lead a life of debauchery. **2.** *v.tr.* to debauch (young pers.).

Debent [de·ˈbɛnt], *m.* **-en/-en,** debtor.

Debet [ˈdeːbɛt], *n.* **-s/-s.** *Book-k:* debit; **im D. stehen,** to be on the debit-side (of an account); **etwas ins D. eines Kontos eintragen,** to enter sth. to the debit(-side) of an account.

Debetbuchung, *f. Book-k:* debit(-entry).

Debetnote, *f. Book-k:* debit note.

Debetposten, *m. Book-k:* debit(-entry).

Debetsaldo, *m. Book-k:* debit balance; **ein Konto, das einen D. in Höhe von soundsoviel aufweist,** an account that shows a debit balance of so much.

Debetseite, *f. Book-k:* debit-side.

debil [de·ˈbiːl], *a.* mentally deficient, feeble-minded.

Debilität [de·bi·li·ˈtɛːt], *f. -/. Med:* mental deficiency, feeble-mindedness.

Debit [de·ˈbi(ː)t], *m.* **-(e)s/.** (retail) sale (of goods).

debitieren [de·bi·ˈtiːrən], *v.tr. Com:* **1.** to debit; **j-n mit einem Betrag d., j-m einen Betrag d.,** to debit s.o. with an amount; **eine Geldsumme einem Konto d.,** to charge a sum to the debit of an account. **2.** to retail; to sell (goods) retail.

Debito [ˈdeːbi·to·], *m.* **-/-,** debt.

Debitor [ˈdeːbi·tor], *m.* **-s/-en** [de·bi·ˈtoːrən], (*a*) debtor; (*b*) *Book-k: pl.* **Debitoren,** accounts receivable (on balance-sheet).

Debitorenkonto, *n. Book-k:* debtor account.

Debitverfahren, *n. Jur:* bankruptcy case.

deblockieren [de·blo·ˈkiːrən], *v.tr.* **1.** (*a*) to raise the blockade of (town, port); (*b*) to release (confiscated goods). **2.** *Rail:* to clear (the line) (*by raising the block signal*). **3.** *Print:* to insert a correct word, words, etc., in place of a quad, quads, etc. (in set type).

Debora [de·ˈboːraː]. *Pr.n.f.* **-s** *& Lit:* **-rens.** Deborah.

debordieren [de·bor·ˈdiːrən], *v.tr. & i.* (*sein*) **1.** (*of water, etc.*) to overflow, brim over, run over. **2.** to exceed, go beyond.

debouchieren [de·bu·ˈʃiːrən], *v.i.* (*sein*) *Mil:* (*of troops, etc.*) to emerge, debouch (from narrow pass, etc.).

debüskieren [de·bys·ˈkiːrən], *v.tr. Mil: A:* to drive (enemy) out of ambush, from under cover.

Debüt [de·ˈbyː], *n.* **-s/-s,** (*a*) first appearance, début (of actor, etc.); **sein D. machen,** to make one's début, one's first appearance; (*b*) beginning, début (of a career, etc.); first speech, maiden speech.

Debütant [de·by·ˈtant], *m.* **-en/-en,** actor, etc., making his first appearance; beginner.

Debütantin [de·by·ˈtantin], *f.* **-/-innen. 1.** actress, etc., making her first appearance; beginner. **2.** débutante, *F:* deb.

debütieren [de·by·ˈtiːrən], *v.i.* (*haben*) to make one's first appearance (on the stage, etc.); to make one's début.

Dec-, dec- [deːk-, deːts-] *cp.* **Dek-, dek-, Dez-, dez-.**

decarbonisieren [de·karbo·ni·ˈziːrən], *v.tr. Ind: Metall:* to decarbonize, decarburize (steel, etc.); *I.C.E:* to decarbonize (engine).

Dechanat [dɛça·ˈnaːt], *n.* **-(e)s/-e. 1.** *R.C.Ch:* (*a*) deanery, (i) office *or* dignity of dean; (ii) dean's residence; (*b*) district under a, the, dean's supervision. **2.** *Sch:*=**Dekanat 1.**

Dechant [dɛˈçant, ˈdɛçant], *m.* **-en/-en. 1.** *R.C.Ch:* (*a*) dean (of chapter); (*b*) rural dean. **2.** *Sch:*= **Dekan 1.**

Dechantei [dɛçanˈtai], *f.* **-/-en,** (*a*) dean's residence; (*b*) district supervised by a rural dean.

Decharge [de·ˈʃarʒə], *f.* **-/-n. 1.** (*a*) unloading, unlading, discharge (of boat, cargo); (*b*) discharge, volley (of musketry, etc.). **2.** *Com: Fin:* discharge, payment (of debts); **j-m, etwas** *dat.*, **D. erteilen,** to discharge s.o., sth.

Dechargeerteilung, *f.* discharge.

dechargieren [de·ʃar·ˈʒiːrən], *v.tr.* **1.** (*a*) to unload, discharge (boat, etc.); (*b*) to discharge, fire (off), let off (firearm, etc.). **2.** to release, acquit (pers.).

Dechenit [de·çe·ˈniːt], *m.* **-(e)s/.** *Miner:* dechenite.

Decher, *m. & n.* **-s/-.** *Meas:* set of ten (pieces, *esp.* pelts).

dechiffrierbar [de·ʃiˈfriːrbaːr], *a.* decipherable.

dechiffrieren [de·ʃiˈfriːrən], *v.tr.* to decipher (cryptogram, etc.).

Dechsel, *f.* **-/-n.** *Tls:* adze.

dechseln, *v.tr. & i.* (*haben*) to adze.

Deci-, deci- [deːtsi·ˈ-, ˈdeːtsi·-] *cp.* **Dezi-, dezi-.**

Decius [ˈdeːtsius]. *Pr.n.m.* **-'.** *A.Hist:* Decius; **die Christenverfolgung des D., unter D.,** the Decian persecution.

Deck, *n.* **-s/-s. 1.** deck (of ship); **glattes D.,** flush deck; **erstes D.,** lower deck; **zweites D.,** middle deck (of three-decker); upper deck (of two-decker); **drittes, oberstes D.,** upper deck; **auf D.,** on deck; **auf, an, D. gehen, kommen,** to go, come, on deck; **auf D. sein,** to be on deck; *F:* **ich bin nicht ganz auf D.,** I'm not feeling very well, I'm a bit off colour, out of sorts, seedy; *see also* **Mann 1** (*b*). **2.** outside, top (deck) (of tram, bus, etc.). **3.** *Av:* deck (of aircraft).

Deck-, *comb.fm. cp.* **Deckungs-.**

Deckadresse, Deckanschrift, *f.* accommodation address.

Deckanstrich, *m.* **1.** final coat, finishing coat (of paint). **2.** (i) paint, (ii) painting, of deck.

Deckaufbau, *m. N.Arch:* superstructure; upper works (of ship); deck-erections.

Deckbalken, *m. N.Arch:* deck beam.

Deckbalkenstütze, *f. N.Arch:* pillar, stanchion.

Deckbalkenunterschlag, *m. N.Arch:* central stringer.

Deckbelastung, *f. Nau:* deck-load.

Deckbeplankung, *f. N.Arch:* deck planking.

Deckbett, *n.* feather-bed (used as eiderdown).

Deckblatt, *n.* **1.** *Bot:* bract. **2.** wrapper, outside leaf, outer leaf (of cigar). **3.** *Mil: etc:* amendment (to an order, etc.). **4.** *Publ:* (*a*) (single) inset; errata slip; (*b*) overlay.

deckblattartig, *a. Bot:* bracteal.

Deckblättchen, *n. Bot:* bracteole.

Deckblätterhülle, *f. Bot:* involucre.

Deckblech, *n.* cover-plate, covering plate.

Deckchen, *n.* **-s/-,** small cloth, *esp.* table-mat, dinner-mat; doily; table-centre; tray-cloth; (*on chair, sofa*) antimacassar.

Deckdienst, *m. Nau:* duty on deck.

Decke, *f.* **-/-n. 1.** covering, cover; (*a*) (woollen) blanket; (travelling) rug, *U.S:* lap robe; (*for horses*) horse-blanket; **eine D. von Schnee,** a blanket of snow; **eine D. von Eis,** a sheet of ice; **eine D. von Blumen,** a carpet of flowers; **unter die D. kriechen,** (i) to go to bed, (ii) to pull the blankets over one's head; *F:* **mit j-m unter einer D. stecken,** to be in league, in collusion, with s.o., to be hand in glove with s.o.; **sich nach der D. strecken,** to cut one's coat according to one's cloth; (*b*) bedspread, coverlet; (*c*) awning (over boat, waggon, etc.). **2.** (*a*) tablecloth; (*b*) altar-cloth. **3.** (*a*) cover, binding (of book); (*b*) wrapper (of cigar): (*c*) *Aut: etc:* outer cover (of tyre); outer tyre. **4.** *Ven:* skin, hide (of deer, wolf, bear). **5.** *Civ.E:* surface (of road). **6.** *Geol:* (*a*) layer, stratum; (*b*) nappe, thrust sheet. **7.** (*a*) *Constr:* ceiling; **kassettierte D.,** coffered, panelled, ceiling; **Zimmer mit hoher, niedriger, D.,** high-, low-ceilinged room; *F:* **vor Freude (bis) an die D. springen,** to be delighted, to be in the seventh heaven (of delight); (*b*) *Min: Geol: etc:* top, roof (of mine, cave, dug-out, etc.). **8.** *Mus:* belly (of violin, etc.).

Deckel, *m.* **-s/-,** (*a*) lid, cover (of box, pot, etc.); cap (of bottle, etc.); lid (of piano); *Tex:* cap (of slay); *Nat.Hist:* (i) operculum; (ii) cup *or* cap (of acorn); *Artil:* apron (of cannon); *Mus:* tampion (of organ-pipe); *see also* **Topf;** (*b*) *Bookb:* (book-)cover; (*c*) *Print:* tympan; (*d*) *Tex:* blade (on carding-machine); (*e*)=**Bierdeckel;** (*f*) *F:* hat, *F:* lid; **eins auf den D. kriegen,** (i) to get a knock on the head, *F:* to get a crack on the nut; (ii) to get a good dressing-down, a good ticking-off.

deckelähnlich, deckelartig, *a.* lid-like; *Nat.Hist:* opercular.

Deckelbecher, *m.* small tankard (with a lid).

Deckelbezug, *m. Bookb:* covering.

Deckelchen, *n.* **-s/-.** *Nat.Hist:* operculum.

Deckeldohle, *f. Civ.E:* closed culvert (with a flat top).

Deckeleisen, *n. Farr:* bar shoe.

Deckelfeder, *f. Sm.a: etc:* cover spring.

Deckelfilz, *m. Paperm:* wet-felt.

Deckelflansch, *m. Mch:* cover flange.

Deckelglas, *n.* (drinking-)glass with a lid; glass tankard (with a lid).

Deckelhalter, *m.* **1.** *Dom.Ec:* lid-rack. **2.** *Print:* frisket (of hand-press).

Deckelkanne, *f.* jug with a lid.

Deckelkapsel, *f. Bot:* pyxidium.

Deckelkarde, *f. Tex:* flat card.

Deckelkorb, *m.* covered basket; basket with a lid; (*for picnics, etc.*) hamper.

Deckelkrug, *m.* tankard (with a lid).

Deckelleiste, *f. Tex:* top riddle plate.

deckellos, *a.* (*of box, etc.*) lidless, without a lid.

deckeln, *v.tr.* **1. etwas d.,** to give sth. a lid *or* cover; **gedeckelt,** lidded; covered; *Ap:* **gedeckelte Wabe, gedeckelte Zelle,** sealed comb, sealed cell. **2.** *F:* **j-n d.,** to take s.o. down a peg, tell s.o. off.

Deckelpresse, *f. Bookb:* arming-press.

Deckelputz, *m. Tex:* carding waste.

Deckelrahmen, *m. Print:* tympan frame; *Paperm:* deckle.

Deckelriemen, *m. Paperm:* deckle (strap).

Deckelriemenwagen, *m. Paperm:* deckle.

Deckelschnecke, *f. Moll:* operculate snail; **Deckelschnecken** *pl*, operculata.

Deckelsieb, *n.* covered sieve.

Deckelspinne, *f. Arach:* trap-door spider, mygale.

Deckelstein, *m.* stone cover, stone lid (over man-hole, etc.); *Constr:* coping-stone.

Deckelstuhl, *m. Print:* gallows (on hand-press).

deckeltragend, *a. Nat.Hist:* operculiferous.

Deckeluhr, *f.* hunter (watch).

decken. I. *v.tr.* **1.** (*a*) to cover; **ihn deckt schon längst der grüne Rasen,** he has long been dead and buried; *abs.* **Farbe, die gut deckt,** paint that covers well; (*b*) *Constr:* **ein Haus d.,** to roof a house; **ein Dach mit Ziegeln d.,** to cover a roof with tiles, to tile a roof; **ein Haus mit Stroh d.,** to thatch a house; (*c*) **ein Tuch über den Tisch d.,** to put a cloth on the table; **den Tisch d.,** to lay, set, the table; **(den Tisch) für drei Personen d.,** to lay for three; **sich an den gedeckten Tisch setzen,** to sit down to a prepared meal; **sie setzt sich gern an den gedeckten Tisch,** (i) she likes to sit down to a prepared meal; (ii) *F:* she likes things to be ready made; she likes to be spoon-fed; (*d*) (*on organ-stops*) **gedeckte Pfeifen,** gedacktwork; *cp.* **gedackt**[1]. **2.** (*a*) to cover, shield, protect, shelter, screen; **j-n d.,** to shield s.o., to defend, stand up for, *F:* stick up for, s.o.; **j-n gegen Verdacht d.,** to shield s.o. from suspicion; **die Pflanzen sind gegen den Wind gedeckt,** the plants are screened, sheltered, from the wind; **die Grenze ist durch eine Festungskette gedeckt,** the frontier is covered, protected, by a chain of forts; *Mil: etc:* **den Rückzug der Armee d.,** to cover the army's retreat; **einen Paß d.,** to guard a pass; *Sp:* **das Tor d.,** to guard, keep, the goal; *abs.* **der Boxer deckt gut,** the boxer has a good defence; *Chess:* **der Turm ist durch den Läufer gedeckt,** the castle is covered by the bishop; (*b*) **j-n, j-s Handlung, d.,** to take responsibility for s.o., s.o.'s action; (*c*) *Sp:* to mark (opponent). **3.** *Com: Fin: etc:* **j-s, seinen, Bedarf d.,** to cover, meet, s.o.'s, one's, needs, requirements; **die Kosten d.,** to cover, meet, defray, the expenses; **ein Defizit d.,** to cover, make up, a deficit; **einen Verlust d.,** to make up, make good, a loss; **eine Schuld d.,** (i) to pay, meet, a debt, (ii) to stand surety, security, for a debt; **der Scheck ist gedeckt, nicht gedeckt,** the cheque is covered, is not covered; **für 1000 Mark gedeckt sein,** to have security for 1000 marks; **der Verkaufspreis deckt kaum die Kosten,** the selling price barely covers the cost. **4.** *Breed:* (*of male animal*) to cover (female); (*of horse*) to serve, cover (mare); **ein Tier d. lassen,** to have an animal mated. **5.** *Ven:* (*of hounds*) to seize and hold fast (prey, *esp.* wild boar). **6.** *Ch:* to purge (crystals); *Sug-R:* (i) to purge, fine (sugar); (ii) to clay (sugar).

II. **sich decken. 1.** *Poet:* **sich mit Blumen, usw., d.,** to cover, deck, adorn, oneself with flowers, etc.; (*of meadow, etc.*) to become covered with flowers, etc. **2.** to take cover; (*of hunter*) to hide oneself, conceal oneself; **sich gegen einen Angriff d.,** to guard oneself against an attack; to shield oneself from an attack; **sich gegen Verdacht d.,** to shield oneself from suspicion; **sich gegen Verlust d.,** to take precautions against loss; to cover oneself against loss; **um gedeckt zu sein, um mich, uns, zu d.,** in order to be on the safe side; *Mil:* **gedeckt vorgehen,** to move forward under cover. **3.** (*of two thgs*) to coincide with one another; *Geom:* (*of two figures*) to be superposable, coincident, congruent; **sich teilweise d.,** to overlap one another; **sein Geschmack deckt sich mit dem meinen,** our tastes are identical, his taste is identical with mine; **ihre Interessen decken sich nicht mit denen ihrer Mutter,** her interests do not coincide with those of her mother; *Geom:* **sich deckende Dreiecke,** superposable, coincident, congruent, triangles; *Log:* **sich deckende Begriffe,** coextensive concepts.

III. *vbl s.* **1. Decken,** *n. in vbl senses.* **2. Deckung,** *f.* (*a*)=II. 1; *also:* protection (of s.o. from sth.); **zur D. unserer Unkosten,** to cover our costs; (*b*) *Geom:* coincidence, congruence (of two figures); **zwei Dreiecke, die sich zur D. bringen lassen,** two triangles which are superposable, coincident, congruent; (*c*) *Geol:* overlap; (*d*) *Constr:* roof; roofing (of house); (*e*) protection, shelter, cover **(gegen etwas,** from sth.); *Box:* defence; *Fenc:* parry; **D. nehmen, in D. gehen,** to take cover; (*f*) *Com: Fin: etc:* cover; surety, security (for sum of money); guarantee (for debt, loan, etc.); provision, necessary funds (for undertaking, etc.); *Fin:* reserve (of gold stocks, etc.); **Auftrag ohne D.,** order without security, without cover; **einen Betrag als D. einzahlen,** to pay in a sum as a security, as a deposit; **zur D. einer Summe,** as cover, security, for a sum; **j-m D. für einen Wechsel anschaffen,** to provide s.o. with cover for a bill; (*g*) *Breed:* service (by male animal).

Deckenanker, m. Mch: crown bar.
Deckenbalken, m. Constr: ceiling beam.
Deckenband, n. 1. Constr: wooden framework supporting a ceiling. 2. Bookb: binding process in which the block and the covers are prepared separately.
Deckenbeleuchtung, f. 1. illumination of a ceiling. 2. ceiling lighting.
Deckenbild, n. Art: (i) ceiling piece, ceiling-panel, ceiling picture; (ii) painting on a ceiling; ceiling fresco.
Deckenfalte, f.=Deckfalte.
Deckenfeld, n. Constr: panel, field, of a ceiling.
Deckenfisch, m. Ich: stromateus, F: pomfret.
Deckengemälde, n. Art: ceiling fresco; painting on a ceiling.
Deckengewebe, n. Biol: epithelium.
Deckengewölbe, n. Arch: vault of a ceiling; cove.
Deckenlampe, f. (flush) ceiling-light, flush ceiling(-light) fitting; Aut: (interior) roof light.
Deckenlicht, n. (a)=Deckenlampe; (b) top light, light shed from above; (c) (window) skylight.
Deckenmalerei, f. Art: painting on a ceiling; ceiling decoration; **Deckenmalereien** pl, ceiling frescoes.
Deckenoberlicht, n. top light, light shed from above.
Deckenputz, m. Constr: ceiling plaster.
Deckenschalung, f. Constr: ceiling-work.
Deckenstrahler, m. inverted lamp (to illuminate a ceiling).
Deckenstrahlungsheizung, f. overhead radiation heating.
Deckenträger, m. 1. Constr: ceiling girder. 2. Mch: crown bar (of fire-box).
Deckenventilator, m. ceiling fan.
Deckenvorgelege, n. Mec.E: overhead countershaft; overhead transmission gear.
Decker, m. -s/-. 1. coverer. 2. roofer.
deckfähig, a. (paint, etc.) of good covering power.
Deckfalte, f. Geol: recumbent fold, overthrust fold.
Deckfarbe, f. (a) Art: etc: covering paint; opaque paint; body-colour; (b) (water-colour) poster paint; (c) Paint: final coat (of paint).
Deckfarbenmalerei, f. Art: painting in body-colour; gouache.
Deckfärbung, f. protective colouring, camouflage (of animals, birds).
Deckfedern, f.pl. Orn: tectrices, (wing-)coverts.
Deckfenster, n. Nau: deck-light, skylight.
Deckfirnis, m. (top) varnish.
Deckfisch, m.=Deckenfisch.
Deckfläche, f. overlap, overlapping.
Deckflügel, m. Ent: elytron, wing-sheath, -case; shard.
Deckflügler, m. -s/-. Ent: coleopter, beetle; die Deckflügler, the coleoptera.
deckflüglerartig, a. Ent: coleopterous; sheath-winged.
Deckfracht, f. Nau: deck-load, deck-cargo.
Deckfrucht, f. Agr: nurse crop, cover crop.
Deckgarn, n.=Decknetz.
Deckgebirge, n. Geol: Min: overburden.
Deckgeld, n. Breed: stud fees.
Deckgestein, n. Geol: surface rock.
Deckglas, Deckgläschen, n. cover-glass, cover-slip (of microscope slide, lantern-slide, etc.).
Deckgut, n. Tobacco Ind: wrapper tobacco.
Deckhammer, m. Tls: slater's hammer.
Deckhaus, n. Nau: deck-house.
Deckhaut, f. Nat.Hist: tegument; integument.
Deckhengst, m. stallion, stud-horse.
Deckkläre, f. -/., **Deckklärsel,** n. -s/. Sug-R: clairce.
Deckklüse, f. Nau: chain-, deck-pipe.
Deckkniee, n.pl. N.Arch: carling-knees.
Deckknochen, m. Anat: membrane bone.
Deckkraft, f. covering power (of paint).
deckkräftig, a. Paint: of good covering power; deckkräftige Farbe, paint that covers well.
Deckladung, f. Nau: deck-load, deck-cargo.
Decklage, f. top layer; Civ.E: surface; surfacing coat.
Decklast, f.=Deckladung.
Decklehm, m. Metall: luting loam.
Decklehne, f. (a) cap of the linchpin; (b) linchpin with a cap.
Deckleiste, f. 1. Carp: covering bead, batten. 2. Mec.E: etc: butt-strap, -strip; flat cover-plate; welt (of butt-joint).
Decklünse, f.=Decklehne.
Deckmantel, m. pretext, pretence; mask; **unter dem D. der Religion, der Tugend,** under the cloak, the pretence, the mask, of religion, of virtue; **unter dem D. der Freundschaft,** under, in, the guise of friendship; under cover of friendship; **seine Frömmigkeit ist nur ein D.,** his piety is only a blind.
Deckmaterial, n. covering; Constr: roofing.
Decknagel, m. Nau: weight-nail, deck-nail.
Deckname, m. (a) pseudonym; assumed name; nom de plume (of an author); (b) alias; assumed name; **unter einem Decknamen reisen,** to travel under an alias; (c) Mil: code name, cover name.
Decknetz, n. Ven: (a) (game-)net, snare; (b) bird-snare.
Deckoffizier, m. Navy: warrant officer.
Deckpapp, m., **Deckpappe,** f. (in calico printing) resist.
Deckpassagier, m. deck passenger.
Deckpflanzung, f. Hort: planting of shrubs for purposes of concealment or protection.
Deckplane, f. awning; tarpaulin (on lorry, etc.).
Deckplanke, f. N.Arch: deck-plank, deck-flat.
Deckplatte, f. Constr: etc: cover-plate, covering plate; coping-stone.
Deckrasen, m. turf for lining slopes, trenches, etc.
Deckrohr, m. thatching reed; thatch.
Deckrüde, m. Breed: (male) dog.
Decks- cp. Deck-.
Decksalon, m. Nau: deck-house.
decksamig, a.=bedecktsamig.
Decksand, m. Geol: outwash sand.
Decksbolzen, m. N.Arch: deck-bolt.
Deckscheibe, f. Anat: knee-cap.
Deckschicht, f. top layer, covering layer; Geol: top stratum, surface stratum.
Deckschild, m. Ann: elytron.
Deckschore, f.=Deckstütze.
Deckschuppe, f. (a) Bot: scale; bract; (b) Ent: elytron.
Deckschwabber, m. Nau: swab.
Deckschwelle, f. Constr: capping, cross-beam (on row of piles, etc.); Hyd.E: capping (of sluice-gate).
Decksel, n. -s/. Sug-R: clairce.
Decksirup, m. Sug-R: syrup obtained in sugar-refining.
Deckspelze, f. Bot: lemna, flowering glume.
Decksprung, m. N.Arch: sheer of the deck.
Deckstein, m. 1. Constr: (a) coping-stone; coping (of wall); cap-stone (of roof); (b) roofing-slab. 2. Clockm: end-stone.
Deckstopfen, m. flanged stopper, flanged cork.
Deckstopper, m. Nau: controller; cable stopper; chain-stopper.
Deckstringer, m. N.Arch: deck stringer.
Deckstroh, n. 1. thatch. 2. straw for covering plants, etc.
Deckstuhl, m. Constr: roofer's trestle.
Deckstütze, f. N.Arch: deck pillar, stanchion.
Decktrockner, m. Nau: squeegee.
Deckung, f. see decken III.
Deckungsbedürfnis, n. Fin: short interest.
Deckungsbestände, m.pl. Fin: cover of notes in circulation.
Deckungsbilanz, f. Fin: balance-sheet showing cover of notes in circulation.
deckungsfähig, a. Fin: (note, draft, etc.) that can be covered.
Deckungsforderungen, f.pl. Fin: (on balance-sheet) assets.
Deckungsgeschäft, n. Com: Fin: covering trans-action.
Deckungsgraben, m. Mil: cover trench, shelter trench.
Deckungskapital, n. Fin: cover of capital; Ins: initiation fee.
Deckungskauf, m. Com: Fin: covering purchase.
Deckungsklausel, f. 1. Com: Fin: cover clause (on bill of exchange or draft). 2. gesetzliche D., clause relating to the gold reserve (of country).
Deckungslager, n. Mil: concealed camp.
Deckungslinie, f. Mil: line of defence.
Deckungsmannschaft, f. Mil: covering party.
Deckungsmittel, n. Fin: etc: (covering) funds; cover.
Deckungsorder, f. Com: covering order.
Deckungspflicht, f. Com: business company's pledge to cover its own debts.
Deckungstruppen, f.pl. Mil: covering forces.
Deckungsverkauf, m. Com: Fin: covering sale.
Deckungswechsel, m. Fin: security credit note.
Deckweiß, n. (a) Art: etc: permanent white; zinc white; (b) lithopone.
Deckwerk, n. 1. Mil: blindage. 2. Hyd.E: pro-tective lining (on canal banks, etc.).
Deckworpen, m.pl. N.Arch: deck transoms.
Deckwort, m. -(e)s/-wörter, code word.
Deckwrangen, f.pl.=Deckworpen.
Deckzange, f. Tls: (roofer's) folding pliers.

Deckzelle, f. Anat: cortical cell, surface cell.
Deckziegel, m. Constr: (a) (brick) coping; (b) roofing-tile.
Décolleté [de·kol'te:], n. -s/-s. Cost: low neck-line, décolletage; **ein tief ausgeschnittenes D.,** a deep décolletage, a plunging neckline; **im D. sein,** to be décolleté; to be wearing a low-cut, décolleté, dress, blouse, etc.
decolletiert [de·kol'ti:rt], a. low-cut, décolleté (evening dress, etc.); adv. **d. gehen,** to be décolleté; to be wearing a low-cut, décolleté, dress, blouse, etc.
decolorieren [de·kolo'ri:rən], v.tr. to decolo(u)-rize.
Decoupiermaschine [de·ku·'pi:rma·ʃinə], f. cut-ting-machine.
decouragieren [de·ku·ra·'ʒi:rən], v.tr. to dis-courage, dishearten (s.o.); to damp (s.o.'s) courage; to take the heart out of (s.o.); to put s.o. out of heart; **decouragiert,** discouraged, disheartened, downcast, despondent.
decrescendo [de·krɛ'ʃɛndo:], adv., **Decrescendo,** n. -s/-s. Mus: decrescendo.
Decylsäure [de·'tsy:l-], f. Ch: decylic acid.
Dedikation [de·di·ka·tsi'o:n], f. -/-en, dedication.
Dedikationsbild, n. dedication picture, presenta-tion picture.
Dedikationsexemplar, n. presentation copy.
dedizieren [de·di·'tsi:rən], v.tr. to dedicate (book, etc.); F: to present, give (sth.) (to s.o.).
Deduktion [de·duktsi'o:n], f. 1. Log: (a) (action) deduction; (b) (thg deduced) deduc-tion, inference. 2. Com: etc: deduction, abatement (of sum of money).
deduktiv [de·duk'ti:f], a. Log: deductive (reason-ing, method).
deduzieren [de·du·'tsi:rən], v.tr. Log: to deduce, infer (result).
Defäkation [de·fɛ·ka·tsi'o:n], f. -/-en. Physiol: defecation.
defamieren [de·fa·'mi:rən], v.tr.=diffamieren.
Defätismus [de·fɛ·'tismus], m. -/. defeatism.
Defätist [de·fɛ·'tist], m. -en/-en, defeatist.
Defekt[1] [de·'fɛkt], m. -(e)s/-e. 1. (a) defect, flaw, fault, imperfection; piece of damage; **einen D. erleiden,** to be damaged; **der Wagen hat einen D.,** something is wrong with the car; (b) deficiency; **einen geistigen D. haben,** to be mentally deficient; (c) A: Com: Fin: deficit. 2. Print: battered letter, F: batter.
defekt[2], a. defective, faulty, imperfect (work, object, etc.); geistig d., mentally deficient; Print: **defekter Buchstabe, defekte Type,** broken letter, battered letter; F: batter.
Defektbuchstabe, m. Print: broken letter, battered letter, F: batter.
Defektelektron, n. Atom.Ph: defect electron.
Defektenprotokoll, n. Fin: (written) statement of deficit.
Defektenverfahren, n. Jur: restitution suit.
defektiv [de·fɛk'ti:f], a. defective, faulty; Gram: defective (verb, etc.).
Defektivität [de·fɛkti·vi·'tɛːt], f. -/-en, defective-ness, faultiness; Gram: defectiveness (of verb, etc.).
Defektivkirche, f. schismatic church.
Defektivum [de·fɛk'ti:vum], n. -s/-va. Gram: defective verb, noun, etc.
Defendend [de·fɛn'dɛnt], m. -en/-en [-'dɛndən]. Jur: defendant.
Defendent [de·fɛn'dɛnt], m. -en/-en. Jur: counsel for the defence.
defendieren [de·fɛn'di:rən], v.tr. to defend.
Defension [de·fɛnzi'o:n], f. -/-en, defence.
defensiv [de·fɛn'zi:f], a. defensive (position, alliance, etc.).
Defensiv-, comb.fm. defensive...; **Defensiv-allianz** f, defensive alliance; **Defensivkrieg** m, defensive war.
Defensive [de·fɛn'zi:və], f. -/-n. Mil: Sp: etc: (a) (action) defence; (b) (state) defensive; Mil. & F: **in der D. sein,** to be on the defensive.
Defensor [de·'fɛnzor], m. -s/-en [-'zo:rən], defender; Jur: counsel for the defence.
Deferent [de·fe·'rɛnt], m. -en/-en. 1. administerer of an oath. 2. Num: mint-mark.
deferieren [de·fe·'ri:rən], v.tr. 1. **j-m den Eid d.,** to administer, tender, the oath to s.o. 2. to accept (application, etc.).
Defiguration [de·fi·gu·ra·tsi'o:n], f. -/-en, dis-figurement, disfiguration.
defigurieren [de·fi·gu·'ri:rən], v.tr. to disfigure (s.o., sth.).
Defilé [de·fi·'le:], n. -s/-s, **Defilee,** n. -s/-n [-s/-'le:ən]. 1. defile, gorge, (mountain) pass. 2. Mil: etc: defiling, march(ing) past.
defilieren [de·fi·'li:rən]. 1. v.i. (haben, sein) Mil:

etc: to march past, to defile. **2.** *v.tr.* to defilade (fortress).

definierbar [de·fi·ˈniːrba·r], *a.* definable.

definieren [de·fi·ˈniːrən], *v.tr.* to define (word, object, etc.).

definit [de·fi·ˈniːt], *a. Gram: etc:* definite.

Definition [de·fi·ni·tsĭˈoːn], *f.* **-/-en. 1.** definition (of word, object). **2.** *Ecc:* definition (of dogma).

definitiv [de·fi·ni·ˈtiːf], *a.* (*a*) definitive, final (resolution, etc.); (*b*) definite (date of arrival, etc.); (*c*) permanent (post, etc.); (*d*) *adv.* definitely.

Definitivfrieden, *m.* final, definitive, declaration of peace.

Definitivum [de·fi·ni·ˈtiːvum], *n.* **-s/-va,** definitive ruling; finality.

Definitivurteil, *n.* final verdict, final judgment, definitive sentence.

Defizient [de·fi·tsĭˈɛnt], *m.* **-en/-en. 1.** defaulter; debtor. **2.** *Austrian:* person, *esp.* clergyman, unfit for service.

Defizit [ˈdeːfi·tsit], *n.* **-s/-e.** *Fin: Com:* deficit; *Adm:* budgetary deficit; **das D. decken,** to make good, make up, the deficit.

Deflagration [de·fla·gra·tsĭˈoːn], *f.* **-/-en.** *Ch: Exp:* deflagration, combustion.

Deflagrator [de·fla·ˈgraːtor], *m.* **-s/-en** [-gra·ˈtoːrən]. *Ch:* deflagrator.

Deflation [de·fla·tsĭˈoːn], *f.* **-/-en.** *Pol.Ec: Geol:* deflation.

deflationistisch [de·fla·tsĭo·ˈnistiʃ], **deflatorisch** [de·fla·ˈtoːriʃ], *a. Pol.Ec:* deflationary (policy, etc.).

Deflektion [de·flɛktsĭˈoːn], *f.* **-/-en,** deflexion, deflection.

Deflektionsmesser, *n.* deflectometer.

Deflektor [deˈflɛktor], *m.* **-s/-en** [-ˈtoːrən]. *Mec.E:* deflector, baffle, baffle-plate.

Defloration [de·flo·ra·tsĭˈoːn], *f.* **-/.** defloration.

Deflorationsanspruch, *m. Jur:* damages claimed for defloration (*in breach of promise case*).

deflorieren [de·flo·ˈriːrən], *v.tr.* to deflower (girl).

deform [de·ˈform], *a.* deformed.

Deformation [de·forma·tsĭˈoːn], *f.* **-/-en,** deformation; distortion; *Mec.E: Mth: etc:* deformation, strain.

deformieren [de·forˈmiːrən], *v.tr.* to deform (sth.); to distort (sth.); to disfigure (s.o.); to deface (building, etc.); **deformiert,** deformed (pers., limb); distorted (thg); **Deformierung** *f,* deformation; distortion, defacement.

Deformität [de·formi·ˈtɛːt], *f.* **-/-en,** deformity.

Defraudant [de·frauˈdant], *m.* **-en/-en,** defrauder, cheat, swindler.

Defraudation [de·frauda·tsĭˈoːn], *f.* **-/-en,** defrauding (of public revenue, etc.).

defraudieren [de·frauˈdiːrən], *v.tr.* to defraud (public revenue, etc.).

deftig, *a.* **1.** (*a*) able, capable, efficient (pers.); sound, solid, strong (peasant, etc.); thorough, hard-working (pers., manner of living, etc.); (*b*) nimble, quick (girl). **2.** (*a*) good, solid, well-made (garment, etc.); (*b*) fat, thick (piece of bread, etc.). **3.** good, suitable, apt (example, etc.); considerable, good (distance, etc.).

Degagement [de·gaːʒəˈmãː], *n.* **-s/-s,** disengagement; release (from obligation, etc.); disentanglement (from intrigue, etc.).

degagieren [de·ga·ˈʒiːrən], *v.tr.* to disengage, release (s.o., sth.) (from obligation, etc.); to disentangle (s.o.) (from intrigue, etc.); *Fenc:* to disengage (the blade); **degagiert,** free, unrestricted.

Degen[1], *m.* **-s/-. 1.** *A:* warrior, soldier; follower in a prince's suite. **2.** *Print:* compositor and printer.

Degen[2], *m.* **-s/-. 1.** (*for duelling, ceremonial dress*) (long, slender) sword; *Fenc: etc:* small-sword, épée; **einen D. führen, tragen,** to wear, carry, a sword; **seinen D. ziehen, zücken, entblößen,** to draw one's sword; **seinen D. ablegen, einstecken,** to put up, sheathe, one's sword; **mit dem D. fechten,** to fight with one's sword; *Fenc:* to fence with the sword, the épée; **mit bloßem, nacktem, D.,** with naked sword; **seinen D. dem Sieger übergeben,** to hand over, deliver, surrender, one's sword to the victor; **j-n vor den D. fordern,** to challenge s.o. to a duel (with swords); **einen Streit mit dem D. ausmachen,** to settle a dispute by the sword. **2.** parting (in horse's mane). **3.** cheese-knife. **4.** *Her:* claymore.

Degenband, *n.* sword-knot.

Degenbinse, *f.*=**Degenkraut** 1.

degenblätt(e)rig, *a. Bot:* ensiform-leaved, sword-leaved.

Degenbrecher, *m. Arm:* sword-breaker.

Degenduell, *n.* duel with swords.

Degeneration [de·ge·ne·ra·tsĭˈoːn], *f.* **-/-en.** *Med: Biol: etc:* degeneration; *Med:* **fettige D. des Herzens,** fatty degeneration of the heart.

Degenerationspsychose, *f. Med:* psychosis consequent on degeneration.

Degenerationszeichen, *n. Med:* symptom of degeneration; stigma.

degenerieren [de·ge·ne·ˈriːrən], *v.i.* (*sein*) to degenerate.

degenfähig, *a. A:* (pers.) who has the right to appear at the royal court.

degenfest, *a.* invulnerable; incapable of being wounded by the sword; *Lit:* proof against steel.

Degenfisch, *m. Ich:* (*a*) sword-fish; (*b*) trichiurus, hair-tail.

degenförmig, *a.* sword-shaped; *Bot: etc:* ensiform.

Degengehänge, *n.*=**Degengehenk.**

Degengehenk, *n.* (*a*) sword-sling; cross-belt, shoulder-belt, baldric; (*b*) sword-belt.

Degengriff, *m.* hilt (of sword).

Degengurt, *m.* sword-belt.

Degenhand, *f.* (*a*) whip-hand (of rider); (*b*) sword-hand, right hand.

Degenhieb, *m.* stroke of the sword, sword-stroke.

Degenkleid, *n.* court-dress.

Degenklinge, *f.* sword-blade.

Degenknopf, *m.* button (of sword).

Degenkoppel, *f.*=**Degengehenk.**

Degenkorb, *m.* hand-guard, shell, basket-hilt (of sword).

Degenkraut, *n. Bot:* **1.** branched bur-reed. **2. die Degenkräuter,** the xyridaceae.

Degenöl, *n. Pharm:* birch oil.

Degenquaste, *f.* sword-knot.

Degenschärfe, *f.* edge of the sword; sword-blade.

Degenscheide, *f.* sheath, scabbard, of a sword.

Degenschleife, *f.* sword-knot.

Degenschlucker, *m.* sword-swallower.

Degenschmied, *m.* sword-cutler.

Degenschwarz, *n. Pharm:* birch oil.

Degenspitze, *f.* point of the sword.

Degenstich, *m.* sword-thrust.

Degenstichblatt, *n.* guard, shell, of a sword.

Degenstock, *m.* sword-stick.

Degenstoß, *m.* sword-thrust.

degommieren [de·goˈmiːrən], *v.tr.* (*a*) to ungum, unstick (sth.); (*b*) to boil off (raw silk); to de-gum (raw silk).

degorgieren [de·gorˈʒiːrən], *v.tr. Wine-m:* to remove the sediment from (champagne).

Degout [de·ˈguː], *m.* **-s/.** disgust, distaste; repugnance.

degoutant [de·gu·ˈtant], *a.* disgusting, sickening; repugnant.

degoutieren [de·gu·ˈtiːrən], *v.tr.* to disgust.

Degradation [de·gra·da·tsĭˈoːn], *f.* **-/-en. 1.** degradation (from office, etc.); *Mil:* degradation, *U.S:* demotion (of officer); reduction (of N.C.O.) to the ranks. **2.** *Ph:* dissipation, degradation, gradual loss (of energy).

degradieren [de·gra·ˈdiːrən], *v.tr.* to degrade, *U.S:* demote, (s.o.) (from office, etc.); *Mil:* to reduce (an N.C.O.) to the ranks.

degra(i)ssieren [de·graˈsiːrən, de·grɛˈsiːrən], *v.tr.* to take the fat from (carcass of animal, etc.); to skim off the fat from (soup, etc.).

Degras [deˈgraː], *n.* **-/.** *Leath:* degras, dubbin(g).

degressiv [de·grɛˈsiːf], *a.* degressive (taxation).

Degustation [de·gusta·tsĭˈoːn], *f.* **-/-en.** *Com:* **1.** tasting (of wines, tea, etc.). **2.** tasting-room.

degustieren [de·gusˈtiːrən], *v.tr.* to taste, sample (wines, tea, etc.).

Dehiszenz [de·hisˈtsɛnts], *f.* **-/.** *Bot:* dehiscence.

dehnbar, *a.* (*a*) (linen, leather, etc.) that stretches; elastic (material, muscles, etc.); extensible, extensile (material, etc.); tensile, ductile (metals, etc.); (vowel) that can be lengthened; (solid) that dilates, swells; dilatable (solid); (*of solid, air, gas*) expansive; expansible; (*b*) elastic, adaptable, loose (ruling, etc.); (idea, etc.) that can be extended; (law, etc.) that can be variously, loosely, interpreted; **Treue ist ein dehnbarer Begriff,** loyalty is a notion that can be variously interpreted; loyalty is a loose notion; *F:* **ein dehnbares Gewissen haben,** to have an elastic conscience.

Dehnbarkeit, *f.* elasticity (of material, muscles, ruling, etc.); ductility (of metal); looseness (of notions, etc.).

dehnen. I. *v.tr.* **1.** (*a*) to stretch (elastic, linen, leather, gloves, shoes, etc.); to draw (out), elongate (metal); to stretch (law, etc.); (*of apparatus, etc.*) to extend, stretch (limb, etc.); (*of heat, etc.*) to expand (solids, gas, etc.); **seine Schuhe durch Tragen d.,** to stretch one's shoes by use; **eine Besprechung in die Länge d.,** to extend, spin out, a discussion; **er wachte auf und dehnte seine Glieder,** he woke up and stretched (himself); (*b*) *Ling:* to lengthen (vowel, syllable, etc.); *Mus:* to hold on, sustain (note); (*c*) to drawl (one's words); to linger on (syllable, etc.); to pronounce (vowel) long; **seine Worte d.,** to drawl; **er spricht seine Vokale gedehnt aus,** he pronounces his vowels long; (*insertion in direct speech*) **'wirklich?' fragte er gedehnt,** 'really?' he asked (i) incredulously, disbelievingly, doubtfully, (ii) hesitantly, (iii) suggestively; **'nein,' sagte er gedehnt,** 'no,' he said (i) significantly, (ii) hesitantly, doubtfully. **2. sich dehnen;** (*a*) (*of pers.*) to stretch oneself, one's limbs, *abs.* to stretch; (*of material, gloves, elastic, etc.*) to stretch; *Ph: etc:* (*of air, gas*) to expand; (*of solid*) to dilate, swell, expand; **sich nach dem Schlafe d.,** to stretch (oneself) after sleeping, on waking; **die Minuten dehnten sich zu Stunden,** the minutes seemed like hours; **seine Brust dehnte sich vor Glück,** his heart expanded with joy; (*b*) (*of countryside, etc.*) to extend, stretch out, spread out; **im Süden dehnte sich das Meer,** to the south lay the expanse of the sea; **die Straße dehnte sich vor uns,** the road stretched out, extended, before us; **nach allen Seiten dehnte sich die ungeheure Wüste,** on all sides spread the vast desert.

II. *vbl s.* **1. Dehnen,** *n. in vbl senses.* **2. Dehnung,** *f.* (*a*)=II. 1; *also:* extension; elongation (of metals, etc.); expansion (of solids, gases, etc.); dilation, dilatation (of solids); *Ling:* lengthening (of vowels, etc.); (*b*) (*state*) stretch; extension, elongation; **elastische D.,** stretch; *Mec:* elastic extension.

Dehnholz, *n.* stretcher (for gloves, shoes, etc.).

Dehnkraft, *f. Mec:* tensile strength.

Dehnkraut, *n. Bot:* lycopod(ium), club-moss.

Dehnlänge, *f. Metall:* linear expansion.

Dehnquerschnitt, *m. Metall:* cross-sectional expansion.

Dehnstrich, *m.* (*diacritical sign*) length-mark (over vowel).

Dehnstufe, *f. Ling:* prolonged grade.

Dehnübung, *f. Gym:* stretching exercise.

Dehnung, *f. see* **dehnen II.**

Dehnungsgrenze, *f. Mec:* elastic limit.

Dehnungs-h, *n. Ling:* h interpolated to lengthen the preceding vowel.

Dehnungskoeffizient, *m.* coefficient of elasticity.

Dehnungskraft, *f. Mec:* tensile strength.

Dehnungsmesser, *m. Mec.E:* extensometer.

Dehnungsmodul, *m.* modulus of elasticity.

Dehnungsmuskel, *m. Anat:* extensor (muscle).

Dehnungsrest, *m. Mec:* permanent extension (of steel rod, etc.).

Dehnungsrohr, *n. Mec.E:* expansion pipe.

Dehnungsstrich, *m.,* **Dehnungszeichen,** *n.*=**Dehnstrich.**

dehydrieren [de·hy·ˈdriːrən], *v.tr.* to dehydrate; **Dehydrierung** *f,* dehydration.

Dei [dai], *m.* **-s/-s & -e.** *Hist:* Dey (of Algiers).

Deianeira [de·ia·ˈnairaː], **Deianira** [de·ia·ˈniːraː]. *Pr.n.f.* **-s** & *Lit:* **-rens.** *Gr.Myth:* Deianira.

Deibel, *m.* **-s/-. 1.** *F:* devil. **2.** *Ich:* chub.

Deich, *m.* **-(e)s/-e. 1.** *Hyd.E:* embankment; dike, dyke (on sea-shore); embankment, bank, levee (of waterway); causeway (across marsh, between mainland and island, etc.); **einen D. bauen, aufführen, aufwerfen,** to build an embankment, a dike, a causeway. **2.** *Min: Geol:* dike, dyke.

Deichacht, *f.* **1.**=**Deichgenossenschaft. 2.** constitution *or* regulations of dike administration.

Deichälteste, *m.* (*decl. as adj.*) member of the dikes committee.

Deichamt, *n.* office dealing with administration of dikes.

Deichanker, *m.* land on which dike is laid.

Deichaufseher, *m.* dike overseer; inspector of dikes.

Deichbau, *m.* building and upkeep of dikes.

Deichbeschauer, *m.*=**Deichaufseher.**

Deichbruch, *m.* **1.** breaking of a dike. **2.** breach in a dike.

Deichdamm, *m. Hyd.E:* protection dike.

deichen, *v.* **1.** *v.i.* (*haben*) (*a*) to build a dike, an embankment; (*b*) to mend, repair, a dike, an embankment. **2.** *v.tr.* to dike (land); to embank (river, etc.).

Deicher, *m.* **-s/-,** diker.

Deichfach, *m.* portion of a, the, dike (for which one man is responsible).

deichfrei, *a.* free of obligation to work on dikes.

Deichgenossenschaft, *f.* league of owners of diked land (controlling dike administration).

Deichgeschworene, *m.* (*decl. as adj.*) dike overseer.

Deichgraf, Deichhauptmann, *m.* dike-reeve, dike-warden, *A:* dike-grave.

Deichinspektor, *m.* inspector of dikes.

Deichkolben, *m. Bot:* cat's-tail, reed-mace.

Deichland, *n.* diked land, land protected by a dike *or* dikes.

Deichlast, *f.* expenses of building and upkeep of dikes.

Deichlücke, *f.* (*a*) hole in a dike; (*b*) gap in a dike (through which traffic can pass).

Deichordnung, *f.* legislation concerning dikes.

Deichpflicht, *f.* obligation for the upkeep of dikes.

Deichrecht, *n.* = **Deichordnung.**

Deichrolle, *f.* dike-register (*with details of ownership, responsibility for upkeep, etc.*).

Deichscharte, *f.* opening in a dike (*closed when floods threaten*).

Deichschau(ung), *f.* official inspection and examination of dikes.

Deichschlag, *m.* = **Deichfach.**

Deichschleuse, *f. Hyd.E:* sluice(-gate), flood-gate (in dike *or* embankment).

Deichschulze, *m.* dike overseer.

Deichsel, *f.* -/-n. **1.** (*a*) pole (of cart, carriage, etc.); (*b*) shafts (of cart, etc.); **ein Pferd in der D.,** a horse in, between, the shafts. **2.** *Her:* pall. **3.** *Tls:* = **Dechsel.**

Deichselarm, *m. Veh:* futchel.

Deichselblech, *n. Veh:* pole-tip.

Deichselende, *n. Veh:* pole-tip; shaft-tip.

Deichselgabel, *f. Veh:* shafts, thills (of cart, etc.).

Deichselkappe, *f. Veh:* pole-tip.

Deichselkette, *f. Harn:* tug-chain, pole-chain.

deichseln, *v.tr.* **1.** = **dechseln. 2.** *F:* to wangle (sth.); **er wird es schon d.,** he'll wangle it somehow.

Deichselnagel, *m. Veh:* thill-pin, shaft-pin.

Deichselpferd, *n.* shaft-horse, thill-horse; wheeler.

Deichselriemen, *m. Harn:* trace.

Deichselschnitt, *m. Her:* **im D. geteilt,** tierced pallwise.

Deichselstein, *m.* stone indicating the middle of the road.

Deichselstück, *n. Her:* gusset.

Deichsiel, *m.* = **Deichschleuse.**

Deichstatut, *n.* = **Deichordnung.**

Deichverband, *m.* = **Deichgenossenschaft.**

Deichvogt, *m. A:* official employed in dike administration.

Deichvorstand, *m.* dikes committee.

Deichweg, *m.* path on *or* beside a dike.

Deifikation [deˑiˑfiˑkaˑtsi'oːn], *f.* -/. deification.

deifizieren [deˑiˑfiˑ'tsiːrən], *v.tr.* to deify (ruler, etc.).

deiktisch ['daiktiʃ], *a. Ling:* deictic; *Sch:* demonstrative (method); **deiktische Lehrform,** visual instruction; object-teaching, -method.

dein, deine, dein. I. *poss.a.* (*written with capital* D *in letters or when addressing the Deity; for use of* **dein** *as opposed to* **Ihr,** *cp.* **du**) **1.** your; (*a*) **dein Freund, deine Freundin, deine Freunde,** your friend, your friends; **einer deiner, meiner, Freunde,** one of your, my, friends, a friend of yours, mine; **das ist deine Sache,** that's your business, affair; **das Haus deines Vaters,** your father's house; **dein Vater und deine Mutter,** your father and mother; **tue dein möglichstes,** do your utmost, do the best you can; (*at end of letter*) **herzliche Grüße, Dein Franz,** with all good wishes from Franz, best wishes, yours, Franz; **mit allen guten Wünschen, Deine Dich liebende Mutter,** with all good wishes, (from) your loving mother; (*b*) **einer von deinen Blinden,** one of your blind people; **ich habe mir ein Paar deiner vielgepriesenen Strümpfe gekauft,** I have bought a pair of those stockings you were praising so highly. **2.** (*in Biblical style; in addressing the Deity; formerly in Quaker language*) thy; (*before a noun or an adj. beginning with a vowel sound*) thine; **Dein Wille geschehe,** Thy will be done; **hast du deine Sünde bereut?** hast thou repented thy sin? **deine Haare sind weiß,** thy hair is white; **dein eigener Sohn,** thine own son; **dein Herz,** thine heart. **3.** (*a*) (*with vbl substantives*) your; **dein Kommen,** your coming; **ich bin mit deinem Lesen nicht zufrieden,** I am not satisfied with your reading; (*b*) *Lit:* (*of you*) **dein Besitz macht mich glücklich, ich bin glücklich in deinem Besitz,** it's happiness to call you mine; **dein Verlust schmerzt mich,** I grieve to have lost you. **4.** *Poet: invariable after noun preceded by definite article* **die Mutter dein,** your mother.

II. **dein, deiner, deine, dein(e)s, deine** (*decl. as adj.*) *poss.pron.* (*for use of capital* D *cp.* I.; *for use of* thine *cp.* I. 2) yours; thine; (*a*) **mein Haus ist größer als dein(e)s, als das deine,** my house is bigger than yours; **ich habe meinen Kamm vergessen — darf ich deinen nehmen?** I have forgotten my comb—may I borrow yours? **das ist dein(s),** that is yours; **hier liegt ein Taschentuch — ist das deins?** here is a handkerchief—is it yours? **wessen Garten ist das? ist es deiner, der deine?** whose garden is that? is it yours? **meine Frau kommt mit — kommt deine, die deine, auch?** my wife is coming with us—is yours coming too? **nimm was dein ist,** take what is yours; **was mein ist, ist dein,** what is mine is yours; *Lit:* **dein ist mein Herz,** my heart is yours, is thine; *Lit. & Hum:* **nimm hin — es sei dein,** take it—it shall be yours; *B:* **Dein ist das Reich,** Thine is the kingdom; *see also* **mein II.** (*a*); (*b*) **das Deine,** your property, your possessions; your affairs, business, etc.; **du mußt das Deine tun,** you must do your share, bit, part; you must pull your weight; **die Deinen,** your people, your family; **Du und die Deinen,** you and yours; **ich bin ganz der Deine,** I am entirely yours, all yours; (*at end of letter*) **stets der Deine,** yours ever.

III. **deiner,** *A. & Lit:* **dein,** *pers. pron. second pers. sg. gen. see* **du.**

deinerseits, *adv.* on your part; on your side.

deinesgleichen, *pron.* (*a*) (of) your own kind; **er ist nicht d.,** he is not (of) your own kind; **du mußt deine Freunde unter d. suchen,** you must look for friends (i) amongst your own kind, (ii) of your own age; **mit d. verkehre ich nicht,** *F:* **gebe ich mich nicht ab,** I don't mix with your kind, *F:* with the likes of you; (*b*) your equal; your equals; **ich bin d.,** I am your equal; **wir sind d.,** we are your equals.

deinesteils, *adv.* on your part.

deinethalben, *adv.* = **deinetwegen.**

deinetwegen, *adv.* (*a*) (i) on your account, because of you; (ii) for your sake; **ich ging d. von zu Hause weg,** I left home (i) on your account, because of you, (ii) for your sake; (*b*) on your behalf; **ich habe mit dem Minister d. gesprochen,** I spoke to the minister on your behalf.

deinetwillen, *adv.* **(um) d.,** (*a*) for your sake; **ich habe es (um) d. getan,** I did it for your sake; **um meinet- und deinetwillen,** for both our sakes; (*b*) because of you, on your account.

deinige, der, die, das, *poss.pron.* (*decl. as adj.*) (*for spelling with capital* D *cp.* **dein I.**) (*a*) yours; thine; (*for use of* thine *cp.* **dein I. 2**) **wem gehören diese Bücher? sind es die deinigen?** whose books are these? are they yours? (*b*) **das Deinige, die Deinigen** = **das Deine, die Deinen,** *q.v. under* **dein II.**

Deining, *f.* -/-en. *Dial:* (*a*) large wave; (*b*) surge, swell.

deinsen, *v.i.* (*haben*) *Nau:* (*of sailing ship*) (*a*) to go astern; (*b*) to drop, fall, astern.

Deise, *f.* -/-n. *North G.Dial:* place in *or* near the chimney for smoking meat.

deisig, *a. North G.Dial:* = **diesig.**

Deismus [de'ˈismus], *m.* -/. deism.

Deist [de'ˈist], *m.* -en/-en, deist.

deistisch [de'ˈistiʃ], *a.* deistic.

Deiwel, Deixel, *m.* -s/-. *F:* devil; **pfui D.!** ugh! how horrid!

Deixis ['daiksis], *f.* -/. *Ling:* deixis, deictic function.

Dejanira [deˑjaˑ'niːraː]. *Pr.n.f.* -s = **Deianeira.**

Dejektion [deˑjɛktsi'oːn], *f.* -/-en. **1.** *Med:* dejection, evacuation (of the bowels). **2.** *pl.* **Dejektionen,** dejecta (of body, etc.); excrements.

Deka ['dɛkaː, 'deːkaː], *n.* -(s)/-. *Meas: Austrian:* decagram(me).

Dekade [deˑ'kaːdə], *f.* -/-n. **1.** (*a*) set, series, of ten; decade; (*b*) *Lit:* **die Dekaden des Livius,** the decades of Livy. **2.** (*a*) decade, period of ten years; **in der zweiten D. des 19. Jahrhunderts,** in the second decade of the 19th century; (*b*) period of ten days; *Fr.Hist:* decade; **nach Abschluß jeder D.,** at the end of every ten days.

dekadent [deˑkaˑ'dɛnt], *a.* decadent.

Dekadenz [deˑkaˑ'dɛnts], *f.* -/. decadence.

Dekadenzdichtung, *f. Hist. of Lit:* literature of decadence; *fin-de-siècle* literature.

Dekadik, die [deˑ'kaːdik], -/. the decimal system.

dekadisch [deˑ'kaːdiʃ], *a.* (*a*) decimal (system, numeration, etc.); (*b*) *Fr.Hist:* decadal.

Dekaeder [deˑkaˑ'eːdər], *n.* -s/-. *Geom:* decahedron.

Dekagon [deˑkaˑ'goːn], *n.* -s/-e. *Geom:* decagon.

dekagonal [deˑkaˑgoˑ'naːl], *a. Geom:* decagonal.

Dekagramm ['deːkaˑgram, deˑkaˑ'gram], *n.* (*abbr.* **Dg,** *in Austria:* **dkg**) *Meas:* decagram(me).

Dekaliter ['deːkaˑˌliːtər, deˑkaˑ'liːtər], *n. Meas:* decalitre.

dekalkieren [deˑkal'kiːrən], *v.tr.* **1.** to transfer (design, coloured picture). **2.** to trace off, to calk (drawing).

Dekalkierpapier, *n.* transfer paper.

Dekalo [deˑ'kaːloː], *m.* -/-li. *Com:* short weight, loss in weight (through shrinkage).

Dekalog, der [deˑkaˑ'loːk], -(e)s/. [-'loːks, -'loːgəs]. *Rel:* the Decalogue.

Dekameron, das [deˑ'kaːmərɔn], -s/. *Lit:* the Decameron.

Dekameter ['deːkaˑˌmeːtər, deˑkaˑ'meːtər], *m. & n. Meas:* decametre.

dekampieren [deˑkam'piːrən], *v.i.* (*haben*) *Mil: A:* to strike camp.

Dekan [deˑ'kaːn], *m.* -s/-e. **1.** (*in German university*) dean (of faculty). **2.** *Ecc:* (*a*) = **Dechant 1**; (*b*) (*in Protestant Church, in some parts of Germany*) superintendent. **3.** *Astrol:* decan.

Dekanat [deˑkaˑ'naːt], *n.* -(e)s/-e. **1.** *Sch: Ecc:* (*a*) office, dignity, of a dean; (*b*) term of office of a dean. **2.** *Sch:* (*place*) dean's office. **3.** (*in Protestant Church*) district under the supervision of a superintendent.

Dekansäure, *f. Ch:* capric acid.

dekantieren [deˑkan'tiːrən], *v.tr.* to decant, pour off (liquid); **Dekantieren** *n,* decantation, decanting.

Dekantiergefäß, *n.* decanting vessel.

dekapieren [deˑkaˑ'piːrən], *v.tr. Metalw:* to pickle, dip (metal objects).

Dekapitation [deˑkaˑpiˑtaˑtsi'oːn], *f.* -/-en. *Obst:* decapitation.

Dekapode [deˑkaˑ'poːdə], *m.* -n/-n. *Crust:* decapod; **die Dekapoden,** the decapoda.

Dekapolis [deˑ'kaːpoˑlis]. *Pr.n.f.* -'. *A.Geog:* Decapolis.

Dekapsulation [deˑkapsuˑlaˑtsi'oːn], *f.* -/-en. *Surg:* decapsulation (of a kidney).

Dekar [deˑ'kaːr], *n.* -s/-e. *Meas:* decare.

dekarbonisieren [deˑkarboˑniˑ'ziːrən], **dekarburieren** [deˑkarbuˑ'riːrən], *v.tr.* = **decarbonisieren.**

Dekaster [deˑkas'tɛːr], *m.* -s/-e & -s. *Meas:* decastere.

Dekateur [deˑkaˑ'tøːr], *m.* -s/-e. *Tex:* (cloth) sponger.

dekatieren [deˑkaˑ'tiːrən], *v.tr. Tex:* to decatize, sponge, steam (cloth); to take the gloss, the finish, off (cloth).

Dekatierer [deˑkaˑ'tiːrər], *m.* -s/-. *Tex:* (cloth) sponger.

Dekatiermaschine, *f. Tex:* sponging-, steaming-, decatizing-machine.

Deklamation [deˑklaˑmaˑtsi'oːn], *f.* -/-en. **1.** (*a*) declamation; recitation, reciting (of poem, etc.); (*b*) (art of) declamation; recitation. **2.** recitation, recital (of poetry, etc.); *Pej:* harangue; mere oratory. **3.** *Mus:* declamation.

Deklamator [deˑkla'ˈmaːtɔr], *m.* -s/-en [-maˑ'toːrən], reciter (of poetry, etc.); *Pej:* person who makes high-flown speeches; ranter.

deklamatorisch [deˑklaˑmaˑ'toːriʃ], *a.* declamatory (speech, etc.); (talent, etc.) for recitation.

deklamieren [deˑklaˑ'miːrən], *v.tr. & i.* (*haben*) to recite (poem); to declaim (speech); *Pej:* to hold forth; to harangue; *P:* to spout; *Hum:* to orate.

Deklamierübung, *f. Sch:* recitation.

Deklarant [deˑklaˑ'rant], *m.* -en/-en. *Cust: etc:* declarer.

Deklaration [deˑklaˑraˑtsi'oːn], *f.* -/-en, declaration; (*a*) proclamation, announcement (of treaty, etc.); (*b*) statement, declaration (of income, etc.); *Cust:* declaring (of dutiable goods); *Com:* statement of value (of goods); (*c*) (customs) declaration; bill of entry.

Deklarationsschein, *m. Cust:* bill of entry; customs declaration.

deklarativ [deˑklaˑraˑ'tiːf], *a.* declarative.

deklarieren [deˑklaˑ'riːrən], *v.tr. Cust: etc:* to declare (dutiable goods, etc.); to make a (written) statement of (income, goods, etc.).

deklassieren [deˑkla'siːrən], *v.tr.* to lower the social position of (s.o.); to bring (s.o.) down in the world; (*of conduct, etc.*) to degrade (s.o.); **Deklassierung** *f,* lowering of one's social position; coming down in the world; degradation.

Deklination [deˑkliˑnaˑtsi'oːn], *f.* -/-en. **1.** *Gram:* declension. **2.** (*a*) *Astr:* declination (of star, etc.); (*b*) *Magn:* **D. des Magnets, magnetische D.,** magnetic variation; **D. der Kompaßnadel,** declination, variation, of the compass.

Deklinationsbussole, *f. Magn:* declination compass.

Deklinationskreis, *m. Astr:* declination circle.

Deklinationsmesser, *m.,* **Deklinatorium** [deˑkliˑnaˑ'toːrium], *n.* -s/-rien. *Magn:* declinometer; declination compass.

deklinierbar [deˑkliˑ'niːrˑ-], *a. Gram:* declinable.

deklinieren [deˑkliˑ'niːrən], *v.* **1.** *v.tr. Gram:* to decline (noun, adjective, etc.). **2.** *v.i.* (*haben*) *Astr: Magn:* (*of star, compass needle*) to deviate.

Deklinograph [deˑkliˑnoˑˈgraːf], *m.* -en/-en. *Magn:* declinometer.

dekohärieren [deˑkoˑhɛˑˈriːrən], *v.tr. W.Tel: A:* to decohere.

Dekokt [deˑˈkokt], *n.* -(e)s/-e. *Pharm:* decoction.

dekolletiert [deˑkolˈtiːrt], *a.*=decolletiert.

dekomponieren [deˑkompoˑˈniːrən], *v.tr.* to decompose; *Tex:* to dissect, analyse (cloth).

Dekomposition [deˑkompoˑziˑtsĭˈoːn], *f.* -/. (*a*) decomposition; *Tex:* dissection, analysis (of cloth); (*b*) *Med:* decomposition; marasmus; (*c*) *Ling:* decomposition.

Dekompositum [deˑkomˈpoːziˑtum], *n.* -s/-ta. *Ling:* decomposite, decompound.

Dekor [deˑˈkoːr], *m.* -s/-s. **1.** decoration, ornamentation (of building, street, etc.). **2.** *Th:* scenery, set(ting), décor.

Dekorateur [deˑkoˑraˑˈtøːr], *m.* -s/-e, (house) decorator, *esp.* curtain fitter; *Com:* window-dresser; *Th:* scene-painter.

Dekoration [deˑkoˑraˑtsĭˈoːn], *f.* -/-en. **1.** (*action*) (*a*) decoration, ornamentation, embellishment (of room, house, etc.); *Com:* (window-)dressing; *Th:* scene-painting; (*b*) decoration (of soldier, eminent pers.). **2.** (*a*) decoration, ornamentation; furnishings (of house, flat); (window) display; **Dekorationen** *pl,* decorations (at festival, party, etc.); (*b*) *Th:* scenery, setting, décor; (*c*) *A. & Hum:* (war, etc.) decoration.

Dekorationsarbeit, *f.* (work of) decoration; **wir führen die Dekorationsarbeiten aus,** we are working on the decoration.

Dekorationsetikett, *n. Com:* display label.

Dekorationsgestein, *n. Constr:* stone used for decorative purposes, *e.g.* incrustation, etc.

Dekorationskarte, *f. Com:* display card.

Dekorationsmaler, *m.* (*a*) house-painter; (*b*) decorative artist; *Th:* scene-painter.

Dekorationsmalerei, *f.* (*a*) decorative painting (of walls and ceilings); (*b*) *Th:* scene-painting.

Dekorationspflanzen, *f.pl.* ornamental, decorative, plants.

Dekorationsstoff, *m. Tex:* furnishing fabric.

Dekorationsstück, *n.* piece of decoration; ornament; *F:* (*pers.*) ornament.

dekorativ [deˑkoˑraˑˈtiːf], *a.* decorative, ornamental.

dekorieren [deˑkoˑˈriːrən]. **I.** *v.tr.* **1.** to decorate (room, house, street, etc.); to ornament (sth.); to fit (room) with furnishings, *esp.* to provide (room) with curtains; *Com:* to dress (a window). **2.** to decorate (s.o.). **II.** *vbl s.* **1. Dekorieren**, *n.* in *vbl senses.* **2. Dekorierung**, *f.* (*a*)=II. 1; *also:* decoration; (*b*) decoration, ornamentation.

Dekort [deˑˈkort], *m.* -(e)s/-e. *Com: etc:* deduction, allowance, abatement, discount.

dekortieren [deˑkorˈtiːrən], *v.tr. Com:* to deduct (sum of money); to make allowance for (sum of money).

Dekortikation [deˑkortiˑkaˑtsĭˈoːn], *f.* -/-en. **1.** decortication (of tree); peeling (of twig). **2.** *Surg:* decortication, *esp.* pulmonary decortication, pleurectomy.

dekortizieren [deˑkortiˑˈtsiːrən], *v.tr.* to decorticate.

Dekorum [deˑˈkoːrum], *n.* -s/. decorum; **das D. wahren,** to observe decorum.

dekreditieren [deˑkrediˑˈtiːrən], *v.tr.*=**diskreditieren**.

Dekrement [deˑkreˑˈmɛnt], *n.* -(e)s/-e, decrement.

Dekrepitation [deˑkreˑpiˑtaˑtsĭˈoːn], *f.* -/-en. *Ch:* decrepitation (of a salt).

dekrepitieren [deˑkreˑpiˑˈtiːrən], *v.i.* (*sein*) *Ch:* (of salt, etc.) to decrepitate.

dekrescendo [deˑkrɛˈʃɛndoˑ], *adv.*=**decrescendo**.

Dekret [deˑˈkreːt], *n.* -(e)s/-e. *Hist: R.C.Ch:* (imperial, papal, etc.) decree.

Dekretale [deˑkreˈtaːlə], *n.* -s/-n & -lien. *R.C.Ch:* decretal; **die Gregorianischen Dekretalen,** the Gregorian Decretals.

dekretieren [deˑkreˈtiːrən], *v.tr.* to decree (sth.); to issue (decision, etc.) as an order; to order (sth.) (in a dictatorial manner).

Dekretist [deˑkreˈtist], *m.* -en/-en. *Ecc.Hist:* decretist.

Dekubitalgeschwür [deˑkuˑbiˑˈtaːl-], *n. Med:* bedsore, decubitus.

dekupieren [deˑkuˑˈpiːrən], *v.tr.* **1.** to cut (sth.) off. **2.** to cut (sth.) out.

Dekupiersäge, *f. Tls:* fret-saw machine.

Dekurie [deˑˈkuːrĭə], *f.* -/-n. *Rom.Ant:* decury.

Dekurio [deˑˈkuːrĭoˑ], *m.* -s & -nen/-nen [deˑkuˑrĭˈoːnən]. *Rom.Ant:* decurion.

dekussiert [deˑkuˈsiːrt], *a. Bot:* decussate.

Dekuvert [deˑkuˑˈvɛːr], *n.* -s/-s. *Fin: St.Exch:* lack of securities; unsecured liability.

dekuvrieren [deˑkuˑˈvriːrən], *v.tr.* to uncover (sth.); to uncover, expose (s.o.); **sich d.,** to reveal oneself.

Delation [deˑlaˑtsĭˈoːn], *f.* -/-en, delation; denunciation.

Delator [deˑˈlaːtor], *m.* -en/-en [-laˑˈtoːrən], delator; denouncer.

delatorisch [deˑlaˑˈtoːriʃ], *a.* delatorian.

Delawarenmöwe [deˑlaˑˈvaːrən-], *f. Orn:* ring-billed gull.

dele [ˈdeːleː]. *Lt.imp.*=**deleatur**[1].

deleatur[1] [deˑleˈaːtur]. *Lt.imp. Print:* delete, dele.

Deleatur[2], *n.* -s/-. *Print:* delete mark; dele.

Delegant [deˑleˈgant], *m.* -en/-en. *Jur:* delegant.

Delegat [deˑleˈgaːt], *m.* -en/-en. **1.** *R.C.Ch:* (papal) delegate. **2.** *Jur:* debtor assigned to a delegate (*in act of assignment*).

Delegatar [deˑleˑgaˑˈtaːr], *m.* -s/-e. *Jur:* delegatee.

Delegation [deˑleˑgaˑtsĭˈoːn], *f.* -/-en. **1.** (*a*) delegation (of authority, etc.); (*b*) *Jur:* assignment, transfer (of debt). **2.** *Coll:* delegation, body of delegates; *Hist:* **die Delegationen,** the (Austro-Hungarian) Delegations.

Delegationschef, *m.* (*a*) leader of a delegation; (*b*) head of a (permanent) delegation.

delegieren [deˑleˈgiːrən], *v.tr.* (*a*) to delegate (s.o.); (*b*) *Com: Jur:* to assign, transfer (a debt).

Delegierte [deˑleˈgiːrtə], *m., f.* (*decl. as adj.*) delegate.

delektieren (sich) [deˑlɛkˈtiːrən], *v.refl.* **sich an etwas** *dat.* **d.,** to take pleasure in sth., to delight in sth.; **sie delektierten sich an den guten Speisen,** they enjoyed, relished, the good food.

deletär [deˑleˈtɛːr], *a. Med: etc:* deleterious; noxious, injurious.

Delfter, *inv.a. & s.n.* -s/. *Cer:* **D. (Fayence, Ware, Porzellan),** Delft ware.

Delftware, *f. Cer:* Delft ware.

Delhi [ˈdeːliː, ˈdɛlhiː]. *Pr.n.n.* -s. *Geog:* Delhi.

Delhibeule, *f. Med:* Delhi boil, Aleppo boil.

Deliberation [deˑliˑbəraˑtsĭˈoːn], *f.* -/-en, deliberation; consideration.

deliberieren [deˑliˑbəˈriːrən], *v.tr.* to deliberate over (a question); to think (sth.) over, to consider (sth.).

Delier [ˈdeːlĭər], *m.* -s/-. *A. Hist:* Delian.

delikat [deˑliˑˈkaːt], *a.* delicate. **1.** (*a*) delicate, exquisite (flavour); delicious (taste); (*b*) delicate (health, colour). **2.** difficult, critical, *F:* delicate (situation, problem, etc.); **eine delikate Angelegenheit, Situation,** a delicate matter, situation. **3.** tactful (manner); **er hat diese Angelegenheit in sehr delikater Weise, behandelt,** *adv.* **sehr d., behandelt,** he treated this matter with great delicacy, with great tact.

Delikatesse [deˑliˑkaˑˈtɛsə], *f.* -/-n. **1.** (*a*) delicacy (of flavour, colour, etc.); **mit D. gemalt,** delicately painted; (*b*) tactfulness (of behaviour, manner, etc.); **mit D.,** tactfully, with tact, with delicacy. **2.** (*food*) delicacy; **Hummer ist eine D.,** lobster is a delicacy; **sie lebt nur von Delikatessen,** she lives purely on delicacies; *Com:* (*on shop-sign, etc.*) 'Delikatessen', 'Delicatessen'.

Delikatessengeschäft, *n.,* **Delikatessenhandlung,** *f.,* **Delikatessenladen,** *m. Com:* delicatessen shop, store; delicatessen.

Delikatessenwaren, *f.pl. Com:* delicatessen.

Delikateßhering, *m. Com:* tinned marinaded herring.

Delikt [deˑˈlikt], *n.* -(e)s/-e. *Jur: etc:* (indictable) offence; **schweres D.,** serious offence; **geringfügiges D.,** minor offence, petty offence.

deliktsfähig, *a. Jur:* (pers.) responsible in law.

Deliktsfähigkeit, *f. Jur:* criminal responsibility.

Delila [deˑˈliːlaː]. *Pr.n.f.* -s & *Lit:* -lens. Delilah.

Delimitation [deˑliˑmiˑtaˑtsĭˈoːn], *f.* -/-en, delimitation.

delimitieren [deˑliˑmiˑˈtiːrən], *v.tr.* to delimitate, demarcate (sth.).

Delinquent [deˑlinˈkvɛnt], *m.* -en/-en. *Jur: etc:* offender, delinquent.

deliqueszieren [deˑliˑkvɛsˈtsiːrən], *v.i.* (*haben*) *Ch:* to deliquesce.

delirant [deˑliˑˈrant], *a. Med: etc:* delirious; raving.

delirieren [deˑliˑˈriːrən], *v.i.(haben)* to be delirious; to rave.

Delirium [deˑˈliːrĭum], *n.* -s/-rien, delirium; **Delirien** *pl,* periods of delirium; **im D. sein,** to be delirious; to rave; **D. tremens** [- ˈtreːmɛns], delirium tremens; **im D. tremens sein, D. tremens haben,** to have delirium tremens, *F:* to have the d.t.'s, the horrors.

delisch [ˈdeːliʃ], *a. A.Geog:* Delian; *Geom:* **das Delische Problem,** the Delian Problem.

deliziös [deˑliˑtsĭˈøːs], *a.* delicious (flavour, scent, etc.).

Delkredere [dɛlˈkreːdərə], *n.* -/-. *Com:* del credere agreement; **D. stehen,** to stand security.

Delkrederefonds, *m. Com:* contingent fund.

Delkrederekonto, *n. Book-k:* contingent account.

Delkredereprovision, *f. Com:* del credere commission.

Delkrederereserve, *f. Com:* contingent fund.

Delkredereversicherung, *f. Ins:* credit insurance.

Delle, *f.* -/-n, shallow depression; dent; hollow, dip (in ground).

Delogement [deˑloˑʒəˈmãː], *n.* -s/-s, (*a*) removal, moving house; (*b*) *Mil:* marching off, decamping.

delogieren [deˑloˑˈʒiːrən]. **I.** *v.* **1.** *v.i.* (*sein*) (*a*) to remove, move house; (*b*) *Mil:* to march off, to decamp. **2.** *v.tr.* to drive (s.o.) out; to evict, turn out (a tenant). **II.** *vbl s.* **Delogierung**, *f.* in *vbl senses; also:* (*a*) removal; (*b*) eviction (of tenant).

Delos [ˈdeːlos]. *Pr.n.n.* -'. *A. Geog:* Delos.

Delphi [ˈdɛlfiː]. *Pr.n.n.* -s. *A.Geog:* Delphi; **die Sibylle von D.,** the Delphic Sibyl.

Delphier [ˈdɛlfiˑər], *m.* **1.** -s/-, man of Delphi. **2.** -s/. **der D.,** the Delphic Apollo.

Delphierin [ˈdɛlfiˑərin], *f.* **1.** -/-innen, woman of Delphi. **2.** -/. **die D.,** the Delphic Sibyl.

Delphin [dɛlˈfiːn], *m.* -s/-e. **1.** *Z: Her:* dolphin; *Z:* **die Delphine,** the delphinidae. **2.** *Astr:* **der D.,** Delphinus, the Dolphin. **3.** *A:* dolphin (of cannon).

Delphinin [dɛlfiˑˈniːn], *n.* -s/. *Ch:* delphinin(e).

Delphinium [dɛlˈfiːnĭum], *n.* -s/-nien & -nia. *Bot:* delphinium.

Delphinus [dɛlˈfiːnus], *m.* -/-phine. **1.** *Fr.Hist:* Dauphin; *see also* in usum Delphini. **2.** *Astr:* Delphinus, the Dolphin.

delphisch [ˈdɛlfiʃ], *a.* Delphian; Delphic; **das Delphische Orakel,** the Delphic Oracle; **die Delphische Sibylle,** the Delphic Sibyl.

Delta [ˈdɛltaː], *n.* **1.** -(s)/-s. *Gr.Alph:* delta. **2.** -s/-s &-ten. *Geog:* delta.

Deltaarm, *m. Geog:* delta distributory.

Deltabildung, *f. Geog:* delta formation.

deltablumig, *a. Bot:* **deltablumige Nelke,** maiden pink.

deltaförmig, *a.* **1.** *Bot: Anat: etc:* deltoid (leaf, muscle, etc.). **2.** (*of river mouth, etc.*) shaped like a delta; deltoid.

Deltaland, *n. Geog:* deltaic land; delta.

Deltametall, *n. Metall:* delta metal.

Deltamuskel, *m. Anat:* deltoid (muscle).

Deltanelke, *f. Bot:* maiden pink.

Deltaschaltung, *f. El.E:* delta connection.

Deltastrahlen, *m.pl. Ph:* delta rays.

Deltoeder [dɛltoˑˈeːdər], *n.* -s/-. *Cryst:* deltahedron.

Deltoid [dɛltoˑˈiːt], *n.* -(e)s/-e [-ˈiːts, -ˈiːdəs/-ˈiːdə]. *Geom:* deltoid.

Deltoiddodekaeder [dɛltoˑiˑtdoˑdeˑkaˑˈeːdər], *m.* -s/-. *Cryst:* deltahedron.

dem *see* **der.**

Demagoge [deˑmaˑˈgoːgə], *m.* -n/-n, demagogue.

Demagogentum, *n.* -s/. demagogism.

Demagogie [deˑmaˑgoˑˈgiː], *f.* -/. demagogy.

demagogisch [deˑmaˑˈgoːgiʃ], *a.* demagogic; **demagogische Umtriebe,** demagogic intrigues.

demanchieren [deˑmanˈʃiːrən], *v.i.* (*haben*) *Mus:* to change position (*on a stringed instrument*).

Demant [ˈdeːmant], *m.* -(e)s/-e. *A. & Poet:* = **Diamant.**

Demantblende, *f. Miner:* eulytite.

demanten [ˈdeːmantən, deˑˈmantən], *a. A. & Poet:*=**diamanten.**

Demantoid [deˑmantoˑˈiːt], *m.* -(e)s/-e [-ˈiːts, -ˈiːdəs/-ˈiːdə]. *Miner:* demantoid.

Demantspat, *m. Miner:* adamantine spar.

Demarche [deˑˈmarʃə], *f.* -/-n, (diplomatic) step, proceeding; démarche; **die nötigen Demarchen machen,** to take the necessary steps; **Demarchen bei j-m machen,** to approach s.o.

Demarkation [deˑmarkaˑtsĭˈoːn], *f.* -/-en, demarcation, delimitation (of frontier, etc.); *Med:* demarcation (of gangrenous area, etc.).

Demarkationslinie, *f.* demarcation line, line of demarcation.

demarkieren [deˑmarˈkiːrən], *v.tr.* to demarcate, delimit; to mark the boundaries of (territory, etc.); **Demarkierung** *f* = **Demarkation.**

demaskieren [deˑmasˈkiːrən], *v.tr.* to unmask (s.o.); **sich d.,** to take off one's mask; *Mil:* **eine Batterie d.,** to unmask a battery.

Demat [ˈdeːmaːt], *m.* -(e)s/-e. *North G.Meas:* land measure, *approx.* between 5,400 and 6,840 square yards.

Demelee [deˑmeˈleː], *n.* -(s)/-s, contention; unpleasant dealings; fight; brawl.

Demen [ˈdeːmən], *m.pl. see* **Demos 2.**
dementgegen [ˈdeːmᵊɛntˈgeːgən], *adv.* against this, that; as opposed to this, that.
Dementi [deˑˈmɛntiː], *n.* **-s/-s.** *Pol: Journ:* (formal) denial, contradiction; **ein D. geben,** to give a (formal) denial.
Dementia [deˑˈmɛntsĭaː], *f.* **-/.** *Med:* dementis; **D. praecox,** dementia praecox.
dementieren [deˑmɛnˈtiːrən], *v.tr. Pol: Journ:* to deny, to give a (formal) denial of (statement, fact, etc.).
dementsprechend [ˈdeːmᵊɛntˈʃprɛçənt], *a.* corresponding; *adv.* correspondingly, accordingly; **ein großes Auto und eine dementsprechende, eine d. große, Garage,** a large car and a correspondingly large garage; **sie hat das Kind von Anfang an verwöhnt, und das Kind hat jetzt ein dementsprechendes, ein d. schlechtes, Benehmen,** she has spoilt the child from the very first, and the child behaves accordingly; **der Junge hat das ganze Jahr nichts für die Schule getan, und sein Zeugnis ist d. schlecht, und er hat ein d. schlechtes Zeugnis,** the boy has not done any work at school all the year and he has a correspondingly bad report; **sie hat sich ein elegantes Jackenkleid gekauft, aber leider hat sie nicht die dementsprechende Figur,** she has bought herself an elegant suit, but unfortunately she has not got the figure for it, the figure that goes with it.
Demenz [deˑˈmɛnts], *f.* **-/.** *Med:* dementia; **angeborene D.,** (congenital) idiocy.
Demerit [deˑmeˑˈriːt], *m.* **-en/-en.** *R.C.Ch:* delinquent priest.
Demeritenanstalt, *f.*, **Demeritenhaus,** *n. R.C.Ch:* reformatory for delinquent priests.
Demeter [deˑˈmeːtər]. *Pr.n.f.* **-s.** *Myth:* Demeter.
Demetrios, Demetrius [deˑˈmeːtriˑos, -triˑus]. *Pr.n.m.* **-'.** Demetrius.
demgegenüber [ˈdeːmgeːgənᵊˈyːbər], *adv.* on the contrary; as opposed to this, that, in opposition to this, that; **d. behauptet er, daß . . . ,** he, on the contrary, maintains that . . . ; **d. steht seine Behauptung . . . ,** in opposition to this, opposed to this, is his assertion . . . .
demgemäß [ˈdeːm-], *a. & adv.* = **dementsprechend.**
Demijohn [ˈdeːmiˑdʒon], *m.* **-s/-s,** demijohn.
Demimonde [dəmiˑˈmõːdə], *f.* **-/.** *demi-monde,* outskirts of society.
deminutiv[1] [deˑmiˑnuˑˈtiːf], *a.* = **diminutiv**[1].
Deminutiv[2], *n.* **-s/-e** [-ˈtiːvə], **Deminutivum** [deˑmiˑnuˑˈtiːvum], *n.* **-s/-va** = **Diminutiv**[2].
Demission [deˑmisĭˈoːn], *f.* **-/-en.** **1.** resignation; **seine D. einreichen,** to tender, send in, hand in, one's resignation, to resign. **2.** dismissal (of employee, etc.).
demissionieren [deˑmisĭoˑˈniːrən], *v.i.* (*haben*) to resign, to tender, hand in, send in, one's resignation.
Demissionsangebot, *n.* offer of resignation.
Demiurg [deˑmiˑˈurk], *m.* **-en** [-ˈurgən] *&* **-s/.** demiurge; creator (of the world).
Demivierge [dəmiˑviˈɛrʒə], *f.* **-/-s.** *Lit:* demivierge.
demnach, *adv. & conj.* according to that; accordingly; consequently; so; **nach der Theorie der Alten war die Erde eine flache Scheibe; d. müßte man an ihren Rand gelangen können,** in ancient theory the earth was a flat disc; according to this one ought to be able to reach the edge; **wir fragten unseren Gastgeber, was er vorhabe, damit wir d. unsere Pläne machen könnten,** we asked our host what his plans were so that we could make ours accordingly; **es erschien ein fantastischer Bericht über Herrn X in der Zeitung; d. wäre sein Rücktritt jeden Tag zu erwarten,** there was an extraordinary report about Mr. X in the newspaper; according to what it said it would seem that his resignation is imminent; **ich hatte heute einen Brief von Frau X; d. geht es ihr sehr gut,** I had a letter from Mrs X today; she seems to be very well.
demnächst, *adv.* (*a*) soon, before long, shortly, in the near future; **er wird d. hierher kommen,** he will be coming here soon, shortly; (*on poster, etc.*) **d. (in diesem Theater),** coming shortly (to this theatre); (*b*) *A:* afterwards.
demobilisieren [deˑmoˑbiˑliˑˈziːrən]. **I.** *v.* **1.** *v.tr.* to demobilize (troops). **2.** *v.i.* (*haben*) to disarm; to disband one's military *or* naval forces.
II. *vbl s.* **Demobilisierung,** *f. in vbl senses; also:* demobilization.
Demobilmachung, *f.* demobilization, demobilizing (of troops).
Demograph [deˑmoˑˈgraːf], *m.* **-en/-en,** demographer.
Demographie [deˑmoˑgraˑˈfiː], *f.* **-/.** demography.
demographisch [deˑmoˑˈgraːfiʃ], *a.* demographic.
demohngeachtet [ˈdeːmᵊoːngəᵊˈaxtət], *adv.* = **dessenungeachtet.**
Demoiselle [deˑmoˑaˑˈzɛl(ə)], *f.* **-/-n** [lən], single woman, unmarried woman.
Demokrat [deˑmoˑˈkraːt], *m.* **-en/-en,** democrat.
Demokratie [deˑmoˑkraˑˈtiː], *f.* **-/-n** [-ˈtiːən], democracy.
demokratisch [deˑmoˑˈkraːtiʃ], *a.* democratic; *adv.* democratically.
demokratisieren [deˑmoˑkraˑtiˑˈziːrən], *v.tr.* to democratize.
Demokrit [deˑmoˑˈkriːt]. *Pr.n.m.* **-s.** Democritus.
demolieren [deˑmoˑˈliːrən]. **I.** *v.tr.* to demolish, pull down (house, defences, etc.); *F:* to ruin, wreck (furniture, etc.); **die Kinder haben mir die ganze Wohnung demoliert,** the children have made an utter wreck of my flat.
II. *vbl s.* **Demolieren** *n.*, **Demolierung** *f. in vbl senses; also:* demolition.
Demolition [deˑmoˑliˑtsĭˈoːn], *f.* **-/.** demolition.
demonetisieren [deˑmoˑneˑtiˑˈziːrən]. **1.** *v.tr.* to demonetize (metal, etc.); to call in, withdraw (coinage, etc.) from circulation. **2.** *vbl s.* **Demonetisierung,** *f.* demonetization; calling in, withdrawal from circulation (of coinage, etc.).
Demonstrant [deˑmonˈstrant], *m.* **-en/-en,** (political, etc.) demonstrator.
Demonstration [deˑmonstraˑtsĭˈoːn], *f.* **-/-en,** demonstration. **1.** (*a*) demonstration, proof (of fact, etc.); (*b*) (practical) demonstration (of apparatus, etc.); *Sch:* demonstration (in anatomy, etc.). **2.** (*a*) (i) (political, etc.) demonstration; (ii) = **Demonstrationszug;** (*b*) *Mil:* demonstration; show of force (*in order to deceive the enemy*).
Demonstrationsart, *f. Ling:* deictic function.
Demonstrationszug, *m.* demonstration march; protest march.
demonstrativ[1] [deˑmonstraˑˈtiːf], *a.* **1.** demonstrative (argument). **2.** ostentatious; pointed; emphatic (action); **ein demonstratives** [deˑmonstraˑˈtiːvəs] **Schweigen,** a pointed silence; a disapproving silence; *adv.* **er verließ d. den Saal,** he left the room in protest, pointedly. **3.** *Gram:* demonstrative (pronoun, etc.).
Demonstrativ[2], *n.* **-s/-e** [-ˈtiːvə]. *Gram:* demonstrative (adjective *or* pronoun).
Demonstrativpronomen, *n. Gram:* demonstrative (pronoun *or* adjective).
Demonstrativum [deˑmonstraˑˈtiːvum], *n.* **-s/-va** = **Demonstrativ**[2].
Demonstrator [deˑmonˈstraːtor], *m.* **-s/-en** [-traˑˈtoːrən]. **1.** demonstrator (of a truth, an apparatus, etc.); *Sch:* demonstrator (in laboratory, etc.). **2.** *occ.* = **Demonstrant.**
demonstrieren [deˑmonˈstriːrən]. **1.** *v.tr.* to demonstrate, prove, establish the truth of (proposition); to illustrate (theory, etc.); to demonstrate (apparatus, etc.). **2.** *v.i.* (*haben*) (*a*) (i) to make a (political, etc.) demonstration; (ii) to take part in a demonstration; (*b*) *Mil:* to make a demonstration (*in order to mislead the enemy*); (*c*) *Sch:* to demonstrate (in anatomy, etc.).
Demontage [deˑmonˈtaːʒə], *f.* **-/-n,** dismantling, dismantlement (of machine, factory, etc.).
demontieren [deˑmonˈtiːrən]. **I.** *v.tr.* to take (sth.) down; to take (sth.) to pieces, to dismantle (sth.); to disassemble (machine, etc.); *Mil:* to strip (rifle).
II. *vbl s.* **Demontieren** *n.*, **Demontierung** *f. in vbl senses; also:* dismantlement (of industrial plant, etc.).
Demoralisation [deˑmoˑraˑliˑzaˑtsĭˈoːn], *f.* **-/.** demoralization; corruption.
demoralisieren [deˑmoˑraˑliˑˈziːrən], *v.tr.* to demoralize; to corrupt; **Demoralisierung** *f,* demoralization; corruption.
Demos [ˈdeːmos], *m.* **-/Demen.** **1.** Demos, the people. **2.** *Gr.Hist:* deme, township.
Demosthenes [deˑˈmosteˑnɛs]. *Pr.n.m.* **-'.** *Gr.Hist:* Demosthenes.
demosthenisch [deˑmosˈteːniʃ], *a.* Demosthenic, Demosthenian.
demotisch [deˑˈmoːtiʃ]. **1.** *a.* demotic; popular. **2.** *a. Pal:* demotic (writing). **3.** *s.* **Demotisch,** *n.* demotic writing; **in D. geschrieben,** written in demotic.
Dempgording, *f. Nau:* leech-line.
demselben *see* **derselbe.**
demungeachtet [ˈdeːmᵊungəᵊˈaxtət], *conj.* = **dessenungeachtet.**
Demut, *f.* **-/.** **1.** humility, humbleness; *B. & Lit:* lowliness (of mind); **christliche D.,** Christian humility; **lasset uns in D. niederknien,** let us kneel in humility. **2.** *Bot:* (*a*) thyme; (*b*) savory.
demütig, *a.* humble; **von Herzen d.,** humble of heart, humble-hearted, *B:* lowly in heart; **ein demütiges Gebet, eine demütige Bitte,** a humble prayer; **ein sehr demütiger Mann,** a very humble man, a man of great humility; **im Anblick der Schönheit der Natur wird man d.,** when confronted with the beauty of nature one feels humble; **das Studium der Naturwissenschaft ist dazu angetan, einen d. zu machen,** the study of science tends to make one humble; *adv.* humbly, in humility; **lasset uns Gott d. um Gnade bitten,** let us humbly ask God for grace.
demütigen. **I.** *v.tr.* (*a*) (*of the Deity*) to humble, abase (s.o.); **Gott demütigt die Stolzen,** God abases the proud; **sich vor Gott d.,** to humble, abase, oneself before God; (*b*) to humiliate, mortify (s.o.); **er demütigte sie durch seinen Spott,** he humiliated her by his mockery; **eine demütigende Erfahrung,** a humiliating experience.
II. *vbl s.* **1. Demütigen,** *n. in vbl senses.* **2. Demütigung,** *f.* (*a*) = II. 1; *also:* humiliation, mortification; abasement; (*b*) humiliation, mortification, *F:* set-down; **er mußte alle Demütigungen hinnehmen,** he had to put up with every humiliation.
Demütigkeit, *f.* = **Demut** 1.
demütiglich, *adv.* humbly, in humility.
Demutspflanze, *f. Bot:* mimosa, *F:* sensitive plant.
demutsvoll, *a.* humble.
demzufolge [ˈdeːmtsuˑˈfolgə]. **1.** *adv.* consequently; accordingly. **2.** *rel.pron.* according to which; **der Bericht, d. die Soldaten die Stadt schon erreicht haben, ist falsch,** the report according to which the soldiers have already reached the town is wrong.
den *see* **der.**
Denar [deˑˈnaːr], *m.* **-s/-e.** *Rom.Ant:* denarius.
denationalisieren [deˑnaˑtsĭoˑnaˑliˑˈziːrən], *v.tr.* to denationalize.
Denaturalisation [deˑnaˑtuˑraˑliˑzaˑtsĭˈoːn], *f.* **-/.** denaturalization.
denaturalisieren [deˑnaˑtuˑraˑliˑˈziːrən], *v.tr.* to denaturalize (s.o.).
denaturieren [deˑnaˑtuˑˈriːrən]. **I.** *v.tr.* to denature (sth.); to adulterate (sth.); **Alkohol d.,** to denature, methylate, alcohol.
II. *vbl s.* **Denaturieren** *n.*, **Denaturierung** *f. in vbl senses; also:* denaturation; adulteration.
Denaturiermittel, *n.* denaturant, denaturing agent.
denazifizieren [deˑnaˑtsiˑfiˑˈtsiˑrən], *v.tr.* to denazify (s.o.); **Denazifizierung** *f,* denazification.
Dendlrose, *f. Bot:* = **Alpenrose.**
Dendrachat [dɛndraˈxaːt], *m. Miner:* tree-agate, dendritic agate.
Dendrit [dɛnˈdriːt], *m.* **-en/-en.** *Miner: Cryst:* dendrite.
Dendritenachat, *m.* = **Dendrachat.**
dendritisch [dɛnˈdriːtiʃ], *a. Miner: Cryst: etc:* dendritic, arborized (markings, etc.).
dendroidisch [dɛndroˑˈiːdiʃ], *a.* dendroid.
Dendrolith [dɛndroˑˈliːt], *m.* **-(e)s/-e** *&* **-en/-en,** dendrolite.
Dendrologie [dɛndroˑloˑˈgiː], *f.* **-/.** dendrology.
Dendrometer, *n.* **-s/-.** *Arb:* dendrometer.
Denegation [deˑneˑgaˑtsĭˈoːn], *f.* **-/-en,** denial.
denen *see* **der.**
Dengelamboß, *m.* scythe-sharpening anvil.
Dengelhammer, *m. Tls:* hammer for sharpening scythes.
Dengelmaschine, *f.* scythe-hammering machine.
dengeln, *v.tr.* to sharpen (scythes); to hammer (scythes) sharp.
Dengelstock, *m.* = **Dengelamboß.**
Denguefieber [ˈdɛŋgeˑ-], *n. Med:* dengue-fever, *F:* dandy-fever, *U.S:* breakbone fever.
Den Haag. *Pr.n.n.* **-s.** *See under* **Haag.**
denitrieren [deˑniˑˈtriːrən], *v.tr.* to denitrify; **Denitrierung** *f,* denitrification.
Denitrifikation [deˑniˑtriˑfiˑkaˑtsĭˈoːn], *f.* **-/.** denitrification.
denitrifizieren [deˑniˑtriˑfiˑˈtsiːrən], *v.tr.* to denitrify.
denjenigen *see* **derjenige.**
Denk-, *comb.fm. cp.* **Gedenk-.**
Denkanmich, *n.* **-s/.** *Bot:* germander.
Denkarbeit, *f.* mental effort.
Denkart, *f.* way of thinking; **das ist wider meine D.,** that goes against my way of thinking; **ein Mann (von) edler D.,** a noble-minded man.
Denkaufgabe, *f.* (mathematical, etc.) problem; brain-twister
denkbar, *a.* **1.** *Phil: etc:* (*a*) (*as opposed to visible*) falling within the province of reason, perceptible to the mind; thinkable, intellectual; (*b*) (*as opposed to real*) imaginable, conceivable.

2. conceivable, imaginable, thinkable; possible; **das ist kaum d.,** that is hardly conceivable, imaginable; **es ist gar nicht d.,** it is quite inconceivable; **ohne Treue ist keine Freundschaft d.,** without loyalty friendship is unthinkable, no friendship is possible. **3.** *adv.* **der d. beste Stil,** the best possible, the best conceivable, style; **in der d. einfachsten Weise leben,** to live in the simplest possible way; **er hat sich die d. größte Mühe gegeben,** he has taken the utmost pains, the greatest possible pains; **in der d. schönsten Umgebung,** in the most beautiful surrounding(s) imaginable; **ich habe es ihm d. leicht gemacht,** I have made it as simple, as easy, as possible for him; **ein d. schlechtes Klima,** the worst climate imaginable; *F:* **er ist d. blöde,** he's absolutely stupid.

Denkbild, *n.* **1.** memorial; monument. **2.** symbol; mental image; mnemonic image.

Denkblümchen, *n. Bot:* pansy.

Denkbuch, *n. A:* memorandum book, *U.S:* (memo) notebook.

denken. (*p.t.* **dachte;** *p.p.* **gedacht**) **I.** *v.tr. & i.* (*haben*) **1.** (*a*) to think; **ich denke, also bin ich,** I think, therefore I am; **laut d.,** to think aloud; **bei sich, für sich, d.,** to think to oneself; **folgerichtig d., logisch d.,** to think logically; **kompliziert d., eine komplizierte Art zu d. haben,** to have a complicated way of thinking; **gut, falsch, gedacht,** well, falsely, reasoned; **selbstständig d.,** to think independently, to think for oneself; **er sagt wenig, aber er denkt viel,** he does not say much but he thinks a lot; **er ist unfähig, logisch zu d.,** he is incapable of logical thought; **sie denkt nicht mit dem Gehirn, sondern mit dem Herzen,** she is guided by her heart rather than by her head; **das Kind denkt langsam,** the child's mind works slowly, the child thinks slowly; **denk, ehe du sprichst,** think before you speak; **handeln, ohne zu d.,** to act without thinking; **jeder denkende Mensch,** every thinking person; **die denkende Vernunft,** reason; **englisch d., in Englisch d.,** to think in English; (*cp.* 2); **etwas d.,** to think about sth.; **große Gedanken d.,** to think great thoughts; **er denkt Böses,** he thinks evil thoughts; **Gott weiß alles, was wir denken,** God knows all our thoughts, God knows all that we think; **er sagt, was er denkt,** he says what he thinks; **einen Gedanken logisch zu Ende d.,** to follow a thought through to its logical conclusion; *Prov:* **was ich denk und tu, trau ich andern zu,** don't judge others by yourself; (*b*) to conceive (sth.) (in one's mind); to have the idea, the concept (of sth.); **denke eine Zahl,** think of a number; **was war die gedachte Zahl?** what was the number you thought of? **sein letzter Entwurf für die Kathedrale ist groß gedacht,** his latest plan for the cathedral is a splendid conception, is splendidly conceived; (*c*) **d., daß . . . ,** to think that . . . ; **ich dachte im Stillen, bei mir, in meinem Herzen . . . ,** I thought to myself, I thought secretly . . . . **2.** (*denoting attitude, character, etc.*) **rechtlich, kleinlich, d.,** to be of an upright, a petty, turn of mind; **ein Mensch, der edel denkt, ein edel denkender Mensch,** a noble-minded man; **wie denkt er überhaupt?** what is his outlook? **englisch d.,** to think, to see things, from an English point of view; to have a nationalistic English viewpoint; **ein europäisch denkender Deutscher,** a German who thinks in terms of Europe; a Europe-minded German; **eine religiös denkende Dame,** a lady of religious convictions, of religious principles. **3.** (*a*) to consider, bear in mind; **wenn man denkt, daß er erst zwanzig ist,** when one considers that he is only twenty; **denke, wieviel du ihr schuldig bist,** think how much you owe her; **du mußt immer d., daß . . . ,** you must always bear in mind that . . . ; (*b*) **das gibt (sehr) zu d.,** it makes you think; **ihr merkwürdiges Verhalten bei der Abreise hat mir zu d. gegeben,** her strange behaviour at the time of departure set me thinking, gave me food for thought. **4.** (*a*) to think, believe; to suppose; to be of the opinion (that . . .); **ich denke, es ist wahr,** I think it is true; **ich denke nicht,** I don't think so; I think not; **ist er schon da? — ich denke nicht, ich denke ja,** is he here already?—I don't think so, I think so; **das dachte ich doch,** I thought so, I thought as much; **glaubst du, daß du es machen könntest? — ich denke ja, ich dächte ja,** do you think you could do it?—I think so, I should think so; **ich weiß, was du denkst, aber du bist sicher im Unrecht,** I know what you are thinking but I am sure you are wrong; **man könnte (fast) d., man wäre in Schottland,** you might (almost) think you were in Scotland; **ich denke, es wird gehen,** I think it will be all right; **man sollte d., das wäre erlaubt,** you would have thought that would be allowed; **der Chef ist noch nicht vierzig; — ich dächte 'doch,** the boss isn't forty yet;—I should have thought he 'was; **wir sind hier schon so lange, ich dächte, es wäre Zeit zu gehen,** we have been here such a long time, I think it's time we went; **man sollte d., er hätte Verstand genug, das zu wissen,** you would have thought he had enough sense to know that; **ist sie zum Arzt gegangen? — ich denke,** has she gone, been, to the doctor?—I think so, I suppose so; **ich dachte, sie zu Haus zu finden,** I thought I should find her, I expected to find her, at home; **sie denkt immer, er werde zurückkommen,** she still hopes he will come back; **ich dachte kaum, daß ich ihn wiedersehen würde,** I little thought I should see him again; (*b*) to think; to imagine; **das läßt sich d.,** I should think so; it's understandable; **wie konnte ich d., daß sie sich ärgern würde?** how could I have imagined that she would get angry? **wer hätte das gedacht!** who would have thought it! **denken Sie bloß nicht, nur nicht, daß ich mir alles gefallen lasse,** don't imagine that I'm going to put up with everything; **ich hatte gedacht, ich könnte mir damit Geld verdienen,** I had thought I could make money by it; **ich dachte, jemanden klopfen zu hören,** I thought I heard a knock, (but I must have imagined it); **wenn man nur denkt, was da hätte geschehen können!** only think what might have happened! **ich dachte, ich sähe nicht recht,** *F:* **ich denke, ich sehe nicht recht,** I thought I wasn't seeing aright; **denk nur!** (just) think! (just) imagine! **schenkst du mir das? — das denkst du wohl so,** *F:* **denkste!** (=**denkst du**), are you going to give me that?—what do 'you think! what an idea! (*c*) **tun Sie, wie Sie denken,** (i) do as you think right; (ii) (*slightly offhand*) please yourself; **sollen wir ausgehen? — wie Sie denken,** shall we go out?—as you please, I don't mind. **5. sich** *dat.* **denken,** (*a*) to think; **sich etwas d.,** to imagine sth.; to believe sth.; **das kann ich mir wohl d.,** I can (well) imagine that; I can believe that; **das habe ich mir gleich gedacht,** I thought so; I thought as much; **ich dachte mir, daß . . . ,** I thought (that) . . . ; **ich dachte mir, sie würde kommen,** I thought, imagined, she would come; **das hättest du dir d. können,** you might have known, imagined, that; **hast du dich über das Auto gefreut? — das kannst du dir (doch) d.!** were you pleased with the car?—of course! **das denkst du dir wohl so!** *F:* **das kannst du dir 'd.!** what an idea! certainly not! (*indignant*) **was denkst du dir eigentlich?** what are you thinking of? what do you think you're doing? (*b*) to imagine; to picture to oneself; **denk dir eine Zahl,** think of a number; **ich dachte mir ihn groß,** I imagined him tall, I thought of him as being tall; **ich denke mir eine Auslandsreise sehr gut für sie,** I can imagine that a journey abroad would be very good for her; **ich hatte mir das so schön gedacht,** I had imagined it all so beautiful, so lovely; **du kannst dir d., wie entsetzt ich war, du kannst dir mein Entsetzen d.,** you can imagine how horrified I was, you can imagine my horror; **denke dir einen Dackel mit langen geraden Beinen, und du weißt, wie mein Hund aussieht,** imagine, picture to yourself, a dachshund with long straight legs, and you know what my dog looks like; (*c*) **das Kind dachte sich nichts Böses dabei,** the child thought no harm in doing it, the child meant no harm, did not mean any harm; **glaubst du, daß jemand sich etwas dabei d. würde?** do you believe that anyone would think anything of it, would think twice about it? do you believe that anyone would see any harm in it, see anything strange in it? **denkst du dir etwas dabei?** (i) do you mean anything special by that? (ii) does it suggest anything to you? **6.** to intend; (*a*) **ich denke, am Dienstag abzureisen,** I intend to leave on Tuesday; **ich dachte, ihn zu überraschen,** I wanted to give him a surprise; **ich denke, nach London zu gehen,** I intend to go to London, I want to go to London; **ich hatte es alles so schön gedacht,** I meant it all to be so lovely; **gedacht, getan,** no sooner said than done; **zur gedachten Stunde,** at the hour agreed upon; *Prov:* **der Mensch denkt, Gott lenkt,** man proposes, God disposes; (*b*) **etwas für j-n d.,** to intend sth. for s.o.; **das Buch habe ich für dich gedacht,** I meant, intended, the book for you; **das war für ihn gedacht,** it was meant for him. **7.** to remember, recall; **solange ich d. kann,** as far back as I can remember. **8.** *A. & Lit:* **j-s d.,** to think of s.o.; to remember s.o.; **ich denke dein,** I am thinking of you.

II. denken, *v.i.* (*haben*) (*used with certain prepositions*) **1. an j-n, etwas** *acc.*, **d.,** (*a*) to think of s.o., sth.; to think about s.o., sth.; **an sich selbst d.,** to think of oneself; **sie denkt nur an sich selbst,** she only thinks of herself; **wir denken an dich, an euch, an Sie,** we are thinking of you; **er denkt nie an seine Mutter,** he never thinks of his mother; he has no thought, no consideration, for his mother; **woran denkst du?** what are you thinking about? *F:* a penny for your thoughts; **woran denken Sie dabei?** (i) what exactly have you in mind? (ii) what does it remind you of? **der Mensch, an den ich denke,** the person (whom) I have in mind; **ich hatte nicht daran gedacht, daß er noch kommen würde,** I didn't think that he would still come; **er konnte nicht schlafen, weil er dauernd an die Kosten d. mußte,** he couldn't sleep for thinking about the expense; **er denkt an nichts anderes als . . . ,** he thinks of nothing else but . . . ; **das Alter kommt heran, ohne daß wir daran denken,** old age comes on without our having given it a thought; **wenn man nur daran denkt, was hätte geschehen können!** only to think what might have happened! **er denkt nur an seinen eigenen Vorteil,** he thinks only of, he is only concerned with, his own advantage; (*b*) to remember sth., to think of sth., not to forget sth.; **daran d., etwas zu tun,** to remember to do sth., to think of doing sth., not to forget to do sth.; **ich habe nicht daran gedacht, dich zu warnen,** I never thought of warning you, I forgot to warn you; **hast du an das Buch gedacht?** did you remember the book? **du denkst aber auch an gar nichts,** you never remember anything, you never think of anything; **man kann nicht an alles d.,** one can't think of, remember, everything; **ich habe dir einen guten Ratschlag gegeben, nun denk auch daran,** I have given you a good piece of advice; do not forget it, bear it in mind; **es tut mir leid, aber ich habe einfach nicht daran gedacht,** I'm sorry, but I just didn't think of it; (*c*) to think of sth., to consider sth.; **daran d., etwas zu tun,** to think of doing sth., to consider doing sth.; **was immer er jetzt auch tut, denke daran, wieviel du ihm zu verdanken hast,** whatever he may do now, consider, bear in mind, how much you have to thank him for; **ich denke daran, morgen abzureisen,** I am thinking of going tomorrow; **ich denke nicht daran,** I wouldn't think of it; I wouldn't dream of it; **ich würde nicht im Traum daran d., es zu tun,** I wouldn't dream of doing it; **ich denke nicht daran, mit ihm auszugehen,** I wouldn't dream of going out with him; **es ist nicht daran zu d., daß er in vierzehn Tagen reisen kann,** it is out of the question, it is not to be thought of, that he can travel in a fortnight; **wir denken daran, das Haus zu vergrößern,** we are thinking of, considering, having the house enlarged; **wir würden nicht daran d., sie einzuladen,** it would never enter our heads to invite them, we would never think of inviting them; **ich hatte eigentlich an einen größeren Tisch gedacht,** I was really thinking of, wanting, a larger table, I really had a larger table in mind. **2.** (*a*) **über etwas** *acc.* **d.,** to think about sth., to ponder sth.; **ich muß noch eine Weile darüber d.,** I must think about it, think it over, for a while; (*b*) **über etwas** *acc.*, **j-n, d.,** to think about sth., s.o.; to think of sth., s.o.; to have an opinion on sth., s.o.; **Gutes, Böses, usw., von j-m d.,** to think kind things, unkind things, etc., about s.o.; **was denken Sie darüber?** what do you think about it? **wie denkst du über dieses Bild?** what do you think of this picture? what is your opinion of this picture? **ich möchte wissen, wie sie über meinen Bruder denkt, was sie von meinem Bruder denkt,** I should like to know what she thinks of my brother; **darüber denke ich genau wie Sie,** I am quite of your way of thinking; **er denkt das Schlimmste von seinem Bruder,** he has the worst possible opinion of his brother; **ich denke nicht sehr gut von ihr,** I don't think very highly of her; (*c*) **das, so etwas, hätte ich von dir nicht gedacht,** I should never have expected, thought, that, such a thing, of you. **3. auf etwas** *acc.* **d.,** to think of, about, sth., to concern oneself, to be concerned, with sth.; **darauf d., etwas zu tun,** to think of a way to do sth.; **wir denken nur darauf, wie wir unseren Sohn glücklich machen können,** our one concern, thought, is how to make our son happy.

III. *vbl s.* **Denken,** *n.* **1.** (*a*) thinking; way of thinking; thought; **tiefes D.,** deep thinking; **freies D.,** free thought, freedom of thought; **freisinniges, freies, D.,** liberal, free, way of thinking; **klares D.,** clear thinking; clear

thought; **abstraktes D.,** abstract thought; abstract way of thinking; **logisches D.,** logical thought; **er ist langsam im D.,** his mind works slowly, he thinks slowly; **Übereinstimmung im D. und Handeln,** harmony in thought and action; **sein D. ist oft verwirrt,** his thinking is often muddled; (*b*) thought; **unser modernes D.,** our modern thought; **im D. des 19. Jahrhunderts,** in the thought of the 19th century; **die Hauptvertreter griechischen Denkens,** the chief exponents of Greek thought; **im kommunistischen D.,** in communist thought. **2.** thoughts; *Poet:* **all mein D.,** all my thoughts.

Denker, *m.* **-s/-,** thinker; **ein großer D.,** a great thinker.

denkerisch, *a.* intellectual (achievement, etc.).

Denkerstirn, *f.* **er hat eine D.,** he has the high forehead of a thinker; **seine D.,** his high forehead.

denkfähig, *a.* (pers.) capable of thought, who can think; **es wird angenommen, daß Tiere nicht d. sind,** it is assumed that animals are incapable of thought, that animals cannot think; **nach zehn Uhr bin ich nicht mehr d.,** I cannot think any more after ten o'clock.

Denkfähigkeit, *f.* (faculty, capability, of) thought; **den Tieren wird die D. abgesprochen,** it is denied that animals have the faculty of thought, that animals can think.

denkfaul, *a.* mentally lazy; too lazy to think.

Denkfaulheit, *f.* mental apathy.

Denkfehler, *m.* fault, flaw, error, in reasoning, in logic; **er hat hier einen entscheidenden D. gemacht,** there is a fundamental error in his logic, in his reasoning, here.

Denkform, *f.* mode of thought.

Denkfreiheit, *f.* freedom, liberty, of thought.

Denkgebäude, *n.* structure of thought; system of thought.

Denkgesetze, *n.pl. Log: etc:* laws of thought.

Denkkraft, *f.* intellect, mental ability; **eine außerordentliche D.,** an extraordinary intellect; **Denkkräfte** *pl,* mental powers; intellect.

Denklehre, *f.* logic.

Denkleistung, *f.* **1.** (action of) thinking. **2.** (*a*) logical achievement; (*b*) intellectual achievement.

Denkmal, *n.* **-s/-mäler** & **-male. 1.** memorial; (*statue, etc.*) monument; **ein D. zur Erinnerung an die im Kriege Gefallenen,** a memorial to the men who fell in the war; **ein D. errichten,** to erect, put up, a monument; **mit diesem Buch hat er sich ein bleibendes D. gesetzt,** this book of his will be a permanent memorial to him. **2.** monument (of art, history, etc.); (historical) document; (historical) relic; **Denkmäler der Architektur, der Literatur,** monuments of architecture, of literature; **das Studium der Kunstgeschichte erfordert eine genaue Kenntnis der Denkmäler,** the study of the history of art demands an accurate knowledge of the works themselves, of the original works; **Denkmäler der Vergangenheit,** relics of the past.

Denkmalamt, *n.* regional office for the recording and preservation of monuments, *approx.*=Royal Commission on Historical Monuments.

Denkmalpflege, *f.* recording and preservation of monuments, including works of art and architecture.

Denkmalpfleger, *m.* curator of monuments.

Denkmalschutz, *m.* protection of monuments; **ein Gebäude unter D. stellen,** to schedule a building as an ancient monument; **unser Haus steht unter D.,** our house is classified as an historical monument.

denkmäßig, *a.* logical.

Denkmünze, *f. Num:* commemorative coin *or* medal.

Denknotwendigkeit, *f. Phil: etc:* logical necessity.

Denkpause, *f.* pause for thought (*in speech etc.*); **er machte eine D.,** he paused for thought.

Denkpsychologie, *f.* experimental psychology (dealing with thought processes).

Denkraum, *m.* range of thought (of pers., nation).

Denkschrift, *f.* **1.** report (with recommendations); memorandum. **2.** (learned, scientific) memoir. **3.** memorial (inscription).

Denksport, *m.* (*a*) mental exercise; mnemonic exercise; (*b*) (*as heading in newspaper*) *approx.*= puzzle corner.

Denksportaufgabe, *f.*=**Denkaufgabe.**

Denkspruch, *m.* maxim; motto.

Denkstein, *m.* (*a*) memorial (stone); (*b*) *A:* tombstone.

Denktätigkeit, *f.* mental activity; **Kaffee regt die D. an,** coffee stimulates mental activity.

Denktypus, *m.* intellectual type; **ein bestimmter D.,** a certain intellectual type, a person of a certain type of intellect.

Denkübung, *f.* mental exercise, exercise of the mind.

Denkungsart, Denkungsweise, *f.* way of thinking, attitude of mind, mental attitude; **ein Mann (von) edler D.,** a noble-minded man.

Denkvermögen, *n.*=**Denkfähigkeit.**

Denkvers, *m.* **1.** rhymed maxim; rhymed motto. **2.** mnemonic (verse).

Denkvorgang, *m.* thought process.

Denkweise, *f.*=**Denkart.**

denkwürdig, *a.* memorable (event, day, etc.); noteworthy (occasion, event, etc.); **ein denkwürdiges Jahr,** a memorable year; an eventful year; **das war ein denkwürdiger Tag,** that was a day we shall never forget.

Denkwürdigkeit, *f.* **1.** memorableness; noteworthiness. **2.** something memorable, worth remembering; memorable occasion, event, etc.; **Denkwürdigkeiten** *pl,* memorabilia (from the life of an eminent person); recollections, memoirs (from one's own life); *Gr.Lit:* **die Denkwürdigkeiten,** the Memorabilia (of Xenophon).

Denkzettel, *m.* **1.** note, memorandum. **2.** *F:* (i) (unpleasant) reminder, (ii) reprimand, reproof; *F:* talking-to; **j-m einen D. geben,** (i) *F:* to haul s.o. over the coals, to give s.o. what for; (ii) to give s.o. a good beating; **er hat einen tüchtigen D. bekommen,** (i) *F:* he got a thorough dressing-down; (ii) he got something nasty to remember.

denn. I. *conj.* **1.** for, because; **wir gingen langsam, d. es war sehr heiß,** we walked slowly, for, because, it was very hot; (*occ. not translated*) **ich kann diese Woche leider nicht kommen, d. ich bin zu beschäftigt,** I can't come this week unfortunately, I'm too busy. **2.** *Lit:* (*with comparative*) than; **er glaubt, größer d. Gott zu sein,** he believes that he is greater than God; (*to avoid repeating* **als**) **er schreibt mehr als Dichter d. als Historiker,** he writes more as a poet than as an historian. **3.** unless; except; **es sei d. . . . ,** except . . .; **es sei d., daß . . . ,** unless; **ich kann nichts für ihn tun, er bessere sich d.,** I cannot do anything for him unless he mends his ways; **ich werde nicht mehr zu ihm gehen, er käme d. zuvor zu mir,** I shall not go to him any more unless he comes to me first; **ich werde sie so bald nicht wiedersehen, es sei d., daß ein Wunder geschehe, geschieht,** I shall not see her for some time unless a miracle happens; *B:* **ich lasse dich nicht, du segnest mich d.,** I will not let thee go, except thou bless me.

II. **denn,** *emotive particle.* **1.** (*used to sum up foregoing remarks, etc.*) then; (*a*) **wenn es d. keine absoluten Werte gibt, . . . ,** if, then, there are no absolute values, . . .; **gut d., ich komme,** all right, then, I'll come; **so gingen wir d. los,** so off we went; **so laßt uns d. Gott um seine Gnade bitten,** let us then ask God's grace; **er ist d. also gekommen,** (so) he has come, then; **was d. könnte schöner sein als . . . ,** for what could be more beautiful than . . .; (*b*) (*used to intensify suggestions, commands, etc.*) **auf d.! also d.!** now then! well then! come on then! **gehen wir d.,** let's go then; **komm herein d.,** all right then, come in; come in then; (*c*) **er hat mich gebeten, zu kommen; ich ging d. auch hin, aber er war nicht zu Hause,** he asked me to come, so I did, but he was not at home; **man hatte ihm das Hotel sehr empfohlen; er fühlte sich d. auch sehr wohl dort,** the hotel had been warmly recommended to him, and he (really) did feel very comfortable there; **und er erhielt d. auch einige Aufträge,** and he got a few commissions too; **ich habe das Buch mit großem Vergnügen gelesen, wie ich d. (auch) die Werke dieses Autors im allgemeinen sehr schätze,** I read the book with great pleasure, as indeed I always appreciate the works of this author. **2.** (*often not translated*) (*a*) **er ist d. doch gekommen,** so he has come after all; **du hast den Schirm d. doch gebrauchen können?** you were able to use the umbrella after all, then? (*b*) **hast du das d. wirklich gern?** do you really like that? **ist es d. (auch) wirklich wahr?** (but) is it really true? **hast du das d. die ganze Zeit gewußt?** but did you ˈreally know that all the time? **ist er d. da gewesen?** was he there, then? **hat er dich d. auch gern?** does he ˈlike you? does he really like you? (*with nuance of encouragement*) **wie heißt du d., Kleiner?** well, and what's ˈyour name, sonny? (*c*) (*almost meaningless*) **was ist d. mit dir los?** what's the matter with you then? **was ist d. heute mit ˈdir los?** what's the matter with ˈyou today? **Mutti! — was d.?** Mummy!—what is it? **man hat es mir gesagt; — wer d.?** I was told so;—by whom? **ich habe ihn gestern gesehen; — wo d.?** I saw him yesterday;—where? **wo bist du d. so lang geblieben?** where ˈhave you been so long? **ich bin nicht gegangen; — ˈwarum d. nicht?** I didn't go;—why didn't you? why not? **meinst du, ich könnte ihn fragen? — warum d. ˈnicht?** do you think I could ask him?—why shouldn't you?—why (ever) not? (*d*) *occ.*=**dann** 3. **3.** (*stressed*) (*with nuance of impatience*) **was ˈd. soll ich tun?** what ˈshall I do, then? **wo ˈd. soll ich noch suchen?** where else shall I look, then?

dennoch [ˈdɛnɔx], *conj.* yet, (but) still, nevertheless, all the same; **er ist ein seltsamer Mensch, (und) d. habe ich ihn gern,** he is a strange person, and yet I like him, but still I like him; **die Medizin schmeckt unangenehm, aber ich muß sie d. trinken, d. muß ich sie trinken,** the medicine tastes unpleasant, but I must drink it all the same, nevertheless I must drink it, but I must drink it nevertheless.

denominal [de·no·mi·ˈnaːl], *a. Ling:* denominative (word).

Denomination [de·no·mi·na·tsiˈoːn], *f.* **-/-en. 1.** denomination, appellation. **2.** *Rel:* (Christian) denomination.

Denominativ [de·no·mi·na·ˈtiːf], *n.* **-s/-ve** [-ˈtiːvə], **Denominativum** [de·no·mi·na·ˈtiːvum], *n.* **-s/-va.** *Ling:* denominative (word).

denominieren [de·no·mi·ˈniːrən], *v.tr.* to denominate, name, designate (s.o., sth.).

denotieren [de·no·ˈtiːrən], *v.tr.* to denote.

denselben *see* **derselbe.**

Densimeter [denzi·ˈmeːtər], *n.* **-s/-.** *Ph:* densimeter.

Densität [dɛnzi·ˈtɛːt], *f.* **-/-en,** density.

dental[1] [dɛnˈtaːl], *a.* (*a*) dental (surgery, etc.); (*b*) *Ling:* dental (consonant).

Dental[2], *m.* **-(e)s/-e, Dentallaut,** *m. Ling:* dental.

dentelieren [dãˑtəˈliːrən, dɛntəˈliːren], *v.tr.* to notch, indent.

Dentin [dɛnˈtiːn], *n.* **-s/.** *Anat:* dentine.

Dentist [dɛnˈtist], *m.* **-en/-en,** dentist (*without university training*).

Dentition [dɛnti·tsiˈoːn], *f.* **-/.** dentition, teething.

Denudation [de·nu·da·tsiˈoːn], *f.* **-/.** *Geol:* denudation.

Denunziant [de·nuntsiˈant], *m.* **-en/-en,** informer, denouncer.

Denunziation [denuntsia·tsiˈoːn], *f.* **-/-en. 1.** denouncing, denunciation (of s.o.); informing (against s.o.). **2.** denunciation; information; **Denunziationen gegen j-n vorbringen,** to inform against s.o.

denunzieren [de·nunˈtsiːrən]. I. *v.tr.* to denounce (s.o.); to inform against (s.o.); **j-n bei der Polizei d.,** to denounce s.o. to the police; to lay information against s.o. with the police.

II. *vbl s.* **1. Denunzieren,** *n. in vbl senses; also:* denunciation. **2. Denunzierung,** *f.* (*a*)=II. 1; (*b*) denunciation; information; **Denunzierungen gegen j-n vorbringen,** to inform against s.o.

Deontologie [de·onto·lo·ˈgiː], *f.* **-/.** *Phil:* deontology.

Departement [de·part(ə)ˈmãː], *n.* **-s/-s.** *Adm: etc:* department.

Dependance [de·pã·ˈdãːs], *f.* **-/-n** [-sən], annex(e) (to a hotel, etc.).

Dependenz [de·pɛnˈdɛnts], *f.* **-/-en,** dependance.

Depesche [de·ˈpɛʃə], *f.* **-/-n,** (*a*) (official) dispatch; (*b*) (telegraphische) **D.,** telegram, *F:* wire.

Depeschenadresse, Depeschenanschrift, *f.* telegraphic address.

Depeschenboot, *n.* dispatch-boat.

Depeschenreiter, *m. Mil:* dispatch-rider; mounted orderly.

Depeschentasche, *f.* dispatch-box, -case.

depeschieren [de·pɛˈʃiːrən]. **1.** *v.tr.* to telegraph, wire (a piece of news). **2.** *v.i.* (*haben*) to telegraph, send a telegram, send a wire, to wire.

dephlegmieren [de·flɛgˈmiːrən], *v.tr. A.Ch:* to dephlegmate.

Depilation [de·pi·la·tsiˈoːn], *f.* **-/-en,** depilation, removal of hair.

Depilatorium [de·pi·la·ˈtoːrium], *n.* **-s/-rien,** depilatory.

depilieren [de·pi·ˈliːrən], *v.tr.* to depilate; to remove the hair from (face, etc.).

Deplacement [de·plas(ə)ˈmãː], *n.* **-s/-s,** displacement; *N.Arch:* **D. eines Schiffes,** displacement of a ship; **leichtes D., D. des leeren Schiffes,** displacement light, light displacement; **geladenes, volles, D., D. des vollen Schiffes,** load displacement, displacement loaded.

Deplacementsschwerpunkt, *m. Nau:* centre of buoyancy.

deplacieren [de·pla'si:rən], **deplazieren** [de·pla-'tsi:rən], *v.tr.* **1.** to displace, shift (sth.); to change the position of (sth., s.o.); *Nau:* to displace (water). **2. deplaciert**, *(of remark, etc.)* out of place, misplaced; *(of pers.)* out of place; **er fühlt sich deplaciert**, he feels out of place.

deplorabel [de·plo·'ra:bəl], *a.* deplorable, lamentable (incident, etc.).

deployieren [de·plo·a·'ji:rən], *v.tr. & i.* (*haben*) *Mil: A:* to deploy.

Depolarisation [de·po·la·ri·za·tsi'o:n], *f.* -/-en. *Opt: El:* depolarization.

depolarisieren [de·po·la·ri·'zi:rən], *v.tr. Opt: El:* to depolarize.

Deponens [de·'po:nɛns], *n.* -/-nenzien [-'nɛntsiən]. *Gram:* deponent (verb).

Deponent [de·po·'nɛnt], *m.* -en/-en. **1.** depositor (of money in bank, etc.). **2.** *Jur:* bailor. **3.** *Jur:* deponent, witness.

deponieren [de·po·'ni:rən]. **I.** *v.tr.* **1.** to deposit; to lay (sth.) down; to leave (sth.) (**bei j-m**, with s.o.); to deposit (money, etc.) (in a safe place). **2.** *Jur: A:* to depose; to give evidence. **II.** *vbl s.* **Deponieren** *n.*, **Deponierung** *f. in vbl senses; also:* deposition.

Deport [de·'port], *m.* -s/-s & -e [-'portə]. *St.Exch:* backwardation.

Deportation [de·porta·tsi'o:n], *f.* -/-en, deportation (of undesirable alien, prisoner, etc.); *Hist:* transportation (of convict).

deportieren [de·por'ti:rən], *v.tr.* to deport (alien, prisoner, etc.); *Hist:* to transport (convict) (overseas); **Deportierung** *f*, deportation; *Hist:* transportation (of convict) (overseas).

Deportierte [de·por'ti:rtə], *m., f.* (*decl. as adj.*) deported person, deportee; transported convict.

Depositalschein [de·po·zi'ta:l-], *m. Bank:* safe-custody receipt, *U.S:* safe-deposit receipt.

Depositar [de·po·zi·'tɛːr], *m.* -s/-e. *Jur: etc:* depositary.

Depositen [de·po·'zi:tən], *n.pl. Bank:* deposits.

Depositenbank, *f.* bank which accepts deposits and gives credits on a short-term basis; deposit bank, bank of deposit.

Depositenbuch, *n. Bank:* deposit book.

Depositengelder, *n.pl. Bank:* deposits; money(s) on deposit.

Depositengeschäft, *n. Bank:* (*a*) depositing business; (*b*) deposit transaction.

Depositenkasse, *f.* sub-branch of a bank.

Depositenkonto, *n. Bank:* deposit account.

Depositenschein, *m.* **1.** deposit receipt, *U.S:* slip. **2.** safe-custody, *U.S:* safe-deposit, receipt.

Deposition [de·po·zi·tsi'o:n], *f.* -/-en. **1.** depositing (of goods, money, etc.). **2.** *Jur:* deposition, evidence, testimony. **3.** *Ecc.Jur:* deprivation, deposition, dismissal (of a priest).

depossedieren [de·pose·'di:rən]. **1.** *v.tr.* (*a*) to dispossess (s.o.); (*b*) to dethrone, depose (monarch). **2.** *vbl s.* **Depossedierung**, *f.* (i) dispossession; (ii) dethronement, deposition (of monarch).

Depot [de·'po:], *n.* -s/-s, (*a*) depository (for valuables, goods, etc.); depot (for goods); storehouse (for furniture, etc.); safe, strong room (in bank); (tram) depot; (bus) garage, depot; *Mil:* depot (for stores); dump (for ammunition); **Möbel ins D. geben**, to put furniture into store, to store furniture; **Möbel in D.**, furniture in store, stored furniture; (*b*) *Com: etc:* store (of goods); **ein D. errichten**, to create a store; (*c*) *Bank:* (i) safe custody, safe keeping, *U.S:* safe deposit; (ii) security, etc., placed on deposit; **etwas in D. geben**, to place sth. on deposit; to place sth. in safe custody, in safe keeping; **Wertpapiere in D. geben, einliefern**, to place securities in safe custody; **verschlossenes D.**, safe deposit; safe custody; **offenes D.**, deposit of securities with a bank on condition that the bank arranges for collection of dividends, etc.

Depotabteilung, *f. Bank:* safe-custody department; securities department.

Depotauszug, *m. Bank:* abstract from the safe-custody register (*sent by bank to depositor for inspection*).

Depotbuch, *n. Bank:* safe-custody register, *U.S:* safe-deposit register.

Depotfund, *m. Archeol:* hoard; (*small*) cache.

Depotgeschäft, *n. Bank:* (*a*) safe-custody business; (*b*) safe-custody transaction.

Depotinsulin, *n. Pharm:* depot insulin.

Depotpenicillin, *n. Pharm:* depot penicillin.

Depotquittung, *f.*, **Depotschein**, *m. Fin: etc:* safe-custody receipt, *U.S:* safe-deposit receipt.

Depotwechsel, *m. Fin:* bill deposited as security against advances.

Depp, *m.* -s/-e. *F: Dial:* fool, blockhead, ass.

Depravation [de·pra·va·tsi'o:n], *f.* -/-en. **1.** (*a*) debasing, debasement (of coinage); (*b*) depravation (of character, etc.). **2.** (*state*) (*a*) debasement (of coinage); (*b*) (moral) depravity.

depravieren [de·pra·'vi:rən], *v.tr.* (*a*) to deprave (character, etc.); (*b*) to debase (coinage).

Depression [de·prɛsi'o:n], *f.* -/-en, depression. **1.** (*a*) depression (in earth's surface); hollow, dip (in ground); (*b*) land below sea level. **2.** *Meteor:* depression; area of low pressure. **3.** *Ph:* depression (of mercury, etc.). **4.** *Astr:* depression (of a star); depression, dip (of the horizon). **5.** *Com: Fin:* depression. **6.** *Med: etc:* (i) depression; (ii) fit of depression; **er fand sie in einem Zustand tiefer D.**, he found her in a state of deep depression; **sie leidet unter Depressionen**, she suffers from fits of depression; **sie hat häufig Depressionen**, she has frequent fits of depression.

Depressionsgebiet, *n. Meteor:* area of low pressure.

Depressionsschuß, *m. Artil:* plunging fire.

Depressionswinkel, *m. Geom: Artil:* angle of depression.

depressiv [de·prɛ'si:f], *a.* depressive (phase, etc.).

Depressor [de·'prɛsor], *m.* -en/-en [-'so:rən]. *Anat:* depressor nerve.

depressorisch [de·prɛ'so:riʃ], *a. Anat:* depressor (muscle).

Depretiation [de·pre·tsia·tsi'o:n], *f.* -/-en. **1.** *Com:* depreciation; fall in value. **2.** under-rating, undervaluing.

deprimieren [de·pri·'mi:rən], *v.tr.* to depress (s.o.); **es deprimiert mich**, it depresses me; **ein deprimierendes Buch**, a depressing book; **er sieht deprimiert aus**, he looks depressed; **das Mittel hat eine deprimierende Wirkung**, the drug has a depressant effect.

Deprivation [de·pri·va·tsi'o:n], *f.* -/-en, (*a*) deprivation (of rights, etc.); (*b*) *Ecc:* deprivation, deposition, dismissal (of priest).

Deputant [de·pu·'tant], *m.* -en/-en, worker paid partly in kind.

Deputat [de·pu·'ta:t], *n.* -(e)s/-e, coal, farm produce, etc., allotted *esp.* to miners and farm workers as part of their wages; free coal, free farm produce, etc.

Deputation [de·pu·ta·tsi'o:n], *f.* -/-en. **1.** deputing, delegation (of s.o.). **2.** deputation; delegation; body of representatives; *A:* (parliamentary) commission.

Deputatist [de·pu·ta·'tist], *m.* -en/-en=**Deputant**.

deputieren [de·pu·'ti:rən], *v.tr.* to depute (s.o.); to delegate (s.o.), to appoint (s.o.) as deputy, as delegate (zu, to).

Deputierte [de·pu·'ti:rtə], *m., f.* (*decl. as adj.*) deputy, delegate, representative.

Deputiertenkammer, *f. Fr.Pol:* Chamber of Deputies.

der, die, das. **I. 1.** *dem.pron.* (*acc. m.* **den**, *f.* **die**, *n.* **das**; *gen. m. & n.* **dessen**, *A:* **des**, *f.* **deren**, (*if followed by rel.pron.*) **derer**; *dat. m. & n.* **dem**, *f.* **der**; *pl. nom. & acc.* **die**; *gen.* **deren**, (*if followed by rel. pron.*) **derer**; *dat.* **denen**) (*a*) (*pers.*) he, she; the one; *pl.* they; those, the ones; (*thg, animal*) that; the one; *pl.* those; the ones; **vertraue auf deinen Vater — wie könnte dich 'der betrügen?** trust your father—how could 'he deceive you? **der, den wir gestern sahen**, (i) (*pers.*) he, the one, the man, whom we saw yesterday, (ii) (*thg*) the one (that) we saw yesterday; **sein Charakter ist liebenswerter als der seines Bruders**, his character is more lovable than that of his brother; **die, welche bei der Hochzeit anwesend waren**, those (who were) present at the wedding; **die, von denen ich rede**, those of whom I speak; **das ist das Buch, das er mir zum Geburtstag schenkte**, this, that, is the book which he gave me for my birthday; **mein Onkel Max? — der ist schon längst gestorben**, my uncle Max?—he died a long time ago; **mit der ist nichts anzufangen**, you can't do anything with 'her; **der — und in die Kirche gehen?** he—go to church! **wer fünf Kinder hat, der weiß, wie teuer das Leben sein kann**, anyone, a person, who has five children knows how expensive living can be; **der, der den Armen gibt**, he who gives to the poor; **ich bin nicht einer von denen, die . . . , ich gehöre nicht zu denen, die . . .**, I am not one of those who . . . : **der Vorteil ist der, daß . . .**, the advantage is that . . .; **von den drei Schlössern der Familie X ist das in Y das schönste**, of the three castles belonging to the X family, the one at Y is the most beautiful; **ich wollte eigentlich den Eigentümer sprechen; — der bin ich**, I want to speak to the owner;—I 'am the owner; **wer von euch ist Maria? — die bin ich**, which of you is Maria?—'I am; **wer ist die da?** who is that woman, that girl? **wer von den Leuten ist Herr X, Frau X?** — **der da, die da**, which of those people is Mr X, Mrs X?—that one (over there); **ich habe mein Buch hier liegen lassen; — ist es das?** — **das ist es**, I left my book here somewhere;—is this it?—that's it; **nehmen Sie diesen Mantel oder den?** are you going to take this coat or that one? **der Esel, der!** the ass! **hol dich der und jener!** the devil take you! **sie ist die Schwester dessen, den wir gestern sahen**, she is the sister of the man (whom) we saw yesterday; **er ging mit seinem Bekannten in dessen Wohnung**, he went with his friend to the latter's, his friend's, flat; **er ist ein sehr aufrechter Charakter, und deren gibt es nicht viele**, he is a very upright character and there are not many of them, of those; **hast du Freunde? — nein, ich habe deren nicht viele**, have you got friends?—no, I haven't many; **eine aus einem Grundstoff abgeleitete Verbindung, die dessen wesentliche Merkmale aufweist**, a compound derived from a basic substance, showing the essential characteristics of this substance, showing its essential characteristics; **die Eltern derer, die mit mir zur Schule gingen**, the parents of those who went to school with me; (*b*) **der und der**, such and such a man; **die und die**, such and such a woman; **das und das**, such and such a thing; **sie sagte, der und der wäre gegangen**, she said such and such a man went; **ich habe das und das gesagt**, I said such and such a thing; (*c*) (*with names of noble families*) **der von Sponheim**, the Lord of Sponheim; **die Gruft derer von Langenau**, the vault of the von Langenau family. **2.** *dem.* (*acc. das, gen. dessen, dat. dem*), that; this; those; these; they; **was ist das?** (i) (*referring to object*) what is this, that? (ii) (*referring to situations, ideas, etc.*) what's (all) this? what's going on? **hast du das gesehen?** (i) have you seen this, that? (ii) did you see that? **das war meine Tochter**, (i) that was my daughter; (ii) it was my daughter who did that; **das waren die Kinder**, (i) those, they, were the children; (ii) it was the children who did that; **wer ist das?** who is that? **was war das?** what was that? **das ist mein Vetter**, that is my cousin; **das sind unsere Verwandten**, those, they, are our relations; **das waren (noch) Zeiten**, those were the days; **das ist mein braves Kind, mein braver Hund**, that's a good boy, girl, a good dog; **das geschah vor zwei Jahren**, that happened two years ago; **das ist es eben**, that's just it, that's just the point; **bist du das?** is that you? **zum Beweis dessen, was er gesagt hatte, zeigte er . . .**, as a proof of what he had said, he showed . . .; **sie ist sehr böse darüber, und das mit Recht**, she is very angry about it, and rightly so, and with good cause; **ist er Arzt? — ja, das ist er**, is he a doctor?—yes, he is (one); **du sagst, er sei ein Held gewesen, aber das war er nie**, you say he was a hero, which he never was, but he never was one; **ist er dumm? — das nicht, aber klug ist er auch nicht**, is he stupid?—no, he's not stupid, but he isn't clever either; **du könntest früher kommen?** — **ja, das könnte ich**, you could come earlier;—so I could; **wie dem auch sei**, however that may be; **er arbeitet nicht viel, aber das, was er schafft, ist gut**, he doesn't do much work, but what he does do is good; **viel Volk war auf dem Platz; das sang und tanzte, das lachte und schrie**, the square was full of people; there was singing and dancing, laughing and shouting. **3.** *dem.a.* (*acc. den, die, das, gen. des, der, des, dat. dem, der, dem; pl. nom. & acc. die, gen. der, dat. den*) (*stressed*) (*a*) that; this; *pl.* those; **der Mann ist mein Vater**, that man is my father; **die Schauspielerin kann ich nicht leiden**, I can't bear that actress; **vergleiche die Ausgabe mit der da**, compare this edition with that one; **ich gehe nicht oft ins Theater, aber das Stück muß ich sehen**, I don't often go to the theatre but I must see that play, but that is a play I must see; **was, die Katze gehört dir?** what? is that cat yours? **mit dem Mantel willst du ins Theater gehen?** do you mean to go to the theatre in 'that coat? **die Leute, die an solchen Sachen Interesse finden**, (those) people who take an interest in such things; (*b*) **der und der Mann**, such and such a man; **die und die Frau**, such and such a woman; **an dem und dem Tag**, on such and such a day. **II. der, die, das**, *def.art.* (*acc. den, die, das, gen. des, der, des, dat. dem, der, dem; pl. nom. & acc. die, gen. der, dat. den*) **1.** the; (*a*) (*particularizing*) **der Tisch**, the table; **die Frau**, the woman,

das Jahr, the year; **die Kinder,** the children; **der Vater und die Mutter,** the father and mother; **an der Ecke,** at the corner; **die Frau des Lehrers, des Lehrers Frau,** the teacher's wife; **der bemerkenswerte Herr X,** the remarkable Mr X; (*with names of rivers*) **der Rhein,** the Rhine; **die Weser,** the Weser; (*emphatic*) **ein gewisser Thomas Mann, — nicht ˈder Thomas Mann,** a certain Thomas Mann—not ˈthe Thomas Mann; **das ist ˈdas Geschäft für Möbel,** that's ˈthe shop for furniture; (*b*) (*generalizing*) **der Hund ist des Menschen bester Freund,** the dog is man's best friend. **2.** (*with nouns formed from adjs*) **der Arme,** (i) (the) poor man, (the) poor chap; (ii) (*general conception*) the, a, poor man; **die Gelehrten,** the learned; **die Armen, die Reichen,** the poor, the rich; **wer ist der Älteste von euch?** who is the oldest among you? **Katharina die Große,** Catherine the Great; **Eduard der Sieb(en)te,** Edward the Seventh; **die Mutter Alexanders des Großen,** the mother of Alexander the Great; **das Komische,** the comic; **das Schöne,** the beautiful; **das Schöne an der Sache ist . . . ,** the nice thing about it is . . . , what is nice about this, it, is . . . . **3.** (*with parts of the body, clothes, etc.*) **den Kopf schütteln,** to shake one's head; **die Achseln zucken,** to shrug one's shoulders; **er hat eine Beule über dem rechten Auge,** he has a lump over his right eye; **er hat den Arm in der Schlinge,** he has his arm in a sling; **zieh dir die Jacke an,** put your jacket on; **sie kam mit einem Buch in der Hand, sie kam, ein Buch in der Hand,** she came with a book in her hand; **die Beine taten ihm weh,** his legs were hurting. **4.** (*distributive*) **zehn Mark der Zentner,** ten marks a hundredweight, the hundredweight; **Eier kosten drei Mark das Dutzend,** eggs cost three marks a dozen. **5.** (*not translated*) (*note: frequently the article is desirable when the noun is in the oblique case*) (*a*) (*with abstract nouns and general conceptions*) **die Natur,** nature; **der Tod,** death; **die Liebe,** love; **wir kämpfen für die Freiheit,** we are fighting for freedom; **die deutsche Dichtung des neunzehnten Jahrhunderts,** German literature of the nineteenth century; **wir müssen den Weltfrieden um jeden Preis erhalten,** we must preserve world peace at any price; **der Mensch,** man; **Gott erschuf den Menschen,** God created man; **die Frau ist die Gefährtin des Mannes,** woman is the companion of man; **das Tier handelt ohne Vernunft,** animals act without reason; **die Pflanze hat weder Vernunft noch Instinkt,** plants have neither reason nor instinct; **er ist der tapferste der Männer,** he is the bravest of men; (*b*) (*with names of persons*) **der Fritz,** Fritz; **die Lotte,** Lotte; **das Lieschen,** Lieschen; **wo ist eigentlich der Peter?** where ˈis Peter? **er spielt mit der Hildegard,** he is playing with Hildegard; **das Schloß der Königin Louise,** the castle of Queen Louise; (*with names of eminent women*) **die Garbo,** Garbo; **die Droste,** Annette von Droste-Hülshoff; (*c*) (*in certain cases with names preceded by adjs*) **der arme Paul,** poor Paul; **die schöne Suleika,** (the) beautiful Zuleika; **der reiche Herr X,** rich Mr X; **der heilige Martin,** Saint Martin; (*d*) (*with names of writers*) **ich habe den Aristoteles nicht ganz gelesen,** I haven't read the whole of Aristotle; (*e*) (*with names of plays and dramatic roles*) **sie führen den Tasso auf,** they are performing Tasso; **wer spielt heute die Iphigenie?** who is playing Iphigenie tonight? (*f*) (*with names of streets, squares, etc.*) **ich wohne in der Goethestraße,** I live in (the) Goethestraße; **in der Oxford Street,** in Oxford Street; **der Friedrichplatz,** (the) Friedrichplatz; **auf dem Trafalgar Square,** in Trafalgar Square; (*with names of mountains*) **der Everest,** (Mount) Everest; **der Sinai,** Mount Sinai; (*g*) (*with names of days and months*) **der Sonntag ist der erste Tag der Woche,** Sunday is the first day of the week; **der Mai ist ein schöner Monat,** May is a lovely month; (*h*) *occ. with names of countries; see under the relevant names.* **6.** (*with vbl substantives*) **das Nähen,** sewing; **das Kochen dieser Speise dauert zwei Stunden,** the cooking of this dish takes two hours; **während des Kochens langsam umrühren,** stir slowly while it is cooking; **während des Kochens öffnen sich die Muscheln,** while cooking the shells open.

III. der, die, das, *rel.pron.* (*acc.* **den, die, das,** *gen.* **dessen, deren, dessen,** *dat.* **dem, der, dem;** *pl.* nom. & *acc.* **die,** *gen.* **deren,** *dat.* **denen**) (*pers.*) who, that; (*thg, animal*) which, that; (*ellipsis of the relative is frequent in Eng.*) (*a*) **der Mann, der so gut singt,** the man who sings so well; **die Karte, die ich dir geschickt habe,** the postcard (that) I sent you; **das Tuch, das sie über den Tisch breitete,** the cloth that, which, she spread over the table; **er ist ein Mann, den niemand achtet,** he is a man whom no one respects; **die Mädchen, mit denen ich arbeite,** the girls with whom I work, the girls I work with; **die Schriftsteller, an die wir denken,** the writers of whom we are thinking, the writers we have in mind; **das Pult, auf dem ich schreibe,** the desk on which I am writing, the desk I am writing on; **die Frau, von der wir reden,** the woman we are talking about; **in den Jahren, in denen er in Köln lebte,** in the years when he was living in Cologne; **in all den Jahren, die er in England lebte,** in all the years that he lived in England; **ich sah ein Mädchen, das aus dem Fenster schaute,** I saw a girl looking out of the window; **ein Mann, der eine Pfeife rauchte, kam uns entgegen,** a man smoking a pipe came towards us; **der Offizier, dessen Befehle ich ausgeführt habe,** the officer whose orders I have carried out; **eine Arme, deren Gebete unerhört bleiben,** a poor woman whose prayers remain unanswered; **das Kind, dessen Bruder gestorben ist,** the child whose brother died; **die Schüler, deren Zeugnisse schlecht sind,** the pupils whose reports are bad; **mein Bruder, in dessen Haus ich wohne,** my brother, in whose house I live; **das war eine Episode, deren ich mit Freude gedenke,** that was an episode which I remember with pleasure; **das Buch, dessen Umschlag zerrissen ist,** the book which has a torn cover, the book the cover of which is torn; **ein Grabstein, dessen Inschrift kaum noch zu lesen war,** a tombstone the inscription on which was scarcely legible, a tombstone whose inscription was scarcely legible; **ein Kessel, dessen Henkel abgebrochen ist,** a kettle with a broken handle; **Briefe, die zu schreiben mir immer schwer fällt,** letters I always find difficult to write; **ich, der ich so alt bin, ich, die ich so alt bin,** I who am so old; **Sie, der Sie so viel gereist sind,** you who have travelled so much; **wir, die wir immer treu waren,** we who were always loyal; *B:* **Vater unser, der du bist im Himmel,** our Father, which art in Heaven; *Lit:* **die du mich liebst,** you who love me; (*b*) **sie ist nicht die Frau, die das tun würde,** she is not the sort of woman to do that; **ich suche einen Mann, der meinen Garten umgräbt,** I am looking for a man to dig up my garden; **er braucht jemanden, mit dem er spielen kann,** he needs someone to play with.

Derangement [deˑrãˑʒəˈmãː], *n.* **-s/-s,** derangement.

derangieren [deˑrãˑˈʒiːrən], *v.tr.* (*a*) to disarrange (papers, etc.); (*of pers.*) **derangiert aussehen,** to look untidy; (*b*) to disturb, trouble, inconvenience (s.o.); **bitte, derangieren Sie sich nicht,** please don't inconvenience yourself, please don't trouble.

derart, *adv.* = **derartig** 2.

derartig. 1. *a.* such; of this kind; of that kind; **derartige Speisen sind sehr ungesund,** such food is very unwholesome; **er fährt mit einer derartigen Geschwindigkeit, daß . . . ,** he drives at such a speed that . . .; **derartige Blumen wachsen nicht in meinem Garten,** flowers of that kind do not grow in my garden; **derartiges, etwas Derartiges, sieht man nicht oft,** one does not often see such things, such a thing, things like that, a thing like that; **in dieser Figur ist ein derartiger Apparat dargestellt,** in this figure an apparatus of this kind is shown. **2.** *adv.* so; in such a way, in such a manner; **sie ist d. schön, daß sich alle in sie verlieben,** she is so beautiful that everyone falls in love with her; **ein d. kleines Zimmer,** such a small room; **er fährt d. schnell, daß . . . ,** he drives at such a speed that . . .; **er hat sich d. schlecht, d., benommen, daß . . . ,** he behaved so badly, in such a manner, that . . . ; **es war d. komisch,** it was ˈso funny.

derb, *a.* **1.** (*a*) coarse, solid (foodstuffs); coarse, rough (cloth); strong, tough (leather); stout, strong, hard-wearing, sound (shoes, boots); thick (stockings); *Miner:* massive (ore, etc.); **derbe Kost,** solid, substantial, food; coarse food; (*b*) (*of pers., etc.*) strong; firm; sturdy, tough; rough; **derbe Fäuste,** strong fists; **ein derber kleiner Junge,** a sturdy, tough, little boy; **eine derbe Umarmung,** a rough embrace; a hearty embrace, a bear-hug; **ein derber Kuß,** a smacking kiss; **sie gab ihm eine derbe Ohrfeige,** she boxed his ears soundly; **seine derbe Gesundheit,** his rude health; **er faßte mich d. am Arm an,** he seized my arm roughly; **faß die Seide nicht so d. an,** don't catch hold of the silk so roughly; **er ist etwas d. mit den Kindern, er geht etwas d. mit den Kindern um,** he is rather rough with the children; **ich brauche jemanden, der d. zupacken kann,** I need someone (i) who can stand up to heavy work, who is not afraid of hard work; (ii) who can take a firm line; **diese Sache darf man nicht d. anfassen,** this matter must be treated delicately, must not be handled in a crude way. **2.** rough, coarse, unpolished, uncouth (pers., manners, etc.); coarse (face, hands, etc.); blunt, plain, unrefined, crude (way of speaking); **ein derber Bauer,** a rough peasant; **eine derbe Frau,** a coarse, rough, woman; **ein derber Bayer,** a rough Bavarian; a plain-spoken, blunt, Bavarian; **derbe Züge,** coarse features; **eine derbe Antwort,** a plain, blunt, answer; **ein derber Brief,** a blunt letter; **derbe Witze,** crude jokes; **derber Humor,** broad humour; **eine derbe Redensart,** a coarse, crude, expression; **ein derber Fluch,** a round oath; **Bauern haben oft einen derben Geschmack,** country people often have a simple, coarse, taste, an unrefined taste; **das war ein derber Spaß,** that was a crude joke; that joke went a bit too far; *adv.* **er drückt sich d. aus,** he expresses himself in plain terms, bluntly.

Derberz, *n. Miner:* massive ore.

Derbgehalt, *n.* solid contents.

Derbheit, *f.* **1.** (*a*) coarseness (of food, etc.); coarseness, roughness (of cloth); toughness, strength (of leather); stoutness, soundness, strength (of shoes, boots); thickness (of stockings); (*b*) roughness, coarseness, uncouthness (of pers., manners, etc.); bluntness, plainness, crudeness (of way of speaking); broadness (of humour). **2.** coarse remark; crude joke; **Derbheiten sagen,** to say coarse, rough, things.

Derbholz, *n. For:* wood of the trunk *or* branches more than 7 cm. in diameter.

Derby [ˈdɛrbiː], *n.* **-(s)/-s, Derbyrennen,** *n. Rac:* (i) (*in England*) **das D.,** the Derby; (ii) (*in Germany*) race for three-year-old horses; (iii) *occ. used for other races, e.g.* **Seifenkisten-D.,** soap-box derby.

dereinst [deːrˀˈainst], *adv. Lit:* **1.** (*in the future*) one day, some day; **wir werden uns d. wiedersehen,** one day we shall see each other again. **2.** (*in the past*) one day; once (upon a time).

dereinsten(s) [deːrˀˈainstən(s)], *adv. Lit:* = **dereinst** 1.

dereinstig [deːrˀˈainstiç], *a. Lit:* future; **mein dereinstiger Erbe,** my future heir.

derelikt [deˑreˑˈlikt], *a.* derelict (house, etc.).

Dereliktion [deˑreˑliktsĭˈoːn], *f.* **-/-en,** dereliction (of property).

deren *see* **der.**

derenthalben. 1. *adv.* = **derentwegen. 2.** *conj.* = **derhalben.**

derentwegen, *adv.* **1.** because of her, on her account; because of them; (*when referring to thgs*) because of this, that; because of those, them. **2.** *rel. use* because of whom, on account of whom, on whose account; (*when referring to thg*) because of which, on account of which.

derentwillen, *adv.* **(um) d. 1.** for her sake; for their sake; (*when referring to thg*) for the sake of that. **2.** *rel. use* for whose sake; (*when referring to thg*) for the sake of which; **die Frau, (um) d. ich so viel ausgestanden habe,** the woman for whose sake I have stood so much; **die Kinder, (um) d. . . . ,** the children for whose sake. . . .

derer *see* **der.**

dergestalt, *adv. Lit:* **1.** in this manner, thus; **und er sprach zu ihr d.: 'fürchte dich nicht',** and he spoke to her thus: 'fear not'. **2.** so, in such a manner; **d. . . . , daß . . . ,** so . . . , that . . . ; **das Bild erfreute ihn d., daß er es immer wieder anschauen mußte,** the picture gave him so much pleasure that he had to keep on looking at it.

dergestaltig, *a. Lit:* such; of that kind; **dergestaltige Anmut sieht man selten,** such charm is rarely seen.

dergleichen [deːrˈglaiçən]. **1.** *dem.pron. inv.* (*a*) such a thing, a thing like that; such things, things like that; **d. habe ich noch nie gehört,** I never heard of such a thing; **d. ist mir noch nie passiert,** a thing like that has never happened to me; **es gibt d. mehr,** there are more of such things; **sie verkauft Zeitschriften, Zeitungen und d.,** she sells magazines, newspapers and the like; **nichts d.,** nothing of the kind, no such thing; **und d. mehr,** and so on and so forth; (*b*) *A:* **d. tun,** to do the same, to do likewise; (*c*) *A:* **d. tun, als ob . . . ,** to pretend that . . . , to give the appearance of . . .; **nicht d. tun,** not to show it; **sie hatte ihn gleich erkannt, tat aber nicht d.,** she had recognized him at once but pretended not to, but did not show it. **2.** *dem.a. inv.* such; of this kind; of that kind; **d. Dinge,** such things; **d. Speisen sind ungesund,** such food is

unwholesome; **d. Zeiten kommen nie wieder,** such times, times like those, will never come again; **d. Lieder singt sie nie,** she never sings such songs, songs of that kind, songs like that; **Spazierstöcke und d. Gegenstände,** walking-sticks and like objects, and similar objects; **in Italien, Spanien und d. Ländern,** in Italy, Spain, and such countries, in such countries as Italy and Spain; **er schenkte ihr Gold, Perlen und d. Dinge mehr,** he gave her gold, pearls and things of that kind; **d. Bilder gibt es noch mehr,** there are more pictures of this kind, of that kind, like this, like that. **3.** *rel.pron.* the like of which; such as; **eine Stoffart, d. man heutzutage nicht mehr sieht,** a cloth the like of which is not seen nowadays; **es wachsen hier Blumen, d. man bei euch nie findet,** flowers grow here such as, the like of which, you never find where you live.

derhalben, *conj. Lit:* because of that, this; for that reason, for this reason; on that, this, account; therefore.

Derivat [de·ri·ˈvaːt], *n.* **-(e)s/-e.** *Ling: Ch: etc:* derivative.

Derivation [de·ri·va·tsĭˈoːn], *f.* **-/-en,** derivation.

Derivationsrechnung, *f. Mth:* differential calculus.

Derivationswinkel, *m. Nau:* drift angle.

derivativ¹ [de·ri·va·ˈtiːf], *a.* derivative.

Derivativ², *n.* **-s/-e** [-ˈtiːfs/-ˈtiːvə], **Derivativum** [de·ri·va·ˈtiːvum], *n.* **-s/-va.** *Ling:* derivative; derived word.

derivieren [de·ri·ˈviːrən], *v.tr.* to derive; **deriviert,** derivative, derived (word, etc.).

derjenige, diejenige, dasjenige (*acc.* **denjenigen, diejenige, dasjenige,** *gen.* **desjenigen, derjenigen, desjenigen,** *dat.* **demjenigen, derjenigen, demjenigen;** *pl.nom.* & *acc.* **diejenigen,** *gen.* **derjenigen,** *dat.* **denjenigen**). **1.** *dem.pron.* (*pers.*) the one; he, she; (*thg*) the one; that, that one; *pl.* those; **derjenige, der zuletzt abfuhr, kam zuerst an,** the one who left last arrived first; **hast du diejenigen gesehen, die . . .?** did you see the ones who . . .? (*referring to thg*) did you see the ones which . . .? **ich möchte denjenigen sehen, der es besser machen kann als ich,** I should like to see the man who can do it better than I can; **die Kinder derjenigen, die das Schulgeld nicht bezahlen können,** the children of those who cannot pay the school fees; **Sieger ist derjenige, der die meisten Punkte hat,** the winner is the one who has the most points; (*in dictionary definition, etc.*) **derjenige, der . . .,** one who . . . . **2.** *dem.a.* that, *pl.* those; **diejenigen Leute, die an solchen Sachen Interesse finden,** those people who take an interest in such things.

derlei. 1. *dem.a.inv.* such; of that kind; **über d. Kleinigkeiten rege ich mich nicht auf,** I don't get excited over such trivialities; **d. Scherze liebe ich nicht,** I don't like tricks like that, I don't like that sort of thing. **2.** *dem.pron.* = **dergleichen 1** (*a*).

Derma [ˈdɛrmaː], *n.* **-s/-ta** [-maˑtaː]. *Anat:* skin, derm(a).

dermal¹ [ˈdeːrmaːl], *adv.* = **dermalen.**

dermal² [dɛrˈmaːl], *a.* dermal, cutaneous; dermic.

dermaleinst [deːrmaːlˀˈainst], *adv.* = **dereinst.**

dermalen [ˈdeːrmaːlən], *adv. A:* (i) at present, now; (ii) at the time, at that time.

dermalig [ˈdeːrmaːliç], *a. A:* (i) present; (ii) of the time; **meine dermalige Überzeugung,** (i) my present opinion; (ii) my opinion at the time; **in meinen dermaligen Umständen konnte ich nichts anderes tun,** in the circumstances in which I found myself at the time I could not do anything else.

dermaßen, *adv.* **1.** *A:* (i) in the same way; similarly; (ii) thus, in this way. **2.** to such a degree, to such an extent; **er ist d. geizig, daß . . .,** he is miserly to such a degree that . . .; **er war d. begeistert, daß . . .,** he was inspired to such a degree, to such an extent, that . . . .

dermatisch [dɛrˈmaːtiʃ], *a.* dermal, cutaneous; dermic.

Dermatitis [dɛrmaˑˈtiːtis], *f.* **-/.** *Med:* dermatitis.

Dermatoid [dɛrmaˑtoˑˈiːt], *n.* **-(e)s/-e** [-s, -ˈiːdəs/-ˈiːdə]. (*R.t.m.*) *Bookb: etc:* dermatoid.

Dermatologe [dɛrmaˑtoˑˈloːgə], *m.* **-n/-n,** dermatologist.

Dermatologie [dɛrmaˑtoˑloˑˈgiː], *f.* **-/.** dermatology.

Dermatoplastik [dɛrmaˑtoˑˈplastik], *f.* **1.** *Surg:* skin grafting, dermatoplasty. **2.** taxidermy.

Dermatose [dɛrmaˑˈtoːzə], *f.* **-/-n.** *Med:* dermatosis.

Dermographie [dɛrmoˑgraˑˈfiː], *f.* **-/.** *Med:* dermographia.

dero, *poss.a.inv. A:* (*used when addressing a superior in the third pers.*) his, her; **ich verbleibe, königliche Majestät, d. ergebenster Diener,** I remain, Your Majesty, your most devoted servant.

Derogation [deˑroˑgaˑtsĭˈoːn], *f.* **-/-en,** derogation (of law, etc.).

derogativ [deˑroˑgaˑˈtiːf], **derogatorisch** [deˑroˑgaˑˈtoːriʃ], *a.* derogatory.

derogieren [deˑroˑˈgiːrən], *v.tr.* to impair (law, etc.); to disparage, belittle (sth.).

derohalben, *adv.* = **derhalben.**

Derrickkran, *m. Mec.E:* derrick crane.

derselbe, dieselbe, dasselbe [deːr-, diː-, dasˈzɛlbə] (*decl. like* **derjenige**) (*written as two words when preceded by a preposition that can be contracted with the article. For differences between contracted and non-contracted forms, compare notes to* **am**). **1.** *dem.pron.* & *a.* the same; **dieselben Worte zweimal wiederholen,** to repeat the same words twice; **ich wohne in demselben Haus wie sie,** I live in the same house as she does; **meine Freundin und ich wohnen im selben Haus,** my friend and I live in the same house; **alle um denselben Tisch sitzend,** all seated round the same table; **ich würde mit ihm nicht mehr am selben Tisch sitzen,** I would not sit at the same table with him any more; **wir gehen in dieselbe Richtung,** we are going in the same direction; **das ist dieselbe (Frau), die wir gestern sahen,** that is the same woman that we saw yesterday; **zu derselben Zeit, zur selben Zeit, als, da, dies geschah,** at the same time that, when, as, this was happening; **sie werden an demselben Tag verkauft, an dem sie ankommen,** they are sold the same day that, as, they come in; **sie liebt dieselben Filme wie ich,** she likes the same films as I (do); **wir haben dieselben Ansichten,** we have the same opinions; **ich bin ganz derselben Meinung wie Sie,** I think just as you do; **der Zweck ist derselbe,** the purpose is the same; **ein und derselbe Mann, eine und dieselbe Frau, ein und dasselbe Kind,** one and the same man, woman, child; **Fritz und der Einbrecher sind ein und derselbe Mann,** Fritz and the burglar are one and the same man; **sie gehören ein und derselben Klasse an,** they belong to one and the same class; **das ist ein(s) und dasselbe,** that's one and the same thing, exactly the same thing; **es kommt alles auf dasselbe heraus, es kommt alles aufs selbe heraus,** it all amounts, comes, to the same thing; **ich stand auf, und er tat dasselbe,** I stood up and he did the same, he did likewise; **mein Mann sagt genau dasselbe,** my husband says just the same thing; **er ist immer derselbe,** he is always the same, he never changes; **die Kinder sind im selben Alter,** the children are of the same age. **2.** *dem.pron.* (*a*) (*the aforesaid*) he, she, it; the same; **ich traf meinen Freund auf der Straße und gab demselben das Buch,** I met my friend in the street and gave him the book; **Kinder säumten die Straße; jedes derselben hatte ein buntes Fähnchen in der Hand,** children crowded the street; each (one) of them had a coloured flag in his hand; *Com:* **bitte, schicken Sie dasselbe, denselben, dieselbe, umgehend zurück,** please send same by return of post; (*b*) *A: pl.* (*in formal address: used like* **Sie**) **ich ersehe daraus, daß Ihnen, werter Herr, mein Buch gefallen, und es Dieselben veranlaßt hat zu . . .,** I perceive from this, Sir, that my book has pleased you and led you to . . . .

derselbige, dieselbige, dasselbige [deːr-, diː-, dasˈzɛlbiˑgə] = **derselbe, dieselbe, dasselbe.**

derwegen, *adv.* = **derentwegen.**

derweil, derweilen [ˈdeːrˈvail(ən)]. **1.** *adv.* meanwhile, (in the) meantime. **2.** *conj.* while.

Derwisch [ˈdɛrviʃ], *m.* **-es/-e,** dervish; **heulender D.,** howling dervish; **tanzender D.,** dancing dervish.

derzeit, *adv.* (i) at this time, at present; (ii) at that time, then.

derzeitig, *a.* (i) present; (ii) of that time; **die derzeitigen Verhältnisse,** (i) the present state of affairs; (ii) the state of affairs at that time.

des¹ *see* **der.**

des², **Des** [dɛs], *n.* **-/-.** *Mus:* (the note) D flat, D♭; **Des-dur, Des-Dur, des-moll, des-Moll, (-Tonart),** (key of) D flat major, D flat minor.

Desannexion [dɛsˀanɛksĭˈoːn], *f.* **-/-en,** disannexation (of territory).

desarmieren [dɛsˀarˈmiːrən], *v.tr.* to disarm (prisoner, etc.).

Desaster [deˑˈzastər], *n.* **-s/-,** disaster.

desavouieren [deˑzavuˑˈiːrən], *v.tr.* to disavow, deny (promise, etc.); to disclaim (authorship, etc.); to disown (offspring).

Desensibilisator [deˑzɛnziˑbiˑliˑˈzaːtor], *m.* **-s/-en** [-zaˑˈtoːrən]. *Phot:* desensitizer.

desensibilisieren [deˑzɛnziˑbiˑliˑˈziːrən], *v.tr. Phot:* to desensitize (plate); *Med:* to desensitize (patient); to render (patient) insensitive (to allergy); **Desensibilisierung** *f,* desensitizing (of photographic plate, allergic pers.).

Deserteur [deˑzɛrˈtøːr], *m.* **-s/-e.** *Mil:* deserter.

desertieren [deˑzɛrˈtiːrən], *v.i.* (*sein*) *Mil:* to desert.

Desertion [deˑzɛrtsĭˈoːn], *f.* **-/-en.** *Mil: Jur:* desertion.

deses, Deses [ˈdɛsɛs], *n.* **-/-.** *Mus:* (the note) D double flat.

desfalls, *adv. A:* in that case; on that account.

desgleichen [dɛsˈglaiçən]. **1.** *dem.pron.* (*a*) such a thing, a thing like that; **d. habe ich noch nie gehört,** I have never heard of such a thing; **d. ist mir noch nie passiert,** a thing like that has never happened to me; (*b*) **d. tun,** to do the same, to do likewise; *B:* **so gehe hin, und tu d.,** go, and do thou likewise. **2.** *rel.pron.* the like of whom, such as; (*referring to thg*) the like of which, such as; **ein Buch, d. noch nie geschrieben worden ist,** a book the like of which has never been written before. **3.** *conj.* likewise, also; in the same way, similarly; **d. sollte gesagt werden, daß . . .,** it should also be stated that . . . .

deshalb. 1. *conj.* (*a*) because of that, this; for that, this, reason; on that, this, account; therefore; **das Leben ist teuer, d. müssen wir sparen,** living is dear, therefore we must economize; **ich würde mich d. freuen, wenn Sie . . . wollten,** I should therefore be glad if you would . . .; **ich hörte, daß sie krank war, d. habe ich sie besucht,** I heard that she was ill, that is why I went to see her; **deine Schwester ist manchmal schlecht gelaunt, und d. willst du das Haus verlassen?** your sister is sometimes bad-tempered—is that the reason why you want to leave home? **sie war ungerecht gegen mich, aber ich bin ihr d. nicht böse,** she was unjust towards me, but I am not angry with her on that account; (*b*) **d. . . . doch,** all the same, nevertheless; **die Puppe ist schon alt; d. kann ich sie doch gern haben,** the doll is old, but I can be fond of it all the same, just the same, but I can still be fond of it; **d., weil ich meinen Mann liebe, brauche ich meine Brüder doch nicht zu hassen, (nur) weil ich meinen Mann liebe, brauche ich d. doch meine Brüder nicht zu hassen,** just because I love my husband I don't need to hate my brothers. **2.** *adv.* **ich habe dich d. gefragt, weil ich mich dafür interessiere,** I asked you because I am interested in it; **ich habe d. nichts gesagt, weil die Kinder dabei waren,** I said nothing because of the children's being there, because the children were there; **ich bin nicht d. gekommen, (um) mich von dir beleidigen zu lassen,** I did not come here to be insulted by you; **ich habe ihn d. kommen lassen, damit, daß, er es selbst sehe,** I got him to come so that he could see it for himself. **3.** *rel. use A:* for which reason.

desiderabel [deˑziˑdəˈraːbəl], *a.* desirable.

Desiderat [deˑziˑdəˈraːt], *n.* **-(e)s/-e, Desideratum** [deˑziˑdəˈraːtum], *n.* **-s/-ta,** desideratum; (*for library books, etc.*) (special) request; suggestion.

Designation [deˑzignaˑtsĭˈoːn], . **-/-en,** designation.

designieren [deˑzigˈniːrən], *v.tr.* to designate (s.o.).

Desillusion [deˑzˀ-, dɛsˀiluˑzĭˈoːn], *f.* **-/-en,** disillusionment.

desillusionieren [deˑzˀ-, dɛsˀiluˑzĭoˑˈniːrən], *v.tr.* to disillusion, undeceive (s.o.).

Desinfektion [deˑzˀ-, dɛsˀinfɛktsĭˈoːn], *f.* **-/.** disinfection; disinfecting.

Desinfektionsanstalt, *f.* disinfecting station.

Desinfektionsgut, *n.* articles to be disinfected.

Desinfektionsmittel, *n.* disinfectant.

Desinfektor [deˑzˀ-, dɛsˀinˈfɛktor], *m.* **-s/-en** [-ˈtoːrən]. **1.** disinfecting officer. **2.** disinfectant.

desinfizieren [deˑzˀ-, dɛsˀinfiˑˈtsiːrən], *v.tr.* to disinfect; **desinfizierendes Mittel,** disinfectant; **desinfizierende Seife,** disinfectant soap.

Desintegrator [deˑzˀ-, dɛsˀinteˑˈgraːtor], *m.* **-s/-en** [-graˑˈtoːrən]. *Civ.E: etc:* disintegrator.

Desinteressement [deˑzˀ-, dɛsˀintərɛs(ə)ˈmãː], *n.* **-s/.** disinterestedness.

desinteressiert [deˑzˀ-, dɛsˀintəreˈsiːrt], *a.* disinterested.

Deskription [deˑskriptsĭˈoːn], *f.* **-/-en,** description.

deskriptiv [deˑskripˈtiːf], *a.* descriptive.

Desman [ˈdɛsmaˑn], *m.* **-s/-e.** *Z:* desman.

Desmer, *m.* **-s/-,** steelyard.

Desmin [dɛsˈmiːn], *m.* **-s/-e.** *Miner:* desmine, stilbite.

Desodoration [deˑzˀ-, dɛsˀoˑdoˑraˑtsĭˈoːn], *f.* **-/-en,** deodorization, deodorizing; sweetening (of breath, etc.).

Desodorationsmittel, *n.* deodorant, deodorizer.

desodorieren [deˑzᵓ-, dɛsᵓoˑdoˑˈriːrən] = **desodorisieren.**

desodorisieren [deˑzᵓ-, dɛsᵓoˑdoˑriˑˈziːrən]. 1. *v.tr.* to deodorize; to sweeten (the breath, etc.); **desodorisierendes Mittel,** deodorant, deodorizer. 2. *vbl s.* **Desodorisieren,** *n.* deodorization, deodorizing.

desolat [deˑzoˑˈlaːt], *a.* desolate.

Desorganisation [deˑzᵓ-, dɛsᵓorgaˑniˑzaˑtsiˈoːn], *f.* -/. disorganization.

desorganisieren [deˑzᵓ-, dɛsᵓorgaˑniˑˈziːrən], *v.tr.* to disorganize.

Desoxydation [deˑz-ᵓ, dɛsᵓoksyˑdaˑtsiˈoːn], *f.* -/. *Ch:* deoxidation, deoxidization, deoxygenation.

desoxydieren [deˑzᵓ-, dɛsᵓoksyˑˈdiːrən], *v.tr. Ch:* to deoxidize, deoxygenate.

despektierlich [deˑ-, dɛspɛkˈtiːrliç], *a.* disrespectful (behaviour, etc.); *adv.* **d. von j-m sprechen,** to speak disrespectfully of s.o.

Desperado [dɛspeˑˈraːdoː], *m.* -s/-s, desperado.

desperat [dɛspeˑˈraːt], *a.* desperate.

Desperation [dɛspeˑraˑtsiˈoːn], *f.* -/. desperation, despair.

Despot [dɛsˈpoːt], *m.* -en/-en. 1. *Hist:* despot. 2. despot, tyrant.

Despotentum [dɛsˈpoːtəntuːm], *n.* -s/. 1. *Hist:* despotism; despotic nature, character (of a ruler, etc.). 2. despotism, tyranny.

Despotie [dɛspoˑˈtiː], *f.* -/-n [-ˈtiːən], despotism, despotic rule; **unter einer D. leben,** to live under a despotism, a despotic rule.

despotisch [dɛsˈpoːtiʃ], *a.* 1. despotic (rule, ruler, etc.). 2. despotic, tyrannical (pers.).

Despotismus [dɛspoˑˈtismus], *m.* -/. despotism, tyranny.

Desquamation [dɛ-, deˑskvaˑmaˑtsiˈoːn], *f.* -/. desquamation.

deß. *A:* = **dessen,** *q.v. under* **der.**

desselben *see* **derselbe.**

dessen *see* **der.**

dessenthalben, *adv. Lit:* = **dessentwegen.**

dessentwegen, *adv. Lit:* 1. **(um) d.** = **deshalb.** 2. *rel. use* because of whom, on whose account; (*when referring to thg*) because of which, on account of which.

dessentwillen, *adv. Lit:* 1. **(um) d.,** for his sake. 2. *rel. use* **(um) d.,** for whose sake; (*when referring to thg*) for the sake of which.

dessenungeachtet, *conj.* regardless (of that, it); nevertheless, none the less, notwithstanding; all the same; **er hat viele Fehler; d. habe ich ihn gern,** he has many faults, but I am fond of him all the same; **auf allen Seiten lauerten Gefahren; d. setzte er seinen Weg fort,** dangers lurked on every side, but he continued on his way none the less, notwithstanding, regardless; **er wußte, daß es ein gefährliches Unternehmen war; d. ließ er sich nicht davon abbringen,** he knew that it was a dangerous undertaking, but nevertheless he refused to be deterred.

Dessert [dɛˈsɛːr, dɛˈsɛrt], *n.* -s/-s, dessert, sweet (course).

Dessertapfel, *m.* dessert apple.

Dessertgabel, *f.* dessert fork.

Dessertlöffel, *m.* dessert spoon.

Dessertmesser, *n.* dessert knife; small knife; (*for fruit, etc.*) fruit knife.

Dessertservice, *n.* dessert service, dessert set.

Dessertteller, *m.* dessert plate.

Dessertwein, *m.* dessert wine.

Dessin [dɛˈsɛ̃ː], *n.* -s/-s. 1. design, pattern; *Tex:* figure (on textiles, etc.). 2. design, plan, scheme.

Dessinateur [dɛsiˑnaˑˈtøːr], *m.* -s/-e. *Tex:* pattern designer; pattern drawer.

dessinieren [dɛsiˑˈniːrən], *v.tr. Tex: Paperm:* to design (pattern); to pattern, figure (fabric); to pattern (paper); **dessinierte Stoffe,** figured, patterned, stuffs.

Destillat [dɛstiˈlaːt], *n.* -s/-e. *Ch: Ind:* distillate.

Destillateur [dɛstilaˑˈtøːr], *m.* -s/-s, distiller (of spirits).

Destillation [dɛstilaˑtsiˈoːn], *f.* -/-en. *Ind:* distillation, distilling; **trockene D.,** dry distillation; **fraktionierte D.,** fractional distillation.

Destillationsanlage, *f. Ind:* distillation plant, distilling plant.

Destillationsblase, *f. Ch: Ind:* distilling retort; still.

Destillationsgefäß, *n.* = **Destilliergefäß.**

Destillationsprodukt, *n.* distillation product; distillate.

Destille [dɛˈstilə], *f.* -/-n. *F:* brandy shop.

Destillierapparat [dɛstiˈliːr-], *m.* (*a*) distilling apparatus, still; (*b*) *Nau:* distilling condenser, fresh-water condenser.

Destillierblase, *f. Ch: Ind:* distilling retort; still.

destillieren [dɛstiˈliːrən], *v.tr. Ind: etc:* to distil (spirits, water); **Destillieren** *n,* **Destillierung** *f,* distillation, distilling.

Destilliergefäß, *n.,* **Destillierkolben,** *m. Ch: Ind:* distilling retort; still.

Destinatar [dɛstiˑnaˑˈtaːr], **Destinatär** [dɛstiˑnaˑˈtɛːr], *m.* -s/-e. *Com:* consignee (of goods).

destituieren [dɛstiˑtuˑˈiːrən], *v.tr.* to dismiss (employee).

Destitution [dɛstiˑtuˑtsiˈoːn], *f.* -/-en, dismissal (of employee).

desto, *adv.* (*A: also* **um d.**) (*preceding an adj. or adv. in the comparative degree*) (*a*) all the (more); **wenn du ganz offen mit ihm bist, wird er dich d. lieber haben,** if you are quite open with him, he will like you all the more; **sein Bruder ist unfreundlich; er ist d. liebenswürdiger,** he is as friendly as his brother is unfriendly, is the reverse; **d. schlimmer für ihn,** so much the worse for him; **ich bin d. erstaunter, als . . .,** I am all the more surprised as . . .; (*b*) (*in correlation with* **je**) **je eher, d. besser,** the sooner the better; **je schärfer die Spitze, d. besser die Nadel,** the sharper the point the better the needle; **je älter sie wurde, d. sonderbarer wurde sie,** the older she grew the stranger she became; **je länger er fortblieb, d. mehr vermißte sie ihn,** the longer he stayed away the more she missed him; **je weniger darüber gesagt wird, d. besser,** the less said about it the better; **man wird ihn d. mehr schätzen, je fleißiger er arbeitet,** the harder he works the more esteemed he will be.

destruieren [dɛstruˑˈiːrən], *v.tr.* to destroy.

Destruktion [dɛstruktsiˈoːn], *f.* -/-en, destruction.

Destruktions-, *comb.fm. Geol:* destructional . . .; **Destruktionsebene** *f,* destructional plane.

destruktiv [destrukˈtiːf], *a.* destructive; **destruktive** [destrukˈtiːvə] **Kritik,** destructive criticism; **eine destruktive Wirkung,** a destructive effect.

desultorisch [deˑzulˈtoːriʃ], *a.* desultory (conversation, etc.).

desungeachtet, *adv.* = **dessenungeachtet.**

deswegen, *conj. & adv.* = **deshalb.**

Deszendent [dɛ-, deˑstsɛnˈdɛnt], *m.* -en/-en, descendant.

Deszendenz [dɛ-, deˑstsɛnˈdɛnts], *f.* -/-en. 1. descent, lineage. 2. *Coll.* descendants.

Deszendenztheorie, *f. Biol:* theory of evolution, of the origin of species; theory of descent.

Deszension [dɛ-, deˑstsɛnziˈoːn], *f.* -/-en. *Astr:* descension (of a star).

Detachement [deˑtaʃ(ə)ˈmɑ̃ː], *n.* -s/-s. *Mil: A:* detachment.

Detachierapparat [deˑtaˈʃiːr-], *m. Nau:* boat unfastening apparatus.

detachieren [deˑtaˈʃiːrən], *v.tr.* 1. to detach, separate; to unfasten, unloose (a boat). 2. *Tex: Dy:* to remove (stain). 3. *Mil: A:* to detach (troops).

Detachiermittel, *n.* stain-remover.

Detail [deˑˈtai], *n.* -s/-s. 1. (*a*) detail (of a plan, a picture, etc.); **im D.,** in detail; **ins D. gehen,** to go into detail; **in allen Details,** in every detail; in the fullest detail; **das feine D. dieses Gemäldes,** the fine detail of this painting; **es ist mit Liebe zum D. gemalt,** it is painted with great care for detail; (*b*) = **Ausschnitt** 3 (*d*). 2. *Com: see* **en detail.**

Detailarbeit, *f. Art: etc:* detail(s).

Detailgeschäft, *n. Com:* 1. retail (trade). 2. retail store.

Detailhandel, *m. Com:* retail (trade).

detaillieren [deˑtaˈjiːrən], *v.tr.* to detail, enumerate (facts, etc.); to relate (sth.) in detail; to specify (request, etc.); **detailliert,** detailed (description, etc.).

Detaillist [deˑtaˈjist], *m.* -en/-en. *Com:* retailer, retail dealer.

Detailpreis, *m. Com:* retail price.

Detailschilderung, *f.* (*a*) (description of, piece of) detail; (*b*) detailed description.

Detailverkauf, *m. Com:* retail sale.

Detektiv [deˑtɛkˈtiːf], *m.* -s/-e [-s/-ˈtiːvə], detective.

Detektivroman, *m.* detective story; crime story; thriller.

Detektor [deˈtɛktor], *m.* -s/-en [-ˈtoːrən]. *W.Tel:* detector; *A:* crystal set.

Detention [deˑtɛntsiˈoːn], *f.* -/. detention, imprisonment, confinement (of s.o.); *Jur:* detention (of property).

Determinante [deˑtɛrmiˑˈnantə], *f.* -/-n. *Mth: Biol:* determinant.

Determination [deˑtɛrmiˑnaˑtsiˈoːn], *f.* -/-en. *Phil: Ph: Mth: etc:* determination; determining.

determinativ¹ [deˑtɛrmiˑnaˑˈtiːf], *a.* determinative.

Determinativ², *n.* -s/-e [-ˈtiːvə]. *Ling: Gram:* determinative (pronoun).

Determinativpronomen, *n. Gram:* determinative (pronoun).

determinieren [deˑtɛrmiˑˈniːrən], *v.tr.* to determine (species, value, area, noun, behaviour, etc.).

Determinismus [deˑtɛrmiˑˈnismus], *m.* -/. *Phil:* determinism.

Determinist [deˑtɛrmiˑˈnist], *m.* -en/-en, determinist.

detestabel [deˑtɛsˈtaːbəl], *a.* detestable.

detestieren [deˑtɛsˈtiːrən], *v.tr.* to detest.

Detonation [deˑtoˑnaˑtsiˈoːn], *f.* -/-en. 1. detonation, explosion. 2. *Mus:* singing out of tune.

Detonator [deˑtoˑˈnaːtor], *m.* -s/-en [-naˑˈtoːrən], detonator.

detonieren [deˑtoˑˈniːrən]. 1. *v.i.* (*sein*) to detonate, explode. 2. *v.i.* (*haben*) *Mus:* to sing out of tune. 3. *vbl s.* **Detonierung,** *f.* detonation, explosion.

Detriment [deˑtriˑˈmɛnt], *n.* -(e)s/-e, detriment; disadvantage.

Detrition [deˑtriˑtsiˈoːn], *f.* -/. *Geol:* detrition.

detto [ˈdɛtoː], *adv.* ditto.

Deube, *f.* -/. *A:* = **Diebstahl.**

Deubel, *m.* -s/. *F:* devil.

deucht *see* **dünken.**

Deukalion [doyˈkaːliɔn]. *Pr.n.m.* -s. *Gr.Myth:* Deucalion.

Deul, *m.* -s/-e. *Metall:* bloom.

Deule, *f.* -/-n = **Düse** 1.

Deut, *m.* -(e)s/-e & -s. *Num: A:* doit; *F:* **ich gebe keinen D. dafür,** I don't care a rap, *A:* a doit, for it; **keinen D., nicht einen D., wert sein,** not to be worth a brass farthing, to be completely worthless; **davon ist nicht ein D. wahr,** there is not a grain of truth in it, not an atom of truth in it.

deutbar, *a.* interpretable, explicable; **die Parabel ist schwer d.,** the parable is hard to interpret, hard to explain.

Deute¹, *f.* -/-n, interpretation.

Deute², *f.* -/-n. *Dial:* = **Tüte.**

Deutefinger, *m.* forefinger, index(-finger).

Deutel, *m.* -s/-. *N.Arch: etc:* treenail-wedge.

Deutelei, *f.* -/-en. 1. pedantic interpreting; niggling, quibbling, splitting hairs, hair-splitting. 2. pedantic interpretation; **kleinliche Deuteleien,** over-meticulous interpretations.

deuteln, *v.i.* (*haben*) to give pedantic interpretations; to split hairs; to niggle, quibble, cavil **(an etwas** *dat.,* about sth.); **daran gibt's nichts zu d.,** there can be no argument about this, that.

deuten. I. *v.* 1. *v.i.* (*haben*) (*a*) to point; **auf j-n d.,** to point at s.o.; **auf etwas** *acc.* **d.,** to point to, towards, sth., to indicate sth.; **er deutete mit dem Finger auf die Tür, zur Tür,** he pointed to, towards, the door, he indicated the door with his finger; **der Wetterhahn deutet gegen, nach, Westen,** the weathercock points to, towards, the west; **ihre Politik deutet in die gleiche Richtung wie die unsere,** their policy points in the same direction as ours; (*b*) to refer, point **(auf j-n, etwas** *acc.,* to s.o., sth.); **diese Bemerkung deutet auf diejenigen, die . . .,** this remark refers to those who . . . . 2. *v.i.* (*haben*) (*A: also v.tr.*) (*a*) **auf etwas** *acc.* **d.,** to indicate, betoken, sth., to give token of sth.; to signify, be a sign of, sth.; to suggest sth.; **diese Antwort deutet auf Intelligenz,** this answer indicates, gives token of, intelligence; **eine hohe Stirn deutet auf Intelligenz,** a high forehead signifies, suggests, intelligence, is a sign of intelligence; **alles im Haus deutet auf einen feinen Geschmack,** everything in the house speaks of, betokens, a refined taste; **nichts in seinem Gebahren deutete darauf, daß er eine Berühmtheit war,** there was nothing in his bearing, there was nothing about him, to indicate, suggest, that he was a celebrity; (*b*) **auf etwas** *acc.* **d.,** to point to sth., to indicate sth.; to portend, (fore)bode, presage, sth.; **alles deutet auf einen glücklichen Ausgang der Verhandlungen,** everything points to a happy issue of the negotiations; **nichts deutete darauf, daß der Winter bevorstand, nichts deutete auf den bevorstehenden Winter,** nothing indicated, suggested, that winter was at hand; **dunkle Wolken, die auf ein Ungewitter deuten,** dark clouds that portend a storm; **einige Zeichen deuteten darauf, daß das Wetter bald wieder besser werden würde,** various signs indicated that the weather would soon improve again; (*c*) *A:* (*of pers.*) to presage, foretell; *B:* **das sagte er aber, zu d., welches Todes er sterben würde,** this he said, signifying what death he should die. 3. *v.tr. A:* **j-m etwas d.,** to point sth. out to s.o., to show s.o. sth. 4. *v.tr.* (*a*) to interpret, explain (text, law, parable, dream, etc.); to read

(the stars); **etwas richtig d.**, to interpret sth. correctly, to give a correct interpretation of sth.; **etwas falsch d.**, to misinterpret sth.; to misconstrue sth., to put a false construction on sth.; (*b*) **j-m etwas übel d.**, to put a bad construction on, to take offence at, s.o.'s action *or* words; **j-m etwas falsch d.**, to misinterpret, misconstrue, s.o.'s action *or* words; **er hat mir diese Bemerkung übel gedeutet**, he took offence at my remark, he took my remark badly, he misconstrued my remark; **sie hat es mir übel gedeutet, daß ich ihre Einladung nicht angenommen habe**, she put a bad construction on my refusal of her invitation; she took offence at, was offended at, my refusal of her invitation.

II. *vbl s.* **1. Deuten**, *n. in vbl senses.* **2. Deutung**, *f.* (*a*)=II. 1; *also:* interpretation, explanation (of text, law, parable, dream, etc.); (*b*) interpretation, explanation; **eine falsche D.**, a misinterpretation; a misconstruction; (*c*) *A:*= **Bedeutung**, *q.v. under* **bedeuten II**.

Deuter, *m.* **-s/-**. **1.** interpreter, explainer (of dreams, etc.). **2.** (*thg*) pointer, indicator. **3.** forefinger, index(-finger).

Deuteragonist [doyte·ra·go·ˈnist], *m.* **-en/-en**. *Gr.Th:* deuteragonist.

Deuterium [doyˈteːrium], *n.* **-s/**. *Ch:* deuterium, heavy hydrogen.

deuterokanonisch [doyte·ro·ka·ˈnoːniʃ], *a. B.Hist:* deuterocanonical.

Deuteron [ˈdoytərɔn], *n.* **-s/-en** [-ˈroːnən]. *Atom. Ph:* deuteron.

Deuteronomion, das [doyte·ro·ˈnoːmiɔn], **Deuteronomium, das** [doyte·ro·ˈnoːmium], **-s**. *B:* Deuteronomy.

Deutewort, *n. Gram:* demonstrative.

-deutig, *comb.fm.* (*suffixed mainly to num. adjs & adjs indicating quantity*) (*word, concept, etc.*) with . . . meaning(s); **eindeutig**, with one meaning, unambiguous; **mehrdeutig**, with several meanings; **verschiedendeutig**, with various meanings.

Deutler, *m.* **-s/-**, quibbler; caviller.

deutlich. **1.** *a.* clear, distinct, plain; (*a*) **eine deutliche Schrift**, a clear, legible, handwriting; **ein deutlicher Widerschein**, a clear reflection; **deutliche Umrisse**, distinct outlines; **ein deutliches Anzeichen**, a clear, plain, indication; (*b*) **eine deutliche Antwort**, a plain answer; **eine deutliche Erklärung**, a lucid explanation; **eine deutliche Erinnerung an etwas**, a distinct, clear, recollection of sth.; **eine deutliche Anspielung auf Herrn X**, an obvious allusion to Mr X; **j-m etwas d. machen**, to make sth. clear to s.o., (i) to explain sth. to s.o., (ii) to make sth. plain to s.o.; **mit j-m d. werden**, to be plain with s.o.; **ich habe es ihr ganz d. gemacht, daß ich nichts mehr mit ihr zu tun haben will**, I have made it quite plain, quite clear, to her that I won't have anything more to do with her; **kannst du mir das etwas deutlicher machen?** can you make that a little clearer to me? can you explain that to me in a little more detail? **wenn er zornig ist, kann er sehr d. werden**, when he is angry he can speak in very plain terms; **das war d. genug**, that was plain, clear, enough. **2.** *adv.* clearly, distinctly, plainly; **d. sprechen**, to speak clearly, distinctly; **d. schreiben**, to write clearly, legibly; to have a clear hand(writing); **ich habe es dir d. gesagt**, I told you clearly, plainly; **es war dunkel, aber ich konnte das Haus d. erkennen**, it was dark but I could distinguish the house clearly; **d. unterscheiden**, to distinguish clearly, to make a clear distinction; **die Küste zeichnet sich immer deutlicher ab**, the coast becomes more and more distinct; **das Plätschern des Bächleins war d. zu hören**, the rippling of the brook was clearly audible; **ich habe Ihnen das klar und d. auseinandergesetzt**, I have explained it to you quite clearly, quite plainly.

Deutlichkeit, *f.* clarity, clearness (of handwriting, explanation, etc.); distinctness (of recollection, etc.); plainness (of indication, answer, etc.); **seine Antwort ließ an D. nichts zu wünschen übrig**, his answer could not have been plainer.

deutsam, *a. A:*=**bedeutsam**.

deutsch. **1.** *a.* German; (*a*) (*spelt with small d*) **die deutsche Sprache**, the German language; **deutsche Erzeugnisse**, German products; **der deutsche Botschafter**, the German Ambassador; **deutsche Schrift**, (i) German script; (ii) *Print:* Gothic text; **der deutsche Homer**, the German Homer, (i) the German translation of Homer; (ii) the Homer of German literature; **ich habe den deutschen Urtext nicht gelesen**, I have not read the original German; *Constr:* **deutscher Verband**, German bond; *see also* **Beefsteak, Schweiz**; (*b*) (*spelt with capital D*) (*in names, titles, etc.*) **das Deutsche Kaiserreich**, the German Empire; *Hist:* **das Heilige Römische Reich Deutscher Nation**, the Holy Roman Empire; **der Deutsche Krieg**, the Prusso-Austrian War (of 1866); **der Deutsche Orden**, the Teutonic Order of Knights; **Deutscher Ritter**, Teutonic Knight; **Deutsches Institut**, (i) German Institute; (ii) (*at University*) Institute of Germanic Languages and Literature; **die Deutsche Bucht**, the German Bight; *Hist:* (*in Nazi period*) **die Deutschen Christen**, the 'German Christians'. **2.** *a.* (*denoting characteristics of the German race*) German; (*sometimes pej.*) Teutonic; **mit typisch deutscher Gründlichkeit**, with typical(ly) German thoroughness; with Teutonic thoroughness; **das Deutsche an diesem Gedicht**, what is German about this poem, the German element in this poem; **was ist d., was ist das typisch Deutsche, in diesem Bild?** what is typically German about this picture? **3.** *adv;* (*a*) German; **d. sprechen**, to speak (in) German. **er spricht nicht d.**, he is not speaking (in German (*cp.* 4 (*a*)); **der Brief ist d. geschrieben**, the letter is (written) in German; **sich d. unterhalten**, to converse, talk, in German (*cp.* 4 (*b*)); **sie redete ihn d. an**, she spoke to him, addressed him, in German; (*b*) *F:* plainly, bluntly; **mit ihm muß man d. reden**, you have to be quite plain, blunt, with him; it's no use mincing matters with him. **4.** (*a*) *s.* **Deutsch**, *n. inv., occ.* **-s**, *Ling:* German; the German language; **das Deutsche** (*decl. as adj.*) the German language; German; **D. sprechen, können**, to speak, know, German; **D. lernen**, to learn German; **Goethes D., das D. Goethes**, Goethe's German; **können Sie D.? sprechen Sie D.?** do you, can you, speak German? **er spricht gut D.**, he speaks German well; **er spricht ein gutes D.**, he speaks good German; **sein D. ist gut**, his German is good; **er kann kein D., er spricht nicht, kein, D.**, he speaks no German, he does not speak German (*cp.* 3 (*a*)); **er kann kein Wort D.**, he doesn't know, can't speak, a word of German; **er beherrscht D., das Deutsche, vollkommen**, he has a perfect command of German; **sie hat in D., im Deutschen, eine gute Note bekommen**, she obtained a good mark in German; **etwas ins Deutsche, aus dem Deutschen, übersetzen**, to translate sth. into German, from German; **im Deutschen sagen wir . . .**, in German we say . . .; *Sch:* **der Lehrstuhl für D.**, the chair of German, the German chair; **Professor für D.**, Professor of German; (*b*) *adv.phr.* (*spelt with small d*) **auf d.**, in German; **etwas auf d. sagen**, to say sth. in German; **das heißt auf d., zu d., . . .**, in German that is called . . .; **sich auf d., in d., unterhalten**, to converse, talk, in German (*cp.* 3 (*a*)); **er hat seine Vorlesung auf d., in d., gehalten**, he gave his lecture in German; **auf gut d.**, (i) in good German; (ii) *F:* plainly, forthrightly, in plain language. **5.** *s.* **Deutsche**, *m., f.* (*decl. as adj.*) German; **er ist (ein) Deutscher, sie ist (eine) Deutsche**, he, she, is (a) German; **die Deutschen**, the Germans.

Deutschamerikaner, *m.* German American.

deutschamerikanisch, *a.* German-American (parentage, etc.).

deutsch-amerikanisch, *a.* (friendship, trade, etc.) between Germany and America; German-American (dictionary, etc.).

Deutschball, *m. Sp:* ball game similar to dodge-ball.

deutschblütig, *a.* (pers.) of German extraction, of German stock.

Deutsche, *m. f. see* **deutsch** 5.

deutscheln, *v.i.* (*haben*) *occ. Pej:* to behave, dress, etc., in a typically German manner.

Deutschenangst, *f.* Germanophobia; fear of the Germans, of Germany.

Deutschenfeind, *m.* anti-German; person who dislikes, hates, the Germans.

deutschenfeindlich, *a.* hostile towards the Germans; anti-German.

Deutschenfresser, *m.* fanatic anti-German.

Deutschenfreund, *m.* pro-German; Germanophile.

deutschenfreundlich, *a.*=**deutschfreundlich**.

deutsch-englisch, *a.* Anglo-German (relations, etc.); German-English (dictionary, etc.).

Deutschenhaß, *m.* hatred of the Germans.

deutschfeindlich, *a.* anti-German.

deutschfranzösisch, *a.* German and French (parentage, etc.).

deutsch-französisch, *a.* Franco-German (relations, etc.); German-French (dictionary, etc.); *Hist:* **der Deutsch-Französische Krieg**, the Franco-Prussian War (1870–1871).

deutschfreundlich, *a.* friendly towards the Germans; pro-German.

Deutschgefühl, *n.* **das D. in mir, mein D.**, the German in me; my German soul.

deutschgesinnt, *a.* German-minded.

Deutschheit, *f.* Germanity; German nature; **sie haben ihre D. vergessen**, they have forgotten that they are German.

Deutschherr, *m. Hist:* Teutonic Knight; **die Deutschherren**, the Teutonic Order of Knights.

Deutschherrenorden, der. *Hist:* the Teutonic Order of Knights.

Deutschkatholiken, *m.pl. Rel.Hist:* German Catholics.

Deutschkunde, *f. Sch:* instruction in German language and literature including cultural history.

deutschkundlich, *a. Sch:* **deutschkundliche Fächer**, subjects relating to German history, geography, language and culture; **deutschkundlicher Unterricht**=**Deutschkunde**.

Deutschland. *Pr.n.n.* **-s**. *Geog:* Germany.

Deutschlandfrage, *f. Pol:* German question.

Deutschlandlied, das, the song 'Deutschland, Deutschland, über alles'.

Deutschlandpolitik, *f.* German policy (*of non-German governments*).

Deutschlehrer, *m. Sch:* German master, German teacher.

Deutschmeister, *m. Hist:* German Master (of the Teutonic Order of Knights).

Deutschordensritter, *m. Hist:* Teutonic Knight.

Deutschritterorden, der. *Hist:* the Teutonic Order of Knights.

Deutschschweizer, *m.* German Swiss.

deutschschweizerisch, *a.* German Swiss (dialect, etc.).

deutsch-schweizerisch, *a.* (relations, traffic, etc.) between Germany and Switzerland; German and Swiss (origin); **die deutsch-schweizerische Grenze**, the border between Germany and Switzerland, the German–Swiss border.

deutschsprachig, *a.* German-speaking (population, etc.); German-language (newspaper, etc.), (newspaper, etc.) in the German language; **deutschsprachiger Unterricht**, instruction given in German.

deutschsprachlich, *a.* **deutschsprachlicher Unterricht**, German classes, German lessons, instruction in the German language.

Deutschsprechen, *n.* speaking German; **sich im D. üben**, to practise speaking German.

Deutschstunde, *f. Sch:* German lesson.

Deutschtum, *n.* **-s/**. **1.** Germanity; German nature; **das D. im Ausland**, German national customs and culture preserved by groups of emigrants (*cp.* 2); **die Einwanderer haben ihr D. bewahrt**, the immigrants have preserved their German language and way of life; the German immigrants have preserved their language and national characteristics. **2.** *Coll.* **das D. im Ausland, in aller Welt**, German people and culture abroad, the world over (*cp.* 1).

Deutschtümelei, *f.* **-/**. *Pej:* (*a*) petty emphasis on Germanity; excessive exhibition of being German, of German nationalism; (*b*) admiration of ancient Teutons; (*c*) Germanomania, Teutomania.

Deutschtümler, *m.* **-s/-**, (*a*) person who displays excessive Germanity; (*b*) Germanomaniac, Teutomaniac.

Deutschunterricht, *m. Sch:* (teaching of) German; instruction in German; German lessons.

Deutschwissenschaft, *f. Sch:* **1.** study of German language and literature. **2.**=**Deutschkunde**.

deutschwissenschaftlich, *a.* relating to the study of German language and literature; **deutschwissenschaftliche Studien**, German studies, Germanistics.

Deutung, *f. see* **deuten II**.

Deutzie [ˈdoytsiə], *f.* **-/-n**. *Bot:* deutzia.

Devalvation [de·valva·tsiˈoːn], *f.* **-/-en**. *Pol.Ec:* devaluation (of the pound, etc.).

devalvieren [de·valˈviːrən], *v.tr. Pol.Ec:* to devalue, devaluate (the pound, etc.).

Devastation [de·vasta·tsiˈoːn], *f.* **-/**. devastation.

devastieren [de·vasˈtiːrən], *v.tr.* to devastate.

Deverbativum [deːverba·ˈtiːvum], *n.* **-s/-va**. *Ling:* deverbal, deverbative.

devestieren [de·veˈstiːrən], *v.tr.* to deprive (s.o.) of a fief; *Ecc:* to unfrock (priest).

Devestitur [de·vɛsti·ˈtuːr], *f.* **-/-en**, depriving (s.o.) of a fief; *Ecc:* unfrocking (of priest).

Deviation [deˑviˑaˑtsiˈoːn], *f.* **-/-en,** deviation (of the compass, stars, etc.).

deviieren [deˑviˑˈiːrən], *v.i.* (*haben*) to deviate.

Devise [deˑˈviːzə], *f.* **-/-n.** **1.** motto; *Her:* device; motto. **2.** *pl.* **Devisen,** *Fin:* foreign exchange; foreign currency; **Devisen beantragen,** to apply for foreign currency; **Devisen anmelden,** to declare foreign currency.

Devisenabteilung, *f. Bank:* foreign exchange department.

Devisenarbitrage, *f. Fin:* arbitration of exchange.

Devisenausländer, *m.* **1.** German national resident abroad (regarded as a foreigner from the point of view of the German bank). **2.** non-resident foreigner in Germany.

Devisenbehörden, *f.pl. Fin:* exchange control authorities.

Devisenberater, *m.* qualified adviser on matters affecting foreign exchange.

Devisenbeschränkung, *f. Fin:* restriction on foreign currency; **wegen der gegenwärtigen D.,** because of the present foreign currency restrictions.

Devisenbestand, *m. Fin:* foreign currency reserve.

Devisenbestimmungen, *f.pl. Fin:* foreign exchange regulations; foreign currency regulations.

Devisenbewirtschaftung, *f. Fin:* exchange control.

Devisenbilanz, *f. Fin:* balance of (foreign exchange) payments.

Devisenbonus, *m.* percentage allowance to earners of foreign currency.

Devisenbörse, *f. Fin:* foreign exchange market.

Devisenbüro, *n. Bank:* foreign exchange department.

Devisenfreibetrag, *m.* foreign currency allowance.

Devisengenehmigung, *f. Fin:* authorization for foreign currency.

Devisengeschäft, *n.* (*a*) *Bank:* foreign exchange business; (*b*)=**Devisenhandel.**

Devisenguthaben, *n. Fin:* foreign exchange assets.

Devisenhandel, *m. Fin:* operations in foreign exchange; foreign currency dealings; foreign exchange dealings.

Devisenhändler, *m. Bank:* foreign exchange dealer.

Deviseninländer, *m.* foreigner resident in Germany (regarded as a national from the point of view of the German bank).

Devisenkontrolle, *f. Fin:* exchange control.

Devisenkurs, *m. Fin:* rate of exchange, (foreign) exchange rate; **zum gegenwärtigen D.,** at the current rate of exchange.

Devisenmakler, *m. Fin:* (foreign) exchange broker.

Devisenmarkt, *m. Fin:* foreign exchange market; **internationale Devisenmärkte,** international exchange markets.

devisenrechtlich. **1.** *a.* relating to (foreign) exchange regulations, to foreign currency regulations; **devisenrechtliche Bestimmungen,** foreign exchange regulations. **2.** *adv.* according to, in accordance with, foreign currency regulations.

Devisenschiebung, *f. Fin:* illegal transference of foreign currency.

Devisenstelle, *f. Adm:* exchange control office.

Devisentermingeschäft, *n. Fin: Com:* forward exchange transaction; *coll.* forward exchange dealings.

Devisenüberwachung, *f. Fin:* exchange control.

Devisenüberwachungsstelle, *f. Adm:* exchange control office.

Devisenwährung, *f. Fin:* currency-exchange standard.

Devisenzuteilung, *f.* foreign currency allocation, foreign currency allowance.

Devisenzwangswirtschaft, *f. Fin:* exchange control.

Devolution [deˑvoˑluˑtsiˈoːn], *f.* **-/-en.** *Jur:* devolution, transmission (of property, etc.); *Ecc:* devolution, lapsing (of benefice).

Devolutionskrieg, der. *Hist:* the War of Devolution.

devolvieren [deˑvolˈviːrən], *v.i.* (*haben*) **1.** *Jur:* (*of property, etc.*) to devolve (to, upon, s.o.); *Ecc:* to lapse. **2.** *Jur:* (*of case*) to be transferred to a higher court.

Devon, das [deˑˈvoːn], **-s/.** *Geol:* the Devonian (system); **das mittlere D.,** the Middle Devonian.

Devonformation, *f. Geol:* Devonian (system).

devonisch [deˑˈvoːniʃ], *a. Geol:* Devonian; **die devonische Formation,** the Devonian system.

devot [deˑˈvoːt], *a.* **1.** devout, religious, pious. **2.** devoted; *Pej:* servile, cringing, abject.

Devotion [deˑvoˑtsiˈoːn], *f.* **-/-en.** **1.** devotion; devoutness, religiousness. **2.** devotion (to a pers., cause, etc.); *Pej:* servility, abjectness.

Devotionalien [deˑvoˑtsioˑˈnaːliən], *f.pl. Com: etc:* devotional articles; devotional helps, devotional aids.

Devotionalienhandel, *m.* sale of devotional articles.

Devotionsbuch, *n.* devotional book.

Dexel, *m.* **-s/-.** *Tls:* adze.

dexeln, *v.tr. & i.* (*haben*) to adze.

Dextrin [dɛksˈtriːn], *n.* **-s/-e.** *Ch: Ind:* dextrin(e).

dextro-, Dextro- [dɛkstroˑˈ-], *comb.fm.* dextro-; **dextrogyr** [dɛkstroˑˈgyːr], dextrogyre, dextrorotatory; **Dextrokardie** [dɛkstroˑkarˈdiː] *f,* dextrocardia.

Dextrose [dɛksˈtroːzə], *f.* **-/.** *Ch:* dextrose.

Dey [dai], *m.* **-(s)/-s.** *Hist:* Dey.

dez-, Dez-, *cp.* **dec-, Dec-.**

dezedieren [deˑtseˑˈdiːrən], *v.i.* (*haben*) to withdraw, retire.

Dezem [ˈdeːtsɛm], *m.* **-s/-s,** tithe.

Dezember [deˑˈtsɛmbər], *m.* **-s & -/-.** December; **im (Monat) D.,** in (the month of) December; *for other phrases cp.* **April.**

dezemberlich, *a.* (i) December, (ii) December-like (weather, etc.); **die dezemberliche Kälte,** the December cold; **das Wetter ist schon richtig d.,** it's real December weather.

Dezemvir [deˑˈtsɛmvir], *m.* **-n & -s/-n.** *Rom.Hist:* decemvir.

Dezemvirat [deˑtsɛmviˑˈraːt], *n.* **-(e)s/-e,** decemvirate.

Dezennium [deˑˈtsɛnium], *n.* **-/-nien,** decennium, decade.

dezent [deˑˈtsɛnt], *a.* (*a*) decent, modest (attire, etc.); respectable (garment); decent (literature, etc.); decent, seemly, proper (behaviour); (*b*) soft, restrained, subdued (music, colour); quiet (colour, dress); chaste (colour); subdued (lighting, etc.); restrained (acting, etc.).

Dezentralisation [deˑtsɛntraˑliˑzaˑtsiˈoːn], *f.* **-/.** decentralization (of administration, etc.).

dezentralisieren [deˑtsɛntraˑliˑˈziːrən], *v.tr.* to decentralize (administration, etc.).

Dezenz [deˑˈtsɛnts], *f.* **-/.** (*a*) decency, modesty (of attire, etc.); decency (of literature); decency, seemliness (of behaviour); (*b*) softness, restraint (of music).

Dezernat [deˑtsɛrˈnaːt], *n.* **-(e)s/-e.** *Adm: etc:* (administrative) department.

Dezernent [deˑtsɛrˈnɛnt], *m.* **-en/-en.** *Adm: etc:* (cultural, etc.) adviser; head of a 'Dezernat', *q.v.*

Dezi, *n.* **-s/-.** *Liquid Meas:* tenth (of a litre).

Dezi-, dezi- [ˈdeːtsiˑ-, deˑtsiˑˈ-], *comb.fm.* deci-; **Dezigramm** *n,* decigram(me); **dezimal,** decimal.

Dezibel [deˑtsiˑˈbɛl], *n.* **-s/-.** *Ph:* decibel, transmission unit of sound.

dezidieren [deˑtsiˑˈdiːrən], *v.tr.* to decide.

Deziliter [ˈdeːtsiˑliːtər, deˑtsiˑˈliːtər], *n. & m. Meas:* decilitre.

dezimal [deˑtsiˑˈmaːl], *a.* decimal (numeration, fraction, system, coinage, etc.); **in dezimaler Schreibweise,** written as a decimal.

Dezimalbruch, *m. Mth:* decimal (fraction).

Dezimale [deˑtsiˑˈmaːlə], *f.* **-/-n.** *Mth:* decimal (place).

Dezimalklassifikation, *f. Library:* Dewey decimal classification.

Dezimallogarithmus, *m. Mth:* Brigg's logarithm, decimal logarithm, common logarithm.

Dezimalrechnung, *f. Mth:* decimal arithmetic; *F:* decimals.

Dezimalschreibung, Dezimalschreibweise, *f. Mth:* decimal notation.

Dezimalstelle, *f. Mth:* decimal (place); **auf fünf Dezimalstellen genau,** correct to five places of decimals.

Dezimalsystem, *n. Mth: etc:* decimal system.

Dezimalwaage, *f.* weigh-bridge.

Dezimalzahl, *f. Mth:* decimal.

Dezimaß [ˈdeːtsiˑ-], *n. Meas:* decimal system of measuring liquid.

Dezimation [deˑtsiˑmaˑtsiˈoːn], *f.* **-/.** decimation.

Dezime [ˈdeːtsiˑmə], *f.* **-/-n.** **1.** *Mus:* (*interval or note*) tenth. **2.** *Pros:* ten-line stanza.

Dezimeter [ˈdeːtsiˑmeːtər, deˑtsiˑˈmeːtər], *m. & n. Meas:* decimetre.

dezimieren [deˑtsiˑˈmiːrən], *v.tr.* to decimate (regiment, etc.); to reduce (population, etc.) (drastically); **die Bevölkerung wurde durch die Pest dezimiert,** the plague decimated, thinned out, the population, took its tithe of the population; **Dezimierung** *f,* decimation.

Dezision [deˑtsiˑziˈoːn], *f.* **-/-en,** decision.

dezisiv [deˑtsiˑˈziːf], *a.* decisive.

Dezisivstimme, *f.* deciding vote; casting vote.

Dezister [deˑtsiˑˈsteːr], *m.* **-s/-e.** *Meas:* decistere.

Dhau, Dhaw [dau], *f.* **-/-en.** *Nau:* d(h)ow.

Di-[1], **di-**, *pref.* (*in foreign words of Greek origin*) *esp.* **1.** *Nat.Hist: etc:* di-; **Didynamia** *n pl,* didynamia; **dichromatisch,** dichromatic; *Cryst:* **Dioktaeder** *n,* dioctahedron. **2.** *Ch:* di-; **Dibenzyl** *n,* dibenzyl; **Dicyan** *n,* dicyanogen; **Dinicotinsäure** *f,* dinicotinic acid.

Di-[2], **di-** =**Dis-, dis-.**

Di(a)-, di(a)-, *pref.* (*in foreign words of Greek origin*) di(a)-; **Diameter** *m,* diameter; **Diapason** *m & n,* diapason; **diaphan,** diaphanous; **Diorama** *n,* diorama; **dioptrisch,** dioptric.

Dia [ˈdiːa], *n.* **-s/-s.** *F:*=**Diapositiv.**

Diabas [diˑaˑˈbaːs], *m.* **-es/-e.** *Miner:* diabase.

Diabetes [diˑaˑˈbeːtes], *m.* **-/.** *Med:* diabetes; (*a*) *in common use*=**D. mellitus,** diabetes mellitus; (*b*) **D. insipidus,** diabetes insipidus.

Diabetiker [diˑaˑˈbeːtikər], *m.* **-s/-.** *Med:* diabetic.

Diabetikerbrot, *n. Med:* bread for diabetics.

Diabetikergebäck, *n.* diabetic rusks.

diabetisch [diˑaˑˈbeːtiʃ], *a. Med:* diabetic.

Diabetrachter [ˈdiːaˑ-], *m. Phot:* slide viewer.

diablastisch [diˑaˑˈblastiʃ], *a. Geol:* diablastic; **diablastische Struktur,** diablastic structure.

diabolisch [diˑaˑˈboːliʃ], *a.* diabolic.

Diabolismus [diˑaˑboˑˈlismus], *m.* **-/.** diabolism.

Diabolo [diˑˈaːboˑloː], *n.* **-/.** *Games:* diabolo.

Diacetyl [diˑˀaˑtseˑˈtyːl], *n.* **-s/.** *Ch:* diacetyl.

Diachronie [diˑaˑkroˑˈniː], *f.* **-/.** *Ling:* diachrony.

diachronitisch [diˑaˑkroˑˈniːtiʃ], *a. Ling:* diachronic.

Diachylon [diˑˈaːçyˑlon], *n.* **-s/.** *Pharm:* diachylon, diachylum.

Diachylonpflaster, *n. Pharm:* lead plaster, diachylum plaster.

Diachylonsalbe, *f. Pharm:* diachylum ointment.

diadelphisch [diˑaˑˈdɛlfiʃ], *a. Bot:* diadelphous, diadelphian.

Diadem [diˑaˑˈdeːm], *n.* **-s/-e.** **1.** diadem. **2.** *Crust:* acorn barnacle.

Diademrotschwanz, *m. Orn:* Moussier's redstart.

Diadoche [diˑaˑˈdoxə], *m.* **-n/-n.** *Gr.Hist:* successor of Alexander the Great, diadochus; **die Diadochen,** the diadochi.

Diageber [ˈdiːaˑ-], *m. TV:* slide scanner.

diagenetisch [diˑaˑgeˑˈneːtiʃ], *a. Geol:* diagenetic; **diagenetische Umwandlung,** diagenetic change, diagenesis.

Diagnose [diˑaˑˈgnoːzə], *f.* **-/-n,** (*a*) diagnosis; **eine D. stellen,** to make a diagnosis; (*b*) (the art of) diagnosis; diagnostics.

diagnosieren [diˑagnoˑˈziːrən], *v.tr.*=**diagnostizieren.**

Diagnostik [diˑaˑˈgnostik], *f.* **-/.** diagnostics, diagnosis.

Diagnostiker [diˑaˑˈgnostikər], *m.* **-s/-,** diagnostician.

diagnostisch [diˑaˑˈgnostiʃ], *a.* diagnostic.

diagnostizieren [diˑagnostiˑˈtsiːrən], *v.tr.* to diagnose (illness, etc.).

diagonal[1] [diˑaˑgoˑˈnaːl], *a.* diagonal; *Geol:* **diagonale Verwerfung,** diagonal fault; *adv. F:* **ein Buch d. lesen,** to skip through a book.

Diagonal[2], *n.* **-s/-e.** *Tex:* diagonal cloth, diagonal.

Diagonalanker, *m. Constr:* diagonal stay.

Diagonalbindung, *f. Tex:* twill weave.

Diagonalboot, *n. Nau:* diagonal-built boat.

Diagonale [diˑaˑgoˑˈnaːlə], *f.* **-/-n.** *Geom:* diagonal; *Constr:* diagonal (rod); diagonal stay; diagonal brace; diagonal strut.

diagonalgeschichtet, *a. Geol:* false-bedded, cross-bedded.

Diagonalköper, *m. Tex:* twill, cotton serge, woven on three shafts.

Diagonalkraft, *f. Mec:* resultant force, resultant.

Diagonallesen, *n. F:* skip-reading.

Diagonalmatrix, *f. Mth:* diagonal matrix.

Diagonalreihe, *f. Mth:* diagonal sequence *or* series.

Diagonalrippe, *f. Arch:* diagonal rib.

Diagonalschichtung, *f. Geol:* current bedding, cross-bedding, false-bedding; oblique lamination.

Diagonalschiene, *f. N.Arch:* diagonal rider; diagonal tie-plate.

Diagonalschnitt, *m.* diagonal section.

Diagonalspant, *m. N.Arch:* diagonal frame.

Diagonalstab, *m.* **1.**=**Diagonalstrebe.** **2.** rod inserted diagonally to measure the capacity of vessels, *esp.* of barrels.

Diagonalstrebe, *f. Constr:* diagonal brace, cross-brace; diagonal stay.

Diagonalstuhl, *m. Tex:* Milan loom.

Diagonaltal, *n. Geol:* diagonal valley.

Diagonalteilung, *f. Tchn:* diagonal pitch (of rivets).

Diagonalverband, m. 1. Constr: diagonal bracing. 2. Constr: diagonal bond. 3. N.Arch: diagonal system of framing. 4. Surg: diagonal bandage.

Diagonalverstrebung, f. Constr: diagonal bracing.

Diagonalverwerfung, f. Geol: diagonal fault.

Diagonalwegerung, f. N.Arch: diagonal ceiling.

Diagramm [di·a·'gram], n. -s/-e, diagram. 1. schematic drawing; (geometrical) diagram, drawing, figure; Surv: A: lay-out. 2. (a) graph (of temperature, pressure, etc.); (statistical, etc.) chart; (b) Mec.E: Mch: diagram.

Diagrammapparat, m. Mch: testing machine (producing diagrams).

diagrammatisch [di·a·gra'ma:tiʃ], a. diagrammatic.

Diagrammfläche, f., **Diagramminhalt,** m. Mch: area of diagram; work area.

Diagrammpapier, n. (a) graph-paper; (b) Mch: Mec.E: indicator card, indicator paper.

Diagraph [di·a·'gra:f], m. -en/-en. Draw: diagraph.

Diagraphie [di·a·gra·'fi:], f. -/-n [-'fi:ən], diagraphics.

Diagraphik [di·a·'gra:fik], f. -/. diagraphics.

diagraphisch [di·a·'gra:fiʃ], a. diagraphic.

Diakaustik [di·a·'kaustik], f. -/-en. Opt: diacaustic.

diakaustisch [di·a·'kaustiʃ], a. Opt: diacaustic (curve, etc.).

Diaklas [di·a·'kla:s], m. -es/-e [-'kla:zəs/-'kla:zə]. Miner: diallage.

Diaklase [di·a·'kla:zə], f. -/-n, **Diaklasis** [di-'a:kla·zis], f. -/-sen [-'kla:zən]. Geol: diaclasis.

diaklastisch [di·a·'klastiʃ], a. Geol: diaclastic.

Diakon [di·a·'ko:n], m. -s & -en/-e(n). Ecc: deacon.

Diakonat [di·a·ko·'na:t], n. -(e)s/-e. Ecc: deaconship, diaconate, deaconry.

Diakonenamt, n. Ecc: deaconship, diaconate, deaconry.

Diakonie [di·a·ko·'ni:], f. -/. Ecc: diaconate.

Diakonikon [di·a·'ko:nikon], n. -s/-ka. Ecc.Arch: diaconicon; sacristy.

Diakonisse [di·a·ko·'nisə], f. -/-n. Ecc: deaconess.

Diakonuspflaster [di·'a:ko·nus-], n.=**Diachylonpflaster.**

Diakope [di·a·'ko:pə], f. -/-n. Surg: diacope.

Diakrise [di·a·'kri:zə], f. -/-n, **Diakrisis** [di-'a:kri·zis], f. -/-sen [-'kri:zən]. Med: diacrisis.

diakritisch [di·a·'kri:tiʃ], a. Gram: diakritisches Zeichen, diacritic(al) sign, mark.

diaktinisch [di·'ak'ti:niʃ], a. Opt: diactinic.

Dialekt [di·a·'lɛkt], m. -(e)s/-e, dialect.

Dialektik [di·a·'lɛktik], f. -/. (a) Phil: (art of) dialectic(s); dialectic method; (b) ich kann gegen seine D. nicht ankommen, I am helpless against the way he presents his arguments.

Dialektiker [di·a·'lɛktikər], m. -s/-, dialectician.

dialektisch [di·a·'lɛktiʃ], a. 1. Ling: dialectal. 2. Phil: dialectic(al).

Dialektologie [di·a·lɛkto·lo·'gi:], f. -/-n [-'gi:ən]. Ling: dialectology.

Diallag [di·a·'lak], m. -(e)s/-e [-'laks, -'la:gəs/-'la:gə]. Miner: diallage.

Diallele [di·a·'le:lə], f. -/-n. Log: dialelus.

Dialog [di·a·'lo:k], m. -(e)s/-e [-'lo:ks, -'lo:gəs/-'lo:gə], dialogue.

Dialogführung, f. dialogue.

dialogisch [di·a·'lo:giʃ], a. dialogic(al); in dialogue; in dialogue form; Sch: dialogische Lehrform, dialogic system of teaching.

dialogisieren [di·a·lo·gi·'zi:rən], v.tr. to turn (sth.) into a dialogue.

Dialogismus [di·a·lo·'gismus], m. -/-men. Rh: Log: dialogism.

Dialypetalen, die [di·a·ly·pe·'ta:lən]=**Choripetalen,** q.v. under **choripetal.**

Dialysator [di·a·ly·'za:tor], m. -s/-en [-za·'to:rən]. Ch: dialyser.

Dialyse [di·a·'ly:zə], f. -/-n. Ch: dialysis.

dialysierbar [di·a·ly·'zi:rba:r], a. Ch: dialysable.

dialysieren [di·a·ly·'zi:rən], v.tr. Ch: to dialyse.

Dialysierpapier, n. Ch: dialysing paper.

dialysisch, dialytisch [di·a·'ly:ziʃ, -'ly:tiʃ], a. Ch: dialytic.

diamagnetisch [di·a·ma'gne:tiʃ], a. diamagnetic.

Diamagnetismus [di·a·magne·'tismus], m. -/-men. Ph: diamagnetism.

Diamant¹ [di·a·'mant], m. -en/-en, diamond; schwarzer D., black diamond, carbonado; geschliffener, ungeschliffener, D., cut, rough, diamond; Diamanten fassen, to set diamonds; F: schwarze Diamanten, coal, F: black diamonds.

Diamant², m. f. Print: diamond; four-point or four-and-a-half-point type.

diamantartig, a. diamondlike, adamantine.

Diamantausgabe, f. Print: diamond edition.

Diamantbohrer, m., **Diamantbohrmaschine,** f. Min: diamond-drill.

Diamantbort, n. Lap: Ind: diamond fragments; Ind: (diamond) bort.

diamanten [di·a·'mantən], a. 1. adamantine; diamond (necklace, etc.); **diamantener Glanz,** adamantine lustre; **diamantene Krone,** diamond crown; **diamantene Hochzeit,** diamond wedding. 2. Lit: hard as diamonds, adamantine; **diamantene Ketten,** adamantine chains.

diamantenführend, a. Miner: diamantiferous.

Diamantengrube, f. Min: diamond mine.

Diamantengrund, m. diamond matrix.

Diamantenmine, f. diamond mine.

Diamantfarbe, f., **Diamantfarbstoff,** m. Ch: Ind: azodye.

Diamantfasan, m. Orn: Lady Amherst's pheasant.

Diamantfeile, f. Tls: diamond file.

Diamantfink, m. Orn: pardalote, diamond sparrow.

Diamantglanz, m. adamantine lustre.

Diamanthändler, m. diamond merchant.

diamantiert [di·a·man'ti:rt], a. Arch: (arch, etc.) with diamond ornament.

Diamantierung [di·a·man'ti:run], f. Arch: diamond ornament (on arches, etc.).

Diamantin [di·a·man'ti:n], n. -(e)s/. Ch: Ind: alundum, aluminium oxide.

Diamantkapsel, f. Gramophones: diamond cartridge.

Diamantkarbonat, n. Miner: carbonado, black diamond.

Diamantkette, f. diamond necklace.

Diamantkitt, m. Lap: Ind: diamond cement; galbanum.

Diamantknoten, m. Nau: diamond-knot.

Diamantpulver, m. diamond-dust.

Diamantquader, m. Constr: rustica diamond facet form.

Diamantring, m. diamond ring.

Diamantsäge, f. Tls: diamond saw.

Diamantscheibe, f. Lap: skive.

Diamantschleifen, n. diamond cutting.

Diamantschleifer, m. (pers.) diamond cutter.

Diamantschleiferei, f. 1. diamond cutting. 2. diamond-cutting workshop.

Diamantschleifscheibe, f. lapidary's mill.

Diamantschliff, m. 1. diamond cutting. 2. diamond cut.

Diamantschmuck, m. Jewel: (i) piece of diamond jewellery; (ii) coll. diamond jewellery, diamonds.

Diamantschnee, m. minute ice crystals in the atmosphere.

Diamantschrift, f. Print:=**Diamant².**

Diamantschwarz, n. diamond black.

Diamantspat, m. Miner: diamond spar, adamantine spar, corundum.

Diamantsplitter, m.pl. diamond sparks, diamond chips; seed-diamonds.

Diamantstahl, m. tool steel.

Diamantstaub, m. 1.=**Diamantpulver.** 2.=**Diamantschnee.**

Diamanttäubchen, n. Orn: diamond dove.

Diamanttinte, f. Ind: hydrofluoric solution used for etching on glass.

Diamantverzierung, f. Arch:=**Diamantierung.**

Diamantvogel, m. Orn: pardalote.

Diamantwerkzeug, n. diamond-tool.

Diameter [di·a·'me:tər, di·'a:me·tər], m. -s/-, diameter.

diametral [di·a·me·'tra:l], a. Geom: diametral, diametrical; d. gegenüberliegende Punkte, diametrically opposed points; d. entgegengesetzt, diametrically opposed.

Diametralebene, f. Geom: Cryst: diametral plane.

diametrisch [di·a·'me:triʃ], a. diametral.

Diamid [di·a·'mi:t], n. -s/. Ch: diamide.

Diamido- [di·'a·mi·do:-], comb.fm.=**Diamino-.**

Diamidobenzol [di·ɔa·mi·do·ben'tso:l], n. Ch: diaminobenzene.

Diamidophenol [di·ɔa·mi·do·fe·'no:l], n. Ch: diaminophenol, diamidophenol.

Diamin [di·ɔa·'mi:n], n. -s/-e. Ch: diamine.

Diaminfarbstoff, m. Dy: diamine dye.

Diamino- [di·ɔa·mi·no·-], comb.fm. Ch: diamino-; diamido-; **Diaminosäure** f, diamino acid; **Diaminodiphenyl** n, diamidodiphenyl.

Diaminogenfarbstoff, m. Ch: etc: disazo dye.

Diaminschwarz, n. Dy: diamine black.

Diaminurie [di·ɔa·mi·nu·'ri:], f. -/. Med: diaminuria.

Diamorphose [di·a·mor'fo:zə], f. -/-n, diamorphosis.

Diana [di·'a:na:]. 1. Pr.n.f. -s & Lit: -nens. Myth: Diana. 2. f. -/-s.=**Dianaaffe.** 3. f. -/. A.Ch: (silver) diana. 4. f. -/-s. Nau: A: morning watch.

Dianaaffe, m. Z: Diana monkey.

Dianaschuß, m. Nau: A: morning gun.

Diandria [di·'a:ndri·a:], n.pl. Bot: diandrous plants, diandria.

diandrisch [di·'andriʃ], a. Bot: diandrous.

Dianenbaum, m. A.Ch: arborescent silver.

Dianentempel, m. temple of Diana.

Dianilfarbstoff [di·ɔa·'ni:l-], m. Dy: dianil dye.

Dianthrenblau [di·ɔan'tre:n-], n. Ch: Dy: indigo blue.

Diapason [di·a·'pa:zon], m. & n. -s/-s & -e [-pa·'zo:nə]. Mus: diapason (in all senses).

Diapedese [di·a·pe·'de:zə], **Diapedesis** [di·a·'pe:de·zis], f. -/. Physiol: diapedesis.

Diapente [di·a·'pɛntə], f. -/-n. Mus: A: diapente.

Diaper ['daiɛpər], n. -s/-. Tex: diaper.

diaphan [di·a·'fa:n], a. diaphanous.

Diaphan(e)ität [di·a·fa·n(e)i·'tɛt], f. -/. diaphaneity.

Diaphorese [di·a·fo·'re:zə], **Diaphoresis** [di·a·'fo:re·zis], f. -/-sen [-fo·'re:zən]. Med: diaphoresis.

diaphoretisch [di·a·fo·'re:tiʃ], a. diaphoretic.

Diaphragma [di·a·'fragma:], n. -s/-men. 1. Anat: diaphragm. 2. Phot: diaphragm, F: stop. 3. El.-Ch: diaphragm.

Diaphragmenstrom, m. El: diaphragm current.

Diaphragmenverfahren, n. El.-Ch: diaphragm process.

Diaphyse [di·a·'fy:zə], f. -/-n. Anat: Bot: diaphysis.

Diapositiv [di·a·po·zi·'ti:f], n. Phot: transparency; (mounted) (lantern-)slide.

Diapositivbetrachter, m. Phot: slide viewer.

Diapositivplatte, f. Phot: diapositive plate.

Diarchie [di·ɔar'çi:], f. -/-n [-'çi:ən], diarchy.

Diärese [di·ɔɛ·'re:zə], f. -/-n. Ling: diaeresis.

Diarium [di·'a:rium], n. -s/-rien, diary; note-book.

Diarrhöe [di·a·'rø:], f. -/-n [-/-'rø:ən]. Med: diarrhoea.

Diarthrose [di·ɔar'tro:zə], **Diarthrosis** [di-'artro·zis], f. -/-sen [-'tro:zən]. Anat: diarthrosis.

diarthrotisch [di·ar'tro:tiʃ], a. Anat: diarthrodial.

Diaspora [di·'aspo:ra:], f. -/. Rel: diaspora.

diastaltisch [di·a·'staltiʃ], a. Physiol: diastaltic.

Diastase [di·a·'sta:zə], f. -/-n. 1. Ch: Bio-Ch: diastase. 2. Surg: diastasis.

Diastasewirkung, f. Bio-Ch: diastatic action.

Diasterstadium [di·'astər-], n. Biol: diaster stage, anaphase.

Diastole [di·a·sto·'le:, di·a·'sto:lə], f. -/-n [di·a·'sto:lən]. Pros: Physiol: diastole.

diastolisch [di·a·'sto:liʃ], a. Physiol: diastolic.

Diastylon [di·'asty·lon], n. -s/-la. Gr.Arch: diastyle.

Diät¹ [di·'ɛt], f. -/-en. 1. diet; nach einer D. leben, to be on a diet; eine strenge D. einhalten, to keep to a strict diet. 2. pl. Diäten, Adm: etc: daily allowance, remuneration (esp. of member of parliament, juryman, delegate, etc.).

diät², adv. d. leben, to live on a diet, to diet.

Diätar [di·'ɛ'ta:r], m. -s/-e. Adm: (junior) official paid on a daily basis.

Diatessaron [di·a·'tɛsa·ron], n. -s/-ra. Mus: B.Lit: diatessaron.

Diätetik [di·ɛ·'te:tik], f. -/-en, dietetics.

Diätetiker [di·ɛ·'te:tikər], m. -s/-, dietician.

diätetisch [di·ɛ·'te:tiʃ], a. dietary, U.S: dietetic.

diatherman [di·a·tɛr'ma:n], a. Ph: diathermic, diathermanous.

Diathermie [di·a·tɛr'mi:], f. -/-n [-'mi:ən]. Med: diathermy.

Diathese [di·a·'te:zə], f. -/-n. Ling: Med: diathesis.

Diäthyl- [di·ɔɛ·'ty:l-], comb.fm. Ch: diethyl-.

Diätist [di·ɛ·'tist], m. -en/-en=**Diätar.**

Diatomee [di·a·to·'me:ə], f. -/-n [-'me:ən]. Algae: diatom; **die Diatomeen,** the diatoms, the diatomeae, the bacillaryophyceae.

Diatomeenerde, f. Miner: kieselguhr, infusorial earth.

Diatomeenschlamm, m. diatom-ooze.

diatomisch [di·a·'to:miʃ], a. Ch: diatomic.

Diatomit [di·a·to·'mi:t], n. -(e)s/. Geol: diatomite; infusorial earth.

Diatonik [di·a·'to:nik], f. -/. Mus: diatonic system.

diatonisch [di·a·'to:niʃ], a. Mus: diatonic (scale, etc.).

Diatribe [di·a·'tri:bə], f. -/-n, diatribe.

Diazethyl- [di·ɔa'tse·ty:l-], comb.fm. Ch: diacetyl-.

Diazeturie [di·ɔa·tse·tu·'ri:], f. -/-n [-'ri:ən]. Med: diacet(on)uria.

Diazo- [di·'a:tso-], comb.fm. Ch: diazo-; **Diazoverbindungen** f pl, diazo compounds; **Diazobenzol** n, diazobenzene; **Diazofarbstoff** m, diazo dye.

Dibbelmaschine, f. Agr: drop drill; dibbling machine, machine dibble, dibbler.

dibbeln, *v.tr. Agr:* to sow (seeds) in clusters; to dibble in (seeds, etc.).

Dibbelsaat, *f. Agr:* (*a*) dibbling; drill-sowing in clusters; (*b*) dibbled seed(s).

Dicarbonsäure [di·karˈboːn-], *f. Ch:* dicarboxylic acid.

dich. 1. *pers.pron. acc.* of **du,** *q.v.* **2.** *refl.pron.* yourself.

Dichasium [diˈçaːzium], *n.* **-s/-sien.** *Bot:* dichasium.

Dichinin [di·çi·ˈniːn], *n.* **-s/.** *Ch:* diquinine.

Dichinol [di·çi·ˈnoːl], *n.* **-s/.** *Ch:* diquinol.

Dichinolin [di·çi·no·ˈliːn], *n.* **-s/.** *Ch:* diquinoline.

Dichinoyl [di·çi·no·ˈyːl], *n.* **-s/.** *Ch:* diquinoyl.

Dichlor- [di·ˌkloːr-], *comb.fm. Ch:* dichloro-; . . . dichloride; **Dichloraceton** *n,* dichloroacetone; **Dichloräthylen** *n,* ethylene dichloride.

dichogam [diço·ˈgaːm], *a. Bot:* dichogamous.

Dichogamen [diço·ˈgaːmən], *pl. Bot:* dichogamous plants.

Dichogamie [diço·ga·ˈmiː], *f.* **-/-n** [-ˈmiːən]. *Bot:* dichogamy.

dichotomal [diço·to·ˈmaːl], *a. Bot:* dichotomous.

Dichotomie [diço·to·ˈmiː], *f.* **-/-n** [-ˈmiːən]. *Astr: Bot: Log: etc:* dichotomy.

dichotomisch [diço·ˈtoːmiʃ], *a. Log: Astr:* dichotomic, dichotomous.

Dichroismus [di·kro·ˈismus], *m.* **-/.** *Cryst:* dichroism.

dichroitisch [di·kro·ˈiːtiʃ], *a. Cryst:* dichroic.

Dichromasie [di·kro·ma·ˈziː], *f.* **-/.** *Med:* dichromic vision, dichromasy.

Dichromat [di·kro·ˈmaːt], **-(e)s/-e. 1.** *n. Ch:*=**Bichromat. 2.** *m. Med:* person with dichromatic vision, dichromat.

dichromatisch [di·kro·ˈmaːtiʃ], *a.* dichromatic.

Dichrosalz [ˈdiːkro·-], *n. Ch:* dichroic salt.

Dichroskop [di·kro·ˈskoːp], *n.* **-s/-e.** *Ph:* dichro(i)-scope.

dicht. I. *a.* **1.** (*a*) *Ph:* (*of body, metal, medium, etc.*) dense; **optisch d.,** optically dense; (*b*) (*of cloth, etc.*) close-woven, of dense texture; (*of fog, darkness, rain, etc.*) dense; (*of fog*) thick; **es fiel dichter Schnee,** the snow fell thickly; (*c*) *Geol:* (*of mass*) compact; (*of rock, etc.*) close-grained, dense-grained; (*d*) *Phot:* dense (negative); (*e*) (*of corn, forest, hair, crowd, etc.*) thick; (*of thicket*) close; **dichte Augenbrauen,** thick, bushy, eyebrows; **eine dichte Menschenmenge,** a thick, dense, crowd; **in dichten Scharen,** in crowds; in hordes; **eine dichte Hecke,** a close-set hedge; (*f*) (*of style, etc.*) concise; compact; (*g*) *Statistics:* **dichtester Wert,** mode. **2.** (*a*) (*of roof, shoes, etc.*) (rain-, water-)proof; **die Stiefel sind nicht mehr d.,** the boots are no longer watertight; (*b*) (*of barrel*) tight; (*of tank, etc.*) leak-proof; (*of piping*) sound; **dichte Nietung,** close, tight, riveting; (*c*) *Nau:* **ein Schiff d. machen,** to make a ship tight, to caulk a ship; (*d*) *F:* **den Laden d. machen,** to close the shop, to lock up; to shut up, lock up, the house.

II. **dicht,** *adv.* **1.** (*also* **dicht-,** *comb.fm.*) (*a*) densely, closely, thickly; **d. gewebt, dichtgewebt,** close-woven, closely woven; (*b*) (growing, etc.) thickly, densely; **d. belaubt, dichtbelaubt,** with thick foliage, thick with leaves; **dichtbehaart,** (*of pers.*) with a thick growth of hair, with thick hair, hairy; (*of animal*) with a thick coat; *see also* **behaart; diese Gegend ist d. besiedelt, bewohnt,** this region is thickly, densely, populated; *see also* **dichtbesiedelt; d. gereiht,** (i) (*of plants*) in close rows; (ii) (*of people*) close-ranked; **das Korn steht d.,** the corn is thick; **die Wiese ist mit Schlüsselblumen d. bestanden,** the meadow is covered with cowslips; **der Kohl ist zu d. gepflanzt,** the cabbages are planted too closely; **d. beschriebene, dichtbeschriebene, Seiten,** closely-written pages; (*c*) (*of material, etc.*) **d. halten,** to be (water-, rain-, sound-)proof; *see also* **dichthalten;** (*of window, door, etc.*) **d. schließen,** to shut tightly; to be draught-proof; **d. schließende Fenster, Türen,** closely fitting windows, doors; **die Fenster waren d. verhängt,** the windows were heavily curtained; **die Fensterläden waren d. verschlossen,** the shutters were tightly shut; *see also* **dichtgeschlossen. 2.** (*a*) close (an, bei, to); **er stand d. am Tisch,** he stood, was standing, close to the table; **bring deinen Stuhl d. ans Feuer,** bring your chair near, close, to the fire; **d. an der Wand stehen,** to stand close to, against, the wall; **sie sind uns d. auf den Fersen,** they are hard on our heels, they are close on us; **d. beisammen,** close together; cheek by jowl; **d. an d., d. bei d.,** (sitting, standing, etc.) close together; **d. daneben,** hard by; close to it, them; **der Bach fließt d. am Haus vorbei,** the brook runs close to the house; **ihre Augen, Zähne, stehen zu d. beieinander,** her eyes are too close-set, her teeth are too close together, rather crowded; *Nau:* **d. am Wind halten,** to hug the wind; **d. beim Wind laufen,** to sail close to the wind; (*b*) **er stand d. vor seinem Examen,** he was about to take his examination, his examination was very near; **d. am Ziel,** near the goal; near the end.

dichtbesiedelt, *attrib. a.* thickly, densely, populated (region, etc.).

dichtbewaldet, *attrib. a.* heavily forested, thickly wooded.

dichtbrennen, *v.tr. sep.* (*conj. like* **brennen**) *Cer:* to vitrify.

Dichte, *f.* **-/. 1.** *Ph: El:* density (of body, gas, etc., *El:* of current); *Ph: Ch:* specific gravity, specific weight; *El:* **magnetische D., D. des magnetischen Feldes,** flux density. **2.** density, thickness (of fog, etc.); density (of population); closeness (of weave); thickness (of wood, hair, etc.); denseness (of building material). **3.** *Phot:* density (of negative). **4.** *Tex: etc:* closeness (of threads).

Dichteisen, *n. Nau:* caulking-iron.

dichteln, *v.i.* (*haben*) to poetize, to dabble in poetry.

Dichtemesser, *m. Ph:* densimeter; areometer, hydrometer.

Dichtemessung, *f. Ph:* densimetry.

dichten[1]. I. *v.tr.* to make (sth.) (water-, air-, steam-, gas-)tight; to caulk, hammer (boiler seams, etc.); *Nau:* to caulk (ship, seams, etc.); *Mec.E: Mch:* to pack (gland, etc.); to tighten (joint, seams, etc.); *Ind: etc:* to lute (retort, crucible, etc.); to seal, joint (pipe, etc.).

II. *vbl s.* **1. Dichten,** *n. in vbl senses.* **2. Dichtung,** *f.* (*a*)=II. 1; (*b*) joint; seal; (packing) gasket; (*c*) *Mec.E: etc:*=**Dichtungsmaterial;** (*d*) *Mec.E:* packing washer; expanding washer.

dichten[2]. I. *v.* **1.** *A:* (*a*) *v.tr.* to think (of, about, sth.); to think, reflect (how to do sth.); to meditate (sth., on sth.); (*b*) *v.i.* (*haben*) **auf etwas** *acc.,* **nach etwas, d.,** to contrive sth.; to think of a way to achieve sth. **2.** *A: v.tr.*=**erdichten. 3.** *v.tr.* to compose, write (poem, novel, etc.); **Verse, Lieder, Dramen, Romanzen, Epen, d.,** to compose, write, verses, songs; to write dramas, romances, epics; *abs.* **d.,** to write poetry.

II. *vbl s.* **1. Dichten,** *n.* (*a*) *in vbl senses of* I. 1, 2; *also:* **sein D. und Trachten auf etwas** *acc.* **richten,** to direct one's efforts, one's thoughts, to(wards) sth.; **all sein D. und Trachten war darauf gerichtet, ging darauf (aus), wie . . . ,** his whole mind was set on the problem how . . . ; *B:* **denn das D. des menschlichen Herzens ist böse von Jugend auf,** for the imagination of man's heart is evil from his youth; (*b*) *in vbl senses of* I. 3; *also:* composition (of verses, etc.). **2. Dichtung,** *f.* (*a*)=II. 1 (*b*); (*b*) imagination; fiction; **das Reich der D.,** the realm of fiction; (*c*) (i) poetry; (ii) (creative) literature; **lyrische, epische, D.,** lyric, epic, poetry; **dramatische D.,** drama; **die französische D. des neunzehnten Jahrhunderts,** (i) French poetry, (ii) French literature, of the nineteenth century; (*d*) *coll.* poetic work; literary writings; **diese Anthologie gibt einen guten Überblick über seine gesamte D.,** this anthology adequately represents his entire poetic work; (*e*) poetic style; **die Besonderheiten Goethescher D.,** the characteristics of Goethe's poetic style; (*f*) poem; poetic work; work (of literature); **eine epische D.,** an epic poem, an epic; **eine dramatische D. in drei Akten,** a drama in three acts; **X liest aus seinen eigenen Dichtungen,** X reads, will read, from his own poems.

Dichter, *m.* **-s/-,** poet; writer (of creative literature), author.

Dichterfeuer, *n.* poetic fire.

dichterisch, *a.* poetic; **dichterisches Werk, Schaffen,** poetic work; literary work; poetry; **dichterische Freiheit,** poetic licence.

Dichterling, *m.* **-s/-e.** *Pej:* poetaster, rhymester.

Dichtermund, *m. Lit:* **aus D.,** from the lips of a, the, poet.

Dichternarzisse, *f. Bot:* poet's narcissus, pheasant's-eye.

Dichteschreiber, *m. Ph:* recording densimeter.

dichtgedrängt, *attrib. a.* closely packed (spectators, etc.); *adv.* **d. stehen,** to stand crowded together, closely packed.

dichtgeschart, *adv.* **d. stehen,** (i) to stand densely packed; (ii) to stand in serried ranks.

dichtgeschlossen, *attrib. a.* closed, serried (ranks, etc.); *see also* **dicht** II. 1.

Dichtgewinde, *n. Mec.E:* sealing thread.

dichthalten, *v.i. sep.* (*strong*) (*haben*) *F:* to hold one's tongue, *F:* to keep one's mouth shut, not to blab, to keep mum; **sie wird schon d.,** don't worry, she won't say anything; *see also* **dicht** II. 1.

Dichthammer, *m. Tls:* caulking-hammer.

Dichtheit, *f.* **1.** density (of fog, etc.); compactness (of mass, etc.); *cp.* **Dichte** 2. **2.** *Mec.E:* tightness (of pipe, cylinder, etc.).

Dichtigkeit, *f.* **1.** *Ph:* density. **2.** imperviousness (of material, etc.). **3.** compactness (of style).

Dichtigkeitsmaximum, *n. Ph:* maximum density (of water, etc.).

Dichtigkeitsmesser, *m.*=**Dichtemesser.**

Dichtkunst, *f.* (art of) poetry; (art of) creative writing; poetic expression.

Dichtmeißel, *m. Tls:* caulking-chisel; caulking-tool.

Dichtung[1], *f. see* **dichten**[1].

Dichtung[2], *f. see* **dichten**[2].

Dichtungsart, *f.* (i) poetic genre, style; (ii) literary genre, style.

Dichtungsbüchse, *f. Mch:* stuffing-box.

Dichtungshaut, *f. Constr:* watertight facing.

Dichtungskern, *m. Civ.E:* watertight core (of wall); *Hyd.E:* core-wall (of dam).

Dichtungsmanschette, *f. Mec.E:* (*a*) (packing) gasket; (*b*)=**Dichtungsmuffe.**

Dichtungsmaterial, *n. Mec.E: etc:* packing, caulking; sealing material.

Dichtungsmuffe, *f. Mec.E:* sealing, packing, sleeve *or* collar; sleeve joint.

Dichtungsring, Dichtungsscheibe, *f. Mec.E:* packing-ring; packing washer; expanding washer; (packing) gasket.

Dichtungsschirm, Dichtungsschleier, *m. Hyd.E:* grout(ing) curtain, diaphragm.

Dichtungsschürze, *f. Hyd.E:*=**Dichtungsvorlage.**

Dichtungsstoff, *m. Mec.E:*=**Dichtungsmaterial.**

Dichtungsvorlage, *f. Hyd.E:* (waterproof) blanket.

Dichtungswand, *f. Tchn:* diaphragm.

Dichtungsweise, *f.*=**Dichtungsart.**

Dichtwerg, *n. Mec.E:* oakum.

Dichtwerk, *n.* poetic work; poem.

dick. I. *a.* **1.** (*of wall, material, thread, tree-trunk, paper, etc.*) thick; (*of book*) thick, bulky; (*of raindrops, etc.*) thick, heavy, large; (*of fruit, etc.*) large, big; (*of pers.*) fat, corpulent, stout; (*of legs, etc.*) thick, fat; (*of lips*) full, thick; (*of maggot, snail, worm, etc.*) fat; **eine dicke Eiche,** a stout oak; **ein dickes Brett,** a thick board; **ein dicker Mantel,** a thick, heavy, warm, coat; **dickes Haar,** (i) coarse hair; (ii) thick hair; **das Brot in dicke Scheiben schneiden,** to cut the bread thick, into thick slices; **der Regen fiel in dicken Tropfen,** heavy drops of rain were falling; **der Schnee fiel in dicken Flocken,** the snow fell in thick flakes; **dicke Tränen rollten ihr die Backen hinunter,** large tears ran down her cheeks; **ein dicker Busen,** a large bosom; **ein dicker Bauch,** a large stomach; (*forthright description*) a big, fat, belly; (*children's, women's or semi-humorous language*) a fat tummy; **dicke Backen,** fat, chubby, cheeks; **eine dicke Backe haben,** to have a swollen cheek; (*of pers.*) **d. werden,** to get, grow, fat, to put on fat, weight; to get stout; **Kartoffeln machen d.,** potatoes are fattening; *F:* **sich d. und satt essen,** to eat one's fill; **einen dicken Kopf haben,** (i) to have a large, big, head; (ii) *F:* to be stubborn; (iii) (*after drinking*) to have a thick head; *F:* **er zog mit einem dicken Kopf ab,** he went off in a huff; **ein dickes Fell haben,** to be insensitive, *F:* to have a thick skin, a thick hide, to be thick-skinned; **ein dicker Geldbeutel,** a fat purse; **ein dicker Unternehmer,** a large industrialist; **dicke Töne reden,** to brag, *F:* to talk big; *see also* **Bohne** 1 (*a*), **Ende** 2 (*a*). **2.** (*dimension*) thick; **einen halben Zentimeter d.,** half a centimetre thick; **eine zwei Fuß dicke Wand,** a wall (that is) two feet thick; **das Brett ist zwei Finger d.,** the board is two fingers thick; **wie d. ist das Eis?** how thick is the ice? **3.** (*a*) (*of liquid*) thick; syrupy; **dicke Tinte,** thick, muddy, ink; **dickes Blut,** thick blood; **dicker Obstsaft,** syrupy fruit juice; **dicke Milch,** (solidified) sour milk; curds; **dicke Erbsensuppe,** thick pea soup; **dicke Soße,** thick sauce; *Cu:* **d. werden,** (*of milk*) to become thick; (*of custard, sauce, etc.*) to thicken; *F:* **mit j-m durch d. und dünn gehen,** to go through thick and thin with s.o.; *Prov:* **Blut ist dicker als Wasser,** blood is thicker than water; (*b*) (*of fog, mist*) thick, heavy, dense; **dicke Luft,** (i) stale, bad, air; smoky air; *F:* fug; (ii) *F:* tense atmosphere; *F:* **hier ist dicke Luft,** trouble is brewing here; feeling is running high; *Nau:* **dickes Wetter,** thick, foggy, weather.

4. *F:* **dicke Freunde, Freundschaft,** close, intimate, friends, friendship; **die Schmidts und die Meiers sind dicke Freunde,** the Schmidts are very thick with the Meiers. **5.** *F:* **das Dicke,** the solid parts (of liquid); the sediment; the dregs; the solid parts, *F:* the solid bits (in soup, etc.); *cp.* **Dicke.**

II. **dick,** *adv.* **1.** thick, thickly, in a thick layer; **der Staub liegt d. auf dem Tisch,** the table is thick with dust; **ein d. mit Butter bestrichenes Brot,** a slice of bread thickly spread with butter; **streich die Butter nicht zu d.,** don't spread the butter too thickly, *F:* too thick; **das Brot d. schneiden,** to cut the bread thick; **Farbe, usw., d. auftragen,** to put paint, etc., on thickly, heavily; *F:* **d. auftragen,** to exaggerate; *F:* to pile it on; to lay it on thick, with a trowel; **sich d. anziehen,** to dress oneself warmly; **d. angezogen,** thickly clad; **sein Knie war d. angeschwollen,** his knee was very swollen; (*of bird*) **sich d. aufplustern,** to puff itself up. **2.** (*of liquid*) **d. fließen,** to run thickly; *Cu:* **etwas d. einkochen lassen,** to boil sth. till it thickens. **3.** *F:* **es d. hinter den Ohren haben,** to be cunning, astute, sly; **es d. haben,** (i) *F:* to be fed up; (ii) to be well off, to live in plenty, to live on the fat of the land; **mit j-m d. befreundet sein,** to be very thick with s.o.; *see also* **dick(e)tun (sich).**

Dickauszug, *m. Ch:* inspissated, thick, extract.

dickbäuchig, *a.* (*of pers.*) corpulent; stout; pot-bellied; (*of vase, jug, etc.*) big-bellied.

dickbeinig, *a.* (*of pers.*) with fat legs.

dickbestanden, *attrib. a.* (*area, etc.*) thickly, closely, set, covered (with shrubs, trees, etc.).

dickbewachsen, *attrib. a.* (*soil, etc.*) covered with thick growth.

Dickblatt, *n. Bot:* (*a*) crassula; (*b*) live-long, orpin(e).

Dickblattgewächse, *n.pl. Bot:* crassulaceae.

Dickbohne, *f. Bot: Cu:* broad bean.

Dickdarm, *m. Anat:* colon, large intestine, *F:* great gut.

Dickdarmentzündung, *f. Med:* colitis.

Dickdolle, *f. Nau:* bollard.

Dickdruckpapier, *n. Paperm:* bulky, bulking, featherweight, paper.

Dicke, *f.* -/. **1.** thickness (of wall, material, thread, tree-trunk, paper, etc.); thickness, bulkiness (of book); fatness, corpulence, stoutness (of pers.); thickness, fatness, largeness (of legs, stomach, etc.); fullness, thickness (of lips); swollenness (of cheek); thickness (of hair); coarseness, strength (of single hair); largeness, size (of hailstones, fruit, etc.). **2.** (*dimension*) thickness; diameter (of screw, nail, wire, rope, etc.); perimeter (of tree-trunk); **die D. der Mauer beträgt zwei Fuß,** the wall is two feet thick, two feet in thickness; **ein Draht von zwei Millimeter D.,** wire two millimetres thick, two millimetres in diameter; **Bretter von einem halben Zoll D.,** half-inch boards, boards half an inch thick; **die D. einer Steinlage,** the thickness of a course; *Carp:* **auf D. hobeln,** to thickness (plank, etc.). **3.** (*a*) thickness, syrupy consistency (of liquid); thickness, denseness (of fog, etc.); (*b*) (relative) thickness, consistency, consistence (of liquid); **die D. der Brühe,** the thickness of the broth. **4.** -/-n. *Metall:* thickness (piece) (of casting).

dicken, *v.tr.* to thicken (liquid); to concentrate, to inspissate (liquid).

Dickenhobelmaschine, *f.* = **Dicktenhobelmaschine.**

Dickenmesser, *m. Tchn:* thickness-gauge; feeler-gauge; set of feelers; slide-gauge; calliper gauge; calliper compass, (pair of) callipers; micrometer; sliding calliper; *Ph:* pachymeter.

Dickenzirkel, *m.* = **Dickzirkel.**

Dickerchen, *n.* -s/-. *F:* fat child, *F:* little dumpling.

dick(e)tun (sich), *v.refl. sep. F:* to give oneself airs, to puff oneself up; **er tut sich gern dick(e),** he likes to show off; **er tut sich gern dick(e) mit seiner Kraft,** he likes to show off his strength.

Dickfarbe, *f.* thick colour; body colour.

dickfellig, *a.* (*a*) *Z:* with a thick skin *or* coat; (*b*) *F:* (*of pers.*) thick-skinned; **d. sein,** (i) to be sluggish, phlegmatic; (ii) to be insensitive; *F:* to be thick-skinned, to have a thick skin, hide.

dickflüssig, *a.* (*of liquid, paste, etc.*) thick, running thickly; semi-liquid; syrupy; viscid; viscous.

Dickflüssigkeit, *f.* thickness (of liquid, etc.); syrupy consistency, semi-liquid state (of liquid, etc.); viscidity; viscosity.

dickfrüchtig, *a.* with large fruit.

Dickfuß, *m.* **1.** *Fung:* boletus pachypus. **2.** *Bot:* (*a*) waterpest; (*b*) pachypodium. **3.** *Orn:* stone curlew.

dickgrell, *a.* (*of pig-iron*) dead-white.

dickgriffig, *a.* (*of paper*) bulky; **d. sein,** to bulk high.

dickhaarig, *a.* with coarse hair; (*of wool*) coarse.

Dickhäuter, *m.* -s/-, (*a*) *Z:* pachyderm; **die Dickhäuter,** the pachyderma; (*b*) *F:* thick-skinned person.

dickhäutig, *a.* thick-skinned, *Z:* pachydermatous; *F:* (*of pers.*) thick-skinned.

Dickheit, *f.* = **Dicke** 1, 3 (*a*).

Dickhorn, *n. Z:* big-horn.

Dickicht, *n.* -(e)s/-e, (*a*) thicket; thick undergrowth; (*b*) *For:* young forest.

Dickkochen, *n.* concentrating, thickening (of liquid) (by heat *or* steam).

Dickkolben, *m.pl. Bot:* amorphophallus.

Dickkopf, *m.* **1.** (*a*) stubborn person; (*b*) **einen D. haben,** to be stubborn, *F:* pigheaded. **2.** *Ich:* chub. **3.** *Ent:* = **Dickkopffalter.**

Dickkopffalter, *m. Ent:* skipper, butterfly of the family *hesperiidae.*

dickköpfig, *a.* stubborn, *F:* pigheaded.

Dickkopfweizen, *m. Agr:* squarehead wheat.

dickleibig, *a.* fat, stout, corpulent; (*of book*) bulky, *F:* fat.

dicklich, *a.* (*a*) (*of legs, etc.*) fattish; (*of pers.*) stoutish; (*of baby*) chubby; (*of child*) plump; (*of fruit, etc.*) largish; (*of paper, material, etc.*) thickish; (*b*) (*of liquid*) (moderately) thick, thickish; running thickly.

dicklippig, *a.* thick-lipped, with full lips.

Dickmaische, *f. Brew:* thick mash.

dickmäulig, *a.* (animal) with a large muzzle *or* snout; *F:* big-mouthed (pers.).

Dickmilch, *f. Cu:* (solidified) sour milk; curds.

Dickmühle, *f. Tex:* fulling mill.

dicknasig, *a.* with, having, a thick, fat, nose.

Dicknuß, *f. Bot:* Constantinople hazel-nut.

Dicköl, *n.* (*a*) thick oil of turpentine; (*b*) stand oil, thickened linseed oil.

Dickölfirnis, *m.* (thick) oil varnish.

Dickpfanne, *f. Ch: etc:* concentration pan.

Dickrübe, *f. Bot: Agr:* beet; mangel-wurzel.

Dicksaft, *m. Sug-R:* concentrated juice, syrup.

Dickschädel, *m. F:* = **Dickkopf 1.**

dickschädelig, *a. F:* = **dickköpfig.**

dickschalig, *a.* (*of fruit*) with a thick skin *or* peel; thick-skinned; (*of egg, etc.*) thick-shelled; (*of grain*) husky.

Dickschlamm, *m. Min:* thick mud.

dickschnäb(e)lig, *a.* (*of bird*) thick-billed.

Dickschnabelkrähe, *f. Orn:* jungle-crow.

Dickschnabellumme, *f. Orn:* Brünnich's guillemot, Brünnich's murre.

Dickschnabelmöwe, *f. Orn:* Pacific gull.

Dickschnabelpinguin, *m. Orn:* Victoria penguin.

Dickschnabelsturmvogel, *m. Orn:* thick-billed prion.

Dickspülung, *f. Min:* fluid mud.

dickstämmig, *a.* (*of tree*) with a thick trunk.

Dickstein, *m. Lap:* table with conic base.

Dickte, *f.* -/-n. **1.** (*a*) *A. & Tchn:* = **Dicke;** (*b*) *Print:* width (of letter). **2.** *Woodw:* (*a*) thin sheet of wood; sliced veneer; (*b*) = **Dicktenhobelmaschine.**

Dickteer, *m.* thick tar, heavy tar.

Dicktenabrichtmaschine, *f. Carp: etc:* timber thicknessing machine.

Dicktenhobelmaschine, *f. Carp:* timber sizer; thicknessing machine.

Dicktenschablone, *f. Mec.E: etc:* feeler-gauge.

Dicktuer, *m.* -s/-, boaster; braggart; self-important person.

Dicktuerei, *f.* -/. boasting, bragging; making oneself self-important.

dicktuerisch, *a.* boastful, bragging, self-important (manner, etc.).

Dicktun, *n.* = **Dicktuerei.**

Dickung, *f.* -/-en. *Ven:* = **Dickicht.**

dickwandig, *a.* thick-walled; with a thick coating, lining.

Dickwanst, *m.* (*a*) big, fat, belly; *F:* pot-belly; (*b*) fat fellow; *F:* pot-bellied chap; *P:* fat-guts.

dickwollig, *a.* (sheep, etc.) with a thick fleece.

Dickwurz, *f.* = **Dickrübe.**

Dickzirkel, *m. Tchn:* outside callipers; **doppelter D.,** double-calliper.

Dickzüngler, *m.* -s/-. *Rept:* agamoid.

Dictum [ˈdiktum], *n.* -s/-ta, dictum, saying.

Dicyan [di·tsy·ˈaːn], *n.* -/. = **Dizyan.**

Didaktik [di·ˈdaktik], *f.* -/. (*a*) didactics; (*b*) didacticism; didactic manner.

Didaktiker [di·ˈdaktikər], *m.* -s/-, didactician; *Pej:* didactic person.

didaktisch [di·ˈdaktiʃ], *a.* didactic; **didaktische Dichtung,** (i) didactic poetry; (ii) didactic poem.

dideldum, *int.* diddle-dee, tra-la-la.

Didelphier, Didelphyer [di·ˈdɛlfi·ər], *m.pl. Z:* didelphia.

Dido [ˈdiːdoː]. *Pr.n.f.* -s. *Lt.Lit:* Dido.

Didym [di·ˈdyːm], *n.* -s/. *Ch:* didymium.

Didyma [ˈdiːdy·maː]. *Pr.n.n.* -s. *A.Geog:* Didyma.

Didymi [ˈdiːdy·miː], *m.pl. Med: A:* testicles.

didymisch [di·ˈdyːmiʃ], *a. Bot:* didymous.

Didymitis [di·dy·ˈmiːtis], *f.* -/. *Med:* orchitis.

Didymoi [ˈdiːdy·moy]. *Pr.n.n.* -s. *A.Geog:* Didyma.

Didymos, Didymus [ˈdiːdy·mos, -mus]. *Pr.n.m.* -'. *B.Hist: Gr.Lit:* Didymus.

die *see* **der.**

Dieb, *m.* -(e)s/-e. **1.** thief; **kleiner D.,** pilferer; filcher; petty thief; **haltet den D.!** stop thief! **D. geistigen Eigentums,** stealer of ideas; *F:* literary magpie; *B:* **wie ein D. in der Nacht,** as a thief in the night; **wie ein D. in der Nacht kommen,** to take s.o. unawares, to steal upon s.o.; *Prov:* **Gelegenheit macht Diebe,** opportunity makes the thief; **die kleinen Diebe hängt man, die großen läßt man laufen,** great rogues get off unscathed and the small fry get hanged; one law for the rich and another for the poor. **2.** *F:* rascal; rogue, knave. **3.** (*on candle*) thief, stranger. **4.** *Hort:* sucker. **5.** *Ent:* ptinus.

-dieb, *comb.fm. m.* ... stealer; ... thief; **Schafdieb,** sheep-stealer; **Hühnerdieb,** chicken-stealer, chicken-thief; **Hoteldieb,** hotel thief; **Museumsdieb,** museum thief.

dieben, *v.tr. & i.* (*haben*) to thieve.

Dieberei, *f.* -/-en, (i) thieving; thievery; (ii) (petty) theft; **seine ständigen Diebereien,** his constant thieving.

Dieb(e)sbande, *f.* band, pack, of thieves.

Dieb(e)sehre, *f.* **1.** honour of a thief. **2.** honour among thieves.

Diebesfalle, *f.* trap for thieves; burglar alarm, thief alarm.

Dieb(e)sfinger, *m. F:* **Diebesfinger** *pl* **haben,** (i) to be lightfingered; (ii) to have nimble fingers.

Dieb(e)sgeselle, *m. Pej:* thief.

Dieb(e)sgesindel, *n.* pack, band, of thieves.

Dieb(e)sglück, *n.* luck of the damned.

Dieb(e)sgut, *n.* stolen goods; booty; *F:* haul, loot, (the) swag.

Dieb(e)shandwerk, *n.* thieving; thievery.

Dieb(e)sschlüssel, *m.* skeleton key; picklock.

diebessicher, *a.* theft-proof; anti-theft; unpickable (lock).

Dieb(e)svolk, *n.* (*a*) race of thieves; (*b*) pack of thieves.

Dieb(e)swerkzeuge, *n.pl.* housebreaking implements, tools.

Diebin, *f.* -/-innen, (female) thief.

diebisch, *a.* thievish; thieving; pilfering; **diebische Elster,** thieving magpie; **d. wie eine Elster,** thievish as a magpie; **ein diebisches Volk,** a thieving people, a race of thieves; **auf diebische Art,** in the manner of thieves; *F:* **diebische Freude,** malicious joy, pleasure; **diebische Kälte,** bitter cold; *adv.* **sich d. (über etwas** *acc.*) **freuen,** to gloat (over sth.).

Diebsameise, *f. Ent:* thief ant.

diebsfest, *a.* = **diebessicher.**

Diebsinseln, die. *Pr.n. Geog:* the Marianas Islands, *A:* the Ladrones.

Diebskäfer, *m. Ent:* ptinus.

Diebskrabbe, *f. Crust:* robber-crab, coconut crab, purse-crab.

Diebsnest, *n.* thieves' kitchen; thieves' den.

Diebspack, *n.* pack of thieves; band of thieves.

Diebssprache, *f.* thieves' cant.

Diebstahl, *m.* -(e)s/=e, (i) larceny, theft; (ii) (act of) larceny, (act of) theft; **einen D., Diebstähle, begehen,** to commit larceny, to commit a theft, to commit thefts; **D. geistigen Eigentums,** stealing of ideas; *Jur:* **einfacher D.,** (simple) larceny; plain theft; **schwerer D.,** aggravated theft, aggravated larceny; robbery; **bewaffneter D.,** armed robbery, robbery under arms; **räuberischer D.,** open, violent, larceny; robbery with violence; **geringfügiger, geringer, D.,** petty larceny, petty theft.

-diebstahl, *comb.fm. m.* -stealing; -theft; theft from ...; **Schafdiebstahl,** sheep-stealing; **Pferdediebstahl,** horse-stealing, horse-theft; **Hühnerdiebstahl,** chicken-stealing; **Hoteldiebstahl,** hotel-theft; **Museumsdiebstahl,** theft from museums.

Diebstahlversicherung, *f.* burglary insurance.

Diebstelegraph, *m.* burglar-alarm (for safes, etc.).

Diechling, *m.* -s/-e. *Arm:* cuisse, thigh-piece.

Diegese [di·ʔe·ˈgeːzə], *f.* -/-n, narrative; statement of the case (in speech); diegesis.

diegetisch [di·ʔe·ˈgeːtiʃ], *a.* narrative; descriptive.

diejenige, *dem.pron. & adj. see* **derjenige.**

Diele, *f.* **-/-n.** **1.** floor(ing)-board; floor-plank (in ship). **2.** *pl.* **Dielen,** (boarded) floor, flooring. **3.** (*a*) (entrance) hall (in flat, house); parlour; (*b*) (ice-cream, coffee, etc.) parlour. **4.** (*in North Germany*) threshing floor.

Dielektrikum [di·ʔe·ˈlɛktri·kum], *n.* **-s/-ken.** *El:* dielectric.

dielektrisch [di·ʔe·ˈlɛktriʃ], *a. El:* dielectric (heating, etc.).

Dielektrizitätskonstante [di·ʔe·lɛktri·tsi·ˈtɛːtskonstantə], *f. Ph:* **relative D.,** dielectric constant, relative permittivity; **absolute D.,** absolute permittivity.

dielen. I. *v.tr.* (*a*) to board over, plank over (deck, etc.); (*b*) to floor, to lay a floor in (room, etc.).
II. *vbl s.* **1. Dielen,** *n. in vbl senses.* **2. Dielung,** *f.* (*a*)=II. 1; (*b*) floor boarding, flooring.

Dielenbalken, *m. Constr:* joist.

Dielenbrett, *n.* floor(ing)-board.

Dielenfußboden, *m.* wooden floor(ing); boarded floor(ing).

Dieler, *m.* **-s/-,** floor-maker, -layer.

Diemat [ˈdiːmaːt], *m.* **-(e)s/-e** =**Demat.**

Dieme, *f.* **-/-n, Diemen,** *m.* **-s/-.** *North G.Dial:* stack, rick (of hay, straw, etc.).

dienen, *v.i.* (*haben*) **1.** (*a*) **j-m d.,** to serve s.o.; **er war ein großer König und viele Ritter dienten ihm,** he was a great king and many knights did him service; *B:* **die eine Königin war, muß nun d.,** she that was princess among the provinces, how she is become tributary; **niemand kann zweien Herren d.,** no man can serve two masters; **ihr werdet nicht d. müssen dem Könige zu Babel,** ye shall not serve the king of Babylon; (*b*) **Gott, seinen Mitmenschen, d.,** to serve God, one's fellow men; **der Sünde, usw., d.,** to be a slave to sin, etc.; *B:* **du sollst Gott, deinen Herrn, anbeten, und ihm allein d.,** thou shalt worship the Lord thy God, and him only shalt thou serve; **wer mir d. will, der folge mir nach,** if any man serve me, let him follow me; **ihr könnt nicht Gott d. und dem Mammon,** ye cannot serve God and mammon. **2.** (*a*) **j-m d.,** to serve s.o. (*as a domestic servant, etc.*); to be a servant to s.o.; to be in service with s.o.; **nach der Schulentlassung ging das Mädchen für einige Jahre d.,** when she had left school, the girl went into, went out to, service for some years; **sie dient bei der Familie X,** she is in service with the X family; **der Junge dient als Stallknecht,** the youth serves as stableboy; **um Geld d.,** to work for money; (*b*) **dem Staat, der Kirche, usw., d.,** to serve the State, the Church, etc.; **er hat dem König jahrelang treu gedient,** for many years he served the king loyally; **er hat sein Leben lang der Kirche gedient,** he devoted his life to the service of the Church, he served the Church all his life; (*c*) **bei der Messe d., Messe d.,** to serve (a priest) at Mass; **im Tempel d.,** to serve in the temple; **am Altar d.,** to serve (at) the altar; **dem Altar, am Altar, d.,** to be a priest; **er diente an der Tafel des Königs,** he served at the king's table; *B:* **und siehe, da traten die Engel zu ihm, und dieneten ihm,** and behold, angels came and ministered unto him. **3.** to serve, to do military service; **bei der Marine, beim Heer, bei der Luftwaffe, d.,** to serve in the navy, in the army, in the air force; **haben Sie gedient?** have you done your military service? *F:* were you in the Forces? **er hatte unter X gedient,** he had served under X; **als gemeiner Soldat d.,** to serve in the ranks; **von der Pike auf d.,** (i) to rise from the ranks; (ii) *F:* to (start from the bottom and) work one's way up; **auf einem Schiff d.,** to serve afloat; **zwölf Jahre d.,** to serve twelve years; **gedienter Soldat,** old soldier, man who has served as a soldier; *see also* **aktiv. 4.** (*a*) **j-m in etwas** *dat.* **d.,** to serve s.o. in sth.; to be of use to s.o. in sth.; **j-m mit etwas d.,** to be of use to s.o. with sth., to help s.o. (out) with sth.; **ich bedaure, daß ich Ihnen in dieser Sache nicht d. kann,** I am sorry, but I can't help you in this matter; **womit kann ich Ihnen d.?** (i) (*in shop*) can I help you? (ii) *Hum:* what can I do for you? **damit kann ich leider nicht d.,** sorry, I can't help you; **wäre Ihnen damit gedient?** would this help you? would this be of any use, help, to you? **mir wäre schon mit 20 Mark gedient,** 20 marks would help me, *F:* 20 would do (me); **er dient einer guten Sache,** he serves a good cause; **es dient einem guten Zweck, einer guten Sache,** it serves, is in aid of, a good cause; **das würde meinen Zwecken d.,** that would serve my purpose; *A. & Hum:* **mein Herr, zu d.,** (i) at your service, sir; (ii) if it please, my lord; *Com. Corr:* **stets bemüht, Ihren Wünschen zu d.,** always anxious to satisfy your wishes; (*b*) (*of thg*) **j-m d.,** to serve, be useful to, s.o.; to stand s.o. in good stead; **der Regenmantel hat mir jahrelang gedient,** my raincoat has served me for years, has stood me in good stead for years. **5.** (*a*) to serve, to be useful (**zu etwas,** for sth.); **ein Werkzeug, das (zu) vielen Zwecken dient,** a tool that is useful for, that serves, many purposes; **wozu dient das?** what is the purpose of this? what is this for? **das dient zu nichts,** this serves no (good) purpose; **die Spenden sollen zum Wiederaufbau der Kathedrale d., sollen dazu d., die Kathedrale wieder aufzubauen,** the contributions are to be used to rebuild, for the rebuilding of, the cathedral; *B:* **wenn doch auch du erkennetest zu dieser deiner Zeit, was zu deinem Frieden dienet!** if thou hadst known, even thou, at least in this thy day, the things which belong unto thy peace! (*b*) **als etwas d.,** to serve as, to be used as sth.; **das Sofa dient als Bett,** the settee serves as a bed, does duty as a bed; (*c*) **zu etwas d.,** to serve as sth.; **das diente ihm zum Vorwand,** this served him as a pretext; **das sollte dir zum Beispiel d.,** this should serve you as an example; **es wird dir nur zum Besten, zu deinem Besten, d.,** it will only be for your good, for your benefit; **das möge dir zur Warnung d., das diene dir zur Warnung,** may this serve as a warning to you, let this be a warning to you.

Diener, *m.* **-s/-.** **1.** servant (of God, state, etc.); **D. des Evangeliums, des Wortes,** minister of the Gospel; *Corr: A:* **Ihr ergebener, untertäniger, D.,** your obedient, most obedient, servant. **2.** (*a*) man-servant; lackey, footman; man; boy; (domestic) servant; *B:* **der Größte unter euch soll euer D. sein,** but he that is greatest among you shall be your servant; *B:* **ich aber bin unter euch wie ein D.,** I am among you as he that serveth; (*b*) *Furn:* **(stummer) D.,** dumb-waiter; cake-stand. **3.** bow; (*of little boy*) **einen D. machen,** to bow.

Dienergefolge, *n.* train, retinue (of servants).

dienerhaft, *a.* (character) like a servant; (manner) of a servant; servile.

Dienerin, *f.* **-/-innen,** (woman-)servant; maid; lady's maid; attendant; *Lit:* maiden; **die Prinzessin im Kreise ihrer Dienerinnen,** the princess surrounded by her ladies; **er betrachtete die Malerei als D. der Architektur,** he considered painting as the handmaid of architecture.

dienern, *v.i.* (*haben*) (*of young boy*) to bow; *F:* (*of pers.*) to bow and scrape.

Dienernatur, *f.* servile nature; servile character.

Dienerschaft, *f.* **-/.** *Coll.* servants; **er hat eine große D.,** he has many servants, he has a large staff (of servants); **die ganze D. war zugegen,** all the servants were present.

Dienerschar, *f.* (body of) servants.

Dienertracht, *f.* (servant's) livery.

dienlich, *a.* (*of thg*) useful, convenient, for (sth.); appropriate for (sth.); **es würde der Sache nicht d. sein,** it would not help (in this matter), it would not further the cause; **ich halte es nicht für d., ihm jetzt einen Brief zu schreiben,** I do not think it advisable, opportune, to write a letter to him now; **es würde dir nicht d. sein, wenn ich in dieser Sache etwas unternähme,** it would not be of any use to you, it would not help, if I did anything in this matter.

Dienlichkeit, *f.* usefulness; convenience; appropriateness.

Dienst, *m.* **-es/-e.** **1.** service; (*a*) **sich, sein Leben, dem Dienste Gottes, der Kirche, widmen,** to devote oneself, one's life, to the service of God, of the Church; **er starb in des Königs D., im D. des Königs,** he died in the king's service; **er war für den D. der Kirche bestimmt,** he was intended for the ministry; **im D. einer guten Sache,** in the service of a good cause; **alle seine Kräfte in den D. einer guten Sache stellen,** to devote all one's strength to the service of a good cause; (*b*) **D. am Volk,** service to the nation, to the people; **im D. an der Freiheit,** in the service of liberty; **D. an seinen Mitmenschen,** service to one's fellow men; **D. am Evangelium, am Wort,** ministry of the Gospel; *Com:* **D. am Kunden,** service to the customer; (assiduous) attention to the customer; 'service with sales'; (*c*) **j-m den D. aufkündigen,** to refuse to serve s.o. any longer; **meine Glieder versagten mir den D.,** I lost the power of my limbs; **der Motor versagte den D.,** the engine wouldn't work. **2.** (*a*) *Mil: etc:* service; duty; **aktiver D.,** service with the colours; regular service; **D. als Bataillonsadjutant tun,** to do duty as a battalion adjutant; **D. unter der Fahne,** service with the colours; **den D. verweigern,** to refuse duty; **D. am Scheinwerfer,** searchlight duty; **Offizier vom D.,** duty *or* orderly officer; *see also* **Waffe;** (*b*) duty; **D. haben,** to be on duty; **seinen D. verrichten,** to do one's work; **außerhalb des Dienstes, außer D.,** off-duty; (*cp.* 3 (*a*)); (*in hospital*) **der Arzt vom D.,** the doctor on duty; **D. in der Küche,** kitchen-duty; **Apotheke vom D.,** pharmacy open (for dispensing of prescriptions); **zum D. antreten,** to report for duty; **wann haben Sie D.?** when are you on duty? **wann beginnt Ihr D.?** when, at what time, do you go on duty? **unziemliches Betragen im D.,** unseemly conduct while on duty; **vom D. abgelöst werden,** to be relieved of one's duties; (*c*) attendance (at court); (*d*) **D. am Altar, D. der Altäre,** ministry; service at the altar; **D. im Tempel,** service in the temple; (*e*) **in D. stellen,** to put (railway carriage, bus, etc.) into service; *Nau:* **ein Schiff in D. stellen,** to commission a ship, to put a ship into service. **3.** (*a*) service; employment; position; **Beamte und Angestellte des öffentlichen Dienstes,** officials and employees of the civil, public, service; **im D. des Staates,** in the service of the state; **in den diplomatischen D. eintreten,** to enter the diplomatic service; **aus dem D. entlassen werden,** to be dismissed from one's post; **außer D.,** *abbr.* **a.D.,** (i) retired (official, officer), official in retirement; (ii) *F:* out of work, *F:* out of a job; **seinen D. antreten,** to take up, enter upon, one's duties, to take up a position, an employment; to start one's work, *F:* one's job; **den D. kündigen,** to resign one's position; **im D. ergrauen,** to grow old in service; **er steht, ist, seit fünfzehn Jahren im D.,** he has been in office fifteen years, he has seen fifteen years' service; **ich bin nicht mehr im D.,** I have retired; (*b*) *Adm:* class; **unterer, einfacher, D.,** *approx.*=minor and manipulative class; **höherer D.,** *approx.*= administrative *or* professional class; (*c*)= **Dienstzeit;** (*d*) service, employment; **in j-s D., Diensten, stehen,** to be in s.o.'s service; *Pej:* to be in s.o.'s pay; **in königlichen, päpstlichen, Diensten, im D. des Königs, des Papstes, stehen, sein,** to be in royal, papal, service, in the king's, Pope's service; **er stand im russischen D., in russischen Diensten,** (i) he worked for Russia; (ii) he was in the pay of Russia; **in j-s D., Dienste, (ein)treten,** to enter s.o.'s service; **j-n in seinen D., in seine Dienste, nehmen,** to take s.o. into one's service, services, into one's employ. **4.** (domestic) service; **D. annehmen,** to go into service; **j-n in seinen D. nehmen,** to take s.o. into (one's) service. **5.** (*service rendered*) (*a*) service; attention; attendance; **die Dienste des Arztes, Rechtsanwalts, usw.,** the services, attentions, of the doctor, the services of the solicitor, etc.; **Dienste eines Priesters, einer Krankenschwester,** ministrations of a priest, of a nurse; **j-m einen D. erweisen, tun,** to render, do, s.o. a service; **er hat bei Herrn X D., Dienste, als Chauffeur getan,** (i) he was in service as chauffeur with Mr X; (ii) he acted as chauffeur to Mr X; **j-s Dienste in Anspruch nehmen, benutzen,** to make use of s.o.'s services; **in Anerkennung Ihrer Dienste,** in recognition of your services; **geleistete Dienste,** services rendered; **würden Sie mir einen großen D. tun?** would you do me a great favour, a great kindness; **j-m einen schlechten D. erweisen,** to do s.o. a disservice; **er hat ihm keinen (guten) D., einen schlechten D., damit erwiesen, daß . . .,** he has not done him a service by . . .; (*b*) *Mediev. Hist:* (*duty owed by tenant to his lord*) service; (*c*) (*of thg*) **D., Dienste, tun, leisten,** to do (good) service, *Lit:* to stand s.o. in good stead; **eine klassische Erziehung wird ihr gute Dienste tun,** a classical education will stand her in good stead; **welche guten Dienste dieser Füllfederhalter mir getan hat!** what good service this pen has done me! **der kleine Koffer wird denselben D., dieselben Dienste, tun,** the small case will do the same service, will do as well; **das Auto ist sehr alt, aber es tut immer noch seine Dienste, seinen D.,** the car is very old, but it still works; **die Badekur hat ihm gute Dienste getan,** the course of treatment at the spa has done him good; **der Magen tut seinen D., seine Dienste, nicht,** the stomach does not work, function, properly; **den Mantel kann ich nicht mehr tragen, er hat seinen D. getan,** I can't wear this coat any longer, it has done its service. **6.** *Arch:* respond; engaged column; **alte Dienste,** engaged columns supporting the transverse arches; **junge Dienste,** engaged columns supporting the ribs. **7. -en/-e(n).** *Swiss:* (domestic) servant.

-dienst, *comb.fm. m.* **1. . . .** service; **Telegraphendienst,** telegraph service; **Suchdienst,** tracing

service (of Red Cross, etc.); **Transportdienst,** transport service; **Gesundheitsdienst,** health service. **2.** . . . service; . . . career; **Kolonialdienst,** colonial service; **Konsulatsdienst,** consular service; **Museumsdienst,** museum career; **Bibliotheksdienst,** librarian's career. **3.** . . . duty, duty . . .; *Mil:* . . . service, . . . duty; **Küchendienst,** kitchen duty; **Nachtdienst,** night duty; **Altardienst,** service at the altar; **Lagerdienst,** camp-duty. **4. Magddienste für j-n tun,** to perform menial services for s.o.; **j-m einen Freundschaftsdienst, Freundschaftsdienste, erweisen,** to render a friendly service, friendly services, to s.o., to render s.o. a true friend's service, services; **Ritterdienst,** knight's service. **5.** . . . service; . . . worship; . . . cult; **Gottesdienst,** divine service; **Götzendienst,** idol worship, worship of idols; **Astartedienst,** Astarte worship, Astarte cult, cult of Astarte.

Dienstablösung, *f.* **1.** relief (of pers. on duty). **2.** (*pers.*) relief.

Dienstabteil, *n. Rail:* guard's van, *U.S:* caboose; guard's compartment; compartment for train personnel.

Dienstadel, *m.* **1.** *Hist:* nobility whose title derives from being in the king's service. **2.**=**Amtsadel.**

Dienstag, *m.* Tuesday; **er kommt jeden D., er kommt immer am D.,** he comes on Tuesdays, he comes every Tuesday; **D. abend, nachmittag, bin ich eingeladen,** I have an invitation for, I am invited out for, Tuesday evening, afternoon; **er ist D. nacht gestorben,** he died Tuesday night; **ich komme D. morgen, D. früh,** I shall come Tuesday morning, early on Tuesday; **D. abends, morgens, gehe ich immer aus,** I always go out on Tuesday evenings, nights, mornings, every Tuesday evening, night, morning.

Dienstagabend, *m.* Tuesday evening; Tuesday night; **am D.,** on Tuesday evening; **an einem D.,** on a Tuesday evening; **jeden D.,** each, every, Tuesday evening; **nächsten D.,** next Tuesday evening.

dienstäglich. 1. *a.* Tuesday, Tuesday's; **unser dienstäglicher Stundenplan,** our Tuesday timetable. **2.** *adv.* on Tuesday(s); every Tuesday; **das Seminar findet d. von zwei bis vier Uhr statt,** the seminar is held on Tuesdays from two to four o'clock.

Dienstagmittag, *m.* Tuesday midday; Tuesday afternoon; **am D.,** at midday on Tuesday; on Tuesday afternoon; **an einem D.,** at midday on a Tuesday; on a Tuesday afternoon; **jeden D.,** each, every, Tuesday (at) midday; each, every, Tuesday afternoon; **nächsten D.,** next Tuesday (at) midday; next Tuesday afternoon; **ich werde ihn am D. anrufen,** I shall telephone him Tuesday lunch-time.

Dienstagmitternacht, *f.* midnight on Tuesday, Tuesday midnight.

Dienstagmorgen, *m.* Tuesday morning; **am D.,** on Tuesday morning; **an einem D.,** on a Tuesday morning; **jeden D.,** each, every, Tuesday morning; **nächsten D.,** next Tuesday morning; **ich werde D. früh kommen,** I shall come early on Tuesday morning.

Dienstagnachmittag, *m.* Tuesday afternoon; **am D.,** on Tuesday afternoon; **an einem D.,** on a Tuesday afternoon; **jeden D.,** each, every, Tuesday afternoon; **nächsten D.,** next Tuesday afternoon.

Dienstagnacht, *f.* Tuesday night; Tuesday evening; **in der D.,** on (the) Tuesday night; **in einer D.,** on a Tuesday night.

dienstags, *adv.* on Tuesday(s); on a Tuesday; **d. abends,** on Tuesday evenings, nights; **ich könnte dich nur d. treffen,** I could only meet you on a Tuesday.

Dienstagvormittag, *m.* Tuesday morning; **am D.,** on Tuesday morning; **an einem D.,** on a Tuesday morning; **jeden D.,** each, every, Tuesday morning; **nächsten D.,** next Tuesday morning.

Dienstalter, *n. Adm: Mil: etc:* seniority; length of service; **nach dem D. befördert werden,** to be promoted by seniority.

dienstälter, *a. Adm: Mil:* senior (officer, etc.); **d. als X sein,** to be senior to X.

dienstälteste(r), -älteste, -älteste(s), *a. Adm: Mil:* (most) senior (officer, etc.); **der dienstälteste Unteroffizier,** the senior N.C.O.

Dienstangelegenheit, *f.* official matter; business matter; matter of business.

Dienstansprüche, *m.pl.* civil servant's rights to remunerations, etc., resulting from his office.

Dienstantritt, *m.* starting of duty; commencement of duties; beginning of work; accession to office, assumption of office.

Dienstanweisung, *f.* instruction(s).

Dienstanzug, *m. Mil: etc:* service uniform; *Mil:* **im D.,** in drill order.

Dienstaufwand, *m. Adm: etc:* ex officio expenditure (for entertainment, etc.).

Dienstaufwandsentschädigung, *f.* allowance (for expenses incurred in course of duty); expenses.

Dienstausrüstung, *f. Mil: etc:* service equipment.

Dienstauszeichnung, *f. Mil: etc:* (service) decoration.

Dienstauto, *n.* official car.

dienstbar, *a.* subject (to s.o., sth.); obedient (to s.o.); tributary (to s.o.); *Hist:* liable to forced *or* statute labour; **j-m d. sein,** to be in s.o.'s servitude; **sich j-n d. machen,** to bring s.o. under one's rule; **der Sünde d.,** a slave to sin; **dienstbarer Geist,** (i) *A:* familiar spirit; ministering spirit *or* angel; (ii) *Hum:* (domestic) servant, *F:* factotum; **das Bemühen der Menschen, sich die Elemente d. zu machen,** man's efforts to become master of the elements; *B:* **der Ältere soll d. werden dem Jüngeren,** the elder shall serve the younger.

Dienstbarkeit, *f.* **1.** subjection; servitude; **in D. geraten,** to lose one's independence, freedom; **j-n in D. halten,** to keep s.o. in subjection, in servitude; **in j-s D. geraten,** to fall into s.o.'s power; **in des Satans D.,** in the power of Satan; **in der Sünde D.,** in the clutches of sin. **2.** *Hist:* bondservice. **3.** *Jur:* easement, *Scot:* servitude.

Dienstbefehl, *m. Mil:* service order; *Adm:* official order.

dienstbeflissen, *a.* (over-)eager, fervent, zealous, in one's duty; over-eager; over-attentive; officious.

Dienstbeflissenheit, *f.* over-eagerness; zealousness; officiousness.

dienstberechtigt, *a. Jur:* entitled to service; (*in contract of employment*) **der Dienstberechtigte,** the employer.

Dienstbereich, *n.* competence, competency (of official); sphere (of duty).

dienstbereit, *a.* (*a*) ready to do one's duty, to be of service; obliging; assiduous; helpful; (*b*) standing by, (being) in readiness; (*c*) (*of pharmacy*) open (for dispensing of prescriptions).

Dienstbereitschaft, *f.* (*a*) readiness to do one's duty; assiduousness; (*b*) readiness; stand-by duty; service (after normal hours, for dispensing, etc.).

Dienstbeschädigung, *f.* injuries received in the course of work, *Mil:* in the course of duty.

Dienstbetrieb, *m.* routine working; routine.

Dienstbezüge, *m.pl.* earnings (including allowances, fees, etc.); emoluments.

Dienstbote, *m.* (domestic) servant; (*in formal speech*) domestic; **die Dienstboten,** the (staff of) servants.

Dienstboteneingang, *m.* back door; tradesmen's entrance.

Dienstbotentreppe, *f.* backstairs, back staircase.

Dienstbriefmarke, *f. Adm:*=**Dienstmarke.**

Dienstbrücke, *f. Civ.E: etc:* service gantry.

Diensteid, *m.* (*a*) oath of allegiance; (*b*)=**Amtseid.**

Diensteifer, *m.* eagerness, zealousness (to perform one's duty); devotion to duty; **(übertriebener) D.,** over-eagerness; officiousness.

diensteifrig, *a.* eager, zealous, in one's duty; **(übertrieben) d.,** over-eager; officious.

Diensteinkommen, *n.*=**Dienstbezüge.**

Diensteinteilung, *f.* work schedule; *Mil:* duty roster; duty list.

Dienstenthebung, *f.* (*a*) suspension (of official); suspension from duty; (*b*)=**Dienstentlassung.**

Dienstentlassung, *f.* dismissal, discharge (from post, from duty).

Dienstentsetzung, *f.* dismissal, removal (of official).

dienstfähig, *a.*=**diensttauglich.**

Dienstfähigkeit, *f.*=**Diensttauglichkeit.**

Dienstfahrplan, *m. Rail:* timetable.

dienstfertig. 1. *a.* eager, zealous, in one's duty. **2.** *adv.* in a zealous manner, zealously; eagerly; **d. nahm er mir das Gepäck ab,** he hastened to take my luggage.

Dienstfertigkeit, *f.* eagerness, zealousness (in one's duty).

dienstfrei, *a.* **1.** *Hist:* immune from bondservice; (*of land*) free of soc(c)age. **2.** (pers., hours, etc.) off duty; off-duty (hours, etc.).

Dienstführung, *f.* execution, performance, of one's duty, of one's duties; administration.

Dienstgeber, *m.*=**Dienstherr** (*b*).

Dienstgebrauch, *m. Adm: Mil:* **'nur für den D.',** 'for official use only', *U.S:* 'restricted'.

Dienstgehalt, *n., occ. m.* salary (of civil servant, etc.); *Mil:* (officers') pay

Dienstgeheimnis, *n.* **1.** official secret. **2.** official secrecy.

Dienstgespräch, *n. Tp:* business call; official call; *Mil: etc:* service call.

Dienstgewalt, *f.* (official) authority.

Dienstgewicht, *n. Rail: etc:* working weight (of engines, etc.).

Dienstgipfelhöhe, *f. Av:* service ceiling.

Dienstgrad, *m.* grade (of civil servant, etc.); *Mil:* rank.

Dienstgradabzeichen, *n. Mil:* badge of rank; rank marking.

Dienstgradbezeichnung, *f.* designation, description, of grade, *Mil:* of rank.

diensthabend, *a.* (pers.) on duty; **der diensthabende Offizier,** the duty officer; **der Diensthabende,** official, officer, on duty.

Diensthandlung, *f.* act performed in the course of one's duty; official act.

Dienstheirat, *f. Anthr:* marriage by service.

Dienstherr, *m.* (*a*) *Hist:* feudal lord; (*b*) master; employer.

Dienstherrschaft, *f.* employers; master and mistress.

Diensthund, *m.* dog trained for police work, customs work, etc.; *esp.* police-dog.

Dienstjahr, *n.* year of (military, civil, etc.) service.

Dienstkleidung, *f.* uniform; *Mil:* service dress.

Dienstkraftfahrzeug, *n.* official (motor-)vehicle.

Dienstlast, *f. Av:* service load.

Dienstlehen, *n. Hist:* soc(c)age.

Dienstleistung, *f.* service (rendered); *Mil:* duty; **ärztliche Dienstleistungen,** medical attention, attendance; doctor's services; **die Dienstleistungen, die von ihr erwartet wurden, standen in keinem Verhältnis zu ihrem Lohn,** the work that was expected of her bore no relation to her pay; **das Kind wurde zu allerlei kleinen Dienstleistungen im Haus angehalten,** the child was encouraged to carry out various little tasks in the home.

Dienstleistungsgewerbe, *n. Pol.Ec:* service industries.

Dienstleitung, *f. Tp:* official line.

Dienstleute, *pl.* (*a*) servants; staff of servants; (*b*) *Hist:* (i) thanes, thegns; ministerials; (ii) retainers, (iii) feudal vassals.

dienstlich, *a.* **1.** (*a*) official; pertaining to one's duty; **dienstliche Mitteilung,** official communication; **dienstlicher Befehl,** official, *Mil:* service, order; (*b*) *adv.* officially; on official business; in an official capacity; **d. verhindert,** detained by official business; **ich habe d. mit Ihnen zu reden,** (i) I have to talk to you in an official capacity; (ii) I have to talk to you about official matters; **d. unterwegs sein,** to be out on official business; **ich bin d. hier,** I am here (i) in an official capacity, (ii) on official business. **2.** *A:*=**dienstbereit. 3.** *A:*=**dienlich.**

Dienstlohn, *m.* wages, pay.

Dienstlokal, *n.* office; police-station.

Dienstmädchen, *n.* maid, domestic servant, help; servant girl, *U.S:* hired girl.

Dienstmagd, *f.*=**Dienstmädchen.**

Dienstmann, *m.* **1. -(e)s/-mannen & -leute,** *Mediev.Hist:* (i) ministerial; (ii) feudal vassal; thane, thegn. **2. -(e)s/-männer,** street-porter.

Dienstmarke, *f. Adm:* official postage-stamp used by government departments.

Dienstmütze, *f. Mil: etc:* uniform cap; service cap.

Dienstordnung, *f. Mil:* service regulations; *Adm:* official regulations.

Dienstort, *m.* town, place, where an official is stationed.

Dienstpersonal, *n.* (railway, etc.) personnel; domestic staff; servants.

Dienstpferd, *n. Mil:* troop-horse; service horse.

Dienstpflicht, *f.* **1.** *Hist:* (i) forced *or* statute labour; (ii) feudal service. **2.** official duty. **3.** (*a*) liability for, to (military, etc.) service; (*b*) *Mil:* (i) (compulsory) military service; (ii) conscription; **seiner D. genügen,** to do one's military service.

dienstpflichtig, *a.* **1.** *Hist:* liable (i) to forced *or* statute labour, (ii) to feudal service. **2.** *Mil: etc:* liable to service; **im dienstpflichtigen Alter sein,** to be of military age.

Dienstplan, *m.* work schedule; roster; *Mil:* detail for duty; duty roster, duty list.

Dienstprämie, *f. Mil:* gratuity.

Dienstrang, *m.* grade (of civil servant, etc.); *Mil:* rank.

Dienstraum, *m.* office.

Dienstreise, *f.* official journey; business journey; *Mil:* travelling in the course of duty.

Dienstreiseausweis, *m. Mil: etc:* travel pass.

Dienstsache, *f.* **1.** official matter, official business. **2.** *Post:* official matter; **gebührenpflichtige D. frei,** official postage paid (*corresponding to O.H.M.S.*); *see also* **gebührenpflichtig.**

Dienstschluß, *m.* end of working hours, office hours; **nach D.,** after work; after (office) hours.

Dienstschreiben, *n.* official letter.

Dienstsiegel, *n. Adm:* official stamp, official seal.

Dienststelle, *f. Adm: etc:* government office; government department; section (of a ministry, etc.); military administrative office; office; centre.

Dienststellenleiter, *m. Adm: etc:* head of a section, of a department.

Dienststempel, *m.* **1.** *Adm:* official stamp. **2.** *Post:* 'official paid' stamp.

Dienststrafe, *f. Adm: Jur:* disciplinary punishment.

Dienststrafrecht, *n.* = **Disziplinarstrafrecht.**

Dienststunden, *f.pl.* office hours; working hours.

diensttauglich, *a.* fit for service, for duty; *Mil:* fit for active service.

Diensttauglichkeit, *f.* fitness for service, for duty, *Mil:* for active service.

Diensttelegramm, *n.* official telegram.

Diensttelegraph, *m. Rail:* railway telegraph.

Diensttelephon, *n.* official telephone; office telephone.

diensttuend, *a.* (officer, official, etc.) on duty.

dienstunfähig, *a.* = **dienstuntauglich.**

Dienstunfähigkeit, *f.* = **Dienstuntauglichkeit.**

dienstuntauglich, *a. Mil: etc:* unfit for service, for duty.

Dienstuntauglichkeit, *f. Mil: etc:* unfitness for service.

Dienstunterricht, *m. Mil:* instruction.

Dienstvergehen, *n. Adm:* offence committed while acting in an official capacity; offence against rules and regulations; *Mil:* offence against military regulations.

Dienstverhältnis, *n.* (contractual) relation between employer and employee; **(zu j-m) im D. stehen,** to be under contract to s.o., to be bound to s.o.; **solange ich noch im D. stehe, . . . ,** as long as I am bound by the terms of my employment . . .; **das D. kündigen,** to dissolve the contract of employment; **lockeres D.,** employment without formal contract.

Dienstvermerk, *m. Adm:* official entry (on file, in record, etc.).

dienstverpflichtet, *a.* (*a*) (*in time of emergency*) under obligation to serve (in factory, etc.); (*b*) *Jur:* liable to service (under contract); (*in contract of employment*) **der Dienstverpflichtete,** the employee.

Dienstverpflichtung, *f.* (*a*) *Adm:* obligation to serve (in factory, etc.); requisition order; (*b*) *Jur:* liability to service (under contract).

Dienstverrichtung, *f.* task (performed in course of duty).

Dienstvertrag, *m. Jur:* contract of service; contract for professional services; contract of employment; **den D. lösen,** to terminate the contract.

Dienstverweigerer, *m.* person, soldier, who refuses duty; recalcitrant.

Dienstverweigerung, *f.* refusal to do duty; recalcitrance.

Dienstvorschrift, *f. Mil:* military manual; service regulations; *Adm:* official regulations.

Dienstwagen, *m.* official car.

Dienstweg, *m. Adm:* **auf dem D.,** officially; through official channels; conforming to official regulations; **den D. einhalten,** to act through the proper, through the usual, channels.

dienstwidrig, *a.* contrary to rules and regulations.

Dienstwidrigkeit, *f.* irregularity (of conduct).

Dienstwohnung, *f.* official quarters; official residence.

Dienstzeit, *f.* **1.** (*a*) (period of) service; period in office; **in meiner langjährigen D.,** during my long years in office; **nach einer D. von drei Monaten,** after three months' service; (*b*) *Mil:* (period of) military service; **seine D. ableisten,** to do one's military service; **zweijährige D.,** two years' military service. **2.** working hours; office hours.

Dienstzwang, *m.* **1.** *Hist:* = **Bauernzwang. 2.** *Mil:* compulsory (military) service; conscription.

Dienstzweig, *m. Adm:* branch of the civil service; government department.

dies[1] *see* **dieser.**

Dies[2] [ˈdiːes], *m.* -/. **D. ater,** black day; *Sch:* (*at German University*) **D. (academicus),** holiday.

diesbezüglich, *a. & adv.* concerning, respecting, regarding, it, this, that, these, those; in respect of, with respect to, relating to, it, this, that, these, those; **die diesbezüglichen Dokumente,** the relevant documents; **diesbezügliche Anfragen sind zu richten an . . . ,** enquiries in this connection should be addressed to . . .; **ich werde Ihnen alle diesbezüglichen Auskünfte gerne erteilen,** I shall be pleased to give you all the relevant information; **d. möchte ich einige Fragen an Sie stellen,** I should like to put some questions to you about this; **ich habe d. noch nichts unternommen,** I have not yet done anything in this matter.

diese[1] *see* **dieser.**

Diese[2] [diˈeːzə], *f.* -/-n. *Mus:* **1.** sharp. **2.** diesis.

Diesel, *m.* -s/. *F:* diesel oil.

Diesel-, *comb.fm.* diesel . . .; *I.C.E:* **Dieselmotor** *m,* diesel engine; **Dieselöl** *n,* diesel oil.

dieselbe *see* **derselbe.**

dieselbige *see* **derselbige.**

dieselelektrisch, *a. & adv. I.C.E:* diesel-electric; *Nau: etc:* **dieselelektrischer Antrieb,** diesel-electric propulsion.

Dieseler, *m.* -/-. *Nau:* diesel(-propelled) vessel.

dieser, diese, dieses, dies (*decl. as adj.*). I. *dem. pron.* **1.** this, this one, *pl.* these; he, she, it, *pl.* they; **welche Bluse möchten Sie?—ich möchte diese da,** which blouse would you like?—I should like this one; **dies(es) ist ein freies Land,** this is a free country; **es gibt Leute, die immer zu spät kommen; ich bin nicht einer von diesen,** there are people who are always late; I am not one of these, not one of them; **er fragte seinen Arzt um Rat; dieser sagte . . . ,** he asked his doctor for advice; he, the latter, said . . .; **dies(es) ist das Buch, das er mir zum Geburtstag schenkte,** this, that, is the book (that) he gave me for my birthday; **ich habe mein Buch hier liegen lassen;—ist es dies(es)?** I left my book here somewhere;—is this it, is this the one? **dies(es) tat er am nächsten Tag,** this he did the next day; **die Sache war diese: . . . ,** it was like this: . . . , the thing was this: . . .; **möchtest du dies oder das, dies(es) oder jenes?** will you have this or that? **die beiden Anrichten sehen gleich aus, aber diese (hier) ist neu, und die, jene, (dort) ist alt,** the two sideboards look very much alike, but this (one) is new and that (one) is old; **'diese oder keine!'** 'I'll marry her or not at all'; *A:* **hol' dich dieser und jener!** (may) the devil take you! **2.** (*a*) **dies, dieses,** this; these; (*referring to pers. or thg*) **dies(es) sind meine Kinder,** these are my children; **wer ist dies?** who is this? **all(es) dies(es) hat er geschrieben,** he has written all this; (*referring to situations, ideas, etc.*) **dies ist es eben,** this is just it; **ist dies der richtige Ort zu streiten?** is this the place to quarrel? **war dies die beste Gelegenheit, das zu besprechen?** was this the (opportune) moment to discuss it? **sie ist sehr böse darüber, und dies mit Recht,** she is very angry about it, and rightly so, and with good cause; **du sagst, er sei ein Held gewesen, aber dies war er nie,** you say he was a hero, which he never was, but he never was one; (*b*) (*with certain prepositions*) *A. & Lit:* **vor diesem wurde das Land von Königen regiert,** up to this time, before this, the country was ruled by kings; **nach diesem wird er vorsichtiger sein,** hereafter, after this, he will be more careful; **mit diesem verließ sie das Zimmer,** thereupon, whereupon, she left the room; **nächst diesem muß sie reich sein,** in addition, next, she must be rich; (*c*) **sie sprachen von diesem und jenem,** they talked of this and that; **er erzählte mir dies und das,** he told me this and that.

II. **dieser, diese, dies(es),** *dem.a.* **1.** (*a*) this, *pl.* these; **dieser Mann ist mein Vater,** this man is my father; **ich gehe nicht oft ins Theater, aber dies(es) Stück muß ich sehen,** I don't often go to the theatre but I must see this play, but this, that, is a play I must see; **diese Schauspielerin kann ich nicht leiden,** I can't bear this (particular) actress; **dieses Mal,** this time; **dies, dieses, eine Mal,** this once; *see also* **diesmal; dieser selbe, dieser nämliche, Punkt,** this very point; **in diesem ihrem ersten Feldzug,** in this their first campaign; **dies(es) dem berühmten Maler zugeschriebene Bild,** this picture, attributed to the famous painter; **ausgerechnet diesen Hut hat sie sich ausgesucht,** she chose this of all hats; **gerade dieses Kind hätte einen Preis bekommen sollen,** this is the one child who should have got a prize; **ich möchte diese Bluse (hier), nicht die (da),** I should like (to have) this blouse, not that one (there); **diese Welt,** this world; **in diesem Leben,** (i) in my life; (ii) in this life; *Com.Corr:* **der Überbringer dieses (Schreibens),** the bearer; (*b*) (*exclamatory*) **diese Überraschung!** what a surprise! **diese Unordnung!** *F:* what a mess! **dieser Dummkopf!** what a fool! **er traut sich nicht, dieser Feigling!** h doesn't dare, the coward (that he is)! **2.** (*a*) (*denoting a period of time*) **ich war Student in diesen Jahren,** I was a student in those days; **am Ende dieses Jahres,** at the end of the year, (i) of this, the current, year, (ii) of that year; **von diesem Tage an,** (i) from that day to this, since that day; (ii) as from that day (on); **seit dieser Nacht,** (i) from this night on(wards), since this, that, night; (ii) from tonight on(wards); **in diesem aufgeklärten Jahrhundert,** in this enlightened age; *Com.Corr:* **Ihr Brief vom 3. dieses (Monats),** your letter of the 3rd inst.; **Ihr Brief vom 10. Februar dieses Jahres,** your letter of the 10th February last; (*b*) (*in adv. phrases*) **diese Nacht,** (i) this night, tonight; (ii) last night; **diesen Morgen, diesen Abend,** this morning; this evening, tonight; **dieser Tage,** (i) in a day or so; (ii) the other day; **ich werde dir dieser Tage schreiben,** I'll write to you in a day or so, within the next few days; **sie wird in diesen Tagen, dieser Tage, hier eintreffen,** she will arrive here in, during, the next few days; **ich habe ihn dieser Tage gesehen,** I saw him the other day; **ich werde es dieser Tage erledigen,** I'll see to it, do it, in, during, the next few days; **ich habe diese Nacht schlecht geschlafen,** I slept badly last night.

dieserhalb, *conj.* = **deshalb.**

dieserlei. 1. *dem.a. inv.* of this kind, sort. **2.** *dem.pron. inv.* (i) this kind, sort; (ii) a thing like this; things like this.

diesfalls, *adv.* in this case.

diesig, *a.* (*a*) (*of weather, etc.*) misty, hazy; (*b*) *F:* (*of pers.*) hazy; dense, silly.

Diesigkeit, *f.* mistiness, haziness.

Diesis [ˈdiːezis], *f.* -/-sen [diˈeːzən] = **Diese**[2].

diesjährig, *a.* of this year, this year's; **diesjähriger Wein,** this year's, fresh, wine; **der diesjährige Sommer,** this summer; **die diesjährigen Schulabgänger,** this year's school-leavers.

diesmal, *adv.* this time; this once; **d. darfst du es noch tun,** you may do it this once, just for (this) once; **für d. haben wir genug getan,** we have done enough for now, for this time; that's all for today.

diesmalig, *a.* this time; **die diesmalige Entscheidung,** the decision in this instance; **unsere diesmalige Jahresversammlung wird im Mai stattfinden,** our annual meeting will take place in May this year.

diesseitig, *a.* **1.** (*a*) on this side; *Lit:* hither; **das diesseitige Ufer des Flusses,** (the bank on) this side of the river, the hither side of the river; (*b*) *A:* on this, on our, on my, side. **2.** of this world; earthly; hither-worldly; **eine diesseitige Einstellung haben,** (i) to be entirely of this world; (ii) to place great emphasis on the things of this world; *adv.* **d. ausgerichtet,** emphasizing things of this world.

Diesseitigkeit, *f.* hither-worldliness; emphasis upon, preoccupation with, things of this world.

diesseits[1]. **1.** *prep.* (+*gen., A:* +*gen., dat.*) on this side; on the one side; **d. des Flusses,** on this side of the river; **die Stadt liegt teilweise d., teilweise jenseits des Flusses,** the town lies partly on this side, partly on the other side of the river; **d. der Vierziger,** this side, on the right side, of forty; **d. der Wahrheit,** this side of truth; (*political or national concept*) **d. des Rheins,** (*from the German viewpoint*) east of the Rhine; **d. der Alpen,** (*from the Italian viewpoint*) south of the Alps; cisalpine; (*from the German viewpoint*) north of the Alps. **2.** *adv.* (*a*) here below, on earth; in this life; (*b*) on this, on our side; **er machte einige Bemerkungen, auf Grund deren man sich d. gekränkt fühlte,** we, on our side, took umbrage at some of the things he said.

Diesseits[2], *n.* -/. this world; **im D.,** here below, on earth; in this life; **Glaube an das D.,** firm attachment to reality.

diesseitsgebunden, *a.* firmly rooted in reality; *Lit:* hither-worldly.

Diesseitsgebundenheit, *f.* firm attachment to reality; *Lit:* hither-worldliness.

Diesseitsglaube, *m.* firm attachment to reality.

Dieter. *Pr.n.m.* -s = **Dietrich** 1.

Dieterich. *Pr.n.m.* -s = **Dietrich** 1.

diet(e)richen, *v.tr.* **eine Tür d.,** to open a door with a skeleton key.

Dietrich. 1. *Pr.n.m.* -s. Dietrich; *G.Myth:* **D. von Bern,** Theoderic the Great. **2.** *m.* -s/-e, skeleton key; picklock.

dieweil [diˈvail]. **1.** *adv.* meanwhile; in the meanwhile, in the meantime. **2.** *conj.* (*a*) as long as, while, whilst; (*b*) *A:* because; since.

Diffamation [difa·ma·tsi̯ˈoːn], *f.* -/-**en**, defamation. **1.** blackening of (s.o.'s) character; bringing (sth.) into disrepute; denigration. **2.** calumny; malicious talk.

Diffamationsklage, *f. Jur:* action of defamation; action for libel *or* slander.

diffamatorisch [difa·ma·ˈtoːriʃ], *a.* defamatory; slanderous; libellous.

Diffamie [difa·ˈmiː], *f.* -/-**n** [-ˈmiːən], calumny; malicious talk.

diffamieren [difa·ˈmiːrən]. **1.** *v.tr.* to defame (s.o.); to blacken (s.o.'s) character; to bring (sth.) into disrepute; *F:* to run (sth., s.o.) down. **2.** *vbl s.* **Diffamierung,** *f.*=**Diffamation.**

differential[1] [difərɛntsiˈaːl], *a.* differential.

Differential[2], *n.* -**s**/-**e. 1.** *Mth:* differential; **partielles, totales, D.,** partial, total, differential. **2.** *Aut:* differential.

Differential-, *comb.fm. Mth: Mec.E: El: etc:* differential . . . .

Differentialbeobachtung, *f. Astr:* differential observation.

Differentialblutbild, *n. Med:* differential blood count.

Differentialdiagnose, *f. Med:* differential diagnosis.

Differentialflaschenzug, *m. Mec.E:* differential pulley.

Differentialgetriebe, *n. Mec.E:* differential gear; *Aut:* differential, compensating, gear.

Differentialgleichung, *f. Mth:* differential equation.

Differentialquotient, *m. Mth:* differential coefficient.

Differentialrechnung, *f. Mth:* differential calculus.

Differentialrelais, *n. El.E:* differential (current) relay.

Differentialrente, *f. Pol.Ec:* differential ground rent.

Differentialschraube, *f.* differential screw.

Differentialstrom, *m. El.E:* differential current.

Differentialtarif, *m.* differential tariff; *Rail:* differential rates.

Differentialwirkung, *f. Mec.E: etc:* differential action.

Differentiation [difərɛntsi̯a·tsi̯ˈoːn], *f.* -/-**en**, differentiation.

differentiell [difərɛntsi̯ˈɛl], *a.* differential; **differentielle Psychologie,** differential psychology.

differentiieren [difərɛntsi·ˈiːrən], *v.tr. & i.* (*haben*) =**differenzieren.**

Differenz [difəˈrɛnts], *f.* -/-**en. 1.** (*a*) difference (between two numbers, quantities, etc.); **die D. beträgt zehn,** the difference is ten, there is a difference of ten; **eine D. von zehn Mark in seiner Rechnung haben,** to have a discrepancy of ten marks in one's account, *F:* to be ten marks short in one's account, to be ten marks out in one's calculations; (*b*) difference, distinction (between people, concepts, etc.); variation (between concepts). **2.** *usu. pl.* **Differenzen,** differences (of opinion, of outlook); disagreements; **mit j-m Differenzen haben,** to disagree with s.o.

Differenzengleichung, *f. Mth:* difference equation.

Differenzenmethode, *f.* **1.** *Log: Statistics:* method of difference; principle of difference; method of concomitant variations. **2.** *Statistics: etc:* method of classification by non-apparent characteristics.

Differenzenrechnung, *f. Mth:* calculus of differences.

Differenzgeschäft, *n.,* **Differenzhandel,** *m. St.Exch:* speculation; buying on margin; time-bargain.

differenzierbar [difərɛnˈtsiːrbaːr], *a.* distinguishable; *Mth:* differentiable.

Differenzierbarkeit, *f.* distinction; *Mth:* differentiability.

differenzieren [difərɛnˈtsiːrən]. **I.** *v.* **1.** *v.tr.* (*a*) *Mth:* to differentiate (function); to obtain the differential (coefficient) of (equation, etc.); (*b*) to differentiate between (two things); to distinguish, to mark the difference, between (two things); to delineate (character, etc.) subtly. **2.** *v.i.* (*haben*) to differentiate, to distinguish; **zwischen zwei Dingen d.,** to differentiate between two things; to distinguish, to mark the difference, between two things; to make distinctions between two things; **man muß d. können,** one should be able to make distinctions; (*of two thgs*) **sich d.,** to differ; *Biol: etc:* to differentiate; to be differentiated.

II. *vbl s.* **1. Differenzieren,** *n. in vbl senses.* **2. Differenzierung,** *f.* (*a*)=II. 1; *also* differentiation; (*b*) development of differences; variation; *Biol: Mth:* differentiation; *Ling:* differentiation, splitting.

Differenziertheit, *f.* distinctiveness.

Differenzmessung, *f. El:* differential measurement.

Differenztarif, *m.*=**Differentialtarif.**

Differenzton, *m. Mus:* differential tone.

differieren [difəˈriːrən], *v.i.* (*haben*) to differ, diverge, to be different (from sth.).

Diffession [difɛsi̯ˈoːn], *f.* -/-**en.** *Jur:* traverse of a (private) deed.

difficil [difiˈtsiːl], *a.*=**diffizil.**

diffident [difi·ˈdɛnt], *a.* distrustful; diffident.

Diffidenz [difi·ˈdɛnts], *f.* -/. distrust; diffidence.

diffidieren [difi·ˈdiːrən], *v.i.* (*haben*) to be distrustful; to be diffident.

diffizil [difi·ˈtsiːl], *a.* difficult, *F:* awkward, ticklish (situation, problem, etc.); delicate (situation); (*of pers.*) difficult; hard to please; awkward.

difform [diˈfɔrm], *a.*=**deform.**

Difformität [difɔrmi·ˈtɛːt], *f.* -/-**en**=**Deformität.**

Diffraktion [difraktsi̯ˈoːn], *f.* -/. *Opt:* diffraction.

Diffraktionsplatte, *f. Opt:* Abbe refractometer.

diffundieren [difunˈdiːrən]. **1.** *v.tr. Opt:* to diffuse, spread, scatter (light); *Sug-R:* to dilute (juice). **2.** *v.i.* (*haben*) (*a*) *Ch:* (*of two fluids, etc.*) **ineinander d.,** to diffuse, mix; (*b*) *Ph:* (*of gases, etc.*) **durch etwas d.,** to diffuse through sth.; **Gase diffundieren,** gases mix.

diffus [diˈfuːs], *a.* diffuse (light); *Opt:* diffused (light); *Med:* (*of aneurism, etc.*) diffuse.

Diffusat [difu·ˈzaːt], *n.* -(**e**)**s**/-**e. 1.** *Ch:* diffusate. **2.** *Sug-R:* diffusion juice.

Diffuseur [dify·ˈzøːr], *m.* -**s**/-**e.** *Sug-R:* diffuser.

Diffusion [difu·zi̯ˈoːn], *f.* -/-**en.** *Ph: Ch: etc:* diffusion.

diffusionsfähig, *a.* diffusible.

Diffusionsfähigkeit, *f.* diffusibility.

Diffusionspumpe, *f. Tchn:* diffusion (air) pump.

Diffusionsrückstände, *f.pl. Sug-R:* exhausted beet slices.

Digallussäure [di·ˈgalus-], *f. Ch:* digallic acid.

Digamie [di·ga·ˈmiː], *f.* -/-**n** [-ˈmiːən]. *Jur:* digamy; *Bot:* dichogamy.

digamisch [di·ˈgaːmiʃ], *a.* dichogamous.

Digamma [di·ˈgamaː], *n.* -**s**-(**s**). *A.Gr.Alph:* digamma.

digen [di·ˈgeːn], *a.* digenous; **digene Fortpflanzung,** digenous reproduction.

Digenie [di·ge·ˈniː], *f.* -/-**n** [-ˈniːən]. *Biol:* digenesis.

digerieren [di·gəˈriːrən], *v.tr. Ch: Pharm:* to digest.

Digesten, die [di·ˈgɛstən], *pl.* the (Justinian) Digest.

digestibel [di·gɛsˈtiːbəl], *a.* digestible.

Digestion [di·gɛsti̯ˈoːn], *f.* -/-**en.** *Physiol: Ch: etc:* digestion.

digestiv [di·gɛsˈtiːf], *a.* digestive.

Digestivmittel, *n. Pharm:* digestive.

Digestor [di·ˈgɛstor], *m.* -**s**/-**en** [-ˈtoːrən]. **1.** *Ch: Pharm: Cu:* digester. **2.** *Ch: Ind:*=**Autoklav.**

Digestorium [di·gɛsˈtoːrĭum], *n.* -**s**/-**rien.** *Ch:* hood.

Digger, *m.* -**s**/-, digger; gold-digger; prospector.

digital [di·gi·ˈtaːl], *a.* digital.

Digitalis [di·gi·ˈtaːlis], *f.* -/. *Bot: Pharm:* digitalis.

Digitalrechner, *m. Electronics:* digital computer.

Diglyph [di·ˈglyːf], *m.* -**s**/-**e, Diglyphe** [di·ˈglyːfə], *f.* -/-**n.** *Arch:* diglyph.

Dignitar [digni·ˈtaːr], *m.* -**s**/-**e,** dignitary.

Dignität [digni·ˈtɛːt], *f.* -/-**en. 1.** dignity. **2.** *pl.* **Dignitäten,** *Ecc:* company of canons.

Digression [di·grɛsi̯ˈoːn], *f.* -/-**en,** digression; *Astr:* digression, elongation.

digyn [di·ˈgyːn], **digynisch** [di·ˈgyːniʃ], *a. Bot:* digynous.

Dihexaeder [di·hɛksa·ˈeːdər], *n.* -**s**/-. *Cryst: etc:* dihexahedron.

dihexagonal [di·hɛksa·go·ˈnaːl], *a. Cryst: etc:* dihexagonal.

Diiambus [di·iˈambus], **Dijambus** [di·ˈjambus], *m.* -/-**ben.** *Pros:* diamb.

Dikabrot [ˈdiːkaː-], *n.* dika bread.

Dikast [diˈkast], *m.* -**en**/-**en.** *Gr.Hist:* dicast.

Dikasterion, Dikasterium [di·kasˈteːrĭon, -ˈteːrĭum], *n.* -**s**/-**rien.** *Gr.Hist:* dicastery.

Dikatopter [di·ka·tˈɔptər], *m.* -**s**/-. *Opt:* camera lucida.

Diketone [di·ke·ˈtoːnə], *f.* -/-**n.** *Ch:* diketone.

diklin [di·ˈkliːn], *a. Bot:* **dikline Blüte,** diclinous, unisexual, flower.

Dikotyle [di·ko·ˈtyːlə], *f.* -/-**n.** *Bot:* dicotyledon.

Dikotyledone [di·ko·ty·le·ˈdoːnə], *f.* -/-**n**=**Dikotyle.**

dikotyledonisch [di·ko·ty·le·ˈdoːniʃ], *a. Bot:* dicotyledonous.

Dikrotie [di·kro·ˈtiː], *f.* -/. *Med:* dicrotism.

dikrotisch [di·ˈkroːtiʃ], *a. Med:* dicrotic.

Diktam [ˈdiktam], *m.* -**s**/.=**Diptam.**

Diktaphon [dikta·ˈfoːn], *n.* -(**e**)**s**/-**e,** dictaphone (*R.t.m.*).

Diktat [dikˈtaːt], *n.* -(**e**)**s**/-**e. 1.** dictation; **nach D. schreiben,** to write, type, at, from, to, (s.o.'s) dictation; to take dictation; **ein Stück, das nach D. niedergeschrieben worden ist,** a passage taken down from dictation; *Sch:* **D. schreiben,** to do, write, dictation. **2.** dictation; dictate; **wir werden uns keinem D. unterwerfen,** we won't submit to dictation; *see also* **Versailler, Versailles.**

Diktatfrieden, *m.* dictated peace.

Diktator [dikˈtaːtor], *m.* -**s**/-**en** [-ta·ˈtoːrən]. *Pol: etc:* dictator.

diktatorisch [dikta·ˈtoːriʃ], *a.* dictatorial; **er hat ein diktatorisches Auftreten,** he is dictatorial in his manner, he has a dictatorial, imperious, manner.

Diktatur [dikta·ˈtuːr], *f.* -/-**en.** *Pol: etc:* dictatorship; **D. des Proletariats,** dictatorship of the proletariat.

diktieren [dikˈtiːrən], *v.tr.* **1.** to dictate (letter, etc.). **2.** (*a*) to dictate (terms of a treaty, etc.); **von der Vernunft diktiert,** dictated by reason; *Jur:* **diktierter Vertrag,** compulsory agreement; (*b*) **ich lasse mir nicht d.,** I won't be dictated to.

Diktiermaschine, *f.* dictating machine.

Diktion [diktsi̯ˈoːn], *f.* -/-**en,** (*a*) way of speaking; manner, mode, of expression; choice of words; manner of speech; (*b*) delivery; diction.

Diktionär [diktsi̯o·ˈnɛːr], *n.* -**s**/-**e,** dictionary.

Diktum [ˈdiktum], *n.* -**s**/-**ta,** dictum; saying.

dilatabel [di·la·ˈtaːbəl], *a.* dilatable, expandable, expansible.

Dilatation [di·la·ta·tsi̯ˈoːn], *f.* -/-**en,** dilatation, dilation; expansion; *Med: Ph:* dilatation.

Dilatationsfuge, *f. Civ.E:* expansion joint.

Dilatator [di·la·ˈtaːtor], *m.* -**s**/-**en** [-ta·ˈtoːrən]. *Anat: Surg:* dilator.

Dilation [di·la·tsi̯ˈoːn], *f.* -/-**en. 1.** delay; procrastination; postponement. **2.** *Ling:* dilation.

Dilatometer [di·la·to·ˈmeːtər], *n.* -**s**/-. *Ph:* dilatometer.

dilatorisch [di·la·ˈtoːriʃ], *a.* dilatory; *Jur:* **dilatorische Einrede,** dilatory exception; *adv.* **etwas d. behandeln,** to treat sth. in a dilatory manner, dilatorily.

Dilemma [di·ˈlɛmaː], *n.* -**s**/-**s** & -**ta.** *Log:* dilemma; *F:* dilemma; embarrassment; **sich in einem D. befinden, in einem D. sein,** to be in a dilemma, *F:* on the horns of a dilemma.

dilemmatisch [di·lɛˈmaːtiʃ], *a.* dilemmatic.

Dilettant [di·lɛˈtant], *m.* -**en**/-**en,** dilettante.

dilettantisch [di·lɛˈtantiʃ], *a.* dilettante; *adv.* **etwas d. tun,** to do sth. in a dilettante fashion.

Dilettantismus [di·lɛtanˈtismus], *m.* -/. dilettantism.

dilettieren [di·lɛˈtiːrən], *v.i.* (*haben*) **in etwas** *dat.* **d.,** to be a dilettante in sth., to do sth. in a dilettante manner.

Diligence [di·li·ˈʒãːs], *f.* -/-**n** [-sən]. *Veh: A:* diligence; stage-coach.

Diligenz [di·li·ˈgɛnts], *f.* -/-**en,** diligence, industry, application.

Dill, *m.* -(**e**)**s**/-**e.** *Bot: Cu:* anethum, (garden) dill; **wilder D.,** spignel.

Dille, *f.* -/-**n. 1.** *Bot:*=**Dill. 2.** nozzle; socket. **3.** *Orn:* myxa.

Dilleniazeen [dile·nĭa·ˈtseːən], *f. pl. Bot:* dilleniads, dillenia family.

Dillenie [diˈleːnĭə], *f.* -/-**n.** *Bot:* dillenia.

Dillenkraut, *n.*=**Dillkraut.**

Dillensauce, *f. Cu:*=**Dillsauce.**

Dillfenchel, *m. Bot:* (common) dill, garden dill.

Dillkraut, *n. Bot:* anethum, dill (leaves).

Dillöl, *n. Pharm:* anethol, dill oil.

Dillsauce, *f. Cu:* dill sauce.

Dilogie [di·lo·ˈgiː], *f.* -/-**n** [-ˈgiːən]. *Rh:* diology.

Dilubock [ˈdiːluː-], *m. Z:* cephalophus, duikerbok.

diluvial [di·lu·vi·ˈaːl], *a. Geol:* pleistocene, glacial, diluvial; **diluviale Ablagerung,** diluvial deposit; **diluvialer Talzug,** glacial valley.

Diluvialzeit, *f. Geol:*=**Diluvium**[2].

Diluvium [di·ˈluːvĭum], *n.* -**s**/-**vien.** *Geol:* **1.** diluvium. **2. das D.,** the Pleistocene epoch, the glacial epoch.

Dimension [di·mɛnzi̯ˈoːn], *f.* -/-**en. 1.** *Mth: etc:* dimension; **lineare D.,** linear dimension; **die vierte D.,** (i) *Mth:* the fourth dimension; (ii) the realm of the departed spirits. **2.** dimension; **Dimensionen** *pl,* dimensions; extent; size; **äußere Dimensionen,** outside, over-all, dimensions; **die Dimensionen eines Körpers bestimmen,** to determine the dimensions, to find the measurements, of a body; **ein Palast von ungeheuren**

Dimensionen, a palace of vast dimensions; **der Rüstungswettlauf nimmt erschreckende Dimensionen an,** the armaments race is assuming frightening proportions.

dimensional [di'mɛnzǐo·'naːl], a. (usu. as second element in compounds) dimensional; **dreidimensional,** three-dimensional; **vierdimensional,** four(th)-dimensional.

Dimensionalität [di'mɛnziona·l'·tɛːt], f. -/-en, dimensionality.

dimensionieren [di'mɛnziǒ·'niːrən], v.tr. Ind: etc: to dimension (sth.).

Dimensionsholz, n. Com: dimension timber.

Dimensionszahl, f. Mth: etc: dimension; dimensionality.

dimer [di'meːr], a. Bot: Ent: dimerous.

Dimeter [di'meːtər], m. -s/-. Pros: dimeter.

Dimethyläther [di'meˑ'tyːlˀˌeːtər], m. Ch: dimethyl ether.

Dimethylbenzol [di'meˑ'tyːlbɛnˌtsoːl], n. Ch: dimethylbenzene.

diminuendo [di'miˑnu·'ɛndoː], adv., **Diminuendo,** n. -s/-s. Mus: diminuendo.

diminuieren [di'miˑnu·'iːrən], v.tr. to diminish, to reduce.

Diminution [di'miˑnu·tsǐ'oːn], f. -/-en, diminution; reduction; Mus: diminution.

diminutiv¹ [di'miˑnu·'tiːf], a. Ling: diminutive; F: diminutive, minute.

Diminutiv², n. -s/-e [-'tiːvə]. Ling: diminutive.

Diminutivsilbe, f. Ling: diminutive syllable.

Diminutivum [di'miˑnu·'tiːvum], n. -s/-va = Diminutiv².

Dimission [di'misǐ'oːn], f. -/-en = Demission.

dimissionieren [di'misio·'niːrən], v.i. (haben) = demissionieren.

Dimity ['dimitiː], m. -s/-. Tex: dimity.

dimorph [di'morf], a. Cryst: Biol: etc: dimorphic, dimorphous.

Dimorphie [di'mor'fiː], f. -/-n [-'fiːən]. Cryst: Biol: etc: dimorphism.

Dimorphismus [di'mor'fismus], m. -/-men = Dimorphie.

Dina ['diːnaː]. Pr.n.f. -s. B: Dinah.

Dinanderie [di'nandə'riː], f. -/-n [-'riːən], dinanderie; brass-ware, copper ware.

Dinar [di'naːr], m. -s/-e. Num: Dinar.

dinarisch [di'naːriʃ], a. Ethn: Dinaric; **die dinarische Rasse,** the Dinaric, Adriatic, race; Geog: **die Dinarischen Alpen,** the Dinaric Alps.

Dinassteine ['diːnas-], m.pl. silica bricks.

Diné, Diner, Dîner [di'neː], n. -s/-s, dinner; **wir geben heute abend ein großes D.,** we are having, giving, a big dinner-party this evening; **wir gehen zum D. zu X,** we are going to dinner, we shall dine, at X's tonight.

Dinformat, Din-Format, n. Ind: paper, etc., of a standardized size; (cp. DIN List of Abbreviations).

Ding¹, n. -s/-e, thing. 1. Phil: thing; entity; **das D. an sich,** the noumenon; the thing in itself; F: **den Weg aller Dinge gehen,** to go the way of all flesh; to die. 2. thing, matter; **die Dinge stehen schlecht,** things are going badly; **wie die Dinge liegen, stehen,** as things are, as matters stand; in the present state of affairs; **du nimmst die Dinge zu ernst,** you take things, matters, too seriously; **nach der Lage der Dinge,** in the circumstances; **den Dingen ihren Lauf lassen,** to let matters take their course; **wenn man die Dinge so, von dieser Seite, sieht, kann man...,** looking at things, matters, from this point of view, one can...; **den Gang der Dinge im Nahen Osten beobachten,** to watch, observe, the course of events, to follow events, in the Near East, to watch the way things are going, developing, in the Near East; **es bereiten sich große Dinge vor,** great events are on the way, are impending; **das ist ein D. der Unmöglichkeit,** that is an impossibility, that is impossible; **das D., ein D., die Dinge, beim rechten Namen nennen,** to call a spade a spade; **jedes D. hat (seine) zwei Seiten,** there are two sides to every question; **vor allen Dingen,** above all things; in the first place; **das geht nicht mit rechten Dingen zu,** here all is not as it should be; F: there is something fishy about this; **(froh und) guter Dinge sein,** to be cheerful, in good spirits; to be of good cheer, of good heart; **unverrichteter Dinge abziehen,** heimkehren, to leave, return, (i) empty-handed, (ii) without success, without achieving one's purpose; B: **bei Gott sind alle Dinge möglich,** with God all things are possible; **bei Gott ist kein D. unmöglich,** with God nothing is impossible; Prov: **aller guten Dinge sind drei,** all good things come in, by, threes. 3. (pl. usu. **Dinger**) F: (a) (inanimate object) **was ist das für ein D.? was sind das für Dinger?** what's that

thing? what are those things? **all die Dinger (da) auf dem Kaminsims,** all those things on the mantlepiece; **was ist das blaue D., das du um deinen Hut hast?** what's that blue thing you've got round your hat? (b) (of women, children, animals) (with adj. expressing pity, contempt, affection, etc.) **armes D.!** poor thing! **die armen kleinen Dinger!** the poor little things! **du dummes D.!** you silly thing; **sie ist ein ekelhaftes D.,** she is a nasty old thing; **ein hübsches kleines D.,** a pretty little thing; cp. **Dings.**

Ding², n. -s/-e. G.Hist: thing, ting; **Ding-,** comb.fm. = Thing-.

Dingel, m. -s/-. Bot: limodorum.

Dingelchen, n. -s/-, little thing; **ein kleines D.,** a tiny little thing; (of woman, child) a dear little thing, a little bit of a thing; F: a nice little thing.

Dingelwurz, f. Bot: epipactis, helleborine.

dingen, v. (p.t. **dingte,** occ. **dang,** p.p. **gedungen,** occ. **gedingt**) 1. v.tr. to hire, engage (s.o.); **gedungener Mörder,** hired assassin; **gedungener, A: gedingter, Knecht,** hired servant. 2. v.i. (haben) A: to bargain (over sth.), to haggle.

Dinger, n.pl. see Ding 3.

Dingerchen, n.pl. little things; **kleine D.,** tiny little things; (of women, children) dear little things, nice little things.

dingfest, a. **j-n d. machen,** to arrest s.o.; to apprehend s.o.; F: to put s.o. behind bars.

Dinggedicht, n. poem in which the poet seeks to penetrate the essential existence of an object in nature.

Dinggeld, n. handsel; earnest (money).

dinghaft, a. Phil: etc: real.

Dinghaftigkeit, f. Phil: etc: reality.

Ding(h)i ['diŋiː], n. -s/-s. Nau: dinghy, dingey.

dinglich, a. 1. Phil: etc: real. 2. Jur: real; **dingliche Klage,** real action; **dingliches Recht,** real right; **dinglicher Vertrag,** real contract. 3. adv. Fin: **d. gesicherte Forderungen,** debts or advances covered by security.

Dingnähe, f. intimate relation with the things of nature.

Dingo ['diŋoː], m. -s/-s. Z: (Australian) dingo.

Dingpfenning, m. = Dinggeld.

Dings, n. -s/-. F: 1. thing; F: thingamy, thingum(a)-bob, thingamajig, thingummy; **wie heißt das D. da?** what's that (i) thing, (ii) place, called? 2. (pers.) **der, die, D. wird es besser wissen (als ich),** Mr what's-his-name, so-and-so, Miss, Mrs, what's-her-name, so-and-so, will know it better than I do; **ich habe gestern die D. getroffen,** I met what's-her-name yesterday.

-dings, comb.fm. 1. suff. (forming advs) **allerdings,** indeed; certainly; **neuerdings,** recently. 2. F: (forming nouns) **was für ein blaues Schleierdings hast du denn da um den Hut?** what's that blue veil thing you've got round your hat?

Dingsbums, n. -/- = Dingsda.

Dingsda, n. -s/-. F: (a) = Dings 1; (b) (pers.) (Mr, Miss, Mrs) so-and-so; what-d'ye-call-him, -her; what's-his, -her, -name; (Mr, Miss, Mrs) thingamy, thingum(a)bob, thingamajig, thingummy; (place) what-d'ye-call-it, what's-its-name.

Dingskirchen, n. -s/-. F: such and such a place; so-and-so; what's-its-name.

Dingstätte, f. = Thingstätte.

Dingwelt, f. Phil: etc: reality.

Dingwort, n. -(e)s/-wörter. Gram: noun, substantive.

dingwörtlich, a. Gram: substantival, nominal.

dinieren [di'niːrən], v.i. (haben) to dine; to take dinner; **Herr X diniert heute abend bei...,** Mr X is dining tonight at..., Mr X is going to a dinner-party tonight at....

dinitrieren [di'ni·'triːrən], v.tr. Ch: to introduce two nitrate groups into (compound).

Dinitrophenol [di'ni·tro·fe·'noːl], n. -s/-. Ch: dinitrophenol.

Dinkaschaf ['diŋka·-], n. Z: Dinka sheep.

Dinkel, m. -s/-. Agr: spelt; German wheat.

Dinoflagellaten [di'no·fla·gɛ·'laːtən], f.pl. Biol: dinoflagellates, peridians.

Dinornis [di'nornis], f. -/-. Paleont: dinornis.

Dinosaurier [di'no·'zauriər], m. -s/-. Paleont: dinosaur(ian).

Dinotherium [di'no·'teːriʊm], n. -s/-rien. Paleont: dinotherium.

Dinozerat [di'no·tse·'raːt], m. -en/-en. Paleont: dinoceras.

Dioch ['diːɔx], m. -s/-s. Orn: red-billed weaver.

Diode [di'oːdə], f. -/-n. W.Tel: etc: diode.

Diodon [di'o·'doːn]. m. -s/-e. Ich: diodon, porcupine-fish, sea-porcupine, globe-fish.

Diodor [di'o·'doːr]. Pr.n.m. -s. Gr.Lit: Diodorus (Siculus).

Diogenes [di'o·'geˑneːs]. Pr.n.m -'. Diogenes; **das Faß des D.,** Diogenes' tub.

Diogeneskrebs, m. Crust: Diogenes crab, hermit-crab, pagurian.

Diökie [di'ø·'kiː], f. -/-n [-'kiːən] = Diözie.

Diokletian [di'o·kle·tsǐ'aːn]. Pr.n.m. -s. Diocletian.

diokletianisch [di'o·kle·tsǐ'aːniʃ], a. Diocletian, of Diocletian; **die Diokletianische Christenverfolgung,** the persecution (of the Christians) under Diocletian.

Dioktaeder [di'ɔkta·'eːdər], n. & m. -s/-, **Dioktaedron** [di'ɔkt'a·eˑdron], -s/-dra. Cryst: dioctahedron.

Diomed [di'o·'meːt], -s, **Diomedes** [di'o·'meːdɛs], -'. Pr.n.m. Gr.Lit: Diomede(s).

Dionäa [di'o·'nɛːaː], f. -/-näen. Bot: dionaea.

Dionys [di'o·'nyːs]. Pr.n.m. -'. Gr.Ant: Dionysius.

Dionysien [di'o·'nyːziən], n.pl. Gr.Ant: Dionysia.

Dionysios [di'o·'nyːzios]. Pr.n.m. -'. Gr.Ant: Dionysius.

dionysisch [di'o·'nyːziʃ], a. 1. (a) Dionysian; (b) Dionysiac (cult, etc.). 2. Chr: Dionysian (era).

Dionysos, Dionysus [di'o·'nyzos, -zus]. Pr.n.m. -'. Gr.Myth: Dionysos.

diophantisch [di'o·'fantiʃ], a. Mth: **diophantische Analysis, Gleichung,** Diophantine analysis, equation.

Diophantos [di'o·'fantos]. Pr.n.m. -'. Hist. of Mth: Diophantos.

Diopsid [di'op'siːt], n. -(e)s/-e [-s, -'siːdəs/-'siːdə]. Miner: diopside.

Dioptas [di'op'taːs], m. -/. dioptase, emerald copper.

Diopter [di'optər], n -s/-, sight-vane, sight (of alidade, sextant, etc.); peep-sight (of rifle); A: view-finder (of camera).

Diopterlineal [di'optərli·ne·ˌaːl], n. Surv: Nau: alidad(e).

Dioptrie [di'op'triː], f. -/-n [-'triːən]. Opt.Meas: diopter, dioptric, dioptry.

Dioptrik [di'optrik], f. -/. dioptrics.

dioptrisch [di'optriʃ], a. dioptric.

Diorama [di'o·'raːmaː], n. -s/-men, diorama, F: peep-show.

dioramisch [di'o·'raːmiʃ], a. dioramic.

Diorismus [di'o·'rismus], m. -/. Log: diorism.

Diorit [di'o·'riːt], m. -(e)s/-e. Geol: diorite.

Dioritgneis, m. Geol: diorite gneiss.

Dioskuren [di'o·'skuːrən]. Pr.n.m.pl. Gr.Myth: the Dioscuri.

Diotima [di'o·'tiːmaː]. Pr.n.f. -s. Gr.Lit: etc: Diotima.

Dioxy- [di'oksy·'-], comb.fm. Ch: dioxy-; **di-hydroxy-; Dioxybenzol** n, dioxybenzene; **Dioxychinon** n, dihydroxyquinone.

Dioxyd [di'o·'ksyːt], n. -(e)s/-e [-'ksyːts, -'ksyːdəs/-'ksyːdə]. Ch: dioxide.

Diözesan [di'o·tse·'zaːn], m. -en/-en. Ecc: diocesan, (i) member of a diocese; (ii) bishop; (in pastoral letter) **geliebte Diözesanen,** dear children in Jesus Christ.

Diözesanverwaltung, f. Ecc: diocesan administration.

Diözese [di'ø·'tseːzə], f. -/-n, diocese.

Diözie [di'ø·'tsiː], f. -/-n [-'tsiːən]. Bot: dioecism.

diözisch [di'ø·tsiʃ], a. Bot: dioecious.

dipetalisch [di·pe·'taːliʃ], a. Bot: dipetalous.

Diphasig [di·fe·'nyːl], n. -s/-. Ch: diphenyl, biphenyl.

diphasisch [di·'faːziʃ], a. El.E: diphase, diphasic.

Diphenyl [di·fe·'nyːl], n. -s/-. Ch: diphenyl, biphenyl.

Dipholisbaum ['diːfo·lis-], m. Bot: bully-tree.

Diphtherie [difte·'riː], f. -/. Med: diphtheria.

diphtherieartig, a. diphtheroid; diphtheria-like.

Diphtheriebakterien, f.pl. Med: diphtherial, diphtheric, bacteria.

Diphtherieschutzimpfung, f. Med: inoculation against diphtheria.

Diphtheritis [difte·'riːtis], f. -/. Med: diphtheria.

diphtheritisch [difte·'riːtiʃ], a. diphtheritic.

Diphthong [dif'toŋ], m. -(e)s/-e. Ling: diphthong.

diphthongieren [diftoŋ'giːrən], v.tr. Ling: to diphthong, to diphthongize (vowels); **Diphthongierung** f, diphthongization; diphthongism.

diphthongisch [dif'toŋiʃ], a. diphthongal; adv. (pronounced, etc.) as a diphthong.

Diphysiten [di·fy·'ziːtən], pl. Ecc.Hist: = Dyophysiten.

Diplegie [di·ple·'giː], f. -/. Med: diplegia.

Dipleidoskop [di·plaido·'skoːp], n. -s/-e. Opt: dipleidoscope.

diplex ['diːplɛks], a. Tg: diplex, duplex.

Duplex-, comb.fm. = Duplex-.

Dipl(o)- [dipl(o·)'-], comb.fm. dipl(o)-; **Diplosom** n, diplosome; **Diplozephalie** f, diplocephaly.

Diplodocus [diˑploˑˈdoːkus], *m.* **-/- & -ci.** *Paleont:* diplodocus.
diploid [diploˑˈiːt], *a. Biol:* diploid.
Diplokokkus [diploˑˈkokus], *m.* **-/-ken.** *Bac:* diplococcus.
Diplom [diˑˈploːm], *n.* **-s/-e.** **1.** (*a*) patent (of nobility); *Sch:* diploma, certificate (of university, degree, etc.); *Com:* diploma (awarded at trade fair); (*b*) *Sch:* diploma; degree. **2.** *Hist: Pal:* diploma.
Diplom-, *comb.fm. Sch:* holding a diploma, certificate; **D.-Ingenieur** *m, abbr.* **Dipl.-Ing.,** academically trained engineer *or* architect, *approx.*=Dip.Tech.(Eng.); **D.-Handelslehrer** *m,* qualified teacher at a college, school, of commerce; **D.-Kaufmann** *m, abbr.* **Dipl.Kfm.,** *approx.*=Bachelor of Commerce (of London University, etc.); **D.-Physiker** *m, approx.*= Bachelor of Science (with specialist qualifications in physics).
Diplomarbeit, *f. Sch:* thesis (submitted for a diploma *or* degree).
Diplomat [diploˑˈmaːt], *m.* **-en/-en,** diplomat; diplomatist; *F:* diplomat.
Diplomatie [diploˑmaˑˈtiː], *f.* **-/-n** [-ˈtiːən]. **1.** (*a*) diplomacy; (*b*) *F:* diplomacy; shrewd tactics; **D. anwenden, um seinen Zweck zu erreichen,** to attain one's ends by diplomacy. **2. die D.,** the diplomatic corps.
Diplomatik [diploˑˈmaːtik], *f.* **-/.** **1.** diplomatics; diplomatology. **2.** *F:* diplomacy.
Diplomatiker [diploˑˈmaːtikər], *m.* **-s/-,** expert in diplomatics.
Diplomatin [diˑploˑˈmaːtin], *f.* **-/-innen,** (woman) diplomat, diplomatist; *F:* diplomat.
diplomatisch [diploˑˈmaːtiʃ], *a.* **1.** (*a*) diplomatic; **das Diplomatische Korps,** the diplomatic corps; **in den diplomatischen Dienst eintreten,** to enter the diplomatic service; **die diplomatische Sprache,** the language of diplomacy; (*b*) diplomatic (answer, person, etc.); **d. sein,** to be diplomatic, to be a good diplomat; *F:* to diplomatize; *adv.* **d. vorgehen,** to act with diplomacy, in a diplomatic manner. **2.** *Pal:* diplomatic.
diplomieren [diˑploˑˈmiːrən], *v.tr.* to grant a diploma to (s.o.).
Diplomprüfung, *f.* examination on which a diploma, etc., is awarded.
Diplopie [diˑploˑˈpiː], *f.* **-/-n** [-ˈpiːən]. *Med:* diplopia.
Dipnoer [diˑˈpnoːər], *m.* **-s/-.** *Ich:* lung-fish, dipnoan; **die Dipnoer,** the dipnoi.
Dipodie [diˑpoˑˈdiː], *f.* **-/-n** [-ˈdiːən]. *Pros:* dipody.
dipodisch [diˑˈpoːdiʃ], *a.* dipodous.
Dipol [ˈdiːpoˑl], *m.* **-s/-e.** *W.Tel:* dipole.
dipolar [diˑpoˑˈlaːr], *a. El: Ph:* dipolar, bipolar, two-pole.
Dippel, *m.* **-s/-** =**Dübel.**
dippen, *v.tr.* **1.** *Nau:* **(die) Flagge d.,** to dip one's flag; *abs.* **d.,** to dip. **2.** *Aut:* **den Vergaser d.,** to tickle *or* flood the carburetter. **3.** *Husb:* **Schafe d.,** to dip sheep.
Dipsazeen [dipsaˑˈtseːən], *f.pl. Bot:* dipsaceae.
Dipsomane [dipsoˑˈmaːnə], *m., f.* **-n/-n,** dipsomaniac.
Dipsomanie [dipsoˑmaˑˈniː], *f.* **-/.** dipsomania.
Diptam [ˈdiptam], *m.* **-s/.** *Bot:* **1.** dittany, fraxinella; **echter, weißer, D.,** false dittany, burning bush, gas-plant. **2. kretischer D.,** dittany of Crete, Cretan dittany.
Diptera [ˈdipteˑraˑ], *f. pl. Ent:* diptera.
Diptere [dipˈteːrə], *f.* **-/-n.** *Ent:* dipter, dipteran.
Dipterologie [dipteˑroˑloˑˈgiː], *f.* **-/.** *Ent:* dipterology.
Dipteros [ˈdipteˑros], *m.* **-/-roi.** *Arch:* dipteros, dipteral temple.
Diptychon [ˈdiptyˑçon], *n.* **-s/-chen & -cha,** diptych.
dir. 1. *pers.pron. dat. of* **du,** *q.v.* **2.** *refl.pron.* yourself.
Directoire, das [diˑrɛktoˑˈaːr], **-s/.** *Fr.Hist:* the Directory; *Furn: Cost:* the Directoire (style).
Directoirestil, der, the Directoire (style).
direkt [diˑˈrɛkt]. **1.** *a.* direct; immediate; **direkte Ursache,** direct, immediate, cause; **direkte Steuern,** direct taxes; **von j-m in direkter Linie abstammen,** to be a direct descendant of s.o.; **in direkter Verbindung mit j-m stehen,** to be in direct communication, in close touch, with s.o.; **direkte Berührung,** direct contact; **in direkter Beziehung zu etwas stehen,** to have a close connection with sth.; to be closely related to sth.; to be closely connected with sth.; **seine Ausdrucksweise ist sehr d.,** he is blunt in his manner of expression; he is outspoken; **ein direkter Hinweis auf etwas** *acc.,* a direct, positive, indication of sth.; *Gram:* **direkte Rede,** direct speech, direct narration, direct oration; *Artil:* **direktes Feuer, direktes Schießen,** direct fire; *Pol:* **direkte Aktion,** direct action; **direkte Wahl,** direct vote; *Rail:* **direkte Fahrkarte,** through ticket; **direkte Verbindung,** through connection, through train. **2.** *adv.* (*a*) direct; straight; directly; **d. von j-m abstammen,** to be directly descended from s.o., to be a direct descendant of s.o.; **ich bin nicht d. betroffen,** I am not directly concerned; **du mußt dich d. an ihn wenden,** you must contact him direct, you must get into direct communication with him; **sie hat es d. von X gehört,** she had it at first hand from X; **Waren d. von der Fabrik beziehen,** to obtain goods direct, *F:* straight, from the factory; **Waren d. an j-n senden,** to dispatch goods direct to s.o.; *El: Mec.E: etc:* **d. gekuppelter Motor,** direct-coupled motor; **d. wirkende Maschine,** direct-acting engine; *Nau:* **d. östlicher Kurs,** due east course; *W.Tel: TV:* **d. senden, übertragen,** to broadcast, transmit, (programme) live; (*b*) *F:* **d. entgegengesetzt,** directly contrary; **er wohnt d. gegenüber der Kirche,** he lives directly opposite the church; **er stand d. hinter dem Baum,** he stood immediately, directly, behind the tree; (*c*) *F:* directly; at once; immediately; **ich komme d.,** I'll come immediately; (*d*) *F:* **da muß man d. wütend werden,** it's enough to make, drive, one wild, mad, crazy; **es ist d. kalt heute,** it's really cold today.
Direktfarbstoff, *m. Dy:* direct (cotton) dye.
Direktion [diˑrɛktsiˈoːn], *f.* **-/-en.** **1.** direction; way; **in welche D. gehen Sie?** in which direction are you going? which way are you going? **2.** direction; running (of business, etc.); management, control (of business house, etc.); directorate (of railways, etc.); administration (of hospital, etc.); headship, headmastership (of school). **3.** director(s); manager(s); board of directors; (board of) management; directorship; administration. **4.** office (of the director, etc.); manager's office; offices (of the board, management, etc.); *Sch:* headmaster's room *or* office.
direktionslos, *a.* without direction.
Direktionssekretärin, *f.* director's secretary.
Direktive [diˑrɛkˈtiːvə], *f.* **-/-n,** directive; *usu. pl.* **Direktiven,** directives; (general) instructions; orders; **Direktiven erhalten,** to receive instructions, directives.
Direktor [diˑˈrɛktor], *m.* **s-/-en** [-ˈtoːrən]. **1.** director (of company, bank, museum, university institute, etc.); head (of industrial concern, etc.); principal (of school of music, etc.); (musical) director; headmaster (of secondary school); *U.S:* principal (of high school, etc.); governor (of prison); **geschäftsführender D.,** managing director; *Sch:* administrative director (of university institute). **2.** *W.Tel:* director.
Direktorat [diˑrɛktoˑˈraːt], *n.* **-(e)s/-e.** **1.** directorate; directorship; managership; management; headmastership, headship, principalship (of school, etc.); governorship (of prison). **2.** (director's, etc.) offices; official quarters (of director, manager, etc.); (prison governor's) office.
direktorial [diˑrɛktoˑriˈaːl], *a.* directorial; managerial.
Direktorial-, *comb.fm.* director's . . .; directors' . . .; directorial . . .; **Direktorialversammlung** *f,* directors' meeting; board meeting; **Direktorialgeschäfte** *npl,* directorial duties.
Direktorin [diˑrɛkˈtoːrin], *f.* **-/-innen,** (woman) director; governor (of women's prison); *Sch:* headmistress; principal.
Direktorium [diˑrɛkˈtoːrium], *n.* **-s/-rien.** **1.** directorate; board of directors, of managers; executive committee (of an association, of a political party, union, etc.); board, governing body (of institution). **2.** *Fr.Hist:* **das D.,** the Directory. **3.** *R.C.Ch:* directory.
Direktrice [diˑrɛkˈtriːsə], *f.* **-/-n,** manageress (*in shop or department for ladies' wear*); head (*of ladies' wear department in store*).
Direktrix [diˑˈrɛktriks], *f.* **-/-izes** [diˑˈrɛktriˑtseˑs]. *Geom:* directrix.
Direktsendung, *f. W.Tel: TV:* live programme; *W.Tel:* live broadcast.
Direktübertragung, *f. W.Tel: TV:* (i) live transmission; (ii) live relay.
Direx [ˈdiːrɛks], *m.* **-(en)/-en.** *Sch: F:* headmaster; *F:* head.
Dirigent [diˑriˑˈgɛnt], *m.* **-en/-en.** **1.** *Mus:* conductor (of orchestra, etc.). **2.** *Nau:*=**Besteder.**
dirigieren [diˑriˑˈgiːrən], *v.tr.* **1.** to direct, give directions to (s.o.); to direct, control, (traffic, etc.); to direct, control, manage, *F:* to run (business, etc.); to control (press, opinion, etc.); **Waren an ihre Bestimmungsorte d.,** to dispatch goods to their destination. **2.** *Mus:* to conduct (an orchestra, etc.).
Dirigierpartitur, *f.* conductor's score.
Dirigismus [diˑriˑˈgismus], *m.* **-/.** *Pol.Ec:* planning; planned economy.
dirigistisch [diˑriˑˈgistiʃ], *a. Pol.Ec:* planned (economy); (policy) of planning; planning (measures).
Dirimentien [diˑriˑˈmɛntsiən], *f.pl. Jur:* diriment impediments (to marriage).
Dirk, *m.* **-s/-e.** **1.** *Nau:* topping-lift. **2.** (*dagger*) dirk.
Dirke [ˈdirkeː]. *Pr.n.f.* **-s.** *Gr.Myth:* Dirce.
dirken, *v.tr. Nau:* to top, peak (a boom).
Dirn, *f.* **-/-en.** *South G. & Austrian Dial:* lass, wench.
Dirnd(e)l, *n.* **-s/-.** **1.** *South G. & Austrian Dial:* (young) girl; young woman; lass. **2.** Austrian and Bavarian traditional women's costume, dirndl dress.
Dirnd(e)lbluse, *f.* dirndl blouse, low-cut blouse with puffed sleeves.
Dirnd(e)lkleid, *n.*=**Dirnd(e)l** 2.
Dirnd(e)lrock, *m.* dirndl skirt, gathered skirt.
Dirnd(e)lschürze, *f.* (*part of dirndl costume*) short apron.
Dirne, *f.* **-/-n.** **1.** *A. & Lit:* maiden; damsel; lass; *A. & Hum:* wench. **2.** prostitute, whore, street-walker; *F:* tart.
Dirnenhaus, *n.* brothel.
Dirnensprache, *f.* street-walkers' cant.
Dirnenviertel, *n.* brothel area (of town); *F:* red light district.
Dirning, *n.* **-s/-s.** *North G. Dial:*=**Dirnd(e)l** 1.
dis, Dis[dis], *n.* **-/-.** *Mus:* (the note) D sharp, D♯; **Dis-dur, Dis-Dur, dis-moll, dis-Moll, (-Tonart),** (key; of) D sharp major, D sharp minor.
dis-, Dis-, *pref.* (*in foreign words of Latin & Greek origin*) (*forming verbs, nouns, adjs*) dis-; **disfigurieren,** to disfigure, disfeature; **diskutieren,** to discuss; **Disfiguration** *f,* disfiguration, disfigurement; **Diskussion** *f,* discussion; **disponibel,** disposable.
Disagio [disˀˈaːdʒoː], *n.* **-/-s.** *Fin:* difference between actual and face value of a security.
Disäure, *f.* **-/-n.** *Ch:* diacid, biacid.
Disazofarbstoff [disˀˈaːtsoː-], *m. Ch: etc:* disazo dye.
Disc- *cp.* **Disk-, Disz-.**
Discantus [disˈkantus], *m.* **-/-ti.** *Mus:* descant.
Diseur [diˑˈzøːr], *m.* **-s/-e, Diseuse** [diˑˈzøːzə], *f.* **-/-n,** monologuist; *diseur, diseuse.*
disgregieren [disˑgreˑˈgiːrən], *v.tr. Ph:* to disgregate (molecules).
Disharmonie [disharmoˑˈniː], *f.* **-/-n** [-ˈniːən], disharmony; misunderstanding; discord; *Mus:* disharmony; dissonance.
disharmonieren [disharmoˑˈniːrən], *v.i.* (*haben*) (*of sounds*) to be discordant, dissonant; (*of colours, opinions, etc.*) to clash; (*of pers.*) **mit j-m d.,** to disaccord, differ, with s.o.; **X und Y disharmonieren,** X and Y are out of harmony, do not get on (together); X and Y are not suited, are at odds, *F:* don't hit it off.
disharmonisch [disharˈmoːniʃ], *a.* disharmonious; discordant, dissonant.
Disilikat [diˑziˑliˑˈkaːt], *n.* **-(e)s/-e.** *Ch:* disilicate.
Disintegrator [disˀinteˑˈgraːtor], *m.* **-s/-en** [-graˑˈtoːrən]=**Desintegrator.**
disis, Disis [ˈdisis], *n.* **-/-.** *Mus:* (the note) D double sharp.
disjungieren [disjuŋˈgiːrən], *v.tr. Log: Gram: etc:* to disjoin, to separate.
disjunkt [disˈjuŋkt], *a. Log:* disjunct.
Disjunktion [disjuŋktsiˈoːn], *f.* **-/-en.** *Log: Gram: etc:* disjunction.
disjunktiv [disjuŋkˈtiːf], *a. Log: Gram: etc:* disjunctive; **disjunktive** [disjuŋkˈtiːvə] **Proposition,** disjunctive proposition, disjunction; **disjunktive Konjunktion,** disjunctive conjunction.
Diskant [disˈkant], *m.* **-(e)s/-e.** *Mus:* (*esp. boy's voice*) soprano, treble.
Diskantflöte, *f.* descant *or* treble flute; descant *or* treble recorder.
Diskantschlüssel, *m. Mus:* C clef.
Diskantviola, *f.* treble *or* descant viol.
Diskobol [diskoˑˈboːl], *m.* **-/-e.** *Gr.Ant:* discobolus, discus-thrower.
Diskont [disˈkont], *m.* **-(e)s/-e.** *Fin:* **1.** discount; bank discount. **2.**=**Diskontsatz.** **3.** discounting.
Diskontbank, *f.* discount bank, discount house.
Diskonten [disˈkontən], *pl. Fin:* discounted bills.
diskontfähig, *a.* discountable.
Diskontgeschäft, *n. Fin:* discount(ing)-business.

Diskonthaus, *n.*=**Diskontbank.**
diskontierbar [diskonˈtiːrbaːr], *a.* discountable.
diskontieren [diskonˈtiːrən]. **1.** *v.tr. Fin:* to discount (bill). **2.** *vbl s.* **Diskontierung,** *f.* discounting; **Diskontierung von Wechseln,** discount-marketing; **Diskontierung von Buchforderungen,** using book-debts as security (for overdraft, loan, etc.).
diskontinuierlich [diskontiˑnuˑˈiːrliç], *a.* discontinuous; intermittent; *Mth:* discontinuous; discrete; **diskontinuierliche Funktion,** discrete function.
Diskontinuität [diskontiˑnuˑiˑˈtɛːt], *f.* -/-en. *Phil: etc:* discontinuity; **die Begriffe von Kontinuität und D.,** the concepts of continuity and discontinuity.
Diskontinuitätsfläche, *f. Meteor:* surface of discontinuity.
Diskontmakler, *m.* bill-broker, bill-discounter.
Diskontpolitik, *f.* discount policy; bank-rate policy.
Diskontrate, *f.*=**Diskontsatz.**
Diskontrechnung, *f. Fin:* statement of charges for discounted bills, including discount.
Diskontsatz, *m. Fin:* (*a*) discount-rate, rate of discount; market-rate; (*b*) bank-rate.
Diskontwechsel, *m. Fin:* discounted bill.
diskordant [diskorˈdant], *a.* discordant; *Geol:* **diskordante Parallelstruktur,** discordant stratification.
Diskordanz [diskorˈdants], *f.* -/-en. *Mus:* discordance; *Geol:* **D. der Schichten,** inconformability of strata.
Diskos [ˈdiskos], *m.* -/- =**Diskus.**
diskreditieren [diskreˑdiˑˈtiːrən], *v.tr.* to discredit (s.o., an opinion); to bring (s.o., oneself, sth.) into disrepute, discredit; (*of pers.*) to throw discredit upon (s.o.); **sein Betragen hat ihn in den Augen der Öffentlichkeit diskreditiert,** his conduct has discredited him with the public; **eine diskreditierte Wissenschaft,** a discredited science.
diskrepant [diskreˑˈpant], *a.* discrepant; different.
Diskrepanz [diskreˑˈpants], *f.* -/-en, discrepancy; disagreement; **eine D. von ...,** a discrepancy, difference, of ....
diskret [disˈkreːt], *a.* **1.** discreet; **er ist durchaus d.,** he is thoroughly discreet; **ein diskretes Schweigen bewahren,** to maintain a discreet silence. **2. diskrete Farben,** quiet colours; **diskrete Eleganz,** quiet elegance; *adv.* **sich d. kleiden,** to dress discreetly, unobtrusively. **3.** *Mth: Log:* discrete.
Diskretion [diskreˑtsĭˈoːn], *f.* -/-en. **1.** discretion; judgment; **D. anwenden,** to use discretion; **ich überlasse es Ihrer D.,** I leave it to your discretion; *Mil:* **sich auf D. ergeben,** to surrender at discretion, to surrender unconditionally. **2.** discretion; secrecy; **vollste D. wahren,** to preserve strictest confidence; **j-n zu äußerster D. verpflichten,** to enjoin the strictest secrecy upon s.o.; **sich auf j-s D. verlassen,** to rely on s.o.'s secrecy, discretion; **Brot a D.,** (*on bills of fare*) unlimited bread, bread *ad lib.*
diskretionär [diskreˑtsĭoˈnɛːr], *a.* discretionary; *Jur:* **diskretionäre Gewalt,** discretionary power.
Diskretionstage, *m.pl. Fin:* days of grace.
Diskriminante [diskriˑmiˑˈnantə], *f.* -/-n. *Mth:* discriminant.
Diskrimination [diskriˑmiˑnaˑtsĭˈoːn], *f.* -/-en. **1.** discrimination (against s.o.). **2.** discrimination; differentiation.
diskriminieren [diskriˑmiˈniːrən]. **1.** *v.i.* (*haben*) to discriminate, differentiate (**zwischen,** between). **2.** *v.tr.* to discriminate against (s.o.); to deal unfairly with (s.o.); *abs.* **d.,** to show preference; **diskriminierende Zölle,** discriminating duties, tariffs. **3.** *vbl s.* **Diskriminierung,** *f.*= **Diskrimination.**
diskurieren [diskuˈriːrən], *v.i.* (*haben*) to discourse, *A:* to hold discourse (**über etwas** *acc.,* upon sth.); to converse.
Diskurs [disˈkurs], *m.* -es/-e, discourse; conversation.
diskursiv [diskurˈziːf], *a.* discursive; *Log:* discursive; deductive.
Diskus [ˈdiskus], *m.* -/-, -se & -ken. **1.** (*a*) *Ant:* disc; plate; (shallow) dish; (*b*) *Sp:* discus. **2.** *Anat:* disc. **3.** *Bot:* thalamus *or* torus.
Diskussion [diskusĭˈoːn], *f.* -/-en, discussion; debate; **die zur D. stehende Frage,** the question under discussion; **die Frage wird morgen zur D. gestellt,** the question will come up for discussion tomorrow; **etwas zur D. stellen,** to put sth. up for discussion; **ohne weitere D. nachgeben,** to comply without further discussion, argument, without arguing.
Diskussionsbasis, *f.* basis for discussion.
Diskuswerfen, *n. Sp:* throwing the discus.
Diskuswurf, *m. Sp:* (*a*) throwing the discus; (*b*) throw (of a discus).
diskutabel [diskuˑˈtaːbəl], *a.* discussible; debatable; **es ist nicht d.,** it is not worth talking about, it is not worth considering.
diskutierbar [diskuˑˈtiːrbaːr], *a.*=**diskutabel.**
diskutieren [diskuˑˈtiːrən], *v.tr. & i.* (*haben*) to discuss (sth.); to debate (sth.); **eine viel diskutierte Frage,** a much discussed question; **über eine Sache d.,** to have a discussion about sth.; **eine Sache zu Ende d.,** to argue out a question; *F:* **darüber läßt sich d.,** that is worth considering.
Dislokation [disloˑkaˑtsĭˈoːn], *f.* -/-en. **1.** *Geol:* dislocation; faulting; deformation; displacement. **2.** *Med: Vet:* dislocation (of bone, etc.).
Dislokationsbeben, *n.* tectonic earthquake.
Dislokationsspalte, *f. Geol:* fault-fissure; lithoclase.
Dismembrator [dismɛmˈbraːtor], *m.* -s/-en [-braˑˈtoːrən]=**Desintegrator.**
Dispachant [dispaˈʃant], *m.* -en/-en =**Dispacheur.**
Dispache [disˈpaʃ(ə)], *f.* -/-n [-ʃən]. *M.Ins:* (*a*) average adjustment, statement; (*b*) average bond.
Dispacheur [dispaˈʃøːr], *m.* -s/-e. *M.Ins:* average-stater, average-adjuster.
dispachieren [dispaˈʃiːrən], *v.i.* (*haben*) *M.Ins:* to adjust an average; to adjust averages.
disparat [dispaˈraːt], *a. Log:* disparate.
Disparität [disparˑiˑˈtɛːt], *f.* -/-en, disparity; incongruity.
Dispens [disˈpɛns], *m.* -es/-e & *f.* -/-en. **1.** (*a*) dispensation (from sth., from doing sth.); exemption (from sth.); (*b*) *Jur: Ecc:* dispensation. **2.** certificate of dispensation; certificate of exemption.
Dispensation [dispɛnzaˑtsĭˈoːn], *f.* -/-en. *Jur: Ecc:* dispensation.
Dispensationsgewalt, *f. Ecc:* dispensing power (of the Pope).
Dispensatorium [dispɛnzaˑˈtoːrĭum], *n.* -s/-rien, dispensatory; pharmacopoeia.
dispensieren [dispɛnˈziːrən], *v.tr.* **1. j-n von etwas d.,** to dispense, exempt, excuse s.o. from doing sth.; **ich bin dispensiert,** I have been excused (from attendance); I have been given leave (of absence); *Ecc:* **j-n vom Fasten d.,** to dispense s.o. from fasting; *abs:* **der Bischof kann d.,** the bishop may dispense; **Dispensierung** *f,* dispensation, exemption (of s.o.) (from doing sth.). **2.** *Pharm:* **Arznei d.,** to dispense, make up, medicine.
Dispergens [dispɛrˈgɛns], *m.* -/-genzien [-ˈgɛntsĭən]. *Ch:* dispersion agent.
dispergierbar [dispɛrˈgiːrbaˑr], *a.* dispersible.
dispergieren [dispɛrˈgiːrən], *v.tr. Opt: etc:* (*of prism, etc.*) to disperse; **dispergierend,** dispersive, dispersing.
dispermatisch [dispɛrˈmaːtiʃ], *a. Biol:* dispermic.
Dispermie [dispɛrˈmiː], *f.* -/-n [-ˈmiːən]. *Biol:* dispermy.
dispers [disˈpɛrs], *a.* disperse, dispersed; *Ch:* **disperses** [disˈpɛrzəs] **System,** disperse system; **disperse Phase,** disperse, dispersed, phase.
Dispersion [dispɛrzĭˈoːn], *f.* -/-en. **1.** dispersion; scattering. **2.** *Ch: Opt:* dispersion.
Dispersionsgrad, *m. Ch: Opt:* degree of dispersion.
Dispersionsmittel, *n. Ch:* (*a*) dispersing medium, dispersion medium, continuous phase; (*b*) dispersive agent.
Dispersität [dispɛrziˑˈtɛːt], *f.* -/-en. *Ch:* dispersity.
Dispersoid [dispɛrzoˑˈiːt], *n.* -s/-e [-ˈiːdə]. *Ch:* dispersoid; dispersed phase.
Disponenda [dispoˑˈnɛndaː], **Disponenden** [dispoˑˈnɛndən], *n.pl. Publ:* books on extended sale or return.
Disponent [dispoˑˈnɛnt], *m.* -en/-en, managing clerk; authorized representative (of a firm).
disponieren [dispoˑˈniːrən]. I. *v.i.* (*haben*) **1. über etwas** *acc.,* **j-n, d.,** (*a*) to have sth., s.o., at one's disposal; **Sie können über mich d.,** I am at your disposal, service; (*b*) to dispose of (s.o.'s fate, etc.); to take charge of sth.; to make arrangements on s.o.'s behalf; to take over s.o.'s affairs; **über etwas** *acc.* **d. können,** to be free to dispose of sth. as one likes; **er kann über seine Zeit d.,** his time is his own; **sie disponiert über mein Haus, als ob es ihres wäre,** she treats my house as though it were her own. **2.** *abs.* to make arrangements; **lassen Sie mich Ihre Pläne wissen, damit ich entsprechend d. kann,** let me know what you plan to do, so that I can make arrangements, can make my plans, accordingly; **wir haben in diesem Sinne disponiert,** we have made arrangements to this effect; **geschickt d.,** to be careful, to plan carefully; to arrange matters cleverly, dextrously.
II. **disponieren,** *v.tr.* **1.** to dispose of (sum of money, etc.). **2.** to arrange, make arrangements for (journey, etc.); to plan (essay, etc.). **3.** *Publ:* to hold (books on sale or return) beyond the agreed period.
III. *p.p. & a.* **disponiert,** *in vbl senses; esp.* (*a*) **d. sein, etwas zu tun,** to feel disposed, inclined, to be in the humour, to do sth.; **ich fühle mich heute nicht d., zu ...,** I don't feel in the mood to ... today, I don't feel like ... today; (*b*) **gut, schlecht, d. sein,** to be in good, bad, form; **der prächtig disponierte Boxer,** the boxer who is, was, in excellent form; (*of artiste, etc.*) **nicht d.,** indisposed; (*c*) *Med:* **für eine Krankheit, usw., d. sein,** to have a tendency, (pre)disposition, to an illness, etc.
Disposition [dispoˑziˑtsĭˈoːn], *f.* -/-en. **1.** disposition; lay-out (of garden, house, essay, etc.); plan (of house, essay, etc.); *Mus:* disposition, specification (of organ stops). **2.** disposal; **etwas zur D. stellen,** to make (funds, etc.) available; to vacate (one's office); **j-m etwas zur D. stellen,** to place sth. at s.o.'s disposal; **zu j-s D. stehen,** to be at s.o.'s disposal; *Adm:* **Stellung zur D.,** sending (of s.o.) into temporary retirement; *Mil:* **Offizier zur D.,** over-age officer (available for re-employment). **3.** (*a*) state (of mind, health, etc.); frame of mind; (*b*) disposition, tendency, predisposition (to an illness, etc.). **4.** *pl.* **Dispositionen,** arrangements; **Dispositionen machen, treffen,** to make arrangements (**für etwas, zu etwas,** for sth., for doing sth.); **Dispositionen über etwas** *acc.* **machen, treffen,** to settle, arrange, what to do with sth.
Dispositionsschein, *m. Fin:* banker's acknowledgement of a credit note.
dispositiv [dispoˑziˑˈtiːf], *a. esp. Jur:* dispositive (law).
Disproportion [disproˑportsĭˈoːn], *f.* -/-en, disproportion.
disproportioniert [disproˑportsĭoˑˈniːrt], *a.* disproportioned; out of proportion.
Disput [disˈpuːt], *m.* -(e)s/-e, dispute; controversy; **sie hatten einen heftigen D. über ...,** they had a fierce argument about ....
disputabel [dispuˑˈtaːbəl], *a.* disputable; controversial.
Disputant [dispuˑˈtant], *m.* -en/-en, disputer, disputant, disputator.
Disputation [dispuˑtaˑtsĭˈoːn], *f.* -/-en. *Sch: etc:* disputation.
disputieren [dispuˑˈtiːrən], *v.i.* (*haben*) to debate, discourse (argumentatively); to have, hold, a debate; *Sch:* to hold a disputation; **über etwas** *acc.* **d.,** to dispute about, on, sth.; to debate, argue, sth.; **mit j-m d.,** to dispute with, against, s.o. (on, about, sth.); *F:* to quarrel, wrangle, argue, with s.o. (over, about, sth.).
Disputiergeist, *m. F:* wrangler; disputatious person; controversialist.
Disputiergesellschaft, *f.*=**Disputierklub.**
Disputierklub, *m.* debating society.
Disputiersucht, *f.* disputatiousness; argumentativeness.
disputiersüchtig, *a.* disputatious; argumentative.
Disqualifikation [diskvaˑliˑfiˑkaˑtsĭˈoːn], *f.* -/-en, disqualification.
disqualifizieren [diskvaˑliˑfiˑˈtsiːrən], *v.tr.* to disqualify (s.o.).
Dissens [diˈsɛns], *m.* -es/-e [-ˈsɛnzəs/-ˈsɛnzə], disagreement; dissent; difference of opinion.
Dissenter [diˈsɛntər], *m.* -s/-s. *Ecc:* Dissenter.
dissentieren [disɛnˈtiːrən], *v.i.* (*haben*) **von j-m, etwas, d.,** to dissent, differ, from s.o., s.o.'s opinion, etc.
disserieren [diseˑˈriːrən], *v.tr. & i.* (*haben*) = **dissertieren.**
Dissertation [disɛrtaˑtsĭˈoːn], *f.* -/-en. *Sch:* dissertation; *esp.*=**Doktorarbeit.**
dissertieren [disɛrˈtiːrən], *v.tr. & i.* (*haben*) **über etwas** *acc.,* **etwas, d.,** to dissert, dissertate, on sth., to deliver a dissertation upon sth.; *Sch:* **über ein Thema d.,** to write a (doctoral) thesis, dissertation, on a subject.
Dissident [disiˈdɛnt], *m.* -en/-en, (*a*) agnostic; (*b*) dissenter (from a national church); dissentient; *Hist:* **die Polnischen Dissidenten,** the Polish Dissidents.
Dissimilation [disiˑmiˑlaˑtsĭˈoːn], *f.* -/-en. *Ling:* dissimilation; *Biol:* dissimilation, catabolism.
dissimilieren [disiˑmiˈliːrən], *v.tr.* **1.** *Biol:* to decompose (substance). **2.** *Ling:* to dissimilate (two sounds). **3.** *vbl s.* **Dissimilierung,** *f.*= **Dissimilation.**

Dissimulation [disi·mu·la·tsi'o:n], *f.* **-/-en.** *Med: etc:* dissimulation.
Dissipation [disi·pa·tsi'o:n], *f.* **-/-en,** dissipation; *Ph:* dissipation, gradual loss (of energy).
Dissipator [disi·'pa:tor], *m.* **-s/-en** [-pa·'to:rən]. *Ind: etc:* dissipator.
dissipieren [disi·'pi:rən], *v.tr.* to dissipate (sth.); **dissipiert,** dissipated.
Dissogonie [diso·go·'ni:], *f.* **-/-n** [-'ni:ən]. *Nat. Hist:* dissogeny.
dissolut [diso·'lu:t], *a.* (*a*) disconnected, disjointed, unconnected, incoherent (ideas, etc.); (*b*) dissolute (conduct, etc.).
Dissonanz [diso·'nants], *f.* **-/-en,** (*a*) *Mus:* dissonance; (*b*) dissonance, discord.
Dissoziation [diso·tsia·tsi'o:n], *f.* **-/-en,** dissociation (*in all senses*).
Dissoziationsdruck, *m. Ph: Ch:* dissociation tension.
Dissoziationsgrad, *m. Ph: etc:* degree of dissociation.
Dissoziationskoeffizient, *m. Ch:* coefficient of dissociation.
Dissoziationsspannung, *f. Ph: Ch:* dissociation tension.
Dissoziationstemperatur, *f. Ph:* temperature of dissociation.
dissoziierbar [diso·tsi·'i:rba:r], dissociable, separable; *Ph: Ch:* dissociable.
dissoziieren [diso·tsi·'i:rən], *v.tr.* to dissociate (person, *Ch:* compound, etc.); **dissoziiert,** dissociated.
distal [dis'ta:l], *a. Nat.Hist:* distal, terminal.
Distanz [dis'tants], *f.* **-/-en. 1.** (*a*) distance; interval; (*b*) distance; aloofness; **(die) D. halten, wahren,** to keep one's distance; (*c*) (artistic, etc.) detachment. **2.** *Turf:* (*a*) distance handicap; (*b*) *approx.*='the distance'. **3.** *Sp:* distance; course.
Distanzenergie, *f. Ph:* potential energy.
Distanzfahrt, *f. Rac: Cy:* long-distance race.
Distanzflug, *m. Av:* long-distance flight.
Distanzfracht, *f. Com:* rateable freight.
Distanzgehen, *n. Sp:* long-distance walk.
Distanzgeschäft, *n. Com:* forward delivery business (outside the area).
distanzieren [distan'tsi:rən], *v.* **1.** *v.tr. Rac: etc:* (*a*) to outdistance, outrun, outstrip, outpace (opponent); (*b*) to put (competitor) in a lower place (*as penalty for infringement of rules*). **2. sich distanzieren,** (*a*) to place oneself at a distance (from sth.); (*b*) to dissociate, disassociate, oneself from (s.o., an action, etc.); to take no part in (sth.); to hold aloof from (a matter); (*c*) **sich von etwas d.,** to look at sth. dispassionately, to view sth. objectively, with detachment.
Distanzkauf, *m.*=**Distanzgeschäft.**
Distanzkompositum, *n. Ling:* separable compound.
Distanzlatte, *f. Surv:* range pole, ranging pole, ranging rod.
Distanzlauf, *m. Sp:* long-distance race.
Distanzmesser, *m. Surv: etc:* telemeter; *Mil: etc:* range-finder.
Distanzpfahl, *m. Rac: Rail:* distance post.
Distanzpfosten, *m. Rac:* distance post.
Distanzpunkt, *m. Opt: etc:* point of distance.
Distanzritt, *m.*=**Dauerritt.**
Distanzschätzen, *n.* estimation of distance.
Distanzscheck, *m. Fin:* cheque not drawn on the bank where the account is held.
Distanzsignal, *n. Rail:* distant, distance, signal.
Distanzton, *m. Med:* heartbeat audible without a stethoscope.
Distanzwechsel, *m. Fin:* bill of exchange payable elsewhere than at the place of issue.
Distanzzeichen, *n. Rail:*=**Distanzpfahl.**
Distel, *f.* **-/-n.** *Bot:* **1.** thistle; **nickende D.,** musk-thistle; *see also* **Acker** 1. **2. welsche D.,** globe artichoke, leaf artichoke.
distelartig, *a.* thistly, thistle-like; *Bot:* **distelartige Flockenblume,** star-thistle.
Disteleisen, *n. Agr:* thistle-hook, weed-hook.
Distelfalter, *m. Ent:* butterfly of the nymphalidae family, *esp.* painted lady.
Distelfeld, *n.* (*a*) thistle-covered field; (*b*) teasel plantation.
Distelfink, *m. Orn:* goldfinch, *U.S:* thistle finch.
distelförmig, *a.* thistle-shaped.
Distelhörnchen, *n. Moll:*=**Distelschnecke.**
distelig, *a.* thistly; thistle-like.
Distelkarde, *f. Bot.*=**Kardendistel.**
Distelkopf, *m.* thistle ball, head of a thistle.
Distelmesser, *n. Agr:* thistle-hook, weed-hook.
Distelorden, der. *Scots Hist:* the Order of the Thistle.
Distelschnecke, *f. Moll:* murex senticosus.
Distelstecher, *m. Tls: Agr:* spud.
Distelvogel, *m.* **1.** *Ent:*=**Distelfalter. 2.** *Orn:*=**Distelfink.**
Distelwolle, *f.* thistle-down.
Disthen [dis'te:n], *m.* **-s/-e.** *Miner:* disthene; cyanite, kyanite.
Distichiasis [disti·'çi:a·zis], *f.* **-.** *Anat:* distichiasis, distichias.
distichitisch [disti·'çi:tiʃ], *a. Pros:* distichal.
Distichon ['disti·çon], *n.* **-s/-chen.** *Pros:* distich.
Distille [dis'tilə], *f.* **-/-n** =**Destille.**
distillieren [disti'li:rən], *v.tr.*=**destillieren.**
distinguieren [distiŋgu·'i:rən], *v.tr.* to distinguish (s.o., sth.).
distinguiert [distiŋgu·'i:rt], *a.* distinguished (pers., appearance, etc.); *adv.* **d. aussehen,** to look distinguished.
distinkt [dis'tiŋkt], *a.* distinct, clear (outline, idea, etc.).
Distinktion [distiŋktsi'o:n], *f.* **-/-en. 1.** distinguishing, distinction. **2.** distinction, difference (**zwischen,** between). **3.** distinction; eminence; **eine Person von D.,** a person of distinction, a distinguished person.
distinktiv [distiŋk'ti:f]. **1.** *a.* distinctive, distinguishing (sign, feature, etc.). **2.** *adv.* (*a*) distinctively (marked, etc.); (*b*) **d. hören, sehen,** to hear, see, distinctly.
Distomatosis [disto·ma·'to:zis], *f.* **-/.** *Vet:* distomiasis, fascioliasis, fluke-disease, (liver-) rot (of sheep, etc.).
Distorsion [distorzi'o:n], *f.* **-/-en. 1.** *Opt:* distortion. **2.** *Med:* sprain (of ankle, etc.).
Distraktion [distraktsi'o:n], *f.* **-/-en. 1.** distraction; diversion. **2.** *Med:* distraction (of fractured bone, etc.).
distribuieren [distri·bu·'i:rən], *v.tr.* to distribute (sth.).
Distribution [distri·bu·tsi'o:n], *f.* **-/-en,** distribution.
distributiv[1] [distri·bu·'ti:f], *a. Log: Gram:* distributive (term, pronoun); **distributives** [distri·bu·'ti:vəs] **Gesetz,** *Mth:* distributive law; *Bio-Ch:* Ehrlich's law of specific chemical affinities.
Distributiv[2], *n.* **-s/-e** [-'ti:və], **Distributivum** [distri·bu·'ti:vum], *n.* **-s/-va.** *Ling:* distributive.
Distrikt [dis'trikt], *m.* **-(e)s/-e,** district; region; area.
disyllabisch [di·zy'la:biʃ], *a.* disyllabic (word, etc.).
Disyllabum [di·'zyla·bum], *n.* **-s/-ba** & **-ben,** disyllable.
diszernibel [distsɛr'ni:bəl], *a.* discernible; perceptible.
diszernieren [distsɛr'ni:rən], *v.tr.* to discern (sth., sth. from sth.); to distinguish (sth., sth. from sth.).
Disziplin [distsi·'pli:n], *f.* **-/-en. 1.** discipline; **eiserne, preußische, D.,** iron discipline; **die Kinder in D. halten,** to keep the children under discipline; **er kann keine D. halten,** he cannot keep discipline; **die D. der Truppen untergraben,** to undermine the discipline of the troops. **2.** branch of learning; *A:* discipline; *Sp:* **die Disziplinen im Schwimmen,** the various types, styles, of swimming. **3.** *Ecc.Hist:* castigation.
Disziplinar- [distsi·pli·'na:r-], *comb.fm. Adm: etc:* disciplinary . . .; **Disziplinarbehörde** *f,* disciplinary authority; **Disziplinar(straf)gewalt** *f, Mil: Adm:* disciplinary power; **Disziplinarstrafordnung** *f, Mil:* disciplinary regulations.
Disziplinarhof, *m. Jur:* court of discipline.
disziplinarisch [distsi·pli·'na:riʃ], *a.* disciplinary (punishment, etc.).
Disziplinarstrafe, *f. Adm: etc:* disciplinary measure.
Disziplinarstrafrecht, *n. Jur: Adm:* disciplinary code (applicable to civil servants).
Disziplinarverfahren, *n. Jur: Adm:* (*a*) disciplinary action *or* proceeding; (*b*) disciplinary procedure.
disziplinell [distsi·pli·'nɛl], *a.* disciplinary.
disziplinieren [distsi·pli·'ni:rən], *v.tr.* **1.** to discipline (pupils, troops, etc.); **sich d.,** to discipline oneself. **2.** to punish, discipline (s.o.).
Ditheismus [di·te·'ismus], *m.* **-/.** ditheism.
dithesisch [di·'te:ziʃ], *a. Bot:* dithecal.
dithionig [di·ti'o:niç], *a. Ch:* dithionous.
Dithionsäure [di·ti'o:n-], *f. Ch:* dithionic acid.
Dithyrambe [di·ty·'rambə], *f.* **-/-n.** *Lit.* & *F:* dithyramb.
dithyrambisch [di·ty·'rambiʃ], *a.* dithyrambic.
Dithyrambos, Dithyrambus [di·ty·'rambos, -bus], *m.* **-/-ben.** *Lit:* dithyramb.
dito ['dito:], *adv.* (*abbr.* **do.**) ditto.
Ditonon ['di:to·non], *n.* **-s/-e** [-'no:nə], **Ditonus** ['di:to·nus], *m.* **-/-ni.** *Mus:* ditone.
Ditroit [di·tro·'i:t], *m.* **-(e)s/.** *Geol:* ditroite.
Ditte, *f.* **-/-n.** *North G. Dial:* dried cow-dung (used as fuel).
ditto ['dito:], *adv.*=**dito.**
Dittographie [dito·gra·'fi:], *f.* **-/-n** [-'fi:ən], dittography.
Diuresis [di·u·'re:zis], *f.* **-/-sen.** *Med:* diuresis.
Diuretikum [di·u·'re:ti·kum], *n.* **-s/-ka.** *Med:* diuretic.
diuretisch [di·u·'re:tiʃ], *a. Med:* diuretic.
Diurnale [di·ur'na:lə], *n.* **-s/-s.** *Ecc:* diurnal.
Diurn(al)ist [di·ur'nist, di·urna·'list], *m.* **-en/-en** =**Diätar.**
Diva ['di:va:], *f.* **-/-s** & **-ven,** (*a*) *Rom.Hist:* diva; (*b*) *Th:* diva; prima donna.
Divan ['di:va·n, di·'va:n], *m.* **-s/-e** [-'va:nə] = **Diwan.**
divergent [di·vɛr'gɛnt], *a.* divergent; *Mth:* **divergente Reihe,** divergent series.
Divergenz [di·vɛr'gɛnts], *f.* **-/-en,** divergence (of lines, rays, opinions, *Bot:* of leaves, *Mth:* of vector, etc.); *Alg:* **D. einer Reihe,** divergence of a series.
Divergenzwinkel, *m. Bot:* angle of divergence (of leaves).
divergieren [di·vɛr'gi:rən], *v.i.* (*haben*) (*of lines, paths, rays, opinions, etc.*) to diverge.
divers [di·'vɛrs], *a.* (*a*) *Com: etc:* diverse, different, varied; sundry; **diverse** [di·'vɛrzə] **Artikel, Diverses, Diversa, Diverse,** sundry goods, miscellaneous goods; sundries; **diverse Ausgaben, Diverses,** sundry expenses; sundries; *Fin:* **Konto pro Diverse,** sundry creditors account; sundry debtors account; (*b*) *F:* various, several; **ich habe noch diverse Angelegenheiten zu erledigen,** I still have various, several, matters to see to; **sie hat ihre diversen Freundinnen besucht,** she visited her various friends; **diverse Leute sahen ihn,** various, several, people saw him.
Diversion [di·vɛrzi'o:n], *f.* **-/-en.** *Mil: etc:* diversion.
divertieren [di·vɛr'ti:rən], *v.tr.* to divert (s.o., sth.).
Divertimento [di·vɛrti·'mɛnto:], *n.* **-s/-ti.** *Mus:* divertimento.
Divertissement [di·vɛrtisə'mã:], *n.* **-s/-s,** (*a*) diversion; entertainment; (*b*) *Th:* divertis(s)ement, *entr'acte*; (*c*) *Mus:* divertimento.
Dividend [di·vi·'dɛnt], *m.* **-en/-en** [-'dɛndən/-'dɛndən]. *Mth:* dividend.
Dividende [di·vi·'dɛndə], *f.* **-/-n.** *Fin:* dividend; **D. auf Aktien,** dividend on shares; **mit, inklusive, einschließlich, D.,** cum dividend, *U.S:* dividend on; **ohne D.,** *abbr.* **o.Div., ex Div., ExD., e.D.,** ex dividend, *U.S:* dividend off; **(seine) Dividenden empfangen,** to draw one's dividends; *see also* **ausschütten I.** 2.
Dividendenabschlag, *m. Fin:* difference between the normal price and the ex-dividend price (of share).
Dividendenpapiere, *n.pl. Fin:* shares, stock, carrying dividend.
Dividendenreserve, *f. Fin:* dividend reserve fund.
Dividendenreservefonds, *m. Fin:* dividend reserve fund.
Dividendensatz, *m. Fin:* dividend rate.
Dividendenschein, *m. Fin:* dividend warrant, coupon.
Dividendenstock, *m. Fin:* dividend reserve fund.
Dividendenwerte, *m.pl. Fin:* shares, stock, carrying dividend.
Dividendus [di·vi·'dɛndus], *m.* **-/-den.** *Mth:* dividend.
dividieren [di·vi·'di:rən], *v.tr. Mth:* to divide; **eine Zahl durch eine andere d.,** to divide one number by another.
Divination [di·vi·na·tsi'o:n], *f.* **-/-en,** divination.
divinatorisch [di·vi·na·'to:riʃ], *a.* divinatory.
Divinität [di·vi·ni·'tɛ:t], *f.* **-/-en,** divinity.
Divis [di·'vi:s], *n.* **-/-** & **-es/-e** [-'vi:zəs/-'vi:zə]. *Print:* hyphen.
Division [di·vi·zi'o:n], *f.* **-/-en. 1.** *Mth: Log:* division. **2.** *Mil: Navy:* division.
Divisionär [di·vi·zio·'nɛ:r], *m.* **-s/-e.** *Mil: A:* divisional commander.
Divisions-, *comb.fm. Mil:* divisional . . ., . . . of a division; **Divisionsadjutant** *m,* chief of divisional administrative staff; **Divisionsarzt** *m,* chief of divisional medical services=Colonel R.A.M.C.; **Divisionsstab** *m,* divisional H.Q. personnel; **Divisionsverband** *m,* combined formations (and co-operating services) of a division.
Divisor [di·'vi:zor], *m.* **-s/-en** [-vi·'zo:rən]. *Mth:* divisor.
Divulsion [di·vulzi'o:n], *f.* **-/-en.** *Med:* divulsion.
Diwan ['di:va·n, di·'va:n], *m.* **-s/-e** [-'va:nə].

1. divan, (i) (Sultan's, etc.) Council; (ii) council room. 2. *Furn:* divan, couch, ottoman. 3. *Persian Lit:* divan.

Dizyan [diˑtsyˑˈaːn], *n. Ch:* dicyanogen.

Djaipur [ˈdʒaipuːr]. *Pr.n.n.* **-s.** *Geog:* Jaipur.

Djerboa [dʒɛrˈboːaː], *m.* **-/-.** *Z:* jerboa.

d-moll, d-Moll, *n. Mus:* (key of) D minor.

do, Do, *n.* **-s/-s.** *Mus:* do(h) (of Fixed *or* Movable Do System).

Döbel[1], **Dobel,** *m.* **-s/-** = **Dübel.**

Döbel[2], *m.* **-s/-.** 1. *Ich:* chub. 2. *Bot:* (bearded) darnel.

döbeln, *v.tr.* = **dübeln.**

Dobermann [ˈdoːbərman], *m.* **-s/-männer, Dobermannpinscher,** *m. Breed:* Dobermann Pinscher.

Doblon [doˑˈbloːn], *m.* **-(e)s/-e** & **-s.** *Num:* doubloon.

Dobostorte [ˈdobos-, ˈdoboʃ-], *f. Cu:* dobostorte, layered sponge cake with cream filling.

Dobrudscha, die [doˑˈbrudʒaː]. *Pr.n.* **-.** *Geog:* the Dobrudja.

Doc- *see* **Dok-, Doz-.**

doch. I. *conj.* (*adversative*) 1. (*a*) but; though; **sie war arm, doch ehrlich, zufrieden,** she was poor, but honest, but happy; **Bande, die stark, doch unsichtbar sind,** bonds, which are strong, though invisible; (*b*) (*introducing a clause*) (*verb is inverted in literary style*) but; however; yet; **er ist nicht hier, doch er wird bald zurückkommen,** he is not here, but, however, he will be back soon; **ich fühle mich nicht wohl, doch bin ich nicht krank,** I am not well, but, yet, I am not ill; **ich werde auf dich warten, doch bleibe nicht zu lange aus,** I'll wait for you, but don't be too long; **sie dachte, es sei falsch, doch sie irrte sich, doch irrte sie sich,** she thought that it was wrong, but she was mistaken; **er gab vor, zuzuhören, doch seine Gedanken waren anderswo, doch waren seine Gedanken anderswo,** he pretended to listen, but his thoughts were elsewhere; **er verspricht viel, doch hält er wenig,** he promises a great deal, but doesn't keep to it; **er scheint ehrlich, doch ich traue ihm nicht, doch traue ich ihm nicht,** he seems honest, (but) yet I don't trust him; **sie hatten alles aufs genaueste vorbereitet, doch der Plan scheiterte,** they prepared everything down to the last detail-however, the plan failed. 2. (*a*) but; nevertheless; though; all the same; (but) still; however; **ich habe es ihm streng verboten, aber er hat es doch getan,** I expressly forbade him to do it, but he did it all the same; **ich möchte doch, daß du hingehst,** all the same, nevertheless, I would like you to go there; **ich möchte doch wissen, wohin wir fahren,** I should like to know all the same where we are going; **ich bin doch ängstlich,** I feel anxious all the same, nevertheless; **er ist ein seltsamer Mensch, (und) doch habe ich ihn gern,** he is a strange person, (but) still I like him; **er hatte versprochen zu kommen, und doch kam er nicht,** he had promised to come; he didn't though, he didn't however; (*b*) (*expressing doubt*) yet; **und doch: es sah aus, als würde es niemals Abend werden,** and yet—it looked as if it never would be evening.

II. **doch,** *adv.* 1. (*a*) (*in answer to negative question*) yes; **bist du noch nicht fertig? — doch!** aren't you ready yet? are you still not ready?—yes, I am (ready); **ist er noch nicht gegangen? — doch!** has he still not gone?—yes (, he has); **du gehst doch nicht wirklich? — doch!** you aren't really going?—yes, I am, certainly I am, *F:* I am though; **er wird nicht darüber hinwegkommen — oh doch!** he won't get over it—of course he will! yes he will! (*b*) (*anticipating negation*) **du hast mir das Leben gerettet; doch, das hast du!** you saved my life; yes you did! **glaubst du, daß er zuverlässig ist? — doch!** do you think he is trustworthy?—yes, I think so.

III. **doch,** *emotive particle* 1. (*stressed*) (*contradictory*) (*a*) but; **ich habe es doch gesehen,** but I ˈdid see it! **es macht doch etwas aus,** (but) it ˈdoes matter; (*b*) (*correcting statement, thought, etc.*) after all; **er kommt doch,** he is coming after all; **es ist doch nicht so weit,** it isn't so far after all, really; **er ist (denn) doch gekommen,** so he has come after all; **also doch!** I knew it! I was right after all! just as I thought! **du wirst also doch heiraten,** you are marrying, going to get married, after all; **er hat doch noch reisen können,** he has been able to make the journey, to travel, after all. 2. (*unstressed*) (*a*) (*urging, encouraging, impatient*) (*rendered in English by stressing the verb*) **sage mir doch, was mit dir los ist,** ˈdo tell me what's the matter; **denk doch!** (i) do think! use your brain! (ii) just think! just imagine! **komm doch herein!** ˈdo come in! **nimm doch Platz,** ˈdo sit down, ˈdo take a seat, ˈdo be seated; **du kannst es doch wenigstens versuchen,** you can at least try, attempt it, you can try, attempt it, anyway; **es ist doch besser als gar nichts,** at any rate it is better than nothing; at least it's something; **beeile dich doch!** do hurry (up)! **sag mir doch schon . . . ,** do tell me now . . .; **was war doch gleich Ihre Branche?** what did you say your line was? **ja doch!** certainly! of course! **nein doch!** of course not! certainly not! **nicht doch!** don't! don't do it! (*b*) (*expressing anxiety or uncertainty*) **er kommt doch?** he is coming, isn't he? he is coming, though? **er ist doch zufrieden?** he is happy, isn't he? he's happy, I hope? **du bist mir doch nicht etwa böse?** you aren't angry with me, are you? **er wird dir aber doch, doch wohl, schreiben, nicht wahr?** but he will write to you, won't he? (*more tinged with anxiety than* **aber doch**) **er wird doch aber schreiben, ja?** he will write, I hope? **ich habe Sie doch schon einmal gesehen,** but I have seen you once, haven't I? **er wird doch noch rechtzeitig ankommen!** I do hope he will come in time! 3. (*used to emphasize the clause; sometimes not translated*) (*a*) **doch; wo doch, wenn doch,** when; **du hast es getan, wo du doch wußtest, daß ich dagegen bin,** you did it, when you knew that I was against it; **warum gehst du sie besuchen, wenn, wo, du doch weißt, daß sie deinen Besuch nicht haben will?** why do you visit her, when you know that she doesn't like it? **warum habe ich mich nicht vorgesehen, wußte ich doch, daß das geschehen würde!** why didn't I take care, when I knew that it would happen! **warum hast du die Blumen abgepflückt, wo sie doch so schnell welken?** why have you picked the flowers, when you know they wither so quickly? (*b*) (*optative*) **doch; o daß doch, wenn doch (nur),** if only; **hättest du es mir doch gesagt! (o) daß du es mir doch gesagt hättest!** if only you had told me! **o daß er doch käme! käme er doch! wenn er doch käme!** if only he would come! **wenn es doch nur nicht regnete!** if only it wouldn't rain! if only it weren't raining! (*c*) (*confident assertion*) **davon müßte ich doch auch gehört haben,** but I would certainly have heard of it; **das müßte ich doch wissen,** but I should surely know, but I should know then; **das müßten Sie doch wissen!** surely you know that! **das können Sie sich doch denken,** (i) obviously! what do you think! (ii) work it out for yourself! (*d*) (*introducing the reason or cause of what precedes*) but; **warum hast du nicht geantwortet? — ich habe doch geschlafen!** why didn't you answer? but I was asleep! **tu etwas! — ich arbeite doch!** do something!—but I am! **ich ˈbin doch nun einmal ängstlich!** but I am a coward! **das dürfen wir doch gar nicht!** but we aren't allowed to! **du kennst aber doch den Weg gar nicht!** but you don't know the way! **du weißt doch genau, daß . . . ,** you know well enough that . . .; **er ist doch höchstens sechs Jahre alt,** he can't be more than six years old; **ich habe dir doch gesagt, daß er kommt,** I have told you he is coming, haven't I? **geh doch selbst!** go yourself! (*e*) (*expressing indignation*) **das ist denn doch die Höhe!** that's the limit! **das möchte ich denn doch mal sehen!** just you try! just let them try! I'd just like to see you, them, try! (*f*) (*summing up previous remarks or reflections*) **das Leben ist doch manchmal grausam,** life is sometimes cruel; **die klügsten Menschen sagen doch manchmal törichte Dinge,** the wisest men ˈdo say foolish things at times; **was ist sie doch für ein hübsches Mädchen!** what a pretty girl she is!

Dochmiose [doxmiˑˈoːzə], *f.* **-/.** *Med:* ankylostomiasis, hookworm disease, miner's anaemia, tunnel disease.

dochmisch [ˈdoxmiʃ], *a. Pros:* dochmiac(al); **dochmischer Vers,** dochmiac verse, dochmiac, dochmius.

Dochmius [ˈdoxmiˑus], *m.* **-/-mien.** *Pros:* dochmius.

Docht, *m.* **-s/-e,** wick (of candle, oil-lamp, oil-stove, etc.); cleaning *or* oiling tow (for rifle); *El:* core (in a carbon); **den D. abschneiden, beschneiden, putzen, schneuzen,** to trim the wick.

Dochtbaumwolle, *f.* wick yarn.

Dochtflasche, *f.* bottle with a wick (for air purification).

Dochtgarn, *n.* = **Dochtbaumwolle.**

Dochtkohle, *f. El:* cored carbon.

Dochthalter, *m.* wick-holder.

Döchting, *n.* **-s/-s.** *North G.Dial:* (*dim. of* **Tochter**) little daughter.

Dochtmaschine, *f. El:* coring machine.

Dochtöler, *m. Mch: etc:* wick-oiler, wick lubricator; oil-box; oil-cup.

Dochtschmierbüchse, *f. Mch: etc:* oil-box.

Dochtschmierung, *f. Mch: etc:* wick-oiling, wick lubrication.

Dochtschraube, *f.* wick-screw, wick-regulator.

Dock, *n.* **-(e)s/-s** & **-e,** dock; *Navy:* naval (dock-) yard, *U.S:* navy yard; **einseitiges D.,** offshore dock; **ein Schiff ins D. bringen,** to put a ship in dock; **ein Schiff aus dem D. bringen,** to take a ship out of dock; (*of ship*) **aus dem D. gehen,** to leave dock; **im D. liegen,** to lie, to be, in dock.

Dockanlagen, *f.pl.* (*a*) docks; (*b*) dock installations.

Dockarbeiter, *m.* dock worker; dock labourer; docker, *U.S:* longshoreman.

Dockbassin, Dockbecken, *n.* dock basin.

Dockboden, *m.* dock apron.

Döckchen, *n.* **-s/-,** (*dim. of* **Docke**[1]) *esp.* skein (of mending wool *or* embroidery silk); roll (of mending wool).

Dockdrempel, *m.* caisson sill of a dock entrance.

Docke[1], *f.* **-/-n.** 1. (*a*) *A. & Dial:* wooden doll; (*b*) stook, shock (of corn); (*c*) skein, hank (of mending wool, embroidery silk); roll (of mending wool); (*d*) coil, roll, twist, pigtail (of chewing tobacco). 2. (*a*) cylindrical piece of wood *or* metal, *esp.* banister; *Mec.E:* (*on lathe*) headstock; tail-stock; poppet-head; *Mus:* jack (of harpsichord); *Lap:* dop, lapidary's stick; (*b*) *Ecc:* (ornamented) pew end.

Docke[2], *f.* **-/-n.** *Z:* sow.

docken[1], *v.* (*a*) *v.tr.* **ein Schiff d.,** to put a ship in dock; to dock a ship; (*b*) *v.i.* (*haben*) (*of ship*) to dock.

docken[2], *v.* 1. *v.i.* (*haben*) *A. & Dial:* to play with dolls. 2. *v.tr.* (*a*) to stook, shock (corn); to bundle (flax); (*b*) to wind (wool, etc.) in skeins; (*c*) to roll, twist (tobacco leaves).

Dockenmaschine, *f. Tex:* bobbin-machine.

Dockenspindel, *f. Mec.E:* mandrel, mandril.

Dockenstock, *m. Mec.E:* headstock *or* tail-stock (of lathe).

Dockgebühren, *f.pl.* dock-dues, dockage.

Dockhafen, *m.* dock-port; port with dock installations.

Dockhaupt, *n.* entrance to dock, dock entrance.

Dockkammer, *f.* = **Dockbassin.**

Dockkehle, *f.* entrance channel of a dock.

Dockmeister, *m.* dock-master.

Dockponton, *m.* floating caisson in a dock entrance.

Dockschleuse, *f.* tide-lock.

Docksohle, *f.* dock bottom, floor of dock.

Dockstufe, *f.* altar (of graving dock).

Dockstütze, *f.* side-shore.

Docktor, *n.* dock gate.

Dockwand, *f.* dock wall, dock side.

Dodecatheon [doˑdeˑkaˑˈteːon], *n.* **-s/.** *Bot:* dodecatheon.

Dodecyl- [doˑdeˑˈtsyːl-], *comb.fm. Ch:* dodecyl-.

Dodek(a)-, dodek(a)- [ˌdoːdeˑk(aˑ)-], *comb.fm.* dodec(a)-; **Dodekarchie** *f,* dodecarchy; **dodekapartit,** dodecapartite.

Dodekadaktylum [ˌdoːdeˑkaˑˈdaktyˑlum], *n.* **-s/.** = **Duodenum.**

Dodekadik [doːdeˑˈkaːdik], *n.* **-s/.** *Mth:* duodecimal system.

dodekadisch [doːdeˑˈkaːdiʃ], *a. Mth:* **dodekadisches System,** duodecimal system.

Dodekaeder [ˌdoːdeˑkaˑˈeːdər], *n.* **-s/-.** *Geom: Cryst:* dodecahedron.

Dodekagon [ˌdoːdeˑkaˑˈgoːn], *n.* **-s/-e.** *Geom:* dodecagon.

dodekagonal [ˌdoːdeˑkaˑgoˑˈnaːl], *a.* dodecagonal.

Dodekandria [doːdeˑˈkandriaː], *n.pl. Bot:* dodecandria.

dodekandrisch [doːdeˑˈkandriʃ], *a.* dodecandrous.

Dodekanes, der [doːdeˑkaˑˈneːs]. *Pr.n.* **-.** *Geog:* the Dodecanese.

Dodekatemorion [doːdeˑkaˑteˑˈmoːrĭon], *n.* **-s.** *Astr:* dodecatemory.

Dodo[1], *m.* **-s/-s.** *Orn:* dodo.

Dodo[2]. *Pr.n.f.* **-s.** (*dim. of* **Dorothea**) Dodo.

Dodona [doˑˈdoːnaː]. *Pr.n.n.* **-s.** *A.Geog:* Dodona.

dodonäisch [doˑdoˑˈnɛːiʃ], *a. A.Geog:* Dodonaean.

Doeskin [ˈdouskin], *n.* **-s/-s.** *Leath:* doeskin.

Doffer, *m.* **-s/-.** *Tex:* doffer (of carding machine).

Dogaressa [doˑgaˑˈrɛsaː], *f.* **-/-ressen.** *Hist:* doge's wife, dogaressa.

Dogat [doˑˈgaːt], *m.* **-(e)s/-e.** *Hist:* dogate, dogeate.

Dogcart [ˈdokart], *m.* **-s/-s.** *Veh:* dog-cart, trap.

Doge [ˈdoːʒə], *m.* **-n/-n.** *Hist:* doge.

Dogenmütze, *f.* **-/-n,** doge's cap.

Dogenpalast, *m.* Doge's Palace, Palace of the Doges, Ducal Palace.

Dogenwürde, *f. Hist:* dogate, dogeate.

Dogessa [doˑˈʒɛsaː], *f.* **-/-gessen.** *Hist:* = **Dogaressa.**

Dogge¹, f. -/-n. Breed: mastiff; F: Great Dane; englische D., mastiff; dänische D., Great Dane; deutsche D., German breed of Great Dane (with cropped ears); schwarzweiß gefleckte D., Harlequin Dane; kleine D., lesser Dane, Dalmatian (dog).
Dogge², f. -/-n. 1. Lap: dop, lapidary's stick. 2. Tex:=Docke¹ 1 (c).
doggen, v.tr. Tex:=docken² 2 (b).
Dogger¹ ['dɔgər], m. -s/-. Nau: dogger(-boat).
Dogger², der, -s. Geol: the Middle, the Brown, Jurassic, the Dogger.
Doggerbank, die. Pr.n. Geog: the Dogger Bank.
Doggerboot, n.=Dogger¹.
Dögling, m. -(e)s/-e. Z: doegling, hyperoödon, bottle-nosed whale, bottle-nose, beaked whale.
Döglingstran, m. doegling oil.
Dogma ['dɔgmaː], n. -s/-men, dogma; Rel: dogma, article of faith; etwas zum D. erheben, erklären, to establish, proclaim, sth. as dogma; ich will keine Dogmen darüber aufstellen, I am not prepared to dogmatize on the subject.
Dogmatik [dɔg'maːtik] f. -/-en, (a) Theol: dogmatics; (b) dogmatic attitude, dogmatic way of speaking; dogmatism.
Dogmatiker [dɔg'maːtikər], m. -s/-, (a) Theol: dogmatician; (b) F: dogmatic person.
dogmatisch [dɔg'maːtiʃ], a. dogmatic (theology, etc.); adv. dogmatically; d. reden, to speak dogmatically; d. festgelegt sein, to be laid down as dogma.
dogmatisieren [dɔgmaˑtiˈziːrən]. 1. v.i. (haben) to dogmatize. 2. v.tr. to establish, proclaim (sth.) as dogma.
Dogmatismus [dɔgmaˈtismus], m. -/. Phil: etc: dogmatism.
Dogmatist [dɔgmaˈtist], m. -en/-en, dogmatist.
Dogmengeschichte, f. history of dogma, of dogmatic theology.
Dohle¹, f. -/-n. Orn: (a) jackdaw, daw; (b) = Alpendohle.
Dohle², f. -/-n=Dole.
Dohlenkrebs, m. Crust: crayfish.
Dohlenrabe, m. Orn:=Dohle¹ (a).
Dohne, f. -/-n. Ven: bird-snare (of horsehair), springe.
Dohnenfang, m. Ven: snaring of birds.
Dohnenschneise, f.=Dohnenstrich.
Dohnensteig. Dohnenstieg, m.=Dohnenstrich.
Dohnenstrich, m. Ven: line of snares; path set with snares.
doktern. F: 1. v.i. (haben) to be under medical care. 2. v.i. (haben) to dabble in medicine. 3. v.tr. to doctor, fake (wine, etc.).
Doktor ['dɔktor], m. -s/-en [-'toːrən]. 1. Sch: Doctor; D. der Rechte, Dr.jur., Doctor of Civil Law, D.C.L. (Oxford), Doctor of Laws, LL.D. (Cambridge); D. beider Rechte, Dr.j.u., Doctor juris atriusque, utriusque juris; Dr. der Theologie, Dr. theol. or D.theol., Doctor of Divinity, D.D.; D. der Medizin, Dr.med., Doctor of Medicine, M.D.; D. der Philosophie, Dr.phil., Doctor of Philosophy, D.Phil. (Oxford), Ph.D. (Cambridge, London); D. ehrenhalber, Dr.h.c. or e.h., Doctor honoris causa; D. der Naturwissenschaften, Dr.rer.nat., Doctor of Philosophy (in Natural Science); D. der Ingenieurwissenschaften, Dr.-Ing., Doctor of Engineering Science, D.Sc. (Eng.); Herr Dr. X, Frau Dr. X, Dr X; Fräulein X ist D. der Philosophie, Miss X is a Doctor of Philosophy; seinen D., den D., machen, F: bauen, to take one's doctor's degree, to proceed doctor; to work for one's doctor's degree; er hat seinen D. gemacht, he has taken his doctor's degree; zum D. promoviert werden, to have the degree of Doctor conferred on one. 2. (medical) doctor; physician; medical practitioner; medical adviser; F: medical man; (Herr) Dr. Schmidt, Doktor Schmidt, Doctor (abbr. Dr) Smith, (specialist) Mr Smith; kommen Sie herein, Herr D., come in, doctor. 3.=Doktorwein. 4. Print: Tex: doctor.
Doktorand [dɔktoˈrant], m. -en/-en [-dən/-dən], doctorand, candidate for a doctorate.
Doktorarbeit, f. Sch: doctoral dissertation; thesis submitted for a doctorate, doctorate thesis.
Doktorat [dɔktoˈraːt], n. -(e)s/-e. Sch: doctorate; degree of Doctor.
Doktordiplom, n. doctor's diploma.
Doktordisputation, f. Sch: maintaining of a thesis for a doctorate.
Doktordissertation, f.=Doktorarbeit.
Doktorexamen, n. G.Sch: oral examination for a doctorate.
Doktorfrage, f. (a) Sch: question that might be

posed to a candidate for a doctorate; (b) question of crucial importance.
Doktorgrad, m. doctorate, doctor's degree; den D. erwerben, to take, gain, one's doctor's degree.
Doktorhut, m. Hist: doctor's bonnet; F: den D. erwerben, to take, gain, one's doctor's degree.
doktorieren [dɔktoˈriːrən], v.i. (haben) Sch: to take one's doctor's degree.
Doktorin [dɔkˈtoːrin], f. -/-innen, (a) woman doctor; (b) doctor's wife.
Doktorpromotion, f. 1. conferring, conferment, of the degree of Doctor. 2. receiving of the degree of Doctor; proceeding to a doctor's degree. 3. ceremony at which doctorates are conferred.
Doktorprüfung, f.=Doktorexamen.
Doktorschrift, f.=Doktorarbeit.
Doktortitel, m. title of doctor, doctor's title; den D. erwerben, to take, gain, one's doctor's degree; j-m den D. verleihen, to confer the degree of Doctor on s.o.
Doktorvater, m. Sch: supervisor (for a doctoral dissertation).
Doktorwein, m. wine from the Berncastel area.
Doktorwürde, f. doctorate; doctorship; j-m die D. verleihen, to confer the degree of Doctor on s.o.
Doktrin [dɔkˈtriːn], f. -/-en, doctrine; eine D. vertreten, to propound, put forward, teach, a doctrine.
Doktrinär¹ [dɔktriˈnɛːr], m. -(e)s/-e. Pol: etc: doctrinarian; Fr.Hist: Doctrinaire.
doktrinär², a. doctrinaire, doctrinarian; doctrinal; doctrinary; adv. doctrinally.
Doktrinarismus [dɔktriˈnaˈrismus], m. -/. doctrinairism, doctrinarianism; doctrinalism.
Dokument [doˈkuˈment], n. -(e)s/-e, (a) document; record; paper; Jur: instrument; Com: document (of title); shipping document; Dokumente, die sich auf den Fall beziehen, die zur Sache gehören, documents relating to the case, to the matter; ein D. beglaubigen lassen, to have a document authenticated; eine Aussage durch Dokumente stützen, to support a statement with documentary evidence; Com: Zahlung gegen Übergabe, Aushändigung, der Dokumente, documents on, against, payment; Akzeptierung gegen Dokumente, documents on, against, acceptance; (b) document; record; expression; dieser Vertrag ist ein D. des guten Willens, this treaty is an expression, demonstration, of goodwill; dieses Buch wird als ein D. der Schande aufbewahrt werden, this book will be preserved as a record of infamy.
Dokumentarbericht [doˈkuˈmɛnˈtaːr-], m. documentary report; documented report; documentary film.
Dokumentarfilm, m. Cin: documentary film, F: documentary.
dokumentarisch [doˈkuˈmɛnˈtaːriʃ], (a) a. documentary; documental; dokumentarische Beweise, documentary evidence; diese Pläne haben keine dokumentarische Unterlage, these maps have no documentary authority; (b) adv. by documents.
Dokumentartratte, f.=Dokumententratte.
Dokumentation [doˈkuˈmɛntaˈtsiˈoːn], f. -/-en. 1. documentation. 2. demonstration, demonstrating, proving (of goodwill, etc.).
Dokumentenakkreditiv, n. Com: Fin: documentary (letter of) credit.
dokumentenecht, a. (of ball-point pen) 'accepted for use on official documents'.
Dokumenteninkasso, n. Fin: collecting of documents (through a bank).
Dokumentenkredit, m. Com: Fin: documentary credit.
Dokumententratte, f. Com: Fin: documentary draft, draft with documents attached.
dokumentieren [doˈkuˈmɛnˈtiːrən], v.tr. 1. to prove (sth.) by documents. 2. to demonstrate, prove (goodwill, faith, etc.); (of thg) sich d., to reveal itself, to be shown.
Dokumentswechsel, m. Com: Fin: documentary bill.
Dolch, m. -es/-e, (i) dagger; poniard; A: misericord(e) dagger; (Malay dagger) kris, creese; (in Burma) kuk(e)ri, Gurkha knife; (ii) (highlander's, midshipman's) dirk; (iii) Fenc: dagger, main gauche; den D. zücken, to draw one's, a, dagger; j-n mit einem D. erstechen, to stab s.o. with a dagger; j-m den D. in die Brust, in den Rücken, stoßen, to stab s.o. in the chest, back, with a dagger; to plunge a dagger into s.o.'s chest, back; seine Blicke waren wie Dolche, (i) his angry looks cut me, him, her, us, them, to the heart, wounded me, him, her, us, them, to the core; (ii) he looked daggers.

dolchartig, a. dagger-shaped, dagger-like.
Dolchmesser, n. hunting-knife, U.S: bowie knife.
Dolchpflanze, f. Bot: yucca, F: Adam's needle.
Dolchstoß, m. (a) dagger-thrust, thrust of a dagger; (b) F: stab in the back; treacherous act.
Dolchstoßlegende, f. Hist: myth of the 'stab in the back'.
Dolchwespen, f.pl. Ent: scolia.
Döldchen, n. -s/-. Bot: umbellule, umbellet.
Dolde, f. -/-n. Bot: umbel, umbella; flowercluster, flower-head; F: cluster; einfache D., simple umbel; zusammengesetzte D., compound umbel.
doldenartig, a. Bot: umbellate, umbellated, umbellar.
doldenblütig, a. umbelliferous.
Doldenblütler, m. -s/-. Bot: umbellifer.
Doldendistel, f. Bot: eryngium, F: eryngo.
doldenförmig, a. Bot: umbelliform, umbellate; F: in clusters; adv. umbellately.
Doldengewächse, n.pl. Bot: umbelliferae.
Doldenmilchstern, m. Bot: star of Bethlehem.
Doldennarzisse, f. Bot: polyanthus narcissus.
Doldenpflanze. f. Bot: umbellifer.
Doldenrebe, f. Bot: ampelopsis; Virginia creeper.
Doldenriesche, f. -/-n. Bot: tradescantia, spiderwort.
Doldenrispe, f. Bot: corymbose cyme.
Doldenstrahlen, m.pl. Bot: rays of an umbel.
Doldentraube, f. Bot: corymb.
doldig, a. Bot: umbellate; doldiger Milchstern, star of Bethlehem.
Doldrums ['dɔldrəms], pl. Geog: Nau: doldrums, calm-belts.
Dole, f. -/-n. Civ.E: drain, culvert, conduit.
Dolerit [doˈleˈriːt], m. -(e)s/-e. Miner: dolerite.
dolichokephal [doˈliˈçoˈkeˈfaːl], a. Anthr: =dolichozephal.
dolichokran [doˈliˈçoˈkraːn], a. Anthr: dolichocranial.
dolichoprosop [doˈliˈçoˈproˈzoːp], a. Anthr: dolichoprosopic.
dolichozephal [doˈliˈçoˈtseˈfaːl], a. Anthr: =dolichocephalic, dolichocephalous.
Dolichozephale [doˈliˈçoˈtseˈfaːlə], m., f. -n/-n. Anthr: dolichocephal.
Dolichozephalie [doˈliˈçoˈtsefaˈliː], f. -/. Anthr: dolichocephaly, dolichocephalism.
dolieren [doˈliːrən], v.tr.=dollieren.
Doline [doˈliːnə], f. -/-n. Geol: dolina, sink(-hole).
doll, a. (a) Dial:=toll; (b) F: doller Husten, bad cough; dolles Glück haben, to have wonderful, marvellous, luck; das ist ja doll! (i) that's shocking, awful, bad! (ii) that's wonderful, marvellous, terrific!
Dollar ['dɔlar], m. -s/-s. Num: U.S: dollar; F: buck; kanadischer D., Canadian dollar; tausend Dollar, a thousand dollars, F: a one, grand, one G., one gee; hundert Dollar, a hundred dollars.
Dollardiplomatie, f. Pol: dollar diplomacy.
Dollarlücke, f. Fin: dollar gap.
Dollarmillionär, m. dollar millionaire.
Dollarraum, m. Fin: dollar area.
Dollarschwund, m. Fin: dollar drain.
Dollarzeichen, n. Fin: dollar sign.
Dollbord, n. Nau: gunwale (of small boat).
Dolle, f. -/-n, (a) Nau: (i) thole-pin; (ii) rowlock; U.S: oarlock; (b) Tchn: metal dowel; Constr: joggle.
Dollenboot, n. Nau: four-oared boat.
Dollerei, f. -/-en. F: 1. fun; aus D., for fun, for a lark. 2. foolish, F: screwy, action.
dollieren [doˈliːrən], v.tr. Leath: to pare, shave, whiten (hides).
Dolliermaschine, f. Leath: whitening machine.
Dolliermesser, n. Leath: whitening knife, parer.
Dölling, m. -(e)s/-e. Ich: (Danubian) pikeperch.
Dolman ['dɔlman], m. -s/-e. Cost: 1. (Turkish) dolman. 2. A.Mil: dolman, (short-skirted) jacket (of hussars, etc.). 3. lady's pelisse, A: dolman.
Dolmen, m. -s/-. Prehist: dolmen, cromlech.
Dolmetsch, m. -es/-e & -en/-en=Dolmetscher.
dolmetschen. 1. v.i. (haben) to interpret, to act as interpreter; für j-n d., to interpret for s.o.; to act as interpreter for s.o.; aus dem Englischen ins Deutsche d., to interpret, translate, from English into German. 2. v.tr. to interpret (speech, etc.); to translate (speech, etc.) (orally); F: j-n d., to interpret s.o.'s speech; to interpret for s.o.
Dolmetscher, m. -s/-, (i) interpreter; (ii) = Dragoman; amtlicher, vereidigter, beeidigter, D., official interpreter, (officially) recognized inter-

preter; sworn interpreter; **einen D. zuziehen,** to call in an interpreter; **als D. fungieren,** to act as an interpreter; **durch einen D. sprechen, reden,** to speak, talk, through an interpreter; *F:* **sich zum D. einer Gruppe, usw., machen,** to appoint oneself spokesman of a group, etc.

Dolmetscherei, *f.* **-/.** interpreting, translating.

Dolmetscherhochschule, *f.* interpreter school, school for interpreters.

Dolmetscherin, *f.* **-/-innen,** (woman) interpreter, interpretress.

Dolmetscher-Institut, *n.* (*a*) interpreter school, school for interpreters; (*b*) (university) institute for interpreters.

Dolmetscherkompanie, *f. Mil:* company of interpreters.

Dolmetscherschule, *f.* interpreter school, school for interpreters.

Dolomit [do·lo·ˈmiːt], *m.* **-(e)s/-e.** *Miner:* dolomite (marble); dolomitic, magnesian, limestone; **gebrannter D.,** calcined dolomite.

Dolomitbildung, *f. Geol:* dolomitization.

Dolomiten, die [do·lo·ˈmiːtən]. *Pr.n.pl. Geog:* the Dolomites.

dolomitisch [do·lo·ˈmiːtiʃ], *a. Miner:* dolomitic.

Dolomitisierung [do·lo·mi·ti·ˈziːruŋ], *f. Geol:* dolomitization.

Dolomitkalk, *m.* **1.** *Miner:* =**Dolomit. 2.** *Constr:* dolomitic lime.

Dolomitmehl, *n.* dolomite powder.

Dolomitofen, *m.* dolomite kiln.

Dolomitstein, *m.* (*a*) *Miner:* dolomite; (*b*) dolomite brick.

dolos [do·ˈloːs], *a. Jur:* dolose, dolous; done with harmful intent.

Dom[1] [doːm], *m.* **-(e)s/-e. 1.** cathedral, cathedral church; **hoher Dom,** noble cathedral; **der Kölner Dom,** Cologne cathedral. **2.** (*a*) *Arch:* dome, cupola; (*b*) *Lit:* vault, canopy (of heaven, trees, etc.). **3.** *Geol:* dome, cupola, pericline. **4.** (*a*) *Mch:* =**Dampfdom;** (*b*) dome (of tank-wagon); (*c*) *Brew:* head (of still). **5.** Hamburg Christmas fair.

Dom[2] [dom], *m.* **-/.** (*title*) Dom.

Doma [ˈdoːmaː], *n.* **-s/-men.** *Cryst:* dome.

Domäne [do·ˈmɛːnə], *f.* **-/-n. 1.** domain, *Jur:* demesne; **staatliche Domäne,** State demesne; (*in England*) Crown land. **2.** *F:* domain; province; field (of work, etc.).

Domänen-, *comb.fm.* demesne . . . , domanial . . . ; . . . of a domain, . . . of domains.

Domänenamt, *n. approx.*=(Office of the) Commissioners of Crown Lands.

Domänenland, *n.* demesne land.

Domänenländereien, *f.pl.* demesne lands.

Domänenpächter, *m.* tenant, leaseholder, of a domain.

Domänenverwaltung, *f.* **1.** administration of a domain, of domains. **2.** =**Domänenamt.**

domanial [do·ma·niˈaːl], *a.* domanial.

Domanial-, *comb.fm.* demesne . . . , domanial . . . ; **Domanialgut** *n,* demesne land.

Dombezirk, *m.* precincts of a cathedral, cathedral precincts.

Domchor, *m.* (*a*) *Arch:* choir of a cathedral; (*b*) (*singers*) cathedral choir.

Domdechant, *m. Ecc:* dean of a cathedral.

Domestikation [do·mɛsti·ka·tsiˈoːn], *f.* **-/.** domestication (of wild animal, savage people); taming (of wild animal); civilizing (of savage people).

Domestik [do·mɛsˈtiːk], *m.* **-en/-en,** domestic.

domestikenhaft, *a.* servile.

domestizieren [do·mɛsti·ˈtsiːrən], *v.tr.* to domesticate, tame (wild animal); to domesticate, civilize (savage).

Domett [do·ˈmɛt], *m.* **-s/-s.** *Tex:* domett(e).

domförmig, *a.* dome-shaped, domed, domelike.

Domfreiheit, *f.* cathedral close.

Domherr, *m. Ecc:* canon.

domherrlich, *a. Ecc:* canonical.

Domherrnpfründe, *f. Ecc:* (*a*) canonry; (*b*) prebend.

Domhof, *m.* (i) parvis of a cathedral; (ii) cathedral close.

dominant [do·mi·ˈnant], *a.* dominant; *Biol:* **dominantes Merkmal,** dominant character, dominant; *see also* **Erbgang;** *adv.* dominantly.

Dominantakkord, *m. Mus:* dominant chord.

Dominante [do·mi·ˈnantə], *f.* **-n/-n.** *Mus:* dominant (note *or* chord).

Dominantseptimenakkord [do·mi·ˌnantˀzɛpˈtiːmənˀakort], *m. Mus:* dominant seventh.

Dominanz [do·mi·ˈnants], *f.* **-/-en.** *Biol:* dominance (of a character).

dominieren [do·mi·ˈniːrən], *v.i.* (*haben*) (*of influence*) to dominate, predominate; (*of pers.*) to dominate; **dominierend,** dominant; *Biol:* **ein Merkmal dominiert über ein anderes,** one character dominates over another.

Dominik [ˈdoːmi·nik]. *Pr.n.m.* **-s.** Dominic.

Dominika [do·ˈmiːni·kaː]. *Pr.n.f.* **-s.** *Geog:* **(die Insel) Dominika,** Dominica.

Dominikaner [do·mi·ni·ˈkaːnər], *m.* **-s/-. 1.** *Ecc:* Dominican (friar), Black Friar. **2.** *Geog:* Dominican; inhabitant of the Dominican Republic.

Dominikaner-, *comb.fm. Ecc:* Dominican . . . ; **Dominikanerbruder** *m,* Dominican friar, Black Friar; **Dominikanerkloster** *n,* Dominican monastery.

Dominikanerin, *f.* **-/-innen.** *Ecc:* Dominican nun.

Dominikaner-Kardinal, *m. Orn:* pope cardinal.

Dominikanermöwe, *f. Orn:* southern black-backed gull.

Dominikanerorden, *m. Ecc:* Dominican order, order of St Dominic.

dominikanisch [do·mi·ni·ˈkaːniʃ], *a.* **1.** *Ecc:* Dominican (rule, etc.). **2.** *Geog:* of the Dominican Republic; **die Dominikanische Republik,** the Dominican Republic.

Dominion [doˈminiən], *n.* **-s/-s & -nien,** dominion.

Domino[1] [ˈdoːmi·noː], *m.* **-s/-s. 1.** (*a*) *Ecc.Cost:* domino, camail; moz(z)etta; (*b*) (i) (*fancy dress*) domino; (ii) domino (mask); **im D., in der Maske, im Kostüm, eines Dominos,** in a domino. **2.** *Orn:* cross-bill.

Domino[2], *n.* **-(s)/-s.** *Games:* **1.** dominoes; **D. spielen,** to play (at) dominoes; **D. machen,** to call 'domino', to make (the) domino. **2.** domino.

Dominomaske, *f.* (*fancy dress*) (i) domino; (ii) domino (mask).

Dominopartie, *f.* game of dominoes.

Dominospiel, *n. Games:* dominoes.

Dominostein, *m.* **1.** domino. **2.** *Cu:* small chocolate-covered cake.

Domitian [do·mi·tsiˈaːn]. *Pr.n.m.* **-s.** *Hist:* Domitian.

Domizil [do·mi·ˈtsiːl], *n.* **-(e)s/-e,** (*a*) domicile; *Com:* domicile, place of payment (of a bill); (*b*) =**Domizilvermerk.**

domizilieren [do·mi·tsi·ˈliːrən]. **1.** *v.i.* (*sein*) **in Frankfurt d.,** (*of pers.*) to be domiciled, to be resident, to live, to reside, in Frankfurt; (*of firm, etc.*) to be located in Frankfurt. **2.** *v.tr. Com:* to domicile (bill of exchange) (**bei,** at a bank, with a banker); **ein domizilierter Wechsel,** a domiciled bill; **in Deutschland domizilierte Wechsel,** bills domiciled in Germany; **Domizilierung** *f,* domiciling, domiciliation (of bill of exchange).

Domizilort, *m. Com:* domicile, place of payment (of bill of exchange).

Domizilprovision, *f. Com:* domicile commission.

Domizilvermerk, *n. Com:* domicile note.

Domizilwechsel, *m. Com:* domiciled bill.

Domkapitel, *n. Ecc:* chapter of canons of a cathedral.

Domkapitular, *m. Ecc:* canon.

Dommel, *f.* **-/-n.** *Orn:* =**Rohrdommel.**

Dompfaff, *m. Orn:* bullfinch; **nordischer D.,** northern bullfinch.

Dompropst, *m. Ecc:* (*in Germany*) provost of a cathedral.

Dompteur [domˈtøːr], *m.* **-s/-e, Dompteuse** [-ˈtøːzə], *f.* **-/-n,** tamer (of wild animals), animal tamer; animal trainer.

Domsänger, *m.* cathedral chorister.

Domschule, *f.* cathedral school.

Domvulkan, *m. Geol:* volcanic dome, lava dome.

Domzeit, *f.*=**Dom**[1] **5.**

Don[1] [don], *m.* **-(s)/-s.** (*Spanish & Italian title*) Don.

Don[2]. *Pr.n.m.* **-s.** *Geog:* (*river*) Don.

Doña [ˈdonjaː], *f.* **-/-s.** (*Spanish title*) Doña, Dona.

Donar [ˈdoːnaːr]. *Pr.n.m.* **-s.** *Myth:* Thor; **Donars Hammer,** Thor's hammer.

Donarkraut, *n. Bot:* eupatorium, hemp agrimony.

Donat [do·ˈnaːt]. **1.** *Pr.n.m.* **-s.** Donatus. **2.** *m.* **-s/-e.** *Hist:* donet.

Donatar [do·na·ˈtaːr], *m.* **-(e)s/-e,** donatory, donee.

Donator [do·ˈnaːtor], *m.* **-s/-en** [-na·ˈtoːrən], donor, donator.

Donatus [do·ˈnaːtus]. *Pr.n.m.* **-'.** Donatus.

Donau, die. *Pr.n.* **-.** *Geog:* the Danube; **Donau-,** *comb.fm.* Danubian . . . ; **der Donauraum, die Donauländer,** the Danubian area, the Danubian countries.

Donaudistel, *f. Bot:* field eryngo.

Donaulachs, *m. Ich:* Danubian salmon, huck.

Donaumonarchie, die. *Hist:* the Austro-Hungarian Empire.

Dönchen, *n.* **-s/-.** *F:* joke, funny anecdote.

Donez, der [ˈdoːnɛts]. *Pr.n.* **-.** *Geog:* the (river) Donetz.

Donja [ˈdonjaː], *f.* **-/-s & -jen. 1.**=**Doña. 2.** *F:* (i) maid(-servant); (ii) girl-friend, *A:* dona(h).

Donjon [dõˈʒõː], *m.* **-s/-s.** *Arch:* donjon, keep, stronghold (of castle); tower; turret.

Don Juan [donju·ˈaːn, donxu·ˈaːn]. **1.** *Pr.n.m.* **- -s.** *Lit:* Don Juan. **2.** *m.* **- -s/- -s.** Don Juan; **er ist ein richtiger Don Juan,** he is a real, regular, Don Juan.

Donkey [ˈdonki·], *m.* **-s/-s,** (*a*) *Nau: Mch:* donkey-engine, donkey-winch; (*b*) *Mch:* donkey-engine.

Donkeykessel, *m. Nau:* donkey-boiler.

Donkeymann, *m.* **-(e)s/-männer,** donkey-man.

Donkeypumpe, *f. Mch:* donkey-pump.

Donkosak [ˈdonko·ˌzak], *m. Ethn:* Don Cossack.

Donna [ˈdonaː], *f.* **-/-s & -nen. 1.** (*Italian title*) Donna. **2.**=**Donja 2.**

Donner[1]. *Pr.n.m.* **-s.** *Myth:* Thor.

Donner[2], *m.* **-s/-,** (i) thunder; (ii) thunderbolt; (iii) *F:* roar, din (of battle); thunder, roar (of waterfall, avalanche, horse's hooves, etc.); **der D. rollte,** the thunder roared; the thunder rumbled, pealed, rolled; **der D. grollte,** the thunder muttered, rumbled; **der D. krachte,** the thunder crashed; **(unter) D. und Blitz,** (amid) thunder and lightning; **der D. seiner Stimme,** the roar of his voice; *F:* **sie war wie vom D. gerührt,** she was thunderstruck, dumbfounded; **da schlag der D. 'rein!** damnation! damn! *P:* blast! *Lit. & F:* **D. und Doria!** confound it!

donnerartig, *a.* like thunder.

Donneraxt, *f. Myth:* Thor's hammer.

Donnerbart, *m. Bot:* **1.**=**Donnerlauch. 2.** livelong, orpin(e).

Donnerbesen, *m.* **1.** *Bot:* mistletoe. **2.** *Bot:* witch-broom, witches'-broom. **3.** *Folkl:* protective symbol (on house) against lightning.

Donnerblech, *n. Th:* thunder sheet.

Donnerbö, *f. Meteor:* black squall.

Donnerbohne, *f. Bot:*=**Donnerbart 2.**

Donnerbüchse, *f. F:* shot-gun; *A:* blunderbuss.

Donnerbusch, *m.*=**Donnerbesen 2.**

Donnerdistel, *f. Bot:* eryngium, field eringo.

Donn(e)rer, *m.* **-s/-.** *Lit:* god of thunder; **der D.,** (*Jupiter*) the Thunder-bearer, the Thunderer, Jupiter Tonans; (*Thor*) god of thunder.

Donnergebrüll, *n. F:* roar(ing) (of lion); howling (of child); **die Kinder kamen mit D. ins Zimmer,** the children came howling into the room.

Donnergepolter, Donnergetöse, *n. F:* clatter; din; **mit D.,** with a (terrific) clatter; with heavy thumps.

Donnergott, *m.* god of thunder; **der D.,** (*Jupiter*) the Thunder-bearer, the Thunderer, Jupiter Tonans; (*Thor*) god of thunder.

Donnergrün, *n. Bot.*=**Donnerlauch.**

Donnerhall, *m.* thunder, roar (of cannon, etc.).

Donnerkäfer, *m. Ent:* stag-beetle.

Donnerkeil, *m.* **1.** *Paleont: F:* belemnite, finger-stone, *F:* thunderbolt. **2.** (*used as int.*)= **Donnerwetter 3.**

Donnerlauch, *m. Bot:* houseleek, Jupiter's beard.

Donnerlegion, *f. Rom.Hist:* (the) Thundering Legion.

Donnerlittchen, Donnerlüttchen, *int. F:* good Heavens! good Lord! my word! whew! *F:* wow!

Donnermaschine, *f. Th:* thunder drum; *A:* bronteon.

donnern. I. *v.* **1.** (*a*) *v.i.* (*haben*) (*of deity*) to make (it) thunder, *A:* to thunder; (*b*) *v.impers.* **es donnert,** it is thundering. **2.** *v.i.* (*haben*) (*of engine, aircraft, etc.*) to roar; (*of applause*) to thunder (forth); (*of avalanche*) to rumble; (*of breaking ice*) to rumble, thunder; (*of pers.*) **gegen j-n, etwas, d.,** to thunder against s.o., sth.; to thunder on, against, sth.; **die Kanonen donnerten,** the cannon thundered, roared, boomed; **das Meer donnert an, gegen, die Felsen,** the sea thunders on the rocks; **sie donnerten an die Tür,** they thundered, hammered (away), pounded (away), on, at, the door; **der Zug donnerte, brauste donnernd, durch den Tunnel, durch die Nacht,** the train thundered through the tunnel, through the night; **die Lawine kam donnernd nieder,** the avalanche came thundering down; **mit donnernder Stimme,** in a thunderous voice, with a voice of thunder; **donnernder Beifall,** thunderous applause; **donnernde Wellen,** thundering, thunderous, crashing, waves; **donnernde Hochrufe,** rousing cheers; **donnernder Lärm,** thundering, thunderous, noise. **3.** *v.tr.* **die Geschütze donnerten Antwort,** the guns thundered a reply; **''raus!' donnerte er,** 'get out!' he thundered, roared.

II. *vbl s.* **Donnern,** *n. in vbl senses; also:* thunder; rumble, rumbling, of thunder; rumble (of volcano, breaking ice); rumble, roar, thunder (of avalanche); roar, roaring (of gale); din (of battle); roar, booming (of guns); **unter D. und Blitzen,** amid thunder and lightning; with thunder and lightning; **die Sekunden vom Aufblitzen bis zum D.,** the seconds between the lightning (flash) and the thunder, *F:* between the flash and the bang; **man hörte das ferne D. eines Gewitters,** one heard, could hear, the distant rumble, muttering, of a storm.

Donnernelke, *f. Bot:* (*a*) Deptford pink; (*b*) sweet-william; (*c*) Carthusian pink; (*d*) maiden pink.

Donnerrebe, *f. Bot:* ground-ivy, cat's-foot.

Donnerruf, *m.* cry like thunder.

Donnerschall, *m.* thunder, roar (of cannon, etc.).

Donnerschlag, *m.* (*a*) thunderbolt; clap, peal, burst, stroke, of thunder; *Poet:* thunder-blast; *F:* **die Nachricht traf ihn wie ein D.,** the news stunned him, bowled him over; (*b*) =**Donnerwetter** 3 (*a*).

Donnerstag, *m.* Thursday; **der Grüne D.,** Maundy Thursday; *for other phrases cp.* **Dienstag.**

Donnerstag-, *comb.fm. cp.* **Dienstag-.**

donnerstags, *adv.* on Thursday(s); on a Thursday.

Donnerstein, *m. Paleont:* belemnite.

Donnerstimme, *f. F:* thundering, thunderous, voice; voice of thunder; stentorian voice; **er brüllte mit D.: 'machen Sie, daß Sie 'rauskommen!',** in a thundering voice he roared: 'get out!'; 'get out!'. he thundered.

Donnerwetter, *n.* **1.** thunderstorm. **2.** *F:* telling-off, blowing-up; **ich hatte ein richtiges D. erwartet,** I had expected a good telling off, *F:* a rocket; **das wird ein D. geben,** that will cause a row, an explosion, *F:* that will raise a stink; **wie ein D. dreinfahren,** to come down on s.o. like a ton of bricks; **er wird ein heiliges D. loslassen,** he will make a frightful row, he will blow up, he will kick up an awful fuss. **3.** *int.* (*a*) (*as comment, surprise*) **Donnerwetter!** my word! by Jove! *F:* wow! (*b*) (*oath*) **D.! zum D.! D. noch mal!** confound it! damn it! damnation! for heaven's sake! **warum, zum D., hast du das erlaubt?** why did you allow it for heaven's sake? **wer zum D. hat dir aufgetragen, das zu tun?** who the devil told you to do that? **zum D.! wo hast du meine Schuhe wieder hingestellt?** confound it, where have you put my shoes this time?

Donnerwurz, *f. Bot:* **1.** aristolochia, birthwort. **2.** (i) greater flea-bane; (ii) ploughman's spikenard, fleawort, flea-bane.

Don Quichotte [donki·ˈʃot]. *Pr.n.m.* - -s =**Don Quixote.**

Donquichotterie [donki·ʃotəˈriː], *f.* -/-n [-ˈriːən], quixotic deed; piece of quixotism; quixotry.

Donquichottismus [donki·ʃoˈtismus], *m.* -/. quixotism, quixotry.

Don Quijote [donki·ˈxoːteː]. *Pr.n.m.* - -s. Don Quixote.

Don Quixote [donki·ˈxoːteː]. *Pr.n.m.* - -s. Don Quixote.

Döns, *f.* -/-en. *North G.Dial:* living-room (in farm-house).

dont[1] [doŋ], *adv. St.Exch:* (*precedes the option rate*) *x* **Aktien zu 180 dont 5% Vorprämie kaufen,** to give 5% for the call of *x* shares at 180.

Dont[2], *n.* -s/-s=**Dontprämie.**

Dontgeschäft, *n. St.Exch:* call option.

Dontprämie, *f. St.Exch:* money paid for a call option.

doof [doːf], *a. F:* dense, stupid, soft, dull-witted (pers.); dull, boring (occasion, etc.).

Doompalme [ˈdoːm-], *f. Bot:*=**Dumpalme.**

dopen [ˈdoːpən], *v.tr. Turf:* to dope (horse); **Dopen** *n*, doping.

Doping [ˈdoːpiŋ], *n.* -(e)s/-s. *Turf:* doping (of horse).

Doppe, *f.* -/-n. **1.** *Lap:* dop, lapidary's stick. **2.**=**Eckerdoppe.**

Doppel[1], *n.* -s/-. **1.** duplicate (of document, etc.). **2.** *Ten:* (i) doubles; (ii) doubles team, tennis pair; doubles partnership; **ein gemischtes D.,** a mixed doubles.

Doppel[2], *m.* -s/-, (*a*) *Th:* double, stand in; **als D. einstehen,** to double for s.o.; (*b*) =**Doppelgänger.**

doppel-, Doppel-, *comb.fm.* double ..., double-; two-; twin ..., twin-; dual ...; duplex ...; bi-; di-; *Rail:* **doppelgleisig,** double-track; *El:* **doppelpolig,** two-pole; *W.Tel:* **doppeldrähtig,** twin-wire; **doppelköpfig,** double-headed, bicephalous; **doppelfarbig,** dichromatic, dichroic; **Doppel-s** *n*, double s; *Brew:* **Doppelbier** *n*, double ale; *Ch:* **Doppelbindung** *f*, double bond; *Sp:* **Doppelsieg** *m*, double victory; *El:* **Doppelstiftstecker** *m*, two-pin plug; *Aut:* **Doppelbereifung** *f*, twin tyres; *Mec.E:* **Doppelkurbel** *f*, duplex crank; *Tg:* **Doppelbetrieb** *m*, duplex telegraphy; *Geom:* **Doppeltangente** *f*, bitangent; *Cryst:* **Doppelfarbigkeit** *f*, dichroism; *I.C.E:* **Doppelzündung** *f*, dual, twin, ignition; *Com:* **Doppelquittung** *f*, duplicate receipt; *prefixed to advs* doubly-; *Ph: Opt:* **doppelbrechend,** doubly-refractive.

Doppelachtfilm, *m. Cin:* double-run eight millimetre film.

Doppelader, *f. Tg: Tp:* twin cable.

Doppeladler, *m. Her: etc:* double-headed eagle; imperial double eagle.

Doppelagent, *m.* double agent.

Doppelanastigmat, *m. Phot:* doublet anastigmat.

Doppelantenne, *f.*=**Dipol.**

doppelarmig, *a.* (*a*) two-armed (lever, etc.); *Rail:* double arm (signal, semaphore); (*b*) *Gym: Sp:* two-handed (lift, etc.); (*c*) *adv.* with two, both, hands.

doppelatmend, *a. Nat.Hist:* dipnoan.

Doppelatmer, *m.pl. Ich:* dipnoi.

doppelatomig, *a. Ph:* diatomic.

Doppelausschalter, *m. El.E:* double cut-out.

Doppelaxt, *f. Tls:* twibill; *Archeol: Myth:* double-axe.

Doppel-♭, *n. Mus:* double flat.

doppelbahnig, *a.* **1.** (hammer) with two faces. **2.** dual (carriageway); two-lane (highway).

Doppelband[1], *m.* two volumes bound in one, double volume.

Doppelband[2], *n.* hinge with two flaps.

Doppelbaß, *m. Mus:* double-bass, contrabass.

Doppelbecher, *m.* (*vessel*) double drinking cup.

Doppelbelichtung, *f. Phot:* double exposure.

Doppelbereifung, *f. Aut:* twin tyres, dual tyres.

Doppelbesteuerung, *f. Fin: Adm:* double taxation.

Doppelbett, *n.* double bed; **Zimmer mit D.,** double bedroom, double room.

Doppelbewicklung, *f. El.E:* compound winding.

Doppelbewußtsein, *n. Psy:* double consciousness.

Doppelbier, *n. Brew:* double ale.

Doppelbild, *n. TV:* double image, *F:* ghost; *Opt:* secondary image, *F:* ghost.

Doppelbildmikrometer, *n.* double-image micrometer.

Doppelbildnis, *n.* picture portraying two people, (*esp.* two friends *or* husband and wife).

Doppelbildseher, *m. Opt:* dipleidoscope.

Doppelbildung, *f.* double formation; *Cryst:* twin formation.

Doppelbindung, *f. Ch:* double bond.

Doppelblattgewächse, *n.pl. Bot:* zygophyllaceae.

Doppelboden, *m. Nau: etc:* double bottom.

Doppelbogen, *m.* (*a*) double bend (in pipe, etc.); (*b*) Grecian bow; (*c*) *Arch:* arch-band; (*d*) *Arch:* twin-arch; (*e*) *Print:* (*proof correction mark*) close up.

doppelbrechend, *a. Ph: Opt:* doubly-refractive, birefringent, birefractive.

Doppelbrechung, *f. Ph: Opt:* double refraction, birefringence.

Doppelbreite, *f.* double width.

Doppelbrief, *m. Post:* overweight letter.

Doppelbruch, *m. Surg:* compound fracture.

Doppelbrücke, *f.* **1.** *El.E:* duplex bridge. **2.** *Civ.E:* twin bridge.

Doppelbüchse, *f. Sm.a:* double-barrelled (sporting) rifle.

Doppelbuchstabe, *m.* (*a*) *Ling:* diphthong; (*b*) *Gram: Print:* digraph; (*c*) *Print: Pal:* ligature.

Doppelbuchung, *f.* double entry (in register, etc.).

Doppelchlorid, *n. Ch:* bichloride, dichloride.

Doppelchor, *n.* **1.** *Arch:* double choir, two choirs; east and west choirs. **2.** *Mus:* double choir.

doppelchörig, *a. Arch:* with two choirs.

Doppelchromat, *n.*=**Bichromat.**

doppelchromsauer, *a. Ch:* bichromate, dichromate, of ....

Doppelchronograph, *m. Clockm:* split-seconds watch.

Doppelcicero, *f. Print:* two-line pica; twenty-four-point type.

Doppeldecker, *m. Av:* biplane; *Veh:* double-decker (bus).

Doppeldeckerbus, *m. Veh:* double-decker (bus).

doppeldeutig, *a.* ambiguous, equivocal (words, etc.); with a double meaning; **eine doppeldeutige Antwort geben,** to give an equivocal answer.

doppeldrähtig, *a. W.Tel:* twin-wire; **doppeldrähtige Antenne,** twin-wire aerial.

Doppeldrehergewebe, *n. Tex:* leno.

Doppeldreier, *m. Skating:* double-three.

Doppeldreizack, *m. Bot:* seaside arrow-grass.

Doppeldribbel, *m.* -s/-. *Basketball:* second dribble.

Doppeldruck, *m. Print:* mackle, blur, slur.

Doppeldruckmaschine, *f. Print:* two-revolution press.

Doppelduo, Doppelduowerk, *n. Metall:* two-high (rolling) mill, two-high rolls.

Doppelehe, *f.* bigamy; bigamous marriage; **in D. leben,** to live bigamously; **in D. lebend,** bigamous; **in D. Lebender** *m*, **Lebende** *f*, bigamist.

Doppelendball, *m. Box:* punch-ball, *U.S:* striking bag (*suspended on rubber springs between floor and ceiling*).

Doppelender, *m.* (*a*) *Mch:* double-ended boiler; (*b*) *Rail: etc:* diesel train, tram, with a driving cabin at each end; *Nau:* double-ended ferry.

Doppeler, *m.* -s/-=**Doppler.**

Doppelerfolg, *m.* double success, double victory; twofold success.

Doppelfagott, *n. Mus:* double-bassoon, contrabassoon.

doppelfarbig, *a.* two-coloured; dichromatic, *Cryst:* dichroic.

Doppelfarbigkeit, *f. Cryst:* dichroism.

Doppelfeder, *f.* elliptic(al) spring.

Doppelfehler, *m. Ten:* double fault.

Doppelfenster, *n.* (*a*) twin-light window; (*b*) double-glazed window.

Doppelfernglas, *n. Opt:* binoculars.

doppelflanschig, *a.* double-flanged (wheel).

Doppelflasche, *f.* double-sized bottle.

Doppelflinte, *f. Sm.a:* double-barrelled shot-gun.

Doppelflöte, *f. Mus:* (i) double flute (with one mouthpiece); (ii) double flute (of organ).

Doppelflugzeug, *n. Av:* composite aircraft.

Doppelfluß, *m. Mch:* double flow.

Doppelform, *f.* double form, duplicate form; *Ling:* doublet, alternative.

Doppelfoul, *n. Sp:* double foul.

Doppelfuge, *n. Mus:* double fugue.

Doppelfüß(l)er, *m.* -s/-. *Arach:* diplopod.

Doppelgänger, *m.* double, *F:* twin; second self, doppelganger; *Th:* double, stand-in.

doppelgängig, *a. Mec.E:* double-threaded (screw, etc.); two-start (thread); *Tls:* **doppelgängiger Schlangenbohrer,** double twist auger.

Doppelgas, *n. Ch:* mixture of water gas and coal gas.

Doppelgegensprechen, *n. Tg:* quadruplex telegraphy.

Doppelgeige, *f. Mus:* viol(a) d'amore.

doppelgeschlechtig, *a. Bot:* bisexual, bisexed.

Doppelgesicht, *n.* dual nature.

Doppelgespann, *n.* pair (of horses, oxen).

Doppelgestaltung, *f. Cryst:* dimorphism.

Doppelgestänge, *n. Tg:* double pole; coupled poles.

Doppelgestirn, *n.* (*a*) *Astr:* double star, binary star; (*b*) *Lit:* (*celebrated artists, etc.*) double star; twin stars.

Doppelgewebe, *n. Tex:* double weave (cloth).

doppeltgewolkt, *a. Her:* nebuly.

Doppelgitterröhre, *f. W.Tel:* double-grid valve.

Doppelglas, *n.* **1.** *Opt:* binoculars. **2.** *Glassm:* flashed glass.

Doppelgleis, *n. Rail:* double track.

doppelgleisig, *a. Rail: etc:* double-track.

Doppelglocke, *f. El:* duplex insulator.

Doppelgriff, *m. Mus:* double-stop; **Doppelgriffe spielen,** to double-stop.

Doppelgriffspiel, *n. Mus:* double-stopping.

Doppelhaken, *m.* (*a*) *Mec.E:* double hook (on lifting tackle); (*b*) *Her:* crampet.

Doppelhakenschlüssel, *m. Tls:* double-ended (open) spanner.

Doppelhaus, *n.* (i) dwelling consisting of two semi-detached houses; (ii) semi-detached house.

Doppelheide, *f. Bot:* cross-leaved heath.

doppelhenk(e)lig, *a.* two-handled (jug, etc.).

Doppelherzstück, *n. Rail:* diamond crossing.

Doppelhieb, *m. Fenc:* double hit; exchanged hit.

Doppelhochzeit, *f.* double wedding.

Doppelhobel, *m. Tls:* double-iron plane.

Doppelhobeleisen, *n. Tls:* double plane-iron.

Doppelhornvogel, *m. Orn:* great hornbill.

Doppelhub, *m. Mch:* up-and-down stroke.

Doppel-Ich, *n. Psy:* dual personality, dissociated personality, split personality.

Doppeljoch, *n.* **1.** *Constr:* double girder. **2.** *Arch:* double bay.
Doppelkabel, *n. Tg: Tp:* twin cable.
Doppelkanon, *m. Mus:* double canon.
Doppelkapelle, *f. Arch:* two-storied chapel (consisting of an upper and a lower chapel).
Doppelkarte, *f.* double-page map, two-page map.
Doppelkegel, *m. Geom:* double cone.
Doppelkeil, *m. Mec.E:* gib and cotter.
Doppelkinn, *n.* double chin.
Doppelkirche, *f. Arch:* two-storied church (consisting of an upper and a lower place of worship).
Doppelknopf, *m.* stud.
doppelkohlensauer, *a.* = **doppeltkohlensauer.**
Doppelkokosnuß, *f. Bot:* double coconut.
Doppelkolbenmotor, *m. I.C.E:* twin(-cylinder) engine.
Doppelkonsonant, *m. Ling:* double consonant.
Doppelkonzert, *n. Mus:* double concerto.
Doppelkopf, *m.* (*German card game*) doppelkopf.
Doppelkopfhörer, *m. W.Tel:* (set of) headphones.
doppelköpfig, *a.* double-headed; bicephalous.
Doppelkopfschiene, *f. Rail:* double-headed rail; bullhead rail.
Doppelkreuz, *n.* **1.** *Mus:* double-sharp. **2.** *Her: etc:* double cross; patriarchal cross; cross of Lorraine. **3.** *Print:* double dagger.
Doppelkrümmer, *m.* (*of pipe, etc.*) double bend.
Doppelkrümmung, *f.* double curvature (of a surface).
Doppelkuppeln, *n. Aut:* double-declutch.
Doppelkurbel, *f. Mec.E:* duplex crank.
Doppellafette, *f. Artil:* twin-mounting.
Doppellauf, *m.* double-barrel (of gun).
doppelläufig, *a.* double-barrelled, twin-barrelled.
Doppellaut, *m. Ling:* diphthong.
Doppelleben, *n.* **1. ein D. führen,** to lead a double life. **2.** *Psy:* double consciousness.
doppellebig, *a. Nat.Hist:* amphibious.
Doppelleitung, *f. Tg: Tp:* double line; twin cable.
Doppellender, *m.* **-s/-.** *Husb:* **1.** fat calf. **2.** porker, fat pig.
Doppellibelle, *f. Surv:* reversible spirit level.
Doppellinien, *f.pl.* double rulings; **auf D. schreiben,** to write between double lines.
Doppellinse, *f. Opt:* doublet (lens).
Doppellitze, *f.* (*a*) double band of trimming; (*b*) *Mil:* double flash; (*c*) *El:* = **Doppelschnur.**
Doppelmagnetzündung, *f. I.C.E:* dual magneto ignition.
Doppelmaschine, *f.* (*a*) *Print:* two-revolution press; (*b*) *Bootm:* twin-machine, sole-laying machine.
Doppelmast, *m. Tg:* double pole.
Doppelmaulschlüssel, *m. Tls:* double-ended spanner; multi-socket wrench.
Doppelmeister, *m. Ten:* doubles champion.
Doppelmesserschalter, *m. El:* double-bladed switch.
Doppelmißbildung, *f. Biol:* double monstrosity.
Doppelmittel, *f. Print:* double English (type), two-line English (type); 28-point type.
Doppelmord, *m.* double murder.
Doppelmutter, *f. Mec.E:* check-nut, jam-nut, lock-nut.
doppeln. **1.** *v.tr.* (*a*) to double; *Gaming:* **seinen Einsatz d.,** to double one's stake; (*b*) *Austrian: Bootm:* to sole (shoe); (*c*) *Nau:* to sheath (ship). **2.** *v.i.* (*haben*) (*a*) *Gaming:* to dice; (*b*) *Th:* **für j-n d.,** to double, stand in, for s.o.
Doppelnadel, *f. El:* **astatische D.,** astatic needles.
Doppelnaht, *f.* double stitching (on shoe, etc.); *Needlew:* French seam.
Doppelname, *m.* (i) double (first) name; (ii) hyphenated surname, *F:* double-barrelled name.
Doppelnashorn, *n. Z:* two-horned rhinoceros.
Doppelnatur, *f.* **1.** double, dual, nature. **2.** *Ph:* dual nature, wave-particle dualism (of light and matter).
Doppelnelson, *m. Wr:* full Nelson.
Doppeloktave, *f. Mus:* double octave.
doppelpaarig, *a. Nat.Hist:* bigeminal.
Doppelpaddel, *n. Row:* double paddle.
doppelpolig, *a. El:* bipolar, dipolar, double-pole, two-pole; **doppelpoliger Schalter,** double-pole, two-pole, switch.
Doppelposten, *m. Mil:* double guard.
Doppelprämiengeschäft, *n. St.Exch:* dealing in double options.
Doppelpunkt, *m.* (*a*) *Print: etc:* colon; (*b*) *Geom:* double point.
Doppelquadrat, *n.* = **Biquadrat.**
Doppelquittung, *f. Com:* receipt in duplicate.
Doppelreifen, *m. Aut:* twin tyres, dual tyres.
Doppelreihe, *f.* (*a*) double row (of trees, etc.); (*b*) *Mth:* double series.
doppelreihig, *a.* consisting of two rows; **doppelreihiger Anzug,** double-breasted suit; **doppelreihige Perlenkette,** double string of pearls; *Mec.E:* **doppelreihige Nietung,** double riveting.
Doppelreim, *m. Pros:* triple rhyme.
Doppelrick, *n. Equit:* double fence.
Doppelrolle, *f. Th: etc:* double role, double part.
Doppelsalto, *m. Gym: etc:* double somersault.
Doppelsalz, *n. Ch:* double salt.
Doppelsame, *m. Bot:* diplotaxis.
Doppelsatz, *m. Print:* double.
Doppelschalter, *m. El:* two-way switch.
doppelschattig, *a.* amphiscian; **die Doppelschattigen,** the amphiscians.
Doppelscheuer, *f. A:* = **Doppelbecher.**
Doppelschicht, *f.* **1.** *Ph: etc:* double layer. **2.** *Ind:* double shift, two shifts.
doppelschichtig, *a.* two-layered; *adv.* in two layers.
Doppelschiebersteuerung, *f. Mch:* double valve-gear.
Doppelschlag, *m.* **1.** *Mus:* turn. **2.** *Num:* double-struck coin.
doppelschlägig, *a. Med:* dicrotic (pulse).
Doppelschlägigkeit, *f. Med:* dicrotism.
Doppelschlangenkreuz, *n. Her:* cross gringolee.
Doppelschleiche, *f. Rept:* amphisbaena.
doppelschlicht, *a.* dead-smooth (file).
Doppelschlichtfeile, *f. Tls:* dead-smooth file.
Doppelschlitz, *m. Arch:* diglyph.
Doppelschlußbewicklung, *f. El.E:* compound winding.
Doppelschlußmotor, *m. El.E:* compound-wound motor.
Doppelschlußwicklung, *f. El.E:* compound winding.
Doppelschnepfe, *f. Orn:* great snipe.
Doppelschnur, *f. El:* (i) twin flex; (ii) two-core flex.
Doppelschraubendampfer, *m.* twin-screw steamer.
Doppelschraubenschlüssel, *m. Tls:* double-ended spanner.
Doppelschuß, *m. Shooting:* double shot, doublet.
doppelschwänzig, *a. Her:* **doppelschwänziger Löwe,** lion with tail forked, lion queue fourchy.
Doppelsechs, *f. Dominoes:* double six.
Doppelsehen, *n. Med:* diplopia, double vision.
Doppelseite, *f. Print:* double-page.
doppelseitig, *a.* double; *Tex:* double-sided, double-faced (material); *Med:* double; bilateral; **doppelseitige Schuldverhältnisse,** mutual indebtedness; *Med:* **doppelseitige Lungenentzündung,** double pneumonia; **doppelseitige Lähmung,** bilateral paralysis, diplegia; *Print:* **doppelseitige Anzeige,** two-page, double-page, spread; *Ling:* **doppelseitige Assimilation,** reciprocal assimilation; *adv.* on both sides; **d. beschrieben,** written on both sides; **d. gelähmt,** paralysed on both sides.
Doppelsichtigkeit, *f.* = **Doppelsehen.**
Doppelsieg, *m.* double victory.
Doppelsieger, *m.* double champion, double winner.
Doppelsinn, *m.* double meaning; two meanings.
doppelsinnig, *a.* ambiguous; equivocal.
Doppelsinnigkeit, *f.* ambiguity; equivocality, equivocalness; equivocation.
Doppelsitzer, *m. Av:* two-seater (aircraft), *U.S:* two-place aircraft.
Doppelsitzventil, *n. Mch:* double beat valve, double seat valve.
Doppelskuller, *m.* = **Doppelzweier.**
Doppelsohle, *f. Bootm:* double sole; clump(-sole).
Doppelsöldner, *m. Mil.Hist:* harquebusier.
Doppelspat, *m. Miner:* Iceland spar.
Doppelspiel, *n.* **1.** *Ten:* doubles (match). **2.** *F:* double game; **ein gefährliches D. treiben,** to play a dangerous double game.
Doppelspielfeld, *n. Ten:* doubles court.
doppelspitzig, *a.* double-pointed; *Bot:* biacuminate.
Doppelsprechen, *n. Tg:* diplex telegraphy.
Doppelsprung, *m. Swim:* double dive; *Rac:* double jump.
Doppelspuraufzeichnung, *f. Tape-recording:* twin-track recording.
Doppelstaater, *m.* **-s/-,** person with dual nationality.
Doppelstecker, *m. El:* adaptor; two-way (plug) adaptor.
Doppelstein, *m. Dominoes:* doublet, double.
Doppelsteppnaht, *f. Needlew:* French seam.
Doppelsteppstich, *m. Needlew:* lock-stitch (on machine).
Doppelstern, *m. Astr:* double star; binary star.
Doppelsternmotor, *m. I.C.E:* two-bank radial engine.
Doppelsteuer, *n. Av: etc:* dual controls; **Flugzeug mit D.,** dual-control aircraft.
Doppelsteuerflugzeug, *n. Av:* dual-control aircraft.
Doppelsteuerung, *f. Av: etc:* dual controls.
Doppelstiftstecker, *m. El:* two-pin plug.
Doppelstrich, *m. Mus:* repeat(-mark); *Morse:* break sign.
Doppelsuperphosphat, *n. Ch:* double superphosphate.
doppelt. **1.** (*a*) *a.* double (quantity, etc.); twice; twofold; **doppelter Boden,** double, false, bottom (of box, etc.), *N.Arch:* double bottom (of ship); **doppelter Whisky,** double whisky; **doppelter Sieg,** twofold victory; double victory; **Schuh mit doppelter Sohle,** shoe with a double sole; **ein doppeltes Geschenk,** a double present; two presents in one; **doppelte Freude,** double pleasure; double joy; **doppeltes Glück haben,** to have double luck; to be doubly lucky; **dieser Stoff liegt in doppelter Breite,** this material is double width; **die Sache hat ein doppeltes Gesicht,** there are two sides to the matter; the affair has two aspects, is two-sided; **der Grund hierfür ist ein doppelter,** the reason for this is twofold; **doppelte Moral,** double set of morals; **ein doppeltes Spiel treiben,** to play a double game; **die doppelte Zahl von Leuten kam,** double, twice, the number of people came; **den doppelten Preis bezahlen,** to pay double the price; *Med:* **doppelte Lungenentzündung,** double pneumonia; *Com:* **doppelte Buchführung,** double-entry bookkeeping; *Com: Adm:* **in doppelter Ausfertigung,** in duplicate; *Nau:* **eine Festmacheleine mit doppeltem Betingschlag festlegen,** to double-bitt a mooring line; *Constr:* **doppeltes Hängewerk,** queen(-post) truss; *Wr:* **doppelter Nackenhebel,** full Nelson; *Dicing:* **doppelte Sechs,** double six; *Prov:* **geteilte Freude ist doppelte Freude,** a joy, pleasure, shared is a double joy, pleasure; (*b*) *adv.* double; twice; doubly; **d. sehen,** to see double; **etwas d. haben,** to have two (copies, sets) of sth.; **d. so groß wie . . .,** twice as large, big, as . . .; **d. so oft,** twice as often; **d. soviel bezahlen,** to pay double, twice, as much; **Papier, Stoff, d. zusammenlegen,** to fold, paper, material, double, in two, to double (up) paper, material, etc.; **dieser Stoff liegt d. breit,** this material is double width; **sie sieht d. so alt aus, wie sie wirklich ist,** she looks twice her real age; **wenn man etwas billig kauft, dann ist es in Wirklichkeit d. teuer,** a cheap buy is doubly, twice as, dear in the long run, a cheap buy is a dear bargain in the long run; **d. soviel wie j-d anders haben,** to have twice as much as s.o. else; **seine Angelrute ist d. so lang wie meine,** his fishing rod is twice the length of, twice as long as, mine; **heute kamen d. so viele Leute wie gestern,** twice as many people came today as yesterday; **eine Tür d. verschließen,** to double-lock a door; **etwas d. vergolden,** to double-gild sth.; *Nau:* **d. reffen,** to double-reef; *Bot: Ling:* **d. zusammengesetzt,** decomposite, decompound; *Com:* (*on receipt*) **'d. für einfach gültig',** 'receipted in duplicate'; *Prov:* **d. genäht hält besser, d. reißt nicht,** it's better to be on the safe side, to play safe; better safe than sorry; another won't hurt; two are better than one; **d. gibt, wer schnell gibt,** he gives twice, who gives without delay; *see also* **gemoppelt;** (*c*) **das Doppelte,** double; **das kostet das Doppelte,** it costs double that amount, twice that sum; (*of price*) **auf das Doppelte steigen,** to double; **es hat mich nur sechs Mark gekostet, aber er hat das Doppelte bezahlt,** it cost me only six marks, but he paid twice as much, twice that sum; **das Doppelte leisten,** to do double the work; to do twice as much work; **Maschinen leisten das Doppelte, wenn man sie gut pflegt,** machines do double, twice, the work when they are well serviced; **er macht vier Stück am Tag, aber andere leisten das Doppelte,** he makes four pieces a day, but others produce double that number, twice that number, twice as many. **2.** *adv.* (*intensive*) (*a*) doubly; twice; **d. glücklich sein,** to be doubly happy; **d. schuldig sein,** to be doubly guilty; **diese Frage wird d. brennend, wenn . . .,** this question becomes doubly pressing if . . .; **es tut mir d. leid, daß . . .,** I am doubly sorry that . . .; (*b*) **d. und dreifach,** twofold; doubled (and trebled); doubly (and trebly); (*of article*) **d. und dreifach verpackt sein,** to be doubly wrapped and packed; **seine Güte wurde ihm d. und dreifach vergolten,** his kindnesses were returned twofold; **unter diesen Umständen zählt das d. und dreifach,** in the circumstances it counts for far more; **sie wurde d. und dreifach belohnt,** she was doubly rewarded.
Doppeltangente, *f. Geom:* bitangent.

Doppel-T-Anker, *m. El.E:* shuttle-type armature, shuttle-wound armature, H armature.
Doppeltaste, *f. Tg:* double-lever sending key.
doppeltbasisch, *a. Ch:* dibasic, bibasic.
doppeltbrechend, *a.* = **doppelbrechend.**
doppeltchromsauer, *a. Ch:* bichromate of (potassium).
Doppelte, *n. see* **doppelt** 1 (*c*).
Doppel-T-Eisen, *f. Tchn:* I bar, I iron.
Doppeltertia, *f. Print:* four-line brevier; 32-point type.
doppeltfiederspaltig, *a. Bot:* bipinnate.
doppeltgefiedert, *a. Bot:* bipinnate.
doppeltgepaart, *a. Nat.Hist:* bigeminal.
doppeltgesägt, *a. Bot:* biserrate.
doppelthohl, *a. Opt:* (*of lens*) biconcave, double concave.
Doppeltier, *n. Ent:* diplozoon.
Doppeltitel, *m.* two titles, two names (of play).
doppeltkohlensauer, *a. Ch:* bicarbonate of . . .; **doppeltkohlensaures Natron,** bicarbonate of soda, sodium bicarbonate.
Doppelton, *m.* double tone; *Physiol:* double murmur.
Doppeltreffer, *m. Shooting:* doublet; right-and-left.
Doppeltriller, *m. Mus:* double shake.
doppeltstehend, *a. Constr:* **doppeltstehender Stuhl,** queen(-post) truss.
Doppeltür, *f.* double door.
doppeltweinsteinsauer, *a. Ch:* bitartrate of . . .; **doppeltweinsteinsaures Kalium,** potassium bitartrate, cream of tartar.
doppeltwirkend, *a. Mec.E: etc:* double-acting, double-action (steam-engine, cylinder, pump, etc.).
Doppelverdiener, *m.* (*a*) person with two jobs; (*b*) *pl.* **Doppelverdiener,** husband and wife who are both earning.
Doppelverhältnis, *n. Mth:* (**nichtharmonisches**) **D.,** double ratio, cross-ratio, anharmonic ratio.
Doppelverkehr, *m. Tg: etc:* two-way communication.
Doppelvers, *m. Pros:* distich.
Doppelversicherung, *f. Ins:* double insurance.
Doppelvierer, *m. Row:* sculling-four.
Doppelvisierfernrohr, *n. Artil:* binocular gun-sight.
Doppelvitriol, *n. Ch: Ind:* Salzburg vitriol; crystalline mixture of iron vitriol and blue vitriol.
Doppelvokal, *m. Ling:* diphthong.
Doppelwägung, *f.* (method of) double-weighing.
Doppelwährung, *f. Pol.Ec:* bimetallism; bimetallic system.
Doppelwand, *f.* double wall; *Constr:* baffle wall.
doppelwandig, *a.* double-walled; *Mch:* **doppelwandiger Kessel,** double-shell boiler; *Civ.E:* **doppelwandiger Träger,** trough-girder.
Doppelwappen, *n. Her:* parted arms; united arms of husband and wife.
Doppelweggleichrichtung, *f. El.E:* full-wave rectification.
Doppelweghahn, *m.* two-way cock.
Doppelzange, *f. Constr:* collar beam; tie beam.
Doppelzentner, *m. Meas:* 100 kilogrammes (= 220.46 lbs).
Doppelzersetzung, *f. Ch:* double decomposition.
Doppelzimmer, *n.* double room, *U.S:* room for two people.
Doppelzugbrücke, *f. Civ.E:* double-leaf lifting-bridge.
Doppelzünder, *m. Artil:* time-and-percussion fuze.
Doppelzündung, *f. I.C.E:* dual ignition, twin ignition.
Doppelzunge, *f. Mus:* double-tonguing.
doppelzüngig, *a.* (*a*) two-tongued (monster, etc.); (*b*) *Pej:* double-tongued, two-faced (pers.); disingenuous (statement, etc.); *adv.* **d. reden,** to speak with two voices.
Doppelzweier, *m. Row:* double-sculler.
Doppelzwilling, *m. Cryst:* twinned crystal.
Doppelzylinderpumpe, *f. Mch:* duplex pump.
doppen, *v.tr.* = **eichen**[3].
Döpper, *m.* **-s/-.** *Tls: Metalw:* (rivet) snap, snap-tool, riveting-die, cup set.
Doppik, *f.* **-/.** *Com:* double-entry book-keeping.
Doppler, *m.* **-s/-.** *Gaming:* gambler; cheat at dice.
Dopplereffekt, *m. Ac: Spectroscopy:* Doppler effect.
Dopplersch, *a. Ac: Spectroscopy:* **Dopplerscher Effekt, Dopplersches Prinzip,** Doppler's principle.
Dorade [do·ˈraːdə], *f.* **-/-n.** *Ich:* **1.** goldfish. **2.** dorado, dolphin. **3.** sea-bream, *esp.* chrysophrys.
Dorado[1], **das** [do·ˈraːdoː]. *Pr.n.* **-s.** (*occ. pl.* **-s**) = **Eldorado.**
Dorado[2]. *Pr.n.m.* **-s.** *Astr:* Dorado, the Swordfish, Xiphias.
Dorant [do·ˈrant], *m.* **-s/-e.** *Bot:* antirrhinum; linaria; gentian; horehound; wild marjoram; **weißer D.,** common, white, horehound; **gelber D.,** yellow toad-flax; **blauer D.,** Calathian violet.
Dorcas-Gazelle [ˈdorkas-], *f. Z:* dorcas (gazelle).
Dorer [ˈdoːrər], *m.* **-s/-.** *A.Hist:* Dorian.
Döres. *Pr.n.m.* **-'.** *Dial:* (*dim. of* **Theodor**) Theodore, Teddy.
Dorf, *n.* **-(e)s/⸚er. 1.** (*a*) village; *U.S:* small town; (*in S.Africa*) dorp; **die Leute vom D.,** country-folk; **auf dem D.,** in the country; **das Leben auf dem Dorf(e),** country life; village life; **in einem D. wohnen,** to live in a village; **sie kommt aus unserem D.,** she is, comes, from our village; **der ist vom D.,** he is a country bumpkin; he is very uncouth in his manner; *F:* **Potemkinsche Dörfer,** (i) façade; blind; (ii) eyewash; **das sind mir böhmische, spanische, Dörfer,** it's all Greek, double Dutch, to me; **auf die Dörfer gehen,** (i) to lower one's standards; to lower one's pretensions; to take a step down; *Th:* to be reduced to playing in small provincial theatres; (ii) *Cards:* to discard; (*b*) (*inhabitants*) **das ganze D. lief zusammen, den Brand zu sehen,** the whole village turned out to see the fire. **2.** *Swiss Dial:* visit.
Dorfanger, *m.* village green.
Dorfbengel, *m.* village lad.
Dorfbewohner, *m.* villager; village-dweller; countryman.
Dörfchen, *n.* **-s/-,** (*dim. of* **Dorf**) small village; (*without a church*) hamlet.
Dorfgeistliche, *m.* (*decl. as adj.*) *R.C.Ch:* village priest.
Dorfgemeinde, *f.* (*a*) village community; rural community; (*b*) country parish.
Dorfgemeinderat, *m.* rural council, parish council.
Dorfgeschichte, *f.* **1.** story of country life; village-tale. **2.** history of a, of the, village.
Dorfidiot, *m.* village idiot.
Dorfjugend, *f. coll.* village youth.
Dorfkind, *n.* village child.
Dorfkirche, *f.* village church.
Dorfkirmes, *f.* village fair, village fête.
Dorfkrug, *m.* = **Dorfschenke.**
Dorfleben, *n.* country life; village life.
Dorflehrer, *m.* village schoolmaster.
Dörflein, *n.* **-s/-** = **Dörfchen.**
Dörfler, *m.* **-s/-.** *Pej:* villager; countryman.
dörflich, *a.* village; **dörfliche Gemeinden,** village communities.
Dorfpfarrer, *m.* country parson; vicar of a country parish; *R.C.Ch:* village priest.
Dorfplatz, *m.* village square.
Dorfschenke, *f.* village inn, village pub.
Dorfschmied, *m.* village blacksmith.
Dorfschöne, *f.* village beauty.
Dorfschule, *f.* village school.
Dorfschulmeister, *m.* village schoolmaster.
Dorfschulze, *m. Hist. & Dial:* mayor of a, the, village.
Dorfschwalbe, *f. Orn:* (barn-)swallow (*hirundo rustica*).
Dorfsimpel, *m.* = **Dorfidiot.**
Dorfstraße, *f.* village street.
Dorfteich, *m.* village pond.
Dorftölpel, *m.* country bumpkin; **der D.,** the village idiot.
Dorfwiese, *f.* village green.
Dorfwirtshaus, *n.* = **Dorfschenke.**
Doria, *int. see* **Donner**[2].
Dorier [ˈdoːriər], *m.* **-s/-** = **Dorer.**
Doris. 1. *Pr.n.f.* **-'.** *Gr.Myth:* Doris. **2.** *Pr.n.f.* **-'.** (*dim. of* **Dorothea**) Doris. **3.** *Pr.n.n.* **-'.** *A.Geog:* Doris. **4.** *f.* **-/Doriden** [do·ˈriːdən]. *Moll:* doris, sea-lemon.
dorisch [ˈdoːriʃ]. **1.** *a. A.Hist:* Dorian (people); Doric (dialect); **die Dorische Wanderung,** the Dorian invasion. **2.** *a. Arch:* Doric; **die dorische Säulenordnung,** the Doric (order); **dorisches Kapitell,** Doric capital. **3.** *a. Mus:* **dorische Tonart,** Dorian mode. **4.** *s.* **Dorisch,** *n. Ling:* Doric.
Dorismus [do·ˈrismus], *m.* **-/-men,** Dorism.
Dorkinghuhn [ˈdorkiŋ-], *n. Husb:* Dorking (fowl).
Dormant [dorˈmãː], *m.* **-s/-s.** *Arch:* window-, door-frame.
Dormeuse [dorˈmøːzə], *f.* **-/-n. 1.** lounge-chair. **2.** *Cost:* night-cap.
dormie [dorˈmiː], *a. Golf:* dormy.
Dormitorium [dormi·ˈtoːrium], *n.* **-s/-rien,** dormitory (*esp.* in monastery).
Dorn, *m.* **I. -(e)s/-en. 1.** *Bot:* (*a*) thorn; prickle; spine; **kleiner D.,** small thorn; *Nat.Hist:* spinule; **in Dornen auswachsende Zweige,** twigs ending in hard spines; **sich** *dat.* **einen D. in den Fuß treten,** to get a thorn in one's foot; *F:* **j-m ein D. im Auge sein,** to be a thorn in s.o.'s side, flesh; (*b*) *usu. pl.* **Dornen,** thorn-bush, brier, briar; thorn-hedge; *F:* **auf Dornen gebettet sein,** to lead a hard life, to suffer hardship; *F:* **Dornen ernten,** to reap no benefit (from it, etc.); *B:* **Dornen und Disteln soll er dir tragen,** thorns also and thistles shall it bring forth to thee. **2.** *Bot:* (*a*) (**gemeiner**) **D.,** hawthorn, whitethorn, may (-bush, -tree); (*b*) = **Dornrose** (*a*); **wohlriechender D.** = **Dornrose** (*b*). **3.** *A:* quill, spine (of porcupine); spine (of dog-fish, etc.).
II. Dorn, *m.* **-(e)s/-e & ⸚er. 1.** *Tchn:* (*a*) arbor, mandrel; bending mandrel; triblet; drift(-pin); punch; awl; pin, pintle (of hinge); plug-gauge; spindle (of door-handle); (*b*) tang, tongue, fang, shank (of blade, etc.); tongue (of buckle); (*c*) bit, web (of key); (*d*) spike (of running shoe, etc.). **2.** *pl.* **Dörner** = **Seigerdörner.**
Dornapfel, *m. Bot:* thorn-apple, stramony, stramonium, *U.S:* jimson weed.
dornartig, *a.* thorn-like, thorn-shaped.
Dornastrild, *m. Orn:* Sydney waxbill.
Dornauszieher, *m. Art:* Boy with a Thorn, Spinario.
Dornbusch, *m.* thorn-bush, brier, briar, bramble; **Moses und der brennende D.,** Moses and the burning bush.
Dorndreher, *m. Orn:* red-backed shrike, butcher-bird.
Dornegge, *f. Agr:* bush-harrow, brush-harrow.
Dorneidechse, *f. Rept:* stellion.
dornen[1], *v.tr. Tchn:* to drift (rivet-hole).
dornen[2], *a.* thorny.
Dornenbalken, *m. Her:* engrailment; **mit D.,** engrailed.
dornenförmig, *a. Nat.Hist:* spiniform.
dornengekrönt, *a.* crowned with thorns; **der Dornengekrönte,** Christ with the crown of thorns.
Dornenhecke, *f.* thorn-hedge, hedge of thorns.
Dornenkrone, *f.* (Christ's) crown of thorns.
dornenlos, *a. Bot:* thornless, without thorns, inerm(ous); *Nat.Hist:* spineless.
dornenreich, *a.* full of thorns; *F:* difficult, hard; **dornenreiche Laufbahn,** difficult career, career beset with difficulties; **dornenreicher Weg,** hard road; **dornenreiches Leben,** hard life.
dornentragend, *a. Bot: Nat.Hist:* spiniferous, spinose, spinous, spiny.
dornenvoll, *a.* full of thorns; *F:* difficult, hard; **dornenvolles Amt,** difficult job, difficult office; **er hat einen dornenvollen Lebensweg gehabt,** he has had a hard life, *F:* he has had a hard row to hoe.
Dornenzaun, *m.* = **Dornenhecke.**
Dornfink, *m. Orn:* pied fly-catcher.
Dornfisch, *m. Ich:* stickleback; *esp.* fifteen-spined stickleback.
Dornfortsatz, *m. Anat:* spinous process.
Dorngesträuch, Dorngestrüpp, *n.* thorn-bushes, brier, briar.
Dorngewächs, *n. Bot:* thorn-bearing plant, prickly plant.
Dorngradierhaus, *n. Saltmaking:* thorn-house.
Dorngrasmücke, *f.,* **Dorngrauschlüpfer,** *m. Orn:* whitethroat, nettle-creeper.
Dorngrundel, *m. & f. Ich:* spined loach, groundling.
Dornhai, *m. Ich:* piked dog-fish, spiny dog-fish.
Dornhecke, *f.* = **Dornenhecke.**
Dornhund, *m.* = **Dornhai.**
dornicht, *a.* = **dornig.**
dornig, *a.* (*a*) with thorns, thorny; *Nat.Hist:* spiniferous; (*b*) **dornige Bahn,** hard road; **dornige Laufbahn,** difficult career; **dornige Fahrt,** hard, difficult, journey.
Dornnuß, *f. Bot:* New Zealand bur.
Dorno-Strahlung, *f. Ph:* Dorno-region.
Dornotter, *m. Rept:* death-adder.
Dornpresse, *f. Tchn:* mandrel press.
Dornrochen, *m. Ich:* thornback.
Dornröschen. *Pr.n.n.* **-s/.** Sleeping Beauty.
Dornröschenschlaf, *m.* hundred years' sleep; *F:* **den, seinen, D. schlafen,** to live in a dream world, to be behind the times; **aus seinem, dem, D. erwachen,** to wake from a long sleep; to wake up to reality; **j-n aus seinem D. wecken,** to bring s.o. back to reality.
Dornrose, *f. Bot:* (*a*) wild rose, dog-rose, briar-rose, wild briar; (*b*) sweet briar, eglantine.
Dornschloß, *m. Locksm:* pin-lock.
Dornschuhe, *m.pl. Sp:* spiked shoes, *F:* spikes; running shoes, track-shoes.

Dornschwanz, *m. Rept:* thorny-tailed, spiny-tailed, lizard.
Dornschwanzhörnchen, *n. Z:* = **Schuppenflughörnchen.**
Dornstein, *m. Saltmaking:* thornstone.
Dornstrauch, *m.* thorn-bush, brier, briar, bramble.
Dornteufel, *m. Rept:* moloch, (Australian) thorn-lizard.
Dornwerk, *n.* faggots (for a thorn-house).
Doronicum [doˑˈroːniˑkum], *n.* **-s/-ca.** *Bot:* doronicum.
Dorothea [doˑroˑˈteːaː], **Dorothee** [doˑroˑˈteː]. *Pr.n.f.* **-s** & *Lit:* **-theens** [-ˈteːəns]. Dorothea, Dorothy.
Dörre, *f.* **-/-n** = **Darre** 2 (*a*), 3.
dorren, *v.i.* (*sein*) to dry; to become dry; to dry up, to wither; to shrivel.
dörren, *v.tr.* to dry, desiccate (foodstuffs, fruit); to dry (fish); to (kiln-)dry, to kiln (hops, etc.); **gedörrtes Obst,** dried fruits; **Dörren** *n,* drying, desiccation (of foodstuffs, fruit).
Dörrkammer, *f.* hemp-kiln.
Dörrobst, *n.* dried fruit(s).
Dörrpflaumen, *f.pl.* (dried) prunes; dried plums.
dorsal[1] [dorˈzaːl], *a. Nat.Hist:* dorsal; *adv.* dorsally.
Dorsal[2] [dorˈzaːl], *n.* **-s/-e, Dorsale** [dorˈzaːlə], *n.* **-/-n.** *Ecc:* back of a choir-stall.
Dorsalflexion, *f. Anat:* dorsiflexion.
Dorsallaut, *m. Ling:* dorsal (consonant).
Dorsalnerv, *m. Anat:* thoracic nerve.
Dorsch, *m.* **-es/-e. 1.** *Ich:* codling; **französischer D.,** whiting-pout, bib, *F:* stink-alive. **2.** *Ich:* (*generic*) gade, gadoid; **die Dorsche,** the gadidae. **3.** *Bot:* = **Wasserrübe.**
Dorschlebertran, *m. Pharm:* cod-liver oil.
dorsoventral [ˌdorzoˑvenˈtraːl], *a. Anat:* dorso-ventral.
dort[1], *adv.* (*space*) (*demonstrative*) there, over there, *Lit:* yonder; **der Baum d.,** that tree (over) there; **warst du schon d.?** have you been there already? **d. steht er!** there he is! **d. geht er ja!** ah, there he goes! **wir haben ihn d. gesehen,** we saw him there; **darf ich d. sitzen, stehen?** may I sit, stand, there? **d. ist viel zu sehen,** there's a lot to be seen (there); **Sie d.!** you (over) there! **das Ding d.,** that thing (over) there; **d. gibt es steile Felsen,** there there are steep rocks; **das Haus ist d. in der Nähe,** the house is there or thereabouts, is somewhere near there; **ich ließ es d., wo ich es fand,** I left it there where I found it; **d. errichteten sie zwei Dämme,** there they built two dams; **an jenem Abend war d. nichts zu erblicken als trübe Dorflichter,** nothing was to be seen there that evening save the dim lights of the village; **bald hier, bald d.,** now here, now there; **hier und d.,** here and there; now and then; **ich kann nicht hier und d. zugleich sein,** I can't be here and there at the same time; **hier und d. sah man strohgedeckte Häuser,** now and then one saw thatched houses; **von d. (aus) fahren wir nach Berlin,** from there, *Lit:* (from) thence, we shall go to Berlin; **von d. ab,** from there on, *Lit:* (from) thence; **von d. ab war der Weg steinig und uneben,** from there on, from that place on, the road was stony and uneven; **er reiste gestern Abend (von) d. ab,** he left there last night; **d. draußen,** outside, out there; **d. drüben,** over there; on the other side; **er lebt in dem Haus d. drüben,** he lives in that house over there; **siehst du den Baum d. drüben über dem Fluß?** can you see the tree on the other side of the river? **d. unten, d. drunten,** down there; down below; under there; **das Dorf liegt d. unten,** the village lies down there, down below; **der Dieb versteckte sich d. unten,** the thief hid down there, under there; **d. heraus,** out of that place, out of there; **sie kam d. heraus und ging in einen anderen Laden,** she came out of there and went into another shop; **er ging da hinein und kam d. heraus,** he went in there and came out (over) there; **d. herum,** round that way; *cp.* **dortherum; d. hinauf,** up that way; up there; **d. hinaus,** out that way, out there; *cp.* **dorthinaus; d. hinein,** in that way, in there; **d. oben,** up there; **ein Scharfschütze hockte d. oben,** a sniper crouched up above; **was tun Sie d. oben?** what are you doing up there? *F:* **d. hat der Zimmermann das Loch gelassen!** there's the door;—get out! *Com:* **franko d.,** carriage paid; **franko Bahnhof d.,** carriage paid to the nearest railway station.
Dort[2], *m.* **-s/-e.** *Bot: F:* (*a*) darnel; (*b*) couch-grass, *U.S:* quack grass.
dorten, *adv. Lit:* = **dort.**
dorther, *adv.* from there, from that place, *A. & Lit:* thence; **ich komme (von) d.,** I come from there.
dortherum, *adv.* thereabout(s); somewhere in that neighbourhood; **das Dorf ist d.,** the village is somewhere around there, somewhere in that area; **er wohnt d.,** he lives somewhere there-abouts, somewhere around there.
dorthin, *adv.* there; to there; to that place; over there; **bis d.,** as far as there; *Lit:* thither; **wie soll man d. kommen?** how is one to get there? how can one get there? **ich gehe bis d.,** I am going as far as there; **wie weit ist es (bis) d.?** how far is it to there, to that place?
dorthinaus, *adv.* out there; **d. geht's nach X,** that's the way to X; *F:* **bis d.,** endlessly, *ad nauseam;* **wir hatten es bis d. geübt,** we had practised it times without number, innumerable times, *ad nauseam.*
dortig, *a.* there; in, of, that place; **die dortigen Verhältnisse,** the conditions there; **die dortigen Schulbehörden,** the school authorities there, in that place; **der dortige Wein,** the wine of that place, the wine there.
dortselbst, *adv.* = **daselbst.**
dortzulande, *adv.* in that country; there, in those parts.
Doryphoros [doˑryːfoˑros, doˑryˑˈfoːros], *m.* **-/-ren** [-ryˑˈfoːrən]. *Art:* doryphorus.
Dösch, *m.* **-es/-e.** *North G.Dial: Ich:* cod.
Döschen, *n.* **-s/-,** (*dim. of* **Dose**) small box; small tin; small case.
Dose[1], *f.* **-/-n. 1.** (lidded) box; container (with a lid); tin, can (of preserved fruit, etc.); tin (of powder, polish, ointment, etc.); pot, jar (of oint-ment, etc.); (powder-)bowl; (needle-)case; (biscuit) tin; *Phot:* (small round) developing tank; **eine D. Kaffee,** a tin of coffee; **Fleisch, Obst, Fisch, usw., in Dosen,** tinned, canned, meat, fruit, fish, etc. **2.** (*a*) *El:* (= **Steckdose**) plug socket; *El.E:* (= **Abzweigdose**) junction-box; (*b*) *Gramophones:* (= **Schalldose**) pick-up, sound-box.
Dose[2], *f.* **-/-n** = **Dosis.**
dösen, *v.i.* (*haben*) *F:* (*a*) to day-dream; to be wool-gathering; **das Kind sitzt den ganzen Tag und döst,** the child sits day-dreaming all day long; **bei seiner Arbeit d.,** to sit idle over one's work; (*b*) to doze, to drowse.
Dosenbier, *n.* canned beer.
Dosenfleisch, *n.* tinned, canned, meat.
Dosenlibelle, *f. Surv:* circular spirit level; water-level; *Phot:* **Sucher mit D.,** view-finder and level combined.
Dosenmilch, *f.* tinned, *U.S:* canned, milk; evapor-ated milk; condensed milk.
Dosenöffner, *m.* tin-opener, *U.S:* can-opener.
Dosenschalter, *m.* = **Drehschalter.**
Dosenschließer, *m.* can-sealer.
Dosensextant, *m. Mth: etc:* box sextant.
dosieren [doˑˈziːrən]. **I.** *v.tr.* **1.** (*of doctor, etc.*) to administer *or* prescribe *or* measure out a certain dose (of medicine); to proportion (medicine); **das Präparat kann folgendermaßen dosiert werden,** the appropriate dose of this preparation can be calculated as follows; **sorgfältig dosierte Mengen,** carefully measured quantities, doses; **wenn richtig dosiert, ist die Droge nicht schädlich,** the drug is harmless if given, administered, in the correct doses; *F:* **j-m die Wahrheit d.,** to let s.o. know the truth gradually; **er dosiert seine Geschenke,** he gives, *F:* doles out, his presents in driblets, in in-stalments, in penny numbers. **2.** *Wine-m:* to liqueur, sweeten, dose (champagne).
II. *vbl s.* **Dosieren** *n.,* **Dosierung** *f. in vbl senses; also:* dosage; (*on label*) **Dosierung,** dose, dosage; **bei richtiger Dosierung ist die Droge nicht schädlich,** the drug is harmless if given, administered, in the correct doses.
dösig, *a. F:* (*a*) dozy, drowsy; **j-n dumm und d. machen,** to make s.o.'s head swim; (*b*) dopey, half-doped; stupid; (*c*) boring; **eine dösige Lektüre,** a boring, tedious, *F:* soporific, piece of reading matter.
Dosimeter [doˑziˑˈmeːtər], *n.* **-s/-.** *Med: X Rays: etc:* dosimeter, quantimeter.
Dosimetrie [doˑziˑmeˑˈtriː], *f.* **-/.** *X Rays:* dosi-metry.
Dosis [ˈdoːzis], *f.* **-/Dosen.** *Med: Pharm: X Rays:* dose; **letale, tödliche, D.,** lethal dose; **eine zu große D. nehmen,** to take an overdose; **j-m etwas in kleinen Dosen verabreichen,** to give s.o. sth. in small doses, to give small doses of sth. to s.o.; to administer sth. to s.o. in small doses; to dose s.o. with small quantities of sth.; *F:* to tell s.o. sth. gradually, a little at a time; *F:* **er hat eine beträchtliche D. Selbstbewußtsein,** he has his full share of self-confidence; **ich kann ihn nur in kleinen Dosen genießen,** I can only stand, take, him in small doses; **in (kleinen) Dosen läßt sich die Wahrheit besser ertragen,** the truth is more bearable, can be better borne, in small doses; **das ist eine starke D.!** that's a bit thick! that's coming it a bit thick! (*of play, book, etc.*) that's pretty strong meat!
Dossier [dosiˈeː], *n.* **-s/-s,** dossier, file (of docu-ments).
dossieren [doˈsiːrən]. **I.** *v.tr.* **1.** to slope (dike, etc.). **2.** to grind down (plate glass); to polish (metal).
II. *vbl s.* **Dossierung,** *f.* (*a*) *in vbl senses;* (*b*) slope (of dike, etc.); taper (of chimney).
Dost, *m.* **-s/-e.** *Bot:* **1.** origan(um); **gemeiner, brauner, roter, D.,** wild marjoram. **2.** wild thyme, shepherd's thyme. **3.** bidens. **4.** hyperi-cum; **gelber D.,** St John's wort. **5.** eupatorium.
Dosten, *m.* **-s/-, Dostenkraut,** *n.* = **Dost 1.**
Dostenöl, *n. Pharm:* origan(um) oil.
Dotalbauer [doˑˈtaːl-], *m.* tenant on church land.
Dotale [doˑˈtaːlə], *m.* **-n/-n** = **Dotalbauer.**
Dotalgrundstück, *n.* dotal property.
Dotalsystem, *n. Jur:* dotal system, marriage settlement in trust, jointure.
Dotation [doˑtaˑtsiˈoːn], *f.* **-/-en,** donation (of money) (to church, etc.); endowment (of church, etc.); (parliamentary) grant for distinguished service to the State; *Adm:* financial allocation, grant (made by the State) to local authority.
dotieren [doˑˈtiːrən]. **I.** *v.tr.* to endow (church, etc.); to make a parliamentary grant to (general, etc.); *Fin:* **einen Fonds d.,** to increase a reserve fund; **eine gut dotierte Stelle,** a well-paid posi-tion; (*in university*) a well-endowed post; **eine reich dotierte Stiftung,** a richly endowed foundation.
II. *vbl s.* **Dotierung,** *f.* **1.** *in vbl senses; also:* donation of money (to church, etc.); endow-ment (of church, etc.); remuneration, pay (of position); *Fin:* allocation (to reserve fund). **2.** donation (of money) (to church, etc.); endowment (of church, etc.); (parliamentary) grant for distinguished service to the State.
Dotter, *m. & n.* **-s/-. 1.** yolk (of egg); *Biol:* vitellus, yolk; **ohne D.,** yolkless; **Ei mit zwei Dottern,** egg with a double yolk. **2.** *m. Bot:* camelina; **echter D.,** gold-of-pleasure.
Dotterblume, *f. Bot:* marsh-marigold.
Dottergang, *m. Biol:* vitelline duct, yolk-duct.
dottergelb, *a.* egg-yellow (colour).
Dotterhaut, *f.* = **Dottersack.**
dott(e)rig, *a.* (*a*) eggy; (*b*) yolk-like.
Dotteröl, *n.* = **Leindotteröl.**
Dottersack, *m. Biol:* yolk-bag, yolk-sac, vitelline membrane.
Dotterweide, *f. Bot:* golden osier, yellow willow, golden willow.
Double [ˈduːbəl], *n.* **-s/-s. 1.** *Th: Cin:* double; stand-in. **2.** *Mus:* double.
Doublé, Doublee [duˑˈbleː], *n.* **-s/-s** = **Dublee** 1, 2.
Doublette [duˑˈblɛtə], *f.* = **Dublette** 2 (*a*).
doublieren [duˑˈbliːrən], *v.tr. Metall:* to plate (metal).
Doubliermaschine, *f. Tex:* lapping machine.
Douglasfichte [ˈduːglas-], **Douglasie** [duˑˈglaːzĭə], *f.* **-/-n.** *Bot:* Douglas fir, Douglas pine, red fir.
Douglastanne, *f.* = **Douglasfichte.**
Doumpalme [ˈduːm-], *f. Bot:* = **Dumpalme.**
Dourine [duˑˈriːnə], *f.* **-/.** *Vet:* dourine,
Dow [dau], *f.* **-/-en** = **Dau.**
Doxale [doˈksaːlə], *n.* **-s/-s.** *Ecc:* (*a*) = **Lettner;** (*b*) choir and organ-loft.
Doxologie [doksoˑloˑˈgiː], *f.* **-/-n** [-ˈgiːən]. *Ecc:* doxology; **die große D.,** the greater doxology; **die kleine D.,** the lesser doxology.
doxologisch [doksoˑˈloːgiʃ], *a.* doxological.
Doyen [doaˈjɛ̃ː], *m.* **-s/-s,** (*a*) doyen (of diplomatic corps); (*b*) = **Altmeister** (*b*).
Dozent [doˑˈtsɛnt], *m.* **-en/-en, Dozentin** [doˑˈtsɛntin], *f.* **-/-innen,** (i) (university) lecturer, *U.S:* assistant professor; (ii) university teacher; **die Dozenten,** (i) the lecturers; (ii) the academic staff (of university, etc.).
Dozentenschaft, *f.* **-/-en,** (*a*) academic staff (of university, etc.); (*b*) university teachers.
Dozentenzimmer, *n.* (lecturers') common-room.
Dozentur [doˑtsɛnˈtuːr], *f.* **-/-en,** lectureship, *U.S:* teaching position (at university).
dozieren [doˑˈtsiːrən], *v.i.* (*haben*) & *v.tr.* (*a*) to lecture, to give lectures, to teach; **er doziert an der Universität X,** he is a lecturer, reader, professor, at X University, he lectures at X University; (*b*) *F:* to pontificate, to hold forth; **in dozierendem Ton vortragen,** to hold forth (in a lofty, pontifical, manner); **er redet nicht, er doziert,** he doesn't talk, he pontificates.
Dozierton, *m.* pontifical tone.
dozil [doˑˈtsiːl], *a.* docile.
Drabe, *f.* **-/-n.** *Bot:* whitlow grass.

Dracäne [dra·ˈtsɛːnə], *f.* **-/-n.** *Bot:* dracaena; dragon-tree.

Drache, *m.* **-n/-n.** **1.** (*a*) *Myth: Her:* dragon; (*b*) *Her:* wyvern; (*c*) *Astr:* **der D.,** Draco, the Dragon; (*d*) *Rept:* **fliegender D.,** flying lizard; (*e*) *F:* (*usu. woman*) dragon; (*woman*) virago, termagant; **sie ist ein alter D.,** she is an old dragon. **2.** *Nau:* =**Drachenanker. 3.** =**Drachenfisch. 4.** *Med:* Guinea-worm. **5.** whirlwind; squall. **6.** *Swiss:* mountain torrent. **7.** =**Drachen.**

Drachen, *m.* **-s/-. 1.** *Toys: etc:* kite; **einen D. steigen lassen,** to fly, send up, a kite. **2.** =**Drache.**

Drachenampfer, *m. Bot:* (*a*) curled dock; (*b*) broad-leaved dock; (*c*) bloody(-veined) dock.

Drachenanker, *m. Nau:* grapnel, hook, grappling-anchor.

Drachenballon, *m.* kite-balloon.

Drachenbaum, *m. Bot:* dracaena; dragon-tree.

Drachenberg, *m. F:* **den D. hinuntergehen,** to go to the bad, *F:* to go to pot.

Drachenblut, *n.* **1.** *A.Pharm:* dragon's-blood. **2.** 'Dragon's-blood' (*a red Rhine wine esp. from the Drachenfels*). **3.** *Bot:* bloody(-veined) dock.

Drachenblutbaum, *m. Bot:* dracaena; dragon-tree.

Drachenblutkraut, *n. Bot:* bloody(-veined) dock.

Drachenblutpalme, *f. Bot:* dracaena; dragon-tree.

Drachenbrut, *f. Lit:* (*a*) dragon's progeny; generation of vipers; (*b*) fruit, outcome, of an evil deed *or* a misguided action.

Drachenfisch, *m. Ich:* (greater) weever, sting-bull.

Drachenfliege, *f. Ent:* dragon-fly.

Drachenflieger, *m.*=**Drachenflugzeug.**

Drachenflugzeug, *n. Hist. of Av:* fixed-wing aircraft.

drachenförmig, *a.* dragon-like, like a dragon; *Her:* dragonné, dragony.

Drachenhure, *f. Ent:* dragon-fly.

Drachenkopf, *m.* **1.** head of a dragon; *Astr: etc:* dragon's head. **2.** *Bot:* dracophalum, dragon's-head. **3.** *Ich:* scorpaena.

Drachenkraut, *n. Bot:* **1.** dracontium; dragonwort, dragon's wort. **2.** hemp agrimony.

Drachenlilie, *f. Bot:* dracaena; dragon-tree.

Drachenlinie, *f. Astr:* line of nodes (of the moon's orbit).

Drachenmonat, *m. Astr:* nodical month, draconitic month.

Drachenpalme, *f. Bot:* dracaena; dragon-tree.

Drachenrot(t)ang, *m. Bot:* calamus draco.

Drachensaat, *f. Myth:* dragon's teeth (*sown by Cadmus*); (*used figuratively*) seeds of discord; (evil) seeds; **die D. des Unfriedens,** the seeds of strife, of discord.

Drachenschlange, *f. Her:* winged dragon (without feet).

Drachenschuß, *m. Med: F:* lumbago.

Drachenschwanz, *m.* **1.** tail of a dragon; *Astr: etc:* dragon's tail; *Her:* **in einen D. auslaufender Löwe,** lion-dragon. **2.** *Bot:*=**Drachenwurz.**

Drachenstation, *f.* weather research station using kites.

Drachensteigen, *n.* kite-flying, flying kites.

Drachenstein, *m. Miner:* draconites, dragonstone.

Drachenwurz, *f. Bot:* **1.** bog arum, water arum, calla. **2.** (common) bistort. **3.** dragonwort, dragon's wort. **4.** houseleek. **5. gelbe D.,** yellow (water) iris. **6.**=**Beifuß. 7.**=**Drachenkraut.**

Drachenzahn, *m.* dragon's tooth; (*used figuratively*) **Drachenzähne säen,** to sow the seeds of discord, to sow dragon's teeth.

Drachme [ˈdraxmə], *f.* **-/-n. 1.** *Pharm.Meas:* dram, drachm, drachma. **2.** *Num:* drachma.

Dragant [dra·ˈgant], *m.*=**Tragant.**

Dragee [dra·ˈʒeː], *f.* **-/-n** & *n.* **-s/-s,** (*a*) dragée; sugar(ed) almond; (*b*) sugar-coated pill.

Dragganker, *m.,* **Dragge,** *f.* **-/-n.** *Nau:* (*a*) grapnel, grappling-anchor, grappling-iron; (*b*) dredging-iron.

draggen[1], *v.tr.*=**dreggen.**

Draggen[2], *m.* **-s/-.** *Nau:* small anchor.

Dragist [dra·ˈʒist], *m.* **-en/-en,** confectioner.

Dragoman [ˈdraːgo·man], *m.* **-s/-s** & **-e,** dragoman.

Dragon [dra·ˈgɔn], *n.* **-s/.** *Bot:* tarragon.

Dragonade [dra·go·ˈnaːdə], *f.* **-/-n.** *Fr.Hist:* dragon(n)ade.

Dragonbeifuß, *m. Bot:* tarragon.

Dragoner [dra·ˈgoːnər], *m.* **-s/-.** *Mil:* dragoon; *F:* (*woman*) masculine type; tough type; (*schoolmistress, etc.*) dragoon; **rangehen wie die Dragoner,** to set to work with a will, *F:* to go at it hammer and tongs.

Dragun [dra·ˈguːn], *n.* **-s/., Dragunbeifuß,** *m. Bot:* tarragon.

Draht, *m.* **-(e)s/⸗e. 1.** wire; (*a*) **D. ziehen,** to draw wire; **gezogener D.,** drawn wire; **isolierter D.,** insulated wire; **verseilter D.,** stranded wire; **elektrischer D.,** wire for electrical purposes; *F:* **er zieht die Drähte,** it is he who pulls the wires; (*b*) **elektrische Drähte,** electric wires; (*c*) *Tg:* **per D.,** by wire; (*d*) *F:* **auf D. sein,** (i) to know one's stuff; (ii) to be up to the mark; **ich bin nicht ganz auf D. heute,** I'm not quite up to the mark today, I'm not at my best today; **etwas auf D. bringen,** to bring sth. into efficient working order, *F:* to bring sth. up to scratch. **2.** wire netting. **3.** *F:* money, *F:* brass, dough.

Drahtabschneider, *m. Tls:* wire-cutter(s).

Drahtadresse, Drahtanschrift, *f.* telegraphic address.

Drahtanker, *m. El:* wire-wound armature.

Drahtantwort, *f.* reply by telegram, by wire; telegraphic reply.

Drahtanweisung, *f.* telegraphic money order.

Drahtarbeit, *f.* (*a*) article made from wire; (*b*) filigree work.

Drahtauslöser, *m. Phot:* cable-release, wire-release.

Drahtband, *n.* **1.** wire gauze ribbon. **2.** flat cable.

Drahtbank, *f. Metalw:* wire-drawer, drawing-frame, wire-drawing bench.

Drahtbauer, *m.* & *n.* wire (bird-)cage.

Drahtbearbeitung, *f.* wirework, wire-making.

Drahtbefestigungsplatte, *f. Av:* wiring-plate.

Drahtbericht, *m.* telegraphic report; *Journ:* **eigener D.,** (wired) from our own correspondent.

Drahtbinder, *m.* tinker.

Drahtblume, *f. Bot:* marsh marigold.

Drahtbürste, *f.* wire brush.

Drahteisen, *n. Metalw:* **1.** wire-drawing die. **2.** wire rod.

Drahtemail, *n. Art:* wire cloisonné.

drahten[1], *v.tr.* to telegraph, to wire (message).

drahten[2], **drähten,** *A:* **drahtern, drähtern,** *a.* (made) of wire.

Drahtfaden, *m.* (thin) wire (for marionettes, etc.).

Drahtfeder, *f.* wire spring.

Drahtfenster, *n.* wire mesh window.

Drahtfernsehen, *n.* wired television.

Drahtfunk, *m. El:* carrier current telegraphy, wired wireless, *U.S:* wired radio.

Drahtgabel, *f.* crook-stick for laying wire.

Drahtgaze, *f.* wire gauze.

Drahtgeflecht, *n.* wire netting; wire mesh; woven wire.

Drahtgerippe, Drahtgerüst, *n.* wire frame (-work) (of handbag, doll, etc.).

Drahtgeschütz, *n. Artil:* wire-wound gun, wire gun.

Drahtgestell, *n.* wire frame (of lampshade, etc.).

Drahtgewebe, *n.* (square mesh) wire cloth; wire mesh; woven wire.

Drahtgitter, *n.* (*a*) wire netting; wire mesh; **einen Hof mit (einem) D. einzäunen,** to surround a yard with wire netting; (*b*) wire grid; *Opt: etc:* wire grating.

Drahtglas, *n.* wired glass, wire-glass.

Drahtgras, *n. Bot:* tufted sedge.

Drahthaar, *n.* wiry hair (of wire-haired dog).

Drahthaardackel, *m.* wire-haired dachshund.

Drahthaarfoxterrier, *m.* wire-haired fox-terrier.

drahthaarig, *a.* wire-haired (terrier, etc.).

Drahthaarterrier, *m.* wire-haired fox-terrier.

Drahtheftmaschine, *f. Bookb:* wire stitcher, wire-stitching machine; stapling machine.

Drahthindernis, *n. Mil:* wire entanglement.

-drähtig, *comb.fm.* **1.** -wired, with . . . wire(s); **dreidrähtig,** three-wired, with three wires. **2.** *Tex:* -stranded, with . . . strands; **dreidrähtiger Faden,** three-stranded thread.

drahtig, *a.* **1.** *occ.* (made) of wire. **2.** wiry (pers., figure).

Drahtkäfig, *m.* wire cage.

Drahtkanone, *f. Artil:* wire-wound gun, wire-gun.

Drahtklemme, *f. El:* terminal, binding post.

Drahtklemmschraube, *f. El:* screw terminal.

Drahtklinge, Drahtklinke, *f.* wire-gauge.

Drahtlehre, *f.* wire-gauge.

Drahtleier, *f. Metalw:* wire-drawing bench with one draw-plate.

Drahtleitung, *f. Tp: Tg:* wire.

drahtlich, *a.* telegraphic.

drahtlos, *a.* wireless, *U.S:* radio; **drahtlose Telegraphie,** wireless telegraphy, *U.S:* radiotelegraphy; **drahtlose Telephonie, drahtloses Fernsprechen,** wireless telephony, *U.S:* radiotelephony; **Nachricht auf drahtlosem Wege,** wireless message; *adv.* **etwas d. melden,** to report sth. by wireless, by radio.

Drahtmaß, *n.* wire-gauge.

Drahtmatratze, *f.* wire mattress.

Drahtmesser, *m.* wire-gauge.

Drahtmühle, *f.* wire-mill, wire-drawing mill.

Drahtnachricht, *f.* telegram.

Drahtnagel, *m.* French nail, wire nail.

Drahtnetz, *n.* wire netting; woven wire; wire gauze.

Drahtpuls, *m. Med:* wiry pulse.

Drahtpuppe, *f.* marionette; puppet.

Drahtreifen, *m.* wired tyre, straight-side tyre.

Drahtrinne, *f. Med:* wire splint.

Drahtrolle, *f.* (*a*) coil of wire; (*b*) roll of wire netting.

Drahtroß, *m. F:* bicycle; *A:* iron steed.

Drahtsaite, *f. Mus:* metal string.

Drahtschere, *f. Tls:* wire-cutter(s); cutting-pliers.

Drahtschlinge, *f.* snare, springe, noose (for trapping small animals).

Drahtschmiele, *f. Bot:* wavy hair-grass.

Drahtschneider, *m. Tls:* wire-cutter(s); cutting pliers.

Drahtseil, *n.* wire rope; cable.

Drahtseilbahn, *f.* cable railway, funicular (railway); cable-car; aerial railway.

Drahtseilbrücke, *f.* suspension bridge.

Drahtseilfähre, *f.* cable ferry.

Drahtseilriese, *f.* aerial railway (for transporting wood, etc.).

Drahtsieb, *n.* wire sieve.

Drahtspanner, *m. Tchn:* wire-strainer, -stretcher, -tightener.

Drahtstift, *m.* French nail, wire nail.

Drahttuch, *n.* wire cloth; wire gauze.

Drahtverbindung, *f.* wire connection; *Tg:* telegraphic connection.

Drahtverhau, *m.* & *n. Mil:* wire entanglement.

Drahtverkehr, *m.* telegraphic communication.

Drahtwalze, *f.* **1.** (*a*) roll of barbed wire; (*b*) roll of wire netting. **2.** *Paperm:* **D. mit Wasserzeichen,** dandy-roller.

Drahtwerk, *n.* **1.** wireworks. **2.**=**Drahtarbeit.**

Drahtwort, *n.* telegraphic address.

Drahtwurm, *m. Ent:* wireworm.

Drahtzange, *f. Tls:* (cutting-)pliers.

Drahtzaun, *m.* wire fence; wire netting surround; **einen Hof mit einem D. umgeben,** to surround a yard with wire netting.

Drahtziegel, *m.* wire netting with brick coating.

Drahtziehbank, *f. Metalw:* wire-drawer, drawing-frame, wire-drawing bench.

Drahtzieheisen, *n. Metalw:* wire-drawing die.

Drahtziehen, *n.* **1.** *Metalw:* wire-drawing. **2.** *F:* wire-pulling.

Drahtzieher, *m.* (*pers.*) **1.** *Metalw:* wire-drawer. **2.** *F:* wire-puller.

Drahtzieherei, *f.* **1.** *Metalw:* wireworks, wire-mill, drawing-mill. **2.** *Metalw:* wire-drawing. **3.** *F:* wire-pulling.

Drainage [drɛ·ˈnaːʒə], *f.* **-/-n** =**Dränage.**

Draisine [drɛ·ˈziːnə], *f.* **-/-n. 1.** *Cy:* dandy-horse. **2.** *Rail:* platelayer's trolley.

Drako [ˈdraːkoː], **Drakon** [ˈdraːkon]. *Pr.n.m.* **-s.** *Gr.Hist:* Draco, Dracon.

drakonisch [dra·ˈkoːniʃ], *a.* (*a*) Draconian; (*b*) *F:* Draconian, harsh, rigorous (measure, etc.); severe (ruling, etc.).

drall[1], *a.* (*a*) firm, strong, tightly twisted (thread, etc.); sturdy (rope, etc.); **d. gespannt,** taut; (*b*) sturdy (girl, horse, etc.); strapping (girl); plump (girl, child, legs, etc.); **eine dralle Bauersfrau,** a plump peasant woman; (*c*) firm (gait).

Drall[2], *m.* **-s/-e. 1.** (*a*) twist; twisting; (*b*) *Mec:* torsion, torque. **2.** *Artil: Sm.a:* (*a*) twist (of rifling of barrel); **gleichbleibender D.,** uniform twist; **zunehmender D.,** increasing twist; (*b*) =**Drallabweichung.**

Drallabweichung, *f. Artil:* drift (of projectile).

Drallabweichungsteilscheibe, *f. Artil:* drift scale plate.

Drallänge, *f. Artil: Sm.a:* length of twist.

Drallheit, *f.* (*a*) firmness, sturdiness (of rope, etc.); (*b*) sturdiness (of girl, horse, etc.); plumpness (of girl, legs, etc.); (*c*) firmness (of gait).

drallieren [dra·ˈliːrən], *v.tr. Tex:* to twist (thread) tightly.

Drama [ˈdraːmaː], *n.* **-s/-men. 1.** (*a*) drama; dramatic play; (*b*) (*incorrectly used*) tragedy; (*c*) *F:* drama; sensation; to-do. **2.** drama (*as a literary genre*); dramatic art.

Dramatik [dra·ˈmaːtik], *f.* **-/.** (*a*) dramatic art, drama; (*b*) drama; dramatic element (in play, novel, etc.); **der dritte Akt bringt den Höhepunkt der D.,** the third act brings the climax of the drama.

Dramatiker [dra·ˈmaːtikər], *m.* **-s/-,** (*a*) dramatist, playwright; (*b*) dramatist; writer, artist, etc., able to produce dramatic effect.

dramatisch [dra·ˈmaːtiʃ], *a.* dramatic (art,

representation, situation, etc.); **dramatische Dichtung,** (i) drama, dramatic literature; (ii) drama; (iii) dramatic poem.

dramatisieren [dra·ma·ti·ˈziːrən]. I. *v.tr.* 1. to dramatize (situation, story, etc.), to give a dramatic, sensational, turn to (situation, story, etc.). 2. to dramatize (novel, etc.), to adapt (novel, etc.) for the stage.

II. *vbl s.* 1. **Dramatisieren,** *n. in vbl senses.* 2. **Dramatisierung,** *f.* (*a*)=II. 1; (*b*) dramatization, adaptation for the stage, stage adaptation (of novel, etc.).

Dramaturg [dra·ma·ˈturk], *m.* **-en/-en** [-ˈturgən]. *Th:* literary adviser (to a theatre).

Dramaturgie [dra·ma·tur·ˈgiː], *f.* **-/.** 1. *Th: Lit:* dramaturgy. 2. *Th:* **(praktisch-szenische) D.,** theatrecraft.

dramaturgisch [dra·ma·ˈturgiʃ], *a.* dramaturgic.

Dramendichter, Dramenschreiber, *m.* dramatist, playwright.

Dramolett [dra·mo·ˈlɛt], *n.* **-s/-e.** *Th:* playlet, short play.

dran (*contraction of* **daran,** *q.v.*), *pron. adv. F:* 1. (*also* **dran-,** *comb.fm.*) on, (on) to, against, at, of, about, in, it, them; **nahe d.,** near to, close to, it, them; *cp.* **daran** 1 (*h*); **denk d.!** don't forget (it)! think of that! **ich denk' nicht d.,** I wouldn't think of it, of doing so; **erinnere mich d.!** remind me of, about, it; **ich glaub' nicht d.,** (i) I don't believe in it, them; (ii) I don't believe it; **es liegt mir nichts d.,** it is of no importance, it doesn't matter, to me; **was liegt uns d.?** what do we care? **an ihm ist nicht viel d.,** there's not much in him, he's not worth much; **es ist was (Wahres) d.,** there's something, some truth, in it; **wenn alle drüber reden, dann muß schon was d. sein,** if everyone is talking about it there must be something, some truth, in it. 2. (*a*) **d. sein,** to have one's turn; **Sie sind jetzt d.,** it's your turn now; **in der Mathematikstunde war er kein einziges Mal d.,** he wasn't asked a single question during the mathematics lesson; *F:* **wenn etwas schief geht, dann bist du d.,** if anything goes wrong you will be blamed, you will be held responsible; (*b*) **gut d. sein,** (i) to be in good health; (ii) to be in a good position, well off; **übel d. sein,** to be in a bad way, (i) to be in bad health, (ii) to be in a bad position; **man weiß nie, wie man mit ihr d. ist,** one never knows what to make of her, what to expect from her; *see also* **all** II. 2 (*d*), **drauf** 1, **drum.** 3. *rel. use*=**daran** 3.

Drän [drɛːn], *m.* **-s/-s,** (*a*) *Agr:* drain(-pipe); (*b*) *Surg:* drain-tube, drain.

Dränage [drɛ·ˈnaːʒə], *f.* **-/-n.** 1. (*a*) *Agr: Nau:* drainage, draining; (*b*) *Surg:* draining, drainage. 2. *Agr:* drainage system.

Dränagesystem, *n. Agr:* drainage system.

drang[1] *see* **dringen.**

Drang[2], *m.* **-(e)s/⸗e.** 1. (*a*) pressure; **im D. der Arbeit,** in the pressure of work; **ich habe es im D. der Ereignisse vergessen,** there was so much going on that I forgot it; everything happened so quickly that I forgot it; *see also* **Sturm;** (*b*) *A. & Lit:* throng; press; **im D. des Kampfes,** in the press of battle. 2. (*a*) urge; strong desire; yearning; **einen D. fühlen, etwas zu tun,** to feel an urge to do sth.; **der D. nach Freiheit,** the urge for freedom; **D. nach Süden,** longing, yearning, for the South; **ein D. zur schöpferischen Arbeit,** an urge for creative activity; **er hat einen unwiderstehlichen D. zum Reisen,** he has an irresistible urge to travel; (*b*) *Physiol:* desire to pass water *or* to evacuate the bowels.

dränge *see* (i) **dringen;** (ii) **drängen.**

drangeben, *v.tr. sep.* (*strong*) =**darangeben.**

drangehen, *v.i. sep.* (*strong*) (*sein*) =**darangehen.**

Drängelei, *f.* **-/-en.** 1. jostling, pushing, shoving. 2. jostle; hustle, scuffle; scrimmage.

drängeln, *v.tr. & i.* (*haben*) (*a*) to jostle (s.o.); to hustle (s.o.); to push, shove; **drängel nicht so!** don't push! (*b*) to pester, bother (s.o.); *F:* to badger (s.o.).

drängen. I. *v.* 1. *v.tr. & i.* (*haben*) (*a*) to thrust, push, shove; to press; **j-n aus dem Wege d.,** to thrust, push, shove, s.o. out of the way; **an die Wand gedrängt sein,** (i) to be pressed (tight) against the wall; (ii) *F:* to be pushed aside; to be made to feel powerless; **bitte nicht d.,** please do not push; **die drängende Menge,** the milling crowd; (*b*) to push; to press; to urge (s.o. to do sth.); **j-n zur Bezahlung d.,** to push s.o. for payment; **von seinen Gläubigern gedrängt sein,** to be pressed by one's creditors; **ich will dich nicht d.,** I don't want to push you; I don't want to rush you; **er drängte auf Antwort,** he pressed for an answer; **die Not drängte ihn dazu,** necessity drove him to it; **die Zeit drängt,** time is running short, is pressing; **es drängt nicht,** it's not urgent, there is no urgency; **ein drängendes Verlangen,** an intense desire; **ihre Bitten wurden drängender,** her entreaties grew more pressing, more intense; **j-n zum Handeln d.,** to urge s.o. to action; **er fühlte sich gedrängt zu sprechen,** he felt an impulse to speak; the spirit moved him to speak; he felt prompted to speak; **es drängt mich, dir die Wahrheit zu gestehen,** I feel I must tell you the truth; I feel forced to tell you the truth; **es drängt mich, Ihnen meinen Dank auszusprechen,** I feel I must thank you; I feel compelled to thank you; **etwas drängte mich vorwärts,** something urged me forwards, something impelled me to go forwards. 2. *A. & Lit:*=**bedrängen.** 3. **sich drängen,** (*a*) to crowd (together); to throng; **die Menschen drängten sich in den Straßen,** the streets were crowded, thronged, with people; **sie drängten sich in dem engen Raum,** they were crowded (together) in the small space; **die Ereignisse drängten sich,** events followed close upon one another; (*b*) to push, thrust, one's way; to push; **sich vorwärts d.,** to push, thrust, oneself forward; **sich durch eine Menge d.,** to push, force, one's way through a crowd; **sich an etwas** *acc.*, **j-n, d.,** to press (oneself) against sth., s.o.; to push up against sth., s.o.; **sie drängten sich dazwischen,** they squeezed in between; **das Blatt drängt sich aus der Knospe,** the leaf is bursting from the bud; **sich um j-n d.,** to crowd, throng, round s.o.; **eine große Menge drängte sich um ihn,** a large crowd pressed round him; **sie drängten sich durch das Tor,** they crowded through the gates; **die Leute drängen sich zum Theater,** the people are crowding, thronging, to the theatre; **Hunderte von Bewerbern drängten sich nach der Stelle,** hundreds of applicants rushed for the job; **er hat sich dazu, danach, gedrängt,** he was very keen on doing it, he was very anxious to do it; **sich in j-s Vertrauen d.,** to force one's way into s.o.'s confidence.

II. *vbl s.* **Drängen,** *n.* 1. *in vbl senses; also:* pressure; **nach langem D. gab er endlich nach,** after much persuasion he eventually gave in. 2.=**Drang**[2] 1, 2 (*a*).

III. *p.p. & a.* **gedrängt,** *in vbl senses; esp.* 1. crowded; **gedrängte Fülle,** thick crowd; abundance; **gedrängt voll,** crowded; **die Straßen waren gedrängt voll von Menschen,** the streets were crowded, thronged, with people. 2. compact, succinct, terse (style); brief (manner of speaking).

Dränger, *m.* **-s/-,** *see* **Stürmer.**

Drängerei, *f.* **-/-en** =**Drängelei.**

Drängnis, *f.* **-/-nisse.** *A:*=**Bedrängnis.**

Drängraben, *m. Agr:* drainage channel; draining ditch.

Drangsal, *f.* **-/-e,** (*a*) distress; anguish; affliction; **in D. sein,** to be in distress; **in der D. meines Herzens,** in the anguish of my heart; **in meiner D. betete ich zu Gott,** in my distress, affliction, I prayed to God; (*b*) tribulation; hardship; affliction; **die Drangsale des Lebens,** the tribulations of life; **wir haben all diese Drangsale überlebt,** we have survived all these afflictions, sufferings.

drangsalen, *v.tr.*=**drangsalieren.**

drangsalieren [draŋza·ˈliːrən], *v.tr.* **j-n d.,** to make s.o.'s life a misery; to torment s.o.; (*of children, etc.*) to harass, plague, s.o.

drangvoll, *a.* 1. intense, ardent. 2. crowded; thronged.

Drängwasser, *n. Nau:* bilge(-water).

dranhalten (sich), *v.refl. sep.* (*strong*) to be quick; to be persistent, to keep at it; **wenn wir uns nicht d., werden wir die Karten nicht bekommen,** if we're not quick we won't get the tickets; **du mußt dich tüchtig d., sonst bekommst du ein schlechtes Zeugnis,** you must keep steadily at it, otherwise you will get a bad report; **er muß sich d., daß er noch etwas bekommt,** he must be quick, persistent, if he wants to get any.

dränieren [drɛ·ˈniːrən], *v.tr. Agr: Surg:* to drain (field, wound); **Dränierung** *f*, drainage, draining.

Dränierpflug, *m. Agr:* draining-plough.

drankommen, *v.i. sep.* (*strong*) (*sein*) 1. to have one's turn; **jetzt komme ich dran,** now it's my turn; **ich bin heute in der Schule dreimal drangekommen,** I had three turns at school today; *F:* **der kommt bald dran,** it'll soon be his turn (to die); *cp.* **daran** 1 (*c*). 2. to reach it, them; to obtain, get hold of, it, them.

dranmachen (sich), *v.refl. sep.*=**daranmachen.**

drannehmen, *v.tr. sep.* (*strong*) *esp. Sch:* 1. **j-n d.,** to let s.o. have a turn; **wen wollen wir jetzt d.?** whom shall we have now? whose turn shall it be now? 2. *occ.* (i) to make (s.o.) work hard; (ii) to scold (s.o.).

Dränrohr, *n.*, **Dränröhre,** *f. Agr:* drain(-pipe).

dransetzen, *v.tr. sep.*=**daransetzen.**

Dränsystem, *n. Agr:* drainage system.

Dränung, *f. Civ.E: Agr:* drainage, draining.

Dränziegel, *m.* drain-tile.

Drap [ˈdrap], *m.* **-s/-s.** *Tex:* twilled woollen cloth.

Draperie [dra·pə·ˈriː], *f.* **-/-n** [-ˈriːən]. 1. *Art: etc:* drapery (of statue, etc.). 2. drapery; curtain; **Draperien,** hangings, draperies.

drapieren [dra·ˈpiːrən], *v.tr.* to drape (article of furniture, cloth, etc.).

drasch, dräsche. *A: see* **dreschen.**

Dräsine [drɛ·ˈziːnə], *f.* **-/-n** =**Draisine.**

Drastikum [ˈdrasti·kum], *m.* **-/-ka.** *Med:* strong purgative.

drastisch [ˈdrastiʃ], *a.* (*a*) drastic (remedy, etc.); **drastische Maßnahmen ergreifen,** to take drastic measures; (*b*) vivid, dramatic (description, etc.).

Draube, *f.* **-/-n**=**Bohrwinde.**

dräuen, *v.i.* (*haben*) *A. & Lit:*=**drohen.**

drauf. 1. *pron. adv. F:*=**darauf; d. und dran sein, etwas zu tun,** to be on the point, on the verge, of doing sth. 2. *adv.* **frisch d.!** come on! go at it! **immer (feste) d.!** go on, let him, them, have it! keep it up!

Draufgabe, *f.* 1.=**Draufgeld.** 2. *Com:* extra weight (granted to customer).

Draufgänger, *m.* dare-devil; reckless person; reckless fellow; (*with regard to money*) spendthrift.

draufgängerisch, *a.* (*of pers., behaviour*) reckless; foolhardy; impetuous; (*with regard to money*) reckless.

Draufgängertum, *n.* recklessness; foolhardiness.

draufgehen, *v.i. sep.* (*strong*) (*haben*) *F:* (*a*) (*of animal*) to die; **dem Bauern ist die Kuh draufgegangen,** the farmer has lost his cow; **dabei kannst du vor Langeweile d.,** you will be bored to death, it will bore you to death; (*b*) **dabei wird sicher viel Geld d.,** a lot of money will go on that.

Draufgeld, *n.* earnest money; part payment in advance; deposit.

drauflegen, *v.tr. sep.* (*a*) to lay, put (sth.) on (top of) it, this, these, them; (*b*) to add (sth.); to give (money) in addition; **ich mußte noch Geld d.,** I had to pay, give, some more for it; **ich habe Geld draufgelegt,** I lost money on it; I sold it for less than I paid for it.

drauflos, *adv.* (*also* **drauflos-,** *comb.fm.*) (i) straight on, straight ahead; (ii) recklessly; **d.!** on with it! go on! **immer d.!** keep at it! go on! **drauflosrennen,** (i) to rush at it, at them; (ii) to rush on recklessly; *F:* to rush one's fences; **drauflos-wirtschaften,** to conduct one's affairs without any planning; to spend recklessly, to be reckless with the money.

drauflosgehen, *v.i. sep.* (*strong*) (*sein*) to go at it; to go ahead; **immer d., unbeirrt d.,** to keep straight ahead, straight forward; **geh nur immer drauflos!** just keep at it! go on!

draufsetzen, *v.tr. F:* to let (s.o.) down.

Draufsicht, *f.* top view, *U.S:* plan view (of machine, group of buildings, etc.).

draus =**daraus.**

drauß. *A:*=**draußen.**

draußen, *adv.* outside. 1. (i) outside the room; (ii) out of doors; **da d.,** out there; **d. bleiben,** to stay outside; **ich habe meinen Hund d. gelassen,** I have left my dog outside; **d. vor der Tür,** (just) outside the door; at the door; **geht d. spielen!** go and play out of doors; **d. im Wald,** out in the woods. 2. (*a*) out of (the) town; in the suburbs; (*b*) out of the country, abroad; (*c*) in the war; on the front; **unsere Männer sind alle d.,** our menfolk are all away in the war; **d. bleiben,** to die on the battlefield, to be killed in the war; (*d*) out at sea. 3. (*preceded by prep.*) **von d.,** from outside; from the outside; *Lit:* from without; **eine Kraft von d.,** a force from outside (ourselves); **ein Haus von d. sehen,** to see a house from the outside; **nach d. gehen,** to go outside; **eine Wirkung nach d.,** an outgoing effect, an outward effect.

Drawida [ˈdraːvi·daː], *m.* **-/-.** *Ethn:* Dravidian.

Drawidasprachen, *f.pl. Ling:* Dravidian languages.

drawidisch [dra·ˈviːdiʃ], *a. Ethn: Ling:* Dravidian.

Drazäne [dra·ˈtsɛːnə], *f.* **-/-n** =**Dracäne.**

Drebel, *m.* **-s/-.** *Fish:* perforated box-like raft for transporting live fish.

Drechselbank, *f. Woodw: etc:* lathe, turning-lathe.

Drechselei, *f.* -/-en. **1.** (piece of) turned work. **2.** *F:* affectation (of manner of speaking, etc.).
Drechselkunst, *f.* turnery.
drechseln. **1.** *v.tr.* (*a*) to turn (wood, ivory, table-leg, etc.); to fashion, shape (sth.) on the lathe; **Kopf und Stiel der Pfeife sind aus einem Stück gedrechselt,** the bowl of the pipe is turned in one piece with the stem; **Holz, das sich gut d. läßt,** wood that turns well; (*b*) *F:* **gedrechselte Redensarten,** stiff, over-formal, expressions; affectations; **gedrechselte Komplimente,** carefully phrased compliments; **hübsch gedrechselte Verse,** prettily turned verses. **2.** *vbl s.* **Drechseln,** *n.* turning (on the lathe); turnery.
Drechselrollschnecke, *f. Moll:* actaeon.
Drechsler, *m.* -s/-, (*pers.*) (lathe-)turner.
Drechslerarbeit, *f. Woodw: etc:* **1.** turnery. **2.** (piece of) turned work.
Drechslerbeitel, *m. Tls:* turning gouge, turning chisel.
Drechslerei, *f.* -/-en. **1.** turnery; lathe-work. **2.** turner's shop.
Drechslerwerkstatt, *f.* turner's shop.
Dreck, *m.* -(e)s/. **1.** dirt; (i) filth, muck; (ii) mud, mire; (iii) excrement(s); droppings; **D. auf den Straßen,** mud, dirt, on the streets; **D. machen,** to make a mess; **im D. sitzen,** to sit in the dirt; to live in a mess; *F:* to be badly off, to be hard up; *F:* **den Karren aus dem D. ziehen,** to clear up the mess; to put, set, things to rights; **aus dem größten D. heraus sein,** to be over the worst; **j-n mit D. bewerfen,** to sling mud at s.o., to throw dirt at s.o.; **j-n, etwas, in den D. ziehen,** to drag s.o.'s name in the mud; to treat sth. with utter contempt; to denigrate sth.; **D. am Stecken haben,** to be not without blemish, to be not entirely innocent; **mach deinen D. alleine!** jolly well do it yourself! **2.** *F:* impurity; scum; *Metall:* dross, scum, slag. **3.** (*a*) *F:* trifle; triviality; **die Nase in jeden D. stecken,** to poke one's nose into everything; **sich um jeden D. kümmern,** to concern oneself with every little thing, every trifle; (*b*) *P:* **ein D.,** nothing (at all); **ich mache mir einen D. daraus,** I don't care two hoots, a straw, (about it); I don't care a damn, give a damn; **das geht ihn einen D. an,** it's none of his business, it's absolutely nothing to do with him; **er kümmert sich keinen D. darum, einen D. darum,** he doesn't care a damn; **die Arbeit ist (ein) D.,** this piece of work is totally useless, is abominable.
Dreckarbeit, *f.* dirty work, rough work.
Dreckbürste, *f. F:* hard shoe-cleaning brush (*for removing mud*).
drecken. *F:* **1.** *v.i.* (*haben*) to make a mess. **2.** *v.impers.* **es dreckt,** it's awful weather; it's dirty weather.
Dreckfink, *m.*=**Dreckspatz.**
Dreckhammel, *m. F:* dirty fellow.
dreckig, *a.* (*a*) dirty (hands, clothes, streets, child, etc.); soiled (hands, clothes); filthy (hovel, etc.); dirty, nasty (weather); (*b*) dirty (laughter, joke, etc.); vulgar (joke); *adv.* **d. lachen,** to give a dirty laugh; to laugh wickedly, mischievously; (*c*) *adv. F:* **es geht ihm d.,** he is in a bad way, things are going badly with him.
Dreckkäfer, *m. Ent: F:* dung-beetle.
Drecklilie, *f. Bot: F:* king's spear, asphodel, *U.S:* Jacob's rod.
Dreckmatz, *m. F:* dirty creature; dirty fellow.
Drecks-, *comb.fm. F:* wretched . . . , beastly . . . ; **wir hätten den Drecksschirm zu Hause lassen sollen,** we should have left the wretched, beastly, umbrella at home.
Drecksack, *m. F:* scoundrel.
Drecksau, *f.* -/⸚e. *P:* dirty creature; dirty fellow.
Dreckschwein, *m.*=**Drecksau.**
Dreckskerl, *m. P:* (dirty) swine; skunk.
Dreckspatz, *m. F:* dirty creature; dirty fellow; (*child*) dirty little beggar; grubby little thing; guttersnipe.
Dreckvogel, *m.*=**Dreckspatz.**
Dreckwetter, *n.* dirty weather.
Dredschanker, *m. Nau:* grapnel, grappling-iron, -anchor.
Dredsche, *f.* -/-n. *Fish:* dredge, drag-net.
Dreesch, *m.* -es/-e, **Dreeschbrache,** *f. Agr:* green fallow, *esp.* used for pasture.
dreesch, *a.*=**brach**[2].
Dreeschling, *m.* -s/-e =**Drieschling.**
Dreeschwirtschaft, *f. Agr:* agricultural system whereby land is used alternately for crop growing and pasture.
Dregganker, *m.,* **Dregge,** *f.* -/-n=**Dragganker.**
dreggen, *v.tr. Nau: etc:* to drag; **einen Anker, Minen, d.,** to drag, sweep, for an anchor, for mines.
Dreh, *m.* -s/. *F:* **im D. sein,** to be in the swing; to be wound up; **ich konnte nicht schlafen; ich war noch so im D.,** I couldn't sleep; I was still all wound up; **den D. 'raushaben,** to have found, got, the knack.
Dreh-, *comb.fm.* **1.** (*a*) rotary . . . ; rotatory . . . ; rotative . . . , rotational . . . ; **Drehbewegung** *f,* (i) rotary motion (of planet, etc.); (ii) rotative movement (of joint, etc.); **Drehkraft** *f,* rotative force, rotational force; *cp.* (*b*); (*b*) torsional . . . ; **Drehkraft** *f,* torsional strength; *cp.* (*a*); (*c*) revolving . . . , rotating . . . , rotary . . . ; swivel-, swivelling . . . ; **Drehofen** *m,* revolving furnace, rotary furnace; **Drehstuhl** *m,* swivel-chair; *Nau:* **Drehturm** *m,* revolving turret; (*d*) . . . of rotation; . . . of revolution; **Drehachse** *f,* axis (of rotation); *Geom:* **Drehfläche** *f,* surface of revolution. **2.** *Tls: etc:* turning . . . , turning-; **Drehröhre** *f,* turning gouge; **Drehstahl** *m,* turning-tool.
Drehachse, *f.* **1.** *Mec.E:* live axle. **2.** axis (of rotation).
Dreharbeit, *f.* **1.** *Metalw: etc:* (*a*) lathe-work, turning; (*b*) (piece of) turned work. **2.** *Cin:* shooting, making (of a film); **die Dreharbeiten haben begonnen,** shooting has begun.
Drehbank, *f. Tls: Metalw: Woodw: etc:* lathe, turning-lathe; **D. mit gekröpftem Bett,** gap lathe.
Drehbankbett, *n.* lathe-bed.
Drehbankfutter, *n.* (lathe-)chuck.
Drehbankherz, *n.*=**Drehherz.**
Drehbankspitze, *f.* lathe-centre.
drehbar, *a.* **1.** (wheel, etc.) that can be turned, rotated; rotating (wheel, etc.); rotary (knob, etc.); revolving (bookcase, etc.); swivelling (stool, etc.); *adv.* **d. gelagert,** pivoted. **2.** (thread, etc.) that can be twisted. **3.** *Metalw: Woodw: etc:* (article, material) that can be turned, that can be shaped, fashioned, on the lathe.
Drehbasse, *f.* -/-n. *Artil: Nau: A:* swivel-gun; *A:* perrier.
Drehbaum, *m.* turnstile.
Drehbeanspruchung, *f. Mec.E:* torsional stress, torsional strain.
Drehbewegung, *f.* **1.** (*a*) rotary motion; rotation; **D. im Uhrzeigersinn,** clockwise rotation; **D. gegen den Uhrzeigersinn,** anti-clockwise rotation; (*b*) rotatory movement (of joint, etc.). **2.** turn (of screw, etc.).
Drehbleistift, *m.* propelling pencil, *U.S:* mechanical pencil.
Drehbogen, *m. Tls:* drill-bow; *Clockm:* turning bow.
Drehbohrer, *m. Tls:* brace and bit.
Drehbolzen, *m. Mec.E: etc:* pivot(-pin); swivel-pin.
Drehbrücke, *f. Civ.E:* swing-bridge, swivel-bridge, turn-bridge, pivot-bridge.
Drehbuch, *n. Cin:* (*a*) (film-)script; (*b*) shooting script.
Drehbuchautor, *m. Cin:* film-script writer.
Drehbühne, *f.* **1.** *Th:* revolving stage. **2.** *Constr: etc:* turntable.
Drehdollen, *f.pl. Row:* swivel rowlocks.
Dreheisen, *n. Tls:* turning-chisel; lathe-tool.
Dreheiseninstrument, *n. El.E:* moving-iron instrument.
drehen. I. *v.tr.* **1.** (*a*) to turn (wheel, handle, etc.); to rotate (wheel, etc.); **den Schlüssel im Schloß d.,** to turn the key in the lock; **die Füße einwärts, auswärts, d.,** to turn in, turn out, one's toes; **einen Leierkasten d.,** to grind a barrel-organ; **die Knöpfe d.,** to turn the knobs (of a wireless set, etc.); **ich hatte kaum den Rücken gedreht, als . . . ,** no sooner had I turned my back than . . . ; *F:* **j-m den Rücken d.,** to turn one's back on s.o.; *F:* **das, sein, Mäntelchen, den, seinen, Mantel, nach dem Wind d., sich nach dem Wind d.,** to trim one's sails to the wind; **man kann die Sache d. und wenden, wie man will; es ist und bleibt unangenehm,** you can look at the thing from whatever angle you like; it's still unpleasant; *see also* **Daumen;** (*b*) *F: v.i.* (*haben*) **an den Knöpfen d.,** (i) to twiddle the knobs; (ii) to twiddle (with) one's buttons, to play with one's buttons; **am Radio d.,** to twiddle the knobs (of the radio); **an etwas** *dat.* **d. und deuteln,** to niggle, quibble, cavil, about sth. **2.** to twist (rope, hair, thread, etc.); to give (sth.) a twist; to lay (rope); **die Haare zu einem Knoten d.,** to twist one's hair into a knot; **j-m etwas aus der Hand d.,** to wrench sth. out of s.o.'s hand; **Locken d.,** to curl hair, to make curls; *F:* **das Recht d.,** to do violence to the law, to twist the law; *F:* **j-m einen Strick aus etwas d.,** to use sth. to trip s.o. up; *F:* **j-m eine Nase d.,** (i) to cock a snook at s.o.; (ii) to play a trick on s.o. **3.** (*a*) to make (sth.) (*by rolling*); **Pillen, Tüten, Papierkügelchen, d.,** to make pills, paper bags, paper pellets; **aus Papier eine Rolle d.,** to make a roll of paper; **eine Zigarette d.,** to roll, make, a cigarette; *F:* (*of burglar, etc.*) **ein Ding d.,** to do a job; *F:* **ich werde das Ding schon d.,** I shall manage all right; (*b*) *Metalw: Woodw: etc:* to turn (sth.) (on the lathe *or* potter's wheel); to fashion, shape (sth.) on the lathe; **gedreht,** turned, made on the lathe; **Metall, das sich gut d. läßt,** metal that turns well. **4.** *Cin:* **einen Film d.,** to make a film; to take, shoot, a film.

II. **sich drehen.** **1.** (*a*) to turn; to rotate; to revolve; to go round; (*fast*) to spin; (*of piano-stool, gun, etc.*) to swivel; **das Rad dreht sich,** the wheel turns, rotates, goes round; **sich im Kreis d.,** to go round in a circle; **sich um eine Achse d.,** (i) to rotate about an axis; (ii) to rotate, revolve, on a spindle, on an axle; (*o pers., thg*) **sich um sich selbst d., sich um seine eigene Achse d., sich um 360° d.,** to turn right round, to turn full circle; to turn right over (*to previous position*); **sich nach rechts, nach links, d.,** to turn to the right, to the left; **sich im Tanz d.,** to dance (round); **der Schlüssel drehte sich im Schloß,** the key turned in the lock; **die Tür dreht sich in den Angeln,** the door turns, swings, on its hinges; **ein sich drehender Körper,** a revolving, rotating, body; **das Kind schaut gern zu, wie sich die Räder drehen,** the child likes to see the wheels go round; **alles dreht sich mir im Kopf,** my head is spinning; **all ihre Gedanken drehen sich um ihn,** all her thoughts revolve round him; **alles dreht sich um ihn,** everything revolves about him, he is the centre of everything; **die ganze Welt dreht sich um die Liebe,** it's love that makes the world go round; (*of pers.*) **sich d. und winden,** to squirm, writhe (with embarrassment, etc.); (*b*) (*of wind*) to turn, veer (right round); (*c*) *v.impers. F:* **es dreht sich um . . . , es dreht sich darum, zu . . . ,** it concerns . . . , it's a matter of . . . , it's a question of . . . ; **es dreht sich darum, einen guten Plan auszudenken,** it's a matter of thinking out a good plan. **2.** to be twisted; to become twisted, to twist; **das Haar dreht sich hinten zu einem Knoten,** her hair is twisted into a knot at the back.

III. *vbl s.* **1. Drehen,** *n. in vbl senses of* I. **2. Drehung,** *f.* (*a*) =III. 1; (*b*) *in vbl senses of* II; *also:* rotation (of wheel, planet, etc.); revolution (of planet); (*c*) torsion (of rope, etc.); *Tex:* twist (of yarn); (*d*) turn; twist; **eine halbe D.,** a half-turn; **eine scharfe D. nach rechts machen,** to turn sharply to the right; **eine leichte D. des Körpers,** a slight twist of the body; (*e*) rotation; revolution; **in vierundzwanzig Stunden macht die Erde eine vollständige D.,** the earth revolves once in twenty-four hours, the earth makes one complete revolution in twenty-four hours.
Dreher, *m.* -s/-. **1.** (*pers.*) turner. **2.** (*a*) knob; (*b*) *Mec.E:* crank-handle; (*c*) hand (of watch, clock). **3.** *Anat:* (*a*) axis, epistropheus; (*b*) rotator (muscle). **4.** *Danc:*=**Ländler.** **5.** *Tex:* (*a*) (*in gauze-weaving*) intersection (of threads); (*b*) gauze.
Drehergewebe, *n. Tex:* gauze.
Drehfeld, *n. El: Magn:* rotating field.
Drehfestigkeit, *f. Mec:* torsional strength.
Drehfeuer, *n.* **1.** *Nau:* revolving light (of lighthouse). **2.** *Pyr:* rotating firework, *esp.* Catherine-wheel.
Drehfläche, *f. Geom:* surface of revolution.
Drehflügel, *m. Av:* rotor.
Drehgabel, *f. Ind:* tilting fork carriage (of fork lift truck).
Drehgelenk, *n. Anat:* pivot-joint, rotatory articulation.
Drehgestell, *n.* revolving frame, pivoted frame; pivot mounting; *Rail:* bogie(-truck).
Drehhaken, *m. Tls: Metalw:* hook-tool (of slide-lathe).
Drehhals, *m. Orn:*=**Wendehals.**
Drehhaspel, *m. Nau:* Spanish windlass.
Drehherz, *n. Mec.E:* lathe-dog, lathe carrier.
Drehkäfer, *m. Ent:* whirligig (beetle).
Drehknopf, *m.* knob (of wireless set, etc.).
Drehkolbenmotor, *m. Mec.E:* (single-rotation) rotary-piston engine.
Drehkolbenpumpe, *f.* rotary pump, rotating pump.
Drehkondensator, *m. El:* variable condenser.
Drehkopf, *m.* **1.** *Vet:* sheep suffering from gid. **2.** *Mec:* revolving tool-holder, capstan, turret.

Drehkörper, *m. Geom:* solid of revolution.
Drehkraft, *f. Mec:* **1.** torsional strength. **2.** rotative force, rotational force.
Drehkran, *m. Mec.E:* revolving crane, swing(ing) crane, slewing crane.
Drehkrankheit, *f. Vet:* gid, sturdy, goggles, (blind) staggers; *F:* **beim bloßen Zusehen kann man schon die D. kriegen,** it makes you giddy, dizzy, just to look at it.
Drehkranz, *m. Artil:* turntable; *Mil.Av:* gun-ring, rotating gun-mounting.
Drehkreis, *m. Aut: etc:* turning circle.
Drehkreuz, *m.* turnstile.
Drehkurve, *f. Rail:* turntable.
Drehlatte, *f. Meas:* surveyor's compass.
Drehleier, *f. Mus: A:* hurdy-gurdy.
Drehleistung, *f. Av:* torque horsepower.
Drehlicht, *n.* revolving light (of lighthouse, etc.).
Drehling, *m.* **-s/-e.** *Fung:* oyster mushroom.
Drehloch, *n.* whirlpool (in river).
Drehm, *m.* **-s/-e.** *Tex:* warp end, thrum.
Drehmangel, *f. Dom.Ec:* mangle.
Drehmaschine, *f.* = **Drehbank.**
Drehmeißel, *m. Tls:* turning-chisel.
Drehmoment, *m. Mec:* torque.
Drehmomentwandler, *n. Mec.E:* torque converter.
Drehmoos, *n. Bot:* funaria.
Drehmuskel, *m. Anat:* rotator (muscle).
Drehofen, *m. Mch:* rotary furnace.
Drehorgel, *f.* barrel-organ, street-organ.
Drehorgelspieler, *m.* organ-grinder.
Drehpflug, *m. Agr:* turnabout, turnover, plough.
Drehpistole, *f.* revolver.
Drehpunkt, *m.* pivot; central point; *Mec: etc:* fulcrum.
Drehreep, *n. Nau:* tie, tye.
Drehröhre, *f. Tls:* turning gouge; woodworking chisel.
Drehrolle, *f.* roller; *Laund:* roller, mangle (for ironing).
Drehsäule, *f. Hyd.E:* heel-post, quoin-post (of lock-gate).
Drehschaf, *n. Vet:* sheep suffering from gid.
Drehschalter, *m. El:* rotary switch.
Drehscheibe, *f.* revolving disk. **1.** potter's wheel. **2.** *Rail: Artil: etc:* turntable. **3.** turntable (of a gramophone). **4.** *Tp:* dial.
Drehscheit, *n. Veh:* splinter-bar, trace-block, swingle-tree.
Drehschemel, *m.* **1.** swivel-stool. **2.** *Veh:* swivelling bolster (of railway truck); swivelling coupling (of articulated lorry unit).
Drehschütz, *n.,* **Drehschütze,** *f. Hyd.E:* drop-gate.
Drehschwindel, *m.* dizziness, giddiness.
Drehseide, *f. Needlew:* silk twist.
Drehseil, *m.* twisted rope.
Drehspäne, *m.pl. Woodw: Metalw: etc:* turnings (from a lathe).
Drehspiegel, *m.* **1.** *Ph:* revolving mirror. **2.** *Furn:* swing-mirror, cheval-glass.
Drehspule, *f. El.E:* moving coil.
Drehspulgalvanometer, *n. El:* moving-coil galvanometer.
Drehstab, *m. Mec.E:* torsion bar.
Drehstahl, *m. Tls:* lathe-tool, turning-tool.
Drehstichel, *m. Tls:* = **Drehstahl.**
Drehstift, *m.* **1.** *(a) Mec.E:* mandrel (of lathe); *(b) Clockm:* turning arbor; **exzentrischer D.,** eccentric arbor. **2.** propelling pencil, *U.S:* mechanical pencil.
Drehstrom, *m. El.E:* three-phase current.
Drehstromdynamomaschine, *f. El.E:* three-phase generator.
Drehstromerzeuger, *m. El.E:* three-phase generator.
Drehstuhl, *m.* **1.** *Tls:* bench lathe; *Clockm:* turn-bench. **2.** swivel-chair.
Drehsucht, *f.* = **Drehkrankheit.**
Drehtransformator, *m. El.E:* phase transformer.
Drehtür, *f.* revolving door.
Drehturm, *m. Mil:* revolving turret (of tank).
Drehung, *f. see* **drehen III.**
Drehungs-, *comb.fm. cp.* **Dreh-.**
Drehungsachse, *f. Geom:* axis (of revolution).
Drehungsfestigkeit, *f. Mec:* torsional strength.
Drehungskörper, *m. Geom:* solid of revolution.
Drehungsmesser, *m.* gyrometer.
Drehungsvermögen, *n. Ph: etc:* rotatory power.
Drehwaage, *f. Ph:* torsion balance.
Drehwähler, *m. El.E:* rotary line switch.
Drehwuchs, *m.,* **Drehwüchsigkeit,** *f. Arb:* twisted growth (of trunks, branches).
Drehwurm, *m. Vet:* stagger-worm (of sheep); *F:* **den D. haben,** to feel giddy.
Drehwurz, *f. Bot:* bindweed, convolvulus.

Drehzahl, *f.* (number of) rotations, revolutions, (*esp.* per minute); speed.
Drehzähler, Drehzahlmesser, *m. Mec:* revolution counter.
Drehzapfen, *m.* **1.** *(a)* pivot(-pin), swivel-pin (of iron gate, etc.); *(b)* gudgeon(-pin) (in piston *or* cross-head). **2.** journal (of shaft, axle).
Drehzeug, *n.* **1.** lathe-tools, turning-tools; turner's tools. **2.** turning *or* twisting implements.
drei, *F:* **dreie.** I. **1.** *cardinal num.a.* three; **d. Wochen,** three weeks; **Nummer d.,** number three; **in d. Tagen,** in three days; **die Bevölkerung dreier großer,** *occ.* **großen, Länder,** the population of three great countries; **die Kinder von dreien dieser Städte,** the children from three of these towns; **zu dreien marschieren,** to march three abreast, in threes; **in Gruppen von d., zu dreien, eintreten,** to enter three by three, in threes; **d. und vier macht, ist, sieben,** three and four make, are, seven; **wir sind zu dreien ins Theater gegangen,** three of us went to the theatre; **er kann nicht bis d. zählen,** (i) he can't count up to three; (ii) *F:* he is a fool, an ass, he is stupid; *F:* **sie sieht aus, als ob sie nicht bis d. zählen könnte,** she looks (i) a bit of a half-wit, (ii) as if butter would not melt in her mouth; **alle d. Sachen zusammen kosten,** *F:* **alles drei zusammen kostet, fünf Mark,** the three things together come to five marks; **Schmidt d. (Schmidt III),** *Mil: Sch: etc:* Smith III; *Sch:* Smith tertius; *Pol:* **die großen D.,** the Big Three; *see also* **Ding 2. 2.** *s.f.* **Drei, -/-en,** *(a)* (figure) three; **eine D., zwei Dreien, schreiben,** to write a three, two threes; **die D. wird als heilige Zahl betrachtet,** three is regarded as a sacred number; *(b) (at dice)* **eine D., zwei Dreien, werfen,** to throw a three, two threes; *Sch:* **eine D. in Latein bekommen,** *(on report, exercise)* to get a satisfactory mark in Latin; *(in examination)* to get a pass in Latin; *F: (of pupil)* **eine D. schreiben,** to write an exercise, essay, of grade three (i.e. 'pass') quality. *(For other phrases cp.* **acht**[1]**.)**
II. **drei-, Drei-,** *comb.fm.* **1.** *(in numerals)* **dreiundzwanzig,** twenty-three; **dreihundert,** three hundred. **2.** three-; with three . . .; in three . . .; triple . . .; tri-; **dreifüßig,** three-footed, with three feet; **dreizähnig,** three-toothed; **Dreiradwagen** *m,* three-wheeler; **dreiteilig,** three-part; in three parts; **Dreischraubendampfer** *m,* triple-screw steamer; **Dreistern** *m,* triple star; **dreibasisch,** tribasic; **Dreieck** *n,* triangle; **Dreirad** *n,* tricycle; **dreimonatlich,** three-monthly, trimestrial. *(For compounds not included cp.* **Acht-, acht-.)**
Dreiachsenwagen, Dreiachser, *m.* **-s/-.** *Aut:* six-wheeler.
dreiachsig, *a. Geom: etc:* triaxial.
Dreiachteltakt, *m. Mus:* three-eight time.
Dreiakter, *m.* **-s/-.** *Th:* three-act play.
dreiaktig, *a. Th:* three-act (play).
Dreiangel, *m.* **-s/-.** *F:* triangle; *Dial:* three-cornered, triangular, tear (in garment).
dreiarten, *v.tr. insep. Agr:* to plough (land) for the third time.
dreiatomig, *a. Ch:* triatomic.
Dreibackenfutter, *n. Mec.E:* fork-chuck.
Dreiball, *m. Golf:* three-ball match.
dreibändig, *a.* three-volume (work); (edition, etc.) in three volumes.
dreibasisch, *a. Ch:* tribasic; **dreibasisches Salz,** triple salt.
Dreibein, *n.* **1.** tripod; three-legged stool *or* stand. **2.** = **Dreischenkel.**
dreibeinig, *a.* three-legged (stool, etc.).
Dreibeinlauf, *m. Sp:* three-legged race.
Dreibeinmast, *m. Nau:* tripod mast.
Dreiberg, *m. Her:* mount treble.
Dreiblatt, *n.* **1.** *Bot: (a)* trefoil, clover; *(b)* = **Bitterklee. 2.** *Arch: Her:* trefoil. **3.** *Cards: (German card game of chance)* dreiblatt.
dreiblätt(e)rig, *a. Bot:* three-leaved, trifoliate.
dreiblumig, dreiblütig, *a. Bot:* three-flowered, triflorous.
Dreibogen, *m. Arch:* triple arch.
dreibrachen, *v.tr. insep.* = **dreiarten.**
Dreibund, der. *Hist:* the Triple Alliance (between Germany, Austria-Hungary, and Italy).
Dreidecker, *m.* **1.** *Nau: A:* three-decker. **2.** *Av:* triplane.
dreidimensional, *a.* three-dimensional (space, effect, etc.).
Dreidimensionalität, *f.* three-dimensional character, nature.
Dreidistel, *f. Bot:* carline thistle.

dreidrähtig, *a. (a) El: etc:* three-wired; *(b) Tex etc:* three-stranded.
Dreieck, *n.* **-(e)s/-e.** *(a) Geom: etc:* triangle; **gleichschenk(e)liges D.,** isosceles triangle; *Astr:* **das nördliche, südliche, D.,** the northern, southern, Triangle; *(b)* triangular, three-cornered, piece, plot of land, etc.; *Arch: etc:* spandrel.
Dreieck-, *comb.fm.* triangular . . .; **Dreieckformation** *f,* triangular formation.
Dreieckfeile, *f. Tls:* three-square file, triangular file.
Dreieckflügel, *m. Av:* delta wing.
dreieckig, *a.* triangular, three-cornered; three-square (file, etc.); *adv.* in the shape of a triangle; triangularly; *F:* **ein dreieckiges Verhältnis,** a three-cornered relationship.
Dreieckkrabbe, *f. Crust:* spider-crab, sea spider.
Dreiecksaufnahme, *f. Surv:* triangulation.
Dreieckschaltung, *f. El:* delta connection.
Dreiecksformation, *f.* triangular formation.
Dreieckshandel, *m. Pol.Ec:* triangular trade.
Dreieckskrabbe, *f.* = **Dreieckkrabbe.**
Dreieckspflanzung, *f. For:* triangular plantation.
Dreieckszwickel, *m. Arch: etc:* spandrel.
Dreiecktuch, *n.* three-cornered scarf, etc.; *Med:* triangular bandage.
dreiehig, *a. Bot:* trigamous.
dreiein, *a.* = **dreieinig.**
dreieinhalb, *cardinal num.a.inv.* three and a half.
Dreieinheit, *f.* = **Dreieinigkeit.**
dreieinig, *a. Theol:* triune (Godhead); **der dreieinige Gott,** the triune God, the Three in One.
Dreieinigkeit, *f. Theol: (a)* triunity; **die D. Gottes,** the triune nature of God; *(b)* **die (heilige) D.,** the (holy, blessed) Trinity.
Dreieinigkeits-, *comb.fm. cp.* **Dreifaltigkeits-.**
Dreielektrodenröhre, *f. W.Tel:* = **Dreipolröhre.**
Dreier, *m.* **-s/-. 1.** *(a)* (figure) three; *Skating:* figure of three; **einen D. schreiben,** to write a three; *(b)* number three (bus, etc.); *(c)* = **drei I. 2** *(b).* **2.** *Num:* three-pfennig piece.
Dreiereinmaleins, das. *Mth:* the three-times table.
Dreiergruppe, *f.* group of three; triad.
dreierlei, *inv.a.* of three kinds, sorts.
Dreierreihe, *f.* row of three; **in Dreierreihen antreten,** to line up in threes; **in Dreierreihen marschieren,** to march three abreast.
dreifach, *a. (a)* triple; treble; threefold; **ein dreifacher Sieg,** a triple, threefold, victory; **ein dreifaches Vergehen,** a triple, treble, offence; **in dreifacher Ausfertigung,** in triplicate; *Mec.E:* **dreifacher Riemen,** three-ply belting; *adv.* **d. eingepackt,** triply wrapped; **Papier d. zusammenlegen,** to fold paper into three; *Tex:* **d. gezwirnt,** three-ply (wool, etc.); *(b)* **das Dreifache nehmen,** to take three times as much, three times the amount; **sechs ist das Dreifache von zwei,** six is three times two; **etwas um das Dreifache vermehren,** to treble sth.; **sich um das Dreifache vermehren,** to treble; to increase threefold; **schon nach dem ersten Jahr wird es den dreifachen Ertrag liefern,** even after the first year it will yield three times the amount.
Dreifach-, *comb.fm.* triple . . .; treble . . .; **Dreifachkabel** *n,* treble cable; **Dreifachdüse** *f,* triple nozzle.
dreifächerig, *a.* three-shelved; *Bot:* trilocular.
Dreifachexpansionsmaschine, *f. Mch:* triple-expansion engine.
Dreifachstecker, *m. El:* three-way (plug) adaptor.
Dreifachsteuerung, *f. Av:* three-control system.
dreifädig, *a.* having three threads; three-ply (wool, etc.).
dreifaltig, *a. Theol:* triune, threefold (Godhead); **der dreifaltige Gott,** the triune God, the Three in One.
dreifältig, *a.* triple, treble, threefold.
Dreifaltigkeit, *f. Theol: (a)* **die D. Gottes,** the threefold nature of God; *(b)* **die Heilig(st)e D.,** the Holy, Blessed, Trinity.
Dreifältigkeit, *f.* triplicity.
Dreifaltigkeitsblume, *f. Bot:* **1.** heart's-ease, wild pansy. **2.** trientalis, star-flower.
Dreifaltigkeitsfest, das. *Ecc:* Trinity Sunday.
Dreifaltigkeitsgläubige, *m., f. (decl. as adj.) Theol:* Trinitarian.
Dreifaltigkeitsorden, der. *Ecc:* the Order of the Holy Trinity.
Dreifaltigkeitssäule, *f. (in Austria)* column *or* pillar with a representation of the Trinity.
Dreifaltigkeitssonntag, *m.* Trinity Sunday.
Dreifarbendruck, *m. Phot: Phot.Engr:* **1.** three-colour process. **2.** three-colour print.
Dreifarbenphotographie, *f.* three-colour(ed) photography, trichromatic photography.

Dreifelderwirtschaft, *f. Agr:* three-course, -field, system.

dreifeldig, *a.* in three panels *or* sections.

dreifingerig, *a.* three-fingered; *Nat.Hist:* tridactyl.

Dreifingerregel, *f. El:* Fleming's rule.

Dreifirner, *m.* three-year-old wine.

dreiflächig, *a. Geom:* trihedral (angle).

Dreiflügelblende, *f. Cin: Phot:* three-bladed shutter.

dreiflüg(e)lig, *a.* **1.** (house, etc.) with three wings. **2.** *Av:* three-blade (airscrew).

dreiförmig, *a.* triform.

Dreifruchtmarmelade, *f.* three-fruit jam.

dreifurchig, *a.* with three grooves *or* furrows; *Biol:* trisulcate.

Dreifuß, *m.* **1.** tripod; three-legged stool *or* stand; **doppelter D.,** cat; **der Delphische D.,** the Tripod at Delphi. **2.** *Bootm:* (triple) hobbing-foot.

Dreifußlafette, *f. Artil:* tripod mounting.

Dreifußstativ, *n. Phot: etc:* tripod (stand).

dreigabelig, *a.* three-forked, three-pronged, trifurcated (lightning, etc.).

Dreigang-, *comb.fm. Aut: etc:* three-speed . . .; three-gear . . . , . . . with three gears; **Dreiganggetriebe** *n,* three-speed gearing.

Dreigespann, *n.* team of three horses; *F: (of close friends, etc.)* trio, threesome.

dreigestaltig, *a.* in three forms, shapes; triform.

Dreigestirn, *n. (a) Astr:* triple star; *(b) F:* triple constellation (of celebrated artists, etc.).

dreigestrichen, *a. Mus:* thrice-accented, three-line (note).

dreigeteilt, *a.* divided into three (parts); tripartite; threefold; *Anat:* **dreigeteilter Nerv,** trigeminal nerve, trifacial nerve.

dreigleisig, *a. Rail:* **dreigleisige Weiche,** three-throw switch.

dreigliedrig, *a.* with three members, three parts; *Bot: Ent: etc:* trimerous; *Mth:* trinomial; **dreigliedriger Ausdruck,** trinomial.

Dreigroschenoper, die. *Mus:* the Threepenny Opera.

dreihauig, *a.* = dreischürig.

Dreiheit, *f. (a)* threefold nature (of Godhead, etc.); *(b)* triad; group of three.

Dreiholz, *n.* gibbet, gallows.

Dreiinselschiff, *n. Nau:* three-island ship.

dreijährig, *a.* **1.** three-year-old (child, horse, etc.). **2.** three-year (appointment, etc.); (appointment, etc.) lasting (for) three years; triennial (reign, etc.).

dreijährlich. **1.** *a.* three-yearly, triennial (meetings, conferences, etc.). **2.** *adv.* every three years; triennially.

Dreikaiserbund, der. *Hist:* the treaty between Wilhelm I of Germany, Franz Joseph I of Austria, and Alexander II of Russia, lasting from 1872 to 1878 and from 1881 to 1886.

Dreikaiserschlacht, die. *Hist:* the Battle of Austerlitz.

Dreikampf, *m. Sp:* triathlon.

Dreikant, *m. -s/-e.* **1.** *Geom:* trihedron. **2.** *Tls:* = Dreikantfeile.

Dreikanter, *m. Geol:* dreikanter.

Dreikantfeile, *f. Tls:* three-square, triangular, file.

dreikantig, *a.* three-square (file, etc.); three-edged (blade, etc.); *Nat.Hist:* triquetrous (stem, etc.); *Geom:* trihedral (angle).

dreikapselig, *a. Bot:* tricapsular.

Dreikäsehoch, *m. -s/-. F: (a)* little chap, *F:* nipper, urchin, whippersnapper; **ein D.,** a bit of a boy; *(b)* short little man, *F:* (little) titch.

Dreiklang, *m. Mus:* triad.

dreiklappig, *a. Nat.Hist:* trivalvular.

Dreiklassenwahlsystem, *n. Hist:* three-class system (of franchise).

dreiklassig, *a.* with three classes; *Sch:* with three forms, classes, *U.S:* grades.

Dreikonchenanlage, *f. Arch:* triconch plan, triconchos.

Dreikönig, *n. F:* = Dreikönige 2.

Dreikönige, die. **1. die (heiligen) D.,** the three Kings, the three Magi. **2.** *Ecc:* **D.,** *F:* **Dreikönigen,** Epiphany; **an Dreikönigen,** at Epiphany.

Dreikönigsabend, *m.* Twelfth-night.

Dreikönigsfest, das. *Ecc:* (the feast of the) Epiphany.

Dreikönigskuchen, *m.* Twelfth-cake.

Dreikönigsschrein, der, the shrine of the Magi (at Cologne).

Dreikönigstag, der. *Ecc:* (the feast of the) Epiphany; Twelfth-day.

dreiköpfig, *a.* **1.** three-headed (giant, etc.); tricephalic, tricephalous (monster, etc.); *Anat: etc:* triceps. **2.** consisting of three persons; **eine dreiköpfige Familie,** a family of three.

dreilappig, *a. Bot: etc:* trilobate.

Dreilaut(er), *m. Ling:* triphthong.

Dreiling, *m. -s/-e.* **1.** *Num:* = Dreier 2. **2.** *Meas:* any of various measures of wine, corn, etc.

Dreimächteabkommen, *n. Pol:* three-power agreement.

dreimähdig, *a.* = dreischürig.

dreimal, *adv.* three times; *A. & Lit:* thrice; **d. soviel,** three times as much; **d. so groß wie . . . ,** three times as big as . . .; **d. heilig,** most holy; **d. gesegnet,** thrice-blest, thrice-blessed.

dreimalig, *a.* (request, apology, etc.) made three times; three (cheers, etc.); **nach dreimaligem Versuch,** after three attempts.

Dreimannhochspiel, *n. Games:* odd-man-out.

dreimännig, *a. Bot:* triandrous.

Dreimarkstück, *n. Num:* (German) three-mark piece.

Dreimaster, *m.* **1.** *Nau:* three-masted ship, three-master. **2.** = Dreispitz 1.

dreimastig, *a. Nau:* three-masted (ship).

Dreimastschoner, *m. Nau:* three-mast(ed) schooner.

Dreimeilengrenze, *f.* three mile limit (of territorial waters).

dreimonatig, *a.* **1.** lasting (for) three months; three-month (period, etc.); (stay, etc.) of three months. **2.** (baby) of three months, three-month(s)-old (baby).

dreimonatlich. **1.** *a.* quarterly; trimestrial. **2.** *adv.* every three months; quarterly.

Dreimonatswechsel, *n. Fin:* bill at three months.

dreimotorig, *a. Av:* three-engined, *U.S:* trimotor (aircraft).

drein, *adv. F:* = darein.

dreinblicken, *v.i. sep. (haben)* **gelassen, traurig, usw., d.,** to have, wear, a calm, sad, etc. expression; **blöde d.,** to stare stupidly.

dreinervig, *a. Bot:* trinervate.

dreinreden, *v.i. sep. (haben) (a)* to interrupt; **du sollst nicht immer d.,** you mustn't keep on interrupting; *(b)* to interfere; **sie redet mir in alles drein,** she interferes in everything I do.

dreinsehen, *v.i. sep. (strong) (haben)* = dreinblicken.

Dreipaß, *m. -passes/-passe. Arch:* trefoil.

Dreiphasen-, *comb.fm. El.E:* three-phase . . .; **Dreiphasen(wechsel)strom** *m,* three-phase current; **Dreiphasendynamomaschine** *f,* **Dreiphasenstromerzeuger** *m,* three-phase generator.

Dreipolröhre, *f. W.Tel:* triode; three-electrode valve, *U.S:* electron tube.

Dreirad, *n.* **1.** tricycle. **2.** *F:* three-wheeled car.

dreiräd(e)rig, *a.* three-wheeled (car, etc.).

Dreiradfahrer, *m.* tricyclist.

Dreiradlieferwagen, *m. Aut:* three-wheeled delivery van.

Dreirud(e)rer, *m. Gr. & Rom.Ant:* trireme.

dreisaitig, *a. Mus:* three-stringed; **dreisaitiges Instrument,** trichord, three-stringed instrument.

Dreisatz, *m.,* **Dreisatzrechnung,** *f. Mth:* rule of three.

Dreisch, *m. -s/-e* = Dreesch.

Dreischenkel, *m. Num: etc:* triskelion, triscele, triskele.

dreischiffig, *a. Arch:* (church) with a nave and two aisles; (hall, etc.) with three aisles, divided into three aisles.

Dreischlag, *m.* **1.** *Mus:* three-beat rhythm; triple time. **2.** *Equit:* uneven trot.

Dreischlitz, *m. Arch:* triglyph.

Dreischneider, *m.* **1.** *Bookb:* three-knife trimmer. **2.** *Tls:* three-lipped twist-drill.

dreischneidig, *a.* three-edged (sword, etc.); *Tls:* three-lipped (borer, etc.).

Dreischneuß, *m. Arch:* flamboyant trefoil.

dreischürig, *a. Agr:* (meadow) mown three times a year.

Dreiseit, *n. -(e)s/-e. Geom:* three-sided figure.

dreiseitig, *a. (a)* three-sided (figure, etc.); trilateral; *(b)* tripartite (agreement, etc.).

dreisilbig, *a.* three-syllable(d), trisyllabic (word).

Dreisitz, *m. Ecc:* stall for the priest and two deacons to sit in during the sung creed.

Dreisitzer, *m. Aut: etc:* three-seater.

dreispaltig, *a. (a) Nat.Hist: etc:* three-cleft, trifid; *(b)* three-column (article, etc.); three-column(ed) (page, etc.); *adv.* (printed, etc.) in three columns.

Dreispänner, *m. -s/-. Veh:* carriage, etc., drawn by three horses; three-horse carriage, etc.

Dreispitz, *m.* **1.** three-cornered (cocked) hat, tricorne. **2.** *Bot:* = Dreizack.

dreisprachig, *a.* trilingual; three-language (dictionary, etc.).

Dreisprung, *m. Sp:* triple jump, hop, step, and jump, *U.S:* hop, skip, and jump.

dreißig. **1.** *cardinal num.a.inv.* thirty; **d. Jahre,** thirty years; **Seite d.,** page thirty. **2.** *s.f.* **Dreißig, -/- & -en,** (number) thirty; **in die D. kommen,** to reach one's thirties; **in den Dreißigen sein,** to be in one's, the, thirties. *(For other phrases see acht, achtzig.)*

dreißiger. **1.** *inv.a. (a)* of *or* relating to a group characterized by the number 30; *(b)* **die d. Jahre,** (i) the thirties (of s.o.'s age); (ii) the thirties (of a century). **2.** *s. m.* **Dreißiger, -s/-,** *(a)* man in his thirties; *(b) pl.* **die Dreißiger,** the thirties (of s.o.'s age); **in den Dreißigern sein,** to be in one's, the, thirties; *(c)* wine of the '30 vintage; *(d)* man born in the year '30; *(e) Mil:* soldier of the 30th Regiment. *(For other phrases cp. achtziger.)*

dreißigjährig, *a.* **1.** thirty-year-old (pers., etc.); **ein dreißigjähriger Mann,** a man of thirty, a thirty-year-old man. **2.** lasting (for) thirty years; *Hist:* **der Dreißigjährige Krieg,** the Thirty Years' war.

dreißigste(r), dreißigste, dreißigste(s), *ordinal num. a.* thirtieth; **am Dreißigsten (des Monats),** on the thirtieth (of the month). *(For other phrases cp. achte(r).)*

dreist, *a.* audacious, impudent, bold (person, action, remark); forward (person); cheeky (child, remark); brazen (person, lie, etc.); barefaced (lie, etc.); **ein dreister Diebstahl,** a bold, daring, robbery; **d. wie eine Elster,** as bold as brass; as cheeky as a cock-sparrow; *adv.* **d. lügen,** to lie brazenly.

Dreisteinwurzel, *f. Bot:* feverwort, feverroot.

dreistellig, *a. Mth:* three-figure (number); three-place (decimal).

Dreistigkeit, *f.* audacity, impudence, boldness (of person, action, remark); forwardness (of person); cheekiness (of child, remark); brazenness (of person, lie, etc.); **eine D. sondergleichen,** confounded impudence, *F:* incredible cheek; **er hatte die D., an mich zu schreiben,** he had the audacity, the cheek, to write to me.

dreistimmig, *a. Mus:* (song, etc.) for three voices, in three parts; (fugue) in three parts; *adv.* **d. singen,** to sing (song) in three voices.

dreistöckig, *a.* three-storied, three-storey (house); *(incorrectly used)* four-storied.

dreistoffig, *a. Ch: etc:* ternary.

dreisträngig, *a.* three-stranded (rope, etc.).

Dreistufenrakete, *f.* three-stage rocket.

Dreistufenschalter, *m.* three-heat switch (on electric blanket, etc.).

dreistündig, *a.* three-hour (examination, etc.); **dreistündige Vorlesung,** (i) three-hour lecture, lecture lasting three hours; (ii) course of lectures consisting of three periods weekly.

dreistündlich. **1.** *a.* three-hourly (bulletins, visits, intervals, etc.). **2.** *adv.* every three hours.

Dreitagefieber, *m. Med:* pappataci fever, sand-fly fever.

dreitägig, *a.* lasting (for) three days; three-day (visit, etc.).

dreitäglich. **1.** *a.* (visits, etc.) at three day intervals. **2.** *adv.* every three days.

Dreitakt, *m. Mus:* triple time, three-part time.

dreitausend, *cardinal num.a.inv.* three thousand.

dreiteilig, *a.* (book, tool, etc.) in three parts; three-part (tool, etc.); three-piece (suit, costume); tripartite (country, etc.); **dreiteiliger Spiegel,** triple mirror; **dreiteiliger Altar, dreiteiliges Altarbild,** triptych; *Mus:* **dreiteiliger Takt,** triple time, three-part time.

Dreiteilung, *f.* division into three (parts); tripartition (of angle, etc.).

Dreitimp, *m. -(e)s/-e. Dial:* = Dreispitz 1.

Dreitritt, *m.* dance in triple time *(e.g. waltz).*

dreiundeinhalb, *cardinal num.a.inv.* three and a half.

Dreiverband, der. *Hist:* the Triple Entente.

dreiviertel. **1.** *attrib.a.inv.* three-quarter; **in d. Lebensgröße,** in three-quarter life size; **in einer d. Stunde,** in three-quarters of an hour. **2.** *adv. (a)* **(um) d. vier,** (at) quarter to four; *(b) (also* **dreiviertel-,** *comb.fm.)* three-quarters; **d. voll, dreiviertelvoll,** three-quarters full; **d. lebensgroß,** in three-quarter life size; **dreiviertellanger Mantel,** three-quarter length coat. **3.** *s.n.* **Dreiviertel,** three-quarters; **wir haben D. des Weges hinter uns,** we are three-quarters of the way there; **ich habe nur D. (davon) getrunken,** I have only drunk three-quarters (of it).

Dreiviertelärmel, *m. Cost:* three-quarter (length) sleeve.

Dreiviertelhose, *f. Cost:* three-quarter length slacks; (calf-length) jeans.

Dreiviertelkreis, *m.* three-quarters of a circle.

Dreiviertelmantel, *m. Cost:* three-quarter length coat.

Dreiviertelmehrheit, *f.* three-quarters majority (in debate, etc.).

Dreiviertelprofil, *n. Phot: Art:* three-quarter face portrait; semi-profile portrait.

Dreiviertelsäule, *f. Arch:* three-quarter column.

Dreiviertelspieler, *m. Rugby Fb:* three-quarter back, three-quarter.

Dreiviertelstab, *m. Arch:* bowtell; three-quarter round.

Dreiviertelstunde, *f.* three-quarters of an hour; **in einer D.,** in three-quarters of an hour.

Dreivierteltakt, *m. Mus:* three-four time.

Dreiwalzwerk, *n. Metall:* three-high mill.

Dreiweg, *m.* meeting of two roads; road-fork.

Dreiweg(e)-, *comb.fm.* three-way . . .; **Dreiweg(e)hahn** *m,* three-way tap; *Rail:* **Dreiwegweiche** *f,* three-way points; *El:* **Dreiwegschalter** *m,* three-way switch.

Dreiwegstück, *n.* T branch; three-limb tube.

dreiweibig, *a. Bot:* trigynous.

dreiwertig, *a. Ch:* trivalent, tervalent; trihydric (alcohol).

Dreiwertigkeit, *f. Ch:* trivalence, tervalence.

dreiwink(e)lig, *a.* triangular.

dreiwöchentlich. 1. *a.* three-weekly (test, etc.). **2.** *adv.* every three weeks.

dreiwöchig, *a.* lasting (for) three weeks; **ein dreiwöchiger Urlaub,** a three-week holiday.

Dreizack, *m.* **-s/-e. 1.** trident (of Neptune, etc.). **2.** *Bot:* arrow-grass.

dreizackig, *a.* with three points; three-pronged (fork, etc.); (crown) with three points, three prongs; (mountain) with three peaks; *Nat.Hist:* tridental; tridentate; *Anat:* tricuspid.

Dreizackpflanzen, die, *pl. Bot:* the arrow-grass family.

Dreizahl, die, (the number) three; **die heilige D.,** the sacred number (of) three.

Dreizahn, *m. Bot:* heath-grass; **niederliegender D.,** decumbent heath-grass.

Dreizahngras, *n. Bot:* spinifex, porcupine-grass.

Dreizehenfaultier, *n. Z:* three-toed sloth.

Dreizehenmöwe, *f. Orn:* kittiwake.

Dreizehenspecht, *m. Orn:* three-toed woodpecker.

dreizehn. 1. *cardinal num.a.inv.* thirteen; **sie ist d. (Jahre alt),** she is thirteen (years old); *F:* **jetzt schlägt's aber d.!** that really is the limit! that's finished it! **2.** *s. f.* **Dreizehn, -/-en,** (number) thirteen. (*For other phrases cp.* **acht.**)

Dreizehner, *m.* **-s/-. 1.** *Mil:* soldier of the 13th Regiment. **2.** wine of the '13 vintage. **2. Dreizehner-,** *comb.fm.* . . . of thirteen; **Dreizehnergruppe** *f,* group of thirteen.

dreizehnjährig, *a.* **1.** thirteen-year-old (child, animal, etc.); **ein dreizehnjähriger Junge, ein Dreizehnjähriger,** a boy of thirteen, a thirteen-year-old boy, *F:* a thirteen-year-old. **2.** lasting (for) thirteen years; thirteen-year (period, etc.).

Dreizehntel, *n.* thirteenth (part); *see also* **-tel.**

dreizehnte(r), dreizehnte, dreizehnte(s), *ordinal num.a.* thirteenth; **das dreizehnte Haus,** the thirteenth house; **Ludwig der Dreizehnte,** Louis the Thirteenth. (*For other phrases cp.* **achte(r)**[1].)

dreizinkig, *a.* three-pronged (fork, etc.).

Dreizweiteltakt, *m. Mus:* three-two time.

Drell, *m.* **-s/-e** =**Drillich.**

Drempel, *m.* **-s/-. 1.** *Constr:* jamb(-wall); attic wall. **2.** (*a*) *Hyd.E:* sill (of lock); caisson sill (of dock entrance); (*b*) *N.Arch:* port-sill.

Drempelwand, *f.* =**Drempel 1.**

Dreschboden, *m.,* **Dreschdiele,** *f.* threshing-floor.

Dresche, *f.* **-/-n.** *F:* **D. kriegen, bekommen,** to get a hiding, a thrashing; **j-m D. geben,** to give s.o. a hiding, a beating, a licking.

dreschen. I. *v.tr.* (*strong*) (*p.t.* **drosch,** *A:* **drasch**) **1.** *Husb:* to thresh (corn, etc.); *F:* **leeres Stroh d.,** to plough the sands; to beat the air; **(leere) Phrasen d.,** to churn out a lot of platitudes, trite remarks. **2.** (*a*) to thrash (s.o.); (*b*) *Cards: F:* **Skat d.,** to play skat; (*c*) *A:* **von häuslichen Sorgen gedroschen sein,** to be beset by household cares.

II. *vbl s.* **Dreschen,** *n. in vbl senses; cp.* **Drusch.**

Drescher, *m.* **-s/-. 1.** (*pers.*) thresher; *F:* **wie ein D. essen,** to eat like a horse, a wolf. **2.** threshing-machine, thresher.

Dreschflegel, *m. Husb:* flail.

Dreschkorb, *m.* sieve (in threshing-machine).

Dreschmaschine, *f.* threshing-machine, thresher.

Dreschtenne, *f.* threshing-floor.

Dresden. *Pr.n.n.* **-s.** *Geog:* Dresden.

Dresd(e)ner. 1. *m.* **-s/-.** *Geog:* inhabitant, native, of Dresden. **2.** *inv.a.* of Dresden, Dresden. . . .

dresd(e)nisch, *a.* of Dresden, Dresden. . . .

Dresseur [drɛ'søːr], *m.* **-s/-e,** animal trainer.

dressieren [drɛ'siːrən]. I. *v.tr.* **1.** to train (animal, *Hum:* husband, etc.); **einen Hund auf etwas** *acc.* **d.,** to train a dog to do sth.; **gut dressiert,** well trained; **dressierte Seehunde, Löwen, usw.,** performing seals, lions, etc. **2.** *Cu:* to truss (up) (fowl); to roll (joint); to skewer (meat). **3.** *Tex:* to comb (floss-silk). **4.** to dress (glove). **5.** *Hatm:* to block (hat).

II. *vbl s.* **Dressieren** *n.,* **Dressierung** *f. in vbl senses; cp.* **Dressur.**

Dressierhalsband, *n.*=**Dressurhalsband.**

Dressiermaschine [drɛ'siːr-], *f. Tex:* combing-machine (for floss-silk).

Dressoir [drɛso·'aːr], *m.* **-s/-s.** *Furn:* sideboard, dresser.

Dressur [drɛ'suːr], *f.* **-/-en. 1.** training (of animals); **Pferd in D.,** horse in training; **D. auf etwas** *acc.,* training to do sth. **2.** (kind of) training; method of training, training method. **3.** dressage.

Dressurhalsband, *n.* spiked collar (*used in training dogs*).

Dressurreiten, *n.* dressage.

dreuen, *v.i.* (*haben*) *A. & Lit:*=**drohen.**

dribbeln, *v.tr. Fb:* to dribble (the ball).

Driesch, *m.* **-s/-e** =**Dreesch.**

Drieschling, *m.* **-s/-e.** *Fung:* (common) mushroom.

Drieschwirtschaft, *f.*=**Dreeschwirtschaft.**

Drift[1], *m.* **-(e)s/-e.** *Dy:* strainer, net (of dyer's vat).

Drift[2], *f.* **-/-en.** *Nau:* drift(-current).

Drifteis, *n. Nau: etc:* drift-ice.

Driftströmung, *f. Oc:* drift-current.

Drilch, *m.* **-(e)s/-e.** *Tex:*=**Drillich.**

Drill[1], *m.* **-s/-e.** *Tex:*=**Drillich.**

Drill[2], *m.* **-(e)s/.** *Mil: etc:* drill; drilling; *Mil: Pej: F:* square-bashing.

Drill[3], *m.* **-(e)s/-e.** *Z:* drill, West-African baboon.

Drillachse, *f. Ph:* (*in quantum theory*) rotator.

Drillbogen, *m. Tls:* drill-bow.

Drillbohrer, *m. Tls:* (spiral) drill.

Drilldocke, *f.* drill-chuck.

Drille, *f.* **-/-n,** rotating cage.

Drillegge, *f. Agr:* drill-harrow.

drillen[1]. I. *v.tr.* **1.** to drill (hole, etc.). **2.** *Tex:* to twist (threads). **3.** *Mil: etc:* to drill (soldiers, etc.); to train (s.o.); **gut gedrillt,** well-drilled; **früher waren die Kinder meist nur auf Auswendiglernen gedrillt,** in the old days children were usually simply made to learn everything by heart.

II. *vbl s.* **1. Drillen,** *n. in vbl senses.* **2. Drillung,** *f.* (*a*) =II. 1; (*b*) torsion; twist.

drillen[2], *v.tr. Agr:* to drill (a field, beets, etc.).

Drillfisch, *m. Ich:* electric eel.

Drillhalle, *f. Mil:* drill hall.

Drillhaus, *n.* **1.**=**Drillhalle. 2.**=**Drillhäuschen.**

Drillhäuschen, *n. Hist:* rotating cage in which an offender was exposed to public ridicule.

Drillich, *m.* **-s/-e.** *Tex:* heavy (*usu.* cotton) twill; drill.

Drillichanzug, *m.* (*a*) (heavy cotton twill) overalls; dungarees; (*b*) *Mil:* fatigue dress.

Drillichhosen, *f.pl.* dungarees; jeans.

Drillichzeug, *n.* **1.**=**Drillich. 2.**=**Drillichanzug.**

Drilling[1], *m.* **-s/-e. 1.** triplet, one of triplets; **Geburt von Drillingen,** birth of triplets; **sie sind Drillinge,** they are triplets. **2.** *Cryst:* tripling. **3.** *Sm.a:* three-barrelled gun (with one smooth bore and two rifled barrels *or vice versa*). **4.** *Fish:* treble hook.

Drilling[2], *m.* **-s/-e.** *Mec.E:* lantern(-wheel, -pinion), trundle(-wheel), wallower(-wheel).

Drillingmaschine, *f. Mch:* triple-cylinder engine.

Drillingsalz, *n. Ch:* triple salt.

Drillingsbalken, *m. Her:* tierce; three bars.

Drillingsblume, *f. Bot:* bougainvillea.

Drillingsbogen, *m. Arch:* triple arch.

Drillingsbruder, *m.* triplet brother.

Drillingsdampfmaschine, *f. Mch:* triple-cylinder engine.

Drillingsfenster, *n. Arch:* triple window, triplet.

Drillingsgeburt, *f.* birth of triplets.

Drillingskind, *n.* triplet, one of triplets.

Drillingskristall, *m. Cryst:* tripling.

Drillingsnerv, *m. Anat:* trifacial (nerve), trigeminal nerve, trigeminus.

Drillingspreßpumpe, *f.* three-piston pump.

Drillingsschwester, *f.* triplet sister.

Drillingsturm, *m. Navy:* triple (gun-)turret.

Drillkäfig, *m.*=**Drillhäuschen.**

Drillkultur, *f. Agr:* drill-planting.

Drillmaschine, *f. Agr:* drill.

Drillpflug, *m. Agr:* drill-plough.

Drillplatz, *m. Mil:* drill-ground.

Drillsaat, *f. Agr:* (*a*) drill-sowing; drilling; (*b*) drill-seed(s).

Drillscheibe, *f. Tls:* drill-plate.

drin, *pron. adv.*=**darin; da d.,** in it; in them; in there; **mitten d.,** in the middle, in the midst; **ich habe den ganzen Tag Kuchen gebacken, und als der Besuch kam, war ich immer noch mitten d.,** I spent the whole day baking cakes, and when the visitors came I was still in the midst, in the middle, of it (all); **wir waren mitten d., die Wohnung auszuräumen, da . . . ,** we were in the midst, in the middle, of turning out the flat when . . .; **wo der Kampf am heftigsten tobte, da war er mitten d.,** he was always in the thick of the battle.

dringen. I. *v.i.* (*strong*) (*sein*) **1.** (*a*) **in etwas** *acc.* **d.,** (*of pers., soldiers, etc.*) to penetrate, make one's way, get, into (house, town, country, etc.), to enter (house, town, country, etc.); (*of crowd*) to surge, throng, into (square, house, etc.); (*of water, etc.*) to penetrate, get, into sth.; **bis an die, bis zu den, Grenzen d.,** to reach, to get as far as, the borders; **sie drangen aus der brennenden Stadt,** they surged, thronged, out of the burning town; **Rauch drang aus allen Fenstern,** smoke was belching out of all the windows; **Geigentöne drangen aus dem offenen Fenster,** the sound of a violin came through the open window; **die Kugel drang tief in den Schenkel,** the bullet penetrated deep into the thigh; **die Feuchtigkeit dringt in, durch, alle Ritzen,** the damp is seeping through all the cracks; **die Nässe dringt einem bis auf die Haut,** the wet penetrates to one's skin; **durch die feindlichen Linien d.,** to penetrate through the enemy lines; **ein lauter Schrei drang durch die Nacht,** a loud cry rang into the night; **ihre fröhlichen Stimmen drangen durch das Haus,** their gay voices rang through the house; **ihre Stimme drang durch den Maschinenlärm,** her voice could be heard above the noise of the machines; **ein Gebet, das durch die Wolken dringt,** a prayer that is heard in heaven; **Musik, die zum Herzen dringt,** music that stirs the soul; **ihre Worte drangen in sein Innerstes,** her words moved him deeply; her words cut deep into his soul; (*of rumour, news, etc.*) **an die Öffentlichkeit d.,** to get abroad, to transpire, to become public, to reach the public; **das Gerücht ist nicht bis zu mir gedrungen,** the rumour has not penetrated to me, has not reached me; (*b*) **in j-n d.,** to press s.o.; to plead with s.o.; to reason with s.o.; to entreat, beg, urge, beseech, s.o. (to do sth.); to try to persuade s.o. (to do sth.); **mit Fragen in j-n d.,** to press, ply, s.o. with questions; **mit Bitten in j-n d.,** to plead with s.o.; **als sie in ihn drang, gestand er,** when she pressed him, when she insisted, he confessed; **wir beschlossen, nicht mehr weiter in ihn zu d. und ihn sein gefährliches Vorhaben ausführen zu lassen,** we decided not to reason, plead, with him any further but to let him carry out his dangerous plans; **sie drangen in ihn zu bleiben,** they entreated, begged, pleaded with, him to stay. **2.** (*haben*) **auf etwas** *acc.* **d.,** to press for sth.; to insist on sth.; **darauf d., daß etwas getan wird, werde,** to press for sth. to be done, to urge that sth. should be done, to insist on sth.'s being done; **bei j-m auf etwas** *acc.* **d.,** to press s.o. for sth.; **die Liberalen dringen auf eine Entscheidung,** the Liberals are pressing for a decision (to be made); **ich muß auf größte Genauigkeit d.,** I must insist on the greatest accuracy; **auf eine Antwort d.,** to press for an answer; **auf Bezahlung d.,** to press for payment.

II. **dringen,** *v.tr.,* **sich dringen** = **drängen** I. 1, 3. *See also* **gedrungen.**

III. *pr.p. & a.* **dringend,** *in vbl senses; esp.* urgent; pressing; **die Sache ist d.,** the case, the matter, is urgent, pressing; **ein dringender Fall,** an urgent case, a case of emergency; an emergency; **die dringendsten Dinge, das Dringendste, zuerst erledigen,** to attend to the most urgent, pressing, things first; **auf ihre dringende Forderung,** at their urgent request; **eine dringende Bitte,** an urgent entreaty; an urgent request; **in dringenden Fällen,** in urgent cases, in cases of emergency, in emergencies; **dringender Verdacht,** strong suspicion; **dringende Gründe,** compelling, cogent, reasons; (*on letter, etc.*) **'d.',** 'urgent'; *Tg:* **dringendes Telegramm** (*abbr.* **D**), priority telegram, urgent telegram; *Tp:* **dringendes Gespräch,** priority call; *adv.* urgently; **etwas d. nötig haben, brauchen,** to need sth. urgently, to be in urgent need of sth., to need, want, sth. badly; **ein Arzt wird d. gebraucht,** a doctor is urgently required; **seine Rückkehr ist dringendst erforderlich,** his return is most urgently required; **j-n d. um etwas bitten,** to beg s.o. for sth.; to implore, beseech, s.o. to give one sth. *or*

to do sth.; **ich muß d. um Ruhe bitten,** I must insist on silence, I must beg you to be silent; **j-n d. (darum) bitten, etwas zu tun,** to ask, request, s.o. urgently to do sth.; **dringender konnte ich ihn nicht bitten,** I couldn't ask him more urgently; **eine d. notwendige Maßnahme,** a measure of pressing necessity; **etwas d. empfehlen, d. empfehlen, etwas zu tun,** to recommend sth. strongly; to advise (s.o.) strongly to do sth.

dringentlich, *a. & adv.*=**dringend,** *q.v. under* **dringen** III.

dringlich, *a.* urgent; pressing; **eine Sache für d. erklären,** to declare a matter to be urgent.

Dringlichkeit, *f.* urgency; **die Anträge werden der D. entsprechend bearbeitet,** the applications are dealt with according to their urgency, in order of priority; **die D. beantragen,** to ask that sth. be dealt with as a matter of urgency; *Parl:* to call for a vote of urgency; **über die Frage der D. entscheiden,** to establish priority; to establish the degree of urgency (of a particular case).

Dringlichkeitsantrag, *m.* application for priority; *Parl:* **den D. stellen,** to call for a vote of urgency.

Dringlichkeitsbescheinigung, *f.* certificate of priority.

Dringlichkeitsfrage, *f.* question of urgency.

drinne, *adv. A. & F:*=**drinnen.**

drinnen. 1. *adv.* (*also* **drinnen-,** *comb.fm.*) inside; indoors; **(da) d.,** in there; **wir wollen im Garten bleiben, d. ist alles noch so unordentlich,** let's stay in the garden—everything is still so untidy indoors, in there; **drinnenbleiben,** to stay in(doors). **2.** *pron. adv.* (*a*) in it, in them; (*b*) *rel. use. A. & Lit:* in which, wherein.

drippeln, *v.i.* (*haben*) *Dial:* (*of liquid*) to dribble; *v.impers.* **es drippelt,** it's spitting (with rain).

Dripsdrill, *m.* **-s/-e.** *F:* dull person; *F:* misery; drip; wet blanket; weary Willy; **er saß den ganzen Abend da wie ein D.,** he sat there all evening like a stuffed dummy, like a dying duck (in a thunderstorm).

drisch *see* **dreschen.**

Drischel, *m.* **-s/-.** *Dial:* flail.

drischst, drischt *see* **dreschen.**

dritt, *adv.* **zu d.,** (the) three of us, you, them; **wir gingen zu d. ins Theater,** (the) three of us went to the theatre; **ihr könnt ein Taxi zu d. nehmen,** (the) three of you can share a taxi; **sie kamen zu d.,** (the) three of them came; all three of them came.

dritt-, Dritt-, *comb.fm.* **1.** third . . .; third-; **die drittgrößte Stadt,** the third largest town; **der dritthöchste, drittgrößte, Turm,** the third highest tower; the third highest steeple; **der, die, das, drittkleinste,** the third smallest; **der drittälteste Sohn,** the third (eldest) son; **der drittjüngste,** the third youngest; **der Drittbeste der Klasse,** the third best in the class; **drittrangig,** third-rate. **2.** *Jur: Com: etc:* . . . by a third party, person; . . . of a third party, person; . . . to, with, a third party; third party . . .; **Drittschaden** *m,* damage suffered by a third party; **Drittverwahrung** *f,* custody of a third party; **Drittverwahrer** *m,* third party having custody (of drafts, deeds, etc.); **Drittverpfändung** *f,* depositing (of drafts, etc.) with a third party as security.

dritt(e)halb, *inv.a.* two and a half.

Dritteil, *n.*=**Drittel I.**

dritteilen, *v.tr.*=**dritteln.**

Drittel. I. *n.* **-s/-,** third (part); **ein D., zwei D., seines Geldes verlieren,** to lose one third, two-thirds, of one's money; **das D. eines Apfels,** a third of an apple; *see also* **-tel.**

II. **drittel,** *inv.a.,* **Drittel-,** *comb.fm.* third (part) of . . .; **ein d. Apfel, ein Drittelapfel,** a third of an apple.

Drittelfaß, *n. A.Meas:* tierce (of wine).

dritteln, *v.tr.* to divide (sth.) into thirds, into three (equal) parts.

Drittelpipe, *f. A.Meas:* tierce (of wine).

drittelsauer, *a. Ch:* tribasic.

Drittelsilber, *n.* silver alloy containing approximately one-third of its weight of silver, tiers-argent.

Drittelwirtschaft, *f. Agr:* third-share farming; 'métayage' system.

Drittenabschlagen, *n. Games:* twos and threes.

drittens, *adv.* thirdly; in the third place.

dritte(r), dritte, dritte(s), *ordinal num.a.* **1.** third; **im dritten Stock,** on the third floor; **an dritter Stelle,** in the third place; **jeden dritten Tag,** every third day; **zum dritten Male,** for the third time; **zum dritten,** thirdly, in the third place; (*at auction*) (for the third time of asking, going, going,) gone! **er kam als dritter oder vierter,** he arrived third or fourth; **in Mathematik ist er Dritter, der Dritte,** he is (the) third best in mathematics; he is third in mathematics; **wir haben noch einen dritten Punkt, ein Drittes, in Betracht zu ziehen,** we have to consider a third point, a third aspect; **bei ihm ist jedes dritte Wort . . . ,** his every third word, his every other word, is . . .; **Hotel dritter Klasse,** third-class hotel; *Rail:* **dritte Klasse,** third class; (*cp.* **erste(r)**); *Com:* **dritte Güte, dritte Wahl,** third quality; **Waren dritter Güte,** thirds; *R.C.Ch:* **der dritte Orden,** the Third Order, the lay order, the Tertiaries; *Games:* **den dritten abschlagen,** *occ.* **abklatschen,** to play twos and threes; *Gram:* **die dritte Person,** the third person; *Sch:* **das dritte Schuljahr,** the third year (in elementary school; *approx.*=the first *or* lower second form of preparatory school); **die dritte Klasse,** (i) (*in elementary school*) =**das dritte Schuljahr;** (ii) (*in secondary school*) *approx.*=the lower fourth form; *see also* **Bund** 1, **Fall**[1] 5, **Grad**[3] 1 (*a*); *cp.* **dritt.** (*For other phrases cp.* **achte(r)**[1]) **2.** (*a*) **ein Dritter, eine dritte Person,** a disinterested person; another person; *Jur: Com:* a third party; *Jur:* a third person; **im Beisein Dritter,** in the presence of other people, before witnesses; **bitte erwähnen Sie diese Sache keinem Dritten gegenüber,** please don't mention this to anyone else, to any other person; **der lachende Dritte,** the outsider who reaps the benefit, the *tertius gaudens*; **eine Summe bei einem Dritten deponieren,** to deposit a sum in the hands of a third party; **Zahlungen zugunsten eines Dritten,** payments in favour of a third party; *Fin:* **der Wechsel kann bei einem Dritten zahlbar gestellt werden,** the draft can be made payable by a third party; *Jur:* **im Namen eines Dritten klagen,** to bring an action in the name of a third person; (*b*) **aus dritter Hand,** (information, etc.) at third hand; third-hand (information, car, etc.).

drittklassig, *a.* third-class (goods, etc.); third-rate (artist, theatre, hotel, etc.); *Com:* **drittklassige Waren,** third-class goods, thirds.

Drittland, *n. Pol:* third country.

drittletzte(r), -letzte, -letzte(s), *a.* last but two; **der drittletzte,** the third from the end; the third from the bottom; the third from last, the last but two; *Pros:* **die drittletzte Silbe,** the antepenultimate, antepenult, syllable.

drittrangig, *a.* third-rate (artist, theatre, hotel, etc.).

Drittschrift, *f.* third copy.

Drittschuldner, *m. Jur:* garnishee.

drob, *pron. adv.*=**darob.**

droben, *adv.* up (there); above; **da d.,** up there; **d. in den Bergen,** up in the mountains; **im Himmel d.,** in the heaven above.

Droge ['dro:gə], *f.* **-/-n,** drug; medicine; pharmaceutical product.

Drogenhandlung, *f.* chemist's shop, *U.S:* drugstore.

Drogenkunde, *f.* pharmacognosy.

Drogerie [dro·gə'ri:], *f.* **-/-n** [-'ri:ən], chemist's shop, *U.S:* drugstore.

Drogeriewaren, *f.pl.* pharmaceutical products.

Drogett [dro·'gɛt], **-(e)s/-e.** *Tex:* drugget.

Drogist [dro·'gist], *m.* **-en/-en,** (retail pharmaceutical) chemist.

Drogistenfachschule, *f.* training school for retail chemists.

Drogue, *f.,* **Droguerie,** *f.,* **Droguist,** *m.*=**Droge, Drogerie, Drogist.**

Drohbrief, *m.* threatening letter.

drohen. I. *v.i.* (*haben*), *occ. v.tr.* (*a*) **j-m mit etwas,** *occ.* **j-m etwas, d.,** to threaten s.o. with sth.; **d., etwas zu tun,** to threaten to do sth.; **j-m mit einem Prozeß d.,** to threaten s.o. with legal proceedings; **er drohte, ihn zu entlassen, er drohte ihm mit Entlassung,** he threatened to dismiss him, he threatened him with dismissal; **j-m mit dem Finger, mit der Faust, d.,** to wag, shake, one's finger at s.o.; to shake one's fist at s.o.; **eine drohende Haltung einnehmen,** to assume a threatening, menacing, attitude; **ein drohender Blick,** a threatening, louring, lowering, look, glance; **dunkle Wolken standen drohend am Himmel,** dark clouds hung louring, lowering, in the sky; **seiner Stimme einen drohenden Klang, Ton, geben,** to put a threatening tone into one's voice; (*b*) (*of danger, event, etc.*) **j-m d.,** to threaten s.o., to impend over s.o., to hang over s.o., over s.o.'s head; *abs.* **d.,** to be impending, imminent; (*of pers., thg*) **zu fallen d.,** to be in danger of falling, to be threatening to fall; **Reich, das zusammenzubrechen droht,** empire in danger of breaking up, empire tottering to its fall; **die Verhandlungen drohten fehlzuschlagen,** the negotiations were in danger of going wrong; **wenn du das tust, droht dir Strafe,** if you do this you risk punishment, you risk being punished, punishment will follow; **eine große Gefahr droht euch,** a great danger hangs over you, over your head; **er warnte sie vor einer drohenden Gefahr,** he warned them of an impending, imminent, a threatening, danger; **es droht zu schneien, zu regnen,** it looks like snow, rain, the sky threatens snow, rain; **ein Gewitter droht,** *occ.* **der Himmel droht ein Gewitter,** a storm is threatening, brewing, the sky threatens a storm.

II. *vbl s.* **1. Drohen,** *n.* (*a*) *in vbl senses;* (*b*) threats; **all sein Bitten und D. war vergeblich,** all his pleas and threats were in vain; **weder mit Bitten noch mit D. konnte er ihn dazu bewegen, zu . . . ,** he couldn't persuade him either by entreaties or by threats to . . . . **2. Drohung,** *f.* (*a*) *in vbl senses; also: Jur:* intimidation; employment of threats; **D. mit Gewalt,** threatening, threat, to use force; intimidation; **einen anderen durch D. zu einer Handlung bewegen,** to incite s.o. to an action by intimidation; to intimidate s.o. into doing sth.; (*b*) threat; menace; **leere Drohungen,** empty threats, idle threats; **eine D. wahrmachen,** to carry out a threat; **Drohungen anwenden,** to use, employ, threats; **j-n mit Drohungen, unter Anwendung von Drohungen, dazu zwingen, etwas zu tun,** to force s.o. by threats to do sth.; to intimidate s.o. into doing sth.; to bully s.o. into doing sth.; **unter Anwendung von Drohungen,** with, by, threats, with employment of threats; **Geld unter Anwendung von Drohungen fordern,** to demand money with menaces; *Jur:* **Drohungen mit gegenwärtiger Gefahr für Leib und Leben anwenden,** to use, employ, threats with immediate danger to life and limb.

Droher, *m.* **-s/-,** threatener, menacer.

Drohne, *f.* **-/-n. 1.** *Ent:* drone. **2.** *F:* drone, parasite, sponger; waster, wastrel; good-for-nothing; **die Drohnen der Gesellschaft,** the drones of society.

dröhnen. I. *v.i.* (*haben*) (*of voice, etc.*) to resound; (*of cannon, drum, etc.*) to roar; (*of voice, cannon*) to boom; (*of air, earth, etc.*) to vibrate, to be resonant (with noise); **es dröhnt mir im Kopf,** my head is buzzing, humming; (*of voice, etc.*) **j-m in die Ohren d.,** to din in s.o.'s ears; **der Motorenlärm dröhnte ihm noch in den Ohren,** the noise of the engines still filled his ears, still roared in his ears; **dröhnende Stimme,** resonant, resounding, booming, voice; **das Tal dröhnte vom Hufschlag ihrer Pferde,** the valley resounded, was resonant, with the sound of their horses' hooves.

II. *vbl s.* **Dröhnen,** *n.* boom (of voice, cannon, drum, etc.); roar (of engines, etc.); vibration (of air, earth, etc.) (with noise); din (of battle, etc.).

drohnenbrütig, *a. Ap:* (*of queen-bee*) laying only drone eggs.

drohnenhaft, *a.* like a drone; parasitic, sponging.

Drohnenschlacht, *f. Ap:* killing of drones by workers.

Drohnentum, *n.* parasitism; sponging.

Drohung, *f. see* **drohen II.**

Drohwort, *n.* **-(e)s/-worte,** threatening word, threat.

Drolerie [dro·lə'ri:], *f.* **-/-n** [-'ri:ən]. *Art:* grotesque ornamentation (in illuminated manuscript, on choir-stalls, etc.).

drollig, *a.* amusing; quaint; comical; *U.S:* cute; **sie hat drollige kleine Löckchen,** she has sweet little curls; **ein drolliges Kind,** a quaint child; **er erzählte ihr drollige Geschichten,** he told her amusing, comical, stories; **ein drolliger Kerl,** an amusing, a quaint, fellow; **ein drolliger Anblick,** a quaint, an amusing, sight.

Drolligkeit, *f.* **1.** quaintness; *U.S:* cuteness. **2.** quaint story *or* action; **das Kind amüsierte alle mit seinen Drolligkeiten,** the child amused everybody with its quaint little ways.

Dromedar [dro·mə'da:r], *n.* **-s/-e.** *Z:* dromedary.

Drommete [dro'me:tə], *f.* **-/-n.** *A. & Poet:* trumpet.

Drongo ['drɔŋgo:], *m.* **-s/-s.** *Orn:* drongo, king-crow.

Dronte, *f.* **-/-n.** *Orn:* dodo.

Drontheim. *Pr.n.n.* **-s.** *Geog:* Trondheim.

dröppeln, *v.i.* (*haben*) =**drippeln.**

Drops, *m.* **-/-,** (fruit, acid, etc.) drop; (boiled) sweet; **saure Drops,** acid drops.

drosch, drösche *see* **dreschen.**

Droschke, *f.* **-/-n. 1.** *Veh:* droshky. **2.** cab; (*a*) *Veh: A:* hackney(-carriage, -coach, -cab); hansom(-cab); (*b*) *Aut:* taxi(-cab).

Droschkengaul, *m.* cab-horse; hackney.

Droschkenhalteplatz, *m.* taxi-rank, cab-rank, *U.S:* cabstand, taxi stand.

Droschkenpferd, *n.*=**Droschkengaul.**

dröseln, *v.tr. Dial:* to twist (thread).

Drosera ['dro:ze·ra:], *f.* **-/.** *Bot:* drosera, sundew.

Droserazeen [dro·ze·ra·'tse:ən], *pl. Bot:* droseraceae.

Drosometer [dro·zo·'me:tər], *n.* **-s/-,** drosometer.

Drossel[1], *f.* **-/-n.** *Orn:* thrush; **bunte D.,** White's thrush, golden mountain-thrush; **Sibirische D.,** Siberian thrush.

Drossel[2], *f.* **-/-n.** *Bot:* green alder.

Drossel[3], *f.* **-/-n. 1.** *Ven:* (i) windpipe; (ii) gullet, throat. **2.** *Mch: I.C.E:* throttle. **3.** *El:* = **Drosselspule.**

Drosselader, *f. Anat:* jugular vein.

Drosselbeere, *f. Bot:* **1.** (*a*) sorb(-apple) (tree), service-tree; (*b*) rowan(-tree), mountain ash. **2.** (*fruit*) (i) sorb(-apple), service-apple, service-berry; (ii) rowan-berry. **3.** = **Drosselkirsche. 4.** wild guelder rose, marsh-elder, water-elder.

Drosselbeerstrauch, *m. Bot:* = **Drosselbeere 4.**

Drosselgrube, *f. Anat:* **1.** jugular fossa. **2.** interclavicular notch.

Drosselkirschbaum, *m.,* **Drosselkirsche,** *f. Bot:* black alder, alder buckthorn.

Drosselklappe, *f. Mch: I.C.E:* throttle(-valve), butterfly valve.

Drosselgarn, *n. Tex:* ring-spun yarn.

Drosselhebel, *m. Mch: I.C.E:* throttle-lever, throttle-control.

Drosselmaschine, *f. Tex:* = **Drosselstuhl.**

drosseln. I. *v.tr.* **1.** *Mch: I.C.E:* to throttle (steam, engine). **2.** *El:* to choke (oscillations). **3.** *F:* to curb (expenditure); to choke back (imports, etc.).

II. *vbl s.* **1. Drosseln,** *n. in vbl senses.* **2. Drosselung,** *f.* (*a*) = II. 1; (*b*) *Mch: I.C.E:* (i) = **Drosselventil;** (ii) = **Drosselhebel;** (*c*) *El:* = **Drosselspule.**

Drosselrohrsänger, *m. Orn:* great reed-warbler.

Drosselspule, *f. El:* choking coil, choke, impedance coil, reactance coil, reactor.

Drosselstuhl, *m. Tex:* ring-frame, ring-spinning frame.

Drosselung, *f. see* **drosseln II.**

Drosselventil, *n. Mch: I.C.E:* throttle(-valve).

Drost, *m.* **-es/-e.** *Hist:* bailiff; magistrate; judge.

Drostei, *f.* **-/-en.** *Hist:* **1.** bailiwick. **2.** bailiff's residence *or* bailiff's court.

drüben, *adv.* **1.** (over) there; yonder; **da d., dort d.,** over there; **er lebt in dem Haus (dort) d.,** he lives in that house over there. **2.** (*a*) on the other side; on the other side of, across, the road, river, valley, border, etc.; **er ist schon d.,** he is already across, on the other side; **ich hatte den Fluß schon überquert, meine Begleiter standen noch d.,** I had crossed the river, but my companions were still on the other side; **siehst du den Baum dort d. über dem Fluß?** can you see the tree on the other side of the river? **von d.,** from the other side; **er kam von d. herüber,** he came from the other side; *see also* **hüben;** (*b*) across the sea; *esp.* across the Atlantic, in America; **er hat viele Jahre d. gelebt,** he has lived in America for many years; **sein Bruder ist gerade von d. gekommen,** his brother has just arrived from America, from across the Atlantic; **unsere Freunde von d.,** our friends from across the Atlantic; **er hat vor, nach d. auszuwandern,** he plans to emigrate to America; **wir wollen nach Australien, Kanada, Amerika, auswandern; mein Mann ist schon d.,** we are going to emigrate to Australia, Canada, America; my husband is already there; (*c*) in the other world; **von d.,** from beyond the grave; **das Drüben,** the beyond; **sie hörte eine Stimme von d.,** she heard a voice calling from beyond the grave, she heard a voice from beyond; **wir werden uns d. wiedersehen,** we shall meet again in the next world.

Druck, *m.* **I. -(e)s/=e. 1.** pressure (of hand, etc.); squeeze (of hand, of a press, etc.); **D. einer Sache auf etwas,** pressure of sth. on sth., pressing of sth. on sth.; **D. auf etwas,** (i) pressing sth.; pressing on sth.; (ii) pressure on sth.; **ein leichter D. seiner Hand beruhigte sie,** the light pressure of his hand reassured her; **mit einem D. seiner Hand versuchte er, ihr seine Anteilnahme zu zeigen,** with a firm handshake he tried to show her his sympathy; **D. des Gewölbes auf die Pfeiler,** pressure of the vaulting on the piers; **Schmerz, der durch den D. eines Knochens auf einen Nerv verursacht wird,** pain caused by a bone pressing on a nerve, by the pressure of a bone on a nerve; **Lähmung, die durch D. auf einen Nervenstamm entsteht,** paralysis caused by pressure (exerted) on a nerve-tree; **die Maschine wird durch einen D. auf den Knopf in Betrieb gesetzt,** the machine is operated by pressing, pushing, a button. **2.** (sensation of) pressure; pressing feeling; oppressive feeling (in one's head, chest, etc.); **einen D. in der Magengrube haben, spüren,** to have a sensation of pressure in the pit of one's stomach. **3.** (*a*) *Ph: Mec: Constr:* pressure; (*surface*) compression; (*axial*) thrust; **hoher, niedriger, D.,** high, low, pressure; **negativer D.,** negative pressure; **kritischer D.,** critical pressure; **osmotischer D.,** osmotic pressure; **D. von fünf Kilogramm pro Quadratzentimeter,** pressure of five kilogrammes to the square centimetre; **Gas unter hohem D.,** gas under high compression; *Meteor:* **atmosphärischer D.,** atmospheric pressure; *Mch:* **unter vollem D.,** at full pressure; **den Kessel unter D. setzen,** to get up pressure, steam; *Mec.E: etc:* **Glied unter D., dem D. ausgesetztes Glied,** member in compression; *Constr: Mec.E:* **den D. auffangen,** to take the thrust; **den D. tragen,** to carry the thrust; (*b*) = **Druckbelastung;** (*c*) = **Drucklager;** (*d*) *Med:* = (i) **Blutdruck;** (ii) = **Pulsdruck. 4. D. auf j-n ausüben,** to bring pressure to bear, to put pressure, on s.o.; **unter D. handeln,** to act under pressure; **unter D. arbeiten,** to work under pressure; **dem D. der öffentlichen Meinung nachgeben,** to yield to the pressure of public opinion; **unter dem D. der Armut,** under the pressure of poverty; **finanzieller D.,** financial pressure; **in unserem Geschäft ist der D. im November am größten,** with us the pressure of business is greatest in November; **im D. der Arbeit,** under the pressure of work; *F:* **(schwer) im D. sein,** (i) to be very rushed; to be (hard) pressed for time; (ii) to be in a quandary; to be hard put to it.

II. Druck, *m.* **-(e)s/-e.** *Print: etc:* **1.** (*a*) printing (of book, etc.); **im D. befindliches Buch, Buch im D.,** book in the press; **das Buch befindet sich, ist, zur Zeit im D.,** the book is in the press now, the book is being printed, is printing, now; **ein Buch zum D. fertig machen,** to get a book ready for the press; (*author's approval of proof*) **'gut zum D.',** 'press'; **wir werden bald mit dem D. beginnen,** we shall start printing soon, we are soon going to press; **etwas in D. geben,** to have sth. printed; **das Buch ist in D. gegeben,** the book has gone to press; **den D. eines Buches übernehmen,** (*of printing firm*) to undertake the printing of a book; (*of publisher*) to undertake the publication of a book, to publish a book; **den D. überwachen,** to supervise the printing, the publication (of book, etc.); to see (book, etc.) through the press; (*in imprint*) **'D. (von) . . .',** 'printed by . . .'; (*b*) (i) (the art of) printing; typography; (ii) textile printing. **2. im D.,** in printed form, in print; **im D. erscheinen,** to appear in print, to be printed, to be published; **ich habe diese Geschichte nie im D. gesehen,** I have never seen this tale in print; **er sieht sich gern im D.,** he likes to see himself in print. **3.** print; type; **großer, kleiner, D.,** large print, type, small print, type; **schwer lesbarer D.,** print difficult to read; **klarer D.,** clear print; **in fettem D.,** in bold type. **4.** (*a*) *Engr: etc:* print; engraving; **eine Sammlung alter Drucke,** a collection of old prints; (*b*) printed book; **frühe Drucke,** early printed books; (*c*) *Tex:* printed material, print; **bunter D.,** coloured print; **D. mit Blumenmuster,** floral print.

Druckakzent, *m. Ling:* stress.

Druckanzug, *m. Av: etc:* pressurized flying suit.

Druckarbeit, *f. Print:* press-work; printing; machining; **(kleinere) Druckarbeiten,** jobbing work, job-work, job-printing (*as distinct from book and newspaper work*); jobs; **die, mit den, Druckarbeiten beginnen,** to start printing.

Druckausgleich, *m.* pressure balance.

Druckausgleichskabine, *f. Av:* pressurized cabin.

Drückbank, *f. Tls:* spinning lathe.

Druckbeanspruchung, *f. Mec.E:* compressive strain; crushing strain.

Druckbehälter, *m.* **1.** = **Druckkammer. 2.** = **Druckwasserspeicher.**

Druckbelastung, *f. Mec.E: Constr: etc:* (compressive) load.

Druckbewilligung, *f.* = **Druckerlaubnis.**

Druckbleistift, *m.* pencil with a retractable point.

Druckbogen, *m. Print:* (printed) sheet.

Druckbrand, *m. Med:* decubitus ulcer, bed-sore.

Druckbuchstabe, *m.* (*a*) *Print:* type; (*b*) block capital, block letter; **in Druckbuchstaben schreiben,** to write in block capitals, in block letters.

druckdicht, *a.* (pressure-)tight; *Av:* pressurized (cabin).

Druckdifferenzverfahren, *n. Surg:* differential pressure anaesthesia.

Drückdrehbank, *f. Tls:* spinning lathe.

Drückeberger, *m.* **-s/-.** *F:* shirker; slacker; (artful) dodger; skulker; *Mil:* malingerer; *Mil: P:* skiver; *Ind:* absentee.

Drückebergerei, *f.* **-/.** *F:* shirking; dodging; skulking; *Mil:* malingering; *Mil: P:* skiving; *Ind:* absenteeism.

Druckeinspritzung, *f. Mec.E: etc:* pump injection; pressure feed.

Druckelektrizität, *f.* piezo-electricity.

Druckempfinden, *n.* pressure sense.

druckempfindlich, *a.* sensitive to pressure; (*of fruit*) easily bruised; (*of velvet*) easily crushed.

Druckempfindlichkeit, *f.* sensitivity to pressure.

Druckempfindung, *f.* **1.** pressure sense. **2.** sensation of pressure, pressing feeling.

drucken[1]. **I.** *v.tr.* **1.** *Print: etc:* to print (book, etc.); to publish (book, etc.); **Visitenkarten d.,** to print visiting-cards; **diese Maschine druckt 80 Blätter in der Minute,** this machine runs off 80 copies a minute; (*of author*) **ein Buch d., d. lassen,** to print, publish, a book, to have a book printed, published; **er sieht sich gerne gedruckt,** he likes to see himself in print; **ich habe diese Geschichte nie gedruckt gesehen,** I have never seen this tale in print; **diese Reden sind gedruckt nicht so interessant,** these speeches are not so interesting in (cold) print; *F:* **lügen wie gedruckt,** to lie like a trooper, like a gas-meter, like a lawyer. **2.** *Tex:* **Muster auf Stoff d.,** to print patterns on material, to print material (with patterns).

II. *vbl s.* **Drucken,** *n. in vbl senses; cp.* **Druck II. 1.**

drücken (*A. & South G. Dial:* **drucken**[2]). **I.** *v.tr.* **1.** to press (sth., s.o.); to squeeze (sponge, etc.); **j-m die Hand d.,** (i) to clasp s.o.'s hand; to press, squeeze, s.o.'s hand; (ii) to shake hands with s.o.; **j-n ans Herz d.,** to press s.o. to one's heart; **den Saft aus einer Zitrone d.,** to squeeze, press, the juice out of a lemon; **Eiter aus einer Wunde d.,** to squeeze pus out of a wound; **etwas durch ein Sieb d.,** to force sth. through a sieve; **etwas in eine Schachtel d.,** to squeeze sth. into a box. **2.** (*a*) **etwas auf etwas** *acc.* **d.,** to impress, (im)print, stamp, sth. (up)on sth.; **ein Siegel auf etwas d.,** to impress, stamp, a seal upon sth.; **einen Stempel auf ein Dokument d.,** to stamp a document; **er drückte ihr einen Kuß auf die Stirn,** he pressed a kiss on her forehead, he kissed her forehead; (*b*) **etwas, j-n, an etwas** *acc.* **d.,** to press sth., s.o., against sth.; **j-n an die Wand d.,** (i) to press s.o. against the wall; (ii) *F:* to push s.o. aside; to make s.o. powerless; **sein Gesicht dicht an die Fensterscheibe gedrückt,** his face pressed close to the window; (*c*) **j-m etwas in die Hand d.,** to give s.o. sth.; to put sth. into s.o.'s hand; to thrust sth. into s.o.'s hand; to slip (money) into s.o.'s hand; (*d*) *Sch: F:* **die Schulbank d.,** to go to school, to be at school. **3.** (*a*) **etwas, j-n, nach unten d.,** to press, push, sth. down; to force s.o. down; (*of burden, etc.*) to weigh s.o. down; **etwas, j-n, nach oben, nach außen, nach innen, zur Seite, d.,** to force sth., s.o., upwards, outwards, inwards, to one side; **j-n zu Boden d.,** to force s.o. to the ground; (*of burden, responsibility, etc.*) to weigh s.o. down; (*b*) to force down (prices, wages, etc.); **die Leistungen d.,** to lower, force down, the standard of work; **die Stimmung d.,** to cast a gloom on the party, to spoil the day; **j-s Stimmung d.,** to make s.o. feel depressed, miserable; to cast a gloom on s.o., to spoil s.o.'s day; *Sp:* **einen Rekord d.,** to lower a record; (*c*) = **bedrücken I.** (*a*); (*d*) *abs.* (*in weight-lifting*) **(beidarmig) d.,** to clean and press; to press. **4.** *Cards:* to discard (cards, suit). **5.** to shape *or* distort (sth.) by pressure; (*a*) **etwas platt, breit, flach, d.,** to flatten sth.; **ein Kind wurde in der Menge zu Tode gedrückt,** a child was crushed to death in the crowd; **wenn der Koffer zu voll ist, werden die Kleider (zu sehr) gedrückt,** if the case is too full the clothes will be crushed; **die Äpfel sind in der Kiste gedrückt worden,** the apples have got bruised in the box; (*b*) *Metalw:* to spin (hollow-ware) (on the lathe).

II. drücken, *v.tr. & i.* (*haben*) **etwas, auf etwas** *acc.,* **d. 1.** to press sth.; to press on sth.; *abs.* to press; **den, auf den, Knopf d.,** to press, push, the button; **auf die Türklinke d.,** to press the door-handle down; **auf seine Feder d.,** to press on one's pen; **nicht zu fest auf den Bleistift d.!** *abs.* **nicht zu fest d.!** don't press too hard on the pencil; don't press too hard; **auf die Tube d.,** (i)

to squeeze the tube, (ii) *Aut: F:* to step on the gas, to step on it. **2.** to press, to be pressing, on sth.; **gegen etwas d.,** to press, to be pressing, against sth.; **ein Knochen drückte auf den Nerv, drückte den Nerv,** a bone was pressing on the nerve; **der Schuh drückt,** the shoe pinches, is too tight; **der Schuh drückt vorne, hinten,** the shoe pinches, is too tight, at the toe, at the heel; *F:* **wissen, wo einen der Schuh drückt,** to know where the shoe pinches. **3. es drückt mein Gewissen,** it weighs on my conscience; **es drückt mein Gewissen, es drückt mich, daß . . . ,** it weighs on my conscience that . . .; **seine Schulden drücken ihn,** his debts weigh him down; **der Gedanke drückt mich,** the thought weighs on my mind; **die Hitze drückt mich,** the heat oppresses me; **das Wetter drückt auf meine Stimmung,** the weather makes me feel depressed, *F:* is getting me down.

III. **sich drücken. 1.** (*a*) **sich in die Ecke d.,** to squeeze (oneself) into the corner; to huddle in the corner; to crouch in the corner; **sich an die Wand d.,** to press against the wall; to flatten oneself against the wall; **die Kinder drückten sich ängstlich in die Ecke,** the children huddled frightened in the corner; **in eine Ecke gedrückt,** huddled, crouched, in a corner; (*b*) (*of clothes, etc.*) to get crushed (in suitcase, etc.); (*c*) (*of thg*) **sich nach unten d.,** to be pressed, forced, pushed, down, to force itself down; **sich nach oben, nach außen, nach innen, zur Seite, d.,** to be forced, to force itself, upwards, outwards, inwards, to one side. **2.** *F:* (*of pers.*) (*a*) to slip away; to steal off; to make oneself scarce; (*b*) **sich vor etwas d.,** to avoid sth., doing sth.; to evade (duty, etc.); to shirk (duty, etc.); to manage to get out of sth.; to back out of sth.; **sich um den, vor dem, Militärdienst d.,** to dodge, shirk, military service; **sich vor, von, der Arbeit d.,** to shirk (hard) work; **sich vor der Verantwortung d.,** to shirk (the) responsibility; **sich vor einer Entscheidung d.,** to shirk, avoid facing, a decision; **ich hoffe, daß ich mich vor der Veranstaltung d. kann,** I hope I can manage to get out of that function; **er versucht, sich davor zu d.,** he is trying to get out of it; he is trying to back out of it; he is trying to shirk it; **sich vor etwas Unangenehmem d.,** to back out of, to dodge, sth. unpleasant.

IV. *vbl s.* **Drücken,** *n.* **1.** *in vbl senses; cp.* **Druck** I. 1. **2.** (sensation of) pressure; pressing feeling; oppressive feeling (in one's head, chest, etc.). **3.** (*in weightlifting*) press.

V. *pr.p. & a.* **drückend,** *in vbl senses; esp.* **1.** heavy (burden, debt, etc.); pressing (debt); **drückende Armut,** dire, wretched, poverty; **drückende Abgaben, drückende Steuerlast,** oppressive taxation; (heavy) burden of taxation. **2.** (*of weather, etc.*) oppressive; close; heavy.

VI. *p.p. & a.* **gedrückt,** *in vbl senses; esp.* **1.** depressed, dejected; **g. sein, in gedrückter Stimmung sein,** to feel depressed, to feel low, to feel very down, to be in low spirits; *adv.* **er ging g. davon,** he went away depressed, in dejection. **2.** *adv.* **g. voll,** crammed full.

Druckentlastung, *f. Mch: Surg: etc:* decompression.

Drucker, *m.* **-s/-.** *Print:* printer; (*for work other than books and newspapers*) job-printer; *Tex:* printer; **D. und Verleger,** printer and publisher.

Drücker, *m.* **-s/-. 1.** *El.E: etc:* push-button (*esp.* for opening door). **2.** *Tchn:* (any) machine component *or* device serving to exert pressure; (*a*) *Tex:* picker stick, driver; (*b*) (*on sewing machine*) presser-bar; presser-foot; (*c*) door-handle, *esp.* lever door-handle; (*d*) Yale-type key; (*e*) *Sm.a:* trigger.

Druckerei, *f.* **-/-en. 1.** printing. **2.** printing-office; printer's; press; printing shop; (*for work other than books and newspapers*) job-office; **D. und Verlag,** printers and publishers; **in einer D. arbeiten,** to work at a printer's; **D. der Universität,** University Press.

Druckereiarbeiter, *m.* worker in the printing trade.

Druckereibesitzer, *m.* (master-)printer.

Druckereigewerbe, *n.* printing trade.

Drückerfuß, *m.* presser-foot (of sewing machine).

Druckerlaubnis, *f. Publ:* imprimatur; *Adm:* licence (to print book, etc.).

Druckermarke, *f. Print:* printer's device, printer's mark.

Druckerpresse, *f.* printing-press.

Druckerschwärze, *f.* printer's ink, printing ink.

Druckerwalze, *f. Print:* impression roller.

Druckerzeichen, *n.* = **Druckermarke.**

druckfähig, *a. Print: etc:* (*a*) (*of paper, material*) impressible; (*b*) = **druckreif.**

Druckfahne, *f. Print:* (galley-)proof.

Druckfarbe, *f. Print:* printing ink, printer's ink; *Tex:* printing colour.

Druckfeder, *f. Mec.E:* compression spring.

Druckfehler, *m.* misprint, printer's error, erratum; literal.

Druckfehlerteufel, der. *Print: F:* the gremlin who creates misprints.

Druckfehlerverzeichnis, *n.* list of errata, 'errata'.

druckfertig, *a. Print:* ready for press; 'press'.

druckfest, *a.* (*a*) *Mec.E: etc:* resistant to compression *or* thrust; (*b*) *Av:* pressurized (cabin, etc.).

Druckfestigkeit, *f.* resistance to pressure; *Mec.E: etc:* compressive strength; crushing strength.

Druckfigur, *f. Physiol:* (pressure) phosphene.

Druckfilz, *m. Print:* cylinder felt.

Druckfirnis, *m. Print:* litho varnish.

Druckfläche, *f.* **1.** *Ph: etc:* pressure plane. **2.** *Meteor:* isobaric surface.

Druckflasche, *f. Ind:* aspirator; siphon.

Druckförderung, *f. Mec.E:* pressure feed.

Druckform, *f.* (*a*) *Print:* forme; (*b*) *Tex:* block; engraved roller; stencil.

Druckfüllstift, *m.* = **Druckbleistift.**

Druckfüßchen, *n.* presser-foot (of sewing-machine).

Druckgas, *n.* pressure gas.

Druckgefälle, *n. Ph: etc:* pressure gradient, pressure drop; *Hyd.E:* head of water; hydraulic head; *Meteor:* pressure gradient, barometric, isobaric, gradient.

Druckgefäß, *n. Ch: Ind: etc:* pressure vessel.

Druckgefühl, *n.* sensation, feeling, of pressure.

Druckgenehmigung, *f.* = **Druckerlaubnis.**

Druckgeschwür, *n. Med:* decubitus (ulcer), bed-sore.

Druckgewerbe, *n.* printing trade.

Druckglied, *n. Mec.E: etc:* member in compression.

Druckguß, *m. Metall:* **1.** (pressure) die-casting. **2.** (pressure) die-castings.

Druckhub, *m. I.C.E:* compression stroke.

Druckhöhe, *f. Ph: etc:* head; *Hyd.E:* hydraulic head; head of water; head of delivery (of pump).

Druckjahr, *n. Publ:* year of publication (of book, etc.).

Druckkabine, *f. Av:* pressurized cabin.

Druckkammer, *f.* **1.** air-drum; air-reservoir; air-chamber (of torpedo, etc.); cylinder (of die-casting machine); *Hyd.E:* air-caisson. **2.** (hydraulic) cylinder.

Druckkasten, *m.* **1.** (toy) printing set. **2.** *Hyd.E:* caisson.

Druckkattun, *m. Tex:* printed calico.

Druckkessel, *m. Ch: Ind:* autoclave.

Druckknopf, *m.* (*a*) press-fastener, snap-fastener, press-stud, press-button, patent fastener, dome-fastener, *F:* popper; (*b*) *El:* push-button; bell-push; *El.E: Clockm: etc:* push-piece.

Druckknopfbetätigung, *f. El.E: Tp: etc:* push-button control.

Druckknopfschalter, *m. El:* push-button switch.

Druckknopfsteuerung, *f. El.E:* push-button control.

Druckkocher, *m. Dom.Ec:* pressure-cooker; *Ind:* pressure-boiler; autoclave.

Druckkolben, *m.* **1.** *Mec.E: Hyd.E:* piston; plunger; ram. **2.** *Ch: etc:* pressure flask.

Druckkosten, *pl.* printing costs.

Druckkraft, *f. Mec.E: etc:* force of compression.

Druckkugelschreiber, *m.* retractable ball-point pen.

Drucklack, *m.* Indian ink, *U.S:* India ink.

Drucklager, *n. Mec.E:* thrust bearing; thrust block.

Drucklähmung, *f. Med:* pressure paralysis.

Drucklast, *f. Mec.E: Constr: etc:* (compressive) load.

Drucklegung, *f. Print:* printing (of book, etc.); going to press; **während der D. dieses Buches . . . ,** while this book was in the press . . . , while this book was being printed, was printing . . .; **rechtzeitig für die D.,** in time for press; **wir werden mit der D. beginnen,** we are going to press; **vor der D.,** before going to press.

Druckleitung, *f.* **1.** *Civ.E: etc:* delivery pipe; *Hyd.E:* penstock. **2.** = **Druckwasserleitung.**

Drucklinie, *f. Mec: Constr:* axis of compression *or* thrust.

Druckluft, *f.* compressed air; **durch D. betrieben, betätigt,** pneumatically operated; pneumatically controlled; **Betätigung durch D.,** pneumatic operation; pneumatic control.

Druckluft-, *comb.fm. Tchn:* pneumatic . . .; air-, compressed air . . .; **Druckluftanlage** *f,* pneumatic plant, compressed air plant; **Druckluftförderer** *m,* pneumatic elevator; **Drucklufthammer** *m,* pneumatic hammer, air-hammer.

Druckluftbehälter, *m.* = **Druckkammer** 1.

druckluftbetätigt, *a.* pneumatically operated; pneumatically controlled; pneumatic (tool, etc.).

Druckluftbohrer, *m. Tls:* pneumatic drill.

Druckluftbremse, *f.* air-brake, pneumatic brake.

Drucklufterzeuger, *m.* (air) compressor.

Drucklufthammer, *m. Tls:* pneumatic hammer, air-hammer.

Druckluftkammer, *f.* = **Druckkammer** 1.

Druckluftkrankheit, *f. Med:* caisson disease.

Druckluftleitung, *f. Mec.E:* delivery pipe; delivery tube.

Druckluftpresse, *f.* pneumatic press; air flattening press.

Druckluftwerkzeuge, *n.pl.* pneumatic tools.

Druckmagnet, *m. Tg:* print magnet.

Druckmaschine, *f. Print: Tex:* printing machine.

Drückmaschine, *f. Metalw:* swaging machine.

Druckmesser, *m.* manometer, pressure-gauge; *Med:* = **Blutdruckmesser.**

Druckminderungsventil, *n. Mec.E:* pressure relief valve.

Druckmittelpunkt, *m.* = **Druckpunkt.**

Drucköl, *n. Mec.E:* pressure-fed oil; forced oil.

Drucköler, *m. Mch: etc:* force-feed oiler; *Aut: etc:* pressure oiler.

Druckölung, *f.* = **Druckschmierung.**

Druckort, *m. Publ:* place of publication (of book, etc.).

Druckpapier, *n. Print:* printing-paper.

Druckplatte, *f.* **1.** *Print:* plate; electrotype, *F:* electro; stereotype (plate); *Engr:* plate. **2.** *Print:* = **Drucktiegel. 3.** *Mec.E: etc:* pressure plate.

Druckposten, *m. F:* soft job, cushy job.

Druckpresse, *f. Print:* printing-press.

Druckprobe, *f.* **1.** *Mec.E:* compression test; pressure test. **2.** *Print:* specimen.

Druckprüfer, *m.* **1.** *Mec.E: etc:* pressure-gauge, pressure-tester; *Aut:* tyre pressure-gauge. **2.** *Print:* (proof-)reader, reviser, corrector of the press.

Druckpumpe, *f.* compression pump; pressure pump; *Hyd.E:* force pump.

Druckpunkt, *m.* **1.** *Mec: Aer: etc:* centre of pressure. **2.** area *or* spot sensitive to pressure; pressure point, pressure spot. **3.** *Sm.a:* **D. nehmen,** to take first pressure.

Druckregler, *m. Mec.E: Mch: etc:* pressure regulator.

druckreif, *a.* (*a*) (*of literary work, etc.*) ready for publication; (*b*) = **druckfertig.**

Druckring, *m. Mec.E:* thrust collar.

Druckrohr, *n.,* **Druckröhre,** *f.* pressure pipe; *Civ.E: etc:* delivery pipe; *Hyd.E:* head-pipe.

Druckrolle, *f. Agr:* press-wheel (of drill).

Drucksache, *f.* **1.** *Post:* printed matter; printed papers, *U.S:* second *or* third class matter; **D. zu ermäßigter Gebühr,** printed papers at reduced rate; **etwas als D. schicken,** to send sth. as printed matter, at printed paper rate. **2.** = **Druckschrift** 2.

Drucksäule, *f. Ph: etc:* head; *Hyd.E:* head of water; hydraulic head; head of delivery (of pump).

Druckschalter, *m.* pressure switch.

Druckscheibe, *f. Mec.E:* thrust washer.

Druckschmerz, *m.* (*a*) pain caused by pressure; (*b*) painful feeling of pressure.

Druckschmierung, *f. Mec.E: etc:* pressure lubrication, forced lubrication, force(d)-feed lubrication; forced feed (of oil).

Druckschmierapparat, *m.* pressure lubricator.

Druckschmierpresse, *f. Mec.E: Aut:* grease-gun, grease-injector.

Druckschraube, *f.* **1.** (*a*) press screw, binding screw, clamp(ing) screw, set screw; (*b*) thrust bolt; thrusting-screw (of a cheese-press). **2.** *Av:* pusher airscrew, *U.S:* pusher propeller; **Flugzeug mit D.,** pusher aircraft.

Druckschrift, *f.* **1.** (*a*) *Print:* type; (*b*) block capitals, block letters; **eine Adresse in D. schreiben,** to write an address in block capitals, block letters, to print an address. **2.** publication, printed work; pamphlet; leaflet; prospectus.

Druckseite, *f.* **1.** compression face; *Av:* **D. des Luftschraubenblattes,** pressure side of the airscrew blade. **2.** *Print:* printed page.

drucksen, *v.i.* (*haben*) *F:* (*a*) to hesitate, *F:* to hum and haw, to shilly-shally; **an einem Brief d.,** to struggle with a letter; **er druckste an der Antwort,** he hummed and hawed over the answer; (*b*) (i) to whimper; (ii) to try to suppress sobs.

Drucksinn, *m.* pressure sense.

Druckspannung, *f. Mec.E:* compressive stress.

Druckspeicher, *m.* **1.** compressed air tank. **2.**=**Druckwasserspeicher.**

Druckspeicherpumpwerk, *n. Hyd.E:* force pump.

Druckstab, *m. Constr:* member in compression.

Druckstelle, *f.* pressure point; (*on fruit*) bruise; (*in carpet, velvet, etc.*) mark (caused by pressure); (*on velvet*) crushed spot.

Druckstempel, *m.* **1.** *Mec.E:* piston; ram; plunger (of pump, etc.); plunger-piston; *Metall:* punch; die. **2.** *Print:* block (for wood-cut).

Druckstift, *m.*=**Druckbleistift.**

Druckstock, *m. Print:* (i) block; (ii) electrotype, *F:* electro.

Druckstoß, *m.* **1.** *Hyd:* water hammer. **2.** *I.C.E:* pressure surge (from injector).

Drucktelegraph, *m. Tg:* printing telegraph, telegraph printing machine, typotelegraph.

Drucktelegraphie, *f. Tg:* printing (telegraph) system, typotelegraphy.

Druckteller, *m.* plate (of press).

Drucktiegel, *m. Print:* platen (of printing-press).

Drucktisch, *m. Tex:* printing table.

Drucktopf, *m.* (*a*) *Ind: Ch: etc:* autoclave; (*b*) *Dom.Ec:* pressure-cooker.

Drucktuch, *n. Print: Tex:* (press-, printing) blanket.

Drucktype, *f. Print:* type.

Druckventil, *n.* delivery-valve (of pump).

Druckverband, *m. Surg:* compression bandage.

Druckverfahren, *n. Print: Tex:* printing process.

Druckverlust, *m. Mec.E:* loss of pressure; *Hyd.E:* loss of head, loss of (water) pressure.

Druckverlusthöhe, *f. Ph: Hyd.E:* friction head.

Druckvermerk, *m.* printer's imprint; (*in early printed books*) colophon.

Druckversuch, *m. Mec.E: etc:* compression test; crushing test (for bricks, etc.).

Druckvorlage, *f. Print:* copy, manuscript; original (from which a block is made).

Druckwalze, *f.* **1.** *Print: Tex: etc:* impression roller. **2.** *Agr: etc:* roller; *Dom.Ec:* top roller (of mangle).

Druckwasser, *n.* water under pressure, pressure water; **Druckwasser-,** *comb.fm.* hydraulic . . .; . . . by hydraulic power; **Druckwasseranlage** *f,* hydraulic plant; **Druckwasserbetrieb** *m,* working by hydraulic power.

Druckwasserbehälter, *m.* (*a*) = **Druckwasserspeicher;** (*b*)=**Druckkammer** 2.

Druckwasserleitung, *f. Hyd.E:* (water) pressure main(s).

Druckwassermaschine, *f.* hydraulic machine; water-engine.

Druckwasserpresse, *f.* hydraulic press.

Druckwasserpumpwerk, *n. Hyd.E:* force pump.

Druckwassersammler, *m. Hyd.E:* hydraulic accumulator.

Druckwassersäule, *f.* hydraulic head.

Druckwasserspeicher, *m. Hyd.E:* hydraulic accumulator.

Druckwelle, *f.* **1.** pressure wave. **2.** *Mec.E:* thrust-shaft.

Drückzange, *f. Tls:* bent-nose pliers.

Druckzwang, *m. Sch:* obligation to have one's doctoral dissertation printed.

Druckzylinder, *m.* **1.** *Mec.E: Hyd.E:* pressure cylinder. **2.** *Print:* impression cylinder.

Drud, *m.* -(s)/-e, elf.

Drude¹, *f.* -/-n, witch; elf.

Drude², *m.* -n/-n. **1.** elf. **2.** (*erroneously*) = **Druide.**

Druden-, *comb.fm. cp.* **Druiden-.**

Drudenbaum, *m.* **1.** witches' tree. **2.** *Bot:* common (British) oak.

Drudenbeere, *f. Bot:* whortleberry, bilberry.

Drudenbeutel, *m. Fung:* puff-ball, fuzz-ball.

Drudenbusch, *m. Bot:* =**Bärlapp.**

Drudeneiche, *f. Bot:* common (British) oak.

Drudenfuß, *m.* **1.** pentagram, pentacle, pentalpha; *Her:* pentalpha. **2.** *Bot:*=**Bärlapp.**

Drudenmehl, *n. Pharm: etc:*=**Bärlappmehl.**

Drudenmistel, *f. Bot:* mistletoe.

Drudenstein, *m.* **1.** Druidical bead, adder stone. **2.**=**Druidenstein.**

Drudenzopf, *m.* elf-lock.

druff, *adv. F:*=**darauf, drauf; immer (feste) d.!** give him, them, what for!

Druide [druˑˈiːdə], *m.* **-n/-n.** Druid.

Druiden-, *comb.fm. cp.* **Druden-.**

Druidenaltar, *m.* Druid's altar; Druid stone.

Druidenamulett, *n.* (*a*) Druidical bead, adder stone; (*b*) Druid's egg.

Druidenstein, *m.* Druid stone; Druid's altar.

Druidentum, *n.* -s/. Druidism.

Druidin, *f.* **-/-innen.** Druidess.

druidisch, *a.* Druidical.

drum. I. *adv., conj. & rel.pron.*=**darum;** *F:* **alles, was so d. und dran ist,** the whole paraphernalia; **ich gebe nichts drum,** I don't care for it; **ich hätte Gelegenheit, jeden Tag ins Kino zu gehen, aber ich gebe nicht viel d.,** I could go to the cinema every day, but I don't care much for it; **drum!** so that's (the reason) why! so that's the reason!

II. **Drum,** *n.* **das D. und Dran,** the things connected with it, the things that go with it; **mit allem D. und Dran,** with everything connected with it, with all the things that go with it, *F:* lock, stock, and barrel; **er kaufte das Haus mit allem D. und Dran,** he bought the house with everything in it, he bought up the house lock, stock, and barrel.

drumlegen, *v.tr. sep.*=**darumlegen.**

Drumlin, *m.* -s/-s. *Geol:* drumlin, drum.

Drumme, *f.* -/-n, wooden culvert.

Drummondsch [ˈdramǝndʃ], *a.* **Drummondsches Licht,** Drummond light.

drunten, *adv.* (down) below; down; **da d., dort d.,** down there; **d. im Tal,** down in the valley.

drunter, *adv.*=**darunter; es ging, alles ging, d. und drüber,** everything was in confusion, there was complete disorder, *F:* chaos; *F:* everything was topsy-turvy; **bei den Müllers geht alles d. und drüber,** everything is at sixes and sevens at the Müllers'.

Drusch, *m.* -(e)s/-e. *Husb:* **1.** threshing (of corn). **2.** (batch of) threshed corn, threshing.

Drüschen [ˈdryːsçǝn], *n.* -s/-. *Biol:* glandule.

Drüschling, *m.* -s/-e. *Fung:* (common) mushroom.

Druse¹, *f.* -/-n. **1.** *Geol:* druse; geode. **2.** *Vet:* strangles. **3.** *A:*=**Drüse. 4.** *Med:* nodule consisting of actinomyces.

Druse², *f.* -/-n, *usu. pl.* **Drusen,** lees (in new wine).

Druse³, *m.* -n/-n. *Ethn:* Druse.

Drüse, *f.* -/-n. *Biol:* gland; *Anat: Med:* **endokrine D., D. mit innerer Sekretion, D. ohne Ausführungsgang,** ductless gland, endocrine; **geschwollene Drüsen haben,** to have swollen glands; *F:* **an (den) Drüsen leiden, Drüsen haben,** (i) to have swollen glands; (ii) to suffer from a disease of the glands.

drüsenartig, *a. Biol: Med:* like a gland; glandular; adenomatous.

Drusenasche, *f.* calcined lees.

Drusenbranntwein, *m. Dist:* marc.

Drüsenentzündung, *f. Med:* adenitis.

Drüsenerkrankung, *f.* glandular affection.

Drüsenfieber, *n. Med:* infectious mononucleosis, glandular fever.

drüsenförmig, *a.* glandiform, glandulous.

Drüsengeschwulst, *f. Med:* adenoma, glandular tumour.

Drüsenglocke, *f. Bot:* adenophora, gland bell-flower.

Drüsenhaar, *n. Bot:* glandular hair, excretory hair.

Drüsenkind, *n. F:* over-fat child (suffering from glandular disturbance).

Drüsenklee, *m. Bot:* psoralea; breadroot.

drusenkrank, *a. Vet:* (horse) suffering from strangles.

drüsenkrank, *a.* suffering from a glandular disease.

Drüsenkrankheit, *f.* glandular disease.

Drüsenleiden, *n.* glandular complaint, glandular disease.

Drüsenmagen, *m. Orn:* proventriculus, glandular stomach, true stomach.

Drusenöl, *n.* oil of wine, oenanthic ether.

Drüsenpest, *f. Med:* bubonic plague.

Drusenschwarz, *n. Art: etc:* Frankfort black.

Drüsenschwellung, *f. Med:* swelling of the glands swollen glands.

Drüsentätigkeit, *f.* working of the glands.

drüsentragend, *a. Bot:* glanduliferous.

Drüsenträger, *m.pl. Bot:* adenophora.

Drüsenverhärtung, *f. Med:* adenosclerosis; bubo.

Drüsenzelle, *f. Anat: Bot:* glandular cell.

drusig, *a.* **1.** *Geol:* containing druses. **2.** *Vet:* (horse) suffering from strangles.

drüsig, *a. Biol:* glandular; glandulous.

Drüswurz, *f. Bot:* **1.** oenanthe, water-dropwort. **2.** buttercup.

Dryade [dryˑˈaːdǝ], *f.* -/-n. **1.** *Myth:* dryad, wood-nymph. **2.** *Bot:* dryas, mountain avens.

Dryanderdistel [dryˑˈandǝr-], *f. Bot:* dryandra carduceus.

Dryandra [dryˑˈandraː], *f.* -/-dren. *Bot:* **distelblättrige D.,** dryandra carduceus.

Dryas [ˈdryːaˑs], *f.* -/-aden [dryˑˈaːdǝn] =**Dryade.**

Dschabalpur [dʒaˑbalˈpuːr]. *Pr.n.n.* -s. *Geog:* Jabalpur.

Dschagannath [dʒaˑgaˑˈnaːt], *m.* -s/. *Rel.Hist:* Juggernaut.

Dschaina [ˈdʒainaː], *m.* -/-. *Hindu Rel:* Jain.

Dschainalehre, *f. Hindu Rel:* Jainism.

Dschaipur [dʒaiˈpuːr]. *Pr.n.n.* -s. *Geog:* Jaipur.

Dschami [ˈdʒaːmiː], *f.* -/. (*mosque*) jami.

Dschamna, die [ˈdʒamnaː], -. *Pr.n. Geog:* the (river) Jumna.

Dschangel [ˈdʒaŋǝl], *m.* -s/- =**Dschungel.**

Dschebel [ˈdʒeːbǝl], *m.* -s/-. *Geog:* jebel.

Dschelada [dʒeˑˈlaːdaː], *m.* -s/-s. *Z:* gelada.

Dschengis Chan [ˈdʒɛŋgis ˈkaːn]. *Pr.n.m.* - -s. *Hist:* Genghis Khan.

Dschibuti [dʒiˑˈbuːtiː]. *Pr.n.n.* -s. *Geog:* Jibuti(l), Djibouti.

Dschiggetai [dʒigǝˈtaːi], *m.* -s/-s. *Z:* dziggetai; wild ass.

Dschihad [dʒiˑˈhaːt], *m.* -/. *Rel.Hist:* Jihad, jehad; holy war.

Dschingis Chan [ˈdʒiŋgis ˈkaːn]. *Pr.n.m.* - -s. *Hist:* Genghis Khan.

Dschinn [dʒin], *m.* -s/-s. *Arab. Myth: Moham.Rel:* jinn(ee); *pl.* **die Dschinns,** the jinn, *F:* the jinns.

Dschiu-Dschitsu [ˈdʒiːuˑˈdʒitsuː], *n.* -s/. jiu-jitsu.

Dschonke [ˈdʒoŋkǝ], *f.* -/-n =**Dschunke.**

Dschungel [ˈdʒuŋǝl], *m. & n.* -s/-, *& f.* -/-n, jungle.

Dschungelfieber, *n. Med:* jungle-fever.

Dschungelhuhn, *n. Orn:* jungle-fowl.

Dschungelkatze, *f. Z:* jungle-cat.

Dschungelkauz, *m. Orn:* jungle owlet.

Dschungelrind, *n. Z:* gaur.

Dschunke [ˈdʒuŋkǝ], *f.* -/-n. *Nau:* junk.

Dsungarei, die [dzuŋgaˑˈrai]. *Pr.n.* -. *Geog:* Zungaria, Dzungaria.

du¹, *pers.pron. second pers. sg. nom.* (*gen.* **deiner,** *A. & Lit:* **dein;** *dat.* **dir;** *acc.* **dich**) (*familiar form of address to relations, intimate friends, children, animals, thgs; for formal address see* **Sie;** *written with capital* D *in letters or when addressing the Deity*) **1.** (*a*) you; **du hast recht,** you are right; **wo bist du?** where are you? **bist du das?** is that you? **warst du es, der das getan hat?** was it you who did that? **du selbst,** you yourself; **j-n du nennen, j-n mit du anreden, du zu j-m sagen,** to use the familiar form of address to s.o.; **du zueinander sagen,** to use the familiar form of address to one another; **mit j-m auf du und du stehen,** to be on familiar terms with s.o.; **ich verstehe dich nicht,** I don't understand you; **er wird dir das Buch geben,** he'll give you the book, he'll give the book to you; **ich will dir keine Ungelegenheiten bereiten,** I don't want to give you any trouble; **scheint dir die Sonne ins Gesicht?** is the sun shining in your eyes? **er wird dir nicht im Wege stehen,** he won't stand in your way; **ich gedenke deiner,** *A. & Lit:* **dein,** I am thinking of you, *A. & Lit:* of thee; **er ist deiner nicht wert,** he is not worthy of you; **es ist deiner nicht würdig,** it is not worthy of you; (*b*) (*in Biblical style; to the Deity in prayers, etc.; in dialect and poetry; formerly in Quaker speech*) thou; **Vater unser, der du bist im Himmel,** our Father, which art in Heaven; *B:* **du sollst nicht töten,** thou shalt not kill; **wir flehen dich an,** we beseech thee; *Ecc:* **wir sagen Dir Dank,** we give Thee thanks, we give thanks (un)to Thee. **2.** (*a*) (*emphasis after imperative*) you, yourself; **sprich du mit ihm!** ˈyou speak to him! **da siehe du zu!** (you) see to it yourself! **kümmre du dich um deine Angelegenheiten!** mind your own business! (*b*) (*in exclamations*) *F:* **du großer Gott!** *F:* (good) Lord! oh Lord! *F:* **ach du Schreck! du liebes bißchen!** *F:* (good) gracious! heavens! *F:* **du ahnst es nicht!** *F:* oh dear! heavens! **und, hast du nicht gesehen, war er um die Ecke!** and he'd rounded the corner in a flash! (*c*) *ethic dat.* **das ist dir ein Kerl!** that's an amazing fellow! there's an amazing fellow for you! **der verdient dir ein Heidengeld!** he earns an unholy amount of money.

Du², *n.* -s/-s, **j-m das Du anbieten,** to suggest the familiar form of address to s.o., to suggest that s.o. should call one 'du'; *Phil:* **die Beziehung zum Du,** the relation to the non-ego.

Dual [ˈduːaːl], *m.* -s/. *Gram:* dual (number, form).

Dualform, *f. Gram:* dual (form).

Dualin [duˑaˑˈliːn], *n.* -s/. *Exp:* dualin.

Dualismus [duˑaˑˈlismus], *m.* -/. dualism.

Dualist [duˑaˑˈlist], *m.* -en/-en, dualist.

dualistisch [duˑaˑˈlistiʃ], *a.* dualistic.

Dualität [duˑaˑliˑˈtɛːt], *f.* -/. duality.

Dualsystem, *n. Mth:* binary (number) system, binary code.

Dualzahl, *f. Mth:* binary number.

Dübel, *m.* -s/-, (*a*) *Carp:* dowel(-pin), coak; *Constr:* dowel, gudgeon, plug, joggle (in stonework, timber); *Sculp:* pin; dowel; **etwas mit Dübeln (an etwas** *dat.***) befestigen,** to fasten sth.

with dowels (to sth.); to dowel sth. on (to sth.); (*b*) *Constr:* plug (*for nail, hook, etc. in wall*).

Dübelgebälk, *n.* dowelled beams.

Dübelloch, *n. Carp: Constr:* dowel-hole.

dubeln, *v.tr. Cin:* to dub (a film).

dübeln, *v.tr. Carp: Constr: etc:* to dowel.

Dübelverbindung, *f. Constr:* joining (of blocks of stone) by means of a gudgeon, a joggle.

Dubiosen [du·bi'oːzən], *f.pl. Com:* doubtful debts, bad debts.

dubitativ [du·bi·ta·'tiːf], *a. Gram:* dubitative.

Duble ['duːbəl], *n.* -s/-s. = **Double.**

Dublee [du·'bleː], *n.* -s/-s. **1.** rolled gold. **2.** *Bill:* stroke off the cushion; **auf D. spielen,** to play off the cushion.

Dubleegold, *n.* rolled gold; **eine Uhr aus D.,** a rolled-gold watch.

Dubleewaren, *f.pl.* gold-plated goods.

Dublette [du·'blɛtə], *f.* -/-n. **1.** duplicate. **2.** (*a*) *Lap: Ling: Opt: etc:* doublet; (*b*) *Mus:* (*organ stop*) doublet. **3.** *Ven:* doublet (shot); right-and-left.

dublieren [du·'bliːrən], *v.tr.* (*a*) to line (a coat, etc.); *Metall:* to plate (metal); (*b*) *Tex:* to draw, to double (the thread); (*c*) *abs. Print:* to mackle, slur; (*d*) *abs. Bill:* to play off the cushion; (*e*) *Th: Cin:* to double (an actor); (*f*) *Nau:* **ein Kap d.,** to double a cape.

Dublierer [du·'bliːrər], *m.* -s/-. *Tex:* (*pers.*) doubler.

Dubliermaschine, *f. Tex:* lapping machine.

Dublone [du·'bloːnə], *f.* -/-n. *Num:* doubloon.

Duchesse [dy·'ʃɛs(ə)], *f.* -/. *Tex:* duchesse satin.

Duchessespitzen, *f.pl.* duchesse lace.

Duchoboren [du·xo·'boːrən], *m.pl. Rel.Hist:* Doukhobors.

Ducht, *f.* -/-en. **1.** strand (of rope). **2.** thwart (of rowing-boat).

Duck [da·k], *m.* -(e)s/-e. *Tex:* duck.

Dückdalbe, *f. usu. pl.* **Dückdalben,** *Nau:* (*group of mooring posts*) dolphin.

ducken, *v.* **1.** *v.tr.* (*a*) to duck (one's head); **er duckte den Kopf, um dem Hieb auszuweichen,** he ducked his head to avoid the blow; (*b*) to duck (s.o.); (*c*) **j-n d.,** to humble, crush, cow, s.o., to break s.o.'s spirit; *F:* to take s.o. down a peg (or two); **ein geducktes Wesen,** (i) a humble, crushed, cowed, nature; (ii) a servile nature. **2.** *v.i.* (*haben*) = **sich ducken,** *q.v. under* 3; **ins Wasser d.,** to dive into the water. **3. sich ducken,** (*a*) to duck; **er duckte sich vor dem Schlag,** he ducked to avoid the blow; **er duckte sich hinter die Hecke, um nicht gesehen zu werden,** he ducked, dodged, behind the hedge so as not to be seen; **sie duckte sich hinter dem Zaun,** she ducked down, crouched, behind the fence; **der Hase duckte sich im Grase,** the hare crouched in the grass; **duck dich!** duck! look out! mind your head! (*b*) **sich (vor j-m) d.,** (i) to bow (to s.o.), (ii) to humble oneself (before s.o.); to cringe (before s.o.).

Duckente, *f. Orn: Dial:* teal.

Ducker, *m.* -s/-. **1.** *Z:* duiker, duikerbok. **2.** = **Düker.**

Dücker, *m.* -s/- = **Düker.**

Duckmäuser, *m.* -s/-, sly, hypocritical, person; servile person; yes-man; (*school language*) goody-goody.

Duckmäuserei, *f.* -/. slyness; hypocrisy; servility.

duckmäuserig, duckmäuserisch, *a.* sly; hypocritical; servile; (*school language*) goody-goody.

Duckstein, *m. North G.Dial:* (*a*) *Geol:* calcareous tufa; (*b*) *Miner:* (i) trass; (ii) dolerite.

Ductus ['duktus], *m.* -/-. **1.** *Anat:* duct; **D. choledochus** [ço·'leːdo·xus], choledoch duct; **D. sudoriferus** [zu·do·'riːfe·rus], sweat-duct. **2.** = **Duktus.**

Dudeldei, Dudeldidel, Dudeldum, *n.* -s/. monotonous sound (made by musical instrument).

Dudelei, *f.* -/-en. *Pej:* (*of music*) tooting, tootling (on wind-instrument); droning.

Dudeler, *m.* -s/-, (*a*) piper, bagpipe-player; (*b*) one who hums, who drools out a song; bad singer; one who toots, tootles, on a wind-instrument; bad player.

dudeln, *v.* **1.** *v.i.* (*haben*) (*a*) to play the bagpipes; (*b*) (*of pers.*) to hum, to drone; to toot, tootle (on a wind-instrument); (*of barrel organ*) to grind away; **den ganzen Tag dudelt er einem die Ohren voll,** he goes on droning out tunes the whole day. **2.** *v.tr.* to hum, *F:* to drool out (tune), to sing (tune) monotonously.

Dudelsack, *m. Mus:* bagpipes; **D., auf dem D., spielen,** to play the bagpipes.

Dudelsackpfeifer, *m.* piper, bagpipe-player.

Dudler, *m.* -s/- = **Dudeler.**

Dudu, *m.* -s/-s. *Orn:* dodo.

Duell [du·'ɛl], *n.* -s/-e, duel; **ein D. mit j-m ausfechten,** to fight a duel with s.o.; **j-n zum D. herausfordern,** to challenge s.o. to a duel, to call s.o. out; **ein D. auf Pistolen,** a pistol duel; **ein D. auf Säbel,** a duel with swords; **ein D. auf Leben und Tod,** a duel to the death; **amerikanisches D.,** drawing of lots to decide which of two persons shall commit suicide.

Duellant [du·ɛ'lant], *m.* -en/-en, dueller, duellist.

duellieren (sich) [du·ɛ'liːrən], *v.refl.* **sich mit j-m d.,** to fight a duel with s.o.

Duenja [du·'ɛnjaː], *f.* -/-s, duenna, chaperon.

Duett [du·'ɛt], *n.* -(e)s/-e. *Mus:* duet.

Duettist [du·ɛ'tist], *m.* -en/-en. *Mus:* duettist.

duff, *a. North G.Dial:* dull.

Düffel, *m.* -s/-. *Tex:* duffel, duffle.

Duft[1], *m.* -(e)s/⸗e. **1.** (*a*) *Poet:* fine vapour; (*b*) foaminess, filminess (of dresses). **2.** (*usu. agreeable*) odour, smell; perfume, fragrance, scent (of flowers, etc.); aroma (of tobacco, wine, etc.). **3.** (*a*) bloom (on fruit); (*b*) white frost.

Duft[2], *f.* -/-en, strand (of rope).

Duftanhang, *m. Dial:* white frost.

Duftbruch, *m.* splitting of boughs by white frost.

dufte, *a. F:* fine, grand, smashing, ripping; **ein dufter Kerl, eine dufte Nummer,** a smashing, ripping, grand, fellow.

duften, *v.i.* (*haben*) **1.** *Poet:* to be vaporous, misty. **2.** (*of flowers, etc.*) to smell, to have a scent, perfume; to be fragrant; (*of tobacco, wine, etc.*) to be fragrant, aromatic; **(süß) d.,** to smell sweet, to exhale a sweet perfume, to have a sweet scent; **(süß) duftend,** sweet-smelling, fragrant; **die Rosen duften,** (i) the roses smell, have a scent; (ii) the roses smell sweet; **diese Blumen duften nicht, das sind keine duftenden Blumen,** these flowers have no smell, scent, these flowers don't smell, are scentless; **der Garten duftet von unzähligen Blumen,** the garden is fragrant with countless flowers; **es duftete herrlich nach Blumen im Zimmer,** there was a wonderful smell of flowers in the room; **duftender Wein,** fragrant wine.

duftig, *a.* **1.** (*of atmosphere, air, cloud, etc.*) fine, light; (*of material*) filmy, gossamer; delicate; (*of dress, nightdress, etc.*) filmy, gossamer; (*of ball dress, bouffant petticoat, lace, etc.*) frothy, foamy; (*of dress, blouse, etc.*) light and dainty. **2.** = **duftend,** *q.v. under* **duften** 2. **3.** (*a*) (*of fruit*) covered with bloom; pruinose; (*b*) frosted, covered with frost.

Duftorgan, *n. Ent:* scent organ.

Duftstoff, *m. Ch:* aroma, aromatic essence, aromatic oil.

Duftstrauch, *m. Bot:* evodia.

Duftwasser, *n.* -s/⸗er, perfume, scent.

Dugong ['duːgɔŋ], *m.* -s/-e & -s. *Z:* dugong, sea-cow.

Dukaten [du·'kaːtən], *m.* -s/-. *Num:* ducat.

Dukatenblume, *f. Bot:* = **Dukatenröschen.**

Dukatenfalter, Dukatenvogel, *m. Ent:* copper (butterfly).

Dukatenröschen, *n. Bot:* mouse-ear hawkweed.

Dukaton [du·ka·'toːn], *m.* -s/-e. *Num:* ducatoon.

Dukdalbe, *f. Nau:* = **Dückdalbe.**

Duk-Duk, *m.* -s/. (*native secret society*) duk-duk.

Düker, *m.* -s/-. *Hyd.E:* siphon.

duktil [duk'tiːl], *a.* ductile.

Duktilität [dukti·li·'tɛːt], *f.* -/. ductility.

Duktor ['duktor], *m.* -s/-en [-'toːrən]. *Tex.Print:* ductor, doctor.

Duktus ['duktus], *m.* -/. lines (of building, etc.); *Calligraphy:* general appearance (of handwriting), *ductus.*

Dulcian [dultsi'aːn], *n.* -(s)/-e. *Mus:* (*a*) bassoon; (*b*) soft reed organ stop.

dulden. I. *v.* **1.** *v.tr.* (*a*) to bear, stand, endure (pain, grief, etc.); *B:* **die Liebe . . . duldet alles,** charity . . . endureth all things; (*b*) to tolerate, suffer, put up with, bear, stand, endure (sth., s.o.); to allow, permit (sth.); **d., daß etwas geschieht,** to allow sth. to happen; **solche Menschen kann man nicht d.,** it is impossible to tolerate such people; **wir werden hier nur geduldet,** we are only here on sufferance; **schlechtes Benehmen wird hier nicht geduldet,** bad behaviour is not tolerated here; **sie dulden alles,** they put up with anything; **sie duldet zu viel,** she puts up with too much, she is too indulgent; **wenn man jetzt die Unartigkeit dieses Kindes duldet, wird es später ein unangenehmer Mensch sein,** if one simply puts up with this child's naughtiness now, if this child is allowed to be so naughty now, it will grow into a very unpleasant person later on; **er duldet keinen Widerspruch,** he won't bear, won't tolerate, contradiction, he brooks no contradiction, he suffers no one to contradict him; **sie duldet keinen Vorwurf,** she won't endure, tolerate, reproach; **werden Sie dieses Unrecht d.?** are you going to tolerate, put up with, this injustice? **etwas stillschweigend d.,** (i) to connive at sth.; (ii) to allow sth., to make no move to stop sth.; **stillschweigend d., daß etwas geschieht,** to allow sth. to be done, to make no move to stop sth.'s being done; **ich kann (es) nicht d., daß man so mit mir umgeht,** I can't tolerate, bear, being treated in this way, I can't allow people to treat me in this way; **die Sache duldet keinen Aufschub,** the matter brooks, allows of, no delay. **2.** *v.i.* (*haben*) (*a*) to suffer; (*b*) to be tolerant; to stand passively by.

II. *vbl s.* **1. Dulden,** *n. in vbl senses.* **2. Duldung,** *f.* (*a*) = II. 1, *also:* toleration, endurance (of sth., s.o.); **stillschweigende D.,** connivance, tacit permission; (*b*) (religious) toleration, tolerance; (*c*) *A:* suffering(s).

Dulder, *m.* -s/-. **1.** (patient) sufferer; long-suffering person; **er ist ein stiller D.,** he suffers in silence. **2.** *occ.* indulgent person; person who tolerates (sth.).

Duldermiene, *f.* patient look, martyred expression; **er zeigte wieder seine D.,** he was wearing his martyred expression again.

Duldersinn, *m.* resignation.

duldsam, *a.* (*a*) tolerant; **sich d. gegen Andersgläubige zeigen,** to be tolerant towards those holding different religious convictions, to be tolerant of other creeds; (*b*) *A:* patient.

Duldsamkeit, *f.* tolerance; toleration; **die D. einer Partei gegen die andere,** one party's toleration of the other, the tolerance of one party towards the other; **D. in Sachen der Religion,** toleration in religious matters; **wenn alle Menschen mehr D. an den Tag legten . . . ,** if everyone showed more tolerance. . . .

Duldung, *f. see* **dulden** II. 2.

Dulie [du·'liː], *f.* -/. *Rel:* dulia; worship of the saints.

Dulkose [dul'koːzə], *f.* -/. *Ch:* dulcite.

Dulldill, *m.*, **Dullkraut,** *n. Bot:* henbane.

Dülle, *f.* -/-n = **Delle.**

Dullerche, *f. Orn:* wood lark.

Dult, *f.* -/-e(n). *South G.Dial:* fair.

Dulzin [dul'tsiːn], *n.* -s/. *Ch:* dulcin.

Dulzinea [dultsi·'neːaː]. **1.** *Pr.n.f.* -s & -neens. *Lit:* Dulcinea. **2.** *f.* -/-neen & -s. *Dulcinea*, lady-love.

Dulzit [dul'tsiːt], *m.* -s/. *Ch:* dulcite.

Duma, *f.* -/-s. *Russ.Hist:* duma, Russian parliament.

Dumdum ['dumdum], *n.* -(s)/-(s). *Mil:* dumdum bullet.

Dumdumgeschoß, *n.* = **Dumdum.**

dumm, *a.* (**dümmer; dümmst**) **1.** (*a*) unintelligent, stupid, *F:* dense, *U.S:* dumb; **meine Schüler sind sehr d.,** my pupils are very stupid, *F:* dense; **er ist nicht so d. wie er aussieht,** he's not as stupid as he looks; **dumme Fragen stellen,** to ask stupid, unintelligent, questions; **sich d. stellen, ein dummes Gesicht machen,** to pretend not to understand; to pretend to know nothing about it; *F:* **d. wie Bohnenstroh, wie die Sünde,** as stupid as an owl, as a donkey; **der ist dümmer als d.,** he's more than stupid; **polizeiwidrig d., dümmer, als die Polizei erlaubt,** impossibly stupid, too stupid to live, too stupid to get out of one's own way; **er will dich d. machen,** he's trying to get the better of you; **die Dummen werden nicht alle,** there are always fools around; **auf eine dumme Frage gehört eine dumme Antwort,** a stupid question deserves a stupid answer; *Prov:* **die dümmsten Bauern haben die größten Kartoffeln,** fortune favours fools; (*b*) confused, giddy; dizzy; **der Lärm in diesem Zimmer macht einen ganz d.,** the noise in this room makes one's head swim, makes one's head go round, makes one stupid; **nachdem sie dreimal Karussell gefahren war, war ihr im Kopf ganz d. davon,** after she had been on the roundabout three times her head began to swim, to go round, she felt quite dizzy, giddy; **er hat mich d. und dämlich geredet,** he talked till my head began to go round, to swim; **ich habe mich d. und dämlich geredet,** I talked myself silly; I talked my head off; **die kann einen d. und dämlich reden,** she'd talk the hind leg off a donkey; **der Kopf ist mir heute ganz d.,** I can't think today, my head is swimming, is going round, today; (*c*) young, green; **damals war er noch ein dummer Junge,** he was only a silly boy, he was still green, in those days. **2.** silly, stupid, foolish, *F:* soft; **du dummer Esel! du dumme Gans!** you silly ass! you silly goose! **sei nicht so d.! laß dir so eine Gelegenheit**

nicht entgehen! don't be so silly, stupid! don't miss an opportunity like that! es war d. von mir, das zu tun, it was stupid, silly, foolish, of me to do that, I was stupid, silly, foolish, to do that; da müßte ich schön d. sein! da mußt du dir einen Dümmeren suchen! no thanks, not me! no thanks, you wouldn't catch me doing that! I wouldn't be such a fool! ich will nicht immer der Dumme sein, I don't want always to be the loser, to get the worst of it; (j-m) eine dumme Antwort geben, to give (s.o.) a stupid *or* evasive answer; frag nicht so d.! du weißt doch, daß es nicht geht! don't be so stupid, silly! you know quite well it's impossible! da hab ich was Dummes gemacht, (i) that was stupid, silly, foolish, of me; (ii) I (have) made a *faux pas*, a gaffe; dummes Zeug! nonsense! rubbish! sie machen, reden, lauter dummes Zeug, they are always, they keep, playing the fool, they do nothing but play the fool; they are always talking, they keep talking, they talk nothing but, nonsense; dumme Witze, silly jokes; man hat mir heute einen dummen Streich gespielt, they played a silly, stupid, joke on me today; das ist eine dumme Geschichte, eine dumme Sache, it's an awkward, annoying, business; es ist zu d., daß du heute Abend nicht kommen kannst, it's too annoying that you can't come this evening; ich will mich nicht bei ihr entschuldigen; es ist mir zu d., es sieht mir zu d. aus, I don't want to apologize to her; it would be too awkward, too embarrassing; du kannst nicht heute wieder zu Herrn X gehen; es sieht zu d. aus, you can't go to Mr X again today; it looks (i) too obvious, (ii) too peculiar; endlich wurde uns die Sache zu d., und wir gingen weg, in the end the whole thing began to bore us, in the end we'd had enough of it, and we went away; diese Sache könnte d. ablaufen, auslaufen, this business could end badly; *see also* August^{2}. 3. *A:* tasteless, spoilt; *B:* wo nun das Salz d. wird, but if the salt have lost his savour. 4. *A:* (*a*) deaf; (*b*) dumb.

Dummbart, *m.* silly, ninny, silly ass; fool; er ist ein D., he's a silly (ass), a ninny, a silly fool.

dummdreist, *a.* impudent.

Dummdreistigkeit, *f.* impudence.

Dummejungenstreich, *m.* (ein Dummerjungenstreich) (*gen.* Dumme(n)jungenstreich(e)s; *pl.* Dumme(n)jungenstreiche;) (boyish) prank, lark; es war keine Bosheit, es war nur ein Dummerjungenstreich, it wasn't done maliciously, it was only a boyish prank, lark; für solche Dummejungenstreiche bist du zu alt, you're too old for larks like that.

Dummerchen, *n.* -s/-, little silly, little ninny, silly little boy, girl; (*of girl*) little goose.

Dummerjan, *m.* -s/-e, (*usu. of children*) silly, ninny.

Dummerling, *m.* -s/-e = Dummerjan.

dummerweise, *adv.* stupidly, foolishly; ich habe d. heute morgen meine Tasche zu Hause gelassen, I stupidly left my bag at home this morning.

Dummheit, *f.* 1. (*a*) stupidity; die D. steht ihm auf der Stirn geschrieben, you can see just by looking at him how stupid he is; ihre D. ist unbeschreiblich, her stupidity is indescribable, she is indescribably stupid; (*b*) foolishness, folly, silliness, stupidity; das hast du deiner eigenen D. zu verdanken, you have only your own folly, stupidity, to thank for that. 2. (*a*) stupid, foolish, thing *or* action; tomfoolery; Dummheiten in der Schule machen, to be up to foolish pranks at school; er macht nichts als Dummheiten, he plays the fool all the time; j-n vor Dummheiten bewahren, to keep s.o. out of mischief; laß mich mit solchen Dummheiten in Ruhe! don't bother me with stupid, silly, foolish, things like that! (*b*) mistake, blunder, foolish action; eine D. begehen, to do sth. foolish, to make a blunder; er macht lauter Dummheiten, he makes mistakes, blunders, all the time; eine D. nach der anderen machen, to make one mistake, blunder, after another.

Dummkoller, *m. Vet:* (sleepy) staggers.

Dummkopf, *m.* stupid, silly, ninny; fool; ass; *F:* blockhead, dunderhead, dunce; er ist ein großer D., he's an awful fool, ass, he's very stupid, an awful stupid; du D.! you silly, ninny, blockhead, dunce! you silly fool, silly ass! er ist ein alter D., he's a silly old fool.

Dummrian, *m.* -s/-e. 1. = Dummerjan. 2. *Bot:* greater fleabane.

Dumpalme, *f.* -/-n. *Bot:* doum, doom-palm.

dumpf, *a.* 1. (*of atmosphere, smell, etc.*) musty, fusty; stale; (*of atmosphere*) stuffy, close, heavy, sultry, oppressive; dumpfe Luft, musty, fusty, stale, air; eine dumpfe Gruft, a damp, dark, vault, grave; ein dumpfes Schulzimmer, a drab and stuffy schoolroom; eine dumpfe Stube, a musty, fusty, room; die dumpfen Gassen der alten Stadt, the musty alleys of the ancient city; dumpfes Heu, mouldy hay. 2. (*of sound*) muffled; dull, hollow; das dumpfe Rollen des Donners, the dull rumble of thunder; man hörte dumpfen Geschützdonner in der Ferne, the rumble of guns was heard in the distance; dumpfes Stöhnen, hollow groan(ing); er hörte das dumpfe Geläut der Glocke, die dumpfe Glocke, he heard the deep, muffled sound, the booming, of the bell; d. tönten die Glocken aus der Ferne, the bells sounded hollowly, dully, from the distance; das dumpfe Gebrüll der Tiere füllte die Arena, the low roaring of the animals filled the arena; mit dumpfem Gebrüll stürzte der Stier in die Arena, with a low bellow the bull rushed into the arena; das dumpfe Rollen der Wagen auf dem Pflaster, the rumble of carriage wheels on the road; dumpfer Schlag, thud, thump; dull blow; er fiel mit dumpfem Geräusch zu Boden, he fell to, he hit, the floor *or* the ground with a (dull) thud. 3. (*of sensation, etc.*) dull, oppressed; numb; torpid, drowsy; ein dumpfer Schmerz, a dull pain; ein dumpfes Gefühl im Kopfe, a heavy, oppressed, feeling in the head; dumpfes Schweigen, heavy, weary, gloomy, silence; dumpfe Gleichgültigkeit, numb, torpid, indifference; in dumpfem Hinbrüten dasitzen, to be lost in gloomy meditation; d. dahinleben, to lead a torpid, drowsy, half-conscious, existence.

Dümpfel, *m.* -s/-. *A:* pool; pond.

Dumpfheit, *f.* 1. mustiness, fustiness, staleness (of atmosphere, smell, etc.); stuffiness, closeness, heaviness, sultriness, oppressiveness (of atmosphere); in der D. ihrer engen Stube, in the musty, fusty, oppressive, atmosphere of her little room. 2. dullness, hollowness (of sound). 3. dullness (of pain, etc.); numbness (of sensation, etc.); torpor, apathy (of mind, etc.); die D. in meinem Kopfe ist noch nicht gewichen, I still have that oppressed feeling in my head.

dumpfig, *a.* 1. musty, fusty, stale (atmosphere, smell, etc.); musty, fusty (taste); stuffy, heavy, close, oppressive, sultry (atmosphere); ein dumpfiger Keller, a damp and musty cellar; dumpfiges Heu, mouldy, damp, hay. 2. *occ.* = dumpf 2.

Dumpfigkeit, *f.* 1. mustiness, fustiness, staleness (of atmosphere, smell, etc.); mustiness, fustiness (of taste); stuffiness, heaviness, closeness, oppressiveness, sultriness (of atmosphere). 2. *occ.* = Dumpfheit 2.

dumpfwarm, *a.* sultry (air).

Dumping ['dampiŋ, dømpiŋ], *n.* -s/. *Com:* dumping.

dun [du:n], *a. North G.Dial:* drunk.

Dune, *f.* -/-n = Daune.

Düne, *f.* -/-n, (sand-)dune, sand-hill, down.

Dünendistel, *f. Bot:* sea-holly.

Dünenhafer, *m. Bot:* (*a*) lyme-grass; (*b*) sea-reed, sea-bent, marram(-grass).

Dünenrose, *f. Bot:* burnet-rose.

Dünenwüste, *f. Geog:* erg (of the Sahara).

Dung, *m.* -(e)s/. *Agr:* (farmyard) manure, dung.

Düngemittel, *n. Agr:* fertilizer; (chemisches, künstliches) D., (chemical, artificial) fertilizer; chemical, artificial, manure.

düngen. I. *v.tr.* to manure, fertilize, dress (land); to dung (land).

II. *vbl s.* Düngen, *n.*, Düngung, *f. in vbl senses; also:* fertilization; bei genügender Düngung sollte etwas aus diesem Boden herauszuholen sein, if sufficiently manured this land should prove productive.

Dünger, *m.* -s/-. *Agr: Hort:* fertilizer, manure; dung; flüssiger D., liquid manure; D. streuen, to spread manure.

Düngergabel, *f. Agr:* dung-fork, manure fork.

Düngergrube, *f.* dung-pit, manure pit.

Düngerhaufen, *m.* dunghill, manure heap.

Düngerstätte, *f.* = Düngerhaufen.

Düngerstreuer, *m.*, **Düngerstreumaschine,** *f. Agr:* manure distributor.

Dungfliege, *f. Ent:* dung-fly.

Dunggabel, *f. Agr:* dung-fork, manure fork.

Dunggrube, *f.* = Düngergrube.

Dunghaufen, *m.* = Düngerhaufen.

Dungkäfer, *m. Ent:* dung-beetle.

Dungstätte, *f.* = Düngerhaufen.

dunkel^{1}, *a.* 1. (*a*) dark; (*of electric bulb, etc.*) dim; es wird d., it's growing, getting, dark; der Himmel wurde d., the sky darkened, grew dark, was overcast; ein dunkles Zimmer, a dark room; diese Tapete macht das Zimmer dunkler, this wall-paper darkens the room, makes the room darker; die hohen Bäume vor dem Haus machen die Wohnung d., the tall trees in front of the house make the flat dark, darken the flat; *abs.* d. machen, (i) to turn out the light; (ii) to draw the curtains, blinds; (iii) to black out; das Zimmer war d., (i) the room was dark; (ii) the room was in darkness; es war d. im Zimmer, it was dark in the room, the room was in darkness; es wurde dunkler und dunkler, immer dunkler, it grew darker and darker; in dunkler Nacht, in the darkness of night; in einer dunklen Nacht, one dark night; das Licht brennt, die Kerzen brennen, d., the light burns, the candles burn, dimly; es wurde ihm d. vor den Augen, his head began to swim, to go round; (*b*) es wurde d. in seinem Geist, his mind grew clouded, began to give way; es wird immer dunkler in seinem Gemüt, he grows more and more gloomy, melancholy; das dunkle Heidentum, the unenlightened heathen; (*c*) dim, faint, vague; eine dunkle Vorstellung, Ahnung, von etwas haben, to have a vague idea of sth.; ich erinnere mich d. daran, ich habe eine dunkle Erinnerung daran, I remember it dimly, vaguely, I have a dim, faint, vague, recollection of it; (*d*) obscure, subconscious; dunkle Gefühle, obscure, subconscious, feelings; ich habe nur einen dunklen Begriff davon, I have only a very unformed, unclear, idea of, I have no clear idea of, it; die dunklen Empfindungen, die in unserem Unterbewußtsein schlummern, the undefined feelings which lie in our subconscious; (*e*) obscure, unknown, doubtful; ein Mann von dunkler Herkunft, a man of obscure origins; der dunkle Erdteil, the Dark Continent; die Dunklen Jahrhunderte, the Dark Ages; die Zukunft liegt d. vor uns, we cannot see into the future; *cp.* 2 (*c*); (*f*) dark, mysterious, obscure; dunkle Anspielungen, dark hints; der dunkle Sinn seiner Rede, the hidden, obscure, meaning of his words; eine dunkle Stelle im Text, an obscure passage in the text; man nannte Heraklit den Dunklen, Heraclitus was called the Dark Philosopher; *B:* wir sehen jetzt durch einen Spiegel in einem dunklen Wort, for now we see through a glass, darkly. 2. (*a*) eine dunkle Farbe, a dark colour, shade; ein dunkles Kleid, ein d. gefärbtes Kleid, a dark dress; dunkle Wolken, dark, black, clouds; dunkles Bier, dark beer; brown ale; dunkle Haare, eine dunkle Gesichtsfarbe, haben, to have dark hair, to have a dark, dusky, swarthy, complexion; von dunkler Hautfarbe sein, to be dark-skinned, swarthy; dunkel-, *comb.fm.* dark . . ., dark-, deep . . .; dunkelblau, dark, deep, blue; dunkelrot, dark, deep, red; dunkelgrau, dark grey; dunkelhaarig, dark-haired; (*b*) dark, black, sombre, gloomy; dunkle Verzweiflung, dark, black, despair; es war der dunkelste Tag ihres Lebens, it was the darkest, blackest, day of her life; eine dunkle Stunde in der Weltgeschichte, a dark, black, hour in the history of the world; (*c*) dark, black; sinister; suspicious, *F:* shady, fishy; dunkle Vorahnungen haben, to have dark premonitions; die Zukunft liegt d. vor uns, the future looks dark, black; *cp.* 1 (*e*); er führt eine dunkle Existenz, he leads a mysterious life; dunkle Pläne aushecken, to be making dark, mysterious, sinister, plans; das ist ein dunkler Punkt in seiner Vergangenheit, that's a doubtful, *F:* a shady, murky, point in his past. 3. dark (vowel); deep (voice, sound, etc.); sombre (sound) (of funeral music, etc.). 4. (*in certain expressions spelt with a small d*) das Dunkle, the dark(ness); (*a*) im Dunkeln sitzen, to sit in the dark, in darkness; Katzen können im Dunkeln sehen, cats can see in the dark; sie geht nicht gern im Dunkeln aus, she doesn't like going out in the dark; j-n im dunkeln lassen, to leave s.o. in the dark; man hat mich darüber völlig im dunkeln gelassen, I was completely left in the dark over it; im dunkeln tappen, to grope, be groping, in the dark; (*b*) ein Sprung ins Dunkle, a leap in the dark; er bleibt, hält sich, im Dunkeln, (i) he keeps in the background, he doesn't want to be in the public eye; (ii) he shuns the light, he works behind the scenes; *Prov:* im Dunkeln ist gut munkeln, it's easy to talk about things you know nothing about; *cp.* Dunkel^{2}, Dunkelheit; (*c*) ein Dunkles, a (glass of) dark beer, brown ale.

Dunkel^{2}, *n.* -s/. 1. darkness; im D. der Nacht, in the darkness of the night; man weiß nie, was im D. der Nacht geschieht, one never knows what happens in the darkness of the night, under cover of the night; in tiefes D. gehüllt, shrouded in darkness; im D. des Waldes, in the darkness of the forest; das ist noch im D. der Zukunft verborgen, that lies hidden in the future; das D.

der Verzweiflung, the darkness of despair; **das D. des Unterbewußtseins,** the dark subconscious. **2.** obscurity; **seine Werke sind im D. versunken,** his works have lapsed into obscurity; **er sank wieder in das D. zurück, aus dem er gekommen war,** he sank back into the obscurity from which he came. **3.** darkness; unenlightenment; **das D. des Heidentums,** heathen darkness; **im D. des Mittelalters,** in the darkness of the Middle Ages; *B:* **Finsternis bedeckt das Erdreich und D. die Völker,** the darkness shall cover the earth, and gross darkness the people. *Cp.* **Dunkelheit.**

Dünkel, *m.* **-s/. 1.** *A:* opinion, *A:* conceit. **2.** conceit, vanity; **er hat einen ungeheuren D.,** he is immensely conceited, vain, he is eaten up with conceit.

Dunkeladaptation, *f. Opt:* adaptation (of the eye) to darkness, dark adaptation.

dunkeläugig, *a.* dark-eyed.

dunkelblau, *a.* dark blue, deep blue.

dunkelblond, *a.* light brown (hair).

Dunkelente, *f. Orn:* black duck.

Dunkelfeldbeleuchtung, *f. Opt:* dark-ground, dark-field, illumination.

Dunkelfuchs, *m.* dark chestnut (horse).

dünkelhaft, *a.* (self-)conceited, vain.

dunkelhäutig, *a.* dark-skinned; swarthy.

Dunkelheit, *f.* **1.** dark, darkness; **bei Einbruch der D.,** at nightfall; **sie geht nicht gern in der D. aus,** she doesn't like going out in the dark; **sie wurden von der D. überrascht,** they were overtaken by darkness, by the dark; **man konnte in der D. nichts erkennen,** it was impossible to distinguish anything in the dark(ness). **2.** darkness (of place, colour); **die D. des Waldes, des Zimmers,** the darkness of the forest, of the room; **das Zimmer war in völliger D.,** the room was in complete darkness; **die Stadt lag in völliger D.,** the town lay in total darkness; **die Blinden leben in immerwährender D.,** the blind live in perpetual darkness. **3.** obscurity, darkness (of prophecy, etc.); **die D. seines Stils,** the obscurity of his style. **4.** obscurity; **in der D. ihrer bescheidenen Existenz,** in the obscurity of her modest life, in her modest and obscure life. **5.** darkness, unenlightened state; **in D. leben,** to be unenlightened; **die D. des Heidentums,** heathen darkness; **in der D. des Wahnsinns,** in mental darkness. *Cp.* **dunkel**[1] 4, **Dunkel**[2].

Dunkelkammer, *f.* (*a*) *Phot:* dark-room; (*b*) *Opt:* camera obscura.

Dunkelmann, *m.* **-(e)s/-männer. 1.** *Lit:* obscurantist. **2.** *F:* back-stage conspirator.

Dunkelmännerbriefe, die. *m.pl. Lit:* the Epistolae Obscurorum Virorum.

dunkelmännisch, *a. Lit:* obscurantist.

dunkeln. I. *v.* **1.** *v.i.* (*haben*) to grow dark, to darken; *v.impers.* **es dunkelt,** it is growing dark. **2.** *v.tr.* to darken, deepen, deaden, dull; *Dy: Paperm:* to sadden (colour).

II. *vbl s.* **Dunkeln,** *n. in vbl senses; also:* **das D. des Abends,** the fall of evening.

Dunkelpause, *f. Cin:* obscuring period, cut-off period.

Dunkelwerden, *n.* **1.** darkening (of light, colour, etc.). **2.** dusk; **nach D.,** after dusk, after dark; **vor D.,** before dusk, before it gets dark.

dünken, *v.* (*pr.t.* **dünkt, deucht;** *p.t.* **deuchte, dünkte;** *p.p.* **gedeucht, gedünkt**). **1.** *v.impers.* to seem, to appear; **mich, mir, dünkt, deucht,** I think, I feel, I have a feeling, it seems to me, I fancy, *A. & Lit:* methinks; **ihn, ihm, dünkt, deucht, sie habe es schon bereut,** he thinks, he fancies, she has already repented it; **mich, mir, dünkt, deucht, ich sehe sie noch,** I seem to see her still, *A. & Lit:* methinks I see her still; **mich, mir, deuchte, ich hätte ein blaues Licht in der Ferne gesehen,** I thought, I fancied, I had seen a will o' the wisp in the distance, *A. & Lit:* methought I saw a will o' the wisp in the distance; **das ist ein vergebliches Bemühen, dünkt mir,** these efforts will all be in vain, I feel, I fancy, it seems to me; **dünkt dir das gut?** does that seem a good idea to you? **2. sich klug, schön, usw., dünken,** to think, imagine, fancy, oneself (to be) clever, beautiful, etc.; **sie dünkt sich eine schöne Frau,** she thinks herself a beautiful woman; **er dünkt sich als Retter seines Volkes zu handeln,** he imagines himself to be acting, he thinks he is acting, as a saviour of his people.

Dünkirchen. *Pr.n.n.* **-s.** *Geog:* Dunkirk.

dünn, *A. & Dial:* **dünne,** *a.* **1.** (*a*) thin (paper, material, skin, etc.); thin, fine, slender (thread); **die dünnen Stellen an einem Kleid,** the thin places in a dress; *F:* **dünn bohren, das Brett an der dünnsten Stelle bohren,** to take the easy way out; (*b*) (*of pers.*) thin, lean, spare; **er ist d. wie ein Faden,** he's as thin as a rake, as a lath; **dünne Beine, Finger,** thin legs, fingers; **dünner werden,** to grow, to become, thinner; to lose flesh; *F:* **sich d. machen,** to make room, to squeeze up; *see also* **dünnmachen. 2.** thin, sparse, scanty (hair, population, vegetation, etc.); thin, straggling (beard); **d. gesät,** (i) sparsely sown; (ii) scarce, rare; few and far between; **eine d. bewachsene Landschaft,** a landscape with sparse vegetation. **3.** (*a*) thin, watery (liquid); thin, rarified, attenuated (air); rare (atmosphere); thin, fine (mist); *Opt:* **das dünne Medium,** the rarer medium; **dünnes Blut,** thin blood; **das Bier dünner machen,** to thin (down), to water (down), to dilute, the beer; **die Sauce, usw., d. machen,** to thin down sauce, etc.; **in der dünnen Luft seiner Philosophie,** in the rarified atmosphere of his philosophy; *Med:* **dünner Stuhl,** fluid faeces; (*b*) thin (sound); **eine dünne Stimme,** a thin, reedy, voice; **der dünne Ton der Violinen,** the thin sound of the violins; (*c*) *F:* weak; **was hältst du von seinem Aufsatz? — ich finde ihn ein bißchen d.,** what do you think of his essay?—I find it a bit thin; **sein Lob war etwas d.,** his praise was rather faint, half-hearted. **4.** *see* **dick** I. 3 (*a*). **5. dünn-,** *comb.fm.* (*a*) thin-, slender-; **dünnhäutig,** thin-skinned; **dünnleibig,** slender(-bodied), thin; (*b*) thin-, thinly . . . , sparse . . . , sparsely . . . ; **dünnhaarig,** with thin, sparse, hair; **dünnbevölkert,** thinly populated, sparsely populated.

Dünnbeil, *n. Carp:* broad axe, chip-axe.

dünnbeinig, *a.* thin-legged, with thin, slender, legs.

dünnbesiedelt, dünnbevölkert, *a.* thinly, sparsely, populated (country).

Dünnbier, *n.* small beer; weak beer.

Dünndarm, *m. Anat:* **der D.,** the small intestine.

Dünndruckausgabe, *f.* thin-paper edition; India paper edition.

Dünndruckpapier, *n.* thin printing paper; India paper.

dünne[1], *a. A. & Dial:* = **dünn.**

Dünne[2], *f.* **-/. 1.** (*a*) thinness (of paper, material, skin, etc.); thinness, fineness, slenderness (of thread); (*b*) thinness, leanness (of pers.); (*c*) thinness, sparseness, scantiness (of hair, population, vegetation, etc.); (*d*) thinness, wateriness (of liquid); (*e*) thinness (of sound); thinness, reediness (of voice). **2.** *F:* diarrhoea.

dünnemachen (sich), *v.refl.* = **dünnmachen (sich).**

dünnen, *v.tr.* = **verdünnen.**

Dünnfaden, *m. Fung:* leptomitus lacteus.

dünnflüssig, *a.* (*of liquid*) thin; watery.

Dünnflüssigkeit, *f.* thin consistency, wateriness (of liquid).

dünnhäutig, *a.* thin-skinned, with a thin skin.

Dünnheit, *f.* = **Dünne**[2].

dünnleibig, *a.* slender(-bodied), thin.

dünnmachen (sich), *v.refl. F:* to make oneself scarce; to clear off; *F:* to hop it, to sling one's hook, to hook it, *U.S:* to scram.

Dünnpfiff, *m. F:* diarrhoea.

Dünnsaft, *m. Sug.-R:* clear juice.

dünnschalig, *a.* (fruit) with a thin skin *or* peel, thin-skinned (orange, etc.); (egg) with a thin shell, thin-shelled (egg).

Dünnschliff, *m.* thin section, microscopic section (of mineral, etc.).

dünnschnäb(e)lig, *a. Orn:* slender-billed, thin-billed.

Dünnschnabelsturmtaucher, *m. Orn:* short-tailed shearwater, mutton-bird.

Dünnschnabelsturmvogel, *m. Orn:* thin-billed prion.

Dünnstein, *m. Lap:* thin table.

Dünntuch, *n.* gauze.

Dünnung, *f.* flank (of animal).

Dunst, *m.* **-es/⸗e. 1.** (*a*) vapour; haze, mist; (fine) spray; **ein leichter D. hing über der Wiese,** a light mist, haze, a fine vapour, hung over the meadow; **ein blauer D. umhüllte das ferne Gebirge,** the distant mountains were enveloped in a blue haze, mist, in blue vapour; **das Wasser des Springbrunnens löst sich in D. auf,** the water of the fountain turns to, dissolves in, fine spray; (*b*) vapour, fume, exhalation; **giftige Dünste stiegen aus dem Sumpf auf,** poisonous vapours, fumes, exhalations, miasmas, arose from the bog; **die Dünste des Weines,** the fumes of wine; *F:* **im Dunst(e) sein,** to be drunk, intoxicated, tipsy; (*c*) (*in kitchen, etc.*) (i) smoke, haze (*after frying*); (ii) steam (*after boiling*). **2. seine Pläne gingen in D. und Rauch auf,** his plans went up in smoke; (*of hopes, illusions, etc.*) **sich in (blauen) D. auflösen,** to melt, vanish, into thin air; *F:* **keinen blassen D. davon haben,** to have not the faintest idea about it, *F:* to have not the foggiest notion, not the ghost of a notion, about it; *see also* **blau** I. 1 (*c*). **3.** *Med: A:* **Dünste,** flatulence, *A:* vapours. **4.** (*a*) *Ven:* (= **Vogeldunst**) dust-shot, small shot, *U.S:* mustard seed; (*b*) *Mil: F:* **D. bekommen,** to be under heavy fire. **5.** *Mill:* (*pl.* **Dunste**) middlings, sharps.

dunsten, *v.i.* (*haben*) to exhale vapour; to give off fumes; to steam; **die dunstenden Wiesen,** the steamy, misty, meadows; **ein dunstender Schwefelsumpf,** a bog exhaling sulphurous vapours, fumes.

dünsten, *v.* **1.** *v.tr. Cu:* to steam (vegetable, fish, etc.); to stew (fruit, meat, fish). **2.** *v.i.* (*haben*) = **dunsten.**

dunstig, *a.* (*a*) hazy (day, etc.); misty (day, weather, etc.); **es ist d. heute,** it is hazy, misty, today; (*b*) **eine dunstige Waschküche,** a steamy washhouse; **es ist d. in der Küche,** the kitchen is full of (i) smoke (*from frying*), (ii) steam (*from boiling*).

Dunstkreis, *m.* (*a*) *Ph: A:* atmosphere; (*b*) (personal) atmosphere, aura; orbit; **im D. der Macht,** in the aura of power.

Dunstobst, *n. Cu:* bottled fruit.

Dunstschleier, *m.* haze.

Dunstzeit, *f. Meteor:* harmattan.

Dünung, *f.* **-/.** (*F: pl.* **Dünungen**) *Nau:* swell, surge (of the sea); **es läuft eine schwere D.,** there is a heavy swell (running).

Duo [ˈduːoː], *n.* **-s/-s.** *Mus:* **1.** (*composition*) duet. **2.** duettists, duet.

duodenal [du·o·de·ˈnaːl], *a. Anat: Med:* duodenal; *comb.fm.* **Duodenal-,** duodenal . . . ; **Duodenalgeschwür** *n,* duodenal ulcer.

Duodenum [du·o·ˈdeːnum], *n.* **-s/.** *Anat:* duodenum.

Duodez [du·o·ˈdeːts], *n.* **-es/.** *Print:* duodecimo twelvemo; *comb.fm.* **Duodez-,** duodecimo . . . , twelvemo . . . , . . . in duodecimo, . . . in twelvemo; *F:* diminutive, tiny (pers., thg); **Duodezausgabe** *f,* duodecimo edition, twelvemo edition, edition in duodecimo, in twelvemo; **Duodezfürst** *m,* duodecimo prince; **Duodezfürstentum** *n,* duodecimo princedom.

duodezimal [du·o·de·tsi·ˈmaːl], *a.* duodecimal.

Duodezimalsystem, *n. Ar:* duodecimal system, duodecimals.

Duodrama, *n. Th:* duologue.

dupieren, düpieren [dy·ˈpiːrən], *v.tr.* to dupe, to gull (s.o.).

Duplet [du·ˈpleː], *n.* **-s/-s.** *Phot:* doublet (lens).

Duplex [ˈduːplɛks], *n.* **-/-plices** [-pli·tse·s]. *R.C. Ch:* double.

Duplex-, *comb.fm.* duplex; **Duplexbrenner** *m,* duplex lamp; *Mec.E:* **Duplexdrehbank** *f,* duplex lathe; **Duplexpumpe** *f,* duplex pump; **Duplextelegraphie** *f,* duplex telegraphy; *Clockm:* **Duplexfinger** *m,* duplex hook; **Duplexhemmung** *f,* duplex escapement; **Duplexrolle** *f,* duplex roller.

duplieren [du·ˈpliːrən], *v.tr.* **1.** = **dublieren** (*a*), (*b*). **2.** *abs. Jur: A:* to make a rejoinder.

Dupliermaschine, *f. Tex:* doubler, doubling frame.

Duplik [du·ˈpliːk], *f.* **-/-en.** *Jur:* (defendant's) rejoinder.

Duplikat [du·pli·ˈkaːt], *n.* **-(e)s/-e,** duplicate; exact copy; **in D.,** in duplicate.

Duplikation [du·pli·ka·tsi·ˈoːn], *f.* **-/-en,** duplication.

Duplikatur [du·pli·ka·ˈtuːr], *f.* **-/-en,** duplication.

duplizieren [du·pli·ˈtsiːrən], *v.tr.* to duplicate (sth.); to make duplicates, a duplicate (of documents, of a document, etc.).

Duplizität [du·pli·tsi·ˈtɛːt], *f.* **-/. 1.** duplexity, doubleness, duplicity; **D. der Fälle,** pair of similar occurrences. **2.** duplicity, double-dealing.

Duplum [ˈduːplum], *n.* **-s/-pla,** duplicate.

Dupont-Lerche [dy·ˈpõː-], *f. Orn:* Dupont's lark.

Düppel, *m.* **-s/-, Düppelstreifen,** *m.pl. Mil.Av:* window, chaff, *U.S:* rope.

Dur, dur, *n.* **-/-.** *Mus:* major (key); **A-dur, A-Dur,** (**-Tonart**), (key of) A major.

durabel [du·ˈraːbəl], *a.* durable.

Durabilität [du·ra·bi·li·ˈtɛːt], *f.* **-/.** durability.

Durakkord, *m. Mus:* major chord.

Duralumin [du·ra·lu·ˈmiːn], *n.* **-s/.** *Metall:* duraluminium, duralumin.

durativ [du·ra·ˈtiːf], *a. Gram:* durative; **durative** [du·ra·ˈtiːvə] **Aktionsart,** durative aspect.

Durbar [durˈbaːr], *n.* **-/-(e),** (*in India*) durbar.

durch. I. *prep.* (+ *acc.*) **1.** through; (*a*) **d. ein Tor gehen,** to go through a gate; **wir gingen d.**

den Wald, we walked through the wood; **d. die Straße gehen,** to go along the street; **er wanderte d. die Straßen,** he wandered through the streets; **er drängte sich d. die Menge,** he pushed his way through the crowd; **er stieß ihm das Schwert d. die Brust,** he ran the sword through his chest; **d. ein Fernrohr sehen,** to look through a telescope; **d. die Nase reden,** to speak through one's nose; (*b*) **ein Gedanke schoß ihm d. den Kopf,** a thought struck him; **die Melodie geht mir fortwährend d. den Kopf,** I have got the tune on my brain; **das Geschrei ging ihm d. Mark und Bein,** the shriek made his blood run cold; **j-m einen Strich d. die Rechnung machen,** to frustrate s.o.'s plans, *F:* to put a spoke in s.o.'s wheel; (*c*) **d. viele Gefahren gehen,** to go through many dangers; **er stand mir d. Not und Trübsal bei,** he stood by me in trouble and in sorrow; **er wanderte ziellos d. die Nacht,** he wandered aimlessly through the night; (*d*) **d. eine lange Zeit (hindurch),** for a long time; over a long period; **d. manche Jahre (hindurch),** for many years; over many years; **d. alle Jahrhunderte,** through all ages; down the ages; **d. sein ganzes Leben,** all through his life, throughout his life; his whole life long; **er schlief d. den ganzen ersten Akt,** he slept throughout, all through, the first act; **d. die (ganze) Nacht,** all night (long), all through the night, throughout the night. **2.** by; (*a*) **die Entdeckung des Penicillins d. Fleming,** the discovery of penicillin by Fleming; **Holofernes wurde d. Judith ermordet,** Holofernes was murdered by Judith; **wir wurden d. das schlechte Wetter verhindert,** we were prevented by the bad weather; (*b*) by (means of); because of; thanks to; through; **er bewog ihn d. Schmeicheleien,** he won him over by (means of) flattery; **wir sind d. unsere eigenen Bemühungen reich geworden,** we have become rich by, thanks to, our own efforts; **etwas d. seine eigene Schuld verlieren,** to have only oneself to blame for losing sth.; **er ist d. Sie zum armen Mann geworden,** it is through you, your fault, thanks to you, that he has become a poor man; **d. Gottes große Güte,** by God's grace; **d. eine glückliche Spekulation,** through a fortunate speculation; (*c*) through, by (the agency of); **ich habe es d. ihn, d. die Zeitung, erfahren,** I came to know of it through him, through the newspaper; **etwas d. j-n erhalten,** to receive sth. through s.o.; **d. die Post,** through the post, by post; **er fiel d. Mörderhand,** he fell at the hand of a murderer; **er starb d. Gift,** he died of poisoning; **zum Tode d. den Strang verurteilt werden,** to be sentenced to die by hanging, to be condemned to death by hanging. **3.** *Mth:* **(dividiert) durch,** divided by; over; **zehn (dividiert) durch drei,** ten divided by three; ten over three; **a durch b,** a over b.

II. **durch,** *adv.* through. **1.** (*a*) **die ganze Nacht d.,** all night (long), all through the night, throughout the night; **die ganze Zeit d.,** the whole time, all the time; **er schlief den ganzen ersten Akt d.,** he slept throughout, all through, during the whole of, the first act; (*b*) (*emphasis*) **d. den Wald d.,** (right) through the wood; (*c*) *Poet:* **die Wolken d.,** through the clouds. **2. d. und d.,** through and through; thoroughly; **d. und d. kalt,** cold through and through; **d. und d. naß,** wet through; **sie ist eine d. und d. ehrliche Frau,** she is a thoroughly honest woman; **er ist Künstler d. und d.,** he's an artist through and through, to the core; **ich kenne Paris d. und d.,** I know Paris through and through, like the back of my hand; **ihr Blick ging mir d. und d.,** she looked me through and through. **3. sechs Uhr d.,** past six o'clock.

III. **durch** (*ellipt. use, with verbal element understood*) (*a*) **ich muß durch (=durchkommen),** I must get through; **er ist durch (=durchgekommen),** he has got through; he has got through, passed (his examinations); **sie ist bei mir unten durch,** I've finished, done, with her, I'm through with her; (*b*) **meine Strümpfe sind an den Knien durch (=durchgewetzt),** my stockings are through, have gone through, worn through, at the knees; (*c*) **er hat das Buch durch (=durchgelesen),** he has finished, gone through, the book; **ist das Fleisch durch (=durchgebraten)?** is the meat done? **der Käse ist durch (=durchgereift),** the cheese is ripe. *See also* **durchhaben.**

durch-, Durch-, *vbl, substantival and adverbial pref.* (*in verbs, where stress falls on first syllable prefix is separable. All intransitive verbs have separate prefix, transitive verbs may be separable or inseparable*) **1.** (*forming verbs, etc., denoting passage through*) (*a*) *v.i. sep.* **durchgehen,** to go, pass, through; **durchbrausen,** to rage, roar, through; **durchdringen,** to penetrate; **durchfliegen,** to fly through; **durchrasen,** to tear through; **durchwandern,** to walk through; **durchsickern,** to filter through; *v.tr.* **durchbrausen** *insep.*, to rage, roar, through (sth.); **durchdringen** *insep.*, to penetrate (sth.); **durchfliegen** *insep.*, to fly through (sth.); **durchrasen** *insep.*, to tear through (sth.); **durchlassen** *sep.*, to let (sth., s.o.) through; *nouns:* **Durchflug** *m*, flight through; **Durchfahrt** *f*, **Durchreise** *f*, journey through; (*b*) *v.refl. sep.* (*denoting penetration*) **sich durcharbeiten,** to work one's way through; **sich durchdrängen,** to push one's way through; **sich durchbohren,** to bore one's way through; **sich durchbetteln,** to beg one's way along; **sich durchfinden,** to find one's way through; (*c*) *v. impers. sep.* **(durchregnen) — es hat durchgeregnet,** the rain has come through; **(durchnässen) — es hat durchgenäßt,** the damp, moisture, has come through; (*d*) *v.tr. sep.* **durchschlagen, durchtreiben, durchreichen, durchziehen,** to knock, drive, hand, pull (sth.) through. **2.** (*right through from beginning to end*) (*a*) *v.tr.* **durchkämpfen** *sep.*, to fight (sth.) out (to the end); **durchlesen** *sep.*, to read (book, etc.) through; **durchspielen** *sep.*, to play (piece of music, etc.) through; **durchmachen** *sep.*, to go through (course of study, difficult time, etc.); **durchblättern** *sep. & insep.*, to leaf through (book); (*b*) *nouns:* **Durchbinder** *m*, through-stone; **Durchbolzen** *m*, through-bolt. **3.** *v.tr.* (*a*) (*penetration of obj.*) **durchbeben, durchzittern,** *insep.*, (*of emotion*) to thrill through (s.o.); (*b*) (*thorough penetration of obj.*) *usu. insep.* **durchnässen,** to soak (sth.) (through); **durchtränken,** to soak, saturate, impregnate (sth.); **durchdringen,** to permeate, pervade (sth.); (*c*) (*thorough treatment of obj.*) *usu. sep.* **durchbacken,** to bake (sth.) thoroughly, through; **durchberaten,** to discuss (sth.) thoroughly; **durchkauen,** to chew (sth.) thoroughly; **durchkneten,** to work, knead (dough, etc.) thoroughly; **durchlüften,** to air (room, etc.) thoroughly. **4.** (*action continued right through period of time*) *v.i. sep.* **durchtanzen,** to dance the whole (of a period of) time; **durchwachen,** to remain awake (throughout a period of time); **durchschlafen,** to sleep (right) through; *v.tr. insep.* **durchtanzen,** to spend (period of time) dancing; **durchwachen,** to remain awake during, to keep watch through (night, etc.); **durchschlafen,** to sleep through (period of time). **5.** (*a*) (*breaking, etc., through, in two*) *v.i. sep.* **durchbrechen,** to break through, apart, asunder, in two; **durchreißen,** to break asunder, to sever; *v.tr. usu. sep.* **durchbeißen,** to bite (sth.) through, in two; **durchbrechen,** to break (sth.) through, in two; **durchreißen,** to tear (sth.) asunder, in two; (*b*) (*breaching of obj.*) *v.tr. usu. insep.* **durchbeißen,** to bite (a hole) through (sth.); **durchbohren,** to bore through (sth.); **durchbrechen,** to breach, break through (sth.); **durchlochen, durchlöchern,** to perforate (sth.), to make holes through (sth.); (*c*) (*wearing through of obj.*) *v.tr. sep.* **durchlaufen,** to wear out (shoes, etc.); **durchreiten,** to wear out (one's trousers) by riding; **durchtanzen,** to wear out (shoes) by dancing. **6.** (*mixing thoroughly*) *v.tr.* **durchmengen** *insep.*, to mix (sth.) (with sth.); **durchmischen** *sep.*, to mix (substances) together; *insep.* to mix (sth.) (with sth.); **durchsetzen** *insep.*, to intersperse, pervade, permeate (sth.) (with sth.); *adv.* **durcheinander,** mixed. **7.** (*searching through*) *v.tr.* **durchsuchen** *sep. & insep.*, **durchstöbern** *insep.*, to search through (house, papers, etc.); **durchwühlen** *sep. & insep.*, to rummage through (drawers, papers, etc.). **8.** (*treatment of objects one after the other*) *v.tr.* **durchprobieren** *sep.*, to try (dishes, etc.), to try on (clothes), one after the other; **durchmustern** *sep.*, to look through (thgs); *insep.* to scrutinize (people, thgs); **durchsehen** *sep.*, to look through (papers, etc.).

durchackern, *v.tr. sep.* (*a*) to plough (field); **ein durchgeackertes Feld,** a ploughed field; (*b*) to do thorough research into (subject); to work through (book, etc.) with great thoroughness.

durcharbeiten[1]. I. *v.sep.* **1.** *v.tr.* (*a*) to work (clay, dough, etc.) thoroughly; (*of sport*) to exercise (body); (*of pers.*) to massage (body) thoroughly; **den Teig d.,** to work the dough, to knead the dough, thoroughly; **beim Schwimmen wird der ganze Körper durchgearbeitet,** swimming exercises the whole body; (*b*) to study (sth.) thoroughly, to make a thorough study of (sth.); **ich habe das Buch durchgearbeitet,** I have made a thorough study of the book; **er hat die Akten noch nicht durchgearbeitet,** he has not studied the files thoroughly yet, he has not worked through, been through, the files properly yet; **sie muß für ihr Examen die englische Geschichte des neunzehnten Jahrhunderts gründlich d.,** for her examination she has to make a thorough study of nineteenth-century English history; (*c*) to work (sth.) out; **Sie haben den Aufsatz nicht genügend durchgearbeitet,** you haven't worked the essay out carefully enough; **der Autor hat die Rollen nicht genügend durchgearbeitet,** the author has not developed the characters sufficiently. **2. sich durch etwas durcharbeiten,** to work one's way through sth.; **sie haben sich durch die Menge durchgearbeitet,** they worked, pushed, elbowed, their way through the crowd; **ich habe mich mit Mühe durch das Buch durchgearbeitet,** I worked through the book with difficulty, *F:* I ploughed through the book. **3.** *v.i.* (*haben*) to work through (a period of time) without stopping, without a break; **wir haben durchgearbeitet,** we didn't have a break, we worked without a break; **die ganze Nacht d.,** to work all night (long), right through the night.

II. *vbl s.* **1. Durcharbeiten,** *n. in vbl senses; also:* (*a*) thorough study (of sth.); (*b*) development (of characters, etc. by author). **2. Durcharbeitung,** *f.* (*a*) =II. 1; (*b*) (*of dough*) being kneaded, worked; (*of body*) (i) being exercised; (ii) being massaged.

durcharbeiten[2], *v.tr. insep.* to work through (period of time); **eine durcharbeitete Nacht,** a night spent working, at work.

durchaus, *adv.* **1.** [ˈdurçᵓˈaus] (*a*) *Lit:* everywhere, all over; **das Kleid war d. mit Perlen besetzt,** the dress was studded all over with pearls; (*b*) entirely, through and through; thoroughly, altogether; **seine Rüstung war d. von Gold,** his armour was made entirely of gold; **das Stück hat mir d. gefallen,** I liked, enjoyed, the play thoroughly; **ein d. zuverlässiger Mann,** a thoroughly, an absolutely, entirely, altogether, reliable man; **er hat d. recht,** he is absolutely, altogether, right; **das Buch ist d. lesbar,** the book is thoroughly, certainly, readable. **2.** [durçᵓˈaus] (*a*) absolutely, quite, completely, entirely; **ich bin d. damit einverstanden, daß er kommt,** I entirely, quite, agree to his coming; **es ist d. möglich, daß ich heute abend ins Theater gehe,** it's quite possible that I shall go to the theatre this evening; **halten Sie das für möglich? — durchaus!** do you think that is possible? — yes, absolutely! yes, certainly! **das können wir d. machen,** we can certainly do that; (*b*) (*in positive statement, if especially emphasized sometimes* ˈdurçᵓˈaus) absolutely; by all means; at all costs; **er will d. recht haben,** he's absolutely certain, convinced, he is right; **sie will d. mit,** she absolutely insists on coming too, she is absolutely determined to come too; **d. nicht,** in no way, by no means, not at all, not in the least; **störe ich Sie? — d. nicht!** am I disturbing you? —not at all! not in the least! by no means! **er ist d. nicht so dumm, wie man meint,** he is by no means, he is not in any way, as stupid as people think; **es ist d. nicht so einfach,** it's by no means so simple; **sie paßt d. nicht in diesen Kreis,** she does not fit into this circle at all; **er wollte es d. nicht gestehen,** he absolutely refused to admit it; **es ist d. nicht unmöglich,** it is by no means, certainly not, impossible.

durchbacken, *v. sep.* (*conj. like* **backen**) **1.** *v.tr.* to bake (sth.) thoroughly, through; **der Kuchen ist noch nicht durchgebacken,** the cake isn't baked through yet; **gut durchgebackenes Brot,** well-baked bread. **2.** *v.i.* (*haben*) **der Bäcker hatte so viel zu tun, daß er die ganze Nacht durchgebacken hat,** the baker had so much to do that he spent the whole night baking, that he baked the whole night through, all night (long).

durchbeben, *v.insep. Lit:* **1.** *v.tr.* (*of emotion*) to thrill through (s.o.); to make (s.o.) quiver, throb; to vibrate, pulsate, tremble, through (s.o.); **ein Gefühl der höchsten Wonne durchbebte ihn,** a feeling of ecstasy thrilled, trembled, through him, thrilled through his veins; **von Wonne, von Angst, durchbebt,** quivering with joy, with fear. **2.** *v.i.* (*haben*) to spend (period of time) in a state of fear; **angstvoll durchbebte Nächte,** nights passed in fear and trembling.

durchbeißen, *v.* (*strong*) I. *v.tr. sep.* **1.** to bite (sth.) through; **der Hund hat die Leine durchgebissen,** the dog bit (right) through the lead, bit the lead (right) through, in two. **2. sich durchbeißen,** (*a*) to bite one's way through (sth.); **die Kaninchen haben sich durch das Netz durchgebissen,** the rabbits escaped by biting a way

through the netting; (*b*) *F:* to fight one's way through, out of (a situation, etc.); **er hat sich durch alle Schwierigkeiten durchgebissen,** he fought his way out of all difficulties; **der Anfang wird schwierig sein, aber da mußt du dich halt d.,** it will be hard at first, but you'll just have to get yourself through it somehow.

II. **durchbeißen,** *v.tr. insep.* to bite (a hole) through (sth.).

durchbekommen, *v.tr. sep.* (*strong*) (*a*) to get (sth.) through (sth.); (*b*) to get (bill) through (Parliament), to get (bill) passed (in Parliament); (*c*) to get (s.o.) through (examination).

durchberaten, *v.tr. sep.* (*strong*) to discuss (a matter) thoroughly, to debate (a matter).

durchbetteln[1] **(sich),** *v.refl. sep.* to make one's living, to live, by begging; **ein fauler Mensch, der sich durchbettelt,** a lazy person who lives by begging, who begs his way through (life); **er hat sich bis nach Italien durchgebettelt,** he begged his way (through) to Italy.

durchbetteln[2], *v.tr. insep.* **er hat das ganze Land durchbettelt,** he has begged his way through, over, the whole country.

durchbiegen. I. *v. sep.* (*strong*) **1.** *v.tr.* (*a*) to bend (sth.) to its fullest extent; to deflect (beam, etc.); (*b*) to break (sth.) by bending (it). **2.** *v.i.* (*sein*) & **sich durchbiegen,** (*of beam, etc.*) to deflect, sag; **durchbiegende Kraft,** deflecting force (on beam).

II. **1. Durchbiegen,** *n. in vbl senses; also:* deflection (of beam, etc.). **2. Durchbiegung,** *f.* (*a*) =II. 1; (*b*) curvature (of lens); *Mec:* deflection; sag.

Durchbiegungskraft, *f.* deflecting force (on beam).

Durchbiegungskurve, Durchbiegungslinie, *f. Mec:* curve of deflection.

Durchbiegungsmesser, Durchbiegungszeichner, *m.* deflectometer.

Durchbinder, *m. Constr:* parpen, bonder, bondstone, through-stone, *U.S:* perpend.

durchblasen, *v.* (*strong*) I. *v.sep.* **1.** *v.tr.* to blow (sth.) through (sth.). **2.** *v.i.* (*haben*) (*of wind, etc.*) **durch etwas d.,** to blow through sth.; **der Wind blies mir durch die Ärmel durch,** the wind blew through my sleeves. **3.** *v.tr.* to play (piece of music) through (on wind instrument); **er hat die ganze Trompetenpartie zweimal durchgeblasen,** he played the whole trumpet part through twice. **4.** *v.i.* (*haben*) to keep blowing (wind instrument) (for period of time); **sie hat auf der Blockflöte bis zum Abend durchgeblasen,** she went on playing her recorder until evening.

II. **durchblasen,** *v.tr. insep.* (*of wind*) to blow through (sth.); **der Wind durchblies die Wälder,** the wind blew through the woods.

Durchblaseventil, *n. Mch:* snifting-valve; blow-valve, air-valve, air-intake (of steam boiler).

durchblättern, *v.tr. sep. & insep.* to leaf through, *U.S:* to page through (book), to turn over the pages (of book); to dip into (book); to glance, skim, through (book).

durchbleuen, *v.tr. sep. F:* to thrash, beat (s.o.), to give (s.o.) a good hiding, drubbing, leathering, to beat (s.o.) black and blue.

Durchblick, *m.* (*a*) view through; **die Häuser am Kai sind so eng zusammengebaut, daß man von der Stadt aus keinen D. auf die See hat,** the houses are built so closely together on the quay-side that one has no view through to, no glimpse of, the sea from the town; (*b*) vista; **von der Allee aus hat man einen herrlichen D. auf den Park,** from the avenue one has a magnificent view of, vista over, of, the park; **der Park ist so angelegt, daß man überall wundervolle Durchblicke hat,** the park is so planned that wherever you stand you have a wonderful vista.

durchblicken, *v.* **1.** *v.i. sep.* (*haben*) (*a*) to look through; **durch etwas d.,** to look through sth.; **er hat durch die Öffnung in der Wand d. können,** he was able to look, see, through the opening in the wall; **hier, wo die Spalte ist, können wir d.,** we can see through here where there's a gap; (*b*) (*of quality, etc.*) to show through; **die innere Güte, die bei allen seinen Handlungen durchblickt,** the genuine kindness which is apparent in all his actions; (*c*) **etwas d. lassen,** to let sth. be seen; to hint at, to intimate, sth.; **sie ließ ihre Mißbilligung d.,** she let her disapproval be seen; **obgleich er nichts Bestimmtes sagte, ließ er d., daß ihm die Sache mißfiel,** although he said nothing definite he let it be seen, he intimated, that the business displeased him. **2.** *v.tr. insep.* = **durchschauen** 3.

durchblitzen, *v.* **1.** *v.i. sep.* (*haben*) to shine, flash, through; **die Sonne blitzt zwischen den Wolken durch,** the sun shines from between the clouds. **2.** *v.tr. insep.* to flash through (sth.); **ein Gedanke durchblitzte sein Hirn,** a thought flashed through his mind.

durchbluten, *v.* **1.** *v.i. sep.* (*haben*) to bleed through; **die Wunde blutete durch,** the blood came through (the bandage). **2.** *v.tr. insep.* (*a*) to bleed through (sth.); **ein durchbluteter Verband,** a blood-stained bandage; (*b*) (*of skin*) **durchblutet werden,** to have the circulation promoted; **durch kalte Abreibungen wird die Haut durchblutet,** the circulation in the skin is promoted by cold rub-downs; **durchblutete Haut,** live skin, skin in which the blood is circulating.

durchbohren, *v.* **1.** *sep.* (*a*) *v.tr.* to bore (right) through (sth.); **ein durchgebohrtes Brett,** a plank that has been bored right through; (*b*) *v.i.* (*haben*) **durch etwas d.,** to bore (right) through sth.; (*c*) **sich d.,** to bore (one's way) through; **der Wurm bohrt sich durch das Holz durch,** the worm bores its way through the wood. **2.** *v.tr. insep.* to bore through (s.o., sth.); to pierce (s.o., sth.) through; **vom Schwerte durchbohrt,** run through with a sword; **sich die Ohrläppchen d. lassen,** to have one's ears pierced; **das Herz wurde ihm von einem Speer durchbohrt,** he was pierced through the heart by a javelin; **j-n mit (seinen) Blicken d.,** to look s.o. through and through.

Durchbolzen, *m. Mec.E: N.Arch:* through-bolt.

durchbrausen, *v.* **1.** *v.i. sep.* (*haben*) to rage, to roar, through; **der Zug brauste durch den Tunnel durch,** the train roared, went roaring, through the tunnel; **der Wind brauste zwischen den Felswänden durch,** the wind raged between the crags. **2.** *v.tr. insep.* (*of wind*) to rage through (trees, etc.).

durchbrechen[1], *v.sep.* (*strong*) I. *v.tr.* **1.** to break (piece of wood, etc.) through, in two; **er hat den Stock in der Mitte durchgebrochen,** he broke the stick through the middle, in half. **2. eine Tür, ein Fenster, usw., (durch eine Mauer) d.,** to make, let in, a door, a window, etc. (in a wall); **eine Verbindungsstraße zwischen zwei Häuserblöcken d.,** to open up a thoroughfare between two blocks of houses; **eine Verbindung zum Nebenhaus d.,** to cut a passage through to the next house.

II. **durchbrechen,** *v.i.* (*sein*) **1.** to break through; to break apart, asunder, in two; **der Damm war an mehreren Stellen durchgebrochen,** the dam had broken, burst, in several places; **die Eisenstange brach in der Mitte durch,** the iron bar broke through the middle, broke in half. **2.** (*a*) **durch etwas d.,** to break through (sth.); *Ven:* (*of game*) to break out (between beaters); **die Sonne bricht durch die Wolken durch,** the sun breaks through the clouds; **die aufgeregte Menschenmenge brach durch die Kette der Polizisten durch,** the excited crowd broke through the police cordon; *Mil:* **(durch die feindlichen Linien) d.,** to break through (the enemy lines); *abs.* **der Feind war an mehreren Stellen durchgebrochen,** the enemy had broken through in several places; (*b*) to break through; to appear, to come to light; (*of teeth*) to come through, to erupt; **seine ersten Zähne sind durchgebrochen,** his first teeth have come through, he has cut his first teeth; **bald werden die Blüten d.,** the buds will be bursting soon; **manchmal bricht ihre wahre Natur durch,** sometimes her true character asserts itself, one gets a glimpse of her true character; **die Wut brach bei ihm durch,** his anger broke loose; **eines Tages wird die Wahrheit d.,** one day the truth will come out, will come to light; (*c*) *Med:* (*of appendix*) **in die Bauchhöhle d.,** to perforate into the peritoneum; **durchgebrochene Blinddarmentzündung,** peritonitis.

III. *vbl s.* **Durchbrechen,** *n. in vbl senses; also:* eruption (of teeth); *cp.* **Durchbruch.**

durchbrechen[2], *v.insep.* I. *v.tr.* to break through (sth.); *Med:* (*of appendix, ulcer, etc.*) to perforate into (bowel, etc.); **eine Wand d.,** to break through, to breach, a wall; **das Wasser hatte den Damm an mehreren Stellen durchbrochen,** the water had breached the dike in several places; **das Auto durchbrach die Absperrkette,** the car broke through the barrier; **die aufgeregte Menschenmenge durchbrach die Kette der Polizisten,** the excited crowd broke through the police cordon; *Mil:* **die feindlichen Linien d.,** to break through, pierce through, the enemy lines; **er durchbricht alle Hindernisse,** he breaks through all obstacles; **er durchbrach alle Regeln des Anstandes,** he violated all the rules of etiquette; **sie durchbrach die Grenzen ihrer kleinbürgerlichen Existenz,** she broke through the barriers of her plebeian existence; **ein Verbot d.,** to ignore a prohibition; **alle Regeln d.,** to break, ignore, all the rules.

II. *vbl s.* **Durchbrechen** *n.*, **Durchbrechung** *f. in vbl senses; also:* breach, violation (of rules); *Med:* perforation (into bowel, etc.).

III. *p.p. & a.* **durchbrochen,** *in vbl senses; esp. Tex: Constr: etc:* openwork; *Needlew:* **durchbrochene Arbeit,** openwork; **durchbrochene Strümpfe,** openwork stockings; *Cer:* **ein Teller mit durchbrochenem Rand,** a plate with a perforated rim; *Her:* **durchbrochenes Kreuz,** cross quarter-pierced; **rund durchbrochenes Kreuz,** cross round-pierced.

durchbrennen[1], *v.sep.* (*conj. like* **brennen**) I. *v.tr.* to burn through (sth.); **die glühenden Kohlen haben den Fußboden durchgebrannt,** the red-hot coals have burnt through the floor.

II. **durchbrennen,** *v.i.* **1.** (*haben*) (*a*) (*of stove, etc.*) to stay alight, to keep burning; **das Licht hat die ganze Nacht durchgebrannt,** the light was left on all night; the light burned all night; (*b*) (*of fire, etc.*) **durch etwas d.,** to burn through sth. **2.** (*sein*) (*of coal, etc.*) to burn through; *F:* (*of coal in boiler, etc.*) to burn right through. **3.** (*sein*) (*a*) to burn through; (*of grate, etc.*) **durchgebrannt sein,** to be burnt through, to have a hole burnt through, to be heated till it breaks; **die Zimmerdecke ist vollkommen durchgebrannt,** the ceiling has been burnt right through, a hole has been burnt right through the ceiling; (*b*) *El.E:* (*of fuse*) to blow; **die Sicherung ist durchgebrannt,** the fuse has blown; *F:* the light has fused; **durchgebrannt,** burnt-out (coil, etc.); blown (fuse). **4.** (*sein*) *F:* to run away, to abscond, *F:* to decamp; (*of daughter, wife*) to elope (with lover); **er ist mit der Frau seines Nachbarn durchgebrannt,** he has run away with his neighbour's wife; **mit der Kasse d.,** to make off with the cash; **er ist von zu Hause durchgebrannt,** he has run away from home.

durchbrennen[2], *v.tr. insep.* (*conj. like* **brennen**) (*of passion, etc.*) to burn through (s.o.).

durchbringen, *v.tr. sep.* (*conj. like* **bringen**) **1.** (*a*) to bring, take, carry, get (s.o., sth.) through; **die Zollbeamten sind sehr streng, — du wirst diesen Wein wohl nicht d. können,** the customs officers are very strict—I don't think you'll be able to get, take, that wine through; **die Tür war sehr eng, aber endlich haben wir alle Möbel durchgebracht,** the door was very narrow, but in the end we managed to get all the furniture through (it); (*b*) to bring, pull (s.o.) through (an illness); to get (s.o.) through (an examination); **er bringt alle seine Schüler durch ihre Prüfungen durch,** he gets all his pupils through their examinations; **eine Gesetzesvorlage (im Parlament) d.,** to get a bill through (Parliament); **einen Antrag d.,** to get a resolution adopted; (*c*) **sich (kümmerlich) d.,** to scrape a living (together); **sich ehrlich d.,** to scrape an honest living; **mit sechs Kindern bringt man sich schwer durch,** if one has six children it is difficult to make ends meet. **2.** (*a*) to spend, to get through (money); **binnen dreier Jahre hatte er sein ganzes Vermögen durchgebracht,** within three years he had got through his entire fortune; (*b*) *A:* to spend (time).

durchbrochen, *a. see* **durchbrechen**[2], III.

Durchbruch, *m.* **1.** opening up (of thoroughfare, etc.); cutting (of door, etc.) through (wall, etc.). **2.** (*a*) breaking through; breaking, bursting (of water) through (dike, etc.); cutting, eruption (of teeth); breakthrough (of enemy troops through lines; of rock-drill into cavity; of scientists, experimenters, to new discovery); *Med:* perforation (of ulcer, etc.) (into bowel, etc.); *Av:* **der D. durch die Schallmauer,** the breaking (through) of the sound-barrier; (*b*) dawn, awakening (of new feelings, etc.); **neuer D.,** revival, re-awakening (of ideas, feelings, etc.); **zum D. kommen,** to break through; **dieser Gedanke ist bei ihm zum D. gekommen,** this thought took shape in his mind; **einer Ansicht zum D. verhelfen,** to help propagate an idea. **3.** gap, opening, aperture (in wall, etc.); breach (in wall, dike, enemy lines, etc.); thoroughfare opened up (between blocks of houses, etc.); road cut through (built up area); *Ph.Geog:* (i) water-gap; (ii) cut-off; *Med:* perforation (in membrane, etc.). **4.** *Needlew:* drawn(-thread)-work. **5.** *A:* diarrhoea.

Durchbrucharbeit, *f. Needlew:* openwork; drawn(-thread)-work; *Constr:* openwork.

Durchbruchstal, *n. Ph.Geog:* transverse valley; water-gap.

durchdenken, *v.tr.* (*conj. like* **denken**) **1.** *sep.* (*a*) to think (sth.) over thoroughly; **wir haben seine Vorschläge sorgfältig durchgedacht,** we have thought his propositions over carefully; (*b*) =2. **2.** *insep.* to think (sth.) out; **jede Handlung ist bei ihm durchdacht,** every action of his is carefully, logically, planned, thought out; **ein fein durchdachter Plan,** a carefully thought out plan; **die Rede war nicht genügend durchdacht,** the speech had not been carefully, logically, enough worked out, thought out; **ich habe den Vorschlag noch einmal durchdacht,** I thought the proposal over carefully once more.

durchdrängen (sich), *v.refl. sep.* to push (one's way) through; **die Menschenansammlung war so groß, man konnte sich kaum d.,** the crowd was so great one could hardly push one's way through (it); **er hat sich durch die Menge durchgedrängt,** he has pushed (his way) through the crowd.

durchdrehen. I. *v.tr. sep.* **1.** to put (meat, etc.) through the mincer, to put (clothes, etc.) through the mangle, to put (coffee) through the grinder; *see also* **durchgedreht. 2.** *Av:* to swing (propeller). **3.** *Aut:* to rev (up) (engine).

II. *v.i. sep.* **1.** (*haben*) *Aut:* (*a*) (*of wheels*) to spin; (*b*) **den Motor d. lassen,** to rev (up) the engine. **2.** (*sein, haben*) *F:* (*of pers.*) to go out of one's mind (with worry, etc.).

durchdringen[1]. I. *v.i. sep.* (*strong*) (*sein*) **1.** to penetrate (**nach, bis, zu,** to; **durch,** through); **das Heer ist bis Berlin durchgedrungen,** the army has penetrated to Berlin; **die Truppen sind durch die feindlichen Linien durchgedrungen,** the troops have penetrated through the enemy lines; **das Wasser drang durch meine Schuhe durch,** the water penetrated (through) my shoes; **das Gerücht ist nicht (bis) zu uns durchgedrungen,** the rumour has not penetrated to, reached, us; **er sieht einen an mit einem Blick, der einem bis ins innerste Mark durchdringt,** he looks at one with eyes that penetrate, that see into, one's very soul. **2.** (*a*) to penetrate, to be penetrating; **bei diesem Lärm kann keine Stimme d.,** no voice can be heard above, can penetrate through, this noise; **ihre Stimme dringt auch im größten Straßenlärm durch,** her voice (is so penetrating that it) can even be heard above the roar of the traffic; **die Kinder sind so laut, daß der Lärm durch alle Wände durchdringt,** the children make so much noise that it can be heard through the walls; **er sang so laut, daß seine Stimme bis ins Nebenhaus durchdrang,** he sang so loudly that his voice could be heard next door; (*b*) **mit seiner Meinung, mit einem Vorschlag, d.,** to win acceptance for one's opinion, for a proposal; **er ist mit seinem Vorschlag bei den Behörden nicht durchgedrungen,** he could not persuade the authorities to accept his proposal.

II. *vbl s.* **Durchdringen,** *n. in vbl senses; also:* penetration (of s.o.) through *or* to (sth.).

III. *pr.p. & a.* **durchdringend,** *in vbl senses, esp.* penetrating (voice, glance); piercing (shriek); pungent (smell); penetrating, acute, incisive (mind); penetrating, incisive, trenchant (judgment); **einen durchdringenden Blick haben,** to have a penetrating eye.

durchdringen[2]. I. *v.tr. insep.* (*strong*) (*a*) to penetrate, to pierce (sth.); (*of water, smell, etc.*) to permeate (sth.); (*of smell*) to pervade (sth.); **sein Schwert durchdrang die Brust seines Feindes,** his sword penetrated, pierced, his enemy's breast; **das Licht durchdrang den finsteren Raum,** the light penetrated the darkness of the room; **Dunkelheit, die das Auge nicht d. konnte,** darkness which the eye could not penetrate; **die Kälte durchdrang allmählich das ganze Haus,** the cold gradually penetrated through, pervaded, the whole house; (*of two substances*) **einander d.,** to (inter)mingle, to (inter)mix; (*b*) *Lit:* to penetrate into, to obtain a thorough knowledge of (a field of learning, etc.); (*c*) *A:* **sich von etwas d.,** to penetrate into (a field of learning, etc.); to become filled, imbued with (an idea); (*d*) (*of idea, emotion, etc.*) to fill, pervade, imbue, penetrate (s.o.); **die Eifersucht durchdrang sein ganzes Wesen,** his whole being was filled with jealousy; **alle seine Schriften sind von diesen Ideen durchdrungen,** all his writings are pervaded, imbued, with these ideas; **er fühlte sich von einer neuen Kraft durchdrungen,** he felt himself infused with a new strength; **von der Wahrheit einer Behauptung durchdrungen sein,** to be convinced of the truth of a statement; **die Propaganda durchdrang die letzten Winkel des Landes,** the propaganda penetrated the remotest corners of the land; **von Liebe, von Angst, durchdrungen,** filled with love, with fear; **sie ist von dem Gefühl ihrer eigenen Wichtigkeit durchdrungen,** she is filled with, imbued with, full of, a feeling of her own importance.

II. *vbl s.* **1. Durchdringen,** *n. in vbl senses; also:* penetration; permeation; pervasion. **2. Durchdringung,** *f.* (*a*) =II. 1; (*b*) penetration, pervasion (of mind, etc.) (by ideas, feelings, etc.); *Pol:* **friedliche D.,** peaceful penetration.

Durchdringungsfähigkeit, *f.* penetrative power.

Durchdringungskurve, *f. Geom:* (line of) intersection (of two planes).

Durchdringungsvermögen, *n.* penetrative power.

Durchdringungszwilling, *m. Cryst:* interpenetrant twin, penetration twin.

durchdröhnen, *v.* **1.** *v.i. sep.* (*haben*) to boom, rumble, resound, ring, through; **der Lärm des Gongs dröhnte durch das Haus durch,** the sound of the gong boomed through the house. **2.** *v.tr. insep.* to fill (sth.) with a booming sound, to boom, rumble, resound, ring, through (sth.); **das vom Lärm des Gongs durchdröhnte Haus,** the house which resounded with the booming of the gong.

durchdrücken, *v.tr. sep.* **1.** (*a*) to press, force, squeeze, push (sth.) through (sth.); **Obst, usw., (durch ein Sieb) d.,** to pass, press, fruit, etc., through a sieve; (*b*) **er hat seinen Willen, seinen Vorschlag, durchgedrückt,** he forced acceptance of his wishes, of his proposal; **ein Gesetz im Parlament d.,** to force a bill through Parliament. **2.** *Gym: etc:* to straighten (one's knees, etc.). **3. sich durchdrücken,** (*a*) to squeeze, push, force one's way, through (sth.); **sich durch eine kleine Öffnung, durch eine Menschenmenge, d.,** to squeeze through a narrow opening, to force one's way, to push, through a crowd of people; (*b*) (*of thg*) to press through (leather, material, etc.) leaving an outline, a bulge; **die Typen haben sich (auf der anderen Seite) durchgedrückt,** the impression of the type has come through (on the other side); **der Stempel hat sich (auf der anderen Seite) durchgedrückt,** the impression of the stamp has come through on the other side; **an den Knien durchgedrückte Hosenbeine,** trousers that have gone baggy, that have bagged, at the knees. **4.** *A:* **sich durchdrücken = sich durchbringen,** *q.v. under* **durchbringen** 1 (*c*).

durchdrungen, *p.p. & a. see* **durchdringen.**

durcheilen, *v.* **1.** *v.i. sep.* (*sein*) to hurry through; **er eilte durch die Stadt durch,** he hurried through the town. **2.** *v.tr. insep.* to hurry **die Straßen d.,** to hurry through the streets. through (sth.);

durcheinander[1], *pron. adv.* **1.** (*a*) mixed; promiscuously, at random, indiscriminately; **in seinen Blumenbeeten wachsen Dahlien und Astern d.,** dahlias and asters grow at random, promiscuously, in his flower-beds; (*b*) in disorder, in confusion, at sixes and sevens, pell-mell, *F:* upside down, topsy-turvy, higgledy-piggledy; **d. liegen,** to be in (a state of) confusion; **alles in ihrem Zimmer war, lag, wie Kraut und Rüben d.,** her whole room was in (a state of) utter confusion, was at sixes and sevens, *F:* upside down, topsy-turvy; **die Papiere lagen d. auf dem Tisch,** the papers lay in disorder, at sixes and sevens, pell-mell, *F:* higgledy-piggledy, on the table; **sie warf alles, Kleider, Schuhe, Bücher, d. in den Koffer,** she threw everything, clothes, shoes, books, pell-mell, *F:* higgledy-piggledy, into the case; *see also* **durcheinanderwerfen;** (*c*) *F:* **er ist ganz d.,** he's all mixed up, confused, muddled, at sixes and sevens, *F:* he's all abroad. **2.** *comb. fm.* **durcheinander-,** (*prefixed to verbs*); **man soll nicht Bier und Wein durcheinandertrinken,** one shouldn't drink beer and wine together, one shouldn't mix, alternate, (drinks of) beer and wine; **durcheinanderlaufen,** (i) (*of people*) to run about in confusion; (ii) (*of colours*) to run; **alle liefen durcheinander auf dem Hofe,** everyone was running about pell-mell, in confusion, everyone was milling around, in the courtyard; **in der Verwirrung schrieen alle durcheinander,** in the confusion everyone was shouting at once; **alles durcheinanderbringen,** (i) to mix everything up, to get everything into a muddle; (ii) to get everything, all one's ideas, mixed (up); **sie hatte alle meine sorgfältig geordneten Bücher wieder durcheinandergebracht,** she had mixed all my carefully sorted books up again, she had got all my carefully sorted books mixed up again; **es hat keinen Zweck, ihm den Plan zu erklären, denn er bringt immer alles durcheinander,** there's no point in explaining the plan to him as he always gets everything mixed up, he always mixes everything up; **j-n durcheinanderbringen,** to confuse s.o., to make s.o. confused; **(die Sachen) durcheinandermengen,** to mix (things) up; **sie hat ihre Sachen mit den meinen durcheinandergemengt,** she got her things all mixed up with mine; **er suchte das Testament im Schreibtisch seines Vaters, und wirbelte alle seine Papiere dabei wild durcheinander,** he looked for the will in his father's desk, and mixed, muddled, all his papers up, and threw all his papers into wild confusion, disorder, in doing so; **durcheinandergehen,** to get all mixed up; **es ging alles durcheinander,** everything was mixed up, was in confusion; **in seiner Rede ging alles durcheinander,** his speech was a complete mix-up.

Durcheinander[2], *n.* **-s/-,** muddle, mess, confusion, disorder, mess-up, mix-up, *F:* chaos; **im Zimmer war ein buntes, wirres, wüstes, D.,** the room was in a state of complete confusion, disorder, *F:* chaos; **auf dem Boden lag ein wüstes D. von Schuhen und Stiefeln, lagen Schuhe und Stiefel in wüstem D.,** on the floor lay a heap of boots and shoes all mixed up, in complete confusion, *F:* lay a chaos of boots and shoes; **ich frage mich, ob ich dieses D. je aufräumen kann,** I wonder whether I shall ever be able to clear up, straighten up, this muddle, mess; **in diesem D. kann man nichts finden,** it's impossible to find anything in this muddle.

durcheinanderwerfen, *v.tr. sep.* (*strong*) (*a*) to throw (thgs, room, etc.) into disorder, to mix (thgs) up, *F:* to turn (room, etc.) upside down; **alles (bunt) d.,** to mix everything up (together), to throw everything into (complete) confusion; **der Zollbeamte hat alle Sachen in meinem Koffer durcheinandergeworfen,** the customs officer mixed all the things in my case up together, threw all the things in my case into confusion; **in der Eile warf sie alles durcheinander,** in her haste she threw everything into confusion, disorder; **es ist nutzlos, die abgefallenen Blätter aufzuhäufen, denn der Wind wird sie doch alle wieder d.,** it's no use collecting the fallen leaves together because the wind will blow them all about again; (*b*) **Begriffe d.,** to get ideas mixed up, to confuse ideas, to get one's ideas mixed, muddled; **er war so aufgeregt, daß er alle Begriffe durcheinanderwarf,** he was so excited that he got everything mixed up, that all his ideas were in confusion.

durchfahren, *v.* (*strong*) **1.** *v.i. sep.* (*sein*) (*a*) (*of pers., vehicle*) to go, pass, travel, through; (*of pers., car*) to drive through; (*of pers., ship*) to go, sail, through; **wir fahren bloß durch,** we are merely travelling, passing, through, *Aut:* driving through; **wir sind mit dem Auto durch Hamburg durchgefahren,** we drove (straight) through Hamburg in the car; **London kenne ich ganz wenig, denn ich bin nur einmal mit dem Bus durchgefahren,** I don't know London very well, as I have only been, passed, through it once by bus; **das Schiff fuhr durch die Meerenge durch,** the ship went, sailed, through the straits; **wenn man von Dover nach Cambridge fährt, muß man durch ganz London d.,** if you go from Dover to Cambridge you have to cross London, you have to travel, go, right across London; (*b*) to go straight through; **der Zug fährt bis X ohne Halt durch,** the train goes straight through to X without stopping; **wir fahren mit dem späteren Zug, denn er fährt durch,** we'll go on the later train, because it goes straight through; **wir fuhren in einem bis Göttingen durch,** we went, travelled, *Aut:* drove, straight through to Göttingen without stopping; **der Zug fährt in Reading durch,** the train doesn't stop at Reading; **ich schlief im Zug ein und bin aus Versehen in Köln durchgefahren,** I fell asleep in the train and so went straight through Cologne by mistake, so failed to get out at Cologne. **2.** *v.tr. insep.* (*a*) to go, travel, drive, through, across (area); to drive through, to traverse (tract of country, etc.); **er hat ganz Deutschland in zwei Tagen durchfahren,** he drove right across, he crossed, Germany in two days; **sie durchfuhren die Lüneburger Heide im Wagen,** they drove across the Lüneburg Heath in their car; **die Meere d.,** to sail (across) the seas; (*b*) (*of shock, emotion, etc.*) to go, pass, through (s.o., sth.); **ein Zittern durchfuhr seinen ganzen Körper,** a shudder passed through, over, him, a shiver ran down his spine; **ein plötzlicher Schreck durchfuhr sie,** she was seized with sudden fear.

Durchfahrt, *f.* **1.** (*a*) journey, passage, through; **die D. durch Berlin dauerte mehrere Stunden,** the journey through, across, Berlin lasted several hours; **die D. durch den Panamakanal,** the passage through the Panama Canal; **'D.**

verboten!' 'keine D.!' 'no thoroughfare!' (*b*) journey, way, through; **ich kenne New York nicht gut; ich habe nur einmal auf der D. dort gehalten,** I don't know New York very well; I only stopped once on the way through; **wir sind hier auf der D. und haben zwei Stunden Zeit,** we are passing through and have two hours to spare; **ich fahre nächste Woche nach Rom und könnte Sie auf der D. in Paris treffen,** I am going to Rome next week and could meet you on my way through Paris; **wir sind bloß auf der D.,** we are merely travelling, passing, through. **2.** way through; gateway; **der Suezkanal ist eine enge D.,** the Suez Canal is a narrow passage.

Durchfahrtshöhe, *f.* headroom (under bridge, etc.) (for passing vehicles).

Durchfahrtsrecht, *n.* right of passage.

Durchfall, *m.* **1.** fall(ing) through. **2.** failure; **D. (durchs Examen),** failure, *F:* plough (in examination). **3.** *Med:* diarrhoea; **D. haben,** to have diarrhoea; **an D. leiden,** to suffer from diarrhoea; **plötzlich D. bekommen,** to have a sudden attack of diarrhoea, *F:* to be taken short. **4.** *Mill: etc:* matter which passes through the sieve, through the riddle; throughs.

Durchfallasche, *f.* riddlings.

durchfallen, *v.i. sep. (strong) (sein)* (*a*) to fall through; (*b*) to fail; **sie ist im, durchs, Examen durchgefallen,** she failed, *F:* she came down, got ploughed, in her examination; **er ist bei der Wahl durchgefallen,** he was not, did not get, elected; he did not get in; **das Theaterstück fiel durch,** the play was a failure, *F:* a flop; **der Plan ist durchgefallen,** the plan failed; **der Antrag fiel durch,** the motion was lost, rejected.

durchfechten, *v.tr. sep. (strong)* (*a*) to fight (duel) out (to the end); **in seinem Zustand wird er das Duell nicht d. können,** in his condition he won't be able to fight the duel out (to the end), he won't be able to finish the duel; (*b*) **seine Ansichten d.,** to fight till one gains acceptance for one's views; **das mußt du alleine d.,** you'll have to fight that out for yourself; (*c*) **sich durchfechten,** (i) to fight one's way through; (ii) to beg one's way through; **er wird sich durchs Leben d. müssen,** he'll have to fight his way through life, he'll have to struggle all his life.

durchfegen, *v.* **1.** *v.tr. & v.i. sep. (haben)* to sweep through; to sweep (sth.) through; **hier ist alles sauber, denn ich habe tüchtig durchgefegt,** everything is clean here, because I've swept thoroughly; **sie fegte das ganze Haus durch,** she swept the whole house through. **2.** *v.tr. insep.* to sweep through (sth.); **der Wind durchfegte die Gassen,** the wind swept down the alley-ways.

durchfeuchten, *v.tr. insep.* to make (sth.) damp (right) through; **das ganze Holz ist vom Regen durchfeuchtet,** all the wood is damp right through from the rain.

durchfinden (sich), *v.refl. sep. (strong)* to find one's way (through); **in dem Gewirr von engen Gäßchen kann man sich schwer d.,** in this maze of narrow streets it is very difficult to find one's way; **das Manuskript hat so viele Verbesserungen, daß der Drucker Schwierigkeiten haben wird, sich durchzufinden,** there are so many corrections in the manuscript that the printer will have difficulty in making it out; **sein Stil ist so kompliziert, daß man Schwierigkeiten hat, sich durch seine Gedankengänge durchzufinden,** his style is so involved that it is difficult to follow his train of thought; **ein Mann, der sich überall durchfindet,** a man who knows what to do in all circumstances.

durchflammen, *v.tr. insep. (of emotion, passion, etc.)* to burn in (s.o., s.o.'s heart, etc.); **Zorn durchflammte ihn, seine Brust,** anger burned within him, in his breast; **von Leidenschaft durchflammt,** inflamed, aflame, with passion.

durchflechten, *v.tr. insep. (strong)* to interweave, intertwine, interlace; (*a*) **ihre Haare waren mit Blumen durchflochten,** her hair was intertwined with flowers, flowers were intertwined with, woven into, her hair; **die Pferde hatten mit bunten Bändern durchflochtene Mähnen,** the horses had coloured ribbons plaited into their manes; (*b*) **seine Reden waren mit vielen Metaphern durchflochten,** his speech was interwoven with a great many metaphors.

durchfliegen, *v. (strong)* **1.** *v.i. sep. (sein)* (*a*) *(of bird, aeroplane, etc.)* to fly through; **er ist von London nach München durchgeflogen,** he flew through from London to Munich; (*b*) **durch etwas d.,** to fly through sth.; **der Stein flog durch das Fenster durch,** the stone flew through the window; **das Flugzeug ist unter der Brücke durchgeflogen,** the aeroplane flew under the bridge; (*c*) *F:* to fail, *F:* to be ploughed (in examinations). **2.** *v.tr. insep.* (*a*) *(of bird, aeroplane, etc.)* to fly through (region, etc.); (*b*) *(of vehicle, etc.)* to race, *F:* to tear, fly, through (region, etc.); **der Schnellzug durchflog die nächtliche Landschaft,** the express train raced through the night; (*c*) **sie hat das Buch durchflogen,** she skimmed through the book.

durchfließen, *v. (strong)* **1.** *v.i. sep. (sein)* (*a*) *(of water, etc.)* to flow (right) through (pipe, area, etc.); **das Wasser fließt durch die Röhren durch,** the water flows through the pipes; **der Rhein fließt mitten durch die Stadt durch,** the Rhine flows through the centre of the town; **die Donau fließt durch ganz Ungarn durch,** the Danube flows right through Hungary; (*b*) to flow through; **das Wasser hatte schon das Badezimmer überschwemmt und begann jetzt, ins Nebenzimmer durchzufließen,** the water had already flooded the bathroom and was now beginning to flow through into the next room. **2,** *v.tr. insep. (of river, etc.)* to flow through (area, etc.); **der Nil durchfließt Ägypten,** the Nile flows through Egypt; **ein von einem Bach durchflossenes Tal,** a valley through which a stream flows.

Durchflug, *m.* flight through; passage through.

Durchfluß, *m.* (*a*) flowing through (of water, etc.), flow (of water) through; (*b*) flow (of water, electric current).

Durchflußgeschwindigkeit, *f.* velocity of flow (through).

Durchflußmenge, *f.* rate of flow (through).

Durchflußmesser, *m.* flow-meter.

Durchflußprofil, *n.* cross-section, sectional area, of water-way (of bridge).

Durchflußquerschnitt, *m.* = **Durchflußprofil.**

Durchflußweite, *f. Civ.E:* water-way (of bridge).

durchfluten, *v.* **1.** *v.sep.* (*a*) *v.i. (sein)* to flow, flood, pour, through; **als der Damm brach, flutete das Wasser durch,** when the dam broke the water flooded, poured, through; (*b*) *v.tr.* to float (sth.) through. **2.** *v.tr. sep.* to flow through (sth.); **ein mächtiger Strom durchflutete das Tal,** a mighty river flowed through the valley; **der Damm war gebrochen, und das Wasser durchflutete die Straßen,** the dike had burst and the water flooded the streets; **der Raum war von Licht durchflutet,** the room was flooded with light; **ein wohliges Gefühl der Wärme durchflutete ihn,** a pleasurable warmth flowed through him.

durchformen, *v.* **1.** *v.tr. sep.* to develop (sth.), to work (sth.) out, thoroughly; **sein Charakter ist noch nicht durchgeformt,** his character is not yet fully developed; **ein durchgeformter Charakter,** a mature character; **er hat den Roman nicht richtig durchgeformt,** his novel was not properly developed, was too sketchily worked out. **2.** *vbl s.* **Durchformung,** *f.* development (of character, novel, etc.).

durchforschen[1], *v.tr. sep.* to examine, investigate (subject) thoroughly, to carry out thorough, exhaustive, research into (subject), to make a complete, an exhaustive, study of (subject); to make a thorough enquiry into (subject).

durchforschen[2]. **I.** *v.tr. insep.* to explore, to search (region, etc.); to explore, to carry out, (thorough) research into (field of study); **er hat zwei Erdteile durchforscht,** he has explored two continents; **wir haben viele Länder nach dieser seltenen Blume durchforscht, wir haben viele Länder durchforscht, um diese seltene Blume zu finden,** we have searched many countries for this rare flower; **er hat das Gebiet der Tierpsychologie gründlich durchforscht,** he has thoroughly explored, he has made extensive researches in, the field of animal psychology; **sich, sein Gewissen, d.,** to search one's heart, one's conscience.

II. *vbl s.* **Durchforschen** *n.,* **Durchforschung** *f. in vbl senses; also:* **1.** exploration (of region, etc.); search (through region, etc.). **2.** (thorough) research (into field of study, etc.).

durchforsten, *v.tr. insep.* to thin (out), to clear (forest); *F:* to weed out the unfit from (society, etc.).

durchfressen, *v. (strong)* **1.** *v.tr. sep.* (*a*) *(of animal)* to eat through (sth.); **die Mäuse haben die Täfelung durchgefressen,** the mice have eaten, gnawed, through the wainscoting; **die Motten haben den Stoff durchgefressen,** the moths have eaten through the material; (*b*) *(of acid, rust, etc.)* to eat through (sth.), to corrode, erode (metal, etc.). **2.** *sep.* **sich durchfressen,** (*a*) *(of animal)* to eat (its way) through; **der Wurm hat sich durch den ganzen Apfel durchgefressen,** the maggot has eaten (its way) right through the apple; (*b*) *F: (of pers.)* to work one's way through (piece of work, etc.); **sie hat sich durch das Buch durchgefressen,** she has waded, ploughed, through the book; (*c*) *F: (of pers.)* to live on other people, to depend on other people for food. **3.** *v.tr. insep. (of rust, etc.)* to eat through (sth.), to corrode, erode (metal, etc.); **das Eisen ist von Rost durchfressen,** the iron has been corroded, eroded, by rust.

durchfrieren, *v. (strong)* **1.** *v.i. sep. (sein)* to freeze (right) through; **ich war ganz durchgefroren,** I was icy (cold), chilled to the marrow, *F:* frozen through, frozen stiff. **2.** *v.tr. insep.* to freeze (sth.) through; to chill (s.o., sth.); **die Kinder kamen durchfroren an,** the children were chilled to the marrow, *F:* frozen through, frozen stiff, when they arrived.

Durchfuhr, *f.* -/-en. *Cust:* transit (of goods).

durchführbar, *a.* practicable, workable, feasible, possible; **Ihr Plan ist leider nicht d.,** unfortunately your plan is not practicable, workable, feasible, unfortunately it won't be possible to carry out your plan.

Durchführbarkeit, *f.* practicability, workability, workableness, feasibility (of plan, etc.).

durchführen. I. *v.tr. sep.* **1.** (*a*) **j-n, etwas, (durch etwas) d.,** to lead, take, s.o., sth., through, across (sth.); **dort führte er die Pferde durch,** that is where he led the horses through; **nachdem er uns durch die ganze Ausstellung durchgeführt hatte . . .,** after he had taken, conducted, us all through, round, the exhibition . . .; **sie führte uns durch das Moor durch,** she led us over, across, the moor; (*b*) to lead (water, etc.) through (place, etc.); to lay, bring (electric cable, etc.) through (place, etc.); **der Fluß soll in ein neues Bett geleitet werden und wird durch unser Tal durchgeführt,** the river is to be given a new course and will be led through our valley; **der Telephondraht soll hier durchgeführt werden,** the telephone wires are going to be brought through here; **der Draht muß durch diese Öffnung durchgeführt werden,** the wire has to be put, has to pass, through this opening; **er führte das Seil durch die Öffnung durch,** he passed, led, the rope through the opening; (*c*) to transport (goods) (through country, etc.); (*d*) to extend (pipe-lines, railway lines, etc.) through to (place); **diese Linie soll nächstes Jahr bis zur Landesgrenze durchgeführt werden,** this line is to be extended as far as the border next year; **ab ersten November wird der Frühzug bis X durchgeführt,** from the first of November the early train will run through to X. **2.** (*a*) to carry out, to carry through, to execute (plan, etc.); to carry out, to enforce (law, etc.); to carry out (experiment, programme, reform, measures); **wenn man so etwas einmal unternimmt, muß man es bis zu Ende d. können,** if one once undertakes a thing of this sort one must be able to carry it through; **er macht immer wieder neue Pläne, aber er führt keinen durch,** he is always making new plans but he never carries any of them out, through; (*b*) to follow through (train of thought); to play (part) (out); **er führte die Rolle eines verarmten Aristokraten bis zu Ende durch,** he played, acted, maintained, the part of an impoverished aristocrat right up to the end; **er ist unfähig, einen Gedankengang bis zu Ende durchzuführen,** he is incapable of pursuing a train of thought, of carrying a train of thought through, to its logical conclusion; (*c*) *Mus: etc:* to develop (theme) (in sonata, etc.).

II. *vbl s.* **1. Durchführen,** *n. in vbl senses.* **2. Durchführung,** *f.* (*a*) = II. 1; *also:* conveyance, *A. & U.S:* transportation (of goods) (through country, etc.); extension (of railway lines, etc.); execution (of plan); enforcement (of law); (*b*) *Mus: (in sonata, etc.)* development; (*c*) *El.E:* bushing (insulator).

Durchfuhrerlaubnis, *f. Cust:* transit permit.

Durchfuhrgebiet, *n.* = **Durchgangsland.**

Durchfuhrhandel, *m.* transit trade.

Durchfuhrtarif, *m.* = **Durchgangstarif.**

Durchführung, *f. see* **durchführen II.**

Durchführungsbestimmung, *f.* regulation (for the implementation of a law *or* an order).

Durchführungsverordnung, *f.* regulations (for the implementation of a law *or* an order).

Durchfuhrzoll, *m. Cust:* transit duty.

durchfurcht [-ˈfurçt], *a.* furrowed (face, etc.); **ein von Leiden durchfurchtes Gesicht,** a face furrowed by suffering.

Durchgabe, *f.* **1.** *in vbl senses of* **durchgeben 2,** *q.v.* **2.** (service) hatch.

Durchgang, *m.* **1.** (*a*) passing, passage, through; crossing (of water, etc.); **'kein D.!' 'D. verboten!'** (i) 'private'; (ii) 'do not pass beyond this point'; (iii) 'no thoroughfare'; **der D. (der Kinder Israels) durch das Rote Meer,** the crossing of the Red Sea (by the Children of Israel); (*b*) transit (of goods, etc.); (*c*) *Astr:* transit; **der D. der Venus durch die Sonne,** the transit of Venus across the sun's disc; **D. eines Sterns durch den Meridian,** transit of a star through the meridian. **2.** (*a*) transition; **diese Stellung ist nur ein D. zu einer besseren,** this post is only a transition to a better one; **der Tod ist der D. zu einem höheren Leben,** death is a transit, a gateway, to a higher life; (*b*) *Mus:* passing note. **3.** way through, passage (through); opening, doorway (connecting buildings, etc.); gangway, *U.S:* aisle (between seats in bus, etc.); *Rail:* (i) corridor; (ii) (concertina) vestibule (between coaches); **den D. frei lassen,** to leave the gangway, corridor, clear; **einen D. frei lassen,** to leave a gangway, passage-way; **dieses Zimmer wird nur als D. zum Wohnzimmer gebraucht,** this room is only used as a passage (through) to the living-room; **unser Haus hat einen D. zum Nebenhaus,** the house next door is accessible from ours. **4.** *Sp:* attempt; run; round.

Durchgänger, *m.* (*a*) runaway, absconder; (*b*) horse liable to bolt, to run away; (*c*) *Atom.Ph:* atomic pile out of control, *F:* runaway.

durchgängig, *a.* **1.** *A:* (house) with a passage through. **2.** permeable; penetrable. **3.** (*a*) general, universal; continual, constant; **eine durchgängige Ansicht,** a universally, generally, held opinion; **die durchgängige Fehlerhaftigkeit seiner Theorien,** the constant fallaciousness of his theories; (*b*) *adv.* universally, generally; at all points, right through, through and through; **d. bruchfest,** resistant to fracture at all points; **das Hotel ist d. modern ausgestattet,** the hotel has every modern convenience.

Durchgängigkeit, *f.* permeability.

Durchgangsbahnhof, *m. Rail:* through station, *U.S:* way station.

Durchgangsgleis, *n. Rail:* through line.

Durchgangshahn, *m.* (intermediate) cock.

Durchgangshandel, *m.* transit trade.

Durchgangsinstrument, *n. Astr:* transit instrument.

Durchgangslager, *n.* transit camp.

Durchgangsland, *n.* country through which goods are conveyed in transit.

Durchgangsstadium, *n.* transition stage, transition period.

Durchgangsstation, *f.* (*a*) *Rail:* through station, *U.S:* way station; (*b*) station on the way through; transition stage; **eine wichtige D. auf seinem Lebensweg,** an important transition stage in his life; **diese Stellung kann eine wichtige D. in seiner Karriere sein,** this post may prove an important transition stage in his career.

Durchgangsstraße, *f.* through road, *esp. U.S:* thoroughfare.

Durchgangstarif, *m. Trans:* transit tariff.

Durchgangston, *m. Mus:* passing note.

Durchgangsventil, *n.* stop-valve.

Durchgangsverkehr, *m.* traffic passing through; through traffic; **'gesperrt für den D.!'** 'no thoroughfare', 'closed to through traffic'; **das Restaurant hatte dieses Jahr gute Einnahmen aus dem D.,** the restaurant made a lot from passing motorists, from people passing through, this year; **Waren im D.,** goods in transit.

Durchgangswagen, *m. Rail:* corridor coach, *U.S:* vestibule car.

Durchgangszimmer, *n.* room giving access to another.

Durchgangszug, *m. Rail:* express train (with corridor coaches).

durchgeben, *v.tr. sep.* (*strong*) **1.** to hand (sth.) through. **2.** *Mil: etc:* to pass on, circulate (message); *W.Tel:* to broadcast (programme, announcement, etc.); to transmit (message, etc.); **eine Meldung, die Nachrichten, d.,** to make an announcement; to read the news; **es wurde durchgegeben, daß . . .,** they said, it was stated, on the radio that . . .; **ein Telegramm telephonisch d.,** (*of sender*) to send a telegram by telephone, to dictate a telegram over the telephone; (*of operator*) to deliver a telegram by telephone; **eine Meldung telephonisch d.,** to telephone a message.

durchgedreht, *a. F:* (*of pers.*) **d. sein,** to be totally, utterly, confused; *see also* **durchdrehen.**

durchgehen[1]. I. *v.i. sep.* (*strong*) (*sein*) **1.** (**durch etwas) d.,** (*a*) (*of pers.*) to go, walk, through (sth.); to pass through (sth.); **hier können wir nicht d.,** we can't go through here; **die Menge wich zurück und ließ ihn d.,** the crowd fell back and let him pass, let him go, pass, through; **bitte d. (im Wagen)!** pass right down the car, please! **durch dichtes Gebüsch d.,** to go, walk, through thick undergrowth; **er ist eben durch die Tür durchgegangen,** he has just gone through the door; **ich bin einmal kurz durch das Buch durchgegangen,** I went once through the book quickly; (*b*) (*of road, pipe-line, etc.*) to go, run, pass, through (sth.); **die Straße geht mitten durch den Wald durch,** the road goes, runs, passes, through the middle of the wood; **der Draht geht durch die zweite Öffnung durch,** the wire goes through the second aperture; (*c*) (*of pers., road, etc.*) to go right through (sth.); to cross, go across (sth.); (*of goods*) to be transported through, across (area, etc.), *abs.* to be in transit; *Astr:* (*of planets, etc.*) to transit (meridian, etc.); **quer durch einen Bach d.,** to go through, to cross, a stream; **ich ging quer durch den ganzen Park durch,** I crossed, walked right across, the park; **ich habe mir die Ausstellung nicht gründlich angesehen; ich bin nur einmal durchgegangen,** I didn't look at the exhibition very thoroughly; I just went through it once; **die Straße geht von einem Ende der Stadt bis zum anderen durch,** the street goes, runs, right through from one end of the town to the other; **die Eisenbahnlinie geht mitten durch die Stadt durch,** the railway line goes, runs, right through the centre of the town; **dieser Gedanke geht durch das ganze Buch durch,** this idea runs through the whole book, runs right through the book; (*d*) (*of application, etc.*) to go through (committee, etc.); (*of property, application, etc.*) **durch mehrere Hände d.,** to pass through several hands; **wer weiß, durch wie viele Hände dieser Antrag d. muß, ehe man wieder etwas davon hört?** who knows through how many hands this application must go, pass, before we hear any more about it? **der Gesetzesentwurf muß durch das Parlament d.,** the bill must pass, go, through Parliament; **der Antrag muß durch alle Instanzen d.,** the application must go through all the authorities concerned, through the usual channels; (*e*) (*of water, etc.*) to go (right) through (sth.), to penetrate (sth.); **das Wasser geht durch meine Schuhe durch,** the water comes through my shoes; **der Regen ging ihr bis auf die Haut durch,** the rain penetrated to her skin, soaked her to the skin; (*f*) to go through (sth.); to get through (sth.) (*without sticking fast*); **der Draht ist zu dick, er wird durch diese Öffnung nicht d.,** the wire is too thick to go through this aperture; **die Tür ist so schmal, daß ein dicker Mann nicht durchgeht,** the door is so narrow that a fat man cannot get through it; **der Gang ist so voll mit Kisten, daß nichts mehr durchgeht,** the corridor is so full of boxes that it is impossible to get anything through it any more. **2.** to go right, straight, through; (*a*) (*of train, carriage*) **bis X d.,** to go right, straight, through to X; **du brauchst in Köln nicht umzusteigen; der Zug geht durch,** you won't have to change at Cologne; the train goes right through, it's a through train; **steig in den ersten Wagen ein; er geht durch bis Mailand,** get into the first coach; it goes right, straight, through to Milan; (*b*) (*of girder, moulding, etc.*) to be continuous, to go right through; (*c*) (*of pers.*) to go straight through; **wenn du gerade durchgehst, wirst du den Zug noch bekommen,** if you go straight through to the station (without stopping) you'll catch the train; **er kümmert sich um keinen Widerstand, er geht in allem gerade durch,** he takes no notice of any opposition but always goes straight ahead. **3.** to go through, to pass, to be passed, to be accepted, adopted; **die Vorlage ging im Parlament durch,** the bill went through, was carried by, the bill was passed by, Parliament; **das Geschäft ging durch,** the deal went through; **der Antrag ging durch,** the motion was carried; **unser Antrag ist durchgegangen,** our application has gone through; **der Vorschlag ging durch,** the plan was adopted. **4.** (*a*) **etwas d. lassen,** to let sth. pass, to overlook sth., *F:* to let (s.o.) get away with sth.; **das läßt er dir nicht d.,** he won't let that pass, *F:* he won't let you get away with that; **man sollte diesem Kinde die Unarten nicht d. lassen, man soll die Unarten dieses Kindes nicht d. lassen,** one shouldn't shut one's eyes to this child's naughtiness, *F:* one shouldn't let this child get away with being so naughty; **er läßt ihr alles d.,** he lets everything she does pass, *F:* he lets her get away with anything; **diesen Fehler können wir ihm nicht d. lassen,** we cannot overlook this mistake of his, *F:* we can't let him get away with this mistake; (*b*) **ihm geht alles durch,** he is always successful, lucky, he is successful in everything, he carries everything off, *F:* everything comes off all right with him. **5.** (*a*) to run away; (*of horse, F: of pers.*) to take the bit between its, one's, teeth; **das Pferd ist (ihm) durchgegangen,** his horse has run away, has bolted; **das Pferd ist (mit) ihm durchgegangen,** he has lost control of his horse, his horse has bolted with him; **seine Frau ist (ihm) durchgegangen,** his wife has run away, has left him, has eloped; **er ist mit meiner Frau durchgegangen,** he has run off with my wife; **ihr Mann ist mit einer anderen Frau durchgegangen,** her husband has gone, run, off with, has left her for, another woman; **er ist mit der Kasse durchgegangen,** he has run away, off, he has absconded, with the cash; (*b*) **seine Nerven gingen mit ihm durch,** he lost control of his nerves; **er läßt seine Einbildungskraft mit sich d.,** he lets his imagination run away with him; **ihr Gefühl ging mit ihr durch,** her feelings ran away with her, got the better of her, she was carried away by her emotions; **ihr Temperament ging mit ihr durch,** her impulsive nature ran away with, got the better of, her; (*c*) *Atom.Ph: etc:* (*of atomic pile, etc.*) to get out of control; (*of furnace*) to burn too fiercely for damping down.

II. **durchgehen,** *v.tr. sep.* (*strong*) **1.** (*sein*) to go (right) through (street, etc.); **er ist alle Straßen durchgegangen, um sie zu suchen,** he went through all the streets in search of her; **gehen Sie diese Straße durch!** go right along, right to the end of, this street. **2.** (*sein & haben*) to go, look, read, through (work, book, etc.); to go through (part, movements, piece of music, etc.); **etwas genau d.,** to go through sth. thoroughly; **(eine Rolle, ein Buch, usw.) noch einmal d.,** to go through, over, (part, etc.) again; to go, look, read, through (book, etc.) again; to re-read (book, etc.); **(eine Rolle, ein Buch, usw.) flüchtig d.,** to run through (part, etc.); to skim, glance, through (book, etc.); **eine Rolle schnell d.,** to run through a part; **ich bin die Aufgaben meiner Schüler schon alle durchgegangen,** I have gone, looked, through all my pupils' exercises already; **er geht immer alle Rechnungen durch, um sicherzugehen, daß keine Fehler darin sind,** he always goes, looks, through bills to make sure there are no mistakes in them; **ein Manuskript auf Schreibfehler (hin) d.,** to look through a manuscript for, in search of, errors; **er ging den Brief genau durch, aber diese Stelle konnte er nicht finden,** he went through the letter carefully, he read the letter through carefully, but he couldn't find the passage; **sie ging im Geiste noch einmal alles durch, was gesagt worden war,** she went over in her mind once more everything that had been said; **wir wollen die Tatsachen noch einmal kurz d.,** let us quickly review, recapitulate, the facts; **er ging die Rolle genau mit mir durch,** he went through the part in detail with me. **3.** (*haben*) to wear out (shoes).

III. *vbl s.* **Durchgehen,** *n. in vbl senses; also:* (*a*) passage through; (*b*) transit (of goods); (*c*) passage (of bill) (through Parliament).

IV. *pr.p. & a.* **durchgehend,** *in vbl senses; esp.* (*a*) (goods) in transit; (*b*) continuous (girder, moulding, etc.); **durchgehender Bolzen,** through-bolt; (*c*) *Rail:* through (train, carriage, ticket); (*d*) *adv.* all through, right through; without exception; from beginning to end, from start to finish, altogether; universally, generally; **die Hotels in dieser Stadt sind d. schlecht,** all the hotels in this town are bad, the hotels in this town are all bad, are altogether bad, without exception bad; **man ist d. der Ansicht, er werde nicht mehr wiederkommen,** it is generally assumed that he won't come back; **die modernen Gelehrten vertreten d. diese Ansicht,** this opinion is universally held among modern scholars.

durchgehen[2], *v.tr. insep.* (*strong*) (*a*) to go through (sth., place, area); (*b*) (*of emotion, etc.*) to go through, to fill (s.o.); (*c*) *occ.*=**durchgehen**[1] II. 2.

durchgehends, *adv.*=**durchgehend,** *q.v. under* **durchgehen**[1] IV. (*d*).

durchgeistigen, *v.tr. insep.* to infuse spiritual life into (sth.); **durchgeistigte Gesichtszüge,** spiritual features; (highly) intelligent features; **er hat ein durchgeistigtes Gesicht,** his face has a spiritual expression, quality.

durchglühen, *v.* **1.** (*a*) *v.tr. sep.* to heat (metal) through (until workable); (*of sun, fire, etc.*) to

heat (sth.), to warm (sth.), through; (*b*) *v.i. sep.* (*sein*) (*of electric bulb*) to burn out. **2.** *v.tr. insep.* (*of emotion, etc.*) to make (s.o.) glow; **von Begeisterung durchglüht,** aglow, fired, with enthusiasm; **er war von dem Gefühl seines Erfolges durchglüht,** he was aglow with the feeling of success.

durchgreifen, *v.sep.* (*strong*) **1.** *v.i.* (*haben*) to reach through, to put one's hand through; **der Dieb schlug das Fenster ein, griff (mit der Hand) durch und nahm die Juwelen,** the thief smashed the window, put his hand through, reached through, and took the jewels. **2.** *v.tr.* to wear (sth.) out with handling. **3.** *v.i.* (*haben*) to take (decisive) action; to take strong, drastic, measures, to take drastic steps; **wenn die Rebellen nicht bleibenden Schaden anrichten sollen, muß die Regierung jetzt gleich d.,** if the rebels are not to do permanent damage the government must take (decisive) action at once; **er hat rücksichtslos durchgegriffen,** he took ruthless measures; **seine Vorgänger ließen alles laufen, er aber griff durch,** his predecessors let everything slide, but he took action; **durchgreifend,** decisive, energetic, vigorous, strong, drastic, effective (measures, etc.); drastic (measures, etc.); drastic (changes); far-reaching (improvements); trenchant (policy).

Durchgriff, *m. Electronics:* durchgriff (of electron valve).

durchhaben, *v.tr. sep.* (*conj. like* **haben**) to have finished (book, etc.).

durchhalten, *v.sep.* (*strong*) **1.** *v.tr.* to keep (sth.) up; **das Tempo d.,** to keep up the pace; **ich konnte es nicht länger d.,** I couldn't keep it up any longer; **diese extravagante Lebensführung wird er nicht lange d. können,** he won't be able to keep up this extravagant way of life for long. **2.** *v.i.* (*haben*) to hold out, *F:* to stick it out, to keep one's end up; **die Truppen werden bis zum letzten Mann d.,** the troops will hold out to the last man; **bis zum äußersten d.,** to hold out to the last, to the end; **bis zum Ende d.,** to hold out, *F:* to stick it out; **halt durch! durchhalten!** keep it up!

Durchhang, *m.* sag, dip (of wire, cable, etc.).

durchhängen, *v.i. sep.* (*conj. like* **hängen**[1]) (*haben*) **1. (durch etwas) d.,** to hang through (sth.). **2.** (*of girder, etc.*) to deflect, sag; **Durchhängen** *n,* deflection (of girder, etc.).

durchhauen[1], *v. sep.* (*conj. like* **hauen**) **1.** *v.tr.* (*a*) to hack, chop, (right) through (sth.); **einen Baum d.,** to hack, chop, through a tree; **ein Stück Holz mit einem Schlage d.,** to chop a piece of wood in half at one blow; **der Gefangene hieb seine Fesseln durch,** the prisoner hacked through his chains; (*b*) **sich d.,** to hack, chop, one's way through, to force one's way through. **2.** *v.tr.* to knock a hole through, to break (glass, etc.). **3.** *v.tr.* to thrash, trounce (s.o.), to give (s.o.) a beating, a good hiding. **4.** *v.i.* (*sein*) *F:* (*of fuse*) to blow.

durchhauen[2], *v.tr. insep.* (*conj. like* **hauen**) to chop, hack, through (sth.); to cleave (sth.).

durchhecheln, *v.tr. sep.* **1.** *Tex:* to hackle, heckle, hatchel (flax, hemp) (thoroughly). **2.** *F:* to gossip about, to discuss (s.o., sth.); *F:* to pick (s.o.) to pieces.

durchhelfen, *v.i. sep.* (*strong*) (*haben*) **1.** (*a*) **j-m durch etwas d.,** to help s.o. (to get) through sth.; **er half ihr durch das Fenster durch,** he helped her (to get) through the window; **j-m durch alle Schwierigkeiten d.,** to help s.o. through all difficulties; (*b*) to help (s.o.) through; **der Flüchtling hatte viele Freunde, die ihm durchhalfen,** the fugitive had many friends who helped him through; **wir werden diesem Studenten wohl weiter d. müssen, denn seine Geldverhältnisse haben sich nicht gebessert,** we shall have to go on helping this student as his financial circumstances have not improved. **2. sich** *dat.* **durchhelfen,** to get by, to manage; **sie hilft sich mit diesem kleinen Gehalt durch,** she gets by, manages, on this small salary; **sie hat sich immer so durchgeholfen,** she has always managed somehow.

Durchhieb, *m.* cutting (in wood), passage cut through (wood); *Min:* cut-through.

durchhocken, *v.i. sep.* (*haben*) *Gym:* to squat through (between arms).

durchirren, *v.tr. insep.* to wander through, over, across (area, country, etc.); **den Wald d.,** to wander through the wood; **die Welt d.,** to wander about the world, *Lit:* to wander the world.

durchkämmen, *v.tr.* **1.** *sep.* to comb (hair) through. **2.** *sep. & insep.* to comb, search (area) **(nach j-m, etwas,** for s.o., sth.).

durchkämpfen, *v.tr.* **1.** *sep.* (*a*) to fight (sth.) out (to the end); **er hat manche Schlacht durchgekämpft,** he has fought (out), come through, many a battle; (*b*) **sich d.,** to fight one's way through; **sich durch die feindlichen Reihen d.,** to fight one's way through the enemy ranks; **sich durchs Leben, durch Schwierigkeiten, d.,** to fight, battle, one's way through life, through difficulties; **sie hat sich immer d. müssen,** she has always had to struggle, to fight her way. **2.** *insep.* to fight through (period of time); **er hat viele in Armut durchkämpfte Jahre hinter sich,** he has many years of struggling with poverty behind him.

durchkauen, *v.tr. sep.* **1.** to chew (food) (thoroughly); *F:* **ein Buch, usw., (in der Schule) d.,** to do, to work on, a book, etc., (in school) for a long time. **2.** to chew through (sth.); to chew (sth.) through; **sich durch etwas d.,** to chew (one's way) through sth.

durchklingen, *v.* (*strong*) **1.** *v.i. sep.* (*haben*) (*of sound*) to penetrate (through) (sth.), to sound through (sth.), to be heard through (sth.); **ihre Stimme klang deutlich durch den Lärm durch,** her voice was heard distinctly above, through, the din; **auch wenn viele zusammen singen, klingt seine Stimme immer noch durch,** even when there are a lot of people singing together his voice penetrates through. **2.** *v.tr. insep.* to sound, ring, through (sth.); **ihr Gesang durchklang das Tal,** their song rang through the valley, the valley rang with their song; **das ganze Gebäude war von Musik durchklungen,** the whole building rang with the sound of music.

durchkneten, *v.tr. sep. & insep.* to work, knead (dough, etc.) (thoroughly); *Metall:* to rabble, work (molten iron).

durchknöpfen, *v.tr. sep.* **1.** to put (button) through (the button-hole). **2.** to button (garment) all the way up; *Dressm:* **ein durchgeknöpftes Kleid,** a button-through dress; a button-front dress.

durchkommen, *v.i. sep.* (*strong*) (*sein*) **1. (durch etwas) d.,** to come, pass, through (sth.); (*a*) **der Fastnachtszug wird hier d.,** the carnival procession will come through here; **er ist durch dieses Loch durchgekommen,** he came, got, through this hole; **es stehen zu viele Menschen im Wege; ich glaube nicht, daß man zu uns d. kann,** there are too many people in the way—I don't think anyone will be able to get through to us; (*b*) **sie ist durch die Prüfung glücklich durchgekommen,** she passed, got through, her examination; **er ist durch den Krieg heil durchgekommen,** he came safely through the war; **durch alle Schwierigkeiten d.,** to come through all difficulties. **2.** (*a*) to come through; **man glaubte, er würde an dieser Krankheit sterben, aber er ist durchgekommen,** they thought he would die of this disease, but he came through it, he pulled through (it); **sie kam mit der vielen Arbeit nicht durch,** she didn't get through all the work she had to do; **mit so wenig Geld werden wir nicht d.,** we shan't be able to get by, to manage, on so little money; (*b*) to get away; to achieve one's ends; **damit kommt er nicht durch,** he won't get away with that; **mit einer so schwachen Ausrede kommen wir bei ihnen nicht durch,** they won't let us get away with such a poor excuse; **mit Lügen wird er nicht d.,** he won't get away with lies, he won't achieve his ends by lying. **3.** (*a*) (*of moisture, etc.*) to come through; **in meinem Zimmer kommt der Regen durch,** the rain is coming through in my room; **bei meinem alten Regenmantel kommt überall der Regen durch,** my old mackintosh lets in the rain everywhere; (*b*) (*of characteristic, etc.*) to appear, to be apparent; **trotz aller städtischen Manieren kommt der Bauer in ihm immer wieder durch,** for all his city manners the farmer in him is always coming through.

durchkomponieren, *v.tr. sep. Mus:* to set (poem) to music with a different setting for every stanza.

durchkosten, *v.tr.* **1.** *sep.* to taste (thgs) one after the other; **sie haben alle Speisen durchgekostet,** they tasted all the dishes one after the other; **er hat alle Freuden und Leiden des Lebens durchgekostet,** he has tasted all the joys and sorrows of life, he has run the gamut of life's joys and sorrows; **sie hat die Freuden des Ruhms gründlich durchgekostet,** she has tasted, enjoyed, all the pleasures of fame. **2.** *insep.* to taste (joys, etc.) (to the full).

durchkreuzen, *v.tr. insep.* **1.** to travel over, across (area, etc.); **er durchkreuzte ganz Asien,** he travelled through all parts of Asia; **er hat alle Meere durchkreuzt,** he has sailed the seven seas; **Blitze durchkreuzten den Himmel,** lightning flashed across the sky. **2. sich, einander, d.,** to cross (one another), to intercross, to intersect; **dort, wo die beiden Straßen sich durchkreuzen,** where the two roads cross, intersect, at the intersection of the roads. **3.** to cross, foil, thwart, frustrate, intercept (plan); **er hat meine Pläne immer wieder durchkreuzt,** he has intercepted, foiled, my plans again and again.

Durchkreuzungszwilling, *m. Cryst:* interpenetrant twin, penetration twin.

durchkriegen, *v.tr. sep. F:* = **durchbekommen.**

Durchlaß, *m.* **-lasses/-lässe. 1. j-m D. gewähren,** to allow s.o. to pass; **D. erhalten,** to obtain permission to pass. **2.** (*a*) way through; gap, opening; (*b*) inlet; outlet; *Civ.E:* culvert; **offener D.,** open culvert; **gedeckter D.,** closed culvert; (*c*) filter, sieve. **3.** = **Durchlaßposten.**

durchlassen, *v.tr. sep.* (*strong*) **1. j-n, etwas, (durch etwas) d.,** to allow s.o., sth., to pass through (sth.); **erst als ich den Paß zeigte, ließ man mich durch,** they did not let me through until I showed my passport; **während die Straßenarbeiten noch im Gang sind, läßt man keine Wagen durch,** while the road repairs are still going on no cars are allowed (to pass) through; **ohne Fahrkarte kann ich Sie nicht durch die Sperre d.,** I can't let you through the barrier without a ticket; **j-n durchs Examen d.,** to pass s.o. in an examination, *F:* to let s.o. through an examination; **die Vorlage wurde im Parlament durchgelassen,** the bill was passed by Parliament. **2.** to let (sth.) through; *Ph: etc:* (*of medium*) to transmit (light), to let (light, etc.) through, to be pervious to (light, etc.); **dieses Sieb läßt nur die kleineren Steine durch,** this sieve only lets through the smaller stones; **die Gardinen lassen das Licht durch,** the curtains let the light through, in; **ein Segel, das den Wind durchläßt,** a sail that lets the wind through; **dieser Stoff läßt kein Wasser durch,** this material is impermeable, impervious, to water; **mein Mantel läßt den Regen durch,** my coat lets the rain through, lets in the rain; **das Dach läßt das Wasser an mehreren Stellen durch,** the roof leaks in several places.

durchlässig, *a.* **1.** pervious (to light, etc.); permeable (to water, gas, etc.); porous. **2.** *Equit:* (horse) which reacts to aids, handy (horse).

Durchlässigkeit, *f.* **1.** perviousness (to light, etc.); permeability (to water, gas, etc.); porousness. **2.** *Equit:* handiness (of horse).

Durchlässigkeitsmesser, *m.* permeameter.

Durchlaßposten, *m. Mil:* control post, check point, check post.

Durchlaucht[1], *f.* **-/-en.** (*title*) (Serene) Highness; **Ihre, Seine, D.,** Your, His, (Serene) Highness; (*to duke*) **Ihre D.,** Your Grace; (*of duke*) **Seine D.,** His Grace.

durchlaucht[2], *a.* **durchlauchter Herr,** Serene Highness.

durchlauchtig, *a.* (*in title*) Serene (Highness); **durchlauchtigst,** Most Serene (Highness).

durchlaufen[1], *v.sep.* (*strong*) **I.** *v.i.* (*sein*) **1. (durch etwas) d.,** (*a*) to run through (sth.); **er lief unter der Brücke durch,** he ran under the bridge; **sie lief durch das dichte Gebüsch durch,** she ran through the thick undergrowth; (*b*) (*of road, pipe-line, etc.*) to run through (sth.); **die Straße läuft mitten durch den Wald durch,** the road runs through the middle of the wood; **der Draht läuft durch die zweite Öffnung durch,** the wire runs through the second aperture; (*c*) (*of pers., road, etc.*) to run right through (sth.); to run right across (sth.); **die Kinder liefen durch das Zimmer durch,** the children ran through the room; **quer durch einen Bach d.,** to run through a stream; **wir liefen quer durch den ganzen Park durch,** we ran right across the park; **die Eisenbahnlinie läuft mitten durch die Stadt durch,** the railway line runs right through the centre of the town; **dieser Gedanke läuft durch das ganze Buch durch,** this idea runs right through the book; (*d*) (*of water, etc.*) to run through; to percolate, filter, seep, through; **das Rohr ist verstopft; das Wasser kann nicht d.,** the pipe is blocked, so that the water cannot run, pass, through (it); **wir sahen einen nassen Fleck an der Decke, wo das Wasser von oben durchgelaufen war,** we saw a wet patch on the ceiling where the water had come, seeped, through from upstairs; (*e*) *Book-k:* **durchlaufende Posten, Gelder,** reimbursements. **2.** (*of girder, moulding, etc.*) to be continuous; **durchlaufender Träger,** continuous girder; *Arch:* **durchlaufendes Gesims,** continuous moulding.

II. **durchlaufen,** *v.tr.* **1.** (*sein*) to run

through (sth.); **ich lief alle Straßen durch, aber den Fremden fand ich nicht wieder,** I ran through all the streets but could not find the stranger again. **2.** (*haben*) to wear out (shoes, etc.); **sich die Schuhe, Strümpfe, d.,** to go through one's shoes, one's stockings; **durchgelaufene Schuhe, Strümpfe,** worn-out shoes, stockings; **sich die Füße d.,** to walk one's feet raw; *F:* to walk one's feet off.

durchlaufen[2], *v.tr. insep.* (*strong*) **1.** (*a*) (*of pers.*) to run, go, pass, travel, through, across (area, etc.); to cover (a distance); (*of star, etc.*) **seine Bahn d.,** to run its course; **der Bach durchläuft das Tal,** the stream runs through the valley; (*b*) **die Schule d.,** to pass through school; **alle Stufen seines Berufes d.,** to go through all the stages of one's career; (*of application, etc.*) **mehrere Dienststellen d.,** to pass through various departments; (*c*) (*of emotion, murmur, etc.*) to run through (s.o., sth.); **ein Schauder durchlief ihn,** a shudder ran through him, a shiver ran down his spine; **das Gerücht durchlief das ganze Land,** the rumour spread through the whole country; **ein Gemurmel durchlief die Versammlung,** a murmur ran, passed, went, through the assembly. **2.** to run, go, look, through, over (sth.), to examine (sth.) (cursorily); **er durchlief (schnell) die Aktenstücke,** he quickly ran through, looked through, the files, he made a quick examination of the files; **sie durchlief in Gedanken alle Gespräche, die sie miteinander gehabt hatten,** in her mind she ran through, over, all the conversations they had had together.

Durchlauferhitzer, *m.* continuous-flow water heater.

Durchlaufgleis, *n. Rail:* through line.

durchläutern *v.tr. insep.* to purify (sth.); **durchläutert,** pure, purified.

durchleben, *v.tr.* **1.** *sep.* to live, go, through (period of time, etc.); **sie hat diese schwere Zeit mit ihm durchgelebt,** she went through, shared, that difficult time with him. **2.** *v.tr. insep.* to pass, to live (through) (period of time); to come, live, go, through (experience); **fröhlich durchlebte Wochen,** weeks happily spent, happy weeks; **es waren angstvoll durchlebte Stunden,** they were anxious hours; **die Zeiten, die wir gerade durchleben,** the times through which we are passing at the moment; **er hat gute und böse Tage durchlebt,** he has seen good days and bad; **ich habe diese Monate sehr bewußt durchlebt,** I lived those months in a state of extreme awareness; **sie hat Schreckliches durchlebt,** she has been through the most terrible experiences.

durchlesen, *v.tr. sep.* (*strong*) to read (sth.) (through); (**einen Brief, usw.**) **flüchtig d.,** to skim, glance, through (a letter, etc.); **könntest du (dir) diesen Bericht bitte d.?** would you mind reading, looking, through this report? **etwas auf Fehler (hin) d.,** to read sth. through in search of mistakes; **etwas (ganz, zu Ende) d.,** to read sth. (right) through, to read sth. through to the end.

durchleuchten[1], *v.i. sep.* (*a*) (*of light, etc.*) to shine, gleam through (sth.); **es gibt so viele Ritzen im Zelt, daß die Sonne überall durchleuchtet,** there are so many tears in the tent that the sun shines through everywhere; **ein Licht leuchtete durch die Äste durch,** a light shone through the branches; **es leuchtete unter der Tür durch,** there was a gleam under the door; (*b*) (*of characteristic, etc.*) to peep through, to be apparent; **trotz seines barschen Äußeren leuchtet in seinen Handlungen immer eine gewisse Menschenfreundlichkeit durch,** in spite of his rough exterior all his actions betray, reveal, a certain kindliness, a certain kindliness is apparent, can be detected, in all his actions.

durchleuchten[2]. I. *v.tr. insep.* **1.** (*a*) (*of pers.*) to search (room, etc.) with the help of a light; (*b*) (*of sun, light, etc.*) to fill, pervade (sth.) with light; (*c*) (*of hope, etc.*) to light up (s.o.'s face), to fill, pervade (s.o.). **2.** (*a*) to test (egg), to test (cheque, etc., for forgery), by subjecting it to a strong light; to candle (egg); *Med:* to X-ray, screen, transilluminate (organ, etc.), to make an X-ray examination of (organ, etc.); to X-ray (s.o.), to give (s.o.) an X-ray; (*b*) *F:* to investigate, to probe into (matter, s.o.'s past, criminal activities, etc.); *F:* to screen (s.o.); to examine (into) (matter, question); **etwas auf etwas** *acc.* **d.,** to analyse sth. for sth.

II. *vbl s.* **1. Durchleuchten,** *n. in vbl senses.* **2. Durchleuchtung,** *f.* (*a*)=II. 1; *also:* investigation (of), examination (of, into) (matter); (*b*) transillumination (of organ, etc.); X-ray examination, fluoroscopic observation (of organ, etc.); (*c*) =**Durchleuchtungsverfahren.**

Durchleuchtungsschirm, *m. X Rays:* fluorescent screen.

Durchleuchtungsverfahren, *n.* radioscopy, fluoroscopy, X-ray examination, fluoroscopic observation.

durchliegen, *v.tr. sep.* (*strong*) **1.** to wear down (mattress, etc.). **2.** *Med:* **sich durchliegen,** to develop bed-sores, decubitus; **Durchliegen** *n,* decubitus, bed-sores.

durchlochen, *v.tr. insep.* to perforate (sth.); to pierce (sth.); to make, bore, holes, through (wood, etc.); to punch holes through (leather, etc.).

durchlöchern, *v.tr. insep.* (*a*) to perforate (sth.); to make, pierce, holes through (sth.); to hole (one's socks, etc.); to prick holes in, through (paper, etc.); **durchlöchert wie ein Sieb,** riddled (like a sieve); **die Tür war von Kugeln durchlöchert (wie ein Sieb),** the door was riddled with bullet-holes; **durchlöcherte Socken,** socks in holes, holey socks; **er trägt durchlöcherte Socken,** his socks are in holes, he has holes in his socks, he is wearing holey socks; **durchlöcherte Schuhe,** shoes in holes; (*b*) *F:* (*of law, regulation*) **durchlöchert,** rendered meaningless (by constant unpunished violation).

durchlüften[1], *v.tr. sep.* to air (sth.) (thoroughly); **wir müssen das Zimmer gut d., um den Zwiebelgeruch loszuwerden,** we must air the room thoroughly to get rid of the smell of onions; **Kleider d.,** to air clothes thoroughly, to give clothes a thorough airing.

durchlüften[2], *v.tr. insep.* **1.** (*a*) to air (room, etc.) (thoroughly); to ventilate (room); (*b*) to aerate (soil, etc.). **2.** *vbl s.* **Durchlüften** *n.,* **Durchlüftung** *f. in vbl senses; also:* ventilation (of room); aeration (of soil, etc.).

durchlumpen, *v.tr. insep. F:* **die Nacht d.,** *F:* to bat around, to make a night of it.

durchmachen, *v. sep.* I. *v.tr.* **1.** *F:* to make (hole, etc.) through (sth.); to put (sth.) through (sth.). **2.** (*a*) to go through (course of study, etc.); **die Schule, die Universität, d.,** to go, pass, through school, through the University; **die Lehrlingszeit d.,** to serve one's apprenticeship; **er hat den Kurs nicht ganz zu Ende durchgemacht,** he did not quite finish, complete, the course; (*b*) to go through (difficult times, etc.); to undergo (suffering, etc.); **er hat viel d. müssen,** he has suffered, been through, a lot; **wenn du nur wüßtest, was ich alles durchgemacht habe!** if you knew all that I have been, gone, through! **wir haben Schweres, schwere Zeiten, zusammen durchgemacht,** we have been through difficult times together; **die ganze Bevölkerung hat im Kriege Schreckliches durchgemacht,** the whole population suffered terribly, underwent terrible suffering, during the war; **sie hat gerade eine schwere Krankheit durchgemacht,** she has just come through, had, a serious illness; **eine schwere Operation durchgemacht haben,** to have undergone, to have had, a serious operation; (*c*) (*of pers., relationship, etc.*) **eine Verwandlung d.,** to change, to undergo a change.

II. **durchmachen,** *v.i.* (*haben*) *F:* **wir machen bis morgen früh, die ganze Nacht, durch,** we'll keep it up till dawn.

Durchmarsch, *m.* **1.** march through (country, etc.); **der D. durch die Stadt,** the march through the town; **beim D. der Soldaten,** while the soldiers were marching through; **Truppen den D. gestatten,** to allow troops to march through. **2.** *F:* diarrhoea.

durchmarschieren, *v.i. sep.* (*sein*) to march through (area, etc.).

durchmengen, *v.tr. sep. & insep.*=**durchmischen.**

durchmessen, *v.tr.* (*strong*) **1.** *sep.* to take all the measurements of (room, etc.); to measure (room, etc.) from one end to the other. **2.** *insep.* to traverse, to travel (over, through, across), to cross (area); to cover (a distance); to traverse, travel (field of knowledge, etc.), to travel (course, etc.); (*of star, etc.*) to travel (through) (space, etc.); **ein Gebiet (zu Fuß) d.,** to cross an area on foot; **eine Strecke (zu Fuß) d.,** to cover a distance on foot, to walk a distance; **er hat die ganze Welt durchmessen, um das Glück zu suchen,** he travelled (round) the whole world in search of happiness; **er durchmaß das Zimmer mit langen Schritten,** (i) he strode through the room, he crossed the room with great strides; (ii) he strode, paced, up and down the room; **das Zimmer mit wenigen Schritten d.,** to cross the room in a few strides.

Durchmesser, *m.* **-s/-,** diameter (of circle, sphere, etc.); **äußerer D.,** outside diameter; **innerer D., lichter D.,** internal diameter (of tube, cylinder, etc.), calibre (of gun, tube, etc.); **zugeordneter D., konjugierter D.,** conjugate diameter; **das Rad hat einen D. von einem Meter, mißt einen Meter im D.,** the wheel is one metre in diameter.

durchmischen, *v.tr.* **1.** *sep.* **zwei Substanzen gut (miteinander) d.,** to mix two substances thoroughly together. **2.** *insep.* to mix (sth.) (with sth.); **Zucker mit Sand d.,** to mix sand with sugar.

durchmustern, *v.tr.* **1.** *sep.* to look through (thgs); **sie musterte ihre Garderobe durch,** she looked through her wardrobe. **2.** *insep.* to scrutinize (persons, thgs); **sie durchmusterte die Menge,** she scrutinized the crowd.

durchnähen, *v.sep.* **1.** *v.tr.* to stitch (right) through (sth.); *Bootm:* to through-seam (shoes). **2.** *v.i.* (*haben*) **durch etwas d.,** to stitch (right) through sth.

Durchnahme, *f.* **-/.** doing, going through (of subject with class, etc.).

durchnässen, *v.* **1.** *v.tr. insep.* to make (sth.) wet through, to soak (sth.) (through), to drench (sth.); **(völlig) durchnäßt,** wet through, drenched, soaked (through), soaking (wet), sodden; **ihre Kleider waren vom Regen durchnäßt,** her clothes had been soaked through by the rain, were soaking from the rain; **wir kamen völlig durchnäßt zurück,** we came back wet through, absolutely drenched, soaked (through), soaking, soaked to the skin. **2.** *sep.* (*a*) *v.tr.* to wet (sth.) right through; (*b*) *v.i.* (*haben*) **der Verband muß erneuert werden; die Wunde hat durchgenäßt,** the bandage must be replaced, as the blood from the wound has soaked through; *impers.* **es hat durchgenäßt,** the damp, moisture, has come through.

durchnehmen, *v.tr. sep.* (*strong*) to do (subject in school, etc.); (*of teacher*) **einen Gegenstand mit der Klasse d.,** to take a class through a subject; **wir werden heute die Quadratwurzeln d.,** we'll learn, do, square roots today; **die ersten beiden Bücher der Aeneis mit j-m d.,** to take s.o. through the first two books of the Aeneid, to do the first two books of the Aeneid with s.o.

durchörtern, *v.tr. insep. Min:* to cut levels through (mountain, etc.).

durchpausen, *v.tr. sep.* to trace (design, etc.); to draw, write, (sth.) through carbon paper; to transfer (design, etc.).

durchprobieren, *v.tr. sep.* to try (dishes, wines, etc.), to try on (clothes), one after the other.

Durchprojektion, *f. Cin:* rear projection.

durchprügeln, *v.tr. sep.* to give (s.o.) a good beating, a good thrashing, a good, thorough, licking; *F:* to lather s.o.

durchpulsen, *v.tr. insep.* (*of blood, feeling, etc.*) to pulse through (s.o.).

durchqueren, *v.tr. insep.* to cross, to traverse, to travel across (country, etc.); to cross (square, room, etc.); **ein Gebiet zu Fuß d.,** to cross an area on foot.

durchrasen, *v.* **1.** *v.i. sep.* (*sein*) to tear, rush, race, dash, through (area, place, etc.); **der Zug raste durch den Bahnhof durch,** the train tore, raced, through the station; **er ist eben auf seinem Fahrrad durchgerast,** he came tearing, racing, dashing, through on his bicycle just now; **er raste durch das Zimmer durch,** he rushed, dashed, through the room. **2.** *v.tr. insep.* to race through (place, country, etc.); (*of wind, fire, etc.*) to rage through (streets, etc.); *Lit:* **eine im Irrsinn durchraste Nacht,** a night spent raving.

durchregnen, *v.impers. sep.* (*a*) **es hat durchgeregnet,** the rain has come through; **es regnet in meinem Zimmer durch,** the rain is coming through (the ceiling) in my room; (*b*) **es hat die (ganze) Nacht durchgeregnet,** it has been raining all (through the) night.

Durchreiche, *f.* **-/-n,** (service) hatch.

durchreichen, *v.tr. sep.* to hand (sth.) through; to pass (sth.) round.

Durchreise, *f.* (*a*) journey through, across; **wie lange dauerte die D. durch Frankreich?** how long did the journey through, across, France last? **j-m die D. gestatten,** to allow s.o. transit (through a country); **bei der D. durch Belgien haben wir drei Pannen gehabt,** on the journey, way, through, across, Belgium we had three breakdowns; (*b*) journey, way, through, across; **er wird uns auf der D. besuchen,** he will visit us on his, the, journey through, way through, as he is passing through; **ich kenne New York nicht gut; ich war nur einmal auf der D. dort,** I don't know New York very well; I only stopped there once on the way through; **wir sind hier**

auf der D. und haben zwei Stunden Zeit, we are passing through and have two hours to spare; **ich fahre nächste Woche nach Rom und könnte Sie auf der D. in Paris treffen,** I am going to Rome next week and could meet you in Paris on my way through.

durchreisen, *v.* **1.** *v.i. sep.* (*sein*) to travel, pass, go, through, *Aut:* to drive through; **ich habe mich in München nie aufgehalten, aber ich bin mehrere Male durchgereist,** I have never stayed in Munich, but I have travelled, been, passed, through (it) several times; **wir reisten mit dem Auto durch,** we went, drove, through in the car. **2.** *v.tr. insep.* to travel over, through, across, to traverse (land, etc.); **er hat ganz Schottland durchreist,** he has travelled right through, across, Scotland.

Durchreisende, *m., f.* (*decl. as adj.*) (*a*) person travelling, passing, through; *U.S:* transient; **die Durchreisenden,** those travelling, passing, through; **das Hotel wird viel von Durchreisenden besucht,** the hotel is much used by people travelling, passing, through, by people on their way through; (*b*) through passenger; **Durchreisende** *pl* **nach Paris,** through passengers to Paris.

Durchreisesichtvermerk, *m. Adm:* transit visa; **D. einmalig, D. mehrmalig,** transit visa for a single journey, for repeated journeys.

Durchreisevisum, *n.* = **Durchreisesichtvermerk.**

durchreißen, *v.* (*strong*) **1.** *sep.* (*a*) *v.tr.* to tear (rope, etc.) (asunder); **etwas (in der Mitte) d.,** to tear sth. in half, in two; **sie hat den Faden durchgerissen,** she tore the thread in half, in two; (*b*) *v.i.* (*sein*) (*of rope, etc.*) to break (asunder), to sever, to snap (asunder); **in der Mitte d.,** to break in half, in two. **2.** *v.tr. insep.* to tear (sth.) in two, in half.

durchreiten, *v.* (*strong*) **1.** *v.i. sep.* (*sein*) (*a*) to ride through (area, etc.), to ride across (fields, etc.), to cross (fields, etc.) on horseback; **das Unterholz ist zu dicht, um durchzureiten,** the undergrowth is too thick to ride through; (*b*) to ride right through, across (area, etc.); **wenn man durch den Wald durchreitet, kommt man an den Fluß,** if you ride (right) through the wood you come to the river. **2.** *v.tr. sep.* (*a*) **die Hose d.,** to wear out one's trousers by riding; **sich d.,** to make oneself sore with riding; (*b*) **ein durchgerittenes Pferd,** a horse trained to respond to aids. **3.** *v.tr. insep.* to ride through (land, etc.), to cross (land, etc.) on horseback.

durchrieseln, *v.* **1.** *v.i. sep.* (*sein*) (*of sand, water, etc.*) to trickle through (opening); (*of water*) to trickle through (ceiling, etc.). **2.** *v.tr. insep.* (*of water, etc.*) to run, trickle, through, across (sth.); (*of emotion*) to run through, pass through, thrill through (s.o.), to pervade (s.o.); (*of cold, warmth, etc.*) to pervade (s.o.); **ein klares Bächlein durchrieselte die Wiese,** a clear little stream rippled across the meadow; **ein leichter Schauder durchrieselte ihn, sein Gebein,** a shiver ran down his spine; **ein wohliges Gefühl der Wärme durchrieselte ihn,** a pleasurable feeling of warmth pervaded him.

durchringen (sich), *v.refl. sep.* (*strong*) to fight one's way through (to sth.); **er hat sich zum Erfolg durchgerungen,** he has fought his way through to success; **sie hat sich endlich zu dem Entschluß durchgerungen, ihn zu verlassen,** after a long struggle with herself she at last decided to leave him.

Durchritt, *m.* riding through; ride through; **beim D. (durch einen Ort),** when riding through (a place); **auf dem D.,** riding through; on the ride through.

durchs, *prep.* (*contraction of* **durch das**; *cp.* **durch** I.) (*for usage of* **durchs** & **durch das** *cp. notes to* **am**) **d. Fenster springen,** to jump through the window; **diese Krankheit begleitete ihn d. ganze Leben,** this illness was with him all his life, throughout his life; **d. Leben gehen,** to go through life.

durchsacken, *v.i. sep.* (*sein*) (*a*) to sag; (*b*) *Av:* (*of aircraft*) to pancake.

Durchsage, *f. W.Tel:* announcement, message.

durchsagen, *v.tr. sep.* **1.** to say (sth.) on the radio *or* over the telephone; to broadcast (statement, etc.) (on the radio); **ein Telegramm telephonisch d.,** (*of sender*) to dictate a telegram over the telephone; (*of operator*) to deliver a telegram by telephone; **eine Meldung, die Nachrichten, d.,** to make an announcement, to read the news (on the radio); **es wurde durchgesagt, daß . . . ,** they said, it was stated, on the radio that . . . . **2.** to say (poem, etc.) right through.

Durchsatz, *m. Ind:* charge (of blast-furnace); throughput (of oil).

durchschaubar [durçˈʃaubaːr], *a.* (**leicht**) **d.,** obvious, transparent (deception, etc.); (deception, trick, etc.) that is easily seen through; **schwer d.,** puzzling, enigmatic (character, etc.); (character, etc.) that is not easily seen through; **seine Pläne, Beweggründe, sind schwer d.,** his plans are not easily seen through, his real motives are not easily detected.

durchschauen, *v.* **1.** *v.i. sep.* (*haben*) = **durchsehen** 1. **2.** *v.tr. sep.* = **durchsehen** 2. **3.** *v.tr. insep.* to see through (s.o., s.o.'s lies, disguise, etc.); to know where one is with (s.o.); to detect (s.o.'s motives, etc.); to know the secret behind (sth.); **Gott durchschaut dein Herz,** God sees into your heart, knows your thoughts; **er ist unfähig, etwas zu verbergen; jeder durchschaut ihn gleich,** he is incapable of hiding anything; one knows at once where one is with him; **sie wollte uns mit Schmeicheleien umgarnen, aber wir durchschauten ihre Absichten,** she wanted to ensnare us with flattery but we saw through her, we saw what she was up to; **er hat den Heuchler gleich durchschaut,** he saw through the hypocrite at once; **ich beginne, die Sache zu d.,** I'm beginning to see through it; **Schliche, die man leicht d. kann,** tricks that are easily seen through; **j-s Beweggründe d.,** to see into s.o.'s motives, to detect s.o.'s real motives; **j-s Spiel d.,** to see through s.o.'s game; **ein Geheimnis d.,** to fathom a secret; **er hat die ganze Sachlage klar durchschaut,** he saw, grasped, the whole situation clearly; **sie hat sein seltsames Benehmen gleich durchschaut,** she saw at once what was behind his strange behaviour.

durchscheinen[1], I. *v.i. sep.* (*strong*) (*haben*) (*a*) (*of sun, light, etc.*) to shine through (sth.); **die Sonne schien durch die Mauerritzen durch,** the sun shone through the cracks in the wall; **das Licht schien unter der Tür durch,** the light shone under the door; **das Licht schien durch die dünnen Vorhänge durch,** the light shone through the thin curtains; (*b*) to show through; **das Unterkleid scheint (durch den durchsichtigen Stoff) durch,** the underskirt shows through (the transparent material); (*c*) (*of characteristic, etc.*) to become evident, apparent, to be seen; **obgleich sie sich freundlich zeigt, scheint ihr Haß doch durch,** although she appears friendly one is aware of her hatred; **ihr ganzes Benehmen ließ ihre Liebe zu ihm d.,** her love for him was revealed, was apparent, in everything she did; **durch sein fröhliches Benehmen scheint zuweilen Schwermut durch,** through his gaiety one sometimes gets a glimpse of melancholy; **bei all seiner Ernsthaftigkeit scheint doch immer sein Humor durch,** for all his earnestness one is always aware of his sense of humour.

II. *pr.p. & a.* **durchscheinend,** *in vbl senses, esp.* translucent; (*of cloth, etc.*) transparent, diaphanous.

durchscheinen[2], *v.tr. insep.* (*of light, etc.*) (*a*) to shine through (sth.); (*b*) to light (sth.) up, to illuminate (sth.), to fill, flood, (sth.) with light.

durchschießen[1], *v. sep.* (*strong*). **1.** *v.i.* (*haben*) to shoot through (sth.); **er schoß durch das Fenster durch,** he shot, took a shot, through the window. **2.** *v.i.* (*sein*) to shoot, race, tear, through (sth.); **das Schleusentor wurde geöffnet und das Wasser schoß durch,** the sluice-gate was opened and the water shot, raced, through. **3.** *v.tr.* (*a*) *Tex:* (**die Schußfäden**) **d.,** to throw the weft-yarn across; (*b*) *Bookb:* to interleave (book).

durchschießen[2], *v.tr. insep.* (*strong*) **1.** to shoot (sth.) through; **sein Helm war überall durchschossen,** his helmet was riddled with bullet-holes; **sein Körper war von mehreren Kugeln durchschossen,** there were several bullet-holes in his body; **seine Brust, von Pfeilen durchschossen, . . . ,** his breast, pierced by arrows, ... **2.** (*of thought, etc.*) to flash through (s.o.'s brain, etc.). **3.** (*a*) *Print:* to lead, space, white out (lines); to space out, set out (type); **durchschossener Satz,** leaded matter; (*b*) *Bookb:* **ein Buch (mit weißem Papier) d.,** to interleave a book; **durchschossene Bände,** interleaved volumes; (*c*) *Tex:* to interweave (sth.) (with sth.); **ein mit Goldfäden durchschossenes Gewebe,** a material interwoven with gold threads; *Lit:* **feines mit lichten Streifen durchschossenes Gewölk,** thin clouds shot through with streaks of light.

durchschimmern, *v.* **1.** *v.i. sep.* (*haben*) to shimmer, glimmer, glisten, gleam, through (sth.); **das kalte Mondlicht schimmerte durch die Vorhänge durch,** the cold moonlight shimmered, gleamed, through the curtains; **ihre schneeweißen Schultern schimmerten durch die Spitzen durch,** her snow-white shoulders gleamed through the lace. **2.** *v.tr. insep.* to shimmer, glimmer, glisten, gleam, through (sth.).

durchschlafen, *v.* (*strong*) **1.** *v.i. sep.* (*haben*) to sleep through; **letzte Nacht hat der Kranke zum erstenmal durchgeschlafen,** last night for the first time the sick man slept right through without waking; **das Kind schläft jetzt von zehn Uhr an durch,** the child sleeps through now from ten o'clock. **2.** *v.tr. insep.* to sleep through (period of time); **die Nacht d.,** to sleep the night through; **durchschlafene Tage,** days spent (in) sleeping.

Durchschlag, *m.* **1.** cutting, driving (of tunnel, etc.); *Min:* joining (of two levels). **2.** *El:* disruptive discharge; breakdown. **3.** opening; *Min:* opening, passage (between two levels); thirl, thirling; junction (of two levels). **4.** (*a*) *Tls:* (nail-)set, (drift-)punch; brad-punch; (*b*) *Dom.Ec:* colander; strainer. **5.** *Typewr:* carbon copy, *F:* carbon.

durchschlagen[1], *v. sep.* (*strong*) I. *v.tr.* **1.** (*a*) to knock a hole through (sth.); **die Wand d.,** to knock a hole in the wall; **eine Fensterscheibe d.,** to smash a window-pane; **die Kugel hat die Scheibe durchgeschlagen,** the bullet went clean through the pane; (*b*) *Fenc: Box:* **j-s Parade d.,** to break through s.o.'s guard. **2.** (*a*) to knock (sth.) through (sth.); **er schlug den Pflock (ganz) durch das Brett durch,** he knocked the peg right through the plank; (*b*) to sieve (fruit, etc.), to pass (fruit, etc.) through a sieve. **3.** *Typewr:* **einen Brief, usw., d.,** to make carbon copies, a carbon copy, of a letter, etc.

II. **durchschlagen,** *v.i.* **1.** (*haben*) (*a*) to go, to come, through (sth.), to penetrate through (sth.); **die Kugel hat durchgeschlagen,** the bullet went through; **der Hagel schlägt durch das Dach durch,** the hail is coming through the roof; (*b*) **d., durchschlagend sein, eine durchschlagende Wirkung haben,** (*of measure, drug, etc.*) to be very, extremely, effective; to have a marked effect; (*of laxative*) to have a drastic effect; **diese Gründe erwiesen sich als durchschlagend, schlugen durch,** these reasons proved convincing; **wir hoffen, daß diese Maßnahmen d. werden, durchschlagend sein werden,** we hope that these measures will have the desired effect; **diesmal schlug er mit seiner Rede durch,** this time his speech took effect, had an effect. **2.** (*sein & haben*) (*a*) (*of ink, moisture, etc.*) to go, come, (right) through; (*of type*) to come through on the other side (of the paper); (*of grease-mark, etc.*) **auf etwas d.,** to come (right) through on to sth.; **die feuchte Stelle in der Wand schlägt immer wieder durch,** the damp patch in the wall always comes through again; **ich benutze dieses dünne Papier nicht, denn die Tinte schlägt durch,** I don't use that thin paper because the ink comes through on the other side; **das Papier schlägt durch,** the paper lets ink through; the print comes through on the other side of the paper; (*b*) (*of characteristic, etc.*) to appear, to come through; **trotz seiner städtischen Manieren schlägt der Bauer in ihm durch,** in spite of his city manners the farmer in him comes through, *F:* crops out; **nach zwei Generationen ist die Krankheit in ihr wieder durchgeschlagen,** after two generations the disease has reappeared in her; *F:* **bei ihr schlägt die Großmutter durch,** she takes after her grandmother, you can see her grandmother in her. **3.** (*sein*) *El:* (*of fuse*) to blow; **die Sicherung ist durchgeschlagen,** the fuse has blown.

III. **sich durchschlagen. 1.** to fight one's way through; **er schlug sich durch die feindlichen Linien durch,** he fought his way through the enemy; **sie haben sich zu ihren eigenen Reihen durchgeschlagen,** they fought their way through to their own lines. **2. sich (durchs Leben) d.,** to get along, to make one's way; **er kann sich allein d.,** he can get along, manage, by himself, he can fend for himself; **mit seinen paar Brocken Französisch hat er sich durch ganz Frankreich durchgeschlagen,** with his little bit of French he managed to make his way right across France; **mit seinem gesunden Humor wird er sich überall d.,** with his healthy sense of humour he'll always get along; **sich kümmerlich d.,** to pinch and scrape; **sich grade so d.,** just to make both ends meet; **man schlägt sich so durch,** one makes ends meet, one gets along, gets by, as well as one can.

durchschlagen[2], *v.tr. insep.* (*strong*) to make, knock, a hole through (sth.), to smash (window, etc.).

Durchschläger, *m. Tls:* = **Durchschlag** 4 (*a*).

Durchschlagpapier, *n. Typewr:* **1.** bank-paper, *F:* flimsy. **2.** carbon paper.
Durchschlagsfestigkeit, *f. El:* dielectric strength, disruptive strength.
Durchschlagskraft, *f.* (*a*) *Ball:* penetrating power, penetration; (*b*) power (of argument, etc.) to convince.
Durchschlagsvermögen, *n. Ball:* penetrating power, penetration.
durchschleichen, *v.* (*strong*) **1.** *v.i. sep.* (*sein*) & **sich durchschleichen,** to creep, slip, steal, through (sth.); **er schlich durch den Gang durch,** he crept, slipped, stole, along the corridor; **das Haus war von Wachen umstellt, aber er schlich sich unbemerkt durch,** the house was guarded by sentries but he slipped through unnoticed. **2.** *v.tr. insep.* to creep, slip, steal, through (sth.).
durchschleusen, *v.tr. sep.* **1.** to pass (ship) through a lock. **2.** to pass (people, etc.) through (transit camp, customs, etc.); *F:* **j-n durchs Examen d.,** to push s.o. through his examination.
Durchschlupf, *m.* hole, way, through (wall, hedge, etc.); *F:* way out; way in; way out (of difficulties).
durchschlüpfen, *v.i. sep.* (*sein*) to slip through.
durchschneiden[1], *v. sep.* (*strong*) **1.** *v.tr.* to cut (sth.) through; to cut (right) across (sth.); **etwas in der Mitte d.,** to cut sth. through the middle, to cut sth. in half, in two; **die neue Straße wird mein Feld in der Mitte d.,** the new road will cut right across the middle of my field; **ein Stück Stoff der Länge nach, quer, d.,** to cut a piece of material lengthwise, across; *F:* **zwischen uns beiden ist das Tischtuch durchgeschnitten,** we have nothing more to do with one another; **hier kann man die Luft mit einem Messer d.,** you could cut the air in here with a knife. **2.** *v.i.* (*haben*) **durch etwas d.,** to cut through sth.; to cut across sth.
durchschneiden[2]. **I.** *v.tr. insep.* (*strong*) **1.** (*a*) to cut (sth.) through, in two; to cut through, across (sth.); to divide (sth.) (into two parts); to intersect (sth.); **die Straße durchschneidet das Feld,** the road cuts, divides, the field in two, cuts through, across, the field; **ein von vielen Wasserwegen durchschnittenes Land,** a land intersected by many waterways; **der Weg durchschneidet den Wald,** the path cuts through the wood; **das Schiff durchschneidet die Fluten,** the ship cuts, ploughs, through the waves; **einen Knoten d.,** to cut (through) a knot; (*b*) (*of pain, grief, etc.*) to pierce (s.o.'s heart, etc.); **es durchschnitt mir das Herz,** it cut, stabbed, me to the heart. **2. sich, einander, d.,** (*of lines, roads, etc.*) to intersect, to cross.
II. *vbl s.* **1. Durchschneiden,** *n.* (*a*) *in vbl senses; also:* division, intersection; (*b*) *Obst:* delivery of the head. **2. Durchschneidung,** *f.* (*a*) = II. 1 (*a*); (*b*) *Surg:* section.
Durchschnitt, *m.* **1.** (*a*) cutting, path, way, through; **einen D. durch einen Wald, durch einen Damm, machen,** to cut a path, a way, to make a cutting, through a wood, to cut, to make a cutting, through an embankment; (*b*) *Folkl:* = **Bilsenschnitt;** (*c*) *Geom: A:* intersection; (*d*) *A:* diameter. **2.** (*a*) section (through building, etc.); *Geol:* section, profile; **ein Gebäude im D. zeichnen,** to draw a building in section; (*b*) *A:* profile (of face). **3.** (*a*) average; mean; **den D. berechnen, finden,** to find the average (of several numbers); **den D. der Ergebnisse nehmen,** to take an average of the results, to average the results; **einen annähernden D. nehmen,** to strike a rough average; **im D.,** on an average; **er arbeitet im D. acht Stunden am Tag,** he works eight hours a day on average; **wir verkaufen im D. tausend Exemplare im Jahr,** we sell on an average, our sales average, a thousand copies a year; **den D. erreichen,** to be up to the average; **ihr Gewinn erreicht einen D. von dreitausend Pfund im Jahr,** their profits average up to three thousand pounds a year; (*b*) **D. der Bevölkerung,** cross-section of the population; **der große D. (der Menschen),** most people, the majority of people, people in general, the (great) bulk of mankind, the common run of people; **die Holländer sind im D. . . . ,** the majority of Dutch people, Dutch people in general, the common run of Dutch people, are . . . , the average Dutchman is . . . ; **der D. der Käufer, die Käufer im D.,** the ordinary run of buyers; **Kandidaten für diese Stelle müssen über dem D. stehen, sein,** candidates for this post must be above the average, must be of more than average ability; **er ist nur D., er gehört nur zum D.,** he has only average ability; **sie ist guter D., sie gehört zum guten D.,** she keeps up a good average; **seine Leistungen liegen über, unter, dem D.,** his achievements are above, below, the average, are more than, less than, average. **4.** *Tls:* punching machine; *Num:* (blank) cutting machine.
durchschnittlich. 1. *a.* (*a*) average; ordinary, normal; **die durchschnittlichen Einnahmen betragen 3000 Mark,** the average, normal, proceeds come to 3000 marks, the proceeds come on an average to, the proceeds average, 3000 marks; **ein Mann von durchschnittlicher Intelligenz,** a man of average, ordinary, normal, intelligence; (*b*) very ordinary, average, limited, insignificant, middling; **ein sehr durchschnittlicher Mensch,** a very ordinary person; **seine Intelligenz ist sehr d.,** he is of limited, of middling, *F:* of very average, intelligence; **mein Einkommen war nie mehr als d.,** my income was never more than average. **2.** *adv.* on an average; normally; **der Baum trägt im Jahre d. einen Zentner Äpfel,** the tree yields on an average, normally yields, one hundredweight of apples a year; **ich gehe d. sechsmal im Jahre dorthin,** I go there on an average, I normally go there, six times a year; **ihr Gewinn erreicht d. dreitausend Pfund im Jahr,** their profits average up to three thousand pounds a year.
Durchschnitts-, *comb.fm.* **1.** . . . of averages; **Durchschnittsrechnung** *f,* (calculation of) averages. **2.** (*a*) average . . . ; mean . . . ; **Durchschnittspreis** *m,* average price; **Durchschnittseinkommen** *n,* average income; **Durchschnittstemperatur** *f,* mean temperature; **der Durchschnittsengländer,** the average Englishman; (*b*) insignificant . . . , very ordinary . . . ; **Durchschnittsleistung** *f,* work showing average, very ordinary, *F:* very average, ability.
Durchschnittsmensch, *m.* (*a*) average person; ordinary person; **der D.,** the common, average, man; (*b*) *Pej:* insignificant, very ordinary, person; **er ist nur ein D.,** he is a very ordinary, insignificant, person, he is nothing out of the common run, the ordinary.
durchschnüffeln, *v.tr. sep. & insep.* to ferret, nose, rummage, through (papers, etc.).
durchschossen *see* **durchschießen**[2].
Durchschreibebuch, *n.* duplicating book.
Durchschreibebuchführung, *f. Book-k:* multiple copy system.
durchschreiben, *v. sep.* (*strong*) **1.** *v.tr.* to make carbon copies, a carbon copy, of (bill, etc.). **2.** *v.i.* (*haben*) (*of pen, etc.*) to make an impression (through carbon paper).
Durchschreibepapier, *n.* carbon paper.
Durchschreibeverfahren, *n.* duplicating.
durchschreiten, *v.* (*strong*) **1.** *v.i. sep.* (*sein*) to walk, stride, through (sth.); **er schritt mit hoch erhobenem Haupte durch,** he walked, strode, through with his head held high in the air. **2.** *v.tr. insep.* to walk, stride, through, across (sth.); to cover (field of knowledge); **er durchschritt mehrere Male das Zimmer,** he paced several times up and down the room.
Durchschrift, *f.* carbon copy, *F:* carbon.
Durchschuß, *m.* **1.** shooting through (sth.); **der D. des Wassers durch den Damm,** the shooting, pouring, of the water through the dam. **2.** shot (right) through; **er hatte einen (glatten) D. durch den Oberschenkel,** he was shot clean through the thigh, the bullet went clean through his thigh. **3.** *Print:* (*a*) spacing out, leading out (of lines); spacing out, setting out (of type); (*b*) space (between type, lines of print); white line; (*c*) lead. **4.** *Bookb:* interleaves. **5.** *Tex:* woof, weft.
Durchschußmaterial, *n. Print:* leads; spaces.
durchschweifen, *v.tr. insep.* to roam, range, rove (through, over, across) (country, etc.), to wander through, over, across (country, etc.); **er durchschweifte die Felder,** he roamed, ranged, wandered, through, over, across, the fields; **das Land d.,** to roam, range, (over) the country; **sein Auge durchschweifte den Himmel,** his eyes ranged, swept, (over) the sky.
durchschwingen, *v. sep.* (*strong*) **1.** *v.tr. Gym:* to swing (arms, legs, etc.) forwards *or* backwards to the fullest extent. **2.** *v.i.* (*haben*) (*a*) *Gym:* to swing forwards *or* backwards to the fullest extent; (*b*) *Golf:* to follow through.
Durchschwung, *m.* (*a*) *Gym:* swing-through; (*b*) *Golf:* follow-through.
durchsegeln, *v.* **1.** *v.i. sep.* (*sein*) (*a*) to sail through (sth.); **zwischen diesen hohen Klippen kann nur das kleinste Schiff d.,** only the very smallest ship can sail between those high cliffs; (*b*) *Sch: F:* to fail, *F:* to be ploughed (in examination). **2.** *v.tr. insep.* to sail over, across (sea, etc.); (*of ship*) **die Meere d.,** to plough the seas.
durchsehen, *v. sep.* (*strong*) **1.** *v.i.* (*haben*) (*a*) to see through (sth.); to look through (sth.); **das Fenster ist beschlagen; man kann nicht d.,** the window is misty; you can't see through (it); **das Wasser war so klar, daß man bis auf den Grund d. konnte,** the water was so clear that you could see right to the bottom; **durch ein Fernrohr d.,** to look through a telescope; **durch eine Maueröffnung d.,** to see, to look, through an opening in the wall; **sie starrte mich an, als ob sie durch mich d. wollte,** she stared at me as though she wanted to look right through me; (*b*) **durch etwas d.,** to get sth. straight; to grasp (the real reason for, the meaning of) sth.; **durch j-n d.,** to see through s.o.; **ich sehe durch ihre Absichten nicht durch,** I can't see what she's up to; **er ist eine so unkomplizierte Natur, daß man gleich durch ihn durchsieht,** he is so uncomplicated that you can read him like a book; **die Sache wird so verworren, daß ich nicht mehr durchsehe,** the whole business is becoming so confused that I can no longer get it straight; **ihre Familienverhältnisse sind so kompliziert, daß man nicht mehr d. kann,** their relationships are so involved that it's impossible to get them straight, *F:* one can't make head or tail of them; (*c*) (*of thg*) to show through, to peep through, to be able to be seen through; **seine Ellbogen sehen durch, die Ellbogen sehen (bei) ihm durch,** his elbows are sticking through (his sleeves); **seine Schuhe waren zerrissen und ließen seine Zehen d.,** his shoes were split and let his toes stick out. **2.** *v.tr.* (*a*) to look, search, through (thgs), to look through, search (sth.); **er sah alle seine Papiere durch, aber den Brief fand er nicht,** he looked, searched, through all his papers, but he couldn't find the letter; **ich habe den ganzen Schreibtisch nach dem Dokument durchgesehen,** I have searched the whole desk for the document; (*b*) to look, go, through, over (sth.); to examine (sth.); to correct (sth.); to revise (sth.); **ich habe die Arbeiten zweimal durchgesehen,** I've looked, been, gone, through, the exercises twice; **er wird die Akten noch einmal d.,** he'll look over, examine, the files once more; **der Lehrer sah die Aufgabe durch und gab mir eine gute Note,** the teacher looked through, corrected, the exercise and gave me a good mark for it; **ein Manuskript auf Schreibfehler (hin) d.,** to look, go, through a manuscript for, in search of, mistakes; **ich muß meine Rolle noch einmal d.,** I must look through my part again; **etwas flüchtig d.,** to look quickly through, to glance through, sth.; *Publ:* **zweite, gründlich durchgesehene Auflage,** second edition revised throughout; (*c*) *A:* **etwas, j-n, d.** = **durch etwas, j-n, d.,** *q.v. under* 1 (*b*).
durchseihen. I. *v.tr. sep.* to filter, strain (liquid); to percolate (liquid)
II. *vbl s.* **Durchseihen** *n.,* **Durchseihung** *f. in vbl senses; also:* filtration.
durchsetzen[1], *v.tr. sep.* **1.** *Metall:* (*a*) to screen, to riddle (ore); (*b*) to smelt (ore). **2.** to get (plan, etc.) carried out, to put through (plan); to achieve (one's end), to obtain (what one wants); **Pläne mit Gewalt d.,** to force one's plans through; **seinen Willen d.,** to get one's (own) way; **seinen Willen (mit Gewalt) bei j-m d.,** to enforce one's will on s.o., to force s.o. to do what one wants; **sie wollen die Reform mit allen Mitteln d.,** they are doing all in their power to bring about the reform; **seine Meinung d.,** to gain acceptance for one's opinion; **seine Überzeugung d.,** to make others see a matter as one sees it; **sie wird ihren Vorschlag bei der Behörde nicht d. können,** she won't get her proposal adopted, accepted, by the authorities; **er kann alles d.,** he can get his (own) way in anything, he can get anything done; **das Kind kann alles beim Vater d.,** the child can get anything he likes out of his father; **d., daß etwas geschieht,** to succeed in getting sth. done; **die Eltern haben durchgesetzt, daß ihre Kinder eine Woche Ferien bekommen, die Eltern haben eine Woche Ferien für ihre Kinder durchgesetzt,** the parents have succeeded in obtaining a week's holiday for their children; **wir haben endlich beim Chef durchgesetzt, daß wir am Samstag frei haben,** we have at last succeeded in persuading, we have at last induced, prevailed upon, the boss to give us Saturday off; **sie haben durchgesetzt, daß der Minister seitnes Ames enthoben wurde, sie haben die Absetzung des Ministers durchgesetzt,** they succeeded in getting the minister relieved of his post. **3. sich durchsetzen,** (*of pers.*) to get one's way; to make one's way; to be successful; (*of opinion, etc.*) to gain acceptance; **er ist nicht**

beliebt, aber er setzt sich überall durch, weil er die Leute einschüchtert, he isn't liked, but he gets the better of people, he gets his own way with people, because he scares them; du wirst dich bei ihm nicht d. können, you won't have any success with him; der Lehrer kann sich in seiner Klasse nicht d., the teacher has no authority in his class; sich mit seiner Meinung d., to gain acceptance for one's opinion; sich (in einer Diskussion) gegen j-n d., to get the better of s.o. (in an argument); er setzt sich überall durch, (i) he can always hold his own; (ii) he carries all before him; um dieses Kind braucht man sich keine Sorgen zu machen; es wird sich schon (im Leben) d., there is no need to worry about this child; he'll always be able to hold his own; er hat sich im Leben durchgesetzt, he has made his way, has been successful; diese Anschauung hat sich erst allmählich durchgesetzt, this view has only gradually gained acceptance, become generally accepted; es wird wohl lange dauern, bis sich die neue Methode (allgemein) durchsetzt, it will be a long time before the new method is generally adopted.

durchsetzen². I. v.tr. insep. to intersperse, pervade, permeate (sth.) (with sth.); to penetrate (sth.); mit etwas durchsetzt sein, to be full of sth.; das Fleisch ist mit Sehnen durchsetzt, the meat is full of sinews; mit Salzen durchsetzt, infiltrated with mineral salts; mit Quarz durchsetzter Schiefer, slate interspersed with quartz; seine Rede war mit lateinischen Zitaten durchsetzt, his speech was interspersed, interlarded, with Latin quotations; das Volk war von Verrätern durchsetzt, traitors were rife among the people; revolutionäre Ideen durchsetzten allmählich die ganze Bevölkerung, revolutionary ideas gradually infiltrated into the whole community; Spione hatten die ganze Armee durchsetzt, spies had penetrated, infiltrated into, the whole army. II. vbl s. **Durchsetzen** n., **Durchsetzung** f. in vbl senses; also: pervasion (of sth.) (by sth.); infiltration (of army, etc.) (by spies, etc.).

Durchsicht, f. 1. going, looking, through, over; examination, inspection (of documents, etc.); correction, correcting (of exercise, etc.); er bekam die Aktenstücke zur D., he was sent the files to go through, look through, he was sent the files for inspection, for examination; sie gab mir fünf Arbeiten zur D., she gave me five exercises to go through, to look through, to correct, for correction; ich schickte ihm meinen Artikel zur D., I sent him my article to look through, for his inspection; zur gefälligen D., for your kind inspection; bei flüchtiger D. der Papiere fiel mir diese Stelle auf, as I was glancing through the papers this passage caught my eye; bei der D. meiner Korrespondenz . . . , when looking through my correspondence . . . . 2. view (through), vista; dann und wann lichtete sich der Wald und wir hatten eine D. auf den See, every now and then the trees became thinner and we could see through, we had a view through, to the lake.

durchsichtig, a. (a) transparent (glass, water, etc.); clear (air, water); transparent, diaphanous (material); (b) clear, lucid (style, etc.); die Sachlage ist mir nicht ganz d., the position isn't quite clear to me; (c) transparent (intentions, etc.).

Durchsichtigkeit, f. transparence, transparency (of glass, material, intentions, etc.); diaphaneity, diaphanousness (of material); clearness (of air, water); clarity, lucidity (of style).

Durchsicht(s)sucher, m. Phot: direct-vision viewfinder.

durchsickern, v.i. sep. (sein) (a) (of liquid) to filter, seep, percolate, ooze, through (sth.); der Eimer war umgefallen, und das Wasser sickerte allmählich durch den Fußboden durch, the pail had been knocked over and the water seeped, oozed, gradually through the floor; das Wasser sickert schnell durch den Sand durch, the water filters, seeps, percolates, quickly through the sand; (b) (of truth, news, etc.) to leak out; die Wahrheit wird allmählich d., the truth will leak out gradually; das Geheimnis sickerte durch, the secret leaked out; viele Einzelheiten über seinen Plan sind schon durchgesickert, a great many details of his plan have already leaked out; Gerüchte sickerten durch, rumours began to spread.

durchsieben, v.tr. sep. to sieve, sift (sth.), to pass (sth.) through a sieve; to sift, sieve, bolt (flour); to screen, riddle (mineral ore).

durchsitzen, v. sep. (strong) 1. v.tr. to wear out (trousers, etc.) by sitting; to wear out (chair, etc.) by sitting on it; er hat seine alte Hose ganz durchgesessen, he has worn right through the seat of his old trousers; ein durchgesessener Stuhl, a chair with a worn-out seat. 2. v.i. (haben) to remain sitting (for a period of time); wir saßen die Nacht durch, we sat up all night; sie hat die Vorlesung durchgesessen, she sat the lecture out; das Parlament hat die ganze Nacht durchgesessen, Parliament was in session all night.

durchspielen, v. sep. 1. v.tr. to play (piece of music, game) through; to play (record) over; er hat das Stück zweimal für sich durchgespielt, he played the piece through to himself twice. 2. v.i. (haben) (die Nacht, usw.) d., to spend the night, etc., playing, to play all night, etc., long.

durchsprechen, v. sep. (strong) 1. v.i. (haben) (durchs Telephon) d., to telephone, to speak over the telephone. 2. v.tr. to discuss (sth.) thoroughly.

durchspringen, v. (strong) 1. v.i. sep. (sein) to jump, leap, through (sth.); der Clown hielt den Reifen hoch, und der kleine Hund sprang durch, the clown held up the hoop and the little dog jumped through (it). 2. v.tr. insep. to jump through, across (fields, etc.).

durchstechen¹, v.tr. & v.i. sep. (strong) (haben) 1. (a) (of pers.) to stick (needle, etc.) through (sth.); (of needle, etc.) to go, come, through (sth.); to stick, be sticking, through (sth.); (die Nadel, mit der Nadel) kräftig (durch den Stoff) d., to stick the needle vigorously through (the material); (b) ein Muster (auf den Stoff, das Papier) d., to pounce a pattern (on to the material, the paper); (c) A: (of colour, etc.) to stand out. 2.=durchstechen². 3. v.i. A: mit j-m d., to be in league, in collusion. with s.o.

durchstechen², v.tr. insep. (strong) (a) to pierce (sth.) (through); to transfix, Lit: to transpierce (s.o., sth.); to run (s.o.) through (with a spear, etc.); to prick holes through (paper, etc.); to puncture (skin, etc.); Med: to pierce (membrane); (b) Civ.E: etc: to pierce, cut through (dike, etc.); to cut through (isthmus, hill, etc.); cp. **Durchstich.**

Durchstecher, m. Mus: cipher (in organ pipe).

Durchstecherei, f. A: intrigue, plot.

durchstehen, v. sep. (strong) 1. v.tr. (a) to go or come through (difficult years, dangers, etc.); to come through (illness); to go or come through (adventures); (b) F: to keep up (pace, etc.). 2. v.i. (haben) to continue standing; ich habe bis nach Paris durchgestanden, I had to stand all the way to Paris.

Durchstein, m. Constr:=**Durchbinder.**

Durchstich, m. 1. Civ.E: etc: cutting through, piercing (of dike, etc.); cutting, driving (of tunnel, etc., through mountain, etc.). 2. Civ.E: cut, cutting; (railway-)cutting; Hyd.E: cut; der D. durch den Sankt Gotthard, the St Gotthard tunnel.

durchstöbern, v.tr. insep. to search, hunt, through (house, etc.); to scour (wood, etc.); to rummage through (drawers, papers, etc.); to ransack (room, pockets, etc.).

Durchstoß, m. 1. Mil: D. (durch die feindlichen Linien), break-through. 2. Tls: punching machine.

durchstoßen¹, v. sep. (strong) 1. v.tr. (a) to push, thrust (s.o., sth.) through (sth.); sie stießen ihn durch die enge Türöffnung durch, they pushed him through the narrow doorway; (b) to knock down, in (door, etc.); to knock a hole through (sth.); to knock (sth.) in two, in half; er stieß die Scheibe mit der Faust durch, he knocked in the pane with his fist; (c) sich dat. die Strümpfe, Schuhe, (vorne) d., to wear through the toes of one's socks, shoes; meine Strümpfe, Schuhe, sind vorne durchgestoßen, my socks, shoes, have holes in the toes. 2. v.i. (haben) to push through; (a) Mil: (durch die feindlichen Linien) d., to break through (the enemy lines); (b) mit der Faust durch etwas d., to knock a hole through sth. with one's fist.

durchstoßen², v.tr. insep. (strong) (a) to pierce (sth.); to make a hole through (sth.); to run (s.o.) through (with sword, etc.); (b) to knock down, in (door, etc.); to knock a hole through (sth.).

Durchstoßmaschine, f. Tls: punching machine.

durchstreichen, v. (strong) 1. v.tr. sep. to strike out, to cross out, to delete, to cancel (word, line, etc.). 2. v.i. sep. (sein) (of wind, etc.) to blow through. 3. v.tr. insep. to rove, roam, wander, through, over, across (countryside, etc.).

durchstreifen, v.tr. insep. to rove, roam, range, wander, through, over, across (countryside, etc.); sein Auge durchstreifte die Versammlung, his eyes ranged, roved, swept, over the gathering.

durchströmen, v. 1. v.i. sep. (sein) to stream, pour, through (sth.); der Deich brach, und das Wasser strömte durch, the dike burst and the water poured through; das Tor wurde geöffnet, und die Menschenmenge strömte durch, the gate was opened and the crowd streamed, poured, through it. 2. v.tr. insep. (of river) to flow through (valley, etc.); (of emotion, etc.) to flow, flood, through (s.o.).

durchsuchen¹. I. v.tr. insep. to search (sth., s.o.), to go through (sth.), to search, scour (a wood, etc.), to search through (thgs), (nach etwas, for sth.); sie durchsuchte das ganze Haus, alle Schubladen, aber sie fand das Geld nicht, she searched the whole house, she ransacked the house, she searched (through), went through, ransacked, all the drawers, but she did not find the money; wir werden ihn, seine Taschen, d. müssen, we shall have to search him, to search, go through, his pockets; die Zollbeamten durchsuchten meine Koffer, the customs officers searched my cases; Jur: ein Haus, j-n, d., to search a house, s.o. II. vbl s. **Durchsuchen,** n. in vbl senses. 2. **Durchsuchung,** f. (a) =II. 1; (b) search; eine D. anordnen, to order a search.

durchsuchen², v.tr. sep. to search, to go through (sth.), to search, scour (a wood, etc.), to search through (thgs), (nach etwas, for sth.).

Durchsuchungsrecht, n. Nau: right of visit and search.

durchtanzen¹, v. sep. 1. v.i. (haben) to dance through (sth.). 2. v.i. (haben) to dance the whole (of a period of) time; sie hat die ganze Nacht durchgetanzt, she danced all night long, the whole night. 3. v.tr. (a) to dance (measure, etc.), through (to the end); diese Figur wollen wir nochmals d., let's dance this figure through once more; (b) to wear out, to wear a hole, holes, through (shoes) by dancing.

durchtanzen², v.tr. insep. (a) to dance through (room, etc.); (b) to spend (period of time) dancing; wir haben die Nächte durchtanzt, we spent our nights dancing; eine durchtanzte Nacht, a night spent dancing, a night of dancing.

durchtoben, v.tr. insep. to rage through (sth.).

durchtränken, v.tr. insep. (a) (of liquid) to soak, saturate, impregnate (sth.); ein mit Öl durchtränkter Lappen, a rag soaked in, saturated, impregnated, with, oil; sein Ärmel war von Blut durchtränkt, his sleeve was soaked in, saturated with, blood; (b) (of book, pers., etc.) von, mit, Gefühl, usw., durchtränkt sein, to be filled with, steeped in, emotion, etc.

durchtreiben, v.tr. sep. (strong) (a) to drive (sth., s.o.) through (sth.); er trieb seine Schafe unter der Brücke durch, he drove his sheep under the bridge (and out on the other side); einen Pflock, usw., durch eine Öffnung d., to drive a peg, etc., through an opening; (b) to put (sth.) through (sieve); (c) to push (plan, etc.) through.

Durchtreiber, m. Tls: drift (punch).

durchtrennen, v.tr. sep. to divide, split (sth.); einen Stoff in der Mitte d., to cut a piece of material into two pieces, in half.

durchtreten. I. v. sep. (strong) 1. v.i. (sein) (a) (of pers.) to walk, step, go, pass, through (sth.); (of liquid, etc.) to pass through (opening, etc.); (of river, etc.) to pass through (narrow gorge, etc.); durch die Tür d., to go through the door; (b) to pass through; Med: (of bone) to stick through (flesh, etc.); (of rupture) to come through (peritoneum, etc.); (of foreign body, etc.) to go, come, through (skin, etc.); Obst: (of foetus) to pass through (birth canal). 2. v.i. (haben) Cy: to pedal hard. 3. v.tr. (a) to put one's foot through (floor-boards, etc.); to wear out (rug, etc.) by walking on it; (b) to tread (sth.) through (sth.); (c) Cy: (of pedals) sich d., to fail to grip; (d) to tread (grapes, etc.) thoroughly. 4. v.tr. sich dat. die Füße d., to get fallen arches. II. vbl s. **Durchtreten,** n. in vbl senses; also: =**Durchtritt.**

durchtrieben [-'tri:bən], a. (of pers.) wily, cunning, artful, sly, guileful; ein durchtriebenes Bürschchen, a sly fellow, F: a downy bird.

Durchtriebenheit, f. wiliness, cunning, artfulness, slyness, guile.

Durchtritt, m. passage (of pers., liquid, river, etc.) through (sth.); Obst: D. des Kindes (durch den Geburtskanal), passage of the baby through the birth canal.

durchwachen, *v.* **1.** *v.tr. insep.* to remain awake during (night, etc.); to keep watch through (night, etc.); **während ihrer Krankheit haben wir drei Nächte nacheinander durchwacht,** during her illness we kept watch, we sat up, for three nights running; **nach einer durchwachten Nacht,** after a sleepless night. **2.** *v.i. sep.* (*haben*) to remain awake (throughout a period of time); **er hat die Nacht durchgewacht,** (i) he remained awake, he didn't sleep, (ii) he watched, kept watch, all night.

Durchwachs, *n.* **-es/⸗er,** & *m.* **-es/⸗e.** *Bot:* hare's-ear, thoroughwax.

durchwachsen[1], *v.i. sep.* (*strong*) (*sein*) to grow through (sth.).

durchwachsen[2], *v.tr. insep.* (*strong*) **1.** to grow through (sth.); **die Ruinen waren mit Farnen und Gräsern durchwachsen,** ferns and grasses had sprung up among the ruins. **2.** *p.p.* & *a.* **durchwachsen,** (*a*) (*of meat*) marbled; streaky; lean; **durchwachsener Speck,** streaky bacon; (*b*) *Bot:* perfoliate (leaf). **3.** *vbl s.* **Durchwachsung,** *f. Bot:* diaphysis.

Durchwachskraut, *n. Bot:* yellow-wort, yellow centaury.

Durchwachsungszwilling, *m. Cryst:* interpenetrant twin, penetration twin.

durchwagen (sich), *v.refl. sep.* to dare to go through (sth.).

durchwalken, *v.tr. sep.* **1.** *Tex:* to full (cloth) thoroughly. **2.** = **durchprügeln.**

durchwandern, *v.* **1.** *v.i. sep.* (*sein*) to walk through, pass through (district, etc.); to hike through (district, etc.); **wir wanderten langsam durch den Wald durch,** we walked, went, slowly through the wood. **2.** *v.tr. insep.* (*a*) to walk through, pass through, (place, area, etc.); to hike through (area, etc.); (*b*) to travel (through) (area, etc.); **er hat ganz Europa durchwandert,** he has travelled all over Europe; **auf seiner letzten Reise hat er den ganzen Schwarzwald durchwandert,** on his last trip he walked all through the Black Forest; **ziellos die Straßen d.,** to wander aimlessly through the streets; (*b*) to walk through (life); to go through (field of knowledge, etc.); to go over (sth.) (in one's mind).

durchwärmen, *v.tr.* (*a*) *sep.* to warm (s.o., sth.) (right) through; (*of pers.*) **sich gut d.,** to get warm, to warm oneself; (*b*) *insep.* to warm (s.o., sth.) (through).

durchwaten, *v.* **1.** *v.i. sep.* (*sein*) to wade through (water, etc.). **2.** *v.tr. insep.* to wade through, across (river, etc.).

Durchweg[1], *m.* way through; passage (through).

durchweg[2], *adv.* all through, from beginning to end; consistently; without exception; altogether; **die Hotels in dieser Stadt sind d. schlecht,** the hotels in this town are all, are without exception, bad; **die Kinder in dieser Klasse sind d. intelligent,** all the children in this class are intelligent; **sein Benehmen ist d. erfreulich,** his behaviour is altogether good; **ihr Fleiß ist d. zufriedenstellend,** her application to her work is consistently satisfactory.

durchwegs, *adv. South G.Dial:* = **durchweg**[2].

durchwetzen, *v.tr. sep.* to wear through, go through (seat of trousers, etc.).

durchwichsen, *v.tr. sep. F:* to give (s.o.) a drubbing, hiding.

durchwirken, *v.tr.* **1.** *sep.* to work (dough, etc.) thoroughly. **2.** *insep. Tex:* to interweave (fabric) (with silk thread, etc.); **ein mit Seidenfäden durchwirkter Stoff,** a material interwoven with silk threads; **mit Gold durchwirkt,** interwoven with gold threads.

durchwühlen, *v.tr.* **1.** *insep.* (*a*) (*of animal, etc.*) to burrow through (earth, etc.); (*b*) to rummage through, to forage about in (drawers, etc.); to root, forage, among, in (papers); (*c*) (*of emotion*) to fill (s.o., s.o.'s breast); **seine Brust war von Leidenschaft durchwühlt,** his breast was torn by passion, his heart was in a turmoil. **2.** *sep.* (*a*) = 1 (*a*), (*b*); (*b*) **sich d.,** to burrow, to work, (one's way) through.

Durchwurf, *m. Civ.E: Min: etc:* **1.** screen. **2.** screened sand, etc.

Durchwurfsieb, *n. Civ.E: Min: etc:* screen.

durchzählen, *v. sep.* **1.** *v.tr.* to count (thgs, persons). **2.** *v.i.* (*haben*) *Mil: etc:* to number (off).

durchzechen, *v.* **1.** *v.i. sep.* (*haben*) **bis zum frühen Morgen d.,** to go on drinking, carousing, till early morning. **2.** *v.tr. insep.* **die Nacht d.,** to spend the night drinking, carousing.

durchzeichnen, *v.tr. sep.* **1.** to trace, to make a tracing of (picture, etc.). **2.** (*of author, etc.*) to draw (character, etc.) (in detail).

durchziehen[1], *v. sep.* (*strong*). I. *v.i.* **1.** (*sein*) to pass, go, come, through (area, etc.); (*of troops*) to march through (country, etc.); **jeden Tag zieht ein Strom von Flüchtlingen hier durch,** every day a stream of refugees passes, comes, through here. **2.** (*haben*) *Cu:* (*a*) (*of vinegar, spices, etc.*) to soak well in, to be thoroughly absorbed (into meat, etc.); (*of tea, coffee, etc.*) to draw; (*b*) **(Fleisch, usw.) d. lassen,** to let (meat, etc.) simmer till well cooked.

II. **durchziehen,** *v.tr.* **1.** (*a*) to pull, draw (sth., s.o.) through (sth.); **er machte das Fenster auf und zog mich durch,** he opened the window and pulled me through; **die Pferde zogen den schweren Wagen durch den Fluß durch,** the horses pulled, drew, the heavy waggon through the river; **man macht eine Schlinge und zieht den Faden durch,** you make a loop and pull the thread through (it); **Gummi, usw., d.,** to pull, draw, elastic, etc., through; *Tex:* **die Kettfäden d.,** to draw in the warp threads; (*b*) to pull, draw, (sth.) (right) through (sth.); (*c*) to draw (line) through (word, passage, etc.); (*d*) = **durchhecheln** 2. **2. sich (durch etwas) durchziehen,** (*a*) (*of stream, road, etc.*) to run, pass, through, across (field, etc.); (*b*) to go, run, through (sth.); to pervade (sth.); **das Motiv zieht sich wie ein roter Faden durch das ganze Werk durch,** this motif runs through the whole work like a red thread.

durchziehen[2], *v.tr. insep.* (*strong*) **1.** to go, travel, through (area, etc.); to travel across, to cross (country, etc.); **die Welt d.,** to travel round the world. **2.** (*a*) (*of stream, etc.*) to flow through (valley, etc.); (*of road, etc.*) to pass, run, through (valley, etc.); (*of stream, road, etc.*) to cross, intersect (field, heath, etc.); (*b*) (*of motif, etc.*) to run through (work, etc.); **das Motiv der Eifersucht durchzieht das ganze Stück,** the motif of jealousy runs through the whole play. **3.** (*of scent, etc.*) to fill, pervade (room, etc.); (*of vinegar, spices, etc.*) to soak well into, to be thoroughly absorbed into, to permeate (meat, etc.). **4.** to streak (sth.) (with sth.); to interweave (sth.) (with sth.); to intersperse (sth.) (with sth.); **ein mit Goldfäden durchzogener Stoff,** a material interwoven with gold threads; **weißer mit roten Adern durchzogener Marmor,** white marble streaked with red; **das Fleisch ist mit Fettstreifen durchzogen,** the meat is streaked with fat; **ein mit grauen Haaren durchzogener Bart,** a beard shot with grey; **ihr Haar war mit Silberfäden durchzogen,** there were strands of silver in her hair; her hair was shot with silver.

Durchzieher, *m.* **-s/-.** *Fenc:* cut across the cheek.

Durchziehgummi, *m.* (narrow) elastic.

Durchziehkordel, *f.* cord (for drawing in top of bag, etc.).

Durchziehnadel, *f.* bodkin.

durchzittern, *v. insep.* **1.** *v.tr.* (*a*) to tremble through (sth.); **der Wind durchzitterte die Pappeln,** the wind trembled through the poplars, made the poplars tremble, quiver; (*b*) (*of sound*) to vibrate through (house, etc.); (*c*) (*of emotion, etc.*) to thrill through (s.o.); to vibrate, tremble, through (s.o.); to make (s.o.) quiver; **von Furcht durchzittert,** quivering with fright. **2.** *v.i.* (*haben*) **die Nacht, usw., d.,** to spend the night, etc., shuddering, shivering, with fright.

durchzogen, *p.p. see* **durchziehen**[2].

durchzucken, *v.tr. insep.* (*a*) to flash through, across (sth.); **Blitze durchzuckten den Himmel,** flashes of lightning lit the sky; (*b*) (*of thought*) to flash through (s.o., s.o.'s mind); (*of emotion, etc.*) to vibrate, shoot, thrill, through (s.o.); **plötzlich durchzuckte mich der Gedanke, daß . . .,** it flashed upon me, across my mind, that . . .; **ein plötzlicher Schrecken durchzuckte mich,** I was seized with sudden fear; **ein heftiger Schmerz durchzuckte sie,** a violent pain shot through her; **ein Gefühl der Wonne durchzuckte ihn,** a feeling of ecstasy thrilled through him.

Durchzug, *m.* **1.** (*a*) (i) passage through, passing through; (ii) journey through, way through; **der D. durch das Rote Meer,** the crossing of the Red Sea; **auf dem D.,** on the journey, way, through; (*b*) (i) marching (of troops) through (country, etc.); (ii) march through (country, etc.); **(einer Armee) den D. gestatten, verweigern,** to allow, to refuse to allow, (an army) passage through, to march through; **beim D. der fremden Truppen,** while the foreign troops were marching through; **beim D. der Truppen hat die Bevölkerung sehr gelitten,** the population suffered greatly when the troops marched through. **2.** *Row:* stroke. **3.** through-draught, draught (right through) (room, etc.); **D. machen,** to make, to create, a through-draught. **4.** (*a*) *Tex:* drawing-frame; (*b*) *Needlew:* hem through which elastic, ribbon, etc., is drawn. **5.** *Constr:* (*a*) continuous girder; (*b*) architrave.

Durchzügler, *m.* **-s/-,** bird of passage, passage-migrant.

Durchzugsrecht, *n. Mil:* right to march through (country).

durchzwängen, *v.tr. sep.* to force (sth.) through (sth.); **sich (durch etwas) d.,** to force one's way, to squeeze (oneself), through (sth.); **die Katze zwängte sich durch das Loch durch,** the cat squeezed (itself) through the hole.

Durdreiklang, *m. Mus:* major triad.

dürfen, *modal aux. v.* (*pr.* **darf, darfst, darf, dürfen, dürft, dürfen;** *p.t.* **durfte;** *p.p.* **gedurft**), **1.** *A. & Lit:* = **bedürfen. 2.** (*a*) **etwas tun d.,** to be allowed, permitted, to do sth.; **ich darf es tun,** I am allowed to do it; **hat sie kommen dürfen? — nein, sie hat nicht gedurft,** was she allowed to come?—no, she wasn't allowed (to do so); **hier darf man nicht rauchen,** one is not allowed, permitted, to smoke here, smoking is not allowed, permitted, here; **so etwas hätte nie geschehen dürfen,** a thing like that should never have happened; **darf ich hereinkommen? — das dürfen Sie (gerne),** may I come in?—you may (with pleasure); **darf ich, dürfte ich, dieses Buch mitnehmen?** may I take, might I take, would you mind if I took, this book with me? **etwas mehr Ruhe, wenn ich bitten darf,** a little quieter, if you please; **wenn ich so sagen darf,** if I may say so; **darf ich Ihnen noch eine Tasse Kaffee anbieten?** may I give you another cup of coffee? (*ironical*) **wenn ich vielleicht auch etwas sagen dürfte . . .,** if I might be allowed, permitted, to speak . . .; **darf ich auch mal was sagen?** might I be allowed to say something? (*said by shopkeeper when weighing out meat, etc.*) **darf's etwas mehr sein?** do you mind if it's a bit over (the weight)? **du darfst dich nicht darüber aufregen,** you mustn't worry about it, you're not to worry about it; **darf ich (Sie) um diesen Tanz bitten?** May I have this dance, please? **darf ich es wagen, Sie für diesen Abend einzuladen?** may I venture to, might I be so bold as to, invite you out this evening? **darf ich es wohl wagen, ihm diesen Vorschlag zu machen?** do you think I could suggest this to him? **'dürfte ich es wagen, allein in das feindliche Lager zu gehen?' fragte er sich,** 'should I risk going alone into the enemy camp?' he wondered; **wer darf ihm das ins Gesicht sagen?** who can, who is the man to, say that to his face? who is bold enough to say that to his face? **wer ist so fehlerlos, daß er sie verurteilen darf? wer darf sie verurteilen?** who is so blameless that he may, that he is in a position to, condemn her? who is in a position to condemn her? **wer darf so etwas schon tun?** who can, who is in a position to, do a thing like that? (*b*) (*command, replacing* **müssen** *in certain negative phrases*) **das darfst du ihm nicht sagen,** you must not tell him that, you are not to tell him that; **sie darf nichts davon wissen,** she must know, she is to know, nothing about it; **du darfst nicht zu spät nach Hause kommen,** you must not, you are not to, come home too late; (*c*) (*elliptical use*) **wir dürfen nicht in die Stadt,** we are not allowed to go into the town; **die Kinder dürfen nicht in den Obstgarten,** the children are not allowed (to go) into the orchard; **ich darf das,** I am allowed to (do so). **3.** (*subjunctive, expressing probability*) **es dürfte sechs Uhr sein,** it must be six o'clock; **der Anzug dürfte zwanzig Pfund gekostet haben,** I should say the suit cost twenty pounds, the suit may well have cost twenty pounds; **das dürfte Herr X sein,** that will be, that must be, Mr X; **wenn er es sagt, dürfte es wohl wahr sein,** if he says so it may well be true, it is very probably true; **es dürfte wahr sein,** it may well be, is probably, true; **das dürfte genug sein,** that should, ought to, be enough; **das dürfte ihm den Tag gründlich verdorben haben,** that will have ruined his day thoroughly for him; **es dürfte jedermann klar sein, daß . . .,** it should be, it ought to be, clear to all that . . .; **es dürfte nicht allzu schwer sein, das zu tun,** it shouldn't, can't, be so very difficult to do that. **4. -dürfen,** *comb.fm.* **hinausdürfen,** to be allowed (to go) out; **heraufdürfen,** to be allowed (to come) up; **darf ich herein?** may I come in? **er darf nicht herein,** he is not allowed (to come) in.

dürftig, *a.* **1.** *A. & Lit:* = **bedürftig** 1. **2.** *A. & Lit:* = **bedürftig** 2. **3.** (*of thg*) poor, wretched, mean, miserable, scant(y), meagre, sorry; **dürftige Kleidung,** scanty, wretched, clothing;

ein dürftiges Mahl, a wretched, scanty, meagre, sorry, meal; **eine dürftige Hütte,** a poor, wretched, mean, miserable, sorry, hovel; **dürftige Kenntnisse,** scanty, *F:* sketchy, knowledge; **dürftige Verse,** poor, sorry, verses; **ein dürftiger Stil,** a bare, barren, style; **der Aufsatz ist ein bißchen d.,** the essay is a bit thin, is rather poor; **eine dürftige Entschuldigung,** a poor, lame, paltry, sorry, excuse.

Dürftigkeit, *f.* 1. *A. & Lit:* =**Bedürftigkeit.** 2. poorness, scantiness (of clothing, meal, knowledge, etc.); *F:* sketchiness (of knowledge); poorness, meanness (of dwelling); bareness, barrenness (of style); poorness, lameness, paltriness (of excuse).

Durian ['du:rïa·n], *m.* **-s/-e.** *Bot:* (*fruit or tree*) durian.

Durine [du·'ri:nə], *f.* **-/.** *Vet:* dourine.

dürr, *a.* 1. (*a*) (*of wood, leaves, etc.*) dry; dead; withered, *Poet:* sere (leaves, etc.); (*of land*) barren, infertile; arid; dry; parched; **dürres Reisig,** dry twigs; **ein dürres Jahr, ein dürrer Sommer,** a year, summer, of drought; *B:* **denn so man das tut am grünen Holz, was will am dürren werden?** for if they do these things in a green tree, what shall be done in the dry? (*b*) (*of pers.*) skinny; spare, thin, lean; gaunt; dried up, desiccated; (*of limb, hand, etc.*) skinny; (*of animal*) skinny; emaciated; thin, lean; **ein langer, dürrer Hals,** a long, scraggy neck; **ein (kleines) dürres Männchen,** a little dried-up man; *F:* **ein (langes) dürres Gestell,** *F:* a beanstalk, a maypole; **d. wie eine Bohnenstange,** as thin as a rake, as a lath, as lean as a shotten herring; *B:* **er . . . sprach zu dem Menschen mit der dürren Hand,** . . . and said to the man which had the withered hand . . .; (*c*) *A:* parching (wind). 2. stark (misery, words, etc.); stark, bare (truth); plain, blunt, straightforward (words, etc.); **mit dürren Worten sagte er, daß . . . ,** he said quite bluntly, he said straight out, without mincing matters, that . . .; he simply stated without further explanation that . . . .

Durra ['dura:], *f.* **-/.** *Agr:* durra.

Dürrbein, *n. Fung:* marasius alliaceus.

Dürre, *f.* **-/-n.** 1. (*a*) dryness, aridity (of land); barrenness, infertility (of land); (*b*) thinness, leanness (of pers.); gauntness (of pers.). 2. drought; **es herrschte überall eine große D. diesen Sommer,** there was a universal drought this summer.

Dürrerz, *n. Miner:* silver ore with no lead content.

Dürrfleckenkrankheit, *f. Bot:* leaf-blight (of fruit-trees, potato plants).

Dürrfutter, *n.* dry fodder.

Durrha ['dura:], *f.* **-/.** *Agr:* durra.

Dürrheit, *f.*=**Dürre** 1.

Dürrkraut, *n. Bot:* erigeron, flea-bane.

Dürrlitzenstrauch, *m. Bot:* cornel(-tree), cornelian cherry.

Dürrwurz, *f. Bot:* (*a*) erigeron, flea-bane; ploughman's spikenard; **weiße D.,** butter-weed, horse-weed; (*b*) =**Dürrwurzalant.**

Dürrwurzalant, *m. Bot:* great flea-bane.

Durst, *m.* **-(e)s/.** thirst. 1. **D. haben,** to be, feel, thirsty, *F:* to be, feel, dry; **D. bekommen,** to become, get, thirsty; **großer D.,** great thirst; **heißer, brennender, D.,** burning, raging, thirst; **ewiger D.,** perpetual thirst, thirstiness; **einen ewigen D. haben,** to have a perpetual thirst; **den, seinen, D. stillen, löschen,** to quench, slake, one's thirst; **D. leiden,** to be thirsty, to suffer thirst; **an (ständigem) D. leiden,** to suffer from (continual) thirst; **an D. sterben,** to die of thirst; *F:* **ich sterbe vor D.,** I'm dying of thirst, I'm terribly thirsty; **diese Arbeit macht D.,** this work makes one thirsty, *F:* this is thirsty work; **Fisch macht D.,** fish makes one thirsty; **Speisen, die D. machen,** dishes that cause thirst, thirst-producing dishes; *F:* **einen über den D. getrunken haben,** to have had one over the eight. 2. **D. nach Wissen,** thirst for, after, knowledge; **brennender D. nach Gerechtigkeit,** craving for, burning thirst for, justice; **seinen D. nach Abenteuern stillen,** to satisfy one's thirst, craving, for adventure; **D. nach Blut,** thirst for blood; **D. nach Blut haben,** to be thirsty, athirst, for blood, to thirst after blood.

-durst, *comb.fm. m.* thirst for, after, . . .; **Blutdurst,** thirst for blood; **Wissensdurst,** thirst for, after, knowledge.

dursten, *occ.* **dürsten,** *v.i.* (*haben*) *Lit:* to go thirsty, *Lit:* to thirst, to be athirst; **sie haben drei Tage lang in der Wüste gedurstet,** they went thirsty, they thirsted, for three days in the desert; *B:* **sie werden weder hungern noch dürsten,** they shall not hunger nor thirst.

dürsten, *occ.* **dursten,** *v.i. & v. impers.* (*haben*) (*A: also v.tr.*) *Lit:* **mich dürstet,** I am thirsty, *Lit:* I thirst, am athirst; *B:* **meine Seele dürstet nach Gott,** my soul thirsteth for God; **nach Blut d.,** *A:* **Blut d.,** to thirst for, to be athirst for, blood; **nach Gerechtigkeit d.,** to thirst after righteousness; **danach d., etwas zu tun,** to thirst, to be thirsting, athirst, to do sth.; **er dürstet danach, sich zu rächen,** he is thirsting for revenge, to revenge himself; **ihn dürstet, es dürstet ihn, nach Rache,** he is thirsting, thirsty, for revenge.

durstig, *a.* thirsty; **d. sein,** to be thirsty; **eine durstige Kehle haben,** to have a dry, parched, throat; **ein durstiger Bruder, eine durstige Seele,** a thirsty person; *F:* **durstiges Wetter,** thirsty weather; **die Durstigen tränken,** to give drink to the thirsty.

-durstig, -dürstig, *comb.fm. a.* thirsty, thirsting, for . . . , thirsting after . . .; -thirsty; longing, yearning, for . . .; **wissensdurstig,** thirsty for knowledge, thirsting after knowledge; **schönheitsdurstig,** yearning for beauty; **blutdürstig,** thirsty, thirsting, for blood; bloodthirsty.

Durstigkeit, *f.* thirst, thirstiness.

durstlöschend, *a.* thirst-quenching, thirst-slaking; **durstlöschende Getränke,** thirst-slaking drinks, *F:* thirst-quenchers.

Durstlöscher, *m.* thirst-quenching drink, fruit, sweet, etc., *F:* thirst-quencher.

durststillend, *a.*=**durstlöschend.**

Durtonart, *f. Mus:* major key.

Duschbad, *n.* shower-bath.

Dusche, *f.* **-/-n.** 1. (*a*) shower(-bath); *Med:* surface douche; **kalte, warme, D.,** hot, cold, shower; *Med:* **schottische D.,** alternating, Scotch, douche; *F:* **j-m eine kalte D. geben,** to throw, pour, cold water on s.o.'s enthusiasm; **ihre Worte wirkten wie eine kalte D. auf ihn,** her words acted like a shower of cold water on him; (*b*) *F:* soaking, dousing; **ich habe eine D. abbekommen,** I got a thorough soaking, I got well and truly soaked. 2. (*attachment or cubicle*) shower; **unter die D. gehen,** to have a shower.

duschen, *v.* 1. *v.tr.* (*a*) to give (s.o.) a shower (-bath); *Med:* to give (s.o.) a (surface) douching, to douche (s.o.); (*b*) *F:* to soak, douse (s.o.). 2. *v.i.* (*haben*) to have a shower(-bath).

Düse, *f.* **-/-n.** 1. nozzle; (*a*) tuyere, twyer, blast-pipe, nozzle, *F:* snout (of blast-furnace); tue-iron (of forge); nose-piece, nozzle (of bellows); (*b*) *I.C.E:* (spray) nozzle; jet. 2. *Av:* jet.

Dusel, *m.* **-s/-.** 1. (*a*) state of confusion; (*b*) sleepiness, drowsiness; sleep, doze; dreamy state; (*c*) intoxication, inebriation, tipsiness; intoxicated, tipsy, state; **im D. sein,** to be intoxicated, inebriated, tipsy. 2. *F:* luck, good fortune; **(einen) D. haben,** to be lucky, *F:* to strike (it) lucky. 3. **-dusel,** *comb.fm.* intoxication, flush; **im ersten Freiheitsdusel,** in the first flush of liberty.

Duselei, *f.* **-/.** 1. *F:* absent-mindedness, abstraction, dreaminess; stupidity, stupid state. 2. befogged state, *F:* fuddle.

dus(e)lig, *a. F:* 1. (*a*) drowsy, sleepy; giddy, dizzy; **mir ist ganz d. im Kopfe,** my head is swimming, *F:* I feel quite dopey; **er hat mich (dumm und) d. geredet,** he talked till my head began to swim; **der Lärm macht mich ganz d. (im Kopf),** the noise makes my head swim, go round; (*b*) befuddled, tipsy. 2.=**dusselig.**

duseln, *v.i.* (*haben*) 1. to doze, to be half asleep, to be drowsy. 2. to wander along in a dreamy, abstracted, state; to maunder along.

Düsen-, *comb.fm. Av:* (i) jet (engine, etc.); (ii) jet-propelled (aircraft).

Düsenantrieb, *m. Av:* jet propulsion; **mit D.,** jet-propelled.

Düsenbomber, *m. Mil.Av:* jet(-propelled) bomber.

Düsenflugzeug, *n.* jet(-propelled) aircraft, *F:* jet.

Düsenjäger, *m. Mil.Av:* jet fighter.

Düsentriebwerk, *n. Av:* jet power plant, jet engine.

Dussel, *m.* **-s/-.** *F:* idiot, imbecile, simpleton.

Dusselei, *f.* **-/.**=**Duselei** 1.

dusselig, *a. F:* absent-minded, dreamy; stupid, silly, foolish.

duster, *a.*=**düster.**

düster[1], *a.* 1. (*a*) dark, gloomy; sombre; **es wird d.,** it is growing dark; **düst(e)res Wetter,** dull, gloomy, weather; **düst(e)rer Himmel,** overcast, gloomy, louring, lowering, sky; **an einem düst(e)ren Tag,** on a gloomy day; **düst(e)re Farben,** sombre colours; **ein düst(e)rer Wald, eine düst(e)re Kirche, ein düst(e)res Gewölbe,** a dark, gloomy, wood, church, vault; **der düst(e)re Schein der Kerzen,** the dim, faint, light of the candles; (*b*) dark, black; **düst(e)re Nacht,** dark, black, night. 2. gloomy, melancholy, sombre, dismal; black; **düst(e)re Gedanken,** gloomy, gloomy, melancholy, sombre, thoughts; **düst(e)re Stimmung,** (i) dismal, gloomy, black, mood; (ii) gloom; **düst(e)res Schweigen,** gloomy silence; **ein düst(e)rer Charakter,** a gloomy, melancholy, character; **düst(e)rer Trauergesang,** sombre dirge; **der düst(e)re Klang der Totenglocke,** the sombre, ominous, sound of the funeral bell; **mit düst(e)rer Stimme,** in a sepulchral, funereal, voice; **düst(e)re Vorahnungen,** dark, dire, forebodings; **in düst(e)res Brüten versunken,** sunk in gloomy meditation. 3. **das Düstere,** the dark; darkness, gloom; **im Düstern sitzen,** to sit in the dark; *B:* **wir sind im Düstern wie die Toten,** we are in desolate places as dead men.

Düster[2], *n.* **-s/.** 1. darkness; **im D. des Waldes,** in the darkness, gloom, of the wood. 2. obscurity.

Düsterheit, Düsterkeit, *f.* 1. darkness. 2. gloom, melancholy; **die D. seines Gemütes,** his gloomy temperament, the gloominess of his temperament.

düstern[1], *a.*=**düster**[1].

düstern[2], *v. Poet:* (*a*) *v.i.* (*haben*) to cast shadows; to spread darkness; to darken; (*b*) *v.impers.* **es düstert,** it is growing dark; (*c*) *v.tr.* to darken (sth.), to make (sth.) dark.

Düsternis, *f.* **-/.** 1. darkness. 2. gloom, melancholy.

Düte, *f.* **-/-n.** *Dial:*=**Tüte.**

Dutt, *m.* **-(e)s/-e.** *Haird: F:* bun.

Dutzend, *n.* **-s/- & -e,** dozen. 1. (*pl.* **Dutzend**) **ein D. Eier,** a dozen eggs; **ein halbes D.,** half a dozen; a half-dozen; **ein halbes D. Apfelsinen,** half a dozen oranges; **ein halbes D. frische Eier,** half a dozen fresh eggs; **geben Sie mir ein halbes D., bitte,** give me half a dozen, a half-dozen, please; **ein großes D.,** a gross; **sechs Dutzend Flaschen Wein,** six dozen bottles of wine; **wieviel Dutzend brauchen Sie?** how many dozen do you require? **einige, mehrere, Dutzend,** a few, several, dozen; **einige Dutzend ihrer Stammkunden, von ihren Stammkunden,** some dozens of their regular customers; **diese Waren werden im D. verkauft,** these articles are sold by the dozen; **im D. sind sie billiger,** they're cheaper by the dozen; **etwa ein D.,** about a dozen; **etwa ein D. Leute waren dabei,** some dozen people were there. 2. (*pl.* **Dutzende**) **Dutzende von Leuten,** dozens of people; **sie kamen zu Dutzenden an,** they came in their dozens; **Dutzende Male,** dozens (and dozens) of times. 3. **Dutzend-,** *comb.fm.* very ordinary . . .; commonplace . . .; run-of-the-mill . . .; **Dutzendmensch,** very ordinary, commonplace, person; **Dutzendbild,** run-of-the-mill picture.

dutzendemal, *adv.* dozens (and dozens) of times.

dutzendmal, *adv.* a dozen times; dozens of times; **ein paar d.,** several dozen times; **ich habe es dir d. gesagt,** I've told you so dozens (and dozens) of times.

Dutzendmensch, *m.* very ordinary, commonplace, person.

Dutzendware, *f.* mass-produced articles; run-of-the-mill goods.

dutzendweise, *adv.* by the dozen; in dozens; **sie sind d. zu haben,** they are to be had by the dozen; **Artikel d. verkaufen,** to sell articles in (sets of) dozens, by the dozen, by dozens; **solche Bilder sieht man d.,** you see dozens, scores, masses, of pictures like that.

Duumvir [du·'umvɪr], *m.* **-n & -s/-n.** *Rom.Hist:* duumvir; **die Duumvirn,** the duumvirs, duumviri.

Duumvirat [du·umvi·'ra:t], *n.* **-s/-e.** *Rom.Hist:* duumvirate.

Duwok, *m.* **-s/.** *Dial: Bot:*=**Schachtelhalm.**

Duzbruder, *m.*=**Duzfreund.**

duzen, *v.tr.* (**du duzest & du duzt**) to use the familiar form of address to (s.o.); to call s.o. 'du'.

Duzfreund, *m.* friend to whom one uses the familiar form of address; personal friend.

Duzfuß, *m.* **mit j-m auf (dem) D. stehen,** to be on familiar terms with s.o.; to call s.o. 'du'.

D-Wagen, *m. Rail:*=**Durchgangswagen.**

dwars, *adv. Nau:* athwart; **achterlicher als d.,** abaft the beam; **vorlicher als d.,** before the beam; **dwars ab (von . . .),** abeam, abreast, of . . .; *cp.* **dwarsab.**

dwarsab, *adv. Nau:* abeam, abreast (**von,** of); **von einem Schiff, von einer Landmarke, d. sein,** to be abreast, abeam, of a ship, of a landmark.

Dwarsfeste, *f.* **-/-n.** *Nau:* breast-rope, breast-fast.

Dwarslinie, *f. Nau:* **in D.,** (in) line abreast.

Dwarsnaht, *f. N.Arch:* butt-seam.

Dwarssaling, f. Nau: cross-trees.
dwarsschiffs, adv. Nau: athwartship(s).
dwarsschlagen, v.i. sep. (strong) (sein) Nau: (of ship) to broach to.
Dwarssee, f. Nau: beam sea.
dwarsstroms, adv. Nau: athwart the stream.
Dweil, m. -s/-e. Nau: swab, mop.
dyadisch [dy·'a:diʃ], a. 1. dyadic. 2. A.Geol: Permian.
Dyas ['dy:as], f. -/. 1. dyad. 2. A.Geol: dyas, Permian system.
Dyn [dy:n], n. -s/. Ph. Meas: dyne.
Dynameter [dy·na·'me:tər], n. -s/-. Opt: dynameter, dynamometer.
Dynamik [dy·'na:mik], f. -/. 1. Mec: dynamics. 2. dynamic force; vitality; Art: tension.
Dynamiker [dy·'na:mikər], m. -s/-, dynamist.
dynamisch [dy·'na:miʃ], a. 1. dynamic(al). 2. dynamic, forceful (personality, etc.); (of composition, lines in painting, etc.) full of tension; full of movement. 3. Med: dynamic, functional (disease). 4. (a) Ling: **dynamischer Akzent**, stress(-accent); (b) Mus: dynamic (accent, etc.).

Dynamismus [dy·na·'mismus], m. -/. dynamism.
Dynamistik [dy·na·'mistik], f. -/. dynamism.
Dynamit [dy·na·'mi:t], n. -(e)s/-e, dynamite; pl. **Dynamite**, types of dynamite.
Dynamo [dy·'na:mo:, 'dy:na·mo:], m. -s/-s. El: dynamo, generator.
dynamoelektrisch, a. dynamo-electric.
Dynamograph [dy·na·mo·'gra:f], m. -en/-en, dynamograph.
Dynamomaschine, f. dynamo, generator.
Dynamometamorphose, f. Geol: dynamo-metamorphism.
Dynamometer [dy·na·mo·'me:tər], n. -s/-. Mec: dynamometer.
Dynast [dy·'nast], m. -en/-en, dynast.
Dynastenfamilie, f. dynasty.
Dynastie [dy·nas'ti:], f. -/-n [-'ti:ən], dynasty.
dynastisch [dy·'nastiʃ], a. dynastic.
Dynatron ['dy:na·tro:n], n. -s/-e [dy·na·'tro:nə]. Electronics: dynatron.
Dyne ['dy:nə], f. -/-n. Ph.Meas: dyne.
Dynode [dy·'no:də], f. -/-n. TV: dynode.
Dyophysiten [dy·o·fy·'zi:tən], m.pl. Ecc.Hist: dyophysites.

Dys-, dys- [dys-], pref. Med: etc: dys-; **Dyschroma(top)sie** f, dyschromatopsia; **Dyslalie** f, dyslaly; **Dyskinesie** f, dyskinesia; **dyspnoeisch**, dyspnoeal, dyspnoeic.
Dysenterie [dysɛntə'ri:], f. -/-n [-'ri:ən], dysentery.
dysenterisch [dysɛn'te:riʃ], a. Med: dysenteric.
Dyskrasie [dyskra·'zi:], f. -/-n [-'zi:ən], dyskrasia.
Dysmenorrhöe [dysme·no·'rø:], f. -/-n [-'rø:ən]. Med: dysmenorrhoea.
Dyspepsie [dyspɛp'si:], f. -/-n [-'si:ən], dyspepsia.
dyspeptisch [dys'pɛptiʃ], a. dyspeptic.
Dyspnoe [dys'pno:e:], f. -/. Med: dyspnoea.
dyspnoeisch [dyspno·'e:iʃ], a. Med: dyspnoeal, dyspnoeic.
Dysprosium [dys'pro:zïum], n. -s/. Ch: dysprosium.
Dystonie [dysto·'ni:], f. -/-n [-'ni:ən]. Med: dystonia.
Dystrophie [dystro·'fi:], f. -/-n [-'fi:ən], dystrophy.
dysuretisch [dysᵊu·'re:tiʃ], a. Med: dysuric.
Dysurie [dysᵊu·'ri:], f. -/-n [-'ri:ən]. Med: dysuria, dysury.
D-Zug, m. contraction of **Durchgangszug**, q.v.
D-Zug-Wagen, m. Rail:=**Durchgangswagen**.

E

E, e [eː], *n.* -/- (*in speech only* -s/-s [eːs]). **1.** (the letter) E, e; *Tp:* **E wie Emil,** E for Edward. **2.** *Mus:* (the note) E; **E-dur, E-Dur, e-moll, e-Moll,** (-Tonart), (key of) E major, E minor. *See also List of Abbreviations.*

Eau [oː], *n. & f.* -/-. (*used only in names of distillates, lotions, etc.*) **Eau de Cologne** [oˈdəkoˈlonjə], eau de Cologne, Cologne water; **Eau de Javel(le)** [oˈdəʒaˈvɛl], potassium chloride water, bleaching water; **Eau-forte** [oˈfort], (i) aqua fortis, nitric acid, (ii) *Engr:* etching, etched engraving; **Eau-de-vie** [oˈdəˈviː] *f,* spirits; brandy.

Ebauche [eˈboˈʃ], *f.* -/-n [-ʃən], rough draft, outline (of plan, novel, etc.); rough sketch (of picture, etc.).

ebauchieren [eboˈʃiːrən], *v.tr.* to sketch, outline (picture, plan, etc.); to outline (novel, etc.).

Ebbe, *f.* -/-n, (*a*) low tide, ebb(-tide), low water; **E. und Flut,** low tide and high tide; ebb and flow, flux and reflux; **the tides; es ist E.,** it is low tide, the tide is out; **bei E.,** at low tide, at ebb-tide; **Hafen mit E. und Flut,** tidal port; **Hafen ohne E. und Flut,** tideless port; (*b*) *F:* **in meiner Kasse ist augenblicklich E.,** my funds are (running) very low at the moment.

Ebb(e)anker, *m. Nau:* ebb anchor.

ebben. I. *v.i.* (*sein*) (*of tide*) to ebb; (*of flood, etc.*) to subside, abate.
II. *vbl s.* **Ebben,** *n. in vbl senses; also:* ebb, reflux (of tide); subsidence, abatement (of flood, etc.).

Ebbestand, *m.* (level of) low tide.

Ebbetor, *n. Hyd:E:* tail-gate, aft-gate (of lock).

Ebbe- und Flutuhr, *f.* tidal clock.

Ebbstrom, *m.* ebb (current); **Richtung des Ebbstroms,** set of the ebb(-tide); **Kentern des Ebbstroms,** turn of the ebb(-tide).

eben¹, *a.* even, flat (surface, ground, etc.); level (ground); smooth (surface, etc.); **ebenes Land,** flat country; **auf ebener Straße,** on a level stretch of road; **zu ebener Erde wohnen,** to live at street level, to live on the ground floor; *see also* **Geometrie, Trigonometrie.**

eben². **I.** *adv.* (*stressed*) **1.** just, precisely, exactly; **an e. dem Ort, zu e. der Zeit,** just, exactly, at that place, at that time, at precisely that place, that time; **e. der Mann,** precisely that man, that very man; **e. der ist es, der e. ist es, der . . .,** it is precisely he who . . ., he is the very one who . . .; **e. das wollte ich sagen,** I was going to say just that, precisely that, that is just, precisely, exactly, what I was going to say; **das e., e. das, weiß ich nicht,** that's just, precisely, exactly, what I don't know. **2.** (*a*) **e., e. noch, e. gerade, gerade e.,** (only) just; **ich habe (nur) e. genug, um davon zu leben,** I have only just enough to live on; **er hat den Zug e. noch erreicht,** he just managed to catch the train; **es war ihm e. noch gelungen, das Auto zum Halten zu bringen,** he (only) just managed to stop the car; **er konnte e. noch dem Taxi ausweichen,** he narrowly, only just, avoided the taxi; **er hat das Examen nur so e. bestanden,** he only just passed the examination; he just scraped through (the examination); (*b*) possibly; **ich schreibe dir, so oft es e. geht,** I write to you as often as I possibly can; **ich kam, so oft ich e. konnte,** I came as often as I possibly could. **3.** (*time*) (*a*) a moment ago; this moment; just now; **er hat e. an dich geschrieben,** he has just written to you; **er ist e. hereingekommen,** he came in just now, this very moment; **er ist e. erst gekommen,** he has only just come, he has only this moment come; **er ist e. fortgegangen,** he has just (this moment) left; **ich habe es e. erst gehört,** I have only just heard of it; **ich habe e. noch mit ihm gesprochen,** I was speaking to him just now, just a moment ago; (*b*) just; **e. vor dem Krieg,** just before the war;

e. bevor ich kam, just before I came; **e. danach,** just after, (i) a moment after, (ii) a short time after; (*c*) just; just then; (at) that moment; **er fing e. an, als ich hereinkam,** he was just beginning when I came in; **ich hatte mich e. erst hingesetzt, als . . .,** I had only just sat down when . . .; **ich wollte e. ausgehen,** I was just about to go out, I was (just) on the point of going out; **e. als die Tür sich öffnete,** just as the door was opening; (*d*) just; exactly; **es ist e. zwölf Uhr,** it is just, exactly, twelve o'clock; **es ist e. eine Woche her, daß . .,** it is just, exactly, a week ago that . . .; **heute sind es e. fünf Jahre her,** it is just five years ago today, on this very day; **du kommst e. recht, um mir zu helfen,** you are just in time to help me; (*e*) *F:* just; **komm mal e. her,** come here just a moment; **ich zeige euch e. mal mein neues Kleid,** I'll just show you my new dress; **ich gehe jetzt mal e. in den Garten,** I am just going into the garden for a moment; **sie will e. mal zum Fleischer gehen,** she just wants to go to the butcher's. **4. eben-,** *comb.fm.* the same . . .; the same . . .; the said . . .; **ebendaher,** (i) from that very place; from that same place; from the said place; (ii) for that very reason; for that same reason; for the said reason; **ebendahin,** to that very place; to that same place; to the said place; **ebendarüber,** (i) above that very, the said, thing, above those very, the said, things (ii) (to speak, etc.) about that very, the said, thing, about those very, the said, things; **ebendarum, ebendeshalb, ebendeswegen,** for that very reason; for that same reason; for the said reason; **ebendort,** at that very place; at that same place; at the said place.
II. eben, *emotive particle.* **1.** (*unstressed*) (*underlining the obvious*) (*a*) simply, just; **wenn er nicht mit uns kommen will, muß er e. zu Hause bleiben,** if he won't come with us, he will simply, just, have to stay at home; **ich werde ihm e. sagen, daß ich nicht ins Theater gehen will,** I shall simply, just, tell him that I do not want to go to the theatre; **er will e. nicht reden,** he just, simply, won't talk; **er hat es e. nicht gewußt,** he simply didn't know it, it is just that he didn't know it; (*b*) **man muß das Leben nehmen, wie es e. ist,** one has to take life as it is; **sie kam, wie sie e. war,** she came just as she was; **wir Offiziere haben es e. nicht leicht,** there it is, we officers don't have an easy time of it; **du mußt es nehmen, wie es e. kommt,** you must take the rough with the smooth. **2.** (*emphatic*) (*a*) (*stressed*) (ja) **e.!** quite (so)! precisely! exactly! **'und wir wollten doch morgen schon da sein!'—'ja e.!'** 'and we wanted to be there tomorrow!'—'yes, quite!' 'yes, exactly!' (*b*) (*unstressed*) **das 'ist es e.!** that is just, precisely, it! er ist e. **'darum!** that's just why! **that's just it! er hatte e. 'doch recht!** he was right all the time! **er ist e. 'doch zu jung!** it just shows that he 'is too young! **'er hat doch sein Examen bestanden?'—'e. 'nicht!'** (ja) **e.!** 'he passed his examination, didn't he?'—'that's just, exactly, what he didn't do!' (*c*) (*unstressed*) **nicht e.,** not exactly; **sie ist nicht e. hübsch,** she is not exactly pretty; **es war nicht e. angenehm,** it was not exactly pleasant; **man kann es nicht e. Feigheit nennen,** one couldn't exactly call it cowardice.

Ebenalen [eˈbəˈnaːlən], *f.pl. Bot:* ebenales.

Ebenazeen [ebənaˈtseːən], *f.pl. Bot:* ebenaceae.

Ebenbau, *m. Agr:* continuous ploughing (*i.e. not in lands*).

Ebenbild, *n.* image; likeness; **Gottes E.,** God's image; **er ist ganz das E. seines Vaters,** he is the very image, the living image, of his father; **ich habe eben einen Mann getroffen, der ganz dein E. ist, der dein ganzes E. ist,** I have just met a man

who is your very image, who is the very image of you.

ebenbürtig, *a.* of equal birth; equal; of equal rank; **er ist dir e.,** he is your equal; **er hatte in ihm einen ebenbürtigen Gegner gefunden,** in him he had found a worthy opponent, an equal, his match; **ich halte ihn den großen Schriftstellern für durchaus e.,** I definitely rank him among the great writers; **ein Ebenbürtiger,** an equal; **du wirst keinen ihm Ebenbürtigen finden, du wirst keinen finden, der ihm e. ist,** you will not find his equal, his peer.

Ebenbürtigkeit, *f.* equality of birth; equality; equal rank.

ebenda, *adv.* at that very place; at the same place; at the said place; (*quoting books*) (*abbr.* ebd.) ibidem (*abbr.* ibid., ib.).

ebendas, -dasjenige -dasselbe *see* **ebenderselbe, ebenderjenige.**

ebendaselbst, *adv.*=ebenda.

ebender, -die, -das = **ebenderselbe, -dieselbe, -dasselbe.**

ebenderjenige, -diejenige, -dasjenige (*decl. like derjenige*). **1.** *dem.pron. & a.* that very, that same (pers., thg). **2.** *dem.pron.* (*the aforesaid*) that same (one); that very one.

ebenderselbe, -dieselbe, -dasselbe (*decl. like derjenige*). **1.** *dem.pron. & a.* the very, the same (pers., thg). **2.** *dem.pron.* (*the aforesaid*) the same (one); the very one.

ebendie, -diejenige, -dieselbe *see* **ebenderselbe, ebenderjenige.**

ebendieser, -diese, -dieses. **1.** *dem.pron. & a.* this very, this same (pers., thg). **2.** *dem.pron.* (*the aforesaid*) this same (one); this very one.

Ebene, *f.* -/-n. **1.** *Geog:* plain; flat open country; **fruchtbare E.,** fertile plain. **2.** (*a*) *Geom: etc:* plane; **horizontale E.,** horizontal plane; *Ph:* **schiefe E.,** inclined plane; *F:* (*of pers.*) **auf die schiefe E. geraten,** to get into bad ways, to go wrong; **durch seine Unehrlichkeit ist er auf die schiefe E. geraten, gekommen, seine Unehrlichkeit hat ihn auf die schiefe E. gebracht,** through his dishonesty he has got into evil ways; (*b*) (intellectual, social, moral, etc.) level, plane; **er steht auf einer höheren gesellschaftlichen E. als sie,** he is on a higher social level, plane, than she; **auf der E. eines Wilden stehen, sein,** to be on the same plane as a savage; **auf der gleichen E. mit etwas stehen, sein,** to be on a level, on the same level, plane, with sth.; to come, amount, to the same (thing); **diese beiden Ideen liegen nicht auf der gleichen, auf derselben, E.,** these two ideas are not on the same, on an equal, plane; **Lügen steht auf der gleichen E. wie, mit, Betrügen,** lying is just as bad as cheating, is no better than cheating; *Pol:* **Gespräche auf hoher E.,** high-level talks; *Pol: Ind: etc:* **Verantwortung auf höchster E.,** responsibility at the highest level.

ebenen, *v.tr.*=ebnen.

Ebenenbündel, *n. Geom: etc:* sheaf of planes.

Ebenenbüschel, *n. & m. Geom: etc:* axial pencil, pencil of planes.

ebenerdig, *a. & adv.* at street level; on the ground floor.

Ebenezer [ebənˈʔeːtsər]. *Pr.n.m.* -s. *B:* Ebenezer.

ebenfalls, *adv.* also, likewise; in the same way; so; **Mutter geht es gut, den Kindern e.,** mother is well, so are the children; **er lehnte ab und sein Partner e.,** he declined and so did his partner, and his partner did likewise; **er beschleunigte seine Schritte, und ich tat es e.,** he quickened his pace and so did I; **ich habe e. drei Kinder,** I, too, I also, have three children; **er nahm e. seinen Hut ab,** he too, he also, took off his hat; **e. sollte gesagt werden, daß . . .,** it should also be stated that . . .; **'ich werde wiederkommen,'**

'ich e.', 'I shall come back,'—'so shall I'; **e.!** (*in answer to good wishes, etc.*) the same to you! **'ich wünsche Ihnen ein glückliches Neues Jahr!'** —**'danke, e.!'** 'a happy New Year to you!'—'thank you, the same to you!'

ebenflächig, *a.* flat-surfaced; *Geom: etc:* plane; with plane, even, surfaces.

Ebenheit, *f.* evenness, flatness (of surface, ground, etc.); levelness (of ground); smoothness (of surface, etc.).

Ebenhoch, *m.* **-(e)s/-s.** *A.Mil:* movable tower, belfry, turret.

Ebenholz, *n.* (*a*) ebony; **schwarzes E.,** black ebony; **rotes E.,** red ebony; **Kästchen aus E.,** ebony box; **schwarz wie E.,** (as) black as ebony; **Eingeborene, die so schwarz wie E. sind,** natives as black as ebony, ebony-black natives; (*b*) *Com:* **blaues E.,** palisander; Brazilian rosewood, purple-wood; **nordisches, abendländisches, E.,** box-wood; **deutsches E.,** yew wood; **falsches E.,** laburnum.

Ebenholzbaum, *m. Bot:* ebony-tree.

Ebenholzgewächse, *n.pl. Bot:* ebenaceae.

ebenieren [e·bə'ni:rən], *v.tr.* (*a*) to inlay (sth.) with ebony; (*b*) to ebonize (wood).

Ebenist [e·bə'nist], *m.* **-en/-en,** ebonist; cabinet-maker.

ebenjener, -jene, -jenes. 1. *dem.pron. & a.* that very, that same (pers., thg). **2.** *dem.pron.* (*the aforesaid*) that same (one); that very one.

Ebenkultur, *f. Agr:* continuous ploughing (*i.e. not in lands*).

Ebenmaß, *n.* harmonious proportion; harmony, harmoniousness; regularity, evenness (of features, etc.); **das E. seines Körpers,** the harmonious proportions of his body; **das wunderbare E. ihrer Gesichtszüge,** the wonderful evenness, regularity, of her features.

ebenmäßig, *a.* in harmonious proportions; harmonious; regular; even; **ebenmäßige Gesichtszüge,** even, regular, features; *adv.* **e. gewellte Landschaft,** evenly, regularly, undulating country.

Ebenmäßigkeit, *f.* harmony, harmoniousness; evenness, regularity (of features, etc.).

ebenpflügen, *v.tr. sep. Agr:* to plough (field) continuously; **Ebenpflügen** *n,* continuous ploughing (*i.e. not in lands*).

ebenso, *adv.* (*also* **ebenso-**, *comb.fm.*) (**ebenso** *may or may not form compounds with advs and undeclined adjs; with declined adjs it never forms compounds*) just as; in the same way; likewise; **dieser Kuchen ist e. gut,** this cake is just as good; **mir ging es e.,** the same thing happened to me; I found myself in the same situation; **Mutter geht es gut, den Kindern e., e. den Kindern,** mother is well, so are the children; **e. . . . wie,** (just) as . . . as; **ich bin e. groß wie du,** I am as tall as you (are); **er weiß e. viel wie du,** he knows as much as you (do); **ich habe ihn e. gern wie sie,** I like him just as much as her; **ich kann es e. gut, ebensogut, wie er,** I can do it (just) as well as he; **dieser Hut gefällt mir e. gut wie der andere,** I like this hat just as much as the other one; **er schreibt e. oft, häufig, wie seine Schwester,** he writes just as often, just as frequently, as his sister; **es waren e. viel, e. viele, Leute da wie gestern,** there were just as many people there as yesterday; **sie war e. gut, wie sie hübsch war,** she was as good as she was pretty; **sie war jetzt e. dick, wie sie früher mager war,** she was now as fat as she had been lean; **am Tage e. wie bei Nacht,** by day as well as by night; **e. wie das Befehlen, so müssen wir auch das Gehorchen lernen,** as we must know how to command, so we must know how to obey; *see also* **ebensogern, ebensogut, ebensohäufig, ebensooft, ebensoviel, ebensowenig.**

ebensogern, *adv.* **ich würde e. Fleisch essen,** I don't mind, meat will do me just as well; **ich würde e. ins Theater gehen,** I would just as soon go to the theatre; *see also* **ebenso.**

ebensogut, *adv.* (just) as well; **man könnte e. sagen, daß schwarz weiß sei,** one might as well say that black is white; **wir hätten e. zu Hause bleiben können,** we might just as well have stayed at home; **Sie hätten e. bis morgen bleiben können,** you could just as well have stayed till tomorrow; *see also* **ebenso.**

ebensohäufig, *adv.* (just) as frequently, (just) as often; **e. kommt er überhaupt nicht nach Hause,** just as frequently, just as often, he does not come home at all; *see also* **ebenso.**

ebensolange, *adv.* (for) just as long; **ich mußte e. warten,** I had to wait just as long.

ebensolch, -solcher, -solche, -solches, *dem.pron. & a.* just, exactly, such a (pers., thg); **ich möchte ebensolch einen Hut, einen ebensolchen Hut,** I want a hat just, exactly, like that, I want just, exactly, such a hat; **deine Tasche ist sehr schön, ich möchte eine ebensolche haben,** your bag is very nice; I would like one just, exactly, like it.

ebensooft, *adv.* (just) as often, (just) as frequently; **e. kommt er überhaupt nicht nach Hause,** just as often, just as frequently, he does not come home at all; *see also* **ebenso.**

ebensosehr, *adv.* (just) as much; **dieser Hut gefällt mir e. wie der andere,** I like this hat just as much as the other one; **er haßt dich e., wie du ihn gern hast,** he hates you as much as you like him; **er würde sich e. darüber freuen,** he would be just as pleased about it; **e. um deinetwillen als um meinetwillen,** as much for your sake as for mine; **es ist e. deine Schuld wie meine,** it is as much your fault as mine.

ebensoviel, *adv.* (just) as much; (just) as many; **sie haben e. gelitten,** they suffered just as much; **er weiß e. wie sein Bruder,** he knows just as much as his brother; **e. Männer wie Frauen,** just as many men as women.

ebensowenig, *adv.* (just) as little; (just) as few; **Herrn X kenne ich nicht, aber e. kenne ich Herrn Y,** I don't know Mr X, but I don't know Mr Y either; **das rote Kleid kannst du ihr e. anbieten wie das blaue,** you can't offer her the red dress any more than the blue one; **diese Lösung bietet e. Schwierigkeiten wie die andere,** this solution presents just as few difficulties as the other one, no more difficulties than the other one; **ich weiß e. darüber wie du,** I know just as little about it as you do, no more about it than you do.

ebensowohl, *adv.* = **ebensogut.**

Ebenstrauß, *m. Bot:* corymb.

Eber, *m.* **-s/-,** boar; **wilder E.,** wild boar; *F:* **wütend wie ein angestochener E.,** (as) fierce as a mad bull; raving mad, in a towering rage.

Eberesche, *f. Bot:* sorb (tree); **gemeine E.,** rowan(-tree), mountain-ash.

Eberfisch, *m. Ich:* boar-fish.

Eberraute, *f.,* **Eberreis,** *n. Bot:* southernwood, abrotanum, *F:* old-man, boy's-love, lad's-love.

Eberwurz, *f. Bot:* carline thistle.

Ebionit [e·bĭo·'ni:t], *m.* **-en/-en.** *Rel:* ebionite.

eblouieren [e·blu'i:rən], *v.tr.* to dazzle.

Ebne, *f.* **-/-n** = **Ebene.**

ebnen. 1. *v.tr.* to level, smooth, even up (ground, etc.); to make (ground, etc.) even, to level (road); to flatten, smooth (surface, etc.); to smooth away, remove (difficulties, etc.); **j-m den Weg e.,** to pave, clear, the way for s.o.; **j-m alle Wege e.,** to smooth all difficulties from s.o.'s path; **die Wege für etwas e.,** to clear the ground for (negotiations, etc.). **2. sich ebnen,** to become level, even, smooth.

Ebonit [e·bo·'ni:t], *n.* **-(e)s/.** *Ch:* ebonite; vulcanite.

E-Boot, *n. Navy:* motor torpedo boat.

Ebräer [e·'brɛ:ər], *m.* **-s/-.** *A:* Hebrew.

ebräisch [e·'brɛ:iʃ], *a. A:* Hebrew.

Ebritz, *f.* **-/-n.** *Dial:* = **Eberraute.**

ebullieren [e·bu'li:rən], *v.i.* (*haben*) **1.** *Ph:* to ebulliate, to boil. **2.** (*of skin, etc.*) to break out into blisters.

Ebullioskop [e·bulĭo·'sko:p], *n.* **-s/-e.** *Ph:* ebullioscope.

ebullioskopisch [e·bulĭo·'sko:piʃ], *a. Ph:* ebullioscopic.

Ebullition [e·buli·tsĭ'o:n], *f.* **-/-en. 1.** *Ph:* ebullition, boiling. **2.** *Med:* eruption (of the skin).

Eburin [e·bu·'ri:n], *n.* **-s/.** *Ch:* eburine.

Eburneation [e·burne·a·tsĭ'o:n], *f.* **-/.** *Med:* eburnation.

Eburonen [e·bu·'ro:nən], *m.pl. Hist:* Eburones.

Ecart [e·'ka:r], *m.* **-s/-s** = **Ekart.**

Ecarté [e·kar'te:], *n.* **-s/-s.** *Cards:* (game of) écarté.

Ecchymose [ɛkçy·'mo:zə], *f.* **-/-n.** *Med:* ecchymosis.

Ecclesiast, der [ɛkle·zi'ast]. *Pr.n.* **-en.** *B:* the Ecclesiast.

Ecclesiastes [ɛkle·zi'astɛs]. *Pr.n.m.* **-'.** *B:* Ecclesiastes.

Ecclesiasticus [ɛkle·zi'asti·kus]. *Pr.n.m.* **-'.** *B.Lit:* Ecclesiasticus.

ecclesiastisch [ɛkle·zi'astiʃ], *a.* ecclesiastic; ecclesiastical.

Echappement [e·ʃap'mã:], *n.* **-s/-s.** *Clockm: etc:* escapement (of clock, piano, etc.).

echappieren [e·ʃa'pi:rən], *v.i.* (*sein*) to escape.

Echarpe [e·'ʃarp], *f.* **-/-n** [-pən]. *Fenc:* diagonal cut.

Echauffement [e·ʃo·f'mã:], *n.* **-s/.** over-excitement.

echauffieren (sich) [e·ʃo·'fi:rən], *v.refl.* to become, get, overheated, hot; to become, get, excited, to excite oneself; **echauffieren Sie sich nicht,** (i) don't get overheated, (ii) don't get excited, don't excite yourself.

Echéance [e·ʃe·'ã:s], *f.* **-/-n** [-'ã:sən]. *Fin: etc:* term, falling due (of bill).

Echelettegitter [e·ʃ(ə)'lɛt-], *n. Opt:* echelette (grating).

Echelon [e·ʃ(ə)'lõ:], *m.* **-s/-s.** *Mil:* echelon (formation); **en é.,** in echelon, echeloned.

échelonieren [e·ʃ(ə)lo·'ni:rən], *v.tr. Mil:* to dispose (troops) in echelon, to echelon (troops).

Echelonspektroskop, *n. Opt:* echelon spectroscope.

Echinit [ɛçi:'ni:t], *m.* **-(e)s/-e & -en/-en.** *Paleont:* echinite, fossil sea-urchin.

Echinoderme [ɛçi·no·'dɛrmə], *m.* **-n/-n.** *Nat. Hist:* echinoderm.

Echinoidee [ɛçi·no·i·'de:ə], *f.* **-/-n.** *Echin:* echinus, sea-urchin, sea-hedgehog, sea-egg.

Echinokokke [ɛçi·no·'kokə], *f.* **-/-n.** *Med:* echinococcus.

Echinokokkenkrankheit, *f. Med:* brain disease caused by echinococcus.

Echinokokkose [ɛçi·no·ko'ko:zə], *f.* **-/-n.** *Med:* echinococcosis.

Echinokokkus [ɛçi·no·'kokus], *m.* **-/-ken.** *Med:* echinococcus.

Echinokokkusblase, *f. Med:* hydatid, echinococcus-cyst.

Echinus [ɛ'çi:nus], *m.* **-/-.** *Arch:* echinus.

Echo ['ɛço:]. **1.** *n.* **-s/-s,** echo (of sound, etc.); repercussion (of event, etc.); **mehrfaches E.,** multiple echo; **das E. eines Rufes zurückwerfen,** to echo back a shout; **Raum, der kein E. hat, Raum ohne E.,** echoless room, room that has no echo, that does not echo; **Filmatelier ohne E.,** echoless film studio, film studio that has no echo; **die Wälder waren erfüllt vom E. des Vogelgesanges,** the woods echoed with the songs of birds; **sein Vorschlag fand ein lebhaftes E.,** his proposal was met with lively approval; **Rede, die ein starkes E. fand,** speech that excited universal interest, that created a big stir. **2.** *Pr.n.f.* **-s.** *Gr.Myth:* Echo.

Echo-, *comb.fm. Med:* echo-; **Echomimie** *f,* echomimia; **Echophrasie** *f,* echophrasia; **Echopraxie** *f,* echopraxia.

echoen, *v.i.* (*haben*) to echo (back), to resound, to re-echo; **seine Stimme echote durch die Halle,** his voice echoed through the hall.

Echogewölbe, *n. Arch:* whispering gallery *or* dome.

Echolalie [ɛço·la·'li:], *f.* **-/.** *Med: Ling:* echolalia.

Echolot, *n.* (*a*) *Oc: Nau:* sonic depth-finder, echo (depth-)sounder; (*b*) *Av:* sonic altimeter.

Echolotung, *f.* (*a*) *Oc: Nau:* sonic depth-finding, echo-sounding; (*b*) *Av:* sonic height-finding.

Echometer [ɛço·'me:tər], *n.* **-s/-,** echometer.

Echowerk, *n. Mus:* echo manual (of organ).

Echse, *f.* **-/-n.** *Rept:* **1.** saurian. **2.** = **Eidechse.**

Echsenadler, *m. Orn:* crested serpent eagle.

Echsenschwanz, *m. Bot:* **nickender E.,** lizard's-tail, breast-weed.

echt. 1. *a.* (*a*) real (gold, stone, leather, etc.); genuine (painting, etc.); genuine, authentic (document, text, etc.); **ein echter Diamant,** a real diamond; **echtes Gold,** real gold; **echte Perlen,** real pearls; **dieser Stein ist nicht e.,** this stone is not real; **echte Seide,** real silk; **echte Kristallgläser,** genuine crystal glasses; **das ist ein echter Rembrandt,** that is a genuine Rembrandt; **echter Burgunder,** genuine Burgundy; **echte Sahne,** real cream; **eine echte Blondine,** a natural blonde; (*b*) true (species, etc.); **der Frosch ist kein echtes Reptil,** the frog is not a true reptile; *Bot:* **echte Dolde,** umbella; **echte Kamille,** (wild) camomile; **echte Tanne,** silver fir; *Bookb:* **echter Bund,** (*non-ornamental*) rib, raised band (on back of book); *Mth:* **echter Bruch,** proper fraction; **echte und unechte Brüche,** proper and improper fractions; (*c*) *Tex: etc:* **echte Farbe,** fast colour, fast dye; (*d*) genuine, unaffected, sincere (pers.); **er ist e.,** he is genuine, sincere, there is nothing affected about him; he is without affectation; he is all right; (*e*) true, genuine, sincere, real (feelings, etc.); **echte Tränen,** real, genuine, tears; **echte Freude,** true joy; unmixed, unalloyed, joy; **seine Gefühle waren e.,** his feelings were genuine; **sein Lachen war niemals e.,** his laughter was never genuine; **der echte Wert der Dinge,** the true, real, value of things; **echte Not,** genuine hardship; **echte Freundschaft,** true, real, friendship; **ein echter Freund,** a true, real, friend; (*f*) true to type, typical; **ein echter Engländer,** a true-born, real, Englishman; a typical Englishman; an Englishman born and bred; **ein echter Bayer,** a real (old) Bavarian; **ein echter Seebär,** a true sea-dog; a real old salt; **wie echte**

Jungen hatten sie . . ., boy-like, like real boys, they had . . .; *F:* **diese Handlung ist e. für ihn,** this action is typical of him, is just like him; **das war wieder einmal e.!** that was typical! **2.** *adv.* **e. Gold,** real gold; **e. christlich,** truly Christian, like a true Christian, like true Christians; **mit e. spanischer Höflichkeit,** with typical(ly) Spanish politeness; *F:* **das ist e. Peter!** that is typically Peter! that is just like Peter! that is Peter all over!

-echt, *comb.fm. Tex:* (*of colours, material*) fast to . . .; **lichtecht,** fast to light; **bügelecht,** fast to ironing; **schweißecht,** fast to sweat; perspiration-resisting; **farbecht,** colour-fast.

Echtfarbe, *f. Tex: etc:* fast colour, fast dye.

Echtheit, *f.* genuineness (of gold, painting, wine, etc.); authenticity (of document, text, painting, etc.); fastness (of colour, dye, etc.); genuineness, sincerity (of pers., feelings, etc.); **die E. eines Diamanten prüfen,** to test whether a diamond is real; **ich bezweifle die E. dieses Gemäldes,** I doubt the genuineness, authenticity, of this painting, I doubt whether this painting is genuine, authentic; **Beweis der E. einer Urkunde,** proof of the authenticity of a document.

Echtheitsbeweis, *m.* proof of genuineness *or* authenticity.

Echtheitsprüfung, *f.* (*a*) test of genuineness *or* authenticity; (*b*) *Tex: etc:* test of colour fastness.

echtlos, *a. Hist:* outlawed, proscribed (pers.); **j-n e. machen,** to outlaw, proscribe, s.o.; **ein Echtloser,** an outlaw, a proscript.

Echtlosigkeit, *f. Hist:* (state of) being outlawed, proscribed; outlawry.

Eck, *n.* **-(e)s/-e(n),** (*a*) *Dial:* corner; *Geog:* **das Deutsche Eck,** the triangle of land at the confluence of the Rhine and the Moselle; (*b*) *used only in the phr.* **über Eck,** cornerwise, across (a corner); diagonally; **etwas über Eck stellen,** to put, place, sth. diagonally; **ein Tischtuch über Eck falten,** to fold a tablecloth corner to corner.

-eck, *comb.fm. n.* **-(e)s/-e.** *Geom:* (*a*) -angle; **Dreieck,** triangle; **Viereck,** quadrangle; **Rechteck,** rectangle; (*b*) -gon; **Siebeneck,** heptagon; **Achtzehneck,** octadecagon; **Vieleck,** polygon.

Eckarmierung, *f. Constr:* corner-stones (of brickwork, etc.).

Eckball, *m. Sp:* corner-kick, -hit, *or* -throw.

Eckband, *n. Constr: Carp: etc:* angle-iron; (flat) corner-plate; corner brace, *U.S:* inside-corner.

Eckbeschlag, *m. Carp: etc:* corner-plate (on wooden chest, etc.).

Eckblatt, *n. Arch:* angle-spur (of column).

Eckbohrdraube, *f.*=**Eckbohrer** (*a*).

Eckbohrer, *m. Tls:* (*a*) ratchet-brace *or* -drill (*for use in corners*); (*b*) angle-brace, corner-brace.

Eckbrett, *n.* corner shelf.

Ecke, *f.* **-/-n. 1.** corner (of table, field, picture, etc.); **die E. einer Visitenkarte knicken,** to turn down the corner of a visiting card; **der Name steht in der linken oberen E. des Briefes,** the name is in the top left-hand corner of the letter; **die Ecken des Buches sind abgenutzt,** the corners of the book are worn; **Einband mit ledernen Ecken,** binding with leather corners; **mit runden, abgerundeten, Ecken,** round-cornered; **es brennt an allen Ecken,** (i) (*of building, etc.*) it is burning from end to end; (ii) *F:* everything is in uproar, everything is in commotion; *F:* **an allen Ecken und Enden,** everywhere, at every turn; here, there, and everywhere; **bei ihnen fehlt es an allen Ecken und Enden,** they are terribly short of everything; **unser Mädchen ist krank, sie fehlt uns an allen Ecken und Enden,** our maid is ill; we are quite lost without her, we miss her at every turn; **ich habe meine Schere verlegt, sie fehlt mir an allen Ecken und Enden,** I have mislaid my scissors, I am quite lost without them. **2.** corner (of street, etc.); **scharfe E.,** sharp corner; **an einer E. gelegenes Grundstück,** property situated at a corner; **ein Geschäft an einer E. übernehmen,** to take a corner shop; **er wohnt um die E.,** he lives round the corner; **der Wagen kam um die E.,** the carriage came, appeared, round the corner; **um die E. gehen, fahren,** to go round the corner, to turn the corner; *F:* **j-n um die E. bringen,** to get rid of s.o., to dispose of s.o.; to do away with s.o., *F:* to bump s.o. off; *see also* **trauen. 3.** (*a*) corner (of room, hall, etc.); **in einer E. des Zimmers stand ein Klavier,** in one corner of the room was a piano; **eine dunkle E.,** a dark corner; **Winkel und Ecken,** nooks and corners; **etwas in allen Ecken und Winkeln suchen,** to look for sth. high and low, in every corner; **in allen Ecken und Winkeln,** in every hole and corner, in every nook and cranny; **von allen Ecken und Enden,** from everywhere under the sun; **ein Kind in die E. stellen,** to put, stand, a child in the corner (*for being naughty*); **etwas in die E. stellen,** (i) to put, stand, sth. in the corner, (ii) *F:* to put sth. aside; to shelve, pigeon-hole, sth.; *F:* **mein Antrag ist in die E. gestellt worden,** my request has been shelved, pigeon-holed; **in die E. gestellte Projekte,** pigeon-holed projects; (*b*) *Box:* corner; **neutrale E.,** neutral corner; (*c*) *Sp:* (i) corner (of goal); (ii) corner (-kick, -hit *or* -throw); **kurze, lange, E.,** near, far, corner (of the goal); **den Ball zur E. abwehren, lenken,** to turn the ball round *or* over for a corner. **4.** (*triangular piece*) (photo) corner; wedge (of cake, etc.); *Cu:* (nut-, etc.) triangle.

Eckeisen, *n. Constr:* angle-iron, (flat) corner-plate; corner brace, *U.S:* inside corner.

Eckenkragen, *m. Cost:* wing collar, butterfly collar.

Eckenrundstoßmaschine, *f. Bookb:* round-cornering machine.

Eckenschützer, *m. Constr:* corner-plate (on wall, etc.).

Eckensteher, *m. F:* (*a*) loiterer; loafer; (*b*) child who has been stood in a corner (*for being naughty*).

Ecker, *f.* **-/-n. 1.** *Bot:* (*a*) beech-nut; (*b*) acorn. **2.** *Cards:* acorn.

Eckerdoppe, *f.* **-/-n. 1.** *Bot:* oak-gall, oak-apple. **2.** *pl.* **Eckerdoppen,** *Com: Tan: etc:* val(l)onia.

Eckfahne, *f. Fb: etc:* corner-flag.

Eckfeld, *n.* corner square (on chessboard, etc.).

Eckfenster, *n.* corner-window.

Eckflagge, *f. Fb: etc:* corner-flag.

Eckflügler, *m.* **-s/-.** *Ent:* vanessa (butterfly).

Eckhaus, *n.* corner house, house on a corner.

Eckholz, *n. Carp:* squared timber; beam.

eckig, *a.* angular; square; square-built, angularly-built (pers.); wooden, jerky (movement); **eckige Schultern,** square shoulders; **mit eckigen Schultern,** square-shouldered; **eckiges Kinn,** square chin; square jaw; **eckiges Gesicht,** angular face; **eckige Handschrift,** angular handwriting; *Av:* **eckiger Flügel,** square wing; *Dressm:* **Mieder mit eckigem Ausschnitt,** bodice with a square neck, square-necked bodice; *adv.* (*of dress, etc.*) **e. ausgeschnitten,** square-cut, square-necked.

-eckig, *comb.fm. a.* (*a*) -cornered; **scharfeckig,** sharp-cornered; **dreieckig,** three-cornered; **rundeckig,** round-cornered; (*b*) *Geom: etc:* -angular; **dreieckig,** triangular; **viereckig,** quadrangular; **rechteckig,** rectangular; (*c*) *Geom: etc:* -gonal; **siebeneckig,** heptagonal; **achtzehneckig,** octadecagonal; **vieleckig,** polygonal.

Eckigkeit, *f.* angularity (of s.o.'s build, handwriting, etc.); squareness (of shoulders, etc.).

Eckkegel, *m.* corner pin (*in game of ninepins*).

Eckknolle, *f. Arch:* angle-spur (of column).

Eckladen, *m.* corner-shop.

Ecklohn, *m. Ind:* standard wage (taken as basis of wage scale).

Eckpfeiler, *m.* corner-pillar; corner-post, angle-post.

Eckpfosten, *m.* corner-post, angle-post.

Eckplatz, *m.* corner seat (in railway carriage, etc.).

Eckpunkt, *m.* vertex, corner (of triangle, etc.); salient (of angle).

Eckraum, *m. Fb:* quarter-circle.

Eckrisalit, *m. Arch:* corner projection, corner ressaut (of building).

Ecksäule, *f.* corner column.

Eckschiene, *f. Constr:* angle-iron.

Eckschlag, *m. Hockey:* corner-hit.

Eckschrank, *m.* corner-cupboard.

Ecksitz, *m.* (*a*) *Furn:* corner seat; (*b*)=**Eckplatz.**

Ecksparren, *m. Constr:* arris-, corner-rafter; hip-rafter.

Ecksporn, *m. Arch:* angle-spur (of column).

Eckstange, *f.* corner-post; *Fb: etc:* corner-flag post.

Eckstein, *m.* **1.** (*a*) *Constr:* corner-stone, head-stone (of house, wall, etc.); *F:* **der E. der Zivilisation,** the corner-stone of civilization; *B:* **der Stein, den die Bauleute verworfen haben, ist zum E. geworden,** the stone which the builders rejected, the same is become the head of the corner; (*b*) guard-stone (*to protect gateway, etc., from vehicles*). **2.** *Cards:* diamond.

Eckstoß, *m. Fb:* corner(-kick).

Eckstrebe, *f. Constr:* strut; *Farr:* bar (of hoof).

Eckstützen, *f.pl.* **1.** (metal) book-ends. **2.** *Constr: etc:* corner support.

Ecktrompe, *f. Arch:* squinch.

Eckturm, *m.* corner tower.

Ecktürmchen, *n.* corner turret; *Her:* **Turm mit E. besetzt,** tower with turrets.

Eckverband, *m. Carp: Constr: etc:* angle-joint.

Eckwinkel, *m. Constr:* angle-iron, (flat) corner-plate; corner brace, *U.S:* inside corner.

Eckwurf, *m. Sp:* corner-throw (*in handball*).

Eckzahn, *m. Anat:* canine (tooth); corner-tooth (of horse).

Eckzapfen, *m. Carp:* angle-tenon, box-tenon.

Eckzier, *f. Arch:* angle-spur (of column).

Eckzimmer, *n.* corner room.

Eckzwickel, *m. Arch:* spandrel; (*on cupola*) pendentive.

Eclair [eˑˈklɛːr], *n.* **-s/-s.** *Cu:* éclair.

Eclat [eˑˈkla], *m.* **-s/-s** =**Eklat.**

Economiser [iˑˈkonomaizər], *m.* **-s/-.** *Ind:* economizer, economizing device; *esp.* exhaust-gas engine.

Ecossais [eˑkoˈsɛː], *m.* **-/.** *Tex:* tartan; plaid.

Ecossaise [eˑkoˈsɛˑzə], *f.* **-/-n.** *Danc: Mus:* écossaise.

ecru [eˑˈkryː], *a. Tex:* (*of material*) unbleached, ecru, natural-coloured.

Ecruseide, *f. Tex:* raw silk; ecru silk.

Ecuador [eˑkvaˑˈdoːr]. *Pr.n.n.* **-s.** *Geog:* Ecuador.

ecuadorianisch [eˑkvaˑdoˑriˈaːniʃ], *a. Geog:* Ecuadorian.

Edamer [ˈeːdamər], *inv.a. & m.* **-s/-. E. (Käse),** Edam (cheese); (red) Dutch cheese.

edaphisch [eˑˈdaːfiʃ], *a. Biol:* edaphic.

Edaphon, das [ˈedaˑfoːn], **-s.** *Biol:* the edaphon.

Edda, *f.* **-/-s & Edden.** *Norse Lit:* Edda; **die ältere E.,** the Older, Poetic, Edda; **die jüngere E.,** the Younger, Prose, Edda.

edel. 1. *a.* (*a*) noble (pers., family, descent, etc.); aristocratic (family); (pers.) of noble birth *or* rank; **aus edlem Geschlecht, von edler Herkunft,** of noble descent, of noble blood, of noble family; **ein edles Pferd,** a noble horse, a thoroughbred; **die edle Kunst des Fechtens,** the noble art of fencing; (*b*) noble (heart, sentiments, deeds, figure, etc.); lofty (soul, demeanour, sentiments, etc.); high-minded, noble-minded (action, nature, etc.); stately (figure, demeanour, etc.); **edle Seele,** noble, high-minded, lofty, soul; (*c*) true, typical (species, etc.); superior, high-class (wine, variety of fruit, food, fish, etc.); dessert (apple, pear, etc.); *Miner:* precious (stones, metal, etc.); rich (ore, etc.); *Ch:* inert, noble, rare (gas); *Miner:* **edler Opal,** precious, noble, opal; **edler Granat,** precious garnet, almandite; pyrope. **2.** *s.* **Ed(e)le,** *m., f.* (*decl. as adj.*) person of noble birth *or* rank; noble (-man), *f.* noblewoman; (*in England*) peer, *f.* peeress; (*as title*) **Edler von . . .,** lord, *Scot:* laird, of . . . .

Edelapfel, *m.* (named variety of) dessert apple.

Edelauge, *n. Arb:* shield-bud; **einem Obstbaum ein E. einsetzen,** to graft a shield-bud on a fruit-tree.

Edelbeere, *f. Vit:* specially selected (over-ripe) grape.

Edelbeerenauslese, *f.* (wine made from) specially selected (over-ripe) grapes.

edelblütig, *a.* of noble blood; of noble descent, of noble family.

edelbürtig, *a.* of noble birth, nobly born; of noble descent, of noble family.

Edeldame, *f.* noblewoman, noble lady.

Edeldampf, *m. Mch:* superheated steam.

edeldenkend, *a.* noble-minded, high-minded.

Edelerden, *f.pl. Ch:* rare earths.

Edelerz, *n. Min:* rich ore.

Edelfalke, *m. Orn:* true falcon; noble falcon.

Edelfasan, *m. Orn:* (common) pheasant.

Edelfäule, *f.* (*a*) *Vit:* over-ripeness, sleepiness (of grapes); 'pourriture noble'; (*b*) mould (on ripe cheese).

Edelfäulepilz, *m. Fung:* (*a*) botrytis cinerea (causing 'pourriture noble' of grapes); (*b*) one of various fungi causing mould on ripe cheese.

Edelfink, *m. Orn:* chaffinch.

Edelfrau, *f.* noblewoman.

Edelfräulein, *n.* (unmarried) noblewoman.

Edelfreie, *m.* (*decl. as adj.*) *Hist:* free-born nobleman; thane.

Edelgas, *n. Ch:* inert gas, noble gas, rare gas.

edelgesinnt, *a.* noble-minded, high-minded.

edelherzig, *a.* noble-hearted; magnanimous.

Edelherzigkeit, *f.* noble-heartedness; magnanimity.

Edelholz, *n.* valuable, luxury, wood.

Edeling, *m.* **-(e)s/-e. 1.** *Hist:* nobleman. **2.** *Arb:* scion, graft; grafted shoot.

Edelkastanie, *f. Bot:* (*a*) (sweet, Spanish) chestnut; (*b*) (sweet) chestnut(-tree).

Edelknabe, *m.* page (attending person of rank).
Edelkoralle, *f.* red coral, precious coral.
Edelkrebs, *m. Crust:* camaron.
Edelkrone, *f.* coronet (of noblemen of the lowest rank).
Edelleute, *pl.* noblemen, nobles.
Edelmann, *m.* **-(e)s/-leute,** nobleman, noble.
Edelmarder, *m. Z:* pine-marten, tree-marten.
Edelmensch, *m.* man of superior breed; 'the better kind of man'.
Edelmetall, *n.* precious metal.
Edelmetallgewicht, *n. Meas:* troy weight.
Edelmist, *m.* farmyard manure.
Edelmut, *m.* noble-mindedness, nobleness of mind; nobility; magnanimity, generosity.
edelmütig, *a.* magnanimous; noble-minded; generous; **sich als e. erweisen,** to show oneself magnanimous.
Edelmütigkeit, *f.* noble-mindedness; magnanimity, generosity.
Edelpassung, *f. Mec.E:* high-class fit.
Edelpilz, *m. Fung:* **1.** meadow mushroom, field mushroom. **2.**=**Edelröhrling.**
Edelpilzkäse, *m.* **Dänischer E.,** Danish Blue (cheese).
Edelrasse, *f.* high-bred race, true-bred race.
Edelraute, *f. Bot:* alpine wormwood.
Edelreife, *f.* (*a*) ripening, maturing (of fruit) (when stored); (*b*) ripeness, maturity (of fruit, cheese, etc.).
Edelreiher, *m. Orn:* large egret, great white heron.
Edelreis, *n. Arb:* scion, graft; grafted shoot.
Edelreisauge, *n. Arb:* shield-bud.
Edelreizker, *m. Fung:* lactarius deliciosus, saffron milk cap.
Edelröhrling, *m. Fung:* edible boletus cep(s).
Edelrost, *m.* patina.
Edelsand, *m. Min:* sand bearing precious stones; gemmiferous sand.
Edelschwein, *n. Breed:* **Deutsches E.,** German breed of large white pig (*related to the Yorkshire*).
Edelsinn, *m.* noble-mindedness, high-mindedness.
edelsinnig, *a.* noble-minded, high-minded.
Edelsinnigkeit, *f.* nobleness of mind, loftiness of mind.
Edelsitz, *m. Hist:* domain; manor.
Edelsorte, *f.* superior variety (of fruit, etc.).
Edelstahl, *m.* high-grade, high-class, steel; high-tensile alloy steel.
Edelstein, *m.* precious stone; gem; jewel; **künstlicher, synthetischer, E.,** artificial stone, artificial gem; **falscher, imitierter,** *F:* **nachgemachter, E.,** imitation stone; **Edelsteine schleifen,** to cut precious stones, gems; **mit Edelsteinen besetzt,** set with precious stones, with jewels; (be)jewelled.
Edelsteinimitation, *f.* imitation jewel; imitation jewelry.
Edelsteinschleifer, *m.* gem-cutter.
Edelsteinschleiferei, *f.* (*a*) gem-cutting; (*b*) (firm of) gem-cutters.
Edeltanne, *f. Bot:* (*a*) silver fir; (*b*) Norfolk Island pine.
Edelwein, *m.* wine of superior quality.
Edelweiß, *n.* **-(es)/-e.** *Bot:* edelweiss.
Edelweißbaum, *m. Bot:* savoy medlar.
Edelwild, *n. Ven:* red deer.
Edelzinn, *m.* pewter plate (*esp. of the period 1570–1640*).
Eden. *Pr.n.n.* **-s.** *B:* **(der Garten) E.,** (the Garden of) Eden.
Edentate [eˑdɛnˈtaːtə], *m.* **-n/-n.** *Z:* edentate; *pl.* edentata.
-eder [-ˈeːdər], *suff. n.* **-s/-.** *Geom: Cryst:* -hedron; **Hexaeder,** hexahedron; **Rhomboeder,** rhombohedron.
Edessa [eˑˈdɛsaː]. *Pr.n.n.* **-s.** *A.Geog:* Edessa.
edessinisch [eˑdɛˈsiːniʃ], *a. A.Geog:* Edessan, of Edessa.
edieren [eˑˈdiːrən], *v.tr.* to edit (text, periodical, etc.); to be the editor of (periodical, etc.).
Edikt [eˑˈdikt], *n.* **-(e)s/-e,** edict; *Hist:* **das E. von Nantes,** the Edict of Nantes.
Ediktalladung, Ediktalzitation [eˑdikˈtaːl-], *f. Jur:* edictal citation, edictal summons.
Edinburg [ˈeːdiˑnburk]. *Pr.n.n.* **-s.** *Geog:* Edinburgh.
Edisonakkumulator [ˈeːdizon-], *m. El. E:* Edison accumulator, Edison (storage) battery.
Edisonfassung, *f. El:* Edison lampholder, Edison screw socket.
Edisongewinde, *n.,* **Edisonsockel,** *m. El:* Edison screw base (on electric bulb).
Edisonzelle, *f. El:* Edison cell.
Edition [eˑdiˑtsĭˈoːn], *f.* **-/-en.** **1.** (*a*) editing (of classical text, book, etc.); (*b*) edition (of book, etc.). **2.** *Jur:* producing of a document (in court, etc.).
Editor [ˈeːdiˑtor], *m.* **-s/-en** [eˑdiˑˈtoːrən], editor (of classical text, book, etc.).
Edle, *m., f. see* **edel** 2.
Edomiter [eˑdoˑˈmiːtər], *m.* **-s/-.** *B.Hist:* Edomite.
-edrisch [-ˈeːdriʃ], *a.suff. Geom: Cryst:* -hedral; **hexaedrisch,** hexahedral; **rhomboedrisch,** rhombohedral.
Eduard [ˈeːduˑart]. *Pr.n.m.* **-s.** Edward.
Edukation [eˑduˑkaˑtsĭˈoːn], *f.* **-/-en,** education; instruction.
Edukt [eˑˈdukt], *n.* **-(e)s/-e.** *Ch:* educt.
E-dur, E-Dur, *n. Mus:* (key of) E-major.
eduzieren [eˑduˑˈtsiːrən], *v.tr. Ch:* to educe (gas, etc.) **(aus,** from).
Efeu, *m.* **-s/.** *Bot:* ivy.
efeuberankt, *a.* ivy-clad, ivy-covered, ivy-mantled.
Efeublatt, *n.* ivy-leaf.
efeublättrig, *a. Bot:* ivy-leaved; **efeublättrige Gundelrebe,** ground-ivy.
Efeuranke, *f.* twine of ivy; *Art: etc:* scroll.
efeuumrankt, *a.*=**efeuberankt.**
Effe, *f.* **-/-n.** *Bot:* elm.
Effeff [ɛfˈɛf], *n.* **-/.** (*abbr.* **ff**) *F:* **etwas aus dem E., ff, verstehen,** to have a thorough knowledge of sth., to be perfectly at home with sth., to know sth. inside out, *F:* to know one's stuff.
Effekt [ɛˈfɛkt], *m.* **-(e)s/-e.** **1.** effect, result; **E. machen,** to have, produce, an effect; to be effective; **einen E. auf etwas haben,** to have an effect on sth., to affect sth.; **ohne E.,** ineffective; without avail; **keinen E. haben,** to be of no effect, to have, produce, no effect; **zu diesem E.,** to this effect, to this end; for this purpose; with this object, end, in view; **meine Warnung hatte den erwünschten E.,** my warning had the desired effect; **der E. seiner Worte war verblüffend,** the effect of his words was staggering. **2.** *Ph:* effect; *Mec.E: etc:* performance, efficiency (of machine, etc.).
Effektbogenlampe, *f. El:* flame arc lamp.
Effekten [ɛˈfɛktən], *pl.* **1.** possessions; belongings; effects; **persönliche E.,** personal effects, personal belongings; goods and chattels. **2.** *Com: Fin:* negotiable instruments; (negotiable) securities; stocks; **festverzinsliche E.,** fixed-interest securities; **E. beleihen,** to advance money on securities; **E. beleihen lassen,** to hypothecate securities.
Effektenabteilung, *f.* securities department (of bank).
Effektenarbitrage, *f. Fin:* arbitrage in securities.
Effektenbank, *f. Fin:* issuing house; investment bank.
Effektenbesitzer, *m.* holder of securities.
Effektenbestand, *m.* holdings (in securities).
Effektenbörse, *f. Fin:* (i) security market; (ii) stock exchange.
Effektenbüro, *n.* securities department (of bank).
Effektengeschäft, *n.* (*a*) transaction, deal, in securities; (*b*) dealing in securities.
Effektenhandel, *m. St.Exch:* dealing in securities; jobbing.
Effektenhändler, *m. St.Exch:* stock-jobber; dealer.
Effektenkommissionsgeschäft, *n. Fin:* stock-exchange deal *or* dealing (on customers' behalf).
Effektenkonto, *n. Fin:* account kept by bank for customers when dealing with stocks and shares on their behalf.
Effektenkredit, *m. Fin:* loan on securities.
Effektenkurs, *m. St.Exch:* market price (of securities); quotation.
Effektenmakler, *m. St.Exch:* stockbroker.
Effektenmarkt, *m. Fin:* (i) security market; (ii) stock exchange.
Effektenpaket, *n. Fin: St.Exch:* block, parcel, of securities.
Effektenscheck, *m. Fin:* document similar to a cheque, used for the transfer of securities.
Effektenstempel, *m. St.Exch:* transfer stamp, contract stamp.
Effektensteuer, Effektenumsatzsteuer, *f. St. Exch:* transfer duty (on securities).
Effektgarn, *n. Tex:* knop-yarn.
Effekthascherei, *f.* straining for effect; showing-off.
effektiv [ɛfɛkˈtiːf]. *a.* **1.** (*a*) effective, efficacious (action, remedy, etc.); **effektiver** [ɛfɛkˈtiːvər] **Schutz,** effective protection; **effektive Blockade,** effective blockade; (*b*) effective; **effektiver Kontrast,** effective contrast; **das Bild ist sehr e.,** the picture is very effective. **2.** (*a*) effective, actual (force, work, etc.); actual (price, weight, measure, etc.); **effektiver Wert,** actual, real, value; **effektiver Bestand,** (i) *Ind: etc:* actual stock (of materials, goods, etc.); (ii) *Com: Fin:* realizable assets; (iii) *Mil:* effective force, total strength (of army, etc.); *Fin: Com:* **die Effektiven,** the realizable assets; *El:* **effektive Spannung,** effective voltage, root-mean-square voltage, R.M.S. voltage; *Mec:* **effektiver Druck,** effective pressure; **effektive Pferdestärke,** effective horse-power; **effektive Leistung,** effective output (of machine, industry, etc.); effective performance (of machine, etc.); (*b*) *Fin:* (*on bill of exchange*) **'e.',** 'to be paid in the specified currency'. **3.** *adv. F:* definitely; distinctly; **der Preis ist e. zu hoch,** the price is definitely too high; **das geht e. zu weit,** that is definitely, really, going too far; **dieses Buch ist e. pazifistisch,** this book is definitely, distinctly, pacifist; **er ist e. verrückt,** he is definitely, distinctly, mad.
Effektivbestand, *m.* (*a*) *Com: etc:* actual stock (of materials, goods, etc.); (*b*) *Fin: Com:* realizable assets; (*c*) *Mil:* effective force, total strength (of army, etc.).
Effektivgeschäft, *n. Com: etc:* (*a*) spot market transaction; (*b*) transaction where goods *or* securities are actually handed over (*i.e. not for the account*).
Effektivklausel, *f. Fin:* clause (on bill of exchange) that payment must be made in the specified currency.
Effektivleistung, *f.* effective output (of machine, industry, etc.); effective performance (of machine, etc.).
Effektivlohn, *m.* net wage; net earnings.
Effektivpreis, *m.* cash price.
Effektivstand, *m. Mil: etc:* effective force, total strength (of army, etc.).
Effektivverzinsung, *f. Com:* net yield (of investment, etc.).
Effektivwert, *m.* **1.** actual, real, value. **2.** *El:* average value (of current).
Effektivzahl, *f.* actual number.
Effektivzahlung, *f. Fin:* payment (of bill of exchange) in the specified currency.
Effektlampe, *f. El:* flame arc lamp.
effektuieren [ɛfɛktuˑˈiːrən], *v.tr.* to effect, carry out, carry into effect, accomplish, execute (scheme, operation, etc.); to effect, make (payment); to carry out, execute (order, etc.); to dispatch, forward, send off (goods, etc.); **Effektuierung** *f,* execution (of order, etc.); dispatch (of goods, etc.).
effektvoll, *a.* effective; striking; **effektvoller Kontrast,** effective, striking, contrast; **effektvolles Bild,** effective picture; **höchst e.,** highly, most, effective; **die Trompetenpartie ist sehr e.,** the trumpet part is very effective; **diese Farbenzusammenstellung ist äußerst, höchst, e.,** this colour scheme is most effective.
effeminieren [ɛfeˑmiˑˈniːrən], *v.tr.* to render (s.o.) effeminate; **effeminiert,** effeminate, unmanly, womanish.
Effeminiertheit, *f.* effeminacy, womanishness,
Ef(f)endi [ɛˈfɛndiː], *m.* **-s/-s,** (*in Turkey, Egypt*) Effendi.
efferveszent [ɛfɛrvɛsˈtsɛnt], *a.* (*of liquid, etc.*) effervescent, sparkling.
Efferveszenz [ɛfɛrvɛsˈtsɛnts], *f.* **-/.** effervescence, sparkling (of liquid, etc.).
efferveszieren [ɛfɛrvɛsˈtsiːrən], *v.i.* (*haben*) (*of liquid, etc.*) to effervesce, to sparkle, *F:* to fizz.
Effet [ɛˈfeː, ɛˈfɛː], *n.* **-s/-s,** effect; *Cr: Ten: etc:* screw, break, twist, spin; *Bill:* side(-screw); **einem Ball E. geben, einen Ball mit E. spielen,** (i) *Cr: Ten: etc:* to put spin, (a) screw, on a ball, to cut a ball; (ii) *Bill:* to put side, (a) screw, on a ball.
Effetstoß, *m. Bill:* shot played with screw.
effilieren [ɛfiˑˈliːrən], *v.tr. Haird:* to thin (hair).
Effilierschere, *f. Haird:* thinning scissors.
effizient [ɛfiˑtsĭˈɛnt], *a.* efficient, effectual (remedy, etc.).
Effizienz [ɛfiˑtsĭˈɛnts], *f.* **-/.** efficacy, effectiveness (of remedy, prayer, etc.); efficiency (of work, machine, etc.).
effizieren [ɛfiˑˈtsiːrən], *v.i.* (*haben*) to have an effect; to be effective, effectual.
Efflation [ɛflaˑtsĭˈoːn], *f.* **-/-en.** *Med:* eructation, bringing up of wind.
Effleurage [ɛflœˑˈraːʒə], *f.* **-/.** *Med:* (*massage*) stroking, effleurage.
Effloreszenz [ɛfloˑrɛsˈtsɛnts], *f.* **-/-en.** **1.** *Bot:* flowering, efflorescence. **2.** *Ch: Min:* efflorescence; bloom (of sulphur on rubber). **3.** *Med:* rash, eruption (on skin).
effloreszieren [ɛfloˑrɛsˈtsiːrən], *v.i.* (*haben*) **1.** *Bot:* to flower, blossom, bloom, *Lit:* to effloresce. **2.** *Ch: Min:* to effloresce.

effluieren [ɛflu·ˈiːrən], *v.i.* (*haben*) (*of liquid, gas, etc.*) to flow out; to emanate; to issue (out of sth.).
Effluvium [ɛˈfluːvium], *n.* **-s/-vien,** effluvium, efflux; emanation; exhalation; *El:* **elektrisches E.,** electric effluvium; silent, dark, discharge.
Effte, *f.* **-/-n.** *Bot:* elm.
Effusat [ɛfu·ˈzaːt], *n.* **-(e)s/-e.** *Ph:* effused substance.
Effusion [ɛfu·ziˈoːn], *f.* **-/-en,** effusion, outpouring, overflowing; *Ph:* effusion (of gas, etc.).
effusiv [ɛfu·ˈziːf], *a. Geol: etc:* effusive (rock, etc.).
Effusivgestein, *n. Geol:* effusive rock.
egal [e·ˈgaːl], *a.* **1.** even, regular (line, etc.); **etwas e. schneiden,** to cut sth. even; *adv.* **e. gesponnener Faden,** evenly spun thread. **2.** (*a*) equal; **die beiden Stücke sind e.,** the two pieces are equal; (*b*) *F:* all the same; **es ist mir ganz e.,** it is all the same, all one, to me; I don't mind; I don't care either way; **ihm ist es e., ob wir kommen oder nicht,** he doesn't mind whether we come or not; **mir ist alles e.,** I don't mind about anything, nothing matters to me, I couldn't care less about anything; **es ist mir ganz e., ob es ihm paßt oder nicht,** I don't care, I couldn't care less, whether he likes it or not; **(das ist) ganz e., er sollte doch um Entschuldigung bitten,** all the same, he ought to apologize. **3.** *adv. Dial. & F:* always; constantly; **sie hat e. Husten,** she always has a cough; **er hat mich e. geschlagen,** he constantly hit me, he kept hitting me.
Egalisator [e·ga·li·ˈzaːtor], *m.* **-s/-en** [-za·ˈtoːrən]. *El:* equalizer.
egalisieren [e·ga·li·ˈziːrən], *v.tr.* to make (sth.) equal; *Sp:* to equalize (score, etc.); to equalize, adjust (pressure, values, conditions, etc.); *abs.* **e.,** *Fb: etc:* to equalize the score; **einen Rekord e.,** to equal a record; **Egalisierung** *f,* equalization, adjustment (of pressure, values, etc.).
Egalität [e·ga·li·ˈtɛːt], *f.* **-/.** (*a*) evenness, regularity (of line, etc.); (*b*) equality.
Egart, *f.* **-/.** *Dial:* meadow land, grassland.
Egart(en)wirtschaft, *f. Agr:* agricultural system whereby land is used alternately for crop growing and for haymaking.
Egel, *m.* **-s/-.** *Ann:* leech.
Egelgras, *n. Bot:* shining-fruited rush.
Egelkrankheit, *f.*=**Egelseuche.**
Egelkraut, *n. Bot:* **1.** (*a*) sundew, drosera; (*b*) round-leaved, common, sundew; moor-grass. **2.** shining-fruited rush. **3.** (*a*) loosestrife, yellow pimpernel; (*b*) moneywort, herb-twopence, creeping jenny. **4.** lesser spearwort.
Egelpfennig, *m.*=**Egelkraut** 3(*b*).
Egelschnecke, *f. Moll:* slug.
Egelseuche, *f. Vet:* distomiasis, fascioliasis, fluke-disease, (liver-)rot (of sheep, etc.).
Egelwürmer, *m.pl. Ann:* hirudinidae, leeches.
Egelzucht, *f.* hirudiniculture, leech-breeding.
Egerling, *m.* **-(e)s/-e.** *Fung:* **1.** agaric. **2.**=**Edelreizker. 3.**=**Edelröhrling.**
Eggartenwirtschaft, *f.*=**Egart(en)wirtschaft.**
Egge, *f.* **-/-n. 1.** *Agr:* harrow; drag; **rotierende E.,** revolving harrow. **2.** *Tex:* selvedge, selvage.
eggen, *v.tr. & i.* (*haben*) *Agr:* to harrow; to drag (field).
Eggenzahn, Eggenzinken, *m. Agr:* tooth, tine (of harrow).
Eglomisémalerei [e·glo·mi·ˈzeː-], *f. Art:* églomisé-work.
églomisieren [e·glo·mi·ˈziːrən], *v.i.* (*haben*) *Art:* to do églomisé-work.
Ego [ˈɛgoː], *n.* **-s/.** (*a*) *Phil:* **das Ego,** the ego; (*b*) **alter Ego,** alter ego, second self.
Egoismus [e·go·ˈismus], *m.* **-/.** (*a*) *Phil:* egoism; (*b*) egoism, selfishness; self-seeking.
Egoist [e·go·ˈist], *m.* **-en/-en,** (*a*) *Phil:* egoist; (*b*) egoist, selfish person.
egoistisch [e·go·ˈistiʃ], *a.* (*a*) *Phil:* egoistic(al); (*b*) egoistic(al), selfish; self-seeking.
Egotismus [e·go·ˈtismus], *m.* **-/.** egotism.
Egotist [e·go·ˈtist], *m.* **-en/-en,** (*a*) egotist; (*b*) author of an autobiographical novel.
egotistisch [e·go·ˈtistiʃ], *a.* egotistic(al).
Egoutteur [e·gu·ˈtøːr], *m.* **-s/-e.** *Paperm:* dandy-roll(er).
egozentrisch [e·go·ˈtsɛntriʃ], *a.* egocentric, self-centred.
egrenieren [e·grə·ˈniːrən], *v.tr. Tex:* to gin (cotton).
Egreniermaschine, *f. Tex:* cotton-gin; boller.
Egyptienne [e·ʒipsiˈɛn], *f.* **-/.** *Print:* **(fette) E.,** Egyptian (type); **halbfette E.,** clarendon.
eh[1]. **1.** *conj.*=**ehe**[1]. **2.** *emotive particle, Austrian Dial:* anyway, anyhow; **ich muß eh dorthin gehen,** I have to go there anyway; **ich hab' es eh gewußt,** I knew it anyway.
eh[2], *int.* **1. eh!** hey! hullo! **2. eh?** eh? what?
Eh-, *comb.fm. cp.* **Ehe-.**
ehaft, *a. A. & Swiss Dial:* legal, lawful (cause, contract, etc.).
Ehaften, *pl. A:* lawful impediments; genuine hardship.
Ehape [e·ha·ˈpeː], *n.* **-s/-s.** *F:* = **Einheitspreisgeschäft.**
ehe[1], *conj.* **1.** (*a*) before; **kommen Sie bei mir vorbei, ehe Sie abreisen,** come and see me before you leave; **es wird lange dauern, ehe wir ihn wiedersehen,** it will be a long time before we see him again; **noch ehe die Nacht hereingebrochen war, hatte ihn die Unglücksbotschaft erreicht,** before nightfall he had received the bad news; **noch ehe ich mich von meiner Überraschung erholen konnte, fuhr er in seinem Bericht fort,** before I got over my surprise he went on with his report; **ehe ich abreiste, mußte ich den Konsul aufsuchen,** prior to my departure, before my departure, I had to see the consul; **ehe er zum Außenminister ernannt wurde, war er Botschafter,** prior to his appointment as foreign minister he was ambassador; *F:* **ehe ich es vergesse, sie erwarten dich heute abend,** before I forget, they expect you this evening; (*b*) (*with expletive* **nicht**) until; **wir können keine weiteren Schritte unternehmen, ehe wir nicht seine Meinung haben,** we cannot make any further move until we have his opinion; **ich werde kein Urteil über das Buch abgeben, ehe ich es nicht gründlich studiert habe,** I shall not pass judgment on the book until I have studied it thoroughly; **kommen Sie nicht herein, ehe ich Sie nicht rufe,** do not come in before, until, I call you. **2. ehe (daß),** rather than; **ehe (daß) ich nachgäbe, würde ich lieber sterben,** I would die rather than yield; rather, sooner, than yield I would die; **ehe er sich etwa einen billigen Photoapparat kauft, schenke ich ihm meinen eigenen,** rather than that he should buy himself a cheap camera I shall give him my own; **ich würde jedes Opfer bringen, ehe ich dich in Schande kommen ließe,** I would sacrifice everything rather than that you should be disgraced.
Ehe[2], *f.* **-/-n. 1.** marriage; matrimony; *Lit. & Jur:* wedlock; **eine Ehe schließen,** (i) to marry, to get married; (ii) (*of priest, registrar, etc.*) to marry, wed, a couple; **mit j-m eine Ehe eingehen,** to contract a marriage with s.o., to marry s.o.; to take s.o. in marriage; to be married to s.o.; **eine zweite Ehe eingehen,** to marry a second time; to marry again, to re-marry; *Lit:* **in den Stand der heiligen Ehe treten,** to be joined in holy matrimony; **die Heiligkeit der Ehe,** the sanctity of marriage; **Ehe zur linken Hand, morganatische Ehe,** morganatic marriage, left-handed marriage; **in glücklicher Ehe leben,** to lead a happy married life, to be happily married; **der Ehe entstammten drei Kinder, die Ehe war mit drei Kindern gesegnet,** there were three children by the marriage, their union was blessed with three children; **ein Kind aus einer früheren Ehe,** a child by, from, a previous marriage; **ungültige Ehe,** invalid marriage; **eine Ehe für nichtig erklären,** to declare a marriage null and void, to annul a marriage; **Nichtigkeitserklärung einer Ehe,** annulment of a marriage; **zerrüttete Ehe,** broken marriage; **die Ehe brechen, die Ehe schänden,** to commit adultery; **eine Ehe scheiden, auflösen,** to dissolve a marriage, to divorce a couple; **nach fünf Jahren wurde ihre Ehe geschieden,** after five years they were divorced, their marriage was dissolved; **in wilder Ehe leben,** to live together (without being married), to live in sin; *see also* **anfechten** I. 1. **2.** union, marriage (of ideas, etc.).
Eheanbahnung, *f.* **1.** introducing of prospective marriage partners to one another (by a marriage bureau). **2.**=**Ehevermittlung** 2.
Eheanfechtbarkeit, *f.* contestability of a, of the, marriage.
Eheaufhebung, *f. Jur:* annulment of marriage.
Eheaufhebungsklage, *f. Jur:* petition for nullity of marriage, nullity suit.
Eheauflösung, *f.* dissolution of marriage; divorce.
ehebaldigst, *adv. A:* as soon as possible.
Eheband, *n.* **-(e)s/-e,** marriage tie; matrimonial bond, marital bond; (the) bond of wedlock.
Eheberater, *m.,* **Eheberaterin,** *f.* marriage guidance counsellor.
Eheberatung, *f.* (*a*) marriage guidance; (*b*) marriage guidance bureau, marriage guidance council.
Eheberatungsstelle, *f.* marriage guidance bureau, marriage guidance council.
Ehebetrug, *m. Jur:* marriage under false pretences; concealment of an impediment to marriage.
Ehebett, *n.* (*a*) marriage-bed, matrimonial bed; (*b*) double bed.
ehebrechen, *v.i.* (*used in inf. only*) to commit adultery; *B:* **du sollst nicht e.,** thou shalt not commit adultery.
Ehebrecher, *m.* **-s/-,** adulterer.
Ehebrecherei, *f.* **-/.** adultery.
Ehebrecherin, *f.* **-/-innen,** adulteress; **Christus und die E.,** Christ and the woman taken in adultery.
ehebrecherisch, *a.* adulterous.
Ehebrief, *m.*=**Ehekontrakt.**
Ehebruch, *m.* adultery; **E. begehen, treiben,** to commit adultery.
ehebrüchig, *a.* adulterous (pers.); **e. werden,** to become an adulterer, an adulteress.
Ehebrüchige, *m., f.* (*decl. as adj.*) adulterer, adulteress.
Ehebund, *m.,* **Ehebündnis,** *n.* marriage; wedlock.
Ehedelikt, *n.* matrimonial offence.
ehedem, *adv.* in former times; formerly; **e. stand ein Schloß auf diesem Berg,** in former times, formerly, there was a castle on this mountain.
Eheerschleichung, *f.*=**Ehebetrug.**
ehefähig, *a.* (*a*) fit to marry; (*b*) free to marry; (*c*)=**ehemündig.**
Ehefähigkeit, *f.* (*a*) fitness to marry; (*b*) freedom to marry; (*c*)=**Ehemündigkeit.**
Ehefrau, *f.* wife.
Ehegartenwirtschaft, *f.*=**Egart(en)wirtschaft.**
Ehegatte, *m.* husband; *Jur:* (*husband or wife*) spouse; **die Ehegatten,** (the) husband and wife.
Ehegattin, *f.* wife.
Ehegelübde, *n.* marriage vows.
Ehegemahl, *m.* husband; *Lit. & Hum:* spouse.
Ehegemahlin, *f.* wife; *Lit. & Hum:* spouse.
Ehegemeinschaft, *f.* marriage, married partnership.
Ehegenoß, *m. A. & Lit:* husband *or* wife.
Ehegenosse, *m. Lit:* husband; *Lit. & Hum:* spouse.
Ehegenossin, *f. Lit:* wife; *Lit. & Hum:* spouse.
Ehegeschenk, *n. Jur:* present *or* property given by one partner to the other during their marriage.
Ehegesetz, *n. Jur:* marriage law; marriage act.
Ehegespons. 1. *m. Lit. & Hum:* husband, spouse. **2.** *n.* wife, spouse.
ehegestern, *adv. A:* the day before yesterday.
Eheglück, *n.* happiness in marriage; married happiness, *F:* married, conjugal, bliss.
Ehegüterrecht, *n. Jur:* law relating to the property of husband and wife.
ehehaft, *a.*=**ehaft.**
Ehehälfte, *f. F:* wife *or* husband.
Ehehalt, *m.* **-en/-en.** *Bavarian Dial:* servant.
Eheherr, *m.* husband.
eheherrlich, *a.* of a husband; **die eheherrliche Gewalt,** the authority of a husband.
Eheherstellungsklage, *f. Jur:* petition for restitution of conjugal rights.
Ehehindernis, *n. Jur:* impediment to marriage; obstacle, bar, to marriage; **trennendes E.,** separating impediment to marriage; **aufschiebendes E.,** suspensive impediment to marriage.
Ehekonsens, *m.* (parents', guardian's) consent to a marriage.
Ehekontrakt, *m.* (*a*) marriage contract; (*b*) (ante-nuptial) marriage settlement.
Ehekreuz, *n. Hum:* husband *or* wife (whom one has to put up with); **mein E.,** *F:* my better half; my old man, my old woman; *F:* (*wife*) my trouble and strife.
Eheleben, *n.* married life.
eheleiblich, *a. A:* legitimate (child).
Eheleute, *pl.* married people; **die E. X,** Mr and Mrs X.
ehelich, *a.* (*a*) legitimate (child, descent, etc.); (child) born in wedlock; **eheliche Nachkommen,** legitimate issue, legitimate offspring; **von ehelicher Abstammung,** of legitimate descent; **j-n für e. erklären,** (i) to legitimate, legitim(at)ize, s.o.; (ii) to declare s.o. legitimate; (*b*) matrimonial; marital, conjugal; **eheliche Verbindung,** matrimony, marriage; **mit j-m eine eheliche Verbindung eingehen,** to contract a marriage with s.o., to marry s.o.; to be joined with s.o. in matrimony, in marriage; **eheliche Gemeinschaft,** married life; matrimony; marital relations; *Jur:* **Aufhebung der ehelichen Gemeinschaft,** separation from bed and board, judicial separation; **Wiederherstellung der ehelichen Gemeinschaft,** restitution of conjugal rights; **eheliche Rechte,** conjugal, marital, rights; **eheliche Pflichten,** conjugal, marital, duties; **ehelicher Verkehr, eheliche Beziehungen,** marital relations; **eheliches Leben,** married life; **eheliche Liebe,**

married love, love between husband and wife; **die eheliche Wohnung,** the matrimonial home, the joint establishment (of husband and wife); **eheliche Treue,** conjugal fidelity, conjugal faithfulness; **Verletzung der ehelichen Treue,** infidelity, unfaithfulness; adultery; *Jur:* **ehelicher Aufwand,** maintenance of wife and children; **eheliches Güterrecht,** law relating to the property of husband and wife.

ehelichen, *v.tr.* (*usu. of man*) to marry, wed (s.o.), to take (s.o.) in marriage; **er ehelichte seine Köchin,** he married his cook.

Ehelichkeit, *f.* legitimacy (of child).

Ehelichkeitsanfechtung, *f.* contestation of (s.o.'s) legitimacy.

Ehelichkeitserklärung, *f. Jur:* (*a*) legitimation (of illegitimate child); (*b*) declaration of legitimacy.

Eheliebste, *f.* (*decl. as adj.*) *Lit. & Hum:* (*wife*) spouse.

ehelos, *a.* (*a*) celibate (monk, etc.); (*b*) unmarried, single (man, woman).

Ehelosigkeit, *f.* (*a*) celibacy (of monk, etc.); (*b*) single life, single state.

Ehemakler, *m.* marriage broker.

ehemalig, *attrib. a.* former, old, ex-, *F:* quondam (teacher, pupil, etc.); **ehemaliger Minister,** former minister, ex-minister; **ein ehemaliger Verbrecher,** a former criminal, an ex-criminal; **in unserer ehemaligen Wohnung,** in our old flat, in the flat we used to have.

ehemals, *adv.* formerly; **Herr X, e. ein Liberaler,** Mr X, formerly a Liberal; **e. Sekretär von...,** formerly secretary to..., ex-secretary to...; **Y, e. Pfarrer dieser Gemeinde,** Y, sometime, at one time, priest of this parish; **e. gehörte dieses Haus dem König,** formerly this house belonged to the king, this house used to belong to the king.

Ehemann, *m.* **-(e)s/-männer,** husband.

ehemündig, *a.* of marriageable age; nubile; **e. sein,** to be of marriageable age, of an age to marry, to be old enough to marry.

Ehemündigkeit, *f.* marriageable age; **die E. erreichen,** to reach the age at which one can marry, to reach marriageable age.

Ehename, *m.* married name (of woman).

Ehenichtigkeit, *f.* nullity of marriage; *Jur:* **Antrag auf E.,** petition for nullity of marriage, nullity suit.

Ehenichtigkeitsantrag, *m. Jur:* petition for nullity of marriage, nullity suit.

Ehenichtigkeitserklärung, *f. Jur:* annulment of marriage; decree of nullity (of a marriage).

Ehenichtigkeitsklage, *f.*=**Ehenichtigkeitsantrag.**

Ehepaar, *n.* married couple; **jungverheiratetes,** *F:* **neugebackenes, E.,** newly-married couple, *F:* newly-weds; **das E. X,** Mr and Mrs X.

Ehepakt, *m. Jur:* (post-nuptial) marriage settlement.

Ehepartner, *m.,* **Ehepartnerin,** *f.* (marriage) partner; *Jur: Lit. & Hum:* spouse.

Eheprozeß, *m. Jur:* matrimonial petition, matrimonial case.

Eher[1], *m.* **-s/-.** *Dial:* male (of animals).

eher[2], *adv.* **1.** earlier, sooner; before; **ich war e. da als du,** I was there earlier than you, I was there before you; **du hättest mir das e. sagen sollen,** you should have told me that before, sooner; **ich konnte nicht e. kommen,** I could not come earlier, before; **nicht e. als fünf Uhr,** not earlier than five o'clock, not before five o'clock; **ich werde nicht e. fortgehen, als bis ich eine Antwort erhalten habe,** I shall not go away until I have received an answer; **je e., desto besser,** the sooner the better; **je e. du anfängst, desto e. wirst du fertig sein,** the sooner you begin the sooner you will be finished. **2.** (*a*) more likely; **er wird das e. wissen als ich,** he is more likely to know that than I am; **es ist e. möglich, daß sie krank ist,** it is more likely that she is ill; **das klingt schon e. danach,** that sounds more like it; **so wird es e. gehen,** this way it will work more easily; **dieses Kleid ist schon e. dein Stil,** this dress is more (like) your style; (*b*) **um so e., als...,** more especially as..., all the more as..., the more so as...; **er wird dir um so e. helfen, als er ja an dieser Sache selbst interessiert ist,** he will help you—more especially as, the more so as, all the more as, he is interested in this business himself; **sie wird um so e. kommen, als sie meinen Mann sowieso zu sprechen wünscht,** she will come—all the more as, more especially as, she wishes to speak to my husband anyway. **3.** (*a*) rather; preferably; **ich möchte e. geliebt als gefürchtet werden,** I would rather be loved than feared; **ich würde e. leiden als lügen,** I would rather suffer than tell a lie; **ich würde e. sterben als nachgeben,** I would die rather than yield; rather, sooner, than yield I would die; **ich würde mich e. umbringen!** I would rather kill myself! **e. den Tod als Sklaverei!** death sooner than slavery! **eher Tod als Schande,** death before dishonour; **ich würde e. jedes Opfer bringen, e. würde ich jedes Opfer bringen, als daß ich dich in Schande kommen ließe,** I would sacrifice everything rather than that you should be disgraced; (*b*) rather; **er ist e. faul als dumm, er ist faul e. als dumm,** he is lazy rather than stupid; **e. lang als kurz,** long rather than short; **es sieht mir e. nach Regen aus,** it looks more like rain to me; it looks rather like rain to me; **e. geht die Welt unter, als daß er tanzen geht,** the heavens will fall before he goes dancing.

Eherecht, *n. Jur:* law of marriage, marriage law.

Ehering, *m.* wedding ring.

ehern, *a.* of ore; brazen, of brass; **ehernes Gefäß,** brazen vessel; **ehernes Standbild,** brazen statue; bronze statue; **die eherne Schlange,** the brazen serpent; **ein ehernes Geschick,** a pitiless fate; **eherner Wille,** iron will; **mit ehernem Mut,** with iron courage; **etwas mit eherner Stirn behaupten,** to state sth. boldly; to make a bold, courageous, statement; **das eherne Gesetz der Notwendigkeit,** the iron law of necessity; *Pol.Ec:* **das eherne Lohngesetz,** (Lassalle's) iron law of wages; *B:* **das eherne Meer,** the brazen sea; *Myth:* **das eherne Zeitalter,** the brazen age.

Ehesache, *f. Jur:* matrimonial petition, matrimonial case.

Eheschänder, *m.* adulterer.

Eheschänderin, *f.* adulteress.

eheschänderisch, *a.* adulterous.

Eheschändung, *f.* adultery.

Ehescheidung, *f. Jur:* divorce; dissolution of marriage.

Ehescheidungsgericht, *n. Jur:* divorce court.

Ehescheidungsgesetz, *n. Jur:* law relating to divorce.

Ehescheidungsgrund, *m. Jur:* ground for divorce.

Ehescheidungsklage, *f. Jur:* petition for divorce, divorce petition.

Ehescheidungsprozeß, *m. Jur:* divorce suit, divorce case.

Ehescheidungsrecht, *n. Jur:* law relating to divorce.

Ehescheidungsurteil, *n. Jur:* divorce decree.

Eheschenkung, *f.*=**Ehegeschenk.**

Eheschließung, *f.* contraction of marriage; marriage ceremony.

Ehesegen, *m. F:* (the) children of a marriage.

ehest. 1. *a.* **eheste(r), eheste, eheste(s),** earliest (opportunity, etc.). **2.** *adv.* **ehest,** soonest; as soon as possible, at the earliest opportunity. **3.** *adv.* **am ehesten,** (*a*) (the) earliest; **er war am ehesten hier,** he was here (the) earliest; (*b*) most likely; **er wird dir am ehesten helfen,** he is the most likely to help you; **so wird es am ehesten gehen,** this way it will work most easily; (*c*) **am ehesten würde ich zu Hause bleiben,** best of all, I would like to stay at home.

Ehestand, *m.* matrimony; (the) married state; **in den E. treten,** to enter into matrimony, into marriage.

ehestens, *adv.* (*a*) at the earliest; **es wird e. nächste Woche sein,** it will be next week at the earliest; (*b*) as soon as possible.

Ehestifter, *m.,* **Ehestifterin,** *f.* matchmaker.

Ehestiftung, *f.* matchmaking.

Ehesuchende, *m.,f.* (*decl. as adj.*) person desirous of marrying, of marriage.

ehetauglich, *a.* fit to marry.

Ehetauglichkeit, *f.* fitness to marry.

Ehetrennung, *f. Jur:* judicial separation, separation from bed and board.

Eheverbot, *n.* (*a*) law *or* decree prohibiting marriage; (*b*) law of celibacy (for monks, etc.).

Eheverfehlung, *f.* matrimonial offence.

Eheverlöbnis, *n.* betrothal, engagement.

Ehevermittler, *m.*=**Heiratsvermittler.**

Ehevermittlung, *f.* **1.**=**Eheanbahnung 1. 2.** marriage bureau, matrimonial agency.

Eheversprechen, *n.* promise of marriage; **Bruch des Eheversprechens,** breach of promise; **Prozeß wegen Bruches des Eheversprechens,** action for breach of promise, *F:* action for breach.

Ehevertrag, *m.* (*a*) marriage contract; (*b*) (antenuptial) marriage settlement.

ehevor, *adv. A:*=**ehemals.**

Ehewappen, *n. Her:* parted arms; united arms of husband and wife.

Eheweib, *n. Lit. & Hum:* (*wife*) spouse.

ehewidrig, *a.* against matrimonial laws; **ehewidrige Beziehungen,** irregular relations, extra-marital relations; **ehewidriges Verhältnis,** extra-marital relationship.

Ehezerrüttung, *f.* breaking up of a, of the, marriage.

Ehni, *m.* **-s/.** *Swiss Dial:* grandfather.

Ehrabschneidung, *f.* slander, vilification, backbiting; *Lit:* denigration.

ehrbar, *a.* honourable, esteemed, respected, worthy (person); respectable (conduct, etc.); **er ist ein ehrbarer Mann,** he is an honourable man, he is a worthy man; **ehrbare Mädchen,** respectable, modest, girls; **ehrbares Alter,** respectable old age; honourable old age; **ein ehrbares Leben führen,** to lead a respectable, worthy, life; **arme, aber ehrbare Leute,** poor but honest people.

Ehrbarkeit, *f.* honourableness (of person); respectability, worthiness (of conduct, etc.).

Ehre, *f.* **-/-n,** honour. **1.** (*a*) **ein Mann von E.,** a man of honour, an honourable man; **er ist die E. selbst,** he is the soul of honour; **die E. seines Landes,** one's country's honour; **das Feld der E.,** the battlefield, the field of honour; **auf dem Felde der E. gefallen,** died on the field of honour, died for his country; **um der E. willen,** for honour's sake; **es ist ein Gebot der E.,** it is a point of honour, honour demands it; **es seiner E. schuldig sein, etwas zu tun,** to be bound in honour, to be honour bound, to do sth.; **seine E. darein setzen, etwas zu tun,** to make it a point, a matter, of honour to do sth.; **seine E. verpfänden, seine E. als Pfand setzen,** to pledge one's honour; **seine E. aufs Spiel setzen,** to stake one's honour; **seine E. wahren,** to guard one's honour, one's good name; **seine E. retten,** to save one's honour, one's good name; **seine E. verlieren,** to lose one's honour; **seine E. wegwerfen,** to fling away one's honour; **j-s E. verletzen, kränken, beleidigen,** to cast a slur on s.o.'s honour; to impugn, besmirch, s.o.'s honour; to defame, vilify, slander, s.o.; **j-n in seiner E. kränken,** to wound s.o.'s honour; **sich in seiner E. gekränkt fühlen,** to feel wounded in one's honour; to feel hurt; **j-m die E. rauben, stehlen, j-n um seine E. bringen,** to rob s.o. of his honour; to ruin s.o.'s honour; **j-n bei seiner E. packen,** to appeal to s.o.'s honour; **er hat keine E. im Leib,** he has no sense of honour; **zu ihrer E. muß gesagt werden, daß...,** it must be said to their honour, to their credit, that...; **das alles ist zu seiner E.,** that is all to his honour, to his credit; **bei seiner E. schwören, daß...,** to swear on one's honour that...; **bei meiner E.! auf E.!** (up)on my (word of) honour! *see also* **abschneiden I. 4;** (*b*) **die E. einer Frau,** a woman's honour; **jungfräuliche E.,** virgin honour, maiden honour; virginity; **er raubte ihr die E.,** he robbed her of her honour, he dishonoured her; (*c*) **seinem Lande, seinen Eltern, E. machen,** to be an honour, a credit, to do credit, to one's country, to one's parents; **es macht ihm alle E., keine E.,** it reflects great credit, no credit, on him; **das tut seinem Mut alle E.,** that speaks well for his courage; **es macht ihm E., es gereicht ihm zur E., er hat E. damit eingelegt,** it does him credit, it reflects great credit on him; **das macht dir keine E.,** this does not redound to your credit, this reflects no credit on you; **ein Schritt, der dir E. macht,** a step that does you credit. **2. etwas in allen Ehren tun,** to do sth. in all good faith; **ich kann dieses Geld nicht in Ehren annehmen,** I cannot in honour accept this money. **3.** glory; **zur (größeren) E. Gottes,** to the (greater) glory of God; **E. sei Gott in der Höhe,** glory to God in the Highest. **4.** (*high esteem*) **j-n in hohen Ehren halten,** to hold s.o. in high honour, in high esteem; **j-s Andenken in Ehren halten,** to honour s.o.'s memory; **seinem Andenken zu Ehren,** in honour of his memory; **etwas, j-n, zu Ehren kommen lassen,** to bring sth., s.o., into honour; **sein Alter, sein weißes Haupt, in Ehren,** all due respect to his age; **Ihre Meinung in Ehren, aber ich glaube dennoch, daß Sie sich irren,** with all due respect to your opinion, I still think you are making a mistake; **ein Standbild zu j-s Ehren errichten,** to put up a statue in honour of s.o.; **zu Ehren des Präsidenten,** in honour of the president; **ein Bankett wurde zu Ehren seiner Ankunft gehalten,** a banquet was held in honour of his arrival; **ein Gastmahl dir zu Ehren,** a dinner in your honour; **ihm gebührt alle E.,** all honour to him; **E. dem Tapferen,** all honour to the brave; **j-m E. erweisen,** to pay, do, honour to s.o.; (*cp.* 5, 6); *F:* **dem Essen alle E. antun,** to do justice to the dinner; *Prov:* **E., wem E. gebührt,** honour to whom honour is due, honour where honour is

due. 5. **j-n mit allen Ehren empfangen,** to receive s.o. with all due honour, with full honours; **akademische Ehren,** academic honours; **mit kriegerischen Ehren,** with the honours of war; **mit allen militärischen, soldatischen, Ehren beigesetzt werden,** to be buried with full military honours; **j-m die letzte E. erweisen,** to pay the last honours to s.o.; **mit Ehren aus einer Sache hervorgehen,** to come out of an affair with honour; **nach Ehren streben,** to aspire to honours. 6. (*a*) (*privilege*) **es als eine E. betrachten, es für eine E. halten, es sich zur E. anrechnen, etwas zu tun,** to consider it an honour, a privilege, to do sth.; **es ist mir eine große E., ich betrachte es als eine große E., Sie hier als meine Gäste empfangen zu dürfen,** I consider it a great honour, I am greatly honoured, to be able to receive you here as my guests; **die E., der Erste zu sein,** the honour of being the first; **ich habe nicht die E., Ihrem Beruf anzugehören,** I have not the honour of belonging to your profession; **ich hatte noch nicht die E., ihm vorgestellt zu werden,** I have not yet had the honour of being introduced to him; **es ist mir eine E., ich habe die E.,** I am (greatly) honoured; **mit wem habe ich die E.?** (i) to whom have I the honour of speaking? (ii) you have the advantage of me, sir; **was verschafft mir die E.?** to what do I owe the honour (of your visit)? **bitte, tun Sie, machen Sie, mir die E., mit mir zu speisen,** please do me the honour of dining with me; **wir geben, erlauben, uns die E., Sie zum . . . einzuladen,** we request the pleasure of your company for . . .; *Com:* **ich bitte um die E. Ihres Besuches,** I shall be honoured to receive your visit; **ich erlaube mir die E., Ihnen einige Muster meiner Stoffe zuzusenden,** I have the honour to submit to you some samples of my materials; (*b*) *Golf: etc:* **die E. haben,** to have the honour; **Sie haben die E.,** your honour.

ehren. I. *v.tr.* to honour (s.o., s.o.'s memory, etc.); to respect (s.o.'s good qualities, sentiments, etc.); (*of action, etc.*) to do credit to, to reflect honour on (s.o.); **Ihre Anwesenheit ehrt mich,** I am (greatly) honoured by your presence; **dein Vertrauen ehrt mich,** your confidence in me is an honour; **ich fühle mich sehr geehrt,** I am greatly, much, honoured; **ich ehre deinen Kummer,** I respect your sorrow; **j-m ein ehrendes Andenken bewahren,** to honour s.o.'s memory; **ehrende Erwähnung, ehrende Anerkennung,** honourable mention; **dieser Schritt ehrt Sie,** this step does you credit; **dein Schweigen ehrt dich,** your silence does you credit, reflects great credit on you; **mein geehrter Kollege,** my respected colleague; *Corr:* **sehr geehrte Herren!** dear Sirs; **sehr geehrter Herr X!** dear Mr X; *B:* **du sollst deinen Vater und deine Mutter e.,** honour thy father and thy mother; *Prov:* **wer den Pfennig nicht ehrt, ist des Talers nicht wert,** take care of the pence and the pounds will take care of themselves.

II. *vbl s.* **Ehrung,** *f.* (*a*) *in vbl senses;* **die E. der Sieger,** the honouring of the victors; (*b*) honour; honourable distinction; **eine hohe E.,** a high honour; **ihm wurden viele Ehrungen erwiesen, zuteil,** he received many honours; many honours were conferred on him.

Ehrenabzeichen, *n.* medal (awarded for honourable distinction); decoration.

Ehrenakzept, *n. Com:* acceptance (of protested bill) for honour, acceptance supra protest.

Ehrenakzeptor, *m. Com:* acceptor (of protested bill) for honour.

Ehrenamt, *n.* honorary function, honorary post.

ehrenamtlich, *a.* honorary (duty, member, membership, etc.); **ehrenamtlicher Präsident,** honorary president; *adv.* **e. bestellter, ernannter, Präsident,** honorary president, president in an honorary capacity.

Ehrenannahme, *f.* = **Ehrenakzept.**

Ehrenbeleidigung, *f.* insult (to s.o.'s honour); *Jur:* **mündliche E.,** slander; **tätliche E.,** assault.

Ehrenbezeigung, Ehrenbezeugung, *f. Mil: etc:* salute; **militärische E.,** military salute; military honours; **eine E. machen,** to give a salute, to salute; **Ehrenbezeigungen,** compliments.

Ehrenbogen, *m.* triumphal arch.

Ehrenbürger, *m.* honorary citizen; freeman (of a city *or* town).

Ehrenbürgerrecht, *n.* freedom (of a city *or* town); **ihm wurde das E. der Stadt verliehen,** he was given the freedom of the town.

Ehrendame, *f.* lady-in-waiting.

Ehrendegen, *m.* sword of honour.

Ehrendienst, *m.* 1. service in an honorary capacity. 2. **j-m den letzten E. erweisen,** to pay the last honours to s.o.

Ehrendoktor, *m. Sch:* 1. honorary doctor, doctor *honoris causa.* 2. = **Ehrendoktorat.**

Ehrendoktorat, *n.* honorary doctorate, doctorate *honoris causa.*

Ehreneintritt, *m. Com:* act of honour.

Ehrenerklärung, *f.* apology (for insult); **eine E. abgeben,** to make the *amende honorable,* to make a full apology.

ehrenfest, *a.* honourable (person).

Ehrenfolgen, *f.pl. Austrian Jur:* penalty involving loss of civil rights.

Ehrenfriedhof, *m.* memorial cemetery, *esp.* military cemetery; cemetery of remembrance.

Ehrengarde, *f.* guard of honour.

Ehrengast, *m.* guest of honour.

Ehrengefolge, *n.* train, retinue, suite (of sovereign, etc.).

Ehrengeleit, *n.* escort (of honour); **j-m das E. geben,** to give s.o. an escort, to escort s.o.

Ehrengericht, *n. Jur:* court of honour; disciplinary court; **ärztliches E.,** (tribunal of the) Medical Council.

ehrengerichtlich, *a. Jur:* **ehrengerichtliches Verfahren,** disciplinary action.

ehrenhaft, *a.* honourable (pers., conduct, etc.); **ein ehrenhafter Mann,** an honourable man, a man of honour; **ein ehrenhaftes Leben führen,** to lead a respectable, a worthy, life; **ehrenhafte Absichten,** honourable intentions; *adv.* **sich e. betragen,** to acquit oneself with honour, honourably.

Ehrenhaftigkeit, *f.* honourableness.

Ehrenhain, *m.* garden of remembrance.

ehrenhalber. 1. *inv.a.* **Doktor e.,** Doctor *honoris causa.* 2. *adv.* for honour's sake; *see also* **Akzept.**

Ehrenhandel, *m.* affair of honour; duel.

Ehrenhof, *m. Arch:* court of honour.

Ehrenintervention, *f. Com:* act of honour.

Ehrenjungfer, *f.* maid of honour.

Ehrenklage, *f. Jur:* action for slander *or* libel.

Ehrenkodex, *m.* code of honour; duelling code.

Ehrenkränkung, *f.* 1. insult. 2. *Jur:* defamation, (i) slander, (ii) libel.

Ehrenkreuz, *n.* cross awarded for distinction; medal.

Ehrenlegion, die, the Legion of Honour.

Ehrenmahl, *n.* dinner *or* lunch in s.o.'s honour.

Ehrenmal, *n.* monument, *esp.* war memorial; **j-m ein E. errichten,** to put up a monument in honour of s.o.

Ehrenmann, *m.* **-(e)s/-männer,** man of honour, honourable man; gentleman.

Ehrenmitglied, *n.* honorary member (of society, etc.).

Ehrenpforte, *f.* triumphal arch.

Ehrenplatz, *m.* place of honour; seat of honour; **den E. einnehmen,** to hold, occupy, the seat of honour; **dieses Buch nimmt auf meinem Bücherbord den E. ein,** this book holds, occupies, stands in, the place of honour on my bookshelf.

Ehrenpreis[1], *m.* (first) prize; **den E. gewinnen,** to win, carry off, the first prize.

Ehrenpreis[2], *m. & n.* **-es/-e.** *Bot:* speedwell, veronica; **echter, echtes, E.,** common speedwell; **efeublättriger, efeublättriges, E.,** ivy-leaved speedwell; winterweed; **gamanderähnlicher, gamanderähnliches, E.,** germander speedwell; bird's-eye.

Ehrenrechte, *n.pl. Jur:* **bürgerliche E.,** civil rights; **Verlust der bürgerlichen E.,** loss of civil rights; *see also* **aberkennen** I, II.

ehrenrührig, *a.* defamatory; slanderous; libellous.

Ehrensäbel, *m.* sword of honour.

Ehrensache, *f.* 1. (*a*) *Jur:* action for slander *or* libel; (*b*) affair of honour; duel. 2. point of honour; **für mich ist es E., daß ich in der Prüfung gut abschneide,** it is a point of honour with me that I should do well in the examination; **es ist E. für ihn,** it is a point of honour with him; **es als E. betrachten, nicht nachzugeben,** to make it a point of honour, to regard it as a point of honour, not to yield; **das ist doch E.!** that is understood! of course!

Ehrensalve, *f.* gun salute (at military funeral).

Ehrenschießen, *n. Mil: Navy:* salute with the guns.

Ehrenschuld, *f.* debt of honour; gambling debt.

Ehrenschüsse, *m.pl. Mil: Navy:* salute; **E. abgeben,** to fire a salute; **E. erwidern,** to return, acknowledge, a salute.

Ehrenschutz, *m.* 1. protection of (s.o.'s) honour. 2. *Austrian:* patronage (of official function); **unter dem E. von . . .,** under the patronage, auspices, of . . . .

Ehrensold, *m. Mil:* special pay for men holding decorations.

Ehrenstelle, . 1. honorary post. 2. *Her:* honour point.

Ehrenstrafe, *f.* 1. *A:* punishment involving the loss of civil rights. 2. punishment involving (personal) disgrace *or* the loss of dignity.

Ehrenstück, *n. Her:* honourable ordinary.

Ehrentag, *m.* day on which s.o. receives special honour; **heute ist ihr E.,** today is her (great) day.

Ehrentat, *f.* honourable deed.

Ehrentitel, *m.* honorary title.

Ehrentod, *m.* honourable death; **den E. sterben,** to die on the field of honour, to die for one's country.

Ehrentor, *n. Fb: etc:* consolation goal.

Ehrenverletzung, *f.* = **Ehrenkränkung.**

ehrenvoll, *a.* honourable; **eine ehrenvolle Tat,** an honourable deed, an honourable action; **ehrenvolles Alter,** respectable old age; **ehrenvoller Frieden,** honourable peace; peace with honour; **ehrenvoller Tod,** honourable death; glorious death; *Mil:* **ehrenvoller Rückzug,** honourable retreat.

Ehrenwache, *f.* guard of honour; **die E. abschreiten,** to inspect the guard of honour.

Ehrenwaffe, *f.* ceremonial weapon.

ehrenwert, *a.* honourable, esteemed, respected, worthy (pers.); respectable, reputable (firm).

Ehrenwort, *n.* **-(e)s/-e,** word of honour; parole; **j-m sein E. geben,** to give s.o. one's word of honour; **(auf) E.!** upon my word (of honour)! I give you my word of honour! *F:* honestly! honest! **einen Gefangenen auf E. entlassen,** to release a prisoner on parole, to put a prisoner on parole.

ehrenwörtlich, *a.* **ehrenwörtliches Versprechen,** solemn promise; *adv.* **etwas e. erklären, versprechen,** to state, promise, sth. on one's honour.

Ehrenzahlung, *f. Com:* payment (of protested bill) for honour.

Ehrenzeichen, *n.* medal (awarded for honourable distinction); decoration; **mit allen Orden und E.,** beribboned and bemedalled.

Ehrenzulage, *f.* = **Ehrensold.**

ehrerbietig, *a.* deferential, respectful (manner, etc.).

Ehrerbietigkeit, *f.* deference; respectfulness.

Ehrerbietung, *f.* deference, respect; **j-m E. erweisen,** to pay, show, deference, respect, to s.o.

Ehrfurcht, *f.* reverence; awe; **in heiliger E.,** in holy awe; **E. vor dem Alter haben,** to have respect, reverence, for old age; **E. vor der Frau,** respect for women; **ein E. gebietender, einflößender, Mann,** an awe-inspiring man, a man who commands respect.

ehrfürchtig, *a.* reverent; reverential; **ehrfürchtiges Schweigen,** reverent silence; **mit ehrfürchtiger Scheu,** with reverential awe; *adv.* **e. berührte sie den Saum seines Gewandes,** reverently, with reverence, she touched the hem of his garment.

Ehrfürchtigkeit, *f.* reverence.

ehrfurchtsvoll, *a.* = **ehrfürchtig.**

Ehrgefühl, *n.* sense of honour; **er hat kein E.,** he has no sense of honour; **mein E. würde es verbieten, würde es nicht zulassen,** it would offend my sense of honour; **j-s E. kränken, verletzen,** to hurt s.o.'s pride.

Ehrgeiz, *m.* (*a*) ambition, ambitiousness; **gesunder E.,** healthy ambition; **von E. verzehrt,** eaten up with ambition; **er hat keinen E.,** he is not ambitious, he lacks ambition; (*b*) ambition; **er hatte den E., um die Welt zu fliegen,** he had an ambition to fly round the world.

ehrgeizig, *a.* ambitious.

ehrlich, *a.* 1. (*a*) honest, straight (pers.); honest, fair, straight (dealings, etc.); **sie sind ehrliche Leute,** they are honest people; **ein ehrliches Mädchen,** an honest, a straight, girl; **ein durchaus, unbedingt, ehrlicher Mann,** a thoroughly, an absolutely, honest man; **er hat ein ehrliches Gesicht, er sieht e. aus,** he has an honest face, he looks honest; **mit ehrlichen Mitteln,** by honest, fair, means; **ehrliches Spiel,** straight, fair, honest, game; **ehrliche Geschäfte,** honest, square, fair, deals; **sein ehrliches Brot verdienen,** to earn an honest living; **einen ehrlichen Beruf haben,** to have an honest trade; **ehrliche Absichten,** honourable intentions; *Prov:* **e. währt am längsten,** honesty pays; (*b*) honest, truthful (pers.); sincere, honest (feelings, opinion, etc.); **mit j-m e. sein,** to be honest, straight, frank, open, with s.o.; **die ehrliche Wahrheit,** the honest truth; **sagen Sie uns Ihre ehrliche Meinung,** tell us your honest opinion; **ehrliches Mitgefühl,** sincere sympathy; **ein ehrliches Verlangen nach Frieden,** a sincere, genuine,

desire for peace; **der ehrliche Wunsch zu helfen,** the sincere, honest, wish to help; *F:* **er ist eine ehrliche Haut,** he always tells the truth, he never lies. **2.** (*a*) **j-n e. machen,** to rehabilitate s.o.; to restore s.o.'s honour, s.o.'s good name; **er möchte das Mädchen gern e. machen,** he wants to make an honest woman of her; (*b*) **ehrliches Begräbnis,** honourable burial, *esp.* Christian burial. **3.** *adv.* (*a*) honestly; **sich e. ernähren,** to earn an honest living; **er hat sich e. geschlagen,** he fought honourably, he fought an honest battle; **e. spielen,** to play a straight game, an honest game; (*b*) honestly, truthfully; sincerely; frankly; **sagen Sie uns e. Ihre Meinung,** tell us your opinion, honestly, frankly, tell us your honest opinion; **ich habe e. geglaubt, daß . . . ,** I honestly believed that . . .; **ich muß ganz e. sagen, daß mir das Kleid nicht gefällt,** I must quite honestly say, to be quite honest I must say, that I don't like the dress; **e. gesagt . . . ,** honestly speaking . . ., to be honest . . .; **ich war e. überrascht,** I was genuinely surprised; **es e. meinen,** (i) to say sth. in all sincerity; (ii) to act in good faith, to act with sincere intentions; **sie hat es e. mit ihm gemeint,** she thought she was acting in his best interests; she meant well by him; **e. gemeinte Ratschläge,** advice given in good faith, with the best (of) intentions; **j-n e. betrauern,** to mourn s.o. sincerely, in all sincerity.

Ehrlichkeit, *f.* (*a*) honesty, frankness, truthfulness (of pers.); sincerity, honesty (of feeling, opinion, etc.); (*b*) honesty, integrity (of pers.); fairness, honesty (of dealings, etc.); **seine unbedingte E.,** his absolute honesty; **Händler von zweifelhafter E.,** tradesman of doubtful honesty.

Ehrlichkeitsversicherung, *f.* *Ins:* insurance against theft, fraud, etc.

Ehrlichmachung, *f.* rehabilitation; restoration of (s.o.'s) honour *or* good name.

ehrlos, *a.* **1.** dishonourable, disreputable, infamous (life, pers., deed); (person) who has no sense of honour; **ehrlose Mädchen,** girls, women, of easy virtue, of loose morals; **ein ehrloses Weib,** a woman of easy virtue; an abandoned woman. **2.** *Hist:* infamous (pers.); (person) who has been branded with infamy; **j-n e. machen,** to brand s.o. with infamy.

Ehrlosigkeit, *f.* **1.** dishonourableness, disreputableness, infamy (of life, pers., deed). **2.** *Hist:* infamy (of pers.).

ehrpusselig, *a.* *F:* = **ehrgeizig.**

ehrsam, *a.* respectable (pers.); **ehrsame Bürger,** respectable citizens.

Ehrsamkeit, *f.* respectability (of pers.).

Ehrsucht, *f.* immoderate ambition.

ehrsüchtig, *a.* immoderately ambitious.

Ehrung, *f. see* **ehren II.**

ehrvergessen, *a.* dishonourable.

Ehrverletzung, *f.* = **Ehrenkränkung.**

ehrwürdig, *a.* **1.** venerable; **ein ehrwürdiger alter Mann, ein ehrwürdiger Greis,** a venerable old man; **Beda der Ehrwürdige,** the Venerable Bede; **eine ehrwürdige alte Kirche,** a venerable old church. **2.** *Ecc:* reverend; **ehrwürdiger Vater,** Reverend Father; **ehrwürdige Mutter,** Reverend Mother Superior; *Freemasonry:* **ehrwürdiger Meister (vom Stuhl),** *F:* **Ehrwürdiger,** Worshipful Master.

Ehrwürdigkeit, *f.* venerability, venerableness.

ei[1], *int.* oh, ah; **ei, wie nett!** oh, how nice! **ei ja,** oh yes; **ei, ja, wir wollen tanzen!** oh, yes, let us dance! **ei freilich!** yes, of course! yes, indeed! (yes,) naturally! **darf ich hereinkommen? — ei freilich!** may I come in?—yes, of course (you may)! **ei, ei,** (*nursery language*) (*when stroking cat, father's face, etc.*) nice pussy, nice daddy, etc.; **ei, ei machen,** to stroke (s.o., s.o.'s face, etc.); (*with a nuance of surprise or annoyance*) **ei, ei!** oho! ha ha! **ei, ei, was sehe ich?** oho! what is this I see? (*indicating annoyance*) **ei je!** oh dear! **ei je, das ist aber dumm!** oh dear, that is annoying! (*indicating surprise or annoyance*) **ei der Tausend!** what the deuce! what the devil! (*indignant repudiation*) **ei was!** nonsense! rubbish! (*indicating annoyance*) **ei, daß dich (der Teufel hole)!** oh, go to hell!

Ei[2], *n.* -(e)s/-er. **1.** (*a*) egg; *Biol:* ovum; **ein Ei legen,** to lay an egg; **frisch gelegtes Ei,** new-laid egg; **faules, schlechtes, Ei,** rotten egg, addled egg; **ein Ei kochen,** to boil an egg; **weichgekochtes, weiches, Ei,** soft-boiled egg; **hartgekochtes, hartes, Ei,** hard-boiled egg; **verlorenes Ei,** poached egg; **j-n mit faulen Eiern bewerfen,** to pelt (actor, speaker, etc.) with rotten eggs; to give s.o. the bird; **sie sehen sich ähnlich, sie gleichen sich, wie ein Ei dem anderen,** they are as like as two peas; *F:* **sie sah aus wie aus dem Ei gepellt, geschält,** she looked as if she had just stepped out of a bandbox; she looked spick and span, as neat as a new pin; **j-n wie ein rohes Ei behandeln,** to handle s.o. gently; to deal tactfully, gently, with s.o., *F:* to handle s.o. with kid gloves; **wie auf Eiern gehen,** (i) to walk gingerly, to walk carefully; (ii) to tread lightly, to tread on delicate ground; **kümmere dich nicht um ungelegte Eier,** (i) don't cross your bridges before you come to them; (ii) mind your own business; *Prov:* **das Ei will klüger sein als die Henne,** go and teach your grandmother, your granny, to suck eggs; (*b*) *usu. pl.* eggs (of insect); spawn (of fish, etc.); (hard) roe (of fish). **2.** (*a*) *Arch:* egg, ovolo, ovum; (*b*) *El.E:* egg-insulator; (*c*) *Clockm:* *F:* **Nürnberger Eier,** early egg-shaped watches, 'Nuremberg eggs'; (*d*) *Mil:* *F:* bomb; (*e*) *F:* **Eier,** money. **3.** *P:* testicle.

-ei, *s.suff.* (*stressed*) [-ˈai], *f.* -/-en. **1.** (*denoting trade or occupation*) (*a*) -y; **Fischerei,** fishery; **Brauerei,** brewery; (*b*) -ing; **Druckerei,** printing; **Malerei,** painting; **Schneiderei,** tailoring. **2.** (*denoting place of business or office*) (*a*) -y; -age; **Bäckerei,** bakery; **Brauerei,** brewery; **Wäscherei,** laundry; **Bücherei,** library; **Einsiedelei,** hermitage; **Abtei,** abbey; **Propstei,** provostry; **Kanzlei,** chancellery, chancellory; office; (*b*) **Druckerei,** printing shop; **Fleischerei, Schlächterei,** butcher's shop; **Sattlerei,** saddler's (work)shop; **Schneiderei,** tailor's (work)shop; **Amtei,** administrative office. **3.** (*denoting action, esp. continuous or intensive*) **Betrügerei,** deception; cheating; **Kuppelei,** procuring; **Schwatzerei,** (continuous) prattling; **Singerei,** singing; **Küsserei,** kissing; **Bummelei,** dawdling. **4.** (*denoting result of action*) (*a*) **Träumerei,** dream; **Liebhaberei,** hobby; **Schlägerei,** fight; **Prahlereien,** boasts; **Verrätereien,** treacherous acts; **Betrügereien,** dishonest acts; (*b*) (*collective concept*) **Barbarei,** barbarism; **Ketzerei,** heresy; (*c*) (*piece of work*) **Malerei,** painting, picture; **Stickerei,** (piece of) embroidery; **Schnitzerei,** carving. **5.** (*denoting district*) **Pfarrei,** parish; **Amtei,** administrative district; (*in names of provinces, etc.*) **Lombardei,** Lombardy; **Mongolei,** Mongolia; **Berberei,** Barbary; **Türkei,** Turkey. **6.** (*denoting professional group*) **Polizei,** police; **Reiterei,** cavalry. **7.** (*denoting organized activity or resulting institution*) **Sklaverei,** slavery; **Tyrannei,** tyranny; **Freimaurerei,** freemasonry.

eia, *int.* (*a*) **eia, eia,** (*nursery language*) (*when stroking cat, father's face, etc.*) nice pussy, nice daddy, etc.; **eia, eia machen,** to stroke s.o., s.o.'s face, etc.; (*b*) **eia popeia,** hushaby baby.

Eiablage, *f.* depositing, laying, of eggs; *Ent:* oviposition.

Eiabstoßung, *f.* *Biol:* *Physiol:* ovulation.

eiapopeia, *int.* hushaby baby.

Eiaustritt, *m.* *Biol:* *Physiol:* ovulation.

Eibe, *f.* -/-n, (*a*) *Bot:* yew(-tree); (*b*) yew-wood.

eiben, *a.* (made) of yew-wood.

Eibenbaum, *m.* *Bot:* yew(-tree).

Eibengewächse, *n.pl.* *Bot:* taxaceae.

Eibenholz, *n.* yew-wood.

Eibenzypresse, *f.* *Bot:* taxodium, swamp cypress.

Eibildung, *f.* *Biol:* oogenesis, ovogenesis.

Eibisch, *m.* -es/-e. *Bot:* (*a*) althea; marshmallow; (*b*) hibiscus; **syrischer E.,** rose of Sharon; **chinesischer E.,** China rose, Indian rose.

Eichamt, *n.* (*a*) *Adm:* Office of Weights and Measures; *U.S:* Bureau of Standards; (*b*) standardizing office.

Eichapfel, *m.* oak-gall, oak-apple.

Eichbaum, *m.* *Bot:* oak-tree, oak.

Eiche, *f.* -/-n. **1.** (*a*) *Bot:* oak, oak-tree; **junge E.** oak-sapling, oaklet, oakling; **gemeine E.,** common (French and British) oak; **weiße E.,** white oak; **immergrüne E.,** evergreen oak, holm-oak, holly-oak, ilex; **österreichische, burgundische, E.,** Turkey oak, Austrian oak; **stark wie eine E.,** (as) firm as a rock; *Prov:* **es fällt keine E. von einem Streiche,** Rome wasn't built in a day; (*b*) oak-wood; **dunkle E.,** dark oak (colour). **2.** (*a*) *Bot:* **afrikanische E.,** African oak; **indische E.,** teak, Indian oak; **neuseeländische E.,** iron-tree; (*b*) *F:* **Marke 'deutsche E.',** inferior war-time tobacco (1914–1918).

Eichel, *f.* -/-n. **1.** (*a*) *Bot:* acorn; (*b*) *Cards:* acorn. **2.** *Anat:* glans (of the penis).

Eichelbecher, *m.* *Bot:* acorn-cup; cupule.

Eichelbohrer, *m.* *Ent:* acorn-weevil.

Eichelentzündung, *f.* *Med:* balanitis.

Eichelernte, *f.* acorn-harvest; acorn-crop.

eichelförmig, *a.* acorn-shaped.

Eichelhäher, *m.* *Orn:* jay.

Eichelkaffee, *m.* coffee substitute (made from acorns).

Eichelkakao, *m.* cocoa containing acorns.

Eichelmast, *f.* *Husb:* acorn-mast, oak-mast; acorn-crop; pannage.

Eichelmaus, *f.* *Z:* lerot, garden dormouse.

eichelnfressend, *a.* acorn-eating.

eichel(n)tragend, *a.* acorn-bearing, balaniferous, glandiferous.

Eichelpilz, Eichelschwamm, *m.* *Fung:* phallus, stink-horn.

Eicheltripper, *m.* *Med:* balanitis.

Eichelwürmer, *m.pl.* *Ent:* acorn worms, enteropneusta, balanoglossida.

Eichelzucker, *m.* *Ch:* quercitol.

Eichen[1], *n.* -s/-, (*dim. of* **Ei**[2]) little egg; *Biol:* ovule.

eichen[2], *a.* oaken, (made) of oak-wood; **eichene Möbel,** oak furniture.

eichen[3]. I. *v.tr.* **1.** (*a*) to standardize, verify (weights, etc.); to gauge (measuring instruments); to calibrate (tubes, etc.); to graduate, calibrate (thermometer, etc.); *Ph:* to rate (light, resistance, etc.); *Astr:* to gauge (stars); *F:* (*of pers.*) **auf etwas** *acc.* **geeicht sein,** to be qualified to deal with sth.; to be versed in sth.; (*b*) *Nau:* to measure the tonnage (of ship). **2.** to stamp, mark (standardized weights, etc.).

II. *vbl s.* **Eichen** *n.*, **Eichung** *f.* **1.** standardization, verification (of weights, etc.); gauging (of measuring instruments); calibration, graduation (of tubes, thermometer, etc.); *Ph:* rating (of light, resistance, etc.); *Astr:* gauging (of stars); *Nau:* measuring of (ship's) tonnage. **2.** stamping, marking (of standardized weights, etc.).

Eichenbaum, *m.* *Bot:* oak-tree, oak.

Eichenblatt, *n.* oak-leaf.

Eichenblattroller, *m.* *Ent:* (*beetle*) attelabus nitens.

Eichenbock, *m.* *Ent:* oak-pruner.

Eichenfarn, *m.* *Bot:* beech-fern.

Eichengallapfel, *m.*, **Eichengalle,** *f.* oak-gall, oak-apple.

Eichengerbsäure, *f.* = **Eichenrindengerbsäure.**

Eichenhain, *m.* oak-grove, oak-plantation.

Eichenhasel, *f.* *Bot:* oak-leaved hazel.

Eichenhefe, *f.* *Fung:* saccharomyces ludwigi.

Eichenholz, *n.* oak-wood, oak-timber; **indisches E.,** wood of chrysophyllum glabrum.

Eichenholzmöbel, *n.pl.* oak furniture.

Eichenkastanie, *f.* *Bot:* oak-chestnut.

Eichenknäuling, *m.* *Fung:* styptic toadstool.

Eichenkranz, *m.* crown of oak-leaves; oak-leaf garland.

Eichenlaub, *n.* oak-leaves.

Eichenmehltau, *m.* *Arb:* oak-blight.

Eichenmistel, *f.* *Bot:* yellow-berried mistletoe.

Eichenreizker, *m.* *Fung:* lactarius quietus, mild toadstool.

Eichenrinde, *f.* *Tan:* *Pharm:* oak-bark; **mit E. gegerbt,** oak-bark tanned.

Eichenrindengerbsäure, *f.* *Tan:* quercitannin, quercitannic acid.

Eichenrose, *f.* oak-gall, oak-apple.

Eichenschälwald, *m.* *For:* oak-coppice.

Eichenspanner, *m.* *Ent:* oak-beauty.

Eichenspinner, *m.* *Ent:* (oak) egger(-moth); processionary moth.

Eichenwald, *m.* oak-wood, oak forest.

Eichenwerftkäfer, *m.* *Ent:* (species of) blister-beetle.

Eichenwickler, *m.* *Ent:* **1.** oak-moth. **2.** = **Eichenblattroller.**

Eichenwurzeltöter, *m.* *Fung:* fungus causing root-rot of oaks.

Eichfelder, *n.pl.* *Astr:* selected areas.

Eichhase, *m.* *Fung:* polyporus umbellatus.

Eichhorn, Eichhörnchen, *n.* *Z:* **1.** squirrel; **graues E.,** grey squirrel; **sibirisches E.,** Siberian squirrel; miniver. **2. fliegendes E.,** (*a*) flying squirrel; (*b*) squirrel phalanger, squirrel opossum.

Eichhornie [-ˈhɔrniə], *f.* -/-n. *Bot:* water hyacinth.

Eichkätzchen, *n.* *Z:* squirrel.

Eichmarke, *f.* **1.** guide mark (in lock, harbour, etc.) indicating a certain water-level. **2.** = **Eichzeichen.**

Eichmaß, *n.* **1.** gauge. **2.** standard (of weights, measures). **3.** *A:* liquid measure (for wine).

Eichochs, *m.* *Ent:* stag-beetle.

Eichordnung, *f.* regulations for the standardization of weights and measures.

Eichpfahl, *m.* guide-post; marker-post; calibration mark; *Hyd.E:* gauge post.

Eichpilz, *m.* *Fung:* polyporus umbellatus.

Eichung, *f. see* **eichen**[3] **II.**

Eichungsamt, *n.* = **Eichamt.**

Eichungsnormal, *n.* standard (of weights, measures).
Eichzeichen, *n. Adm:* official stamp, mark (on standardized weights, measuring instruments, etc.).
Eid, *m.* **-es/-e,** (solemn) oath; **einen Eid ablegen, schwören, leisten,** to swear, make, an oath, to take an oath; **Ablegung, Leistung, eines Eides,** taking of an oath; **falscher Eid,** false oath; perjury; **einen falschen Eid schwören,** to swear a false oath; to commit perjury; **j-m den Eid abnehmen,** to put s.o. on his oath; to administer the oath to s.o.; **j-n seines Eides entbinden,** to release, relieve, s.o. from his oath; **seinen Eid brechen,** to break one's oath; to commit perjury; **Verletzung, Bruch, eines Eides,** violation, breaking, of an oath; perjury; **promissorischer Eid,** promissory oath; **assertorischer Eid,** assertory oath; **j-m einen Eid zuschieben,** to tender an oath to s.o.; **j-m einen Eid zurückschieben,** to tender back an oath to s.o.; **ich würde einen Eid darauf ablegen, schwören, ich würde es auf meinen Eid nehmen,** I would take my oath on it; **ich lege einen Eid darauf ab, ich schwöre einen Eid darauf, daß es so geschah, wie ich sage,** on my (Bible) oath it happened as I am telling you; **durch (einen) Eid gebunden,** oath-bound; **unter Eid,** on, upon, under, oath; **etwas unter Eid aussagen,** to declare, state, sth. on oath; **den Eid verweigern,** to refuse to take the oath, to object to taking the oath; **Versicherung, Erklärung, an Eides Statt,** solemn affirmation (in lieu of an oath); statutory declaration; **eine Versicherung, eine Erklärung, an Eides Statt abgeben,** to make a statutory declaration.
Eidam, *m.* **-(e)s/-e.** *A:* son-in-law.
Eidbrecher, *m.* oath-breaker; perjurer.
Eidbruch, *m.* violation, breaking, of an oath; perjury.
eidbrüchig, *a.* (person) who has broken his oath.
Eidbrüchige, *m., f.* (*decl. as adj.*) oath-breaker; perjurer.
Eidechse, *f.* **-/-n. 1.** *Rept:* lizard; **gemeine E.,** sand-lizard; **grüne E.,** green lizard. **2.** *Astr:* **die E.,** (the constellation) Lacerta.
eidechsenartig, *a.* like a lizard; lacertian, lacertiform.
Eidechsenpflanze, *f. Bot:* sauromatum.
Eidechsenschwanz, *m.* **1.** lizard's tail. **2.** *Bot:* **nickender E.,** lizard's tail, breast-weed.
Eidechsenschwanzpflanzen, *.pl. Bot:* saururaceae, plants of the lizard's-tail family.
Eidechsenwurz, *f. Bot:* sauromatum.
Eider, *m.* **-s/-** & *f.* **-/-n.** *Orn:* eider(-duck).
Eiderdaunen, *f.pl.* eider-down.
Eiderente, *f.*, **Eidergans,** *f.*, **Eidervogel,** *m. Orn:* eider(-duck).
Eidesantrag, *m. Jur:* application for the administration of an oath to s.o.
Eidesbelehrung, *f. Jur:* caution (to pers. about to take the oath).
Eidesbrecher, *m.* oath-breaker; perjurer.
Eidesbruch, *m.* = **Eidbruch.**
eidesbrüchig, *a.* = **eidbrüchig.**
Eidesdelation, *f. Jur:* tendering of an oath (to s.o.).
eidesfähig, *a. Jur:* capable of taking an oath; oathworthy.
Eidesfähigkeit, *f. Jur:* capability of taking an oath; oathworthiness.
Eidesformel, *f. Jur: etc:* oath formula; wording of the, of an, oath.
eidesgleich, *a. Jur:* **eidesgleiche Beteuerung,** solemn affirmation (*substituted for oath by reason of religious scruples*).
Eideshelfer, *m. Hist:* compurgator, oath-helper.
Eidesleister, *m.* taker, swearer, of an oath; *Hist: etc:* juror.
Eidesleistung, *f.* taking of an, of the, oath.
eidesmündig, *a. Jur:* of age to take an oath.
Eidesmündigkeit, *f. Jur:* age at which one is allowed to take an oath.
Eidesnorm, *f. Jur:* set oath formula.
Eidesnotstand, *m. Jur:* special circumstances mitigating a false statement on oath.
Eidespflicht, *f. Jur:* obligations of a witness on oath; **Verletzung der E.,** violation of the oath.
eidesstattlich, *a. Jur: etc:* in lieu of an oath; **eidesstattliche Versicherung, Erklärung,** (solemn) affirmation (in lieu of an oath); statutory declaration; **eine eidesstattliche Erklärung abgeben,** to make a statutory declaration.
eidesunfähig, *a. Jur:* incapable of taking an oath.
Eidesunfähigkeit, *f. Jur:* incapability of taking an oath.
Eidesversicherung, *f. Jur: etc:* statement on oath, sworn statement; (*in writing*) affidavit.
Eidesverwarnung, *f.* = **Eidesbelehrung.**
Eidesverweigerer, *m. Jur: etc:* person who refuses to take an oath.
Eidesverweigerung, *f. Jur: etc:* refusal to take an oath; objection to taking an oath.
Eideszuschiebung, *f.* = **Eidesdelation.**
Eidetik [ai'deːtik], *f.* **-/.** *Psy:* theory *or* study of eidetic imagery.
Eidetiker [ai'deːtikər], *m.* **-s/-.** *Psy:* (*pers.*) eidetic.
Eidetikertyp, *m. Psy:* eidetic type.
eidetisch [ai'deːtiʃ], *a. Psy:* eidetic; **eidetischer Typus,** eidetic type; **eidetische Anschauungsbilder,** eidetic images.
eidgebunden, *a.* bound by an oath, oath-bound.
Eidgenosse, *m.* **1.** confederate. **2.** Swiss citizen.
Eidgenossenschaft, *f.* **die Schweizerische E.,** the Swiss Confederation; Switzerland.
eidgenössisch, *a.* **1.** Federal. **2.** Swiss.
Eidhelfer, *m. Hist:* compurgator, oath-helper.
eidlich, *a. Jur: etc:* on, upon, under, oath; **eidliche Aussage,** statement on oath, sworn statement; **eine eidliche Erklärung abgeben,** to make a statement, a declaration, on oath; (*in writing*) to swear an affidavit; *adv.* **etwas e. aussagen,** to declare, state, sth. on oath; **e. gebunden, e. verpflichtet,** bound by an oath, oath-bound; **seine Aussage e. bekräftigen, erhärten,** to take an oath on one's evidence, to swear to one's evidence.
Eidograph [aido·'graːf], *m.* **-en/-en.** *Draw:* eidograph.
Eidolon ['aido·lon], *n.* **-(s)/-la,** idolum, phantom, image.
Eidotter, *m.* & *n.* yolk (of egg); *Biol:* vitellus.
Eidschwur, *m.* (solemn) oath.
eidvergessen, *a.* (person) who has broken his oath.
Eieralbumin, *n. Biol: Ch:* egg-albumin, ovalbumin.
Eierapfel, *m. Bot:* aubergine, egg-fruit.
Eierbecher, *m.* egg-cup.
Eierbovist, *m. Fung:* (kind of) puff-ball.
Eierbriketts, *n.pl. Com:* (coal) ovoids.
Eierfarbe, *f.* dye for colouring (Easter) eggs.
eierförmig, *a.* egg-shaped; oviform, ovoid.
Eierfrau, *f.* egg-woman.
Eierfrucht, *f. Bot:* egg-fruit, aubergine.
Eierhandgranate, *f. Mil:* egg-shaped hand-grenade.
Eierhändler, *m.* egg-dealer, egg-man.
ei(e)rig, *a.* egg-shaped; **er hat einen ei(e)rigen Kopf,** he has an egg-shaped head; **ein ei(e)riges Rad,** a wheel that is no longer fully circular.
Eierkette, *f. El.E:* chain of egg-insulators.
Eierkopf, *m. F:* egg-shaped head.
Eierkuchen, *m. Cu:* (*a*) pancake; (*b*) *occ.* omelette.
Eierkuchenmesser, *n.*, **Eierkuchenwender,** *m. Dom.Ec:* egg-slice, pancake turner.
Eierkunde, *f. Orn:* oology.
Eierlampe, *f.* ooscope.
Eierlandung, *f. Av:* three-point landing.
Eierlaufen, *n. Games:* egg-and-spoon race.
Eierlegen, *n.* (*a*) egg-laying; *Ent:* oviposition; **manche Hühnerrassen fangen früh mit dem E. an,** some breeds of fowl start laying (eggs) early; (*b*) *Mil: F:* bombing, dropping bombs.
eierlegend, *a. Nat.Hist:* egg-laying; oviparous.
Eierleger, *m.* (egg-)layer.
Eierlikör, *m.* liqueur with egg yolks, *esp.* advokaat.
Eierlöffel, *m.* egg-spoon.
Eiermann, *m.* **-(e)s/-männer,** egg-man, egg-dealer.
Eiermehl, *n. Cu:* egg-powder.
eiern, *v.i.* (*haben*) (*of wheel, etc.*) to move bumpily (*through distortion from circular shape*).
Eiernudeln, *f.pl. Cu:* egg-noodles.
Eieröl, *n. Ch:* egg-oil.
Eierpfanne, *f. Dom.Ec:* egg-pan (with separate compartments).
Eierpfannkuchen, *m. Cu:* pancake.
Eierpflanze, *f. Bot:* aubergine, egg-plant.
Eierpflaume, *f. Hort:* large egg-shaped plum.
Eierpilze, *m.pl. Fung:* oomycetes.
Eierprüfer, *m.* (*device*) ooscope.
Eierpulver, *n. Cu:* dried egg.
Eierpunsch, *m.* egg-flip, egg-nog.
Eiersack, *m.*, **Eiersäckchen,** *n. Crust:* egg-sac.
Eiersalat, *m. Cu:* egg salad.
Eiersauce, *f.* egg sauce.
Eierschachtel, *f.* egg-carrier, egg-box.
Eierschale, *f.* egg-shell.
Eierschalenporzellan, *n. Cer:* egg-shell porcelain, egg-shell china.
Eierschnee, *m. Cu:* beaten white of egg.
Eierschneeschläger, *m. Dom.Ec:* egg-whisk, egg-beater.
Eierschneider, *m. Dom.Ec:* egg-slicer, egg-cutter.
Eierschrank, *m. Dom.Ec:* egg-stand.
Eierschwamm, *m. Fung:* chanterelle, egg-mushroom.
Eierspeise, *f. Cu:* **1.** egg dish. **2.** *Austrian:* scrambled eggs.
Eierspiegel, *m.* ooscope.
Eierstab, *m. Arch:* egg and dart moulding, egg and anchor moulding, egg and tongue moulding.
Eierständer, *m. Dom.Ec:* egg-stand.
Eierstein, *m. Miner: Geol:* oolite.
Eierstich, *m. Cu:* cooked-egg garnish (for soup).
Eierstock, *m. Anat: Bot:* ovary; *Anat:* oophore.
Eierstockband, *n. Anat:* ligament of the ovary.
Eierstockentfernung, *f. Surg:* ovariotomy.
Eierstockentzündung, *f. Med:* ovaritis, oophoritis.
Eierstockgeschwulst, *f. Med:* ovarian tumour.
Eierstockgeschwür, *n. Med:* ovarian abscess.
Eierstockhormon, *n. Physiol:* ovarian hormone.
Eierstockschwangerschaft, *f. Med:* ovarian pregnancy.
Eierstockzyste, *f. Med:* ovarian cyst.
Eiertanz, *m.* egg-dance; *F:* **wir mußten einen regelrechten E. aufführen,** we had to tread very warily.
eiertragend, *a. Nat.Hist:* oviferous, ovigerous.
Eieruhr, *f.* egg-timer.
Eierverkäufer, *m.* egg-dealer, egg-man.
Eierwärmer, *m.* egg-cosy.
Eifer, *m.* **-s/.** eagerness, enthusiasm; zeal; fervour; **religiöser E.,** religious zeal, religious fervour; **von heiligem E. erfüllt,** filled with holy zeal; **glühender E.,** ardour; passion; **fanatischer E.,** fanatic zeal; **blinder E.,** blind enthusiasm; **in E. geraten,** to become heated; to be moved to enthusiasm; **E. bei etwas zeigen,** to show eagerness, enthusiasm, in doing sth.; **mit E. studieren,** to be a keen student; **mit E. an eine Arbeit gehen, sich mit E. an eine Arbeit machen,** to attack a piece of work with enthusiasm, with zeal; to put one's heart and soul into a piece of work; **sein E. erlahmte, erkaltete, schnell,** his enthusiasm, his eagerness, cooled off quickly; **mit neuem E., mit erneutem E.,** with renewed zeal, enthusiasm, eagerness.
Eiferer, *m.* **-s/-,** zealot; fanatic; **religiöser E.,** religious zealot; **Simon der E.,** Simon the Zealot.
eifern, *v.i.* (*haben*) **1. für eine Sache e.,** to agitate, campaign, for a cause, to strive in the cause of sth.; to devote oneself to a cause; **gegen etwas e.,** to agitate, campaign, against sth.; to strive against sth.; **um j-s Liebe e.,** to strive for s.o.'s love; to compete, vie, for s.o.'s love; **mit j-m um die Wette e.,** to compete, vie, with s.o. **2.** *A. & Dial:* to be jealous, envious; **mit j-m e.,** to be jealous of s.o.; *B:* **die Liebe eifert nicht,** charity envieth not.
Eifersucht, *f.* **-/.** jealousy; **aus E. begangenes Verbrechen,** crime due to jealousy.
Eifersüchtelei, *f.* (*a*) jealousy; (*b*) *usu. pl.* **Eifersüchteleien,** jealous acts; **seine ewigen Eifersüchteleien,** his constant jealousy.
eifersüchteln, *v.i.* (*haben*) to be jealous.
eifersüchtig, *a.* jealous; **auf j-n, etwas, e. sein,** to be jealous of s.o., sth.; **auf j-s Erfolg e. sein,** to be jealous of s.o.'s success; **j-n e. machen,** to make s.o. jealous; **ein eifersüchtiger Ehemann,** a jealous husband; *adv.* **e. über j-m wachen,** to watch jealously over s.o., to keep a jealous eye on s.o.; **sie wachte e. über ihre Rechte,** she guarded her rights jealously.
Eifersüchtigkeit, *f.* jealousy.
Eifersuchtsanfall, *m.* fit of jealousy; **in einem E. tötete er seine Frau,** he killed his wife in a fit of jealousy.
Eifersuchtsverbrechen, *n.* crime due to jealousy.
Eifersuchtswahn, *m.* insane jealousy.
Eiffelturm, der, the Eiffel tower.
Eiform, *f.* egg-shape.
eiförmig, *a.* egg-shaped; oviform, ovoid.
eifrig, *a.* eager, enthusiastic; zealous; keen; **ein eifriger Schüler,** an eager, a keen, pupil; **eifriger Sportler,** keen, enthusiastic, sportsman; **ein eifriger Golfspieler,** a keen golfer, a golf enthusiast; **allzu e.,** over-eager, over-enthusiastic; over-zealous; *adv.* **e. bei einer Sache sein,** (i) to be busy with sth.; to be busy doing sth.; (ii) to show keen interest in sth.; **er war e. bei der Arbeit,** he was busily working, he was busy at work: **sie war e. bemüht, alle ihre Bücher in eine große Kiste zu packen,** she was busy packing all her books into a big box; **e. lernen,** to learn eagerly, to be an eager, a keen, pupil; **die Kinder hörten e. zu,** the children listened eagerly, attentively.
Eifrigkeit, *f.* eagerness, keenness; enthusiasm; zeal.
Eifurchung, *f. Biol:* cleavage, segmentation (of egg).

Eigang, *m. Nat.Hist:* oviduct.

Eigelb, *n.* yolk (of egg); *Cu:* **man nehme zwei Eigelb,** take the yolk of two eggs.

eigen[1], *a.* **1.** *(a)* own; **mein eigener Bruder, meine eigene Schwester,** my own brother, my own sister; **eines meiner eig(e)nen Kinder,** one of my own children; **sein eigenes, sein e., Fleisch und Blut,** his own flesh and blood; **das Haus ist mein eigenes,** the house is my own; **ihr eigenes Geld,** her own money; **ein kleines Ding, aber mein eigenes,** a small thing, but my own; **ich habe es mit (meinen) eigenen Augen gesehen,** I saw it with my own eyes; **das waren seine eigenen Worte,** those were his own words, his very words; **hier kann man sein eigenes Wort nicht hören, nicht verstehen!** one cannot hear oneself speak here! one cannot hear a word anyone is saying here! **kümmere dich um deine eigenen Angelegenheiten, um deine eigenen Sachen!** mind your own business! **etwas aus eigener Tasche bezahlen,** to pay sth. from one's own pocket; **in eig(e)ner Person,** in (one's own) person; personally; **der König kam in eigner Person,** the king came in person; **einen Brief dem Empfänger zu eigenen Händen abgeben,** to deliver a letter to the addressee in person; **'(dem Empfänger) zu eigenen Händen abzugeben',** 'to be delivered to the addressee in person'; **sein eigener Herr sein,** to be one's own master; to be independent; **auf eigenen Füßen stehen,** to stand on one's own feet, to be independent; **in seinem eigenen Namen, im Namen eines anderen, handeln,** to act in one's own, s.o. else's, name; **etwas auf eigene Verantwortung tun,** to do sth. on one's own responsibility; **mit eigenem Antrieb,** self-driven, self-powered (machine, etc.), self-propelled (vehicle, etc.); **etwas aus eigenem Antrieb tun,** to do sth. of one's own accord, of one's own free will; **auf eigene Gefahr,** at one's own risk; **Betreten des Grundstückes auf eigene Gefahr,** persons entering this property do so at their own risk; **auf eigene Kosten, für, auf, eigene Rechnung,** at one's own expense, on one's own account; **in seinem eigenen Interesse handeln,** to act for, in, one's own interest; **auf seinen eigenen Vorteil bedacht sein,** to have a care for one's own interest, to look to one's own interests; **ich spreche aus eigener Erfahrung,** I speak from my own, from personal, experience; **für den eigenen Bedarf, Gebrauch,** (i) for personal use, for personal requirements; for personal consumption; (ii) *Com: etc:* for home consumption; *Journ:* **'eigener Bericht',** 'from our own correspondent'; *Com: Fin:* **eigener Wechsel,** promissory note, note of hand; *Hist:* **eigene Leute,** bond(s)men, bond(s)women; serfs, thralls; *Prov:* **eigner Herd ist Goldes wert,** (be it ever so humble) there's no place like home; *(b)* of one's, my, his, their, etc., own; **ich habe keine eigenen Mittel,** I have no resources of my own; **er hat keinen eigenen Willen,** he has no will of his own; **sie hat keine eigenen Ideen,** she has no ideas of her own; **wir haben keine eigene Wohnung,** we have no home of our own. **2.** *(invariable) (a) (substantival use)* **das Haus ist mein e.,** the house is my own; **ein kleines Ding, aber mein e.,** a small thing, but my own; **etwas sein e. nennen,** to call sth. one's own; to own sth.; **hier ist nichts, was ich mein e. nennen könnte,** there is not a thing here that I could call my own; *(b) (vbl phrases)* **etwas zu e. haben,** to own sth., to possess sth.; to have sth. for one's own; **j-m etwas zu e. geben,** to give sth. to s.o. (for his own); **sich j-m zu e. geben,** to give oneself to s.o.; to devote oneself to s.o.; **sich Gott zu e. geben,** to give oneself to God, to give, devote, one's life to God; **er gab ihm den Ring zu e.,** he gave him the ring for his (very) own; **sich** *dat.* **etwas zu e. machen,** (i) to make sth. one's own; to acquire sth., to bring sth. into one's possession; (ii) to adopt (theory, view, etc.); to agree with (s.o.'s opinion, etc.); **ich erwarte nicht, daß Sie sich meine Ansicht vorbehaltlos zu e. machen,** I do not expect you to agree with my opinion without reservation. **3.** (+*dat.*) peculiar (to s.o., sth.); characteristic (of s.o., sth.); **eine Haltung, die ihm e. ist, eine ihm eigene Haltung,** an attitude (which is) peculiar to him, characteristic of him; **mit der ihm eigenen Sorgfalt,** with the care which is characteristic of him; **Geruch, der einem Tier e. ist,** smell peculiar to an animal. **4.** peculiar, odd; strange, queer; **ihr war e. (zu Mute),** she felt strange, peculiar, odd, queer; **die Landschaft hat eine eigene Schönheit,** the landscape has a peculiar beauty (of its own); **wie e., daß er es vergessen hat!** how odd, peculiar, strange, that he should have forgotten it; **das ist sehr e.!** that's very odd, peculiar, strange, queer; *F:* **er, sie, ist ein wenig, etwas, e.,** he, she, is a little peculiar, strange, odd, queer. **5.** *F:* particular; careful; tidy; **in seiner Kleidung e. sein,** to be particular in one's dress; **sie ist sehr e. in ihren Sachen,** she is very careful, very tidy, with her things; **im Essen e. sein,** to be particular, fussy, about one's food.

Eigen[2], *n.* **-s/.** =**Eigentum** 2.

-eigen, *comb.fm. a.* belonging to . . .; property of . . ., . . . property; **bahneigen,** belonging to the railway, railway property; **staatseigen,** belonging to the state, property of the state, state property; state-owned; **fabrikseigene Tennisplätze,** factory tennis courts.

Eigenantrieb, *m. Mch: etc:* **mit E.,** self-propelling (vehicle, etc.), self-driven, self-powered (machine, etc.).

Eigenart, *f.* peculiarity, singularity; peculiar nature (of sth.); **es war eine seiner Eigenarten, eine seiner Eigenarten war, beim Lesen die Lippen zu bewegen,** a peculiarity of his, one of his peculiarities, was that he moved his lips while reading; **die Fähigkeit, seine Hautfarbe zu verändern, ist eine charakteristische E. des Chamäleons,** a characteristic peculiarity of the chameleon is its ability to change the colour of its skin.

eigenartig, *a.* peculiar, singular; odd, strange, queer; **eigenartiger Geschmack,** peculiar, strange, flavour; **eigenartiges Benehmen,** strange, peculiar, odd, behaviour; **ein eigenartiges Mädchen,** a peculiar, strange, girl; **er ist ein eigenartiger Mensch,** he is a peculiar, an odd, a queer, person; **ihr war e. zu Mute,** she felt peculiar, strange, odd, queer; **diese eigenartigen Ansichten,** these singular, peculiar, opinions; **die Landschaft hat eine eigenartige Schönheit,** the landscape has a peculiar beauty (of its own); **sie trägt die eigenartigsten Hüte,** she wears the strangest, the most peculiar, hats; **wie e., daß er es vergessen hat!** how odd, how strange, how peculiar, that he should have forgotten it! **das ist sehr e.!** that is very odd, peculiar, strange, queer; **das Eigenartige daran ist, daß er es nicht einmal wußte,** the odd, strange, thing about it is that he did not even know it.

eigenartigerweise, *adv.* oddly, strangely (enough); **e. wußte keiner etwas davon,** oddly enough, strangely enough, nobody knew anything about it; **e. traf ich ihn in London,** oddly enough, strangely enough, I met him in London.

Eigenartigkeit, *f.* peculiarity, strangeness, oddness, queerness (of conduct, style, dress, etc.).

Eigenbedarf, *m. (a)* personal requirements; *(b)* home requirements (of a country, etc.).

Eigenbericht, *m. Journ:* **'E.',** 'from our own correspondent'.

Eigenbesitz, *m. (a)* proprietorship, (personal) ownership; *(b)* proprietary possession; (personal) property.

Eigenbesitzer, *m.* proprietary possessor; proprietor; owner.

Eigenbewegung, *f. Mec: etc:* proper motion; individual motion; *Astr:* **E. eines Fixsternes,** (actual) proper motion, peculiar motion, real movement, of a star; **E. des Sonnensystems,** solar motion.

Eigenblutbehandlung, *f. Med:* autohemotherapy.

Eigenbrenner, *m.* private distiller (*not licensed to sell*).

Eigenbrödler, Eigenbrötler, *m.* **-s/-,** *(a)* solitary, lonely, person; recluse; *F:* lone wolf; *(b)* peculiar, odd, queer, person; crank.

eigenbrödlerisch, eigenbrötlerisch, *a. (a)* solitary, lonely (pers., life); *(b)* peculiar, odd, queer (pers.).

Eigendünkel, *m.* self-conceit, self-importance; presumption; bumptiousness.

Eigenerregung, *f. El:* self-excitation, self-excitement.

Eigenfinanzierung, *f. Com: Fin:* financing out of (person's *or* firm's) own capital.

Eigengeschäft, *n. Com:* business *or* transaction carried out on one's own account.

eigengesetzlich, *a.* having its own laws; acting in accordance with inherent laws of its being.

Eigengesetzlichkeit, *f.* determination by inherent laws; untrammelled individuality (of mind, etc.).

Eigengewässer, *n.pl. Pol: etc:* territorial waters.

Eigengewicht, *n.* (own) weight (of container, object, etc.); dead load, weight (of bridge, building, etc.); tare weight (of vehicle); *Nau:* light weight, unladen weight (of ship).

Eigengift, *n. Med: Physiol:* autotoxin.

Eigenhalbleiter, *m. El:* intrinsic semiconductor.

Eigenhandel, *m.Com:* trade, business, carried out on one's own account.

eigenhändig, *a. & adv. (a)* with one's own hands; personally; **etwas e. tun,** to do sth. with one's own hands; **ich habe das Auto e. geputzt,** I polished the car with my own hands, myself; **j-m etwas e. abgeben,** to deliver sth. to s.o. personally, in person; **etwas e. schreiben,** to write (letter, etc.) in one's own hand, to write (will, etc.) in holograph; **eigenhändiges Dokument, e. geschriebenes Dokument,** document in the author's own hand; holograph, holographic document; *Jur:* **eigenhändiges Testament,** will in the testator's own handwriting; holograph(ic will); **eigenhändiges Manuskript,** autograph; **eigenhändige Unterschrift,** personal signature; **etwas e. unterschreiben,** to sign sth. personally; *(b) Post:* **'(dem Empfänger) e. abzugeben',** 'to be delivered to the addressee in person'.

Eigenhändler, *m. Com:* businessman, firm, trading on his, its, own account.

Eigenheim, *n.* house (inhabited and owned by one family); **ein E. kaufen,** to buy one's own house.

Eigenheit, *f.* **1.** peculiarity, singularity; peculiar nature (of sth.). **2.** peculiarity, strangeness, oddness, queerness (of s.o.).

Eigenhilfe, *f.* self-help.

eigenhörig, *a. Hist: (of pers.)* in bondage; **ein Eigenhöriger,** a bond(s)man, a serf, a thrall.

Eigenhörigkeit, *f. Hist:* serfdom, serfage; bondage; thraldom.

Eigenimpfstoff, *m. Med:* autovaccine.

Eigenjagd, *f. Ven:* right of hunting on one's own estate.

Eigenkapital, *n. Com: Fin:* (person's *or* firm's) own capital.

Eigenkätner, *m.* cottager; *Scot:* cottar, cotter.

Eigenkirche, *f. Hist:* church with advowson held by the landlord.

Eigenkloster, *n. Hist:* monastery under the jurisdiction of a feudal landlord.

Eigenleben, *n.* (a person's, community's, etc.) own way of life; **jeder hat das Recht auf ein E.,** everybody is entitled to lead his own life.

Eigenlehner, *m.* **-s/-.** *Min:* private proprietor of a mine.

Eigenleute, *pl. Hist:* bond(s)men, bond(s)women; serfs; thralls.

Eigenliebe, *f.* **1.** self-love; egoism. **2.** *Psy:* narcissism.

Eigenlob, *n.* self-praise; *Prov:* **E. stinkt,** self-praise is no recommendation.

Eigenlöhner, *m.* **-s/-** =**Eigenlehner.**

Eigenmacht, *f.* (self-given) authority; *Jur:* **verbotene E.,** unlawful interference; trespass.

eigenmächtig, *a.* high-handed (pers., action, decision, etc.); arbitrary (decision, action); (action) taken without official authority, backing, sanction; *adv.* **etwas e. tun,** to do sth. without having (official) authority, *F:* off one's own bat; **er hat diese Verordnung e. erlassen,** he gave out this order on his own authority; **die Mieter dürfen bauliche Veränderungen nicht e. vornehmen,** the tenants must not carry out structural alterations without the owner's consent.

Eigenmächtigkeit, *f. (a)* high-handedness; **er machte sich durch seine E. unbeliebt,** he was unpopular because of his high-handedness; *(b)* action taken without official authority *or* sanction.

Eigenmann, *m.* **-(e)s/-leute.** *Hist:* bond(s)man; serf; thrall.

Eigenname, *m. Gram:* proper name, proper noun.

Eigennutz, *m.* self-interest; selfishness; **etwas aus E. tun,** to do sth. from selfishness, from self-interest; *Jur:* **strafbarer E.,** unlawful action performed for personal profit.

eigennützig, *a.* self-interested (pers.); selfish (pers., motive, etc.).

Eigennützigkeit, *f.* selfishness (of pers., motive, etc.).

Eigenpersönlichkeit, *f.* personality; **er hat eine starke E.,** he has a strong personality.

Eigenrechnung, *f. Com:* **auf E.,** (transaction, etc.) on his own account.

eigens, *adv.* especially; expressly; purposely; **e. für diesen Zweck,** for this express purpose, for this very purpose; **e. dafür gemacht,** made for that very purpose; **das Geld ist e. dafür bestimmt,** the money is for this express purpose, is specially intended for this purpose; **der Mann ist e. dazu angestellt, die Hunde zu füttern und zu pflegen,** the man's sole occupation is to feed and care for the dogs; **der Käfig wurde e. für den Löwen gebaut,** the cage was built especially for

the lion; **ich ging e. dorthin, um sie zu sehen,** I went there specially, purposely, to see them.
Eigenschaft, *f.* **-/-en.** **1.** quality (of s.o.); property (of sth.); **er hat viele gute Eigenschaften,** he has many good qualities, points; **die Eigenschaften eines Diktators,** the qualities of a dictator; **er hat die E., einem Vertrauen einzuflößen,** he has the quality of inspiring confidence; **die natürlichen Eigenschaften der Kohle,** the natural properties of coal; **Pflanzen mit heilenden Eigenschaften,** plants with healing properties; **ein Magnet besitzt die E., Eisen anzuziehen,** a magnet has the property of attracting iron. **2.** capacity; **in seiner E. als Anwalt,** in his capacity of advocate; as an advocate; **in seiner E. als Vormund handeln,** to act in one's capacity as guardian; **in meiner E. als Präsident schrieb ich ihm einen Brief,** as president, I wrote him a letter; **ich bin hier in meiner E. als Priester,** I am here in my capacity as a priest. **3.** = **Eigenhörigkeit.**
Eigenschaftswort, *n.* **-(e)s/-wörter.** *Gram:* adjective; **als E. gebraucht,** used as an adjective, used adjectivally.
eigenschaftswörtlich, *a. Gram:* adjectival; **eigenschaftswörtlicher Gebrauch,** adjectival use; *adv.* **e. gebrauchtes Wort,** word used as an adjective, word used adjectivally.
Eigenschwingung, *f. Ph:* free oscillation (of violin string, etc.).
Eigenserumbehandlung, *f.* *Med:* autoserotherapy.
Eigensetzung, *f.* *Civ.E:* *etc:* natural setting, settling (of soil, etc.).
Eigensinn, *m.* **1.** obstinacy, stubbornness, *F:* mulishness, pigheadedness; **das ist purer E.,** that is sheer, rank, obstinacy. **2.** *F:* obstinate child.
eigensinnig, *a.* obstinate, stubborn, *F:* mulish, pigheaded; wilful; headstrong; **e. sein,** to be obstinate, stubborn; to show obstinacy; **eigensinnige Weigerung,** obstinate, stubborn, refusal; *adv.* **e. auf einer Meinung bestehen,** to persist obstinately in an opinion; **er weigert sich e. zu essen,** he obstinately, stubbornly, refuses to eat.
Eigensinnigkeit, *f.* obstinacy, stubbornness, *F:* mulishness, pigheadedness.
eigenständig, *a.* independent.
Eigensucht, *f.* selfishness; egoism.
eigensüchtig, *a.* selfish; egoistic(al).
Eigensüchtigkeit, *f.* selfishness; egoism.
Eigentemperatur, *f.* = **Eigenwärme.**
eigentlich. I. *a.* actual; real; proper; **sein eigentlicher Name ist Peter,** his real name is Peter; **es ist kein eigentlicher Fehler,** it is not an actual, a real, mistake, it is not actually, really, a mistake; **der eigentliche Sinn des Wortes,** the real, true, proper, meaning of the word; **das eigentliche Problem ist die Unwissenheit der Bevölkerung,** the real problem is the ignorance of the population; **wir wohnen nicht im eigentlichen Hotel, sondern in einem Annex,** we do not live in the actual hotel, in the hotel itself, in the hotel proper, but in an annex(e); **die eigentliche Feier dauerte nur zwanzig Minuten, aber . . .,** the actual ceremony, the ceremony itself, as such, the ceremony proper, lasted only twenty minutes, but . . . .

II. **eigentlich.** **1.** *adv.* (*a*) actually, really, in actual fact; in reality; **diese Tasche gehört e. meiner Tante, sie hat sie mir nur geliehen,** in actual fact, actually, this bag belongs to my aunt, this bag really belongs to my aunt, she only lent it to me; **er hieß e. Peter,** he was really called Peter, in actual fact, in reality, he was called Peter; **e. wollten wir nach Frankreich fahren,** really, originally, we wanted to go to France; (*b*) strictly speaking; in actual fact, actually, really; **e. müßte ich jetzt schon im Büro sein,** strictly speaking, in actual fact, really, I should be at the office by now; **e. ist das eine Sache für den Direktor,** that is really a matter for the director; **e. soll er überhaupt nicht aufstehen, aber für heute hat es ihm der Doktor erlaubt,** strictly speaking, really, he should not leave his bed at all, but the doctor allowed him to get up today. **2.** *emotive particle* (*unstressed*) (*sometimes not translated*) (*a*) (*expressing curiosity*) **was ist e. mit ihm los?** what is actually the matter with him? what really ˈis the matter with him? **warum hat er e. nie geheiratet?** why did he never marry (I wonder)? **weiß er e., daß wir hier sind?** by the way, does he know that we are here? **lebt er e. noch?** is he still alive (I wonder)? **hat er e. auch ein Auto?** has he got a car too? (*b*) (*expressing impatience or annoyance*) **was willst du e. von mir?** (just) what ˈdo you want from me? *F:* what the dickens ˈdo you want from me? **was denkt er sich e.?** what ˈdoes he think he is doing? what on earth does he think he is doing? (*c*) (*summing up a situation*) **du hast e. ganz recht,** actually, really, you are quite right; **es ist e. doch ganz schön, daß er gekommen ist,** it is (really) quite nice after all that he came; **es ist e. nicht so schlimm,** really it's not as bad as all that.
Eigentöne, *m.pl.* *Ph:* *etc:* individual notes *or* tones.
Eigentor, *n. Fb:* *etc:* own goal.
Eigentum, *n.* **-(e)s/⸗er.** **1.** ownership; proprietorship; property; **das E. an etwas haben,** to own sth., to have the ownership of sth.; **das E. an etwas erwerben,** to acquire the ownership of sth.; *Jur:* **E. ohne Nutznießung,** bare ownership, ownership without usufruct; *Com:* **gewerbliches E.,** proprietary right. **2.** property; possession(s); **privates, öffentliches, E.,** private, public, property; **persönliches E.,** personal property; personal belongings, possessions, effects; **das Haus ist mein E.,** the house is my own, is my property; **dieser Sessel ist mein persönliches E.,** this armchair is my personal property, belongs to me, is my own; **feindliches E.,** enemy property; **fremdes E.,** other people's property; **sich an fremdem E. vergreifen,** to steal; **mit fremdem E. großzügig umgehen,** to be free, generous, with other people's property; **geistiges E.,** literary property; (author's, composer's, artist's) work protected by copyright; *see also* **beweglich** 2 (*b*).
Eigentümer, *m.* **-s/-,** owner; proprietor; **der rechtmäßige E.,** the rightful owner; **alleiniger E.,** sole owner; **E. eines Hotels,** proprietor of a hotel; **die Eigentümer eines Schiffes,** the owners of a ship; **der E. dieses Grundstückes,** the owner of this piece of land.
Eigentümergrundschuld, *f.* *Jur:* owner's land charge.
Eigentümerhypothek, *f.* owner's mortgage.
Eigentümerin, *f.* **-/-innen,** owner, proprietress.
Eigentümerkapital, *n.* private capital of the owner (of firm, farm, etc.).
Eigentümerrecht, *n.* *Jur:* *etc:* owner's right *or* privilege.
Eigentümerschaft, *f.* ownership, proprietorship.
eigentümlich, *a.* **1.** (+*dat.*) peculiar (to s.o., sth.), characteristic (of s.o., sth.); **eine Haltung, die ihm e. ist, eine ihm eigentümliche Haltung,** an attitude (which is) peculiar to him, characteristic of him; **mit der ihm eigentümlichen Sorgfalt,** with the care which is characteristic of him; **Geruch, der einem Tier e. ist,** smell peculiar to an animal. **2.** peculiar, singular; odd, strange, queer; **eigentümlicher Geschmack,** peculiar, odd, flavour; **ihr war e. zu Mute,** she felt peculiar, strange, odd, queer; **die Landschaft hat eine eigentümliche Schönheit,** the landscape has a peculiar beauty; **sie trägt die eigentümlichsten Hüte,** she wears the strangest, the most peculiar, hats; **das Eigentümliche daran ist, daß er es nicht einmal wußte,** the odd, strange, thing about it is that he did not even know it.
eigentümlicherweise, *adv.* oddly, strangely (enough); **e. wußte keiner etwas davon,** oddly enough, strangely enough, nobody knew anything about it.
Eigentümlichkeit, *f.* **1.** peculiarity, characteristic (of s.o., sth.). **2.** peculiarity, strangeness, oddness, queerness (of s.o., sth.).
Eigentumsanspruch, *m. Jur:* (*a*) claim of ownership; (*b*) title to property.
Eigentumsaufgabe, *f.* giving up, relinquishing, of ownership.
Eigentumsdelikte, *n.pl.* *Jur:* offences against property.
Eigentumserwerb, *m.* acquisition of (i) ownership, (ii) property.
Eigentumsfreiheitsklage, *f.* *Jur:* action for trespass.
Eigentumsgrundschuld, *f.* *Jur:* owner's land charges.
Eigentumsklage, *f. Jur:* action claiming property for its owner.
Eigentumsmeere, *n.pl. Pol:* *etc:* territorial waters.
Eigentumsrecht, *n.* *Jur:* (right of) ownership; proprietary right; title; **das E. an etwas erwerben,** to acquire the ownership of sth.; **das E. an seinem Grundstück behalten,** to retain the property in, the ownership of, one's estate; *Com:* **gewerbliches E.,** proprietary right.
Eigentumsstörung, *f.* *Jur:* private nuisance; trespass.
Eigentumsstörungsklage, *f.* *Jur:* action for trespass.
Eigentumstitel, *m. Jur:* title to property.
Eigentumsübergang, *m.* passing of (i) ownership, (ii) property (to s.o. else).
Eigentumsübertragung, *f.* transfer of (i) ownership, (ii) property.
Eigentumsurkunde, *f. Jur:* title-deed.
Eigentumsverhältnisse, *n.pl. Jur:* *etc:* question of ownership; **die E. klären,** to settle the question of ownership.
Eigentumsverletzung, *f. Jur:* damaging of s.o.'s property; trespass.
Eigentumsvermutung, *f.* *Jur:* presumption of ownership.
Eigentumsverzicht, *m.* giving up, relinquishing, of ownership; renunciation of property.
Eigentumsvorbehalt, *m. Com:* *etc:* reservation of proprietary rights.
Eigentumswohnung, *f. approx.* = freehold flat.
Eigenvakzin, *n. Med:* autovaccine.
Eigenverbrauch, *m. El.E:* current consumption by the instrument.
Eigenverständigung, *f. Av:* *etc:* intercommunication system, *F:* intercom.
eigenwarm, *a. Nat.Hist:* warm-blooded (animal).
Eigenwärme, *f. Nat.Hist:* body temperature (of warm-blooded animal); *Geol:* interior heat (of earth).
Eigenwechsel, *m.* *Com:* *Fin:* promissory note, note of hand.
Eigenwert, *m.* **1.** actual value (of sth.); intrinsic value (of sth.); value (of sth.) in itself; (s.o.'s) value as a person(ality). **2.** *Ph:* eigen value.
Eigenwille, *m.* self-will.
eigenwillig, *a.* (pers.) of independent mind; highly individual (style, etc.); **ein eigenwilliger Junge,** a boy with a will of his own, who knows what he wants, who goes his own way; **eigenwillige Behandlung eines Themas,** highly individual treatment of a subject.
Eigenwilligkeit, *f.* independence of mind; individuality (of style, etc.).
eignen. I. *v.* **1.** *v.i.* (*haben*) (*a*) *A:* to belong to (s.o., sth.); (*b*) (*of behaviour, attitude of mind, etc.*) to be characteristic of, to be peculiar to (s.o.). **2. sich eignen, geeignet sein,** to be suited, suitable (to, for, s.o., sth.); (*a*) **sich für etwas, für einen Zweck, e., für etwas, für einen Zweck, geeignet sein,** to be suited, suitable, for sth., for a purpose; **das eignet sich vortrefflich für meine Zwecke, das ist vortrefflich für meine Zwecke geeignet,** that is most suitable for my purposes, that suits my purposes perfectly; **dieses Geschenk eignet sich kaum für ein Kind, ist kaum für ein Kind geeignet,** this present is hardly suitable for a child; **ist es ein Buch, das sich für ein junges Mädchen eignet, eignen würde?** is it a book suitable for a young girl? **das Fahrzeug eignet sich nicht für Bergfahrten, ist nicht für Bergfahrten geeignet,** the vehicle is not suited to, not suitable for, mountain touring; **sich für einen Beruf e., für einen Beruf geeignet sein,** to be suited for a profession; **er eignet sich schlecht, nicht gut, für diese Rollen, er ist für diese Rollen schlecht, nicht gut, geeignet,** he is not suited, is ill suited, for these parts; (*b*) **sich als etwas, zu etwas, e., zu etwas, als etwas, geeignet sein,** to be suited, suitable, *F:* cut out, for sth., to be sth.; **er eignet sich nicht zum Pastor, er ist nicht zum Pastor geeignet,** he is not suited for, to be, a parson, *F:* he is not cut out for a parson; **das Bild würde sich gut als Geschenk e., das Bild wäre als Geschenk geeignet,** the picture would be suitable as a present, the picture would make a good present; **dieses Gebäude eignet sich nicht als Hotel. zum Hotel, dieses Gebäude ist nicht geeignet als Hotel,** this building is not suitable for a hotel; **zur Photographie geeignet,** photogenic.

II. *vbl s.* **Eignung,** *f.* suitability; **E. eines Bewerbers für eine Stelle,** suitability of a candidate for, to, a post; **ich bezweifle seine E. zum Pastor,** I doubt whether he would be suited for, to be, a parson; **bei E. für diesen Zweck,** if suitable for this purpose.
Eigner, *m.* **-s/-,** owner, proprietor.
Eignungsprüfung, *f. Ind:* *etc:* aptitude test.
Eihandgranate, *f.* = **Eierhandgranate.**
Eihaut, *f.* egg-membrane.
Eihülle, *f.* egg-membrane; chorion.
eiig, *a. F:* eggy, smeared with egg.
Eiisolator, *m. El.E:* egg-insulator.
eijeh, *int.* oh dear! **e., das ist aber dumm!** oh dear, that ˈis annoying.
Eikapsel, *f. Ich:* egg-case (of shark, skate, etc.); sea-purse (of skate).
Eikern, *m. Biol:* egg-nucleus, female pronucleus; ovocentre.

Eiklar, *n. Cu: Austrian:* white of egg.
Eiland, *n.* -(e)s/-e. *Poet:* island, *Poet:* isle.
Eiländer, *m.* -s/-. *Poet:* islander.
eilbedürftig, *a. Jur:* urgent.
Eilbestellung, *f. Post:* express delivery, *U.S:* special delivery.
Eilbote, *m.* (*a*) *Post:* express messenger, *U.S:* special delivery messenger; 'durch Eilboten', 'by express messenger', 'express', *U.S:* 'by special delivery'; (*b*) messenger boy.
Eilbotenlauf, *m. Sp: A:* relay race.
Eilbotschaft, *f. Post: etc:* express letter, telegram, etc.
Eilbrief, *m. Post:* express letter, *U.S:* special delivery letter.
Eile, *f.* -/. haste, hurry; **E. haben, in E. sein,** to be in a hurry, to be in haste; **keine E. haben,** to be in no hurry; **die Sache hat keine E., es hat keine E. damit,** there is no (special) hurry (about it); **sie ist immer in E.,** she is always in a hurry; **in meiner E. vergaß ich es,** in my hurry I forgot it; **in größter, höchster, E.,** in great haste, in a great, *F:* tearing, hurry; hastily, hurriedly; **in größter E. packte sie ihre Sachen,** hastily, hurriedly, in great haste, she packed her belongings; **in überstürzter E.,** in breathless haste; **in aller E. schreiben,** to write in a hurry; **ich erhielt einen Zettel, der in aller E. geschrieben worden war, ich erhielt einen in aller E. geschriebenen Zettel,** I received a note which had been written in a hurry, in haste, I received a hasty note; (*at end of letter*) 'in E.', 'in haste'.
Eilein, *n.* -s/-, (*dim. of Ei*) little egg.
Eileiter, *m. Nat.Hist:* oviduct; (*in mammals*) Fallopian tube; salpinx.
Eileiterentzündung, *f. Med:* salpingitis.
Eileiterschwangerschaft, *f. Med:* tubal pregnancy.
eilen, *v.* **1.** *v.tr. A:* to hurry, hasten (s.o.). **2.** *v.i.* (*sein*) (*a*) to hurry, hasten; to move quickly; **sie eilte nach Hause,** she hurried, hastened, home; she went home as quickly as possible; **j-m zu Hilfe e.,** to hurry, hasten, to s.o.'s help, to s.o.'s assistance; **er eilte zur Tür, aber sie war verschlossen,** he rushed, dashed, to the door but it was locked; **er ging eilenden Schrittes, mit eilenden Schritten, die Straße entlang,** he walked quickly, with quick, hurrying, steps, along the road; *Prov:* **eile mit Weile,** more haste less speed; slow and steady wins the race; *F:* easy does it; (*b*) to be urgent, pressing; **die Sache eilt, es eilt mit der Sache,** the matter is urgent, pressing; **es eilt nicht damit,** there is no (special) hurry about it; it is not urgent; **es eilt mir nicht damit,** I am not in a hurry for it; **es eilt ihm gar nicht mit dem Abreisen,** he is in no hurry to leave; *Post: etc:* 'eilt', 'urgent'. **3. sich eilen,** to hasten, make haste, to hurry (up); to be quick; **eil(e) dich!** hurry up! look sharp! *F:* buck up! **ihr müßt euch e., wenn ihr zur Zeit ankommen wollt,** you will have to hurry (up) if you want to arrive in time; **sich mit etwas e.,** to hurry over sth.; **etwas tun, ohne sich zu e.,** not to hurry over sth.; to do sth. without haste, in a leisurely fashion; **sich e., etwas zu tun,** to hasten, make haste, to do sth.; to lose no time in doing sth.; **sie eilte sich, nach Hause zu kommen,** she hurried, hastened, home.
eilends, *adv.* hurriedly, hastily; quickly; **sie ging e. nach Hause,** she hurried, hastened, home; she went home quickly; **e. hinausgehen,** to go out in a hurry; **sich e. anziehen,** to dress hurriedly, quickly, in a hurry; to hurry into one's clothes.
eilf, *num.a. A:* eleven.
Eilfracht, *f.*=Eilgut.
Eilfrachtbrief, *m. Rail: Com:* special consignment note for goods sent by fast goods, express freight, service.
Eilgut, *n. Rail:* goods sent by fast goods, express freight, service; **etwas per E. schicken,** to send sth. by fast goods, express freight, service.
Eilgüterzug, *m. Rail:* fast goods, express freight, train.
eilig. **1.** *a.* (*a*) hurried; quick; **ein paar eilige Worte,** a few hurried words, a few words in haste; **nach einer eiligen Besichtigung des Schlosses,** after a quick, short, hurried, look round the castle; **e. sein,** to be in a hurry, to be hurried; (*b*) urgent, pressing (matter, etc.); **ein eiliger Brief,** an urgent letter; **es ist ein eiliger Fall, der Fall ist e.,** the case is urgent, pressing; **ein sehr eiliger Fall,** a very urgent case; an emergency; **die Sache, es, ist nicht e.,** there is no (special) hurry (about it); **ich muß zuallererst noch eine sehr eilige Sache, etwas sehr Eiliges,**

erledigen, first of all, I must attend to a very urgent, a very important, matter; **die eiligsten Sachen zuerst erledigen,** to attend to the most pressing, most urgent, things first; **trotz seiner Warnung hatte sie nichts Eiligeres zu tun, als (dennoch) dorthin zu gehen,** in spite of his warning, the very first thing she did was to go there after all. **2.** *adv.* hurriedly, hastily; quickly; **sie ging e., eiligst, nach Hause,** she hurried, hastened, home; she went home quickly; **sich e. anziehen,** to dress hurriedly, quickly, in a hurry; to hurry into one's clothes; **eiligst packte sie ihre Sachen,** hurriedly, hastily, in great haste, she packed her belongings; **es e. haben,** to be in a hurry, to be in haste; **sie hat es immer sehr e.,** she is always in a hurry; **warum so e.? hast du's aber e.!** what's the hurry? **er hatte es gar nicht e. abzureisen, er hatte es gar nicht e. mit dem Abreisen,** he was in no hurry to leave; **es zu e. haben mit dem Geldverdienen,** to be in too great a hurry to make money.
Eiligkeit, *f.* urgency (of letter, matter, etc.).
Eilmarsch, *m. Mil:* forced march; **in Eilmärschen vorrücken,** to advance by forced marches.
Eilpost, *f. Post:* express delivery, *U.S:* special delivery; **durch E.,** by express messenger, *U.S:* by special delivery.
Eilschrift, *f.* high-speed shorthand.
Eilschritt, *m.* **im E. gehen,** to walk quickly, fast.
Eilsendung, *f. Post: etc:* letter, parcel, etc., sent by express messenger.
Eiltempo, *n. F:* **im E.,** quickly, fast; hurriedly; at high speed.
Eilüberweisung, *f. Bank:* direct transfer (of money).
Eilung, *f.* -/-en. *Meteor:* gust of wind immediately before a thunderstorm.
Eilzug, *m. Rail:* semi-fast train; limited stop train.
Eilzugtempo, *n. F:* **im E.,** at high speed, at express speed.
Eilzugzuschlag, *m. Rail:* supplement, extra fare, excess fare (payable on semi-fast trains).
Eilzuschrift, *f.* immediate reply (to advertisement, etc.).
Eilzustellung, *f. Post:* express delivery, *U.S:* special delivery.
Eilzustellvermerk, *m. Post:* 'express' label, stamp, *or* marking (on letter, packet).
Eimembran, *f.* egg-membrane.
Eimer, *m.* -s/-. **1.** (*a*) bucket; pail; (milking-)pail; (slop-)pail; (coal-)scuttle; (ash-, rubbish-)bin; large can (for honey, jam, etc.); *Ecc:* bucket; **einen E. Wasser bringen,** to bring a bucket of water, a bucketful, a pailful, of water; *F:* **es regnet, gießt, wie mit Eimern,** it is pouring (with rain); *F:* it is raining buckets, it is raining cats and dogs; **in den E. gucken, sehen,** to be left out in the cold; **schön im E. sein,** to be in the cart, in a fix, in the soup; **wenn er nicht kommt, ist unser ganzer Plan im E.,** if he doesn't come, our whole plan will be wrecked, *F:* will be down the drain, up the spout; (*b*) *Tchn:* bucket (of dredger, conveyor, etc.); (*c*) *Nau: F:* ship, *F:* tub. **2.** *A.Meas:* approx.=14 gallons.
Eimerbagger, *m.*=Eimerkettenbagger.
Eimerchen, *n.* -s/-, (*dim. of Eimer*) small bucket, pail (*esp. for children*); large tin (for honey, jam, etc.) (*with a capacity of* 5–10 *lbs*); **E. und Schaufel,** bucket and spade.
eimerförmig, *a.* bucket-shaped (bag, etc.).
Eimerkette, *f.* (*a*) *Tchn:* chain of buckets, bucket-chain (of dredger, etc.); (*b*) (*of firemen, etc.*) eine **E. bilden,** to form a bucket-chain.
Eimerkettenbagger, *m.* (*a*) *Hyd.E:* bucket(-ladder)-dredger; (*b*) *Civ.E:* bucket-conveyor, -elevator; paternoster(-elevator).
Eimerkettenförderer, *m.*=Eimerkettenbagger.
Eimerleiter, *f.* bucket-ladder (of dredger, etc.).
Eimerspritze, *f.* bucket-pump.
eimerweise, *adv.* in buckets, in bucketfuls; **wir haben e. Wasser aus dem Keller geschöpft,** we baled out bucketfuls of water from the cellar.
Eimerwerk, *n. Civ.E:* bucket-conveyor, -elevator; paternoster(-elevator).
ein[1], **eine, ein** (*acc.* **einen, eine, ein,** *gen.* **eines, einer, eines,** *dat.* **einem, einer, einem,** *pl.* **die einen,** *q.v. under* III. 1 (*c*)). **I.** **1.** *num.a.* one; (*a*) **Familien mit einem Kind,** families with one child; **seine eine Sorge,** his one care; **nicht ein Mann rührte sich,** not a single man moved, not one man moved; **nur ein Paar Schuhe,** nur ein **einziges Paar Schuhe,** only one (single) pair of shoes; **ein oder zwei Leute sahen es,** one or two people saw it; **das Kind ist ein Jahr alt,** the child is a year, one year, old; **Kinder von einem bis zu zwölf Jahren, von ein bis zwölf Jahren,** children aged from one to twelve; **in ein und einem halben**

Jahr, in einem und einem halben Jahr, (i) within a year and a half, (ii) in a year and a half's time; **eine Mark sechzig (Pfennig),** one mark and sixty pfennigs; **ein und ein halbes Pfund,** a pound and a half, one pound and a half, one and a half pounds; **ein Uhr,** one o'clock; **ungefähr um ein Uhr,** at about one (o'clock); **die Reise dauert ein bis zwei Stunden,** the journey takes one to two hours; **er zögerte nicht einen Augenblick,** he did not hesitate one (single) moment, he did not think twice; **in einem Stück gegossene Zylinder,** cylinders cast in one (piece); **auf einen Zug,** at one draught; *F:* at one go; (**alle) wie ein Mann,** as one man; **sie rückten vor wie ein Mann,** they advanced as one man; **sie sind ein Herz und eine Seele,** they are the best of friends; they are hand in glove; (*b*) one; the same; **sie waren alle auf einem Platz zusammengekommen,** they had all gathered in one spot; **alle in einer Richtung,** all in one direction; **ich beschränke mich nicht auf Bücher aus einem Verlag allein,** I do not limit myself to the books issued by any one publishing firm; **einer Meinung sein,** to be of one, of the same, opinion; **sie sind in einer Klasse,** they are in one class, in the same class; **sie wohnen alle in einem Haus, in ein und demselben Haus,** they all live in the same house; **ein(e) und dieselbe Frau,** one and the same woman; **wir hatten ein und denselben Gedanken,** one and the same thought came into our minds; *F:* **in einer Tour,** continuously, without a break; *F:* in one go; **er redete in einer Tour,** he talked continuously, without ceasing, without a break; (*c*) **er trank ein Glas nach dem anderen,** he drank, had, one glass after the other; **ein Jahr ums andere, ein Jahr nach dem anderen,** one year after the other, every year; **ein Tag geht um den anderen hin, nach dem anderen hin,** one day follows the other; **einen um den anderen, einen über den anderen, Tag,** every other day, every second day; **er kommt einen um den anderen Tag,** he comes one day out of two, every other day; *see also* **allemal** 1. **2.** *num.pron.* one; (*a*) **einer hielt Wache, während alle anderen schliefen,** one kept watch while all the others slept; **ich bemerkte zwei Männer, einer hinkte,** I noticed two men; one (of them) walked with a limp; **einer meiner Freunde,** one of my friends; **nur einer kann uns jetzt helfen,** only one (person) can help us now; **einer allein kann es nicht tun,** no one man can do it, one man alone, one single man, cannot do it; **nicht einer rührte sich,** not a single man moved, not one man moved; **einer für alle, alle für einen,** one for all and all for one; **einer zu viel,** one too many; **einer nach dem anderen,** one after the other; one by one; **eins nach dem anderen,** one thing after the other; **einer, eine, eins, von ihnen,** one of them; **von jeder Sorte einer, eine, eins,** one of each (kind); **eins von zwei Dingen,** one of two things; **noch eins,** one other thing; **ich möchte eins von diesen Kätzchen,** I would like one of these kittens; **es ist nur einer, eine, eins, übrig,** there is only one left; **zwei Bände in einem,** two volumes in one; **eins gefällt mir an ihr,** one thing I like about her; **er war ihr ein und alles,** he was all in all to her, everything to her; (*b*) **in einem,** *Austrian Dial:* unter einem, at the same time; **sie lachte und weinte in einem,** she was laughing and crying at the same time; **das könnte ich alles in einem machen,** I could do all that at the same time; **das geht in einem hin,** that's no extra trouble; **in einem fort, weg,** continuously, without a break; **er redete in einem fort,** he talked continuously, without ceasing, without a break.

II. **ein, eine, ein,** *indef. art.* **1.** (*before a consonant*) a, (*before a vowel sound*) an; (*a*) **eine Frau und Mutter,** a wife and mother; **ein Mann und eine Frau,** a man and (a) woman; **ein Tag, eine Woche, ein Jahr,** a day, a week, a year; **ein geschichtlicher Roman,** a, an, historical novel; **ein Hotel,** a, an, hotel; **eine Stunde,** an hour; **eine Einheit,** a unit; **einen großen Mund haben,** to have a big mouth; **er hat ein neues Auto,** he has a new car; **wir fanden die Spur eines Elefanten,** we found the trail of an elephant; **sie ist die Tochter einer berühmten Schauspielerin,** she is the daughter of a famous actress; **ich gab das Geld einem Bettler, einer Bettlerin,** I gave the money to a beggar, to a beggar-woman; **er ist ein einziges Kind,** he is an only child; **ich traf nicht einen einzigen Menschen,** I did not meet a single person; **nicht ein einziges Wort sagen,** not to say a single word; **ein gewisser Herr X,** a certain Mr X; **in einem gewissen Sinne hat er**

recht, in a certain sense, in a way, he is right; (*b*) **so ein, solch ein,** such a; **so ein, solch ein, guter Mann,** such a good man; **so eine schwere Aufgabe,** such a hard task; **er war so ein, solch ein, gehorsamer Junge,** he was such an obedient boy; **an solch einem, so einem, Tage, an einem solchen Tage,** on such a day; **bei so einer, solch einer, Gelegenheit, bei einer solchen Gelegenheit,** on such an occasion; (*c*) **was für ein, eine, ein . . . ,** (i) what sort of, kind of, (a) . . . ? (ii) (*exclamatory*) what a . . . ! **was für ein Mann ist er?** what sort of, kind of, a man is he? **was für eine Blume ist das?** what kind of flower is that? **was für ein Auto hast du?** what make of car have you? **was für einen Ball möchtest du?** what sort of (a) ball do you want? **was für ein Lärm!** what a noise! **was für ein schönes Hotel!** what a nice hotel! **was für eine Menge Leute!** what a lot of people! **was für eine dumme Frage!** what a stupid question! **was für eine Antwort!** what an answer! *see also* **jeder** 1, 2, **jeglicher** 1, 2. **2.** (*generalizing*) (*a*) **einen Tiger kann man sehr schwer zähmen,** it is very difficult to tame a tiger; **eine Katze kann auch im Dunkeln sehen,** a cat can see in the dark, cats can see in the dark; **eine Pflanze hat weder Vernunft noch Instinkt,** plants have neither reason nor instinct; **ein Kaktus braucht viel Sonne und wenig Wasser,** a cactus needs a lot of sun and little water; (*b*) **nur ein Millionär kann sich so etwas leisten,** only a millionaire can afford anything like that; **von einem Lehrer hätte ich das nicht erwartet,** I would not have expected that from a teacher; **einem Offizier sollte so etwas nicht passieren,** a thing like that should not happen to an officer; **ein Metzger ist ihnen nicht gut genug für ihre Tochter,** (they think) a butcher is not good enough for their daughter; **ein Armer ist oft im Nachteil,** a poor man is often at a disadvantage; (*c*) **wollen wir einen Kaffee trinken?** shall we have some coffee, a cup of coffee? what about a coffee? **in der Gegend bekommt man einen ausgezeichneten Wein,** you can get an excellent wine, some first-rate wine, in that district; **sie kocht einen vorzüglichen Kaffee,** she makes excellent coffee; (*d*) (*with names of famous persons*) **ein Adonis ist er gerade nicht,** he is not exactly an Adonis, *F:* he's no oil-painting; **er hält sich für einen Shakespeare,** he fancies himself a sort of Shakespeare; **ein vollständiger Hölderlin,** a complete set of Hölderlin's works, a complete Hölderlin; **eine Garbo kann man nicht jeden Tag sehen,** it is not every day that one can see a Garbo; **es brauchte einen Dickens, um das soziale Gewissen Englands im 19. Jahrhundert aufzurütteln,** it took a Dickens to awaken the social conscience of England in the 19th century. **3.** (*intensive*) (*usu. not translated*) (*a*) **das war eine Hitze!** the heat was terrific! it was boiling hot! **das war ein Spaß!** it was such fun! what fun it was! **wir hatten einen Hunger, einen Durst!** we were terribly hungry, terribly thirsty; **ich hatte vielleicht eine Angst!** I was terribly frightened, scared; **hast du eine Ahnung!** that's what you think! **eine Frechheit ohnegleichen!** what (a) confounded cheek! **er hatte einen Schwips, — er konnte kaum gehen!** he was so tight he could hardly walk! **das war ein Wein! das war ein Weinchen!** that was a lovely wine! what a wine that was! *F:* that 'was a wine, that was! (*b*) **dann gab's ein Singen und Tanzen und Lachen,** then they sang and danced and laughed; **sowie die Lehrerin das Zimmer verlassen hatte, begann ein aufgeregtes Flüstern,** as soon as the teacher had left the room an excited whispering started; **es wäre mir ein Leichtes,** it would be easy for me.

III. **einer, eine, ein(e)s. 1.** *indef.pron.* one; (*a*) **ich habe keinen Bleistift, hast du einen?** I haven't a pencil, have you one? **sein Vater war ein Matrose, und er möchte auch einer werden,** his father was a sailor and he wants to be one too; **er schickte mir ein Paket und meinem Bruder auch eins,** he sent me a parcel and one to my brother too; **diese Tasche ist hübsch, so eine möchte ich auch haben,** this bag is nice, I want one like it; **was für ein seltsamer Hund, so einen habe ich noch nie gesehen,** what a peculiar dog—I have never seen one like that; **der Plan ist nicht einer von denen, die . . . ,** the plan is not one of those that . . . ; **Sie finden es sicher in einem der anderen Läden in der Stadt,** you are sure to find it in one of the other shops in the town; (*b*) **ich habe noch nie so einen wie ihn gesehen,** I never saw such a one as him; **er ist auch so einer,** he is one of that kind too; he's like that too; he's another of them, *F:* he's just another; **manch einer,** many a man, many a one; **ich will die Meinung von einem, der besser urteilen kann,** I want the opinion of someone better able to judge; **diese Undankbarkeit von einem, den er so gut kannte,** this ingratitude on the part of one he knew so well; **so einer wie ihr würde ich nie Geld leihen,** I would never lend money to anyone like her; **du bist mir, vielleicht, aber, einer, eine!** you're a fine one! **einer, der mir leid tut, eine, die mir leid tut, ist . . . ,** one whom I pity is . . . ; **ich bin nicht einer, der . . . ,** I am not (the) one to . . . ; **sie war nicht eine, die ihren Ärger aufspeicherte,** she was not one, not the sort of person, to nurse a grievance; *F:* **er spielt Tennis wie nur einer,** he is a wizard tennis player; (*c*) **der eine sagt dies, der andere das,** (the) one says this, the other that; **die einen sagen dies, die anderen das,** some say this, the others (say) that; **wenn man die Dummheit des einen mit der Intelligenz des anderen vergleicht,** when you contrast the stupidity of the one with the intelligence of the other; **weder der, die, das, eine noch der, die, das, andere,** neither (the) one nor the other; neither; **ich kenne weder den einen noch den anderen,** I don't know either of them; **man kann nicht das eine, nicht eins, ohne das andere haben,** you can't have one (thing) without the other; **der, die, das, eine oder der, die, das, andere,** one or the other; either (of the two); **der eine oder andere,** one or two; a few; **der eine oder andere der Gefangenen versuchte zu entfliehen,** one or two of the prisoners, some, certain, of the prisoners, tried to escape; **auf der einen Seite . . . auf der anderen Seite,** on the one hand . . . on the other hand; (*d*) **wenn einer Geduld hat, ist es ganz einfach,** if one has the patience, if you have the patience, it is quite easy; **wenn einer genug Geld hat, kann er das tun,** if one has enough money one can do it, if you have enough money you can do it; **das kann einen ja um den Verstand bringen! das kann einen ja verrückt machen!** that's enough to drive one, drive you, mad! **diese Übersicht versetzt einen in die Lage, allen Argumenten zu begegnen,** this synopsis puts one in a position to answer any arguments; **so etwas muß einem ja gefallen,** a thing like that cannot fail to please one; **das bringt einem nur Sorgen,** that only brings one, brings you, worry; **wie soll einer das anstellen?** how is one supposed to manage that? (*e*) (*in certain phrases, elliptical*) **laßt uns eins** (= **ein Lied**) **singen,** let us sing a song; **einen, eins, trinken gehen, einen** (= **einen Krug**) **heben gehen,** to go for a drink, to go and have one; **wir wollen noch eins, einen, trinken,** let's have another drink; *F:* **einen über den Durst trinken,** to have one too many, one over the eight; *F:* **j-m eins auf die Nase geben,** to give s.o. one on the nose; *F:* **j-m eine** (= **eine Ohrfeige**) **'runterhauen,** to give s.o. a box on the ear; *F:* **sich eins ins Fäustchen lachen,** to laugh up one's sleeve; *F:* **einen** (= **einen Furz**) **streichen lassen, fahren lassen,** to pass wind, *P:* to fart, do a fart; (*f*) **es ist mir alles eins,** it is all the same, all one, to me; I don't care either way; I don't mind. **2.** *indef.a.* (*used to form adverbial element of time*) (*a*) (*gen.*) **eines Tages, Morgens, Abends,** (i) (*in past*) one day, one morning, one evening, (ii) (*in future*) one day, morning, evening, some day, morning, evening; one of these (fine) days, mornings, evenings; **eines Tages wird er ein reicher Mann sein,** one day, some day, he will be a rich man; **eines Abends traf ich ihn im Park,** one evening I met him in the park; **eines Sonntags, als . . . ,** one Sunday, when . . . ; (*b*) (*acc.*) (*past & future*) **einen Winter, einen Frühling,** one winter, one spring; **einen Sommer fuhr ich mit ihr nach Italien,** one summer I went to Italy with her; **einen Nachmittag gingen wir nach X,** one afternoon we went to X; **komm und besuche mich einen Montag, einen Abend,** come and see me one Monday, one evening, some Monday, some evening; **ein Wochenende wird er uns besuchen,** one weekend he is going to visit us.

ein[2], *adv.* **ein und aus,** in and out; **sie gehen ein und aus,** they go in and out; **bei j-m ein und aus gehen,** to be a regular caller, visitor, at s.o.'s house; **nicht ein noch aus wissen,** not to know what to do; **er weiß nicht ein noch aus, weder ein noch aus, weder aus noch ein,** he doesn't know which way to turn, he has no idea what to do.

ein-[1], **Ein-,** *comb.fm.* **1.** (*forming numerals*) (*a*) -one; **einundfünfzig,** fifty-one, *A:* one and fifty; **einhundert,** one hundred; **eintausendundeins,** one thousand and one, a thousand and one; **einundzwanzig Äpfel,** twenty-one apples, *A:* one and twenty apples; (*b*) **der einunddreißigste,** the thirty-first; **am einundzwanzigsten April,** on the twenty-first of April. **2.** (*forming adjs and nouns*) (*a*) one-; **einarmig,** one-armed; **einäugig,** one-eyed; **einstöckig,** one-storied; **Einbahnstraße** *f,* one-way street; (*b*) single-; **eindrähtig,** single-wire; **einscheibig,** single-pulley (block); **eingängig,** single-threaded (screw); **Einsitzer** *m, Aut: Av:* single-seater; (*c*) mono-; **einsilbig,** monosyllabic; **einphasig,** monophase (current); **Eintönigkeit** *f,* monotony; *Ch:* **einwertig,** monovalent; (*d*) uni-; **einblumig,** uniflorous; **einschalig,** univalve; **eingeschlechtig,** unisexual; **Einklang** *m,* unison.

ein-[2], *pref.* I. *vbl pref. sep.* (*cp. Note to* **ab-**) **1.** (*denoting motion towards or into sth.*) (*Note: in older German the pref.* **ein-** *is frequently used in the meanings of this section where* **hinein-** *or* **herein-** *are now more usual*) (*a*) (*motion inwards from outside*) (i) (*forming tr. vbs*) **etwas eintauchen,** to dip sth. in; **etwas in etwas** *acc.* **eintauchen,** to dip sth. into sth.; **etwas in etwas** *acc.* **einblasen,** to blow sth. into sth.; **etwas einsenden, einschicken,** to send in (application, etc.); **eine Nadel in etwas** *acc.* **einführen,** to insert a needle into sth.; **sich in etwas** *acc.* **einzwängen,** to squeeze (oneself) into sth.; (ii) (*forming intr. vbs*) **eintreten,** to enter, to come in; **in ein Zimmer, usw., eintreten,** to enter, come into, a room, etc.; **einsinken,** to sink in; **in ein Land einrücken, einmarschieren,** to march into a country; (*b*) (*forming intr. vbs*) (*arrival in a place*) **in den Hafen einsegeln,** to sail into port, to come sailing into port; (*of train, ship*) **eindampfen,** to steam in, to come steaming in; (*of train, letters*) **einlaufen,** to come in, to arrive; **einwandern,** to immigrate; (*c*) (*forming tr. vbs*) (*placing sth. inside sth.; insertion*) **etwas in etwas** *acc.* **einkleben,** to glue, stick, paste, sth. into sth.; **etwas in etwas** *acc.* **einpacken,** to pack sth. into sth.; **etwas in etwas** *acc.* **einfüllen,** to fill sth. into sth.; **etwas in etwas** *acc. & dat.* **einpflanzen,** to plant sth. in sth.; (*d*) (*forming tr. vbs*) (*inserting, fitting, sth. into sth.; inserting sth. between other thgs*) **etwas in etwas** *acc.* **einfügen,** to fit sth. into sth.; **einer Maschine ein Teil einsetzen, ein Teil in eine Maschine einsetzen,** to fit a part into a machine; (*e*) (*forming tr. vbs*) (*making pattern, mark, etc., in sth. by process implied in the simplex*) **etwas in etwas** *acc.* **einbrennen,** to burn (mark, etc.) into sth.; **etwas in etwas** *acc.* **einritzen,** to scratch sth. into sth.; **ein Loch in etwas** *acc.* **einbohren,** to drill, bore, a hole into sth.; (*f*) (*forming tr. vbs*) (*motion towards subject*) (**sich** *dat.*) **Geld einstecken,** to put money into one's pocket; **j-n einladen,** to invite s.o.; **Medizin einnehmen,** to take medicine; **die Ernte einbringen,** to gather in the harvest; (*of investment, etc.*) **Geld einbringen,** to bring in money; (*g*) (*forming tr. vbs*) (*motion into subject*) **etwas einatmen,** to breathe sth. in, to inhale sth.; **etwas einsaugen,** to suck sth. in; **etwas einschlürfen,** to drink in (soup, etc.); (*h*) (*forming tr. vbs*) (*with sense of inclusion*) **etwas in etwas** *acc.* **einarbeiten,** to work sth. into sth.; **etwas in etwas** *acc.* **einmischen,** to mix sth. in with sth.; to mix sth. into sth.; **etwas in etwas** *acc.* **einschließen, einbeziehen,** to include sth. in sth.; (*i*) (*forming tr. vbs*) (*surrounding sth. with thg implied in the simplex*) **etwas einhüllen,** to envelop sth.; **etwas einwickeln,** to wrap sth. up; **etwas einmauern,** to wall sth. up, in; **Land eindeichen,** to dike land; **eine Stadt einnebeln,** to put a town under a fog-screen; (*j*) (*forming intr. vbs*) (*implying position inside*) **in etwas** *dat.* **einliegen,** to be enclosed in sth.; to be inside sth. **2.** (*forming tr. vbs*) (*intensifying*) **etwas einstudieren, einüben,** to study, practise, sth.; **j-m etwas eindrillen,** to drill s.o. in sth.; **j-m etwas einbleuen,** to knock sth. into s.o.'s head, to ram, drum, sth. into s.o. **3.** (*a*) (i) (*forming tr. vbs*) (*forcing sth. inwards by action implied in the simplex*) **ein Fenster einwerfen,** to break a window by throwing something through it; **etwas einblasen,** to blow sth. in, down; **die Tür einschlagen,** to batter down the door; **etwas einfahren,** to knock sth. down by driving against it; **j-m den Brustkorb eindrücken,** to cave in s.o.'s ribs; **j-m die Zähne einschlagen,** to knock s.o.'s teeth in; (ii) (*forming intr. vbs*) (*to collapse*) **einfallen, einstürzen,** to fall in, to cave in, to collapse; (*b*) (*forming tr. vbs*) (*shaping of object in a form implied in the simplex*) **etwas einbuchten,** to indent sth.; to scallop sth.; **etwas eindellen,** to make a dent *or* dents in sth.; **etwas einkerben,** to notch sth.; **etwas eindrücken,** to make a dent *or* dents in sth. (by pressing it). **4.** (*forming tr. vbs*) (*a*) (*getting s.o. or oneself used to an activity or a condition*)

j-n, sich, einarbeiten, to make s.o., oneself, familiar with new work; **ein Pferd einreiten,** to break in, train, a horse; **Rekruten einexerzieren,** to train recruits; **sich einsingen,** to get oneself into voice; **sich einleben,** to become acclimatized; **sich eingewöhnen,** to settle in; (*b*) (*marking the start of sth.*) **einsingen,** to sing in (the new year, etc.); **einläuten,** to ring in (Sunday, new year, etc.). **5.** (*diminution by process implied in the simplex*) (*a*) (*forming tr. vbs*) **etwas eindampfen, eindünsten,** to evaporate sth. down; **etwas einschrumpfen,** to shrivel sth. up, to shrink sth.; **etwas einkochen, eindicken,** to boil sth. down, to thicken sth.; (*b*) (*forming intr. vbs*) **eindampfen, eindunsten,** to evaporate; **einschrumpfen,** to shrivel (up), to shrink; (*of garment, etc.*) **einlaufen, eingehen,** to shrink. **6.** (*forming tr. vbs*) (*application of the substance implied in the simplex*) **etwas einsalzen,** to put sth. in salt *or* brine; **etwas einschmutzen,** to dirty sth.; **etwas einölen,** to oil sth., to lubricate sth.; to rub oil into sth.; **etwas einfetten,** to grease sth. **7.** (*a*) (*forming tr. vbs*) (*inducing sleep by method implied in the simplex*) **j-n einschläfern,** to make s.o. fall asleep; **j-n einwiegen,** to rock s.o. to sleep; **j-n einsingen,** to sing s.o. to sleep; (*of wind*) **j-n einsäuseln,** to fan s.o. to sleep; (*b*) (*forming intr. vbs*) (*to go to sleep*) **einschlafen,** to go to sleep, to fall asleep; **eindämmern, einnicken,** to fall into a doze, a snooze.

II. **ein-, Ein-** (*prefixed to nouns, adjs, advs*) **1.** (*forming verbal nouns, adjs, and advs corresponding in meaning to the verbs from which they are derived*) (*a*) (*retaining vbl senses*) **Einbruch** *m*, breaking in; **Einwanderung** *f*, immigration; **Einführung** *f*, introduction; (*of transaction, etc.*) **einträglich,** bringing in money, (financially) rewarding, successful; (*b*) **Eingang** *m*, entrance, way in; **Eindruck** *m*, impression; **Einband** *m*, binding, cover (of book); **einwärts,** inwards. **2.** (*implying position inside*) **Eingeweide** *npl*, intestines; bowels; **Einwohner** *m*, inhabitant; **eingedenk,** keeping, bearing, in mind.

ein, *suff.* into...; **waldein,** into the wood; **querfeldein,** across the fields; **jahraus, jahrein,** year in, year out; *see also* **darein, herein, hinein, worein.**

Einachsanhänger, *m. Aut: etc:* single-axle trailer; two-wheel trailer.

einachsig, *a.* (*a*) *Cryst: Bot:* uniaxial, monaxial; (*b*) single-axle (trailer, etc.).

einackern, *v.tr. sep. Agr:* to plough in (manure, etc.).

Einakter, *m. Th:* one-act play *or* opera.

einaktig, *a. Th:* one-act (play, opera).

einand [aiˈnant], *pron.adv. A:* = **einander.**

einander [aiˈnandər], *pron.adv.* (*a*) one another, each other; **sie kennen e.,** they know one another, each other; **liebet e.,** love one another; **die beiden hassen e.,** the two hate one another, each other; **gleiche Pole stoßen e. ab,** like poles repel one another; **e. zum Trotz,** in defiance of one another, in mutual defiance; (*b*) **-einander,** *comb.fm.* ... each other, ... one another; **sie sind füreinander wie geschaffen,** they are made for one another, each other; **sie streiten ständig miteinander,** they are always quarrelling with one another; *see also* **aneinander, aufeinander, füreinander,** *etc.*

Einankerumformer, *m. El.E:* rotary converter.

einarbeiten, *v.tr. sep.* **1. j-n e.,** to make s.o. familiar with new work; to train s.o. (for a job); **der Vorarbeiter wird die Neuen e.,** the foreman will train the newcomers; **sich in etwas** *acc.* & *dat.* **e.,** to get into sth.; to get into the way of doing sth.; *F:* to get the hang of sth.; **sich in ein Fach e.,** to become familiar with, to get into, a subject; **er hat sich in seiner neuen Stellung gut eingearbeitet,** he has settled down well in his new job; **wenn du dich ein wenig eingearbeitet hast, wird es bei dir auch schneller gehen,** when you have got into your job a little, *F:* when you have got the hang of things a little, you will be quicker at it too; **er wird sich schon e.,** he'll get into it all right. **2. etwas in etwas** *acc.* **e.,** to work sth. into sth.; **das Muster ist in den Stoff eingearbeitet,** the pattern is worked into the material; **mit in den Schuß eingearbeiteten Silberfäden,** with silver threads worked into the woof; (*in recipe*) **'den Rest des Mehles gut (in den Teig) e.',** 'work remaining flour well into the pastry'; **neue Tatsachen in eine Abhandlung e.,** to work new facts into a treatise, to incorporate new facts in a treatise; **einen Vorfall in ein Buch e.,** to work an incident into a book; **der Verfasser konnte die letzten Entdeckungen nicht mehr e.,** the author could not incorporate the most recent discoveries.

einärmeln, *v.tr. sep. F:* **j-n e., sich bei j-m e.,** to take s.o.'s arm, to link arms with s.o.

einarmig, *a.* (*a*) one-armed, having only one arm; *Sp:* **einarmiges Stoßen,** one-hand jerk; (*b*) *Mec:* **einarmiger Hebel,** lever of the second order, kind; *Nau:* **einarmiger Anker,** anchor with only one fluke.

einäschern. I. *v.tr. sep.* **1.** (*a*) to reduce, burn, (sth.) to ashes; to incinerate (sth.); **eine Stadt e.,** to reduce a town to ashes, to lay a town in ashes; (*b*) to cremate (dead body). **2.** = **äschern** 1.

II. *vbl s.* **1. Einäschern,** *n. in vbl senses; also:* (*a*) incineration; (*b*) cremation (of dead body). **2. Einäscherung,** *f.* (*a*) = II, 1; (*b*) cremation; **die E. fand am letzten Montag statt,** the cremation took place last Monday.

Einäscherungshalle, *f.* crematorium.

Einäscherungsofen, *m.* crematorium, cremator, cremating furnace.

Einatemventil, *n.* inlet valve (of respirator).

einatmen. I. *v.sep.* **1.** *v.tr.* to breathe (sth.) in; to inhale (sth.); *Med: etc:* to inhale, breathe in (ether, oxygen); **die frische Luft e.,** to breathe in, to inhale, the fresh air; **er atmete den Duft der Rosen tief ein,** he breathed in deeply the scent of the roses; **Rauch, giftige Gase, e.,** to breathe in smoke, poisonous fumes. **2.** *v.i.* (*haben*) to breathe in, to inhale; **man soll tief e. und langsam wieder ausatmen,** one should breathe in, inhale, deeply and breathe out, exhale, again slowly.

II. *vbl s.* **Einatmen** *n.*, **Einatmung** *f. in vbl senses; also:* inhalation; **das Einatmen, die Einatmung, von Rauch und Auspuffgasen ist gesundheitsschädlich,** breathing in, inhaling, of smoke and exhaust fumes is detrimental to health.

einatomar, einatomig, *a. Ph:* monatomic.

einätzen, *v.tr. sep.* **etwas in etwas** *acc.* **e.,** to etch sth. into sth.; **das Muster ist eingeätzt,** the pattern is etched in.

einäugeln, *v.tr. sep. Hort:* to graft (scion) into (tree, etc.).

einäugig, *a.* (*a*) one-eyed; **ein Einäugiger,** a one-eyed man; *Prov:* **im Reich der Blinden ist der Einäugige König,** in the country of the blind the one-eyed man is king; (*b*) *Phot:* single-lens (camera).

Einback, *m.* -(e)s/-e. *Cu:* milk-roll.

einbacken, *v.tr. sep.* (*conj. like* **backen**) **etwas in etwas** *acc.* **e.,** to bake sth. into sth.; **eine Münze in einen Kuchen e.,** to bake a cake with a coin in it; **Kuchen mit einer eingebackenen Münze,** cake with a coin baked in it.

Einbadfarben, *f.pl. Dy:* single-bath dyes.

einbahnig, *a.* (*a*) single-lane (road, race-track, etc.); single-line (traffic); (*b*) one-way (street, traffic, etc.); (*c*) single-face (hammer, etc.).

Einbahnstraße, *f.* one-way street.

einballen, *v.tr. sep.* = **einballieren.**

einballieren, *v.tr. sep.* to pack (cotton, etc.) in bales, to bale (cotton, etc.).

einballig, einbällig, *a. Bootm:* (boot, shoe) made to fit either foot.

einbalsamieren, *v.tr. sep.* to embalm (corpse); **Einbalsamierung** *f*, embalming, embalmment.

Einbalsamierer, *m.* -s/-, embalmer (of corpses).

Einband, *m.* -(e)s/⸚e. *Bookb:* binding (of book); book-cover; **E. mit Lederecken,** binding with leather corners.

Einbanddecke, *f. Bookb:* book-cover.

Einbandentwurf, *m.* bookbinding design; **E. von...,** binding designed by....

einbändig, *a.* one-volumed (novel, work), (novel, work) in one volume.

Einbandstoff, *m. Bookb:* (binding) cloth.

einbasig, einbasisch, *a. Ch:* monobasic (acid, salt).

einbatschen, *v.tr. sep. Tex:* to batch (jute).

Einbau, *m.* -(e)s/. **1.** building in, fitting (of cupboard, etc.) (into a wall, etc.); installation, fitting (of engine, etc.) (in car, etc.); **beim E. des Motors in ein Flugzeug,** when installing, fitting, the engine in an aircraft. **2.** (*pl.* **Einbauten**) *Constr: etc:* built-in element; (internal) fitting; addition (to the internal structure).

Einbauantenne, *f. W.Tel:* built-in aerial, built-in antenna.

Einbaubadewanne, *f.* (*a*) tub for a built-in bath unit; (*b*) built-in bath(-tub).

einbauen, *v.tr. sep.* **etwas in etwas** *acc.* **e.,** to build (cupboard, pipe, safe, etc.) into (wall, etc.); to install (engine, etc.) in (car, etc.); to mount (gun, etc.) permanently on (ship, platform, etc.); to work, incorporate sth. into (treatise, etc.); **den Motor in ein Auto, in ein Flugzeug, e.,** to install the engine in a car, in an aircraft, to fit the engine into a car, into an aircraft; **sich** *dat.* **einen Schrank e. lassen,** to have a cupboard built in; **eingebauter Schrank,** built-in cupboard; **Fahrrad mit eingebautem Geschwindigkeitsmesser,** bicycle with a built-in speedometer; **eingebaute Badewanne,** built-in bath(-tub); **Werkarbeit sollte in größerem Maße in den Lehrplan eingebaut werden,** handicraft should be more extensively incorporated in the curriculum.

einbaufertig, *a. Constr: etc:* ready for fitting, ready to be fitted.

Einbauküche, *f.* built-in kitchen; fitted kitchen.

Einbaum, *m.* **1.** dug-out (canoe); pirogue. **2.** *Min:* (rough) ladder.

Einbaumöbel, *n. pl.* built-in furniture.

Einbaumotor, *m. El.E: Mec.E:* (*a*) built-in motor; (*b*) motor ready to be built in.

Einbauschrank, *m. Furn:* built-in cupboard; fitted cupboard.

Einbeere, *f. Bot:* Paris; **vierblättrige E.,** herb Paris, (herb) true-love.

einbeeren, *v.tr. sep.* to bait (bird-snare, etc.) with berries.

einbegreifen, *v.tr. sep.* (*strong*) to include, contain, comprise, embrace (sth.); **etwas in etwas** *acc.* **e.,** to include sth. in sth.; **in etwas** *dat.* & *acc.* **einbegriffen sein,** to be included in sth.; **das Frühstück ist im Preis einbegriffen,** the terms are inclusive of breakfast; **Männer über siebzig sind in dieser, in diese, Zahl nicht einbegriffen,** men over seventy are not included in this number; **in diesem einen Satz sind alle unsere Probleme einbegriffen,** this sentence embraces all our problems, sums up all our problems in a nutshell, all our problems are summed up in this one sentence.

einbehalten. I. *v.tr. sep.* (*strong*) to retain, keep back, withhold (money, property, etc.); **j-s Lohn e.,** to retain, hold back, withhold s.o.'s wages; **zehn Prozent vom Lohn eines Dienstboten e.,** to keep back, withhold, ten per cent from a servant's wages; **die Steuern werden vom Arbeitgeber einbehalten,** the taxes are deducted by the employer.

II. *vbl s.* **Einbehalten** *n.*, **Einhaltung** *f. in vbl senses; also:* retention (of money, property, etc.); deduction (of taxes) (by employer).

Einbeinfahrgestell, *n. Av:* single-strut undercarriage, cantilever-type undercarriage.

einbeinig, *a.* one-legged; **ein einbeiniger Mann, ein Einbeiniger,** a one-legged man.

einbeißen, *v. sep.* (*strong*) **1.** *v.i.* (*haben*) **in etwas** *acc.* **e.,** to bite into sth. **2. sich in etwas** *acc.* **einbeißen,** (*a*) (*of pers., animal*) to sink one's, its, teeth into sth.; to hold on to sth. with one's, its, teeth; (*b*) (*of acid*) to bite into, eat into (metal, etc.).

einbekennen, *v.tr. sep.* (*conj. like* **kennen**) to admit (sth., guilt, etc.); *abs.* **e.,** *Austrian:* to declare, return, one's income; **Einbekennung** *f*, declaration, return, of income, income-tax return.

Einbenennung, *f. Jur:* **E. eines unehelichen Kindes,** legitimation of an illegitimate child by a husband who is not the father.

einberufen. I. *v.tr. sep.* (*strong*) (*a*) to summon, call together, convoke (assembly); to convene, call (meeting, etc.); **eine Versammlung kurzfristig e.,** to convene, call, a meeting at short notice; **das Parlament wieder e.,** to recall parliament; (*b*) *Mil:* to call up (s.o.), *U.S:* to draft (s.o.); to call up, conscript (men); to call up, call out (reservists, etc.); **j-n zur Fahne e.,** to call s.o. to the colours; **er wurde zum Heer, zum Heeresdienst, einberufen,** he was called up into, for, the army; **zur Marine einberufen werden,** to be called up into, for, the navy.

II. *vbl s.* **1. Einberufen,** *n. in vbl senses.* **2. Einberufung,** *f.* (*a*) = II. 1; *also:* convocation (of assembly); *Mil:* call-up, conscription (of men); (*b*) *Mil:* call-up, *U.S:* draft; **auf seine E. warten,** to wait for one's call-up, *U.S:* to wait for the draft; **die ersten Einberufungen erfolgten im Dezember,** the first recruits were called up in December; (*c*) = **Einberufungsbefehl.**

Einberufene, *m.* (*decl. as adj.*) man called up for military service; conscript; *U.S:* enlisted man.

Einberufungsbefehl, *m. Mil:* call-up order(s).

einbetonieren, *v.tr. sep.* to set (sth.) in concrete.

einbetten. I. *v.tr. sep.* **etwas in etwas** *acc.* **e.,** (*a*) to lay sth. in sth., to put sth. into sth.; to embed sth. in sth.; (*of weighty object*) **sich in etwas** *acc.* **e.,** to (em)bed itself (in earth, wood, etc.); **in Stroh eingebettet,** packed, wrapped, bedded, in straw; **der Ring war in Watte eingebettet,** the ring was bedded in cotton-wool; **ins Fruchtfleisch eingebettete Kerne,** pips *or* stones embedded in the fleshy part of a fruit; **die**

Stadt liegt in das Tal eingebettet, the town nestles in the valley; **in ein Tal, in einen Wald, zwischen Bäumen, eingebettetes Dorf,** village nestling in a valley, in a wood, among trees; **das Geschoß hatte sich, war, tief in die Erde eingebettet,** the projectile had embedded itself, had buried itself, deep in the earth; **das Wrack war, hatte sich, tief in den Schlamm eingebettet,** the wreck was deeply embedded in the mud; (*b*) to embed, bed (stone, etc.) (in cement, etc.); **in Beton eingebettet,** embedded in concrete; **in Mörtel oder Zement eingebetteter Stein,** stone embedded in mortar or cement; **der Mörtel, in welchen der Stein eingebettet ist,** the mortar embedding the stone; **ein Kabel in Sand e.,** to embed a cable in sand; **ein in Quarz eingebetteter Edelstein,** a precious stone embedded in quartz; (*c*) to embed (microscopic substance) (in wax, paraffin, etc.).

II. *vbl s.* **1. Einbetten,** *n. in vbl senses; also:* embedment; **E. von mikroskopischen Präparaten,** embedding of microscopic substances. **2. Einbettung,** *f.* (*a*)=II. 1; (*b*) embedment; bed.

einbeulen. I. *v.tr. sep.* to dent (sth.), to make a dent *or* dents in (sth.); **eingebeulter Hut,** battered hat; *Aut:* **eingebeulter Kotflügel,** dented wing, dented mudguard.

II. *vbl s.* **1. Einbeulen,** *n. in vbl senses.* **2. Einbeulung,** *f.* (*a*)=II, 1; (*b*) dent; **der Kotflügel wies mehrere Einbeulungen auf,** the mudguard had several dents in it.

einbeziehen. I. *v.tr. sep.* (*strong*) **etwas in etwas** *acc.* **e.,** to include sth. in sth.; to incorporate (land, etc.) into (estate, etc.); **in etwas** *acc. & dat.* **einbezogen sein,** to be included in sth.; **das Frühstück ist im Preis, in den Preis, einbezogen,** the terms are inclusive of breakfast; **Männer über siebzig sind in diese Zahl nicht einbezogen,** men over seventy are not included in this number; **der Verfasser hat auch medizinische Probleme in seine Abhandlung einbezogen,** the author has also included medical problems in his treatise; **Werk, das alle neuesten Entdeckungen einbezieht,** work that incorporates all the latest discoveries.

II. *vbl s.* **Einbeziehen** *n.*, **Einbeziehung** *f. in vbl senses; also:* inclusion; incorporation.

einbiegen. I. *v.sep.* (*strong*) **1.** *v.tr.* to bend (sth.) inwards; *Her:* **unten eingebogen,** arched in base. **2.** *v.i.* (*sein*) (*a*) (*of road, river bank, etc.*) to curve inwards; (*b*) (*of pers., car, etc.*) to take a turning; **in eine andere Straße e.,** to turn into, to take, another road; **er bog (nach) links ein,** he turned to the left; **ich bog in die Regent Street ein,** I turned into, down, Regent Street; **das Auto bog in den Hof ein,** the car turned into the courtyard; **biegen Sie in die erste Straße rechts ein,** take the first street, the first turning, on the right; **biegen Sie links ein,** take the turning on the left; turn, bear, (to th lefte).

II. *vbl s.* **1. Einbiegen,** *n. in vbl senses.* **2. Einbiegung,** *f.* (inward) bend, curve; **das Ufer macht hier eine E.,** the bank curves inwards here.

einbilden (sich). I. *v.refl. sep.* **sich** *dat.* **etwas e.,** (*a*) to imagine, fancy, suppose, think, sth.; **er bildet sich ein, er sei ein Millionär,** he thinks he is a millionaire, he imagines himself to be a millionaire; **sie bildet sich ein, daß jedermann sie bewundert,** she thinks, fancies, that everybody admires her; **er bildet sich ein, daß jemand ihn vergiften will,** he thinks, imagines, he has the fixed idea, that someone wants to poison him; **ich bildete mir ein, es hätte geklopft,** I thought, imagined, fancied, I heard a knock; **sie bildet sich ein, eine schöne Frau zu sein,** she thinks herself a beautiful woman; **er bildet sich ein, als Retter seines Volkes zu handeln,** he imagines himself to be acting, he thinks he is acting, as a saviour of his people; **du mußt dir nicht e., daß . . .,** you must not imagine, fancy, think, that . . .; **bilden Sie sich nicht etwa ein, ich sei zufrieden,** do not imagine, *F:* don't kid yourself, that I am satisfied; **was bildest du dir eigentlich ein?** who do you think you are? what do you think you are doing? (*b*) to be (self-)conceited, to fancy oneself, *F:* to think a lot of oneself; to give oneself airs; **sich etwas auf etwas** *acc.* **e.,** to be (over-)proud of (one's abilities, etc.), to be conceited about (one's wealth, etc.); **sich viel auf etwas e.,** to be terribly conceited, *F:* terribly stuck-up, about sth.; **darauf brauchst du dir nichts einzubilden,** that's nothing to be proud of; **darauf kannst du dir etwas e.,** you can be proud of that, that is something to be proud of; *F:* that's a feather in your cap; **bilde dir bloß nicht so viel ein,** don't be so conceited, so stuck up, don't put on such airs; **er bildet sich zuviel ein,** he thinks too much, no end, *F:* a precious sight too much, of himself; **er bildet sich eine Menge, viel, auf seine rednerischen Fähigkeiten ein,** he fancies himself as a speaker, he thinks a lot of himself as a speaker.

II. *vbl s.* **Einbildung,** *f.* (*a*) imagination; **etwas in seiner E. sehen,** to see sth. in one's imagination, in one's mind's eye; **das Haus ist nur in seiner E. vorhanden, das Haus existiert nur in seiner E.,** the house exists only in his imagination; (*b*) fancy; imagination; hallucination; **ihr Leiden ist reine E.,** her illness is pure imagination; **das ist nur E.,** that is only imagination, fancy; **war es E., oder hat es wirklich an der Tür geklopft?** was it my imagination or was there really a knock on the door? **er hat seltsame Einbildungen,** he has strange fancies; **an Einbildungen leiden,** to suffer from hallucinations; **er hat dauernd Einbildungen,** he is always imagining things; **alles das sind vergebliche Einbildungen,** all these are vain imaginings; (*c*)= **Eingebildetheit**; (*d*)=**Einbildungskraft.**

III. *p.p. & a.* **eingebildet,** *in vbl senses; esp.* **1.** imaginary; **eingebildete Krankheit,** imaginary illness; **eingebildeter Kranker,** imaginary invalid; **eingebildete Reichtümer,** imaginary riches; *Med:* **eingebildete Schwangerschaft,** nervous pregnancy. **2.** (self-)conceited, vain; **e. sein,** to be (self-)conceited, vain; to fancy oneself, *F:* to think a lot, no small beer, of oneself; to give oneself airs; to be stuck-up; **er ist unglaublich e.,** he is unbearably conceited, he is full of (self-)conceit, he thinks no end of himself; **sei bloß nicht so e.,** don't be so conceited, so stuck-up, don't put on such airs; **er sieht sehr e. aus,** he looks very conceited; **ein eingebildeter junger Mann,** *F:* **ein eingebildeter Affe,** a conceited young man, *F:* a conceited puppy, a conceited ass.

Einbildungskraft, *f.* imagination; fantasy; **lebhafte, fruchtbare, E.,** lively, fertile, imagination; **seiner E. freien Lauf lassen,** to give free rein to one's imagination.

Einbildungsvermögen, *n.*=**Einbildungskraft.**

einbinden, *v.sep.* (*strong*) **1.** *v.tr.* (*a*) **etwas in etwas** *acc.* **e.,** to tie sth. into sth.; to tie sth. up in sth.; **Spargelgrün in einen Blumenstrauß e.,** to tie in asparagus fern with a bunch of flowers; **Rosen in einen Kranz e.,** to work roses into a wreath; **junge Bäume mit Stroh e.,** to wrap straw round young trees; (*b*) *Bookb:* to bind (books); **in Pappe eingebunden,** bound in boards; **in Leinen eingebunden,** bound in cloth, cloth-bound; **in Leder eingebunden,** bound in leather, leather-bound; (*c*) *Coop:* to hoop (barrel); to shoe, tyre (wheel); (*d*) *Constr:* to bond (bricks, stones); (*e*) *Nau:* to furl (sail); (*f*) *Surv:* to tie on (line) (in+*acc.*, to). **2.** *v.tr. A:*=**einschärfen.** **3.** *v.i.* (*sein*) *Constr:* (*of wall, etc.*) to key in.

Einblaseapparat, *m. Med: etc:* insufflator.

einblasen. I. *v.tr. sep.* (*strong*) **1.** (*of wind, etc.*) to blow down (shed, wall, etc.); to blow in (window-pane, etc.); **die Wände des Hauses sind so dünn, daß der Wind sie leicht e. könnte,** the walls of the house are so thin that the wind could easily blow them down. **2.** (*a*) **etwas in etwas** *acc.* **e.,** to blow (air, gas, etc.) into (balloon, bladder, etc.); *Med: etc:* to insufflate (lungs, throat, etc.) with (air, gas, powder, etc.); to spray (throat, nostrils, etc.) with (lotion, powder, etc.); *B:* **und er blies ihm ein den lebendigen Odem in seine Nase,** and breathed into his nostrils the breath of life; (*b*) **j-m etwas e.,** to whisper sth. to s.o., (i) to insinuate sth. to s.o., to make insinuations to s.o.; (ii) to make flattering remarks to s.o., to flatter s.o.; (iii) to prompt (schoolboy, etc.).

II. *vbl s.* **Einblasen** *n.*, **Einblasung** *f. in vbl senses; also: Med: etc:* insufflation.

Einbläser, *m.* **1.** (*pers.*) (i) insinuator; (ii) prompter. **2.** (*device*) *Med: etc:* insufflator.

Einblaskopf, *m.* deflector, cowl (of chimney, etc.).

Einblasungsapparat, *m. Med: etc:* insufflator.

Einblatt, *n. Bot:* adder's-tongue, ophioglossum.

Einblattdruck, *m.* broadsheet, broadside.

einblatten, *v.tr. sep.* **1.** *Carp:* to scarf, graft (timbers); to join (timbers) by mortises. **2.** *Rail:* to chair (sleeper).

Einblattholzschnitt, *m. Lit.Hist:* broadsheet, broadside (from a woodcut).

Einblattluftschraube, *f. Av:* single-blade air-screw.

einblättrig, *a. Bot:* one-leaved, monophyllous, unifoliate.

einblenden, *v.tr. sep.* (*a*) *Art: etc:* to blend (colours); **eine Farbe in eine andere e.,** to blend one colour with another; (*b*) *Ph:* to focus, concentrate (rays); (*c*) *Cin:* to fade in (a scene); *W.Tel:* to fade in (an effect, a melody, etc.).

einbleuen, *v.tr. sep. F:* **j-m etwas e.,** to impress sth. upon s.o., *F:* to ram, drum, knock, sth. into s.o.; **einem Jungen Latein e.,** to bang, knock, drum, Latin into a boy's head, to hammer, drum, knock, Latin into a boy; **ich kann es ihm nicht e.,** I can't get it, drive it, beat it, into his head; **ich habe ihm eingebleut, daß er nicht auf der Straße spielen darf,** I told him again and again, *F:* I rammed it into him, that he must not play in the street.

Einblick, *m.* insight (into a situation, etc.); **in eine Sache E. nehmen, tun,** to look into a matter; **(einen) E. in etwas gewinnen, bekommen, sich** *dat.* **E. in etwas verschaffen,** to get, gain, an insight into sth.; **einen tieferen E. in etwas bekommen,** to get a deeper insight into sth.; **j-m E. in etwas gewähren,** to give, afford, grant, s.o. an insight into sth.; **seine Arbeit gewährte ihm, verschaffte ihm, E., durch seine Arbeit bekam er einen E., in die Verhältnisse, in denen viele Leute leben mußten,** his work afforded, gave, him an insight into the conditions in which many people had to live.

Einblickfenster, *n. Phot:* eyepiece (of range-finder).

einbohren, *v.tr. sep.* **1.** to bore, drill (hole) in(to) (plank, wall, etc.); **Löcher e.,** to drill in holes. **2. sich einbohren,** to bore into (sth.); **diese Insekten bohren sich in das Holz ein,** these insects bore (themselves) into the wood; **das Geschoß bohrte sich in die Erde ein,** the projectile bored itself into the ground, buried itself in the ground.

einbrechen, *v.sep.* (*strong*) I. *v.tr.* **1.** to break in, break down, break open (door, etc.); to break, smash (ice, window-pane, etc.). **2.** to break in, train (horse); **Pferd, das noch nicht eingebrochen ist,** horse not yet broken in, unbroken, untrained, horse.

II. **einbrechen,** *v.i.* (*sein*) **1.** (*a*) (*of structure, support, etc.*) to collapse; to fall in; to give way; to break; (*of roof, ground, etc.*) to cave in; **der Fußboden brach unter seinem Gewicht ein,** the floor-boards broke, collapsed, gave way, under his weight; **das Eis brach unter ihr ein,** the ice broke, gave way, under her; **mit lautem Krachen brach die hölzerne Brücke ein,** the wooden bridge collapsed with a loud crash; (*b*) (*of pers.*) to break through (ice, floor-boards, etc.); **ich brach gestern beim Schlittschuhlaufen (auf dem Eis) ein,** when I was skating yesterday I broke through, *F:* went through, the ice. **2.** (*a*) **in etwas** *acc.* **e.,** (*of enemy, troops, etc.*) to invade, enter, march into (country, etc.); (*of sea, etc.*) to encroach, advance (on the land); (*b*) (*sein & haben*) (*of burglar, etc.*) to break into (a house, etc.); *F:* to burgle (a house); **die Diebe waren durch das Küchenfenster eingebrochen,** the burglars had broken in through the kitchen window; **bei uns ist vorige Woche eingebrochen worden, bei uns haben sie vorige Woche eingebrochen,** our house was broken into last week; we had burglars last week; *F:* our house was, we were, burgled last week; **gestern sind Diebe in unsere Wohnung eingebrochen,** thieves broke into our flat yesterday. **3.** (*of dusk, night, etc.*) to set in, to close in, to fall; (*of cold, heat, etc.*) to set in; **die Nacht bricht ein,** night is falling, closing in; **strenge Kälte brach ein,** severe cold set in; **bei einbrechender Nacht,** at nightfall, when night (i) closes in, sets in, (ii) closed in, set in; **bei, mit, einbrechender Dunkelheit,** at dusk, (i) when it gets dark, when darkness comes, (ii) when it got dark, when darkness came. **4.** *Min:* (*of ore*) to occur in gangue.

III. *vbl s.* **Einbrechen,** *n. in vbl senses; cp.* **Einbruch.**

Einbrecher, *m.* housebreaker; burglar.

Einbrecheralarm, *m.* burglar alarm.

einbrecherisch, *a.* burglarious; **einbrecherischer Versuch,** burglarious attempt; attempt to burgle (a house, etc.); **in einbrecherischer Absicht,** with intent to commit a burglary.

Einbrenn, *f.* **-/-en** =**Einbrenne.**

Einbrenne, *f.* **-/-n.** *Cu:* roux; **helle E.,** light roux; **dunkle E.,** dark roux, browned flour (*for making brown gravy, etc.*); **eine E. machen,** to make a roux; to brown flour.

einbrennen, *v.tr. sep.* (*conj. like* **brennen**) **1.** (*a*) **etwas in etwas** *acc.* **e.,** to burn sth. into sth.; **einem Tier, einem Sklaven, ein Zeichen e.,** to burn a mark into an animal's, a slave's, skin; to brand an animal, a slave; *Art:* **eingebrannte Holzmalerei,** pyrography, pyrogravure, poker-work; **eingebrannte Wachsmalerei.** encaustic;

(*b*) *Ind:* to stove (enamel); *Cer:* to harden, fix (colours, glaze, etc.) by firing; (*c*) *Cu:* **Mehl e.,** to brown flour (*in order to make a roux*); (*d*) to match, sulphur, fumigate (cask). **2.** *Leath:* to tallow (skin).

Einbrennlack, *m. Ind:* stove enamel; *Cer:* baking varnish.

einbrennlackiert, *a. Ind:* stove enamelled.

Einbrennlackierung, *f. Ind:* **1.** stove enamelling. **2.** stove enamel, baked on enamel.

Einbrennsauce, *f. Cu:* brown sauce *or* gravy (*made with browned flour*).

Einbrennsuppe, *f. Cu:* soup made with browned flour.

einbringen. I. *v.tr. sep.* (*conj. like* **bringen**) **1.** (*a*) to bring in (sth., s.o.); **das Getreide e.,** to bring in, get in, the corn; **die Ernte e.,** to get in the crops, the harvest; **das Schiff (in den Hafen) e.,** to bring the ship into port; to get, put, into port; **das Schiff sicher in den Hafen e.,** to bring the ship safely into port; to get safe into port, to reach port safely; **die Soldaten brachten zehn Gefangene ein,** the soldiers brought in, brought back, ten prisoners; **nach dem Kampf wurden viele Verwundete eingebracht,** after the battle many wounded were brought in, were carried in; **einen Verbrecher ins Gefängnis e.,** to put a criminal in(to) prison; **Kapital in eine Gesellschaft e.,** to bring capital into a company; *Print:* **Raum e.,** to make room (for an insertion); *Jur:* **eingebrachtes Gut,** estate brought in (by husband *or* wife upon marriage); **das Eingebrachte,** the dowry; *Jur:* **eingebrachte Sachen,** articles of personal property introduced into a hotel by a guest, into a dwelling by a tenant; (*b*) **etwas in etwas** *acc.* **e.,** to get sth. into sth.; **Zement e.,** to fill in, pour in, cement (into a hole); **Farbstoff unter die Haut e.,** to inject a dye under the skin; (*c*) to send in, submit (application, etc.); to bring, lodge (complaint, claim, etc.); to present (bill); to propose, bring forward, put (motion); *Parl:* **einen Gesetzesantrag e.,** to bring in, to introduce, a bill; to present a bill; (*d*) **etwas wieder e.,** to make up for (lost time, etc.); to make up for, make good, retrieve (loss, etc.); **die verlorene Zeit wieder e.,** to make up for lost time, to redeem the lost time; **wenn Sie ihm Zeit gäben, könnte er das Versäumte leicht wieder e.,** if you gave him time he could easily make up for what he missed, he could easily catch up. **2.** (*a*) (*of investment, business, transaction, etc.*) to bring in, bear, yield, produce (profit, etc.); **Zinsen e.,** to bring in, bear, yield, interest; **Kapitalanlage, die 5 Prozent (Zinsen) einbringt,** investment that brings in, bears, yields, returns, 5 per cent; **dieses Grundstück bringt ihm ein Einkommen von zehntausend Mark ein,** this land brings him in an income of ten thousand marks; **diese kleinen Arbeiten bringen mir zwei oder drei Pfund in der Woche ein,** these little jobs bring me in two or three pounds a week; **das Geschäft hat ihm viel eingebracht,** the deal brought him in a lot of money, gave him a big profit, proved very profitable for him; he made a big profit by the deal; **das Geschäft bringt einen schönen Gewinn ein,** the business yields a handsome profit; **ein Geschäft, das viel einbringt,** a profitable, paying, lucrative, business; **das bringt nicht viel ein,** there's not much profit in it, it doesn't pay; (*b*) (*of action, conduct, etc.*) **j-m Ehre, usw., e.,** to gain, bring, s.o. credit, to do s.o. credit; to add to s.o.'s reputation; **das bringt dir keine Ehre ein,** this does you no credit, you will gain no credit by this; **seine Handlungsweise brachte ihm viele Freunde, viel Anerkennung, ein,** his conduct gained, won, him many friends, much praise; **seine Unerbittlichkeit brachte ihm viele Feinde ein, brachte ihm die Feindschaft vieler Leute ein,** his relentlessness made him many enemies.

II. *vbl s.* **Einbringen** *n.*, **Einbringung** *f. in vbl senses; also:* submission (of application, etc.); lodgment (of complaint, claim, etc.); proposal (of motion); *Parl:* presentation, introduction (of bill).

einbringlich, *a.* profitable, paying (business, investment, transaction, work, etc.); lucrative (business, etc.).

einbröckeln, *v.sep.* **1.** *v.i.* (*sein*) (*of wall, etc.*) to crumble, to fall to pieces. **2.** *v.tr.*=**einbrocken** (*a*).

einbrocken, *v.tr. sep.* (*a*) **Brot in die Suppe, in die Milch, e.,** to break, crumble, bread into the soup, into the milk; (*b*) **sich** *dat.*, **j-m, etwas e.,** to get oneself, s.o., into trouble, into a fix, into a mess; **er hat sich, uns, was Schönes eingebrockt,** he's landed himself, us, in a nice fix, in a nice mess, he's got himself, us, into a nice pickle, into a nice packet of trouble; **das hast du dir selber eingebrockt,** you've only yourself to thank for the trouble, the mess, you are in; you've been asking for it; **ich wußte, ahnte, nicht, was ich mir da einbrockte,** I didn't know what I was letting myself in for; *Prov:* **was man sich eingebrockt, muß man auch auslöffeln,** as you make your bed so you must lie on it; you must drink as you have brewed.

Einbruch, *m.* **1.** (*a*) breaking (down), falling in, collapse (of structure, support, etc.); caving in, collapse (of roof, ground, etc.); *Min:* fall (of roof); *Geol:* down-faulting, (down-)sinking, subsidence (of soil); (*b*) *St.Exch:* break, drop, fall, decline, slump (in prices); **scharfer E. in Baumwollpreisen,** heavy drop, heavy fall, heavy slump, in cotton prices; collapse of cotton prices. **2.** (*a*) intrusion, encroachment (of sea, etc.); *Geol:* incursion, ingress (of sea); **feindliche Einbrüche (in ein Land),** enemy incursions (into a country); (*b*) *Jur:* breach of close, of domicile; breaking and entering (with intent to commit a felony); (*at night*) burglary; (*in the day-time*) housebreaking; **einen E. verüben,** to commit a burglary; **bewaffneter E.,** armed burglary; **in dieser Gegend sind kürzlich mehrere Einbrüche verübt worden,** there have been several burglaries recently in this area, *F:* several houses have recently been burgled in this area. **3. bei E. der Nacht, der Dunkelheit,** at nightfall, when night (i) closes in, sets in, (ii) closed in, set in; **bei E. der Kälte sollte das Wasser nachts abgestellt werden,** when the cold (weather) sets in, the water should be turned off at night. **4.** *Her:* ba(s)ton (couped); *F:* bar sinister.

Einbruchsbecken, *n. Geol:* trough, syncline.

Einbruchscaldera, *f. Geol:* caldera; volcanic sink.

Einbruchsdiebstahl, *m. Jur:* (*at night*) burglary; (*in the day-time*) theft by breaking and entering, *F:* daylight burglary.

Einbruchsfeld, *n. Geol:* depression.

Einbruchskrater, *m. Geol:* volcanic sink; sink-hole.

Einbruchsmeer, *n. Geol:* sea caused by the overflowing of a subsided area.

einbruch(s)sicher, *a.* burglar-proof.

Einbruchstal, *n. Geol:* rift valley.

Einbruchsversicherung, *f. Ins:* burglary insurance.

Einbruchsversuch, *m.* (*a*) attempt to commit burglary, attempted burglary; (*b*) attempt to invade (a country, etc.); attempted invasion (of a country, etc.).

Einbruchswerkzeuge, *n.pl.* housebreaking tools, housebreaking implements.

einbrüderig, *a. Bot:* monadelphous; **einbrüderige Pflanze,** monadelph.

einbuchten. I. *v.tr. sep.* **1.** (*a*) to indent (sth.); to hollow (sth.) out; (*b*) **sich einbuchten,** to form a bay, a recess; to be indented. **2.** *F:* to lock (s.o.) up; to put (s.o.) in prison, *F:* jug.

II. *vbl s.* **1. Einbuchten,** *n. in vbl senses.* **2. Einbuchtung,** *f.* (*a*)=II. 1; (*b*) indentation; bay; recess.

einbuddeln, *v.tr. sep. F:*=**eingraben.**

einbürgern. I. *v.tr. sep.* **1.** to naturalize (alien); to settle (s.o.) (in town, etc.); to naturalize (word, custom, etc.); to naturalize, acclimatize (plant, animal); **eine seit vielen Jahren in X eingebürgerte Familie,** a family which has lived in X for many years, which settled in X many years ago. **2. sich einbürgern,** (*of pers.*) to settle, establish oneself (in town, etc.); (*of word, custom, etc.*) to become naturalized, to take root; (*of plant, animal*) to become naturalized, acclimatized; **dieses Wort hat sich bei uns eingebürgert,** this word has been, has become, naturalized, established, here, has taken root here, this word has been adopted here.

II. *vbl s.* **1. Einbürgern,** *n. in vbl senses.* **2. Einbürgerung,** *f.* (*a*)=II. 1; *also:* naturalization (of alien); settlement, establishment (of s.o.) (in town, etc.); naturalization (of word, custom, plant, animal, etc.); acclimatization (of plant, animal); (*b*) *Adm:* naturalization; **einen Antrag auf E. stellen,** to apply for naturalization.

Einbürgerungsantrag, *m. Adm:* application for naturalization.

Einbuße, *f.* loss, forfeiture (of money, influence, honour, etc.); **eine E. an etwas** *dat.* **erleiden,** to suffer loss of sth.; to forfeit sth.; to suffer damage to (health, etc.); **durch diesen Vertrag erlitt, erfuhr, er eine empfindliche E. an Geld,** because of this contract he suffered, sustained, a severe loss of money; **er tat es unter E. seiner Ehre,** he acted at the cost, expense, of his honour, with the loss of his honour; **er rettete sie unter E. seines eigenen Lebens,** he saved them at the cost, expense, loss, of his own life; *Com:* **E. an Kundschaft, an Kunden,** loss of custom; **E. an Handel,** loss of trade.

einbüßen. I. *v.tr. sep.* to lose, forfeit (money, influence, honour, one's life, a right, etc.); **ich habe bei diesem Geschäft viel Geld eingebüßt,** I lost, *F:* dropped, a lot of money on this deal, I suffered a heavy loss, heavy losses, on this deal; **er büßte bei der Schlägerei ein Auge ein,** he lost an eye in the fight; **sein Ansehen e.,** to lose, (people's) esteem, to lose face; **durch seine Handlungweise büßte er seine Ehre ein,** he acted at the cost, expense, of his honour, with the loss of his honour; **er büßte seine Gesundheit dabei ein,** he lost his health doing it.

II. *vbl s.* **Einbüßen** *n.*, **Einbüßung** *f. in vbl senses; also:* loss, forfeiture (of money, influence, honour, one's life, a right, etc.); **unter Einbüßung seines eigenen Lebens,** at the cost, expense, loss, of his own life; *Com:* **Einbüßung von Kundschaft, von Kunden,** loss of custom; *cp.* **Einbuße.**

eindachen, *v.tr. sep.* to roof (house, etc.).

eindämmen. I. *v.tr. sep.* **1.** (*a*) to (em)bank (river, etc.); to dike (land); to impound (water); (*b*) to dam (up), stem, check (flood-water, etc.); to check, restrain (developments); **das Wasser, die Fluten, e.,** to stem the waters; **eine Seuche e.,** to stem, check, limit, an epidemic, to stay the progress, to restrict the spread, of an epidemic; **j-s Redefluß e.,** to dam up, to stem the torrent of, s.o.'s eloquence; **j-s Enthusiasmus e.,** to stem, restrain, s.o.'s enthusiasm. **2.** to tamp (down) (earth, sand, etc.).

II. *vbl s.* **1. Eindämmen,** *n. in vbl senses.* **2. Eindämmung,** *f.* (*a*)=II. 1; (*b*) dam; embankment; dike.

eindämmern, *v.i. sep.* (*sein*) to fall into a doze; to fall into a light sleep.

Eindampfapparat, *m. Ch: Ind:* evaporating apparatus, evaporator; concentrator.

eindampfen, *v.sep.* **1.** *v.i.* (*sein*) (*of train, ship, etc.*) to steam in, come steaming in. **2.** *v.i.* (*sein*) (*of liquid*) to boil down; to thicken (by evaporation). **3.** *v.tr.*=**eindämpfen I.**

eindämpfen. I. *v.tr. sep.* to boil down, to evaporate down (liquid); to concentrate (liquid) by evaporation; to inspissate (liquid).

II. *vbl s.* **Eindämpfen** *n.*, **Eindämpfung** *f. in vbl senses; also:* evaporation; concentration (by evaporation); inspissation.

Eindampfer, *m.* **-s/-** =**Eindampfapparat.**

Eindampfgefäß, *n.* evaporating dish, basin, pan.

Eindampfgerät, *n.*=**Eindampfapparat.**

Eindampfpfanne, Eindampfschale, *f.* = **Eindampfgefäß.**

eindecken. I. *v.tr. sep.* **1.** (*a*) to cover (sth.) up, to cover (sth.) over; **Kartoffeln mit Stroh e.,** to cover (over) potatoes with straw; **Rosen mit Reisig e.,** to cover (up) roses with branches (*as protection against frost*); (*b*) *Constr:* to cover (roof); to roof (house, etc.); **ein Dach mit Ziegeln e.,** to tile a roof; **ein Haus, ein Dach, mit Stroh e.,** to thatch a house, a roof; (*c*) *Mil:* to provide (trench, dugout) with an overhead cover, with a roof; **sich e.,** to dig oneself in. **2. j-n mit etwas e.,** to provide s.o. with sth.; **sich mit etwas e.,** to provide oneself with sth.; to lay in, take in, a stock, a supply, of sth.; to stock up with sth.; **sich mit Vorräten für den Winter e.,** to lay in one's winter stocks, to lay in stocks, stores, for the winter, to stock up for the winter; **sich mit Kartoffeln, mit Äpfeln, e.,** to get in, lay in, one's stock of potatoes, of apples, to stock up with potatoes, with apples; **sich mit Haushaltswäsche gut e.,** to lay in a good stock of household linen; **die Geschäftsleute decken sich mit Weihnachtsartikeln ein,** the tradesmen are getting in their Christmas goods, their Christmas stocks, the tradesmen are stocking up with Christmas goods; **sich mit Kohlen genügend eingedeckt haben, mit Kohlen genügend eingedeckt sein,** to be well provided with coal, to have a sufficient stock of coal; **wir haben uns für die Feiertage gut mit Büchern eingedeckt,** we have laid in a good stock, a good supply, of books for the holidays.

II. *vbl s.* **1. Eindecken,** *n. in vbl senses.* **2. Eindeckung,** *f.* (*a*)=II. 1; *also:* provision, supply (with stocks, stores, etc.); (*b*) cover, covering; *Constr:* roof, roofing; **E. aus Stroh,** thatched roof; thatch; (*c*) *Mil:* (i) overhead cover, roof (of dugout, etc.); (ii) dugout, *F:* bolt-hole; **bombensichere E.,** bomb-proof dugout.

Eindecker, *m.* (*a*) *Av:* monoplane; (*b*) *Nau:* single-deck ship, single-decker.

Eindeckschiff, *n. Nau:* single-deck ship, single-decker.

eindeichen, *v.tr. sep.* to dike (land), to protect (land) with dikes; **Eindeichung** *f*, dike.

eindellen, *v.tr. sep.* to make a dent, dents, in (sth.); to dent (sth.); (*of hollow object, hat, etc.*) **eingedellt sein,** to be dented.

eindeutig, *a.* clear, plain; with one meaning; unambiguous; unequivocal; **eine eindeutige Antwort geben,** to give a clear, a plain, an unequivocal, answer; **auf eindeutige Weise ausgedrückt,** expressed in clear, plain, terms; **die Sache ist ganz e.,** the matter is perfectly clear, plain, there is no doubt about the matter; **eine eindeutige Handbewegung,** an unmistakable gesture, a gesture leaving no doubt as to its meaning; **eindeutiger Fall von Bestechung,** clear case of bribery; *adv.* **e. ausgedrückt,** expressed in clear, plain, terms; **es war e. seine Stimme,** it was certainly his voice, there is no doubt (that), without (a) doubt, without question, it was his voice.

Eindeutigkeit, *f.* singleness of meaning; unambiguity, unequivocality, unequivocalness; **seine Handbewegung war von unmißverständlicher E.,** his gesture was unmistakable.

eindeutschen. I. *v.tr. sep.* (*a*) to Germanize (word, one's name, race, area, etc.); (*b*) *occ.* to translate (sth.) into German.

II. *vbl s.* **1. Eindeutschen,** *n. in vbl senses.* **2. Eindeutschung,** *f.* (*a*)=II. 1; *also:* Germanization; (*b*) Germanized word *or* name; (*c*) *occ.* translation (into German).

eindicken. I. *v.sep.* **1.** *v.tr.* to boil down, reduce (liquid); to thicken (sauce, etc.); to concentrate (solution, etc.); to condense, inspissate (liquid); to body, give body to (oil, paint, etc.); **eingedickte Milch,** condensed milk; evaporated milk. **2.** *v.i.* (*sein*) (*of liquid*) to thicken, to become thick; (*of solution, etc.*) to become concentrated; (*of paint, etc.*) to liver; to get body, to get thick.

II. *vbl s.* **Eindicken** *n.*, **Eindickung** *f. in vbl senses; also:* concentration (of solution, etc.); condensation, inspissation (of liquid).

eindimensional, *a.* one-dimensional, unidimensional.

eindorren, *v.i. sep.* (*sein*) to shrink in drying, to dry up.

eindosen, *v.tr. sep.* to tin, can (fruit, meat, sardines, etc.); to preserve, conserve, (fruit, meat, etc.) in tins, cans.

eindösen, *v.i. sep.* (*sein*) to doze off, to fall into a doze.

Eindrahtantenne, *f. W.Tel:* single-strand aerial.

eindrähtig, *a. El.E:* single-wire (line, etc.).

Eindrahtleitung, *f. El.E:* single-wire line.

eindrängen (sich), *v.refl. sep.* to force, push, oneself in; to squeeze (oneself) in; to force one's way in; **sich bei j-m e.,** to force oneself upon s.o.; **er hat sich bei uns eingedrängt,** he forced, intruded, himself (up)on us; **er wollte sich in das Gebäude e., aber ein Polizist hielt ihn zurück,** he was about to force, push, his way into the building but a policeman held him back; **er hatte sich in die Versammlung eingedrängt,** he had intruded himself, he had forced his way, into the meeting; **das Wasser drängte sich durch die Ritzen in der Tür ein,** the water came in through the cracks in the door; **er wurde von den eindrängenden Wassermassen fortgerissen,** he was swept away by the inrush of water.

eindrehen, *v.tr. sep.* to screw (sth.) in; **etwas in etwas** *acc.* **e.,** to screw sth. into sth.; to twist, spin, (silver thread, etc.) in with (wool, etc.); **eine Glühbirne e.,** to screw in, put in, an electric light bulb; **j-m, sich** *dat.*, **Locken e.,** to curl s.o.'s, one's, hair.

eindrillen, *v.tr. sep.* **1.** to drill, bore (hole) (into sth.). **2.** (*a*) *Mil: etc:* to drill, train (recruits, etc.); (*b*) *F:* **j-m etwas e.,** to train s.o. in sth.; *F:* to ram, drum, sth. into s.o.; **j-m e., was er sagen soll, tun soll,** to drill s.o. in what he has to say, do; *Sch:* **den Kindern französische Verben e.,** to drill the children in French verbs, to drum French verbs into the children.

eindringen. I. *v.i. sep.* (*strong*) (*sein*) **1. in etwas** *acc.* **e.,** (*a*) (*of pers., soldiers, etc.*) to penetrate, make one's way, force one's way, get, into (house, town, country, etc.); (*of soldiers, etc.*) to enter (town, country, etc.); to invade (country); (*of crowd*) to surge into, throng into, *F:* invade (building, etc.); (*of water, light, etc.*) to penetrate, get, into sth.; (*of water*) to rush into (building, etc.); (*of pointed or sharp object, foreign body, poison, etc.*) to penetrate into sth.; **er drang in den Wald ein,** he penetrated into the forest; **er drang in das Gemach des Königs ein,** he forced his way into the king's cabinet; **die Kugel drang tief in den Schenkel ein,** the bullet penetrated deep into the thigh; **die Feuchtigkeit dringt durch alle Ritzen ein,** the damp is seeping in through all the cracks; **das Wasser war überall eingedrungen,** the water had got in, had penetrated, everywhere; **Wasser dringt in poröre Körper ein,** water penetrates into, impregnates, porous bodies; **die eindringende Feuchtigkeit,** the damp that is seeping in; **die eindringenden Feinde,** the enemy who is thrusting in upon us; the enemy who has penetrated into our territory; (*b*) **in ein Geheimnis e.,** to penetrate, fathom, a secret; **ihre Worte drangen tief in sein Innerstes ein,** her words moved him deeply; her words cut deep into his soul; **er ist tief in die Probleme dieser Sache eingedrungen,** he has gone deeply into the problems of this matter, he has studied closely the problems of this matter; **versuchen, in die Zukunft einzudringen,** to try to see into the future. **2. auf j-n e.,** (*a*) to attack s.o.; *F:* to mob s.o.; *Mil:* to make an assault on, to charge, storm, attack, rush (enemy, etc.); **die Männer drangen mit gezogenen Säbeln auf ihn ein,** the men attacked him, rushed at him, with drawn swords; (*b*) to press s.o.; to plead with s.o.; to reason with s.o.; to entreat, beg, urge, beseech, s.o. (to do sth.); to try to persuade s.o. (to do sth.); **mit Fragen auf j-n e.,** to press, ply, s.o. with questions; **mit Bitten auf j-n e.,** to plead with s.o.; **wir beschlossen, nicht mehr weiter auf ihn einzudringen und ihn sein gefährliches Vorhaben ausführen zu lassen,** we decided not to reason, plead, with him any further but to let him carry out his dangerous plans.

II. *vbl s.* **Eindringen,** *n. in vbl senses; also:* penetration (of chemical, light, bullet, etc.); **E. von Giftgas,** penetration of poison gas; **um das E. von Luft, von Licht, in den Behälter zu verhindern,** to prevent penetration of air, of light, into the container, to prevent air, light, from penetrating, from getting, into the container.

eindringlich, *a.* urgent (warning, entreaty, etc.); **mit eindringlichen Worten schilderte er die Not der Leute,** with moving words he described the plight of the people, he described the plight of the people vividly; *adv.* urgently; **er warnte ihn e., seine Pläne aufzugeben,** he warned him urgently to give up his plans, he urged him to give up his plans; **sie empfahl uns e., nicht ohne Führer auf das Moor zu gehen,** she advised us strongly, she urged us, impressed upon us, not to go on the marshes without a guide; **er spricht immer so e.,** he is always so intense in everything he says; **ich verbot ihm eindringlichst, auf das eindringlichste, auf die Straße zu gehen,** I forbade him most strictly, most sternly, to go into the street; I impressed upon him that he must not go into the street.

Eindringlichkeit, *f.* urgency (of warning, entreaty, etc.); **er sprach mit großer E.,** he spoke with great intensity.

Eindringling, *m.* **-s/-e,** intruder; (*at party, etc.*) uninvited guest, intruder, *F:* gate-crasher; **sich wie ein E. vorkommen,** to feel like an intruder, to feel as if one were intruding.

Eindringungstiefe, *f.* (*a*) *Ball:* (depth of) penetration (of projectile); (*b*) *Mil.Av:* radius of action (of aircraft over enemy territory).

Eindruck, *m.* I. **-(e)s/⸚e.** **1.** impress(ion), imprint; **sie fanden den verwischten E. eines Fußes,** they found the blurred imprint of a foot, a blurred footprint; **E. von Schuhen im Sand,** impression of shoes in the sand; **der E. ihres Kopfes im Kissen,** the impress(ion) of her head on the cushion. **2.** (mental) impression; (*a*) **E. machen,** to make an impression; to be impressive; **j-m E. machen, E. auf j-n machen,** to make an impression on s.o.; to impress s.o.; **mit etwas E. machen,** to make an impression with sth.; **tiefen E. machen,** to make a deep impression; **es hat in, bei, mir einen bleibenden, unauslöschlichen, E. hinterlassen,** it left a lasting impression on me; **um auf die Unwissenden E. zu machen,** in order to impress the ignorant; **seine Standhaftigkeit machte E. auf sie,** his firmness impressed them; **seine Rede machte großen E.,** his speech made, created, a great impression, his speech was most impressive; *F:* his speech went home; **keinen E. machen,** to make no impression, to fail to make an impression, to fail to impress; *F:* to cut no ice (with s.o.); **es machte keinen, nicht den geringsten, E. auf ihn,** it made no impression on him (at all); **was für einen E. machte, hatte, es auf ihn?** what impression did it make on him? **was für einen E. machte sie auf dich? was für einen E. hattest du von ihr?** what impression did you have of her? how did she impress you? how did she strike you? **einen guten, schlechten, E. auf j-n machen,** to make a good, bad, impression on s.o., to impress s.o. favourably, unfavourably; **er macht immer einen schlechten, ungünstigen, E.,** he always gives a bad, unfavourable, impression; **die Reisenden standen noch ganz unter dem E. dieses gewaltigen Anblicks,** the travellers were still under the spell of this majestic sight; **die Überlebenden des Unglücks standen noch vollständig unter dem E. ihres schrecklichen Erlebnisses,** the minds of the survivors of the accident were still filled with vivid memories of their terrible experience; (*b*) **die Stadt macht einen traurigen E.,** the town gives an impression of sadness; **er macht den E. eines sehr besorgten Menschen,** he gives the impression of a very worried man; **ich habe den E., daß . . . ,** it is my impression that . . .; **den E. hervorrufen, vermitteln, machen, als ob . . . ,** to create, give, the impression that . . .; **ich stand lange unter dem E., daß das Haus Herrn X gehörte,** for a long time I was under the impression that the house belonged to Mr X; (*c*) **seine Eindrücke schildern, beschreiben,** to describe one's impressions; **all die verschiedenen Eindrücke stürmten auf sie ein,** all the different impressions crowded in on her; **seine Eindrücke austauschen,** to exchange impressions, *F:* to compare notes.

II. **Eindruck,** *m.* **-(e)s/-e.** **1.** *Print:* printing in (of colour, etc.); *Tex:* (*in calico printing*) grounding in, blocking in (of colours). **2.** *Print:* passage, etc., printed in the text, inserted into the (printed) text.

eindrucken, *v.tr. sep.* (*a*) **etwas in etwas** *acc. & dat.* **e.,** (i) to print sth. in sth., (ii) to imprint sth. on sth.; to emboss sth. on sth.; **die Farben e.,** to print in the colours; **in einem Kapitel einen falschen Absatz e.,** to print a wrong paragraph in a chapter; **Briefpapier mit eingedruckter Adresse,** notepaper with embossed address, embossed notepaper; (*b*) *Tex:* (*in calico printing*) to ground in, block in (colour).

eindrücken, *v.tr. sep.* **1.** (*a*) **etwas e.,** to press, push, sth. in; to stave sth. in; to flatten, squash, crush (box, etc.); **eine Fensterscheibe e.,** to push in, press in, a window-pane; **durch die Explosion wurden viele Fensterscheiben eingedrückt,** many windows were broken, shattered, by the explosion; **bei dem Unfall wurde ihm der Brustkorb eingedrückt,** his chest was crushed in the accident; **aus seinen Boxertagen hatte er eine eingedrückte Nase,** he had a flattened nose from his boxing days; **eingedrückter Hut,** dented hat; battered hat; **die Seite des Schiffes war vollständig eingedrückt,** the side of the ship was completely stove in, completely smashed; *Aut:* **der Kühler war eingedrückt,** the radiator was stove in; *Mil:* **die feindlichen Reihen, die feindliche Front, e.,** to make a breach in the enemy's lines, in the enemy front; (*b*) *Ven:* to beat (game). **2. etwas in etwas** *acc.* **e.,** to press sth. into sth.; to press sth. down in sth.; **Butter in ein Gefäß e.,** *abs.* **Butter e.,** to press butter into a dish; **Sauerkraut in Fässer e.,** to press, pack, sauerkraut into casks. **3. etwas in etwas** *acc.* **e.,** to impress, imprint, sth. on sth.; **er drückte seine Hände in den nassen Sand ein,** he pressed his hands into the wet sand; **in den Sand eingedrückte Fußspuren,** footmarks imprinted on the sand; **er drückte sein Siegel in das Wachs ein,** he impressed his seal into, (up)on, the wax. **4. sich eindrücken,** to become impressed, imprinted, stamped (on sth.); **das Muster hat sich in das Leder eingedrückt,** the pattern has been imprinted, impressed, (up)on the leather; **seine Finger haben sich in den weichen Ton eingedrückt,** his fingers left their imprint, their impression, in the soft clay, he left the imprint, impress, impression, of his fingers in the soft clay.

eindrücklich, *a.* impressive.

eindrucksfähig, *a.* impressionable; sensitive.

Eindruckskunst, *f. Art:* impressionism.

Eindruckskünstler, *m. Art:* impressionist.

eindrucksvoll, *a.* impressive; **eindrucksvolles Gebäude,** impressive building; **höchst e.,** most impressive; **die Feier war sehr e., es war eine sehr eindrucksvolle Feier,** the ceremony was very impressive.

eindübeln, *v.tr. sep.* to dowel (sth.) in; **etwas in etwas** *acc.* **e.,** to dowel sth. into sth.

eindunsten, *v. sep.* **1.** *v.i.* (*sein*) (*of liquid*) to evaporate; **Eindunstung** *f*, evaporation. **2.** = **eindünsten.**

eindünsten, *v.tr. sep.* to evaporate (down) (liquid); **Eindünstung** *f*, evaporating (down), evaporation.

eine *see* **ein**[1].
einebnen, *v.tr. sep.* **1.** to level, even up(ground, site, etc.); to make (ground, etc.) even; to level (road, etc.); to flatten, smooth (surface, etc.); **ein Terrain, ein Baugrundstück, e.,** to level an area, a site; **die Stadt wurde völlig eingeebnet,** the town was flattened, was razed to the ground; **alle gesellschaftlichen Unterschiede wurden eingeebnet,** all social distinctions were levelled out, away, were evened out. **2.** (*of ground, etc.*) **sich einebnen,** to become level, even, smooth.
eineggen, *v.tr. sep. Agr:* to cover up (seed, etc.) by harrowing.
Einehe, *f.* monogamy; **in E. leben,** to live in monogamy; **in E. Lebender,** monogamist.
einehig, *a.* monogamous (pers., tribe, etc.); **e. leben,** to live in monogamy.
eineiig, *a. Biol:* uniovular, uniovulate; **eineiige Zwillinge,** identical twins, uniovular twins.
eineindeutig, *a. Mth: etc:* one-to-one (relation, correspondence).
eineinhalb, *cardinal num.a. inv.* one and a half; **e. Pfund,** a pound and a half, one and a half pounds.
Eineinhalbdecker, *m. Av:* sesquiplane.
eineinhalbmal, *adv.* one and a half times; **e. soviel,** one and a half times as much.
Einemsen, *n. Orn:* anting.
einen, *v.tr.* **1.** to unite (people, country, etc.); to unify (people, etc.); **die Bedrohung des Friedens einte das Land,** the threat to peace unified, united, the country; **ein geeintes Volk,** a united people; **Einung** *f,* unification. **2. sich einen,** to unite; to become united, unified.
Einender, *m. Nau:* single-ended marine boiler.
einengen. I. *v.tr. sep.* **1.** to narrow (sth.); to make (sth.) narrower; to limit, restrict, confine (sth.); to set bounds, limits, to (s.o.'s power, rights, etc.); **die Bedeutung eines Wortes auf einen bestimmten Sinn e.,** to restrict a word to a particular sense; **ihr Tätigkeitsfeld ist eingeengt auf . . .,** their sphere of activity is restricted, limited, to . . .; **seine Forschungen auf ein kleineres Gebiet e.,** to narrow down, restrict, confine, one's research to a smaller field. **2.** (*a*) **j-n e.,** to constrict, restrict, confine, s.o.'s movements; **das Kleid engt mich ein,** the dress cramps, restricts, my movements; (*b*) **sich eingeengt fühlen,** (i) to feel hampered, restricted; (ii) to feel tight in the chest; (iii) to feel oppressed, hemmed in, shut in. **3.** = **abdampfen** I. 3.
II. *vbl s.* **Einengen** *n.*, **Einengung** *f. in vbl senses; also:* limitation, restriction; constriction; **Einengung eines Gesetzes durch neue Bestimmungen,** limiting, limitation, restricting, restriction, of a law by new clauses.
einenteils, *adv.* = **einesteils.**
einer[1] *see* **ein**[1].
Einer[2], *m.* **-s/-.** **1.** *Mth:* unit; **die Zahl dreiundsechzig hat sechs Zehner und drei Einer,** the number sixty-three has six tens and three units. **2.** *Row:* single-sculler.
einerlei. **1.** *inv.a.* (*a*) of one sort, kind; of the same kind; **es gab nur e. Wein,** there was only one sort of, kind of, wine; (*b*) **es ist alles e.,** it's all one, all the same; it makes no difference; it doesn't matter; **mir ist alles e.,** it is all one, all the same, to me; I don't care one way or the other; **es ist mir ziemlich e., ob . . .,** it matters little to me, it makes little difference to me, I don't care very much, whether . . . ; **ihm ist es e., ob wir kommen oder nicht,** he doesn't mind whether we come or not. **2.** *s.* **Einerlei,** *n.* **-s,** monotony; sameness; humdrum, humdrumness (of one's existence, etc.); **das (ewige) E. des täglichen Lebens, des Alltags,** the humdrum of daily life; the daily grind.
einernten, *v.tr. sep.* to harvest, gather (crops); *F:* to reap, gain, earn (fame, praise, etc.).
einerseits, *adv.* on the one hand; in one respect; **e. . . . and(e)rerseits,** on the one hand . . . on the other hand; **e. möchte ich sehr gern wieder nach Italien fahren, aber and(e)rerseits lockt mich doch Spanien noch mehr,** on the one hand I should love to go to Italy again, but on the other hand, Spain attracts me even more; **e. hat er ganz recht, aber and(e)rerseits kann man auch den Standpunkt seiner Gegner verstehen,** in one respect he is quite right, but on the other hand, one can also understand the point of view of his opponents.
Einerstelle, *f. Mth:* unit's place.
Einerzelt, *n.* one-man tent.
einesteils, *adv.* on the one hand; in one respect; **e. . . . ander(e)nteils,** on the one hand . . . on the other hand.
einexerzieren, *v.tr. sep.* (*a*) *Mil: etc:* to drill, train (recruits, etc.); (*b*) **j-m etwas e.,** to train s.o. in sth.; to drill s.o. in sth., to do sth.
einfach. I. *a.* **1.** (*a*) single; **einfache Breite,** single width; **Schuh mit einfacher Sohle,** shoe with a single sole; **den Faden e. nehmen,** to take a single thread; *Rail: etc:* **einfache Fahrkarte,** single, *U.S:* one-way, ticket; **einfacher Fahrpreis, einfache Fahrt,** single fare; single journey; *Constr:* **einfacher Bogen,** single arch; *Mus:* **Instrument mit einfachem Rohrblatt,** single-reed instrument; *see also:* **Buchführung**; (*b*) simple, uncompounded; *Ch: etc:* **einfacher Körper,** simple, elementary, body; *Ph: etc:* **einfache Farben,** primary colours; *Bot:* **einfache Blüte,** single flower; **Pflanze mit einfachen Blättern,** plant with simple leaves; *Gram:* **einfacher Satz,** simple sentence; **einfache Zeit,** simple tense; *Com:* **einfacher Zins,** simple interest. **2.** (*uncomplicated*) simple; easy; **eine einfache Aufgabe,** a simple task; **ich kann mir nichts Einfacheres vorstellen,** I can't think of anything more simple, easier; **das Problem ist einfach zu lösen,** the problem is easy to solve; **das ist gar nicht so einfach,** that's not so simple, easy; that requires, takes, some doing; **es wird am einfachsten sein, wenn du selbst hingehst,** it will be simplest if you go there yourself; *Med:* **einfacher Knochenbruch,** simple fracture; *Mth:* **einen Bruch auf die einfachste Form bringen,** to reduce a fraction to its lowest terms; *F:* **um es auf den einfachsten Nenner zu bringen,** to put it in a nutshell. **3.** ordinary (people, etc.); simple (folk, life, tastes, etc.); plain (people, dress, food, etc.); plain, homely (meal, etc.); **ein einfacher Stil,** a plain, unlaboured, unaffected, style; **das einfache Landvolk,** plain country-folk; **die einfache Klugheit gebietet, daß . . .,** simple, ordinary, elementary, prudence demands that . . .; **einfaches Holz,** plain wood; **ein einfaches Leben führen,** to lead a simple life; **der einfache Mann,** the common man; **der einfache Soldat,** the ordinary soldier; the private; **die einfachen Soldaten,** the ordinary soldiers; the rank and file; *adv.* **e. leben,** to live simply; **e. sprechen, sich e. kleiden,** to speak, dress, simply.
II. **einfach,** *emotive particle* simply; just; **es ist e. eine Frage der Zeit,** it is simply, just, a matter of time; **ich sagte ihm (ganz) e., daß . . .,** I just, simply, told him that . . . ; **du siehst e. reizend aus,** you look simply lovely; **du 'mußt e.,** you simply 'must; **das ist e. unmöglich,** that is simply impossible; **die Sache ist e. die, daß . . .,** the matter is simply that . . .; **es ist e. Wahnsinn,** it is sheer madness; **es ist e. Zeitverschwendung,** it's a pure, sheer, waste of time; **er wurde e. John genannt,** he was simply called John.
einfach-, Einfach-, *comb.fm.* single-, single . . .; *Ch:* mono-; *Mec.E:* **einfachwirkend,** single-acting, single-action (machine, motor, etc.); *Ch:* **Einfachbromjod,** iodine monobromide; **Einfachchlorjod,** iodine monochloride; **Einfachchlorschwefel,** sulphur monochloride; **einfachkohlensaures . . .,** neutral carbonate of . . . .
einfachbasisch, *a. Ch:* monobasic.
Einfachbetrieb, *m. Tp: Tg:* simplex operation.
Einfachbier, *n.* small beer, table beer.
einfachbrechend, *a. Opt:* singly refracting.
Einfachbrechung, *f. Opt:* simple, single, refraction.
Einfachdampfraumkessel, *m.* boiler with a single steam-space.
einfächerig, *a.* (*a*) undivided (box, etc.); (box, etc.) not divided into sections; (*b*) *Bot:* unilocular, uniloculate.
einfachfrei, *a. Ch:* univariant, monovariant.
Einfachheit, *f.* **1.** *Phil: etc:* elementary nature (of substance, etc.). **2.** simplicity (of method, task, etc.); **der E. halber, wegen,** for the sake of simplicity; to make it easier, to make it less complicated; **das ist die E. selber,** it is simplicity itself. **3.** simplicity (of dress, customs, style, etc.); plainness (of dress, furniture, style, etc.); **E. der Lebensführung,** simplicity of (s.o.'s way of) life; **die E. und Genügsamkeit der Landbevölkerung,** the simplicity and contentment of the rural population; **er besitzt die E., die ein Kennzeichen der Größe ist,** he has the simplicity which goes with greatness.
Einfachhobeleisen, *n. Tls:* uncut plane iron.
Einfachkabel, *n. El.E:* single (-core, -conductor) cable.
Einfachleitung, *f. El:* single conductor; simplex circuit; *Tp: etc:* single line.
Einfachobjektiv, *n. Phot:* single lens, landscape lens.
Einfachschnur, *f. El.E:* single(-conductor) cord *or* flex.
Einfachschraubenschlüssel, *m. Tls:* single-ended spanner.
Einfachstrombetrieb, *m. El.E:* single-current working.
Einfachstromturbine, *f. Av: etc:* turbo-jet (unit).
Einfachtarifzähler, *m. El:* single-tariff meter, single-rate meter.
einfädeln, *v.tr. sep.* **1.** to thread (needle); *abs.* **e.,** to thread a needle; to thread (up) a sewing-machine. **2.** *F:* to set (sth.) on foot; to start the ball rolling, to set the ball rolling; **wir müssen die Sache schlau, klug, e.,** we must go about, set about, the matter subtly; we must be subtle about it; **ich weiß, wie man es e. muß,** I know how to go about it, set about it. **3.** *Mil:* to filter (vehicles into traffic, troops into column, etc.).
Einfadenaufhängung, *f. El.E:* unifilar suspension.
Einfadenlampe, *f. El:* single filament lamp.
einfädig, *a.* single-stranded; *El: etc:* unifilar.
Einfädler, *m.* **-s/-,** (needle-)threader.
einfahren, *v.sep.* (*strong*) I. *v.i.* (*sein*) **in etwas** *acc.*, *occ. dat.*, **e.,** (*of pers.*) to drive into (courtyard, etc.), to enter (courtyard, etc.) (*by vehicle*); *Min:* to go down (mine-shaft), to descend (pit); (*of vehicle*) to drive into, enter (courtyard, etc.); (*of train*) to come into, enter (station); (*of ship*) to enter (harbour); to sail into (harbour); **der Zug fuhr gerade ein,** the train was just coming in; **die Gäste fuhren gerade ein,** the guests were just driving in; *Ven:* (*of fox, etc.*) **in den Bau e.,** to go to earth, to go, run, to ground.
II. **einfahren,** *v.tr.* **1.** to get in, gather in, bring in, take in (the harvest, etc.) (*in cart, etc.*). **2.** (*a*) to close (pontoon bridge); (*b*) *Av:* to retract (undercarriage, flaps). **3.** to break in (horse) (for driving); *Aut:* to run in (motor-car, etc.); (*notice*) **'wird eingefahren', 'running in'**; *Ski: etc:* **die Bahn ist noch nicht eingefahren,** the run has not yet worn smooth. **4.** to knock down (door, gate, wall, etc.) (*by driving against it*); (*of motorist*) **j-m den Kühler e.,** to crush s.o.'s radiator (*in collision*). **5. sich einfahren,** (*of pers.*) to get used to driving (motor-car, etc.); to get used to riding (bicycle); (*of motor-car, etc.*) to (be) run in.
III. *vbl s.* **Einfahren,** *n. in vbl senses; also:* entry (into courtyard, station, harbour, etc.); *Min:* descent (into the pit); *cp.* **Einfahrt.**
Einfahrgleis, *n. Rail:* arrival line, arrival track.
Einfahrgruppe, *f. Rail:* receiving yard.
Einfahrschuh, *m. Rail:* rerailing ramp.
Einfahrsignal, *n. Rail:* home signal.
Einfahrstraße, *f. Rail:* arrival line; incoming line.
Einfahrt, *f.* **1.** entry (into courtyard, station, harbour, etc.); *Min:* descent (into the pit); **das Unglück geschah bei der E. des Zuges in den Bahnhof,** the accident happened when the train was coming into, entering, the station; **der Zug aus Düsseldorf hat E. auf, in, Gleis 2,** the train from Düsseldorf is now coming into Platform 2; **wir beobachteten die E. der Gäste in den Schloßhof,** we watched the guests driving into, entering, the courtyard of the castle; **bei der E. in die Grube, in den Schacht, beobachteten sie . . .,** during their descent of the pit, as they were descending the pit, while they were going down the shaft, they observed . . . . **2.** getting in, gathering in, bringing in, taking in (of the harvest, etc.) (*by cart, etc.*). **3.** closing (of pontoon bridge). **4.** (carriage-)entrance, (carriage-)gate, gateway (to, of, building, etc.); way in (of, building, town, etc.); entrance (to, of, tunnel, harbour), mouth (of tunnel, harbour); access (road) (to motorway); *Min:* pit-head; *Ven:* entrance to the burrow (of fox, etc.); (*traffic sign*) 'way in', 'entrance'; **das Gebäude wird eine breitere E. erhalten,** the building will be given a broader entrance, carriage-gate, gateway; **die E. ist frei,** the entrance is clear; **'bitte E. freihalten!'** 'please keep entrance clear'; **'keine E.!'** 'no entry'.
Einfahrtsboje, *f. Nau:* entrance buoy.
Einfahrtsignal, *n. Rail:* home signal.
Einfahrtstonne, *f. Nau:* entrance buoy.
Einfahrzylinder, *m. Av:* jack (of undercarriage).
Einfall, *m.* **1.** collapsing, collapse (of building, bridge, wall, etc.); caving in (of roof, ground). **2.** entrance (*esp.* from above); *Opt:* incidence (of light, etc.). **3. E. (in ein Gebiet, usw.),** invasion (of territory, etc.); incursion (into territory, etc.); raid (into territory, etc.); **wir müssen mit neuen Einfällen des Feindes rechnen,** we must expect new invasions of our territory, new incursions, raids, by the enemy. **4.** (sudden) idea; **glücklicher, lustiger, E.,** fortunate,

amusing, idea; **sonderbarer, merkwürdiger, E.,** strange, odd, idea; queer notion; **er ist voll von geistreichen und witzigen Einfällen,** he is full of bright and witty ideas; **auf diesen E. wäre ich nie gekommen,** this idea would never have occurred to me; **plötzlich kam ihm der E., ins Kino zu gehen,** he suddenly took it into his head to go to the cinema; **was für ein E.!** what an idea! **einem plötzlichen E. folgend rief er seinen Freund an,** a sudden whim made him telephone his friend; on a sudden impulse he telephoned his friend.

Einfallebene, f. Opt: Geol: etc:=**Einfallsebene.**

einfallen. I. v.i.sep. (strong) (sein) **1.** (of building, roof, bridge, wall, etc.) to fall in; to collapse; to give way; to fall down, tumble down; (of roof, ground, etc.) to cave in; (of ground, building, etc.) to founder; **viele Häuser fielen während des Erdbebens ein,** many houses fell in, collapsed, during the earthquake; **einzufallen drohen,** to be in danger of collapse. **2.** (of features, etc.) to sink in, to become hollow, gaunt, haggard; (of pers.) **eingefallen sein,** to be wasted, haggard, gaunt; **eingefallene Augen,** sunken, hollow, eyes; **eingefallene Wangen,** gaunt, hollow, sunken, cheeks; **eingefallene Gesichtszüge,** pinched, haggard, gaunt, hollow, sunken, features; **nach der langen Krankheit sah sie sehr eingefallen aus,** after the long illness she looked very haggard, gaunt, peaked. **3.** (a) to enter (esp. from above); Ven: (of fowl) to settle down, alight (on water, etc.); to come in to water; Opt: etc: **einfallender Strahl,** incident ray; Min: **einfallende Wetter,** intake air; (b) Geol: Min: (of stratum, coal-seam, gallery, etc.) to dip, pitch; to underlay, hade; to plunge; **einfallender Schacht,** incline(-shaft); **einfallende Strecke,** dip; **steil einfallendes Flöz,** steeply inclined coal-seam; **Einfallende** f, grade-heading, dip(-road), dip-heading; (c) (of lock) to click to, to engage. **4.** to break in (on a conversation), F: to cut in, butt in; Mus: (of voices, instruments, etc.) to come in, join in. **5.** (a) (of night, etc.) to fall; (of storm) to arise; (of frost, rain, etc.) to set in; (b) (in ein Land, usw.) **e.,** to invade, overrun (country, etc.); to make a raid (into enemy country, etc.); to make incursions (into enemy country, etc.); (c) (of trains, buses, etc.) **in X e.,** to arrive in X. **6. j-m e.,** (a) to occur to s.o., to s.o.'s mind; to come to s.o.'s mind; to strike s.o.; **da fällt mir gerade ein, daß . . .,** the thought has just struck me, it just comes to my mind that . . .; it just occurs to me that . . .; **sie sagte, was ihr gerade einfiel,** she said the first thing that came into her head, mind; **dabei fällt mir ein, daß ich noch einen Brief zu schreiben habe,** that reminds me that I have still got a letter to write; **in diesem Augenblick fiel mir das Kind ein,** at that moment I remembered the child; **jetzt ist es mir wieder eingefallen,** now I remember (again); **es fällt mir im Augenblick nicht ein,** I can't remember at the moment; **es wird dir schon wieder e.,** it will come back to you soon; (b) F: to enter s.o.'s head; **es fällt mir nicht ein, mich ausnützen zu lassen,** I have no intention of letting myself be exploited; **so etwas würde mir niemals e.,** such an idea would never enter my head; **ich weiß nicht, was ihm da wieder eingefallen ist,** I don't know what he has got into his head this time; **was fällt dir ein!** what do you mean by that? what's the idea? **es wäre mir im Traum nicht eingefallen, daß . . .,** it would never have entered my head that . . .; **das fällt mir im Traum nicht ein,** I wouldn't dream of it; **das sollte mir e.!** **fällt mir gar nicht ein!** I wouldn't dream of it! F: not (blooming) likely! **(es) sich e. lassen, etwas zu tun,** to entertain the idea of doing sth.; to try to do sth.; **laß dir das ja nicht e.,** don't you dare to do such a thing! you'd better not! **laß es dir nicht e., ihn um Rat zu bitten,** don't try to ask him for advice; **du könntest dir etwas Besseres e. lassen,** you might think of something better. **7.** v.tr. **sich** dat. **etwas e.,** to break (one's skull, etc.) by a fall.

    II. vbl s. **Einfallen,** n. in vbl senses; also: collapse; Opt: etc: incidence (of light, etc.); Min: inclination; dip, pitch; underlay, hade; grade; **zum E. bringen,** to cause (sth.) to fall in, collapse; cp. **Einfall.**

Einfallklinke, f. Mec.E: catch; pawl.

Einfallpforte, f. Opt: etc: port of entry (of radiation, etc.).

Einfallsböschung, f. Geol: dip slope.

Einfallschnalle, f. Clockm: rack hook.

Einfallsebene, f. Opt: plane of incidence; Geol: etc: plane of the dip.

Einfallsfeld, n. Opt: etc: plane of entry (of radiation, etc.).

einfallslos, a. lacking in ideas; **er ist gänzlich e.,** he is entirely lacking in ideas.

Einfallslosigkeit, f. paucity of ideas; lack of imagination, unimaginativeness; **seine E. ist nicht zu übertreffen,** no one could be more lacking in ideas than he.

Einfallslot, n. Opt: perpendicular, normal (line) (to plane of incidence of light).

Einfallspforte, f. gateway.

einfallsreich, a. full of ideas, rich in ideas.

Einfallsreichtum, m. fertility of ideas; **der E. dieses Dichters, dieses Werks, ist unerschöpflich,** this poet, this work, shows an endless fertility of ideas.

Einfallsstrahl, m. Opt: incident (ray).

Einfallstor, n. gateway.

Einfall(s)winkel, m. Ph: angle of incidence; Ball: etc: angle of descent; Geol: Min: angle of dip; angle of hade.

Einfalt, f. -/. (a) simplicity; naïvety; artlessness; **E. des Herzens,** singleness of heart, single-heartedness; **er besitzt die E. eines Kindes,** he has the simplicity, the artlessness, of a child; he is as artless as a child; **klassische Kunst zeichnet sich durch edle E. aus,** classical art is distinguished by its noble simplicity; (b) simpleness, simple-mindedness; stupidity; **seine E. geht mir auf die Nerven,** his stupidity gets on my nerves; **heilige E.!** what innocence! blissful ignorance! **sie gibt sich als die E. vom Lande aus,** she acts the simple country-girl.

einfalten, v.tr. sep. to fold (sth.) (up); to turn in (the sides of a piece of paper, etc.); to turn down (the corner of a piece of paper, etc.).

einfältig, a. **1.** single; simple. **2.** (a) simple; simple-hearted; naïve; artless; **einfältigen Herzens,** single-hearted, simple-hearted; adv. with simplicity; (b) simple; simple-minded; stupid; **einfältige Bemerkungen machen,** to make artless, naïve, remarks; **ich bin nicht so e., das zu glauben,** I am not so stupid, simple, as to believe that; **was für eine einfältige Seele er ist!** what a simple soul he is! **hören Sie auf mit Ihrem einfältigen Geschwätz!** stop talking rubbish! **sie lächelte e.,** she smiled stupidly.

Einfältigkeit, f. **1.** singleness; simplicity. **2.** (a) simplicity; naïvety; artlessness; **E. des Herzens,** singleness of heart, single-heartedness; (b) simpleness, simple-mindedness; stupidity; **seine E. geht mir auf die Nerven,** his stupidity gets on my nerves.

einfältiglich, adv. A. & B: with simplicity.

Einfaltspinsel, m. F: simpleton, ninny.

einfalzen, v.tr. sep.—**falzen** I. 1, II. 2 (a).

Einfamilienhaus, n. house (suitable for one family); one-family unit, one-family dwelling.

Einfang, m. Atom.Ph: capture, trapping.

einfangen, v.tr. sep. (strong) **1.** (a) to catch (s.o., sth.); to capture (s.o., sth.); to seize (s.o., sth.); Atom.Ph: to capture, trap (electrons); **mit dem Lasso e.,** to lasso (animal); **einen Bienenschwarm e.,** to hive a swarm of bees; **es gelang ihnen, den Verbrecher wieder einzufangen,** they succeeded in re-catching, re-capturing, the criminal; (b) Nau: (of sail) to catch (the wind); (c) to catch, capture (a mood, an expression, etc.); **in dieser Schilderung ist die friedliche Abendstimmung wirkungsvoll eingefangen,** in this description the peaceful mood of the evening is effectively caught, captured, portrayed. **2.** (of animal) **sich (in etwas** acc.) **einfangen,** to bury its fangs (in sth.).

Einfarbdrossel, f. Orn: Tickell's thrush.

einfärben, v.tr. sep. (a) to dye (dress, material, etc.) (in order to obliterate pattern, to hide stain, etc.); to get the dye well into (material, etc.); **etwas rot e.,** to dye sth. red; (b) Print: etc: to ink (forme).

einfarbig, a. unicolour, unicoloured; plain (material, dress, etc.); single-coloured (flower, etc.); (decoration, trimming, etc.) in one colour; Ph: etc: monochromatic (light, etc.); **einfarbige Seidenstoffe,** plain silks.

Einfarbigkeit, f. uniformity of colour.

Einfarbstar, m. Orn: spotless starling.

Einfaßband, n. binding (ribbon); (bias) binding; (decorative) edging.

einfassen. I. v.tr.sep. **1.** (a) to surround, encompass, bound (sth.) (with sth.); to edge, line, border (road, etc.) (with hedges, etc.); to enclose (sth.), to close (sth.) in (by wall, etc.); (ein Grundstück) mit einer Hecke, einem Zaun, einer Mauer, **e.,** to hedge in, fence in, wall in (piece of ground); **eine Quelle e.,** to kerb, curb, a well; **von Blumenbeeten eingefaßter Rasen,** lawn surrounded, bounded, bordered, by flower-beds, edged with flower-beds; (b) to put a border, an edging, on (sth.); to edge, border, bind, hem (material, etc.); to pipe (material, etc.); to braid (material, etc.); to edge, border, bind (hat) (with ribbon); to welt (glove, shoe); to bind (brim of a hat); to frame (page of a book, etc.) (with an ornamental border); to set, mount (precious stone); **etwas mit einer Spitze e.,** to edge, border, sth. with lace. **2.** (Mehl, usw.) **in Säcke, Tüten, e.,** to put (flour, etc.) into sacks, bags, etc.; to sack (flour, etc.); to bag (up) (flour, etc.).

    II. vbl s. **1. Einfassen,** n. in vbl senses. **2. Einfassung,** f. (a)=II. 1; (b) border (of piece of ground, etc.); lip, kerb, curb(-stone) (of well); edge, edging, border (of material, etc.); welt (of glove, shoe); framing, (ornamental) border (in book, manuscript, etc.); setting, mount(ing) (of precious stone); bezel (of precious stone); frame (of mirror, etc.).

Einfaßschiene, f. binding strip; edging strip.

Einfassungsband, n. binding (ribbon); (bias) binding; (decorative) edging.

Einfassungsmauer, f. surrounding wall; retaining wall (of well).

einfetten, v.tr.sep. to grease (parts of machine, one's skin, boots, etc.); to lubricate (parts of machine, etc.); to smear (leather, etc.) (with sth.); to dub (leather); **sich** dat. **die Haut, seine Haut, sich, mit Creme e.,** to rub cream into one's skin; **die Kuchenform e.,** to grease the cake-tin; (of water-fowl) **sich e.,** to apply oil from the preen gland.

einfeuchten, v.tr.sep. to damp, moisten, wet (sth.); Ind: to spray (pulp, etc.); **Wäsche e.,** to damp, sprinkle, linen (for ironing).

einfeuern, v.i.sep. (haben) **1.** to light a fire (in a stove, grate, etc.). **2. auf j-n, etwas, e.,** to fire at (the enemy, enemy ship, etc.). **3. j-m e.,** to make things, it, hot for s.o.

einfieren, v.tr.sep. Nau: to slack (rope).

einfinden (sich), v.refl.sep. (strong) **1.** to come (bei j-m, an einem Ort, to s.o., to a place); to appear, to turn up (an einem Ort, zu etwas, at a place, for sth.); to arrive (zur verabredeten Zeit, at the appointed time); to present oneself (for an examination, etc.); **sich wieder e.,** (of pers.) to come back, to return; (of lost object) to be found, turn up (again); **er fand sich pünktlich um acht Uhr ein,** he came, appeared, arrived, turned up, punctually at eight; **er fand sich zur verabredeten Zeit vor dem Rathaus ein,** he came to the town hall at the appointed time, he appeared, arrived, outside the town hall at the appointed time; **er versäumte es, sich zu der Feier einzufinden,** he failed to come to, for, to appear for, at, the ceremony, to be present, to present himself, to turn up, at the ceremony. **2. sich in etwas e.,** to grow familiar with (situation, work, etc.), to familiarize oneself with (situation, work, etc.).

Einflächer, m. -s/-. Av: monoplane.

einflammig, a. (gas-cooker, etc.) with one ring, burner; Mch: single-flame (boiler, etc.).

Einflammrohrkessel, m. Mch: single-flue, Cornish, boiler.

einflechten, v.tr. sep. (strong) **etwas in etwas e.,** (a) to twist sth. into sth.; to plait sth. into sth.; to weave sth. into sth.; **Blumen in eine Girlande e.,** to twist flowers into a garland; **buntes Stroh e.,** to weave in coloured straw; **ein Band ins Haar e.,** to plait a ribbon into one's hair; (b) to work in, insert (remarks, jokes, etc.) (into one's speech, etc.); to include (remarks, jokes, etc.) (in one's speech, etc.); to weave, insert, introduce (episodes, etc.) (into novel, etc.).

einflicken, v.tr. sep. (a) to insert (a patch in a garment); (b) to interpolate (word, phrase, passage, etc.) (in text, etc.); **diese Stelle muß nachträglich eingeflickt worden sein,** this passage must have been interpolated later on; **hie und da flickte er ein Zitat in seine Rede ein,** now and again he worked a quotation into his speech.

einfliegen, v.sep. (strong) **1.** v.i. (sein) (of aircraft, etc.) to fly in; **in ein Gebiet e.,** to fly into a territory. **2.** v.tr. to break (window, etc.) (by flying through, at, it). **3.** v.tr. Mil.Av: **Truppen e.,** to fly in troops. **4.** v.tr. Av: (a) **eine Maschine e.,** to carry out test-flights with an aircraft, to test-fly an aircraft, to fly an aircraft in; (b) **eine Strecke e.,** to fly a line for the first time. **5.** (of pers.) **sich einfliegen,** to get used to flying.

Einflieger, m. test pilot.

einfließen. I. v.i. sep. (strong) (sein) **1. in etwas e.,** (a) (of liquid, air) to flow into sth.; (of river,

etc.) to flow into (the sea, etc.), to enter (the sea, etc.); **frische Luft kann e.,** fresh air can flow in; **einfließend,** inflowing; (*b*) *Lit:* (*of ideas, etc.*) to enter (into s.o.'s life, judgment, etc.). **2.** (*of funds*) to come in. **3. etwas e. lassen,** to throw out, let fall, drop, a hint (in the course of the conversation, etc.); to slip a remark (into one's speech, etc.); to work in, insert (remarks, quotations, etc.) (into one's speech, etc.); to include (remarks, quotations, etc.) (in one's speech, etc.); **e. lassen, daß . . . ,** to make it understood that . . . ; **er ließ einige Bemerkungen über die schlechten Manieren gewisser Leute in seine Rede e.,** he slipped a few remarks about certain people's bad manners into his speech; **er ließ ins Gespräch e., daß er beabsichtige . . . ,** in the course of the conversation he gave a hint of his intention to . . . ; in the course of the conversation he threw out, let fall, dropped, a hint of his intention to, that he intended to . . . .

II. **Einfließen,** *n. in vbl senses; also:* inflowing, influx (of water, air, etc.); *cp.* **Einfluß 1**

einflößen, *v.tr. sep.* **j-m (etwas) e.,** (*a*) to pour (medicine, brandy, etc.) into s.o.'s mouth; to feed (patient, etc.) with (soup, etc.); (*b*) to infuse, instil, put, (a feeling, principle, etc.) into s.o.; to impart (a feeling, principle, etc.) to s.o.; to inspire s.o. (with a feeling, principle, etc.); **j-m Mitleid, Verdacht, Interesse, e.,** to arouse s.o.'s compassion, suspicion, interest; **Achtung, Bewunderung, e.,** to command, to inspire, respect, admiration; **j-m Vertrauen e.,** to inspire s.o.'s confidence; **j-m Mut e.,** to infuse, instil, put, courage into s.o.; to impart courage to s.o.; to inspire s.o. with courage; to excite, arouse, raise, s.o.'s courage; to encourage s.o.; **von Jugend auf waren ihm diese Grundsätze eingeflößt worden,** from youth these principles had been instilled into him.

einfluchten, *v.tr. sep.* to bring (object) into line; to align, line up (objects); to lay out, set, (objects) in a line.

Einflug, *m.* **1.** flying in; **der E. in das Feindgebiet ist gelungen,** aircraft successfully penetrated enemy territory; **wir beobachteten den E. der Bienen in den Stock,** we watched the bees flying into, entering, the hive. **2. E. in etwas,** flight into sth.; **sie unternahmen zahlreiche Einflüge in das Feindgebiet,** they made numerous flights into enemy territory. **3.** entrance (to bee-hive, pigeon-house, etc.).

einflüg(e)lig, *a.* having one wing; **einflüg(e)lige Tür,** single-wing door; *Rail:* **einflüg(e)liges Signal,** single-arm semaphore; *Min:* **einflüg(e)liger Abbau,** winning in a single direction.

Einflugschneise, *f. Av:* air corridor; flying lane.

Einfluß, *m.* **1.** inflow, influx (of water, air, etc.); **kurz vor dem E. ins Meer erweitert sich der Fluß,** the river widens shortly before it flows into, enters, the sea. **2.** inlet; orifice, opening (*through which water, etc., enters*). **3.** influence (on, upon, over, s.o., sth.); effect (on, upon, s.o., sth.); influence (with s.o., at court, etc.); (*of pers.*) **E. (bei j-m) haben,** to have influence (with s.o.); **(einen) E. (auf j-n, etwas) haben,** to influence (s.o., sth.), to have, exercise, an influence (on, over, s.o., sth.), to have an effect (on, upon, s.o., sth.); (*of thg*) to affect (s.o., result, event, etc.); (*of pers.*) **einen E. auf j-n ausüben,** to exercise, exert, have, an influence over, on, s.o.; to bring influence to bear on s.o.; to influence s.o.; **(einen) E. (auf j-n, etwas) nehmen,** to influence (s.o., sth.); **seinen E. (zu j-s Gunsten, Nachteil) geltend machen,** to use one's influence (in favour, to the disadvantage, of s.o.); **seinen ganzen E. geltend machen, um zu . . . ,** to bring every influence to bear in order to . . . ; **unter j-s, E., unter dem E. von etwas, stehen,** to be under the influence, sway, of s.o., sth.; to be influenced by s.o., sth.; **großen E. im Parlament haben,** to have great influence, sway, in the House; **seinen E. mißbrauchen,** to abuse one's influence; **äußere Einflüsse, Einflüsse von außen,** outside influences; **guter, günstiger, wohltuender, schlechter, E.,** good, favourable, beneficial, bad, influence, effect; **unter dem E. von Alkohol,** under the influence of drink, alcohol; **wenn sie unter dem E. des Hypnotiseurs stand,** when the influence of the hypnotist was upon her; **E. bei Hofe,** influence, credit, at court; **sein Name hat großen E.,** his name carries great weight; **ein Mann von E.,** a man of influence, consequence; **er hat (einen) E. auf den Gang der Untersuchung,** he can influence the course of the enquiry; **Einflüsse, die im Leben des Dichters eine Rolle spielten,** influences which played a part in the poet's life; **Leidenschaften sollten keinen E. auf deine Entscheidungen haben,** passions should not (be allowed to) influence your decisions.

Einflußgebiet, *n. Dipl: etc:*=**Einflußsphäre.**

Einflußlinien, *f.pl. Mec: etc:* lines of influence.

einflußlos, *a.* without influence; uninfluential; **er spielte einmal eine wichtige Rolle, jetzt aber ist er ganz e.,** he played an important part at one time, but now he is quite without influence; **das ist e. auf meine Entscheidung,** that doesn't influence my decision.

Einflußlosigkeit, *f.* lack of influence; **er ist in dieser Position zur E. verurteilt,** in this position he is unable to exercise any influence.

Einflußnahme, *f.* -/. influencing; **eine E. auf den Ablauf der Ereignisse ist jetzt unmöglich,** it is now impossible to influence the course of events.

einflußreich, *a.* influential (pers., position); (pers.) of influence, consequence; **einflußreiche Freunde haben,** to have influential friends; **einflußreiche Persönlichkeiten auf dem Gebiet der Kunst,** persons of influence in the world of art; **einflußreiche Position,** influential position.

Einflußrohr, *n.* inflow pipe; inlet pipe.

Einflußsphäre, *f. Dipl: etc:* sphere of influence; **die französische E. in Afrika,** the French sphere of influence in Africa.

einflüstern. I. *v.tr. sep.* **j-m etwas e.,** to whisper (word, etc.) to s.o.; **einem Mitschüler e.,** to prompt a classmate; **nicht e.!** no prompting! **diese Lügen muß dir dein sauberer Freund eingeflüstert haben,** it must have been that nice friend of yours who told you these lies; **der Teufel muß ihm eingeflüstert haben, das zu tun,** he must have been prompted by the devil to do that; **das hat ihm seine Frau eingeflüstert,** it was his wife who put the idea into his head.

II. *vbl s.* **1. Einflüstern,** *n. in vbl senses.* **2. Einflüsterung,** *f.* (*a*)=II. 1; (*b*) prompting; whispered temptation (of the devil, etc.); **hören Sie nicht auf seine Einflüsterungen,** don't listen to his insinuations.

einfluten, *v.i. sep.* (*sein*) (*of water, sunlight, etc.*) to flood in; to stream in; **das Wasser flutete von allen Seiten in das sinkende Schiff ein,** the water flooded, streamed, into the sinking ship from all sides.

einforderbar, *a.* claimable, demandable.

einfordern, *v.tr. sep.* to call in (debt, etc.), to demand payment of (debt, etc.) (from s.o.); to claim (debt, etc.) (from s.o.); **wir müssen die ausstehenden Beträge e.,** we must call in, demand payment of, claim, the outstanding sums; *Fin:* **nicht eingefordertes Kapital,** uncalled capital.

einförmig, *a.* (*a*) *Lit:* uniform; (*b*) monotonous, unvarying (landscape, surroundings, style, life, etc.).

Einförmigkeit, *f.* (*a*) *Lit:* uniformity; (*b*) monotony; sameness.

einforsten, *v.tr. sep. A:* **einen Wald e.,** to prohibit, ban, public use of a wood.

einfräsen, *v.tr. sep. Mec.E:* **eine Rinne in ein Werkstück e.,** to mill a groove into a piece of work; **ein Gesenke e.,** to sink a die.

einfressen, *v.tr. sep.* (*strong*) **1.** (*a*) **etwas e.,** to swallow sth.; *F:* **die Arbeiter müssen viel Staub e.,** the workers have to swallow a lot of dust; **seinen Ärger e.,** to swallow one's anger; (*b*) (*of acid, etc.*) **etwas e.,** to eat into sth.; **die Säure frißt die Magenwand ein,** the acid eats into, erodes, the wall of the stomach; (*c*) (*of acid, etc.*) **Löcher, usw., in etwas** *acc.* **e.,** to eat holes, etc., in (material, etc.). **2. sich in etwas einfressen,** (*of insect, worm*) to eat into, to eat its way into (wood, etc.); (*of acid*) to eat into (metal, etc.); to eat away (metal, etc.); to corrode, erode, pit (metal, etc.); (*of metal parts, etc.*) **eingefressen,** corroded, eroded, pitted; **die Säure frißt sich in das Eisen ein,** the acid eats into the iron, eats away, corrodes, erodes, the iron; **der Haß fraß sich ihm in die Seele ein, fraß sich in seine Seele ein,** hatred was gnawing at his heart; **das Gefühl der Enttäuschung beginnt sich einzufressen,** the feeling of disappointment is beginning to take firm hold.

einfried(ig)en. I. *v.tr. sep.* to enclose, close in (piece of ground, etc.) (with wall, fence, etc.); to fence (in) (piece of ground, etc.).

II. *vbl s.* **1. Einfried(ig)en,** *n. in vbl senses.* **2. Einfried(ig)ung,** *f.* (*a*)=II. 1; (*b*) enclosed piece of ground, enclosure; (*c*) enclosure; fence.

Einfried(ig)ungsmauer, *f.* enclosure wall; surrounding wall.

einfrieren, *v.sep.* (*strong*) **1.** *v.i.* (*sein*) to freeze (up); to freeze in; (*of ship, harbour*) to become icebound; (*of molten metal, solution, etc.*) to freeze, solidify, congeal; *Fin:* (*of capital, etc.*) to freeze, to be blocked; **der Kühler fror ein,** the radiator froze (up); **die Wasserleitung ist eingefroren,** the water-pipes are frozen; **das Lächeln fror auf seinen Lippen ein,** the smile froze on his lips; **das Schiff ist eingefroren,** the ship is frozen in, icebound, locked in the ice, iced up. **2.** *v.tr.* (*a*) to (deep-)freeze (vegetables, etc.); (*b*) *F:* to freeze (capital, etc.).

einfrüchtig, *a. Bot:* monocarpic.

einfuchsen, *v.tr. sep. F:* **j-m etwas e.,** to drum sth. into s.o.; **er ist darauf eingefuchst,** he has had this drummed into him.

einfugen, *v.tr. sep. Carp:* to join (parts of a piece of furniture, etc.) (by mortising, scarfing, rabbeting, etc.).

einfügen. I. *v.tr. sep.* **1.** (*a*) **etwas in etwas** *acc.* **e.,** to fit sth. into sth.; to set sth. into sth.; **eine Gedenktafel in eine Mauer e.,** to set, fit, set, a commemorative tablet into a wall; (*b*) *Carp:*= **einfugen;** (*c*) to insert sth.; to interpolate (word, phrase, passage, etc.); **eine Klausel, Bedingung, in eine Urkunde e.,** to insert a clause, a condition, in a document. **2. sich einfügen,** to fit in; **sich (in etwas** *acc.***) e.,** to adapt oneself (to sth.); **Leute, die sich nicht e. wollen, können wir hier nicht brauchen,** we can't have people here who won't fit in, who won't adapt themselves; **er fügte sich sehr gut in seine neue Umgebung ein,** he adapted himself very well to his new surroundings.

II. *vbl s.* **1. Einfügen,** *n. in vbl senses.* **2. Einfügung,** *f.* (*a*)=II. 1; *also:* insertion (of sth. into sth.); interpolation (of word, phrase, passage, etc.); (*b*) inserted word, passage, etc., insertion; interpolated word, passage, etc., interpolation.

Einfügungssatz, *m. Gram:* incidental, parenthetical, clause.

einfühlen (sich), *v.refl. sep.* **sich in j-n, in j-s Seele, e.,** to achieve a sympathetic understanding of s.o.; to project oneself into the mind of s.o.; **sich in etwas** *acc.* **e.,** to get into the spirit of sth.; **er vermag sich in die Seele des Kindes einzufühlen,** he can project himself into the mind of the child, into the child's mind; **sich in das Werk eines Dichters e.,** to get into the spirit of a writer's work; *Psy: Lit:* **Einfühlung** *f,* empathy.

Einfühlungsvermögen, *n.* capacity for projecting oneself into another's mind, for getting into the spirit of sth.; *Psy: Lit:* (power of) empathy; **er hat kein E.,** he is incapable of projecting himself into another person's mind.

Einfuhr, *f.* -/-en. *Com:* **1.** import, importation, importing (of goods, etc.); **die E. von Baumwolle,** the import of cotton. **2.** import(s); **Einfuhren** *pl,* imports (of a country); goods imported; **die E. und Ausfuhr eines Landes,** the imports and exports of a country; **unsichtbare E.,** invisible imports; **'Einfuhr',** 'inwards'.

Einfuhrartikel, *m. Com:* import; imported article; article for import.

einführbar, *a. Com:* importable (goods, etc.).

Einfuhrbeschränkung, *f. Adm:* import restriction.

Einfuhrbestimmungen, *f.pl. Adm:* import regulations.

Einfuhrbewilligung, *f. Adm:* (*a*) permission to import; (*b*) import licence, import permit.

Einfuhrdeklaration, *f. Cust:* (bill of) entry, entry inwards.

einführen. I. *v.tr. sep.* **1.** (*a*) to introduce (sth., the use of sth.); to establish (new tax, law, fashion, etc.); to institute (law, tax, etc.); to bring in (fashion, tax, law, etc.); to initiate (method, policy, reform, fashion, etc.); to set (a fashion); to inaugurate (new system, feast, etc.); to set in force, set up (regulation, etc.); **eine neue Sitte einführen,** to introduce, establish, inaugurate, a new custom; **an allen Schulen wurden neue Bücher eingeführt,** new books were introduced into all the schools; **eine Mode wieder einführen,** to revive a fashion; *F:* **er führte die Mode ein, jeden Tag zehn Minuten zu spät zu kommen,** he started the fashion of coming ten minutes late every day; (*b*) to introduce (s.o.) (to s.o., to society, into a family, etc.); to present (s.o.) (to s.o., at court); **er wurde bei Lady X eingeführt,** he was introduced, presented, to Lady X; **ich werde Sie in diese Familie e.,** I shall introduce you into this family; **er ist in den besten Kreisen eingeführt,** he has his place in, is accepted in, the best social circles; **alle Hauptpersonen werden im ersten Akt des Dramas eingeführt,** all the main characters are introduced, presented, in the first act of the drama; **der Dichter führt sich selbst als handelnde Person in die Erzählung ein,** the poet introduces himself into the story as one of the characters; **die Erzeugnisse unserer Firma sind**

auf diesem Markt gut eingeführt, the products of our firm are well-established, have a good reputation, on this market; **ein gut eingeführtes Geschäft,** a well-established business; (*c*) to introduce (s.o.) (to work, a process, to a science, office, etc.); to initiate (s.o.) (in a science, an art, etc.); to induct (s.o.) (into an office); to admit (s.o.) (to an office); to install (s.o.) (in an office); **im einführenden Kapitel,** in the introductory, introductive, chapter; **nach einigen einführenden Worten,** after a few introductory words; *Ecc:* **einen Geistlichen in sein Amt e.,** to induct a clergyman to a living. **2.** *Com:* to import (goods, etc.); to bring in (goods, etc.); **Waren in ein Land e.,** to import, bring, goods into a country; **aus England eingeführt,** imported from England. **3.** to introduce (sth.) (into sth.); to insert (sth.) (into sth.); *Typewr:* to feed (paper) in, to insert (paper) (into the machine); *Med:* to introduce (catheter, etc.) (into the bladder, etc.); *El.E:* to lead in (cable, etc.); **ein Kabel in ein Haus e.,** to lead a cable into a house. **4.** to bring in (load of hay, etc.). **II.** *vbl s.* **1. Einführen,** *n. in vbl senses.* **2. Einführung,** *f.* (*a*)=II. 1; *also:* (i) introduction (of sth., the use of sth.); establishment (of new tax, law, fashion, etc.); institution (of a law); initiation (of method, policy, reform, fashion, etc.); inauguration (of new system, feast, etc.); (ii) introduction (of s.o.) (to s.o., to society, into a family, etc.); presentation (of s.o.) (to s.o., at court); (iii) introduction (into a science, a job, etc.); initiation (of s.o.) (in a science, an art); induction (of an official to his duty, work, etc., of a clergyman to a living); (iv) *Com:* importation (of goods, etc.); (v) introduction (of sth.) (into sth.); insertion (of sth.) (into sth.); (*b*) introduction (to s.o., to society); presentation (to s.o., at court); **er mußte lange Zeit auf seine E. bei Hofe warten,** he had to wait for a long time before he was presented at court; (*c*) introduction (to sth.); **eine Einführung in die Geometrie veröffentlichen,** to publish an introduction to geometry; (*d*) *W.Tel: etc:* lead-in.
Einführer, *m. Com:* importer.
Einfuhrerklärung, *f. Cust:*=**Einfuhrdeklaration.**
Einfuhrerlaubnis, Einfuhrgenehmigung, *f. Adm:* (*a*) permission to import; (*b*) import licence, import permit.
Einfuhrgut, *n. Com:* import.
Einfuhrhafen, *m.* port of importation.
Einfuhrhandel, *m. Com:* import trade.
Einfuhrhändler, *m. Com:* importer.
Einfuhrkontingent, *n. Adm: Com:* import quota.
Einfuhrland, *n. Pol.Ec: Com:* importing country.
Einfuhrliste, *f. Adm: Com:* import list.
Einfuhrlizenz, *f. Adm:* import licence, import permit.
Einfuhrmonopol, *n. Pol.Ec: Com:* import monopoly.
Einfuhrprämie, *f. Adm:* import bounty, import premium.
Einfuhrquota, Einfuhrquote, *f.* **1.** *Pol.Ec:* import rate. **2.**=**Einfuhrkontingent.**
Einfuhrschein, *m. Adm:* preferential import licence (*granted as a privilege, esp. to grain exporting firms*).
Einfuhrtarif, *m. Rail:* special transport rates, tariff, for certain imports.
Einfuhrüberschuß, *m. Pol.Ec:* import surplus.
Einführung, *f. see* **einführen** II.
Einführungsdraht, *m. W.Tel: etc:* lead(ing)-in wire, lead-in.
Einführungsgesetz, *n. Jur:* introductory act.
Einführungsgestänge, *n. El.E:* leading-in pole.
Einführungskabel, *n. El.E:* lead(ing)-in cable.
Einführungsmuffe, *f. Mch: etc:* inlet sleeve.
Einführungsrohr, *n. W.Tel: etc:* lead(ing)-in tube.
Einführungsschreiben, *n.* letter of introduction.
Einführungsunterricht, *m.* introductory teaching; preliminary instruction.
Einführungswalze, *f. Tchn:* feed-roll.
Einfuhrverbot, *n. Pol.Ec:* import ban, import prohibition; **das E. für Getreide wurde aufgehoben,** the ban on the import of grain was lifted.
Einfuhrware, *f. Com:* import; import commodity; imported article; article for import.
Einfuhrzoll, *m. Cust:* import duty.
Einfuhrzuschuß, *m. Pol.Ec:* import subsidy.
einfüllen, *v.tr. sep.* **etwas (in etwas** *acc.***) e.,** to put sth. (into container, etc.); to pour sth. (into container, etc.); to charge, fill (accumulator, blast-furnace, etc.) (with acid, ore, etc.); **(Wein, usw.) in Fässer e.,** to barrel, cask, tun (wine, etc.); **(Wein, usw.) in Flaschen e.,** to bottle (wine, etc.); **(Korn, usw.) in Säcke e.,** to sack (corn, etc.); **Öl e.,** to put in, pour in, oil.

Einfüllhahn, *m. Mch: etc:* filling cock; feed-cock.
Einfüllstopfen, *m. Mec.E:* filler plug.
Einfüllstutzen, *m. I.C.E: etc:* filler(-pipe) (of fuel tank, radiator, sump, etc.).
Einfülltrichter, *m. Ind: etc:* (charging, loading) funnel, hopper.
Einfüllverschraubung, *f.* screw cap (of oil-tank, etc.).
Einfunkenzündung, *f. I.C.E:* single-spark ignition.
einfurchen. I. *v.tr. sep.* **1. etwas e.,** to make a furrow, groove, furrows, grooves, in sth. **2. sich einfurchen,** (*a*) to become grooved; **das befruchtete Ei furcht sich ein,** the fertilized ovum develops furrows, grooves; *Geol:* **eingefurchter Kegel,** trenched cone; (*b*) (*of thg*) **sich in etwas** *acc.* **e.,** to make a furrow, groove, in sth.; **das Flußbett hat sich tief in das Tal eingefurcht,** the river has cut its bed deep into the valley. **II.** *vbl s.* **1. Einfurchen,** *n. in vbl senses.* **2. Einfurchung,** *f.* (*a*)=II. 1; (*b*) furrow; groove.
einfüßig, *a.* **1.** one-footed, monopode, monopodous. **2.** *Civ.E: etc:* **einfüßige Böschung,** one-to-one slope.
Eingabe, *f.* application; petition; **eine E. (um, für, etwas) bei einem Ministerium, usw.) machen,** to make an application, to present a petition (for sth.) (to a ministry, etc.).
Eingabefrist, *f.* time limit for application(s); **die E. läuft am 20. Mai ab,** the time limit for applications expires on 20th May.
eingabeln, *v.tr. sep. Artil:* to bracket, straddle (target).
Eingabetermin, *m.* last date, closing date, for application(s); **der E. ist der 20. Mai,** the last date, closing date, for applications is 20th May.
Eingang, *m.* **1.** entering; coming in; (*a*) entry; coming in; **'E. verboten',** 'no entry', 'no admittance'; *see also:* **Ausgang 1;** (*b*) arrival (of goods, mail, report, etc.); receipt (of instalment due, letter, etc.); **der E. dieses Berichts verursachte große Verwirrung,** the arrival of this report caused great confusion; **den E. eines Briefes bestätigen,** to acknowledge receipt of a letter; **nach, bei, E. Ihres Briefes,** on receiving your letter, on receipt of your letter; **nach, bei, E. des Wechsels,** on receipt of the draft; *Com:* **'E. vorbehalten',** 'subject to the account's being paid in due course'. **2.** (*a*) (*gen.,* **zu, in**+*acc.,* of, to) entrance (to, of, building, valley, cave, etc.); gate(way) (of building, etc.); door(way) (of building, etc.); way in (to building, etc.); mouth (of tunnel, harbour, cave, etc.); inlet (to bay, harbour, etc.); *Min:* pit-head; **'kein E.',** 'verbotener E.', 'no entry', 'no admittance'; **der Tod ist der E. zu einem höheren Leben,** death is the gateway to a higher life; (*b*) beginning (of poem, letter, speech, epoch, etc.); introduction. introductory passage (of poem, letter, speech, etc.); preamble (of letter, speech, etc.); (*at religious service, etc.*) **zum E. singen wir ein Lied,** let us begin by singing a hymn; **zu, im, E. seiner Rede bemerkte er, daß . . .,** at the beginning of, in the introduction to, in the introductory passages of, his speech he observed that . . .; **am E. des vorigen Jahrhunderts,** at the beginning of the last century. **3.** (*in vbl phrases*) (*of pers.*) **E. in etwas** *acc.* **finden,** to gain entry, access, to (society, etc.); to find favour with, gain the favour of (the highest social circles, etc.); (*of product, etc.*) **E. in ein Land, in einem Land, finden,** to find a market in a country; to make its way into a country; **E. (bei j-m) finden,** (*of request, etc.*) to find favour (with s.o.); (*of rumour, suspicion, etc.*) to gain, find, acceptance (with s.o.); (*of play, etc.*) **E. beim Publikum finden,** to find acceptance with the public, to find, meet with, a favourable reception from the public, to be well received by the public; **sich E. verschaffen,** to manage to get in; to force one's way in; **j-m E. verschaffen,** to clear a way, a path, for s.o.; **j-m E. (in etwas** *acc.,* **zu etwas, bei Hofe, usw.) verschaffen,** to obtain access for s.o. (to society, to the court, etc.); **etwas** *dat.* **E. verschaffen,** to introduce, bring in (novelty, etc.); **etwas** *dat.* **E. beim Publikum, in einem Land, in ein Land, usw., verschaffen,** to bring (novelty, etc.) to the public, into a country, etc.; **die neue Mode hat überall E. gefunden,** the new fashion has been accepted, adopted, everywhere; **diese Eindrücke haben E. in das Werk des Dichters gefunden,** these impressions have found a place in the author's work; **er hat allen möglichen Mißbräuchen E. verschafft,** he has opened the door to all sorts of abuses; **er verschaffte sich E. bei Hofe,** he

managed to gain access to court; **er verschaffte sich nur mit Mühe E.,** he hardly managed to get in, to force his way in; **unsere Erzeugnisse haben nun auch im Ausland E. gefunden,** now our products have also found a market abroad. **4.** *pl.* **Eingänge,** (*a*) *Fin: Com:* incomings, receipts; **die Ausgänge sind höher als die Eingänge,** the outgoings exceed the incomings; (*b*) *Com:* incoming mail, goods, etc.; goods, etc., received; arrivals (of goods, etc.); deliveries; **wir hatten heute keine Eingänge zu verzeichnen,** we had no deliveries today; (*on letter tray*) 'Eingänge', 'in'.
Eingänger, *m. Ven:* solitary old boar.
eingängig[1], *a. Mec.E:* (screw, etc.) with a single thread; **eingängiges Gewinde,** single thread; **eingängiger Fräser,** single start cutter.
eingängig[2], *a.* comprehensible; **etwas in einer eingängigen Form darstellen,** to present (theory, etc.) in a comprehensible form.
Eingängigkeit, *f.*=**Eingänglichkeit.**
eingänglich, *a.*=**eingängig**[2].
Eingänglichkeit, *f.* comprehensibility (of theory, etc.).
eingangs, *adv. & prep.* (+*gen.*) at the beginning; **gleich e. erwähnte er, daß . . .,** at the very beginning, he mentioned that . . .; **wie e. erwähnt,** as mentioned at the beginning.
Eingangsabgaben, *f.pl. Cust: etc:* import dues.
Eingangsabfertigung, *f. Cust: etc:* customs examination, clearance (of incoming goods).
Eingangsanzeige, *f. Com:* acknowledgement of receipt.
Eingangsarm, *m. Clockm:* engaging pallet.
Eingangsbestätigung, *f. Com:* acknowledgement of receipt.
Eingangsbilanz, *f. Com:*=**Eröffnungsbilanz.**
Eingangsbuch, *n. Com:* register of articles, letters, etc., received; goods inward book.
Eingangsdeklaration, *f. Com:*=**Einfuhrdeklaration.**
Eingangsenergie, *f. El.E:* input.
Eingangsfakturenbuch, *n. Com:* invoice book.
Eingangsgewicht, *n. Com:* weight inwards; weight delivered.
Eingangshafen, *m.* port of entry.
Eingangshalle, *f.* (entrance-)hall; booking-hall (of railway-station).
Eingangsjournal, *n. Com:*=**Eingangsbuch.**
Eingangsklaue, *f. Clockm:* entry pallet stone.
Eingangsklemme, *f. El.E:* input terminal.
Eingangsleistung, *f. El.E:* input (of generator).
Eingangslied, *n. Ecc:* introit.
Eingangsrede, *f.* opening speech.
Eingangsspannung, *f. El.E:* input voltage.
Eingangsstromkreis, *m. El:* input circuit.
Eingangstor, *n.* entrance (door) (of fortress, palace, etc.); gate (of town, fortress, palace, etc.); gateway (of fortress, palace, etc.); portal (of large house, etc.).
Eingangstür, *f.* entrance door, *esp.* front door, street door.
Eingangsweiche, *f. Rail:* entry points.
Eingangswiderstand, *m. El:* input resistance.
Eingangsworte, *n.pl.* opening words (of book, speech, etc.).
Eingangszoll, *m. Cust: etc:*=**Einfuhrzoll.**
eingarnen, *v.tr. sep. F:* **j-n e.,** to take s.o. in; to pull the wool over s.o.'s eyes; **sich (von j-m, von j-s Lügen, usw.) e. lassen,** (to allow oneself) to be taken in (by s.o., by s.o.'s lies, etc.).
eingeben. I. *v.tr. sep.* (*strong*) **1.** to present, hand in (petition, application, etc.); **j-n für eine Auszeichnung, zur Beförderung, usw., e.,** to put s.o.'s name, s.o., forward for a decoration, for promotion, etc. **2. j-m etwas e.,** (*a*) to administer (medicine, food, poison, etc.) to s.o.; to feed (patient, etc.) with (soup, etc.); **diese Medizin muß tropfenweise eingegeben werden,** this medicine should be administered a few drops at a time; (*b*) to inspire s.o. with sth.; to put sth. into s.o.'s heart; **j-m e., etwas zu tun,** to inspire s.o. to do sth.; to suggest to s.o. to do sth.; to prompt s.o. to do sth.; **die Antwort wurde dem Propheten im Traum eingegeben,** the answer was given to the prophet in his dream; **die Schrift wurde den Propheten und Aposteln eingegeben,** the prophets and apostles received the Scripture from God; **die Schrift wurde vom Heiligen Geist eingegeben,** the Scripture was inspired by the Holy Ghost; **diesen Gedanken gab ihm der Teufel ein,** the devil put this idea into his head; **sein Schutzengel muß ihm eingegeben haben, an jenem Tag zuhause zu bleiben,** his guardian angel must have suggested to him, inspired him, put it into his heart, to stay at home that day; **der Geist gab dem Propheten ein,**

was er tun sollte, the Spirit told the prophet, guided the prophet in, what he was to do. **3.** *v.i.* (*haben*) **um etwas e.,** to apply, make an application, for (scholarship, dispensation, etc.).

II. *vbl s.* **1. Eingeben,** *n. in vbl senses; also:* presentation (of petition, application, etc.); administration (of medicine, etc.). **2. Eingebung,** *f.* (*a*)=II. 1; *also:* inspiration; **die E. der Schrift durch den Heiligen Geist,** the inspiration of the Scripture by the Holy Spirit; (*b*) inspiration; dictate; impulse; **eine Eingebung von oben,** an inspiration from above; **höhere, göttliche, E.,** divine inspiration; afflatus; **der Prophet hatte eine E.,** the prophet had a divine inspiration; **höre nicht auf die Eingebungen der Leidenschaft,** do not listen to the voice, dictates, of passion; **eine plötzliche E. haben,** to have a sudden inspiration; **einer plötzlichen E. folgend,** following a sudden impulse.

eingebildet, *p.p. & a. see* **einbilden** III.

Eingebildetheit, *f.* self-conceit; self-importance; priggishness; **ich kann ihre E. nicht ausstehen,** I can't bear her self-conceit, self-importance, priggishness; **er ist von einer unerträglichen E.,** he is unbearably conceited, priggish.

Eingebinde, *n.* **-s/-.** *A. & Lit:* christening present.

eingeboren[1], *a. Theol: B:* **der eingeborene Sohn,** the only begotten Son.

eingeboren[2], *a.* **1.** innate, inborn, inherent (quality, etc.); **das sittliche Gefühl ist dem Menschen e.,** moral sense is innate, inborn, inherent, in mankind; *Phil:* **eingeborene Ideen,** innate ideas. **2.** native (population, etc.) (of colony, foreign country, etc.); aboriginal (population, etc.) (*esp. of Australia, New Zealand*).

Eingeborene[1], **der.** *Theol:* the only begotten Son.

Eingeborene[2], *m., f.* (*decl. as adj.*) native (*esp.* of foreign country, colony); aboriginal; **die Eingeborenen Südafrikas,** the natives of South Africa; **die Eingeborenen Australiens,** the aborigines of Australia.

Eingeborenenaufstand, *m.* native (up)rising.

Eingeborenenstaat, *m.* native state.

Eingeborenentruppen, *f.pl.* native troops.

eingedenk, *pred.a.* (+*gen.*) bearing (sth.) in mind, remembering (sth.); **einer Sache e. sein, bleiben,** to bear, keep, sth. in mind; **j-s e. sein, bleiben,** to keep s.o.'s memory green; to keep s.o. in one's memory, one's thoughts; **stets meiner Pflicht e.,** ever mindful of my duty; **e. der Wohltaten, die er uns erwies, werden wir . . . ,** bearing in mind, remembering, the kindnesses he did us, we shall . . . ; **e. der Tatsache, daß . . . ,** in view of the fact that . . . ; **wir werden dessen e. sein, daß wir ihm alles verdanken,** we shall bear, keep, in mind that we owe him everything.

eingefahren, *p.p. & a. see* **einfahren.**

eingefallen, *p.p. & a. see* **einfallen.**

eingefaßt, *p.p. & a. see* **einfassen.**

eingefleischt, *a.* (*a*) *A:* incarnate (genius, devil, ghost, etc.); (*b*) *F:* (*of pers.*) confirmed; thoroughgoing; staunch; **ein eingefleischter Junggeselle,** a confirmed bachelor; **ein eingefleischter Revolutionär,** a thoroughgoing, die-hard, revolutionary; **ein eingefleischter Sozialist,** a staunch socialist; **ein eingefleischter Ire,** a dyed-in-the-wool Irishman; **er ist ein eingefleischter Ire,** he is Irish to the core, bone; (*c*) *F:* (*of prejudices, habits, etc.*) deep-rooted; ingrained; confirmed.

eingehäkelt, *p.p. & a. see* **einhäkeln.**

eingehakt, *p.p. & a. see* **einhaken.**

eingehängt, *p.p. & a. see* **einhängen.**

eingehen, *v.sep.* (*strong*) I. *v.i.* (*sein*) **1.** (*a*) *Lit: B:* to come in, to enter in; **in das Himmelreich, in das ewige Leben, usw., e.,** to enter into heaven, into eternal life, etc.; **in den ewigen Frieden e.,** to enter into, find, eternal peace; **diese Eindrücke sind in das Werk des Dichters eingegangen,** these impressions have found a place in the author's work; **seine Werke werden in die Ewigkeit e.,** his works will live for ever; *B:* **was zum Munde eingehet, das verunreiniget den Menschen nicht,** not that which goeth into the mouth defileth a man; (*b*) (*of funds*) to come in; to be received; to be paid; to come to hand; (*of mail, goods, etc.*) to arrive; to come in; to be received; **die eingegangenen Spenden wurden für wohltätige Zwecke verwendet,** the contributions which came in were used for charity; **es gingen zahlreiche Spenden ein,** contributions came pouring in, flowed in; **eingehende Post, Waren, Gelder, usw.,** incoming mail, goods, funds, etc.; *Com:* **eingehende Rechnungen, Fakturen,** inward invoices; **eingehendes Gewicht,** delivered weight; weight inwards. **2.** (*of line, etc.*) to close in; *Geom: Fort:* **eingehender Winkel,** re-entrant angle. **3.** (*of facts, words, etc.*) **j-m e.,** to be credible to s.o.; to be understandable to s.o.; **es will mir nicht e., daß er das getan haben soll,** it is incredible to me that he should have done it; **es ging ihm schwer ein, daß er diesmal seinen Willen nicht durchsetzen konnte,** he found it hard to realize that this time he could not have his own way; **das geht mir ein, aber . . . ,** I can see that, but . . . ; **die lateinische Grammatik ging ihm schwer, hart, ein,** he found Latin grammar difficult; Latin grammar came hard to him; **diese Regeln gehen mir einfach nicht ein,** I simply cannot grasp these rules; **das ging ihm glatt ein,** (i) he grasped it easily; (ii) *F:* he lapped it up; **diese Worte gingen ihm süß ein,** these words were sweet music to his ears. **4. auf etwas e.,** (*a*) to enter into (details); to go into (details, question, matter, etc.); **auf einen Vorschlag, ein Angebot, usw., (näher) e.,** to go into, consider the details of, a proposal, an offer; **er ging auf ihre Entschuldigungen gar nicht erst ein,** he did not even listen to her apologies; **eine eingehende Schilderung,** a detailed, comprehensive, description; **ein eingehender Bericht,** a detailed, comprehensive, circumstantial, account; **eine eingehende Suche, Untersuchung,** a thorough, close, search, inquiry; **ein eingehendes Studium einer Sache,** a thorough, close, profound, comprehensive, detailed, study of a subject; **nach eingehender Prüfung Ihres Angebots,** after a close examination of your offer; **nach eingehender Überlegung,** after careful consideration; **sich mit einer Sache eingehend, aufs eingehendste, befassen,** to go closely, thoroughly, into a matter; **die Frage wurde eingehend diskutiert,** the question was thoroughly discussed; (*b*) to accept, to agree to, consent to (conditions of a treaty, arrangement, demand, request, etc.); to fall in with (demand, request, arrangement, etc.); to submit to (conditions of a treaty, etc.); to be agreeable to, to accede to, comply with (demand, request, etc.); **darauf e., etwas zu tun,** to agree, to consent, to do sth.; **wenn er derartige Vorschläge machen sollte, gehen Sie nur nicht darauf ein,** if he should put forward such proposals, don't accept them whatever you do; **der Kläger ging auf keinen Vergleich ein,** the plaintiff would not agree to, accept, any arrangement; **auf einen Scherz, Spaß, e.,** to join in a joke; **er ging auf den leichten Ton der Unterhaltung ein,** he fell in with the light tone of the conversation. **5.** (*of material, etc.*) to shrink; **das Kleid ist beim Waschen eingegangen,** the dress has shrunk in the wash, in washing. **6.** (*of animal, P: of pers.*) to die, perish (from disease, cold, heat, etc.); (*of plant*) to die (off); (*of firm, etc.*) to cease to exist, *F:* to pack up; (*of society, etc.*) to cease to exist; to dissolve; (*of periodical, etc.*) to cease to appear, to be published; to cease publication; **etwas e. lassen,** to close down (factory, periodical, etc.); **sie sahen sich gezwungen, die Zweigstelle in X e. zu lassen,** they saw themselves forced to give up the branch in X; *F:* **ich wäre vor Langeweile beinahe eingegangen,** I nearly died of boredom. **7.** *Dial:* to be caught (with sth.); **da bin ich schön eingegangen,** I was badly caught there; **mit dem neuen Auto bin ich richtig eingegangen,** I have been badly caught with the new car.

II. **eingehen,** *v.tr.* **1.** (*sein, occ. haben*) to enter into (contract, bargain, obligation, etc.); to conclude (marriage, contract, bargain); to strike, make, clinch (bargain); to assume, contract (obligation); to incur, run, take (risk); to take (chances); to make, lay, take (up) (bet, wager); to accept (contract, obligation, risk); **eine Ehe, eine eheliche Verbindung, mit j-m e.,** to contract a marriage with s.o., to be joined with s.o. in matrimony, in marriage; **verschiedene Stilelemente sind in diesem Roman eine Verbindung eingegangen,** various elements of style have combined in this novel; **die eingegangenen Verpflichtungen waren ihm eine schwere Last,** the obligations which he had assumed were a heavy burden to him; **ich gehe jede Wette darauf ein, daß . . . ,** I'll bet you anything (you like) that . . . ; *Jur: etc:* **eine Bürgschaft e.,** to stand, go, surety; to stand as guarantor; **einen Vergleich e.,** to enter into an agreement, arrangement; to accept an agreement, arrangement, to agree to an arrangement; to come to terms, to an agreement, arrangement; to compromise; (*of creditor*) to compound (with debtor); **die beiden Parteien gingen schließlich einen Vergleich ein,** the two parties reached a settlement, entered into, accepted, agreed to, an arrangement in the end; the two parties came to terms, to an agreement, arrangement, in the end; the two parties compromised in the end. **2.** (*haben*) *Ven:* to ring in, close in, encircle (quarry).

III. *vbl s.* **1. Eingehen,** *n. in vbl senses; also:* (*a*) arrival (of mail, goods, etc.); receipt (of funds, mail, goods); *cp.* **Eingang** 1; (*b*) **E. auf etwas,** consideration of (details, etc.); acceptance of, agreement, consent, to (conditions, arrangement, demand, request, etc.); submission to (conditions of a treaty, etc.); **ein E. auf diesen Vorschlag würde bedeuten, daß . . . ,** an acceptance of this proposal would mean that . . . , if we should accept this proposal, it would mean that . . . ; (*c*) death (of plant, animal); dissolution (of firm, etc.); extinction (of firm, etc.); cessation of publication, disappearance (of periodical, etc.); (*d*) shrinkage (of material, etc.); (*e*) **E.** +*gen.*, acceptance of (obligation, contract, risk, wager, etc.); conclusion of (marriage, contract, bargain, etc.); **das E. einer Bürgschaft will wohl überlegt sein,** the acceptance of surety has to be carefully considered; **das E. eines solchen Risikos wäre unvernünftig,** it would be silly to take such a risk. **2. Eingehung,** *f.*=III. 1 (*e*).

eingehenkelt, *p.p. & a. F: see* **einhenkeln.**

eingemeinden, *v.tr. sep.* **ein Dorf, einen Vorort, usw., e.,** to incorporate a village, suburb, etc., in(to) a community; **vor kurzer Zeit wurde dieser Vorort (der Stadt, in die Stadt) München eingemeindet,** a short time ago this suburb was incorporated into the town of Munich; **Eingemeindung** *f,* incorporation (of village, suburb, etc.) (into a community).

eingenommen, *p.p. & a. see* **einnehmen.**

Eingenommenheit, *f.* prejudice (**gegen,** against; **für,** in favour of); bias (**gegen,** against; **für,** in favour of, towards).

Eingerichte, *n.* **-s/-,** ward (of lock).

Eingesandt, *n.* **-s/-s.** *Journ:* letter (to the editor).

eingesattelt, *a.* saddle-shaped, saddle-backed (hill, etc.).

eingeschlechtig, *a.* unisexual, with one sex; *Biol:* **eingeschlechtige Fortpflanzung,** parthenogenesis; *Bot:* **eingeschlechtige Blüte,** diclinous, unisexual, flower.

eingeschlechtlich, *a.* **1.** *Gram:* genderless (adjective, etc.). **2.** *occ.*=**eingeschlechtig.**

eingeschossig, *a.* (building) with one storey; single-storey (building).

eingesessen, *a.* old-, long-established (family, farmer, etc.) (*in a particular place*); **die eingesessenen Bürger,** the old-established inhabitants.

eingestanden, *p.p. & a. see* **eingestehen.**

eingestandenermaßen, *adv.* by (s.o.'s) own admission; on (s.o.'s) own confession; confessedly; **er ist e. ein Mitwisser dieser verräterischen Pläne gewesen,** he was on his own confession, by his own admission, an accessory to these treasonable plans.

eingeständig, *a.*=**geständig.**

Eingeständnis, *n.* confession, admission, acknowledgement (of mistake, one's guilt, etc.).

eingestehen. I. *v.tr. sep.* (*strong*) to confess (mistake, crime, one's guilt, etc.); to admit, own, acknowledge (mistake, crime, one's guilt, etc.); to own (up) to (mistake, crime, etc.); **ich muß dir e., daß . . . ,** I must confess, admit, to you that . . . ; **er gestand ein, es getan zu haben,** he confessed, admitted, acknowledged, that he had done it; he owned (up) to having done it; **ich muß dir etwas e.,** I have something to confess to you; **man muß sich** *dat.* **seine Fehler e.,** one must admit one's faults to oneself; **er wollte sich** *dat.* **nicht e., daß . . . ,** he did not want to admit to himself that . . . ; **ich muß meine Unwissenheit e.,** I have to confess, admit, own, my ignorance; **wenn du alles ehrlich eingestanden hättest, wäre die Sache halb so schlimm,** if you had honestly confessed (to), admitted, everything, things wouldn't be half so bad.

II. *vbl s.* **Eingestehen** *n.,* **Eingestehung** *f. in vbl senses; also:* confession, admission, acknowledgement (of mistake, crime, one's guilt, etc.); *cp.* **Eingeständnis.**

eingestrichen, *a. Mus:* **eingestrichene Oktave,** once-accented, one-line, octave; **eingestrichenes c,** middle C.

Eingeweide, *n.* **-s/-,** *usu. pl.* **Eingeweide,** *Anat:* viscera, *F:* innards; (*loosely*) intestines, bowels, *P:* guts (of human being); entrails (of animal, bird, etc.); guts (of fish); *Lit:* bowels (of the earth); **die E. (eines Tieres) herausnehmen,** to eviscerate (an animal); to disembowel (an animal); to gut (fish, rabbit, etc.); to draw (fowl).

Eingeweidebeschauer, *m. Rom. Ant:* extispex, haruspex.

Eingeweidebeschauung, *f. Rom.Ant:* = **Eingeweideschau.**

Eingeweidebruch, *m. Med:* hernia, rupture.

Eingeweidegicht, *f. Med:* abarticular, irregular, gout.

Eingeweidelehre, *f. Med:* splanchnology.

Eingeweidenerv, *m. Anat:* splanchnic nerve.

Eingeweideschau, *f. Rom.Ant:* (*a*) extispicy, haruspicy; (*b*) haruspication.

Eingeweideschlagader, *f. Anat:* coeliac artery.

Eingeweidesenkung, *f. Med:* enteroptosis, visceroptosis.

Eingeweidevorfall, *m. Med:* prolapse, prolapsus.

Eingeweidewurm, *m. Ann: Med:* intestinal worm; helminth; **die Eingeweidewürmer,** the enthelmintha, enthelminthes.

eingewöhnen, *v.tr. sep.* **j-n, ein Tier, e.,** to accustom s.o., an animal, to new surroundings; to make s.o. feel at home (in new surroundings); **sich e.,** to accustom oneself to new surroundings; to get, become, accustomed, used, to new surroundings; to get, become, acclimatized (to new surroundings); to settle down (in a new place of work, etc.); **wir müssen versuchen, das Kind in seine neue Umgebung einzugewöhnen,** we must try to accustom the child to its new surroundings, to make the child feel at home in its new surroundings; **er gewöhnte sich dort nur schwer ein,** it was a long time before he felt at home there; **er hat sich hier gut eingewöhnt,** he has settled down here very nicely; **sich in einen Beruf e.,** to settle into a job; **nach kurzer Zeit war er bei uns eingewöhnt,** after a short time he felt quite at home with us.

eingezogen, *p.p. & a.* (*of life, etc.*) secluded, retired; *adv.* **e. leben,** to live in seclusion, to live retired; *see also* **einziehen.**

Eingezogenheit, *f.* seclusion; **in E. leben,** to live in seclusion.

eingießen. I. *v.tr. sep.* (*strong*) **1. etwas in etwas** *acc.* **e.,** to pour, run, sth. into (vessel, mould, etc.); *Metall:* to pour, run, (molten metal) into (mould); **den Tee, den Wein, e.,** to pour (out) the tea, the wine; **würden Sie mir bitte eine Tasse Tee e.?** would you please pour (out) a cup of tea for me? **2.** *Metall: etc:* to set, fix, (iron bar, etc.) (with cement, lead, etc.); to cast in (iron bar, etc.); **etwas in etwas e.,** to set, fix, (iron bar, etc.) (with cement, lead, etc.) into (stone, etc.); to cast (iron bar, etc.) into (moulding-box, etc.); **Werkstück mit eingegossenen Rinnen,** piece with cast-in grooves; **etwas mit Blei e.,** to lead sth. in; *Mec.E:* **eingegossenes Gegengewicht,** cast-on balance weight.

II. *vbl s.* **1. Eingießen,** *n. in vbl senses.* **2. Eingießung,** *f.* (*a*) = II. 1; (*b*) *Med:* infusion; *cp.* **Einguß.**

eingipsen, *v.tr. sep.* (*a*) to bed, fasten, fix, (sth.) in with plaster; **eine Eisenstange in eine Mauer e.,** to bed, fasten, fix, an iron bar into a wall; (*b*) to plaster up (hole, crack); (*c*) *Med:* to put (arm, leg, etc.) in plaster.

eingittern, *v.tr. sep.* to fence in, enclose, (piece of ground, etc.) with lattice-work, with railings.

Eingitterröhre, *f. W.Tel:* triode, three-electrode valve.

Einglas, *n.* monocle; (single) eye-glass.

einglasen, *v.tr. sep.* to glaze (window, greenhouse, picture, etc.); **wir müssen das Fenster neu e. lassen,** we must get new glass put in the window.

eingleichen, *v.tr. sep.* (*strong*) to put (sth.) in line with sth.; to put (things) in line with one another.

eingleisen, *v.tr. sep.* (*a*) *Rail: etc:* to rerail (engine, etc.); (*b*) *F:* to put (sth.) right (again); **das wird sich schon wieder e.,** things will come out all right again.

eingleisig, *a. Rail:* **eingleisige Strecke,** single (-track) line; **eingleisiger Betrieb,** single-track working.

Eingleisungsrampe, *f. Rail:* rerailing ramp.

eingleiten, *v.i. sep.* (*strong*) (*sein*) (*of machine part*) to slide in; to glide in; **in etwas** *acc.* **e.,** to glide into (groove, etc.); to slide into (groove, etc.).

eingliedern. I. *v.tr. sep.* to fit in (details, etc.); to insert (details, etc.); **etwas in etwas** *acc.* **e.,** to fit, incorporate, (details, findings, facts, etc.) into (system, etc.); to insert (details, findings, facts, etc.) into (system, etc.); to incorporate (institution, etc.) into (organization, etc.); **sich e.,** to fit in; **sich in etwas** *acc.* **e.,** to fit into sth.; **eine Polizeieinheit der Wehrmacht, in die Wehrmacht, e.,** to incorporate a police unit into the army; **j-n in den Arbeitsprozeß e.,** to find employment for s.o.; **j-n, etwas, in einen Arbeitsprozeß e.,** to incorporate s.o., sth., into a working process.

II. *vbl s.* **Eingliedern** *n.*, **Eingliederung** *f. in vbl senses; also:* incorporation (of details into a system, of institution into an organization, etc.); insertion (of details into a system, etc.).

eingliedrig, *a. Mth:* monomial; **eingliedriger Ausdruck,** monomial (expression), single term.

Eingottglaube, *m.* monotheism.

eingraben, *v. sep.* (*strong*) I. *v.tr.* **1.** (*a*) to bury (sth.); **viele Bewohner des Dorfes hatten Vorräte in die Erde eingegraben,** many of the inhabitants of the village had buried supplies in the ground; **der Mörder grub die Leiche im Wald ein,** the murderer buried the corpse in the forest; (*b*) *Constr: etc:* to drive in, ram in, sink (in) (pile, etc.); **einen Pfahl in die Erde e.,** to drive, ram, sink, a pile into the ground. **2. eine Inschrift, usw., in etwas e.,** to cut, incise, an inscription, etc., into (metal, stone); to engrave an inscription, etc., on (metal, stone); to carve an inscription, etc., on (stone).

II. **sich eingraben. 1.** (*a*) (*of hibernating animal, etc.*) to dig itself in; *Mil:* to dig oneself in, to entrench oneself; **sich in seine Arbeit e.,** to bury oneself in one's work; (*b*) **das Geschoß grub sich in die Erde ein,** the projectile buried, embedded, itself in the ground. **2.** to engrave itself on sth.; **diese Worte haben sich in mein Gedächtnis eingegraben,** these words have engraved themselves on my memory; **die Spuren der Witterung haben sich in den Felsen eingegraben,** the weather has carved its traces on the rock.

eingravieren, *v.tr. sep.* **ein Muster, usw., in etwas** *acc.* **e.,** to engrave a design, etc., on (metal, stone, etc.); to cut, incise, a design, etc., into (metal, stone, etc.); **eine Platte mit einer eingravierten Inschrift,** a plate engraved with an inscription.

Eingreifdivision, *f. Mil:* counter-attack division.

eingreifen. I. *v.i. sep.* (*strong*) (*haben*) **1.** *Mec.E: etc:* (*of toothed wheel, etc.*) to be in gear, in mesh (**in etwas** *acc.*, with sth.); to come into gear, into mesh (**in etwas** *acc.*, with sth.); to engage (**in etwas** *acc.*, sth.); to mesh, gear (**in etwas** *acc.*, with sth.); to pitch (**in etwas** *acc.*, into sth.); to catch, to tooth; (*of screw, etc.*) to bite; (*of anchor*) to bite, hold, grip; **ineinander e.,** (*of parts*) to lock into one another; to fit into one another; to interlock; (*of toothed wheels, etc.*) to interlock; to gear into, with, one another; to engage one another; to mesh with one another; to be in mesh, contact, with one another; to cog; to mate; **ein Zahnrad e. lassen,** to bring, throw, put, a toothed wheel into engagement, mesh, gear; to engage, mesh, gear, a toothed wheel; **die Balken greifen in die Mauer ein,** the ends of the beams are locked into the wall; **die Speichen greifen in die Löcher der Felge ein,** the spokes lock into the holes of the felly. **2.** to intervene; to interfere; **in j-s Rechte e.,** to encroach, infringe, trespass, intrude, on s.o.'s rights; to invade s.o.'s rights; **in den Gang der Ereignisse e.,** to influence the course of events; to change the course of events; **ein Ereignis, das tief in den Gang ihres Lebens eingriff,** an event which had a radical effect on the course of her life, which cut sharply across the normal course of her life; **die Diskussion verlief ruhig, bis er in die Debatte eingriff,** the discussion went on calmly until he intervened, interfered, in the debate; **die Polizei weigerte sich einzugreifen,** the police refused to take action, to act, interfere, intervene; **in dieser, in diese, Angelegenheit kann ich nicht e.,** I cannot interfere, intervene, in this matter; **es ist, wird, Zeit einzugreifen,** it is time to act; **eingreifende Maßnahmen,** strong, radical, drastic, energetic, effective, measures.

II. **Eingreifen,** *n. in vbl senses; also:* **1.** *Mec.E:* engagement, mesh(ing), pitch(ing), gearing (of toothed wheel, etc.); *cp.* **Eingriff** 1. **2.** intervention; interference; **jedes E. in dieser, in diese, Angelegenheit würde die Situation nur verschlechtern,** any action, intervention, interference, in this matter would only worsen the situation; *cp.* **Eingriff** 2 (*a*).

eingrenzen, *v.tr. sep.* **1.** (*a*) to enclose, close in (piece of ground, etc.) (with wall, fence, etc.); (*b*) to localize (epidemic, fire, etc.). **2.** to delimit, define (powers); to define, narrow down (field of research).

Eingriff, *m.* **1.** *Mec.E:* (*a*) engagement, meshing, pitching, gearing (of toothed wheel, etc.); contact (of toothed wheel, etc.); **Zahnräder, usw., in E. bringen,** to bring, throw, put, toothed wheels, etc., into engagement, mesh, gear; to engage, mesh, gear, connect, toothed wheels, etc.; (*of toothed wheels, etc.*) **miteinander im E. stehen,** to interlock; to gear into, with, one another; to engage one another; to mesh with one another; to be in mesh, contact, with one another; to cog; to mate; **mit einem Zahnrad im E. stehen,** to be in gear, mesh, contact, with a toothed wheel; to mesh, gear, with a toothed wheel; to pitch into a toothed wheel; **Zahnräder, usw., außer E. bringen, setzen,** to throw, bring, toothed wheels, etc., out of gear, mesh; to ungear, disengage, toothed wheels, etc.; **in E. kommen,** to come into gear, mesh; (*b*) (*of tools*) **im E.,** in actual contact with the piece; in attack. **2.** (*a*) encroachment, trespass, intrusion (**in j-s Rechte,** on s.o.'s rights); infringement, invasion (**in j-s Rechte,** of s.o.'s rights); *cp.* **eingreifen** II, 2; (*b*) interference (in natural development, etc.); disruption (of s.o.'s life, etc.); **dieses Ereignis war ein schmerzlicher E. in seinem Leben,** this event cut painfully across his normal life; *Med:* **(operativer) E.,** operation; **einen E. machen, vornehmen,** to operate, to perform an operation; **verbotener, unerlaubter, E.,** illegal operation. **3.** *Ven:* spoor (of fleeing deer). **4.** notch (in lockbolt, etc.).

Eingriff(s)bogen, *m. Mec.E:* pitch-arc.

Eingriff(s)linie, *f. Mec.E:* line of action; pitch-line (of toothed wheel).

Eingriffsrippe, *f. Mec.E:* engaging rib (on piston ring, etc.).

Eingriff(s)winkel, *m. Mec.E:* angle of action (of toothed wheel, gear, etc.).

Eingriff(s)zirkel, *m. Mec.E: Clockm:* depthing tool (for toothed wheels).

Einguß, *m.* **1.** (*a*) pouring in, running in (of molten metal, plaster, etc.); (*b*) *Med:* infusion. **2.** *Metall: etc:* setting, fixing (of iron bar, etc.) (with cement, lead, etc.); casting in (of iron bar, etc.). **3.** *Metall:* (in)gate; runner; sprue(-gate). **4.** *Metall:* ingot mould.

Eingußform, *f. Metall:* casting mould.

Eingußkanal, *m. Metall:* sprue(-gate).

Eingußkasten, *m. Metall:* feed-box.

Eingußtrichter, *m. Metall:* sprue(-gate).

Eingußvorrichtung, *f. Metall:* pouring device.

einhacken, *v.sep.* **1.** *v.i.* (*haben*) **auf etwas** *acc.* **e.,** to hack at sth.; (*of bird*) to peck at sth.; *F:* **auf j-n e.,** to keep, go, on at s.o. **2.** *v.tr.* (*of animal, bird*) **die Krallen in etwas** *acc.* **e.,** to dig its claws into sth. **3.** *v.tr.* to hack (hole, etc.) (in sth.); (*of bird*) to peck (hole, etc.) (in bark of tree, etc.).

einhageln, *v.sep.* **1.** *v.i.* (*sein*) **auf j-n, etwas, e.,** (*of blows*) to fall as thick as hail on s.o., sth.; (*of bullets*) to hail on s.o., sth.; **Schläge hagelten nur so auf uns ein,** blows fell as thick as hail on us, hailed on us, rained on us; **Kugeln hagelten auf sie ein,** bullets were hailing on them. **2.** *v.tr.* (*usu. used in passive or impers.*) **eingehagelt werden,** to be smashed by hail; **es hat fast alle Scheiben des Glashauses eingehagelt,** almost all the glass of the greenhouse has been smashed by the hail.

einhäkeln, *v.tr. sep.* **1.** to edge, border, (handkerchief, napkin, etc.) with crochet(ing). **2. sich einhäkeln,** (*a*) (*of animal*) to dig its claws in; (*b*) *F:* to take s.o.'s arm; (*of several people*) to link arms.

einhaken, *v.sep.* **1.** *v.tr.* (*a*) to fasten (sth.) (by means of a hook, clasp, clip); to attach (coupling device, etc.); to hitch (trailer, etc.) on; **die Sicherheitskette e.,** to put the chain on (the door); **wir müssen die Fensterläden e.,** we must fasten the shutters back; (*b*) *F: v.i.* (*haben*) & **sich e.,** to take s.o.'s arm; (*of several people*) to link arms; **sie gingen eingehakt,** they went, walked, arm in arm; **ich hakte mich bei ihm ein,** I took his arm, put, linked, my arm in his. **2.** *v.i.* (*haben*) to cut in, break in (at point of speech, etc.) (*in order to attack*); **der Verteidiger hakte bei dem Widerspruch in der Aussage des Zeugen ein,** counsel for the defence seized on the contradiction in the witness's statement; **an diesem Punkt hakte er ein,** at this point he broke in, cut in.

einhalbmal, *adv.* **e. eine Strecke, usw.,** half the way, etc.; **e. soviel,** half as much.

einhallen, *v.tr. sep. Av:* to park (aircraft) in a hangar.

einhalsen, *v.tr. sep. Metalw:* to neck (metal cylinder, etc.).

Einhalt, *m.* -(e)s/. **j-m, etwas** *dat.*, **E. gebieten, tun,** to stop s.o., sth.; to put a stop to sth.; **ich werde seinem Treiben E. gebieten, bevor er weiteres Unheil anrichtet,** I shall put a stop to his activities before he does any more damage.

einhalten, *v.sep.* (*strong*) I. *v.tr.* **1.** to keep to, adhere to, *F:* stick to (time-table, conditions,

contract, fixed date, etc.); to observe (conditions, contract, etc.); to perform, abide by (contract); to keep up (payments); to hold, keep (one's course); **er hielt seine Zahlungen immer pünktlich ein,** he always kept up his payments punctually. **2.** to take in (dress, etc.); to pull in (curtain, etc.); **der Vorhang wirkt besser, wenn er an dieser Stelle ein wenig eingehalten wird,** the curtain looks nicer if it is pulled in a little here. **3.** to retain, hold (one's urine, etc.). **4. sich einhalten,** (*a*) *Dial:* to hold tight; **halt dich jetzt fest ein,** hold tight now; (*b*) *A:* to stay at home.

II. **einhalten,** *v.i.* (*haben*) to stop; to pause; **mit etwas e.,** to stop doing sth.; *Lit:* **haltet ein, er ist unschuldig!** hold, stay, he is innocent! **er hielt mitten im Satz ein, als er ihn hereinkommen sah,** he stopped in the middle of a sentence when he saw him coming in.

III. *vbl s.* **Einhalten** *n.*, **Einhaltung** *f.* (+*gen.*) *in vbl senses of* I; *also:* observation (of sth.), adherence (to sth.); **unter Einhaltung einer Frist von . . .,** subject to a term of . . . .

einhämmern, *v.tr. sep.* to drive (post, etc.) in with a hammer, to hammer (post, etc.) in; **etwas in etwas** *acc.* **e.,** to drive (post, etc.) into (the ground, etc.) with a hammer, to hammer (post, etc.) into (the ground, etc.); *F:* **j-m etwas e.,** to hammer sth. into s.o.

einhandeln, *v.tr. sep.* **etwas (von, bei, j-m) e.,** to buy sth. (from, of, s.o.); to bargain (with s.o.) for sth.; **etwas gegen etwas e.,** to barter sth. for sth.; **er hat diese Ware günstig eingehandelt,** he bought these goods at a favourable price; **er handelte das Zaumzeug mit ein,** he got the harness as well, into the bargain.

einhändig, *a.* **1.** (*of pers.*) one-handed. **2.** *adv.* with one hand; **e. radfahren,** to ride a bicycle with one hand; **e. Klavier spielen,** to play the piano with one hand.

einhändigen, *v.tr. sep.* to hand (sth.) in; **j-m etwas e.,** to hand sth. in, over, to s.o.; to deliver sth. to s.o.; **er händigte ihm die versprochene Summe ein,** he handed over, delivered, the promised sum to him.

Einhängeblende, *f. Opt:* interchangeable diaphragm.

Einhängemaschine, *f. Bookb:* casing-in machine.

einhängen, *v.sep.* (*conj. like* **hängen**[2]). **1.** *v.tr.* to hang, suspend (sth.) in position, to hang (door, window, bell); to attach (coupling device, etc.); to couple up, on (carriage); to hitch on (trailer, etc.); to replace (suspension file); to lay (roof-tiles); *Rail:* to set, lock (coupling); **die Sicherheitskette e.,** to put the chain on (the door); *Tp:* **den Hörer e.,** *abs.* **e.,** to replace the receiver, *abs.* to hang up, ring off; *Nau:* **das Steuerruder e.,** to hang, ship, the rudder; *Bookb:* **den Buchblock in die Buchdecke e.,** to attach the book to its cover, case; to case the book in. **2. sich einhängen,** to take s.o.'s arm; (*of several people*) to link arms; **sie gingen eingehängt,** they went, walked, arm in arm; **ich hängte mich bei ihm ein,** I took his arm, put, linked, my arm in his, linked arms with him.

Einhängetasche, *f.* (*office equipment*) suspension file.

einhängig, *a. Constr:* **einhängiges Dach,** lean-to roof, pent-roof.

einhauchen, *v.tr. sep.* **j-m, etwas** *dat.*, **Leben, Unsterblichkeit, usw., e.,** to breathe, *Lit:* inspire, life, immortality, etc., into s.o., sth.; **Gott hat dem Menschen eine unsterbliche Seele eingehaucht,** God has breathed an immortal soul into man; **der Dichter vermochte seinen Figuren Leben einzuhauchen,** the poet succeeded in breathing life into his characters.

einhauen, *v.sep.* (*conj. like* **hauen**) **1.** *v.tr.* (*a*) to break open (door); to break down (door, wall, etc.); (*b*) **eine Öffnung, usw., in etwas** *acc.* **e.,** to make, hew, an opening, etc., in sth.; **einen Tunnel in einen Felsen e.,** to hew a tunnel into a rock; (*c*) **etwas in etwas** *acc.* **e.,** to cut (groove, etc.) in (stone, etc.); to carve (inscription, etc.) in (stone, rock, etc.); to hew (figure, etc.) in (rock); **eine roh in den Felsen eingehauene Inschrift,** an inscription roughly carved in the rock. **2.** *v.i.* (*haben*) **auf j-n, etwas, e.,** to strike at s.o., sth. (with whip, sword, etc.); to strike blows at s.o., sth.; to attack, fall (up)on, s.o. (with sword, etc.); **der Kutscher hieb wütend auf sein Pferd ein,** the coachman struck furiously at his horse; **sie hieben mit ihren Schwertern auf die Feinde ein,** they attacked, fell upon, the enemy with their swords; **tüchtig, wacker, e.,** (i) to fight bravely; (ii) *F:* to tuck into one's food.

Einhaus, *n.* farm-house with stables, etc., under one roof,

einhäusig, *a. Bot:* monoecious; **einhäusige Pflanze,** monoecian; **einhäusige Pflanzen,** monoecia.

Einhäusigkeit, *f. Bot:* monoecism.

einheben, *v.tr. sep.* (*strong*) to lift (sth.) in; to lift (sth.) into position; to hang (door, window).

einheften, *v.tr. sep.* **1. etwas in etwas** *acc.* **e.,** to put (document, extra sheet, etc.) into (loose-leaf file); to sew (extra sheet) into (book, copy-book, etc.); to staple (extra sheet) into (copy-book, etc.). **2.** *Dressm:* to tack in, baste on (sleeves, lining, etc.).

einhegen, *v.tr. sep.* = **einfriedigen.**

einheimisch, *a.* home (trade, product, industry, etc.); home-produced (goods, etc.); local (population, trade, product, industry, customs, etc.); home-grown (fruit, etc.); home-bred (farm-stock, etc.); indigenous, native (population, plant, animal, product, etc.); resident (population, etc.); *Nat.Hist:* endemic (plant, animal, etc.); **die einheimischen Bürger,** the local population, the inhabitants, the residents (of town, village, etc.); **die Einheimischen,** the natives; the locals; **in den Tropen einheimische Pflanzen,** plants native, indigenous, to the tropics.

einheimsen, *v.tr. sep.* to garner (harvest, fruits, etc.); to reap (reward of other people's labours, etc.); **den Ruhm für sich e.,** to take the glory for oneself; **er läßt andere die Arbeit tun und möchte selbst den Gewinn, die Lorbeeren, e.,** he lets others do the work but wants to reap the profit, take the laurels, himself; **die Bienen heimsen den Honig ein,** the bees gather (in) the honey; *F:* **eine hübsche Summe Geld e.,** to rake in a pretty sum of money.

Einheirat, *f.* **E. (in ein Geschäft, usw.),** marriage into a business, etc.; (*in advertisement*) **'E. erwünscht',** 'would be interested in marrying into a family business'.

einheiraten, *v.i. sep.* (*haben*) **in eine Familie, ein Geschäft, e.,** to marry into a family, a business.

Einheit, *f.* **1.** (*a*) unit (of measure, value, etc.); *Phil:* unity; monad; *Mth:* unit; unity; **die Familie ist die kleinste E. in einem Gemeinwesen,** the family is the smallest unit in a community; *Mth:* **einen Koeffizienten auf die E. zurückführen,** to reduce a coefficient to unity; *Alg:* **E. (der Zahlenlinie, eines Vektorraums),** unit point (of the number scale, a vector space); (*b*) *Mil:* unit; **taktische E.,** tactical unit; **strategische E.,** strategical unit; (*c*) *Golf:* bogey; **Spiel gegen E.,** play against bogey. **2.** (*a*) unity, oneness (of God, the universe, etc.); (*b*) unity (of style, thought, work of art, etc.); continuity (of train of thought, etc.); *Lit:* unity (of action, place, time); **die dramatischen Einheiten,** the dramatic unities; **Teile zu einer E. verschmelzen,** to weld parts into a homogeneous, an integrated, whole; **sich zu einer E. zusammenschließen, zu einer E. verschmelzen, eine E. bilden,** to unite to form an integrated whole; (*of husband and wife*) **eine E. bilden,** to be as one; **zu einer E. verschmelzen,** to become as one; **die ganze Bevölkerung, eine Partei, zu einer E. zusammenschließen,** to unify the whole population, a party; (*c*) unity (of the Church, a state, etc.); **nationale E.,** national unity.

einheitlich. 1. *a.* (*a*) homogeneous, integrated (whole); homogeneous (structure, construction of play, design, etc.); uniform (philosophical system, style, etc.); coherent (train of thought, etc.); **das Stück hat keine einheitliche Handlung,** there is no unity of action in this play; **dieses Werk des Dichters weist eine einheitliche Gestaltung auf,** this work of the poet shows unity of form; **ich konnte kein einheitliches Bild der Lage gewinnen,** I could not get a uniform, coherent, consistent, picture of the situation; **sie handelten ohne einen einheitlichen Plan,** they acted with no concerted plan; **ein einheitliches Volk,** a homogeneous people; **die Truppen unterstehen einem einheitlichen Kommando,** the troops are under a centralized command; **eine einheitliche Front bilden,** to present a united front; (*b*) standard (price, tariff, etc.); uniform (standard, quality, tariff, rate of pay, etc.); **einheitliche Maßstäbe anwenden,** to apply uniform standards; **die Schüler tragen einheitliche Kleidung,** the pupils wear uniform clothing, a uniform, are dressed alike; **es wurden einheitliche Preise für bestimmte Waren festgesetzt,** a standard price was fixed for a certain type of goods; **einheitliche Größenregelung,** standardization (of sizes); **Waren von einheitlicher Güte,** goods of uniformly, consistently, good quality. **2.** *adv.* uniformly; consistently; **Maßnahmen e. durchführen,** to apply measures uniformly; to carry out measures consistently; **einen Plan e. durchführen,** to keep consistently to one's plan (in constructing a novel, a building, etc.); **dieses Motiv ist im ganzen Werk e. durchgeführt,** this motif runs consistently through the whole work; *Geol:* **e. gebauter Vulkan,** monogenic volcano.

Einheitlichkeit, *f.* (*a*) unity (of action, form, etc.); uniformity (of philosophical system, style, etc.); integrity (of a whole); homogeneity (of structure, design, construction of play, etc.); coherence (of train of thought, etc.); consistency (of measures, plan, train of thought, etc.); (*b*) uniformity (of price, tariff, rate of pay, standard, quality, etc.).

Einheits-, *comb.fm.* **1.** standard . . .; standardized . . .; uniform . . .; **Einheitstarif** *m*, standard tariff; **Einheitsware** *f*, standard, standardized, article(s); **Einheitsformat** *n*, standard size; **Einheitsmietvertrag** *m*, standard form of rent agreement; **Einheitssatz** *m*, uniform rate; **Einheitszoll** *m*, uniform rate of duty; *Tchn:* **Einheitsgewinde** *n*, standard thread. **2.** unit . . .; unit-; **Einheitslänge** *f*, unit length; *Mth:* **Einheitsvektor** *m*, unit-vector; *Ph:* **Einheitspol** *m*, unit magnetic pole. **3.** unitary . . .; united . . .; **Einheitstendenz** *f*, unitary tendency; **Einheitsfront** *f*, united front.

Einheitsbestrebung, *f. usu. pl.* **Einheitsbestrebungen,** unitary tendencies, tendencies towards unification.

Einheitsbewegung, *f.* movement towards unity, unitary movement.

Einheitsboot, *n.* one-design (sailing) boat.

Einheitselement, *n. Mth:* identity (of a group).

Einheitsform, *f.* uniform type (of building, etc.); standard form; *Alg:* primitive polynomial.

Einheitsfront, *f. Pol:* bloc, united front (of parties).

Einheitsgetriebe, *n. Aut: etc:* unit gearing.

Einheitsgewerkschaft, *f.* unified trade union.

Einheitsgewicht, *n.* (*a*) standard weight; (*b*) unit weight; *Av: I.C.E:* power-weight ratio (of engine).

Einheitsgewinde, *n. Mec.E:* standard thread.

Einheitsgranate, *f. Artil:* combined high-explosive and shrapnel shell.

Einheitskleidung, *f.* (*a*) standardized clothing; uniform (clothing) (of pupils, prisoners, etc.); (*b*) utility clothing.

Einheitskreis, *m. Mth:* unit circle; **Bogenlänge eins im E.,** radian.

Einheitskugel, *f. Mth:* unit sphere.

Einheitskurs, *m.* **1.** *St.Exch:* adjusted rate. **2.** *Fin:* medium rate of exchange.

Einheitskurzschrift, *f.* standard shorthand system.

Einheitslänge, *f.* unit length.

Einheitsmaß, *n.* standard measure; standard (of weight, etc.).

Einheitsmasse, *f. Ph:* unit mass.

Einheitsmatrix, *f. Alg:* unit matrix, identity matrix.

Einheitsmonat, *m. Statistics:* month adjusted for calendar variation.

Einheitsoperator, *m. Alg:* unity operator.

Einheitspol, *m. Ph:* unit magnetic pole.

Einheitspreis, *m.* (*a*) standard price; uniform price; unit price; **alle zu einem E. von einer Mark,** all at the same price, at the uniform price, of one mark; (*b*) (*at auction*) reserve price.

Einheitspreisgeschäft, *n.* one-price store.

Einheitssatz, *m.* **E. (für etwas),** standard rate (of fares, postage, etc.).

Einheitsschlüssel, *m. Mus:* single clef.

Einheitsschule, *f.* comprehensive school.

Einheitsspiel, *n. Golf:* bogey play.

Einheitsstaat, *m. Pol:* state with central government, centralized state.

Einheitsstrecke, *f.* unit (of) distance.

Einheitstarif, *m. Rail: Post: etc:* uniform, standard, tariff.

Einheitsvektor, *m. Mth:* unit-vector.

Einheitsversicherung, *f. Ins:* all risks insurance.

Einheitsvolumen, *n. Ph:* unit volume.

Einheitswaren, *f.pl.* standardized goods; utility goods.

Einheitswert, *m.* **1.** unit value; standard value. **2.** *Adm:* rat(e)able value (of house, etc.).

Einheitszeit, *f.* standard time.

Einheitszoll, *m. Cust:* uniform rate of duty.

einheizen, *v.i. sep.* (*haben*) to light a fire; *occ. v.tr.* to light (stove); **in einem Zimmer e.,** *occ. v.tr.* **ein Zimmer e.,** to light, have, a fire in a room; to heat a room; *F:* **j-m e.,** to make things, it, hot

for s.o.; *F:* **er scheint tüchtig eingeheizt zu haben,** he seems to have had a good deal to drink, he looks as if he had had a few.

einhelfen, *v.tr. sep.* (*strong*) *Dial:* **j-m e.,** to prompt (fellow-pupil, etc.).

einhellig, *a.* unanimous; **man spendete ihm einhelliges Lob,** they were unanimous in their praise of him; *adv.* unanimously; by common consent, with one consent; **sie faßten e. den Beschluß, den Verbündeten zu Hilfe zu eilen,** they took the unanimous decision, they unanimously decided, they decided by common consent, to come to the help of their allies.

Einhelligkeit, *f.* unanimity.

einhenk(e)lig, *a.* (jug, etc.) with one handle, one-handled (jug, etc.).

einhenkeln, sich, *v.refl. sep. F:*=**einhängen** 2.

einher-, *comb.fm.* (*expletive, with a general implication of progress*) along; **einhergehen,** to walk along; **einherfahren,** to drive along; **einherstolzieren,** to strut along; to stalk along; **er stolziert einher, als ob er ein Fürst wäre,** he stalks along as if he were a prince; **der Hahn stolziert einher,** the cock struts along; **die Teilnehmer der Prozession schritten feierlich einher,** the people in the procession walked along solemnly; **das Bächlein rauscht einher,** the brook goes babbling along; **die Wolken ziehen einher,** the clouds go their way.

einherbsten, *v.tr. sep.* to gather (in) (grapes, etc.).

Einherier, Einherjer, *m.* **-s/-.** *Norse Myth:* fallen warrior in Valhalla.

Einhieb, *m. For:*=**Einschlag** 9.

einhieven, *v.tr. sep. Nau:* to heave in, haul in (cable, etc.).

einhöckerig, *a. Z:* one-humped; *see also* **Kamel.**

einholen. I. *v.tr. sep.* **1.** (*a*) to take, bring, get, in (harvest, etc.); to (go out and) buy (food, etc.); **e. gehen,** to go shopping; (*b*) **Auskunft (über j-n, etwas) e.,** to seek information, to make enquiries (about s.o., sth.); to enquire into (sth.); **Auskunft bei j-m e.,** to seek information from s.o.; **j-s Rat, Erlaubnis, Zustimmung, e.,** to ask for, seek, s.o.'s advice, permission, consent; to get, to procure, s.o.'s advice, permission, consent; **Instruktionen, Befehle, e.,** to apply for, get, instructions, orders; **ein Rechtsgutachten e.,** to get a legal opinion; to take counsel's opinion; **das Gutachten eines Fachmanns e.,** to call for, obtain, an expert's report. **2.** (*of welcoming committee, etc.*) **j-n e.,** to arrange a ceremonial entry for s.o.; **sie holten den Sieger feierlich ein,** they received the victor with due ceremony and escorted him home. **3.** to take in (sail, etc.); to haul in, heave in (rope, etc.); to strike, lower, haul down (sail, flag); to run in, rig in (bowsprit, etc.). **4. j-n, ein Fahrzeug, usw., e.,** to catch s.o., a vehicle, etc. (up); to catch up, come up, draw level, with s.o., a vehicle, etc.; to rejoin s.o., a group of people, etc.; **ein anderes Fahrzeug e.,** to catch up with another car; **wenn du läufst, könntest du ihn e.,** you may catch him if you run; **ich nahm den nächsten Dampfer und holte die anderen in Köln ein,** I took the next boat and caught up with the others at Cologne; **er holte uns im Dorf ein,** he caught us up at the village; **sich von j-m e. lassen,** to let oneself be caught by s.o.; (*b*) **verlorene Zeit e.,** to make up for, to recover, lost time; **es wird für das Kind schwierig sein, das Versäumte einzuholen,** it will be difficult for the child to catch up with what he has missed; **die Versäumnisse der Jugendjahre sind nicht einzuholen,** the omissions of one's youth cannot be repaired; **ich werde die verlorene Zeit leicht e.,** I shall easily make up the time I have lost.

II. *vbl s.* **Einholen** *n.,* **Einholung** *f. in vbl senses; also:* **feierliche Einholung der Fahne,** ceremonial lowering of the flag.

Einholer, *m.* **-s/-.** *Nau:* inhaul.

Einholmflügel, *m. Av:* single-spar wing, monospar wing.

Einholtasche, *f.* shopping-bag.

Einhorn, *n.* **1.** *Myth: Her:* unicorn. **2.** *Z:* (*a*) single-horned rhinoceros; (*b*) sea-unicorn, unicorn-fish, unicorn-whale, narwhal. **3.** *Astr:* **das E.,** Monoceros, the Unicorn.

einhörnig, *a. Z:* single-horned; unicorn, unicornous.

Einhufer, *m.* **-s/-.** *Z:* soliped, solipede.

einhufig, *a. Z:* soliped, solidungulate, whole-hoofed.

einhüftig, *a. Arch:* **einhüftiger Bogen,** rampant arch.

einhüllen, *v.tr. sep.* to wrap (s.o., sth.) (up); to enclose, encase (sth.); **j-n, etwas, in etwas** *acc.* **e.,** to wrap s.o., sth., (up) in (cloth, paper, etc.); **er hüllte das Kind warm ein,** he wrapped the child up warmly; **er hüllte sich fest, dicht, in seine Decke ein,** he wrapped his blanket closely round, about, him; he wrapped himself (up) tightly in his blanket; **dicht in Pelze eingehüllt sein,** to be all wrapped up, to be completely enveloped, in furs; **in einen Schal eingehüllt,** wrapped, swathed, in a shawl; **eine Leiche in das Leichentuch e.,** to shroud a corpse; **der Nebel hüllte die Straßen in Finsternis ein,** the fog wrapped, shrouded, enveloped, the streets in darkness; **eine in Nebel eingehüllte Landschaft,** a landscape (en)shrouded in mist; a landscape enveloped, enfolded, in mist; **in Finsternis eingehüllt,** shrouded in gloom; **sich in seine Würde e.,** to stand on one's dignity; **er hüllte sich in seine Professorenwürde ein,** he stood on his professorial dignity; he retired into professorial aloofness; *Civ.E:* **Steine in Teer e.,** to coat stones with tar; *Geom:* **einhüllende Kurve, einhüllende Fläche, Einhüllende** *f,* envelope.

einhundert, *num.a. inv.* one hundred, a hundred; **£100, in Worten einhundert Pfund,** £100, in words one hundred pounds.

einig, *a.* **1.** (*a*) united (people, family, etc.); **e. sein,** to be united; **seid e.!** be of one mind! (*b*) **(sich** *dat.***) in einer, über eine, Angelegenheit e. sein,** to be of one mind in, about, a matter; to be of the same opinion in, about, a matter; to agree, to be agreed, to be in agreement, in, about, a matter; **(sich** *dat.***) über die Bedingungen, den Preis, usw., e. sein,** to agree, to be agreed, to be in agreement, on the conditions, the price, etc.; to have settled on the, a, price; **(sich** *dat.***) mit j-m e. sein,** to be of one mind with s.o., to be of the same mind as s.o., to be of s.o.'s mind; to be of the same opinion as s.o., to be of s.o.'s opinion; to agree, to be agreed, to be in agreement, with s.o.; **(sich** *dat.***) (mit j-m) e. werden,** to come to, arrive at, reach, an agreement (with s.o.); **sie konnten (sich) über die Bedingungen nicht e. werden,** they could not agree on the conditions; **er konnte mit ihm nicht über den Preis e. werden,** he could not agree on a price with him; **bist du jetzt endlich mit dir e., bist du dir jetzt endlich e.?** have you finally made up your mind? **er ist immer noch nicht mit sich darüber e.,** he is still in two minds about it, he still hasn't made up his mind about it; **über diesen, in diesem, Punkt sind (sich) alle e.,** all are unanimous on this point; all are agreed on this point; **wir sind (uns) also darin, darüber, e., daß . . . ,** so we agree that . . .; **darüber sind die Gelehrten sich noch nicht e.,** scholars are not agreed on that; *F:* that is an open question; **man war (sich) nicht darüber e., was jetzt zu tun sei,** opinions were divided as to what should be done now; **wir werden (uns) niemals e. werden,** we shall never agree, come to an agreement; **in diesem Punkt bin ich völlig mit Ihnen e.,** I quite, entirely, agree with you on that point; **alle waren (sich) e. in der Überzeugung, daß . . . ,** all shared the conviction that . . . . **2.** *A:* only; one; **sein einiger Sohn,** his only son; *B:* **der Herr, unser Gott, ist ein einiger Gott,** the Lord our God is one Lord.

einige *see* **einiger, einige, einiges.**

einigeln (sich), *v.refl. sep.* (*a*) *F:* (*of pers.*) to curl oneself up in a ball; (*b*) *Mil:* to take up a position of all-round defence, *F:* to form a hedgehog.

einigemal, *adv.* a few times; once or twice.

einigen. I. *v.tr. sep.* **1.** to unite (people, etc.); to unify (people, etc.); **die Bedrohung des Friedens einigte das Land,** the threat to peace unified, united, the country; **ein geeinigtes Volk,** a united people. **2. sich (mit j-m) (in einer, über eine, Angelegenheit, über den Preis, die Bedingungen, usw.) e.,** to come to an agreement, to terms, to an understanding (with s.o.) (in, about, a matter, on the price, the conditions, etc.); **sich auf etwas** *acc.* **e.,** to agree on (a certain price, certain conditions, etc.); **wir haben uns (darüber) geeinigt, daß . . . ,** we have agreed that . . .; **sie hatten sich daraufhin geeinigt, daß . . . ,** they had agreed that . . .; they had come to an agreement that . . .; **sie hatten sich noch nicht darüber geeinigt, ob . . . ,** they still had not come to, reached, an agreement as to whether . . .; **ich habe mich mit ihr über den Preis geeinigt,** I have agreed, come to an agreement, on the price with her; **einigt euch doch schon endlich,** do make up your minds (and come to an agreement).

II. *vbl s.* **1. Einigen,** *n. in vbl senses.* **2. Einigung,** *f.* (*a*)=II. 1; *also:* unification (of a people, etc.); (*b*) agreement; **eine E. erreichen, erzielen, zu einer E. kommen,** to come to an agreement, to terms, to an understanding; **eine E. zwischen zwei Parteien zustande bringen, erreichen, erzielen,** to bring two parties to an agreement.

einiger, einige, einiges. I. *indef. a.* **1.** (*a*) some; **in einiger Entfernung,** some distance away; **einige Zeit standen wir schweigend,** for some time, for a little while, we stood silent; (*b*) (*pl.*) some; a few; **eine Regel mit einigen Ausnahmen,** a rule subject to some exceptions; **vor einigen Tagen,** some days ago; **in einigen (wenigen) Minuten,** in a few minutes; **einige wenige Getreue bleiben,** a faithful few remain; **einige wenige dachten anders,** a few thought otherwise; **ich wartete einige (wenige) Minuten,** I waited some, a few, minutes; **wir werden nur einige wenige sein,** we shall only be a (select) few; **einige mehr,** a few more; **es wird einige Minuten dauern,** it will take a few, some, minutes, a minute or two; **ich bin einige Male dort gewesen,** I have been there a few times; **er und einige andere,** he and some others; **einige Gramm darüber,** a few odd grammes over; (*c*) (+*num.*) (i) several (hundred, thousand, etc.); a few (hundred, thousand, etc.); (ii) some (twenty, thirty, etc.); (twenty, thirty, etc.) odd; about (twenty, thirty, etc.); **einige Hundert, einige Tausend,** several hundred, several thousand; a few hundred, a few thousand; **einige Tausende,** several thousand; a few thousand; **einige Hundert Schafe,** several hundred sheep; a few hundred sheep; **einige zwanzig, dreißig, Pfund,** some twenty, thirty, pounds; twenty, thirty, pounds odd; about twenty, thirty, pounds; **einige fünfzigtausend,** some fifty thousand; fifty thousand odd; about fifty thousand. **2. eine Stadt von einiger Bedeutung,** a town of some importance; **es braucht einigen Mut, das zu tun,** it needs some (little) courage to do that; **diese Angelegenheit verursachte mir einiges Kopfzerbrechen, einige Mühe,** this matter caused me no little headache, trouble.

II. *indef.pron.* (*a*) *pl.* **einige,** some; a few; **einige stimmen mit uns überein, andere nicht,** some agree with us, and some disagree; **einige ihrer Freunde sagten ihr, daß . . . ,** some of her friends told her that . . .; **ich möchte einige von diesen Äpfeln,** I want a few, some, of these apples; **ich kenne einige von ihnen,** I know some, a few, of them; **möchten Sie noch einige?** do you want (any) more, some more, a few more? (*b*) *neuter* **einiges,** something; some; some, a few, things; **er versteht einiges auf diesem Gebiet,** he knows quite a lot in this field; he knows something in this field; **ich habe ihm einiges zu sagen,** I have some, a few, things to tell him; **einiges davon,** part of it, some of it; **nur einiges aus seiner Arbeit ist wirklich brauchbar,** only parts of his work are really useful; **einiges von der Welt gesehen haben,** to have seen something of the world; **sein Plan hat einiges für sich,** his plan has something in it, there is something in his plan, there is something to be said for his plan.

einigermaßen, *adv.* to some, to a certain, in some, degree; to some, to a certain, extent; in some measure; somewhat; rather, fairly, quite, *F:* pretty; **e. wichtig sein,** to be fairly, rather, important; **e. überrascht, enttäuscht, sein,** to be somewhat, rather, fairly, surprised, disappointed; **ein e. ausführlicher Bericht,** a quite, fairly, detailed report; **wir besorgten einen e. guten Wein,** we got a fairly good wine, quite a good wine; **es ist e. sicher, daß . . . ,** it is fairly, pretty (well), certain that . . .; **ist er e. zuverlässig?** is he fairly reliable? **kaum hatte ich mich e. von dem Schreck erholt, als . . . ,** I had only just recovered a little, to some extent, from the shock when . . .; **wissen Sie jetzt e. Bescheid, worum es geht?** have you some idea now, have you an inkling now, of what it is all about? **wenn man (auch nur) e. intelligent ist, sieht man . . . ,** if you have any intelligence at all, you can see . . . .

einiggehen, *v.i. sep.* (*strong*) (*sein*) **mit j-m in einer Angelegenheit e.,** to agree with s.o., to be agreed, in agreement, with s.o., in a matter; to be of the same mind as s.o., of one mind with s.o., to be of s.o.'s mind, in a matter; to be of the same opinion as s.o., to be of s.o.'s opinion, in a matter; **ich gehe mit ihnen darin einig, daß . . . ,** I agree with them that . . . .

Einigkeit, *f.* (*a*) unity, union, concord, harmony; **miteinander in völliger E. leben,** to live together in perfect unity, union, harmony, concord; **E. der Nation,** national unity; *Prov:* **E. ist Stärke,** unity is strength; (*b*) unanimity; **es herrschte E. in allen, über alle, wesentlichen Fragen,** there was unanimity on all the important questions.

Einigungsamt, *n.* conciliation board (*in industrial dispute*); arbitration board (*in industrial dispute*); arbitration tribunal.
Einigungswerk, *n.* work of unification.
einimpfbar, *a. Med:* inoculable.
einimpfen. I. *v.tr. sep.* **j-m etwas e.,** to inoculate s.o. with (vaccine, etc.); *F:* to inoculate s.o. with (doctrine, idea, feeling, etc.); to implant in s.o. (doctrine, idea, feeling, etc.); to instil (doctrine, idea, feeling, etc.) into s.o.
II. *vbl s.* **Einimpfen** *n.*, **Einimpfung,** *f. in vbl senses; also:* inoculation (of vaccine, idea, etc.) (into body, mind).
einjagen, *v.tr. sep.* **1. j-m Schrecken, Angst, Furcht, e.,** to give s.o. a fright, to scare s.o.; *F:* to put the wind up s.o.; **dieser Anblick jagte ihm Schrecken, Furcht, ein,** this sight gave him a sudden fright, threw him into terror; **ihre Worte jagten ihm eine furchtbare Angst, einen furchtbaren Schrecken, ein,** her words gave him a dreadful fright; **du hast mir einen schönen Schrecken, eine schöne Angst, eingejagt,** you gave me a proper fright, you 'did scare me, 'did give me a scare. **2. sich** *dat.* **einen Splitter e.,** to get a splinter (in one's finger, etc.). **3. einen Jagdhund e.,** to break in a hound.
einjährig, *a.* **1.** (one-)year old (child, animal, etc.); **ein einjähriges Fohlen,** a yearling (foal). **2.** one-year (appointment, etc.); (appointment, etc.) lasting (for) one year; a, one, year's (training, friendship, etc.); (friendship, etc.) of one year; **heute kann der Verein auf ein einjähriges Bestehen zurückblicken,** today the society has been in existence for a, one, year; **nach einjähriger glücklicher Ehe,** after a, one, year of happy married life; *Mil:* **einjährige Dienstzeit,** a year's military service, one-year term of conscription. **3.** *Bot:* annual; **einjährige Pflanzen,** annual plants, annuals. **4. Einjährige** *m, Mil: A:* volunteer (with certain educational qualifications) opting for one year's military service (with subsequent obligation as a reservist). **5.** *Sch: A. & F.* **das Einjährige,** *approx.* = General Certificate of Education (at Ordinary Level).
Einjährig-Freiwillige, *m.* (*decl. as adj.*) *Mil: A:* volunteer (with certain educational qualifications) opting for one year's military service (with subsequent obligation as a reservist).
einjochen, *v.tr. sep.* to yoke (oxen).
einkacheln, *v.tr. sep.* **1.** (*a*) to line (bathroom, etc.) with (Dutch) tiles, to tile (bathroom, etc.); (*b*) to tile in (bath, kitchen-range, etc.). **2.** *F:* to burn (coal, etc.); *abs.* **tüchtig e.,** to make a roaring fire.
einkalken, *v.tr. sep. Agr:* to sprinkle (the ground, etc.) with lime; to lime (the ground, etc.); to lime-wash (fruit-trees, etc.): *Tan:* to lime (skins).
einkälken, *v.tr. sep.* = **einkalken.**
einkämmen, *v.tr. sep.* **1.** to comb (sth.) in; **etwas in etwas** *acc.* **e.,** to comb (brilliantine, etc.) into (one's hair, etc.). **2.** *Carp:* to join (beams, etc.) by cogging, to cog (beams, etc.); *Mec.E:* to mesh (gears).
Einkammerkessel, *m. Mch:* single header boiler.
Einkammersystem, *n. Pol:* unicameral system, single-chamber system.
einkampfern, *v.tr. sep.* **Kleider e.,** to put clothes in mothballs *or* moth-powder.
einkapseln, *v.tr. sep.* to enclose (sth.) in a capsule; *Biol: Med:* to encapsulate (organism); *Ling:* to incapsulate (element); **sich e.,** to become enclosed in a capsule *or* cyst; (*of tuberculosis germ, etc.*) to become encapsulated (within fibrous area, etc.); (*of tumour, parasite, etc.*) to encyst, to become encysted; (*of pers.*) to retire into one's shell; **eingekapselte Trichinen,** encysted trichinae; **Einkapselung** *f,* encystation, encystment; encapsulation.
einkassieren. I. *v.tr. sep.* to collect (contributions, moneys due, etc.); to recover (outstanding debt, etc.); *Com: etc:* to take (sum as daily total, etc.); *Sch:* to confiscate (toys, etc.); **wir müssen die Außenstände e.,** we have to recover the outstanding debts; **Beiträge werden monatlich einkassiert,** contributions are, will be, collected monthly; **er kassierte das Geld stillschweigend ein, ohne zu fragen, woher es kam,** he took, accepted, the money silently without asking where it came from.
II. *vbl s.* **Einkassieren** *n.*, **Einkassierung** *f. in vbl senses; also:* collection (of contributions, moneys due, etc.); recovery (of outstanding debt, etc.).
einkasteln, *v.tr. sep. F:* to put (s.o.) in prison, *F:* in jug, in clink, to jug s.o.
Einkauf, *m.* **1.** buying, purchasing, purchase; **beim E. von Vorräten,** when buying, purchasing, supplies; **Einkauf und Verkauf,** purchase and sale. **2.** (*thing bought*) purchase; **einen E. tätigen,** to make a purchase; **seine Einkäufe erledigen, besorgen, machen,** to do one's shopping; **ich habe einige Einkäufe zu erledigen,** I have some shopping to do; I have to make some purchases.
einkaufen. I. *v.tr. sep.* **1.** to buy, purchase (sth.); **e. gehen,** to go shopping; **im großen, en gros, e.,** to buy wholesale. **2. sich in etwas** *acc.* **einkaufen,** to buy a place *or* a share in sth.; **sich in ein Altersheim e.,** to buy a place in an old people's home; **sich in eine Versicherung e.,** to pay premiums on an endowment; **sich in eine Sterbeversicherung e.,** to pay premiums on a burial insurance.
II. *vbl s.* **Einkaufen,** *n. in vbl senses; also:* purchase (of sth.).
Einkäufer, *m. Com:* buyer (for business house, etc.).
Einkaufsabteilung, *f.* buying department, purchasing department (of firm, etc.).
Einkaufsbuch, *n. Com:* invoice book.
Einkaufsgeld, *n. A:* = **Anzugsgeld.**
Einkaufsgenossenschaft, *f. Com:* co-operative wholesale society.
Einkaufsgeschäft, *n. Com:* purchase.
Einkaufskommission, *f. Com:* **1.** purchase made by a commission agent in his own name for a principal. **2.** commission (*taken by commission agent*).
Einkaufskorb, *m.* shopping-basket.
Einkaufskosten, *pl. Com:* expenses arising in connection with a purchase (*e.g. commission to purchasing agent, etc.*).
Einkaufsleiter, *m. Com:* head of buying, purchasing, department; chief buyer.
Einkaufsnetz, *n.* string-bag.
Einkaufspreis, *m. Com:* purchase price.
Einkaufsprovision, *f. Com:* = **Einkaufskommission** 2.
Einkaufsrechnung, *f.* invoice presented by purchasing agent to his principal.
Einkaufsselbstkosten, *pl. Com:* purchase price plus charges (*cost of freight, insurance, etc.*).
Einkaufsspesen, *pl. Com:* = **Einkaufskosten.**
Einkaufstasche, *f.* shopping-bag.
Einkehle, *f. Constr:* valley(-channel, -gutter).
einkehlen. I. *v.tr. sep. Constr:* to groove, channel (sth.); to cut, make, a cove in (sth.); to make a neck in (pipe, tube, etc.); to make a hollow moulding in (architrave, etc.).
II. *vbl s.* **1. Einkehlen,** *n. in vbl senses.* **2. Einkehlung,** *f.* (*a*) = II. 1; (*b*) channel, groove; cove; neck (of pipe, tube, etc.); hollow moulding (in architrave, etc.); hollow (of moulding, etc.).
Einkehr, *f.* -/. **1.** (*a*) *A:* (i) stop (made at an inn) (for food, drink, etc.); (ii) stay (at an inn) (for the night, etc.); (*b*) *vbl phr.* (*of joy, peace, care, poverty, etc.*) **bei j-m E. halten,** to come to s.o.; **Friede hielt E. in ihren Herzen,** peace entered, came into, their hearts; (*c*) **(innere) E.,** self-examination; self-communion; **bei sich E. halten, E. in sich, in sein Inneres, halten,** to search one's heart; to look into one's heart; to commune with oneself. **2.** *A:* inn.
einkehren, *v.i. sep.* (*sein*) (*a*) **bei j-m e.,** (i) to call on s.o.; (ii) to stay overnight at s.o.'s house; **bei einem Wirt, in einem Gasthaus,** *occ.* **in ein Gasthaus, e.,** *abs.* **e.,** (i) to stop at an inn (for food, drink); (ii) to put up at an inn (for the night), to stop, stay, at an inn (for the night); **sie kehrten mehrere Male ein,** they stopped at several inns; (*b*) (*of joy, peace, care, poverty, etc.*) **bei j-m e.,** to come to s.o.; **Friede kehrte in ihre Herzen ein,** peace entered, came into, their hearts; (*c*) **in sich, bei sich, e.,** to search one's heart; to look into one's heart; to commune with oneself.
einkeilen, *v.tr. sep.* to wedge (piece of wood, etc.) in; **etwas in etwas** *acc.* **e.,** to wedge sth. in sth.; *F:* **er war zwischen zwei dicken Frauen eingekeilt,** he was sandwiched, wedged, in between two fat women; *Surg:* **eingekeilter Bruch,** impacted fracture; *Dent:* **eingekeilter Zahn,** impacted tooth.
einkeimblättrig, *a. Bot:* monocotyledonous; **einkeimblättrige Pflanze,** monocotyledon.
einkellern, *v.tr. sep.* to store, stock up (potatoes, coal, etc.) (*in the cellar*); to lay in (stock of potatoes, coal, etc.) (*in the cellar*).
einkerben. I. *v.tr. sep.* (*a*) to cut a notch, notches, in (sth.); to notch (sth.); to make a tommy-hole in (screw-head); to notch, nick, score (tally-stick, etc.); to make grooves on (top of loaf, etc.); (*b*) **etwas in etwas** *acc.* **e.,** to cut (a notched design, etc.) into (piece of wood, etc.); to chip-carve (design) in (piece of wood).
II. *vbl s.* **1. Einkerben,** *n. in vbl senses.* **2. Einkerbung,** *f.* (*a*) = II. 1; (*b*) notch; nick; score; tommy-hole (in screw-head); groove.
Einkerbprobe, *f. Mec.E:* notch test.
einkerkern, *v.tr. sep.* to throw (s.o.) into a dungeon; to incarcerate (s.o.); to immure (s.o.) (in a tower, etc.); to imprison (s.o.); **die Seele ist im Körper eingekerkert,** the soul is imprisoned in the body; **er war zehn Jahre eingekerkert,** he was imprisoned, incarcerated, for ten years.
einkernig, *a. Biol:* mononuclear.
einkesseln, *v.sep.* **1.** *v.tr. Ven:* to ring in, close in, encircle (quarry); *Mil:* to encircle, hem in, pocket (enemy troops). **2.** *Ven:* (*of wild boar*) **sich einkesseln,** to lair.
Einketten, *n.* -s/. *Surv:* method of surveying by running chains of triangles.
einkimmen, *v.tr. sep. Coop:* (*a*) to croze (cask stave, etc.); (*b*) to fit (the head) into the croze.
einkitten, *v.tr. sep.* to putty (sth.) in; to cement (sth.) in; to fix (sth.) in with putty *or* cement, with mastic *or* lute.
einklagbar, *a. Jur:* suable (debt, etc.).
Einklage, *f. Jur:* **E. einer Schuld,** suing for a debt.
einklagen, *v.tr. sep. Jur:* to sue for (outstanding debt, etc.).
einklammern, *v.tr. sep.* to put (words, passage, *Mth:* term) in, between, brackets, to bracket (words, passage, *Mth:* term); to put (words, passage) in parentheses; **eingeklammert,** bracketed; in brackets; in parentheses.
Einklang, *m.* (*a*) *Mus:* unison; (*b*) consonance, agreement, accordance (of ideas, facts, etc.); concord, harmony (of ideas, facts, hearts, etc.); **miteinander im E. stehen,** (*of ideas, facts, etc.*) to be consonant, to agree, to be in accord, to concord, to harmonize; (*of pers.*) to be of one mind; to be of the same opinion; to agree, to be agreed, in agreement; to be in accord; (*of ideas, facts, etc.*) **mit etwas im, in, E. stehen,** to be consonant, to agree, to be in accord, in accordance, to accord, to concord, to harmonize, to be in tune, in keeping, with sth.; (*of pers.*) **mit j-m im, in, E. stehen,** to be of one mind with s.o., to be of the same mind as s.o., to be of s.o.'s mind; to be of the same opinion as s.o., to be of s.o.'s opinion; to agree, to be agreed, to be in agreement, with s.o.; to be in accord with s.o.; **etwas (mit etwas) in E. bringen,** to harmonize (ideas, colours, etc.), to bring (ideas, etc.) into harmony (with sth., with one another); **ihre Herzen standen miteinander im E.,** their natures were attuned to each other; **diese Handlungsweise steht nicht im, in, E. mit seinem Charakter,** this action is not consonant, not in consonance, does not accord, is not in keeping, is incompatible, with his character; **seine Handlungsweise mit seinen Prinzipien in E. bringen,** to square one's practice with one's principles; **du versuchst, unvereinbare Gegensätze in E. zu bringen,** you are trying to reconcile contradictions; **das ist nicht in E. zu bringen, steht nicht im E., mit seinen Worten,** that does not agree, is not in accordance, is quite out of keeping, incompatible, with what he said; **wie bringst du das in E. mit deinem Gewissen?** how do you square it, reconcile it, with your conscience? **die Form steht in völligem E. mit dem Gehalt,** the form is perfectly attuned to the matter.
einklarieren, *v.tr. sep. Cust: Nau:* to clear (inward-bound ship); **Einklarierung** *f,* clearance inwards, entry inwards.
einklatschen, *v.tr. sep. Med: etc:* to pat in (ointment).
einklauben, *v.tr. sep. A. & Dial:* to collect (fruit, etc.) (in basket, etc.).
einkleben, *v.tr. sep.* to stick (sth.) in; to glue, paste (sth.) in; **etwas in etwas** *acc.* **e.,** to stick sth. into sth.; to glue, paste, sth. into sth.; **Briefmarken, Photos, e.,** to put in, stick in, stamps, photos.
einkleiden, *v.tr. sep.* (*a*) *Ecc:* to clothe (aspirant to noviciate) in the habit of the order; *Mil:* to fit (recruit) out (with uniform clothing); *F:* **j-n (neu) e.,** to provide s.o., to fit s.o. out, with a new set of clothes; **Einkleidung** *f, Ecc:* clothing (ceremony); *Mil:* fitting out; (*b*) **etwas in Verse e.,** to put (rules, etc.) into rhyme; to clothe (ideas, sentiments) in verse; **seine Lehre in Gleichnisse e.,** to couch one's teachings in the form of parables; *Mth:* **eingekleidete Rechenaufgabe,** problem.
Einkleidungsgeld, *n. Mil:* outfit allowance.

einklemmen. I. *v.tr. sep.* to force *or* squeeze (sth.) into sth. so that it is held tight; **etwas in etwas** *acc.* **e.,** to clamp sth. in (pair of tongs, vice, etc.); to grip (paper, etc.) in (holder, etc.); **ein Stück zwischen zwei andere e.,** to clamp a piece between two others; **sich** *dat.* **die Finger, seine Finger, seinen Mantel, in die Türe, in der Türe, e.,** to nip, pinch, shut, one's fingers in the door, to get one's fingers jammed in the door, to shut, catch, one's coat in the door; **er klemmte sich die Finger zwischen zwei Holzklötze ein,** he got his fingers jammed, caught, wedged, between two logs; **die Zange, die das Eisen einklemmt,** the pincers that hold the iron; **sich e.,** (*of machine part, etc.*) to jam, to get, become, jammed; *Med:* (*of hernia, etc.*) to become incarcerated *or* strangulated; (*of gall-stone, etc.*) to become impacted; **die Schublade ist eingeklemmt,** the drawer is jammed; *F:* **er war zwischen zwei dicken Frauen eingeklemmt,** he was sandwiched, wedged, in between two fat women; *Med:* **eingeklemmter Bruch,** incarcerated *or* strangulated hernia.

II. *vbl s.* **1. Einklemmen,** *n. in vbl senses.* **2. Einklemmung,** *f.* (*a*)=II. 1; (*b*) *Med:* strangulation (of hernia); incarceration (of hernia); constriction (of intestines, etc.); impaction (of gall-stone, etc.).

einklettern, *v.i. sep.* (*sein*) **in ein Haus, usw., e.** to climb into a house, etc.; **der Dieb muß durch ein offenes Fenster eingeklettert sein,** the thief must have climbed in through an open window.

einklinken, *v.sep.* **1.** *v.tr.* (*a*) to latch (door); **ist die Türe eingeklinkt?** is the door latched, on the latch? (*b*) *Mec.E:* to engage (catch, etc.); (*c*) *Carp: Metalw:* to lap-joint (boards, edges of metal sheets). **2.** *v.i.* (*sein*) to click to, to engage.

einklopfen, *v.tr. sep.* to knock in (nail, etc.); **etwas in etwas** *acc.* **e.,** to knock (nail, etc.) into (piece of wood, etc.).

einkneifen, *v.tr. sep.* (*strong*) (*a*) **die Lippen e.,** to pull one's mouth into a straight line; **die Augen e.,** to half-close one's eyes; (*b*) (*of dog, etc.*) **den Schwanz e.,** to put its tail between its legs; *F:* **er zog mit eingekniffenem Schwanz ab,** he went off with his tail between his legs; *Her:* **Löwe mit eingekniffenem Schwanz,** lion coward, lion with its tail between its legs.

einknicken. I. *v.sep.* **1.** *v.tr.* to bend, kink (wire, etc.), to make a bend in (wire, etc.); to fold in, nip in (paper, etc.); to break (stick, etc.) (partially); to snap (stick, etc.); *Mec.E: etc:* to buckle (support, etc.); **ein Blatt Papier e.,** to dog-ear a page; to fold down a sheet of paper. **2.** *v.i.* (*sein*) (*of wire, etc.*) to bend, kink; (*of paper, etc.*) to be folded in, nipped in; (*of stick, etc.*) to break (partially); to snap; *Mec.E: etc:* (*of support, etc.*) to buckle; **die Balken knickten wie Streichhölzer ein,** the beams broke, snapped, like matchwood; **die Knie knickten ihm ein,** his knees gave way; **mit eingeknickten Knien gehen, in den Knien e.,** to bend one's legs as one walks; **sein Fußgewölbe ist eingeknickt,** the arch of his foot has fallen.

II. *vbl s.* **1. Einknicken,** *n. in vbl senses.* **2. Einknickung,** *f.* (*a*)=II. 1; (*b*) bend; kink; break; *Med:* infraction.

Einknolle, *f. Bot:* **echte E.,** musk orchis.

einknöpfbar, *a.* (lining, etc.) that can be buttoned in; button-in (lining, etc.).

einknöpfen, *v.tr. sep.* to button in (lining, etc.); **etwas in etwas** *acc.* **e.,** to button (lining, etc.) into (coat, etc.).

einknüpfen, *v.tr. sep.* to knot (ribbons, etc.) in; **etwas in etwas** *acc.* **e.,** to knot (ribbons, etc.) in (horse's mane, etc.), into (mat, etc.).

Einkochapparat, *m. Dom.Ec:* sterilizing apparatus; fruit-preserver.

einkochen. I. *v.sep.* **1.** *v.tr.* (*a*) to boil down (liquid); to evaporate (down) (liquid); (*b*) to preserve (fruit, vegetables, meat, etc.); to bottle *or* tin (fruit, vegetables, meat, etc.); **Marmelade e.,** to make jam; **wir haben dieses Jahr dreißig Pfund Äpfel eingekocht,** (i) we have preserved, bottled, thirty pounds of apples this year; (ii) we have made apple purée out of thirty pounds of apples this year. **2.** *v.i.* (*sein*) (*of liquid*) to boil down; to boil away; to evaporate; (*of vegetables, etc.*) to boil dry; **etwas e. lassen,** to reduce sth. (by boiling); to boil sth. down; to evaporate (liquid) (down); **wenn man nicht vorsichtig ist, kocht der ganze Saft ein,** if one is not careful all the juice will boil away.

II. *vbl s.* **Einkochen,** *n. in vbl senses; also:* (*a*) evaporation (of liquid); (*b*) preservation (of fruit, vegetables, meat, etc.).

Einkochglas, *n. Dom.Ec:* preserving jar.

Einkochring, *m. Dom.Ec:* rubber ring (for preserving jar).

einkoffern, *v.tr. sep.* to box (sth.) in; *Civ.E:* to pack (sth.) in a layer of stones; *Hyd.E:* to coffer (well, etc.).

einkommen[1], *v.i. sep.* (*strong*) (*sein*) **1.** (*a*) (*of money, mail, etc.*) to come in; **einkommend,** incoming (money, mail, etc.); inward (cargo, freight, etc.); (*b*) *A:* to enter. **2. bei einer Behörde, usw., um etwas e.,** to apply, make an application, to an authority, etc., for (leave, grant, etc.); **um seinen Abschied e.=seinen Abschied einreichen,** *q.v. under* **einreichen.**

Einkommen[2], *n.* **-s/-,** income; earnings; revenue (from estates, etc.); **E. aus Kapital(vermögen),** income from capital, unearned income; **effektives, tatsächliches, E.,** real income; **festes E.,** settled, fixed, income; regular, steady, income; **Feststellung des Einkommens,** assessment of income; **Leute mit höheren Einkommen,** people with larger incomes; **er hat ein gutes, hohes, E.,** he has a good, large, income; **mein E. reicht für unsere Bedürfnisse aus,** my income is, my earnings are, sufficient for our wants.

Einkommensteuer, *f.* income-tax; **progressive E.,** graduated income-tax.

Einkommensteuererklärung, *f.* income-tax return, *U.S:* statement.

einkommensteuerpflichtig, *a.* liable to income-tax.

Einkommensteuersatz, *m.* rate of income-tax.

Einkommensteuertabelle, *f.* income-tax table.

einköpfen, *v.tr. sep. Fb:* **einen Ball e.,** to head a ball into the goal.

einköpfig, *a.* (*a*) one-headed; *Bot:* monocephalous; (*b*) **eine einköpfige Besatzung,** a crew of one.

einkoppeln, *v.tr. sep.* to fence in (meadow, etc.).

Einkorn, *n. Agr:* one-grained spelt.

einkrallen (sich), *v.refl. sep.* (*of animal*) to dig in its claws; **sich in etwas** *acc.* **e.,** (*of animal*) to dig its claws into (s.o.'s coat, etc.); *F:* (*of pers.*) to dig one's nails into (s.o.'s flesh, etc.).

einkräuseln, *v.tr. sep. Dressm:* to gather in (dress, etc.); to gauge, shirr (dress, etc.).

Einkreisempfänger, *m. W.Tel:* single-circuit receiver.

einkreisen, *v.tr. sep. Ven:* to ring in, close in, encircle (quarry, hunting-ground, etc.); *Mil:* to encircle, surround (enemy troops, town, etc.); *Pol:* to encircle (country) (by alliances); **Einkreisung** *f,* encirclement.

Einkreisungsgespenst, das. *Hist:* the spectre of encirclement.

Einkreisungspolitik, *f. Pol:* policy of encirclement.

einkühlen, *v.tr. sep. Austrian:* to cool (beer, wine).

Einkünfte, *f.pl.* earnings (of pers., commercial undertaking, etc.); income (of pers., from investment, work, estate, etc.); revenue (from estate, taxes, etc.); proceeds (of charitable enterprise, etc.); *Com:* receipts; takings; **E. aus Kapital(vermögen),** income from capital, unearned income; **feste E.,** settled, fixed, income; regular, steady, income.

einkuppeln, *v.i. sep.* (*haben*) *Aut:* to let in the clutch.

einkuscheln (sich), *v.refl. sep. F:* **sich ins Bett, in die Decken, e.,** to snuggle up in bed, in one's blankets; **sich bei j-m e.,** to snuggle up to s.o.

Einladebahnhof, *m. Rail:* loading station; station of origin; *Mil:* entraining station.

einladen[1]. I. *v.tr. sep. strong*) **etwas in einen Lastwagen, ein Schiff, e.,** to load (goods, etc.) on to a lorry, into a ship; *Nau:* to ship, lade (goods, etc.); *abs.* **e.,** to load; **sie laden noch ein,** they are still loading.

II. *vbl s.* **Einladen** *n.,* **Einladung** *f. in vbl senses; also:* shipment (of goods, etc.).

einladen[2]. I. *v.tr. sep.* (*strong*) (*a*) to invite (s.o.); **j-n zum Mittagessen e.,** to invite s.o. for, to, lunch; to ask s.o. to lunch; **ich habe ihn fürs Wochenende eingeladen,** I have asked him for the week-end; **sich selbst e.,** to invite oneself; (*b*) **j-n e., etwas zu tun,** to invite, ask, s.o. to do sth.; **j-n e., näherzutreten,** to invite, ask, s.o. to come closer; **j-n e., einem Treffen beizuwohnen, ein Amt zu übernehmen,** to invite, ask, s.o. to attend a meeting, to take up an office; *abs.* **das schöne Wetter lud zu einem Spaziergang ein,** the fine weather made you want to go for a walk; **unbeschränkte Freiheit lädt zu Mißbräuchen ein,** unrestricted freedom invites, asks for, abuse.

II. *vbl s.* **1. Einladen,** *n. in vbl senses.* **2. Einladung,** *f.* (*a*)=II.1; (*b*) invitation; **schriftliche E.,** written invitation; **eine E. erhalten,** to receive, get, an invitation; to be invited; (*c*) party; reception.

III. *pr.p. & a.* **einladend,** *in vbl senses; esp.* inviting, tempting (weather, dish, etc.); **nicht sehr e.,** not very inviting, tempting; **mit einer einladenden Geste forderte er ihn auf einzutreten,** with a welcoming gesture he signed to him to come in; **dieser Sessel sieht e. aus,** this armchair looks inviting; *adv.* **ein Gericht e. herrichten,** to make a dish look attractive.

Einlader, *m. Sm.a:* single-loader.

Einladungskarte, *f.* invitation card.

Einladungsschreiben, *n.* (letter of) invitation; written invitation.

Einladungswettbewerb, *m. Sp:* invitation event.

Einlage, *f.* **1.** (*a*) insertion (of sth.) (into sth.); (*b*) *Fin:* investment (of capital); **eine E. von 10 000 Mark in dieses Unternehmen,** an investment of 10,000 marks in this undertaking, a contribution of 10,000 marks to this undertaking. *Cp.* **einlegen** II. **2.** *Bank:* deposit; *Fin:* initial share (in undertaking); initial contribution (to undertaking); capital invested; investment; *Games: Gambling:* stake; *Bank:* **eine E. machen,** to pay in, make, a deposit. **3.** (musical, humorous, etc.) item inserted in the programme; interlude; intermezzo (between acts of drama, etc.); **lyrische Einlagen in einem Drama,** lyrical passages in a play. **4.** inserted piece, insertion; component inserted in a main structure; *esp.* (*a*) *Dent:* temporary filling (of tooth); (*b*) enclosure (in letter); (*c*) *usu.pl.* **Einlagen,** set of loose leaves (for folder, copy-book, etc.); (*d*) *Med:* (arch-)support; **Einlagen tragen,** to wear (arch-)supports; (*e*) stiffening (of tie, hat, etc.); padding (of hat, etc.); interfacing (of dress, etc.); (*f*) filler (of cigar); (*g*) *Mec.E: etc:* insert; lining; shim; reinforcement; *Civ.E:* iron mesh reinforcement (in concrete road, etc.); (wood, marble, etc.) inlay. **5.** *Cu:* garnish (for soup) (*e.g. vegetables, meatballs, noodles, etc.*).

Einlageblatt, *n.* loose leaf; additional loose leaf.

Einlagebuch, *n. Bank:* pass-book, bank-book.

Einlagefeld, *n. Mil:* insertion bay (in bridge).

Einlagekapital, *n. Fin:* capital invested; initial share, contribution.

Einlagerer, *m.* **-s/-,** depositor (of goods in warehouse, repository, etc.).

Einlageripper, *m.* **-s/-.** *Cigar-making:* (*pers.*) filler stripper.

einlagern. I. *v.tr. sep.* **1.** to store (provisions); to lay in (provisions). **2.** *Geol: Ch: Physiol:* (*of substance*) **sich in etwas** *acc. & dat.* **einlagern.** to form a deposit, a layer, an intercalation (in rock, bone, compound, etc.); *Geol:* **eingelagert,** embedded; interstratified; **Schichten mit eingelagertem Kalkstein,** strata intercalated with limestone; **eingelagerter Schieferton,** interstratified shale; **eingelagerte Schichten,** intercalary strata.

II. *vbl s.* **1. Einlagern,** *n. in vbl senses.* **2. Einlagerung,** *f.* (*a*)=II. 1; *also:* (i) storage (of provisions); (ii) *Geol: Ch:* intercalation; *Physiol:* introsusception, intussusception; (*b*) *Geol:* intercalary stratum, intercalation; embedded stone, shale, etc.; *Physiol: etc:* deposit (of calcium, etc.); *Ch:* intercalation (in compound).

Einlagerungsverbindung, *f. Ch:* intercalation compound.

Einlagestoff, *m. Tail:* stiffening material.

einlangen, *v.sep.* **1.** (*a*) *v.tr. A. & Dial:* to present, hand in (application, etc.); (*b*) *v.i.* (*haben*) *Austrian:* **um etwas e.,** to present, hand in, an application for sth.; **bei einer Behörde, usw., um etwas e.,** to apply, make an application, to an authority, etc., for sth. **2.** *v.i.* (*sein*) *Austrian:*= **eintreffen 1.**

einlappen, *v.tr. sep. Ven:*=**ablappen.**

Einlaß, *m.* **-lasses/-lässe. 1.** admittance; access (**beim König, bei Hofe, usw.,** to the king, to the court, etc.); admission (**ins Theater, usw.,** to the theatre, etc.); **j-m E. gewähren,** to let s.o. in; **sich** *dat.* **E. verschaffen,** to get admitted; to gain entry; to gain admission; **eine schmale Öffnung gewährte ihnen E.,** a narrow opening permitted them to enter, afforded them entry; **ein Fremder bat um, begehrte, E.,** a stranger asked to be let in, asked for admittance; **er verschaffte sich mit Gewalt E.,** he forced his way in; **mein Freund verschaffte mir E. in das Botschaftsgebäude,** my friend got me admitted, gained me admittance, to the embassy; **traurigen Gedanken E. gewähren,** to admit sad thoughts; *Th:* **E. eine halbe Stunde vor Spielbeginn,** doors open half an hour before the performance. **2.** (*a*) entrance; wicket(-gate, -door); (*b*) *Mec.E: etc:* inlet (for water, steam, etc.).

Einlaßbohrung, *f. Oil-drilling:* intake well.

einlassen, *v.sep.* (*strong*) I. *v.tr.* **1.** to let (s.o.) enter; to let (s.o., sth.) in; to admit (s.o., sth.); **j-n, etwas, in etwas** *acc.* **e.,** to let s.o., sth., into sth.; to admit s.o., sth., to, into, sth.; **j-n ins Haus e.,** to let s.o. into the house; **ich gab Anweisung, ihn nicht einzulassen,** I gave orders that he was not to be let in, admitted; **Schuhe, die Wasser e.,** shoes that let in, take, water; **das Wasser (in die Badewanne) e.,** to run water, let the water run, into the bath-tub; to run the bath; **die Fenster lassen nicht genügend Luft ein,** the windows do not let in, admit, enough air. **2.** to let in, set in (pillar, etc.); to let in, fit in, insert, embed (slab, etc.); to set, chase, mount (gem, etc.); **etwas in etwas** *acc.* **e.,** to let (pillar, etc.) into (bed, concrete, etc.); to set, sink, (pillar, etc.) in (bed, concrete, etc.); to embed (pillar, slab, etc.) in (concrete, wall, etc.); to let, fit, insert, (slab, etc.) into (wall, etc.); to set (gem, etc.) in (mount, etc.); **in den Schwertgriff waren Diamanten eingelassen,** the sword-handle was set with diamonds; **in die Schnalle ist ein Rubin eingelassen,** a ruby is set in the buckle; **ein in den Boden eingelassenener Steinblock,** a block of stone sunk in, set in, embedded in, let into, the ground; **die Reliquien sind in der Mitte des Altares eingelassen,** the relics are enclosed in the middle of the altar. **3.** *Austrian:* **den Fußboden e.,** to wax the floor.

II. **sich einlassen,** (*a*) **sich auf etwas** *acc.* **e.,** to let oneself in for sth.; to let oneself get involved in (discussion, enterprise, etc.); to let oneself get mixed up in (politics, quarrels, conspiracy, etc.); to accept (excuses, conditions, etc.); **sich in etwas** *acc.* **e.,** to let oneself get involved in (discussion, etc.); to let oneself get mixed up in (politics, quarrels, conspiracy, etc.); **ich kann mich nicht darauf e., daß das Geschäft ohne seine Zustimmung abgeschlossen wird,** I can't allow the transaction to be settled without his consent; **ich kann mich nicht auf Erklärungen, Einzelheiten, e.,** I can't go into explanations, details; **er hat sich da auf, in, eine böse Sache eingelassen,** he has got himself involved in something bad, got himself mixed up in something shady; **bevor wir uns auf diese Frage e.,** before going into this problem; **auf so ein schlechtes Geschäft lasse ich mich nicht ein,** I won't let myself in for such a bad deal; **das ist eine gefährliche Sache, auf die ich mich nicht e. möchte,** this is a dangerous matter in which I have no wish to be involved; **ich wußte nicht, auf was ich mich einließ,** I did not know what I was letting myself in for; **auf bloße Versprechungen kann ich mich nicht e.,** I won't be satisfied with mere promises; **darauf kann ich mich leider nicht e.,** I am sorry, but I can't do *or* accept that; I am sorry, but that won't do; *Jur:* (*of accused*) **sich auf eine Klage e.,** to defend a charge; to enter an appearance; **Einlassung** *f,* (entering of an) appearance; **im Fall einer rügelosen Einlassung,** in case the accused enters an appearance without objecting to the charge; (*b*) **sich mit j-m e.,** to enter into relations with s.o.; to get mixed up with s.o.; to have an affair with (woman, man); to get entangled with (woman, man); **laß dich nicht mit diesen Leuten ein,** have nothing to do with those people; **es ist gefährlich, sich mit ihm einzulassen,** it is dangerous to get mixed up, to get involved, with him; **laß dich nicht zu weit mit ihm ein,** don't get too involved with him; don't become too familiar with him.

Einlaßgrund, *m. Paint:* sealer.

Einlaßhub, *m. Mch: I.C.E:* induction stroke, admission stroke.

Einlaßkarte, *f.* admission ticket.

Einlaßleitung, *f. Mch: I.C.E:* inlet pipe, admission pipe; inlet manifold, admission manifold, induction manifold.

einläßlich, *a. Swiss:* thorough (discussion, enquiry, etc.).

Einlaßsonde, *f. Oil-drilling:* input well.

Einlaßstutzen, *m. I.C.E:* water inlet (of radiator).

Einlaßventil, *n. Mch: I.C.E:* inlet valve, induction valve, admission valve.

Einlauf, *m.* **1.** *Com:* incoming mail, goods, etc.; goods, etc., received; arrival (of goods, etc.); delivery. **2.** *Cu:* thickening (for soup) (*consisting of milk, flour, egg*). **3.** *Ven:* gap (in fence) (*to allow deer to pass through*). **4.** *Med:* rectal injection, enema; **j-m einen E. machen,** to give s.o. an enema. **5.** *Mec.E:* admission channel, inlet (for air, etc.); *I.C.E:* lead (of supercharger).

einlaufecht, *a. Tex:* unshrinkable; shrink-resistant; fully shrunk; pre-shrunk.

einlaufen, *v .sep.* (*strong*) I. *v.i.* (*sein*) **1.** (*a*) (*of runner, skier*) to run in; **soeben ist der Sieger ins Ziel eingelaufen,** the winner has just passed the winning-post; **ins Stadium e.,** to run into the stadium; *Ven:* (*of game*) **ins Netz e.,** to run into, be caught in, the net; (*b*) (*of train*) to come in, pull in; to arrive; (*of ship*) to sail in, to enter the harbour; **in den Bahnhof e.,** to come into, enter, the station; **der Zug wird um sechs Uhr abends in Paris e.,** the train will arrive in Paris, reach Paris, at six o'clock in the evening; (*c*) (*of road, etc.*) **in eine andere Straße e.,** to lead into, run into, join, another road; (*d*) (*of water, etc.*) to run in; to flow in; to flood in, stream in; **in etwas** *acc.* **e.,** to run into (bath-tub, etc.); to flow into (pool, etc.); to flood into, stream into (sinking ship, etc.); **das Bad, das Badewasser, e. lassen,** to run the bath; (*e*) (*of funds*) to come in; to be received; to be paid; to come to hand; (*of mail, goods, etc.*) to arrive; to come in; to be received; **die eingelaufenen Spenden wurden für Wohltätigkeitszwecke verwendet,** the contributions which came in were used for charity; **einlaufende Post, Waren, Gelder, usw.,** incoming mail, goods, funds, etc.; **zahlreiche Spenden liefen ein,** contributions came pouring in, flowed in; *Com:* **einlaufende Rechnungen,** inward invoices. **2.** (*of material, etc.*) to shrink.

II. **einlaufen,** *v.tr.* **1.** **etwas e.,** to knock sth. down by running against it; *F:* **j-m das Haus, die Türe, e.,** to come and pester s.o. with requests; to pester s.o. with unwanted visits; **der Vertreter lief mir (beinahe) die Türe ein,** the salesman was everlastingly on my doorstep, at my door; **die Zeitungsreporter liefen ihm das Haus ein,** the reporters lived on his doorstep. **2.** **neue Schuhe e.,** to break in a new pair of shoes. **3.** **sich einlaufen,** (*of runner, skier*) to practise to regain running form; to warm up; (*of motor-car, engine, etc.*) to (be) run in; (*of new plan, system, etc.*) to get going; **die Sache muß sich erst e.,** the thing has to get going first; **wenn sich der Plan einmal eingelaufen hat,** once the plan runs smoothly; **die Maschine ist noch nicht eingelaufen,** the engine is not yet run in.

Einläufer, *m.* **1.** single-barrelled gun *or* rifle. **2.** *Ven:* solitary old boar.

Einlaufgleis, *n. Rail:* = **Einfahrgleis.**

einläufig, *a.* **1.** single-barrelled (gun, rifle). **2.** *Constr:* **einläufige Treppe,** straight flight of stairs.

einläuten, *v.tr. sep.* to ring in (Sunday, new year, festival, etc.).

einleben (sich), *v.refl. sep.* (*a*) to accustom oneself to new surroundings, to get, become, accustomed, used, to new surroundings; to get, become, acclimatized (to new surroundings); to settle down (in a new place of work, etc.); **er lebte sich dort nur schwer ein,** it was a long time before he felt at home there; **er hat sich hier gut eingelebt,** he has settled down well here; **Sie müssen versuchen, sich einzuleben,** you must try to accustom yourself to your new surroundings, to acclimatize yourself; **sich in einen Beruf e.,** to settle into a job; **er hat sich schon ganz in die Familie eingelebt,** he is quite at home with the family now; (*b*) **sich in j-n, in j-s Seele, e.,** to project oneself into the mind of s.o.; **sich in etwas** *acc.* **e.,** to get into the spirit of sth.; **er vermag sich in die Seele des Kindes einzuleben,** he can project himself into the mind of the child, into the child's mind; **sich in das Werk eines Dichters e.,** to get into the spirit of a writer's work.

Einlegearbeit, *f.* inlaid work; marquetry; (*on marble, etc.*) incrustation.

Einlegekeil, *m. Mec.E: etc:* sunk key.

Einlegelauf, *m.* (*a*) *Sm.a:* Morris tube; (*b*) *Artil:* sub-calibre barrel; liner.

Einlegemesser, *n.* pen-knife; clasp-knife.

einlegen. I. *v.tr. sep.* **1.** (*a*) to put, place, lay, (sth.) in; to insert (sth.); **etwas in etwas** *acc.* **e.,** to put sth. into sth.; to place, lay, sth. in sth.; to insert sth. into sth.; to deposit (money) with (bank); to pay (money) into (bank); to put (money) in (savings-bank); **Geld, eine Quittung, usw., in einen Brief e.,** to enclose money, a receipt, etc., with a letter; **ein Blatt in ein Ringbuch e.,** to put, insert, a leaf into a file; **Fließpapier zwischen die Blätter e.,** to put, insert, blotting-paper between the sheets; **einen Pfeil e.,** to put an arrow to the bow; **eine Patrone e.,** to put in a cartridge; **einen Film e.,** to put in, insert, load, a film; *Tail:* **Watte in die Schultern eines Mantels, usw., e.,** to pad the shoulders of a coat, etc.; *Print: Typewr:* **das Papier (in die Maschine) e.,** to insert, feed, the paper (into the machine); *Nau:* **die Riemen e.,** to (i) ship, (ii) lay in, unship, the oars; **einlegen!** unship oars! *Aut:* **einen Gang e.,** to engage a gear; (*b*) to fit in, put in (pause, extra lesson, etc.); to insert (musical intermezzo, etc.); **einen Zug, einen Omnibus, usw., e.,** to put on an extra train, a relief bus; (*c*) **Vorräte e.,** to store, stock, provisions; to lay in provisions; to stock up with provisions; (*d*) *Cu:* **Heringe, usw., (in Salzlake) e.,** to put herrings, etc., in brine, to brine herrings, etc.; **Fleisch, Fisch, rote Beete, usw., in Beize, Marinade, e.,** to marinade meat, fish, beetroot, etc.; to souse meat, fish, etc.; **Gurken (in Essig, Salzlake) e.,** to pickle gherkins; **Eier e.,** to put down, preserve, eggs; **eingelegte Eier,** preserved eggs; (*e*) to inlay (ivory, mother of pearl, rosewood, etc.); **ein Möbelstück, usw., mit Elfenbein, Perlmutter, Rosenholz, usw., e., Elfenbein, Perlmutter, Rosenholz, usw., in ein Möbelstück, usw., e.,** to inlay a piece of furniture, etc., with ivory, mother of pearl, rosewood, etc.; **eine Wand, usw., mit Marmor e.,** to incrust a wall, etc., with marble; **Tisch mit Perlmutter eingelegt,** table inlaid with mother of pearl; **eingelegte Arbeit,** inlaid work; marquetry; incrustation, incrusted work; **eingelegte Emailarbeit, Ornamente,** inlaid enamel work, ornaments; **eingelegter Fußboden,** inlaid floor; **Schwertgriff mit Diamanten eingelegt,** sword-handle set with diamonds; (*f*) = **legen** . **2.** (*a*) **Beschwerde (gegen j-n, etwas) e.,** to lodge, lay, make, a complaint (against s.o., sth.); **Protest, Verwahrung, gegen etwas e.,** to make, enter, a protest against sth.; **sein, ein, Veto gegen etwas e.,** to put, place, set, one's veto, a veto, on sth.; to veto sth.; **bei j-m ein gutes Wort, Fürbitte, für j-n e.,** to put in a (good) word with s.o. for s.o.; to intercede with s.o. for s.o.; to plead with s.o. for s.o.; *see also* **berufen** II. 2 (*g*); (*b*) **mit etwas Ehre, Schande, e.,** to bring honour, shame, upon oneself with sth.; **damit legst du keine (große) Ehre ein,** this does you no credit, this doesn't reflect much credit on you; **mit ihm kann die Schule Ehre e.,** he is a credit to the school; **damit kannst du nur Schande, Unehre, e.,** this can only bring shame on you; **mit ihm kannst du keine Ehre e.,** he'll do you no credit.

II. *vbl s.* **Einlegen** *n.,* **Einlegung** *f. in vbl senses; also:* (*a*) insertion (**von etwas in etwas** *acc.,* of sth. into sth.; of sth. in sth.); (*b*) storage (of provisions); *cp.* **Einlage.**

Einlegeplatte, *f.* insertable leaf, shelf, board, etc.; (extension) leaf (of table).

Einleger, *m.* **1.** *Ind:* (*pers. or device*) feeder. **2.** inlayer (of wood, etc.). **3.** *Bank:* depositor.

Einlegerohr, *n.* (*a*) *Sm.a:* Morris tube; (*b*) *Artil:* sub-calibre barrel; liner.

Einlegeschranke, *f. Rail:* rod barrier.

Einlegesohle, *f.* insole, sock (in boot, shoe).

Einlegestück, *n.* insertable piece; piece to be inserted; *Mec.E: etc:* inset; lining; shim; reinforcement.

Einlegetisch, *m. Print:* feed-board.

einleiten. I. *v.tr. sep.* **1.** **etwas in etwas** *acc.* **e.,** to lead (water, etc.) into (reservoir, etc.). **2.** (*a*) to initiate (negotiations, relations, etc.); to open (negotiations); to institute, set up (inquiry); **die einleitenden Schritte tun,** to take the preliminary steps; to arrange the preliminaries; *Jur:* (*of public prosecutor*) **ein Verfahren gegen j-n e.,** to order proceedings to be taken against s.o., to initiate, institute, proceedings against s.o.; (*b*) to write an introduction to (book, etc.); to introduce, initiate, *F:* usher in (new epoch, etc.); **etwas mit etwas e.,** to begin, commence, start, (treatise, speech, ceremony, etc.) with (general remarks, hymn, etc.); **einleitend,** introductory (words, speech, etc.); **die Ereignisse, die die Krise einleiteten,** the events with which the crisis started; **ein Bombardement leitete die Schlacht ein,** a bombardment preluded the battle.

II. *vbl s.* **Einleiten,** *n. in vbl senses.* **2. Einleitung,** *f.* (*a*) = II. 1; *also:* introduction, initiation (of negotiations, relations, etc.); (*b*) introduction; prelude; **als E. dienen,** to serve as an introduction; **eine E. schreiben,** to write an introduction; **einige Scharmützel, die E. zum Kampf,** a few skirmishes, the prelude to the battle.

Einleiterantenne, *f. El.E:* single-wire aerial.

Einleiterkabel, *n. El.E:* single(-core) cable.

Einleiterwandler, *m. El.E:* single-turn transformer.

Einleitung, *f. see* **einleiten** II.

Einleitungsbeschluß, *m. Jur:* decision to institute proceedings.

Einleitungsformel, *f.* introductory formula; *Jur:* caption (of a deed).

einlenken, *v.sep.* **1.** *v.tr.* **den Wagen, usw., in eine Seitenstraße, nach links, usw., e.**, to turn one's car, etc., into a side-road, to the left, etc. **2.** *v.i.* (*a*) (*haben, sein*) **in eine Seitenstraße, nach links, usw., e.**, to turn into a side-road, to the left, etc.; (*b*) (*haben*) to make a conciliatory gesture; **seine heftigen Worte taten ihm leid, und er lenkte ein**, he regretted his violent words and showed himself conciliatory.

einlernen, *v.tr. sep.* = einstudieren I.

einlesen[1], *v.tr. sep.* (*strong*) **1.** to gather in, collect (fruit, etc.); **etwas in etwas** *acc.* **e.**, to collect (fruit, etc.) in (basket, etc.). **2.** *Tex:* **das Muster e.**, to read in; **das Blatt e.**, to lease.

einlesen[2] **(sich)**, *v.refl. sep.* (*strong*) **sich in eine Fremdsprache e.**, to get into a foreign language (by reading); to get used to reading a foreign language; **sich in einen Autor e.**, to get used to the style of an author; **sich in ein Buch e.**, to get into a book, into the spirit of a book.

einleuchten, *v.i. sep.* (*haben*) **j-m e.**, (*of argument, etc.*) to be (clearly) evident to s.o.; **einleuchtend**, (thoroughly) comprehensible (example, argument, etc.); obvious (example, etc.); **es leuchtet ein, es ist einleuchtend, daß . . .**, it stands to reason that . . .; it is plain, clear, that . . .; **es leuchtet mir nicht ein, warum ich das tun soll**, I don't see why I should do that; I don't see the point, the advantage, of doing that; **es muß jedermann e., daß er das nicht tun konnte**, everybody must understand that he could not do that; **das leuchtet mir ein, aber . . .**, I can see that, but . . .

einliefern, *v.tr. sep.* (*a*) **etwas in etwas** *acc.* **e.**, to deliver (goods, etc.) to (depot, etc.); (*b*) **j-n ins Gefängnis e.**, to take s.o. to prison; **j-n in das Gefängnis zu X e.**, to take s.o. to X prison; **j-n ins Krankenhaus e.**, to take s.o. to hospital; **ins Krankenhaus eingeliefert werden**, to be taken to hospital; to be admitted to (the) hospital.

Einlieferungsschein, *m.* (certificate of) receipt; *Post:* certificate of posting.

einliegen, *v.i. sep.* (*strong*) (*haben*) (*of thg*) **etwas** *dat.* **e.**, to be enclosed with sth.; **einliegend**, enclosed (document, etc.); **einliegend sende ich . . .**, I enclose . . ., please find enclosed . . . .

einlochen, *v.tr. sep.* **1.** *Golf:* to putt, hole (ball); *abs.* to hole (out). **2.** *F:* **j-n e.**, to put s.o. in prison, *F:* to put s.o. in jug, in clink, to jug s.o.

einlogieren, *v.tr. sep.* **j-n bei j-m e.**, to lodge s.o. at s.o.'s house; **sich bei j-m e.**, to take lodgings *or* a room at s.o.'s house; *F:* to install oneself at s.o.'s house; **sich in einem Hotel e.**, to take a room *or* rooms at an hotel.

einlösbar, *a.* (*of pledge, mortgage, etc.*) redeemable; (*of goods, etc.*) collectable; (*of bill, cheque, etc.*) payable; due to be paid; **in Gold einlösbare Banknoten**, bank-notes convertible into gold.

einlösen. I. *v.tr. sep.* (*a*) to ransom (prisoner); (*b*) to redeem (pledge, mortgage, goods held up by customs, etc.); to take (sth.) out of pawn; to collect (luggage left at the cloakroom); **seine Uhr e.**, to redeem one's watch (from pawn); (*c*) **sein Versprechen, sein Wort, e.**, to carry out, make good, one's promise; (*d*) *Com:* to honour (bill); **einen Wechsel nicht e.**, to dishonour a bill; **seine Akzepte e.**, to meet one's acceptances, one's drafts; *Bank:* **Banknoten e.**, to pay cash in exchange for bank-notes, to cash bank-notes; (*e*) to cash (cheque, postal order, etc.).

II. *vbl s.* **Einlösen** *n.*, **Einlösung** *f. in vbl senses; also:* (*a*) ransom (of prisoner); (*b*) redemption (of pledge, mortgage, etc.).

Einlösungspflicht, *f.* **1.** *Bank:* obligation (of bank) to cash bank-notes. **2.** *Fin:* obligation to honour a bill.

einlotsen, *v.tr. sep.* (*a*) *Nau:* to pilot (ship) in; **ein Schiff in den Hafen e.**, to pilot a ship into harbour; (*b*) *Mil: Av:* (*of pathfinder aircraft*) to guide (bombers) into the target area.

einlullen, *v.tr. sep.* to lull (s.o.) asleep, to sleep; *F:* to lull (s.o., s.o.'s suspicions).

Einmachapparat, *m. Cu:* sterilizing apparatus; fruit-preserver.

einmachen. I. *v.tr. sep. Cu:* to preserve (fruit, vegetables); **etwas (in Gläser, in Flaschen) e.**, to bottle (fruit, vegetables); **etwas (in einen Topf) e.**, to pot (fruit, vegetables); **Marmelade e.**, to make jam; **wir haben zehn Gläser Kirschen eingemacht**, we have preserved, bottled, ten jars of cherries; **Gurken (in Essig) e.**, to pickle gherkins; **Bohnen, usw., in Steintöpfe e.**, to preserve beans, etc., in earthenware jars; *see also* **Büchse.**

II. *vbl s.* **Einmachen**, *n. in vbl senses; also:* preservation (of fruit, vegetables).

III. *p.p. & a.* **eingemacht**, preserved (fruit, vegetables); bottled *or* tinned, *U.S:* canned (fruit, vegetables); **Eingemachtes**, preserved fruit *or* vegetables; bottled fruit *or* vegetables; tinned, *U.S:* canned, fruit *or* vegetables.

Einmachglas, *n. Dom. Ec:* preserving jar.

Einmachhaut, *f. Dom.Ec:* cellophane cover (for jam-pot, etc.).

Einmachring, *m. Dom.Ec:* rubber ring (for preserving jar).

einmaischen, *v.tr. sep. Brew:* to mash in (malt).

einmal. **1.** *adv.* (*a*) (*stressed*) once; **e. fünf ist fünf**, once five is five, one times five is five; **mehr als e.**, more than once; **e. in der Woche, in vierzehn Tagen**, once a week, a fortnight; **e. im Jahr, des Jahres**, once a year; **e. und nicht wieder**, once but never again; never again; **e. für allemal**, once (and) for all, for good and all, quite finally; **e. ist keinmal**, once won't hurt; **e. ein Dieb, immer ein Dieb**, once a thief, always a thief; **er fragte sich nicht e., wozu das führen könnte**, he never once asked himself what it could lead to; **das ist mir nur e. passiert**, it happened to me only once; **ich habe das nicht nur e. beobachtet**, I have seen that more than once; **das gibt's nur e.**, there is nothing like it; it happens only once; (*b*) **schon e.**, once before; before; **ich muß ihn irgendwo schon e. gesehen haben**, I must have met him somewhere before; **wieder e.**, once again; **er ist wieder e. zu spät (daran)**, he is late once again; **noch e.**, (once) again; once more; **ich möchte ihn noch e. sehen, bevor er fortgeht**, I should like to see him once again, once more, before he leaves; **sag das noch e.**, say that (once) again, once more; **tu das nicht noch e.**, don't do it again; **so etwas wird nicht noch e. vorkommen**, such a thing will never happen again; **noch e. so groß, so schwer, so langsam**, twice as large, as heavy, as slow; as large, as heavy, as slow, again; **noch e. soviel**, twice as much; as much again; **noch e. soviel Wasser**, twice as much water; as much water again; **er ist noch e. so alt wie du**, he is twice as old as you, twice your age; **noch e. so schön**, twice as nice; (*c*) **wenn . . . e.**, (if) once; (when) once; **wenn du ihn e. aus den Augen verlierst, ist es schwierig, ihn wiederzufinden**, if once you lose sight of him, it's a job to find him again; **wenn du das (erst) e. verstehst, wird alles einfach**, once you have grasped this fact everything becomes clear; (*d*) **e. . . ., e. . . .**, now . . ., now . . .; now . . ., then . . .; now . . . and again; sometimes . . ., sometimes . . .; at one time . . ., at another (time) . . .; **e. hier, e. dort**, now here, now there; now here, then there; **e. in Paris, e. in London**, sometimes in Paris, sometimes in London; at one time in Paris, at another (time) in London; now in Paris, now in London; now in Paris, then in London; **e. der eine, e. der andere**, sometimes the one, sometimes the other; at one time the one, at another (time) the other; **e. so, e. anders sagen**, to say sometimes one thing and then the other, to say first one thing and then another; **e. lachten, e. weinten sie**, they laughed and cried by turns; **e. ja, e. nein sagen**, to say yes one moment and no the next; **e. über das andere, e. um das andere**, again and again, time and again; (*e*) **e., weil . . ., sodann, weil . . .**, for one thing . . ., for another . . .; **ich habe diesen Plan aufgegeben, e., weil die Sache zu teuer kommt, sodann, weil die Zeit zu kurz ist**, I have given up this plan; for one thing it is too expensive, for another, the time is too short. **2.** *adv.* (*stressed*) **auf e.**, (*a*) at once, at the same time, at a time, at one go; **sprecht nicht alle auf e.**, don't all speak at once; **verschiedene Dinge auf e. tun**, to do several things at once, at the same time, *F:* to have several things on at once; **sechs Durchschläge auf e. machen**, to make six carbons at one go, at a time; **die ganze Flasche auf e. trinken**, to drink the whole bottle at once, at one go; **man kann nicht zwei Dinge auf e. tun**, one can't do two things at once; (*b*) all at once, suddenly, all of a sudden; **auf e. öffnete sich die Türe, und . . .**, suddenly, all of a sudden, the door opened and . . . . **3.** *adv.* (*always unstressed*) **nicht e.**, not even; **ich habe nicht e. mein Fahrgeld**, I haven't even, as much as, my fare; **er wollte es nicht e. ansehen**, he would not even, *F:* not so much as, look at it; **er hat nicht e. zu meinem Geburtstag geschrieben**, he did not even write for my birthday; **nicht e. richtig schreiben kann er!** he cannot even write properly! **4.** *adv.* (i) at one time; once (upon a time); one day; *Lit:* time was when; (ii) one day; (at) some (future) day; some time; **ein e. beliebtes Buch**, a book popular at one time, a one-time popular book; **das war e. anders**, at one time it used not to be so; it was different years ago; *Lit:* time was when things were different; **es war, lebte, e. . . ., e., vor langer Zeit, in alten Zeiten, lebte . . .**, once (upon a time) there was . . .; **ein Kragen, der e. weiß war**, a collar that was once white; **e. wird der Tag kommen, da . . .**, once, some time, the day will come when . . .; **das wirst du noch e. bereuen**, you will regret that some day, one day; **wenn du ihn e. treffen solltest**, if you should meet him some time; **irgend(wann) e.**, some time (or other). **5.** *emotive particle* (*always unstressed*) (*usu. not translated*) (*a*) (*summing up foregoing remarks, thoughts, etc.*) **das ist nun e. so im Leben**, life is like that; *F:* such is life, such is the world; **ich bin nun e. so**, that's how I am made; **es tut mir leid, aber ich kann ihn nun e. nicht ausstehen**, I am sorry, but I just can't stand him; **es ist (nun) e. nichts mit ihm anzufangen**, one just can't do anything with him; (*b*) (*with imperative, intensifying*) **hör e., schau e., sieh e.**, listen, *F:* look here; **sagen Sie e., wie lange haben Sie daran gearbeitet?** do tell me, how long did you work at this? **lies das nur e.!** just read that! **hör nur e.! schau nur e.!** just listen! just look! **denken Sie sich nur e., er hat . . .**, just imagine, he has . . .; just think, he has . . .; **na hör e.!** really! I say! *U.S:* say! **komm e. her!** now come here! **nun sag e., wo bist du gewesen?** now then, where have you been? **nun sag e., was ist denn los mit dir?** now (tell me) what's the matter with you? well now! now then! what's the matter with you? **nun paß e. auf!** now listen! now pay attention! **sag e., wie kommt es, daß . . .**, tell me, how is it that . . .; (*c*) (*with imperative, with nuance of impatience*) **laß mich doch erst e. zur Ruhe kommen!** do let me have a rest first! **nun sei doch (endlich) e. still!** now do be quiet! do shut up! **nun hört (schon) (endlich) e. mit dem Streiten auf!** now do give over quarrelling! **hat er jetzt endlich e. geantwortet?** has he now answered at last? (*d*) (*almost meaningless*) **du bist mir e. einer, unsere Verabredung einfach zu vergessen!** you really are a nice one forgetting our date! **er hätte schon längst e. zum Arzt gehen sollen**, he should have gone to the doctor long ago; **da wir (nun) (schon) e. hier sind, können wir ja das Museum besuchen**, as we have come here we may just as well visit the museum; **wenn wir erst e. dort sind**, once we are there.

Einmalbehälter, *m.* disposable container.

Einmaleins, *n. Ar: Sch:* multiplication table(s); **das kleine E.**, (the) multiplication tables up to ten; **das große E.**, (the) multiplication tables up to twenty-five; **E. mit der Drei**, three-times table.

einmalig, *a.* (*a*) single; non-recurring (expenditure, etc.); **ein einmaliges Versehen ist kein Grund, ihn zu entlassen**, a single mistake is no reason for dismissing him; **nach einmaligem Durchprobieren konnte sie das Stück fehlerfrei spielen**, after one, a single, run-through she could play the piece without a mistake; (*b*) unique; **eine einmalige Gelegenheit**, a unique opportunity; a chance in a thousand; *F:* the chance of a lifetime; **ein einmaliges Naturschauspiel**, a unique natural phenomenon; (*c*) *Civ.E: etc:* **einmalige Böschung**, one-to-one slope.

Einmalpackung, *f.* disposable packet, package.

Einmann-, *comb.fm.* one-man (operation, vehicle, etc.); **Einmannbus**, *m*, one-man bus; **Einmannsäge** *f*, one-man crosscut saw.

Einmarsch, *m.* marching in (of troops, etc.); entry (of troops, etc.); **beim E. in die Stadt**, when marching into the town, when entering the town; **der E. der feindlichen Truppen in unser Gebiet**, the entry of the enemy troops into our territory.

einmarschieren, *v.i. sep.* (*sein*) (*of troops, etc.*); to march in; to enter; **in eine Stadt e.**, to march into, to enter, a town; **in ein Gebiet e.**, to enter a territory.

Einmaster, *m. Nau:* single-masted ship, single-master.

einmauern, *v.tr. sep.* (*a*) to let, fit, insert, (slab, etc.) into a wall, to embed (slab, etc.) in a wall; (*b*) to enclose (document, relic, etc.) in a wall; to wall in, immure (document, relic, prisoner, victim, etc.); **etwas in den Fußboden, in eine Wand, in den Altar, usw., e.**, to enclose (document, relic, etc.) in the floor, in a wall, in the altar, etc.; **die Gründungsurkunde wurde hinter dem Altar eingemauert**, the foundation document was enclosed in the wall *or* floor behind the altar, was immured, walled in, behind the altar.

einmäulig, *a. Tls:* **einmäuliger Schraubenschlüssel**, single-ended spanner, *U.S:* wrench.

einmehrdeutig, *a. Mth:* one-too-many (relations).

einmeißeln, *v.tr. sep.* to carve (inscription, etc.) in

(with a chisel); to chisel (inscription, etc.); **etwas in etwas** *acc.* **e.**, to cut, carve, (inscription, etc.) into (stone, etc.), to chisel (inscription, etc.) in (stone, etc.).

einmengen, *v. sep.*=**einmischen.**

einmieten[1], *v.tr. sep.* **j-n bei j-m e.**, to get, obtain, lodgings for s.o. with s.o.; **sich bei j-m e.**, to take lodgings with s.o.

einmieten[2], *v.tr. sep. Agr:* to clamp *or* silo (potatoes, etc.).

Einmieter, *m. Biol:* commensal, guest, inquiline.

einmischen. I. *v.sep.* **1.** *v.tr.* to mix in (ingredient, etc.); **etwas in etwas** *acc.* **e.**, to add sth. to (substance, etc.); to mix sth. into, in with (other ingredients, etc.). **2. sich einmischen,** to interfere, intermeddle; to butt in; to join in; *F:* to put in one's oar, to stick one's oar in; **sich in etwas** *acc.* **e.**, to meddle in, with, to interfere in (other people's affairs, etc.); to nose, poke one's nose, into (other people's business, etc.); to join in (conversation); to butt into, butt in on (conversation); **sich in Dinge e., die einen nichts angehen,** to meddle with things that do not concern one; **ich habe es nicht gerne, wenn man sich in meine Angelegenheiten einmischt,** I don't like people interfering in my affairs; **'ich habe das auch gesehen', mischte er sich ein,** 'I saw it, too,' he joined in.

II. *vbl s.* **1. Einmischen,** *n. in vbl senses.* **2. Einmischung,** *f.* (*a*)=II. 1; (*b*) interference; **fremde E.,** (i) outside interference; interference from other people; (ii) foreign interference; **ich verbitte mir jede E. in meine Angelegenheiten,** I'll brook no interference in my affairs.

Einmischungsklage, *f. Jur:* intervention.

einmitten, *v.tr. sep. Typewr:* to centre (heading); *Opt:* to centre, adjust (lens).

einmotorig, *a. Av:* single-engined (aircraft).

einmotten, *v.tr. sep.* to put (clothes, etc.) in mothballs; *F: Navy:* to mothball (a ship).

einmummeln, *v.tr. sep. F:* to wrap, muffle, (s.o., oneself) up; **sich in die Decken e.**, to snuggle up in one's blankets.

einmummen, *v.tr. sep.* to wrap, muffle, (s.o., oneself) up; **in dicke Pelze eingemummt,** muffled up in thick furs.

einmünden. I. *v.i. sep.* (*sein*) **in etwas** *acc.* **e.**, (*of river, etc.*) to flow into, enter (the sea, etc.); (*of road, etc.*) to lead into, run into, join (another road, etc.); (*of pipe, etc.*) to run into (opening, another pipe, etc.); *Anat:* (*of blood-vessel*) to inosculate, anastomose, with (artery, etc.); **Straßen, die in den Marktplatz einmünden,** roads that open on to, that run into, lead into, the market place; **die Rhone mündet ins Mittelmeer ein,** the Rhone empties itself, flows, discharges, into the Mediterranean.

II. *vbl s.* **Einmünden** *n.*, **Einmündung** *f. in vbl senses; also:* junction (of roads); *Anat:* **Einmündung eines Blutgefäßes in eine Arterie,** inosculous, inosculation, anastomosis, of a blood-vessel with an artery.

einmünzen, *v.tr. sep.* to coin, mint (gold, silver, etc.), to convert (gold, silver, etc.) into coinage; **alte Geldstücke e.**, to recoin, remint, old coinage.

Einmut, *f.* -/. harmony; concord; unity.

einmütig, *a.* (*a*) unanimous; *adv.* unanimously; by common consent, with one consent; **sie faßten den einmütigen Beschluß,** *adv.* **e. den Beschluß, den Verbündeten zu Hilfe zu eilen,** they took the unanimous decision, they unanimously decided, they decided by common consent, to come to the help of their allies; **man spendete ihm einmütiges Lob,** *adv.* **e. Lob,** they were unanimous in their praise of him; (*b*) harmonious, united (family, etc.); *adv.* harmoniously; unitedly; in harmony, concord, unity; **sie leben e. zusammen,** they live together in harmony.

Einmütigkeit, *f.* (*a*) unanimity; (*b*) harmony; concord; unity.

einnageln, *v.tr. sep.* to nail (sth.) in, to fasten (sth.) with nails; **etwas in etwas** *acc.* **e.**, to fasten (clothes-hook, etc.) in (wall, etc.).

einnähen, *v.tr. sep.* **1.** to sew (sth.) up; **etwas in etwas** *acc.* **e.**, to sew sth. up in (bag, etc.); **in einen Beutel eingenähtes Geld,** money sewn up in a bag. **2.** to sew in (name-tape, etc.); **etwas in etwas** *acc.* **e.**, to sew (name-tape, etc.) into (dress, etc.); to put (patch, etc.) in (sheet, dress, etc.). **3. ein Kleid e.**, to take a dress in; to make a tuck in a dress.

Einnahme, *f.* -/-n. **1.** (*a*) taking (of meal, medicine, etc.); (*b*) taking (of money); receipt (of taxes, etc.); (*c*) seizure, capture (of town, fortress, etc.); (*d*) taking up (of defensive position, etc.). **2.** *usu. pl.* **Einnahmen,** earnings (of pers., commercial undertaking, etc.); income (of pers.; from investment, work, estate, etc.); revenue (from estate, taxes, etc.); proceeds (of charitable enterprise, etc.); *Com:* receipts; takings; **Einnahmen und Ausgaben,** income and expenditure; **die Einnahmen sind gut,** the receipts, takings, are good; **meine Einnahmen reichen für unsere Bedürfnisse aus,** my earnings are, my income is, sufficient for our needs; **mit dieser E. können wir jetzt nicht mehr rechnen,** we can't count on this source of income any longer.

Einnahmequelle, *f.* source of income; source of revenue.

einnebeln, *v.tr. sep. Mil:* **etwas e.**, to shroud, blanket, (factory, area, etc.) in fog, to lay a smoke screen over (area); (*of troops*) **sich e.**, to surround themselves with a smoke screen.

einnehmbar, *a.* (*of fortress, etc.*) capable of being taken; pregnable.

einnehmen. I. *v.tr. sep.* (*strong*) **1.** to take (meal, medicine, etc.); to have (meal); **er nimmt seine Mahlzeiten im Hotel ein,** he takes, has, his meals in the hotel; **das Mittel muß tropfenweise eingenommen werden,** the remedy must be taken in drops. **2.** *Nau:* to take in, take on (supply of water, etc.); to take (freight, etc.) on board, aboard; to ship, lade (freight, etc.). **3.** *Com: etc:* (*of business, shop, etc.*) to take (money); (*of artist, businessman, etc.*) to make, pick up (money); *Adm:* (*of state, etc.*) to receive (taxes, etc.); **er nimmt von seinen Besitzungen 10 000 Mark im Jahr ein,** he gets, has, an income of 10,000 marks a year from his estates; **der Staat nimmt täglich Tausende von Mark an Vergnügungssteuern ein,** the state collects, receives, thousands of marks in entertainment tax every day; *F:* **er hat diese Woche ein hübsches Sümmchen eingenommen,** he has collected a nice sum of money this week, made a nice profit this week. **4.** (*a*) to take, seize, capture (fortress, town, etc.); **eine Festung im Sturm e.**, to take, seize, capture, a fortress by storm; **die letzten Positionen des Feindes e.**, to carry, seize, capture, take, the enemy's last positions; (*b*) to take (one's seat) (in train, etc.); to assume, take up (position); **nehmen Sie Ihre Plätze ein!** take your seats! take your places! **das Tier nahm eine Abwehrstellung ein,** the animal took up a defensive position; *Navy:* (*of ship*) **seinen Standort vorne, achtern, e.**, to take up position ahead, astern. **5.** (*a*) (*of pers.*) to occupy, hold (position, etc.); *Mil: Navy: etc:* to hold (rank); (*of thg*) to hold (place, rank, etc.); **er nimmt eine hohe Stellung in der Gesellschaft ein,** he occupies, holds, a high position in society; **j-s, etwas** *gen.*, **Stelle e.**, to take the place of s.o., sth., to replace s.o., sth.; **die Astronomie nahm die Stelle der Astrologie ein,** astronomy took the place of, replaced, astrology; (*b*) to take up, occupy, fill (space); **der Tisch nimmt die Hälfte des Korridors ein,** the table occupies, fills, takes up, half the corridor; **der Aufsatz nimmt sechs Seiten ein,** the essay fills, takes up, six pages; **diese Frage nimmt einen breiten Raum in seinen Forschungsarbeiten ein,** this problem takes up, occupies, a large part of his research work. **6.** (*of pers.*) **j-n für sich e.**, to captivate s.o. (by one's charm, etc.); to gain s.o.'s favour, heart (by one's good manners, etc.); to gain s.o.'s favour, to prepossess s.o. in one's favour (by flattery, etc.); (*of good manners, etc.*) **j-n für j-n e.**, to prepossess s.o. in s.o.'s favour; (*of considerations, etc.*) **j-n für etwas e.**, to prepossess s.o. in favour of (plan, idea, etc.); **er nahm alle Menschen, alle(r) Herzen, durch sein gewinnendes Wesen (für sich) ein,** he gained everyone's favour, heart, by his charm; **seine guten Manieren nehmen (jedermann) für ihn ein,** his good manners prepossess everyone in his favour, make everyone take to him; **er nimmt jedermann gegen sich ein durch seine schlechten Manieren,** his bad manners prejudice everyone against him; **diese Überlegungen nahmen mich gegen den Plan ein,** these considerations prepossessed, prejudiced, me against the plan, turned me against the plan. **7.** to take in (dress, sleeve, seam, etc.); **ein Kleid in der Taille e.**, to take in a dress at the waist. **8.** *Nau:* to take in (sail, etc.); to run in, rig in (bowsprit, etc.); to ship (oars).

II. *pr.p. & a.* **einnehmend,** *in vbl senses; esp.* prepossessing, engaging, captivating, winning, taking (appearance, manners, ways, etc.); **ein einnehmendes Wesen haben,** (i) to have taking manners, ways; (ii) *Hum:* to be greedy; to take all one can get.

III. *p.p. & a.* **eingenommen,** *in vbl senses; esp.* **für j-n e. sein,** to be well disposed towards s.o.; to be prepossessed in s.o.'s favour; to be biased, have a bias, towards s.o.; **von j-m e. sein,** to be taken with s.o.; to like s.o.; **gegen j-n e. sein,** to be ill disposed towards s.o.; to be prepossessed against s.o.; to be prejudiced, biased, to have a bias, against s.o.; **für etwas e. sein,** to be well disposed towards (plan, idea, etc.); **von etwas e. sein,** to be taken with (plan, idea, etc.); to be intrigued by (plan, idea, etc.); to be prejudiced, biased, to have a bias, in favour of (plan, idea, etc.); **gegen etwas e. sein,** to be ill-disposed towards (plan, idea, etc.); to be prejudiced, biased, to have a bias, against (plan, idea, etc.); **von sich e. sein,** to be full of one's own importance; to be conceited; to be taken up with oneself, to fancy oneself, *F:* to think a lot, no small beer, of oneself; **er ist sehr von sich e.**, he is very conceited, full of self-conceit, full of his own importance, he thinks no end of himself, he is very much taken up with himself.

einnicken, *v.i. sep.* (*sein*) to fall into a doze; to doze off.

einnieten, *v.tr. sep. Metalw:* to rivet (in); **eingenieteter Bolzen,** riveted bolt.

einnisten (sich), *v.refl. sep.* (*of bird*) to build its nest, to nest (in barn, etc.); (*of vermin*) to settle in; *F:* (*of pers.*) to park (oneself); *F:* **die Schlamperei, die sich eingenistet hat, muß ein Ende finden,** the slovenliness which has set in must come to an end; **er hat sich bei uns eingenistet,** he has parked himself on us.

einnorden, *v.tr. sep.* to orientate (map, plan).

Einöde, *f.* **1.** wilderness; desert; **in dieser E. kann ich es nicht aushalten,** I cannot live in this desert. **2.** isolated farm.

Einödhof, *m.* isolated farm.

einohrig, *a.* one-eared (rabbit, etc.).

einölen, *v.tr. sep.* to oil (machine, boots, etc.); to lubricate (machine, etc.); to smear (leather, etc.) with oil; *Tex:* to oil, grease (wool); **sich** *dat.* **die Haut, seine Haut, sich, e.**, to rub oil into one's skin, to oil one's skin.

einordnen, *v.tr. sep.* to put (sth.) in its place; to fit (detail, etc.) in; to arrange (objects) in proper order; to classify (animals, plants, etc.); to file (letter, etc.); **etwas richtig, falsch, e.**, to put (book, etc.) (back) in the right, wrong, place; to classify, class, sth. correctly, wrongly; to file (letter, etc.) correctly, wrongly; **etwas an der richtigen, falschen, Stelle e.**, to put sth. in the right, wrong, place; **etwas in etwas** *acc.* **e.**, to put sth. in its proper place in (drawer, file, etc.); to fit (detail, fact, etc.) into (system, etc.); to arrange (objects) in (drawer, etc.); to put (document, etc.) into (file, etc.); **sich e.**, to fit in; to fall, drop, into place; to fall into line; (*of pers.*) to take one's place (in queue, etc.); *Aut:* to get into the correct traffic lane; **Akten, Briefe, Karteikarten, usw., alphabetisch e.**, to file documents, letters, index-cards, etc., in alphabetical order; **ein Tier in die Klasse der Säugetiere, unter die Säugetiere, e.**, to classify an animal as a mammal; **ein Buch unter die Romane e.**, to class a book as a novel; **ein Buch unter die Romane, den Romanen, e.**, to put a book among the novels; **ein Mensch, der sich schwer einordnet,** a person who finds it difficult to fit in.

einpacken. I. *v.tr. sep.* (*a*) to pack (up) (goods, one's clothes, etc.); to pack (goods), to put (goods) up; to wrap (sth.) up; *abs.* to pack (up); **etwas in etwas** *acc.* **e.**, to pack sth. in (case, etc.), to put sth. into (case, etc.); to pack (goods) in (shavings, etc.); to do, put, (goods) up in (paper, etc.); to wrap sth. (up) in (paper, etc.); **j-n, sich, in etwas** *acc.* **e.**, to wrap s.o., oneself, up in (blanket, etc.); **Waren in Kisten, Schachteln, e.**, to case goods (up); to box (goods) (up); **ich habe vergessen, meine Schuhe einzupacken,** I have forgotten to pack my shoes; **der Hausierer packte seine Waren ein,** the hawker packed (up) his wares; **pack dich warm ein!** wrap yourself up warm(ly)! **er packte sich fest, dicht, in seine Decke ein,** he wrapped himself (up) tightly in his blanket; he wrapped his blanket closely round, about, him; **dicht in Pelze eingepackt sein,** to be all wrapped up, to be completely enveloped, in furs; *F:* **seine Siebensachen e.**, to pack (up) one's few belongings, to pack up one's traps; *Med:* **einen Patienten in feuchte Tücher e.**, to pack a patient; (*b*) *F:* **er ist ein solches Genie, daß alle anderen e. können,** he is such a genius that all the others might as well give up, pack up and go; **der kann nach diesem letzten Vorfall e.**, he may as well pack up and go after this last affair; **mit diesen Ausreden kannst du e.**, you can keep your excuses.

II. *vbl s.* **1. Einpacken,** *n. in vbl senses.*

2. Einpackung, *f.* (*a*)=II. 1; (*b*) *Med:* **(feuchte) E.,** wet pack.

einpalmen, *v.tr. sep. Nau:* **ein Tau e.,** to haul in a rope hand over hand.

einpaschen, *v.tr. sep. F:* to smuggle (goods, etc.) in; **etwas in ein Land e.,** to smuggle (goods, etc.) into a country.

einpassen, *v.tr. sep.* to fit sth. in; **etwas in etwas** *acc.* **e.,** to fit sth. into (opening, etc.); *Clockm:* **das Uhrwerk in das Gehäuse e.,** to box in the watch-movement.

einpassieren, *v.sep.* **1.** *v.i.* (*sein*) (*of ship, etc.*) to enter, pass in; *F:* (*of soldier, etc.*) to return to barracks; to rejoin his unit (after holiday, etc.); **in den Hafen e.,** to enter the harbour, pass into the harbour. **2.** *v.tr. Tex:* **die Kettfäden e.,** to draw, draft, enter, pass, the warp threads.

einpauken, *v.tr. sep. Sch:* **j-m etwas e.,** to hammer, knock (Latin, vocabulary, etc.) into (pupil); to grind (pupil, etc.) in (Latin, etc.); **eine Lektion mit j-m e.,** to hammer away at a lesson with s.o.; to cram, drum, a lesson into s.o.; **j-n e.,** to cram (candidate) (for examination); **(sich** *dat.***) etwas e.,** to swot up, grind away at (Latin verbs, etc.).

einpeitschen, *v.tr. sep.* (*a*) **auf j-n, auf ein Pferd, usw., e.,** to whip, lash, s.o., a horse, etc.; (*b*) *F:* **j-m etwas e.,** to drub sth. into s.o.

Einpeitscher, *m. Parl:* whip, *U.S:* floor leader.

einpelzen, *v.tr. sep. Hort: Arb:*=**einpfropfen.**

einpendeln, *v.tr. sep.* to adjust (pendulum); **sich e.,** (*of pendulum*) to fall into its normal swing; (*of prices, etc.*) to settle down, to even out; to find their own level.

Einpendler, *m.* commuter who travels into a town.

einpfeffern, *v.tr. sep.* to pepper (meat, etc.).

einpferchen, *v.tr. sep.* (*a*) to fold (sheep); to pen (sheep); (*b*) to crowd, cram (people) (into small room, etc.); **drei Familien waren in einen kleinen Raum eingepfercht,** three families were crowded into one small room; **er war zwischen zwei dicken Frauen eingepfercht,** he was wedged in between, sandwiched (in) between, two fat women.

einpflanzen. I. *v.tr. sep.* (*a*) to plant (tree, flower, vegetable); (*b*) **j-m etwas e.,** to implant, engraft, (principle, idea, etc.) in s.o.'s mind; to infuse, instil, (principle, idea, etc.) into s.o.; to impart (principle, idea, etc.) to s.o.

II. **Einpflanzen** *n.*, **Einpflanzung** *f. in vbl senses; also:* implantation (of principle, idea, etc.); instillation, infusion (of principle, idea, etc.).

einpflastern, *v.tr. sep.* **1.** to pave over (courtyard, etc.). **2.** to set (post, etc.) in pavement.

einpfropfen, *v.tr. sep. Arb: Hort:* to graft (scion, etc.); **etwas in etwas** *acc.* **e.,** to graft (scion, etc.) into (stock, etc.).

Einphasenstrom, *m. El:* single-phase current.

einphasig, *a.* monophase, monophasic, uniphase single-phase.

einpichen, *v.tr. sep.* to pitch (sth.), to coat (sth.) with pitch; *Nau:* to pay (ship).

einpinseln, *v.tr. sep.* **etwas mit etwas e.,** to paint sth. with (iodine, etc.); **sich e.,** to lather one's face (with a brush).

einplanieren, *v.tr. sep.* to level, even up (ground, etc.); to make (ground, etc.) even; to level (road, etc.); to flatten, smooth (surface, etc.).

einplanken, *v.tr.sep.* to board in (building-site, etc.).

einpökeln, *v.tr.sep.* (*a*) to salt (down) (meat, fish); to cure (meat, fish) (by salting); to brine, souse (meat, fish); to pickle (meat, fish); to corn (meat); (*b*) *Leath:* to cure (skins).

Einpolgenerator, *m. El.E:* unipolar generator.

einpolig, *a. El.E: etc:* unipolar.

Einpoligkeit, *f. El.E: etc:* unipolarity

einpolymerisieren, *v.tr. sep. Ch: Plastics:* to co-polymerize (compounds); **Einpolymerisieren** *n,* co-polymerization.

einprägen. I. *v.tr. sep.* (*a*) **etwas in etwas** *acc.* **e.,** to imprint, impress, stamp, (inscription, etc.) on (medal, etc.); (*of pattern, etc.*) **sich in etwas** *acc.* **e.,** to become imprinted, impressed, stamped, on (medal, etc.); (*b*) **j-m etwas e.,** to imprint, implant, plant, fix, (idea, principle, etc.) in s.o.'s mind; to impress (idea, principle, etc.) upon s.o.; to infuse, instil, (principle, idea, etc.) into s.o.; **j-m e., etwas zu tun,** to enjoin (on) s.o. to do sth.; to give s.o. strict instructions to do sth.; to instruct s.o. to do sth.; (*of memory, etc.*) **sich j-m, in j-s Seele, e.,** to imprint, impress, stamp, itself on s.o., on s.o.'s mind; to engrave itself on s.o.'s mind; **sich j-m ins Gedächtnis e., sich in j-s Gedächtnis, sich j-m, e.,** to imprint, impress, stamp, engrave, itself on s.o.'s memory; **etwas seinem Gedächtnis, sich** *dat.* **etwas, e.,** to imprint, impress, engrave, (details, etc.) on one's memory; *F:* to fix sth. in one's memory; **präge dir das gut ein,** fix that in your mind; **Verse prägen sich leichter (ins Gedächtnis, dem Gedächtnis) ein als Prosa,** verse is easier to remember, makes a more lasting impression, than prose; **diese Kindheitserinnerungen waren unauslöschlich in seine Seele eingeprägt,** these childhood memories were ineradicably imprinted, impressed, stamped, engraved, on his mind; **dieses Symbol prägt sich dem Auge ein,** this symbol leaves a visual impression on the mind; **Sie müssen ihm e., daß . . . ,** you must impress on him that . . . ; **von Jugend auf waren ihm diese Grundsätze eingeprägt worden,** these principles had been impressed, imprinted, inculcated, implanted, in him, instilled into him, from his youth.

II. *vbl s.* **Einprägen** *n.*, **Einprägung** *f. in vbl senses; also:* **E. in etwas** *acc.*, (*a*) impression (of pattern, etc.) on (medal, etc.); (*b*) impression (of idea, principle, etc.) on (s.o.'s mind); inculcation (of idea, principle, etc.) in (s.o.'s mind); instillation (of idea, principle, etc.) into (s.o.'s mind).

einprasseln, *v.i. sep.* (*sein*) (*of hail, rain, etc.*) **auf etwas, j-n, e.,** to come pouring down on sth., s.o.; **Schläge prasselten auf ihn ein,** blows rained down on him; **ein Wortschwall prasselte auf uns ein,** a flood of words swept over us.

einpressen, *v.tr. sep.* **1.** to press (drawing-pin, etc.) in; to squeeze, force, sth. in; **etwas in etwas** *acc.* **e.,** to press (drawing-pin, etc.) into (board, etc.); to squeeze, force, sth. into sth.; *Constr:* to inject (concrete) (into a wall, etc.); **ein Muster in einen Stoff e.,** to press a pattern into a material; **seinen Körper in ein Korsett e.,** to force, squeeze, oneself into a corset; **etwas zwischen zwei Gegenstände e.,** to wedge sth. between two things; to squeeze sth. in between two things; **er war zwischen zwei dicken Frauen eingepreßt,** he was sandwiched, wedged, in between two fat women; *Bookb:* **den Buchblock e.,** to put the book in the press. **2.** *abs. Constr:* to grout under pressure; **Einpressung** *f,* injection, pressure grouting.

Einpreßgas, *n. Oil-drilling:* input gas.

Einpreßloch, *n. Constr:* grout hole.

Einpreßsonde, *f. Oil-drilling:* input well.

Einpreßverfahren, *n. Constr:* pressure grouting, (grout) injection process.

einprobieren, *v.tr. sep.* to rehearse (play, part, etc.).

einpudern, *v.tr. sep.* **etwas, j-n, e.,** to powder sth., s.o.; to sprinkle powder on sth.; *Metall:* to dust (mould); **sich e.,** to dust oneself with (talcum) powder, to powder oneself.

einpumpen, *v.tr. sep.* to pump (sth.) in; **etwas in etwas** *acc.* **e.,** to pump sth. into sth.

einpuppen (sich), *v.refl. sep. Ent:* to pupate.

einquartieren. I. *v.tr. sep.* **j-n bei j-m e.,** to get lodgings for s.o. with s.o.; *Mil:* to quarter (troops) (with s.o., in, on, a town); to billet (troops, refugees) (on s.o., in, on, a town); **sich bei j-m e.,** to take lodgings with s.o.; *F:* to billet, quarter, oneself on s.o.; **bei j-m einquartiert sein,** to have lodgings with s.o., in s.o.'s house; to be quartered with s.o., billeted on s.o.

II. *vbl s.* **1. Einquartieren,** *n. in vbl senses.* **2. Einquartierung,** *f.* (*a*)=II. 1; (*b*) *Mil:* soldiers quartered with s.o., billeted on s.o.; *F:* unwanted, unwelcome, guests; **wir haben E.,** (i) we have soldiers billeted on us; (ii) *F:* we have had visitors dumped on us.

Einquartierungsschein, Einquartierungszettel, *m. Mil:* billeting paper.

einquetschen, *v.tr. sep.* **etwas in etwas** *acc.* **e.,** to get (one's fingers, etc.) squeezed in (door, etc.); **sich** *dat.* **die Finger, seine Finger, in die Türe, in der Türe, e.,** to catch, shut, nip, pinch, one's fingers in the door, to get one's fingers jammed, crushed, in the door; **sich** *dat.* **eine Rippe e.,** to crush a rib, to break a rib; **ich habe mir die Finger eingequetscht,** I have got my fingers caught; **er quetschte sich den Fuß zwischen zwei Holzklötze ein,** he got his leg jammed, caught, wedged, between two logs; **er war zwischen zwei dicken Frauen eingequetscht,** he was sandwiched, wedged, in between two fat women; **j-m den Brustkorb e.,** to crush s.o.'s chest (in).

einracken, *v.tr. sep. Nau:* to parrel (yard), to fasten (yard) by a parrel.

Einrad, *n. Cy:* monocycle.

einraffen, *v.tr. sep.* **1.** to gather (dress, etc.) (at the side, etc.). **2.** *Nau:* to reef (sail).

einrahmen, *v.tr. sep.* to frame (picture, mirror, etc.); to frame (picture, page of book, etc.) (with an ornamental border, etc.); **das Städtchen ist von Weinbergen eingerahmt,** the little town is surrounded by vineyards; **die Feier wurde von musikalischen Darbietungen eingerahmt,** the ceremony was put in a musical setting; *Iron:* **das kannst du dir e. (lassen)!** why don't you have it framed?

einrammen, *v.tr. sep.* to ram (down), drive (in), drive (home), sink (pile, etc.); **etwas in etwas** *acc.* **e.,** to ram, drive, sink, (pile, etc.) into (ground, etc.).

einrangieren, *v.tr. sep.* to fit (sth.) in; **etwas in etwas** *acc.* **e.,** to fit sth. into sth.

einrasten, *v.sep.* **1.** *v.tr.* to engage (catch, etc.); to lock (lever, etc.) into position. **2.** *v.i.* (*sein*) to snap into position; to snap home; to lock; to catch.

einräumen. I. *v.tr. sep.* **1.** to put (sth.) in its place; to stow (away) (objects); to put (things) into a cupboard, drawer, etc.; to put (furniture) into a room, etc.; **etwas in etwas** *acc.* **e.,** to put (objects) into (drawer, etc.); to arrange (objects) in (drawer, etc.); to put (furniture) into (room, etc.); **der Hausierer hatte seine Waren schon eingeräumt,** the hawker had already packed (up), stowed away, his goods. **2.** (*a*) **j-m ein Vorrecht, einen Vorteil, ein Recht, usw., e.,** to concede, grant, accord, a privilege, an advantage, a right, to s.o.; **j-m den Gebrauch von etwas e.,** to let s.o. have the use of (garage, etc.); **ich mußte den Flüchtlingen eines meiner Zimmer e.,** I had to let the refugees have one of my rooms, I had to give up one of my rooms to the refugees; **dem Feind eine Stellung e.,** to abandon, yield, a position to the enemy; *Com: Fin:* **j-m Kredit e.,** to give s.o. credit; **j-m einen Diskont, usw., e.,** to allow s.o. a discount, etc.; (*b*) to concede, grant, admit, acknowledge (fact); **ich räume ein, einen Fehler gemacht zu haben, daß ich einen Fehler gemacht habe,** I admit, own, (to) having made a mistake, I allow, concede, grant, own, that I have made a mistake, I acknowledge having made a mistake; **ich räume ein, daß das wahr ist,** I allow that to be true; *Gram:* **einräumendes Bindewort, einräumender Satz,** concessive conjunction, clause.

II. *vbl s.* **Einräumen** *n.*, **Einräumung** *f. in vbl senses; also:* allowance (of credit); concession (of privilege, etc.); admission (of fact).

Einräumungssatz, *m. Gram:* concessive clause.

einrechnen, *v.tr. sep.* to count, reckon, (sth.) in; to include (sth.) (in one's calculations, in a number, etc.); to allow for (sth.); to take (sth.) into account, to take account of (sth.); **Männer über siebzig sind nicht in dieser Zahl eingerechnet,** men above seventy are not included in this number; **das Frühstück ist (im Preis) nicht eingerechnet,** breakfast is not included (in the charge); **die Verpackung ist nicht eingerechnet,** packing is not allowed for; **in diesem Budget sind ausstehende Gelder nicht eingerechnet,** in this budget moneys owing to us are not taken into account; **alles eingerechnet sind wir noch gut davongekommen,** all things considered, taking everything into account, we have come out of it well; **die Möglichkeit von Verspätungen ist eingerechnet,** possible delays are allowed for.

Einrede, *f.* **1.** *Jur:* exception, incidental plea (of defence); (statement of) defence; **peremptorische, dauernde, E.,** peremptory plea, special plea; demurrer; plea in bar; traverse; **dilatorische, aufschiebende, E.,** dilatory plea, dilatory exception; **E. erheben,** to raise an objection in law; to put in a plea; to take exception; to demur; to traverse; to set up a defence. **2.** objection; contradiction.

einreden, *v.sep.* **1.** *v.tr.* **j-m etwas e.,** to make s.o. believe sth.; to persuade s.o. of (the truth of) sth.; to put (foolish ideas, etc.) into s.o.'s head; **j-m e., daß . . . ,** to talk s.o. into believing that . . . ; to make s.o. believe that . . . ; to persuade s.o. that . . . ; **du wirst mir das doch nicht e. wollen,** surely you don't want to make me believe that? surely you won't have me believe that? **er wollte uns e., daß . . . ,** he would have us believe that . . . ; he tried to persuade us that . . . ; **sich** *dat.* **etwas e.,** to make oneself believe sth.; to persuade oneself of sth.; to imagine sth.; **das redest du dir nur ein,** you are only trying to make yourself believe it; you are only imagining it; **sich** *dat.* **e., daß . . . ,** to make oneself believe that . . . ; to persuade oneself that . . . ; to imagine that . . . ; **er redete sich ein, daß nun alles in Ordnung sei,** he persuaded himself that all was now well; **er redete es sich solange ein, bis er es selber glaubte,** he persuaded himself of it until at last he believed it; in the end he succeeded in persuading himself,

convincing himself, that the thing was true; **er ließ sich e., daß es am besten sei, die Sache totzuschweigen,** he let himself be talked into thinking, let himself be persuaded, that it would be best to keep the matter quiet. **2.** *v.i.* (*haben*) **auf j-n e.,** to speak, talk, (persuasively *or* insistently) to s.o.; to try to persuade s.o.; to reason with s.o.; **alle redeten zugleich auf ihn ein,** they were all talking to him at once; **sie redete eine halbe Stunde auf ihn ein,** she talked to him, kept on at him, for a full half-hour.

einreefen, einreffen, *v.tr. sep. Nau:* to reef (sail).

einregeln, *v.tr. sep.* to adjust (measuring instrument, etc.); **Einregelung** *f*, adjustment.

einregistrieren, *v.tr. sep.* to insert (sth.) in the file; to file (sth.); to register, record, file (document, etc.); to register, record, enter (incoming mail) (in entry book, etc.); to register, enter (name, etc.) (in book, etc.).

einregnen, *v.sep.* **1.** *v.impers.* **an dieser Stelle regnet es ein,** rain comes in here; **es hat in den Dachboden eingeregnet,** the rain has come through into the loft; **es hat durch das offene Fenster eingeregnet,** the rain has come in through the open window. **2.** *v.i.* (*sein & haben*) *F:* to rain on s.o.; **Schläge regneten auf ihn ein,** blows rained upon him; **Einladungen regnen nur so auf uns ein,** invitations are pouring in (on us). **3.** *v.i.* (*sein*) *F:* (*of pers.*) (i) to be soaked by the rain; (ii) to be trapped, caught, by the rain; **wir sind richtig eingeregnet,** (i) we were thoroughly soaked by the rain; (ii) we were trapped, caught, by the rain. **4.** *v.impers.* **es regnet sich ein,** the rain seems to be settling in; **es hat sich eingeregnet,** the rain has settled in.

Einreibemittel, *n. Med:* liniment; embrocation.

einreiben. I. *v.tr. sep.* (*strong*) **j-n, einen Körperteil, (mit etwas) e.,** to rub s.o., a part of the body, with oil, ointment, liniment, etc.; to rub oil, ointment, liniment, etc., into s.o., a part of the body; *Med:* to embrocate a part of the body; **Öl, Salbe, in die Haut e.,** to rub oil, ointment, into the skin; to rub in oil, ointment; **seine Haut, sich, mit Creme e., sich** *dat.* **die Haut mit Creme e.,** to rub one's skin, oneself, with cream; **Fleisch mit Salz, Pfeffer, usw., e.,** to rub salt, pepper, etc., into meat; **eine Salatschüssel mit Knoblauch e.,** to rub a salad bowl with garlic; **Leder mit Fett e.,** to rub grease into leather; to dub leather; **Schuhe mit Creme e.,** to apply polish to shoes; **soll ich dich heute abend e.?** shall I rub your back, shoulder, etc., (with liniment) tonight?

II. *vbl s.* **1. Einreiben,** *n. in vbl senses.* **2. Einreibung,** *f.* (*a*)=II. 1; *also:* application (of ointment, etc.); **E. der Haut mit Öl, E. von Öl in die Haut,** application of oil to the skin; (*b*) embrocation; application of ointment, etc.; **der Arzt hat drei Einreibungen am Tag angeordnet,** the doctor has ordered the ointment to be applied three times a day.

Einreiber, *m.* (casement-)window catch.

Einreibungsmittel, *n. Med:* liniment; embrocation.

einreichen, *v.tr. sep.* to present, hand in, submit (petition, etc.); to submit, send in, *U.S:* file (application); **Rechnungen bei einer Versicherung, usw., e.,** to send in bills to an insurance office, etc.; **seine Papiere e.,** to send in, forward, one's papers; **um etwas e.,** to apply for, make an application for (scholarship, etc.); **seinen Abschied, sein Abschiedsgesuch, e.,** to tender one's resignation; to ask to be relieved of one's duties; to give notice; *Mil: Navy:* to send in one's papers; to ask to be placed on the retired list.

einreihen, *v.tr. sep.* **1.** to insert (sth.) (in its place); to fit (sth.) in; **etwas, j-n, in etwas** *acc.* **e.,** to insert sth. in (catalogue, etc.); to fit sth. into sth.; to enlist, enrol, s.o. in (organization, etc.); **sich e.,** to fit in; to fall, drop, into place; to fall into line; (*of pers.*) to take one's place (in queue, etc.); **sich in eine Organisation e.,** to join an organization; **sich in die Marschkolonne e.,** to fall into line, to fall in; **Briefe, Karteikarten, usw., alphabetisch e.,** to file letters, index-cards, etc., in alphabetical order; **ein Tier in die Klasse der Säugetiere, unter die Säugetiere, e.,** to classify an animal as a mammal; **ein Buch unter die Romane e.,** (i) to put a book among the novels; (ii) to class a book as a novel; **als Biographen reihe ich ihn unter die Besten ein,** as a biographer I place him among the first; **j-n unter die großen Männer e.,** to rank, range, s.o. among the great men; **mit diesem Werk reihte er sich unter die großen Schriftsteller ein,** this work placed him among the great writers. **2.** *Tex:*=**einpassieren** 2. **3.** *Dressm:*=**einkräuseln.**

Einreiher, *m.* **-s/-,** single-breasted suit.

einreihig, *a. Tail:* single-breasted (jacket, etc.).

Einreise, *f.* **E. in ein Land, nach England, usw.,** entering a country, England, etc.; entry into a country, into England, etc.; **bei der E. habe ich Schwierigkeiten mit meinem Paß gehabt,** on entering the country, on my entry into the country, I had difficulty over my passport; *Adm:* **j-m die E. verweigern,** to refuse s.o. entry into a, the, country.

Einreiseerlaubnis, Einreisegenehmigung, *f. Adm:* entry permit.

einreisen, *v.i. sep.* (*sein*) **(in ein Land) e.,** to enter (a country).

Einreisesichtvermerk, *m. Adm:* entry visa.

einreißen, *v.sep.* (*strong*) I. *v.tr.* **1.** to tear (sth.) (at the edge); to make a tear in (sth.); to score (rock, metal, etc.); **ich habe mir das Kleid am Ärmel eingerissen,** I have torn my dress at the edge of the sleeve; **sich** *dat.* **den Fingernagel e.,** to split a nail; **sich** *dat.* **die Haut e.,** to gash oneself; **der Gletscher hat tiefe Furchen in den Felsen eingerissen,** the glacier has scored deep into the rock. **2.** to pull down, break down, demolish (house, etc.); to take down, break down (wall, etc.); **durch seinen Leichtsinn hat er eingerissen, was wir in Jahren mühevoller Arbeit aufgebaut haben,** by his carelessness he has destroyed what we have built up in years of hard work.

II. **einreißen,** *v.i.* (*sein*) **1.** to tear; to get torn; **der Rock ist am Saum eingerissen,** the skirt has got torn, has a tear, at the hem; **die Banknote ist eingerissen,** the bank-note is torn, has a tear in it. **2.** (*of discontent, abuse, etc.*) to spread; **die eingerissene Schlamperei muß aufhören,** this widespread slovenliness will have to stop.

einreiten, *v.sep.* (*strong*) **1.** *v.i.* (*sein*) to ride in; **in den Schloßhof e.,** to ride into the castle courtyard. **2.** *v.tr.* to break in (horse).

einrenken, *v.tr. sep.* (*a*) *Med:* to set, reduce (dislocated limb, fracture); **Einrenkung** *f* **eines Bruches,** setting, reduction, of a fracture; (*b*) **das werden wir schon wieder e.,** we shall be able to put that right, to rights, to straighten that out; **die Sache wird sich schon wieder e.,** the matter will right itself, will straighten itself out.

einrennen, *v.sep.* (*conj. like* **rennen**) **1.** *v.i.* (*sein*) **auf j-n, etwas, e.,** to run at s.o., sth. **2.** *v.tr.* **etwas e.,** to knock (down) (fence, etc.) by charging into it; **er rannte die Fensterscheibe mit dem Kopf ein,** he broke the window with his head; **sich** *dat.* **(an etwas** *dat.***) den Schädel e.,** to crack one's skull (by running into sth.); *F:* to run, beat, one's head against a brick wall; **an seinem Eigensinn wirst du dir den Schädel e.,** you will be knocking your head against a brick wall if you try to overcome his stubborness; *F:* **offene Türen e.,** to force an open door; to flog a dead horse; **j-m die Türe e.=j-m die Türe einlaufen,** *q.v. under* **einlaufen** II. 1.

einrichten. I. *v.tr. sep.* **1.** (*a*) **etwas e.,** to arrange (meeting between two people, etc.); **etwas nach etwas e.,** to make (one's life, conduct, etc.) conform to (certain principles, etc.); to arrange, dispose, (one's plans, etc.) according to (s.o.'s suggestions, etc.); to proportion (one's expenditure, etc.) to (one's income, etc.), to regulate (one's expenditure, etc.) according to (one's income, etc.); **es so e., daß . . .,** to arrange it so that . . .; **ich werde das schon e.,** I shall arrange it, manage it; **er richtete das sehr schlau ein,** he arranged, managed, it very cleverly; **wenn ich es irgend e. kann,** if I can see how to arrange, manage, it; **ich richtete es so ein, daß niemand von seiner Abreise erfuhr,** I so arranged it that nobody knew of his departure; **die Zeit seiner Ankunft so e., daß sie mit der der übrigen zusammenfällt,** to time one's arrival to coincide with that of the others; **ich richtete es so ein, daß er in mein Bataillon kam,** I managed to have him put in my battalion; (*b*) **sich e.,** to adapt, adjust, accommodate, oneself to circumstances; to manage; to economize, retrench; *F:* to make both ends meet; **er weiß sich einzurichten,** he knows how to manage; (*c*) **sich auf etwas** *acc.* **e.,** to make arrangements for sth.; to make (one's) preparations for sth.; to prepare for sth.; **auf etwas eingerichtet sein,** to be prepared for sth.; **ich bin nicht darauf eingerichtet,** I am not prepared for it; **teile mir die Zeit deiner Ankunft mit, damit ich mich darauf e. kann,** let me know the time of your arrival so that I can make arrangements, arrange matters, accordingly; **wir müssen uns auf eine Hungerzeit e.,** we must prepare, be prepared, for a famine. **2.** (*a*) to furnish (house, room, etc.); to equip (house, kitchen, workshop, etc.); to fit up (apartment, workshop, etc.); to fit out (office, workshop, kitchen, etc.); **sich e.,** to furnish one's home; **sich geschmackvoll, elegant, e.,** to furnish one's home with taste, elegantly; **er ist fürstlich eingerichtet,** he has furnished his home in a princely style; **j-m ein Haus, eine Wohnung, e.,** to furnish a house, a flat, for s.o.; **j-m eine Praxis, ein Geschäft, e.,** to equip, fit up, fit out, a surgery, a shop, for s.o.; **die Eltern haben das junge Ehepaar vollständig eingerichtet,** the parents have provided the young couple with all the furniture; **ein gut, schlecht, eingerichtetes Zimmer,** a well-furnished, an ill-furnished, room; **eine bequem, luxuriös, elegant, eingerichtete Wohnung,** a comfortably, an expensively, elegantly, furnished flat; an elegantly appointed flat; **diese Werkstatt ist nicht sehr zweckmäßig eingerichtet,** this workshop is not very well, very efficiently arranged; **ein Zimmer als Büro e.,** to adapt a room to office use; to convert a room into an office; to fit a room up, out, as an office; *Mil:* **eine Stellung e.,** to prepare a position; (*b*) **sich e.,** to settle in; **sich in etwas** *dat.* **e.,** to settle in (new house, etc.). **3.** *Mus:* **ein Stück für Klavier, Violine und Flöte, für Orchester, e.,** to arrange a work for piano, violin and flute, for orchestra. **4.** (*a*) to fix, fasten, attach (part of machine, etc.); *Mil:* to bring (gun) to bear; (*b*) *Med:* to set, reduce (dislocated limb, fracture, etc.); (*c*) *Mth:* to reduce (mixed number) to an improper fraction. **5.** to set up (agency, school, hospital, shop, irrigation system, defence works, etc.); to start (shop, etc.); to found (school, hospital, scholarship, new chair, etc.); to establish (agency, new route, new chair, etc.); to institute (office, etc.); **es wurden überall im Land neue Schulen eingerichtet,** everywhere in the country new schools were set up, established, founded.

II. *vbl s.* **1. Einrichten,** *n. in vbl senses; also: Med:* reduction (of dislocated limb, fracture, etc.); *Mth:* reduction (of mixed number). **2. Einrichtung,** *f.* (*a*) *in vbl senses; also:* equipment (of house, kitchen, workshop, etc.); foundation (of school, hospital, scholarship, new chair, etc.); establishment (of agency, new route, new chair, etc.); institution (of office, etc.); arrangement (of reference book, work for piano, etc.); (*b*) institution; **ich halte nichts von diesen neumodischen Einrichtungen,** I don't believe in those new-fangled institutions, ideas; **eine karitative E.,** a charitable institution; **eine stehende E.,** a permanent institution; a standing custom; **öffentliche Einrichtungen,** public institutions; public services; **der Postbote ist eine wohlbekannte E. geworden,** the postman has become a well-known institution; **dieser Teil der Fabrik ist eine ganz neue E.,** this part of the factory is quite a new arrangement, institution; *F:* **er ist dort eine feste E. geworden,** he has become a fixture there; (*c*) device; contrivance; **die neue Maschine ist eine sehr nützliche E.,** the new machine is a very useful device; **eine E. zum Papierschneiden,** a paper-cutting device; (*d*) arrangement; lay-out (of workshop, etc.); **er bewunderte die zweckmäßige E. dieser Werkstatt,** he admired the practical lay-out of this workshop; (*e*) furniture (of house, room, etc.); equipment (of house, kitchen, workshop, etc.); furnishings (of house, room, etc.); **wir haben eine ganz neue E. gekauft,** we have bought entirely new furniture; (*f*) *pl.* **Einrichtungen,** (electrical, sanitary, technical, etc.) installations.

Einrichtungsgegenstand, *m.*, **Einrichtungsstück,** *n.* piece of furniture; piece of equipment (in office, etc.).

einriegeln, *v.tr. sep.* to bolt (s.o.) in; **sich e.,** to bolt oneself in.

Einriß, *m.* rent, tear, slit (in material, etc.); cleft, split (in rock); score, fissure (in rock, etc.).

einritzen, *v.tr. sep.* (*a*) to scratch (surface of sth., one's skin, etc.); to make a slight incision in (skin, etc.); to score (stone, metal, etc.); to incise (stone, etc.); **der Arzt ritzt die Haut leicht ein,** the doctor makes a slight incision in the skin, scratches the skin; (*b*) **etwas in etwas** *acc.* **e.,** to cut, incise, (figure, inscription, etc.) in sth.; to scratch (pattern, etc.) on (stone, metal, etc.); **er ritzte seinen Namen in die Baumrinde ein,** he scratched his name on the bark of the tree; **die Inschrift war roh in den Stein eingeritzt,** the inscription was roughly scratched on the

stone; **ein Stein mit eingeritzten Buchstaben,** a stone scratched with letters.

einrollen, *v.tr. sep.* **1.** *Sp:* to roll (ball) in; **den Ball ins Feld e.,** to roll the ball on to the field. **2.** to roll (up) (piece of paper, etc.); **sich e.,** (*of paper*) to roll up, curl up; (*of leaves*) to curl up; (*of cat, hedgehog*) to curl (itself) up, to roll (itself) up in a ball; **eingerolltes Blatt,** curled leaf; *Bot:* involute leaf.

einrosten, *v.i. sep.* (*sein*) (*a*) to become covered with, in, rust; (*b*) (*of screw, part of machine, etc.*) to rust in; (*of lock, machine, gun, etc.*) to rust inside, to become rusty; (*of pers., thg*) *F:* to rust; to get rusty; **seine Kenntnisse e. lassen,** to allow one's knowledge to rust; **mit sechzig beginnen einem die Gelenke einzurosten,** at sixty one's joints begin to get rusty; **mein Französisch ist eingerostet,** my French is rusty; **er konnte einmal singen, aber jetzt ist seine Stimme eingerostet,** he could sing once, but now his voice has become rusty; **ich habe keine Lust, in diesem Dorf einzurosten,** I don't want to rust away in this village.

einrücken, *v.sep.* I. *v.tr.* **1.** *Print: etc:* to indent (line, word, etc.); **eingerückte Zeile, eingerückter Absatz,** indented line, paragraph. **2. eine Anzeige e.,** to put, insert, an advertisement in a paper. **3.** *Mec.E:* to start (machine), to set (machine) in action, motion; to engage, connect (part); to throw (part) into gear.

II. **einrücken,** *v.i.* (*sein*) (*a*) (*of troops, etc.*) to march in; to enter; **unsere Truppen sind in Feindgebiet, in der Stadt, in die Stadt, eingerückt,** our troops have entered enemy territory, have entered, marched into, the town; (*b*) (*of soldier*) **in die Kaserne e.,** to return to barracks (after leave, etc.); (*c*) **(zum Militär) e.,** to enter the forces; to go for one's military service; to be called up; (*d*) **in seine Rechte e.,** (*of heir*) to come into one's inheritance; **die Natur rückte in ihre Rechte ein,** nature claimed her own; **in j-s Stelle e.,** to move into the place vacated by s.o.; to take s.o.'s place; to supplant s.o.

III. *vbl s.* **1. Einrücken,** *n. in vbl senses; also:* (*a*) *Print: etc:* indention, indentation (of line, word, etc.); (*b*) **das E. einer Anzeige in eine Zeitung,** the insertion of an advertisement in a paper; (*c*) entry (of troops, etc.) (into enemy territory, etc.); **E. in die Kaserne,** return to barracks. **2. Einrückung,** *f in vbl senses of* I.

Einrücker, *m.* **-s/-.** *Mec.E:* engaging lever.

Einrückgabel, *f. Rail:* re-engaging lever, re-setting lever.

Einrückhebel, *m. Mec.E:* engaging lever.

einrühren, *v.tr. sep. Cu: etc:* to stir (sth.) in; **ein Ei in die Suppe e.,** to stir an egg into the soup; *F:* **sich, j-m, etwas e.,** to get oneself, s.o., into a mess, into a fix; **er hat sich, uns, was Schönes eingerührt,** he's landed himself, us, in the soup, in a nice mess, in a fix, he's got himself, us, into a nice pickle, into a nice packet of trouble.

einrüsten, *v.tr. sep. Constr:* (*a*) to erect scaffolding around *or* in (building), to scaffold (building); (*b*) to centre (arch).

einrutschen, *v.i. sep.* (*sein*) (*of embankment, etc.*) to slip, to collapse.

eins[1]. **1.** *cardinal num.* one; (*a*) (number) one; **von e. bis zehn zählen,** to count from one to ten; **Kinder von e. bis zwölf,** children aged from one to twelve; **e. und e. ist zwei, e. und e. gleich zwei, e. und e. macht zwei,** one and one are two, make two; **Nummer e.,** number one; **Seite e.,** page one, first page; **Kapitel e.,** chapter one, first chapter; **Linie e.,** number one bus *or* tram; *Th:* **Akt e.,** act one, first act; *Sp: etc:* **e., zwei, drei, los!** one, two, three, go! (*b*) one o'clock; **es ist bald e.,** it is nearly one (o'clock); **um e.,** at one (o'clock); **zehn (Minuten) nach e.,** ten (minutes) past one; **von e. bis zwei arbeiten,** to work from one to two; **ich werde zwischen e. und zwei kommen,** I shall come between one and two (o'clock); (*c*) **e. sein mit Gott,** to be one with God; **e. werden,** to become one, to be made one; **am Horizont wurden Himmel und Erde e.,** at the horizon the sky and the earth became one; **(sich** *dat.***) mit j-m e. sein,** to be (at) one with s.o., to be in agreement with s.o.; **wir sind (uns) e. darin,** we are one in the matter, we are in perfect agreement on the matter; *F:* **es ist alles e., es kommt alles auf e. heraus,** it is all one, all the same, it makes no difference; **mir ist alles e.,** it is all one, all the same, to me, I don't care one way or the other; *F:* **ihn sehen und kehrtmachen war e.,** the sight of him meant an immediate about-turn; **die gestohlenen Äpfel fortwerfen und davonlaufen war e.,** it was the work of a single moment to throw the stolen apples away and run for it; *B:* **ich und der Vater sind e.,** I and my father are one. **2.** *s.f.* **Eins, -/-en,** (*a*) (figure) one; **eine römische E.,** a Roman one; **elf wird mit zwei Einsen geschrieben,** eleven is written with two ones; (*b*) (*at dice*) **eine E., zwei Einsen, werfen,** to throw a one, two ones; (*c*) *F:* **die E.,** number one tram; **er muß mit der E. fahren,** he has to go on the number one tram; (*d*) *Sch:* **im Aufsatz eine E. schreiben, bekommen,** to get full marks, an alpha, for an essay; **eine E. in Latein bekommen,** (*on report, exercise*) to get a 'very good', an alpha, in Latin; (*in examination*) to get a distinction in Latin; **eine Prüfung mit E. bestehen,** to get a grade one in an examination; (*at university*) to get a first class, *F:* a first, in an examination; *F:* (*of pupil*) **eine E. schreiben,** to write an exercise, essay, of grade one (*i.e.* distinction) quality.

eins[2], *indef.pron. see* **ein**[1] I. 2 (*a*), III.

Einsaat, *f.* **1.** sowing, dissemination (of seed). **2.** (sown) seed.

einsacken, *v.sep.* **1.** *v.i.* (*sein*) (*of platform, roof, etc.*) to sag; (*of pers.*) **in den Knien e.,** to sag at the knees. **2.** *v.tr.* to sack (potatoes, grain, wool, etc.); to pack (wool, etc.) into bags; *F:* **eine hübsche Summe Geld e.,** to rake in a pretty sum of money. **3. sich einsacken,** (*of tumour, etc.*) to become encysted, to encyst; (*of bowel, etc.*) to invaginate; **Einsackung** *f,* encystment; invagination.

einsäen, *v.tr. sep.* to sow, scatter (seed).

einsagen, *v.tr. sep.* **j-m etwas e.,** to whisper (word, etc.) to s.o.; **einem Mitschüler e.,** to prompt a classmate; **nicht e.!** no prompting!

einsägen, *v.tr. sep.* **etwas e.,** to saw into sth.; *Bookb:* **(die Bünde) e.,** to saw (book).

einsalben, *v.tr. sep.* **j-n e.,** to rub s.o. with ointment, to rub ointment into s.o.; **j-n, einen Körperteil, (mit etwas) e.** to rub s.o., a part of the body (with oil, etc.); to rub (oil, etc.) into s.o., into a part of the body; to apply (oil, etc.) to a part of the body; *Med:* to embrocate (affected part of the body, etc.); **sich** *dat.* **die Haut, seine Haut, sich, mit Öl e.,** to rub oil into one's skin.

einsalzen, *v.tr. sep.* (*a*) to salt (down) (meat, fish, etc.); to salt (herring); to cure (meat, fish, etc.) (by salting); to brine, souse (meat, fish, etc.); to pickle (meat, fish, gherkins, etc.); **eingesalzenes Fleisch,** salt meat, salted meat, (*b*) *Leath:* to cure (skins).

einsam, *a.* lonely (place, life, cottage, pers., etc.); solitary (pers., life, etc.); secluded (place, life, etc.); *Lit:* lone, lonesome (pers., place, life, etc.); **einsame Lage,** retired, secluded, position (of house, etc.); **ein einsamer Flecken,** a lonely, secluded, spot; **in einsames Gebet versunken sein,** to be deep in solitary prayer; **sich e. fühlen,** to feel lonely, *Lit. & F:* to feel lonesome; **er saß da e. und allein,** he sat there all by himself; **ein einsames Leben führen, e. leben,** to live in solitude, in seclusion; to lead a lonely life; **e. gelegen,** lonely, solitary; *Nat. Hist:* **e. lebend,** solitary.

einsamenlappig, *a. Bot:* monocotyledonous; **einsamenlappige Pflanze,** monocotyledon.

Einsamkeit, *f.* (*a*) solitude; loneliness; secluded position, seclusion (of house, etc.); **die E. lieben,** to be fond of solitude, to like being alone; **in E. leben,** to live in solitude, in seclusion; **Wunsch nach E.,** desire for solitude; **er litt unter seiner E.,** he suffered from (his) loneliness; **in der E.,** *Lit:* **den Einsamkeiten, schlafloser Nächte,** in the solitude of sleepless nights; (*b*) lonely place; **in dieser E. kann ich nicht leben,** I cannot live in this lonely place.

einsammeln, *v.tr. sep.* to collect (money); to collect, gather (rents, contributions, etc.); *A. & Lit:* to gather in (harvest); *Sch:* (*of pupil*) to collect (up) (exercise-books, etc.); (*of teacher*) to collect in (exercise-books, etc.).

einsargen, *v.tr. sep.* to put (corpse) in a coffin; to coffin (corpse); **in einem dunklen Kellergeschoß eingesargt leben,** to live confined in a dark basement; **seine Hoffnungen e.,** to bury one's hopes; *F:* **du kannst dich e. lassen!** go and shoot yourself! go and bury yourself! **ehe ich das täte, würde ich mich lieber gleich e. lassen,** I would die rather than do it! I would sooner die!

Einsattlung, *f.* pass, col, saddle(-back) (of mountain).

Einsatz, *m.* **1.** insertion (of sth.); inserting of sth.); putting in, fixing (of sth.); *Dressm: etc:* putting in, letting in, insertion (of piece of material, etc.). **2.** (*a*) wagering, betting (of sum of money); depositing (of sum of money) (for sth.); risking (of one's life, etc.); **der E. des Lebens für eine Idee,** risking, the risk of, the risking of, one's life for an idea; **unter E. seines Lebens,** at the risk of one's life; **der E. einer hohen Summe lohnt sich,** it pays to wager a high stake; **durch den E. einer bestimmten Summe garantiert der Entleiher die Rückgabe des Gegenstandes,** the borrower gives security for the return of the article by depositing a certain sum of money; (*b*) stake; deposit (on bottles, books, etc.); pledge; risk; **ein Menschenleben ist ein zu hoher E.,** a human life is too high a stake; **seinen E. zurückziehen,** to withdraw one's stake; **machen Sie Ihre Einsätze,** put down your stakes, place your bets; (*c*) *Cards: etc:* pool. **3.** (*a*) use, employment (of labour, machines, troops, police, one's resources, etc.); **E. aller Kräfte,** summoning up of all one's powers, mustering of all one's energies; **der E. aller unserer Kräfte ist Voraussetzung für das Gelingen,** we must summon up every ounce of our energy to achieve success; **dieser Beruf verlangt den E. der ganzen Persönlichkeit,** this profession requires complete dedication on the part of the individual; (*b*) **zum E. bringen,** to use, employ (labour, etc.); to bring (machines) into use, to put (machines) into operation; **zum E. kommen,** (*of labour, etc.*) to be brought into action; (*of machines, etc.*) to be brought into use; to come into operation; **Maschinen im vollen E.,** machines in full operation; (*c*) *Mil: Navy: Av:* operation; *Mil: Navy:* action; engagement; *Mil.Av:* sortie; **Truppen, Polizei, Panzer, Flugzeuge, usw., zum E. bringen,** to bring, put, troops, police, tanks, aircraft, etc., into action; **zum E. kommen,** (*of troops, police, tanks, aircraft, etc.*) to be brought into action; **im E.,** (*of guns, tanks, etc.*) in action; in operation; (*of personnel*) on active service; *Mil.Av:* (*of personnel, aircraft*) on operational duties; **zum E. bereit,** (*of personnel*) ready for action; in operational readiness; (*of tanks, aircraft, etc.*) ready for use, ready for operations; **beim E.,** when in action; when going into action; under operational conditions; *Mil:* **bei besonderem E.,** on active service; **sie standen zwölf Stunden in pausenlosem E.,** they were in action for twelve hours on end; they saw continuous action for twelve hours; *Mil.Av:* **einen E. fliegen,** to fly a sortie; to fly a mission; **der E. war erfolgreich,** the sortie, the mission, was a success. **4.** (*a*) *Mus:* coming in, entry, joining in (of instrument, voice choir); entry (of theme in fugue, etc.); beginning; **der E. der Geige erfolgte zu früh,** the violin came in too early; **ein falscher E. kann das ganze Stück verderben,** (i) an entry at the wrong time, (ii) a false beginning, can spoil the whole piece; (*b*) *Mus:* sign to come in (for instrument, voice, choir) (*given by conductor or written on score*); **dem Chor einen falschen E. geben,** to bring in the choir at the wrong time; (*c*) *Mus:* entry; **der Chor verdarb alle Einsätze,** the choir spoiled all the entries; (*d*) *Ling:* initial glide; **fester E.,** rough glide; **leiser E.,** soft glide. **5.** *Row:* **E. der Ruder (ins Wasser),** attack; catch; **beim E. der Ruder ist zu beachten, daß ...,** in catching the stroke care should be taken that ...; **richtiger E. der Ruder,** correct attack, catch. **6.** filling *or* charge (to be) put into sth., *esp.* (*a*) filling (of respirator canister); (*b*) *Metall:* charge (for furnace, etc.). **7.** piece *or* part (to be) inserted; insert; insertion; *esp.* (*a*) *Dressm: Tail: etc:* piece let in; insertion; inset; panel; (man's) (false) shirt-front, *F:* dicky; (woman's) bodice-front, modesty-vest; gusset; (*b*) *Mus:* crook (of horn); (*c*) interchangeable, exchangeable, part; exchangeable point (of compasses); filler, renewable face (of hammer); (*d*) extra leaf, extension-leaf, extension(-piece) (of table); (*e*) removable pan, tray, etc.; removable stand; (*f*) *Mch: I.C.E:* liner (of cylinder); (*g*) *Mec.E:* tool, cutter, bit (*to be inserted in chuck*).

Einsatzbefehl, *m. Mil: etc:* operational order.

einsatzbereit, *a. Mil: etc:* (*of troops, tanks, etc.*) ready for action; (*of aircraft*) ready to take off; (*of ambulance, lifeboat, etc.*) ready for use, for service; **an alle Soldaten erging der Befehl, sich e. zu halten,** an order was sent out, issued, given, to all soldiers to stand by.

Einsatzbereitschaft, *f.* (*a*) willingness (to be of service); (*b*) *Mil: etc:* readiness for action (of troops, tanks, etc.); readiness for use, for service (of ambulance, lifeboat, etc.); **um die E. unserer Truppen zu erhöhen ...,** in order to increase the fighting efficiency of our troops.

Einsatzbericht, *m. Mil:* report on operation(s).

Einsatzbesprechung, *f. Mil: Mil.Av:* conference (*before operation*); *Mil.Av:* briefing.

Einsatzblende, *f. Phot:* interchangeable diaphragm.

einsatzfähig, *a. Mil: etc:* (*of troops, tanks, etc.*) fit for action; (*of aircraft*) fit for operational use; serviceable; (*of ambulance, lifeboat, etc.*) fit for use; available.

Einsatzfähigkeit, *f. Mil: etc:* fitness for action (of troops, tanks, etc.); fitness for use (of ambulance lifeboat, etc.).

Einsatzfahrzeug, *n. Fire-fighting: etc:* operations vehicle.

Einsatzgebeit, *n. Mil: Mil.Av:* operational area.

Einsatzhafen, *m. Navy:* base harbour; *Mil.Av:* operational airfield.

einsatzhärten, *v.tr. insep. Metall:* to case-harden (steel); to cement (steel); to carburize (steel); **im Zyanbad e.,** to cyanide (steel); **Einsatzhärten** *n*, **Einsatzhärtung** *f*, case-hardening; cementation; carburizing; cyaniding.

Einsatzleiter, *m. Navy:* gunnery control officer.

Einsatzmittel, *n. Metall:* case-hardening compound.

Einsatzofen, *m. Metall:* case-hardening furnace; carburizing furnace.

Einsatzraum, *m. Mil: Mil.Av:* operational area.

Einsatzring, *m. Mec.E: etc:* inserted ring; fitted ring.

Einsatzstahl, *m.* **1.** *Metall:* case-hardened steel; case-hardening steel. **2.** *Tls:* (cutter) bit; bit (of lathe tool).

einsatzstählen, *v.tr. insep. Metall:* = **einsatzhärten.**

Einsatzstück, *n.* piece (to be) inserted; insert; insertion; *Constr:* distance- piece; *cp.* **Einsatz** 7.

Einsatzteich, *m.* fish-pond (for preserving fish); fish-preserve.

Einsatzteil, *m.* = **Einsatzstück.**

Einsatzverpflegung, *f. Mil:* iron rations.

Einsatzzeichen, *n. Mus:* sign (for singer, instrument, choir) to come in (*given by conductor or on score*); signal to begin.

Einsatzzirkel, *m.* compasses with detachable legs.

einsäuern, *v.tr. sep. Ch: etc:* to acidify; *Agr:* **Futter e.,** to ensilage, ensile, silo (fodder); *Cu:* to pickle (cabbage, gherkins, etc.); *Bak:* to leaven (dough, bread); **Einsäuerung** *f*, *Ch: etc:* acidification; *Agr:* ensilage, ensilation (of fodder); *Cu:* pickling (of cabbage, gherkins, etc.); *Bak:* leavening (of bread).

Einsäuerungsbad, *n. Ch: etc:* acid bath.

Einsaug(e)mittel, *n.* absorbent.

einssaugen, *v.sep.* (*weak & strong*) **1.** *v.tr.* (*of pump, etc.*) to suck in, up, to draw in, up (air, liquid); (*of vacuum cleaner*) to suck in, take up (dust, etc.) (*of sponge, etc.*) to suck up, soak up, to absorb (water, etc.); (*of flower, etc.*) to drink in, take in, absorb (dew, etc.); (*of bees, etc.*) to suck (honey, etc.); (*of ground, etc.*) to drink in, imbibe, absorb (water, etc.); (*of wall, etc.*) to soak up (paint, liquid); (*of pers.*) to imbibe (fresh air, knowledge, ideas, etc.); **etwas mit der Muttermilch e.,** to suck in sth. with one's mother's milk; **j-s Worte gierig e.,** to suck in s.o.'s words. **2. sich einsaugen,** (*a*) (*of leeches, etc.*) to fasten on, to cling; (*of suction disc*) to cling, stick on; (*b*) (*of liquid, paint*) to soak in.

Einsaugungsmittel, *n.* absorbent.

einsäumen, *v.tr. sep.* to hem (garment, etc.); **etwas mit etwas e.,** to edge, hem, border, sth. with (lace, ribbon, etc.); **eine Straße mit Pappeln e.,** to border a road with poplars; **eine von, mit, Pappeln eingesäumte Straße,** a road bordered, edged, with poplars,

einsäurig, *a. Ch:* monoacid.

einschaben, *v.tr. sep. Tchn:* to scrape (sth.) to the required shape.

einschachteln. I. *v.tr. sep.* **1.** to box (sth.) in, to box (sth.) up; to put (sth.) in a box. **2. etwas in etwas** *acc.* **e.,** to fit, insert, sth. into sth.; **Gegenstände ineinander e.,** to fit things into one another, to nest (boxes, etc.); **etwas zwischen zwei Gegenstände e.,** to sandwich sth. between two things; **ineinander eingeschachtelt sein,** to be enclosed *or* to lie one within another; *Gram:* **eingeschachtelter Satz,** incapsulated clause; *Biol: A:* **Theorie der eingeschachtelten Urkeime,** encasement theory.

II. *vbl s.* **1. Einschachteln,** *n. in vbl senses.* **2. Einschachtelung,** *f.* (*a*)=II. 1; (*b*) *Gram:* incapsulated clause; **ein Satz voller Einschachtelungen,** an incapsulated sentence.

Einschachtelungstheorie, *f. Biol: A:* encasement theory.

einschalen. I. *v.tr. sep. Constr:* to encase, case in (sth.) (with boards, etc.); to lag (centre for arch); *Min: etc:* to coffer, plank, line (shaft, gallery).

II. *vbl s.* **1. Einschalen,** *n. in vbl senses.* **2. Einschalung,** *f.* (*a*)=II. 1; (*b*) *Constr:* boarding, planking (of roof, etc.); lagging (of centre for arch); framework, framing, shuttering (for concrete work, etc.); *Min:* casing, frame-work (of shaft, gallery).

einschalig, *a.* having, with, one skin *or* shell; *Moll:* univalve, univalvular; *Geom:* (hyperboloid) of one sheet.

Einschaltbild, *n. Print:* inset.

Einschaltblatt, *n. Print:* interpolated sheet; inset.

einschalten. I. *v.tr. sep.* **1.** (*a*) to insert (word, passage, etc.) (in book, etc.); to put in, interpolate (remarks, corrections, etc.) (in text); to ask (s.o.) to join (discussion, etc.), to invite (s.o.) (into discussion); to call in, use (s.o.) as mediator, etc.); to call upon (s.o.'s) good offices; **j-n in die Verhandlungen e.,** to call s.o. in on the negotiations; *Gram:* **eingeschalteter Satz,** interpolated clause; parenthetical clause, incidental clause; *Geol:* **eingeschaltete Schichten,** intercalary strata; (*b*) *Chr:* to intercalate (day, month, year); **eingeschalteter Tag, Monat, eingeschaltetes Jahr,** intercalary day, month, year. **2.** (*a*) *El.E:* to cut in, switch in (resistance); **einen Kondensator in den Stromkreis e.,** to insert a condenser in the circuit; (*b*) *El.E:* to switch on (current, machine, etc.), *abs.* to switch on; (*c*) *Aut:* **die Kupplung e.,** to let in the clutch; **den ersten Gang e.,** to go into first, bottom, gear. **3. sich einschalten,** (*a*) *El.E:* (*of current, machine, etc.*) to switch itself on (automatically); (*b*) (*of pers.*) to intervene; *F:* to step in; to join in (a conversation, discussion, etc.); **nachdem die Verhandlungen gescheitert waren, schaltete sich Herr X ein,** after the negotiations had broken down, Mr X stepped in, intervened.

II. *vbl s.* **1. Einschalten,** *n. in vbl senses.* **2. Einschaltung,** *f.* (*a*)=II. 1; *also:* insertion, interpolation (of word, passage, etc.) (in book, etc.); intercalation (of day, etc.); (*b*) interpolation, interpolated passage; insertion, inserted passage; *Gram:* interpolated clause, parenthesis; (*c*) *Chr:* intercalation.

Einschalter, *m. El.E:* circuit-closer; switch.

Einschalthebel, *m.* starting lever.

Einschaltier, *n. Moll:* univalve.

Einschaltknopf, *m. El.E:* push-button switch.

Einschaltmotor, *m. El.E:* starting motor.

Einschaltstellung, *f. El.E:* on-position.

Einschaltstrom, *m. El.E:* starting current.

Einschaltungszeichen, *n. Print:* insertion mark; caret.

Einschaltvorrichtung, *f. El.E:* switchgear.

einschanzen, *v.tr. sep. Mil:* to entrench (position, etc.); **sich e.,** to entrench oneself.

einschärfen, *v.tr. sep.* **j-m etwas e.,** to inculcate, impress, sth. on s.o., s.o.'s mind; **j-m dringend e., etwas zu tun,** to impress strictly upon s.o. to do sth., to give s.o. strict instructions to do sth.; **ich hatte ihm dringend eingeschärft, daß er kommen sollte,** I had strictly impressed upon him that he should come; **du mußt (es) ihm e., daß . . . ,** you must impress upon him that . . . .

einscharig, *a.* **1.** *Agr:* single(-furrow) (plough). **2.** *Geom:* **einscharige Regelfläche,** singly ruled surface.

einscharren, *v.tr. sep.* **1.** to bury (s.o., sth.) hastily; to hide (sth.) in the ground; to cover (sth., corpse) over (thinly) with earth; (*of cat, dog*) to scratch earth over (sth.) **2.** (*of animal*) **sich einscharren,** to dig, burrow, itself in.

einschattig, *a. Geog:* heteroscian; **die Einschattigen,** the Heteroscians.

einschätzen. I. *v.tr. sep.* to value, to appraise (sth.); to estimate (the value of sth.); to form an estimate of (s.o.'s capabilities); **j-n, etwas, hoch, niedrig, e.,** to have a high, poor opinion of s.o.; to set great, little, store by sth.; **j-n, etwas, falsch, richtig, e.,** to form a false, true, estimate of s.o., sth.; **wie schätzen Sie ihn ein?** what is your opinion of him? **er schätzt sich zu hoch ein,** he has too high an opinion of himself.

II. *vbl s.* **1. Einschätzen,** *n. in vbl senses.* **2. Einschätzung,** *f.* (*a*)=II. 1; *also:* valuation, appraisal (of sth.); assessment, estimation (of s.o.'s capabilities, etc.); (*b*) estimation, estimate; opinion; **meine E. hat sich als richtig erwiesen,** my estimate proved to be correct.

einschaufeln, *v.tr. sep.* **1.** to shovel in (earth, etc.); to shovel (earth, etc.) into (hole, etc.). **2.** to bury (sth., *F:* s.o.).

einschaukeln, *v.tr. sep.* **1.** to rock (s.o.) to sleep; to lull (s.o.). **2.** *Av.: F:* **j-n e.,** to take s.o. on his first flight as a passenger; **eingeschaukelt werden,** to get used to flying.

Einscheibe, *f. Mec.E:* single(-sheave) pulley.

Einscheibenkupplung, *f. Aut:* single-plate clutch.

einschenken, *v.tr. sep.* **1.** to pour out (wine, water, etc.); **j-m ein Glas e.,** to pour out a glass for s.o., to fill s.o.'s glass; **er schenkte mir noch einmal ein,** he poured me out another glass, he filled up my glass again; *B:* **Du schenkest mir voll ein,** my cup runneth over; *F:* **j-m reinen Wein e.,** to tell s.o. the truth; to come out into the open. **2.** *Sp:* to pass (the ball).

einscheren, *v.tr. sep.* (*strong*) **1.** *Carp:* to mortise (one piece of wood to another); to join, clamp, together (two pieces of wood) with a tenon and mortise. **2.** *Nau:* to reeve (a rope).

einschichten, *v.tr. sep.* to put, arrange, (thgs) in layers; to arrange (sth.) in, fit (sth.) in (*among layers of other thgs*); **etwas in einen Schrank e.** to put, stack, sth. away in a cupboard (*among layers of other thgs*); *Geol:* **Sandstein mit eingeschichtetem Quarz,** sandstone interstratified, intercalated, with quartz.

einschichtig, *a.* (*a*) having one layer, *Geol:* one stratum; (*b*) *F:* single, unmarried; **e. leben,** to live alone.

einschicken, *v.tr. sep.* to send in, send up (application, money, bill, etc.); **wir schicken Ihnen unsere Rechnung ein,** we are forwarding our account to you.

Einschieb(e)brett, *n.* movable shelf (of bookcase, etc.); extra leaf, extension-leaf (of table).

einschieben. I. *v.tr. sep.* (*strong*) (*a*) **etwas in etwas e.,** to slide, push, sth. into sth.; **eine Schublade e.,** to close a drawer; **etwas in den Backofen e.,** to put sth. into the oven; *Typewr:* **das Papier e.,** to insert, feed, the paper (into the machine); (*b*) to insert (sth. into sth.); to push, *F:* shove (sth. into sth.); to interpolate (words, passage) (into text); **etwas zwischen andere Dinge e.,** to put sth. in among *or* between other things; **diese Stelle ist später eingeschoben,** this passage is a later interpolation; **eine besondere Mahlzeit e.,** to fit in an extra meal (between other meals); **eine Vorlesung e.,** to fit in, put in, an extra lecture; **eine Bedingung in einen Kontrakt e.,** to insert a clause into a contract; *Gram:* **eingeschobener Satz,** interpolated clause, parenthetical clause, incidental clause; *Ling:* **eingeschobener Konsonant,** inserted, epenthetic, consonant.

II. *vbl s.* **1. Einschieben,** *n. in vbl senses.* **2. Einschiebung,** *f.* (*a*)=II. 1; *also:* insertion, interpolation (of sth. into sth.); (*b*) inserted piece, passage; insertion; interpolated piece, passage; interpolation; *Gram:* interpolated clause; parenthetical clause, incidental clause.

Einschieb(e)satz, *m. Gram:* incidental clause, parenthetical clause.

Einschiebsel, *n.* **-s/-,** insertion, interpolation; inserted, interpolated, passage.

einschienen, *v.tr. sep. Surg:* to splint (a limb), to put (a limb) in splints.

Einschienenbahn, *f. Rail:* monorail.

Einschienenhängebahn, *f. Rail:* overhead monorail.

einschießen. I. *v.tr. sep.* (*strong*) **1.** (*a*) *Artil:* **ein Geschütz e.,** to range a gun; **ein Gewehr e.,** to break in a (new) rifle; *F:* **auf etwas eingeschossen sein,** to be experienced in sth., well versed in sth.; to know all the tricks of the trade; (*b*) *Artil:* **sich e.,** to range (a gun) **(auf ein Ziel,** on a target), to find the range (of a target); to register. **2.** to breach, make a breach in, (walls, etc.) by gunfire; to batter down, demolish, destroy, (walls, etc.) by gunfire. **3.** to give, contribute (money) (to an enterprise, etc.). **4.** (*a*) to set (bread) in the oven; (*b*) to load (a ship) (with ballast); (*c*) *Bookb:* **ein Blatt e.,** to insert a leaf. **5.** *Tex:* **den Schuß e.,** to pick; to shoot the weft. **6.** *Fb:* to shoot (the ball) (into goal).

II. **einschießen,** *v.i.* (*sein*) (*of water, etc.*) to rush in, to come rushing in; **in etwas** *acc.* **e.,** to rush into sth.

III. *vbl s.* **Einschießen,** *n. in vbl senses; also:* (*a*) *Artil:* registration; (*b*) demolition, destruction, (of walls, etc.) by gunfire.

Einschießofen, *m. Bak:* peel oven.

Einschießverfahren, *n. Artil:* registration; ranging.

Einschießziel, *n. Artil:* registration target.

einschiffen. I. *v.tr. sep.* to embark (troops, goods, etc.); to ship (goods, etc.); to bring, take, (supplies, etc.) on board; **hundert Kisten sind eingeschifft worden,** a hundred crates have been shipped, taken on board; **sich e.,** to go on board (a ship); to embark; to take passage **(nach,** for) (country, port); **er schiffte sich nach Amerika ein,** he embarked for America; **er schiffte sich in Hamburg ein,** he boarded a ship

at Hamburg; **er schiffte sich in Southampton nach Afrika ein,** at Southampton he boarded a ship for Africa.

II. *vbl s.* **Einschiffen** n., **Einschiffung** *f. in vbl senses; also:* embarkation (of troops, goods, etc.); shipment, embarkment (of goods, etc.).

einschiffig, *a. Arch:* **einschiffige Kirche,** church consisting of a nave only; **einschiffiger Saal,** undivided hall.

Einschiffungserlaubnis, *f.* loading permit; (*for pers.*) permission to embark.

Einschiffungshafen, *m.* port of embarkation.

Einschiffungskosten, *pl.* shipping charges.

Einschiffungsoffizier, *m.* embarkation officer.

einschirren, *v.tr. sep.* to harness (horse, etc.) (to cart, etc.); to hook in (horse).

einschlachten, *v.tr. sep.* to kill, slaughter (an animal, *esp.* pig) (for one's own use).

einschlafen, *v.i. sep.* (*strong*) (*sein*) (*a*) to fall asleep; to go to sleep; *F:* to drop, doze, off; **wieder e.,** to go back to sleep again; **nicht e. können,** to be unable to get to sleep; (*b*) to die (peacefully), to pass away (peacefully); (*c*) (*of limbs*) to go to sleep, to become numb; **das Bein ist mir eingeschlafen,** my leg has gone to sleep, *F:* I have got pins and needles in my leg; (*d*) (*of correspondence*) to cease (gradually), to be (gradually) discontinued; (*of friendship*) to cease (gradually), to peter out, to die a natural death; (*of conversation*) to die down, to flag; (*of wind*) to die down, to slacken, to abate; (*of custom*) to die out, to fall into disuse; **dieser Brauch ist langsam eingeschlafen,** this custom gradually died out; **eine Angelegenheit e. lassen,** to let an affair peter out, die a natural death; **damit schlief die Sache ein,** there the matter rested, dropped.

einschläfern, *v.tr. sep.* (*a*) to lull (s.o.) to sleep; to send (s.o.) to sleep; to make (s.o.) drowsy; **diese Musik hat eine einschläfernde Wirkung,** this music is soporific; *Med:* **einschläferndes Mittel,** narcotic; soporific; opiate; **einschläfernder Trank,** sleeping draught; (*b*) *Vet:* **ein Tier e.,** to put an animal to sleep; **ein Tier e. lassen,** to have an animal put to sleep; (*c*) **j-n durch falsche Hoffnungen, Versprechungen, usw., e.,** to lull s.o. with false hopes, promises, etc.; **j-n durch Schmeicheleien e.,** to lull s.o. (into a sense of false security) by flattery; **sein Gewissen e.,** to soothe, salve, one's conscience; **j-s Verdacht e.,** to allay s.o.'s suspicions.

einschläfrig, *a. Furn:* **einschläfriges Bett,** single bed.

Einschlag, *m.* **1.** (*a*) striking, hitting (of lightning, bomb, projectile) (on sth.); burst (of bomb, shell); *Artil: etc:* impact (of bomb, projectile) (on sth.); **nach dem Gewitter wurden vier Einschläge gemeldet,** after the storm, the lightning was reported to have struck four times; (*b*) hole, scar (on building, wall, etc.) (made by projectile, bomb, etc.); (*c*) *Golf:* putt. **2.** handshake (after bargain is made); **nach dem E. galt der Handel als abgeschlossen,** a handshake clinched the bargain. **3.** *Constr:* (door-, window-)aperture (in building). **4.** *Dressm:* **einen E. machen,** (i) to make a tuck (in dress, etc.); (ii) to turn up the hem (of dress, skirt). **5.** (paper) cover (for book). **6.** *Tex:* (*a*) weft, woof, filling; (*b*) machine-spun twist, mule-twist. **7.** *Wine-m:* preparation for clarifying wine; pearl. **8.** *For:* nursery (for young trees). **9.** *For:* (*a*) felling (of trees, timber); cutting (of wood, timber); (*b*) amount (of wood, timber) felled *or* to be felled; cut (of wood, timber); fell; felling rate. **10.** infusion; admixture; element; **ein Roman mit starkem religiösen E.,** a novel with a strong element of religion; **ein Drama mit lyrischem E.,** a drama with lyrical elements; **ein Gesicht mit stark orientalischem E.,** a face showing marked oriental characteristics; **das Gedicht hat einen E. ins Preziöse,** the poem has a touch, hint, of preciosity; **die Bevölkerung hat stark negroiden E.,** the population has a strong infusion of negro blood; **er sprach Deutsch mit starkem sächsischen E.,** his German was heavily tinged with Saxon.

Einschlag(e)garn, *n. Tex:* weft-yarn.

Einschlag(e)grube, *f. Agr: Hort:* trench (for plants, young trees, etc.).

Einschlag(e)messer, *n.* clasp-knife, pocket-knife.

einschlagen, *v. sep.* (*strong*) I. *v.tr.* **1.** (*a*) to knock in, hammer in, drive in (nail, wedge, post etc.); to drive home (a nail); **einen Nagel in etwas** *acc.* **e.,** to knock, hammer, drive, a nail into sth.; **die Katze schlug ihre Krallen tief in sein Fleisch ein,** the cat dug its claws deep into his flesh; (*b*) *Tex:* **den Schuß e.,** to pick; to shoot the weft; (*c*) *Cu:* **Eier (in Suppe, usw.) e.,** to break eggs (into soup, etc.); (*d*) *Print: etc:* to drive, press (stamp, etc.) (into matrix, etc.); (*e*) *Golf:* to hole (the ball); to drive (the ball) (into hole). **2. Pflanzen e.,** to put plants (temporarily) in the earth; **Möhren im Keller e.,** to store carrots in the cellar (*keeping them covered with earth*). **3.** to wrap up, envelop (sth.) (in paper, cloth, etc.); **jedes Stück ist in Papier eingeschlagen,** each piece is wrapped in paper; **soll ich's e.?** shall I wrap it? **4. den Boden eines Fasses e.,** to stave in the bottom of a cask; **j-m die Fenster e.,** to break s.o.'s windows; **j-m den Schädel e.,** to crack s.o.'s skull, *F:* to bash s.o.'s head in; **die Tür e.,** to batter down, burst open, the door. **5.** to take (a road, direction); **er schlug die Richtung nach dem Dorf ein,** he took the path towards the village; **den kürzesten Weg e.,** to take the shortest way, road; **einen falschen Weg e.,** (i) to take a wrong turning; to get on the wrong track; to stray from the right path; to make a wrong choice (of profession, etc.); (ii) to use the wrong method; **er blieb auf dem einmal eingeschlagenen Weg,** he kept to the road once he had taken it; he held to his course; **einen anderen Weg e.,** (i) to take another road; (ii) to try another way, a different method; **den Weg der Tugend e.,** to follow, choose, the path of virtue; **eine Laufbahn e.,** to enter upon a career; **einen schnelleren Schritt e.,** to quicken one's pace (when walking). **6.** to fold (sth.) over, down; to fold, turn, (sth.) up; **ein Blatt in einem Buch e.,** to turn down a page in a book; *Dressm:* **den Saum eines Kleides e.,** to turn up the hem of a dress. **7.** *Wine-m:* to match (wine); to clarify (wine) with pearl. **8.** *For:* to fell (trees, timber); to cut (wood, timber). **9.** *Aut:* to lock (road wheels, steering wheel) over; *abs.* **(stark) nach links, rechts, e.,** to lock (hard) over to the left, right.

II. **einschlagen,** *v.i.* **1.** (*haben*) **auf j-n, auf ein Tier, usw., e.,** to belabour, to rain blows on, s.o., an animal, etc.; **er schlug unbarmherzig auf das Pferd ein,** he beat the horse unmercifully. **2.** (*haben*) **in etwas** *acc.* **e,,** (*a*) (*of claw, etc.*) to dig into (flesh, etc.); (*b*) (*occ. sein*) (*of lightning, bomb, projectile*) to strike, hit, sth.; (*of shell, bomb*) to land somewhere, on sth.; **der Blitz ist, hat, in das Haus eingeschlagen,** the house has been struck by lightning; **eine Bombe, ein Geschoß, ist in das Haus eingeschlagen,** a bomb, a shell, has hit the house; **der Blitz, es, hat viermal eingeschlagen,** the lightning struck four times; **diese Nachricht schlug wie eine Bombe ein,** this news came like a bombshell, like a bolt from the blue; (*c*) (*of book, etc.*) to have reference to sth., to concern sth.; to be of relevance to sth.; **das schlägt nicht in mein Fach ein,** that's not my department, province, *F:* that's off my beat, that's not (in) my line. **3.** to shake, clasp, hands (on a bargain); to agree to a proposal; **eingeschlagen!** agreed! *F:* it's a deal! **er hat eingeschlagen,** (i) he gave me his hand on the bargain, on it; (ii) he has agreed, accepted; **schlagen Sie ein!** shake hands on it! it's a bargain! **4.** (*haben*) *Tex:* to pick; to shoot the weft. **5.** (*haben*) (*of paint*) to soak in and become flat, dull. **6.** (*haben*) *Constr:* (*of beams, etc.*) to sag. **7.** (*haben, sein*) (*of thg*) to be a success, *F:* to take, catch, on; (*of pers.*) to be a success; **die Ernte ist gut eingeschlagen,** the crop is a success; **diese Weizensorte hat, ist, hier nicht eingeschlagen,** this sort of wheat has not been a success, has not taken on, here.

III. *vbl s.* **Einschlagen,** *n. in vbl senses; also:* impact; *cp.* **Einschlag.**

Einschlag(e)tuch, *n.* wrapping cloth, wrapper (for delivering goods); shawl (for baby).

Einschlagfaden, *m. Tex:* weft, weft-yarn, weft thread.

Einschlagfutter, *n. Mec.E:* socket-chuck.

Einschlaggarnspulen, *n. Tex:* weft-winding.

Einschlagheft, *n. Tls.* handle of a folding knife *or* tool.

einschlägig, *a.* (*a*) relevant, pertinent (literature, passage, authority, etc.); (chapters, etc.) concerned; **einschlägige Literatur,** literature relevant to the subject: relevant literature; (*b*) *Com:* **in allen einschlägigen Geschäften zu haben,** obtainable from all stockists, from your dealer; **alle einschlägigen Artikel,** the whole range of articles (in a certain line).

Einschlagpapier, *n.* wrapping-paper, packing-paper; brown paper.

Einschlagpunkt, *m. Ball: etc:* point of impact.

Einschlagseide, *f. Tex:* tram(-silk).

Einschlagspuler, *m. Tex:* weft-winder.

Einschlagwecker, *m. Tg: etc:* single-stroke bell.

Einschlagwinkel, *m.* **1.** *Ball:* angle of impact. **2.** *Aut:* **E. der Lenkung,** angle of lock (of steering).

einschlämmen, *v.tr. sep.* to saturate the ground with water around ((i) young plant, tree, (ii) pile or stake being driven); *Civ.E: etc:* to sluice (the ground) with water (*to consolidate it*).

einschleichen (sich), *v.refl. sep.* (*strong*) **sich in etwas** *acc.* **e.,** to creep, steal, slip, *F:* sneak, into sth.; **in seine Übersetzung haben sich verschiedene Fehler eingeschlichen,** various errors have crept into his translation; **Sorge schlich sich in ihre Herzen ein,** anxiety crept, stole, into their hearts: **Agenten fremder Mächte haben sich in unser Land eingeschlichen,** agents of foreign powers have infiltrated, smuggled themselves, into our country; **sich in j-s Gunst e.,** to worm one's way into s.o.'s favour; **sich in j-s Herz e.,** to win s.o.'s heart, affections; to insinuate oneself into s.o.'s affections; **sich bei j-m e.,** (i) to worm one's way into s.o.'s confidence; (ii) to creep into s.o.'s home.

einschleifen, *v.tr. sep.* (*strong*) **1. etwas in etwas** *acc.* **e.,** to grind, cut, (pattern, groove, etc.) into, in, on (glass, metal, etc.). **2.** *I.C.E: etc:* **ein Ventil e.,** to grind (in) a valve, to reseat a valve; *Mec.E:* **den Kolben e.,** to grind in the piston; *El.E:* **die Bürsten e.,** to bed the brushes (of dynamo, etc.).

Einschliefer, *m.* grinding-tool, grinder.

Einschleifpaste, *f. Metalw:* grinding-paste, grinding-compound.

einschleppen. I. *v.tr. sep.* (*a*) to tow (boat, etc.) in; **einen Dampfer in den Hafen e.,** to tow a steamer into port; (*b*) to introduce, bring in, carry in (pest, contagious disease, etc.); **aus Frankreich eingeschleppte Kartoffelkäfer,** Colorado beetles carried in from France.

II. *vbl s.* **Einschleppen** *n.*, **Einschleppung** *f. in vbl senses; also:* introduction (of pest, contagious disease, etc.).

einschleusen. I. *v.tr. sep.* **etwas, j-n, in etwas** *acc.* **e.,** (*a*) to pass, channel, let, sth., s.o., into sth.; **Flüchtlinge in ein Lager e.,** to pass, channel, refugees into a camp; **Spione in ein Land, in eine Organisation, e.,** to infiltrate spies into a country, into an organisation, *F:* to feed spies into an organisation; **Geld in den Wirtschaftskreislauf e.,** to pump money into the economic system; (*in E.E.C.*) **Waren e.,** to let goods in on payment of the import levy; (*b*) to pass, let, sth., s.o., into sth.; **ein Schiff in ein Dock e.,** to pass a ship into a dock; *Hyd.E:* **j-n, etwas in eine Arbeitskammer e.,** to let s.o., sth., into a working chamber through an air lock.

II. *vbl s.* **Einschleusung,** *f. in vbl senses; also:* infiltration (of spies into a country); introduction (of s.o., sth., into sth.); (*in E.E.C.*) entry (of goods) on payment of the import levy.

Einschleusungspreis, *m.* (*in E.E.C.*) 'sluice-gate' price.

einschließen. I. *v.tr. sep.* (*strong*) **1.** (*a*) to lock (s.o., sth.) in, up; to shut (s.o., sth.) in, up; *Jur:* to put (s.o.) into prison, to imprison (s.o.); **ein Kind, einen Hund, in ein, in einem, Zimmer e.,** to lock, shut, up a child, a dog, in a room; **sich e.,** to lock, shut, oneself in; to shut oneself up (in room, etc.); *A. & F:* to closet oneself (in one's room); **sie schloß sich in ihr, in ihrem, Zimmer ein,** she locked herself in her room; **in seinem Zimmer eingeschlossen,** shut up, *F:* closeted, in his room; (*b*) **etwas in Klammern e.,** to put, enclose, (word, etc.) in brackets; to bracket (word, etc.); to put (word, etc.) in parentheses. **2.** to enclose (sth.) (**mit etwas,** in, with, by, sth.); to surround, encircle (sth.) (**mit etwas,** with, by, sth.); to encompass (sth.) (**mit etwas,** by sth.); to girdle (sth.) (**mit etwas,** with sth.); *Mil:* to surround, encircle, invest (town, etc.); *Pol:* to enclave (land, territory) (in other territory); **einen Garten mit einer Hecke e.,** to enclose, surround, a garden with a hedge, to hedge in a garden; **die Mauern, welche die Stadt einschließen,** the walls that surround, encircle, girdle, encompass, the town; **ein von Bergen eingeschlossener See,** a lake surrounded by, set among, mountains; **von Felsen eingeschlossen,** shut in, enclosed, by rocks; *Lit:* rock-girt; **ein Lager mit Palisaden e.,** to surround a camp with palisades, to palisade a camp; **eine Festung e.,** to surround, encircle, a fort; **das Schiff ist vom Eis eingeschlossen,** the ship is hemmed in by the ice, is trapped, caught, in the ice; **drei Bergleute sind noch in der Grube eingeschlossen,** three miners are still trapped in the pit. **3.** (*a*) to include,

embrace, contain, comprise (sth.) (in sth.); **etwas in etwas** *acc.* **e.,** to include sth. in sth.; **in etwas** *dat.* **eingeschlossen sein,** to be included in sth.; **das Frühstück ist im Preis eingeschlossen,** the terms are inclusive of breakfast; **schließen Sie mich in ihr Gebet ein,** remember me in your prayers; **dieser eine Satz schließt alle unsere Probleme ein, in diesem einen Satz sind alle unsere Probleme eingeschlossen,** this sentence embraces all our problems, sums up all our problems in a nutshell, all our problems are summed up in this one sentence; (*b*) *Ch:* (*of substance*) to occlude (gas, compound).

II. *vbl s.* **1. Einschließen,** *n. in vbl senses; also:* inclusion (of sth.) (in sth.); enclosure of land) (in estate, etc.); *Ch:* occlusion (of gas, compound). **2. Einschließung,** *f.* (*a*)=II. 1; (*b*) *Mil: etc:* encirclement (of town, etc.); (*c*) *Jur:* imprisonment; *cp.* **Einschluß.**

einschließlich. 1. *adv.* including; inclusive; inclusively; **bis Seite zwangig e.,** up to and including page twenty, *U.S:* through page twenty; **vom vierten bis zwölften Februar e.,** from the fourth to the twelfth of February inclusive(ly), *U.S:* (from) the fourth through the twelfth of February. **2.** *prep.* (+*gen.*) inclusive (of), including; **Preis e. Porto und Verpackung,** price inclusive of, including, postage and packing; **Preise e. (der) Bedienung,** terms inclusive of service; **im Wagen waren fünf Leute e. des Fahrers,** there were five people in the car including the driver.

einschlitzen, *v.tr. sep.* to slit, slash (cloth, garment); to make a slit in (cloth, etc.).

einschlucken, *v.tr. sep.* (*a*) to swallow (food, etc.); (*b*) **eine Beleidigung e.,** to swallow, put up with, *F:* stomach, an insult; (*c*) (*of soil, etc.*) to absorb (liquid).

einschlummern, *v.i. sep.* (*sein*) (*a*) to fall asleep, to fall into a slumber; (*b*) *Poet:* to die (peacefully), to pass away (peacefully).

einschlüpfen, *v.i. sep.* (*sein*) to slip, slide, in; to slip, slide (into room, etc.).

einschlürfen, *v.tr. sep.* to sip (drink); to drink in (a liquid); **gierig e.,** to gulp down (a liquid).

Einschluß, *m.* **1.** (*a*) *Mil: etc:* encircling, encirclement (of town, etc.); *Pol: etc:* enclavement (of territory); (*b*) inclusion (of sth.) (in sth.); enclosure (of land) (in estate, etc.); (*c*) *Ch:* occlusion (of gas, compound); *cp.* **einschließen** II. **2.** (*adv. phrase*) **mit E.** +*gen.*, **unter E.** +*gen.*, inclusive of; including; with the inclusion of; **Preise mit E. der Bedienung,** terms inclusive of service; **der Preis ist fünf Mark mit E. der Verpackung,** the price is five marks including, inclusive of, packing; **die interessierten Staaten unter E. Ägyptens waren zur Konferenz eingeladen,** the countries interested, concerned, including Egypt, were invited to the conference. **3.** (*a*) words in brackets; parenthesis; (*b*) *A:* enclosure (in letter). **4.** (*a*) *Geol:* inlier; (*b*) *Miner: Geol:* enclosure, inclusion; xenolith; xenocryst; **endogener E.,** endogenous enclosure; **exogener E.,** exogenous enclosure.

Einschlußblennorrhöe, *f. Med:* gonorrhoeal conjunctivitis; purulent ophthalmia.

Einschlußgebiet, *n.* enclave.

Einschlußklammer, *f. Print:* bracket; parenthesis.

Einschlußlack, *m. Microscopy:* varnish used for ringing cells.

Einschlußmittel, *n. Microscopy:* embedding medium; mounting medium; supporting medium.

Einschlußrohr, *n. Ch: etc:* sealed tube.

Einschlußthermometer, *n. Med. etc:* enclosed-scale thermometer.

Einschlußverbindung, *f. Ch:* adduct; inclusion compound, occlusion compound, clathrate compound (or urea, etc.).

einschlußweise, *adv.* parenthetically; by way of parenthesis.

Einschlußzeichen, *n. Print:* bracket parenthesis.

einschmalzen, *v.tr. sep.* (*a*) to oil, grease, lubricate (machine, etc.); (*b*) *Tex:* to oil, grease (wool).

Einschmalztrog, *m. Tex: etc:* oiling-trough, greasing-trough.

einschmeicheln (sich), *v.refl. sep.* **sich bei j-m e.,** to worm oneself into s.o.'s good graces; to ingratiate oneself with s.o.; **sich in j-s Gunst e.,** to curry favour with s.o., to worm oneself into s.o.'s favour; **sich in j-s Herz e.,** to win s.o.'s heart, affections; **einschmeichelndes Wesen,** ingratiating, insinuating, ways, manner.

einschmeichlerisch, *a.* (*of manner, etc.*) insinuating, ingratiating.

einschmeißen, *v.tr. sep.* (*strong*) *F:* to break. smash (windows, etc.); to smash in (windows, etc.); **j-m die Fenster e.,** to break, smash, s.o.'s windows.

einschmelzen. I. *v.sep.* **1.** *v.i.* (*strong*) (*sein*) (*of substance*) to melt; to melt away. **2.** *v.tr.* (*strong, occ. weak*) (*a*) to melt down (metal object); to fuse, smelt (pig-metal, etc.); (*b*) to fuse, seal, (sth.) in (by melting process); (*c*) *Geol:* (*of rock*) to assimilate (neighbouring type of rock).

II. *vbl s.* **Einschmelzen** *n.*, **Einschmelzung** *f. in vbl senses; also:* fusion (of pig-metal, etc.).

Einschmelzflasche, *f. Ch: etc:* bottle with the aperture fused over.

Einschmelzglas, *n.* fusible glass.

Einschmelzkolben, *m.* melting flask.

Einschmelzprobe, *f. Metall:* melt-down test.

Einschmelzrohr, *n.*, **Einschmelzröhre,** *f. Ch:* sealed tube.

Einschmelzschlacke, *f. Metall:* first slag.

Einschmelzstelle, *f. Metall:* seal.

einschmiegen (sich), *v.refl. sep.* **das Städtchen schmiegt sich in die Bucht ein, liegt in die Bucht eingeschmiegt,** the little town nestles around the curve of the bay, follows the curve of the bay.

einschmieren, *v.tr. sep.* to oil, grease, lubricate (machine, etc.); to put polish on (shoes); *F:* to smarm (one's hair) (with brilliantine, etc.); **Leder, usw., mit Fett, Öl, e.,** to rub leather, etc., with grease, oil, to grease, oil, leather, etc.; **Leder, usw., mit Talg e.,** to tallow leather, etc.; **seine Steifel e.,** (i) to grease one's boots; (ii) to put polish on one's boots; **sich mit Sonnenöl e.,** to rub oneself with sun-tan oil; *F:* **er hat sich das Haar mit Brillantine eingeschmiert,** he has smarmed down his hair with brilliantine, has plastered his hair with brilliantine.

einschmuggeln, *v.tr. sep.* to smuggle in (goods, etc.); to import (goods, etc.) illegally; **eingeschmuggelte Waren,** smuggled goods; *Adm: etc:* contraband; **j-n in ein Land, in ein Haus, in eine Versammlung, usw., e.,** to smuggle s.o. into a country, a house, a meeting, etc.; **sich in ein Land, usw., e.,** to smuggle oneself into a country, etc.; to enter a country, etc., illegally; **sich in eine Versammlung e.,** to attend a meeting uninvited, *F:* to gate-crash, *U.S:* to crash, a meeting.

einschmutzen, *v.tr. sep.* **etwas e.,** to soil, dirty, sth. (completely); to get, make, sth. (very) dirty; **eingeschmutzt sein,** to be filthy.

einschnappen, *v.i. sep.* (*sein*) (*a*) (*of latch, catch, etc.*) to snap, click (home); to close, to fall into place (with a snap); (*of latch, fastening, etc.*) to catch; *Mec.E:* (*of catch in machine*) to engage; **die Tür schnappte ein,** the door closed with a click; **die Falle schnappt ein,** the trap snaps closed; (*b*) *F:* (*of pers.*) **eingeschnappt sein,** to be offended; to be sulking, *F:* to have the sulks; to have shut up like a clam; **sie ist leicht eingeschnappt, sie schnappt leicht ein,** she is very touchy; she takes offence very easily; she is very thin-skinned.

Einschnappfeder, *f.* snap-spring (of lock, etc.).

einschnarchen, *v.i. sep.* (*sein*) to fall asleep and snore; to fall asleep and start snoring.

einschneiden, *v. sep.* (*strong*) I. *v.tr.* **1.** (*a*) **etwas, ein Muster, usw., in etwas** *acc.* **e.,** to cut, incise, sth., a pattern, etc., in, into, sth.; to engrave, carve, a pattern, etc., on sth.; **seinen Namen in einen Baum, in eine Baumrinde, e.,** to carve one's name on a tree, in the bark of a tree; (*b*) **etwas e.,** to make a cut, notch, an incision, in sth.; to jag sth.; to score (joint of pork); *Surg:* **das Fleisch oberflächlich e.,** to make a superficial incision, superficial incisions, in the flesh; to scarify the flesh; *Mec.E:* **Kerben in ein Rad e.,** to notch a wheel **die Zähne eines Rads e.,** to cog a wheel; to cut the teeth of a cog-wheel; *Bookb:* **ein Buch e.,** to saw-cut (the back of) a book; *Cu:* **die Schwarte kreuzweise e.,** to make criss-cross cuts in the rind (of joint of pork); (*of cog-wheels, leaves, etc.*) **eingeschnitten,** notched; serrated; jagged; indented; *Her:* **lang eingeschnitten,** indentill(e)y; (*c*) *Artil:* to dig in (gun, battery); **eingeschnittene Batterie,** dug-in battery. **2.** (*a*) to cut (sth.); to cut up (sth.); **Holz nach den Angaben des Käufers e.,** to cut, cut up, timber to, according to, the customer's requirements; (*b*) *A:* to cut, harvest (corn, etc.).

II. **einschneiden,** *v.i.* (*haben*) **1. in etwas e.,** (*a*) (*of pers.*) to cut into sth.; *Surg:* **in das Fleisch e.,** to make an incision in the flesh; (*b*) (*of thg*) **in etwas e.** & *v.refl.* **sich in etwas e.,** to cut into sth.; **die Fesseln schnitten ihm tief in das Fleisch ein,** the chains, fetters, cut deep into his flesh; **im Laufe der Zeit hat sich der Fluß tief in den Fels eingeschnitten,** in the course of time the river has cut deeply into the rock; **ein tief eingeschnittenes Flußbett,** a deep river-valley; **tief eingeschnittenes Tal,** deep, steep-sided valley; canyon; (*c*) (*of events, measures, etc.*) to affect (s.o.'s life, etc.) profoundly; to cut right across (s.o.'s life, etc.); to make a decisive break, a great upheaval (in s.o.'s life, etc.); **ein Ereignis, das tief in ihr Leben einschnitt,** an event that meant a great upheaval in her life, that profoundly affected the course of her life, that had far-reaching consequences for her; (*d*) *Obst:* (*of child's head, etc.*) to appear between the labia (when about to be born). **2.** *Surv: Artil: etc:* to take cross-bearings.

III. *vbl s.* **1. Einschneiden,** *n. in vbl senses: also:* (*a*) incision (of sth.); (*b*) *Surv: Artil: etc:* location by cross-bearings; (*c*) *Obst:* appearance (of child's buttocks, etc.) between the labia; crowning (of child's head). **2. Einschneidung,** *f.*=III. 1 (*a*), (*b*).

IV. *pr.p.* & *a.* **einschneidend,** *in vbl senses; esp.* radical (change, measure, etc.); incisive (measure, etc.); fundamental (change, etc.); profound (effect, etc.); **das war für ihn ein einschneidendes Ereignis, Erlebnis,** this event, experience, had a most profound effect on him.

Einschneidesäge, *f. Bookb:* (bookbinder's) saw.

einschneidig, *a.* (*of blade, tool, sword, etc.*) one-edged, single-edged.

einschneien, *v.tr. sep.* (*usu. in passive*) **eingeschneit sein, werden,** to be, to become, covered with snow, to be snowed up, *U.S:* snowed under, to become, to get, snowed up, snowbound, *U.S:* snowed under; **das Auto wurde auf dem Wege zur Stadt eingeschneit,** on the way to the town the car became snowbound; the car was, got, snowed up on the way to the town; **wir waren tagelang, mehrere Wochen, eingeschneit,** we were snowed up for days, for several weeks.

Einschnitt, *m.* **1.** (*a*) incision; cut; **einen E. in die Haut machen,** to make an incision in the skin; **sofort nach dem E. muß die Wunde verbunden werden,** the wound must be bandaged immediately after the incision has been made; **oberflächlicher E. (in die Haut),** superficial incision (in the skin); scarification; **E. mit der Säge,** saw-cut; (*b*) *Tchn:* cut; (*in head of screw*) slot; (*in blade of penknife*) thumbnail notch; *Locksm:* ward (of key-bit); *Bot:* notch; serration (on leaf, etc.); **kerbenförmiger E.,** notch; nick; **(offener) E.,** opening; slot; **(zahnförmiger) E.,** indentation; tooth (on cog-wheel, etc.); *Her:* **mit langen Einschnitten versehen,** indentill(e)y; (*c*) *Civ.E: Rail:* cutting; cut; *Geol:* cleft; gorge; ravine. **2.** (*a*) *Pros:* caesura; *Rh: etc:* pause, break (in period, etc.), (*b*) break (in s.o.'s life, etc.); interruption, hiatus (in course of events, etc.); **die Heirat ist ein tiefer E. im Leben der Frau,** marriage cuts right across a woman's life; **die Übersiedlung nach Amerika bedeutete einen tiefen E. in ihrem Leben,** emigrating to America meant a great upheaval in their lives.

einschnittig, *a. Metalw: etc:* single-shear (joint); **einschnittige Nietung, Vernietung,** single-shear rivet joint.

Einschnittmeißel, *n. Tls:* ripping-chisel.

Einschnittmesser, *n. Surg:* bistoury.

einschnitzen, *v.tr. sep.* to cut, carve, incise (sth.) **(in, auf, etwas,** *acc.*, into, on, sth.).

einschnüren. I. *v.tr. sep.* (*a*) to tie up (package, etc.) (with string, etc.); to cord, cord up (bales); *Bookb:* to tie up (book); *Pyr:* to choke (rocket, etc.); (*b*) (*of tight garment, etc.*) ro constrict, restrict (s.o., part of body, etc.); *Med:* to strangulate, constrict (an organ); **sich e.,** (*of pers.*) to tight-lace oneself; to corset oneself; to lace oneself up (in a corset); to lace up one's corset, *A.* & *F:* one's stays; *Biol:* (*of cell, etc.*) to segment; **eingeschnürt,** (*of pers.*) strait-laced; *Bot:* (*of pod*) angiospermous; (*of pod, root, etc.*) constricted, moniliform; (*of cell*) segmented; (*c*) *Mil:* to encircle, hem in (body of troops, etc.).

II. *vbl s.* **1. Einschnüren,** *n. in vbl senses.* **2. Einschnürung,** *f.* (*a*)=II. 1; *also:* contriction, restriction (of part of body, etc.); tight-lacing; encirclement (of troops, etc.); *Med: Bot: etc:* strangulation (of organ, pod, etc.); *Biol:* segmentation (of cell); (*b*) bottleneck (in thoroughfare, etc.); narrow channel (in sth.); narrow point (in sth.); neck (in pipe, etc.).

einschränkbar, *a.* (*a*) (power, expenditure, etc.) that can be restricted, limited; (*b*) modifiable (statement, rule, etc.).

einschränken. I. *v.tr. sep.* **1.** (*a*) to limit, restrict, reduce, cut down (one's expenditure, expenses, etc.); to retrench (one's expenses); to restrain, curb (one's, s.o.'s, generosity, etc.); to

restrict (s.o.'s movement, freedom, etc.); **j-s Machtbefugnisse auf ein gewisses Gebiet e.,** to confine s.o.'s authority (to) within certain limits, (to) within a certain sphere; to limit s.o.'s authority to a certain sphere; to curtail s.o.'s authority; **wir müssen unsere Ausgaben auf ein vernünftiges Maß e.,** we must keep our expenditure within reasonable limits; **ich muß meinen Zigarettenverbrauch e.,** I have to cut down on cigarettes; **einschränkende Maßnahmen,** restrictive measures; **einschränkende Handelsgesetze,** restrictive trade laws; (*b*) to modify, qualify (rule, statement, condition, etc.); **die Bedingungen eines Testaments, eines Kontrakts, eines Vertrags, durch eine Klausel e.,** to modify, qualify, the terms of a will, a contract, a treaty, by means of a clause; **einschränkende Klausel,** modifying, qualifying, clause; **einschränkende Bedingungen,** modifying, qualifying, conditions; *Gram:* **einschränkende Partikel,** restrictive particle; modificative (particle); qualificative (particle). **2. sich einschränken,** to reduce one's standard, style, of living; to economize; to retrench; **sich auf das Nötigste e.,** to restrict, confine, limit, oneself to what is most essential, to the essentials; **ich muß mich zur Zeit sehr e.,** I have to live very frugally, I have to economize, at present, *F:* I have to tighten my belt now.

II. *vbl s.* **1. Einschränken,** *n. in vbl senses.* **2. Einschränkung,** *f.* (*a*)=II. 1; *also:* limitation, restriction, reduction (of s.o.'s expenses, expenditure, etc.); limitation, curtailment (of s.o.'s authority, etc.); modification, qualification (of terms, rule, statement, conditions, etc.); **E. der Ausgaben,** retrenchment; **ohne E.,** (to say, confirm, sth.) without reservation, unreservedly; (*b*) restriction, limit (on one's expenditure, etc.); **sich** *dat.* **Einschränkungen auferlegen,** to impose limits on one's expenditure; **nach Jahren von Einschränkungen und Entbehrungen,** after years of scraping and saving and doing without, after years of scraping and self-denial, after years of scrimping and pinching.

Einschränkungsmaßnahme, *f.* economy measure; measure to cut down expenditure.

Einschraub-, *comb.fm. Mec.E: etc:* screw-in . . . , screw-on . . . ; **Einschraubteil** *n,* screw-in, screw-on, part; **Einschraubthermometer** *n,* screw-in thermometer.

einschraubbar, *a.* screw-on, screw-in (machine part, etc.); **einschraubbarer Stöpsel,** screw plug; **einschraubbare Glühbirne,** screw-in electric light bulb.

einschrauben, *v.tr. sep.* to screw (sth.) on, in; to fasten (sth.) on, in, with a screw; **etwas in etwas** *acc.* **e.,** to screw sth. into sth.; **eine Glühbirne e.,** to screw in, put in, an electric light bulb; **dieser Maschinenteil kann aus- und eingeschraubt werden,** this part of the machine can be taken out and put back again, is removable.

Einschraublänge, *f. Mec.E:* length, depth, of engagement (of screw).

Einschrauböse, *f.* eye-bolt; screw-ring, screw-eye.

einschreibbar, *a. Geom:* inscribable.

Einschreib(e)brief, *m. Post:* registered letter.

Einschreib(e)gebühr, *f.* (*a*) *Adm: etc:* registration fee; enrolment fee; (*b*) *Post:* registration fee, *U.S:* registry fee; charge for registering a letter, etc.; registered post rate.

Einschreib(e)geld, *n.*=**Einschreib(e)gebühr.**

einschreiben. I. *v.tr. sep. (strong)* **1.** (*a*) to write in, put in, put down, enter (name, item, etc.); **etwas in ein Buch, in eine Liste, usw., e.,** to write, put, inscribe, sth. in a book, on a list, etc.; *Com:* to book, enter (item, etc.); **er schrieb seinen Namen, sich, in das Gästebuch ein,** he signed, entered, his name in the visitors' book *or* hotel register; **sich in eine Liste, usw., e.,** to enter, put down, one's name on a list, etc.; (*b*) to enrol (s.o.) (in club, etc.); to put down (child, etc.) (for school, etc.); to register (s.o., oneself) (at a university, etc.); to enter (s.o., horse, etc.) (for competition, race, etc.); **sich, j-n, als Mitglied eines Vereins e.,** to enrol oneself, s.o., as a member of a club; **sich e. lassen,** to give in one's name; to enrol oneself; to put oneself down (for course of study, etc.); to register (at university, etc.). **2.** *Post:* to register (letter, parcel, etc.); **eingeschriebener Brief, eingeschriebenes Paket,** registered letter, parcel; **einen Brief e. lassen,** to send a letter by registered post; to register a letter. **3.** *Geom:* to inscribe (figure) (within another figure); **einen Kreis in ein Polygon e.,** to inscribe a circle within a polygon; **eingeschriebener Kreis,** inscribed circle; **Mittelpunkt eines eingeschriebenen Kreises,** in-centre. **4. eine Feder e.,** to break in a (new) (fountain-)pen.

II. *vbl s.* **1. Einschreiben,** *n.* (*a*) *in vbl senses; also:* entry (of name, item, etc.) (on list, in ledger, etc.); inscription (of name, etc.) (on list, etc.); (*b*) *Post:* registered packet; **einen Brief per E. schicken,** to send a letter by registered post; (*on letter, etc.*) **'Einschreiben',** 'registered'. **2. Einschreibung,** *f. in vbl senses; also:* enrolment (of s.o.) (into club, etc.); registration (of s.o.) (at university, etc.).

Einschreib(e)paket, *n. Post:* registered parcel.

Einschreib(e)porto, *n. Post:* postal and registration charges; registered post rate; fee for postage of registered letter, parcel, etc.

Einschreiber, *m. Adm:* registrar; recorder.

Einschreib(e)sendung, *f. Post:* registered packet.

einschreiten. I. *v.i. sep. (strong) (sein)* **1.** to walk in, stride in (solemnly). **2.** to intervene; to interpose; to step in; to take action; *Sp:* (*of referee*) to intervene; **es wäre Zeit, daß die Polizei hier einschritte,** it is about time that the police took action, intervened, in this matter; **die Polizei schritt gegen die Demonstranten ein,** the police took action against the demonstrators; **energisch gegen etwas e.,** to take drastic measures, action, against sth.; to take drastic steps against sth.; *Jur:* **gerichtlich gegen j-n e.,** to go to law with s.o.; to take legal proceedings, measures, against s.o.; to proceed against s.o.; to take s.o. to court; to sue s.o.; (*of official body*) to prosecute s.o.

II. *vbl s.* **Einschreiten,** *n. in vbl senses; also:* intervention.

Einschrieb, *m.* **-(e)s/.** *Swiss: Post:* registration (of packet).

einschroten, *v.tr. sep.* to let down, lower, shoot (cask) (into cellar) (*by means of a parbuckle*).

einschrumpeln, *v.i. sep. (sein) F:*=**einschrumpfen.**

einschrumpfen. I. *v.i. sep. (sein)* (*of leaf, parchment, etc.*) to shrivel, shrivel up; (*of parchment, etc.*) to crinkle up; (*of wood, metal, etc.*) to shrink; to contract; (*of apple, face, pers.*) to become wrinkled, wizened; (*of limb*) to shrivel; (*of income, resources*) to shrink; to be depleted; *Med:* (*of organ, etc.*) to atrophy; to be contabescent; **ein eingeschrumpfter Apfel,** a wizened apple; **eine eingeschrumpfte alte Frau,** a wizened, dried-up, (little) old woman; **ihre eingeschrumpften, verknöcherten Hände,** her shrivelled, bony hands; **sein Gesicht war eingeschrumpft wie bei einer Mumie,** his face was shrivelled like a mummy's; *Geol:* **eingeschrumpfter See,** shrunken lake.

II. *vbl s.* **1. Einschrumpfen,** *n. in vbl senses.* **2. Einschrumpfung,** *f.* (*a*)=II. 1; *also:* shrinkage (of wood, metal, etc.); *Med:* atrophy (of an organ); contabescence (of organ, etc.); (*b*) shrinkage.

Einschub, *m.* **1.** insertion (of sth.); interpolation (of sth.). **2.** inserted piece, passage; insertion; interpolated piece, passage; interpolation. **3.** *Ling:* epenthesis. **4.** *Constr: etc:* insert; inserted piece (of wood, etc.); piece inserted (between other thgs). **5.** *El.E:* exchangeable unit (in high-frequency apparatus, etc.).

Einschubdecke, *f. Constr:* false ceiling; sound-boarded ceiling.

Einschubelement, *n. Ling:* parasitic element.

Einschubschwarte, *f.*=**Einschubdecke.**

Einschubvokal, *m. Ling:* epenthetic vowel; glide.

einschüchtern. I. *v.tr. sep.* to intimidate (s.o.); to frighten (s.o.) (by threats); (*of s.o.'s riches, social standing, etc.*) to overawe (s.o.); **ich werde mich nicht e. lassen,** I will not let myself be, allow myself to be, intimidated; **durch Drohungen nicht eingeschüchtert,** undaunted, unintimidated, not intimidated, by threats; **leicht eingeschüchtert,** easily intimidated; **sie war durch seine Überlegenheit eingeschüchtert,** she was, she felt, overawed by his superiority; **die Pracht um ihn her schüchterte ihn ein, er war durch die Pracht um ihn her eingeschüchtert,** he was overawed at, by, the splendour around him.

II. *vbl s.* **1. Einschüchtern,** *n. in vbl senses.* **2. Einschüchterung,** *f.* (*a*)=II. 1; *also:* intimidation (of s.o.); (*b*) intimidation; threat; **j-n durch Einschüchterungen zu etwas bewegen, j-n durch Einschüchterungen dazu bewegen, etwas zu tun,** to intimidate s.o. into doing sth.

Einschüchterungsprinzip, *n. Pol:* principle of intimidation.

Einschüchterungssystem, *n. Pol:* system of intimidation.

Einschüchterungsversuch, *m. Pol: etc:* attempt at intimidation; attempt to intimidate (pers., country, etc.).

einschulen, *v.tr. sep.* **1.** to train (s.o., horse, etc.); to school (s.o.) (in an activity, etc.). **2.** *Adm:* to take (children) on the school rolls; **zu Ostern eingeschult werden,** to start school at Easter; (*of parents*) **ein Kind einschulen lassen,** to send a child to school (for the first time); **Einschulung** *f,* enrolment (in elementary school).

Einschur, *f. Husb:* (*a*) shearing (of sheep) (once a year); (*b*)=**Einschurwolle.**

einschürig, *a. Husb:* **einschüriges Schaf,** sheep shorn once a year; *Agr:* **einschürige Wiese,** meadow mown once a year.

Einschurwolle, *f. Husb:* fleece from sheep shorn once a year.

Einschuß, *m.* **1.** *Fin:* (*a*) money, capital, funds, invested (in an enterprise, etc.); share, investment (in enterprise, business, etc.); (*b*) deposit; payment; payment on account; (*c*) *St.Exch:* margin (for buying orders); **einen E. leisten,** to margin. **2.** (*a*) bullet-hole; point of entry (of bullet); entry wound; **einen E. feststellen,** to find a bullet-hole (in sth., s.o., animal, etc.); to register a shot (on aircraft, tank, etc.); (*b*) *Fb:* shot (into the goal). **3.** *Tex:* weft; woof; filling. **4.** *Vet:* phlegmon; inflammatory swelling (on leg of horse, udder of cow, etc.). **5.** admixture (of liquid); tinge (of quality, etc.). *Also in vbl senses of* **einschießen I.** 2.

Einschußfaden, *m. Tex:* weft-yarn.

Einschußmaterial, *n. Tex:* weft material.

Einschütte, *f.* feather-mattress; feather-bed.

Einschütt(e)kasten, *m. Ind:* charging box; charging hopper.

Einschütt(e)loch, *n. Ind:* charging hole (of blast furnace, boiler, etc.).

einschütten, *v.tr. sep.* to pour in (sth.); **etwas in etwas** *acc.* **e.,** to pour sth. into sth.; to put (corn, coal, etc.) into (sacks); **Koks in den Hochofen e.,** to feed, charge, the blast furnace with coke, to feed coke into the blast furnace.

Einschütttrichter, *m. Ind: etc:* (charging) funnel, hopper (of furnace).

einschützig, *a. Tex:* (*a*) single-shuttle (loom); (*b*) single-weft (plush, etc.).

einschwalben, einschwalken, *v.tr. sep. Carp:* to dovetail (two pieces of wood).

einschwärzen, *v.tr. sep.* (*a*) to make (sth.) black: to blacken (sth.) (with dye, soot, dirt, etc.); *Print: Engr:* to ink (plate, forme); *Metalw:* to coat (mould) with black-wash, to black-wash (mould); (*b*) *F:* to smuggle in (goods, etc.).

Einschwärzfarbe, Einschwärztinte, *f. Print: Engr:* (printing, printer's) ink.

einschwätzen, einschwatzen, *v.sep.* **1.** *v.i. (haben)* **auf j-n e.,** to chatter away at s.o., to run on at s.o. **2.** *v.tr.* **j-m etwas e.**=**j-m etwas einreden,** *q.v. under* **einreden** 1.

einschwefeln, *v.tr. sep.* to sulphur (cask); to match (wine, cask).

einschwenken, *v.sep.* **1.** *v.tr.* **etwas in etwas** *acc.* **e.,** to swivel, swing, (gun-barrel, instrument, etc.) into (a certain position). **2.** *v.i.* (*sein, haben*) (*of gun barrel, instrument, etc.*) to swivel, swing, into (a certain position); (*of pers., vehicle*) **in eine Seitenstraße, usw., e.,** to turn into a side-street, etc.; **nach rechts, links, e.,** to turn to the right, left; (*of cart-horse, etc.*) to wheel (to the) right, left; *Mil:* (*of column, etc.*) to wheel right, left; **nach links schwenkt ein!** left wheel!

einschwichten, *v.tr. sep. Nau:* to swift, snake (shrouds).

Einschwimmerflugzeug, *n. Av:* single-float seaplane.

einschwingen, *v.i. sep. (strong) (sein)* **1.** *Gym:* (*on parallel bars*) **nach vorn, nach hinten, e.,** to swing oneself forwards, backwards, between the bars. **2. sich einschwingen,** (*a*) *Ph:* (*of pendulum*) to find its normal rhythm; (*of magnetic field, etc.*) to build up; (*b*) *Ven:* (*of game-bird*) to settle (on tree, etc.).

Einschwingvorgang, *m. Ph:* building-up process.

einschwöden, *v.tr. sep. Tan:* to lime (skins).

einsegeln, *v.i. sep. (sein)* (*of sailing vessel*) to sail in; **in den Hafen e.,** to sail, come sailing, into harbour, port.

Einsegelungsmarken, *f.pl. Nau:* landmarks, leading marks.

einsegnen, *v.tr. sep.* **1.** (*a*) *R.C.Ch:* to bless (new building, grave, etc.); (*b*) (*in Protestant Church*) to confirm (young pers.). **2.** *vbl s.* **Einsegnung,** *f.* (*a*) *R.C.Ch:* blessing (of new building, grave, etc.); (*b*) (*in Protestant Church*) confirmation.

einsehbar, *a.* **1.** (*a*) (books, documents, etc.) open to, available for, inspection, examination; (*b*) *Mil:* (area, road, etc.) open to (enemy) observation. **2.** understandable (motive, etc.).

einsehen, *v. sep. (strong)* I. *v.tr.* **1.** (*a*) to look at

examine, inspect (documents, books, samples, etc.); to consult (books, documents, etc.); to study (manuscript, documents, etc.); to see (manuscripts, papers, etc.); **ich konnte das Manuskript nicht e.,** I was not able to see, to examine, *F:* to get a look at, the manuscript; **ich habe die einschlägigen Texte eingesehen,** I have looked through, read through, read, the relevant texts; **die Fachliteratur e.,** to study the relevant literature, the special literature; **die Akten e.,** to examine, study, look at, the documents, papers; **j-s Papiere e.,** to look through s.o.'s papers; **bevor wir unsere Wahl treffen, möchten wir die Muster e.,** before we make our choice we would like to inspect, look over, have a look at, the patterns; (*b*) *Mil:* to observe; **die Straße konnte vom Feind eingesehen werden,** the road could be observed by the enemy, the enemy was able to see on to the road. **2. etwas einsehen,** to see, to realize, sth.; to understand sth.; **ich sehe nicht ein, warum gerade er das tun soll,** I cannot see why he of all people should do that; **ich sehe den Sinn der Sache nicht ein,** I don't see the sense of the thing (at all); **ich kann den Zweck seiner Handlungsweise nicht e.,** I cannot see the purpose of his action; **Sie werden wohl e., daß ich im Augenblick nichts versprechen kann,** you will of course understand, realize, that I can promise nothing at the moment; **siehst du nicht ein, daß du das nicht tun darfst?** don't you realize, understand, you can't do that? **er hat seinen Irrtum eingesehen,** he has seen, realized, *Lit:* perceived, his error; **ich sehe (gar) nicht ein, warum ich das tun soll,** I see no reason (at all) why I should do that, I don't see why, *F:* why on earth, I should do that.

II. **einsehen,** *v.i.* (*haben*) **1. mit j-m in ein Buch, usw., e., bei j-m e.,** to share, look over, s.o.'s book, etc. **2. bei j-m e.,** to look in on s.o.; to pay s.o. a fleeting visit; to call in, *F:* to drop in, on s.o. (for a few moments).

III. *vbl s.* **1. Einsehen,** *n.* (*a*) *in vbl senses; also:* inspection (of samples, manuscripts, etc.); examination (of manuscripts, documents, etc.); (*b*) sense; understanding; **ich hoffe, sie haben ein E.,** I hope they show some sense; (*c*) consideration, understanding; **ein E. haben,** to show consideration, understanding; to make allowances; **hab doch ein E!** do show some consideration! **haben Sie doch ein E. mit ihm und vergessen Sie den Zwischenfall!** please make allowances for him, please show some understanding, and forget the incident; **ich hoffe, der Richter wird ein E. haben und den Jungen nicht zu streng bestrafen,** I hope the judge will make allowances, will show some understanding, and not punish the boy too severely; **hoffentlich hat der Himmel, das Wetter, ein E.,** let's hope the weather will be favourable, will be kind. **2. Einsehung,** *f.* = III. 1 (*a*).

IV. *pr.p. & a.* **einsehend,** *A:* = **einsichtig.**

Einseifbecken, *m.* shaving-basin, lather-bowl.

einseifen, *v.tr. sep.* **1.** to soap (sth.); to rub (sth.) with soap; to rub soap into (sth.); **die Wäsche e.,** to soap the wash, the dirty linen; **j-n e.,** (i) to lather, soap (s.o.) (in bath, etc.); (ii) to lather s.o.'s face (before shaving); **sich e.,** (i) to lather, soap, oneself (in bath, etc.); (ii) to lather one's face (before shaving); **den Hund e.,** to soap, to shampoo, the dog. **2.** *F:* **j-n e.,** (*a*) to softsoap s.o.; to slander s.o.; to cheat, swindle, fleece, s.o.; (*b*) to get s.o. tight, sozzled.

Einseitenband-, *comb.fm. W.Tel:* single-side band ...; **Einseitenbandempfänger** *m,* single-side band receiver.

einseitig, *a.* **1.** one-sided; unilateral; having one side; (fixed, applied, etc.) on one side; *Tex:* one-face, non-reversible (material); *Tls:* single-head, single-end (wrench, etc.); **einseitiger Druck,** (i) pressure (applied) from one side; pressure on one side; (ii) *Print:* printing on one side of the page; **ihre Freundschaft ist ein wenig e.,** their friendship is a bit one-sided; *Mth:* **einseitige Fläche,** one-sided, unilateral, surface; *Med:* **einseitige Lähmung,** paralysis on one side (of body, part of body); **einseitiger Vertrag,** (i) *Jur:* nude contract, nude pact; (ii) *Pol:* unilateral treaty; *Jur:* **einseitiger Antrag,** ex parte application; **einseitige Verzichtserklärung,** renunciation, withdrawal, by one party (in lawsuit); **einseitige Rechtsgeschäfte,** unilateral (legal) procedure. **2.** one-sided (pers., development, training, etc.); asymmetrical, lopsided (development, etc.); ill-balanced (course of study, etc.); biased, prejudiced, partial (attitude, opinion, treatment, etc.); **er ist ein einseitiger Mensch, er ist e.,** he is very one-sided; *F:* he has a one-track mind. **3.** *adv.* (*a*) on one side; to one side; unilaterally; **e. beschrieben,** (sheet, page) written on on one side; (manuscript) with sheets, folios, written on on one side only; **e. bedruckt,** (material, page, etc.) printed on one side; *Print:* not backed; (*b*) **ein Thema e. behandeln,** to treat a subject one-sidedly; to be one-sided, biased, prejudiced, in one's treatment of a subject; **zu e. auf etwas** *acc.* **eingestellt sein,** to be too one-sided in one's attitude to sth.; to think of nothing but one thing.

Einseitigkeit, *f.* one-sidedness (of pers., of thg); limitedness (of s.o.'s interests, etc.); biased, prejudiced, character (of s.o.'s attitude, etc.); biased, prejudiced, quality (of s.o.'s judgment, etc.).

Einseitkiemer, *m. Moll:* monopleurobranch; *pl.* **Einseitkiemer,** monopleurobranchiata.

einsenden. I. *v.tr. sep.* (*conj. like* **senden**) to send in (application, money, bill, article, etc.); to submit (article, etc.); **einen Brief, einen Artikel, an eine Zeitung e.,** to send in a letter, an article, to a newspaper, to submit an article to a newspaper; **er hat seinen Antrag der betreffenden Behörde, an die betreffende Behörde, eingesandt,** he has sent in, sent up, his application to the appropriate authority.

II. *vbl s.* **1. Einsenden,** *n. in vbl senses.* **2. Einsendung,** *f.* (*a*) = II. 1; *also:* **gegen E. einer Anzahlung von zwanzig Mark werden wir Ihnen den gewünschten Gegenstand liefern,** on receipt of, on your sending in, an initial payment of twenty marks, we will deliver to you the article desired; **wir hoffen, daß wir nach E. des fälligen Betrags Ihre Lieferung in Kürze erhalten werden,** we hope to obtain delivery shortly after we have transmitted (to you) the sum due; (*b*) (*thg sent in*) entry (for competition); sum of money (sent in) (as payment), remittance; contribution (to charity, to newspaper, etc.); application (sent to authority, etc.).

Einsender, *m.* person who sent in, sent up (letter, bill, etc.); submitter (of article, etc.); sender (of article, *Com:* of bill, money, etc.).

einsengen, *v.tr. sep.* to burn, brand, in (mark, etc.); **etwas in etwas** *acc.* **e.,** to burn, brand, (mark, etc.) into sth.

einsenken. I. *v.tr. sep.* **1. etwas in die Erde, usw., e.,** to sink sth. in, into, the earth, etc.; to lower (coffin) into the earth; to lay (coffin) in the earth. **2. sich einsenken,** (*a*) (*of heavy object*) **sich in die Erde, usw., e.,** to sink into the earth, etc.; *Geol:* **eingesenkter Fluß,** sunken river; (*b*) (*of beam, etc.*) to sag; (*of wall, etc.*) to subside.

II. *vbl s.* **1. Einsenken,** *n. in vbl senses.* **2. Einsenkung,** *f.* (*a*) = II. 1; (*b*) sagging (of beam, etc.); subsidence (of wall, etc.); (*c*) depression, dip (in ground); trough (in ground).

Einser, *m.* **-s/-** = **Eins,** *q.v. under* **eins**[1] 2.

einsetzbar, *a.* (thg) that can be inserted, put in; removable (part, etc.); (part, etc.) that can be renewed, replaced; interchangeable (tool head, blade, etc.).

einsetzen, *v.sep.* I. *v.tr.* **1.** (*a*) to put in (sth.); to insert (sth.); to fix in (sth.); *Nau:* to step (mast); to ship (boat, rudder); to hang (rudder); **etwas in etwas** *acc.* **e.,** to put, insert, fix, sth. into sth.; to set, place, lay, sth. in sth.; to install (engine, etc.) (in car, plane, etc.); **etwas für etwas (anderes) e.,** to substitute sth. for sth. (else); **setze für dieses Wort, an Stelle dieses Wortes, ein anderes ein,** substitute another word for, in place of, this word; **eine neue Glasscheibe e.,** to put in, insert, a new pane of glass; **einen Teil einer Maschine e.,** to put in, fix in, insert, a part of a machine; **j-m ein Glasauge, usw., e.,** to fit s.o. with a glass eye, etc.; **ein Puppenauge e.,** to fix in, put in, a doll's eye; **Speichen in ein Rad e.,** to spoke a wheel; *Coop:* **den Boden in ein Faß e.,** to bottom a cask, a barrel; to head (up) a barrel; *Tex:* **den Spannstab e.,** to set the temple; (*b*) *Tail: Dressm:* to put in, let in, insert (piece of material, gusset, etc.) (in garment); **einen Ärmel e.,** to set in a sleeve; **einen Hosenboden e.,** to seat a pair of trousers; **eingesetztes Stück,** piece let in; inserted piece; insert. **2.** (*a*) **Fische in einen Teich e.,** to stock a pond; **Karpfen in einen Teich e.,** to stock a pond with carp; (*b*) to set (out) (plants, etc.); **Pflanzen in die Erde e.,** to put plants in the ground; (*c*) *Ind:* **das Metall in den Ofen e.,** to charge the furnace; (*d*) *Nau:* to hoist in (boat). **3.** to stake, to bet; to wager (money, etc.); to risk (one's life, one's honour, etc.); **Geld in die Lotterie e.,** to have a stake in the lottery; to put money into the lottery; **etwas als Pfand e.,** to pledge sth. as security; to pawn sth.; **sein Leben für j-n, für das Vaterland, e.,** to risk one's life for s.o., for one's country. **4.** to use, to make use of (body of troops, police, workmen, etc.); to call in (troops, police, etc.) (during strike, etc.); to call out (militia, etc.) (during riots, etc.): to bring, send, (troops, vehicles, aircraft, ships, etc.) into action; to use (one's influence, one's resources, etc.), to bring (one's influence, one's resources, etc.) to bear; **gegen die Demonstranten mußte Polizei eingesetzt werden,** police had to be used, called in, against the demonstrators; **seine besten Kräfte e.,** to summon up all one's strength, one's powers, to muster all one's energies; **sich für j-n, etwas, e.,** to support s.o., sth.; to stand up, speak up, *F:* stick up, for s.o., sth.; **seinen Einfluß für j-n e.,** to use one's influence on behalf of s.o.; **er hat sich für sie beim Chef eingesetzt,** he used his influence with the boss on her behalf; **er hat sich für die (Sache der) Menschlichkeit eingesetzt,** he supported the cause of humanity. **5.** *Rail:* (*a*) to make up (a train); to start (a train); **der Zug wird in X eingesetzt,** the train starts at X; (*b*) **ein neues Zugpaar auf einer Strecke e.,** to start, to put on, a new service on a line. **6.** to appoint (official, committee, etc.); to establish, appoint (new government, etc.); to establish, institute (feast, holiday, etc.); to set up (commission, committee, new government, court of inquiry, etc.); **j-n als etwas e.,** to appoint s.o. (as) sth.; **j-n in ein Amt e.,** to appoint, nominate, s.o. to an office; to install s.o. in an office; **einen Bischof feierlich in sein Amt e.,** to enthrone a bishop; **j-n zum Erben, als seinen Erben, e.,** to appoint s.o. one's heir, to make s.o. one's heir; **j-n in seine Rechte wieder e.,** to reinstate, re-establish, s.o. in his *or* her rights, to restore s.o. to his *or* her rights; **einen Treuhänder e.,** to appoint a trustee; **eine Kommission zur Erforschung der Flüchtlingsfrage e.,** to appoint, set up, a commission for the investigation of the refugee problem; **Christus hat das Altarsakrament mit den Worten eingesetzt ...,** Christ instituted the Sacrament with the words .... **7.** *Metall:* to case-harden (iron, steel); to cement (iron, steel); to carburize (iron, steel).

II. **einsetzen,** *v.i.* (*haben*) (*a*) (*of story, play, etc.*) to begin, to start, to open; (*of cold, hot, weather, of season, fashion, etc.*) to set in; to start; (*of gale*) to blow up; (*of storm*) to break; **mit etwas e.,** to begin, open, start off, with sth.; **die Ouvertüre setzte mit einem Trommelwirbel ein,** the overture began with a roll of drums; **der Sommer setzte mit einer Hitzewelle ein,** the summer started off, began, with a heat-wave; **diese Mode hat gerade erst eingesetzt,** this fashion has only just come in; **dann setzte der Sturm mit voller Wut ein,** then the gale blew up in all its fury; **die Handlung des Films setzt mitten in einer Kampfszene ein,** the action of the film begins with a battle scene; **er setzte mit seiner Erzählung wieder ein,** he resumed his story; **das Fieber setzte wieder ein,** the fever recurred; (*b*) *Mus:* (*of instrument, voice*) to come in, to enter; **falsch e.,** to come in at the wrong time; to come in on a wrong note; **zu hoch, zu tief, e.,** to come in on too high, too low, a note.

III. *vbl s.* **1. Einsetzen,** *n. in vbl senses; also:* (*a*) insertion (of sth.) (in, into, sth.); installation (of engine, etc.) (in car, plane, etc.); substitution (of one word for another, etc.); (*b*) use (of troops, police, of one's resources, etc.); *cp.* **Einsatz;** (*c*) start, beginning (of heat-wave, etc.); (*d*) case-hardening (of iron, steel). **2. Einsetzung,** *f. in vbl senses of* I; *also:* appointment (of official, committee, trustee, etc.); establishment (of feast, holiday, etc.); **die E. des Altarsakraments,** the institution of the Sacrament.

Einsetzkran, *m. Metall:* charging crane (for blast furnace).

Einsetzlöffel, *m. Metall:* (hand-)ladle.

Einsetzrahmen, *m.* **1.** removable frame. **2.** slide frame (for epidiascope, etc.).

Einsetzschaufel, *m. Ind:* (hand-)ladle; peel.

Einsetzung, *f. see* **einsetzen** III.

Einsetzungsworte, die, *n.pl.* the words with which Christ instituted the sacrament.

Einsicht, *f.* **1.** (*a*) **E. in etwas** *acc.,* examination, inspection (of sth.); consultation (of book, etc.); **E. in etwas** *acc.* **nehmen,** to look at, look through, consult (documents, books, papers, etc.); *Com:* **E. in die Bücher nehmen,** to inspect the books; **j-m die Bücher zur E. vorlegen,** to show s.o. the books, to let s.o. see the books; (*b*) insight; **j-m E. in eine Sache gewähren,** to give s.o. an insight into a matter. **2.** understanding; discernment;

insight; (good) judgment; judiciousness; **ein Mann von großer E.,** a man of great understanding, discernment, insight; **keine E. haben,** to have no understanding, discernment; **die E. kommt mit den Jahren,** we grow wiser as we grow older; **handeln Sie nach bester E.,** do what you think (is) best, do as you think best.

einsichtig, *a.* (*of pers.*) understanding; discerning; having good judgment; judicious; **ein einsichtiger Mann,** a man of insight.

Einsichtigkeit, *f.* understanding; discernment; good judgment.

Einsichtnahme, *f.* **-/-n, E. in etwas** *acc.*, inspection, examination, of sth.; consultation of (books, documents, etc.); **ich bitte, beiliegenden Brief nach E. zurückzusenden,** please return the enclosed letter after having read it; **'zur E.',** 'for your attention.'

einsichtslos, *a.* (*of pers.*) undiscerning; lacking in insight; lacking in (good) judgment.

Einsichtslosigkeit, *f.* lack of discernment; lack of insight; lack, want, of judgment.

einsichtsvoll, *a.*=**einsichtig.**

einsickern. I. *v.i. sep.* (*sein*) (*of liquid*) to soak in; to soak away; to seep in, away; **in etwas** *acc.* **e.,** to soak into sth.; to seep, ooze, into sth.; to trickle into sth.; to infiltrate into sth.; **das Wasser ist durch eine Ritze im Dach eingesickert,** the water has seeped in, trickled in, through a crack in the roof; **fremde Einflüsse waren überall eingesickert,** foreign influences had infiltrated everywhere.

II. *vbl s.* **Einsickern** *n.*, **Einsickerung** *f. in vbl senses; also:* seepage; infiltration.

Einsiedeglas, *n. Austrian: Dom.Ec:* preserving jar.

Einsiedelei, *f.* hermitage.

einsiedeln, *v.i.* (*haben*) = **einsiedlern.**

einsieden, *v.sep.* (*conj. like* **sieden**) **1.** *v.tr.* (*a*) to boil down (liquid); to evaporate (down) (liquid); (*b*) to preserve (fruit, vegetables, etc.); to bottle (fruit, vegetables, etc.). **2.** *v.i.* (*sein*) (*of liquid*) to boil down; to boil away; to evaporate; **etwas e. lassen,** to reduce sth. by boiling; to boil sth. down; to evaporate (liquid) down.

Einsiedler, *m.* **1.** (*a*) hermit; recluse; anchorite; solitary; **er lebt wie ein E.,** he lives the life of a hermit; he leads the life of a recluse; (*b*) animal, etc., living apart from its own kind. **2.** *Orn:* (*a*) hermit humming-bird; (*b*) solitaire.

Einsiedlerbiene, *f. Ent:* solitary bee.

Einsiedlerdrossel, *f. Orn:* hermit-thrush.

Einsiedlerin, *f.* **-/-innen,** (woman) hermit; recluse; anchoress.

einsiedlerisch, *a.* (*a*) hermit-like, solitary (life, etc.); (*b*) (animal, etc.) living apart from its own kind; (*c*) *Prot:* (*of spore*) producing only one sporozoite; monozoic.

Einsiedlerkrebs, *m. Crust:* hermit-crab, pagurian.

Einsiedlerleben, *n.* life as a hermit, a recluse; life (like that) of a hermit, a recluse; hermit-like existence.

einsiedlern, *v.i.* (*haben*) to live as a hermit; to live like a hermit; to live, lead, the life of a hermit.

Einsiedlerspiel, *n. Games:* solitaire.

Einsiedlerzelle, *f.* hermit's cell.

Einsilber, *m.* **-s/-,** word of one syllable, one-syllable(d) word; monosyllable.

einsilbig, *a.* **1.** *Ling:* monosyllabic (word); **einsilbiges Wort,** word of one syllable; monosyllabic word; monosyllable. **2.** *F:* monosyllabic (reply, etc.); (*of pers.*) taciturn; **eine einsilbige Unterhaltung,** a conversation in monosyllables.

Einsilbigkeit, *f.* **1.** *Ling:* monosyllabism (of word). **2.** *F:* taciturnity (of pers.).

Einsilbler, *m.* **-s/-**=**Einsilber.**

einsingen, *v.tr. sep.* (*strong*) **1.** to sing (s.o.) to sleep; to lull (s.o.) to sleep (by singing). **2. sich einsingen,** to get oneself into voice; (*of opera singer, etc.*) **sich in eine Rolle e.,** to sing oneself into a rôle.

einsinken. I. *v.i. sep.* (*strong*) (*sein*) to sink; to sink in; (*of building, ground, etc.*) to subside; (*of earth over hole, etc.*) to cave in; to collapse; **in etwas** *acc.* **e.,** to sink into sth.; **der Karren war tief in den Schlamm eingesunken,** the cart had sunk deep into the morass; **im Moor, usw., e.,** to sink down in the fen, etc.; **wir waren bis über die Knie eingesunken,** we had sunk in to above our knees; **der Boden sank ein,** the floor *or* ground caved in, gave way; **eingesunkene Augen,** sunken, hollow, eyes.

II. *vbl s.* **Einsinken,** *n. in vbl senses; also:* subsidence (of building, of ground, etc.).

Einsitzer, *m. Aut: Av: etc:* single-seater.

Einskuller, *m. Row:* single-sculler.

einsmals, *adv. Dial:* suddenly.

Einsonderungsdrüse, *f. Anat:* endocrine gland.

einspaltig, *a. & adv.* **einen Bogen e. beschreiben,** to write on the left- *or* right-hand side only of a sheet; *Print:* **einspaltiger Satz,** composition to full measure; page set as one column.

Einspannapparat, *m. Carp:* clamp.

einspannen, *v.tr. sep.* **1.** (*a*) to fix, clamp (sth.) into position; **etwas in etwas** *acc.* **e.,** to fix, clamp (piece of work, etc.) (on to lathe, etc.); to mount (piece of work, etc.) (on lathe, frame, etc.); to set (piece of work, etc.) (in vice, frame, etc.); to clamp, fix (piece of work, etc.) (in vice, etc.); to grip (piece of metal, etc.) (in vice, chuck, etc.); **eine Zeitung e.,** (*in reading room, etc.*) to fix, put, a newspaper into the holder; *Typewr:* **das Papier e.,** to insert, feed, the paper into the machine; **bitte spannen Sie ein,** please put the paper, some paper, into the machine, the typewriter; (*b*) *Bookb:* **ein Buch e.,** to tie up a book. **2.** (*a*) to put, harness, (horses, etc.) to the carriage, etc.; *abs.* to put the horses to; to yoke (oxen); **einen Wagen e.,** to put, harness, a horse *or* horses to a carriage, cart; (*b*) *F:* **j-n (für eine Arbeit) e.,** to rope s.o. in (for a job, a task).

Einspänner, *m.* **-s/-.** **1.** carriage drawn by one horse; one-horse carriage. **2.** (*a*) *F:* person living alone; bachelor; single woman; recluse; (*b*) *A:* miner who works a mine alone; (*c*) *A:* small farmer, driver, owning only one horse. **3.** *Austrian:* black coffee with whipped cream.

einspännig, *a.* one-horse (carriage, etc.); *adv.* **e. fahren,** to drive with one horse.

Einspannlappen, *m.* fixing flange, holding flange.

Einspannschraube, *f.* set screw, clamping-screw, locking-screw.

einsparen, *v.tr. sep.* I. **etwas e.,** to save (money, time, space, etc.) (*by cutting down on sth.*); to save (material) (*by economical layout, etc.*); to cut down, to reduce (expenditure, etc.) (*in order to balance one's budget, etc.*); to make a saving; to make economies; **eine Stelle e.,** to abolish, to dispense with, an office, a post (*for reasons of economy*); **wo könnten wir etwas e.?** where could we economize, make economies? **eine Summe e., um sie für andere Zwecke verwenden zu können,** to save a sum of money in order to dispose of it elsewhere; to economize in order to use the money for another purpose; **im letzten Jahr konnten wir keine größeren Summen e.,** last year we could not make any major economies; *Print:* **eine Zeile e.,** to save a line.

II. *vbl s.* **1. Einsparen,** *n. in vbl senses.* **2. Einsparung,** *f.* (*a*)=II. 1; (*b*) saving (in time, money, etc.); economy; time, space, etc., saved; money saved (*by cutting down expenses*); **das bedeutete für uns eine große E.,** that was a great saving for us; **eine E. von zehn Minuten,** a saving of ten minutes; **im letzten Jahr konnten wir keine größeren Einsparungen machen,** last year we could not make any major economies.

einsperren, *v.tr. sep.* **1.** to shut (s.o.) up, to lock (s.o.) up; to confine (s.o.) (in room, etc.); to shut up (animal, etc.) (in cage, etc.); *F:* to imprison (s.o.), to jail (s.o.), to lock (s.o.) up in prison; **sich in sein Zimmer e.,** to shut oneself up in one's room. **2.** *St.Exch:* to corner (shares, commodity, etc.); to make a corner in (commodity, etc.).

einspielen, *v.tr. sep.* **1.** (*a*) **ein Instrument e.,** to get an instrument into good playing order by practising on it; (*b*) to level out, balance (out) (scales, pointer, etc.). **2. sich einspielen,** (*a*) (*of project, etc.*) to get going (properly); to get into full swing; to get into proper working order; (*b*) (*of pers.*) to get into practice (in sth.); *Sp:* to play oneself in; **sich auf einem Instrument e.,** to get the feel of an instrument by playing it, by practising on it; **sich in eine Rolle e.,** to get the feel of a rôle, a part, by acting *or* rehearsing it; *F:* to get under the skin of a part (by rehearsing it); **die Spieler des Orchesters müssen sich besser e.,** the orchestra players must get (into) the feel of the music more; (*c*) **auf etwas** *acc.* **eingespielt sein,** to have got the hang of sth.; **sich aufeinander e.,** (*of members of team, orchestra, etc.*) to play, to practise playing, together (until they play as one, in perfect co-ordination); (*of work team, etc.*) to learn to work together as a team, to become co-ordinated; **gut aufeinander eingespielt sein,** (*of sports team*) to work together as a perfect team, to be well co-ordinated; (*of musicians*) to play together as one; (*of work team, etc.*) to work together in thorough co-ordination; **sie sind fabelhaft aufeinander eingespielt,** their teamwork is marvellous; **die Mitglieder des Orchesters müssen sich besser aufeinander e.,** the members of the orchestra must learn to keep together better. **3.** (*of pers., company, etc.*) to take (money) (at cinemas, theatres, etc.); **in einem Monat haben wir eine Million Mark eingespielt,** we have taken a million marks in one month (with our production(s)); (*of film, etc.*) to bring in (money) (from its performances); **der Film hat insgesamt 250 Millionen Mark eingespielt,** the film has brought in a total of 250 million marks (from its performances).

einspinnen, *v.tr. sep.* (*strong*) **1.** (*a*) (*of spider*) to spin a web round (fly, etc.); (*b*) *F:* (*of police, etc.*) to imprison, *F:* jug (s.o.); (*c*) *Tex:* **etwas in etwas** *acc.* **e.,** to spin sth. into sth. **2. sich einspinnen,** (*a*) (*of silkworm*) to cocoon, to spin a cocoon round itself, to surround itself with a cocoon; (*b*) (*of pers.*) to seclude oneself; to shut oneself away from the world; **in sein, in seinem, Studium eingesponnen sein,** to be wrapped up in one's studies.

einsporig, *a. Bot:* monospored, monosporous.

Einsprache, *f.* **1.** objection; protest; *cp.* **Einspruch.** **2.** *Mil: F:* mouthpiece (of field telephone). **3.** *Swiss:*=**Einrede 1.**

einsprachig, *a.* monolingual, unilingual (pers., dictionary, etc.).

einsprechen, *v.sep.* (*strong*) **1.** *v.tr.* **j-m Mut e.,** to instil courage into s.o., to inspire s.o. with courage (by talking to him *or* her); to encourage s.o.; **j-m Trost e.,** to speak comfortingly to s.o., to speak words of comfort to s.o., to comfort s.o., to console s.o. **2.** *v.i.* (*haben*) (*a*) **auf j-n e.**=**auf j-n einreden,** *q.v. under* **einreden** 2; (*b*) *A:* **gegen etwas** *acc.* **e.**=**Einspruch gegen etwas erheben,** *q.v. under* **Einspruch;** (*c*) *A:* **für j-n e.,** to intercede for s.o.; to speak up for s.o.; to use, exert, one's influence on behalf of s.o.; (*d*) *A:* **bei j-m e.,** to pay s.o. a visit; to stop at s.o.'s home (for the night *or* for a short stay).

einsprengen, *v.sep.* I. *v.tr.* **1. etwas mit etwas e.,** to sprinkle sth. with sth.; to sprinkle sth. over sth.; **die Wäsche e.,** to damp the washing, to sprinkle the washing with water (before ironing). **2.** *Miner:* **Stein mit eingesprengtem Kupfer,** rock containing scattered, disseminated, deposits of copper. **3. eine Öffnung in den Felsen e.,** to blast an opening in the rock. **4.** *Ven:* **das Wild e.,** to drive the game (into preserve, etc.).

II. **einsprengen,** *v.i.* (*sein*) **auf den Feind, usw., e.,** to rush, to rush upon, to charge, the enemy, etc. (on horseback).

III. *vbl s.* **1. Einsprengen,** *n. in vbl senses.* **2. Einsprengung,** *f.* (*a*)=III. 1; (*b*) *Miner:* scattered deposit (of ore); **Stein mit Einsprengungen von Kupfer,** rock containing scattered, disseminated, deposits of copper.

Einsprengling, *m.* **-s/-e.** *Miner:* scattered deposit (of ore, etc.); xenolith; xenocryst.

einspringen, *v. sep.* (*strong*) I. *v.i.* (*sein*) **1.** (*a*) to jump in; to leap in; to spring in; **in etwas** *acc.* **e.,** to jump into sth.; to leap into sth.; to spring into sth.; (*b*) **auf j-n e.,** to spring (up)on s.o.; to pounce (up)on s.o.; to fall upon s.o.; to dash at s.o.; to rush at s.o. **2. für j-n e.,** to step in (in place of s.o.); to take s.o.'s place (voluntarily); **während ich krank war, sprang er für mich ein,** while I was ill he took my place, he deputized for me; **als Ersatz e.,** to step in, go in, as a substitute (for s.o.) (*as member of team, in game, etc.*). **3.** *Tchn:* (*of lock, etc.*) to catch; (*of spring, etc.*) to snap; (*of catch on machine, etc.*) to engage. **4.** *Tex:* (*of fabric*) to shrink (in width) (during weaving). **5.** (*of skin*) to chap; to crack; (*of wall, glass, etc.*) to crack. **6.** *Constr: Arch:* (*of wall, window, etc.*) to recede; **einspringend,** recessed; set back (in sth.); **einspringender Zentrier(ungs)ring,** recessed centring ring; *Geom: Mil:* **einspringender Winkel,** re-entrant angle.

II. **einspringen,** *v.tr.* **1.** to break, smash, (sth.) in (by jumping on it). **2. ein Pferd e.,** to train a horse in jumping over obstacles, to get a horse accustomed to jumping over obstacles.

III. *vbl s.* **Einspringen,** *n. in vbl senses; also:* *Tex:* shrinkage (in width) (of fabric during weaving); *cp.* **Einsprung.**

Einspritzdruck, *m. I.C.E:* injection pressure.

einspritzen. I. *v.tr. sep.* (*a*) *Med: etc:* to inject (sth.); to spray (sth.) in; **j-m Morphium, usw., e.,** to give s.o. an injection of morphia, etc.; **j-m etwas ins Ohr e.,** to inject sth. into s.o.'s ear; to spray, to syringe, sth. into s.o.'s ear; (*b*) *Tchn:* **etwas in etwas** *acc.* **e.,** to inject sth. into sth.; to syringe sth. into sth.; to spray sth. into sth.; *F:* to squirt sth. into sth.; (*c*) **die Wäsche e.,** to damp the washing, to sprinkle the washing (with water) (before ironing); (*d*) **etwas e.,** to get sth. spattered, filthy (with mud, dirt, etc.).

II. *vbl s.* **1. Einspritzen,** *n. in vbl senses.* **2. Einspritzung,** *f.* (*a*)=II. 1; *also:* injection (of sth.) (into sth.); (*b*) *Med:* injection.
Einspritzhahn, *m.* injection cock.
Einspritzkarburetter, *m.*=**Einspritzvergaser.**
Einspritzklappe, *f. Mch:* injection valve.
Einspritzkondensation, *f. Mch:* jet condensation.
Einspritzkondensator, *m. Mch:* jet condenser.
Einspritzkühlung, *f.* jet cooling, injection cooling.
Einspritzmaschine, *f.* **1.** *Mch: etc:* injector. **2.** (diesel) engine with airless injection of fuel.
Einspritzmotor, *m. I.C.E:* fuel-injection engine, spark-injection engine.
Einspritzpumpe, *f.* **1.** *Mch:* injection pump. **2.** *Med:* enema pump.
Einspritzrohr, *n.*, **Einspritzröhre,** *f. Mch: I.C.E: etc:* injection pipe, injection tube.
Einspritzschieber, *m. Mch:* injection slide.
Einspritzventil, *n. Mch: etc:* injection valve.
Einspritzverdichter, *m. Mch:* jet condenser.
Einspritzvergaser, *m. I.C.E:* spray carburetter, jet carburetter.
Einspritzvorrichtung, *f.* injection device; spraying device; spray; *I.C.E:* primer (of the engine).
Einspruch, *m.* objection; protest; *Jur: Adm:* appeal (against decision, etc.); **E. (gegen etwas) erheben,** to object (to sth.); to protest (against sth.); to oppose (sth.); to appeal (against decision, etc.); **kein E. erfolgte, es erhob sich kein E.,** no protest was made; no objection was raised; **der Vorschlag wurde ohne E. angenommen,** the proposal, the motion, was carried unanimously; *Jur:* **E. erheben, einlegen,** to lodge an appeal; to lodge, file, an objection; **schriftlichen E. erheben,** to make a written protest; **einen E. aufrechterhalten,** to sustain an objection.
Einsprung, *m.* **1.** (*a*) jump, leap (**in etwas** *acc.*, into sth.); (*b*) *Sp:* (*in figure skating*) preliminary jump (before cutting figure); (*c*) *Ven:* entrance, opening (*enabling deer, etc., to enter park enclosure, but not to leave*). **2.** *Arch:* turn, return, angle (of wall); recess (in wall).
einspülen, *v.tr. sep.* to saturate the ground with water around (pile, stake, etc.); *Civ.E: etc:* to sluice the ground with water (*to consolidate it*).
einspulig, *a. El.E:* single-coil (instrument, etc.).
einspunden, einspünden, *v.tr. sep. Coop:* to bung (cask, barrel).
einspuren, *v.tr. sep. Nau:* to step (mast).
einspurig, *a. Rail:* single-line, single-track (railway).
Einssein, *n.* (*a*) oneness, unity (of God, etc.); (*b*) **E. mit der Natur, usw.,** unity, oneness, with nature, etc.
einst, *adv.* **1.** (*past*) formerly; once; once upon a time; in the past; in times past; in olden times; long ago; **e. war es Brauch, zu . . . ,** it was the custom formerly, in times past, in olden times, to . . . ; **e. ging ich spazieren, als . . . ,** one day I was walking, when . . . ; **ein Buch, das e. so beliebt war,** a book which was once, at one time, so popular; **X, e. ein berühmter Maler,** X, once a famous painter; (*in story*) **in Florenz lebte e. ein Arzt,** in Florence there once lived a doctor; **e. wie jetzt,** (now) as ever; **das Leben ist dasselbe, e. wie jetzt,** life is the same as it ever was; **wie e.,** as in the past; *Lit:* as of yore; **sie ist nicht mehr so schlank wie e.,** she is no longer as slim as she used to be, as she was (once), *Hum:* as of yore; **von e.,** of the past; of old; of long ago; of former times; of former days; **Sitten von e.,** bygone customs; **die Ritter von e.,** the knights of old; **die Frauen von e.,** the women of former days; **Menschen von e.,** men of olden times; **dies ist nicht mehr das England von e.,** this is no longer the England of the past; England is not what it was; *Hum:* **ein Kragen, der e. weiß war,** a collar that was once white. **2.** (*future*) one day; some day; in times to come; **e. wird er einsehen, daß ich recht hatte,** some day he will realize that I was right; **wenn ich e. gestorben bin,** one day when I am gone; **e. werden wir die Wahrheit unverhüllt erkennen,** one day the veil will be drawn aside and we shall see the truth; **jetzt und e.,** now and in the future; *Lit:* **e. wird kommen der Tag), wo . . .),** the day will dawn (when . . .); the day will come (when . . .). **3.** *s.* **das Einst, -/.** (*a*) the past; **das E. mit dem Jetzt vergleichen,** to compare the past with the present; (*b*) (i) the future; (ii) the other world; **im E. werden wir uns wiedersehen,** we shall meet in the beyond, in the life to come, in the other world.
einstallen, *v.tr. sep.* to stall (cattle); to stable (horses); to pen (sheep); to put (pig) in a sty.
einstämmig, *a.* **1.** *Bot:* (plant) with one stem. **2.** *Ling:* (verb) with one stem.
einstampfen, *v.tr. sep.* (*a*) to ram (down), to tamp (earth); to press (fruit, etc.) down; *Cu:* to press (vegetables for preserving) well down; **etwas in etwas** *acc.* **e.,** to press sth. into sth.; to ram sth. into (the ground); to trample sth. into (the ground); (*b*) *Paperm:* to pulp (books, paper).
Einstampfmaschine, *f. Paperm:* pulping machine.
Einstampfpapier, *n. Paperm:* pulping paper; waste paper.
Einstand, *m.* **1.** (i) entry; taking up of, entry into, a job (*esp. on a farm*); beginning of, entry into, entering upon, an apprenticeship, etc.; (ii) setting up of one's own home, establishment; **seinen E. geben, feiern,** (i) to celebrate one's start in one's new job, on one's apprenticeship, etc.; (ii) (*of newly-married couple*) to give a house-warming party. **2.** footing; fees *or* dues (payable on admission to a society, etc.); **seinen E. geben, entrichten,** to pay (for) one's footing. **3.** *Jur: A:*=**Einstandsrecht. 4.** *Com:*=**Einstandspreis. 5.** *Ten:* deuce.
Einständerhammer, *m.* single-framehammer.
Einständermaschine, *f.* open-side planing machine.
Einstandspreis, *m. Com:* price delivered.
Einstandsrecht, *n. Jur: A:* (right of) pre-emption; refusal.
einstanzen, *v.tr. sep.* **ein Muster in Metall, Leder, usw., e.,** to impress a design on, into, metal, leather, etc. (*with a punch or die*); to stamp a design into metal, leather, etc.; **eingestanzte Muster,** impressed patterns.
einstauben, *v.sep.* **1.** *v.i.* (*sein*) (*of thg*) to become very dusty; **eingestaubt sein,** to be covered with dust. **2.** *v.tr.* to make (sth.) dusty; to cover (sth.) with dust; **sich** *dat.* **die Schuhe, Kleider, e.,** to get one's shoes, clothes, dusty.
einstäuben, *v.tr. sep.* **1.** to cover (sth.) with dust. **2.** to dust, to powder, to sprinkle (sth.); **einen Kuchen mit Puderzucker e.,** to dust, powder, sprinkle, a cake with icing sugar.
Einstaubverfahren, *n. Phot:* powder process, dusting-on process.
Einstechahle, *f. Tls:* stabbing-awl.
Einstechbogen, *m. Print:* tympan-sheet.
einstechen, *v.sep.* (*strong*) **1.** *v.tr.* (*a*) **eine Nadel, usw., in etwas** *acc.* **e.,** to stick a needle, etc., into sth.; to stab a needle, etc., into sth.; **die Nadel tief e.,** to stick the needle right in; (*b*) **ein Muster in Papier e.,** to prick a design in paper; **eine Rille in eine Röhre e.,** to cut a neck in a tube, to recess a tube; **Löcher in etwas** *acc.* **e.,** to prick holes in sth., to prick sth. **2.** *v.i.* (*haben*) (*a*) (*of needle, etc.*) **in etwas** *acc.* **e.,** to stick into sth.; to sink into sth.; **die Nadel stach tief ein,** the needle sank in, went in, deep; (*b*) (*of pers.*) **mit der Nadel, usw., in etwas** *acc.* **e.,** to stick the needle, etc., into sth.; to stab the needle into sth.; (*c*) **auf j-n e.,** to stab at s.o.; **sie stachen aufeinander ein,** they stabbed at one another.
Einstechgarn, *n. Bootm:* welting thread.
Einstechmaschine, *f. Bootm:* welting machine, welter.
Einstechrahmen, *m. Bootm:* welt (of boot, shoe).
Einstechschleifen, *n. Mec.E:* plunge-cut grinding.
Einstechschloß, *n.* mortise lock.
Einstechstahl, *m. Tls:* recessing tool.
Einstechwerkzeug, *n. Tls:* recessing tool.
Einsteckamboß, *m. Tls: Metalw:* stake(-anvil).
einsteckbar, *a.* insertable, attachable.
Einsteckblende, *f. Phot:* insertable diaphragm.
Einsteckbogen, *m. Bookb:* inset.
einstecken, *v.tr. sep.* (*a*) **etwas in etwas** *acc.* **e.,** to put sth. into, in, sth.; to insert sth. into (a hole); *Bookb:* to insert (inset) in (book); **den Schlüssel (ins Schloß) e.,** to insert the key in the lock; **Nadeln in etwas** *acc.* **e.,** to stick pins into sth.; **das Schwert e.,** to sheathe, to put up, one's sword; **den Stecker, ein elektrisches Gerät, e.,** to put the plug in (the socket), to plug in an electrical appliance; **einen Brief (in den Briefkasten) e.,** to drop a letter into the letter-box, to post, to mail, a letter; *F:* **schmutzige Wäsche (zum Einweichen in Lauge) e.,** to put the dirty washing (in) to soak; *F:* **j-n e.,** to put, clap, s.o. in prison, *F:* to jug s.o.; (*b*) to put (sth.) into one's pocket, bag, etc.; to pack (sth.); to take (sth.) (*along with one*); *Hum: Pej:* to pocket (money, etc.); **jemand hat meinen Tabak eingesteckt,** someone has pocketed my tobacco; **er steckte gewöhnlich die Hälfte unserer Einnahmen ein,** he used to pocket half our takings; **hast du deinen Schlafanzug eingesteckt?** have you packed, taken, got, your pyjamas? (*c*) to swallow (an insult, a defeat, etc.); *F:* to take (an insult, a defeat, etc.) lying down; **ich werde diese Beleidigung nicht e.,** I do not mean to put up with that insult; **das wird er nicht e.,** he won't take that lying down; **einen Tadel e.,** to take a rebuke (calmly, meekly, etc.); **einen Schlag e.,** to take a blow.
Einsteckgriff, *m.* attachable, insertable, handle.
Einsteckkamm, *m.* hair-comb; back-comb; side-comb.
Einsteckkurbel, *f. Mec.E:* insertable crank.
Einstecklauf, *m.* (*a*) *Sm.a:* Morris tube; (*b*) *Artil:* liner; sub-calibre barrel.
Einsteckmagazin, *n. Mil: Sm.a:* (loading-)clip.
Einsteckschloß, *n.* mortise lock.
einstehen, *v.i. sep.* (*strong*) (*sein*) **1.** *A:* **in eine Stellung e.,** to take a job, to go into service (*esp. on a farm*). **2. für j-n e.,** to take, fill, s.o.'s place; to deputize for s.o.; (*at public functions, etc.*) to act in s.o.'s stead; to officiate for s.o. **3. für j-n, etwas, e.,** to vouch for s.o., sth.; to answer for s.o., sth.; to be answerable for sth.; to warrant sth.; to guarantee sth.; to take, accept, responsibility for sth.; to pledge oneself for sth.; **für die Folgen e.,** to answer for the consequences; **für seine Überzeugung e.,** to stand up for one's convictions; **für seine Handlungen e.,** to be answerable for one's actions; **sie kann für sein gutes Benehmen e.,** she can vouch, answer, for his good conduct; **ich stehe dafür ein, daß ihm kein Schaden geschieht,** I pledge myself, vouch for it, answer for it, warrant, that he won't come to any harm; **ich stehe dafür ein, daß die Summe bezahlt wird,** I warrant that the sum shall be paid; **ich will für seine Sicherheit e.,** I will be responsible, answer, for his safety.
Einsteher, *m.* **-s/-.** *Mil: A:* substitute.
einstehlen (sich), *v.refl. sep.* (*strong*) **sich in etwas** *acc.* **e.,** to steal, slip, creep, *F:* sneak, into sth.; to insinuate oneself into sth.; **er hat sich nachts eingestohlen,** he stole in, slipped in, crept in, sneaked in, at night; **sich in j-s Gunst, Vertrauen, e.,** to insinuate oneself, to creep, to worm one's way, into s.o.'s favour, confidence.
Einsteigebrücke, *f. Rail: etc:* gangway; ramp.
Einsteigeloch, *n.* man-hole.
Einsteig(e)luke, *f.* hatch, access door (of aircraft, armoured vehicle, etc.).
einsteigen, *v.i. sep.* (*strong*) (*sein*) (*a*) to get in; to climb in; *Mil:* (*of troops*) to entrain; to emplane; **in etwas** *acc.* **e.,** to get into sth.; to climb into (house, etc.); to get on, into (bus); to get into (train, coach, car, etc.); to board (plane, bus); **(ins Schiff) e.,** to board, go on board, go aboard (ship); to embark; **sie stiegen durch ein Fenster in das Haus ein,** they climbed through a window into the house; **die Einbrecher waren durch das Küchenfenster eingestiegen,** the burglars had got in, climbed in, broken in, through the kitchen window; (*asked by bus-conductor, etc.*) **wo sind Sie eingestiegen?** where did you get in, on? *Rail: etc:* **(bitte) einsteigen!** all aboard! (*on underground station*) hurry along, please! (*b*) *F:* **in ein Geschäft, eine Branche, usw., e.,** to get in on, into, a firm, line of business, etc. (as a partner, shareholder, etc.).
Einsteigeschacht, *m.* man-hole.
Einsteinium [ainˈʃtainĭum], *n.* **-s/.** *Ch:* einsteinium.
Einstell-, *comb.fm.* (*a*) *Mec.E: etc:* adjusting . . . ; setting . . . ; **Einstellschlüssel** *m*, adjusting wrench; **Einstellspindel** *f*, adjusting, setting, spindle; **Einstellehre** *f*, setting gauge; (*b*) *Phot: Opt:* focusing . . . ; **Einstellupe** *f*, focusing glass, focusing magnifier; **Einstellmikroskop** *n*, focusing microscope; **Einstelltuch** *n*, focusing cloth.
einstellbar, *a.* adjustable; **einstellbarer Auslöser,** adjustable release; **einstellbare Luftschraube,** variable pitch, adjustable pitch, air-screw.
Einstellbarkeit, *f.* adjustability.
Einstellbüchse, *f. Mec.E:* adjusting ring; set collar.
Einstellebene, *f. Surv: etc:*=**Bezugsebene.**
einstellen, *v. sep.* I. *v.tr.* **1. etwas in etwas** *acc.* **e.,** to put sth. into, in, sth.; **Bücher e.,** to put books (back) on the shelf; (*of library assistant*) to shelve books; **das Auto (in die Garage) e.,** to put the car in (the garage), to put the car away; **etwas bei j-m e.,** to deposit (goods, etc.) with s.o., to leave sth. at s.o.'s house, flat, establishment, etc. (for storage); to put (horse, cattle) in s.o. else's stall; to stall (cattle, horse); to stable (horse) at s.o.'s house, establishment, etc.; to put up (horse) in s.o.'s stable; *Tex:* **die Kette ins Blatt e.,** to set, slay, the warp in the reed. **2.** to take on (worker, etc.); to engage (s.o.); to hire (workman, etc.); to enrol (soldier, etc.); **j-n in sein Geschäft e.,** to give s.o. employment, to give s.o. a post, a job, in one's business,

one's firm. 3. (*a*) to adjust (tool, instrument, motor, etc.); to set (instrument, tool, etc.); *W.Tel:* to tune (in) (set); *abs.* to tune in; *Opt: Phot:* to focus (instrument, camera, image); to bring (image) into focus; *I.C.E: Mch:* to time, tune (ignition, valve); **ein Instrument, usw., auf etwas** *acc.* **e.,** to adjust, set, an instrument, etc., to sth.; **das Grammophon auf 78 U/min e.,** to set the gramophone at, to, 78 r.p.m.; **etwas neu, wieder, e.,** to readjust, reset, sth.; **einen Scheinwerfer e.,** to focus a headlamp *or* searchlight; **das Fernglas ist für mich nicht richtig eingestellt,** the binoculars are not properly focused for me; *W.Tel:* **das Empfangsgerät auf eine bestimmte Wellenlänge e.,** to tune (in) the set to a given wave-length; **auf einen Sender e.,** to tune in (to) a station; *Phot:* **die Entfernung e.,** to focus the camera; **(den Apparat) auf einen Gegenstand e.,** to focus (the camera) on an object; **auf unendlich e.,** to focus on, for, to set at, to, infinity; (*b*) **etwas auf etwas** *acc.* **e.,** to concentrate (one's efforts, etc.) on sth.; to focus (propaganda, etc.) on sth.; to adapt (style, etc.) to (a certain public, etc.); **er hat sein Leben ganz auf die Arbeit eingestellt,** his whole life is centred on his work; *cp.* II. 2. 4. to stop (work, working, payments, etc.); to cease (working); to discontinue (payments); to stop, leave off (doing sth.); to break off (relations, negotiations); **die Arbeit e.,** (i) to stop work; (ii) to down tools, *U.S:* to quit working; **die Arbeiten, Zahlungen, zeitweilig e.,** to suspend work, payments, temporarily; to stop, cease, work, payments, temporarily; **eingestellt werden,** to cease; (*of payments*) to be discontinued, to stop, to cease; **das Feuer, die Feindseligkeiten, e.,** to cease fire, hostilities; (*of paper, periodical*) **das Erscheinen e.,** to cease publication, to cease to be published, to appear; *Jur:* **das Verfahren e.,** to stay, to stop, proceedings; not to proceed with the prosecution; **das Verfahren gegen j-n e.,** to stop the proceedings against s.o.; to drop the charge against s.o.; *Sp: etc:* **einen Rekord e.,** to equal a record; *see also* **Betrieb** 1 (*a*).

II. **sich einstellen.** 1. (*of pers.*) to come (**bei j-m, an einem Ort,** to s.o., to a place); to appear, to turn up, *F:* to show up, (**an einem Ort,** at a place); (*of lost object*) to be found, to turn up (again); (*of conditions, difficulties, etc.*) to arise; (*of symptom*) to appear; to occur; (*of fit*) to come on; to occur; (*of love, etc.*) to arise; to come (into being); **sich wieder e.,** to come back; to return; to reappear; (*of fit*) to recur; **er stellte sich zur verabredeten Zeit bei mir ein,** he came to see me at the time we had arranged; **sich im richtigen Augenblick e.,** to appear, to turn up, at the right moment; **die Nachfrage nach diesem Artikel wird sich bald e.,** the demand for this article will soon arise; **(die) Aufträge stellen sich allmählich ein,** orders are gradually coming in; **der Winter hat sich dieses Jahr frühzeitig eingestellt,** winter has set in early this year; **nach zwei Stunden stellte sich bei dem Patienten ein heftiges Fieber ein,** after two hours the patient developed a high temperature. 2. **sich auf etwas** *acc.*, **j-n, e.,** (i) to attune oneself to sth.; to attune oneself to s.o.'s personality; to adapt oneself to sth.; to adapt oneself to s.o.'s personality; (ii) to prepare oneself (mentally *or* physically) for sth.; to get oneself in the right frame of mind, in the right mood, for sth., to deal with s.o.; **auf etwas** *acc.*, **j-n, eingestellt sein,** (i) to be attuned to sth.; to be adapted to sth.; to be attuned to s.o.'s personality; (ii) to be prepared (mentally *or* physically) for sth.; to be in the right frame of mind, in the right mood, for sth., for dealing with s.o.; (*cp.* IV); **wir sind nicht auf Gäste eingestellt,** we are not prepared for guests; we have no (proper) accommodation for guests; **sie ist ganz auf Heiraten eingestellt,** all her thoughts are centred on marriage; **Schulbücher, die auf das moderne Leben eingestellt sind,** school-books that are in keeping with, are adapted to, modern conditions.

III. *vbl s.* 1. **Einstellen,** *n. in vbl senses.* 2. **Einstellung,** *f.* (*a*) *in vbl senses; also:* (i) engagement (of workers, etc.); enrolment (of soldiers, etc.); (ii) adjustment (of tool, instrument, motor, etc.); *Opt: Phot:* focusing; **E. auf Null,** adjustment, setting, to zero; (iii) stoppage (of work, payments, etc.); cessation (of work, hostilities, etc.); discontinuation (of payments, etc.); **zeitweilige E. der Arbeit, der Zahlungen,** suspension, temporary stoppage, of work, of payments; **E. des Feuers,** cease-fire; *Jur:* **E. des Verfahrens,** stay, discontinuance, of proceedings; (*b*) *Mec.E: Opt:* adjustment; *Opt: Phot:* focusing, focus; **die E. überprüfen,** to check the focus; **das Fernglas hat nicht die richtige E. für mich,** the binoculars are not properly focused for me; (*c*) attitude; outlook; **seine politische, religiöse, E.,** his political, religious, attitude, outlook; **seine E. dem Leben gegenüber,** his attitude towards, his outlook upon, life; **seine E. zu dem Problem, zu seinen Eltern, ist falsch,** his attitude towards the problem, towards his parents, is wrong; **bei seiner E. kommen wir zu keinem Entschluß,** his attitude makes any decision impossible; **keine E. zu etwas haben,** to have no definite views on sth.; **kritische E.,** critical attitude; **die richtige E. zu seiner Arbeit haben,** to have the right approach to one's work; *F:* **das ist keine E.,** that is not the right, that is the wrong, that is no sort of, attitude; (*d*)=**Einsteller** 2.

IV. *p.p. & a.* **eingestellt,** *in vbl senses; esp.* **konservativ e. sein,** to be conservative, to be of a conservative cast of mind; *Pol:* to have conservative leanings; **praktisch e.,** practically minded; **materialistisch e. sein,** to be a materialist; **gegen j-n, etwas, e. sein,** to be against s.o., sth.; to be badly, unfavourably, disposed towards s.o., sth.

Einsteller, *m.* 1. (*pers.*) setter; adjuster; 2. (*device*) adjuster; adjusting, setting, device.

Einstellfassung, *f. Phot:* focusing mount.

Einstellhebel, *m. Mec.E:* adjusting lever.

einstellig, *a. Mth:* single, one-figure (number); one-place (decimal).

Einstellknopf, *m.* adjusting knob; *Phot:* focusing knob.

Einstellring, *m. Mec.E:* adjusting ring; *Phot:* focusing ring.

Einstellscheibe, *f. Mec.E: etc:* adjusting disc, setting disc; *I.C.E:* timing disc; *Artil:* dial (of dial sight); *Phot:* focusing screen; focusing glass.

Einstellschraube, *f. Mec.E: etc:* adjusting screw; set screw; regulating, regulation, screw; *Phot:* focusing screw.

Einstellskala, *f. Mec.E: etc:* adjustment, setting, scale; *Phot:* focusing scale; *Typewr:* front scale, lateral scale.

Einstellung, *f. see* **einstellen III.**

Einstellvorrichtung, *f. Mec.E: etc:* adjusting device, setting device; *Phot:* focusing device.

Einstellwinkel, *m. Opt: Av: etc:* angle of incidence; *Mec.E:* adjusting angle.

einstemmen, *v.tr. sep.* 1. **etwas in etwas** *acc.* **e.,** (*a*) to fix (blade of tool, etc.) into (hole in handle, etc.); to drive (pole, etc.) in, into, sth.; to ram down, pack, (oakum, etc.) into (opening) (*with caulking-iron*); to caulk (in) (rivet, etc.); (*b*) to make, cut, (hole) in sth. (*with punch, etc.*); **Zapfenlöcher (in etwas** *acc.*) **e.,** to cut mortises (in sth.), to mortise (sth.). 2. (*a*) **die Arme in die Hüften e.,** to brace one's arms on one's hips; **mit eingestemmten Armen,** (to stand) with one's arms akimbo; (*b*) *Ski:* to stem, to make a point-inward angle; **den rechten, linken, Fuß e.,** to stem with the right, left, foot.

einstens, *adv.*=**einst.**

einsteuern, *v.sep.* 1. *v.i.* (*sein*) (*of vessel, etc.*) to sail into (harbour, etc.); to steer into (harbour, etc.); to pilot one's way into (harbour, etc.); (*of vehicle, pers.*) to turn into (side-road, etc.). 2. *v.tr.* (*a*) to sail (vessel, etc.) into (harbour, etc.); to steer (vessel, etc.) into (harbour, etc.); to sail, steer, (vessel, etc.) in; *see also* **Hafen**[1]; (*b*) to steer (telescope, searchlight, etc.) (on to sth.).

Einstich, *m.* 1. (*a*) sticking, stabbing, (of needle, etc.) (into sth.); insertion (of needle, etc.) (into sth.); pricking (of hole, etc.); cutting in (of neck) (in tube, etc.); (*b*) sticking in, sinking in (of needle, etc.). 2. prick (of needle, etc.); small hole, puncture; *Surg:* puncture; **einen E. (in etwas** *acc.*) **machen,** to make a puncture (in sth.).

einsticken, *v.tr. sep.* **etwas in etwas** *acc.* **e.,** to embroider, work, (pattern, etc.) on (material); **sein Name, in Gold eingestickt,** his name embroidered in gold; **Tischdecke mit eingesticktem Muster,** tablecloth with an embroidered pattern.

Einstieg, *m.* **-s/-e.** 1. *in vbl senses of* **einsteigen,** *q.v.* 2. entrance (to bus, car, cockpit of aircraft, etc.); entrance, way in (to air-raid shelter, etc.); **Bus mit seitlichem E.,** bus with a side entrance.

Einstiegluke, *f.*=**Einsteig(e)luke.**

Einstieler, *m.* **-s/-.** *Av:* single-bay machine; single-strutter.

einstig, *a.* 1. former; (people, customs, etc.) of old, of olden times, *Lit:* of yore; sometime (teacher, etc.); *Lit:* erstwhile (friend, lover, etc.); **meine einstigen Schüler,** my former pupils; **sein einstiger Freund X,** his former, one-time, *Lit:* erstwhile, friend X; X, who had once been his friend; **die einstigen Ritter,** the knights of old. 2. future; prospective (heir, etc.); **die einstigen Besitzer des Hauses,** the future owners of the house.

einstimmen, *v.sep.* 1. *v.i.* (*haben*) (*a*) (**in etwas** *acc.*) **e.,** to join in (singing, song, shouts of joy, etc.); to chime in (song, shouts, etc.); **einer sang ein Lied, bald stimmten alle ein,** one sang a song, soon all the rest joined in; (*b*) to consent (to sth.); to agree (to sth.); (*c*) *A:* to agree (with sth.). 2. *v.tr.* **Instrumente aufeinander e.,** to tune instruments to each other; (*of pers.*) **aufeinander eingestimmt sein,** to be attuned to one another.

einstimmig. 1. *a.* (*a*) *Mus:* (song, etc.) for one voice; unison (singing, song, etc.); unisonant (singing, etc.); *Gr.Mus:* monophonic, monophone (music); (*b*) unanimous (resolution, refusal, praise, etc.). 2. *adv.* (*a*) *Mus:* in unison; (*conductor's direction, etc.*) unisono; (*b*) unanimously; with unanimity; with one voice; with one accord; by one, common, consent; **j-n e. wählen,** to elect s.o. unanimously, by common consent, *Parl: etc:* without one dissentient voice; **sie weigerten sich e., die Bedingungen anzunehmen,** they refused with one voice, with one accord, as one man, to accept the conditions; **der Beschluß wurde e. angenommen,** the resolution was carried, passed, unanimously.

Einstimmigkeit, *f.* (*a*) *Mus:* unison; *Gr.Mus:* monody; (*b*) unanimity; agreement; **es herrschte, bestand, E. in allen Punkten, in der Beurteilung der Angelegenheit,** there was agreement on all points, they agreed, were unanimous, in their views on the matter; **es war schwierig, E. zu erzielen,** it was difficult to reach an agreement, to achieve unanimity.

einstippen, *v.tr. sep. F:* to dip, *U.S:* to dunk, (bread, cake, etc.) in (coffee, milk, etc.).

einstmalig, *a. Lit:*=**einstig** 1.

einstmals, *adv.* 1. (*past*) formerly; one day; at one time; once. 2. (*future*) some day; one day; in times to come.

einstöckig, *a.* one-storied (building); **einstöckiges Haus,** (i) one-storied house, one-storey house; bungalow; (ii) (*incorrectly used*) two-storied house; **einstöckige Bauweise,** single-storey construction.

einstöpseln, *v.tr. sep.* to plug in (electric appliance).

einstoßen, *v.tr. sep.* (*strong*) 1. **etwas in etwas** *acc.* **e.,** to push sth. into sth.; to thrust sth. into sth.; to force sth. into sth.; to ram (post, etc.) (into ground). 2. to break, knock in (window-pane, etc.); to smash in, stave in, batter in (door, etc.); to knock down (wall, etc.); to stave in (bottom of cask, etc.).

Einstrahlung, *f. Meteor:* insolation.

einstreichen, *v.sep.* (*strong*) 1. *v.tr.* **etwas in etwas** *acc.*, *occ.* **etwas mit etwas, e.,** to rub (ointment, etc.) into sth.; to smear sth. with sth.; to smooth (ointment, etc.) into sth.; **Kitt, usw., in eine Fuge, einen Spalt, e.,** to fill up, to stop, a joint, a crack, with putty, etc. 2. *v.tr.* to rake in (money, profits, dividends, interest, etc.); to scoop (profits, dividends, interest, etc.); **ihm geht es nur darum, die Provision einzustreichen,** all he cares about is pocketing, raking in, the commission. 3. *v.tr. Metalw: etc:* to file a notch, a nick, in (sth.); to nick (sth.); to slit a groove in (sth.). 4. *v.i.* (*sein*) *Ven:* (*of partridges, etc.*) to go to cover.

Einstreichfeile, *f. Tls:* slitting-file; feather-edged file.

Einstreu, *f. Husb:* litter.

einstreuen. I. *v.tr. sep.* 1. **etwas in etwas** *acc.* **e.,** to strew sth. in sth.; to scatter (seed, etc.) in (seed-box, etc.); **Zweifel in j-s Herz e.,** to sow doubt in s.o.'s mind; **Stroh (in den Stall) e.,** to litter (down) the stable; *abs.* **den Pferden e.,** to litter (down) the horses. 2. **etwas in etwas** *acc.* **e.,** to intersperse (conversation, speech) with (quotations, witty remarks); to insert (quotations, witty remarks) (into speech); to include (quotations, witty remarks) (in speech); to insert, introduce, weave (episodes, etc.) (into novel, etc.); **auf (einen) dunklen Grund waren rote Blumen eingestreut,** red flowers were strewn on a dark ground.

II. *vbl s.* **Einstreuen** *n.*, **Einstreuung** *f. in vbl senses; also:* insertion (of quotations, witty remarks) (into a speech); insertion, introduction (of episodes, etc.) (into a novel, etc.).

Einstrich, *m.* **1.** *Locksm:* ward (of key-bit); notch, nick; slot (of screw-head). **2.** *Min:* cross-beam; bunton; spreader.
einstricken, *v.tr. sep.* **etwas in etwas** *acc.* **e.,** to knit (pattern, threads, sleeve, etc.) in sth.
einströmen. I. *v.i. sep.* (*sein*) (*of water, etc.*) to stream in, pour in, rush in; (*of light, steam, gas, etc.*) to pour in, stream in, flow in; (*of crowd of people, etc.*) to stream in, pour in; to rush in; **das Wasser strömte in den Keller ein,** the water was pouring into the cellar; **die einströmende Flut,** the flood pouring in, the inrushing, inpouring, flood; **der Dampf strömt durch das Loch in das Rohr ein,** the steam flows through the hole into the tube; **Wasser, Dampf, Gas, usw., e. lassen,** to allow water, steam, gas, etc., to flow in; *Mch: I.C.E:* to admit steam, gas; **die einströmende Luft,** the inflowing air; **das einströmende Sonnenlicht,** the sunlight streaming in; **die einströmende Menge,** the crowd (that comes, came) rushing in; the incoming crowd.
II. *vbl s.* **Einströmen** *n., occ.* **Einströmung** *f. in vbl senses; also:* (i) influx, inflow (of water, gas, etc.); (ii) *Mch: I.C.E:* admission, induction (of steam, gas, etc.).
Einströmperiode, *f. I.C.E:* admission stroke, induction stroke.
Einströmungsöffnung, *f. Mch: I.C.E:* admission port, inlet port, induction port.
Einströmungsrohr, *n. Mch: I.C.E:* admission pipe, inlet pipe, induction pipe.
Einströmungsventil, *n. Mch: I.C.E:* admission valve, inlet valve, induction valve, intake valve.
einstückeln, *v.tr. sep.* **etwas in etwas** *acc.* **e.,** to patch (piece of material) into sth.
einstudieren. I. *v.tr. sep.* to study (rôle, gestures, etc.) thoroughly, to make a thorough study of (rôle, piece of music, etc.), to learn (rôle, piece of music, poem, etc.) thoroughly; **ein Musikstück, eine Rolle, ein Gedicht, mit j-m e.,** to go through a piece of music, a part, a poem, with s.o. (very carefully, over and over again); **j-m, sich** *dat.*, **etwas e.,** to teach s.o. sth.; to learn sth. (*by constant repetition*); *Th:* **eine Rolle mit j-m e.,** to coach s.o. in a part, in his part (in a play); to rehearse, to go through, a part with s.o.; **alle seine Bewegungen sind einstudiert,** all his movements are studied.
II. *vbl s.* **1. Einstudieren,** *n. in vbl senses.* **2. Einstudierung,** *f.* (*a*)=II. 1; *also:* study (of part, etc.); *Th:* direction (of play); (*b*) **wir sahen Hamlet in einer auffallend modernen E.,** we saw a strikingly modern production of Hamlet.
einstufen. I. *v.tr. sep.* **j-n, etwas, e.,** to classify s.o., sth., to put s.o., sth., in a certain class; to grade (students, etc.) (according to ability); to grade (goods, etc.) (according to quality, etc.); **j-n in eine bestimmte Gruppe e.,** to put s.o. in a certain grade; **j-n, etwas, neu, wieder, e.,** to reclassify s.o., sth.; to regrade s.o., sth.; *Adm:* **j-n in eine höhere Steuergruppe, eine höhere Gehaltsgruppe, e.,** to put s.o. in a higher tax group, salary group.
II. *vbl s.* **1. Einstufen,** *n. in vbl senses.* **2. Einstufung,** *f.* (*a*)=II. 1; *also:* classification (of people, goods, etc.); (*b*) class; grade; **Einstufungen vornehmen,** to make classifications; to establish grades.
einstülpen. I. *v.sep.* **1.** *v.tr.* to turn (bag, finger of glove, etc.) inside out; to push in (finger of glove, ball, balloon, etc.); to turn in, to tuck in (sleeve, etc.); *Surg: etc:* to invaginate, to introsuscept, intussuscept, to introvert (bowel, etc.); **etwas in etwas** *acc.* **e.,** to push sth. into sth. **2. sich einstülpen,** (*of bag, sac, etc.*) to get turned inside out; (*of ball, balloon, hat, etc.*) to get pushed in; (*of hat, ball, sac, etc.*) to dent; *Nat.Hist: Med:* (*of bowel, scolex of tapeworm, wall of blastula, eye-cup, optic capsule, etc.*) to invaginate; (*of bowel*) to become introsuscepted, intussuscepted, introverted; (*of uterus*) to become retroverted.
II. *vbl s.* **1. Einstülpen,** *n. in vbl senses.* **2. Einstülpung,** *f.* (*a*)=II. 1; *also: Nat.Hist: Med: etc:* invagination (of bowel, scolex of tapeworm, wall of blastula, bladder, etc.); introsusception, intussusception, introversion (of bowel); retroversion (of uterus); (*b*) indentation; dent (in hat, ball, balloon, etc.); *Nat.Hist: Med: etc:* invagination (in wall of bladder, blastula, etc.); sac.
einstündig, *a.* (speech, etc.) lasting one hour; one-hour (examination, etc.); *Sch:* **einstündige Vorlesung,** course of lectures of one hour weekly.
einstürmen, *v.i. sep.* (*sein*) **1. in etwas** *acc.* **e.,** to storm, rush, burst, into (place, building, etc.). **2. auf j-n, etwas** *acc.*, **e.,** to rush at, on, to bear down on (opponent, etc.); *Mil:* to make an assault on, to charge, storm, attack (enemy, position, etc.). **3. auf j-n e.,** (*a*) (*of pers.*) to bombard, to assail, s.o. (with questions, requests, etc.); (*b*) (*of feelings, doubts, temptations, etc.*) to assail s.o.; to crowd in on s.o.; (*of impressions, thoughts, etc.*) to swarm, crowd, in upon s.o.; **Zweifel stürmten auf ihn ein,** doubts assailed him, he was assailed by doubts; **mannigfache Eindrücke stürmten auf ihn ein,** manifold impressions swarmed in upon him, crowded in on him; **von allen Seiten stürmten Schwierigkeiten auf ihn ein,** he was assailed on all sides by difficulties; difficulties crowded in, pressed in, on him from all sides.
Einsturz, *m.* collapse, collapsing (of building, wall, roof, etc.); falling in (of building, trench, etc.); foundering (of ground, building, etc.); caving in (of roof, ground, etc.).
Einsturzbeben, *n. Seismology:* earthquake due to underground subsidence.
einstürzen, *v.sep.* **1.** *v.i.* (*sein*) (*of building, roof, bridge, wall, etc.*) to collapse; to fall in; to give way; to fall down; to tumble down; (*of ground, building, etc.*) to founder; (*of roof, ground, etc.*) to cave in; **das Haus droht einzustürzen,** the house is in danger of collapse, collapsing; **die Decke stürzte über uns ein,** the ceiling fell about our ears, caved in upon us. **2.** *v.i.* (*sein*) **auf j-n e.,** (*of feelings, etc.*) to assail s.o.; **die Ereignisse stürzten gewaltsam auf ihn ein,** events crowded in on him violently. **3.** *v.tr.* to cause (sth.) to collapse, to fall in, to tumble down; to cave (sth.) in; to batter down (wall, etc.).
Einsturzgefahr, *f.* danger of collapse, collapsing; **das Haus muß wegen E. geräumt werden,** the house must be cleared, as it is in danger of collapsing, as it is unsafe; *P.N:* **'Vorsicht, E.!'** 'danger—building unsafe!'
Einsturztrichter, *m. Geol: etc:* sink-hole.
einstweilen [ainst'vailən], *adv.* for the present; for the time being; temporarily; meanwhile; in the meantime; **bleibe e., wo du bist,** stay where you are for the time being; **ich muß mich e. mit dem begnügen, was ich habe,** I have to be satisfied with what I have got for the time being, for the present; **unser Haus ist im Herbst fertig; e. leben wir im Hotel,** our house will be ready in the autumn; meanwhile, in the meantime, we are living in a hotel; **ich weiß nicht, in welches Zimmer ich den neuen Schrank stellen werde; ich habe ihn e. in die Diele gestellt,** I don't know in which room I am going to put the new cupboard; I've put it in the hall for the time being, temporarily, for the moment.
einstweilig, *a.* temporary (arrangement, address, regulation, accommodation, etc.); provisional (arrangement, etc.); interim (regulation, etc.); *Jur:* **einstweilige Verfügung,** interim order; (interim) injunction.
Einswerden, *n.* becoming one, unification (with nature, etc.).
eintägig, *a.* (feast, etc.) lasting one day; day-old (chick, etc.); ephemeral (flower, etc.).
Eintagsblume, *f. Bot:* ephemeral flower.
Eintagsfieber, *n.* ephemeral fever.
Eintagsfliege, *f.* **1.** *Ent:* ephemera, ephemeron; may-, day-fly. **2.** *F:* (*pers.*) ephemera.
Eintagsküken, *n.* day-old chick.
Eintagstid, *f. Dial:* diurnal tide.
Eintagswesen, *n.* ephemeral being; short-lived being; creature of a (single) day.
eintanzen (sich), *v.refl. sep.* (*a*) (*of ballet-dancer, etc.*) to do a few steps (to get into practice); **nach dem Unfall dauerte es lange, bis er sich wieder eingetanzt hatte,** after the accident it took him a long time to get used to dancing again; (*b*) (*of couple*) **sich aufeinander e.,** to get used to dancing together, to become practised in dancing together; **sie sind aufeinander eingetanzt,** they are used to, practised in, dancing together; they dance well together, they are well partnered.
Eintänzer, *m.* (professional male) dancing partner; gigolo.
eintauchen, I. *v.sep.* **1.** *v.tr.* to dip, *U.S:* to dunk, (bread, cake, etc.) in (coffee, milk, etc.); **die Feder e.,** to dip one's pen in the ink; **j-n, etwas, in etwas** *acc.* **e.,** to dip, plunge, s.o., sth., into (water, etc.); to immerse s.o., sth., in (liquid, etc.); (*of ship*) to pitch (her head) into (sea); **die Hände, usw., in eine Flüssigkeit e.,** to dip, to plunge, one's hands, etc., into a liquid. **2.** *v.i.* (*sein*) (*a*) (*of ship*) to pitch into (trough of wave, etc.); (*of pers., animal, etc.*) **mit dem Kopf, usw., zuerst e.,** to plunge in head, etc., first; *Swim:* to enter the water head, etc., first; *Mec.E:* **eintauchende Achse,** pitching, plunging, axis; (*b*) to become immersed.
II. *vbl s.* **Eintauchen** *n.*, **Eintauchung** *f. in vbl senses; also:* (*a*) immersion (of s.o., sth.) (in liquid); *Theol:* **Taufe durch E.,** baptism by immersion; (*b*) entry (into the water).
Eintauchmikroskop, *n. Opt:* microscope with immersion objective.
Eintauchrefraktometer, *n. Ph:* immersion refractometer, dipping refractometer.
Eintausch, *m.* exchange, exchanging (of sth.); barter (of goods); truck, trucking, *F:* swap, swapping, *U.S: F:* trade, trading (of sth.); **E. einer Ware gegen eine andere,** exchange, barter, of one commodity for another; **achten Sie beim E. Ihres Gutscheins bitte auf die Nummer,** when exchanging your coupon please make a note of its number.
eintauschen, *v.tr. sep.* to exchange, to barter (goods, etc.); **etwas gegen, für, etwas e.,** to exchange, barter, truck, *Com. & U.S: F:* trade, *F:* swap, sth. for sth.; **sie tauschten ihre Waren gegen Lebensmittel ein,** they exchanged, bartered, their goods for foodstuffs; **tauschen Sie Ihre Aktien gegen neue ein,** exchange your shares for new ones; **ich habe meinen alten Wagen gegen ein neueres Modell eingetauscht,** I have exchanged my old car for a more recent model; **ein kleines Übel gegen ein größeres e.,** to get rid of a small evil and saddle oneself with a greater one.
eintausend, *num. a. inv.* one thousand, a thousand; **£1000, in Worten eintausend Pfund,** £1,000, in words one thousand pounds.
einteilen. I. *v.tr. sep.* **1.** (*a*) **Tiere, Pflanzen, usw., in Arten, Gattungen, usw., e.,** to class, to classify, animals, plants, etc., into species, genera, etc.; **Menschen in Gruppen, usw., e.,** to divide people into groups, etc.; **die Würmer sind in drei Gruppen eingeteilt,** worms are divided into three groups; **die Bevölkerung nach der Höhe ihres Einkommens in Klassen e.,** to class, to grade, the population according to income; **ein Meßinstrument in Grade e.,** to graduate, to calibrate, a measuring instrument; **ein Buch in Kapitel e.,** to divide a book into chapters; **eine Stadt in Bezirke e.,** to divide a town into wards; **eine Strecke in gleiche Abschnitte e.,** to divide a line into equal sections; (*b*) to plan (out) (room, surface to be decorated, etc., page, expenditure, etc.); **sein Geld e.,** to plan one's expenditure; **seine Vorräte für die ganze Woche e.,** to plan out one's rations for the whole week; **sich** *dat.* **seine Arbeit, sein Studium, (gut, schlecht) e.,** to plan out, to organize, one's work, one's studies, (well, badly); **sich** *dat.* **seine Zeit e.,** to plan how to spend, how to divide up, one's time; (*of housewife, etc.*) **sie kann nicht e.,** she is a bad manager; **wenn du mit deinem Geld auskommen willst, mußt du besser e. lernen,** if you want to make both ends meet you must learn to manage (your money) better; **es ist nicht mehr viel davon da, wir müssen es e.,** there is not much of it left, so we have to go carefully with it, we have to use it economically. **2.** *Mil: etc:* **j-n zu einer Arbeit, einem Dienst, e.,** to detail, tell off, s.o. for a duty.
II. *vbl s.* **1. Einteilen,** *n. in vbl senses.* **2. Einteilung,** *f.* (*a*)=II. 1; *also:* division (of sth.) (**in etwas** *acc.*, into sth.); graduation (of scale, etc.); classification (of plants, etc.); **E. der Arbeit,** planning of work; (*b*) division; classification; category; graduation (of thermometer, etc.); **E. der Erde in Breitengrade,** division of the earth into latitudes; **eine E. nach einem bestimmten Gesichtspunkt vornehmen,** to make a classification, *Log:* to establish a division, according to a given point of view; **der Aufsatz, die Rede, hat keine E.,** the essay, the speech, has no proper plan; (*c*) *F:* (*of pers.*) **keine E. haben,** to have no sense of planning; to be a bad manager (in financial matters).
einteilig, *a.* one-piece (bathing-costume, etc.); *Tchn:* solid (bearing, etc.).
Einteilungsgrund, *m. Log: fundamentum divisionis,* principle of division.
Eintel, *n.* **-s/-.** *Mth:* (*in speech only*) **ein, zwei, usw., Eintel,** one, two, etc., over one.
eintönig, *a.* monotonous (voice, recitation, literary style, scenery, etc.); monotonous, humdrum, dull, tedious (existence, work, etc.).
Eintönigkeit, *f.* monotony (of recitation, voice, literary style, scenery, etc.); sameness (of scenery, existence, work, etc.); monotony, humdrumness, dullness, tediousness (of existence, work, etc.).
Eintopf, *m.*, **Eintopfgericht,** *n. Cu:* dish of

vegetables, potatoes and meat, cooked together; hot-pot; stew.

Eintracht, *f.* -/. harmony; concord; unity; **E. stiften, herstellen,** to establish harmony, concord; **in friedlicher E. nebeneinander leben,** to live side by side in perfect harmony; **überall herrscht E.,** everywhere harmony reigns; **die E. erhalten,** to keep, to maintain, the peace; *Prov:* **E. bringt Macht,** unity is strength; **E. vermehrt, Zwietracht zerstört,** united we stand, divided we fall.

einträchtig. 1. *a.* harmonious, united (family, etc.). **2.** *adv.* harmoniously; unitedly; in harmony, concord, unity; **sie leben e. zusammen,** they live together in harmony.

einträchtiglich, *adv.*=**einträchtig** 2.

Eintrag, *m.* **-(e)s/⸗e. 1.** entry (in account-book, diary, register, etc.); *Com:* **einen E. in ein Buch machen, vornehmen,** to make an entry in a book; **ein falscher E.,** a wrong entry, a misentry. **2. (etwas** *dat.*, **j-m,) E. tun,** to damage (s.o., sth.); to wrong (s.o.); to inflict an injury, a loss, on (s.o.); to be detrimental, injurious, prejudicial, hurtful, to (s.o., s.o.'s interests, s.o.'s reputation); to hurt, injure (s.o.'s interests, cause, etc.); to detract from (value, s.o.'s interests, reputation, rights, etc.); to impair (s.o.'s health, authority, reputation, etc.); **j-s Interessen, Autorität, Ruf, E. tun,** to hurt, injure, damage, s.o.'s interests, reputation; to impair s.o.'s authority; **die lange Trennung tat ihrer Freundschaft keinen E.,** the long separation did not hurt, harm, their friendship, did not affect their friendship; **gelegentliche Verluste können unserem Geschäft keinen E. tun,** occasional losses cannot be injurious to our business; **ihre altmodische Kleidung tat ihrer Schönheit keinen E.,** her old-fashioned clothes in no way detracted from her beauty. **3.** *Tex:*=**Einschuß** 3.

eintragen. I. *v.tr. sep.* (*strong*) **1.** to gather (in) (the harvest, etc.); **die Bienen tragen den Blütenstaub ein,** the bees gather the pollen; **etwas in etwas** *acc.* **e.,** to carry sth. into (room, etc.). **2.** (*a*) **etwas (in etwas** *acc.*) **e.,** to write down, to put down, to enter (details, facts, observations, etc.) (in one's note-book, diary, etc.); to write down, to put down, to enter, to register (name, item, etc.) (on list, in register, etc.); to register, to enter (birth, marriage, deed, property, ship, patent, etc.) (in register); to record (fact, etc.) (in diary, book, etc.); *Book-k:* to book, to enter (up) (an order, etc.); to enter (up), to post, to pass (items) (in ledger, etc.); to make an entry of (a transaction) (in account-book, etc.); **sich in eine Liste e.,** to write down, to put down, to enter, to register, one's name on a list; **sich ins Gästebuch e., sich e.,** to sign the visitors' book, to sign, write something in, the guest book; **sich e.,** (*at hotel*) to sign the (hotel) register; **sich als Journalist e.,** to put, set, oneself down as a journalist; *Book-k:* **etwas falsch e.,** to make a wrong entry, a misentry; **der Posten wurde auf Ihr Konto eingetragen,** the item was entered to your account; *Com: Jur:* **eine Gesellschaft (ins Handelsregister) e. lassen,** to register a company (in the Commercial Register, Trade Register); **(handelsgerichtlich) eingetragene Gesellschaft,** registered company; incorporated company; **eingetragener Verein** (*abbr.* **e.V.**), registered society *or* association; **eingetragenes Warenzeichen, Muster,** registered trade-mark, design; *Jur:* **einen Geschworenen in die Schöffenliste e.,** to impanel, empanel, a juror; *Nau:* **einen Matrosen in die Musterrolle e.,** to enter a seaman on the ship's books; (*b*) to write in (place-name), to put in (place-name, feature) (on map); to put in, add in (colour) (in painting); (*c*) *Mth: etc:* to plot (point, curve, etc.); **die Abszisse, die Ordinate, eines Punktes e.,** to plot the abscissa, the ordinate, of a point; (*d*) *Tex:* **den Schuß e.,** to pick; to shoot the weft. **3.** (*a*) (*of investment, business, transaction, etc.*) to bring in, bear, yield (profit, etc.); **das Amt, das Geschäft, trägt wenig ein,** the position is not a lucrative one, is unremunerative, not at all remunerative; the business yields little profit, brings little in; **ein Geschäft, das viel einträgt,** a profitable, paying, lucrative, business; **das trägt nicht viel ein,** there's not much profit in it, it does not pay well; (*b*) **seine Handlungsweise trug ihm viele Freunde, viel Anerkennung, ein,** his conduct gained him many friends, much praise; **seine Hartnäckigkeit trug ihm die Feindschaft vieler Leute ein,** his pertinacity made him many enemies; **es trug ihm nichts als Spott ein,** he gained, earned, nothing by it, reaped nothing from it, but ridicule; **seine Gefälligkeit trug ihm nur Undank ein,** his kindness gained him, reaped, nothing but ingratitude. **4.** *v.i.* (*haben*) *A:* **j-m e.**=**j-m E. tun,** *q.v. under* **Eintrag** 2.

II. *vbl s.* **1. Eintragen,** *n. in vbl senses.* **2. Eintragung,** *f.* (*a*)=II. 1; *also:* entry (of name, etc.) (on list, in book, etc.); **E. in ein öffentliches Verzeichnis, Register,** registration; entry (of birth, marriage, land, patent, etc.) (in public register); enrolment (of new member); *Book-k:* entry (of items) (in a ledger); (*b*)= **Eintrag** 1.

einträglich, *a.* lucrative, remunerative, profitable (trade, occupation, etc.); paying (concern, etc.); **das Amt ist nicht e.,** the position is not a lucrative one, is unremunerative, not at all remunerative; **ein einträgliches Geschäft,** a profitable, paying, lucrative, business.

Einträglichkeit, *f.* lucrativeness, remunerativeness, profitableness (of trade, occupation, etc.).

eintränken, *v.tr. sep.* **1.** *Metall:* to steep (silver, etc.) (in molten lead, etc.). **2.** *F:* **j-m etwas e.,** to pay, serve, s.o. out for sth., to pay s.o. back for sth.; **ich werde es ihm schon noch e.,** I'll pay, serve, him out for that, I'll pay him back for that; I'll make him smart for it; I'll be even with him yet; **ich werde ihm seine Unverschämtheit e.,** I'll make him pay, smart, for his impudence.

einträufeln. I. *v.tr. sep.* **etwas in etwas** *acc.* **e.,** to introduce (liquid) drop by drop into sth.; to instil (liquid) into sth.; to put (lotion) drop by drop into (eye, etc.); **j-m etwas e.,** to give s.o. drops of sth.; **die Tropfen müssen in die Nase eingeträufelt werden,** the drops have to be put up the nose.

II. *vbl s.* **Einträufeln** *n.*, **Einträuf(e)lung** *f. in vbl senses; also:* instillation (of liquid) (into sth.); introduction (of liquid) drop by drop (into sth.).

eintreffen. I. *v.i. sep.* (*strong*) (*sein*) **1.** (*of pers., goods, vehicle, ship, letter, etc.*) to arrive; **in Köln, England, e.,** to arrive at Cologne, to arrive in, reach, Cologne, England; **bei j-m e.,** (*of pers.*) to arrive at s.o.'s house, office, etc.; (*of goods, letter, etc.*) to reach s.o.; **er traf rechtzeitig am Bestimmungsort ein,** he arrived at, reached, his destination in good time; **ich erwarte, daß er morgen, hier, dort, eintrifft,** I expect he'll get here, there, tomorrow; **er wird voraussichtlich nächste Woche e.,** he is expected to arrive next week; **sobald er in Köln eintraf,** as soon as he arrived in, reached, Cologne; **benachrichtigen Sie uns bitte, sobald der Brief, das Paket, eintrifft,** please let us know as soon as the letter, the parcel, arrives, comes to hand; **der Zug wird voraussichtlich mit zehn Minuten Verspätung e.,** the train is expected to arrive ten minutes late; **der Zug trifft um sieben Uhr in Berlin ein,** the train arrives, is due, at Berlin at seven o'clock; **ein Telegramm aus London ist für Sie eingetroffen,** a telegram from London has arrived, come, for you; **die Zahlungen, die Güter, werden vor Monatsende bei Ihnen e.,** the payments, the goods, will reach you before the end of the month; **aus Amerika traf die Nachricht ein, daß . . .,** from America news came that . . .; (*notice in shop*) **Ananas, frisch eingetroffen,** pineapples, newly arrived. **2.** (*a*) (*of dream, prophecy, fears, etc.*) to come true; (*of predicted event*) to happen, *Lit:* to come to pass; **seine Voraussagung traf ein,** his prediction came true, proved correct, true; **seine Träume, seine Befürchtungen, trafen ein,** his dreams, his fears, came true; what he had dreamt of, feared, happened, came to pass; **alles traf genau so ein, wie sie es vorausgesagt hatte,** everything happened exactly as she had predicted; (*b*) *A:* **mit etwas e.,** (*of events*) to coincide with sth.; (*of actions*) to correspond, conform, be consistent, be in accordance, be in conformity, with sth.

II. *vbl s.* **Eintreffen,** *n. in vbl senses; also:* arrival; **bei meinem E.,** on arriving, on my arrival.

eintreibbar, *a. Com:* recoverable (debt).

eintreiben. I. *v.sep.* (*strong*) **1.** *v.tr.* **etwas in etwas** *acc.* **e.,** (*a*) to drive (peg, wedge, nail, pile, etc.) into sth.; to ram (pile, etc.) into ground, etc.); **einen Pflock, einen Keil, usw., e.,** to drive in a peg, wedge, etc.; to drive a peg, wedge, etc., home; (*b*) to drive (sheep, etc.) into (pen, etc.); **das Vieh e.,** to drive the cattle home. **2.** *v.tr. Com: Jur:* to recover, to call in (money outstanding); to recover, to collect, to get in (debts, taxes, etc.); to exact (taxes, money, tolls, etc.); **sorgen Sie bitte dafür, daß unsere Außenstände eingetrieben werden,** please take steps to ensure the recovery of outstanding debts due to us, of money owed to us. **3.** *v.i.* (*sein*) (*of boat, etc.*) to run, sail (into bay, harbour, etc.); to drift (into bay, harbour, etc.).

II. *vbl s.* **Eintreiben** *n.*, **Eintreibung** *f. in vbl senses of* I. 1, 2; *also:* recovery, collection (of debts, taxes); exaction (of taxes, etc.).

eintreten, *v.sep.* (*strong*) **I.** *v.i.* (*sein*) **1.** (*a*) *of pers.*) to enter, to come in; to go in; to walk in; **in ein Zimmer, usw., e.,** to enter a room, etc.; **treten Sie bitte ein!** please come in! (*on office door*) **bitte e. ohne anzuklopfen!** please enter without knocking, please walk (straight) in; **er trat durch einen Seiteneingang ein,** he entered, came in, went in, by a side entrance; (*b*) (*of thgs*) to enter; to pass in; **in etwas** *acc.* **e.,** to enter, pass into, sth.; **dort, wo der Fluß in die Ebene eintritt,** (the place) where the river enters the plain; **die Kugel trat durch die Schläfe ins Gehirn ein,** the bullet entered the brain through the temple; *Astr:* **wenn die Sonne in das Zeichen des Steinbocks eintritt,** when the sun passes into the sign of Capricorn; **ein Planet tritt in den Schatten eines anderen ein,** a planet passes into the umbra of another. **2. in etwas** *acc.* **e.,** (*a*) to join (association, society, federal union, party, etc.); **in das Heer e.,** to enter, to join, the army; **in einen geistlichen Orden, in ein Kloster, e.,** to join a religious order; to enter a monastery *or* convent; **bei j-m, in eine Firma, als Teilhaber e.,** to enter, go, into partnership with s.o.; to become a partner in a firm; **in das Geschäft seines Vaters e.,** to enter, go into, join, one's father's firm; (*b*) to take up, to start (a job); **in j-s Dienst e.,** to enter into s.o.'s service; **wann treten Sie bei uns ein?** when do you start (work) with us? **er trat in die diplomatische Laufbahn ein,** he entered upon a diplomatic career; (*c*) to enter (up)on, to start (discussions, negotiations, etc.); to join (discussions, negotiations, etc.); (*of third party*) **in einen Streit e.,** to join a dispute; **als Amerika in den Krieg eintrat,** when America entered the war; (*d*) **in j-s Rechte, Pflichten, e.,** to enter into s.o.'s rights; to take over s.o.'s obligations; *Jur:* **in eine Erbfolge e.,** to succeed to an inheritance, to an estate; (*e*) (*of pers., disease, undertaking, action, etc.*) **in eine neue Phase, in ein neues Stadium, e.,** to enter a new phase, a new stage; **der Krieg ist in eine neue Phase, ein neues Stadium, eingetreten,** the war has entered a new phase, a new stage; **er ist in sein sechzigstes Lebensjahr eingetreten,** he has entered upon his sixtieth year. **3.** (*a*) **für j-n e.,** to take, fill, s.o.'s place; to deputize for s.o.; to act in s.o.'s stead; to officiate for s.o.; (*b*) **für j-n, etwas, e.,** to support s.o., sth.; to stand up, speak up, *F:* stick up, for s.o., sth.; to take s.o.'s part, s.o.'s side; to champion s.o.'s cause; to intercede for s.o.; to plead for s.o., sth.; **bei j-m für j-n, für j-s Sache, e.,** to use one's influence with s.o. on s.o.'s behalf; to intercede with s.o. for s.o., on s.o.'s behalf; to plead with s.o. for s.o.; to plead s.o.'s cause with s.o.; **für eine Sache, eine Idee, eine Lehre, e.,** to support a cause, an idea, a doctrine; to champion a cause; **für seine Überzeugungen e.,** to stand up for one's convictions; **für seine Freunde e.,** to stand up, *F:* to stick up, for one's friends; **für die Durchführung einer bestimmten Maßnahme e.,** to advocate the carrying out of a certain measure; **er trat dafür ein, daß die Flüchtlinge aufgenommen würden,** he advocated that the refugees should be taken in. **4.** to occur, to happen; to take place; (*of difficulties, conditions, etc.*) to arise; *F:* to crop up; (*of rains, winter, darkness, etc.*) to set in; **der Tod trat plötzlich ein,** death came, ensued, suddenly; **der Tod trat um fünf Uhr ein,** death occurred at five o'clock; **bei eintretendem Frost, Tauwetter,** when frost, thaw, sets in; **falls keine Verwicklungen e.,** if no complications arise, set in; **es ist keine Besserung im Befinden des Kranken eingetreten,** there has been no improvement in the state of the patient; **inzwischen ist eine günstige Wendung eingetreten,** meanwhile there has been a change for the better; **für einen Augenblick trat Stillschweigen ein,** silence fell for a moment; **in diesem Zeitraum traten wichtige Ereignisse ein,** important events took place in this period; **nach zwei Stunden trat bei dem Patienten ein heftiges Fieber ein,** after two hours the patient developed a high temperature; **das Ereignis trat früher ein, als man erwarten konnte,** it happened sooner than could be expected; **wenn der Fall e. sollte, daß . . .,** should it happen, should the case arise, occur, that . . .; *Com:* **bei eintretendem Bedarf,** when the demand arises; when, if, required.

II. eintreten, *v.tr.* **1.** to tread (sth.) in; to tread down, trample down (earth around plant, etc.); **etwas in etwas** *acc.* **e.,** to tread sth. into (earth, etc.); **sich** *dat.* **einen Dorn, usw., e.,** to run a thorn, etc., into one's foot. **2.** to kick (sth.) in; **die Türe e.,** to kick the door in. **3. seine Schuhe e.,** (i) to wear one's shoes down on the inside; (ii) to break one's shoes in. **III.** *vbl s.* **Eintreten,** *n. in vbl senses; also:* (*a*) entrance; entry; (*b*) intercession (**bei j-m,** with s.o.); **für j-n,** on s.o.'s behalf); advocacy, championship, espousal (**für eine Sache,** of a cause). *Cp.* **Eintritt.**

eintretendenfalls, *adv.* should the case arise, occur; in case of need; should it so happen.

Eintretensdebatte, *f. Parl: etc: Swiss:* preliminary debate.

Eintretensfrage, *f. Parl: etc: Swiss:* previous, preliminary, question.

eintrichtern, *v.tr. sep. F:* **j-m., sich** *dat.,* **etwas e.,** to drum, hammer, (lesson, etc.) into s.o.'s, one's, head; **j-m e., was er sagen oder tun soll,** to drill s.o. in what he has to say or to do.

Eintritt, *m.* **1.** (*a*) entering; entrance; entry; coming in; going in; passing in; **j-m den E. verwehren,** to refuse s.o. entry; **E. in einen Ort,** entering of a place; entrance, entry, into a place; **'kein E.', 'E. verboten',** 'no admittance'; 'private'; **bei seinem E.,** when he entered, came in, went in; (*b*) *Astr:* immersion (of planet); **E. der Sonne in das Zeichen des Steinbocks,** passing of the sun into the sign of Capricorn. **2.** (*a*) entrance, entry, into (association, society, army, convent, etc.); entering, joining, of (association, society, federal union, army, religious order, party, etc.); accession to (party, etc.); **sein E. ins Kloster erfolgte nicht freiwillig,** he did not enter the monastery voluntarily; **der E. eines Staates in einen Bundesstaat,** entry of a state into a confederation; entering, joining, of a confederation by a state; *Com:* **E. in eine Firma (als Teilhaber, usw.),** entering, coming into, a firm, joining of a firm (as a partner, etc.); (*advertisement*) **die Firma X sucht zum baldigen E. einen Ingenieur,** engineer required at an early date by the firm of X; **unser Unternehmen bietet einem erfahrenen Geschäftsmann baldigen E. als tätiger Teilhaber,** our firm offers an experienced man of business the opportunity to join us at an early date as an active partner; (*b*) **E. in eine Stellung,** taking up of, starting of, a job; entering into service; **E. in eine Laufbahn,** entering (up)on a career; (*c*) entering (up)on (discussions, negotiations, etc.); joining of (discussions, negotiations, etc.); entering (of third party, etc.) into (dispute, etc.); **E. eines Landes in den Krieg, in die Weltpolitik,** entry, entering, of a country into the war, into world politics; *Mus:* **E. eines Themas in einer Fuge,** entry of a theme in a fugue; (*d*) **E. in ein neues Stadium, eine neue Phase,** entering (of pers., disease, action, etc.) into a new stage, a new phase; **E. ins Mannesalter,** entering upon, accession to, manhood; **E. ins Greisenalter,** passing into old age; (*e*) **E. in j-s Rechte, Pflichten,** entry into s.o.'s rights; taking over of s.o.'s obligations; *Jur:* **E. in eine Erbfolge,** succession to an inheritance, an estate. **3.** onset, setting-in, beginning (of rains, winter, night, etc.); **nach E. der Dunkelheit,** after dark; after nightfall; **bei E. der Dunkelheit,** when it gets dark; when darkness sets in, falls; at nightfall; **nach E. der kalten Jahreszeit,** after the beginning of the cold season; after the cold season has, had, set in. **4.** entrance; admission (**für, in, etwas** *acc.,* to sth.); entrance-fee; admission-fee; **'E. frei',** 'admission free'; **Kinder haben freien E.,** children are admitted free; **wir haben zwei Mark E. bezahlt,** we paid two marks admission, we paid an entrance-fee of two marks.

Eintrittsebene, *f. Opt:* **=Einfallsebene.**

Eintrittsgeld, *n.* entrance-fee; admission-fee; entrance-money; door-money.

Eintrittskarte, *f.* admission ticket *or* card.

Eintrittspreis, *m.* admission-fee; entrance-fee; **der E. beträgt zwei Mark,** admission is two marks.

eintrocknen, *v.i. sep.* (*sein*) (*a*) (*of ink, gelatine, etc.*) to dry (up); (*of bog, pond, etc.*) to dry (up), to go dry; (*of stream, etc.*) to dry (up); (*b*) (*of skin, berries, etc.*) to shrivel (up).

eintröpfeln, *v.tr. sep.* **=einträufeln.**

eintrüben (sich), *v.refl. sep. Meteor:* (*of weather*) to grow dull; **Eintrübung** *f,* (onset of) dull weather, dullness; **eine allmähliche Eintrübung wird eintreten,** general conditions will gradually become dull.

eintunken, *v.tr. sep.* to dip, *U.S:* to dunk (bread, cake, etc.) in (coffee, milk, etc.); **die Feder e.,** to dip one's pen in the ink; **etwas in etwas** *acc.* **e.,** to dip sth. into (liquid); **j-n (ins Wasser) e.,** to put s.o. bodily into the water.

einüben, *v.tr. sep.* to practise, learn (piece of music, part, dance, figure in skating, etc.); **ein Musikstück, einen Tanz, eine Rolle, eine Figur, mit j-m e.,** to practise a piece of music, a dance, a part, a figure, with s.o.; to coach s.o. in a part, in his part (in a play); **sich** *acc.,* **j-n, e.,** to train oneself, to train s.o.; **sich** *dat.,* **j-m, etwas e.,** to teach oneself, s.o., sth. by practising hard; **eine Mannschaft e.,** to practise, train, *Sp:* coach, a team, a crew.

einundeinhalb, *cardinal num. a.* **=eineinhalb.**

Einung, *f. see* **einen.**

einverleiben. I. *v.tr. sep. & insep.* **etwas etwas** *dat.,* **etwas in etwas** *acc.,* **e.,** to incorporate sth. in sth.; to annex (territory) to (another territory); **sich** *dat.* **etwas e.,** (*of state, etc.*) to incorporate (province, territory, etc.); to annex (territory); *F:* (*of pers.*) to eat *or* drink sth., *F:* to put oneself outside (food, etc.), to down, knock back (drink); **er hat das Stück seiner Sammlung einverleibt,** he has added the piece to his collection; *Ling:* **einverleibende Sprachen,** agglomerating, polysynthetic, incapsulating, incorporating, languages. **II.** *vbl s.* **Einverleiben** *n.,* **Einverleibung** *f. in vbl senses; also:* incorporation (of sth.) (into sth.); annexation (of territory) (to a state).

Einvernahme, *f.* **-/-n.** *Austrian: Swiss:* interrogation, questioning (of s.o.); *Jur: etc:* examination (of witness); interrogation (of prisoner).

Einvernehmen [1]**,** *n.* understanding; agreement; concord; harmony; entente; **mit j-m in gutem, in bestem, E. stehen,** to be on friendly, on good, on the best of, terms with s.o.; to be in full agreement with s.o.; **in gutem E. miteinander leben,** to live together in harmony; to live together on friendly, on good, terms; **sich mit j-m ins E. setzen,** to come to terms, an understanding, an arrangement, with s.o.; to come to, arrive at, an agreement with s.o.; **unser gutes E. mit England,** our good understanding with England; **in gegenseitigem E. mit . . . ,** in mutual understanding, agreement, with . . . ; **das gute E. unter den Nationen,** concord among nations; the comity of nations.

einvernehmen [2]**,** *v.tr. sep.* (*strong*) *Austrian: Swiss:* **j-n e.,** to interrogate, question, s.o.; *Jur: etc:* to examine (witness, etc.); to interrogate (prisoner, etc.).

einverstanden, *pred.a.* **e. sein,** to agree, to consent; **mit etwas e. sein,** to agree to, consent to, approve of, *F:* be agreeable to, sth.; **mit j-m e. sein,** (i) to approve of s.o.; to be pleased with s.o.; (ii) to agree, be at one, be in agreement, with s.o.; to be of the same mind as s.o., of a mind with s.o.; **nicht e. sein,** to disagree; to disapprove; **mit etwas nicht e. sein,** to disagree with sth.; to disapprove (of) sth.; **mit j-m nicht e. sein,** (i) to disapprove of s.o.; to be out of sympathy with s.o.; (ii) to disagree, be in disagreement, with s.o.; to be at variance with s.o.; to dissent from s.o.'s opinion; **sich e. erklären, etwas zu tun,** to agree, consent, to do sth.; **sich mit etwas e. erklären,** to assent to sth.; to agree, consent, to sth.; to express one's approval of sth.; **damit e. sein, daß etwas geschieht, daß jemand etwas tut,** to agree, consent, to sth.'s being done, to agree, consent, to s.o.'s doing sth.; to approve of sth.'s being done, to approve of s.o.'s doing sth.; **ich bin mit allem e.,** I agree, consent, to everything; I agree with everything; **ich bin mit allem e., was er vorschlägt,** I agree to everything he proposes; I agree with, approve of, everything he proposes; **mit einer Maßnahme, einem Vorschlag, e. sein,** to be in agreement with a measure, a proposal; **ich bin damit e., daß er zu uns kommt,** I'm quite agreeable to his coming to us; **wenn du damit e. bist,** if that is agreeable to you; if that is all right with you; **ich bin mit Ihren Bedingungen e.,** I agree to, assent to, your conditions; **einverstanden! agreed! quite so! very well! all right!** *F:* right oh! O.K.! **einverstanden? agreed? do you agree? all right?** *F:* O.K.?

einverständlich, *a. Austrian:* (action) undertaken by common consent; *adv.* (to act) by common consent.

Einverständnis, *n.* (*a*) consent; assent; approval; *Jur: etc:* **schriftliches E.,** written consent; **mündliches E.,** verbal assent; **j-s E. einholen,** to obtain s.o.'s consent; **sein E. erklären,** to give one's consent; to declare one's approval; **es**

geschah mit seinem E., it was done with his approval, his consent; (*b*) understanding; agreement; accord; **geheimes, stillschweigendes, E.,** tacit understanding, agreement; *Pej:* connivance; collusion; **es herrschte, bestand, vollkommenes E. zwischen ihnen,** there was perfect understanding, full agreement, between them; **im E. mit j-m handeln,** to act in agreement with s.o.; *Pej:* to act in collusion with s.o.; **ein geheimes E. mit dem Feinde haben, in geheimem E. mit dem Feinde stehen,** to have a secret agreement with the enemy; to be in collusion, in league, with the enemy.

Einwaage, *f.* **-/.** **1.** weight lost (in weighing out). **2.** (*esp. in compounds*) content (by weight); 'Nettogewicht 200 g, Fleischeinwaage 150 g', 'net weight 200 g, meat content 150 g'.

einwachsen [1]**,** *v.i. sep.* (*strong*) (*sein*) (*of toe-, finger-nail, etc.*) to grow in; **in etwas** *acc.* **e.,** (*of toe-, finger-nail*) to grow into (flesh); (*of plant*) to grow into (crevice, etc.); **eingewachsener Fußnagel,** ingrowing, ingrown, toe-nail.

einwachsen [2]**,** *v.tr. sep.* (*weak*) to (wax-)polish, put (wax-)polish (on floor, piece of furniture, etc.); to wax (floor, skis, etc.).

Einwand, *m.* objection (**gegen etwas,** to sth.); **einen E. machen, erheben,** to make, to raise, an objection; **Einwände gegen etwas erheben, vorbringen,** to raise objections, to object, to sth.; to argue against sth.; **einen E. widerlegen,** to refute an objection; to dispose of an objection; **er machte keinen weiteren E.,** he made no further objection; he made no further demur; *cp.* **Einwendung,** *q.v. under* **einwenden II. 2.**

Einwanderer, *m.* immigrant.

einwandern. I. *v.i. sep.* (*sein*) **in ein Land, ein Gebiet, e.,** (*of pers.*) to come into, to enter, a country, an area, (as a settler); *abs.* to immigrate; (*of tribes, beasts*) to migrate into a country, an area; **die Ostgoten wanderten in Italien ein,** the Ostrogoths came and settled in Italy; **die Hugenotten sind in Preußen eingewandert,** the Huguenots came to Prussia. **II.** *vbl s.* **Einwandern** *n.,* **Einwanderung** *f. in vbl senses; also:* immigration (of settler).

einwandfrei, *a.* faultless; unimpeachable (conduct, character, evidence, etc.); impeccable, irreproachable (conduct, quality, style, etc.); incontestable, indubitable (proof, evidence, etc.); (*of skater*) **in einwandfreier Haltung eine Figur ausführen,** to execute a figure in a faultless attitude; **ein einwandfreies Alibi haben,** to have a perfect alibi; **die Waren befinden sich in einwandfreiem Zustand,** the goods are in perfect condition; **ich habe es aus einwandfreier Quelle,** I have it from an unimpeachable source; **nicht e.,** faulty; (*of proof, evidence, etc.*) contestable; (*of character*) impeachable; dubious; questionable; shady; **er ist nicht ganz e.,** (i) he is a somewhat shady character; (ii) he is politically not quite reliable; **ein Witz, der nicht ganz e. ist,** a doubtful joke; *adv.* **es steht e. fest,** it is beyond question.

einwärts, *adv.* **einwärts-,** *comb.fm.* inward(s); **die Füße einwärtssetzen, einwärtsstellen,** to turn one's toes in; **mit e. gerichteten, gestellten, Füßen gehen,** to walk pigeon-toed, with one's toes turned in; **einwärtsbiegen,** to bend, flex, (sth.) inward(s).

-einwärts, *comb.fm.* into . . . ; **landeinwärts,** into the country; **feldeinwärts,** into the field; **waldeinwärts,** into the wood.

einwärtsdrehen, *v.tr. sep.* to turn (sth.) inwards; to introvert (sth.); *Med: etc:* to pronate (hand, etc.); **Einwärtsdrehung** *f,* turning inwards; inward turn; introversion; *Med: etc:* pronation (of hand, etc.).

einwärtsgehen, *v.i. sep.* (*strong*) (*sein*) (*of pers.*) to walk pigeon-toed, with one's toes turned in.

einwärtskehren, *v.tr. sep.* to introvert (toes, etc.); **Einwärtskehrung** *f, Surg:* introversion (of eyelid).

einweben, *v.tr. sep.* (*weak & strong*) to weave in, to work in (gold thread, ornament, etc.); **etwas in etwas** *acc.* **e.,** to weave, to work, (silk, gold thread, design, etc.) into (fabric); *F:* to weave, to work, (episodes, parables, rhymes, etc.) into (story, etc.); **ein dunkler Stoff mit eingewebten Silberfäden,** a dark material interwoven, wrought, with silver threads; **ein Blumenmuster in Seide, Tuch, e.,** to weave a floral design into silk, cloth; to weave, to damask, silk, cloth, with a floral design.

einwechseln, *v.sep.* **1.** *v.tr.* to change (foreign currency, bank-note, etc.); **etwas gegen, für, etwas anderes e.,** to (ex)change one thing for another. **2.** *v.i.* (*sein*) *Ven:* (*of game*) in **ein anderes Revier e.,** to move to a new haunt.

einwecken, *v.tr. sep.* to preserve (fruit, meat, vegetables, etc.); to bottle (fruit, vegetables) (in sterilizing apparatus).

Einweg-, *comb.fm. Com:* non-returnable . . .; **Einwegflasche** *f*, non-returnable bottle; **Einwegglas** *n*, non-returnable jar.

Einweghahn, *m. Tchn:* one-way cock.

Einwegschalter, *m. El.E:* one-way switch.

einweibig, *a. Bot: Z: etc:* monogynous.

Einweibigkeit, *f. Bot: Z: etc:* monogyny.

einweichen, *v.tr. sep.* (*weak*) to soak (dried vegetables, prunes, etc.); to steep (dried fruit, bread, etc.); to macerate (herbs, etc.); **etwas in etwas** *acc.* **e.,** to soak, steep, sth. in (liquid); **die schmutzige Wäsche e.,** to soak, steep, the dirty washing, to put the dirty washing (in) to soak, steep.

einweihen. I. *v.tr. sep.* **1.** (*a*) to inaugurate, *U.S:* to dedicate (building, monument, statue, etc.); *Ecc:* to consecrate (church, etc.); **seine neue Wohnung, sein neues Haus, e.,** to give, have, a house-warming; (*b*) *F:* to use, wear, (sth.) for the first time; *F:* to christen (object); **unserem Gast zu Ehren werde ich heute abend mein neues Kleid e.,** I shall wear my new dress for the first time to-night in honour of our guest. **2. j-n in etwas** *acc.* **e.,** to initiate s.o. in (a science, an art, mysteries, etc.), into (an office, a secret, etc.); **j-n in ein Geheimnis e.,** to initiate s.o. into a secret, to let s.o. into a secret; **eingeweiht sein,** to be in the secret, *F:* in the know; **er wurde in den Plan, in die Verschwörung, eingeweiht,** he was let into the plan, into the plot; **in eingeweihten Kreisen berichtet man, daß . . .,** it is reported in well-informed quarters that . . .; **Eingeweihte** *m, f,* initiate; *F:* person in the know; **den Eingeweihten spielen,** to pretend to be in the know.

II. *vbl s.* **1. Einweihen,** *n. in vbl senses.* **2. Einweihung,** *f.*=II. 1; *also:* (*a*) inauguration, *U.S:* dedication (of building, monument, etc.); *Ecc:* consecration (of church, etc.); (*b*) initiation (of s.o.) (in, into, sth.).

Einweihungsfeier, *f.* inaugural ceremony, *U.S:* dedication ceremony; consecration (of church, etc.).

Einweihungsfest, *n.* inaugural celebration; house-warming.

Einweihungsrede, *f.* inaugural address.

einweisen. I. *v.tr. sep.* (*strong*) (*a*) **j-n in etwas** *acc.* **e.,** to introduce s.o. to (new duties, etc.); to instruct s.o. in (his duties, etc.); **j-n in sein Amt e.,** (i) to introduce s.o. to (the functions of) his appointment; (ii) to install s.o. in his office; to institute *or* induct (parish priest); (*b*) (*at car-park, airport, etc.*) to direct (s.o., car, aircraft, etc.) in; *Adm:* **j-n in eine Wohnung e.,** to assign a flat *or* house to s.o.; **j-n in ein Lager e.,** to send s.o. to, to assign s.o. to, a camp; **j-n in den Besitz einer Sache e.,** to assign a property to s.o.

II. *vbl s.* **1. Einweisen,** *n. in vbl senses.* **2. Einweisung,** *f.*=II. 1; *also:* introduction (of s.o.) (to a new job); instruction (of s.o.) (in sth.); installation (of s.o.) (in an office); institution *or* induction (of parish priest).

einwenden. I. *v.tr. sep.* (*conj. like* **wenden**; *usu. p.t.* **wandte ein,** *p.p.* **eingewandt**) **etwas e.,** to raise, make, an objection; **e., daß . . .,** to object that . . .; **man, er, wandte ein, daß . . .,** it was objected, he objected, made the objection, that . . .; **ich wandte ein, daß wir nicht genug Zeit hätten,** I objected, pointed out, that there was not enough time; **er wußte nichts darauf einzuwenden,** he had no reply (to make) to it; **etwas gegen j-n, etwas, e.,** to raise, make, an objection to s.o., sth.; to object (sth.) to s.o., sth.; **was haben Sie gegen ihn einzuwenden?** what objection have you got to him? why do you object to him? **ich habe gegen deinen Vorschlag nichts einzuwenden,** I have no objection to (make to), nothing to say against, your proposal; **es läßt sich nichts gegen sein Argument e.,** there is no reply to his argument; **gegen ein Glas Bier hätte ich nichts einzuwenden,** I wouldn't mind, I wouldn't say no to, a glass of beer.

II. *vbl s.* **1. Einwenden,** *n. in vbl senses.* **2. Einwendung,** *f.* (*a*)=II. 1; (*b*) objection; *Jur:* plea in bar; **rechtsvernichtende E.,** plea by way of traverse; **rechtshindernde E.,** plea by way of confession and avoidance; **Einwendungen gegen etwas erheben,** to raise objections, to object, to sth.; *Jur:* to raise objections (in law) to (witness, indictment, etc.). *Cp.* **Einwand.**

einwerfen, *v.tr. sep.* (*strong*) **1.** to throw in (sth.); **etwas in etwas** *acc.* **e.,** to throw sth. into sth.; **eine Münze (in einen Automaten) e.,** to insert a coin (in a slot-machine); **einen Brief e.,** to post, mail, a letter (in a letter-box); *Fb: etc:* **den Ball (ins Spiel) e.,** to throw in the ball; *abs.* **e.,** to throw in. **2.** to break, smash, knock out (window-pane, etc.) (*by throwing stones, etc.*). **3.** (*a*) to interpose (remark, etc.); (*b*) *abs.* to object; **er warf ein, daß mein Argument nicht stichhaltig sei,** he objected that my argument did not hold water.

einwertig, *a. Mth:* single-valued (function); *Ch:* monovalent; univalent; monohydric (alcohols).

Einwertigkeit, *f. Mth:* single value (of function); *Ch:* monovalency, monovalence; univalency, univalence.

einwickeln, *v.tr. sep.* (*a*) to wrap (sth., s.o.) (up); **einen Gegenstand in Papier e.,** to wrap (up), do up, an article in paper; **ein Kind in ein Umschlagetuch e.,** to wrap a baby (up) in a shawl; **sich fest in seinen Mantel e.,** to wrap oneself up well in one's overcoat; **sein Finger war in einen großen Verband eingewickelt,** his finger was swathed in a big bandage; (*b*) *F:* **j-n e.,** to get round s.o.; **sie hat ihn völlig eingewickelt,** she has twisted him round her little finger; **er ist ein durchtriebener Bursche, aber ich lasse mich nicht von ihm e.,** he is a cunning fellow, but I won't let him get the better of me; **ich lasse mich nicht von deinen schönen Worten e.,** I am not to be taken in, won over, by your fine words; you can't get round me with your fine words; **sie haben ihn derartig eingewickelt, daß er ein neues Testament gemacht hat,** they inveigled him into making a new will.

einwiegen, *v.tr. sep.* to rock (child, etc.) to sleep; **j-n mit falschen Hoffnungen, Versprechungen, e.,** to lull s.o. with false hopes, promises.

einwilligen. I. *v.i. sep.* (*haben*) to consent; to agree; **in etwas** *acc.* **e.,** to consent, agree, to sth.; **in j-s Vorschläge, Bedingungen, e.,** to agree, consent, to s.o.'s proposals, conditions; to accept s.o.'s conditions; **wenn sie (darin) einwilligt, mir ihr Haus zu überlassen,** if she agrees to let me have her house.

II. *vbl s.* **1. Einwilligen,** *n. in vbl senses.* **2. Einwilligung,** *f.* (*a*)=II. 1; (*b*) consent; **seine E. zu etwas geben, erteilen,** to give one's consent, to consent, to sth.; **mit E. des Vaters,** with the consent of the father; **j-s E. einholen,** to obtain s.o.'s consent; **seine E. zu etwas verweigern, vorenthalten,** to refuse to consent, one's consent, to sth.; to withold one's consent.

einwintern, *v.sep.* **1.** *v.tr.* to winter (plants, etc.); **Kartoffeln, Rüben, e.,** to protect potatoes, turnips, against frost. **2.** *v.i.* (*sein*) **in einem Ort e.,** to winter at, in, a place.

einwirken[1]. I. *v.i. sep.* (*haben*) **auf etwas** *acc.*, **j-n, e.,** to have an effect on sth., s.o.; to influence sth., s.o.; to exercise, to have, an influence on sth.; to exert, exercise, an influence on s.o.; to work on s.o., on s.o.'s mind; (*of thgs*) to affect (result, event); (*of stimulants, etc.*) to act (up)on (brain, heart, etc.); *Ch: etc:* **(wechselseitig) aufeinander e.,** to act upon each other; to interact; **auf j-n, etwas** *acc.*, **günstig e.,** to have, exercise, a good effect, influence, on s.o., sth.; **wirken Sie bitte dahingehend auf ihn ein, daß . . .,** please bring your influence to bear on him to . . .; **eine Veränderung in der Umwelt, eine Kraft, wirkt auf ein Organ ein,** a change in environment, a force, affects, acts on, an organ.

II. *vbl s.* **1. Einwirken,** *n. in vbl senses.* **2. Einwirkung,** *f.* (*a*)=II. 1; (*b*) influence, effect (**auf etwas** *acc.*, **j-n,** (up)on sth., s.o.); effect, action (of heat, current, water, etc.) (on sth., s.o.); *Ch: etc:* **gegenseitige, wechselseitige, E.,** action upon each other; interaction; **unter der E. von Morphium,** under the influence of morphia; **telepathische Einwirkungen,** telepathic influences; **die E. des Lichtes,** the effect of (the) light; **die E. der Sonne auf die Erde,** the action, effect, of the sun on the earth; **die E. eines Reizes auf ein Organ,** the action of a stimulus on an organ.

einwirken[2], *v.tr. sep.* to weave in, work in (gold thread, design, etc.); **etwas in etwas** *acc.* **e.,** to weave, work, (gold thread, design, etc.) into (fabric).

Einwohner, *m.* **-s/-,** inhabitant (of country, town, etc.); resident (of town, etc.); **eine Stadt von 10 000 Einwohnern,** a town of 10,000 inhabitants.

Einwohnermeldeamt, *n. Adm:* registration office (keeping records of residents).

Einwohnerschaft, *f.* inhabitants; population (of town, village, etc.).

Einwohnerzahl, *f.* number of inhabitants; **die E. stieg um 5%,** the population increased by 5%.

einwölben, *v.tr. sep. Constr:* to vault (ceiling, room, cellar, etc.).

Einwurf, *m.* **1.** throwing in (of sth.); **E. einer Münze in einen Automaten,** insertion of a coin in a slot-machine; **'Einwurf 1 Mark',** 'insert 1 mark'; *Fb: etc:* throw-in. **2.** slit (of letter-box, etc.); slot (of slot-machine, etc.). **3.** (i) interjection; interposition; (ii) objection; **einen E. machen, vorbringen,** (i) to make an interjection; (ii) to make, raise, an objection, to object; **einen E. widerlegen,** to refute, dispose of, an objection.

einwurzeln, *v.i. sep.* (*sein*) (*a*) (*of plants*) to take root (**in etwas** *dat.*, in sth.); (*of pers.*) **in einem Ort eingewurzelt sein,** to be rooted in a place; to be established in a place; (*b*) (*of evil, bad habits, etc.*) **tief eingewurzelt sein,** to be deeply rooted; to be inveterate; **ein tief eingewurzelter Brauch,** a deep-rooted custom; **eine tief eingewurzelte Abneigung gegen j-n,** a deep-rooted aversion to s.o.; **ein Gedanke, der tief bei ihm eingewurzelt ist,** a thought deep-rooted in his mind.

Einzahl, *f. Gram:* singular; **in der E.,** in the singular.

einzahlen. I. *v.tr. sep.* to pay in (money); **Geld bei einer Bank e.,** to pay in, to deposit, money at a bank; **eine Geldsumme auf ein Konto e.,** to pay money into an account; *Fin:* **voll eingezahlte Aktien,** fully paid(-up) shares.

II. *vbl s.* **1. Einzahlen,** *n. in vbl senses.* **2. Einzahlung,** *f.* (*a*)=II. 1; *also:* payment (of money); (*b*) payment; (*at bank, etc.*) deposit; **eine E. machen,** to pay money in; to deposit money.

Einzahler, *m.* payer; *Bank:* depositor.

Einzahlung, *f. see* **einzahlen II.**

Einzahlungsbuch, *n. Bank:* paying-in book, *U.S:* bankbook.

Einzahlungsschein, *m. Bank:* pay(ing)-in slip, *U.S:* deposit slip.

einzahnen, *v.tr. sep. Tchn:* to cut teeth in (timbers, etc.); to dovetail (timbers).

einzapfen, *v.tr. sep. Carp:* to insert (end of timber) into a mortise; to tenon and mortise (timbers), to join (timbers) by tenon and mortise; *Mec.E:* to fix (lug of machine-part) into (boring).

einzäunen. I. *v.tr. sep.* to fence (in), to hedge in, to enclose (piece of ground, etc.); **ein eingezäuntes Feld,** an enclosed, a fenced-in, field; **das Grundstück ist nicht eingezäunt,** the piece of ground is unfenced, unenclosed, open.

II. *vbl s.* **1. Einzäunen,** *n. in vbl senses.* **2. Einzäunung,** *f.* (*a*)=II. 1; *also:* enclosure (of piece of ground, etc.); (*b*) fence; enclosure.

einzeichnen, *v.tr. sep.* (*a*) to draw in (details, etc.) (on picture, plan, etc.); *Surv: etc:* to plot (levels, position, etc.) (on plan, map, etc.); *Mth: Geom:* to plot (curve, etc.); to inscribe (polygon, etc.) (in square, etc.); (*b*) **sich** *acc.* **in etwas** *acc.* **e.,** to write (down) one's name (on list, etc.); (*of subscriber*) to put oneself down (for sth.).

Einzeiler, *m.* **-s/-.** *Pros:* monostich.

einzeilig, *a.* one-line, single-line (entry, etc.); *Pros:* monostich (verse); *adv. Typewr:* **e. geschrieben,** single-spaced.

Einzel, *n.* **-s/-.** *Ten:* singles.

Einzel-, *comb.fm.* individual . . .; single . . .; isolated . . .; **Einzelausbildung** *f,* individual training; *Med:* **Einzelgabe** *f,* single dose; *Tp:* **Einzelanschluß** *m,* single line; **Einzelerscheinung** *f,* isolated phenomenon.

Einzelabteil, *n. Rail:* single compartment.

Einzelanfertigung, *f. Ind:* job-work; production of single parts, specialized production.

Einzelantrieb, *m. Mec.E:* individual drive.

Einzelaufhängung, *f. Mec.E:* independent suspension.

Einzelaufzählung, *f.* detailed enumeration.

Einzelausgabe, *f. Publ:* separate edition.

Einzelbeispiel, *n.* (*a*) individual example; (*b*) isolated instance.

Einzelbett, *n.* single bed.

Einzelbild, *n. Cin:* (*a*) frame; (*b*) still.

Einzeldarstellung, *f.* (*a*) individual handling; detailed presentation; (*b*) individual study (of small field of knowledge); monograph.

Einzelexemplar, *n.* **1.** (*a*) unique copy (of book, etc.); (*b*) single volume, fascicule, etc. (of serial, publication, etc.). **2.** (*a*) special piece; odd piece (of set, etc.); (*b*) unique specimen.

Einzelfall, *m.* (*a*) isolated instance, case; (*b*) individual case; particular, special, case.

Einzelfeuer, *n. Mil: etc:* independent fire; single rounds (of fire) (from machine-gun, etc.).

Einzelfirma, *f. Com:* one-man firm.

Einzelgänger, *m.* **1.** (i) *Ven:* old boar; (ii) rogue (elephant, buffalo, etc.). **2.** person who goes his own way; solitary person; *F:* lone wolf.

Einzelgesang, *m. Mus:* solo (song).

Einzelhaft, *f.* solitary confinement.

Einzelhandel, *m. Com:* retail trade; **Waren im E. verkaufen, vertreiben,** to sell goods (by) retail.

Einzelhandelspreis, *m. Com:* retail price.

Einzelhändler, *m. Com:* retail trader, retail dealer, retailer.

Einzelhaus, *n.* detached house.

Einzelheit, *f.* detail; particular; **Einzelheiten anführen,** to give particulars (of sth.); to particularize; **die Einzelheiten eines Vorgangs,** the details, particulars, of an event; **eine Angelegenheit in allen Einzelheiten erörtern,** to discuss a matter in detail; **wegen näherer Einzelheiten wenden Sie sich an . . .,** for further particulars, details, apply to . . .; **auf alle Einzelheiten eingehen,** to go into all the details, all the particulars; **etwas in allen Einzelheiten berichten, erzählen,** to give a detailed, circumstantial, account of sth.; to relate sth. in detail; **sich in Einzelheiten verlieren,** to get lost in the details; to get bogged down in detail(s); **ich kenne die Angelegenheit in allen Einzelheiten,** I know all the details of the matter; *F:* I know all the ins and outs of the matter; I know the matter inside-out.

Einzelhof, *m.* isolated farm.

Einzelkampf, *m.* single combat; *Sp:* individual contest.

Einzelkaufmann, *m. Com:* sole trader.

Einzelkind, *n.* only child.

Einzellader, *m. Sm.a:* single-loader.

Einzeller, *m.* **-s/-.** *Biol:* unicellular organism; protist.

einzellig, *a.* (*a*) *Biol:* unicellular; **Einzellige** *pl*, unicellular organisms; protista; (*b*) *Bot:* unilocular, one-celled (ovary).

Einzelmensch, *m.* individual.

einzeln. 1. (*a*) *a.* individual; single; separate (parts, etc.); odd (glove, stocking, etc.); *adv.* singly; individually; separately; one by one; **der einzelne Mensch,** the individual man, the individual; **die einzelnen Bände eines Werkes, ein einzelner Band,** the separate, individual, volumes of a work; a single, an individual, volume; **die einzelnen Teile eines Ganzen,** the individual, separate, parts of a whole; **in seiner Zusammenfassung umriß er noch einmal kurz die einzelnen Punkte,** in his summary he again briefly outlined the individual, separate, points; **ein einzelnes Haus,** a solitary house; **eine einzelne Kiefer,** a single, isolated, lone, pine; **jeder einzelne Fall wird sorgfältig geprüft werden,** each individual case will be carefully examined; **jedes einzelne Kind erhielt ein Geschenk,** each child, every one of the children, received a present; **er führte Beispiele an, um jeden einzelnen Punkt seiner Ausführungen zu beweisen,** he gave examples to prove each and every point of his statements; **ich möchte mit den Mitgliedern e. sprechen,** I should like to speak to the members individually; **die Bände können nicht e. verkauft werden,** the volumes cannot be sold singly, separately; **die Zeugen e. befragen,** to question the witnesses individually, singly; **die Kandidaten traten e. in das Zimmer ein,** the candidates entered the room one by one; **die Besucher wurden e. eingelassen,** the visitors were admitted one at a time; (*b*) *a.* **einzelne Punkte in einem Bericht gesondert behandeln,** to treat a few points in a report separately; **wir können nur einzelne Bewerbungen annehmen,** we can only accept a few applications; **in der Sammlung sind nur einzelne Gemälde bemerkenswert,** only a few isolated paintings in the collection are worthy of note. **2.** *indef.pron.* (*a*) **der einzelne,** the individual; **jeder einzelne,** each one; each individual; (*stressed*) every single, individual, one; **jeder einzelne von uns muß seine Pflicht erfüllen,** every single one of us has to do his duty; **der einzelne ist machtlos,** the individual is powerless; (*b*) **das einzelne,** detail(s); **im einzelnen,** in detail; **im einzelnen auf etwas eingehen,** to enter, go, into the details, into the particulars, of sth., to go into sth. in detail; **ein bis ins einzelne gehender Bericht,** a detailed account; **im einzelnen kann ich mich nicht mehr erinnern,** I cannot remember in detail; **alles einzelne erzähle ich dir später,** I'll tell you all the details later; **vom Einzelnen ins Ganze gehen,** to pass from details to the whole; (*c*) **einzelne,** a few (people, things); some (people, things); **einzelnes,** a few (things); **einzelne von uns,** some few of us; **einzelne erklärten, daß . . .,** a few, some (people), stated that . . .; **in einem Bericht einzelnes hervorheben,** to stress a few points in a report; **ich erinnere mich nur noch an einzelnes,** I remember only a few things, one or two points.

einzelnstehend, *a.* (house, etc.) standing alone; isolated (house, etc.); *Bot:* solitary, lone, isolated (flower, pine, etc.).

Einzelperson, *f.* single person; individual (person).

Einzelrichter, *m. Jur:* judge *or* magistrate sitting alone.

Einzelspiel, *n. Ten: etc:* singles (match); *Golf:* single.

Einzelstück, *n.* (*a*) special piece; odd piece (of set, etc.); (*b*) unique piece.

Einzelteile, *n.pl.* single, individual, parts (of machine, etc.); component parts, components.

Einzelverkauf, *m. Com:* retail (sale); **im E. 5 Mark,** retail price 5 marks.

Einzelwesen, *n.* individual (being).

Einzelzelle, *f.* **1.** *Biol:* single, isolated, cell. **2.** (*a*) single cell; (*in prison*) solitary (confinement) cell; (*b*) individual cubicle.

Einzelzimmer, *n.* single (bed)room; (*in hospital*) private room.

einziehen, *v.sep.* (*strong*) **I.** *v.tr.* **1.** (*a*) to draw in (sth.); to pull in (sth.); to take in (sail, etc.); to retract (part of body, etc.); **ein Kabel e.,** to draw in, haul in, a cable; **ein Tau e.,** to haul in a rope; **der Fischer zieht seine Netze ein,** the fisherman pulls in, hauls in, his nets; **den Kopf e.,** (*of pers.*) to draw in one's head; to duck one's head; (*of tortoise*) to withdraw its head; (*of snail, cat*) **die Fühlhörner, die Krallen, e.,** to draw in, retract, its horns, its claws; **den Schwanz e.,** (i) (*of animal*) to put its tail between its legs; (ii) *F:* (*of pers.*) to retreat (ignominiously); **er schlich mit eingezogenem Schwanz davon,** he slunk off with his tail between his legs; **zieh den Bauch ein!** draw your stomach in! *F:* pull in your tummy! **die Flagge e.,** to haul down the flag; *Nau:* **die Segel e.,** to furl, take in, the sails; **die Ruder e.,** to ship the oars; **den Anker e.,** to haul in the anchor, to take the anchor aboard; *Av:* **das Fahrgestell e.,** to retract the undercarriage; (*b*) (*of plants, absorbent substance, etc.*) to draw in, absorb, take in, soak in (moisture, etc.); (*of pers., etc.*) to inhale (air, tobacco-smoke, etc.); to sniff in (fresh air, scent, etc.). **2.** (*a*) **etwas in etwas** *acc.* **e.,** to insert sth. into sth.; to put sth. into sth.; **eine Schnur, usw., in etwas** *acc.* **e.,** to insert a cord, etc., in (hem, etc.); to pass, thread, a cord, etc., through (hem, etc.); **ich muß das Gummiband wieder e.,** I must re-thread the elastic; *Tex:* **die Kettenfäden in den Kamm e.,** to pass, draw, enter, the warp threads through the reed; (*b*) *Constr: etc:* **Scheiben, Balken, e.,** to put panes, beams, in; to insert panes, beams; **Wände e.,** to erect partition-walls; (*c*) **sich einen Splitter (in die Hand, usw.) e.,** to run a splinter into one's hand, etc.; to get a splinter (in one's hand, etc.). **3.** (*a*) *Constr:* to recess, set back (façade, etc.); *Print:* to indent (line); (*b*) *Metalw:* to reduce (metal sheets). **4.** (*a*) to withdraw (publication, s.o.'s driving licence, passport, etc.); to call in (currency, bank-note, etc.); to retire, withdraw, take up (bill, note, etc.); **Aktien e.,** to withdraw shares; **Münzen e.,** to withdraw coins from circulation; (*b*) **eine Dienststelle e.,** to abolish, wind up, a government, an army, etc., office; **ein Stipendium e.,** to withdraw, discontinue, stop, a scholarship; (*c*) *Jur: etc:* to confiscate, seize (goods, property, etc.); **sein Besitz wurde vom Staat eingezogen,** his property was confiscated by, seized by, forfeited to, the state. **5.** (*a*) to collect, get in (debts, taxes, rents, etc.) (**von j-m,** from s.o.); *Fin: Com:* to encash, collect (bills, etc.); (*of bank*) **einen Scheck e.,** to collect a cheque; **seine Außenstände e.,** to call in one's money outstanding; (*b*) to collect, gather (information, etc.); **Erkundigungen über etwas** *acc.*, **j-n, e.,** to make inquiries about sth., s.o.; to seek information about sth., s.o.; **die eingezogenen Erkundigungen ergaben, daß . . .,** the information obtained showed, proved, that . . .; (*c*) *Mil:* to call (s.o.) up; **zum Militärdienst eingezogen werden,** to be called up, to be called to the colours; **einen bestimmten Jahrgang e.,** to call up a certain age group.

II. einziehen, *v.i.* (*sein*) **1.** (*a*) (*of pers., army, etc.*) **in eine Stadt, usw., e.,** to come into, to enter, a town, etc.; to make one's entrance, one's entry, into a town, etc.; **die Truppen zogen in die Stadt ein,** the troops made their entry into, entered, the town; **der Frühling ist eingezogen, zieht ins Land ein,** spring has made its appearance, spring is making its appearance in the country; (*b*) **in eine neue Wohnung e.,** to move into a new house, flat; *abs.* **e.,** to move in; **bei j-m e.,** to move into s.o.'s house; to take lodgings, to take up residence, with s.o.; **wann ziehen Sie bei uns ein?** when do you move in with us? **2.** (*of moisture, flavour, etc.*) **in etwas** *acc.* **e.,** to penetrate, permeate, sth.; (*of paint, liquid*) to soak into sth.; *abs.* **e.,** to soak in; **der Farbstoff muß e. können,** the dye must be allowed to soak in, to sink in; **die Feuchtigkeit ist in die Wände eingezogen,** the moisture has seeped, percolated, into the walls. *See also* **eingezogen.**

III. *vbl s.* **1. Einziehen,** *n. in vbl senses; also:* (*a*) retraction (of claws, horns, etc.); *Av:* **E. des Fahrgestells,** retraction of the undercarriage; (*b*) absorption (of moisture, etc.); inhalation (of air, tobacco-smoke, etc.); (*c*) insertion (of cord, etc.) (**in etwas** *acc.*, in sth.); (*d*) *Metalw:* reduction (of metal sheets); *Print:* indentation (of line); (*e*) withdrawal (of currency, publication, passport, etc.); *Fin:* retirement, withdrawal (of bill, note, etc.); abolishment, abolition (of public service, etc.); withdrawal, discontinuation, stoppage (of scholarship, etc.); *Jur:* confiscation, seizure (of goods, property, etc.); (*f*) collection (of information, etc.); collection (of debts, taxes, rents, etc.) (**von j-m,** from s.o.); *Fin: Com:* encashment, collection (of bills, etc.). **2. Einziehung,** *f.* (*a*)=III. 1; (*b*) *Constr:* recess (in wall, etc.).

Einzieher, *m. Tex:* warp-drawer; drawer-in; reacher-in.

Einziehhaken, *m. Tex:* heddle-hook.

Einziehschacht, *m. Min:* intake shaft.

Einziehstrebe, *f. Av:* radius rod (of undercarriage).

Einziehung, *f. see* **einziehen III.**

einzifferig, *a. Math:* single-figure, one-figure (entry, decimal, etc.).

einzig. 1. *a.* (*a*) only, sole, single (specimen, etc.); **sein einziger Sohn,** his only son, (*stressed*) his one and only son; **das ist seine einzige Sorge,** that is his one, only, sole, care; **ein einziger Blick genügte,** a single glance sufficed; **seine einzige Waffe war sein Spazierstock,** his only weapon was his walking-stick; **sein einziger Halt,** his sole support; **ein einziges Mal muß ich sie noch sehen,** I must see her just once again; **ich hatte keine einzige Patrone mehr,** I hadn't a single cartridge left; **er konnte nicht eine einzige, keine einzige, Frage beantworten,** he couldn't answer a single question, one question; **das ist meine einzige Hoffnung,** that is my one and only hope; **mein einziger Kragen,** my one and only collar; (*b*) (*of talent, beauty, etc.*) unique; unrivalled; unparalleled; peerless; **sie ist e. in ihrer Art,** she is unique, alone, of her kind; **er ist e. auf seinem Gebiet,** he is without his equal, no one can match up to him, in his field; *Lit:* **mein einziger Liebling,** my own darling; *F:* **du bist e.!** (i) you're the limit! (ii) you are wonderful! **ist das nicht e.!** (i) have you ever heard of such nonsense! (ii) isn't that wonderful, marvellous! **2.** *adv.* (*a*) only; **e. und allein,** solely, entirely, uniquely; **das ist das e. Richtige (zu tun),** that is the only thing that can be done; **das ist das e. Wahre,** that is the only truth; **das e. Gute daran ist . . .,** the only good thing about it is . . .; **es ist e. und allein seinen Bestrebungen zu verdanken, daß . . .,** it is due entirely, solely, to his efforts that . . .; (*b*) **seine Leistung steht e. da,** his achievement is unique; **dieser Vorfall steht e. da in der Geschichte unseres Landes,** this incident stands alone, is unique, in the history of our country; **sie ist e. schön,** she is singularly beautiful. **3.** *indef.pron.* **ein einziger,** one only, one person only; only one, only one person; **nicht ein einziger, kein einziger,** not a single one, not one, none whatever; **er war der einzige, der es bemerkte,** he was the only one who noticed it; he alone noticed it; **sie waren die einzigen, die gerettet wurden,** they were the only ones to be saved; **du bist nicht die einzige, die von ihm betrogen wurde,** you are not the only person, the only one, who has been cheated by him; **einem einzigen habe ich alles erzählt,** I have told everything just to one person; **nicht ein einziges meiner Kinder,** not a single one of my children; **Peter ist unser Einziger,** Peter is our only son, only child; **das einzige,** the only thing; **das ist das einzige, was wir für Sie tun können,** that is the only thing we can do for you; *F:* **das einzige daran ist, es ist ziemlich teuer,** the only thing is that it is rather expensive.

einzigartig, *a.* unique, singular, uncommon, unparalleled (event, phenomenon, etc.); unique, singular (man, etc.); singular, remarkable, extraordinary (beauty, merit, etc.); **das ist eine einzigartige Gelegenheit,** that is a unique opportunity, *F:* a most unique opportunity; **seine einzigartigen Verdienste auf dem Gebiete der Medizin,** his outstanding, extraordinary, merits in the sphere of medicine; **dies ist ein**

einzigartiger Beweis für . . ., this is a remarkable proof of . . ., this is a unique proof of . . . .

Einzigartigkeit, *f.* uniqueness, uniquity, singularity (of man, event, phenomenon, etc.); singularity, remarkableness, extraordinariness (of talent, merits, beauty, etc.).

Einzigkeit, *f.* uniqueness; singleness; oneness.

einzuckern, *v.tr. sep.* to cover (sth.) with sugar; to sugar (sth.); to candy (fruit).

Einzug, *m.* **1.** (*a*) entrance, entry (of pers., army, etc.) (into town, etc.); entry, appearance, coming (in) (of spring, etc.); **(seinen) E. halten,** (*of pers., army, etc.*) to make one's, its, entrance, entry, **(in eine Stadt, usw.,** into a town, etc.); (*of spring, etc.*) to make its appearance, to come; **der E. (Christi) in Jerusalem,** Christ's entry into Jerusalem; **gestern hielt unser neues Mädchen seinen E.,** our new maid made her appearance yesterday; (*b*) moving in; **der E. in eine neue Wohnung,** moving into a new house *or* flat; (*c*) *Tex:* **E. der Kettenfäden,** passing, drawing in, entering, of the warp threads (through the reed, etc.). **2.** (*a*) *Fin:* collection, encashment (of bills, etc.); (*b*) *Constr:* recessing, setting back (of façade, etc.); *Print:* indentation (of line). **3.** (*a*) *Tex:* draught (of warp); (*b*) *Constr:* recess (in wall, etc.); *Print:* indentation (in line).

Einzüger, *m.* **-s/-.** *Adm: Swiss:* collector (of rates, etc.).

Einzugsgebiet, *n. Hyd.E: Ph.Geog:* catchment area, catchment basin; drainage area, drainage basin.

einzwängen, *v.tr. sep.* **etwas, j-n, in etwas** *acc.* **e.,** to force, squeeze, jam, wedge, sth., s.o., into sth.; **sich** *acc.* **in ein enges Kleid, ein Korsett, e.,** to squeeze oneself into a tight dress, a corset; **seine Füße in enge Schuhe e.,** to force, squeeze, one's feet into tight shoes.

Einzylindermotor, *m. I.C.E:* single-cylinder, one-cylinder, engine.

Eipilze, *m.pl. Fung:* oomycetes.

Eipulver, *n. Cu:* dried egg.

eirund[1], *a.* oval, egg-shaped, oviform.

Eirund[2], *n.* oval.

Eis[1], *n.* **-es/.** **1.** ice; **mit Eis bedeckt,** ice-covered, covered with ice; (*of water, etc.*) **sich in Eis verwandeln,** to turn to ice; to freeze; (*of ship, etc.*) **vom Eis(e) eingeschlossen,** trapped, caught, in the ice; hemmed in by the ice; icebound; **aufs Eis gehen,** (i) to go on the ice; (ii) to go skating; **Tauwetter setzte ein, und das Eis brach,** a thaw set in and the ice broke; *F:* **endlich war das Eis gebrochen,** at last the ice was broken; *F:* **j-n aufs Eis führen,** to lead s.o. on to thin ice, on to dangerous ground; **(etwas) auf Eis legen,** (i) to put (sth.) into cold storage; to put (food, drink, etc.,) on (the) ice; (ii) to put, lay, aside (work, project, etc.) (temporarily); *F:* to put (work, project, etc.) into cold storage; **Champagner auf Eis,** champagne on ice. **2.** *Cu:* ice-cream; ice; **gemischtes Eis,** mixed ice-cream; **Eis essen,** to eat an ice-cream *or* ices, ice-creams; **zwei Eis, bitte,** two ices, two ice-creams, please.

eis[2], **Eis** ['eːis], *n.* **-/-.** *Mus:* (the note) E sharp, E♯.

Eisabscheuerung, *f. Geol:* glacial scouring.

Eisachat, *m. Miner:* translucent agate, uncoloured agate.

Eisalabaster, *m. Miner:* translucent alabaster.

Eisalaun, *m.* rock-alum.

Eisalk, *m. Orn:* razor-bill.

Eisammer, *f. & m. Orn:* snow-bunting.

Eisanhang, *m.* layer, deposit, of ice (on walls, trees, etc.); ice crust (on walls, trees, etc.).

Eisanker, *m. Nau:* ice anchor.

Eisansatz, *m.* layer, deposit, of ice.

Eisapfel, *m. Bot:* winter-apple; **sibirischer E.,** Siberian crab(-tree), cherry-apple (tree).

Eisarnika, *f. Bot:* icy arnica.

Eisausdehnung, *f. Geol:* extent of the ice; glaciation.

Eisaxt, *f.* ice-axe.

Eisbahn, *f.* ice (for skating); (ice-, skating-)rink; slide (on ice); **künstliche E.,** artificial rink; **überdachte E.,** covered rink.

Eisbalken, *m. Hyd.E: Nau:* fender-beam (of ice-breaker); ice-fender; ice-beam.

Eisband, *n. Mount:* ledge of ice.

Eisbank, *f.* ice-field.

Eisbär, *m. Z:* polar bear, white bear.

Eisbaum, *m. Hyd.E:* fender-beam (of ice-breaker); ice-fender; ice-beam.

Eisbecher, *m.* **1.** ice-cream glass *or* cup; sundae glass. **2.** coupe (of ice-cream).

eisbedeckt, *a.* ice-covered, covered with ice.

Eisbedeckung, *f.* (process of) covering (sth.) with ice, becoming covered with ice; glaciation.

Eisbeere, *f. Bot:* snowberry.

Eisbehälter, *m.* ice-chamber.

eisbehangen, *a.* hung with icicles.

Eisbeil, *n.* ice-axe.

Eisbein, *n.* **1.** *Cu:* pickled knuckle of pork in its own jelly. **2.** *Anat: Cu:* ice-bone, share-bone. **3.** *pl.* **Eisbeine,** *F:* cold feet.

Eisbelag, *m.* coating of ice (on wires, etc.).

Eisbelastung, *f.* load of ice (on wires, etc.).

Eisbereitung, *f.* ice manufacture, ice-making.

Eisberg, *m.* iceberg.

Eisbericht, *m. Meteor: Nau:* ice report.

Eisbeutel, *m. Med:* ice-bag; ice-pack.

Eisbewegung, *f. Geol:* ice movement, movement of the ice.

Eisbildung, *f.* ice formation, formation of ice.

Eisbirne, *f. Hort:* white doyenné (pear).

Eisblase, *f.* = **Eisbeutel.**

Eisblick, Eisblink, *m. Meteor:* iceblink.

Eisblock, *m.* (*a*) ice-block; large ice-floe; (*b*) *Ind:* block of ice.

Eisblume, *f.* **1.** *Bot:* = **Eispflanze. 2.** *pl.* (*a*) **Eisblumen,** frost-flowers, frost-work (on window, etc.); (*b*) (*of paint, varnish, etc.*) **Eisblumen bilden,** to frost.

Eisblumenbildung, *f.* reticulation (of paint, varnish, etc.).

Eisblumenglas, *n.* frosted glass.

Eisblumenlack, *m.* crystal lacquer.

Eisbock, *m. Hyd.E:* ice-breaker, ice-apron, ice-fender, starling (on bridge, etc.).

Eisboden, *m. Geol:* permafrost.

Eisbohrer, *m.* ice-auger.

Eisbombe, *f. Cu:* *bombe glacée*, ice-pudding.

Eisboot, *n.* ice-boat, ice-yacht.

Eisbootsegeln, *n.* ice-yachting.

Eisbosseln, *n. Games:* (ice-sport similar to) curling.

Eisbrechdampfer, *m.* = **Eisbrecher** 2.

Eisbrecher, *m.* **1.** (*a*) ice-fender, ice-apron, starling (of bridge, etc.); (*b*) ice-beam (of ship). **2.** ice-breaker (ship).

Eisbruch, *m.* **1.** breaking (up) of the ice. **2.** *Geol:* ice-fall.

Eisbrücke, *f. Geol:* (natural) bridge of ice.

Eisbrunnen, *m. Geol:* glacial pot-hole, moulin.

Eischale, *f.* egg-shell.

Eiscreme, *f.* ice-cream.

Eisdamm, *m. Geol:* glacial dam, ice dam.

Eisdecke, *f.* (*a*) sheet, layer, of ice (on lake, etc.); frozen surface (of lake, etc.); (*b*) *Geol:* ice-sheet.

Eisdiele, *f.* ice-cream parlour.

Eisdopplung, *f. Nau:* reinforced bow-plates (*as protection against ice*).

Eisdorn, *m. Echin:* asterlas,

Eisdrift, *f. Geol:* glacial drift (movement).

Eiseimer, *m.* ice-bucket, ice-pail.

eisen[1]. **1.** *v.tr.* to ice (sth.); to turn (sth.) to ice; *F:* **j-s Blut e.,** to make s.o.'s blood run cold. **2.** *v.i.* (*a*) (*sein*) to turn to ice; (*of pond, etc.*) to freeze (over); (*b*) (*haben*) to go fishing on the ice. **3.** *v.impers.* **es eist,** it is freezing hard.

Eisen[2], *n.* **-s/-.** **1.** *Metall: etc:* iron; **weiches E.,** soft iron; **brüchiges E.,** short iron; **gegossenes E.,** cast iron; **hämmerbares, schmiedbares, E.,** malleable iron; **geschmiedetes E.,** wrought iron; **(galvanisch) verzinktes E.,** galvanized iron; **altes E.,** old iron, scrap-iron, *F:* junk; *F:* **etwas zum alten E. werfen,** to throw sth. on the scrap-heap, to scrap sth.; to discard sth.; to shelve (plan, etc.); *U.S:* to junk sth.; **j-n zum alten E. werfen,** to cast s.o. aside; to discard s.o.; to put (official, etc.) on the shelf, to shelve (official, etc.); **man hat ihn zum alten E. geworfen, getan,** he is on the shelf; **er gehört zum alten E.,** he is past his work, he's no longer any use; **ein Deckel, ein Band, aus E.,** an iron lid, an iron hoop; **es ist aus E.,** it is made of iron; **er hat eine Gesundheit (wie) aus E.,** he has an iron constitution, he is made of iron; **er ist wie von E.,** (i) he is made of iron; (ii) he has an iron will; **er hat Muskeln (wie) aus E.,** he has muscles like iron; **hart wie E.,** as hard as iron; **etwas mit E. beschlagen,** to fit, mount, sth. with iron; **einen Stock mit E. beschlagen,** to put a ferrule on a stick; **mit E. beschlagener Stock,** iron-shod stick; **mit E. beschlagene Tür,** (i) door sheathed, faced, with iron, (ii) door studded with iron nails; **mit E. beschlagene Schuhe,** (i) hobnailed shoes, (ii) shoes fitted with iron plates; *Prov:* **Not bricht E.,** needs must when the devil drives; necessity knows no law; *see also* **gediegen** 1 (*a*); **halbieren I.** (*b*). **2.** *Med:* iron; **E. (ein)nehmen,** to take iron. **3.** *Metalw:* (*a*) (piece of) iron (to be worked); *Prov:* **man muß das E. schmieden, solange es heiß, warm, ist,** strike while the iron is hot; make hay while the sun shines; go while the going is good; *F:* **zwei, mehrere, Eisen im Feuer haben,** to have two, several, irons in the fire; to have more than one string to one's bow; **ich habe noch ein E. im Feuer,** I have another plan to fall back upon; I have still one string to my bow; I've still got a shot in the locker; **zu viele Eisen im Feuer haben,** to have too many irons in the fire; **das ist ein heißes E.,** it's a tricky business; (*b*) (worked piece of) iron; iron beam; iron section; **T-E.,** T iron. **4.** horseshoe; (*of horse*) **ein E. abwerfen,** to cast a shoe. **5.** *pl.* **Eisen,** irons, chains, fetters. shackles, *Lit:* gyves; **in Eisen liegen,** to be in irons, fetters; to be fettered; **einen Mann in Eisen legen,** to put a man in irons, in fetters; to fetter a man. **6.** (*a*) sword; dagger; knife; **durchs E. sterben,** to perish by the sword; **Frage, die nur durch Blut und E. zu entscheiden ist,** problem that can only be resolved by the sword, by armed force; **Politik von Blut und E.,** policy of blood and iron; (*b*) firearm; gun; rifle; pistol; *F:* shooting-iron. **7.** *Tls: etc:* (*a*) iron (cutting) tool *or* iron blade of a tool; axe(-blade, -head); plough(-share); scythe(-blade); cutting-iron, blade (of a plane), plane-iron; chisel; crowbar; (*b*) branding-iron; *Med:* searing-iron, cauterizing-iron; (*c*) *Dom.Ec: etc:* iron; flat-iron, laundry iron; **elektrisches E.,** electric iron; (*d*) *Golf:* (*club*) iron; **Eisen II, III,** number two iron, number three iron. **8.** *Ven:* trap; **Eisen** *pl* **stellen,** to set traps.

Eisen-, *comb.fm.* iron (bridge, rod, wire, etc.); *Miner: etc:* ferruginous (earth, etc.); chalybeate (spring, water); *Metall:* ferro-(alloy, etc.); *Ch:* (*in names of compounds*) iron . . .; (*with trivalent iron*) ferric . . ., iron (III) . . .; ferri-; (*with divalent iron*) ferrous . . ., iron (II) . . .; ferro-; *Miner:* **Eisenbitterkalk** *m,* ferruginous dolomite; **Eisensand** *m,* ferruginous sand; *Metall:* **Eisenbronze** *f,* ferro-bronze; **Eisenchrom** *n,* ferro-chrome; **Eisenvanadin** *n,* ferro-vanadium; *Ch:* **Eisenverbindung** *f,* iron compound; **Eisenchlorid** *n,* ferric chloride; **Eisenchlorwassersäure** *f,* ferrichloric acid; **Eisenchlorür** *n,* ferrous chloride; **Eisenzyanür** *n,* ferrous cyanide; **Eisenzyankalium** *n,* potassium ferrocyanide.

Eisenabfall, *m.*, **Eisenabfälle**, *m.pl. Metall:* (*a*) scrap-iron, iron scrap; (*b*) iron filings.

Eisenabgang, *m. Ind:* scrap-iron, iron scrap.

Eisenalaun, *m. Ch:* iron alum.

Eisenammoniakalaun, *m. Ch:* ferric ammonium sulphate.

Eisenantimonglanz, *m. Miner:* berthierite.

Eisenarbeit, *f.* ironwork.

Eisenarbeiter, *m.* ironworker.

eisenarm, *a.* (ore, country, etc.) poor in iron.

eisenartig, *a.* iron-like; *Ch: etc:* ferruginous.

Eisenarznei, *f. Med:* medicine containing iron, preparation of iron; **E. einnehmen,** to take iron.

Eisenasbest, *m. Metall:* fibrous silica.

Eisenbahn, *f.* **1.** railway, *U.S:* railroad; **eingleisige, einspurige, zweigleisige, zweispurige, E.,** single-track, double-track, railway; **elektrische E.,** electric railway; **in, auf, der E.,** (i) on, in, the train; (ii) in (the) trains; (iii) on the railways; **mit der E. fahren,** to go, travel, by train, by rail; **etwas mit der E., per E., befördern,** to send, forward, sth. by rail, per rail; **er arbeitet bei der E.,** he works on the railways; *Com:* **frei E.,** free on rail, *abbr.* f.o.r.; *U.S:* free on board, *abbr.* f.o.b.; *Hum:* **es ist, wird, (die) höchste E.,** time presses; **es wird aber auch höchste E.!** and about time too! **es ist höchste E., daß . . .,** it is about time, it is high time, that . . .; **Eisenbahn-,** *comb. fm.* railway, *U.S:* railroad (bridge, journey, official, ticket, etc.); rail (journey, ticket, traffic, etc.). **2.** (*Swiss also m.*) (railway-) train.

Eisenbahnanschluß, *m.* **1.** railway connection (with ship, etc.). **2.** railway junction.

Eisenbahnarbeiter, *m.* railway employee, railwayman.

Eisenbahnbau, *m.* railway construction.

Eisenbahnbauunternehmer, *m.* railway contractor.

Eisenbahnbeamte, *m.* railway official.

Eisenbahnbetrieb, *m.* **1.** railway service. **2.** working, operation, of a railway, of railways.

Eisenbahnbrücke, *f.* railway bridge; (railway) viaduct.

Eisenbahndamm, *m.* railway embankment.

Eisenbahndirektion, *f.* **1.** (*in Germany*) Regional Administration (of the Federal Railways). **2.** railway directorate; board of directors (of a railway).

Eisenbahneinschnitt, *m.* railway cutting.

Eisenbahnendpunkt, *m.* railhead.

Eisenbahner, *m.* **-s/-.** *F:* railwayman, railway employee.

Eisenbahnergewerkschaft, *f.* union of railwaymen, railwaymen's union.
Eisenbahnfähre, *f.* train ferry.
Eisenbahnfahrt, *f.* railway journey, train journey, journey by rail.
Eisenbahngelände, *n.* (*land*) railway property.
Eisenbahngeleise, *n.* railway track, railway lines.
Eisenbahngeschütz, *n. Artil: A:* railway gun.
Eisenbahngesellschaft, *f.* railway company.
Eisenbahngleis, *n.* railway track, railway lines.
Eisenbahnhof, *m.* railway station.
Eisenbahnknotenpunkt, *m.* railway junction.
Eisenbahnkreuzung, *f.* railway crossing.
Eisenbahnlähmung, *f. Med:* railway spine.
Eisenbahnlinie, *f.* railway line; railway route; **eingleisige, zweigleisige, E.,** single-track, double-track, railway line; **die großen Eisenbahnlinien,** the great railway routes, tracks.
Eisenbahnnetz, *n.* railway network, system.
Eisenbahnoberbau, *m. Rail:* permanent way, road-bed, superstructure.
Eisenbahnpostwagen, *m. Rail:* mail-van.
Eisenbahnschiene, *f. Rail:* rail.
Eisenbahnschwelle, *f. Rail:* sleeper, *U.S:* tie.
Eisenbahnstation, *f.* railway station.
Eisenbahnstrecke, *f.* **1.** section, *U.S:* division (of railway). **2.** *F:* stretch of railway(-line).
Eisenbahntransport, *m.* railway transport.
Eisenbahnübergang, *m. Rail:* level crossing, *U.S:* grade crossing; **bewachter, unbewachter, E.,** guarded, unguarded, (level) crossing, gated, ungated, (level) crossing.
Eisenbahnübersichtskarte, *f.* railway map.
Eisenbahnunfall, *m.* railway accident, accident on the railway.
Eisenbahnunglück, *n.* railway accident; railway disaster; train crash.
Eisenbahnunterbau, *m. Rail:* bed, substructure.
Eisenbahnverband, *m.* railway association.
Eisenbahnverkehr, *m.* railway traffic, rail traffic.
Eisenbahnverkehrsordnung, *f. Adm:* Railway Traffic Regulations.
Eisenbahnwagen, *m. Rail:* (*a*) (*for passengers*) (railway) carriage; (*b*) (goods) truck; wagon.
Eisenbahnzug, *m.* railway-train.
Eisenband, *n. Constr: etc:* iron band; iron hoop; iron strap; **Beton mit Eisenbändern,** iron-banded concrete.
Eisenbarren, *m. Metall:* iron bar; ingot, billet (of iron).
Eisenbau, *m.* -(e)s/. **1.** erection, building, of iron structures; ironwork. **2.** (*pl.* **Eisenbauten**) iron structure; structural, constructional, ironwork.
Eisenbaum, *m. Bot:* sideroxylon, ironwood(-tree).
Eisenbauunternehmer, *m.* ironwork contractor.
Eisenbauwerk, *n.*=**Eisenbau** 2.
Eisenbeißer, *m.*=**Eisenfresser.**
Eisenbeize, *f. Dy:* iron liquor, iron mordant.
Eisenbereifung, *f. Veh:* iron tyre(s); **Räder mit E.,** iron-tyred wheels.
Eisenbergwerk, *n.* iron-mine.
Eisenbeschlag, *m.* iron fitting(s); iron mounting.
Eisenbeton, *m. Constr:* ferro-concrete, reinforced concrete, armoured concrete.
Eisenbetonbau, *m.* ferro-concrete construction.
Eisenbett, *n.* iron bed.
Eisenbettgestell, *n.* iron bedstead.
Eisenbitterkalk, *m. Miner:* ferruginous dolomite.
Eisenblau, *n. Miner:*=**Eisenblauspat.**
Eisenblauerde, *f. Miner:* (earthy) vivianite.
eisenblausauer, *a. Ch:* ferrocyanide of . . . .
Eisenblausäure, *f. Ch:* ferrocyanic acid.
Eisenblauspat, *m. Miner:* vivianite.
Eisenblech, *n. Metalw:* (*a*) sheet-iron; (*b*) plate iron (for boilers, etc.); boiler-plate.
Eisenblock, *m.* block of iron; *Metall:* (i) ingot, billet (of iron), (ii) bloom.
Eisenblüte, *f. Miner:* aragonite.
Eisenbor, *n. Ch:* iron boride.
Eisenbronze, *f. Metall:* ferro-bronze, iron bronze.
Eisenchlorid, *n. Ch:* iron chloride, ferric chloride.
Eisenchlorür, *n. Ch:* ferrous chloride.
Eisenchrom, *n.* **1.** *Metall:* ferro-chrome, chrome iron. **2.** *Miner:* chromite.
Eisendraht, *m.* iron wire.
Eisenerde, *f.* **1.** *Miner:* ferruginous earth; (clay) iron-stone; **blaue E.,** (earthy) vivianite. **2.** *Cer:* iron-stone ware, iron-stone china.
Eisenerz, *n. Miner:* iron ore.
Eisenfeilicht, Eisenfeilsel, *n. Metalw:* iron filings; iron file-dust.
Eisenfellspäne, *m. pl. Metalw:* iron filings.
Eisenfleck, *m.* iron-mould.
Eisenfleckigkeit, *f. Agr:* (*disease of potatoes*) stain.
Eisenfresser, *m. F:* (*a*) dare-devil; (*b*) fire-eater; braggart, swaggerer, swashbuckler.
Eisenfrischer, *m. Metall:* (*pers.*) iron (re)finer.
Eisenfrischerei, *f. Metall:* (*a*) iron (re)fining; (*b*) iron (re)finery.
Eisengang, *m. Min:* lode of iron.
Eisengans, Eisenganz, *f. Metall:* pig (of iron).
Eisengarn, *n. Needlew: etc:* extra-strong thread.
Eisengehalt, *m. Ch: Miner:* iron-content; **Gestein mit hohem E.,** rock with high iron-content, rock that contains a high percentage of iron.
Eisengerippe, Eisengerüst, *n. Constr:* iron frame(work); iron skeleton (of building, etc.); structural ironwork.
Eisengießer, *m.* (*pers.*) iron-founder.
Eisengießerei, *f.* **1.** iron-foundry, ironworks. **2.** iron-founding.
Eisengitter, *n.* iron bars; iron railing; iron fence; iron grating; grille.
Eisenglanz, *m. Miner:* iron-glance, specular iron ore, haematite.
Eisenglimmer, *m. Miner:* micaceous haematite.
eisengrau, *a.* iron-grey.
Eisengraupen, *f.pl. Miner:* granular bog-iron ore.
Eisengrube, *f.* iron-mine.
Eisenguß, *m. Metall:* **1.** (*process*) iron casting. **2.** (*a*) (*product*) iron casting; (*b*) cast iron; **Eisenguß-,** *comb.fm.* cast-iron (articles, etc.).
eisenhaltig, *a.* containing iron; *Miner: etc:* ferruginous (earth, rock, spring, water, etc.); chalybeate (spring, water).
Eisenhammer, *m.* **1.** *Tls:* forge-hammer. **2.** *Metall: A:* forge.
Eisenhammerschlag, *m. Metalw:* hammer-scale(s), anvil dross.
Eisenhandel, *m.* (*a*) iron trade; (*b*) ironmongery business, hardware business.
Eisenhandlung, *f.* ironmonger's shop, hardware shop.
eisenhart[1], *a.* (as) hard as iron.
Eisenhart[2], *m.* -(e)s/-e. *Bot:* verbena, vervain.
Eisenholz, *n.* **1.** =**Eisenholzbaum. 2.** *Com:* (*a*) ironwood; (*b*) **weißes E.,** fiddlewood (timber).
Eisenholzbaum, *m. Bot:* sideroxylon, ironwood.
Eisenhut, *m.* **1.** *Arm:* (visorless) helmet. **2.** *Bot:* aconite, *esp.* monk's-hood; **gelber E.,** wolf's-bane. **3.** *Miner:* gossan, iron cap, iron hat (of metallic vein).
Eisenhütchen, Eisenhütlein, *n.* **1.**=**Eisenhut** 2. **2.** *Her: pl.* **Eisenhütchen, Eisenhütlein,** vair; **mit E. besetzt,** vairy.
Eisenhütte, *f.*=**Eisenhüttenwerk.**
Eisenhüttenkunde, *f.* metallurgy of iron.
Eisenhüttenwerk, *n. Ind:* ironworks; iron and steel works.
Eisenhydroxyd, *n. Ch:* ferric hydroxide.
Eisenhydroxydul, *n. Ch:* ferrous hydroxide.
Eisenindustrie, *f.* iron industry; heavy industry.
Eisenkalialaun, *m. Ch:* ferric potassium sulphate.
Eisenkalk, *m. Miner:* ankerite.
Eisenkern, *m. El.E: etc:* iron core.
Eisenkernspule, *f. El.E:* iron-core inductance (-coil).
Eisenkernverlust, *m. El.E:* core losses.
Eisenkies, *m. Miner:* iron pyrites.
Eisenkitt, *m.* iron-cement.
Eisenklumpen, *m.* (*a*) block, lump, of iron; (*b*) *Metall:*=**Eisensau.**
Eisenkonstrukteur, *m.* constructional iron-worker.
Eisenkonstruktion, *f.* **1.** iron structural work, iron construction. **2.** iron structure; structural ironwork.
Eisenkram, *m.* ironmongery, hardware.
Eisenkrämer, *m.* ironmonger, hardware dealer.
Eisenkraut, *n. Bot:* **1.** verbena, vervain. **2.** *F: popular name for various plants, esp.* (*a*) lady's mantle; (*b*) rest-harrow; (*c*) corn gromwell; (*d*) brown radiant knapweed.
eisenkrautartig, *a. Bot:* verbenaceous.
Eisenkrautgewächse, *n.pl. Bot:* verbenaceae.
Eisenladen, *m.* ironmonger's shop, hardware shop.
Eisenlebererz, *n. Miner:* hepatic iron ore.
Eisenlegierung, *f. Metall:* ferrous alloy; ferro-alloy.
Eisenluppe, *f. Metall:* (*a*) bloom; puddle-ball; (*b*) ingot, billet (of iron).
eisenmagnetisch, *a.* ferromagnetic.
Eisenmangan, *n. Metall:* ferromanganese.
Eisenmittel, *n. Pharm:* medicine containing iron; *F:* iron tonic.
Eisenmohr, *m. Miner:* earthy magnetite.
Eisenmörtel, *m. Constr:* reinforced cement *or* concrete.
Eisenmulm, *m. Miner:* earthy iron ore.
Eisennährpräparat, *n. Pharm:* iron blood-tonic.
Eisennickel, *n. Metall:* ferro-nickel, nickel iron.
Eisen-Nickel-Akkumulator, *m. El.E:* nickel-iron accumulator.
Eisenofen, *m.* **1.** (cast-)iron stove. **2.** *Metalw:* forging furnace.
Eisenoolith, *m. Miner:* iron oolite; oolitic iron ore.
Eisenoxyd, *n. Ch:* ferric oxide.
Eisenoxydul, *n. Ch:* ferrous oxide.
Eisenoxyduloxyd, *n. Ch:* ferroso-ferric oxide, magnetic iron oxide.
Eisenportlandzement, *m. Constr:* Portland blast-furnace cement.
Eisenpräparat, *n. Pharm:* preparation of iron.
Eisenprobe, *f. Hist:* ordeal by hot iron.
Eisenquelle, *f.* chalybeate spring, ferruginous spring.
Eisenrahm, *m. Miner:* porous haematite.
Eisenrindenbaum, *m. Bot:* iron-bark (tree), red-gum.
Eisenrogenstein, *m. Miner:* oolitic iron ore.
Eisenrost[1], *m.* iron grate.
Eisenrost[2], *m.* rust.
Eisenrostzement, *m.* rust-cement.
Eisensäge, *f. Tls:* hack-saw.
Eisensalz, *n. Ch:* iron salt.
Eisensand, *m. Miner:* ferruginous sand.
Eisensau, *f. Metall:* iron bear, sow, salamander, shadrach.
eisensauer, *a. Ch:* ferrate of . . .; **eisensaures Salz,** ferrate.
Eisensäuerling, *m.* chalybeate, ferruginous, (mineral) water.
Eisensäure, *f. Ch:* ferric acid.
eisenschaffend, *a.* iron-producing (industry).
Eisenschaum, *m.* **1.** *Metall:* kish. **2.** *Miner:* porous haematite.
Eisenschiene, *f.* **1.** iron rail. **2.** *Surg:* iron (splint *or* brace).
Eisenschimmel, *m.* iron-grey horse.
Eisenschlacke, *f. Metall:* clinker, scoria, slag (from furnace).
Eisenschlag, *m. Golf:* iron shot.
Eisenschläger, *m. Golf:* iron club, iron.
Eisenschmelzhütte, *f.* iron-foundry, ironworks.
Eisenschmied, *m.* ironsmith, ironworker.
Eisenschmiede, *f. Metall:* forge; ironworks.
Eisenschrott, *m. Metall: etc:* scrap-iron, iron scrap.
eisenschüssig, *a. Miner:* ferruginous (rock, clay).
Eisenschutzfarbe, *f.* anti-rust paint.
Eisenschutzmittel, *n.* anti-rust composition, rust preventive.
Eisenschwamm, *m. Metall:* spongy iron.
Eisenschwärze, *f.* **1.** graphite, black-lead, plumbago. **2.** *Dy:* iron liquor.
Eisenspäne, *m.pl. Metalw:* iron chips; iron turnings; iron filings.
Eisenspat, *m. Miner:* siderite; spathose iron(-ore).
Eisenstab, *m.* iron rod; iron bar.
Eisenstange, *f.* iron bar.
Eisenstaub, *m.* (very fine) iron filings.
Eisenstein, *m. Miner:* iron-stone; **spatiger E.,** siderite.
Eisensulfat, *n. Ch:* ferrous sulphate, *Ind:* green vitriol, copperas.
Eisente, *f. Orn:* long-tailed duck, old squaw, *U.S:* winter duck.
Eisenträger, *m.* iron girder.
Eisentropfen, *m.pl. Pharm:* iron drops, steel drops.
Eisenveilchenbaum, *m. Bot:* blue gum(-tree).
eisenverarbeitend, *a.* iron-using (industry).
Eisenverlust, *m. El.E:* iron losses; core losses.
Eisenvitriol, *n. Ch: Ind:*=**Eisensulfat.**
Eisenwaren, *f.pl.* ironmongery, hardware.
Eisenwarenhändler, *m.* ironmonger, hardware dealer.
Eisenwarenhandlung, *f.* ironmonger's shop, hardware shop.
Eisenwasser, *n. Miner: etc:* chalybeate, ferruginous, water.
Eisenwerk, *n. Ind:* ironworks.
Eisenwolfram, *n. Metall:* ferro-tungsten.
Eisenzeit, die. *Prehist:* the Iron Age.
Eisenzyanid, *n.* (i) ferrous cyanide; ferrocyanide; (ii) ferric cyanide; ferricyanide.
Eisenzyankalium, *n. Ch:* potassium ferrocyanide.
Eisenzyanür, *n. Ch:* ferrous cyanide.
Eiserich, *m.* -s/-e. *Bot:* verbena, vervain.
eisern, *a.* **1.** (made) of iron; iron; **eiserner Kasten,** box made of iron, iron box; **eisernes Tor,** iron gate; **eiserner Vorhang,** (i) (*in theatre*) fire-proof curtain, safety curtain; (ii) *Pol:* iron curtain; **hinter dem Eisernen Vorhang,** behind the Iron Curtain; **eiserne Hochzeit,** seventieth *or* seventy-fifth wedding anniversary; *Bot: F:* **eiserner Heinrich,** verbena, vervain; *Geog:* **das Eiserne Tor,** the Iron Gates (of the Danube);

Prehist: **das eiserne Zeitalter,** the Iron Age; *Hist:* **die Eiserne Krone,** the Iron Crown (of Lombardy); **Götz mit der eisernen Hand,** Götz with the iron, artificial, hand; **die Eiserne Jungfrau,** (*instrument of torture*) the Iron Maiden; *Hist:* **das Eiserne Kreuz (erster, zweiter, Klasse),** the Iron Cross (first class, second class); *see also* **Lunge. 2.** (*a*) of great (physical) strength; **er hat eine eiserne Gesundheit, Konstitution,** he has an iron constitution, he is made of iron; **eiserne Muskeln,** muscles like iron; **einen eisernen Magen haben,** to have the digestion of an ostrich; (*b*) inflexible, unyielding; implacable; strict, stern, severe; unrelenting, relentless; stubborn (defiance, will, etc.); unwearying, unremitting (industry, etc.); untiring, tireless, unflagging (energy, etc.); **eiserne Notwendigkeit,** iron, inescapable, inevitable, necessity; **eisernes Gesetz,** iron, immutable, law; *see also* **Gesetzmäßigkeit; das eiserne Gesetz der Notwendigkeit,** the iron law of necessity; **eiserne Grundsätze,** rigid, *F:* cast-iron, principles; **eiserne Logik,** irrefutable logic; **eiserne Disziplin,** iron, stern, discipline; **eiserner Fleiß,** unwearying diligence, unremitting industry; **eiserne Sparsamkeit,** rigid economy; rigid parsimony; **eisernes Herz,** heart of steel; **eiserner Wille,** will of iron, iron will; stubborn will; **mit eisernem Griff,** with a grip of iron; **mit eiserner Hand regieren,** to rule with an iron hand, with a rod of iron; *see also* **Besen** 1; **j-n mit eiserner Faust niederhalten,** to keep s.o. down relentlessly; to hold s.o. in a grip of iron; **er hatte eine eiserne Miene aufgesetzt,** his face was set like a rock; he had put on a stony look; **mit eiserner Stirn,** (i) with the utmost determination, resolution, (ii) brazenly; **mit eiserner Stirn bot er den Feinden Trotz,** he defied his enemies with great resolution; **mit eiserner Stirn log er weiter,** he continued to lie brazenly, he went on lying with the utmost effrontery; *Hist:* **der Eiserne Kanzler,** the Iron Chancellor, Bismarck; **der Eiserne Herzog,** the Iron Duke, the Duke of Wellington; *adv.* resolutely; with the utmost resolution; stubbornly; **sie beharrte, bestand, e. auf ihrer Meinung,** she stuck stubbornly to her opinion; **e. sparen,** (i) to save rigorously; to save every possible penny; (ii) *Adm:* to save under a compulsory savings scheme; (*c*) *Jur: A:* inalienable (property); **eisernes Vieh,** permanent herd (of cattle); (*d*) (*of stocks, reserves*) for emergency use only; **eiserner Bestand,** emergency stock(s), reserve stock(s); *Fin:* reserve fund; *Mil: etc:* **eiserne Portion, eiserne Ration,** iron ration(s), emergency ration(s); *Adm:* **eiserne Sparguthaben,** savings deposits with restricted withdrawal facilities.

Eiserosion, *f. Geol:* glacial erosion.
Eiseskälte, *f.* icy cold, icy coldness.
Eisessig, *m. Ch:* glacial acetic acid.
Eisfabrik, *f.* (*a*) ice-manufacturing plant, ice-factory; (*b*) ice-cream factory.
Eisfall, *m.* ice-fall, ice-cascade.
Eisfalter, *m. Ent:* (*a*) limenitis; (*b*) **kleiner E.,** white admiral (butterfly).
Eisfeld, *n.* ice-field.
Eisfender, *m. Nau:* ice-fender.
Eisfigurenlaufen, *n.* figure-skating.
Eisfisch, *m. Z:* Greenland whale, arctic whale.
Eisfläche, *f.* (*a*) frozen surface; sheet *or* expanse of ice; (*b*) ice-field.
Eisfront, *f. Geol:* ice-front, glacier-front.
Eisfuchs, *m.* arctic fox, white fox.
Eisfuß, *m.* **1.** *Geol:* ice-foot. **2.** *F:* **ich habe Eisfüße,** my feet are like ice, are cold as ice.
Eisgabel, *f. Dom.Ec:* ice-pick, ice-fork.
Eisgang, *m.* (i) breaking up of the ice; débâcle; (ii) ice-drift; **Fluß mit starkem E.,** river full of, heavy with, floating ice.
Eisgebirge, *n.* ice-mountains; chain of glaciers.
eisgekühlt, *a.* ice-cooled; ice-cold; chilled; (*of melon, drink, etc.*) iced, *frappé.*
Eisgewächs, *n. Bot:* ice-plant.
Eisglas, *n.* frosted glass.
Eisglätte, *f.* icy surface (on road, etc.).
Eisgrat, *m.* ice-ridge; ice-covered ridge.
eisgrau, *a.* grey; hoary; aged (pers.); **eisgraues Alter,** hoary old age.
Eisgrenze, *f. Geol:* glacial limit; glacial boundary; ice limit.
Eisgrube, *f.* ice-pit.
Eisgürtel, *m.* ice-belt; belt of ice.
Eishai, *m. Ich:* Greenland shark.
Eishaken, *m.* (climber's) ice-hook.
Eishase, *m. Z:* arctic hare.
Eishaut, *f.* = **Eisdopplung.**
Eisheiligen, die. *Pr.n.m.pl.* the Ice Saints, (*11th–14th May when the weather often turns cold*).
Eishockey, *n. Sp:* ice-hockey.
Eishockeyplatz, *m. Sp:* ice-hockey rink.
Eishockeyscheibe, *f. Sp:* puck.
Eishufeisen, *n. Farr:* calkin, frost-nail.
eisig, *a.* (*a*) icy; cold as ice, ice-cold; frosty; **eisiges Wasser,** icy(-cold) water; **eisiger Wind,** icy wind; **meine Füße sind e.,** *adv.* **e. kalt,** my feet are icy, icy-cold; *Lit:* **der eisige Hauch des Winters,** winter's icy breath; (*b*) (*of look, etc.*) icy, freezing; (*of manner, etc.*) icy, frigid; (*of reception, smile, etc.*) icy, glacial; **sie war e.,** her manner was icy; **eisige Höflichkeit,** icy, chilly, chilling, frigid, politeness.
eisigkalt, *attrib. a.* icy-cold (day, weather, water, etc.).
Eisjacht, *f.* ice-boat, ice-yacht.
Eiskaffee, *m.* coffee with ice-cream; iced coffee.
Eiskalorimeter, *n. Ph:* ice calorimeter.
Eiskalotte, *f.* ice-cap (of mountain, etc.).
eiskalt, *a.* ice-cold, cold as ice; icy; freezing; **meine Füße sind e.,** my feet are like ice, are frozen; **es ist e. draußen,** it is icy cold out(side).
Eiskälte, *f.* icy cold, icy coldness.
Eiskammer, *f.* ice-chamber; refrigerating-chamber.
Eiskante, *f. Geol:* ice-foot.
Eiskappe, *f.* ice-cap.
Eiskaskade, *f.* ice-fall (in glacier).
Eiskasten, *m.* ice-box; ice-chest.
Eiskegeln, *n.* = **Eisbosseln.**
Eiskeller, *m.* ice-cellar; **natürlicher E.,** ice-cave; **mein Zimmer ist wie ein E.,** my room is like an ice-box.
Eiskessel, *m.* ice-bucket, ice-pail.
Eisklub, *m.* ice-club, skating club.
Eiskluft, *f. Arb:* (*in timber*) frost-cleft; frost-crack; frost-rib; frost-shake.
eisklüftig, *a.* (*of tree, etc.*) frost-cleft; frost-cracked; frost-riven.
Eisklumpen, *m.* lump of ice; *F:* **meine Füße sind wie Eisklumpen,** my feet feel like (lumps of) ice, are cold as ice.
Eiskompresse, *f. Med:* ice-pack.
Eiskrachen, *n.* ice-quake.
Eiskrampe, *f.* (climber's) crampon.
Eiskraut, *n. Bot:* ice-plant.
Eiskruste, *f.* ice crust; crust of ice.
Eiskübel, *m.* ice-bucket, ice-pail.
Eiskühlung, *f.* ice-cooling, ice refrigeration.
Eiskunstlauf, *m.* figure-skating.
Eiskunstläufer, *m.* figure-skater.
Eislast, *f.* ice-load; load of ice (on wires, etc.).
Eislauf, *m.* skating.
Eislaufbahn, *f.* skating rink.
eislaufen, *v.i. sep.* (*strong*) (*sein*) to skate.
Eisläufer, *m.* skater.
Eislawine, *f.* ice-avalanche.
Eislimonade, *f.* iced lemonade.
Eisloch, *n.* hole in the ice; ice-hole.
Eislöffel, *m.* ice-cream spoon.
Eismann, *m.* **-(e)s/-männer. 1.** iceman. **2. die Eismänner,** the Ice Saints, the Icemen.
Eismantel, *m. Geol:* (continental) ice-sheet.
Eismaschine, *f.* (*a*) ice-machine; ice-maker; (*b*) ice-cream machine, ice-cream freezer.
Eismasse, *f.* mass of ice; body of ice; (*on water*) ice-floe.
Eismeer, *n. Geog:* polar sea; **das Nördliche, Südliche, E.,** the Arctic, Antarctic, Ocean.
Eismeermuschel, *f. Moll:* yoldia arctica.
Eismonat, Eismond, *m. A. & Poet:* January.
Eismöwe, *f. Orn:* glaucous gull, burgomaster gull.
Eisnadel, *f. Geol:* sérac (of glacier); ice-pinnacle.
Eisnagel, *m.* (*a*) *Farr:* calkin, frost-nail; (*b*) ice-nail (on boots).
Eisnebel, *m. Meteor:* ice-fog.
Eispackung, *f. Med:* ice-pack.
Eispapier, *n.* frosted paper.
Eispfahl, *m.* = **Eisbalken.**
Eispfeiler, *m. Geol:* sérac (of glacier).
Eispflanze, *f. Bot:* ice-plant.
Eispfriem, *m.* ice-pick.
Eispicke, *f.*, **Eispickel,** *m.* ice-pick; ice-axe.
Eisprung, *m. Biol: Physiol:* ovulation.
Eispyramide, *f. Geol:* sérac (of glacier); ice pyramid.
Eisrand, *m. Geol:* ice-margin, glacier margin (of continental glacier).
Eisregen, *m.* sleet.
Eisriese, *f. For:* ice-covered timber-slide.
Eisrinde, *f.* (*a*) = **Eiskruste;** (*b*) **die E. um sein Herz schmolz,** the ice round his heart melted.
Eiß, *m.* **-es/-e.** *South G. & Swiss Dial:* = **Eiterbeule.**
Eissäge, *f.* ice-saw.
Eisscheide, *f.* ice-shed.
Eisscheuerung, *f. Geol:* glacial scouring.
Eisschießen, *n.* = **Eisbosseln.**
Eisschiff, *n.* ice-boat, ice-yacht.
Eisschimmer, *m.* = **Eisblick.**
Eisschliff, *m. Geol:* (*a*) glacial scouring; (*b*) *usu. pl.* **Eisschliffe,** (i) ice-smoothed rock surfaces; (ii) glacial striae, glacial striations.
Eisschmelzkegel, *m. Geol:* sérac (of glacier).
Eisschnellauf, *m. Sp:* speed skating.
Eisscholle, *f.* ice-floe.
Eisschrank, *m.* refrigerator, *F:* fridge; ice-box; ice-chest.
Eisschranke, *f.* ice-barrier.
Eisschrumpfung, *f. Geol:* glacial shrinkage.
Eisschutz, *m. Nau:* ice-fender; bowgrace.
Eiße, *f.* **-/-n.** *South G. & Swiss Dial:* = **Eiterbeule**
Eissee, *m. Geol:* glacial dam, glacier dam; ice lake.
Eisseetaucher, *m. Orn:* great northern diver, loon; **weißschnäbliger E.,** white-billed diver.
Eissegelboot, *n.* ice-boat, ice-yacht.
Eissegeln, *n.* ice-yachting.
Eissohle, *f. Geol:* ice sole.
Eisspat, *m. Miner:* adularia.
Eisspieß, *m.* = **Eisnadel.**
Eisspitze, *f.* **1.** ice-covered mountain peak. **2.** (*a*) ice-nail, ice-spur (for boots); (*b*) *Farr:* calkin, frost-nail.
Eissporn, *m.* (*a*) (*for boots*) ice-spur; crampon; (*b*) *Farr:* calkin; frost-nail.
Eissport, *m.* ice-sport; game (played) on ice.
Eissproß, *m.*, **Eissprosse,** *f. Ven:* bay-antler, bez antler.
Eisstadion, *n. Sp:* ice stadium.
Eisstaub, *m. Miner:* cryoconite.
Eisstausee, *m.* = **Eissee.**
Eisstein, *m. Miner:* cryolite, Greenland spar.
Eisstock, *m.* (wooden) curling-stone.
Eisstoß, *m. Austrian:* piled-up ice (at river-bend).
Eisstrom, *m. Geol:* ice-flow.
Eisstülpfalten, *f.pl. Geol:* frost lifting.
Eissturmvogel, *m. Orn:* fulmar.
Eistafel, *f. Geol:* glacier table.
Eistaucher, *m. Orn:* common loon, great northern diver; **gelbschnäbeliger E.,** yellow-billed loon.
Eistisch, *m.* = **Eistafel.**
Eistorte, *f. Cu:* ice-cream gateau.
Eistreiben, *n.*, **Eistrift,** *f.* drifting of the ice; ice-drift.
Eistüte, *f.* ice-cream cone, ice-cream cornet.
Eisumschlag, *m. Med:* ice-pack.
Eisverkäufer, *m.* ice-cream seller, ice-cream man.
Eisvogel, *m.* **1.** *Orn:* (*a*) kingfisher; (*b*) dipper. **2.** *Ent:* **kleiner E.,** white admiral (butterfly).
Eisvorstoß, *m. Geol:* ice advance; ice invasion.
Eiswaffel, *f.* (*a*) ice-cream wafer; (*b*) wafer (-biscuit) (for ice-cream); (*c*) cream wafer (biscuit).
Eiswall, *m. Geol:* ice rampart (on lake shore).
Eiswand, *f. Geol:* wall of ice; ice-cliff.
Eiswarndienst, *m. Meteor: Nau:* ice warning system.
Eiswasser, *n.* ice-water.
Eiswein, *m.* ice-wine, wine made from grapes exposed to frost.
Eiswerk, *n.* ice-works, ice-factory.
Eiswolke, *f. Meteor:* ice cloud.
Eiswürfel, *m.* ice cube.
Eiswüste, *f.* frozen waste(s).
Eiszacken, *m.* icicle.
Eiszange, *f. Dom.Ec:* ice-tongs; *Ind:* **Eiszangen** *pl,* ice-claw.
Eiszapfen, *m.* icicle.
Eiszeit, *f. Geol:* ice-age; glacial period, epoch; boulder-period.
Eiszeitklima, *n. Meteor:* glacial climate.
eiszeitlich, *a. Geol:* glacial; pertaining to *or* belonging to the ice age, the glacial period; **eiszeitlicher See,** glacier lake, glacial lake.
Eiszone, *f.* frigid, glacial, zone.
Eiszucker, *m. Cu:* (*a*) icing sugar; (*b*) white icing.
eitel, *a.* **1.** (*usu. inv.*) *A. & Lit:* pure, sheer; **e. Gold,** pure gold; *adv.* merely, only; **das Leben ist nicht e. Freud und Sonnenschein,** *F:* life is not all beer and skittles. **2.** *a.* (*of pers.*) vain; **e. wie ein Pfau, e. wie ein Affe,** as vain as a peacock; **ein eitler Affe, Geck,** a dandy, *Lit. & A:* a coxcomb; **ein eitles Äffchen,** a vain little thing; **e. auf etwas sein,** to be vain of, about, sth. **3.** *a.* vain (pleasure, hope, etc.); empty (words, etc.); idle (wishes, talk, etc.); futile (ideas, amusements, etc.); **eitles Geschwätz,** empty words, idle talk; **eitler Tand,** vain trifles, vanities; *B:* **es ist alles ganz e.,** all is vanity.
Eitelkeit, *f.* **1.** (*a*) vainness, vanity (of amusements, ideas, etc.); emptiness (of pleasures, etc.); futility (of human achievements, etc.); **die E. dieser Welt,** the vanity of this world; (*b*) **sich von den Eitelkeiten der Welt abwenden,** to forsake the vanities of the world. **2.** vanity, vain-

ness; **etwas aus E. tun,** to do sth. out of vanity; **j-s E.** *dat.* **schmeicheln, j-s E. kitzeln,** to tickle s.o.'s vanity; **j-s E.** *dat.* **Nahrung geben,** to feed s.o.'s vanity; **gekränkte E.,** injured vanity.

Eiter, *m.* **-s/.** *Med:* pus, matter; **E. absondern,** to discharge pus; **Absonderung von E.,** discharge of pus; **E. bilden,** to generate pus; **E. erregen,** to cause the formation of pus.

Eiterabsonderung, *f. Med:* **1.** discharge of pus. **2.** purulent discharge.

Eiteransammlung, *f. Med:* collection of pus, gathering (of pus).

eiterartig, *a. Med:* pus-like.

Eiterbecken, *n. Med:* pus basin.

Eiterbeule, *f. Med:* abscess, boil, gathering.

eiterbildend, *a. Med:* pyogenic.

Eiterbildung, *f. Med:* formation of pus, suppuration; purulence.

Eiterbläschen, *n. Med:* pustule.

Eiterblase, *f. Med:* pustule.

Eiterbrust, *f. Med:* empyema, pyothorax.

Eitererreger, *m. Med:* pus-organism.

Eiterfieber, *n. Med: F:* pyaemia.

Eiterflechte, *f. Med: F:* impetigo.

Eiterfluß, *m. Med:* pyorrhea, suppurative blennorrhoea.

Eitergang, *m. Med:* suppurative tract; sinus.

Eitergeschwulst, *f. Med:* = **Eiterbeule.**

Eitergeschwür, *n. Med:* abscess, boil, gathering; ulcer.

Eitergrind, *m. Med:* = **Eiterflechte.**

Eiterharn, *m. Med:* **1.** purulent urine. **2.** pyuria.

Eiterharnen, *n. Med:* pyuria.

Eiterherd, *m. Med:* suppurative focus.

Eiterhöhle, *f. Med:* abscess cavity.

eiterig, *a. Med:* = **eitrig.**

Eiterkanal, *m. Med:* = **Eitergang.**

Eiterkokken, *m.pl. Bac:* pyococci.

Eiterkörperchen, *n. Med:* pus corpuscle, leucocyte.

eitern. I. *v.i.* (*haben*) *Med:* (*of wound, etc.*) to discharge pus; to suppurate; to ulcerate; (*of wound, sore*) to run; (*of wound*) to fester; **eiternd,** suppurating; running (sore, wound); festering (wound).

II. *vbl s.* **1. Eitern,** *n. in vbl senses.* **2. Eiterung,** *f.* (*a*) = II. 1; *also:* discharge of pus; suppuration; purulence; ulceration; (*b*) purulent discharge.

Eiternessel, *f. Bot:* perennial nettle, small nettle.

Eiterpflock, *m.*, **Eiterpfropf,** *m. Med:* core (of boil, abscess, etc.).

Eiterpöckchen, *n. Med:* whitehead.

Eitersack, *m. Med:* cyst containing pus.

Eiterschale, *f. Med:* pus basin.

Eitersenkung, *f. Med:* burrowing of pus.

Eiterstock, *m. Med:* = **Eiterpflock.**

Eiterung, *f. see* **eitern** II.

Eitervergiftung, *f. Med:* pyaemia.

eitrig, *a. Med:* purulent, suppurating, suppurative, pussy; **eitriger Ausfluß,** purulent discharge; **eitriger Auswurf,** purulent expectoration; **eitrige Mandelentzündung,** suppurative tonsillitis.

Eiweiß, *n.* (*a*) white of egg, egg-white; *Bookb:* glair; *Cu:* **drei E.,** the whites of three eggs; **E. zu Schnee schlagen,** to beat the white of egg until it is stiff; (*b*) *Ch:* protein; *Biol: Ch:* (*soluble in water, dilute acid or alkali*) albumin; (*soluble in water*) albumen; **tierisches E.,** animal albumin; **pflanzliches E.,** vegetable albumin.

Eiweißabbau, *m. Physiol:* breaking down, decomposition, of protein.

eiweißähnlich, *a.* like albumin; albuminoid.

eiweißartig, *a.* albuminoid; albuminous.

Eiweißbedarf, *m. Physiol:* protein requirement.

Eiweißbestimmung, *f. Med:* test for the presence of albumin.

Eiweißdrüse, *f. Anat:* albuminous gland.

Eiweißfaser, *f. Plastics:* fibre derived from protein.

eiweißförmig, *a.* albuminous.

Eiweißgehalt, *m.* albumin *or* protein content.

eiweißhaltig, *a.* containing albumen *or* protein; albuminous, albuminose.

Eiweißharn, *m. Med:* **1.** urine containing albumin. **2.** albuminuria.

Eiweißharnen, *n. Med:* albuminuria.

Eiweißhaushalt, *m. Physiol:* protein metabolism; (regulation of) protein supply (of the body).

Eiweißkörner, *n.pl. Bot: Ch:* protein grains, aleuron(e) (grains).

Eiweißkörper, *m. Biol: Ch:* protein; albuminoid; albuminous body.

Eiweißkraftfutter, *n. Agr:* protein-concentrated feeding stuffs.

Eiweißkunststoff, *m. Ind:* protein plastic.

Eiweißleim, *m.* gluten glue, gluten protein.

Eiweißmilch, *f. Med:* protein milk, casein milk.

Eiweißprobe, *f. Med:* test for the presence of albumin *or* protein; albumin test; protein test.

eiweißspaltend, *a. Physiol:* (agent) that breaks down proteins; proteolytic (agent, etc.).

Eiweißspaltung, *f. Physiol:* breaking down, cleavage of proteins; proteolysis.

Eiweißstoff, *m. Ch: Biol:* protein; **einfache Eiweißstoffe,** simple proteins; **zusammengesetzte Eiweißstoffe,** conjugated proteins.

Eiweißstoffwechsel, *m. Physiol:* = **Eiweißhaushalt.**

Eiweißtrübung, *f. Brew:* albumin clouding, albumin turbidity.

Eiweißüberzug, *m. Bookb:* glairage.

Eiweißumsatz, *m. Physiol:* = **Eiweißhaushalt.**

Eiweißverbindung, *f. Ch:* protein; albuminous compound; albuminate.

Eiweißverdauung, *f. Physiol:* assimilation of albumin.

Eizahn, *m. Orn: Rept:* egg-tooth.

Eizelle, *f. Biol:* egg-cell; ovum.

Ejakulat [e·ja·ku·ˈlaːt], *n.* **-(e)s/-e.** *Physiol:* ejaculum, *esp.* seminal fluid.

Ejakulation [e·ja·ku·la·tsĭˈoːn], *f.* **-/-en.** **1.** *Physiol:* ejaculation. **2.** (*a*) *Ecc:* ejaculation, short prayer; (*b*) ejaculation, exclamation.

ejakulieren [e·ja·ku·ˈliːrən], *v.tr.* **1.** *Physiol:* to ejaculate (fluid). **2.** *F:* to ejaculate (cry, etc.); to exclaim.

Ejektion [e·jɛktsĭˈoːn], *f.* **-/-en.** **1.** *Jur:* expulsion (from place, property), ejectment. **2.** ejection (of steam, sand, ashes, etc.).

ejektiv [e·jɛkˈtiːf], *a. Ling:* ejective (consonant).

Ejektor [e·ˈjɛktor], *m.* **-s/-en** [-ˈtoːrən], (*a*) *Sm.a: etc:* ejector; (*b*) *Mch:* jet pump.

ejizieren [e·ji·ˈtsiːrən], *v.tr.* **1.** to expel (s.o.) by force, to oust (s.o.). **2.** to eject (steam, sand, ashes, etc.).

Eka- [ˌe·ka·-], *comb.fm. Ch:* (*in names of certain elements*) eka-; **Ekabor** [ˌe·ka·ˈboːr] *n*, ekaboron; **Ekazäsium** [e·ka·ˈtsɛːzĭum] *n*, ekacaesium; **Ekasilizium** [e·ka·zi·ˈliːtsĭum] *n*, ekasilicon.

Ekart [e·ˈkaːr], *m.* **-s/-s.** *Fin:* margin of profit; *St.Exch:* (*in option deal*) margin between price of future delivery and option price.

Ekarté [e·karˈteː], *n.* **-s/-s** = **Ecarté.**

Ekbatana [ɛkˈbaːta·naː]. *Pr.n.n.* **-s.** *A.Geog:* Ecbatana.

Ekchymose [ɛkçy·ˈmoːzə], *f.* **-/-n** = **Ecchymose.**

Ekel[1], *m.* **-s/.** (*a*) **E. (vor etwas** *dat.*, **j-m),** aversion (for, to, sth., s.o.); loathing (for sth., s.o.); disgust (at, for, towards, sth., s.o.); repulsion (for sth., s.o.); repugnance (to sth.); **einen E. vor Fleisch haben,** to have an aversion to, for, meat; **ein Gefühl des Ekels stieg in ihr hoch,** she was overcome by a feeling of nausea; her gorge rose; **E. vor etwas** *dat.*, **j-m, empfinden,** to feel an aversion to, for, sth., s.o., to feel disgust at, for, towards, sth., s.o.; to feel repulsion for sth., s.o.; to feel repugnance to sth., s.o., to find sth., s.o., repugnant; **beim bloßen Anblick kommt einen der Ekel an,** the mere sight is nauseating, fills one with disgust, repulsion, makes one feel sick; **etwas bis zum E. wiederholen,** to repeat sth. *ad nauseam;* (*b*) **Spinnen sind mir ein E.,** I have a horror of spiders, I loathe spiders; *F:* spiders give me the creeps, the willies.

Ekel[2], *n.* **-s/-.** *F:* (*of pers.*) **er ist ein E.,** he is disgusting, repulsive; he is loathsome, extremely unpleasant; **du E.!** you horror, beast!

ekel[3], *a.* **1.** *A. & Lit:* repellent, repulsive, repugnant; loathsome. **2.** *A:* (*of pers.*) squeamish; (*of pers., of sense of smell, etc.*) fastidious.

ekelerregend, *a.* repellent, repulsive, repugnant, revolting (ulcers, sight, etc.).

Ekelgefühl, *n.* feeling of nausea, sick feeling.

ekelhaft, *a.* **1.** revolting, repulsive, repellent, disgusting (smell, sight, etc.); offensive (smell); **ekelhafte Speisen,** revolting, repulsive, food; **seine ekelhaften Gesichtszüge,** his repugnant, repulsive, features. **2.** revolting, repulsive, repellent, disgusting (behaviour, manner, etc.); **seine ekelhafte Prahlerei,** his appalling, atrocious, awful, bragging; **er ist ein ekelhafter Kerl,** he is a horrible, nasty, fellow; **das war e. von dir,** that was nasty, *F:* beastly, of you; *adv.* **sich e. benehmen,** to behave in an atrocious, *F:* beastly, manner; **es tut e. weh,** it hurts horribly, terribly; **er ist e. unterwürfig,** he is disgustingly, revoltingly, repulsively, obsequious.

Ekelhaftigkeit, *f.* **1.** offensiveness (of smell); repulsiveness (of features, food, etc.); disgustingness (of food, sight, etc.). **2.** atrociousness, nastiness; *F:* beastliness. **3.** (*actions, behaviour, etc.*) **ihre Ekelhaftigkeiten trieben ihn aus dem Haus,** her nastiness, *F:* beastliness, drove him out of the house.

ekelig, *a.* = **eklig.**

ekeln. 1. *v.impers.* **mir, mich, ekelt, es ekelt mich, mich ekelt's, mir ekelt's,** I am nauseated; I feel disgust, horror, loathing; I shudder; **es ekelt mich, das zu tun,** it fills me with nausea, makes me feel sick, *F:* it gives me the creeps, to do it; **dabei ekelt mich, mir,** it makes me feel sick, nauseates me, fills me with horror, repulsion; **bei diesem Anblick ekelt mich,** this sight repels me, nauseates me; **schon beim bloßen Gedanken daran ekelt('s) mich,** the mere thought of it makes me feel sick, nauseates me, repels me. **2. sich vor etwas** *dat.*, **vor j-m, ekeln,** to feel an aversion to, for, sth., s.o., to feel disgust at, for, towards, sth., s.o.; to feel repulsion for sth., s.o.; to feel repugnance to sth.; **ich ek(e)le mich vor Fleisch,** I have an aversion to, for, meat; **ich ek(e)le mich vor seinen Händen,** I find his hands repellent.

Ekkl- *cp.* **Eccl-.**

Ekklesia [ɛˈkleːzĭaː], *f.* **-/-sien. 1.** *Gr.Ant:* ecclesia. **2.** the Church, Ecclesia.

Ekklesiarch [ɛkle·zĭˈarç], *m.* **-en/-en,** ecclesiarch.

Ekklesiarchie [ɛkle·zĭarˈçiː], *f.* **-/-n** [-ˈçiːən], ecclesiarchy, government by ecclesiastics.

Ekkrisis [ɛˈkriːzis], *f.* **-/-sen.** *Med:* eccrisis.

Eklampsie [ɛklampˈsiː], *f.* **-/-n** [-ˈsiːən]. *Med:* eclampsia; *F:* convulsions.

Eklat [e·ˈkla], *m.* **-s/-s** [e·ˈklaːs]. **1.** *A. & F:* commotion, stir; **einen E. machen,** to cause a stir. **2. mit E.,** (i) splendidly; with *éclat;* (ii) *Iron:* (*of play, examination candidate, etc.*) **mit E. durchfallen,** to fail dismally, to be a resounding failure, to be an utter flop; *A:* **sie hängten ihn mit E.,** they hanged him as high as Haman.

eklatant [e·kla·ˈtant], *a.* striking; blatant; **ein eklatanter Betrug,** a barefaced swindle; **ein eklatanter Fall von Bestechung,** a blatant case of corruption.

Eklektik [ɛkˈlɛktik], *f.* **-/.** *Phil: etc:* eclectic method; eclecticism.

Eklektiker [ɛkˈlɛktikər], *m.* **-s/-,** eclectic.

eklektisch [ɛkˈlɛktiʃ], *a.* eclectic.

Eklektizismus [ɛklɛktiˈtsismus], *m.* **-/.** eclecticism.

eklig, *a.* **1.** revolting, repulsive, repellent, disgusting (smell, sight, etc.); offensive (smell); **er ist mir e.,** I find him repulsive, *F:* he gives me the creeps. **2.** (*of pers., behaviour, etc.*) revolting, repulsive, repellent, disgusting; atrocious, appalling, nasty; *F:* beastly; **e. zu j-m sein,** to be nasty, *F:* beastly, towards s.o.; **sich e. benehmen,** to behave atrociously, abominably, *F:* in a beastly manner. **3.** *F:* **eklig vor etwas** *dat.*, **j-m, sein** = **sich vor etwas** *dat.*, **vor j-m, ekeln,** *q.v. under* **ekeln** 2.

Eklipse [ɛˈklipsə, e·ˈklipsə], *f.* **-/-n.** *Astr:* eclipse; **totale, partielle, ringförmige, E.,** total, partial, annular, eclipse.

Ekliptik [ɛˈkliptik, e·ˈkliptik], *f.* **-/-en.** *Astr:* ecliptic.

ekliptisch [ɛˈkliptiʃ, e·ˈkliptiʃ], *a. Astr:* ecliptic.

Ekloge [ɛkˈloːgə, e·ˈkloːgə], *f.* **-/-n.** *Lit:* eclogue.

Ekonomiser [i·ˈkono·maizər], *m.* **-s/-.** *Mch:* (fuel) economizer; **Dampfmaschine mit E.,** exhaust-gas engine.

Ekossaise [e·koˈsɛːzə], *f.* **-/-n** = **Ecossaise.**

Ekphorie [ɛkfo·ˈriː], *f.* **-/-n** [-ˈriːən]. *Biol:* ecphory.

Ekphrase [ɛkˈfraːzə], *f.* **-/-n, Ekphrasis** [ˈɛkfra·zis], *f.* **-/-sen** [-ˈfraːzən], ecphrasis.

Ekrasit [e·kra·ˈziːt], *n.* **-(e)s/.** *Exp:* ecrasite.

ekrü [e·ˈkryː], *a.* = **écru.**

Ekrüseide, *f. Tex:* raw silk.

Ekstase [ɛkˈstaːzə], *f.* **-/-n. 1.** *Theol:* ecstasy; *Psy:* trance, ecstasy. **2.** *F:* ecstasy, rapture, extreme exaltation, transport; **j-n in E. versetzen,** to throw s.o. into ecstasies, raptures; **über etwas** *acc.* **in E. geraten,** to go into raptures, into ecstasies, over sth.; **in E. sein,** to be enraptured, entranced, (to be transported (with joy).

Ekstatiker [ɛkˈstaːtikər], *m.* **-s/-,** ecstatic.

ekstatisch [ɛkˈstaːtiʃ], *a.* **1.** *Theol: Psy:* ecstatic. **2.** *F:* ecstatic; rapturous; enraptured.

Ektase [ɛkˈtaːzə], *f.* **-/-n.** *Pros:* ectasis.

Ektasie [ɛkta·ˈziː], *f.* **-/-n** [-ˈziːən]. *Med:* ectasis, ectasia.

Ektasis [ˈɛkta·zis], *f.* **-/-sen** [-ˈtaːzən]. *Pros:* ectasis.

ekto-, Ekto- [ɛkto·-], *pref.* ecto-; **ektodermal,** ectodermal; **Ektoparasit** [ˌɛkto·para·ˈziːt] *m*, ectoparasite; **Ektozoon** [ˌɛkto·ˈtsoːon] *n*, ectozoon.

Ektoderm [ɛkto·ˈdɛrm], *n.* **-s/-e.** *Biol:* ectoderm.

ektodermal [ɛkto·dɛrˈmaːl], *a. Anat:* ectodermal, ectodermic.

Ektomie [ɛkto·ˈmiː], *f.* **-/-n** [-ˈmiːən]. *Surg:* excision; *comb.fm.* **-ektomie,** -ectomy; **Tonsillektomie,** tonsillectomy.

Ektopie [ɛkto·ˈpiː], *f.* **-/-n** [-ˈpiːən]. *Med:* ectopia.
ektopisch [ɛkˈtoːpiʃ], *a. Med:* ectopic.
Ektoplasma [ɛkto·ˈplasmaː], *n. Biol:* ectoplasm.
Ektropium [ɛkˈtroːpium], *n.* **-s/.** *Med:* ectropion; eversion of the eyelid.
Ekuador [e·ku·a·ˈdoːr]. *Pr.n.n.* **-s.** *Geog:* Ecuador.
Ekuadorianer [e·ku·a·do·riˈaːnər], *m.* **-s/-.** *Geog:* Ecuadorian.
ekuadorianisch [e·ku·a·do·riˈaːniʃ], *a. Geog:* Ecuadorian.
Ekzem [ɛkˈtseːm], *n.* **-s/-e.** *Med:* eczema.
ekzematisch [ɛktse·ˈmaːtiʃ], *a. Med:* eczematous.
Elaborat [e·la·bo·ˈraːt], *n.* **-(e)s/-e.** *Pej:* (literary, etc.) product; laboured exposition.
elaborieren [e·la·bo·ˈriːrən], *v.tr.* to elaborate, work out (plan, etc.).
Elagabal [e·la·ga·ˈbaːl]. *Pr.n.m.* **-s.** *Rom.Hist:* Heliogabalus, Elagabalus.
Elamit [e·la·ˈmiːt], *m.* **-en/-en.** *A.Hist:* Elamite.
elamitisch [e·la·ˈmiːtiʃ], *a. A.Hist:* Elamite.
Elan [e·ˈlãː], *m.* **-s/.** energy, vigour, impetus; **sich mit E. in eine Arbeit stürzen,** to attack a job with great vigour.
Eläolith [e·lɛ·o·ˈliːt], *m.* **-(e)s/-e** *&* **-en/-en.** *Miner:* elaeolite.
Eläoplast [e·lɛ·o·ˈplast], *m.* **-s/-e.** *Biol:* elaioplast.
Elastik [e·ˈlastik], *f.* **-/-en** *&* *n.* **-s/-s.** *Tex:* elastic material.
Elastikreifen, *m. Aut:* solid rubber tyre.
Elastin [e·lasˈtiːn], *n.* **-s/.** *Biol: Ch:* elastin.
elastisch [e·ˈlastiʃ], *a.* **1.** *(a)* elastic (solid); resilient, flexible (wood, metal); springy, pliant, supple (wood); *Ph:* **elastische Formänderung,** elastic deformation; *Ph:* **elastische Linie,** elastic line; *Surg:* **elastische Binde,** elastic bandage; *(b) Pol. Ec:* **elastische Nachfrage,** elastic demand. **2.** *F:* springy (movement, step, etc.); supple (limbs, muscles, etc.); buoyant, elastic (step); adaptable (mind); **mit elastischem Schritt die Treppe hinaufgehen,** to climb the stairs with a springy, buoyant, step; **er fühlte sich wieder kräftig und e.,** he felt strong and full of bounce again; *Pej:* **ein elastisches Gewissen haben,** to have an elastic conscience; *adv.* **er paßt sich e. den veränderten Umständen an,** he adapts himself easily to changed circumstances; **die Verordnung wurde sehr e. gehandhabt,** the regulation was applied very loosely.
Elastizität [e·lasti·tsi·ˈtɛːt], *f.* **-/.** **1.** *(a)* elasticity (of solid); flexibility, resilience (of wood, metal, etc.); springiness, suppleness (of wood); *(b) Pol.Ec:* **E. der Nachfrage,** elasticity of demand. **2.** *F:* springiness (of gait, step); suppleness (of limbs, muscles); buoyancy, elasticity (of mind, disposition); **seine geistige E. verlieren,** to lose one's elasticity of mind.
Elastizitätsgrenze, *f. Ph:* elastic limit, limit of elasticity.
Elastizitätskoeffizient, *m. Ph:* coefficient of elasticity.
Elastizitätsmodul, *m.,* **Elastizitätszahl,** *f. Mec:* modulus of elasticity, Young's modulus.
Elastometrie [e·lasto·me·ˈtriː], *f.* **-/.** *Ph:* elastometry.
Elatere [e·la·ˈteːrə], *f.* **-/-n.** *Bot:* elater; *pl.* **Elateren,** elaters.
Elaterenträger, *m. Bot:* elaterophore.
Elateridae [e·la·te·ˈriːdɛː], *f.pl. Ent:* elateridae, click-beetles.
Elaterit [e·la·te·ˈriːt], *m.* **-(e)s/.** *Miner:* elaterite, elastic bitumen.
Elaterium [e·la·ˈteːrium], *n.* **-s/.** *Pharm:* elaterium.
Elatine [e·la·ˈtiːnə], *f.* **-/-n.** *Bot:* elatine, water-wort.
Elativ [ˈeːla·tiːf, e·la·ˈtiːf], *m.* **-s/-e** [-tiːvə]. *Gram:* elative.
Elba [ˈɛlbaː]. *Pr.n.n.* **-s.** *Geog:* (the island of) Elba.
elbabwärts, *adv.* down the (river) Elbe.
elbaufwärts, *adv.* up the (river) Elbe.
Elbbutt, *m. Ich:* flounder.
Elbe[1], *f.* **-/-n.** *A:* = **Elfe.**
Elbe[2], **die.** *Pr.n.* **-.** *Geog:* the Elbe.
Elb(e)athen. *Pr.n.n. Lit. & Hum:* Dresden, 'Athens on the Elbe'.
Elbflorenz. *Pr.n.n. Lit. & Hum:* Dresden, 'Florence on the Elbe'.
Elbkahn, *m.* **1.** barge on the Elbe. **2.** *F:* large shoe; *F:* boat, barge, beetle crusher.
Elbkatze, *f.* = **Iltis.**
Elbling, *m.* **-s/-e.** *Vit:* Elbling grape.
Elbschiffahrt, *f.* navigation on the Elbe.
Elbstrom, der. *Geog:* the Elbe.
Elch, *m.* **-(e)s/-e.** *Z:* elk; moose.
Elchhornfarn, *m. Bot:* common elk's-horn fern, stag's-horn fern.
Elchhund, *m. Ven:* elk-hound.
Eldorado [ɛldo·ˈraːdoː]. *Pr.n.n.* **-s** *& s.n.* **-s/-s.** El Dorado.

Elea [ˈeːle·aː]. *Pr.n.n.* **-s.** *A.Geog:* Elea.
Eleasar [e·le·ˈaːza·r]. *Pr.n.m.* **-s.** *B.Hist:* Eleazar.
Eleate [e·le·ˈaːtə], *m.* **-n/-n.** *Phil:* eleatic philosopher, eleatic.
eleatisch [e·le·ˈaːtiʃ], *a. Phil:* eleatic (school, etc.).
elec-, Elec- *cp.* **elek-, Elek-.**
Electrit [e·lɛkˈtriːt], *n.* **-(e)s/.** *Ind:* alundum.
Electuarium [e·lɛktu·ˈaːrium], *n.* **-s/-rien.** *Pharm:* electuary.
Eleer [e·ˈleːər], *m.* **-s/-.** *A.Hist:* Elean.
Elefant [e·le·ˈfant], *m.* **-en/-en.** **1.** *(a) Z:* elephant; *F:* **aus einer Mücke einen Elefanten machen,** to make a mountain out of a mole-hill; *(b) F:* clumsy person; *F:* baby elephant; **er ist wie ein E. im Porzellanladen,** he is like a bull in a china-shop. **2.** *Paperm: (size of paper)* elephant. **3.** *Chess:* castle.
Elefantenapfelbaum, *m. Bot:* elephant's-apple tree, feronia.
elefantenartig, *a.* elephantine.
Elefantenbein, *n. Med: Vet:* elephantiasis, elephant's leg.
Elefantenbulle, *m. Z:* bull elephant.
Elefantenfarn, *m. Bot:* crape fern.
Elefantenfell, *n.* = **Elefantenhaut.**
Elefantenführer, *m.* elephant-driver, mahout.
Elefantenfuß, *m. Bot:* elephant's foot, tortoise plant, testudinaria.
Elefantengras, *n. Bot:* elephant grass.
Elefantenhaut, *f. (a)* elephant hide; *(b) F:* **eine E. haben,** to have a skin like a rhinoceros, to have a thick skin, hide.
Elefantenkalb, *n. Z:* calf elephant, elephant calf; *F:* baby elephant.
Elefantenknochen, *m.* **1.** elephant's bone. **2.** *A:* ivory.
Elefantenkrankheit, *f.* = **Elefantiasis.**
Elefantenkuh, *f. Z:* cow elephant.
Elefantenküken, *n. F:* clumsy teenager, tubby girl, baby elephant.
Elefantenlaus, *f. Bot: (a)* cashew (nut tree); *(b)* cashew nut.
Elefantennuß, *f. Bot:* ivory nut, corozo nut.
Elefantenorden, der, *(decoration)* the Order of the Elephant.
Elefantenrobbe, *f. Z:* sea-elephant, elephant-seal.
Elefantenrüssel, *m.* elephant's trunk, proboscis.
Elefantenschildkröte, *f. Rept:* Galapagos giant tortoise.
Elefantenspitzmaus, *f. Z:* elephant shrew.
Elefantentreiber, *m.* elephant-driver, mahout.
Elefantenzahn, *m.* **1.** elephant's tusk. **2.** *Moll:* elephant's tusk shell.
Elefant-Folio, *n. Paperm: (size of paper)* large elephant.
Elefantiasis [e·le·fanˈtiːa·zis], *f.* **-/.** *Med:* elephantiasis.
elegant[1] [e·le·ˈgant], *a. (a)* elegant (dress, woman, room, etc.); smart (dress, woman); *adv.* **e. gekleidet,** elegantly dressed; *(b)* neat (demonstration of theorem, etc.); graceful, elegant (style, movements, etc.); **der elegante Flug der Möwe,** the graceful flight of the sea-gull; *adv. F:* **das war e. gemacht,** that was neat.
Elegant[2] [e·leˈgãː], *m.* **-s/-s,** man of fashion; *F:* swell, dandy, beau.
Eleganz [e·le·ˈgants], *f.* **-/.** *(a)* elegance (of dress, woman, room, etc.); smartness (of dress, woman); *(b)* elegance, gracefulness (of style, expression, manner, movement); neatness (of style, expression).
Elegiambus [e·le·giˈambus], *m.* **-/-ben.** *Gr. & Lt. Pros:* elegiambus.
Elegie [e·le·ˈgiː], *f.* **-/-n** [-ˈgiːən]. *Lit:* elegy.
Elegiker [e·ˈleːgikər], *m.* **-s/-,** elegiac poet, elegist.
elegisch [e·ˈleːgiʃ], *a.* **1.** *Pros:* elegiac; **elegische Verse, Rhythmen,** elegiacs; **elegischer Dichter,** elegiac poet, elegist; **elegisches Gedicht,** elegiac (poem), elegy. **2.** mournful (poem); *F:* melancholy, plaintive (pers., expression, etc.).
Elektawolle [e·ˈlɛktaː-], *f. Tex:* first-class wool.
elektiv [e·lɛkˈtiːf], *a.* selective, favoured.
Elektor [e·ˈlɛktor], *m.* **-s/-en** [-ˈtoːrən]. *G.Hist:* Elector.
Elektorat [e·lɛkto·ˈraːt], *n.* **-(e)s/-e.** *G.Hist:* Electorate.
Elektra [e·ˈlɛktraː]. *Pr.n.f.* **-s** *& Lit:* **-trens.** Electra.
Elektret [e·lɛkˈtreːt], *m.* **-s/-e.** *Ph:* electret.
Elektrifikation [e·lɛktri·fi·ka·tsiˈoːn], *f.* **-/-en,** electrification (of railway, etc.).
elektrifizieren [e·lɛktri·fi·ˈtsiːrən]. *v.tr.* to electrify (railway, plant, etc.); **Elektrifizierung** *f,* electrification (of railway, etc.).
Elektrik [e·ˈlɛktrik], *f.* **-/.** (science of) electricity.
Elektriker [e·ˈlɛktrikər], *m.* **-s/-,** electrician.
elektrisch [e·ˈlɛktriʃ]. **1.** *a. (a) (charged with or capable of developing electricity)* electric (current, battery, lighting, etc.); **elektrischer Heizofen,** electric fire, stove; **elektrischer Ventilator,** electric fan; **elektrischer Rasierapparat,** electric razor, shaver; **elektrische Leitung,** (i) electric wiring *or* wires; (ii) electric cable *or* wire; (iii) electricity supply; **die elektrische Leitung in einem Haus (ver)legen,** to wire a house (for electricity); *Ich:* **elektrischer Fisch,** gymnotus, *F:* electric eel, electric ray; *(b) (relating to electricity)* electrical (unit, machinery, supplies, engineering); **mit elektrischem Antrieb,** electrically driven. **2.** *adv.* electrically; (driven, etc.) by electricity; **e. gesteuert,** electrically controlled; **e. geladen,** electrically charged; live (wire); *F:* electric (atmosphere).
Elektrische [e·ˈlɛktriʃə], *f. (decl. as adj.) F:* (electric) tram.
elektrisierbar [e·lɛktri·ˈsiːr-], *a.* electrifiable (substance).
elektrisieren [e·lɛktri·ˈziːrən]. **I.** *v.tr.* to electrify (substance, *F:* audience); **sich e., elektrisiert werden,** to get an electric shock; *Med:* **j-n e.,** to give s.o. electric treatment; *F:* **er sprang wie elektrisiert auf,** he shot, leapt, to his feet as if electrified, galvanized.
II. *vbl s.* **Elektrisieren** *n.,* **Elektrisierung** *f., in vbl senses; also:* electrification (of substance, *F:* of audience, etc.).
Elektrisiermaschine, *f.* electrostatic machine.
Elektrizität [e·lɛktri·tsi·ˈtɛːt], *f.* **-/-en,** electricity; **positive, negative, E.,** positive, negative, electricity.
Elektrizitäts-, *comb.fm.* electricity ...; electric ...; electro-; **Elektrizitätszähler** *m,* electricity meter; **Elektrizitätsentladung** *f,* electric discharge; **Elektrizitätszeiger** *m,* electroscope.
Elektrizitätserzeugung, *f.* generation of electricity, of (electric) power.
Elektrizitätslehre, *f.* science of electricity, electrology.
Elektrizitätsleiter, *m.* conductor (of electricity).
Elektrizitätsleitung, *f.* **1.** conduction (of electricity). **2.** electric (supply) cable.
Elektrizitätsmesser, *m.* electrometer.
Elektrizitätsmessung, *f.* electrometry.
Elektrizitätsnetz, *n.* electricity grid.
Elektrizitätsversorgung, *f.* electricity supply.
Elektrizitätswerk, *n.* electricity works, power (generating) station.
Elektrizitätswirtschaft, *f.* electric power industry.
Elektrizitätszähler, *m.* electricity meter, electric meter.
Elektro-, elektro- [e·ˌlɛktro·-], *pref.* electro-; **Elektrochemie** *f,* electro-chemistry; **elektrochemisch,** electro-chemical; **elektropositiv,** electro-positive.
Elektroabscheider, *m.* = **Elektrofilter.**
Elektroakustik, *f.* electro-acoustics.
Elektroanalyse, *f.* electro-analysis.
Elektroantrieb, *m.* electric drive, electric traction.
Elektrobioskopie [e·lɛktro·bi·o·sko·ˈpiː], *f.* **-/.** electrobioscopy.
Elektroblech, *n. Metall:* electrical sheet-steel.
Elektrochemie, *f.* electro-chemistry.
elektrochemisch, *a.* electro-chemical.
Elektrochirurgie, *f.* electro-surgery.
Elektrode [e·lɛkˈtroːdə], *f.* **-/-n,** electrode.
Elektrodenhalter, *m.* electrode holder.
Elektrodenkohle, *f.* electrode carbon.
Elektrodenspannung, *f.* electrode potential.
Elektrodiagnostik, *f. Med:* electro-diagnostics.
Elektrodose, *f. Gramophones:* electro-magnetic pick-up.
Elektrodynamik, *f.* electrodynamics.
elektrodynamisch, *a.* electro-dynamic(al); **elektrodynamischer Lautsprecher,** electro-dynamic loudspeaker.
Elektrodynamometer, *n.* electrodynamometer.
Elektroenergie, *f.* electrical energy.
Elektroenzephalographie, *f. Med:* electro-encephalography.
Elektrofilter, *n. & m.* electrostatic precipitator.
elektrogalvanisch, *a.* electrogalvanic.
Elektrogerät, *n.* electric appliance.
Elektrographie [e·lɛktro·gra·ˈfiː], *f.* **-/.** electrography.
Elektrohängebahn, *f.* electric suspension railway, telpher.
Elektrohochofen, *m.* electric blast furnace.
Elektroindustrie, *f.* electrical industry.
Elektroingenieur, *m.* (qualified) electrical engineer.
Elektroinstallateur, *m.* electrician, electrical fitter.
Elektrokardiogramm, *n. (abbr.* EKG) *Med:* electro-cardiogram, *(abbr.* ECG).

Elektrokardiographie, *f.* -/. *Med:* electrocardiography.
Elektrokarren, *m.* electrically driven truck, *F:* electric truck.
Elektrokaustik, *f. Med:* electrocautery, galvanocautery.
Elektrokinetik, *f.* electro-kinetics.
Elektrokorund, *m.* electro-corundum, fused alumina.
Elektrolokomotive, *f. Rail:* electric locomotive.
Elektrolot, *n. Nau:* electric depth sounder.
Elektrolyse [eˑlɛktroˑˈlyːzə], *f.* **-/-n,** electrolysis.
elektrolysieren [eˑlɛktroˑlyˑˈziːrən], *v.tr.* to electrolyse.
Elektrolyt [eˑlɛktroˑˈlyːt], *m.* **-(e)s/-e & -en/-en.** *El:* electrolyte.
elektrolytisch [eˑlɛktroˑˈlyːtiʃ], *a.* electrolytic; **elektrolytisches Bad,** electrolytic bath; electrobath; four-cell bath.
Elektrolytkupfer, *m.* electrolytic copper.
Elektromagnet, *m.* electro-magnet.
elektromagnetisch, *a.* electro-magnetic.
Elektromagnetismus, *m.* electro-magnetism.
Elektromechanik, *f.* electro-mechanics.
Elektromechaniker, *m.* electrician.
Elektromeister, *m.* (qualified) electrician.
Elektrometallurgie, *f.* electro-metallurgy.
elektrometallurgisch, *a.* electro-metallurgic.
Elektrometeore, *m.pl.* atmospheric phenomena caused by electric disturbances.
Elektrometer, *n.* **-s/-,** electrometer; **geeichtes E.,** calibrating electrometer.
Elektrometrie, *f.* -/. electrometry.
Elektromobil, *n. Veh:* electrically driven (road-) vehicle, *F:* electric motor car; electric van.
Elektromonteur, *m.* electrician, electrical fitter.
Elektromotor, *m.* electric motor, electromotor.
elektromotorisch, *a.* electromotive; **elektromotorische Kraft,** electromotive force; **elektromotorische Gegenkraft,** counter-electromotive, back-electromotive, force.
Elektron[1] [eˑˈlɛktron], *n.* **-s/-en** [-ˈtroːnən]. *Atom.Ph: etc:* electron.
Elektron[2] [ˈeˑlɛktron, eˑˈlɛktron], *n.* **-s/.** = **Elektrum.**
elektronegativ, *a.* electro-negative.
Elektronen- [eˑlɛkˈtroːnən-], *comb.fm.* electron(ic) . . .; **Elektronentheorie** *f,* electron(ic) theory; **Elektronenhülle** *f,* electron cloud.
Elektronenausstrahlung. *f.* emission of electrons, thermionic emission.
Elektronenbild, *n.* electron image.
Elektronenemission, *f.* = **Elektronenausstrahlung.**
Elektronenfernrohr, *n.* electron telescope.
Elektronengehirn, *n.* electronic brain.
Elektronenlehre, *f.* electron(ic) theory; (science of) electronics, electronic science.
Elektronenlinse, *f.* electron lens.
Elektronenmikroskop, *n.* electron microscope.
Elektronenoptik, *f.* electron optics.
Elektronenröhre, *f. W.Tel: etc:* electron(ic) valve, *U.S:* tube; thermionic valve, *U.S:* tube.
Elektronenschleuder, *f. Atom.Ph:* betatron.
Elektronenstoß, *m. Atom.Ph:* electronic impact.
Elektronenstrahl, *m.* electron beam, ray; cathode ray.
Elektronenstrom, *m.* stream of electrons.
Elektronentheorie, *f.* electronic theory, theory of electronics.
Elektronenvolt, *n. Atom.Ph:* electron volt.
Elektronik [eˑlɛkˈtroːnik], *f.* -/. electronics.
elektronisch [eˑlɛkˈtroːniʃ], *a.* electronic; **elektronische Musik,** electronic music.
Elektroofen, *m.* electric furnace.
Elektrooptik, *f.* electro-optics.
Elektroosmose, *f.* electric osmosis, electro-osmosis.
Elektrophor [eˑlɛktroˑˈfoːr], *m.* **-en/-en,** electrophorus.
Elektrophorese [eˑlɛktroˑfoˑˈreːzə], *f.* **-/-n,** electrophoresis.
Elektrophysik, *f.* electrophysics.
Elektrophysiologie, *f.* electro-physiology.
elektrophysiologisch, *a.* electro-physiological.
elektroplattieren, *v.tr.* to electroplate; **Elektroplattierung** *f,* electroplating.
elektropositiv, *a.* electro-positive.
Elektrorasierer, *m. Toil:* electric shaver, razor.
Elektroschalldose, *f. Gramophones:* electromagnetic pick-up.
Elektroschock, *m. Med:* electro-shock; electric convulsion.
Elektrosilage, *f. Agr:* electric ensilage.
Elektroskop [eˑlɛktroˑˈskoːp], *n.* **-s/-e,** electroscope.
Elektrostahl, *m. Metall:* electric steel.
Elektrostatik, *f.* electrostatics.
elektrostatisch, *a.* electrostatic(al).
Elektrotechnik, *f.* electrotechnics, electrical technology; electrical engineering.
Elektrotechniker, *m.* electro-technician; electrical engineer.
elektrotechnisch, *a.* electrotechnic(al).
elektrotherapeutisch, *a. Med:* electrotherapeutic(al).
Elektrotherapie, *f. Med:* electrotherapy, electrotherapeutics, electropathy.
Elektrothermie [-tɛrˈmiː], *f.* -/. electro-thermancy, electro-thermy.
elektrothermisch, *a.* electro-thermic, electrothermionic, electro-thermal, thermo-electric(al).
Elektrotomie [-toˑˈmiː], *f.* **-/-n** [-ˈmiːən]. *Surg:* electrotomy.
Elektrotonus [eˑlɛktroˑˈtoːnus], *m.* -/. *Physiol:* electrotonus.
Elektrotrockenrasierer, *m. Toil:* electric dry shaver, electric razor.
Elektrotypie, *f.* -/. = **Galvanoplastik.**
Elektrum [eˑˈlɛktrum], *n.* **-s/.** **1.** *Miner:* electrum. **2.** *A:* amber, electrum.
Elektuarium [eˑlɛktuˑˈaːrĭum], *n.* = **Electuarium.**
Element [eˑləˈmɛnt, eˑleˑˈmɛnt], *n.* **-(e)s/-e.** **1.** (*a*) element; **die vier Elemente,** the four elements; **das Toben, Wüten, der Elemente,** the raging, tumult, of the elements; **die Gewalt der Elemente,** the force(s) of nature, the elemental forces; **den Elementen trotzen,** to brave the elements; **Wasser ist das E. der Fische,** water is the fishes' element; *F:* **in seinem E. sein,** to be in one's element; (*b*) *Ch:* element. **2.** *pl.* **Elemente,** elements, first principles (of a science); **j-n in den Elementen einer Wissenschaft unterrichten,** to instruct s.o. in the elements of a science, to give s.o. a grounding in a science. **3.** (*a*) element (of structure, *El:* of battery, electric iron, etc.); member, component (of machine, structure, etc.); cell (of electric battery); *Mth:* element (of determinant, magnitude, etc.); *Psy:* element; *Pol.Ec:* unit of labour (in piece-work); *Astr: etc:* datum, element; **galvanisches E.,** galvanic, primary, cell; **das E. des Tragischen im griechischen Drama,** the tragic element in Greek drama; *F:* **üble, asoziale, Elemente,** undesirable, antisocial, elements; (*b*) *Theol:* **die eucharistischen Elemente,** the eucharist elements.
elementar [eˑləmɛnˈtaːr, eˑleˑmɛnˈtaːr], *a.* **1.** elemental (force, etc.); **elementare Gewalt, Kraft,** elemental force; force of nature; **das Ereignis brach mit elementarer Gewalt über sie herein,** the event overtook her with elemental, overpowering, force; **die elementare Gewalt der Liebe,** the elemental force of love; **elementare Größe,** elemental grandeur. **2.** (*a*) *Ch: etc:* simple, uncompounded; pure; non-decomposable, elemental (substance); **elementarer Kohlenstoff,** uncombined carbon; **im elementaren Zustand,** in the free state; (*b*) fundamental, basic, elementary (rule, right, instinct, etc.); **die elementaren Menschenrechte,** the basic human rights; **elementare Bedürfnisse,** basic needs; **elementare Wahrheiten,** elemental, basic, truths; **elementare Pflichten des Einzelnen gegenüber der Gemeinschaft,** elementary, fundamental, duties of the individual towards the community; (*c*) elementary, rudimentary, primary (instruction, knowledge, algebra, etc.); **er hat nur elementare Kenntnisse in der Mathematik,** he has only an elementary knowledge of mathematics.
Elementaranalyse, *f. Ch:* elementary, organic, analysis.
Elementarberechnung, *f. Pol.Ec:* computation of piece-work rates (on the basis of units of labour).
Elementarbildung, *f.* elementary education.
Elementarereignis, *n.* (*a*) natural occurrence; natural disturbance, manifestation (of the power) of the elements; (*b*) event of overpowering, overwhelming, force.
Elementargefühl, *n. Psy:* elementary, primary, emotion.
Elementargeist, *m.* elemental spirit, elemental.
Elementargewalt, *f.* force of nature, elemental force.
elementarisch [eˑləmɛnˈtaːriʃ, eˑleˑmɛnˈtaːriʃ], *a.* = **elementar.**
Elementarkörnchen, *n. Physiol:* blood dust.
Elementarkörperchen, *n.pl. Bac:* chlamydozoa.
Elementarkraft, *f.* (*a*) = **Elementargewalt;** (*b*) *Tchn:* energy from a natural source.
Elementarladung, *f. Atom.Ph:* elementary charge.
Elementarmagnet, *m. Ph:* molecular magnet.
Elementarprozeß, *m. Atom.Ph:* process involving elementary particles.
Elementarquantum, *n. El: Ph:* elementary quantum.
Elementarschule, *f.* primary school, elementary school.
Elementarstoff, *m. Ch:* elementary matter, element.
Elementarteilchen, *n. Atom.Ph:* elementary particle.
Elementarteiler, *m. Mth:* elementary divisor.
Elementarunterricht, *m. Sch:* primary, elementary, instruction.
Elementarwelle, *f. Ph:* Huyghens' wavelet, secondary wave; motion of the particles of a medium.
Elementenpaar, *n. Mec:* pair (of elements).
Elementenpsychologie, *f.* structural psychology.
Elementglas, *n. El:* battery jar.
Elementkohle, *f. El:* cell carbon.
Elemi [eˑˈleːmiː], *n.* **-s/., Elemigummi,** *m.*, **Elemiharz,** *n.* (gum) elemi.
Elen, *n. & m.* **-s/-.** *Z:* elk; moose.
Elenantilope, *f. Z:* eland.
Elenchus [eˑˈlɛnçus], *m.* **-/-chi.** *Log:* elench(us), refutation.
Elend[1], *n.* **-(e)s/-e.** *Bot:* = **Ellend.**
Elend[2], *n.* **-(e)s/.** **1.** *A:* foreign land; exile, banishment; **ins E. gehen,** to go into exile. **2.** (*a*) extreme poverty, destitution, want, distress; misery; squalor; **ins E. geraten,** to be reduced to poverty, to become, to be rendered, destitute; **j-n ins E. stürzen, bringen,** to render, leave, s.o. destitute, in distress; **im E. umkommen,** to die destitute, in destitution, in squalor; to die a dog's death; **im E. leben,** to live in destitution, in want; **in den Gassen herrschte unbeschreibliches E.,** there was indescribable, untold, squalor in the streets; **in diesen Häusern wohnt das E.,** misery dwells in these houses; (*b*) distress, wretchedness, misery; **E. über j-n bringen,** to bring misery to s.o., to inflict misery on s.o.; **menschliches E.,** human misery; **das E. des menschlichen Lebens,** the wretchedness, misery, of human existence; *F:* **das graue E. überkam ihn, kam ihn an,** he was filled with blank despair, despondency, wretchedness, *F:* he got the blues; **er kriegte das heulende E.,** he got lachrymose (*e.g.* with drink), he got maudlin, *F:* he got a fit of the blues, of the dismals; **er sitzt da wie ein Häufchen E.,** he sits there looking a picture of misery; (*c*) **es ist ein rechtes E. mit dem Kind,** the child is a great trial; the child is heart-breaking.
elend[3], *a.* (*a*) poverty-stricken, miserable (existence, life, surroundings, conditions); distressed (circumstances); wretched, miserable (dwellings, etc.); squalid (dwellings); **eine elende Baracke,** a (wretched) shack, a shanty, a hovel; **sie lebte in elenden Verhältnissen,** she lived in distressed circumstances, in dire poverty; **den Armen und Elenden helfen,** to help the poor and the needy; (*b*) (*of pers.*) miserable, wretched, distressed; **sie fühlte sich e. und verlassen,** she felt miserable and lonely; **der Krieg hat viele Menschen e. gemacht,** war has inflicted misery on many; *B. & Lit:* **die Elenden,** the afflicted; *A:* **du Elender!** you poor, miserable, wretch! (*cp.* (*e*)); (*c*) **er sieht e. aus,** he looks very ill; he looks pale, wan, *F:* he looks seedy; **mir ist ganz e. zumute,** I feel ill, sick; (*d*) **der elende Sünder,** the wretched sinner; **vergib uns elenden Sündern, uns Elenden!** forgive us poor miserable sinners! (*e*) contemptible, mean (action, behaviour, etc.); **das ist ein elender Betrug,** this is a mean fraud; **er ist ein elender Schurke,** he is a vile wretch, despicable creature; **elender Schurke! Elender!** you wretch! **ein elendes Gesindel,** a despicable crew, *F:* bunch; (*f*) poor, sorry (performer, play, etc.); *F:* rotten (performance, etc.); **er ist ein elender Schauspieler,** he is a deplorable, sorry, actor; *F:* **was für ein elendes Nest!** what a beastly, wretched, hole (of a place)! **es ist elende Ausbeutung,** it is shameful exploitation; (*g*) **elende Schinderei,** sheer slavery, drudgery; **elende Hitze,** terrible heat; *adv.* **ich habe mich e. in ihm getäuscht,** I was terribly mistaken in him; *F:* **es tut e. weh,** it hurts awfully, terribly, *F:* it hurts like hell.
Elende, *f.* **-/-n,** deserted settlement.
elendig, *a.* = **elend**[3], *esp.* (*a*).
elendiglich, *adv.* distressedly, miserably; **e. umkommen, zugrunde gehen,** to perish miserably, in poverty.
Elendsquartier, *n.* (*a*) squalid dwelling; shack, shanty; hovel; (*b*) = **Elendsviertel.**
Elendsviertel, *n.* slum (quarter); shanty-town; **die Pariser Elendsviertel,** the slums of Paris; **Sanierung der Elendsviertel,** slum-clearance.
Elendswohnung, *f.* squalid dwelling; shack, shanty; hovel.

Elenhirsch, *m.*=**Elen.**
Elenkraut, *n. Bot:* field eryngo.
Elenktik [e·ˈlɛŋktik], *f.* -/. *Log:* elenctic art, method.
Elentier, *n.*=**Elen.**
Eleocharis [e·le·o·ˈça:ris], *f.* -/-**ren.** *Bot:* eleocharis, spike rush.
Eleonore [e·le·o·ˈno:rə]. *Pr.n.f.* **-s** & *Lit:* **-ns.** Eleanor(e), Elinor.
Eleonorenfalke, *m. Orn:* Eleonora's falcon.
Elephant [e·le·ˈfant], *m.* **-en/-en**=**Elefant.**
Elephantiasis [e·le·fanˈti:a·zis], *f.* -/. *Med:*=**Elefantiasis.**
Eleusine [e·loyˈzi:nə], *f.* **-/-n.** *Bot:* eleusine.
Eleusinien, die [e·loyˈzi:niən], *n.pl. Gr.Ant:* the Eleusinia, the Eleusinian mysteries.
eleusinisch [e·loyˈzi:niʃ], *a. Gr.Ant:* Eleusinian; **die Eleusinischen Mysterien,** the Eleusinian mysteries.
Eleusis [e·ˈloyzis]. *Pr.n.n.* **-'.** *Geog:* Eleusis.
Eleutherien [e·loyˈte:riən], *n.pl. Gr.Ant:* Eleutheria.
eleutheropetal [e·loyte·ro·pe·ˈta:l], *a. Bot:* eleutheropetalous.
Elevation [e·le·va·tsiˈo:n], *f* **-/-en.** **1.** *Ecc:* **E. der Hostie,** elevation of the Host. **2.** *Psychics:* levitation; locomotion at a distance. **3.** *Astr:* altitude, elevation (of star). **4.** *Artil:* elevation (of gun).
Elevationswinkel, *m. Artil:* angle of elevation.
Elevator [e·le·ˈva:tor], *m.* **-s/-en** [-va·ˈto:rən]. **1.** *Anat:* elevator (muscle). **2.** *Tchn:* (*a*) bucket conveyer; bucket elevator; paternoster (elevator); (*b*) (grain) elevator.
Elevatorbecher, *m.,* **Elevatoreimer,** *m. Tchn:* elevator bucket.
Eleve [e·ˈle:və], *m.* **-n/-n,** student (*esp.* of forestry); pupil; apprentice.
Elevin [e·ˈle:vin], *f.* **-/-innen,** (girl) student; pupil; apprentice; girl trainee.
elf[1], *F:* **elfe. 1.** *cardinal num.a.* eleven; **e. Tage,** eleven days; **Kapitel, Seite, e.,** chapter, page, eleven; **eine Familie von elf(en),** a family of eleven; **sie waren zu elf(en),** there were eleven of them. **2.** *s.f.* **Elf, -/-en,** *F:* **Elfe, -/-n,** (*a*) (figure) eleven; **eine E., zwei Elfen, schreiben,** to write an eleven, two elevens; (*b*) *Sp: Fb:* (*team*) eleven. (*For other phrases cp* **acht**[1].) **3. elf-, Elf-,** *comb. fm.* (*a*) (*in numerals*) **elfhundert,** eleven hundred; **elfeinhalb,** eleven and a half; (*b*) eleven-; having, with, eleven . . .; of eleven . . .; in eleven . . .; *Geom: etc:* hendec(a)-; **elfsilbig,** eleven-syllable(d), hendecasyllabic; **elfstellig,** eleven-figure (number); *Geom:* **Elfeck** *n,* hendecagon, undecagon; **elfeckig,** having eleven angles, hendecagonal. (*For compounds not listed above cp.* **acht**[1] 3.)
Elf[2], *m.* **-en/-en.** *Myth:* elf; fairy; imp.
elfe[1], *cardinal num.a. pred. see* **elf.**
Elfe[2], *f.* **-/-n.** *Myth:* elf; fairy; sprite; pixie, pixy; brownie.
elfeinhalb, *cardinal num.a.inv.* eleven and a half.
Elfenbein, *n.* **1.** ivory; **weiches, hartes, E.,** soft, hard, ivory; **fossiles E.,** fossil ivory; odontolite; **vegetabilisches E.,** vegetable ivory; **ein Kamm aus E.,** an ivory comb; **ihre Hände hatten die Farbe von E.,** her hands were the colour of ivory; **sein Gesicht war wie aus E. geschnitzt,** his features were like an ivory carving. **2.** ivory carving, ivory; **eine Sammlung von Elfenbeinen,** a collection of ivories.
Elfenbeinarbeit, *f.* ivory carving, ivory.
elfenbeinen, elfenbeinern, *a.* ivory, of ivory; *Ecc:* **elfenbeinerner Turm,** Tower of Ivory.
elfenbeinfarbig, *a.* ivory-coloured.
Elfenbeinhändler, *m.* ivory-dealer.
Elfenbeinkamm, *m.* ivory comb.
Elfenbeinkarton, *m. Paperm:* ivory board.
Elfenbeinkästchen, *n.,* **Elfenbeinkasten,** *m.* ivory casket.
Elfenbeinküste, die. *Pr.n.f. Geog:* the Ivory Coast.
Elfenbeinmasse, *f.* synthetic ivory.
Elfenbeinmöwe, *f. Orn:* ivory gull.
Elfenbeinnuß, *f. Bot:* ivory nut, corozo nut.
Elfenbeinpalme, *f. Bot:* ivory(-nut) palm, corozo(-palm).
Elfenbeinpapier, *n. Paperm:* ivory paper.
Elfenbeinporzellan, *n.* ivory porcelain.
Elfenbeinschnecke, *f. Moll:* ivory shell, eburna.
Elfenbeinschnitzerei, *f.* ivory carving, ivory.
Elfenbeinschwarz, *n.* ivory black, bone black.
Elfenbeinskulptur, *f.* ivory carving, ivory.
Elfenbeinturm, *m.* ivory tower.
elfenhaft, *a.* elfin; elfish.
Elfenkönig, *m.* fairy-king; *Lit:* King of the fairies, elves.
Elfenkönigin, *f.* fairy-queen; *Lit:* Queen of the fairies.
Elfenreich, *n.* elf-land.
Elfenreigen, *m.* round dance of the fairies.
Elfenring, *m.*=**Elfentanzplatz.**
Elfenschuh, *m. Bot:* columbine.
Elfentanzplatz, *m.* fairy-ring (of mushrooms, toadstools).
Elfer, *m.* **-s/-. 1.** (figure) eleven. **2.** (*a*) wine of the '11 vintage: (*b*) *Mil:* soldier of the 11th Regiment. **3.** *Fb: F:* penalty (kick).
Elfereinmaleins, *n. Mth:* eleven times table.
Elferprobe, *f. Mth:* casting out elevens.
Elferrat, *m.* committee of eleven (*esp. to organize Rhineland Shrovetide celebrations*).
Elferrest, *m. Mth:* excess of elevens (in casting out elevens).
elffach, *a.* (*a*) elevenfold; (*b*) **zweiundzwanzig ist das Elffache von zwei,** twenty-two is eleven times two; **sich um das Elffache vermehren,** to increase elevenfold.
elffältig, *a.* elevenfold.
Elfflach, *n. Geom:* hendecahedron.
elfflächig, *a. Geom:* hendecahedral.
elfisch, *a.* elfin.
elfjährig, *a.* **1.** eleven-year-old (child, animal, etc.); **ein elfjähriger Junge, ein Elfjähriger,** a boy of eleven, an eleven-year-old boy, *F:* an eleven-year-old. **2.** lasting (for) eleven years.
elfmal, *adv.* eleven times; **e. soviel,** eleven times as much; **e. so groß wie . . . ,** eleven times as big as . . . .
Elfmeter, *m. Fb:* penalty (kick); **einen E. verschießen,** to miss a penalty.
Elfmeterpunkt, *m. Fb:* penalty spot.
Elfmeterraum, *m. Fb:* penalty area.
Elfmeterstoß, *m. Fb:* penalty kick.
Elfsilber, *m.* **-s/-.** *Pros:* hendecasyllable.
elfstellig, *a. Mth: etc:* eleven-figure (number); eleven-place (decimal).
elft, *adv.* **zu e.,** (the) eleven of us, you, them; **wir gingen zu e. zum Bahnhof,** (the) eleven of us went to the station; **sie lebten zu e. in einer Wohnung,** (the) eleven of them lived in one flat.
elft-, Elft-, *comb.fm.* eleventh . . .; **die elftgrößte Stadt,** the eleventh largest town; **er ist der Elftbeste in seiner Klasse,** he is the eleventh best pupil in his form.
elftausend, *cardinal num.a.inv.* eleven thousand; **die heilige Ursula und die e. Jungfrauen,** Saint Ursula and the Eleven Thousand Virgins.
Elftel. I. *n.* **-s/-,** eleventh (part); **ein E., zwei E., des Wertes verlieren,** to lose one eleventh, two elevenths, of the value; *see also* **-tel.**
II. **elftel,** *inv.a.* eleventh (part) of . . .; **ein e. Meter,** an eleventh of a metre.
elftens, *adv.* in the eleventh place.
elfte(r), elfte, elfte(s), *ordinal num.a.* eleventh; **im elften Kapitel,** in the eleventh chapter; **an elfter Stelle,** in the eleventh place; **zum elften Mal,** for the eleventh time; **in elfter Stunde,** at the eleventh hour; **Ludwig der Elfte,** Louis the Eleventh; **am Elften im Elften,** on the eleventh of the eleventh. (*For other phrases cp.* **achte(r).**)
Elger, *m.* **-s/-.** *Fish:* fish-gig; eel-spear, eel-prong.
Eli [ˈe:li:]. *Pr.n.m.* **-s.** *B.Hist:* Eli.
Elia [e·ˈli:a:]. *Pr.n.m.* **-s** & **-liä.** *B:* Elijah.
Elias [e·ˈli:as]. *Pr.n.m.* **-'** & **-liä.** *B:* Elijah.
Eliasapfel, *m. Bot:* colocynth, bitter-apple.
Eliasfeuer, *n.*=**Elmsfeuer.**
elidieren [e·li·ˈdi:rən], *v.tr. Ling:* to elide (vowel).
Elieser [e·li·ˈe:zər]. *Pr.n.m.* **-s.** *B:* Eliezer.
Eligius [e·ˈli:gius]. *Pr.n.m.* **-'.** *Rel.Hist:* Eligius.
Elihu [e·ˈli:hu:]. *Pr.n.m.* **-s.** *B:* Elihu.
Elimination [e·li·mi·na·tsiˈo:n], *f.* **-/-en,** elimination.
eliminieren [e·li·mi·ˈni:rən], *v.tr.* to eliminate, remove; *Alg:* **eine Unbekannte e.,** to eliminate an unknown (quantity).
Elisa[1] [e·ˈli:za:]. *Pr.n.f.* **-s** & *Lit:* **-sens.** Eliza, Elsie.
Elisa[2] [e·ˈli:za:]. *Pr.n.m.* **-s.** *B:* Elisha.
Elisabeth [e·ˈli:za·bɛt]. *Pr.n.f.* **-s.** Elizabeth.
Elisabethaner [e·li·za·be·ˈta:nər], *m.* **-s/-.** *Eng. Hist:* Elizabethan.
elisabethanisch [e·li·za·be·ˈta:niʃ], *a.* Elizabethan (drama, style, etc.).
Elisabethorden, der, the Order of Elizabeth.
Elisabethpol [e·li·za·bɛtˈpo:l]. *Pr.n.n.* **-s.** *Geog:* Gandzha, *A:* Elisavetpol.
Elisäus [e·li·ˈzɛ:us]. *Pr.n.m.* **-'.** *B:* Elisha.
elisch [ˈe:liʃ], *a.* Elian; *Gr.Phil:* **die Elische Schule,** the Elian School.
Elise [e·ˈli:zə]. *Pr.n.f.* **-s** & *Lit:* **-ns.** Eliza, Elsie.
Elision [e·li·ziˈo:n], *f.* **-/-en.** *Ling:* elision.
Elite [e·ˈli:tə], *f.* **-/-n,** élite; flower, pick (of society, army, etc.); **eine E. heranbilden,** to create an élite.
Elitecorps, *n.* corps d'élite.
Elitesaat, *f.,* **Elitesaatgut,** *n. Agr:* highest quality seed.
Eliteschicht, *f.* élite.
Elitetruppe, *f. Mil:* corps d'élite; crack regiment; *pl.* **Elitetruppen,** picked troops.
Elitezucht, *f. Breed:* reselected strain.
Elixier, Elixir [e·liˈksi:r], *n.* **-s/-e.** *Alch: Pharm:* elixir.
Elk, *m.* **-(e)s/-e.** *Z:* **1.** Canadian elk. **2.** *Dial:*=**Iltis.**
Ellagengerbsäure [ɛla·ˈge:n-], *f. Ch:* ellagic acid.
Ellaubwurzel, *f. Bot:* (root of) field eryngo.
Ellbogen, *m.* **-s/-.** *Anat:* elbow; **sich auf die Ellbogen stützen, die Ellbogen, sich mit den Ellbogen, aufstützen,** to prop oneself, to lean, rest, on one's elbows; **die Ellbogen auf den Tisch aufstützen,** to put, lean, rest, one's elbows on the table; **j-n mit den Ellbogen anstoßen,** to elbow s.o.; to nudge s.o.; **ich muß meine Ellbogen frei haben,** I need elbow-room; I need free play, a free hand, free scope; **seine Ellbogen gebrauchen,** (i) to use one's elbows; (ii) to push ahead ruthlessly; to shove, elbow, one's way (ahead); **er weiß seine Ellbogen zu gebrauchen,** he knows how to push ahead ruthlessly (in his career); **sein Mantel ist an den Ellbogen durchgestoßen,** his coat is out at the elbows.
Ellbogenfortsatz, *m. Anat:* olecranon process.
Ellbogenfreiheit, *f.* elbow-room.
Ellbogenfühlung, *f.* **in, auf, E.,** side by side, close together; *Mil:* in close formation.
Ellbogengelenk, *n. Anat:* elbow-joint.
Ellbogenhöcker, *m.*=**Ellbogenfortsatz.**
Ellbogenhöhe, *f.* **in E.,** at elbow level; (width, etc.) at the elbows.
Ellbogenkachel, *f. Arm:* elbow guard, cubitière.
Ellbogenknochen, *m. Anat:* ulna, cubitus.
Ellbogennerv, *m. Anat:* ulnar nerve.
Ellbogenraum, *m.* elbow-room.
Ellbogenstück, *n. Arm:* elbow guard, cubitière.
Elle, *f.* **-/-n. 1.** *Anat:* ulna. **2.** (*a*) *A.Meas:* ell (*usu. about* 25 *inches*); cubit; **englische E.,** yard; (*b*) (*measuring stick*) ell; yard-stick; **mit der E. messen,** to measure by the yard-stick; **er geht, als ob er eine E. verschluckt hätte,** he walks as if he had swallowed a poker.
Ellenbogen, *m.* **-s/-**=**Ellbogen.**
Ellend, *n.* **-(e)s/-e.** *Bot:* eryngium, field eringo.
ellenlang, *a.* (*a*) an ell *or* a yard long; (*b*) *F:* very long; tediously long, interminable, endless; **er mußte sich eine ellenlange Geschichte anhören,** he had to listen to an interminable, endless, story.
Ellenmaß, *n.* ell; yard-stick.
Ellenmesser, *m. A:* alnager.
Ellenstock, *m.*=**Ellenmaß.**
ellenweise, *adv.* by the ell *or* by the yard.
Eller, *f.* **-/-n.** *Bot:* alder.
Ellgriff, *m. Gym:* rotated grasp.
Ellhorn, *n. Bot:* common elder tree.
Ellipse [ɛˈlipsə], *f.* **-/-n. 1.** *Gram:* ellipsis. **2.** *Geom:* ellipse.
ellipsenförmig, *a.* having the form of an ellipse, elliptic(al).
Ellipsenzirkel, *m.,* **Ellipsograph** [ɛlipso·ˈgra:f], *m.* **-en/-en.** *Draw:* ellipsograph, trammel, elliptic compass.
Ellipsoid [ɛlipso·ˈi:t], *n.* **-(e)s/-e** [**-s, -ˈi:dəs/-ˈi:də**]. *Geom:* ellipsoid; **dreiachsiges E.,** ellipsoid with three unequal axes.
ellipsoidisch [ɛlipso·ˈi:diʃ], *a.* ellipsoid(al).
elliptisch [ɛˈliptiʃ], *a. Gram: Geom:* elliptic(al).
Elliptizität [ɛlipti·tsi·ˈtɛ:t], -/. *Astr:* ellipticity.
Ellok [ˈɛllok], *f.*=**E-lok.**
Ellritze, *f.* **-/-n.** *Ich:* minnow.
Elmo [ˈɛlmo:]. *Pr.n.m.* **-s.** (Saint) Elmo.
Elmsfeuer, *n. Meteor:* **(Sankt-)E.,** Saint Elmo's fire, corposant.
-eln, *vbl suff.* **1.** (*indicating reiterated movement or sound*) **rütteln,** to shake (pers., tree, etc.); **watscheln,** to waddle; **zappeln,** (*of child, etc.*) to wriggle; (*of fish*) to flounder about; **stammeln,** to stammer, to stutter; **lispeln,** to lisp; **rascheln,** to rustle. **2.** (*reducing the action implied in the simplex to an isolated or restricted form*) **lächeln,** to smile; **hüsteln,** to cough a little, to give a slight cough; **gärteln,** to do gardening in a small way. **3.** (*as verbalizing suffix, often with pej. nuance*) **witzeln,** to quip; **frömmeln,** to affect piety; **französeln,** to imitate the French *or* the French language.
Eloah [e·ˈlo:a:]. *Pr.n.m.* **-(s)/Elohim.** *B:* Eloah.
Eloge [e·ˈlo:ʒə], *f.* **-/-n,** eulogy.
Elogium [e·ˈlo:gium], *n.* **-s/-gien.** *Lt.Lit:* elogium, *F:* eulogy.
Elohim [e·lo·ˈhi:m]. *B.Lit:* **1.** *Pr.n.m.* **-s.** (*God* Elohim. **2.** *m.pl.* (*heathen gods*) Elohim.

Elohist [e·lo·'hist], m. -en/. B.Lit: Elohist.
E-Lok, f. (abbr. of **Elektrolokomotive**) electric locomotive.
Elokution [e·lo·ku·tsi·'o:n], f. -/-en, elocution.
Elongation [e·loŋga·tsi·'o:n], f. -/-en, elongation, lengthening; Astr: elongation, digression of planet; Ph: displacement (of pendulum from equilibrium).
elongieren [e·loŋ'gi:rən], v.tr. to elongate.
eloquent [e·lo·'kvɛnt], a. eloquent.
Eloquenz [e·lo·'kvɛnts], f. -/. eloquence.
Eloxal [e·lo·'ksa:l], n. -s/. Ch: eloxal, protective coating on aluminium surfaces.
Eloxalverfahren, n. Ch: eloxal process.
eloxieren [e·lo·'ksi:rən], v.tr. to anodize (metal).
Elritze, f. -/-n. Ich: minnow.
Elsa. Pr.n.f. -s & Lit: -sens. Eliza, Elsie.
Elsaß, das. Pr.n. - & -sasses. Geog: Alsace.
Elsässer. 1. m. -s/-. Alsatian. 2. inv.a. Alsatian.
elsässisch, a. Alsatian.
Elsaß-Lothringen. Pr.n.n. -s. Geog: Alsace-Lorraine.
Elsbeerbaum, m. Bot: (a) wild service-tree; (b) bird-cherry (tree).
Elsbeere, f. Bot: 1.=**Elsbeerbaum**. 2. (a) (fruit) sorb(-apple), service-apple, service-berry, swallow-pear; (b) bird-cherry.
Else¹, f. -/-n. 1. Bot: (a) alder; (b) bird-cherry. 2. Ich: shad. 3. Tls: Nau: sail-maker's awl, marline-spike, marlin(g)spike.
Else². Pr.n.f. -s & Lit: -ns. Eliza, Elsie.
Elsebeerbaum, m.=**Elsbeerbaum**.
Elsebeere, f.=**Elsbeere**.
Elster, f. -/-n. Orn: magpie; sie ist geschwätzig wie eine E., she chatters like a magpie, F: she talks nineteen to the dozen; see also **diebisch**.
Elsterchen, n. -s/-. (dim. of **Elster**) Orn: 1. little magpie. 2. African mannikin.
Elsterkormoran, m. Orn: pied cormorant.
Elster(n)auge, n. Med: F: corn (on the toe or foot).
Elsternspecht, m. Orn: white-backed woodpecker.
Elsterschnepfe, f. Orn: oyster-catcher.
Elsterstar, m. Orn: pied mynah.
Elten, m. -s/-. Ich: chub.
Elter, m. & n. -s/-n. Biol: Statistics: parent; see also **Eltern**.
elterlich, a. parental; das elterliche Haus, der elterliche Herd, the house of one's parents, the parental hearth; elterliche Pflichten, parental duties; Jur: elterliche Gewalt, parental authority.
Eltermutter, f. A. & Dial: grandmother.
Eltern, pl. parents; ein Kind von armen E., a child of poor parents; F: (of thg, achievement, etc.) nicht von schlechten E. sein, to be not at all bad, F: to be pretty classy.
Elternabend, m. Sch: parents' evening.
Elternausschuß, m., **Eltern(bei)rat**, m. Sch: parents' council.
Elternhaus, n. home (of one's childhood), one's parents' home; Schule und E., home and school (as influences on a child); (of young pers.) das E. verlassen, to leave home; er hat ein gutes E. gehabt, he had a good home (as a child).
Elternliebe, f. 1. parental love. 2. filial love.
elternlos, a. parentless, orphaned; Biol: elternlose Zeugung, spontaneous generation, autogenesis.
Elternmord, m. parricide, parenticide.
Elternmörder, m. parricide, parenticide.
Elternpaar, n. parents; die beiden Elternpaare, the two sets of parents.
Elternpflicht, f. parental duty, duty as a parent.
Elternrat, m. see **Elternausschuß**.
Elternrecht, n. parental right.
Elternrente, f. Adm: pension to parents (of servicemen).
Elternschaft, f. -/. 1. parenthood. 2. Coll. parents (of pupils of a school, etc.).
Elternteil, m. parent; beide Elternteile, both parents.
Elternvertretung, f.=**Elternausschuß**.
Elternzeugung, f. Biol: tocogony, parental generation.
Eluat [e·lu·'a:t], n. -(e)s/-e. Ch: eluate.
eluieren [e·lu·'i:rən], v.tr. Ch: to elute.
Elution [e·lu·tsi·'o:n], f. -/. Ch: elution.
eluvial [e·lu·vi·'a:l], a. Geol: eluvial.
Eluvialboden, m. Geol: residual soil.
Eluvium [e·'lu:vium], n. -s/. Geol: eluvium.
Elymäer [e·ly·'mɛ:ər], m. -s/.=**Elamit**.
elymäisch [e·ly·'mɛ:iʃ], a.=**elamitisch**.
Elymus [e:ly·mus], m. -/. Bot: elymus, lyme-grass.
elysäisch [e·ly·'zɛ:iʃ], a.=**elysisch**.
elysisch [e·'lyziʃ], a. Elysian; Myth: die elysischen Gefilde, the Elysian fields.
Elysium [e·'ly:zium]. Pr.n.n. -s. Myth: Elysium.

Elz(e)beere, f.=**Elsbeere**.
Elzevi(e)r ['ɛlzəvi:r]. 1. Pr.n.m. -s. Elzevir. 2. f. -/-e. Print: Elzevir (edition, type).
Elzevi(e)rdruck, m. Elzevir (edition).
Elzevi(e)rschrift, f. Print: Elzevir (type).
Elzeviriana [ɛlzəvi·ri·'a:na:], n.pl. Elzevir editions, Elzevirs.
Email [e·'mai], n. -s/-s. 1. (a) enamel; durchsichtiges E., translucent, transparent, enamel; undurchsichtiges E., opaque enamel; farbiges E., coloured enamel; (b) enamel coat, enamel lining. 2. enamel work; enamel painting; enamel; die byzantinischen Emails, the Byzantine enamels.
Emailarbeit, f. enamel work, enamel.
Emailbecher, m. enamel(led) mug.
Emailbelag, m. enamel coat, enamel lining.
Emaildraht, m. enamel (insulated) wire.
Emailfarbe, f. (a) vitrifiable paint, enamel colour; (b) enamel paint.
Emaillack, m. enamel varnish.
emaillackiert, a. enamelled.
Emaille [e·'maljə, e·'mai], f. -/-n. 1. (a) enamel; (b) enamel coat, enamel lining. 2. enamel work, enamel.
Emailleur [e·mal'jø:r, e·ma·'jø:r], m. -s/-e. Jewel: etc: enameller.
Emaillierarbeit [e·mal'ji:r-, e·ma·'ji:r-], f. enamel work.
emaillieren [e·mal'ji:rən, e·ma·'ji:rən]. I. v.tr. to enamel; emaillierter Kochtopf, enamelled saucepan.
II. vbl s. 1. **Emaillieren**, n. in vbl senses. 2. **Emaillierung**, f. (a)=II.1; (b) enamel (coat, lining).
Emaillierer [e·mal'ji:rər, e·ma·'ji:rər], m. -s/-, enameller.
Emailliermühle, f. enamel mill.
Emaillierofen, m. enamel furnace.
Emailmaler, m. enamel-painter.
Emailmalerei, f. enamel-painting.
Emailminiaturmalerei, f. miniature enamel-painting.
Emailphotographie, f. enamel photograph.
Emailsoda, f. Ind: pulverized cryolite.
Emailüberzug, m. enamel coat, enamel lining.
Emailverfahren, n. Print: amerikanisches E., process of photographic copper or zinc etching in the manufacture of half-tone blocks.
Emailware, f. enamel-ware.
Emailzifferblatt, n. Clockm: enamelled dial.
Emanation [,e·ma·na·tsi·'o:n], f. -/-en. Phil: emanation; Ph: Ch: emanation, efflux; Ch: (element) emanation.
Emanationslehre, f. Phil: doctrine of emanation.
Emanationstheorie, f.=**Emissionstheorie**.
Emanationstherapie, f. Med: emanotherapy, radiotherapy.
Emanatismus [e·ma·na·'tismus], m. -/. Phil: doctrine of emanation, emanationism.
Emanatorium [e·ma·na·'to:rium], n. -s/-rien. Med: emanatorium.
emanieren [e·ma·'ni:rən], v. 1. v.i. (sein) to emanate. 2. v.tr. to emit, to send forth.
Emanuel [e·'ma:nu·el]. Pr.n.m. -s. B.Lit: Immanuel, Emmanuel.
Emanzipation [e·mantsi·pa·tsi·'o:n], f. -/-en, emancipation; Hist: manumission (of slave).
emanzipatorisch [e·mantsi·pa·'to:riʃ], a. emancipatory (movement, etc.).
emanzipieren [e·mantsi·'pi:rən], v.tr. to emancipate (women, slaves, etc.); Hist: to manumit (slave); sich e., to become emancipated; to break away, to cut loose (from sth., s.o.); sich von kleinbürgerlichen Anschauungen e., to break away from the bourgeois view of life; emanzipiert, emancipated; **Emanzipierung** f, emancipation; Hist: manumission (of slave).
Emaskulation [e·masku·la·tsi·'o:n], f. -/-en, emasculation, castration.
Emaskulator [e·masku·'la:tor], m. -s/-en [-la·'to:rən] Vet: (instrument) emasculator.
Emballage [ã·ba·'la:ʒə], f. -/-n, (a) packing, wrapping (of parcel, goods, etc.); (b) cost of packing.
emballieren [ã·ba·'li:rən], v.tr. to pack (goods, etc.).
Embargo [ɛm'bargo:], n. & m. -s/-s, embargo; ziviles E., civil embargo; internationales, völkerrechtliches, E., hostile embargo; ein Schiff mit E. belegen, E. auf ein Schiff legen, to lay an embargo on a ship; das E. aufheben, to take off, raise, the embargo; mit E. belegt sein, to be under (an) embargo.
embarrassieren [ã·bara·'si:rən], v.tr. A: (a) to embarrass (s.o.); (b) to embarrass, encumber, hamper.

Embaterien [ɛmba·'te:riən], n.pl. Gr.Lit: embateria.
Emberitze [ɛmbe·'ritsə], f. -/-n. Orn: bunting.
Emblem [ɛm'ble:m], n. -s/-e & -ata, (a) emblem; badge; (b) emblem, symbol; der Ölzweig ist das E. des Friedens, the olive branch is the emblem of peace.
emblematisch [ɛmble·'ma:tiʃ], a. emblematic(al); symbolic.
emblematisieren [ɛmble·ma·ti·'zi:rən], v.tr. to emblematize; to symbolize.
Emblica ['ɛmbli·ka:], f. -/. Bot: emblic.
Embolektomie [ˌɛmbo·lekto·'mi:], f. -/-n [-'mi:ən]. Surg: embolectomy.
Embolie [ɛmbo·'li:], f. -/-n [-'li:ən]. Med: embolism.
embolisch [ɛm'bo:liʃ], a. Med: embolic.
Embonpoint [ã·bõpo·'ɛ̃], n. -s/. (a) embonpoint, plumpness, stoutness; (b) ein E. haben, to be corpulent, F: to have a corporation.
Embritze [ɛm'britsə], f. -/-n=**Emberitze**.
embrouillieren [ã·brul'ji:rən, ã·bru·'ji:rən], v.tr. to confuse, muddle (s.o.).
Embryo ['ɛmbry·o:], m. -s/-s & -nen [-s, -'o:nən]. Biol: embryo.
embryogen [ɛmbry·o·'ge:n], a. Biol: embryogenic.
Embryogenie [ɛmbry·o·ge·'ni:], f. -/. Biol: embryogeny.
Embryologe [ɛmbry·o·'lo:gə], m. -n/-n, embryologist.
Embryologie [ɛmbry·o·lo·'gi:], f. -/. Biol: embryology.
embryologisch [ɛmbry·o·'lo:giʃ], a. Biol: embryologic(al).
embryonal [ɛmbry·o·'na:l], a. Biol: embryonic, embryonary (period, stage); F: seine Pläne befanden sich noch im embryonalen Zustand, his plans were still in embryo, in the embryonic state.
Embryonalgewebe, n. Bot: merismatic tissue, meristem.
Embryonalhülle, f. Biol: embryonic membrane.
embryonisch [ɛmbry·'o:niʃ], a.=**embryonal**.
Embryosack, m. Bot: embryo-sac.
Embryotomie [ɛmbry·o·to·'mi:], f. -/-n [-'mi:ən]. Surg: embryotomy.
Emd, n. -es/., **Emde**, n. -s/. Swiss: Agr: after-grass, aftermath.
Emendation [e·mɛnda·tsi·'o:n], f. -/-en, emendation (of text).
Emendator [e·mɛn'da:tor], m. -s/-en [-da·'to:rən], emender, emendator.
emendieren [e·mɛn'di:rən], v.tr. to emend (text); **Emendierung** f, emendation.
Emergenz [e·mer'gɛnts], f. -/-en, emergence.
Emergenzwinkel, m. Seismology: angle of emergence.
emeritieren [e·me·ri·'ti:rən], v.tr. to relieve (official, etc.) of his active duties; Sch: to give (professor) emeritus status; emeritiert, retired (official); (professor) emeritus; **Emeritierung** f, (honourable) discharge (of official); Sch: award of emeritus status (to professor).
Emeritus [e·'me:ri·tus], m. -/-ti, (professor) emeritus.
Emersion [e·merzi·'o:n], f. -/-en. Astr: emersion (of star).
Emetikum [e·'me:ti·kum], n. -s/-ka. Med: emetic.
Emetin [e·me·'ti:n], n. -s/. Pharm: emetin(e).
emetisch [e·'me:tiʃ], a. Med: emetic.
Emigrant [e·mi·'grant], m. -en/-en, emigrant, émigré.
Emigrantentum, n. -(e)s/. 1. emigration; (the) émigré question. 2. Coll. emigrants, émigrés.
Emigration [e·mi·gra·tsi·'o:n], f. -/-en. 1. emigration (esp. for political reasons); in die E. gehen, to emigrate; in der E. leben, to live in exile; 'innere E.', passive resistance (to the régime). 2. Physiol: Med: emigration.
emigrieren [e·mi·'gri:rən], v.i. (sein) to emigrate (esp. for political reasons); **Emigrierung** f, emigration.
Emil ['e:mi:l]. 1. Pr.n.m. -s. Aemilius, Emil. 2. m. -s/-s & -e. Mil.Av: F: pilot.
Emilia [e·'mi:lia:]. 1. Pr.n.f. -s & Lit: -liens. Emilia, Emily. 2. Geog: die E., Emilia.
Emilianer [e·mi·li·'a:nər], m. -s/. Emilian.
emilianisch [e·mi·li·'a:niʃ], a. Geog: Emilian.
Emilie [e·'mi:liə]. Pr.n.f. -s & Lit: -ns. Emilia, Emily.
eminent [e·mi·'nɛnt], a. eminent, prominent, distinguished; eine Frage von eminenter Bedeutung, Wichtigkeit, adv. eine e. wichtige Frage, a question of prime, extreme, importance; an extremely important question.
Eminenz [e·mi·'nɛnts], f. -/-en. Ecc: (title of cardinal) Eminence; seine E., der Kardinal von X., his Eminence, the Cardinal of X.; Hist: &

F: **die graue E.,** the Eminence Grise; the Grey Eminence; the power behind the throne.
Emir ['eːmir, eˑ'miːr], *m.* -s/-e ['eːmiːrə, eˑ'miːrə], Emir, Ameer.
Emirat [eˑmiˑ'raːt], *n.* -(e)s/-e, emirate.
Emissär [eˑmi'sɛːr], *m.* -s/-e, emissary.
Emissarium [eˑmi'saːrium], *n.* -s/-ria. *Anat:* emissary vein.
Emission [eˑmisi'oːn], *f.* -/-en. 1. *Ph: Ch:* emission (of light, waves, etc.). 2. *Fin:* issue (of shares, debentures).
Emissionsabteilung, *f. Fin:* issue department.
Emissionsbank, *f. Fin:* issuing house.
Emissionsfähigkeit, *f. Ph:* emissivity.
Emissionsgeschäft, *n. Fin:* (*a*) issuing transaction; issuing; (*b*) *esp. Swiss:* underwriting business.
Emissionsgesetz, *n. Adm: Fin:* Issue Law.
Emissionskonsortium, *n. Fin:* (*a*) issuing syndicate; (*b*) *esp. Swiss:* underwriting syndicate (*in connection with issues of securities*).
Emissionskontrolle, *f. Fin:* control of capital issue.
Emissionskredit, *m. Fin:* credit obtained through an issue of securities.
Emissionskurs, *m. Fin:* issue price.
Emissionsstempel, *m. Fin:* stamp duty (on the issue of securities).
Emissionstheorie, *f. Ph:* emission theory (of light), corpuscular theory (of light).
Emissionsüberhang, *m. Fin:* excess issue (of bonds).
Emittent [eˑmi'tɛnt], *m.* -en/-en. *Fin:* issuing establishment (*e.g. bank, syndicate*).
emittieren [eˑmi'tiːrən], *v.tr.* 1. to emit, send forth, send out (ray of light, sound wave, etc.). 2. *Fin:* to issue (shares, debentures).
Emma. *Pr.n.f.* -s. Emma.
Emmaus ['ɛmaˑus]. *Pr.n.n.* -'. *A.Geog:* Emmaus.
Emmausjünger, *m.* disciple to whom the risen Christ appeared on the road to Emmaus.
Emmenagoga [ɛmɛnaˑ'goːgaː], *n.pl. Pharm:* emmenagogues.
Emmensit [ɛmɛn'ziːt], *n.* -(e)s/. *Exp:* emmensite.
Emmental, das. *Pr.n. Geog:* the Emmental.
Emmentaler. 1. *m.* -s/-, (*a*) inhabitant of the Emmental; (*b*) Gruyère cheese. 2. *inv.a.* (of the) Emmental; **Emmentaler Käse,** Gruyère cheese.
Emmer[1], *m.* -s/-, (*a*) *North G.Dial:* bucket; (*b*) *Austrian: Meas:* bucket(ful).
Emmer[2], *m.* -s/-, **Emmerkorn,** *n. Agr:* emmer, amelcorn.
Emmerling, *m.* -s/-e. *Orn:* bunting.
Emmersegel, *n. Nau:* sprit-sail.
e-moll, e-Moll, *n. Mus:* (key of) E minor.
Emollientium [eˑmɔli'ɛntsium], *n.* -s/-tia. *Pharm:* emollient.
Emolument [eˑmoˑluˑ'mɛnt], *n.* -(e)s/-e, *usu.pl.* **Emolumente,** emoluments.
Emotion [eˑmoˑtsi'oːn], *f.* -/-en, (*a*) emotion; (*b*) emotion, excitement.
emotional [eˑmoˑtsioˑ'naːl], *a.* emotional.
Emotionalismus [eˑmoˑtsioˑnaˑ'lismus], *m.* -/. emotionalism.
emotionell [eˑmoˑtsioˑ'nɛl], *a.* emotional.
emotiv [eˑmoˑ'tiːf], *a.* emotive.
Emotivität [eˑmoˑtiˑviˑ'tɛːt], *f.* -/. emotivity, emotiveness, emotionality.
Emotivpartikel, *f. Ling:* emotive particle.
Emouchette [eˑmuˑ'ʃɛtə], *f.* -/-n, fly-net (for horses).
empaillieren [ãˑpaˑ'jiːrən], *v.tr.* to pack (goods, etc.) in straw; to stuff (dead animal).
Empaistik [ɛm'paistik], *f.* -/.=**Empästik.**
empalieren [ɛmpaˑ'liːrən], *v.tr.* to impale.
Empaste [ɛm'pastə], *f.* -/-n. *Art:* impasto.
Empästik [ɛm'pɛːstik], *f.* -/. *Metalw:* (art of) chasing, embossing, repoussé-working.
Empedokles [ɛm'peːdoˑklɛs]. *Pr.n.m.* -'. Empedocles.
empfahen, *v.tr. A:*=**empfangen.**
empfahl, empfhäle *see* **empfehlen.**
empfand, empfände *see* **empfinden.**
Empfang, *m.* -(e)s/⸗e. 1. receipt (of letter, goods, order, etc.); **etwas in E. nehmen,** to accept (present, etc.); *Com:* to accept, take, delivery of (goods); *Com:* **den E. einer Sendung bestätigen,** to acknowledge receipt of a consignment; **bei E.,** on receipt, delivery; **vor E.,** previous to receipt, delivery; **nach E.,** on, after, receipt, delivery; **zahlbar bei E.,** payable on receipt, delivery. 2. (*a*) reception (of guests); **j-m einen freundlichen, herzlichen, E. bereiten,** to give s.o. a kind, cordial, reception; **ein kühler, frostiger, E.,** a cold, icy, reception; **die Straßen waren zum E. des hohen Gastes geschmückt,** the streets were decorated to greet, to welcome, the distinguished guest; (*b*) *W.Tg: W.Tp:* reception; **drahtloser E.,** wireless reception; **störungsfreier E.,** reception without interference; **auf E. bleiben,** to stand by (to receive). 3. reception; levee, drawing-room (at court); at-home; **einen E. geben,** to hold, give, a reception. 4. (*at hotel*) reception desk *or* office; 'reception'; **gehen Sie bitte zum E.,** please go to reception.
empfangbar, *a. Com:* acceptable (goods); (goods) fit for acceptance.
Empfangbarkeit, *f. Com:* acceptability, acceptableness (of goods).
empfangen, *v.tr.* (*strong*) 1. (*a*) to receive, get (gift, present, alms, etc.); **eine Auszeichnung e.,** to receive an award; **er empfing die Nachricht sehr gelassen,** he received, took, the news with great composure, very calmly; **was für Eindrücke haben Sie auf Ihrer Reise empfangen?** what impressions did you get on your journey? **von j-m Befehle e.,** to take, receive, orders from s.o.; *Com.Corr:* **wir haben Ihr Schreiben vom 10. d.M. empfangen,** we are in receipt of, have received, your letter of the 10th inst.; **wir haben den ausstehenden Betrag noch nicht empfangen,** we have not yet received the outstanding amount; (*b*) *W.Tel:* to receive (station); **ich kann auf meinem Apparat eine große Anzahl von Sendern e.,** I can get a large number of stations on my radio; (*c*) *Ecc: etc:* to receive (blessing, sacrament, etc.); **die (heilige) Taufe, Firmung, Kommunion, usw., e.,** to receive baptism, confirmation, holy communion, etc. 2. to receive (guest, etc.); **j-n mit offenen Armen e.,** to receive, welcome, s.o. with open arms; **j-n herzlich e.,** to receive s.o. cordially; **j-n kühl, frostig, e.,** to receive s.o. coldly, frostily; **der Dirigent wurde mit stürmischem Applaus e.,** the conductor was received, greeted, with enthusiastic applause; *abs.* **jede Woche e.,** to hold a weekly reception; to have an at-home every week; **sie empfängt heute nicht,** she is not at home today, this is not her at-home day. 3. *Biol:* (*of woman*) to conceive (child); (*of woman, mammal*) to become pregnant with (young); *abs.* to conceive; to become pregnant.
Empfänger, *m.* -s/-. 1. (*pers.*) recipient, receiver; addressee (of letter, telegram); beneficiary (of legacy, etc.); *Com:* consignee; *Fin:* payee (of cheque, etc.); *Med:* recipient (of blood); *Com:* **E. bezahlt,** cash on delivery. 2. (*device*) *W.Tel:* receiver, receiving set.
Empfängerröhre, *f. W.Tel:* receiving valve, receiving tube.
empfänglich, *a.* 1. susceptible (**für etwas,** *A:* **etwas** *gen.*, to sth.); **für infektiöse Krankheiten e. sein,** to be susceptible to, prone to (catch), liable to (catch), infectious diseases; **für neue Eindrücke, Ideen, e. sein,** to be receptive to new impressions, ideas; **sie ist sehr e. für das Schöne,** she is keenly alive to the beautiful; **für schlechte Einflüsse e. sein,** to be open to, an easy prey to, evil influences; **sie ist für Schmeicheleien sehr e.,** she is very susceptible to flattery. 2. *Biol:* **Frau, die sehr e. ist,** woman who conceives easily, with whom conception occurs easily, who easily becomes pregnant.
Empfänglichkeit, *f.* 1. susceptibility, proneness (to diseases); susceptibility, receptiveness (to impressions, ideas, influences). 2. *Biol:* tendency to conceive easily; **die E. ist zu einem bestimmten Zeitpunkt höher als zu einem anderen,** conception, pregnancy, is likely to occur more easily at one period than at another.
Empfangnahme, *f.* -/. receipt; taking delivery (of goods).
Empfängnis, *f.* -/-nisse, conception (of child); *Theol:* **die Unbefleckte E.,** the Immaculate Conception.
empfängnisfähig, *a. Biol:* capable of conceiving, of becoming pregnant.
Empfängnishügel, *m. Biol:* fertilization cone.
Empfängnisoptimum, *n. Biol:* optimum for fertilization.
empfängnisverhütend, *a.* contraceptive; **empfängnisverhütende Mittel,** contraceptives.
Empfängnisverhütung, *f.* contraception.
Empfängniszeit, *f. Biol: Jur:* period of possible conception.
Empfangsantenne, *f. W.Tel:* receiving aerial.
Empfangsanzeige, *f.* notice of receipt, acknowledgement of receipt.
Empfangsapparat, *m.*=**Empfänger** 2.
Empfangsbahnhof, *m. Rail:* station to which goods, etc., are consigned; receiving station.
empfangsbedürftig, *a. Jur:* **empfangsbedürftige Willenserklärung,** declaration of intention requiring communication.
empfangsberechtigt, *a.* authorized to receive (goods, etc.); **Empfangsberechtigte** *m, f, Com: Jur:* legitimate consignee.
Empfangsberechtigung, *f.* authorization to receive (goods, etc.).
Empfangsbereich, *m. W.Tel:* reception area; service area.
Empfangsbescheinigung, *f.,* **Empfangsbestätigung,** *f.* receipt, acknowledgement of receipt.
Empfangschef, *m.* (*a*) *Com:* shop-walker; (*b*) (*in hotel*) reception clerk, *U.S:* room clerk.
Empfangsdame, *f.* (*in hotel, office*) receptionist.
Empfangseinrichtung, *f. W.Tel:* receiver, receiving apparatus; receiving system.
Empfangsfrequenz, *f. W.Tel:* receiving frequency.
Empfangsgebäude, *n.* (*a*) reception building (at port, airport, etc.); (*b*) main building (of railway station).
Empfangsgerät, *n. W.Tel:* receiver, receiving apparatus, receiving set.
Empfangshalle, *f.* reception hall.
Empfangssalon, *m.* reception room; drawing room.
Empfangsschein, *m. Com:* receipt.
Empfangsstation, *f.* 1.=**Empfangsbahnhof.** 2. *W.Tel:* receiving station.
Empfangsstörung, *f. W.Tel:* interference.
Empfangstag, *m.* (*a*) at-home day; receiving day; (*b*) *Com:* day of delivery.
Empfangsvermögen, *n. W.Tel:* receiving power.
Empfangsverstärker, *m. W.Tel:* receiving amplifier.
Empfangszimmer, *n.* reception room.
Empfehl, *m.* -(e)s/-e. *A:*=**Empfehlung,** *q.v. under* **empfehlen** II.
empfehlen. I. *v.tr.* (*strong*) 1. **j-n, etwas, j-m e.,** to commend s.o., sth., to the care of s.o., to s.o.'s care; **sich, seine Seele, Gott e.,** to commend oneself, one's soul, to God. 2. (*a*) **j-m etwas e.,** to recommend sth. to s.o.; **der Arzt hat mir empfohlen, in die Schweiz zu fahren,** the doctor has advised me to go to Switzerland; **es empfiehlt sich, einen Regenschirm mitzunehmen,** it is advisable to take an umbrella; (*b*) to recommend (s.o., sth.); **diesen Bewerber kann ich Ihnen e.,** I can recommend this candidate to you; **lassen Sie sich diesen Bewerber empfohlen sein,** let me recommend this candidate to you; **können Sie mir einen Gärtner e.?** can you recommend a gardener to me? **das Buch ist für junge Menschen nicht zu e.,** the book is not recommended for young people; **dieses Hotel ist wegen seiner guten Küche zu e., dieses Hotel empfiehlt sich durch seine gute Küche,** this hotel is to be recommended for its good cuisine; **ein empfehlendes Äußeres haben,** to have a prepossessing appearance; (*c*) **empfehlen Sie mich Ihren Eltern!** remember me to your parents! give my (kind) regards to your parents! 3. (*of pers.*) **sich empfehlen,** to take one's leave, to say goodbye; to retire (at night, etc.); **ich empfehle mich,** (I wish you) good-bye, good evening, etc.
II. *vbl s.* 1. **Empfehlen,** *n. in vbl senses.* 2. **Empfehlung,** *f.* (*a*)=II. 1; (*b*) recommendation; advice; **nach eingehender Untersuchung brachte der Ausschuß seine Empfehlungen vor,** after a thorough investigation the committed submitted its recommendations; **er befolgte die Empfehlungen seines Arztes sehr gewissenhaft,** he followed the advice of his doctor very conscientiously, (*c*) (letter of) recommendation; testimonial; (letter of) introduction; **gute Empfehlungen werden Ihnen bei der Bewerbung nützlich sein,** good references will be useful to you when you make your application; **er wurde auf die E. seines Onkels (hin) angestellt,** he was employed on the recommendation of his uncle; (*d*) commendatory letter (in book, etc.); (*e*) **meine E., Empfehlungen, an den Herrn Vater!** my (kind) regards, my compliments, to your father! *Corr:* **mit (den) besten Empfehlungen,** (I, we, remain) yours truly.
empfehlenswert, *a.* (*a*) advisable, recommendable; **es scheint nicht e., diese Aktien zu erwerben,** it does not seem advisable to buy these shares; (*b*) (*of quality, candidate, thgs*) recommendable; worthy of commendation; **der Film ist für Jugendliche nicht e.,** the film is not to be recommended for young people.
empfehlenswürdig, *a.*=**empfehlenswert.**
Empfehlung, *f. see* **empfehlen** II. 2.
Empfehlungsbrief, *m.* (i) letter of recommendation; testimonial; letter of introduction; (ii) commendatory letter (in book, etc.).
Empfehlungsschreiben, *n.* letter of recommendation; testimonial; letter of introduction.
empfiehlst, empfiehlt *see* **empfehlen.**

empfindbar, *a.* (*a*) perceptible; sensible; (*b*) *A:* sensitive; feeling.
Empfindbarkeit, *f.* (*a*) sensibility; perceptibility; (*b*) *A:* sensitiveness.
empfindeln, *v.i.* (*haben*) to sentimentalize.
empfinden. I. *v.* (*strong*) **1.** *v.tr.* (*a*) to perceive (sth.) (*with the senses*); to feel, have a sensation of (pain, hunger, cold, etc.); **er empfand die Wärme sehr wohltuend,** he found the warmth very comforting; **im vergangenen Jahr haben wir die Kälte sehr empfunden,** we felt the cold badly last year; (*b*) to feel (joy, love, sorrow, repentance, etc.); **er empfand dein Verhalten als eine tiefe Kränkung,** he was deeply hurt by, offended by, your behaviour; **der Verlust unseres Kollegen wird von allen schmerzlich empfunden,** the loss of our colleague is painfully felt by all, everybody feels the loss of our colleague deeply; (*c*) to be aware of, conscious of (sth.); to be sensible of (sth.); **alle empfanden die Bedeutung dieser Stunde,** all were aware of the importance of this hour; **er empfand seine Fehler sehr deutlich,** he was very sensible, acutely aware, of his defects; **wie empfinden Sie in dieser Angelegenheit?** what are your sentiments on this matter? **er konnte sogleich die Feindseligkeit der anderen e.,** he could sense the hostility of the others immediately; **ich empfinde sehr deutlich, daß Sie mir damit eine Ehre erweisen wollen,** I am well aware that you want to do me an honour by it; **deine Bemerkung bestätigte, daß ich richtig empfunden hatte,** your remark showed that my feelings had been right, that I had been right in my feelings. **2.** *v.i.* (*haben*) **mit, für, j-n e.,** to feel for s.o.; to share s.o.'s feelings; to sympathize with s.o.; **jeder empfindende Mensch,** every person with any feeling; **ein empfindendes Herz, eine empfindende Seele,** a feeling heart. **3. sich glücklich empfinden,** to feel happy; **sich als Dichter e.,** to feel oneself to be a poet.
II. *vbl s.* **1. Empfinden,** *n.* (*a*) *in vbl senses;* (*b*) **meinem E. nach,** in my opinion; to my mind; **das E. haben, daß . . . ,** to feel, to have a feeling that . . .; **ich hatte das deutliche E., daß noch jemand im Raum sei,** I clearly felt, I was conscious of, another person's presence in the room; **er hatte das deutliche E., daß dieser Mann ein gefährlicher Gegner war,** he sensed that this man was a dangerous opponent, he sensed a dangerous opponent in this man; **es wird sich bald zeigen, daß mein E. mich nicht trügt,** it will soon be clear that my feelings do not, my instinct does not, deceive me. **2. Empfindung,** *f.* (*a*) *in vbl senses; also:* **in der E., daß . . . ,** feeling that . . .; **in der deutlichen E. der Größe seines Verbrechens,** sensible of the enormity of his crime; **deine Äußerung bestätigt, daß meine E. richtig war,** your remark shows that my feeling, instinct, was right; (*b*) feeling, sensation; **es schmerzt nicht, es ist nur eine unangenehme E.,** it does not hurt, it is merely an unpleasant sensation; (*c*) feeling, sentiment; **er machte aus seinen Empfindungen kein Hehl,** he did not conceal his feelings; **die Empfindungen, die diese Nachricht bei mir auslöste,** the feelings this news aroused in me; **wie sind Ihre Empfindungen in dieser Angelegenheit?** what are your feelings in this matter? **meine Empfindungen in dieser Sache,** my feelings, sentiments, in this matter; **seine Landschaften sind voller E.,** his landscapes are full of feeling; **sie spielt Klavier mit E.,** she plays the piano with feeling; **voll edler Empfindungen,** full of noble sentiment.
III. *p.p. & a.* **empfunden,** *in vbl senses;* **seine Reue war nicht wirklich, nicht echt, e.,** his contrition was not genuine; *cp.* **tiefempfunden.**
Empfindler, *m.* **-s/-,** sentimentalist.
empfindlich, *a.* **1.** (*a*) sensitive (to sth.); susceptible (to sth.); delicate (material, etc.); sensitive (photographic plate, scales, etc.); **empfindliche Ohren haben,** (i) to have delicate ears; (ii) to be easily shocked (by bad language, etc.); (iii) to have a sensitive ear, a keen sense of hearing; **das ist nicht für ihre empfindlichen Ohren,** that is not for her tender ears; **eine empfindliche Haut haben,** to have a sensitive skin; **gegen Kälte, usw., e. sein,** to feel the cold, etc.; **gegen Schmerz e. sein,** to be susceptible to pain; **ein empfindliches Kleid,** a dress that marks, fades, tears, etc., easily; **ein empfindlicher Kleiderstoff,** a delicate dress-material; *Phot:* **eine Emulsion, die für alle Farben e. ist,** an emulsion that is sensitive to all colours; *Ball:* **empfindlicher Zünder,** graze fuse; (*b*) (*painful or sore when touched*) sensitive, tender (spot, etc.); sensitive (pers.); touchy (pers.); **empfindliche Füße,** tender feet; **er hat am Arm eine empfindliche Stelle,** he has a tender spot on his arm; **j-n an seiner empfindlichen Stelle treffen,** to touch s.o. on his tender spot, *F:* to tread on s.o.'s pet corn; **deine Bemerkung traf ihn an seiner empfindlichsten Stelle,** your remark touched him on the raw; **sei nicht so e.!** don't be so touchy, sensitive! **in Ehrensachen ist er sehr e.,** he is very sensitive, particular, on points of honour; **gegen Spott ist er sehr e.,** he is very sensitive to ridicule. **2. die Kälte im vergangenen Winter war e.,** the cold was severe last winter; **j-m einen empfindlichen Schlag versetzen,** to deal s.o. a heavy blow; **empfindliche Verluste erleiden,** to suffer, sustain, heavy losses; **eine empfindliche Lücke,** a noticeable gap; *adv.* **es war e. kalt,** it was extremely, bitterly, cold.
-empfindlich, *comb.fm. a.* (*a*) (*of measuring instrument, material, etc.*) sensitive to . . .; -sensitive; (*of material, etc.*) susceptible to . . .; (*of seismograph, etc.*) **erschütterungsempfindlich,** sensitive to vibration; (*of emulsion*) **farbempfindlich,** colour-sensitive; (*of plant, etc.*) **frostempfindlich,** susceptible to frost; (*b*) (*of pers.*) susceptible to . . .; **schmerzempfindlich,** susceptible to pain.
Empfindlichkeit, *f.* (*a*) sensitivity, sensitiveness (**gegen, für, etwas,** to sth.); susceptibility (**für etwas,** to sth.); sensitiveness (of scales, etc.); *Phot:* speed, sensitivity (of plate, film, emulsion, etc.); **die Empfindlichkeit einer photographischen Platte kann in Scheiner gemessen werden,** the speed of a photographic plate can be measured in Scheiner; (*b*) sensitiveness, tenderness (of spot, etc.); sensitiveness (of pers.); touchiness (of pers.); **eine krankhafte E. haben,** to be hypersensitive; to be very touchy.
-empfindlichkeit, *comb.fm. f.* sensitiveness to . . .; sensitivity to . . .; susceptibility to . . .; **Erschütterungsempfindlichkeit,** sensitivity to vibration (of seismograph); **Farbempfindlichkeit,** sensitivity, sensitiveness, to colour (of emulsion, etc.); **Frostempfindlichkeit,** susceptibility to frost (of plant, etc.); **Schmerzempfindlichkeit,** susceptibility to pain (of pers.).
Empfindlichkeitsbestimmung, *f. Phot: etc:* sensitometry.
Empfindlichkeitsgrenze, *f.* limit of sensitivity (of scales, etc.).
Empfindlichkeitsmesser, *m. Phot:* sensitometer.
Empfindlichkeitsmessung, *f. Phot:* sensitometry.
Empfindnis, *n.* **-nisses/-nisse.** *A:* = **Empfindung,** *q.v. under* **empfinden II.**
empfindsam, *a.* sentimental; guided by sentiment; **ein empfindsamer Mensch,** a sentimentalist; **empfindsame Literatur,** sentimental literature.
Empfindsamkeit, *f.* sentimentalism, sentimentality (of pers., literature, etc.).
Empfindung, *f. see* **empfinden II.**
Empfindungsdissoziation, *f. Med:* partial sensory paralysis.
Empfindungseigenheit, *f. Med: Psy:* idiosyncrasy.
Empfindungserreger, *m. Physiol:* sense stimulus.
Empfindungserregung, *f. Physiol:* sense stimulation.
empfindungsfähig, *a.* (*a*) sensitive; susceptible; perceptive; (*b*) capable of feeling, emotion.
Empfindungsfeld, *n. Anat:* **optisches E.,** visuosensory area.
Empfindungskreis, *m. Physiol:* area, circle, of sensation.
Empfindungslähmung, *f. Med:* sensory paralysis.
Empfindungslaut, *m. Gram:* interjection.
empfindungsleer, *a.* void of feeling.
Empfindungsleere, *f.* utter absence of feeling.
empfindungslos, *a.* (*a*) insensible, numb (limb, etc.); (*b*) (*of pers.*) unfeeling, callous.
Empfindungslosigkeit, *f.* (*a*) numbness (of limb, etc.); (*b*) callousness (of pers.).
Empfindungsnerv, *m. Anat:* sensory nerve.
Empfindungsorgan, *n.* sense organ, sensory organ.
Empfindungsspiegelung, *f. Psy: déjà vu* phenomenon, *entendu* phenomenon.
Empfindungstemperatur, *f. Air-conditioning:* effective temperature.
Empfindungsvermögen, *n.* faculty of perception, of sensation.
Empfindungswort, *n.* **-(e)s/-wörter.** *Gram:* interjection.
Empfindungszelle, *f. Anat:* sensory cell.
empföhle, empfohlen *see* **empfehlen.**
empfunden *see* **empfinden.**
Emphase [ɛm'faːzə], *f.* **-/-n.** *Rh:* emphasis.
emphatisch [ɛm'faːtiʃ], *a.* emphatic; *Ling:* **emphatischer Akzent,** emphatic stress.
Emphysem [ɛmfy·'zeːm], *n.* **-s/-e.** *Med:* emphysema.
emphysematisch [ɛmfy·ze·'maːtiʃ], **emphysematös** [ɛmfy·ze·ma·'tøːs], *a.* emphysematous.
Emphyteuse [ɛmfy·'toyzə], *f.* **/-n, Emphyteusis** [ɛm'fyːtoyzis], *f.* **-/-sen** [-fy·'toyzən]. *Jur:* emphyteusis.
Empire, *n.* **-s/.** **1.** [ã·'piːr], (*a*) *Fr.Hist:* Empire; (*b*) (*also comb.fm.* **Empire-**) **E., Empirestil** *m,* Empire (style); **dieser Schreibtisch ist E., ist ein Empireschreibtisch,** this desk is an Empire (piece). **2.** ['ɛmpaiər], **das britische E.,** the British Empire.
Empirem [ɛmpi·'reːm], *n.* **-s/-e.** *Phil:* empirically known fact.
Empirestil, *m. Art:* Empire style.
Empirie [ɛmpi·'riː], *f.* **-/., Empirik** [ɛm'piːrik], *f.* **-/.** empiricism.
Empiriker [ɛm'piːrikər], *m.* **-s/-,** empiric, empiricist.
Empiriokritizismus [ɛmpi·rio·kri·ti·'tsismus], *m.* **-/.** *Phil:* empiriocriticism.
empirisch [ɛm'piːriʃ], *a.* empiric(al).
Empirismus [ɛmpi·'rismus], *m.* **-/.** empiricism.
Empirist [ɛmpi·'rist], *m.* **-en/-en,** empiricist.
empiristisch [ɛmpi·'ristiʃ], *a.* empiric(al).
Emplacement [ã·plas'mãː], *n.* **-s/-s.** *Mil: A:* (gun) emplacement.
empor [ɛm'poːr], *adv.,* **empor-, Empor-,** *comb.fm.* up, upwards; up above; **die Herzen e.!** lift up your hearts! **zum Licht e.!** to the light! (*of plant*) **emporsprießen,** to spring up, to shoot up; **Emporkömmling,** *m,* upstart, parvenu.
emporarbeiten, *v.tr. sep.* to work up (business, etc.); **sich e.,** to work one's way up; **er hat sich mit eigener Kraft emporgearbeitet,** he has made his own way up; **sich aus kleinsten Anfängen e.,** to work one's way up from small beginnings; **er hatte sich zum Direktor emporgearbeitet,** he had worked his way up to a directorship.
empordringen, *v.i. sep.* (*strong*) (*sein*) to rise (up); *Lit:* (*of song, prayer, etc.*) to rise (to heaven).
Empore [ɛm'poːrə], *f.* **-/-n.** *Arch:* gallery.
empören. I. *v.tr.* **1.** (*of action, etc.*) to fill (s.o.) with indignation, to make (s.o.) indignant; **über etwas empört sein, sich über etwas e.,** to be, feel, indignant at, about, sth.; **über j-n empört sein,** to be indignant with s.o.; **sein Verhalten empörte mich, ich war über sein Verhalten empört,** I was indignant at, about, his behaviour, his behaviour filled me with indignation; **darüber empört sein, daß . . . ,** to be indignant that . . . , to be full of indignation that . . .; **das ist eine empörende Zumutung,** that is an outrageous suggestion; **sein Benehmen ist empörend,** his behaviour is infuriating, shocking. **2. sich empören,** to rebel, to rise in rebellion, to revolt; *Mil: etc:* to mutiny; **sich gegen,** *A. & Lit:* **wider, etwas e.,** to rise, revolt, against (proposal, etc.); **mein ganzes Wesen empört sich gegen diese Ungerechtigkeit,** my whole being revolts at, against, this injustice; **sich gegen die Staatsgewalt e.,** to rebel against the authority of the state.
II. *vbl s.* **Empörung,** *f.* **1.** indignation (**über etwas,** at, sth.); **in E. geraten,** to grow, become, indignant, to be filled with indignation; **ein Sturm der E. brach los,** a storm of indignation broke out; **eine Welle der E. erfaßte das ganze Volk,** a wave of indignation seized the whole nation. **2.** insurrection, revolt, rebellion; *Mil: etc:* mutiny.
Emporenkirche, *f. Arch:* church with a gallery.
Empörer, *m.* **-s/-,** insurgent; insurrectionist; *Mil: etc:* mutineer.
empörerisch, *a.* rebellious, rioting, insurgent (populace, elements); rebellious (activities).
emporfahren, *v.i. sep.* (*strong*) (*sein*) to start up (involuntarily); to give a jump, a sudden start; **vom Stuhl e.,** to start up, jump up, from one's chair; **aus dem Schlaf e.,** to wake up with a start, to start up from one's sleep.
emporheben, *v.tr. sep.* (*strong*) to lift (sth.) up; to raise (glass, arm, etc.); **die Augen zum Himmel e.,** to cast up one's eyes to heaven; **die Hand e.,** to lift, raise, one's hand (in salute, to take an oath, etc.).
Emporium [ɛm'poːrium], *n.* **-s/-rien,** mart; storehouse; *A:* emporium.
emporkeimen, *v.i. sep.* (*sein*) to germinate; (*of plant*) to shoot, spring, sprout, up; **emporkeimende Liebe,** dawning, budding, love.
Emporkirche, *f.* = **Emporenkirche.**
emporkommen, *v.i. sep.* (*strong*) (*sein*) (*a*) to come up, come to the surface; (*b*) to rise in the world, in life; to make one's way; **er war nur auf sein Emporkommen bedacht,** he thought only of his advancement.
Emporkömmling, *m.* **-s/-e,** upstart, parvenu.
emporragen, *v.i. sep.* (*haben*) (*of building, etc.*) to

tower (up); **das Gebirge ragte vor ihnen empor,** the mountains towered, rose, before them.

emporranken, *v.i. sep.* (*sein*) *&* **sich emporranken,** (*of plant*) to creep, to climb; (**sich**) **an einer Mauer e.,** to creep up, climb up, a wall.

emporrecken, *v.tr. sep.* to stretch (sth.) upwards; **die Hände, die Arme, zum Himmel e.,** to stretch up one's hands, arms, towards Heaven; **den Hals e.,** to crane one's neck.

emporrichten, *v.tr. sep.* to put, set, stand, (sth.) upright; **sich e.,** (*of pers., plant, etc.*) to straighten (up); (*of pers.*) to draw oneself up (to one's full height); **sich stolz e.,** to draw oneself up proudly.

emporschauen, *v.i. sep.* (*haben*) to look up; **zum Himmel e.,** (i) to look up at the sky; (ii) to look up to Heaven; **zu j-m e.,** (i) to look up at s.o.; (ii) to look up to s.o.

emporschleudern, *v.tr. sep.* to throw, fling, cast, hurl, (sth.) up, into the air.

emporschrauben, *v.tr. sep.* (*of plane*) **sich e.,** to spiral up; to rise vertically.

emporschwingen, *v.tr. sep.* (*strong*) **1.** to swing (sth.) up(wards). **2. sich emporschwingen,** (*a*) to swing (oneself, itself) up(wards); (*b*) (*of bird, etc.*) to soar; *F:* **er hat sich zum Direktor des Betriebes emporgeschwungen,** he has risen to be director of the firm.

emporsteigen, *v.i. sep.* (*strong*) (*sein*) (*of smoke, balloon, sound, etc.*) to rise, ascend; (*of mist*) to rise from the ground; **die Sonne stieg schon am Himmel empor,** the sun was already rising in the sky, climbing the sky; **er fühlte einen ohnmächtigen Zorn in sich e.,** he felt an impotent rage rising, mounting, within him.

emporstreben, *v.i. sep.* (*a*) (*sein*) (*of building, etc.*) to rise, tower up(wards); to soar up; **emporstrebende Pfeiler,** soaring pillars; (*b*) (*haben*) (*of pers.*) to strive (upwards); **ein emporstrebender Geist,** an aspiring spirit.

emporstrecken, *v.tr. sep.* to raise, stretch up (one's hands, etc.); **die Arme zum Himmel e.,** to stretch up one's arms to heaven.

emportürmen (sich), *v.refl. sep.* to tower up; **das Gebirge türmte sich mächtig vor uns empor,** the mountains towered up grandly before us.

Empörung, *f. see* **empören II.**

emporwachsen, *v.i. sep.* (*strong*) (*sein*) to grow up; to spring up, shoot up.

emporwogen, *v.i. sep.* (*sein*) (*of sea, waters, etc.*) to rise up; to surge, swell, billow (up).

emporziehen, *v.tr. sep.* (*strong*) to pull, draw, (sth.) up; to hoist (sth.) up; **die Augenbrauen e.,** to raise, lift, one's eyebrows.

emporzüngeln, *v.i. sep.* (*sein*) (*of flames*) to leap up, to spring up; **Flammen züngelten an den Wänden empor,** flames were licking the walls.

Empyem [ɛmpy·ˈeːm], *n.* **-s/-e.** *Med:* empyema.

empyreisch [ɛmpy·ˈreːiʃ], *a.* empyreal, empyrean.

Empyreum [ɛmpy·ˈreːum], *n.* **-s/-reen,** empyrean.

Empyreuma [ɛmˈpyːroymaː], *n.* **-/-mata** [ɛmpy·ˈroyma·taː], empyreuma.

empyreumatisch [ɛmpy·royˈmaːtiʃ], *a.* empyreumatic(al).

Emse, *f.* **-/-n.** *A. & Dial:* = **Ameise.**

emsig, *a.* industrious, diligent, assiduous; busy, active; **die emsige Biene,** the busy bee; *adv.* **sie hatte den ganzen Tag e. genäht,** she had been busy sewing all day.

Emsigkeit, *f.* industry, diligence, assiduity; activity.

Emu [ˈeːmuː], *m.* **-s/-s.** *Orn:* emu.

Emulgator [e·mulˈgaːtor], *m.* **-s/-en** [-ga·ˈtoːrən]. *Ch:* emulsifier, emulsifying agent

emulgierbar [e·mulˈgiːr-], *a.* emulsifiable.

emulgieren [e·mulˈgiːrən], *v.tr.* to emulsify, emulsionize.

Emulsin [e·mulˈziːn], *n.* **-s/.** *Ch:* emulsin.

Emulsion [e·mulziˈoːn], *f.* **-/-en,** emulsion.

emulsionieren [e·mulzio·ˈniːrən] = **emulgieren.**

Emulsionsfarbe, *f.* emulsion paint.

Emulsionskolloid, *n.* *Ch:* emulsion colloid, emulsoid.

Emulsoid [e·mulzo·ˈiːt], *n.* **-(e)s/-e** [-s, -ˈiːdəs/-ˈiːdə]. *Ch:* emulsoid, emulsion colloid.

Emunktorium [e·muŋkˈtoːrium], *n.* **-s/-ria.** *Physiol:* emunctory.

-en¹, *a. suff.* (*suffixed to nouns*) of . . .; made of . . .; -en; (*a*) **samten,** made of velvet; of velvet; **golden,** golden; made of gold; gold (bracelet, etc.); **metallen,** made of metal; metallic (object); **hanfen, hänfen,** made of hemp; hemp, hempen (cord); (*b*) (*only* **-n** *suffixed to nouns already ending in* **-e**) **eichen,** oaken; **buchen,** beech (-wood) (furniture, etc.); *A. & Lit:* beechen; **birken,** made of birch(-wood); **irden,** earthen; **seiden,** silk (dress, etc.); made of silk; *A:* silken.

-en², *vbl suff.* **1.** (*ending of infinitive*) **lesen,** to read; **beginnen,** to begin, to commence; **lieben,** to love. **2.** *vbl s. n.* (*a*) **-s/.** (*denoting vbl action: no pl.*) -ing; -ion; -tion. (*Note: all German verbs have a vbl s. usage corresponding to the English gerund in* -ing; *throughout the Dictionary the English words in* -ing *have not been listed in the* '*vbl s.*' *section of the article as their existence is self-evident.*) (i) **Sterben,** dying; **Reisen,** travelling; **Filmen,** filming; **Waschen,** washing; (ii) **Übersetzen,** translating, translation (of book, etc.); **Vorstellen,** introducing, introduction (of s.o.); **Einstufen,** classifying, classification; **Wiederholen,** repeating, repetition (of sth.); **Erzeugen,** producing, production; (*b*) **-s/-.** (*originally vbl s., but now with predominantly nominal flavour and therefore capable of pl. use*) **Leiden,** (i) suffering, (ii) ailment; **die Leiden,** (i) the sufferings, (ii) the ailments; **Schreiben,** letter; communication; **die Schreiben,** the letters; the communications; **Beben,** earthquake; **die Beben,** the earthquakes.

Enak [ˈeːnak]. *Pr.n.m.* **-s.** *B.Lit:* Anak.

Enakskinder, *n. pl.*, **Enakssöhne,** *m. pl.* (*a*) *B.Lit:* sons of Anak; (*b*) *F:* giants.

Enallage [ɛnˀala·ˈgeː, e·ˈnala·geː], *f.* **-/.** *Rh:* enallage.

Enanthem [ɛnˀanˈteːm, e·nanˈteːm], *n.* **-s/-e.** *Med:* enanthema.

enantiomorph [e·nantsio·ˈmorf], *a.* *Cryst: Ch:* enantiomorphous, enantiomorphic.

enantiotrop [e·nantsio·ˈtroːp], *a. Ph.Ch:* enantiotropic.

Enantiotropie [e·nantsio·tro·ˈpiː], *f.* **-/.** enantiotropy.

Enarthrose [ɛnˀarˈtroːzə, e·narˈtroːzə], *f.* **-/-n.** *Anat:* enarthrosis, ball-and-socket joint.

en avant [ɑ̃·a·ˈvɑ̃ː]. *Fr.phr.* come on! let's go! *Mil: etc:* forward! advance!

en bloc [ɑ̃·ˈblok]. *Fr. adv. phr.* en bloc; **etwas en bloc kaufen,** to buy sth. in bulk, en bloc.

Enchiridion [ɛnçi·ˈriːdion], *n.* **-s/-dien,** enchiridion; handbook.

encouragieren [ɑ̃·ku·ra·ˈʒiːrən], *v.tr.* to encourage, to put courage into (s.o.); **j-n zu etwas e., j-n e., etwas zu tun,** to encourage s.o. to do sth.

End-, *comb.fm.* (*in combination with numerals, indicating a person's age*) **Endzwanziger** *m*, person in his late twenties; man in his late twenties; **Endzwanzigerin** *f*, woman in her late twenties; **Endvierziger** *m*, person in his late forties; man in his late forties.

-end, *suff.* **1.** (*ending of present participle*) -ing; (*a*) **a. erschreckend,** terrifying; **singend,** singing; (*b*) *vbl s. m., f.* (*decl. as adj.*) (i) **Sterbende,** dying person; **die Sterbenden,** the dying; **Lebende,** living person; **die Lebenden,** the living; **Liebende,** person who is in love; lover; **die Liebenden,** the lovers; (the) people who are in love; (ii) **Reisende,** traveller; **die Reisenden,** the travellers; **Überlebende,** survivor; **die Überlebenden,** the survivors; **Badende,** bather; **die Badenden,** the bathers. **2.** (*Ending of* '*gerundive*' *developed from old infinitive form; used to denote that something is yet to be done*) **der zu schreibende Brief,** the letter (that is) to be written; **die zu lesenden Bücher,** the books (that are) to be read.

Endarterie, *f. Anat:* end artery.

Endbahnhof, *m. Rail:* terminus; terminal (station); rail-head (of line).

Endbuchstabe, *m.* final (letter).

Endchen, *n.* **-s/-,** (*dim. of* **Ende**) small piece, scrap, bit (of string, etc.); *F:* **j-n ein E. begleiten,** to accompany s.o. a short, a little, way.

Enddarm, *m.* (*a*) *Anat:* rectum; (*b*) *Nat. Hist:* proctodaeum (of invertebrate).

Ende, *n.* **-s/-n. 1.** (*a*) end (of stick, line, street, etc.); termination (of line, bus route, etc.); **das äußerste E. eines Astes,** the extremity of a branch; **die beiden Enden eines Balkens,** the two ends of a beam; **von einem E. (bis) zum anderen, von Anfang bis zu E.,** from end to end, from one end to the other; from beginning to end; **das obere, das untere, E.,** the upper, the lower, end; the head, the foot (of table, etc.); the top, the bottom (of stairway, etc.); **die Enden von Balken aneinanderfügen,** to join beams end to end; **ganz am E. der Straße,** at the far end, at the bottom, of the road; **am anderen E. des Dorfes,** at the other end of the village; **ein Wagen am E. des Zuges,** a carriage at the back, at the rear, of the train; **das E. des Pfades,** the end of the path; **das E. der Erde, das E. der Welt,** the ends of the earth, (*cp.* 2); **ich folge dir bis ans E. der Welt,** I shall follow you to the ends of the earth; *F:* **er wohnt am anderen E. der Welt,** he lives at the back of beyond, in the middle of nowhere; *F:* **etwas am falschen E. anfassen, anpacken,** to go, set, about sth. (in) the wrong way; *F:* to begin, start, sth. at the wrong end; to put the cart before the horse; (*b*) *Ven:* prong, tine, point (of antler); (*c*) **an allen Enden,** everywhere; *F:* **an allen Ecken und Enden,** everywhere; at every turn; here, there, and everywhere; **bei uns fehlt es an allen Ecken und Enden,** we are terribly short of everything; **unser Mädchen ist krank; sie fehlt uns an allen Ecken und Enden,** our maid is ill; we are quite lost without her, we miss her at every turn. **2.** (*a*) end (of month, work, meeting, lawsuit, etc.); end, termination, close (of period of time, action, speech, etc.); end, conclusion (of book, chapter, etc.); end, termination (of business connection, career, letter, etc.); end, finish (of life); (*at end of book, etc.*) finis; the end; *Sp: etc:* finish (of match, race, presentation, etc.); **am E.,** (i) at the end (of speech, period of time, etc.); (ii) in the end; finally; ultimately; eventually; (iii) *F:* in the upshot; **am E. des Jahres,** at the end, at the close, of the year; **am E. sagte er . . .,** in the end, finally, he said . . .; *F:* **am E. meint er noch . . .,** he might end up by thinking . . .; **E. Januar,** (i) at the end of January; (ii) towards the end of January; **E. der dreißiger Jahre,** in the late thirties; towards the end of the thirties; **gegen E. des Sommers,** towards the end of the summer, in late summer; **das E. der Welt, aller Dinge,** the end of the world, of all things; (*cp.* 1 (*a*)); **bis ans E. der Zeiten,** till the end of time; until the crack of doom; **das E. des Menschen,** the end of man; **ein schönes, ein friedliches, E. haben,** to make a good end; to have a peaceful end; **sein Leben neigt sich dem E. zu,** his life is drawing to an end, to a close; **er fand sein E. im Kampf,** he met his death in battle; **einer Sache ein E. machen, bereiten, setzen,** to make an end of sth., to put an end, a stop, to sth.; **der Tod machte, setzte, den Eroberungen Alexanders ein E.,** death put an end to the conquests of Alexander; **bis zum bitteren E. standhalten, etwas bis zum bitteren E. durchkämpfen,** to go on, to persevere, to the bitter end; to fight (sth. out) to the bitter end, to a finish; **ganz bis zum E.,** to the very end, to the finish, the very last; **Geschichten ohne E.,** never-ending, long-winded, interminable, endless, stories; **ein Schrecken ohne E.,** an endless terror; *B:* **ich bin das A und das O, der Anfang und das E.,** I am Alpha and Omega, the beginning and the ending; *Prov:* **E. gut, alles gut,** all's well that ends well; *F:* **das dicke E. kommt (noch) nach,** the worst is still to come; it is all very well so far but there is still a snag to come; the sting is in the tail; **und was war das E. vom Lied?** and what was the end of the story? **das E. vom Lied war, daß er zurücktrat,** the upshot of it all was that he resigned; *F:* **letzten Endes,** after all (is said and done); **letzten Endes bin ich doch nicht dein Dienstmädchen,** after all, I am not your maid; (*b*) *vbl phr.* **zu E. gehen** (*of period of time, war, etc.*) to come to an end; to draw to an end, to a close; to near its end; (*of supplies, money, etc.*) to come to an end; (i) to run out, to give out; (ii) to run low; (*of period of time, war, supplies, etc.*) **zu E. sein,** to be at an end; **etwas zu E. führen, bringen,** to bring (undertaking, speech, etc.) to an end, to a close; to end, to finish (off), to complete, to conclude (piece of work, etc.); (*of period of time, pers., etc.*) **ein E. nehmen, finden,** to come to an end; **mit etwas ein E. machen,** to make an end of sth., to put an end, a stop, to sth.; **das Jahr geht zu E.,** the year is drawing to an end, to a close; the year is nearing its end; **mit dem Alten geht es zu E.,** the old man is nearing his end; **sein E. naht,** his end is approaching, nigh; **die Ferien sind zu E.,** the holidays are at an end, are over; **der Krieg ist zu E.,** the war is at an end, is over; **meine Geduld ist zu E.,** my patience is at an end, is exhausted; **unser Benzin ist zu E.,** we are at the end of our petrol, we are out of petrol; **mein Urlaub ist zu E.,** my leave is up; **eine Angelegenheit zu einem guten E. führen,** to bring a matter to a successful issue, conclusion; to carry a matter through; **die Tagung nahm ein plötzliches E.,** the meeting came to an abrupt end; **alles muß einmal ein E. nehmen,** all good things, everything, must come to an end sometime; **alles hat, nimmt, einmal ein E.,** there is an end to everything; **es wird mit ihm noch ein böses E. nehmen,** he will come to a bad end; **das Gerede, Staunen, nahm kein E.,** there was endless gossip, there was no end of gossip, of astonishment; **das nimmt kein E.,** there's no end to it; **wir müssen damit ein E.**

machen, we must make an end of it, we must finish it; **das ist ein für alle Mal zu E.,** that is over and done with; that is finished for good; *F:* **er war mit seiner Weisheit, mit seinem Latein, mit seiner Kunst, zu E.,** he was at his wit's end; (*of pers.*) *F:* **am E. sein,** to be at the end of one's resources, of one's tether; to be finished; *F:* **da ist das E. von weg!** it's fantastic, extraordinary, beyond belief! **3.** end, purpose, aim, object; **zu diesem E.,** to this end; for this purpose; with this object, end, in view; **zu welchem E.,** to what end, for what purpose, object; **was ist das E. unserer Erdenfahrt?** what is the end, the purpose, of life's journey? **am E. seiner Reise sein,** to be at the end of one's journey. **4.** *F:* piece (of ribbon, etc.); **ein E. Stoff, ein E. Schnur,** a length of material, a piece of string; **ein E. Wurst,** a piece of sausage; **es ist noch ein gutes E. bis zum Bahnhof,** it is still a good way (to go) to the station, the station is still a good way off; **wir waren ein gutes E. gegangen, als . . .,** we had gone a good way when . . .; **wir gingen ein E. zusammen,** we went part of the way together.

Endebildchen, *n. Cin:* end-frame.

Endeffekt, *m.* final effect; *F:* **im E.,** in the upshot; in the last, final, analysis.

Endel, *n.* **-s/-.** *Tex: Austrian:* selvedge.

endeln, *v.tr. Needlew: Austrian:* to oversew (edge, etc.).

Endemie [ɛnde·ˈmiː], *f.* **-/-n** [-ˈmiːən]. *Med:* endemic.

endemisch [ɛnˈdeːmiʃ], *a. Bot: Med:* endemic.

enden. I. *v.* **1.** *v.i.* (*haben*) (*a*) (*of period of time, road, etc.*) to end; to finish; to terminate; to come to an end; (*of term, treaty, etc.*) to expire; **das erste Kapitel endet mit einem Mord,** the first chapter ends with a murder; **die Zusammenkunft endete mit, in, einer Schlägerei,** the meeting finished in a brawl; **er hatte noch nicht geendet, als . . .,** he had not yet finished, *F:* done, speaking when . . .; **der Tag endete mit einem Mißklang,** the day ended on a discordant note; **das Spiel endete unentschieden,** the game resulted in a draw; **der Abend endete mit Musik,** the evening ended with, concluded with, music; **wie endet die Geschichte, das Stück?** how does the story, the play, end (up)? **das goldene Zeitalter endet mit Ovid,** the golden age ends, comes to an end, with Ovid; **er endete in der Verbannung,** he ended his days in exile; **ich weiß nicht, wie das e. soll,** I do not know how things will end; **es endete damit, daß . . .,** the upshot of it was that . . .; **wie soll das noch e.?** how will it end (up), what will be the end of it? **nicht e. wollender Beifall,** unending applause, acclamations; (*b*) (*of word, etc.*) to terminate, end, (**auf etwas** *acc.*, **in, mit, etwas** *dat.*, in, with, sth.); (*of pyramid, etc.*) **in einer Spitze e.,** to end, terminate, finish, in a point; **das Wort endet auf einen, mit einem, Konsonanten,** the word ends, terminates, in, with, a consonant; **dieser Weg endet bei der Landstraße,** this path ends at the high road; **sein ganzes Denken endet in Gott,** his thoughts all terminate in God. **2.** *v.tr.* to end, to finish, to conclude, to terminate (sth.); **seine Tage in Frieden e.,** to end one's days in peace; **ende meine Qualen,** end my sufferings; **einen Konflikt e.,** to end a conflict, to put an end to a conflict.

II. *vbl s.* **1. Enden,** *n. in vbl senses.* **2. Endung,** *f.* (*a*)=II. 1; (*b*) *Gram:* ending, termination (of word).

ender, *comb.fm. m.* **-s/-. 1.** *Mch: etc:* -ended boiler; **Einender,** single-ended marine boiler; *cp.* **Doppelender. 2.** *Ven:* -pronger; -tined stag; **Zehnender** *m*, five-pronger; ten-tined stag; ten-pointer.

Endergebnis, *n.* final, ultimate, result; end-result.

en detail [ɑ̃· de·ˈtai], *adv.* in detail; *Com:* retail.

Endetitel, *m. Cin:* end-frame.

Endfläche, *f.* end face, terminal face (of crystal, etc.).

Endgeschwindigkeit, *f.* final, terminal, velocity (of projectile).

Endglied, *n.* final member (of equation, etc.); end link (of chain, etc.); terminal segment (of finger, etc.).

endgültig, *a.* definitive, final (resolution, judgment, result, answer, etc.); ultimate (decision, answer, result); **endgültiger Bestimmungsort,** ultimate destination; *Publ:* **endgültige Ausgabe,** definitive, final, edition; *adv.* finally; definitively; **er ist e. abgereist,** he has gone away for good (and all); **es steht e. fest, daß . . .,** (i) it has been established beyond doubt that . . .; (ii) it is final that . . .; **sie hat e. mit ihm gebrochen,** she has broken with him for good and all.

Endgültigkeit, *f.* finality, definitiveness (of resolution, utterance, etc.).

Endhaar, *n. Anat:* terminal hair.

endigen, *v.tr. & i.* (*haben*)=**enden.**

Endivie [ɛnˈdiːviə], *f.* **-/-n.** *Bot: Hort:* endive.

Endkampf, *m.* final struggle; *Sp: etc:* final (contest); *Box:* final bout.

Endknospe, *f. Bot:* terminal bud.

endlich. I. *a.* **1.** ultimate, final, eventual (judgment, etc.). **2.** (*a*) *Phil: etc:* finite (space, nature, being, etc.); **das Endliche und das Unendliche,** the finite and the infinite; (*b*) *Mth:* finite (numbers, etc.); **eine endliche Größe,** a finite magnitude; **endlicher Dezimalbruch,** terminate decimal fraction.

II. **endlich,** *adv.* (*a*) at last; at long last; at length; finally; **e. antwortete er,** at last, in the end, finally, at length, he answered; **e. wurde es Tag,** daylight came at last, at long last; **e. verstehe ich dich,** at last, now at last, I understand you; **e. willigte er ein,** at length, finally, he gave his consent; **da bist du ja e.!** here you are at last! **endlich!** at last! **er sollte e. wissen,** he ought to know by now; (*b*) (*in enumeration, etc.*) lastly; finally; ultimately. *See also* **schließlich.**

Endlichkeit, *f.* finiteness, finitude (of space, time, capacity, etc.); *Phil:* **die E. und die Unendlichkeit,** the finite and the infinite; **die E. irdischen Seins,** the finite nature of earthly existence.

endlos, *a.* (*a*) endless, infinite, boundless, unbounded (space, etc.); endless (ribbon, journey, etc.); **die Ebene erstreckt sich ins Endlose,** the plain stretches out endlessly, extends without end; (*b*) endless, interminable, never-ending, unending (stories, discussions, etc.); endless, infinite (mercy, etc.); *adv.* **e.,** *adv.phr.* **(bis) ins Endlose,** endlessly, indefinitely, *F:* ad infinitum.

Endlosigkeit, *f.* endlessness, infiniteness, boundlessness (of space, etc.); endlessness (of ribbon, journey, etc.).

Endlösung, *f. Nazi Terminology:* final solution.

Endluft, *f. Hor:* end-shake.

Endmaß, *n.* **1.** *Mec:* end measurement. **2.** *Tls:* end standard; gauge-block.

Endmast, *m. El:* terminal pole.

Endmoräne, *f. Geol:* terminal moraine, end moraine.

endo-, Endo- [ɛndo·-], *pref.* endo-; ento-; *Bot:* **endospor** [ɛndo·ˈspoːr], endosporous; *Ch:* **endotherm** [ɛndo·ˈtɛrm], endothermic (reaction); *Bot:* **Endodermis** [ɛndo·ˈdɛrmis] *f*, endodermis; **Endokarp** [ɛndo·ˈkarp] *n*, endocarp; *Biol:* **Endoplasma** [ɛndo·ˈplasmaː] *n*, endoplasm; **Endoparasit** [ɛndo·pa·ra·ˈziːt] *m*, endoparasite, entoparasite.

Endogamie [ɛndo·ga·ˈmiː], *f.* **-/.** *Anthr:* endogamy; inbreeding; breeding in and in.

endogen [ɛndo·ˈgeːn], *a. Bot: Med:* endogenous (plant, contagion); *Biol:* endogenetic; *Geol:* **endogenes Gestein,** endogenetic rock.

Endokard [ɛndo·ˈkart], *n.* **-(e)s/-e** [-s, -ˈkardəs/-ˈkardə]. *Anat:* endocardium.

Endokarditis [ɛndo·karˈdiːtis], *f.* **-/.** *Med:* endocarditis.

endokrin [ɛndo·ˈkriːn], *a. Anat:* endocrine, ductless (gland).

Endokrinologie [ɛndo·kri·no·lo·ˈgiː], *f.* **-/.** *Physiol:* endocrinology.

Endolymphe [ɛndo·ˈlymfə], *f.* **-/-n.** *Anat:* endolymph.

Endometritis [ɛndo·me·ˈtriːtis], *f.* **-/.** *Med:* endometritis.

Endometrium [ɛndo·ˈmeːtrium], *n.* **-s/-trien.** *Anat:* endometrium.

endomorph [ɛndo·ˈmɔrf], *a. Geol:* endomorphic, endomorphous.

Endophyt [ɛndo·ˈfyːt], *m.* **-en/-en.** *Bot:* entophyte.

Endoskop [ɛndo·ˈskoːp], *n.* **-s/-e.** *Med:* endoscope.

Endoskopie [ɛndo·sko·ˈpiː], *f.* **-/-n** [-piːən]. *Med:* endoscopy.

Endosmose [ɛndɔsˈmoːzə], *f.* **-/-n.** *Ph:* endosmose, endosmosis.

endosmotisch [ɛndɔsˈmoːtiʃ], *a. Ph:* endosmotic.

Endosperm [ɛndo·ˈspɛrm], *n.* **-(e)s/-e.** *Bot:* endosperm.

Endospore [ɛndo·ˈspoːrə], *f.* **-/-n.** *Fung:* endospore.

Endothel [ɛndo·ˈteːl], *n.* **-s/-e.** *Physiol:* endothelium.

endothelial [ɛndo·te·li·ˈaːl], *a. Physiol:* endothelial.

Endplatte, *f.* end plate, terminal plate.

Endprodukt, *n.* end product; final product.

Endpunkt, *m.* (*a*) final, last, point; end; (*b*) extremity; terminus, terminal point (of line, etc.).

Endreim, *m.* end-rhyme.

Endröhre, *f. W.Tel:* output valve.

Endrunde, *f. Sp: etc:* final round; final; *Rac:* final heat.

Endsee, *m. Geol:* lake without outlet (in steppe, etc.).

Endsilbe, *f.* terminal, last, syllable; end syllable.

Endspannung, *f.* final tension; *El.E:* terminal voltage.

Endspiel, *n.* **1.** *Sp: etc:* final game, final match; final. **2.** *Mec.E:* **E. in Längsrichtung,** end-play.

Endspurt, *m. Sp. & F:* final spurt.

Endstadium, *n.* final stage; terminal stage.

Endstation, *f. Rail: etc:* terminus; terminal (point) (of line, etc.).

Endstellung, *f. Gram:* end-position, final position (of verb, etc.).

Endstück, *n.* (*a*) final piece; (*b*) endpiece (of cheese, etc.).

Endstufe, *f.* final stage.

Endsumme, *f.* total (sum).

Endtermin, *m.* final date; closing date.

Endung, *f. see* **enden** II.

Endursache, *f. Phil:* final cause.

Endurteil, *n. Jur: etc:* final judgment; final verdict.

Endverstärker, *m. W.Tel:* terminal amplifier.

Endwert, *m.* final value.

Endzeit, *f. Theol:* last days, last times; last state (of the world).

endzeitlich, *a. Theol:* eschatological (doctrine).

Endziel, *n.* (*a*) final, ultimate, object; final, ultimate, aim; final, ultimate, purpose; end; (ultimate) objective; (*b*) ultimate destination, ultimate goal; end (of journey).

Endzug, *m. Row:* finish of the stroke; follow-through.

Endzweck, *m.* final, ultimate, purpose, object; *Phil:* finality.

Energetik [e·nɛrˈgeːtik], *f.* **-/.** energetics.

Energie [e·nɛrˈgiː], *f.* **-/-n** [-ˈgiːən]. **1.** *Ph: Mch: etc:* energy; *pl.* **Energien,** types of energy; **potentielle E.,** potential energy; **kinetische, aktuelle, E.,** kinetic, active, actual, energy; **die Erhaltung der E.,** the conservation of energy; **zugeführte E.,** input of energy; **E. erzeugen,** to generate energy; *Ind: etc:* **E. und Brennstoff,** power and fuel. **2.** energy; vigour; *F:* go; vim; drive; punch (of pers., etc.); **geistige E.,** mental energy; **keine E. haben,** to have no energy, to lack energy, *F:* go, vim; **voller E. sein, viel E. haben,** to be full of energy, to have plenty of energy, *F:* go, vim; to be very energetic; **E. entfalten,** to display energy; **seine E. vergeuden,** to dissipate, waste, one's energy, one's energies; **mit großer E. an eine Aufgabe herangehen,** to set about a task with great energy, with great vigour, very energetically, very vigorously. *See also* **aufspeichern.**

Energieabgabe, *f.* release of energy; output of energy.

Energieaufspeicherung, *f.* storage of energy, accumulation of energy.

Energieaufwand, *m.* expenditure of energy.

Energieentwertung, *f. Ph:* dissipation, gradual loss, of energy.

Energiehaushalt, *m. Physiol: etc:* regulation of the supply of energy.

energielos, *a.* without energy, lacking in energy; languid (pers.); **e. sein,** to be without energy, to lack energy, *F:* go, vim; to be lacking in energy; *F:* to have no drive, no punch.

Energielosigkeit, *f.* lack of energy, *F:* lack of go, of vim.

Energiequelle, *f.* source of energy.

Energieübertragung, *f. Ph:* transmission of energy.

Energieumwandlung, *f. Ph:* transformation of energy.

Energieverbrauch, *m.* consumption of energy.

Energieverlust, *m.* loss of energy.

Energieversorgung, *f.* supply of energy.

Energiewirtschaft, *f.* economics, economy, of energy; *Ind:* economy of power.

energisch [e·ˈnɛrgiʃ], *a.* vigorous; forceful; determined, resolute, firm (pers., etc.); strong, energetic (measures, etc.); **in energischem Ton,** in a determined, resolute, firm, tone; **ein energisches Kinn, einen energischen Gang, haben,** to have a determined, firm, chin, an energetic and determined step; *adv.* **er bestritt e., daß . . .,** he stoutly denied that . . .; he emphatically denied that . . .; **e. mit j-m verfahren,** to deal firmly with s.o.; to deal forcefully with s.o.

Enervation [e·nɛrva·tsiˈoːn], *f.* **-/.** enervation.

enervieren [e·nɛrˈviːrən], *v.tr.* to enervate, weaken (body, mind).

enfilieren [ɑ̃·fi·ˈliːrən], *v.tr. Mil:* to enfilade, rake (trench, etc.).

Enfilierfeuer [ɑ̃·fi·ˈliːr-], *n. Mil:* enfilading fire, raking fire.

Enfleurage [ã·flø·ˈraːʒə], *f.* -/. enfleurage (of fats and oils).

eng. 1. *a.* (*a*) narrow (valley, passage, staircase, etc.); confined, cramped, narrow (space); tight (boots, clothes); **ein enges Zimmer,** a small, cramped, room; **auf engem Raum,** in a cramped, small, space; **ein enger Rock,** (i) a narrow, slim, skirt; (ii) a tight skirt; (*of passage, etc.*) **e. werden,** to become narrow, to narrow; (*of garment, etc.*) **zu e. werden,** to become too tight, overtight; **etwas enger machen,** to narrow (opening, etc.), to make (opening, etc.) narrower; to make (garment, etc.) tighter; to take in (garment); **es wurde mir zu e. im Zimmer,** (i) I felt cramped in the room; (ii) I felt oppressed in the room; *Med:* **enges Becken,** narrow pelvis; *B:* **die enge Pforte,** the strait gate; *Lit:* **es wurde mir e. ums Herz,** I had a sudden tight feeling in my chest; *adv.* (*of dress, etc.*) **e. ansitzen, e. anliegen, e. anschließen,** to be tight-, close-fitting; to cling to the figure; to fit like a glove; **e. geschnürt,** tight-laced (corset, pers.); *F:* **den Gürtel enger schnallen,** to tighten one's belt; (*b*) **in engen Grenzen,** within narrow limits, bounds; **im engsten Sinne,** in the narrowest, strictest, sense; **einen engen Wirkungskreis haben,** to have a narrow, restricted, limited, sphere of action; **im engen Kreise der Familie,** in one's immediate family circle; in the intimacy of one's family circle; **in engen Verhältnissen leben,** to live in narrow circumstances; to live in cramped conditions; to live in a small way; (*c*) **engerer Ausschuß,** select committee; **engere Wahl,** interim selection (*from which final selection is to be made*); short list (*of possible candidates for appointment*); **in die engere Wahl kommen,** to be put on the short list; to get into the finals (in competition, etc.); (*d*) narrow, restricted (outlook, existence, etc.); **enge Ansichten haben,** to have narrow, *F:* hidebound, views; to be narrow-minded. **2.** (*a*) *a.* close (relationship, connection, friendship, etc.); **seine engsten Mitarbeiter, Berater,** his closest colleagues, his closest advisers; **enge Zusammenarbeit,** close co-operation; **im engen Zusammenhang mit dieser Frage,** in close connection with this question; **ihre enge Freundschaft,** their close, intimate, friendship; *adv.* **e. verbunden, verknüpft, mit,** closely connected, bound, linked, with; **freundschaftliche Bande enger knüpfen,** to draw closer the bonds of friendship; **e. miteinander befreundet sein,** to be close friends; to be bosom friends; (*b*) *adv.* **zwei e. beschriebene Seiten,** two closely written pages; **e. schreiben,** to write closely; to cramp one's writing; **e. (beieinander) stehen, e. sitzen,** to stand, sit, close together; (*of people, houses, etc.*) **e. zusammengedrängt sein,** to be huddled together; **sich e. an den Text, an das Original, halten,** to keep close to the text, to the original.

Engadin, das [ˈɛŋga·diːn]. *Pr.n.* -s. *Geog:* the Engadine.

Engagement [ã·ga·ʒ(ə)ˈmãː], *n.* -s/-s. **1.** engagement; *Fin:* commitment; **ein E. eingehen,** to enter into a commitment. **2.** *Th: etc:* engagement; **ein festes E. haben,** to have a permanent engagement (as leading lady, etc.); **ohne E. sein, kein E. haben,** to be disengaged, *F:* out of a job; *Th: F:* to be resting. **3.** *Fenc:* engagement, engaging (of sword).

engagieren [ã·ga·ˈʒiːrən]. I. *v.tr.* **1.** (*a*) to engage, take on (employee, *Th:* actor); **j-n als Sekretär e.,** to engage s.o. as a secretary; (*b*) **sind Sie für den nächsten Walzer schon engagiert?** are you engaged for the next waltz? **ich bin schon engagiert für heute abend,** I am engaged for to-night, I already have an engagement for to-night; (*c*) *Fin:* **engagiertes Kapital,** tied-up, locked-up, capital; (*d*) *Fenc:* **die Klinge e.,** to engage the sword; *abs.* to engage.

II. *vbl s.* **Engagieren** *n.*, **Engagierung** *f. in vbl senses; also:* engagement (of s.o.).

enganliegend, *a.* (*of garment*) tight-, close-fitting; clinging; **e. über den Hüften,** close-fitting over the hips, fitting closely over the hips.

enganschließend, *a.* **1.** adjoining. **2.** = **enganliegend.**

engbefreundet, *attrib.a.* (people) who are close friends, who are bosom friends.

engbegrenzt, *attrib.a.* very restricted, limited, narrow (sphere of action, number, etc.).

engbrüstig, *a.* **1.** narrow-chested (pers.). **2.** short-winded, wheezy (pers., horse); broken-winded (horse).

Engbrüstigkeit, *f.* **1.** narrowness of the chest. **2.** shortness of breath; short-windedness (of pers., horse).

enge[1], *a. occ.* = **eng.**

Enge[2], *f.* -/-n. **1.** (*a*) narrowness (of path, space, life, etc.); tightness (of garment); **der E. des Alltags entfliehen,** to escape from the narrowness, from the restrictions, of everyday life; (*b*) closeness (of relations, etc.). **2.** (*a*) narrow space; narrow place; narrow way; *Ph.Geog:* (*in mountains*) defile; (*in sea*) narrows; strait(s); (*b*) **j-n in die E. treiben,** to corner s.o., to drive s.o. into a corner; to press s.o. hard, closely; *F:* to drive s.o. to the wall; **in die E. getrieben sein, in die E. geraten sein,** to be cornered, to be driven into a corner; *F:* to be in a tight corner, in a tight spot.

Engel, *m.* -s/-, angel; **der E. des Herrn, des Lichtes,** the angel of the Lord, of light; **der E. des Todes, der Finsternis,** the angel of death, of darkness; **schön, rein, wie ein E. sein,** to be beautiful, pure, as an angel; **sein rettender E., sein guter E.,** his guardian angel, his good angel; **sein böser E.,** his evil angel; his evil genius; **sie ist ein E.,** she is an angel; she is angelic; **du bist ein E.!** you are an angel; **mein E.,** (my) angel, darling, sweetheart; *F:* **die Engel im Himmel pfeifen, singen, hören,** *F:* to see stars; *F:* **ein Engel geht, fliegt, durchs Zimmer,** (*said to break a silence*) there's an angel flying overhead.

Engelamt, *n. R.C.Ch:* first mass (of the three masses) at Christmas.

Engelaut, *m. Ling:* fricative; spirant.

Engelchen, *n.* -s/-, little angel; cherub.

Engelehe, *f.* unconsummated marriage.

Engelfisch, *m. Ich:* angel-fish, angel-shark, monkfish, fiddle-fish.

engelgleich, *a.* angelic(al); angel-like, like an angel.

Engelhaar, *n.* white floss (*for decorating Christmas-trees, etc.*).

engelhaft, *a.* angelic(al); angel-like, like an angel; **mit engelhafter Geduld,** with angelic patience; with the patience of Job, of a saint.

Engelhai, *m.* = **Engelfisch.**

Engelkraut, *n. Bot: Pharm:* arnica; mountain tobacco.

Engelland. *Pr.n.n.* -s. *A:* = **England.**

Engelmacherin, *f.* -/-innen. *Pej:* baby-farmer, *A:* angel-maker.

Engelrot, *n.* = **Englischrot.**

Engelsblümchen, *n. Bot:* cat's-foot, mountain cudweed.

Engelsburg, die. *Pr.n.* the Castle of St Angelo (at Rome).

Engelschar, *f.* angelic host, host of angels.

Engelsgeduld, *f.* angelic patience; **eine E. haben,** to have the patience of Job, of a saint; to have endless patience (**mit j-m,** with s.o.).

Engelstaler, *m. Num: A:* angel.

Engelsüß, *n.* -/-e. *Bot:* common polypody; wall fern.

Engel(s)zunge, *f. B:* **wenn ich mit Menschen- und mit Engelzungen redete,** though I speak with the tongues of men and of angels; *F:* **mit Engelszungen reden,** to speak with the tongues of men and angels; to speak honeyed words.

Engelverehrung, *f.* angelolatry, angel-worship.

Engelwurz, *f. Bot:* angelica; **kleine E.,** aegopodium, gout-weed, bishop's weed.

engen, *v.tr.* **1.** *A:* = **beengen. 2. sich engen,** to narrow; to become narrower.

Engerling, *m.* -s/-e. *Ent:* cockchafer-grub; may-bug grub.

Engführung, *f. Mus:* stretto (*in fugue*).

enghalsig, *a.* narrow-necked (bottle, etc.).

Engheit, *f.* -/. **1.** (*a*) narrowness (of space, etc.); tightness (of garment); (*b*) closeness (of relations, etc.). **2.** narrowness, narrow-mindedness (of pers., views).

engherzig, *a.* ungenerous, petty; unsympathetic.

Engherzigkeit, *f.* lack of generosity, pettiness; lack of sympathy.

Engigkeit, *f.* = **Engheit 1** (*a*).

England. *Pr.n.n.* -s, (*a*) *Geog:* England; *Hist:* (South) Britain; (*b*) (*loosely used*) (Great) Britain, the British Isles.

Engländer, *m.* -s/-. **1.** (i) Englishman (*as opposed to Scotsman, Welshman*); (ii) (*loosely used*) Briton; **die Engländer,** (i) the English (people); (ii) (the) Englishmen; (iii) (the) Britons; **er ist ein geborener, gebürtiger, E., er ist E. von Geburt,** he is English-born, he is English by birth. **2.** *Tls:* screw spanner, monkey-wrench, shifting spanner, adjustable spanner.

Engländerei, *f.* -/. Anglomania.

Engländerer, *m.* -s/-. Anglomaniac.

Engländerin, *f.* -/-innen, (i) Englishwoman; (ii) (*loosely used*) British woman; **eine junge E.,** a young Englishwoman; an English girl; **sie ist E.,** she is English.

Englandfeind, *m.* Anglophobe.

englandfeindlich, *a.* Anglophobe; anti-British.

Englandfeindlichkeit, *f.* Anglophobia; anti-British attitude.

Englandfreund, *m.* Anglophile, person of pro-English, pro-British, sympathies.

englandfreundlich, *a.* Anglophile; pro-English; pro-British.

Englandfreundlichkeit, *f.* Anglophilia, Anglophilism; pro-English *or* pro-British attitude.

englisch[1]. **1.** *a.* (*a*) English; (*loosely used*) British; **die englische Sprache,** the English language; **englische Geschichte,** English history; **englische Erzeugnisse,** English products; **ein englisches Mädchen,** an English girl; (*b*) **das englische Parlament,** the English Parliament; **ein englischer Garten, Park,** a landscape garden; **englisches Vollblut,** British thoroughbred; *Constr:* **englischer Verband,** Old English bond; *Med:* **die englische Krankheit,** rachitis, *F:* rickets; **englisches Pflaster,** court-plaster. **2.** *adv.* English; **e. sprechen,** to speak (in) English; **sie redete ihn e. an,** she spoke to him, addressed him, in English. **3.** (*a*) *s.* **Englisch,** *n. inv., occ.* -s, *Ling:* English; the English language; **das Englische** (*decl. as adj.*) the English language; English; **E. sprechen, können,** to speak, know, English; **E. lernen,** to learn English; **Chaucers E., das E. Chaucers,** Chaucer's English; **können Sie E.? sprechen Sie E.?** can you, do you speak English? **er spricht ein gutes E.,** he speaks, good English; he speaks English well; **er beherrscht das Englische vollkommen,** he has a perfect command of English; **einen Satz aus dem Englischen ins Deutsche übersetzen,** to translate a sentence from English into German; (*b*) *adv. phr.* (*spelt with small e*) **auf e.,** in English; **sich auf e., in e., unterhalten,** to converse, talk, in English; **was sagt man auf e. für . . .?** what is the English for . . .? *For other phrases cp.* **deutsch. 4. englisch-,** *comb.fm.* English-; Anglo-; **die englischsprechenden Völker,** the English-speaking nations; **englischamerikanische Literatur,** Anglo-American literature; **englisch-amerikanischer Handelsvertrag,** Anglo-American trade agreement; **englisch-deutsch,** Anglo-German (relations, etc.); English-German (dictionary, etc.).

englisch[2], *a.* angelic(al); *Ecc:* **der Englische Gruß,** the Angelic Salutation.

Englischblau, *n. Dy: etc:* royal blue.

Englischgelb, *n. Dy: etc:* cassel yellow.

Englischhorn, *n. Mus:* cor anglais, English horn, tenor oboe.

Englischleder, *n. Tex:* moleskin.

Englischrot, *n. Dy: etc:* English red, Venetian red, colcothar.

englisieren [ɛŋli·ˈziːrən], *v.tr.* = **anglisieren** 2.

englumig [ˈɛŋlu·miç], *a. Bot:* (wood) with small pores; small (wood-vessel, etc.).

engmaschig, *a.* close-meshed (net, fabric, etc.).

Engobe [ã·ˈgoːbə], *f.* -/-n. *Cer:* engobe.

engobieren [ã·go·ˈbiːrən], *v.tr. Cer:* to coat (pottery, etc.) with an engobe.

Engpaß, *m.* **1.** (narrow) pass, defile (between mountains); bottle-neck (in road); *Hist:* **der E. der Thermopylen,** the pass of Thermopylae; *P.N:* **'Engpaß',** 'road narrows'. **2.** *Ind:* bottle-neck (in production, supply, etc.); **in einen E. geraten sein,** (*of production, etc.*) to have reached a bottle-neck; (*of pers.*) to be in a tight corner, a tight spot.

Engramm [ɛŋˈgram], *n.* -s/-e. *Biol: Psy:* engram.

en gros [ã·ˈgroː]. *Fr.phr. Com:* wholesale.

Engroshandel, *m. Com:* wholesale trade.

Engroshändler, *m. Com:* wholesale dealer, wholesaler.

Engrospreis, *m. Com:* wholesale price.

engstirnig, *a.* narrow(-minded), *F:* hidebound (pers.); narrow, restricted, *F:* hidebound (views).

Engstirnigkeit, *f.* narrow-mindedness, narrowness (of pers., views, etc.); narrowness of mind.

enharmonisch [ˌɛnharˈmoːniʃ], *a. Mus:* enharmonic (note, modulation, etc.); **enharmonische Verwechslung-** enharmonic change.

Enjambement [ã·ʒã·bəˈmãː], *n.* -s/-s. *Pros:* enjambement, overflow.

Enkaustik [ɛŋˈkaustik, ɛnˈkaustik], *f.* -/. *Art:* encaustic.

enkaustisch [ɛŋˈkaustiʃ, ɛnˈkaustiʃ], *a. Art:* encaustic (icon, tile, etc.).

Enkel[1], *m.* -s/-, grandson; (male) grandchild; **Enkel** *pl,* (i) grandsons; (ii) (*male and female*) grandchildren; **unsere Enkel,** our grandchildren; our descendants, posterity.

Enkel[2], *m.* -s/-. *Anat:* ankle.

Enkelin, *f.* -/-innen, grand-daughter.

Enkelkind, *n.* grandchild.
Enkelsohn, *m.* grandson.
Enkeltafel, *f.* table of descendants.
Enkeltochter, *f.* grand-daughter.
Enklave [ɛŋ-, ɛn'klaːvə], *f.* -/-n. *Pol:* enclave.
Enklise, Enklisis [ɛŋ'kliːzə, -zis, ɛn'kliːzə, -zis], *f.* -/-klisen. *Ling:* enclisis.
Enklitikon [ɛŋ'kliːti·kon], *n.* -s/-ka & -ken. *Gram:* enclitic.
enklitisch [ɛŋ'kliːtiʃ], *a. Gram:* enclitic.
Enkomiast [ɛŋko·mi'ast], *m.* -en/-en, encomiast.
Enkomion [ɛŋ'koːmion], **Enkomium** [ɛŋ'koːmium], *n.* -s/-mien & -mia, encomium.
Enkrinit [ɛŋkri·'niːt], *m.* -en/-en. *Geol:* encrinite.
en miniature [ã·mi·nia·'tyːr]. *Fr.phr.* in miniature; on a small scale.
Enoch ['eːnox]. *Pr.n.m.* -s. Enoch.
Enophthalmus [e·nof'talmus], *m.* -/. *Med:* enophthalmus.
enorm [e·'norm], *a.* enormous; huge, vast, immense; *F:* tremendous; **er hatte einen enormen Erfolg,** he had a tremendous success; *adv.* **e. viel,** a vast amount (of); *F:* a tremendous lot (of); **e. große Füße,** enormous, *F:* enormous great, feet; **ein e. großes Haus,** an enormous house, a house of enormous, stupendous, size; *F:* **ich habe mich e. amüsiert,** I enjoyed myself hugely, tremendously; I had a great time.
en personne [ã·pɛr'son]. *Fr.phr.* in person.
en profil [ã·pro·'fiːl]. *Fr.phr.* in profile; **en p. dargestellt,** shown in profile, shown side-face.
Enquete [ã·'kɛːt(ə)], *f.* -/-n [-tən], (official) investigation, inquiry.
enragiert [ã·ra·'ʒiːrt], *a.* (*of pers.*) enraged, worked up, *F:* in a state.
Ensemble [ã·'sãːbəl], *n.* -s/-s. **1.** *Cost: Mus: etc:* ensemble. **2.** *Mus: etc:* ensemble; *Th: etc:* company; troupe.
Ensete [ɛn'zeːtə], *f.* -/-n. *Bot:* ensete, Abyssinian banana.
Ensilage [ã·si·'laːʒə], *f.* -/. *Agr:* ensilage, ensilation.
ent-, *insep. pref.* I. *forming vbs.* **1.** (*from vbs, intensifying meaning of simplex*) **enthalten,** to contain; **entblößen,** to bare; to denude. **2.** (*from vbs, denoting correspondence, reciprocity, or requital*) **entsprechen,** to correspond; to comply; **entrichten,** to pay (sum of money); **entbieten,** to offer, present, send (greetings, etc.); **entgelten,** to pay for (sth.). **3.** (*expressing deprivation or reversal of thg, state or action denoted in the simplex*) de-; dis-; un-; (*a*) (*from vbs*) **entwickeln,** to develop; **entweihen,** to desecrate, to profane; to defile; **entdecken,** to discover; **enttäuschen,** to disappoint; to disillusion; **entkleiden,** to undress; to disrobe; **enthüllen,** to uncover; to disclose, reveal; to unveil; **entfalten,** to unfold; to unfurl (roll); **entsiegeln,** to unseal; (*b*) (*from nouns*) **enthülsen,** to dehusk; **enthaaren,** to depilate; **entvölkern,** to depopulate; **entlausen,** to delouse; **entthronen,** to dethrone; **entmenschen,** to dehumanize; **entjungfern,** to deflower; **enthaupten,** to decapitate, to behead; **entblättern,** to defoliate; **entkörpern,** to disbody, to disembody; **entschleiern,** to unveil; **entnerven,** to unnerve; (*c*) (*from adjs*) **entsittlichen,** to demoralize; **entchristlichen,** to dechristianize; **entstaatlichen,** to denationalize; **entmutigen,** to discourage; to dishearten; **etwas entbittern,** to eliminate, remove, the bitter components, substances, etc., from sth. **4.** (*from vbs, denoting removal from object or subject*) (*a*) (*forming intr. vbs*) **entschwinden,** to disappear, to vanish; **entlaufen,** to run away, to escape; **j-m entkommen,** to escape from s.o.; **etwas** *dat.* **entsteigen,** to emerge from sth.; (*b*) (*forming tr. vbs*) **j-n entführen,** to abduct s.o.; **j-n, etwas, entfernen,** to remove s.o., sth.; **j-m etwas entziehen,** to deprive s.o. of sth.; **j-m etwas entlocken,** to coax sth. out of s.o.; **j-m etwas entringen,** to wrest sth. from s.o.; **j-n etwas** *gen.* **entheben,** to relieve s.o. of sth.; **sich etwas** *gen.* **enthalten,** to abstain from sth.; to refrain from sth.; (*c*) (*forming tr. vbs*) **j-n entlassen,** to dismiss s.o.; **j-n entsenden,** to send s.o. out (on a mission). **5.** (*from vbs, denoting emergence from sth.*) (*forming intr. vbs*) **etwas** *dat.* **entblühen,** to blossom forth from sth.; **etwas** *dat.* **entkeimen,** to germinate, to sprout, from sth.; **etwas** *dat.* **entstammen,** to stem from sth.; **etwas** *dat.* **entsprießen,** to sprout from sth. **6.** (*from vbs, denoting entrance into a state*) (*a*) (*forming tr. vbs*) **entfachen,** to kindle (flame, passion, etc.); **entzünden,** to kindle (fire, passion); to inflame (wound, passion); (*b*) (*forming intr. vbs*) **entbrennen,** to kindle; **entschlafen,** to fall asleep; to pass away; **entschlummern,** to fall asleep, to doze off; to pass away.

II. *forming adjs, adverbs & preps,* **entzwei,** in two; **entgegen,** against; **entlang,** along.

III. *forming vbl nouns and vbl adjs* (*corresponding to all meanings of the vbs from which they are formed*) **Entzücken** *n,* delight; **Entgegnung** *f,* reply; **Entzug** *m,* deprivation; **entzündlich,** inflammable; **entsetzlich,** terrible.

entaktivieren [ɛntˀakti·'viːrən], *v.tr. Ch: etc:* to make, render, (sth.) inactive, to deactivate, inactivate (serum, etc.).
entarten, *v.i.* (*sein*) to degenerate; **entartet,** degenerate; **Entartung** *f,* degeneration; degeneracy.
Entase [ɛn'taːzə], *f.*, **Entasis** ['ɛnta·zis], *f.* -/-tasen [-'taːzən]. *Arch:* entasis.
entäußern, *v.tr.* **1.** *A:* to give (sth.) up; to alienate (sth.); **Entäußerung** *f,* giving up; alienation (of property, etc.). **2. sich etwas** *gen.* **entäußern,** to give sth. up; to relinquish sth.; to renounce, forgo, sth.; to divest oneself of sth.; **sich seiner Rechte e.,** to forgo, renounce, one's rights; **er entäußerte sich all seines Besitzes,** he gave up, relinquished, all his possessions.
entbasten, *v.tr. Tex:* to degum (ramie, etc.); *Ser:* to remove the gum from, to degum (raw silk); to boil off (silk); **Entbasten** *n,* **Entbastung** *f,* degumming; stripping.
entbehren. I. *v.* **1.** *v.tr.* (*A: v.tr. & v.i.* (*haben*) +*gen.*) to do without (sth., s.o.), to dispense with (sth., s.o.); to spare (sth., s.o.); to go without (sth.); *abs.* to live in want, to live in privation; **wenn du das Buch e. kannst, leih es mir bitte,** if you can spare this book, do lend it to me; **ich kann ihn heute nicht e.,** I can't spare him today; **ich habe mich so an mein Radio gewöhnt, ich könnte es nicht mehr e.,** I have got so used to my radio that I couldn't do without it any more; **sie hat in ihrer Kindheit so viel e. müssen, daß . . . ,** she had to go without so many things when she was a child that . . .; **er entbehrt nichts,** he goes short of nothing, he lacks nothing; he denies himself nothing; **ich kann es, ihn, e.,** I can spare it; I can manage without it, him; *Iron:* I can do without it, him. **2.** *v.i.* (*haben*) (+*gen.*) to lack, to be lacking (sth.); to be without (sth.); **dieses Gerücht entbehrt jeglicher Grundlage,** this rumour is without any foundation, has no foundation whatsoever; **die Situation entbehrte nicht einer gewissen Komik,** the situation was not completely lacking in, did not completely lack, was not without, comedy, the situation had its comical side; **ihr Verhalten entbehrt jeder Würde,** her conduct completely lacks, is completely lacking in, dignity, is without dignity. **3.** *v.tr.* to miss (s.o., sth.); **das Kind entbehrt seine Mutter,** the child misses his mother; **ich entbehre ihn sehr,** I miss him terribly; **er entbehrte sein tägliches Glas Bier mit seinen Freunden,** he missed his daily glass of beer with his friends.

II. *vbl s.* **1. Entbehren,** *n.* = II. 2 (*a*). **2. Entbehrung,** *f.* (*a*) (living in) want, (living in) privation; **Hunger und E. hatten ihn vorzeitig altern lassen,** hunger and privation had aged him prematurely; (*b*) privation; **die Entbehrungen des Krieges,** the privations of wartime; **sich** *dat.* **Entbehrungen auferlegen,** to impose privations upon oneself; to deny oneself; **er war seit früher Kindheit an Entbehrungen gewöhnt,** from early childhood he was accustomed to go without.

entbehrlich, *a.* dispensable; superfluous; (pers.) who can be dispensed with, who can be spared; (thg) that can be spared, that can be dispensed with, that one can do without; **sie hat alle entbehrlichen Kleidungsstücke weggegeben,** she has given away all the clothes she can spare.
Entbehrlichkeit, *f.* dispensability; superfluousness.
entbeinen, *v.tr.* to bone (meat).
entbieten, *v.tr.* (*conj. like* **bieten**) **1. j-m etwas e.,** (*a*) *A:* to inform, apprise, advise, s.o. of sth.; to make sth. known to s.o., to bring sth. to s.o.'s knowledge; to notify s.o. of sth.; (*b*) to present, offer, send, (greetings) to s.o. **2. j-n zu sich e.,** to summon s.o. (to attend); to send for s.o. **3.** *A:* **sich entbieten,** to offer oneself (as sth.).
entbinden. I. *v.tr.* (*strong*) **1.** (*a*) to untie, unbind (sth.); *Lit:* **j-n von seinen Ketten e.,** to free s.o. from his chains; (*b*) *Ch: Ph:* to release, liberate, set free (gas, heat, etc.); *Lit:* to release, to set free, to free (the spirit, etc.). **2. j-n etwas** *gen.*, **von etwas, e.,** (*a*) to absolve s.o. (from sin); (*b*) to release, absolve, s.o. (from a pledge, a vow, an obligation, etc.); to relieve s.o. of, to let s.o. off (duty, a task); **j-n seines Eides, von seinem Eide, e.,** to release s.o. from his oath. **3.** *Obst:* (*of doctor, etc.*) to deliver (a woman); (*of woman*) **entbunden werden,** to be confined; to be delivered, *A:* brought to bed (**von,** of); **von einem Knaben entbunden werden,** to give birth to a boy; **sie ist soeben entbunden worden,** her confinement is just over, the baby has just arrived.

II. *vbl s.* **1. Entbinden,** *n. in vbl senses.* **2. Entbindung,** *f.* (*a*) = II. 1; *also:* release; *Ch: Ph:* liberation (of gas, heat, etc.); *Obst:* delivery (of woman); (*b*) *Obst:* confinement; childbirth; **eine schwierige E.,** a difficult confinement, a difficult birth; **glückliche E.,** successful confinement; **sie steht unmittelbar vor der E.,** her confinement is expected daily; **sie starb bei der E.,** she died in childbirth; (*of doctor, midwife*) **die E. vornehmen,** to deliver the child.

Entbindungsanstalt, *f.* maternity hospital, maternity clinic; *Adm:* maternity centre.
entblättern, *v.tr.* to defoliate (plant); to strip (flower) of its petals; **sich e.,** (*of plant, tree*) to shed its leaves; (*of flower*) to drop its petals; *Hum:* (*of pers.*) to take one's clothes off; to strip; *F:* to shed one's clothes; **Entblätterung** *f,* defoliation.
entblocken, *v.tr. Rail:* to clear (the block section).
entblöden (sich), *v.refl.* **sich nicht e.,** *A:* **sich e., zu . . . ,** to have the audacity, *F:* the cheek, to . . .; **er entblödete sich nicht, mir zu schreiben,** he had the cheek to write to me.
entblößen. I. *v.tr.* **1.** to bare, uncover (part of body); *Lit:* to bare (one's soul, etc.); **seinen Körper e.,** to take off one's clothes, to strip; **sein Haupt e.,** to remove one's hat, to bare one's head; to uncover one's head, *abs.* to uncover; **sein Schwert e.,** to bare one's sword. **2. j-n, etwas, etwas** *gen.*, **von etwas, e.,** to strip s.o., sth., of sth.; to deprive s.o. of sth.; to denude sth. of sth.; **der Adel, aller Macht, von aller Macht, entblößt, . . . ,** the nobility, stripped of all its authority, . . .; **aller Mittel entblößt,** stripped of all means; **eine Festung, ein Land, usw., von Truppen e.,** to withdraw the troops from a fortress, from a country, etc.; to strip a fort, a country, etc., of troops; *Mil:* **die Flanke e.,** to expose one's flank. **3. sich entblößen,** (*a*) (i) to take one's clothes off, to strip; (ii) to remove one's hat, to bare, uncover, one's head, *abs.* to uncover; (*b*) *Lit:* to lay oneself bare, to bare one's soul, one's thoughts; (*c*) to strip oneself bare; **sich etwas** *gen.*, **von etwas, e.,** to strip oneself of (money, etc.); to deprive oneself of sth.; (*of country, etc.*) **sich von Truppen e.,** to strip itself of all its troops; **wir dürfen nicht alles verschenken, wir können uns doch nicht ganz e.,** we must not give away everything—after all, we can't strip ourselves bare.

II. *vbl s.* **Entblößen** *n.*, **Entblößung** *f. in vbl senses; also:* **Entblößung einer Festung, eines Landes, usw., von Truppen,** withdrawal of the troops from a fort, a country, etc.; stripping of a fort, a country, etc., of troops.

entbrennen, *v.i.* (*sein*) (*conj. like* **brennen,** *occ. p.t.* **entbrennte,** *p.p.* **entbronnen**) **1.** *A. & Poet:* (*of flame, etc.*) to kindle, to be kindled; to begin to burn; **entbrannt sein,** to be burning. **2.** (*a*) (*of fight, quarrel, argument, etc.*) to break out; (*of anger, fury, etc.*) to be excited, aroused (**gegen j-n, etwas,** against s.o., sth.); to kindle; (*of passion, love, desire, zeal, hatred, etc.*) to be aroused, excited; to kindle; **der Kampf entbrannte von neuem,** fighting broke out again; the fight flared up again; **eine heftige Liebe zu ihr entbrannte in ihm, in seinem Herzen,** his heart was inflamed with passion for her, he was seized with an ardent passion for her; (*b*) (*of pers.*) **von, in, Leidenschaft, Haß, Zorn, Wut, usw., e.,** to be seized with passion, hatred, anger, fury, etc.; **von, in, Leidenschaft, Haß, Zorn, Wut, usw., entbrannt sein,** to burn, to be burning, with passion, hatred, anger, fury, etc.; **in Liebe zu j-m e.,** to fall in love with s.o.; to be seized with a passion for s.o.; **in Liebe zu ihr entbrannt,** inflamed with love for her; *A. & Lit:* **gegen j-n e.,** to be seized with anger against s.o.; (**über j-n, etwas**) **e.,** to yearn for s.o., sth., to be filled with desire for s.o., sth.; *B:* **mein Herz ist entbrannt in meinem Leibe,** my heart was hot within me.
Entchen, *n.* -s/-, (*dim. of* **Ente**) duckling; *Her:* duck.
entchristlichen, *v.tr.* to dechristianize (s.o., society, etc.).
entdeckbar, *a.* discoverable; (*of error, etc.*) detectable; (*of distant object*) discernible.
entdecken. I. *v.tr.* **1.** (*a*) to discover, find out

(plot, crime, the truth, etc.); to expose (plot); to detect (error); to bring (crime, etc.) to light; **ich entdeckte zu spät, daß . . .**, I discovered too late that . . .; **ich habe mehrere Fehler entdeckt,** I have detected several mistakes; **das Verbrechen wurde erst nach Monaten entdeckt,** the crime was only discovered, only came to light, months later; **einige merkwürdige Tatsachen sind entdeckt worden,** some curious facts have been discovered, have come to light; (*b*) to discover (sth. hitherto unknown); to be the first to find (sth.); **ein neues Gas, die Ursache einer Krankheit, eine Insel, e.,** to discover a new gas, the cause of a disease, an island; **er entdeckte in dem verstaubten Laden des Althändlers ein wertvolles Manuskript,** in the dusty junk-shop he discovered a valuable manuscript, brought a valuable manuscript to light, unearthed a valuable manuscript; *F:* **wir haben einen guten Chauffeur entdeckt,** we have found, *F:* discovered, a good chauffeur; (*c*) *Th: Cin: etc:* to discover (s.o.); **die Schauspielerin X wurde entdeckt, als . . .**, the actress X was discovered when . . . . 2. to discern, descry (sth., s.o.); to make out (sth., s.o.); *F:* to spot (sth., s.o.); **ich konnte ihn in der Menge nirgendwo e.,** I couldn't spot him anywhere in the crowd; **sie entdeckten am Horizont ein Licht,** they saw, made out, discerned, a light on the horizon; **in der Ferne entdeckten sie ein Schiff,** they descried, discerned, a ship in the distance. 3. *Lit:* **j-m etwas e.,** to disclose sth. to s.o., to make sth. known to s.o.; to reveal sth. to s.o.; **j-m ein Geheimnis e.,** to tell s.o. a secret, *A. & Lit:* to discover a secret to s.o.; **j-m sein Herz e.,** to open, to lay bare, one's heart to s.o. 4. *Lit:* **sich entdecken,** (*a*) (*of idea, scientific fact, etc.*) to reveal itself; to become known; (*b*) (*of pers.*) **sich j-m e.,** (i) to confide in s.o.; to confide one's intentions to s.o.; to open one's heart to s.o.; (ii) to disclose one's identity to s.o., *A. & Lit:* to discover oneself to s.o.

II. *vbl s.* 1. **Entdecken,** *n. in vbl senses;* **die Freude des Entdeckens,** the joy of discovering something, the joy of discovery. 2. **Entdeckung,** *f.* (*a*) *in vbl senses; also:* discovery (of plot, crime, the truth, etc.); exposure (of plot, etc.); detection (of error); *Lit:* disclosure, revelation, *A. & Lit:* discovery (of secret, etc.); (*b*) **der E. entgehen,** (*of criminal, etc.*) to escape detection; (*of error*) to escape detection, to escape notice; **sich der E. entziehen,** (*of criminal, etc.*) to avoid discovery, detection, to avoid being found (out); (*of error*) to fail to be discovered, to go undetected, unnoticed; **die Furcht vor der E.,** the fear of detection, discovery, the fear of being found (out); (*c*) discovery (of sth. hitherto unknown); **die E. Australiens,** the discovery of Australia; (*d*) discovery; **eine E. machen,** to make a discovery; **die Entdeckungen der letzten Jahre,** the discoveries of the last few years; (*of actor, etc.*) **eine große E. sein,** to be a big discovery; **(in einem Gebiet, einer Stadt, einem Haus, usw.) auf Entdeckungen ausgehen, ausziehen,** to explore, to go and explore (a district, a town, a house, etc.); *abs.* to go exploring.

Entdecker, *m.* **-s/-.** 1. discoverer (of America, of a new gas, etc.); explorer; **die großen Entdecker auf dem Gebiete der Atomforschung,** the great discoverers in the field of atomic research; **Nansen, einer der großen Entdecker,** Nansen, one of the great explorers. 2. detector (of error, etc.); person who discovers, finds out (crime, plot, etc.); *A:* discoverer (of plot, etc.).

Entdeckerfreude, *f.* joy of discovery.

Entdeckung, *f. see* **entdecken II.**

Entdeckungseifer, *m.* zest for discovery; zest for exploration.

Entdeckungsfahrt, *f.* = **Entdeckungsreise.**

Entdeckungsreise, *f.* (*a*) voyage of discovery; voyage of exploration; expedition, journey of exploration; (*b*) *F:* exploration; **auf Entdeckungsreisen ausgehen,** to go exploring; to explore, to go to explore **(in einer Stadt, usw.,** (in) a town, etc.).

Entdeckungsreisende, *m., f.* (*decl. as adj.*) explorer.

entdunkeln, *v.tr.* to remove the black-out in (room, etc.).

Ente, *f.* **-/-n.** 1. *Orn:* duck; **Türkische E.,** Muscovy duck, Barbary duck, musk-duck; *Cu:* **gebratene E.,** roast duck; *F:* **gehen, watscheln, wie eine E.,** to waddle like a duck; **schwimmen wie eine bleierne E.,** to swim badly, *F:* to swim like a stone; **tanzen wie eine bleierne E.,** to dance like a sack of potatoes; **aussehen wie eine E. wenn's donnert,** to look like a dying duck in a thunderstorm; *Navy: F:* (*of submarine*) **eine E. machen,** to crash-dive. 2. *F:* (*pers., ship, etc.*) **eine lahme E.,** a lame duck. 3. (*drink*) **kalte E.,** (a kind of) white wine cup. 4. *F:* false report, hoax, *F:* canard. 5. *Med: F:* (bed) urinal. 6. *Av:* = **Entenflugzeug.**

entehren. I. *v.tr.* (*a*) (*of pers.*) to bring dishonour disgrace, upon (s.o., one's family, etc.); (*of action, etc.*) to degrade (s.o.); (*of pers., action*) to destroy (s.o.'s, one's family's) honour; **er hat den Namen seines Vaters entehrt,** he brought dishonour upon his father's name; **er ist entehrt,** he stands dishonoured; **er hat sein Mönchsgewand entehrt,** he has disgraced his cowl; **die Art, wie sie es tat, hat sie in meinen Augen entehrt,** the way she did it debased, degraded, her in my eyes; **sich entehrt fühlen,** to feel degraded; **eine entehrende Strafe,** (i) a degrading punishment; (ii) a punishment entailing the loss of civic rights; **eine entehrende Handlung,** a dishonourable action; **ein entehrendes Ansinnen,** a degrading suggestion; **ein entehrender Vertrag,** a dishonourable, degrading, treaty; (*b*) *Lit:* **eine Frau, eine Jungfrau, e.,** to violate, ravish, dishonour, *A:* defile, a woman, a virgin; to deflower a virgin; **das Bett e.,** to defile the marriage bed.

II. *vbl s.* 1. **Entehren,** *n. in vbl senses.* 2. **Entehrung,** *f.* (*a*) = II. 1; *also:* (i) deprivation of civic rights; (ii) violation, defloration (of girl); (*b*) **er litt unter der E. seines Namens,** he suffered greatly from the dishonour brought upon his name; **die E., die mit dieser Strafe verbunden ist,** the degradation that this punishment brings with it; (*c*) dishonour; disgrace; degradation; **er hat Schmähungen und Entehrungen auf sich nehmen müssen,** he had to put up with insults and degradation.

enteignen, *v.tr.* 1. *A:* **j-n, sich, etwas** *gen.* **e.,** to deprive s.o., oneself, of sth.; to rob s.o., oneself, of sth.; to divest s.o., oneself, of sth.; to dispossess s.o. of sth., to expropriate s.o. from sth. 2. *Jur:* to expropriate (owner, property); to dispossess (owner) of property; to requisition (movable goods); **enteigneter Bergbaubetrieb, Grundbesitz,** expropriated mine, estate; **enteignete Gesellschaft, enteignete Bauern,** dispossessed company, farmers; **der Enteignende,** the expropriating authority, the expropriator; the dispossessor; **Enteignung** *f,* expropriation (of owner, property); dispossession (of owner).

Enteignungsentschädigung, *f. Jur:* compensation for expropriated property.

Enteignungsrecht, *n. Jur:* right to expropriate owner *or* property.

Enteignungsverfahren, *n. Jur:* expropriation proceedings.

enteilen, *v.i.* (*sein*) *Lit:* to flee; to hurry, haste, away, *Lit:* to depart in haste; (*of time*) to fly, to speed away; to fly by; **j-m e.,** to flee from s.o.; to hurry, haste, away from s.o.; to escape from s.o.; (*of s.o.'s time*) to speed away, to fly by.

enteisen, *v.tr.* to defrost (refrigerator); *Av: Rail: etc:* to de-ice (wings, track, etc.).

enteisenen, *v.tr.* to deferrize (drinking water, etc.); **Enteisenung** *f,* deferrization.

Enteiser, *m.* **-s/-.** *Av: Rail: etc:* de-icer.

Enteisungsanlage, *f. Av: Rail: etc:* de-icing apparatus, de-icing equipment.

Enteisungsgerät, *n. Av: Rail: etc:* de-icer; de-icing apparatus, de-icing equipment.

entelechial [ɛnteˑleçiˈaːl], *a. Phil:* (principle, etc.) of entelechy.

Entelechie [ɛnteˑlɛˈçiː], *f.* **-/-n** [-ˈçiːən]. *Phil:* entelechy.

entenähnlich, *a.* duck-like, like a duck.

Entenbeere, *f. Swiss Dial: Bot:* raspberry.

entenbeinig, *a.* with legs like a duck, duck-legged.

Entenbeize, *f.* duck-shooting.

Entenbraten, *m. Cu:* roast duck.

Entencholera, *f. Vet:* duck cholera.

Entendunst, *m. Ven:* duck-shot.

Entenei, *n.* duck egg, duck's egg.

Entenfall, *m. Ven:* place where wild ducks regularly come in to water at dawn or dusk.

Entenfang, *m.* 1. catching of ducks. 2. *Ven:* decoy(-pond).

Entenfett, *n. Cu:* duck grease, duck fat.

Entenflinte, *f. Sm.a:* duck-gun.

Entenfloß, *n.* **-es/., Entenflott,** *n.* **-(e)s/.** *Bot:* duckweed, water lentil.

Entenflugzeug, *n. Av:* canard; tail-first machine.

Entenfuß, *m.* 1. duck's foot. 2. *Bot:* podophyllum; **schildblättriger E.,** mandrake, may-apple.

Entengras, *n. Bot:* float-grass, manna-grass.

Entengries, *n.,* **Entengrün,** *n.,* **Entengrütze,** *f. Bot:* duckweed, water lentil.

Entenjagd, *f.* duck-shooting; **auf die E. gehen,** to go duck-shooting.

Entenklaffmuschel, *f. Moll:* lantern shell.

Entenlinse, *f. Bot:* duckweed, water lentil.

Entenmuschel, *f.* 1. *Crust:* (goose-)barnacle, lepas. 2. *Moll:* pond mussel.

Entenpfuhl, *m.,* **Entenpfütze,** *f.* duck-pond.

Entenschmalz, *n. Cu:* duck grease, duck fat.

Entenschnabel, *m.* 1. duck's bill. 2. *Moll:* wedge shell. 3. *A.Cost:* (*shoe*) duck-bill.

Entenschnabelweizen, *m. Agr:* duck-bill (wheat).

Entenschrot, *m. & n.* duck-shot.

Entensturmvogel, *m. Orn:* prion, whale-bird.

Entente [ãˑˈtãːt(ə)], *f.* **-/-n** [-tən], entente; *esp. Dipl:* entente cordiale; **die Kleine E.,** the Little Entente.

Ententeich, *m.* duck-pond.

Ententeichmuschel, *f. Moll:* pond mussel.

Entenwal, *m. Z:* hyperoödon, bottle-nosed whale, bottle-nose, beaked whale.

Enter, *m.* **-s/-.** *North G.Dial:* yearling colt.

Enterbeil, *n. A. Nau:* grappling iron.

enterben. I. *v.tr.* to disinherit (s.o.), to cut (s.o.) out of one's will, *Jur:* to exheredate (s.o.); **die Enterbten,** (i) those who have been disinherited, the disinherited ones; (ii) *Lit:* the outcasts of fortune; the underprivileged classes.

II. *vbl s.* 1. **Enterben,** *n. in vbl senses.* 2. **Enterbung,** *f. in vbl senses; also:* disinheritance, *Jur:* exheredation.

Enterbrücke, *f. A.Nau:* boarding bridge.

Enterdragge, *f.,* **Enterdregg,** *m.* **-s/-en** = **Enterhaken.**

Enterhaken, *m. Nau:* grappling iron, grapnel.

Enterich, *m.* **-s/-e.** *Orn:* drake.

enterisch [ɛnˈteːriʃ], *a. Med:* enteric.

Enteritis [ɛnteˑˈriːtis], *f.* **-/.** *Med:* enteritis.

Entermesser, *n. Nau: A:* cutlass.

entern. 1. *v.tr. Nau:* to board, to grapple (ship) (in battle). 2. *v.i.* (*haben, sein*) (*a*) *Nau:* to climb up the rigging, the shrouds; (*b*) *Gym:* to climb, swarm up, a rope.

Entero- [ˌɛnteˑroˑ-], *comb.fm. Med:* entero-; **Enteroanastomose** [ˌɛnteˑroˑˀanastoˑˈmoːzə] *f,* enteroanastomosis; **Enterocele** [ˌɛnteˑroˑˈtseːlə] *f,* enterocele; **Enterokinase** [ˌɛnteˑroˑkiˑˈnaːzə] *f,* enterokinase; **Enteroklyse** [ˌɛnteˑroˑˈklyːzə] *f,* enteroclysis.

Enterocolitis [ˌɛnteˑroˑkoˑˈliːtis], *f.* **-/.** *Med:* enterocolitis.

Enterolith [ɛnteˑroˑˈliːt], *m.* **-en/-en.** *Med:* enterolith.

Enterologie [ˌɛnteˑroˑloˑˈgiː], *f.* **-/.** enterology.

Enteropneusten [ˌɛnteˑroˑˈpnoystən], *pl.* = **Eichelwürmer.**

Enteroptose, Enteroptosis [ɛnteˑropˈtoːzə, -ˈtoːzis], *f.* **-/-tosen.** *Med:* enteroptosis, visceroptosis.

Enterorrhagie [ˌɛnteˑroˑraˑˈgiː], *f.* **-/-n** [-/-ˈgiːən]. *Med:* enterorrhagia.

Enterotomie [ˌɛnteˑroˑtoˑˈmiː], *f.* **-/-n** [-/-ˈmiːən]. *Surg:* enterotomy.

entfachen, *v.tr.* to kindle (fire, passions); to fan (fire, discontent, hatred, etc.); to inflame, excite, rouse (passions); to stir up, foment (hatred, discord, etc.); **eine Leidenschaft zu heller Glut e.,** to fan a passion into flame.

entfahren, *v.i.* (*strong*) (*sein*) **j-m e.,** (*of remark, etc.*) to escape s.o., s.o.'s lips, to slip out; (*of cry, etc.*) to escape s.o., s.o.'s lips; **sie hat das nicht ernst gemeint, es ist ihr nur so entfahren,** she didn't mean it seriously, it just slipped out; **ein Schrei entfuhr ihm, seinen Lippen,** a cry escaped him, his lips, a cry burst from his lips; **die Bemerkung ist ihm im Zorn entfahren,** he let the remark fall in the heat of anger.

Entfall, *m.* waste, loss.

entfallen, *v.i.* (*strong*) (*sein*) 1. (*a*) (*of thg*) **j-m, j-s Händen, e.,** to fall from s.o.'s hands; to slip from s.o.'s hands; **das Messer entfiel ihr, entfiel ihren Händen,** the knife fell, slipped, from her hands; (*b*) (*of word, event, etc.*) **j-m, j-s Gedächtnis, e.,** to escape s.o., to slip, escape, s.o.'s memory; **Ihr Name ist mir entfallen,** your name has slipped my memory, I cannot remember your name, I have forgotten your name; **es war mir entfallen,** it had escaped, slipped, my memory, it had gone out of my mind; (*c*) *occ.* (*of word, etc.*) **j-m e.,** to escape s.o., s.o.'s lips, to slip out; (*d*) *A. & Lit:* **der Mut entfiel ihm,** his courage left him, he lost courage. 2. *Adm:* (*of regulation, etc.*) (*a*) to be dropped; to be cancelled; (*b*) (*entry against question on official form*) **'entfällt',** 'not applicable', *abbr.* 'n.a.' 'N/A.' 3. **auf j-n e.,** (*of share, etc.*) to fall to

s.o.; to be given to s.o.; (*of money, etc.*) to fall to s.o.'s share; **Anteil, der auf die Erben von väterlicher Seite entfällt,** share that falls to the heirs on the father's side; **auf jeden Teilnehmer entfallen 10 Mark,** 10 marks fall to every participant's share, each participant receives 10 marks; **der auf jeden entfallende Anteil,** each person's share; **bei gerechter Verteilung entfallen auf dich x Mark,** with an equitable distribution you will receive, get, *x* marks, your share will be *x* marks; **bei einer Geburtenzahl von 3000 entfallen auf jede Familie 2 Kinder,** if the number of births is 3000 it will work out at, it will make, an average of 2 children per family.

entfalten. I. *v.tr.* (*p.p.* **entfaltet**) **1.** (*a*) to unfold, open out, spread out (newspaper, handkerchief, etc.); to unfurl (flag, sail, roll, scroll); to display (flag); to spread (sails, wings); *Mil:* to deploy (troops) (initially), to put (troops) into initial deployment; (*of flower*) **ihre Blätter e.,** to open; (*b*) to display, show (a quality, etc.); **er entfaltete eine angestrengte Tätigkeit,** he displayed great activity; **sie entfaltete eine vielseitige Tätigkeit,** she engaged in a wide range of activities; **er entfaltete seine ganze Beredsamkeit,** he displayed all his eloquence; **er entfaltete ungeahnten Mut,** he displayed, showed, unexpected courage; **Ludwig XIV. entfaltete eine ungeheure Pracht,** Louis XIV surrounded himself with great splendour; **seine Kräfte, Fähigkeiten, voll e.,** (i) to develop one's powers, faculties, fully; (ii) to have full scope for displaying one's powers, faculties; **sie hat ihre Persönlichkeit nie (frei) e. können,** she was never able to display her full personality. **2. sich entfalten,** (*a*) (*of sail, flag, scroll, etc.*) to unfurl; (*of flower, parachute*) to open; (*of wings*) to spread; **die Blüte entfaltete sich zu voller Schönheit,** the flower opened to full beauty; (*b*) (*of beauty, character, etc.*) to develop (**zu,** into); to unfold; **ihre Schönheit hatte sich voll entfaltet,** her beauty had come to full bloom; **man soll die Persönlichkeit des Kindes sich frei e. lassen,** the child should have full scope to develop its personality.

II. *vbl s.* **1. Entfalten,** *n. in vbl senses.* **2. Entfaltung,** *f.* (*a*) *in vbl senses; also:* display (of a quality, etc.); development (of a faculty, of beauty, etc.); *Mil:* initial deployment (of troops); (*b*) (*vbl phrases*) **seine, j-s, Kräfte, Fähigkeiten, zur E. bringen,** (i) to develop one's, s.o.'s, powers, faculties; (ii) to give one's, s.o.'s, powers, faculties, (full) scope; (*of the faculties, etc.*) **zur E. kommen,** to develop; to unfold; **seine, j-s, Kräfte, Fähigkeiten, zur E. kommen lassen,** (i) to allow one's, s.o.'s, powers, faculties, to develop; (ii) to give one's, s.o.'s, powers, faculties, scope; **ihre Schönheit war zu voller E., voll zur E., gekommen,** her beauty had come to full bloom.

entfärben. I. *v.tr.* to remove the colour *or* dye from, to take the colour *or* dye out of (sth.); to remove (old) dye from (hair), to bleach (hair); to strip (cloth); *Ch: Sug-R: Glassm:* to decolo(u)rize (crude sugar, glass, etc.), to treat (crude sugar, glass, etc.) with a decolo(u)rizing agent; **sich e.,** (*of thg*) to lose its colour *or* dye; (*of crude sugar, glass, etc.*) to become free of coloured impurities; (*of pers., face*) to grow (suddenly) pale; *Ch: etc:* **entfärbendes Mittel = Entfärbungsmittel.**

II. *vbl s.* **Entfärben** *n.,* **Entfärbung** *f. in vbl senses; also: Ch: etc:* decolo(u)rization.

Entfärber, *m.* **-s/- = Entfärbungsmittel.**

Entfärbungsmesser, *m. Ch: Sug-R:* decolorimeter.

Entfärbungsmittel, *n.* dye-remover; colour-remover; *Ch: Sug-R: Glassm:* decolo(u)rizing agent, decolo(u)rant, decolo(u)rizer.

entfasern, *v.tr. Tex:* to extract the fibre from (stem, leaf).

entfernen. I. *v.tr.* **1.** to move (sth.) to a distance, away; **etwas von etwas e.,** to move sth. away from sth.; **einen Gegenstand von einem andern weiter e.,** to move an object further away, to place an object at a greater distance, from another; **diese Diskussion hat uns von unserem Thema weit entfernt,** this discussion has led us far away from our subject. **2.** (*a*) to remove (sth.); to take (sth.) away; to take off (sth.); **Hühneraugen, lästige Haare, usw., e.,** to remove corns, superfluous hair, etc.; **Flecken e.,** to remove, take out, stains; **die Rinde e.,** to remove, strip off, peel off, the bark; to remove, take off, the rind; **ein Hindernis e.,** to remove an obstacle; to clear away an obstacle; **j-s Namen von einer Liste e.,** to remove, strike off, s.o.'s name from a list; (*b*) **einen Beamten aus dem Dienst e.,** to dismiss an official, to remove an official from his office; **einen Offizier aus dem Heer, aus der Marine, e.,** to discharge an officer with ignominy, ignominiously, to dismiss, to remove, an officer from the army, the navy; **j-n aus seinem Amt e.,** to dismiss, remove, s.o. from his office; **j-n vom Hofe e.,** to dismiss s.o. from the court; (*c*) to remove, liquidate (rival, etc.). **3. sich entfernen,** (*a*) (*of moving object*) to move away; to move off; to move (slowly) out of sight; (*of pers., moving object*) **sich von etwas e.,** to move away from sth.; **wir blickten dem Schiff nach, wie es sich langsam vom Ufer entfernte,** we watched the ship as it moved slowly away from the shore; **wir hatten uns schon weit vom Festland entfernt,** we were already far away from the mainland; **man hatte den Kindern gesagt, sie sollten sich nicht zu weit vom Haus e.,** the children had been told not to move too far away from the house; (*b*) **sich mit seinen Anschauungen von j-m, von einer Doktrin, usw., e.,** to diverge, deviate, in one's opinions from s.o., from a doctrine, etc.; **sich vom Original e.,** to depart from the original (*in copying*); **sich vom Thema e.,** to depart, deviate, wander, from the subject; **als er dieses Buch schrieb, hatte er sich schon weit von den Dogmen der Kirche entfernt,** when he wrote this book he had already departed, divagated, deviated, greatly from the dogmas of the Church; (*c*) (*of pers.*) to withdraw, to go away; to go out (of a room); **der Diener entfernte sich geräuschlos,** the servant withdrew noiselessly; **er entfernte sich, ohne ein Wort zu sagen,** he went away, he went out, without saying a word; **sich eilends e.,** to hurry away, to withdraw hastily.

II. *vbl s.* **1. Entfernen,** *n. in vbl senses.* **2. Entfernung,** *f.* (*a*) *in vbl senses; also:* (i) removal (of stains, superfluous hair, corns, etc.); (ii) dismissal (of official) (from service); *Mil: Navy:* **E. aus dem Heer, der Marine,** ignominious discharge; (*b*) deviation, divergence (from doctrine, etc.); departure (from the original, from the subject); (*c*) *Mil:* **unerlaubte E.,** absence without leave; (*d*) distance; **E. zwischen zwei Orten,** distance between two places; **eine E. abschätzen,** to judge, estimate, a distance; **in einer E. von . . .,** at a distance of . . ., . . . (away) from; **auf eine E. von x Metern an etwas herantreten,** to approach sth. to within a distance of *x* metres; **auf, für, große, kurze, Entfernungen berechnet sein,** to be calculated for, calculated to cover, long, short, distances; **aus, bei, dieser E. kann man nichts sehen,** one can see nothing from that distance; **j-m in einiger E. folgen,** to follow s.o. at a distance, at a short distance; **in London sind alle Entfernungen so groß,** in London all distances are so great; **auf kurze Entfernungen sieht er gut, aber nicht auf große,** he can see close things very well, but not distant ones; **es ist keine E.,** it is no distance (away); *see also* **einstellen** I. 3 (*a*); (*e*) *Ball:* range; **die E. messen, schätzen,** to take, estimate, the range; **auf eine E. von . . .,** at a range of . . .; **auf kurze E.,** at close range.

III. *p.p. & a.* **entfernt,** *in vbl senses; esp.* **1.** (*a*) distant; away (from); (away) from; at a distance; **drei Kilometer e.,** three kilometres away, at a distance of three kilometres; **nicht weit e. von . . .,** not far (away, distant) from . . .; at no great distance from . . .; **unsere Häuser liegen zu weit (voneinander) e.,** our houses are, lie, too far away from one another, too far apart; **das Haus liegt weit von der Straße e.,** the house lies far away, lies remote, from the road; **wie weit ist London vom Meer e.?** how far is London from the sea? how far away from the sea is London? **Wissenschaften, die weit voneinander e. sind,** sciences remote from each other; **ein Bericht, der von der Wahrheit weit e. ist,** an account that is far from the truth; **sein Gefühl war von Liebe nicht weit e.,** his feeling was not far removed from love; **weit (davon) e. sein, etwsa zu tun, zu glauben,** to be far from doing, believing, sth.; **weit davon e., ihn zu bewundern, verachtet er ihn (sogar),** far from admiring him, he loathes him; **weit davon e. nachzulassen, griff die Seuche immer mehr um sich,** far from subsiding, the epidemic spread further and further; **ich bin nicht unzufrieden, weit davon e., aber . . .,** I am not dissatisfied, far from it, but . . .; (*b*) far (away); remote; outlying (districts, etc.); **in den entferntesten Winkeln der Erde,** in the most remote, in the remotest, corners of the earth; *Gram:* **entfernteres Objekt,** indirect object, enlargement. **2.** distant (resemblance, relation, etc.); remote, vague, faint (resemblance, etc.); *adv.* distantly (related); remotely, vaguely (similar); **er ist ein entfernter Verwandter von mir, er ist e. mit mir verwandt,** he is a distant relation of mine, he is distantly related to me; **nicht im entferntesten,** not in the least; in no way; not at all; never; **er hat nicht im entferntesten daran gedacht, daß du darüber beleidigt sein könntest,** he never thought, the thought never came to him, it never entered his head, it never occurred to him, that you might feel hurt about it; **das stört mich nicht im entferntesten,** it doesn't disturb me in the least, it doesn't disturb me at all; **sie haben nicht die entfernteste Ähnlichkeit miteinander, sie sehen sich nicht im entferntesten ähnlich,** they don't look the least bit alike, at all alike, they don't resemble each other at all, in any way, they haven't the slightest, the faintest, resemblance to one another; **wenn ich auch nur e., im entferntesten, gedacht, geglaubt, hätte, ich würde ihn damit kränken,** if I had had the faintest idea I would hurt him by it.

Entfernung, *f. see* **entfernen** II.

Entfernungsfehler, *m. Artil: etc:* error in range, range error.

Entfernungslineal, *n. Surv:* stadia rod.

Entfernungsmesser, *m. Surv: etc:* telemeter; *Mil: Phot: etc:* rangefinder; **stereoskopischer E.,** stereoscopic telemeter.

Entfernungsmeßfaden, *m. Surv:* stadia line.

Entfernungsmeßmann, *m. Artil:* range-taker.

Entfernungsmessung, *f.* (*a*) measuring of distances; *Artil: etc:* range-finding; **Entfernungsmessungen vornehmen,** to measure distances; *Artil: etc:* to take ranges; (*b*) telemetry.

Entfernungsskala, *f. Phot:* focusing scale.

Entfernungsskizze, *f. Artil:* range card.

Entfernungsvorhalt, *m. Artil:* (*esp. anti-aircraft*) range correction; lead, aim-off.

entfesseln, *v.tr.* to unleash (passions, fury, etc.); to let loose (anger); to raise (a storm); **einen Sturm der Entrüstung e.,** to raise a storm of indignation; **(allgemeine) Heiterkeit e.,** to raise a storm of laughter, to set everyone laughing; **einen Krieg e.,** to unleash a war; *Lit:* to let loose the dogs of war; **die entfesselte Gewalt des Sturms,** the uncontrolled fury of the storm; **den entfesselten Elementen preisgegeben sein,** to be exposed to the fury of the elements; *Lit:* **der entfesselte Prometheus,** Prometheus unbound.

entfestigen, *v.tr.* **1.** to dismantle, demolish, the fortifications of (town, etc.). **2.** *Metall:* to soften (metal).

entfetten. I. *v.tr.* to remove the grease from (sth.); to remove the fat from (sth., s.o.); *esp.* (*a*) *Ch: Ind: etc:* to degrease (hide, hair, metal, etc.); *Tex:* to scour (wool); *Ser:* to boil off (silk); **die Milch e.,** to extract the fat from the milk; **Seife entfettet die Haut,** soap dries the skin, makes the skin dry; **stark entfettende Seife,** soap that dries the skin; (*b*) *Cu:* to skim the fat off (soup).

II. *vbl s.* **1. Entfetten,** *n. in vbl senses.* **2. Entfettung,** *f.* (*a*) = II. 1; *also:* removal of grease *or* fat from (sth.); (*b*) *Med:* reducing slimming.

Entfettungskur, *f. Med:* reducing diet *or* treatment, slimming diet *or* treatment; slimming course.

Entfettungsmittel, *n.* (*a*) *Ch: Ind: etc:* degreasing agent; (*b*) *Med:* anti-fat remedy, slimming remedy, reducing preparation.

entfeuchten, *v.tr.* to desiccate (sth.).

Entfeuchter, *m.* **-s/-,** desiccator.

entflammbar, *a.* (*a*) (*of substance*) (in)flammable; ignitable; easily set on fire; (*b*) **leicht e.,** (*of passion, etc.*) easily kindled, roused, excited; (*of pers.*) (i) inflammable; easily fired with enthusiasm; (ii) easily inflamed with passion, easily roused to passion; (pers.) who easily falls in love.

Entflammbarkeit, *f.* (in)flammability, (in)flammableness; ignitability.

entflammen. **1.** *v.tr.* (*a*) to inflame, ignite (substance); (*b*) to inflame, excite, rouse (passions); to inflame, stir up, foment (hatred, discord, etc.); to kindle (enthusiasm); (*of passion, hatred, etc.*) to rouse, excite, stir, kindle, inflame, fire (s.o.); (*of passion*) to set (s.o.) afire; (*of enthusiasm*) to fire (s.o.); **j-n zu Begeisterung e.,** to rouse s.o. to, to fire s.o. with, enthusiasm; to kindle s.o.'s enthusiasm; **j-n zu großen Taten e.,** to stir s.o. to great deeds; **sein Lied entflammte sie zu wilder Leidenschaft,** his song roused violent passion in them, fired them with violent passion; **j-n mit Leidenschaft, usw.,**

e., to inflame s.o. with passion, etc.; to rouse, inflame, stir (up), s.o.'s passion; **Begeisterung entflammte alle Herzen,** enthusiasm fired all hearts; **j-n dazu e., etwas zu tun,** to rouse s.o. to do sth. **2.** *v.i.* (*sein*) (*a*) (*of substance*) to inflame, to ignite; (*of kerosene, etc.*) to flash; (*b*) (*of passion, desire, hatred, enthusiasm, etc.*) to be (a)roused, excited, to kindle; (*of anger, fury, etc.*) to be excited, (a)roused; (*of pers.*) **von Leidenschaft, Haß, Begeisterung, usw., entflammt sein,** to burn, to be burning, to be inflamed, a-flame, with passion, hatred, etc.; to be fired with, roused to, enthusiasm; **in Liebe zu j-m e.,** to fall in love with s.o.; to be seized with a passion for s.o. **3. sich entflammen,** (*of passion, desire, hatred, etc.*) to be (a)roused, excited, to kindle; **sich an etwas** *dat.* **e.,** (*of enthusiasm, passion, feeling*) to be roused, stirred, kindled, by sth.; (*of pers.*) to kindle at, to, sth.

Entflammprüfung, *f.*, **Entflammungsprobe,** *f. Ch: etc:* flash-test.

Entflammungspunkt, *m. Ch: etc:* flash-point, flashing-point.

entflattern, *v.i.* (*sein*) (*of bird, butterfly, etc.*) to flutter away, off; to fly off; (*of bird*) to take wing; **etwas** *dat.* **e.,** to flutter, fly, out of, away from, sth.

entflechten, *v.tr.* (*strong*) (*a*) to undo (hair, wickerwork, etc.); to unplait (hair); to unbraid (hair); (*b*) to disentangle (threads, network, intricate business, etc.); (*c*) *Pol.Ec:* to break up (trusts, cartels); **Entflechtung** *f* **von Kartellen,** decartelization, *U.S: F:* trust-busting.

entfleischen, *v.tr.* **1.** *A. & Lit:* to tear the flesh from (bones, animal); **entfleischte Knochen,** bare bones; **entfleischte Glieder,** fleshless limbs. **2.** *Leath:* to flesh, scrape (hide).

Entfleischmaschine, *f. Leath:* fleshing-machine.

entfliegen, *v.i.* (*strong*) (*sein*) (*of bird, butterfly, etc.*) to fly off, away; (*of bird*) to take wing; **etwas** *dat.* **e.,** (*of bird, etc.*) to fly away from sth.; to fly out of sth.; (*of arrow*) to shoot, speed, from (the bow); **ihr Kanarienvogel ist ihr entflogen,** her canary has disappeared, flown away; (*in advertisement*) **'entflogen, blauer Wellensittich',** 'escaped, blue budgerigar'.

entfliehen, *v.i.* (*strong*) (*sein*) to flee, fly; to run away; to slip away; to escape; (*of hours, days, etc.*) to fly by; **j-m, etwas** *dat.*, **e.,** (*of pers., animal*) to escape s.o., sth.; to escape from s.o., sth.; (*of word, cry*) to escape s.o., s.o.'s lips; **aus einem Ort e.,** to escape from, out of, a place; to flee, fly, from a place; **aus dem Gefängnis e.,** to escape from, out of, prison; **zu j-m, nach Amerika, usw., e.,** to flee, fly, to s.o., to flee to America, etc.; **der Gefahr e.,** to escape (the) danger; **dem Gewitter e.,** to escape from the storm; **sein Glück war entflohen,** his luck had left him, deserted him; **man kann seinem Schicksal nicht e.,** one cannot escape one's fate; **ein entflohener Gefangener,** an escaped prisoner, an escapee; **er gedachte der entflohenen Jahre seiner Jugend,** he thought of the vanished years of his youth.

entfließen, *v.i.* (*strong*) (*sein*) **etwas** *dat.*, **aus etwas, e.,** to flow from sth.; to flow out of sth.; **Tränen entflossen ihr, ihren Augen,** tears streamed from her eyes.

entflocken, *v.tr. Ch:* to deflocculate (colloidal substance); **Entflockung** *f*, deflocculation.

entfremden. I. *v.tr.* **1.** *A:* **j-m etwas e.,** to take sth. away from s.o., to rob s.o. of sth.; **j-n etwas** *gen.* **e.,** to deprive, rob, s.o. of sth. **2. j-n j-m e.,** to alienate s.o. from s.o.; to estrange s.o. from s.o.; to turn s.o. away from s.o.; **j-n sich** *dat.* **e.,** to alienate s.o.; to estrange s.o.; **j-m entfremdet werden, sich j-m e.,** to become a stranger to s.o.; **durch diese Handlung hat er sich alle seine Verwandten entfremdet,** by this action he alienated, estranged, all his relations; **sein Verhalten hatte ihm seine Freunde entfremdet,** his conduct had estranged, alienated, him from his friends, had turned his friends away from him; **seine Heirat hatte ihn seinen Freunden entfremdet,** his marriage alienated him from his friends, lost him his friends; **durch die lange Trennung waren sie (sich) ganz entfremdet,** the long separation had made them strangers to one another, through long separation they had become strangers to one another; **der Krieg zwischen ihren beiden Ländern hatte die Freunde entfremdet, durch den Krieg zwischen ihren beiden Ländern waren (sich) die Freunde entfremdet,** the war between their two countries had estranged the friends, the friends had become estranged through the war between their two countries; **ich will mich nicht für lange Zeit von meinem Kind trennen, damit es mir nicht entfremdet wird, damit es sich mir nicht entfremdet,** I do not want to be separated from my child for a long period, for fear it may become a stranger to me.

II. *vbl s.* **Entfremdung,** *f.* alienation; estrangement; **ihre E., die E. zwischen ihnen, war durch den Krieg verursacht,** their estrangement was caused by the war; they had become alienated through the war, the war had made them strangers to one another.

entfritten, *v.tr. W.Tel:* to decohere; **Entfrittung** *f*, decoherence.

Entfritter, *m.* **-s/-.** *W.Tel:* decoherer.

entfrosten, *v.tr.* to defrost (windscreen, refrigerator, etc.).

Entfroster, *m.* **-s/-.** *Aut: etc:* defroster.

entführen. I. *v.tr.* **1.** to kidnap (s.o.); to abduct, to run away with, *Poet:* to rape (girl, woman); *Jur:* to abduct (a minor); (*of girl, woman*) **sich von j-m e. lassen,** to elope with s.o., to run away with s.o.; **er wurde ins Nachbargebiet, nach X, entführt,** he was (kidnapped and) carried off to neighbouring territory, to X. **2.** to carry (sth.) away, off (by force); *A. & Hum:* **j-m etwas e.,** to take sth. away from s.o.; to steal sth. from s.o.

II. *vbl s.* **1. Entführen,** *n. in vbl senses.* **2. Entführung,** *f. in vbl senses; also:* abduction, *Poet:* rape (of girl, woman); *Jur:* kidnapping (of s.o.); abduction (of a minor); **E. wider Willen (durch List, Drohung oder Gewalt),** abduction by fraud, menace or force; **E. mit Willen,** abduction by consent; *Th:* **die E. aus dem Serail,** *F:* **die E.,** Il Seraglio (*opera by Mozart*).

Entführer, *m. Jur:* kidnapper; abductor (of a minor).

Entführungsheirat, *f.* marriage after abduction; marriage after elopement; runaway marriage, runaway match.

entfuseln, *v.tr. Dist:* to remove fusel-oil from (spirits).

entgasen, *v.tr.* to remove gas from (sth.); to degas (*Ind:* coal, etc., *Mil:* confined space); *Mch:* to de-aerate (feed water); **Entgasung** *f*, *Ind:* degasification, degasifying, destructive distillation (of coal, etc.); *Mil: etc:* degassing; *Mch:* de-aeration (of feed water).

entgegen, *adv.* (*also with prepositional functions*) (+*dat.*), **entgegen-,** *comb.fm.* (*forming sep. verbs, vbl nouns and vbl adjs*) **1.** toward(s); to; -ward(s); **dem Süden e.,** towards the south, southwards; **den Bergen e.,** towards the mountains, mountainwards; **dem Wind e.,** into the wind, in the teeth of the wind, head on to the wind; **dem Feind e.!** at the enemy! **auf, ihm e.!** let us go to meet him, let us go towards him; **j-m, etwas** *dat.*, **entgegenziehen,** to march, go, towards s.o., sth.; to go, march, to meet s.o.; **j-m entgegenreiten,** to ride out to meet s.o.; **j-m, etwas** *dat.*, **entgegeneilen,** to hurry towards s.o., sth.; to hurry to meet s.o.; **j-n j-m entgegenschicken,** to send s.o. to meet s.o.; (*of sound*) **j-m entgegenhallen,** to come echoing over to s.o.; **j-m entgegenströmen,** (*of water*) to flow towards s.o.; (*of smell, sound*) to meet s.o.; (*of river*) **dem Meer entgegenströmen,** to flow towards the sea; **j-m entgegenjubeln,** to greet s.o. with shouts of joy; **die Lichter des Dorfes blinkten, leuchteten, dem einsamen Wanderer freundlich entgegen,** the friendly lights of the village greeted the lonely wanderer; **aus der Ferne blinkte, leuchtete, ihm ein Licht entgegen,** a distant light was winking at him; **die Öde seines Zimmers starrte ihm entgegen,** he was met by the blank dreariness of his room; **aus dem Dunkel starrten ihm zwei glühende Augen entgegen, glühten ihm zwei Augen entgegen,** two glowing eyes stared at him from the darkness; **ein strahlender Frühlingsmorgen lachte ihm entgegen,** a bright spring morning greeted him; **die Sonne lachte uns entgegen,** the sun smiled down on us; **ein kalter Wind blies ihm entgegen,** a cold wind blew in his face. **2.** against (s.o., sth.); contrary to (sth.); **seinem Willen e., e. seinem Willen,** against his wishes, contrary to his wishes; **dem Rat seiner Eltern e., e. dem Rat seiner Eltern,** against, contrary to, his parents' advice; **seinen sonstigen Gewohnheiten e., e. seinen sonstigen Gewohnheiten,** contrary to his usual habits; **allen Regeln e.,** against, contrary to, all rules; **aller Vernunft e.,** against, contrary to, all reason; **der Natur e.,** against, contrary to, nature; **e. dem Uhrzeiger, dem Sinn des Uhrzeigers,** anti-clockwise, counter-clockwise; **etwas** *dat.*, **j-m, entgegensein,** to be against sth., s.o.; to stand, be, in the way of sth., in s.o.'s way; **der Wind ist uns entgegen,** the wind is against us; **dem ist nichts entgegen,** there is nothing against it, in the way of it; **j-m entgegenreden,** to contradict s.o.; to speak up to s.o.; *see also* **dementgegen.**

entgegenarbeiten, *v.i. sep.* (*haben*) **j-m, etwas** *dat.*, **e.,** to work against s.o., sth.; **j-s Plänen e.,** to interfere with s.o.'s plans, to counter s.o.'s plans, designs; **einer Wirkung, einem Einfluß, e.,** to counteract an effect, an influence.

entgegenblicken, *v.i. sep.* (*haben*) = **entgegensehen.**

entgegenbringen, *v.tr. sep.* (*conj. like* **bringen**) (*a*) **j-m etwas e.,** to bring sth. to s.o.; to carry sth. to s.o.; (*b*) **j-m, etwas** *dat.*, **etwas e.,** to show, have (sympathy, goodwill, understanding, etc.) towards s.o., for (s.o.'s problems, work, etc.); to approach s.o., sth., with (sympathy, understanding, etc.); to have an (understanding, etc.) approach towards s.o., sth.; **seiner Arbeit Interesse e.,** to show interest in one's work; **j-m Vertrauen e.,** to show trust in s.o.

entgegenführen, *v.tr. sep.* (*a*) **j-n j-m e.,** to lead s.o. towards, up to, s.o.; **j-n glücklichen Zeiten, dem Verderben, usw., e.,** to lead s.o. on to happy times, to disaster, etc.; **er hofft, sein Volk einer glücklicheren Zukunft entgegenzuführen,** he hopes to lead his country to a happier future; (*b*) **eine Arbeit der Vollendung e.,** to carry a work to its completion.

entgegengehen, *v.i. sep.* (*strong*) (*sein*) (*a*) **j-m e.,** to go to meet s.o.; to go towards s.o.; **sie ging ihm ein Stück Weges entgegen,** she went part of the way to meet him; **sie gingen der sinkenden Sonne entgegen,** they walked towards, into, the setting sun; (*b*) **etwas** *dat.* **e.,** to be heading for (happy times, disaster, etc.); **wir gehen glücklichen Zeiten, einer glücklichen, ungewissen, Zukunft, entgegen,** happy times are, a happy, an uncertain, future is, lying ahead of us, we are heading for happy times, for a happy, an uncertain, future; **sie wußten, daß sie dem sicheren Tod entgegengingen,** they knew they were going to certain death, that certain death awaited them; **der Alte ging seinem Ende entgegen,** the old man was nearing his end.

entgegengesetzt, *a.* contrary (interest, direction, etc.); opposite (direction, etc.); opposed (interest, opinion, etc.); **in entgegengesetzter Richtung,** in the opposite direction; **in die entgegengesetzte Richtung gehen,** to go off in the opposite direction, the opposite way; **diametral e.,** diametrically opposed; **e. dem Sinn des Uhrzeigers,** anti-clockwise, counter-clockwise; **im entgegengesetzten Sinn,** (i) in the opposite, contrary, inverse, direction; (ii) in the opposite sense, meaning; **er hat Anschauungen, die den meinen ganz e. sind,** his opinions are quite contrary, opposed, to my own; **er tut immer das Entgegengesetzte von dem, was man ihm sagt,** he always does the opposite to what he is told; *Mth:* **entgegengesetztes Element eines Gruppenelementes,** inverse (element) of a group element; *adv.* **die Krankheit hat sich e. entwickelt, als der Arzt erwartet hatte,** the illness developed contrary to the doctor's expectation; *see also* **entgegensetzen.**

entgegenhalten, *v.tr. sep.* (*strong*) **1. j-m etwas e.,** to hold sth. out to s.o.; to stretch out (one's hand, etc.) to, towards, s.o. **2. etwas** *dat.* **etwas e.,** to reply sth. to sth.; to say sth. in answer, in reply, to sth.; **j-m etwas e.,** to point sth. out to s.o. (in reply to sth.); **seiner Behauptung konnte ich e., daß . . . ,** I could answer his statement by saying that . . . , by pointing out that . . . ; **dem ist nichts entgegenzuhalten,** there is nothing to be said in reply to this; **wenn er mich darum bitten sollte, kann ich ihm immer e., daß er mir noch nie einen Gefallen getan hat,** should he ask me for it I can always reply, point out to him, that he has never done anything to please me.

entgegenhandeln, *v.i. sep.* (*haben*) = **zuwiderhandeln.**

entgegenkommen. I. *v.i. sep.* (*strong*) (*sein*) **1. j-m e.,** (*of pers.*) to come to meet s.o.; (*of pers., car, etc.*) to approach s.o. (from the opposite direction); to come from the opposite direction; (*of sound, etc.*) to meet s.o., s.o.'s ear; **die Kinder kamen ihm ans Gartentor entgegen,** the children met, welcomed, greeted, him at the garden gate; **er kam mir ein Stück (Weges) entgegen,** he came part of the way to meet me; **schon an der Tür kam uns der Geruch von Kohl entgegen,** at the very door we were met by a smell of cabbage; **das Wasser kam uns auf der Treppe entgegen,** we were met by the water pouring down the stairs; **als ich die Tür öffnete, kam mir ein seltsames Geräusch entgegen,** as I opened the door a strange noise met my ear, I was met by a strange noise. **2. j-m, j-s Wünschen, e.,** to meet s.o.; to oblige s.o.; to

make s.o. concessions; **j-m auf halbem Wege e.,** to meet s.o. half-way; **ich werde mein Bestes tun, Ihnen entgegenzukommen,** I will do my best to meet you, to oblige you; **er hat es getan, um uns entgegenzukommen,** he did it to oblige us; **mehr kann ich Ihnen wirklich nicht e.,** I really cannot make you any further concessions; **ich würde Ihnen gerne in dieser Sache e.,** I should like to oblige you in this matter; **wir müssen uns bemühen, jedem Geschmack entgegenzukommen,** we must try to cater for every taste; *Com.Corr:* **stets bereit, Ihren Wünschen entgegenzukommen, . . . ,** always willing to oblige you, to meet your wishes, ...

II. *vbl s.* **Entgegenkommen,** *n.* obligingness; complaisance; willingness to please; accommodating attitude; **E. zeigen,** to be accommodating, obliging, willing to oblige; **er hat uns immer großes E. gezeigt,** he was always very accommodating towards us, he was always willing to make us concessions, willing to meet us, to oblige us; **wir danken Ihnen für Ihr freundliches E.,** thank you for your kindness; **dank des Entgegenkommens der Herren X . . . ,** thanks to the obligingness of Messrs X . . .

III. *pr.p. & a.* **entgegenkommend,** *in vbl senses; esp.* **1.** (pers., vehicle, etc.) coming, approaching, from the opposite direction; oncoming (traffic, vehicle). **2.** accommodating, obliging, willing to oblige; willing to please; complaisant; **stets e. sein, sich stets e. zeigen,** to be always willing to oblige, to be always obliging; **ein entgegenkommender Mann,** an obliging, accommodating, man; **Herr X hat uns in entgegenkommender Weise sein Haus zur Verfügung gestellt,** Mr X obligingly put his house at our disposal; *adv.* **sich e. verhalten,** to be, to show oneself, obliging, complaisant, accommodating.

entgegenlaufen, *v.i. sep. (strong) (sein)* **1. j-m e.,** to run towards s.o.; to run to meet s.o.; (*of water*) to come running, rushing, towards s.o.; **die Kinder liefen ihm ein Stück entgegen,** the children ran a little way to meet him; **das Wasser lief uns auf der Treppe entgegen,** we were met by the water rushing down the stairs. **2.** (*of action, etc.*) **etwas** *dat.* **e.,** to go against, run counter to (interests, conventions, orders, etc.); **eine Tendenz, die der modernen Entwicklung entgegenläuft,** a tendency that runs counter to modern developments.

Entgegennahme, *f.* accepting, acceptance (of present, gift, homage, contributions to a charity, etc.); receiving (of orders, congratulations, etc.); taking (of orders); **E. von Spenden auch außerhalb der Dienststunden,** gifts will also be accepted outside office hours.

entgegennehmen. I. *v.tr. sep. (strong)* to accept (gifts, present, goods, contributions to a charity, order, etc.); to receive (congratulations, orders, etc.) (*personally*); to take (orders); **Huldigungen e.,** to accept homage; **ein Geschenk gnädig e.,** to be graciously pleased to accept a present; **Aufträge werden jederzeit entgegengenommen,** orders are taken at any time; **er nahm schweigend den Befehl entgegen,** he took, received, his order in silence; **Spenden aller Art werden gerne entgegengenommen,** we will be pleased to accept gifts of any kind.

II. *vbl s.* **Entgegennehmen,** *n.*=**Entgegennahme.**

entgegenschauen, *v.i. sep. (haben)*=**entgegensehen.**

entgegenschlagen, *v.i. sep. (strong) (sein)* **1.** *F:* **j-m e.,** (*of strong smell, smoke, fumes*) to come surging at s.o.; (*of flames*) to leap out at s.o.; (*of loud noise*) to strike s.o.'s ear. **2.** *Lit:* **aller Herzen schlugen ihm entgegen,** (i) all hearts went out to him (in sympathy); (ii) the thought of seeing him made everyone's heart beat faster; **ihr Herz schlug ihm freudig entgegen,** her heart leapt with joy at the thought of being with him; **ihr Herz schlug erwartungsvoll der Stunde entgegen, da sie ihn wiedersehen würde,** her heart throbbed with eagerness for the moment when she would see him again.

entgegensehen, *v.i. sep. (strong) (haben)* **einem glücklichen Leben, einer glücklichen Zukunft, e.,** to look forward to a happy life, a happy future; **der Zukunft mit Bangen e.,** to look to the future with apprehension, apprehensively; **einer Entscheidung gelassen, mit gemischten Gefühlen, e.,** to await a decision calmly, with mixed feelings; **sie sahen seiner Ankunft mit Freude, mit Bangen, entgegen,** they awaited his arrival with joy, with apprehension; **dem Tod ruhig, gelassen, e.,** to face the thought of death calmly, with composure.

entgegensetzen, *v.tr. sep.* **der Gewalt der Fluten einen Damm e.,** to oppose a dike to the fury of the waves; **j-m, etwas** *dat.*, **Widerstand e.,** to put up resistance to s.o., sth.; to oppose s.o., sth.; **er setzte dem Vorschlag heftigen Widerstand entgegen,** he put up, offered, a vigorous resistance to the proposal, he opposed the proposal vigorously; **einer Autorität eine andere e.,** to set one authority against another; *see also* **entgegengesetzt.**

entgegenstehen, *v.i. sep. (strong) (haben)* **1. j-m, etwas** *dat.*, **e.,** to oppose s.o., sth.; to be opposed to s.o., sth.; to stand in s.o.'s way; to stand in the way of (scheme, etc.); **ich will deinen Wünschen nicht e.,** I won't oppose your wishes, I won't obstruct your wishes; **ich will deinem Glück nicht e.,** I won't stand in the way of your happiness; **dem steht nichts entgegen,** there is no objection to it; *Jur:* **entgegenstehende Rechte, Ansprüche,** conflicting rights, claims. **2. etwas** *dat.* **e.,** to contrast with sth.; **den mageren Ergebnissen steht der große Kostenaufwand entgegen,** the meagre results are in marked contrast with the great expenditure.

entgegenstellbar, *a. Nat. Hist:* **entgegenstellbare Zehen,** divergent toes.

entgegenstellen, *v.tr. sep.* **1. etwas** *dat.* **etwas e.,** to set sth. against sth.; **einer Behauptung eine andere e.,** to set one statement against another. **2. sich j-m, etwas** *dat.*, **e.,** to oppose s.o., sth.; to put up, offer, resistance to s.o., sth.; **er stellte sich diesen Vorschlägen energisch entgegen,** he opposed these proposals vigorously, he put up, offered, a vigorous resistance to these proposals.

entgegenstrecken, *v.tr. sep.* **j-m etwas e.,** to hold sth. out to s.o.; to stretch out (one's hands) to, towards, s.o.; **sie streckte ihm ihre Hände hilfeflehend entgegen, ihre Hände streckten sich ihm hilfeflehend entgegen,** she stretched out her hands to him imploringly.

entgegentreten, *v.i. sep. (strong) (sein)* (*a*) **j-m e.,** to step up to s.o., to go, come, advance, towards s.o.; (*b*) **dem Feind, der Gefahr, e.,** to face the enemy, danger; (*c*) **j-m, etwas** *dat.*, **e.,** to oppose s.o., sth.; to put up, offer, resistance to s.o., sth.; to resist sth.; to set oneself against sth.; to take steps against (abuse, etc.); **einem Projekt e.,** to set oneself against, to oppose, a scheme; **Forderungen e.,** to oppose demands; to reject demands; **dieser Unsitte muß energisch entgegengetreten werden,** vigorous steps must be taken against this abuse; **j-s Ansichten e.,** to oppose, to stand up against, s.o.'s opinions.

entgegenwirken, *v.i. sep. (haben)* **etwas** *dat.* **e.,** to act, work, against sth.; to counteract (effect, influence); to interfere with, to counter (s.o.'s designs, etc.).

entgegnen. I. *v.* **1.** *v.i. (sein) A:* **j-m, etwas** *dat.*, **e.,** (*a*) to approach s.o., sth.; to go towards s.o., sth.; to come towards s.o., sth.; to face (danger, etc.); (*b*) to meet s.o., sth. **2.** *v.tr. & i. (haben)* to reply, to answer; to make a reply, to give an answer; to retort; **j-m etwas e.,** to make s.o. a reply, to give s.o. an answer; **er entgegnete nichts,** he made no reply, he gave no answer, he answered nothing; **etwas auf etwas** *acc.* **e.,** to reply sth. to sth.; to make a reply to sth.; **er konnte mir darauf nichts e.,** he could not make me any reply to this; **was haben Sie darauf zu e.?** what have you to say in reply to this? **auf meine Frage entgegnete sie, daß . . . ,** in reply to my question she said that . . . , her answer to my question was that . . . ; **er entgegnete, daß ich unrecht habe,** he answered, replied, that I was wrong; **auf meine Anschuldigungen wußte er nichts zu e.,** he had no reply to make to my accusations; **'das ist meine Sache', entgegnete er,** 'that is my business', he retorted, returned; **'Sie haben unrecht', entgegnete er,** 'you are wrong', he replied, answered.

II. *vbl s.* **Entgegnung,** *f.* reply, answer; response; retort; rejoinder; **er beantwortete den Angriff mit einer zwei Seiten langen E.,** he wrote a two-page reply to the attack made on him; **er erhielt eine Antwort, auf die keine (weitere) E. mehr möglich war,** he received an answer to which no rejoinder was possible; **eine E. machen, schreiben,** to make, write, a reply; to give an answer; to write a rejoinder; **seine E. wurde in Buchform veröffentlicht,** his rejoinder was published as a book.

entgehen, *v.i. (strong) (sein)* (*a*) **j-m e.,** (*of pers., remark, etc.*) to escape s.o.; **diese Tatsache ist mir, meiner Aufmerksamkeit, entgangen,** this fact escaped me, has escaped my attention; I have overlooked this fact; **kein Wort ist ihm entgangen,** he did not miss a single word; **ihm entgeht nichts,** nothing escapes him; **er soll mir nicht e.!** I won't let him escape! **es wird niemandem, niemandes Aufmerksamkeit, entgangen sein, daß . . . ,** it will not have escaped the notice of anyone that . . . ; **diese Bemerkung ist mir entgangen,** I failed to hear that remark, I missed that remark; (*b*) **etwas** *dat.* **e.,** to avoid, dodge (difficulty, etc.); to avoid (unpleasant situation, etc.); to escape (destiny, death); **ich habe versucht, dieser peinlichen Situation zu e.,** I tried to avoid this embarrassing situation; **man kann seinem Schicksal nicht e.,** one cannot escape one's fate, destiny; **dem Tode kann niemand e.,** nobody can escape death; (*c*) **sich** *dat.* **etwas e. lassen,** to let slip sth.; to let sth. escape; **sich** *dat.* **eine Gelegenheit e. lassen,** to let slip an opportunity, to miss an opportunity; **dieses Vergnügen habe ich mir leider e. lassen,** unfortunately I missed that treat; **er läßt sich nichts e.,** he misses nothing, he does not miss anything.

entgeisten, *v.tr. Ch: etc:* to remove spirit *or* alcohol from (mixture, etc.); to dealcoholize.

entgeistert, *a. & adv.* petrified, paralysed (with fear); flabbergasted, dumbfounded, thunderstruck (with astonishment); **er starrte sie e. an,** he looked at them flabbergasted.

Entgelt, *n.* **-s/.** payment; monetary reward; fee; **gegen E.,** against payment; for a consideration; **ohne E.,** gratis, for nothing, free of charge; **gegen ein geringes E.,** for a small fee; against payment of a small sum; for a small consideration; **der Arzt behandelt arme Patienten ohne E.,** the doctor treats poor patients free of charge.

entgelten, *v.tr. (strong)* **etwas e.,** to pay for sth.; to pay the penalty of sth.; **j-n etwas e. lassen,** to make s.o. pay for sth.; **das soll er mir e.!** he shall pay for this, I'll make him pay for this!

entgeltlich, *a. & adv.* against payment; *Jur:* **entgeltliche Verträge,** contracts in which consideration on both sides is involved.

entgerbern, *v.tr. Ind:* to wash, scour (wool).

entgiften, *v.tr.* to free (sth.) of poison, to remove the poison from (sth.); to decontaminate (sth.); to free (body) of toxic matter, to detoxicate (body).

entglasen, *v.tr.* to devitrify (glass); **Entglasung** *f*, devitrification.

entgleisen. I. *v.i. (sein)* (*a*) *Rail: etc:* (*of train, tram*) to leave the rails, to be derailed; **einen Zug e. lassen,** to derail a train; **der Zug war nicht entgleist,** the train was not derailed, the train kept the rails; (*b*) *F:* (*of pers.*) (i) to go off, to run off, the rails; to go wrong; (ii) to slip up; to make a slip, a *faux pas*.

II. *vbl s.* **1. Entgleisen,** *n. in vbl senses; also:* derailment; **einen Zug zum E. bringen,** to derail a train. **2. Entgleisung,** *f.* (*a*)=II. 1; (*b*) *F:* slip; gaffe; *faux pas*; **eine peinliche E.,** an embarrassing slip.

Entgleisungsweiche, *f. Rail:* derailing points, trap points.

entgleiten, *v.i. (strong) (sein)* **1.** (*a*) (*of thg*) **j-m, j-s Hand, j-s Händen, e.,** to slip from s.o.'s hands; to slip from s.o.'s fingers; **das Messer entglitt ihm, seiner Hand,** the knife slipped from his hand; **die Feder entglitt ihr, ihrer Hand,** the pen slipped from her fingers; **sein schwerer Körper entglitt ihr, ihren Händen,** his heavy body slipped from her grasp; (*b*) (*of pers.*) **j-m e.,** to grow, drift, away from s.o.; **sie entglitt ihm immer mehr,** she grew more and more away from him. **2.** *abs.* (*of ship, etc.*) to glide away.

entgöttern, *v.tr.* to deprive (world, etc.) of deities; **die griechischen Philosophen haben den Olymp entgöttert,** the Greek philosophers banished, expelled, the gods from Olympus; **die rationalistische Weltanschauung hat die Natur entgöttert,** rationalism has removed the gods from nature; **eine entgötterte Welt,** a world without gods. **2.**=**entgöttlichen.**

entgöttlichen, *v.tr.* to deprive, strip, (deity) of its divine nature; to deprive (nature) of its divinity

entgrannen, *v.tr.* to awn (barley, etc.).

Entgranner, *m.* **-s/-.** *Agr:* awn-removing device (on threshing-machine).

entgraten, *v.tr. Metalw:*=**abgraten.**

entgräten, *v.tr.* to bone (fish); to fillet (fish).

entgummieren, *v.tr. Ser:* to degum, boil off (silk).

enthaaren, *v.tr.* to depilate, to remove the hair from (sth.); *Leath:* to unhair, scrape, grain (skins); *Toil:* to remove (one's, s.o.'s) superfluous hair; **enthaarend,** depilatory (ointment, etc.); **Enthaarung** *f*, *Leath:* unhairing, scraping, graining; *Toil:* removal of superfluous hair.

Enthaarungsmittel, *n. Leath:* unhairing agent; *Toil:* depilatory, (superfluous) hair remover.

Enthalpie [ɛntalˈpiː], *f.* -/-n [-ˈpiːən]. *Ph:* enthalpy.

enthalten. I. *v.tr.* (*strong*) **1.** to contain; to comprise; to include; **in etwas** *dat.* **enthalten sein,** to be contained, included, in sth.; *Mth:* (*of number*) to go into, to be contained in (another number); **das Frühstück ist im Preis nicht enthalten,** breakfast is not included in the price; **in diesem Satz sind alle unsere Probleme enthalten,** this sentence embraces all our problems, sums up all our problems in a nutshell, all our problems are summed up in this one sentence; **Artikel, der die folgenden Bestimmungen enthält,** article that embodies, contains, the following regulations; **Buch, das viele Wahrheiten enthält,** book that contains many truths; **Gestein, das einen hohen Prozentsatz Eisen enthält,** rock that contains, rock containing, a high percentage of iron; **Substanz, die Arsen enthält, Arsen enthaltende Substanz,** substance that contains, substance containing, arsenic; **in seinem philosophischen System sind alle geistigen Strömungen seiner Zeit enthalten,** his philosophy comprises, includes, embodies, all the various trends of thought current in his time; **wie oft ist 5 in 30 enthalten?** how many times does 5 go into 30? **5 ist in 30 6 mal enthalten,** 5 goes into, is contained in, 30 6 times. **2. sich enthalten,** (*a*) to contain oneself; to restrain oneself; **sich (davon) e., etwas zu tun,** to refrain from doing sth.; **er konnte sich nicht e. zu lächeln, er konnte sich eines Lächelns nicht e.,** he could not refrain from smiling, he could not help smiling; **man kann sich nicht e., seine Arbeit zu bewundern, man kann sich der Bewunderung für seine Arbeit nicht e.,** it is impossible to refrain from admiring his work, one cannot help admiring his work; **sie konnte sich der Tränen nicht e., sie konnte sich nicht e. zu weinen,** she could not keep back, hold back, her tears; **sie konnte sich nicht länger e. und fing an zu lachen,** she could not contain herself any longer and started laughing; **sich der Stimme e.,** *Pol:* to abstain (from voting); *F:* to abstain from giving one's opinion; **sich eines Urteils e., sich e. zu urteilen,** to abstain, refrain, from forming *or* expressing a judgment; (*b*) **sich etwas** *gen.*, *occ.* **von etwas, e.,** to abstain from (alcohol, meat, women, etc.); **sich des Fleischgenusses e.,** to abstain from (eating) meat; **sich des Alkoholgenusses, des Alkohols, e.,** to abstain from alcohol, from drink.

II. *vbl s.* **Enthaltung,** *f.* **1.** (*a*) abstaining, abstention (**von,** from); **E. vom Fleischgenusse,** abstention from (eating) meat; (*b*) *A:* abstention; restraint. **2.** *Pol:* abstention (*in voting*); **fünfzehn Stimmen gegen drei bei zwei Enthaltungen,** fifteen votes to three with two abstentions.

enthaltsam, *a.* abstemious; continent; temperate; moderate; (*in sexual matters*) continent; chaste; **ein enthaltsames Leben führen,** *adv.* **e. leben,** to live continently; **völlig e. leben,** to live in complete chastity; **e. im Hinblick auf Alkohol sein,** to abstain from alcohol, to be an abstainer; **man sollte in allen Dingen e. sein,** one ought to be moderate, temperate, in all things.

Enthaltsamkeit, *f.* abstemiousness; temperateness; moderation; continence, continency; (*with regard to alcohol*) abstention; (*in sexual matters*) continence; chastity; **der Arzt hat völlige E. im Hinblick auf Alkohol empfohlen,** the doctor advised total abstention (from alcohol); **E. in allen Dingen,** moderation in all things; **in E. leben, ein Leben der E. führen,** to live continently; **in völliger E. leben,** to live in complete chastity; **E. üben,** to practise continence, chastity.

Enthaltung, *f. see* **enthalten II.**

enthärten, *v.tr.* to soften (water).

Enthärter, *m.* **-s/-, Enthärtungsmittel,** *n.* softening agent, softener (*for water*).

entharzen, *v.tr.* to remove the resin from (substance), to deresinify (substance).

Enthauchung, *f. Ling:* deaspiration.

enthaupten. I. *v.tr.* to behead, decapitate (s.o.), to cut (s.o.'s) head off; *F:* to decapitate (flower); **j-n e. lassen,** to have s.o. beheaded.

II. *vbl s.* **Enthauptung,** *f.* beheading, decapitation; **Hinrichtung durch E.,** (execution by) decapitation; **die E. Johannes des Täufers,** the beheading of St John the Baptist; **das Fest der E. Johannes, Johannes' E.,** the Feast of the Decollation of St John the Baptist.

enthäuten, *v.tr.* to skin (eel, rabbit, etc.); to flay (large animal); *Cu:* to skin (brains, liver, etc.); (*of reptile, insect*) **sich e.,** to cast (off) its skin, slough, to slough its skin, to slough.

entheben, *v.tr.* (*strong*) **j-n etwas** *gen.* **e.,** to relieve s.o. of (obligation, worry, doubts, etc.); to release, absolve, s.o., to set s.o. free, from (an obligation); to save s.o. sth.; to spare s.o. sth.; **j-n seines Amtes e.,** to relieve s.o. of his post, office, to dismiss s.o.; **j-n davon e., etwas zu tun,** to release s.o. from doing sth.; to make it unnecessary for s.o. to do sth.; **j-n der Mühe e., etwas zu tun,** to save s.o. the trouble of doing sth.; **das hat ihn vieler Unannehmlichkeiten enthoben,** this has saved him much trouble; **sein Besuch hat mich einer Reise enthoben,** his visit spared, saved, me a journey; **j-n der Notwendigkeit e., etwas zu tun,** to relieve s.o. of the necessity of doing sth.; **das enthebt mich jeglicher Verantwortung,** it relieves me of all responsibility; **niemand kann Sie Ihrer Verantwortung e.,** nobody can relieve you of, release you from, your responsibility; **das würde sie aller Sorgen e.,** it would relieve her of all her worries, it would take away all her worries; **ich fühle mich jeder Verpflichtung enthoben,** I feel free from all obligation, I feel under no obligation; **seine Antwort hat mich davon enthoben, weitere Schritte in dieser Sache zu unternehmen,** his answer has made it unnecessary for me to take further steps in this matter, has relieved me of the necessity of taking further steps in this matter.

entheiligen, *v.tr.* to profane (sth. sacred); **den Sabbat, den Sonntag, e.,** to profane the Sabbath (-day); **Entheiligung** *f*, profanation.

Entheiliger, *m.* **-s/-,** profaner (of the Sabbath-day, etc.).

Enthelminthen [ɛnthɛlˈmintən], *pl. Ann:* enthelmintha, enthelminthes, intestinal worms.

enthemmen, *v.tr. Psy:* to disinhibit (s.o.); **Enthemmung** *f*, disinhibition.

enthüllbar, *a.* revealable.

enthüllen. I. *v.tr.* (*a*) to bare, uncover (part of body, etc.); to unveil (monument, etc.); **j-m seine Seele e.,** to reveal, lay bare, one's soul to s.o.; (*b*) to reveal, disclose, divulge (secret, plan, the truth, etc.); to bring (crime, etc.) to light; (*of truth, etc.*) **sich e.,** to be revealed, disclosed; **ihr Brief enthüllte mir alles,** her letter told me all; **eines Tages wird die Wahrheit sich uns e.,** the truth will be revealed to us some day, one day we shall see the truth unveiled; (*c*) to reveal (sth.) (*unintentionally*); **sich j-m, j-s Blicken, e.,** (*of sight, etc.*) to be revealed to s.o.'s eyes; (*of scenery, etc.*) to be revealed to s.o.'s gaze, to lie open to s.o.'s gaze, to lie in front of s.o.; **blitzartig enthüllte sich mir die Wahrheit, enthüllte sich die Wahrheit meinem geistigen Auge,** the truth burst (in) upon me, the truth flashed upon me; **die Landschaft enthüllte sich in ihrer ganzen Schönheit,** the scenery revealed itself in all its beauty.

II. *vbl s.* **1. Enthüllen,** *n. in vbl senses.* **2. Enthüllung,** *f.* (*a*)=II. 1; *also:* revelation, disclosure (of secret, plan, the truth, etc.); **feierliche E. eines Denkmals,** ceremonial unveiling of a monument; (*b*) revelation; disclosure; **Enthüllungen machen,** to make revelations; to make disclosures; **seine Enthüllungen über die Zustände in der Polizei,** his disclosures about the state of affairs in the police force.

enthülsen, *v.tr.* (*a*) to husk, hull (peas, barley, rice, etc.); (*b*) to shell (peas); to pod (beans).

Enthülser, *m.* **-s/-.** *Agr:* husking, hulling, device (on threshing-machine).

Enthülsungsmaschine, *f.* husking machine, hulling machine.

enthüpfen, *v.i.* (*sein*) (*of bird, F: of pers.*) to hop off.

enthusiasmieren [ɛntuˑziasˈmiːrən], *v.tr.* to fire (s.o.) with, rouse (s.o.) to, enthusiasm; to enrapture (s.o.); **sich e.,** to become enthusiastic, to be moved to enthusiasm; **sich über etwas** *acc.* **e.,** to be enthusiastic about sth., to go into raptures over sth., *F:* to enthuse over sth.

Enthusiasmus [ɛntuˑziˈasmus], *m.* -/. enthusiasm; rapture; **mit jugendlichem E.,** with the enthusiasm of youth; **ich kann keinen großen E. dafür aufbringen,** I cannot feel much enthusiasm for it, I cannot be very enthusiastic about it, I cannot go into raptures over it; **sein E. wird sich bald abkühlen,** his enthusiasm will soon cool; **etwas voller E., mit großem E., tun,** to do sth. with great enthusiasm, enthusiastically.

Enthusiast [ɛntuˑziˈast], *m.* **-en/-en,** enthusiast.

enthusiastisch [ɛntuˑziˈastiʃ], *a.* enthusiastic; **ein enthusiastischer Bewunderer Wagners,** a Wagner enthusiast; **leicht, schnell, e. werden, sein,** to be easily moved to enthusiasm; *adv.* enthusiastically; **etwas e. annehmen, aufnehmen,** to accept, receive, sth. enthusiastically, with enthusiasm.

Enthymem [ɛntyˑˈmeːm], *n.* **-s/-e.** *Log:* enthymeme.

Entität [ɛntiˑˈtɛːt], *f.* -/-en. *Phil:* entity.

entjochen, *v.tr.* to unyoke (oxen, *F:* a people); to unharness (draught-horse).

entjungfern, *v.tr.* to deflower (girl); **Entjungferung** *f*, defloration.

entkalken. I. *v.tr.* **1.** *Ind: etc:* to delime (substance), to free (substance) from lime. **2.** *Med: Geol:* to decalcify (bone, rock).

II. *vbl s.* **Entkalken** *n.*, **Entkalkung** *f.* **1.** *Ind: etc:* deliming. **2.** *Med: Geol:* decalcification.

entkeimen. I. *v.* **1.** *v.i.* (*sein*) (*of seed*) to germinate; to come up; to sprout; **der Erde e.,** to come out of the earth), to sprout. **2.** *v.tr.* (*a*) to remove the sprouts from, to take the sprouts off (potatoes); (*b*) to extract the germ from (wheat, etc.). **3.** *v.tr.* to sterilize (sth.); to pasteurize (milk).

II. *vbl s.* **Entkeimen** *n.*, **Entkeimung** *f. in vbl senses; also:* **1.** germination (of seed). **2.** removal of the sprouts (from potatoes); extraction of the germ (from wheat, etc.). **3.** sterilization; pasteurization (of milk).

entkernen, *v.tr.* to stone (cherries, dates, raisins, etc.); to seed (grapes, raisins, etc.).

entkieseln, *v.tr.* to desilicify; **Entkieselung** *f*, desilicification.

entkleiden. I. *v.tr.* **1.** to undress (s.o.); **sich e.,** to undress (oneself), to take one's clothes off; to strip. **2. j-n etwas** *gen.*, *occ.* **von etwas, e.,** to divest s.o. of (an office, his dignity, a right, etc.); **alles Irdischen entkleidet,** stripped of all earthly things; (*of thoughts, etc.*) free from all mundane things; **seiner Göttlichkeit entkleidet,** stripped of his divinity; **seiner Würde, seiner Ehre, entkleidet,** bared, stripped, divested, of his dignity, his honour; **aller irdischen Güter entkleidet,** stripped of all earthly goods; **die Bäume standen nackt, ihrer Blätter entkleidet,** the trees were stripped, denuded, bared, of their leaves.

II. *vbl s.* **1. Entkleiden,** *n. in vbl senses;* **j-m beim E. helfen,** to help s.o. to undress. **2. Entkleidung,** *f.* (*a*)=II. 1; *also:* **die E. Christi,** the disrobing of Christ; (*b*) (state of) being stripped, bared, divested (**von etwas,** of sth.); bareness.

Entkleidungsnummer, *f. Th:* strip-tease act.

Entkleidungsrevue, *f. Th:* strip-tease show.

entkletten, *v.tr. Tex:* to remove the burs from (wool).

Entklettungsmaschine, *f. Tex.* bur-picking machine.

entknechten, *v.tr.* to free (s.o., a people) from slavery, from bondage.

entkohlen, *v.tr. Ind: Metall:* to decarbonize, decarburize (steel, etc.); *I.C.E:* to decarbonize (engine); **Entkohlung** *f*, decarbonization, decarburization.

Entkohlungsmittel, *n. Ind: Metall:* decarbonizer, decarburizer; *I.C.E:* decarbonizer.

entkommen. I. *v.i.* (*strong*) (*sein*) to escape, to get away; **j-m e.,** to escape from s.o.; to escape s.o.; **seinen Wärtern e.,** to escape (from) one's keepers; **aus dem Gefängnis e.,** to escape from prison; **ins Gebirge e.,** to escape, to get away, to the mountains; **die Einbrecher entkamen mit 1000 Mark,** the burglars got away with 1000 marks; **zwei der Verbrecher wurden gefaßt, der dritte entkam,** two of the criminals were caught; the third one got away; **ich lasse ihn nicht e.,** I won't let him get away, escape.

II. *vbl s.* **Entkommen,** *n.* escape; **ein Ort, von dem es kein E. gibt,** a place from which there is no escape, which offers no escape.

entkoppeln, *v.tr. W.Tel:* to decouple, uncouple (valve, etc.); **Entkoppelung** *f*, decoupling, uncoupling.

Entkoppelungswiderstand, *m.* decoupling resistance.

entkorken, *v.tr.* to uncork, open (bottle).

entkörperlicht, *a.* spiritualized (features, etc.).

entkörpern, *v.tr.* to free (the soul) from the body, to disembody (the soul); (*of soul*) **sich e.,** to be disembodied; **die entkörperte Seele, der entkörperte Geist,** the disembodied soul, spirit; **die Entkörperung der Seele,** the disembodiment of the soul.

entkräften. I. *v.tr.* **1.** (*of illness, hunger, etc.*) to weaken (s.o.), to make (s.o.) feeble; to sap (s.o.'s) strength; to debilitate (s.o.); (*of climate, etc.*) to enervate (s.o.); **durch die lange Krankheit entkräftet,** weakened by his, her, long illness. **2.** to weaken, invalidate (evidence, argument, etc.); to lessen (suspicion); **j-s Aussage zu e. versuchen,** to try to invalidate, weaken, s.o.'s statement *or* evidence.

II. *vbl s.* **1. Entkräften,** *n. in vbl senses.*

2. Entkräftung, *f.* (*a*) *in vbl senses; also:* invalidation (of evidence, argument, statement, etc.); (*b*) (physical) debility; (physical) collapse; feebleness, weakness; (state of) starvation; **in einem Zustand völliger E.,** in a state of complete collapse; **an, vor, E. sterben,** to die of physical exhaustion (*brought about by starvation, exposure, etc.*); to die of general debility.
entkräftigen, *v.tr. A:* = **entkräften.**
entkriechen, *v.i.* (*strong*) (*sein*) **etwas** *dat.* **e.,** to creep, crawl, out of sth.; (*of bird, larva, etc.*) **dem Ei e.,** to emerge from the egg.
entkrusten, *v.tr.* (*a*) to remove the crust from (bread); (*b*) to remove the incrustation from (sth.); to scale (boiler, tube, etc.).
entkuppeln, *v.tr. Mec.E: etc:* to disconnect, disengage, uncouple (machine parts, etc.); *Rail:* to uncouple (trucks, etc.); **Entkuppelung** *f, Mec.E: etc:* disconnection, disengagement, uncoupling (of machine parts, etc.); *Rail:* uncoupling (of trucks, etc.).
Entlade-, *comb.fm. cp.* **Entladungs-.**
Entladegebühr, *f.* unloading charge(s).
Entladegrenze, *f. El:* discharge voltage limit.
Entladehub, *m. I.C.E:* exhaust stroke.
entladen, *v.* (*strong*) I. *v.tr.* **1.** (*a*) to unload (lorry, truck, train, etc.); to unlade, discharge (boat); (*b*) *A:* **j-n etwas** *gen.*, **von etwas, e.,** to relieve s.o. of (burden, responsibility, etc.); to release s.o., free s.o., from (responsibility, etc.); to release s.o. from (task). **2.** (*a*) to discharge, fire (off), let off (firearm, gun); (*b*) to vent (one's anger); (*c*) to unload (revolver, etc.); to remove, withdraw, the charge from (revolver, cartridge, mine, etc.); to empty (shell). **3.** *El:* to discharge (accumulator, battery, cell, etc.).
II. **sich entladen. 1.** (*of gun, etc.*) to go off; to discharge. **2.** *El:* (*of storage battery, etc.*) to run down; to discharge. **3.** (*of storm*) to break; (*of anger*) to discharge itself, vent itself; to be vented; to break out; (*of pent-up energy*) to be released, to be let loose; **das Gewitter entlud sich über der Stadt, über uns,** the storm broke over the town, over our heads; **sein ganzer Zorn wird sich über uns e.,** the full force of his anger will be vented on us, we shall receive the full force of his anger. **4.** *A:* **sich etwas** *gen.*, **von etwas, e.,** to get rid of sth., to rid oneself of sth.; to free oneself from (burden, responsibility, etc.); to be relieved of (responsibility, etc.); to put down, lay down (burden); to carry out (commission).
III. *vbl s.* **1. Entladen,** *n. in vbl senses; also:* (*a*) discharge (of boat); (*b*) removal, withdrawal, of the charge from (revolver, cartridge, mine, etc.). **2. Entladung,** *f.* (*a*) = III. 1; *also: El:* discharge (of accumulator, battery, cell, etc.); (*b*) *El:* discharge; **dunkle, stille, E.,** dark, silent, discharge; **langsame E.,** slow discharge; **plötzliche, disruptive, E.,** disruptive discharge, spark discharge.
Entlader, *m.* **1.** (*pers.*) unloader. **2.** *El:* (*device*) discharger, (static) exciter; spark-arrester.
Entladespannung, *f. El:* discharge voltage.
Entladestock, *m. A.Artil: Sm.a:* wad-hook, worm.
Entladestrom, *m. El:* discharge current.
Entladewiderstand, *m. El:* discharge resistance.
Entladung, *f. see* **entladen III.**
Entladungs-, *comb.fm. cp.* **Entlade-.**
Entladungslampe, *f. El:* discharge lamp.
Entladungsröhre, *f. El:* discharge tube.
entlang, *adv. & prep.*, **entlang-,** *comb.fm.* (+ *preceding acc. or* + **an** + *dat., occ.* + *preceding or following dat. or* + *following gen.*) along; **am Fluß e., den Fluß e.,** along the river; **das ganze Dorf e.,** along the outskirts of the village; **dicht an der Mauer e.,** close to the wall; **die ganze Mauer e.,** all along the wall; **eine Straße entlanggehen,** to go, walk, along, down, a street, a road; **die ganze Straße entlanggehen,** to go, walk, the length of the street, road; **eine Straße entlangfahren,** to drive, travel, along a road; **die Küste, an der Küste, entlangfahren,** (*of ship, pers.*) to sail along the land, the coast; (*of pers., car, etc.*) to drive, travel, along the coast; **die Mauer, an der Mauer, entlangkriechen,** to creep, crawl, along the wall; **er kroch auf der Mauer entlang,** he crawled, was crawling, along the top of the wall; **sie lief den ganzen Zug, am ganzen Zug, entlang,** she ran the whole length of the train; **der Weg führt am Wald entlang,** the path runs along the edge of the wood, skirts the wood.
entlarven, *v.tr.* to unmask (s.o.); **einen Betrüger e.,** to unmask, expose, show up, an impostor; **Entlarvung** *f,* unmasking, exposure (of impostor, etc.).
entlassen. I. *v.tr.* (*strong*) **1.** (*a*) to dismiss (s.o.), to send (s.o.) away, to let (s.o.) go; **der König entließ ihn mit einigen freundlichen Worten,** the king dismissed him with a few gracious words; **er entließ seinen Kammerdiener und begab sich zur Ruhe,** he dismissed his valet, he sent his valet away, and retired to bed; *B: Ecc:* **nun entlässest du, Herr, deinen Diener in Frieden,** Lord, now lettest thou thy servant depart in peace; (*b*) to dismiss (assembly, troops, etc.); to disband (troops, an army). **2.** (*a*) to discharge (soldier, patient, prisoner); to pay off, discharge (crew); to release (prisoner); **einen Patienten aus dem Krankenhaus, einen Soldaten aus dem Heeresdienst, e.,** to discharge a patient from hospital, a soldier from the service; **er wurde gestern aus dem Krankenhaus entlassen,** he was discharged from hospital yesterday; **j-n als geheilt e.,** to give s.o. his, her, final discharge (from hospital, home, etc.); **j-n aus der Haft e.,** to release s.o. from custody; **einen Schüler aus der Schule e.,** to allow a pupil to leave school; **entlassen werden,** (*of soldier, prisoner, patient, etc.*) to be discharged; to get one's discharge; (*of pupil*) (i) to leave school, (ii) to be let out of school; *Jur:* **j-n vorläufig e.,** to discharge s.o. conditionally; **j-n bedingt, auf Widerruf, (aus einer Anstalt, usw.) e.,** to give s.o. a provisional discharge (from an institution, etc.); to discharge s.o. on licence; *see also* **Ehrenwort**; (*b*) to dismiss, *F:* sack (servant, employee, official); to give (servant, employee, official) the sack; **einen Beamten aus dem Dienst,** *A:* **des Dienstes, e.,** to relieve an official of his post, to dismiss an official; **(aus dem Amt, aus dem Dienst) entlassen werden,** to be, get, dismissed, *F:* to be sacked, to get the sack; **j-n fristlos e.,** to dismiss, discharge, s.o. without notice; *Mil: Navy:* **j-n (aus dem Dienst) e.,** to dismiss s.o. from the service; to cashier, break (officer); **(aus dem Dienst) entlassen werden,** to be dismissed the service; (*c*) *A:* **j-n etwas** *gen.* **e.,** to release, free, s.o. from (obligation, responsibility); to discharge s.o. from, of (obligation).
II. *vbl s.* **Entlassung,** *f.* **1.** (*a*) dismissal (of servant, assembly, troops); disbanding (of troops); (*b*) *Ecc:* (*part of the mass*) dismissal. **2.** (*a*) discharge (of soldier, patient, prisoner) (from the army, from hospital, prison); release (of prisoner) (from custody); **E. aus der Schule,** leaving school; **um seine E. bitten, seine E. beantragen,** to ask for one's discharge; **seine E. erhalten,** to get one's discharge; **nach seiner E. aus dem Krankenhaus, Gefängnis,** after his discharge from hospital, prison; **E. auf Ehrenwort,** release on parole; *Jur:* **vorläufige E.,** conditional discharge; **bedingte E., E. auf Widerruf (aus einer Anstalt, usw.),** provisional discharge (from an institution, etc.); discharge on licence; (*b*) dismissal, *F:* sacking (of servant, employee, official); the sack; *Mil: Navy:* dismissal (of s.o.); cashiering, breaking (of officer); **j-m mit (der) E. drohen,** to threaten s.o. with dismissal, with the sack; **die Firma bestand auf seiner E.,** the firm insisted on his dismissal; **Entlassungen werden unvermeidlich sein,** dismissals, sackings, will be unavoidable; *Mil:* **E. aus dem Heer,** dismissal from the army. **3.** *Sch:* = **Entlassungsfeier** 1.
Entlassungsfeier, *f.* **1.** *Sch:* school-leaving ceremony. **2.** *Ecc:* (*part of the Mass*) dismissal.
Entlassungspapiere, *n.pl.* discharge papers.
Entlassungsschein, *m.* certificate of discharge.
Entlassungsstelle, *f. Mil:* demobilization centre.
entlasten. I. *v.tr.* **1.** to remove, lift, the burden from (s.o., sth.); *esp.* (*a*) *Jur:* to exonerate, exculpate (s.o.); to clear (s.o.) of suspicion; **Zeugenaussage, die Sie entlastet,** evidence that exonerates you; **entlastende Zeugenaussage,** exonerating evidence; (*b*) **den Vorstand e.,** to give formal approval to the actions of the chairman *or* board; **den Schatzmeister e.,** to accept the treasurer's account; **einen ausscheidenden Beamten, Angestellten, usw., e.,** to approve the activities of an outgoing official, employee, etc.; (*c*) *Com:* **j-n für einen Betrag, j-s Konto um, für, einen Betrag, e.,** to credit s.o.'s account with a sum, to credit a sum to s.o.'s account. **2.** to relieve (s.o.) (of part of his responsibilities, duties, etc.); to ease, lighten (s.o.'s) burden; to give (s.o.) relief; to relieve the strain on (sth.); to take the strain *or* weight off (sth.); to ease the load on (electric power system, railway, telephone, etc., service, motor, etc.); *Mil:* to relieve the pressure (of the enemy) on (unit, position, etc.); **j-n, sich, von etwas e.,** to ease s.o., oneself, of (a burden); to relieve s.o., oneself, of (a responsibility, etc.); **sein Gewissen e.,** to ease one's conscience; **den Verkehr e.,** to ease the traffic; **die Eisenbahn(en) e.,** to relieve (the pressure on), to ease the load on, the railways; **er half zuweilen im elterlichen Geschäft, um seinen Vater zu e.,** he occasionally helped to relieve his father in his parents' firm; **das Einstellen der Zahlung gewisser Hilfsgelder wird den Staat (finanziell) e.,** the cancelling of certain subsidies will be a financial relief to the State, will ease the financial burden on the State; *Mch: Mec.E:* **entlastet,** balanced (valve, expansion joint, etc.).
II. *vbl s.* **1. Entlasten,** *n. in vbl senses.* **2. Entlastung,** *f.* (*a*) *in vbl senses; also: Jur:* exoneration, exculpation (of accused); (*b*) relief; **es wird eine große (finanzielle) E. für den Staat bedeuten,** it will mean a considerable relief to the State, it will ease the financial burden on the State considerably, it will be a great lightening of the (financial) burden on the State; **zur E. des Direktors wurde ein neuer Assistent eingestellt,** a new assistant was employed to take some of the burden off the director; **zur E. des elektrischen Leitungsnetzes,** (in order) to ease the load on the electric network; (*c*) **j-m die E. erteilen,** to approve the activities of (outgoing official, employee, etc.); to give formal approval to the actions of (chairman *or* board); to accept the (treasurer's) accounts.
Entlastungsangriff, *m. Mil:* attack made to relieve some other point from enemy pressure; *U.S:* relief attack.
Entlastungsanzeige, *f. Com:* credit note.
Entlastungsbalken, *m.* (*a*) *Constr:* relieving beam; (*b*) *N.Arch:* sweep (of tiller).
Entlastungsbogen, *m. Constr: Civ.E:* relieving arch.
Entlastungsgewölbe, *n. Civ.E:* relieving vault (of bridge).
Entlastungshahn, *m. Mch:* relief cock.
Entlastungshebel, *m. Mch:* easing gear lever (of safety valve).
Entlastungskanal, *m. Hyd.E:* spill-channel.
Entlastungskolben, *m. Mch:* balance piston.
Entlastungsrahmen, *m. Mch: etc:* back pressure valve.
Entlastungsschieber, *m. Mch:* balance slide-valve.
Entlastungsventil, *n. Mch:* relief valve.
Entlastungswehr, *n. Hyd.E:* spill-way.
Entlastungszeuge, *m. Jur:* witness for the defence.
Entlastungszeugnis, *n. Jur:* evidence for the defence, exonerating evidence.
Entlastungszug, *m. Rail:* relief train.
entlauben, *v.tr.* (*of autumn, wind*) to strip, denude, bare, (tree, forest) of its leaves; **sich e.,** (*of tree*) to shed its leaves; (*of forest*) to be stripped of its leaves; **entlaubte Bäume,** trees stripped, denuded, bared, of their leaves.
entlaufen, *v.i.* (*strong*) (*sein*) (*of dog, cat, pers.*) to run away; **j-m e.,** to run away from s.o.; **ein entlaufener Sträfling, Sklave,** a runaway convict, slave; **ein entlaufener Soldat,** a deserter; (*in advertisement*) **'entlaufen, schwarzer Pudel',** 'lost, black poodle'.
entlausen, *v.tr.* to delouse; **Entlausung** *f,* delousing.
Entlausungsanstalt, *f. Adm: Mil:* delousing station.
entledigen (sich), *v.refl.* **sich etwas** *gen.* **e.,** (*a*) to get rid of sth., to rid oneself of sth.; to free oneself, to get free, from sth.; to put down, lay down (a burden); **sich eines Rivalen e.,** to rid oneself of a rival; to dispatch a rival; **sich seines Mantels e.,** to take off one's coat, *Hum:* to disburden oneself of one's coat; (*b*) **sich einer Aufgabe, eines Auftrags, e.,** to fulfil, carry out, acquit oneself of, a task; to carry out a commission; **sich seiner Pflichten e.,** to fulfil, discharge, one's duties; **er hat sich seiner Aufgabe glänzend entledigt,** he carried out his task admirably, he acquitted himself admirably.
entleeren. I. *v.tr.* **1.** to empty (sth.); to drain (cask, pipes, water-tank, etc.); to drain (off) (pond); *Mch:* to run down, blow off (boiler); *Post:* to clear (letter-box); *Med: Physiol:* to evacuate, clear (the bowels); to empty (the bladder, the stomach); **etwas in etwas** *acc.* **e.,** to empty sth. into sth. **2. sich entleeren,** to empty; to become empty; *Med: Physiol:* (*of bowels*) to be evacuated, cleared; (*of bladder, stomach*) to empty; **sich in etwas** *acc.* **e.,** to empty into sth.
II. *vbl s.* **1. Entleeren,** *n. in vbl senses.* **2. Entleerung,** *f.* (*a*) = II. 1; *also: Med: Physiol:* evucation (of the bowels); (*b*) *Post:* collection;

clearing (of letter-box); **nächste E.**, next collection; **täglich drei Entleerungen**, three collections daily.

Entleerungshahn, *m. Mch: etc:* drain-cock, drip-cock.

Entleerungsrohr, *n.*, **Entleerungsröhre**, *f.* drain-pipe.

entlegen, *a.* far away, remote, isolated, out-of-the-way, lonely, unfrequented, secluded (place, spot); sequestered (spot); **im entlegensten Teil Asiens**, in the remotest part of Asia; **in den entlegeneren Dörfern**, in the remoter, more isolated, villages; **seine Zitate stammen aus ganz entlegenen Quellen, Schriftstellern**, his quotations come from quite remote, out-of-the-way, sources, from quite remote authors.

Entlegenheit, *f.* remoteness, isolation, loneliness, seclusion (of a place, spot).

entlehnen. I. *v.tr.* **etwas etwas** *dat.*, **von, aus, etwas, e.**, to borrow (idea, motif, etc.) from (literary source, model, etc.); **einen Ausdruck (aus) Vergil e.**, to borrow, take, an expression from Virgil; **ein (aus) dem Lateinischen entlehntes Wort**, word taken from the Latin; **seine Motive sind (aus) verschiedenen klassischen Bildwerken entlehnt**, his motifs are borrowed, taken, from various classical monuments.

II. *vbl s.* **1. Entlehnen**, *n. in vbl senses.* **2. Entlehnung**, *f.* (*a*)=II. 1; (*b*) idea, motif, etc., borrowed; **das Wort ist eine E. aus dem Lateinischen**, the word is taken from, is a borrowing from, the Latin; the word is a Latin loan-word; **in diesem Werk lassen sich viele Entlehnungen aus älteren Vorbildern feststellen**, in this work we find much that has been borrowed from earlier models; **fast alle seine Ideen sind Entlehnungen aus anderen Autoren**, almost all his ideas are borrowed from other authors.

Entlehner, *m.* **-s/-**, borrower.

entleiben, *v.tr. Lit:* to kill (s.o.); **sich (selbst) e.**, to kill oneself, to commit suicide.

entleihen, *v.tr.* (*strong*) **etwas von j-m e.**, to borrow sth. from s.o.; **Bücher aus, von, der Bibliothek e.**, to borrow books from the library.

Entlein, *n.* **-s/-**, (*dim. of* Ente) duckling; **das häßliche junge E.**, the ugly duckling.

entloben (sich), *v.refl. F:* to break off one's engagement.

entlocken, *v.tr.* **j-m etwas e.**, to wheedle, coax, sth. out of s.o.; **j-m ein Geheimnis, ein Geständnis, e.**, to elicit a secret, a confession, from s.o.; to wheedle a secret, a confession, out of s.o.; **j-m Tränen e.**, to bring tears to s.o.'s eyes; to squeeze tears out of s.o.; **einem Musikinstrument Töne e.**, to draw, extract, sounds from a musical instrument; **er versuchte, der alten Geige eine Melodie zu e.**, he tried to coax a tune out of the old fiddle.

entlohnen. I. *v.tr.* to pay (workman, servant, etc.) (for work done); to pay wages to (s.o.).

II. *vbl s.* **1. Entlohnen**, *n. in vbl senses.* **2. Entlohnung**, *f.* (*a*)=II. 1; *also:* (*action*) payment (of workman, etc.) (for work done); (*b*) payment, pay.

entlöschen, *v.tr. Nau:* to discharge (ship).

entlüften. 1. *v.tr.* to ventilate; to bleed (hydraulic brakes, etc.); *Ind:* to de-aerate (introcellulose, viscose solution, etc.). **2.** *vbl s.* **Entlüftung**, *f.* (*a*) *in vbl senses; also:* ventilation; *Ind:* de-aeration; (*b*) (air-)vent; priming funnel (of pump).

Entlüfter, *m.* ventilator; vent; extractor fan; bleeder (of hydraulic brakes, etc.).

Entlüftungseinrichtung, *f.* ventilating device; vent.

Entlüftungsschraube, *f.* air-release plug (of compressed air apparatus).

Entlüftungsventil, *n.* air-release valve; vent; bleeder valve (of hydraulic brakes, etc.).

entmachten, *v.tr.* to deprive (government, etc.) of (its) power.

entmagnetisieren. 1. *v.tr.* (*a*) *Ph:* to demagnetize; (*b*) *Navy: etc:* to degauss (ship). **2.** *vbl s.* **Entmagnetisierung**, *f.* (*a*) *Ph:* demagnetization; (*b*) *Navy: etc:* degaussing (of ship).

Entmagnetisiergerät, *n. Navy: etc:* degaussing apparatus.

entmannen, *v.tr.* to emasculate, castrate (man); **Entmannung** *f*, emasculation, castration.

entmasten, *v.tr.* to dismast, unmast (ship); to take down the masts of (ship).

entmenschen, *v.tr.* to dehumanize, brutalize (s.o., a people); **entmenscht**, brutalized; brutal, inhuman; **Entmenschung** *f*, (i) brutalizing; (ii) brutality.

Entmenschtheit, *f.* brutality.

entmilitarisieren, *v.tr. Adm:* to demilitarize (area); **Entmilitarisierung** *f*, demilitarization.

entminen, *v.tr. Mil:* to clear (area) of mines.

entmischen, *v.tr. Ch: etc:* to decompose, dissociate; **Entmischung** *f*, decomposition, dissociation.

entmündigen, *v.tr. Jur:* to declare (s.o.) incapable of managing his affairs, to incapacitate (s.o.); **entmündigt**, under disability, declared incapable of managing one's affairs, incapacitated; **Entmündigung** *f*, declaration of (s.o.'s) disability; incapacitation.

Entmündigungsverfahren, *n. Jur:* incapacitation proceedings.

entmutigen. I. *v.tr.* to discourage, dishearten (s.o.); **er läßt sich leicht e.**, he easily loses heart, he easily gets discouraged; **man soll sich nie e. lassen**, one should never lose heart, courage; **laß dich nicht e.**, don't lose heart, don't get discouraged, *F:* keep your chin up! **entmutigend**, discouraging, disheartening.

II. *vbl s.* **Entmutigung**, *f.* discouragement; dejection, despondency; **für ihn gibt es keine E.**, he has never known discouragement; **tiefe E. hatte ihn ergriffen**, he was seized with deep despondency.

entmythologisieren, *v.tr.* to demythologize (religion, etc.); **Entmythologisierung** *f*, demythologizing.

Entnahme, *f.* **-/-n. 1.** (*a*) taking (of sth.) (from sth., out of sth.); drawing (of sth.) (from sth.); using, use (of electricity, gas, water); **widerrechtliche E. von Strom**, illegal use of electricity, stealing of electricity; *Med:* **E. von Blut (aus der Vene, usw.)**, drawing of blood (from the vein, etc.); *Mch:* **E. von Dampf**, extraction, *F:* bleeding, of steam; (*b*) *Com:* **E. eines Betrags auf j-n**, drawing (of a bill) (up)on s.o. for a certain sum. **2.** (*thg taken*) (*a*) *Com: etc:* money withdrawn (from the bank, from takings of a business, for living expenses, etc.); article retained for personal use or other non-business purposes; **Entnahmen** *pl*, drawings; (*b*) passage, etc., taken, lifted (from a book, an author); **der Dichter hat mehrere Entnahmen bei Vergil gemacht**, the poet took several passages *or* lines from Virgil; **diese Stelle ist eine E. aus Schiller**, this passage is taken from Schiller; (*c*) *Com:* draft.

Entnahmekreis, *m. El:* load circuit.

Entnahmeventil, *n. Mch:* extraction valve, bleeder valve.

entnationalisieren [ɛntna·tsĭo·na·li·ˈziːrən], *v.tr.* to denationalize; **Entnationalisierung** *f*, denationalization.

entnazifizieren [ɛntna·tsi·fi·ˈtsiːrən], *v.tr.* to denazify; **Entnazifizierung** *f*, denazification.

entnebeln, *v.tr.* to clear (chemical factory, etc.) of fumes.

entnehmen, *v.tr.* (*strong*) **1.** (*a*) **etwas etwas** *dat.*, **aus etwas, e.**, to take sth. from sth.; to take sth. out of sth.; to draw sth. from, out of, sth.; **er entnahm seiner Börse ein Goldstück**, he took a gold piece from his purse; **er entnahm seiner Brieftasche ein Schriftstück**, he took, drew, a document from his wallet; **er öffnete die Kassette und entnahm ihr ein Bündel Geldscheine**, he opened the casket and took out a bundle of notes; **Geld aus der Ladenkasse e.**, to take money from the till; **elektrischen Strom, Gas, Wasser, e.**, to use electric current, electricity, gas, water; **elektrischen Strom widerrechtlich e.**, to use electricity illegally, to steal electricity; *Mch:* **Dampf e.**, to extract, *F:* bleed, steam; *Med:* **Blut (aus der Vene, usw.) e.**, to draw blood (from the vein, etc.); (*b*) *Com:* **einen Betrag auf j-n e.**, to draw (a bill) (up)on s.o. for a certain sum; **500 Mark auf j-n e.**, to draw (a bill) (up)on s.o. for 500 marks; (*c*) **eine Stelle einem, aus einem, Buch, Schriftsteller, e.**, to take, lift, a passage from a book, from an author; **dieser Vers ist Vergil entnommen**, this line is taken from Virgil; **er hat alle seine Motive Shakespeare entnommen**, he has taken all his motifs from Shakespeare; **das Architekturmotiv ist einem antiken Wandgemälde entnommen**, the architectural motif is taken from a classical wall painting. **2. etwas etwas** *dat.*, **aus etwas, e.**, to infer, conclude, deduce, sth. from sth.; to understand sth. from sth.; to gather sth. from sth.; **daraus entnahm ich, daß . . .**, from this I inferred, concluded, understood, deduced, from this I drew the conclusion, the inference, that . . .; **eine bestimmte Absicht war aus ihrem Verhalten nicht zu e.**, one could not infer a definite intention from her behaviour; **das ist alles, was ich ihrem, von ihrem, Gespräch e. konnte**, that is all I could infer, conclude, understand, deduce, from their conversation; **ich entnehme Ihrem Brief, daß . . .**, I understand, I take it, from your letter that . . .; **aus seinen Mitteilungen läßt sich nicht e., was wirklich vorgegangen ist**, it cannot be seen, it is not clear, from what he told us what really happened.

Entnehmer, *m.* user (of electricity, etc.); *Com:* drawer (of bill).

entnerven, *v.tr.* to weaken (s.o.); to drain, sap, (s.o.'s) strength; to wear (s.o.) down; (*of climate, etc.*) to enervate (s.o.); **ein entnervender Lärm**, a nerve-racking noise; **entnervendes Klima**, enervating climate; **das entnervende Leben der Großstadt**, the enervating life of the city; **er war völlig entnervt durch ein Leben der Üppigkeit**, his strength had been sapped by a life of indulgence.

ento-, Ento- [ɛnto·-], *pref.* ento-; endo-; **Entoderm** *n*, entoderm, endoderm; **Entoparasit** [ɛnto·pa·ra·ˈziːt] *m*, entoparsite, endoparasite.

Entoblast [ɛnto·ˈblast], *n.* **-(e)s/-e.** *Biol:* entoblast, endoblast.

Entoderm [ɛnto·ˈdɛrm], *n.* **-s/-e.** *Biol:* entoderm, endoderm.

Entomologe [ɛnto·mo·ˈloːgə], *m.* **-n/-n**, entomologist.

Entomologie [ɛnto·mo·lo·ˈgiː], *f.* **-/.** entomology.

entomologisch [ɛnto·mo·ˈloːgiʃ], *a.* entomological.

entomophag [ɛnto·mo·ˈfaːk], *a.* entomophagous.

Entomophage [ɛnto·mo·ˈfaːgə], *m.* **-n/-n**, entomophagous animal *or* plant.

entomophil [ɛnto·mo·ˈfiːl], *a.* entomophilous.

Entomophile [ɛnto·mo·ˈfiːlə], *m.* **-n/-n**, entomophilous plant.

Entophyt [ɛnto·ˈfyːt], *m.* **-en/-en.** *Bot:* entophyte.

entopisch [ɛnˈtoːpiʃ], *a.* entopic.

Entoplasma [ɛnto·ˈplasmaː], *n.* endoplasm.

entoptisch [ɛntˀˈoptiʃ], *a.* entoptic (vision).

entotisch [ɛntˀˈoːtiʃ], *a.* entotic (hearing).

Entourage [ã·tu·ˈraːʒə], *f.* **-/-n**, entourage; suite (of king, etc.).

Entozoon [ɛnto·ˈtsoːon], *n.* **-(s)/-zoen** & **-zoa** [-ˈtsoːən, -ˈtsoːaː]. *Z:* entozoon; *pl.* entozoa.

entpersönlichen. I. *v.tr.* to take away (s.o.'s) individuality; to make (s.o.) lose (his) individuality; to deprive, rob, strip, (s.o.) of (his) personality, individuality; to make (relationship, etc.) impersonal; **sich e., entpersönlicht werden**, (*of pers.*) to lose one's individuality; to lose, to be deprived, stripped, of one's personality, one's individuality; (*of relationship, etc.*) to become impersonal; **die Uniform entpersönlicht den Menschen, durch die Uniform wird der Mensch entpersönlicht**, uniform strips a man of his individuality; **das Ziel der Meditation ist, sich zu e., entpersönlicht zu werden**, the aim of meditation is the surrender of personality.

II. *vbl s.* **Entpersönlichung**, *f.* **1.** *in vbl senses.* **2.** loss of individuality; loss of personality; surrender of individuality, personality; **das Ziel der Meditation ist völlige E.**, the aim of meditation is the complete surrender of personality.

entpesten, *v.tr.* to disinfect (area); to free (area) from vermin.

entpflichten, *v.tr.* to relieve (official, etc.) of his active duties; *Sch:* to give (professor) emeritus status; **Entpflichtung** *f*, (honourable) discharge (of official); *Sch:* award of emeritus status (to professor).

entpfropfen, *v.tr.* to uncork, open (bottle).

entphosphoren, *v.tr. Metall:* to dephosphorize (iron); **Entphosphorung** *f*, dephosphorization.

Entpolarisation [ɛntpo·la·ri·za·tsĭˈoːn], *f. Opt: El:* depolarization.

entpolarisieren [ɛntpo·la·ri·ˈziːrən], *v.tr. Opt: El:* to depolarize; **Entpolarisierung** *f*, depolarization.

Entpolymerisation [ɛntpo·ly·me·ri·za·tsĭˈoːn], *f.*, **Entpolymerisierung** [ɛntpo·ly·me·ri·ˈziːruŋ], *f.* depolymerization.

entpuppen (sich), *v.refl.* (*a*) (*of butterfly*) to emerge from the chrysalis; (*of silkworm*) to emerge from the cocoon; **die häßliche Raupe hatte sich zum schönen Schmetterling entpuppt**, the ugly caterpillar had emerged as a beautiful butterfly; (*b*) *F:* (*of pers., thg*) **sich als etwas e.**, to reveal oneself, itself, (as) sth., to show oneself, itself, (to be) sth.; to turn out (to be) sth.; to come out as sth.; **er hat sich als ausgezeichneter Koch entpuppt**, he revealed himself (as), he showed himself, turned out (to be), he came out as, an excellent cook; **er hat sich als Feigling entpuppt**, he showed himself (to be) a coward; he turned out to be a coward; **die Sache hat sich als Schwindel entpuppt**, it turned out to be a fraud;

er hat sich als der Sohn meines alten Freundes entpuppt, he turned out to be my old friend's son.

entquellen, *v.i.* (*strong*) (*sein*) **etwas** *dat.* **e.,** (*of water*) to spring from, well out of (rock, earth); to flow, stream, from, to spout out of, to spurt, squirt, from (rock, opening); (*of blood*) to squirt, spurt, stream, from (wound); (*of light*) to stream out of (window, etc.); (*of sound*) to flow, pour forth, from (instrument, etc.); (*of emotion*) to well up from (one's heart); **Tränen entquollen ihren Augen,** tears started, welled, from her eyes; **immer neue Melodien entquollen ihrer Kehle,** melody after melody poured forth from her throat; **ein Gefühl tiefer Dankbarkeit entquoll seinem Herzen,** a feeling of deep gratitude welled, flowed, streamed, from him; **dicker Rauch entquoll dem Schornstein,** thick smoke was pouring from the chimney.

entraffen, *v.tr.* **1.** *Lit:* to snatch (s.o.) away, to carry (s.o.) off; **der Tod hat ihn uns vor der Zeit entrafft,** death has snatched him from us before his time. **2.** *A.Lit:* (*of pers., spiritual force, etc.*) **sich etwas** *dat.* **entraffen,** to free oneself, itself, from sth.; to shake off (one's, its, fetters).

entrahmen, *v.tr.* to take the cream off (milk), to cream (off) (milk); to skim (milk); (*in machine*) to separate (milk); **entrahmte Milch, Frischmilch,** skim milk, creamed milk; **Entrahmung** *f*, (i) skimming, (ii) separating (of milk).

Entrahmer, *m.* **-s/-, Entrahmungsmaschine,** *f.* cream separator, creamer.

entraten, *v.i.* (*strong*) (*haben*) (*occ. v.tr.*) *Lit:* **etwas** *gen.* **e. können, müssen,** to be able to, to have to, do without sth., dispense with sth.; **etwas** *gen.* **nicht e. können, nicht e. wollen,** not to be able, not to wish, to do without sth., dispense with sth.; **er kann unserer Hilfe nicht e.,** he cannot do without our help; **er wollte, mochte, ihrer Gesellschaft nicht mehr e.,** he did not want to be without her, he could not do without her company, any longer; **er mußte mancher Bequemlichkeiten e.,** he had to go, do, without many a comfort.

enträtseln, *v.tr.* to puzzle out (sth.); to solve (mystery); **die Geheimnisse der Natur, die Natur, e.,** to discover the secrets of nature; to solve the mysteries of nature; **er versuchte, ihr Gesicht zu e.,** he tried to get at the secret behind her expression; **Frauen sind schwer zu e.,** women's minds are a mystery, women are difficult to understand; **geheimnisvolle Schriftzeichen, die niemand e. konnte,** mysterious characters that nobody could decipher.

entratten, *v.tr.* to derat; **Entrattung** *f*, deratization.

Entreakt [ã·tərᵓˈakt, ã·ˈtrakt], *m.* **-s/-e.** *Th:* entr'acte, interlude.

Entrechat [ã·tərˈʃa(:)], *m.* **-s/-s.** *Danc:* entrechat.

entrechten. I. *v.tr.* to deprive (s.o.) of (his, her) rights; **das Volk e.,** to deprive the people of its rights; **die entrechteten Klassen, die Entrechteten,** the underprivileged classes.

II. *vbl s.* **Entrechtung,** *f.* **1.** *in vbl senses.* **2.** (state of) being deprived of one's rights; **in völliger E. leben,** to live deprived of all rights.

Entrecote [ã·tərˈkoːt], *n.* **-(s)/-s.** *Cu:* entrecote, *F:* rib of beef.

Entree [ã·ˈtreː], *n.* **-s/-s. 1.** entrance; (entrance) hall; vestibule. **2.** admission (fee), entrance fee. **3.** *Cu:* entrée.

entreißen, *v.tr.* (*strong*) **j-m etwas e.,** to take sth. away from s.o. (by force); to snatch sth. (away) from s.o.; to snatch sth. out of s.o.'s hands; to tear sth. from s.o.; **er entriß dem Tier seine Beute,** he snatched the animal's prey from it; **sie konnte der Katze das Fleisch noch rechtzeitig e.,** she was just able to snatch the meat from the cat in time; **er entriß ihr das Kind,** he snatched the child from her; **ihr Kind war ihr früh entrissen worden,** (i) her child had been torn from her at an early age; (ii) her child had died, had been taken from her, when very young; **der Tod hat ihn uns entrissen, er wurde uns durch den Tod entrissen,** death has taken him away, has snatched him, has torn him, from us; **mit dieser mutigen Tat entriß er ihn dem Tode,** by this courageous deed he snatched him from the jaws of death.

Entrelacs [ã·tərˈlaː], *n.* **-/-.** *Art:* interlacing, interlaced design, tracery; strap-work.

Entremets [ã·tərˈmeː], *n.* **-/-** [-ˈmeː/-ˈmeːs]. *Cu:* entremets, dish served between courses.

entre nous [ã·tərˈnuː]. *Fr.phr.* (*a*) (be it said) between ourselves, between you and me, *F:* between you and me and the gate-post; (*b*) **wir werden ganz e. n. sein,** we shall be by ourselves.

Entrepot [ã·tərˈpoː], *n.* **-/-s,** warehouse, store; *Cust:* bonded warehouse.

Entrepreneur [ã·tərprəˈnøːr], *m.* **-s/-e,** contractor; *Pol.Ec:* entrepreneur.

Entreprise [ã·tərˈpriːzə], *f.* **-/-n,** (industrial, etc.) enterprise; (business) undertaking.

Entresol [ã·tərˈsol], *n.* **-s/-s.** *Arch:* entresol, mezzanine (floor).

entrichten. I. *v.tr.* to pay (sum of money, contributions, taxes, duties, etc.) (**j-m, an j-n,** (to) s.o.); **j-m seinen Dank e.,** to extend, offer, one's thanks to s.o.; **die Summe von *x* Mark ist an die zuständige Behörde zu e.,** the sum of *x* marks is to be paid to the appropriate authority; **die Bauern hatten dem Grundherrn jährliche Abgaben zu e.,** the farmers had to render annual dues to the landlord.

II. *vbl s.* **Entrichten** *n.*, **Entrichtung** *f.* *in vbl senses; also:* payment (of sum of money, contributions, taxes, duties, etc.).

entriegeln, *v.tr.* to unbolt (door, etc.); *Artil:* to unlock the breech mechanism of (gun, etc.).

entrieren [ã·ˈtriːrən], *v.tr.* to enter into (negotiations, contract, business, etc.); to initiate, start (negotiations, business transactions, etc.).

entrinden, *v.tr.* to strip the bark off, to bark (tree); to decorticate (tree); to peel (twig); to remove the crust from (bread); to remove the rind from (cheese); **Entrindung** *f*, barking (of tree); decortication (of tree); peeling (of twig); removal of the crust (from bread); removal of the rind (from cheese).

entringen[1], *v.tr.* = **abringen**[1].

entringen[2], *v.tr.* (*strong*) *Lit:* **j-m etwas e.,** to wrest sth. from s.o.; to wrench sth. from s.o.; to wring sth. from, out of, s.o.; **ein Seufzer entrang sich ihrer Brust,** a sigh broke from her.

entrinnen, *v.i.* (*strong*) (*sein*) **1.** *Lit:* (*of water, etc.*) **etwas** *dat.* **e.,** to flow from, run from, out of, sth. **2.** (*of time*) to flee, to fly by; **die Tage, die Jahre, die Stunden, entrinnen,** the days, years, hours, fly by, slip by; **die Stunden entrinnen uns,** the hours fly by, slip by. **3.** (*of pers.*) **j-m, etwas** *dat.*, **aus etwas, e.,** to escape s.o., sth.; to escape from s.o., sth.; **einer Gefahr e.,** to escape a danger; to escape from a danger; **dem Tode e.,** to escape death; **er war dem Tode um Haaresbreite entronnen,** he had escaped death by a hair's-breadth; **diesem Schicksal war er glücklich entronnen,** he had succeeded in escaping this fate; **seinen Verfolgern e.,** to escape (from) one's pursuers; **der Hölle e.,** to escape hell; **er war der Hölle der Schlacht entronnen,** he had escaped from the hell of battle.

II. *vbl s.* **Entrinnen,** *n.* escape; **davon, daraus, gibt es kein E.,** there is no escape from it.

entrippen, *v.tr.* = **ausrippen.**

Entrochit [εntroˈxiːt], *n.* **-(e)s & -en/-en.** *Paleont:* entrochite, trochite.

entrollen, *v.* **1.** *v.tr.* to unroll (map, etc.); to unfurl (flag, roll, scroll); **sein Bericht entrollte ein furchtbares Bild menschlicher Gemeinheit,** his report revealed a dreadful picture of human depravity. **2. sich entrollen,** (*of map, etc.*) to come unrolled, to unroll; (*of flag, roll, scroll*) to come unfurled, to unfurl; **eine anmutige Landschaft, ein anmutiges Landschaftsbild, entrollte sich vor uns, vor unseren Augen,** a delightful landscape, scene, unfolded (itself), stretched out, before us, before our eyes. **3.** *v.i.* (*sein*) (*a*) (*of ball, stone, etc.*) to roll away; to roll (down); **j-m, etwas** *dat.*, **e.,** to roll away from s.o.; to roll from (s.o.'s hands, etc.); **Tränen entrollten ihr, ihren Augen,** tears were rolling down her cheeks; (*b*) (*of time*) to roll by.

Entropie [εntroˑˈpiː], *f.* **-/-n** [-ˈpiːən]. **1.** *Ph:* entropy. **2.** *Med:* entropion.

Entropium [εnˈtroːpĭum], *n.* **-s/.** *Med:* entropion.

entrosten, *v.tr.* to remove the rust of (sth.), to take the rust off (sth.); **Entrostung** *f*, removal of rust.

Entrostungsmittel, *n.* rust remover.

entrücken, *v.tr.* *Lit:* to carry (s.o.) off, to take (s.o.) away; **j-n j-s Blicken, von j-s Blicken, e.,** to remove s.o. from s.o.'s sight; **er wurde zum Himmel entrückt,** he was carried up to heaven; **er war (von) ihren Blicken entrückt,** he was removed from their sight; **er lebte der Welt, allem Irdischen, entrückt,** he lived quite apart from the world, from all earthly things; **der Tod hat ihn aller Sorge entrückt,** death has put him beyond all cares.

entrümpeln, *v.tr.* to clear (attic, loft, etc.) of lumber, rubbish; **Entrümpelung** *f*, clearance (of attic, loft, etc.) of lumber, rubbish.

Entrundung, *f.* *Ling:* unrounding, delabialization.

entrüsten. I. *v.tr.* to fill (s.o.) with indignation, to make (s.o.) indignant; **über etwas entrüstet sein, sich über etwas e.,** to be, feel, grow, indignant at, about, sth.; to be full of indignation at, about, sth.; to feel indignation at, about, sth.; **darüber entrüstet sein, sich darüber e., daß . . . ,** to be indignant that . . . ; **sich moralisch e., moralisch entrüstet sein,** to feel moral indignation; **er war über ihr Verhalten entrüstet, ihr Verhalten entrüstete ihn,** her conduct made him indignant, aroused his indignation.

II. *vbl s.* **Entrüstung,** *f.* indignation; **in gerechter, moralischer, E.,** in righteous, moral, indignation; **wir hören mit E., daß . . . ,** we are indignant to hear, we hear with indignation, that . . . ; **seine Worte lösten einen Sturm der E. aus,** his words provoked a storm of indignation; **ein Sturm der E. brach los,** there was a storm of indignation; **er lehnte den Vorschlag mit E. ab,** he turned down the proposal indignantly.

Entrüstungssturm, *m.* storm of indignation.

entsaften, *v.tr.* *Dom.Ec:* to extract the juice from (fruit, etc.).

Entsafter, *m.* **-s/-.** *Dom.Ec:* juice extractor.

entsagen. I. *v.i.* (*haben*) **etwas** *dat.* **e.,** (*a*) to renounce (earthly things, sin, etc.); to forego (pleasures); to give up (a habit); **der Welt e.,** to renounce the world; **dem Trunk e.,** to give up drink; **einem Anspruch e.,** to renounce, withdraw, waive, forego, a claim; **dem Thron e.,** to renounce the throne; *abs.* **e. lernen,** to learn renunciation, to learn to forego; (*b*) *A:* to abnegate (one's religion, etc.); to renounce (one's faith).

II. *vbl s.* **Entsagen** *n.*, **Entsagung** *f.* **1.** *A: in vbl senses;* **E. eines Anspruchs, auf einen Anspruch,** renouncement, renunciation, waiving, foregoing, withdrawal, of a claim. **2.** renunciation; self-denial; **ein Leben des Entsagens, der Entsagung, voller Entsagungen, führen,** to live a life of renunciation, of constant self-denial; **sich Entsagungen auferlegen,** to deny oneself.

entsagungsvoll, *a.* (life) full of renunciation, of (constant) self-denial; **mit entsagungsvoller Miene, mit entsagungsvollem Blick,** with a resigned look.

entsanden, *v.tr.* to remove sand from (river-bed, etc.); to clean (casting, etc.).

Entsander, *m.* **-s/-.** *Hyd.E:* sand-trap.

Entsatz, *m.* **-es/.** *Mil:* relief, relieving (of a town, fortress, etc.); **er sandte ein Heer zum E. der Stadt,** he sent out an army to the relief of the town, to relieve the town.

Entsatzarmee, *f.*, **Entsatzheer,** *n.* relief army, relieving army.

Entsatztruppen, *f.pl.* relief troops, relieving troops.

entsäuern, *v.tr.* *Ch:* to remove acid from (liquid, etc.); to deoxidize; **Entsäuerung** *f*, removal of acid (from liquid); deoxidization.

entschädigen. I. *v.tr.* to compensate (s.o.); to indemnify (s.o.); **j-n für etwas e.,** to compensate, indemnify, recoup, s.o. for sth.; *Jur:* to compensate s.o. for (loss); to pay s.o. damages for (physical injuries); **sich für etwas e.,** to recoup oneself for sth.; **j-n für einen Verlust e.,** to compensate, recoup, recompense, s.o. for a loss; to make good a loss to s.o.; **keine Summe wäre groß genug, ihn für seinen Verlust zu e.,** no sum would be large enough to compensate him for his loss; **nichts kann ihn für den Verlust seiner Sehkraft e.,** nothing can compensate him, can make up, for the loss of his sight; **die Natur hat ihn für seine schwachen Augen durch einen besonders fein entwickelten Tastsinn entschädigt,** nature compensated him for his weak eyesight by a particularly finely developed sense of touch.

II. *vbl s.* **1. Entschädigen,** *n.* *in vbl senses.* **2. Entschädigung,** *f.* (*a*) *in vbl senses; also:* compensation, indemnification (of s.o.) (for sth.); (*b*) compensation; *Jur:* (*for loss*) compensation; indemnity; indemnification; (*for physical injuries*) damages; **E. für Enteignung,** compensation, indemnity, for expropriation; **als E.,** as, by way of, compensation, indemnification; **j-m eine E. zahlen,** to pay s.o. compensation *or* damages; **eine E. in Höhe von *x* Mark,** a compensation of *x* marks; *x* marks damages; **die Höhe der E. festsetzen,** to fix the amount of compensation *or* damages; **j-n zu einer E. verurteilen,** to order s.o. to pay compensation *or* damages; **einen Antrag auf E. stellen, E. beantragen,** to claim, to put in a claim for, compensation *or* damages.

Entschädigungsanspruch, *m.* *Jur:* claim to compensation *or* damages.

Entschädigungsantrag, *m.* *Jur:* claim for compensation *or* damages.

entschädigungsberechtigt, *a.* *Jur:* entitled to compensation *or* damages.

Entschädigungsklage, *f. Jur:* action for damages.

entschädigungspflichtig, *a. Jur:* liable to (pay) compensation *or* damages.

Entschädigungssumme, *f. Jur:* compensation; indemnity; damages.

entschälen, *v.tr. Ser:* to degum, boil off (silk).

entschärfen, *v.tr.* to unprime (shell); to render (mine, unexploded bomb, etc.) harmless; to remove the detonator of (bomb, etc.).

Entschärfungskommando, *n. Mil: etc:* bomb- *or* mine-disposal squad.

entschäumen, *v.tr.* to remove the foam from (liquid); to skim, scum (molten metal, etc.).

Ehtschäumer, *m.* **-s/-,** (*device*) skimmer, scummer; (*agent*) foam remover, antifoam agent.

Entschäumungsmittel, *n.* antifoam agent, foam remover.

Entscheid, *m.* **-(e)s/-e.** *Jur: Adm:* decision.

entscheidbar, *a.* that can be decided, decidable.

entscheiden. I. *v.tr., v.i.* (*haben*) & **sich entscheiden** (*strong*) 1. (*a*) to decide, settle (question, quarrel, dispute, etc.); **die Sache ist entschieden,** the matter is decided; **die Sache ist noch nicht entschieden,** the matter is not yet settled, has not yet been settled, decided; **nur ausgedehnte Versuche werden e., es wird sich nur durch ausgedehnte Versuche e., welcher der beiden Prozesse der bessere ist,** only extensive experiments will decide which of the two processes is the better; **über eine Sache, in einer Sache, e.,** to make, give, a decision on, as to, regarding, a matter; **der Richter hat zu unseren Gunsten entschieden,** the judge gave a decision in our favour, gave a ruling in favour of us; **der Richter entschied, daß . . . ,** the judge ruled that . . . ; **er wußte lange Zeit nicht, wie er den Streit e. sollte,** he did not know for a long time how to decide, settle, the dispute, quarrel, what decision to give in the dispute; **eine Frage ein für alle mal e.,** to settle a question once and for all; (*b*) to decide, fix, settle, determine (sth.); *abs.* **e.,** to be decisive; **sein Schicksal wird sich heute e.,** his fate will be decided, determined, today; **es ist noch nichts entschieden, es hat sich noch nichts entschieden,** nothing is fixed, decided, settled, yet; **die Artillerie hat die Schlacht, den Ausgang der Schlacht, entschieden,** the artillery decided the battle; **er schoß das Tor, das das Spiel entschied, durch das das Spiel entschieden wurde,** he shot the goal that decided the game; **das Los soll e.,** the matter must be settled by drawing lots; **sein Wunsch entscheidet, hat zu e.,** the matter must be decided by his wishes, his wishes must decide the matter; the decision must be in accordance with his wishes; **Notwendigkeit allein entscheidet,** necessity must decide, will force a decision; (*c*) to decide, to make up one's mind; **du mußt selbst e.,** it is for you to decide; **e., sich e., etwas zu tun,** to decide, to make up one's mind, to do sth.; **nicht wissen, wie man sich e. soll,** not to know what decision to make; **ich habe (mich) noch nicht entschieden, ich bin noch nicht entschieden, was ich tun soll, was ich antworten werde, ob ich gehen werde,** I have not yet decided, I have not yet made up my mind, what to do, what answer I shall give, whether I shall go. 2. **für etwas, j-n, e., sich für etwas, j-n, e.,** to decide (up)on sth., to resolve upon, determine on, fix upon, settle (up)on, sth.; to decide for, in favour of, s.o.; **gegen etwas, j-n, sich gegen etwas, j-n, e.,** to decide against sth., s.o.; **sich dafür e., etwas zu tun,** to decide on doing sth.; **(sich) für eine Handlungsweise, Arbeitsmethode, e.,** to decide upon, settle upon, a course of action, a method of working; **wir haben uns für ein Klavier entschieden,** we have decided, settled, (up)on a piano; **die Versammlung entschied für Krieg,** the assembly decided upon war. *See also* **entschieden.**

II. *vbl s.* 1. **Entscheiden,** *n. in vbl senses of* 1 (*a*), (*b*). 2. **Entscheidung,** *f.* (*a*) *in vbl senses; also:* decision, settlement (of question, quarrel, dispute, etc.); determination (of sth.); **eine Frage zur E. bringen,** to bring a question to a decision; **j-m eine Angelegenheit zur E. vorlegen,** to submit a matter to s.o.'s decision, to ask s.o. to give a decision in a matter; **eine Sache zur E. stellen,** to ask for a decision in a matter; **die Frage, die Sache, die hier zur E. steht,** the question, matter, submitted for decision, the matter at issue; (*b*) decision; **eine E. in einer Sache fällen,** to give a decision on a case; **seine E. ist zu unseren Gunsten, günstig für uns, ausgefallen,** his decision was in our favour; he has decided in favour of us; he has given a decision favourable to us; *Jur:* **gerichtliche E.,** judicial decision; (*c*) decision; **eine E. herbeiführen,** to bring about a decision; **eine Sache zur E. bringen,** to bring a matter to a head; **eine E. mit Gewalt herbeiführen,** to force a decision; to bring matters to a head; **sein Tor führte zur E. (des Spiels), führte die E. (des Spiels) herbei,** his goal decided the match; **die E. ist gefallen,** the outcome (of the match, battle, etc.) is decided, the result (of the match, battle, etc.) is settled; **der Abend brachte die E. (der Schlacht), am Abend fiel die E.,** the decision (in the battle) came in the evening, the evening brought the decision; (*d*) decision; determination; **eine E. treffen, zu einer E. kommen,** to come to, make, arrive at, reach, a decision (**über etwas** *acc.*, on, as to, regarding, sth.); to make up one's mind (**über etwas** *acc.*, about sth.); **vor einer wichtigen, schweren, E. stehen,** to face a difficult decision; **in der Stunde der E.,** in the hour of decision; in the crucial hour; in the hour of crisis.

III. *pr.p. & a.* **entscheidend,** *in vbl senses; esp.* decisive (battle, question, argument, factor, etc.); crucial (point, test, etc.); **die entscheidende Schlacht,** the decisive, deciding, battle; **diese Frage ist für uns e.,** this question is decisive for us; this is a crucial question for us; **dieser Vorfall war für seine Laufbahn e.,** this incident was decisive for his career, decided, determined, his career; **eine Frage von entscheidender Bedeutung,** a question of prime, decisive, importance; **die Notwendigkeit allein ist e.,** necessity must decide; **den entscheidenden Schritt tun,** to take the decisive step, *F:* to take the plunge; **im entscheidenden Augenblick, Moment,** at the critical, crucial, moment, *F:* when it comes, came, to the pinch; **entscheidende Stimme,** (i) decisive vote; (ii) casting vote; *Sp:* **entscheidendes Spiel,** deciding game; decider.

Entscheidungsfrage, *f.* categorical question, question demanding the answer 'yes' or 'no'.

Entscheidungsgrund, *m. Jur:* reason for a judicial decision.

Entscheidungskampf, *m.* (*a*) decisive struggle; decisive battle; (*b*) *Sp:* final.

Entscheidungslauf, *m. Sp:* (*a*) (*after dead heat*) decider; (*b*) final.

Entscheidungsrennen, *n. Sp:* (*a*) (*after dead heat*) decider; (*b*) final.

Entscheidungsschlacht, *f.* decisive, deciding, battle.

Entscheidungsspiel, *n. Sp: Games:* (*a*) deciding game; decider; *Cards:* deciding rubber; (*b*) final.

entschieden. 1. *a.* (*a*) decided, decisive (manner, tone, etc.); resolute, firm (tone); **eine entschiedene Weigerung, ein entschiedenes Nein,** a decided, firm, categorical, peremptory, refusal, a decided, definite, 'no'; (*b*) decided, firm, declared (opponent of sth.); confirmed, staunch (adherent, supporter, of sth.); (*c*) decided, undeniable; marked, pronounced; definitive, positive; **ein entschiedener Fortschritt,** a decided, undeniable, step forward; a definite, decided, marked, improvement; **eine entschiedene Wendung zum Besseren,** a decided, marked, undeniable, definite, positive, turn for the better. 2. *adv.* (*a*) decidedly, resolutely; firmly; strongly; in a decided, resolute, firm, manner *or* tone; **ich muß das ganz e., aufs entschiedenste, bestreiten,** I deny this categorically, in the strongest possible terms; **ich bin e. dagegen,** I am firmly, *F:* dead, against it; **ich bin (ganz) e. dafür,** I am strongly in favour of it, I am all for it; **sich e. für, gegen, etwas aussprechen,** to pronounce strongly, decisively, in favour of sth.; to pronounce firmly, emphatically, in strong terms, against sth.; (*b*) decidedly; undeniably; positively; definitely; **er ist e. der Beste,** he is decidedly, undeniably, the best; **es geht ihm e. besser,** he is decidedly, definitely, better; **er ist ihm e. überlegen,** he is decidedly, definitely, superior to him; *F:* **er ist e. verrückt,** he is definitely, positively, mad; *F:* **ich habe e. kein Glück,** I 'am unlucky, and no mistake. *See also* **entscheiden.**

Entschiedenheit, *f.* (*a*) resoluteness, firmness (of manner, tone, etc.); **die E. seiner Weigerung,** the firmness, decisiveness, of his refusal; **die E. seines Tons, seine E., überraschte mich,** his firm, decided, tone surprised me; (*b*) *adv.phr.* **mit E.,** decidedly, resolutely; firmly; strongly; in a decided, resolute, firm, manner *or* tone; **er bestritt es mit aller E.,** he denied it categorically, in the strongest possible terms; **er hat sich mit E. dagegen ausgesprochen,** he pronounced strongly, emphatically, against it; **sich mit E. für etwas einsetzen,** to advocate sth. vigorously, strongly.

entschlacken, *v.tr.* (*a*) to skim, scum (molten metal); to remove the slag from (metal), the dross from (iron); (*b*) *F:* to purge (the body).

entschlafen, *v.i.* (*strong*) (*sein*) 1. *A:* to fall asleep. 2. *Lit:* to pass away, to die; *B:* to fall asleep; **sanft e.,** to pass away peacefully; **im Herrn e.,** to fall asleep in the Lord, in Christ; **die Entschlafenen,** the dead, the departed; *B:* **wir werden nicht alle e., wir werden aber alle verwandelt werden,** we shall not all sleep, but we shall all be changed.

entschlagen (sich), *v.refl.* (*strong*) *Lit:* **sich etwas** *gen.* **e.,** to rid oneself of, to free oneself from, sth.; to throw off, get out of, break off (habit); to cast aside, off (habit, thoughts); to put (thoughts, wishes) out of one's head; to banish (fear, care); to renounce (sin, earthly things, etc.); **dieses Gedankens kannst du dich getrost e.,** you may safely put that thought out of your head; **sich der Sünde, des Übels, e.,** to renounce sin, evil; **sich aller Wünsche e.,** to renounce all wishes.

entschlammen, *v.tr.* to clear (street, ditch, etc.) of mud *or* slime; to sluice (sewer); to clean (out) (cistern, *Mch:* boiler); *Min:* to wash (coal, ore); to trunk, clean, sluice, buddle (ore).

entschleiern, *v.tr.* to unveil (face, etc.); **sich e.,** (*of pers.*) to take off, drop, one's veil, to unveil; (*of face*) to appear unveiled; (*of truth, etc.*) to be revealed, disclosed; **die entschleierte Wahrheit,** the truth unveiled.

entschleimen, *v.tr.* to clear (sth.) of slime; *Med:* to clear (respiratory tract, etc.) of mucus.

entschlichten, *v.tr. Tex:* to remove the size, sizing, dressing, from (linen, cotton, etc.); to de-size (linen, cotton, etc.); to boil the sizing, dressing, out of (linen, cotton, etc.); **entschlichtetes Leinen,** linen free of dressing, sizing, dressing-free linen.

Entschlichtungsbad, *n.*, **Entschlichtungsflotte,** *f. Tex:* de-sizing bath, de-sizing liquor.

entschließen (sich), *v.refl.* (*strong*) (*a*) to make up one's mind; to come to a decision; **er kann sich nie e.,** he can never make up his mind; he is always undecided; **endlich hat er sich entschlossen,** at last he has made up his mind, he has come to a decision; **er entschließt sich schnell, schwer,** he makes up his mind quickly, with difficulty, he is quick, slow, to make up his mind; (*b*) **sich zu etwas e., sich (dazu) e., etwas zu tun,** to make up one's mind, to decide, to do sth.; to decide on doing sth.; to determine to do sth., on doing sth.; to resolve upon sth., on doing sth., to do sth.; *U.S: F:* to fix to do sth.; **ich habe mich entschlossen, nach Italien zu fahren,** I have decided, resolved, to go to Italy; **sie entschlossen sich zum Kauf eines Autos,** they decided to buy a car, they decided on the purchase of a car; **nach langem Zögern entschloß er sich endlich, mit uns zu reisen,** after long hesitation he at last made up his mind, decided, to travel with us; **ich kann mich heute zu nichts e.,** I can't make up my mind to anything, bring myself to do anything, today; **er konnte sich nicht dazu e. zu gehen,** he couldn't bring himself to go; **wir haben uns dazu e. müssen, unser Auto zu verkaufen,** there was nothing else for it—we had to sell our car; **er konnte sich nur schwer dazu e., seine Zustimmung zu geben,** he agreed very reluctantly; **er wird sich dazu e. müssen,** he'll have to do it (however reluctantly); **ich würde mich sehr freuen, wenn Sie sich dazu e. könnten, dem jungen Mann zu helfen,** I should be very happy if you could see your way to helping the young man. *See also* **entschlossen.**

II. *vbl s.* **Entschließung,** *f.* resolution; **eine E. annehmen,** to pass, carry, a resolution; to adopt a resolution. *Cp.* **Entschluß.**

entschlossen, *a.* 1. (*a*) resolute, determined (pers., character, etc.); (pers.) of decision, determination; **mit entschlossener Miene,** with a look of resolution, determination, decision, with a determined look; **eine entschlossene Miene aufsetzen,** to put on a firm look; to assume an air of determination; **ein entschlossenes Auftreten haben,** to have an air of determination (about one), to look determined; to have a resolute manner; **eine entschlossene Haltung einnehmen,** to take a firm stand; *adv.* **e. handeln,** to act with decision, determination; to act resolutely; **wenn man e. auftritt, erreicht man mehr,** one achieves more if one has a firm, determined, resolute, manner, air; **er zögerte einen Augenblick an der Tür, dann trat er e. ein,** he hesitated for a moment at the door, then went firmly in, then resolutely went in; **sich e. an die Arbeit machen,** to go resolutely to work, to

set to work with determination; (*b*) **kurz e.,** without a moment's, the slightest, hesitation; without faltering; unhesitatingly; **kurz e. kaufte er sich eine Fahrkarte nach Rom,** without a moment's thought he bought a ticket to Rome; **kurz e. stand er auf und verließ das Zimmer,** with sudden determination, without a moment's hesitation, he stood up and left the room; **kurz e. trat er in das Geschäft und kaufte den Verlobungsring,** without thinking twice he walked into the shop and bought the engagement ring. **2.** (*a*) **e. sein,** to have one's mind made up, to be decided, determined; **sie war e.: sie mußte gehen,** her mind was made up: she had to go; **ich bin noch nicht e.,** I am not yet decided, I am still undecided, I have not yet made up my mind, my mind is not made up yet; **er war entschlossener als, denn, je,** he was more determined than ever; (*b*) **zu etwas e. sein, e. sein, etwas zu tun,** to be determined, decided, resolved on sth., on doing sth., to do sth.; **sie war fest e., nicht ohne ihn zu reisen,** she was firmly resolved not to travel without him; **er war zum Äußersten e.,** he was determined on extreme measures; he was resolved to risk everything; **ich bin fest dazu e.,** I am quite determined, decided, on it, on doing it; my mind is made up to do it; **ich bin e., diese Beleidigung nicht auf mir sitzen zu lassen,** I don't mean to put up with that insult. *See also* **entschließen.**

Entschlossenheit, *f.* **1.** decision (of character), determination, resolution; firmness; **ein Mann von E. und Charakterstärke,** a man of decision, determination, resolution, and strength of character; **mit E. handeln,** to act with decision, determination, resolution; **sich mit E. an die Arbeit machen,** to go resolutely to work, to set to work with determination; **mit E. auftreten,** to have a firm, determined, resolute, manner, air, to have an air of determination (about one). **2.** determination, resolution (to do sth.); **seine E. nicht nachzugeben war unerschütterlich,** his determination not to yield, give way, was unshakeable; **seine E. zu bauen,** his determination to build.

entschlüpfen, *v.i.* (*sein*) (*a*) to escape; to slip away; **j-m e.,** (*of pers.*) to escape s.o.; (*of time*) to slip away from s.o.; to slip by; (*of word, remark*) to escape s.o., s.o.'s lips; **eine Gelegenheit e. lassen,** to let an opportunity slip; **die Bemerkung ist ihr nur so entschlüpft,** the remark just slipped out; (*b*) (*of caterpillar, bird*) **dem Ei e.,** to emerge from the egg.

Entschluß, *m.* -schlusses/-schlüsse, resolution, decision; **einen E. fassen,** to make a decision, resolution; **zu einem E. kommen,** to come to a decision; to arrive at, reach, a decision; to make up one's mind; **j-n in seinem E. bestärken,** to strengthen s.o.'s resolution; to strengthen s.o. in his, her, decision; **j-n in seinem E. wankend machen,** to shake s.o.'s determination (to do sth.); **in seinem E. wankend werden,** to falter in one's decision, to weaken; **den E. fassen, etwas zu tun,** to decide, resolve, make up one's mind, to do sth.; **er hat den festen E. gefaßt, seine Stelle aufzugeben,** he has made a firm resolution, decision, he has firmly decided, to give up his job; **mein E. ist gefaßt, steht fest,** my mind is made up; **sein E. war schnell gefaßt,** his mind was quickly made up, his decision was quickly made; **von einem E. abgehen,** to reverse a decision; to change one's mind; to go back on a decision; **er geht nie von einem einmal gefaßten E. ab,** he never changes his mind once it is made up; once he has made up his mind, once he has made a decision, he never budges; **er ist unerschütterlich in seinem E.,** his decision is unshakeable; he will not budge from his decision.

Entschlußkraft, *f.* decision, determination, resolution; **Mangel an E.,** lack of resolution.

entschlußlos, *a.* (*of pers.*) irresolute, undecided; lacking in resolution; unable to make up one's mind.

Entschlußlosigkeit, *f.* irresoluteness, irresolution; lack of resolution; inability to make up one's mind.

entschuldbar, *a.* **1.** excusable. **2.** *Jur:* (farm, estate) that can be disencumbered.

entschulden, *v.tr. Jur:* to free (estate, farm) of debts, to disencumber (estate, farm); **Entschuldung** *f,* disencumbering, disencumberment.

entschuldigen. I. *v.tr.* **1.** (*a*) to excuse (s.o., s.o.'s conduct, etc.); to pardon (s.o.); to exculpate, exonerate (s.o.); to free (s.o.) from blame; **j-n für seine Faulheit e., j-s Faulheit e., e., daß j-d faul ist,** to excuse s.o.'s laziness, to excuse s.o. his laziness, to excuse s.o. for his laziness, to excuse s.o.'s being lazy; **j-n, sich, j-s Verhalten, sein Verhalten, mit etwas e.,** to excuse s.o., oneself, s.o.'s, one's, conduct, by referring to sth., to offer sth. as an excuse for s.o., s.o.'s, one's, conduct; to make sth. one's excuse; **sich mit seiner Jugend, mit Unwissenheit, e.,** to plead the inexperience of youth, to plead ignorance, to offer the inexperience of youth, to offer ignorance, as an excuse (for one's conduct, action, etc.); **seine Jugend entschuldigt ihn, entschuldigt ihn nicht,** his youth excuses him, is no excuse; **sein Verhalten läßt sich nicht e., ist durch nichts zu e., nichts kann sein Verhalten e.,** nothing can excuse his conduct, there is no excuse for his conduct, his conduct admits of no excuse, nothing can be said in excuse for him, his conduct; **Unwissenheit entschuldigt nicht,** ignorance is no excuse; **sich damit e., daß . . . ,** to excuse oneself on the ground that . . . ; **das entschuldigt nicht, daß er nicht schreibt,** that is no excuse for his not writing; **das entschuldigt seine Faulheit nicht,** that is no excuse for his laziness, for his being lazy; **sie hat seine Fehler immer entschuldigt,** she always found excuses for his faults; **j-s Fernbleiben, j-s Abwesenheit, e.,** to excuse s.o.'s absence, s.o.'s non-attendance; **bitte entschuldigen Sie meine Verspätung, bitte entschuldigen Sie, daß ich zu spät komme,** please excuse my being late; **bitte entschuldigen Sie, daß ich gestern nicht kommen konnte, bitte entschuldigen Sie mein Fernbleiben gestern,** please excuse, accept my apologies for, my absence yesterday, please excuse me for not coming yesterday; **bitte entschuldigen Sie, daß, wenn, ich so schnell fortgehe,** please excuse me for hurrying away; **entschuldigen Sie, wenn ich Ihnen widerspreche,** pardon, excuse, my contradicting you; **wenn Sie den Ausdruck e. (wollen),** if you will excuse the expression; **entschuldigen Sie! entschuldige!** (i) excuse me! (ii) sorry! **entschuldigen Sie, könnten Sie mir bitte das Salz reichen?** excuse me, could you please pass me the salt? **entschuldigen Sie die Störung, entschuldigen Sie, daß, wenn, ich (Sie) störe,** sorry to trouble you; excuse the interruption; **wer sich entschuldigt, klagt sich an,** excuses always proceed from a guilty conscience; (*b*) **j-n e.,** (i) to excuse s.o. from attendance *or* from doing sth.; (ii) to make s.o.'s excuses for s.o.; *Sch:* to excuse s.o.; **sich e.,** to make *or* send one's excuses; to send one's apologies; to ask to be excused from attendance; *U.S:* to send regrets; **ich möchte mich für heute abend e.,** I should like to be excused from coming tonight; **sich e. lassen,** to send one's excuses, apologies, for not coming; to ask s.o. to make, to convey, one's excuses for one; **sich mit Arbeit e.,** to make work one's excuse; **j-n für entschuldigt halten,** to consider s.o. excused; **bitte halten Sie mich für entschuldigt,** I must ask you to consider me excused; **bitte entschuldigen Sie mich für einen Augenblick,** please excuse me for a moment; **j-n beim Gastgeber, beim Lehrer, e.,** to excuse s.o. to the host, to the teacher; **sie war gestern entschuldigt, aber heute fehlt sie unentschuldigt,** she was excused yesterday, but today she has stayed away without any excuse; **sie begannen alle, sich zu e.,** they all began to make excuses, *Lit:* excuse. **2. sich entschuldigen,** to apologize, to make an apology, one's apology, apologies **(bei j-m,** to s.o.); **sich für etwas e.,** to apologize for sth.; (*in letter*) **ich muß mich für mein langes Schweigen bei Ihnen e.,** I have to apologize to you for not having written for such a long time; **er hat sich sehr dafür entschuldigt,** he was very apologetic about it; he was full of apologies; **sich (bei j-m) für j-n e., für j-s Betragen e.,** to apologize for s.o., for s.o.'s conduct, (to s.o.); **sich für seinen Anzug e.,** to apologize for one's dress.

II. *vbl s.* **Entschuldigung,** *f.* **1.** (*a*) excuse; **zur E. seiner schlechten Laune, als E. für seine schlechte Laune,** as an excuse for his bad temper; in excuse of his bad temper, (in order) to excuse his bad temper; **nichts kann zu seiner E., zur E. seines Verhaltens, gesagt werden,** there is nothing to be said in excuse for him, for his conduct, his conduct admits of no excuse; **für sein Verhalten gibt es keine E.,** there is no excuse for his conduct; **es gibt keine E. dafür, daß er nicht geschrieben hat,** there is no excuse for his not writing; **er konnte nichts zu seiner E. vorbringen,** he could say nothing to excuse himself, in excuse of his conduct; **Unwissenheit ist keine E.,** ignorance is no excuse; **etwas als E. angeben,** to offer sth. as an excuse; to make sth. one's excuse; **als E. gab er an, daß . . . ,** by way of excuse he alleged that . . . ; **eine E. für etwas finden,** to find an excuse for sth.; **Entschuldigungen vorbringen,** to make excuses, to offer excuses; **eine glaubwürdige E. vorbringen,** to offer a reasonable, valid, excuse; **ich hätte gerne eine E. für heute Abend gefunden,** I should have liked to find an excuse for tonight; **Entschuldigung!** excuse me! (*cp.* 2); (*b*) excuse (*for non-attendance, for not doing sth.*); **ohne E. fehlen,** to be absent without any excuse, without being excused; **ohne E. zu spät kommen,** to be late without (valid) excuse; (*c*) *Sch: etc:* letter *or* note of excuse; **j-m eine E. schreiben,** to write a note of excuse for s.o.; **eine schriftliche E. vorlegen,** to bring *or* send a written excuse. **2.** apology; **j-n um E. bitten,** to apologize to s.o., to offer s.o. an apology, one's apologies, to make one's apologies to s.o.; **du mußt sofort um E. bitten,** you must apologize at once, you must say at once you are sorry; **er hat mich für sein Benehmen um E. gebeten,** he has apologized to me for his behaviour; **j-n für j-n, für j-s Verhalten, um E. bitten,** to apologize for s.o., for s.o.'s conduct, to s.o.; **j-s E. annehmen,** to accept s.o.'s apology; **Entschuldigung!** sorry! (I beg your) pardon! (*cp.* 1 (*a*)); **bitte um E.!** if you will pardon, excuse, the expression; **eine E. verlangen,** to demand an apology.

Entschuldigungsbrief, *m.* **1.** letter of apology, (written) apology; **er schrieb einen E.,** he wrote to apologize, to say he was sorry. **2.** *Sch: etc:* letter of excuse, note of excuse.

Entschuldigungsgrund, *m.* excuse; **Müdigkeit ist kein E.,** tiredness is no excuse; **etwas als E. angeben,** to make sth. an, one's, excuse, to offer sth. as an excuse.

Entschuldigungsschreiben, *n.* letter of apology, (written) apology.

Entschuldigungszettel, *m. Sch: etc:* note of excuse.

Entschuldung, *f. see* **entschulden.**

entschuppen, *v.tr.* to scale (fish).

entschweben, *v.i.* (*sein*) (*of soap bubble, balloon, spirit, F: of pers.*) to float away.

entschwefeln, *v.tr. Ch: Ind:* to desulphurize; **Entschwefelung** *f,* desulphurization.

Entschwefelungsmittel, *n.* desulphurizing agent.

entschweißen, *v.tr. Tex:* to scour (wool).

entschwinden, *v.i.* (*strong*) (*sein*) to vanish, disappear; (*of time*) to vanish away; **j-s Blicken e.,** to vanish from sight, to fade from sight, from s.o.'s eyes, to disappear from s.o.'s sight; **(aus) dem Sinn, dem Gedächtnis, e.,** to fade from memory; **das Schiff entschwand unseren Blicken,** the ship faded, vanished, from sight; **die Stunden entschwinden,** the hours vanish away; **entschwundene Hoffnungen,** vanished hopes.

entseelen, *v.tr.* **1.** to destroy (s.o.'s) soul; to make (civilization, etc.) soulless; **die entseelende Wirkung der Mechanisierung,** the soul-destroying effect of mechanization; **eine entseelte Kunst,** an art without soul. **2.** *Lit:* to kill (s.o.); **sie sank entseelt zu Boden,** she fell dead, lifeless, to the ground.

entsehnen, *v.tr.* to remove the sinews from (meat).

entsenden, *v.tr.* (*conj. like* **senden**) to send out (s.o.); to dispatch (messenger); (*of sun*) to send forth (rays); (*of plant*) to send out, forth (leaves); **j-n an einen Ort e.,** to send s.o. to a place.

entsetzen. I. *v.tr.* **1.** to relieve (town, fortress); **er sandte ein Heer aus, die Stadt zu e.,** he sent out an army to relieve the town, for the relief of the town. **2. j-n seines Amtes e.,** to relieve s.o. of his post, office, to dismiss s.o.; **j-n des Thrones e.,** to cast s.o. from his throne, to dethrone s.o. **3.** (*a*) to horrify (s.o.), to fill (s.o.) with horror; to appal (s.o.); **der Anblick, der Gedanke, entsetzte ihn,** the sight, the thought, filled him with horror, horrified him, appalled him; he was horrified, appalled, at the sight, at the thought; (*b*) **sich über etwas** *acc.*, **j-n, e.,** to be horrified at, about, sth., at s.o.'s actions, behaviour, at s.o.; **sich bei einem Anblick, Gedanken, e.,** to be horrified, appalled, at a sight, a thought; **sich vor etwas, j-m e.,** to be seized with a horror, to have a horror, of sth., of doing sth., of s.o.

II. *vbl s.* **1. Entsetzen,** *n.* horror; **starr vor E.,** paralysed with horror; horror-stricken; **zu meinem E.,** to my horror; **von E. ergriffen werden,** to be seized with horror; to be horror-stricken; **sich mit E. (von etwas) abwenden,** to turn away in horror; **voller E.,** horror-stricken; **mit einem Schrei des Entsetzens,** with a shriek of horror,

with a horrified shriek. **2. Entsetzung,** *f.* (*a*)=**Entsatz;** (*b*) **E. vom Amt,** dismissal; (*c*) *A:*=II. 1.

III. *p.p. & a.* **entsetzt,** *in vbl senses; esp.* horrified; in horror, horror-stricken; appalled; **e. von diesem, über diesen, Anblick,** horrified, appalled, at the sight; **bei diesem Anblick wich sie e. zurück,** when she saw this she recoiled in horror; **er floh e.,** he fled in horror, horror-stricken; **sich e. (von etwas) abwenden,** to turn away in horror, horror-stricken; **die entsetzte Menge,** the horrified, horror-stricken, crowd; **in entsetztem Schweigen,** in horrified silence, in a silence full of horror; **wir waren ganz e., als wir die Geschichte hörten,** we were altogether horrified, quite appalled, when we heard the story.

entsetzlich. **1.** *a.* (*a*) horrible, horrifying; terrible; **es war ein entsetzlicher Anblick, es war e. anzusehen,** it was horrible to look at, it was a horrifying, horrible, gruesome, ghastly, sight; **ein entsetzliches Schicksal traf ihn,** he met with a terrible, horrible, fate; **eine entsetzliche Krankheit,** a horrible disease; (*b*) *F:* horrid, horrible, terrible; dreadful, awful; frightful; shocking, appalling; **was für eine entsetzliche Frau!** what a horrid, horrible, dreadful, woman! **er hatte entsetzliche Angst,** he was horribly, dreadfully, terribly, frightened; **entsetzliches Wetter,** horrible, terrible, dreadful, awful, shocking, appalling, weather; **er hatte eine entsetzliche Erkältung,** he had a terrible, frightful, shocking, cold; **ein entsetzlicher Lärm,** a horrid, terrible, horrible, dreadful, frightful, noise; **seine dauernde Nörgelei ist e.,** his constant complaining is, his constant complaints are, terrible, awful; **er starb in entsetzlichen Schmerzen,** he died in agonies. **2.** *adv.* horribly, terribly; dreadfully, awfully; frightfully; shockingly, appallingly; **es ist e. kalt,** it is terribly, horribly, frightfully, dreadfully, awfully, cold; **er ist e. erkältet,** he has a terrible, frightful, shocking, cold; **sie geht mir e. auf die Nerven,** she gets terribly on my nerves; **sie sieht e. (schlecht) aus,** she looks terribly, dreadfully, ill, she looks awful, appalling; **in diesem Kleid sieht sie e. aus,** she looks awful, frightful, a fright, in this dress; **es sah e. aus,** it looked horrible, terrible; **sie spielt e. (schlecht),** she plays terribly badly, shockingly (badly); **sich e. (schlecht) benehmen,** to behave terribly badly; **e. gefährlich,** terribly dangerous.

Entsetzlichkeit, *f.* **1.** horrible nature (of disease, crime, etc.); horribleness (of sight, etc.). **2.** horrible thing, deed, etc.; horror; atrocity.

entsetzt, *a. see* **entsetzen III.**

Entsetzung, *f. see* **entsetzen II.**

entseuchen, *v.tr.* to disinfect; **Entseuchung** *f,* disinfection.

entsichern, *v.tr.* **1.** to cock (firearm); to release the safety device of (gun, rifle, etc.); to arm (mine, bomb, etc.). **2.**=**entschärfen.**

entsiegeln, *v.tr.* **1.** to unseal, open, break open (letter); to unseal, break the seal of (document); *Lit:* to open (door). **2.** *Lit:* to solve (mystery, puzzle); to reveal (secret); to reveal, unseal (the future); to unseal (s.o.'s lips).

entsilbern, *v.tr. Metall:* to desilverize (lead).

entsinken, *v.i.* (*strong*) (*sein*) *Lit:* (*a*) (*of thg*) **j-m, j-s Händen, e.,** to fall from s.o.'s hands; (*b*) **ihm entsank der Mut,** his courage failed him.

entsinnen (sich), *v.refl.* (*strong*) **sich etwas** *gen.*, **j-s, e.,** to remember, recall, sth., s.o.; to recollect sth.; **sich e., daß . . . ,** to remember, recollect, recall, that . . .; **ich kann mich (dessen) nicht e.,** I don't remember it; **ich entsinne mich nicht, daß du es mir erzählt hast,** I don't remember your telling me so; **soviel, soweit, ich mich entsinne, wenn ich mich recht entsinne,** to the best of my recollection; as far as I remember, recollect; if I remember rightly, aright; **ich entsinne mich dessen, seiner, nur noch dunkel,** I remember it, him, only vaguely; I have only a dim recollection of it, him; **ich entsinne mich, es, ihn, gesehen zu haben,** I remember seeing it, him; **ich entsinne mich, daß er eines Tages von Hause fortging,** I remember his going away from home one day.

entspannen. I. *v.tr.* **1.** (*a*) to slacken, relax, loosen (sth. that is taut); to unbend (bow); to relax, loosen up (the muscles); to uncock (rifle); **eine Feder e.,** (i) to let down, loosen, release the tension on, (ii) to release, a spring; **ein Seil e.,** to slacken a rope; **den Geist e.,** *abs.* **e.,** to relax, give relaxation to, the mind; *abs.* to be relaxing, to have a relaxing effect; **die Nerven e.,** *abs.* **e.,** to steady the nerves; *abs.* to have a soothing effect; **die politische Lage e.,** to ease the political situation; **diese Beschäftigung ist entspannend, hat eine entspannende Wirkung, entspannt,** this occupation is a relaxation for one's mind, has a relaxing effect; **entspannende Lektüre,** relaxing reading; (*b*) *Mch: etc:* to expand (steam, gas); to cut off (steam); (*c*) *Ph.Ch:* (*of chemical agent in detergent*) **das Wasser e.,** to reduce the surface tension of the water; **Wasser entspannendes, seifenfreies Reinigungsmittel,** (surface active) detergent. **2. sich entspannen,** (*a*) (*of thg*) to become slack, to slacken, to relax; (*of muscle*) to relax, to loosen up; **meine Nerven entspannen sich,** my nerves are calming down; **der Geist entspannt sich,** one relaxes, I relax (mentally); **sein Gesicht entspannte sich, seine Züge entspannten sich,** his face relaxed; **die politische Lage hat sich entspannt,** the political situation has eased, has become a little easier; (*b*) (*of pers.*) to relax; to find relaxation; to take some relaxation; **ich lese, um mich zu e.,** I read to relax my mind, I read for relaxation; (*c*) *Mch: etc:* (*of steam, gas*) to expand.

II. *vbl s.* **1. Entspannen,** *n. in vbl senses of* I. 1. **2. Entspannung,** *f.* (*a*)=II. 1; *also:* relaxation (of the muscles, the nerves, etc.); *Mch: etc:* expansion (of gas, steam); **zur E. der Nerven,** for the relaxation of the nerves, to steady the nerves; **Übungen zur E. der Muskeln,** exercises to loosen up, relax, the muscles; (*b*) *in vbl senses of* I. 2; *also: Mch: etc:* expansion (of steam, gas); *Pol:* relaxation of tension, détente; **das wird zur E. der politischen Lage beitragen,** this will contribute to the easing of the political situation; this will help to ease the political situation; **eine E. (zwischen den beiden Ländern) ist eingetreten,** the situation has become less strained, has become easier (between the two nations); there is an improvement in the situation; (*c*) relaxation; **E. in Büchern suchen,** to seek relaxation in books; **E. nach des Tages Arbeit,** relaxation after the day's toil; **Angeln ist seine einzige E.,** fishing is his only relaxation; **diese kleinen Arbeiten bedeuten eine E. für mich,** these little jobs are a relaxation for my mind; **als eine E.,** as a relaxation.

Entspannungsglühen, *n. Metall:* stress-relieving annealing.

Entspannungsmittel, *n.* **1.** means of relaxation. **2.** (*a*) means of releasing tension; (*b*) *Ph.Ch:* wetting agent; surface-active agent, *U.S:* surfactant.

Entspannungsübungen, *f.pl. Gym:* loosening-up exercises (*for the muscles*); *Psy:* exercises in (mental) relaxation.

entspiegeln, *v.tr. Phot:* to eliminate reflection from (a surface); **entspiegeltes Objektiv,** coated lens.

entspinnen, *v.tr.* (*strong*) **1.** *A:*=**anspinnen** 3 (*a*). **2. sich entspinnen,** (*of conversation, etc.*) to start; (*of relations*) to develop, to come into being; (*of friendship, intimacy, rivalry, quarrel, etc.*) to spring up; **nach einer Weile entspann sich ein lebhaftes Gespräch zwischen ihnen,** after a while a lively conversation started between them; **allmählich entspann sich eine zarte Freundschaft zwischen ihnen,** gradually a tender friendship sprang up between them; **es entspann sich ein heftiger Kampf,** a violent struggle developed.

entspitzen, *v.tr. Hort:* (i) to top (plant); to nip the top off (plant); (ii) to nip off the buds of (plant).

entsprechen. I. *v.i.* (*strong*) (*haben*) (*a*) **etwas** *dat.* **e., entsprechend sein,** to correspond to, with, sth.; to be corresponding to sth.; to agree, to be in agreement, with sth.; to tally, square, with sth.; to suit, meet, answer (requirements, etc.); to accord with sth.; to answer, correspond to, *F:* come up to (a standard); to be consistent with sth.; (*of part*) to conform, correspond, to (another part, etc.); **sein Bericht entspricht nicht den Tatsachen, ist nicht den Tatsachen entsprechend,** his report does not agree with, is not in agreement with, does not correspond with, is not true to, not in accordance with, the facts; **Artikel, die unseren Bedürfnissen entsprechen, entsprechend sind,** articles that meet, suit, answer, our needs, requirements, articles adapted to our needs, requirements; **diese Interpretation entspricht nicht dem Geist des Vertrags, ist nicht dem Geist des Vertrags entsprechend,** this interpretation does not correspond with, to, does not accord with, the spirit of the treaty; **seine Handlungen entsprechen seinen Prinzipien, sind seinen Prinzipien entsprechend,** his actions conform with, accord with, are consistent with, in accordance with, in conformity with, his principles; **Verhalten, das seiner Natur nicht entspricht, entsprechend ist,** conduct not consistent with, not in accordance with, his nature; **dem Zweck e., dem Zweck entsprechend sein,** to answer the purpose; **j-s Erwartungen e., entsprechend sein,** to answer, satisfy, come up to, be equal to, s.o.'s expectations; **den Erwartungen nicht e., nicht entsprechend sein,** to fall short of expectations; (*of two thgs*) **sich, einander, e., einander entsprechend sein,** to correspond, be corresponding, to conform; to tally; (*b*) (*of pers.*) **j-s Wünschen, usw., e.,** to conform with, comply with, fall in with, s.o.'s wishes, etc.; **wir sind gerne bereit, Ihren Wünschen zu e.,** we shall be most willing to comply with your wishes; **Ihren Wünschen entsprechend haben wir die Waren per Bahn an Sie gesandt,** in compliance, in accordance, with your wishes we have sent you the goods by rail; **Ihren Anordnungen entsprechend,** in compliance, conformity, accordance, with your instructions. *Cp.* III.

II. *vbl s.* **Entsprechung,** *f.* (*a*) correspondence, agreement (between thgs); (*b*) parallel; analogy; **es gibt keine genaue E. zu diesem Phänomen,** there is no exact parallel, analogy, to this phenomenon, this phenomenon has no exact parallel, analogy; there is nothing quite comparable to this phenomenon; **er hat zahlreiche Entsprechungen gefunden,** he has found numerous parallels.

III. *pr.p. & a.* **entsprechend,** *in vbl senses; esp.* that is in accordance with (sth.); that accords with (sth.); according (*dat.*, to); true (*dat.*, to); appropriate, suitable; corresponding, analogous (part, etc.); *Geom:* corresponding, homologous; *adv.* correspondingly; accordingly; **wenn man in die Tropen fährt, muß man (die) entsprechende Kleidung tragen, muß man sich e. anziehen,** when you go to the tropics you have to wear appropriate clothes, you have to dress accordingly; **sie trug ein der Gelegenheit entsprechendes Kleid,** she wore a dress suitable to, appropriate for, the occasion; **er führte ein seiner Philosophie entsprechendes Leben, ein Leben seiner Philosophie e.,** he led a life that conformed with his philosophy; **wenn man viel reisen will, muß man die entsprechenden Mittel haben,** if one wants to travel a lot one must have adequate means; **wenn man ein großes Haus hat, muß man die entsprechenden Möbel haben,** if one has a large house one has to have suitable furniture; **ich nehme Ihren Vorschlag an und habe eine entsprechende Änderung in meinen Plänen vorgenommen, und habe meine Pläne e. geändert,** I accept your suggestion and I have altered my plans accordingly; **wir haben Ihre neue Adresse zur Kenntnis genommen und haben einen entsprechenden Vermerk in unseren Akten gemacht,** we have received notice of your new address and have made a corresponding entry in our files; **dem Alter, der Größe, e.,** according to age, according to size *or* height; **wir geben unseren Mitteln e.,** we give according to our means; **wir haben Ihrem Auftrag e. gehandelt,** we acted in accordance with your order; **ich habe eine Erkältung und fühle mich e. (schlecht),** I have a cold and feel like it; **sie sahen bald, was geschehen war, und verhielten sich e.,** they soon saw what had happened and behaved accordingly; **sie saßen den ganzen Abend in der Bar und tranken e. (viel),** they sat in the bar all evening and drank accordingly; **du mußt dich deinem Alter e. benehmen,** you must behave as befits your age. *Cp.* I; *see also* **dementsprechend.**

entsprießen, *v.i.* (*strong*) (*sein*) (*a*) (*of plants*) **(der Erde) e.,** to spring up, to come up; to grow; (*b*) (*of pers.*) **einem,** *occ.* **von, aus, einem, edlen Geschlecht entsprossen sein,** to come, to be descended, to spring, to be sprung, to issue, from a noble family, race.

entspringen, *v.i.* (*strong*) (*sein*) **1.** (*of river, etc.*) to rise, to have its source; **der Rhein entspringt auf dem St. Gotthardt,** the Rhine rises, has its source, on Mount St Gotthardt. **2.** (*a*) *A. & Lit:* **j-m, einer Familie, usw., e.,** to spring from, to be sprung from, to issue from, s.o., a family, etc.; (*b*) (*of virtue, vice, feeling, need, etc.*) **etwas** *dat.*, **aus etwas, e.,** to spring from, (a)rise from, sth.; to originate from sth.; to originate in sth.; **der Streit entsprang (aus) einem Mißverständnis,** the quarrel (a)rose, sprang, from a misapprehension; **alle diese Laster entspringen (aus) der gleichen Wurzel,** all these vices spring from the same root; **nichts Gutes kann daraus e.,** nothing good can come of it. **3.** (*of prisoner, captured animal, etc.*) to escape, to run away; **aus dem**

Gefängnis e., to escape from prison; to break prison; (*of animal*) **aus dem Zoo e.**, to escape from the zoo; **ein entsprungener Sträfling**, an escaped, a runaway, convict.
entsprossen, *v.i.* (*sein*)=**entsprießen.**
entspunden, *v.tr.* to draw the bung from, to unbung (barrel, cask).
Entspunder, *m.* **-s/-**. *Tls:* bung-drawer.
entstaatlichen, *v.tr.* to free (school, etc.) from state control; to denationalize (industry, etc.); to disestablish (church); **Entstaatlichung** *f*, removal of state control (from school, etc.); denationalization (of industry, etc.); disestablishment (of church).
entstählen, *v.tr. Metall:* to unsteel (lamina).
entstammen, *v.i.* (*sein*) (*a*) to be descended, to be sprung, to issue (*dat.*, *occ.* **von**, from); **er entstammt einem Bauerngeschlecht**, he comes of peasant stock; **er entstammt einer armen Familie**, he comes of a poor family, he is born of poor parents; **einem adligen Geschlecht e.**, to be of noble descent, birth; **die Kinder, die dieser Ehe entstammen**, the children issuing from this marriage; **dieser Ehe entstammten drei Kinder**, there were three children from this marriage; this marriage produced three children; **das Buch entstammt seiner Feder**, the book comes from his pen; (*b*) (*of words*) **einer gemeinsamen Wurzel e.**, to be derived, to derive, from a common root.
entstauben, entstäuben, *v.tr. Ind: etc:* to free (sth.) from dust, to remove the dust from (sth.); **Entstaubung** *f*, dust-removal, freeing from dust.
entstehen, I. *v.i.* (*strong*) (*sein*) (*a*) to originate; to come into being; (*of ideas, civilization, etc.*) to come to birth, to be born; to emerge; (*of friendship, quarrel, etc.*) to arise, spring up; (*of fears, hopes, etc.*) to be born, to (a)rise, to spring up; (*of difficulty*) to emerge, to arise, to spring up; (*of work of art*) to be made, to be created; **aus etwas e.**, to originate in sth.; to originate from sth.; to arise, spring (up), from sth.; **plötzlich e.**, to spring, come suddenly, into existence; **langsam, allmählich, e.**, to emerge slowly, gradually; **der Streit entstand aus einem Mißverständnis**, the quarrel (a)rose, sprang, from a misapprehension; **der Streik entstand aus der Forderung nach . . .**, the strike originated in the demand for . . .; **Krieg und alle Übel, die daraus entstehen**, war and all the evils that proceed from it; **wie konnte solch ein Mißverständnis e.?** how could such a misunderstanding come about? **eine innige Freundschaft entstand zwischen ihnen**, an intimacy, a close friendship, sprang up between them; **das Feuer entstand unter dem Fußboden**, the fire originated under the floor; **einige griechische Philosophen waren der Ansicht, die Erde sei aus Schlamm entstanden**, some Greek philosophers believed the earth to have originated from mud; **die Frucht entsteht aus dem Fruchtknoten**, the fruit is formed, develops, from the ovary; **überall entstanden neue Gebäude**, everywhere new buildings arose, rose, came into being; **die Handschrift ist im 11. Jahrhundert in Köln entstanden**, the manuscript was made, was written, in Cologne in the 11th century; **zahlreiche Kunstwerke entstanden in dieser Zeit unter dem Einfluß der Antike**, at this time numerous works of art were produced under the influence of antiquity; **während dieser Jahre entstanden des Malers, des Dichters, beste Werke**, he painted his best pictures, he wrote his best works, in those years; **die griechische Kunst ist nicht aus dem Nichts entstanden**, Greek art was not created *ex vacuo*; (*b*) to result, arise; (*of heat, gas, etc.*) to be generated, to be developed, produced; **aus etwas, durch etwas, e.**, to result from sth.; to arise from sth.; to come of, from, sth.; to be caused by sth.; **Erkrankungen, die durch falsche Ernährung entstehen**, illnesses that arise from, resulting from, caused by, a wrong diet; **die Übel, die aus der Unmäßigkeit entstehen**, the evils that result, ensue, follow, from intemperance; **viel Unheil ist daraus entstanden**, much harm resulted from it; **nichts Gutes kann dabei, daraus, e.**, nothing good can come of it; **Lebensbedingungen, die durch den Krieg entstanden sind**, living conditions arising out of the war; **niemand weiß, was noch daraus e. kann**, no one knows what it may lead to; **bei dem Feuer entstand ungeheurer Schaden**, the fire caused immense damage; **der entstandene Schaden**, the resulting damage; **das Feuer entstand durch die Unachtsamkeit eines Angestellten**, the fire was caused by the negligence of one of the employees; **bei diesem Prozeß entsteht Wärme**, in this process heat is generated, developed, produced; **die Kosten, die dabei entstehen, die dabei entstehenden Kosten**, the costs arising, resulting, from it; **wir werden Ihnen die dabei entstandenen Unkosten ersetzen**, we shall reimburse you for expenses incurred; **entstehende Zinsen**, accruing interest; **möglicherweise entstehende Kosten**, expenses that may arise; **möglicherweise entstehende Schwierigkeiten**, potential difficulties, difficulties that may arise, spring up, emerge; **die daraus entstehenden Folgen**, the resulting consequences.
II. *vbl s.* **1. Entstehen**, *n. in vbl senses;* **im E. (begriffen) sein**, to be in the process of creation; to be in embryo, in an embryonic state; to be nascent; (*of ideas, civilization, etc.*) to be coming to birth; *Sch:* **Realgymnasium im E.**, 'Lyzeum' (*q.v.*) which is being progressively converted into a 'Realgymnasium' (*q.v.*). **2. Entstehung**, *f. in vbl senses; also:* origination; rise; origin; genesis; birth; generation, development (of heat, gas, etc.); **in der E. (begriffen) sein**=**im Entstehen (begriffen) sein**, *q.v. under* II. 1; **die E. neuer Industrien**, the coming into being of new industries; **die E. neuer Ideen**, the rise, emergence, of new ideas; the birth of new ideas; **plötzliche, langsame, allmähliche, E.**, sudden, slow, gradual, emergence; **Geschichte in ihrer E.**, history in the making; **die E. einer Idee beobachten**, to watch the genesis, birth, of an idea; **die Geschichte der E. der Welt**, the history of the first beginnings of the world; **die E. der Frucht aus dem Fruchtknoten**, the formation, development, of the fruit from the ovary; **die E. der Tragödie**, the origins, birth, of tragedy; **die E. der Arten**, the origin of species; **der Zeitpunkt der E. des Romans, des Bildes, ist ungewiß**, it is uncertain when the novel was written, the picture was painted; **der Ort der E.**, the place of origin; **um die E. von Gerüchten zu vermeiden**, to prevent rumours (from arising); **um die E. von Schäden, die E. unnötiger Ausgaben, zu vermeiden**, to avoid damage, unnecessary expense; **dieser Prozeß befördert die E. von Wärme**, this process promotes the generation, development, of heat.
Entstehungsart, *f.*=**Entstehungsweise.**
Entstehungsgeschichte, *f.* history of origins; history of development; genesis (of idea, work of art, etc.); **die E. der attischen Tragödie**, the history of the origins of Attic Tragedy.
Entstehungsweise, *f.* mode of origin; mode of formation; mode of development.
Entstehungszeit, *f.* **1.** time taken (by sth.) to come into being *or* emerge. **2.** date (of work of art, etc.).
Entstehungszustand, *m.* state of emergence; *Ch: etc:* nascent state; *Biol: etc:* embryonic state; *Ch:* **Körper, Element, im E.**, nascent body, element.
entsteigen, *v.i.* (*strong*) (*sein*) **etwas** *dat.*, *occ.* **aus etwas, e.**, to get out of, climb out of (car, bed, etc.); to rise from (depth, etc.); (*of smell, fumes, etc.*) to come up from, to rise from, sth.; **sie war soeben dem Bad entstiegen**, she had just come out of the bath; **Venus, dem Meer entstiegen**, Venus risen from the sea; **ein Seufzer entstieg ihrer Brust**, she heaved a sigh; **Schwefeldünste entstiegen dem Krater**, sulphurous fumes were rising from the crater.
entsteinen, *v.tr.* to stone, *U.S:* to pit (plums, dates, etc.).
Entsteinmaschine, *f.* stoning machine.
entstellen. I. *v.tr.* (*a*) to disfigure, deform (sth., s.o.); to distort (face, etc.); to deface (statue, etc.) (*by destroying the surface*); to mar (face, beauty); **eine entstellende Narbe**, a disfiguring scar; **mit vor Wut entstelltem Gesicht**, with a face distorted by rage; **eine Einzelheit, die das Bild entstellt**, a detail that mars, spoils, the picture; **die Fabrikschornsteine entstellen die Landschaft**, the factory chimneys disfigure, spoil, mar, the view; **Druckfehler, die das Buch entstellen**, misprints that disfigure the book; **die Kirche ist durch die neuen Fenster ganz entstellt**, the church is completely spoiled, disfigured, by the new windows; (*b*) to distort (facts, truth, language, meaning, etc.); **entstellter Text (eines Telegramms, usw.)**, corrupt text (of a telegram, etc.).
II. *vbl s.* **1. Entstellen**, *n. in vbl senses.* **2. Entstellung**, *f.* (*a*)=II. 1; *also:* disfigurement, deformation (of sth., s.o.); defacement (of statue, etc.); distortion (of truth, facts, language, meaning, etc.); (*b*) (state of) being disfigured; disfigurement; distortion; (*c*) disfigurement; deformity; **der Arzt hofft, daß keine dauernde E. zurückbleibt**, the doctor hopes that no permanent disfigurement will ensue; **häßliche Entstellungen**, ugly disfigurements.
Entsteller, *m.* **-s/-**, person who disfigures, deforms (sth., s.o.); distorter (of truth, facts, etc.).
entstielen, *v.tr.* to remove the stalks from (fruit).
entstöpseln, *v.tr.* to unstopper (bottle, etc.).
entstören, *v.tr. W.Tel:* to suppress interference from (electrical apparatus, etc.); to suppress (electrical apparatus, etc.); *Aut:* **einen Motor e.**, to fit suppressors to an engine; **Entstörung** *f*, suppression (of interference).
Entstörer, *m. W.Tel:* interference suppressor.
Entstörgerät, *n. W.Tel:* anti-interference device.
Entstörkappe, *f. Aut:*=**Entstörstecker.**
Entstörkondensator, *m. W.Tel:* anti-interference capacitor, suppression capacitor.
Entstörstecker, *m. Aut:* suppressor (terminal) cap (for sparking plug).
Entstörung, *f. see* **entstören.**
Entstörwiderstand, *m. W.Tel:* suppression resistor.
entströmen, *v.i.* (*sein*) **etwas** *dat.* **e.**, (*of water, etc.*) to flow, stream, from, to pour from, out of (source, rock, opening); (*of blood*) to stream, flow, pour, from (wound, etc.); to stream, flow, from (s.o.'s mouth, nose, etc.); **Tränen entströmten ihren Augen**, tears started, welled, from her eyes; **ein Redeschwall entströmte seinem Mund**, he poured forth a torrent of words; **dicker Rauch entströmte dem Schornstein**, thick smoke was pouring from the chimney.
entstützen, *v.tr.* to unshore (ship in dry-dock, etc.).
entsühnen, *v.tr.* to purify (sth., s.o., defiled with crime, etc.); **sich e.**, to purify oneself; to be purified; **Entsühnung** *f*, purification.
entsündigen, *v.tr. B. & Lit:*=**entsühnen.**
enttäuschen. I. *v.tr.* to disappoint (s.o., s.o.'s hopes, etc.); to disillusion (s.o.); **über etwas, j-n, enttäuscht sein**, to be disappointed with sth.; to be disappointed in, with, s.o.; **ich war über ihren Mangel an Verständnis enttäuscht, ihr Mangel an Verständnis hat mich enttäuscht**, I was disappointed at her lack of understanding, her lack of understanding disappointed me; **angenehm enttäuscht sein**, to be agreeably disappointed; **er war schwer, bitter, enttäuscht**, he was sorely, bitterly, disappointed; **er war sehr darüber enttäuscht, daß er nicht eingeladen war**, he was very disappointed at not having been invited; **ich hoffe, Sie werden mich nicht e.**, I hope you won't disappoint me, let me down; **das Leben hat sie enttäuscht**, life has disillusioned her; **in der Liebe enttäuscht sein**, to be disappointed in love; **aus enttäuschter Liebe Selbstmord begehen**, to commit suicide out of disappointed love; **enttäuschter Ehrgeiz**, disappointed ambition; **sie sah sich in ihren Hoffnungen enttäuscht**, her hopes were disappointed, dashed; **die Aufführung war enttäuschend**, the performance was disappointing; **seine Arbeit war enttäuschend**, his work was disappointing, disappointingly bad; **sie sah ihn enttäuscht an**, she looked at him disappointedly; **er starb im Alter von siebzig Jahren, enttäuscht und verbittert**, he died at the age of seventy, disillusioned and bitter.
II. *vbl s.* **Enttäuschung**, *f.* disappointment; disillusionment, disillusion; **j-m eine E., Enttäuschungen, bereiten**, to disappoint s.o.; **viele Enttäuschungen erfahren**, to suffer many disappointments; **E. in der Liebe**, disappointment in love; **ihre Kinder haben ihr nichts als Enttäuschungen bereitet, gebracht**, her children have been a great disappointment to her; **eine schwere E.**, a keen disappointment; **a great** disappointment; **ein Gefühl der E. zurücklassen**, to leave a feeling of disappointment; **ihre E. darüber war groß**, her disappointment (at it) was great; **das Kind ist eine E.**, the child is a disappointment.
entthronen, *v.tr.* to dethrone; **Entthronung** *f*, dethronement.
enttrümmern, *v.tr.* **eine Stadt e.**, to clear away the debris from a town.
entvölkern, *v.tr.* to depopulate (country, etc.); **entvölkert werden**, to become depopulated, to lose its population; **der Krieg hatte weite Landstriche entvölkert**, the war had depopulated vast regions; *F:* **im heißen Sommer ist die Stadt entvölkert**, in the heat of summer the town is deserted; **Entvölkerung** *f*, depopulation.
entwachsen, *v.i.* (*strong*) (*sein*) **1.** (*of plant*) **der Erde, usw., e.**, to grow out of the earth; (*of flower*) **der Knospe e.**, to grow from the bud. **2.** (*of pers.*) **den Kinderschuhen entwachsen sein**, to be out of one's infancy; to be no longer a child; to be grown up; **kaum den Kinderschuhen entwachsen**, hardly out of one's infancy; hardly

more than a child; **der Schule entwachsen sein,** to have left one's school-days behind one.

entwaffnen, *v.tr.* to disarm (s.o.); **die Gefangenen wurden entwaffnet,** the prisoners were disarmed; **er hat ihn durch seine Güte entwaffnet,** he disarmed him with his kindness; **ein entwaffnendes Lächeln,** a disarming smile; **Entwaffnung** *f,* disarming.

entwalden, *v.tr.* to deforest, untimber (land); to clear (country) of trees; **Entwaldung** *f,* deforestation.

entwarnen, *v.i.* (*haben*) *Civil Defence:* to give, sound, the 'all clear'; **Entwarnung** *f,* (i) cancellation of warning; (ii) 'all clear' (signal).

Entwarnungssignal, *n.* 'all clear' signal.

entwässern. I. *v.tr.* 1. *Agr:* to drain (soil, etc.); to reclaim, drain (land); to dry up (ground). 2. *Ch:* (*a*) to dehydrate; to desiccate; (*b*) to rectify (alcohol); to concentrate (solution). II. *vbl s.* **Entwässern** *n.,* **Entwässerung** *f.* in *vbl senses; also:* 1. *Agr:* drainage (of soil, etc.). 2. *Ch:* (*a*) dehydration; desiccation; (*b*) rectification (of alcohol); concentration (of solution).

Entwässerungsanlagen, *f.pl.* drainage installations.

Entwässerungsflansch, *m. Mch:* emptying outlet (of turbine).

Entwässerungsgebiet, *n. Ph.Geog: Hyd.E:* drainage area; catchment area.

Entwässerungsgraben, *m. Agr:* drain, drainage ditch.

Entwässerungshahn, *m. Mch:* drain-cock, drip-cock.

Entwässerungskanal, *m.=* **Entwässerungsgraben.**

Entwässerungsmittel, *n. Ch:* dehydrating agent.

Entwässerungsrohr, *n.,* **Entwässerungsröhre,** *f. Mch: etc:* drain-pipe; *Agr:* agricultural drain, field drain; *U.S:* drain-tile.

Entwässerungsschacht, *m.* drain-shaft.

Entwässerungssystem, *n.* drainage system.

Entwässerungsventil, *n. Mch:* drain-valve.

entweder, *conj. & adv.* **e. . . . oder,** either . . . or; **e. du oder dein Bruder,** either you or your brother; **e. komm herein oder geh hinaus, komm e. herein oder geh hinaus,** either come in or go out; **e. alles oder gar nichts,** either the whole lot or nothing at all; **e. ganz, e. richtig, oder gar nicht,** either do the job properly or leave it alone; **du mußt e. – oder sagen,** you have to decide one way or the other; **hier gibt es nur ein Entweder – Oder,** a clear decision (one way or the other) is called for, you just have to make up your mind (one way or the other).

Entwehrung, *f. Jur:* eviction (of property).

entweichen. I. *v.i.* (*strong*) (*sein*) 1. to flee; to escape; **aus dem Gefängnis e.,** to escape from prison; **die Gefangenen waren entwichen,** the prisoners had escaped, had got away; *Lit:* **die Nacht entweicht (dem Tage),** the night is drawing to an end; night yields to day. 2. *Ch: etc:* (*of gas, vapour, etc.*) to be given off; to escape. II. *vbl s.* **Entweichen** *n.,* **Entweichung** *f.* in *vbl senses; also:* 1. escape; flight. 2. *Ch: etc:* escape (of gas, vapour, etc.).

Entweichungsklappe, *f.* escape-valve.

Entweichungsrohr, *n.,* **Entweichungsröhre,** *f.* escape-pipe.

Entweichungsventil, *n.* escape-valve.

entweihen, *v.tr.* to profane (sth. sacred, art, etc.); to desecrate (sacred place); **den Sonntag, Sabbat, e.,** to profane the Sabbath(-day); **Entweihung** *f,* profanation (of sth. sacred, art, etc.); desecration (of sacred place).

Entweiher, *m. -s/-,* profaner; desecrator.

entwenden. I. *v.tr.* (*conj. like* wenden, *but usu. weak*) to misappropriate, embezzle (funds); to steal, make away with, abstract (sth.); **j-m etwas e.,** to steal, filch, abstract, sth. from s.o.; to embezzle (money) from s.o.; **ein Buch aus einer Bibliothek e.,** to filch, steal, a book out of a library. II. *vbl s.* **Entwenden** *n.,* **Entwendung** *f.* in *vbl senses; also:* abstraction (of sth.); misappropriation, embezzlement (of funds).

entwerfen, *v.tr.* (*strong*) 1. (*a*) to sketch, draw, outline (plan, pattern, picture, etc.); to sketch, outline (design, essay, novel, etc.); to make a skeleton of (novel, etc.); to draw up (document, etc.); to draft, make a draft of (document, etc.); to rough out (design, plan, picture); to rough in (picture); to sketch, make a sketch for (sculpture, mural, etc.); to make a cartoon for (tapestry, mosaic, etc.); **etwas flüchtig, im Groben, e.,** to make a rough sketch of sth.; to make a rough draft of (essay, etc.); **das Bild ist gut entworfen, aber liederlich ausgeführt,** the composition *or*

the drawing of the picture is good, but it is badly executed; (*b*) to design (building, machine, clothes, etc.); to invent, produce (textile-design, etc.); to plan, design (garden, etc.); **Bucheinbände e.,** to design book-bindings; **eine gut entworfene Maschine,** a machine of well worked out design, a well designed machine; (*c*) **j-m ein Bild von etwas e.,** to draw a (mental) picture of sth. for s.o.; to give s.o. a (graphic) description of sth.; **sie hat mir ein anschauliches Bild von der Lage entworfen,** she gave me a graphic picture of the situation. 2. to make, work out (plan); to prepare, design (project); **sie hatte ihre Ferienpläne bis in alle Einzelheiten entworfen,** she had planned her holidays in every detail.

Entwerfer, *m. -s/-,* designer; drafter (of document, etc.).

entwerten. I. *v.tr.* 1. (*a*) to lower the value of (sth.); to depreciate (sth.); **entwertet werden,** to lose (its) value, to fall in value; to depreciate; **das Haus würde durch den Bau einer Fabrik in unmittelbarer Nähe entwertet werden,** the house would fall in value if a factory were to be built in its immediate neighbourhood; **seine Unzuverlässigkeit hat seine Aussage stark entwertet,** his unreliability considerably diminished the value of his evidence; **moralische Begriffe e.,** to lessen the value of moral concepts; **etwas völlig e.,** to render sth. valueless; (*b*) *Pol.Ec:* to devaluate (currency); *Hist:* to debase (coinage). 2. *Post:* to cancel, deface (stamp); **entwertete Briefmarke,** cancelled, used, stamp. II. *vbl s.* 1. **Entwerten,** *n.* in *vbl senses.* 2. **Entwertung,** *f.* (*a*) depreciation (of sth.); (*b*) *Pol.Ec:* devaluation (of currency); *Hist:* debasement (of coinage); (*c*) *Post:* cancellation (of stamp); (*d*) loss in value, decrease in value; **die völlige E. moralischer Begriffe,** the complete devaluation of moral concepts.

Entwertungsstempel, *m. Post:* cancellation (on stamp); postmark.

entwesen, *v.tr.* to free (place, etc.) from vermin; to disinfest; **Entwesung** *f,* disinfestation.

entwickeln. I. *v.tr.* 1. (*a*) to develop (the faculties, etc.); **Gymnastik entwickelt die Muskeln,** gymnastics develops, strengthens, the muscles; **seine Kräfte, Fähigkeiten, voll e.,** to develop one's powers, faculties, fully; (*b*) to develop (thought, doctrine, etc.); to expound, enlarge on (subject); to evolve (plan, etc.); **j-m seine Pläne e.,** to tell, unfold, one's plans to s.o.; (*c*) **etwas weiter e.,** to develop sth. further; to expand (branch of industry, etc.); **einen Gedanken weiter e.,** to work out an idea (in detail), to elaborate, enlarge upon, an idea; **wir wollen dieses Modell weiter e.,** we want to develop this model more fully. 2. *Mil:* to deploy (troops) (finally), to put (troops) into final deployment. 3. to display, show, develop (a quality, etc.); **er entwickelte ungeahnten Mut,** he displayed, showed, developed, unexpected courage; **der Wagen entwickelte eine große Geschwindigkeit,** the car developed great speed; **eine lebhafte Tätigkeit e.,** to display great activity; **einen Geschmack für etwas e.,** to acquire, develop, a taste for sth. 4. *Phot:* to develop (negative, film, print). II. **sich entwickeln.** 1. (*a*) (*of the body, the faculties, etc.*) to develop; **wir müssen die Dinge sich e. lassen,** we must let things develop; **in diesem Alter ist der Charakter noch nicht voll entwickelt, hat sich der Charakter noch nicht voll entwickelt,** at this age the character is not yet fully developed; **eine hoch entwickelte Kultur,** a highly developed civilization; **die Industrie ist in dieser Gegend nicht so hoch entwickelt wie die Landwirtschaft,** in this district industry is not as highly developed as agriculture; **sich weiter e.,** to develop further; **sich langsam, schnell, e.,** to develop slowly, rapidly; **das Kind entwickelt sich rasch,** the child is developing, *F:* is coming on, rapidly; (*b*) (*of race, species, etc.*) to evolve; to develop; **sich aus etwas e.,** to evolve from sth.; to develop from sth.; **die Theorie, daß sich eine Art stufenweise entwickelt hat,** the theory that a species has evolved gradually; **seine Lehre ist nicht plötzlich entstanden, sondern hat sich allmählich entwickelt,** his teaching did not emerge all at once but evolved gradually; **aus der Blüte entwickelt sich die Frucht,** the fruit develops from the flower; **daraus könnte sich eine unangenehme Situation e.,** that might grow into an awkward situation; (*c*) **sich zu etwas e.,** to develop, grow, into sth.; **sie hatte sich zu einem schönen Mädchen entwickelt,** she had grown into a fine girl; **er hatte sich zum Mann entwickelt,** he had

grown into a man; **London entwickelte sich zum Handelszentrum Europas,** London developed into the general mart of Europe; **die Situation könnte sich leicht zu einer allgemeinen Krise e.,** the situation might easily develop into a general crisis. 2. (*of gas, vapour, etc.*) to form, evolve, to be developed, produced. III. *vbl s.* 1. **Entwickeln,** in *vbl senses of* I. 2. **Entwick(e)lung,** *f.* (*a*)=III. 1; *also:* development (of body, the faculties, etc.); enlargement (of idea, etc.); expansion (of project, idea, etc.); *Mil:* final deployment (of troops); *Phot:* development, developing (of film, negative, print); (*b*) in *vbl senses of* II; *also:* development; growth; evolution (of events); **seine, j-s, Kräfte, Fähigkeiten, zur E. bringen,** to develop one's, s.o.'s, powers, faculties; **zur E. kommen,** to develop; **seine, j-s, Kräfte, Fähigkeiten, zur E. kommen lassen,** to allow one's, s.o.'s, powers, faculties, to develop, to grow; **zu voller E. kommen,** to develop fully; (*of plant, etc.*) to attain full growth; **in der E. sein, stehen,** to be in the course of development, to be in a stage of development; **ein Kind in seiner E. hemmen, die E. eines Kindes hemmen,** to hamper the development of a child; **die E. stören,** to interfere with the development; **die E. aufhalten,** to stop, halt, the development, growth; **das würde eine Störung in der E. des Kindes bedeuten,** that would mean an interruption of the child's development; **den Gang der E. beobachten,** to watch how things develop; (*c*) evolution (of species, theories, etc.); **die E. der Frucht aus der Blüte,** the development of the fruit from the flower; **die E. einer höheren Art aus einer niederen,** the evolution of a higher species from a lower one; (*d*) development; turn (of events); **eine neue E. ist eingetreten,** a new development occurred; **weitere Entwicklungen abwarten,** to await further developments.

Entwickler, *m. -s/-.* 1. *Phot:* developer, developing agent. 2. *Ch: etc:* (gas) generator.

Entwicklerflüssigkeit, *f. Phot:* developing liquid, developer.

Entwicklerschale, *f. Phot:* developing dish *or* tray.

Entwicklung, *f. see* **entwickeln** III.

Entwicklungsablauf, *m.* (course of) development; (course of) evolution.

Entwicklungsbad, *n. Phot:* developing bath.

Entwicklungsbottich, *m. Phot:* developing tank.

Entwicklungsdose, *f. Phot:* small developing tank.

Entwicklungserscheinung, *f.* sign, symptom, of development.

entwicklungsfähig, *a.* capable of development.

Entwicklungsfaktor, *m.* factor in the development.

Entwicklungsflüssigkeit, *f. Phot:* developing liquid, developer.

Entwicklungsgang, *m.=***Entwicklungsablauf.**

Entwicklungsgebiet, *n. Pol.Ec:* development area.

Entwicklungsgefäß, *n.* 1. *Ch: etc:* generating vessel, (gas) generator. 2. *Phot:* developing tank *or* tray.

Entwicklungsgeschichte, *f.* 1. history of development. 2. biogenetics.

entwicklungsgeschichtlich, *a.* 1. associated with *or* seen from the point of view of the history of development. 2. biogenetic.

Entwicklungshilfe, *f. Pol.E:* development aid.

Entwicklungsjahre, *die,* the years of development; the formative years.

Entwicklungskolben, *m. Ch:* generating flask.

Entwicklungskrankheit, *f.* developmental ailment.

Entwicklungsland, *n. Pol.Ec:* developing country.

Entwicklungslehre, *f. Biol: Phil:* theory of evolution.

Entwicklungspapier, *n. Phot:* developing (out) paper, *abbr.* D.O.P.

Entwicklungsphysiologie, *f.* developmental physiology.

Entwicklungsprozeß, *m.* (process of) development; (process of) evolution, evolutionary process.

Entwicklungspsychologie, *f.* developmental psychology.

Entwicklungsrahmen, *m. Cin:* developing rack.

Entwicklungsreihe, *f.* line of evolution.

Entwicklungsroman, *m.* novel portraying the development of an individual's character.

Entwicklungsstörungen, *f.pl.* developmental disturbances.

Entwicklungstheorie, *f. Biol: Phil:* theory of

evolution; evolutionism; **Anhänger der E.,** evolutionist.

Entwicklungstrog, *m. Phot:* developing tank.

Entwicklungsunterbrechung, *f.* interruption in the development; *Biol:* epistasis.

Entwicklungsverfahren, *n. Phot:* developing process; developing method.

Entwicklungsvorgang, *m.* = **Entwicklungsprozeß.**

Entwicklungszeit, *f.* **1.** period of development. **2.** *Phot:* developing time.

entwinden, *v.tr.* (*strong*) **j-m etwas e.,** to wrench sth. from s.o.; **sich j-m, j-s Armen, e.,** to wrench oneself free from s.o.; **sich j-s Griff e.,** to wrench oneself from s.o.'s grasp.

entwipfeln, *v.tr.* to top, pollard (tree).

entwirren, *v.tr.* to disentangle, unravel (threads, skein, tangle, etc.); to tease (out) (wool); to comb out (hair); to clear up, disentangle, unravel, sort out (situation, matters); **sich e.,** (*of threads, skein, tangle, etc.*) to become disentangled, to disentangle, unravel; (*of situation, etc.*) to disentangle, unravel; to sort itself out; **Entwirrung** *f*, unravelling, disentanglement (of threads, skein, tangle, situation, etc.).

entwischen, *v.i.* (*sein*) to escape, to get away; to slip off; **j-m e.,** to escape s.o.; to escape from s.o.; to give s.o. the slip.

entwitschen, *v.i.* (*sein*) *F:* = **entwischen.**

entwöhnen. I. *v.tr.* **1.** to wean (child, lamb, etc.). **2. j-n etwas** *gen.*, **von etwas, e.,** to disaccustom s.o. to sth.; to break s.o. of (a habit, the habit of doing sth.); to wean s.o. from (alcohol, drugs, etc.); to make s.o. leave off, to cure s.o. of (drinking, drugs, etc.); **sich etwas** *gen.*, **von etwas, e.,** to grow unused to sth., to become disaccustomed to sth.; to break oneself of (a habit, the habit of doing sth.); to give up, leave off, cure oneself of (drinking, drugs, etc.); **man muß den Süchtigen langsam e.,** one has to wean the addict gradually; **ein Volk, das der Freiheit längst entwöhnt ist,** a nation long disaccustomed, grown unused to, freedom; **ich habe mich solcher Sentimentalitäten längst entwöhnt,** I have cured myself of, weaned myself from, such sentimentalities long ago; **das Kind war der Zärtlichkeit so sehr entwöhnt, daß . . . ,** the child had grown so unused to affection that . . . .

II. *vbl s.* **1. Entwöhnen,** *n. in vbl senses.* **2. Entwöhnung,** *f.* (*a*) = II. 1; (*b*) (state of) being weaned; (state of) being cured (of drinking, drugs, etc.); **nach völliger E.,** when completely weaned; when the desire has been completely overcome.

entwölken, *v.tr.* (*of wind, etc.*) to clear (up) (the sky); (*of event etc.*) to brighten (s.o.'s brow); **sich e.,** (*of sky*) to clear up; (*of situation, etc.*) to become brighter, to brighten; **seine Stirn entwölkte sich,** his face brightened, his brow cleared.

entwürdigen, *v.tr.* to degrade, debase (s.o.); **Trunkenheit entwürdigt den Menschen,** drunkenness robs a man of his dignity, degrades a man; **eine entwürdigende Zumutung,** a degrading suggestion; **Entwürdigung** *f*, degradation, debasement.

Entwurf, *m.* -(e)s/⸗e. **1.** (*a*) sketching, outlining (of plan, design, pattern, picture, essay, novel, etc.); drawing (of plan, pattern, picture, etc.); roughing out (of design, plan, picture, novel, etc.); roughing in, sketching out, blocking out (of picture, etc.); sketching (of sculpture, mural, etc.); drawing up (of document, etc.); drafting (of bill, etc.); **flüchtiger E.,** rough-sketching (of sth.); (*b*) designing (of building, machine, clothes, etc.); planning, designing (of garden, etc.); invention, production (of textile-design, etc.). **2.** (*a*) (rough) draft (of document, bill, contract, literary work, etc.); skeleton, outline (of novel, etc.); **erster E. eines Romans,** first draft of a novel; **das Buch ist im E. fertig,** the book is finished in outline, the plan of the book is complete; **die verschiedenen Entwürfe zu einem Drama,** the various (preliminary) drafts of a play; **den E. zu einem Schriftstück machen,** to draft, make a draft of, a document; (*b*) *Art:* sketch; (preliminary) drawing; cartoon (for tapestry, mosaic, etc.); *Arch: etc:* rough plan, rough sketch; **vorläufiger, flüchtiger, E.,** rough sketch; rough plan; rough outlines (of portrait, etc.); **Entwürfe zu einem, für ein, Wandgemälde,** sketches, drawings, for a mural; **den Entwurf zu einem Gemälde machen,** to sketch, make a sketch for, a painting; to rough out, block out, a painting; (*c*) *Arch: etc:* plan (of building, garden, etc.); *Ind: etc:* design (for machine, furniture, clothes, bookbinding, etc.); *Sculp: maquette,* clay model (of statue); *Th:* (stage-)design; **das Flugzeug ist über das Stadium der Entwürfe nie hinausgekommen,** the aircraft never passed the planning stage, never left the drawing-board; **Michelangelos Entwürfe für St. Peter,** Michelangelo's plans for St. Peter's.

entwurzeln. I. *v.tr.* (*a*) to uproot (tree), to tear up (tree) by the roots; (*b*) to uproot (s.o.); to tear (s.o.) from his usual surroundings; **entwurzelt,** uprooted; torn from one's usual surroundings; *déraciné.*

II. *vbl s.* **Entwurzelung,** *f. in vbl senses; also:* uprootal.

entzaubern, *v.tr.* (*a*) (*of sorcerer, etc.*) to free (s.o., sth.) from a magic spell, to disenchant (sth.); (*b*) to break the spell of, to take the spell from (sth., s.o.); (*of thg*) **entzaubert werden,** to lose its charm; to lose its spell; to lose its magic; **plötzlich war seine Kindheit für ihn entzaubert,** suddenly his childhood had lost its spell, its magic, for him; **im hellen Sonnenlicht lag der Wald, der ihm in der Nacht so unheimlich erschienen war, entzaubert vor ihm,** the wood that had seemed to him so uncanny the night before, now looked completely ordinary in the bright sunlight.

entzerren, *v.tr. Phot:* to rectify (distorted photograph, etc.); *W.Tel: Tp: Tg:* to correct, counteract (distortion); **Entzerrung** *f*, rectification; *W.Tel: Tp: Tg:* compensation; correcting, correction (of distortion); equalization; **Entzerrung der Dämpfung,** attenuation compensation.

Entzerrer, *m.* **-s/-.** *Phot:* rectifier; *W.Tel: Tp: Tg:* compensator, equalizer.

Entzerrerkette, *f. W.Tel: Tp: Tg:* equalizing network.

Entzerrung, *f. see* **entzerren.**

Entzerrungsgerät, *n. Phot:* rectifier.

entziehen. I. *v.tr.* (*strong*) **1. j-m etwas e.,** to take sth. away from s.o.; to deprive s.o. of sth.; to withdraw sth. from s.o.; to withhold sth. from s.o.; to dock s.o. of sth.; *Ch: etc:* **etwas** *dat.* **etwas e.,** to extract sth. from sth.; **j-m sein Vertrauen, seine Gunst, seine Freundschaft, e.,** to withdraw one's confidence, one's favour, one's friendship, from s.o.; **j-n einem Einfluß e.,** to withdraw s.o. from an influence; **j-n j-s Rache e.,** to put s.o. out of the reach of s.o.'s vengeance; **j-n der gerechten Strafe e.,** to protect s.o. from just punishment; **j-m das Wort e.,** to impose silence on s.o.; **einem Redner das Wort e.,** to direct a speaker to discontinue; **j-m den Besitz e.,** to dispossess s.o.; **j-m ein Recht e.,** to deprive s.o. of a right; **j-m das Benutzungsrecht an etwas** *dat.* **e.,** to withdraw from s.o. the right to use sth.; **einem Kind zur Strafe das Taschengeld e.,** to stop, withhold, cut off, a child's pocket-money as a punishment; **j-m die Nahrung, e.** to deprive s.o. of food (*as a punishment*); to cut off s.o.'s food; **j-m den Alkohol, ein Rauschgift, e.,** to deprive s.o. of alcohol, of a drug; **man hat ihm seine Pension entzogen,** his pension has been taken away from him, has been stopped, he has been docked of his pension; **j-m die Konzession e.,** to cancel, revoke, withdraw, s.o.'s licence; **j-m den Führerschein e.,** to revoke, take away, s.o.'s driving licence; to ban s.o. from driving; **j-m den Oberbefehl e.,** to deprive s.o. of the command; **etwas j-s Zugriff e.,** to put sth. out of s.o.'s reach, grasp, to prevent s.o. from getting at sth.; **sie entzog ihm ihre Hand,** she drew her hand away from his; **einem Körper Wärme e.,** to take heat from a body; (*of plant, etc.*) **dem Boden alle Nährkräfte e.,** to take all the nourishment out of the soil; **einem Gerücht die Grundlage, den Boden, e.,** to knock the bottom out of a rumour; **eine Wolke entzog das Flugzeug unseren Blicken,** a cloud hid the aircraft from our sight. **2. sich entziehen,** (*a*) (*of pers.*) **sich etwas** *dat.* **e.,** to avoid, elude, escape, sth.; to dodge, shirk, evade (responsibility, etc.); (*of fact, etc.*) **sich j-m, sich der Erkenntnis, e.,** to elude s.o., to elude knowledge; **sich der Strafe e.,** to avoid, evade, punishment; **sich der gerichtlichen Verfolgung e.,** to evade justice; to abscond; **sich den Nachforschungen der Polizei e.,** to hide from the police; to keep out of the reach of the police; **sich einer Diskussion, einer Verpflichtung, e.,** to back out of a discussion, of an obligation; to shirk, evade, a discussion, an obligation; **er hat sich der Festnahme durch die Flucht entzogen,** he evaded arrest by absconding; **sich dem Militärdienst e.,** to avoid, evade, *F:* dodge, military service; **sich j-s Zugriff e.,** to elude s.o.'s grasp; **sie entzieht sich mir,** she holds aloof from me; **ich sehe nicht, wie ich mich dieser Verantwortung, Verpflichtung, e. kann,** I see no way of evading this responsibility, of getting out of this obligation; **sich j-s Blicken e.,** (*of pers.*) to disappear, vanish, from s.o.'s sight; to hide from s.o.'s sight; (*of thg*) to be hidden from s.o.'s sight; to disappear, vanish; **sie entzog sich den Blicken der Neugierigen,** she withdrew herself from the gaze of the curious; **eine Felswand türmte sich vor uns auf, und der Gipfel entzog sich wieder unseren Blicken,** a wall of rock towered up before us and the peak vanished again from our sight; **die Ursachen dieser Krankheit entziehen sich noch ärztlicher Erkenntnis,** the causes of this disease have so far eluded medical knowledge; **das entzieht sich meiner Kenntnis,** I don't know (anything about it); **es entzieht sich meiner Kenntnis, ob . . . ,** I don't know whether . . . ; (*b*) (*of pers.*) **sich j-s Umarmung e.,** to free oneself from s.o.'s embrace; **sich j-s Griff e.,** to escape from s.o.'s hold; **er hielt sie so fest, daß sie sich seinem Griff, dem Griff seiner Hand, nicht e. konnte,** he held her so firmly that she could not shake off his hand.

II. *vbl s.* **Entziehen** *n.*, **Entziehung** *f.* = **Entzug.**

entzifferbar, *a.* decipherable (inscription, handwriting, etc.).

Entzifferer, *m.* **-s/-,** decipherer (of inscription, etc.).

entziffern, *v.tr.* to decipher, make out, puzzle out (inscription, etc.); to make out, decipher (handwriting); to decipher (cryptogram); **ich kann den Brief nicht e.,** I can't read the letter; **Entzifferung** *f*, deciphering, decipherment, making out (of inscription, etc.).

entzinnen, *v.tr. Metalw:* to detin; **Entzinnung** *f*, detinning.

entzücken. I. *v.tr.* to enrapture (s.o.), to carry (s.o.) away; to delight (s.o.), to fill (s.o.) with delight; **von etwas entzückt sein,** to be filled with delight by sth.; to be delighted with sth.; to be overjoyed at sth.; **sie war nicht sehr entzückt von dieser Idee,** she was not greatly taken with the idea; the idea did not greatly appeal to her; **der Anblick entzückte sie, sie war entzückt von dem Anblick,** the sight filled her with delight; **ich bin entzückt, Sie hier zu sehen,** I am delighted to see you here; **'wie schön', rief sie entzückt,** 'how lovely', she cried with delight; **in entzücktem Staunen,** in delighted wonder; **er ließ sich von der Musik e.,** he let himself be carried away, be enraptured, by the music.

II. *vbl s.* **1. Entzücken,** *n.* (*a*) delight; joy; **zu meinem E.,** to my delight; **zu der Kinder großem E.,** much to the delight of the children, to the children's great delight, joy; **er stellte mit E. fest, daß . . . ,** he noticed with delight that . . . ; **wer kann sich mein E. vorstellen, als . . . ,** who can imagine my delight, joy, when . . . ; **der Garten war ihr ganzes E.,** the garden was her great delight, joy; (*b*) rapture; **in seligem E.,** in raptures of delight; in joyous rapture; **in staunendem E.,** in (en)raptured wonderment; **zum E.,** charming; ravishing; **zum E. schön,** ravishingly beautiful; **in E. geraten,** to go into raptures; to be carried away; **sie geriet darüber in höchstes E.,** she went into raptures of delight over it; **j-n in E. versetzen,** to send s.o. into raptures. **2. Entzückung,** *f. Lit:* = II. 1 (*b*).

III. *pr.p. & a.* **entzückend,** delightful; charming; ravishing; enchanting; *adv.* delightfully; charmingly; ravishingly; **in diesem Kleid sieht sie e. aus,** she looks charming in this dress; **e. schön,** ravishingly beautiful; **eine entzückende Landschaft,** a delightful, charming, landscape; **eine entzückende Stimme,** a charming, delightful, enchanting, voice; **ein entzückendes Kind,** a charming child; **sie haben eine entzückende kleine Wohnung,** they have a charming, delightful, little flat; **e. angezogen sein,** to be charmingly, ravishingly, dressed.

Entzug, *m.* -(e)s/. taking away (of sth.); withdrawal, withdrawing (of friendship, favour, licence, etc.); revoking, cancelling, cancellation (of licence, etc.); deprivation (of drug, food, command, etc.); cutting off (of food, alcohol, etc.); stopping (of allowance, ration, etc.); docking (of pension, etc.); *Ch: etc:* extraction (of oxygen, etc.); **j-n durch E. der Nahrung bestrafen,** to punish s.o. by depriving him of food; **bei einem völligen E. von Licht würde die Pflanze eingehen,** if you deprived the plant completely of light it would die; **plötzlicher E. von Morphium ist gefährlich,** sudden deprivation of morphia is dangerous.

entzündbar, *a.* = **entflammbar.**

Entzündbarkeit, *f.* = **Entflammbarkeit.**

entzünden. I. *v.tr.* **1.** to light (lamp, fire, candle, etc.); to kindle (flame, etc.); to ignite, inflame

(substance); to set fire to (sth.); to set (sth.) on fire; **ein Streichholz e.,** to strike a match; **eine Kerze an einer anderen e.,** to light one candle from another. **2.** to inflame, excite, rouse (passions); to inflame, stir up, foment (hatred, etc.); to kindle (enthusiasm); (*of passion, hatred, etc.*) to (a)rouse, stir, kindle, inflame, fire (s.o.); (*of passion*) to set (s.o.) afire; (*of enthusiasm*) to fire (s.o.); **sein Lied entzündete sie zu wilder Leidenschaft, entzündete wilde Leidenschaft in ihnen,** his song roused violent passion in them, fired them with violent passion; **Begeisterung entzündete alle Herzen,** enthusiasm fired all hearts; **von Leidenschaft, Begeisterung, usw., entzündet sein,** to burn, to be burning, to be inflamed, with passion, etc.; to be fired with, roused to, enthusiasm.

II. **sich entzünden.** **1.** (*of substance*) to inflame, ignite; (*of kerosene, etc.*) to flash; (*of fire, etc.*) to light; to catch alight, to kindle; **sich von selbst e.,** to catch fire spontaneously; **sich an etwas e.,** to catch fire from sth.; to catch alight on (gas-fire, etc.). **2.** (*of passion, desire, etc.*) to be (a)roused, excited; to kindle; **sich an etwas e.,** (*of passion, enthusiasm, etc.*) to be (a)roused, stirred, kindled, by sth.; (*of pers.*) to kindle at, to, sth.; **er entzündete sich an ihrer Begeisterung,** he caught her enthusiasm. **3.** *Med:* (*of wound, etc.*) to become inflamed, to inflame; **entzündete Augen,** inflamed eyes; **entzündet sein,** to be inflamed.

III. *vbl s.* **1. Entzünden,** *n. in vbl senses of* I. **2. Entzündung,** *f.* (*a*)=III. 1; (*b*) *in vbl senses of* II; *also:* inflammation, ignition (of substance); *I.C.E:* ignition; **eine Substanz zur E. bringen,** to cause a substance to ignite; (*c*) *Med:* inflammation; **E. der Augenlider,** inflammation of the eyelids; **eine E. verursachen,** to cause an inflammation.

entzündlich, *a.* **1.** (*of substance*) (in)flammable; ignitable; **(leicht) entzündliche Stoffe,** inflammables; **hoch e.,** highly inflammable. **2.** *Med:* (*of wound, etc.*) inflammable, easily inflamed.

Entzündlichkeit, *f.* (in)flammability, (in)flammableness; ignitability.

Entzündung, *f. see* **entzünden III.**

Entzündungsfieber, *n. Med:* inflammatory fever.

Entzündungsherd, *m. Med:* centre of inflammation.

Entzündungsprobe, *f.* ignition test; flash-test.

Entzündungspunkt, *m.* ignition point; burning point, flash-point (of kerosene, etc.).

entzündungswidrig, *a. Med:* antiphlogistic.

entzurren, *v.tr. Nau: etc:* to unclamp *or* to unleash (gear, etc.).

entzwei, *adv.,* **entzwei-,** *comb.fm.* in two; asunder; in pieces; broken; **entzweibrechen,** to break in two; to break asunder; to break into pieces; **entzweibersten,** to burst in two, asunder; **entzweigehen,** to break (in two); to break into pieces; to fall to pieces; to come asunder; (*of friendship, etc.*) to break up; **entzweischlagen,** to smash; **entzweischneiden,** to cut (asunder); to cut in two; to cut into pieces, to cut up; **entzweispringen,** to burst in two, asunder; to snap asunder; to crack (open); **die Vase war e.,** the vase was broken, was in pieces; **die Betrunkenen schlugen sämtliche Stühle entzwei,** the drunks smashed all the chairs; **ihre Freundschaft war längst entzweigegangen,** their friendship had broken up a long time ago; **sei vorsichtig, damit das Buch nicht entzweigeht,** take care the book does not fall to pieces.

entzweien. I. *v.tr.* to disunite, divide (a people, etc.); to bring discord, disunity, division, into (a people); to set (people) at variance; **sich e.,** to become disunited, divided; to quarrel; to fall out; **sich mit j-m e.,** to quarrel with s.o.; to fall out with s.o.; **sich mit j-m entzweit haben, mit j-m entzweit sein,** to be on bad terms with s.o.; to have fallen out with s.o.; to be at loggerheads with s.o.; to be at variance with s.o.; **ein entzweites Volk,** a divided people.

II. *vbl s.* **1. Entzweien,** *n. in vbl senses.* **2. Entzweiung,** *f.* (*a*)=II. 1; *also:* division (of a people); (*b*) discord; disunity; division; **E. verursachen,** to bring about discord.

Enukleation [eˑnuˑkleˑaˑtsĭ'oːn], *f.* -/-**en.** *Surg:* enucleation (of tumour, eyeball, etc.).

enuklëieren [eˑnuˑkleˑ'iːrən], *v.tr. Surg:* to enucleate (tumour, tonsils, etc.).

Enumeration [eˑnuˑmərаˑtsĭ'oːn], *f.* -/-**en,** enumeration.

enumerieren [eˑnuˑmə'riːrən], *v.tr.* to enumerate.

Enunziation [eˑnuntsĭaˑtsĭ'oːn], *f.* -/-**en. 1.** enunciation, stating, declaring, expressing, asserting, assertion (of thought, fact, etc.). **2.** *Gram:* clause of statement.

Enurese [eˑnuˑ'reːzə], *f.* -/., **Enuresis** [eˑnuˑ'reːzis], *f.* -/. *Med:* enuresis, *esp.* nocturnal enuresis, bed-wetting.

Enveloppe [ãˑvə'lɔp(ə)], *f.* -/-**n** [-pən]. **1.** envelope (of letter, etc.); wrapper, cover(ing) (of document, etc.). **2.** *Geom:* envelope (of system of curves).

Envers [ãˑ'vɛːr], *m.* -/- [-'vɛːr(s)/-'vɛːrs], reverse (side) (of coin, medal, flag, etc.); wrong side, reverse, back (of material, etc.).

en vogue [ãˑ'voːg(ə)]. *Fr.adj.phr.* **en vogue sein,** to be popular, fashionable, in fashion, in vogue, *F:* all the rage, all the go.

Enzeht [ɛn'tseːt], *f.* -/-**en** =**Ensete.**

Enzephalitis [ɛntseˑfaˑ'liːtis], *f.* -/. *Med:* encephalitis, inflammation of the brain; **epidemische E., E. epidemica, lethargica,** encephalitis lethargica, *F:* sleepy sickness.

enzephalitisch [ɛntseˑfaˑ'liːtiʃ], *a. Med:* encephalitic.

Enzephalographie [ɛntseˑfaˑloˑgraˑ'fiː], *f.* -/. *Med:* encephalography.

Enzephalomalazie [ɛntseˑfaˑloˑmaˑlaˑ'tsiː], *f.* -/. *Med:* encephalomalacia, softening of the brain.

Enzephalozele [ɛntseˑfaˑloˑ'tseːlə], *f.* -/-**n.** *Med:* encephalocele, hernia of the brain.

Enzian, *m.* -(e)s/-**e.** *Bot:* **1.** gentian; **gelber, großer, E.,** yellow gentian, bitterwort; **bayrischer E.,** Bavarian gentian; **bitterer E.,** felwort, autumn gentian; **gefranster E.,** fringed gentian; **stengelloser E.,** gentianella. **2. weißer E.,** laserpitium, laser-wort. **3.** swertia. **4.**=**Enzianbranntwein.**

Enzianbitter, *n. Pharm:* gentian-bitter.

Enzianbranntwein, Enzianschnaps, *m. Dist:* Enzian.

Enzianviolett, *n. Med:* gentian-violet.

Enzianwurzel, *f. Pharm:* gentian-root.

Enzootie [ɛntsoˑoˑ'tiː], *f.* -/-**n** [-'tiːən]. *Vet:* enzootic disease, enzootic.

enzootisch [ɛntsoˑ'oːtiʃ], *a. Vet:* enzootic.

Enzyklika [ɛn'tsyːkliˑkaː], *f.* -/-**ken.** *R.C.Ch:* encyclic, encyclical.

enzyklisch [ɛn'tsyːkliʃ], *a. R.C.Ch:* encyclic(al); **enzyklischer Brief,** encyclic, encyclical.

Enzyklopädie [ɛntsyˑkloˑpɛˑ'diː], *f.* -/-**n** [-'diːən], encyclopaedia.

Enzyklopädiker [ɛntsyˑkloˑ'pɛːdikər], *m.* -s/-, encyclopaedist.

enzyklopädisch [ɛntsyˑkloˑ'pɛːdiʃ], *a.* encyclopaedic.

Enzyklopädist [ɛntsyˑkloˑpɛˑ'dist], *m.* -**en**/-**en,** encyclopaedist.

Enzym [ɛn'tsyːm], *n.* -(e)s/-**e.** *Ch:* enzym(e).

enzymatisch [ɛntsyˑ'maːtiʃ], *a.* enzymic.

Enzymologie [ɛntsyˑmoˑloˑ'giː], *f.* -/. enzymology.

enzystieren (sich) [ɛntsys'tiːrən], *v.refl. Biol: Med:* (*of tumour, etc.*) to become encysted, to encyst; **Enzystierung** *f,* encystation, encystment.

Eocen, das [eˑoˑ'tseːn], -**s**=**Eozän**[2].

eo ipso ['eːoː 'ipsoː]. *Lt.adv.phr.* ipso facto.

Eolith [eˑoˑ'liːt], *m.* -**en**/-**en.** *Prehist:* eolith; celt.

Eolithikum, das [eˑoˑ'liːtiˑkum], -**s.** *Prehist:* the Eolithic period.

eolithisch [eˑoˑ'liːtiʃ], *a. Prehist:* eolithic.

Eos ['eːɔs]. *Pr.n.f.* -'. *Gr.Myth:* Aurora.

Eosin [eˑoˑ'ziːn], *n.* -**s**/-**e.** *Ch:* eosin.

eosinieren [eˑoˑziˑ'niːrən], *v.tr.* to dye (sth.) with eosin.

eosinophil [eˑoˑziˑnoˑ'fiːl], *a.* eosinophil(e), eosinophilic.

Eosinophilie [eˑoˑziˑnoˑfiˑ'liː], *f.* -/. *Med:* eosinophilia.

eozän[1] [eˑoˑ'tsɛːn], *a. Geol:* Eocene.

Eozän[2], **das,** -**s.** *Geol:* the Eocene.

Eozänformation, *f. Geol:* Eocene formation; Eocene strata.

Eozoikum, das [eˑoˑ'tsoːiˑkum], -**s.** *Geol:* the Pre-Cambrian (group, era), the Eozoic (group, era).

eozoisch [eˑoˑ'tsoːiʃ], *a. Geol:* eozoic (system, sediment, etc.).

Ep-, ep- [ɛp(ᵊ)-], *pref.* ep-; *Ling:* **epexegetisch** [ɛpᵊɛkseˑ'geːtiʃ], epexegetic(al).

Epagoge [ɛp(ᵊ)aˑgoˑ'geː], *f.* -/. *Log:* epagoge; (argument by) induction.

epagogisch [ɛp(ᵊ)aˑ'goːgiʃ], *a. Log:* epagogic, inductive; **epagogische Beweisführung,** inductive reasoning.

Epakridazeen [eˑpaˑkriˑdaˑ'tseːən], **Epakrideen** [eˑpaˑkriˑ'deːən], *f.pl. Bot:* epacridaceae.

Epakris [eˑ'paːkrıs], *f.* -/-. *Bot:* epacris.

Epakte [ɛpᵊ'aktə, ɛ'paktə], *f.* -/-**n.** *Chr: Astr:* epact.

Epanalepse [ɛpᵊanaˑ'leːpsə, -'lɛpsə], **Epanalepsis** [ɛpᵊana'leːpsis, -'lɛpsis], *f.* -/-**sen.** *Ling:* epanalepsis.

Epanaphora [ɛpᵊa'nafoˑraː], *f.* -/-**rä.** *Rh:* anaphora.

Eparch [ɛpᵊ'arç, ɛ'parç], *m.* -**en**/-**en,** eparch.

Eparchie [ɛp(ᵊ)ar'çiː], *f.* -/-**n** [-'çiːən]. *Gr.Adm: Hist: Ecc:* eparchy.

Epaulett [eˑpoˑ'lɛt], *n.* -(e)s/-s =**Epaulette.**

Epaulette [eˑpoˑ'lɛtə], *f.* -/-**n.** *Mil: etc:* epaulette, epaulet.

Epeira [eˑ'pairaː], *f.* -/-**ren.** *Arach:* epeirid, araneus, garden spider.

Epeirogenese [eˑpairoˑgeˑ'neːzə], *f.* -/. *Geol:* epeirogeny, epeirogenesis.

epeirogenetisch [eˑpairoˑgeˑ'neːtiʃ], *a. Geol:* epeirogenic.

Epen ['eːpən], *n.pl. see* **Epos.**

Ependym [ɛp(ᵊ)ɛn'dyːm], *n.* -(e)s/-**e, Ependyma** [ɛpᵊ'ɛndyˑmaː], *n.* -**s**/-**men** [-'dyːmən]. *Anat:* ependyma.

Epenthese [ɛp(ᵊ)ɛn'teːzə], *f.* -/-**n.** *Ling:* epenthesis.

epenthetisch [ɛp(ᵊ)ɛn'teːtiʃ], *a. Ling:* epenthetic.

Epexegese [ɛpᵊɛkseˑ'geːzə], *f.* -/-**n.** *Ling:* epexegesis.

Ephebe [ɛ'feːbə], *m.* -**n**/-**n.** *Gr.Ant:* ephebe.

Ephedra [ɛ'feːdraː], *f.* -/-**ren.** *Bot:* ephedra, shrubby horsetail.

Ephedrin [ɛfeˑ'driːn], *n.* -**s**/. *Pharm:* ephedrin(e).

Ephelide [ɛfeˑ'liːdə], *f.* -/-**n.** *Med:* ephelis, freckle.

ephemer [ɛfeˑ'meːr], *a.* ephemeral.

Ephemera[1] [ɛ'feːmeˑraː], *n.pl. Med:* ephemeral fever.

Ephemera[2] [ɛ'feːmeˑraː], *f.* -/-**ren** [ɛfeˑ'meːrən]. **1.**=**Ephemeride** 1. **2.** *Bot: pl.* **Ephemeren,** diurnal flowers.

Ephemeride [ɛfeˑmeˑ'riːdə], *f.* -/-**n** *&* -**rida. 1.** *Ent:* ephemera, ephemeris, ephemeron, may-fly, day-fly; **die Ephemeriden,** the ephemeridae, the may-flies, day-flies. **2.** ephemeris; (*a*) *Astr:* astronomical table; nautical almanac; (*b*) diary; almanac; (*c*) periodical (publication).

Ephemeris [ɛ'feːmeˑris], *f.* -/-**riden** [ɛfeˑmeˑ'riːdən] =**Ephemeride** 2.

ephemerisch [ɛfeˑ'meːriʃ], *a.* ephemeral.

Epheser ['ɛfeˑzər], *m.* -s/-. *A.Hist:* Ephesian.

Epheserbrief, der. *B:* the Epistle to the Ephesians.

ephesisch [ɛ'feːziʃ], *a. A.Hist:* Ephesian.

Ephesos, Ephesus ['ɛfeˑzɔs, -zus]. *Pr.n.n* -'. *A.Geog:* Ephesus.

Epheu, *m.* -**s**/. *Bot: A:* ivy.

Ephidrosis [ɛfiˑ'droːzis], *f.* -/. *Med:* ephidrosis, excessive perspiration.

Ephippium [ɛ'fipĭum], *n.* -**s**/-**pien.** *Ent:* ephippium.

Ephod [eˑ'fɔːt], *n.* -**s**/-**e** [-'foːdə]. *Jew.Ant:* ephod.

Ephor [ɛ'foːr], *m.* -**en**/-**en.** *Gr.Ant:* ephor.

Ephorat [ɛfoˑ'raːt], *n.* -(e)s/-**e.** *Gr.Ant:* ephoralty, ephorate.

Ephore [ɛ'foːrə], *m.* -**n**/-**n.** *Gr.Ant:* ephor.

Ephorie [ɛfoˑ'riː], *f.* -/-**n** [-'riːən]. *Ecc:* district under superintendent's charge; diocese.

Ephorus ['ɛfoˑrus], *m.* -/-**ren** [-'foːrən]. **1.** =**Ephor. 2.** *Ecc:* (*a*) superintendent (*in Reformed Church*); (*b*) head (of a theological college, etc.).

Ephräm ['ɛfrɛˑm]. *Pr.n.m.* -**s.** *Ecc.Hist:* **E. der Syrer,** Ephraim, Ephraem, the Syrian.

Epi-, epi- [eˑpiˑ-], *pref.* epi-; **Epikrise** *f,* epicrisis.

Epiblast [eˑpiˑ'blast], *n.* -(e)s/-**e.** *Biol:* epiblast, ectoderm.

Epibolie [eˑpiˑboˑ'liː], *f.* -/-**n** [-'liːən]. *Biol:* epiboly, epibolic invagination.

epibolisch [eˑpiˑ'boːliʃ], *a. Biol:* epibolic.

Epicalyx [eˑpiˑ'kaːlyks], *m.* -(es)/-**e.** *Bot:* calycle, calyculus.

Epicanthus [eˑpiˑ'kantus], *m.* -/-**thi.** *Med:* epicanthus.

Epidauros, Epidaurus [eˑpiˑ'dauros, -rus]. *Pr.n.n.* -'. *A.Geog:* Epidaurus.

epideiktisch [eˑpiˑ'daiktiʃ], *a. Ling:* epideictic, deictic.

Epidemie [eˑpiˑdeˑ'miː], *f.* -/-**n** [-'miːən]. *Med:* epidemic.

Epidemiologie [eˑpiˑdeˑmĭoˑloˑ'giː], *f.* -/. epidemiology.

epidemisch [eˑpiˑ'deːmiʃ], *a. Med:* epidemic(al).

Epidendron [eˑpiˑ'dɛndrɔn], *n.* -**s**/-**dra.** *Bot:* epidendrum.

Epidermis [eˑpiˑ'dɛrmis], *f.* -/-**men.** *Anat:* epidermis, cuticle; *Bot:* epidermis; *Art:* epidermis; surface of the naked part of the body (in sculpture, portrait, etc.).

epidermisch [eˑpiˑ'dɛrmiʃ], *a.* epidermal, epidermic.

Epidermistransplantation, *f. Surg:* skin grafting.

epidermoidal [eˑpiˑdɛrmoˑiˑ'daːl], *a.* epidermoid(al).

Epidermolysis [eˑpiˑdɛrmoˑ'lyːzis], *f.* -/. *Med:* epidermolysis.

Epidermophyt [e·pi·dɛrmo·ˈfyːt], *m.* **-en/-en.** *Fung:* epidermophyton; ringworm fungus.

Epidiaskop [e·pi·di·a·ˈskoːp], *n.* **-(e)s/-e.** *Opt:* epidiascope.

epidiaskopisch [e·pi·di·a·ˈskoːpiʃ], *a. Opt:* epidiascopic.

Epididymis [e·pi·ˈdiːdy·mis], *f.* **-/-miden** [-di·dy·ˈmiːdən]. *Anat:* epididymis.

Epididymitis [e·pi·di·dy·ˈmiːtis], *f.* **-/.** *Med:* epididymitis.

Epidot [e·pi·ˈdoːt], *m.* **-(e)s/-e.** *Miner:* epidote, pistacite.

epidural [e·pi·du·ˈraːl], *a. Anat:* epidural.

epigäisch [e·pi·ˈgɛːiʃ], *a. Bot:* epigeous, epigeal.

epigastrisch [e·pi·ˈgastriʃ], *a. Anat:* epigastric.

Epigastrium [e·pi·ˈgastrĭum], *n.* **-s/-strien.** *Anat:* epigastrium.

Epigenese [e·pi·ge·ˈneːzə], **Epigenesis** [-ˈgeːne·zis], *f.* **-/.** *Biol:* epigenesis.

epigenetisch [e·pi·ge·ˈneːtiʃ], *a. Geol:* epigenetic.

Epiglottis [e·pi·ˈglotis], *f.* **-/-tes.** *Anat:* epiglottis.

Epigone [e·pi·ˈgoːnə], *m.* **-n/-n,** (weak) successor of a great period (of history, art, literature, etc.); epigonus, epigon(e).

epigonenhaft, *a.* epigonous.

Epigramm [e·pi·ˈgram], *n.* **-(e)s/-e,** epigram.

Epigrammatiker [e·pi·gra·ˈmaːtikər], *m.* **-s/-,** epigrammatist.

epigrammatisch [e·pi·gra·ˈmaːtiʃ], *a.* epigrammatic; *adv.* epigrammatically.

Epigrammatist [e·pi·grama·ˈtist], *m.* **-en/-en,** epigrammatist.

Epigrammdichter, *m.* epigrammatist.

Epigraph [e·pi·ˈgraːf], *n.* **-s/-e,** epigraph; inscription; motto.

Epigraphik [e·pi·ˈgraːfik], *f.* **-/.** epigraphy.

Epigraphiker [e·pi·ˈgraːfikər], *m.* **-s/-,** epigraphist.

epigraphisch [e·pi·ˈgraːfiʃ], *a.* epigraphic.

epigyn [e·pi·ˈgyːn], *a. Bot:* epigynous (flower).

Epigynie [e·pi·gy·ˈniː], *f.* **-/.** *Bot:* epigyny.

Epik [ˈeːpik], *f.* **-/.** (i) epic poetry; (ii) narrative literature.

Epikanthus [e·pi·ˈkantus], *m.* **-/-thi.** *Med:* epicanthus.

Epikarp [e·pi·ˈkarp], *n.* **-(e)s/-e, Epikarpium** [e·pi·ˈkarpĭum], *n.* **-s/-pien.** *Bot:* epicarp.

Epikedeion [e·pi·ˈkeːdaion], *n.* **-s/-deia.** *Gr.Lit:* epicedium, funeral song *or* ode.

Epiker [ˈeːpikər], *m.* **-s/-,** (i) epic poet; (ii) narrative author.

Epiklese [e·pi·ˈkleːzə], *f.* **-/-n.** *Ecc:* epiklesis, epiclesis.

Epikrise [e·pi·ˈkriːzə], *f.* **-/-n.** *Med:* epicrisis.

Epiktet [e·pi·ˈkteːt]. *Pr.n.m.* **-s.** *Gr.Phil:* Epictetus.

Epikur [e·pi·ˈkuːr]. *Pr.n.m.* **-s.** *Gr.Phil:* Epicurus.

Epikureer [e·pi·ku·ˈreːər], *m.* **-s/-.** *Gr.Phil:* Epicurean; *F:* epicurean.

epikureisch [e·pi·ku·ˈreːiʃ], **epikurisch** [epi·ˈkuːriʃ], *a. Gr.Phil:* Epicurean; *F:* epicurean.

Epikurismus [e·pi·ku·ˈrismus], *m.* **-/.** Epicureanism, Epicurism.

Epikuros [e·pi·ˈkuːros]. *Pr.n.m.* **-'.** = **Epikur.**

Epikykloide [e·pi·ky·klo·ˈiːdə], *f.* **-/-n** = **Epizykloide.**

Epilation [e·pi·la·tsĭ·ˈoːn], *f.* **-/.** depilation, epilation; removal of (superfluous) hair; plucking (of eyebrows).

Epilepsie [e·pi·lɛ·ˈpsiː], *f.* **-/.** *Med:* epilepsy.

Epileptiker [e·pi·ˈlɛptikər], *m.* **-s/-,** epileptic.

epileptisch [e·pi·ˈlɛptiʃ], *a. Med:* epileptic; **epileptischer Anfall,** epileptic fit.

epilieren [e·pi·ˈliːrən], *v.tr.* to depilate, epilate; to remove (superfluous) hair; to pluck (eyebrows).

Epilobium [e·pi·ˈloːbĭum], *n.* **-s/.** *Bot:* epilobium, willow-herb.

Epilog [e·pi·ˈloːk], *m.* **-s/-e** [-ˈloːgə], epilogue.

Epimorphose [e·pi·mor·ˈfoːzə], *f.* **-/-n.** *Miner:* pseudomorphism by incrustation.

Epinastie [e·pi·nas·ˈtiː], *f.* **-/.** *Bot:* epinasty.

epinastisch [e·pi·ˈnastiʃ], *a. Bot:* epinastic; **epinastisches Wachstum,** epinasty.

Epinglé [e·pɛ̃·ˈleː], *m.* **-s/-s.** *Tex:* terry, uncut velvet.

Epinikion [e·pi·ˈniːkĭon], *n.* **-s/-kien.** *Gr.Lit:* epinicion, song in honour of a victor.

Epipaläolithikum, das [e·pi·pa·lɛ·o·ˈliːti·kum], **-s.** *Prehist:* the Epipaleolithic period.

Epipedon [e·ˈpiːpe·don], *n.* **-s/-den** [e·pi·ˈpeːdən] & **-da** [e·ˈpiːpe·daː]. *Geom:* plane.

Epiphania(s) [e·pi·ˈfaːnĭaː, -ˈfaːnĭas], *f.* **-/.** *Ecc:* Epiphany.

Epiphaniasfest, *n. Ecc:* Epiphany.

Epiphaniassonntage, *m.pl. Ecc:* Sundays after Epiphany.

Epiphanie [e·pi·fa·ˈniː], *f.* **-/-n** [-ˈniːən], epiphany (of a divinity); *Ecc:* Epiphany.

Epiphanienfest [e·pi·ˈfaːnĭən-], *n. Ecc:* Epiphany.

Epiphänomen [e·pi·fɛ·no·ˈmeːn], *n.* **-s/-e.** *Med:* epiphenomenon.

Epiphonem [e·pi·fo·ˈneːm], *m.* **-s/-e.** *Rh:* epiphonema.

Epiphora [e·ˈpi·fo·raː], *f.* **-/-ren** [-ˈfoːrən]. **1.** *Rh:* epiphora; epistrophe. **2.** *Med:* epiphora, watering of the eyes.

epiphyllisch [e·pi·ˈfyliʃ], *a. Bot:* epiphyllous.

Epiphyllum [e·pi·ˈfylum], *n.* **-s/-la & -len.** *Bot:* epiphyllum.

Epiphyse [e·pi·ˈfyːzə], *f.* **-/-n.** *Anat:* epiphysis.

Epiphysenlösung, *f. Med:* epiphyseolysis, separation of epiphysis.

Epiphyt [e·pi·ˈfyːt], *m.* **-en/-en.** **1.** *Bot:* epiphyte. **2.** *Med:* vegetable parasite on the body.

epiphytisch [e·pi·ˈfyːtiʃ], *a. Bot:* epiphytal, epiphytic.

Epiphytismus [e·pi·fy·ˈtismus], *m.* **-/.** *Bot:* epiphytatism.

epiploisch [e·pi·ˈploːiʃ], *a. Anat:* epiploic, omental (vein, etc.).

Epiploitis [e·pi·plo·ˈiːtis], *f.* **-/.** *Med:* epiploitis, inflammation of the epiploon.

Epiploon [e·ˈpi·plo·on], *n.* **-s/-ploen & -ploa.** *Anat:* epiploon, omentum.

Epirogenese [e·pi·ro·ge·ˈneːzə], *f.* **-/-n.** *Geol:* epeirogeny, epeirogenesis.

epirogenetisch [e·pi·ro·ge·ˈneːtiʃ], *a. Geol:* epeirogenic.

Epirot [e·pi·ˈroːt], *m.* **-en/en.** *A.Hist:* Epirot(e).

epirotisch [e·pi·ˈroːtiʃ], *a. A.Hist:* Epirotic.

epirrhizisch [e·pi·ˈriːtsiʃ], *a. Bot:* epir(r)hizous.

episch [ˈeːpiʃ], *a.* (i) epic; (ii) narrative; **epische Dichtung,** (i) epic poetry; (ii) epic (poem); (iii) narrative literature.

Episkop [e·pi·ˈskoːp], *n.* **-(e)s/-e.** *Opt:* episcope; projector for opaque objects.

episkopal [e·pisko·ˈpaːl], *a. Ecc:* episcopal; **Episkopale** *m, f,* Anglican; *Scot: U.S:* Episcopalian.

Episkopalismus [e·pisko·pa·ˈlismus], *n.* **-/.** *Ecc:* (*a*) episcopacy; government of the church by bishops; (*b*) *R.C.Ch:* episcopalism.

Episkopalist [e·pisko·pa·ˈlist], *m.* **-en/-en.** *Ecc:* Anglican; *Scot: U.S:* Episcopalian.

Episkopalkirche, *f. Ecc:* Anglican Church; *Scot: U.S:* Episcopal Church.

Episkopalsystem, *n.* = **Episkopalismus** (*a*).

Episkopat [e·pisko·ˈpaːt], *m. & n.* **-(e)s/-e.** *Ecc:* **1.** episcopate; office of bishop; **unter dem E. von . . . ,** under the episcopate of . . . . **2.** episcopacy, episcopate, (the) bishops.

Episkopie [e·pisko·ˈpiː], *f.* **-/.** *Opt:* projection of opaque objects, episcopic projection.

episkopisch[1] [e·pi·ˈskoːpiʃ], *a. Ecc:* episcopal.

episkopisch[2], *a. Opt:* episcopic (projection, etc.).

Episode [e·pi·ˈzoːdə], *f.* **-/-n,** episode; incident.

Episodenfilm, *m. Cin: A:* serial film.

episodisch [e·pi·ˈzoːdiʃ], *a.* episodic(al).

Episporium [e·pi·ˈspoːrĭum], *n.* **-s/-rien.** *Bot:* epispore (of fern).

Epistel [e·ˈpistəl], *f.* **-/-n,** (*a*) *B.Lit:* epistle (of apostle); (*b*) *Ecc:* epistle; *F:* **j-m gehörig die E. lesen,** to lecture, scold, reprimand, s.o., *F:* to give s.o. a good dressing-down; (*c*) *F:* letter, *esp.* long letter, *F:* epistle; **eine lange E. nach Hause schreiben,** to write a long letter, *F:* a long epistle, home.

Epistelseite, *f. Ecc:* epistle-side, south-side (of altar).

Epistemologie [e·piste·mo·lo·ˈgiː], *f.* **-/.** *Phil:* epistemology.

Epistolar [e·pisto·ˈlaːr], *n.* **-s/-e.** *Ecc:* (epistle) lectionary, epistolary.

epistolisch [e·pi·ˈstoːliʃ], *a.* epistolary.

Epistolograph [e·pisto·lo·ˈgraːf], *m.* **-en/-en,** epistolographer.

Epistolographie [e·pisto·lo·gra·ˈfiː], *f.* **-/.** epistolography; the art of letter-writing.

Epistrophe [e·ˈpistro·feː, e·pi·ˈstroːfə], *f.* **-/-n** [e·pi·ˈstroːfən]. *Rh:* epistrophe.

Epistropheus [e·ˈpistro·foys], *m.* **-/.** *Anat:* epistropheus, axis.

Epistyl [e·pi·ˈstyːl], *n.* **-s/-e.** *Arch:* epistyle, architrave.

Epitaph [e·pi·ˈtaːf], *n.* **-s/-e, Epitaphium** [epi·ˈtaːfĭum], *n.* **-s/-phien.** **1.** epitaph. **2.** memorial stone; memorial plaque (in church).

Epitasis [e·ˈpi·ta·zis], *f.* **-/** *.Gr.Drama:* epitasis.

Epithalamion, Epithalamium [e·pi·ta·ˈlaːmĭon, -ĭum], *n.* **-s/-mien.** *Lit:* epithalamium.

Epithel [e·pi·ˈteːl], *n.* **-s/-e.** *Anat:* epithelium.

epithelartig, *a. Anat: Bot:* epithelial (cells, etc.).

Epithelgewebe, *n. Anat:* epithelial tissue.

epithelial [e·pi·te·lĭ·ˈaːl], *a. Anat:* epithelial.

Epithelialkrebs, *m. Med:* epithelial cancer, epithelioma.

Epitheliom [e·pi·te·lĭ·ˈoːm], *n.* **-s/-e.** *Med:* epithelioma, epithelial cancer.

Epithelium [e·pi·ˈteːlĭum], *n.* **-s/-lien.** *Anat:* epithelium.

Epithelkörperchen, *n. Anat:* epithelial body, parathyroid gland.

Epithelzyste, *f. Med:* epithelial, dermoid, cyst.

Epithem [e·pi·ˈteːm], *n.* **-s/-a.** *Pharm:* epithem.

Epithese [e·pi·ˈteːzə], *f.* **-/-n.** *Ling:* epithesis.

Epithet [e·pi·ˈteːt], *n.* **-s/-a** [e·ˈpi·te·taː], epithet.

epithetisch [e·pi·ˈteːtiʃ], *a.* epithetic(al); *adv.* epithetically.

Epitheton [e·ˈpi·te·ton], *n.* **-s/-ta,** epithet; **E. ornans,** decorative epithet.

Epitomator [e·pi·to·ˈmaːtor], *m.* **-s/-en** [-ma·ˈtoːrən], epitomist.

Epitome [e·ˈpi·to·meː], *f.* **-/-n** [e·pi·ˈtoːmən], epitome (of book, etc.).

epitomisieren [e·pi·to·mi·ˈziːrən], *v.tr.* to epitomize, to abridge.

Epitrachelion [e·pi·tra·ˈxeːlĭon], *n.* **-s/-lien.** **1.** *Arch:* colarin, neck, frieze (of Doric and Tuscan column). **2.** *Ecc:* epitrachelion, stole (worn by priests of the Eastern Church).

Epitrope [e·ˈpi·tro·peː], *f.* **-/-n** [e·pi·ˈtroːpən[. *Rh:* epitrope.

Epitrophie [e·pi·tro·ˈfiː], *f.* **-/.** *Bot:* epitrophy.

Epizentrum [e·pi·ˈtsɛntrum], *n.* **-s/-ren.** *Geol:* epicentre, epicentrum (of earthquake).

epizön [e·pi·ˈtsøːn], *a.* **1.** *Gram:* epicene. **2.** *Nat. Hist:* hermaphrodite, hermaphroditic.

Epizoon [e·pi·ˈtsoːon], *n.* **-s/-zoen & -zoa.** *Nat.Hist:* epizoon, external parasite.

Epizootie [e·pi·tso·o·ˈtiː], *f.* **-/-n** [-ˈtiːən]. *Vet:* epizootic disease, epizooty.

epizootisch [e·pi·tso·ˈoːtiʃ], *a. Vet:* epizootic (disease, etc.).

Epizykel [e·pi·ˈtsyːkəl], *m.* **-s/-.** *Geom: Astr:* epicycle.

epizyklisch [e·pi·ˈtsyːkliʃ], *a. Geom: etc:* epicyclic.

epizykloidal [e·pi·tsy·klo·i·ˈdaːl], *a. Geom: Mec.E:* epicycloidal.

Epizykloide [e·pi·tsy·klo·ˈiːdə], *f.* **-/-n.** *Geom:* epicycloid.

Epizykloidenverzahnung, *f. Mec.E:* epicyclic gearing.

epochal [e·po·ˈxaːl], *a.* epochal, epoch-making, epoch-marking.

Epoche [e·ˈpoxə], *f.* **-/-n,** epoch; **E. machen,** to make, mark, an epoch.

epochemachend, *a.* epoch-making, epoch-marking (discovery, event, etc.); **von epochemachender Bedeutung,** epoch-making, epoch-marking.

Epode [ɛp(ˀ)ˈoːdə], *f.* **-/-n.** *Pros: Cl.Lit:* epode.

Eponym [ɛp(ˀ)o·ˈnyːm], *n.* **-s/-e,** surname, apellation.

Eponymie [ɛp(ˀ)o·ny·ˈmiː], *f.* **-/.** eponymy.

eponymisch [ɛp(ˀ)o·ˈnyːmiʃ], *a.* (*a*) eponymous (hero, etc.); (*b*) eponymic.

Eponymus [ɛp(ˀ)ˈoːny·mus], *m.* **-/-men** [-o·ˈnyːmən]. *Cl.Ant:* eponym.

Epopöe [e·po·ˈpøː(ə)], *f.* **-/-n** [-ˈpøːən]. *A:* epopee, epic poem.

Epos [ˈeːpos], *n.* **-/Epen** [ˈeːpən], (*a*) epos, epic, epic poem; **höfisches E.,** court epic; (*b*) narrative work (in prose).

Eppich, *m.* **-(e)s/-e.** *Bot:* **1.** (*a*) celery; (*b*) lesser celandine, pilewort; (*c*) horse-parsley; (*d*) mountain-parsley; (*e*) = **Attich.** **2.** *Poet:* = **Efeu.**

Eprouvette [e·pru·ˈvɛtə], *f.* **-/-n.** *Ch: etc: Austrian:* test-tube, test-glass.

Epsilon [ˈɛpsi·lon], *n.* **-(s)/-s.** *Gr.Alph:* epsilon.

Epsomer [ˈɛpsomər], *inv.a. Pharm:* **E. Salz,** Epsom salts.

Epsomit [ɛpso·ˈmiːt], *n.* **-s/.** *Pharm:* Epsom salts.

Epsomsalz [ˈɛpsəm-], *n. Pharm:* Epsom salts.

Equidae [e·ˈkviːdɛː], *m.pl. Z:* equidae, the horses.

equilibrieren [e·kvi·li·ˈbriːrən], *v.tr.* = **äquilibrieren.**

Equilibrist [e·kvi·li·ˈbrist], *m.* **-en/-en** = **Äquilibrist.**

Equine [e·ˈkviːnə], *f.* **-/-n.** *Vet:* horse-pox.

Equipage [e·k(v)i·ˈpaːʒə], *f.* **-/-n.** **1.** (*a*) *Veh:* equipage, carriage and horses; (*b*) retinue, suite, train; (*c*) equipment. **2.** *Nau:* crew; **die E.,** the ship's company, *F:* the hands.

Equipe [e·ˈk(v)iːp], *f.* **-/-n** [-pən]. *Sp: etc:* team of riders, equestrian team.

equipieren [e·k(v)i·ˈpiːrən], *v.tr. Mil: etc:* to equip (s.o., sth.); to fit (s.o., sth.) out; **Equipierung** *f,* fitting out, equipment (of soldiers with uniform, kit, etc.; of ship with armaments, etc.).

Equisetum [e·kvi·ˈzeːtum], *n.* **-s/.** *Bot:* equisetum, *F:* horse-tail.

Equitation [e·kvi·ta·tsĭ·ˈoːn], *f.* **-/.** equitation, riding; horsemanship.

Equitationsschule, *f.* riding-school.

er, *pers.pron. third person sg. nom. m.* (*gen.* **seiner,** *A. & Lit:* **sein;** *dat.* **ihm;** *acc.* **ihn) 1.** (*a*) (*of pers.*) he; (*of animal, bird, etc., that is masc. in German*) it; (*occ. of male animal*) he; **er liebt,** he loves; **er sah mich nicht,** he didn't see me; **was sagt er?** what is he saying? **er und ich,** he and I; *F:* him and me; **ich bin so groß wie er,** I am as tall as he (is); **er ist es,** it is he, *F:* him; **wenn ich er wäre,** if I were he, *F:* him; **hier kommt er,** here he comes; **der Hund blieb stehen, er hatte den Mann gesehen,** the dog stopped; it, he, had seen the man; **der Hecht ist ein Raubfisch, er frißt kleinere Fische,** the pike is a cannibal; it eats smaller fish; **ich gedenke seiner,** *A. & Lit:* **sein, in Dankbarkeit,** I think of him with gratitude; **sie ist seiner nicht wert,** she is not worthy of him; **ich gab ihm das Buch,** I gave him the book, I gave the book to him; **das kann ich ihm nicht antun,** I can't do that to him; **es geht ihm gut,** he is well; **kennen Sie ihn?** do you know him? (*stressed*) **'ihn möchte ich nicht als Lehrer haben,** I would not like (to have) 'him for a teacher, I would not like 'him to be my teacher; (*b*) (*of the Deity, often written or printed as* **Er,** *or* ER) He; **Er wird uns nicht verlassen,** He will not forsake us; **betet zu Ihm,** pray to Him; **wir glauben an Ihn, den Erlöser,** we believe in Him, the Saviour; (*c*) (*of thgs that are masc. in German*) it; **ich kaufte einen Apfel, aber er war schlecht,** I bought an apple, but it was bad; **der Rhein ist einer der größten deutschen Flüsse, er entspringt in der Schweiz,** the Rhine is one of the largest German rivers; it has its source in Switzerland; **der Mond ging auf, er war beinahe voll,** the moon rose, it, *Poet:* she, was nearly full; **der Apfelbaum stand beim Brunnen, ich kann mich seiner noch gut erinnern,** the apple-tree grew by the fountain; I can remember it very well; **der Film war höchst interessant, ich würde ihn sehr gern noch einmal sehen,** the film was most interesting; I would very much like to see it again; **der Everest ist der höchste Berg der Welt, nur wenige haben ihn bestiegen,** Mount Everest is the highest mountain in the world; only few people have climbed it. **2. Er,** (*old-fashioned address, used to inferiors*) you; **was will Er da?** what do you want there? **zeige Er mir den Brief!** show me the letter! **ich werde Ihm morgen meine Entscheidung mitteilen,** I will let you know my decision tomorrow; **das geht Ihn gar nichts an,** that is none of your business. **3.** (*as substantive*) **ein Er,** a he, a male; **es ist ein Er,** (*of new-born child*) it's a boy, a he, (*of kitten, puppy, etc.*) it's a he, a male, (*of kitten*) it's a tom

er-, *pref.* **I.** *vbl pref. insep.* **1.** (*denoting motion upwards or outwards*) (*from vbs*) (*a*) (*forming tr. vbs*) **etwas errichten, erbauen,** to build sth. up, to erect sth.; **etwas erheben,** to lift up, raise (up), sth.; **Kinder erziehen,** to bring up children; (*b*) (*forming intr. vbs*) **erstehen,** to rise (up); (*c*) (*forming tr. vbs*) **etwas erschließen,** to open up sth.; **etwas erbrechen,** to break sth. open. **2.** (*a*) (*forming tr. vbs*) (*bringing about the state implied in the simplex*) (i) (*from adjs & vbs*) **erfrischen, erquicken,** to refresh; **erweitern,** to widen, make wider; **ermutigen,** to encourage; **erniedrigen,** to lower; **erhöhen,** to make higher, to raise; **erleichtern,** to relieve; **erweichen,** to soften; **ernüchtern,** to make sober, to sober; **erhärten,** to harden; **erwärmen,** to warm; **ermäßigen,** to modify; to moderate; **erklären,** to make clear, plain, to explain; (ii) (*from nouns*) **erhitzen,** to heat; (*b*) (*forming intr. vbs*) (*attaining the state implied in the simplex*) (i) (*from vbs*) **erglühen,** to glow, to become aglow; **erstaunen,** to become astonished; **erblühen,** to blossom, to bloom; **erwachen,** to awake(n); (ii) (*from adjs*) **ergrünen,** to become green; **erröten,** to become, grow, red; to blush; **erblassen, erbleichen,** to become, grow, pale, to pale; **erblinden,** to go blind; **erkranken,** to become ill, sick, to sicken; **ermüden,** to tire; to become, grow, tired; **erstarken,** to become, grow, strong; (*c*) (*forming refl. vbs*) (*from adjs*) **sich erdreisten, erfrechen,** to have the cheek (to do sth.); **sich erkühnen,** to have the audacity (to do sth.). **3.** (*forming tr. vbs*) (*from vbs*) (*undergoing, suffering, sth.*) **etwas ertragen,** to bear sth.; **etwas erleiden, erdulden,** to suffer sth. **4.** (*forming tr. vbs*) (*from vbs*) (*a*) (*achieving a result by method implied in the simplex*) **j-n erretten,** to save s.o.; **etwas erproben,** to test sth.; **j-n, etwas, erwählen,** to choose s.o., sth.; **j-n, etwas, erwecken,** to awaken s.o., sth.; **etwas erzeugen,** to produce sth.; (*b*) (*denoting desire for sth.*) **etwas erstreben,** to strive for sth.; **etwas ersehnen,** to long for sth.; **j-n, etwas, erwarten,** to wait for s.o., sth.; to await, expect, s.o., sth.; **etwas erhoffen,** to hope for sth.; (*c*) (*killing by method implied in the simplex*) **j-n erschießen,** to shoot s.o. dead; **j-n erstechen,** to stab s.o. to death; **j-n, sich, erhängen,** to hang s.o., oneself; **j-n ermorden,** to murder s.o.; **eine Katze ertränken, ersäufen,** to drown a cat; **einen Wurm, eine Blume, ertreten,** to kill a worm, a flower, by treading on it; (*d*) (*forming intr. vbs*) (*dying in the manner implied in the simplex*) **erfrieren,** to freeze to death; **ertrinken,** to drown, to be drowned; **ersticken,** to suffocate. **5.** (*forming tr. vbs*) (*a*) (*from intr. vbs or from the intr. meaning of vbs which can be either tr. or intr.*) (*gaining or achieving sth. by method implied in the simplex*) **etwas erbetteln,** to get sth. by begging; **etwas erkämpfen,** to get sth. by fighting for it, to fight for sth.; **etwas ersparen,** to get sth. by saving, to save sth.; **etwas erarbeiten,** to get sth. by working for it, to work for sth.; **j-n, etwas, erfassen, ergreifen,** to grasp, seize, s.o., sth.; **etwas erblicken,** to see, perceive, sth.; **j-n, etwas, erspähen,** to espy s.o., sth.; **etwas erleben,** to experience sth.; **etwas erfahren,** to hear, to learn, sth.; **sich nach j-m, etwas, erkundigen,** to enquire after s.o., sth.; (*b*) (*from tr. vbs, with a different object from that governed by the simplex*) **etwas erbitten,** to ask, beg, for sth.; **etwas erzwingen,** to get sth. by force; **den Weg erfragen,** to find one's way by asking, to ask the way; **j-n erpressen,** to blackmail s.o.; **sich erholen,** to recover; (*c*) (*from vbs*) (*production of sth. by mental activity, usu. implied in the simplex*) **etwas erträumen,** to dream sth. up; **etwas erfinden,** to make sth. up, to invent sth.; **etwas erlügen,** to make sth. up, to trump up sth.; to lie about sth.

II. 1. Er-, (*forming vbl nouns*) (*a*) (*corresponding in meaning to the vbs from which they are derived*) **Erguß** *m,* (i) pouring out, forth; (ii) outburst; **Erlaß** *m,* edict; **Erweis** *m,* proof; **Erwerb** *m,* acquisition; **Ermordung** *f,* (i) murdering, murder; (ii) being murdered, murder; (*b*) (*with independent meaning*) **Ertrag** *m,* yield; **Erlös** *m,* proceeds (of collection, etc.); **Erfolg** *m,* success. **2. er-,** (*forming vbl adjs corresponding in meaning to the vbs from which they are derived*) **erträglich,** bearable; **erklärlich,** explainable; **erkennbar,** recognizable; **erhältlich,** obtainable; **ersprießlich,** fruitful; **erstaunlich,** astonishing; **leicht ermüdbar,** easily tired; **erholsam,** restful, refreshing.

-er[1], *s.suff. m.* **-s/-. 1.** (*persons*) (*denoting profession, occupation, etc.*) (*a*) -er; -(s)man; . . . man; **Gärtner,** gardener; **Lehrer,** teacher; **Bäcker,** baker; **Tänzer,** dancer; **Sänger,** singer; **Fahrer,** driver; **Schriftsteller,** writer; **Jäger,** hunter, huntsman; **Ruderer,** rower, oarsman; **Heizer,** stoker, *Rail:* fireman; **Händler,** trader; tradesman; **Reiter,** rider, horseman; **Arbeiter,** worker, workman, working man; **Kämpfer,** fighter, fighting man; **Golfspieler,** golfer; **Sportler,** sportsman; **Bremser,** brakeman; **Fischer,** fisherman; (*b*) -ist; **Botaniker,** botanist; **Physiker,** physicist; **Chemiker,** chemist; **Geiger,** violinist; **Radler, Radfahrer,** cyclist; (*c*) -or; **Verräter,** traitor; **Schauspieler,** actor; **Kanzler,** chancellor; **Übersetzer,** translator; **Erzieher,** tutor; (*d*) -ian; **Akademiker,** academician; **Musiker,** musician; **Politiker,** politician; **Elektriker,** electrician; **Patrizier,** patrician; **Magier,** magician; (*e*) -ic; **Epileptiker,** epileptic; **Rachitiker,** rachitic; **Fanatiker,** fanatic; **Häretiker,** heretic. **2.** (*referring to geographical origin*) (*a*) *s.m.* (i) native, inhabitant, of . . .; man from . . .; **Kölner,** native, inhabitant, of Cologne; **Warschauer,** native, inhabitant, of Warsaw; **Prager,** native, inhabitant, of Prague; (ii) -er; **Londoner,** Londoner; **Isländer,** Icelander; **Neuseeländer,** New Zealander; **Neuyorker,** New Yorker; **Hamburger,** Hamburger; (iii) -an; **Mexikaner,** Mexican; **Deutscher,** German; **Toskaner,** Tuscan; **Afrikaner,** African; **Amerikaner,** American; (iv) -ian; -iard; **Inder,** Indian; **Österreicher,** Austrian; **Pariser,** Parisian; **Glasgower,** Glaswegian; **Elsässer,** Alsatian; **Italiener,** Italian; **Schlesier,** Silesian; **Australier,** Australian; **Spanier,** Spaniard; (v) -man; **Holländer,** Dutchman; **Engländer,** Englishman; **Irländer,** Irishman; (vi) -ese; **Wiener,** Viennese; **Japaner,** Japanese; (*b*) *inv.a.* (i) of, from, . . .; **ein Amsterdamer Einwohner,** an inhabitant of Amsterdam; **ein Hamburger Fischer,** a fisherman from Hamburg; **eine Wiener Schauspielerin,** an actress from Vienna; (ii) (*translated by using the adj. derived from the place name*) **Holländer Käse,** Dutch cheese; **Schweizer Berge,** Swiss mountains; **Wiener Walzer,** Viennese waltzes; **Pariser Aussprache,** Parisian accent; **Elsässer Tracht,** Alsatian costume; (iii) (*translated by the place name used adjectivally*) **Brüsseler Spitzen,** Brussels lace; **Wiener Würstchen,** Vienna sausages; **Dresdener Porzellan,** Dresden china; **Pariser Moden,** Paris fashions; **der Kölner Dom,** Cologne cathedral; **die Londoner Untergrundbahn,** the London underground (railway); **die Oxforder, Heidelberger, Universität,** Oxford, Heidelberg, university. **3.** *Nat.Hist:* (*denoting species, usu. pl.*) **Zweiflügler,** diptera; **Kurzhörner,** brachycera; **Warmblüter,** warm-blooded animals; **Doppelatmer,** dipnoi; **Spaltschlüpfer,** orthorrapha. **4.** (*thg, device, agent*) (*a*) **Eindampfer,** evaporating apparatus; **Entfärber,** decolourizing agent; **Sortierer,** sorting device; (*b*) -er; **Klopfer,** knocker; **Kocher,** cooker; **Teppichklopfer,** carpet-beater; **Dampfer,** steamer; **Entferner,** remover; **Doppeldecker,** double-decker; **Fünfer,** fiver; **Dreipfünder,** three-pounder; **Köpfer** (=**Kopfsprung**), header; (*c*) **Bohrer,** drill; **Schalter,** switch; **Tennisschläger,** tennis-racquet; **Zahnstocher,** toothpick; **Kugelschreiber,** ball-point pen.

-er[2], *a. & adv. suff. forming comparatives.* **1.** (*adjs*) -(e)r; more . . .; (*a*) **tiefer,** deeper; **kleiner,** smaller; **klarer,** clearer; **teu(e)rer,** dearer; **hübscher,** prettier; **lockiger,** curlier; **bleicher,** paler; **schöner,** more beautiful; **angenehmer,** more pleasant; **ernster,** more serious; **schwieriger,** more difficult; **zufriedener,** more satisfied; (*b*) (*modifying the vowel of the positive*) **wärmer,** warmer; **höher,** higher; **härter,** harder; **größer,** greater; bigger; taller; **länger,** longer; **röter,** redder. **2.** (*advs*) (*a*) more +*adv.*; **leichter,** more easily; **schneller,** more quickly; **deutlicher, klarer,** more clearly, more plainly; **gieriger,** more greedily; (*b*) -er; **länger warten,** to wait longer; **schneller laufen,** to run faster; **eher kommen,** to come sooner, earlier; **sich besser fühlen,** to feel better.

erachten. I. *v.tr.* **etwas für gut e.,** to consider, think, believe, deem, sth. to be good; **es für richtig, ratsam, nötig, e., etwas zu tun, daß etwas getan werden soll,** to think, consider, deem, it proper, advisable, necessary, to do sth., that sth. should be done; **die Maßnahmen, die für nötig erachtet werden,** the measures considered necessary; **ich erachte es als eine Ehre, Ihnen dienen zu dürfen,** I consider, deem, it an honour to serve you; **ich erachte es als meine Pflicht,** I consider it my duty.

II. *vbl s.* **Erachten,** *n.* **meines, unseres, Erachtens** (*abbr.* **m. E., u. E.**), **meinem, unserem, E. nach,** in my, our, opinion, estimation, view; to my, our, mind; as I, we, consider, take, see, it; **meines Erachtens, meinem E. nach, sollte er kommen,** in my opinion he ought to come; **seines Erachtens bestand keine Gefahr,** in his opinion there was no danger; **ihres Erachtens, ihrem E. nach, wird er niemals wiederkommen,** she is of the opinion, her opinion is, that he will never come back; **meines Erachtens ist das ein ausgezeichneter Ratschlag,** in my opinion, view, that is excellent advice, that, to my mind, is excellent advice.

Eradiation [e·ra·dĭa·tsĭ'oːn], *f.* **-/-en,** radiation, *Lit:* eradiation.

eradieren [e·ra·'diːrən], *v.tr.* to erase (word, etc.).

eradiieren [e·ra·di·'iːrən], *v.i.* (*haben*) to radiate, *Lit:* to eradiate.

Eradikation [e·ra·di·ka·tsĭ'oːn], *f.* **-/-en,** eradication, extirpation.

eradizieren [e·ra·di·'tsiːrən], *v.tr.* to eradicate, extirpate, root out (evil, etc.).

erahnen, *v.tr.* to imagine (sth.); **selbst in ihren wildesten Phantasien konnten sie das nicht e.,** even in their wildest fantasies they could not have imagined this.

Eranthis [e·'rantis], *f.* **-/.** *Bot:* eranthis.

erarbeiten, *v.tr.* **etwas e.,** to get sth. by working for it; to work for sth.; to acquire (knowledge, etc.) by one's own efforts; **(sich** *dat.***) etwas schwer, sauer, e.,** to work hard for sth.; to get sth. by hard work, by the sweat of one's brow; **schwer, sauer, erarbeitetes Geld,** money earned by hard work; **schwer erarbeiteter Reichtum,** hard-won fortune; **mühsam erarbeitetes Wissen,** hard-won knowledge; **einer muß sich das Wissen mühsam e., dem anderen fliegt es zu,** some people have to acquire their knowledge by hard work, to others it comes easily; **er ist jetzt ein wohlhabender Mann, aber er hat sich seinen Reichtum schwer e. müssen,** he is a rich man now,

but he had to work hard for it, but he got his wealth by hard work.

Erasmianer [eˑrasmiˈaːnər], *m.* **-s/-.** Erasmian.

erasmisch [eˑˈrasmiʃ], *a.* Erasmian.

Erasmus [eˑˈrasmus]. *Pr.n.m.* **-'.** Erasmus.

Erastianer [eˑrastiˈaːnər], *m.* **-s/-.** *Rel.Hist:* Erastian.

erastianisch [eˑrastiˈaːniʃ], *a. Rel.Hist:* Erastian.

Erastianismus [eˑrastiaˑˈnismus], *m.* **-/.** *Rel.Hist:* Erastianism.

Erastus [eˑˈrastus]. *Pr.n.m.* **-'.** *Rel.Hist:* Erastus.

eräugen, *v.tr.* **j-n, etwas, e.,** to espy s.o., sth.; to catch sight of s.o., sth.; *F:* to spot s.o., sth.

Erbabweichung, *f. Biol:* mutation (of type).

Erbadel, *m.* **1.** hereditary title (of nobility). **2.** hereditary nobility; the peers.

Erbamt, *n. Hist:* hereditary office.

Erbänderung, *f. Biol:* mutation (of type).

Erbanfall, *m. Jur:* inheritance; succession, reversion, of an estate.

Erbanfallsteuer, *f.* =**Erbschaftssteuer.**

Erbanlage, *f.* **1.** *Biol:* gene. **2.** *Med:* (i) hereditary, (ii) inherited, disposition *or* inclination (to characteristic, disease, etc.).

Erbanspruch, *m. Jur:* title, claim, to an inheritance; **bedingter E.,** contingent remainder.

Erbanteil, *m.* =**Erbteil.**

Erbanwartschaft, *f. Jur:* expectation, expectancy, of an inheritance; **bedingte E.,** contingent remainder.

Erbärmdebild, *n. Art:* (representation of the) Man of Sorrows.

Erbarmedich, *n.* **-/-.** *Ecc:* kyrie (eleison).

erbarmen. I. *v.tr.* **1.** to move (s.o.) to pity; to arouse pity, compassion (in s.o.); **sein Elend erbarmte mich,** his misery moved me to pity, aroused my pity; *F:* **das möchte einen Stein e.,** it would melt a heart of stone; **sie schreit, daß es Gott erbarm, daß es einen Stein e. könnte,** her screams are heart rending; *see also* **Hund. 2.** (*impers. construction*) **es erbarmte mich seiner, mich erbarmte seiner,** I felt pity, felt sorry, for him. **3. sich j-s, etwas** *gen.*, **e.,** to take pity on s.o., sth.; to have pity, compassion, mercy, on s.o., sth.; **sie erbarmte sich des weinenden Kindes,** she took pity on the weeping child; **er erbarmte sich des verletzten Hundes und trug ihn in das Haus,** he took pity on the injured dog and carried it into the house; **erbarme dich unser, seiner,** have pity, mercy, on us, on him; (*in prayer*) **Herr, erbarme dich unser,** Lord, have mercy upon us; *F:* **es ist noch ein Stück Kuchen übrig, — will sich keiner e. (und es essen)?** there is one piece of cake left—will no one take pity on it (and eat it)?

II. *vbl s.* **Erbarmen,** *n., occ.* **Erbarmung,** *f.* pity, compassion; mercy; **Erbarmen mit j-m haben, mit j-m, für j-n, E. fühlen,** to have pity on s.o., to feel pity, compassion, for s.o.; **habt Erbarmen mit ihm,** have pity, mercy, on him, be merciful to him; **er kannte kein Erbarmen, er war ohne Erbarmen,** he knew no pity, he was without pity, mercy, he was pitiless, merciless; **voller Erbarmen, voller Erbarmung,** full of pity, of compassion; **um, ums, Erbarmen! um Erbarmung!** for pity's sake! for mercy's sake! **Gott in seinem unendlichen Erbarmen, in seiner unendlichen Erbarmung,** God in his infinite mercy; **es ist zum Erbarmen,** it is pitiable, pitiful; **er sah zum Erbarmen aus,** he was a pitiful, pitiable, sight, it was pitiful to see him; *F:* **er singt zum Erbarmen,** he is a wretched, deplorable, singer, he sings deplorably.

Erbarmer, der, -s, the merciful God, (God) the Merciful.

erbärmlich, *a.* (*a*) pitiable, pitiful, piteous; lamentable; poor; wretched; **er war in einem erbärmlichen Zustand,** he was in a pitiful, pitiable, lamentable, sorry, very poor, state; **eine erbärmliche Hütte,** a wretched, miserable, poor, hovel; **ein erbärmliches Leben führen,** to lead a pitiful, pitiable, miserable, wretched, existence; *adv.* **er sah e. aus,** he was a pitiful, pitiable, sorry, sight; he was a picture of misery; **der Hund jaulte e.,** the dog whined piteously; **wir froren e.,** we were wretchedly, miserably, cold; (*b*) wretched; abominable, despicable, contemptible (conduct, etc.); poor (excuse, quality, etc.); **dieser Kaffee ist e.,** this coffee is abominable, very poor, this coffee is wretched stuff; **erbärmliches Papier,** very poor, abominable, paper; **was für erbärmliches Wetter!** what wretched, miserable, weather! **erbärmliche Kälte,** wretched, terrible, cold; **ein erbärmlicher Wicht,** a despicable fellow, a despicable wretch; **erbärmlicher Schriftsteller,** wretched, very poor, writer; *adv.* **er hat sich e. benommen,** he behaved abominably, despicably, his conduct was abominable, despicable; **sie waren e. schlecht gekleidet,** they were very poorly, very shabbily, wretchedly, dressed; **er singt e.,** he is a wretched, deplorable, singer, he sings deplorably.

Erbärmlichkeit, *f.* pitiableness, pitifulness, piteousness; wretchedness.

erbarmungslos, *a.* pitiless, merciless, hard-hearted (pers.); cruel (pers., wind, cold, etc.); **er war e.,** he knew no pity, he was without pity, mercy, he was pitiless, merciless; *adv.* pitilessly, mercilessly, without mercy; cruelly; **der Frost tötete e. die jungen Knospen,** the frost mercilessly, cruelly, killed the young buds.

Erbarmungslosigkeit, *f.* pitilessness, mercilessness; cruelty.

erbarmungsvoll, *a.* compassionate, pitiful, merciful; full of pity, compassion.

erbarmungswürdig, *a.* pitiable, pitiful, piteous; **er war in einem erbarmungswürdigen Zustand,** he was in a pitiable, pitiful, lamentable, wretched, sorry, state.

Erbarmungswürdigkeit, *f.* pitiableness, pitifulness, piteousness.

erbauen. I. *v.tr.* **1. etwas e.,** to build (house, church, etc.); to erect, set up (temple, etc.); **das von dem berühmten Architekten erbaute Opernhaus,** the opera-house built by the famous architect; *Prov:* **Rom ist nicht an einem Tage erbaut worden,** Rome was not built in a day. **2.** (*a*) (*of sermon, book, etc.*) to edify (s.o.); to have an edifying effect (on s.o.); (*b*) (*of pers.*) **sich an etwas** *dat.* **e.,** to be edified by sth.; to be uplifted by sth.; **er erbaute sich am frischen Grün der Felder, am Gesang der Vögel,** his heart was uplifted by the fresh green of the fields, by the song of the birds; (*c*) *F:* **von etwas nicht sehr erbaut sein,** to be not pleased, not delighted, with, about, sth.; **sie waren von dieser Nachricht nicht eben, nicht gerade, erbaut,** they were not exactly pleased, delighted, with this news, they were not exactly overjoyed at this news; **wir waren nicht sehr erbaut davon, ihn in unserem Abteil sitzen zu sehen,** we were not exactly pleased, not at all pleased, to see him sitting in our compartment.

II. *vbl s.* **Erbauung,** *f.* (*a*) *in vbl senses of* 1; *also:* erection (of temple, etc.); (*b*) (moral) edification; moral improvement; (moral) uplift; **eine Predigt zu unserer E.,** a sermon for our edification.

Erbauer, *m.* **-s/-. 1.** builder; constructor; architect; **eine Statue des Erbauers der Kirche,** a statue of the builder of the church; **die Erbauer der Kathedrale,** the builders of the cathedral; **der E. des Dammes,** the constructor of the dam. **2.** edifier.

erbaulich, *a.* edifying (sermon, book, talk, etc.); heart-warming, uplifting (sight, etc.); *F:* **ein Anblick, der nicht gerade e. war, ein nicht gerade erbaulicher Anblick,** a spectacle that was not exactly edifying.

Erbaulichkeit, *f.* edifying nature (of sermon, book, etc.).

Erbausschlagung, *f. Jur:* renunciation, relinquishment, of a succession, of an inheritance.

Erbauung, *f. see* **erbauen** II.

Erbauungsbuch, *n.* improving book; *Rel:* devotional book.

Erbauungslektüre, *f.* improving literature.

Erbbauern, *m.pl.* **1.** farmers holding their land in fee-simple. **2.** *Hist:* villein-socmen.

Erbbaurecht, *n. Jur:* hereditary right to erect *or* maintain a building on s.o. else's property; superficies.

Erbbauzins, *m. Jur:* rent paid for the right to erect *or* maintain a building on s.o. else's property.

Erbbegräbnis, *n.* family grave; family vault.

erbberechtigt, *a. Jur:* (*of pers.*) entitled to inherit, entitled to an, to the, inheritance; **Erbberechtigte** *m, f,* person entitled to inherit; person who has the (right of) succession; successor.

Erbberechtigung, *f. Jur:* title, right, of inheritance; (right of) succession; heirship.

Erbbescheinigung, *f.* =**Erbschein.**

Erbbesitz, *m.* inheritance; (corporeal) hereditament; **dieses Grundstück war ein E. der Familie,** this property was a family inheritance.

Erbbild, *n. Biol:* **1.** genotype. **2.** diagram showing the working of heredity-factors.

erbbildlich, *a. Biol:* genotypical (constitution, etc.).

Erbbiologe, *m.* geneticist.

Erbbiologie, *f.* genetics.

erbbiologisch, *a.* genetic.

Erbcharakter, *m. Biol:* hereditary character.

Erbe[1], *m.* **-n/-n.** *Jur: etc:* heir; universal successor; **leiblicher E.,** heir of the body; **gesetzlicher E.,** legal heir, heir-at-law, general heir; **rechtmäßiger E.,** rightful heir; **testamentarischer E.,** devisee, heir by devise; **alleiniger, einziger, E.,** sole heir; **mutmaßlicher E.,** heir presumptive; **j-n zum Erben, als seinen Erben, einsetzen, j-n zu seinem Erben machen,** to appoint, make, s.o. one's heir; **der E. eines Besitzes sein,** to be heir to an estate; **sich als würdiger E. einer Tradition erweisen,** to prove a worthy heir, successor, to a tradition.

Erbe[2], *n.* **-s/.** *Jur: etc:* inheritance, heritage; **elterliches, väterliches, E.,** patrimony; **sein väterliches E. vergeuden, verschwenden,** to squander one's patrimony, one's inheritance; **in sein E. kommen,** to come into one's inheritance, into one's own; **ein E. ausschlagen, auf ein E. verzichten,** to refuse, turn down, an inheritance; to renounce, relinquish, a succession; **das gemeinsame E. eines Volkes,** the common inheritance, heritage, of a nation, the patrimony of a nation; **unser geistiges E.,** our spiritual inheritance, heritage, our (spiritual) patrimony; **ein E. der Scham,** a legacy of shame; **das E. der Sünde,** the legacy of sin; *see also* **antreten** II. 4 (*a*), **Antritt** 2.

erbeben, *v.i.* (*sein*) to tremble, quiver, shake; to quake; **die Erde erbebte unter unseren Füßen,** the earth shook, quaked, under our feet.

erbeigen, *a.* inherited (property, etc.); (property, etc.) belonging to s.o. by right of inheritance.

erbeingesessen, *a.* old-, long-established (family, farmers, etc.).

Erbeinheit, *f. Biol:* gene.

Erbeinsetzung, *f. Jur:* appointment of an, of one's, heir.

Erbeinsetzungsvertrag, *m.* =**Erbvertrag.**

erben, *v.tr.* to inherit (sth.); **ein Haus, einen Titel, e.,** to inherit a house, a title; **ein Vermögen e.,** to inherit, succeed to, come into, a fortune, to be left a fortune; **er erbte den Besitz,** he came into, inherited, the property, the property was left to him; **etwas von j-m e.,** to inherit sth. from s.o.; to be left sth. by s.o. (in his will); *F:* to be given (worn clothes, etc.) by s.o., *F:* to inherit (worn clothes, etc.) from s.o.; **er hat diese Möbel von seiner Mutter geerbt,** he inherited this furniture from his mother; **einen Charakterzug, eine Vorliebe für etwas, von seinem Vater e.,** to inherit a characteristic, a taste for sth., from one's father; **er hat seine Schüchternheit von seiner Mutter geerbt,** he has inherited, he gets, his shyness from his mother; *F:* **hier ist nichts zu e.,** there is nothing to be got here, there will be nothing in it for me, you, us, etc.

Erbengemeinschaft, *f. Jur:* (community of) joint heirs.

Erbenhaftung, *f. Jur:* responsibility of the heir *or* heirs for the liabilities of the predecessor.

Erbeserbe, *m. Jur:* heir of an heir; reversionary heir.

erbetteln, *v.tr.* **etwas e.,** to get, obtain, sth. by begging; **von j-m Geld e.,** to beg money from s.o.; to wheedle money out of s.o.; **er erbettelte sich von seinem Vater die Erlaubnis, länger aufbleiben zu dürfen,** he begged until his father gave way and let him stay up longer.

erbeuten. I. *v.tr.* **etwas e.,** to seize, take, carry off, sth. (as booty); to carry off, seize (prize, etc.); to capture, take (tank, gun, ship, etc.); (*of thg*) **von j-m erbeutet werden,** to be captured, seized, taken, by s.o., to fall into s.o.'s hands; **die Soldaten erbeuteten mehrere feindliche Geschütze,** the soldiers captured several enemy guns, several enemy guns fell into the hands of the soldiers; **wir erbeuteten drei Waggons mit Proviant und Decken,** we captured, took, seized, three wagons with food and blankets; **der Einbrecher erbeutete eine wertvolle Kette,** the burglar took, *F:* got away with, a valuable necklace; **die Kinder hatten die Speisekammer geplündert, aber sie erbeuteten nur ein paar Kekse,** the children had raided the larder but their haul only consisted of a few biscuits.

II. *vbl s.* **Erbeuten** *n.*, **Erbeutung** *f. in vbl senses; also:* capture, seizure.

erbfähig, *a. Jur:* legally capable of inheriting; heritable (pers.).

Erbfähigkeit, *f. Jur:* (person's) legal capacity of inheriting.

Erbfaktor, *m. Biol:* gene.

Erbfall, *m. Jur:* arising, creation, of a succession.

Erbfallschulden, *f.pl. Jur:* liabilities falling to the heir *or* heirs on the death of the predecessor.

Erbfehler, *m. Breed:* inherited fault; *Biol:* inherited defect.
Erbfeind, *m.* traditional enemy.
Erbfeindschaft, *f.* traditional enmity.
Erbfolge, *f. Jur:* (universal) succession; inheritance; **gesetzliche E.,** succession by common law; **gewillkürte E.,** testate succession.
Erbfolgekrieg, *m. Hist:* war of succession; **der Spanische E.,** the War of the Spanish Succession; **der Österreichische E.,** the War of the Austrian Succession.
Erbfolgeordnung, *f. Jur:* canon of inheritance.
Erbformeln, *f.pl. Biol:* formulas *or* theories of inheritance.
Erbforschung, *f. Biol:* genetic research.
Erbgang, *m.* **1.** *Jur:* succession; inheritance. **2.** *Biol:* (mode of) inheritance; **dominanter E.,** inheritance of dominant characteristics; **rezessiver E.,** inheritance of recessive characteristics.
erbgesessen, *a.* old-, long-established (family, farmers, etc.).
erbgesund, *a.* free from hereditary disease; of sound, healthy, stock.
Erbgesundheit, *f.* freedom from hereditary disease.
Erbgraf, *m.* heir to an earldom.
Erbgrind, *m. Med:* favus.
Erbgroßherzog, *m.* heir to a Grand Duchy.
Erbgut, *n.* **1.** (*a*) freehold estate of inheritance; fee-simple; (*b*) heritable estate, property; inheritance, patrimony; **das gemeinsame E. eines Volkes,** the common inheritance, the patrimony, of a nation. **2.** *Biol:* genotype; idioplasm.
Erbhof, *m.* estate of specified size held in fee-tail special.
Erbhofbauer, *m.* farmer of an 'Erbhof' (*q.v.*).
erbieten. I. *v.tr.* (*strong*) **1.** *A:* **j-m etwas e.,** to offer sth. to s.o.; **j-m Ehre e.,** to show respect to s.o.; **j-m seine Dienste e.,** to offer one's services to s.o. **2. sich erbieten,** to offer (to do sth.); **er erbot sich, meinem Freund das Paket abzugeben,** he offered to deliver the parcel to my friend; **sie erbot sich, ihm den Weg zu zeigen,** she offered to show him the way.
II. *vbl s.* **Erbieten,** *n.* offer; **er nahm ihr E. an,** he accepted her offer.
erbietig, *a. A:* =**erbötig.**
Erbin, *f.* **-/-innen,** heiress.
Erbinerde [ɛrˈbiːn-], *f. Ch:* erbium oxyde, erbia.
Erbinmetalle [ɛrˈbiːnmeˌtalə], *n.pl. Ch:* erbium metals.
erbitten, *v.tr.* (*strong*) **(sich** *dat.***) etwas e.,** to ask for sth.; to request sth.; to beg, plead, for sth.; **sich Rat e.,** to ask for, request, advice; **(sich) Erlaubnis für etwas e.,** to ask for, to request, permission to do sth.; **sich Gehör e.,** to ask, plead, beg, to be heard; **sich von j-m eine Gunst e.,** to ask, request, a favour of s.o., to ask s.o. for a favour; **sie erbat sich drei Tage Bedenkzeit,** she asked for three days to think it over; **er erbat sich vom Pförtner den Schlüssel zum Turm,** he asked the porter for the key to the tower.
erbittern. I. *v.tr.* (*a*) to embitter (s.o.); to make (s.o.) feel bitter; **es erbitterte ihn, daß selbst seine Freunde sich von ihm abwandten,** it embittered him, it made him feel bitter, it filled him with bitterness, that even his friends turned away from him; (*b*) to arouse a feeling of resentment in (s.o.); to fill (s.o.) with inward fury; **ihre Gleichgültigkeit erbitterte ihn, er war über ihre Gleichgültigkeit erbittert,** he was inwardly furious at her indifference; (*c*) **es war ein erbittertes Ringen, ein erbitterter Kampf,** it was a stubborn struggle, fight; **erbittert kämpfen,** to put up a stubborn fight; **um die Stellung wird noch erbittert gekämpft,** a stubborn battle is going on for the position; **erbitterter Konkurrenzkampf,** cut-throat competition.
II. *vbl s.* **Erbitterung,** *f.* (*a*) bitterness; **er fühlte keine E.,** he felt no bitterness; (*b*) resentment; inward fury; (*c*) **sie kämpften mit E.,** they put up a stubborn fight.
Erbium [ˈɛrbium], *n.* **-s/.** *Ch:* erbium.
Erbiumoxyd, *n. Ch:* erbium oxyde, erbia.
Erbkrankheit, *f. Med:* hereditary disease.
Erblande, *n.pl. Hist:* patrimonial lands (*esp.* of the German Emperor).
erblassen, *v.i.* (*sein*) (*of pers., light, star, etc.*) to become, grow, pale; (*of pers.*) to pale, to blanch; to turn, go, white; **vor Schreck, Furcht, e.,** to turn pale, white, with horror, fright; to blanch with horror, fright; **er erblaßte, als er ihn sah,** his face, he, grew, turned, pale, white, when he saw him; **vor j-m e.,** (i) to turn pale before s.o.; (ii) to be overshadowed by s.o.; **sein Ruhm erblaßte vor dem seines Sohnes,** his fame was overshadowed by that of his son.
Erblasser [ˈɛrpˀlasər], *m.* **-s/-.** *Jur:* predecessor; testator, devisor.
Erblasserin, *f.* **-/-innen,** (female) predecessor; testatrix.
Erblehen, *n.* hereditary fief.
Erblehre, *f. Biol:* genetics.
erbleichen, *v.i.* (*sein*) (*p.t.* **erbleichte** *&* **erblich;** *p.p.* **erbleicht**) (*of pers.*) (i) to become, grow, turn, pale, white; to pale, blanch; (ii) *Lit:* (*p.p.* **erblichen**) to die.
Erbleiden, *n.* =**Erbkrankheit.**
erblich[1], *see* **erbleichen.**
erblich[2], *a.* hereditary (right, disease, etc.); (in)heritable (property, etc.); (disease) that runs in the family; *Biol:* genotypical (constitution, etc.); **erbliche Belastung,** hereditary taint, (i) liability to develop a hereditary disease, (ii) hereditary disease, disease that runs in the family, (iii) *F:* inclination towards sth. that runs in the family; **e. belastet sein,** to be afflicted with a hereditary taint, (i) to be liable to develop a hereditary disease, (ii) to suffer from a hereditary disease, (iii) *F:* to have an inclination towards sth. that runs in the family.
Erblichkeit, *f. Jur:* (in)heritability (of a right, property, etc.); *Biol:* inheritableness, (in)heritability, inheritance (of a characteristic, disease, etc.).
erblicken, *v.tr.* to catch sight of, to see (s.o., sth.); to set eyes (up)on (s.o., sth.); to sight (s.o., sth.); *Lit:* to behold (s.o., sth.); **plötzlich erblickte sie ihren Vater in der Menschenmenge,** suddenly she saw, caught sight of, her father in the crowd; **sowie er uns erblickte, lief er fort,** the moment he saw us, caught sight of us, at the sight of us, he ran away; **ich erblicke hierin einen großen Vorteil,** I see a great advantage in this; **das Licht der Welt e.,** to be born, to come into the world.
erblinden. I. *v.i.* (*sein*) to go, become, blind; *Poet:* to be blinded (**an etwas** *dat.*, by sth.); **auf einem Auge erblindet,** blind in one eye.
II. *vbl s.* **Erblinden** *n.*, **Erblindung** *f. in vbl senses; also:* **nach seinem Erblinden, nach seiner Erblindung,** after he had gone blind; **völlige Erblindung eines Auges,** complete blindness in one eye.
Erblinie, *f.* pedigree.
erblos, *a.* heirless, without an heir.
erblühen, *v.i.* (*sein*) (*of flower*) to open, blossom (out); (*of plant, flower*) to bloom, blossom, blow; to come, burst, into bloom, into flower; *Lit:* to effloresce; **voll erblühte Blume,** flower in full bloom, full-blown flower; *Lit:* **sie war zu einem schönen Mädchen erblüht,** she had grown into a beautiful girl; **sie war zu ihrer vollsten Schönheit erblüht,** she was in the full bloom of her loveliness.
Erbmangel, *m. Breed: etc:* hereditary fault, hereditary infirmity.
Erbmarschall, *m. Hist:* (hereditary) Earl Marshal.
Erbmasse, *f.* **1.** *Jur:* estate (of deceased person); assets (of deceased person); inheritance. **2.** *Biol:* genotype; idioplasm; *F:* **bei ihm hat die E. nicht gereicht,** in him the breed seems exhausted; with him there is a sad falling off.
Erbmonarchie, *f.* hereditary monarchy.
erbosen, *v.tr.* to annoy, provoke, infuriate (s.o., animal); to anger, vex (s.o.); **sich über etwas e.,** to get annoyed, angry, cross, about sth.; **über j-n, etwas, sehr erbost sein,** to be very much annoyed, very angry, furious, with s.o., about sth.; **er neckte den Hund mit einem Stock, bis das erboste Tier ihn in den Arm biß,** he teased the dog with a stick until the angry, infuriated, animal bit him in the arm.
erbötig, *a.* willing, ready; **e. sein, sich e. zeigen, etwas zu tun,** to be ready, willing, to do sth.; to show oneself willing to do sth.; to offer to do sth.
Erbpacht, *f.* heritable tenancy; fee-tail.
Erbplasma, *n. Biol:* idioplasm, germ-plasm.
Erbprinz, *m.* heir to a Duchy *or* Principality; *F:* **unser E.,** our son and heir.
erbrausen, *v.i.* (*sein*) (*of sea, wind, etc.*) to rise to a roar; **in die Stille hinein erbrauste die Orgel,** the silence was broken by the mighty swell of the organ.
erbrechen. I. *v.* (*strong*) **1.** *v.tr.* to break (sth.) open; to force (door, lock, etc.); to break (seal); **eine Tür, einen Geldschrank, e.,** to break open, to force, a door, a safe; **einen Brief e.,** to break open, to open, to tear open, a letter; **er fand die Kassette erbrochen,** he found that the cash-box had been forced (open). **2.** *v.tr. Med:* to vomit (blood, mucus, etc.); to bring up (food, etc.); **Erbrochenes** *n*, vomit. **3.** *v.i.* (*haben*) *&* **sich erbrechen,** *Med:* to vomit, to be sick; **er fing an (sich) zu e.,** he began to vomit.
II. *vbl s.* **Erbrechen,** *n.* **1.** breaking open, forcing (of door, lock, etc.); breaking (of seal). **2.** *Med:* vomiting; being sick; sickness; **morgendliches E.,** morning sickness (during pregnancy); **schwarzes E.,** melaena, black vomit.
Erbrecht, *n.* **1.** *Jur:* law of inheritance, law of succession. **2.** *Jur:* title, right, of inheritance, (right of) succession; heirship. **3.** hereditary, (in)heritable, right.
erbringen, *v.tr.* (*conj. like* **bringen) den Beweis, Beweise, für etwas e.,** to produce, adduce, proof of sth., evidence for sth.; to prove sth.; **er erbrachte den Beweis, daß die Urkunden gefälscht waren,** he produced proof, he proved, that the documents were forgeries; **Erbringung** *f* **eines Beweises, Erbringung von Beweisen,** production, adduction, of evidence, of proof.
Erbschaft, *f.* **-/-en,** inheritance; **eine E. machen,** to come into an inheritance; **eine E. erwarten,** to have expectations (of an inheritance); **eine E. ausschlagen, auf eine E. verzichten,** to renounce, relinquish, a succession, to refuse, turn down, an inheritance; *see also* **antreten** II. 4 (*a*), **Antritt** 2.
Erbschaftsanfall, *m. Jur:* inheritance; succession, reversion (of an estate); **durch E.,** by accession to an inheritance, to an estate.
Erbschaftsanspruch, *m. Jur:* claim to an inheritance.
Erbschaftsanwärter, *m. Jur:* expectant heir, heir in expectancy.
Erbschaftsausschlagung, *f. Jur:* renunciation, relinquishment, of a succession, of an inheritance.
Erbschaftsbesitz, *m. Jur:* ownership of the estate (to be inherited).
Erbschaftsbesitzer, *m. Jur:* owner of the property to be inherited.
Erbschaftsklage, *f. Jur:* legal dispute concerning an inheritance.
Erbschaftsmasse, *f. Jur:* estate (of deceased person).
Erbschaftssteuer, *f. Adm:* estate duties, death duties, *U.S:* inheritance tax, estate tax.
Erbschaftsvermächtnis, *n. Jur:* universal fideicommissum.
Erbschaftsverwalter, *m. Jur:* trustee of an estate.
Erbschein, *m. Jur:* certificate of inheritance.
Erbschen, *n.* **-s/-,** (*dim. of* **Erbse**) small pea; *Cu:* **Erbschen** *pl*, young peas; petits pois; **Erbschen und Möhrchen,** young peas and carrots.
erbschleichen, *v.i. insep.* (*strong*) (*haben*) to angle for a legacy.
Erbschleicher, *m.* **-s/-,** legacy-hunter; *Jur:* captator.
Erbse, *f.* **-/-n.** *Hort: Cu:* pea; **junge Erbsen,** young peas; **grüne Erbsen,** (i) fresh green peas; (ii) dried green peas; **getrocknete Erbsen,** dried peas; **geschälte Erbsen,** split peas; **wilde E., graue E.,** field pea, grey pea; *F:* **wie auf Erbsen gehen,** to walk as if one had stones in one's shoes; **hier geht man wie auf Erbsen,** it hurts one's feet to walk here; it's like walking on sharp stones.
Erbsel, *f.* **-/-n, Erbseldorn,** *m. Bot:* barberry.
Erbsenbaum, *m. Bot:* caragana, pea-tree.
Erbsenbein, *n. Anat:* pisiform (bone).
Erbsenblüte, *f. Bot:* pea-flower.
Erbsenbohne, *f. Bot:* pigeon pea.
Erbsenbrei, *m. Cu:*=**Erbsenpüree.**
erbsenförmig, *a.* pea-shaped; pisiform.
erbsengroß, *a.* (of) the size of a pea.
Erbsenkäfer, *m. Ent:* pea-beetle, -bug, -weevil.
Erbsenmehl, *n. Cu:* pease-flour, -meal.
Erbsenmüdigkeit, *f. Agr:* soil exhaustion caused by too frequent growing of peas.
Erbsenpüree, *n. Cu:* pease-pudding; *U.S:* (split) pea purée.
Erbsenschote, *f.* pea-pod, pea-shell.
Erbsenstein, *m. Miner:* pisolite, peastone.
Erbsenstrauch, *m.* =**Erbsenbaum.**
Erbsenstroh, *n.* pea-straw.
Erbsensuppe, *f. Cu:* pea-soup; *F:* pea-souper (fog).
Erbsenwickler, *m. Ent:* pea-moth.
Erbsenzähler, *m. F:* (*a*) pedantic person; (*b*) miser.
erbsförmig, *a.* pea-shaped.
Erbskohle, *f. Com:* small coal; fines, peas.
Erbssuppe, *f. Cu:* pea-soup.
Erbstaaten, *m.pl.* =**Erblande.**
Erbstück, *n.* heirloom, inheritance.

Erbsubstanz, *f. Biol:* idioplasm, germ-plasm.

Erbsünde, *f. Theol:* original sin.

Erbswurst, *f. Cu:* seasoned pease-flour compressed into sausage shape (*for making soup*).

Erbteil, *n., Jur: m.* (share in an, the) inheritance.

Erbteilung, *f. Jur:* division of an, of the, inheritance; **Güter, die durch E. zu klein geworden sind,** properties grown too small through division on inheritance.

Erbübel, *n.* inherited failing; inherited ailment; ingrained defect; **Uneinigkeit, das E. der Deutschen,** disunity, Germany's never-ending (cause of) trouble.

erbunfähig, *a. Jur:* (legally) incapable of inheriting.

Erbunfähigkeit, *f. Jur:* (legal) incapacity of inheriting.

Erbuntertänigkeit, *f. Hist:* serfdom.

erbunwürdig, *a. Jur:* incapable of inheriting (by reason of having committed a criminal act).

Erbunwürdigkeit, *f. Jur:* incapacity of inheriting (by reason of having committed a criminal act).

Erbvergleich, *m. Jur:* agreement between co-heirs about the distribution of the inheritance.

Erbvermächtnis, *n.* = Erbschaftsvermächtnis.

Erbvertrag, *m. Jur:* contract of inheritance; testamentary contract.

Erbverzicht, *m. Jur:* renunciation, relinquishment, of a succession, of an inheritance.

Erbzelle, *f. Biol:* zygote.

Erdabhang, *m. Civ.E: etc:* earth-slope.

Erdableitung, *f. El.E:* **1.** earth-connection. earth, *U.S:* ground connection, ground. **2.** earth-leakage, earth-fault, *U.S:* ground.

Erdableitungswiderstand, *m. El:* earthing resistance.

Erdabwehr, *f. Mil:* ground defences.

Erdachse, *f.* axis of the earth.

Erdachsenschwankung, *f. Astr:* variation of latitude.

Erdalkalien, *n.pl. Ch:* alkaline earths.

Erdalkalimetalle, *n.pl. Miner:* alkaline-earth metals.

Erdalter, *n.* geological era, age of the earth.

Erdaltertum, das. *Geol:* the Palaeozoic (group, era).

Erdamarant, *m. Bot:* **gemeiner E.,** wild amarant(h).

Erdamsel, *f. Orn:* ring-ouzel.

Erdanker, *m. Av:* ground-anchor.

Erdanschluß, *m. El.E:* earth-connection, earth, *U.S:* ground-connection, ground.

Erdantenne, *f. W.Tel:* ground aerial, *U.S:* ground antenna.

Erdapfel, *m. Bot:* **1.** *esp. Austrian:* potato. **2.** Jerusalem artichoke.

Erdäpfelsalat, *m. Austrian Cu:* potato salad.

Erdarbeiten, *f.pl. Civ.E:* earthwork(s), excavation work.

Erdarbeiter, *m.* navvy, digger, excavation labourer.

Erdart, *f.* **1.** *Ch:* = Erde 2 (c). **2.** *Agr: Hort:* type of soil.

Erdartischocke, *f. Bot:* Jerusalem artichoke.

Erdatmosphäre, *f. Astr:* (earth's) atmosphere.

Erdaufklärung, *f. Mil:* ground reconnaissance.

Erdaufwurf, *m.* (earth-)bank, mound; *Mil:* earth-parapet (of trench).

Erdbahn, *f. Astr:* orbit, path, of the earth.

Erdball, *m.* = Erdkugel.

Erdbauten, *m.pl.* **1.** = Erdarbeiten. **2.** earth-, mud-huts.

Erdbauunternehmer, *m.* earthworks contractor.

Erdbeben, *n.* earthquake, seism; **tektonisches E.,** tectonic earthquake; **vulkanisches E.,** volcanic earthquake; **unterseeisches, submarines, E.,** submarine earthquake.

erdbebenarm, *a.* (country, etc.) relatively free from earthquakes.

Erdbebendislokation, *f.* dislocation of earth's crust due to an earthquake.

Erdbebenerschütterung, *f.* = Erdbebenschock.

Erdbebenflut, *f.* seismic sea-wave, tidal wave.

Erdbebenforschung, *f.* seismometry.

erdbebenfrei, *a.* earthquake-free (country, region, etc.).

Erdbebengebiet, *n.* (*a*) earthquake district, earthquake region, seismic region; (*b*) region stricken by an earthquake.

Erdbebengeographie, *f.* distribution of earthquake areas over the world.

Erdbebenherd, *m.* focus, centre, of an earthquake, seismic focus.

Erdbebenkarte, *f.* earthquake map, seismic map.

Erdbebenkunde, *f.* seismology.

Erdbebenland, *n.* earthquake country; earthquake region.

Erdbebenmesser, *m.* seismometer; seismograph.

Erdbebenregistrierinstrument, *n.* seismograph.

Erdbebenregistrierung, *f.* seismography.

Erdbebenschock, *m.* earthquake shock, seismic shock; earth-tremor.

Erdbebenschwarm, *m.* earthquake cluster.

erdbebensicher, *a.* (*a*) earthquake-proof (building, etc.); (*b*) (region, etc.) free from earthquakes.

Erdbebentätigkeit, *f.* frequency of earthquakes (in a country *or* region).

Erdbebenwarte, *f.* seismological station.

Erdbebenwelle, *f.* earthquake wave, seismic wave.

Erdbeerbaum, *m. Bot:* arbutus, strawberry-tree, cane-apple.

Erdbeerbeet, *n.* strawberry bed.

Erdbeerbrand, *m. Hort:* strawberry leaf-spot, strawberry leaf-blight.

Erdbeere, *f. Bot: Hort:* strawberry; **wilde, gemeine, E.,** wild strawberry, wood strawberry; **hochstengelige E.,** hautbois (strawberry).

Erdbeereis, *n.* strawberry ice(-cream).

erdbeerfarben, *a.* strawberry (coloured).

Erdbeerhimbeere, *f. Bot:* strawberry-raspberry.

Erdbeerköpfchen, *n. Orn:* Nyasa lovebird.

Erdbeermarmelade, *f.* strawberry jam.

Erdbeerpocken, *f.pl. Med:* framboesia, yaws, pian.

Erdbeerspinat, *m. Bot:* strawberry blite, strawberry spinach.

Erdbeerstecher, *m. Ent:* strawberry-weevil.

Erdbeerstrauch, *m. Bot:* calycanthus (floridus), *U.S:* strawberry bush, shrub, Carolina allspice.

Erdbeschleunigung, *f. Ph:* acceleration due to, of, gravity, gravitational acceleration.

Erdbestattung, *f.* burial, inhumation, interment.

Erdbewegung, *f.* **1.** *Astr:* movement, motion, of the earth; *esp.* revolution of the earth about the sun. **2.** *Meteor:* dislocation of the earth's crust (due to earthquake, etc.). **3.** *usu.pl.* **Erdbewegungen,** excavation (of earth); earthworks.

Erdbiene, *f. Ent:* andrena.

Erdbirne, *f. Bot:* **1.** Jerusalem artichoke. **2.** *Dial:* potato.

Erdboden, *m.* ground, earth; **eine Stadt dem E. gleichmachen,** to flatten a town, to raze a town to the ground; *F:* **etwas aus dem E. stampfen,** to conjure sth. up, to produce sth. out of a hat.

Erdbogen, *m. Constr:* inverted arch, invert.

Erdbohne, *f. Bot:* **1.** = Erdnuß 1. **2.** tuberous pea, earth-nut pea, heath pea.

Erdbohrer, *m. Min: Civ.E: etc:* borer, drill, auger.

Erdbrot, *n. Bot:* manna lichen.

Erddamm, *m.* (earthwork) embankment; (earth-)bank; *Hyd.E:* earth-dam.

Erddämpfe, *m.pl. Ph:* exhalations from the ground.

Erddeckungen, *f.pl. Mil:* earthworks.

Erddichte, *f. Ph:* density of the earth.

Erddraht, *m. El.E:* earth-wire, *U.S:* ground wire.

Erddrän, *m. Agr: etc:* underground drainage channel.

Erddrossel, *f. Orn:* White's thrush, golden mountain-thrush.

Erddruck, *m. Constr: etc:* earth pressure, earth force, pressure of the earth.

Erddurchmesser, *m. Astr: etc:* diameter of the earth.

Erde, *f. -/-n,* earth. **1.** (*a*) *Astr: Geol: etc:* earth; **Drehung der E.,** rotation of the earth; **die Kruste der E.,** the earth's crust, the lithosphere; **das Innere der E.,** the interior of the earth, *Lit:* the bowels of the earth; **Mutter E.,** Mother Earth; (*b*) world, earth; **auf der ganzen E.,** in the whole world; **überall auf der E.,** all over the world, all the world over; **auf dieser E.,** in this world; **auf der E., auf Erden,** on earth; here below; **nirgendwo auf Gottes Erden, auf Gottes weiter E.,** nowhere on God's earth; **das wäre der Himmel auf Erden,** that would be heaven on earth; *B:* **wie im Himmel, also auch auf Erden,** on earth as it is in heaven; *see also* Himmel 2 (*a*), Salz. **2.** (*a*) (i) earth, ground; (ii) *F:* floor; **auf der E. liegen,** (i) to lie on the ground, (ii) to lie on the floor; **auf der E. schlafen,** (i) to sleep on the ground, (ii) to sleep on the floor; **er warf die Münze auf die E.,** he threw, dashed, the coin to the ground; **zu ebener E. wohnen,** to live at street level, to live on the ground-floor; **in fremder E. begraben sein,** to be buried in alien soil, in a foreign land; **über der E.,** above ground; **Zweige, Vorhänge, die bis auf die, bis zur, E. hängen,** branches which hang down to the ground, curtains which hang down to the floor; **unter der E.,** (i) below the ground, under-

ground; (ii) in the grave; *F:* **j-n unter die E. bringen,** to bring s.o. to the grave; *F:* **mit beiden Beinen auf der E. stehen,** to have both feet (firmly) on the ground; *F:* **ich kann es doch nicht aus der E. stampfen,** I can't produce it, get it, out of a hat, I can't conjure it up; (*b*) *Agr: etc:* soil, earth; land; **gute, fruchtbare, E.,** fertile soil; **unfruchtbare E.,** poor, barren, soil, infertile land; **trockene E.,** dry soil, dry earth; **steinige E.,** stony soil, stony ground; **sandige E.,** sandy soil; **lehmige E.,** clay soil; **eine Grube mit E. auffüllen,** to fill a pit with earth; *B:* **denn du bist E. und sollst zu E. werden,** for dust thou art and unto dust shalt thou return; **E. zu E.,** ashes to ashes; *see also* Staub; (*c*) *Ch:* earth; **alkalische Erden,** alkaline earths; **seltene Erden,** rare earths; *Miner:* **E. von Siena,** sienna; **englische E.,** rotten-stone, Tripoli powder; **grüne E., Veroneser E.,** green earth, Verona green, Verona earth; *Bot:* **japanische E.,** catechu, *Com:* cutch, Japonic earth; **feuerfeste E.,** fire-clay; *A.Med:* **lemnische E.,** Lemnian earth, Lemnian bole. **3.** *El.E:* (i) earth, earth-wire, -lead, *U.S:* ground, ground wire, ground lead; (ii) earth, earth-connection, earth-circuit, *U.S:* ground, ground connection, ground circuit; **an E. legen, mit der E. verbinden,** to earth, to connect to earth, *U.S:* to ground.

Erdeessen, *n. Anthr: Med:* geophagy.

Erdefeu, *m. Bot:* ground-ivy.

Erdeichel, *f. Bot:* **1.** = Erdnuß 1. **2.** tuberous pea, earth-nut pea. **3.** dropwort. **4.** = Erdkastanie.

Erdeichhörnchen, *n.* = Erdhörnchen.

Erdeinbruch, *m.* subsidence, collapse, of ground.

Erdeinschießziel, *n. Artil:* ground registration target.

Erdelektrizität, *f. Ph:* terrestrial electricity.

erdelos, *a.* **erdelose Pflanzenzucht,** soilless plant culture.

erden. **I.** *v.tr. El.E:* to earth, to connect to earth, *U.S:* to ground; **gut geerdet,** well earthed; **geerdeter Leiter,** earthed conductor; **geerdete Rückleitung,** earth-circuit, *U.S:* grounded circuit; earth-return, *U.S:* ground return. **II.** *vbl s.* **1. Erden,** *n. in vbl senses.* **2. Erdung,** *f.* (*a*) *in vbl senses;* (*b*) = Erde 3.

Erdenbürger, *m.* inhabitant of the earth; (baby) **ein junger, neuer, E.,** a new addition to the human race.

erdenkbar, *a.* = erdenklich.

erdenken, *v.tr.* (*conj. like* denken) to think up, make up, invent (sth.); **eine erdachte Geschichte,** an invented, a made up, fictitious, story; a work of fiction; **ein erdachter Charakter,** an invented, a fictitious, an imaginary, character.

erdenklich, *a.* imaginable, conceivable, thinkable, possible; **er hat sich alle erdenkliche Mühe gegeben,** he has taken the utmost pains, the greatest possible pains; **alle erdenklichen Mittel,** all means conceivable, imaginable, all possible means; **alles Erdenkliche tun,** to do everything possible, to do all one possibly can.

Erdenkloß, *m. Lit:* mortal (man), *Lit:* lump of mortal clay.

Erdenleben, *n.* life on earth, earthly existence.

Erdennähe, *f.* = Erdnähe.

Erdenrei h, *n.* world, earth; **im ganzen E.,** in the whole world.

Erdenrund, *n.* globe, world, terrestrial sphere; **auf dem ganzen E.,** in the whole (wide) world.

Erdensohn, *m.* son of (the) earth; mortal.

Erdenwurm, *m. Lit:* (poor) mortal.

Erdenzian, *m. Bot:* gentianella.

Erder, *m. -s/-. El.E:* earth, earth-wire, -lead, *U.S:* ground, ground wire, ground lead.

Erderbse, *f. Bot:* Bambar ground-nut.

Erderschütterung, *f.* earth-tremor.

Erdeule, *f. Ent:* agrotis.

Erdfall, *m. Geol:* dolina, (sink-) hole, swallow-hole.

Erdfarbe, *f. Miner:* earth colour, earth pigment, mineral pigment.

erdfarben, *a.* earth-coloured.

Erdfehler, *m. El.E:* earth-leakage, earth-fault, *U.S:* ground.

Erdferkel, *n. Z:* orycteropus, aardvark; **kapisches E.,** Cape aardvark, Cape ant-eater.

Erdferne, *f. Astr:* apogee (of moon); **in E.,** (*of star, etc.*) far from the earth; (*of moon*) in apogee; **der Mond ist in (der größten) E.,** the moon is in apogee.

Erdfeste, *f. Geol:* land areas of the globe.

Erdfließen, *n. Geol:* creeping of the soil; solifluction.

Erdfloh, *m. Ent:* flea-beetle.

Erdfrüchter, *m.pl.* = Erdfrüchtler.

Erdfrüchtigkeit, *f. Bot:* geocarpism (of plants).

Erdfrüchtler, *m.pl. Bot:* geocarpic plants.
Erdfunkstelle, *f. W.Tel:* ground radio station.
Erdgas, *n. Ch: Ind:* natural gas, rock-gas.
Erdgasbrunnen, *m.* natural gas well.
erdgebunden, *a. Lit:* earth-bound; earthly.
Erdgeist, *m.* **1.** *Myth:* gnome. **2.** (the) Earth-Spirit.
Erdgeruch, *m.* earthy smell; smell of earth.
Erdgeschichte, *f.* history of the earth; geology.
erdgeschichtlich, *a.* geological.
Erdgeschoß, *n.* ground-floor, *U.S:* first floor (of house); **im E. wohnen,** to live on the ground-floor.
Erdglas, *n. Miner:* selenite; crystalline *or* foliated gypsum.
Erdglasuren, *f.pl. Cer: etc:* mineral glazes.
Erdglobus, *m. Sch: etc:* terrestrial globe.
Erdgottheit, *f.* chthonian deity; god of the underworld.
Erdgrün, *n. Miner:* green earth, Verona green, Verona earth.
Erdgürtel, *m. Geog:* zone.
Erdhacke, *f. Tls: Agr:* two- *or* three-pronged hoe; Canterbury hoe.
Erdhälfte, *f. Geog: etc:* hemisphere; **die nördliche, südliche, E.,** the northern, southern, hemisphere.
Erdharz, *n. Miner:* native bitumen; **gelbes E.,** (i) amber; (ii) pitchstone, retinite.
Erdhaue, *f. Tls: Agr:* mattock, grubbing-hoe.
Erdhaus, *n.* **1.** earth-, mud-hut. **2.** *Hort:* hot-house partly sunk into the ground.
Erdhörer, *m. Geophysics: Min: etc:* geophone.
Erdhörnchen, *n. Z:* ground-squirrel, chipmunk.
Erdhügel, *m.* mound (of earth).
Erdhülle, *f. Geol:* envelope of the earth (*consisting of lithosphere, hydrosphere, and atmosphere*).
Erdhunde, *m.pl. Ven:* dogs that hunt game underground (*e.g. terriers, dachshunds*).
erdicht, *a. A. & Lit:*=**erdig.**
erdichten. I. *v.tr.* to think up, make up, invent, fabricate (story, etc.); **es ist alles erdichtet,** it is all made up, invented.
II. *vbl s.* **1. Erdichten,** *n. in vbl senses.* **2. Erdichtung,** *f.* (*a*)=II. 1; *also:* invention, fabrication (of a story, etc.); (*b*) invented, made up, story; **das ist ja reine E.,** it is pure invention, pure fabrication, it is all invented, made up.
erdig, *a.* earthy; **erdiger Geschmack,** earthy taste; **einen erdigen Geruch haben,** to have an earthy smell; *Miner:* **erdige Masse, erdiges Erz,** earthy material, earthy ore; **erdige Kohle,** earthy coal; dirty coal; **erdige Säuerlinge,** earthy (mineral) waters.
Erdigkeit, *f.* earthiness (of mineral, coal, etc.).
Erdinduktor, *m. El.E:* earth inductor.
Erdinnere, *n.* (*decl. as adj.*) *Geol:* interior of the earth, *Lit.* bowels of the earth.
Erdkabel, *n. El.E:* underground cable, buried cable.
Erdkampf, *m. Mil:* ground fighting.
Erdkampfflugzeug, *n. Mil.Av:* ground-attack aircraft.
Erdkarte, *f. Geog:* map of the world.
Erdkastanie, *f. Bot:* pig-nut, earth-nut, carum bulbocastanum.
Erdkeimer, *m. Bot:* geoblast.
Erdkern, *m. Geol:* core of the earth.
Erdklemme, *f. El.E:* earth-terminal, *U.S:* ground(-ing) terminal.
Erdklosett, *n. Hyg:* earth-closet.
Erdklumpen, *m.* clod, lump of earth.
Erdkobalt, *m. Miner:* earthy cobalt; **roter E.,** cobalt bloom, erythrite; **schwarzer E.,** asbolite, asbolan; bog manganese.
Erdkohle, *f. Min:* earthy brown coal.
Erdkohlrabi, *m. Agr:* Swedish turnip, swede.
Erdkontakt, *m. El.E:* **1.** earth-connection, earth, *U.S:* ground connection, ground. **2.** earth-leakage, earth-fault, *U.S:* ground.
Erdkrebs, *m.* **1.** *Ent:* mole-cricket. **2.** *For:* canker of coniferous trees caused by agaricus melleus.
Erdkreis, *m.* earth, world; **ein Ereignis, das den E. erschütterte,** an event which shook the world.
Erdkrokodil, *n. Rept:* skink.
Erdkröte, *f. Amph:* common toad.
Erdkrume, *f. Agr:* surface soil, topsoil, tilth.
Erdkruste, *f. Geol:* earth's crust, lithosphere
Erdkugel, *f. Astr:* globe, terrestrial sphere; world; *Sch: etc:* **(künstliche) E.,** terrestrial globe.
Erdkunde, *f.* geography; **allgemeine E.,** general geography; **spezielle E.,** regional geography; **physische, physikalische E.,** physical geography; **biologische E.,** biogeography; **staatsbürgerliche, politische, E.,** political geography.
Erdkundebuch, *n. Sch:* geography book.
Erdkundestunde, *f. Sch:* geography lesson.
Erdkundeunterricht, *m. Sch:* (i) teaching of geography; (ii) geography (lessons).
Erdkundler, *m.* **-s/-,** geographer.
erdkundlich, *a.* geographical; *Sch:* **erdkundlicher Unterricht,** (i) teaching of geography; (ii) geography (lessons).
Erdleiter, *m. El.E:* earthed, *U.S:* grounded, conductor.
Erdleitung, *f. El.E:* (i) earth, earth-wire, -lead, *U.S:* ground, ground wire, ground lead; (ii) earth-connection, earth-circuit, earth, *U.S:* ground connection, ground circuit, ground; (iii)=**Erdrückleitung.**
Erdleitungsdraht, *m. El.E:* earth-wire, *U.S:* ground wire.
Erdlicht, *n. Astr:* (*a*) zodiacal light; (*b*)=**Erdschein** (*a*).
Erdloch, *n.* hole in the ground; *Mil:* fox-hole, funk-hole.
erdmagnetisch, *a. Ph:* concerning terrestrial magnetism; **erdmagnetische Elemente,** magnetic elements.
Erdmagnetismus, *m. Ph:* terrestrial magnetism: **Elemente des E.,** magnetic elements.
Erdmandel, *f. Bot:* **1.** =**Erdnuß** 1. **2.** Jerusalem artichoke. **3.** tuberous pea, earth-nut pea. **4.** chufa.
Erdmännchen, *n.* **1.** *Myth:* gnome. **2.** (root of) mandragora, mandrake.
Erdmantel, *m. Geol:* mantle of the earth.
Erdmarder, *m.* (*a*) *Z:* kolinsky; (*b*) *Com:* kolinsky (fur).
Erdmasse, *f.* **1.** *Astr:* mass of the earth. **2.** *pl.* **Erdmassen,** masses of earth; **große Erdmassen mußten bewegt werden,** great masses of earth had to be shifted; **ungeheure Erdmassen versperrten die Straße,** huge masses of, *F:* tons of, earth blocked the road.
Erdmast, *f.* food-substances rooted up by wild boars.
Erdmaus, *f. Z:* field-vole, field-mouse, meadow-mouse.
Erdmeridian, *m. Geog:* meridian.
Erdmessung, *f.* (*a*) *Mth:* geodesy; (*b*) (i) measuring of the earth, (ii) measurement(s) of the earth.
Erdmetall, *n. Ch:* earth-metal.
Erdmine, *f. Mil: etc:* land-mine.
Erdmittelalter, das. *Geol:* the Mesozoic (group, era).
Erdmittelpunkt, *m.* centre of the earth.
erdnah, *a. Astr: etc:* close to the earth; (*of moon*) in perigee.
Erdnähe, *f.* **1.** *Astr:* perigee (of moon); **in E.,** (*of star, etc.*) close to the earth, in the vicinity of the earth; (*of moon*) in perigee. **2.** *Av:* low altitude.
Erdnetz, *n. El.E:* earth(-return) circuit, *U.S:* ground (return) circuit.
Erdneuzit, die. *Geol:* the C(a)enozoic (group, era).
Erdnuß, *f. Bot:* **1.** peanut, earth-nut, ground-nut, monkey-nut. **2.**=**Erdkastanie.** **3.** tuberous pea, earth-nut pea. **4. amerikanische E.,** apios, ground-nut. **5.** *A:* potato.
Erdnußbutter, *f.* peanut butter.
Erdnußöl, *n.* peanut oil, earth-nut oil, ground-nut oil.
Erdoberfläche, *f. Geol:* surface of the earth, earth's surface.
Erdöl, *n.* petroleum; mineral oil; **rohes E.,** crude petroleum, crude oil; **raffiniertes E.,** refined petroleum, refined oil, rectified petroleum; **auf E. stoßen,** to strike oil.
Erdöläther, *m. Ch:* petrolic ether, petroleum ether.
Erdölbrunnen, *m.* oil-well.
erdolchen, *v.tr.* to stab (s.o.) to death (with a dagger); *F:* **j-n mit seinen Blicken e.,** to look daggers at s.o.; to cast a withering glance at s.o., to give s.o. a withering look.
Erdölfeld, *n.* petroleum-field, oil-field.
erdölführend, *a. Geol:* petroliferous, oil-bearing, petroleum-bearing (strata, etc.).
Erdölgebiet, *n. Geol:* oil-belt; *Ind:* oil-producing region.
erdölhöffig, *a. Min:* offering good prospects for oil.
Erdölindustrie, *f.* oil-industry.
Erdöllager, *n. Geol:* oil-sheet, sheet of petroleum; oil-belt.
Erdölquelle, *f. Geol:* petroleum-spring, oil-spring; oil-well; **auf eine E. stoßen,** to strike oil.
Erdölschacht, *m.* oil-well.
Erdölvorkommen, *n.* source of (mineral) oil.
Erdölzone, *f. Geol:* oil-belt.
Erdorgeln, *f.pl.*=**Erdpfeifen.**
Erdpapagei, *m. Orn:* kakapo, owl-parrot, night-parrot.
Erdpech, *n. Miner:* mineral pitch, Jew's pitch, asphalt; **elastisches E.,** elaterite, elastic bitumen.
Erdperiode, *f.* geological era, age of the earth.
Erdpfeifen, *f.pl. Geol:* sand-pipes, sand-galls.
Erdpfeiler, *m.*=**Erdpyramide.**
Erdpistazie, *f.*=**Erdnuß** 1.
Erdplatte, *f. El.E:* earth-plate, *U.S:* ground plate.
Erdplattenstrom, *m. El:* earth-current.
Erdpol, *m. Geog:* pole.
Erdpotential, *n. El:* earth potential.
Erdprimel, *f. Bot:* common primrose.
Erdpyramide, *f. Geol:* erosion column, earth pillar; chimney-rock.
Erdrauch, *m. Bot:* fumitory, fumaria.
Erdraupe, *f. Ent:* cutworm.
Erdreich, *n.* **1.**=**Erdenreich.** **2.** earth, soil; **das E. lockern,** to loosen, break up, the soil; **fruchtbares E.,** fertile soil.
erdreisten (sich), *v.refl.* to have the audacity, the impudence, *F:* the nerve, the cheek (to do sth.); **er erdreistete sich, eine Unterredung mit mir zu verlangen,** he had the audacity, the impudence, *F:* the nerve, the cheek, to demand an interview with me.
Erdriese, *f. For:* timber-slide, -shoot.
Erdrinde, *f.*=**Erdkruste.**
Erdritterling, *m. Fung:* earthy toadstool.
erdröhnen, *v.i.* (*sein*) (*of cannon, etc.*) to begin to boom, to roar; (*of voice, drum, etc.*) to boom out; (*of air, room, etc.*) to (begin to) vibrate, to be resonant (with noise); **plötzlich erdröhnte die Stimme des Kapitäns aus dem Lautsprecher,** suddenly the captain's voice boomed out from the loudspeaker; **das Tal erdröhnte vom Hufschlag ihrer Pferde,** the valley resounded, was resonant, was filled, with the sound of their horses' hooves.
Erdrosseler, *m.* **-s/-,** strangler.
erdrosseln, *v.tr.* to strangle, throttle (s.o.); to garrotte (prisoner); to choke (s.o.) to death; **Erdrosseln** *n,* **Erdrosselung** *f,* **Erdroßlung** *f,* strangling, strangulation, throttling, garrotting (of s.o.).
Erdroßler, *m.* **-s/-,** strangler.
Erdrotation, *f. Astr:* rotation of the earth.
Erdrübe, *f. Agr:* Swedish turnip, swede.
erdrücken. I. *v.tr.* to crush (s.o.) to death; (*of mental burden, etc.*) to weigh (s.o.) down, to overcome, overwhelm (s.o.); **er wurde von dem fallenden Balken erdrückt,** he was crushed to death by the falling beam; **er erdrückte sie fast mit seiner Umarmung,** he nearly crushed her with his embrace; **von der Last der Arbeit fast erdrückt werden,** to be overwhelmed, *F:* snowed under, with work, to be up to one's eyes in work; **von Kummer erdrückt,** overcome, weighed down, with grief, bowed down, borne down, by grief; **von Sorgen, von der Last der Sorgen, erdrückt,** weighed down with worries; **von seinen Schulden, von der Last seiner Schulden, fast erdrückt werden,** to be nearly crippled with debts; **erdrückende Übermacht,** overwhelmingly superior numbers (of enemy, etc.); **angesichts des erdrückenden Beweismaterials gestand er,** in the face of, faced with, the overwhelming evidence he confessed.
II. *vbl s.* **Erdrücken,** *n. in vbl senses; also:* **der Raum, der Saal, war zum E. voll,** the room, the hall, was crowded, packed, crammed, to suffocation.
Erdrückleitung, *f. El.E:* earth-return (circuit), *U.S:* ground return (circuit).
Erdrusch, *m.* **-(e)s/.** yield of corn from threshing.
Erdrutsch, *m.* landslide, landslip; earth-fall.
Erdsänger, *m. Orn:* erithacus.
Erdsappe, *f. Mil:* sap; **flüchtige E.,** flying sap; **völlige E.,** full sap, single sap.
Erdsatellit, *m. Astr: etc:* earth satellite; **künstlicher E.,** artificial earth satellite, artificial moon; sputnik.
Erdsäuren, *f.pl. Ch:* highest oxides of the elements of the vanadium family.
Erdschalter, *m. El.E:* earthing switch.
Erdscharre, *f. Min: Tls:* fluke, spoon (for bore-holes).
Erdschatten, *m. Astr:* shadow of the earth (on the moon).
Erdscheibe, *f.* **1.** *Hist. of Astr:* disc of the earth. **2.** *Bot:* cyclamen, sowbread.
Erdschein, *m. Astr:* (*a*) earth-light, earth-shine (of the moon); (*b*) **nächtlicher E.,** zodiacal light.
Erdschellack, *m. Ch:* acaroid resin; *Com:* yellow gum.

Erdschicht, *f. Geol:* bed, layer, stratum (of earth, soil).
Erdschieber, *m. Fung:* fleecy toadstool.
Erdschlipf, *m.* **1.** landslide, landslip; rockslide; fall, slip, slide (of earth, rock, etc.). **2.**=**Erdtrichter.**
Erdschluß, *m. El.E:* earth-leakage, accidental earth-connection; fault, *U.S:* ground; **vollständiger E.,** dead earth; **unvollständiger E.,** partial earth.
Erdschlußanzeiger, *m. El.E:* leakage indicator; fault-finder.
Erdschlußfehler, *m. El.E:* earth-leakage, earth-fault, *U.S:* ground.
Erdschlußstrom, *m. El:* earth-current, current (flowing) to earth.
Erdschnake, *f. Ent:* tipula, crane-fly, *F:* daddy-long-legs.
Erdschnecke, *f. Moll:* (small) slug, *esp.* field slug.
Erdscholle, *f.* clod, lump of earth.
Erdschwalbe, *f. Orn:* sand-martin.
Erdschwein, *n.*=**Erdferkel.**
Erdsittich, *m. Orn:* ground-parakeet.
Erdspalte, *f.* fissure in the ground; chasm.
Erdsphäre, *f.* **1.** *Astr:* terrestrial sphere, globe; world. **2.** *Hist. of Astr:* sphere of the earth.
Erdsporn, *m. Artil:* trail-spade (of gun).
Erdstamm, *m. Bot:* rhizome, root-stock.
Erdstampfbau, *m. Constr:* cobwork, pisé-work.
Erdstampfer, *m. Civ.E: etc:* earth rammer, punner.
Erdstern, *m. Fung:* earth-star.
Erdstoß, *m.* earth tremor, (earthquake) shock.
Erdstrahlen, *m.pl. Ph:* earth rays.
Erdstrahlung, *f. Ph:* earth radiation.
Erdstraße, *f.* unsurfaced road; cart-track, cart-road; *U.S:* dirt road.
Erdstrom, *m. Ph: El:* earth-current.
Erdteer, *m. Miner:* mineral tar, maltha, pissasphalt.
Erdteil, *m. Geog:* continent; **der dunkle E.,** the Dark Continent, Africa.
Erdtelegraphie, *f. Mil:* earth induction telegraphy.
Erdtrabant, *m.*=**Erdsatellit.**
Erdtrichter, *m. Geol:* dolina, sink(-hole), swallow-hole.
erdulden, *v.tr.* to bear, endure, suffer (pain, grief, etc.); **sie erduldete ihr Leiden ohne Klagen,** she endured, suffered, bore, her illness without complaint; **während dieser Zeit mußten sie viel e.,** during this time they had to suffer much, they had to bear, endure, much suffering.
Erdumdrehung, *f. Astr:* rotation of the earth.
Erdumfang, *m. Astr:* circumference of the earth, terrestrial circumference.
Erdumlauf, *m. Astr:* **E. um die Sonne,** revolution of the earth about the sun.
Erdumsegelung, *f.* circumnavigation of the globe.
Erdung, *f. see* **erden.**
Erdungsdraht, *m. El.E:* earth-wire, *U.S:* ground wire.
Erdungskreis, *m. El.E:*=**Erdnetz.**
Erdungsleitung, *f. El.E:*=**Erdleitung** (i), (ii).
Erdverbindung, *f. El.E:* earth-connection, earth, *U.S:* ground connection, ground.
erdverlegt, *a.* underground, buried (cable, etc.).
Erdvermessung, *f.* geodesy.
Erdverwerfung, *f. Geol:* fault.
Erdvorlage, *f. Mil:* earth parapet (of trench, etc.).
Erdwachs, *n.* ozocerite, ozokerite; mineral wax; fossil wax.
Erdwall, *m.* earth-bank; earthworks; mound; earth-wall; *Mil:* earthworks, earth-parapet (of trenches, etc.).
Erdwalze, *f. Mil:* full sap, single sap.
Erdwärme, *f. Ph:* temperature of the earth's interior.
Erdweg, *m. Post:* **auf dem E.,** by surface mail.
Erdweite, *f. Astr:* mean distance of the earth from the sun.
Erdweizen, *m. Bot:* melampyrum, cow-wheat.
erdwendig, *a. Bot:* geotropic (plant).
Erdwendigkeit, *f. Bot:* geotropism.
Erdwerke, *n.pl. Mil:* earthworks.
Erdwolf, *m. Z:* aardwolf.
Erdzeitalter, *n.* geological era, age of the earth.
Erdziel, *n. Mil:* ground target.
Erebos, Erebus, der ['eːre·bos, -bus], **-.** *Gr.Myth:* Erebus.
Erechtheion, Erechtheum, das [e·rɛç'taion, -'teːum], **-s,** the Erechtheion, Erechtheum.
ereifern (sich), *v.refl.* to become, grow, get, heated, agitated, excited; **sich über etwas** *acc.* **e.,** to get excited, heated, agitated, worked up, about sth.; to fly into a passion about sth.; **ereifere dich nicht gleich so!** don't get so worked up, so excited! don't get all hot and bothered! *F:* keep your shirt, your hair, on! **'aber das geht doch nicht'! ereiferte sie sich,** 'but that is impossible!' she said heatedly.
ereignen (sich), *v.refl.* to happen, occur; to take place; to come about, to come to pass; **die Sache ereignete sich vor zehn Jahren,** the incident occurred, happened, took place, ten years ago; **die Dinge, die sich ereignet haben,** the events which have taken place, have come to pass, which have occurred; **dieser Fall hat sich tatsächlich ereignet,** this case actually happened, occurred; **der Zusammenstoß ereignete sich um Mitternacht,** the collision occurred at midnight; **der Unfall ereignete sich, als das Auto einen Lastwagen zu überholen versuchte,** the accident happened, occurred, when the car tried to overtake a lorry.
Ereignis, *n.* **-nisses/-nisse,** event, happening, occurrence; incident; **ein seltsames, sonderbares, merkwürdiges, E.,** a singular, peculiar, odd, occurrence; **ein trauriges, schmerzliches, E.,** a sad event; **wichtige, bedeutende, Ereignisse,** important events, important happenings; **dem Gang der Ereignisse folgen,** to follow the course of events; **die Ereignisse der letzten Wochen haben ihnen recht gegeben,** the events of the past weeks proved them right; **die Fülle der Ereignisse,** the rush of events; **künftige Ereignisse voraussagen,** to forecast, prophesy, future events; **große Ereignisse werfen ihre Schatten voraus,** important events cast their shadows before; **das ist ein E.,** that's quite an event; *F:* **ein freudiges E.,** a happy event.
ereignislos, *a.* uneventful, eventless.
ereignisreich, *a.* eventful (life, day, etc.); memorable (day, etc.); **ereignisreiche Woche, ereignisreiches Jahr,** eventful week, eventful year.
ereilen, *v.tr.* (*of evil fate, etc.*) to overtake (s.o.); **der Tod, sein Geschick, ereilte ihn bei einem Fluchtversuch,** his fate overtook him, he met his death, his fate, while he was attempting to escape; **da ereilte ihn das Schicksal,** then fate intervened.
erektil [e·rɛk'tiːl], *a. Physiol:* erectile (tissue, etc.).
Erektion [e·rɛktsi'oːn], *f.* **-/-en.** *Physiol:* erection.
erektionsfähig, *a. Physiol:* erectile (tissue, etc.).
Erektionsvermögen, *n. Physiol:* erectility.
Eremit [e·re·'miːt], *m.* **-en/-en. 1.** hermit; recluse; anchorite; **wie ein E. leben,** to live like a hermit, to live, lead, a hermit's life, the life of a recluse. **2.**=**Eremitenkrebs.**
Eremitage [e·re·mi·'taːʒə], *f.* **-/-n,** hermitage; **die E.,** the Hermitage (at Leningrad).
eremitenhaft, *a.* hermit-like, eremitic(al), solitary (life, etc.).
Eremitenkrebs, *m. Crust:* hermit-crab, pagurian.
eremitisch [e·re·'miːtiʃ], *a.*=**eremitenhaft.**
Eren, *m.* **-/-.** *Dial:* (entrance) hall (of house).
ererben, *v.tr.* **etwas e.,** to inherit sth.; **ererbter Besitz,** inherited property; inheritance; **ererbte Krankheit,** inherited disease.
erethisch [e·'reːtiʃ], *a. Med:* erethic.
Erethismus [e·re·'tismus], *m.* **-/.** *Med:* erethism; excessive irritability.
erfahren. I. *v.tr.* (*strong*) **1.** to hear, learn (sth.); **eine Nachricht e.,** to hear, learn, a piece of news; **die Wahrheit e.,** to learn, hear, the truth; **etwas über j-n e.,** to learn sth. about s.o.; **ich habe es aus zuverlässiger Quelle erfahren,** I have it from a reliable source, I have it on good authority; **ich konnte keine Einzelheiten, nichts Näheres, e.,** I was unable to learn any details, I could not find out any details; **ich habe erfahren, daß . . . ,** I have learned, heard, it has come to my knowledge, that . . . ; **am Bahnhof erfuhren wir, daß der Zug drei Stunden Verspätung haben würde,** at the station we learned, heard, we were told, that the train would be three hours late. **2.** to experience (sth.); to suffer (loss, etc.); **etwas am eigenen Leibe e.,** to experience sth. personally; to learn sth. from personal experience; **er erfuhr im Hause seines Onkels nur Liebe,** he received, was shown, only affection in his uncle's house; **sie hat in ihrem Leben nicht viel Gutes erfahren,** she has experienced, encountered, known, few good things in her life; **eine Demütigung e.,** to experience, suffer, a humiliation; to be humiliated; **einen Verlust e.,** to meet with a loss, to suffer a loss; **eine Niederlage e.,** to suffer defeat, to be defeated.

II. *vbl s.* **Erfahrung,** *f.* **1.** *vbl phr.* **etwas in E. bringen,** to hear, learn, sth.; **wir haben in E. gebracht, daß . . . ,** we have learned, it has come to our knowledge, that . . . . **2.** (*a*) *Phil:* empirical knowledge; (*b*) experience; **praktische E.,** practical experience; **viel E. haben,** to have had much experience, to be experienced; **ihm fehlt die E.,** he lacks experience; **E. in (der) Buchhaltung,** experience in book-keeping, book-keeping experience; **E. im Unterrichten haben,** to have experience of teaching; **etwas aus (eigener) E. wissen,** to know sth. from (personal) experience; **ich weiß aus bitterer E., daß . . . ,** I know from bitter experience that . . . ; **ich spreche aus (eigener) E.,** I speak from experience; **aus eigener E., aus meiner eigenen E., kann ich das bestätigen,** I can confirm that from personal experience; **durch E. wird man klug,** we learn from experience; *Rel:* **innere E.,** (religious) experiences; (*c*) **mit j-m, etwas, eine schlechte Erfahrung machen,** to find s.o., sth., unsatisfactory; to be disappointed in s.o., with sth.; **mit diesem Geschäft habe ich immer nur gute Erfahrungen gemacht,** I have always got satisfaction at that shop; **Erfahrungen sammeln,** to get experience, to gather experience; **frühere Erfahrungen haben bewiesen, daß . . . ,** previous experience has, previous experiences have, proved that . . . ; **mit einer Behandlungsweise ausgezeichnete Erfahrungen machen,** to achieve excellent results with a method of treatment; **ich habe mit diesem Material nur gute Erfahrungen gemacht,** in my experience this material has always been good; **er hat mit diesem Restaurant schlechte Erfahrungen gemacht,** his experience of this restaurant has been disappointing, he has fared badly with this restaurant.

III. *p.p. & a.* **erfahren,** (*a*) *in vbl senses;* (*b*) experienced; versed, practised, proficient, well up (in sth.); conversant (with sth.); **in etwas** *dat.* **e. sein,** to be experienced, practised, in sth.; to be versed, proficient, in sth.; to have had experience in sth.; **in Geschäftssachen e. sein,** to be experienced, well versed, well up, in business matters; **wenig e. im Umgang mit Menschen,** with little experience of how to deal with people; **er ist noch nicht sehr e.,** he is not very experienced as yet, he still lacks experience; **ein erfahrener Reiter,** an experienced rider; **eine in Buchhaltung erfahrene Sekretärin,** a secretary (who is) experienced in book-keeping, a secretary who has had experience in book-keeping; **Erfahrene** *m, f,* experienced person; **der Erfahrene, ein Erfahrener, kennt alle diese Anzeichen,** an experienced person knows all these signs.
Erfahrenheit, *f.* experience; proficiency; **seine E. in Geschäftssachen,** his experience in business matters.
Erfahrungsbeweis, *m. Phil:* proof *a posteriori.*
erfahrungsgemäß, *adv.* from (previous) experience; *Phil:* empirically; **e. tritt die Krankheit meist im Winter auf,** it is known, we know, from previous experience that the disease is most prevalent in winter; **e. sind diese Anzeichen nicht zuverlässig,** previous experience has shown, has proved, that these signs are not reliable.
Erfahrungsheillehre, *f. Hist. of Med:* empiricism.
Erfahrungskreis, *m.* (sphere of) experience; **aus meinem E.,** from my (own, personal) experience.
Erfahrungskunde, Erfahrungslehre, *f. Phil:* empiricism.
erfahrungslos, *a.* inexperienced, without experience.
erfahrungsmäßig. 1. *a.* according to, in accordance with, experience; empirical (knowledge, etc.). **2.** *adv.*=**erfahrungsgemäß.**
erfahrungsreich, *a.* experienced (pers.); (life, etc.) rich in, full of, experiences.
Erfahrungswissen, *n. Phil:* empirical knowledge, knowledge gained through experience.
Erfahrungswissenschaft, *f. Phil:* empiricism.
erfassen. I. *v.tr.* **1.** (*a*) to seize (s.o., sth.); to grasp (s.o., sth.), to lay hold, take hold, catch hold of (s.o., sth.); **er erfaßte ihre Hand,** he grasped, took hold of, her hand; **sie konnte ihn gerade noch am Hemdenzipfel e.,** she just managed to catch hold of him, to seize him, by the tail of his shirt; **der Wind erfaßte seinen Hut und trug ihn davon,** the wind caught his hat and carried it away; **das Boot, der Schwimmer, wurde von der Strömung erfaßt,** the boat, the swimmer, was caught by the current; **der Fußgänger wurde vom Auto erfaßt,** the car caught the pedestrian; (*b*) (*of fear, desire, etc.*) to seize, overcome (s.o.); (*of pers.*) **von Angst, Furcht, erfaßt werden,** to be seized, overcome, with fear; **Grausen erfaßte sie, sie wurde von Grausen erfaßt,** she was overcome, seized, with horror; **von Mitleid erfaßt werden,**

to be moved to pity; **er wurde von einer tiefen Leidenschaft zu ihr erfaßt,** he fell passionately in love with her; **tiefe Trauer erfaßte ihn,** a feeling of great sadness came over him; **er wurde vom Schwindel erfaßt,** he was overcome by, seized with, dizziness; **wilde Begeisterung erfaßte die Menge,** the crowd was moved to wild enthusiasm, wild enthusiasm gripped the crowd; **von Begierde nach etwas erfaßt werden,** to be seized with a desire, longing, for sth.; (*c*) to grasp, understand, comprehend (sth.); to take (sth.) in; **sie konnte die Sache einfach nicht e.,** she simply could not grasp, understand, the matter, the matter was simply beyond her; **ich hab's erfaßt,** I've got it, I've got the idea (of it), *F:* I've got the hang of it. **2.** to include, take in (s.o., sth.); **bei der Impfung sollen alle Kinder unter zehn Jahren erfaßt werden,** it is hoped to include all children under ten years of age in the vaccinations; **dieses System ermöglicht es, bei der geplanten Ausdehnung des Stromnetzes selbst die entlegensten Dörfer zu e.,** this system makes it possible to include even the most isolated villages in the planned extension of the grid; **dem neuen Gesetz zufolge werden alle achtzehnjährigen Männer für den Wehrdienst erfaßt,** in accordance with the new law all eighteen-year-old men will be called up for military service; **eine Altersgruppe statistisch e.,** to make a statistical survey of an age group.

II. *vbl s.* **Erfassung,** *f. in vbl senses; also:* inclusion; **die geplante E. aller Schulkinder für Röntgenuntersuchungen,** the plan to include all school children in X-ray examinations; **eine statistische E. aller Minderjährigen wird durch die nomadischen Gewohnheiten der Bewohner dieser Gegend erschwert,** the nomadic habits of the people in this area make it difficult to include all minors in a statistical survey.

erfechten, *v.tr. (strong)* **1. etwas e.,** to get, gain, sth. by fighting; to fight for sth.; **die Soldaten erfochten einen herrlichen Sieg,** the soldiers gained a wonderful victory. **2.** *F:* to get, obtain, (sth.) by begging; to beg for sth.

erfinden. I. *v.tr. (strong)* (*a*) to invent, devise, contrive (machine, etc.); **die von ihm erfundene Vorrichtung,** the contrivance invented, devised, by him; *F:* **er hat das Pulver nicht erfunden, das Pulver hat er nicht erfunden,** he is no genius, no great brain; *F:* he will never set the Thames on fire, *U.S:* he will never set the woods on fire; (*b*) to invent, make up, fabricate (story, excuse, etc.); to coin (new word, etc.); **Lügen über j-n e.,** to invent calumnies about s.o.; **es ist alles erfunden,** it is all invented, all made up, it is pure invention, pure fabrication; **die Geschichte ist frei erfunden, ist von A bis Z erfunden,** the story is pure invention, pure fabrication; **erfundene Geschichte,** invented, made-up, story.

II. *vbl s.* **1. Erfinden,** *n. in vbl senses.* **2. Erfindung,** *f.* (*a*)=II. 1; *also:* invention (of machine, story, etc.); fabrication (of story, etc.); **eine Mausefalle seiner eigenen E.,** a mousetrap of his own invention; (*b*) invention; **eine höchst nützliche E.,** a most useful invention; **die neuesten Erfindungen wurden auf der Messe gezeigt,** the latest inventions were shown at the fair; **eine E. patentieren lassen,** to take out a patent for an invention; (*c*) fabrication, invention; **diese Geschichte ist reine E.,** this story is pure invention, pure fabrication; **das ist ja alles E.,** it is all invented, all made up, it is all pure invention, pure fabrication.

Erfinder, *m.* -s/-, inventor; **der E. dieser Maschine,** the inventor of this machine.

erfinderisch, *a.* inventive (talent, mind, etc.); resourceful, imaginative, ingenious (pers.); **ein erfinderischer Kopf,** an inventive mind; **sie war sehr e. in der Zubereitung leckerer Speisen,** she was very resourceful in concocting tasty dishes; **Not macht e.,** necessity is the mother of invention.

Erfinderrecht, *n. Jur:* patent rights.

Erfindung, *f. see* **erfinden II.**

Erfindungsgabe, *f.* inventive ability, inventive talent; inventiveness; ingenuity.

Erfindungspatent, *n. Adm: Jur:* (letters) patent.

erfindungsreich, *a.* resourceful; ingenious.

erflehen, *v.tr.* **etwas von j-m e.,** (i) to beg, implore, sth. of s.o.; (ii) to obtain sth. from s.o. by entreaties; **sie erflehten Gottes Gnade,** they implored God's mercy.

Erfolg, *m.* -(e)s/-e. **1.** result, issue, outcome, effect (of an undertaking, etc.); **der E. unserer Bemühungen,** the result, outcome, success, of our labours; **der E. war, daß . . . ,** the result, effect, consequence, was that . . . ; **der einzige E. des Streiks war, daß die Industrie viele neue Aufträge verlor,** the only effect, result, of the strike was that the industry lost many new orders; **meine Warnung hatte den gewünschten E.,** my warning had the desired effect; **diese Eröffnungen hatten den E., daß die Regierung stürzte,** these revelations resulted in the fall of the government; **guter, schlechter, E.,** good, bad, success; favourable, unfavourable, issue, outcome, result; **mit gutem E. arbeiten,** to work with good result, with good success; to work to good purpose; **ein zweiter Versuch hatte keinen besseren E.,** a second attempt met with no better success, brought no better result; **ohne bleibenden E.,** without lasting, permanent, effect. **2.** (*a*) (*favourable result*) success; **E. haben,** to achieve success, to meet with success, to be successful; **einen E. erringen,** to score a success; **große Erfolge erringen,** to achieve great successes, great triumphs; **wir wünschen dir E.,** we wish you success; **seinen E. verdankte er dem Zufall,** his success was due to chance; **von E. zu E. schreiten,** to advance from success to success; **vollen E. haben, von vollem E. begleitet sein,** to be entirely successful; **bei den Wahlen E. haben,** to be successful at the polls; **junger Mann, der E. haben wird,** young man who will succeed, who will get on in the world; **er hat in allem E., alles, was er unternimmt, ist von E. gekrönt,** he is successful in everything; **unsere Bemühungen hatten E., waren von E. gekrönt,** our efforts were successful; **ich sehe keine Möglichkeit, in dieser Sache zum E. zu gelangen,** I see no possibility of success, of succeeding, in this matter; **eine Aufgabe mit E. erledigen,** to deal successfully with a task; **ohne E.,** without success, unsuccessful(ly); **ohne E. zurückkehren,** to return without any success; to return empty-handed; **Wiederbelebungsversuche blieben ohne E., waren ohne E.,** artificial respiration was applied without success, without avail; **wir protestierten ohne E., — der Baum wurde gefällt,** we protested in vain, it was in vain that we protested—the tree was cut down; **sich ohne E. um eine Stellung bewerben,** to apply for a post unsuccessfully, without success, to make an unsuccessful application for a post; (*b*) success; **ein E. sein,** (*of play, venture, pers., etc.*) to be, turn out, prove, a success, (*of play, book, etc.*) to be, make, a hit; **sein Besuch war kein E.,** his visit was not a success; **der Abend war ein großer E.,** the evening was a great success; **es war ein großer E.,** it was a great, *F:* a huge, success, it was most successful; **als Hamlet war er ein großer E.,** he was a great success as Hamlet.

erfolgen, *v.i. (sein)* **1.** to follow, ensue; **auf etwas** *acc.* **e.,** to follow sth.; to be the result, the consequence, of sth.; to be due to sth.; to be caused by sth.; to ensue (up)on, from, sth.; **der Tod erfolgte durch Herzschlag,** death was due to, ensued from, heart failure; **auf diese Eröffnungen hin erfolgte der Sturz der Regierung,** these revelations resulted in the fall of the government; **was erfolgte darauf?** what happened afterwards? what ensued? **auf seinen Brief erfolgte sehr bald eine Antwort,** a reply was received very soon after his letter; **auf meine Mahnung erfolgte lange Zeit gar nichts,** nothing happened for a long time after my warning; **er wartete, aber keine Antwort erfolgte,** he waited but there was no answer, but no answer came. **2.** to take place, to happen, to occur; **ihre Verlobung erfolgte bald darauf,** their engagement took place soon after; **die Explosion erfolgte einige Minuten später,** a few minutes later the explosion occurred; **sein Eintritt in diese Firma kann frühestens nächste Woche e.,** he can start, take up, his job in this firm next week at the earliest; **Bezahlung erfolgte in Dollars,** payment was made, effected, in dollars; **nach erfolgtem Abzug der Truppen,** after the troops had left, after the departure of the troops; **nach erfolgter Untersuchung,** after the examination; **nach, bei, erfolgter Bezahlung,** after payment; **bei, nach, erfolgter Einspritzung des Vakzins,** after the injection of the vaccine, after the vaccine has, had, been injected.

erfolglos, *a.* unsuccessful; vain, fruitless; without success; **e. sein,** to be unsuccessful; **ein erfolgloser Versuch,** an unsuccessful, a vain, a fruitless, attempt; **der erfolglose Bewerber,** the unsuccessful (i) candidate, (ii) suitor; **die Verhandlungen waren e.,** the negotiations were unsuccessful; **die Suche blieb e.,** the search was in vain; **Wiederbelebungsversuche waren, blieben, e.,** artificial respiration was applied without success, without avail; **es war e., daß wir protestierten, — der Baum wurde gefällt,** it was in vain that we protested, we protested in vain—the tree was cut down; *adv.* **e. zurückkehren,** to return without any success; to return empty-handed; **sich e. um eine Stellung bewerben,** to apply for a post unsuccessfully, without success, to make an unsuccessful application for a post.

Erfolglosigkeit, *f.* want of success, ill-success; failure; miscarriage (of plan, etc.); **Unternehmen, das von vornherein zur E. verurteilt war,** enterprise foredoomed to failure; ill-starred venture.

erfolgreich, *a.* successful; **erfolgreiche Kandidaten,** successful candidates; **erfolgreiches Stück,** successful play; **e. sein,** (*of pers.*) (i) to be successful, to achieve success, to meet with success; to score a success; (ii) to be, prove, a success; (*of attempt, search, etc.*) to be successful; (*of play, venture, etc.*) to be successful, to be, turn out, prove, a success; (*of play, book, etc.*) to be, make, a hit; **in jeder Hinsicht e. sein,** to be successful in every respect, to be entirely successful; **bei etwas e. sein,** to be successful in (doing) sth., to succeed in sth.; **er ist in allem e.,** he is successful in everything; **ich glaube, er wird e. sein,** I believe he will be successful, he will succeed; **bei den Wahlen e. sein,** to be successful at the polls; **der Trick ist immer e.,** that trick is always successful; **eine Operation zu einem erfolgreichen Ende führen,** to bring an operation to a successful conclusion; **die Operation war e.,** *Mil: Navy:* the action, the operation, was successful; *Med:* the operation was successful; *adv.* **sich e. um eine Stellung bewerben,** to apply for a post successfully, to make a successful application for a post; **sich e. einer Prüfung unterziehen,** to undergo a test successfully; to pass an examination, a test: **eine Aufgabe e. erledigen,** to deal successfully with a task.

Erfolgsanteilsystem, *n. Com: etc:* profit sharing scheme; bonus system.

Erfolgshonorar, *n.* contingent fee.

Erfolgskonto, *n. Com:* profit and loss account.

Erfolgsrechnung, *f. Com:* profit and loss accounting.

erfolgversprechend, *a.* promising; **erfolgversprechender Anfang,** promising beginning; **erfolgversprechendes Unternehmen,** promising undertaking; **die Zukunft, die Ernte, sieht e. aus,** the future, the harvest, looks promising, the prospects for the future, for the harvest, are good, promising.

erforderlich, *a.* necessary, required, requisite; needed; **die erforderliche Geldsumme, die erforderlichen Mittel, haben,** to have the money required; **es fehlt ihnen das erforderliche Kapital,** they lack the required, requisite, necessary, capital; **das erforderliche Alter,** the required age; **die erforderlichen Eigenschaften besitzen, haben,** to have the required qualities; **die erforderlichen Maßnahmen treffen,** to take the necessary, requisite, measures; **zu dieser, für diese, Arbeit ist viel Geduld, viel Zeit, e.,** this work requires, demands, a great deal of patience, of time, a great deal of patience, of time, is required, needed, for this work; **Kurzschriftkenntnisse sind für diese Stelle nicht e.,** a knowledge of shorthand is not required for this post; **eine Armee wäre e., um diese Festung einzunehmen,** the fort would require an army to take it, it would require, need, an army, an army would be necessary, needed, to take the fort; **falls e.,** if required; **zur Einreise in die Schweiz ist ein Visum nicht e.,** no visa is required, necessary, needed, to enter Switzerland; **diese neuen Tatsachen machen eine weitere Nachforschung e.,** these new facts necessitate a further enquiry; **ich werde alles Erforderliche tun,** I shall do everything necessary, everything that is required, whatever is required, I shall take the requisite measures, the necessary steps.

erforderlichenfalls, *adv.* if required, if needed, if necessary; in case of need; **e. wird er selbst kommen,** he will come himself if necessary, if need be, if needs must, if required.

erfordern, *v.tr.* (*of thg*) to require, need, demand, take (time, money, patience, etc.); to call for (tact, care, etc.); **diese Sache wird viel Zeit, viel Geld, e.,** this matter will require, need, take, a great deal of time, of money; **das erfordert Mut,** that takes, needs, courage; **die Situation erfordert Takt, Geduld,** the situation requires, demands, calls for, tact, patience; **es erforderte seine ganze Aufmerksamkeit,** it required his

whole attention; **Arbeit, welche große Präzision erfordert**, work that requires, needs, demands, great precision; **es erforderte seine ganze Kraft, sie zurückzuhalten**, it took, required, needed, all his strength to hold them back; **seine Wunde erfordert sehr wenig Pflege**, his wound requires, needs, very little care; **diese Tatsachen erfordern keinerlei Erklärung**, these facts need no comment.

Erfordernis, *n.* -nisses/-nisse, requirement, demand; exigence, exigency; **allen Erfordernissen genügen**, to comply with, to meet, all requirements; to satisfy all conditions; **j-s Erfordernissen entsprechen, genügen**, to meet s.o.'s requirements; **den Erfordernissen der Zeit genügen**, to meet the exigencies of the time.

erforschen. I. *v.tr.* (*a*) to explore (country, etc.); to try to find out, to try to discover (sth.); to search for, search into, enquire into, study (causes, etc.); **die Geheimnisse des Meeres e.**, to explore the secrets of the sea; **eine Höhle e.**, to explore, investigate, a cave; **noch nicht erforschte Gegenden**, unexplored regions; **sein Gewissen e.**, to search, examine, one's conscience; (*b*) to discover, find out (sth.); **er wollte die Hintergründe dieses Falles e.**, he wanted to find out, to discover, the facts behind this case; **sie hatten es sich zur Aufgabe gemacht, die Ursachen dieser Krankheit zu e.**, they had set themselves to discover the causes of this disease. **II.** *vbl s.* **Erforschen** *n.*, **Erforschung** *f.* in *vbl senses*; *also*: exploration (of country, cave, etc.); investigation (of cave, etc.); investigation, enquiry (into causes, etc.); examination (of one's conscience, etc.).

Erforscher, *m.* -s/-, explorer (of country, etc.).

erfragen, *v.tr.* to ask for (sth.); **den Weg e.**, to find one's way by asking; to ask the way; **Einzelheiten sind bei Herrn X zu e.**, for details apply to Mr. X.

erfrechen (sich), *v.refl.* to have the impudence, *F:* the cheek, the nerve (to do sth.).

erfreuen. I. 1. *v.tr.* to please (s.o.); to delight (s.o.); to gladden, cheer (s.o.); to give (s.o.) pleasure, joy; **dieses Geschenk erfreute ihn sehr**, this present gave him great, much, pleasure; **es erfreute sie, daß . . .**, she was pleased, glad, that . . . , it gave her great pleasure that . . . ; **j-n mit einem Brief e.**, to give s.o. pleasure by writing him *or* her a letter; (*of music, colourful sight, etc.*) **das Ohr, das Auge, e.**, to please, delight, enchant, the ear, the eye; **es erfreut das Auge**, it pleases, delights, the eye, it is pleasing to the eye; **Musik, die das Ohr erfreut**, music that pleases, delights, the ear; **der Wein erfreut des Menschen Herz**, wine maketh glad the heart of man. **2. sich erfreuen**, (*a*) **sich an etwas** *dat.* **e.**, to delight in sth., to take, find, delight, pleasure, in sth.; to be pleased, delighted, enchanted, by sth.; **sich am Duft der Blumen e.**, to be delighted, enchanted, by the scent of the flowers; to delight in the scent of the flowers; **sich an Musik e.**, to take, find, pleasure in (listening to) music; **die Bücher, an denen sich so viele Leute erfreuen**, the books which please, delight, give pleasure to, so many, the books delighted in by so many; **daran erfreut sich das Auge**, it pleases, delights, the eye, it is pleasing to the eye; (*b*) **sich etwas** *gen.* **e.**, to enjoy (good health, a good reputation, etc.); **er erfreut sich bester Gesundheit**, he enjoys good, excellent, health, he is in the best of health; **sich eines sehr guten Rufes e.**, to enjoy a high reputation, to have a high reputation, to be held in high repute; **sich höchster Achtung e.**, to be held in the highest esteem; **er erfreut sich keines guten Rufes**, he has a bad reputation; **er erfreute sich des Rufes, ein ausgezeichneter Jäger zu sein**, he enjoyed, had, the reputation of being an excellent hunter; **Theater, das sich eines guten Rufes erfreut**, theatre of good repute; **Ort, der sich keines guten Rufes erfreut**, place of ill repute; **das Restaurant erfreut sich guten Zuspruchs**, the restaurant is well patronized, well frequented. **II.** *p.p. & a.* **erfreut**, (*a*) *in vbl senses*; (*b*) pleased, glad; delighted; **über etwas** *acc.* **e. sein**, to be pleased, glad, about sth.; to be delighted about sth., with sth.; **erfreutes Lächeln**, pleased, delighted, smile; **sie war über die Nachricht sehr e.**, she was very pleased, glad, she was delighted, to hear it, to hear the news; **ich bin sehr e., daß er kommt**, I am very pleased, glad, that he is coming; **wir wären sehr e., wenn Sie uns besuchen könnten**, we would be very pleased, we would be delighted, it would give, afford, us great pleasure, if you could

visit us; (*on being introduced to s.o.*) (**sehr**) **e.!** pleased to meet you! **alles andere als e. sein**, to be anything but pleased; **wir waren nicht eben e.**, we were not exactly pleased; *adv.* **er sah uns e. an**, he looked at us delightedly.

erfreulich, *a.* pleasing; pleasant; **er hat erfreuliche Fortschritte gemacht**, he has made pleasing, gratifying, progress, good progress; **erfreulicher Anblick**, sight that pleases the eye, sight pleasing to the eye; **erfreuliche Nachrichten**, good news, welcome news; **eine erfreuliche Veränderung**, a pleasing, pleasant, nice, welcome, change; **das ist eine höchst erfreuliche Tatsache**, that is a most encouraging fact; **eine erfreuliche Erfahrung**, a pleasant experience; **eine erfreuliche Zunahme an Käufern**, a pleasing increase, an encouraging increase, a gratifying increase, in the number of buyers; **ein wenig erfreulicher Vorfall**, a not very nice, pleasant, edifying, incident; a disagreeable incident; **das ist sehr e.**, I am very pleased, glad, to hear that, about that; that is very gratifying; **was ich von seinem Lehrer hörte, war nicht sehr e.**, what his teacher told me was not very encouraging, not very satisfactory; **das Erfreulichste an der Sache ist, daß . . .**, the best, the most gratifying, thing about the matter is that . . . ; **ich kann leider nur wenig Erfreuliches über ihn sagen**, (i) I regret I can say nothing very agreeable about him; (ii) I'm afraid I can't say anything very encouraging about him.

erfreulicherweise, *adv.* **e. ging es ihm besser**, I was pleased, glad, to find him better; **e. hatten wir sogar noch Zeit, das Museum zu besichtigen**, to our great satisfaction, pleasure, we even had time to visit the museum; **e. hatten uns unsere Gastgeber sogar ein Radio zur Verfügung gestellt**, we were very pleased to find that our hosts had even put a radio at our disposal.

erfrieren. I. *v.* (*strong*) **1.** *v.i.* (*sein*) (*a*) (*of pers., animal*) to freeze to death; (*of plant*) to be killed by the frost, to be frostbitten, frost-nipped; **die Bergsteiger waren in der eisigen Kälte erfroren**, the climbers had frozen to death in the icy cold; **letztes Jahr ist unser Apfelbaum erfroren**, last year our apple-tree was killed by the frost; **alle unsere Rosen sind in einer Nacht erfroren**, the frost, the cold, killed all our roses in one night; *F:* **ich bin halb erfroren**, I'm frozen (to death), I'm freezing; **ich bin fast erfroren, während ich auf dich wartete**, I have got frozen waiting for you; **sie waren ganz erfroren, als sie endlich hier ankamen**, they were absolutely frozen when they finally arrived here; (*b*) (*of limb, nose, etc.*) to become frostbitten; **erfrorene Füße haben**, to have frostbitten feet, to have frostbite in one's feet; **er hatte drei erfrorene ¶Finger**, he had frostbite in three fingers, three of his fingers were frostbitten. **2.** *v.tr.* **sich** *dat.* **die Nase, die Füße, e.**, to get one's nose, one's feet, frostbitten; **er hat sich zwei Zehen erfroren**, two of his toes are frostbitten. **II.** *vbl s.* **1. Erfrieren**, *n. in vbl senses;* **Tod durch E.**, death by freezing. **2. Erfrierung**, *f.* (*a*)=II. 1; *also*: allgemeine **E.**, freezing; **örtliche E.**, frostbite; (*b*) *usu. pl.* **Erfrierungen**, injuries through frostbite; **er hatte schwere Erfrierungen an beiden Füßen**, he suffered from severe frostbite in both feet.

Erfrierungstod, *m.* death by freezing.

erfrischen. I. *v.tr.* (*of drink, rest, etc.*) to refresh (s.o.); to revive, reinvigorate (s.o.); **den Geist e.**, to refresh the mind; **sich e.**, to refresh oneself; **sich an einem, mit einem, Getränk e.**, to refresh oneself with a drink; **das Auge erfrischt sich an den grünen Wiesen und Wäldern**, the eye is refreshed by the green of the meadows and woods; **der Regen erfrischte die durstenden Felder**, the rain refreshed, freshened, the parched fields; **ich fühle mich erfrischt nach meinem Bad**, I feel refreshed after my bath; **sie kam sehr erfrischt aus den Ferien zurück**, she returned from her holiday very much refreshed, rested; **erfrischt aufwachen**, to awake refreshed, rested; **erfrischender Schlaf**, refreshing sleep; **ein erfrischendes Getränk**, a refreshing drink; **erfrischender Humor**, refreshing humour; **erfrischende Offenheit**, refreshing frankness; **erfrischende Naivität**, refreshing innocence. **II.** *vbl s.* **1. Erfrischen**, *n. in vbl senses; also*: refreshment. **2. Erfrischung**, *f.* (*a*)=II. 1; **zur E.**, for refreshment; as a refreshment; (*b*) refreshment, *esp.* refreshing drink; **eine E. zu sich nehmen**, to take some refreshment; to have sth. to drink; **Erfrischungen**, refreshments

(*at a dance, meeting, etc.*); **Erfrischungen wurden gereicht**, refreshments were handed round; refreshments were available; **der Verkauf von Erfrischungen ist sonntags erlaubt**, the sale of refreshments is permitted on Sundays.

Erfrischungshalle, *f.* refreshment room (at station, etc.); refreshment tent *or* stall (at fair, etc.).

Erfrischungsraum, *m.* refreshment room.

erfror, erfroren *see* **erfrieren**.

erfüllbar, *a.* (wish, promise, etc.) that can be fulfilled; **leicht, schwer, e.**, easily, not easily, fulfilled; **sein Wunsch ist leider nicht e.**, unfortunately his wish cannot be fulfilled.

erfüllen. I. *v.tr.* **1.** to fill; (*a*) **Kochdunst erfüllte das Haus**, an odour of cooking filled the house; **mit Rauch erfülltes Zimmer**, room filled with, full of, smoke; **sie erfüllten die Luft mit ihrem Geschrei**, they filled the air with their cries; (*b*) **die Nachricht erfüllte uns mit tiefer Trauer**, the news filled us with great sadness, the news distressed us deeply; **von tiefem Schmerz erfüllt sein**, to be grief-stricken; **er, sein Herz, war von Dankbarkeit erfüllt**, he, his heart, was filled with, was full of, gratitude; **von seiner eigenen Wichtigkeit erfüllt sein**, to be filled with, full of, one's own importance; **seine waghalsigen Experimente erfüllten sie mit Bewunderung**, his daring experiments filled them with admiration; **von Furcht, Schrecken, erfüllt**, filled with, full of, fear, horror; **von einer Idee erfüllt sein**, to be possessed with an idea; **er war ganz erfüllt von seinen Eindrücken, von seinen Erlebnissen**, he was filled with his impressions, his experiences. **2.** *Lit:* **sein Leben, seine Zeit, wird bald erfüllt sein**, his life, his time, is nearing its end; *B:* **oder Alte, die ihre Zeit nicht erfüllen**, nor an old man that hath not filled his days; **als die Zeit erfüllet war, sandte Gott seinen Sohn**, when the fullness of the time was come, God sent forth his Son; **denn meine Zeit ist noch nicht erfüllet**, for my time is not yet full come. **3.** (*a*) to fulfil, carry out, perform (promise, duty, etc.); to discharge (a duty, an obligation, etc.); to comply with, accede to (request, etc.); to fulfil, comply with (clause in contract, s.o.'s wishes, etc.); to fulfil, perform, implement (contract, etc.); to meet (requirements); to conform to, satisfy (condition, etc.); to satisfy (desire, etc.); **seine Pflicht e.**, to do, perform, fulfil, one's duty; **einen Auftrag e.**, to carry out a commission; to fulfil an order; to perform, carry out, a mission; **eine Bitte e.**, to comply with, fall in with, accede to, a request; to grant a request; **bereit, jeden Wunsch seines Herrn zu e.**, ready to comply with every wish of his master; **sein Wunsch erfüllte sich bald darauf**, his wish was fulfilled soon after that; **er hat sein Versprechen nicht erfüllt**, he has not fulfilled his promise, he has gone back on his promise; (*b*) to fulfil (prediction, dream, hopes, expectations, etc.); to answer, satisfy, come up to, be equal to (s.o.'s expectations); to make (prediction, dream, etc.) come true; **die Prophezeiung wurde erfüllt, erfüllte sich**, the prophecy was fulfilled, came true; **diese Hoffnung wird sich wohl niemals e.**, I doubt whether this hope will ever be realized; **die Maschine hat unsere Erwartungen nicht erfüllt**, the machine has not come up to our expectations, the machine fell short of (our) expectations; *B:* **dann wird erfüllet werden das Wort**, then shall be brought to pass the saying; (*c*) **seine Bestimmung e.**, (*of pers.*) to fulfil one's destiny; to fulfil oneself; (*of thg*) to fulfil its purpose, to answer, serve, its purpose; to serve the purpose in view; **ihr Buch hat seinen Zweck erfüllt: es hat die Leute zum Nachdenken bewegt**, her book has achieved its purpose: it has made people think; **es wird seinen Zweck schon e.**, it will serve its, the, purpose, it will serve; **der Mann hat seinen Zweck erfüllt, jetzt müssen wir ihn beseitigen**, the man has served our purpose, the man has served his purpose, now we must get rid of him. **II.** *vbl s.* **1. Erfüllen**, *n. in vbl senses*. **2. Erfüllung**, *f.* (*a*)=II. 1; *also*: fulfilment (of promise, duty, clause in contract, s.o.'s wishes, etc.); performance (of promise, duty, etc.); compliance (with clause in contract, s.o.'s wishes, etc.); discharge (of duty, obligation, etc.); performance, implementation (of contract, etc.); satisfaction (of condition, desire, etc.); **die E. seines Wunsches wird nicht leicht sein**, it will not be easy to fulfil his wish; **bei E. aller dieser Bedingungen**, if all these conditions are fulfilled, are complied with; **in der E. seiner Pflicht**, in the execution, discharge, of his duty;

Jur: Com: **effektive E.,** specific performance; **E. Zug um Zug,** contemporaneous, simultaneous, performance; **an Erfüllungs Statt,** in lieu of performance; (*b*) fulfilment (of prediction, desire, dream, etc.); realization (of hopes, etc.); **in E. gehen,** (*of prediction, wish, dream, etc.*) to be fulfilled, to come true; (*of hopes, etc.*) to be fulfilled, to be realized, to materialize; to come to fruition; **die Prophezeiung ging in E.,** the prophecy was fulfilled, came true; **sein Wunsch ging bald darauf in E.,** his wish was fulfilled soon after that; **diese Hoffnung wird wohl nie in E. gehen,** I doubt whether this hope will ever be realized; **die Geburt seines Sohnes brachte ihm die E. aller seiner Wünsche,** the birth of his son was the fulfilment of all his wishes; *B:* **so ist nun die Liebe des Gesetzes E.,** therefore love is the fulfilment of the law.

Erfülltheit, *f.* (state of) being filled (with an emotion, etc.); enthusiasm.

Erfüllung, *f., see* **erfüllen** II.

Erfüllungsanspruch, *m.* claim for performance (of a contract, etc.).

Erfüllungseid, *m. Jur:* suppletory oath, *Scot:* oath in supplement.

Erfüllungsgehilfe, *m. Jur:* (debtor's) agent.

erfüllungshalber, *adv. Com:* in order to discharge an obligation; *Jur:* **Hingabe e.,** dation in payment.

Erfüllungsort, *m. Com: Jur:* place of fulfilment *or* performance (of contract); place of payment, settlement (in financial transaction); place of delivery (of purchase).

Erfüllungspolitik, *f. Hist:* policy of unconditional fulfilment of the reparations clauses of the Versailles Treaty.

Erfüllungstag, *m. Com:* settlement day.

erfunden, *p.p & a. see* **erfinden.**

Erg[1], *m.* **-s/Äreg.** *Geog:* erg (of the Sahara).

Erg[2], *n.* **-s/-.** *Ph.Meas:* erg.

ergänzen. I. *v.tr.* to complement (sth.); to supplement (sth.); to complete (collection, etc.); to replenish (stores, wardrobe, etc.); to complete, finish (sentence, etc.); to supply (missing word, letter); to restore (mutilated statue, text, etc.); **einander e., sich e.,** to be complementary to one another; to form a whole; **die Streitkräfte wurden durch fünf deutsche Divisionen ergänzt,** the armed forces were supplemented by five German divisions; **diese Briefmarke ergänzte seine Sammlung französischer Kolonialmarken,** this stamp completed his collection of French colonial stamps; **die Nase ist in Gips ergänzt,** the nose has been restored in plaster; **die Statue ist falsch als Ceres ergänzt,** the statue has been incorrectly restored as Ceres; **Fragmente zu einer Gruppe der drei Grazien ergänzen,** to reconstruct a group of the three Graces from fragments; **die beiden Bände ergänzen einander,** the two volumes complement one another; **'wenn wir jetzt nicht bald gehen', begann sie, — 'dann kommen wir beide zu spät', ergänzte er,** 'if we don't go soon,' she started—'then we shall both be late,' he completed, finished, the sentence for her; *Geom:* **die Winkel ergänzen einander zu** (i) **90°,** (ii) **180°,** the angles are (i) complementary, (ii) supplementary; *F:* (*of married couple, etc.*) **sie ergänzen einander sehr gut,** they are a perfect complement to one another; **ergänzend,** complementary (colour, angle, etc.); **ergänzend möchte ich zu der Rede meines Kollegen nur noch sagen, daß . . . ,** there is just one thing left that I would like to add to my colleague's remarks, namely . . . ; *Gram:* **ergänzender Satz,** completive clause; **ergänzendes Element,** extension; complement; object; **ergänztes Element,** determinated element.

II. *vbl s.* **1. Ergänzen,** *n. in vbl senses.* **2. Ergänzung,** *f.* (*a*) *in vbl senses; also:* completion (of collection, sentence, etc.); replenishment (of stores, wardrobe, etc.); restoration (of mutilated statue, text, etc.); reconstruction (of statue, etc.) (from fragments); **er brauchte nur noch ein Bild zur E. seiner Sammlung,** he needed only one more picture to complete his collection; (*b*) completing part (of collection, etc.); supplement (to book, periodical, etc.); *Gram:* extension, complement; object; *Log:* complement (of logarithm); *Geom:* **E. eines Winkels,** (i) complement, (ii) supplement, of an angle; (*c*) restoration, restored part (of statue, text, etc.); reconstruction, reconstructed form (of group of statuary, etc.); **die Statue, der Text, weist mehrere moderne Ergänzungen auf,** the statue, the text, has been restored at several points in modern times.

Ergänzungsband, *m.* supplementary volume, supplement (to encyclopaedia, etc.).

Ergänzungseid, *m. Jur:* suppletory oath, *Scot:* oath in supplement.

Ergänzungseinheit, *f. Mil: A:* reserve training unit.

Ergänzungsfarbe, *f. Opt:* complementary colour.

Ergänzungsheft, *n.* supplementary issue (of periodical, etc.), supplement (to periodical, etc.); supplementary fascicle (of work published in parts).

Ergänzungsnährstoffe, *m.pl. Bio-Ch:* vitamins.

Ergänzungsoffizier, *m. Mil: A:* re-employed officer.

Ergänzungsparallelogramm, *n. Geom:* complement, completive parallelogram.

Ergänzungssatz, *m. Gram:* completive clause.

Ergänzungsstrich, *m. Print:* (abbreviating) dash.

Ergänzungswinkel, *m. Geom:* (i) complementary, (ii) supplemental, angle.

Ergänzungswort, *n.* **-(e)s/-wörter.** *Gram:* suppletory word.

Ergänzungszwillinge, *m.pl. Cryst:* mimetic twins, pseudo-symmetric twins.

ergattern, *v.tr. F:* to contrive to get hold of (sth.); **ich habe noch das letzte Stück Kuchen ergattert,** I managed to get, *F:* grab, the last piece of cake; **irgendwo hatten die Kinder ein altes Fahrrad ergattert,** somewhere the children had picked up, had unearthed, an old bicycle, the children had managed to get an old bicycle from somewhere; **sie hat sich endlich einen Mann ergattert,** at last she has managed to hook a man, to get herself a husband.

ergaunern, *v.tr. F:* to get (sth.) by trickery; **von einem gutgläubigen Händler ergaunerte er ein Auto,** he stung a trusting dealer for a car; **er hat zweitausend Pfund von ihr ergaunert,** he did her, tricked her, chiselled her, out of two thousand pounds; **das hat er alles ergaunert,** he got it all by trickery, *F:* he got it all on the crook.

ergeben, *v.* (*strong*) I. *v.tr.* (*of experiment, etc.*) to establish (fact, etc.); to show, prove (sth.); to result in (sth.); **Resultate e.,** to yield, show, results; **eine genaue Prüfung der Bücher ergab ein Defizit von 2000 Mark,** a close examination of the books showed, established, (that there was) a deficit of 2000 marks; **das ergibt insgesamt 10 Mark,** that amounts, comes, to 10 marks in all, that totals 10 marks; **die Untersuchung ergab, daß er einen Tumor hatte,** the examination showed, established, that he had a tumour; (*of fact, state of affairs, etc.*) **sich aus etwas e.,** to be the result, the consequence, of sth.; to arise out of, to spring from, sth.; to ensue from sth.; **die Rechnung ergab folgendes Resultat, aus der Rechnung ergab sich folgendes Resultat,** the calculation gave, yielded, showed, the following result; **die Dokumente ergaben seine Unschuld, aus den Dokumenten ergab sich seine Unschuld, ergab sich, daß er unschuldig war,** the documents established, proved, his innocence, established, showed, proved, that he was innocent; **daraus ergibt sich, daß . . . ,** it shows, establishes, that . . . ; hence it follows that . . . ; **aus dieser Sache werden sich Unannehmlichkeiten ergeben,** this matter will result in unpleasantness.

II. **sich ergeben. 1.** (*a*) to surrender (oneself); **sich dem Feind e.,** to surrender, yield, to the enemy; **sich auf Gnade und Ungnade e.,** to surrender unconditionally, to surrender at discretion; **die belagerte Stadt ergab sich nach drei Wochen,** after three weeks the beleaguered town surrendered; **ergib dich! ergebt euch!** surrender! hands up! (*b*) (*of woman*) **sich einem Mann e.,** to give, surrender, oneself to a man; **in jener Nacht ergab sie sich ihm,** that night she gave herself to him, she yielded to him. **2.** (*a*) **sich in sein Schicksal, sein Geschick, e.,** to resign oneself to one's fate; to commit oneself to, to throw oneself on, Providence; **sich in Gottes Willen e.,** to surrender oneself, resign oneself, to God's will; **sich in das Unvermeidliche e.,** to submit to the inevitable; (*b*) **sich etwas** *dat.* **e.,** to surrender oneself to, give oneself up to (vice, etc.); to become addicted to, take to (drink, etc.); **sich der Sünde e.,** to yield to sin; **er hatte sich dem Teufel ergeben,** he had sold himself, his soul, to the devil; **sich dem Trunk e.,** to take, become addicted, to drink; **sich dem Schlaf e.,** to surrender oneself to sleep.

III. *vbl s.* **Ergebung,** *f.* **1.** *Theol:* resignation, submissiveness; **E. in Gottes Willen,** resignation, submissiveness, to God's will. **2.** surrender.

IV. *p.p. & a.* **ergeben,** *in vbl senses; esp.* (*a*) resigned (to God's will, etc.); (*b*) addicted to, given to (drink, vice, etc.); **dem Trunk e. sein,** to be addicted, to have taken, to drink; (*c*) devoted, loyal (to s.o.); **j-m e. sein,** to be devoted to s.o.; **sie war ihrer Herrin treu e.,** she was devoted to her mistress; *adv.* **seinem Herrn e. dienen,** to serve one's master devotedly, with devotion; *Corr:* (*esp. Com. & Adm.*) (*usu. used by inferior to superior*) **Ihr (sehr) ergebener . . . , Ihr ergebenster . . . , ergebenst . . . ;** (*more formal*) **Ihr ganz ergebener . . . , ganz ergebenst . . . ,** (i) (*without previous acquaintance*) yours faithfully . . . , yours truly . . . , (ii) (*with personal acquaintance*) yours sincerely . . . ; *A:* **Ihr ergebener Diener . . . ,** your (most) obedient servant. . . .

Ergebenheit, *f.* (*a*) resignation, submissiveness (to God's will, etc.); (*b*) devotion, devotedness, loyalty (to s.o.).

Ergebnis, *n.* **-nisses/-nisse,** (*a*) result, outcome, effect (of an undertaking, etc.); **das E. unserer Bemühungen,** the outcome, effect, of our labours; **gute Ergebnisse erzielen, zeitigen,** to achieve good results; **günstiges E.,** favourable result, issue; **das E. war schlecht, ungünstig,** the result was unfavourable; **mageres E.,** poor result; **seine Schwäche ist das E. eines Unfalls,** his infirmity is the result of an accident; **das E. war, daß . . . ,** the result, effect, outcome, consequence, was that . . . ; **er hat gegen das Urteil Berufung eingelegt mit dem E., daß er jetzt noch mehr bezahlen muß,** he appealed against the decision with the result, effect, that he now has to pay even more; **zu einem E. kommen,** to arrive at, come to, a conclusion; **sie kamen zu dem E., daß der Plan unmöglich wäre,** they came to the conclusion that the plan was impossible; **die Ergebnisse bekanntgeben,** to announce, give out, the results (of a competition, elections, etc.); (*b*) *Mth: etc:* result; solution, answer; **das E. einer Addition heißt Summe,** the result of an addition is a sum; **Arithmetikbuch mit Ergebnissen,** arithmetic (book) with answers.

ergebnislos, *a.* unsuccessful, fruitless, vain; without result; **ergebnislose Bemühungen,** vain, fruitless, unsuccessful, efforts; **die Verhandlungen waren e.,** the negotiations were unsuccessful; **die Suche blieb e.,** the search was unsuccessful, was in vain.

ergebnisreich, *a.* fruitful, successful (research, experiment, etc.).

Ergebung, *f. see* **ergeben** III.

ergehen. I. *v.i.* (*strong*) (*sein*) **1.** (*of decree, etc.*) to be issued; **Einladungen sind an alle Mitglieder ergangen,** invitations have been issued, sent, to all members; **ein Aufruf erging an die Bevölkerung der Stadt,** an appeal was made to the population of the town; **an alle Soldaten erging der Befehl, sich einsatzbereit zu halten,** an order was sent out, was issued, given, to all soldiers to stand by; **eine Verordnung e. lassen,** to issue a decree; **an ihn ist ein Ruf an die Universität X ergangen,** he has been offered a professorship, a chair, at X university. **2. Gnade für Recht, Gnade vor Recht, e. lassen,** to be lenient, to show leniency; **dieses Mal werde ich noch einmal Gnade für Recht e. lassen,** this time I will deal leniently, I will be lenient, with you. **3. etwas über sich** *acc.* **e. lassen,** to suffer sth. (passively, without protest); **er ließ ihre Schmähungen über sich e.,** he suffered her abuse without protest; **j-s Liebkosungen über sich e. lassen,** to suffer s.o.'s caresses (passively); **sie mußte seinen Zorn, seinen Zornesausbruch, über sich e. lassen,** she had to suffer, bear, his fury; **wir mußten ihren Redeschwall über uns e. lassen,** we had to submit to the torrent of her words; **er ließ alles geduldig über sich e.,** he suffered everything patiently. **4.** *impers.* **es ist ihr gut ergangen,** things, everything, went well with her; **wie wird es ihm dort wohl e.?** I wonder how it will, how things will, go with him there, how it will fare with him there, how he will get on there; **es ist ihm sehr schlecht ergangen,** things did not go well with him; he has had a bad time; **er erzählte ihnen, wie es ihm im Ausland ergangen war,** he told them how he had fared abroad, he told them about his life, his experiences, abroad; **wie ist er dir bei der Prüfung ergangen?** how did you get on, fare in, the examination? *U.S. & F:* how did you make out in the exam? **es wird ihm schlecht e., wenn er sich nicht zusammennimmt,** it will go hard with him if he does not pull himself together; **wenn du versagst, wird es dir schlecht e.,** if you fail, it will go hard with you; *B:* **auf daß es dir wohl ergehe und du lange lebest auf Erden,** that it fare well with thee and that thy days may be long upon the earth. **5. sich ergehen,** (*a*) *Lit:* to

take a walk; **nach dem Mahl ergingen sie sich im Garten,** after the meal they took a stroll, they strolled, in the garden; (*b*) **sich in einer langen Rede, in langen Reden, über etwas** *acc.* **e.,** to hold forth at length about sth., to expatiate (up)on sth.; **sie erging sich in Schmähungen,** she let forth, broke out into, a stream of abuse; **er erging sich in Lobpreisungen über das Bild,** he was profuse in his praise of the picture, he praised the picture profusely; **sich in Dankesbezeugungen e.,** to thank s.o. profusely, to be profuse in one's gratitude, to express one's gratitude in most profuse terms; **sich in lauten Beteuerungen seiner Unschuld e.,** to make loud protestations of one's innocence; **er erging sich in begeisterten Schilderungen der schönen Landschaft,** he gave enthusiastic descriptions of the beautiful landscape, he enthused, went into raptures, about the beautiful landscape.

II. *vbl s.* **Ergehen,** *n.* condition; **ich weiß nichts über sein E.,** I don't know how he is, how things are going with him, how he is faring, how he is getting on; **er erzählte ihnen von seinem E. im Ausland,** he told them how he had fared abroad, he told them about his life, his experiences, abroad.

ergetzen, ergetzlich. *A:* = **ergötzen, ergötzlich.**

ergiebig, *a.* productive (soil, mine, tree, etc.); rich, fertile (soil, etc.); rich (mine, source, etc.); abundant, plentiful (source, etc.); **ergiebige Ernte,** plentiful, rich, bounteous, bountiful, harvest; **auf eine ergiebige Ölquelle stoßen,** to strike a rich source of oil; **er hat in seinem Vater eine ergiebige Geldquelle,** in his father he has a plentiful source of money.

Ergiebigkeit, *f.* productiveness (of soil, mine, tree, etc.); fertility (of soil, etc.); richness (of soil, mine, source, etc.); abundance (of source, etc.).

ergießen (sich), *v.refl.* (*strong*) (*of water, etc.*) to pour, flow (into sth., over sth.); **der Wein ergoß sich über das Tischtuch,** the wine flowed all over the tablecloth; **der Eimer kippte um, und das Wasser ergoß sich über seine Schuhe,** the bucket tipped over and all the water poured over his shoes; **Fluß, der sich ins Meer ergießt,** river that pours, flows, into the sea; **helle Röte ergoß sich über ihre Wangen,** a blush spread to her cheeks, came, rose, to her cheeks; **sein Zorn ergoß sich über sie, über ihr Haupt,** he let loose his fury upon her, upon her head, his fury vented itself upon her.

erglänzen, *v.i.* (*sein*) to (begin to) gleam, glisten, shine; **die ersten Sterne erglänzten am Himmel,** the first stars glistened, sparkled, in the sky; **hell e.,** to shine brightly.

erglimmen, *v.i.* (*strong*) (*sein*) (*of fire, light, etc.*) to (begin to) glimmer, to glow; (*of light, dying fire, etc.*) to flicker up; **ein Streichholz erglomm in der Dunkelheit,** a match flickered up in the darkness.

erglühen, *v.i.* (*sein*) to (begin to) glow; **der Horizont erglühte in der untergehenden Sonne,** the horizon glowed in the setting sun; **mit erglühenden Wangen sah sie ihn an,** she looked at him with a blush rising in her cheeks; **er erglühte vor Scham,** he blushed with shame; **er erglühte in Liebe zu ihr,** his heart was afire with love for her.

ergo [ˈɛrgoː]. *Lt.conj.* ergo, therefore.

Ergostat [ɛrgoˑˈstaːt], *m* -(e)s/-en. *Med:* ergostat.

Ergosterin [ɛrgoˑsteˑˈriːn], *n.* -s/. *Ch:* ergosterol, ergosterine.

Ergotamin [ɛrgoˑtaˑˈmiːn], *n.* -s/. *Ch:* ergotamine.

Ergotin [ɛrgoˑˈtiːn], *n.* -s/. *Pharm:* ergotine.

Ergotismus [ɛrgoˑˈtismus], *m.* -/. *Med:* ergotism, ergotic poisoning.

ergötzen. I. *v.tr.* (*a*) *Lit:* to divert, delight (company, audience, etc.); to edify (company, etc.); **das Auge, das Ohr, e.,** to delight, please, the eye, the ear; **sich an etwas** *dat.* **e.,** to take a delight in sth.; (*b*) to amuse (s.o.); to entertain, divert (s.o.); to delight (s.o.); **der kleine Affe ergötzte die Zuschauer mit seinen Kunststücken,** the little monkey amused, delighted, the audience, the little monkey kept the audience amused, with his antics; **sich an etwas** *dat.* **e.,** to be amused, entertained, by sth.; **sie ergötzte sich an meiner Verwirrung,** she was amused by my confusion.

II. *vbl s.* **Ergötzen** *n.*, **Ergötzung** *f.* amusement, delight; delectation; **zu unserem Ergötzen, zu unserer Ergötzung,** to our amusement, to our delight; **zum Ergötzen der Kinder lief der Hund auf zwei Beinen,** to the amusement, delight, of the children the dog walked on two legs; **zum großen Ergötzen der Gesellschaft,** to the great amusement, much to the entertainment, of the company.

ergötzlich, *a.* (*a*) *Lit:* diverting; *Lit:* delectable; *A:* edifying; (*b*) amusing; entertaining, diverting; delightful; *Hum:* delectable; **es war ein ergötzlicher Anblick,** it was an amusing, a delightful, sight, it was amusing to see; it was a pleasing sight; **die Kunststücke des kleinen Affen waren höchst e.,** the antics of the little monkey were highly entertaining, most amusing.

Ergötzlichkeit, *f. Lit:* delectableness.

ergrauen, *v.i.* (*sein*) (*of pers., of the hair*) to go, grow, grey, *U.S:* gray; (*of the hair*) to turn grey; to be touched with grey; **er ist schon früh ergraut,** he has gone grey very early; **sein Haar ist an den Schläfen ergraut,** his hair has gone grey at the temples; **ergrauendes Haar,** greying hair, hair growing, going, turning, grey; (*of pers., F: of thg*) **in Ehren ergraut sein,** to have seen long service; (*of pers.*) **im Dienst e.,** to grow old in service.

ergreifen. I. *v.tr.* (*strong*) **1.** (*a*) to seize, grasp (s.o., sth.); to lay hold, take hold, catch hold, of (s.o., sth.); to capture, seize (thief, etc.); **j-s Hand e., j-n bei der Hand e.,** to take hold of, grasp, s.o.'s hand; to take s.o. by the hand; **ich ergriff ihn beim Arm,** I grasped his arm, I seized him by the arm; **die Feder e.,** to take up one's pen (to write); **er ergriff sein Schwert,** he seized his sword; **sie ergriffen den Dieb und übergaben ihn der Polizei,** they seized, held, captured, the thief and handed him over to the police; **die Flammen ergriffen die Kirche, die Kirche wurde von den Flammen ergriffen,** the flames, the fire, caught the church; **die Zügel der Regierung e.,** to assume, take up, the reins of government; (*b*) to grasp, seize (opportunity, etc.); to take (measures, precautions, etc.); to take (possession of sth.); to seize (power); to take up (profession, etc.); **die Flucht e.,** to take flight, to flee, *F:* to take to one's heels; **die Diebe ergriffen die Flucht,** the thieves fled; **die Gelegenheit e., etwas zu tun,** to take the opportunity to do, of doing, sth.; **die Gelegenheit beim Schopf e.,** to take time by the forelock; to seize, grasp, avail oneself of, snatch at, the opportunity (to do sth.); **ich möchte diese Gelegenheit e., Ihnen für Ihre Gastfreundschaft zu danken,** I would like to take this opportunity to thank you for your hospitality; **für j-n Partei e., j-s Partei e.,** to take s.o.'s side, s.o.'s part, to take sides, to side, with s.o.; to stand up, *F:* stick up, for s.o.; **das Wort e.,** to begin to speak; (*at public meeting*) to take the floor; **nachdem der Präsident gesprochen hatte, ergriff Herr X das Wort,** after the president had spoken, Mr X rose, got up, to speak, made a speech. **2.** (*of fear, desire, etc.*) to seize, overcome (s.o.); **Furcht, Angst, ergriff sie, sie wurde von Furcht, Angst, ergriffen,** she was seized, overcome, with fear; **wilde Begeisterung ergriff die Menge,** the crowd was moved to wild enthusiasm, wild enthusiasm gripped the crowd. **3.** (*of speech, spectacle, etc.*) to move (s.o.); **ihre Geschichte hat ihn sehr ergriffen, er war sehr von ihrer Geschichte ergriffen,** her story moved him deeply, he was very much moved by her story; **der Film ergreift mich jedesmal von neuem, ich finde den Film jedesmal von neuem ergreifend,** I am always moved by the film, the film moves me, every time I see it; **eine ergreifende Geschichte,** a moving tale; **mit ergreifenden Worten schilderte er die Not dieser Leute,** in moving words he described the plight of these people; **von etwas ergriffen sein,** to be moved, touched, affected (with emotion), by sth.; **tief ergriffen sein,** to be deeply moved, touched, affected; **die Musik ergriff ihn so sehr, er war von der Musik so sehr ergriffen, daß ihm die Tränen kamen,** he was moved to tears by the music, the music moved him to tears; **wir waren von dem Anblick sehr ergriffen,** we were overcome with emotion, deeply moved, at the sight; *adv.* **ergriffen lauschten wir seinen Worten, der Musik,** deeply moved we listened to his words, to the music.

II. *vbl s.* **Ergreifen** *n.*, **Ergreifung** *f. in vbl senses; also:* seizure, capture (of criminal, etc.); seizure (of power).

ergriffen, *p.p. & a. see* **ergreifen** I. 3.

Ergriffenheit, *f.* emotion; **in tiefer E.,** overcome with emotion, deeply moved, deeply touched.

ergrimmen, *v.i.* (*sein*) *Lit:* to become angry, furious.

ergründbar, *a.* = **ergründlich.**

ergründen, *v.tr.* to fathom, sound (abyss, mystery, etc.); to penetrate (sth.); to get to the bottom, the root, of (mystery, matter, etc.); **ein Geheimnis e.,** to fathom a secret; **eine Sache e.,** to get to the bottom, the root, the core, of a matter; **etwas zu e. (ver)suchen,** to probe into sth., to examine sth.; to go deeply, thoroughly, into sth.; **er versuchte, das Rätsel zu e.,** he tried to fathom the mystery, he tried to get to the bottom of the mystery; **die Vergangenheit zu e. versuchen,** to probe into the past; **das menschliche Herz zu e. versuchen,** to probe deeply into the human heart.

ergründlich, *a.* (mystery, etc.) that can be fathomed; **nicht e.,** unfathomable, unsoundable (sea, etc.); unfathomable (abyss, mystery, etc.).

Erguß, *m.* **1.** flowing, pouring (of water, etc.); outpouring, outburst (of thoughts, feelings, etc.); *Med:* extravasation, effusion (of blood); *Physiol:* ejaculation (of semen). **2.** (*a*) flow (of water, words, etc.); flood (of tears, abuse, etc.); effusion (of emotions, etc.); outpourings (of the heart); **E. von Schmähungen,** outburst, torrent, of abuse; **wir mußten ihren E., ihre Ergüsse, über uns ergehen lassen,** we had to submit to the torrent of her words; **welcher E.!** what a flood of words! what an outburst! (*b*) *Med:* contusion; haematoma; bruise.

Ergußgestein, *n. Geol:* eruptive rock.

erhaben, *a.* **1.** raised, elevated, embossed (letter, figure, etc.); anaglyptic (print); (*of figure, etc.*) **e. sein,** to stand out in relief; **erhabene Arbeit,** raised work; embossed work; work in relief; **erhabene Stellen auf der Haut,** raised marks on the skin. **2.** (*a*) sublime, lofty, exalted (thoughts, etc.); exalted, uplifted (state of mind, etc.); lofty, noble (style, etc.); **ein erhabener Anblick,** a noble, magnificent, sight; **erhabenes Gefühl,** exalted, uplifted, feeling, feeling of exaltation; **das Erhabene,** the sublime; **vom Erhabenen zum Lächerlichen ist (es) nur ein Schritt,** it is but one step from the sublime to the ridiculous; (*b*) **über etwas** *acc.* **e. sein,** to be above sth.; to be superior to sth.; **über jede Kritik e.,** above criticism; **über alles Lob e.,** beyond all praise; **über allen Zweifel e.,** beyond doubt; **du mußt zeigen, daß du über Vorurteile e. bist,** you must show yourself (to be) above prejudice; **über Schmeicheleien e. sein,** to be superior to, to be above, flattery; **über jeden Verdacht (hoch) e. sein,** to be above (all) suspicion; to be beyond the reach of calumny; **er ist über jede Heuchelei e.,** he is above deception; **sie ist über solch kleinliche Dinge hoch e.,** she is above petty things like that, (i) petty things like that cannot touch, affect, her, (ii) she would not do, stoop to, petty things like that; **ich bin über so etwas (hoch) e.,** I am above doing that, I would not lower, abase, myself by doing that.

Erhabenheit, *f.* **1.** *Art:* elevation, (standing out in) relief (of figure, letter, etc.). **2.** (*a*) sublimity, loftiness (of thoughts, etc.); grandeur (of spectacle, etc.); nobility (of character, thoughts, etc.); (*b*) superiority (over sth.); **du mußt deine E. über Vorurteile zeigen,** you must show yourself (to be) above prejudice.

Erhalt, *m.* -(e)s/. receipt (of letter, goods, order, etc.); *Com:* **den E. einer Sendung bestätigen,** to acknowledge receipt of a consignment.

erhaltbar, *a.* **1.** capable of being preserved, maintained. **2.** = **erhältlich.**

Erhaltbarkeit, *f.* preservability.

erhalten. I. *v.tr.* (*strong*) **1.** to receive, get (letter, salary, gift, news, answer, etc.); **jedes Kind erhielt einen Apfel,** every child received, got, was given, an apple; **sie erhielt den dritten Preis,** she won, received, got, the third prize; **ich erhielt noch kein Gehalt,** I did not yet get a salary, I was not yet in receipt of a salary; **etwas von j-m e.,** to receive, get, sth. from s.o., to be given sth. by s.o.; **(die) Erlaubnis e., etwas zu tun,** to get, obtain, permission to do sth.; **Bescheid e.,** to be informed (of sth.); *Corr:* **ich habe Ihren Brief vom 8. Mai erhalten,** I have received your letter, *Com:* I am in receipt of your letter, of 8th May; **sein Teil e.,** to get what is due to one; to get one's share; **bei der Taufe erhielt er den Namen Johannes,** he was christened John, he was given the name John; **nach der Bemalung erhalten die Vasen noch eine Glasur,** after being painted the vases are glazed; **das Abendmahl e.,** to receive communion, to receive the sacrament; **Besuch e.,** to have a visitor, visitors; **er erhielt drei Tage Urlaub,** he was given, granted, three days' leave; **Genugtuung e.,** to get satisfaction (for an insult, etc.). **2.** (*a*) to keep (s.o.); to support (s.o.) (financially); **er muß seine Frau und drei Kinder**

e., he has to support a wife and three children; **er verdient nicht genug, um sich selbst zu e.**, he does not earn, get, enough to keep, support, himself, to live (up)on; **in seinem Alter müßte er sich selbst e. können**, at his age he should be able to keep, support, himself; (*b*) to keep, protect (s.o.); to keep, preserve, maintain (health, strength, etc.); **Gotte erhalte dich!** God keep you! **Gott wird uns e.**, God will keep us; **j-n in der Gefahr e.**, to keep s.o. safe in a time of peril; **sich gesund e.**, to keep well, fit; to keep in good health, to keep up one's health; **j-n am Leben e.**, to keep s.o. alive; **trotz seiner schweren Verwundungen konnte er am Leben erhalten werden**, despite his terrible wounds he survived, he was saved; **erhalte dir deine Kräfte, erhalte dich bei Kräften**, keep up, preserve, your strength; **sich durch Schwimmen jung e.**, to keep young by swimming; **erhalte dir deinen Mut!** keep up your courage! **wir werden versuchen, ihn bei guter Laune zu e.**, we shall try to keep him in a good mood; (*c*) to preserve, take care of (building, furniture, etc.); to preserve, conserve (ancient monument, etc.); to keep, maintain, retain (rights, situation, etc.); to maintain, keep (up) (temperature, etc.); to conserve (energy, etc.); (*of thg*) to keep, retain (shape, etc.); **einen alten Brauch e.**, to keep up an old custom; **der Frieden muß auf jeden Fall erhalten werden**, the peace must be kept, maintained, at all cost; **die Straßen in gutem Zustand e.**, to maintain, keep, the streets in good condition; **ein Haus in gutem baulichen Zustand e.**, to keep a house in good repair; **die Fresken in dem Saal sollen beim Umbau nach Möglichkeit erhalten bleiben**, if possible, it is hoped to keep, save, the frescoes in the hall when it is rebuilt; **leider hat sich keine Handschrift dieses Werkes erhalten**, unfortunately, no manuscript of this work has come down to us, has survived; **die Temperatur muß gleichmäßig erhalten werden**, an even temperature must be maintained; *cp.* **aufrechterhalten.**

II. *vbl s.* **Erhaltung,** *f. in vbl senses; also:* **1.** (*a*) (financial) support, maintenance (of family, parents, etc.); protection (of s.o., s.o.'s life, etc.); (*b*) maintenance (of streets, building, even temperature, etc.); preservation (of building, work of art, health, etc.); retention (of custom, situation, etc.); **zur E. des Friedens**, in order to preserve, maintain, peace; *Ph:* **E. der Energie, der Kraft**, conservation of energy, of force. **2. Zustand der E.**, state of preservation (of building, work of art, etc.).

III. *p.p. & a.* **erhalten,** *in vbl senses; esp.* (*a*) (*of building, work of art, etc.*) surviving; (*of pers.*) alive; **e. bleiben**, (*of pers., building, work of art, etc.*) to survive; **nur zwei ihrer fünf Kinder blieben ihnen e.**, only two of their five children survived; **von den drei Kirchen der Stadt blieb nur eine e.**, of the three churches in the town only one remained undamaged, only one survived; **nur wenige Gemälde dieses großen Künstlers sind uns e. geblieben**, only a few paintings by this great artist have survived; **die wenigen erhaltenen altchristlichen Handschriften**, the few surviving early Christian manuscripts; (*b*) **gut, schlecht, e. sein,** (*of building, car, etc.*) to be in good, poor, condition; (*of building*) to be in good repair, to be in a poor state of repair; (*of archaeological find, etc.*) to be well, badly, preserved, to be in good, poor, condition; **das Fahrrad war sehr gut e., in sehr gut erhaltenem Zustand**, the bicycle was in very good condition; **sehr gut erhaltener Mantel**, coat in very good condition; **bei den Ausgrabungen wurden mehrere bestens erhaltene Statuen gefunden**, during the excavations several very well preserved statues, several statues in excellent condition, were found; **das Gemälde war nicht sehr gut, war schlecht, e.**, the painting was not in very good condition, was in poor condition, was not very well preserved, was badly preserved, was not in a good state of preservation.

erhaltenswert, *a.* (*of ancient monument, painting, etc.*) worthy of preservation.

Erhalter, *m.* **-s/-**, (*a*) (*God*) preserver; protector, guardian; (*b*) bread-winner, supporter, maintainer (of a family, etc.).

erhältlich, *a.* obtainable; (goods, etc.) that can be bought, obtained; **schwer erhältlicher Artikel**, article that is difficult to buy, to get, article that is not easily obtainable; **Fahrpläne sind am Schalter e.**, timetables can be obtained, bought, at the counter; **'Prospekte hier e.'**, 'prospectuses sold here', 'get your prospectus here'; **'X-Schuhe hier e.'**, 'X shoes stocked here', 'X shoes sold here'.

Erhaltung, *f. see* **erhalten II.**

Erhaltungsfutter, *n. Husb:* maintenance ration (of fodder).

Erhaltungshaus, *n. Hort:* conservatory.

Erhaltungstrieb, *m.* instinct of self-preservation; will to survive.

Erhaltungszustand, *m.* state of preservation (of building, work of art, etc.).

erhandeln, *v.tr. Lit:* to get (sth.) by bargaining; to buy (sth.); **sich** *dat.* **eine Frau e.**, to buy oneself a wife.

erhängen. I. *v.tr.* (*weak*) to hang (s.o., oneself); **als Pirat erhängt werden**, to be hanged for a pirate; **er erhängte sich aus Verzweiflung**, he hanged himself out of despair; **er wurde an einem Laternenpfahl erhängt**, he was hanged, *F:* strung up, on a lamp-post; **Erhängte** *m, f,* person who has been hanged *or* who has hanged himself.

II. *vbl s.* **1. Erhängen,** *n.* hanging (of criminal, etc.); execution (of s.o.) by hanging; **Tod durch E.**, death by hanging, death on the gallows; **Selbstmord durch E. verüben**, to hang oneself, to commit suicide by hanging oneself. **2. Erhängung,** *f.* (*a*)=II. 1; (*b*) **mehrere Erhängungen fanden dort statt**, several people were hanged there, several executions by hanging took place, were carried out, there.

erharten, *v.* **1.** *v.i.* (*sein*)=**erhärten** I. 2. **2.** *v.tr. occ.*=**erhärten** I. 1.

erhärten. I. *v.* **1.** *v.tr.* (*a*) to harden (sth.), to make (sth.) hard; to indurate (sth.); *Metall:* to harden (steel); to chill (casting, etc.); **die Muskeln e.**, to harden the muscles; **Alkohol erhärtet die Blutgefäße**, alcohol hardens the blood-vessels; (*b*) **eine Aussage eidlich, durch einen Eid, e.**, to take an oath that one's evidence is true, to swear to one's evidence; **seine Meinung durch Tatsachen e.**, to strengthen, reinforce, substantiate, one's opinion by facts. **2.** *v.i.* (*sein*) to harden, to grow, become, get, hard; to indurate; (*of clay, etc.*) to become indurated; (*of cement, etc.*) to harden; to set; (*of tissue, etc.*) to harden; to ossify.

II. *vbl s.* **Erhärten** *n.*, **Erhärtung** *f. in vbl senses; also:* induration (of clay, etc.); ossification (of tissue, etc.); *Metall:* **Prozeß zur Erhärtung**, hardening process.

Erhärtungseid, *m. Jur:* oath taken on one's evidence.

Erhärtungsprozeß, *m. Metall:* hardening process.

erhaschen, *v.tr.* (*a*) to catch (s.o., sth.); **sie konnte ihn gerade noch beim Hemdenzipfel e.**, she just managed to catch hold of him by the tail of his shirt; (*b*) to catch, meet (s.o.'s eye, s.o.'s glance); **er versuchte, einen Blick von ihr zu e.**, he tried to catch a glance from her, he tried to catch her eye.

erheben. I. *v.tr.* (*strong*) **1.** (*a*) to raise, lift (up) (an arm, the eyes, etc.); **sein Glas an die Lippen e.**, to raise one's glass to one's lips; **er erhob den Kopf**, he raised (up) his head; **seine Augen, den Blick, zu j-m e.**, to raise one's eyes to s.o., to look up at s.o.; **er erhob die Hand zum Gruß**, he raised his hand in a salute; **seine Hände zum Himmel e.**, to raise (up), lift up, one's hands to heaven; **die Hand gegen j-n e.**, to raise, lift, one's hand against s.o., to offer to strike s.o.; **mit erhobenen Händen**, with hands raised; **mit hoch erhobenem Kopfe**, with head held high, erect; *F:* **j-n in den Himmel e.**, to laud, praise, s.o. to the skies; (*b*) to raise, promote (s.o.); to elevate (s.o.); **j-n zur Macht e.**, to raise s.o. to power; **j-n auf den Thron e.**, to put, seat, install, s.o. on the throne; **j-n in einen höheren Rang e.**, to raise, elevate, s.o. to a higher rank; **j-n in den Adelsstand e.**, to raise s.o. to noble rank, to ennoble s.o.; (*in England*) to raise s.o. to the peerage; to knight s.o.; **eine Baronie zum Herzogtum e.**, to erect a barony into a dukedom; **die Osteopathie in die Reihe der medizinischen Wissenschaften e.**, to accept osteopathy as one of the medical sciences; to recognize osteopathy as (having the status of) a medical science; *Hist:* **j-n auf den Schild e.**, to raise s.o. on a shield (and thereby acknowledge him as leader); (*c*) *Mth:* **eine Zahl zur dritten Potenz e.**, to raise a number to the third power, to cube a number; **eine Zahl zur zweiten Potenz e.**, to square a number; **drei zur vierten Potenz erhoben**, three raised to the fourth power, three to the fourth; (*d*) to edify (s.o.); **den Geist e.**, to elevate, edify, the mind; **dieser Anblick muß jeden e.**, this sight must have an edifying, uplifting, effect on everyone; **erhebend,** edifying (sermon, book, sight, etc.); heart-warming, uplifting (sight, etc.); **dieser erhebende Anblick**, this edifying sight; this exalting, magnificent, sight; this stirring sight; **erhebendes Gefühl**, feeling of exaltation; **erhebende Feier**, solemn ceremony; moving ceremony; (*e*) **einen Vorschlag zum Beschluß e.**, to adopt a proposal as a resolution; **wir wollen diesen Spruch zu unserem Motto e.**, we shall adopt this proverb as our motto, we shall make this proverb our motto. **2.** (*a*) to raise (an objection, etc.); to make, put in, put forward (claim, etc.); to bring (case); to make (accusation, etc.); **seine Stimme e.**, to lift up one's voice; to (begin to) speak, to speak up; **keiner erhob seine Stimme**, nobody spoke (up); **mit erhobener Stimme**, with raised voice, in a raised voice; **sie erhoben ein großes Geschrei**, they set up a loud shout; they raised a great cry; **Protest e.**, to make, set up, a protest; **gegen etwas Einspruch e.**, to raise an objection to sth., to object to sth.; to lodge an objection to sth.; **gegen etwas keinen Einspruch e.**, to make no objection to, against, sth.; **Anspruch auf etwas** *acc.* **e.**, to lay claim to sth., to claim sth.; to make, put in, a claim for sth.; **Zweifel** *pl*, **Bedenken** *pl*, **an etwas** *dat.* **e.**, to raise doubts about sth.; **eine falsche Beschuldigung gegen j-n e.**, to bring a false accusation against s.o.; *see also* **Klage**; (*b*) to levy, impose (tax, toll, etc.); to make (monetary charge, etc.); to charge (fee); to collect (data); **eine Steuer auf Zucker e.**, to impose a tax on sugar; **eine kleine Gebühr soll für die Benutzung des Parkplatzes erhoben werden**, a small charge is to be made for the use of the car park. **3. sich erheben,** (*a*) (*of pers.*) to rise, to get up; (i) to get up, rise (from sitting, lying, position), to raise oneself (from lying position); (ii) *Lit:* to get up (from bed); to rise; **sich früh e.**, to rise, get up, early; **er hatte sich erst spät erhoben**, he had not got up till late; **sich vom Stuhl e.**, to get up, rise, from the chair; **als er eintrat, erhoben wir uns**, when he entered we rose to our feet, we stood up; **der Vorsitzende erhob sich, und alle schwiegen**, the chairman rose to his feet, got up, and all were silent; **er erhob sich mühsam vom Boden und schüttelte den Staub von seinen Kleidern**, he got up painfully from the ground and shook the dust from his clothes; **bei ihrem Eintritt hatten sich alle Gäste erhoben**, all the guests had risen, got to their feet, when she entered; (*b*) (*of hill, tower, etc.*) to rise; **Bäume, die sich dreißig Meter hoch über die Ebene erheben**, trees rising thirty metres above the plain; **in der Ferne erhebt sich ein Schloß**, a castle rises in the distance; **hinter den Häusern erhebt sich das Gebirge**, behind the houses the mountains rise up; **das Gebirge erhebt sich hier zu beträchtlicher Höhe**, the mountains rise here to a considerable height; (*c*) (*of wind, etc.*) to rise, to spring up; (*of question, difficulty, quarrel, etc.*) to arise; **ein Sturm erhob sich**, a storm arose; **eine leichte Brise erhob sich**, a light breeze sprang up; **es erhebt sich die Frage, ob . . .**, the question arises, crops up, whether . . . ; **ein lautes Geschrei erhob sich**, there arose a great cry, loud shouting, loud shouts; **ein Murmeln, ein Streit, erhob sich**, a murmur, a quarrel, arose; **lautes Gelächter erhob sich, als er geendet hatte**, there was a shout, a burst, of laughter when he had ended; **ein Zweifel erhob sich in ihm**, a doubt arose, sprang up, in his mind; (*d*) (*of people*) to rise (in revolt, in rebellion); to revolt (**gegen j-n**, against s.o.); **das ganze Volk erhob sich gegen den Tyrannen**, the whole country rose against the tyrant; (*e*) **sich über etwas** *acc.* **e.**, to rise above sth.; **er versucht immer, sich über andere zu e.**, he always tries to be superior to others; **sich über die Versuchung e.**, to rise above, to rise superior to, temptation; **dieser Film erhebt sich nicht über das Gewöhnliche**, this film does not rise above the ordinary; *cp.* **erhaben** 2 (*b*).

II. *vbl s.* **1. Erheben,** *n. in vbl senses.* **2. Erhebung,** *f.* (*a*) *in vbl senses; also:* promotion, elevation (to higher rank, etc.); imposition (of a tax, etc.); **seine E. in den Adelsstand**, his elevation to the nobility; (*b*) rise in the ground; high ground; elevation; eminence; **die Bergkette steigt bei X zu ihrer höchsten E. an**, the range rises to its highest elevation at X; **der Brocken ist die höchste E. im Harz**, the Brocken is the highest elevation, the highest mountain, in the Harz; **eine E. schränkte die Aussicht ein**, rising ground, a rise in the ground, limited the view; **Kirche, die auf einer E. steht**, church

standing on a rise, on high ground, on an eminence; (*c*) elevation (of mind); uplift (of the soul); (*d*) revolt, rising (of a people); uprising; (*e*) *pl.* **Erhebungen,** enquiries; **Erhebungen über etwas** *acc.* **anstellen,** to make enquiries about sth.; to hold an inquiry into sth.

erheblich. 1. *a.* considerable, important, large (sum, etc.); considerable, large (quantity, etc.); handsome (sum, fortune, dowry, etc.); substantial (increase, etc.); considerable, extensive (damage); *Lit:* goodly (fortune, etc.); *F:* sizeable, tidy (sum, fortune, etc.); **Schäden von erheblichem Ausmaß, erhebliche Schäden,** considerable, extensive, damage; **erhebliche Schulden,** heavy debts. **2.** *adv.* **e.,** *adv.phr.* **um ein erhebliches,** considerably; **die Unfallsziffer ist e., um ein erhebliches, gestiegen,** the accident rate has risen considerably.

Erheblichkeit, *f.* importance, considerable size (of sum, fortune, etc.); extensiveness, considerable extent (of damage).

Erhebung, *f. see* **erheben** II.

erheischen, *v.tr.* to demand (sth.); **die Ehre erheischt (es), daß wir ablehnen,** honour demands that we should refuse.

erheitern. I. *v.tr.* to amuse, entertain (s.o.); **sich e.,** to become gay, cheerful; to cheer up; **ihre Aufregung schien ihn zu e.,** her excitement seemed to amuse him; **ein erheitertes Lächeln,** an amused smile.

II. *vbl s.* **1. Erheitern,** *n. in vbl senses.* **2. Erheiterung,** *f.* (*a*)=II. 1; *also:* amusement; **zu ihrer E.,** for their amusement, (in order) to amuse them; (*b*) **zur großen E. der Volksmenge,** much to the amusement, entertainment, of the crowd; **zur allgemeinen E. fiel er ins Wasser,** to everybody's amusement he fell into the water.

erhellen. 1. *v.tr.* to light (up), illuminate (sth.); to throw light upon (mystery, etc.); **die Straßen werden von Gaslampen erhellt,** the streets are lit by gas lamps; **Feuerschein erhellte die Nacht,** the glow of fire lit up, illuminated, the night; **der Vollmond erhellte den Weg,** the full moon shone upon the road, made the road bright; **erhellte Fenster,** lit-up windows; **das Dokument erhellt einige dieser geheimnisvollen Vorgänge,** the document throws light upon some of these mysterious incidents. **2. sich erhellen,** to become, grow, light(er); (*of sky, etc.*) to clear, to become clear, bright; **nach dem Gewitter erhellte sich der Himmel ganz plötzlich,** after the storm, the sky suddenly brightened, cleared, grew light; **ihr Gesicht erhellte sich,** her face lit up. **3.** *v.impers.* **daraus erhellt, es erhellt daraus, daß . . . ,** from this it appears, would appear, would seem, that . . . ; **aus den Dokumenten erhellt, daß er unschuldig ist,** the documents show, prove, it is evident from the documents, that he is innocent.

erheucheln, *v.tr.* **1.** to obtain (sth.) by pretence. **2.** to feign, sham, pretend, put on (an emotion, etc.); **erheuchelte Liebenswürdigkeit,** artificial, put-on, charm; **erheuchelte Fröhlichkeit,** assumed, artificial, put-on, gaiety; **erheuchelte Frömmigkeit,** assumed piety, sham piety; **erheuchelte Tränen,** artificial, false, tears, *F:* crocodile tears; **mit erheuchelter Kaltblütigkeit,** with feigned calmness; **erheucheltes Wohlwollen,** feigned, assumed, sham, benevolence; **erheuchelte Überraschung,** feigned, pretended, surprise.

erhitzen. I. *v.tr.* to heat (water, metal, etc.); (*of wine, exercise, etc.*) to heat (s.o., the blood, the mind, etc.); **eine Flüssigkeit auf 70° C e.,** to heat a liquid up to (a temperature of) 70° C, to raise the temperature of a liquid to 70° C; **sich e.,** to get heated, to get, grow, hot; (*of hay, etc.*) to heat; (*of pers.*) to get heated, hot, overheated (with running, anger, etc.), to heat oneself (with running, etc.); **das Wasser erhitzt sich auf 70° C, wird auf 70° C erhitzt,** the temperature of the water rises to 70° C, the water heats up to (a temperature of) 70° C; **vom schnellen Laufen erhitzt sein,** to be hot, heated, from running fast; **bade nicht, wenn du erhitzt bist,** do not bathe when heated; **der Wein hatte ihre Gemüter erhitzt,** the wine had heated, excited, stirred up, their minds; **vom Wein erhitzt,** heated, flushed, with wine; **erhitzte Gemüter, erhitzte Geister,** heated, excited, minds; hot-heads; (*of pers.*) **leicht erhitzt sein,** to be hot-headed, quick to anger, quick to flare up; **erhitzte Auseinandersetzung,** heated, fierce, argument; **erhitzte Debatte,** heated debate.

II. *vbl s.* **1. Erhitzen,** *n. in vbl senses.* **2. Erhitzung,** *f.* (*a*)=II. 1; (*b*) becoming heated, hot; **man darf bei starker E. nicht baden,** one should not bathe when one is very hot, heated; **bei übermäßiger E. des Heues besteht die Gefahr eines Feuers,** should the hay become excessively hot, heated, there is a risk of fire.

erhoffen, *v.tr.* to hope for (sth.); to wish for, desire (sth.); **das ist nicht das Ergebnis, das ich erhofft hatte,** that is not the result I had hoped for; **wir alle erhofften schönes Wetter,** we were all hoping for good weather; (**sich** *dat.*) **zu viel von etwas e.,** to expect, hope for, too much from sth.; **wir hatten uns von diesem Plan viel mehr erhofft,** we had hoped for, expected, much more from this plan; **der erhoffte Sieg blieb aus,** the hoped-for victory did not materialize; **der erhoffte Sohn und Erbe,** the hoped-for, longed-for, son and heir.

erhöhen. I. *v.tr.* **1.** (*a*) to make (sth.) higher; to raise (sth.); **eine Mauer e.,** to raise, heighten, a wall; **ein Haus um zwei Stockwerke e.,** to raise a house two stories, to make a house two stories higher; (*b*) to raise, promote (s.o.); to elevate (s.o.); **j-n im Rang e.,** to raise, elevate, s.o. to a higher rank; *B:* **wer sich selbst erhöhet, der soll erniedrigt werden; und wer sich selbst erniedriget, der wird erhöhet werden,** every one that exalteth himself shall be abased; and he that humbleth himself shall be exalted; (*c*) *Mus:* to raise (a note) a semitone, to sharpen, sharp (note); **eine Note doppelt e.,** to raise a note by a whole tone. **2.** to increase, raise (prices, taxes, wages, production, etc.); to increase (speed, interest, etc.); to advance, put up (prices, etc.); to put up (wages, etc.); to increase, enhance (price, pleasure, beauty, etc.); to heighten (interest, etc.); **den Preis von etwas e.,** to raise, increase, advance, put up, the price of sth.; **j-s Gehalt e.,** to increase, raise, s.o.'s salary; to give s.o. a rise (in salary); **wenn Sie die Summe auf tausend Pfund e. könnten,** if you could raise, increase, the sum to a thousand pounds; **die Temperatur e.,** to raise the temperature; **die Temperatur auf 100° e.,** to raise the temperature to 100°; **seine Wachsamkeit, seine Anstrengungen, e.,** to increase one's vigilance, one's efforts; **diese Juwelen erhöhen ihre Schönheit,** these jewels enhance, set off, her beauty; **die Produktion auf das Maximum e.,** to increase, raise, production to the maximum; *Nau:* **die Fahrt auf zwanzig Knoten e.,** to increase speed to twenty knots. **3. sich erhöhen,** (*of prices, taxes, wages, production, speed, etc.*) to increase; to be increased, raised; (*of tension, interest, etc.*) to grow, to be increased, heightened; (*of pleasure, etc.*) to be enhanced, increased; (*of number, production, price, etc.*) to rise, to go up, to advance; **die Preise haben sich bedeutend erhöht,** prices have risen, gone up, considerably; **die Zahl der Opfer hat sich auf zwanzig erhöht,** the number of victims has risen to twenty.

II. *vbl s.* **1. Erhöhen,** *n. in vbl senses.* **2. Erhöhung,** *f.* (*a*)=II. 1; *also:* promotion, elevation (of pers.); increase, rise (in prices, wages, production, etc.); increase (of speed, vigilance, interest, etc.); advancement (of prices, etc.); enhancement, increase (of pleasure, etc.); **eine E. der Preise führt zu einer E. der Lebenshaltungskosten,** an increase in prices leads to an increase in the cost of living; (*b*) high ground, rising ground; rise (of the ground); elevation, eminence, height; hill; mound; (*c*) *Astr:* exaltation (of planet); (*d*)=**Erhöhungswinkel.**

III. *p.p. & a.* **erhöht,** *in vbl senses; esp.* (*a*) raised (platform, print, etc.); **der Redner stand auf einer erhöhten Tribüne,** the speaker stood on a raised platform; (*b*) *Mus:* raised, sharpened, sharp (note); **erhöhtes F,** F sharp; **doppelt erhöhtes F,** F double sharp; (*c*) increased, raised (prices, wages, taxes, production, etc.); increased (speed, vigilance, interest, etc.); heightened (interest, etc.); enhanced (prices, pleasure, beauty, etc.); **erhöhte Lebenshaltungskosten,** increased cost of living; **mit erhöhter Kraft,** with increased strength; **eine erhöhte Tätigkeit begann,** an increased activity began; **erhöhte Sorgfalt brauchen,** to require increased care; **mit erhöhter Aufmerksamkeit,** with increased attention, concentration; *Med:* **erhöhte Temperatur,** raised temperature, temperature above normal; **erhöhter Blutdruck,** increased blood pressure.

Erhöhung, *f. see* **erhöhen** II.

Erhöhungswinkel, *m. Artil:* angle of elevation.

Erhöhungszeichen, *n. Mus:* **E. (für einen halben Ton),** sharp; **E. für einen ganzen Ton,** double sharp.

erholen. I. **1.** *v.i.* (*haben*) *A:* **sich** *dat.* **etwas** *gen.* **e.,** to get, obtain, sth.; **sich** *dat.* **bei j-m Rat e.,** to get advice from s.o. **2. sich erholen,** (*a*) (*of pers.*) to recover (one's health), to get well again, to pick up again, to be restored to health (after illness, etc.); to convalesce, to recuperate; to have a rest, to recover one's strength (after hard work, etc.); to recover (after shock, financial failure, etc.); **sich von einer Krankheit e.,** to recover from an illness; **sich von den Nachwirkungen eines Krieges e.,** to recover from the after-effects of a war; **sich von seinem Staunen e.,** to recover from one's astonishment, to get over one's astonishment; **er wird sich von dem Schreck nie mehr e.,** he will never recover from, get over, the shock; **sich nach einem geschäftlichen Fehlschlag e.,** to recover from a business setback; **er erholte sich nur langsam,** he recovered only slowly, he made a slow recovery; **völlig erholt sein,** to be fully, quite, recovered; **sie kam gut erholt aus den Ferien zurück,** she returned from her holiday much rested; **er sieht gut, sehr, erholt aus,** he looks very much rested, he looks very well again, very fit again; (*b*) (*of prices, shares, etc.*) to recover; (*of trade, etc.*) to revive, look up, pick up; *St.Exch:* (*of market*) to rally; **die Preise haben sich erholt,** prices have recovered; **diese Aktien haben sich erholt,** these shares have looked up, have recovered; **die Baumwollindustrie hat sich gut erholt,** the cotton industry has made a good recovery. **3.** *Com:* **sich bei j-m, an j-m, für etwas erholen,** to reimburse oneself upon s.o.; to recover from s.o.; **sich bei j-m für seine Unkosten e.,** to recover one's expenses from s.o.

II. *vbl s.* **Erholung,** *f.* (*a*) recovery; convalescence, recuperation; **seine E. geht gut voran,** he is making a good recovery; (*b*) rest; recreation; **er braucht dringend E.,** he badly needs a rest, a holiday; **zur E. an die See fahren,** to go to the seaside for a rest, for a holiday; **einige Augenblicke der E.,** a few moments of recreation, of rest; **E. finden,** to find rest.

erholsam, *a.* restful (holiday, surroundings, etc.); peaceful (surroundings, etc.); refreshing (sleep, etc.); **eine erholsame Beschäftigung,** a restful occupation; **erholsame Ruhe,** beneficial quiet, restful quiet.

Erholung, *f. see* **erholen** II.

Erholungsaufenthalt, *m.* rest-cure; holiday, *U.S:* vacation.

erholungsbedürftig, *a.* in need of a rest, of a holiday; **erholungsbedürftige Leute, Erholungsbedürftige** *pl,* people in need of a rest, *F:* people needing a change of air.

Erholungsheim, *n.* convalescent home; holiday home for people in need of rest.

Erholungsort, *m.* spa; holiday resort.

Erholungssuchende, *m., f.* (*decl. as adj.*) person seeking rest and quiet.

Erholungsurlaub, *m.* (i) (normal) holiday leave; leave for rest and recreation; *U.S:* vacation; (ii) convalescent leave.

erhören, *v.tr.* **1.** *A:* to hear (sth.); *F:* **das ist nicht erhört!** that's the limit! that beats all! **2.** to grant, give ear to, hear, answer (s.o.'s prayer, etc.); to fulfil, grant (wish, etc.); to grant (a suitor) his desire, to accept (a suitor); **j-n e., j-s Bitte e.,** to grant s.o.'s request; **sein Gebet wurde erhört,** his prayer was granted, answered; **erhöre mich! erhöre mein Gebet!** hear my prayer!

erhungern. 1. *v.tr.* to get, save, (money, etc.) by starving oneself. **2.** *v.i.* (*sein*) *A:* to die of starvation.

Eriaseide ['eːrĭaː-], *f. Tex:* eria(-silk).

Erica, *f.* -/. *Bot:* heather, heath.

Erich. *Pr.n.m.* **-s.** Eric.

Eriesee, der ['iːriː-]. *Pr.n. Geog:* Lake Erie.

Erigeron [e·'riːgəron], *n.* **-s/.** *Bot:* erigeron, flea-bane.

erigibel [e·ri·'giːbəl], *a. Physiol:* erectile (tissue, etc.).

erigieren [e·ri·'giːrən], *v.i.* (*haben*) *Physiol:* (*of organ*) to become erected; (*of man*) to have an erection; **erigiert,** in a state of erection.

Erika. 1. *Pr.n.f.* **-s.** Erica. **2.** *f.* **-/-ken.** *Bot:* heather, heath.

Erikalen [e·ri·'kaːlən], *f.pl. Bot:* ericales.

Erikazeen [e·ri·ka·'tseːən], *f.pl. Bot:* ericaceae.

erikoid [e·ri·ko·'iːt], *a. Bot:* ericaceous.

Erin ['eːrin]. *Pr.n.n.* **-s.** *A. & Poet:* Ireland, Erin.

erinnerlich, *a.* (*of incident, etc.*) **j-m e. sein,** to be remembered by s.o.; **das ist mir nicht e.,** I cannot remember it, it has escaped, slipped, my memory, it has gone out of my memory;

soviel, soweit, mir e. ist, as far as I (can) remember, to the best of my recollection, as far as I recollect; **mir ist nur noch e., daß . . . ,** I can only remember, recollect, that . . . , all I can remember, recollect, is that . . . ; **es ist mir nicht e., daß du es mir erzählt hast,** I cannot remember your telling me.

erinnern. I. *v.tr.* **1.** to remind (s.o.); **j-n an etwas** *acc.* **e.,** to remind s.o. of sth., to recall sth. to s.o.'s mind; *F:* to jog s.o.'s memory about sth.; **j-n daran e., etwas zu tun,** to remind s.o. to do sth.; **erinnere mich bitte (daran), an ihn zu schreiben,** please remind me to write to him; **gut, daß du mich daran erinnert hast,** it's a good thing that you have reminded me of it; **Reisende werden daran erinnert, daß . . . ,** passengers are reminded that . . . ; **ich wurde an mein Versprechen erinnert,** I was reminded of my promise; **das erinnert mich an . . . ,** that reminds me, puts me in mind, of . . . ; **er erinnert mich an seinen Vater,** he reminds me of, puts me in mind of, his father; **sie erinnert mich an einen Fuchs,** she reminds me, puts me in mind, of a fox; **alles hier erinnert mich an meine Jugend,** everything here reminds me of, brings back, carries me back to, my youth; *abs.* **Szenen, die an Holland erinnern,** scenes that remind one, make one think, put one in mind, of Holland; scenes with something Dutch about them; **das Bild erinnert an Constable,** the picture reminds one of Constable; **Melodien, die an Alt-Wien erinnern,** tunes reminiscent of, that recall memories of, Old Vienna. **2. sich erinnern,** to remember, to recollect, to recall to mind; **sich an etwas** *acc.*, **an j-n, e., sich etwas** *gen.*, **j-s, e.,** to remember, recall, sth., s.o., to recollect sth.; **sich an Dinge e. können, die vor langer Zeit geschehen sind,** to be able to remember things that happened a long time ago; **ich kann mich im Augenblick seines Namens, an seinen Namen, nicht e.,** I can't remember, recall, recollect, his name for the moment; **erinnern Sie sich nicht an mich? erinnern Sie sich meiner nicht?** don't you remember me? **ich kann mich der Sache, an die Sache, einfach nicht mehr e.,** I simply cannot remember, recollect, the matter; **ich erinnere mich dessen, seiner, nur noch dunkel,** I remember, recollect, it, him, only vaguely, I have only a dim recollection of it, of him; **wenn ich mich recht erinnere,** if I remember rightly, aright, if my memory serves me right; **soviel, soweit, ich mich e. kann,** as far as I (can) remember, to the best of my recollection; **jetzt erinnere ich mich (daran), es zu Hause gelassen zu haben,** now I remember that I left it at home, now I remember leaving it at home; **ich erinnere mich, es gesehen zu haben,** I remember seeing it; **ich kann mich nicht (daran) e., daß du es mir erzählt hast,** I cannot remember your telling me. **3.** *v.tr. North German:* **etwas, j-n, e.,** to remember, recall, sth., s.o., to recollect sth.; **ich kann die Sache einfach nicht mehr e.,** I simply cannot remember the matter; **ich erinnere, daß du es mir erzählt hast,** I remember your telling me. **4.** *v.tr. A:* **etwas e.,** to raise, make, an objection; **wir fanden, hatten, nichts dazu zu e.,** we had no objections to make against it.

II. *vbl s.* **1. Erinnern,** *n.* (*a*) reminding (of s.o.); (*b*) remembering (of sth.). **2. Erinnerung,** *f.* (*a*) remembrance, memory (**an etwas** *acc.*, **an j-n,** of sth., of s.o.); **zur E. an . . . ,** in memory, remembrance, of . . . ; as a souvenir of (visit, journey, etc.); **zur freundlichen E. an deine Freundin Anna,** to remind you of your friend Anna; **zur E. an meine Reise,** as a memento, souvenir, of my trip; (*b*) memory; **etwas in (der) E. behalten,** to keep, retain, sth. in one's memory, to remember sth.; **etwas in klarer E. behalten,** to retain a clear memory of sth., to have a clear recollection of sth., to remember sth. clearly; **j-n in freundlicher E. behalten, haben,** to remember s.o. kindly; **ich habe es jedenfalls so in (der) E.,** in any case, that is how I remember it; **ich habe jene Tage in schöner E.,** I have a wonderful memory, recollection, of those days; **es ist mir ganz deutlich in (der) E. geblieben,** I remember it quite clearly, it stands out quite clearly in my memory; **ich habe es nicht mehr in E.,** I cannot remember it, it has escaped, slipped, my memory, it has gone out of my memory; **die E. an etwas** *acc.* **auffrischen,** to refresh one's memory of, about, sth.; **j-m etwas in E. bringen,** to bring, recall, sth. to s.o.'s recollection; to remind s.o. of sth.; **ich möchte Ihnen den Sachverhalt in E. bringen,** I would like to remind you of the facts; **bei j-m in guter E. stehen,** to be remembered kindly by s.o.; (*c*) memory, recollection; reminiscence; **alte Erinnerungen austauschen,** to exchange reminiscences; **Erinnerungen aus der Kindheit,** childhood memories, childhood recollections, reminiscences of childhood; **aus meinen frühesten Erinnerungen,** from my earliest memories; **sie lebt von ihren Erinnerungen,** she lives on her memories; **traurige Erinnerungen,** sad memories; **es rief viele Erinnerungen in mir wach,** it brought many memories, recollections, to my mind; (*d*) token of remembrance; memento; keepsake; souvenir (of visit, journey, etc.); **das ist eine schöne E. an unsere Ferien,** that is a pleasant souvenir of our holiday; **das wird eine E. an dich sein,** that will be something to remember you by; **Photos sind immer schöne Erinnerungen,** photos always make pleasant mementos. **3.** *Jur:* appeal (against payment of costs, etc.).

Erinnerungsaphasie, *f. Med:* verbal amnesia.

Erinnerungsbild, *n.* visual memory, visual remembrance; *Psy:* memory image.

Erinnerungsfälschung, *f. Med:* false recollection; paramnesia.

Erinnerungsillusion, *f.* = **Erinnerungsfälschung.**

Erinnerungslosigkeit, *f. Med:* amnesia, absence of memory.

Erinnerungslücke, *f. Med: etc:* gap in s.o.'s, one's, memory.

Erinnerungsposten, *m. Book-k:* amount entered in a depreciation reserve account.

Erinnerungsschreiben, *n. Com: etc:* (letter of) reminder.

Erinnerungsschwäche, *f. Med:* weakness of memory.

Erinnerungstafel, *f.* memorial plaque (in church, etc.).

Erinnerungstäuschung, *f. Med:* mnesic delusion.

Erinnerungsverlust, *m. Med:* loss of memory; amnesia.

Erinnerungsvermögen, *n.* memory; power of recollection.

Erinnye [eˈrinjə, eˈrinyə], **Erinnys** [eˈrinys]. *Pr.n.f.* -/**Erinnyen.** *Gr.Myth:* Erinys, one of the Erin(n)yes; **die Erinnyen,** the Erin(n)yes, the Furies.

Eriometer [erioˈmeːtər], *n.* -s/-. *Opt:* eriometer.

Eristik [eˈristik], *f.* -/. *Phil:* eristic.

Eristiker [eˈristikər], *m.* -s/-. *Phil:* eristic (philosopher).

eristisch [eˈristiʃ], *a. Phil:* eristic; Megarian.

Eritrea [eriˈtreːaː]. *Pr.n.n.* -s. *Geog:* Eritrea.

eritreisch [eriˈtreːiʃ], *a. Geog:* Eritrean.

Eritrichium [eriˈtriːçium], *n.* -s/. *Bot:* eritrichium.

Erizinen [eriˈtsiːnən], *f.pl. Bot:* ericales.

erjagen, *v.tr.* to hunt (animal, etc.); *F:* to gain, achieve (honour, etc.); **versuchen, das Glück zu e.,** to chase after happiness *or* success.

erkalten, *v.i.* (*sein*) to get, grow, cold; to get cool; (*of heated mass, emotion, passion, zeal, etc.*) to cool (down, off); (*of love*) to grow cold; (*of zeal*) to abate, slacken; **das ließ seine Begeisterung e.,** that chilled, damped, his enthusiasm; **nach dem völligen Erkalten der Masse,** when the mixture has thoroughly cooled, has become quite cold; **seine erkaltende Zuneigung,** his cooling affection; **die Asche erkaltender Leidenschaft,** the embers of a dying passion; **erkaltete Liebe,** love grown cold; **erkaltete Leidenschaft,** dead passion; *Lit:* **im Tode e.,** to die.

erkälten. I. *v.tr.* **1.** *Lit:* to make (sth.) cold; to cool (sth.) (down); to chill (enthusiasm, etc.). **2. sich** *dat.* **die Blase, den Magen, usw., e.,** to get a cold on the bladder, on the stomach, etc. **3. sich erkälten,** to catch (a) cold; to catch a chill; **erkältet sein,** to have a cold; to have a chill; **sich in der Zugluft e.,** to catch cold from the draught.

II. *vbl s.* **1. Erkälten,** *n. in vbl senses.* **2. Erkältung,** *f.* (*a*) = II. 1; (*b*) cold; chill; **eine schwere, schlimme, E. haben,** to have a heavy, a bad, cold; to have a heavy, a bad, chill; **sich** *dat.* **eine E. holen, zuziehen,** to catch (a) cold; to catch a chill; **ich kann meine E. nicht loswerden,** I can't get rid of my cold; **sich gegen Erkältungen schützen,** to protect oneself from colds; **die E. hat sich mir auf die Nieren gelegt, ist auf die Nieren gegangen, geschlagen,** the chill has got on to my kidneys; **E. im Magen, des Magens,** cold in the stomach.

Erkältungskrankheit, *f.* (illness caused by a) cold.

erkämpfen, *v.tr.* **(sich** *dat.***) etwas e.,** to gain sth. by fighting for it; to gain sth. by strenuous effort; **er hat sich seinen Erfolg schwer e. müssen,** he has had to fight, struggle, hard for his success.

erkaufen, *v.tr.* **etwas mit etwas e.,** to buy sth. with sth.; to buy sth. at the price of sth.; **die Freiheit mit seinem Blut e.,** to buy, purchase, freedom with one's blood; **ein teuer erkaufter Sieg,** a dear-bought, dearly-bought, victory; **sie hat (sich) den Erfolg teuer erkauft,** she has paid a high price for her success, bought her success at a high price; her success has cost her dear, has been dearly bought.

erkecken (sich), *v.refl.* = **erdreisten (sich).**

erkennbar, *a.* **1.** (*a*) recognizable; distinguishable; detectable; discernible; perceptible; perceivable; **die Küste war durch den Nebel kaum e.,** the coast was hardly distinguishable, recognizable, discernible, through the mist; one could hardly see the coast through the mist; **dem Auge, für das Auge, noch e.,** still perceptible to, perceivable by, the eye; still visible, discernible; **kein erkennbarer Unterschied,** no perceivable, perceptible, detectable, discernible, distinguishable, difference; **ein Anflug von Selbstgefälligkeit ist in diesen Memoiren e.,** a touch of complacency is discernible in these memoirs; (*b*) *Phil:* that can be known; knowable; cognizable; **nach Kant sind die Dinge an sich nicht e.,** according to Kant noumena are unknowable, we can have no cognition of noumena; **der Ursprung des Lebens ist für den menschlichen Verstand nicht e.,** the human mind has no knowledge, no cognition, of the origins of life; **der Bereich des Erkennbaren,** the realm of the knowable. **2.** recognizable; identifiable; **er ist leicht an seiner Narbe e.,** he is easily known, easily recognizable, by his scar; **der Vogel ist an seinem gelben Schnabel e.,** the bird can be identified by its yellow beak.

Erkennbarkeit, *f.* (*a*) recognizability (of distant object, target, etc.); **bei der leichten E. des Unterschieds,** as the difference is so easily perceptible, recognizable, discernible, distinguishable; **die schwere E. der Krankheit verhindert oft ein rechtzeitiges Eingreifen,** the fact that the disease is difficult to diagnose, recognize, very often makes it impossible to treat it in the early stages; (*b*) *Phil: etc:* cognizability; **Kant bestreitet die E. der Dinge an sich,** Kant denies that noumena can be known, according to Kant noumena are unknowable, we can have no cognition of noumena.

erkennen. I. *v.* (*conj. like* **kennen**) **1.** *v.tr.* (*a*) to discern, distinguish, make out, perceive, recognize (distant object, etc.); to realize, recognize, perceive (danger, difference, importance *or* value of sth.); to detect (difference, fault, etc.); to appreciate (value of sth.); to be alive to (danger, importance of sth.); to make out (reason for sth., importance of sth.); **ich kann die einzelnen Buchstaben auf diese Entfernung nicht e.,** I cannot discern, distinguish, make out, recognize, read, the individual letters from this distance; **man konnte die Kirchturmspitze in der Ferne noch e.,** one could still discern, make out, see, the spire in the distance; **er erkannte, daß er im Unrecht war,** he saw, realized, that he was wrong; **ein Mensch, dessen wahren Wert man niemals erkannte,** a man who was never appreciated at his true worth, a man whose true worth was never recognized; **ich habe meinen Fehler erkannt,** I have realized my mistake; **ich erkannte zu spät, daß . . . ,** I realized, discovered, found out, too late that . . . ; **daran erkannte ich, daß er die Wahrheit sprach,** by this I knew that he was telling the truth; **wir haben ihn längst als Lügner erkannt,** we discovered, found out, realized, long ago that he is a liar; **es läßt sich nicht e., ob diese Handschrift echt oder gefälscht ist,** one cannot tell whether this manuscript is genuine or not; **seine Worte lassen e., daß er es ernst meint,** his words show, make it plain, that he is in earnest; **er gab seine Absicht nur zu deutlich zu e.,** he showed his intention only too clearly; **er gab zu e., daß . . . ,** he indicated that . . . ; *F:* **dich habe ich erkannt!** I am up to your tricks! I know your little game! (*b*) *Phil: etc:* to know; to cognize; to recognize; **erkenne dich selbst,** know thyself; **nach Kant können wir die Dinge an sich nicht e.,** according to Kant noumena are unknowable, we can have no cognition of noumena; **den Ursprung des Lebens wird der Mensch niemals e.,** man will never know the origin of life. **2.** *v.tr.* to recognize, know (s.o., s.o.'s voice, etc.); to identify (s.o., animal, etc.); **j-n, etwas, an etwas** *dat.* **e.,** to recognize, know, s.o., sth., by sth.; to identify, tell, s.o., sth., by sth.; **sich (j-m) zu e. geben,** to make oneself known (to s.o.); to disclose one's identity (to

s.o.); *A. & Lit:* to discover oneself (to s.o.); **sie erkannte ihn von weitem,** she knew, recognized, him from afar; **j-n an seinem Gang e.,** to know, recognize, s.o. by his walk; **ich konnte ihn in der Menge nicht e.,** I could not distinguish him among the crowd; **man erkennt ihn leicht an seiner Stimme,** he is easily known by his voice, one can easily tell him by his voice; **ich erkannte ihn als Deutschen,** I recognized, *F:* spotted, him as a German, I knew him for a German; *B:* **an ihren Früchten sollt ihr sie e.,** by their fruits ye shall know them. **3.** *v.tr. Book-k:* **ein Konto (mit einem Betrag) e.,** to credit an account (with an amount). **4.** *v.tr. B:* (*of man*) to know (woman) (*carnally*). **5.** *v.tr. A:*=**anerkennen I. 1. 6.** *v.i.* (*haben*) *Jur:* **auf etwas** *acc.* **e.,** to pass sentence of (death, a month's imprisonment, etc.); **auf Freispruch e.,** to acquit the accused; **auf Schadenersatz e.,** to award damages; **auf eine Geldstrafe e.,** to impose a fine; **zu j-s Gunsten, gegen j-n, e.,** to bring in a finding for, against, s.o.; to find for, against, s.o.; to give judgment in favour of s.o., against s.o.; **zu Recht, für Recht, e.,** to decide (**daß,** that); to find (**daß,** that).

II. *vbl s.* **Erkennen,** *n., occ.* **Erkennung,** *f. in vbl senses; also:* (*a*) perception, recognition, realization (of danger, difference, mistake, etc.); appreciation (of value, etc.); diagnosis (of disease); (*b*) *Phil:* cognition; perception; recognition; knowledge (of truth, etc.); **Fähigkeit des Erkennens,** (power of) cognition; (*c*) *Phil: etc:* (range *or* power of) cognition; knowledge; **das menschliche Erkennen ist begrenzt,** human knowledge, cognition, is limited.

erkenntlich, *a.* **1.**=**erkennbar** 2. **2. sich j-m e. zeigen,** to show s.o. one's appreciation; to show oneself grateful to s.o.; **ich werde mich ihm schon e. zeigen,** I shall do something for him to show my appreciation, I shall see he doesn't lose by it.

Erkenntlichkeit, *f.* **1.** *A:* = **Erkennbarkeit. 2.** gratitude; appreciation; **als Zeichen meiner E.,** as a sign of my gratitude, appreciation. **3.** token of gratitude, of appreciation.

Erkenntnis. I. *f.* **-/-nisse. 1.** (*a*) perception, recognition, realization (of danger, difference, mistake, etc.); appreciation (of value, etc.); (*b*) *Phil: etc:* cognition; perception; recognition; knowledge (of truth, etc.); **der Baum der E. (des Guten und Bösen),** the tree of knowledge (of good and evil); (*c*) *Phil: etc:* (range *or* power of) cognition; knowledge; **die menschliche E. ist begrenzt,** human knowledge, cognition, is limited. **2.** knowledge; **die Erkenntnisse eines langen Lebens,** the knowledge of a lifetime, the accumulated experience of a long life: **diese E. kam zu spät,** the realization came too late.

II. **Erkenntnis,** *n.* **-nisses/-nisse. 1.** *A:* =**Erkenntnis I. 2.** *Jur:* decision (of court); judgment; sentence; finding; award (of arbitration tribunal).

Erkenntnisdrang, *m.* thirst for knowledge.

Erkenntnisgegenstand, *m. Phil: Psy:* object of knowledge; object of cognition.

Erkenntnislehre, *f.*=**Erkenntnistheorie.**

Erkenntnisprozeß, *m. Phil: Psy:* process of knowing, of knowledge; process of cognizing.

Erkenntnispsychologie, *f. Psy: Phil:* psychology of cognition.

erkenntnistheoretisch, *a. Phil:* epistemological.

Erkenntnistheorie, *f. Phil:* theory of knowing, of knowledge, of cognition; epistemology.

Erkenntnisvermögen, *n. Phil: Psy:* cognitive faculty; cognition.

Erkennung, *f. see* **erkennen II.**

Erkennungsdienst, *m. Adm:* (police) records department.

Erkennungskarte, *f.* name-card; card with (child's) name and address.

Erkennungsmarke, *f. Mil: etc:* identification marking; identity disc, *U.S:* identification tag.

Erkennungsmerkmal, *n.* distinguishing mark; distinguishing characteristic.

Erkennungssignal, *n. Mil: etc:* recognition signal.

Erkennungsszene, *f. Th: etc:* recognition scene.

Erkennungstuch, *n. Mil.Av:* ground strip, ground panel

Erkennungswort, *n.* **-(e)s/-wörter &-worte.** *Mil: etc:* watchword; password, countersign.

Erkennungszeichen, *n.* (*a*) sign by which a person *or* thing can be identified; symptom (of disease, etc.); *Mil: etc:* recognition marking (on aircraft, etc.); **als E. werde ich eine rote Rose im Knopfloch tragen,** you will recognize me by the red rose in my buttonhole; **ein sicheres E. dieser Krankheit,** a sure symptom of this disease; (*b*) *Mil: etc:*=**Erkennungssignal.**

Erker, *m.* **-s/-. 1.** *Arch:* bay(-window); *Mediev. Arch:* oriel; **Zimmer mit einem großen E.,** room with a large bay(-window). **2.** *F:* nose.

Erkerfenster, *n. Arch:* bay-window; (*curved*) bow-window; (*semi-circular*) compass-window; *Mediev.Arch:* oriel-window.

Erkerstube, *f.* room with a bay-window.

Erkerturm, *m. Mediev.Arch:* oriel.

Erkerzimmer, *n.* room with a bay-window.

erkiesen, *v.tr.* (*p.t.* **erkor,** *A:* **erkieste;** *p.p.* **erkoren,** *A:* **erkiest**) to choose.

erklärbar, *a.*=**erklärlich.**

erklären. I. *v.tr.* **1.** (*a*) to explain (sth.); to account for (fact, one's conduct, etc.); to interpret (text, law, dream, etc.); to comment on (text, etc.); to expound (passage of Scripture, etc.); *Gram:* to analyse (sentence, etc.); to parse (word, sentence, etc.); **j-m etwas e.,** to explain sth. to s.o.; **das ist leicht zu e., das läßt sich leicht e.,** that is easily explained; **ich weiß mir nicht zu e., kann mir nicht e., warum ...,** I am at a loss to understand, I can't understand, make out, why ...; **etwas falsch e.,** to explain sth. wrongly; to misinterpret (text, etc.); **erklären Sie sich deutlicher,** explain yourself (more clearly); **'das ist ein alter Brauch hier', erklärte der Fremdenführer,** 'it is an old local custom', explained the guide; **erklärend,** explanatory (statement, note, etc.); (*b*) *A:* **sich mit j-m e.,** to have it out with s.o.; **sich mit j-m über eine Angelegenheit e.,** to clear up a matter with s.o. **2.** to declare (war, one's intention, one's willingness to do sth., etc.); to state, announce, affirm (one's intention to do sth., etc.); **j-m, einem Lande, den Krieg e.,** to declare war on s.o., a country; **er erklärte feierlich, daß die Bedingungen des Vertrags gewissenhaft erfüllt würden,** he declared, affirmed, solemnly that the conditions of the treaty would be conscientiously fulfilled; **einem Mädchen seine Liebe e.,** to make a declaration of love to a girl; **seinen Austritt aus einem Verein, usw., e.,** to resign (formally) from a club, etc.; **er erklärte, nichts gesehen zu haben,** he declared he had seen nothing; **j-n für einen Lügner e.,** to declare s.o. a liar; **etwas für eine Lüge, für ungültig, e.,** to declare sth. a lie, invalid; **eine Sitzung für eröffnet, geschlossen, e.,** to declare a session open, closed; **j-n, sich, zum,** *A:* **als, Erben e.,** to declare s.o., oneself, heir; **sich (für) besiegt e.,** to admit oneself defeated, to admit defeat; **sich bereit e., etwas zu tun,** to express, declare, oneself willing, prepared, ready, to do sth., to express, declare, one's willingness, readiness, to do sth.; (*of lover*) **sich e.,** to declare oneself; **sich für, gegen, j-n, etwas, e.,** to declare oneself for, against, s.o., sth.; **j-n, sich, bankrott e.,** to adjudge, adjudicate, declare, s.o. bankrupt; to declare oneself insolvent; *Hist:* **j-n für vogelfrei e.,** to outlaw s.o.; *Jur:* **j-n, sich, für schuldig, unschuldig, e.,** to declare s.o., oneself, (to be) guilty, innocent; **j-n für unzurechnungsfähig e.,** to declare s.o. irresponsible; **j-n für volljährig e.,** to declare s.o. to be of age; **an Eides Statt, eidesstattlich, e., daß ...,** to make a statutory declaration that ..., to affirm (solemnly) that ...; **eidlich, unter Eid, e., daß ...,** to make a statement, a declaration, on oath that ..., to declare, state, on oath that ...; **eine Hypothek für verfallen e.,** to foreclose a mortgage; *Nau:* **ein Schiff für seeuntüchtig e.,** to condemn a ship; *Fin:* **eine Dividende e. (auf+*acc.*),** to declare a dividend (on ...).

II. *vbl s.* **1. Erklären,** *n. in vbl senses.* **2. Erklärung,** *f.* (*a*)=II. 1; *also:* explanation; interpretation (of text, law, dream, etc.); comment (on text, etc.); commentation (of text, etc.); exposition (of text, etc.); *Gram:* analysis (of sentence, etc.); *Theol:* exegesis (of Holy Scripture); (*b*) explanation; **Erklärungen für sein Verhalten geben,** to give explanations of one's conduct; **ich kann mich nicht auf lange Erklärungen einlassen,** I cannot enter into long explanations; (*c*) statement; affirmation; announcement; declaration; asseveration; *Jur:* deposition; **eine offizielle E. an die Presse,** an official statement to the press; **eine E. abgeben, veröffentlichen,** to make, publish, a statement; **eine E. der Regierung,** a declaration, an announcement, by the government; **eine feierliche E. abgeben,** to make a solemn statement, declaration, assertion, affirmation, asseveration; *Hist:* **E. der Menschen- und Bürgerrechte,** Declaration of the Rights of Man and of the Citizen; *see also* **Eid, eidlich, eidesstattlich.**

III. *p.p. & a.* **erklärt,** *in vbl senses; esp.* declared; avowed, professed, open (atheist, enemy of the Government, etc.); acknowledged (favourite); **er ist ein erklärter Sozialist,** he is a declared, an avowed, a professed, socialist; **seit diesem Erfolg ist er der erklärte Liebling des Publikums,** since this success he has been the acknowledged favourite of the public.

Erklärer, *m.* **-s/-,** explainer; expositor (of text, etc.); commentator (on text, etc.).

erklärlich, *a.* explainable; explicable; **das ist leicht e.,** that is easily explained, easily explainable, easily explicable; that is easily accounted for; **nicht e.,** unexplainable; inexplicable; **jetzt ist mir e., warum er meinen Fragen immer auswich,** now I know, now I can see, why he always avoided my questions; **aus (leicht) erklärlichen Gründen wollte er seinen Namen nicht genannt wissen,** for obvious, understandable, quite explicable, reasons he did not wish his name to be mentioned; **sein Verhalten ist mir nicht e.,** I find his conduct inexplicable.

erklärlicherweise, *adv.* for obvious, understandable, quite explicable, reasons.

Erklärung, *f. see* **erklären II.**

erklärungsbedürftig, *a.* needing (an) explanation; **diese Behauptung ist e.,** this statement needs explanation.

Erklärungstag, *m. St.Exch:* contango-day.

Erklärungsversuch, *m.* attempt at an explanation, attempted explanation.

erklecken, *v.i.* (*haben*) *A. & Dial:* to be sufficient; to be of use.

erklecklich, *a.* considerable (amount of money, profit, expenses, etc.); *F:* respectable (sum, profit, etc.); **er hat eine erkleckliche Summe zusammengespart,** he has saved up a quite considerable, handsome, amount of money, a pretty fair sum; **er hat eine erkleckliche Leistung vollbracht, Erkleckliches geleistet,** he has put up a very respectable performance; **eine erkleckliche Anzahl von ...,** a goodly number of ....

erklettern, *v.tr.* to climb (up) (mountain, tree, wall, etc.); **sie erkletterten die Steilwand in drei Stunden,** they climbed the steep face of the rock in three hours.

erklimmen, *v.tr.* (*strong*) to climb (mountain, stairs, etc.); to mount to, climb (up) to, go up to (top of a hill, etc.); to mount (hill, stairs, wall, etc.); to scale (mountain, etc.); **den Gipfel der Macht e.,** to climb, attain, reach, the summit of power; **er hatte die höchste Stufe seiner Laufbahn erklommen,** he had reached the summit of his career.

erklingen, *v.i.* (*strong*) (*sein*) (*of musical instrument*) to (begin to) sound, to (begin to) resound; (*of bell, music*) to (begin to) ring out, to (begin to) sound; (*of voice, song*) to break the silence; to ring out, to sound (forth); (*of valley, wood, etc.*) **vom Gesang der Vögel, usw., e.,** to (re)sound, ring, echo, with the song of birds, etc.; **die Geige e. lassen,** to let the fiddle sound (forth); **ein Lied e. lassen,** to let a song ring out; **seine Stimme e. lassen,** to let one's voice ring out, ring forth, resound; to strike up a song; **die Hirten ließen das Tal mit fröhlichem Gesang e.,** the shepherds made the valley resound with their merry singing; **die Glöckchen in der Mähne des Pferdes erklangen bei jedem Schritt,** the bells in the horse's mane sounded, resounded, tinkled, jingled, rang out, with each step; **alle Glocken erklangen, als sich die Prozession in Bewegung setzte,** all the bells began to ring, sound, as the procession moved off; **hell erklangen ihre lustigen Lieder,** their songs rang out merrily; **liebliche Musik erklang,** sweet music sounded; **laßt ein Lied e.!** strike up a song! **der Wind ließ die Saiten der Äolsharfe e.,** the wind drew music from the strings of the Aeolian harp; **das Lob Gottes e. lassen,** to sound, speak, the praise of God.

erklirren, *v.i.* (*sein*) to (begin to) rattle; **der Wind ließ die Fensterscheiben e.,** the wind made the windows rattle.

erklügeln, *v.tr. occ.*=**ausklügeln.**

erkor, erkoren *see* **erkiesen, erküren.**

erkranken. I. *v.i.* (*sein*) to be taken, fall, get, ill, *U.S:* to take, get, sick; (*of animal, plant, organ, etc.*) to become diseased; to become affected; **an etwas** *dat.* **erkrankt sein,** (*of pers.*) to be ill, *F:* down, with (a disease); (*of animal, plant*) to be affected with (a disease); **an (der) Gelbsucht e.,** to fall ill, to be taken ill, with jaundice; to develop jaundice; **er erkrankte unheilbar an**

Krebs, he developed an incurable cancer; lebensgefährlich erkrankt, dangerously ill; erkrankte Teile einer Pflanze, erkrankte Organe, diseased parts of a plant; diseased organs; sein rechter Lungenflügel ist erkrankt, his right lung has become, is, affected; ein Kind, das vernachlässigt wird, muß seelisch e., the mind of a neglected child is bound to suffer.

II. *vbl s.* 1. Erkranken, *n. in vbl senses.* 2. Erkrankung, *f.* (*a*)=II. 1; im Fall der plötzlichen E. eines der Kinder, in case one of the children is taken ill, falls ill, suddenly; nach Scharlach muß einer E. der inneren Organe vorgebeugt werden, after scarlet fever one must take precautions against any affection of the internal organs; (*b*) affection (of pers., animal, plant, organ); es handelt sich um eine schwere E. der Nieren, there is a serious affection of the kidneys, the kidneys are seriously affected; seine leichte E. wird bald vorübergehen, his slight illness, indisposition, will soon pass; dauernde Vernachlässigung eines Kindes muß seine seelische E. zur Folge haben, the mind of a constantly neglected child is bound to suffer.

erkühnen (sich), *v.refl. Lit:* sich einer Tat *gen.* einer Frage *gen.*, e., to dare to do a deed; to venture (upon) a question; to make bold to ask a question; wessen, *occ.* was, erkühnst du dich! how dare you! sich e., etwas zu tun, to dare to do sth.; to have the audacity, to make bold, to do sth.; to venture to do sth.

erkunden. I. *v.tr.* (*a*) to explore (ground, area); *Mil: Av: Navy:* to reconnoitre (ground, terrain, area); *abs.* to scout; (*b*) to explore, investigate (problem).

II. *vbl s.* Erkunden *n.*, Erkundung *f. in vbl senses; also:* (*a*) exploration (of ground, area); *Mil: Av:* (ground) reconnaissance, *F:* (ground) recce; scouting; *Navy:* reconnaissance; gewaltsame Erkundung, reconnaissance in force; (*b*) exploration, investigation (of problem).

Erkunder, *m.* -s/-. *Mil.Av:*=Erkundungsflugzeug.

erkundigen. I. *v.* 1. *v.tr. A:* etwas e., to find sth. out; to find out about (matter); to explore (country, etc.). 2. sich erkundigen, to make enquiries; sich nach j-m e., to enquire about, after, s.o., to ask about, after, s.o.; to ask (i) how s.o. is (getting on, faring), (ii) where s.o. is; sich über j-n, etwas, e., to make enquiries about s.o., sth.; to ask about s.o., sth.; sich nach etwas e., to ask, enquire, about sth.; to ask (the way, the time); ich werde mich nach dem Preis e., I'll ask, enquire, about the price, I'll try to find out the price; er erkundigte sich bei mir nach deiner Gesundheit, he asked me about your health, he enquired about your health; die Mutter erkundigte sich beim Lehrer über die Leistungen ihres Sohnes, the mother asked the teacher to tell her how her son was doing (in his school work); sich e., ob . . . , wie . . . , to enquire, ask, whether . . . , how . . . .

II. *vbl s.* Erkundigung, *f.* enquiry; information; Erkundigungen (über j-n, etwas *acc.*) einziehen, einholen, to make enquiries (about s.o., sth.); to gather information (about s.o., sth.); to enquire into (s.o.'s financial position, s.o.'s work, etc.); to inform oneself about (s.o., s.o.'s financial position, s.o.'s work, etc.); bei wem haben Sie Erkundigungen eingeholt? from whom did you seek information? genaue Erkundigungen einziehen, to make detailed enquiries; to get detailed information.

erkundschaften, *v.tr.*=auskundschaften.

Erkundung, *f. see* erkunden II.

Erkundungsauftrag, *m. Mil: Mil.Av:* reconnaissance mission.

Erkundungsfahrzeug, *n. Mil:* reconnaissance vehicle; scout vehicle.

Erkundungsflug, *m. Mil.Av:* reconnaissance flight.

Erkundungsflugzeug, *n. Mil.Av:* reconnaissance aircraft; scout (aircraft).

Erkundungstrupp, *m. Mil:* reconnaissance detachment.

Erkundungsvorstoß, *m. Mil: Mil.Av:* reconnaissance raid; scouting raid.

erkünsteln, *v.tr.* to feign (sth.); to affect (indifference, interest, cheerfulness, etc.); erkünstelt, affected, feigned, pretended (indifference, interest, cheerfulness, etc.); constrained, forced (smile, laugh, etc.).

erküren, *v.tr.* (*p.t.* erkor; *p.p.* erkoren)=erkiesen.

-erl, *s.suff.* -s/-(n). *South G. Dial: (forming diminutives, often implying affection, & always rendering noun neuter)* Hunderl, little dog; Haserl, little hare; Bürscherl, chap.

erlaben, *v.tr.*=laben

Erlagschein, *m. Austrian:*=Zahlkarte.

erlahmen, *v.i.* (*sein*) (*of hand, foot, wing, etc.*) to weary, tire; to fail; (*of zeal, enthusiasm*) to abate, flag; (*of attention, interest, strength, etc.*) to flag; to fail; (*of energy*) to slacken; *Mil:* (*of attack, resistance*) to slacken; (*of resistance*) to crumble; die Pferde begannen zu e., the horses were tiring, wearying, beginning to give out; er hatte alle seine Kräfte verbraucht, und Hände und Füße erlahmten ihm, he had used up all his strength, and his hands and feet were failing him; die Kräfte erlahmten ihm, seine Kräfte erlahmten, his strength was flagging, failing; sie erlahmte nicht im Guten, she was untiring in her good works; sein Eifer ist erlahmt, his zeal has abated, flagged.

erlangbar, *a.* that can be attained; that can be obtained; attainable; obtainable.

Erlangbarkeit, *f.* attainability; obtainability.

erlangen. I. *v.tr.* 1. *A:* to (be able to) reach (apple, etc.) (*with one's hand*); to seize, grasp (sth.) (*with one's hand*); to reach (s.o., animal) (*with one's spear, arrow, etc.*). 2. *A:* to reach, attain (summit of a mountain, old age, etc.). 3. to attain, get (power, fame, wealth, etc.); to attain to, achieve (power, fame); Gnade bei j-m e., to find mercy with s.o.; to get mercy from s.o.; Gnade bei Gott e., to find favour in the eyes of God.

II. *vbl s.* Erlangen *n.*, Erlangung *f. in vbl senses; also:* attainment; zur Erlangung seines Zweckes, for the attainment of his purpose, to attain his purpose.

erlängen, *v.tr. A:* to make (sth.) longer; to lengthen, prolong (sth.); sich e., to become longer; to be lengthened, prolonged; *Min:* eine Strecke e., to drive a gallery.

Erlaß, *m.* -lasses/-lasse. 1. (+*gen.obj.*) (*a*) remittal, remission (of penalty, debt, fees, etc.); release (from penalty, debt, fees, etc.); exemption (from penalty, fees, etc.); exemption, dispensation (from examination, etc.); *Jur:* acquittal (of a debt); *Com: Jur:* acquittance (of a debt); ein E. dieser Gebühren wird nicht gewährt, no exemption from these fees can be granted; er ersuchte um E. der mündlichen Prüfung, he asked for exemption, dispensation, from the oral examination; (*b*) remission (of a sin), remittal (for a sin). 2. (+*gen.obj.*) issuing (of amnesty, order, decree, etc.); laying down, setting up (of regulation, etc.); enaction, enactment (of a law). 3. *Adm: etc:* decree; edict; order; ordinance; enaction, enactment; (official) regulation; (official) announcement; *Ecc: etc:* rescript; nach einem E. des Kultusministeriums, in accordance with a decree, an order, an enactment, of the Ministry of Education.

erlaßbar, *a.* (*a*) remissible (debt, fine, etc.); dispensable (vow); (*b*) remissible (sin).

erlassen. I. *v.tr.* (*strong*) 1. (*a*) j-m etwas e., to let s.o. off (from), release s.o. from, grant s.o. a release from, acquit s.o. of, excuse s.o. (debt, penalty, etc.); to relieve s.o. of (obligation, debt, etc.); to forgive s.o. (debt); to dispense s.o. from, absolve s.o. from (examination, task, debt, obligation, etc.); to exempt s.o. from (tax, fees, penalty, examination, etc.); j-m e., etwas zu tun, to let s.o. off from doing sth.; to dispense s.o. from doing sth.; to excuse s.o. from doing sth.; to exempt s.o from doing sth.; erlassen Sie es mir, Einzelheiten zu schildern, erlassen Sie mir die Schilderung von Einzelheiten, don't ask me to go into details; allow me to refrain from going into details; diesmal sei dir die Strafe erlassen, this once you shall go unpunished; *Jur:* eine Schuld, eine Steuer, e., to release a debt, a tax; (*b*) to remit (sin). 2. to issue (amnesty, order, decree, etc.); to set up, lay down (regulation, etc.); to enact (a law); *Mil:* to issue (order); *Jur:* einen Haftbefehl gegen j-n e., to issue a warrant for the arrest of s.o. 3. *A:* to release (prisoner, etc.).

II. *vbl s.* Erlassen *n.*, Erlassung *f.*=Erlaß 1, 2.

Erlaßjahr, *n.* 1. *R.C.Ch:* jubilee year. 2. *B.Hist:* year of release.

erläßlich, *a.*=erlaßbar.

Erlaßsünde, *f. Theol:* venial sin.

Erlassung, *f. see* erlassen II.

Erlassungsjahr, *n.*=Erlaßjahr.

Erlaßvergleich, *m. Jur:* composition (between debtor and creditor, to avoid bankruptcy proceedings).

Erlaßvertrag, *m.* agreement between creditor and debtor as to the acquittal of a debt.

erlauben, *v.tr.* 1. (*a*) to allow (sth.); to permit (sth.); j-m etwas e., to allow s.o. sth.; to permit s.o. sth.; j-m e., etwas zu tun, to allow, permit, s.o. to do sth.; es wurde mir erlaubt, das Werk zu besuchen, I was permitted, allowed, to visit the works; der Genuß von Wein ist mir erlaubt, I am allowed, permitted, wine; erlauben Sie, daß ich mich setze, erlauben Sie mir, mich zu setzen, allow me to sit down; erlauben Sie mir, Sie zu begleiten, gnädige Frau, allow me to escort you, madam; erlauben Sie mir, Ihnen meinen Bruder vorzustellen, allow, permit, me to introduce my brother to you; may I introduce my brother? sie erlaubte ihm nicht, ein einziges Wort zu seiner Verteidigung zu sagen, she would not allow, suffer, him to say a single word in his (own) defence; erlauben Sie! (i) allow me! (ii) excuse me! *F:* erlauben Sie mal! what do you mean by that? what's the idea? I beg your pardon? Sie erlauben doch? I hope you don't mind? (please) may I? erlaubt, allowed, permitted; allowable; permissible; legitimate; lawful; erlaubt ist, was gefällt, anything that pleases is allowable; sie hielten für erlaubt, was ihren Zwecken diente, they considered permissible everything that served their purpose; wir werden alle erlaubten Mittel anwenden, we shall employ all legitimate means; *see also* Grenze 2 (*b*); (*b*) (*of condition, circumstances, weather, etc.*) j-m e., etwas zu tun, to allow, permit, s.o. to do sth., to allow, permit, of s.o.'s doing sth.; sein Zustand erlaubte es ihm nicht, auszugehen, his condition would not allow of, permit, his going out, allow, permit, him to go out; sobald die Umstände es erlauben, as soon as circumstances allow, permit; wenn es das Wetter erlaubt, (wind and) weather permitting, if the weather allows, permits, if the weather will let us; in einem Ton, der keinen Widerspruch erlaubte, in a tone which permitted, allowed, of no reply; die Angelegenheit erlaubt keine Verzögerung, the matter admits, allows, of no delay; die Stelle erlaubt mehrere Auslegungen, the passage admits of several interpretations. 2. (*a*) sich *dat.* etwas erlauben, to indulge in (extravagance, pleasures, insolent remarks, etc.); to allow, permit, oneself (another cigar, insolent remarks, etc.); to take (liberties); to adopt (a tone of insolence); to venture an opinion, a guess); sich *dat.* e., etwas zu tun, to take the liberty to do, of doing, sth.; to beg to do sth.; to beg, take, leave to do sth.; to venture to do sth.; to make bold, make so bold as, to do sth.; sich Freiheiten j-m gegenüber, mit j-m, e., to take liberties with s.o.; bei mir können Sie sich so etwas nicht e., I don't allow that kind of thing; mit mir können Sie sich so etwas nicht e., you can't take that kind of liberty with me; you can't do that kind of thing to me; bei seiner Mutter kann er sich alles e., he can get away with everything as far as his mother is concerned; wenn ich mir e. darf, Sie darauf aufmerksam zu machen, daß . . . , if I may be so bold as to draw your attention to the fact that . . . ; if I may take the liberty of drawing your attention to the fact that . . . ; if I may venture to draw your attention to the fact that . . . ; was erlauben Sie sich? how dare you! I beg your pardon? erlauben Sie sich ja nicht zu viel! don't take too many liberties! don't go too far (with me)! darf ich mir e.? may I? ich erlaube mir, Ihnen mitzuteilen, daß . . . , I beg to inform you that . . . ; I take the liberty of informing you that . . . ; (*b*) sich *dat.* etwas e. können, to be able to afford sth.; ich kann mir das nicht e., I can't afford it; ich kann mir, kann mir nicht, e., großzügig zu sein, I can, cannot, afford to be generous; ich kann mir keinen Gärtner e., ich kann es mir nicht erlauben, einen Gärtner zu halten, I cannot afford (to keep) a gardener, I cannot go to the expense of keeping a gardener.

Erlaubnis, *f.* -/-nisse, (*a*) permission; leave (to do sth.); j-m die E. erteilen, geben, etwas zu tun, to give s.o. permission to do sth.; to give, grant, s.o. leave to do sth.; E. einholen, to get, obtain, permission; um E. bitten, etwas tun zu dürfen, to ask for permission to do sth.; to beg leave to do sth.; mit Ihrer (freundlichen, gütigen) E., with your (kind) permission; by your leave, with your leave; j-s E. erhalten, etwas zu tun, to get, obtain, s.o.'s permission, leave, consent, to do sth.; ohne auch nur um E. zu fragen, without even asking permission; without even saying by your leave, with not even a by your leave; (*b*)=Erlaubnisschein.

Erlaubnisschein, *m.* (written) permission; permit; licence.

erlaubt, *p.p. & a. see* erlauben, *esp.* 1 (*a*).

Erlaubtheit, *f.* permissibility, permissiblenese

(of action, etc.); admissibility (of argument, etc.).

erlaucht, *a.* illustrious (family, personage, deed, etc.); noble (personage, assembly, deed, etc.); *Hist:* (*form of address to a Count*) **Erlaucht,** your Lordship; **Erlaucht möchte . . . ,** his Lordship desires . . . .

erlauern, *v.tr.* **j-n, etwas, e.,** to lie in wait (for s.o.); to be on the look-out, on the watch, for (s.o., opportunity, etc.); to waylay (s.o.); to watch for (opportunity, etc.); **endlich hatte er die Gelegenheit erlauert zu . . . ,** he had found the long-awaited opportunity to . . . .

erlauschen, *v.tr.* to get to know (secret, etc.) by listening intently, by careful observation.

erläutern. I. *v.tr.* to explain (question, passage, etc.); to elucidate (question, passage, etc.); to comment on, to make a commentary on (a text); **eine Regel an Hand von Beispielen e.,** to explain, illustrate, a rule by (giving) examples, to exemplify a rule.

II. *vbl s.* **1. Erläutern,** *n. in vbl senses.* **2. Erläuterung,** *f.* (*a*)=II. 1; *also:* explanation (of question, passage, etc.); elucidation (of question, passage, etc.); **E. an Hand von Beispielen,** explanation with illustrative examples; exemplification; (*b*) *usu.pl.* **Erläuterungen,** explanatory remarks *or* notes; explanations; **einen Text mit Erläuterungen versehen,** to comment on a text, to make a commentary on a text; **wir danken dem Redner für seine Erläuterungen zu unserem Thema,** we thank the speaker for his (enlightening) comments on our subject.

Erle[1], *f.* **-/-n.** *Bot:* alder; **gemeine, rote, schwarze, E.,** common alder.

Erle[2], *f.* **-/-n.** *Tls: etc:* tang (of knife-, tool-blade).

erleben, *v.tr.* (*a*) to experience, have (good times, difficult times, adventures, crisis, disappointment, surprise, etc.); to see (good times, difficult times, changes, etc.); to live through, go through, pass through (good times, difficult times, adventures, crisis, changes, etc.); to undergo (loss, crisis, etc.); **wer ins Ausland geht, erlebt vieles,** foreign travel brings variety of experience; **ich habe (schon) merkwürdigere Dinge erlebt,** I have known stranger things to happen; **manche Schlacht erlebt haben,** to have been in, been through, seen, many a battle; **das Schiff hat manchen Sturm erlebt,** the ship has gone through, lived through, seen, many a storm; **ich habe es erlebt, man hat (es) erlebt, daß . . . ,** I have known it (to), seen it, happen. it has been known to happen, that . . . ; **ich habe es selbst, an mir (selbst), erlebt, was das heißt,** I have gone through it myself and know what it means, I know from experience what that means; **so etwas habe ich noch nicht erlebt!** I never saw *or* heard anything like it; **so etwas hast du noch nicht erlebt!** you never saw *or* heard anything like it; **wir mußten es e., daß all unsere Arbeit in einem Augenblick zunichte gemacht wurde,** we saw all our work destroyed in a moment; **ich möchte das nicht noch einmal e.,** (i) I should not like to go through that again; (ii) (*admonition*) don't let that happen again; **ich glaube, ich werde es noch e., daß er ein böses Ende nimmt,** I believe I shall see him come to a bad end yet; *F:* **wenn du jetzt nicht sofort den Mund hältst, kannst du etwas e.,** if you don't shut up immediately you may have cause to regret it; shut up now, or I'll make you sorry you spoke; **Freude an etwas** *dat.* **e.,** to take, find, pleasure in sth.; **ein Kind, an dem die Mutter ihre Freude erlebte,** a child who was a constant source of joy to his mother; **an dem Jungen wird die Mutter keine Freude e.,** that boy won't give much pleasure to his mother; **mit ihm, an ihm, wirst du noch dein blaues Wunder e.,** one day he will give you an eye-opener; **eine erlebte Geschichte,** a true story; a real-life story; **Erlebtes,** actual (personal) experience; *Stylistics:* **erlebte Rede,** interior monologue, *style indirect libre*; (*b*) to live to see (sth.); (*of book, etc.*) to go through (many editions, etc.); (*of play, etc.*) to see (many performances, etc.); **ich werde es nicht mehr e.,** I shall not, never, live to see it; **der Kranke wird den nächsten Tag kaum mehr e.,** the patient will hardly live to see another day; **das Buch hat zehn Auflagen erlebt,** the book has gone through, seen, ten editions; **die Versicherungssumme wird nur beim Erleben eines bestimmten Alters ausgezahlt,** the policy money is payable only if the person insured survives to a certain age; (*c*) to feel oneself essentially at one with (sth.); to feel oneself an essential part of (sth.); (*of artist*) **er hat diese Landschaft wirklich erlebt,** he has really seen this landscape from the inside; **es kommt auf das wirkliche Erleben des Kunstwerkes an,** one has to sink oneself in a work of art.

Erlebensfall, *m. Ins:* **im E. zahlbare Summe,** sum payable if the person insured survives (to a certain date).

Erlebensfallversicherung, *f. Ins:* pure endowment assurance.

Erlebenswahrscheinlichkeit, *f. Statistics: Ins:* probability of survival (to a specified date).

Erlebnis, *n.* **-nisses/-nisse,** experience; event; occurrence; adventure; **ein seltsames E.,** a strange experience; a strange adventure; **er erzählte uns alle seine Erlebnisse,** he told us all his adventures; **ein alltägliches, ein einmaliges, E.,** an everyday occurrence, experience, a singular occurrence, experience; **seelisches E.,** spiritual experience; **die Erlebnisse seiner Kindheit,** the experiences of his childhood; **die Reise wurde ihr zum E.,** the journey was a memorable experience for her; **das (unvergeßliche) E. der ersten Liebe, der Heimkehr, der Trennung,** the unforgettable experience of first love, home-coming, separation: **das E., das hinter jeder großen Dichtung steht,** the valid personal experience that lies behind all great literature; *Psy:* **verdrängte Erlebnisse,** (mental) experiences that have been repressed.

Erlebnisdichtung, *f.* poetry *or* literature *or* work based on valid personal experience.

Erlebnisfähigkeit, *f. Psy: etc:* capability of experience.

Erlebnispsychologie, *f. Psy:* psychology based on self-observation.

erlebnistranszendent, *a. Psy: Phil:* (reality) not accessible to experience.

Erlebnisunterricht, *m. Sch:* 'making it live' method of teaching.

erledigen. I. *v.tr.* **1.** to settle (matter); to handle, manage (matter); to put, set, (matter) right, in order; to adjust, arrange (matter); to do (piece of work); to deal with, attend to, see to (matter, piece of work); to dispose of, dispatch (matter, piece of work); to finish with (matter); to finish (off) (piece of work); to get (matter, piece of work) finished, off one's hands; to clear off (arrears of work, etc.); to get through (a great deal of work, etc.); **etwas durch j-n e. lassen,** to get sth. done, seen to, by s.o.; **etwas in der Stadt zu e. haben,** to have something to do in town; **ich möchte die Sache erledigt wissen,** I want to know that the matter is settled; **ich konnte diese Arbeit noch nicht e.,** I have not been able to do, deal with, attend to, that job yet; **das muß noch erledigt werden, das ist noch zu e.,** that still wants doing; that's still to be done; **das ist schon erledigt,** that's been done (already); **ich weiß nicht, was ich zuerst e. soll,** I don't know what to put my hand to first; **Ihr Gesuch wird sobald wie möglich erledigt werden,** your application will be dealt with, attended to, seen to, as soon as possible; **erledigt das unter euch,** settle, arrange, that among yourselves; **das erledigt jeden etwa noch bestehenden Einwand, Zweifel,** this removes, settles, clears, disposes of, dispatches, every objection, doubt, which may still exist; **und damit ist der Fall, die Sache, die Angelegenheit, erledigt, und damit muß der Fall, die Sache, die Angelegenheit, erledigt sein,** and that is, will be, the end of the matter; and that's that; and that will be that; so that's that; and that's an end of it; and there's an end of it; **der Fall ist, wäre, also erledigt,** so that is settled then; so everything is settled, all right now; so it's all settled; so the matter is settled; *F:* so that's all over and done with, so it is ended and done with; **sich e.,** (*of matter, question*) to settle itself; to be settled; (*of matter*) to be finished, ended; (*of objection*) to settle itself; to be settled (*of doubt*) to be settled; **damit erledigt sich die Frage,** that settles it; **damit erledigt sich die Angelegenheit,** that settles, finishes, ends, the matter; by this the matter is settled, finished, ended; by this the matter settles itself; **damit hat sich der Fall, ist der Fall, erledigt,** so the matter has settled itself, has been settled; so the matter is now settled, in order; **diese Frage wird sich von selbst e.,** this question will settle itself; **dieser Einwand läßt sich nicht in einem Satz e.,** this objection cannot be settled, disposed of, in one sentence; *Com:* **wir werden den Auftrag zu Ihrer vollen Zufriedenheit e.,** your order shall have our best attention. **2.** *F.* **j-n e.,** (*of pers., misfortune, etc.*) to settle s.o., *F:* to settle s.o.'s hash; to do for s.o.; to finish s.o. (off); to account for s.o.; (*of pers.*) to dispose of s.o.; (*of heat, etc.*) to take it out of s.o.; **erledigt sein,** (i) to be finished; to be (dead and) done for; to be out; *F:* to have had it; to be played out; (ii) to be done up; to be dead-beat, whacked, *U.S:* bushed; to be worn out, all in; **ich bin ganz, völlig, erledigt,** I'm (absolutely) worn out, all in; I'm (absolutely) done for, done in; I'm properly done up; I'm dead-beat, whacked; **er ist ein erledigter Mann, er ist erledigt,** he is finished, played out; he is a has-been; *F:* he's had it; **diese Theorie ist heutzutage erledigt,** this theory is played out; **nach diesem Skandal ist er erledigt,** this scandal has finished him, *F:* done for him, has cooked his goose; **ein junger Kritiker erledigte ihn mit ein paar Artikeln,** a young critic settled him, settled his hash, finished him (off), disposed of him, in a few articles; **er ist, du bist, für mich erledigt,** I have done with him, you; I am through with him, you; I have finished with him, you; I have had enough of him, you; I am fed up with him, you. **3.** *A:* (*of benefice, position, office, etc.*) **sich erledigen,** to fall vacant; *A:* to fall void; **ein erledigtes Amt, eine erledigte Pfründe,** a vacant, *A:* void, position, benefice. **4.** *A:* (*a*) to free, set free, liberate (s.o., a people); **j-n, sich, j-s, etwas** *gen.*, **e., j-n, sich, von j-m, von etwas, aus etwas, e.,** to free s.o., oneself, from s.o., sth.; to escape from (prison, etc.); (*b*) **sich etwas** *gen.*, **von etwas, e.**=**sich etwas entledigen,** *q.v. under* **entledigen (sich)** (*a*).

II. *vbl s.* **1. Erledigen,** *n. in vbl senses.* **2. Erledigung,** *f.* (*a*)=II. 1; *also:* settlement (of matter); arrangement, adjustment (of matter); disposal (of matter, piece of work, etc.); dispatch (of matter, piece of work, etc.); *A: Ecc:* voidance (of benefice); *A:* release (of prisoner, etc.); **es ist immer jemand im Büro zur E. der laufenden Geschäfte,** there is always somebody at the office for the dispatch of current business; (*on office file, tray, etc.*) **'zur E.',** 'to be dealt with', *Adm:* 'action'; **nach E. dieser Angelegenheit,** after this matter has been settled, arranged, adjusted, disposed of; **Sie können sich auf die prompte E. Ihrer Aufträge verlassen,** you can rely on it that your orders will be attended to without delay; (*b*) **eine E., Erledigungen, machen,** to do, finish, some business, some pieces of business.

erlegen[1], *v.tr.* **1.** to pay (down) (sum); **gegen Erlegung einer geringfügigen Summe,** on payment of a negligible sum. **2.** to kill, bring down (deer, etc.); to shoot (deer, etc.); to kill (one's opponent, etc.) (in a duel, etc.).

erlegen[2], *p.p. see* **erliegen.**

-erlei, *suff.* (*with numeral prefixed*) of . . . sorts, kinds, varieties; **tausenderlei,** of a thousand sorts, kinds, varieties; *see also* **achterlei, allerlei, einerlei, mancherlei, vielerlei, zweierlei.**

erleichtern. I. *v.tr.* **1.** to ease, lighten (burden); *Nau:* to lighten (ship); **sie mußten den Tragtieren die Lasten e.,** they had to ease, lighten, the pack-animals' burden. **2.** to make (s.o.'s task, suffering, etc.) easier; to lighten (s.o.'s task, griefs, one's conscience, etc.); to ease, relieve (s.o.'s suffering, pain, one's conscience, etc.); to alleviate, assuage, allay (pain, suffering, etc.); to help, aid, assist, facilitate, make easy (spreading of a new doctrine, etc.); to facilitate (payment, task, etc.); **sich, sein Herz, e.,** to unburden oneself; to relieve one's feelings; to unburden, unload, one's heart; to disburden one's mind; **j-m etwas e.,** to make s.o.'s (task, work, etc.) easier; to grant s.o. facilities for (payment, etc.); **j-s Los, j-m sein Los, e.,** to ease, lighten, s.o.'s burden, misery, suffering; **sich erleichtert fühlen,** to feel easier; to feel some relief; **erleichtert aufatmen, aufseufzen,** to heave, breathe, a sigh of relief; **diese Methode wird Ihnen Ihre Aufgabe sehr e.,** this method will make your task much easier, will greatly facilitate your task, will greatly ease, lighten, your task; **ich bin sehr erleichtert, das zu hören,** I am much relieved to hear it; *F:* **j-n um eine hübsche Summe e.,** to relieve s.o. of a tidy sum; **sich e.,** to relieve nature, oneself.

II. *vbl s.* **1. Erleichtern,** *n. in vbl senses.* **2. Erleichterung,** *f.* (*a*)=II. 1; *also:* relief; alleviation (of pain, etc.); (*b*) relief; **einen Seufzer der E. ausstoßen,** to heave, breathe, a sigh of relief; **einige E. verspüren,** to feel some relief; **die Medizin brachte, verschaffte, ihm einige E.,** the medicine brought him some relief; **man gewährte den Gefangenen einige**

Erleichterungen, they granted the prisoners some slight reliefs; **einem Kranken E. verschaffen,** to give a patient relief; to ease a patient; **zu seiner E. vernahm er, daß . . . ,** to his relief he heard that . . . ; **wir gewähren alle denkbaren Erleichterungen bei der Abzahlung der geliehenen Summe,** we grant all possible facilities for the repayment of the loan.

erleiden, *v.tr.* (*strong*) (*a*) to suffer, meet with (loss, defeat, injury, accident, etc.); to sustain (loss, defeat, injury, etc.); to undergo (loss, defeat, etc.); **den Tod e.,** to meet with, suffer, death; to meet one's death; (*of pers., ship*) **Schiffbruch e.,** to suffer shipwreck; to be shipwrecked; **im Leben Schiffbruch e.,** to make shipwreck of one's life; **er erlitt eine schwere Einbuße an seinem Vermögen,** he suffered a severe diminution of his fortune; **er erlitt einen Nervenzusammenbruch, einen Schlaganfall,** he suffered, had, a nervous breakdown, a stroke; **der Fahrer erlitt Verbrennungen an Händen und Armen,** the driver suffered burns to his hands and arms; **das Bataillon erlitt schwere Verluste,** the battalion suffered severe losses, suffered severely; **die Maschine erlitt schwere Schäden,** the engine suffered severely, was severely damaged; **er verlangte eine hohe Summe für den erlittenen Schaden,** he demanded a large sum for the damage he had suffered, sustained; (*b*) to suffer (penalty, pain, wrong, etc.) (patiently); to endure, bear (pain, wrong, penalty, etc.); **die Strafe für seine Missetaten e.,** to suffer, endure, bear, the penalty of one's misdeeds; **er erlitt standhaft alle Schmerzen,** he suffered, endured, bore, all the pain with fortitude.

erlen, *a.* (made) of alderwood.

Erlenbruch, *m. & n.* alder-swamp.

Erlenholz, *n.* alder-wood, alder-timber.

Erlenkönig, *m.*=**Erlkönig.**

Erlenzeisig, *m. Orn:* siskin, aberdevine.

erlernbar, *a.* that can be learned; learnable; **leicht, schwer, e.,** easy, difficult, to learn; **Rhythmus ist nicht e.,** rhythm is something that one cannot learn.

erlernen, *v.tr.* to learn (trade, craft, the rudiments of grammar, etc.); to acquire (language, the rudiments of grammar, etc.); *see also* **Beruf.**

erlesen[1]**. 1.** *v.tr.* (*strong*) *A:* to choose; to pick; to select. **2.** *p.p. & a.* **erlesen,** excellent, choice (food, etc.); choice, selected (fruit); select (company, etc.); exquisite (food, wines, taste, enjoyments, etc.); precious (gems, etc.); **Waren von erlesener Qualität,** goods of the very best quality; **erlesene Leckerbissen,** choice dainties; **erlesene Kostbarkeiten,** choice and precious things.

erlesen[2]**,** *v.tr.* (*strong*) **sich** *dat.* **Kenntnisse e.**=**sich Kenntnisse anlesen,** *q.v. under* **anlesen 2.**

erleuchten. I. *v.tr.* (*a*) to light, to illuminate, *Lit:* to illumine (sth.); (*of sun, etc.*) to give light to, to illuminate, to light (planet, etc.); **ein jäher Blitz erleuchtete den Himmel, die Dunkelheit,** a sudden flash of lightning lit up, illuminated, the sky, the darkness; **Hunderte von Lampions erleuchteten den Park,** hundreds of fairy-lamps lit up, illuminated, the park; **hell, festlich, erleuchtet,** brightly, festively, lit; brightly, festively, illuminated; **zu einer bestimmten Zeit ist der von der Sonne erleuchtete Teil des Mondes der Erde zugekehrt,** at a certain time the part of the moon that is lit by the sun faces the earth; (*b*) to illumine, enlighten (s.o., s.o.'s mind, etc.); to illuminate, lighten (s.o.'s mind, etc.); to inspire (prophet, s.o.'s mind, etc.); **Gott erleuchtete seinen Geist,** God illumined, illuminated, his mind; **die erleuchteten Propheten des Alten Testaments,** the inspired prophets of the Old Testament; **plötzlich kam ihm ein erleuchtender Gedanke,** suddenly he had an illuminating idea, a flash of inspiration, suddenly a brilliant idea illumined his mind; **ein Erleuchteter,** an illuminate; *Rel. Hist:* **die Erleuchteten,** the Illuminati.

II. *vbl s.* **1. Erleuchten,** *n. in vbl senses.* **2. Erleuchtung,** *f.* (*a*)=II. 1; *also:* illumination (of sth., s.o., s.o.'s mind, etc.); enlightenment, inspiration (of s.o., s.o.'s mind, etc.); (*b*) illumination; inspiration; *F:* **plötzlich kam ihm eine E.,** suddenly he had an illuminating idea, a flash of inspiration; suddenly he saw the light. he saw daylight.

erliegen. I. *v.i.* (*strong*) (*sein*) (*a*) to succumb to (opponent, temptation, etc.); to be overpowered, overcome, by (opponent, etc.); **der Versuchung e.,** to succumb, give in, give way, yield, to temptation; **der Übermacht e.,** to be overcome by superior force; **er erlag seinem Gegner nach einem kurzen Kampf,** he was defeated, worsted, overpowered, by his opponent after a short fight; **er drohte, der Last dieses furchtbaren Geheimnisses zu e.,** he was in danger of succumbing, of giving way, under the strain of this terrible secret; (*b*) to die; **einer Krankheit e.,** to die from a disease, to be killed, carried off, by a disease, to succumb to a disease; **er ist seinen Verletzungen erlegen,** he has died from his injuries.

II. *vbl s.* **Erliegen,** *n.* **zum E. kommen,** (*of mine, business, etc.*) to close down, to shut down; (*of traffic, etc.*) to be brought to a standstill; (*of strength, efforts, etc.*) to flag, to weaken; (*of strength, etc.*) to fail, to give way; **seine Kräfte kamen bald zum E.,** his strength soon failed, gave way, he soon lost all strength; **bald kam es zum vollständigen E. des Bergwerkes,** soon the mine shut down, closed down, completely, soon the mine was completely idle, completely abandoned.

erlisten, *v.tr.* to get, obtain, (sth.) by stealth *or* cunning.

Erlkönig, der. *Myth:* the Erl-king.

erlogen, *a.* false, made-up, trumped-up (story, etc.); **es ist alles e., es ist von A bis Z e.,** *F:* **es ist alles erstunken und e.,** it is all made up, invented, it is all a lie, it is made up from beginning to end, there is not a grain of truth in it; **erlogener Bericht,** false, untrue, report; *see also* **erlügen.**

Erlös, *m.* **-es/-e,** proceeds (of sale, etc.); **der E. der Tombola ist für karitative Zwecke bestimmt,** the proceeds of the **tombola** are intended to be used for charitable **purposes; der E. der Auktion überstieg alle Erwartungen,** the proceeds of the auction, the amount realized from the auction, surpassed all expectation; **er verkaufte sein Radio, um sich von dem E. ein Fahrrad anzuschaffen,** he sold his radio in order to buy a bicycle with the proceeds, with the money.

erlosch, erloschen *see* **erlöschen.**

erlöschen. I. *v.i.* (*strong*) (*sein*) (*a*) (*of fire, light, etc.*) to go out, *Lit:* to expire; (*of fire, epidemic, etc.*) to die down; (*of love, passion, etc.*) to die; (*of race, family, etc.*) to die out, to become extinct; **plötzlich erlosch das Licht,** suddenly the light went out; **das Feuer ist erloschen,** the fire is out; **der Vulkan ist schon seit vielen Jahren erloschen,** the volcano has been extinct, has not been active, for many years; **erloschener Vulkan,** extinct, spent, burnt-out, volcano; **mit seinem Tode erlischt dieses alte Geschlecht,** with his death this old family will become extinct, will die out; **aller Haß in seinem Herzen war erloschen,** all the hatred had gone out of his heart; **mit erlöschender Kraft,** with failing, ebbing, strength; **mit erlöschender Stimme bat er um Wasser,** with an expiring, a failing, voice, with an ever weaker, feebler, voice, he asked for water; **sein erlöschendes Auge,** his dying eye; (*b*) (*of firm, etc.*) to cease to exist, to go out of existence; to be dissolved; (*of contract, claim, membership, insurance policy, law, treaty, etc.*) to expire, to lapse; (*of right, patent, etc.*) to lapse; (*of debt, etc.*) to be cancelled; **die Gültigkeit dieses Passes erlischt am . . . ,** (the validity of) this passport will expire on . . . ; **ein Recht e. lassen,** to allow a right to lapse, to forfeit a right; *Bank:* **dieser Kreditbrief ist erloschen,** this letter of credit has expired; *Ins:* **erloschene Police,** expired policy.

II. *vbl s.* **Erlöschen,** *n. in vbl senses; also:* (*a*) extinction (of fire, light, race, etc.); **ein Feuer, eine Leidenschaft, ein Geschlecht, usw., zum E. bringen,** to extinguish a fire, a passion, a race, etc.; to bring about the extinction of a race; (*b*) expiration, lapse (of contract, claim, membership, law, treaty, etc.); lapse (of right, patent); **E. einer Schuld, eines Schuldverhältnisses,** cancellation of a debt; **einen Vertrag, ein Gesetz, ein Recht, zum E. bringen,** to extinguish a contract *or* a treaty, a law, a right; to cause a contract *or* a treaty, a law, a right, to lapse; *Ins:* **E. einer Police,** expiration of a policy.

erlösen. I. *v.tr.* **1.** (*a*) to release, deliver (s.o.) (from imprisonment, fear, etc.); to set (s.o.) free, to liberate (s.o.); *Theol:* to deliver, redeem, save (mankind, etc.) (from sin, etc.); **j-n von seinen Banden e.,** to free, loose, release, s.o. from his bonds; **j-n von, aus, einem Leben der Knechtschaft e.,** to deliver s.o. from a life of servitude; **j-n von einem Fluch e.,** to release, free, s.o. from a curse, to break the curse on s.o.; **der Prinz erlöste die schlafende Prinzessin durch seinen Kuß,** with his kiss the prince released the sleeping princess from the spell, the prince broke the spell over the sleeping princess with his kiss; *B:* **erlöse uns von dem Übel,** deliver us from evil; (*b*) (*of God*) to release (s.o.) (from suffering, etc.); **er wurde gestern nach langem Leiden erlöst,** he died yesterday after long suffering; **er ist erlöst,** death, God, has released him from his sufferings; (*c*) to free, relieve (s.o.) (of burden, etc.); **j-n von einer Last, einer Sorge, e.,** to free s.o. of a burden, of a worry; **sich von einer schweren Last erlöst fühlen,** to feel relieved of a great weight; **ein Land von Banditen, von der Banditenplage, e.,** to rid, clear, a country of bandits; **von aller Angst erlöst,** relieved from all anxiety; **ein erlöstes Gefühl,** a feeling of release; **erlöst aufatmen,** to heave a sigh of relief. **2.** *Com:* to realize (money) (from a sale, etc.); **aus einer Auktion erlöstes Geld,** money realized from an auction, proceeds of an auction; **das aus der Tombola erlöste Geld ist für karitative Zwecke bestimmt,** the proceeds of the tombola are intended to be used for charitable purposes.

II. *vbl s.* **1. Erlösen,** *n. in vbl senses.* **2. Erlösung,** *f.* (*a*) *in vbl senses; also:* (*action of*) release, deliverance, liberation (of s.o.) (from imprisonment, etc.); *Theol:* redemption, salvation (of mankind) (from sin, etc.); (*b*) release, liberation; *Theol:* redemption; salvation; **nach ihrer E. aus der Hand ihrer Feinde,** after their release, liberation, from the hands of their enemies; **die Opfer des Zauberers warteten auf ihre E.,** the victims of the sorcerer waited for their release; **ihr Tod war eine E.,** her death was a happy release; *B:* **und gebe sein Leben zu einer E. für viele,** and to give his life a ransom for many.

III. *pr.p. & a.* **erlösend,** *in vbl senses; esp.* **erlösendes Wort, erlösendes Lachen,** word, laughter, that breaks, relieves, the tension.

Erlöser, *m.* **-s/-,** (*a*) liberator, deliverer; rescuer; **die befreiten Gefangenen dankten ihrem E.,** the released prisoners thanked their liberator, their rescuer; (*b*) *Theol:* redeemer, saviour; **Christus ist unser E.,** Christ is our Saviour; *B:* **ich weiß, daß mein E. lebt,** I know that my redeemer liveth.

Erlöserorden, *m. Gr.Hist:* Order of the Redeemer.

Erlösung, *f. see* **erlösen II.**

Erlösungsreligion, *f.* redemptive religion.

erlügen, *v.tr.* (*strong*) **1.** to invent, make up, fabricate (story, etc.). **2.** to get, obtain, (sth.) by lying. *See also* **erlogen.**

erlustieren (sich) [ɛrlus'tiːrən], **erlustigen (sich),** *v.refl. Lit:* **sich an etwas** *dat.* **e.,** to take a delight in sth.; **sich im Garten e.,** to take a walk in the garden.

ermächtigen. I. *v.tr.* **1. j-n zu etwas e., j-n (dazu) e., etwas zu tun,** to empower s.o., to authorize s.o., to give s.o. authority, to do sth.; **zu etwas ermächtigt sein, ermächtigt sein, etwas zu tun,** to be empowered, authorized, to do sth., to have authority, full powers, to do sth.; **zum Handeln ermächtigt sein,** to be empowered, authorized, to act, to have authority, full powers, to act; **nicht ermächtigt,** unauthorized, not authorized; **durch diesen Erlaß ist er dazu ermächtigt, zu handeln,** this decree authorizes, enables, him to act. **2. sich einer Sache ermächtigen,** to lay, take, hold of sth., to seize upon sth.; to take possession of sth.; **sich des Thrones e.,** to seize, usurp, the throne.

II. *vbl s.* **1. Ermächtigen,** *n. in vbl senses.* **2. Ermächtigung,** *f.* (*a*)=II. 1; *also:* authorization (of s.o. to do sth.); (*b*) authorization; authority, (full) powers (to do sth.); **um E. bitten, Frieden schließen zu dürfen,** to ask for powers to conclude peace.

Ermächtigungsgesetz, *n. Pol: etc:* enabling act.

ermahnen. I. *v.tr.* **1.** to admonish, exhort (s.o.) (**etwas zu tun,** to do sth.); *Sch: etc:* to give (s.o.) a warning, a (mild) reprimand; **j-n e., seine Pflicht zu tun,** to admonish s.o. to do his duty, to urge s.o. to do his duty; to remind s.o. to do his duty; **er ermahnte sie, stets ihrer Heimat zu gedenken,** he exhorted, urged, them always to remember their country; **j-n zu etwas e.,** to exhort, urge, admonish, s.o. to sth., to do sth.; **j-n zur Vorsicht, zur Mäßigkeit, e.,** to urge caution, moderation, upon s.o., to admonish, urge, s.o. to be cautious, moderate; **j-n zum Gehorsam, zum Fleiß, e.,** to admonish, urge, s.o. to be obedient, diligent; **j-n zur Zahlung e.,** to request payment of s.o., to urge

s.o. to pay his debts; **ermahnende Worte,** admonitory, monitory, words; **kannst du dir nicht einmal die Hände waschen, ohne daß ich dich (dazu) e. muß?** can't you even wash your hands without my having to remind you? **2.** *occ.* **j-n an etwas** *acc.* **e.,** to remind s.o. of sth.

II. *vbl s.* **1. Ermahnen,** *n. in vbl senses.* **2. Ermahnung,** *f.* (*a*)=II. 1; *also:* admonishment, admonition (of s.o.); (*b*) admonition, admonishment; exhortation; warning; *Sch: etc:* (mild) reprimand, warning; **eine freundliche, ernste, E.,** a friendly, serious, admonition; **eine scharfe E.,** a sharp admonition, a sharp warning; **j-m Ermahnungen, eine E., geben,** to admonish s.o.; to warn s.o.; to give s.o. a warning; **seine Ermahnungen, Gutes zu tun,** his exhortations to good deeds; **j-s Ermahnungen nicht beachten, in den Wind schlagen,** to disregard, make light of, ignore, s.o.'s admonitions, s.o.'s warnings.

Ermahner, *m.* **-s/-,** admonisher, admonitor; warner.

ermangeln. I. *v.i.* (*haben*) **1. etwas** *gen.*, **einer Sache, e.,** to lack, be lacking, sth.; to be short of, to be in need of, want of (money, provisions, etc.); **er ermangelt des Mutes,** (*impers. construction*) **es ermangelt ihm an Mut,** he lacks, is lacking in, courage, he has no courage; **es ermangelte ihnen an Gelegenheit,** they lacked the opportunity, they had no opportunity. **2. e., etwas zu tun,** to fail to do sth.; **ich werde nicht e., alles gut auszuführen,** I shall not fail to carry out everything satisfactorily.

II. *vbl s.* **Ermangelung,** *f.* **in E.**+*gen.*, for want of, lack of, sth.; in the absence of sth.; **in E. eines geeigneten Gefäßes trugen sie die Pilze in ihren Mützen,** for want of a suitable container they carried the mushrooms in their caps; **in E. eines Besseren,** for want of, in default of, lack of, something better; **in E. genauer Anweisungen,** in the absence of, lacking, failing, definite instructions.

ermannen (sich), *v.refl.* to pull oneself together, (i) to regain one's self-control, to recover oneself; (ii) to take courage, to take heart; to brace oneself.

ermäßigen. I. *v.tr.* to reduce, diminish, lower (prices, rates, taxes, duty, etc.); to cut (prices, etc.); **den Preis eines Artikels e.,** to reduce, lower, bring down, cut, *U.S:* cut down, the price of an article, to make a reduction on an article; to mark down (the price of) an article; **Preise stark e.,** to reduce prices drastically, *F:* to slash prices; **stark ermäßigte Preise,** greatly, much, reduced prices; **alles zu ermäßigten Preisen,** everything reduced, everything at reduced, cut, prices; **ermäßigter Fahrpreis, ermäßigter Eintrittspreis,** reduced fare, reduced entrance fee; **Fahrkarten zu ermäßigten Preisen, ermäßigte Fahrkarten,** tickets at reduced rates, reduced, cheap, tickets.

II. *vbl s.* **1. Ermäßigen,** *n. in vbl senses.* **2. Ermäßigung,** *f.* (*a*)=II. 1; *also:* reduction (of price, taxes, etc.); (*b*) reduction, cut (in prices, taxes, duty, etc.); *Adm:* (tax) allowance (for dependant, etc.); **E. bei Mengenabnahme,** discount, reduction, for quantities; **eine E. gewähren,** to allow a discount, a reduction; **eine E. von 25%,** a reduction, discount, of 25%, a 25% reduction, discount; **starke Ermäßigungen,** great reductions, big cuts (in price).

ermatten. I. *v.i.* (*sein*) (*a*) (*of pers., limbs*) to weary, to tire; to become, grow, weak(er); (*of pers.*) to lose one's strength; **sie ermattete zusehends,** her strength was failing visibly; **ermattet,** (*of pers., limbs*) weary, tired, weak; (*of pers.*) fatigued; worn out, exhausted; **sein Arm war bald ermattet,** his arm soon grew weary, tired; **von der Anstrengung ermattet,** worn out, tired out, exhausted, from the exertion; **von der Hitze ermattet,** exhausted from the heat; limp with the heat; (*b*) (*of pers.*) **in etwas** *dat.* **e.,** to flag, weary, in (one's efforts, etc.); **er ermattete bald in seinem Eifer,** his zeal soon began to flag; (*c*) *v.tr. A:* to tire, weaken, exhaust (s.o.).

II. *vbl s.* **1. Ermatten,** *n. in vbl senses.* **2. Ermattung,** *f.* (*a*)=II. 1; (*b*) weariness; fatigue, tiredness; weakness; exhaustion.

ermeßbar, *a.*=**ermeßlich.**

ermessen. I. *v.tr.* (*strong*) (*a*) to measure (dimensions, quantity, etc.); to calculate, estimate (sth.); to judge (sth.); **der Schaden ist schwer, kaum, zu e.,** it is difficult to calculate, assess, the extent of the damage; **wir können gar nicht e., es ist nicht zu e., welche Folgen ein solcher Schritt haben würde,** we have no way, there is no way, of telling, knowing, what consequences such a step would have; **keiner kann das Leid eines Heimatlosen e., das Leid eines Heimatlosen ist nicht zu e.,** nobody can realize, comprehend, fathom, the sorrow of a homeless person; **du kannst sicher selbst e., wieviel Schaden du mit deiner Handlung hättest anrichten können,** you yourself can surely realize, judge, imagine, how much damage you might have done by acting like that.

II. *vbl s.* **Ermessen,** *n.* (*a*) estimation, judgment; discretion; **nach meinem E.,** in my view, estimation, opinion, judgment; to my mind, as I see it; **ich werde nach meinem eigenen E. handeln,** I shall act at, I shall use, my own discretion; **etwas in j-s E. stellen, etwas j-s E. überlassen,** to leave sth. to s.o.'s discretion, to s.o.'s judgment; **ich überlasse es ganz Ihrem E., ich überlasse es Ihrem freien E., ich stelle es in Ihr freies E.,** I leave it entirely to you (to judge), I leave it entirely to your discretion, your judgment; **nach menschlichem E. können sie nicht mehr am Leben sein,** as far as is humanly possible to judge, tell, say, by all human conjecture, they can no longer be alive; (*b*) *Jur:* **richterliches E.,** judicial discretion; **etwas dem E. des Richters überlassen,** to leave sth. to the discretion of the judge; **nach dem E. des Gerichts,** at the, left to the, within the, discretion of the court; **Geldstrafe, die dem E. des Richters überlassen ist,** fine at, left to, the discretion of the judge; **Ausübung des Ermessens,** exercise of discretion.

Ermessensfehler, *m.*=**Ermessensmißbrauch.**

Ermessensfrage, *f.* matter of discretion.

Ermessensmißbrauch, *m. Jur:* abuse of power (of discretion).

Ermessensrecht, *n. Jur:* (right of) discretion; discretionary power; **Ausübung des Ermessensrechts,** exercise of discretion.

ermeßlich, *a.* (damage, extent, etc.) that can be calculated, estimated; **schwer ermeßliche Folgen,** consequences that are difficult to foresee.

Ermitage [ɛrmiˈtaːʒə], *m.* -/-, (*wine*) hermitage.

ermitteln. I. *v.tr.* to establish (fact, s.o.'s identity, etc.); to trace (s.o., s.o.'s whereabouts, etc.); to ascertain, find out, discover (fact, s.o.'s name, etc.); to elicit (fact, etc.); *Mth: etc:* to determine (a value, etc.); **wir haben seine Adresse bisher noch nicht e. können,** we have so far been unable to find out his address; **die Polizei versucht, etwaige Verwandte des Verletzten zu e.,** the police are trying to trace any relatives of the injured man; **die Täter e.,** to find, discover, the culprits; **inzwischen konnte ermittelt werden, daß das Auto in X gestohlen worden war,** it has meanwhile been established that the car had been stolen in X; **e., ob eine Firma zahlungsfähig ist,** to find out whether a firm is solvent; **etwas zu e. versuchen,** to try to find out sth.; to make enquiries about sth.; to investigate sth.

II. *vbl s.* **1. Ermitteln,** *n. in vbl senses.* **2. Ermitt(e)lung,** *f.* (*a*)=II. 1; *also:* ascertainment (of fact, etc.); *Mth: etc:* determination (of a value, etc.); **zur E. der Tatsachen,** in order to ascertain, find out, establish, the facts; (*b*) *pl.* **Ermitt(e)lungen,** investigations, enquiries; **Ermittlungen anstellen,** to instigate, start, investigations, to start, make, enquiries; to hold, institute, an inquiry; **umfangreiche Ermittlungen,** extensive investigations, enquiries; **polizeiliche Ermittlungen blieben erfolglos,** investigations by the police produced, brought forth, no result(s), were without results.

Ermittlungsbeamte, *m.* (*decl. as adj.*) *Jur:* investigating officer (in judicial inquiry).

Ermittlungsergebnis, *n. Jur:* result of a, of the, judicial inquiry.

Ermittlungsverfahren, *n. Jur:* judicial inquiry; **ein E. einleiten,** to institute, hold, a judicial inquiry; **die im E. erwiesenen Tatsachen,** the facts established by the inquiry.

ermöglichen. I. *v.tr.* to make (sth.) possible; **j-m etwas e.,** to make it possible for s.o. to do sth., to enable s.o. to do sth.; **nur durch seine freundliche Hilfe wurde uns der Besuch der Fabrik ermöglicht,** our visit to the factory was made possible only through his kind assistance; **die gründlichen Vorbereitungen ermöglichten einen reibungslosen Ablauf der Veranstaltung,** the thorough preparations made it possible for the function to go off smoothly, without a hitch; **der gesteigerte Umsatz hat es uns ermöglicht, neue Maschinen anzuschaffen,** the increased turnover has enabled us, has made it possible for us, to buy new machines; **dieses Vermächtnis ermöglichte es ihm, sich zur Ruhe zu setzen,** this legacy enabled him to retire; **die Eltern sparten jahrelang, um ihr ein Universitätsstudium e. zu können,** her parents saved for years to give her a university education; **seine Tante ermöglichte ihm das Studium,** his aunt enabled him to study, made it possible for him to study; **ich würde ihr gern die Reise e.,** I should like to make it possible for her to go on the journey.

II. *vbl s.* **Ermöglichen** *n.*, **Ermöglichung** *f. in vbl senses; also:* **ein Stipendium zur Ermöglichung seines Studiums,** a grant to enable him to study, to make it possible for him to study.

ermorden. I. *v.tr.* to murder (s.o.); to assassinate (king, political opponent, etc.); **er war ermordet worden,** he had been murdered; **Ermordete** *m, f,* murdered person, person murdered, murder victim; **der Ermordete war ein reicher Kaufmann,** the murdered man, the (murderer's) victim, was a rich merchant.

II. *vbl s.* **1. Ermorden,** *n. in vbl senses* **2. Ermordung,** *f.*=II. 1; *also:* murder; assassination; **die E. des Königs,** the assassination, murder, of the king; **nach seiner E.,** after his assassination, after he had been assassinated, murdered.

ermüdbar, *a.* (*of child, etc.*) **leicht e.,** easily tired.

ermüden. I. *v.* **1.** *v.tr.* to tire (s.o.), to make (s.o.) tired, weary; to wear (s.o.) out; to tire, strain (one's eyes, etc.); **das viele Sprechen hatte sie ermüdet,** all the talking had tired her, worn her out; **seine Augen, (sich** *dat.*) **die Augen, durch zu vieles Lesen e.,** to strain, try, one's eyes by reading too much; **ermüdend,** tiring, wearying, tedious; fatiguing; tiresome; **diese Arbeit ermüdet einen sehr, diese Arbeit ist sehr ermüdend,** this work is very tiring, wearying, tedious, this work makes one very tired, tires one very much, wears one out. **2.** *v.i.* (*sein*) to tire; to become, get, grow, tired, weary, fatigued; **der Patient ermüdet leicht,** the patient gets tired very easily; **die Pferde ermüdeten,** the horses were tiring, wearying; **sie war vom vielen Sprechen ermüdet,** she was tired from so much talking, all the talking had tired her, worn her out; **meine Augen ermüden schnell,** my eyes get tired, strained, very quickly; **sie waren alle stark ermüdet,** they were all very tired, very weary, tired out, worn out.

II. *vbl s.* **1. Ermüden,** *n. in vbl senses.* **2. Ermüdung,** *f.* (*a*)=II. 1; (*b*) tiredness, weariness; fatigue; **die Ursache seines Anfalls war starke E.,** his attack was caused by extreme tiredness, fatigue, by overtiredness; (*c*) *Tchn:* fatigue (of materials); **E. des Metalls,** fatigue of metals, metal fatigue.

Ermüdungsbruch, *m. Mec.E: Med:* fatigue fracture.

Ermüdungserscheinungen, *f.pl.* (*a*) signs of weariness, of fatigue; (*b*) *Tchn:* signs of fatigue (in metals, materials).

Ermüdungsgefühl, *n.* feeling of tiredness, of weariness.

Ermüdungsgrenze, *f.* (*a*) *Tchn:* fatigue point (of metals, etc.); (*b*) fatigue point (of pers.).

Ermüdungsrausch, *m. Med:* fatigue narcosis.

Ermüdungsstoff, *m.*, **Ermüdungstoxin,** *n.* fatigue toxine.

Ermundure [ɛrmunˈduːrə], *m.* **-n/-n.** *Hist:* one of the Hermunduri; **die Ermunduren,** the Hermunduri.

ermuntern. I. *v.* **1.** *v.tr.* (*a*) to cheer, *F:* buck, (s.o.) up; to put new heart, new life, into (s.o.); to rouse (s.o.) from lethargy; **ein ermunternder Brief,** a heartening, cheering, cheerful, letter; (*b*) to encourage, prompt (s.o.) (to do sth., say sth.); **j-n zur Arbeit e.,** to encourage, induce, incite, s.o. to work; **sie ermunterte ihn mit einem Lächeln weiterzuerzählen,** she encouraged him with a smile to continue his tale; **mit einem leisen Zuruf ermunterte er das Pferd zum Springen,** he spoke softly to the horse to encourage it to jump; **'erzähle mir mal, was du gestern getan hast', ermunterte sie den Knaben,** 'tell me what you did yesterday,' she encouraged, prompted, the boy; **ermunternde Zurufe,** encouraging shouts, shouts of encouragement. **2. sich ermuntern,** to wake up, to come to (*after sleep, etc.*).

II. *vbl s.* **1. Ermuntern,** *n. in vbl senses.* **2. Ermunterung,** *f.* (*a*)=II. 1; *also:* encouragement; **zur E.,** in order to encourage (s.o.); in order to cheer (s.o.) up; (*b*) encouragement; **eine E.,** something to cheer one, s.o., up; something to encourage one, s.o.; **er braucht eine kleine E.,** he needs a little encouragement, he needs something to encourage him.

ermutigen. I. *v.tr.* to give (s.o.) courage, to put courage into (s.o.); to put (s.o.) in good heart, to put spirit, *F:* pluck, into (s.o.); to encourage, hearten (s.o.); **j-n zu etwas e.,** to encourage s.o. to do sth., to give s.o. (the) courage to do sth.; **der freundliche Ton des Briefes ermutigte ihn dazu, seine Bitte zu wiederholen,** the friendly tone of the letter encouraged him, gave him the courage, to repeat his request; **ich war von seiner Antwort nicht sehr ermutigt,** I did not find his answer very encouraging, heartening, I was not encouraged by his answer; **von dieser Entwicklung ermutigt, setzte er seine Arbeit mit erneutem Eifer fort,** encouraged, heartened, by this development he continued his work with renewed enthusiasm; **ermutigende Nachrichten,** encouraging, heartening, news; **das Resultat war nicht sehr ermutigend,** the result was not very encouraging.

II. *vbl s.* **1. Ermutigen,** *n. in vbl senses.* **2. Ermutigung,** *f.* (*a*)=II. 1; *also:* encouragement (of troops, etc.); **zur E.,** as an encouragement, in order to encourage (oneself, s.o.); (*b*) encouragement; **ohne diese E. hätte ich es nie getan,** without this encouragement, without these encouraging words, I should never have done it.

Ermutiger, *m.* **-s/-,** person who encourages, gives (s.o.) courage; heartener.

Ern, *m.* **-/-** =**Eren.**

-ern[1], *a.suff.* (*usu. suffixed to nouns of one syllable*) of . . . ; made of . . . ; -en; **bleiern,** (made) of lead; leaden; **hölzern,** (made) of wood; wooden; **beinern,** (made) of bone; bone (spoon, etc.); **gläsern,** (made) of glass; glass (dish, etc.); **tönern,** (made) of clay; clay (pipe, etc.); **steinern,** (made) of stone; stone (jug, etc.).

-ern[2], *vbl suff.* (*usu. indicates reiterated movement or sound*) **flattern,** to flutter; **wandern,** to wander; **zittern,** to tremble; **stottern,** to stutter; **klappern,** to rattle; **zwitschern,** to twitter.

Erna. *Pr.n.f.* **-s.** Ernestine, Erna.

ernähren. I. *v.tr.* (*a*) to feed (s.o., animal, etc.); to nourish (s.o., plant, etc.); **sich von etwas e.,** (*of pers.*) to live on sth.; (*of animal*) to feed on sth.; **j-n mit etwas e.,** to feed s.o. with, on, sth., to nourish s.o. with sth.; **sich von Fleisch e.,** to live on (a diet of) meat, to eat meat; **sich gut e.,** to eat well; **die Eingeborenen ernähren sich größtenteils von Fisch,** the natives eat mainly fish, the natives live mainly on fish, the natives' diet consists mainly of fish; **sich von pflanzlicher Kost e.,** (*of pers.*) to live on a vegetarian diet, to be a vegetarian; (*of animal*) to be herbivorous; **gut ernährte Kinder,** well-fed, well-nourished, children; **schlecht ernährte Leute,** ill-fed, underfed, undernourished, people; (*b*) to keep, maintain (s.o.); to support (s.o., family, etc.); **er hat sechs Kinder zu e.,** he has to keep, feed, provide food for, six children; **seine Familie e.,** to maintain, support, one's family; **sich von seiner Hände Arbeit e.,** to live by the work of one's hands; **seine Feder ernährt ihn, er ernährt sich von seiner Feder,** he lives by his pen, by his writing, he makes his living by his pen, by writing; **dieser Beruf ernährt seinen Mann nicht mehr,** you cannot make your living in this trade any more, in this trade you no longer make, earn, enough (money) to live upon.

II. *vbl s.* **1. Ernähren,** *n. in vbl senses.* **2. Ernährung,** *f.* (*a*)=II. 1; *also:* nourishment (of s.o.); alimentation (of plants, animals, etc.); **künstliche E.,** artificial feeding; **E. durch die Nase,** feeding through the nose; **intravenöse E.,** feeding by intravenous injections; (*b*) *Physiol: etc:* nutrition; **Vorgänge der E.,** processes of nutrition, nutritive processes; **ungenügende, mangelhafte, E.,** inadequate nutrition, malnutrition, undernourishment; **richtige, falsche, E.,** correct, wrong, diet; **die E. war schlecht,** the food was bad; (*c*) maintenance (of family, etc.).

Ernährer, *m.* **-s/-,** provider; supporter, breadwinner (of family); **Gott, der E.,** God the Provider.

Ernährungsabfälle, *m.pl. Physiol:* waste products of nutrition.

Ernährungsamt, *n. Adm:* Food Office.

Ernährungsbehandlung, *f. Med:* dietetic treatment.

Ernährungsfachmann, *m.* nutrition expert, nutritionist; dietician, dietist.

Ernährungsflüssigkeit, *f. Physiol:* lymph.

Ernährungslehre, *f.* (science of) dietetics.

Ernährungsminister, *m. Adm:* =Minister of Agriculture, Fisheries, and Food.

Ernährungsschicht, *f. Biol:* trophoblast.

Ernährungsstörung, *f. Med:* dystrophy; disorder of the alimentary system.

Ernährungssubstanz, *f.* (*a*) nutrient; (*b*) *Biol:* trophoplasm.

Ernährungstherapie, *f. Med:* dietetic treatment.

Ernährungsweise, *f.* form of nutrition; diet; feeding habits (of animals); **richtige, falsche, E.,** correct, wrong, diet.

ernährungswichtig, *a.* **ernährungswichtige Industrien,** essential food industries.

Ernährungswirtschaft, *f.* economics of food supply.

Ernährungswissenschaft, *f.* (science of) dietetics.

ernennen. I. *v.tr.* (*conj. like* **nennen**) to appoint, nominate, name (s.o.) (to an office *or* a post); **j-n zum Direktor e.,** to make s.o. a director, to appoint s.o. as director; **neu ernannte Minister,** newly-appointed ministers.

II. *vbl s.* **1. Ernennen,** *n. in vbl senses.* **2. Ernennung,** *f.* (*a*)=II. 1; *also:* appointment, nomination (of s.o.) (to an office *or* a post); (*b*) **nach seiner E. zum Minister,** after his appointment as minister, after he had been made a minister; **seine E. zum Minister, usw., erhalten,** to receive one's appointment as minister, etc.; (*c*)=**Ernennungsurkunde.**

Ernennungsurkunde, *f.* certificate of appointment (to an office *or* a post).

Ernestinisch [ɛrnɛs'tiːniʃ], *a. Hist:* **die Ernestinische Linie,** the Ernestine branch (of the house of Frederick of Saxony, etc.).

erneuen. I. *v.tr.* (*a*) to renew (promise, etc.); to renew, resume (efforts, hostilities, etc.); **sich e.,** to be renewed; **die Angriffe gegen ihn erneuten sich,** the attacks against him were renewed, resumed; fresh, new, attacks were made upon him; (*b*) (*of God, etc.*) to renew (nature, etc.); to revive (s.o.'s spirit, s.o.'s strength, etc.); **sich e.,** (*of nature, etc.*) to renew itself, to be renewed; (*of spirit, etc.*) to revive, to be revived; **die Natur erneut sich jedes Jahr,** nature renews itself every year; *B:* **du erneuest die Gestalt der Erde,** thou renewest the face of the earth.

II. *p.p. & a.* **erneut. 1.** *in vbl senses; esp.* renewed; **erneute Tätigkeit,** renewed activity; **erneute Hoffnung,** renewed, new, hope; **erneuter Ausbruch eines Vulkans,** renewed eruption of a volcano; **mit erneutem Eifer,** with renewed zeal; **mit erneuten Kräften, mit erneuter Kraft,** with renewed strength, with renewed vigour; **erneute Angriffe,** renewed, new, fresh, attacks; **erneuter Versuch,** renewed, new, attempt. **2.** *adv.* again; anew, afresh; **eine Arbeit e. in Angriff nehmen,** to attack a task anew, afresh; **sie versuchten e., den Kasten zu heben,** they tried again, anew, they made another attempt, to lift the box; **er wies e. auf die Gefahren des Unternehmens hin,** (once) again, once more, he pointed out the dangers of the undertaking; **sie drangen e. auf das Gebäude ein,** again, once more, they surged towards the building.

erneuern. I. *v.tr.* **1.** (*a*) to renew, replace (part of machine, etc.); to repair, mend (road, etc.); to restore, renovate (damaged painting, building, statue, etc.); to retouch, touch up (painting, paintwork, etc.); **das abgenutzte, beschädigte, Rad muß erneuert werden,** the worn, damaged, wheel has to be replaced; **seine Reifen e.,** to renew one's tyres; **den Straßenbelag e.,** to resurface a road; **den Hosenboden in einer Hose e.,** to put a new seat in a pair of trousers, to reseat a pair of trousers; **den Bezug eines Sessels e.,** to put a new cover on an armchair, to re-cover an armchair; **der Fußboden wurde vollständig erneuert,** a completely new floor was put in; **die Batterie muß von Zeit zu Zeit erneuert werden,** from time to time the battery has to be (i) replaced, (ii) recharged; **einen Verband e.,** to renew a bandage; *Phot:* **das Fixierbad e.,** to renew the fixing bath; *Aut:* **das Öl e.,** to change the oil; (*b*) to renew (promise, treaty, alliance, lease, acquaintance, etc.); to renew, resume (efforts, hostilities, etc.); **einen Paß e.,** to renew a passport; **sein Abonnement, seine Mitgliedschaft, e.,** to renew one's subscription, one's membership; **das Taufgelübde e.,** to renew the baptismal vows; **die Bekanntschaft mit j-m e.,** to renew one's acquaintance with s.o.; **die Freundschaft, freundschaftliche Beziehungen, mit j-m e.,** to renew, resume, one's friendship, friendly relations, with s.o.; *Com: Fin:* **einen Wechsel e.,** to renew a bill. **2. sich erneuern,** to be renewed; (*of spirit, etc.*) to revive, to be revived; **die Haut einer Schlange erneuert sich jedes Jahr,** the skin of a snake is renewed, is replaced by a new one, every year.

II. *vbl s.* **1. Erneuern,** *n. in vbl senses.* **2. Erneuerung,** *f.* (*a*)=II. 1; *also:* renewal, replacement (of part of machine, etc.); restoration, renovation (of damaged painting, building, statue, etc.); renewal (of promise, treaty, alliance, lease, friendship, etc.); revival (of custom, etc.); **E. eines Gelübdes,** renewal of a vow; **E. des Abonnements, der Mitgliedschaft,** renewal of the subscription, of membership; **E. der Bekanntschaft,** renewal of acquaintance; **E. des Hausanstrichs,** repainting, redecorating, of a house; **alle drei Monate wird eine E. der Glühbirne nötig,** every three months the bulb has to be replaced, every three months replacement of the bulb becomes necessary; *Com: Fin:* **E. eines Wechsels,** renewal of a bill; (*b*) **an einem Hause Erneuerungen ausführen,** to repair, renovate, a house; **an der Maschine sind verschiedene Erneuerungen notwendig,** several parts of the machine need replacing; (*c*) (spiritual, etc.) revival, renascence; *Theol:* **E. der Seele,** renovation of the soul; *B:* **das Bad der Wiedergeburt und E. des heiligen Geistes,** the washing of regeneration and the renewing of the Holy Ghost.

Erneuerungsfonds, *m. Com: Fin:* reserve funds for replacements.

Erneuerungskonto, *n. Book-k:* reserve account for replacements.

Erneuerungsschein, *m. Com: Fin:* talon (of sheet of coupons).

erneut, *a. & adv. see* **erneuen II.**

erniedrigen. I. *v.tr.* **1.** (*a*) to lower, reduce, diminish (prices, rates, taxes, duties, etc.); to cut (prices, etc.); **den Preis eines Artikels e.,** to reduce, lower, bring down, cut, the price of an article, to make a reduction on an article; **alles zu erniedrigten Preisen,** everything reduced, everything at reduced, cut, prices; (*b*) *Mus:* to flatten (note); to mark (note) with a flat; **erniedrigte Note,** flattened note; **erniedrigtes E,** E flat; **doppelt erniedrigtes E,** E double flat; (*c*) *Her:* **erniedrigt,** in base; **erniedrigter Sparren,** chevron in base. **2.** to degrade, abase, debase (s.o.); to humiliate, mortify, humble (s.o.); **sich e.,** to abase, debase, lower, demean, degrade, oneself; **sich zu etwas e., sich dazu e., etwas zu tun,** to demean, lower, oneself so far, to stoop so low, as to do sth., to stoop to sth.; **zu so etwas werde ich mich nicht e.,** I will not, I refuse to, stoop to such a thing; **sich in den Augen anderer e.,** to degrade oneself in other people's eyes; **du würdest dich durch diese Arbeit durchaus nicht e.,** you would not lower, demean, yourself in the least by doing this job; **erniedrigend,** degrading; humiliating; **er empfand es als sehr erniedrigend, daß man ihn nicht eingeladen hatte,** he found it very humiliating, it was a great humiliation to him, he felt it as a great humiliation, that he had not been invited; *see also* **erhöhen** I. 1 (*b*).

II. *vbl s.* **1. Erniedrigen,** *n. in vbl senses.* **2. Erniedrigung,** *f.* (*a*)=II. 1; *also:* reduction (of prices, etc.); (*b*) degradation, abasement, debasement (of s.o.); humiliation, mortification (of s.o.); **ein Leben der E. führen,** to lead a life of degradation; (*c*) degradation; humiliation, humiliating remark *or* action; **eine E. erfahren, erleiden,** to suffer a humiliation, an affront.

Erniedrigungszeichen, *n. Mus:* **E. (für einen halben Ton),** flat; **E. für einen ganzen Ton,** double flat.

Ernst[1]. *Pr.n.m.* **-s.** Ernest.

ernst[2]. **1.** *a.* (*a*) serious, serious-minded, earnest (pers.); solemn, serious, grave (face, tone, mood, etc.); **ein ernstes Kind,** a serious, solemn, child; **er ist immer so e.,** he is always so serious, so earnest, so much in earnest; **mit ernstem Gesicht, mit ernster Miene,** (i) with a serious, grave, face, look; (ii) with a straight face; **er sprach in ernstem Ton,** he spoke seriously, gravely, his tone was serious, grave; **ein ernstes Wort mit j-m sprechen,** to speak seriously to s.o., to have a serious talk with s.o.; to speak to s.o. in earnest; **ein ernster Verweis,** a severe reprimand; **ernste Mahnung,** solemn warning; solemn admonition; **es ist ein ernstes Buch,** it is a serious book; **ernste Musik,** serious music (*as opposed to light music*); **ich habe mir noch nie ernste Gedanken darüber gemacht,** I have never thought seriously about it, I have never given it, the subject, serious thought; (*b*) serious (intentions, attempt, etc.); **earnest** (request, effort, desire, etc.); serious, earnest,

genuine (offer); **ernste Absichten haben,** (i) to have serious intentions (of doing sth.); (ii) to have honourable intentions; (*c*) grave, weighty, serious, important (matter, etc.); grave, serious, severe (illness, damage, etc.); grave serious, dangerous, critical (situation, illness, etc.): stern (fact, necessity, reality); **sein Zustand ist e.,** his condition is serious; **ernste Nachrichten,** grave news; **es wäre sehr e., es wäre eine sehr ernste Sache, wenn . . .,** it would be very serious, a very serious matter, if . . .; **die Sache wird e., jetzt wird es e.,** the matter, it, is getting serious; things are getting serious; **das ist eine sehr ernste Sache, Geschichte,** that is a very serious business; **bevor er ernsteren Schaden anrichten kann,** before he can cause more serious damage. **2.** *adv.* (*a*) gravely; with gravity; solemnly; earnestly; in earnest; seriously; **er sah e. aus,** he looked serious, grave; he had an earnest look about him; **sie sah uns e. an,** she looked at us gravely, solemnly; she looked earnestly at us; **sie sagte uns e., daß keine Hoffnung auf Rettung mehr bestünde,** she told us gravely that there was no more hope of rescue; **ich muß einmal e. mit dir reden,** now I want to have a serious talk with you; **sich e. halten, e. bleiben,** to remain serious; to keep a straight face; (*b*) **die Sache, die Lage, sieht e. aus,** the matter, the situation, looks serious; (*c*) **etwas, j-n, e. nehmen,** to take sth., s.o., seriously; **nimm die Sache nicht zu e.,** don't take the matter too seriously; don't take it too hard; **die Krankheit ist unbedingt e. zu nehmen,** the illness must be taken, treated, seriously, must not be treated lightly; **man kann ihn nie e. nehmen,** one can never take him quite seriously; he is never quite serious, quite in earnest; he continually, always, has his tongue in his cheek; you can never take him at his word; **das war nicht e. gemeint,** that was not meant seriously; *cp.* **ernstgemeint.**

Ernst[3], *m.* -(e)s/. (*a*) seriousness, gravity (of pers., face, etc.); earnestness (of pers., mind, etc.); serious-mindedness (of pers.); gravity, seriousness, weightiness, importance (of matter, etc.); gravity, seriousness (of illness, situation, etc.); severity (of illness, etc.); **angesichts des Ernstes der Lage,** in view of the seriousness, gravity, of the situation; **der E. des Lebens,** the serious side of life, life in all its seriousness; **jetzt fängt der E. des Lebens an,** now life begins in earnest; (*after holiday, etc.*) **jetzt fängt der E. des Lebens wieder an,** back to the grindstone! (*b*) **etwas in allem E., allen Ernstes, sagen,** to say sth. in all seriousness, in sober earnest; **er hat allen Ernstes geglaubt, daß . . .,** he believed in all seriousness, in good earnest, he quite seriously believed, that . . .; **wir werden jetzt im E. damit beginnen,** we shall now start seriously with it, we shall now make a serious start with it; we shall now set to work in earnest; **ist das dein E.? ist es dir E. damit?** are you in earnest? are you serious? do you really, earnestly, seriously, mean that? **glaubst du, er meinte es im E.? glaubst du, es war ihm E. mit dem, was er sagte?** do you think he meant what he said? do you think he was serious, in earnest, when he said that? **es ist mein E., es ist mir E. damit,** I mean it, I am quite serious, I am in earnest, about it; **es ist mein bitterer, blutiger, tödlicher, E., es ist mir bitter E. damit,** I am dead serious, in dead earnest, very much in earnest, about it; **das ist doch nicht dein E.!** you don't (earnestly, seriously) mean that! you can't be serious (about that)! **es wird E., jetzt wird es E.,** the matter, it, is getting serious, things are getting serious; this is the real thing, this is it; **das ist kein Spiel, sondern bitterer, blutiger, E.,** this is no game but a very serious matter; this is deadly earnest, dead serious; **mit etwas E. machen,** to put (plan, promise, etc.) into effect; to get down to (preparations, etc.); **er wird mit seiner Drohung E. machen,** his words are not an empty threat, he will certainly do what he threatens; **denkt er im E. daran, sein Haus zu verkaufen?** is he seriously thinking of selling his house?

Ernstfall, *m.* **im E.,** (i) in case of emergency; (ii) *Mil:* in case of war; **für den E. gerüstet sein,** to be ready for an emergency.

ernstgemeint, *attrib. a.* sincerely-meant (offer, advice, etc.); serious, genuine (offer); serious, genuine (application, etc.); (threat, etc.) that is meant seriously; **das sind ernstgemeinte Drohungen,** these are no empty threats; *cp.* **ernst**[2] 2 (*c*).

ernsthaft. 1. *a.* (*a*) serious(-minded), earnest, solemn (pers.); solemn, serious, grave (face, tone, etc.); **er ist immer so e.,** he is always so serious, so earnest, so much in earnest; **ein ernsthaftes Kind,** a serious, solemn, child; **mit ernsthaftem Gesicht, mit ernsthafter Miene,** (i) with a serious, grave, face, look; (ii) with a straight face; **ein ernsthaftes Wort mit j-m sprechen,** to speak seriously to s.o., to have a serious talk with s.o.; to speak to s.o. in earnest; **ein ernsthaftes Buch,** a serious book; **eine ernsthafte Angelegenheit,** a serious matter; (*b*) serious (intentions, attempt, etc.); earnest (request, effort, desire, etc.); serious, earnest, genuine (offer); **ernsthafte Absichten haben,** (i) to have serious intentions (of doing sth.); (ii) to have honourable intentions; **er hatte die ernsthafte Absicht, Maler zu werden,** he had the serious intention of becoming a painter, he seriously intended to become a painter. **2.** *adv.* (*a*) gravely; with gravity; solemnly; earnestly; in earnest; seriously; **er nickte e.,** he nodded gravely, earnestly; **er sagte es ganz e.,** he said it quite earnestly, seriously, in all seriousness; **(ganz) e. bleiben,** to remain serious; to keep a straight face; (*b*) = **ernstlich** 2.

Ernsthaftigkeit, *f.* seriousness, earnestness, solemnity (of pers.).

ernst-heiter, *a.* (*of pers.*) serious yet cheerful.

ernstlich. 1. *a.* (*a*) serious (intention, etc.); **es ist mein ernstlicher Wunsch,** it is my serious, sincere, wish; (*b*) serious, grave (danger, etc.); **das Haus ist in ernstlicher Gefahr einzustürzen,** the house is in serious, grave, danger of collapse; **in ernstlicher Verlegenheit sein,** (i) to be seriously embarrassed; (ii) to be in serious difficulties. **2.** *adv.* seriously; in earnest; **e. daran denken, etwas zu tun,** to think seriously of doing sth., to have serious intentions of doing sth.; **wir werden e. an die Weihnachtsvorbereitungen denken müssen,** we shall have to start seriously, we shall have to make a serious start, with our preparations for Christmas, we shall have to get down to our preparations for Christmas; **sich** *dat.* **etwas e. überlegen,** to think seriously about sth., to consider sth. seriously, to give serious thought to sth.; **ich habe mir e. überlegt, ob ich mir nicht doch ein Auto kaufen sollte,** I have seriously considered, I have been thinking seriously, whether I should not buy a car after all; **ich habe noch nie e. darüber nachgedacht,** I have never thought seriously about it, I have never given it, the subject, serious thought; **er hat e. geglaubt, daß . . .,** he believed earnestly, in all seriousness, in sober earnest, he quite seriously believed, that . . .; **er riet ihr e., das Haus zu verkaufen,** he earnestly advised her to sell the house; **e. in Verlegenheit sein,** (i) to be seriously embarrassed; (ii) to be in serious difficulties; **e. erkrankt, e. krank,** seriously, gravely, ill; **e. verletzt,** seriously, badly, injured; **e. böse sein,** to be seriously displeased, to be seriously annoyed.

Ernte, *f.* -/-n. **1.** (i) harvesting, gathering, reaping (of crop, corn, etc.); picking (of fruit, etc.); vintaging (of grapes, etc.); (ii) harvest time, harvest season; **während der E.,** during the harvest, at harvest time; **bald beginnt die E.,** the harvest will soon begin, harvest time will begin soon. **2.** harvest; crop(s); vintage; **die E. einbringen,** to gather in, get in, win, the harvest, the crops; **E. auf dem Halm,** standing crop; **eine gute, reiche, E.,** a good harvest, a good crop; **eine schlechte E.,** a bad, poor, crop; **die E. ist verregnet,** the harvest has, the crops have, been ruined by rain; **verhagelte E.,** crop ruined by hail; *F:* **ihm ist die E. verhagelt,** his hopes have been blighted; **reiche E. halten,** to reap a good harvest, a good crop; *Lit:* **der Tod, die Seuche, hielt reiche, furchtbare, E.,** death, disease, took a heavy toll; *Prov:* **wie die Saat, so die E.,** we reap as we sow, we reap what we have sown.

-ernte, *comb.fm. f.* (i) harvesting of . . ., . . . harvest; (ii) time of . . . harvest; (iii) . . . crop, . . . harvest; **Tabakernte,** (i) tobacco harvest; (ii) time of the tobacco harvest; (iii) tobacco crop, tobacco harvest; **Olivenernte,** (i) olive harvest(ing); (ii) time, season, of the olive harvest; (iii) olive crop, olive harvest.

Ernteameise, *f. Ent:* harvesting, agricultural, ant.

Erntearbeit, *f.* harvesting work, harvesting.

Erntearbeiter, *m.* harvester, reaper, harvestman, harvest-hand.

Ernteball, *m.* = **Erntetanz.**

Erntedankfest, *n.* (*in Germany held on the first Sunday after Michaelmas Day*) harvest thanksgiving *or* festival; harvest-home.

Erntedanktag, *m.* (*in Germany the first Sunday after Michaelmas Day*) harvest thanksgiving day; *U.S:* Thanksgiving Day.

Ernteertrag, *m. Agr:* produce, yield (of field, etc.).

Erntefest, *n.* **1.** = **Erntedankfest. 2.** = **Erntetanz.**

Erntefieber, *n. Med:* harvest fever.

Erntefläche, *f. Agr:* area under cultivation; sown area.

Erntekranz, *m.* harvest crown, harvest wreath.

Erntekrätze, *f. Med:* trombidiasis.

Erntekrone, *f.* harvest crown.

Erntelager, *n.* harvest camp.

Erntemahl, *n.* harvest-home (dinner).

Erntemaschine, *f.* reaping machine, harvesting machine, harvester, reaper; **Erntemaschinen,** harvesting machinery.

Erntemilbe, *f. Ent:* harvest-mite, -bug, -tick, -louse, chigger, jigger, red bug.

Erntemonat, Erntemond, *m. A. & Lit:* August.

ernten, *v.tr.* (*a*) to harvest, reap, gather (in) (crop, corn, etc.); to pick (fruit, berries, etc.); to harvest, pick, vintage (grapes); **den Weizen, das Heu, e.,** to harvest the wheat, the hay; **Erdbeeren e.,** to gather, pick, strawberries; **von dem Apfelbaum haben wir nicht viel geerntet,** we did not get a good crop, we did not get many apples, from that apple-tree; *B:* **was der Mensch sät, das wird er e.,** whatsoever a man soweth that he shall also reap; **wer Wind säet, wird Sturm e.,** he who sows the wind shall reap the whirlwind; **die mit Tränen säen, werden mit Freuden e.,** they that sow in tears shall reap in joy; *Prov:* **wir ernten, was wir gesäet haben,** we reap as we sow, we reap what we have sown; (*b*) to reap (praise, glory, etc.); to earn, win (praise, gratitude, reputation, etc.); to win, gain (fame, reputation, etc.); **er hat viel Lob geerntet,** he earned, won, much praise; **Lorbeeren e.,** to win, reap, laurels; **die Früchte seiner Arbeit e.,** to reap the fruits of one's labour; **Beifall e.,** to win applause; **er wird keinen Dank dafür e.,** he will not get any thanks for it; **für seine Mühe erntete er nur Undank, nur Spott,** for all his troubles he earned only ingratitude, only scorn; **ich erntete nur Schläge und Beschimpfungen,** all I got out of it was blows and insults.

Ernter, *m.* -s/-, harvester, reaper, harvestman, harvest-hand.

Erntetanz, *m.* harvest-home dance.

Erntewagen, *m.* harvest-waggon, harvest-wain.

Erntewetter, *n.* harvest weather; **gutes, schlechtes, E.,** good, bad, weather for the harvest.

Erntezeit, *f.* harvest time; **in der E.,** during the harvest, at harvest time.

Ernting, *m.* -(e)s/. *A. & Lit:* August.

ernüchtern. I. *v.tr.* (*a*) to sober (down) (intoxicated pers., etc.); to make (s.o.) sober; to bring (s.o.) to his senses; **sich e.,** to sober down, to sober up, to become sober; to come to one's senses; **die frische Luft ernüchterte ihn sofort,** the fresh air sobered him immediately, immediately cleared his head; (*b*) to disillusion, disenchant (romantic, enthusiast, etc.); **sich e.,** to be disillusioned, disenchanted; **diese Nachricht ernüchterte ihn, wirkte ernüchternd auf ihn,** this news sobered him, had a sobering effect on him; **nach seinen Erlebnissen war er vollständig ernüchtert,** he was completely disillusioned after his experiences.

II. *vbl s.* **1. Ernüchtern,** *n. in vbl senses.* **2. Ernüchterung,** *f.* (*a*) = II. 1; *also:* disillusionment, disenchantment; (*b*) disillusionment, disenchantment; disappointment; **es war eine große E. für ihn,** it was a grave disillusionment for him, he was very disillusioned, disappointed.

Eroberer, *m.* -s/-, conqueror; *Hist:* **Wilhelm der E.,** William the Conqueror.

erobern. I. *v.tr.* to conquer (country, town, etc.); to capture, take (town, fort, etc.); *F:* to capture, captivate (s.o., s.o.'s affection, etc.); to conquer, win (s.o.'s love, etc.); to make a conquest of (s.o., s.o.'s heart, etc.); **Gallien wurde von Caesar erobert,** Gaul was conquered by Caesar; **erobertes Gebiet,** conquered territory; **eine Festung im Sturm e.,** to take a fort by storm, by assault; *F:* **alle Herzen im Sturm e.,** to take all hearts by storm, to conquer, win, capture, all hearts; **die Sänger eroberten die Stadt im Sturm,** the singers took the town by storm; **sie hat ihn erobert,** she has won his heart; *Com:* (*of industry, firm, etc.*) **neue Märkte e.,** to capture new markets.

II. *vbl s.* **1. Erobern,** *n. in vbl senses.* **2. Eroberung,** *f.* (*a*) = II. 1; *also:* conquest (of country, town, *F:* s.o.'s heart, s.o.'s love.

etc.); capture (of town, fort, etc.); capture, captivation (of s.o., s.o.'s affection, etc.); (*b*) conquest; **eine E. machen,** to make a conquest; *F:* **da hast du wieder eine E. gemacht,** you have made another conquest, you have conquered, captured, captivated, won, another heart; (*of man or woman*) **auf Eroberungen ausgehen,** to be out to make conquests; **Eroberungen machen,** to make conquests.

Eroberungskrieg, *m.* war of conquest.

eroberungslustig, *a.* (*of ruler, etc.*) lusting for conquests; *F:* (*of man or woman*) out to make conquests.

Eroberungsrechte, *n.pl. Mil:* rights of conquest.

erodieren [e·ro·ˈdiːrən], *v.tr.* (*of acid, rust, glacier, water, etc.*) to erode, abrade, eat away, wear away (rocks, metals, etc.); **erodierend,** erosive (action, effect, etc.).

eröffnen. I. *v.tr.* **1.** (*a*) to open (box, tomb, etc.); to open, unseal, break open (letter, etc.); **ein Testament e.,** to open a will; to read a will; (*b*) to open (new shop, school, etc.); to open, inaugurate (institution, etc.); **ein neues Geschäft, eine neue Zweigstelle, e.,** to open (up), to set up, to start, a new shop, a new branch; **die Schule soll morgen feierlich eröffnet werden,** the school is to be opened, inaugurated, tomorrow with all due ceremony; **eine neue Straße für den Verkehr e., eine neue Straße dem Verkehr e.,** to open a new road to traffic; (*c*) to open up (new prospects, possibilities, etc.); (*of prospects, etc.*) **sich e.,** to open out, open up; **diese Entdeckung eröffnet den Ärzten ganz neue Behandlungsmethoden, durch diese Entdeckung eröffnen sich den Ärzten ganz neue Behandlungsmethoden,** this discovery opens up completely new methods of treatment to doctors. **2.** to open, begin, start (discussion, meeting, etc.); **eine Unterhaltung, eine Debatte, e.,** to open, begin, start, a conversation, a debate; **den Ball e.,** to open the ball; **Verhandlungen e.,** to set negotiations on foot, to open, start, begin, negotiations; **eine Feier e.,** to open a ceremony; **die Sitzung wurde mit einer kurzen Ansprache eröffnet,** the session opened, was opened, with a short address; **die Saison e.,** to open the season; **das Parlament e.,** to open Parliament; *Mil:* **das Feuer, die Feindseligkeiten, e.,** to open fire, to start hostilities; **eine Offensive e.,** to open, start, an offensive; *Bank:* **ein Konto e.,** to open an account; *Jur:* **die Verhandlung e.,** to open the proceedings; *Fin:* **den Konkurs e.,** to institute bankruptcy proceedings. **3. j-m etwas e.,** to disclose sth. to s.o.; to inform s.o. of sth.; **sich j-m e.,** to open one's heart, to open oneself, to s.o.; **j-m seine Gedanken e.,** to open one's mind to s.o., to reveal, disclose, one's thoughts to s.o.; **er eröffnete mir seine Pläne, seine Absichten,** he told me, informed me of, his plans, his intentions; **sie eröffnete mir, daß . . .,** she revealed to me that . . .; **als wir ankamen, wurde uns eröffnet, eröffnete man uns, daß die Verhandlungen abgebrochen worden waren,** when we arrived we were informed, they informed us, that the negotiations had been broken off; **ich weiß nicht, wie ich ihm e. soll, daß . . .,** I have no idea how I am going to tell him, to break it to him, that. . . .

II. **eröffnen,** *v.i.* (*haben*) (*of season, etc.*) to open, to start; **die Saison eröffnete mit 'Aida',** the season opened with (a performance of) 'Aida'; *St.Exch:* **die Börse eröffnete ruhig,** the market opened quietly.

III. *vbl s.* **1. Eröffnen,** *n. in vbl senses.* **2. Eröffnung,** *f.* (*a*)=II. 1; *also:* inauguration (of new school, etc.); *Fin:* institution (of bankruptcy proceedings); **E. einer neuen Zweigstelle, einer neuen Straße,** opening of a new branch, of a new road; **nach E. der Debatte, der Sitzung,** after the opening of the debate, of the session; **bei E. eines Kontos,** when opening an account; **E. der Saison,** opening of the season; **E. eines Testaments,** opening of a will; reading of a will; (*b*) disclosure; information; (*surprising or disagreeable*) announcement; **j-m eine E. machen,** to announce sth. to s.o.; to inform s.o. of sth.; **als wir ankamen, wurde uns die E. gemacht, machte man uns die E., daß die Verhandlungen abgebrochen worden waren,** when we arrived we were informed, they informed us, that the negotiations had been broken off; **diese Eröffnungen überraschten mich,** these disclosures, these announcements, surprised me, were a surprise to me; this news astonished me.

Eröffnungsbilanz, *f. Com:* initial statement of affairs (at beginning of financial year, at opening of new business, etc.).

Eröffnungsfeier, *f.* opening ceremony, ceremony of inauguration, (ceremonial, solemn) inauguration (of new school, etc.).

Eröffnungskurs, *m. St.Exch:* opening price.

Eröffnungsperiode, *f. Obst:* first stage of labour, period of dilatation.

Eröffnungsrede, *f.* inaugural address, inaugural speech; *Jur: etc:* opening speech.

Eröffnungstag, *m.* opening day (of new shop, etc.); inauguration day (of new school, etc.); first day (of shooting season, etc.).

erogen [e·ro·ˈgeːn], *a. Physiol: etc:* erogenous, erogenic; **erogene Zonen,** erogenous areas (of the body).

Eroika, die [e·ˈroːi·kaː], -. *Mus:* the Eroica (*Beethoven's third symphony*).

erörtern. I. *v.tr.* to discuss, argue (question, case, etc.); to consider, examine (matter); **die Frage wurde ausführlich, gründlich, erörtert,** the question was discussed in great detail, was considered, examined, thoroughly; **etwas des längeren e.,** to discuss, debate, sth. at length; **im zweiten Kapitel erörtert der Autor verschiedene Fragen,** in the second chapter the author discusses, treats, deals with, various questions.

II. *vbl s.* **1. Erörtern,** *n. in vbl senses.* **2. Erörterung,** *f.* (*a*)=II. 1; *also:* discussion (of question, case, etc.); consideration, examination (of matter); **ausführliche, gründliche, E. einer Frage,** detailed, thorough, discussion of a question; **etwas zur E. bringen,** to bring sth. up for discussion; (*of matter, question, etc.*) **zur E. kommen,** to come up for discussion; to be discussed, debated; (*b*) discussion; argument; debate; **die Erörterungen waren noch im Gange,** the discussion, debate, was still going on; the matter was still under discussion, under consideration, the matter was still being discussed, debated, considered.

Eros [ˈeːrɔs]. **1.** [*also* ˈɛrɔs] *Pr.n.m.* -'. *Gr.Myth: Astr:* Eros. **2.** *m.* -/. *Psy:* Eros, libido. **3.** *m.* -/Eroten [e·ˈroːtən]. *Art: usu. pl.* **Eroten,** Cupids.

Erosion [e·ro·zi·ˈoːn], *f.* -/-en. **1.** *Geol: etc:* (*a*) erosion; eating away, wearing away; denudation; (*b*) coastal erosion; corrosion. **2.** *Med:* abrasion (of mucous membrane, etc.); erosion (of teeth).

Erosionstal, *n. Geog:* valley formed by erosion.

Erosionstopf, *m. Geog:* pot-hole, *F:* kettle(-hole), giant's kettle.

Eroten [e·ˈroːtən], *m.pl. see* **Eros** 3.

Erotik [e·ˈroːtik], *f.* -/. **1.** eroticism; sensuality, *F:* sexiness. **2.** erotic; doctrine of love. **3.** erotic literature.

Erotiker [e·ˈroːtikər], *m.* -s/-. **1.** erotic person, erotic; person preoccupied with sex. **2.** erotic writer; erotic poet.

erotisch [e·ˈroːtiʃ], *a.* (*a*) erotic (poem, etc.); **erotische Dichtung,** erotic poetry; (*b*) erotic (pers., etc.); highly-sexed (pers.); sexy (film, book, etc.).

Erotomane [e·ro·to·ˈmaːnə], *m.* -n/-n. *Med:* erotomaniac, *F:* sex-maniac.

Erotomanie [e·ro·to·ma·ˈniː], *f.* -/. *Med:* erotomania, *F:* sex-mania.

Erpel, *m.* -s/-. *Orn:* drake.

erpicht, *a.* **auf etwas** *acc.* **e. sein,** to have set one's heart on sth., to be set, bent, on sth.; to want sth.; **darauf e. sein, etwas zu tun,** to have set one's heart on doing sth., to be set on doing sth.; **er ist sehr aufs Geldverdienen e.,** he is very keen on money-making, he is dead set on money-making; **sie war nicht sehr aufs Kochen e.,** she was not very keen on cooking; **er war sehr darauf e., daß sein Sohn Lehrer werden sollte,** he was very keen, he had set his heart on it, that his son should become a teacher; **ich bin durchaus nicht darauf e., zu dieser Gesellschaft zu gehen,** I am not at all keen on, I am not looking forward at all to, going to this party.

Erpichtheit, *f.* keenness, eagerness (for sth., to do sth.).

erpressen. I. *v.tr.* (*a*) *Jur:* **j-n e.,** to blackmail s.o.; **erpreßt werden,** to be blackmailed; **von j-m etwas e.,** to blackmail s.o. for sth.; to demand (money, etc.) from s.o. with menaces; **Erpreßte** *m, f,* person who is being blackmailed, victim of blackmail; (*b*) **von j-m etwas e.,** to extort (money, information, etc.) from s.o.; to bleed s.o. for (money); **von j-m ein Versprechen, ein Geständnis, e.,** to extort a promise, a confession, from s.o.; **erpreßtes Geständnis,** extorted confession, confession extorted by threats, by blackmail.

II. *vbl s.* **1. Erpressen,** *n. in vbl senses.* **2. Erpressung,** *f.* (*a*)=II. 1; *also:* extortion; *Jur:* blackmail; **etwas durch E. bekommen,** to get sth. by blackmail; (*b*) (case of) blackmail.

Erpresser, *m.* -s/-, blackmailer; extorter.

erpresserisch, *a.* blackmailing, extortionary (methods, etc.); *Jur:* **erpresserischer Kindesraub,** kidnapping for the purpose of ransom.

Erpressungsbrief, *m.* blackmailing letter.

Erpressungsversuch, *m.* attempt to blackmail s.o., attempted blackmail.

erproben. I. *v.tr.* to test, try, prove (sth.); to put (s.o., s.o.'s loyalty, etc.) to the test; to try (out) (new machine, new remedy, etc.); *Mil: Artil: Av:* to prove (tank, aircraft, gun); **j-s Mut e.,** to test s.o.'s courage, to put s.o.'s courage to the test; **dieser Stoff ist ein erprobtes Material für Regenmäntel,** this cloth has proved a reliable material for raincoats; **ein erprobtes Mittel gegen Grippe,** an established, proved, proven, remedy for influenza; **die erprobte Formel für größte Festigkeit,** the well-tried, (old-)established, formula for maximum stability; **es sind alles erprobte Leute,** they are all people who have proved themselves, who have shown themselves (to be) reliable.

II. *vbl s.* **1. Erproben,** *n. in vbl senses.* **2. Erprobung,** *f. in vbl senses; also:* test; trial; try-out.

erprobt, *p.p. & a. see* **erproben** I.

Erprobtheit, *f.* reliability (of pers., method, etc.); efficacy (of medicine, etc.).

Erprobung, *f. see* **erproben** II.

Erprobungsflug, *m. Av:* proving flight; test flight; trial flight.

Erprobungsgelände, *n. Mil: Artil:* proving ground; *Artil:* experimental range.

Erprobungsstelle, *f. Mil: Artil:* proving station; experimental station; testing ground.

erquicken. I. *v.tr.* (*of drink, rest, etc.*) to refresh (s.o.); to revive, reinvigorate (s.o.); **sich e.,** to refresh oneself; **sich an einem, mit einem, Getränk e.,** to refresh oneself with a drink; **sich an einem schönen Anblick, an einem schönen Gedicht, e.,** to be uplifted by a beautiful sight, by a beautiful poem; **das Auge erquickt sich an den grünen Wiesen und Wäldern,** the eye is refreshed by the green of the meadows and woods; **der Regen erquickte die durstenden Felder,** the rain refreshed, freshened, the parched fields; **ich fühle mich erquickt nach meinem Bad,** I feel refreshed after my bath; **erquickt aufwachen,** to awake refreshed, rested; **erquickender Schlaf,** refreshing sleep; **erquickendes Getränk,** refreshing drink; **erquickende Luft,** refreshing air, reinvigorating air; **erquickender Anblick,** refreshing sight; uplifting sight; *B:* **kommet her zu mir alle, die ihr mühselig und beladen seid, ich will euch e.,** come unto me, all ye that labour and are heavy laden, and I will give you rest; *B:* **Er erquicket meine Seele,** He restoreth my soul.

II. *vbl s.* **1. Erquicken,** *n. in vbl senses; also:* refreshment. **2. Erquickung,** *f.* (*a*)=II. 1; **zur E.,** for refreshment; (*b*) refreshment; **das Bad war eine rechte E.,** the bath was a real refreshment, was most refreshing, reinvigorating; **die grünen Wiesen und Wälder sind dem Auge eine E., sind eine E. für das Auge,** the green of the meadows and woods is a pleasure, a joy, to the eye, refreshes the eye, the eye is refreshed by the green of the meadows and woods; **der Regen brachte den durstenden Feldern E.,** the rain refreshed, brought new life to, the parched fields.

erquicklich, *a.* refreshing (humour, story, etc.); heart-warming, uplifting (sight, etc.); edifying (book, sermon, talk, etc.); *Iron:* **ein Anblick, der nicht gerade e. war,** a sight that was not exactly edifying.

erraffen, *v.tr.* to snatch, seize, grab (sth.); (**sich** *dat.*) **ein Vermögen e.,** to make a fortune hand over fist, *F:* to get rich quick.

Errata [ɛˈraːtaː], *n.pl. see* **Erratum.**

erratbar, *a.* guessable; **leicht, schwer, e.,** easy, difficult, to guess.

erraten, *v.tr.* to guess (sth.) (right); **ein Rätsel, ein Geheimnis, e.,** to guess a riddle, a secret; **du hast es erraten!** you've guessed it! you've guessed right! you've got it! **j-s Absicht e.,** to guess s.o.'s intention, to guess what s.o. intends *or* intended to do; **etwas aus j-s Benehmen e.,** to guess sth. from s.o.'s manner; **es ist schwer, seine Gedanken zu e.,** it is difficult to guess his thoughts, to guess what he is thinking; **das war leicht zu e.,** that was easy to guess, that was an easy guess.

erratisch [ɛˈraːtiʃ], *a.* erratic; *Geol:* **erratischer Block,** erratic block, erratic; boulder.

Erratum [ɛˈraːtum], *n.* -s/-ta. *Print: etc:* erratum; misprint.

errechnen. I. *v.tr.* to calculate, work out, compute

(price, distance, amount, etc.); to arrive at (price, number, etc.); *Mth:* to calculate, find, work out, compute (value, quantity, etc.); **den Inhalt eines Zylinders e.,** to find, work out, calculate, the capacity of a cylinder; **die Entfernung kann mit dieser Methode leicht errechnet werden,** the distance can be calculated, worked out, easily by this method; **die errechnete Summe,** the sum arrived at, the calculated, computed, sum.

II. *vbl s.* **Errechnen** *n.*, **Errechnung** *f. in vbl senses; also:* calculation; computation; **zur Errechnung des Inhalts eines Rechtecks,** in order to find, work out, calculate, the area of a rectangle.

erregbar, *a.* (*of pers., Physiol: of muscle, nerve, etc.*) excitable; (*of pers.*) irritable; **er ist leicht e.,** he is very excitable, easily excited; he is quick to flare up, he is hot-headed; **überaus e.,** over-excitable.

Erregbarkeit, *f.* excitability (of pers., *Physiol:* of muscle, nerve, etc.); irritability, hot-headedness (of pers.); *Med: etc:* over-excitability; erethism.

erregen. I. *v.tr.* **1.** (*a*) *El:* to generate, produce (electricity, etc.); *Ch:* (*of bacteria, etc.*) to produce, cause (mould, pus, etc.); to cause (fermentation, putrefaction, disease, etc.); (*b*) to excite, provoke, cause, arouse, stir up (envy, curiosity, etc.); to excite, arouse, create (interest, etc.); to cause, provoke (mirth, etc.); to cause (astonishment, etc.); to call forth (admiration, etc.); to arouse, provoke (anger, hatred, etc.); to arouse (pity, suspicion, fear, mistrust, etc.); **allgemeine Neugier e.,** to arouse universal curiosity; **j-s Mißfallen e.,** to incur s.o.'s displeasure; **Mitleid e.,** to arouse compassion, pity; **j-s Mitleid e.,** to move s.o. to pity, to compassion, to arouse, move, s.o.'s pity; **seine Bemerkung erregte große Heiterkeit,** his remark caused, provoked, aroused, great mirth, caused, aroused, loud laughter; *see also* **Anstoß, Ärgernis, aufsehen** II. **2.** (*a*) *Physiol:* to stimulate (organ, nerve, etc.); to excite (organ, nerve, etc.); to apply a stimulus to (nerve, etc.); **j-n geschlechtlich e.,** to excite s.o. sexually, to rouse s.o.; *Med:* **erregendes Mittel,** excitant; stimulant; (*b*) *El:* to excite, energize (dynamo, etc.); to excite (magnetic field, etc.); (*of dynamo, core of coil, etc*) **sich e.,** to energize; (*c*) to excite (s.o.); to rouse, agitate (s.o., the people, etc.); to stir up (the people); (*of discussion, wine, etc.*) to excite, heat (the mind, the heart, etc.); (*of pers.*) **sich e., erregt werden,** to become, get, grow, excited, agitated, heated; **sich über etwas** *acc.* **e.,** to get excited about sth., to get heated about sth.; **er war sehr erregt, stark erregt,** he was very excited, agitated, he was in a state of great excitement, agitation; he was in a high state of emotion; **die Sinne e.,** to excite the senses; **der Wein hatte ihre Gemüter erregt,** the wine had heated, excited, stirred up, their minds; **erregte Gemüter, erregte Geister,** heated, excited, minds; **leicht erregt sein,** to be hot-headed, to be easily roused to anger, quick to flare up; **mit erregter Stimme,** in a voice quivering with emotion; in an excited, agitated, voice; **erregte Worte,** heated words; **erregte Auseinandersetzung,** heated, fierce, argument; **erregte Debatte,** heated debate; **die erregte Menge,** the excited crowd; **eine erregende Nachricht,** an exciting piece of news, a sensational piece of news; *adv.* **sie sprach erregt auf ihn ein,** she talked to him excitedly, in great agitation; (*d*) to stir (up) (waves, etc.); **die erregten Wogen werden sich wieder glätten,** the troubled waves will become smooth again; *B:* **es errege sich das Wasser mit webenden und lebendigen Tieren,** let the waters bring forth abundantly the moving creature that hath life.

II. *vbl s.* **1. Erregen,** *n. in vbl senses.* **2. Erregung,** *f.* (*a*)=II. 1; *also:* (i) generation (of electricity, etc.); provocation (of envy, curiosity, anger, hatred, etc.); (ii) *Physiol:* stimulation, excitation, excitement (of organ, nerve, etc.); (*b*) *El:* excitation, energization (of dynamo, etc.); **gemischte E.,** compound excitation; **remanente E.,** residual excitation; **schwache E.,** poor excitation; (*c*) *Physiol:* (state of) excitement (of organ, nerve, etc.); **in geschlechtlicher E.,** in a state of sexual excitement; (*d*) (state of) excitement, agitation; **er war in großer, in höchster, E.,** he was in a state of great excitement, agitation, he was very agitated, excited; he was in a high state of emotion; **die Menge war in wilder, höchster, E.,** the crowd was wildly excited, was wild with excitement, was seething with excitement; **ich fand ihn in großer E.,** I found him greatly excited; **ihre E. wuchs,** her excitement, agitation, grew, she grew, became, more and more excited, agitated; **in ihrer E. vergaß sie es,** in her excitement, agitation, she forgot it; **er konnte vor E. kaum sprechen,** he was so excited, agitated, that he could hardly speak, he could hardly speak for emotion; **mit vor E. zitternder Stimme,** in a voice quivering, shaking, with excitement, with emotion.

-erregend, *comb.fm. a.* (*a*) causing, provoking, arousing (envy, fear, anger, etc.); -able; -fying; **aufsehenerregend,** causing, creating, a stir, a sensation; **mitleiderregend,** pitiable, pitiful; **neiderregend,** that arouses envy, arousing envy; enviable; **furchterregend,** terrifying, horrifying; (*b*) *Ch: Med: etc:* causing, producing (disease, mould, etc.); *Ch:* -tive; *Med:* -genic; **fäulniserregend,** causing putrefaction, putrefactive; **gärungserregend,** causing fermentation, fermentative; **krankheitserregend,** pathogenic; **eitererregend,** pyogenic.

Erreger, *m.* **-s/-. 1.** exciter, instigator. **2.** *El:* exciter, exciting dynamo. **3.** *Med: Ch:* causal agent, exciting agent (of disease, fermentation, etc.); *Med:* pathogen, pathogenic agent, pathogenic organism, exciting cause (of disease); **die Erreger von Schimmel sind verschiedene Pilze,** mould is caused, produced, by various fungi; **Robert Koch entdeckte den E. der Cholera,** Robert Koch discovered the pathogenic organism of cholera, discovered the cholera bacillus.

-erreger, *comb.fm. m. Med: etc:* (micro-)organism causing . . .; **Eitererreger,** pus organism, exciter of suppuration; **Choleraerreger,** cholera bacillus, cholera organism; **Fäulniserreger,** organism causing putrefaction; putrefactive agent.

Erregerbatterie, *f. El:* exciting battery.

Erregerdynamo, *m.*, **Erregerdynamomaschine,** *f.*=**Erreger** 2.

Erregerfeld, *n. El:* exciting field.

Erregerkreis, *m. El:* exciting circuit.

Erregerkultur, *f. Med:* culture of pathogenic bacteria.

Erregermaschine, *f. El:* exciter, exciting dynamo.

Erregerspannung, *f. El:* exciting voltage.

Erregerspule, *f. El:* field coil, exciting coil, exciter coil.

Erregerstrom, *m. El:* exciting current, field current.

Erregerstromkreis, *m. El:* exciting circuit.

Erregerwicklung, *f. El:* exciting winding.

erregt, *p.p. & a. see* **erregen** I. 2 (*c*).

Erregtheit, *f.* excitement, agitation; **in ihrer E. vergaß sie es,** in her excitement, agitation, she forgot it; **er konnte vor E. kaum sprechen,** he was so excited, agitated, that he could hardly speak, he could hardly speak for excitement, for emotion.

Erregung, *f. see* **erregen** II.

Erregungsmittel, *n. Med:* excitant; stimulant.

Erregungszustand, *m. Physiol:* state of (*esp.* sexual) excitement (of organ, etc.).

erreichbar, *a.* (*a*) within reach (of s.o., one's hand, etc.); within range (of searchlight, gun, etc.); **zu Fuß leicht e.,** within easy walking distance; **leicht erreichbares Ziel,** goal easy to attain; easily reached goal; **nicht e.,** out of reach; **Hilfe war nicht e.,** no help was within reach; **ein Hotel, das vom Bahnhof leicht e. ist,** hotel within easy reach of the station; **Versailles ist von Paris leicht e.,** Versailles is within easy reach of Paris; **der Ort ist mit dem Auto leicht e.,** the place is easily reached by car; (*b*) **ein Arzt muß Tag und Nacht e. sein,** a doctor must be available day and night; **ich bin täglich in meinem Büro e.,** you can get in touch with me every day at my office; **er ist nie e.,** one can never get hold of him; **telephonisch e. sein,** to be on the telephone; **ich bin unter der Nummer 160 telephonisch e.,** you can get me, get in touch with me, by telephoning 160; my telephone number is 160.

erreichen. I. *v.tr.* (*a*) to reach (sth.) (with one's hand, etc.); to reach, hit (target, etc.); to reach, arrive at (town, etc.); *Nau:* to fetch (harbour, shore, etc.); **ich kann das oberste Brett gerade e.,** I can just about reach the top shelf; **das andere Ufer e.,** to gain, reach, the other, the further, shore; **den Gipfel des Berges e.,** to reach, attain, the summit of the mountain; **sein Reiseziel e.,** to reach, arrive at, the end of one's journey; to reach, arrive at, one's destination; **wir werden Paris am Abend e.,** we shall get to, arrive at, reach, Paris in the evening; **das Ende seines Lebens erreicht haben,** to have reached the end of one's life; (*b*) (*of pers.*) to get in touch with (s.o.), to reach (s.o.); to catch (train, bus, etc.); (*of letter, parcel, news, etc.*) to reach (s.o.); **dein Brief erreichte mich heute,** your letter reached me today; **dieser Brief hat ihn nie erreicht,** this letter never reached him, he never got this letter; **diese Nachricht erreichte ihn, als er auf Urlaub war,** this news reached him, he got this news, while he was on leave; **das Telegramm wird ihn nicht mehr e.,** the telegram will not reach him, he will not get the telegram; **j-n telephonisch e.,** to get in touch with s.o. by telephone; to get s.o. on the telephone; **kann ich Sie telephonisch e.? sind Sie telephonisch zu e.?** can I get in touch with you by, get you on the, telephone? are you on the telephone? **ich fürchte, wir werden den Zug nicht mehr e.,** I am afraid we shall not catch the train, I am afraid we shall miss the train; **ich habe meinen Anschluß in Köln gerade noch erreicht,** I only just got my connection at Cologne; (*c*) to reach, attain (age, speed, etc.); *Sp:* to equal (record); **ein hohes Alter e.,** to live to an old, a great, age; **sein sechzigstes Lebensjahr e.,** to reach, attain, the age of sixty; (*of vehicle, plane, etc.*) **eine hohe Geschwindigkeit e.,** to reach, attain, a high speed; **in diesem Jahr wurde der vorjährige Rekord im Hochsprung nicht erreicht,** last year's record in the high jump was not reached this year; **Buch, das die sechste Auflage erreicht hat,** book that has reached its sixth edition; **das Buch hat zehn Auflagen erreicht,** the book has seen, gone through, ten editions; (*d*) to achieve, attain (sth.); to obtain (what one wants); **seine Absicht e.,** to achieve, attain, one's end; **mit Ausdauer kann man viel e., läßt sich viel e.,** one can achieve a good deal by persistence; **bei j-m etwas e.,** to have success with s.o.; to get somewhere with s.o.; **e., daß etwas geschieht,** to succeed in bringing sth. about; **die Eltern haben erreicht, daß ihre Kinder eine Woche Ferien bekommen,** the parents have succeeded in obtaining a week's holiday for their children; **wir haben endlich beim Chef erreicht, daß wir am Samstag frei haben,** we have at last succeeded in persuading, we have at least induced, prevailed upon, the boss to give us Saturday off; **sie haben erreicht, daß der Minister seines Amtes enthoben wurde,** they succeeded in getting the minister relieved of his post; **ich ging heute zum Konsulat, habe aber nichts erreicht, ohne etwas zu e.,** I went to the consulate today but I achieved nothing, but without success.

II. *vbl s.* **Erreichen** *n.*, **Erreichung** *f. in vbl senses; also:* arrival (in town, etc.); attainment (of age, speed, etc.); achievement, attainment (of sth., one's end, etc.); **zur Erreichung seines Zieles,** for the attainment of his purpose, (in order) to attain his purpose; **bei Erreichung des sechzigsten Lebensjahres,** on reaching, on attaining, one's sixtieth year.

erretten. I. *v.tr.* to rescue, save (s.o.); *Theol:* to redeem, deliver, save (s.o., s.o.'s soul, etc.); **j-n aus einer Gefahr e.,** to save, rescue, s.o. from a danger; **j-n vom Tode e.,** to rescue, save, deliver, s.o. from death; **j-n vom Ertrinken, vom Tode des Ertrinkens, e.,** to save, rescue, s.o. from drowning; **j-n von allen seinen Sünden e.,** to deliver s.o. from all his sins; **die Erretteten,** the rescued.

II. *vbl s.* **Erretten** *n.*, **Errettung** *f. in vbl senses; also:* rescue; *Theol:* salvation, redemption; **Errettung vom Tode,** rescue from imminent death; **Errettung vom Tode des Ertrinkens,** rescue from drowning.

Erretter, *m.* **-s/-,** rescuer; *Theol:* saviour, redeemer.

errichten. I. *v.tr.* (*a*) to erect, set up, raise (statue, temple, mast, etc.); to construct, build, erect (tower, building, etc.); to erect, put up (scaffolding, etc.); to throw up (barrier, parapet, etc.); to found (empire, institution, etc.); **eine Schreckensherrschaft e.,** to establish, set up, a reign of terror; (*b*) *Geom:* **eine Senkrechte auf einer Geraden e.,** to erect a perpendicular on a line.

II. *vbl s.* **Errichten** *n.*, **Errichtung** *f. in vbl senses; also:* erection (of statue, temple, mast, scaffolding, *Geom:* of perpendicular, etc.); construction (of building, tower, etc.); foundation (of empire, institution, etc.); establishment (of system, etc.).

Errichter, *m.* **-s/-,** erector (of statue, temple, mast, scaffolding, etc.); constructor (of building, tower, etc.).

erringen. I. *v.tr.* (*strong*) to achieve, gain (victory,

etc.); to achieve (success, etc.); to achieve, attain, gain (honour, etc.); to acquire, attain, gain, win (position, knowledge, etc.); to gain, establish (reputation, etc.); to acquire (property, etc.); **durch diese Tat errang er öffentliches Ansehen,** this action won him public regard, the esteem of the public; **schwer errungener Sieg,** hard-won victory; *Jur:* **errungene Güter,** acquest; acquired goods.

II. *vbl s.* **1. Erringen,** *n. in vbl senses.* **2. Erringung,** *f.* (*a*)=II. 1; *also:* achievement, attainment (of honour, success, etc.); acquisition, attainment (of position, knowledge, etc.); (*b*)=**Errungenschaft.**

erröten. I. *v.i.* (*sein*) to redden; to grow red; to blush; to turn, go, red (in the face); to flush (red); **vor Scham e.,** to blush for shame, to go red with shame; **über und über e.,** to blush to the roots of one's hair, to blush, flush, up to the ears; to blush furiously; **bei einer Bemerkung e.,** to blush at a remark; **sie errötete beim bloßen Gedanken daran,** she blushed, a blush rose to her cheeks, at the mere thought of it; **sie antwortete errötend,** she answered blushing(ly), with a blush.

II. *vbl s.* **Erröten,** *n.* blushing, blush; **mit E.,** blushing, blushingly; **mit jungfräulichem, mädchenhaftem, E.,** with a maidenly, girlish, blush.

Errungenschaft, *f.* **-/-en. 1.** acquired property; acquisition; *Jur:* acquest, property acquired in common (by husband and wife); *F:* **komm und sieh dir meine neuen Errungenschaften an,** come and see my new acquisitions. **2.** achievement, attainment, acquirement; acquired knowledge; **seine geistigen, sprachlichen, Errungenschaften,** his intellectual, linguistic, attainments, acquirements; **Errungenschaften der Forschung,** scientific achievements; **es war eine seiner größten Errungenschaften,** it was one of his greatest achievements; **mit allen Errungenschaften der modernen Technik versehen, ausgestattet,** equipped with every modern technical device.

ersättigen, *v.tr. A:*=**sättigen.**

ersättlich, *a. A:* satiable.

Ersatz, *m.* **-es/. 1.** (*a*) replacement, replacing; substitution; **der E. von Butter durch Margarine,** the substitution of margarine for butter; (*b*) replacement (of sth. lost *or* damaged); **ich muß auf dem E. der zerbrochenen Teller bestehen,** I must insist that the broken plates be replaced *or* paid for; (*c*) compensation (for loss of earnings, etc.); indemnification (for loss). **2.** (*a*) (*thg*) replacement; **Sie können für jedes Stück des Services in ihrem Fachgeschäft E. bekommen,** you can buy a replacement for every piece of the set from your stockist, *U.S:* dealer; (*b*) (*pers.*) substitute; replacement; *Ind:* spare hand; *Sp:* reserve; substitute; *Artil: etc:* spare number (of gun-crew, etc.); **als E. für j-n einspringen,** to step in as a substitute for s.o.; **für die verstorbene Sekretärin fand sich kein E.,** no replacement was found for the secretary who had died. **3.** substitute (for foodstuff, etc.); *F:* ersatz; **Margarine ist kein vollwertiger E. für Butter,** margarine is not an adequate substitute for butter; **als E. für Kautschuk wird vielfach synthetisches Gummi verwendet,** synthetic rubber is often used in place of, in lieu of, caoutchouc. **4.** *Jur:* indemnity, compensation, damages, restitution; **E. fordern,** to claim damages; **zum E. verpflichtet sein,** to be liable for compensation; **E. leisten,** to pay damages; to make compensation, restitution. **5.** *Mil:* (*a*) recruitment, intake; (*b*) draft *or* drafts.

Ersatz-, *comb.fm.* (*a*) replacement . . . ; substitute . . . ; alternative . . . ; *Com:* **Ersatzbeschaffung** *f,* replacement purchase; **Ersatzfaser** *f,* substitute fibre; **Ersatzstrafe** *f,* alternative punishment; (*b*) spare . . . ; **Ersatzbereifung** *f,* spare tyres; (*c*) *Mil:* recruiting (and training) . . . ; depot . . . ; **Ersatzbezirk** *m,* recruiting district; **Ersatzbataillon** *n,* depot battalion.

ersatz, *m. comb.fm.* . . . substitute; *F:* ersatz . . . ; **Kaffee-Ersatz,** coffee substitute, *F:* ersatz coffee; **Gummiersatz,** rubber substitute; **Benzinersatz,** petrol substitute.

Ersatzabteilung, *f. Artil:* depot battery.

Ersatzanspruch, *m.* claim for damages, claim for, of, indemnification.

Ersatzaussonderungsrecht, *n. Jur:* creditor's prior right to compensation for goods that were under reputed ownership of a bankrupt and are sold in realization of the bankrupt's estate.

Ersatzbataillon, *n. Mil:* depot battalion.

Ersatzbatterie, *f. El:* refill (for electric torch, *U.S:* flashlight, etc.); spare battery.

Ersatzbedienung, *f. Mil:* spare numbers (of gun-crew, etc.); spare gunners.

Ersatzbehörde, *f. Mil:* recruiting authority.

ersatzberechtigt, *a. Jur:* entitled to damages.

Ersatzberechtigung, *f.* title to damages.

Ersatzbewegung, *f. Med:* substituted movement.

Ersatzdehnung, *f. Ling:* compensatory lengthening.

Ersatzdienst, *m. Mil:* alternative service (for conscientious objectors).

Ersatzdienststelle, *f. Mil:* recruiting centre.

Ersatzerbe, *m. Jur:* substitute heir.

Ersatzflügeltiefe, *f. Av:* mean aerodynamic chord.

Ersatzfreiheitsstrafe, *f. Jur:* imprisonment as a substitute for failure to pay a fine.

Ersatzgeldstrafe, *f. Jur:* payment of a fine as a substitute for imprisonment.

Ersatzgewicht, *n. Ch:* equivalent weight.

Ersatzglied, *n.* artificial limb; *Surg:* prosthesis.

Ersatzheer, *n. Mil:* training army.

Ersatzkasse, *f.* (recognized) private sickness insurance society (*offering better services than compulsory schemes*).

Ersatzliga, *f. Fb:* reserve league.

Ersatzmann, *m.* **-(e)s/-männer,** replacement, substitute; deputy; *Sp:* reserve; substitute; *Mil: A:* substitute; **einen E. stellen,** to provide a substitute.

Ersatzmannschaft, *f.* (*a*) *Sp:* reserve team; (*b*) *Mil: pl.* **Ersatzmannschaften,** drafts, replacements.

Ersatzmine, *f.* refill, spare lead (for propelling, *U.S:* automatic, pencil).

Ersatzmittel, *n.* substitute; surrogate.

Ersatzpferd, *n. Mil:* remount.

Ersatzpflicht, *f. Jur:* liability to pay damages; onus of recompense.

ersatzpflichtig, *a.* liable for compensation, damages.

Ersatzpflichtige, *m., f.* (*decl. as adj.*) person liable for compensation, damages.

Ersatzrad, *n. Veh:* spare wheel.

Ersatzregiment, *n. Mil:* training regiment.

Ersatzreifen, *m. Veh:* spare tyre.

Ersatzreserve, *f. Mil:* supplementary reserve.

Ersatzspieler, *m. Th:* understudy; *Sp:* reserve; substitute; *Mus:* (*in orchestra*) substitute player.

Ersatzstoff, *m.* substitute.

Ersatzstück, *n.* spare part, spare.

Ersatzsystole, *f. Med:* extrasystole.

Ersatzteil, *n.* spare part, spare.

Ersatztruppen, *f.pl. Mil:* depot troops.

Ersatztruppenteil, *m. Mil:* depot unit.

Ersatzwahl, *f. Pol:* by-election.

Ersatzwesen, *n. Mil:* recruitment.

Ersatzwiderstand, *m. El:* equivalent resistance.

Ersatzzahn, *m. Anat:* permanent tooth.

Ersatzzustellung, *f. Jur:* substituted service.

ersaufen, *v.i.* (*strong*) (*sein*) (*a*) (*of animal, F: of pers.*) to be, *F:* get, drowned; to drown; **sie ließen ihn jämmerlich e.,** they left him to drown miserably; (*b*) (*of field, etc.*) to be flooded, inundated; (*of mine, carburetter, etc.*) to be flooded; (*of hay, etc.*) to be swamped (in water); **ersoffene Felder,** waterlogged, drowned, fields.

ersäufen, *v.tr.* to drown (animal, *F:* pers.); *F:* **seinen Kummer im Wein e.,** to drown one's sorrows in wine; **Ersäufung** *f,* drowning; *Fr.Hist:* (collective) execution by drowning; noyade.

erschaffen[1], *v.tr.* (*strong*) (*usu. of God*) to create, make (the world, man, etc.); **gezeugt, nicht erschaffen,** begotten, not made; **Erschaffung** *f,* creation (of the world, man, etc.).

erschaffen[2], *v.tr.* (*weak*) (**sich** *dat.*) **etwas e.,** to get sth. by working for it.

Erschaffer, der, -s, (*God*) the Creator, the Maker of all.

Erschaffung, *f. see* **erschaffen**[1].

erschallen, *v.i.* (*weak & strong*) (*sein*) (*a*) to (begin to) sound, to (begin to) resound; (*of voice, laughter, song*) to ring out, to sound forth; (*of trumpet, etc.*) to sound out; **das Tal erschallte, erscholl, vom Klang der Hörner,** the valley echoed, rang, resounded, with the sound of the horns; (**die Trompete**) **e. lassen,** to sound (the trumpet); **plötzlich erscholl, erschallte, eine Stimme,** suddenly a voice was heard; **laut erschallte ihr Lachen,** her laughter rang out loudly; *Lit:* **laßt eure Lieder e.!** let your songs resound! **lasset die Stimmen e. zum Lobe des Herrn!** let your voices be raised in praise of the Lord! **das Lob des Herrn erschalle durch alle Lande,** let the praise of the Lord ring through every land; **das Lob Gottes e. lassen,** to sound, speak, the praise of God; (*b*) *A:* (*of tidings, rumour, etc.*) to become known, to (be) spread; *B:* **die Rede erscholl in das ganze jüdische Land,** the rumour went forth throughout all Judea.

erschaudern, *v.i.* (*sein*) to shudder, quiver, tremble; **ich erschauderte vor dem Anblick,** I shuddered at the sight; **schon bei dem Gedanken daran muß man e.,** the very thought of it makes one shudder.

erschauen, *v.tr. A. & Lit:* to see, behold (s.o., sth.).

erschauern, *v.i.* (*sein*) to thrill; to quiver, vibrate (with emotion); **j-s Herz e. machen, lassen,** to thrill s.o.'s heart; **in, vor, Ehrfurcht e.,** to thrill with awe, to be awestruck; **seine gewaltigen Worte ließen jeden e.,** his powerful words thrilled, gripped, everyone.

erscheinen. I. *v.i.* (*strong*) (*sein*) **1.** (*a*) to appear, become visible; (*of star, moon, etc.*) to appear, come out; (*of ghost, spectre, etc.*) to appear, show itself; **j-m e.,** to appear to s.o.; **der Herr erschien ihm im Traum,** the Lord appeared to him in a dream; **plötzlich erschien vor uns der schneebedeckte Gipfel,** suddenly the snow-covered peak appeared before us; **die ersten Veilchen waren schon erschienen,** the first violets were already out, had already appeared, come out, made their appearance; **ein Ausschlag erschien auf ihrem Arm,** a rash appeared, made its appearance, came out, on her arm; (*b*) (*of phenomenon, word, etc.*) to appear, occur; **das Wort erscheint zum ersten Mal bei Tacitus,** the word appears, occurs, for the first time in Tacitus; **der Name erscheint in der Urkunde mehrere Male,** the name appears several times in the document; **dieser Posten erscheint auf der Passivseite der Bilanz,** this item appears on the debit side of the account; (*c*) (*of book, etc.*) to be published, to come out; (*of periodical*) to appear, come out; *St.Exch:* (*of security*) to be issued; **erscheinend demnächst,** (*of book, etc.*) to be published shortly; (*of periodical*) appearing shortly, out soon; (*of article*) appearing shortly; **ein Buch e. lassen,** to publish, bring out, a book; **das Buch ist in unserem Verlag erschienen,** the book has been published, brought out, by our firm; **das Buch ist noch nicht erschienen,** the book is not yet published, out, in print; **das Buch ist soeben erschienen,** the book has just been published, has just come out; (*d*) (*of pers.*) to appear, to make one's appearance (on the stage, in society, etc.); **vor, in, der Öffentlichkeit e.,** to appear in public; **zum ersten Male auf der Bühne, in der Gesellschaft, als Redner, e.,** to make one's debut on the stage, in society, as a speaker; **erscheinen Sie bitte pünktlich zur Untersuchung,** please present yourself punctually for the examination; **der Polizist erschien im rechten Augenblick am Tatort,** the policeman appeared, *F:* turned up, on the scene at the right moment; *F:* **auf der Bildfläche e.,** to appear on the scene; *Jur:* **vor Gericht e.,** to appear, *Scot:* to compear, before a court of justice; to appear in court; **als Zeuge e.,** to appear as a witness. **2.** to appear, seem; **der Ort erschien ihm vertraut,** the place seemed, appeared, familiar to him, *F:* struck him as familiar; **dadurch erscheint die Angelegenheit in einem anderen Licht,** the matter thus appears in a different light, this throws a different light on the matter; **es erscheint im höchsten Grade unwahrscheinlich, daß . . . ,** it appears extremely unlikely that . . .

II. *vbl s* **1. Erscheinen,** *n. in vbl senses; also:* (*a*) appearance (of ghost, etc.); (*b*) *Publ:* publication, appearance (of book, etc.); *St.Exch:* issue (of security); **wöchentliches, tägliches, E.,** weekly, daily, appearance, publication; **die Zeitung wird ihr E. demnächst einstellen,** the newspaper will soon cease to be published, publication of the newspaper will soon be discontinued; *St.Exch:* **Handel per E.,** selling of stocks in advance subject to their being actually issued; (*c*) appearance (in court, in society, on the stage); **er hat sein E. zugesagt,** he has agreed to come, to be present; he has promised to put in an appearance. **2. Erscheinung,** *f.* (*a*) *in vbl senses; also:* appearance; **in E. treten,** to appear; to become visible; to show (up); (*of characteristic, intention, etc.*) to appear, become evident; (*of effect, etc.*) to make itself felt; (*of pers.*) to show oneself; **seine wahren Absichten traten erst nachher in E.,** his true intentions only came out, came to light, afterwards; *F:* **die jüngste Tochter tritt fast überhaupt nicht in E.,** the youngest daughter keeps very much in the background; *Ecc:* **die E. Christi,** the appearance of Christ, the

Epiphany; **das Fest der E. (Christi),** Epiphany; (*b*) phenomenon, fact; occurrence; *Phil:* phenomenon; **Erdbeben sind in diesem Lande keine seltene E.,** earthquakes are no rare occurrence in this country; **es ist eine seltsame E., daß . . . ,** it is a curious phenomenon that . . . ; **diese Krankheit ist eine typische E. der Nachkriegszeit,** this disease is a typical feature, symptom, of post-war times; **diese Gebrechen sind Erscheinungen des Greisenalters,** these infirmities are symptoms of senility; (*c*) appearance; visitation; **die Erscheinungen Christi nach seinem Tode,** the appearances of Christ after his death; **eine E. haben,** to have a vision; to have a visitation; (*d*) apparition, vision, ghost, spectre; (*e*) **er ist eine angenehme E.,** he is a man of pleasing appearance; **er ist eine imposante E.,** he is an imposing figure, he has an imposing appearance, presence.

Erscheinungsbild, *n. Biol:* phenotype.

Erscheinungsform, *f.* form of manifestation, appearance (of disease, etc.); *Phil: Theol:* hypostasis; *Biol:* phenotype.

Erscheinungslehre, *f. Phil:* phenomenology.

Erscheinungspflicht, *f. Jur: etc:* duty to appear (in court).

Erscheinungstag, *m.* **1.** *Publ:* day of publication (of book, etc.); *St.Exch:* day of issue (of security). **2.** *Ecc:* Epiphany.

Erscheinungswelt, *f. Phil:* tangible world; world of phenomena.

erschießen. I. *v.tr.* (*strong*) **1. j-n e.,** to shoot s.o. dead; **sich e.,** to shoot oneself, *F:* to blow one's brains out; **erschossen werden,** to be shot (dead); *F:* **erschossen sein,** to be exhausted, dead-beat, done up, worn out, whacked, *U.S:* bushed; *Mil:* **j-n standrechtlich e.,** to shoot s.o. by order of a court martial. **2.** *Artil:* **die Tageseinflüsse e.,** to carry out a meteor shoot; **erschossene Tabellen,** range tables established by trial firing.

II. *vbl s.* **1. Erschießen,** *n. in vbl senses; also:* (*a*) **Tod durch E.,** death by shooting; (*b*) *Artil:* **E. der Tageseinflüsse,** meteor shoot (to eliminate error of the day). **2. Erschießung,** *f.* (*a*) *in vbl senses; also:* **standrechtliche E.,** execution by a firing squad; (*b*) **es fanden viele Erschießungen statt,** there have been many shootings.

Erschießungskommando, *n. Mil:* firing squad.

erschimmern, *v.i.* (*sein*) *Poet:* (*of sea, etc.*) to (begin to) shimmer; (*of star, etc.*) to glimmer; (*of diamond, etc.*) to sparkle.

erschlaffen. I. *v.i.* (*sein*) (*of muscle*) to become slack, relaxed, to lose tone; (*of bowels*) to become sluggish; (*of pers.*) to become enervated; to tire, to become tired; (*of zeal, interest, courage*) to flag, abate, fall off.

II. *vbl s.* **1. Erschlaffen,** *n. in vbl senses.* **2. Erschlaffung,** *f.* (*a*)=II. 1; (*b*) slackness (of muscle, etc.); *Med:* atony, enervation (of muscle); sluggishness (of bowels).

Erschlaffer, *m.* **-s/-.** *Anat:* **der E. des Trommelfells,** the laxator tympani.

erschlagen. I. *v.tr.* (*strong*) **1.** to slay, kill (s.o.); **j-n mit dem Schwert, der Axt, e.,** to slay, kill, s.o. with a sword, an axe; **Siegfried erschlug den Drachen,** Siegfried slew the dragon; (*of pers., animal*) **vom Blitz erschlagen werden,** to be killed by lightning. **2.** *A:* to beat down, flatten down (crop); **der Regen hat das Korn erschlagen,** the rain has beaten down, flattened, laid, the corn.

II. *p.p. & a.* **erschlagen,** *in vbl senses; esp. F:* (*a*) **e. sein,** to be exhausted, worn out, *F:* dead-beat, done up, whacked, *U.S:* bushed; (*b*) **über diese Neuigkeit war ich völlig erschlagen,** I was completely bowled over, struck dumb, by this news.

erschleichen, *v.tr.* (*strong*) to obtain (sth.) by undue influence, by insidious means, in an underhand way; to obtain (sth.) by trickery, guile; **j-s Vertrauen e.,** to insinuate oneself, worm one's way, into s.o.'s confidence; **j-s Gunst e.,** to creep into s.o.'s good graces, to worm one's way into s.o.'s favour; **eine Erbschaft e.,** to obtain a legacy by intrigue, artifice; *Log:* **einen Beweisgrund e.,** to beg a question.

Erschleicher, *m.* **-s/-,** person who obtains something by trickery, guile, artifice.

erschließbar, *a.* (*a*) (market, country, etc.) capable of being opened up; developable (country); (*b*) inferable, deducible (fact); conjecturable (form, etc.).

erschließen. I. *v.tr.* (*strong*) **1.** (*a*) **j-m sein Herz, sein Inneres, e., sich j-m e.,** to open one's heart to s.o.; (*b*) to open up (new market, etc.); to (begin to) work, to (begin to) exploit, to open up (coal-mine); to develop (district, coal-area, etc.); **neue Absatzmärkte e.,** to open up new markets; **moderne Verkehrsmittel haben das Innere des Kontinents erschlossen,** modern means of communication have made the interior of the continent accessible; **viel Kapital wird noch nötig sein, um dieses Land zu erschließen,** much capital will still be needed to develop this country; **diese Landstriche sind dem Fremdenverkehr noch nicht erschlossen,** these regions have not yet been opened up to the tourist trade. **2.** to deduce, infer, conclude (sth.); to conjecture (original form of fragmentary work of art, poem, unrecorded linguistic form, etc.); **aus früheren Erfahrungen läßt sich e., daß . . . ,** from previous experiences it can be concluded that . . . ; **erschlossene Form,** conjectural form (of work of art, poem, word).

II. *vbl s.* **Erschließen** *n.*, **Erschließung** *f. in vbl senses; also:* (*a*) development (of country, etc.); exploitation (of mine, etc.); **zur Erschließung des Landes werden große Summen nötig sein,** the development of the country will require large sums of money; **man hat hier noch nicht mit der Erschließung der Bodenschätze begonnen,** the natural resources are not yet being exploited here; (*b*) deduction; establishing (of original form, etc.) by conjecture.

erschmeicheln, *v.tr.* to obtain (sth.) by flattery; **sich** *dat.* **von j-m etwas e.,** to wheedle, cajole, sth. out of s.o., from s.o.; **sich** *dat.* **j-s Gunst e.,** to worm one's way into s.o.'s favour.

erschmeizen, *v.tr.* (*strong*) **Metall aus Erz e.,** to extract metal from ore by smelting.

erschnappen, *v.tr.* to catch (sth.) (as it falls, in mid-air); **der Hund erschnappte den Knochen,** the dog caught the bone as it fell.

erschöpfbar, *a.* exhaustible.

Erschöpfbarkeit, *f.* exhaustibility.

erschöpfen. I. *v.tr.* **1.** (*a*) to exhaust, use up, consume (provisions, stores, etc.); to exhaust (means, resources, patience, strength); to work out, deplete, exhaust (natural resources, etc.); **meine Energie war fast erschöpft,** my energy was almost exhausted, spent; **unsere Vorräte sind beinahe erschöpft,** our stores are running low, getting short, giving out, running out, are almost exhausted; **die Möglichkeiten dieses Schauspielers sind mit wenigen Rollen erschöpft,** the talents of this actor are limited to a few parts; **meine Geduld ist erschöpft,** my patience is exhausted, is at an end; **erschöpfende Auskunft geben,** to give exhaustive information; **ein Thema erschöpft haben,** to have exhausted a subject; **ein Thema erschöpfend behandeln,** to treat a subject exhaustively; (*b*) *Ch: Ind: etc:* to exhaust, spend (liquor, bath, wood-ashes, etc.); **den Boden e.,** to exhaust, impoverish, the soil; *El:* **erschöpfte Batterie,** run-down battery. **2.** to exhaust (s.o., oneself), to tire (s.o., oneself) out, to wear (s.o., oneself) out; to drain (s.o.) of his strength; **die geringste Anstrengung erschöpfte ihn, seine Kräfte,** the least exertion wore him out, tired him; **er hatte sich bei dieser Arbeit völlig erschöpft,** he had thoroughly exhausted himself, worn himself out, over this task; (*of pers.*) **erschöpft sein,** to be exhausted; to be worn out, tired out; **er machte einen erschöpften Eindruck,** he looked tired, worn out.

II. *vbl s.* **1. Erschöpfen,** *n. in vbl senses.* **2. Erschöpfung,** *f.* (*a*)=II. 1; *also:* exhaustion (of provisions, stores, means, resources, patience, strength, etc.); depletion (of natural resources, etc.); (*b*) (state of) exhaustion, prostration; *Med:* exhaustion, lassitude; **er befand sich in einem Zustand völliger E.,** he was in a state of complete exhaustion, complete collapse; **ich war nahe daran, vor E. umzufallen,** I was ready to drop with exhaustion.

erschöpft, *a. see* **erschöpfen** I.

Erschöpftheit, *f.*=**Erschöpfung,** *q.v. under* **erschöpfen** II. 2 (*b*).

Erschöpfung, *f. see* **erschöpfen** II.

Erschöpfungsdelirium, *n. Med:* delirium due to inanition.

Erschöpfungspsychose, *f. Med:* exhaustion psychosis.

Erschöpfungstod, *m.* death from exhaustion.

Erschöpfungszustand, *m.* state of exhaustion.

erschrak, erschräke *see* **erschrecken** I. 2.

erschrecken. I. *v.* **1.** *v.tr.* (*weak*) to startle (s.o., animal); to frighten, scare (s.o., animal); to alarm (s.o.); to shock (s.o.); **der Schuß erschreckte die Rehe,** the shot startled the deer, the deer took fright at the shot; **habe ich dich erschreckt?** did I frighten you? **ihr Aussehen erschreckte mich,** her appearance alarmed me; **er erschreckte mich so sehr, daß ich kein Wort hervorbrachte,** I was so terrified by him that I could not utter a word. **2.** *v.i.* (*strong*) (*sein*) to be startled; to be, get, frightened, scared; to take fright; to be terrified; to be horrified; **über etwas** *acc.*, **j-n, e.,** to be frightened, startled, by sth., s.o.; **vor etwas** *dat.*, **j-m, e.,** to be frightened at sth., s.o., at seeing, hearing, sth.; **erschrick nicht über den Anblick,** don't let the sight shock you; **er erschrak über ihr Aussehen,** he was alarmed at her appearance; **würdest du vor einem Gespenst e.?** would you be frightened at, of, a ghost? **warum erschrickst du vor mir?** why are you frightened of me? **3. sich erschrecken** (*p.t.* **erschreckte,** *p.p.* **erschrocken),** to be startled; to be, get, frightened, scared; to take fright; to be terrified; **sich über etwas** *acc.*, **j-n, e.,** to be frightened, startled, by sth., s.o.; **sich vor etwas** *dat.*, **j-m, e.,** to be frightened, startled, at sth., s.o., at seeing, hearing, sth.

II. *vbl s.* **Erschrecken,** *n. in vbl senses; also:* fright, scare; terror; alarm.

III. *pr.p. & a.* **erschreckend,** frightening, terrifying; alarming; terrible, dreadful; appalling (news, ugliness, etc.); **die Unglücksstätte bot ein erschreckendes Bild,** the scene of disaster offered a terrible sight; **mit erschreckender Deutlichkeit wurde ihm klar, daß . . . ,** he realized with terrible clarity that . . . ; **die Jugendkriminalität hat ein erschreckendes Ausmaß angenommen,** juvenile delinquency has assumed frightening, appalling, proportions; *adv.* **e. häßlich,** terribly, frightfully, appallingly, alarmingly, ugly; **die Einnahmen sind e. zurückgegangen,** there has been an appalling drop in the takings.

IV. *p.p. & a.* **1. erschreckt,** *in vbl senses of* I. 1; *esp.* terrified (child, etc.); startled (bird, deer, child, etc.); **sie fuhr auf wie ein erschrecktes Reh,** she jumped up like a startled deer. **2. erschrocken,** *in vbl senses of* I. 2, 3; *esp.* **das Kind war zu Tode e.,** the child was frightened to death, was frightened, terrified, out of his wits; **über so viel Unwissenheit war ich ganz e.,** I was quite horrified at so much ignorance; **mit erschrockenem Gesicht, mit erschrockener Stimme, sagte sie . . . ,** with a frightened, terrified, look, she said . . . ; in a terrified voice, in a voice trembling with fright, she said . . . ; *adv.* **er hielt e. inne,** he paused in alarm.

erschrecklich, *a. Lit:* =**erschreckend,** *q.v. under* **erschrecken** III.

Erschrecknis, *n.* **-nisses/-nisse.** *A:* fright, scare; terror.

erschreckt *see* **erschrecken** I. 1, IV. 1.

erschrocken, *p.p. & a. see* **erschrecken** IV. 2.

Erschrockenheit, *f.* frightened, terrified, state; (state of) fright; horrified state (of mind); (state of) alarm.

erschröcklich, *a. A:*=**erschrecklich.**

erschürfen, *v.tr.* (*a*) *Min:* (*of prospector*) to discover, open up (bed of ore, seam of coal, etc.); (*b*) *Lit:* to rummage out (facts, information, etc.).

erschüttern. I. *v.tr.* (*a*) to shake (sth.); to make (sth.) quiver, tremble, shake, quake; to make (sth.) rock, totter; **das Erdbeben hat die Grundmauern des Hauses erschüttert,** the earthquake has shaken the foundations of the house; **eine heftige See erschütterte das Boot,** a heavy sea set the boat quivering, shook the boat, made the boat shudder; **Detonationen erschütterten die Luft,** detonations shook the air, made the air quiver; (*b*) to disturb (sth.), to have a disturbing effect on (sth.); to shake (health, credit, authority, faith, trust, etc.); to upset, unsettle (political situation, activity, etc.); **das Klima hat seine Gesundheit erschüttert,** the climate has undermined his health; **der Krieg hat die Stabilität der Währung erschüttert,** the war has unsettled, upset, the stability of the currency; **seine Stellung ist durch diesen Vorfall stark erschüttert worden,** this incident has disturbed his position profoundly, has made his situation very uncertain, *F:* very shaky; (*c*) to shake (s.o.) (up), to give (s.o.) a shaking up; to disturb (s.o.); to upset (s.o.); **die Nachricht hat ihn erschüttert** the news has shaken him badly, has disturbed him profoundly, has given him a nasty shock; **es war ein erschütternder Anblick,** it was a deeply moving sight; *F:* **das kann ihn doch nicht e.,** that won't worry him; **er läßt sich durch nichts e.,** nothing ever ruffles him.

II. *vbl s.* **1. Erschüttern,** *n. in vbl senses.* **2. Erschütterung,** *f.* (*a*)=II. 1; (*b*) vibration (of ground, railway carriage, *Mec.E:* of engine, bed, etc.); tremor (of earth, ground, etc.);

shock (from sudden impact, earthquake, etc.); jolt (of carriage, etc.); *Med:* concussion (of the brain); **ihr Kopf schmerzte bei jeder E.,** her head ached with every jolt; (*c*) shock, emotional upset; **er hat sich von der seelischen E. noch nicht erholt,** he has not yet recovered from the emotional upset; **alle wurden von tiefer E. erfaßt,** everybody was deeply moved.

erschütterungsfest, *a.* shock-proof, proof against vibration.

erschütterungsfrei, *a. Mec.E: etc:* free from vibration.

Erschütterungsgebiet, *n. Geol:* region of seismic disturbance, disturbed area.

Erschütterungsladung, *f. Exp:* cracking charge.

Erschütterungsmesser, *m. Ph:* vibrograph, vibration recorder.

Erschütterungsmessung, *f.* seismography.

Erschütterungsreiz, *m. Physiol:* contact stimulus.

Erschütterungssinn, *m.* sense of vibration (of animal, etc.).

Erschütterungswelle, *f.* earthquake wave.

Erschütterungszeiger, *m. Ph:* seismograph.

erschweren. I. *v.tr.* **1.** to make (work, etc.) (more) difficult; to hinder (work, etc.); to impede (progress, etc.); **die hohen Zölle erschweren den Außenhandel,** the high duties are a hindrance, an impediment, to foreign trade; **schlechte Sicht erschwerte die Suche nach den Verunglückten,** bad visibility hindered, hampered, the search for the victims; **er erschwert sich die Arbeit unnötig,** he makes work unnecessarily difficult for himself; **die Arbeit mußte unter erschwerten Bedingungen fortgesetzt werden,** work had to be continued under less favourable conditions; **der Fortgang der Verhandlungen wurde dadurch erschwert,** this made it more difficult to continue negotiations; **das erschwert die Lage nur noch mehr,** this only makes the situation more difficult, this only complicates the situation. **2.** to aggravate (crime); **erschwerende Umstände,** aggravating circumstances. **3.** *Tex:* to weight (silk).

II. *vbl s.* **1. Erschweren,** *n. in vbl senses.* **2. Erschwerung,** *f.* (*a*)=II. 1; (*b*) (added) difficulty; impediment, hindrance; **das bedeutet eine zusätzliche E. meiner Arbeit,** this is an added difficulty in my work, this adds another difficulty to my work; (*c*) aggravation (of crime).

erschwindeln, *v.tr.* (*a*) **(sich** *dat.***) etwas e.,** to get sth. by swindling; **er hat (sich) sein ganzes Vermögen erschwindelt,** he has got his whole fortune by swindling; **er hat (sich) 100 Mark von ihr erschwindelt,** he has swindled 100 marks out of her; (*b*) to invent, make up (story); **das ist alles erschwindelt,** that is pure fabrication, that's all lies.

erschwingen, *v.tr.* (*strong*) **1.** (*a*) *A. & Lit:* to attain, gain (fame, fortune, etc.); to rise to (high position, etc.); (*b*) to be able to afford (sth.); **die Miete ist so hoch, wir können sie kaum e.,** the rent is so high that we can hardly afford it, run to it, rise to it; **das ist für uns nicht zu e.,** it is beyond our means, it is not within our means, we can't run, rise, to it, we can't afford it. **2.** *A:* (*of bird, song, etc.*) **sich erschwingen,** to rise into the air; to soar.

erschwinglich, *a.* (purchase, price, rent, etc.) that is within one's means, that one can afford; **wir bieten Ihnen unsere Waren zu erschwinglichen Preisen an,** we offer you our goods at reasonable prices, at prices that you can afford (to pay); **das Auto ist für uns nicht e.,** the car is beyond, not within, our means.

ersehen, *v.tr.* (*strong*) **1.** (*a*) *A:* to see, behold (sth.); (*b*) (*also v.i. (haben)*) *A:* **(sich** *dat.***) eine Gelegenheit, einen Vorteil, einer Gelegenheit, eines Vorteils, e.,** to see, recognize, an opportunity, advantage; (*c*) **etwas aus etwas e.,** to see, learn, understand, sth. from sth.; **aus Ihrem Brief habe ich ersehen, daß . . . ,** from your letter I saw, learnt, that . . . ; **wie aus Ihrem Brief zu e. ist,** as can be seen, learnt, from your letter . . . ; **aus Ihrem Schreiben ist leider nicht zu e., ob . . . ,** unfortunately your letter does not indicate, show, does not make it clear, whether . . . ; **aus Ihrem Verhalten läßt sich leicht e., daß . . . ,** your behaviour shows clearly that . . . **2.** to choose, elect (s.o.).

ersehnen, *v.tr.* **(sich** *dat.***) etwas e.,** to long for sth., to yearn for, after, sth.; **den Frieden e.,** to long for peace; **Reichtum e.,** to desire wealth, to long for wealth; **endlich bot sich die lange ersehnte Gelegenheit,** the long-desired opportunity finally came.

ersetzbar, *a.* replaceable; (loss, damage, etc.) that can be made good, that can be compensated for; *Lit:* reparable (loss, injury).

ersetzen. I. *v.tr.* **1.** (*a*) to take, fill, the place of (s.o., sth.); to serve as a substitute for (s.o., sth.); to do duty for (s.o., *F:* sth.); **niemand kann meine frühere Köchin e.,** nobody can take, fill, the place of my former cook; **niemand kann eine Mutter e.,** no one can take the place of a mother, no one can replace a mother; **diese Maschine ersetzt drei Arbeitskräfte,** this machine does the work of three men; (*b*) to make up for (sth.); to make good (sth.); **nichts kann mir diesen Verlust e.,** nothing can make good this loss to me. **2.** (*a*) to provide, supply, a suitable substitute for (sth., s.o.); **etwas, j-n, durch etwas, j-n,** *occ.* **mit etwas, j-m, e.,** to replace sth., s.o., by sth., s.o.; to substitute sth. for sth., s.o. for s.o.; **Seide wird in steigenden Maße durch synthetische Fasern ersetzt,** silk is being replaced more and more by synthetic fibres; **ein schwer zu ersetzender Arbeiter,** a workman (who is) difficult to replace; **Butter durch Margarine e.,** to substitute margarine for butter; (*b*) to replace, to provide, supply, a replacement for (a lost *or* broken object); to refund, reimburse (expenses); **j-m den Schaden e.,** to compensate s.o. for the damage; to make good the damage suffered by s.o.; **j-m den Verdienstausfall e.,** to compensate s.o. for loss of earnings *or* wages; **Sie werden mir die zerrissenen Bettücher e. müssen,** you will have to replace *or* pay me for the torn sheets, the sheets that have been torn; **wir ersetzen Ihnen alle Auslagen,** we shall refund all your disbursements (to you), we shall reimburse you (for) all your expenses.

II. *vbl s.* **Ersetzen** *n.*, **Ersetzung** *f.*=**Ersatz** 1.

ersetzlich, *a.*=**ersetzbar.**

ersichtlich, *a.* apparent, manifest, obvious (fact, etc.); evident, clear; **aus Ihrem Brief ist e., daß . . . ,** your letter makes it clear, obvious, that . . . , your letter shows that . . . ; **daraus ist klar e., daß . . . ,** this shows clearly that . . . .

Ersichtlichkeit, *f.* clearness, plainness; obviousness.

ersinnen, *v.tr.* (*strong*) to think out, think up, contrive, devise (plan, etc.); to invent, think up (story, etc.).

ersisch [ˈɛrzɪʃ]. **1.** *a.* Erse (language, etc.). **2.** *s.* **Ersisch,** *n. Ling:* Erse.

ersitzen. I. *v.tr.* (*strong*) **1.** *Jur:* to acquire (sth.) by (positive) prescription, usucap(t)ion; **ein ersessenes Recht,** a right acquired by (positive) prescription. **2.** *Hum:* **(sich** *dat.***) eine Professur e.,** to obtain a professorship by sheer length of service.

II. *vbl s.* **Ersitzen** *n.*, **Ersitzung** *f. Jur:* (positive) prescription, usucap(t)ion.

Ersitzungsfrist, *f. Jur:* prescriptive period, period of prescription.

ersparen, *v.tr.* **1.** (*a*) **(sich** *dat.***) etwas e.,** to save (up) (money, etc.); **sie lebten nur von dem Ersparten,** they lived entirely on their savings; (*b*) to save (time, labour, etc.); **der Tunnel erspart einen Weg von 200 Kilometern,** the tunnel saves a distance of 200 kilometres; **eine Zeit ersparende Vorrichtung,** a time-saving device. **2. j-m etwas e.,** to spare s.o. sth.; **erspare mir diese peinliche Begegnung,** spare me this embarrassing meeting; **nichts blieb ihm erspart,** he was spared nothing; **deine Bemerkungen kannst du dir e.,** you can keep your remarks to yourself; **erspare dir diese Mühe,** spare, save, yourself the trouble, *F:* don't bother; *F:* **den Rest kannst du dir e.,** you need not do *or* say any more.

Ersparnis, *f.* **-/-nisse. 1.** (*also comb.fm.* **-ersparnis**) **E. an Zeit, Arbeit, Zeitersparnis, Arbeitsersparnis,** saving in time, in labour; **E. an Arbeitskräften,** saving in manpower, in labour. **2.** *usu.pl.* **Ersparnisse,** savings.

ersprießen, *v.i.* (*strong*) (*sein*) (*a*) *A:* (*of plant, etc.*) to spring up; (*b*) *A:* **j-m, etwas** *dat.*, **e.,** to be fruitful for s.o., sth., to be profitable, beneficial, to s.o., sth.; (*c*) *F:* **aus etwas e.,** to arise, result, follow, from sth.; **daraus kann nichts Gutes e.,** nothing good can come of it.

ersprießlich, *a.* fruitful, profitable, beneficial (activity, etc.).

Ersprießlichkeit, *f.* fruitfulness, profitableness, beneficial nature (of activity, etc.).

erst, *adv.* **1.** (*a*) first; **er hat das Recht, e. zu sprechen,** he has the right to speak first; **geht ihr e.!** you go first! (*b*) first, at first; **e. die Arbeit, dann das Spiel,** work first and play afterwards; business before pleasure; **e. muß ich meine Mutter fragen,** I shall have to ask my mother first; (*c*) **das muß ich mir e. einmal überlegen,** I shall have to think that over first; **das muß e. noch bewiesen werden,** that still remains to be proved; **¹der Mann müßte e. (noch) geboren werden,** such a man has yet to be born; there has never been such a man yet; *see also* **nachmachen** 1 (*a*). **2.** only, (only) just; **ich habe es ihm doch eben e. gesagt,** but I only told him a short while ago; **es ist e. halb sieben,** it is only half past six; **wir können es e. im nächsten Jahr erfahren,** we shall not know until next year; **bist du e. jetzt mit der Arbeit fertig?** have you only just finished your work? **wenn du nur e. wieder gesund wärest!** if only you were well again! **ich gebe dir das Geld e. dann, wenn ich weiß, daß du es nicht vertust,** I'll give you the money only when, I won't give you the money until, I'm sure you won't waste it; **dann e. gab er ihr das Geld,** only then did he give her the money. **3.** (*emotive particle*) (*emphasizing statement*) (*a*) really; just; **das gab e. eine Aufregung,** that really caused excitement; **der Herbst war schon kalt genug, aber der Winter e.!** the autumn was quite cold enough, but it was nothing compared with the winter; **sie ist hübsch, aber du solltest e. ihre Schwester sehen!** she is pretty, but you should just see her sister! (*b*) **nun müssen wir e. recht vorsichtig sein,** now we shall have to be doubly careful, even more careful (than before); **wenn man es ihm verbietet, tut er es e. recht,** if it is forbidden him he is absolutely certain to (go and) do it; **das würde ihm e. recht nicht gefallen,** he most certainly would not like that; he would like that even less.

erstarken, *v.i.* (*sein*) to grow strong(er); to gather strength, to gain strength; **wieder e.,** to regain strength, to recover (strength); **im Glauben e.,** to grow strong in the faith.

erstarren. I. **1.** *v.tr. A:* to benumb (s.o.'s limbs, etc.). **2.** *v.i.* (*sein*) (*a*) (*of fluids, etc.*) to become solid, to solidify, consolidate, set; to freeze; (*of oil, etc.*) to congeal, solidify; (*of lava*) to solidify; *Cu:* (*of jelly, etc.*) to set; *F:* **das Blut erstarrte ihr in den Adern,** her blood froze (in her veins), her blood ran cold; (*b*) (*of limb, etc.*) to grow stiff, to stiffen; to become rigid, to rigidify; to go numb; **ihre Finger sind vor Kälte erstarrt,** her fingers are stiff, numb, with cold; **mit vor Kälte erstarrten Fingern,** with fingers stiff with cold; **seine erstarrten Glieder,** his stiffened, rigid, limbs; **die Leiche ist erstarrt,** the body has become rigid, has stiffened, is stiff; **seine Gesichtszüge waren zu einer Maske erstarrt,** his features had set in a mask; **das Lächeln erstarrte auf seinen Lippen,** the smile froze on his lips; **vor Entsetzen e.,** to be paralysed, petrified, with fear; (*c*) (*of concept, idea, art, style, etc.*) to grow, become, rigid, to rigidify; (*of style*) to become set; **in den erstarrten Formen der Tradition,** in rigid traditional forms; in an ironbound tradition; **erstarrte Form,** (i) rigid form, (ii) *Ling:* fossilized form.

II. *vbl s.* **1. Erstarren,** *n. in vbl senses; also:* solidification (of oil, etc.); congelation, congealment (of fluid). **2. Erstarrung,** *f.* (*a*)=II. 1; **E. der künstlerischen Form,** rigid formalization of artistic form; (*b*) **Zustand der E.,** congealed state (of fluid); solidified, frozen, state; stiffness, rigidity, numbness (of limb, etc.).

Erstarrtheit, *f.* stiffness, rigidity; numbness.

Erstarrung, *f. see* **erstarren** II.

Erstarrungsdiagramm, *n. Ch:* solidification diagram.

Erstarrungsgestein, *n. Geol:* igneous, pyrogenic, rock.

Erstarrungskruste, *f. Geol:* original, primitive, crust.

Erstarrungspunkt, *m. Ph:* point of solidification; freezing point.

Erstarrungsrinde, *f. Geol:*=**Erstarrungskruste.**

Erstarrungswärme, *f. Ch:* heat evolved on solidification.

Erstarrungszustand, *m.* congealed state, state of congelation (of fluid, etc.); solidified state; state of rigidity (of limb, etc.).

erstatten. I. *v.tr.* **1.** (*a*) to refund, return (expenses, amount overpaid); to make restitution of (money); **j-m die Unkosten e.,** to reimburse s.o. (for) his expenses, to refund, repay, s.o.'s expenses; (*b*) *A:* to give (sth.) back; to restore (sth.); to make good (sth.). **2. Bericht e.,** to report; to make, give, a report; **über etwas Bericht e.,** to report on sth.; **Anzeige e.,** to give notification. *See also* **Anzeige** 2, **Bericht.**

II. *vbl s.* **1. Erstatten,** *n. in vbl senses.* **2. Erstattung,** *f.* (*a*)=II. 1; *also:* restitution, reimbursement (of expenses, sum overpaid,

etc.); (*b*) (sum paid as) restitution, reimbursement; refund; **für etwas E. erlangen**, to obtain restitution of sth.; to get a refund of (deposit, etc.), to get (deposit, etc.) refunded.

Erstattungsanspruch, *m.* claim for restitution, for refund.

Erstattungsantrag, *m.* application for restitution, for refund.

Erstattungsverfahren, *n. Jur:* restitution suit.

Erstaufführung, *f. Th: etc:* first performance, first night (of play, etc.).

erstaufgeführt, *p.p. Th: etc:* (play, etc.) performed for the first time (in a town); **das Stück wurde gestern in Hamburg e.**, the play had its first performance in Hamburg last night

erstaunen. I. **1.** *v.i.* (*sein*) (*occ.* **sich erstaunen**) **über etwas** *acc.*, **j-n, e.**, **erstaunt sein**, to be surprised at sth.; to be astonished, astounded, amazed, at sth., s.o.; **alle erstaunten über solche Kühnheit**, all marvelled at such audacity; **ich bin (darüber) erstaunt, daß . . .**, I am astonished, astounded, that . . . ; **ich bin erstaunt, dich hier zu treffen**, I am surprised to find you here; **höchst, höchlich**, *F:* **baß, erstaunt sein**, to be most, greatly, surprised, astonished, amazed; **ich bin erstaunt über dich!** I am surprised at you! you astonish me! **erstaunt vernahm er, daß . . .**, with astonishment, amazement he heard that . . . ; **auf seine erstaunte Frage erwiderte ich . . .**, to his astonished question I replied . . . ; **er machte ein sehr erstauntes Gesicht**, he looked greatly surprised, *F:* quite mystified. **2.** *v.tr.* to surprise (s.o.); to astonish (s.o.); to astound, amaze (s.o.); **es erstaunt mich, daß . . .**, I am astonished, amazed, that . . . ; **was mich daran am meisten erstaunt, ist . . .**, what surprises, astonishes, me most about it is . . . ; the greatest wonder about it is . . . ; what strikes me most (about it) is . . . ; **das würde mich nicht weiter e.**, I shouldn't be surprised at it, it wouldn't surprise me.

II. *vbl s.* **Erstaunen**, *n.* astonishment, surprise; amazement; **zu meinem großen E.**, to my great surprise, to my great astonishment, amazement; **in E. geraten**, to be astonished, amazed, to be filled with astonishment, amazement; **j-n in E. (ver)setzen**, to astonish s.o., to fill s.o. with amazement; **seine Kunststücke setzten uns in E.**, his tricks amazed us.

erstaunenswert, erstaunenswürdig, *a.* astounding, astonishing, amazing.

erstaunlich, *a.* astonishing, amazing, astounding; surprising; *F:* stupendous, prodigious; **mit erstaunlicher Geschicklichkeit**, with surprising, astonishing, astounding, skill; **er hat auf diesem Gebiet Erstaunliches geleistet**, he has done amazing things in this field; *adv.* **für diese Jahreszeit ist es e. kalt**, it is astonishingly cold for this time of the year; **von dieser Sache ist e. viel Aufhebens gemacht worden**, there has been an amazing, *F:* a prodigious, amount of fuss about this business.

Erstausbildung, *f. Mil: Mil.Av:* initial training.

Erstausfertigung, *f. Adm:* original (copy) (of document).

Erstausführung, *f. Veh: etc:* prototype; (original) model; original pattern.

Erstausgabe, *f. Publ:* first edition.

Erstausrüstung, *f. Mil:* initial equipment.

Erstausstattung, *f.* initial equipment, outfit; *Mil:* initial issue; *Fin:* initial allocation of currency (*after currency reform in Germany in* 1948).

erstbeste(r), -beste, -beste(s), *a.*=**erste(r) beste(r), erste(s) beste(s)**, *q.v. under* **beste(r)** 1 (*a*).

erste, *a. see* **erste(r)**.

erstechen, *v.tr.* (*strong*) to stab (s.o.) to death.

erstehen, *v.* (*strong*) I. *v.i.* (*sein*) (*a*) *Lit:* to rise (again), to return from the dead; **Christ ist erstanden**, Christ has risen; (*b*) to arise, spring up; **neue Städte sind überall erstanden**, new towns have risen, sprung up, everywhere; (*c*) (*of difficulty, etc.*) to arise, result (**aus etwas**, from sth.); **daraus können nur Schwierigkeiten e.**, nothing but difficulties will result from it.

II. **erstehen**, *v.tr.* **1.** *A:* to go through (sth.), to get through (trying period, etc.). **2.** to acquire, buy (sth.); **ich habe diese Äpfel billig erstanden**, I got these apples cheap, these apples were a bargain.

Ersteher, *m.* **-s/-**, buyer, purchaser (at auction).

ersteigbar, *a.* climbable (mountain, etc.).

ersteigen, *v.tr.* (*strong*) to climb, scale (mountain, wall, etc.); to go up (stairs, etc.); to mount (ladder); **einen Gipfel e.**, to climb a peak, *Lit:* to ascend, make the ascent of, a peak; **Ersteigung** *f*, ascent (of mountain, etc.).

erstellen, *v.tr.* to make (sth.) available; to provide (sth.); **für den Transport müssen fünfzig Güterwagen erstellt werden**, fifty wagons will have to be made available for the transport; **Erstellung** *f*, provision (of sth.).

erstemal, *n.* **das e.**=**das erste Mal**; **zum erstenmal**=**zum ersten Mal(e)**; *q.v. under* **erste(r)**.

erstens, *adv.* first, firstly, in the first place.

erste(r), erste, erste(s), *ordinal num.a.* first; (*a*) **das erste Mal**, the first time; **zum ersten Mal(e)**, for the first time; **wann hast du ihn zum ersten Mal(e) gesehen?** when did you see him for the first time? **der erste Weltkrieg**, the First World War, *F:* World War I; **die erste Etage**, the first floor, *U.S:* the second story; (*at auction*) **zum ersten, zum zweiten, zum dritten**, going, going, gone; **an erster Stelle**, in the first place, first; first and foremost; **die Geldfrage steht immer an erster Stelle**, money is always the first consideration; **in erster Linie**, first and foremost, above all; **am ersten**, (i) first; (ii) in the first place; **als erster ankommen**, to arrive first; **er war einer der ersten, die ankamen**, he was one of the first arrivals, he was one of the first to arrive; **er ist der Erste in Latein**, he is the first in Latin, he takes the lead in Latin; **er ist der Erste in seiner Klasse**, he is top of his class, top boy; **der erste Chirurg in London**, the first, leading, surgeon in London; **eines der ersten Modehäuser in Paris**, one of the leading fashion houses of Paris; **die ersten Familien der Stadt**, the first families of the town; **die Ersten des Landes**, the first (people) in the land; **ein Wissenschaftler ersten Ranges**, a prominent, first-rate, *F:* top, scientist; **das war eine Vorführung ersten Ranges**, that was a performance of the first order, that was a first-class performance; **ein Hotel erster Klasse**, a first-class hotel; **er betrachtete es als seine erste Pflicht**, he considered it his first duty; **der erste Januar**, the first of January; **am nächsten Ersten**, on the first of next month, *Com:* on the first prox.; **vom ersten Tage an**, from the first day, from the first; *Th:* **erster Rang**, dress circle; *Geom: Mapm:* **erste Projektion**, horizontal projection; **erste Projektionsebene**, horizontal projection plane; *Fin:* **erster Kurs, erster Preis**, opening price; *Parl:* **erste Lesung**, first reading (of bill); *Sch:* **das erste Schuljahr**, (i) the first year at school; (ii)=**die erste Klasse**; **die erste Klasse**, (i) (*in German elementary school*) the first form, class, *U.S:* grade; (*in English elementary school*) *approx.* the third form, class; (*in English private or junior school*) the lower second (form); (*in U.S. elementary school*) the first grade; (ii) (*in German and English secondary schools*) the first form; (*in English secondary school with junior school attached*) the upper third *or* lower fourth (form); (*in U.S. elementary school*) the fifth grade; (iii) (*in German and English secondary schools*) the sixth form; (*in U.S. senior High school*) the twelfth grade; *Ling:* **erste Lautverschiebung**, first sound-shift, first consonant-shift; *Jur:* **erste Instanz**, first instance; **Gerichtsbarkeit erster Instanz**, jurisdiction of first instance, original jurisdiction; **Gericht erster Instanz**, court of first instance; *Com:* **erste Güte, erste Wahl**, first, finest, top(-grade), quality; **Waren erster Wahl**, top-grade goods; firsts; *Rail: etc:* **erste Klasse**, first class; *U.S: approx.*=Pullman; **erster Klasse**, *F:* **Erster, reisen**, to travel first (class), *U.S:* Pullman; *see also* **Fall**[1] 5, **Gang**[1] 8, **Geige, Hand** 1 (*f*), **Person**; (*b*) **in den ersten Tagen des Januar, in den ersten Januartagen**, in the early part of January; **die ersten Monate des Jahres**, the early months of the year; **die ersten drei Jahre, die drei ersten Jahre**, the first three years; **in der ersten Zeit**, at first, in the early days; **beim ersten Morgengrauen**, at the first light of dawn, at first light; **ich werde bei der ersten Gelegenheit bei Ihnen vorsprechen**, I shall call on you at the first opportunity; **fürs erste**, for now, for the moment, for the time being; **damit mußt du dich fürs erste behelfen**, you will have to make this do for now; *see also* **beste(r)** 1 (*a*).

ersterben, *v.i.* (*strong*) (*sein*) (*a*) *A:* (*of pers.*) to be (gradually) dying; (*of limb, etc.*) (i) to mortify; (ii) to become insensible, insensitive; to grow numb; *B:* **sein Herz erstarb ihm im Leibe**, his heart died within him; (*b*) *A:* (*of plant, tree, etc.*) to die off, to wither away; (*c*) **er erstarb fast vor Ehrfurcht**, he was awestruck, awestricken, he was benumbed with awe; *Corr: A:* **ich ersterbe in tiefster Ehrfurcht, Ihr . . .**, your most humble and obedient servant . . . ; (*d*) *Lit:* (*of sound, voice, etc.*) to die away (gradually); (*of smile*) to fade; (*of hatred, love, etc.*) to die (gradually); (*of hope, etc.*) to die, vanish; **das Geräusch erstarb in der Ferne**, the noise died away in the distance; **das Lächeln erstarb auf ihren Lippen**, the smile faded from, died on, her lips; **mit ersterbender Stimme**, with an expiring voice.

erstere(r), erstere, erstere(s), *a.* (the) former; **von beiden Möglichkeiten würde ich die erstere vorziehen**, of the two possibilities I should prefer the former.

ersterwähnt, *attrib.a.* first-mentioned.

Erstfinderrecht, *n. Jur: Min:* right of the discoverer.

erstgebärend, *a. Med:* primiparous, giving birth for the first time.

Erstgebärende, *f.* (*decl. as adj.*) *Med:* primipara, woman giving birth for the first time.

erstgeboren, *attrib.a.* first-born (child).

Erstgeburt, *f.* **-/-.** **1.** *B: etc:* first-born (child); *coll.* **alle Erstgeburt**, all first-born. **2.** primogeniture; birthright; *B:* **verkaufe mir heute deine E.**, sell me this day thy birthright; *F:* **seine E. verkaufen**, to sell one's birthright; to sell (sth.) for a mess of pottage.

Erstgeburtsrecht, *n. Jur:* right of primogeniture.

erstgenannt, *attrib.a.* first-named; first-mentioned.

ersticken. I. *v.* **1.** *v.i.* (*sein*) (*a*) (*of pers.*) to suffocate, stifle, choke (to death); (*of plant, flame*) to be stifled, to die (*from lack of oxygen*); (*of plant*) to be suffocated, stifled, choked (by weed, etc.); **im Rauch e.**, to be suffocated, stifled, choked to death, by smoke; **an dem Bissen wäre er fast erstickt**, the piece of food nearly choked him; **vor Husten wäre er fast erstickt**, he nearly choked to death with coughing; **vor Lachen e.**, to choke with laughter; **ich glaubte, ich müßte e.**, I thought I was going to suffocate; *F:* **ich ersticke in Arbeit**, I am up to my neck in work; (*b*) (*of feeling, aspiration, etc.*) to be smothered, quenched, quelled; (*of sound, voice, etc.*) to be smothered, stifled; **mit halb erstickter Stimme**, in a stifled, strangled, voice. **2.** *v.tr.* (*a*) to suffocate, smother, stifle, choke (s.o.); to asphyxiate (s.o.); to smother, choke (fire, etc.); to suffocate, choke (plant); **der Rauch erstickte alle Kühe**, all the cattle were asphyxiated by the smoke; **j-n mit seinen Umarmungen, Küssen, e.**, to smother s.o. with one's embraces, kisses; **erstickende Hitze**, stifling heat; **es war erstickend heiß**, it was (stifling) hot; *Min:* **erstickende Wetter** *pl*, choke-damp; *Mil:* **erstickender Kampfstoff**, asphyxiating (war) gas; (*b*) to smother, stifle (sound, voice, etc.); to quell, suppress, stifle (revolt, etc.); to suppress, smother (feeling, aspiration, etc); **der Schnee erstickte das Geräusch ihrer Fußtritte**, the snow muffled the sound of their footsteps; **ihre Stimme war von Tränen erstickt**, her voice was choked with tears; **jede menschliche Regung wurde sogleich erstickt**, any human feeling was immediately quenched, quelled, stifled; *see also* **Keim** 2.

II. *vbl s.* **1. Ersticken**, *n. in vbl senses; also:* (*a*) suffocation; asphyxia; **Tod durch E.**, death from, due to, suffocation, asphyxia; **es war zum E. heiß**, it was hot to the point of suffocation, it was stifling(ly) hot; **die Luft im Saal war zum E.**, the air in the hall was stifling; (*b*) suffocation (of s.o.); suppression (of revolt, feeling, etc.). **2. Erstickung**, *f.*=II. 1; *also: Med:* **innere E.**, asphyxia due to the inhalation of asphyxiating gases; **äußere E.**, asphyxia due to strangulation.

Erstickungsanfall, *m.* attack of choking.

Erstickungsgefahr, *f.* danger of suffocation.

Erstickungsschimmel, *m. Bot:* choke.

Erstickungstod, *m.* death from, due to, suffocation.

erstinken, *v.tr. & i.* (*strong*) *used only in p.p.* **erstunken**, *q.v.*

erstinstanzlich ['eːrstˀinˌʃtantslɪç], *a. Jur:* (verdict, etc.) of the court of first instance.

erstklassig, *a.* first-class, first-rate, top-rate, excellent; **das ist eine erstklassige Arbeit**, this is a first-class, first-rate, excellent, piece of work; **eine erstklassige Sekretärin**, a first-rate secretary; *Fin:* **erstklassige Wertpapiere**, first-class stock, gilt-edged stock; **eine erstklassige Obligation**, a prime bond.

erstlich, *adv.* in the first place; firstly; first.

Erstling, *m.* **-(e)s/-e.** *Lit:* (*a*) first-born (child); (*b*) firstling (of flock, etc.); (*c*) first fruit; earliest fruit (of the season); **Erstlinge**, first fruits; *Ecc.Hist:* annates; (*d*)=**Erstlingswerk.**

Erstlings-, *comb.fm.* **1.** first . . . ; beginner's . . . ; **Erstlingsroman** *m*, first novel (of young author); **Erstlingsversuch** *m*, first attempt, beginner's

attempt; first work, first product. **2.** infant's . . . , baby's . . . ; **Erstlingshemdchen** *n*, infant's, baby's, vest.
Erstlingsarbeit, *f.* first product; first work (of scholar, etc.).
Erstlingsausstattung, *f.* layette (*for baby*).
Erstlingschaft, *f.* -/. **1.** *Jur:* primogeniture. **2.** *Coll.* (the) first-born.
Erstlingsdruck, *m. Print:* first production (of a printer *or* a press).
Erstlingsrede, *f.* first speech; *Parl: etc:* maiden speech.
Erstlingswäsche, *f.* clothing for a newborn baby.
Erstlingswerk, *n.* first work (of writer, scholar, artist, etc.); first product (of artist).
Erstluft, *f. Ind:* (*in blast furnace*) primary air.
Erstmädchen, *n.* first maid, head maid; lady's maid.
erstmalig. 1. *a.* first. **2.** *adv.*=**erstmals.**
erstmals, *adv.* (for) the first time.
Erstmeldung, *f. Journ:* exclusive news report, *F:* scoop.
Erstmilch, *f. Physiol:* colostrum; *Vet:* beestings.
erstrahlen, *v.i.* (*sein*) to (begin to) shine, glitter; **die Sonne erstrahlte in hellem Glanze,** the sun shone brilliantly; **ihre Augen erstrahlten vor** Freude, her eyes lit up with joy.
erstrangig, *a.* first-class, first-rate, top-rate.
erstreben, *v.tr.* **1.** *A:* to obtain (sth.) (by one's efforts). **2.** to endeavour, aim, to get *or* bring about (sth.); to strive for, after (sth.); to aspire to, after (fame, wealth, etc.); **es wird erstrebt, daß . . . ,** the aim is that . . . .
erstrebenswert, *a.* (aim, object) worth striving for; **eine engere Zusammenarbeit ist e.,** closer cooperation is to be aimed at; **das ist nicht einmal e.,** that is not even desirable.
erstrecken. I. *v.tr.* **1.** (*a*) *A:* to stretch out (limbs, etc.); (*b*) *A:* to extend (lease, etc.); (*c*) **etwas auf etwas** *acc.*, **auf j-n, e.,** to extend sth. to sth., to s.o. **2. sich erstrecken,** (*a*) **sich über etwas** *acc.* **e.,** to extend, stretch, across, over, sth.; **sich bis an etwas e.,** to extend, stretch, to sth.; **der Wald erstreckte sich bis an das Meer,** the forest extended, stretched, to the sea; **das Gebirge erstreckt sich von . . . bis . . . ,** the mountains extend, stretch, from . . . to . . . ; **die Verbrennungen erstreckten sich über seinen ganzen Rücken,** the burns extended over, covered, the whole of his back; **sein Einfluß erstreckt sich weit über die Grenzen seines Heimatlandes,** his influence extends, reaches, far beyond the frontiers of his own country; **unsere Versuche erstreckten sich über mehrere Jahre,** our experiments extended, ranged, over several years; (*b*) (*of activity, knowledge, etc.*) **sich auf etwas** *acc.* **e.,** to include, comprise, embrace, sth.; to be concerned with sth.; (*of law, regulation, etc.*) **sich auf j-n e.,** to extend to s.o., to apply to s.o., to concern s.o.; **seine Forschungen erstrecken sich nur auf dieses begrenzte Feld,** his researches do not extend beyond, are confined to, this limited field; **unser Gespräch erstreckte sich auf alle wichtigen Fragen,** our talk dealt with, covered, all important questions; **dieses Gesetz erstreckt sich nur auf Minderjährige,** this law applies only to minors, covers only the case of minors.
II. *vbl s.* **Erstreckung,** *f.* extension, extent; *Min:* **Erzlager großer E.,** extensive ore deposits.
Erstschwarm, *m. Ap:* first swarm, virgin swarm.
erststellig, *a. Fin:* **erststellige Hypothek,** first mortgage.
Erststimme, *f. Pol:* first vote (on ballot-paper).
Ersttagsbrief, *m. Philately:* first-day cover.
Ersttagsstempel, *m.* first-day date stamp.
erstunken, *p.p. F:* **das ist e. und erlogen,** that is all trumped up, sheer, pure, invention; that's a pack of lies; **es sind schon viele erfroren, aber es ist noch keiner e.,** better a stuffy atmosphere than to risk freezing to death.
erstürmen. I. *v.tr. Mil:* to storm, carry (fortified position, etc.); to take (fortified position, etc.) by storm, by assault; **eine Festung e.,** to storm a fortress, to take a fortress by storm; to escalade a fortress.
II. *vbl s.* **Erstürmen** *n.*, **Erstürmung** *f. in vbl senses; also:* seizure, capture, (of fortress, etc.) by storm, by assault.
Erstversicherer, *m. Ins:* original insurer.
ersuchen. I. *v.tr.* **j-n e., etwas zu tun,** to ask, request, s.o. to do sth.; **j-n um etwas e.,** to ask, request, sth. of s.o.; **die Fahrgäste werden ersucht, ihre Fahrkarten an der Sperre abzugeben,** passengers are requested to give up their tickets at the barrier; **ich muß Sie dringend e., . . . ,** I must urgently request you . . . ; *Jur:* **ersuchter Richter,** judge specially appointed (to hear a particular case).
II. *vbl s.* **1. Ersuchen,** *n.* request, entreaty; **auf dringendes E. von . . . ,** at the urgent request of . . . . **2. Ersuchung,** *f.*=II. 1.
Ersuchungsschreiben, *n. Jur:* official request (to an authority to take a certain action).
ertappen, *v.tr.* to catch (s.o.) unawares, unprepared; **j-n bei etwas e.,** to catch s.o. (in the act of) doing sth.; **j-n beim Stehlen, bei einem Diebstahl, e.,** to catch s.o. (in the act of) stealing; **j-n auf frischer Tat e.,** to catch s.o. in the (very) act, red-handed, *flagrante delicto*; **j-n bei einer Lüge e.,** to catch s.o. (out) in a lie; **ich ertappte ihn dabei,** I caught him at it; **ich ertappte ihn dabei, wie er sie küßte,** I caught him (in the act of) kissing her; **man darf sich nicht e. lassen,** you must not get yourself caught, be caught, be found out; **ich ertappte mich dabei, daß ich weinte,** I caught myself crying; **ich ertappe mich manchmal bei dem Gedanken, daß . . . ,** I sometimes catch myself thinking that . . . .
ertasten, *v.tr.* (**sich** *dat.*) **etwas e.,** to make out sth. by feel, touch; *F:* to feel, grope, one's way towards understanding sth.
erteilen. I. *v.tr.* to give (permission, information); to grant (permission); to impart (information) (**über etwas** *acc.*, on sth.); **j-m Rat, eine Antwort, e.,** to give s.o. advice, an answer; **j-m die Erlaubnis (für, zu, etwas) e.,** to give s.o. permission (to do sth.); to grant s.o. permission (to do sth.); **j-m eine Auskunft e.,** to give s.o. a piece of information; **j-m ein Patent e.,** to grant a patent to s.o.; **j-m einen Befehl e.,** to give s.o. an order; to issue an order to s.o.; **j-m ein Lob e.,** to praise s.o., to give s.o. praise; **j-m einen Verweis e.,** to administer a reproof, a reprimand, to s.o., to reprove, reprimand, s.o.; *Sch: etc:* to admonish s.o.; **j-m eine scharfe Rüge e.,** to administer a sharp rebuke to s.o., to rebuke s.o. sharply; to reprimand s.o. severely; **j-m eine Lektion e.,** to teach s.o. a lesson; **j-m Vollmacht für etwas e.,** to give s.o. authority to do sth., to authorize, empower, s.o. to do sth.; **j-m Unterricht e.,** to give s.o. lessons, tuition; to instruct, teach, s.o.; *A:* **j-m den Abschied e.,** to retire s.o., pension s.o. off, superannuate s.o.; *Com:* **j-m Prokura e.,** to confer powers of attorney on s.o.; *Ecc:* **j-m die Absolution e.,** to give, grant, s.o. absolution; **j-m die Sterbesakramente e.,** to give, administer, the last sacraments to s.o.: *see also* **Auftrag** 1.
II. *vbl s.* **Erteilen** *n.*, **Erteilung** *f. in vbl senses; also:* administration (of last sacraments, etc.).
Erteiler, *m.* -s/-, giver (of order, etc.).
ertönen, *v.i.* (*sein*) (*of voice, music, song, bells, etc.*) to ring out; to be heard; (*of valley, wood, etc.*) **vom Gesang der Vögel e.,** to (begin to) (re)sound, ring, with the song of birds; **als die ersten Klänge ertönten,** when the first sounds were heard; **plötzlich ertönte ein Schuß,** suddenly a shot rang out; *Lit:* **laßt frohe Jubellieder ertönen,** let songs of joy resound.
ertöten. I. *v.tr.* **1.** *A:* **j-n e.,** to kill s.o., to put s.o. to death. **2.** to deaden (sentiments, passions); to extinguish (one's passions); to kill (ambition); to mortify (one's flesh, passions); **die Begierden des Fleisches e.,** to mortify the desires of the flesh; **seine Grausamkeit ertötete in mir jedes Gefühl für ihn,** his cruelty killed, deadened, any feeling I had for him; **der Krieg hatte jede menschliche Regung in ihm ertötet,** the war had extinguished all human feelings in him; **der Schmerz ertötete jede Empfindung in ihr,** her grief left her utterly numbed.
II. *vbl s.* **Ertöten** *n.*, **Ertötung** *f. in vbl senses; also:* mortification (of the flesh, of passions); extinction (of passions).
Ertrag, *m.* -(e)s/⸗e, yield (of field, fruit-tree, mine, investment, etc.); return(s), profit (from enterprise, etc.); proceeds (from goods sold, etc.); revenue (from an estate, an annuity, etc.); **der E. unserer Arbeit,** the fruits of our labour; **den E. steigern,** to increase the yield (of one's farm, etc.); to increase one's returns, one's profit; **der jährliche E. von Arbeit und Kapital,** the annual return(s), profit, income, earnings, from labour and capital; **vom E. seines Geschäfts, seiner Aktien, leben,** to live on the income from one's business, from one's shares; **E. bringen, einen E. geben,** to yield; to yield profit; to bring in returns; **dieser Obstbaum bringt guten E.,** this fruit-tree yields well, is a good bearer.
ertragen, *v.tr.* (*strong*) to bear, endure, stand (pain, heat, misfortune, etc.); to tolerate (contradiction, rude behaviour, etc.); **er erträgt sein schweres Geschick mit Gleichmut,** he bears, endures, his hard fate with equanimity; **er erträgt keinen Widerspruch,** he will not bear, tolerate, suffer, stand, contradiction; **ich kann den Gedanken daran, den Anblick, nicht e.,** I cannot bear the idea, the sight, of it, I cannot bear to think of it, to see it; **sie konnte es nicht e., daß er sie auslachte,** she could not bear him to laugh at her, she could not stand, tolerate, his laughing at her; **wie lange kannst du dieses Leben noch e.?** how much longer can you stand, *F:* stick, this kind of life? **ich kann ihn nicht e.,** I cannot bear, stand, tolerate, suffer, endure, abide, *F:* stick, stomach, him; **j-s Launen geduldig e.,** to bear patiently with s.o.'s moods, to tolerate, suffer, s.o.'s moods with patience; **die Ungewißheit läßt sich nicht länger e.,** the uncertainty is no longer bearable, the uncertainty has become unbearable, intolerable, unendurable; **das ist nicht zu e.,** that is not to be borne, endured, that is unbearable, intolerable, unendurable, insupportable, beyond endurance.
ertragfähig, *a.* (soil, tree, mine, etc.) capable of yielding; (enterprise) capable of yielding return(s), profit.
Ertragfähigkeit, *f.* yield-capacity (of forest, soil, mine, etc.); return potential, earning capacity (of enterprise).
erträglich, *a.* (*a*) bearable, tolerable, endurable, supportable (pains, heat, etc.); **die Hitze ist kaum e.,** the heat is hardly bearable; (*b*) tolerable, passable, *F:* fair to middling; **es ist ganz e.,** it's not too bad, it's tolerably good; *F: adv.* tolerably well; fairly well; **es geht mir e.,** I am tolerably well.
Erträglichkeit, *f.* bearableness, tolerableness, endurableness, supportableness, supportability (of pains, heat, etc.).
Erträglichkeitsgrenze, *f.* limit of supportability; limit of tolerance.
ertraglos, *a.* unproductive, non-productive (land, capital, labour, enterprise, etc.); unprofitable (labour, enterprise, etc.).
Erträgnis, *n.* **-nisses/-nisse=Ertrag.**
erträgnisreich, *a.*=**ertragreich.**
ertragreich, *a.* that yields well; productive (land, tree, etc.); profitable, lucrative, paying (business, etc.); **ein ertragreiches Jahr,** a fruitful year; **e. sein,** (*of land, etc.*) to yield abundantly, richly, to show a rich yield; (*of business, etc.*) to be profitable, to show a good profit.
Ertragslage, *f. Pol.Ec:* (situation with regard to) earnings and profits.
Ertragsrechnung, *f.*=**Erfolgsrechnung.**
Ertragssteigerung, *f.* increase in yield; increase in return(s), profit.
Ertragssteuer, *f. Pol.Ec:* tax on profit(s).
Ertragswert, *m. Fin: Pol.Ec:* capitalized value of potential yield; capitalized value of potential return(s), profit; **voraussichtlicher E.,** expectation value (of crop, etc.).
ertränken, *v.tr.* **j-n, ein Tier, e.,** to drown s.o., an animal; **sich e.,** to drown oneself; *F:* **seine Sorgen, seinen Kummer, im Wein, im Alkohol,** *P:* **im Suff, e.,** to drown one's sorrows in wine, in alcohol, in drink.
erträumen, *v.tr.* (**sich** *dat.*) **etwas e.,** (i) to dream of, about, sth.; (ii) to imagine sth., to see sth. in one's imagination; **ein Haus, wie ich es mir schöner nicht hätte e. können,** a house of unimaginable beauty, *F:* a real dream (of a) house; **soviel Glück hätte ich mir nie erträumt,** I would never have dreamt of such happiness *or* good fortune; **ihre lang erträumte Wiedervereinigung,** their long dreamt-of reunion; **nie erträumte Seligkeit,** undreamt-of bliss.
ertrinken, *v.i.* (*strong*) (*sein*) to be drowned, to drown; **im Meer e.,** to be drowned, to drown, in the sea; *Nau: F:* to go to Davy Jones's locker; **er ertrank beim Baden,** he was drowned while bathing; **er wäre beinahe e.,** he was nearly drowned, he nearly drowned; **ein Ertrunkener, eine Ertrunkene,** a drowned man, woman; **ein Ertrinkender,** a drowning person; **Ertrinken** *n*, drowning; **Tod durch Ertrinken,** death by drowning; *see also* **erretten II.**
ertrotzen, *v.tr.* (**sich** *dat.*) **etwas e.,** to get, obtain, (s.o.'s consent, etc.) by sheer stubbornness, obstinacy, defiance.
ertüchtigen. I. *v.tr.* (*of physical exercise, etc.*) **j-n e.,** to toughen s.o. up, to make s.o. tough, fit, to harden s.o.; **sich e.,** to toughen (up), to become tough, fit, hardened (by training).

II. *vbl s.* **Ertüchtigen** *n.*, **Ertüchtigung** *f.* *in vbl senses; esp.* **körperliche Ertüchtigung,** physical toughening(-up), hardening; physical training.

Ertüchtigungslehrgang, *m. Mil: etc:* toughening-up course.

erübrigen. 1. *v.tr.* (*a*) to save, put by (money, provisions, etc.); **etwas erübrigt haben,** to have sth. left over, to have sth. put by, to have saved sth.; **ich habe davon keinen Pfennig erübrigt,** I have not got a penny left; (*b*) to spare (time, money, etc.) (**für j-n, für etwas,** for s.o., for sth.); **kannst du eine Stunde für mich e.?** can you spare me an hour? **2.** *v.i.* (*haben*) to remain; **es erübrigt noch, darauf hinzuweisen, daß . . . ,** it remains for us to point out that . . . . **3. sich erübrigen,** to be superfluous; to be unnecessary; to be useless; **es erübrigt sich, zu . . . ,** it is superfluous to . . . ; **unter den veränderten Umständen erübrigt es sich, zu . . . ,** under the changed circumstances it is superfluous, no longer necessary, unnecessary, to . . . ; **jeder weitere Versuch erübrigt sich,** any further attempt is useless, pointless.

Erudition [e·ru·di·tsi'o:n], *f.* -/. erudition, learning, scholarship.

eruieren [e·ru·'i:rən], *v.tr.* to elicit, bring out (facts, meaning of sth., etc.); *Austrian:* to trace; to establish the identity of (culprit).

Eruktation [e·rukta·tsi'o:n], *f.* -/-en, eructation.

eruktieren [e·ruk'ti:rən], *v.i.* (*haben*) to eruct, eructate.

Eruption [e·ruptsi'o:n], *f.* -/-en. **1.** eruption (of volcano, water, passion, etc.); *Med:* eruption, breaking out (of rash, etc.); (*of volcano*) **zur E. kommen,** to erupt. **2.** *Med:* eruption, rash (on the skin).

Eruptionskanal, *m. Geol:* volcanic vent, funnel.

eruptiv [e·rup'ti:f], *a. Geol:* eruptive (rock, etc.).

Eruptivgestein, *n. Geol:* eruptive rock; igneous rock.

Erve, *f.* -/-n. *Bot:* bitter vetch, ers.

erwachen. I. *v.i.* (*sein*) **1.** (*a*) (*of pers., nature, etc.*) to awake(n), to wake (up); **als ich erwachte,** when I awoke, woke up; **aus einem unruhigen Schlaf e.,** to (a)wake from a troubled sleep; **von dem Geräusch erwachte ich,** the noise woke me up; **aus seiner Teilnahmslosigkeit, aus einem Wahn, e.,** to awake from one's lethargy, from an illusion; **vom Tode e.,** to come back to life, to revive; **die ganze Natur erwacht,** all nature awakes, wakes up; **sobald der Tag erwacht,** as soon as the day breaks, dawns; (*b*) (*of the senses, instinct, memories, etc.*) to awake(n); (*of emotion, hope, etc.*) to awake(n), to be awakened; to be roused; to stir; **sein Gewissen erwachte,** his conscience awoke; **in ihr erwachte die Reue,** she began to feel remorse; remorse began to stir within her; **seine Eifersucht erwachte aufs neue,** his jealousy was aroused afresh; **in ihr erwachte die Frau,** the woman in her awoke; **ihre Neugierde erwachte,** her curiosity was awakened, aroused, stirred; **in ihm erwachten väterliche Gefühle,** fatherly feelings awoke in him, were aroused in him.

II. *vbl s.* **Erwachen** *n.*, *occ.* **Erwachung** *f. in vbl senses;* **beim Erwachen,** on waking, when I (a)woke, woke up; **das Erwachen der Natur,** the awakening of nature; **das war ein grausames Erwachen,** that was a rude awakening; **das Erwachen der Sinne,** the awakening of the senses; **welches Erwachen!** what an awakening!

erwachsen. I. *v.i.* (*strong*) **1.** (*of seed*) to grow; (*of pers.*) to grow (up); **zu etwas e.,** to grow, develop, into sth.; **aus dem Kirschkern ist ein Baum erwachsen,** a tree has grown from the cherry-stone; (*b*) **zwischen ihnen erwuchs eine bleibende Freundschaft,** a lasting friendship developed, sprang up, between them. **2.** to arise; to accrue; to result; to proceed; **j-m e.,** (*of expenses, obligations*) to be incurred by s.o.; (*of advantages, interest*) to accrue to s.o.; **die Vorteile, die der Gesellschaft aus der Vereinbarung erwuchsen,** the advantages that accrued to the society from the agreement; **aus dem Geschäft erwuchsen der Firma nur Unannehmlichkeiten,** the deal only brought the firm trouble; **die Kosten, die uns daraus erwachsen, die daraus erwachsenden Kosten,** the expenses which we incur by it, the expenses arising, resulting, from it; **aus deiner Einstellung wird dir nur Schaden e.,** your attitude will only damage you; **aus dieser Verbindung wird uns Nutzen e.,** this association will bring us advantage.

II. *p.p & a.* **erwachsen,** *in vbl senses; esp.* adult, grown-up, full-grown (pers.); **ein erwachsener Mensch,** a grown-up person, an adult; **wenn du e. bist,** when you are grown up; when you grow up; **Erwachsene** *m, f,* adult, grown-up (person); **'nur für Erwachsene',** 'adults only'; **die Erwachsenen,** the grown-ups, the adults; **sich wie ein Erwachsener,** *adv.* **sich e., benehmen,** to behave like a grown-up, like an adult, in an adult fashion.

Erwachsenenbildung, *f.* adult education.

Erwachsenentaufe, *f. Ecc:* adult baptism.

erwägen. I. *v.tr.* (*strong, occ. weak*) to consider, weigh, ponder, think over (matter, offer, etc.); to deliberate on, over, to ponder over, to reflect on (question, etc.); to turn (question, etc.) over in one's mind; **das Für und Wider einer Sache e.,** to weigh the pros and cons of a matter; **wir haben alle Möglichkeiten reiflich erwogen,** we have considered, weighed, all the possibilities carefully, we have taken all the possibilities into careful consideration; **ich habe ernstlich erwogen, das Angebot anzunehmen,** I have seriously considered accepting the offer; **unser Urteil ist wohl erwogen,** we have weighed, pondered, our verdict carefully; our verdict is the result of careful consideration; **das sollte man schon e.,** that is worth thinking about; that is worth considering, worthy of consideration; that should be given careful consideration; **e., ob . . . ,** to consider whether . . . , to deliberate if, as to whether, . . . , to think over whether . . . .

II. *vbl s.* **1. Erwägen,** *n. in vbl senses.* **2. Erwägung,** *f.* (*a*) *in vbl senses; also:* consideration; **etwas in E. ziehen** to consider, think about (offer, etc.); **in E. ziehen, etwas zu tun,** to consider, think about, doing sth.; **wenn man alles in E. zieht,** taking all things into consideration, into account; all things considered; **der E. wert sein,** to be worthy of consideration, to be worth considering; **in der E., daß . . . ,** in view of the fact that . . . ; **nach reiflicher E.,** after careful, mature, consideration, after due deliberation, after careful thought; (*b*) consideration; deliberation; reflection; **seine Erwägungen führten zu keinem Schluß,** his deliberations led to no conclusion; **ich kann deinen Erwägungen nicht folgen,** I cannot follow your reasoning.

erwägenswert, *a.* (offer, etc.) worthy of consideration, worth considering, worth consideration, worth thinking about.

erwählen. I. *v.tr.* **etwas, j-n, e.,** to choose sth., s.o.; **j-n zum König e.,** to choose s.o. (for) king, to call s.o. to be king; **Gott hat ihn erwählt,** God has chosen, elected, him; **sie hat den richtigen Beruf erwählt,** she has chosen the right profession; **er hat den besseren Teil, das bessere Teil, erwählt,** he has chosen the better part.

II. *vbl s.* **1. Erwählen,** *n. in vbl senses.* **2. Erwählung,** *f.* (*a*)=II. 1; *also:* choice (of s.o., sth.); election (of s.o.); (*b*) *Theol:* election; **an seiner E. zweifeln,** to doubt one's election.

III. *p.p. & a.* **erwählt,** *in vbl senses; esp.* chosen, elected (pers., etc.); **ein Erwählter,** one chosen (by God, etc.); *Theol:* **die Erwählten,** the elect, the chosen; **der Erwählte des Herrn,** the Lord's elect.

erwähnen. I. *v.tr., A: also v.i.* (*haben*) **j-n, etwas,** *A:* **j-s, etwas** *gen.*, **e.,** to mention s.o., sth., to make mention of s.o., sth.; **eine Tatsache e.,** to mention, make mention of, a fact; to refer to, make reference to, a fact; **etwas beiläufig e.,** to mention sth. in passing, incidentally; **das hat er uns gegenüber nie erwähnt,** he has never mentioned it to us; **er erwähnte keine Namen,** he mentioned no names; **j-n in seinem Testament e.,** to mention s.o. in one's will; **dieser germanische Brauch wird zuerst bei Tacitus erwähnt,** the first mention of this Germanic custom is to be found in Tacitus; **in dem Bericht wird nichts dergleichen erwähnt,** nothing of the kind is mentioned, is referred to, in the report, no mention of, no reference to, anything of the kind is made in the report; **j-n ehrend e.,** to make honourable mention of s.o.; **wie oben erwähnt,** as mentioned above; as aforesaid; *Mil:* **j-n im Tagesbericht e.,** to mention s.o. in dispatches.

II. *vbl s.* **1. Erwähnen,** *n. in vbl senses.* **2. Erwähnung,** *f.* (*a*)=II. 1; *also:* **j-s, etwas** *gen.*, **E. tun,** to make mention of s.o., of sth., to mention s.o., sth.; **der E. wert sein,** to be worth mentioning, to be worthy of mention; (*b*) mention; **eine ehrenvolle E.,** an honourable mention; *Mil:* **E. im Tagesbericht,** mention in dispatches.

erwähnenswert, *a.* (fact, etc.) worth mentioning, worthy of mention; mentionable (event, etc.).

erwähntermaßen, *adv.* as already mentioned.

Erwähnung, *f. see* **erwähnen II.**

erwandern, *v.tr.* (**sich** *dat.*) **etwas e.,** to get to know (district, etc.) by travelling through it (*esp. on foot*); **er hat (sich) den Schwarzwald erwandert,** through his many rambles in the Black Forest he has got to know it well.

erwarmen, *v.i.* (*sein*) to get warm; to grow warm; to warm up.

erwärmen. I. *v.tr.* **1. etwas, j-n, e.,** to warm sth., s.o., (up); **eine Flüssigkeit e.,** to warm up, heat up, a liquid; **eine Flüssigkeit auf 80° e.,** to warm up a liquid to 80°, to raise the temperature of a liquid to 80°; **ein Zimmer e.,** to warm (up), heat, a room; **seine kalten Hände vor dem Feuer e.,** to warm one's cold hands before the fire; **die Sonne erwärmt die Erdoberfläche,** the sun warms (up) the surface of the earth; **sich e.,** (*of pers.*) to warm oneself (by the fire, by exercise), to warm oneself up (by exercise, etc.); (*of ground, etc.*) to warm up, to become warm, to grow warm; (*of liquid*) to warm up, to become warm; **das Land erwärmt sich leichter als das Meer,** the land warms up more easily than the sea; **die Luft erwärmt sich um 10°,** the temperature of the air rises by 10°, the air warms up by 10°, becomes 10° warmer. **2. j-n für etwas, für j-n, e.,** to arouse s.o.'s interest in sth., to get s.o. interested in s.o.; to arouse s.o.'s sympathy for s.o.; to arouse s.o.'s enthusiasm for sth., for s.o.; **sich für etwas, für j-n, e.,** to warm to sth., to s.o.; to take to sth., to s.o.; **sich für einen Plan, für eine Idee, e.,** to warm to a plan, to an idea; to take to a plan, to an idea; **ich kann mich für seinen Vorschlag nicht e.,** I cannot feel any enthusiasm for his proposal; **ich konnte mich für ihn nicht e.,** I couldn't take to him; my heart didn't warm to him.

II. *vbl s.* **1. Erwärmen,** *n. in vbl senses of* I. 1 (*a*). **2. Erwärmung,** *f.* (*a*)=II. 1; (*b*) **die allmähliche E. des Bodens,** the gradual warming up of the ground; **eine E. um 10°,** a rise in temperature of 10°.

Erwärmungskraft, *f. Ph:* (*a*) warming power (of sun, etc.); calorific power (of fuel); (*b*) calefaction (of stove, etc.).

erwarten. I. *v.tr.* **1.** (*a*) to expect (s.o., sth.); **j-n zum Essen e.,** to expect s.o. to dinner; **wir erwarten Besuch,** we are expecting visitors; **es war, stand, zu e., daß . . . ,** it was to be expected that . . . ; **ich wußte, was ich zu e. hatte,** I knew what to expect; **das ist nicht das Ergebnis, das ich erwartete, das ist nicht das erwartete Ergebnis,** that is not the result I expected, anticipated, that is not the expected, anticipated, result; **er kann wohl e., daß . . . ,** he can surely expect that . . . ; **sie hatten nicht erwartet, mich hier zu finden,** they had not expected to find me here; **wir erwarten Gast in der nächsten Woche,** we are expecting our guest, our guest is expected to arrive, next week; **das habe ich schon erwartet,** I expected as much; I thought as much, I thought so; **ein Kind e.,** to be expecting a baby; (*b*) **etwas von j-m e.,** to expect sth. of s.o.; **das hatte ich nicht von ihr erwartet,** (i) I did not expect that from her; (ii) I did not expect that of her; **ich weiß, daß man viel von ihm erwartet,** I know that much is expected of him; **von ihm hast du nichts Gutes zu e.,** (i) you cannot expect (to get) anything good from him; (ii) you cannot expect any good of him; **ich habe vom Leben nichts mehr zu e.,** I have nothing more to expect of, from, life; **ich erwarte von dir, daß du deine Pflicht erfüllst,** I expect you to do your duty. **2.** (*of pers.*) to await, wait for (sth.); (*of thg*) to await (s.o.); to be waiting for (s.o.); (*of fate, etc.*) to be in store for (s.o.); **das Schicksal, das ihn erwartete,** the fate that awaited him, that was in store for him; **den Tod e.,** to await death; **mich erwartet zu Hause ein krankes Kind, viel Arbeit,** I have a sick child, a lot of work, waiting for me at home; **er kann ihre Rückkehr kaum e.,** he can hardly await, wait for, her return; **die Kinder können die Ferien kaum e.,** the children can hardly wait for the holidays.

II. *vbl s.* **1. Erwarten,** *n.* **über E.,** beyond expectation; **wider E.,** contrary to (all) expectation(s); **alles ging über E. gut,** everything went far better than expected. **2. Erwartung,** *f.* (*a*) expectation; **in ständiger E. leben,** to live in constant expectation; **die Kinder lebten tagelang in freudiger E.,** the children lived for days in joyful expectation; **in der freudigen E.**

Ihres Besuches, looking forward to your visit, to seeing you; **in der E., daß . . . ,** expecting that . . . ; **in gespannter E.,** in eager expectancy, expectation; **j-n voller E. anblicken,** to look at s.o. expectantly, full of expectancy; *Corr:* **'in E. Ihrer Antwort',** 'awaiting your reply', 'looking forward to your reply'; (*b*) **mathematische E.,** mathematical expectation; (*c*) *pl.* **Erwartungen,** expectations; **allen Erwartungen entgegen, zum Trotz,** contrary to all expectations; **j-s Erwartungen entsprechen, erfüllen,** to come up to, to answer, fulfil, s.o.'s expectations; **j-s Erwartungen enttäuschen, nicht entsprechen,** to disappoint, fall short of, s.o.'s expectations; **alle Erwartungen übertreffen,** to exceed all expectation(s); **er sah sich in seinen Erwartungen getäuscht,** he was disappointed, things did not come up to his expectations.

erwartungsvoll, *a.* expectant (pers., etc.); (pers., etc.) full of expectation(s); **erwartungsvolles Schweigen,** expectant silence; *adv.* **j-n e. anblicken,** to look at s.o. expectantly.

Erwartungswert, *m. Statistics:* expectation value.

erwecken. I. *v.tr.* (*a*) **j-n (aus dem Schlaf) e.,** to awake(n), wake(n), s.o., to (a)rouse s.o. (from sleep); to wake s.o. up; **j-n aus seiner Lethargie, aus seiner Stumpfheit, e.,** to arouse s.o. from his lethargy; **j-n von den Toten, vom Tode, e.,** to raise s.o. from the dead; (*b*) to awaken, arouse, excite, stir up (emotion, passion, suspicion, interest, etc.); to awaken, wake, stir up, call forth (memories, etc.); **ein heftiges Verlangen in j-m e.,** to awaken, arouse, excite, a violent desire in s.o.; **Furcht, Hoffnung, e.,** to awaken, raise, give rise to, anxiety, hope; **Mitleid e.,** to arouse pity; **Vertrauen e.,** to inspire confidence; **den Anschein e., als ob . . . ,** to create the impression that . . . ; to look as if . . . ; **sein Verhalten erweckte sogleich meinen Argwohn,** his behaviour immediately aroused my suspicion(s); **er konnte die schlimmsten Instinkte im Menschen e.,** he could arouse a man's worst instincts. **II.** *vbl s.* **1. Erwecken,** *n.* in vbl senses. **2. Erweckung,** *f.* (*a*)=II. 1; (*b*) *Rel:* **religiöse E.,** (i) religious awakening (of individual); (ii) religious revival.

Erwecker, *m.* -s/-, (a)wakener (of conscience, etc.).

Erweckung, *f. see* erwecken II.

Erweckungsbewegung, *f. Rel:* revivalist movement.

Erweckungsprediger, *m. Rel:* revivalist.

erwehren (sich), *v.refl.* (*a*) **sich j-s, etwas** *gen.,* **e.,** to offer resistance to s.o., sth.; to keep s.o. at bay; to ward off s.o.; **er konnte sich seiner Angreifer nicht länger e.,** he could no longer keep his attackers at bay; **er versuchte vergeblich, sich seiner Zweifel zu e.,** he tried in vain to put his doubts from him, out of his mind; **ich konnte mich seiner Zudringlichkeiten, seiner Zärtlichkeiten, nicht e.,** I was defenceless, helpless, against his insistence, against his demonstrations of affection; **ich konnte mich seiner Bitten nicht länger e.,** I could not resist his entreaties any longer; (*b*) **sich etwas** *gen.* **e.,** to refrain from sth., from doing sth.; **ich konnte mich eines Lächelns nicht e.,** I couldn't help, refrain from, keep from, smiling; **ich konnte mich des Verdachts, des Gedankens, nicht e., daß . . . ,** I couldn't help suspecting, thinking, that . . . ; **sie konnte sich nur mit Mühe der Tränen e.,** she found it difficult to refrain from tears; she found it difficult to keep back, hold back, her tears; **ich kann mich des Eindrucks nicht e., daß . . . ,** I cannot help feeling that . . . ; **er konnte sich des Schlafes nicht e.,** he could not keep awake; he succumbed to sleep.

erweichbar, *a.* (substance) that can be softened.

erweichen. I. *v.* (*strong*). **1.** *v.tr.* (*a*) to soften sth.; (*b*) to soften (s.o.) up; **sich e. lassen,** to let oneself be softened; to relent; **er versuchte vergeblich, mich durch Bitten zu e.,** he tried in vain to soften me, to move me, by his entreaties; **der Anblick hätte einen Stein e. können,** the sight of it would have softened, melted, a heart of stone; **er ließ sich nicht e.,** he would not relent; he would not budge; **sie ließ sich endlich e., mir zu helfen,** at last she relented, gave in, and helped me. **2.** *v.i.* (*sein*) (*a*) (of substance) to soften, to become, go, soft; *Med:* **erweichte Knochen,** softened bones; (*b*) (of pers.) to soften. **II.** *vbl s.* **1. Erweichen,** *n.* in vbl senses. **2. Erweichung,** *f.* (*a*)=II. 1; (*b*) *Med:* softening (of the bones, etc.); **E. des Gehirns,** soften-

ing of the brain; (*c*) softened area, softened part.

III. *pr.p & a.* **erweichend,** in vbl senses; *esp. Pharm: Med:* emollient (remedy); **erweichender Umschlag,** emollient poultice; **erweichende Mittel,** emollients.

Erweichungsmittel, *n. Pharm:* emollient (remedy).

Erweis, *m.* -es/-e, proof; **den E. für etwas erbringen,** to produce proof of sth.; to prove (efficiency, etc.); to prove, demonstrate, establish (truth of proposition, etc.).

erweisen. I. *v.tr* (*strong*) **1.** (*a*) to prove (the truth of sth.); to demonstrate, establish (truth of proposition, etc.); **sich als etwas e.,** (*of pers.*) to prove (oneself) (to be) sth.; to show oneself, to turn out, (to be) sth.; (*of matter, thg*) to prove (to be) sth.; to turn out (to be) sth.; **seine Unschuld ist noch nicht erwiesen, hat sich noch nicht erwiesen,** his innocence is not yet established, proved; his innocence has not yet been established, proved; **es ist eindeutig erwiesen, es hat sich eindeutig erwiesen, daß . . . ,** it is, it has been, proved beyond doubt, conclusively, that . . . ; **das muß noch erwiesen werden, das muß sich noch e.,** that remains to be proved; **es erwies sich, daß . . . ,** it turned out that . . . ; **er erwies sich als ein wahrer Freund,** he proved (himself), he showed himself (to be), a true friend; **das Dokument erwies sich als (eine) Fälschung,** the document proved to be a forgery; **die Nachricht erwies sich als falsch,** the information proved (to be), turned out to be, false; **sich dankbar e.,** to show oneself grateful; to give proof of one's gratitude; **sich (als) nützlich, vorteilhaft, e.,** to prove (to be) useful, advantageous; (*b*) (*of pers.*) to show (one's kindness, etc.); to prove (one's usefulness, etc.). **2. j-m etwas e.,** to render s.o. (a service, etc.); to do, render, s.o. (a kindness, etc.); **j-m Ehre e.,** to pay, do, s.o. honour; **j-m Wohltaten e.,** to do s.o. kindnesses; to confer benefits upon s.o.; **j-m einen Gefallen e.,** to do s.o. a favour; **j-m Achtung e.,** to pay, show, deference to s.o.; **j-m die letzte Ehre e.,** to pay the last honours, one's last respects, to s.o.; **damit hast du ihm einen schlechten Dienst erwiesen,** you have done him a disservice, a bad turn by this; **sie hat uns nur Gutes erwiesen,** she has never shown us anything but kindness; **er hat dem Land große Dienste erwiesen,** he has rendered the country great services; **wir danken Ihnen für die erwiesenen Beileidsbezeugungen,** we thank you for your kind expressions of sympathy. **II.** *vbl s.* **Erweisen** *n.,* **Erweisung** *f.* in vbl senses; *also:* demonstration, establishment (of the truth of proposition, etc.).

erweislich, *a.* that can be proved, that is capable of being proved, provable; demonstrable (proposition, etc.).

erweitern. I. *v.* **1.** *v.tr.* (*a*) to widen (road, channel, valley, etc.); to widen, enlarge, open out (opening, hole, etc.); to ream out (hole); to expand (tube); to dilate (pupil of eye, etc.); *Med:* to enlarge (heart, liver); to distend, dilate (stomach); **die Mündung eines Flusses e.,** to widen, enlarge, open out, the mouth of a river; *Med:* **sein Herz ist krankhaft erweitert,** he has an enlarged heart; (*b*) to expand, extend (business, estate, etc.); to extend, widen (sphere of influence, etc.); to extend (concept, meaning of word, etc.); **wir wollen unseren Betrieb e.,** we want to expand, extend, our business; we want to increase the scope of our business; **seinen Bekanntenkreis e.,** to extend, enlarge, one's circle of acquaintances; **im erweiterten Sinne des Wortes,** in the wider, extended, sense of the word; *Gram:* **erweiterter Infinitiv,** extended infinitive, infinitive followed by an adjunct; (*c*) to extend, widen (range of knowledge, of ideas, etc.); to broaden (one's outlook); **seine Kenntnisse e.,** to extend, improve, one's range of knowledge; **durch Reisen seinen (geistigen) Horizont, seinen Gesichtskreis, e.,** to broaden one's horizon, one's outlook, by travelling; (*d*) *Alg:* **einen Bruch e.,** to reduce a fraction to higher terms. **2. sich erweitern,** (*a*) (*of road, valley, channel, etc.*) to widen, to open out; (*of opening, etc.*) to widen, to enlarge; (*of tube*) to expand; (*of pupil of eye, etc.*) to dilate; *Med:* (*of stomach*) to distend, become distended; (*of heart, etc.*) to enlarge, become enlarged; **die Pupille erweitert sich im Dunkeln,** the pupil dilates in the dark; (*b*) (*of sphere of influence, range of ideas, etc.*) to widen, to extend; (*of business, etc.*) to expand, extend; (*c*) (*of knowledge, outlook, etc.*) to broaden.

II. *vbl s.* **1. Erweitern,** *n.* in vbl senses of **I. 1. 2. Erweiterung,** *f.* (*a*)=II. 1; *also:* enlargement (of opening, territory, etc.); expansion (of tube, etc.); *Mth:* **E. eines Bruches,** reduction of a fraction to higher terms; (*b*) in vbl senses of I. 2; *also:* (i) dilation (of pupil of eye, etc.); *Med:* enlargement, dilation (of heart, etc.); distension, dilation (of stomach); (ii) expansion (of business, range of knowledge, etc.); (*c*) enlargement, expansion (in channel, road, tube, etc.); (*d*) extension, addition (to firm, etc.); extension (to building); (*e*) extension (of concept, meaning of word).

Erweiterungsbau, *m.* (*pl.* **-bauten**) (building-) extension; addition to building; annexe.

Erweiterungsbohrer, *m. Tls:* broaching-bit; reamer(-bit).

Erweiterungskleid, *n.* maternity dress.

Erwerb, *m.* -(e)s/-e. **1.** acquisition, acquiring (of money, object, etc.); obtainment, obtaining (of rights); **E. durch Erbschaft,** acquisition by inheritance. **2.** earnings; earned income; **sein E. ist gering,** his earnings are small. **3.** living, livelihood; **er muß seinem E. nachgehen,** he has to earn his living; he has (to go) to work.

erwerben. I. *v.tr.* (*strong*) (*a*) to acquire (property, money, fortune, knowledge, etc.); to acquire, obtain (rights); **sich** *dat.* **kümmerlich sein Brot e.,** to make a precarious living, to earn a precarious living; **etwas käuflich e.,** to acquire sth. by purchase, to purchase sth.; **etwas durch Arbeit, durch Kauf, e.,** to acquire, gain, sth. by work; to acquire sth. by purchase; **er hat sein Vermögen nach dem Krieg erworben,** he acquired, made, his fortune after the war; **er hat das Grundstück käuflich erworben,** he has acquired the piece of ground by purchase, he has bought, purchased, the piece of ground; **wir haben das Urheberrecht erworben,** we have acquired, obtained, the copyright; **die englische, deutsche, Staatsbürgerschaft e.,** to acquire British, German, citizenship, to become a British subject, a German national; **er hat seine Fachkenntnisse im Ausland erworben,** he has acquired, gained, his expert knowledge abroad; **erworbene Kenntnisse,** acquired knowledge; **angeborene und erworbene Eigenschaften,** innate and acquired characteristics; (*b*) to win, earn (glory, respect, fame, favour, etc.); (sich *dat.*) **j-s Vertrauen, Zuneigung, e.,** to win, earn, gain, s.o.'s confidence, affection; **er hat sich große Verdienste um die Firma erworben,** the firm is greatly indebted to him for his valuable services; **er hat sich viele Freunde erworben,** he has won, gained, made, many friends; **er hat sich als Arzt einen guten Ruf erworben,** he has gained a good reputation as a doctor, he has made himself a good name as a doctor.

II. *vbl s.* **1. Erwerben,** *n.* in vbl senses. **2. Erwerbung,** *f.* (*a*)=II. 1; *also:* acquisition (of money, property, rights, knowledge, etc.); obtainment (of rights); (*b*) (*thg acquired*) acquisition; purchase.

Erwerber, *m.* -s/-, acquirer (of object, rights, etc.); purchaser, buyer; *Jur:* vendee; **gutgläubiger E.,** purchaser in good faith.

erwerbsam, *a.* (*of pers.*) industrious; keen on making a living.

Erwerbsamkeit, *f.* industriousness, industry; keenness on making a living.

erwerbsbeschränkt, *a.* (*of pers.*) partially disabled; not capable of full employment; **ein Erwerbsbeschränkter,** a partially disabled person; a person not capable of full employment.

Erwerbsbeschränktheit, *f.* **1.** partial incapacity (for full employment). **2.** *Jur:* limitation of right to acquire, purchase (land, etc.).

erwerbsfähig, *a.* (pers.) capable of gainful employment.

Erwerbsfähigkeit, *f.* capability of gainful employment; **Beeinträchtigung der E.,** impaired earning capacity.

erwerbslos, *a.* unemployed, out of work, out of a job, idle; **e. werden,** to become unemployed, to lose one's employment, one's job; to lose one's living, one's livelihood; **j-n e. machen,** to render s.o. unemployed, to throw s.o. out of work, to put s.o. out of a job; to deprive s.o. of his living, his livelihood; **Erwerbslose** *m, f,* unemployed person; **die Erwerbslosen,** the unemployed, the workless.

Erwerbslosenfürsorge, *f. Adm:* national assistance for the unemployed.

Erwerbslosenunterstützung, *f. Adm:* unemployment benefit, unemployment pay; **E. beziehen,**

to draw unemployment benefit, *F:* to be on the dole.

Erwerbslosenversicherung, *f. Adm:* unemployment insurance.

Erwerbsminderung, *f.* reduction of working capacity.

Erwerbsquelle, *f.* source of income.

Erwerbssinn, *m.* **1.** (natural) business sense; commercial acumen. **2.** *Phren:* acquisitiveness.

Erwerbssteuer, *f. Pol.Ec:* tax on profit(s) *or* gains.

erwerbstätig, *a.* gainfully employed (pers.); **e. sein,** to be gainfully employed; to have a paid job; to earn, work for, one's living; **Erwerbstätige** *m, f,* gainfully employed person.

Erwerbstätigkeit, *f.* gainful employment.

erwerbsunfähig, *a.* (pers.) incapable of gainful employment; disabled (pers.); **dauernd e. sein,** to be permanently unfit for gainful employment; to be permanently disabled.

Erwerbsunfähigkeit, *f.* inability to earn a living; **dauernde E.,** permanent disability.

Erwerbszweig, *m.* line of business (of pers.); line of trade, of industry (of town, etc.).

Erwerbung, *f. see* **erwerben II.**

erwidern. I. *v.tr.* **1.** to reply, answer; to make a reply, to give an answer; to rejoin; to retort; **etwas e.,** to say sth. in reply; to make some reply; **etwas auf etwas** *acc.* **e.,** to make a reply to sth.; **er erwiderte nichts,** he made no reply, he gave no reply, he said nothing in reply, he answered nothing; **auf meine Frage erwiderte sie, daß . . . ,** in reply to my question she said that . . . ; her answer to my question was that . . . ; **er konnte darauf nichts e.,** he could not make any reply to this; **was haben Sie darauf zu e.?** what have you to say in reply to this? **auf meine Vorwürfe wußte er nichts zu e.,** he had no reply to make to my reproaches; **'kümmere dich um deine Angelegenheiten', erwiderte sie,** 'mind your own business', she retorted, she rejoined; **'danke schön', erwiderte sie lächelnd,** 'thank you,' she responded with a smile. **2.** to return (sentiment, compliment, insult, etc.); to reciprocate (sentiment); **etwas mit etwas e.,** to return sth. with sth.; **j-s Liebe e.,** to return, reciprocate, s.o.'s love; **meine Liebe wird nicht erwidert,** my love is not returned, is unreturned; **einen Besuch, einen Gruß, e.,** to return a visit, a salutation; **einen Dienst e.,** to return, requite, a service; **er erwiderte den Gruß mit einer höflichen Verbeugung,** he returned the salutation with a polite bow; *Mil:* **das Feuer des Feindes e.,** to return the enemy's fire, to reply to, to answer, the enemy's fire.

II. *vbl s.* **1. Erwidern,** *n. in vbl senses.* **2. Erwiderung,** *f.* (*a*)=II. 1; *also:* (i) **in E. auf Ihren Brief,** in answer, in reply, to your letter; (ii) return (of sentiment, insult, visit, etc.); reciprocation (of sentiment); (*b*) **ihre Liebe fand keine E.,** her love was not returned, was unreturned, her love met with no response; (*c*) reply, answer; rejoinder; retort; response.

erwiesenermaßen, *adv.* as has been proved, demonstrated, established.

erwirken, *v.tr.* to obtain, procure (s.o.'s consent, permission, release, etc.); to bring about, effect (s.o.'s release, etc.); **ich habe endlich die Scheidung erwirkt,** I have at last obtained a divorce; **er erwirkte den Freispruch des Angeklagten, er erwirkte, daß der Angeklagte freigesprochen wurde,** he obtained the acquittal of the accused; **wir müssen sein Einverständnis e.,** we have to obtain his consent; **er erwirkte eine Verlängerung des Visums,** he obtained, succeeded in obtaining, an extension of the visa; **bei j-m eine Gnade e.,** to succeed in obtaining a favour from s.o. (*for oneself or for another*); **bei seinem Vorgesetzten Urlaub (für sich) e.,** to succeed in getting one's superior to grant one leave; **der Konsul hat beim Gouverneur die Freilassung der Gefangenen erwirkt,** at the request of the consul the governor has agreed to release the prisoners; **eine gerichtliche Verfügung gegen j-n e.,** to obtain an injunction against s.o.

erwirtschaften, *v.tr.* to get, obtain, (sth.) by careful management, by good economy; to make (profits, etc.) by careful management, by good economy; **wir haben in diesem Jahr einen Überschuß erwirtschaftet,** by careful management we made a surplus this year.

erwischen, *v.tr.* to catch (s.o., sth.); to catch, get hold of (s.o., sth.); (*a*) **einen Dieb e.,** to catch, get hold of, lay hands on, *F:* cop, nab, pinch, a thief; **von der Polizei erwischt werden, sich von der Polizei e. lassen,** to get caught, *F:* copped, nabbed, by the police; **j-n beim Stehlen, bei einem Diebstahl, e.,** to catch s.o. (in the act of) stealing; **j-n auf frischer Tat e.,** to catch s.o. in the (very) act, red-handed, in flagrante delicto; **man darf sich nicht e. lassen,** you must not let yourself be caught, you must not get yourself caught, you must not be found out; **du wirst mich nicht noch einmal e.,** you won't catch me again; **ich erwischte ihn dabei,** I caught him in the act, I caught him at it; (*b*) **er erwischte sie bei den Zöpfen,** he caught her, got hold of her, by the plaits; *F:* **ich habe den Zug noch gerade erwischt,** I just managed to catch the train; *Hum:* **die Grippe hat ihn erwischt,** the 'flu has got (hold of) him; *F:* **der Regen hat uns noch erwischt,** we got caught in the rain; **es hat ihn an der linken Schulter erwischt,** he has caught it, he has got it, in his left shoulder; **ihn hat's erwischt,** (i) he has got it badly; *F:* he has copped it badly; (ii) *F:* he has had it.

erwünschen, *v.tr.* to wish for, desire (sth.); **es wäre zu e., daß . . . ,** it would be desirable that . . . ; **die erwünschte Wirkung, das erwünschte Ergebnis,** the desired effect, result; **es ist zu e., es ist erwünscht, daß . . . ,** it is desirable that . . . ; **wie erwünscht senden wir Ihnen . . . ,** as desired, as requested, we are sending you . . . ; **dein Besuch, diese Gelegenheit, ist mir sehr erwünscht, kommt mir sehr erwünscht,** your visit, this occasion, is most opportune (for me), comes most opportunely for me; your visit, this occasion, is most welcome to me; **deine Gegenwart ist hier nicht erwünscht,** you are not wanted here; **'Besuch(e), Besucher, nicht erwünscht!'** 'no visitors, please!'; (*in advertisement, etc.*) **Kurzschrift erwünscht, aber nicht Bedingung,** shorthand desirable, an advantage, but not essential; **praktische Erfahrungen erwünscht,** practical experience an advantage; practical experience required.

Erwünschtheit, *f.* desirability, desirableness (of opportunity, course of action, etc.); opportuneness (of visit, etc.).

erwürgen. I. *v.* **1.** *v.tr.* to strangle, throttle (s.o.) (*usu.* by hand); to choke (s.o.) to death; to gar(r)otte (prisoner, etc.); **die Tränen erwürgten sie fast,** she was almost choking with tears. **2.** *v.i.* (*sein*) to choke; **an etwas** *dat.* **e.,** to choke on sth.; *F:* **an dem Bissen soll er e.!** I hope this mouthful chokes him!

II. *vbl s.* **Erwürgen** *n.,* **Erwürgung** *f. in vbl senses; also:* strangulation (of s.o.).

Erwürger, *m.* **-s/-,** strangler; gar(r)otter.

erymanthisch [eˑryˑˈmantiʃ], *a. A.Geog:* Erymanthian; *Myth:* **der Erymanthische Eber,** the Erymanthian boar.

Eryngium [eˑˈryŋgĭum], *n.* **-s/-gien.** *Bot:* eryngium, *F:* eringo.

Erysipel [eˑryˑziˑˈpeːl], *n.* **-s/.** *Med:* erysipelas.

erysipelatös [eˑryˑziˑpeˑlaˑˈtøːs], *a. Med:* erysipelatous.

Erythem [eˑryˑˈteːm], *n.* **-s/-e.** *Med:* erythema.

Erythräa [eˑryˑˈtrɛːaː]. *Pr.n.n.* **-s.** *Geog:* Eritrea.

Erythräer [eˑryˑˈtrɛːər], *m.* **-s/-.** *Geog:* Eritrean, native of Eritrea; inhabitant of Eritrea.

erythräisch [eˑryˑˈtrɛːiʃ], *a. Geog:* Eritrean; **das Erythräische Meer,** the Erythraean Sea.

Erythrin [eˑryˑˈtriːn]. **1.** *n.* **-s/.** *Ch:* erythrin. **2.** *m.* **-s/.** *Miner:* erythrite, red cobalt.

Erythrit [eˑryˑˈtriːt], *n.* **-(e)s/.** *Ch:* erythrite.

erythrokarpisch [eˑryˑtroˑˈkarpiʃ], *a. Bot:* erythrocarpous.

Erythronium [eˑryˑˈtroːnĭum], *n.* **-s/-nien.** *Bot:* erythronium, dog's tooth, dogtooth, (violet).

Erythrosin [eˑryˑtroˑˈziːn], *n.* **-s/.** *Ch:* erythrosin.

Erythrozyt [eˑryˑtroˑˈtsyːt], *m.* **-en/-en,** erythrocyte, red blood-corpuscle.

Erz, *n.* **-es/-e. 1.** *Min: Miner:* ore; **refraktorische, strengflüssige, widerspenstige, Erze,** refractory ores; **Erz aufbereiten,** to dress, prepare, ore. **2.** *A. & Lit:* bronze; brass; **Standbild aus Erz,** bronze *or* brazen statue; **Tür aus Erz,** bronze door; *F:* **wie in, aus, Erz gegossen,** like a (brazen) statue; **er stand da wie aus, in, Erz gegossen,** he stood there like a (brazen) statue, as though carved out of rock; *B:* **so wäre ich ein tönend Erz oder eine klingende Schelle,** I am become as sounding brass or a tinkling cymbal.

Erz-, erz-, *comb.fm.* **1.** (*a*) *Min: Miner:* ore . . . , ore-; of ore; **Erzgrube** *f,* ore-pit; **Erzhaltigkeit** *f,* ore content (of rock); **erzführend,** ore-bearing (soil); **Erzwäsche** *f,* washing of ore; (*b*) *A. & Lit:* bronze . . . ; of bronze; brass . . . ; brazen, of brass; **Erzstandbild** *n,* bronze *or* brazen statue; **Erztür** *f,* bronze door; **erzbeschlagen,** studded with bronze. **2.** (*a*) arch-; archi-; **Erzdiakon** *m,* archdeacon; **Erzkanzler** *m,* arch-chancellor; **Erzfürst** *m,* arch-prince; **erzbischöflich,** archiepiscopal; (*b*) arch-; arrant . . . ; utter . . . ; complete . . . ; **Erzverräter** *m,* arch-traitor; **Erzdummkopf** *m,* arch-dunce, utter fool; **Erzlügner** *m,* arch-liar, arrant liar; **Erzspitzbube** *m,* arrant knave; **Erzfaulenzer** *m,* complete, utter, lazybones; (*c*) utterly . . . ; extremely . . . ; **erzdumm,** utterly stupid; **erzböse,** utterly evil, wicked; **erzfaul,** extremely lazy, bone-lazy.

Erzabfall, *m. usu. pl.* **Erzabfälle,** *Min:* tailings.

Erzabt, *m. R.C.Ch:* president of a monastic congregation.

Erzader, *f. Min:* vein, lode, streak, lead, of ore; **auf eine E. stoßen,** to strike a vein of ore.

erzählbar, *a.* relatable, tellable (story, etc.); (story, etc.) that can be told.

erzählen. I. *v.tr. & i.* (*haben*) (*a*) to tell (sth.); *Lit:* to narrate (sth.); **j-m etwas e.,** to tell s.o. sth., to tell sth. to s.o.; **j-m von etwas, von j-m, e.,** to tell s.o. of, about, sth., s.o.; **einem Kind eine Geschichte, ein Märchen, e.,** to tell a story, a fairy-tale, to a child; **er erzählte die Geschichte sehr überzeugend,** he told the story very convincingly, he narrated the story very convincingly; **etwas ausführlich e.,** to tell sth. in detail; to recount, relate, sth. in detail; **eine Begebenheit ausführlich e.,** to give a detailed account of a happening; **der Historiker, der von diesen Ereignissen erzählt,** the historian who relates, recounts, these events; **sie erzählte uns oft von meinem Vater,** she used to tell us often about my father; **erzähle uns aus deiner Jugend,** tell us about your youth; **er erzählte von fremden Ländern,** he talked about foreign countries; **das alte Haus könnte viel e.,** the old house could tell a great deal; **auf dem Bild wird erzählt, wie . . . ,** the picture tells how . . . ; **das Buch erzählt . . . ,** the book tells, relates, . . . ; **er erzählt gern Geschichten,** (i) he likes to tell stories; (ii) he enjoys telling a yarn; **er hat ein bewegtes Leben gehabt und kann viel e.,** he has had an eventful life and has a lot to tell; **ich werde dir später alles e.,** I shall tell you all about it later; **sie erzählte mir, daß . . . ,** she told me that . . . ; **sie erzählte, daß . . . ,** she said that . . . ; she told me, him, us, etc., that . . . ; **man erzählt (sich), daß . . . ,** the story goes that . . . ; they, people, say that . . . ; **man hat mir erzählt, ich habe mir e. lassen, daß . . . ,** I have been told that . . . ; *F:* **erzähle keine Märchen, keine Geschichten!** don't tell (me) tales, stories! **du kannst mir doch nichts e.,** don't tell me that! tell me another! *U.S: F:* don't give me that! *B:* **die Himmel erzählen die Ehre Gottes,** the heavens declare the glory of God; (*b*) *abs.* to tell a story, stories; to talk; **gut e. (können),** to tell a story, stories, well, to tell a good story, to be a good story-teller; to talk well, to be a good talker; **erzähle!** do tell me, him, us, etc.! *F:* **los, erzähle!** fire away, go ahead! **wir haben die ganze Nacht erzählt,** we told each other stories all night; we talked all night; **ich höre sie gern e.,** I like to hear her tell a story, stories; I like to hear her talking about things.

II. *vbl s.* **1. Erzählen,** *n. in vbl senses; also:* narration, relation (of story, etc.); recital (of facts, events, etc.); **die Kunst des Erzählens,** the art of narration; **beim E.,** while telling, narrating, a story, stories, in story-telling; while talking. **2. Erzählung,** *f.* (*a*)=II. 1; (*b*) (*oral*) narration; (*written*) narrative; **Stifter ist ein Meister der E.,** Stifter is a master of narrative; (*c*) **ich könnte stundenlang seinen Erzählungen zuhören,** I could listen for hours to his stories, his tales; (*d*) *Lit:* story, tale; **Erzählungen und Märchen,** stories and fairy-tales; **Erzählungen für Kinder,** tales, stories, for children; **die E. ist gut geschrieben,** the story is well written.

III. *pr.p & a.* **erzählend,** *in vbl senses; esp.* narrative (style, poem, etc.); **erzählende Dichtung,** narrative poetry; **der erzählende Teil eines Gedichtes,** the narrative part, the narration, of a poem; **erzählende Darstellungsweise,** narrative style, manner, of representation.

erzählenswert, *a.* (story, etc.) worth telling, relating, narrating, recounting, worthy of relation, of narration.

Erzähler, *m.* **-s/-,** narrator, relater, teller (of stories, etc.); narrative writer; **er ist ein guter E.,** he is a good story-teller; he is a good talker; **er ist ein meisterhafter E.,** he is a masterly narrator, a master of narration; **dieser Schriftsteller ist ein E. ersten Ranges,** this author is a narrative writer of the best kind.

erzählerisch, *a.* narrative.

Erzählkunst, *f.* art of narration, (art of) narrative; **Stifter ist ein Meister der E.**, Stifter is a master of narrative.

Erzählung, *f. see* **erzählen** II.

Erzamt, *n. Hist:* high imperial office (of German Elector, etc.).

Erzaufbereitung, *f. Min:* dressing, preparation, of ore.

Erzbergbau, *m. Min:* ore mining.

Erzbergwerk, *n. Min:* ore mine, ore working.

Erzbetrüger, *m.* arch-deceiver, arch-swindler.

Erzbischof, *m. Ecc:* archbishop.

erzbischöflich, *a. Ecc:* archiepiscopal.

Erzbistum, *n. Ecc:* archbishopric, archdiocese, archsee; archiepiscopate.

Erzblüte, *f. Ch: Metall:* verdigris.

Erzbösewicht, *m.* arrant rogue; arch-scoundrel.

Erzbrecher, *m. Min:* ore-crusher; ore-breaker.

Erzbruderschaft, *f. Ecc:* archconfraternity.

Erzdiözese, *f. Ecc:* archdiocese.

erzeigen, *v.tr.* **1. j-m etwas e.**, to show s.o. (kindness, etc.); to render s.o. (a service, etc.); to do, render, s.o. (a kindness, etc.); **Gott hat uns seine Barmherzigkeit erzeigt**, God has shown his mercy to us. **2. sich als etwas erzeigen**, to show oneself (to be) sth.; **er hat sich als wahrer Freund erzeigt**, he showed himself (to be) a true friend; **sich dankbar e.**, to show oneself grateful, to express one's gratitude.

erzen[1], *v.tr.* **(du erzest & erzt)** *A:* **j-n e.**, to address s.o. in the third person.

erzen[2], *a.* of, made of, bronze *or* brass; brazen (vessel, etc.).

Erzengel, *m.* archangel.

erzeugen. **I.** *v.tr.* **1.** to produce; to procreate; *(usu. of father)* to beget (offspring); **im Ehebruch erzeugte Kinder**, children begotten in adultery; **Kinder, die in der zweiten Ehe erzeugt wurden**, children born of the second marriage. **2.** to produce (sth.); *(a)* to produce (foodstuffs, meat, chemicals, industrial products, etc.); to manufacture, make (industrial products, chemicals, etc.); *F:* to produce (work of art, etc.); **Deutschland erzeugte dieses Jahr mehr Wein als im Vorjahr**, Germany produced more wine this year than last; **die Lederwarenindustrie erzeugte weniger, als erwartet wurde**, the leather-goods industry produced, manufactured, less than expected; **die chemischen Produkte, die wir erzeugen**, the chemical products made by us; *(b) El: Ph: etc:* to generate, produce (electricity, steam, etc.); to raise (steam); to produce, generate, develop (heat); **Dampfkraft, die durch Kohle erzeugt wird**, steam power generated from coal; **Strom, der durch einen Dynamo erzeugt wird**, current generated, produced, by a dynamo; **Elektrizität e.**, to generate, produce, electricity; **Reibung erzeugt Wärme**, friction produces, generates, heat; **ein Vakuum e.**, to produce a vacuum; *(c) Geom:* to generate (surface, etc.); **der Rauminhalt, der durch diese Fläche erzeugt wird**, the volume generated by this surface; *(d)* to produce, engender, bring forth (effect); to engender, breed (disease); to produce, generate, engender, give birth to, breed, beget (hatred, etc.); **das Morphium erzeugte in ihm ein Gefühl der Zufriedenheit**, the morphia produced a feeling of contentment in him. **II.** *vbl s.* **1. Erzeugen**, *n.* in vbl senses. **2. Erzeugung**, *f. (a)* in vbl senses; *also:* (i) production; procreation (of offspring); (ii) production (of agricultural produce, industrial products, chemicals, etc.); manufacture (of industrial products, chemicals, etc.); *F:* production (of literary work, etc.); (iii) *El: Ph: etc:* generation, production (of electricity, steam, etc.); production, generation, development (of heat); **die E. von Dampf**, steam-raising, the generation of steam; **die E. von Elektrizität ist teuer**, the generation, production, of electricity is expensive; (iv) *Geom:* generation (of surface, etc.); (v) production (of effect); generation (of hostile feelings, etc.); *(b)* production; **die E. dieses Jahres ist höher als der Verbrauch**, this year's production is higher than consumption. **III.** *pr.p. & a.* **erzeugend**, in vbl senses; *esp. (a)* productive, producing (force, etc.); *(b)* generative, generating (power of organ, etc.); *(c) Geom:* **Erzeugende** *f*, generating line (of surface); generatrix, generator; element, ruling (of a cone).

Erzeuger, *m.* -s/-. **1.** procreator, begetter; father (of child); **der E. des Kindes wurde gerichtlich ermittelt**, the identity of the child's

father was established by legal means; **wir müssen dem Herrn, unserem E., danken**, we have to thank the Lord, our maker, our creator. **2.** *Com:* producer (of agricultural produce, industrial products, chemicals, etc.); **E. und Verbraucher**, producer and consumer. **3.** *Ind:* generator, (steam-, gas-, electricity-, etc.) generating machine; (gas) producer.

Erzeugergroßmarkt, *m. Com:* central market (with direct deliveries from producers).

Erzeugerland, *n. Com:* country of origin.

Erzeugerpreis, *m. Com:* producer's price.

Erzeugnis, *n.* -nisses/-nisse, product; **landwirtschaftliche Erzeugnisse**, agricultural produce, farm produce; **die Erzeugnisse eines Landes**, the products of a country; **ausländische Erzeugnisse**, foreign products; goods of foreign origin; **dieses Medikament ist ein deutsches E.**, this medicine is a German product; **die besten Erzeugnisse der Textilindustrie**, the best products, manufactures, of the textile industry; *(on label)* '**deutsches E.**', (i) *(on wine-bottle, etc.)* 'produce of Germany'; (ii) *(on manufactured article)* 'manufactured in Germany', 'made in Germany'.

Erzeugung, *f. see* **erzeugen** II.

Erzeugungskosten, *pl. Com:* cost of production; production costs.

Erzeugungskraft, *f. (a)* productive power (of country, etc.); *(b)* generative force (of dynamo, etc.).

Erzeugungsort, *m. Com:* place of production.

Erzeugungsschlacht, die. *(Nazi term)* the battle of production.

Erzfall, *m. Min:* ore content (of lode); grade, content, of ore.

Erzfeind, *m.* arch-enemy; archfiend; **der E.**, the archfiend, Satan.

Erzflöz, *n. Min:* ore-seam.

Erzförderung, *f. Min:* output of ore.

erzführend, *a. Min:* ore-bearing (soil).

Erzführung, *f. Min:* ore content (of soil).

Erzgang, *m. Min:* vein, lode, streak, lead, of ore.

Erzgauner, *m.* arrant knave; arch-rogue.

Erzgebirge, das. *Pr.n. Geog:* the Erzgebirge.

erzgebirgisch, *a. Geog:* of the Erzgebirge; **das erzgebirgische Becken**, the Erzgebirge basin.

Erzgehalt, *m. Min:* ore content (of soil).

Erzgewinnung, *f. Min:* ore winning; ore production.

erzhaltig, *a. Min:* ore-bearing (soil), (soil) containing ore; **e. sein**, to contain ore, to be ore-bearing.

Erzherzog, *m.* archduke.

Erzherzogin, *f.* archduchess.

erzherzoglich, *a.* archducal.

erzhöffig, *a. Min:* (rock) promising a rich yield of ore.

erziehbar, *a.* trainable; educable, educatable (pers.); **der Junge ist schwer e.**, the boy is difficult to bring up, to train (up); the boy is a problem, a problem child; **Heim für schwer erziehbare Kinder**, home for difficult children, for problem children.

erziehen. **I.** *v.tr.* (strong) **1.** *A:* to pull (coach, etc.). **2.** *(a) A:* to rear (animal, child, plant); *(b)* to bring up, *U.S:* raise (child); to train (young person, animal); to educate (child); **du hast deinen Sohn gut, streng, schlecht, erzogen**, you have brought up your son well, strictly, badly; **er wurde in Frankreich erzogen**, he was brought up in France; he was educated in France; **sie wurde in einer Klosterschule erzogen**, she was brought up in a convent school; she was educated at a convent school; **im christlichen Glauben erzogen worden sein**, to have been brought up in the Christian faith; **sie hat ihre Kinder zu fleißigen Menschen erzogen**, she has brought up her children to be industrious; **ich habe meine Kinder frühzeitig zur Sparsamkeit erzogen**, I brought up my children to be economical from an early age; **sich zu etwas e., sich (dazu) e., etwas zu tun**, to train oneself for, to train oneself to do, sth.; to educate oneself to do sth.; **sein Ohr dazu e., verschiedenartige Laute zu unterscheiden**, to train one's ear to distinguish various sounds; **der Junge ist schwer zu e.**, the boy is difficult to bring up, to train (up); the boy is difficult, is a problem child; **ein wohl, gut, schlecht, erzogenes Kind**, a well brought up, well-trained, well-mannered, well-bred, well-behaved, child; a badly brought up, badly trained, ill-mannered, ill-bred, ill-behaved, child; **ein wohl erzogenes Kind gehorcht sofort**, a well brought up, well-behaved, child obeys immediately; **das kleine Mädchen saß wohl erzogen auf seinem Stuhl**, the

little girl sat well-behaved on her chair; **er ist schlecht erzogen**, he is badly brought up, he has no manners. **II.** *vbl s.* **1. Erziehen**, *n.* in vbl senses; *also:* upbringing (of child); education (of young person). **2. Erziehung**, *f. (a)* = II. 1; *(b)* education; training; upbringing; **sittliche E.**, moral education; **körperliche E.**, physical education; physical training; **die E. der Jugend durch Schule und Elternhaus**, the education of the young at school and in the home; **seinen Kindern eine gute E. geben**, to give one's children a good education; **eine gute E., eine sorgfältige E., erhalten, genossen, haben**, to have had a good upbringing; to have received a good, careful, education; **er hat eine gute E. genossen**, he is well-bred, well brought up; he has enjoyed a good education; **ihr fehlt jegliche E.**, she lacks good breeding, she has no manners whatsoever; she lacks any sort of education; **seine E. macht sich bemerkbar**, his breeding shows; **vergiß deine gute E. nicht!** don't forget your manners!

Erzieher, *m.* -s/-, *(a)* educator; instructor; **die Erzieher der Jugend**, the educators, the instructors, of youth; **das verantwortungsvolle Amt des Erziehers**, the responsible office of the educator; *(b)* tutor; **er geht nicht zur Schule, er hat einen E.**, he does not go to school, he has a private tutor.

Erziehergabe, *f.* educative talent; pedagogic gift, talent.

Erzieherin, *f.* -/-innen, *(a)* educator; instructress; **meine Lehrerin war eine ausgezeichnete E.**, my teacher was an excellent educator; **die Natur, unsere E.**, Nature, our instructress; *(b)* **das kleine Mädchen hat eine E.**, the little girl has a governess.

erzieherisch, *a.* educational (work, etc.); educative, instructive (measures, etc.); **erzieherische Methoden**, educational, pedagogic, methods; **für erzieherische Zwecke**, for educational purposes; **aus erzieherischen Gründen**, for educational reasons; for the sake of the child's education *or* training; **die erzieherische Aufgabe der Schule**, the educational task of the school; *adv.* **e. wirken**, to have an educative effect.

erziehlich, *a.* educational; educative, instructive; *adv.* **e. wirken**, to have an educative effect.

Erziehung, *f. see* **erziehen** II.

Erziehungsanstalt, *f.* educational establishment, educational institution; school.

Erziehungsbeihilfe, *f.* educational grant; grant to parents of children receiving education.

Erziehungsberechtigte, *m., f.* (decl. as adj.) *Jur:* parent *or* guardian.

Erziehungslehre, *f.* = **Erziehungswissenschaft**.

Erziehungsmethode, *f.* method of bringing up children; educational, pedagogic, method.

Erziehungsminister, *m.* Minister of Education *(in countries other than Germany).*

Erziehungsministerium, *n.* Ministry of Education *(in countries other than Germany).*

Erziehungsroman, *m.* 'novel of education'; novel portraying the development of an individual's character.

Erziehungswesen, *n.* educational matters; **das deutsche E.**, German education, education in Germany.

Erziehungswissenschaft, *f. Sch:* science of education, educational science; pedagogics.

erzielen. **I.** *v.tr. (a)* to achieve, obtain (result, etc.); to reach, arrive at (agreement, etc.); *Sp: etc:* to score (points, etc.); **ein Übereinkommen e.**, to reach, arrive at, an agreement; **es war schwierig, Übereinstimmung zu e.**, it was difficult to reach an agreement, to achieve unanimity; **wir erzielten gute Ergebnisse mit dem Experiment**, we achieved, obtained, good results with the experiment; **er erzielte einen großen Erfolg**, he achieved, *F:* scored, a great success; **Fb:** **ein Tor e.**, to score, kick, a goal; *(b)* to make (profit); to obtain (price); *(of goods, etc.)* **einen bestimmten Preis e.**, to fetch, make, realize, a certain price; **die im Vorjahr erzielten Gewinne**, the profits made, realized, last year; **wir erzielten einen angemessenen Preis für das Haus**, we obtained, got, a reasonable price for the house; **Baumwolle erzielte einen günstigen Preis**, cotton fetched, realized, a favourable price; **die Preise, die gestern für Wolle erzielt wurden**, the prices obtained, made, yesterday for wool. **II.** *vbl s.* **Erzielen** *n.*, **Erzielung** *f.* in vb senses; *also:* achievement (of result).

erzittern, *v.i.* (sein) *(of pers.)* to (begin to) tremble, quiver, shake; to (begin to) quake;

(*of earth*) to (begin to) quake, shake, vibrate; (*of leaves, etc.*) to (begin to) tremble, quiver, vibrate; **sie erzitterte bei seinem Anblick,** she began to tremble, to shake, at the sight of him; **die Blätter erzitterten im Wind,** the leaves trembled, quivered, in the wind; **der Boden erzitterte unter seinen schweren Schritten,** the ground shook under his heavy steps.

Erzkörper, *m. Min:* ore body.

Erzlager, *n. Min:* ore-bed.

Erzlagerstätte, *f. Min:* ore-deposit.

Erzpriester, *m.* archpriest.

Erzscheider, *m.* **-s/-.** *Min:* ore separator.

Erzscheidung, *f. Min:* separation of ore; **E. auf feuchtem Wege,** wet separation of ore.

Erzschurke, *m.* arch-villain.

Erzstatue, *f. A. & Lit:* bronze *or* brazen statue.

Erzstock, *m. Geol: Min:* ore-stock.

erzürnen, *v.* (*a*) *v.tr.* **j-n e.,** to make s.o. angry, to annoy s.o., to anger s.o.; to irritate s.o.; **erzürnt,** angry, annoyed, irritated (pers.); **über j-n, etwas** *acc.*, **erzürnt sein,** to be angry, annoyed, with s.o., about sth.; (*b*) **sich e.,** to get angry, annoyed, to lose one's temper; to become irritated; **sich mit j-m e.,** to fall out with s.o.

Erzvater, *m.* (biblical) patriarch.

erzwingen. I. *v.tr.* (*strong*) to obtain, get, (s.o.'s consent, etc.) by force; **eine Aussage, ein Geständnis, e.,** to obtain a statement, a confession, by force; **ein Versprechen, Geld, von j-m e.,** to wring, wrest, extort, a promise from s.o., to force a promise out of s.o.; to extract, exact, extort, money from s.o., to get money from s.o. by force; **sich den Eintritt in ein Haus e.,** to force one's way into a house; **Achtung, Bewunderung, läßt sich nicht e.,** respect, admiration, cannot be compelled; **der Feind erzwang mit Waffengewalt die Übergabe der Stadt,** the enemy compelled the town to surrender by force of arms; **ein erzwungenes Geständnis,** a forced confession.

II. *vbl s.* **Erzwingen** *n.*, **Erzwingung** *f. in vbl senses; also:* extortion (of money, confession); exaction (of money).

es¹, *pers.pron. third person sg. nom. & acc. neuter* (*gen.* **seiner,** *A. & Lit:* **sein;** *dat.* **ihm**) **1.** (*referring to inanimate object*) it; (*certain inanimate objects, e.g. ships, vehicles, countries, etc., which are neuter in German and therefore represented by a neuter pronoun, may in English be referred to as either* 'it' *or* 'she'. *Some German words indicating persons, esp. diminutives and groups of persons, are neuter, and the corresponding pronoun is therefore* '**es**'; *the pronoun is translated as* 'he,' 'she,' 'they,' *acc.* 'him,' 'her,' 'them,' *according to the sex or number of the persons indicated. A child—in German neuter and having a corresponding neuter pronoun—is in English usually referred to as* 'he' *or* 'she,' *acc.* 'him,' 'her'; 'it,' *acc.* 'it,' *is used* (i) *in referring to an infant about whose sex the speaker is uncertain,* (ii) *in situations where the child is not envisaged as a distinct personality. Animals may likewise be called* 'it' *in English, but are frequently familiarly called* 'he' *or* 'she') **das Haus ist klein, aber es gehört mir,** the house is small but it is my own; **ich gebe dir das Buch zurück, sobald ich es ausgelesen habe,** I shall return the book to you as soon as I have finished it; **das Leben ist kurz, nütze es,** life is short, make the best of it; **das Boot, das Auto, ist zwar alt, aber es ist noch gut erhalten,** the boat, the car, is indeed old, but it, she, is still in good condition; **das Mädchen gefällt mir, weil es ehrlich ist,** I like the girl because she is honest; **mein Brüderchen ist krank, es hat die Masern,** my little brother is ill, he has the measles; **das Kind blieb stehen, als es seine Mutter sah,** the child stopped when it, he *or* she, saw its, his *or* her, mother; **das Kleine hat Hunger, gib ihm die Flasche,** the baby is hungry, give him *or* her the bottle; **das Volk hungert, es ist mutlos und erschöpft,** the people are starving, they are discouraged and exhausted; **wir haben dem Ehepaar Kleidungsstücke geschenkt, um ihm zu helfen,** we gave clothes to the couple in order to help them; **wir haben ein zahmes Eichhörnchen, es ist im Garten,** we have a tame squirrel; it, he *or* she, is in the garden; **das Rotkehlchen wird erfrieren, wenn wir uns seiner nicht annehmen,** the robin will freeze to death if we don't take care of it, *F:* of him. **2.** (*impers. and expletive uses*) (*a*) **es ist zehn Uhr,** it is ten o'clock; **es sind noch vierzehn Tage bis Weihnachten,** there is still a fortnight to go until Christmas; **es war an einem Montag,** it was on a Monday; (*b*) **es ist selten, daß . . . ,** it is rare, seldom, that . . . ; **es macht nichts,** it doesn't matter; **es stimmt,** it is true; **es steht geschrieben, daß . . . ,** it is written that . . . ; **in den Bestimmungen heißt es . . . ,** it says in the regulations . . . ; **es fragt sich, ob . . . ,** the question is whether . . . ; (*c*) **es gibt,** there is; there are; **es gibt Menschen, die . . . ,** there are people who . . . ; **es gibt nichts, was er nicht kennt,** there is nothing he doesn't know; **es gab, es waren, einige unter ihnen, die . . . ,** there were some among them who . . . ; (*d*) **es geschah alles, wie er es gesagt hatte,** everything happened as he had said; **es bleibt mir nichts anderes übrig, als . . . ,** there is nothing I can do but . . . ; **es wird eine gute Ernte geben,** there will be a good harvest; **es ist jemand an der Tür,** there is someone at the door; **es waren ihrer zu viele,** there were too many of them; **es war einmal ein König,** there was once a king, once upon a time there was a king; **es wird einmal die Zeit kommen, wenn, wo, . . . ,** there will come a time when . . . , the time will come when . . . ; **es lebe der König!** long live the king! **es lebe die Liebe!** vive l'amour! **es lebe Schottland!** Scotland forever! (*e*) (*with vbs of sensation, etc.*) **es friert mich,** I am cold; **es gefällt ihr hier,** she likes it here; **wie geht es dir?** how are you? (*f*) (*as subject, anticipating subsequent clause*) **es tut mir leid, daß . . . ,** I am sorry that . . . ; **es freut mich, daß . . . ,** I am glad that . . . ; **es wundert mich, daß . . . ,** I am surprised that . . . ; **es reut ihn, daß . . . ,** he regrets that . . . ; **es überraschte uns, daß . . . ,** it surprised us that . . . ; **es ärgerte ihn, daß . . . ,** it annoyed him that . . . ; **es war mir, als ob ich träumte,** it seemed to me that I was dreaming; **es gelang, glückte, ihm, zu . . . ,** he succeeded, was successful, in + *gerund.* **3. bist du es, Vater?** is it you, Father? **ich bin es, dein Bruder,** it is I, *F:* it's me, your brother; **ist es ein Junge oder ein Mädchen? — es ist ein Junge,** is it a boy or a girl?—it's a boy; **wer ist es gewesen? — es waren die Kinder,** who was it?—it was the children; **er war es, der . . . ,** it was he who . . . ; **es war ein Franzose und nicht ein Deutscher, der . . . ,** it was a Frenchman and not a German who . . . . **4.** (*with vbs used impersonally*) (*a*) **es regnet,** it is raining (now, again); it rains (every day, etc.); **es schneit,** it is snowing (now, again); it snows (in January, etc.); **es dunkelt,** it is getting dark; **es brennt,** there is a fire; **es spukt hier,** this place is haunted; (*b*) (*unidentified agent*) **es klopft,** there is a knock; **es klingelt,** (i) the bell is ringing; (ii) the telephone is ringing; **es pfiff,** there was a whistle; (*c*) (*passive formulation*) **es wurde gesungen und getanzt,** there was singing and dancing; **es wurde viel gelacht,** there was a lot of laughter, people laughed a great deal; **es wird erzählt, daß . . . ,** it is said that . . . , people, they, say that . . . ; the story goes that . . . ; **es wird von ihm gesagt, daß er . . . ,** it is said of him that he . . . , he is said to . . . ; **es wird allgemein anerkannt, daß . . . ,** it is generally recognized, acknowledged, that . . . ; (*d*) (*impersonal reflexive*) **hier sitzt es sich gut,** it's pleasant sitting here; **hier läßt es sich gut sein,** life is good here; **aus diesem Glas trinkt es sich gut,** this is a good glass to drink out of. **5.** (*as provisional object*) (*a*) **sie halten es für ihre Pflicht,** they believe it their duty; **ich halte es für wahrscheinlich, daß . . . ,** I think it (is) likely that . . . ; (*b*) (*as vague object in vbl phr.*) (*usu. not translated*) **es mit j-m verdorben haben,** to have lost favour with s.o.; **es gut (mit j-m) meinen,** to mean well (by s.o.); **es auf etwas abgesehen haben,** to be aiming at sth.; to have sth. in view, in contemplation, *F:* to be keen on sth.; **es mit j-m zu tun, zu schaffen, haben,** to (have to) deal with s.o.; **es gut, schlecht, haben,** to have a good, a bad, time; to be fortunate, unfortunate; to be lucky, unlucky; **er ist es gewohnt, daß man alles für ihn tut,** he is used to having everything done for him; **wir sind es leid, daß er immer zu spät kommt,** we have had enough of his constant late-coming; **es zufrieden sein, daß . . . ,** to be content that . . . ; *F:* **da hast du's!** there you are! (*c*) (*referring to an idea expressed in the previous sentence*) **wenn ich es nun tun würde?** supposing I did so? supposing I were to do it? **ich habe es dir ja schon einmal gesagt,** I have already told you so once before; **er wird deine Erwartungen nicht enttäuschen; — ich hoffe es,** he will not disappoint your expectations;—I hope not; **wird er wieder gesund werden? — ich hoffe es; — ich glaube es nicht,** will he recover?—I hope so;—I don't think so; **wird er heute abend kommen? — ich weiß es nicht,** will he come to-night?—I don't know; **er war krank und war es schon seit langem,** he was ill and had been so for a long time; **du bist reich, er ist es nicht,** you are rich, he isn't.

Es², *n.* **-/-.** *Psy:* id; **das Ich und das Es,** the ego and the id.

es³, Es [ɛs], *n.* **-/-.** *Mus:* (the note) E flat, E♭; **Es-dur, Es-Dur, es-moll, es-Moll,** (**-Tonart**), (key of) E flat major, E flat minor.

Esau [ˈeːzau]. *Pr.n.m.* **-s.** Esau; *F:* **er ist ein haariger E.,** he is as hairy as an ape.

Esch, *m.* **-es/-e.** *Agr:* field(s) under cultivation.

Eschatologie [ɛsça·to·lo·ˈgiː], *f.* **-/-n** [-ˈgiːən]. *Theol:* eschatology.

eschatologisch [ɛsça·to·ˈloːgiʃ], *a. Theol:* eschatological.

Esche, *f.* **-/-n. 1.** *Bot:* ash(-tree). **2.** ash (-timber, -wood).

Eschel, *m.* **-s/.** *Glassm:* finest pulverized smalt.

eschen, *a.* made of ash; ash (furniture); ashen.

Eschenbaum, *m. Bot:* ash-tree.

Escheneule, *f. Ent:* blue underwing (butterfly).

Eschenholz, *n. Com:* ash(-timber, -wood).

Eschenwurzel, *f. Bot:* (white) dittany.

Eschlauch, *n. Bot: Hort:* shallot, *Dial:* scallion.

Eschscholtzie [ɛʃɔˈʃɔltsiə], *f.* **-/-n.** *Bot:* eschscholtzia; **kalifornische E.,** Californian poppy, Noah's night-cap.

Escorial, der [ɛsko·riˈaːl]. *Pr.n.* **-s,** the Escorial, Escurial.

Esel, *m.* **-s/-,** (*a*) ass, donkey; **Bileams E.,** Balaam's ass; *F:* (*of pers.*) **beladen, bepackt, sein wie ein E.,** to be loaded like a donkey, like a mule; **er ist störrisch wie ein E.,** he is as stubborn as an ass, as a donkey, as a mule; **so dumm wie ein E.,** as stupid as a donkey; **der E. in der Löwenhaut,** the ass in the lion's skin; *Prov:* **wenn's dem E. zu wohl wird, geht er aufs Eis (tanzen),** over-confidence is risky; (*b*) *F:* **du alter E.,** you silly ass! you old duffer, you old fool! **du bist ein richtiger E.,** you are a perfect ass; **ich E.!** I ˈam an ass, a donkey, a fool!

Eselei, *f.* **-/-en,** foolish act *or* remark, piece of stupidity; **eine E. begehen,** to do something asinine, idiotic, to do a stupid, a silly, thing; **solche Eseleien!** such stupidity, such foolishness!

Eselfüllen, *n.* ass's foal, ass's colt.

eselhaft, *a.* (*a*) like an ass, a donkey, asinine; (*b*) *F:* asinine, idiotic, stupid, foolish.

Eselhengst, *m.* he-ass, he-donkey, jackass, stallion-ass.

Eselin, *f.* **-/-innen,** she-ass, she-donkey; **Bileams E.,** Balaam's ass.

Eselsbank, *f. Sch:* dunce's seat.

Eselsbrücke, *f. F:* **1.** (*a*) *Sch:* crib, *U.S:* pony; key (to school-book); **eine E. benutzen,** to crib, to use a crib; (*b*) mnemonic; *F:* donkey-bridge. **2.** *Geom: F: pons asinorum,* the asses' bridge.

Eselsdistel, *f. Bot:* (*a*) musk thistle; (*b*) Scotch thistle, cotton thistle.

Eselsfüllen, *n.* ass's foal, ass's colt.

Eselsgurke, *f. Bot:* squirting cucumber.

Eselshaupt, *n. Nau:* cap (of mast).

Eselslattich, *m. Bot:* coltsfoot.

Eselsmilch, *f.* **1.** ass's milk. **2.** *Bot:* leafy spurge.

Eselsohr, *n.* **1.** ass's ear. **2.** *F:* turned-down corner, *F:* dog's ear, dog-ear (of book, etc.); **Eselsohren, ein E., in ein Buch machen,** to dog's-ear, dog-ear, a book. **3.** *Bot:* = **Aasblume. 4.** *Fung:* otidea onotida.

Eselspinguin, *m. Orn:* gentoo penguin.

Eselsrücken, *m.* **1.** *Arch:* ogee arch; keel arch. **2.** *Rail:* hump (in marshalling yard).

Eselsstute, *f.* she-ass, she-donkey.

Eseltreiber, *m.* donkey-, ass-driver; donkey-boy.

eses, Eses [ˈɛs ɛs], *n.* **-/-.** *Mus:* (the note) E double flat.

Eskader [ɛsˈkaːdər], *f.* **-/-s.** *Navy: A:* squadron.

Eskadron [ɛska·ˈdroːn], *f.* **-/-en.** *Mil: A:* squadron (of cavalry).

Eskadronsführer, *m. Mil: A:* (cavalry) major.

Eskalade [ɛska·ˈlaːdə], *f.* **-/-n,** escalade.

Eskapade [ɛska·ˈpaːdə], *f.* **-/-n. 1.** *Equit:* caper (of horse). **2.** escapade (of pers.); **Eskapaden machen,** to commit escapades.

Eskariol [ɛska·riˈoːl], *m.* **-s/-e.** *Bot: Hort:* broad-leaved endive, Batavian endive, broad-leaved chicory.

Eskarpe [ɛsˈkarpə], *f.* **-/-n.** *Fort:* (e)scarp.

eskarpieren [ɛskarˈpiːrən], *v.tr. Fort:* to (e)scarp (glacis).

Eskimo [ˈɛski·moː], *m.* **-s/-s.** *Ethn: Geog:* Eskimo, *U.S:* Husky; **die Eskimos,** the Eskimo(e)s, the Eskimo.

Eskimobrachvogel, *m. Orn:* Eskimo curlew.
Eskimofrau, *f.* Eskimo woman.
Eskimohund, *m.* Eskimo dog, husky.
eskimoisch [ˈɛskiˑˌmoːiʃ], *a.* Eskimo.
Eskimosprache, *f. Ling:* Eskimo (language), Husky.
Eskompte [ɛsˈkõːt, ɛsˈkɔmpt(ə)], *m.* **-s/-s. 1.** = **Diskont. 2.** *Fin:* anticipation (of changes in discount rates, etc.).
eskomptieren [ɛskõˑˈtiːrən, ɛskɔmpˈtiːrən], *v.tr.* **1.** = **diskontieren. 2.** *Fin:* to anticipate (change in discount rates, etc.).
Eskont [ɛsˈkɔnt], *m.*° **-(e)s/-e** = **Diskont.**
eskontieren [ɛskɔnˈtiːrən], *v.tr.* = **diskontieren.**
Eskorial, der [ɛskoˑrĭˈaːl]. *Pr.n.* **-s,** the Escorial, Escurial.
Eskorte [ɛsˈkɔrtə], *f.* **-/-n.** *Mil: etc:* escort; *Navy:* convoy.
eskortieren [ɛskɔrˈtiːrən], *v.tr.* to escort (s.o.); *Navy:* to convoy, escort (ship).
Esoteriker [eˑzoˑˈteːrikər], *m.* **-s/-,** esoter(ic)ist, esoteric person.
esoterisch [eˑzoˑˈteːriʃ], *a.* esoteric(al).
Espagnoletteverschluß [ɛspanjoˑˈlɛt(ə)-], *m.* espagnolette, hasp (of French window).
Esparsette [ɛsparˈzɛt(ə)], *f.* **-/.** *Bot: Agr:* sainfoin, cockshead.
Esparto [ɛsˈpartoː], *m.* **-s/.** *(a) Ind:* esparto; *(b)* = **Espartogras** *(a).*
Espartogras, *n. (a) Bot:* esparto-grass, alfa grass, Spanish grass; *(b) Ind:* esparto.
Espe, *f.* **-/-n.** *Bot:* aspen, trembling poplar.
espen, *a.* aspen, made of aspen-wood.
Espenblatt, *m.* aspen leaf.
Espenlaub, *n.* aspen foliage, aspen leaves; *F: (of pers.)* **zittern wie E.,** to tremble like an aspen leaf.
esperantisch [ɛspeˑˈrantiʃ], *a. Ling:* Esperantist; Esperanto (word, etc.).
Esperantist [ɛspeˑranˈtist], *m.* **-en/-en.** *Ling:* Esperantist.
Esperanto [ɛspeˑˈrantoː], *n.* **-(s)/.** *Ling:* Esperanto.
Esplanade [ɛsplaˑˈnaːdə], *f.* **-/-n,** esplanade.
Espresso [ɛsˈprɛsoː]. **1.** *m.* **-s/-s** *&* **-si,** espresso coffee. **2.** *n.* **-s/-s,** espresso bar.
Espressomaschine, *f.* espresso machine.
Esprit [ɛsˈpriː], *m.* **-s/-s,** esprit, sparkling wit; **ein Mann mit E.,** a man of esprit.
Esquilin, der [ɛskviˑˈliːn]. *Pr.n.* **-s,** the Esquiline (Hill) (in Rome).
esquilinisch [ɛskviˑˈliːniʃ], *a.* **der Esquilinische Hügel,** the Esquiline (Hill) (in Rome).
Esra [ˈɛsraː]. *Pr.n.m.* **-s.** *B:* Ezra; **das Buch E.,** the Book of Ezra.
Essäer [ɛˈsɛːər], *m.* **-s/-.** *B.Lit:* Essene.
Essai [ɛˈsɛː], *m.* **-s/-s** = **Essay.**
Eßapfel, *m.* eating apple; dessert apple; **ein guter E.,** a good eating apple, a good eater.
Essay [ˈɛseː, ɛˈseː], *m.* **-s/-s.** *Lit:* essay.
Essayist [ɛseˑˈist], *m.* **-en/-en.** *Lit:* essayist.
eßbar, *a.* edible; eatable; fit to eat; **eßbare Pilze,** edible fungi; **eßbare Kastanien,** edible chestnuts; **etwas Eßbares,** something to eat, *F:* something edible; **wir konnten nichts Eßbares im Haus finden,** we couldn't find anything to eat in the house; **das Fleisch war etwas zäh, aber es war so eben e.,** the meat was somewhat tough, but it was just eatable; **der Kuchen war kaum e.,** the cake was scarcely eatable, *F:* edible.
Eßbarkeit, *f.* edibility (of fungus, etc.).
Eßbesteck, *n.* (single set of) knife, fork, and spoon; **Eßbestecke** *pl,* table-cutlery.
Esse, *f.* **-/-n. 1.** chimney. **2.** forge, smith's hearth. **3.** *Geol:* (lava) chimney, (lava) conduit, (lava) pipe.
Eßecke, *f.* dining area *or* recess.
essen. I. *v. (strong) (p.t.* **aß;** *p.p.* **gegessen) 1.** *v.tr. (a)* to eat (bread, apple, meal, etc.); **j-m etwas zu e. geben,** to give s.o. sth. to eat; to give s.o. (some) food; **nichts zu e. haben,** to have nothing to eat; **viel e.,** to eat a great deal; to be a big eater; **wenig e.,** to eat little; to be a small eater; **was haben Sie zu Mittag, zu Abend, gegessen?** what did you have for lunch, for supper, dinner? *F:* **du mußt deinen Teller leer e.,** you must eat everything on your plate, you must clear your plate; **j-n arm e., j-m die Haare vom Kopf e.,** to eat s.o. out of house and home; *(b) abs.* to eat; **von etwas e.,** to eat of sth.; **zu Mittag e.,** to lunch, to have lunch; **zu Abend e.,** to have supper; to have dinner, to dine; **haben Sie schon zu Abend gegessen?** have you already had supper, dinner? have you dined already? **wir essen um sieben Uhr,** we have supper, dinner, at seven o'clock; we eat at seven o'clock; **auswärts e.,** to eat out; **im Restaurant e.,** to eat in a restaurant; to have a meal *or* one's meals in a restaurant; **gut e. und (gut) trinken,** to eat and drink well; **wir gaben ihm zu e. und zu trinken,** we gave him food and drink, something to eat and drink; **er ißt für drei,** he eats enough for three (people); *F:* **wir haben tüchtig gegessen,** we made a hearty meal, *F:* we had a good feed; **e. wie ein Scheunendrescher,** (i) to eat like a horse; (ii) to wolf one's food; *B:* **von dem Baum der Erkenntnis des Guten und Bösen sollst du nicht e.,** of the tree of the knowledge of good and evil, thou shalt not eat of it; *Prov:* **wer nicht arbeiten will, soll auch nicht e.,** no work, no dinner; *(c)* **sich an etwas** *dat.* **satt e.,** to eat one's fill of sth.; *F:* to fill up on sth.; **sich satt e.,** *F:* **sich dick und rund e.,** to eat one's fill. **2.** *v.i. (haben)* **an etwas** *dat.* **e.,** to eat sth.; **an diesem Braten werden wir drei Tage lang e.,** we shall be eating this roast for three days. **3. sich essen,** *(of food, fruit, etc.)* **sich gut, schlecht, e.,** to be easy, difficult, to eat; **mit einem Löffel ißt es sich besser,** it's easier to eat with a spoon; **so ein Kuchen ißt sich schnell,** a cake like that is soon eaten, *F:* soon goes.

II. *vbl s.* **Essen,** *n.* **1.** *in vbl senses; also:* **beim E. sollst du nicht sprechen,** you shouldn't talk with your mouth full (cp. 2 *(b)*); **er vergaß darüber E. und Trinken,** he was so absorbed in it that he forgot to eat and drink, that he forgot food and drink; *Prov:* **der Appetit kommt beim E., mit dem E., über dem E.,** (i) once you start eating you soon get hungry; (ii) the more a man gets the more he wants; the appetite grows with what it feeds on. **2.** *(a)* food; victuals; *F:* grub; **gutes, schlechtes, E.,** good, bad, food; **einen bestimmten Betrag für E. und Kleidung ausgeben,** to spend a certain sum of money on food and clothing; **beständig am E. mäkeln,** to grumble incessantly about, over, the food; *Mil:* **E. fassen,** to draw rations; *(b)* meal; **während des Essens, beim E., sollst du nicht sprechen,** you shouldn't talk at meals; **das E. zubereiten,** to prepare the meal, to make the meal; **sie ruht gewöhnlich nach dem E.,** she usually rests after meals; **pünktlich zum E. erscheinen,** to be punctual at meals, at meal-times; **j-n zum E. einladen,** to invite s.o. to, for, a meal; to invite s.o. to, for, lunch *or* supper *or* dinner; **er blieb zum E.,** he stayed for the meal; *Pharm:* **nach dem E. einzunehmen,** to be taken after meals; *(c)* dinner; banquet; **ein E. geben,** to give a dinner *or* a banquet; **die deutsche Botschaft gab ein E. zu Ehren des Präsidenten,** the German Embassy gave a dinner, banquet, in honour of the president; **zu einem offiziellen E. eingeladen sein,** to be invited to an official dinner. **3. -essen,** *comb.fm. (a)* eating (of) . . . ; **beim Kirschenessen,** when eating cherries; *(b)* meal of . . . ; feast of . . . , feast on . . . ; **bei uns war gestern großes Forellenessen,** yesterday we had a feast of trout; **ein Pfannkuchenessen veranstalten,** to have a pancake feast; to give a pancake party.
Essener[1] [ˈɛsənər]. **1.** *m.* **-s/-.** *Geog:* inhabitant of Essen, native of Essen. **2.** *inv.a.* of Essen . . . ; **das E. Münster,** Essen Cathedral.
Essener[2] [ɛˈseːnər], *m.* **-s/-.** *B.Lit:* Essene.
essenisch [ɛˈseːniʃ], *a. B.Lit:* Essenian.
Essenismus [ɛseˑˈnismus], *m.* **-/.** Essenism.
Essenkehrer, *m.* chimney-sweep.
Essensaufzug, *m.* dinner-lift, service-lift; service-hoist; plate-hoist.
Essenszeit, *f.* meal-time; lunch-time; supper-time; dinner-time.
essentiell [ɛsɛntsĭˈɛl], *a.* essential.
Essenträger, *m.* **1.** *Mil: (pers.)* ration carrier. **2.** dinner-can, dinner-pail.
Essenz [ɛˈsɛnts], *f.* **-/-en. 1.** *Phil: Theol:* essence; **die wahre E. aller Dinge,** the true essence of all things; *F:* **die E. des Buches,** the essence of the book. **2.** *(a) Ch:* essence; (essential) oil (of laurel, etc.); attar (of roses); *(b) Cu:* essence.
Essenzessig, *m. Cu:* concentrated vinegar.
Esser, *m.* **-s/-,** eater; **ein schlechter, ein guter, E.,** a bad, a good, eater; **ein schwacher, starker, E.,** a small, a big, eater; **ein mäßiger E.,** a moderate eater; **unnütze Esser können wir nicht gebrauchen,** we can't have people who eat and don't work, we don't want useless mouths to feed.
Esserei, *f.* **-/.** eating; way of eating; **ich kann eure beständige E. nicht ausstehen,** I cannot stand your constant eating, *F:* guzzling.
Eßfeige, *f.* common fig, edible fig.
Eßgabel, *f.* table-fork.
Eßgerät, *n.* (i) implement *or* utensil, (ii) *coll.* implements and utensils, used for eating.
Eßgeschirr, *n.* **1.** *coll.* plates and dishes, table-service. **2.** *Mil: etc:* mess-tin, -kettle; canteen; billy-can; *F:* dixie, dixy.
Eßgier, *f.* craving for food.
Essig, *m.* **-s/-e. 1.** vinegar; **zu E. werden,** to turn into vinegar, to acetify. **2.** *F:* **damit ist es nun E.,** it has come to nothing; it has fallen through; **es ist E. mit dem Ausflug,** the excursion has fallen through.
Essigälchen, *n. Ann:* vinegar-eel.
Essigäther, *m. Ch:* acetic ether; ethyl acetate.
Essigbakterie, *f.* acetic acid bacillus.
Essigbaum, *m. Bot:* Canadian sumac; *Dy:* **echter E.,** tanner's sumac, Sicilian sumac.
Essigbeere, *f. Bot:* barberry.
Essigbildner, *m. Ch: etc:* acetifier.
Essigbildung, *f. Ch: etc:* acetification.
Essigdorn, *m. Bot:* barberry(-bush).
Essigessenz, *f.* concentrated vinegar.
Essigfabrikation, *f.* vinegar making.
Essigfliege, *f. Ent:* vinegar-fly.
Essiggärung, *f.* acetic fermentation.
Essiggurke, *f. (a) Cu:* (pickled) gherkin; pickled cucumber; *(b) Hort:* small cucumber for pickling.
Essigkaraffe, *f.* vinegar-cruet.
Essigkräutersauce, *f. Cu:* vinegar sauce.
Essigmesser, *m. Ind:* acetimeter.
Essigmutter, *f. Ch: Ind:* mother of vinegar.
Essigpflaume, *f. usu.pl.* **Essigpflaumen,** *Cu:* plums preserved in vinegar with sugar and cinnamon-bark.
Essigpilz, *m.* acetic acid bacillus.
Essigprüfer, *m. Ind:* acetimeter.
essigsauer, *a. (a)* acetous; *Ch:* acetic; . . . acetate; **essigsaure Salze,** acetates; **essigsaure Tonerde,** aluminium acetate; *(b) F:* **mit essigsaurer Miene,** with a vinegary, vinegarish, (expression of) face, vinegar-faced.
Essigsäure, *f. Ch:* acetic acid.
Essigsumach, *m.* = **Essigbaum.**
Eßkastanie, *f. (nut)* edible chestnut; *(tree or nut)* sweet chestnut, Spanish chestnut.
Eßkastanienbaum, *m.* sweet chestnut, Spanish chestnut (tree).
Eßkohle, *f. Ind:* forge coal.
Eßkorb, *m.* hamper; picnic-basket.
Eßlöffel, *m.* tablespoon *or* large dessert spoon; **zwei Eßlöffel voll,** two tablespoonfuls.
eßlöffelweise, *adv.* by tablespoonfuls; **e. einzunehmen,** to be taken in tablespoonfuls.
Eßlust, *f.* appetite; desire to eat.
Eßmesser, *n.* table-knife.
Eßnapf, *m.* (small) bowl, basin; *Mil: etc:* mess-tin.
Eßobst, *n.* dessert fruit.
Eßplatz, *m.* (i) eating place; (ii) dining area *or* recess.
Eßsaal, *m.* dining-hall.
Eßschokolade, *f.* eating chocolate.
Eßsucht, *f. Med:* mania for food.
Eßtisch, *m.* dining-table.
Eßunlust, *f.* lack of appetite; loss of appetite; *Med:* inappetence; anorexia.
Eßwaren, *f.pl.* comestibles, eatables, edibles; food; provisions.
Eßwerkzeug, *n. (a)* eating implement; *(b) Anat:* organ for eating.
Eßzeit, *f.* = **Essenszeit.**
Eßzimmer, *n. (a)* dining-room; *(b) Furn:* dining-room suite.
Eßzimmereinrichtung, *f. Furn:* dining-room suite.
Eßzimmerschrank, *m.* sideboard; dresser.
Eßzimmertisch, *m.* dining-table.
Estafette [ɛstaˑˈfɛtə], *f.* **-/-n,** estafette; *Mil:* mounted orderly; dispatch-rider.
Estampe [ɛˈstãːp(ə)], *f.* **-/-n** [-pən], engraving; print.
Este, *m.* **-n/-n.** *Geog:* Esthonian.
Ester, *m.* **-s/-.** *Ch:* ester.
Esther. *Pr.n.f.* **-s.** Esther.
Estland. *Pr.n.n.* **-s.** *Geog:* Esthonia.
Estländer, *m.* **-s/-.** *Geog:* Esthonian.
estländisch, *a. Geog:* Esthonian.
estnisch. 1. *a.* Esthonian (language, literature, etc.). **2.** *s.* **Estnisch,** *n. Ling:* Esthonian.
Estrade [ɛsˈtraːdə], *f.* **-/-n,** estrade.
Estragon [ˈɛstraˑgɔn], *m.* **-s/.** *Bot: Cu:* tarragon.
Estragonessig, *m. Cu:* tarragon vinegar.
Estrich, *m.* **-s/-e. 1.** (bare) earth-, stone-, *or* asphalt-floor. **2.** loft.
Estrichgips, *m. Constr:* flooring-plaster; tiling-plaster, hard finish plaster.
Eszett [ɛsˈtsɛt], *n.* **-/- & -s/-s,** (the letter) ß.
Eta [ˈeːtaː], *n.* **-(s)/-s.** *Gr.Alph:* eta.
etablieren [eˑtaˑˈbliːrən], *v.tr.* to establish, set up (business house, etc.); **sich e.,** to establish oneself; to become established **(in etwas** *dat.,*

in sth.); **er hat sich als Juwelier in X etabliert,** he set up as a jeweller in X; **diese Einrichtung ist fest etabliert, hat sich fest etabliert,** this institution is firmly established, has become firmly established; **Etablieren** *n*, **Etablierung** *f*, establishing, establishment (of business house, etc.).

Etablissement [e·ta·blis(ə)ˈmã:], *n.* **-s/-s,** (*night-club, etc.*) establishment.

Etage [e·ˈta:ʒə], *f.* **-/-n. 1.** floor, stor(e)y (of house); **wir wohnen auf der dritten E.,** we live on the third floor, three flights up, *U.S:* on the fourth story; **wir wohnen auf der gleichen E.,** we live on the same floor; **ein Haus mit zwei Etagen,** a two-storied house. **2.** (*a*) tier; range; step; **in Etagen übereinander angeordnet,** arranged in tiers (above each other); (*b*) *Geol:* stage.

etagenförmig, *a. & adv.* (arrangement, arranged) in tiers; **die Weinberge lagen e. übereinander,** the vineyards rose in tiers, rose up one above the other.

Etagengeschäft, *n.* shop on the first floor *or* on the upper floors.

Etagenheizung, *f.* central heating serving one flat.

Etagenwohnung, *f.* self-contained flat, *U.S:* apartment.

Etagere [e·ta·ˈʒɛ:rə], *f.* **-/-n,** etagere, what-not; (set of) shelves.

Etalage [e·ta·ˈla:ʒə], *f.* **-/-n,** display, show (of goods); window-display.

Etalon [e·ta·ˈlõ:], *m.* **-s/-s,** etalon; standard (of weights, measures).

etalonnieren [e·ta·loˈni:rən], *v.tr.* to standardize, verify (weights, measures).

Etamin [e·ta·ˈmi:n], *n.* **-s/.** *Tex:* etamine.

Etappe [e·ˈtapə], *f.* **-/-n. 1.** *A:* mart, emporium. **2.** (*a*) stage (of journey, etc.); *Sp:* stage, leg (of road-race, etc.); **eine Strecke in Etappen zurücklegen,** to cover a distance in stages; (*b*) *Mil: etc:* (i) halting-place; (ii) distance between two halting-places; day's march. **3.** *Mil:* **die E.,** the lines of communication(s), *F:* the L. of C.; the base; **in der E. sein, in der E. liegen,** to be behind the lines, to be at base.

Etappenanfangsort, *m. Mil:* advanced base of supplies.

Etappengebiet, *n. Mil:* lines of communication(s) area, *F:* L. of C. area.

Etappenhauptort, *m. Mil:* main road post (on line of communication).

Etappenhengst, *m. Mil: F:* base wallah.

Etappenlazarett, *n. Mil:* clearing-station, -hospital.

Etappenort, *m. Mil:* road-post (on line of communication); field base.

Etappenschwein, *n. Mil: F:* base wallah.

etappenweise, *a. & adv.* by stages.

Etat [e·ˈta:], *m.* **-s/-s. 1.** *Fin: Parl:* budget; **veranschlagter E.,** estimates; **ordentlicher E.,** ordinary budget; **außerordentlicher E.,** extraordinary budget; **den E. aufstellen,** to draw up the budget; **den E. überschreiten,** to exceed the budget; **Ausgaben, die im E. vorgesehen sind,** expenses provided for in the budget, budgeted for. **2.** *Mil: Adm:* establishment (of military unit, official organization); *Mil:* strength (of regiment, etc.).

Etatdefizit, *n. Fin:* deficit in the budget.

etatisieren [e·ta·ti·ˈzi:rən], *v.tr. Fin:* to budget for (certain expenditure), to include (certain expenditure) in the budget.

etatmäßig, *a.* **1.** *Fin:* (expenditure, etc.) in accordance with the budget, with the estimates, (expenditure, etc.) that has been budgeted for. **2.** *Adm:* (post) on the establishment; (post) provided for in the establishment.

Etatrecht, *n. Parl:*=**Haushaltsrecht.**

Etatsjahr [e·ˈta:s-], *n. Fin:* fiscal year, financial year, budgetary year.

Etatsposten, *m. Fin:* item included in the budget.

Etazismus [e·ta·ˈtsismus], *m.* **-/.** *Gr.Ling:* etacism.

Eteokles [e·ˈte:o·klɛs]. *Pr.n.m.* **-'.** *Gr.Lit:* Eteocles.

etepetete [ˌe·təpəˈte:tə], *a. F:* finicky; pernickety; pseudo-refined; over-particular, over-fastidious; over-nice (pers., behaviour, etc.); **sie tut immer so e.,** she is always so finicky; she always tries to be so very refined.

Eternit [e·tɛrˈni:t], *n. & m.* **-(e)s/.** (*R.t.m.*) *Constr:* asbestos cement sheeting.

Etesien [e·ˈte:ziən], *pl. Nau:* Etesian winds.

Etesienklima, *n.* Etesian climate.

Ethik [ˈe:tik], *f.* **-/. 1.** (*a*) ethics; moral philosophy; (*b*) *Gr.Lit:* (*pl.* **-en**) **die Nikomachische E.,** the Nicomachean Ethics. **2.** ethics; ethical sense, moral sense; ethical values, principles; moral values, principles.

Ethiker [ˈe:tikər], *m.* **-s/-,** (*a*) ethicist; (*b*) ethic philosopher.

ethisch [ˈe:tiʃ], *a.* **1.** ethical (pers., values, etc.); **unvereinbar mit seinen ethischen Grundsätzen,** incompatible with his ethical principles. **2.** *Gram:* **der ethische Dativ,** the ethic dative.

Ethnarch [ɛtˈnarç], *m.* **-en/-en,** ethnarch.

Ethnarchie [ɛtnarˈçi:], *f.* **-/-n** [-ˈçi:ən], ethnarchy.

ethnisch [ˈɛtniʃ], *a.* **1.** *Rel.Hist:* ethnic(al), gentile. **2.** ethnic (influence, characteristic).

Ethnograph [ɛtno·ˈgra:f], *m.* **-en/-en,** ethnographer.

Ethnographie [ɛtno·gra·ˈfi:], *f.* **-/.** ethnography.

ethnographisch [ɛtno·ˈgra:fiʃ], *a.* ethnographic(al).

Ethnologe [ɛtno·ˈlo:gə], *m.* **-n/-n,** ethnologist.

Ethnologie [ɛtno·lo·ˈgi:], *f.* **-/.** ethnology.

ethnologisch [ɛtno·ˈlo:giʃ], *a.* ethnological.

Ethologe [e·to·ˈlo:gə], *m.* **-n/-n,** ethologist.

Ethologie [e·to·lo·ˈgi:], *f.* **-/.** ethology.

ethologisch [e·to·ˈlo:giʃ], *a.* ethological.

Ethos [ˈe:tos], *n.* **-/.** (*a*) *A.Rh: etc:* ethos; (*b*) ethos; ethical sense, moral sense; ethical values, principles; **ein hohes E. haben,** to have a highly developed ethical sense, to have a highly developed sense of moral values.

Etikett [e·ti·ˈkɛt], *n.* **-(e)s/-e,** label (on bottle, garment, etc.); tag (on garment, etc.); price-ticket, -tag (on article for sale); **etwas mit einem E. versehen,** to label sth.; to label, ticket, tag (article for sale).

Etikette [e·ti·ˈkɛtə], *f.* **-/-n. 1.** etiquette; **es ist gegen die E., zu . . . ,** it is not etiquette, not good form, it is bad form, to . . . ; **gegen die E. verstoßen,** to commit a breach of etiquette; **die Regeln der E. beachten,** to observe the rules of etiquette. **2.**=**Etikett.**

etikettieren [e·ti·kɛˈti:rən], *v.tr.* to label (bottles, etc.); to label, ticket, tag (article for sale); *F:* to label (s.o.).

Etiolement [e·tĭoləˈmã:], *n.* **-s/.** *Bot:* etiolation (of plant).

etiolieren [e·tĭo·ˈli:ren], *v.* **1.** *v.tr.* to etiolate (plant). **2.** *v.i.* (*sein*) to etiolate.

etliche *see* **etlicher.**

etlichemal, *adv.* several times, a number of times.

etlicher, etliche, etliches. 1. *indef.a. sg.* some; **nach etlicher Zeit,** after some time; **mit etlicher Mühe,** with some difficulty. **2.** *indef.a. pl.* (*a*) several, a number of; some; a few; **vor etlichen Wochen,** several weeks ago, some weeks ago; a few weeks ago; **etliche Male,** several, a number of, times; (*b*) (+*num.*) **etliche hundert,** several hundred; a few hundred; some hundreds; **etliche tausend Bücher,** several thousand books; a few thousand books; (*c*) (+*num.*) **etliche zehn Tage,** about ten days, some ten days; ten days odd; **es sind ihrer etliche zwanzig,** there are some, about, twenty of them; there are twenty odd of them. **3.** *indef.pron.* (*a*) *pl.* **etliche,** several, a number, some; a few; **etliche von euch,** several of you, a number of you; some of you; a few of you; **es sind ihrer etliche, die . . . ,** there are several, a number, of them who . . . , there are some of them who . . . ; there are a few of them who . . . ; (*b*) *neut.* **etliches,** several things, a number of things; some things; a few things; *Lit:* sundry things; **etliches gefiel ihm,** he liked several, a number of, things; he liked some things; he liked a few things; **er kann etliches davon erzählen,** he has quite a lot to tell about it; **sie ist um etliches älter als er,** she is considerably older than he is.

Etmal, *n.* **-(e)s/-e.** *Nau:* **1.** period of time from noon to noon. **2.** ship's run, sailing, in 24 hours; day's run.

Etrurien [e·ˈtru:rĭən]. *Pr.n.n.* **-s.** *A.Geog:* Etruria.

Etrurier [e·ˈtru:rĭər], *m.* **-s/-.** *Hist:* Etrurian, Etruscan.

etrurisch [e·ˈtru:riʃ], *a. Hist:* Etrurian, Etruscan.

Etrusker [e·ˈtruskər], *m.* **-s/-.** *Hist:* Etruscan.

etruskisch [e·ˈtruskiʃ]. **1.** *a. Hist:* Etruscan (art, language, etc.). **2.** *s.* **Etruskisch,** *n. Ling:* Etruscan.

Etruskologe [e·trusko·ˈlo:gə], *m.* **-en/-en.** Etruscologist.

etsch[1], *int.*=**ätsch.**

Etsch[2], **die.** *Pr.n* **-.** *Geog:* the (river) Adige.

Etschland, das. *Geog:* South Tirol.

Etüde [e·ˈty:də], *f.* **-/-n.** *Mus:* étude, study.

Etui [e·ty·ˈi:, e·ˈtvi:], *n.* **-s/-s,** case (for spectacles, cigars, cigarettes, drawing instruments, etc.).

etwa. I. *adv.* **1.** (+*num.*) **etwa zehn, fünfhundert, usw.,** about ten, five hundred, etc.; some ten, five hundred, etc.; ten, five hundred, etc., or so; **e. 600 Personen,** about 600 people, 600 people or so, or thereabouts; some, approximately, 600 people; **in e. einem Jahr,** in about a year's time, in something like a year, in a year or so; **die Summe beträgt e. 200 Mark,** the sum amounts to about, around, approximately, something like, 200 marks; **sie ist e. dreißig Jahre alt,** she is about thirty. **2.** *adv.phr.* **in e.,** to a certain extent, to some extent, to some degree; **ich kann es in e. verstehen, daß . . . ,** I can understand to a certain extent, to some extent, to some degree, that . . . ; **sie mag in e. recht haben,** she may be right to some extent.

II. **etwa,** *emotive particle.* **1.** (*expressing uncertainty*) (*a*) perhaps; **wann paßt dir mein Besuch, — Montag abend e.?** when would it be convenient for me to visit you—Monday evening perhaps? **kennen Sie ihn e.?** do you happen to know him? do you by any chance know him? **hat er Sie e. belästigt?** did he by any chance molest you? (*b*) (*with nuance of indignation, surprise, etc.*) **hast du es e. vergessen?** (do) you mean to say you forgot? **hat er Sie e. auch betrogen?** (do) you mean to say he deceived you too? **kennen Sie ihn e. auch?** (i) you don't mean to say you know him too? (ii) do you happen to know him too? (*c*) (*in conditional clauses*) **sollte ich es e. vergessen . . . ,** should I happen to forget, should I by any chance forget, in case I forget, . . . ; **sollte er es e. haben,** should he happen to have it. **2. nicht e.,** (*with nuance of expostulation, reluctance to accept idea, etc.*) (*a*) surely; **du glaubst das doch nicht e.?** surely you don't believe that? **Sie erwarten doch nicht e., daß ich mit Ihnen gehe?** you surely don't expect me to go with you? **Sie wollen doch nicht e. sagen, daß . . . ?** you surely don't mean to say that . . . ? you don't really mean to say that . . . ? **denken Sie nicht e., daß . . . ,** you mustn't think that . . . ; (*b*) **nicht e., daß ich ihn fürchte,** not that I am really afraid of him; **es war nicht e. so, daß sie ihm etwas schuldete,** there was no question of her owing him anything; (*c*) **und nicht e.,** and not as you might think, expect, assume, suppose; **er hat sein Vermögen der Kirche und nicht e. seiner Familie vermacht,** he left his fortune to the church and not, as you might think, as you might expect, to his family; **er hat es nicht e. aus Nächstenliebe getan,** he certainly didn't do it for altruistic reasons.

etwaig, *a.* possible (expenses, claims, losses, etc.); (expenses, claims, losses, etc.) that may occur, arise; **bei etwaigen Schwierigkeiten,** should any difficulties occur, arise, in case of any difficulties.

etwas. 1. *indef.pron.* (*a*) something; anything; **sonst e.,** something else; anything else; **irgend e.,** something; anything; **kaum e.,** hardly anything, scarcely anything; **ich möchte dir e. erzählen,** I want to tell you something; **sag doch e.!** do say something! **um e. zu trinken bitten,** to ask for something to drink; **sein Plan hat e. für sich,** his plan has its points, there is something to be said for his plan; **er hat e. an sich, das mir nicht gefällt,** there is something about him I don't like; **es muß e. an der Sache sein,** there must be something in it; **er wird es in seinem Beruf noch zu e. bringen,** he will get somewhere in his job; **nun, das ist immerhin e.!** well, that's something anyway! **das ist schon e.!** (i) that really 'is something! that's something worth while! *F:* that's something like! (ii) that's getting somewhere! now we are getting somewhere! **irgend e. klappte nicht,** something (or other) went wrong; **irgend e. passiert immer gerade, wenn ich ausgehen will,** something always happens just when I want to go out; **hat er dir e. erzählt?** did he tell you something, anything? **ohne mir e. zu sagen,** without telling me anything; **sonst noch e., mein Herr?** anything else, something else, sir? **kann ich (irgend) e. für Sie tun?** is there anything (at all) I can do for you? **haben Sie e. zum Schreiben bei sich?** have you anything to write with on you? (*b*) **so e.,** a thing like that; a thing of this, of that, sort; something of the sort, of the kind; **so e. habe ich noch nicht gesehen,** I have never seen anything like it; **haben Sie je so e. gehört?** did you ever hear of such a thing, did you ever hear anything like it? **er ist so e. wie ein Heiliger für sie,** he is something like a saint for her; **er ist ein Gelehrter oder so e.,** he is a scholar or something of the kind; **nein so e.!** would you believe it! **2.** *indef.a.* **e. anderes,** something else; something different; **e. Schreckliches, Schönes, Unerklärliches,** something awful, beautiful, inexplicable; **kannst du nicht an e. anderes denken?** can't you think of something, anything, else? **das ist e. ganz anderes,** that is

quite a different thing, that is quite another matter; **sie hat e. Gewöhnliches an sich,** there is something common about her; **es ist e. Wahres daran,** there's some truth in it; **so e. Dummes!** what a stupid thing, what a stupid business! **3.** (*a*) *indef.a.* a little; some; **ich habe noch e. Zeit,** I still have a little time, some time (to spare); **e. Geld,** a little money, some money; **er spricht e. Englisch,** he speaks some English, he speaks a little English; (*b*) *adv.* a little; somewhat; **e. mehr,** a little more; **e. weniger,** a little less; **mit e. mehr Geduld,** with a little more patience; **ich war e. überrascht, enttäuscht,** I was a little, somewhat, surprised, disappointed; **es geht mir e. besser,** I feel a little better, I feel rather better; **das kommt mir e. plötzlich,** that is rather too sudden for me; *F:* **das ist e. stark,** that's a bit thick, that's rather too much (of a good thing), *F:* that's coming it a bit strong; (*c*) **im ganzen waren es e. über hundert Personen,** all told there were something, a little, over a hundred people; **er ist e. über vierzig,** he is something, a little, over forty; (*d*) *adv. F:* a short while; *F:* a bit; **ich gehe noch e. spazieren,** I am going for a short walk, for a bit of a walk; **er ging noch e. in den Garten,** he went for a short while into the garden; **ich muß noch e. üben,** I must have a bit more practice, I must practise a bit longer; **kannst du noch e. herauskommen?** can you come out for a short while, for a bit? (*e*) *adv.phr. A:* **in e.,** to some, to a certain, extent; to some degree. **4. Etwas** *n,* (*a*) something; **ein unerklärliches Etwas,** an inexplicable something; **jenes, dieses, Etwas, das sich nicht erklären läßt,** that, this, certain something that cannot be explained; **ihm fehlt jenes gewisse Etwas,** he lacks that certain something; *F:* **sie hat das gewisse Etwas,** she's got that certain something; *F:* she's got 'it'; (*b*) **solch ein winziges Etwas,** such a tiny little thing.

etwelche(r), etwelche, etwelche(s), *indef.a. & pron. A:* some; *pl.* some; a few.

etwelchermaßen, *adv. Swiss:* = **einigermaßen.**

Etymologe [e·ty·mo·ˈloːgə], *m.* **-n/-n,** etymologist.

Etymologie [e·ty·mo·lo·ˈgiː], *f.* **-/-n** [-ˈgiːən], etymology.

etymologisch [e·ty·mo·ˈloːgiʃ], *a.* etymological.

etymologisieren [e·ty·mo·lo·gi·ˈziːrən], *v.tr.* to etymologize (word).

Etymon [ˈeːty·mon], *n.* **-s/-ma.** *Ling:* etymon, root (of a word).

Etzeichen [ɛt-], *n. Print:* ampersand; &.

Etzel [ˈɛtsəl]. *Pr.n.m.* **-s.** *Hist:* Attila.

etzlicher, etzliche, etzliches, *indef.a. & pron. A:* = **etlicher, etliche, etliches.**

Eu-, eu- [ɔy-], *pref.* eu-; **Eugenik** *f,* eugenics; **Euphonie** *f,* euphony; **eupeptisch,** eupeptic.

Euander [ɔyˈandər], **-s, Euandros** [ɔyˈandros], **-'.** *Pr.n.m. Rom.Myth:* Euandros.

Euböa [ɔyˈbøːaː]. *Pr.n.n.* **-s.** *Geog:* Euboea.

Euböaner [ɔybøˈaːnər], *m.* **-s/-.** *Geog:* Euboean.

euböisch [ɔyˈbøːiʃ], *a. Geog:* Euboic, Euboean; **das Euböische Meer,** the Euboic Sea.

Eucain [ɔyka·ˈiːn], *n.* **-s/.** *Pharm:* eucaine.

euch. 1. (*a*) *pers.pron. acc. & dat. of second pers.pl., see* **ihr**[1] 1; (*b*) **Euch,** *A. & Lit: acc. & dat. of* **Ihr** *q.v. under* **ihr**[1] 2. **2.** *refl.pron.* (*a*) yourselves; (*b*) **Euch,** *A. & Lit:* yourself.

Eucharis [ɔyˈçaris], *f.* **-/-.** *Bot:* eucharis.

Eucharistie [ɔyçaris'tiː], *f.* **-/.** (*a*) *A.Ecc:* eucharistic liturgy; (*b*) *R.C.Ch:* **die E.,** the Eucharist.

eucharistisch [ɔyça'ristiʃ], *a.* eucharistic; *R.C.Ch:* **der eucharistische Heiland,** the Eucharist.

Euchet [ɔyˈçeːt], *m.* **-en/-en.** *Rel.Hist:* Euchite, Messalian.

Euchinin [ɔyçi·ˈniːn], *n.* **-s/.** *Pharm:* euquinine.

Euchlor [ɔyˈkloːr], *n.* **-s/.** *Ch:* euchlorine.

Eudämon [ɔyˈdɛːmon], *m.* **-s/.** eudemon, eudaemon.

Eudämonismus [ɔydɛ·mo·ˈnismus], *m.* **-/.** eudemonism.

Eudämonist [ɔydɛ·mo·ˈnist], *m.* **-en/-en,** eudemonist.

eudämonistisch [ɔydɛ·mo·ˈnistiʃ], *a.* eudemonic.

Eudiometer [ɔydi·o·ˈmeːtər], *n.* **-s/-.** *Ch:* eudiometer.

Eudiometrie [ɔydi·o·me·ˈtriː], *f.* **-/.** eudiometry.

eudiometrisch [ɔydi·o·ˈmeːtriʃ], *a.* eudiometric(al).

euer, eu(e)re, euer, *poss.a. & pron.* (*written with capital* E *in letters or with titles*) (*for use of* **euer** *as opposed to* **Ihr,** *cp.* **ihr**[2] III). I. **1.** *poss.a.* your; (*referring to several persons*) **euer Freund, eure Freundin, eure Freunde,** your friend; your friends; **euer Kind, eure Kinder,** your child, your children; **einer eurer Bekannten,** one of your acquaintances, an acquaintance of yours; **das ist eure Sache,** that's your business, affair; **euer Vater und eure Mutter,** your father and mother; (*in letter*) **Euer Sohn,** your son; **herzliche Grüße, Euer Hans, Eure Grete,** with all good wishes from Hans, from Grete, all good wishes, yours (ever), Hans, Grete. **2.** (*in formal address referring to one pers. only*) **Euer, Eu(e)re, Euer,** (*a*) *pers.pron. A. & Lit: sg. form of formal address, q.v. under* **ihr**[1] 2; (*b*) *poss.pron.* (*with titles*) **Eure, Euer, Exzellenz,** Your Excellency; **der Bote Eurer, Euer, Exzellenz,** your Excellency's messenger; **Euer, Eure, Majestät,** Your Majesty; **Euer Gnaden,** Your Grace.

II. **euer, eu(e)rer, eu(e)re, eu(e)res, eu(e)re,** *poss.pron.* (*decl. as adj.*) (*usu. referring to several persons; may also in older German, in formal address, refer to one pers. only*) (*a*) yours; **unser Haus ist größer als eures, als das eure,** our house is bigger than yours; **das ist eures,** that is yours; **wessen Garten ist das? ist es eurer, der eure?** whose garden is that? is it yours? (*b*) **das Eu(e)re,** your property, your possessions; your affairs, business, etc.; **ihr müßt das Eure tun,** you must do your share, part, bit; you must pull your weight; (*c*) **die Euren, die Euern,** your people; your family.

III. **euer,** *pers.pron. gen. of second pers.pl. see* **ihr**[1] 1.

euer-, euers-, euert-, *comb.fm.* = **eurer-, eures-, euret-.**

Eugen [ɔyˈgeːn]. *Pr.n.m.* **-s.** Eugene.

Eugenetik [ɔyge·ˈneːtik], *f.* **-/.** = **Eugenik.**

eugenetisch [ɔyge·ˈneːtiʃ], *a.* = **eugenisch.**

Eugenglanz [ˈɔygən-], *m. Miner:* polybasite.

Eugenia, Eugenie [ɔyˈgeːniaː, -niə]. *Pr.n.f.* **-s** & *Lit:* **-niens.** Eugenia.

Eugenik [ɔyˈgeːnik], *f.* **-/.** eugenics.

eugenisch [ɔyˈgeːniʃ], *a.* eugenic (problem, question, etc.).

Eugenius [ɔyˈgeːnius]. *Pr.n.m.* **-'.** Eugene.

Eugenol [ɔyge·ˈnoːl], *n.* **-s/.** *Ch:* eugenol.

Eugensäure, *f. Ch:* eugenic acid.

Euhemerismus [ɔyhe·məˈrismus], *m.* **-/.** Euhemerism.

euhemeristisch [ɔyhe·məˈristiʃ], *a.* Euhemeristic.

Euhemeros [ɔyˈheːməros]. *Pr.n.m.* **-'.** *Gr.Phil:* Euhemerus.

Eukalyptol [ɔyka·lyp'toːl], *n.* **-s/.** *Pharm:* eucalyptol.

Eukalyptus [ɔyka·ˈlyptus], *m.* **-/- & -ten. 1.** *Bot:* eucalyptus(-tree); gum(-tree). **2.** *Pharm:* eucalyptus (oil, lozenges, etc.).

Eukalyptusbaum, *m. Bot:* eucalyptus-tree; gum-tree.

Eukalyptusöl, *n. Pharm:* eucalyptus oil, *F:* eucalyptus.

Euklid [ɔyˈkliːt]. *Pr.n.m.* **-s.** Euclid.

euklidisch [ɔyˈkliːdiʃ], *a.* Euclidean; **euklidische Geometrie,** Euclidean geometry, *F:* Euclid.

Eulalia, Eulalie [ɔyˈlaːliaː, -liə]. *Pr.n.f.* **-s** & *Lit:* **-liens.** Eulalia.

Eule, *f.* **-/-n. 1.** *Orn:* owl; **junge Eule,** young owl, owlet; *F:* **sie sieht wie eine alte Eule aus,** she looks like a stuffed owl; *Prov:* **Eulen nach Athen tragen,** to carry coals to Newcastle. **2.** *Ent:* = **Eulenfalter. 3.** hand-broom; wall-broom; long-handled feather-broom. **4.** *Nau: F:* (*of ship*) **eine Eule fangen,** to broach to; to be taken aback; to be in irons.

eulenartig, *a.* owl-like; owlish.

eulenäugig, *a.* owl-eyed (pers., etc.).

Eulenfalter, *m. Ent:* noctua, noctuid, owlet-moth.

Eulenflucht, *f. Lit:* owl-light, dusk.

eulenhaft, *a.* owl-like; owlish; *adv.* **e. aussehen,** to look owlish, to look like an owl.

Eulennest, *n.* owl's nest.

Eulenpapagei, *m. Orn:* kakapo, owl-parrot, night-parrot.

Eulenspiegel. *Pr.n.m.* **-s.** *Lit:* Owl-glass.

Eulenspiegelei, *f.* **-/-en,** prank, roguish trick, piece of knavery.

eulenspiegeln, *v.i. insep.* (*haben*) to play pranks, roguish tricks.

Eulersch, *a. Mth:* Eulerian (constant, equation, etc.).

Eumeniden, die [ɔyme·ˈniːdən]. *Pr.n.f.pl. Gr. Myth:* the Eumenides.

Eunuch [ɔyˈnuːx], *m.* **-en/-en,** eunuch.

eunuchenhaft, *a.* (*of pers.*) eunuch-like, like a eunuch; (*of pers., voice*) effeminate.

Eunuchoidie [ɔynu·xo·i·ˈdiː], *f.* **-/.** = **Eunuchoidismus.**

Eunuchoidismus [ɔynu·xo·i·ˈdismus], *m.* **-/.** eunuchoidism.

Eupatorium [ɔypa·ˈtoːrium], *n.* **-s/-rien.** *Bot:* eupatorium.

Eupatride [ɔypa·ˈtriːdə], *m.* **-n/-n.** *Gr.Hist:* Eupatrid.

Eupen-Malmedy [ˌɔypənˈmalmədiː]. *Pr.n.n.* **-s.** *Geog:* Eupen and Malmédy.

Eupepsie [ɔypɛpˈsiː], *f.* **-/.** eupepsia, eupepsy.

eupeptisch [ɔyˈpɛptiʃ], *a.* eupeptic.

Euphemia [ɔyˈfeːmia]. *Pr.n.f.* **-s** & *Lit:* **-miens.** Euphemia.

Euphemismus [ɔyfe·ˈmismus], *m.* **-/-men,** euphemism.

euphemistisch [ɔyfe·ˈmistiʃ], *a.* euphemistic.

Euphonie [ɔyfo·ˈniː], *f.* **-/-n** [-ˈniːən], euphony.

euphonisch [ɔyˈfoːniʃ], *a.* euphonic, euphonious.

Euphonium [ɔyˈfoːnium], *n.* **-s/-nien.** *Mus:* euphonium.

Euphorbia [ɔyˈforbiaː], *f.* **-/-bien.** *Bot:* euphorbia.

Euphorbiazee [ɔyforbia·ˈtseːə], *f.* **-/-n** [-ˈtseːən]. *Bot:* (any) one of the euphorbiaceae; **die Euphorbiazeen,** the euphorbiaceae.

Euphorbie [ɔyˈforbiə], *f.* **-/-n** = **Euphorbia.**

Euphorbium [ɔyˈforbium], *n.* **-s/.** *Pharm: Vet:* euphorbium.

Euphorie [ɔyfo·ˈriː], *f.* **-/.** *Med:* euphory.

euphorisch [ɔyˈfoːriʃ], *a. Med:* euphoric.

Euphrasia [ɔyˈfraːziaː], *f.* **-/-sien.** *Bot:* euphrasy.

Euphrat, der [ˈɔyfrat]. *Pr.n.* **-(s).** *Geog:* the (river) Euphrates.

Euphrosyne [ɔyfro·ˈzyːnə]. *Pr.n.f.* **-s** & *Lit:* **-ns.** *Gr. Myth:* Euphrosyne.

Euphuismus [ɔyfu·ˈismus], *m.* **-/.** *Lit.Hist:* euphuism.

Euphuist [ɔyfu·ˈist], *m.* **-en/-en,** euphuist.

euphuistisch [ɔyfu·ˈistiʃ], *a.* euphuistic.

Eupnoe [ɔyˈpnoːeː], *f.* **-/.** *Med:* eupnoea.

Eurafrikaner [ɔyra·fri·ˈkaːnər], *m.* Eurafrican.

Eurasien [ɔyˈraːziən]. *Pr.n.n.* **-s.** *Geog:* Eurasia.

Eurasier [ɔyˈraːziər], *m.* **-s/-. 1.** *Ethn:* Eurasian. **2.** *Hist:* supporter of the Eurasian movement.

eurasisch [ɔyˈraːziʃ], *a.* **1.** *Ethn:* Eurasian. **2.** *Hist:* **die eurasische Bewegung,** the Eurasian movement.

Euratom [ɔyra·ˈtoːm], *n.* **-s.** (= **Europäische Atomgemeinschaft**) Euratom (= European Atomic Community).

eu(e)re, *poss.a. & pron. see* **euer.**

eurerseits, *adv.* on your part; on your side.

euresgleichen, *pron.* (*a*) (of) your own kind; **er ist nicht e.,** he is not (of) your own kind; **mit e. verkehre ich nicht,** I don't mix with your kind, with people like you, *F:* with the likes of you; (*b*) your equal; your equals; **ich bin e.,** I am your equal; **wir sind e.,** we are your equals.

eurethalben, *adv.* = **euretwegen.**

euretwegen, *adv.* (*a*) (i) on your account, because of you; (ii) for your sake; **ich ging e. von zu Hause weg,** I left home (i) on your account, because of you, (ii) for your sake; (*b*) on your behalf; **ich habe e. mit dem Minister gesprochen,** I spoke to the minister on your behalf.

euretwillen, *adv.* (um) e., (*a*) for your sake; **ich habe es (um) e. getan,** I did it for your sake; (*b*) on your account, because of you.

Eurhythmie [ɔyrytˈmiː], *f.* **-/. 1.** *Mus: Med: Arch: etc:* eurhythmy. **2.** *Danc:* eurhythmics.

eurhythmisch [ɔyˈrytmiʃ], *a.* eurhythmic.

eurige, der, die, das, *poss.pron.* (*decl. as adj.*) (*spelt in letters with capital* E) (*a*) yours; **wem gehören diese Bücher, sind es die eurigen?** whose books are these? are they yours? (*b*) **das Eurige, die Eurigen** = **das Eu(e)re, die Euren, die Euern,** *q.v. under* **euer** II.

euripideisch [ɔyri·pi·ˈdeːiʃ], *a.* Euripidean (tragedy, style).

Euripides [ɔyˈriːpi·deˑs, ɔyˈriːpi·dɛs]. *Pr.n.m.* **-'.** *Gr.Lit:* Euripides.

Euripos, Euripus [ˈɔyri·pos, ˈɔyri·pus]. *Pr.n.n.* **-'.** *A.Geog:* Euripus.

Europa [ɔyˈroːpaː]. *Pr.n.* **-s,** *A. & Lit:* **-pens. 1.** *f. Gr.Myth:* Europa. **2.** *n. Geog:* Europe.

Europäer [ɔyro·ˈpɛːər], *m.* **-s/-.** *Geog:* European.

europäid [ɔyro·pɛ·ˈiːt], *a.* = **europid.**

europäisch [ɔyro·ˈpɛːiʃ], *a. Geog:* European; **das Europäische Rußland,** the European part of Russia; **die Europäische Türkei,** Turkey in Europe, the European part of Turkey; **die Europäische Gemeinschaft für Kohle und Stahl,** the European Coal and Steel Community; *adv.* **e. denken,** to think as a European.

europäisieren [ɔyro·pɛ·i·ˈziːrən], *v.tr.* to Europeanize; to westernize; **sich e.,** to become Europeanized, westernized; **Europäisierung** *f,* Europeanization, westernization.

europamüde, a. tired, weary, of Europe; **Europamüde** m, f, person who is tired, weary, of Europe.
Europarat, Europa-Rat, der, the Council of Europe.
Europaunion, Europa-Union, die, the European Union.
europid [oyro·'piːt], a. Anthr: (pers., type) with European racial characteristics; white (pers., race).
Europide [oyro·'piːdə], m. -n/-n. Anthr: person with European racial characteristics; member of a white race; white.
Europium [oy'roːpĭum], n. -s/. Ch: europium.
Euryalos, Euryalus [oy'ryːa·los, oy'ryːa·lus]. Pr.n.m. -'. Lt.Lit: Euryalus.
Euryanthe [oyry·'antə]. Pr.n.f. -s & Lit: -ns. Euryanthe.
Eurydike [oy'riːdi·keː, oy'ryːdi·keː]. Pr.n.f. -s & Lit: -ns. Gr.Myth: Eurydice.
euryhalin [oyry·ha·'liːn], a. Biol: euryhaline.
Euryskop [oyry·'skoːp], n. -s/-e. Phot: euryscope.
Eurystheus [oy'rystoys]. Pr.n.m. -'. Gr.Myth: Eurystheus.
eurytherm [oyry·'tɛrm], a. eurythermal, eurythermic.
Eusebianer [oyze·bĭ'aːnər], m. -s/-. Rel.Hist: Eusebian.
eusebisch [oy'zeːbiʃ], a. Rel.Hist: Eusebian.
Eusebius [oy'zeːbĭus]. Pr.n.m. -'. Rel.Hist: Eusebius.
Euskara [oy'skaːra·], n. -s/. Ling: Euskarian, Basque.
Eustach [oys'tax]. Pr.n.m. -s. Eustace.
Eustachisch [oys'taxiʃ], a. Anat: **die Eustachische Röhre,** the Eustachian tube.
Eustachius [oys'taxĭus]. Pr.n.m. -'. Eustace.
Eutektikum [oy'tɛkti·kum], n. -s/-ka. Ch: eutectic.
eutektisch [oy'tɛktiʃ], a. Ch: eutectic.
Euter, n. -s/-, udder, dug (of cow, etc.).
Euterpe [oy'tɛrpə]. 1. Pr.n.f. -s & Lit: -ns. Gr.Myth: Euterpe. 2. f. -/-n. Bot: euterpe.
Euthanasie [oyta·na·'ziː], f. -/. euthanasia.
Eutrop [oy'troːp]. Pr.n.m. -s. Lt.Lit: Eutropius.
eutroph [oy'troːf], a. Med: eutrophic.
Eutrophie [oytro·'fiː], f. -/. Med: eutrophy.
Eutropius [oy'troːpĭus]. Pr.n.m. -'. Lt.Lit: Eutropius.
Eutyches [oy'tyːçe·s]. Pr.n.m. -'. Rel.Hist: Eutyches.
Eutychianer [oyty·çĭ'aːnər], m. -s/-. Rel.Hist: Eutychian.
eutychianisch [oyty·çĭ'aːniʃ], a. Rel.Hist: Eutychian.
Euxanthinsäure [oyksan'tiːn-], f. Ch: euxanthic acid.
Euxanthon [oyksan'toːn], n. -s/. Ch: euxanthone.
Euxenit [oykse·'niːt], m. -(e)s/. Miner: euxenite.
Euxinus [oy'ksiːnus], a. see Pontus Euxinus.
euzyklisch [oy'tsyːkliʃ], a. Bot: eucyclic, complete (flower).
Eva [eːva·]. Pr.n.f. -s. Eva; B: Eve.
Evagination [e·va·gi·na·tsĭ'oːn], f. -/-en. Med: Physiol: evagination (of sheathed organ).
Evakuant [e·va·ku·'ant], m. -en/-en. Mus: evacuant (of organ bellows).
Evakuation [e·va·ku·a·tsĭ'oːn], f. -/-en. 1. evacuation (of area, space). 2. Mil: etc: evacuation (of troops, wounded, population, etc.); withdrawal (of troops, etc.).
evakuieren [e·va·ku·'iːrən]. I. v.tr. 1. to evacuate (area, space). 2. Mil: etc: to evacuate (troops, wounded, population, etc.); to withdraw (troops, etc.); **evakuiert werden,** to be evacuated; **während des Krieges wurden wir aufs Land evakuiert,** during the war we were evacuated into the country; **evakuierte Personen, Evakuierte,** evacuated persons, evacuees. II. vbl s. 1. **Evakuieren,** n. vbl senses; also: evacuation. 2. **Evakuierung,** f. (a)=II. 1; (b) evacuation (of area, space, troops, wounded, population, etc.); **seit unserer E.,** since our evacuation, since we were evacuated; (c) pl. **Evakuierungen in großem Ausmaß,** large-scale evacuation measures; **gestern wurden die ersten Evakuierungen vorgenommen,** yesterday a start was made with the evacuation of certain areas.
Evakuierungskessel, m. Mec.E: vacuum boiler.
Evander [e·'vandər]. Pr.n.m. -s. Rom.Myth: Evander.
Evangeliar [e·vaŋge·lĭ'aːr], n. -s/-e & -ien [-ĭən]. **Evangeliarium** [-'aːrĭum], n. -s/-rien, gospel-book, gospels, evangeliary.
Evangelienabschnitt [e·vaŋ'geːlĭən-], m. section, passage, of the gospels.
Evangelienbuch, n. gospel-book, gospels.
Evangelienharmonie, f. harmony of the four Gospels, gospel-harmony.

Evangelienkonkordanz, f. (a) concordance of the Gospels; (b) concordance to the Gospels.
Evangelienpult, n. Ecc: lectern.
Evangelienseite, f. Ecc: gospel-side, north side (of altar).
Evangelimann [e·vaŋ'geːli·-], m. -(e)s/-männer. A: (esp. in Austria) bible-reading and hymn-singing mendicant.
Evangelisation [e·vaŋge·li·za·tsĭ'oːn], f. -/-en, evangelization, evangelizing (of area, etc.); **E. treiben,** to evangelize.
evangelisch [e·vaŋ'geːliʃ], a. 1. Ecc: evangelic; according to the Gospel; **die evangelische Botschaft,** the evangelic message, the message of the Gospel. 2. Rel: Lutheran protestant (church, etc.); (of pers.) **e. sein,** to be Lutheran; to be a Protestant; **Evangelische** m, f, Protestant.
evangelisch-lutherisch, a. Rel: Lutheran (church, etc.).
evangelisch-reformiert [-re·for'miːrt], a. Rel: Reformed (church, etc.).
Evangelist [e·vaŋge·'list], m. -en/-en. 1. B.Lit: Evangelist; **der E. Johannes, Johannes, der E.,** the Evangelist John, John the Evangelist. 2. evangelist (amongst the heathen or in a Christian community); evangelizer (of the heathen).
Evangelistar [e·vaŋge·lis'taːr], n. -(e)s/-e. Ecc: (gospel-)lectionary, evangelistary.
Evangelistensymbole, n.pl. symbols of the evangelists.
Evangelium [e·vaŋ'geːlĭum], n. -s/-lien, gospel; (a) **das E. des Markus,** St Mark's Gospel, the Gospel according to St Mark; **die synoptischen Evangelien,** the Synoptic Gospels; **das E. verkünden,** to preach the gospel; **auf das E. schwören,** to take an oath on the Gospel; F: **er glaubt daran wie an das, an ein, E., es ist für ihn (ein) E.,** he takes it all for gospel (truth); **sein Wort ist für sie (ein) E.,** his every word is as gospel for her; **eine Enzyklopädie ist kein E.,** an encyclopaedia is not to be taken as gospel; (b) Ecc: **das E. (des Tages),** the gospel (for the day), the pericope; **das E. verlesen,** to read the gospel (for the day).
Evaporation [e·va·po·ra·tsĭ'oːn], f. -/-en, evaporation; evaporating (of moisture).
Evaporationskraft, f. evaporative power (of the atmosphere, a fuel, etc.).
Evaporator [e·va·po·'raːtor], m. -s/-en [-ra·'toːrən]. Ind: evaporator.
evaporierbar [e·va·po·'riːr-], a. evaporable.
evaporieren [e·va·po·'riːrən], v.i. (sein) (of liquids) to evaporate; **eine Flüssigkeit e. lassen,** to evaporate, dry off, a liquid; **evaporierte Milch,** evaporated milk.
Evaporimeter [e·va·po·ri·'meːtər], **Evaporometer** [e·va·po·ro·-], n. -s/-, evaporimeter.
Evasion [e·va·zĭ'oːn], f. -/-en. 1. evasion (of sth.). 2. evasion; **Evasionen machen,** to make evasions.
evasiv [e·va·'ziːf], a. evasive.
evasorisch [e·va·'zoːriʃ], a. evasive.
Evastochter ['eːvaːs-], f. F: daughter of Eve; **sie ist eine echte E.,** she is a real daughter of Eve, she is all woman.
Evchen ['eːvçən]. Pr.n.f. -s, little Eva.
Evektion [e·vɛktsĭ'oːn], f. -/-en. Astr: evection.
Eveline [e·ve·'liːnə]. Pr.n.f. -s & Lit: -ns. Evelyn.
eventual [e·vɛntu·'aːl], a. (claims, etc.) that may occur, arise; possible (claims, etc.).
Eventualanspruch, m. Jur: auxiliary claim(s).
Eventualantrag, m. Jur: auxiliary petition, by(e) petition.
Eventualaufrechnung, f. Jur: alternative balancing off, alternative setting off (of claims).
Eventualforderung, f. Com: contingent claim.
Eventualität [e·vɛntu·a·li·'tɛːt], f. -/-en, possibility; contingency; eventuality; possible event; **du mußt für alle Eventualitäten Vorkehrungen treffen,** you must provide for all possibilities, for all contingencies, emergencies, eventualities; **wir haben alle Eventualitäten erwogen,** we have carefully considered everything that may occur, arise, we have carefully considered all contingencies, all possibilities.
eventualiter [e·vɛntu·'aːli·tər], adv. (a)=**eventuell** (b); (b) Jur: alternatively; as an alternative.
Eventualverbindlichkeiten, f.pl. Com: Fin: contingent liabilities.
eventuell [e·vɛntu·'ɛl], (a) a. possible (losses, claims, etc.); (losses, claims, etc.) that may occur, arise; **bei eventuellen Schwierigkeiten,** should any difficulties arise, occur; in case of difficulty; (b) adv. perhaps; should the occasion arise; if necessary; **würdest du dich e. bereit erklären, ihm zu helfen?** would you, if the occasion arose, say you were prepared to help

him? **du kannst e. bei uns wohnen,** you might possibly stay with us.
Everest, der ['eːvə·rest]. Pr.n. -(e)s. Geog: Everest.
Evertebrat [e·vɛrte·'braːt], m. -en/-en. Nat. Hist: invertebrate; **Evertebraten,** invertebrata.
evident [e·vi·'dɛnt], a. evident, obvious, manifest, clear, plain.
Evidenz [e·vi·'dɛnts], f. -/. (a) evidence, evidentness; manifestness (of facts, etc.); **etwas zur E. erheben,** to accept something as evident; (b) **eine Liste in E. halten,** to keep a list up to date.
Evidenzhaltung, f. keeping (of list, facts, etc.) up to date.
Eviktion [e·viktsĭ'oːn], f. -/-en. Jur: eviction, dispossession, ejectment (of tenant).
evinzibel [e·vin'tsiːbəl], a. A: 1. demonstrable. 2. Jur: evictable (tenant).
evinzieren [e·vin'tsiːrən], v.tr. Jur: A: to evict, dispossess, eject (tenant).
Eviration [e·vi·ra·tsĭ'oːn], f. -/-en, eviration; emasculation.
Eviszeration [e·vistse·ra·tsĭ'oːn], f. -/-en, evisceration.
eviszerieren [e·vistse·'riːrən], v.tr. to eviscerate, disembowel (pers.).
evoe [eːvo·'eː], int. Gr.Ant: evoe.
Evokation [e·vo·ka·tsĭ'oːn], f. -/-en. Jur: A: 1. summons, citation (of pers.). 2. evocation (of cause).
evolut [e·vo·'luːt], a. evolute (curve).
Evolute [e·vo·'luːtə], f. -/-n. Geom: evolute (curve).
Evolution [e·vo·lu·tsĭ'oːn], f. -/-en. 1. Biol: etc: evolution; development. 2. Geom: evolution (of curve). 3. Mil: Navy: A: evolution, manœuvre.
Evolutionismus [e·vo·lu·tsĭo·'nismus], m. -/. Biol: evolutionism.
evolutionistisch [e·vo·lu·tsĭo·'nistiʃ], a. Biol: etc: evolutionary (process, etc.).
Evolutionstheorie, f. Biol: doctrine of evolution.
Evolvente [e·vol'vɛntə], f. -/-n. Geom: evolvent; involute. Mec.E: involute.
Evolventenrad, n. Mec.E: involute gear.
Evolventenverzahnung, f. Mec.E: involute (toothed) gearing.
evolventisch [e·vol'vɛntiʃ], a. Geom: Mec.E: involute.
evolvieren [e·vol'viːrən], v.tr. to evolve (theory, curve, etc.).
evomieren [e·vo·'miːrən], v.tr. to vomit.
Evonymus [e·'voːny·mus], m. -/. Bot: euonymus, spindle-tree.
Evorsion [e·vorzĭ'oːn], f. -/-en. Geol: pot-hole.
evozieren [e·vo·'tsiːrən], v.tr. Jur: A: to summon (s.o.) (before the court); to issue a writ against (s.o.).
Ewe[1], f. -/-n. Poet: age, epoch.
Ewe[2] ['eːve·]. 1. Pr.n.m.pl. Ethn: Ewe, Ewe. 2. n. -/. Ling: Ewe, Ewe.
Ewenke [e·'vɛnkə], m. -n/-n & -ki. Ethn: Tungus, Tunguz.
Ewer, m. -s/-. Nau: sailing-barge; wherry; lighter.
Ewerführer, m. Nau: bargeman, bargee; wherry-man; lighterman.
Ewerkahn, m. Nau: lighter.
ewig. 1. a. (a) eternal (life, truth, etc.); everlasting, perpetual, unending, never-ending, endless (joy, bliss, etc.); **der ewige Gott, der ewige Vater, der Ewige,** God Eternal, the Eternal Father, the Father Eternal, the Eternal; **das ewige Leben,** (the) eternal, everlasting, life; **ewige Wahrheiten,** eternal truths, eternal verities, eternities; **das Ewige,** the eternal; eternal things, the things of eternity; **der ewige Wechsel der Gezeiten,** the eternal changing of the tides; **die Ewige Stadt,** the Eternal City (i.e. Rome); **sie schworen sich ewige Freundschaft,** they swore eternal friendship; **zum ewigen Andenken,** (i) to remind you always; (ii) to the everlasting, immortal, memory (of s.o.); **ewiger Schnee,** perpetual, everlasting, eternal, snow; **der Ewige Jude,** the Wandering Jew, Ahasuerus; **ein ewiger Student,** a perpetual student; **das ewige Licht,** the light of eternity, the light perpetual; Ecc: **die Ewige Lampe, das Ewige Licht,** the sanctuary-lamp; Fin: **ewige Anleihe,** perpetual bond; **ewige Rente,** perpetual annuity, perpetuity; G.Hist: **der Ewige Landfriede,** the Perpetual Peace (of 1495); Swiss Hist: **die Ewige Richtung,** the Perpetual Settlement (of 1474); Min: **ewige Teufe,** unlimited depth; Bot: **ewiger Klee,** lucerne, alfalfa; **ewige Zwiebel,** (i) Welsh onion, stone-leek; (ii) shallot, Dial: scallion; see also **Jagdgrund** 2, **Kalender**[1]

2, **Ruhe** 1 (*a*); (*b*) *F:* constant, endless, perpetual (strife, chatter, etc.); **ein ewiges Einerlei,** an unending monotony; **nach ewigem Hin und Her kamen sie endlich zu einem Entschluß,** after endless chopping and changing they finally reached a decision; **ich bin deine ewigen Beschwerden leid,** I am tired of your everlasting, endless, complaints; **laßt euer ewiges Gezänk!** stop your eternal bickering! **2.** *adv.* (*a*) for ever; for evermore; always; **sein Andenken wird ewig fortleben,** his memory will last for ever, will never fade; **ich werde ihn ewig lieben,** I shall love him always; **das wird mir ewig leid tun,** I shall always regret, be sorry for, it; **auf ewig, auf immer und ewig,** for ever, for evermore, for ever and ever; *Lit:* **das tut mir ewig leid,** I am very sorry about it; (*b*) *F:* **ewig und drei Tage,** for ever and a day; **ich hab ihn ewig nicht gesehen,** it is ages, an age, since I saw him, I have not seen him for ages; **das dauert ewig,** that takes *or* will take ages; that will take a month of Sundays; **zankt euch doch nicht ewig!** don't keep quarrelling!

Ewiggeld, *n. Fin:* = **ewige Rente,** *q.v. under* **ewig** 1 (*a*).

Ewigkeit, *f.* **1.** eternal existence, eternity (of God, laws, truth, etc.); eternalness, eternality, everlastingness (of laws, truth, fame, etc.). **2.** eternity; **in alle E.,** for ever and ever; in all eternity; to, for, in perpetuity; **von E. zu E.,** from everlasting to everlasting; (*in prayer formula*) for ever and ever; (*prayer formula*) **wie es war im Anfang, . . . und von E. zu E., . . . und in E.,** as it was in the beginning, . . . world without end; **in die, zur, E. eingehen,** to pass into eternity; to enter into eternal life; *F:* **jede Minute wurde mir zur E.,** every minute seemed an eternity, an age, to me; *F:* **das wird eine E. dauern,** that will take an age, ages, that will take a month of Sundays.

Ewigkeitsblume, *f. Bot:* everlasting (flower), immortelle.

ewiglich, *adv.* for ever, for evermore.

Ewig-Weibliche, das. *Lit. & F:* the Eternal Feminine.

ex [ɛks], *prep.* out; out of; from; without; (*a*) (*in Lt. adv. phr.*) *ex improviso,* suddenly; *ex officio,* ex officio, by virtue of one's office; (*b*) (*in adv. phr.*) *Fin:* **ex Dividende,** ex dividend; **ex Coupon,** ex coupon, without interest; **diese Aktien werden ex Dividende notiert,** these shares are quoted ex dividend; (*c*) *F:* **damit ist es ex!** that's over, that's the end of it! **ex!** drink up! down the hatch! bottoms up!

ex-, Ex-, *pref.* **1.** (*a*) ex-; **exhumieren,** to exhume; **Exfoliation** *f*, exfoliation; (*b*) dis-; *Surg:* **Exartikulation** *f*, disarticulation. **2.** ex-, former . . . ; **Exminister** *m*, ex-minister; **Exkaiser** *m*, ex-emperor, former emperor; *F:* **Exgeliebte** *f*, ex-mistress.

exact [ɛksᵊlakt, ɛˈksakt], *a.* = **exakt.**

Exactheit, *f.* = **Exaktheit.**

Exaggeration [ɛks(ᵊ)ageˈraˑtsĭˈoˑn], *f.* -/-en, exaggeration; overstatement; aggravation (of disease, etc.).

exaggerieren [ɛks(ᵊ)ageˈriˑrən], *v.tr.* to exaggerate (sth.).

exakt [ɛksᵊlakt, ɛˈksakt], *a.* exact, accurate (result, calculation, etc.); precise, accurate (information, description, etc.); **eine exakte Wiedergabe,** a close, true, exact, copy; **die exakten Wissenschaften,** the exact sciences; *adv.* **er arbeitet sehr e.,** his work is very accurate, exact.

Exaktheit, *f.* exactness, exactitude, accuracy (of statement, calculation, etc.); closeness (of copy, etc.).

Exaktion [ɛks(ᵊ)aktsĭˈoˑn], *f.* -/-en. **1.** exaction (of tax, etc.). **2.** extortion.

Exaltado [ɛksalˈtaˑdo], *m.* -s/-s. **1.** *Spanish Hist:* Exaltado. **2.** *F:* hot-head, fanatic; fire-eater.

Exaltation [ɛksaltaˑtsĭˈoˑn], *f.* -/. **1.** *Astr:* exaltation (of planet). **2.** (*a*) exaltation, rapture; (*b*) over-enthusiasm.

exaltiert [ɛksalˈtiˑrt], *a.* (*a*) uplifted, exalted, rapturous (state of mind); (*b*) *F:* (over-)excited; (over-)enthusiastic; *adv. F:* **e. tun, sich e. gebärden,** to indulge in fussy sentiment; to gush; **e. über etwas sprechen,** to enthuse, gush, about sth.

Examen [ɛˈksaˑmən], *n.* -s/- & -mina, examination, *F:* exam; **mündliches E.,** oral examination, viva (voce), *F:* oral; **schriftliches E.,** written examination; **ein E. ablegen, machen,** to go in for, sit (for), an examination; **ein E. bestehen,** to pass (in) an examination; **ein E. nicht**

bestehen, *F:* **in einem E. durchfallen, durch ein E. fallen,** to fail an examination; *F:* **ins E. steigen,** to go in for the examination.

Examensarbeit, *f.* **1.** (i) examination paper; (ii) thesis presented for an examination. **2.** work for an examination.

Examensaufgabe, *f.* examination question *or* test; (piece of) work required for an examination.

Examensfieber, *n. F:* exam(ination) fever.

Examenskandidat, *m.* (examination) candidate, examinee.

Examinand [ɛksaˑmiˈnant], *m.* -en/-en [-ˈnandən], examinee.

Examination [ɛksaˑmiˈnaˑtsĭˈoˑn], *f.* -/-en, examination.

Examinator [ɛksaˑmiˈnaˑtor], *m.* -s/-en [-naˈtoˑrən], examiner.

Examinatorium [ɛksaˑmiˈnaˈtoˑrĭum], *n.* -s/-ria. **1.** examining board, (board of) examiners. **2.** revision course.

examinieren [ɛksaˑmiˈniˑrən], *v.tr.* to examine (candidate); to investigate, inspect, scrutinize (facts, etc.); to examine, *F:* go over (patient).

Exanthem [ɛks(ᵊ)anˈteˑm], *n.* -s/-e. *Med:* exanthem, exanthema.

exanthematisch [ɛks(ᵊ)anteˈmaˑtiʃ], *a. Med:* exanthematous.

Exaration [ɛks(ᵊ)aˈraˑtsĭˈoˑn], *f.* -/-en. *Geol:* exaration; glacial erosion.

exarch[1], [ɛksᵊlarç], *a. Bot:* exarch.

Exarch[2], *m.* -en/-en. *Hist:* exarch.

Exarchat [ɛksᵊarˈçaˑt], *n.* -(e)s/-e. *Hist:* exarchate.

Exartikulation [ɛks(ᵊ)artiˑkuˑlaˑtsĭˈoˑn], *f.* -/-en. *Surg:* disarticulation, disjointing; amputation through the joint.

Exasperationsprinzip [ɛksaspeˈraˑtsĭˈoˑns-], *n. Jur:* (principle of) increasing the severity of punishment.

Exaudi [ɛksᵊlaudĭ], *m.* -/. *Ecc:* Exaudi (Sunday).

exc- *cp.* **exz-.**

ex cathedra [ɛksˈkateˈdraˑ]. *Lt. adv.phr.* ex cathedra, infallibly; **ex cathedra sprechen,** (i) (*of pope*) to speak ex cathedra, (ii) to speak with authority; *F:* to speak in a dogmatic, doctrinaire, way.

Exe [ˈɛksə], *f.* -/-n. *A:* axe.

Exeat [ˈɛks(ᵊ)eˈat], *n.* -s/. *Ecc:* exeat, permission to leave the diocese.

Exedra [ˈɛkseˈdraˑ], *f.* -/-dren. *Arch:* ex(h)edra.

Exegese [ɛkseˈgeˑzə], *f.* -/-n. *Theol:* exegesis.

Exeget [ɛkseˈgeˑt], *m.* -en/-en. *Theol:* exegete.

Exegetik [ɛkseˈgeˑtik], *f.* -/. *Theol:* exegetics.

exegetisch [ɛkseˈgeˑtiʃ], *a. Theol:* exegetic(al).

Exekration [ɛkseˈkraˑtsĭˈoˑn], *f.* -/-en = **Exsekration.**

exekutabel [ɛkseˈkuˈtaˑbəl], *a. Jur:* executable, enforceable (measure, etc.).

exekutieren [ɛkseˈkuˈtiˑrən], *v.* **1.** *v.tr.* (*a*) to execute, carry out (orders, etc.); to enforce (the law); (*b*) to execute (criminal), put (criminal) to death; (*c*) *Jur:* to distrain upon (debtor). **2.** *v.i.* (*haben*) *St.Exch:* (i) to buy in; (ii) to sell out.

Exekution [ɛkseˈkuˈtsĭˈoˑn], *f.* -/-en, (*a*) execution, performance, carrying out (of orders, etc.); (*b*) execution (of criminal); (*c*) *Jur:* distraint, distress, execution; (*d*) *St.Exch:* (i) buying in, (ii) selling out.

Exekutionsauftrag, *m. St.Exch:* (i) order to buy in; (ii) order to sell out.

Exekutionsbefehl, *m. Jur:* writ of execution, elegit.

exekutionsfrei, *a. Jur:* **exekutionsfreies Vermögen,** property that cannot be distrained, property not distrainable.

Exekutionskauf, *m. St.Exch:* buying in.

Exekutionskommando, *n. Mil: etc:* execution squad; firing squad.

Exekutionsmannschaft, *f.* troops charged with a military, etc., execution.

Exekutionsstück, *n. St.Exch:* security bought in (for compulsory fulfilment of contract).

Exekutionsverkauf, *m. St.Exch:* selling out.

exekutiv [ɛkseˈkuˈtiˑf], *a. Pol: Jur:* executive; **die exekutive Staatsgewalt, die Exekutive** [ɛkseˈkuˈtiˑvə], the executive (power).

Exekutivgewalt, die. *Pol:* the executive power.

Exekutivorgan, *n. Adm:* executive organ.

Exekutivrat, *m. Adm:* Executive Council.

Exekutor [ɛkseˈkuˑtor], *m.* -s/-en [-kuˈtoˑrən]. *Jur: A:* bailiff.

exekutorisch [ɛkseˈkuˈtoˑriʃ], *a. Jur:* (recovery, etc.) by way of restraint.

Exempel [ɛˈksɛmpəl], *n.* -s/. **1.** example, instance; *F:* **ein E. statuieren,** to set a warning example,

F: to give a horrid warning. **2.** *Mth:* problem, sum; **(die) Probe aufs E. machen,** (i) to check (the result) back; (ii) *F:* to put sth. to a test, to put sth. to trial.

Exemplar [ɛksɛmˈplaˑr], *n.* -s/-e, (*a*) specimen, sample, piece; example; **das schönste E. in seiner Sammlung,** the finest specimen, piece, in his collection; **ein seltenes E.,** a rare specimen; **dieser Typ hat sich nur in wenigen Exemplaren erhalten,** only a few examples of this type have survived; (*b*) copy (of book, engraving, etc.); **der Autor erhält zehn Exemplare,** the author receives ten copies.

exemplarisch [ɛksɛmˈplaˑriʃ], *a.* exemplary (punishment, etc.).

Exemplarismus [ɛksɛmplaˈrismus], *m.* -/. *Phil:* exemplarism.

Exemplifikation [ɛksɛmpliˑfiˑkaˑtsĭˈoˑn], *f.* -/-en. **1.** exemplification, illustration by examples. **2.** *A:* attested copy (of document).

exemplifizieren [ɛksɛmpliˑfiˈtsiˑrən], *v.tr.* to exemplify (sth.); **etwas an einem Fall e.,** to use a case as an example of sth., to use a case to illustrate sth.

exemt [ɛksᵊlɛmt, ɛˈksɛmt], *a.* exempt (from tax, jurisdiction, etc.).

Exemtion [ɛksɛmˈtsĭˈoˑn], *f.* -/-en, exemption (from tax, jurisdiction, etc.); *Ecc:* exemption from the jurisdiction of a bishop.

Exenteration [ɛks(ᵊ)enteˈraˑtsĭˈoˑn], *f.* -/-en. *Surg:* exenteration.

Exequatur [ɛkseˈkvaˑtuˑr], *n.* -s/. *Jur:* (consul's) exequatur.

Exequialmesse [ɛksekvĭˈaˑl-], *f. R.C.Ch:* exequial mass.

Exequien [ɛˈksekvĭən], *n.pl. R.C.Ch:* exequial mass.

exequieren [ɛkseˈkviˑrən], *v.tr.* **1.** to execute (orders, etc.). **2.** *Jur:* to distrain upon (a pers.).

Exerzieranzug, *m. Mil:* drill uniform.

Exerzierausbildung, *f. Mil: etc:* drill.

exerzieren [ɛksɛrˈtsiˑrən], *v.* **I.** *v.* **1.** *v.i.* (*haben*) to drill. **2.** *v.tr.* to drill (soldiers, etc.).
II. *vbl s.* **Exerzieren,** *n.* **1.** drilling (of soldiers). **2.** drill.

Exerziergeschoß, *n. Artil:* dummy shell.

Exerzierhalle, *f. Mil:* drill hall.

Exerzierhaus, *n. Mil:* drill shed.

Exerzierknochen, *m. Med:* rider's bone; myositis ossificans.

Exerziermunition, *f. Mil: Navy:* dummy ammunition.

Exerzierpatrone, *f. Mil:* dummy (cartridge).

Exerzierplatz, *m. Mil:* parade ground, *F:* (the) square.

Exerzierreglement, *n. Mil: A:* drill regulations.

Exerzierschritt, *m. Mil: A:* ceremonial march; goose-step.

Exerziertorpedo, *n. Navy:* dummy torpedo.

Exerziervorschrift, *f.* (*a*) regulation governing drill; (*b*) drill book.

Exerzitium [ɛksɛrˈtsiˑtsĭum], *n.* -s/-tien. **1.** *Sch:* (written) exercise. **2.** *pl.* **Exerzitien,** *R.C.Ch:* religious exercises.

Exfoliation [ɛksfoˈlĭaˈtsĭˈoˑn], *f.* -/-en. *Physiol: etc:* exfoliation.

Exhalation [ɛkshaˈlaˈtsĭˈoˑn], *f.* -/-en. *Physiol: Geol: etc:* exhalation.

Exhaustion [ɛkshaustsĭˈoˑn], *f.* -/. *esp. Mth:* exhaustion.

Exhaustionsmethode, *f. Mth:* method of exhaustion; **geometrische E.,** method of geometric exhaustion.

Exhaustor [ɛksˈhaustor], *m.* -s/-en [-ˈtoˑrən], (gas-)exhaustor, suction fan.

exheredieren [ɛkshereˈreˈdiˑrən], *v.tr.* to exheredate, disinherit (s.o.).

exhibieren [ɛkshiˈbiˑrən], *v.tr.* (*a*) to produce, present, submit (documents, etc.); (*b*) to exhibit, show (pictures, etc.).

Exhibit [ɛkshiˈbiˑt], *n.* -(e)s/-e, application, petition (in writing).

Exhibition [ɛkshiˈbiˑtsĭˈoˑn], *f.* -/-en, (*a*) producing, production (of document, etc.); (*b*) exhibition (of picture, etc.).

Exhibitionismus [ɛkshiˑbiˑtsĭoˈnismus], *m.* -/. *Jur: Psy:* exhibitionism, *esp. Jur:* indecent exposure.

Exhibitionist [ɛkshiˑbiˑtsĭoˈnist], *m.* -en/-en. *Jur: Psy:* exhibitionist.

exhumieren [ɛkshuˈmiˑrən], *v.tr.* to exhume, disinter (body); **Exhumierung** *f*, exhumation, disinterment.

Exigenz [ɛksiˈgɛnts], *f.* -/-en, exigency, exigence; requirement(s), demand(s).

exigieren [ɛksiˑˈgiːrən], *v.tr.* to demand (payment, etc.).

Exil [ɛˈksiːl], *n.* **-s/-e**, exile; **ins E. gehen,** to go into exile; **im E. leben,** to live in exile.

exilieren [ɛksiˑˈliːrən], *v.tr.* to exile (s.o.).

Exilregierung, *f.* government in exile.

eximieren [ɛksiˑˈmiːrən], *v.tr.* **j-n von etwas e.,** to exempt s.o. from sth.

Exine [ɛˈksiːnə], *f.* **-/-n.** *Bot:* exine.

existent [ɛksisˈtɛnt], *a.* existing, existent.

existential [ɛksistɛntsĭˈaːl], *a. Phil:* existential.

Existentialismus [ɛksistɛntsĭaˑˈlismus], *m.* **-/.** *Phil:* existentialism.

Existentialist [ɛksistɛntsĭaˑˈlist], *m.* **-en/-en.** *Phil:* existentialist.

existentialistisch [ɛksistɛntsĭaˑˈlistiʃ], *a. Phil:* existentialist.

Existentialität [ɛksistɛntsĭaˑliˑˈtɛːt], *f.* **-/.** *Phil:* existentiality.

Existentialphilosophie [ɛksistɛntsĭˈaːlfiˑloˑzoˑˌfiː], *f.* existential philosophy, existentialism.

existentiell [ɛksɪstɛntsĭˈɛl], *a.* existential.

Existenz [ɛksiˈstɛnts], *f.* **-/-en. 1.** existence; **an der E. Gottes zweifeln,** to doubt the existence of God, to doubt whether God exists; **die bloße E. dieses Phänomens genügt, zu beweisen, daß . . . ,** the mere existence of this phenomenon is sufficient to prove that . . . **2.** *(a)* life, existence; **j-s E. bedrohen,** to threaten s.o.'s very existence; **sich in seiner E. bedroht fühlen,** to feel that one's very existence is threatened, is in jeopardy, is at stake; **es ist eine Frage der E.,** it is a matter of life and death; *(b)* (material) existence; means of existence; subsistence; **eine kümmerliche E.,** a miserable existence; **diese Stellung bietet Ihnen eine gesicherte E.,** this position offers you a secure living; **eine auskömmliche E. haben,** to have enough to live on, to subsist upon; **ihre E. war durch den Tod ihres Mannes gefährdet,** her material existence was jeopardized by the death of her husband; **er wanderte aus, um sich in Amerika eine neue E. aufzubauen,** he emigrated in order to build a new life for himself in America. **3.** *(pers.)* **eine merkwürdige E.,** a remarkable personality; a curious individual; **dunkle, zweifelhafte, Existenzen,** shady, dubious, individuals; **eine verkrachte E.,** a person who has made shipwreck of his life.

Existenzbeweis, *m.* proof of the existence (of sth., *Mth:* of a quantity).

existenzfähig, *a.* capable of existing, of maintaining a separate existence; *Biol: Obst:* viable (organism, child).

Existenzfrage, *f.* matter of life and death.

Existenzgrundlage, *f.* basis of subsistence; basis of existence.

existenzial [ɛksistɛntsĭˈaːl], *a.* = **existential.**

Existenzialismus [ɛksistɛntsĭaˑˈlismus], *m.* **-/.** = **Existentialismus.**

Existenzialurteil, *n. Log:* existential proposition.

Existenzkampf, *m.* struggle for existence, for life.

Existenzminimum, *n.* (bare) subsistence level; *Pol.Ec:* living wage.

Existenzmittel, *n.* means of subsistence; *pl.* **Existenzmittel,** basic means of subsistence; basic livelihood; *Pol.Ec:* basic goods and services.

Existenzphilosophie, *f.* = **Existentialphilosophie.**

existieren [ɛksisˈtiːrən], *v.i.* *(haben)* **1.** to exist; **er zweifelt daran, daß Gott existiert,** he doubts whether God exists, he doubts the existence of God; **existiert dieser Name überhaupt?** does this name exist at all? **2. e. können,** *(a)* to be able to exist, live; **die Pflanze kann in diesem Klima nicht e.,** the plant cannot exist, survive, in this climate; **in einem so schmutzigen Haus könnte ich nicht e.,** I could not manage to exist in a house as dirty as that; *(b) F:* to subsist; to (manage to) keep alive; **sein Gehalt ist nicht hoch genug, daß er (davon) e. könnte,** his salary is not enough for him to subsist on, *F:* not enough to keep him alive.

Exitus [ˈɛksiˑtus], *m.* **-/.** *(a)* end, close, conclusion; *(b) Med:* death, exitus.

Exkardination [ɛkskardiˑnaˑtsĭˈoːn], *f.* **-/-en.** *R.C.Ch:* excardination (of a cleric).

Exkavation [ɛkskaˑvaˑtsĭˈoːn], *f.* **-/-en. 1.** excavation, excavating. **2.** excavation, hollow.

Exkavator [ɛkskaˑˈvaːtor], *m.* **-s/-en** [-vaˑˈtoːrən], *(a) Civ.E: etc:* digging machine, digger, excavator, grub; mechanical navvy; steam-navvy; *(b) Dent.Surg:* *(instrument)* excavator.

exkavieren [ɛkskaˑˈviːrən], *v.tr.* to excavate, dig out.

Exklamation [ɛksklaˑmaˑtsĭˈoːn], *f.* **-/-en,** exclamation.

exklamieren [ɛksklaˑˈmiːrən], *v.tr.* to exclaim (sth.).

Exklave [ɛksˈklaːvə], *f.* **-/-n.** *Pol:* exclave.

exkludieren [ɛkskluˑˈdiːrən], *v.tr.* to exclude (s.o., sth.).

Exklusion [ɛkskluˑzĭˈoːn], *f.* **-/-en,** exclusion (of s.o., sth.); expulsion (of s.o.).

exklusiv [ɛkskluˑˈziːf], *a.* *(a)* exclusive, sole (right, etc.); *(b)* exclusive, select (society, club, circle, party); exclusive (hotel).

exklusive [ɛkskluˑˈziːvə], *(abbr.* **exkl.**) *adv.* exclusive; exclusive of, excluding; **fünf Personen, Fahrer e.,** five persons excluding, exclusive of, the driver; **der Preis versteht sich e. Verpackung,** the price does not include packing, is exclusive of packing; **vom 10. bis zum 15. e.,** from the 10th to the 14th inclusive; **von Kapitel 10 bis 20 e.,** chapters 10 to 19 inclusive.

Exklusivität [ɛkskluˑziˑviˑˈtɛːt], *f.* **-/.** exclusiveness (of club, circle, etc.).

Exkommunikation [ɛkskomuˑniˑkaˑtsĭˈoːn], *f.* **-/-en.** *R.C.Ch:* excommunication; **kleine, große, E.,** lesser, greater, excommunication.

exkommunizieren [ɛkskomuˑniˑˈtsiːrən], *v.tr.* *R.C.Ch:* to excommunicate (s.o.); **Exkommunizierte** *m, f,* excommunicated person.

Exkoriation [ɛkskoˑriˑaˑtsĭˈoːn], *f.* **-/-en,** excoriation, abrasion (of skin).

exkoriieren [ɛkskoˑriˑˈiːrən], *v.tr.* to excoriate, abrade (skin, etc.); to flay (animal).

Exkrement [ɛkskreˑˈmɛnt], *n.* **-(e)s/-e.** *Physiol: etc:* excrement.

Exkret [ɛksˈkreːt], *n.* **-(e)s/-e.** *Physiol:* excreted matter; excretion; *pl.* **Exkrete,** excreta.

Exkretion [ɛkskreˑtsĭˈoːn], *f.* **-/-en.** *Physiol:* **1.** excreting, excretion. **2.** excreted matter, excretion.

Exkretionsorgan, *n. Anat:* excretory organ.

Exkulpation [ɛkskulpaˑtsĭˈoːn], *f.* **-/-en,** exculpation, exoneration.

exkulpieren [ɛkskulˈpiːrən], *v.tr.* to exculpate, exonerate (s.o.).

Exkurs [ɛksˈkurs], *m.* **-es/-e,** excursus.

Exkursion [ɛkskurzĭˈoːn], *f.* **-/-en,** *(a) Sch:* (i) *(short)* excursion, study outing; (ii) study trip, study tour; *(b) F:* **eine E. in die Geschichte machen,** to make an excursion into history.

exlex [ˈɛkslɛks], *a.* outlawed.

Exmatrikel [ɛksmaˑˈtrikəl], *f.* **-/-n.** *Sch:* (i) certificate of withdrawal from the register of students; (ii) certificate of completion of studies.

Exmatrikulation [ɛksmaˑtrikuˑlaˑtsĭˈoːn], *f.* **-/-en.** *Sch:* removal *or* withdrawal (of s.o.'s *or* one's name) from the register of students *(on completion of studies or when changing to another university)*.

exmatrikulieren [ɛksmaˑtrikuˑˈliːrən]. *Sch:* **1.** *v.tr.* to remove (s.o.'s name) from the register of students. **2.** *v.i.* *(haben)* & **sich exmatrikulieren,** to have one's name removed from the register of students. **3.** *vbl s.* **Exmatrikulieren** *n,* **Exmatrikulierung** *f* = **Exmatrikulation.**

Exmission [ɛksmisĭˈoːn], *f.* **-/-en.** *Jur:* evictment, ejection (of tenant).

exmittieren [ɛksmiˈtiːrən], *v.tr. Jur:* to evict, eject (tenant).

exo-, Exo- [ɛksoˑ-], *pref.* exo-; **exogam,** exogamous; **Exoplasma** *n,* exoplasm.

Exodermis [ɛksoˑˈdɛrmis], *f.* **-/-men.** *Biol:* exoderm.

Exodium [ɛks(ʔ)ˈoːdĭum], *n.* **-s/-dien.** *Rom.Th:* exodium.

Exodos [ˈɛksoˑdos], *m.* **-& -doi.** *Gr.Th:* *(a)* final stasimon; *(b)* exode, exodium.

Exodus [ˈɛksoˑdus], *m.* **-/. 1.** *B.Hist:* exodus (of the Israelites). **2.** *B:* **der E.,** (the book of) Exodus. **3.** = **Exodos.**

ex officio [ɛks oˈfiːtsĭoː]. *Lt. adv.phr.* officially, *ex(-)officio;* **ex officio handeln,** to act in virtue of one's office.

exogam [ɛksoˈgaːm], *a. Anthr:* exogamous.

Exogamie [ɛksoˑgaˑˈmiː], *f.* **-/.** *Anthr:* exogamy.

exogen [ɛksoˈgeːn], *a. Bot:* exogenous; *Geol:* exogenetic.

exogenetisch [ɛksoˑgeˑˈneːtiʃ], *a. Geol:* exogenetic.

Exokarp [ɛksoˑˈkarp], *n.* **-(e)s/-e.** *Bot:* exocarp.

Exomphalus [ɛksʔˈomfaˑlus], *m.* **-/-li.** *Med:* exomphalos, umbilical hernia.

Exoneration [ɛks(ʔ)oˑneˑraˑtsĭˈoːn], *f.* **-/-en,** exoneration.

exonerieren [ɛks(ʔ)oˑneˑˈriːrən], *v.tr.* to exonerate (s.o.).

Exophthalmie [ɛks(ʔ)oftalˈmiː], *f.* **-/-n** [-ˈmiːən]. *Med:* exophthalmia, exophthalmus.

exophthalmisch [ɛks(ʔ)ofˈtalmiʃ], *a. Med:* exophthalmic.

exorbitant [ɛks(ʔ)orbiˑˈtant], *a.* exorbitant.

Exorbitanz [ɛks(ʔ)orbiˑˈtants], *f.* **-/-en,** exorbitance.

Exordium [ɛksʔˈordĭum], *n.* **-s/-dien.** *Rh:* exordium.

exorzieren [ɛks(ʔ)orˈtsiːrən], **exorzisieren** [ɛks(ʔ)ortsiˑˈziːrən], *v.tr. Ecc:* to exorcise, cast out (demon); to expel (evil spirit).

Exorzismus [ɛks(ʔ)orˈtsismus], *m.* **-/-men.** *Ecc:* exorcism.

Exorzist [ɛks(ʔ)orˈtsist], *m.* **-en/-en.** *Ecc:* exorcist, exorcizer.

Exosmose [ɛks(ʔ)oˈsmoːzə], *f.* **-/-n.** *Ph:* exosmosis.

exosmotisch [ɛks(ʔ)osˈmoːtiʃ], *a. Ph:* exosmotic.

Exosphäre [ɛksoˑˈsfɛːrə], *f.* **-/.** *Meteor: Rocketry:* exosphere: last zone of the earth's atmosphere.

Exospore [ɛksoˑˈspoːrə], *n.* **-s/-n.** *Fung:* exospore.

Exostose [ɛks(ʔ)osˈtoːze], *f.* **-/-n.** *Med:* exostosis.

Exot [ɛˈksoːt], *m.* **-en/-en, Exote** [ɛˈksoːtə], *m.* **-n/-n. 1.** *(a)* exotic (plant, animal); *(b)* exotic (pers.). **2.** *Fin:* foreign share *or* bond.

Exoteriker [ɛksoˑˈteːrikər], *m.* **-s/-,** exoteric, uninitiated person.

exoterisch [ɛksoˑˈteːriʃ], *a.* exoteric (doctrine, disciples).

exotherm [ɛksoˑˈtɛrm], *a. Ch:* exothermic (reaction, etc.).

Exotik [ɛˈksoːtik], *f.* **-/.** exoticism.

exotisch [ɛˈksoːtiʃ], *a.* exotic.

Expander [ɛksˈpandər], *m.* **-s/-. 1.** *Gym:* (chest) expander. **2.** *Telecom:* (volume) expander.

Expanderverstärker, *m. Telecom:* volume expander.

expandieren [ɛkspanˈdiːrən], *v.tr.* *(a) Ph:* to expand, dilate (gases, solids, etc.); *(b)* to expand, extend (trade, etc.); *(c) Ph: etc:* **sich e.,** to expand.

expansibel [ɛkspanˈziːbəl], *a. Ph: etc:* expansible, expandable.

Expansibilität [ɛkspanziˑbiˑliˑˈtɛːt], *f.* **-/.** expansibility, expandibility.

Expansion [ɛkspanzĭˈoːn], *f.* **-/-en,** *(a) Ph: etc:* expansion, dilatation, dilation (of gases, solids, etc.); *Mch:* expansion (of steam); *(b)* expansion (of trade, of an empire).

Expansionist [ɛkspanzĭoˑˈnist], *m.* **-en/-en,** expansionist.

expansionistisch [ɛkspanzĭoˑˈnistiʃ], *a.* expansionist.

Expansionsbestrebung, *f. Pol.Ec: etc:* effort(s) to expand; expansionist tendencies.

Expansionsblatt, *n. Tex:* expanding reed.

Expansionsdampfmaschine, *f. Mch:* expansion (steam-)engine.

Expansionsdorn, *m. Mec.E:* expanding mandrel.

Expansionsdrang, *m. Pol.Ec: etc:* urge to expand; expansionist tendencies.

Expansionsgefäß, *n. Mch:* expansion chamber.

Expansionsgelüst, *n. Pol.Ec: etc:* appetite for expansion; expansionist tendencies.

Expansionsgeschoß, *n. Sm.a: A:* expanding bullet, dum-dum bullet.

Expansionsgrad, *m. Ph: etc:* degree of expansion.

Expansionskälte, *f. Ph:* cooling effect in adiabatic expansion; Joule-Thompson effect.

Expansionskamm, *m. Tex:* expanding reed.

Expansionskraft, *f. Ph: etc:* expansive force.

Expansionskurve, *f. Ph:* expansion curve.

Expansionsmaschine, *f. Mch:* expansion (steam-) engine.

Expansionsmuffe, *f. Mec.E:* expansion joint.

Expansionspolitik, *f.* policy of expansion, expansionist policy.

Expansionsreservoir, *n. Plumb:* expansion tank.

Expansionsriet, *n. Tex:* expanding reed.

Expansionsrohr, *n. Mec.E:* expansion pipe.

Expansionsschalter, *m. El.E:* expansion circuit breaker.

Expansionsschieber, *m. Mch:* expansion slide valve.

Expansionssteuerung, *f. Mch:* expansion valve gear.

Expansionsventil, *n. Mch:* expansion valve.

expansiv [ɛkspanˈziːf], *a.* expansive (growth, etc.).

Expansivkraft, *f. Ph:* = **Expansionskraft.**

Expatriation [ɛkspaˑtrĭaˑtsĭˈoːn], *f.* **-/-en,** expatriation.

expatriieren [ɛkspaˑtriˑˈiːrən], *v.tr.* to deprive (s.o.) of citizenship; to banish, exile (s.o.); to expatriate (s.o.).

Expectorans [ɛksˈpɛktoˑrans], *n.* **-/-rantia & -rantien** [-ˈrantsĭaː & -ˈrantsĭən] = **Expektorantium.**

Expedient [ɛkspeˑdĭˈɛnt], *m.* **-en/-en.** *Com:* (forwarding) clerk.

expedieren [ɛkspeˑˈdiːrən], *v.tr.* to dispatch, send

(off) (letter, goods, *F:* pers.); to forward (letter, goods); to ship (goods, consignment) (*by sea, F: by road or rail*).

Expedit [ɛkspeˈdiːt], *n.* **-(e)s/-e.** *Com: Austrian:* dispatch department.

Expedition [ɛkspe·di·tsĭˈoːn], *f.* **-/-en.** **1.** (*a*) dispatch(ing), forwarding (of goods, parcel, letter, etc.); **E. per Schiff,** shipping, shipment; (*b*) dispatch department. **2.** (*a*) (military) expedition; (*b*) (exploring, archaeological) expedition; (archaeological) mission; **die E. zum Südpol,** the expedition to the South Pole; **die E. bestand aus fünf Mitgliedern,** the expedition consisted of five members. **3.** *A:* office, bureau (of newspaper, etc.).

Expeditionstruppen, *f.pl.* *Mil:* expeditionary troops.

Expektorantium [ɛkspɛkto·ˈrantsĭum], *n.* **-s/-tien.** *Pharm:* expectorant.

Expektoration [ɛkspɛkto·ra·tsĭˈoːn], *f.* **-/-en.** **1.** *Med:* (*a*) expectoration, expectorating, coughing up (of phlegm); (*b*) expectoration, expectorated matter. **2.** *F:* (long-winded) outpouring.

expektorieren [ɛkspɛkto·ˈriːrən], *v.tr.* **1.** *Med:* to expectorate (phlegm). **2.** *Lit:* **sich expektorieren,** to pour out one's heart, to unbosom oneself.

Expensen [ɛksˈpɛnzən], *pl.* *Com:* expenses, costs; (legal) fees.

Experiment [ɛkspe·ri·ˈmɛnt], *n.* **-(e)s/-e,** experiment; **chemisches E.,** chemical experiment; **Experimente an, mit, Tieren,** experiments (up)on, with, animals; **mit etwas Experimente machen, anstellen,** to experiment with sth., to make, try, experiments with sth.

experimental [ɛkspe·ri·mɛnˈtaːl], *a.* experimental.

Experimental-, *comb.fm.* experimental . . . ; **Experimentalchemie** *f,* experimental chemistry; **Experimentalphysik** *f,* experimental physics; **Experimentalpsychologie** *f,* experimental psychology.

Experimentator [ɛkspe·ri·mɛnˈtaːtor], *m.* **-s/-en** [-ta·ˈtoːrən]. **1.** experimenter, experimentalist. **2.** *Sch: etc:* demonstrator.

experimentell [ɛkspe·ri·mɛnˈtɛl], *a.* experimental; *adv.* **e. gewonnene Erkenntnisse,** knowledge gained experimentally, by experiment; empirical knowledge.

experimentieren [ɛkspe·ri·mɛnˈtiːrən], *v.i.* (*haben*) to experiment; **mit etwas e.,** to experiment, make experiments, with sth.; **an Tieren, usw., e.,** to experiment (up)on animals, etc.

Experimentierfreudigkeit, *f.* pleasure in experimenting.

Expert[1] [ɛksˈpɛrt], *m.* **-en/-en, Experte** [ɛksˈpɛrtə], *m.* **-n/-n,** expert; **auf, in, einem Gebiet E. sein,** to be an expert in a field; **in rechtlichen Fragen ist er E.,** he is an expert on legal questions.

expert[2], *a.* expert (advice, etc.); **in etwas e. sein,** to be (an) expert in sth.

Expertise [ɛkspɛrˈtiːzə], *f.* **-/-n,** expertise (on picture, etc.); expert's report; **eine E. geben, anfertigen, schreiben,** to give, write, an expertise.

expertisieren [ɛkspɛrti·ˈziːrən], *v.tr.* to give an expertise on (picture, etc.).

Explanation [ɛkspla·na·tsĭˈoːn], *f.* **-/-en,** explanation.

Expletivum [ɛksple·ˈtiːvum], *n.* **-s/-va, Expletivwort,** *n.* **-(e)s/-wörter.** *Gram:* expletive

Explikation [ɛkspli·ka·tsĭˈoːn], *f.* **-/-en,** explication, explanation, interpretation; *Log:* explication (of principle, etc.).

explizieren [ɛkspli·ˈtsiːrən], *v.tr.* to explain (sth.); to interpret (theory, etc.); *Log:* to explicate (principle, etc.); **sich e.,** to make one's meaning clear.

explizit [ɛkspli·ˈtsiːt], *a.* *Mth:* explicit (function).

explizite [ɛksˈpliːtsi·teː], *adv.* explicitly, clearly, plainly.

explodierbar [ɛksplo·ˈdiːr-], *a.* explodable; explosive (gas, etc.); explosible (mine, etc.).

Explodierbarkeit, *f.* explosiveness.

explodieren [ɛksplo·ˈdiːrən], *v.i.* (*sein*) (*of bomb, shell, gun*) to explode, burst; (*of mine, powder-magazine, boiler, etc.*) to blow up, explode; *F:* **ich könnte vor Wut e.!** I could burst with rage!

Exploitation [ɛksplo·a·ta·tsĭˈoːn], *f.* **-/-en,** exploitation (of mine, human labour, etc.).

Exploiteur [ɛksplo·a·ˈtøːr], *m.* **-s/-e,** exploiter.

exploitieren [ɛksplo·a·ˈtiːrən], *v.tr.* (*a*) to exploit (mine, etc.); (*b*) to exploit, take (unfair) advantage of, (human) labour.

Exploration [ɛksplo·ra·tsĭˈoːn], *f.* *Med:* exploration.

Explosion [ɛksplo·zĭˈoːn], *f.* **-/-en,** explosion (of bomb, gun, shell; *I.C.E:* of mixture; *Ling:* of consonant); exploding, bursting (of boiler, etc.); **mehrere Explosionen erfolgten gleichzeitig,** there were several explosions at the same time; *F:* **sein Zorn entlud sich in einer gewaltigen E.,** his rage exploded in one wild burst.

explosionsartig, *a.* like an explosion.

Explosionsbereich, *m.* area of the, an, explosion.

Explosionsdruck, *m.* blast (pressure).

explosionsfähig, *a.* explosive.

Explosionsfähigkeit, *f.* explosiveness.

Explosionsgas, *n.* explosive gas.

Explosionsgefahr, *f.* danger of explosion.

Explosionsgemisch, *n.* explosive mixture.

Explosionsgrenze, *f.* explosion limit, explosive limit.

Explosionskraft, *f.* explosive power.

Explosionsmaschine, *f.,* **Explosionsmotor,** *m.* internal combustion engine.

Explosionspilz, *m.* mushroom (from atomic explosion).

Explosionsraum, *m.* *I.C.E:* combustion chamber.

Explosionsröhre, *f.,* **Explosionsschlot,** *m.* *Geol:* (eruptive) pipe.

explosionssicher, *a.* proof against explosion, explosion-proof.

Explosionstemperatur, *f.* temperature of explosion.

Explosionswelle, *f.* explosion wave.

Explosionswolke, *f.* cloud arising from an explosion.

explosiv [ɛksplo·ˈziːf], *a.* explosive (gas, etc.; *Ling:* consonant); explodable, explosible (mine, etc.).

Explosivbalken, *m.* *Mil.Exp:* Bangalore torpedo.

Explosive [ɛksplo·ˈziːvə], *pl.* *Ling:* explosives.

Explosivkraft, *f.* = **Explosionskraft.**

Explosivlaut, *m.* *Ling:* plosive.

Explosivstoff, *m.* explosive (substance); **brisanter E.,** shattering, disruptive, explosive.

Explosivum [ɛksplo·ˈziːvum], *n.* **-s/-va** & **-ve.** *Ling:* = **Explosivlaut.**

Exponent [ɛkspo·ˈnɛnt], *m.* **-en/-en.** **1.** exponent, representative (of party, movement, etc.). **2.** *Mth:* exponent; (power) index.

Exponentenbewertung, *f.* *Mth:* exponential evaluation.

exponential [ɛkspo·nɛntsĭˈaːl], *a.* *Mth:* exponential.

Exponentialfunktion, *f.* *Mth:* exponential function.

Exponentialgleichung, *f.* *Alg:* exponential equation.

Exponentialgröße, *f.* *Mth:* exponential (quantity).

Exponentialkurve, *f.* *Mth:* exponential curve.

Exponentialreihe, *f.* *Mth:* exponential series.

Exponentialtrichter, *m.* *El.Ac:* exponential horn.

exponentiell [ɛkspo·nɛntsĭˈɛl], *a.* *Mth:* exponential.

exponieren [ɛkspo·ˈniːrən], *v.tr.* **1.** to set forth, set out, develop, unfold (theory, etc.). **2.** *Phot:* to expose (negative). **3. j-n, sich, exponieren,** to lay s.o., oneself, open to criticism, attacks, etc.; **an exponierter Stelle,** in an exposed position.

Export [ɛksˈport], *m.* **-(e)s/-e.** **1.** export, exporting (of goods, etc.); **freier E.,** free export; **der E. von Baumwolle,** the export of cotton. **2.** export(s); **Exporte** *pl,* exports, goods exported; **die Exporte sind im vergangenen Jahr um 20 Prozent zurückgegangen,** exports have decreased by 20 per cent during the last year; **Baumwolle ist der wichtigste E. dieses Landes,** cotton is the chief export of this country.

Exportabteilung, *f.* *Com:* export department; export section.

Exportagent, *m.* *Com:* export agent.

Exportartikel, *m.* *Com:* export; exported article; article for export; export article.

Exportbestimmungen, *f.pl.* *Adm:* export regulations.

Exportbewilligung, *f.* *Adm:* = **Exportgenehmigung.**

Exportbier, *n.* *Brew:* export ale.

Exportdeklaration, *f.* *Cust:* entry outwards.

Exporterklärung, *f.* = **Exportdeklaration.**

Exporterlaubnis, *f.* *Adm.* = **Exportgenehmigung.**

Exporteur [ɛksporˈtøːr], *m.* **-s/-e.** *Com:* exporter.

Exportfreudigkeit, *f.* keenness (of industry) to export.

Exportgenehmigung, *f.* *Adm:* (*a*) permission to export; (*b*) export licence, export permit.

Exportgeschäft, *n.* *Com:* **1.** (*a*) export trade; (*b*) export transaction. **2.** (*firm*) export business.

Exportgut, *n.* *Com:* (i) export; (ii) *coll.* exports.

Exporthafen, *m.* port of exportation.

Exporthandel, *m.* *Com:* export trade.

exportieren [ɛksporˈtiːrən], *v.tr.* to export (goods, etc.); **Exportieren** *n,* **Exportierung** *f,* export, exporting, exportation.

Exportindustrie, *f.* export industry.

Exportkaufmann, *m.* **1.** exporter. **2.** (*in firm*) export official *or* clerk.

Exportkontingent, *n.* *Adm:* *Com:* export quota.

Exportland, *n.* *Pol.Ec:* *Com:* **1.** exporting country. **2.** country of destination of exports.

Exportleiter, *m.* *Com:* export manager.

Exportliste, *f.* *Adm:* *Com:* export list.

Exportlizenz, *f.* *Adm:* export licence, export permit.

Exportmonopol, *n.* *Pol.Ec:* *Com:* export monopoly.

Exportprämie, *f.* *Adm:* export bounty, export premium.

Exportquota, Exportquote, *f.* **1.** *Pol.Ec:* export rate. **2.** = **Exportkontingent.**

Exportsachbearbeiter, *m.* *Com:* export clerk.

Exportsubvention, *f.* *Pol.Ec:* export subsidy.

Exporttarif, *m.* *Rail:* special transport rates, tariff, for certain exports.

Exporttaxe, *f.* *Adm:* levy on exports; export duty.

Exportüberschuß, *m.* *Pol.Ec:* export surplus.

Exportverbot, *n.* *Pol.Ec:* export ban, export prohibition.

Exportvergütung, *f.* **1.** *Cust:* drawback (on certain goods). **2.** *Adm:* tax rebate (to exporters).

Exportware, *f.* *Com:* (i) export; export commodity; article for export; export article; (ii) *coll.* exports.

Exportzoll, *m.* *Cust:* export duty.

Exposé [ɛkspo·ˈzeː], *n.* **-s/-s,** exposé, exposition.

Exposition [ɛkspo·zi·tsĭˈoːn], *f.* **-/-en.** **1.** (*a*) *A:* exhibition, show (of works of art, etc.); (*b*) *Ecc:* exposition (of the sacrament). **2.** (*a*) exposition (of views, theories, etc.); (*b*) *Lit:* *Mus:* exposition (of drama, sonata, etc.). **3.** aspect, exposure (of house, etc.). **4.** *Phot:* exposure (of negative).

Expositur [ɛkspo·zi·ˈtuːr], *f.* **-/-en.** **1.** *A:* (*a*) *Com:* branch, branch office; (*b*) *Ecc:* branch house; *R.C.Ch:* chapel of ease. **2.** *Sch:* *Austrian:* overflow premises.

Expositus [ɛksˈpoːzi·tus], *m.* **-/-ti.** *R.C.Ch:* *A:* priest at a chapel of ease.

Expostulation [ɛkspostu·la·tsĭˈoːn], *f.* **-/-en,** expostulation, dispute, argument.

Expreß[1] [ɛksˈprɛs], *m.* **-presses/-presse.** **1.** *Rail:* express (train). **2.** *adv.phr.* **per E.,** *Rail:* by express, *occ. Post:* by express, *U.S:* by special delivery; **Waren per E. senden,** to send goods by express.

expreß[2], *a.* *F:* express, distinct, explicit (prohibition, etc.); *adv.* specially, on purpose; **sie hat es e. deswegen getan,** she has done it for that very purpose.

Expreßbote, *m.* express messenger.

Expreßbrief, *m.* *Post:* express letter.

Expreßbüchse, *f.* *Sm.a:* express rifle.

Expresse [ɛksˈprɛsə], *m.* **-n/-n.** *A:* express (messenger).

Expreßgut, *n.* *Rail:* express parcel(s); **etwas als E. schicken,** to send sth. (by) express, to express sth.

Expreßgutbeförderung, *f.* conveyance of express parcels.

Expreßgutverkehr, *m.* *Rail:* express parcel traffic.

Expression [ɛksprɛsĭˈoːn], *f.* **-/-en,** expression; *Mus:* expression stop (of harmonium).

Expressionismus [ɛksprɛsĭo·ˈnismus], *m.* **-/-men.** *Art:* *Lit:* expressionism.

Expressionist [ɛksprɛsĭo·ˈnist], *m.* **-en/-en.** *Art:* *Lit:* expressionist.

expressionistisch [ɛksprɛsĭo·ˈnistiʃ], *a.* expressionist.

expressiv [ɛksprɛˈsiːf], *a.* expressive, full of expression; **expressiver** [ɛksprɛˈsiːvər] **Tanz** = **Ausdruckstanz.**

Expressivorgel, *f.* *Mus:* (early form of) harmonium.

Expresso [ɛksˈprɛsoː], *m.* & *n.* **-s/-s** = **Espresso.**

Expreßzug, *m.* *Rail:* express train.

Expropriation [ɛkspro·prĭa·tsĭˈoːn], *f.* **-/-en,** expropriation (of property, owner); dispossession (of owner).

expropriieren [ɛkspro·pri·ˈiːrən], *v.tr.* to expropriate (owner, property); to dispossess (owner) of property.

Expulsion [ɛkspulzĭˈoːn], *f.* **-/-en.** **1.** *Jur:* eviction,

dispossession (of tenant farmer); expulsion (of alien, etc.). **2.** *Med:* expulsion.

expulsiv [ɛkspul'ziːf], *a. Med:* expulsive, expelling (drug, etc.).

exquisit [ɛkskvi·'ziːt], *a.* exquisite (taste, etc.).

Exsekration [ɛks(z)e·kra·tsi'oːn], *f.* -/-en, malediction, curse, *A:* execration.

exsekrieren [ɛks(z)e·'kriːrən], *v.tr.* to curse, pronounce a curse upon (s.o., sth.); *A:* to execrate (s.o., sth.).

Exsequatur [ɛks(z)e·'kvaːtuːr], *n.* -s/-s = Exequatur.

Exsikkation [ɛks(z)ika·tsi'oːn], *f.* -/-en, exsiccation.

Exsikkator [ɛks(z)i'kaːtor], *m.* -s/-en [-ka·'toːrən]. *Ch: etc:* desiccator, exsiccator.

Exsikkose [ɛks(z)i'koːzə], *f.* -/-n. *Med:* exsiccated condition, exsiccation (of tissue).

Exspektanz [ɛks(s)pɛk'tants], *f.* -/-en. *R.C.Ch:* right of succession.

Exspektation [ɛks(s)pɛkta·tsi'oːn], *f.* -/-en, expectation.

exspektativ [ɛks(s)pɛkta·'tiːf], *a.* expectative; *Med:* **exspektative** [ɛks(s)pɛkta·'tiːvə] **Behandlung,** expectative treatment.

exspektieren [ɛks(s)pɛk'tiːrən], *v.tr.* to expect (sth.).

Exspiration [ɛks(s)pi·ra·tsi'oːn], *f.* -/-en. *Physiol:* expiration.

exspiratorisch [ɛks(s)pi·ra·'toːriʃ], *a. Anat:* expiratory (organ, etc.); *Ling:* **exspiratorischer Akzent,** stress-accent, stress.

exspirieren [ɛks(s)pi·'riːrən]. **1.** *v.tr.* to breathe out (air). **2.** *v.i. (sein) (a)* to breathe out, expire; *(b) (of lease, etc.)* to come to an end, expire; *(c)* to die.

Exspoliation [ɛks(s)po·lia·tsi'oːn], *f.* -/-en, spoliation.

exspoliieren [ɛks(s)po·li·'iːrən], *v.tr.* to despoil, rob (s.o.); to despoil, plunder (house, tomb, etc.).

Exstase [ɛks'(s)taːzə], *f.* -/-n = Ekstase.

Exstirpation [ɛks(s)tirpa·tsi'oːn], *f.* -/-en, eradication, extirpation (of people, etc.); *Surg:* extirpation, complete removal (of growth, etc.).

Exstirpator [ɛks(s)tir'paːtor], *m.* -s/-en [-pa·'toːrən]. *Agr:* extirpator.

Exsudat [ɛks(z)u·'daːt], *n.* -(e)s/-e. *Med:* exudation, exuded matter.

Exsudation [ɛks(z)u·da·tsi'oːn], *f.* -/-en. *Med:* exudation.

exsudativ [ɛks(z)u·da·tiːf], *a. Med:* exudative.

exsudieren [ɛks(z)u·'diːrən], *v.tr.* to exude (moisture. etc.).

Extemporale [ɛkstempo·'raːlə], *n.* -s/-lien [-liən] = Extempore.

Extempore [ɛks'tempoːreː], *n.* -s/-(s), *(a) Sch:* extempore, extemporary, written exercise; *(b)* extemporization, improvisation; extemporized extra, improvised extra (in musical, etc., performance); improvised insertion.

ex tempore. *Lt. adv.phr.* extempore, impromptu.

extemporieren [ɛkstempo·'riːrən]. **1.** *v.tr.* to extemporize (speech, etc.). **2.** *v.i. (haben)* to extemporize; to play *or* speak *or* perform extempore; *Mus:* to improvise, extemporize.

Extended [ɛks'tɛndid], *f.* -/. *Print:* extended-letter (type).

extendieren [ɛkstɛn'diːrən], *v.tr.* to extend, spread, stretch (sth.).

Extension [ɛkstɛnzi'oːn], *f.* -/-en, extension; *Surg:* extension, traction (of broken limb).

Extensionsverband, *m. Surg:* skin traction.

Extensität [ɛkstɛnzi·'tɛːt], *f.* -/. *Psy: etc:* extensity.

extensiv [ɛkstɛn'ziːf], *a.* extensive, vast, wide (area, etc.); *Agr:* **extensive** [ɛkstɛn'ziːvə] **Landwirtschaft,** extensive farming; *Log:* **extensive Größe,** extensive quantity.

Extensivrasse, *f. Husb:* race of domestic animal suitable for extensive stock rearing.

Extensor [ɛks'tɛnzor], *m.* -s/-en [-'zoːrən]. *Anat:* extensor (muscle).

Extenuation [ɛkste·nu·a·tsi'oːn], *f.* -/-en, extenuation *(in all senses).*

Exterieur [ɛkste·ri'øːr], *n.* -s/-e, exterior (of house, etc.); (outward) appearance, looks; **das E. eines Pferdes,** the exterior, the points, of a horse.

Exteriorität [ɛkste·ri·ori·'tɛːt], *f.* -/-en, exteriority, externality.

Extermination [ɛkstɛrmi·na·tsi'oːn], *f.* -/-en. **1.** *A:* extermination, expulsion, driving out (of s.o.). **2.** extermination, eradication, extirpation (of race, heresy, etc.).

exterminieren [ɛkstɛrmi·'niːrən], *v.tr.* **1.** *A:* to exterminate, drive out, banish (s.o.). **2.** to ex-

terminate, eradicate, extirpate (race, heresy, etc.).

extern [ɛks'tɛrn], *a.* external, outside; **externe Schüler, Schülerinnen,** day-pupils (at boarding-school).

Externat [ɛkstɛr'naːt], *n.* -(e)s/-e, day-school.

Externe [ɛks'tɛrnə], *m. f., (decl. as adj.) Sch:* **1.** day-pupil (at boarding-school). **2.** private study candidate; external candidate.

Externist [ɛkstɛr'nist], *m.* -en/-en. **1.** *Med:* specialist in external diseases. **2.** *Sch: Austrian:* = Externe.

exterritorial [ɛkstɛri·to·ri'aːl], *a.* extraterritorial.

Exterritorialität [ɛkstɛri·to·ri·a·li·'tɛːt], *f.* -/. extra-territoriality.

Extinkteur [ɛkstiŋk'tøːr], *m.* -s/-e, fire-extinguisher.

Extinktion [ɛkstiŋk tsi'oːn], *f.* -/-en. *Opt:* extinction (of light).

Extinktionskoeffizient, *m. Opt:* extinction coefficient.

extorquieren [ɛkstor'kviːrən], *v.tr.* to extort (promise, money, etc.).

Extorsion [ɛkstorzi'oːn], *f.* -/-en, extortion (of money, promise, etc.).

extra[1] ['ɛkstraː]. **1.** *adv. (a)* extra, separately, apart; over and above; in addition; **Getränke werden e. berechnet,** drinks are charged extra, separately; **alle Unkosten, die e. berechnet werden,** all expenses charged separately, all extras; *F:* **damit will er sich etwas e. verdienen,** he wants to earn a little extra money by this, *F:* he wants to make a little money on the side by this; *(b) F:* specially; on purpose; **e. deswegen,** for the very purpose; **e. dafür gemacht,** made specially for the purpose; **du hast das e. getan,** you did that on purpose, out of spite. **2.** *inv. a. F:* extra, additional; special; **ein e. Gedeck auflegen,** to lay an extra, additional, cover; *(incorrect use)* **sie will immer etwas Extra(e)s für sich,** she always wants something special for herself.

Extra[2], *m.* -s/-s. *Cin:* supernumary, *F:* extra.

extra-, Extra- [ɛkstraː-], *pref.* **1.** *(in words of foreign origin) (outside)* extra-; **extraperitoneal** [ɛkstraːpe·ri·to·ne·'aːl], extraperitoneal; **extraparochial** [ɛkstraːpa·roxi'aːl], extraparochial, outside the parish; **Extrapolation** *f,* extrapolation. **2.** ['ɛkstraː]- *(intensive)* extra-, extra . . . ; additional . . . ; **Extrakosten** *pl,* extra cost; additional cost; **Extraversicherung** *f,* extra, additional, insurance; **extrastark,** extra-strong.

Extraausgabe, *f.* **1.** extra expense, extra. **2.** special edition (of book, etc.); extra number (of periodical, magazine).

Extrablatt, *n.* extra edition (of newspaper), extra.

extradieren [ɛkstra·'diːrən], *v.tr. Jur:* to extradite.

Extradition [ɛkstra·di·tsi'oːn], *f.* -/-en. *Jur:* extradition.

Extradividende ['ɛkstra·di·vi·ˌdɛndə], *f. Fin:* bonus, extra dividend; *U.S:* melon.

Extrados [ɛks'traːdos], *m.* -/-. *Arch:* extrados, back of an arch.

extradossiert [ɛkstra·do'siːrt], *a. Arch:* extradosed (arch).

extrafein, *a.* extra-fine, superfine.

extragalaktisch [ɛkstra·ga·'laktiʃ], *a. Astr:* extragalactic (nebula).

extragenital [ɛkstra·ge·ni·'taːl], *a. Anat:* extra-genital.

Extrahent [ɛkstra·'hɛnt], *m.* -en/-en. **1.** *Com:* person who makes an abstract, a statement (of account, etc.). **2.** *Jur:* person at whose request a writ is issued.

extrahierbar [ɛkstra·'hiːr-], *a.* extractable.

extrahieren [ɛkstra·'hiːrən], *v.tr. (a)* to take, extract, passages (from book, etc.); *Com:* to make an abstract (from an account); to draw up a statement of (an account); *(b) Ch: Pharm: etc:* to extract, draw out (oils, etc.); to leach out, to leach away (salts, etc.).

extrajudizial [ɛkstra·ju·di·tsi'aːl], *a. Jur:* extra-judicial.

Extrakosten, *pl.* extra cost(s) *or* charges, extras; additional cost(s) *or* charges.

Extrakt [ɛks'trakt], *m. & n.* -(e)s/-e. **1.** *(a)* extract, excerpt, extracted passage (from book, etc.); *(b) Ch: Pharm: etc:* extraction (of oils, etc.); **-extrakt,** *comb.fm.:* . . . extract; **Fleischextrakt,** meat extract; **Malzextrakt,** malt extract. **2.** *Tex:* extract wool, extract.

Extraktbestimmung, *f. Brew: etc:* determination of extract.

Extraktgehalt, *m. Brew: etc:* extract content.

Extraktion [ɛkstraktsi'oːn], *f.* -/-en, *(a)* extraction, excerpting (of passage from book, etc.); *(b) Surg:* extraction, pulling out (of tooth,

etc.); *Obst:* extraction (of child from womb); *(c) Ch: Pharm: etc:* extraction (of oils, etc.).

Extraktionsanlage, *f. Ind:* extraction plant.

Extraktionsapparat, *m. Ind:* extractor, extraction apparatus.

Extraktionsmittel, *n. Ch: Ind:* extracting agent.

Extraktivstoff [ɛkstrak'tiːf-], *m. Ch: Ind: etc:* extractive matter, extractive substance, extractive.

Extraktwolle, *f. Tex:* extract wool, extract.

extramental [ɛkstra·mɛn'taːl], *a. Phil: etc:* extramental.

extramundan [ɛkstra·mun'daːn], *a. Phil: etc:* extramundane.

extran [ɛks'traːn], *a.* extraneous; foreign, strange.

Extraneer [ɛks'traːne·ər], **Extraner** [ɛks'traːnər], *m.* -s/-. *Sch:* day-pupil.

extraordinär [ɛkstra·ʔordi·'nɛːr], *a.* extraordinary.

Extraordinariat [ɛkstra·ʔordi·na·ri'aːt], *n. Sch:* extraordinary professorship, *approx.* = (university) readership, *U.S:* associate professorship.

Extraordinarium [ɛkstra·ʔordi·'naːrium], *n. Pol. Ec:* extraordinary budget.

Extraordinarius [ɛkstra·ʔordi·'naːrius], *m. Sch:* professor extraordinarius, extraordinary professor, *approx.* = (university) reader, *U.S:* associate professor.

Extrapolation [ɛkstra·po·la·tsi'oːn], *f.* -/-en. *Mth:* extrapolation.

extrapolieren [ɛkstra·po·'liːrən], *v.tr. & i. (haben) Mth:* to extrapolate.

Extrapost, *f. A:* special post; special mail coach.

Extrastrom, *m. El:* extra-current, self-induction current.

Extrasystole ['ɛkstra·zys·toːlə], *f. Med:* extra-systole.

Extratara ['ɛkstra·ˌtaːra], *f. Com:* extra tare.

Extratour ['ɛkstra·ˌtuːr], *f.* extra tour, walk, trip; *F:* **er will immer eine E.,** he always wants something special, something extra.

extrauterin [ˌɛkstra·ʔu·te·'riːn], *a. Anat:* extra-uterine.

Extrauteringravidität [ɛkstra·ʔu·te·'riːngra·vi·di·ˌtɛːt], *f. Med:* extra-uterine pregnancy.

extravagant [ɛkstra·va·'gant], *a.* extravagant (pers., opinion, claim, conduct, etc.); wild (claim, utterance, action, etc.); fantastic (claim, dress, etc.).

Extravaganz [ɛkstra·va·'gants], *f.* -/-en. **1.** extravagance (of pers., opinion, claim, conduct, etc.); wildness (of claim, utterance, action); fantastic nature, fantasticalness (of pers., claim, dress, etc.). **2.** extravagant action *or* notion, extravagance; **er war ihrer Extravaganzen müde,** he was weary of her extravagances.

Extravasat [ɛkstra·va·'zaːt], *n.* -s/-e. *Med:* extravasation, extravasated fluid.

Extraversion [ɛkstra·verzi'oːn], *f.* -/-. *Psy:* extroversion.

extravertiert [ɛkstra·ver'tiːrt], *a. Psy:* extrovert; **ein extravertierter Typ,** an extrovert.

Extrawurst, *f. (a) Cu: Austrian:* (kind of) mild pork sausage; *(b) F:* **j-m eine E. braten,** to give s.o. sth. extra; **er will immer eine E. haben,** he must always have something different, special.

Extrazug, *m. Rail:* extra train. special train.

extrem[1] [ɛks'treːm], *a.* extreme (point, limit, cold, measures, views, etc.); farthest, utmost (point, limit, etc.); intense (cold, stupidity, hatred, etc.); **ein extremer Fall,** an extreme case; **zu extremen Mitteln greifen,** to have recourse to extreme, drastic, measures, to take drastic steps; *Mth: Meteor: etc:* **extreme Werte,** extreme values; *Pol:* **die extreme Linke,** the extreme left.

Extrem[2], *n.* -s/- e, extreme (limit); *Mth:* extreme (value); **von einem E. ins andere fallen,** to go from one extreme to another; **etwas bis ins E. verfolgen,** to carry something to extremes, to go to extremes with something; **(die) Extreme berühren sich,** extremes meet; **too far east is west;** *Meteor:* **absolute, mittlere, Extreme,** absolute, mean, extremes.

Extremale [ɛkstre·'maːlə], *f.* -/-n. *Mth:* extremal.

Extremismus [ɛkstre·'mismus], *m.* -/-. extremism.

Extremist [ɛkstre·'mist], *m.* -en/-en, extremist.

Extremität [ɛkstre·mi·'tɛːt], *f.* -/-en, *(a)* extremity, end; *(b) usu. pl.* **Extremitäten,** *Nat. Hist: Anat:* limbs, extremities.

Extremthermometer, *n. Med: Meteor: etc:* maximum and minimum thermometer.

Extremum [ɛk'streːmum], *n.* -s/-ma. *Mth:* extreme (value) (of function).

Extroversion [ɛkstro·verzi'oːn], *f.* -/-en = Extraversion.

extrovertiert [ɛkstro·ver'tiːrt], *a.* = extravertiert.

Extrusion [ɛkstruˑziˈoːn], f. -/-en. Geol: extrusion.
extrusiv [ɛkstruˈziːf], a. Geol: extrusive (rock).
Exulant [ɛksuˈlant], m. -en/-en, exiled, banished, person; exile.
Exulzeration [ɛksultseˑraˑtsiˈoːn], f. -/-en. Med: exulceration.
exulzerieren [ɛksultseˈriːrən], v.tr. Med: to exulcerate.
ex usu [ɛks ˈuːzuː]. Lt. adv.phr. Jur: from usage, from practice.
Exuvien [ɛksᵓˈuːviən], pl. (a) Nat.Hist: exuviae (of snails, insects, etc.); (b) A: garments of saints kept as relics; (c) A: pillage, spoils, booty.
ex voto [ɛks ˈvoːtoː]. Lt.phr. ex voto, according to one's vow.
Exvoto [ɛksˈvoːtoː], n. -s/-s & -voten, ex-voto; votive offering.
Exzedent [ɛkstseˈdɛnt], m. -en/-en. 1. A: evildoer, malefactor; transgressor, offender. 2. Ins: surplus (in reinsurance).
exzellent [ɛkstseˈlɛnt], a. excellent.
Exzellenz [ɛkstseˈlɛnts], f. -/-en, (title of honour) Excellence, Excellency; Ihre E., your Excellency; **dürfte ich Ihre E. bitten . . .**, may I ask your Excellency. . . .
exzellieren [ɛkstseˈliːrən], v.i. (haben) to excel.
Exzenter [ɛksˈtsɛntər], n. -s/-. Mec.E: eccentric; Tex: tappet; Clockm: snail.
Exzenterbügel, m. Mec.E: eccentric strap, eccentric hoop.
Exzentergetriebe, n. Mec.E: eccentric gear.

Exzenterhub, m. Mec.E: throw of the eccentric.
Exzenterpresse, f. Mec.E: eccentric press.
Exzenterscheibe, f. Mec.E: eccentric disc, eccentric sheave.
Exzenterstange, f. Mec.E: eccentric rod.
Exzentrik[1] [ɛksˈtsɛntrik], m. -s/-s = **Exzentriker** (a).
Exzentrik[2], f. -/. Th: (art of) grotesque comedy (on variety stage or in circus).
Exzentrik[3], n. -s/-s. Mec.E: eccentric.
Exzentriker [ɛksˈtsɛntrikər], m. -s/-, (a) Th: grotesque comedy artist (on variety stage or in circus); (b) (pers.) eccentric.
exzentrisch [ɛksˈtsɛntriʃ], a. 1. eccentric (circle, ellipse, orbit, etc., Mec.E: rod, wheel, pulley, etc.); (of wheel) out of true; Clockm: **exzentrische Scheibe**, kidney-piece. 2. eccentric; peculiar, (rather) queer.
Exzentrizität [ɛkstsɛntriˑtsiˈtɛːt], f. -/. 1. eccentricity (of circle, ellipse, orbit, etc., Mec.E: of rod, wheel, pulley, etc.); Geom: **(lineare) E. eines Kegelschnitts**, distance of a focus from the centre of a conic section; **numerische E. eines Kegelschnitts**, eccentricity of a conic section. 2. eccentricity (of pers., conduct, etc.); peculiarity, queerness (of pers., conduct).
Exzeption [ɛkstsɛptsiˈoːn], f. -/-en. A: exception; Jur: exception, plea in defence.
exzeptionell [ɛkstsɛptsioˈnɛl], a. exceptional.
exzeptiv [ɛkstsɛpˈtiːf], a. exceptive.
exzerpieren [ɛkstsɛrˈpiːrən], v.tr. to excerpt, make excerpts from (literary work, etc.).

Exzerpt ɛksˈtsɛrpt], n. -(e)s/-e, excerpt (from literary work).
Exzeß [ɛksˈtsɛs], m. -zesses/-zesse. 1. excess; immoderation; **bis zum E.**, to excess, excessively; **Alkoholgenuß im E. ist schädlich**, excessive, immoderate, consumption of alcohol is harmful. 2. excess; outrage; violation of the law; **er war bekannt für seine Exzesse**, he was notorious for his excesses; he was known for loose living. 3. (a) Trig: **sphärischer E.**, spherical excess (of triangle); (b) Statistics: excess, kurtosis (of frequency curve).
exzessiv [ɛkstseˈsiːf], a. (a) excessive; Geog: **exzessives** [ɛkstseˈsiːvəs] **Klima**, continental climate; (b) excessive; outrageous; immoderate (drinking, mirth, etc.).
exzidieren [ɛkstsiˈdiːrən], v.tr. Surg: to excise, cut out, dissect out (tumour, etc.).
exzipieren [ɛkstsiˈpiːrən], v.tr. to except, make an exception of (sth.).
Exzision [ɛkstsiziˈoːn], . -/-en. Surg: excision (of tumour, etc.).
exzitabel [ɛkstsiˈtaːbəl], a. excitable.
Exzitabilität [ɛkstsiˑtaˑbiˑliˈtɛːt], f. -/. excitability.
Exzitans [ˈɛkstsiˑtans], n. -/-tanzien & -tantia [-ˈtantsiən & -ˈtantsiaː]. Med: excitant, stimulant.
Exzitation [ɛkstsiˑtaˑtsiˈoːn], f. -/-en, excitation.
exzitieren [ɛkstsiˈtiːrən], v.tr. to excite, stimulate (s.o., the circulation, etc.).
Eyresee, der [ˈɛːr-]. Pr.n.m. Geog: Lake Eyre.
Ezechiel [eˑˈtsɛçiˑəl]. Pr.n.m. -s. B.Hist: Ezekiel.